INTERNATIONAL
AUTHORS AND WRITERS
WHO'S WHO

INTERNATIONAL AUTHORS AND WRITERS WHO'S WHO

Publisher:
Nicholas S Law

Consultant Editors:
David Cummings
Dennis K McIntire

Senior Editor:
Jocelyn Timothy

Assistant Editors:
Barbara Cooper
Janine Lawrence

All communications to: International Authors and Writers Who's Who
International Biographical Centre
Cambridge CB2 3QP, England

INTERNATIONAL AUTHORS AND WRITERS WHO'S WHO

FIFTEENTH EDITION

Consultant Editors:
David Cummings
Dennis K McIntire

Routledge
Taylor & Francis Group

LONDON AND NEW YORK

This edition published 2014 by Routledge
2 Park Square, Milton Park, Abingdon, Oxon, OX14 4RN
711 Third Avenue, New York, NY 10017

Routledge is an imprint of the Taylor & Francis Group, an informa business

First published 1934
Second Edition 1935
Third Edition 1948
Fourth Edition 1960
Fifth Edition 1963
Sixth Edition 1972
Reprinted 1972
Seventh Edition 1976
Eighth Edition 1977
Ninth Edition 1982
Tenth Edition 1986
Eleventh Edition 1989
Twelfth Edition 1991
Thirteenth Edition 1993
Fourteenth Edition 1995
Fifteenth Edition 1997

ISBN 978-0-948-87572-4 (hbk)

FOREWORD

The **International Authors and Writers Who's Who** was first published in 1934, and subsequently went through thirteen more editions. With this *Fifteenth Edition* the Consultant Editors have overseen the most extensive revision in its history. Several thousand new and/or completely revised entries have been included in this edition, making it the most accurate and up-to-date one-volume biographical source of its kind in the world.

For this exhaustive revision, innumerable notable writers in all of the major genres, including fiction, non-fiction, poetry, and drama, have been included. A special effort has been made to expand the coverage of non-fiction writers, ranging from historians and political scientists to philosophers and theologians. While the entrants are primarily those who write in English, this edition has expanded its scope to embrace many writers whose work has been widely disseminated with English translations.

As in previous editions, every biographee was sent a typescript of his or her entry for amending and approval, and the necessary corrections and updates have been incorporated in the final copy. While every care is taken to ensure accuracy, it is inevitable that errors will find their way into print. We apologize in advance for such errors and will make a good faith effort to make amends in the next edition.

We thank all those who have leant their assistance in the production of this new edition. We are grateful to Publisher Nicholas Law for kindly allowing us to serve as Consultant Editors, and we are especially grateful to Senior Editor Jocelyn Timothy and her staff for their patience, co-operation and efficiency.

David Cummings
Consultant Editor
UK, Commonwealth & Europe

March 1997

Dennis K McIntire
Consultant Editor
Canada & USA

March 1997

INTERNATIONAL BIOGRAPHICAL CENTRE RANGE OF REFERENCE TITLES

From one of the widest ranges of contemporary biographical reference works published under any one imprint, some IBC titles date back to the 1930's. Each edition is compiled from information supplied by those listed, who include leading personalities of particular countries or professions. Information offered usually includes date and place of birth; family details; qualifications; career histories; awards and honours received; books published or other creative work; other relevant information including postal address. Naturally there is no charge or fee for inclusion.

New editions are freshly compiled and contain on average 80-90% new information. New titles are regularly added to the IBC reference library.

Titles include:

Dictionary of International Biography

Who's Who in Australasia and the Pacific Nations

Who's Who in Western Europe

Dictionary of Scandinavian Biography

International Who's Who in Art and Antiques

International Authors and Writers Who's Who

International Leaders in Achievement

International Who's Who in Community Service

International Who's Who in Education

International Who's Who in Engineering

International Who's Who in Medicine

International Who's Who in Music and Musicians' Directory - Volume One - Classical and Light Classical

International Who's Who in Music - Volume Two - Popular Music

Men of Achievement

The World Who's Who of Women

The World Who's Who of Women in Education

International Youth of Achievement

Foremost Women of the Twentieth Century

International Who's Who in Poetry and Poets' Encyclopaedia

Enquiries to:
International Biographical Centre
Cambridge CB2 3QP, England

CONTENTS

Biographies

A

AALAVANDAAR. See: **GOPALACHAR Aalavandar.**

AARDEMA Verna Geneva, b. 6 June 1911, New Era, Michigan, USA. Elementary Teacher; Journalist. m. (1) Albert Aardema, 30 May 1936, dec 1974, 1 son, 1 daughter, (2) Dr Joel Vugteveen, 3 Aug 1975. Education: BA, Michigan State College (now University), 1934. Appointments: Publicity Chairman, Juvenile Writers' Workshop, 1955-69; Staff Correspondent, Muskegon Chronicle. Publications: Tales for the Third Ear, 1969; Behind the Back of the Mountain, 1975; Why Mosquitoes Buzz in People's Ears, 1975; Who's in Rabbit's House?, 1977; Riddle of the Drum, 1978; Bringing the Rain to Kapiti Plain, 1981; What's So Funny, Ketu?, 1982; The Vingananee & the Tree Toad, 1983; Oh, Kojo! How Could You!, 1984; Bimwili & the Zimwi, 1985; Princess Gorilla and a New Kind of Water, 1988; Anansi Finds a Fool, 1992; A Bookworm Who Hatched, 1993; Sebgugu the Glutton, 1993; Misoso: Tales from Africa, 1993. Honours: Caldecott Award, 1976; Lewis Carroll Shelf Award, 1978; Parents' Choice Awards, 1984, 1985, 1989, 1991; Junior Library Guild Selection, 1991; Redbook Award, 1991; American Library Association Notable Book, 1991. Memberships: Juvenile Writers' Workshop; Childrens' Reading Round Table, Chicago; National and Michigan Education Associations; Womens' National Book Association. Literary Agent: Curtis Brown Ltd. Address: 784 Via Del Sol, North Fort Myers, Florida, USA.

AAZIM Muzaffar, b. 29 Apr 1934, Kashmir, India. Poet; Author; Educationist. m. Padshah Jan, 14 Oct 1956, 2 sons. Education: University of Kashmir. Publications: Zolana, poems 1964; Man-i-Kaman, poems 1974; Many poems translated into various European Languages; Author of many plays, articles, papers and translations. Contributions to: Radio, TV, Magazines and Periodicals including Poetry Review, AAj Kal; Neb, Kashmiri Shairi. Honours: Best Book Prize, Jammu and Kashmir Academy of Art, Culture and Languages, 1965, 1976; Soviet Land Nehru Award for the translation of War and Peace, 1978. Memberships: Sahitya Akademi (National Academy of Letters, India); Kashmir Academy of Art, Culture and Languages; Brontë Society of England; Historical & Cultural Society; Advisory Committee, Kashmir University; National Authors Registry, USA, 1994. Literary Agent: Akhtar Purvez, PO Box 318, Alkharj 11942, Saudi Arabia. Address: 1733 Gosnell Road #202, Vienna, VA 22182, USA.

ABALUTA Constantin, b. 8 Oct 1938, Bucharest, Romania. Writer. m. Gabriela, 1989. Education: Master of Architecture, 1961. Publications: The Rock (poems), 1968; Objects of Silence (poems), 1979; Air: Directions for Use (poems), 1982; To Stay Upright (prose), 1986; The Cyclops' Solitude (selected poems), 1995; Others: Symetric Planet (prose); Glider, The Same Same Sands, Marine in a Brain (poems). Contributions to: Contemporanul magazine; poems, essays, translations in Romanian and foreign magazines & journals. Honours: Prize of Breve revue, Napoli, 1970; Prix des Poètes Francophones, 1973. Memberships: Romanian Writers Union, Council Member; Constantza Haiku Society, Romania. Address: Str Arh D Hirjeu 76, Sect 2, 73281 Bucharest, Romania.

ABBAS (Khwaja) Ahmad, b. 7 June 1914, Panpit, Punjab, India. Novelist. Education: BA, 1933, LLB, 1935, Aligarph Muslim University. Appointments: Proprietor, Naya Sansar film production company, Bombay, 1951-. Publications: Tomorrow is Ours!, 1943, as Divided Heart, 1968; Defeat for Death: A Story Without Names, 1944; Blood and Stones, 1947; Inqilab, 1955; When Night Falls, 1968; Mera Naam, Joker, 1970; Maria, 1972; Boy Meets Girl, 1973; Bobby, 1973; Distant Dream, 1975; The World is My Village, 1983; Short stories: Not All Lies!, 1945; Rice and Other Stories, 1947; Cages of Freedom and Other Stories, 1952; One Thousand Nights on a Bed of Stones and Other Stories, 1957; The Black Son and Other Stories, 1963; The Most Beautiful Woman in the World, 1968; The Walls of Glass, 1977; Men and Women, 1977; The Thirteenth Victim, 1986; Several plays, screenplays and non-fiction works. Honour: Padma Shree, 1969. Address: c/o Blitz Publications, Canada Building, 3rd Floor, D N Road, Bombay 400 001, India.

ABBENSETTS Michael, b. 8 June 1938, British Guiana (British citizen, 1974). Writer. Education: Queen's College, Guyana, 1952-56; Stanstead College, Quebec; Sir George Williams University, Montreal,

1960-61. Appointments: Security Attendant, Tower of London, 1963-67; Staff Member, Sir John Soane Museum, London, 1968-71; Resident playwright, Royal Court Theatre, London, 1974; Visiting Professor of Drama, Carnegie Mellon University, Pittsburgh, 1981. Publications: Plays: Sweet Talk (produced London, 1973, New York, 1974); Alterations (produced London and New York, 1978; revised version produced London 1985); Samba (produced London, 1980); In the Mood (produced London, 1981); Outlaw (produced Leicester and London, 1983); El Dorado (produced London, 1984); Writer for radio and television. Novel: Empire Road (novelization of television series), 1979. Honours: George Devine Award, 1973; Arts Council Bursary, 1977; Afro-Caribbean Award, 1979. Literary Agent: Anthony Sheil Associates, London. Address: Sheil Associates, 43 Doughty Street, London WC1N 2LF, England.

ABBOTT John B Jr, b. 25 Feb 1956, Plainfield, New Jersey, USA. Mystery Writer. m. Maria G Di Tommaso, 3 Oct 1992. Education: BA, English, 1985; MEd, 1995, Rutgers University; Attending EdD Program, Graduate School of Education, Rutgers University. Appointments: Writing Tutor, English Department, 1988-94; Visiting Professional Lecturer, Rutgers University, 1989-; Adjunct Instructor, Mercer County Community College, Trenton, New Jersey, 1993-94; Writing Tutor, Middlesex County College, Edison, NJ, 1994-95. Publications: Knight Moves, 1990; Interactive Murder Mystery Scripts: All in the Game; Two for the Money; The Botsford Inn Mystery; The Kris Kringle Kaper; How the West was Fun and Birthdays Can Be Murder; Smithsonian's Knight, 1992. Memberships: Mystery Writers of America; New Jersey College English Association; National Council of Teachers of English; New Jersey Institute for Collegiate Learning and Teaching; New Jersey Association for Developemental Education. Address: 22 Church Street, PO Box 439, Kingston, NJ 08528-0439, USA.

ABISH Walter, b. 24 Dec 1931, Vienna, Austria. Writer. m. Cecile Abish. Publications: Duel Site, 1970; Alphabetical Africa, 1974; Minds Meet, 1975; In the Future Perfect, 1977; How German Is It, 1980; The New Meaning, 1990; Eclipse Fever, 1993. Contributions to: Antaeus; Conjunctions; Granta; Manuskripte; New Directions Annual; Paris Review; Partisan Review; Tri-Quarterly; Salmagundi. Honours: Ingram Merrill Foundation Grant, 1977; National Endowment for the Arts Fellowships, 1979, 1985; PEN-Faulkner Award, 1981; Guggenheim Fellowship, 1981; Deutscher Akademischer Austauschdienst Residency, Berlin, 1987; John D and Catharine T MacArthur Foundation Fellowship, 1987-92; Award of Merit Medal, American Academy of Arts and Letters, 1991; Lila Wallace-Reader's Digest Fellowship, 1992-95; Honorary Doctor of Letters, State University College of ONEONTA, New York, 1996. Membership: PEN. Address: PO Box 485, Cooper Square, NY 10276, USA.

ABLEMAN Paul, b. 13 June 1927, Leeds, Yorkshire, England. Writer. Education: King's College, London. Publications: Even His Enemy (with Gertrude Macauley), 1948; I Hear Voices, 1958; As Near As I Can Get, 1962; Green Julia (play), 1966; Tests (playlets), 1966; Vac, 1968; Blue Comedy: Madly in Love, Hawk's Night, 1968; The Twilight of the Vilp, 1969; Bits: Some Prose Poems, 1969; Tornado Pratt, 1977; Shoestring (novelization of TV play), 1979; Porridge (novelization of screen play), 1979; Shoestring's Finest House, 1980; County Hall (novelization of TV series), 1981; The Anatomy of Nakedness, 1982; The Doomed Rebellion, 1983. Address: Flat 37, Duncan House, Fellows Road, London NW3, England.

ABRAHAM Claude (Kurt), b. 13 Dec 1931, Lorsch, Germany. Professor of French; Writer; Editor; Translator. m. Marcia Phillips, 3 June 1956, 1 son, 3 daughters. Education: BA, 1953, MA, 1956, University of Cincinnati; PhD, Indiana University, 1959. Appointments: Instructor, 1959-61, Assistant Professor, 1961-64, University of Illinois; Associate Professor, 1964-70, Professor of French, 1970-75, University of Florida at Gainesville; Professor of French, University of California at Davis, 1975-; Guest Lecturer, University of Paris, 1992. Publications: Gaston d'Orléans et sa cour, 1963, revised edition, 1975; The Strangers: The Tragic World of Tristan L'Hermite, 1966; Enfin Malherbe: The Influence of Malherbe on French Lyric Prosody, 1605-1674, 1971; Pierre Corneille, 1972; Théâtre de Tristan L'Hermite (editor with J Schweitzer and J V Baelen), 1975; Le Théâtre Complet de Tristan L'Hermite, 1975; Jean Racine, 1977; Tristan L'Hermite, 1980; Norman Satirists of the Age of Louis XIII, 1983; On the Structure of Molière's Comedies-Ballets, 1984; Actes de Davis (editor), 1988. Contributions to: Scholarly journals. Honours: National Endowment for the Humanities Grant, 1969; Guggenheim Fellowship, 1982-83;

Humboldt Prize, 1982; Knight, French Academie de Plames, 1984; Phi Beta Kappa Teaching Award, 1988. Address: 1604 Westshore Street, Davis, CA 95616, USA.

ABRAHAM Henry J(ulian), b. 25 Aug 1921, Offenbach am Main, Germany. Political Scientist. m. Mildred Kosches, 13 Apr 1954, 2 sons. Education: AB, Kenyon College, 1948; AM, Columbia University, 1949; PhD, University of Pennsylvania, 1952. Appointments: Instructor, 1949-53, Assistant Professor, 1953-57, Associate Professor, 1957-62, Professor, 1962-72, of Political Science, University of Pennsylvania; Henry L and Grace Doherty Memorial Foundation Professor in Government and Foreign Affairs, 1972-78, James Hart Professor in Government and Foreign Affairs, 1978-, University of Virginia; Visiting Lecturer and Visiting Professor at many universities and colleges in the US and abroad. Publications: Compulsory Voting, 1955; Government as Entrepeneur and Social Servant, 1956; Elements of Democratic Government (with J A Corry), 3rd edition, 1958, 4th edition, 1964; Courts and Judges: An Introduction to the Judicial Process, 1959; The Judicial Process: An Introductory Analysis of the Courts of the United States, England, and France, 1962, 6th edition, 1993; The Judiciary: The Supreme Court in the Governmental Process, 1965, 10th edition, 1996; Essentials of American National Government with J C Phillips), 2nd edition, 1966, 3rd edition, 1971; Freedom and the Court: Civil Rights and Liberties in the United States, 1967, 6th edition (with B A Perry), 1994; Justices and Presidents: A Political History of Appointments to the Supreme Court, 1974, 3rd edition, 1992; American Democracy, 1983, 3rd edition (with W J Keefe et al), 1989. Contributions to: Numerous chapters in books, articles, monographs and essays. Honours: Fulbright Lecturer, 1959-60; American Philosophical Society Fellow, 1960-61, 1970-71, 1979; Rockefeller Foundation Resident Scholar, Bellagio, Italy, 1978; Thomas Jefferson Award, University of Virginia, 1983; First Lifetime Achievement Award, Organized Section on Law and Courts, American Political Science Association, 1996; Phi Beta Kappa; Pi Gamma Mu; Pi Sigma Alpha. Memberships: American Judicature Society; American Political Science Association, vice-president, 1980-82; American Society for Legal History; International Political Science Association; National Association of Scholars; Southern Political Science Association; Many editorial boards. Address: 906 Fendall Terrace, Charlottesville, VA 22903, USA.

ABRAHAMS Peter (Henry), b. 19 Mar 1919, Vrededorp, Johannesburg, South Africa. Novelist. m. Daphne Elizabeth Miller, 3 children. Education: Church of England mission schools and colleges. Appointments: Controller, West Indian News, Jamaica, 1955-64; Chairman, Radio Jamaica, Kingston, 1977-80. Publications: Song of the City, 1945; Mine Boy, 1946; The Path of Thunder, 1948; Wild Conquest, 1950; A Wreath for Undomo, 1956; A Night of Their Own, 1965; This Island Now, 1966; The View from Coyaba, 1985; Short stories: Dark Testament, 1942; Verse: A Black Man Speaks of Freedom, 1938. Address: Red Hills, PO Box 20, St Andrew, Jamaica.

ABRAHAMS Roger (David), b. 12 June 1933, Philadelphia, Pennsylvania, USA. Professor of Folklore and Folklife; Writer. Education. BA, Swarthmore College, 1955; MA, Columbia University, 1958; PhD, University of Pennsylvania, 1961. Appointments: Instructor, 1960-63, Assistant Professor, 1963-66, Associate Professor, 1966-69, Professor of English and Anthropology, 1969-79, Chairman, English Department, 1974-79, University of Texas at Austin; Alexander H Kenan Professor of Humanities and Anthropology, Pitzer College and Scripps College, Claremont, California, 1979-85; Professor of Folklore and Folklife, University of Pennsylvania, 1985-; Various visiting professorships. Publications: Deep Down in the Jungle: Negro Narrative Folklore from the Streets of Philadelphia, 1964, revised edition, 1970; Anglo-American Folksong Style (with George W Foss, Jr), 1968; Positively Black, 1970; Deep the Water, Shallow the Shore: Three Essays on Shantying in the West Indies, 1974; Talking Black, 1976; Afro-American Folk Culture: An Annotated Bibliography, 1977; Between the Living and the Dead: Riddles Which Tell Stories, 1980; The Man-of-Words in the West Indies, 1983; Singing the Master: The Emergence of African-American Culture in the Plantation South, 1992. Honours: Guggenheim Fellowship, 1965-66; American Folklore Society Fellow, 1970; National Humanities Institute Fellow, 1976-77; Lifetime Achievement Award, American Folklore Society, 1989. Memberships: American Folklore Society, president, 1978-79; International Society for Folk Narrative Research; Phi Beta Kappa. Address: University of Pennsylvania, Philadelphia, PA 19104, USA.

ABRAMS M(eyer) H(oward), b. 23 July 1912, Long Branch, New Jersey, USA. Writer; Professor of English Emeritus. m. Ruth Gaynes, 1 Sept 1937, 2 daughters. Education: AB, 1934, MA, 1937, PhD, 1940, Harvard University; Graduate Studies, Cambridge University, 1934-35. Appointments: Instructor in English, 1938-42, Research Associate, Psycho-Acoustic Laboratory, 1942-45, Harvard University; Assistant Professor, 1945-47, Associate Professor, 1947-53, Professor of English, 1953-61, Frederic J Whiton Professor, 1961-73, Class of 1916 Professor, 1973-83, Professor Emeritus, 1983-, Cornell University; Visiting Lecturer at several institutions of higher learning. Publications: The Milk of Paradise: The Effects of Opium Visions on the Works of De Quincey, Crabbe, Francis Thompson and Coleridge, 1934, 2nd edition, 1970; The Mirror and the Lamp: Romantic Theory and the Critical Tradition, 1953; A Glossary of Literary Terms, 1957, 6th edition, 1993; The Correspondent Breeze: Essays in English Romanticism, 1984; Doing Things With Texts: Essays in Criticism and Critical Theory, 1989. Editor: The Poetry of Pope, 1954; Literature and Belief, 1958; English Romantic Poets: Modern Essays in Criticism, 1960, 2nd edition, revised, 1975; The Norton Anthology of English Literature, 1962, 6th edition, 1993; Wordsworth: A Collection of Critical Essays, 1972; William Wordsworth: Prelude, 1979. Contributions to: Several volumes. Honours: Rockefeller Foundation Fellowship, 1946-47; Ford Foundation Fellowship, 1953; Fulbright Scholarship, 1954; Guggenheim Fellowships, 1958, 1960; Fellow, Center for Advanced Study in the Behavioral Sciences, 1967; James Russell Lowell Prize, Modern Language Association of America, 1971; Visiting Fellow, All Soul's Colllege, Oxford, 1977; Award in Humanistic Studies, American Academy of Arts and Sciences, 1984; Distinguished Scholar Award, Keats-Shelley Association, 1987; American Academy and Institute of Arts and Letters Award, 1990. Memberships: American Academy of Arts and Sciences; American Association of University Professors; American Philosophical Society; British Academy, corresponding fellow; Modern Language Association of America; Founders' Group, National Humanities Center. Address: 378 Savage Farm Drive, Ithaca, NY 14850, USA.

ABSE Dannie, b. 22 Sept 1923, Cardiff, Glamorgan, Wales. Medical Specialist; Writer. m. Joan Mercer, 1951, 1 son, 2 daughters. Education: St Illtyd's College, Cardiff; University of South Wales and Monmouthshire, Cardiff; King's College, London; Westminster Hospital, London; qualified as physician 1950, MRCS, LRCP; Served in the RAF 1951-54: Squadron Leader. Career: Specialist in charge of chest clinic, Central London Medical Establishment, 1954-; Senior Fellow in Humanities, Princeton University, New Jersey, 1973-74. Publications: Verse: Corgi Modern Poets in Focus 4, (with others, edited by Jeremy Robson), 1972; Funland and Other Poems, 1973; Lunchtime, 1974; Penguin Modern Poets 26, (with D J Enright and Michael Longley), 1975; Collected Poems 1948-76,1977; Way Out in the Centre, 1981, as One-Legged on Ice, Athens, 1981; Recordings: Poets of Wales, Argo, 1972; The Poetry of Dannie Avse, McGraw Hill; Dannie Abse, Canto, 1984; Plays: Gone in January (produced London, 1978), published in Madog, 1981; Various plays for radio; Novels: Ash on a Young Man's Sleeve, 1954; Some Corner of an English Field, 1956; O Jones, O Jones, 1970; Voices in the Gallery, 1986; The Music Lover's Literary Companion, 1988; The Hutchinson Book of Post-War British Poets, 1989; Various other published works. Honours: Foyle Award, 1960; Welsh Arts Council Award for verse, 1971, for play 1980. Membership: President, Poetry Society, 1978-. Literary Agent: Anthony Sheil Associates Ltd, 2-3 Morwell Street, London WC1B 3AR. Address: 85 Hodford Road, London NW11 8NH, England.

ACHEBE (Albert) Chinua(lumogu), b. 16 Nov 1930, Ogidi, Nigeria. Writer; Poet; Editor; Professor. m. Christie Chinwe Okoli, 10 Sept 1961, 2 sons, 2 daughters. Education: University College, Ibadan, 1948-53; BA, London University, 1953; Received training in broadcasting, BBC, London, 1956. Appointments: Producer, 1954-58, Controller, Eastern Region, Enugu, Nigeria, 1958-61, Founder-Director, Voice of Nigeria, 1961-66, Nigerian Broadcasting Corp, Lagos; Senior Research Fellow, 1967-72, Professor of English, 1976-81, Professor Emeritus, 1985-, University of Nigeria, Nsukka; Professor of English, University of Massachusetts, 1972-75; Editor, Okike: A Nigerian Journal of New Writing, 1971-; Director, Okike Arts Centre, Nsukka, 1984-; Founder-Publisher, Uwa Ndi Igbo: A Bilingual Journal of Igbo Life and Arts, 1984-; Pro-Chancellor and Chairman of the Council, Anambra State University of Technology, Enugu, 1986-88; Visiting Professor and Lecturer at universities in Canada and the US; Charles P Stevenson Professor, Bard College, New York, 1990-. Publications: Novels: Things Fall Apart, 1958; No Longer at Ease, 1960; Arrow of God, 1964; A Man of the People, 1966; Anthills of the

Savannah, 1987. Other Fiction: The Sacrificial Egg and Other Stories, 1962; Girls at War (short stories), 1973. Juvenile Fiction: Chike and the River, 1966; How the Leopard Got His Claws (with John Roaganachi), 1972; The Flute, 1978; The Drum, 1978. Poetry: Beware, Soul-Brother and Other Poems, 1971; Christmas in Biafra and Other Poems, 1973. Essays: Morning Yet on Creation Day, 1975; The Trouble With Nigeria, 1983; Hopes and Impediments, 1988. Editor: Don't Let Him Die: An Anthology of Memorial Poems for Christopher Okigbo (with Dubem Okafor), 1978; Aka Weta: An Anthology of Igbo Poetry (with Obiora Udechukwu), 1982; African Short Stories (with C L Innes), 1984; The Heinemann Book of Contemporary African Short Stories (with C L Innes), 1992. Contributions to: New York Review of Books; Transition; Callaloo. Honours: Margaret Wrong Memorial Prize, 1959; Nigerian National Trophy, 1961; Jock Campbell/New Statesman Award, 1965; Commonwealth Poetry Prize, 1972; Neil Gunn International Fellow, Scottish Arts Council, 1975; Lotus Award for Afro-Asian Writers, 1975; Nigerian National Order of Merit 1979; Order of the Federal Republic of Nigeria, 1979; Commonwealth Foundation Senior Visiting Practitioner Award, 1984; Booker Prize Nomination, 1987; 26 honorary doctorates, 1972-96. Memberships: American Academy of Arts and Letters, Honorary Member; Association of Nigerian Authors, Founder and President, 1981-86; Commonwealth Arts Organization; Modern Language Association of America, Honorary Fellow; Fellow, Royal Society of Literature, London, 1981; Writers and Scholars International, London; Writers and Scholars Educational Trust, London. Literary Agent: David Bolt and Associates. Address: Bard College, Annadale on Hudson, NY 12504, USA.

ACHUGAR Hugo J, b. 9 Feb 1944, Uruguay. Editor; Writer. m. Marta Del Huerto Diaz, 23 Jan 1967, 1 son, 3 daughters. Education: Literature, IPA, Uruguay, 1969; PhD, University of Pittsburgh, USA, 1980. Appointments: Editor, Brecha, 1968-69; Editorial Board, Fragmentos, 1976-83; Revista de Estudios Hispanicos, 1985-; Cuadernos de Marcha, 1986-. Publications: Poetry: Las Mariposas Tropicales, 1987; Con Bigote Triste, 1971; El Derrumbe, 1969; Textos Para Decir Maria, 1976; Todo Lo Que Es Solido Se Disuelve En El Aire, 1989; Poesia y Sociedad. Contributor to: Marcha; Casa de Las Americas; Eco; Triquarterly. Honours: Banda Oriental Prize, 1969; National Literary Award, Poetry, 1969; Feria de Libros, 1973. Memberships: ASESUR; PEN; MMLA; LASA. Address: Hispanic Studies, Northwestern University, Evanston, IL 60208, USA.

ACKERMAN Diane, b. 7 Oct 1948, Waukegan, Illinois, USA. Writer. Education: BA, English, Pennsylvania State University, 1970; MFA, Creative Writing 1973, MA, English 1976, PhD, 1978, Cornell University. Appointments: Writer-in-Residence, College of William & Mary 1982, Ohio University 1983, Washington University, 1983; Director, Writers programme, Washington University, St Louis, 1984-86; Visiting Writer, Cooper Union, 1984, New York University 1986, Columbia University 1986, 1987, Cornell University, 1987. Publications: Poetry: Jaguar of Sweet Laughter, 1990; Lady Faustus, 1984; Wife of Light, 1978; The Planets: A Cosmic Pastoral, 1976; Prose: On Extended Wings, 1985, 1987; Twilight of the Tenderfoot, 1980; Reverse Thunder, 1989; A Natural History of the Senses, 1990; The Moon by Whale Light, 1990; A Natural History of Love, 1994. Contributions to: New Yorker; Life; New York Times; Parade; National Geographic. Honours: National Endowment for the Arts Grant, 1986; Peter I B Lavan Award, Academy of American Poets, 1985; Advisory Board, Planetary Society, 1980-; Board of Directors, Associated Writing Programs, 1982-85; Poetry Panel, New York Foundation for the Arts, 1985; Poetry judge, various awards and festivals; Panellist, various bodies. Literary Agent: Morton Janklow, 598 Madison Avenue, New York, NY 10022, USA.

ACKROYD Peter, b. 5 Oct 1949, London, England. Writer. Education: MA, Cambridge University, 1971; Mellon Fellowship, Yale University, 1971-73; Hon D Litt, Exeter University, 1992. Appointments: Literary Editor, Spectator, 1973-77; Lead Reviewer, Times, 1976-. Publications: Dressing Up: Transvestism and Drag: The History of an Obsession, 1979; Ezra Pound and His World, 1981; The Great Fire of London, 1982; The Last Testament of Oscar Wilde, 1983; Hawksmoor, 1985; Chatterton, 1987; Dickens, 1990; Introduction to Dickens, 1991; English Music, 1992; The House of Doctor Dee, 1993; Dan Leno and the Limehouse Golem, 1994; Blake, 1995. Honours: Somerset Maugham Award, 1984; Whitbread Prize for Biography, 1985; Royal Society of Literatures WE Heinemann Award, 1985; Whitbread Prize for Fiction, 1986; Guardian Fiction Award, 1986. Membership: Royal Society of Literature. Literary Agent: Anthony Sheil Associates.

Address: c/o Anthony Sheil Ltd, 43 Doughty Street, London WC1N 2LF, England.

ACKROYD Peter (Runham), b. 15 Sept 1917, Derby, England. Religious Scholar; Professor. m. Evelyn A Nutt, 25 July 1940, 2 sons, 3 daughters. Education: BA, 1938, MA, 1942, PhD, 1945, Cambridge University; BD, 1940, MTh, 1942, New College, London. Appointments: Congregational Minister, Essex, 1943-47, London, 1947-48; Lecturer in Old Testament and Biblical Hebrew, University of Leeds, 1948-52; Lecturer in Divinity, Cambridge University, 1952-61; Hulsean Lecturer, Cambridge, 1960-62; Ordained, Anglican Priest, 1958; Samuel Davidson Professor of Old Testament Studies, 1961-62, Professor Emeritus, Dean of the Faculty of Theology, 1968-69, Fellow, 1969-, University of London, King's College; Visiting Professor and Lecturer at various universities in the UK and abroad. Publications: Freedom in Action, 1951; The People of the Old Testament, 1959; Continuity: A Contribution to the Study of the Old Testament Religious Tradition, 1962; Chronicles I and II: A Contribution to the Study of the Old Testament Religious Tradition, 1962; The Old Testament Tradition 1963; Exile and Restoration: A Study of Hebrew Thought of the Sixth Century, BC, 1968; Israel Under Babylon and Persia, 1970; Chronicles I and II: Ezra, Nehemiah, Ruth, Jonah, I and II Maccabees, 1970; First Book of Samuel, 1971; Second Book of Samuel, 1977; Doors of Perception: Guide to Reading the Psalms, 1983; The Major Prophets: A Commentary on Isaiah, Jeremiah, Lamentations, Ezekiel, Daniel, 1983; Studies in the Religious Tradition of the Old Testament, 1987; The Chronicler in his Age, 1991. Editor: Bible Key Words, 5 volumes, 1961-64; Words and Meanings (with Barnabas Lindars), 1968; Cambridge History of the Bible: From the Beginnings to Jerome (with others), 1970; Studies in Biblical Theology (with others), 1971. Honour: DD, St Andrews University, 1970. Memberships: Commission on Religious Education in Schools, 1967-70; Palestine Exploration Fund, chairman; Society for Old Testament Study, president, 1972, foreign secretary, 1985-89. Address: 155 Northumberalnd Road, North Harrow HA2 7RB, England.

ACLAND Alice. See: WIGNALL Anne.

ACZEL Tamas, b. 16 Dec 1921, Budapest, Hungary. Novelist; Professor of English. m. 5 Aug 1959, 1 son, 1 daughter. Education: BA, University of Budapest, 1948; MA, Eotvos Lorant Universit, Budapest, 1950; DLitt, 1992. Appointments: Editor in Chief; Szikra, 1948-59, Csillag, 1950-52; Secretary, Hungarian Writers Association, 1953-54; Editor, Hungarian Literary Gazette, London, 1957-63; Professor, English, University of Massachusetts. Publications: Novels: In the Shadow of Liberty, 1948; Storm and Sunshine, 1950; The Revolt of the Mind, 1959; The Ice Age, 1966; Underground Russian Poetry, 1973; Illuminations, 1980; The Hunt, 1991; Poetry: Song on the Ship, 1941; Vigilance and Faith, 1948; In Lieu of a Report, 1950; Flames and Ashes, 1955; On the Secret, 1956. Contributions to: Preuves; Encounter; Poesie; Monat; Forum; Massachusetts Review. Honours: Kossuth Prize for Literature, 1949; Stalin Prize for Literature, 1952; National Endowment for the Arts Award, 1977; Fulbright Scholar, Hungary, 1991-92. Memberships: Vice President, PEN in Exile, American Branch. Literary Address: Department of English, University of Massachusetts, Amherst, MA 01003, USA.

ADAIR Ian (Hugh), b. 20 Dec 1942, Scotland. Writer. Appointments: Writer; Partner, Supreme Magic Company, Devon, England; President, Ideas Associated; Former Television Announcer and Presenter, STV, Westward Television. Publications: Adair's Ideas, 1958; Magic with Doves, 1958; Dove Magic, Parts 1 and 2, 1959; Dove Magic Finale, 1960; Ideen, 1960; Television Dove Magic, 1961; Television Card Manipulations, 1962; Television Puppet Magic, 1963; Doves in Magic, 1964; Doves from Silks, 1964; New Doves from Silks, 1964; Dove Classics, 1964; More Modern Dove Classics, 1964; Further Dove Classics, 1964; Classical Dove Secrets, 1964; Diary of a Dove Worker, 1964; Magic on the Wing, 1965; Balloon-o-Dove, 1965; Spotlite on Doves, 1965; Watch the Birdie, 1965; Dove Dexterity, 1965; Rainbow Dove Routines, 1965; Heads Off!, 1965; Tricks and Stunts with a Rubber Dove, 1965; Television Dove Steals, 1965; A La Zombie, 1966; Pot Pourri, 1966; Magical Menu, 3 volumes, 1967; Encyclopedia of Dove Magic, vols 1 and 2, 1968, vol 3, 1973, vol 4, 1977, vol 5, 1980; Magic with Latex Budgies, 1969; Paddle Antics, 1969; Conjuring as a Craft, 1970; Magic Step by Step, 1970; Party Planning and Entertainment, 1972; Oceans of Notions, 1973; Papercraft-Step by Step, 1975; Card Tricks, 1975; Glove Puppetry, 1975; The Know How Book of Jokes and Tricks, 1977; Complete Party Planner, 1978; Complete Guide to Conjuring, 1978; Magic, 1979;

Complete Guide to Card Conjuring, 1980; Swindles: The Cheating Game, 1980. Address: 20 Ashley Terrace, Bideford, Devon, England.

ADAIR Jack. See: **PAVEY Don.**

ADAIR James Radford, b. 2 Feb 1923, Asheville, North Carolina, USA. Writer. Appointments: Editor, Power for Living, Free Way, Teen Power and Counselor weekly churchpapers, 1949-77; Senior Editor, Victor Books Division, Scripture Press Publications Inc, Wheaton, 1970-. Publications: Saints Alive, 1951; Editor, God's Power Within, 1961; We Found Our Way (edited with T Miller), 1964; Editor, Teen with a Future, 1965; Editor, God's Power to Triumph, 1965; The Old Lighthouse, 1966; The Man from Steamhouse, 1967, 1988; Editor, Tom Skinner Top Man of the Lords and Other Stories, 1967; M R DeHaan: The Man and His Ministry, 1969; Editor, Hooked on Jesus, 1971; Escape from Darkness (edited with Ted Miller), 1982; Surgeon on Safari (autobiography, Paul J Jorden MD), 1976, 1985; A Greater Strength (autobiography, Paul Anderson; co-authored with Jerry Jenkins), 1975, 1990; 101 Days in the Gospels, Oswald Chambers, compiled with Harry Verploegh, 1992; 101 Days in the Epistles with Oswald Chambers, compiled with Harry Verploegh, 1994. Address: 703 Webster Avenue, Wheaton, IL 60187, USA.

ADAM SMITH Patricia (Patsy) Jean, b. 31 May 1926, Gippsland, Victoria, Australia. Author. Appointments: Adult Education Officer, Hobart, Tasmania, 1960-66; Manuscripts Field Officer, State Library of Victoria, 1970-82; President, Federal Fellowship of Australian Writers, 1973-75. Publications: Hear the Train Blow, 1963; Moon Bird People, 1964; There Was a Ship, 1965; Tiger Country, 1966; The Rails Go Westward, 1967; Folklore of Australian Railmen, 1969; No Tribesmen, 1970; Tasmania Sketchbook, 1972; Launceston Sketchbook, 1972; Port Arthur Sketchbook, 1973; Carcoo Salute, 1973; The Desert Railway, 1974; Romance of Australian Railways, 1974; The Anzacs, 1978; Outback Heroes, 1981; The Shearers, 1982; Australian Women at War, 1984; Heart of Exile, 1986; Prisoner of War from Gallipoli to Korea, 1992; Goodbye Girlie, 1994. Honour: Officer of the Order of the British Empire, 1980; Triennial Award; Order of Australia. Address: 47 Hawksburn Road, South Yarra, Victoria 3141, Australia.

ADAMS Alice, b. 14 Aug 1926, Fredericksburg, Virginia, USA. Author. m. 1946, div 1958, 1 son. Education: BA, Radcliffe College, 1945. Publications: Careless Love (in UK as The Fall of Daisy Duke), 1966; Families and Survivors, 1975; Listening to Billie, 1978; Beautiful Girl (short stories), 1979; Tich Rewards, 1980; Superior Women, 1984; Return Trips, 1985; Second Chances, 1988; After You're Gone, 1989; Caroline's Daughters, 1991; Mexico, 1991; Almost Perfect, 1993. Contributions to: New Yorker; Atlantic Monthly; Redbook; McCalls; Paris Review. Honour: American Academy of Arts and Letters Award, 1992. Address: 2661 Clay Street, San Francisco, CA 94115, USA.

ADAMS Chuck. See: **TUBB E(dwin) C(harles).**

ADAMS Clifton, (Jonathon Gant, Matt Kinkaid, Clay Randall), b. 1 Dec 1919, Commanche, Oklahoma, USA. Author; Musician; Freelance Writer. Publications: Western Novels: The Desperado, 1950; A Noose for the Desperado, 1951; Six Gun Boss (as Clay Randall), 1952; The Colonel's Lady, 1952; When Oil Ran Red (as Clay Randall), 1953; Two Gun Law, 1954; Gambling Man, 1955; Law of the Trigger, 1956; Outlaw's Son, 1957; Boomer (as Clay Randall), 1957; Killer in Town, 1959; Stranger in Town, 1960; The Legend of Lonnie Hall, 1960; Day of the Gun, 1962; Reckless Men, 1962; The Moonlight War, 1963; The Dangerous Days of Kiowa Jones, 1963; The Oceola Kid (as Clay Randall), 1963; Hardcase for Hire (as Clay Randall), 1963; Amos Flagg Series, 6 vols (as Clay Randall), 1963-69; Doomsday Creek, 1964; The Hottest Fourth of July in the History of Hangtree County, 1964 (in UK as The Hottest Fourth of July, 1965); The Grabhorn Bounty, 1965; Shorty, 1966; A Partnership with Death, 1967; The Most Dangerous Profession, 1967; Dude Sheriff, 1969; Tragg's Choice, 1969; The Last Days of Wolf Garnett, 1970 (in UK as Outlaw Destiny, 1972); Biscuit-Shooter, 1971; Rogue Cowboy, 1971; The Badge and Harry Cole, 1972 (in UK as Lawman's Badge, 1973); Concannon, 1972; Hard Times and Arnie Smith, 1972; Once an Outlaw, 1973; The Hard Time Bunch, 1973; Hasle and the Medicine Man, 1973; Crime Novels: Whom Gods Destroy, 1953; Hardcase (as Matt Kinkaid), 1953; Death's Sweet Song, 1955; The Race of Giants (as Matt Kinkaid), 1956; Never Say No to a Killer (as Jonathon Gant), 1956; The Very Wicked, 1960, The Long Vendetta (as Jonathon Gant), 1963. Address:

c/o Ace Books, Berkeley Publishing Group, 200 Madison Avenue, New York, NY 10016, USA.

ADAMS Daniel. See: **NICOLE Christopher Robin.**

ADAMS Deborah, b. 22 Jan 1956, Tennessee, USA. Writer. Publications: Poetry: Propriety, 1976; Looking for Heroes, 1984; Mystery: All the Great Pretenders, 1992; All the Crazy Winters, 1992; All the Dark Disguises, 1993; All the Hungry Mothers, 1994. Memberships: Sisters in Crime; MWA; Appalachian Writers' Association. Address: Rt 4, Box 664, Waverly, TN 37185, USA.

ADAMS Douglas (Noel), b. 11 March 1952, Writer; Producer. Education: BA, MA, St Johns College, Cambridge. Appointments: Radio Producer, BBC, London, 1978; Script Editor, Doctor Who, BBC TV, 1978-80. Publications: The Hitch Hiker's Guide to the Galaxy, 1978; The Restaurant at the End of the Universe, 1980; The Meaning of Life, 1984; So Long, And Thanks for All the Fish, 1984; The Utterly Itterly Merry, 1986; Comic Relief Christmas Book, 1986; The Long Dark Tea Time of the Soul, 1988; Last Chance to See, 1990; Mostly Harmless, 1991. Address: c/o Ed Victor Ltd, 6 Bayley Street, London WC1B 3HB, England.

ADAMS Harold, b. 20 Feb 1923, Clark, South Dakota, USA. Executive. m. Betty E Skogsberg, 17 Sept 1959, div Apr 1965, 1 daughter. Education: BA, University of Minnesota, 1950. Publications: Murder, 1981; Paint the Town Red, 1982; The Missing Moon, 1983; The Naked Liar, 1985; The Fourth Widow, 1986; When Rich Men Die, 1987; The Barbed Wire Noose, 1987; The Man Who Met the Train, 1988; The Man Who Missed The Party, 1989; The Man Who Was Taller Than God, 1992; A Perfectly Proper Murder, 1993; A Way with Widows, 1994; The Ditched Blonde, 1995. Honours: Minnesota Book Award, Mystery and Detective, 1993; Shamus Award, Best Private Eye Novel, 1992. Memberships: Author's Guild; Mystery Writers of America. Literary Agent: Ivy Fischer Stone. Address: 12916 Greenwood Road, Minnetonka, MN 55343, USA.

ADAMS Hazard, b. 15 Feb 1926, Cleveland, Ohio, USA. University Professor. m. 17 Sept 1949, 2 sons. Education: BA, Princeton University, 1948; MA, 1949, PhD, 1953, University of Washington. Appointments: Instructor, Cornell University, 1952-56; Assistant Professor, University of Texas, 1956-59; Associate Professor to Professor, Michigan State University, 1959-64; Fulbright Lecturer, Trinity College, Dublin, 1961-62; Professor and Founding Chair of English, University of California, Irvine, 1964-77; Byron W and Alice L Lockwood Professor of Humanities, University of Washington, 1977-; Professor of English, University of California, Irvine, 1990-94. Publications: Poems by Robert Simeon Adams, 1952; Blake and Yeats: The Contrary Vision, 1955; William Blake - A Reading, 1963; The Contexts of Poetry, 1963; Poetry: An Introductory Anthology, 1968; Fiction as Process, 1968; The Horses of Instruction, novel, 1968; The Interests of Criticism, 1969; The Truth About Dragons, novel, 1971; Critical Theory Since Plato, 1972, revised edition, 1992; Lady Gregory, 1973; Philosophy of the Literary Symbolic, 1983; The Book of Yeats's Poems, 1990; Antithetical Essays on Literary Criticism and Liberal Education, 1990; Critical Essays on William Blake. Contributions to: Numerous poetry, scholarly and critical journals, 1954-. Membership: American Conference for Irish Studies. Address: 3930 North East 157th Place, Seattle, WA 98155, USA.

ADAMS James MacGregor David, b. 22 Apr 1951, Newcastle, England. Journalist; Author. m. Rene Thatcher Riley, 1 July 1990, 1 daughter. Education: Harrow, 1964-69; Neuchâtel University, 1979-71. Publications: The Unnatural Alliance, 1984; The Financing of Terror, 1986; Secret Armies, 1988; Ambush (the War Between the SAS and the IRA) with Robin, Morgan and Anthony Bambridge, 1988; Merchants of Death, 1990; The Final Terror, 1991; Bull's Eye, 1992; Taking the Tunnel, 1993. Contributions to: Sunday Times; Washington Post; Los Angeles Times; Atlantic. Literary Agent: Janklow Nesbit. Address: c/o The Sunday Times, 1 Pennington Street, London E1 9XW, England.

ADAMS Joanna Z. See: **KOCH Joanne Barbara.**

ADAMS Perseus, b. 11 Mar 1933, Cape Town, South Africa. Writer; Journalist; Poet; Teacher. Education: BA, University of Cape Town, 1952; Cert Ed, 1961. Appointments: Journalist; English Teacher. Publications: The Land at My Door, 1965; Grass for the Unicorn, 1975; Cries and Silences, 1996. Contributions to: Numerous, mostly to Contrast, Cape Town, South Africa. Honours: South Africa State Poetry Prize, 1963; Festival of Rhodesia Prize, 1970; Keats Memorial International Prize, 1971; Bridport Arts Festival Prize, 1984; Co-Winner, Writing Section, Bard of the Year, 1993; Nominated for the Forward Prize for the Outstanding Poem in the UK, for Eros Desperatus, 1994-95. Address: 21 Mapesbury Road, Kilburn, London NW2, England.

ADAMS Richard George, b. 9 May 1920, Newbury, Berkshire, England. Author. m. Barbara Elizabeth Acland, 26 Sept 1949, 2 daughters. Education: MA, Worcester College, Oxford, 1948. Publications: Watership Down, 1972; Shardik, 1974; Nature Through the Seasons (co-author Max Hooper), 1975; The Tyger Voyage, narrative poem, 1976; The Plague Dogs, 1977; The Ship's Cat, 1977; Nature Day & Night, 1978; The Iron Wolf, 1980; The Girl in a Swing, 1980; Voyage Through the Antarctic, (with Ronald Lockley), 1982; Maia, 1984; The Bureaucats, 1985; A Nature Diary, 1985; Occasional Poets, anthology, 1986; The Legend of Te Tuna, narrative poem, 1986; Traveller, 1988; The Day Gone By, autobiography, 1990. Contributions to: Numerous Journals and Magazines. Honours: Carnegie Medal, 1972; Guardian Award of Childrens Literature, 1972; Medal, CA Young Readers Association, 1977. Memberships: Royal Society of Literature; RSPCA. Literary Agent: David Higham Associates Ltd. Address: Benwells, 26 Church Street, Whitchurch, Hampshire RG28 7AR, England.

ADAMSON Robert Harry, b. 17 May 1943, Sydney, New South Wales, Australia. Poet; Publisher. m. (1) Cheryl Adamson, 1973, (2) Juno Adamson, 19 Feb 1989, 1 son. Appointments: Editorial positions, New Poetry Magazine, Sydney, 1968-77; Editor and Director, Prism Books, Sydney, 1970-77; Founding Editor and Director (with Dorothy Hewett), Big Smoke Books, Sydney, 1979-. Publications: Canticles on the Skin, 1970; The Rumour, 1971; Swamp Riddles, 1973; Cross the Border, 1977; Selected Poems, 1977; The Law at Heart's Desire, 1982; The Clean Dark, 1989; Wards of the State, 1991. Contributions to: Various periodicals. Honours: Grace Levin Prize for Poetry, 1977; Kenneth Slessor Award, 1990; Turnbull-Fox Philips Poetry Prize, 1990; C J Dennis Prize for Poetry, 1990. Memberships: Australian Society of Authors; Poetry Society of Australia, president, 1970-80. Address: PO Box 59, Brooklyn, New South Wales 2083, Australia.

ADCOCK Fleur, b. 1934, New Zealand. Poet. Publications: The Eye of the Hurricane, 1964; Tigers, 1967; High Tide in the Garden, 1971; The Scenic Route, 1974; The Inner Harbour, 1979; Below Loughrigg, 1979; Selected Poems, 1983; The Virgin and the Nightingale, 1983; The Incident Book, 1986; Time Zones, 1991; Editor: The Oxford Book of Contemporary New Zealand Poetry, 1982; The Faber Book of 20th Century Women's Poetry, 1987. Translator and Editor: Hugh Primas and the Archpoet, 1994. Honour: Order of the British Empire, 1996. Membership: Fellow, Royal Society of Literature. Address: 14 Lincoln Road, London N2 9DL, England.

ADDINGTON Larry H(olbrook), b. 16 Nov 1932, Charlotte, North Carolina, USA. Professor of History Emeritus; Writer. Education: BA, 1955, MA, 1956, University of North Carolina at Chapel Hill; PhD, Duke University, 1962. Appointments: Assistant Professor, San Jose State College, 1962-64; Assistant Professor, 1964-66, Associate Professor, 1966-70, Professor, 1970-94, Professor Emeritus, 1994-, of History, The Citadel; Visiting Professor, Duke University, 1976-77. Publications: From Moltke to Hitler: The Evolution of German Military Doctrine, 1865-1939, 1966; Firepower and Manuever: The European Inheritance in the Two World Wars, 1967; Firepower and Manuever: Historical Case Studies, 1969; The Blitzkrieg Era and the German General Staff, 1865-1941, 1971; The Patterns of War Since the Eighteenth Century, 1984, revised edition, 1994; The Patterns of War Through the Eighteenth Century, 1990. Contributions to: Encyclopedias, books and scholarly journals. Honour: AMI Award for Best Seminal Work, 1984. Memberships: American Historical Association; Society for Military History; Phi Beta Kappa. Address: 1341 New Castle Street, Charleston, SC 29407, USA.

ADELBERG Doris. See: **ORGEL Doris.**

ADELI Hojjat, b. 3 June 1950, Southern Shore of Caspian Sea, Iran. Engineering Educator; Author. m. Nahid Dadmehr, Feb 1979, 2 sons, 2 daughters. Education: BS, MS, University of Tehran, 1973; PhD, Stanford University, USA, 1976. Appointments: Founder, Editor-in-Chief, International Journal of Microcomputers in Civil Engineering, 1986-; Editor-in-Chief, Heuristics, The Journal of

Knowledge Engineering, 1991-93; Founder, Editor-in-Chief, Integrated Computer-Aided Engineering, 1993-; Plenary Lecturer, international conferences in Italy, Mexico, Japan, China, USA, Canada, Portugal, Germany, Morocco, Singapore. Publications: Interactive Microcomputer-Aided Structural Design, 1988; Expert Systems for Structural Design (with K V Balasubramanyam), 1988; Parallel Processing in Structural Engineering (with O Kamal), 1993; Machine Learning - Neural Networks, Genetic Algorithms, and Fuzzy Systems (with S L Hung), 1995; Editor, 10 books. Contributions to: Over 250 articles to 40 research journals. Honours: Numerous awards including: Lichtenstein Award for Faculty Excellence, 1990; Lumely Research Award, Ohio State University, 1994. Memberships: Fellow, World Literary Academy; Editorial Board, 22 journals. Address: 1540 Picardae Court, Powell, OH 43065, USA.

ADHIKARI Santos Kumar, b. 24 Nov 1923, India. Writer; Author; Retired College Principal. m. Sadhona. Education: Calcutta University; Indian Institute of Bankers. Publications: Clouds on the Horizon, 1960; Novels: Rakta Kamal, 1967; Nirjan Sikhar, 1971; Banking Law and Practice; Lending Banker; Paari Collection of Poems, 1986; Vidyasager and the New National Consciousness, 1990; Netaji Subhas Chandra, 1990; Vidyasager - Educator, Reformer and Humanist, 1995. Author of over 24 titles including anthologies, collections of poems, novels, short stories and biographies. Contributions to: Major Journals, Calcutta; All Indian Radio. Honours: PRASAD Award, 1986; Invited, and delivered, Vidyasagar Lectures, University of Calcutta, 1979; Invitation, Bengal Studies Conference, University of Chicago, USA, 1990. Memberships: Vidyasagar Research Centre; Asiatic Society; National Council of Akhil Bharat Bhasha Sahitya Sammelan. Address: Vidyasagar Research Centre, 81 Raja Basanta Roy Road, Calcutta 700 029, India.

ADICKES Sandra, b. 14 July 1933. Professor of English; Writer. Education: BA, Douglass College, 1954; MA, Hunter College, 1964; PhD, New York University, 1977. Publications: The Social Quest, 1991; Legends of Good Women, 1992; Others: To Be Young Was Very Heaven: Women in New York Before World War I, forthcoming. Contributions to: The Legacy of the Mississippi Freedom Schools - Radical Teacher; Mind Among the Spindles, Women's Studies. Address: 579 West 7th Street, Winona, MN 55987, USA.

ADISA Opal Palmer, b. 6 Nov 1954, Kingston, Jamaica. Teacher. m. V K Tarik Farrar, 12 Aug 1989, 1 son, 2 daughters. Education: BA, Hunter College, City University of New York, 1975; MA, English, San Francisco State University, 1981; MA, Drama, 1986; PhD, University of California, 1992. Appointments: Head Teacher, Booker T Washington Child Development Center, San Francisco, 1978-79; Teacher, Counselor, Lucinda Weeks Center, San Francisco, 1979-81; Instructor, City College of San Francisco, 1980-84; Lecturer, San Francisco State University, 1981-87; Writer, Development Studies Center, San Ramon, California, 1991; Lecturer, University of California, Berkeley, 1992; Associate Professor and Chair of Ethnic Studies, California College of Arts and Crafts, 1993-. Publications: Tamarind and Other Mango Women; Traveling Women; Bake Face and Other Guava Stories; Pina: The Many Eyed Fruit. Contributions to: Frontiers; Berkeley Poetry Review. Honours: Master Folk Artist; Pushcart Prize; Affirmative Action Dissertation Year Fellowship; Feminist Institute and Gender Study Research Grant; PEN Oakland/Josephine Miles Award. Memberships: Modern Language Association; Society for the Study of Multi Ethnic Literature of the US; Diasponic Representative of CAFRA. Address: PO Box 10625, Oakland, CA 94610, USA.

ADKINS Arthur William Hope, b. 17 Oct 1929, Leicester, England. Professor; Writer. Education: BA, 1952, MA, 1955, PhD, 1957, Merton College, Oxford. Appointments: Assistant, Humanity Department, University of Glasgow, 1954-56; Lecturer in Greek, Bedford College, University of London, 1956-61; Fellow, Classical Languages and Literature, Exeter College, Oxford, 1961-65; Professor of Classics, University of Reading, 1966-74; Visiting Senior Fellow, Society for the Humanities, Cornell University, Ithaca, New York, 1969-70; Edward Olson Professor, Depts of Classical Languages, Literature, Philosophy and Early Christian Literature; Chairman, Committee on Ancient Mediterranean World, University of Chicago, 1974-82. Publications: Merit and Responsibility: A Study in Greek Values, 1960; From the Many to the One: A Study of Personality and Views of Human Nature in the Context of Ancient Greek Society, Values and Beliefs, 1970; Moral Values and Political Behaviour in Ancient Greece, 1972; Polupragmosune and Minding One's Own Business: A Study in Greek Social and Political Values, 1976; Poetic

Craft in the Early Greek Elegists, 1985; Joint Editor, University of Chicago, Readings in Western Civilization, Vol I, The Greek Polis. Memberships: American Philological Association; Classical Association of Great Britain; Society, Promotion of Hellenic Studies; American Philosophical Association. Address: Department of Classics, University of Chicago, 1050 East 59th Street, Chicago, IL 60637, USA.

ADLER C(arole) S(chwerdtfeger), b. 23 Feb 1932, Long Island, New York, USA. Children's Book Author. m. Arnold R Adler, 22 June 1952, 3 sons. Education: BA, Hunter College, 1952; MS, Russell Sage College, 1964. Publications: The Magic of the Glits, 1979; The Silver Coach, 1979; In Our House Scott is My Brother, 1980; The Cat That Was Left Behind, 1981; Down By the River, 1981; Shelter on Blue Barns Road, 1981; Footsteps on the Stairs, 1982; The Evidence That Wasn't There, 1982; The Once in a While Hero, 1982; Some Other Summer, 1982; The Shell Lady's Daughter, 1983; Get Lost Little Brother, 1983; Roadside Valentine, 1983; Shadows on Little Reef Bay, 1984; Fly Free, 1984; Binding Ties, 1985; With Westie and the Tin Man, 1985; Good-Bye Pink Pig, 1985; Split Sisters, 1986; Kiss the Clown, 1986; Carly's Buck, 1987; Always and Forever Friends, 1988; If You Need Me, 1988; Eddie's Blue Winged Dragon, 1988; One Sister Too Many, 1989; The Lump in the Middle, 1989; Help Pink Pig!, 1990; Ghost Brother, 1990; Mismatched Summer, 1991; A Tribe for Lexi, 1991; Tuna Fish Thanksgiving, 1992; Daddy's Climbing Tree, 1993; Willie, the Frog Prince, 1994; That Horse Whiskey, 1994; Youn Hee and Me, 1995; Court Yard Cat, 1995; What's to be Scared of, Suki?, 1996; More Than a Horse, 1997; Her Blue Straw Hat, 1997. Honours: William Allen White Award, 1980; Golden Kite Award, 1980; American Library Association Best Young Adult Book, 1984; Children's Book Award, Child Study Committee, 1986; IRA Children's Selections, 1987, 1991. Memberships: SCBW, Authors Guild. Address: 7041 N Cathedral Rock Place, Tucson, AZ 85718, USA.

ADLER Margot Susanna, b. 16 Apr 1946, Little Rock, Arkansas, USA. Journalist; Radio Producer; Talk Show Host; New York Bureau Chief -Correspondent, National Public Radio. Education: BA, University of California, Berkeley, 1968; MS, Columbia School of Journalism, 1970; Nieman Fellow, Harvard University, 1982. Publication: Drawing Down the Moon: Witches, Druids, Goddess-Worshippers & Other Pagans in America Today, 1979, revised edition, 1986; A 1960's Memoir: Heretics Heart. Memberships: Authors Guild; American Federation of Radio and Television Artists. Literary Agent: Jane Rotrosen. Address: 333 Central Park West, New York, NY 10025, USA.

ADLER Mortimer J(erome), b. 28 Dec 1902, New York, New York, USA. Philosopher; Author. m. (1) Helen Leavenworth Boynton, 2 May 1927, div 1961, 2 sons, (2) Caroline Sage Pring, 22 Feb 1963, 2 sons. Education: PhD, Columbia University, 1928; BA, Columbia College, 1983. Appointments: Instructor, Columbia University, 1923-30; Assistant Director, People's Institute, New York City, 1927-29; Associate Professor of the Philosophy of Law, 1930-42, Professor, 1942-52, University of Chicago; Visiting Lecturer, 1937-85, Visting Lecturer Emeritus, 1985-, St John's College, Maryland; Director, Institute for Philosophical Research, Chicago, 1952-95; President, San Francisco Productions Inc, 1954-94; Chairman, Board of Editors, 1974-95, Chairman Emeritus, 1995-, Encyclopaedia Britannica; Co-Founder and Honorary Chairman, Center for the Study of Great Ideas, 1990-. Publications: Dialectic, 1927; Crime, Law and Social Science (with Jerome Michael), 1933; Diagrammatics (with Maude Phelps Hutchins), 1932; Art and Prudence: A Study in Practical Philosophy, 1937; revised edition as Poetry and Politics, 1965; What Man Has Made of Man, 1938; How to Read a Book: The Art of Getting a Liberal Education (with Charles Van Doren), 1940; A Dialectic of Morals, 1941; The Capitalist Manifesto (with Louis Kelso), 1958; The New Capitalists, 1961; The Revolution in Education (with Milton Mayer), 1958; The Idea of Freedom, 2 volumes, 1958, 1961; Great Ideas from the Great Books, 1961; The Conditions of Philosophy, 1965; The Difference of Man and the Difference It Makes, 1967; The Time of Our Lives, 1970; The Common Sense of Politics, 1971; The American Testament (with William Gorman), 1975; Some Questions About Language: A Theory of Human Discourse, 1976; Philosopher at Large: An Intellectual Autobiography, 1977; Reforming Education, 1977; Aristotle for Everybody, 1978; How to Think About God, 1980; Six Great Ideas, 1981; The Angels and Us, 1982; The Paideia Proposal, 1982; Paidia Program, 1984; A Vision of the Future, 1984; Ten Philosophical Mistakes, 1985; A Guidebook to Learning: For the Lifelong Pursuit of Wisdom, 1986; We Hold These Truths: Understanding the Ideas and Ideals of the Constitution, 1987;

Reforming Education: The Opening of the American Mind, 1989; Intellect: Mind Over Matter, 1990; Truth in Religion, 1990; Haves Without Have-Nots, 1991; Desires Right and Wrong, 1991; A Second Look at the Rearview Mirror, 1992; The Great Ideas: A Lexicon of Western Thought, 1992; The Four Dimensions of Philosophy, 1993; Art, the Arts and the Great Ideas, 1994; Adler's Philosophical Dictionary, 1995. Editor-in-Chief: Great Books of the Western World, 2nd edition, 1990 et seq. Memberships; American Catholic Philosophers Association; American Maritain Association; International Listening Association. Address: Institute for Philosophical Research, 310 S Michigan Avenue, 7th Floor, Chicago, IL 60604, USA.

ADLER Renata, b. 19 Oct 1938, Milan, Italy. Writer. Education: AB, Bryn Mawr College, 1959; Dd'ES, Sorbonne, Paris, 1961; MA, Harvard University, 1962; Law Degree, Yale University. Appointments: Writer-Reporter, New Yorker magazine, 1962-68, 1970-82; Fellow, Trubull College, Yale University, 1969-72; Associate Professor of Theatre and Cinema, Hunter College of the City University of New York, 1972-73. Publications: Toward a Radical Middle: Fourteen Pieces of Reporting and Criticism, 1969; A Year in the Dark: Journal of a Film Critic, 1968-69, 1970; Speedboat (novel), 1976; Pitch Dark (novel), 1983; Reckless Disregard: Westmoreland v. CBS et al: Sharon v. Time, 1986. Contributions to: Many periodicals. Honours: Guggenheim Fellowship, 1973-74; First Prize, O Henry Short Story Awards, 1974; American Academy and Institute of Arts and Letters Award, 1976; Ernest Hemingway Prize, 1976. Memberships: American Academy and Institute of Arts and Letters; PEN. Address: 178 East 64th Street, New York, NY 10021, USA.

ADLER Warren, b. 16 Dec 1927, New York, USA. Author. m. Sonia Kline, 5 May 1951, 3 sons. Education: BA, New York University, 1947; New School for Social Research, New York City. Appointments: Editor, Queens Pose, Forest Hills, New York; President, advertising and public relations agency, Washington, DC, 1959-78. Publications: Options, 1974; Banquet Before Dawn, 1976; The Henderson Equation, 1976; Trans-Siberian Express, 1977; The Sunset Gang, 1978; The Casanova Embrace, 1978; Blood Ties, 1979; Natural Enemies, 1980; The War of the Roses, 1981; American Quartet, 1982; American Sextet, 1983; Random Hearts, 1984; Twilight Child, 1989; Immaculate Deception, 1991; Senator Love, 1991; Private Lies, 1992; The Witch of Watergate, 1992; The Ties That Bind, 1994. Memberships: Authors Guild; Authors League of America; Mystery Writers of America. Address: 45 Hucklberry Drive, Jackson Hole, WY 83001, USA.

ADNAN Etel, b. 24 Feb 1925, Beirut, Lebanon. Poet; Writer; Painter; Tapestry Designer. Education: Sorbonne, University of Paris; University of California, Berkeley; Harvard University. Appointments: Teacher, Philosophy of Art and Humanities, Dominican College, San Rafael, California, 1958-72; Cultural Editor, Al-Safa newspaper, Lebanon, 1972-79; Paintings exhibited around the world. Publications: Poetry: Moonshots, 1966; Five Senses for One Death, 1971; From A to Z, 1982; The Indian Never Had a Horse and Other Poems, 1985; The Arab Apocalypse, 1989; The Spring Flowers Own and the Manifestations of the Voyage, 1990. Novel: Sitt Marie-Rose, 1982. Other: Journey to Mount Tamalpais, 1986; Of Cities and Women, 1993; Paris, When It's Naked, 1993. Contributions to: Poems and short stories in many publications. Honour: France-Pays-Arabes Prize, 1978. Membership: Poetry Center, San Francisco. Address: 35 Marie Street, Sausalito, CA 94965, USA.

ADOFF Arnold, b. 16 July 1935, New York, New York, USA. Poet; Writer; Literary Agent. m. Virginia Hamilton, 19 Mar 1960, 2 children. Education: BA, City College of New York, 1956; Columbia University, 1956-58; New School for Social Research Poetry Workshops, New York City, 1965-67. Appointments: Teacher, New York City Public Schools, 1957-69; Literary Agent, Yellow Springs, Ohio, 1977-; Distinguished Visiting Professor, Queens College, 1986-87; Guest Lecturer in many US venues. Publications: Poetry: Black Is Brown Is Tan, 1973; Make a Circle Keep Us In: Poems for a Good Day, 1975; Big Sister Tells Me That I'm Black, 1976; Tornado!: Poems, 1977; Under the Early Morning Trees, 1978; Where Wild Willie, 1978; Eats: Poems, 1979; I Am the Running Girl, 1979; Friend Dog, 1980; OUTside INside Poems, 1981; Today We Are Brother and Sister, 1981; Birds, 1982; All the Colors of the Race, 1982; The Cabbages Are Chasing the Rabbits, 1985; Sports Pages, 1986; Flamboyan, 1988; Greens, 1988; Chocolate Dreams, 1989; Hard to Be Six, 1990; In for Winter, Out for Spring, 1991. Other: Malcolm X (biography), 1970; MA nDA LA, picture book, 1971. Editor: I Am the Darker Brother: An Anthology of Modern Poems by Negro Americans,

1968; Black on Black: Comentaries by Negro Americans, 1968; City in All Directions: An Anthology of Modern Poems by Black Americans, 1970; Brothers and Sisters: Modern Stories by Black Americans, 1970; It Is the Poem Singing into Your Eyes: An Anthology of New Young Poets, 1971; The Poetry of Black America: An Anthology of the 20th Century, 1973; My Black Me: A Beginning Book of Black Poetry, 1974; Celebrations: A New Anthology of Black American Poetry, 1978. Contributions to: Articles and reviews in periodicals. Honours: Children's Book of the Year Citations, Child Study Association of America, 1968, 1969, 1986; American Library Association Notable Book Awards, 1968, 1970, 1971, 1972, 1979; Best Children's Book Citations, School Library Journal, 1971, 1973; Notable Children's Trade Book Citation, Children's Book Council-National Council for Social Studies, 1974; Jane Addams Peace Association Special Certificate, 1983; Children's Choice Citation, International Reading Association-Children's Book Council, 1985; National Council of Teachers of English Poetry Award, 1988. Address: Arnold Adoff Agency, PO Box 293, Yellow Springs, OH 45387, USA.

ADORJAN Carol (Madden), (Kate Kenyon), b. 17 Aug 1934, Chicago, Illinois, USA. Writer; Teacher. m. William W Adorjan, 17 Aug 1957, 2 sons, 2 daughters. Education: BA, English Literature, Magna Cum Laude, Mundelein College, 1956. Appointments: Fellow, Midwest Playwrights Lab, 1977; Writer in Residence, Illinois Arts Council, 1981; Writer in Residence, National Radio Theatre, 1980-81. Publications: Someone I Know, 1968; The Cat Sitter Mystery, 1972; Eighth Grade to the Rescue (as Kate Kenyon), 1987; A Little Princess (abridgment), 1987; Those Crazy Eighth Grade Pictures (as Kate Kenyon), 1987; WKID: Easy Radio Plays (co-author): Yupi Rasovsky, 1988; The Copy Cat Mystery, 1990; That's What Friends Are For, 1990; Radio and Stage Plays: Julian Theater, BBC, National Radio Theatre, etc. Contributions to: Redbook; Woman's Day; North American Review; Denver Quarterly; Four Quarters; Yankee. Honours: Josephine Lusk Fiction Award, Munderlein College, 1955; Earplay, 1972; Illinois Arts Council Completion Grant, 1977-78; Dubuque Fine Arts Society National One-Act Playwriting competition, 1978; Ohio State Award, 1980. Memberships: Dramatists Guild; Society of Midland Authors; Poets and Writers; Children's Reading Roundtable. Literary Agent: Denise Marcil; Shelly Power (Abroad). Address: 1667 Winnetka Road, Glenview, IL 60025, USA.

ADRIAN Frances. See: POLLAND Madelaine Angela.

ADUNIS (Ali Ahmad Said), b. 1930, Syria. Poet. Education: University of Damascus, 1950-54; PhD, St Joseph University Beirut, 1973. Appointments: Professor, Lebanese University, Beirut, 1971-85. Publications: Delilah, 1950; The Earth Has Said, 1952; First Poems, 1957; Resurrection and Ashes, 1958; Leaves in the Wind, 1958; The Stage and the Mirrors, 1968; A Time Between Ashes and Roses, 1970; A Tomb for New York, 1971; The Complete Works: Poetry, 1971; The Blood of Adonis, 1971; Mirrors, 1976; Transformations of the Lover, 1982; Victims of a Map, 1984; The Book of the Siege, 1985; An Introduction to Arab Poetics, 1990; Sophism and Surrealism, 1992. Honour: Jean Malrieu Prize, 1991. Address: c/o Al Saqi Books, 26 Westbourne Grove, London W2 5RH, England.

AFONINA Nina Yourjevna, b. 2 Apr 1949, St Petersburg, Russia. Musicologist. Education: Music College, N A Rimsky-Korsakov, 1964-68; Diploma of Musicologist, Teacher (musical theory and history), Lecturer, S P Conservatory, 1968-73; Postgraduate course under Professor E A Ruchjevskaja, 1973-76; Doctor of Musicology degree, 1984. Publications: Variability of Music Metre in West-European Music, in the book Theoretical Problems of Classical and Modern Music, 1977; Variability of Music Metre, Its Formbuilding and Expressive Significance, dissertation, 1983; About Interdependence of Music Metre and Syntax (From Baroque to Classicism), in the book Form and Style, 1990; Rhythmical Education in Theoretical Courses, in the book Theoretical Disciplines of Music College, 1993; Some Aspects of Semantic and Etymology of Music Terminology (A Problem of Space and Time), in Transactions of the Faculty of Music Theory, 1995. Address: Kosmonavtov av 52 K 4, Apt 77, St Petersburg 196233, Russia.

AFRICANO Lillian, (Nora Ashby, Lila Cook, Jessica March), b. 7 June 1935, Paterson, New Jersey, USA. Author; Columnist. Divorced, 2 sons, 1 daughter. Education: BA, summa cum laude, Barnard College, 1953-57; Columbia University Graduate Schoo, 1958. Appointments: Arts Editor, The Villager, 1971; News Editor, Penthouse/Forum, 1973; Columnist, New York Times Syndicate, 1977;

Woman's World, 1980. Publications: Businessman's Guide to the Middle East, 1977; Doctor's Walking Book (co-author), 1980; Something Old, Something New, 1983; Passions, 1985; Gone From Breezy Hill (as Nora Ashby), 1985; Illusions (as Jessica March), 1988; Consenting Adults (as Lila Cook), 1988; Temptations (as Jessica March), 1989; Obsessions, 1990. Contributions to: New York Times; New York News; Reader's Digest; Harper's Bazaar; Woman's Day; Woman's World; National Review; Nation. Honour: Phi Beta Kappa, 1956. Memberships: Drama Desk, Vice President, Secretary; Outer Critics' Circle; American Society of Journalists and Authors; Authors Guild. Address: 95 West RiverRoad, Rumson, NJ 07760, USA.

AGEE Jonis, b. 31 May 1943, Omaha, Nebraska, USA. Writer; Poet; Teacher. 1 daughter. Education: BA, University of Iowa, 1966; MA, 1969, PhD, 1976, State University of New York at Binghampton. Appointments: Teacher, College of St Catherine, St Paul, Minnesota, 1975-95; Literary Consultant, Walker Arts Center, Minneapolis, 1978-84; Adjunct Teacher, Macalester College, St Paul, Minnesota, 1980-88; Teacher and Editor, Literary Post Program for Senior Citizen Writers, 1986-89; Professor, University of Michigan, 1995-; Many poetry readings. Publications: Houses (poem), 1976; Mercury (poems), 1981; Two Poems, 1982; Border Crossings (editor), 1984; Stiller's Pond (editor), 1988, expanded edition, 1991; Bend This Heart (stories), 1989; Pretend We've Never Met (stories), 1989; Sweet Eyes (novel), 1991; Strange Angels (novel), 1993; A .38 Special and a Broken Heart (stories), 1995; South of Resurrection (novel), forthcoming. Contributions to: Anthologies and periodicals. Honours: Minnesota State Arts Board Award, 1977; National Endowment for the Arts Fellowship, 1978; Loft-McKnight Awards, 1987, 1991. Memberships: Literary Guild. Address: 503 South First Street, Ann Arbor, MI 48103, USA.

AGUIRRE Eugenio, b. 31 July 1944, Mexico City, Mexico. Writer. m. 6 Aug 1971, 1 son, 1 daughter. Education: BA Law, MA Literature, Universidad Nacional Autonoma de Mexico. Appointments: Lecturer: University of Lawrence, Kansas, USA; Wabash College, USA; Writers Association of Panama; Several bank and government offices, Mexico. Publications: Novels: Jesucristo Perez, 1973; Pajar de Imaginacion, 1975; El caballero de las espadas, 1978; Gonzalo Guerrero, 1980; El testamento del diablo, 1981; En el campo, 1982; Cadaver exquisito, 1984; El rumor que llego del mar, 1985; Pajaros de fuego, 1986; Un mundo de nino lleno de mar, 1986; Pasos de sangre, 1988; Amor de mis amores, 1988; De cuerpo entero, 1991; El guerrero del sur, 1991; Cosas de angeles y otros cuentos, 1992; Los ninos de colores, 1993;Elena o el laberinto de la lujuria, 1994; El demonio me visita, 1994; La fascinacion de la bestia, 1994; Desierto ardiente, 1995; Ruiz Massieu: el mejor enemigo, 1995. Contributions to: Excelsior; Uno & Uno; El Cuento; Plural; Vaso Comunicante; Contenido; El Buho; All Mexico City; Also Angoleta, Venezuela; Paris Atlantic, France; Revista Siempre!. Honours: Great Silver Medal, International Academy of Lutece, Paris, France, 1981; Finalist, 1st crime novel, Plaza de Janes, 1985; Finalist, Fuentes Mares Prize for Literature, 1986; Finalist, 1st International Award, Diana Publishers, 1986. Memberships: Past president, Asociacion de Escritores de Mexico; Board, Sociedad General de Escritores de Mexico; International PEN Club. Address: Buhos no 32, Fracc Loma de Guadalupe, Mexico DF 01720, Mexico.

AHERNE Owen, See: CASSILL R(onald) V(erlin).

AHLSEN Leopold, b. 12 Jan 1927, Munich, Germany. Author. m. Ruth Gehwald, 1964, 1 son, 1 daughter. Publications: 13 Plays, 23 radio plays, . 42 television plays, 5 novels. Honours: Gerhart Hauptmann Prize; Schiller-Forderungspreis; Golden Bildschirm; Horspielpreis der Kriegsblinden; Silver Nymph of Monaco. Address: Waldschulstrasse 58, 8000 Munich 82, Germany.

AHRENS Bridget, b. 9 Jan 1958, Buffalo, New York, USA. Writer. m. 1 Aug 1981, 1 son, 1 daughter. Education: BA, Medical Technology, State University of New York, 1980; MPH, University of California, 1981; MFA, Writing, Vermont College, 1990. Appointments: Instructor, Fiction and Non-Fiction Writing, Lebanon College, 1990-; Associate Editor, AIDS and Society: An International Research and Policy Bulletin. Publications: Our Lady of the Keyboard, 1989; The Problems and Pitfalls of Writing about Sex, 1989; A Woman's Place is Intuition, 1990; The Art of Baking, The Politics of Love, 1991; The Eye of the Needle, 1991; Atlas's Revenge, 1992. Honours: Fellowship, Vermont Council on the Arts, 1992. Membership: Poets and Writers. Address: 78 Brigham Hill Road, Norwich, VT 05055, USA.

AICHINGER Ilse, b. 1 Nov 1921, Vienna, Austria. Novelist; Playwright. Education: University of Vienna, 1945-48. Appointments: Member of Grupe 47, 1951-. Publications: Die Grössere Hoffnung, 1948; Rede Unter dem Galgen, 1953; Eliza, Eliza, 1965; Selected Short Stories and Dialogue, 1966; Nachricht und Tag: Erzählungen, 1970; Schlechte Worter, 1976; Meine Sprache und Ich Erzählungen, 1978; Spiegelesichte: Erzählungen und Dialoge, 1979; Plays, Zu Keiner Stunde, 1957, 1980; Besuch im Pfarrhaus, 1961; Auckland: 4 Horspiele, 1969; Knopfe, 1978; Weisse Chrysanthemum, 1979; Radio Plays, Selected Poetry and Prose of Ilse Aichinger, 1983; Collected Works, 8 volumes, 1991. Honours: Belgian Europe Festival Prize, 1987; Town of Solothurn Prize, 1991. Address: c/o Fischer Verlag, Postfach 700480, 6000 Frankfurt, Germany.

AIDOO (Christina) Ama Ata, b. 1942, Abeadzi Kyiakor, Ghana. Writer. 1 daughter. Appointments: Lecturer, University of Cape Coast, Ghana, 1970-83; Minister of Education, Ghana, 1982-83; Chair, Africa Regional Panel of Commonwealth Writers Prize, 1990-91. Publications: Changes, A Love Story; The Dilemma of a Ghost; Anowa; No Sweetness Here; Our Sister Killjoy; Someone Talking to Sometime; The Eagle and the Chickens; Birds and Other Poems; Short Stories. Contributions to: BBC African Service; MS Magazine; South Magazine; Kumapipi; Rapport; Chapman Review. Address: PO Box 4930, Harare, Zimbabwe.

AIKEN Joan Delano, b. 4 Sept 1924, Rye, Sussex, England. Writer. m. (1)Ronald George Brown, Dec 1955, 1 son, 1 daughter. (2)Julius Goldstein, 2 Sept 1976. Appointments: Librarian, United Nations London Information Centre, 1945-49; Features Editor, Argosy Magazine, 1955-60; Freelance Writer, Full Time, 1961-. Publications: 21 Books for adults; Over 50 for Children; Selected titles, adult and juvenile: The Fortune Hunters, 1965; Died on a Rainy Sunday, 1972; Deception, 1987; A Harp of Fishbones, stories, 1972; The Mooncusser's Daughter, 1973; The Skin Spinners, poems, 1976; The Teeth of the Gale, 1988; Give Yourself a Fright, 1989; Mortimer and Arabel, 1992; A Creepy Company, 1993; Eliza's Daughter, 1994; The Winter Sleepwalker, 1994; Cold Shoulder Road, 1995; Emma Watson, 1996; The Cockatrice Boys, 1996; The Jewel Seed, 1997. Contributions to: New Statesman; Washington Post; Good Housekeeping; Womans Journal; Childrens Literature in Education. Honours: Guardian Award, 1969; Lewis Carroll Award, 1970. Memberships: Society of Authors; Writers Guild; Mystery Writers of America; Crime Writers Association. Literary Agent: A M Heath Ltd. Address: The Hermitage, East Street, Petworth, West Sussex GU28 0AB, England.

AITMATOV Chingiz (Torekulovich), b. 12 Dec 1928, Sheker, Kirghizstan. Novelist. Education: Gorky Literary Institute, Moscow, 1956-58. Appointments: Deputy, Supreme Soviet, 1966-89; Ambassador, Luxembourg, 1990. Publications: Melody, 1959; Milky Way, 1963; The First Master, 1963; Short Novels, 1964; The Son of a Soldier, 1970; The White Ship, 1972; The Lament of a Migrating Bird, 1973; The Soldier, 1974; Night Dew, 1975; Collected Works, 2 volumes, 1978; The Legend of the Horned Mother Deer, 1979; Short Stories, 1982; Collected Works, 3 volumes, 1982-84; Echo of the World, 1985; The Place of the Skull, 1989; Mother Earth and Other Stories, 1989. Honours: Lenin Prize, 1963; Hero of Socialist Labour, 1978; Member, World Academy of Art & Science, 1987. Address: Russian Writers Union, Moscow, Russia.

AJIBADE (Ade)Yemi (Olanrewaju), b. 28 July 1939, Nigeria. Actor; Playwright; Director. m. Gwendoline Augusta Ebonywhite, May 1973, 2 daughters. Education: Diplomas, Dramatic Arts Film Technique; British Drama League Diploma, Theatre Production; Associate of Drama Board; MA, London University, 1985. Appointments: Tutor, Producer, Drama, Panel of Inner London Education Authority; Visiting Director, Actors Workshop, London; Artistic Director, Pan-African Players, Keskidee Centre, London; Assistant Advisor to Earl of Snowdon on Mary Kingsley; Senior Arts Fellow and Artistic Director, Unibadan Masques, Acting Company of Ibadan University, Nigeria; Artist in Residence, Colby College, Waterville, Maine, USA, 1987. Publications: Lagos, Yes Lagos, BBC Radio; Award (Keskidee Centre); The Black Knives (ORTF, Paris); The Big One, Parcel Post (Royal Court, London); Behind the Mountain, Mokai, The Girl from Bulawayo (Arts Theatre, Ibadan University); Fingers Only (Black Theatre Cooperative, London); Para Ginto (black version of Peer Gynt), commissioned by Birmingham Repertory Theatre; Waiting for Hannibal (Black Theatre Co-op), 1986. Honours: British Arts Council Bursary Award for Playwriting, 1976, 1977, 1981,

1984. Memberships: Fellow, Royal Society of Arts; British Kinematographic Society; Theatre Writers Union; Black Writers Association. Literary Agent: Michael Imison Playwrights, London. Address: 29 Seymour House, Churchway, London NW1, England.

AKAVIA Miriam, b. 20 Nov 1927, Krakow, Poland. Novelist; Translator. m. 3 Dec 1946, 2 daughters. Appointments: Co-editor of some bulletins. Publications: Adolescence of Autumn, 1975; Ha mechir (The Price), 1978; Galia & Miklosh, 1982; Karmi Sheli (My Own Vineyard), 1984; Adventure on a Bus, 1986; Ma Vigne A Moi, 1992; The Other Way, The Story of a Group, in Hebrew, 1992. Contributions to: Various literary magazines. Honours: Dvorsecki Prize; Korczak Prize, SEK Prize (Sociéte Européen de Culture); Amicus Polonie; Cracovians Prize. Literary Agent: Lipman, AG, CG-8044 Zürich, Switzerland. Address: PO 53050, 61530 Tel-Aviv, Israel.

AKEN Paul Van, b. 20 Nov 1948, Reet, Belgium. Teacher; Literary Critic. Education: Free University, Brussels, 1966-70. Publications: Features of the Essay; Lettermarker, A History of Dutch Literature; Paul De Wispelaer; About Sugar by Hugo Claus; About Lucifer by Vondel; About the Wall by Jos Vandeloo. Contributions to: Nieuw Vlaams Tydschrift; De Vlaamse Gids; Yang; Kunst & Cultuur; Kruispunt; Ons Erfdeel; Creare; Septentrion. Memberships: PEN; FLANDERS. Address: Dirk Martensstraat 60, 9300 Aalst, Belgium.

AKERS Alan Burt, See: **BULMER Henry Kenneth.**

AKHMADULINA Bella Akhatovna, b. 10 Apr 1937, Moscow, Russia. Poet. m. Boris Messerer, 1974. Education: Gorky Literary Institute, Moscow, 1960. Appointments: Secretary, Union of Soviet, Russian Writers, 1986-. Publictions: Fire Tree, 1958; String, 1962; Tale of the Rain, 1963; My Genealogy, 1963; Adventure in an Antique Store, 1967; Fever and Other Poems, 1968; Snowstorm, 1968; Music Lessons, 1969; Candle, 1977; Three Russian Poets, 1979; The Garden, 1987; Seashore, 1991. Screenplay: Clear Ponds, 1965. Honours: American Academy of Arts and Letters, 1977. Address: Cherniachovskoho Street 4, Apt 37, 125319 Moscow, Russia.

AKSENOV Vasilii (Pavlovich), b. 20 Aug 1932, Kazan, Russia. Novelist. m. Maia Karmen, 1979. Education: Povlov Medical Institute, 1956. Appointments: Exiled to USA, 1980; Writer-in-Residence, University of Michigan, University of Southern California and George Washington University; Returned Russia, 1992. Publications: Colleagues, 1961; Oranges from Morocco, 1963; Catapult, 1964; Its Time My Friend Its Time, 1969; Surplussed Barrelware, 1972; Samson and Samsoness, 1972; Around the Clock Non-Stop, 1976; In Search of a Genre, 1977; The Steel Bird and Other Stories, 1979; Our Golden Ironburg, 1980; The Burn, 1984; The Island of Crimea, 1983; The Paperscape, 1983; The Day of the First Snowfall, 1990; Capital Displacement, 1990; The Yolk of an Egg, 1990; Moscow Saga, 1991; Rendezvous, 1991; Plays: Kollegi, 1962; Always on Sale, 1965; Your Murderer, 1977; The Four Temperaments, 1979; Aristophaniana and the Frogs, 1981; The Heron, 1984; Screenplays: The Blues with a Russian Accent, 1987; In Search of Melancholy Baby, 1987. Address: Krasnoirmeskaia Str 21, Apt 20, 125319 Moscow, Russia.

AL-AZM Sadik J, b. 7 Nov 1934, Damascus, Syria. University Professor. m. Fawz Touqan, 2 July 1957, 2 sons. Education: American University, Beirut, 1953-57; Yale University, 1957-61. Appointments: Visiting Professor, Princeton University, 1988-90, 1991-92; Visiting Fellow, Woodrow Wilson International Centre for Scholars, 1992-93; Chairman, Department of Philosophy and Sociology, Damascus University, 1993-; Visiting Professor, University of Oldenburg, Germany, 1995. Publications: Kant's Theory of Time: The Origins of Kant's Arguments in the Antinonnies; Critique of Religious Thought; Studies in Modern Western Philosophy; Of Love and Arabic Courtly Love; Materialism and History: A Defense; Unbehagen in Der Moderne: Aufklarung im Islam, 1993; The Tabooing Mentality: Salman Rushdie and the Truth of Literature, 1992, 2nd edition, 1994; Sadik Al-Azm: Mot Hevdvunne Sannheter, 1995. Contributions to: Orientalism and Orientalism in Reverse; Sionisme Une Entreprise de Colonisation; Der Palastinensiche Widerstand neu Durchdacht; Palestinian Zionism; The Importance of Being Earnest About Salman Rushdie; South Asia Bulletin. Address: Department of Philosophy, Faculty of Letters, Damascus University, Damascus, Syria.

AL-KHARRAT Edwar, b. 16 Mar 1926, Alexandria, Egypt. Writer. 2 sons. Education: LLB, Alexandria University, 1946. Appointments: Editor, Gallery 68 Magazine, 1968; Editor, Afro Asian

Writings Magazine, 1968; Edited, Special Issue, Egyptian Literature of AL Karmal Magazine, 1984. Publications: High Walls, 1959; Hours of Pride, 1972; Ramah and the Dragon, 1980; Suffocations of Love and Mornings, 1983; The Other Time, 1985; City of Saffron Arabic, 1986; Girls of Alexandria, 1990; Waves of Nights, 1991; Appollos Ruins, 1992; Penetrations of Love and Perdition, 1993; My Alexandria, 1993; The New Sensibility, 1994; From Silence to Rebellion, 1994; Transgeneric Writing, 1994; Ripples of Salt Dreams, 1994; Fire of Phantasies, 1995; Hymn to Density, 1995; 7 Interpretations (poetry), 1996; Wings of Your Bird Struck Me (poetry), 1996; Why?: Extracts of a Love Poem, 1996; Soaring Edifices (novel), 1997; Cry of the Unicorn (poetry), forthcoming; The Certitude of Thirst, forthcoming. Contributions to: Many Arab Literary Magazines. Honours: Arts and Letters Medal, 1972; State Prize for Short Story, 1972; Franco Arab Friendship Award, 1989; UWAIS Award for Fiction, 1995. Memberships: Egyptian Writers Union; Gezira Sporting Club; Egyptian PEN Club. Address: 45 Ahmed Hishmat Street, Zamalak 11211, Cairo, Egypt.

AL-SHAROUNI Youssef, b. 14 Oct 1924, Menuf, Egypt. Ministry of Information. m. Nargis S Basta, 2 Oct 1952, 1 son, 1 daughter. Education: BA, Cairo University. Appointments: Under-Secretary, High Council of Arts, 1978-83; Professor for Postgraduate Courses, Cairo University, 1979-81; Ministry of Information, Oman, 1985-92. Publications: The Five Lovers: A Message to a Woman; The Last Eve; Studies on Love and Friendship in Arabic Tradition; Complete Short Stories, volume 1, 1992, volume 2, 1993. Contributions to: Al Adib; Al Adab; Al Arabi; Al Muntada; Al Ahram; Al Quissa. Honours: Egyptian State Prizes in Short Story, 1970, and Literary studies, 1978; First Grade Order of Science and Arts, Arab Republic of Egypt, 1970; Order of the Republic, 1978; Fellow, German Academic Exchange Service, Free University of Berlin, 1976, Netherlands Organisation for Advancement of Pure Research, 1981-82. Memberships: Story Club, Cairo, Board, 1970-; Writers' Union, Cairo; Pen Club; Fiction Committee at High Council of Culture, 1963-83. Address: 12 El-Sad El Aali Street, El-Maadi, PC 11431, Cairo, Egypt.

ALBANY James. See: RAE Hugh Crauford.

ALBEE Edward (Franklin III), b. 12 Mar 1928, Virginia, USA. Playwright. Education: Trinity College, Hartford, Connecticut, 1946-47. Appointments: Lecturer at various US colleges and universities. Publications: Plays: The Zoo Story, 1958; The Death of Bessie Smith, 1959; The Sandbox, 1959; The American Dream, 1960; Who's Afraid of Virginia Woolf?, 1962; Tiny Alice, 1963; A Delicate Balance, 1966; Box, 1970; Quotations from Chairman Mao, 1970; All Over, 1971; Seascape, 1975; Counting the Ways, 1976; Listening, 1977; The Lady from Dubuque, 1979; Finding the Sun, 1982; The Man Who Had Three Arms, 1983; Walking, 1984; Marriage Play, 1987; Three Tall Women, 1991; Fragments, 1993. Adaptions of: Carson McCuller's The Ballad of the Sad Café, 1963; James Purdy's Malcolm, 1965; Giles Cooper's Everything in the Garden, 1967; Vladimir Nabokov's Lolita, 1980. Honours: Pulitzer Prizes in Drama, 1967, 1975, 1994; American Academy and Institute of Arts and Letters Gold Medal, 1980; Theater Hall of Fame, 1985; Memberships: Dramatists Guild Council; Edward F Albee Foundation, president; International Theatre Institute, president. Address: 14 Harrison Street, New York, NY 10013, USA.

ALBERT Gábor, b. 30 Oct 1929, Hungary. Writer; Essayist. m. Zuzsanna Marek, 30 Oct 1954, 1 son, 1 daughter. Education: Eötvös Lorand University, 1955. Appointments: Editor-in-Chief, Uj Magyarország, 1991-92; Editor in Chief, Magyarok Világlapja, 1992-; Editor, The Pointer, 1994. Publications: Dragon and Octahedron: After Scattering, Essays; Where Are Those Columns; In a Shell; Book of Kings; Heroes of the Failures; Atheist; Final Settlement of a Wedding; Stephen King's Tart Wine, 1993; ...We Have Survived Him, 1996. Memberships: Association of Hungarian Writers; Association of D Berzsenyi. Address: Erdő u 150, H 2092 Budakeszi, Hungary.

ALBEVERIO MANZONI Solvejg, b. 6 Nov 1939, Arogno, Switzerland. Painter; Writer. m. Sergio Albeverio, 7 Feb 1970, 1 daughter. Education: Textile Designer, Diploma, Como, Italy, 1960; Art Courses, Zürich, 1969; Drawing and Etching Statens - Kunsthåndverkskole, Oslo, 1972-77. Publications: Da stanze chiuse; Il pensatore con il mantello come meteora; Controcanto al chiuso; Il fiore, il frutto, triandro donna; Frange di solitudine. Contributions to: Poems and Drawings in Literary Journals and Reviews; Exhibitions, Many Countries. Honours: Premio Ascona, 1987; Pro Helvetia Prize, 1995. Memberships: Swiss Society of Painters, Sculptors and Architects; Swiss Society of Writers; PEN; Associazione Scrittori della Svizzera Italiana. Address: Auf dem Aspei 55, D-4630 Bochum, Germany.

ALBRIGHT Daniel, b. 29 Oct 1945, Chicago, Illinois, USA. Professor of English; Writer. m. Karin Larson, 18 June 1977, 1 daughter. Education: BA, Rice University, 1967; MPhil, 1969, PhD, 1970, Yale University. Appointments: Assistant Professor, 1970-75, Associate Professor, 1975-81, Professor, 1981-87, University of Virginia; Visiting Professor, University of Munich, 1986-87; Professor, 1987-, Richard L Turner Professor in the Humanities, 1995-, University of Rochester. Publications: The Myth against Myth: A Study of Yeats' Imagination in Old Age, 1972; Personality and Impersonality: Lawrence, Woolf, Mann, 1978; Representation and the Imagination: Beckett, Kafka, Nabokov and Schoenberg, 1981; Lyricality in English Literature, 1985; Tennyson: The Muses' Tug-of-War, 1986; Stravinsky: The Music-Box and the Nightingale, 1989; W B Yeats: The Poems (editor), 1990, 3rd printing, revised, 1994; Quantum Poetics: Yeats, Pound, Eliot, and the Science of Modernism, 1997. Contributions to: Various periodicals. Honours: Phi Beta Kappa, 1966; National Endowment for the Arts Fellowship, 1973-74; Guggenheim Fellowship, 1976-77. Address: 121 Van Voorhis Road, Pittsford, NY 14534, USA.

ALCOCK (Garfield) Vivien, b. 23 Sept 1924, Worthing, England. Author. m. Leon Garfield, 23 Oct 1948, 1 daughter. Education: Oxford School of Art. Publications: The Haunting of Cassie Palmer, 1980; The Stonewalker, 1981; The Sylvia Game, 1982; Travellers by Night, 1983; Ghostly Companions, 1984; The Cuckoo Sister, 1985; The Mysterious Mr Ross, 1987; The Monster Garden, 1988; The Trial of Anna Cotman, 1989; A Kind of Thief, 1991. Membership: Authors Society. Literary Agent: John Johnson. Address: 59 Wood Lane, London N6 5UD, England.

ALDEN Michele. See: AVALLONE Michael (Angelo Jr).

ALDERSEY-WILLIAMS Hugh Arthur, b. 17 June 1959, London, England. Journalist; Author. m. Moira Morrissey, 2 Sept 1989. Education: St John's College, Cambridge, BA, 1980; MA, 1984. Publications: New American Design, 1988; World Design: Nationalism and Globalism in Design, 1992; The Most Beautiful Molecule: The Discovery of the Buckyball, 1995; Monographs on Leading Designers & various book chapters. Contributions to: The Independent; Independent on Sunday. Memberships: Society of Authors; Royal Society of Arts. Literary Agent: Caroline Davidson & Robert Ducas Literary Agency.

ALDISS Brian Wilson, b. 18 Aug 1925, East Dereham, England. Writer. m. (1) 1 son, 1 daughter. (2)Margaret Manson, 11 Dec 1965, 1 son, 1 daughter. Appointments: Literary Editor, Oxford Mail, 1958-69; Managing Director, Avernus Ltd; President, World SF, 1980-82. Publications: The Brightfount Diaries, 1955; Non-Stop, 1958; Hothouse, 1962; The Horatio Stubbs Trilogy, 1970; Frankenstein Unbound, 1973; Forgotten Life, 1988; Best SF Stories of Brian W Aldiss, 1965; Cities and Stones, A Traveller's Yugoslavia, 1966; This World and Nearer Ones, 1979; The Helliconia Trilogy, 1985; Bury My Heart at W H Smiths, a Writing Life, 1990; Remembrance Day, 1993; Somewhere East of Life, 1994; At the Caligula Hotel, 1995; The Secret of This Book, 1995. Contributions to: SF Studies. Honours: Hugo Awards; Nebula Award. Memberships: FRSL; Writers in Oxford; Society of Authors; IAFA. Literary Agent: Michael Shaw, Curtis Brown. Address: Hambleden, 39 St Andrews Road, Old Headington, Oxford OX3 9DL, England.

ALDRIDGE (Harold Edward) James, b. 10 July 1918. Author; Journalist. m. Dina Mitchnik, 1942, 2 sons. London School of Economics. Appointments: Herald & Sun, Melbourne, 1937-38; Daily Sketch, Sunday Dispatch, London, 1939; Australian Newspaper Service & North American Newspaper Alliance, Finland, Norway, Middle East, Greece, USSR, 1939-45; Correspondent, Time and Life, Teheran, 1944. Publications: Signed with their Honour, 1942; The Sea Eagle, 1944; Of Many Men, 1946; The Diplomat, 1950; The Hunter, 1951; Heroes of the Empty View, 1954; Underwater Hunting for Inexperienced Englishmen, 1956; I Wish He Would Not Die, 1958; Gold and Sand, 1960; The Last Exile, 1961; Captive in the Land, 1962; The Statesman's Game, 1966; My Brother Tom, 1966; The Flying 19, 1966; Living Egypt, 1969; Cairo, Biography of a City, 1970; A Sporting Proposition, 1973; The Marvellous Mongolian, 1974; Mockery in Arms, 1974; The Untouchable Juli, 1975; One Last Glimpse, 1977; Goodbye Un America, 1979; The Brokern Saddle,

1982; The True Story of Lilli Stubek, 1984; The True Story of Spit MacPhee, 1986. Honours: Rhys Memorial Award, 1945; Lenin Peace Prize, 1972. Address: c/o Curtis Brown, 28/29 Haymarket, London SW1Y 4SP, England.

ALDRIDGE John Watson, b. 26 Sept 1922, Sioux City, Iowa, USA. Literary Critic; Educator. m. (2) Patricia McGuire Eby, 16 July 1983, 5 sons, previous marriage. Education: BA, University of California, Berkeley, 1947. Appointments: Lecturer, Christian Gauss seminars in criticism, Princeton University, 1953-54; Breadloaf Writers Conference, 1966-69; Rockefeller Humanities Fellowship, 1976; Book Critic, MacNeil/Lehrer TV News, 1983-84. Publications: After the Lost Generation, criticism, 1951; In Search of Heresy, criticism, 1956; The Party at Cranton, novel, 1960; Time to Murder and Create, criticism, 1966; In the Country of the Young, social commentary, 1970; The Devil in the Fire, criticism, 1972; The American Novel and the Way We Live Now, criticism, 1983; Talents and Technicians, criticism, 1992; Classics and Contemporaries, criticism, 1992. Literary Agent: Gerard F McCauley. Address: 1050 Wall Street, No 4C, Ann Arbor, MI 48105, USA.

ALDRIDGE Sarah. See: **MARCHANT Anyda.**

ALDYNE Nathan. See: **McDOWELL Michael.**

ALEGRIA FLAKOLL Claribel, (Claribel Alegria), b. 12 May 1924, Esteli, Nicaragua. Writer. m. Darwin J Flakoll, 29 Dec 1947, 1 son, 3 daughters. Education: BA Philosophy and Letters, George Washington University, Washington DC, USA. Publications: Cenizas de Izalco, novel, co-author, 1966; Suma y Siqua, poetry, 1982; Nicaragua: la revolucion sandinists, history, 1982; No me agarran viva, testimony, 1983; Woman of the River, poetry, 1989; Y esta poema-rio, poetry, 1989; Family Album, 3 novellas, 1990; Total of 30 books in five languages. Contributions to: Many magazines and journals. Honour: Casa de las Americas poetry prize for Sobrevivo, 1978. Literary Agent: Alexander Taylor, Curbstone Press. Address: Aptdo Postal A-36, Managua, Nicaragua.

ALEMANY-VALDEZ Herminia M, b. 16 June 1961, Chicago, Illinois, USA. Spanish and Literature Instructor. m. Juan Irizarry-Rivera, 22 Mar 1986. Education: BA, 1986, MA, 1991, Universidad de Puerto Rico, Mayagüez; PhD, Universidad Nacional Autonoma de Mexico. Appointment: El Cuervo's Board of Editors, Universidad de Puerto Rico, Aguadilla, 1996. Publications: Galeria de mujeres: La mujer en Album de familia y Papeles de Pandora, 1994; Abriendo la caja de Pandora: La obra de Rosario Castellanos y Rosario Ferré; El proceso de la creacion en la recreacion: lo mitico indigena en la obra de Rosario Castellanos. Contributions to: Periodicals and journals. Address: PO Box 5640, College Station Mayagüez, Puerto Rico 00681-5640, USA.

ALEX Peter. See: **HAINING Peter Alexander.**

ALEXANDER Caroline Elizabeth, b. 13 Mar 1956, Florida, USA. Writer. Education: BA, Florida State University, 1977; BA, Oxford University, 1980; PhD, Columbia University, 1991. Appointments: Editorial Board, American Oxonian. Publications: One Dry Season: In the Footsteps of Mary Kingsley, 1990; The Way to Xanadu, 1994; Battle's End. Contributions to: New Yorker; Smithsonian; Independent; Sunday Telegraph Weekend Magazine; Others. Honours: Mellon Fellowship; Rhodes Scholarship. Memberships: American Philological Society; Royal Geographical Society. Address: c/o Anthony Sheil, 43 Doughty Str, London WC1 N2LF, England.

ALEXANDER Christine Anne, b. 9 July 1949, Hastings, New Zealand. University Lectuer. m. Peter Fraser Alexander, 18 June 1977, 1 son, 1 daughter. Education: BA, 1970, MA, 1971, University of Canterbury; PhD, University of Cambridge, 1978. Appointments: Assistant Lectureship, University of Canterbury, 1972; Tutor, 1978-83, Lecturer, 1986-88, Senior Lecturer, 1988-92, Associate Professor, 1993-, University of New South Wales, Australia. Publications: Bibliography of the Manuscripts of Charlotte Brontë, 1982; The Early Writings of Charlotte Brontë, 1983; An Edition of the Early Writings of Charlotte Brontë, 3 vols, 1987-; The Art of the Brontës, 1994. Contributions to: Books: Charlotte Brontë at Roe Head; Search after Love; Articles and reviews in various Journals; Authorial Voice, 1990. Honours: New Zealand Postgraduate Scholarships; New Zealand

University Womens Fellowship; Travel Grants; Special Research Grants; British Academy Rose Mary Crawshay Prize, 1984; Australian Research Council Senior Research Fellowship; Fellow, Australian Academy of the Humanities, 1995. Memberships: Brontë Society; Australasian Language and Literature Association; Australian Victorian Studies Association; Australian and South Pacific Association for Comparative Literary Studies; Cambridge Society; Jane Austen Society; Association for the Study of Australian Literature; Bibliographical Society of Australia and New Zealand; Society for Textual Scholarship; Society for the History of Authorship, Reading and Publishing. Address: School of English, University of New South Wales, Sydney, New South Wales 2052, Australia.

ALEXANDER Doris Muriel, b. 14 Dec 1922, Newark, NJ, USA. Professor; Writer. Education: BA, University of Missouri, 1944; MA, University of Pennsylvania, 1946; PhD, New York University, 1952. Appointments: Instructor, Rutgers University, 1950-56; Associate Professor, then Department Chairman, CUNY, 1956-62. Publications: The Tempering of Eugene O'Neill, 1962; Creating Characters with Charles Dickens, 1991; Eugene O'Neill's Creative Struggle, 1992; Creating Literature Out of Life, 1996; Others: Many articles in reviews. Honours: Penfield Fellowship, New York University, 1946; Fulbright Professor, University of Athens, 1966-67. Memberships: Trustee, Dickens Society; Association of Literary Scholars and Critics; Eugene O'Neill Society. Literary Agent: Gunther Stuhlmann. Address: San Trovaso 1116, Dorsoduro, 30123 Venice, Italy.

ALEXANDER Gary (Roy), b. 18 Jan 1941, Bremerton, Washington, USA. Writer. m. Shari, 9 Aug 1969, 3 daughters. Education: Olympic Community College; University of Washington. Publications: Pigeon Blood, 1988; Unfunny Money, 1989; Kiet and the Golden Peacock, 1989; Kiet and the Opium War, 1990; Deadly Drought. 1001; Dead Dinosaurs, 1994. Contributions to: Many stories in magazines. Membership: Mystery Writers of America. Address: 6709 South 238th Place, H-102, Kent, WA 98032, USA.

ALEXANDER Lloyd (Chudley), b. 30 Jan 1924, Philadelphia, Pennsylvania, USA. Writer. m. Janine Denni, 8 Jan 1946, 1 daughter. Education: West Chester State Teachers College, 1942; Lafayette College, 1943; Sorbonne, University of Paris, 1946. Appointment: Author-in-Residence, Temple University, 1970-74. Publications: And Let The Credit Go, 1955; My Five Tigers, 1956; Janine is French, 1958; My Love Affair with Music, 1960; Park Avenue Vet (with Louis Camuti), 1962; Fifty Years in the Doghouse, 1963; My Cats and Me: The Story of an Understanding, 1989; Juvenile Books: Border Hawk: August Bondi, 1959; Aaron Lopez and the Flagship Hope, 1960; Time Cat: The Journeys of Jason and Gareth, 1963; Coll and His White Pig, 1965; The Truthful Harp, 1967; The Marvelous Misadventures of Sebastian, 1970; The King's Fountain, 1971; The Four Donkeys, 1972; The Foundling and Other Tales of Prydain, 1973; The Cat Who Wished to Be A Man, 1973; The Wizard in the Tree, 1975; The Town Cats and Other Tales, 1977; The First Two Lives of Lukas-Kasha, 1978; The Remarkable Journey of Prince Jen, 1991; The Fortune-Tellers, 1992; The House Gobbaleen, 1995; The Arkadians, 1995. Honours: Newbery Honor Book, 1965; Newbery Medal, 1969; National Book Award, 1971; Drexel Awards, 1972, 1976; American Book Award, 1982; Austrian Children's Book Award, 1984; Regina Medal, Catholic Library Association, 1986; Church and Synagogue Library Association Award, 1987; Lifetime Achievement Award, Pennsylvania Center for the Book in Philadelphia, 1991; Horn Book Award, 1993. Memberships: Amnesty International; Authors Guild; Authors League of America; PEN. Address: 1005 Drexel Avenue, Drexel Hill, PA 19026, USA.

ALEXANDER Louis George, b. 1932. Writer. Publications: Sixty Steps, 1962; Poetry and Prose Appreciation, 1963; A First Book in Comprehension, 1965; Essays and Letter Writing, 1965; The Carters of Greenwood, 1966; Detectives from Scotland Yard, 1966; April Fools Day, 1966; New Concept English (4 volumes), 1967; Worth a Fortune, 1967; Question and Answer, 1967; For and Against, 1968; Look, Listen and Learn, Sets 1-4, 1968-71; Reading and Writing English, 1969; Car Thieves, 1969; K's First Case, 1975; Good Morning, Mexico!, 1975; Operation Janus, 1976; Clint Magee, 1976; Dangerous Game, 1977; Some Methodological Implications of Waystage and Threshold Level, Council of Europe, 1977; Follow Me, 1979; Survive in French/Spanish/German/Italian, 1980; Conversational French/Spanish/German/Italian, 1981; Excel, 1985-87; Plain English, 1987-88; Longman English Grammar, 1988-89; Longman English Grammar Practice, 1990; Step by Step 1-3, 1991; Longman Advanced Grammar, 1993; The Essential English Grammar, 1993; Right Word,

Wrong Word, 1994. Address: Garden House, Weydown Road, Haslemere, Surrey, England.

ALEXANDER Meena, b. 17 Feb 1951, Allahabad, India. Writer; Poet; Professor. m. David Lelyveld, 1 May 1979, 1 son, 1 daughter. Education: BA, Khartoum University, 1969; PhD, Nottingham University, 1973. Appointments: Lecturer, Miranda House, Delhi University, 1974, Jawaharlal Nehru University, 1975, Central Institute of English and Foreign Languages, Hyderabad, 1975-77; Lecturer, 1977-79, Reader, 1979, University of Hyderabad; Assistant Professor, Fordham University, 1980-87, Hunter College, 1987-89; Associate Professor, Member, Graduate Faculty, City University of New York, 1989-92; Lecturer in Poetry, Columbia University, 1991-; Professor of English and Women Studies, Hunter College and the Graduate Center, City University of New York, 1992-. Publications: The Bird's Bright Ring (poem), 1976; In the Middle Earth (play), 1977; Without Place, 1977; I Root My Name, 1977; The Poetic Self: Towards a Phenomenology of Romanticism, 1979; Stone Roots, 1980; House of a Thousand Doors (poetry and prose), 1988; Women in Romanticism: Mary Wollstonecraft, Dorothy Wordsworth and Mary Shelley, 1989; The Storm: A Poem in Five Parts, 1989; Nampally Road (novel), 1991; Night-Scene: The Garden (poem), 1992; Fault Lines (memoir), 1993; River and Bridge (poems), 1995, expanded edition, 1996; Sandhya Rosenblum (novel), 1996; The Shock of Arrival: Post-Colonial Reflections, 1996; Manhattan Music (novel), 1997. Contributions to: Poetry and prose in various publications. Honours: Altrusa International Award, 1973; MacDowell Fellow, 1993; International Writer-in-Residence, Arts Council of England, 1995; Lila Wallace Writer-in-Residence, Asian American Renaissance, Minneapolis, 1995; Various grants. Memberships: Modern Languages Association; PEN American Centre. Literary Agent: Louise Quayle, Ellen Levine Agency. Address: 730 Fort Washington Avenue, No 2B, New York, NY 10040, USA.

ALEXANDER Sue, b. 20 Aug 1933, Tucson, Arizona, USA. Writer. m. 2 sons, 1 daughter. Education: Drake University, 1950-52; Northwestern University, 1952-53. Publications: Small Plays for You and a Friend, 1973; Nadir of the Streets, 1975; Peacocks Are Very Special, 1976; Witch, Goblin and Sometimes Ghost, 1976; Smalls Plays for Special Days, 1977; Marc the Magnificent, 1978; More Witch, Goblin and Ghost Stories, 1978; Seymour the Prince, 1979; Finding Your First Job, 1980; Whatever Happened to Uncle Albert? and Other Plays, 1980; Witch, Goblin and Ghost in the Haunted Woods, 1981; Witch, Goblin and Ghost's Book of Things to Do, 1982; Nadia the Willful, 1983; Dear Phoebe, 1984; World Famous Muriel, 1984; Witch, Goblin and Ghost Are Back, 1985; World Famous Muriel and the Scary Dragon, 1985; America's Own Holidays, 1986; Lila on the Landing, 1987; There's More - Much More, 1987; World Famous Muriel and the Magic Mystery, 1990; Who Goes Out on Halloween?, 1990; Sara's City, 1995. Literary Agent: Marilyn E Marlow/Curtis Brown Ltd. Address: 6846 McLaren, Canoga Park, CA 91307, USA.

ALEXIS Paul. See: HOLLO Anselm.

ALFRED William, b. 16 Aug 1922, New York, USA. Dramatist; Professor of English. Education: BA, Brooklyn College, 1948; MA, 1949, PhD, 1954, Harvard University. Appointments: Associate Editor, American Poet magazine, Brooklyn, 1942-44; Instructor, 1954-57, Assistant Professor, 1957-59, Associate Professor, 1959-63, Professor of English, 1963-, Harvard University. Publications: Plays: The Annunciation Rosary, 1948; Agamemnon, 1953; Hogan's Goat, 1965, revised as Cry for Us All, 1970; The Curse of an Aching Heart, 1979; Holy Saturday, 1980. Editor: Complete Prose Works of John Milton, Vol I (with others), 1953. Translator: Beowulf, 1963. Honours: Brooklyn College Literary Association Award, 1953; Amy Lowell Traveling Poetry Scholarship, 1956; Brandeis University Creative Arts Award, 1960; American Academy and Institute of Arts and Letters Grant, 1965. Address: 31 Athens Street, Cambridge, MA 02138, USA.

ALLABY John Michael, b. 18 Sept 1933, Belper, Derbyshire, England. Author; Editor. m. Ailsa Marthe McGregor, 3 Jan 1957, 1 son, 1 daughter. Publications: Inventing Tomorrow, 1976; Dictionary of the Environment, 1977, 4th edition, 1994; The Oxford Dictionary of Natural History, 1980; A Year in the Life of a Field, 1981; Animal Artisans, 1982; The Greening of Mars, 1984; The Concise Oxford Dictionary of Earth Sciences, 1986; All the National Trails in England and Wales, 1987; Conservation at Home, 1988; Guide to Gaia, 1989; Elements: Air, 1992; Elements: Water, 1992; Elements: Fire, 1993; Elements: Earth, 1993; The Concise Oxford Dictionary of Ecology,

1994; Facing the Future, 1995. Contributions to: Newspapers and magazines. Memberships: Association of British Science Writers; New York Academy of Sciences; Society of Authors. Address: Penquite, Fernleigh Road, Wadebridge, Cornwall Pl27 7BB, England.

ALLAN Elkan. b. 8 Dec 1922, London, England. Journalist. Appointments: Writer, Odhams Press, 1950-55; Writer, Producer, Executive and Head of Entertainment, Rediffusion Television, 1955-66; Television Columnist, Sunday Times, 1966-82; Editor, Video Viewer, 1982-83; Columnist, Video Week, 1983-; Listings Editor, 1986-88, Senior Editor, 1988-, The Independent. Publications: Quiz Team, 1945; Editor, Living Opinion, 1946; Good Listening: A Survey of Broadcasting, (with D M Robinson), 1948; The Sunday Times Guide to Movies on Television, (with A Allan), 1973, 1980; Editor, Video Year Book, 1984, 1985; 10 monographs on Silent Films Makers, 1990-. Contributions to: Senior Editor, The Independent. Honours: Triple Berlin TV Awards, 1965; British Press Awards, 1988. Address: The Independent, 40 City Road, London EC1Y 2DB, England.

ALLAN Keith, b. 27 Mar 1943, London, England. Academic. m. Wendy F Allen, 1 Jan 1993, 2 daughters. Education: BA Hons, Leeds University, 1964; MLitt 1970, PhD 1977, Edinburgh University. Publications: Linguistic Meaning, 2 vols, 1986; Euphemism and Dysphemism: Language Used as Shield and Weapon, with Kate Burridge, 1991. Contributions to: Many articles in professional journals on various topics in linguistics. Honour: Fellow, Austrian Academy of Humanities, 1995-. Address: Linguistics Department, Monash University, Clayton, 3168, Australia.

ALLAN Mabel Esther, (Jean Estoril, Priscilla Hagon, Anne Pilgrim), b. 11 Feb 1915, Wallasey, Cheshire, England. Author. Publications: A Dream of Hunger Moss, 1983; The Pride of Pine Street, 1985; The Rod to Huntingland, 1986; The Crumble Lane Mystery, 1987; Up the Victorian Staircse, 1987; First Term at Ash Grove, 1988; Drina Ballerina, 1991; Over 150 Other Books. Contributions to: Over 320 Short Stories; Articles; Poetry. Honours: Various Honours and Awards. Literary Agent: Curtis Brown & John Farquharson Ltd. Address: 11 Oldfield Way, Heswall, Wirral L60 6RQ, England.

ALLBEURY Ted. See: ALLBEURY Theodore Edward le Bouthillier.

ALLBEURY Theodore Edward le Bouthillier, (Ted Allbeury, Richard Butler, Patrick Kelly), b. 20 Oct 1917. Author. Publications: A Choice of Enemies, 1973; Snowball, 1974; The Special Collection, 1975; Palomino Blonde, 1975; The Only Good German, 1976; Moscow Quadrille, 1976; The Man with the President's Mind, 1977; The Lantern Network, 1978; Consequence of Fear, 1979; The Alpha List, 1979; The Twentieth Day of January, 1980; The Reaper, 1980; The Other Side of Silence, 1981; The Secret Whispers, 1981; All Our Tomorrows, 1982; Shadow of Shadows, 1982; Pay Any Price, 1983; The Judas Factor, 1984; No Place To Hide, 1984; The Girl from Addis, 1984; Children of Tender Years, 1985; The Choice, 1986; The Seeds of Treason, 1986; The Crossing, 1987; A Wilderness of Mirrors, 1988; Deep Purple, 1989; A Time Without Shadows, 1990; Other Kinds of Treason, 1990; Dangerous Edge, 1991; Show Me a Hero, 1992; The Line Crosser, 1993; As Time Goes By, 1994; Beyond the Silence, 1995; The Long Run, 1996. As Patrick Kelly: Codeword Cromwell, 1980; The Lonely Margins, 1981. As Richard Butler: Where All the Girls are Sweeter, 1975; Italian Assets, 1976. Membership: Society of Authors. Literary Agent: Blake Friedmann Literary Agency. Address: Cheriton House, Furnace Lane, Lamberhurst, Kent, England.

ALLCOT Guy. See: POCOCK Tom.

ALLDRITT Keith, b. 10 Dec 1935, Wolverhampton, England. Professor of English; Writer. m. Joan Hardwick, 10 Apr 1980, 1 son, 1 daughter. Education: BA, MA, St Catherine's College, Cambridge. Publications: The Making of George Orwell, 1969; The Visual Imagination of D H Lawrence, 1970; The Good Pit Man, 1975; The Lover Next Door, 1977; Elgar on the Journey to Hanley, 1978; Poetry as Chamber Music, 1978; Modernism in the Second World War, 1989; Churchill the Writer: His Life as a Man of Letters, 1992; The Greatest of Friends: Franklin Roosevelt and Winston Churchill 1939-45, 1995. Honour: Fellow, Royal Society of Literature. Memberships: Arnold Bennett Society; Society of Authors; D H Lawrence Society; International Churchill Society; Modern Language Association. Literary

Agent: Murray Pollinger Agency. Address: 48 Church Street, Lichfield, Staffordshire WS13 6ED, England.

ALLEN Blair H, b. 2 July 1933, Los Angeles, California, USA. Writer; Poet; Artist. m. Juanita Aguilar Raya, 27 Jan 1968, 1 son, 1 daughter. Education: AA, San Diego College, 1964; Studied, University of Washington, 1965-66; BA, San Diego State University, 1970. Appointments: Book Reviewer, Los Angeles Times, 1977-78; Special Feature Editor, Cerulean Press & Kent Publications, 1982-. Publications: Televisual Poems for Bloodshot Eyeballs, 1978; Malice in Blunderland, 1974; N/Z, 1979; The Atlantis Trilogy, 1982; Dreamwish of the Magician, 1983; Right through the Silver Lined 1984 Looking Glass, 1984; The Magical World of David Cole (editor), 1984; Snow Summits in the Sun, (editor), 1988; Trapped in a Cold War Travelogue, 1991; May Burning into August 1992; The Subway Poems, 1993; When the Ghost of Cassandra Whispers in My Ears, 1996; Editor: The Cerulan Anthology of Sci-Fi/Outer Space/Fantasy/Poetry and Prose Poems, 1995; Bonfire on the Beach, 1993; 5 Other Small Chapbooks & Poetry. Contributions to: Numerous periodicals. Honours: First Prize for Poetry, Pacificus Foundation Competition for 1992; Various Honours and Awards. Memberships: Beyond Baroque Foundation; Medina Foundation; California State Poetry Society; Association of Applied Poetry. Address: 9651 Estacia Court, Cucamonga, CA 91730, USA.

ALLEN Diogenes, b. 17 Oct 1932, Lexington, Kentucky, USA. Clergy; Professor. m. Jane Billing, 8 Sept 1958, 3 sons, 1 daughter. Education: BA with high distinction, University of Kentucky, 1954; BA Honours 1957, MA 1961, Oxford University, England; BD 1959, MA 1962, PhD 1965, Yale University. Publications: Reasonableness of Faith, 1968; Finding Our Father, 1974, re-issued as Path of Perfect Love, 1992; Between Two Worlds, 1977, re-issued as Temptation, 1984; Traces of God, 1981; Three Outsiders, 1983; Mechanical Explanations and the Ultimate Origin of the Universe According to Leibniz, 1983; Philosophy for Understanding Theology, 1985; Love, 1987; Christian Belief in a Postmodern World, 1989; Quest, 1990; Spirit, Nature, Community (with Eric O Springsted), 1994. Contributions to: About 50 magazines and journals. Honours: Phi Beta Kappa, 1953; Rhodes Scholar, 1955-57, 1963-64; Rockefeller Doctoral Fellow, 1962-64; Outstanding Educator of America, 1974; Research Fellowship, Association of Theological Schools, 1975-76; PEW Evangelical Scholar, 1991-92; Research Fellow, Center Theological Inquiry, 1984-86, 1994-95. Memberships: Executive Board, Society of Christian Philosophers; Executive Board, American Well Society; Advisory Committee of Center of Theological Inquiry; Leibniz Gesellschaft. Address: Princeton Theological Seminary, Princeton, NJ 08542, USA.

ALLEN John. See: **PERRY Ritchie.**

ALLEN Malcolm Dennis, b. 20 Oct 1951, Wakefield, England. Academic. m. Susan Beatrice Anne Whitehead, 24 Nov 1979, 2 sons, 2 daughters. Education: BA Hons, English & French Studies, University of Lancaster, England, 1974; MA, English, Louisiana State University, 1975; PhD, English, Pennsylvania State University, 1983. Publication: The Medievalism of Lawrence of Arabia, 1991. Contributions to: Twelve articles in academic journals, 15 book reviews in academic journals. Membership: Association of Literary Scholars and Critics. Address: University of Wisconsin, Fox Valley, 1478 Midway Road, Menasha, WI 54952-8002, USA.

ALLEN Oliver E, b. 29 June 1922, Cambridge, Massachusetts, USA. Writer. m. Deborah Hutchison, 8 May 1948, 3 sons, 2 daughters. Education: AB, Harvard University, 1943. Publications: New York, New York; Gardening with the New Small Plants; Wildflower Gardening; Decorating With Plants; Pruning & Grafting; Shade Gardens; Winter Gardens; The Windjammers; The Airline Builders; The Pacific Navigators; Building Sound Bones & Muscles; The Atmosphere; Secrets of a Good Digestion; The Vegetable Gardener's Journal; The Tiger, 1993. Contributions to: Horticulture Magazine; American Heritage; Smithsonian. Literary Agent: Curtis Brown Ltd. Address: 42 Hudson Street, New York, NY 10013, USA.

ALLEN Paula Gunn, b. 1939, Cubero, New Mexico, USA. Writer; Poet; University Lecturer. Education: BA; MFA; PhD. Appointments: Lecture, San Francisco State University, University of New Mexico, Fort Lewis College, University of California at Berkeley. Publications: The Blind Lion, 1974; Sipapu: A Cultural Perspective, 1975; Coyote's Daylight Trip, 1978; A Cannon Between My Knees,

1981; From the Center: A Folio of Native American Art and Poetry (editor), 1981; Shadow Country, 1982; Studies of American Indian Literature: Critical Essays and Course Designs (editor), 1983; The Woman Who Owned the Shadows, 1983; The Sacred Hoop: Recovering the Feminine in American Indian Traditions (essays), 1986, new edition, 1992; Skins and Bones, 1988; Spider Woman's Granddaughters: Traditional Tales and Contemporary Writing by Native American Women (editor), 1989; Grandmothers of the Light: A Medicine Woman's Sourcebook, 1991; Columbus and Beyond, 1992; Voice of the Turtle, 1994. Honours: American Book Award, 1990; Ford Foundation Grant; National Endowment for the Arts Award. Address: c/o Diane Cleaver Inc, 55 Fifth Avenue, 15th Floor, New York, NY 10003, USA.

ALLEN Roberta, b. 6 Oct 1945, New York, New York, USA. Writer. Appointments: Creative Writing Instructor, Parsons School of Design, 1986; Guest Lecturer, Murdoch University, Perth, Australia, 1989; Instructor, The Writer's Voice, 1992-95, 1996, The New School, 1993-95, 1996, New York University, 1996, Continuing Education, 1993-95. Publications: The Traveling Woman, 1986; The Daughter, 1992; Amazon Dream, 1993; Certain People, 1996; Anthologies: Contemporary American Fiction, 1983; Wild History, 1985; Between C & D, 1988; Mondo Barbie, 1993; Border Lines, 1993; Stories: House Hunting; Certain People; The Unbearables, 1995; Microfiction, 1996. Contributions to: Fiction International, 1993; Chelsea, 1991, 92, 93; Die Reisende, Akzente, Munich, 1992; The Sophisticated Traveler; The New York Times Magazine. Honours: LINE grant, 1985; Yaddo, 1987; Yaddo, 1993; VCCA, 1994. Membership: PEN. Literary Agent: Georges Borchadt Inc. Address: 5 West 16th Street, New York, NY 10011, USA.

ALLEN Stephen Valentine, (Steve Allen, William Christopher Stevens), b. 26 Dec 1921, New York, USA. Entertainer. m. Jayne Meadows, 4 sons. Education: First year: Drake University, Des Moines, Iowa; Second year: Arizona University. Publications: Dumbth, 1989; Meeting of Minds, Vol I, 1978, Vol II, 1979, Vol II, 1989, Vol IV, 1989; Murder on the Glitter Box, 1989; Murder in Manhattan, 1990; Passionate Nonsmokers' Bill of Rights, 1989; The Public Hating, 1990; Steve Allen on the Bible, Religion and Morality, 1990; Murder in Vegas, 1991; Hi-Ho, Steverino: My Adventures in the Wonderful Wacky World of TV, 1992; How To Be Funny (re-release), 1992; The Murder Game, 1993; More Steve Allen on the Bible, Religion and Morality, Book Two, 1993; Make 'em Laugh, 1993; Reflections, 1994; Compositions: Written over 4,700 songs. Contributions to: Numerous articles to magazines and newspapers. Address: Meadowlane Entertainment Inc, 15201 Burbank Boulevard, Suite B, Van Nuys, CA 91411, USA.

ALLENDE Isabel, b. 2 Aug 1942, Lima, Peru. Writer. m. William C Gordon, 17 July 1988, 1 son, 1 daughter. Publications: The House of the Spirits, 1985; Of Love and Shadows, 1987; Eva Luna, 1988; The Stories of Eva Luna, 1992; The Infinite Plan, 1995. Literary Agents: Carmen Balcells. Address: c/o Carmen Balcells, Diagonal 580, Barcelona 21, Spain.

ALLISON Gaylene Dolores, b. 2 Aug 1948, Saskatchewan, Canada. English and E S L Teacher; Editor; Poet. m. Geoff Hancock, 6 Aug 1983, 1 daughter. Education: BA, BEd, University of British Columbia; MA, University of Toronto. Appointments: Co-founder, Woman's Writing Collective, 1975; Poetry Editor, Landscape, 1976; Founding Editor, Fireweed Feminist Journal, 1977; Poetry Editor, Waves Literary Journal, 1983; Fiction Editor, The Canadian Forum: Literary and Political Magazine, 1984; Advisory Board: Tiger Lily, 1985. Publications: Women and Their Writing I and II, anthology, 1975, 1976; Landscape, anthology, 1977; Life: Still, poetry, 1981; The Unravelling, 1987; In the Valley of the Butterflies, 1989; Fungus Lady. Contributions to: Landscape; Fireweed; Canadian Literature; Island; Canadian Forum; Women and Their Writing I/II; PCR; Writers' Quarterly; Femme Plurielle; Prairie Fire; Dandelion; Poetry Toronto; Waves; Room of One's Own; Anthologies: Sp/elles; Women and Words, 1984; Canadian Poetry by Women, 1986; Canadian Women Studies, 1987. Honours: Poetry Awards, Ontario Teachers Federation, 1982, 1987; Nominated for Pat Lowther Poetry Award, 1987. Memberships: League of Canadian Poets; Amnesty International. Address: Fiction Editor, 109 Brunswick Street, Stratford, Ontario N5A 3L9, Canada.

ALLISON Michael John, b. 30 June 1940. Consultant. m. Janette Eaves Morse, 10 Mar 1967, 2 sons. Education: Ord Ctf in Mechanical Engineering, Ipswich Civic College, England, 1956-58;

HND in Mechanical Engineering, NE Essex Teaching College, England, 1958-61; Fellowship Diploma in Mechanical Engineering, 1974-76; Graduate Diploma in Quality Technology, AOQ Prize, 1976-79, RMIT; Cert Quality Engineer, American Society for Quality Control. Appointments include: Project Engineer, Product Engineering, Ford Motor Company, Geelong, 1964-67; Manufacturing Research Engineer, Boeing Co, Seattle, USA, 1967-70; Manager of Product Engineering & Quality Control, Flexdrive Inds Pty Ltd, Melbourne, 1971-78; Class 2 through to Prin Engineer, 1978-88; Supervising Engineer, TQM Dev, TNE Metro, 1988-90; Australian Telecomms Corp, Melbourne; Consultant for various industries, Stockdales Pty Ltd, Melbourne, 1990-; Visiting Lecturer, Auckland Institute of Technology. Publications: Author of numerous articles, books, tapes & software packages on quality including: Counting Out Random Numbers, in Your Computer, 1989; Quality Systems, audio tape, 1992; Productivity Improvement Through Quality Management, 1993; The Conversion Kit: The Guide to Problem Busting, book, 1994; Service Quality Systems, audio tape, 1995; Eng, 1996. Honours: Managing Director's Prize, Ransomes & Rapier Ltd, Eng; Shilkin Prize for Literature in the Field of Quality, 1994. Memberships: Chairman of Certification Committee, Council, Australian Organization for Quality, Victoria Division; Australian Society of Authors; American Society for Quality Control. Hobby: Computer Programming. Address: 8 Brixton Avenue, Eltham, Vic 3095, Australia.

ALLOTT Miriam, b. 16 June 1920, London, England. University Lecturer. m. Kenneth Allott, 2 June 1951, dec 1973. Education: MA, 1946, PhD, 1949, Liverpool University. Appointments: William Noble Fellowship, English Literature, 1946-48; Lecturer, Senior Lecturer, Reader, English Literature, 1948-73, Andrew Cecil Bradley Professor, Modern English Literature, 1973-81, Liverpool University; Professor of English, Birkbeck College, London University, 1981-85; Honorary Senior Fellow, Liverpool University; Professor Emeritus, London University. Publications: The Art of Graham Green, (with Kenneth Allott), 1951; Novelists on the Novel, 1959; Complete Poems of John Keats, 1970; Complete Poems of Matthew Arnold, 2nd edition 1979 (1st edition, Kenneth Allott, 1965); Matthew Arnold, (with R H Super), 1986; Numerous essays and articles on 19th and 20th century novelists and poets, notably Keats, Shelley, Arnold, Clough, the Brontës, George Eliot, Henry James, James Joyce, Graham Greene, Iris Murdoch, William Golding; Currently completing: E M Forster's Alexandria, a History and a Guide, and Pharos and Pharillon, edited for the New Abinger edition of Forster's writings; Critical biography of Clough; Poets on Poetry. Membership: Executive Committee, English Association. Address: 21 Mersey Avenue, Liverpool L19 3QU, England.

ALLSOPP (Harold) Bruce, b. 4 July 1912, Oxford, England. Author; Artist. m. Florence Cyrilla Woodruffe, 29 Dec 1936, dec 1991, 2 sons. Education: BA, 1933, Dip CD, 1935, Liverpool University. Appointments: Senior Lecturer, 1969-73; Reader, 1973-77, University of Newcastle-upon-Tyne. Publications: General History of Architecture, 1955; Art and the Nature of Architecture, 1952; Civilization, The Next Stage, 1969; A Modern Theory of Architecture, 1970; The Country Life Companion to British and European Architecture, 1977; Social Responsibility and the Responsible Society, 1985; Spirit of Europe, A Subliminal History, 1997. Contributions to: Various Journals. Memberships: Athenaeum; Art Workers Guild Master; MRTPI; FSA; Society of Architectural Historians. Address: Ferndale, Mount View,Stocksfield, Northumberland NE43 7HL, England.

ALLWOOD Martin Samuel, b. 13 Apr 1916, Jonkoping, Sweden. Author; Professor. m. Enelia Paz Gomez, 20 Dec 1976, 2 sons, 3 daughters. Education: MA, Cantab; MA, Columbia, 1949; Dr Rer Pol Technische Hochschule Darmstadt, 1953. Appointments: President, Anglo-American Centre, Sweden; Professor, Nordic College of Journalism. Publications: The Cemetery of the Cathedrals, 1945; The Swedish Crime, play, 1976; New English Poems, 1981; Valda Svenska Dikter, 1982; Meet Will Shakespeare, 1985; Essays on Contemporary Civilization, 1988; The Roots of Western Civilization, 1990; The Empress and Her Lover, 1993; Verona Bratesch, 1993; The Big Book of Humo(u)r From Britain and America, 1993; The Empress and Her Lover, plays, 1994. Contributions to: Numerous articles. Honour: Kaj Munk Society Award, 1992. Memberships: Gothenburg Society of Authors; Swedish Society of Immigrant Authors. Address: Anglo-American Centre, 56532 Mullsjo, Sweden.

ALMQUIST Gregg Andrew, b. 1 Dec 1948, Minneapolis, Minnesota, USA. Actor; Novelist; Playwright. Education: BA, University

of Minnesota, 1971. Publications: Beast Rising, 1988 (published in France under the title L'eveil de la bete); Wolf Kill, 1990; Plays (produced): The Duke; The Eve of Saint Venus (adapted from Burgess); The Winter That Ended in June; Pavan for a Dead Princess. Address: ICM, 40 West 57th Street, New York, NY 10019, USA.

ALONSO ALVAREZ Emilio, (Andrenio), b. 2 July 1940, Minera de Luna, Leòn, Spain. Naval Architect. m. Mercedes Pueyo, 29 July 1966, 1 son. Education: Naval Architecture, Escuela Técnica Superior de Ingenieros Navales, 1965. Publications: Coplas de la Transiciòn, De Franco a Tejero, poetry, 1986; Octavas Reales Callejeras sin Ton ni Son, poetry, 1987; An anonymous libel against the Gulf War - El Amor Petrolero es Signo de Mal Agüero, theater, 1991; El Condòn Encantado, theater, not published. Contributions to: El Cocodrilo; El Independiente; El Mundo. Honour: Casa Villas Poetry Award, Madrid, 1983. Address: Juan Ramon Jimenez 24, 28036 Madrid, Spain.

ALPERN David M. Senior Editor, Newsweek. Education: Studied History, Columbia University, New York. Appointments: New York City Reporter, United Press International, 3 years; New York Correspondent, 1966, Periscope Writer, 1967, Associate Editor in Nation, 1968, New York Bureau Chief, 1972, General Editor in National Affairs, 1973, News Media Editor, 1977, Senior Editor in National Affairs, 1978, Senior Editor and Deputy National Affairs Editor, 1979, Newsweek, 1966-: Editor or Writer of cover stories and features on such topics as anti-nuclear movement, welfare, Watergate, CIA, KGB, Presidential campaigns, crime, and the roles of money and media in politics; Co-Host, Newsweek on Air, broadcast on over 100 stations of AP Radio Network; Supervises the advance excerpting of books appearing in Newsweek including books by Dan Quayle, Boris Yeltsin and Nancy Reagan; Also in charge of the Newsweek Poll, a public-opinion survey on social and political issues. Honours: 2 McKnight Journalism Awards, Daily Spectator (school newspaper); National Award of Merit for cover story, Living With Crime, USA, Association of Trial Lawyers, 1973; Writing Award for cover story, The Concorde Furor, Aviation and Space Writers Association, 1976; Honors, National Association of Realtors' Journalism Awards Competition for inside report, A City Revival?, 1979; Silver Gavel Award for cover story, All About Impeachment, American Bar Association, 1975; Winner for report on Cuban refugees, Lincoln University Unity Award for Political Reporting, 1981; First Prize, Golden Hammer Award for cover profile of Felix Rohatyn, National Association of Home Builders, 1982; Co-Recipient, Citation for The Watergate Legacy, Freedoms Foundation, Valley Forge, 1983. Address: c/o Newsweek, 251 West 57th Street, New York, NY 10019-1894, USA.

ALPERS Antony, b. 10 Sept 1919, New Zealand. Writer. Appointments: Journalist, Editor, New Zealand, 1936-66; Professor of English, Queen's University, Kingston, Ontario, 1966-82 (now Emeritus). Publications: Katherine Mansfield: A Biography, 1953; Dolphins, 1960; Maori Myths and Tribal Legends, 1964, 2nd edition 1996; Legends of the South Sea, 1970, as The World of the Polynesians, 1987; The Life of Katherine Mansfield, 1980; The Stories of Katherine Mansfield, 1984; Confident Tomorrows, A Biographical Self Portrait of O T J Alpers, 1993. Honours: Honorary Doctor of Laws, Queens University, Kingston, Ontario, Canada, 1984. Address: 46 Memorial Avenue, Christchurch 5, New Zealand.

ALPHONSO-KARKALA John B, b. 30 May 1923, South Kanara, Mysore State, India. Writer; Poet; Professor of Literature. m. Leena Anneli Hakalehto, 20 Dec 1964, 3 children. Education: BA, 1950, MA, 1953, Bombay University; University of London, 1954-55; PhD, Columbia University, 1964. Appointments: Visiting Lecturer, City College of the City University of New York, 1963; Assistant Professor, 1964-65, Associate Professor, 1965-68, Professor of Literature, 1969-, State University of New York at New Paltz; Visiting Professor, Columbia University, 1969-70. Publications: Indo-English Literature in the Nineteenth Century, 1970; Anthology of Indian Literature (editor), 1971, revised edition as Rishis Buddha, Acharyas, Bhaktas and Mahatma, 1987; Bibliography of Indo-English Literature, 1800-1966 (editor with Leena Karkala), 1974; Comparative World Literature: Seven Essays, 1974; Passions of the Nightless Night (novel), 1974; Jawaharlal Nehru: A Literary Portrait, 1975; When Night Falls (poems), 1980; Vedic Vision (editor), 1980; Joys of Jayanagara (novel), 1981; Indo-English Literature: Essays (co-author Leena A Karkala), 1994 . Memberships: American Oriental Society; Association for Asian Studies; International Congress of Comparative Literature; International Congress of Orientalists; Modern Language Association of America. Address: 20 Millrock Road, New Paltz, NY 12561, USA.

ALSTON William (Payne), b. 29 Nov 1921, Shreveport, Louisiana, USA. Professor of Philosophy; Writer. m. (1) Mary Frances Collins, 15 Aug 1943, div, 1 daughter, (2) Valerie Tibbetts Barnes, 3 July 1963. Education: BM, Centenary College, 1942; PhD, University of Chicago, 1951. Appointments: Instructor, 1949-52, Assistant Professor, 1952-56, Associate Professor, 1956-61, Professor, 1961-71, Acting Chairman, 1961-64, Director of Graduate Studies, 1966-71, Department of Philosophy, University of Michigan; Professor of Philosophy, Douglass College, Rutgers University, 1971-76, University of Illinois at Urbana-Champaign, 1976-80, Syracuse University, 1980-; Visiting Lecturer, Harvard University, 1955-56; Fellow, Center for Advanced Studies in the Behavioral Sciences, 1965-66; Austin Fagothey Visiting Professor of Philosophy, Santa Clara University, 1991. Publications: Religious Belief and Philosophical Thought, 1963; Readings in Twentieth Century Philosophy (with G Nakhnikian), 1963; The Philosophy of Language, 1964; The Problems of Philosophy: Introductory Readings (with R B Brandt), 1967, 3rd edition, 1978; Divine Nature and Human Language, 1989; Epistemic Justification, 1989; Perceiving God, 1991; The Reliability of Sense Perception, 1993; A Realist Conception of Truth, 1996. Editor: Philosophical Research Archives, 1974-77; Faith and Philosophy, 1982-90; Cornell Studies in the Philosophy of Religion, 1987-. Contributions to: Scholarly books and journals. Honour: Chancellor's Exceptional Academic Achievement Award, Syracuse University, 1990. Memberships: American Academy of Arts and Sciences; Society for Philosophy and Psychology, president, 1976-77; American Philosophical Association, president of Central Division, 1978-79; President, Society of Christian Philosophers, 1978-81. Address: c/o Department of Philosophy, Syracuse University, Syracuse, NY 13244, USA.

ALTER Jonathan. Senior Editor. m. Emily Lazar, 1 son, 2 daughters. Education: BA with Honours, History, Harvard University, 1979. Appointments: Freelance Writer for various publications including New Republic, Esquire, Rolling Stone, and New York Times; Editor, Washington Monthly, 1981-83; Associate Editor in Nation section, 1983, Media Critic, 1984-, Senior Writer, 1987, Senior Editor, writes the Between the Lines column, 1991-, Newsweek; Covered the Presidential campaigns for Newsweek, 1984, 1988, 1992, 1996; Contributing Correspondent, NBC News (includes NBC Nightly News, Today, MSNBC), 1996-; Television appearances including shows on CNN, BBC, ABC's Nightline, and This Week with David Brinkley, PBS's MacNeil/Lehrer NewsHour, and Charlie Rose, and MTV. Publications: Co-Author, Selecting a President; Co-Editor, Inside the System; Author of weekly publication, Conventional Wisdom Watch; Editor of various publications including Newsweek's 60th Anniversary issue. Honours: Many awards for media criticism including: Lowell Mellett Award, 1987; 2 New York State Bar Association Media Awards; Winner, Gerald Loeb Award for Distinguished Business Reporting, 1987; Many awards for his political columns including: National Headliner Award for Consistently Outstanding Feature Column, 1993; Clarion Award for Best Magazine Opinion Column, Women in Communications, 1994. Address: c/o Newsweek, 251 West 57th Street, New York, NY 10019-1894, USA.

ALTER Robert B(ernard), b. 2 Apr 1935, New York, New York, USA. Professor; Literary Critic. m. Carol Cosman, 17 June 1974, 3 sons, 1 daughter. Education: BA, Columbia College, 1957; MA 1958, PhD 1962, Harvard University. Appointments: Instructor, Assistant Professor, English, Columbia University, 1962-66; Associate Professor, Hebrew and Comparative Literature, 1967-69, Professor of Hebrew and Comparative Literature, 1969-89, Class of 1937 Professor, 1989-, University of California, Berkeley. Publications: Partial Magic, 1975; Defenses of the Imagination, 1978; Stendhal: A Biography, 1979; The Art of Biblical Narrative, 1981; Motives for Fiction, 1984; The Art of Biblical Poetry, 1985; The Pleasures of Reading in an Ideological Age, 1989; Necessary Angels, 1991; The World of Biblical Literature, 1992; Hebrew and Modernity, 1994; Genesis: Translation and Commentary, 1996. Contributions to: Commentary; New Republic; New York Times Book Review; London Review of Books; Times Literary Supplement. Honours: English Institute Essay Prize, 1965; National Jewish Book Award for Jewish Thought, 1982; Present Tense Award for Religious Thought, 1986; Award for Scholarship, National Foundation for Jewish Culture, 1995. Memberships: American Comparative Literature Association; Association of Literary Scholars and Critics; Council of Scholars of the Library of Congress; American Academy of Arts and Sciences. Literary

Agent: Georges Borchardt. Address: 1475 Le Roy Avenue, Berkeley, CA 94708, USA.

ALTHER Lisa, b. 23 July 1944, Tennessee, USA. Author. m. Richard Alther, 26 Aug 1966, 1 daughter. Education: BA, Wellesley College, 1966. Appointments: Staff Member, Atheneum Publishers, New York City; Lecturer, St Michael's College, Burlington, 1980. Publications: Kinflicks, 1976; Original Sins, 1981; Other Women, 1984; Bedrock, 1990; Five Minutes in Heaven, 1995. Contributions to: New York Times Magazine; New York Times Book Review; Natural History; New Society; Arts and Antiques; Boston Globe; Washington Post; Los Angeles Times; San Francisco Chronicle; Southern Living. Memberships: PEN; Authors Guild; National Writers Union. Literary Agent: Gloria Loomis. Address: Watkins-Loomis, 133 East 35th Street, No 1, New York, NY 10016, USA.

ALTICK Richard Daniel, b. 19 Sept 1915, Lancaster, Pennsylvania, USA. Writer. m. Helen W Keller, 15 Aug 1942, 2 daughters. Education: AB, Franklin and Marshall College, 1936; PhD, University of Pennsylvania, 1941. Appointments: Faculty 1945, Regent's Professor of English 1968-82, Regent's Professor Emeritus of English 1982-, Ohio State University, Columbus. Publications: Preface to Critical Reading, 1946, 6th revised edition, 1984; The Cowden Clarkes, 1948; The Scholar Adventurers, 1950; The English Common Reader: A Social History of the Mass Reading Public, 1800-1900, 1957; The Art of Literary Research, 1963, 4th revised edition, 1992; Lives and Letters: A History of Literary Biography in England and America, 1965; Carlyle: Past and Present (editor), 1965; Browning's Roman Murder Story (with J F Loucks), 1968; To Be in England, 1969; Victorian Studies in Scarlet, 1970; Browning: The Ring and the Book (editor), 1971; Victorian People and Ideas: A Companion for the Modern Reader of Victorian Literature, 1973; The Shows of London, 1978; Paintings from Books: Art and Literature in Britain 1760-1900, 1985; Deadly Encounters: Two Victorian Sensations (in UK as Evil Encounters), 1986; Writers, Readers and Occasions, 1989; The Presence of the Present: Topics of the Day in the Victorian Novel, 1991; Punch: The Lively Youth of a British Institution 1841-51, 1997. Honours: Guggenheim Fellowship, 1975; Phi Beta Kappa's Christian Gauss Award, 1991. Address: 276 West Southington Avenue, Worthington, OH 43085, USA.

ALTMAN Philip, b. 6 Jan 1924, Kansas City, Missouri, USA. Editor; Administrator. m. Lillian Berlinsky, 1 Sept 1946, 1 son, 1 daughter. Education: BA, University of Southern California, 1948; MSc, Western Reserve University, 1949. Appointments: Director, Editor, Office of Biological Handbooks, 1959-79; Executive Director, Council of Biology Editors, 1981-; Executive Editor, Biology Databook Series, 1983-86. Publications: Handbook of Respiration, 1958; Handbook of Circulation, 1959; Blood and Other Body Fluids, 1961; Growth, 1962; Biology Data Book, 1964, 2nd edition, 3 vols, 1972-74; Environmental Biology, 1966; Metabolism, 1968; Respiration & Circulation, 1971; Cell Biology, 1976; Human Health and Disease, 1977; Inbred and Genetically Defined Strains of Laboratory Animals, 1979; Pathology of Laboratory Mice and Rats, 1985. Contributions to: Scientific journals and other publications. Address: Council of Biology Editors, 9650 Rockville Pike, Bethesda, MD 20814, USA.

ALUKO Timothy Mofolorunso, b. 14 June 1918, Ilesha, Nigeria. Novelist. m. Janet Adebisi Fajemisin, 1948, 6 children. Education: BSc, University of London, 1950; PhD in Public Health Engineering, University of Lagos, 1976. Appointments: Senior Lecturer, University of Ibadan, 1966; Commissioner of Finance, Government of Western Nigeria, 1971-73. Publications: One Man, One Wife, 1959; One Man, One Matchet, 1964; Kinsman and Foreman, 1966; Chief the Honourable Minister, 1970; His Worshipful Majesty, 1973; Wrong Ones in the Dock, 1982; A State of Our Own, 1986; Conduct Unbecoming, 1993; Uncollected short story: The New Engineer, 1968. Honours: Officer of the Order of the British Empire, 1963; OON, 1964. Address: 53 Ladipo Oluwote Road, Apapa, Lagos, Nigeria.

ALVAREZ Alfred, b. 5 Aug 1929, London, England. Poet; Author. m. 7 Apr 1966, 2 sons, 1 daughter. Education: BA, 1952, MA, 1956, Corpus Christi College, Oxford. Appointments: Poetry Critic and Editor, The Observer, 1956-66; Advisory Editor, Penguin Modern European Poets, 1964-76. Publications: The Shaping Spirit, 1958; The School of Donne, 1961; The New Poetry, 1962; Under Pressure, 1965; Beyond All the Fiddle, 1968; Penguin Modern Poets No 18, 1970; Apparition, 1971; The Savage God, 1971; Beckett, 1973; Hers, 1974;

Faber Book of Modern European Poetry, 1992; Night, 1995. Contributions to: Numerous Magazines and Journals. Honours: Vachel Lindsay Prize for Poetry, 1961. Memberships: Climbers; Alpine; Beefsteak. Address: c/o Aitken & Stone, 29 Fernshaw Road, London SW10 0TG, England.

AMADI Elechi, b. 12 May 1934, Aluu, Nigeria. Novelist. m. Doah Ohlae, 1957, 8 children. Education: BSc in Mathematics and Physics, University College, Ibadan, 1959. Appointments: Writer-in-Residence and Dean of the Faculty of Arts, College of Education, Port Harcourt, 1984-87; Commissioner of Education, 1987-89, and Commissioner of Lands and Housing, 1989-90, Rivers State. Publications: The Concubine, 1966; The Great Ponds, 1969; The Slave, 1978; Estrangement, 1986; Plays: Isiburu, 1969; Peppersoup, and The Road to Ibadan, 1977; Dancer of Johannesburg, 1979; Other works including Hymn and Prayer books. Honour: International Writers Program Grant, University of Iowa, 1973. Address: Box 331, Port Harcourt, Nigeria.

AMADO. See: **ARTAZA PAZ Roberto Alejandro.**

AMANSHAUSER Gerhard, b. 2 Jan 1928, Salzburg, Austria. Writer. Education: Technical University of Graz; Universities of Vienna, Austria and Marburg; Dr H C, 1993. Publications: Aus der Leben der Quaden, 1968; Der Deserteur, 1970; Ärgernisse eines Zauberers, 1973; Schloss mit späten Gäten, 1975; Grenzen Essays, 1977; Aufzeichnungen einer Sonde, 1979; List der Illusionen, 1985; Gedichte, 1986; Fahrt zur verbotenen Stadt, 1987; Der Ohne Namen See, Chinese Impressions, 1988; Moloch Horridus, 1989; Lektüre, 1991; Gegensätze, 1993; Das Erschlagen von Stechmücken, 1993. Contributions to: Literatur und Kritik; Neues Forum; Protokolle; Neue Rundschau. Honours: Georg Trakl Promotion Prize, 1952; Theodor Körner Prize, 1970; Rauriser Literaturpreis, 1973; Förderungspreis der Stadt Salzburg, 1975; Preis der Salzburger Wirtschaft, 1985; Alma Johanna Koenig Preis, 1987; Würdigungspreis für Literatur, Bundesministeriums für Wissenschaft, Forschung und Kunst, 1994. Address: Brunnhausgasse 10, 5020 Salzburg, Austria.

AMB Daniel. See: **ANDERSEN Baltser.**

AMBLER Eric, b. 28 June 1909, London, England. Author; Screenwriter. m. (1) Louise Crombie, 1939, div 1958, (2) Joan Harrison, 1958. Education: London University. Publications: The Dark Frontier, 1936; Uncommon Danger, 1937; Epitaph for a Spy, 1938; Cause for Alarm, 1938; The Mask of Dimitrios, 1939; Journey Into Fear, 1940; The October Man, 1948; Judgement on Deltcher, 1951; The Schirmer Inheritance, 1953; The Night Comers, 1956; Passage of Arms, 1959; The Light of Day, 1962; The Ability to Kill, and Other Pieces, 1963; A Kind of Anger, 1964; The Intriguers, 1965; Dirty Story: A Further Account of the Life and Adventures of Arthur Abdel Simpson, 1967; The Intercom Conspiracy, 1969; The Levanter, 1972; Doctor Frigo, 1974; Send No More Roses, 1977; The Care of Time, 1981; Here Lies: An Autobiography, 1985; Waiting for Orders: Short Stories, 1991; The Story So Far (stories and reminiscences), 1993. Honours: Golden Dagger Awards, Crime Writers Association, 1959, 1962, 1967, 1973; Edgar Allan Poe Awards, Mystery Writers of America, 1975; Diamond Dagger Award, Crime Writers Association, 1989. Address: 14 Brynaston Square, London W1H 7FF, England.

AMBROSE David Edwin, b. 21 Feb 1943, Chorley, Lancs, England. Playwright; Screenwriter; Novelist. m. Lawrence Huguette Hammerli, 13 Sept 1979. Education: Degree in Law, University of Oxford, Merton College, 1965. Publications: Novels: The Man Who Turned Into Himself, 1993, 1994; Mother of God, 1995; Hollywood Lies; Many TV Plays and Screenplays in Hollywood and Worldwide; also Seige, Cambridge Theatre, London, 1972. Honours: 1st Prize Screenplay, Sitges Film Festival, 1980, for The Survivor. Membership: Dramatists' Club, London. Literary Agent: William Morris Agency. Address: 31 Soho Square, London, W1V 5DG, England.

AMBROSE John. See: **CALVOCORESSI Peter.**

AMBROSE Stephen E(dward), b. 10 Jan 1936, Decatur, Illinois, USA. Historian; Writer; Professor. m. (1) Judith Dorlester, 6 June 1957, dec Oct 1966, 1 son, 1 daughter, (2) Moira Buckley, 30 Sept 1967. Education: BS, University of Wisoncsin, 1957; MA, Louisiana State University, 1958; PhD, University of Wisconsin, 1963. Appointments: Assistant Professor, Louisiana State University, 1960-64; Associate Professor, Johns Hopkins University, 1964-69; Ernest J King Professor, Naval War College, Newport, Rhode Island, 1969-70;

Dwight D Eisenhower Professor of War and Peace, Kansas State University, 1970-71; Professor, 1971-, Alumni Distinguished Professor, 1982-, University of New Orleans; Mary Ball Washington Professor, University College, Dublin, 1981-82; Visiting Professor, University of California at Berkeley, 1986, US Army War College, Carlisle, Pennsylvania, 1990. Publications: Halleck: Lincoln's Chief of Staff, 1962; Upton and the Army, 1964; Duty, Honor, Country: A History of West Point, 1966; Eisenhower and Berlin, 1945; The Decision to Halt at the Elbe, 1967; Institutions in Modern America: Innovation in Structure and Process (editor), 1967; The Papers of Dwight D Eisenhower: The War Years (assistant editor), 5 volumes, 1970; The Supreme Commander: The War Years of General Dwight D Eisenhower, 1970; Rise to Globalism: American Foreign Policy since 1938, 1971, 6th edition, revised, 1991; The Military and American Society (with James Barber), 1972; Crazy Horse and Custer: The Parallel Lives of Two American Warriors, 1975; Ike's Spies: Eisenhower and the Espionage Establishment (with Richard Immerman), 1981; Eisenhower: Soldier, General of the Army, President-Elect, 1890-1952, 1983; Milton S Eisenhower: Educational Statesman (with Richard Immerman), 1983; Eisenhower: The President, 1984; Pegasus Bridge: 6 June 1944, 1985; Nixon: The Education of a Politician, 1913-1962, 1987; Nixon: The Triumph of a Politician, 1962-1972, 1989; The Wisdom of Dwight D Eisenhower: Quotations from Ike's Speeches and Writings, 1939-1969 (editor), 1990; Nixon: Ruin and Recovery, 1973-1990, 1991; Band of Brothers: E Company, 506th Regiment, 101st Airborne, from Normandy to Hitler's Eagle's Nest, 1992; Eisenhower and the German POWs: Fact against Falsehood, editor, 1992; Undaunted Courage: Meriwether Lewis, Thomas Jefferson, and the Opening of the American West, 1996. Contributions to: Books, journals and television documentaries. Honour: National Book Award, Freedom, Foundation, 1984. Memberships: American Committee on World War II; American Historical Association; American Military Institute; Southern Historical Association. Address: c/o Ambrose Tubbs Inc, 1606 Hauser Boulevard, Helena, MT 59601, USA.

AMERY Carl, b. 9 Apr 1922, Munich, Germany. Writer. m. Marijane Gerth, 10 Apr 1950, 3 sons, 2 daughters. Education: Humanistisches Gymnasium, 1940; Literary and Language Studies, Munich and Washington, DC, 1946-50. Appointments: Editor, Bavarian Radio, 1950, 1962; Director, Munich Library System, 1967-71. Publications: Novels: Die Grosse Deutsche Tour, 1959; Das Koenigsprojekt, 1974; Die Wallfahrer, 1986; Das Geheimnis der Krypta, 1990. Essays: Die Kapitulation, 1963; Das Ende der Vorshung, 1972. Honour: Cross of Merit, Germany, 1988. Memberships: German Writer's Association; PEN Center, Germany. Address: Draechslstrasse 7, D-8 Munich 90, Germany.

AMES Leslie. See: **RIGONI Orlando Joseph.**

AMICHAI Yehuda, b. 1924, Würzburg, Germany (Israeli citizen). Poet. m. Chang Sokolov. Education: Hebrew University, Jerusalem. Appointments: Visiting Poet, University of California, Berkeley, 1976, New York University, 1987. Publications: Now and in Other Days, 1955; Two Hopes Away, 1958; In The Park, 1959; Now in the Turmoil, 1968; And Not in Order to Remember, 1971; Songs of Jerusalem and Myself, 1973; Behind All This Lies Great Happiness, 1974; Amen, 1978; On New Years Day, Next to a House Being Built, 1979; Time, 1979; Love Poems, 1981; Hour of Charity, 1982; Great Tranquility: Questions and Answers, 1983; From Man You Came, and to Men You Will Return, 1985; The Selected Poetry of Yehuda Amichai, 1986; Poems of Jerusalem, 1987; Even a Fist was Once an Open Palm with Fingers, 1991. Honour: Honorary Doctorate, Hebrew University, 1990. Address: 26 Malki Street, Yemin Moshe, Jerusalem, Israel.

AMICOLA José, b. 15 Feb 1942, Buenos Aires. Professor. Education: Licenciado en Letras, Universidad de Buenos Aires, Argentina; Dr Philosophiae, Universität Göttingen, Germany, 1982. Publications: Sobre Cortazar, 1969; Astrologia y Fascismo en la Obra de Arlt, 1984; Manuel Puig y La Tela Que Atrapa Al Lector, 1992; Dostoievski, 1994; De La Forma a La Informacion, 1997. Honour: Premio Banco Mercantil, 1992. Memberships: Instituto Intern Literatura Iberoamericana, Pittsburgh. Address: Las Heras, 3794 - 11A, 1425 Buenos Aires, Argentina.

AMIN Sayed-Hassan, b. 25 Nov 1948, Persia. University Professor Emeritus; Author; Advocate. m. 2 sons, 2 daughters. Education: LLB, 1970; LLM, 1975; PhD, 1979; Scottish Bar Exams, 1980-82; Mufti-at-large in Islamic Law. Appointments: Lecturer, 1979;

AMIN Sayed-Hassan, b. 25 Nov 1948, Persia. University Professor Emeritus; Author; Advocate. m. 2 sons, 2 daughters. Education: LLB, 1970; LLM, 1975; PhD, 1979; Scottish Bar Exams, 1980-82; Mufti-at-large in Islamic Law. Appointments: Lecturer, 1979; Senior Lecturer, 1981; Reader, 1984; Professor, 1991, Glasgow Caledonian University; President, Islamic Institute of International and Comparative Law, 1994-. Publications: 36 Books including: Philosophy of Mulla Sadra; International and Legal Problems of the Gulf; Middle East Legal Systems; Law and Justice in Contemporary Yemen; Islamic Law and its Implications for the Modern World; Legal System of Iraq; Legal System of Kuwait; Law of Intellectual Property in Developing Countries. Contributions to: International and Comparative Law Quarterly; Oil and Gas Law and Taxation Review; Kayhan-e Andisheh. Memberships: Society of Authors; Executive Council: Scottish Branch; Royal Institute of International Affairs; Faculty of Advocates; Council for National Academic Awards; Patron, Prisoners Abroad, Past Director and Representative, World Development Movement; Fellow, Islamic Academy. Address: Faculty of Advocates, Parliament House, Edinburgh EH1 1RF, Scotland.

AMIS Martin Louis, b. 25 Aug 1949, Oxford, England. Author. Education: BA, Exeter College, Oxford. Appointments: Fiction and Poetry Editor, Times Literary Supplement, 1974; Literary Editor, New Statesman, 1977-79; Special Writer, The Observer Newspaper, 1980-. Publications: The Rachel Papers, 1973; Dead Babies, 1975; Success, 1978; Other People: A Mystery Story, 1981; Invasion of the Space Invaders, 1982; Money, 1984; London Fields, 1989; Time's Arrow; Einstein's Monsters: Five Stories, 1987; The Information, 1995. Honour: Somerset Maugham Award, 1974. Address: c/o Peters Fraser & Dunlop, 5th Floor, The Chambers, Chelsea Harbour, Lots Road, London SW10 0XP, England.

AMMONS A(rchie) R(andolph), b. 18 Feb 1926, Whiteville, North Carolina, USA. Poet; Professor of English. m. Phyllis Plumbo, 26 Nov 1949, 1 son. Education: BS, Wake Forest College, 1949; University of California at Berkeley, 1950-52. Appointments: Principal, Elementary School, Hatteras, North Carolina, 1949-50; Executive Vice President, Friedrich and Dimmock Inc, Millville, New Jersey, 1952-62; Poetry Editor, Nation, New York City, 1963; Assistant Professor, 1964-68, Associate Professor, 1968-71, Professor of English, 1971-73, Goldwin Smith Professor of English, 1973-, Cornell University; Visiting Professor, Wake Forest University, 1974-75. Publications: Ommateum, with Doxology, 1955; Expressions of Sea Level, 1964; Corsons Inlet, 1965; Tape for the Turn of the Year, 1965; Northfield Poems, 1966; Selected Poems, 1968; Uplands, 1970; Briefings, 1971; Collected Poems, 1951-1971, 1972; Sphere: The Form of a Motion, 1973; Diversifications, 1975; For Doyle Fosso, 1977; Highgate Road, 1977; The Snow Poems, 1977; The Selected Poems, 1951-1977, 1977, expanded edition, 1987; Breaking Out, 1978; Six-Piece Suite, 1978; Selected Longer Poems, 1980; Changing Things, 1981; A Coast of Trees, 1981; Worldly Hopes, 1982; Lake Effect Country, 1982; Sumerian Vistas, 1987; The Really Short Poems of A R Ammons, 1991; Garbage, 1993. Contributions to: Periodicals. Honours: Guggenheim Fellowship, 1966; Levinson Prize, 1970; National Book Awards for Poetry, 1973, 1993; Bollingen Prize for Poetry, 1974-75; John D and Catharine T MacArthur Foundation Prize, 1981-86; National Book Critics Circle Award, 1982; North Carolina Award for Literature, 1986; Frost Silver Medal, Poetry Society of America. Address: Department of English, Cornell University, Ithaca, NY 14853, USA.

AMOROSO Bruno, b. 11 Dec 1936, Rome, Italy. Associate Professor in Economic Policy. Education: MD, University La Sapienza, Rome, 1966. Publications: Lo Stato Imprenditore, 1978; Rapporto Dalla Scandinavia, 1980; European Industrial Relations, 1990; Macroeconomic Theories and Policies for the 1990s, 1992; Scandinavian Perspectives on European Integration, 1990. Contributions to: Comparative Labour Law Journal; International Journal of Human Resource Management; Economia Pubblica. Memberships: Vice President, European Inter-University Association on Society, Science and Technology, Brussels; European Culture Association, Venice. Address: Webersgade 28, Copenhagen DK-2100, Denmark.

ABRAMS Meyer Howard, b. 1912. Publications: The Mirror and The Lamp, 1953; A Glossary of Literary Terms, 1957; English Romatic Poets: Modern Essays in Criticism, 1960; The Norton Anthology of English Literature (editor), 1962 et al; Natural Supernaturalism, 1971; Wordsworth, 1972; The Correspondent Breeze: Essays, 1984; Doing

Things With Texts, 1989. Honours: Fellow, American Academy and Institute of Arts & Letters, 1990.

AN Tai Sung, b. 3 Feb 1931, Seoul, Korea. College Professor; Author. m. Sihn Ja Lee, 23 Aug 1969, 2 daughters. Education: BA, Indiana University, Bloomington, USA, 1956; MA, Yale University, New Haven, USA, 1957; PhD, University of Pennsylvania, USA, 1963. Appointments: Professor of Political Science, 1963-73, Everett E Nuttle Professor, Political Science, Washington College, Chestertown, 1973-. Publications: Mao Tse Tung's Cultural Revolution; The Sino Soviet Territorial Dispute; The Lin Piao Affair; North Korea in Transition: From Dictatorship to Dynasty; North Korea: A Political Handbook: The Vietnam War; About 80 articles. Honours: Lindback Award for Distinguished Teaching; Sears Roebuck Foundation Teaching Excellence and Campus Leadership Award. Memberships: American Political Science Association; Association for Asian Studies; Asia Society; Korean Association of Oriental History and Civilization; American Association of University Professors. Address: Department of Political Science and International Studies, Washington College, 300 Washington Avenue, Chestertown, MD 21620, USA.

ANAND Mulk Raj, b. 12 Dec 1905, Peshawar, India. Novelist. m. (2) Shirin Vajifdar, 1950, 1 daughter. Education: BA (Hons), Punjab University, 1924; PhD, University College, University of London, 1929; Cambridge University, 1929-30. Appointments: Director, Kutub publishers, Bombay, 1946-; Taught at the Universities of Punjab, Benares, and Rajasthan, Jaipur, 1948-66. Publications: Untouchable, 1935; The Coolie, 1936; Two Leaves and a Bud, 1937; The Village, 1939; Lament on the Death of a Master of Arts, 1939; Across the Black Waters, 1940; The Sword and the Sickle, 1942; The Big Heart, 1945; Seven Summers: The Story of an Indian Childhood, 1951; Private Life of an Indian Prince, 1953; The Old Woman and the Cow, 1960; The Road, 1961; Morning Face, 1968; Confession of a Lover, 1976; The Bubble, 1984; Death of a Hero, 1995; Also: Various short stories and other works. Honours: Sahitya Academy Award, 1974. Address: 25 Cuffe Parade, Bombay 400 005, India.

ANANIA Michael (Angelo), b. 5 Aug 1939, Omaha, Nebraska, USA.Author; Poet. Literary Appointments: Co-ordinating Council of Literary Magazines, Bibliographer, Lockwood Library, State University of New York, Buffalo, 1963-64; Editor, Audit, 1963-64; Co-editor, Audit/Poetry, Buffalo, 1963-67; Instructor in English, State University of New York, Fredonia, 1964-65, Northwestern University, Evanston, Illinois, 1965-68; Literary Editor, Swallow Press, Chicago, 1968-; Professor of English, University of Illinois, Chicago, 1970-. Publications: New Poetry Anthology I and II, 1969, 1972; The Colour of Dust, 1970; Sets/Sorts, 1974; Riversongs, 1978; The Red Menace, 1984; Constructions/Variations, 1985; The Sky at Ashland, 1986; In Plain Sight, 1991; In Plain Sight: Obsessions, Morals & Domestic Laughter, 1993; Selected Poems, 1965-1994, 1994. Address: 5755 Sunset Avenue, La Grange, IL 60525, USA.

ANDELSON Robert V, b. 19 Feb 1931, Los Angeles, USA. Professor Emeritus of Philosophy. m. Bonny Orange Johnson, 7 June 1964. Education: AB equivalent, University of Chicago, 1952; AM, University of Southern California, 1954; PhD, University of Southern California, 1960. Appointment: Assistant Professor to Professor Emeritus of Philosophy, Auburn University, 1965-92; Distinguished Research Fellow, American Institute for Economic Research, 1993-. Publications: Imputed Rights: An Essay in Christian Social Theory, 1971; Critics of Henry George, editor/co-author, 1979; Commons Without Tragedy, editor/co-author, 1991; From Wasteland to Promised Land, joint author with J M Dawsey, 1992; Land-Value Taxatiion Around the World, editor/co-author, 1997. Contributions to: Articles in the Personalist, Modern Age, American Journal of Economics & Sociology, Southern Journal of Philosophy. Honours: George Washington Honor Medals, Freedoms Foundation, 1970, 1972; Research Awards: Foundation for Social Research, 1959; Relm Foundation, 1967. Address: 534 Cary Drive, Auburn, Alabama, 36830-2502, USA.

ANDERSEN Baltser, (Daniel Amb), b. 3 Jan 1956, Ribe, Denmark. Schoolteacher; Author. m. Magdaline Mattak, 26 Dec 1984, 2 daughters. Education: Student, Tonder, 1975; Student, Aarhus, 1976, 1986-88. Appointments: Teacher, Tonder, 1981; Teacher, Greenland, 1982-87; Leader, Greenlandic Peacemovement, Sorsunnata, 1984-87. Publications: Poems: Interlocking Hands, 1973; To Be Awake, 1977; Grey Asphalt, 1979; Travelling Spaceship, 1992; Angantyr and the Black Sword, 1993; Greenland; A Pawn in the Play; Encounter to the

Book; Essay, In the Name of Democracy. Contributions to: Many articles and essays about political and cultural matters in leftwing Danish newspapers. Memberships: Leader, Norse Mythologican Circle, Alfheim; The Danish Writers' Union; Socialist Peoples Party, 1976-93; Red-Green Alliance, 1993-. Address: Krusaavej 33 Alslevb, 6240 Logumkloster, Denmark.

ANDERSEN Benny Allan, b. 7 Nov 1929, Copenhagen, Denmark. Author. m. Cynthia La Touche Andersen, 28 Dec 1981. Publications: Den Musikalske al, 1960; Den Indre Bowlerhat, 1964; Portraetgaller, 1966; Tykke Olsen M Fl, 1968; Her i Reservatet, 1971; Himmelspraet, 1979; Tiden og Storken, 1985; Chagall & Skorpiondans, 1991; Denne Kommen og Gaen, 1993. Contributions to: Anthologies: Poetry Now; Prism International; West Coast Review; Literary Review; Scandinavian Review; Liberte; Svetova Literature. Address: Kaerparken 11, 2800 Lyngby, Denmark.

ANDERSEN Jolanta Buch, b. 9 Apr 1939, Miejsce Piastowe, Poland. President; Chief Executive Officer. m. Erling Buch Andersen, 6 Oct 1962. Education: BBA, 1974, 1982. Publications: Samfundsfjende, 1986; Samfundsven, 1987; Business Plan, Alex to Proste, 1994; How Easy. Contributions to: Various books and journals. Honour: Merkonomprisen, 1987. Membership: Danske Forfattforening. Address: Vejlesoparken 31, DK-2840 Holte, Denmark.

ANDERSON Barbara, b. 14 June 1926, New Zealand. Writer; Playwright. m. Neil Anderson, 1951, 2 sons. Education: BA, University of Otago, 1946; BA, Victoria University, Wellington, 1983. Publications: The Peacocks; Uncollected Short Stories, 1985; I Think We Should Go Into The Jungle (short stories), 1989; Girls High, 1990; We Could Celebrate, 1991; Portrait of the Artist's Wife, 1992; All The Nice Girls, 1993; The House Guest, 1995; Several radio plays; Many short stories. Honours: John Cowie Reid Memorial Award (play), 1986; Ansett/Sunday Star Short Story Award, 1988; Timaru Herald/Aorak Short Story Award, 1990; Victoria University Fellowship, 1991; Goodman Fielder Wattie Award, 1992; Scholarship of Letters, 1994. Membership: Committee member, PEN (New Zealand), 1992-94. Literary Agent: Caroline Dannay, Peters Frazer & Dunlop, The Chambers, Chelsea Harbour, Lots Road, London SW10 OXF. Address: Victoria University Press, Victoria University, PO Box 600, Wellington, New Zealand.

ANDERSON David D(aniel), b. 8 June 1924, Lorain, Ohio, USA. Professor; Writer. m. Patricia Ann Rittenhour, 1 Feb 1953. Education: BS, 1951, MA, 1952, Bowling Green State University; PhD, Michigan State University, 1960. Appointments: Distinguished University Professor, Department of American Thought and Language, Michigan State University, East Lansing, 1957-; Editor, Midwestern Miscellany Annual; Executive Secretary, Society for the Study of Midwestern Literature, 1971-73. Publications: Louis Bromfield, 1964; Critical Studies in American Literature, 1964; Sherwood Anderson, 1967; Sherwood Anderson's Winesburg, Ohio, 1967; Brand Whitlock, 1968; Editor-in-Chief, The Black Experience, 1969; Abraham Lincoln, 1970; The Literary Works of Abraham Lincoln, 1970; The Dark and Tangled Path (with R Wright), 1971; Sunshine and Smoke, 1971; Robert Ingersoll, 1972; Mid-America I-XIV, 1974-87; Sherwood Anderson: Dimensions of His Literary Art (essays), 1976; Woodrow Wilson, 1978; Sherwood Anderson: The Writer at his Craft, 1979; Ignatius Donnelly, 1980; William Jennings Bryan, 1981; Critical Essays on Sherwood Anderson, 1981; Michigan: A State Anthology, 1982; Route Two, Titus, Ohio, 1993. Address: Department of American Thought and Language, Michigan State University, East Lansing, MI 48821, USA.

ANDERSON Kenneth Norman, b. 1921, USA. Writer. Appointments: Executive Editor, Publishers Editorial Services; President, Editorial Guild; Editor, Holt, Rinehart and Winston Inc, New York, 1965-70; Executive Director, Coffee Information Institute, New York, 1970-. Publications: Co-author, Lawyer's Medical Cyclopedia, 1962; The Family Physician (with Robert Addison), 1963; Today's Health Guide (with William Baver), 1965; Pictorial Medical Guide (with Robert Addison), 1967; Field and Stream Guide to Physical Fitness, 1969; Home Medical Encyclopedia (with Paul Kuhn), 1973; Sterno Guide to the Outdoors, 1977; Eagle Claw Fish Cookbook, 1977; The Newsweek Encyclopedia of Family Health and Fitness, 1980; Banham Medical Dictionary (with Walter Glanze), 1980; How Long Will You Live, 1981; Dictionary of Dangerous Pollutants, Ecology and Environment (with David Tver), 1981; The Pocket Guide to Coffees and Teas, 1982; Orphan Drugs, 1983; Longman Dictionary of Psychology and Psychiatry (with Walter Glanze and Robert

Goldenson), 1984; History of the US Marines (with Jack Murphy), 1984; Prentice-Hall Dictionary of Nutrition and Health (with Lois Harmon Anderson), 1985; Mosby Medical Encyclopedia (with Lois Harman Anderson and Walter Glanze), 1985; The International Dictionary of Food and Nutrition (with Lois Anderson), 1993; International Menu Speller (with Lois Anderson), 1993. Address: Coffee Information Institute, 60 East 42nd Street, New York, NY 10017, USA.

ANDERSON Leone Castell, b. 12 Aug 1923, Los Angeles, California, USA. Writer; Owner and Operator of Lee's Booklover's. m. J Eric Anderson, 17 Aug 1946, 3 sons. Education: Austin Academy of Music, 1942-43. Appointments: Copy-writer, Russell Seeds, Advertising, Chicago, Illinois, USA, 1944-46; Free-lance Writer, 1946-49; Member of library staff, Elmhurst Public Library, Illinois, 1969-74; Free-lance Writer, 1974-; Owner and Operator of Lee's Booklover's, 1979-. Publications: Publications for children: The Good-By Day, 1984, reprinted as Moving Day, 1987; My Friend Next Door, 1984; Contributor to Christmas Handbook, 1984; Surprise at Muddy Creek, 1984; How Come You're So Shy? 1987; My Own Grandpa, 1987; Other works: Glendenna's Dilemma (readers' theatre), first performed in Chicago, Illinois, 1979; Come-Uppance (readers' theatre) first performed in Stockton, Illinois, 1986. Contributions to: Columns in Elmhurst Press and Stockton Herald News (author); Magazines and Newspapers. Memberships: Society of Children's Book Writers (Midwest representative, 1981-87); Children's Reading Round Table; Authors Guild; Off-Campus Writer's Workshop. Address: Lee's Booklover's, 127 South Main, Stockton, IL 61085, USA.

ANDERSON Matthew Smith, b. 23 May 1922, Perth, Scotland. Historian; Retired Professor. m. Olive Ruth Gee, 10 July 1954, 2 daughters. Education: MA, 1947, PhD, 1952, University of Edinburgh. Appointments: Assistant Lecturer in History, University of Edinburgh, 1947-49; Assistant Lecturer, 1949-53, Lecturer, 1953-61, Reader, 1961-72, Professor of International History, 1972, now retired, London School of Economics and Political Science, University of London. Publications: Britain's Discovery of Russia, 1553-1815, 1958; Europe in the Eighteenth Century, 1713-1783, 1961, 3rd edition, 1987; The Eastern Question, 1966; Eighteenth Century Europe, 1966; The Great Powers and the Near East, 1774-1923, 1970; The Ascendancy of Europe, 1815-1914, 1972, 2nd edition, 1985; British Parliamentary Papers Relating to Russia, 1800-1900: A Critical Commentary, 1973; Peter the Great, 1978; The Historiograohy of Eighteenth-Century Europe, 1979; Wars and Society in Europe of the Old Regime, 1618-1789, 1988; The Rise of Modern Diplomacy, 1450-1919, 1993; The War of the Austrian Succession, 1740-1748, 1995. Contributions to: Numerous historical periodicals. Memberships: Royal Historical Society; Economic History Society; Past and Present Society. Address: 45 Cholmeley Crescent, Highgate, London N6 5EX, England.

ANDERSON Michael Falconer, b. 16 Jan 1947, Aberdeen, Scotland. Author; Journalist. m. Hildegarde Becze, 16 Apr 1970, 2 sons. Appointments: Newspaper and Magazine Editor; Chief Sub-Editor of a national weekly; Sub-Editor of a daily newspaper; Showbusiness Writer; Reporter; Correspondent in newspapers, television and radio. Publications: The Woodsmen, 1986; The Unholy, 1987; God of a Thousand Faces, 1987; The Covenant, 1988; Black Trinity, 1989; The Clan of Golgotha Scalp, 1990; Numerous short stories and plays for radio and television. Contributions to: Feature articles on everything from travel to history, the environment to books, in newspapers and magazines around the world. Memberships: Society of Authors; National Union of Journalists. Address: Portlehen, Aberdeen, Scotland.

ANDERSON Poul William, b. 25 Nov 1926, Bristol, Pennsylvania, USA. Writer. m. Karen Kruse, 12 Dec 1953, 1 daughter. Education: BS, University of Minnesota, 1948. Publications: Brain Wave, 1954; The High Crusade, 1960; Guardians of Time, 1961; Three Hearts and Three Lions, 1961; Tau Zero, 1971; The Broken Sword (revised edition), 1971; Hrolf Kraki's Saga, 1973; A Midsummer's Tempest, 1974; The Atavar, 1978; The Merman's Children, 1979; Orion Shall Rise, 1983; The Boat of a Million Years, 1989; Harvest of Stars, 1993; The Stars Are Also Fire, 1994. Contributor to: Analog; Magazine of Fantasy and Science Fiction; Destinies; National Review; Boy's Life and others. Honours: Hugo Awards, 1961, 1964, 1968, 1971, 1973, 1978, 1982; Nebula Awards, 1971, 1972, 1981; Knight of Mark Twain, 1971; Mythopoeic Award, 1975; J R R Tolkien Memorial Award, 1978. Memberships: Science Fiction Writers of America, president,

1972-73; Baker Street Irregulars. Literary Agent: Chichak Inc, New York. Address: 3 Las Palomas, Orinda, CA 94563, USA.

ANDERSON Quentin, b. 21 July 1912, Minnewaukan, North Dakota, USA. Writer. Education: AB, 1937, PhD, 1953, Columbia University; MA, Harvard University, 1945. Appointments: Columbia University, 1939-82; University of Sussex, 1966-67; University of Barcelona, 1985. Publications: Selected Short Stories by Henry James, 1950; The American Henry James, 1957; The Proper Study: Essays on Western Classics (with Joseph A Mazzeo), 1962; The Imperial Self: An Essay in American Literary and Cultural History, 1971; Art, Politics and Will: Essays in Honor of Lionel Trilling (with others), 1977; Making Americans: An Essay on Individualism and Money, 1992. Honours: National Endowment for the Humanities, Senior Fellow, 1973; Paley Lecturer, Hebrew University of Jerusalem, 1982; Fellow, National Humanities Center, 1979-80; Fellow, New York Institute for the Humanities, 1981-95. Address: 29 Claremont Avenue, New York, NY 10027, USA.

ANDERSON Rachel, b. 18 Mar 1943, Hampton Court, Surrey, England. Writer: Novels, Short Stories, Plays. m. David Bradby, 4 children. Publications: Books for adults: Pineapple, 1965; The Purple Heart Throbs, A Survey of Popular Romantic Fiction, 1850-1972, 1974; Dream Lovers, 1978; For the Love of Sang, 1990; Books for small children: Tim Walks, 1985; The Cat's Tale, 1985; Wild Goose Chase, 1986; Jessy Runs Away, 1988; Best Friends, 1991; Jessy and The Long-Short Dress, 1992; Tough as Old Boots, 1991; Little Lost Fox, 1992; For older children: Moffatt's Road, 1978; The Poacher's Son, 1982; The War Orphan, 1984; Little Angel Comes to Stay, 1985; Little Angel, Bonjour, 1988; French Lessons, 1988; Renard The Fox (with David Bradby), 1986; The Boy Who Laughed, 1989; The Bus People, 1989; Paper Faces, 1991; When Mum Went to Work, 1992; The Working Class, 1993; Jessy and the Long Short Dress, 1993. Honours: Medical Journalists Association Award for The Love of Sang, 1990; 25th Anniversary Guardian Children's Fiction Award for Paper Faces, 1992. Address: c/o Oxford University Press, Oxford OX2 6DP, England.

ANDERSON Robert Woodruff, b. 28 Apr 1917, New York, New York, USA. Playwright; Screenwriter; Novelist. Education: AB, Magna Cum Laude, 1939 MA, 1940, Harvard University. Publications: Plays: Tea and Sympathy, 1953; All Summer Long, 1954; Silent Night Lonely Night, 1959; The Days Between, 1965; You Know I Can't Hear When the Water's Running, 1967; I Never Sang for My Father, 1968; Solitaire/Double Solitaire, 1971; Free and Clear, 1983; Co-author, Elements of Literature, 1988; Novels: After, 1973; Getting Up and Going Home, 1978; Screenplays: Tea and Sympathy, 1956; Until They Sail, 1957; The Nun's Story, 1959; The Sand Pebbles, 1966; I Never Sang For My Father, 1970; Play: The Last Act is a Solo, TV, 1991; Absolute Strangers, TV, 1991. Honours: Awards for, I Never Sang for My Father, Writer's Guild, 1970; The Ace Award for The Last Act Is A Solo, 1991. Memberships: Dramatists Guild, president, 1971-73; Authors League Council; Writers Guild of America West; American Playwrights Theatre, Board of Trustees; Theatre Hall of Fame, 1981; PEN. Literary Agent: William Morris. Address: Transylvania Road, Roxbury, CT 06783, USA.

ANDREE Alice. See: **CLUYSENAAR Anne.**

ANDRENIO. See: **ALONSO ALVAREZ Emilo.**

ANDRESKI Stanislav Leonard, b. 18 May 1919, Czestochowa, Poland. Writer. 2 sons, 2 daughters. Education: BSc, 1st Class Honours, 1943, MSc 1947, Economics, PhD 1953. Appointments: Professor Emeritus, University of Reading and Polish University in London, Editorial Board, Journal of Strategic Studies. Publications: Military Organisation & Society, 1954, 2nd edition 1968; Elements of Comparative Sociology, 1964; Parasitism & Subversion: The Case of Latin America, 1966, 2nd edition, 1969; The African Predicament: A Study in Pathology of Modernisation, 1968; Social Sciences as Sorcery, 1972; The Prospects of a Revolution in the USA, 1973; Max Weber's Insights & Errors, 1984; Syphilis, Puritanism and Witch Hunts: Historical Explanations in the Light of Medicine and Psychoanalysis with a Forecast About Aids, 1989; Wars, Revolutions, Dictatorships, 1992; Editor: Herbert Spencer: Principles of Sociology, 1968; Herbert Spencer: Structure, Function and Evolution, 1971; The Essential Comte, 1974; Reflections on Inequality, 1975; Max Weber on Capitalism, Bureaucracy and Religion, 1984. Contributions to: Approximately 90 articles in learned journals. Memberships: Writers'

Guild; Institute of Patentees and Inventors. Address: Farriers, Village Green, Upper Basildon, Berkshire RG8 8LS, England.

ANDREW Prudence (Hastings), b. 23 May 1924, London, England. Author. Education: Honours degree in history, St Anne's College, Oxford, 1946. Publications: The Hooded Falcon, 1960; Ordeal by Silence, 1961; Ginger Over the Wall, 1962; A Question of Choice, 1963; Ginger and Batty Billy, 1963; The Earthworms, 1964; Ginger and No 10, 1964; The Constant Star, 1964; A Sparkle from the Coal, novel, 1964; Christmas Card, 1966; Mr Morgan's Marrow, 1967; Mister O'Brien, 1972; Rodge, Sylvie and Munch, 1973; Una and Grubstreet, 1973; Goodbye to the Rat, 1974; The Heroic Deeds of Jason Jones, 1975; Where Are You Going To, My Pretty Maid? 1977; Robinson Daniel Crusoe, 1978 (in USA as Close Within My Own Circle, 1980); The Other Side of the Park, 1984. Address: c/o Heinemann Limited, 10 Upper Grosvenor Street, London W1X 9PA, England.

ANDREWS Allen, b. 25 Apr 1913, London, England. Author. Education: MA, Oxford University, 1935. Publications: Proud Fortress: Gibraltar, 1958; Earthquake (sociology), 1963; The Mad Motorist (exploration), 1964; Those Magnificent Men in Their Flying Machines (humour), 1965; Monte Carlo or Bust (humour), 1969; Quotations for Speakers and Writers, 1969; I Did It My Way (biography as Billy Cotton), 1970; Intensive Inquiries (criminology), 1973; The Follies of King Edward VII, 1975; Kings and Queens of England and Scotland, 1976; The Whisky Barons (biography), 1977; An Illustrated Dictionary of Classical Mythology, 1978; The Cards Can't Lie, 1978; The Royal Coats of Arms of England, 1982; Castle Crespin (novel), 1982; The People of Rome (verse), 1984; Straight Up, 1984; Impossible Loyalties (novel), 1985. Address: 4 Hazelmere Road, London NW6 6PY, England.

ANDREWS Elmer, b. 26 Jan 1948, Northern Ireland. Senior Lecturer in English. m. 20 June 1976, 2 daughters. Education: BA, 1970, MA, 1973, PhD, 1976, Queens University, Belfast. Appointments: Thessaloniki University, Greece, 1972-74; Mohammed V University Rabat, Morocco, 1976-80; Queens University, Belfast, 1980-81; University of Ulster, 1981-. Publications: The Poetry of Seamus Heaney; All The Realms of Whisper; Seamus Heaney: A Collection of Critical Essays; Contemporary Irish Poetry; The Art of Brian Frièl: Neither Reality nor Dreams. Contributions to: Many journals and magazines on Irish and American literature and culture. Honours: Porter Scholarship; Foundation Scholarship. Address: Department of English, University of Ulster, Coleraine, Northern Ireland.

ANDREWS Graham, b. 3 Feb 1948, Belfast, Northern Ireland. Freelance Writer. m. Agnes Helena Ferguson, 10 Apr 1982. Education: BA, History & Psychology, Open University, Milton Keynes, England, 1979-86. Literary Appointments: Associate Editor, Extro Science Fiction Magazine, 1980-81; Staff Writer, World Association for Orphans & Abandoned Children, 1990-91. Publications: The Fragile Future, 1990; The Wao Vocational Training Programme, 1990; Darkness Audible (science fiction novel), 1991; St Jame's Guide to Fantasy Writers (contributor), 1996; Two Just Men: Richard S Prather & Shell Scott (forthcoming). Contributions to: Belfast Telegraph; Brussels Bulletin; The Guardian; Interzone; Million Vector Foundation Book & Magazine. Honour: Aisling Gheal (Bright Vision) Award, Irish Science Fiction Association, 1980. Memberships: Society of Authors; Royal Society of Literature; British Science Fiction Association. Address: Avenue Du Merle 37, 1640 Rhode-Saint-Genese, Belgium.

ANDREWS Lucilla Matthew, (Diana Gordon, Joanna Marcus), Writer. Publications: The Print Petticoat, 1954; The Secret Armour, 1955; The Quiet Wards, 1956; The First Year, 1957; A Hospital Summer, 1958; My Friend the Professor, 1960; Nurse Errant, 1961; The Young Doctors Downstairs, 1963; Flowers for the Doctor, 1963; The New Sister Theatre, 1964; The Light in the Ward, 1965; A House for Sister Mary, 1966; Hospital Circles, 1967; A Few Days in Endel (as Diana Gordon), 1968; Highland Interlude, 1968; The Healing Time, 1969; Edinburgh Excursion, 1970; Ring o' Roses, 1972; Silent Song, 1973; In Storm and in Calm, 1975; No Time for Romance: An Autobiographical Account of a Few Moments in British and Personal History (non-fiction), 1977; The Crystal Gull, 1978; One Night in London, 1979; Marsh Blood (as Joanna Marcus), 1980; A Weekend in the Garden, 1981; In an Edinburgh Drawing Room, 1983; After a Famous Victory, 1984; The Lights of London, 1985. Address: c/o Heinemann Ltd, 10 Upper Grosvenor Street, London W1X 9PA, England.

Lecturer, American Literature, University of Leicester, 1965-88; Visiting Professor of English, Indiana University, Bloomington, 1978-79; Poetry Critic, The Sunday Times, London, 1968-79. Publications: Ash Flowers, 1958; Fugitive Visions, 1962; The Death of Mayakovsky and Other Poems, 1968; Kaleidoscope: New and Selected Poems, 1973. Address: Flat 4-32, Victoria Centre, Nottingham NG1 3PA, England.

ANGEL Leonard Jay, b. 20 Sept 1945. Writer; Lecturer. m. Susan, 1 son, 1 daughter, 1 stepdaughter. Education: BA, Philosophy, McGill University, 1966; MA, Philosophy 1968, MA, Creative Writing and Theatre 1970, PhD, Philosophy 1974, University of British Columbia. Appointments: Department of Creative Writing, University of British Columbia, 1981-82; University of Victoria, 1984-86. Publications: Antietam, 1975; Isadora and G B, 1976; The Unveiling, 1981; The Silence of the Mystic, 1983; Eleanor Marx, 1985; How to Build a Conscious Machine, 1989; Englightenment East & West, 1994. Contributions to: Dialogue and Dialectic, Dialogue, 1991; Six of One, 1985. Honours: 1st Prize, Short Fiction, McGill Daily, 1963; 1st Prize (joint), Playhouse Theatre Award, 1971; Canada Council Artist B Grants, 1979, 1982; Nominee Jessie Award, Best New Play, 1982. Memberships: Playwrights Canada 1976-88; Chairman, British Columbia Region, Guild of Canadian Playwrights 1978-79; Regional Representative 1980-81. Address: 865 Durward Avenue, Vancouver, British Columbia V5V 2Z1, Canada.

ANGELOU Maya, b. 4 Apr 1928, St Louis, Missouri, USA. Poet; Writer; Professor. m. (1) Tosh Angelou, div, (2) Paul Du Feu, 1973, div, 1 son. Education: Studied music; Received training in modern dance from Martha Graham, Pearl Primus, and Ann Halprin, in drama from Frank Silvera and Gene Frankel. Appointments: Taught modern dance, Rome Opera and Hambina Theater, Tel Aviv, 1955; Appeared in Off-Broadway plays; Northern Coordinator, Southern Christian Leadership Conference, 1959-60; Assistant Administrator, School of Music and Drama, Institute of African Studies, University of Ghana, 1963-66; Lecturer, University of California at Los Angeles, 1966; Writer-in-Residence, University of Kansas, 1970; Distinguished Visiting Professor, Wake Forest University, 1974, Wichita State University, 1974, California State University at Sacramento, 1974; 1st Reynolds Professor of American Studies, Wake Forest University (lifetime appointment), 1981-; Many television appearances in various capacities. Publications: Poetry: Just Give Me a Cool Drink of Water 'fore I Die, 1971; Oh Pray My Wings Are Gonna Fit Me Well, 1975; And Still I Rise, 1978; Shaker, Why Don't You Sing?, 1983; Poems: Maya Angelou, 1986; I Shall Not Be Moved, 1990; On the Pulse of Morning, for the inauguration of President Bill Clinton, 1993; The Complete Poems of Maya Angelou, 1994; Phenomenal Woman: Four Poems Celebrating Women, 1995. Fiction: Mrs. Flowers: A Moment of Friendship, 1986; Short stories; stage, film and television plays. Non-Fiction: I Know Why the Caged Bird Sings, 1970; Gather Together In My Name, 1974; Singin' and Swingin' and Gettin' Merry Like Christmas, 1976; The Heart of a Woman, 1981; All God's Children Need Traveling Shoes, 1986. Contributions to: Many publications. Honours: Yale University Fellowship, 1970; Rockefeller Foundation Scholarship for Italy, 1975; Member, American Revolution Bicentennial Comission, 1975-76; Woman of the Year in Communications, 1976; Matrix Award, 1983; North Carolina Award in Literature, 1987; Distinguished Woman of North Carolina, 1992; Horatio Alger Award, 1992; Grammy Award for One the Pulse of Morning, 1994. Memberships: Directors Guild; Harlem Writers Guild; Women's Prison Association, advisory board. Address: c/o Dave La Camera, Lordly and Dame Inc, 51 Church Street, Boston, MA 02116, USA.

ANGHELAKI-ROOKE Katerina, b. 22 Feb 1939, Athens, Greece. Poet; Translator. Education: Universities of Nice, Athens, Geneva, 1957-63. Appointments: Freelance Translator, 1962-; Visiting Professor (Fulbright), Harvard University, 1980; Visiting Fellow, Princeton University, 1987. Publications: Wolves and Clouds, 1963; Poems, 1963-69, 1971; The Body is the Victory and the Defeat of Dreams, 1975; The Scattered Papers of Penelope, 1977; The Triumph of Constant Loss, 1978; Counter Love, 1982; The Suitors, 1984; Beings and Things on Their Own, 1986; When the Body, 1988; Wind Epilogue, 1990; Empty Nature, 1993; Translations of Works by Shakespeare, Albee, Dylan Thomas, Beckett and Nikos Kazantzakis. Honours: Greek National Poetry Prize, 1985. Address: Synesiou Kyrenes 4, 114 71 Athens, Greece.

ANGLUND Joan Walsh, b. 1926, USA. Children's Writer. Publications: A Friend is Someone Who Likes You, 1958; Look Out the Window, 1959; The Brave Cowboy, 1959; Love is a Special Way of

Feeling, 1960; In a Pumpkin Shell: A Mother Goose ABC, 1960; Christmas Is a Time of Giving, 1961; Cowboy and His Friend, 1961; Nibble Nibble Mousekin: A Tale of Hansel and Gretel, 1962; Cowboy's Secret Life, 1963; Spring is a New Beginning, 1963; Childhood Is a Time of Innocence, 1964; A Pocketful of Proverbs (verse), 1964; A Book of Good Tidings from the Bible, 1965; What Color is Love? 1966; A Year is Round, 1966; A Cup of Sun: A Book of Poems, 1967; A Is for Always: An ABC Book, 1968; Morning Is a Little Child (verse), 1969; A Slice of Snow: A Book of Poems, 1970; Do You Love Someone? 1971; The Cowboy's Christmas, 1972; A Child's Book of Old Nursery Rhymes, 1973; Goodbye, Yesterday: A Book of Poems, 1974; Storybook, 1978; Emily and Adam, 1979; Almost a Rainbow, 1980; A Gift of Love, 5 vols, 1980; A Christmas Cookie Book, 1982; Rainbow Love, 1982; Christmas Candy Book, 1983; A Christmas Book, 1983; See the Year, 1984; Coloring Book, 1984; Memories of the Heart, 1984; Teddy Bear Tales, 1985; Baby Brother, 1985; All About Me! 1986; Christmas is Here! 1986; Tubtime for Thaddeus, 1986; A Mother Goose Book, 1991; A Child's Year, 1992; Love is a Baby, 1992; The Way of Love, 1992; Bedtime Book, 1993; The Friend We Have Not Met, 1993; Peace is a Circle of Love, 1993. Address: c/o Random House, 201 East 50th Street, New York, NY 10022, USA.

ANGREMY Jean-Pierre, (Pierre-Jean Remy), b. 21 Mar 1937, Angouleme, France. Diplomat; Author. m. Odile Cail, 1963, div 1979, 1 son, 1 daughter. m. (2) Sophie Schmit, 1986, 1 son. Education: Institut d'Études Politiques, 1955-60; Brandeis University, 1958-59; École Nationale d'Administration, 1960-63. Appointments: Diplomatic Service, Hong Kong, 1963; Second Secretary, Beijing, 1964, London, 1966; First Secretary, London, 1968; Counsellor, Ministry of Foreign Affairs, 1971; Director and Programme Coordinator, ORTF, 1972; Cultural Counsellor, French Embassy, London, 1975-79, French Ministry of Culture, 1979-81; Consul General de France, Florence, 1985-87; Director General, Cultural Exchanges, Ministry of Foreign Affairs, 1987-90; French Ambassador to UNESCO, 1990-93; Director, French Academy, Rome, 1994-97; President, French National Library, 1997. Publications: Et Gulliver mourut de sommeil, 1961; Midi ou l'attentat, 1962; Gaugins a gogo, 1971; La sac du palais d'ete, 1971; Urbanisme, 1972; Une mort sale, 1973; La vie d'Adrian Putney, 1973; Ava, La mort de Floria Tosca, memoires secrets pour servir a l'histoire de ce siècle, 1974; Rever la vie, 1975; La figure dans la pierre, 1976; Chine: Un itineraire, 1977; Les Enfans du parc, 1977; Si j'etais romancier, 1977; Callas: Une vie, 1978; Les nouvelles aventures du Chevalier de la Barre, 1978; Orient Express, 1979; Cordelia ou l'Angleterre, 1979; Don Giovanni, 1979; Pandora, 1980; Slaue pour moir le monde, 1980; Un voyage d'hiver, 1981; Don Juan, 1982; Le dernier été, 1983; Mata Hari, 1983; La vie d'un hero, 1985; Une ville immortelle, 1986; Des Chatevoux Allamagne, 1987; Toscanes, 1989; Algerie bords-de-Seine, 1990; Un cimitière rouge en Nouvelle Angleterre, 1991; Desir d'Europe, 1995; Le Rose et le Blanc, 1997. Honours: Officier, Légion d'Honneur; Officier, Ordre National du Merité; Commandeur des Arts et des Lettres. Membership: Academie Française, member, 1987. Address: Biblitheque Nationale de France, 58 Rue de Richelieu, 75002, Paris, France.

ANGUS Ian. See: **MACKAY James Alexander**.

ANGUS Tom. See: **POWELL Geoffrey Stewart**.

ANMAR Frank. See: **NOLAN William F(rancis)**.

ANSCOMBE Isabelle Mary, b. 4 Oct 1954. Author; Journalist; Scriptwriter; Broadcaster. m. Howar Grey, 17 Dec 1981, 1 daughter. Education: MA, Newnham College, Cambridge. Publications: Not Another Punk Book, 1978; Arts & Crafts in Britain and America, 1978; Omega And After, 1981; A Woman's Touch, 1860 to the Present Day, 1984; Arts and Crafts Style, 1991. Contributions to: Sunday Times; Independent; Daily Telegraph; Cosmopolitan. Memberships: Society of Authors; Romantic Novelists Association. Literary Agent: AM Heath Ltd. Address: c/o AM Heath, 79 St Martins Lane, London WC2N 4AA, England.

ANSELL Jonathan. See: **WOLFF Tobias**.

ANTHONY Evelyn, b. 3 July 1928, England. m. Michael Ward-Thomas, 1955. Education: Convent of Sacred Heart, Roehampton. Publications: Imperial Highness, 1953; Curse Not the King, 1954; Far Flies the Eagle, 1955; Anne Boleyn, 1957; Victoria and

ANTHONY Evelyn, b. 3 July 1928, England. m. Michael Ward-Thomas, 1955. Education: Convent of Sacred Heart, Roehampton. Publications: Imperial Highness, 1953; Curse Not the King, 1954; Far Flies the Eagle, 1955; Anne Boleyn, 1957; Victoria and Albert, 1958; Elizabeth, 1960; Charles the King, 1961; The Heiress, 1964; The Rendezvous, 1967; Anne of Austria, 1968; The Legend, 1969; The Assassin, 1970; The Tamarind Seed, 1971; The Occupying Power, 1973; The Malaspiga Exit, 1974; The Persian Ransom, 1975; The Silver Falcon, 1977; The Return, 1978; The Grave of Truth, 1979; The Defector, 1980; The Avenue of the Dead, 1981; Albatross, 1982; The Company of Saints, 1983; Voices on the Wind, 1985; No Enemy but Time, 1987; The House of Vandekar, 1988; The Scarlet Thread, 1989; The Relic, 1991; The Doll's House, 1992; Exposure, 1993; Bloodstones, 1994. Honours include: US Literary Guild Award for Anne Boleyn; Yorkshire Post Fiction Prize for the Occupying Power. Address: Horham Hall, Thaxted, Essex, England.

ANTHONY James R(aymond), b. 18 Feb 1922, Providence, Rhode Island, USA. Professor; Musicologist. m. Louise MacNair, 24 May 1952, 1 son, 2 daughters. Education: BS, 1946, MA, 1948, Columbia University; Diploma, Sorbonne, University of Paris, 1951; PhD, University of Southern California at Los Angeles, 1964. Appointments: Faculty, University of Montana, 1948-50; University of Arizona, 1952-. Publications: French Baroque Music from Beaujoyeul to Rameau, 1973, revised edition, 1978; Edited music by Baroque composers. Contributions to: Church Music in France, 1661-1750, New Oxford History of Music (with N Dufourq), 1975; More than 40 articles in The New Grove Dictionary of Music and Musicians, 1980; Many journals, including Acta Musicologia; Early Music; Journal of the American Musicological Society; Notes. Honours: Research Grants; J Heyer, editor, Jean-Baptist Lully and the Music of the French Baroque: Essays in Honour of James Anthony, 1988. Memberships: American Musicological Society, council member, 1975-77, 1983-85; American Association of University Professors; Société Française de Musicologie. Address: 800 North Wilson Avenue, Tucson, AZ 85719, USA.

ANTHONY Michael, b. 10 Feb 1930, Mayaro, Trinidad and Tobago. Writer. m. Yvette Francesca, 8 Feb 1958, 2 sons, 2 daughters. Education: Mayaro Roman Catholic School; Junior Technical College, San Fernando, Trinidad. Appointments: Sub Editor, Reuters News Agency, London, 1964-68; Assistant Editor, Texas Star, Texaco Trinidad, Pointe-a-Pierre, Trinidad and Tobago, 1972-78; Teacher of Creative Writing, University of Richmond, Virginia, USA, 1992. Publications: Novels: The Games Were Coming, 1963; The Year in San Fernando, 1965; Green Days by the River, 1967; Streets of Conflict, 1976; All That Glitters, 1981; Bright Road to Eldorado, 1982. Stories: Cricket in the Road and Other Stories, 1973; Sandra Street and Other Stories, 1973; Folk Tales and Fantasies, 1976; The Chieftain's Carnival and Other Stories, 1993. Other: Glimpses of Trinidad and Tobago, with a Glance at the West Indies, 1974; King of the Masquerade, 1974; Profile Trinidad: A Historical Survey from the Discovery to 1900, 1975; The Making of Port-of-Spain, 1757-1939, 1978; Port-of-Spain in a World War, 1939-45, 1984; First in Trinidad, 1985; Heroes of the People of Trinidad and Tobago, 1988; Parade of the Carnivals of Trinidad, 1839-1989, 1989; The Golden Quest: The Four Voyages of Christopher Columbus, 1992. Editor: The History of Aviation in Trinidad and Tobago, 1913-1962, 1987. Contributions to: Various periodicals. Address: 99 Long Circular Road, St James, Port-of-Spain, Trinidad and Tobago.

ANTIN David, b. 1 Feb 1932, New York, New York, USA. Professor of Visual Arts; Poet. m. Eleanor Fineman, 1960, 1 son. Education: BA, City College, New York City, 1955; MA in Linguistics, New York University, 1966. Appointments: Chief Editor and Scientific Director, Research Information Service, 1958-60; Curator, Institute of Contemporary Art, Boston, 1967; Director, University Art Gallery, 1968-72, Assistant Professor, 1968-72, Professor of Visual Arts, 1972-, University of California at San Diego. Publications: Definitions, 1967; Autobiography, 1967; Code of Flag Behavior, 1968; Meditiations, 1971; Talking, 1972; After the War, 1973; Talking at the Boundaries, 1976; Who's Listening Out There?, 1980; Tuning, 1984; Poemas Parlés, 1984; Selected Poems 1963-73, 1991; What it Means to be Avant Garde, 1993. Contributions to: Periodicals. Honours: Longview Award, 1960; University of California Creative Arts Award, 1972; Guggenheim Fellowship, 1976; National Endowment for the Humanities Fellowship, 1983; PEN Award for Poetry, 1984. Address: PO Box 1147, Del Mar, CA 92014, USA.

ANTOINE Yves, b. 12 Dec 1941, Port-au-Prince, Haiti. Professor. 1 daughter. Education: MEd, 1972, LittD, 1988, University of Ottawa. Publications: La Veillée, 1964; Témoin Oculaire, 1970; Au gré des heures, 1972; Les sabots de la nuit, 1974; Alliage, 1979; Libations pour le soleil, 1985; Sémiologie et personnage romanesque chez Jacques S Alexis, 1993; Polyphonie, poetry and prose, 1996. Contributions to: Une affligeante réalité, Le Droit, Ottawa, 1987; L'indélébile, Symbiosis, Ottawa, 1992. Honour: Guest, Harambee Foundation Society, 1988. Memberships: Union of Writers, Quebec; Ligue des Droits et Liberté; Association des auteurs de l'Outaouais québécois. Address: 200 boul Cité des Jeunes, app 403, Hull, Quebec J8Y 6M1, Canada.

ANTROBUS John, b. 2 July 1933, Woolwich, London, England. Writer. m. Margaret McCormick, 1958, div 1980, 2 sons, 1 daughter. Education: King Edward VII Nautical College; Royal Military Academy, Sandhurst, Camberley, Surrey. Appointments: Apprentice Deck Officer, Merchant Navy, 1950-52; Served in British Army, East Surrey Regiment, 1952-55; Supply Teacher and Waiter, 1953-54; Freelance Writer 1955-. Publications: Plays: The Bed-Sitting Room, with Spike Milligan (also co-director; produced London, 1963); Captain Oate's Left Sock, 1969; Walton on Thames, Surrey, Hobbs, 1970, revised version as The Bed-Sitting Room 2 (also director, produced London, 1983); Crete and Sergeant Pepper, 1972; Jonah (also director, produced Cambridge, 1979); Hitler in Liverpool, One Orange for the Baby, Up in the Hide (produced London, 1980), London, Calder and New York; When Did You Last See Your Trousers? with Ray Galton, adaptation of a story by Galton and Alan Simpson (produced Mold, Clwyd, 1986); Screenplays: Carry on Sergeant, with Norman Hudis, 1958; Idol on Parade, 1959; The Wrong Arm of the Law, with others, 1962; The Big Job, with Talbot Rothwell, 1965; The Bed-Sitting Room, with Charles Wood, 1969; Children's Books: The Boy with Illuminating Measles, 1978; Help I'm a Prisoner in a Toothpaste Factory, 1978; Ronnie and the Haunted Rolls Royce, 1982; Ronnie and the Great Knitted Robbery, 1982; Ronnie and the High Rise, 1992; Ronnie and the Flying Fitted Carpet, 1992; Writer for radio and television. Honours: George Devine Award, 1970; Writers Guild Award, 1971; Arts Council Bursary, 1973, 1976, 1980, 1982; Room at the Bottom 1 with Ray Galton, BANFF TV Festival Award, Best Comedy, 1987; Finalist, International Emmy Awards, 1987. Memberships: Writers Guild of Great Britain; Writers Guild of America, West Inc. Literary Agent: c/o Pat White, Rogers Coleridge and White, Address: 20 Powis Mews, London W11 1JN, England.

ANYIDOHO Kofi, b. 1947, Wheta, Ghana. Lecturer in English; Poet. Education: MA in Folklore, Indiana University, Bloomington; PhD in Comparative Literature, University of Texas at Austin. Appointment: Lecturer in English, University of Ghana. Publications: Elegy for the Revolution, 1978; A Harvest of our Dreams, 1984; Earthchild, 1984; Brain Surgery, 1984. Co-editor: Our Soul's Harvest, 1979; Interdisciplinary Dimensions of African Literature, 1985; The Fate of Vultures: New Poetry of Africa, 1989. Honours: Langston Hughes Award (Ghana); Fania Kruger Fellowship. Address: Department of English, University of Ghana, PO Box 25, Legon, Near Accra, Ghana.

APFEL Necia H(alpern), b. 31 July 1930, Mt Vernon, New York, USA. Science Writer. m. Donald A Apfel, 7 Sept 1952, dec, 1 son, 1 daughter. Education: BA magna cum laude, Tufts University, 1952; Radcliffe College Graduate School, 1952-53; Northwestern University Graduate School, 1962-69. Publications: Astronomy One (with J Allen Hynek), 1972; Architecture of the Universe (with J Allen Hynek), 1979; It's All Relative; Einstein's Theory of Relativity, 1981; The Moon and Its Exploration, 1982; Stars and Galaxies, 1982; Astronomy and Planetology, 1983; Soft-cover Edition, Astronomy Projects for Young Scientists, 1984; Calendars, 1985; It's All Elementary From Atoms to the Quantum World of Quarks, Leptons, and Gluons, 1985; Space Station, 1987; Space Law, 1988; Nebulae: The Birth and Death of Stars, 1988; Voyager to the Planets, 1991; Orion the Hunter, 1995. Contributions to: Various articles to Odyssey magazine; Ask Ulysses, and I/O Port monthly columns. Honours: Phi Beta Kappa, 1952; Nebulae chosen as 1 of 100 Best Children's Books, 1988. Memberships: Society of Midland Authors; Society of Children's Book Writers; Astronomical Society of the Pacific; American Association for the Advancement of Science; Planetary Society. Address: 3461 University Avenue, Highland Park, IL 60035, USA.

APOSTOLOU John L, b. 4 Jan 1930, Brooklyn, New York, USA. Writer. Education: City College, New York, 1948-50; Columbia University, 1950-51; BA, University of Southern California, 1956.

Publications: Murder in Japan, 1987; The Best Japanese Science Fiction Stories, 1989. Contributions to: Detective and Mystery Fiction, 1985; Twentieth Century Crime and Mystery Writers, 1991; Armchair Detective; Extrapolation. Address: 532 North Rossmore Avenue, #114, Los Angeles, CA 90004, USA.

APPELFELD Aharon, b. 1932, Czernowitz, Poland (Israeli citizen). Novelist. Education: Hebrew University, Jerusalem. Appointments: Lecturer, Be'er Shev'a University, 1984. Publications: In the Wilderness, 1965; Frost in the Land, 1965; At Ground Level, 1968; Five Stories, 1970; The Skin and the Gown, 1971; My Master the River, 1971; Like the Pupil of an Eye, 1972; Years and Hours, 1975; Lika a Hundred Witnesses: A Selection, 1975; The Age of Wonders, 1978; Badenheim, 1939, 1980; Tzili, The Story of a Life, 1983; The Shirt and the Stripes, 1983; The Retreat, 1985; At One and the Same Time, 1985; To the Land of the Cattails, 1986; The Immortal Bartfuss, 1988; Tongues of Fire, 1988; For Every Sin, 1989; Katerina, 1992; The Railway, 1991; Essays in First Person, 1979; Writing and the Holocaust, 1988. Honours: H H Wingate Literary Award, 1989. Address: c/o Keter Publishing House, PO Box 7145, Jerusalem 91071, Israel.

APPIAH Anthony, b. 8 May 1954, London, England. Philosopher; Novelist; Professor. Education: BA, 1975, PhD, 1982, Clare College, Cambridge University. Publications: In My Father's House, 1992; Necessary Questions, 1989; Avenging Angel, 1990; Nobody Likes Letita, 1994; For Truth in Semantics, Assertion and Conditionals. Contributions to: Times Literary Supplement; New York Times Book Review; WA Post; Book World; New Republic. Honours: Greene Cup, 1975; Annisfield Wolf Book Award, 1993; Herskovitz Book Award, 1993; James Russell Lowell Prize Finalist, 1993. Memberships: African Studies Association; American Philosophical Association; Modern Language Association. Literary Agent: Brandt & Brandt, 1501 Broadway, New York, NY 10036, USA. Address: 1430 Massachusetts Avenue, 4th Floor, Cambridge, MA 02135, USA.

APPIAH Peggy, b. 21 May 1921, England. Children's Writer. Publications: Ananse the Spider, 1966; Tales of an Ashanti Father, 1967; The Pineapple Child and Other Tales from Ashanti, 1969; Children of Ananse, 1969; A Smell of Onions, 1971; Why Are There So Many Roads?, 1972; Gift of the Mmoatia, 1973; Ring of Gold, 1976; A Dirge Too Soon, 1976; Why the Hyena Does Not Care for Fish and Other Tales, 1977; Young Readers Afua and The Mouse, Alena and the Python, Kofi and the Crow, The Twins, 1991; Poems of Three Generations, 1978. Literary Agent: David Higham Associates. Address: PO Box 829, Kumasi, Ashanti, Ghana.

APPLE Jacki, b. 11 Dec 1941, New York, New York, USA. Writer; Artist; Producer. Education: Syracuse University; Parsons School of Design. Appointments Contributing Editor, 1984-95, Media Arts Editor, High Performance Magazine, 1993-95; Faculty Member, Art Center College of Design, Pasadena, CA, 1993-; Instructor, Screenwriting, University of California, San Diego, 1995, 1996, 1997. Publications: Trunk Pieces; Doing it Right in LA; The Mexican Tapes; Swan Lake; Voices in the Dark; The Culture of Disappearance; The Garden Planet Revisited; The Amazon, The Mekong, The Missouri and The Nile; One Word at a Time; Thank You for Flying American, CD, 1995; Ghost Dances/on the event horizon, CD, 1996. Contributions to: High Performance; Artweek; LA Weekly; Media Arts; Visions; Public Art Review; Drama Review; Performing Arts Journal; Art Jounal. Honour: VESTA Award. Memberships: International Association of Art Critics; National Writers Union; College Art Association. Address: 3827 Mentone Avenue, No 3, Culver City, CA 90232, USA.

APPLEMAN M(arjorie) H(aberkorn), b. Fort Wayne, Indiana, USA. Dramatist; Poet. m. Philip Appleman. Education: BA, Northwestern University; MA, Indiana University; Degré Supérieur, Sorbonne, University of Paris. Appointments: Professor of English and Playwriting, New York University, Columbia University; International Honors Program, Indiana University. Publications: Plays: Seduction Duet, 1982; The Commuter, 1985. Other: Over 25 plays given in full productions or staged readings, 1971-97. Poetry: Against Time, 1994. Opera libretto: Let's Not Talk About Lenny Anymore, 1989. Contributions to: Numerous anthologies and journals. Honours: Several playwriting awards. Memberships: Academy of American Poets; Authors League of America; Circle Repertory Company Playwrights Unit; Dramatists Guild; League of Professional Theatre; PEN American Center; Poets and Writers. Address: PO Box 39, Sagaponack, NY 11962, USA.

APPLEMAN Philip (Dean), b. 8 Feb 1926, Kendallville, Indiana, USA. Writer; Poet; Distinguished Professor of English Emeritus. m. Marjorie Ann Haberkorn, 19 Aug 1950. Education BS, 1950, PhD, 1955, Northwestern University; AM, University of Michigan, 1951. Appointments: Fulbright Scholar, University of Lyon, 1951-52; Instructor to Professor, 1955-67, Professor, 1967-84, Distinguished Professor of English, 1984-86, Emeritus, 1986-, Indiana University; Director and Instructor, International School of America, 1960-61, 1962-63; Visiting Professor, State University of New College at Purchase, 1973, Columbia University, 1974; Visiting Scholar, New York University, University of Southern California at Los Angeles; John Steinbeck Visiting Writer, Long Island University at Southampton, 1992. Publications: Novels: In the Twelfth Year of the War, 1970; Shame the Devil, 1981; Apes and Angels, 1989. Poetry: Kites on a Windy Day, 1967; Summer Love and Surf, 1968; Open Doorways, 1976; Darwin's Ark, 1984; Darwin's Bestiary, 1986; Let There Be Light, 1991; New and Selected Poems, 1956-96, 1996. Non-Fiction: The Silent Explosion, 1965. Editor: 1859: Entering an Age of Crisis, 1959; Darwin, 1970, 2nd edition, revised, 1979; The origin of Species, 1975; An Essay on the Principal of Population, 1976. Contributions to: Numerous publications. Honours: Ferguson Memorial Award, Friends of Literature Society, 1969; Christopher Morley Awards, Poetry Society of America, 1970, 1975; Castanola Award, Poetry Society of America, 1975; National Endowment for the Arts Fellowship, 1975; Pushcart Prize, 1985. Memberships: Academy of American Poets; American Association of University Professors; Authors Guild of America; Modern Language Association; National Council of Teachers of English; PEN American Center; Poetry Society of America; Poets and Writers. Address: PO Box 39, Sagaponack, NY 11962, USA.

APTHEKER Bettina Fay, b. 2 Sept 1944. Teacher; Writer. 1 son, 1 daughter. Education: BA, University of California, Berkeley, 1967; MA, San Jose State University, 1976; PhD, University of California, Santa Cruz, 1983. Publications: Tapestries of Life: Women's Work, Women's Consciousness and the Meaning of Daily Experience, 1989; Woman's Legacy: Essays on Race, Sex and Class in American History, 1982; The Morning Breaks: The Trial of Angela Davis, 1976; Academic Rebellion in the US: A Marxist Appraisal; With Angela Y Davis: If They Come in the Morning: Voices of Resistance, 1971. Contributions to: Journals. Address: Women's Studies, Kresge College, University of California, Santa Cruz, CA 95064, USA.

ARCHER Fred, b. 30 Apr 1915, Ashton Underhill, England. Publications: The Distant Scene, 1967; Under the Parish Lantern, 1969; Hawthorn Hedge Country, 1970; The Secrets of Bredon Hill, 1971; A Lad of Evesham Vale, 1972; Muddy Boots and Sunday Suits, 1973; Golden Sheaves and Black Horses, 1974; The Countryman Cottage Life Book, 1974; When Village Bells were Silent, 1975; Poachers Pie, 1976; By Hook and By Crook, 1978; When Adam was a Boy, 1979; A Hill Called Bredon, 1983; Fred Archer Farmer's Son, 1984; The Village Doctor, 1986; Evesham to Bredon in Old Photographs, 1988; The Village of My Childhood, 1989; Country Sayings, 1990. Address: 54 Stanchester Way, Curry Rivel, Langport, Somerset TA10 0PU, Gloucestershire, England.

ARCHER Jeffrey Howard, (Lord Archer of Weston Super Mare)b. 15 Apr 1940, Mark, Somerset, England. Author; Politician. m. Mary Weeden, 2 sons. Education: Brasenose College, Oxford. Publications: Plays: Not a Penny More, Not a Penny Less, 1975; What Shall We Tell the President?, 1977; Kane & Abel, 1979; A Quiver Full of Arrows, 1980; The Prodigal Daughter, 1982; First Among Equals, 1984; A Matter of Honour, 1986; A Twist in the Tale, 1988; As The Crow Flies, 1991; Honour Among Thieves, 1993; Twelve Red Herrings, 1994; The First Estate, 1997. Contributions to: Numerous Journals and Magazines. Honours: Queen's Birthday Honours, 1992; Lord Archer of Weston Super Mare. Address: Alembic House, 93 Albert Embankment, London SE1 7TY, England.

ARCHERY Helen. See: ARGERS Helen.

ARCHIBALD Rupert Douglas, b. 25 Apr 1919, Port of Spain, Trinidad. Author; Playwright. Education: BA, McGill University, 1946. Appointments: Editor, Progress Magazine, 1952; Member, Editorial Board, Clarion Newspaper, 1954-56. Publications: Junction Village, 1954; Anne Marie, 1958; The Bamboo Clump, 1962; The Rose Slip, 1962; Old Maid's Tale, 1965; Island Tide, 1972; Defeat with Honour, 1973; Isidore and the Turtle (novel), 1973. Address: 7 Stephens Road, Maraval, Trinidad and Tobago, West Indies.

ARDAI Charles, b. 25 Oct 1969, New York, New York, USA. Author; Editor. Education: BA, English, summa cum laude, Columbia University, 1991. Appointments: Contributing Editor, Computer Entertainment and K-Power, 1985; Editor, Davis Publications, 1990-91. Publications: Great Tales of Madness and the Macabre, 1990; Kingpins, 1992; Futurecrime, 1992. Contributions to: Alfred Hitchcock's Mystery Magazine; Ellery Queen's Mystery Magazine; Twilight Zone; The Year's Best Horror Stories; Computer Gaming World; and others. Honour: Pearlman Prize for Fiction, Columbia University, 1991. Membership: Active Member, Mystery Writers of America. Address: 350 East 52 Street, New York, NY 10022, USA.

ARDEN John, b. 26 Oct 1930, Barnsley, Yorkshire, England. Playwright. m. Margaratta Ruth D'Arcy, 4 sons, 1 dec. Education: Kings College, Cambridge; Edinburgh College of Art. Publications include: Plays Produced: All Fall Down, 1955; The Waters of Babylon, 1957; Live Like Pigs, 1958; Serjeant Musgraves' Dance, 1959; Soldier, Soldier, 1960; The Workhouse Donkey, 1963; Ironhand, 1963; Left Handed Liberty, 1965; The Bagman, 1970; To Put It Frankly, 1979; Garland for a Hoar Head, 1982; The Old Man Sleeps Alone, 1982; With M D'Arcy: The Happy Haven, 1986; A Suburban Suicide, 1994; Other: The Royal Pardon, 1966; The Hero Rises Up, 1968; Island of the Mighty, 1972; The Non Stop Connolly Cycle, 1975; The Little Gray Home in the West, 1978; Whose is the Kingdom, 1988; Essays: To Present the Pretence, 1977; Awkward Corners, (with M D'Arcy), 1988; Novels: Silence Among the Weapons, 1982; Awkward Corners, 1988; Books of Bale, 1988; Cogs Tyrannic, 1991; Jack Juggler and the Emperor's Whore, 1995. Address: c/o Casarotto Ramsay Ltd, National House, 60-66 Wardour Street, London W1V 3HP, England.

ARDEN William. See: LYNDS Dennis.

ARDLEY Neil Richard, b. 26 May 1937, Wallington, Surrey, England. Writer. m. Bridget Mary Gantley, 3 Sept 1960, 1 daughter. Education: BSc, Bristol University, 1959. Publications: How Birds Behave, 1971; Atoms and Energy, 1975; Birds of Towns, 1975; Birds of the Country, 1975; Birds of Coasts, Lakes and Rivers, 1976; Birdwatching, 1978; Man and Space, 1978; Birds, 1978; Birds of Britain and Europe, 1978; Birds and Birdwatching, 1980; 1001 Questions and Answers (with Bridget Ardley), 1981; The World of Tomorrow Series, 1981-82; Transport on Earth, 1981; Out Into Space, 1981; Tomorrow's Home, 1981; School, Work and Play, 1981; Our Future Needs, 1982; Health and Medicine, 1982; Future War and Weapons, 1982; Fact or Fantasy? 1982; Computers, 1983; Action Science Series, 1983-84; Working with Water, 1983; Using the Computer, 1983; Hot and Cold, 1983; Sun and Light, 1983; Making Measurements, 1983; Exploring Magnetism, 1983; Making Things Move, 1984; Discovering Electricity, 1984; Air and Flight, 1984; Sound and Music, 1984; Simple Chemistry, 1984; Force and Strength, 1984; My Favourite Science Encyclopedia, 1984; Just Look At...Flight, 1984; Sinclair ZX Spectrum User Guide, 1984; Just Look At...The Universe, 1985; The Science of Energy, 1985; Music-An Illustrated Encyclopedia, 1986; My Own Science Encyclopedia, 1987; The Universe - Exploring the Universe, 1987; The Inner Planets; The Outer Planets; The Way Things Work, (with David Macaulay), 1988; The World of the Atom, 1989; Music (Eyewitness Guide), 1989; India, 1989; Greece, 1989; Twentieth Century Science, 1989; The Giant Book of the Human Body, 1989; How We Build Bridges; Dams; Oil Rigs, 1989; Language and Communications, 1989; Sound Waves to Music, 1990; Wings and Things, 1990; Snap Happy, 1990; Tune In, 1991; Bits and Chips, 1991; How It Works, 1991; The Way It Works, Light, 1991; The Way It Works, Electricity, 1991; My Science (A Series of 15 Science Books), 1991-92; 101 Great Science Experiments, 1993; Dictionary of Science, 1994; How Things Work, 1995; A Young Person's Guide to Music (with Poul Ruders), 1995; The Oxford Childrens' A-Z of the Human Body (with Bridget Ardley), 1996. Contributions to: Caxton Yearbook; Macmillan Children's Encyclopedia; Collins Music Dictionary; Joy of Knowledge; Children's Illustrated Encyclopedia. Honours: Fellow, Royal Society of Arts, 1982; Science Book Prize (under 16), 1989; Times Educational Supplement Senior Information Book Award, 1989. Address: Lathkill House, Youlgrave, Derbyshire DE45 1WL, England.

ARDMORE Jane Kesner, b. 12 Sept 1915, Chicago, Illinois, USA. Author; Journalist. m. Albert Ardmore, 10 Nov 1951, 1 daughter. Education: PhB, University of Chicago. Publications: Novels: Women Inc, 1946; Julie, 1952; To Love Is To Listen, 1967; Biographies: Take My Life, Eddie Cantor, 1957; The Self Enchanted, Mae Murray, 1959; The Dress Doctor, Edith Head, 1959; Portrait of Joan, Joan Crawford,

1962. Contributions to: Good Housekeeping; McCall's; Family Circle; Redbook; Woman, UK; Woman's World, UK; Woman's Own, UK. Honours: Fiction prize, Indiana Writers Conference, 1942; Fiction Award, California Press Women, 1967; Headliner Award, Women in Communications, 1968. Membership: Hollywood Women's Press Club. Address: 10469 Dunleer Drive, Los Angeles, CA 90064, USA.

ARGERS Helen, (Helen Archery), b. New Jersey, USA. Writer; Novelist; Playwright. Education: BA from a US University, graduate studies. Appointment: Conference Lecturer, 1996. Publications: A Lady of Independence (novel), 1982; A Scandalous Lady (novel), 1991; A Captain's Lady (novel), 1991; An Unlikely Lady, 1992; A Season of Loving (novel), 1992; The Age of Elegance (novel), 1992; Lady Adventuress (novel), 1994; Duel of Hearts (novel), 1994; Noblesse Oblige, 1994. Contributions to: Library Journal, article on First Novel, 1981. Honours: Writer's Digest Short Story Award, Weisbrod Award, 1987; Resolution of Honor from New Jersey State, 1994. Literary Agent: Margit Bolland, Creatorwrites Literary Agency. Address: Creatorwrites Literary Agency, 78 Woodbine Avenue, Newark, NJ, USA.

ARGIRIDIS Michalis, b. Larissa, Greece, 1952. Education: Studied, Pedagogical Academy of Larissa. Appointment: Teacher, 23rd Primary School of Larissa. Publications include: Circle of Greek Children's Book; Union of Children's Book Writers; Author, Books for Children and Young People, 1991. Honour: Panhellenic Prize, Konstantinos Demertziz. Address: 68-70 Ipsilantou St, Larissa 41223, Greece.

ARGUETA Manilo, b. 24 Nov 1935, San Miguel, El Salvador. Poet; Novelist. Education: Universidad Nacional, San Salvador. Publitions: Fiction: El Valle des Hamacas, 1970; Caperucita en la Zona Rosa, 1977; One Day of Life, 1980; Cuzcatalan, Where the Southern Sea Beats, 1987; Verse: Poemas, 1967; En el Costado de la Luz, 1979; El Salvador, 1990; Editor: Poesia de El Salvador, 1983. Honours: University of Central America Prize, 1980. Address: c/o Chatto and Windus, 20 Vauxhall Bridge Road, London SW1N 2SA, England.

ARIAS SARAVIA Leonor, b. 29 June 1941, Salta, Argentina. University Professor. Education: Literature Professor Graduate, magna cum laude, Universidad Nacional de Tucuman. Appointments: Congress of Linguistic and Literature, Argentina, 1978-96, Brazil, 1990, Mexico, 1993, Venezuela and Colombia, 1996, Germany, 1986, France, 1992. Publications: Oficio del lenguaje, 1992; Estudio socio-economico y cultural de Salta, 1982; Contributor: Teorizaciones sobre 'lo fantastico'; desde la literatura argentina, 1990; Hitos en la exaltacion y la descalificacion del modelo espanol, 1994; Radiogradda de la pampa, 1995; El Recurso a la definicion, 1996. Contributions to: La poesia de S San Martin; El drama de C Matorras; E Mallea: la palabra y el silencio; El desenmascaramiento en E O'Neill. Memberships: ILLI; AIH; CELCIRP; ALFAL. Address: Alsina 1043, 4400 Salta, Argentina.

ARIDJIS Homero, b. 6 Apr 1940, Mexico. Poet; Novelist. m. Betty Ferber, 1965, 2 daughters. Education: Autonomous University of Mexico, 1961. Appointments: Director, Festival Internacional de Poesia, 1981-87. Publications: Verse: Los Ojos Desdoblados, 1960; Antes del Reino, 1963; La Dificil Ceremonia, 1963; Quemar Las Naves, 1975; Antologa, 1976; Vivir Para Ver, 1977; Construir la Muerte, 1982; Republicia de Poetas, 1985; Obra Poetica, 1960-86, 1987; Imagenes Para el Fin del Milenio, 1990; Fiction: Mirandola Dormir, 1964; Persefone, 1967-86; El Encantador Solitario, 1972; Playa Nudista; El Ultimo Adan, 1982; Memorias del Nuevo Mundo, 1988. Honours: Novela Novedades Prize, 1988. Address: Sirra Jiutepec 1558, Lomas Barrilaco, Mexico City 11010, Mexico.

ARLEN Leslie. See: NICOLE Christopher Robin.

ARLEN Michael (John), b. 9 Dec 1930, London, England. Author. m. Alice Albright, 1972, 4 daughters. Education: BA, Harvard University, 1952. Publications: Living-Room War, 1969; Exiles, 1970; An American Verdist, 1972; Passage to Ararat, 1974; The View From Highway One, 1975; Thirty Seconds, 1980; The Camera Age, 1982; Say Goodbye to Sam, 1984. Contributions to: New Yorker magazine. Honours: National Book Award, 1975; Le Prix Bremond, 1976; Honorary DLitt, 1984. Memberships: Authors Guild; PEN. Address: 1120 Fifth Avenue, New York, NY 10128, USA.

ARMAH Ayi Kwei, b. 1938, Takoradi, Ghana. Novelist. Education: AB in Social Studies, Harvard University, Massachusetts; Columbia University, New York. Appointments: Scriptwriter for Ghana Television; Teacher at Teacher's College, Dar-es-Salaam, and Universities of Massachusetts, Amherst, Lesotho, and Wisconsin, Madison. Publications: The Beautiful Ones Are Not Yet Born, 1968; Fragments, 1970; Why Are We So Blest?, 1972; Two Thousand Seasons, 1973; The Heales, 1978; Uncollected short stories: A Short Story, 1965; Yaw Manu's Charm, 1968; The Offal Kind, 1969; Doctor Kamikaze, 1989. Address: c/o Heinemann Educational, Ighorado Road, Jericho PMB 5205, Ibadan, Oyo State, Nigeria.

ARMES Roy (Philip), b. 16 Mar 1937, Norwich, England. Author; Lecturer. m. Margaret Anne Johnson, 12 Aug 1960, 1 son, 2 daughters. Education: BA, University of Bristol, 1959; Teacher's Certificate, University of Exeter, 1960; PhD, University of London, 1978. Appointments: Teacher, Royal Liberty School, Romford, 1960-69; Associate Lecturer in Film, University of Surrey, 1969-72; Research Fellow, 1969-72, Lecturer, 1972-73, Hornsey College of Art; Senior Lecturer, 1973-78, Reader in Film and Television, 1978-; Middlesex Polytechnic; Visiting Lecturer at many colleges and universities. Publications: French Cinema since 1946, 2 volumes, 1966, 2nd edition, 1970; The Cinema of Alain Resnais, 1968; French Film, 1970; Patterns of Realism, 1972; Film and Reality: An Historical Survey, 1974; The Ambiguous Image, 1976; A Critical History of British Cinema, 1978; The Films of Alain Robbe-Grollet, 1981; French Cinema, 1984; Third World Film Making and the West, 1987; Action and Image: Dramatic Structure in Cinema, 1994. Contributions to: Many books and periodicals. Address: 19 New End, Hampstead, London NW3, England.

ARMITAGE G(ary) E(dric), (Robert Edric), b. 14 Apr 1956, Sheffield, England. Writer. m. Sara Jones, 12 Aug 1978. Education: BA, 1977, PhD, 1980, Hull University. Publications: Winter Garden, 1985; A Season of Peace, 1985; A New Ice Age, 1986; Across the Autumn Grass, 1986. As Robert Edric: A Lunar Eclipse, 1989; In the Days of the American Museum, 1990; The Broken Lands, 1992; Hallowed Ground, 1993; The Earth Made of Glass, 1994; Elysium, 1995. Contributions to: Various periodicals. Honours: James Tait Black Memorial Award, 1985; Trask Award, 1985; Society of Authors Award, 1994; Arts Council Bursary, 1995. Address: The Lindens, Atwick Road, Hornsea, North Humberside, England.

ARMITAGE Ronda (Jaqueline), b. 11 Mar 1943, Kaikoura, New Zealand. Author; Teacher; Family Therapist. m. David Armitage, 1966, 2 children. Education: Teacher's Certificate, 1962, Teacher's Diploma, 1969, Hamilton Teacher's College. Appointments: Schoolteacher, Duchavelles, New Zealand, 1964-66, London, England, 1966, Auckland, New Zealand, 1968-69; Advisor on Children's Books, Dorothy Butler Ltd, Auckland, 1970-71; Assistant Librarian, Lewes Priory Comprehensive School, Sussex, England, 1976-77; Teacher, East Sussex County Council, England, 1978-; Family Therapist. Publications: Let's Talk About Drinking, 1982; New Zealand, 1983. Juvenile Fiction: The Lighthouse Keeper's Lunch, 1977; The Trouble With Mr Harris, 1978; Don't Forget, Matilda!, 1978; The Bossing of Josie, 1980, in the USA as The Birthday Spell, 1981; Ice Creams for Rosie, 1981; One Moonlit Night, 1983; Grandma Goes Shopping, 1984; The Lighthouse Keeper's Catastrophe, 1986; The Lighthouse Keeper's Rescue, 1989; When Dad Did the Washing, 1990; Watch the Baby, Daisy, 1991; Looking After Chocolates, 1992; A Quarrel of Koalas, 1992; The Lighthouse Keeper's Picnic, 1993. Honour: Esther Glen Award, New Zealand Library Association, 1978. Address: Old Tiles Cottage, Church Lane, Hellingly, East Sussex BN27 4HA, England.

ARMOUR Peter James, b. 19 Nov 1940, Fleetwood, Lancashire, England. University Professor. Education: PhL, English College and Gregorian University, Rome, Italy, 1961; BA (Hons), University of Manchester, 1966; PhD, Leicester, 1980. Publications: The Door of Purgatory, 1983; Dante's Griffin and the History of the World, 1989; Chapters in: G Aquilecchia et al, Collected Essays, K Speight, 1971; D Nolan, Dante Commentaries, 1977 and Dante Soundings, 1981; RA Cardwell and J Hamilton, Virgil in a Cultural Tradition, 1986; G Barblan, Dante e la Bibbia, 1988; T O'Neill, The Shared Horizon, 1990; J R Dashwood and J E Everson, Writers and Performers in Italian Drama, 1991; J C Barnes and J Petrie, Word and Drama in Dante, 1993; P Boyde and V Russo, Dante e la scienza, 1995; J Cherry, Mythical Beasts, 1995; Dante, The Divine Comedy, 1995. Contributions to: The Year's Work in Modern Language Studies; Italian Studies, volumes 34, 38, 48, 49; Lectura Dantis; Deutsches Dante-Jahrbuch, vol 67; Letture classensi, volume 22; Romance Studies, no 23; Dante Studies, volume 112; Reviews in Italian Studies; Modern Language Review; Medium Aevum; Filologia e Critica; Translations in Journal of Garden History, volumes 1, 3 and 5; The Genius of Venice. Memberships: Società Dantesca Italiana; Dante Society of America; Society for Italian Studies; Modern Humanities Research Association; London Medieval Society; Middlesex County Cricket Club. Address: Department of Italian, Royal Holloway, University of London, Egham Hill, Egham, Surrey TW20 0EX,England.

ARMSTRONG Alice Catt, b. Fort Scott, Kansas, USA. Author; Editor; Publisher. 1 son. Education: LittD, St Andrews University, England, 1969; St Pauls College and Seminary, Italy, 1970. Publications: 17 books including: California Biographical and Historical Series, 1950-; Dining & Lodging on the North American Continent, 1958; And They Called It Society, 1961-62; Editor, special issue, 200th Anniversary of California, 1968; Also radio skits, travel guides, children's stories including Princess McGuffy and the Little Rebel. Honours: National Travel Guide Award, National Writers Club, 1958; Dame Grand Cross, Order of St Jaurent; Outstanding Citizen. Memberships: National Society of Magna Charta Dames; Los Angeles World Affairs Council; National Writers Club; Historical Los Angeles Association; Art Patrons Association of America. Address: 1331 Cordell Views, Cordell Place, Los Angeles, CA 90069, USA.

ARMSTRONG Jeannette Christine, b. 5 Feb 1948, Canada. Writer; Educator. m. Robert Bonneau, 12 Apr 1969, dec, 1 son, 1 daughter.Education: Diploma Fine Arts, Okanagan College, 1975; BFA, University Victoria, 1978. Appointment: Adjunct Professor, University of Victoria, 1989-. Publications: Neekna and Chemai, childrens fiction, 1984; Slash, fiction novel, 1985; Native Creative Process, non-fiction, 1991; Breath Tracks, poetry collection, 1991; Looking at the Words of Our People, 1993; Others: Enwhisteetkwa, 1982. Honour: Children's Book Centre, Choice Award, 1983. Memberships: Writers Union of Canada; PEN International. Literary Agent: BRFB Young Inc; Theytus Books. Address: Theytus Books, 257 Brunswick Street, Penticton, British Columbia, V2A 5P9, Canada.

ARMSTRONG John Alexander, b. 4 May 1922, Saint Augustine, Florida, USA. Professor Emeritus of Political Science; Author; Consultant. m. Annette Taylor, 14 June 1952, 3 daughters. Education: PhB 1948, MA 1949, University of Chicago; Frankfurt University, West Germany, 1949-50; PhD, Public Law and Government 1953, Certificate of Russian Institute 1954, Columbia University. Appointments: Research Analyst, War Documentation Project, Alexandria, Virginia, 1951, 1953-54; Assistant Professor, University of Denver, 1952; Visiting Assistant Professor, Russian Institute, Columbia University, 1957; Assistant Professor to Philippe de Commynes Professor of Political Science (presently Emeritus), University of Wisconsin, Madison, 1954-86. Publications: Ukrainian Nationalism, 1955, 3rd edition, 1990; The Soviet Bureaucratic Elite, 1959; The Politics of Totalitarianism, 1961; Ideology, Politics and Government in the Soviet Union, 1962, 4th edition, 1978; Soviet Partisans in World War II (editor), 1964; The European Administrative Elite, 1973; Nations Before Nationalism, 1982. Address: 40 Water Street, Saint Augustine, FL 32084, USA.

ARMSTRONG Karen Andersen, b. 14 Nov 1944, Stourbridge, Worcestershire, England. Writer; Broadcaster. Publications: Through the Narrow Gate, 1981; The First Christian: St Paul's Impact on Christianity, 1994; The Gospel According to Woman, 1986; Holy War: The Crusades and Their Impact on Today's World, 1988; Muhammad: A Western Attempt to Understand Islam, 1991; A History of God, 1993; A History of Jerusalem: One City, Three Faiths, 1996; In the Beginning: A New Interpretation of Genesis, 1996. Contributions to: Sunday Times; Daily Telegraph; New Statesman; Observer. Literary Agent: Felicity Bryan. Address: 2A North Parade, Banbury Road, Oxford, OX2 6PE, England.

ARMSTRONG Patrick Hamilton, b. 10 Oct 1941, Leeds, Yorkshire, England. University Lecturer. m. Moyra E J Irvine, 8 Aug 1964, 2 sons. Education: BSc, 1963, Dip Ed, 1964, MA, 1966, University of Durham; PhD, 1970. Publications: Discovering Ecology, 1973; Discovering Geology, 1974; The Changing Landscape, 1975; A Series of Children's Book for Ladybird Books, 1976-79; Ecology, 1977; Reading and Interpretation of Australian and New Zealand Maps, 1981; Living in the Environment, 1982; The Earth: Home of Humanity, 1984; Charles Darwin in Western Australia, 1985; A Sketch Map Geography of Australia, 1988; A Sketch Map Physical Geography for Australia, 1989; Darwin's Desolate Islands, 1992. Contributions to: New Scientist; Geographical Magazine; East Anglian Magazine; Geography; Cambridgeshire Life; Eastern Daily Press; Work and Travel Abroad; West Australian Newspaper; Weekly Telegraph. Address: Department of Geography, University of Western Australia, Nedlands, WA 6907, Australia.

ARMSTRONG Richard B, b. 29 Nov 1956, Winston-Salem, North Carolina, USA. Writer; Training Developer. m. Mary Willems Armstrong, 23 May 1981. Education: BA, Telecommunications, 1979, MSc, Instructional Systems Technology, 1981, Doctorate of Education in Instructional Systems Technology, 1993, Indiana University. Publications: The Movie List Book: A Reference Guide to Film Themes, Settings and Series (with Mary Willems Armstrong), 1990, 2nd edition, 1994. Contributions to: Reviews published in Film Quarterly and Film Fax; Training Development articles published in Performance Improvement Quarterly, and Armor magazine. Honour: Article of the Year Award for, The TIP Theory: Prescriptions for Designing Instruction for Teams, Performance Improvement Quarterly, 1993. Address: c/o McFarland and Co Inc, Publishers, Box 611, Jefferson, NC 28640, USA.

ARNOLD Arnold, b. 6 Feb 1928, Germany. m. (1) Eve Arnold, 1942, (2) Alison Pilpel, 1982. Education: St Martins School of Art, London, 1937-38; Pratt Institute, New York, 1938-39; New York University, Columbia University, 1939-42. Appointments: Graphic Toy and Industrial Designer, 1946; Director, Workshop School, New York, 1949-52; President, Arnold Arnold Design Inc, 1960-66; President, Manuscript Press Inc, 1963-66; Designer of Childrens Play, Learning Materials and Programs; Consultant Editor, Rutledge Books, New York, 1962-65; Cyberneticist, Writer, Consultant, Systems Analysis and Operational Research, London, 1980-. Publications: How To Play with Your Child; Your Child's Play; Your Child and You; The World Book of Children's Games; The World Book of Arts and Crafts for Children; The Corrupted Sciences; The I Ching and the Theory of Everything. Contributions to: Several Journals and Newspapers and Reviews. Honour: Fellow, Boston University; Leverhulme Fellow. Address: c/o Andrew Mann Ltd, 1 Old Compton Street, London W1V 5PH, England.

ARNOLD Eleanor Parsons, b. 4 May 1929, Indiana, USA. Farm homemaker; Editor. m. Clarence E Arnold, 26 Dec 1948, 1 son, 2 daughters. Education: Clayton High School, valedictorian Indiana University, 1946; BA, English, Honours, 1950. Publications: Voices of American Homemakers, 1985; Series: Memories of Hoosier Homemakers, including books as follows: Feeding Our Families, 1983; Party Lines, Pumps and Privies, 1984; Budgies and Bad Times, 1985; Girlhood Days, 1987; Going to Club, 1988; Living Rich Lives, 1990. Contributions to: Interpreting Women's Culture; American Association of State and Local History; Hoosier Hoemakers; National Oral History; Voices of American Homemakers; National Extension Homemakers. Honours: Sagamore of the Wabash (Indiana award), Commendation: AASLH. Memberships: American Association of State and Local Hiistory; National Oral History Association; Indiana Oral History Roundtable; Indianapolis Press Club. Address: 1744 North 450 East, Rushville, IN 46173, USA.

ARNOLD Emily. See: **McCULLY Emily Arnold.**

ARNOLD Heinz Ludwig, b. 29 Mar 1940, Essen, Ruhr, Germany. Writer; Critic; Editor. Education: University of Göttingen. Appointments: Editor, Text und Kritik, 1963; Kritisches Lexikon zur Deutschsprachigen Gegenwartsliteratur, 1978; Kritisches Lexikon zur Fremdsprachigen Gegenwartsliteratur, 1983. Publications: Brauchen wir noch die Literatur? 1972; Gespräche mit Schriftstellern, 1975; Gespräch mit F Durrenmatt, 1976; Handbuch der Deutschen Arbeiterliteratur, 1977; Als Schriftsteller leben, 1979; Vom Verlust der Scham und Dem Allmaehlichen Verschwinden der Demokratie, 1988; Krieger Waldgaenge, Anarch Versuch über E Jünger, 1990; Querfahrt mit Durrenmatt, 1990; Die Drei Sprunge der Westdeutschen Gegenwartsliteratur, 1993; Die Deutsche Literatur 1945-1960, 4 volumes, 1995. Contributions to: Die Zeit; Deutsches Allgemeines Sonntagblatt; Frankfurter Allgemeine Zeitung; Various Radio Stations. Honour: Honorary Professor, University of Göttingen. Memberships: Association of German Writers; PEN; OH Tulip Order. Address: Tuckermannweg 10, 37085 Göttingen, Germany.

ARNOLD Margot. See: **COOK Petronelle Marguerite Mary.**

ARONSON Theo, b. 13 Nov 1930, South Africa. Writer. Education: BA, University of Cape Town, 1950. Publications: The Golden Bees, 1965; Royal Vendetta, 1967; The Coburgs of Belgium, 1968; The Fall of the Third Napoleon, 1970; The Kaisers, 1971; Queen Victoria and the Bonapartes, 1972; Grandmama of Europe, 1973; A Family of Kings, 1975; Victoria and Disraeli, 1977; Kings Over the Water, 1979; Princess Alice, 1981; Royal Family, 1983; Crowns in Conflict, 1986; The King in Love, 1988; Napoleon and Josephine, 1990; Heart of a Queen, 1991; The Royal Family at War, 1993; Prince Eddy, 1994; Princess Margaret, 1997. Contributions to: Various Journals and Magazines. Literary Agent: Andrew Lownie. Address: North Knoll Cottage, 15 Bridge Street, Frome, Somerset BA11 1BB, England.

ARRABAL Fernando, b. 11 Aug 1932, Melilla, Morocco. Writer; Poet; Dramatist. m. Luce Moreau, 1958, 1 son, 1 daughter. Education: University of Madrid. Appointments: Political prisoner in Spain, 1967; Co-Founder, Panique Movement. Publications: Novels: Baal Babylone, 1959; L'Enterrement de la Sardine, 1961; Fêtes et Rites de la Confusion, 1965; La Torre Herida por el Rayo, 1983; Poetry: Le Pierre de la Folie, 1963; 100 Sonnets, 1966; Les Evêques se Noient, 1969; Poèmes, 1982; Lanzarote, 1988. Plays: Numerous, both published and unpublished. Honours: Ford Foundation Fellowship, 1960; Société des Auteurs Prize, 1966; Grand Prix du Théâtre, 1967; Grand Prix Humour Noir, 1968; Obie Award, Village Voice newspaper, New York City, 1976; Premio Nadal (novel), 1983; World's Theatre Prize, 1984; Prix du Théâtre, Académie Française, 1993; Prix International Nabokov (novel), 1994; Premio Espasa de Ensayo, 1994. Address: 22 Rue Jouffroy d'Abbans, Paris 75017, France.

ARREOLA Juan José, b. 12 Sept 1918, Ciudad Guzman, Jalisco, Mexico. Novelist. Education: Paris, 1945. Appointments: Founding Member, Actor, Poesia en Voz Alta Group. Publications include: Gunther Stapenhorst: Vinetas de Isidoro Ocampo, 1946; Varia Invencion, 1949, 1971; Cinco Cuentes, 1951; Confabulario and Other Inventions, 1952-64; Besitario, 1958; Punta de Plata, 1958; Le Feria, 1963; Cuentos, 1969; Antologia de Juan José Arreola, 1969; Palindroma, 1971; Mi Confabulario, 1979; Confabulario Personal, 1980; Imagen Obra Escogida, 1984; Estas Paginas Mias, 1985. Address: Editorial Joaquin Mortiz, Avenue Insurgentes Sur 1162-3, Col del Valle, 03100 Mexico City, Mexico.

ARROW Kenneth (Joseph), b. 23 Aug 1921, New York, New York, USA. Professor of Economics Emeritus; Writer. m. Selma Schweitzer, 31 Aug 1947, 2 sons. Education: BS, City College of New York, 1940; MA, 1941, PhD, 1951, Columbia University. Appointments include: Acting Assistant Professor, 1949-50, Associate Professor, 1950-53, Professor of Economics, 1953-68, Joan Kenney Professor of Economics, 1979-91, Professor Emeritus, 1991-, Stanford University; Professor of Economics, 1968-74, James Bryant Conant University Professor, 1974-79, Harvard University. Publications: Social Choice and Individual Values (co-author), 1951; Mathematical Studies in Inventory and Production (co-author), 1958; Studies in Linear and Nonlinear Programming (co-author), 1958; Time Series Analysis of Inter-industry Demands (co-author), 1959; Essays in the Theory of Risk Bearing (co-author), 1971; Public Investment, the Rate of Return and Optimal Fiscal Policy (co-author), 1971; General Competitive Analysis (co-author), 1971; The Limits of Organization (co-author), 1974; Studies in Resource Allocation Processes (co-author), 1977; Collected Papers, 6 volumes, 1983-85; Social Choice and Multicriterion Decision Making (co-author), 1985. Contributions to: Professional journals. Honours: John Bates Clark Medal, American Economic Association, 1957; Nobel Memorial Prize in Economic Science, 1972; Guggenheim Fellowship, 1972-73; 18 honorary doctorates. Memberships: President, American Economic Association, 1973; Vice President, 1979-81, 1991-93, American Academy of Arts and Sciences; American Philosophical Society; Corresponding Member, British Academy; Econometric Society; President, International Economic Association, 1983-86. Address: c/o Department of Economics, Stanford University, Stanford, CA 94305, USA.

ARTAZA PAZ Roberto Alejandro, (Amado), b. 25 June 1977, Rosario de la Frontera. Student. Education: Degree, Computer Operator, Perito Mercantil. Appointments: Third Latin American Culture, Fine Arts, Science & Education Conference, 1993; Exhibition of Paintings and Literacy Works in Prose About Rosario de la Frontera, 1995; Sixth Cultural October Conference in Metan City, 1995; First Department Book Show, 1996; Andian Seminar of Latin American Literature Jalla-E Students Representation, 1996. Publications: The

Train of Solitude; Roots, poems book; Selection of Argentinian Authors. Contributions to: Cervantes magazine; El Tribuno, newspaper. Honours: First City Council Award Juana M Gorriti, 1995; International Young Poets Award, Bilbao, Spain, 1995. Address: Pasaje Los Crisantemos No 180, Barrio Santa Teresita, Rosario de la Frontera, Salta, Argentina.

ARTHUR Elizabeth Ann, b. 15 Nov 1953, New York, USA. Writer. m. Steven Bauer, 19 June 1982. Education: BA, English, University of Victoria, 1978; Diploma, Education, 1979. Appointments: Visiting Instructor, Creative Writing, University of Cincinnati, 1983-84; Assistant Professor, English, Miami University, 1984-85; Assistant Professor, English, 1985, Associate Professor, 1992-96, IUPUI, Indianapolis; Visiting Associate Professor of English, Miami University, 1996-. Publications: Island Sojourn, 1980; Beyond the Mountain, 1983; Bad Guys, 1986; Binding Spell, 1988; Looking for the Klondike Stone, 1993; Antarctic Navigation, novel, 1995. Contributor to: New York Times; Outside; Backpacker; Ski-XC; Shenandoah. Honours: William Sloane Fellowship, Bread Loaf Writers' Conference, 1980; Writing Fellowship, Ossabaw Island Project, 1981; Grant in Aid, Vermont Council on the Arts, 1982; Fellowship in Prose, National Endowment for the Arts Fellowship, 1988-89; Antarctic Artists and Writers Grant, National Science Foundation, 1990; Critics Choice Award for Antarctic Navigation, 1995; Notable Book, New York Times Book Review, 1995. Membership: Poets and Writers. Literary Agent: Jean Naggar. Address: Bath, IN 47010, USA.

ARZILLE Juliette (d'), b. 23 Nov 1932, La Neuveille, Switzerland. Writer. m. Walter Friedemann, 26 Sept 1955, 1 son, 1 daughter. Education: Studies of music and autodidactical literary education. Appointment: Member, Literature Committee of the Canton of Neuchatel, 1993-. Publications: Le Deuxieme Soleil, 1973; Identite suivi de les Embellies, 1976; Une Innocence Verte, 1982; Nocturne, 1984; Esquisses et Propos, 1986; D'Ici et d'Ailleurs, 1989. Contributions to: Swiss French Magazines and Newspapers. Honour: French Lierature Award of the Canton Bern, 1982. Memberships: PEN International; Swiss Society of Writers; AENJ. Address:En Arzille, CH-1788 Praz, Switzerland.

ASANTE Molefi Kete, b. 14 Aug 1942, Vaidosta, California, USA. Professor. m. Kariamu Welsh, 1981, 2 sons, 1 daughter. Education: BA, Oklahoma Christian University, 1964; MA, Peppendine University, 1965; PhD, University of California at Los Angeles, 1968. Appointment: Vice President, African Writers Union, 1994-. Publications: Afrocentricity, 1980; The Afrocentric Idea, 1987; Kemet, Afrocentricity and knowledge, 1992; Classical Africa, 1992; African American History, 1995; African Intellectual Heritage, 1996. Contributions to: Journal of Black Studies; Academe; The World and I. Honours: Honorary degrees, citations and awards, more than 100 awards. Literary Agent: Barbara Lowenstein. Address: Temple University, Philadelphia, PA 19122, USA.

ASCH Frank, b. 6 Aug 1946, Somerville, New Jersey, USA. Education: BA, Cooper Union. Publications: George's Store, 1969; Elvira Everything, 1970; The Blue Balloon, 1971; I Met a Penguin, 1972; In the Eye of the Teddy, 1973; Gia and the $100 Worth of Bubblegum, 1974; Good Lemonade, 1975; The Inside Kid, 1977; Macgoose's Grocery, 1978; Country Pie, 1979; The Last Puppy, 1980; Just Like Daddy, 1981; Happy Birthday Moon, 1982; Mooncake, 1983; Moongame, 1984; Baby in the Box, 1990; Journey to Terezor, 1991; Here Comes the Cat, 1991; Little Fish, Big Fish, 1992; Short Train, Long Train, 1992; Dear Brother, 1992; The Flower Faerie, 1993; Moonbear's Books, 1993; Moonbear's Canoe, 1993; Moonbear's Friend, 1993; The Earth & I, 1994. Address: c/o McGraw-Hill Inc, 1221 Avenue of the Americas, New York, NY 10020, USA.

ASCHER Sheila, (Ascher/Straus), b. New York, USA. Writer. Education: MA, Columbia University. Publications: Letter to an Unknown Woman; The Other Planet; The Menaced Assassin; Red Moon/Red Lake. Contributions to: Chicago Review; Paris Review; Epoch; Top Stories; Chelsea; Exile; Calyx; Zone; Confrontation; Central Park; New American Writing; Asylum Annual; Top Top Stories (anthology); 15 Years in Exile (anthology); Likely Stories (anthology); The Living Underground (anthology). Honours: Panache Experimental Fiction Prize; Pushcart Prize; Caps Fellowship. Address: PO Box 176, Rockaway Park, NY 11694, USA.

ASCHERSON Neal, b. 5 Oct 1932, England. Journalist; Editor. m. (1) Corinna Adam, 1958, div 1982. (2) Isobel Hilton, 1984.

Education: Eton College; King's College, Cambridge. Appointments: Reporter and Correspondent with the Observer, 1960-85, Associate Editor, 1985-89; Assistant Editor, The Independent on Sunday, 1990-. Publications: The King Incorporated, 1963; The Polish August, 1981; The Struggles for Poland, 1987; Games with Shadows, 1988; Black Sea, 1995. Honours: Reporter of the Year, 1982; Journalist of the Year, 1987; George Orwell Award, 1993; Golden Insignia, Order of Merit (Poland), 1992. Address: 27 Corsica Street, London, N5 1JT, England.

ASH John, b. 29 June 1948, Manchester, England. Writer; Poet; Teacher. Education: BA, University of Birmingham, 1969. Publications: The Golden Hordes: International Tourism and the Pleasure Periphery (with Louis Turner), 1975; Casino: A Poem in Three Parts, 1978; The Bed and Other Poems, 1981; The Goodbyes, 1982; The Branching Stairs, 1984; Disbelief, 1987. Contributions to: Periodicals. Honour: Ingram Merrill Foundation Grant, 1985. Address: c/o Carcanet Press Ltd, 208 Corn Exchange Buildings, Manchester M4 3BQ, England.

ASHANTI Baron James, b. 5 Sept 1950, New York, USA. Poet;Writer; Editor; Critic; Lecturer. m. Brenda Cummings, 11 Sept 1979, 1 son, 1 daughter. Appointments: Literary Editor, Impressions Magazine, 1972-75; City and Third World Editor, Liberation News Service, 1974-79; Contributing Editor, The Paper, 1978; Lecturer; Director, Arts-in-Education Program, Frederick Douglass Creative Arts Center, New York City, 1988-. Publications: Nubiana, 1977; Nova, 1990. Contributions to: Many periodicals. Honours: Killen Prize for Poetry, St Peter's College, 1982; PEN Fellowships, 1985, 1987; Pulitzer Prize in Poetry Nomination, 1991. Address: 274 West 140th Street, Apt No 45, New York, NY 10030, USA.

ASHBY Nora. See: AFRICANO Lillian.

ASHDOWN Dulcie Margaret, b. 24 Feb 1946, London, England. Writer; Editor. Education: BA, Bristol University, 1967. Publications: Christmas Past, 1976; Ladies in Waiting, 1976; Princess of Wales, 1976; Royal Children, 1980; Royal Weddings, 1981; Victoria and the Coburgs, 1981; 4 Other books. Contributions to: Majesty; Heritage; Writers' Monthly; The Lady. Address: c/o National Westminster Bank, 1302 High Road, Whetstone, London N20, England.

ASHE Geoffrey Thomas, b. 29 Mar 1923, London, England. Writer; Lecturer. m. Dorothy Irene Train, 3 May 1946, dec, 4 sons, 1 daughter, (2) Maxine Lefever, 8 Dec 1992, div. Education: BA, University of British Columbia, Canada, 1943; BA, Trinity College, Cambridge University, 1948. Appointment: Associate Editor, Arthurian Encyclopaedia, 1986. Publications: King Arthur's Avalon, 1957; From Caesar to Arthur, 1960; Land to the West, 1962; The Land and The Book, 1965; Gandhi, 1968; The Quest for Arthur's Britain, 1968; Camelot and the Vision of Albion, 1971; The Art of Writing Made Simple, 1972; The Finger and the Moon, 1973; The Virgin, 1976; The Ancient Wisdom, 1977; Miracles, 1978; Guidebook to Arthurian Britain, 1980; Kings and Queens of Early Britain, 1982; Avalonian Quest, 1982; The Discovery of King Arthur, 1985; Landscape of King Arthur, 1987; Mythology of the British Isles, 1990; King Arthur: The Dream of a Golden Age, 1990; Dawn Behind the Dawn, 1992; Atlantis, 1992. Contributions to: Numerous magazines and journals. Honour: Fellow, Royal Society of Literature, 1963. Memberships: Medieval Academy of America; Secretary, Camelot Research Committee. Address: Chalice Orchard, Well House Lane, Glastonbury, Somerset BA6 8BJ, England.

ASHLEY Bernard, b. 2 Apr 1935, London, England. Writer. Education: Teachers Certificate; Advanced Diploma, Cambridge Institute of Education. Publications: The Trouble with Donovan Croft, 1974; Terry on the Fence, 1975; All My Men, 1977; A Kind of Wild Justice, 1978; Break in the Sun, 1980; Dinner Ladies Don't Count, 1981; Dodgem, 1982; High Pavement Blues, 1983; Janey, 1985; Running Scared, 1986; Bad Blood, 1988; The Country Boy, 1989; The Secret of Theodore Brown, 1989; Clipper Street, 1990; Seeing off Uncle Jack, 1992; Cleversticks, 1993; Three Seven Eleven, 1993; Johnnie's Blitz, 1995; I Forgot, Said Troy, 1996; A Present for Paul, 1996. Contributions to: Books for Your Children; Junior Education; Books for Keeps; Times Educational Supplement; School Librarian. Honours: The Other Award, 1976; Runner Up, Carnegie Medal, 1979, 1986; Royal TV Society Best Childrens Entertainment Programme, 1993. Membership: Writers Guild. Address: 128 Heathwood Gardens, London SE7 8ER, England.

ASHLEY Leonard (Raymond Nelligan), b. 5 Dec 1928, Miami, Florida, USA. Professor Emeritus of English; Author; Editor. Education: BA, 1949, MA, 1950, McGill University; AM, 1953, PhD, 1956, Princeton University. Appointments: Instructor, University of Utah, 1953-56; Assistant to the Air Historian RCAF, 1956-58; Instructor, University of Rochester, 1958-61; Faculty, New School for Social Research (part-time), 1962-72; Faculty, Brooklyn College of the City University, New York, 1961-95. Publications: What's in a Name?; Elizabethan Popular Culture; Colley Cibber; Nineteenth-Century British Drama; Authorship & Evidence in Renaissance Drama; Mirrors for Man; Other People's Lives; The Complete Book of Superstition, Prophecy and Luck; The Complete Book of Magic and Witchcraft; The Complete Book of Devils and Demons; The Complete Book of the Devil's Disciples; Ripley's Believe It Or Not Book of the Military; The Air Defence of North America; A Military History of Modern China (collaborator); Shakespeare's Jest Book; George Peele: The Man and His Work; Language in Contemporary Society (co-editor); Geolinguistic Perspectives (co-editors); Phantasms of the Living, 2 volumes (editor). Contributions to: Books. Honours: The Shakespeare Gold Medal; American Name Society Best Article Award; Fellowships and Grants. Memberships: The American Name Society, Executive Board; International Linguistics Association, former Secretary; American Association of University Professors, former President; American Society of Geolinguistics, President, Brooklyn College Chapter; Princeton Club of New York; Modern Language Association; American Dialect Society. Address: Department of English, Brooklyn College, City University of New York, Brooklyn, NY 11230, USA.

ASHTON Christina Julia Allen, b. 16 Sept 1934, Brooklyn, New York, USA. Writer; Teacher. m. 21 Aug 1954, 1 daughter. Education: BA, English 1957, Washington State University; MS, Special Education 1975, Dominican College. Publications: Words Can Tell, A Book About Our Language, 1988; The First Defender of France (article), 1991; Codes and Ciphers, 1993. Contributions to: Calliope Magazine. Honours: English Honours, University of Oregon, 1954; Second Prize, California Writers Club, short story, 1991; Second Prize, National Writers Club, short story, 1991; Honorable Mention, National Writers Club, non-fiction book, 1992. Memberships: National Writers Club; California Writers Club, member, secretary, Peninsular Branch. Literary Agent: Norma Lewis Agency, New York. Address: 4009 Kingridge Drive, San Mateo, CA 94403, USA.

ASHTON Robert, b. 21 July 1924, Chester, England. Retired University Professor. m. Margaret Alice Sedgwick, 30 Aug 1946, 2 daughters. Education: Magdalen College School, Oxford, 1938-40; University College, Southampton, 1946-49; BA, First Class Honours, London, 1949; London School of Economics, 1949-52, PhD, 1953. Appointments: Assistant Lecturer, Lecturer, Senior Lecturer, Nottingham University, 1952-63; Visiting Associate Professor, University of California, Berkeley, 1962-63; Professor, 1963-89, Emeritus Professor, 1989-, University of East Anglia; Visiting Fellow, All Souls College, Oxford, 1974-75, 1987. Publications: The English Civil War: Conservatism and Revolution 1603-49, 1978, 2nd edition, 1989; The Crown and the Money Market 1603-40, 1960; James I by his Contemporaries, 1969; The City and the Court 1603-1643, 1979; Reformation and Revolution, 1558-1660, 1984; Counter Revolution: The Second Civil War and its Origins 1646-1648, 1994. Contributions to: Articles in Economic History Review; Bulletin of Institute of Historical Research; Past and Present; Historical Journals. Honours: Vice President, 1983-85, Fellow, 1961-, Royal Historical Society. Membership: Royal Historical Society. Address: The Manor House, Brundall, Norwich NR13 5JY, England.

ASIMOV Janet O Jeppson, b. 6 Aug 1926, Ashland, Pennsylvania, USA. Physician; Writer. m. Isaac Asimov, 30 Nov 1973. Education: BA, Stanford University, 1948; MD, New York University College of Medicine, 1952; Diploma, Psychoanalysis, William Alanson White Institute, 1960. Publications: The Second Experiment, 1974; The Last Immortal, 1980; The Mysterious Cure, 1985; Mind Transfer, 1988; With Isaac Asimov: How to Enjoy Writing; Laughing Space, 1982; Norby, the Mixed-Up Robot, 1983; Norby's Other Secret, 1984; Norby and the Lost Princess, 1985; Norby and the Invaders, 1985; Norby and the Queen's Necklace, 1986; Norby Finds a Villain, 1987; The Package in Hyperspace, 1988; Norby and Yobo's Great Adventure, 1989; Norby and the Oldest Dragon, 1990; Norby Down to Earth, 1991; Norby and the Court Jester, 1991. Contributions to: Several journals. Honour: Phi Beta Kappa, 1948. Memberships: Science Fiction Writers of America; William Alanson White Society; American Academy of Psychoanalysis; American Psychiatric Association. Address: 10 West 66th Street, New York, NY 10023, USA.

ASMUNDSDOTTIR Steinunn, b. 1 Mar 1966, Reykjavik, Iceland. Environmental Educator. Education: General Education. Publications: Poems published in various collections from 1985; Book for Children, 1986; Solo on the Rainbow, 1989; Words of the Musas, 1993; A House on the Moore, 1996. Contributions to: Editor, Litterature Magazine Andblaer (Breeze), 1995-. Membership: Icelandic Writers Union, 1994-. Address: Egilsstadir I, PO Box 85, 700 Egilsstadir, Iceland.

ASPENSTROM Werner, b. 13 Nov 1918, Norrbarke, Sweden. Poet; Playwright. m. Signe Lund, 1946. Education: BA, University of Stockholm, 1945. Publications: Verse: The Scream and the Silence, 1946; Snow Legend, 1949; Litany, 1952; The Dogs, 1954; Poems Under the Trees, 1956; The Stairs, 1964; Within, 1969; Meanwhile, 1972; Earth Cradle Sky Ceiling, 1973; Dictionary, 1976; Early One Morning Late on Earth, 1976-80; You and I and the World, 1980; Murmur, 1983; Beings, 1988; Plays: A Clown Must Have Lost His Way, 1949; The Snare, 1959; Television Plays: Theatre I, 1959; Theatre II, 1963; The Carpet, 1964; The Spiders and a Short Play, 1966; With Ones Own Eyes, 1967; Poor Job, 1969; The Nose, 1971; Not So Young Anymore, 1972; Those Who Wait, 1976; Radio Play, Sidelights: A Selection of Prose, 1989. Honours: Honorary Doctorate, University of Stockholm, 1976. Address: c/o Bonniers Forlag, Box 3159, 103 63 Stockholm, Sweden.

ASPLER Tony, b. 12 May 1939, London, England. Writer. 1 son, 1 daughter. Education: BA, McGill University, Canada, 1959. Publications: With Gordon Page: Chain Reaction, 1978; The Scorpion Sanction, 1980; The Music Wars, 1983; Sole Author: Streets of Askelon, 1972; One of my Marionettes, 1973; Vintage Canada, 1983, updated edition, 1992; The Wine Lover Dines, International Guide to Wine; Titanic (novel), 1989; Blood is Thicker than Beaujolais (novel), 1993; Cellar and Silver (with Rose Murray), 1993; Aligote to Zinfandel, 1994; The Beast of Barbaresco (novel), 1996; Guide to New World Wines. Contributions to: Editor: Winetidings; City Food, Toronto Star; Decanter. Membership: Founding Chairman, Crime Writers of Canada, 1982-84. Literary Agent: Livingston Cooke. Address: 27B Claxton Boulevard, Toronto, Ontario M6C 1L7, Canada.

ASPREY Robert B, b. 16 Feb 1923, Sioux City, Iowa, USA. Writer. Education: University of Iowa; New College, Oxford University; University of Vienna, Austria; University of Nice, France. Publications: The Panther's Feast; The First Battle of the Marne; Once a Marine; At Belleau Wood; Semper Fidelis; War in the Shadows; Operation Prophet; Frederick the Great - the Magnificent Enigma; The German High Command at War. Contributions to: Marine Corps Gazette; New Yorker; Naval Institute Proceedings; Brassey's Annual; Army Quarterly; New York Times; Army (magazine). Honours: Recipient of one of the first Fulbright Scholarships, New College, Oxford, England; Served in two World Wars as commissioned officer in the US Marine Corps; Guest Speaker, Western Front Association, 1993. Memberships: Authors Guild; Oxford University Society; New College Society; Army and Navy Club, Washington DC; Special Forces Club, London. Address: Robert Gottlieb, William Morris Agency, 1350 Avenue of the Americas, New York, NY 10019, USA.

ASSAAD Fawzia, b. 17 July 1929, Cairo, Egypt. Author. m. Dr Fakhry Assaad, 17 Dec 1959, 1 son, 2 daughters. Education: BA, 1949, PhD, 1956, Sorbonne, Paris; Franch Baccalaureate, Cairo, 1946; Arabic Baccalaureate, Cairo, 1957. Appointments: Lecturer in Philosophy, University of Ain Shams, Cairo, 1957, 1964, University of Taipei, Taiwan, 1964-65. Publications: Soren Kierkegaard, essay, 1960; L'Egyptienne, novel, 1975; Des Enfants et des Chats, novel, 1987; Les Préfigurations Egyptiennes de la Pensée de Nietzsche, essay, 1986; La Grande Maison de Louxor (novel), 1992. Contributions to: Philosophical essays. Honours: Prix de l'association des Ecrivains de Genève, 1985, 1991. Memberships: PEN International; Representative, PEN, Commission of Human Rights, United Nations, Geneva; Association des Critiques Litteraires. Address: 2 ch. de Sous-Cherre, 1245 Collonge-Bellerive, Geneva, Switzerland.

ASSELINEAU Roger Maurice, (Maurice Herra), b. 24 Mar 1915, Orleans, France. Emeritus Professor, American Literature. Education: Licence es Lettres, Agregation, English, 1938, Docteur es Lettres, 1953, Sorbonne, Paris. Publications: L'Evolution de Walt Whitman, 1954; The Literary Reputation of Mark Twain, 1964; Poesies Incompletes, 1959; E A Poe, 1970; Transcendentalist Constant in

American Literature, 1980; St John de Crevecoeur: The Life of an American Farmer, (with Gay Wilson Allen), 1987; Poésies incomplètes (II), 1989; Poètes anglais de la Grande Guerre, 1991; As Maurice Herra, Poèmes de Guerre 1939-1944, 1991. Contributions to: Etudes Anglaises; Revue de Litterature Comparee; Forum; Dialogue; Calamus; Walt Whitman Review. Honours: Walt Whitman Prize, Poetry Society of America; Honorary doctorate, University of Poznan. Memberships: Honorary President, French Association for American Studies; Honorary member, Modern Language Association; Hemingway Society; International Association of University Professors of English; Societe des Gens de Lettres. Address: 114 Avenue Leon Blum, 92160 Antony, France.

ASTLEY Thea, (Beatrice May), b. 25 Aug 1925, Brisbane, Queensland, Australia. Novelist. m. Edmund John Gregson, 1948, 1 son. Education: BA, University of Brisbane, 1947. Appointments: Senior Tutor, then Fellow in English, Macquarie University, Sydney, New South Wales, 1968-85. Publications: Girl With a Monkey, 1958; A Descant for Gossips, 1960; The Well-Dressed Explorer, 1962; The Slow Natives, 1965; A Boat Load of Home Folk, 1968; The Acolyte, 1972; A Kindness Cup, 1974; An Item from the Late News, 1982; Beachmasters, 1985; It's Raining in Mango, 1987; Reach Tin River, 1990; Short stories: Hunting the Wild Pineapple, 1979; Also various uncollected short stories. Honours: Age Book of the Year Award, 1975; Patrick White Award, 1989. Address: c/o Elise Goodman, Goodman Associates, 500 West End Avenue, New York, NY 10024, USA.

ASTOR Gerald (Morton), b. 3 Aug 1926, New Haven, Connecticut, USA. Writer. m. Sonia Sacoder, 23 Nov 1949, 3 sons. Education: AB, Princeton University, 1949; Columbia University, 1949-51. Publications: The New York Cops: An Informed History, 1971; "...And a Credit to His Race": The Hard Life and Times of Joseph Louis Barrow, a.k.a. Joe Louis, 1974; The Charge is Rape, 1974; A Question of Rape, 1974; Hot Paper, 1975; Photographing Sports: John Zimmerman, Mark Kauffman and Neil Leifer (with Sean Callahan), 1975; Brick Agent: Inside the Mafia for the FBI (with Anthony Villano), 1977; The Disease Detectives: Deadly Medical Mysteries and the People Who Solved Them, 1983; The "Last" Nazi: The Life and Times of Dr. Joseph Mengele, 1985; The Baseball Hall of Fame Anniversary Book, 1988; The PGA World Golf Hall of Fame Book, 1991; Hostage: My Nightmare in Beirut (with David Jacobsen), 1991; A Blood-Dimmed Tide: The Battle of the Bulge by the Men Who Fought It, 1992; Battling Buzzards: The Odyssey of the 517th Regimental Parachute Combat Team, 1943-1945, 1993; June 6, 1944: The Voices of D-Day, 1994; Operation Iceberg: The Invasion and Conquest of Okinawa in World War II: An Oral History, 1995; Crisis in the Pacific: The Battles for the Philippines, 1996; The Mighty Eighth: The Air War in Europe by the Men Who Fought It, forthcoming. Contributions to: Periodicals. Memberships: Authors Guild; Authors League of America. Address: 50 Sprain Valley Road, Scarsdale, NY 10583, USA.

ATHANASSIADIS Tassos, b. 1 Nov 1913, Salichli of Asia Minor, Turkey. Author; Novelist; Essayist; Biographer. m. Maria Dimitropoulou, 1979. Education: Law and Foreign Languages, Law School of Athens University, 1931-36. Publications: The Panthei Saga, 1948-61; The Guards of Achaia, 1974; The Last Grandchildren, 1981-84; Niobe's Children, 1985-88; Three Children of the Century; Essays: Recognitions, 1965; Certainties and Doubts, 1980; From Ourself to Others, 1992; Novels Translated into French, Italian, Swedish, Portuguese, Romanian and German; Holy Youth, 1993. Honours: State Literary Awards, 1955, 1961, 1963; The Athens Academy Award, 1961; Ipeski Prize of Greek Turkish Friendship, 1989; Doctor Honoris Causa of Athens University, 1994. Memberships: Athens Academy; PEN; Greek Lyric Opera; Greek National Theatre. Address: 83 Drossopoulou Street, Athens 112 57, Greece.

ATKINS Stephen E, b. 29 Jan 1941, Columbia, Missouri, USA. Librarian; Professor. m. Susan Starr Jordan, 9 June 1966, 1 son, 1 daughter. Education: BA (Honours), European History, 1963, MA (Honours), French History, 1964, University of Missouri-Columbia; PhD, French History, 1976, MA, Library Science, 1983, University of Iowa. Appointments: Political Science Specialist, Education and Social Science Library, Associate Professor, University of Illinois, Urbana-Champaign, 1983-89; Head of Collection Development, Sterling C Evans Library, 1989-, Professor, 1994-, Texas A&M University, College Station. Publications: Arms Control and Disarmament, Defense and Military, International Security and Peace: An Annotated Guide to Success, 1980-1987, 1989; The Academic Library in the American University, 1991; Terrorism: A Reference

Handbook, 1992. Contributions to: National Forum, 1986; Library Trends, 1988; Proceedings of the Western Society for French History; Several others. Honour: Peace Award, American Library Association, 1992. Memberships: Western Society for French History, Executive Board 1984-87; American Library Association, Chairperson, Law and Political Science Section, 1989-90; ACCESS: A Security Information Service, Secretary, Board of Directors, 1991-94, Chair, Activities Council 1994-95; Association of College and Research Libraries; Social Science History Association; Library Administration and Management Association. Address: 2724 Normand Circle, College Station, TX 77845, USA.

ATKINSON James, b. 27 Apr 1914, Tynemouth, Northumberland, England. Retired Professor of Theology. m. Laura Jean Nutley, dec 1967, 1 son, 1 daughter. Education: BA, 1936, MA, 1938, M Litt, 1950, University of Durham; DTh, University of Münster, Germany, 1955. Publications: Library of Christian Classics, 1962; Rome and Reformation, 1966; Luther's Works, Vol 44, 1967; Luther and the Birth of Protestantism, 1968; The Reformation, 1968; The Trial of Luther, 1971; Martin Luther, Prophet to Church Catholic, 1983; The Darkness of Faith, 1987. Contributions to: Learned Journals; Part author of several books; Many articles. Memberships: Society for the Study of Theology; Society of the Study of Ecclesiastical History; L'Academie Internationale des Sciences Religieuses. Address: Leach House, Hathersage, Sheffield, S30 1BA, England.

ATKINSON Mary. See: HARDWICK Mollie.

ATLAN Liliane, b. 14 Jan 1932, Montpellier, France. Writer. m. June 1952, div 1976, 1 son, 1 daughter. Education: Diploma Philosophy; CAPES Modern Literature. Publications: Plays: Mr Fugue of Earth Sick; The Messiahs, The Carriage of Flames and Voices; Poetry: L'Amour Elementaire; Lapsus, 1971; Bonheur mais sur quel fon le dire, 1996. Videotext: Même les oiseaux ne peuvent pas toujours planner, 1979; The Passerby, 1989 (France), 1993 (USA), play 1997; An Opera for Terezin, 1989, 1992, 1993, play 1997; Quelques pages arrachées all grand livre des rêves, 1994; Bonheur mais sur quel ton le dire, poems, 1996; Many Books and Plays have been broadcast by France Culture. Honours: Prix Habimah, 1972; Prix Wizo, 1980; Chevalier de l'Ordre des Arts et des Lettres, 1984; Prize Villa Medicis Outside the Walls, 1992. Memberships: Writers Union of France; AMOAL. Address: 70 Rue du Javelot, 75645 Paris, Cedex 13, France.

ATODA Takashi, b. 13 Jan 1935, Tokyo, Japan. Author. m. 1965, 2 sons, 1 daughter. Education: Graduate, Literary Department, Waseda University, 1961. Publications: Napoleon Crazy, 1979; Do You Know Greek Mythology?, 1981; You Resemble Somebody, 1984; The New Illiad, 1994; The Fantasy of Azuchi Castle, 1996. Honours: Mystery Writers of Japan Award, for The Visitor, 1979; Naoki Award, for Napoleon Crazy, 1979; Yoshikawa Eiji Award, for The New Illiad, 1998. Memberships: Japan Writers Association; Japan Pen Club; Mystery Writers of Japan; Mystery Writers of America. Literary Agent: Woodbell Co Ltd. Address: 3-1-18 Takaido-Higashi, Suginami-ku, Tokyo, Japan.

ATTENBOROUGH David Frederick, b. 8 May 1926, London, England. Broadcaster; Naturalist. m. Jane Elizabeth Ebsworth Oriel, 11 Feb 1950, 1 son, 1 daughter. Education: Wyggeston Grammar School, Leicester; Clare College, Cambridge. Publications: Zoo Quest to Guiana, 1956; Zoo Quest for a Dragon, 1957; Zoo Quest in Paraguay, 1959; Quest in Paradise, 1960; Zoo Quest to Madagascar, 1961; Quest Under Capricorn, 1963; The Tribal Eye, 1976; Life on Earth, 1979; The Living Planet, 1984; The First Eden, 1987; Atlas of Living World, 1989; The Trials of Life, 1990. Honours: Silver Medal, Zoological Society of London, 1966; Gold Medal, Royal Geographical Society; Kalinga Prize, UNESCO; Honorary Degrees: Leicester, London, Birmingham, Liverpool, Heriot-Watt, Sussex, Bath, Ulster, Durham, Bristol, Glasgow, Essex, Cambridge, Oxford. Memberships: Fellow, Royal Society; Honorary Fellow, British Academy of Film and Television Arts. Address: 5 Park Road, Richmond, Surrey, England.

ATWOOD Margaret (Eleanor), b. 18 Nov 1939, Ottawa, Ontario, Canada. Poet; Author; Critic. Education: BA, Victoria College, University of Toronto, 1961; AM, Radcliffe College, Cambridge, Massachusetts, 1962; Attended Harvard University, 1962-63, 1965-67. Appointments: Teacher, University of British Columbia, 1964-65, Sir George Williams University, Montreal, 1967-68, University of Alberta, 1969-70, York University, 1971-72; Writer-in-Residence, University of Toronto, 1972-73, University of Alabama, Tuscaloosa, 1985,

Macquarie University, Australia, 1987; Holder, Berg Chair, New York University, 1986. Publications: Poetry: Double Persephone, 1961; The Circle Game, 1964; Kaleidoscopes Baroque, 1965; Talismans for Children, 1965; Speeches for Doctor Frankenstein, 1966; The Animals in That Country, 1968; The Journals of Susanna Moodie, 1970; Procedures for Ungerground, 1970; Oratorio for Sasquatch, Man and Two Androids, 1970; Power Politics, 1971; You Are Happy, 1974; Selected Poems, 1976; Marsh Hawk, 1977; Two-Headed Poems, 1978; True Stories, 1981; Notes Towards a Poem That Can Never Be Written, 1981; Snake Poems, 1983; Interlunar, 1984; Selected Poems II: Poems Selected and New, 1976-1986, 1986; Selected Poems 1966-1984, 1991; Margaret Atwood Poems 1965-75, 1992; Morning in the Burned House, 1995. Fiction: The Edible Woman, 1969; Surfacing, 1972; Lady Oracle, 1976; Dancing Girls, 1977; Life Before Man, 1979; Bodily Harm, 1981; Encounters With the Element Man, 1982; Murder in the Dark, 1983; Bluebeard's Egg, 1983; Unearthing Suite, 1983; The Handmaid's Tale, 1985; Cat's Eye, 1988; Wilderness Tips, 1991; Good Bones, 1992; The Robber Bride, 1993; Alias Grace, 1996. Non-Fiction: Survival: A Thematic Guide to Canadian Literature, 1972; Days of The Rebels 1815-1840, 1977; Second Words: Selected Critical Prose, 1982; The Oxford Book of Canadian Verse in English (editor), 1982; The Best American Short Stories (co-editor with Shannon Ravenel), 1989; Strange Things: Fictions of the Malevolent North in Canadian Literature, 1995. Contributions to: Books in Canada; Canadian Literature; Globe and Mail; Harvard Educational Review; The Nation; New York Times Book Review; Washington Post. Honours: Guggenheim Fellowship, 1981; Companion of the Order of Canada, 1981; Fellow, Royal Society of Canada; Foreign Honorary Member, American Academy of Arts and Sciences, 1988; Order of Ontario, 1990; Centennial Medal, Harvard University, 1990; Commemorative Medal, 125th Anniversary of Canadian Confederation, 1992; Honorary degrees. Memberships: Writers Union of Canada, President, 1981-82; PEN International, President, 1985-86. Address: c/o Oxford University Press, 70 Wynford Drive, Don Mills, Ontario M3C 1J9, Canada.

AUBERT Alvin (Bernard), b. 12 Mar 1930, Lutcher, Louisiana, USA. Professor of English Emeritus; Poet. m. (1) Olga Alexis, 1948, div, 1 daughter, (2) Bernardine Tenant, 1960, 2 daughters. Education: BA, Southern University, Baton Rouge, Louisiana, 1959; AM, University of Michigan, 1960; University of Illinois at Urbana-Champaign, 1963-64, 1966-67. Appointments: Instructor, 1960-62, Assistant Professor, 1962-65, Associate Professor of English, 1965-70, Southern University; Visiting Professor of English, University of Oregon at Eugene, 1970; Associate Professor, 1970-74, Professor of English, 1974-79, State University of New York at Fredonia; Founder-Editor, Obsidian magazine, 1975-85; Professor of English, 1980-92, Professor Emeritus, 1992-, Wayne State University, Detroit. Publications: Against the Blues, 1972; Feeling Through, 1975; South Louisiana: New and Selected Poems, 1985; If Winter Come: Collected Poems, 1994; Harlem Wrestler, 1995. Honours: Bread Loaf Writers Conference Scholarship, 1968; National Endowment for the Arts Grants, 1973, 1981; Coordinating Council of Literary Magazines Grant, 1979; Annual Callaloo Award, 1989. Address: 18234 parkside Avenue, Detroit, MI 48221, USA.

AUBURN Hugues. See: **BLACKBURN Gaston.**

AUCHINLOSS Louis Stanton, b. 27 Sept 1917, Lawrence, New York, USA. Lawyer; Author. m. Adele Lawrence, 1957, 3 sons. Education: Yale University; University of Virginia; Admitted, New York Bar, 1941. Publications: The Indifferent Children, 1947; The Injustice Collectors, 1950; Sybil, 1952; A Law for the Lion, 1953; The Romantic Egoists, 1954; The Great World and Timothy Colt, 1956; Venus in Sparta, 1958; Pursuit of the Prodigal, 1959; House of Five Talents, 1960; Reflections of a Jacobite, 1961; Portrait in Brownstone, 1962; Powers of Attorney, 1963; The Rector of Justin, 1964; Pioneers and Caretakers, 1965; The Embezzler, 1966; Tales of Manhattan, 1967; A World of Profit, 1969; Motiveless Malignity, 1969; Edith Wharton: A Woman in her Time, 1971; I Come as a Thief, 1972; Richelieu, 1972; The Partners, 1974; A Winter's Capital, 1974; Reading Henry James, 1975; The Winthrop Convenant, 1976; The Dark Lady, 1977; The Country Cousin, 1978; Persons of Consequence, 1979; Life, Law and Letters, 1979; The House of the Prophet, 1980; The Cat and the King, 1981; Watchfires, 1982; Exit Lady Masham, 1983; The Book Clan, 1984; Honorable Men, 1985; Diary of a Yuppie, 1987; The Golden Calves, 1989; Fellow Passengers, 1990; J P Morgan, 1990; False Gods, 1992; Family Fortunes: 3 Collected Novels, 1993; Three Lives, 1993; The Style's the Man, 1994. Contributions to: New York Review

of Books; New Criterion. Membership: National Institute of Arts and Letters. Address: 1111 Park Avenue, New York, NY 10028, USA.

AUERBACH Nina (Joan), b. 24 May 1943, New York, New York, USA. Professor of English; Writer. Education: BA, University of Wisconsin at Madison, 1964; MA, 1967, PhD, Columbia University. Appointments: Adjunct Professor of English, California State University at Los Angeles, 1970-72; Assistant Professor, 1972-77, Associate Professor, 1977-83, Professor, 1983-, of English, University of Pennsylvania. Publications: Communities of Women: An Idea in Fiction, 1978; Woman and the Demon: The Life of a Victorian Myth, 1982; Romantic Imprisonment: Women and Other Glorified Outcasts, 1985; Ellen Terry: Player in Her Time, 1987; Private Theatrical: The Lives of the Victorians, 1990; Forbidden Journeys: Fairy Tales and Fantasies by Victorian Women Writers (editor with U C Knoepflmacher), 1992; Our Vampires, Ourselves, 1995. Contributions to: Books and periodicals. Honours: Ford Foundation Fellowship, 1975-76; Radcliffe Institute Fellowship, 1975-76; Guggenheim Fellowship, 1979-80; National Book Critics Circle Nomination for Criticism, 1982; Phi Beta Kappa; Phi Beta Phi. Memberships: Modern Language Association of America; Victorian Society of America. Address: Department of English, University of Pennsylvania, Philadelphia, PA 19104, USA.

AUGUST Marcus. See: **BANTOCK Gavin.**

AUMBRY Alan. See: **BAYLEY Barrington (John).**

AUSTER Paul, b. 3 Feb 1947, Newark, New Jersey, USA. Writer; Poet. m. (1) Lydia Davis, 6 Oct 1974, div 1979, 1 son, (2) Siri Hustvedt, 16 June 1981, 1 daughter. Education: BA 1969, MA 1970, Columbia University. Appointment: Lecturer, Princeton University, 1986-90. Publications: Novels: City of Glass, 1985; Ghosts, 1986; The Locked Room, 1986; In the Country of Last Things, 1987; Moon Palace, 1989; The Music of Chance, 1990; Leviathan, 1992; Mr Vertigo, 1994. Poetry: Unearth, 1974; Wall Writing, 1976; Fragments from Cold, 1977; Facing the Music, 1980; Disappearances: Selected Poems, 1988. Non-Fiction: White Spaces, 1980; The Invention of Solitude, 1982; The Art of Hunger, 1982, augmented edition, 1992. Editor: The Random House Book of Twentieth-Century French Poetry, 1982. Films: Smoke, 1995; Blue in the Face, 1995. Contributions to: Numerous periodicals. Honours: National Endowment for the Arts Fellowships, 1979, 1985; Chevalier, l'Ordre des Arts et des Lettres, France; Prix Medicis Etranger, 1993. Membership: PEN. Address: c/o Carol Mann Agency, 55 Fifth Avenue, New York, NY 10003, USA.

AUSTIN Brett. See: **FLOREN Lee.**

AUSTIN William W(eaver), b. 18 Jan 1920, Lawton, Oklahoma, USA. Musicologist. Education: BA, 1939, MA, 1940, PhD, 1951, Harvard University. Appointments: Assistant Professor, 1947-50, Associate Professor, 1950-60, Professor, 1960-69, Goldwin Smith Professor of Musicology, 1969-80, Given Foundation Professor of Musicology, 1980-90, Professor Emeritus, 1990-, Cornell University. Publications: Music in the 20th Century From Debussy Through Stravinsky, 1966; Susanna, Jeanie, and The Old Folks At Home: Meanings and Contexts of the Songs of Stephen C Foster From His Time to Ours, 1975, 2nd edition, 1987. Editor: New Looks at Italian Opera: Essays in Honour of Donald J Grout, 1968. Translator: Carl Dahlhaus's Musikästhetik as Esthetics of Music, 1982. Honours: Guggenheim Fellowship, 1961-62; Fellow, American Academy of Arts and Sciences. Membership: American Musicological Society. Address: 205 White Park Road, Ithaca, NY 14850, USA.

AVALLONE Michael (Angelo Jr), (Michele Alden, James Blaine, Nick Carter, Troy Conway, Priscilla Dalton, Mark Dane, Jean-Anne de Pre, Fred Frazer, Dora Highland, Amanda Jean Jarrett, Stuart Jason, Steve Michaels, Memo Morgan, Dorothea Nile, Edwina Noone, John Patrick, Vance Stanton, Sidney Stuart, Lee Davis Willoughby), b. 27 Oct 1924, New York, New York, USA. Writer. m. (1), 1 son, (2) Frances Weinstein, 27 May 1960, 1 son, 1 daughter. Education: New York City Schools. Publications: Novels: All the Way, 1960; The Little Black Book, 1961; Stag Stripper, 1961; Never Love a Call Girl, 1962; Sex Kitten, 1962; Lust at Leisure, 1963; And Sex Walked In, 1963; The Man from A.V.O.N., 1967; My Secret Life with Older Women, 1968; Missing!, 1969; The Night Before Chaos, 1971; The Beast with Red Hands, 1973; Death Is a Dark Man, 1974; Devil, Devil, 1975; Only One More Miracle, 1975; Red Roses Forever, 1983; The Rough Riders, 1984; Numerous others, including the Ed

Noon series, 1953-78. Other: Various film and television novelizations, short stories, and articles. Contributions to: Many periodicals. Honours: Literary Luminary of New Jersey, 1977; Many scrolls. Memberships: Authors League, 1975-78; Mystery Writers of America, board member, 1958-70. Address: 80 Hilltop Boulevard, East Brunswick, NJ 08816, USA.

AVERY Gillian (Elise), b. 30 Sept 1926, England. Writer; Editor. Appointments: Junior Reporter, Surrey Mirror, Redhill, Surrey, 1944-47; Staff, Chambers Encyclopaedia, London, 1947-50; Assistant Illustrations Editor, Clarendon Press, Oxford, 1950-54. Publications: Victorian People in Life and Literature, 1970; A Likely Lad, 1971; Ellen's Birthday, 1971; Jemima and the Welsh Rabbit, 1972; The Echoing Green: Memories of Victorian and Regency Youth, 1974; Ellen and the Queen, 1974; Book of Strange and Odd, 1975; Childhood's Pattern: A Study of the Heroes and Heroines of Children's Fiction, 1770-1850, 1975; Freddie's Feet, 1976; Huck and Her Time Machine, 1977; Mouldy's Orphan, 1978; Sixpence, 1979; The Lost Railway, 1980; Onlookers, 1983; The Best Type of Girl, 1991. Editor: Many books. Address: 32 Charlbury Road, Oxford OX2 6UU, England.

AVGERINOS Cecily T Grazio, b. 16 Apr 1945, New York, USA. Poet; Novelist. m. Robert T Avgerinos, 24 May 1969, 2 sons, 1 daughter. Education: BA, New York University, 1966. Publications: Poems: My Tatterdemalion, 1985; Sunrises, 1985; Eternity, 1986; Summer Fantasy, 1986; My Prayer, 1986; Lunch in the Park, 1986; Circle Of Gold, 1986; Lord, I Wonder, 1986; The Fig Tree, 1987; Fishing, 1987; Septecential, 1987; Loss, 1987; Bridge Across Tomorrow, 1987; To My Children, 1987; The Stringless Guitar, 1988; Pink Socks, 1988; My Dogwood-Love's Analogy, 1989; Merry-Go-Round, 1989; Strawsticks, 1989. Contributions to: Numerous anthologies. Honours: 25 Awards of Merit, World of Poetry, 1985-; 4 Golden Poet Awards, 1985-. Address: 173 Momar Drive, Ramsey, NJ 07446, USA.

AVICE Claude (Pierre Marie), (Pierre Barbet, David Maine, Oliver Sprigel), b. 16 May 1925, Le Mans, France. Science Fiction Writer. m. Marianne Brunswick, 23 July 1952, 2 sons, 1 daughter. Education: Diplomas in Bacteriology, Serology and Parasitology, 1954, PhD, Summa cum laude, in Pharmacy, 1955, Institut Pasteur, University of Paris. Appointments: Pharmacist, Paris, 1952-81; Science Fiction Writer, 1962. Publications: Over 70 books including: Les Grognards d'Eridan, 1970, English translation as The Napoleons of Eridanus, 1976; A quoi songent les psyborgs?, 1971, English translation as Games Psyborgs Play, 1973; L'Empire du Baphomet, 1972, English translation as Baphomet's Meteor, 1972; La Planete enchantée, 1973, English translation as Enchanted Planet, 1975; Liane de Noldaz, 1973, English translation as The Joan-of-Arc Replay, 1978; L'Empereur d'Eridan, 1982, English translation as The Emperor of Eridanus, 1983. Contributions to: Many publications both fiction and non-fiction. Honour: Gold Medal, International Institute of Science Fiction, Poznan, Poland. Memberships: Association Internationale des Critiques litteraires; European Academy of Arts, Letters and Science; European Society of Science Fiction; Science Fiction Writers of America; Society of Doctors in Pharmacy; Société francophone de Science-Fiction; World Science Fiction. Address: 4 Square de l'Avenue du Bois, 75116 Paris, France.

AVISON Margaret (Kirkland), b. 23 Apr 1918, Galt, Ontario, Canada. Poet; Translator. Education: BA in English, University of Toronto, 1940. Appointments: Writer-in-Residence, University of Western Ontario, 1972-73; Staff, Mustard Seed Mission, Toronto, 1978-. Publications: History of Toronto, 1951; Winter Sun, 1960; The Research Compendium, 1964; The Dumbfoundling, 1966; Sunblue, 1978. Co-translator: The Plough and the Pen: Writings from Hungary, 1930-1956, 1963; Acta Sanctorum and Other Tales, 1970. Honours: Guggenheim Fellowship, 1956; Governor-General's Award, 1961. Address: c/o Mustard Seed Mission, Toronto, Ontario, Canada.

AWOONOR Kofi Nyidevu, b. 13 Mar 1935, Wheta, Ghana. Diplomat. 4 sons, 1 daughter. Education: Zion College of West Africa, 1951-54; Achimota Secondary School, 1955-56; University College of Ghana, 1957-60; University College of London, 1967-68; State University of New York at Stony Brook, 1969-72. Publications: Rediscovery, 1964; Night of My Blood, 1971; This Earth My Brother, 1972; Ride Me Memory, 1973; Guardian of the Sacred Word, 1974; Breast of the Earth (essays), 1974; House by the Sea, 1978; Until the Morning After (poetry), 1988; Ghana: A Political History, 1990; Comes the Voyager At Last (fiction), 1992; Latin American and Caribbean

Notebook (poetry), 1993. Honours: Translation Award, Columbia University, 1972; Ghana Book Award, 1978; Dillons Commonwealth Award, 1989; Ghana Association of Writers Distinguished Authors Award, 1992. Address: Permanent Mission of Ghana to the United Nations, 19 East 47th Street, New York, NY 10017, USA.

AXTON David. See: KOONTZ Dean R.

AYCKBOURN Alan, b. 12 Apr 1939, London, England. Theatre Director; Playwright; Artistic Director. Plays: Mr Whatnot, 1963; Relatively Speaking, 1965; How the Other Half Loves, 1969; Time and Time Again, 1971; Absurd Person Singular, 1972; The Norman Conquests, 1973; Absent Friends, 1974; Confusions, 1975; Bedroom Farce, 1975; Just Between Ourselves, 1976; Ten Times Table, 1977; Joking Apart, 1978; Sisterly Feelings, 1979; Taking Steps, 1979; Season's Greetings, 1980; Way Upstream, 1981; Intimate Exchanges, 1982; A Chorus of Disapproval, 1984; Woman in Mind, 1985; A Small Family Business, 1986; Henceforward, 1987; Man of the Moment, 1988; The Revenger's Comedies, 1989; Time of My Life, 1992; Dreams From a Summer House, 1992; Communicating Doors, 1994; Hunting Julia, 1994; The Musical Jigsaw Play, 1994. Honours: Hon DLitt, Hull, 1981, Keele, 1987, Leeds, 1987, York, 1992, Bradford, 1994; Commander of the Order of the British Empire, 1987; Cameron Mackintosh Professor of Contemporary Theatre, 1992. Memberships: Garrick Club; Royal Society of Arts. Literary Agent: Casarotto Ramsay Ltd. Address: c/o Casarotto Ramsay Limited, National House, 60-66 Wardour Street, London W1V 3HP, England.

AYDY Catherine. See: TENNANT Emma Christina.

AYERST David (George Ogilvy), b. 24 July 1904, London, England. Appointments: Editorial Staff Member, 1929-34, Historian, 1964-73, The Guardian, Manchester and London; H M Inspector of Schools, 1947-64. Publications: Europe in the 19th Century, 1940; Understanding Schools, 1967; Records of Christianity (editor with A S T Fisher), 1970, 1977; Guardian: Biography of a Newspaper (in US as The Manchester Guardian), 1971; The Guardian Omnibus (editor), 1973; Garvin of the Observer, 1985. Address: Littlecote, Burford, Oxford OX18 4SE, England.

AYIM May. See: OPITZ May.

AYLEN Leo (William), b. 15 Feb 1935, Vryheid, South Africa. Writer; Poet. m. Annette Battam. Education: MA, New College, Oxford, 1959; PhD, University of Bristol, 1962. Appointments: Producer, BBC-TV, London, 1965-70; Poet-in-Residence, Fairleigh Dickinson University, USA, 1972-74; Hooker Distinguished Visiting Professor, McMaster University, Canada, 1982; Numerous appearances as a poet on radio and TV in the UK, USA and South Africa. Publications: Greek Tragedy in the Modern World, 1961; Greece for Everyone, 1976; The Greek Theatre, 1985. Poetry: Discontinued Design, 1969; I, Odysseus, 1971; Sunflower, 1976; Return to Zululand, 1980; Jumping-Shoes, 1983; Rhymoceros, 1989. Play: Red Alert: This is a God Warning, 1981. Children's opera: The Apples of Youth, 1980. Contributions to: Many anthologies. Honours: C Day-Lewis Fellowship, 1979-80; Runner-up Prizewinner, Arvon International Competition, 1992. Memberships: Poetry Society of Great Britain; Poetry Society of America; Writers Guild of Great Britain; Writers Guild of America. Address: 13 St Saviour's Road, London, SW2 5HP, England.

AYLING Stanley (Edward), b. 15 Mar 1909, London, England. Retired History Teacher; Writer. m. Gwendoline Hawkins, 17 Dec 1936, 2 sons. Education: BA, 1931, MA, 1934, Emmanuel College, Cambridge. Appointments: Grammar school teacher, Exeter and London, 1932-45; Senior history master, Sandown Grammar School, Isle of Wight, England, 1945-69. Publications: Twele Portraits of Power: An Introduction to Twentieth Century History, 1961, 5th edition, 1971; Georgian Century, 1971; Nineteenth Century Gallery: Portraits of Power and Rebellion, 1970; George the Third, 1972; The Elder Pitt, Earl of Chatham, 1976; John Wesley, 1979; A Portrait of Sheridan, 1985; Edmund Burke: His Life and Opinions, 1988; Fox: The Life of Charles James Fox, 1991. Membership: Fellow, Royal Society of Literature, 1980-. Address: The Beeches, Middle Winterslow, Salisbury, Wiltshire, England.

AYLMER Gerald Edward, b. 30 Apr 1926, England. Historian. Education: BA, MA, 1950, PhD, 1955, Oxford University. Appointments: J E Proctor Visiting Fellow, Princeton University, NJ, 1950-51; Junior Research Fellow, Balliol College, Oxford, 1951-54;

Assistant Lecturer, 1954-57, Lecturer, 1957-62, University of Manchester; Professor and Head of Department, University of York, 1963-78; Master, St Peters College, Oxford, 1978-91; Editorial Board, History of Parliament, 1968-, Chairman, 1989-; Member, 1978-, Chairman, 1989-94, Commission on Historical Manuscripts. Publications: The King's Servants, 1625-1642, 1961; The Diary of William Lawrence, 1961; The Struggle for the Constitution 1603-1689, 1963; The Interregnum 1646-1660, 1972; The State's Servants, 1649-1660, 1973; The Levellers in the English Revolution, 1975; A History of York Minster, 1977; Rebellion or Revolution 1640-1660, 1986. Honour: Fellow of the British Academy, 1976. Memberships: Royal Historical Society, Vice President, 1973-77, President, 1984-88, Honorary Vice President, 1988; Historical Association, Honorary Vice President, 1992-. Address: 18 Albert Street, Jericho, Oxford OX2 6AZ, England.

AYRES Philip (James), b. 28 July 1944, South Australia. Writer; Lecturer. m. (1) Maruta Sudrabs, 11 Dec 1965, div 1981, (2) Patricia San Martin, 28 Nov 1981, 1 son. Education: BA, 1965, PhD, 1971, University of Adelaide. Appointments: Lecturer, 1972-79, Senior Lecturer, 1979-, Monash University. Publications: The Revenger's Tragedy, 1977; The English Roman Life, 1980; Malcolm Fraser: A Biography, 1987. Editor: Ben Jonson: Sejanus His Fall, 1990. Contributions to: English Literary Renaissance; Modern Philiology; Studies in Bibliography; Studies in English Literature; Studies in Philology. Honour: Fellow, Royal Historical Society. Address: 13 Harris Avenue, Glen Iris, Victoria 3146, Australia.

B

B Dick. See: **BURNS Richard Gordon.**

B Thomas. See: **JENKINS Dan.**

BAANTJER Albert Cornelis, b. 16 Sept 1923, Urk, Holland. Police Officer. m. Marretje van der Vaart, 3 Dec 1952. Education: Police High School, 1945. Publications: Dr Kok and the Sorrowing Tomcat; Dr Kok and the Brothers of the Easy Death; Dr Kok and the Mask of Death; Murder in Amsterdam. Contributions to: Nieuws van de Dag; Margriet; Libelle. Honours: Winner, Short Story Competition, 1961; Silver Medal, 1979; Television Book Award, 1985. Literary Agent: John Bakkenhoven. Address: Poortweydt 4, 1671RC Medemblik, Holland.

BABB Sanora, b. 21 Apr 1907, Leavenworth, Kansas, USA. Writer. m. James Wong Howe, 12 Sept 1949, dec 1976. Education: Kansas State University. Publications: The Lost Traveler, 1958; An Owl on Every Post, 1970, 1972; The Dark Earth, stories, 1987; Cry of the Tinamou, 1997. Contributions to: Short stories, articles, poems, 1930s. Honours: Barestone Mountain Poetry Award, 1967; Best American Short Stories, 1950, 1960; Cross Section of American Literature, 1945, 1948; American Childhoods, 1987. Membership: Authors Guild. Literary Agent: McIntosh and Otis, 310 Madison Avenue, New York, NY 10017, USA. Address: 1562 Queen's Road, West Hollywood, CA 90069, USA.

BABINEAU Jean Joseph, b. 10 Aug 1952, Moncton, New Brunswick, Canada. Teacher; Writer. m. Gisèle Ouellette, 27 Aug 1993, 1 son. Education: BA, 1977; BA, French, 1981; BEd, 1985. Publication: Bloupe, 1993. Contributions to: Éloizes; Mots en Volet; Littéréalité. Honour: Canada Council Exploration Grant, 1989. Memberships: Entrecroisements; UNEQ. Address: Boîte 1516, Robichaud, New Brunswick E0A 2S0, Canada.

BABINGTON Anthony Patrick, b. 4 Apr 1920, Cork, Ireland. Education: Reading School: Inns of Court Law School; Called to Bar, 1948; Circuit Judge, London, 1972-90. Publications: For the Sake of Example; No Memorial; Military Intervention in Britain; A House in Bow Street; The Rule of Law in Britain; The Devil to Pay; The Power to Silence; The English Bastille; Shell-Shock. Memberships: PEN; Society of Authors; Garrick. Address: 3 Gledhow Gardens, Kensington, London SW5 0BL, England.

BABSON Marian, American. Writer. Appointment: Secretary, Crime Writers Association, London, 1976-86. Publications: Cover-up Story, 1971; Murder on Show, 1972; Pretty Lady, 1973; The Stalking Lamb, Unfair Exchange, 1974; Murder Sails at Midnight, There Must Be Some Mistake, 1976; Untimely Guest, 1976; The Lord Mayor's Death, Murder Murder Little Star, 1977; Tightrope for Three, 1978; So Soon Done For, The Twelve Deaths of Christmas, 1979; Dangerous to Know, Queue Here for Murder, 1980; Bejewelled Death, 1981; Death Warmed Up, Death Beside the Seaside, 1982; A Fool for Murder, 1983; The Cruise of a Deathtime, A Trail of Ashes, Death Swap, 1984; Death in Fashion, Weekend for Murder, 1985; Reel Murder, 1986; Fatal Fortune, 1987; Guilty Party; Encore Murder, 1989; Past Regret, 1990. Address: c/o William Collins Sons & Co Ltd, 8 Grafton Street, London W1X 3LA, England.

BACHMAN Richard. See: **KING Stephen Edwin.**

BACOCK Robert Joseph (Brennan), b.22 Feb 1926, Newcastle upon Tyne, England. Senior Teacher in English, Retired. Education: BA, Open University, 1986. Appointments: Several teaching positions in Schools and Colleges in the north of England. Contributions to: Newspapers, periodicals and literary journals including: Times; Daily Express; Observer; Evening Standard; Newcastle Evening Chronicle. Address: 27 Elliott Terrace, Fenham, Newcastle upon Tyne NE4 6UP, England.

BADAWI Mohamed Mustafa, b. 10 June 1925, Alexandria, Egypt. Lecturer. Education: BA, Alexandria University, 1946; BA, 1950, PhD, 1954, London University. Appointments: Research Fellow, 1947-54, Lecturer, 1954-60, Assistant Professor, 1960-64, Alexandria University, Egypt; Lecturer, Oxford University, and Brasenose College,

1964-92; Fellow, St Antony's College, Oxford, 1967-; Editor, Journal of Arabic Literature, Leiden, 1970; Advisory Board Member, Cambridge History of Arabic Literature. Publications: An Anthology of Modern Arabic Verse, 1970; Coleridge as Critic of Shakespeare, 1973; The Saint's Lamp and other Stories by Yahya Haqqi, 1973; A Critical Introduction to Modern Arabic Poetry, 1975; Sara, by AM El Aqqad, 1978; Background to Shakespeare, 1981; The Thief and the Dogs by Naguib Mahfouz, 1984; Modern Arabic Literature and the West, 1985; Modern Arabic Drama in Egypt, 1987; Early Arabic Drama, 1988; Cambridge History of Arabic Literature, Modern Arabic Literature (editor), 1992; A Short History of Modern Arabic Literature, 1993. Honour: King Faisal International Prize for Arabic Literature. Memberships: Ministry of Culture, Egypt; Unesco Expert on Modern Arabic Culture. Address: St Antony's College, Oxford, England.

BADER-MOLNAR Katarina Elisabeth, b. Berlin, Germany. Retired Teacher, Professor; Freelance Writer. m. Imre Molnar, div. Education: Diploma, Librarian, Berlin, 1934; English Literature Studies, Liverpool, England; MA, French Philology, Kopernikus University, 1950; English Philosophy Diploma, 1950; DLitt, Albert Einstein International Academy Foundation, 1965. Appointments: Professor and Librarian, Toruń, Grudziądz, Dantzig, Zürich; Freelance Writer. Publications: L'idée d'humanité dans l'oeuvre de Voltaire jusqu'en y, 1750, 1950; Lyriden (poems), 1976; Romantisches Gefuege (poems and stories), 1978; Teufelskreis und Lethequelle (novel), 1979; Karola contra Isegrim und Reineke (story), 1980; Da waren Träume noch süss (novel), 1988; Vom Leuchten der Liebe (novel), 1990; Gehn und Sein (selected poems), 1991; Bruderkriegy Neue Gedichte (poems), 1994; Various poems, stories for journals, for children and for anthologies in 3 languages. Honours: Gold Medal, Diploma, Académie Internationale de Lutèce, Paris, 1984, 1986; Silver Medal, Académie Universelle de Lausanne, 1984; Shield of Valor, ABI, USA, 1992; Diploma of Honour, Life Research Fellow IBC, Cambridge, England, 1993; International Award of Recognition, 1993; International Order of Merit, 1993. Memberships: Schweizerischer Schriftsteller-Verband Zürich; PEN Zentrum Bern; Schriyftsteller-Verband Zürich, Literarischer Club, Zürich; Mozart Gesellschaft; Académie Internationale de Lutèce et Paris, Life Fellow. Address: Tobelhofstr 6, CH-8044, Zurich, Switzerland.

BADMAN May Edith, (May Ivimy), b. 10 Nov 1912, Greenwich, London. Local Government Officer (retired); Writer. m. Raymond Frank Badman, 18 Oct 1968, 1 son, 1 daughter. Publications: Collections of Poems: Night is Another World, 1964; Midway This Path, 1966; Parting the Leaves, 1984; Strawberries in the Salad, 1992; The Best Part Of the Day, 1992; Late Swings; My House. Contributions to: Time and Tide, Literary Review, Poetry Review, Pembroke State University, Magazine USA, The Independent Arts Co, New Poetry, Radio 3 and 4, many poetry magazines, anthologies including for schools. Honour: Howard Sergeant Memorial Award for Services to Poetry. Memberships: Council member 7 years, Treasurer, 4 years, Poetry Society; Society of Women Writers and Journalists, former committee member; Founded Ver Poets, 1966, organiser to present day; Member, Royal Society of Literature. Address: Haycroft, 61/63 Chiswell Green Lane, St Albans, Herts, AL2 3AL, England.

BAERWALD Hans H(erman), b. 18 June 1927, Tokyo, Japan. Professor Emeritus of Political Science; Writer. Education: BA, 1950, MA, 1952, PhD, 1956, University of California at Berkeley. Appointments: Assistant Professor, 1956-61, Associate Professor, 1961-62, of Government, Miami University, Oxford, Ohio; Lecturer, 1962-65, Associate Professor, 1965-69, Professor, 1969-91, of Political Science, University of California at Los Angeles. Publications: The Purge of Japanese Leaders Under the Occupation, 1959; American Government: Structure, Problems, Policies (with Peter H Odegard), 1962; Chinese Communism: Selected Documents (with Dan N Jacobs), 1963; The American Republic, Its Government and Politics (with Peter H Odegard), 1964, revised edition (with William Harvard), 1969; Japan's Parliament: An Introduction, 1974; Party Politics in Japan, 1986. Contributions to: Asian Survey. Honour: Order of the Sacred Treasure with Gold and Silver Star, Japan, 1989. Address: 2221 Barnett Road, St Helens, CA 94574, USA.

BAIGELL Matthew, b. 27 Apr 1933, New York, New York, USA. Professor of Art History; Writer. m. Renee Moses, 1 Feb 1959, 2 daughters. Education: BA, University of Vermont, 1954; MA, Columbia University, 1955; PhD, University of Pennsylvania, 1965. Appointments: Instructor, 1961-65, Assistant Professor, 1965-67, Associate Professor of Art, 1967-68, Ohio State University; Associate

Professor, 1968-72, Professor, 1972-78, Distinguished Professor of Art History, 1978-, Rutgers, the State University of New Jersey at New Brunswick. Publications: A History of American Painting, 1971; A Thomas Hart Benton Miscellany (editor), 1971; The American Scene: American Painting in the 1930's, 1974; Thomas Hart Benton, 1974; Charles Burchfield, 1976; The Western Art of Frederic Remington, 1976; Dictionary of American Art, 1979; Albert Bierstadt, 1981; Thomas Cole, 1981; A Concise History of American Painting and Sculpture, 1984; The Papers of the American Artists' Congress (1936), 1985; Artists Against War and Fascism (editor with J Williams), 1986; Soviet Dissident Artists: Interviews After Perestroika (with Renee Baigell), 1995. Address: c/o Department of Art History, Rutgers, the State University of New Jersey at New Brunswick, New Brunswick, NJ 08903, USA.

BAIGENT Beryl, b. 16 Dec 1937. Writer; Teacher. m. Alan H Baigent, 19 Jan 1963, 3 daughters. Education: Grove Park Grammar School, Wrexham, Wales; BA, Physical Education; MA, English Literature, University of Western Ontario, London, Canada. Appointments: Director, Canadian Poetry Association, 1993-94; LCP Ontario Representative, 1994-95, 1995-96. Publications: The Quiet Village, 1972; Pause, 1974; In Counterpoint, 1976; Ancestral Dreams, 1981; The Sacred Beech, 1985; Mystic Animals, 1988; Absorbing the Dark, 1990; Undress Stress, 1991; Hiraeth: In Search of Celtic Origins, 1994; Triptych: Virgins, Victims, Votives, 1996. Contributor to: Poetry Toronto; Poetry Canada Review, CV II; Canadian Author and Bookman; Chester Poetry Anthology; Canadian Humanist; Herspectives; Poet International; Plowman; Pom Seed; Wayzgoose Anthology; Poets Gallery; Public Works; Amethyst Review; Sage Woman; Kairos; The Muse; Hecate's Loom; Prairie Journal; Bite to Eat Place; Magic Tree; Eramose Anthology; An Invisible Accordion; Writing Towards 21st Century. Address: 137 Byron Avenue, Thamesford, Ontario N0M 2M0, Canada.

BAIL Murray, b. 22 Sept 1941, Adelaide, South Australia, Australia. Novelist. m. Margaret Wordsworth, 1965. Education: Norwood Technical High School, Adelaide. Publications: Homesickness, 1980; Holden's Performance, 1987; Short stories: Contemporary Portraits and Other Stories, 1975; Uncollected short stories: Healing, 1979; Home Ownership, 1984. Membership: Council, Australian National Gallery, Canberra, 1976-81; Editor, The Faber Book of Contemporary Australian Short Stories, 1988. Honours: The Age Book of the Year Award, 1980; Victorian Premier's Award, 1988. Address: 39/75 Buckland Street, Chippendale, New South Wales 2008, Australia.

BAILEY Anthony (Cowper), b. 5 Jan 1933, Portsmouth, England. Author; Journalist. Education: BA, 1955, MA, 1956, Merton College, Oxford. Appointment: Staff Writer, New Yorker magazine, 1956-92. Publications: Making Progress, 1959; The Mother Tongue, 1961; The Inside Passage, 1965; Through the Great City, 1967; The Thousand Dollar Yacht, 1968; The Light in Holland, 1970; In the Village, 1971; A Concise History of the Low Countries, 1972; Rembrandt's House, 1978; Acts of Union: Reports on Ireland, 1973-79, 1980; America, Lost and Found, 1981; Along the Edge of the Forest: An Iron Curtain Journey, 1983; England, First and Last, 1985; Spring Jaunts: Some Walks, Excursions, and Personal Explorations of City, Country and Seashore, 1986; Major André, 1987; The Outer Banks, 1989; A Walk Through Wales, 1992; Responses to Rembrandt, 1994; A Coast of Summer: Sailing New England Waters from Shelter Island to Cape Cod, 1994. Honour: Overeas Press Club Award, 1974. Memberships: Authors Guild; International PEN; Society of Authors. Address: c/o Donadio and Ashworth Inc, 231 West 22nd Street, New York, NY 10011, USA.

BAILEY D(avid) R(oy) Shackleton, b. 10 Dec 1917, Lancaster, England. Professor Emeritus of Latin Language and Literature; Writer; Editor; Translator. m. (1) Hilary Ann Bardwell, 1967, diss 1974, (2) Kristine Zvirbulis, 1994. Education: BA, 1939, MA, 1943, LittD, 1957, Cambridge University. Appointments: Fellow, 1944-55, Paralector, 1954-55, Fellow and Deputy Bursary, 1964, Senior Bursar, 1965-68, Gonville and Gaius College, Cambridge; University Lecturer in Tibetan, Cambridge University, 1948-68; Fellow and Director of Studies in Classics, Jesus College, Cambridge, 1955-64; Visiting Lecturer in Classics, Harvard College, 1963; Professor of Latin, 1968-74, Adjunct Professor, 1989-, University of Michigan; Andrew V Raymond Visiting Professor, State University of New York at Buffalo, 1973-74; Professor of Greek and Latin, 1975-82, Pope Professor of Latin Language and Literature, 1982-88, Professor Emeritus, 1988-, Harvard University;

Editor, Harvard Studies in Classical Philology, 1978-84; Visiting Professor, Peterhouse College, Cambridge, 1980-81. Publications: The Sátapañcsátka of Mátrceta, 1951; Propertiana, 1956; Towards a Text of Cicero ad Atticum, 1960; Ciceronis Epistulae ad Atticum IX-XVI, 1961; Cicero's Letters to Atticus, volumes I and II, 1965, volume V, 1966, volume VI, 1967, volumes III and IV. 1968, volume VII, 1970; Cicero, 1971; Two Studies in Roman Nomenclature, 1976; Cicero: Epistulae ad Familiares, 2 volumes, 1977; Cicero's Letters to Atticus, 1978; Cicero's Letters to His Friends, 2 volumes, 1978; Towards a Text of Anthologia Latina, 1979; Selected Letters of Cicero, 1980; Cicero: Epistulae ad Q Fratrem et M Brutum, 1981; Profile of Horace, 1982; Anthologia Latina I.I, 1982; Horatius, 1985; Cicero: Philippics, 1986; Ciceronis Epistulae, 4 volumes, 1987-88; Lucanus, 1988; Onomasticon to Cicero's Speeches, 1988; Quintilianus: Declamationes minores, 1989; Martialis, 1990; Back from Exile, 1991; Martial, 3 volumes, 1993; Homoeoteleuton in Latin Dactylic Verse, 1994; Onomasticon to Cicero's Letters, 1995; Onomasticon to Cicero's Treatises, 1996; Selected Classical Papers, 1996. Contributions to: Scholarly periodicals. Honours: Charles Goodwin Prize, American Philological Association, 1978; National Endowment for the Humanities Fellowship, 1980-81; Hon LittD, University of Dublin, 1984; Kenyon Medal, British Academy, 1985. Memberships: American Academy of Arts and Science, fellow, 1979-; American Philosophical Society; British Academy, fellow. Address: 303 North Division, Ann Arbor, MI 48104, USA.

BAILEY Martin, b. 26 Oct 1947, London, England. Journalist. Education: PhD, London School of Economics, 1974. Appointment: The Observer, 1983-. Publications: Freedom Railway, 1976; Oilgate: The Sanctions Scandal, 1979; A Green Part of the World, 1984; Young Vincent: Van Gogh's Years in England, 1990; Van Gogh: Letters from Provence, 1990; Van Gogh in England: Portrait of the Artist as a Young Man, 1992. Honour: Journalist of the Year, 1979. Literary Agent: A D Peters. Address: The Observer, Chelsea Bridge House, Queenstown Road, London SW8 4NN, England.

BAILEY Paul, b. 16 Feb 1937, London, England. Writer. Education: Central School of Speech and Drama, 1953-56. Appointment: Actor, 1953-63. Publications: At the Jerusalem, 1967; Trespasses, 1971; A Worthy Guest, A Distant Likeness, 1973; Peter Smart's Confessions, 1977; Old Soldiers, 1980; An English Madam: The Life and Work of Cynthia Payne, 1982; Gabriel's Lament, 1986; An Immaculate Mistake, 1990; Hearth and Home, 1990. Honours: Maugham Award, 1968; Arts Council Award, 1968; E M Forster Award, 1974; Orwell Memorial Prize, 1978; Fellow, Royal Society of Literature, 1982. Address: 79 Davisville Road, London W12 9SH, England.

BAILYN Bernard, b. 10 Sept 1922, Hartford, Connecticut, USA. Professor Emeritus of History; Writer. m. Lotte Lazarsfeld, 18 June 1952, 2 sons. Education: AB, Williams College, 1945; MA, 1947, PhD, 1953, Harvard University. Appointments: Instructor, 1953-54, Assistant Professor, 1954-58, Associate Professor, 1958-61, Professor of History, 1961-66, Winthrop Professor of History, 1966-81, Adams University Professor, 1981-93, Director, Charles Warren Center for Studies in American History, 1983-94, James Duncan Phillips Professor of Early American History, 1991-93, Professor Emeritus, 1993-, Harvard University; Colver Lecturer, Brown University, 1965; Phelps Lecturer, New York University, 1969; Trevelyan Lecturer, 1971, Pitt Professor of American History, 1986-87, Cambridge University; Becker Lecturer, Cornell University, 1975; Walker-Ames Lecturer, University of Washington, 1983; Curti Lecturer, University of Wisconsin, 1984; Lewin Visiting Professor, Washington University, St Louis, 1985; Thompson Lecturer, Pomona College, 1991; Fellow, British Academy, and Christ's College, Cambridge, 1991; Montgomery Fellow, Dartmouth College, 1991. Publications: The New England Merchants in the Seventeenth Century, 1955; Massachusetts Shipping, 1697-1714: A Statistical Study (with Lotte Bailyn), 1959; Education in the Forming of American Society: Needs and Opportunities for Study, 1960; Pamphlets of the American Revolution, 1750-1776, Vol 1 (editor), 1965; The Apologia of Robert Keayne: The Self-Portrait of a Puritan Merchant (editor), 1965; The Ideological Origins of the American Revolution, 1967, new edition, 1992; The Origins of American Politics, 1968; The Intellectual Migration: Europe and America, 1930-1960 (editor with Donald Fleming), 1969; Religion and Revolution: Three Biographical Studies, 1970; Law in American History (editor with Donald Fleming), 1972; The Ordeal of Thomas Hutchinson, 1974; The Great Republic: A History of the American People (with others), 1977, 4th edition, 1992; The Press and the American Revolution (editor with John B Hench). 1980; The Peopling of British North America: An Introduction, 1986; Voyagers to the West: A Passage in the Peopling of America on the Eve of the Revolution, 1986; Faces of Revolution: Personalities and Themes in the Struggle for American Independence, 1990; Strangers within the Realm: Cultural Margins of the First British Empire (editor with Philip B Morgan), 1991; The Debate on the Constitution: Federalist and Antifederalist Speeches, Articles and Letters during the Struggle over Ratification, 2 volumes, 1993. Contributions to: Scholarly journals. Honours: Robert H Lord Award, Emmanuel College, 1967; Bancroft Prize, 1968; Pulitzer Prizes in History, 1968, 1987; National Book Award in History, 1975; Saloutos Award, Immigration History Society, 1986; Triennial Book Award, 1986; Thomas Jefferson Medal, American Philosophical Society, 1993; Henry Allen Moe Prize, 1994; Honorary doctorates. Memberships: American Academy of Arts and Sciences; American Historical Association, president, 1981; American Philosophical Society; National Academy of Education; Royal Historical Society. Address: 170 Clifton Street, Belmont, MA 02178, USA.

BAINBRIDGE Beryl Margaret, b. 21 Nov 1934, Liverpool, England. Education: Merchant Taylors School, Liverpool. Appointments: Actress, Repertory Theatres in UK, 1949-60; Clerk, Gerald Duckworth & Company Ltd, London, 1971-73. Publications: A Weekend with Claude, 1967; Another Part of the Wood, 1968; Harriet Said, 1972; The Dressmaker, 1973; The Bottle Factory Outing, 1974; Sweet William, 1975; A Quiet Life, Injury Time, 1976; Young Adolf, 1978; Winter Garden, 1980; English Journey or the Road to Milton Keynes, Watson's Apology, 1984; Mum & Mr Armitage, 1985; Forever England, 1986; Filthy Lucra, 1986; An Awfully Big Adventure, 1989; The Birthday Boys, 1991. Honours: Guardian Fiction Award, 1974; Whitbread Award, 1977; Fellow, Royal Society of Literature, 1978; DLitt, University of Liverpool, 1986. Address: 42 Albert Street, London NW1 7NU, England.

BAINBRIDGE Cyril, b. 15 Nov 1928, Bradford, West Yorkshire, England. Author; Journalist. m. Barbara Hannah Crook, 20 Jan 1953, 1 son, 2 daughters. Education: Negus College, Bradford. Appointments: Reporter, Bingley Guardian, 1944-45; Reporter, Yorkshire Observer & Bradford Telegraph, 1945-54; The Press Association, 1954-63; Assistant News Editor, 1963-88, News Editor, 1967-69, Regional News Editor, 1969-77, Managing News Editor, 1977-82, Assistant Managing Editor, 1982-88, The Times. Publications: Pavilions on the Sea; Brass Triumphant; The Brontës and Their Country; North Yorkshire and North Humerside; One Hundred Years of Journalism; The News of the World Story, 1993. Contributions to: Various Feature, Travel Articles; Book Reviews. Memberships: Brontë Society; Chartered Institute of Journalists; Society of Authors. Literary Agent: Laurence Pollinger. Address: 6 Lea Road, Hemingford Grey, Huntingdon, Cambs PE18 9ED, England.

BAITZ Jon Robin, b. 1961, Los Angeles, California, USA. Playwright. Plays: The Film Society, 1987; Dutch Landscape, 1989; The Substance of Fire, 1991; Three Hotels, 1993; The End of the Day, 1993. Contributions to: Anthologies. Honour: Fellow, American Academy and Institute of Arts and Letters, 1994. Address: c/o William Morris Agency Inc, 1350 Avenue of the Americas, New York, NY 10019, USA.

BAKER David (Anthony), b. 27 Dec 1954, Bangor, Maine, USA. Associate Professor of English; Poet; Editor. m. Ann Townsend, 19 July 1987. Education: BSE, 1976, MA, 1977, Central Missouri State University; PhD, University of Utah, 1983. Appointments: Poetry Editor, 1980-81, Editor-in-Chief, 1981-83, Quarterly West; Visiting Assistant Professor, Kenyon College, 1983-84; Assistant Editor, 1983-89, Poetry Editor/Consulting Poetry Editor, 1989-94, Poetry Editor, 1994-, Kenyon Review; Assistant Professor of English, 1984-90, Associate Professor of English, 1990-, Denison University; Visiting Telluride Professor, Cornell University, 1985; Contributing Editor, The Pushcart Prize, 1992-; Visiting Associate Professor, University of Michigan, 1996; Many poetry readings. Publications: Poetry: Looking Ahead, 1975; Rivers in the Sea, 1977; Laws of the Land, 1981; Summer Sleep, 1984; Haunts, 1985; Sweet Home, Saturday Night, 1991; Echo for an Anniversary, 1992; After the Reunion, 1994; Holding Katherine, 1996. Editor: The Soil is Suited to the Seed: A Miscellany in Honor of Paul Bennett, 1986; Meter in English: A Critical Engagement, 1996. Contributions to: Anthologies and periodicals. Honours: Margaret Bridgman Scholar of Poetry, Bread Loaf, 1982; Outstanding Writer, Pushcart Press, 1982, 1984, 1985, 1986, 1990, 1991, 1994, 1995; James Wright Prize for Poetry, Mid-American Review, 1983; National

Endowment for the Arts Fellowship, 1985-86; Bread Loaf Poetry Fellow, 1989; Pushcart Prize, 1992; Mary Carolyn Davies Award, Poetry Society of America, 1995; Thomas B Fordham Endowed Chair in Creative Writing, Denison University, 1996. Memberships: Associated Writing Programs; Modern Languages Association; National Book Critics Circle; Poetry Society of America; Poets and Writers. Address: 135 Granview Road, Granville, OH 43023, USA.

BAKER Houston Alfred Jr, b. 22 Mar 1943, Louisville, Kentucky, USA. Professor; Writer. m. Charlotte Pierce, 1 son. Education: BA, Howard University, 1965; MA, 1966, PhD, 1968, University of California at Los Angeles; Graduate Studies, Edinburgh University, 1967-68. Appointments: Instructor, Howard University, 1966; Instructor, 1968-69, Assistant Professor, 1969, Yale University; Associate Professor, 1970-73, Professor of English 1973, University of Virginia, Charlottesville; Director of Afro-American Studies 1974-77, Professor of English 1977-82, Albert M Greenfield Professor of Human Relations 1982-, University of Pennsylvania, Philadelphia. Publications: Black Literature in America, 1971; Long Black Song: Essays in Black American Literature and Culture, Twentieth Century Interpretations of Native Son, 1972; A Many-Coloured Coat of Dreams: The Poetry of Countee Cullen, Singers of Daybreak; Studies in Black American Literature, 1974; Reading Black: Essays in the Criticism of African, Caribbean and Black American Literature, 1976; No Matter Where You Travel, You Still Be Black, 1979; The Journey Back: Issues in Black Literature and Criticism, 1980; Spirit Run, 1982; Blue, Ideology and Afro-American Literature: A Vernacular Theory, 1984; Blues Journeys Home, 1985; Modernism and the Harlem Renaissance, 1987; Long Black Song; Black Studies, Rap, and the Academy, 1993. Address: Department of English, University of Pennsylvania, Philadelphia, PA 19104, USA.

BAKER Kenneth (Wilfred), b. 3 Nov 1934, England. m. Mary Elizabeth Muir, 1963, 1 son, 2 daughters. Education: Magdalen College, Oxford. Career includes: MP for Acton, 1968-70, St Marylebone, 1970-83, Mole Valley, 1983-97; Secretary of State for Education and Science, 1986-89; Home Secretary, 1990-92. Publications include: I Have No Gun But I Can Spit (editor), 1980; London Lines (editor), 1982; The Faber Book of English History in Verse (editor), 1988; Unauthorized Versions: Poems and Their Parodies (editor), 1990; The Faber Anthology of Conservatism (editor), 1993; The Turbulent Years, My Life in Politics, 1993; The Prime Ministers - An Irreverent Political History in Cartoons, 1995. Honours include: CH, 1992. Address: c/o House of Commons, London, SW1A 0AA, England.

BAKER Lillian, (Liliane L Baker, Miss Elbee), b. 12 Dec 1921, Yonkers, New York, USA. Writer; Poet; Editor. m. Roscoe Albert Baker, 1 son, 1 daughter. Education: El Camino College, 1952; University of California, Los Angeles, 1968. Appointments: Continuity Writer, WINS Radio, New York City, 1945-46; Columnist, Freelance Writer, Reviewer, Gardena Valley News, 1964-76; Editor, Points newsletter, 1977-; Columnist, World War II Times, 1994-. Publications: Creative and Collectible Miniatures, 1984, revised edition, 1991; War-Torn Woman, 1985; Fifty Years of Collectible Fashion Jewelry, 1925-1975, 1986, 3rd edition, 1991; Dishonoring America: The Collective Guilt of American Japanese, 1988; American and Japanese Relocation in World War II: Fact, Fiction, and Fallacy, 1989, revised edition, 1991; The Japanning of America: Redress and Reparations Demands by Japanese-Americans, 1991; Twentieth Century Fashionable Plastic Jewelry, 1992; The Common Doom, 1992; The Coming of Dawn (poems), 1993. Contributions to: Anthologies. Honours: Freedoms Foundation Award, 1971; Award of Merit, Scholarship Category, Conference of California Historical Societies, 1983; Award, Hoover Institution on War, Revolution and Peace, 1985; Golden Poet Award, International Poets Society, 1989; George Washington Honour Medal, Freedoms Foundation, 1991; Semi-Finalist, North American Poetry Contest, 1993; Commendation, Artist for 1994 Olympics. Memberships: Co-Founder, Americans for Historical Accuracy, 1972; Art Students League of New York; Founder, International Club for Collectors of Hatpins and Hatpin Holders, 1977; National Historical Society; National League of American Pen Women; National Trust for Historic Preservation; National Writers Club; Society of Jewelry Historians of the USA; Honorary Member, Centre for World War II Civilian Internees, 1995. Address: 15237 Chanera Avenue, Gardena, CA 90249, USA.

BAKER Margaret Joyce, b. 21 May 1918, Reading, Berkshire, England. Education: King's College, London, 1936-37. Publications:

The Fighting Cocks, 1949; Four Farthings and a Thimble, 1950; A Castle and Sixpence, 1951; The Family That Grew and Grew, 1952; Lions in the Potting Shed, 1954; The Wounderful Wellington Boots, 1955; Anna Sewell and Black Beauty, 1956; The Birds of Thimblepins, 1960; Homer in Orbit, 1961; The Cats of Honeytown, 1962; Castaway Christmas, 1963; Cut off from Crumpets, The Shoe Shop Bears, 1964; Home from the Hill, 1968; Snail's Place, 1970; The Last Straw, 1971; Boots and the Ginger Bears, 1972; The Sand Bird, 1973; Lock Stock & Barrel, 1974; Sand in Our Shoes, 1976; The Gift Horse, 1982; Catch as Catch Can, 1983; Beware of the Gnomes, 1985; The Waiting Room Doll, 1986; Fresh Fields for Daisy, 1987. Address: Prickets, Old Cleeve, Nr Minehead, Somerset TA24 6HW, England.

BAKER Paul Raymond, b. 28 Sept 1927, Everett, Washington, USA. Professor. m. Elizabeth Kemp, 1 child. Education: AB, Stanford University, 1949; MA, Columbia University, 1951; PhD, Harvard University, 1960. Appointments: Professor of History, 1965-, Director of American Civilization Program, 1972-92, New York University. Publications: Views of Society and Manners in America, by Frances Wright D'Arusmont, 1963; The Fortunate Pilgrims: Americans in Italy 1800-1860, 1964; The Atomic Bomb: The Great Decision, 1968; The American Experience, 5 volumes, 1976-79; Richard Morris Hunt, 1980; Stanny: The Gilded Life of Stanford White, 1989; Around the Square, contributor, 1982; Master Builders, 1985; The Architecture of Richard Morris Hunt, 1986. Address: c/o Department of History, New York University, 19 University Place, Room 523, New York, NY 10003, USA.

BAKOLAS Nikos, b. 26 July 1927, Thessaloniki, Greece. Retired Journalist. m. Helene Issidorou, 6 Sept 1957, 2 sons. Education: University of Thessaloniki; University of Michigan. Appointment: Artistic Manager, National Theatre of Northern Greece, 1980-81, 1990-. Publications: The Big Square; Mythology; The Prince's Garden; Trepass; Don't Cry Darling; Marches; Death Sleep. Contributions to: Numerous. Honours: Plotin Literary Award; National Book Award. Memberships: Greek Literary Society; Journalists Union of Macedonia. Address: 16 Papadiamandi Street, 546 45 Thessaloniki, Greece.

BAKR Salwa, b. June 1949, Cairo. Egypt. Novelist. Education: BA, 1972, BA, 1976, Ayn Shams University, Cairo. Appointments: Founder, Hagar journal, 1993. Publications: Zinat at the President's Funeral, 1986; Atiyyah's Shrine, 1986; About the Soul that was Spirited Away, 1989; The Wiles of Men and Other Stories, 1992; Monkey Business, 1992; Depicting the Nightingale, 1993; The Golden Chariot Does Not Ascend to Heaven, 1994. Address: c/o Atelier of Writers, Karim al-Dawla Street, Talat Harb Square, Cairo, Eygpt.

BALAAM. See: **LAMB Geoffrey Frederick.**

BALABAN John, b. 2 Dec 1943, Philadelphia, Pennsylvania, USA. Professor of English; Writer; Poet; Translator. m. 28 Nov 1970, 1 daughter. Education: BA, Penn State University, 1966; AM, Harvard University, 1967. Appointments: Instructor in Linguistics, University of Can Tho, South Vietnam, 1967-68; Instructor, 1970-73, Assistant Professor, 1973-76, Associate Professor, 1976-82, Professor, 1982-92, of English, Penn State University; Professor of English, Director of Creative Writing, University of Miami, 1992-. Publications: Vietnam Poems, 1970; Vietnamese Folk Poetry (editor and translator), 1974; After Our War, poems, 1974; Letters From Across the Sea, poems, 1978; Ca Dao Vietnam: A Bilingual Anthology of Vietnamese Folk Poetry (editor and translator), 1980; Blue Mountain, poems, 1982; Coming Down Again, novel, 1985, revised edition, 1989; The Hawk's Tale, children's fiction, 1988; Three Poems, 1989; Vietnam: The Land We Never Knew, 1989; Words for My Daughter, poems, 1991; Remembering Heaven's Face, memoir, 1991; Vietnam: A Literary Companion (editor with Nguyen Qui Duc), 1996; New and Selected Poems and Translations, 1997. Contributions to: Anthologies, books, scholarly journals and periodicals. Honours: National Endowment for the Humanities Younger Humanist Fellow, 1971-72; Lamont Selection, Academy of American Poets, 1974; Fulbright-Hays Senior Lectureship in Romania, 1976-77; Steaua Prize, Romanian Writers Union, 1978; Fulbright Distinguished Visiting Lectureship in Romania, 1979; National Endowment for the Arts Fellowships, 1978, 1985; Vaptsarov Medal, Union of Bulgarian Writers, 1980; National Poetry Series Book Selection, 1990; Pushcart Prize XV, 1990. Memberships: American Literary Translators Association, president, 1994-; National Endowment for the Arts Translation Panel, chair, 1993-94. Address:

Department of English, University of Miami, PO Box 248145, Coral Gables, FL 33124, USA.

BALADO-LOPEZ Daniel Francis Stephen, b. 27 Nov 1969, Hoddesdon, Hertfordshire, England. Copy Editor. Education: BA Hons in English Language and Literature, St Edmund's College, 1981-88; King's College, London, 1989-92. Contributions to: Verbatim; The Edmundian. Address: 82 Stanstead Road, Hoddesdon, England.

BALCOMB Mary Nelson, b. 29 April 1928, Ontonagon, Michigan, USA. Artist (painter-etcher); Author. m. Robert S Balcomb, 3 July 1948, 1 son, 1 daughter. Education: AA, American Academy of Art, 1948; BFA cum laude, 1961, Univ of New Mexico, 1967; MFA, University of Washington, 1971. Publications: Nicolai Fechin Russian and American Artist, 1975; Les Perhacs Sculptor, 1978; William F Reese American Artist, 1984; Robin-Robin, A Journal, 1995. Contributions to: American Artist; Southwest Art; Staus. Honours: Rounce & Coffin Club, Occidental College, California, 1975, 1984; Books travelled for two years to library exhibits. Memberships: The Authors Guild, Inc, New York, 1980-; Phi Kappa Phi honor society. Address: POB 1922, Silverdale, WA 98383, USA.

BALL B(rian) N(eville), b. 19 June 1932, Cheshire, England. Writer. Education: BA, London University, 1960; MA, Sheffield University, 1968. Appointments: Staff Member, subsequently Senior Lecturer in English, Doncaster College of Education, 1965-81; Chairman, Doncaster Prose and Poetry Society, 1968-70. Publications: Mr Tofat's Term, Tales of Science Fiction, 1964; Sundog, 1965; Basic Linguistics for Secondary Schools, 3 vols, 1966-67; Paris Adventures, 1967; Timepiece, Timepivot and Timepit, 1968-71; Lay Down Your Wife for Another, Lesson for the Damned, 1971; Night of the Robots (in the US as The Regiments of Night), Devil's Peak, The Probability Man, 1972; Planet Probability, Singularity Station, 1973; Death of a Low Handicap Man, Montenegrin Gold, The Venomous Serpent (in the US as The Night Creature), 1974; The Space Guardians, Keegan: The No-Option Contract, Princess Priscilla, 1975; Jackson's Friend, Jackson's House, Jackson's Holiday, 1975-77; Keegan: The One-Way Deal, Witchfinder: The Mark of the Beast, 1976; Witchfinder: The Evil at Monteine, 1977; Jackson and the Magpies, 1978; The Witch in Our Attic, Young Person's Guide to UFO's, 1979; Dennis and the Flying Saucer, 1980; The Baker Street Boys, The Starbuggy, 1983; The Doomship of Drax, 1985; Truant from Space, 1985; Look Out, Duggy Dog!, 1987; BMX Billy, 1986; Frog Island Summer, 1987; I'm Lost, Duggy Dog! 1987; The Quest for Queenie, 1988; Cat in the Custard, 1988; Stone Age Magic, 1989; Hop It, Duggy Dog!, 1989; Bella at the Ballet, 1990; Cat in the Classroom, 1990; Come Back, Duggy Dog, 1991; Magic on the Tide; Bella's Concert, 1994; What's That, Duggy Dog?, 1994; Trouble in Store, 1995; Bella and the Beanstalk, 1996; Mrs Potts' New Pets, in Let's Join In, The 'Jenny' tales, in Here Comes Pob and Pob and Friends and various others in anthologies in the US and the UK; Various reviews and articles for the Guardian and Times Educational Supplement, BBC, Jackanory...televising of The Witch in Our Attic, 1979 and Magic on the Tide, 1995; Channel 4, in Pob's Programme, televising of the Jenny's stories, 1987-88; BBC Education various playlets in the Let's Join In, programme, 1979. Address: c/o Hamish Hamilton Ltd, 27 Wrights Lane, London W8 5TZ, England.

BALLANTYNE Sheila, b. 26 July 1936, Seattle, Washington, USA. Writer; Teacher. m. Philip Speilman, 22 Dec 1963, 1 son, 1 daughter. Education: BA, Mills College. Appointments: Dominican College, 1983; Mills College, 1984-; Bay Area Writers Workshop, 1988, 1989. Publications: Norma Jean the Termite Queen; Imaginary Crimes; Life on Earth. Contributions to: New Yorker; American Review; Prize Stories: O Henry Awards; Short Story International; Aphra. Honours: O'Henry Award; MacDowell Colony Fellowship; Guggenheim Fellowship; National Women's Political Caucus Distinguished Achievement Award. Memberships: Authors Guild; National Writers Union; PEN. Address: Department of English, Mills College, 5000 MacArthur Boulevard, Oakland, CA 94613, USA.

BALLARD James Graham, b. 15 Nov 1930, Shanghai, China. Novelist; Short Story Writer. m. Helen Mary Mathews, 1954, dec 1964, 1 son, 2 daughters. Education: BA, King's College, Cambridge. Publications: The Drowned World, 1963; The Terminal Beach, 1964; The Drought, 1965; The Crystal World, 1966; The Disaster Area, 1967; Crash, 1973; Vermilion Sands, 1973; Concrete Island, 1974; High Rise, 1975; Low Flying Aircraft, 1976; The Unlimited Dream Company, 1979; Myths of the Near Future, 1982; Empire of the Sun, 1984; The

Day of Creation, 1987; Running Wild, 1988; War Forever, 1990; The Kindness of Women, 1991. Honours: Guardian Fiction Prize, 1984; James Tait Black Prize, 1984. Address: 36 Old Charlton Road, Shepperton, Middlesex, England.

BALLARD Juliet Lyle Brooke, b. 6 Feb 1913. Poet; Editor; Prose Writer. Education: AB, Randolph-Macon Woman's College, 1934; Certificate of Social Case Work, Richmond Professional Institute, 1938. Appointments: Associate Editor, Association for Research and Enlightment Journal, 1966-70; Associate Editor, Association for Research and Enlightenment Children's Magazine, 1970; Editor, Treasure Trove (Association for Research and Enlightenment Children's Quarterly), 1971-73. Publications: Under a Tropic Sun, 1945; Winter Has Come, 1945; The Ballad of the Widow's Flag (official poem of the Star-Spangled Banner Flag House Association, Baltimore, Maryland), 1956; Prose Works: The Hidden Laws of Earth, 1979; Treasures from Earth's Storehouse, 1980; The Art of Living, 1982, retitled Unto the Hills, 1987; Research Bulletin, Pilgrimage into the Light, Vols I, II and III, 1988, Vol IV, 1989; translation of The Hidden Laws of Earth into Japanese by Chuo Art Shuppan Sha, 1989. Address: 2217 Wake Forest Street, Virginia Beach, VA 23451-1420, USA.

BALLE Solvej, b. 16 Aug 1962, Denmark. Prose Writer. m. Ole Kiehn, 9 Sept 1990. Education: Studies in Philosophy, Literature, University of Copenhagen, 1984-; The Writers' School, Copenhagen, 1987-89. Appointment: Co-Editor, Den Bla Port, Literary Magazine, 1994-. Publications: Lyrefugl, 1986; Prose Poetry, 1990; According to the Law, short stories, 1993. Membership: Danish PEN. Literary Agent: L & R, Kristianiagade 14, 2100 Copenhagen, Denmark. Address: Bakkehuset, Rahbeks Allé 23, 1801 Frederiksberg C, Denmark.

BALLEM John Bishop, b. 2 Feb 1925, New Glasgow, Nova Scotia, Canada. Lawyer. m. Grace Louise Flavelle, 31 Aug 1951, 2 sons, 1 daughter. Education: BA 1946, MA 1948, LLB 1949, Dalhousie University, Halifax, Nova Scotia; LLM 1950, Harvard University Law School, Boston, Massachusetts. Publications: The Devil's Lighter, 1973; Dirty Scenario, 1974; Judas Conspiracy, 1976; The Moon Pool, 1978; Sacrifice Play, 1981; Marigot Run, 1983; Oilpatch Empire, 1985; The Oil and Gas Lease in Canada, textbook, 2nd edition, 1985; Death Spiral, 1989; The Barons, 1991; short stories and poems. Contributions to: Numerous legal articles in: Canadian Bar Review; Alberta Law Review; and others. Honours: Queen's Counsel, 1966; Honorary Doctor of Laws Degree, University of Calgary, 1993. Memberships: Writers Guild of Alberta; Writer's Union of Canada; Crime Writers of Canada; Calgary Writers Association; International Bar Association; Bars of Nova Scotia, Ontario and Alberta; Law Society of Alberta; Phi Delta Theta. Address: High Trees, Box 20, Site 32, RR # 12, Calgary, Alberta T3E 6W3, Canada.

BALY Elaine Vivienne. See: BROWNING Vivenne.

BANCROFT Anne, b. 17 Apr 1923, London, England. Author. 2 sons, 2 daughters. Education: Sidney Webb Teacher's Training College, 1961-63. Publications: Twentieth Century Mystics and Sages, 1976, republished 1989; Religions of the East, 1974; Zen: Direct Pointing to Reality, 1980; The Luminous Vision, republished 1989; Six Medieval Mystics, 1981; Chinse New Year, 1984; Festivals of the Buddha, 1984; The Buddhist World, 1984; The New Religious World, 1985; Origins of the Sacred: The Spiritual Way in Western Tradition, 1987; Weavers of Wisdom, 1989. Contributions to: The Middle Way; Everyman's Encyclopedia; Women in the World's Religions. Memberships: Society of Authors; Society of Women Writers and Journalists. Address: 1 Grange Villas, The Street, Charmouth, Bridport, Dorset DT6 6QQ, England.

BANCROFT Iris (May Nelson), (Julia Barnright, Iris Brent, Andrea Layton), b. 26 May 1922, King Chow, China. Writer. m. (1) Robert Koenig, 1945, div 1962, (2) Keith O Bancroft, 1 son. Education: BEd, Chicago Teachers College, 1945; MEd, Northwestern University, 1962. Appointments: Public School Teacher, elmhurst, Illinois, 1957-61, Chicago, 1961-62; Writer, Photographer, Editor, Elysium Publications and American Art, Los Angeles, 1962-77. Publications: Novels: Love's Gentle Fugitive, 1978; So Wild a Rapture, 1978; Midnight Fires, 1979; Love's Burning Flame, 1979; Rapture's Rebel, 1980; Rebel's Passion, 1981; Dawn of Desire, 1981. Other: The Sexually Exciting Female, 1971; The Sexually Superior Male, 1971; Swinger's Diary, 1973; My Love Is Free, 1975; Whispering Hope, 1981; The Five-Minute Phobia Cure (with Roger Callahan), 1984; Any Man

Can (with William Hartman and Marilyn Fithian), 1984; Sex and the Single Parent (with Mary Mattis), 1986; Reaching Intimacy (with Jerry DeHaan), 1986. Memberships: Mensa; PEN. Address: c/o Teal and Watt Literary Agency, 8033 Sunset Boulevard, Los Angeles, CA 90046, USA.

BANDELE THOMAS Biyi, b. 13 Oct 1967, Kafanchan, Nigeria. Education: Dramatic Arts, Obafemi Awolowo University, ILE IFE, 1987-90. Appointments: Associate Writer, Royal Court Theatre, London, 1992-; Writer in Residence, Talawa Theatre Company, 1993. Publications: The Man Who Came in From the Back of Beyond; The Sympathetic Undertaker and Other Dreams; Incantations On The Eve of An Execution; Plays: Rain; Marching for Fausa; Death Catches the Hunter; Screenplay: Not Even God is Wise Enough, 1993; Radio: The Remale God, 1993; The Will of Allah, 1994. Contributions to: West Africa. Honours: International Student Playscript Competition; Arts Council Writers Bursary; LWT plays for Stage Award, 1993. Memberships: Society of Authors; Writers Guild; PEN. Literary Agent: MBA. Address: 45 Fitzroy Str, London W1P 5HR, England.

BANI-SADR Abol-Hassan, b. 22 Mar 1933, Hamadan, Iran. Researcher; Writer; Economist; Politician. Appointments: Ministry of the Economy; Ministry of Foreign Affairs, Iran 1979; President of the Republic, Iran 1980. Education: Degrees in Islamic Law and Economic Sciences, Tehran University. Publications: The Betrayed Hope; Women and Conjugal Life (in the Koran); The Koran and Human Rights; The Directing Principles of Islam; My Turn to Speak; Petrol and Violence; Which Revolution for Iran? Asian Politics (collective works); Totalitarisme and Democracy. Contributions to and founder of the newspaper, Islamic Revolution, 1979-. Address: 5 Rue du General Pershing, 78000 Versailles, France.

BANKOFF George. See: MILKOMANE George Alexis Milkomanovich.

BANKS Brian (Robert), b. 4 Oct 1956, Carshalton, Surrey, England. Antiquarian Bookseller. m. Catherine Walton, 28 Sept 1987, 1 son, 2 daughters. Education: Westminister College; Middlesex Polytechnic. Publications: The Image of J-K Huysmans, 1990; Phantoms of the Belle Epoque, 1993; Atmosphere and Attitudes (poems), 1993; Contributor to Encyclopaedia of the 1980s, 1993. Contributions to: (Yeats Society); Nuit Iris; Book and Magazine Collector. Memberships: Societe de J K Huysmans, Paris; 1890's Society. Address: c/o 4 Meretune Court, Martin Way, Morden, Surrey SM4 4AN, England.

BANKS James Albert, b. 1941, American. Professor. Appointments: Assistant Professor 1969-71, Associate Professor 1971-73, Professor of Education 1973-, Chairman of the Department of Curriculum and Instruction, 1982-, University of Washington, Seattle; National Council for the Social Studies, 1982. Publications: Teaching the Black Experience: Methods and Materials, March Toward Freedom: A History of Black Americans, 1970, 2nd edition (with Cherry A Banks), 1978; Teaching Social Studies to Culturally Different Children (edition with William W Joyce), Teaching the Language Arts to Culturally Different Children (with W Joyce), 1971; Black Self-Concept (edition with Jean D Grambs), 1972; Teaching Ethnic Studies, Teaching Strategies for the Social Studies, 1973, 3rd edition 1985; Teaching Strategies for Ethnic Studies, 1975, 4th edition 1987; Curriculum Guidelines for Multiethnic Education (with others), 1976; Multiethnic Education: Practices and Promises, 1971; Multiethnic Education: Theory and Practice, 1981, 1988; Education in the 80's: Multiethnic Education, 1981; We Americans: Our History and People, 2 volumes (with Sebesta), 1982; Multicultural Education in Western Societies (with James Lynch), 1986; An Introduction to Multiculture Education, 1993. Address: 115 Miller Hall-DQ-12, University of Washington, Seattle, WA 98195, USA.

BANKS Lynne Reid, b. 31 July 1929, London, England. Writer; Journalist; Playwright. m. Chaim Stephenson, 1965, 3 sons. Education: Overseas; Italia Conti Stage School, 1946; Royal Academy of Dramatic Art, 1947-49. Appointments: Actress, 1949-54; Reporter and Scriptwriter, Independent Television News, London, 1955-62; English Teacher, Western Galilee, Israel, 1963-71; Writer, Lecturer, Journalist, 1971-. Publications: The L-Shaped Room, 1960; An End to Running, 1962; Children at the Gate, 1968; The Backward Shadow, 1970; Two is Lonely, 1974; Dark Quartet: The Story of the Brontës, 1976; Path to the Silent Country: Charlotte Brontë's Years of Fame, 1977; Defy the Wilderness, 1981; Torn Country: An Oral History of the Israeli War of

Independence, 1982; The Warning Bell, 1984; Casualities, 1986. Juvenile: One More River, 1973, revised edition, 1993; Sarah and After: The Matriarchs, 1975; The Adventures of King Midas, 1976, revised edition, 1994; The Farthest-Away Mountain, 1977; My Darling Villain, 1977; I, Houdini: The Autobiography of a Self-Educated Hamster, 1978; Letters to My Israeli Sons: The Story of Jewish Survival, 1979; The Indian in the Cupboard, 1980; The Writing on the Wall, 1981; Maura's Angel, 1984; The Fairy Rebel, 1985; Return of the Indian, 1985; Melusine: A Mystery, 1988; The Secret of the Indian, 1988; The Magic Hare, 1992; The Mystery of the Cupboard, 1993; Broken Bridge, 1994; Harry the Poisonous Centipede, 1996; Angela and Diabola, forthcoming. Plays: It Never Rains, 1954; All in a Row, 1956; The Killer Dies Twice, 1956; Already, It's Tomorrow, 1962; The Wednesday Caller (television), 1963; The Last Word on Julie (television), 1964; The Gift, 1965; The Stowaway (radio), 1967; The Eye of the Beholder (television), 1977; The Real Thing, 1977; Lame Duck (radio), 1978; Purely from Principal (radio), 1985; The Travels of Yoshi and the Tea-Kettle (children), 1993. Anthologies: Is Anyone There?, 1978; Women Writing 3, 1980; A Treasury of Jewish Stories, 1996; Ballet Stories, forthcoming. Contributions to: Short stories and articles in various publications. Honours: Best Books for Young Adults Award, American Library Association, 1977; Outstanding Books of the Year Award, New York Times, 1981; Notable Books Award, New York Times, 1986; Children's Books of the Year Award, 1987; Rebecca Caudill Young Reader's Books Award, Illinois Association for Media in Education, 1988; Several children's Choice Awards. Address: c/o Watson, Little Ltd, Capo di Monte, Windmill Hill, Hampstead, London NW3 6RJ, England.

BANKS Russell, b. 28 Mar 1940, Newton, Massachusetts, USA. Novelist. 4 daughters. Education: BA, highest honours, English, University of North Carolina. Publications: Searching for Survivors, 1975; Family Life, 1975; Hamilton Stark, 1978; The New World, 1978; The Book of Jamaica, 1980; Trailerpark, 1982; The Relation of My Imprisonment, 1984; Continental Drift, 1985; Success Stories, 1986; Affliction, 1989; Sweet Hereafter, 1992; Rule of the Bone, 1995. Contributions to: New York Times Book Review; Washington Post; American Review; Vanity Fair; Antaeus; Partisan Review; New England Review; Fiction International; Boston Globe Magazine. Honours: Best American Short Stories, 1971, 1985; Fels Award, fiction, 1974; Prize story, O Henry Awards, 1975; Guggenheim Fellow, 1976; National Endowment for the Arts Fellowships, 1977, 1983; St Lawrence Award, fiction, 1976; John dos Passos Award, 1986; Pulitzer Prize nominee, 1986; Award, American Academy of Arts and Letters, 1986. Memberships: Executive, PEN American Centre; Board, 1968-71, Secretary, 1970-71, Coordinating Council of Literary Magazines. Literary Agent: Ellen Levine. Address: c/o Ellen Levine Literary Agency Inc., Suite 1801, 15 East 26th Street, New York, NY 10010-1505, USA.

BANNON Paul. See: DURST Paul.

BANTOCK Gavin (Marcus August), b. 1939, England. Retired Professor; Poet. Appointments: Professor of English, Reitaku University, Japan, 1969-94. Publications: Christ: A Poem in Twenty-Six Parts, 1965; Juggernaut, The Last of the Kings: Frederick the Great, 1968; A New Thing Breathing, 1969; Anhaga, 1970; Gleeman, 1972; Eirenikon, 1973; Isles, 1974; Dragons, 1979. Address: c/o Peter Jay, 69 King George Street, London SE10 8PX, England.

BANTOCK Geoffrey Herman, b. 12 Oct 1914, Blackpool, England. Emeritus Professor of Education. m. Dorothy Jean Pick, 6 Jan 1950. Education: BA, 1936, MA, 1942, Emmanuel College, Cambridge. Appointments: Lecturer to Professor of Education, University of Leicester, 1958-76. Publications: Freedom and Authority in Education, 1952; L H Myers, A Critical Study, 1956; Education and Values, 1965; Education, Culture and The Emotions, 1967; Culture, Industrialisation and Education, 1968; Education in an Industrial Society, 1968; T S Eliot and Education, 1970; Dilemmas of the Curriculum, 1980; Studies in the History of Educational Theory, Volume I, 1980, Volume II, 1984; Parochialism of the Present, 1981. Contributions to: Scrutiny; Cambridge Journal; Essays in Criticism; ELH; TES; Listener. Honour: Book Prize of Standing Conference in Education Studies for Best Book on Education Published in 1984. Address: 1807 Melton Road, Rearsby, Leicestershire LE7 4YS, England.

BANTOCK Nick, b. 1950, Worcestershire, England. Writer; Book Jacket Illustrator. m. Kim Kasasian, 4 children. Publications: There

Was an Old Lady, 1990; Wings: A Pop-Up Book of Things That Fly, 1990; Griffin and Sabine: An Extraordinary Correspondence, 1991; Sabine's Notebook: In Which the Extraordinary Correspondence of Griffin and Sabine Continues, 1992; Runners, Sliders, Bouncers, Climbers: A Pop-Up Look at Animals in Motion (with Stacie Strong), 1992; The Walrus and the Crpenter, 1992; The Golden Mean: In Which the Extraordinary Correspondence of Griffin and Sabine Concludes, 1993; The Egyptian Jukebox: A Conundrum, 1993; Robin Hood: A Pop-Up Rhyme Book, 1993; Averse to Beasts: Twenty-Three Reasonless Rhymes, 1994. Address: c/o Chronicle Books, Chronicle Publishing Company, 275 Fifth Street, San Francisco, CA 94103, USA.

BANVILLE John, b. 8 Dec 1945, Wexford, Ireland. Author. m. Janet Dunham, 2 sons. Education: Christian Brothers School; St Peters College, Wexford. Appointment: Literary Editor, Irish Times, Dublin, 1988. Publications: Nightspawn, 1971; Birchwood, 1973; Doctor Copernicus, 1976; Kepler, 1983; The Newton Letter: An Interlude, 1985; Mefisto, 1987; The Book of Evidence, 1989; Ghosts, 1993; Athena, 1995. Contributions to: Reviews for the Observer; New York Review of Books; Irish Times. Literary Agent: Anthony Sheil, Sheil Land Associates Ltd.

BARAKA Amiri. See JONES (Everett) LeRoi.

BARAŃCZAK Stanislaw, b. 13 Nov 1946, Poznan, Poland. Professor of Polish Language and Literature; Poet; Writer; Editor; Translator. m. 2 children. Education: MA 1969, PhD 1973, Adam Mickiewicz University, Poznan. Appointments: Assistant Professor, Institute of Polish Philology, Adam Mickiewicz University, 1969-77, 1980; Co-Founder and Member, KOR, human rights group, 1976-81; Associate Professor of Slavic Languages and Literatures, 1981-84, Alfred Jurzykowski Professor of Polish Language and Literature, 1984-, Harvard University; Co-Editor, Zeszyty Literackie, 1982-; Associate Editor, 1986-87, Editor-in-Chief, 1987-90, The Polish Review. Publications: Poetry: Selected Poems: The Weight of the Body, 1989; 18 other books in Polish, 1968-96. Criticism and essays: Breathing Under Water, and Other East European Essays, 1990; 14 other books in Polish, 1971-96. Other: 43 books translated from English into Polish, 1974-96. Contributions to: Many scholarly journals and periodicals. Honours: Alfred Jurzykowski Foundation Literary Award, 1980; Guggenheim Fellowship, 1989; Terrence Des Pres Poetry Prize, 1989; Chivalric Cross of the Order of Polonia Restituta, 1991; Special Diploma for Lifetime Achievement in Promoting Polish Culture Abroad, Polish Minister of Foreign Affairs, 1993; PEN and Book-of-the-Month Club Award for the Best Literary Translation, with Clare Cavanagh, 1996. Memberships: American Association for Advancement of Slavic Studies; American Association for Polish-Jewish Studies; PEN Polish Centre; Polish Institute of Arts and Sciences in America. Address: c/o Department of Slavic Languages and Literatures, Harvard University, 301 Boylston Hall, Cambridge, MA 02138, USA.

BARBALET Margaret (Evelyn Hardy), b. 19 Dec 1949, Adelaide, South Australia. Writer. m. Jack Barbalet, 12 May 1970, div 10 Jan 1989, 3 sons. Education: MA, Adelaide University, 1973. Appointments: Historian, Adelaide Children's Hospital, 1973-74; Research Officer, Adelaide City Council, 1973-75; Research Consultant, Commonwealth Schools Commission, 1984-88; Staff, Department of Foreign Affairs and Trade, Australia, 1990-. Publications: Far From a Low Gutter Girl: The Forgotten World of State Wards, 1983; Blood in the Rain (novel), 1986; Steel Beach (novel), 1988; The Wolf (children's book), 1991; Lady, Baby, Gypsy, Queen (novel), 1992. Honours: Literature Grant, 1985; New Writers Fellowship, 1986; Vogel Award Shortlist, 1988; Children's Book of the Year Award Shortlist, 1992. Memberships: Amnesty International; Australian Society of Authors. Address: c/o Penguin Books, PO Box 257, Ringwood, Victoria 3134, Australia.

BARBER Charles Laurence, b. 20 Apr 1915, Harold Wood, Essex, England. University Teacher, Retired. m. Barbara Best, 27 July 1943, 2 sons, 2 daughters. Education: BA, St Catharines College, Cambridge University, 1937; MA, 1941; Teachers Diploma, University of London, 1938; PhD, University of Gothenburg, Sweden, 1957. Appointments: Lecturer, University of Gothenburg, 1947-56, Queen's University of Belfast, 1956-59, University of Leeds, 1959-80. Publications: Best Known: The Idea of Honour in the English Drama, 1957; The Story of Language, 1964; Linguistic Change in Present Day English, 1964; Early Modern English, 1976; Poetry in English, An Introduction, 1983; The Theme of Honours Tongue, 1985; The English

Language: A Historical Introduction, 1993; Others, Editor of Works by Thomas Middleton, A Trick to Catch the Old One, 1968; Women Beware Women, 1969; A Chaste Maid in Cheapside, 1969; Shakespeare, Henry V, 1980; As You Like It, 1981; Richard III, 1981; Richard II, 1987. Contributions to: Numerous Articles in Learned Journals. Address: 7 North Parade, Leeds, West Yorkshire LS16 5AY, England.

BARBER Lynn, b. 22 May 1944, England. Journalist. m. David Cloudesley Cardiff, 1 Sept 1971, 2 daughters. Education: BA Honours, English, Oxford University. Appointments: Assistant Editor, Penthouse Magazine, 1968-73; Staff Feature Writer, Sunday Express Magazine, 1984-89; Feature Writer, Independent on Sunday, 1990-. Publications: How to Improve Your Man in Bed, 1970; The Penthouse Sexindex, 1973; The Single Women's Sexbook, 1975; The Heyday of Natural History, 1980. Honours: British Press Awards as Magazine Writer of the Year, 1986, 1987. Address: Independent on Sunday, 40 City Road, London EC1Y 2DH, England.

BARBER Richard William, b. 30 Oct 1941. Publisher; Author. m. Helen Tolson, 7 May 1970, 1 son, 1 daughter. Education: Trevelyan Scholar, BA, MA, PhD, 1982; Corpus Christi College, Cambridge University. Publications: Arthur of Albion, 1961; The Knight and Chivalry, 1972; Edward Prince of Wales & Aquitaine, 1976; Companion Guide to South West France, 1977; Tournaments, 1978; The Arthurian Legends, 1979; The Penguin Guide to Medieval Europe, 1984; Fuller's Worthies, 1987; The Worlds of John Aubrey, 1988; Pilgrimages, 1991. Contributions to: Arthurian Literature. Honours: Somerset Maugham Award, 1972; Times Higher Educational Supplement Book Award, 1978. Memberships: Royal Society of Literature; Royal Historical Society; Society of Antiquaries. Address: Stangrove Hall, Alderton, Nr Woodbridge, Suffolk IP12 3BL, England.

BARBET Pierre. See: **AVICE Claude (Pierre Marie).**

BARBOSA Miguel, b. 22 Nov 1925, Lisbon, Portugal. Writer; Painter. Appointments: Moulin de l'Ecluse - Le Mur de la Poesie, Carnac, France, 1993; Poesia Pace, Milano, Italia, 1994; Jeux Floreaux d'Aquitaine, Bordeaux, France, 1995. Education: Economics and Finance, University of Lisbon. Publications: Short Stories: Retalhos de Vida, 1955; Manta de Trapos, 1962; Plays: O Palheiro, 1963; Os Carnivoros, 1964; O Piquenique, 1964; O Insecticida, 1965; A Mulher que Paris a France, 1971; Los profetas de la Paja, 1973; How New York was Destroyed by Rats, 1977; The Materialisation of Love, 1978; Novels: Trineu do Morro, 1972; Mulher Macumba, 1973; A Pileca no Poleiro, 1976; As Confissoes de Um Cacador de Dinossauros, 1981; Esta Louca Profissao de Escritor, 1983; Cartas a Um Fogo-Fatuo, 1985; Poetry: Dans un Cri de Couleurs, 1991; Um Gesto no Rosto da Utopia, 1994; Prima del Verbo, 1995; Mare di Illusioni Naufragate, 1995; Prelúdio Poético de um Vagabundo da Madrugada, 1996; Mouthfuls of Red Confetti and the Hunt for God's Skull, 1996; O Teu Corpo na Minha Alma, 1996. Contributor to: Various publications. Honours: 1st Prize, Maria Terza Alves Viana Theatre, Sao Paulo, Brazil; Prix Nu, Jubile Mondial d'arts Plastiques, Nice, France, 1984; Honourable Mention, Le Quadriennale Mondiale des Beaux Arts, Lyon, France, 1985; Medaille D'Argent, Academie de Lutece, Paris, 1987; Prix de La Revue D'Art, La Cote des Arts, Cannes, 1990. Memberships: Society of Portuguese Authors; Instituto de Sintra, Portugal; Accademia Italiana Gli Etruschi, Italy; Accademia Internazionale Greci-Marino di Lettere, Arti e Scienze. Address: Avenue Joao Crisostomo 91-2, Lisbon 1050, Portugal.

BARBOUR Douglas, b. 21 Mar 1940, Winnipeg, Manitoba, Canada. Professor of English; Poet; Writer. m. M Sharon Nicoll, 21 May 1966. Education: BA, Acadia University, 1962; MA, Dalhousie University, 1964; PhD, Queen's University, Kingston, Ontario, 1976. Appointments: Teacher, Alderwood Collegiate Institute, 1968-69; Assistant Professor 1969-77, Associate Professor 1977-82, Professor of English, 1982-, University of Alberta. Publications: Poetry: Land Fall, 1971; A Poem as Long as the Highway, 1971; White, 1972; Song Book, 1973; He and She and, 1974; Visions of My Grandfather, 1977; Shore Lines, 1979; Vision/Sounding, 1980; The Pirates of Pen's Chance (with Stephen Scobie), 1981; The Harbingers, 1984; Visible Visions: Selected Poems, 1984; Canadian Poetry Chronicle, 1985. Other: Worlds Out of Words: The Science Fiction Novels of Samuel R Delany, 1978; The Maple Laugh Forever: An Anthology of Canadian Comic Poetry (editor with Stephen Scobie), 1981; Writing Right: New Poetry by Canadian Women (editor with Marni Stanley), 1982; Tesseracts 2 (editor with Phyllis Gollieb), 1987; B P Nichol and His

Works, 1992; Daphne Marlatt and Her Works, 1992; John Newlove and His Works, 1992; Michael Ondaatje, 1993. Memberships: Association of Canadian University Teachers; League of Canadian Poets, Co-Chairman, 1972-74. Address: c/o Department of English, University of Alberta, Edmonton, Alberta T6G 2E5, Canada.

BARCLAY Robert Leslie, b. 17 July 1946, London, England. Conservator; Trumpet-maker. m. Janet Mair Fenwick, 21 Jan 1971, 2 sons, 2 daughters. Education: City & Guilds of London, Science Laboratory Technology, 1969; BA, Honours, University of Toronto, 1975. Publications: The Care of Musical Instruments in Canadian Collections, 1982; Anatomy of an Exhibition: The Look of Music, 1983; The Art of the Trumpet-maker, 1992; Recommendations for the Conservation of Musical Instruments, 1993. Contributions to: Museum International, Studies in Conservation; Historic Brass Society Journal; Galpin Society Journal. Honour: Nicholas Bessaraboff Prize, AMIS, 1995. Address: Canadian Conservation Institute, 1030 Innes Road, Ottawa, Ontario K1A 0M5, Canada.

BARDIS Panos D(emetrios), b. 24 Sept 1924, Lefcohori, Arcadia, Greece. Professor of Sociology; Writer; Poet; Editor. m. Donna Jean Decker, 26 Dec 1964, 2 sons. Education: Panteios University, Athens, 1945-47; BA, Bethany College, West Virginia, 1950; MA, Notre Dame University, 1953; PhD, Purdue University, 1955. Appointments: Instructor to Associate Professor of Sociology, 1955-59, Acting Head, Sociology Department, 1958-59, Albion College, Michigan; Associate Professor, 1959-62, Professor, 1963, of Sociology, University of Toledo; Editor, Social Science, 1959-81; Co-Editor, 1970-72, Book Review Editor, 1995-, Revue Internationale de Sociologie; Editor, Book Review Editor, International Social Science Review, 1982-; Founder, Editor-in-Chief, International Journal on World Peace, 1983-. Publications: Non-Fiction: The Family in Changing Civilizations, 1967; Encyclopedia of Campus Unrest, 1971; History of the Family, 1975; The Future of the Greek Language in the United States, 1976; The Family in Asia (editor with Man Das), 1978; Sociology as a Science, 1980; History of Thanatology, 1981; Atlas of Human Reproductive Anatomy, 1983; Evolution of the Family in the West, 1983; Global Marriage and Family Customs, 1983; Dictionary of Quotations in Sociology, 1985; Marriage and Family: Continuity, Change and Adjustment, 1988; History of Sociology, 1988; South Africa and the Marxist Movement, 1989; Urania Smiles Now!: Universal Peace and Cosmic Harmony, 1993; Cronus in the Eternal City: Scientific, Social and Philosophical Aspects of Time in Ancient Rome, 1995. Fiction: Ivan and Artemis, novel, 1957. Poetry: Nine Oriental Muses, 1983; A Cosmic Whirl of Melodies, 1985; Ode to Orion: An Epic Poem in Twenty Rhapsodies, 1994; Ho Orionas: To Phengobolema Mias Chrysocenteies Astrothalassas, epic poem, 1996. Contributions to: Numerous publications. Honours: Many poetry awards and prizes. Memberships: American Association for the Advancement of Science; American Sociological Association; American Association of University Professors; Academy of American Poets; International Poets Academy; World Academy of Scholars; International Institute of Arts and Letters; Institut International de Sociologie. Address: 2533 Orkney Drive, Ottawa Hills, Toledo, OH 43606, USA.

BAREHAM Terence, b. 17 Oct 1937, Clacton-on-Sea, Essex, England. University Professor. Education: Open Scholar and State Scholar 1959-62, BA (Hons) 1962, MA 1969, Lincoln College, Oxford University, England; DPhil, Ulster University, Northern Ireland, 1977. Publications: George Crabbe: A Critical Study, 1977; George Crabbe: A Bibliography (joint author), 1978; The Art of Anthony Trollope, 1980; Anthony Trollope (Casebook Series), 1982; Tom Stoppard (Casebook Series), 1989; Malcolm Lowry, 1989; Charles Lever: New Evaluations (editor), 1991; York Notes, Monographs on Robert Bolt, T S Eliot, Shakespeare. Contributions to: Numerous on literature of 17th - 20th Century. Address: c/o Department of English, University of Ulster, Coleraine, County Derry, Northern Ireland.

BARER Burl, b. 8 Aug 1947, Walla Walla, Washington, USA. Writer. m. Britt Johnsen, 2 Mar 1974, 1 son, 1 daughter. Education: Communications, University of Washington. Publications: Selections from the Holy Quran, 1987; The Saint, 1993; Maverick, 1994; Man Overbaord: The Counterfeit Resurrection of Phil Champagne, 1994. Contributions to: The Epistle; Oxford Companion to Mystery and Detective Fiction. Honour: Edgar Award, 1994. Membership: Mystery Writers of America. Literary Agent: Gelfman/Schnieder. Address: 1839 Crestline Drive, Walla Walla, WA 99362, USA.

BARGER Timothy Knox, b. 4 Jan 1958, Edwards AFB, California, USA. Writer; Editor. Education: BA, Humanities, Hendrix College, 1978; BJ, Magazine Journalism, Texas, Austin, 1987; MLIS, Library Science, Texas, Austin, 1994; Doctoral Studies, Mass Communication, Syracuse University, 1994-. Appointments: Associate Editor, The Austin Light, Austin, Texas, 1987-88; Coordinating Editor, Butterworth Legal Publishers, Austin, Texas, 1989-92; Writer and Researcher, The Reference Press, Austin, Texas, 1992-94. Publications: Co-author: Hoover's Handbook of American Business, 1993, 1994, 1995; Hoover's Handbook of World Business, 1993; Hoover's Guide to the Book Business, 1993; Hoover's Handbook of Emerging Companies, 1993-94; Hoover's Guide to Private Companies, 1994-95; The Bay Area 500, 1994; The Texas 500, 1994. Contributions to: Austin American-Statesman; Austin Chronicle; Austin Light. Honours: Phi Kappa Phi, 1993; Beta Phi Mu, 1996; Syracuse University Graduate Fellow, 1994-97. Memberships: Austin Writers' League; Society of Professional Journalists; Association for Education in Journalism and Mass Communications; American Library Association. Address: 256 Thurber Street, Apt 8, Syracuse, NY 13210-3655, USA.

BARKER Audrey Lilian, b. 13 Apr 1918, St Pauls Cray, Kent, England. Author. Appointments: Staff, Amalgamated Press, 1936; Reader, Cresset Press, 1947; Secretary, Sub Editor, BBC, London, 1948-78. Publications: Innocents, 1947; The Middling, 1967; John Brown's Body, 1969; Life Stories, 1981; No Word of Love, 1985; The Gooseboy, 1987; The Woman Who Talked to Herself, 1989; Any Excuse for a Party: Selected Stories, 1991; Zeph, 1991. Contributions to: Many short story Anthologies including: Twelve Stories by Famous Women Writers; Tales to Make the Flesh Creep; Magazines including: Harper's; Good Housekeeping; Woman and Beauty. Honours: Atlantic Award in Literature, 1946; Somerset Maugham Award, 1947; Cheltenham Festival Award, 1963; Arts Council Award, 1970; SE Arts Creative Book Award, 1981. Memberships: Fellow, Royal Society of Literature; English PEN. Literary Agent: Jennifer Kavanagh. Address: 103 Harrow Road, Carshalton, Surrey, England.

BARKER Dennis (Malcolm), b. 21 June 1929, Lowestoft, England. Journalist; Novelist. m. Sarah Katherine Alwyn, 1 daughter. Education: National Diploma in Journalism, 1959. Appointments: Reporter and Sub-Editor, Suffolk Chronicle & Mercury, Ipswich, 1947-48; Reporter, Feature Writer, Theatre and Film Critic, 1948-58, East Anglian Daily Times; Estates and Property Columnist, 1958-63, Express & Star, Wolverhampton; Midlands Correspondent, 1963-67, Reporter, Feature Writer, Columnist, The Guardian, 1967-91 (contributor). Publications: Novels: Candidate of Promise, 1969; The Scandalisers, 1974; Winston Three Three Three, 1987; Non-fiction: The People of the Forces Trilogy (Soldiering On, 1981, Ruling the Waves, 1986, Guarding the Skies, 1989); One Man's Estate, 1983; Parian Ware, 1985; Fresh Start, 1990. Contributions to: BBC; Punch; East Anglian Architecture & Building Review (editor and editorial director, 1956-58); The Guardian, 1991-. Memberships: National Union of Journalists, secretary, Suffolk Branch, 1953-58, Chairman 1958; Chairman, Home Counties District Council, 1956-57; Life Member, 1991; Life Member, Newspaper Press Fund; Writers Guild of Great Britain; Broadcasting Press Guild; Society of Authors. Address: 67 Speldhurst Road, London W4 1BY, England.

BARKER Howard, b. 28 June 1946, London, England. Playwright. Education: MA, Sussex University, 1968. Appointment: Resident Dramatist, Open Space Theatre, London, 1974-75. Publications: Stripwell, with Claw, 1977; Fair Slaughter, 1978; That Good Between Us with Credentials of a Sympathiser, The Love of a Good Man with All Bleeding, 1980; The Hand of the Gaol with Heaven, Two Plays for the Right: Birth on a Hard Shoulder and the Loud Boy's Life, No End of Blame: Scenes of Overcoming, 1981; The Castle/Scenes from an Execution, Victory, 1984; Crimes in Hot Countries/Fair Slaughter, The Power of the Dog: Movements in History and Anti-History, A Passion in Six Days/Downchild, 1985; Don't Exaggerate, 1986; The Possibilities, 1987; The Bite of the Night, 1987; The Last Supper, 1988; Women Beware Women, 1988; Seven Lears/Golgo, 1989; The Europeans/Judith, 1990; Collected Plays, Volume I, 1990; Poems - The Breath of the Crowd, 1987; Garry the Thief, 1988; Lullabies for Impatient, 1988; The Ascent of Monte Grappa, 1990. Address: Judy Daish Associates, 83 Eastbourne Mews, Brighton, Sussex, England.

BARKER Nicola, b. 30 Mar 1966, Ely, Cambridgeshire, England. Writer. Education: Read Philosophy and English, Cambridge University, 1988. Appointments: Regular Reviewer, The Observer. Publications: Love Your Enemies (short stories), 1992; Reversed Forecast (novel), 1994; Small Holdings (novel), 1995; Heading Inland (short stories), 1996. Contributions to: The Time Out Book of London Short Stories; Food With Feeling, story adapted for BBC Radio 4. Honours: David Higham Prize for Fiction; Joint Winner, Macmillan Silver PEN Award for Fiction. Address: c/o Rogers, Coleridge and White Ltd, 20 Powis Mews, London W11 1JN, England.

BARKER Patricia Margaret, b. 8 May 1943, Thornaby on Tees, England. Writer. m. 29 Jan 1977, 1 son, 1 daughter. Education: BSc, London School of Economics, 1965. Appointment: Patron, New Writing North. Publications: Union Street, 1982; Blow Your House Down, 1984; The Century's Daughter, 1986; The Man Who Wasn't There, 1989; Regeneration, 1991; The Eye in the Door, 1993; The Ghost Road, 1995; The Century's Daughter, retitled Liza's England, 1996. Honours: One of Best of Young British Novelists, 1982; Joint Winner, Fawcett Prize, 1982; Hon M Litt University Teesside, 1993; Guardian Fiction Prize, 1994; Northern Electric Special Arts Award, 1994; Booker Prize, 1995; Hon DLitt, Napier University, 1996; Nonorary Doctorate, Open University, 1997; Honorary DLitt, Durham University, 1997. Memberships: Society of Authors; PEN; Royal Society of Literature. Address: c/o Aitken & Stone, 29 Fernshaw Road, London SW10 0TG, England.

BARKER Paul, b. 24 Aug 1935, Halifax, Yorkshire, England. Writer; Broadcaster. m. Sally Huddleston, 3 sons, 1 daughter. Education: MA, Oxford University. Appointments: Editor, New Society, 1968-86; Director, Advisory Editor, Fiction Magazine, 1982-87; Social Policy Editor, Sunday Telegraph, 1986-88; Columnist, London Evening Standard, 1987-92, Social Policy commentator, 1992-; Associate Editor, The Independent Magazine, 1988-90; Visiting Fellow, University of Bath, 1986-; Trustee, 1991-, Fellow, 1992, Senior Fellow, Institute of Community Studies; Fellow, Royal Society of Arts, 1990; Leverhulme Research Fellow, 1993-95. Publications: A Sociological Portrait, 1972; One for Sorrow, Two for Joy, 1972; The Social Sciences Today, 1975; Arts in Society, 1977; The Other Britain, 1982; Founders of the Welfare State, 1985; Britain in the Eighties, 1989; Towards a New Landscape, 1993; Young at Eighty, 1995; Gulliver and Beyond, 1996; Living as Equals, 1996. Address: 15 Dartmouth Park Avenue, London NW5 1JL, England.

BARLOW Frank, b. 19 Apr 1911, Wolstanton, England. Emeritus Professor. m. Moira Stella Brigid Garvey, 1 July 1936, 2 sons. Education: MA, D Phil, Hon D Litt, Exon; St Johns College, Oxford, 1929-36. Publications: The Letters of Arnulf of Lisieux, 1939; Durham Annals and Ducouments of the Thirteenth Century, 1945; Durham Jurisdictional Peculiars, 1950; The Feudal Kingdom of England, 1955; Vita Aedwardi Regis, 1962; The English Church, 1000-1066, 1963, 1066-1154, 1979; William I and the Norman Conquest, 1965; Edward the Confessor, 1970; William Rufus, 1983; Introduction to Devonshire Domesday Book, 1991; English Episcopal Acta, XI, XII: Exeter 1046-1257, 1996. Contributions to: Various Professional Journals. Honours: D Litt, 1981; Commander of the Order of the British Empire, 1989. Memberships: British Academy; Royal Society of Literature; Royal Historical Society. Address: Middle Court Hall, Kenton, Exeter EX6 8NA, England.

BARLTROP Robert (Arthur Horace), b. 6 Nov 1922, Walthamstow, England. Writer. m. Mary Gleeson, 18 July 1947, 3 sons. Education: Teacher's Certificate, Forest Training College, 1950. Appointments: Editor, Socialist Standard, 1972-78, Cockney Ancestor, 1983-86. Publications: The Monument, 1974; Jack London: The Man, the Writer, the Rebel, 1977; The Muvver Tongue, 1980; My Mother's Calling Me, 1984; A Funny Age, 1985; Bright Summer, Dark Autumn, 1986; The Bar Tree, 1979; Revolution - Stories and Essays by Jack London (editor), 1981. Contributor to: Weekly columns and features, Recorder Newspapers, 1985-; Guardian Newspapers; Root; Essex Countryside. Membership: Institute of Journalists. Address: 77 Idmiston Road, Stratford, London E15 1RG, England.

BARNABY (Charles) Frank, b. 27 Sept 1927, Andover, Hampshire, England. Author. m. 12 Dec 1972, 1 son, 1 daughter. Education: BSc, 1951, MSc, 1954, PhD, 1960, London University. Publications: Man and the Atom, 1970; Nuclear Energy, 1975; Future Warfare, 1983; Prospects for Peace, 1981; The Automated Battlefield, 1986; Star Wars Brought Down to Earth, 1986; The Invisible Bomb, 1989; The Gaia Peace Atlas, 1989; The Role and Control of Arms in the 1990's, 1993; How Nuclear Weapons Spread, 1993. Contributions to: Ambio; New Scientist; Technology Review. Honour: Hon Doctorate, Free University, Amsterdam, University of Southampton, 1996. Literary Agent: June Hall. Address: Brandreth, Station Road, Chilbolton, Stockbridge, Hampshire SO20 6HW, England.

BARNARD Christiaan (Neethling), b. 8 Nov 1922, Beaufort West, Cape Province, South Africa. Physician; Professor of Surgical Science Emeritus; Senior Consultant and Scientist-in-Residence; Writer. m. (1) Aletta Gertruida Louw, 6 Nov 1948, diss 1970, 1 son dec. 1 daughter, (2) Barbara Maria Zoellner, 1970, diss 1980, 2 sons, (3) Karin Setxkon, 1988, 1 son. Education: MB, ChB, 1946, MD, 1953, MMed, 1953, University of Cape Town; MS, PhD, 1958, Universit of Minnesota. Appointments: Private Practice, South Africa, 1948-51; Senior Resident Medical Officer, City Fever Hospital, Cape Town, 1951-53; Registrar, Groote Schuur Hospital, 1953-55; Research Fellow in Surgery, University of Cape Town, 1953-55; Charles Adams Memorial Scholar and Dazian Foundation for Medical research Scholar, University of Minnesota, 1956-58; Lecturer, 1959-63, Associate Professor, 1963-68, Professor of Surgical Science, 1968-83, Professor Emeritus, 1983-, University of Cape Town; Senior Cardiothoracic Surgeon, Groote Schuur Hospital, 1958-83; Senior Consultant and Scientist-in-Residence, Oklahoma Heart Center, Baptist Medical Center, 1985-; Performed first human heart transplant operation, 1967, and first human double-heart transplant operation, 1974. Publications: The Surgery of the Common Congenital Cardiac Malformation (with Velva Schrire), 1968; Christiaan Barnard: One Life (with Curtis Bill Pepper), 1970; Heart Attack: You Don't Have to Die, 1971; The Unwanted (with Siegfried Stander), novel, 1974; South Africa: Sharp Dissection, 1977; In the Night Season (with Siegfried Stander), novel, 1977; The Best Medicine, 1979; Good Life, Good Death: A Doctor's Case for Euthanasia and Suicide, 1980; The Arthritis Handbook, 1984. Contributions to: Many medical journals. Honours: Numerous. Address: 18 Silwood Road, Rondebosch 7700, South Africa.

BARNARD Robert, b. 23 Nov 1936, Burnham on Crouch, Essex, England. Crime Writer. m. Mary Louise Tabor, 7 Feb 1963. Education: Balliol College, Oxford, 1956-59; Dr Philos, Bergen University, Norway, 1972. Publications: Death of an Old Goat, 1976; Sheer Torture, 1981; A Corpse in a Gilded Cage, 1984; Out of the Blackout, 1985; Skeleton in the Grass, 1987; At Death's Door, 1988; Death and the Chaste Apprentice, 1989; Masters of the House, 1994; As Bernard Bastable: Dead, Mr Mozart, 1995; Too Many Notes, Mr Mozart, 1995. Honours: Seven Times Nominated for Edgar Awards. Memberships: Crime Writers Association; Brontë Society; Society of Authors. Literary Agent: Gregory & Radice. Address: Hazeldene, Houghley Lane, Leeds LS13 2DT, England.

BARNES Christopher J(ohn), b. 10 Mar 1942, Sheffield, England. Professor of Slavic Languages and Literatures; Writer. m. Alexa H Dey, 26 July 1975, 2 daughters. Education: BA, 1963, MA, 1967, PhD, 1970, Corpus Christi College, Cambridge. Appointments: Lecturer in Russian Languages and Literature, University of St Andrews, Scotland, 1967-89; Professor and Chairman of the Department of Slavic Languages and Literatures, University of Toronto, 1989-. Publications: Studies in Twentieth-Century Russian Literature (editor), 1976; Boris Pasternak: Collected Short Prose (editor and translator), 1977; Boris Pasternak: The Voice of Prose (editor and translator) 2 volumes, 1986, 1990; Boris Pasternak: A Literary Biography, Vol 1, 1890-1928, 1989; Boris Pasternak and European Literature (editor), 1990; Proceedings of the Pasternak Centenary Conference, 1990, 1991. Contributions to: Scholarly journals. Memberships: American Association for the Advancement of Slavic Studies; American Association of Teachers of Slavic and East European Languages; British Royal Musical Association; British Universities Association of Slavists; Canadian Association of Slavists; Modern Language Association of America. Address: c/o Department of Slavic Languages and Literatures, University of Toronto, Toronto, Ontario M5S 1A1, Canada.

BARNES Clive (Alexander), b. 13 May 1927, London, England. Journalist; Dance and Theatre Critic. m. (2) Patricia Amy Evelyn Winckley, 26 June 1958, 1 son, 1 daughter. Education: King's College, London; BA, St Catherine's College, Oxford, 1951. Appointments: Co-Editor, Arabesque, 1950; Assistant Editor, 1950-58, Associate Editor, 1958-61, Executive Editor, 1961-65, Dance and Dancers; Administrative Officer in Town Planning, London County Council, 1952-61; Chief Dance Critic, 1961-65, New York Correspondent, 1970, The Times, London; Dance Critic, 1965-78, Drama Critic, 1967-78,

New York Times; Associate Editor and Chief Dance and Drama Critic, New York Post, 1978-. Publications: Ballet in Britain Since the War, 1953; Frederick Ashton and His Ballets, 1961; Ballet Here and Now (with A V Coton and Frank Jackson), 1961; Ballett, 1965: Chronik und Bilanz des Balletjahres (editor with Horst Koegler), 1965; Ballett 1966: Chronik und Bilanz des Balletjahres (editor with Horst Koegler), 1966; Fifty Best Plays of the American Theatre from 1787 to the Present, (editor), 4 volumes, 1969; Best American Plays: Sixth Series, 1963-1967 (editor with John Gassner), 1971; Best American Plays: Seventh Series (editor), 1975; Inside American Ballet Theatre, 1977; Nureyev, 1982; Best American Plays: Eighth Series, 1974-1982 (editor), 1983; Best American Plays: Ninth Series, 1983-1992 (editor), 1993. Contributions to: Many periodicals. Honours: Knight of the Order of Dannebrog, Denmark, 1972; Commander of the Order of the British Empire, 1975. Address: 825 West End Avenue, New York, NY 10025, USA.

BARNES Jonathan, b. 26 Dec 1942, England. Professor of Ancient Philosophy; Writer. m. Svetlana Babushkina 20 April, 1994. 2 daughters. Education: Balliol College, Oxford. Appointments: Fellow, Oriel College, 1968-78, Balliol College, 1978-94, Oxford; Visiting positions, Institute for Advanced Study, Princeton, New Jersey, 1972, University of Texas, 1981, Wissenschaftskolleg zu Berlin, 1985, University of Alberta, 1986, University of Zürich, 1987, Istituto Italiano per gli studi filosofici, 1988; Professor of Ancient Philosophy, Oxford University, 1989-94, University of Geneva, 1994-. Publications: The Ontological Argument, 1972; Aristotle's Posterior Analytics, 1975; The Presocratic Philosphers, 1979; Aristotle, 1982; Early Greek Philosophy, 1987; The Toils of Scepticism, 1991; A Companion to Aristotle, 1995. Address: 1, place de la Taconnerie, 1204 Geneva, Switzerland.

BARNES Julian Patrick, (Dan Kavanagh, Basil Seal), b. 19 Jan 1946, Leicester, England. Writer. Education: Magdalen College, Oxford, 1964-68. Appointments: Lexicographer, Oxford English Dictionary Supplement, 1969-72; TV Critic, 1977-81, Assistant Literary Editor, 1977-79, New Statesman; Contributing Editor, New Review, 1977-78; Deputy Literary Editor, Sunday Times, 1979-81; TV Critic, The Observer, 1982-86. Publications: Metroland Duffy, 1980; Before She Met Me, 1982; Fiddle City, 1983; Flaubert's Parrot, 1984; Putting the Boot In, 1985; Staring at the Sun, 1986; History of the World in Ten & a Half Chapters, 1989; Talking it Over, 1991. Address: The Chambers, Chelsea Harbour, Lots Road, London SW10 0XF, England.

BARNES Peter, b. 10 Jan 1931, London, England. Writer. m. 28 Aug 1963. Publications: The Ruling Class, 1969; Red Noses, 1985; Collected Plays, Volumes I, II, III, 1989-96; Nobody Here But Us Chickens, 1990; The Spirit of Man, 1990; Sunsets and Glories, 1990. Honours: John Whiting Award, 1969; Evening Standard Award, 1969; Giles Cooper Award, 1981; Olivier Award, 1985; Royal Television Award, 1989. Literary Agent: Casarotto Ramsay. Address: 7 Archery Close, Connaught Street, London W2, England.

BARNETT A(rthur) Doak, b. 8 Oct 1921, Shanghai, China. Political Scientist; Professor Emeritus. m. Jeanne Hathaway Badeau, 22 Mar 1954, 1 son, 2 daughters. Education: BA, 1942, MA, 1947, Yale University. Appointments: Fellow, Institute of Current World Affairs in China and South East Asia, 1947-50, 1952-53; Correspondent, Chicago Daily News, 1947-50, 1952-55; Consul and Public Affairs Officer, American Consulate-General, Hong Kong, 1951-52; Head, Department of Foreign Area Studies, Foreign Service Institute, US Department of State, 1956-57; Research Fellow, Council on Foreign Relations, 1958-59; Professor of Political Science, Columbia University, 1961-69; Senior Fellow, 1969-82, Senior Fellow Emeritus, 1982-, Brookings Institution; Professor of Chinese Studies, 1982-89, Professor Emeritus, 1989-, School of Advanced International Studies, Johns Hopkins University. Publications: Turn East Towards Asia, 1958; Communist Economic Strategy: The Rise of Mainland China, 1959; Communist China and Asia: Challenge to American Policy, 1960; Communist China in Perspective, 1962; Communist Strategies in Asia: A Comparative Analysis of Governments and Parties (editor), 1963; China on the Eve of Communist Takeover, 1963; Communist China: The Early Years, 1949-55, 1964; Cadres, Bureaucracy and Political Power in Communist China, 1967; China after Mao, 1967; Chinese Communist Politics in Action (editor), 1969; The United States and China: The Next Decade (editor with Edwin O Reischauer), 1970; A New United States Policy Toward China, 1971; Uncertain Passage: China's Transition to the Post-Mao Era, 1974; China Policy: Old Problems and New Challenges, 1977; China and the Major Powers in

East Asia, 1977; China and the World Food System, 1979; China's Economy in Global Perspective, 1981; The FX Decision, 1981; US Arm Sales: The China-Taiwan Tangle, 1982; Modernizing China: Post-Mao Reform and Development (with Ralph N Clough), 1983; The Making of Foreign Policy in China: Structure and Process, 1985; After Deng, What? Will China Follow the USSR?, 1991; China's Far West: Four Decades of Change, 1993. Contributions to: Books and journals. Honours: Phi Beta Kappa; LLD, Franklin and Marshall College, 1967; LittD, Washington College; DHL, Monmouth College, 1990. Memberships: American Political Science Association; Council on Foreign Relations; Institute of Current World Affairs; National Committee on China-US Relations, Board of Directors, 1966-93, Chairman, 1968-69; UN Association. Address: School of Advanced International Studies, Johns Hopkins University, 1740 Massachusetts Avenue North West, Washington DC 20036, USA.

BARNETT Correlli (Douglas), b. 28 June 1927, Norbury, Surrey, England. Author. m. Ruth Murby, 30 Dec 1950, 2 daughters. Education: BA, 1951, MA, 1955, Exeter College, Oxford. Appointments: Keeper of the Churchill Archives Centre and Fellow, Churchill College, 1977-95; Defence Lecturer, Cambridge University, 1980-84. Publications: The Hump Organisation, 1957; The Channel Tunnel (co-author), 1958; The Desert Generals, 1960, new enlarged edition 1984; The Swordbearers, 1963; The Great War (co-author), 1964; The Lost Peace (co-author), 1966; Britain and Her Army, 1970; The Collapse of British Power, 1972; The Commanders, 1973; Marlborough, 1974; Strategy and Society, 1975; Bonaparte, 1978; The Great War, 1979; The Audit of War, 1986; Engage the Enemy More Closely: The Royal Navy in the Second World War, 1991; The Lost Victory: British Dreams, British Realities 1945-1950, 1995. Honours: Best Television Documentary Script Award, Screenwriter's Guild, for The Great War; Royal Society of Literature Award for Britain and Her Army; Chesney Gold Medal of the Royal United Services Institute for Defence Studies, 1991; Yorkshire Post Book of the Year Award for Engage the Enemy More Closely, 1991; DSc Honoris Causa, Cranfield University, 1993. Literary Agent: Bruce Hunter, David Higham Associates, 5-8 Lower John Street, Golden Square, London W1R 4HA. Address: Catbridge House, East Carleton, Norwich NR14 8JX, England.

BARNETT Paul (le Page), (Dennis Brezhnev, Eve Devereux, John Grant, Armytage Ware, Freddie Duff-Ware), b. 22 Nov 1949, Aberdeen, Scotland. Writer; Freelance Editor. m. Catherine Stewart, 7 July 1974, 1 daughter, plus 1 other daughter. Education: Kings & University Colleges, London (no degree), 1967-68. Publications: As John Grant: Book of Time (with Colin Wilson), 1979; Aries 1, 1979; Directory of Discarded Ideas, 1981; Directory of Possibilities, with Colin Wilson, 1981; A Book of Numbers, 1982; Dreamers, 1983; The Truth About the Flaming Ghoulies, 1983; Sex Secrets of Ancient Atlantis, 1985; The Depths of Cricket, 1986; Encyclopedia of Walt Disney's Animated Characters, 1987, 2nd edition, 1997; Earthdoom (with David Langford), 1987; The Advanced Trivia Quizbook, 1987; Great Mysteries, 1988; Introduction to Viking Mythology, 1989; Great Unsolved Mysteries of Science, 1989; Eclipse of the Kai (with Joe Dever), 1989; The Dark Door Opens (with Joe Dever), 1989; Sword of the Sun (with Joe Dever), 1989; Hunting Wolf (with Joe Dever), 1990; Albion, 1991; Unexplained Mysteries of the World, 1991; The Claws of Helgedad (with Joe Dever), 1991; The Sacrifice of Ruanon (with Joe Dever), 1991; The World, 1992; Monsters, 1992; The Birthplace (with Joe Dever), 1992; The Book of the Magnakai (with Joe Dever), 1992; Legends of Lone Wolf Omnibus (with Joe Dever), 1992; The Tellings (with Joe Dever), 1993; The Lorestone of Varetta (with Joe Dever), 1993; Technical Encyclopedia of Science Fiction, by John Clute and Peter Nicholls (editor), 1993; A Thog the Mighty Text (history book), 1994; The Secret of Kazan-Oud (with Joe Dever), 1994; The Rotting Land (with Joe Dever), 1994; The Hundredfold Problem, 1994; Dr Jekyll and Mr Hyde, 1995; Encyclopedia of Fantasy Art Techniques (with Ron Tiner). 1996; Frankenstein, 1997; Encyclopedia of Fantasy (co-editor, with John Clute), 1997. As Paul Barnett: Translation and Expansion, Electric Children: Roots and Branches of Modern Folk-Rock, 1976; Planet Earth: An Encyclopedia of Geology (co-editor, with A Hallam and Peter Hutchinson); Phaidon Concise Encyclopedia of Science and Technology (contributing editor), 1978; Strider's Galaxy, 1997. Eve Devereux: Book of World Flags, 1992; Ultimate Card Trick Book, 1994; Pamper Your Pooch, 1996; Cosset Your Cat, 1996. As Armytage Ware (joint pseudonym with Ron Tiner): Parlour Games, 1992; Conjuring Tricks, 1992; Juggling and Feats of Dexterity, 1992; Card Games, 1992. As Freddie Duff-Ware (joint pseudonym with Ron Tiner): Practical Jokes, 1993. Membership: West Country Writers'

Association. Literary Agent: Robert Kirby (Sheila Land). Address: 17 Polsloe Road, Exeter, Devon EX1 2HL, England.

BARNRIGHT Julia. See: **BANCROFT Iris.**

BARON J W. See: **KRAUZER Steven M.**

BARR Densil Neve. See: **BUTTREY Douglas N.**

BARR Patricia Miriam, b. 25 Apr 1934, Norwich, Norfolk, England. Writer. Education: BA, University of Birmingham; MA, University College, London. Publications: The Coming of the Barbarians, 1967; The Deer Cry Pavilion, 1968; A Curious Life for a Lady, 1970; To China with Love, 1972; The Memsahibs, 1976; Taming the Jungle, 1978; Chinese Alice, 1981; Uncut Jade, 1983; Kenjiro, 1985; Coromandel, 1988; The Dust in the Balance, 1989. Honour: Winston Churchill Fellowship for Historical Biography, 1972. Membership: Society of Authors. Literary Agent: David Higham Associates, 5 Lower John Street, London W1R 4HA. Address: 6 Mount Pleasant, Norwich NR2 2DG, England.

BARRERA Carlos, b. 11 Aug 1962, Burgos, Spain. University Professor and Journalist. Education: PhD, Public Communication, University of Navarra, Spain, 1991. Publications: La Informacion como Relato, co-editor, 1991; Historia del Periodismo Espanol, co-author, 1992; Periodismo y Franquismo, 1995; Sin Mordaza Veinte Años de Prensa en Democracia, 1995; El Diario Madrid: Realidad y Simbolo de Una Epoca, 1995. Contributions to: Several articles in scientific reviews, mainly Historia 16 and Comunicacion y Sociedad. Memberships: Asociacion de Historiadores de la Comunicacion; AIERI-IAMCR (History Section); AEJMC (History Section). Address: Department of Public Communication, University of Navarra, 31080 Pamplona, Spain.

BARRETT Cathlene Gillespie, b. 14 Aug 1962, Utah, USA. Poet; Publisher; Editor. m. Kevin Barrett, 29 Aug 1981, 1 son, 1 daughter. Education: College. Appointment: Publisher, Editor, Midge Literary Magazine, 1991-. Contributions to: Anthologies and periodicals. Honours: Golden Poet Award; Honorable Mention, Poet of the Year, Utah State Poetry Society. Membership: Utah State Poetry Society. Address: 2330 Tierra Rose Drive, West Jordan, UT 84084, USA.

BARRETT Charles Kingsley, b. 4 May 1917, Salford, England. Retired University Professor. m. Margaret E Heap, 16 Aug 1944, 1 son, 1 daughter. Education: BA 1938, MA 1942, BD 1948, DD 1956. Cambridge University, England. Appointments: Lecturer, 1945-58, Professor, 1958-82, University of Durham. Publications: The Holy Spirit and the Gospel Tradition, 1947; The Epistle to the Romans, 1957, new edition 1991; From First Adam to Last, 1962; The First Epistle to the Corinthians, 1968; The Signs of an Apostle, 1970; The Second Epistle to the Corinthians, 1973; The Gospel According to St John, 1955, new edition, 1978; Freedom and Obligation, 1985; Paul: An Introduction to His Thought, 1994; The Acts of the Apostles, Volume 1, 1994. Contributions to: Many learned journals. Honours: Fellow, British Academy, 1961; Burkitt Medal for Biblical Studies, 1966; Honorary DD, Hull University, 1970; Aberdeen University, 1972; DTheol, Hamburg University, 1981. Memberships: Studiorum Novi Testamenti Societas, President, 1973-74; Society for Old Testament Study; Royal Norwegian Society of Sciences and Letters, 1991. Address: 22 Rosemount, Pity Me, Durham DH1 5GA, England.

BARRETT Susan (Mary), b. 24 June 1938, Plymouth, England. Writer. m. Peter Barrett, 18 June 1960, 1 son, 1 daughter. Publications: Louisa, 1969; Moses, 1970; The Circle Sarah Drew (with Peter Barrett), 1970; The Square Ben Drew (with Peter Barrett), 1970; Noah's Ark, 1971; Private View, 1972; Rubbish, 1974; The Beacon, 1981; Travels with a Wildlife Artist: Greek Landscape and Wildlife (with Peter Barrett), 1986; Stephen and Violet, 1988; A Day in the Life of a Baby Deer: The Fawn's First Snowfall (with Peter Barrett), 1996. Address: c/o Toby Eady Associates Ltd, Orme Court, 3rd Floor, London W2 4RL England.

BARRINGTON Judith Mary, b. 7 July 1944, Brighton, England. Poets; Critic. Education: BA 1978, MA 1980. Appointments: West Coast Editor, Motheroot Journal, 1985-86; Poet in the Schools, Oregon, 1986-87. Publications: Deviation, 1975; Why Children (co-author), 1980; Trying to Be an Honest Woman, 1985; History and Geography, 1989; An Intimate Wilderness (editor). 1991; Anthologies:

Work in: One Foot on the Mountain, 1979; Hard Feelings, 1982; Beautiful Barbarians, 1986; The World Between Women, 1987. Contributions to: Contemporary Literary Criticism; Northwest Magazine; San Francisco Chronicle; Ottawa Citizen; MS Magazine. Honours: Fairlie Place Essay Prize, 1963; Jeanette Rankin Award for Feminist Journalism, 1983; Metropolitan Arts Commission Grant, 1985, 1987; Oregon Institute of Literary Arts Fellowship (Creative Nonfiction), 1989 and Poetry, 1992. Memberships: Poetry Society of America; National Writers; Union; National Book of Critics Circle. Address: 622 South East 29th Avenue, Portland, OR 97214, USA.

BARRON Judith (Welch), b. 3 Aug 1939, Youngstown, Ohio, USA. Lyricist; Author. m. John Ronald Barron, 12 Sept 1959, 1 son, 1 daughter. Education: Grove City College; BEd, Youngstown State University, 1969. Publication: There's a Boy in Here, 1992. Honour: Christopher Award, 1993. Membership: American Society of Composers, Authors and Publishers. Literary Agent: Jed Mattes. Address: 529 West 42nd Street, No 7F, New York, NY 10036, USA.

BARROS Joseph De, b. 22 July 1921, Goa. History Research; Writer. Education: MA, PhD, DLitt. Appointments: Professor, Principal, National Lyceum, Goa; Doctoral Research Teacher, Goa University; General Secretary, Institute Menezes, Braganza. Publications: Geography of Goa; History of Goa; Buddhism and World Peace; Francisco Luis Gomes - The Historian. Contributions to: Navhind Times; Herald; Institute Menezea Braganza; Bulletin; R C Acau; Gomantak Times. Memberships: Indian Academy of Science; Academia Portuguesa da Historia; Academia Canadense de Historia; Geographic Society, Lisbon; Royal Asiatic Society of London; Indian History Congress, New Delhi; World Academy of Arts and Culture; Institute Menezes Braganza. Address: PO Box 221, Institute Menezes Braganza, Panaji Gao, India.

BARROW Iris (Lena), b. 8 Oct 1933, Auckland, New Zealand. Psychological Counsellor; Human Resources Consultant; Author. m. Robert Barrow, 1 son, 4 daughters. Education: ATCL, Speech and Communications, 1952. Appointment: Head, Seminar/Counselling Agency; Human Resources Consultant. Publications: Your Marriage Can Work, 1979; Relax and Come Alive (with Helen Place), 1981; Know Your Strengths and Be Confident, 1982; You Can Communicate, 1983; 15 Steps to Overcome Anxiety and Depression, 1985; From Strength to Strength, 1988; Make Peace with Yourself, 1990; You Can Do It, 1993; How to Lead and Motivate Others, 1995. Other: Radio plays; 8 self-help personal and interpersonal skills-training tapes, 1981-89; Video training tape: Celebrating Life with Iris Barrow, 1990. Contributions to: Various periodicals. Memberships: New Zealand PEN. Address: 334 Onemana Drive, Onemana Beach, Whangamata, New Zealand.

BARROW Robin St Clair, b. 18 Nov 1944, Oxford, England. Professor of Education; Author. Education: BA, MA, 1967, Oxford University; Postgraduate Certificate in Education, Institute of Education, London, 1968; PhD, University of London, 1972. Appointments: Lecturer in Philosophy of Education, 1972-80, Personal Readership in Education, 1980-82, University of Leicester; Visiting Professor of Philosophy of Education, University of Western Ontario, 1977-78; Professor of Education, 1982-, Dean of Education, 1992-, Simon Fraser University, Burnaby, British Columbia. Publications: Athenian Democracy, 1973, 2nd edition, 1976; An Introduction to the Philosophy of Education, 1974, 3rd edition, 1987; Sparta, 1975; Plato, Utilitarianism and Education, 1975; Moral Philosophy for Education, 1975; Greek and Roman Education, 1976; Plato and Education, 1976; Common Sense and the Curriculum, 1976; Plato's Apology, 1978; The Canadian Curriculum: A Personal View, 1978; Radical Education, 1978; Happiness, 1979; The Philosophy of Schooling, 1981, 2nd edition. 1983; Injustice, Inequality and Ethics, 1982; Language and Thought: Rethinking Language Across the Curriculum, 1982; Giving Teaching Back to Teachers: A Critical Introduction to Curriculum Theory. 1984; A Critical Dictionary of Educational Concepts: An Appraisal of Selected Ideas and Issues in Educational Theory and Practice. 1986, 2nd edition, 1990; Understanding Skills: Thinking, Feeling and Caring, 1990; Utilitarianism: A Contemporary Statement, 1991; Beyond Liberal Education (editor with Patricia White), 1993; Language, Intelligence and Thought, 1993. Contributions to: Books and scholarly journals. Memberships: Philosophy of Education Society of Great Britain. vice chairman, 1980-83; Northwestern Philosophy of Education Society of North America, president, 1984-85; Canadian Philosophy of Education Society. president, 1990-91; Royal Society of

Canada, fellow, 1996-. Address: Faculty of Education, Simon Fraser University, Burnaby, British Columbia V5A 1S6, Canada.

BARRY James P, b. 23 Oct 1918, Alton, Illinois, USA. Writer; Editor. m. Anne Elizabeth Jackson, 16 Apr 1966. Education: BA cum laude, Ohio State University. Appointments: Director, Ohioana Library Association, 1977-88; Editor, Ohioana Quarterly, 1977-88. Publications: Georgian Bay: The Sixth Great Lake, 1968, 3rd edition, 1995; The Battle of Lake Erie, 1970; Bloody Kansas, 1972; The Noble Experiment, 1972; The Fate of the Lakes, 1972; The Louisiana Purchase, 1973; Ships of the Great Lakes: 300 Years of Navigation, 1973, revised edition, 1996; Wrecks and Rescues of the Great Lakes, 1981; Georgian Bay: An Illustrated History, 1992; Old Forts of the Great Lakes, 1994. Honours: American Society of State and Local History Award, 1974; Great Lakes Historian of the Year, Marine History Society of Detroit, 1995. Membership: Ohioana Library Association. Address: 353 Fairway Boulevard, Columbus, OH 43213, USA.

BARRY Mike. See: **MALZBERG Barry.**

BARRY Sebastian, b. 5 July 1955, England. Writer. Education: LCC, Newend, London; Catholic University School, Dublin; BA, Trinity College, Dublin, 1977. Appointments: Iowa International Writing Fellowship, 1984; Writer in Association, Abbey Theatre, Dublin, 1989-90; Director of Board, Abbey Theatre, 1989-90. Publications: The Engine of Owl-Light, 1987; Boss Grady's Boys, play, 1989; Fanny Hawke Goes to the Mainland Forever, verse, 1989. Contributions to: Antaeus; London Review of Books; Stand; Observer. Honours: Arts Council Bursary, 1982; Hawthornden International Fellowships, 1985, 1988; BBC/Stewart Parker Award, 1989. Memberships: Irish Writers' Union; Aosdana; Half Moon Swimming Club. Literary Agent: Curtis Brown Ltd, Haymarket House, 28-29 Haymarket, London. Address: c/o The Abbey Theatre, Abbey Street, Dublin 1, Ireland.

BARSTOW Stan(ley), b. 28 June 1928, Horbury, Yorkshire, England. Author; Playwright; Scriptwriter. m. Constance Mary Kershaw, 8 Sept 1951, 1 son, 1 daughter. Publications: Novels: A Kind of Loving, 1960; Ask Me Tomorrow, 1962; Joby, 1964; The Watchers on the Shore, 1966; A Raging Calm, 1968; The Right True End, 1976; A Brother's Tale, 1980; Just You Wait and See, 1986; B-Movie, 1987; Give Us This Day, 1989; Next of Kin, 1991. Short Stories: The Desperados, 1961; A Season with Eros, 1971; The Glad Eye and Other Stories, 1984. Plays: Listen for the Trains, Love, 1970; Stringer's Last Stand (with Alfred Bradley), 1971. Other: Television plays and scripts. Honours: Best British Dramatization Award, Writers Guild of Great Britain, 1974; Best Drama Series Award, British Broadcasting Press Guild, 1974; Writer's Award, Royal Television Society, 1975; Honorary MA, Open University, 1982; Honorary Fellow, Bretton College, 1985. Address: c/o Lemon, Unna and Durbridge Ltd, 24 Pottery Lane, London W11 4LZ, England.

BARTH John (Simmons), b. 27 May 1930, Cambridge, Maryland, USA. Professor Emeritus; Author. m. (1) Harriette Anne Strickland, 11 Jan 1950, div 1969, 2 sons, 1 daughter, (2) Shelly Rosenberg, 27 Dec 1970. Education: Juilliard School of Music; AB, 1951, MA, 1952, Johns Hopkins University. Appointments: Instructor, 1953-56, Assistant Professor, 1957-60, Associate Professor, 1960-65, of English, Penn State University; Professor of English, 1965-71, Edward H Butler Professor of English, 1971-73, State University of New York at Buffalo; Alumni Centennial Professor of English and Creative Writing, 1973-90, Professor Emeritus, 1990-, Johns Hopkins University. Publications: Fiction: The Floating Opera, 1956, revised edition, 1967; The End of the Road, 1958, revised edition, 1967; The Sot-Weed Factor, 1960, revised edition, 1967; Giles, Goat-Boy: or, the Revised New Syllabus, 1966; Lost in the Funhouse: Fiction for Print, Tape, Live Voice. 1964; Chimera, 1972; LETTERS, 1979; Sabbatical: A Romance, 1982; Tidewater Tales: A Novel, 1987; The Last Voyage of Somebody the Sailor, 1991; Once Upon a Time: A Floating Opera, 1994; On with the Story (short stories), 1996. Non-Fiction: The Literature of Exhaustion, and the Literature of Replenishment, 1982; The Friday Book: Essays and Other Nonfiction, 1984; Don't Count on It: A Note on the Number of 1001 Nights, 1984; Further Fridays: Essays, Lectures, and Other Nonfiction, 1984-1994, 1995. Contributions to: Books and many periodicals. Honours: Brandeis University Creative Arts Award, 1965; Rockefeller Foundation Grant, 1965-66; National Institute of Arts and Letters Grant, 1966; National Book Award, 1973. Memberships: American Academy and Institute of Arts and Letters; American Academy of Arts and Sciences. Address: 5630 Langford Bay Road, Chestertown, MD 21620, USA.

BARTH J(ohn) Robert, b. 23 Feb 1931, Buffalo, New York, USA. College Dean; Writer. Education: AB, 1954, MA, 1956, Fordham University; PhL, Bellarmine College, 1955; STB, 1961, STL, 1962, Woodstock College; PhD in English, Harvard University, 1967. Appointments: Society of Jesus; Assistant Professor of English, Canisius College, Buffalo, 1967-70; Assistant Professor of English, Harvard University, 1970-74; Associate Professor of English, 1974-77, Professor of English, 1977-88, Chairman, Department of English, 1980-83, University of Missouri-Columbia; Thomas I Gasson Professor of English, 1985-86; Dean, College of Arts and Sciences, Boston College, 1988-. Publications: Coleridge and Christian Doctrine, 1969; Religious Perspectives in Faulkner's Fiction Yoknapatawpha and Beyond (editor), 1972; The Symbolic Imagination: Coleridge and the Romantic Tradition, 1977; Marginalia: The Collected Works of Samuel Taylor Coleridge (co-editor with George Whalley), 1984-; Coleridge and the Power of Love, 1988; Coleridge, Keats and the Imagination: Romanticism and Adam's Dream-Essays in Honor of Walter Jackson Bate (co-editor with John L Mahoney), 1990. Contributions to: Books and journals. Honour: Book of the Year Award, Conference on Christianity and Literature, 1977. Memberships: American Association of University Professors; Conference on Christianity and Literature; English Institute; Keats-Shelley Association; Modern Language Association; Wordsworth-Coleridge Association, President, 1979. Address: Office of the Dean, College of Arts and Sciences, Boston College, Chestnut Hill, MA 02167, USA.

BARTHELME Frederick, b. 10 Oct 1943, Houston, Texas, USA. Professor of English; Writer; Editor. Education: Tulane University, 1961-62; University of Houston, 1962-65, 1966-67; Museum of Fine Art, Houston, 1965-66; MA, Johns Hopkins University, 1977. Appointments: Assistant Director, Kornblee Gallery, New York, 1967-68; Creative Director, BMA Advertising, Houston, 1971-73; Senior Writer, GDL&W Advertising, Houston, 1973-76; Teaching Fellow, Johns Hopkins University, 1976-77; Professor of English, Director, Center for Writers, Editor, Mississippi Review, University of Southern Mississippi, Hattiesburg, 1977-. Publications: Rangoon (stories), 1970; War & War, 1971; Moon Deluxe (stories), 1983; Second Marriage, 1984; Tracer, 1985; Chroma (stories), 1987; Two Against One, 1988; Natural Selection, 1990; The Brothers, 1993; Painted Desert, 1995. Screenplays: Second Marriage, 1985; Tracer, 1986-87. Contributions to: Periodicals. Honour: National Endowment for the Arts Grant, 1980. Memberships: Associated Writing Programs; Author's Guild; Coordinating Council of Literary Magazines; PEN; Writers Guild. Address: 203 Sherwood Drive, Hattiesburg, MS 39402, USA.

BARTHELMESS Klaus, b. 4 Sept 1955, Cologne, Germany. Historian; Whaling Expert. m. Helga Kietzmann, 1992, 1 son. Education: MA, University of Cologne, 1989 (PhD pending). Appointments: Kendall Whaling Museum, Sharon, Massachusetts, 1987; German Maritime Museum, Bremerhaven, 1991; Cologne Historic Museum, 1996. Publications: Das Bild des Wals, 1982; Monstrum Horrendum (with Joachim Münzing), 1991; Whaling - Con & Pro, 1994; Dozens of scholarly articles on whaling, sealing, the history of cetology. Memberships: Editorial Board of Historisch-Meereskundliches Jahrbuch, Berlin & Hamburg; International Network for Whaling INWR Digest, Edmonton, Alberta. Address: PO Box 620255, 50695 Cologne, Germany.

BARTHOLET Jeffrey Ives. Tokyo Bureau Chief, Newsweek. Education: Graduate Degree in Middle East Studies; Diploma in Arabic Language Studies, American University, Cairo; BA, Philosophy and Political Science, University of Vermont; Studied at Birzeit University, Israeli-occupied West Bank. Appointments: Reporter, Norwich Bulletin, Connecticut, 1981, 1982; Freelance Special Correspondent, Washington Post, Cairo; Writer, Newsweek, Chicago Tribune and Boston Globe; Middle East Correspondent, Reuters News Agency, 1987-89; Nairobi Bureau Chief, 1989, Jerusalem Bureau Chief, 1993-96, Tokyo Bureau Chief, 1996-, Newsweek. Honours: Co-Winner, Lincoln University of Missouri Unity Award. Address: c/o Newsweek, 251 West 57th Street, New York, NY 10019-1894, USA.

BARTKOWIAK Tadeusz Ludwik, b. 19 Aug 1942, Tomaszow Mazowiecki, Poland. Journalist. m. 30 Dec 1968, 1 son. Education: Diploma, Poznan Teachers College, 1962; Diploma, Philosophical and Historical Faculty, Adam Mickiewicz University, Poznan, 1967; Diploma, Evening University of Marxism-Leninism, 1985. Appointment: Editorial Staff, Poznan Newspaper, 1972-. Publications: The Western Watch-Tower, 1922-1939; New Materials on the Battle of Poznan,

1945; A Chronicle of Poznan City; The Polish Association of Philatelists in Poznan, 1969-74; The Poznan Newspaper, 2.V.87-9.VI.87; The Union of Poles in Germany, 1922-87; Almanac of Polish Emigrants Society, 1985. Honours: 5 awards, Polish Journalists Association, 1976-85. Memberships: Polish Journalists Association; International Union of Philatelic Journalists; Polish Club of Marine Painters and Writers. Address: Osiedle Rzeczypospolitej 14 m 33, 61-397 Poznan, Poland.

BARTLETT Christopher John, b. 12 Oct 1931, Bournemouth, England. University Professor of International History. m. Shirley Maureen Briggs, 7 Aug 1958, 3 sons. Education: University College, Exeter, 1950-53; 1st Class Honours, History (London External), PhD, International History, London School of Economics. Publications: Great Britain and Sea Power 1815-53, 1963; Castlereagh, 1966; The Long Retreat (British Defence Policy 1945-70), 1972; The Rise and Fall of the Pax Americana, 1974; A History of Postwar Britain, 1945-74, 1977; British Foreign Policy in the Twentieth Century, 1989; The Special Relationship: A Political History of Anglo-American Relations Since 1945, 1992; Defence and Diplomacy: Britain and the Great Powers, 1815-1914, 1993; The Global Conflict, 1880-1990, 1994; Peace, War and the European Great Powers 1814-1914, 1996. Contributions to: English Historical Review; History; Annual Register. Memberships: Fellow, Royal Historial Society; Fellow, Royal Society of Edinburgh. Address: History Department, The University, Dundee DD1 4HN, Scotland.

BARTLETT Elizabeth, b. 28 Apr 1924, Deal, Kent, England. Poet. Education: Dover County School for Girls, 1935-39. Appointment: Lecturer, Workers Education Association, Burgess Hill, 1960-63. Publications: A Lifetime of Dying, 1979; Strange Territory, 1983; The Czar is Dead, 1986; Look, No Face, 1991; Instead of a Mass, 1991; Two Women Dancing, 1994. Honours: Cheltenham Poetry Competition Prize, 1982; Arts Council Bursary, 1985; Cholmondeley Award, Society of Authors, 1996. Address: 17 St John's Avenue, Burgess Hill, West Sussex RH15 8HJ, England.

BARTOSZEWSKI Wladyslaw, b. 19 Feb 1922, Warsaw, Poland. Writer; Historian; Diplomat. Education: Doctor honoris causa, Polish University in exile, London, 1981; Baltimore Hebrew College, USA, 1984. Appointments: Vice President, Institute for Polish Jewish Studies, Oxford, England; Visiting Professor, Munich, Eichstaett, Augsburg, 1983-90; Voted Chairman, International Council of the Museum, Auschwitz, 1990; Polish Ambassador in Vienna, 1990-95; Polish Foreign Minister, 1995. Publications: Warsaw Death Ring, 1939-44, 2nd edition, 1970; The Samaritans, Heroes of the Holocaust (with Z Lewin), 1970; 1859 Days of Warsaw, 1974; The Warsaw Ghetto As It Really Was, 1983; Days of the Fighting Capital: A Chronicle of the Warsaw Uprising, 1984; On the Road to Independence, 1987; Experiences of My Life, 1989. Contributions to: Various Catholic Magazines and Papers. Honours: Polish Military Cross, 1944; Medal and Title of the Righteous Among the Nations, the Martyrs and Heroes Remembrance Yad Vashem, Jerusalem, 1963; Prize, Alfred Jurzykowski Foundation, New York, 1967; Prize, Polish Pen, Warsaw, 1975; Herder Prize, Vienna, 1983; Peace Prize, German Publishers' and Booksellers Association, 1986; Commander, Polonia Restituta (with Star), London, 1986; Honorary Citizen of the State of Israel, 1991; Distinguished Service Cross, Order of Merit of Germany, 1991; Austrian Cross of Honour for Science and Art, 1st Class, 1992; R Guardini Prize, Munich, 1995; Mitteleuropa Prize, Vienna, 1995; Brücken Prize, Regensburg, 1995; St Vincent de Paul Award, Chicago, 1995; Order of the White Eagle, Warsaw, 1995; Grand Decoration of Honour in Gold with Sash for Services to the Republic of Austria, Vienna, 1995; Heinrich Heine Prize, Düsseldorf, 1996; Honorary Doctorate, University of Wroclaw, Poland, 1996. Memberships: Polish PEN, Secretary General, 1972-83, Board Member, 1988-90, Vice President, 1995-; Associate Member, French PEN. Address: ul Karolinki 12, 02 635 Warsaw, Poland.

BARTSCH William Henry, b. 18 Jan 1933, Washington, DC, USA. Military Historian; Development Economist. m. Lila Sepehri, 5 Aug 1965, 1 son, 1 daughter. Education: BA, Washington and Lee University, 1955; Fulbright Fellow to Sweden, 1956-57; MA, University of Virginia, 1959; PhD, University of London, 1970. Publications: Problems of Employment Creation in Iran, 1970; Draft Chapters of Human Resources for Development Plans of Fiji, Marshall Islands and Federated States of Micronsia, 1975, 1986-90; Employment and Technology Choice in Asian Agriculture, 1977; Doomed at the Start, 1992. Contributions to: Articles on employment problems and planning in developing countries, 1971-90. Honour: Phi Beta Kappa, 1955. Address: 2434 Brussels Court, Reston, VA 22091-2508, USA.

BARTUSIAK Marcia Frances, b. 30 Jan 1950, Chester, Pennsylvania, USA. Science Writer; Author. m. Stephen A Lowe, 10 Sept 1988. Education: BA, Communications, American University, 1971; MS, Physics, Old Dominion University, Norfolk, 1979. Appointments: Writer, Science News, 1979; Discover Magazine, 1980-82; Contributing Editor, Discover, 1990-; Contributor, The New York Times Book Review, 1986-. Publications: Thursday's Universe; Through a Universe Darkly. Contributions to: Discover; Science Digest; Omni; Popular Science; Air & Space; Reader's Digest. Honours: American Institute of Physics Science Writing Award; Astronomy Book of the Year; NASA Journalist in Space Finalist. Memberships: Authors Guild; National Association of Science Writers; Sigma Xi Honor Society. Literary Agent: Scovil Chichak Galen Literary Agency. Address: c/o Scovil Chichak Galen Literary Agency, 381 Park Avenue South, Suite 1112, New York, NY 10016, USA.

BARZUN Jacques (Martin), b. 30 Nov 1907, Créteil, France (US citizen, 1933). Historian; Educator. m. (1) Mariana Lowell, Aug 1936, dec 1979, 2 sons, 1 daughter, (2) Marguerite Davenport, June 1980. Education: AB, 1927, MA, 1928, PhD, 1932, Columbia University. Appointments: Lecturer, 1927-29, Assistant Professor, 1938-42, Associate Professor, 1942-45, Professor, 1945-67, Dean, Graduate Faculties, 1955-58, Dean, Faculties and Provost, 1958-67, Professor Emeritus, 1967-, Columbia University; Literary Advisor, Charles Scribner's Sons, publishers, New York City, 1975-93. Publications: The French Race: Theories of Its Origins and Their Social and Political Implications Prior to the Revolution, 1932; Race: A Study in Modern Superstition, 1937, revised edition as Race: A Study in Superstition, 1956; Of Human Freedom, 1939, revised edition, 1964; Darwin, Marx, Wagner: Critique of a Heritage, 1941, revised edition, 1958; Romanticism and the Modern Ego, 1943, 2nd edition, revised, as Classic, Romantic, and Modern, 1961; Introduction to Naval History (with Paul H Beik, George Crothers and E O Golob), 1944; Teacher in America, 1945; Berlioz and the Romantic Century, 1950, 3rd edition, revised, 1969; God's Country and Mine: A Declaration of Love Spiced with a Few Harsh Words, 1954; Music in American Life, 1956; The Energies of Art: Studies of Authors, Classic and Modern, 1956; The Modern Researcher (with Henry F Graff), 1957, 5th edition, 1993; Lincoln the Literary Genius, 1959; The House of Intellect, 1959, 2nd edition, 1975; Science: The Glorious Entertainment, 1964; The American University: How It Runs, Where It Is Going, 1968; On Writing, Editing and Publishing: Essays Explicative and Horatory, 1971; A Catalogue of Crime (with Wendell Hertig Taylor), 1971; The Use and Abuse of Art, 1974; Clio and the Doctors: Psycho-History, Quanto-History and History, 1974; Simple and Direct: A Rhetoric for Writers, 1975; A Stroll with William James, 1983; A Word or Two Before You Go..., 1986; The Culture We Deserve, 1989; Begin Here: On Teaching and Learning, 1990; An Essay on French Verse, 1991. Other: Editor and translator of several books. Contributions to: Scholarly and non-scholarly periodicals. Honours: Chevalier de la Légion d'Honneur, France; George Polk Memorial Award, 1967. Memberships: American Academy and Institute of Arts and Letters, president, 1972-75, 1977-78; American Academy of Arts and Sciences; American Philosophical Society; Phi Beta Kappa; Royal Society of Fine Arts, fellow; Royal Society of Literature; Society of American Historians. Address: 18 Wolfton Way, San Antonio, TX 78218, USA.

BASINGER Jeanine (Deyling), b. 3 Feb 1936, Ravenden, Arkansas, USA. Professor of Film Studies; Curator; Writer. m. John Peter Basinger, 22 Sept 1967, 1 daughter. Education: BS, 1957, MS, 1959, South Dakota State University. Appointments: Instructor, South Dakota State University, 1958-59; Teaching Associate, 1971-72, Adjunct Lecturer, 1972-76, Adjunct Associate Professor, 1976-80, Associate Professor, 1980-84, Professor, 1984-88, Corwin-Fuller Professor of Film Studies, 1988-, Wesleyan University; Founder-Curator, Wesleyan Cinema Archives, 1985-. Publications: Working with Kazan (editor with John Frazer and Joseph W Reed), 1973; Shirley Temple, 1975; Gene Kelly, 1976; Lana Turner, 1977; Anthony Mann: A Critical Analysis, 1979; Anatomy of a Genre: World War II Combat Films, 1986; The It's A Wonderful Life Book, 1986; A Woman's View: How Hollywood Saw Women, 1930-1960, 1993; American Cinema: 100 Years of Filmmaking, 1994. Contributions to: Books and periodicals. Honours: Best Film Book of the Year Nomination, National Film Society, 1976; Distinguished Alumni Award, 1994 and Honorary PhD, 1996, South Dakota State University;

Outstanding Teaching Award, Wesleyan University, 1996. Memberships: Trustee, American Film Institute; Phi Kappa Phi. Address: 133 Lincoln Street, Middletown, CT 06457, USA.

BASS Jack, b. 24 June 1934, Columbia, South Carolina, USA. Writer. m. Carolyn Mclung, 3 Mar 1957, div 1984, (2) Alice Calsaniss, 22 June 1984, 2 sons, 1 daughter. Education: AB, 1956, MA, 1976, Harvard University. Appointments: Bureau Chief, Knight Newspapers, Columbia, South Carolina, 1966-73; Visiting Research Fellow, Institute of Policy Sciences and Public Affairs, Duke University, 1973-75; Writer-in-Residence, South Carolina State College, 1975-78; Research Fellow, Director of American South Special Projects, University of South Carolina, 1979-85. Publications: The Orangeburg Massacre (with Jack Nelson), 1970; You Can't Eat Magnolias (co-author), 1972; Porgy Comes Home, 1972; The Transformation of Southern Politics (with Walter DeVires), 1978; Unlikely Heroes, 1981; The American South Comes of Age, 1985; Taming the Storm, 1993. Address: 2327 Terrace Way, Columbia, SC 29205, USA.

BASS Rick, b. 7 Mar 1958, Fort Worth, Texas, USA. Writer. Education: BS, Utah State University, 1979. Publications: The Deer Pasture, 1985; Wild to the Heart, 1987; Oil Notes, 1989; The Watch: Stories, 1989; Platte River, 1994; The Lost Grizzlies, 1995; In the Loyal Mountains: Stories, 1995; The Book of YAAK, 1996. Contributions to: Anthologies and periodicals. Honours: Pushcart Prize; O Henry Award; PEN-Nelson Award, 1988. Address: 3801 Vinal Lake Road, Troy, MT 59935, USA.

BASS Thomas (Alden), b. 9 Mar 1951, Chagrin Falls, Ohio, USA. Writer. Education: AB, University of Chicago, 1973; PhD, University of California, 1980. Publications: The Eudaemonic Pie, 1985; Camping with the Prince and Other Tales of Science in Africa, 1990; Reinventing the Future: Conversations with the World's Leading Scientists, 1993. Contributions to: Audubon; New York Times; Smithsonian. Memberships: Authors Guild; PEN. Address: 31 Rue Saint Placide, Paris 75006, France.

BASSETT Ronald Leslie, (William Clive), b. 10 Apr 1924, London, England. Writer. Appointments: Served with King's Royal Rifle Corps, 1938-1939, Royal Navy, 1940-54; Full-time Author, Documentary and medical film scriptwriter, 1958-. Publications: The Carthaginian, 1963; The Pompeians, 1965; Witchfinder General, 1966; Amorous Trooper, 1968; Rebecca's Brat, 1969; Kill the Stuart, 1970; Dando on Delhi Ridge (as W Clive), 1971; Dando and the Summer Palace (as W Clive), 1972; Dando and the Mad Emporer (as W Clive), 1973; The Tune That They Play (as W Clive), 1974; Blood of an Englishman (as W Clive), 1975; Fighting Mac (as W Clive), 1976; Tinfish Run, 1977; Pierhead Jump, 1978; Neptune Landing, 1979; Guns of Evening, 1980; Battle-Cruisers, 1982. Address: 19 Binstead Drive, Blackwater, Camberley, Surrey, England.

BATARDE Eduarde. See: **THOMPSON Tom.**

BATCHELOR John Barham, b. 15 Mar 1942, Farnborough, England. University Teacher. m. Henrietta Jane Letts, 14 Sept 1968, 2 sons, 1 daughter. Education: MA, 1964, PhD, 1969, Magdalene College, Cambridge; MA, University of New Brunswick, 1965. Appointments: Lecturer in English, Birmingham University, 1968-76; Fellow and Tutor, New College, Oxford, 1976-90; Joseph Cowen Professor of English Literature, University of Newcastle upon Tyne, 1990-. Publications: Mervyn Peake, 1974; Breathless Hush (novel), 1974; The Edwardian Novelists, 1982; Lord Jim (World's Classics Edition), 1983; H G Wells, 1985; Victory (World's Classics Edition), 1986; Lord Jim (Unwin Critical Library), 1988; Virginia Woolf, 1991; The Life of Joseph Conrad: A Critical Biography, 1994; Editor, The Art of Literary Biography, 1995. Contributions to: Reviews for: Times Literary Supplement; Observer; Economist; Articles in English, Yearbook of English Studies; Review of English Studies. Membership: International Association of Professors of English. Literary Agent: Felicity Bryan, 2a North Parade, Oxford. Address: Department of English, University of Newcastle, Newcastle upon Tyne NE1 7RU, England.

BATE Jonathan, b. 26 June 1958, England. Professor of English; Critic. m. Paula Byrne, 1996. Education: MA, PhD, St Catharine's College, Cambridge. Career: Fellow of Trinity Hall, Cambridge, and Director of Studies in English, 1985-90; King Alfred Professor of English Literature at the University of Liverpool, 1991-. Publications include: Shakespeare and the English Romantic

Imagination, 1986; Charles Lamb: Essays of Elia (editor), 1987; Shakespearean Constitution: Politics, Theatre, Criticism 1730-1830, 1989; Romantic Ecology: Wordsworth and the Environmental Tradition, 1991; The Romantics on Shakespeare (editor), 1992; Shakespeare and Ovid, 1993; The Arden Shakespeare: Titus Andronicus (editor), 1995; Shakespeare: An Illustrated Stage History (editor), 1996; The Genius of Shakespeare, 1997. Address: Department of English, PO Box 147, Liverpool, L69 3BX, England.

BATE Walter Jackson, b. 23 May 1918, Mankato, Minnesota, USA. Professor of English; Writer. Education: AB, 1939, MA, 1940, PhD, 1942, Harvard University. Appointments: Faculty, 1946-56, Professor of English, 1956-, Chairman, Department of English, 1956-63, 1966-68, Abbott Lawrence Lowell Professor of the Humanities, 1962-79, Kingsley Porter University Professor, 1979-, Harvard University; Various guest professorships. Publications: Negative Capability, 1939; The Stylistic Development of Keats, 1945; From Classic to Romantic, 1946; Criticism: The Major Texts, 1952; The Achievement of Samuel Johnson, 1955; Prefaces to Criticism, 1959; The Writings of Edmund Burke, 1960; John Keats, 1963; The Yale Edition of the Works of Samuel Johnson (co-editor), Vol II, 1963, Vols III-V, 1969; Coleridge, 1968; The Burden of the Past and the English Poet, 1970; Samuel Johnson, 1977; The Collected Works of Samuel Taylor Coleridge: Biographia Literaria (co-editor), 1982; British and American Poets, 1985; Harvard Scholars in English, 1991. Contributions to: Books and professional journals. Honours: Guggenheim Fellowships, 1956, 1965; Christian Gauss Awards, 1956, 1964, 1970; Pulitzer Prizes in Biography, 1964, 1978; Notable Book Award, 1978; Notable Book Critics Circle Award, 1978; Various honorary doctorates. Memberships: American Academy of Arts and Sciences; American Philosophical Society; British Academy; Phi Beta Kappa. Address: c/o Warren House, Harvard University, Cambridge, MA 02138, USA.

BATES Milton J(ames), b. 4 June 1945, Warrensburg, Missouri, USA. Professor of English; Writer. m. 6 May 1972, 1 son, 1 daughter. Education: BA, St Louis University, 1968; MA, 1972, PhD. 1977, University of California at Berkeley. Appointments: Assistant Professor of English, Williams College, 1975-81; Assistant Professor, 1981-86, Associate Professor, 1986-91, Professor, 1991-, of English, Marquette University. Publications: Wallace Stevens: A Mythology of Self, 1985; Sur Plusieurs Beaux Sujects: Wallace Stevens' Commonplace Book, 1989; Wallace Stevens: Opus Posthumous, revised edition, 1989; The Wars We Took to Vietnam: Cultural Conflict and Storytelling, 1996. Contributions to: Articles and book reviews in journals and periodicals. Honours: Notable Book of the Year, New York Times Book Review, 1985; Outstanding Achievement in Literature, Wisconsin Library Association, 1985; National Book Critics Circle Award Nomination, 1985; Guggenheim Fellowship, 1989-90. Memberships: Modern Language Association; Wallace Stevens Society, secretary, 1990-. Address: Department of English, Marquette University, Milwaukee, WI 53201, USA.

BATTESTIN Martin C(arey), b. 25 Mar 1930, New York, New York, USA. Professor of English; Author. m. Ruthe Rootes, 14 June 1963, 1 son, 1 daughter. Education: BA, 1952, PhD, 1958, Princeton University. Appointments: Instructor, 1956-58, Assistant Professor, 1958-61, Wesleyan University; Assistant Professor, 1961-63, Associate Professor, 1963-67, Professor, 1967-75, William R Kenan, Jr, Professor of English, 1975-, Chairman, Department of English, 1983-86, University of Virginia; Visiting Professor, Rice University, 1967-68; Associate, Clare Hall, Cambridge, England, 1972. Publications: The Moral Basis of Fielding's Art: A Study of "Joseph Andrews", 1959; The Providence of Wit: Aspects of Form in Augustan Literature and the Arts, 1974; New Essays by Fielding: His Contributions to "The Craftsman" (1734-39) and Other Early Journalism, 1989; Henry Fielding: A Life, with Ruthe R Battestin, 1989-90, corrected edition, 1993. Editor: Henry Fielding: Joseph Andrews and Shamela, 1961; Henry Fielding: The History of the Adventures of Joseph Andrews, 1967; Tom Jones: A Collection of Critical Essays, 1968; Henry Fielding: The History of Tom Jones, a Founding (with Fredson Bowers), 2 volumes, 1974, corrected edition, 1975; Henry Fielding: Amelia, 1983; British Novelists, 1660-1800, 1985; The Correspondence of Henry and Sarah Fielding (with Clive T Probyn), 1993. Contributions to: Books and scholarly journals. Honours: American Council of Learned Societies Fellowships, 1960-61, 1972; Guggenheim Fellowship, 1964-65; Council of the Humanities Senior Fellow, Princeton University, 1971-; Centre for Advanced Studies, University of Virginia, 1974-75; National

Endowment for the Humanities Bicentennial Research Fellow, 1975-76; Festschrift, 1997. Memberships: Association of Literary Critics and Scholars; American Society of 18th Century Studies; International Association of University Professors of English; The Johnsonians; Modern Language Association. Address: 1832 Westview Road, Charlottesville, VA 22903, USA.

BATTIN B W (S W Bradford, Alexander Brinton, Warner Lee, Casey McAllister), b. 15 Nov 1941, Ridgewood, New Jersey, USA. Writer. m. Sandra McCraw, 14 Feb 1976. Education: BA, University of New Mexico, 1969. Publications: as B W Battin: Angel of the Night, 1983; The Boogeyman, 1984; Satan's Servant, 1984; Mary, Mary, 1985; Programmed for Terror, 1985; The Attraction, 1985; The Creep, 1987; Smithereens, 1987; Demented 1988; as Warner Lee: Into the Pit, 1989; It's Loose, 1990; Night Sounds, 1992; as S W Bradford: Tender Prey, 1990; Fair Game, 1992; as Alexander Brinton: Serial Blood, 1992; as Casey McAllister: Catch Me if You Can, 1993. Literary Agent: Dominick Abel, New York. Address: 711 North Mesa Road, Belen, NM 87002, USA.

BATTISCOMBE E(sther) Georgina (Harwood), b. 21 Nov 1905, London, England. Biographer. m. Lt Col C F Battiscombe, 1 Oct 1932, 1 daughter. Education: St Michael's School, Oxford; BA Honours, History, Lady Margaret Hall, Oxford. Publications: Charlotte Mary Yonge, 1943; Mrs Gladstone, 1956; John Keble, 1963; Queen Alexandra, 1970; Lord Shaftesbury, 1974; Reluctant Pioneer, Life of Elizabeth Wordsworth, 1978; Christina Rossetti, 1981; The Spencers of Althorp, 1984; Winter Song, 1992. Contributions to: Times; Sunday Telegraph; Times Literary Supplement; Spectator; Country Life; Books & Bookmen; History Today. Honour: James Tait Black Prize, 1963. Memberships: Fellow, Royal Society of Literature; Society of Authors. Literary Agent: A M Heath & Company. Address: 40 Phyllis Court Drive, Henley-on-Thames, Oxfordshire RG9 2HU, England.

BATTLES Roxy (Edith Baker), b. 29 Mar 1921, Spokane, Washington, USA. Writer; Poet; Children's Author; Teacher. m. Willis Ralph Battles, 2 May 1941, 1 son, 2 daughters. Education: AA, Bakersfield Junior College, 1940; BA, California State University, 1959; MA, Pepperdine University, 1976. Appointments: Elementary Teacher, Torrance Unified Schools, 1959-85; Instructor, Torrance Adult School, 1968-88, Pepperdine University, 1976-79; Instructor, Creative Writing, Los Angeles Harbor College, 1995. Publications: Over the Rickety Fence, 1967; The Terrible Trick or Treat, 1970; 501 Balloons Sail East, 1971; The Terrible Terrier, 1972; One to Teeter Totter, 1973; Eddie Couldn't Find the Elephants, 1974; What Does the Rooster Say, Yoshio?, 1978; The Secret of Castle Drai, 1980; The Witch in Room 6, 1987; The Chemistry of Whispering Caves, 1989; The Lavender Castle, stage play, 1996. Contributions to: Numerous periodicals. Honours: National Science Award, 1971; United Nations Award, 1978; Author-in-Residence, American School of Madrid, Spain, 1991. Membership: Southwest Manuscripters. Address: 560 South Helberta Avenue, Redondo Beach, CA 90277, USA.

BAUER Caroline Feller, b. 12 May 1935, Washington, DC, USA. Author; Lecturer. m. 21 Dec 1969, 1 daughter. Education: BA, Sarah Lawrence College, 1956; MLS, Columbia University, 1958; PhD, University of Oregon, 1971. Publications: My Mom Travels a Lot, 1981; This Way to Books, 1983; Too Many Books, 1984; Celebrations, 1985; Rainy Day, 1986; Snowy Day, 1986; Midnight Snowman, 1987; Presenting Reader's Theater, 1987; Windy Day, 1988; Halloween, 1989; Read for the Fun of It, 1992; New Handbook for Storytellers, 1993; Putting on a Play, 1993; Valentine's Day, 1993; Thanksgiving Day, 1994; The Poetry Break, 1995; Leading Kids to Books Through Magic, 1996. Honours: ERSTED Award for Distinguished Teaching; Christopher Award; Dorothy McKenzie Award for Distinguished Contribution to Children's Literature. Memberships: American Library Association; Society of Children's Book Writers. Address: 10155 Collins Avenue, #402, Miami Beach, FL 33154, USA.

BAUER Steven (Albert), b. 10 Sept 1948, Newark, New Jersey, USA. Professor of English; Writer; Poet. m. Elizabeth Arthur, 19 June 1982. Education: BA, Trinity College, Hartford, Connecticut, 1970; MFA, University of Massachusetts, Amherst, 1975. Appointments: Instructor, 1979-81, Assistant Professor, 1981-82, Colby College, Waterville, Maine; Assistant Professor, 1982-86, Associate Professor, 1986-96, Professor, 1996-, of English, Director of Creative Writing, 1986-96, Internal Director of Creative Writing, 1996-, Miami University, Oxford, Ohio. Publications: Satyrday, novel, 1980; The River, novel, 1985; Steven Spielberg's Amazing Stories, 2 volumes, 1986; Daylight

Savings, poems, 1989; The Strange and Wonderful Tale of Robert McDoodle (Who Wanted to be a Dog), children's verse collection, 1997. Contributions to: Essays, stories and poems in many periodicals. Honours: Strouse Award for Poetry, Prairie Schooner, 1982; Master Artist Fellowship Award, Indiana Arts Council, 1988; Peregrine Smith Poetry Prize, 1988. Address: c/o Department of English, Miami University, Oxford, OH 45056, USA.

BAUER Yehuda, b. 6 Apr 1926, Prague, Czechoslovakia. Historian; Professor. m. Shula White, 20 Dec 1955, 2 daughters. Education: BA, 1948, MA, 1950, University of Wales; PhD, Hebrew University, Jerusalem, 1960. Appointments: Served in Palmach Forces of the Haganah (Jewish Underground), 1944-45, and in Israel's War of Independence, 1948-49; Lecturer, 1961-73, Head of Division of Holocaust Studies, 1968-95, Associate Professor, 1973-77, Head, 1973-75, 1977-79, Professor, 1977-95, Institute of Contemporary Jewry, Hebrew University; Founder-Chairman, Vidal Sassoon International Center for the Study of Antisemitism, Hebrew University, 1982-95; Editor, Journal of Holocaust and Genocide Studies, 1986-95; Visiting Professor, University of Honolulu at Manoa, 1992, Yale University, 1993; Distinguished Visiting Professor, Ida E King Chair of Holocaust Studies, Richard Stockton College, New Jersey, 1995-96; Director, International Center for Holocaust Studies, Yad Vashem, Jerusalem, 1996-. Publications: (in English): From Diplomacy to Resistance: A History of Jewish Palestine, 1939-1945, 1970; My Brother's Keeper, 1974; Flight and Rescue, 1975; The Holocaust in Historical Perspective, 1978; The Jewish Emergence From Powerlessness, 1979; The Holocaust as Historical Experience (editor), 1981; American Jewry and the Holocaust, 1982; History of the Holocaust, 1984; Jewish Reactions to the Holocaust, 1988; Out of the Ashes, 1989; Jews for Sale?: Nazi-Jewish Negotiations, 1939-1945, 1994. Contributions to: Scholarly books, yearbooks and journals. Address: c/o International Center for Holocaust Studies, Yad Vashem, PO Box 3477, Jerusalem 91034, Israel.

BAUMAN Janina, b. 18 Aug 1926, Warsaw, Poland. Writer. m. Zygmunt Bauman, 18 Aug 1948, 3 daughters. Education: Academy of Social Sciences, 1951; University of Warsaw, 1959. Appointments: Script Editor, Polish Film, 1948-68. Publications: Winter in the Morning: A Dream of Belonging; Various other publications. Contributions to: Jewish Quarterly; Oral History; Polin; British Journal of Holocaust Education. Honour: Award by Polityka Weekly, Poland, 1991. Address: 1 Lawnswood Gardens, Leeds LS16 6HF, Yorkshire, England.

BAUMAN Zygmunt, b. 19 Nov 1925, Poznan, Poland. Sociologist. m. Janina Bauman, 18 Aug 1948, 3 daughters. Education: MA, 1954; PhD, 1956. Appointments: Warsaw University, 1953-68; Tel Aviv University, 1968-75; University of Leeds, 1971-91. Publications: Modernity & the Holocaust; Legislators & Interpreters; Intimations of Postindermity; Thinking Sociologically; Modernity & Ambivalence; Freedom; Memories of Class; Culture as Praxis; Between Class & Elite; Mortality, Immortality & Other Life Strategies. Contributions to: Times Literary Supplement; New Statesman; Professional Periodicals. Honours: Amalfi European Prize for Sociology. Memberships: British Sociological Association; Polish Sociological Association. Address: 1 Lawnswood Gardens, Leeds LS16 6HF, England.

BAUMBACH Jonathan, b. 5 July 1933, New York, USA. Writer; Professor. 3 sons, 1 daughter. Education: AB, Brooklyn College, 1955; MFA, Columbia University, 1956; PhD, Stanford University, 1961. Appointments: Instructor, Stanford University, 1958-60; Assistant Professor, Ohio State University, 1961-64; Director of Writing, New York University, 1964-66; Professor, English, Brooklyn College, 1966-; Visiting Professorships, Tufts University, 1970, University of Washington, 1978, 1983. Publications: The Landscape of Nightmare, 1965; A Man to Conjure With,1965; What Comes Next, 1968; Reruns, 1974; Babble, 1976; Chez Charlotte & Emily, 1979; (Stories): Return of Service, 1979; My Father More or Less, 1984; The Life and Times of Major Fiction, 1987; Separate Hours, 1990; Seven wives, 1994. Contributions to: Movie Critic, Partisan Review, 1973-82; Articles, Fiction in Esquire; New American Review; Tri Quarterly; Iowa Review; North American Review; Fiction. Honours: National Endowment of the Arts Fellowship, 1978; Guggenheim Fellowship, 1980; O Henry Prize Stories: included 1980, 1984, 1988; Best American Short Stories, included 1978. Memberships: Pen; Teachers and Writers Collaborative, Board of Directors; National Society of Film Critics, Chairman, 1982-84. Literary Agent: Robert Cornfield. Address: 320 Stratford Road, Brooklyn, NY 11218, USA.

BAUSCH Richard (Carl), b. 18 Apr 1945, Fort Benning, Georgia, USA. Author; Professor of English. m. Karen Miller, 3 May 1969, 2 sons, 1 daughter. Education: BA, George Mason University, 1974; MFA, University of Iowa, 1975. Appointment: Professor of English, George Mason University, 1980-. Publications: Real Presence, 1980; Take Me Back, 1981; The Last Good Time, 1984; Spirits and Other Stories, 1987; Mr Field's Daughter, 1989; The Fireman's Wife and Other Stories, 1990; Violence, 1992; Rebel Powers, 1993; Rare and Endangered Species: A Novella and Stories, 1994; The Selected Stories of Richard Bausch, 1996. Honours: PEN-Faulkner Award Nominations, 1982, 1988; Guggenheim Fellowship, 1984. Membership: Associated Writing Programs. Address: Department of English, George Mason University, 4400 University Drive, Fairfax, VA 22030, USA.

BAWDEN (KARK) Nina Mary, b. 19 Jan 1925. Novelist. m. (1) Henry Walton Bawden, 1946, (2) Austen Steven Kark, 1954, 2 sons, 1 dec, 1 daughter, 2 stepdaughters. Education: MA, Somerville College, Oxford 1946. Publications: Main Books: Carrie's War, 1975; Afternoon of a Good Woman, 1976; The Peppermint Pig, 1976; Circles of Deceit; Family Money, 1991; Total 21 novels, 18 children's books, 3 picture books; In My Own Time, autobiography, 1994; Granny the Pig, 1995. Contributions to: Reviews for: Daily Telegraph; Evening Standard. Honours: Guardian Award Children's Books, 1975; Yorkshire Post Novel of the Year, 1976; UK Nominee, Ibby Hans Andersen Award, 1996. Memberships: PEN, executive; Council, Royal Society of Literature; President, Society of Women Writers and Journalists; Council, Society of Authors. Literary Agent: Curtis Brown. Address: 22 Noel Road, London N1 8HA, England.

BAXT George, b. 11 June 1923, Brooklyn, New York, USA. Mystery Writer. Education: City College; Brooklyn College. Publications: Films: Circus of Horrors, The City of the Dead (Horror Hotel), 1960; The Shadow of the Cat, Payroll, 1961; Night of the Eagle (Burn Witch Burn), 1962; Strangler's Webb, Thunder in Dixie, 1965; Books: A Queer Kind of Death, 1966; Swing Low Sweet Harriet, A Parade of Cockeyed Creatures, Did Someone Murder Our Wandering Boys? 1967; Topsy and Evil, 1968; I! Said the Demon, 1969; The Affair of Royalties, 1971; Burning Sappho, 1972; Process of Eliminations, The Dorothy Parker Murder Case, 1984; The Alfred Hitchcock Murder Case: An Unauthorized Novel, 1986; The Tallulah Bankhead Murder Case, 1987; Who's Next?, 1988; The Talking Picture Murder Case, 1990; The Greta Garbo Murder Case, 1992; The Noel Coward Murder Case, 1993; The Mae West Murder Case, 1993; The Marlene Dietrich Murder Case, 1993; A Queer Kind of Love, The Bette Davis Murder Case, 1994; 40 short stories, Ellery Queen Mystery Magazine. Honour: Mystery Writers of America (nomination), 1967. Address: c/o St Martin Press, 175 Fifth Avenue, New York, NY 10010, USA.

BAXTER Craig, b. 16 Feb 1929, Elizabeth, New Jersey, USA. Professor of Politics and History; Author; Consultant. m. Barbara T Stevens, 28 May 1984, 1 son, 1 daughter. Education: BA, 1951, AM, 1954, PhD, 1967, University of Pennsylvania. Appointments: Vice Consul, Bombay, 1958-60, Political Officer, New Delhi, 1961-64, Deputy Principal Officer and Political Officer, Lahore, 1965-68, Analyst for India, 1968-69, Senior Political Officer for Pakistan and Afghanistan, 1969-71, Visiting Associate Professor in Social Sciences, United State Military Academy, 1971-74, Political Counselor, Accra, 1974-76, and Dhaka, 1976-78, Officer-in-Charge, International Scientific Relations for the Near East, South Asia, and Africa, 1978-80, US Foreign Service; Adjunct Lecturer, University of Virginia, Falls Church, 1969-71; Lecturer, Mount Vernon College, Washington, DC, 1981; Visiting Professor of Political Science and Diplomat-in-Residence, 1981-82, Professor of Politics and History, 1982-, Chairman, Department of Political Science, 1991-94, Juniata College, Huntingdon, Pennsylvania; Consultant to various organizations. Publications: The Jana Sangh: A Biography of an Indian Political Party, 1969; District Voting Trends in India: A Research Tool, 1969; Bangladesh: A New Nation in an Old Setting, 1984; Zia's Pakistan: Politics and Stability in a Frontline State (editor and contributor), 1985; Government and Politics in South Asia (with Yogendra K Malk, Charles H Kennedy, and Robert C Oberst), 1987, 3rd edition, 1993; Historical Dictionary of Bangladesh (with Syedur Rahman), 1989, 2nd edition, 1996; Pakistan Under the Military: Eleven Years of Zia ul-Haq (with Shahid Javed Burki), 1990; Pakistan: Authoritarianism in the 1980s (editor with Syed Razi Wasti and contributor), 1992; Bangladesh: From a Nation to a State, 1996. Contributions to: Books, encyclopedias, and scholarly journals. Memberships: American Foreign Service Association; Association for

Asian Studies; Bengal Studies Conference; Middle East Institute; Research Committee on the Punjab, executive comittee, 1986-90. Address: RR No 4, Box 103, Huntingdon, PA 16652, USA.

BAXTER John, b. 14 Dec 1939, Sydney, New South Wales, Australia. Writer. Education: Waverly College, Sydney, 1944-54. Appointments: Director of Publicity, Australian Commonwealth Film Unit, Sydney, 1968-70; Lecturer in Film and Theatre, Hollins College, 1974-78; Freelance TV Producer and Screenwriter, 1978-87; Visiting Lecturer, Mitchell College, 1987. Publications: The Off Worlders, 1966, in Australia as The God Killers, Adam's Woman (adaptor), Hollywood in the Thirties, 1968; The Pacific Book of Australian Science Fiction, The Australian Cinema, Science Fiction in the Cinema, The Gangster Film, 1970; The Cinema of Josef von Sternburg, The Cinema of John Ford, The Second Pacific Book of Australian Science Fiction, 1971; Hollywood in the Sixties, 1972; Sixty Years of Hollywood, An Appalling Talent: Kent Russell, 1973; Stunt: The Story of the Great Movie Stunt Men, 1974; The Hollywood Exiles, The Fire Came By (with Thomas R Atkins), King Vidor, 1976; The Hermes Fall, 1978; The Bidders (in UK as Bidding), 1979; The Kid, 1981; The Video Handbook (with Brian Norris), The Black Yacht, 1982; Who Burned Australia? The Ash Wednesday Fires, 1984; Filmstruck, 1987; Bondi Blues, 1993, Fellini, 1993, Buñuel, 1994; Steven Spielberg: The Unauthorised Biography, 1996; Feature Film Scripts: The Time Guardian, 1988; TV Series: The Cutting Room, 1986; First Take, 1986; Filmstruck, 1986. Address: c/o Curtis Brown Literary Agents, Haymarket House, 28-29 Haymarket, London SW1Y 4SP, England.

BAYATI Abed Al-Wahab, b. 1926, Baghdad, Iraq. Poet. Education: Baghdad Teachers Training College. Appointments: Cultural Adviser, Ministry of Culture and Fine Arts, Baghdad. Publications: Angels and Devils, 1950; Broken Pitchers, 1954; Glory Be to Children and the Olive, 1956; Poems in Exile, 1957; 15 Poems from Vienna, 1958; 20 Poems from Berlin, 1959; Words that Never Die, 1960; Fire and Words, 1964; The Book of Poverty and Revolution, 1965; That Which Comes and Does Not Come, 1966; Death in Life, 1968; Dead Dogs' Eyes, 1969; The Writing on Clay, 1970; Love Poems on the Seven Gates of the World, 1971; Collected Poems, 1971; Lilies and Death, 1972; The Moon of Shiraz, 1975; The Singer and the Moon, 1976; Eye of the Sun, 1978; Kingdom of the Spike, 1979; Love in the Rain, 1985; Love, Death and Exile, 1990; Book of Elegies, 1995. Play: Trial in Nishapur, 1963. Works have been translated into many languages including: English, French, German, Russian, Spanish. Honour: Sultan Al-Owais Poetry Award, United Arab Emirates, 1995 Address: PO Box 927293, Amman, Jordan.

BAYBARS Taner, (Timothy Bayliss), b. 18 June 1936, Cyprus. Writer; Winegrower. 1 daughter. Education: Private, Turkish Lycée. Publications: To Catch a Falling Man, 1963; A Trap for the Burglar, 1965; Plucked in a Far-Off Land, 1970; Narcissus in a Dry Pool, 1978; Pregnant Shadows, 1981; A Sad State of Freedom, 1990; Fox and the Cradle Makers, 1997; Critical Quarterly, Ambit; Orte; Détours d'Ecritures; Hudson Review; Others. Memberships: Club de Vin d'Angoulême; Poetry Society of London. Literary Agent: MBA Literary Agents. Address: Les Epardeaux, St Amant de Bonnieure, 16230 Mansle, France.

BAYLEY Barrington (John), (Alan Aumbry, P F Woods), b. 9 Apr 1937, Birmingham, England. Author. m. Joan Lucy Clarke, 31 Oct 1969, 1 son, 1 daughter. Publications: Star Virus, 1970; Annihilation Factor, 1972; Empire of Two Worlds, 1972; Collision with Chronos, 1973; The Fall of Chronopolis, 1974; The Soul of the Robot, 1974; The Garments of Caean, 1976; The Grand Wheel, 1977; The Knights of the Limits, 1978; Star Winds, 1978; The Seed of Evil, 1979; The Pillars of Eternity, 1982; The Zen Gun, 1984; The Forest of Peldain, 1985; The Rod of Light, 1985. Honour: Seiun Award for Best Foreign Science Fiction Novel Published in Japan, 1984-85. Membership: Science Fiction Foundation. Address: 48 Turreff Avenuem, Donnington, Telford, Shropshire TF2 8HE, England.

BAYLEY John (Oliver), b. 27 March 1925, England. m. Dame Jean Iris Murdoch, 1956. Education: 1st Class Hons in English and Tutor in English, New College, Oxford, 1955-74; Warton Professor of English Literature and Fellow of St Catherine's College, University of Oxford, 1974-92. Publications: In Another Country (novel), 1954; The Romantic Survival: A Study in Poetic Evolution, 1956; The Characters of Love, 1961; Tolstoy and the Novel, 1966; Pushkin, A Comparative Commentary, 1971; The Uses of Division: Unity and Disharmony in Literature, 1976; An Essay on Hardy, 1978; Shakespeare and Tragedy,

1982; The Order of Battle at Trafalgar, 1987; The Short Story: Henry James to Elizabeth Bowen, 1988; Housman's Poems, 1992; Alice (novel), 1994; The Queer Captain (novel), 1995. Address: c/o St Catherine's College, Oxford.

BAYLEY Peter (Charles), b. 25 Jan 1921, Gloucester, England. Professor Emeritus; Writer. Education: MA, Oxford University, 1947. Appointments: Fellow, University College, 1947-72; Praelector in English, 1949-72, University Lecturer, 1952-72, Oxford University; Master, Collingwood College, University of Durham, 1972-78; Berry Professor and Head of English Department, 1978-85, Berry Professor Emeritus, 1985-, University of St Andrews, Fife. Publications: Editor, The Faerie Queene, by Spenser, Book II 1965, Book 1 1966, 1970; Edmund Spenser, Prince of Poets, 1971; Loves and Deaths, 1972; A Casebook on Spenser's Faerie Queene, 1977; Poems of Milton, 1982; An ABC of Shakespeare, 1985. Address: 63 Oxford Street, Woodstock, Oxford OX20 1TJ, England.

BAYLISS Timothy. See: BAYBARS Taner.

BEACHCROFT Ellinor Nina, b. 10 Nov 1931, London, England. Writer. m. Dr Richard Gardner, 7 Aug 1954, 2 daughters. Education: Wimbledon High School, 1942-49; 2nd Class Hons Degree in English Literature, St Hilda's College, Oxford, 1953. Publications: Well Met by Witchlight, 1972; Under the Enchanter, 1974; Cold Christmas, 1974; A Spell of Sleep, 1975; A Visit to Folly Castle, 1976; A Farthing for the Fair, 1977; The Wishing People, 1978; The Genie and Her Bottle, 1983; Beyond World's End, 1985. Memberships: Society of Authors; Children's Writers' Group, twice a Committee Member. Literary Agent: David Highams. Address: 9 Raffin Green Lane, Datchworth, Herts SG3 6RJ, England.

BEALES Derek (Edward Dawson), . b. 12 June 1931, Felixstowe, England. Education: BA, 1953, MA, PhD, 1957, Cambridge University. Appointments: Research Fellow, 1955-58, Fellow, 1958-, Tutor, 1961-70, Vice Master, 1973-75, Sidney Sussex College; Assistant Lecturer, 1962-65, Lecturer, 1965-80, Chairman, Faculty Board of History, 1979-81, Professor of Modern History, 1980-, Cambridge University; Member of Council, Royal Historical Society, 1984-87; Editor, Historical Journal, 1971-75; British Academy Representative, Standing Committee for Humanities, European Science Foundation, 1993-. Publications: England and Italy 1859-60, 1961; From Castlereagh to Gladstone, 1969; The Risorgimento and the Unification of Italy, 1971; History and Biography, 1981; History, Society and the Churches (editor with G F A Best), 1985; Joseph II: In the Shadow of Maria Theresa 1741-80, 1987; Mozart and the Habsburgs, 1993; Sidney Sussex College Quatercentenary Essay, (editor, with H B Nisbet), 1996. Honours: Doctor of Letters, 1988; Fellow of the British Academy, 1989; Stenton Lecturer, University of Reading, 1992; Birkbeck Lecturer, Trinity College, Cambridge, 1993. Address: Sidney Sussex College, Cambridge CB2 3HU, England.

BEAR Greg(ory Dale), b. 20 Aug 1951, San Diego, California, USA. Writer. m. (1) Christina Nielsen, 12 Jan 1975, div Aug 1981, (2) Astrid Anderson, 18 June 1983, 1 son, 1 daughter. Education: AB, San Diego State College, 1969. Publications: Hegira, 1979; Psychlone, 1979; Beyond Heaven's River, 1980; Strength of Stones, 1981; The Wind From a Burning Woman, 1983; Corona, 1984; The Infinity Concerto, 1984; Eon, 1985; Blood Music, 1985; The Serpent Mage, 1986; The Forge of God, 1987; Sleepside Story, 1987; Eternity, 1988; Hardfought, 1988; Early Harvest, 1988; Tangents, 1989; Queen of Angels, 1990; Heads, 1990; Anvil of Stars, 1992; Moving Mars, 1993; Legacy, 1995. Honours: Awards from Science Fiction Writers of America. Membership: Science Fiction Writers of America, President, 1988-90. Address: 506 Lakeview Road, Alderwood Manor, WA 98036, USA.

BEARDSLEY J(ohn) Douglas, b. 27 Apr 1941, Montreal, Quebec, Canada. Writer; Poet; Editor; Reviewer; Teacher. Education: BA, University of Victoria, British Columbia, 1976; MA, York University, Toronto, Ontario, 1978. Appointments: Chief Editor, Gregson Graham Ltd, 1980-82; Senior Instructor, Department of English, University of Victoria, 1981-; Writer, Editor and Graphic Designer, Osborne, Beardsley and Associates, Victoria, 1982-85; Writer, Editor and Proofreader, Beardsley and Associates, Victoria, 1985-. Publications: Going Down into History, 1976; The Only Country in the World Called Canada, 1976; Six Saanich Poems, 1977; Play on the Water: The Paul Klee Poems, 1978; Premonitions and Gifts (with Theresa Kishkan), 1979; Poems (with Charles Lillard), 1979; Pacific Sands, 1980; Kissing the Body of My Lord: The Marie Poems, 1982; Country on Ice, 1987; A Dancing Star, 1988; The Rocket, the Flower, the Hammer and Me (anthology of Canadian hockey fiction) (editor), 1988; Free to Talk, 1992; Inside Passage, 1994; Wrestling with Angels (Selected Poems, 1960-95), 1996; My Friends the Strangers, 1996. Contributions to: Anthologies, newspapers, magazines, and periodicals. Honours: Canada Council Arts Award, 1978; British Columbia Book Prize for Poetry Nomination, 1989. Address: 1074 Lodge Avenue, Victoria, British Columbia V8X 3A8, Canada.

BEASLEY W(illiam) G(erald), b. 22 Dec 1919, England. Professor Emeritus; Writer. Education: BA, 1940, PhD, 1950, University of London. Appointment: Professor of History of the Far East, School of Oriental and African Studies, 1954-83, Professor Emeritus, 1983-, University of London. Publications: Great Britain and the Opening of Japan 1833-1858, 1951; Select Documents on Japanese Foreign Policy 1853-1868 (editor and translator), 1955; Historians of China and Japan (editor with E G Pulleyblank), 1961; The Modern History of Japan, 1963, 3rd edition, 1981; The Meiji Restoration, 1972; Modern Japan: Aspects of History, Literature and Society (editor), 1975; Japanese Imperialism 1894-1945, 1987; The Rise of Modern Japan, 1990; Japan Encounters the Barbarian, Japanese Travellers in America and Europe, 1995. Address: 172 Hampton Road, Twickenham TW2 5NJ, England.

BEASLEY-MURRAY George Raymond, b. 10 Oct 1916, London, England. Professor. m. Ruth Weston, 4 Apr 1942, 3 sons, 1 daughter. Education: BD 1941, MTh 1945, PhD 1952, King's College; DD, London University, 1963; MA 1954, DD 1963, Cambridge University. Appointments: Lecturer, Spurgeon's College, London, 1950-56; Professor of Greek New Testament, Rüschlikon Zürich, 1956-58; Principal, Spurgeon's College, London, 1958-73; Professor, 1970-80, Senior Professor, 1980-92, Southern Baptist Seminary, Louisville, Kentucky. Publications: Jesus and the Future, 1954; A Commentary on Mark Thirteen, 1957; Baptism in the New Testament, 1962; The Book of Revelation, New Century Bible, 1974; Jesus and the Kingdom of God, 1996; John, in Word Biblical Commentary, 1987; Gospel of Life: Theology in the Fourth Gospel, 1991; Jesus and the Last Days, 1993; Preaching the Gospel from the Gospels, 1996. Memberships: Society of Biblical Literature; Studiorum Novi Testamenti Societas; Catholic Biblical Association of America. Address: 4 Holland Road, Hove, East Sussex BN3 1JJ, England.

BEATTIE Ann, b. 7 Sept 1947, Washington, DC, USA. Education: BA, American University, 1969; MA, University of Connecticut, 1970. Publications: Chilly Scenes of Winter, 1976; Distortions, 1976; Secrets and Surprises, 1978; Falling in Place, 1980; The Burning House, 1982; Love Always, 1985; Where You'll Find the Other Stories, 1986; Picturing Will, 1990; What Was Mine, 1991. Contributions to: New Yorker. Address: c/o Janklow & Nesbit, 598 Madison Ave, New York, NY 10022, USA.

BEATY (Arthur) David, b. 28 Mar 1919, Hatton, Ceylon. Author. m. Betty Joan Campbell Smith, 29 Apr 1948, 3 daughters. Education: MA History, Merton College, Oxford University, England, 1940; MPhil Psychology, University College, 1965; Airline Transport Pilot's Licence; Navigation and Radio Licences. Appointments: RAF, 1940-46; Squadron Leader, British Overseas Airways Corporation, Senior Captain, Principal Atlantic Routes, 1946-53; Foreign Office, 1966-74. Publications: The Take Off, 1948; The Heart of the Storm, 1954; The Proving Flight, 1956; Cone of Silence, 1958; Call Me Captain, 1959; Village of Stars, 1960; The Wind off the Sea, 1962; The Siren Song, 1964; Milk and Honey, 1964; Sword of Honour, 1965; The Human Factor in Aircraft Accidents, 1969; The Temple Tree, 1971; Electric Train, 1974; The Water Jumper: History of North Atlantic Flight, 1976; Excellency, 1977; The Complete Sky Traveller, 1978; The White Sea Bird, 1979; Wings of the Morning, with Betty Beaty, 1982; Strange Encounters, 1982; The Stick, 1984; The Blood Brothers, 1987; Eagles, 1990; The Naked Pilot, 1991; Light Perpetual, Airmen's Memorial Windows, 1995. Honours: MBE for services to aviation, DFC at Bar. Membership: Royal Aeronautical Society. Address: Manchester House, Church Hill, Slindon, Near Arundel, West Sussex BN18 0RD, England.

BEATY Betty Joan Campbell Smith, (Karen Campbell, Catherine Ross). British. m. (Arthur) David Beaty, 29 Apr 1943, 3 daughters. Appointments: WAAF Officer; Airline Hostess; Medical Social Worker, London. Publications: Maiden Flight, 1956; South to the Sea, 1956; Amber Five, 1958; The Butternut Tree, 1958; From This

Day Forward, 1959; The Colours of the Night, 1962; The Path of the Moonfish, 1964; The Trysting Tower, 1964; Miss Miranda's Walk, 1967; Suddenly in the Air, 1969; Thunder on Sunday, 1971; The Swallows of San Fedora, 1973; Love and the Kentish Maid, 1973; Head of Chancery, 1974; Master at Arms, 1975; Fly Away Love, 1976; Death Descending, 1976; Exchange of Hearts, 1977; The Bells of St Martin, 1979; Battle Dress, 1979; Wings of the Morning (with David Beaty), 1982; The Missionary's Daughter, 1983; Matchmaker Nurse, 1983. Address: Manchester House, Church Hill, Slindon, Near Arundel, West Sussex BN18 0RD, England.

BEAUMONT Roger Alban, b. 2 Oct 1935, Milwaukee, Wisconsin, USA. Professor of History. m. 8 Dec 1974, 1 son, 2 daughters. Education: BS, 1957; MS, University of Wisconsin, Madison, 1960; PhD, Kansas State University, 1973. Publications: Military Elites, 1974; Sword of the Raj, 1977; The Nerves of War, 1986; Special Operations & Elite Units: A Reference Guide, 1988; Joint Military Operations, 1993; War, Chaos and History, 1994; 4 monographs. Contributions to: 61 articles and 17 book chapters; Co-founder and North American Editor, Defence Analysis, 1983-89. Honours: Senior Honors, University of Wisconsin, Madison, 1957; Department of the Army Patriotic Civilian Service Award, 1987; Secretary, The Navy Fellow, US Naval Academy, 1989-90. Address: History Department, Texas A&M University, College Station, TX 77843, USA.

BEAVER Bruce (Victor), b. 14 Feb 1928, Sydney, New South Wales, Australia. Freelance Journalist. Publications: Under The Bridge, 1961; Seawall and Shoreline, 1964; The Hot Spring, 1965; You Can't Come Back, 1966; Open at Random, 1967; Letters to Live Poets, 1969; Lauds and Plaints, 1968-72, 1974; Odes and Days, 1975; Death's Directives, 1978; As It Was, Selected Poems, 1979; Prose Sketches, 1986; Charmed Lives, 1988; New and Selected Poems, 1960-90, 1991. Honours: FAW, Christopher Brennan Award; Patrick White Literary Award, 1982; New South Wales, State Special Literary Award, 1990; Captain Cook Bi-Centenary Prize; Grace Leven Prize; Poetry Society of Australia Award; AM Award, 1991. Address: 14 Malvern Avenue, Manly, New South Wales 2095, Australia.

BEAVER Paul Eli, b. 3 Apr 1953, Winchester, England. Journalist; Author; Broadcaster. m. Ann Middleton, 20 May 1978, div June 1993. Education: Sheffield City Polytechnic; Henley Management College. Appointments: Editor, IPMS Magazine, 1976-80, Helicopter World, 1981-86, Defence Helicopter World, 1982-86, Jane's Videotape, 1986-87; Assistant Compiler, Jane's Fighting Ships, 1987-88; Managing Editor, Jane's Defence Yearbooks, 1988-89; Publisher, Jane's Defence Weekly, 1989-93; Senior Publisher, Jane's SENTINEL, 1993-94; Defence and Aerospace Correspondent, European Business News (TV).Publications: Ark Royal - A Pictorial History, 1979; U-Boats in the Atlantic, 1979; German Capital Ships, 1980; German Destroyers and Escorts, 1981; British Aircraft Carrier, 1982; Fleet Command, 1984; Invincible Class, 1984; NATO Navies of the 1980s, 1985; Missile Systems, 1985; Nuclear-Powered Submarines, 1986; Modern British Missiles, 1986; Encyclopaedia of Aviation, 1986; Modern Royal Navy Warships, 1987; British Aircraft Carrier, 3rd edition, 1987; Modern Military Helicopters, 1987; Attack Helicopters, 1987; Encyclopaedia of the Fleet Air Arm Since 1945, 1987; Today's Army Air Corps; The Modern Royal Navy; Today's Royal Marines; Jane's World Naval Aviation; The Gulf States Regional Security Assessment, 1993; The Balkans Regional Security Assessment, 1994; D-DAY: Private Lines, 1994; The South China Sea Regional Security Assessment, 1994; The CIS Regioanl Security Assessment, 1994; The North Africa Regional Security Assessment, 1994; The China and North East Asia Regional Security Assessment, 1995; Baltics and Central Europe Regional Security Assesment, 1996; The Modern Royal Navy, 1996. Author of more than 100 articles. Address: Avenir House, Barton Stacey, Winchester, Hampshire, SO21 3RL, England.

BEBB Prudence, b. 20 Mar 1939, Catterick, England. Writer. Education: BA; Dip Ed. Publications: The Eleventh Emerald; The Ridgeway Ruby; The White Swan; The Nabob's Nephew; Life in Regency York; Butcher, Baker, Candlestick Maker; Life in Regency Harrogate, 1995. Membership: English Centre of International PEN. Address: 12 Brackenhills, Upper Poppleton, York YO2 6DH, England.

BECHMANN Roland (Philippe), b. 1 Apr 1919, Paris, France. Architect; Historian; Writer. m. Martine Cohen, 18 July 1942, 6 daughters. Education: Licencié és Lettres, 1938; Government Architect Diploma, 1944; Doctor (3C) in Geography, 1978. Appointments:

Architect; Chief Editor, Amenagement et Nature, 1966-. Publications: Les Racines des Cathedrales, L'architecture gothique, expression des conditions du milieu, 1981, 4th edition, 1996; Des Arbres et des Hommes: La foret au Moyen Age, 1984, English translation as Trees and Man: The Forest in the Middle Ages, 1990; Carnet de Villard de Honnecourt XIII e siècle (joint author), 1986; Villard de Honnecourt Disegni (joint author), 1987; Villard de Honnecourt: La pensée technique au XIIIe siècle et sa communication, 1991, 2nd edition, 1993. Contributions to: Journals. Honours: Croix de guerre, 1994; Chevalier de la Légion d'Honneur, 1952. Membership: Association des Journalistes de l'Environnement. Address: 21-23 rue du Conseiller Collignon, 75116 Paris, France.

BECK Tatyana, b. 21 Apr 1949, Moscow, Russia. Poet; Writer. m. div. Education: Diploma of a Literary Editor, Moscow State University, Journalist Department, 1967-72. Publications: Skvoreshniky, 1974; Snegir, 1980; Zamysel, 1987; Poetry: Mixed Forest, 1993. Contributions to: Poems and Articles in: Novymir; Znamya; Oktyabr; Voprosy; Literatury; Literatyrnoe Obozrenie; Ogoniek; others. Memberships: Writers Union (former USSR), Secretary and Member, Russian PEN Centre. Address: Krasnoarmeiskaya Street, House No 23, Apartment 91, Moscow 125319, Russia.

BECKER Gary Stanley, b. 2 Dec 1930, Pottsville, Pennsylvania, USA. Professor of Economics and Sociology. m. (1) Doria Slote, 19 Sept 1954, dec, (2) Guity Nashet, 31 Oct 1979, 2 sons, 2 daughters. Education: AB summa cum laude, Princeton University, 1951; AM, 1953, PhD, 1955, University of Chicago. Appointments: Board of Publications, University of Chicago Press, 1971-75; Professor, Economics, Sociology, 1983-, Chairman, Department of Economics, 1984-85, University of Chicago; Columnist, Business Week, 1985-. Publications: The Economics of Discrimination, 1957, 2nd edition, 1971; Human Capital, 1964, 3rd edition, 1993; Human Capital and the Personal Distribution of Income: An Analytical Approach, 1967; Economic Theory, 1971; Essays in the Economics of Crime and Punishment (edited with William M Landes), 1974; The Allocation of Time and Goods Over the Life Cycle (with Gilbert Ghez), 1975; Essays in Labor Economics in Honor of H Gregg Lewis (editor), 1976; The Economic Approach to Human Behavior, 1976; A Treatise on the Family, 1981, expanded edition, 1991; Several translated into other languages. Contributions to: American Economic Review; Journal of Political Economy; Quarterly Journal of Economics; Journal of Law and Economics; Journal of Population Economics; Econometrica; Business Economics; Others; Several books. Honours: Nobel Prize for Economic Science, 1992; 7 honorary doctorates. Memberships: Phi Beta Kappa, 1950; Economic History Association; National Academy of Sciences; Distinguished Fellow, Past President, American Economic Association; Fellow: American Statistical Association; Econometric Society; American Academy of Arts and Sciences; National Association of Business Econometrics. Address: Department of Economics, University of Chicago, 1126 East 59th Street, Chicago, IL 60637, USA.

BECKER Stephen David, b. 31 Mar 1927, Mt Vernon, New York, USA. Novelist; Translator. m. Mary Elizabeth Freeburg, 24 Dec 1947, 2 sons, 1 daughter. Education: AB, Harvard College, 1947; Yenching University, Beijing, 1947-48. Appointments: Occasional teaching and lecturing at several universities. Publications: Novels: The Season of the Stranger, 1951; Shanghai Incident, 1955; Juice, 1959; A Covenant with Death, 1965; The Outcasts, 1967; When the War is Over, 1970; Dog Tags, 1973, reissue 1987; The Chinese Bandit, 1975; The Last Mandarin, 1979; The Blue-Eyed Shan, 1982; A Rendezvous in Haiti, 1987; Non-fiction: Comic Art in America, 1959; Marshall Field III, 1964; Translations: The Colours of the Day, 1953; Mountains in the Desert, 1954; The Sacred Forest, 1954; Faraway, 1957; Someone Will Die Tonight in the Caribbean, 1958; The Last of the Just, 1961; The Town Beyond the Wall, 1964; The Conquerors, 1976; Diary of My Travels in America, 1977; Ana No, 1980; The Aristotle System, 1985; Cruel April, 1990; Between Tides, 1991; The Forgotten, 1992. Contributions to: Dozens of short stories, essays, reviews, columns, introductions. Honours: Rotary Fellowship to Peking, 1947; Guggenheim Fellowship, fiction, 1954; National Endowment for the Arts grant in translation, 1984; Judge, Hopwood Awards, fiction, University of Michigan, 1989. Literary Agent: Russell & Volkening, New York. Address: 1281 North East 85th Street, Miami, FL 33138, USA.

BECKET Henry S A. See: **GOULDEN Joseph C.**

BECKETT Kenneth Albert, b. 12 Jan 1929, Brighton, Sussex, England. Horticulturalist; Technical Advisor; Editor. m. Gillian Tuck, 1 Aug 1973, 1 son. Education: Diploma, Horticulture, Royal Horticulture Society. Appointments: Technical Editor, Gardener's Chronicle, Reader's Digest; Retired. Publications: The Love of Trees, 1975; Illustrated Dictionary of Botany, 1977; Concise Encyclopaedia of Garden Plants, 1978; Amateur Greenhouse Gardening, 1979; Growing Under Glass, 1981; Complete Book of Evergreens, 1981; Growing Hardy Perennials, 1981; Climbing Plants, 1983; The Garden Library, 4 volumes: Flowering House Plants, Annuals and Biennials, Roses, Herbs, 1984; The RHS Encyclopaedia of House Plants, 1987; Evergreens, 1990; Alpine Garden Society Encyclopaedia of Alpines, 2 volumes, 1993-94. Contributions to: The Garden; The Plantsman. Honours: Veitch Memoiral Medal, Royal Horticultural Society, 1987; Lyttel Trophy, AGS, 1995; Clarence Elliott Memorial Award, AGS, 1995. Memberships: Scientific Committee, Royal Horticultural Society; Australasian Plant Society; Botanical Society of the British Isles; Plantsman; International Dendrology Society; Butterfly Conservation; Alpine Garden Soicety. Address: Bramley Cottage, Stanhoe, King's Lynn, Norfolk PE31 8QF, England.

BECKLES WILLSON Robina Elizabeth, b. 26 Sept 1930, London, England. Writer. m. Anthony Beckles Wilson, 1 son, 1 daughter, Education: BA, 1948, MA, 1952, University of Liverpool. Appointments: Teacher, Liverpool School of Art, 1952-56; Ballet Rambert Educational School, London, 1956-58. Publications: Leopards on the Loire, 1961; A Time to Dance, 1962; Musical Instruments, 1964; A Reflection of Rachel, The Leader of the Band, 1967; Roundabout Ride, 1968; Dancing Day, 1971; The Last Harper, The Shell on Your Back, 1972; What a Noise, 1974; The Voice of Music, 1975; Musical Merry-go-Round, 1977; The Beaver Book of Ballet, 1979; Eyes Wide Open, Anna Pavlova: A Legend Among Dancers, 1981; Pocket Book of Ballet, Secret Witch, 1982; Square Bear, Merry Christmas, Holiday Witch, 1983; Sophie and Nicky series, 2 volumes, Hungry Witch, 1984; Music Maker, Sporty Witch, 1986; The Haunting Music, 1987; Mozart's Story, 1991; Just Imagine, 1993. Address: 44 Popes Avenue, Twickenham, Middlesex TW2 5TL, England.

BECKWITH Lillian, b. 25 Apr 1916, Ellesmere Port, England. Author. m. Edward Thornthwaite Comber, 3 June 1937, 1 son, 1 daughter. Education: Ornum College, Birkenhead. Publications: The Hebridean Stories: The Hill is Lonely, 1959; The Sea for Breakfast, 1961; The Loud Halo, 1964; A Rope in Case, 1968; Beautiful Just!, 1975; Lightly Poached, 1973; The Spuddy, 1974; Green Hand, 1967; About My Father's Business, 1971; The Lillian Beckwith Hebridean Cookbook (Anecdotes and recipes), 1976; Bruach Blend, 1978; A Shine of Rainbows, 1984; The Bay of Strangers, 1988; A Proper Woman, 1986; The Small Party, 1989; An Island Apart, 1992. Contributions to: Countryman; Woman's Own and various other magazines for women. Memberships: Society of Authors; Mark Twain Society; Women of the Year Association, Consultative Committee. Address: c/o Curtis Brown Ltd, 4th Floor Haymarket House, 28/29 Haymarket, London SW1Y 4SP.

BEDAU Hugo Adam, b. 23 Sept 1926, Portland, Oregon, USA. Professor of Philosophy; Author. m. (1) Jan Mastin, 1952, div 1988, 3 sons, 1 daughter, (2) Constance Putnam, 1990. Education: BA, University of Redlands, 1949; MA, Boston University, 1951; MA, 1953, PhD, 1961, Harvard University. Appointments: Instructor, Dartmouth College, 1953-54; Lecturer, Princeton University, 1954-57, 1958-61; Associate Professor, Reed College, 1962-66; Professor of Philosophy, Tufts University, 1966-. Publications: Victimless Crimes: Two Views (with Edwin M Schur), 1974; The Courts, the Constitution, and Capital Punishment, 1977; Current Issues and Enduring Questions (with Sylvan Barnet), 1987, 4th edition, 1996; Death is Different: Studies in the Morality, Law, and Politics of Capital Punishment, 1987; In Spite of Innocence (with Michael Radelet and Constance Putnam), 1992; Critical Thinking, Reading, and Writing (with Sylvan Barnet), 1993, 2nd edition, 1996; Thinking and Writing About Philiosophy, 1996; Making Mortal Choices, 1996. Editor: The Death Penalty in America, 1964, 4th edition, 1997; Civil Disobedience: Theory and Practice, 1969; Justice and Equality, 1971; Capital Punishment in the United States (with Chester M Pierce), 1976; Civil Disobedience in Focus, 1991. Contributions to: Many books, journals, and magazines. Honours: Visiting Fellow, Clare Hall/Cambridge University, 1980, 1989, Max Planck Institutes, Heidelberg and Freiburg im Breisgau, 1988, Wolfson College, Oxford, 1989; Romanell-Phi Beta Kappa Professor of Philosophy, 1995. Memberships: American Association of University Professors; American Philosophical Association; American Society for

Political and Legal Philosophy. Address: Department of Philosophy, Tufts University, Medford, MA 02155, USA.

BEDE. See: **JOHNSON Paul**

BEDFORD Sybille, b. 16 Mar 1911, Carlottenburg, Germany (British). Novelist. m. Walter Bedford, 1935. Education: Private education in Italy, England and France. Appointments: Worked as a Law Reporter for the Observer, London, and the Saturday Evening Post, Philadelphia; Life Magazine, 1963-65. Publications: A Legacy, 1956; A Favourite of the Gods, 1963; A Compass Error, 1968; Official Biography: Aldous Huxley, 2 volumes, 1973-74; Jigsaw: An Unsentimental Education, 1989; Uncollected short stories: Compassionata at Hyde Park Corner, 1963; Une Vie de Château, 1989; Various non-fiction works. Honours: Society of Authors Travelling Scholarship, 1989; Fellow, Royal Society of Literature, 1964; Vice President, English PEN; Officer of the Order of the British Empire, 1981; Companion of Literature, C.Lit, 1994. Address: Lutyens and Rubenstein, 231 Westbourne Park Road, London W11 1EB, England.

BEECHING Jack, b. 8 May 1922, Hastings, Sussex, England. Writer. Publications: Poetry: Aspects of Love, 1950; The Polythene Maidenhead, in Penguin Modern Poets, 1969; Twenty Five Short Poems, 1982; The View From the Balloon, 1990; Novels: Let Me See Your Face, 1958; The Dakota Project, 1967; Death of a Terrorist, 1982; Tides of Fortune, 1988; History: The Chinese Opium Wars, 1975; An Open Path: Christian Missionaries 1515-1914, 1979; The Galleys at Lepanto, 1982. Literary Agent: Tessa Sayle. Address: c/o Tessa Sayle, 11 Jubilee Place, London SW3 3CE, England.

BEER Patricia, b.4 Nov 1924, Exmouth, Devon, England. Writer; Poet. m. (2) John Damien Parsons, 1964. Education: BA, University of London; BLitt, St Hugh's College, Oxford. Appointments: Lecturer in English, University of Padua, 1946-48, Ministero Aeronautica, Rome, 1950-53; Senior Lecturer in English, Goldsmiths' College, University of London, 1962-68. Publications: Loss of the Magyar and Other Poems, 1959; New Poems (editor with Ted Hughes and Vernon Scannell), 1962; The Survivors, 1963; Just Like the Resurrection, 1967; Mrs Beer's House (autobiography), 1968; The Estuary, 1971; An Introduction to the Metaphysical Poets, 1972; Spanish Balcony, 1973; Reader, I Married Him, 1974; Driving West. 1975; Moon's Ottery, 1978; Poems 1967-79, Selected Poems, 1979; The Lie of the Land, 1983; Wessex, 1985; Collected Poems, 1988. Contributions to: Listener; London Review of Books. Address: Tiphayes, Up Ottery, Near Honiton, Devon, England.

BEERS Burton F(loyd), b. 13 Sept 1927, Chemung, New York, USA. Professor of History; Writer. m. Pauline Cone Beers, 6 Sept 1952, 1 son, 1 daughter. Education: AB, Hobart College, 1950; MA, 1952, PhD, 1956, Duke University. Appointments: Instructor, 1955-57, Assistant Professor, 1957-61, Associate Professor, 1961-66, Professor, 1966-96, North Carolina State University. Publications: Vain Endeavor: Robert Lansing's Attempts to End the American-Japanese Rivalry, 1962; The Far East: A History of Western Impacts and Eastern Responses, 1830-1875 (with Paul H Clyde), 4th to 6th editions, 1966-75; China in Old Photographs, 1981; North Carolina's China Connection 1840-1949 (with Lawrence Kessler and Charles LaMonica), 1981; North Carolina State University: A Pictorial History (with Murray S Downs), 1986; The Vietnam War: An Historical Case Study (with Rose Ann Mulford), 1997. Contributions to: Textbooks, books, scholarly journals, and periodicals. Honours: Alexander Quarles Holladay Medal for Excellence, North Carolina State University Board of Trustees, 1992; Medal for Excellence, Hobart and William Smith Colleges, 1994. Memberships: American Historical Association; Association for Asian Studies; Association of Historians in North Carolina; Historical Society of North Carolina; Phi Alpha Theta; Phi Beta Kappa; Phi Kappa Phi; North Carolina Literary and Historical Society; Sigma Iota Rho; Society for Historians of American Foreign Relations; Southern Historical Association. Address: 629 South Lakeside Drive, Raleigh, NC 27606, USA.

BEEVOR Antony, b. 14 Dec 1946, London, England. Historian; Novelist. m. Artemis Cooper, 2 Feb 1986, 1 son, 1 daughter. Education: Winchester College; Grenoble University; Royal Military Academy, Sandhurst. Publications: The Spanish Civil War, 1982; The Enchantment of Christina Von Retzen, novel, 1988; Inside the British Army, 1990; Crete-The Battle and the Resistance, 1991; Paris After the Liberation 1944-49, 1994. Contributions to: Times Literary Supplement; Times; Telegraph; Independent, Spectator. Honour:

Runciman Award, 1992. Memberships: Society of Authors; Royal Geographical Society; Anglo Hellenic League. Literary Agent: Andrew Nurnberg. Address: 54 Saint Maur Road, London SW6 4DP, England.

BEGLEY Louis, b. 6 Oct 1933, Stryj, Poland. Lawyer; Writer. m. (1) Sally Higginson, 11 Feb 1956, div May 1970, 2 sons, 1 daughter, (2) Anne Muhlstein Dujarric dela Riviere, 30 Mar 1974. Education: AB, 1954, LLB, 1959, Harvard University. Appointments: Specialist in international corporate law; writer; lecturer. Publications: Novels: Wartime Lies, 1991; The Man Who Was Late, 1993; As Max Saw It, 1994; About Schmidt, 1996. Contributions to: Periodicals. Honours: Irish Times-Aer Lingus International Fiction Prize, 1991; PEN/Ernest Hemingway First Fiction Award, 1992; Prix Medicis Etranger, 1992; Jeanette-Schocken Preis, Bremerhaven Bürgerpreis für Literatur, 1995; American Academy of Letters Award in Literature, 1995. Memberships: Bar Association of the City of New York; Council on Foreign Relations; Union Internationale des Avocats. Address: c/o Georges Borchardt, 136 East 57th Street, New York, NY 10022, USA.

BEGLEY Sharon. Senior Writer, Newsweek. m. 1 son, 1 daughter. Education: BA, Yale University. Appointments: Editorial Assistant in Science, 1977, Senior Editorial Assistant, 1979, Assistant Editor, 1979, Associated Editor, 1980, General Editor, 1983, Senior Writer in Science Department, 1990-, Newsweek. Honours: Global Award for Media Excellence, Popular Institute, 1991; Benjamin Fine Award, National Association of Secondary School Principals, 1991; Media Award, American Society on Aging, 1992; Premier Award, Aviation and Space Writers Association, 1993; Distinguished Achievement Award, Educational Press Association, 1994. Address: c/o Newsweek, 251 West 57th Street, New York, NY 10019-1894, USA.

BEGUIN Bernard, b. 14 Feb 1923, Sion, Valais, Switzerland. Journalist. m. Antoinette Waelbroeck, 1948, 2 sons, 2 daughters. Education: Les L, Geneva University; Graduate, Institute of International Studies. Appointments: Correspondent, UN European Headquarters, 1946-70; Foreign Editor, 1947, Editor-in-Chief, 1959-70, Journal de Geneve; Diplomatic Commentator, Swiss Broadcasting System, 1954-59, Swiss TV, 1959-70; Head of Programmes, Swiss-French-Speaking TV, 1970-73; Deputy Director, Radio and TV, 1973-86. Honours: Honorary Member, Swiss Press Association, 1974-; Visiting Professor, Professional Ethics, University of Neuchatel, 1984-88. Memberships: Central President, Swiss Press Council, 1985-90; Federal Commission on Cartels, 1964-80; Board, Swiss Telegraphic Agency, 1968-71; President, Independent Authority on Complaints dealing with Radio and Television, 1991-92; UNESCO Consultant on Media Situation in Belarus, 1994. Address: 41 Avenue de Budé, 1202 Geneva, Switzerland.

BÉGUIN Louis-Paul, b. 31 Mar 1923, Amiens, France. Writer. Education: BA, Amiens Lille Sorbonne University, Paris; Terminology Diploma, New York, USA. Appointment: Cultural Agent, 1970-92. Publications: Miroir de Janus, 1966; Impromptu de Québec, 1974; Un Homme et son langage, 1977; Problèmes de langage, 1978; Idoles et Paraboles, 1982; Yourcenar, 1982; Poèmes et pastiches, 1985; Parcours parallèles, 1988; L'Ange Pleureur, 1991; Poèmes depuis la tendre enfance, 1995; The Weeping Angel, 1996. Contributions to: Newspapers and magazines. Honours: Poetry Award, 1967; Prix Montcalm, 1974. Memberships: PEN, Quebec; Quebec Writers Union. Address: 1800 rue Bercy App 1218, Montreal, Quebec H2K 4K5, Canada.

BEHLEN Charles (William), b. 29 Jan 1949, Slaton, Texas, USA. Poet. 1 daughter. Education: New Mexico Junior College, 1968-70. Publications: Perdition's Keepsake; Three Texas Poets; Dreaming at the Wheel; Uirsche's First Three Decades; The Voices Under the Floor. Contributions to: Bloomsbury Review; Cedar Rock; New Mexico Humanities Review; Poetry Now; Puerto del Sol; The Smith; Texas Observer; Borderlands; New Texas '91; New Texas '95. Honours: Pushcart Prize (nominee); Ruth Stephan Reader; Manuscripts Displayed and Placed in Time Capsule by San Antonio Museum of Art. Membership: Texas Association of Creative Writing Teachers. Address: 501 West Industrial Drive, Apartment 503-B, Sulphur Springs, TX 75482, USA.

BEHR Edward (Samuel), b. 7 May 1926, Paris, France. Journalist; Editor; Writer. m. Christiane Wagrez, 1 Apr 1967. Education: BA, 1951, MA, 1953, Magdalene College, Cambridge. Appointments: Correspondent, Reuters, 1950-54, Time Inc, 1957-63;

Contributing Editor, Saturday Evening Post, 1963-65; Reporter-Director, Cinq Colonnes a la Une TV Programme, 1963-65; Paris Correspondent, 1965-66, Hong Kong Bureau Chief, 1966-68, Paris Bureau Chief, 1968-72, European Editor, Paris, 1973-83, Cultural Editor, 1984-87, Contributing Editor, 1987-, Newsweek Magazine. Publications: The Algerian Problem, 1961; Lai Ying: The Thirty-Sixth Way: A Personal Account of Imprisonment and Escape from Red Chine (translator and editor with Sydney Liu), 1969; Bearings: A Foreign Correspondent's Life Behind the Lines, 1978 (in the UK as Anyone Here Been Raped and Speaks English?, 1981); Getting Even, novel, 1980; The Last Emperor, novel based on the film, 1987; Hirohito: Behind the Myth, 1989; The Complete Book of Les Miserables, 1990; Indonesia: A Voyage Through the Archipelago, 1990; The Story of Miss Saigon (with Mark Steyn), 1991; Kiss the Hand You Cannot Bite: The Rise and Fall of the Ceausescus, 1991; The Good Frenchman: The True Story of the Life and Times of Maurice Chevalier, 1993. Honour: Gutenberg Prize, 1988. Address: c/o Newsweek, 162 Faubour St Honore, Paris 75008, France.

BEILBY Alexander John, (Alec Beilby), b. 4 Jan 1938, London, England. Appointments: Daily Mail, 1966-71; Financial Times, 1971-80; Sunday Express/Daily Express, 1980-89. Publications: To Beat The Clipper, 1976; Rough Passage, 1986; Survival At Sea, 1989; Heroes All!, 1992, reprinted 1992, 1994. Contributions to: Country Life; Field; Yachtsman; Sunday Express Magazine; Australian Life. Memberships: Yachting Journalists Association. Address: Bow Cottage, Ermington, Ivybridge, Devon, PL1 2LP, England.

BEIM Norman, b. 2 Oct 1923, Newark, New Jersey, USA. Playwright; Actor; Director. div. Education: Ohio State University; Hedgerow Theatre School, Philadelphia; Institute of Contemporary Art, Washington, DC. Publications: Productions: The Deserter, 1979; Theatre includes 11 off-Broadway productions, 1950-70; Success (Holland), 1982, 1983; Pygmalion & Galatea (Holland), 1983; Archie's Comeback (California, 1986); Six Award Winning Plays, 1994; Plays at Home and Abroad, 1996. Honours: 1st Prize, Double Image/Samuel French Award; On a Darkling Plain, Winner, David James Ellis Memorial Award, best play of season at Theatre Americana, 1990; Dreams, Winner, new play competition, No Empty Space Theatre, New York, 1992; Shakespeare Revisited, Winner Maxim Mazumdar Competition, Alleyway Theatre, New York. Memberships: Dramatists Guild; Actors Equity Association; Literary Managers and Dramatists; Screen Actors Guild; Federation of TV and Radio Artists. Literary Agent: Francis Lonnee, International Drama Agency, Amsterdam, Holland. Address: 425 West 57th Street, Apartment 2J, New York, NY 10019, USA.

BEISSEL Henry, b. 12 Apr 1929, Cologne, Germany. Poet; Dramatist; Writer; Translator; Editor; Teacher. m. (1) 2 daughters, (2) Arlette Francière, 3 Apr 1981, 1 daughter. Education: University of London, 1949; MA, University of Toronto, Canada, 1960. Appointments: Teacher, University of Edmonton, 1962-64; University of Trinidad, 1964-66, Concordia University, Montreal, 1966-96; Founder-Editor, Edge Journal, 1963-69. Publications: Poetry: Witness the Heart, 1963; New Wings for Icarus, 1966; The World is a Rainbow, 1968; Face on the Dark, 1970; The Salt I Taste, 1975; Cantos North, 1980; Season of Blood, 1984; Poems New and Selected, 1987; Ammonite, 1987; Stones to Harvest, 1987; Dying I Was Born, 1992. Plays: Inook and the Sun, 1974; Goya, 1978; Under Coyote's Eye, 1980; The Noose, 1989; Improvisations for Mr X, 1989. Fiction: Winter Crossing (novel in progress), 1971-; The Sniper (novel in progress), 1978-. Other: Kanada: Romantik und Wirklichkeit, 1981; Raging Like a Fire: A Celebration of Irving Layton (editor with Joy Bennett), 1993; Translations of poetry and plays. Contributions to: Journals. Honours: Epstein Award, 1958; Davidson Award, 1959; Deutscher Akademischer Austauschdienst Fellowship, 1977; Walter-Bauer Literaturpreis, Germany, 1994. Memberships: International Academy of Poets; League of Canadian Poets, President, 1980-81; PEN; Playwrights Canada. Address: Box 339, Alexandria, Ontario K0C 1A0, Canada.

BEKEDEREMO J P Clark. See: CLARK John Pepper.

BEKRI Tahar, b. 7 July 1951, Gabes, Tunisia. Writer; Poet; Maître de conferences Paris X. m. Annick Lethoer, 16 Jan 1987. Education: Licence French Litt, University of Tunisia, 1975; Dr French Litt, Sorbonne, Paris, 1981. Publications: Le Laboureur du soleil, 1983; Le Chant du roi errant, 1985; Le coeur rompu aux oceans, 1988; Les Chapelets d'attache, 1994; Litteratures de Tunisie et du Maghreb,

1994; Others: Malek Haddad, Harmattan, 1986; Poemes a Selma, Harmattan, 1996. Contributions to: La Presse, Le Temps, Al-Massar (Tunisia); Croissance; Notre Librairie, Europe, Esprit, Gemmes, Sapriphages, Sud (France). Honour: Officier Mérite Cultural, Tunisia, 1993. Memberships: SGDL (France); UET (Tunisia). Address: 32 Rue Pierre Nicole, 75005 Paris, France.

BELCZYNSKA Barbara, b. 3 Sept 1947, Mlynary, Poland. Writer. Education: Coll in Bydgoszcz, 1970; Econ. Appointments: Econ, 1971-90; Writer, 1990-. Publications: The Silver Wind, 1990; Nobody's Pearls, 1991; The Tear Among Stars, 1992; The Diogenesis Lantern, 1993; The Conjure, 1995; The Matrimonial Announcement, 1997. Contributions to: Metafora. Membership: Lit Soc, Klin. Literary Agent: Book Office, Festina. Address: ul Nawrof 72 M 25, 90-045 Lodz, Poland.

BELIC Oldrich, b. 9 June 1920, Nasedlovice, Czech Republic. Professor. m. Zdenka Neubauerova, 1996, 1 son, 1 daughter. Education: Masaryk University Brno, Romance and Slavonic Philology, 1947, Dr of Philology, 1947, Dr of Philological Sciences, 1963. Appointments: Assistant, University of Olomuc, 1947; Assistant Professor, Olomouc, 1954, Prague, 1958; Professor of Spanish and Spanish-American Literature, University of Prague, 1963. Publications: The Spanish Picaresque Novel and the Realism, 1963; Spanish Literature, 1968; Structural Analysis of Hispanic Texts, 1969, 1977; The Essence of the Spanish Verse, 1975; Introduction to the Theory of Literature, with J Hrabak, 1983, 1988. Contributions to: Numerous essays on Spanish and Spanish-American Literature, in Spanish published mostly in: Philologica Pragensia, Romanistica Pragensia; Ibero-Americana Pragensia. Honour: Commander of the Order of Elisabeth the Catholic, 1991. Address: Vranovska 108, 614 00, Brno, Czech Republic.

BELITT Ben, b. 2 May 1911, New York, New York, USA. Professor of Literature and Languages; Poet; Writer. Education: BA, 1932, MA, 1934, Postgraduate Studies, 1934-36, University of Virginia. Appointments: Assistant Literary Editor, The Nation, 1936-37; Faculty Member to Professor of Literature and Languages, Bennington College, Vermont, 1938-. Publications: Poetry: Wilderness Stair, 1955; The Enemy Joy: New and Selected Poems, 1964; Nowhere But Light: Poems, 1964-1969, 1970; The Double Witness: Poems, 1970-1976, 1977; Possessions: New and Selected Poems, 1938-1985, 1986; Graffiti, 1990. Other: School of the Soldier, 1949; Adam's Dream: A Preface to Translation, 1978; The Forged Feature: Toward a Poetics of Uncertainty, 1994. Editor and translator of several volumes. Contributions to: Books. Honours: Shelley Memorial Award in Poetry, 1936; Guggenheim Fellowship, 1947; Brandeis University Creative Arts Award, 1962; National Institute of Arts and Letters Award, 1965; National Endowment for the Arts Grant, 1967-68; Ben Belitt Lectureship Endowment, Bennington College, 1977; Russell Loines Award for Poetry, American Academy and Institute of Arts and Letters, 1981; Rockefeller Foundation Residency, Bellagio, Italy, 1984; Williams/Derwood Award for Poetry, 1986. Memberships: Authors Guild; Phi Beta Kappa; PEN; Vermont Academy of Arts and Sciences, fellow. Address: PO Box 88, North Bennington, VT 05257, USA.

BELL James Edward, b. 12 May 1941, Chicago, Illinois, USA. College Professor. m. Ruth Wilder Bell, 5 Sept 1964, 1 son, 1 daughter. Education: BA summa cum laude, University of Minnesota, 1963; PhD, University of Minnesota, 1967. Publications: A Guide to Library Research in Psychology, 1971; Co-author, Research and Ideas on Teaching, A Bit of a Handbook, 1976; Sharpen Your Critical Thinking Skills, 1991, 2nd edition, 1995; Evaluating Psychological Information: Sharpen Your Critical Ideas and Issues in Psychology, editor and author, 7th edition, 1994. Contributions to: Numerous articles in professional journals and conference proceedings. Honour: Teaching Award, American Psychological Association, 1982. Address: 5411 Storm Drift, Columbia, MD 21045, USA.

BELL Madison Smartt, b. 1 Aug 1957, Nashville, Tennessee, USA. Author; College Teacher. m. Elizabeth Spires, 15 June 1985. Education: AB, Princeton University, 1979; MA, Hollins College, 1981. Appointments: Lecturer, Poetry Center of the 92nd Street YMHA, New York City, 1984-86; Writer-in-Residence, Director of the Creative Writing Program, Goucher College, 1984-86, 1988-; Visiting Lecturer, University of Iowa, 1987-88; Visiting Associate Professor, Johns Hopkins University, 1989-95. Publications: Fiction: The Washington Square Ensemble, 1983; Waiting for the End of the World, 1985; Straight Cut, 1986; Zero db, 1987; The Year of Silence, 1987; Soldier's

Joy, 1989; Barking Man, 1990; Doctor Sleep, 1991; Save Me, Joe Louis, 1993; All Souls' Rising, 1995; Ten Indians, 1996. Non-Fiction: Readers' guides on various authors, 1979-83; The History of the Owen Graduate School of Management, 1988. Contributions to: Fiction in many anthologies and periodicals; Essays, book reviews, etc. Honours: Lillian Smith Award, 1989; Guggenheim Fellowship, 1991; George A and Eliza Gardner Howard Foundation Award, 1991-92; National Endowment for the Arts Fellowship, 1992; National Book Award Finalist, 1995; PEN/Faulkner Award Finalist, 1996. Address: 6208 Pinehurst Road, Baltimore, MD 21212, USA.

BELL Marvin Hartley, b. 3 Aug 1937, New York, New York, USA. Poet; Teacher. m. Dorothy Murphy, 2 sons. Education: BA, Alfred University, 1958; MA, Literature, University of Chicago, 1961; MFA, Literature, University of Iowa, 1963. Appointments: Faculty, 1965-, Flannery O'Connor Professor of Letters, 1986-, University of Iowa; Visiting Lecturer, Goddard College, 1970; Visiting Professor, University of Hawaii, 1981-82. Publications: A Probable Volume of Dreams, 1969; The Escape into You, 1971; Residue of Song, 1974; Stars Which See, Stars Which Do Not See, 1977; These Green-Going-To-Yellow, 1981; Segues: A Correspondence in Poetry (with William Stafford), 1983; Old Snow Just Melting; Essays and Interviews, 1983; Drawn by Stones, by Earth, by Things That Have Been in the Fire, 1984; New and Selected Poems, 1987; Iris of Creation, 1990; The Book of the Dead Man, 1994; A Marvin Bell Reader, selected poetry and prose, 1994. Contributor to: Professional journals. Honours: Lamont Award, Academy of American Poets, 1969; Bess Hokin Award, Poetry magazine, 1969; National Book Finalist, 1977; Guggenheim Fellowship, 1977; National Endowment for the Arts Fellowships, 1978, 1984; American Poetry Review Prize, 1982; Senior Fulbright Scholar, 1983, 1986; American Academy of Arts and Letters Award, 1994. Address: Writers' Workshop, EPB, University of Iowa, Iowa City, IA 52242, USA.

BELLAMY David James, b. 18 Jan 1933, England. Botanist; Writer. m. Rosemary Froy, 1959, 2 sons, 3 daughters. Education: Chelsea College of Science and Technology; PhD, Bedford College, London University. Appointments: Lecturer, Botany, 1960-68, Senior Lecturer, Botany, 1968-82, Honorary Professor, Adult Education, 1982-. University of Durham; Television and radio presenter, scriptwriter of series including: Bellamy's New World, 1983; Seaside Safari, 1985; The End of the Rainbow Show, 1986; Bellamy on Top of the World, 1987; Turning the Tide, 1987; Bellamy's Bulge, 1987-88; Bellamy's Birds Eye View, 1988; Moa's Ark, 1989-90; Special Professor of Botany, University of Nottingham, 1987-; Visiting Professor, Natural Heritage Studies, Massey University, New Zealand, 1989-91; Director, Botanical Enterprises, David Bellamy Associates, National Heritage Conservation Fund (NZ), Conservation Foundation, London. Publications: The Great Seasons, 1981; Discovering the Countryside with David Bellamy, 4 volumes, 1982-83; The Mouse Book, 1983; The Queen's Hidden Garden, 1984; Bellamy's Ireland, 1986; Bellamy's Changing World, 4 volumes, 1988; England's Last Wilderness, 1989; How Green are You?, 1991; Tomorrow's Earth, 1991; World Medicine, 1992; Various books connected with Television series. Honours: Officer of the Order of the British Empire; Dutch Order of the Golden Ark; UNEP Global 500 Award; Duke of Edinburgh's Award for Underwater Research; British Academy of Film and Television Arts; BSAC Diver of the Year; Richard Dimbleby Award; Chartered Institute of Water and Environmental Management, fellow. Memberships: Fellow, Linnaean Society; Founder-Director, Conservation Foundation; President, WATCH, 1982-83; President, Youth Hostels Association, 1983; President, Population Concern; President, National Association of Environmental Education. Address: Mill House, Bedburn, Bishop Auckland, County Durham DL13 3NW, England.

BELLI Gioconda, b. 1948, Nicaragua. Poet. Education: Studied in Europe and the USA. Publications: Sobre la grama, 1974; Linea de fuego, 1978; Truenos y arco iris, 1982; Amor insurrecto, 1984; From Eve's Rib, 1987; Poesia reunida, 1989; Novels: La Mujer Habitada, 1988, translated into English, German, Italian, Dutch, Danish, Finnish, Greek and Turkish; Sofia, 1990; Poems: The Eye of the Woman, collected poems from 1970-90, 1991. Honours: Casa delas Americas Prize, 1978; Best Political Novel of the Year, Friederich Ebhert Foundation, 1989. Address: c/o Curbstone Press, 321 Jackson Street, Willimantic, CT 06226, USA.

BELLOW Saul, b. 10 June 1915, Lachine, Quebec, Canada. Writer. m. (1) Anita Goshkin, div, 1 son, (2) Alexandra Tschacbasov,

1956, div, 1 son, (3) Susan Glassman, 1961, div, 1 son, (4) Alexandra Ionesco Tuleca, 1974, div, (5) Janis Freedman, 1989. Education: University of Chicago, 1933-35; BS, Northwestern University, 1937. Appointments: Instructor, Pestalozzi-Froebel Teachers College, Chicago, 1938-42; Editorial Department, Great Books of the Western World, Encyclopaedia Britannica, Chicago, 1943-46; Instructor, 1946, Assistant Professor, 1948-49, Associate Professor, 1954-59, University of Minnesota; Visiting Lecturer, New York University, 1950-52; Creative Writing Fellow, Princeton University, 1952-53; Teacher, Bard College, 1953-54; Grunier Distinguished Services Professor, University of Chicago, 1962-; Lecturer, Oxford University, 1990. Publications: Fiction: Dangling Man, 1944; The Victim, 1947; The Adventures of Augie March, 1953; Seize the Day, 1956; Henderson the Rain King, 1959; Herzog, 1964; Mr Sammler's Planet, 1970; Humboldt's Gift, 1975; The Dean's December, 1982; More Die iof Heartbreak, 1986; A Theft, 1989; The Bellarosa Connection, 1989. Stories: Mosby's Memoirs and Other Stories, 1968; Him With His Foot in His Mouth and Other Stories, 1984; Something to Remeber Me By: Three Tales, 1991; Occasional Pieces, 1993. Plays: The Wrecker, 1954; The Last Analysis, 1964; Under the Weather, 1966. Non-Fiction: To Jerusalem and Back: A Personal Account, 1976; It All Adds Up: From the Dim Past to the Uncertain Future, 1994. Contributions to: Many periodicals. Honours: Guggenheim Fellowship, 1948; National Book Awards, 1954, 1964, 1970; Nobel Prize for Literature, 1976; Pulitzer Prize in Fiction, 1976; American Academy of Arts and Letters Gold Medal, 1977; Brandeis University Creative Arts Award, 1978; Commander, Legion of Honour, 1983, Order of Arts and Letters, 1985, France; National Medal of Arts, 1988; National Book Award Lifetime Achievement Award, 1990. Membership: American Academy of Arts and Letters. Address: 1126 East 59th Street, Chicago, IL 60637, USA.

BELOFF Lord, (Max), b. 2 July 1913, London, England. Historian. m. Helen Dobrin, 20 Mar 1938, 2 sons. Education: St Paul's School, 1926-32; Corpus Christi and Magdalen Colleges, Oxford, 1932-37, MA Oxon 1937, DLitt 1974. Publications: The Foreign Policy of Soviet Russia, 1947; The American Federal Government, 1959; New Dimensions in Foreign Policy, 1961; Imperial Sunset - vol 1, Britain's Liberal Empire, 1969; The Intellectual in Politics, 1970; Wars and Welfare, Britain 1914-45, 1987; Imperial Sunset - vol 2, Dream of Commonwealth, 1989; Joint Author: The Government of the UK, 1985; An Historian in the Twentieth Century, 1992; Joint Editor: L'Europe du XIX siècle et XX siècle (1960-66); Britain and European Union: dialogue of the deaf, 1996. Contributions to: The National Interest; Jewish Journal of Sociology; Minerva; Times Literary Supplement; History Today. Honours: Knighted, 1980; Life Peer, 1981; Six honorary doctorates. Memberships: Fellow, British Academy; Fellow, Royal Historical Society; Royal Society of Arts, fellow. Address: House of Lords, London SW1A 0PW, England.

BEN JELLOUN Tahar, b. 1 Dec 1944, Fes, Morocco. Writer; Poet; Dramatist. m. Aicha Ben Jelloun, 8 Aug 1986, 1 daughter. Education:University of Rabat, 1963-68; PhD, University of Paris, 1975. Publications: Fiction: Harrouda, 1973; La Réclusion solitaire, 1976, English translation as Solitaire, 1988; Moha le fou, Moha le sage, 1978; La Prière de l'absent, 1981; Muha al-ma'twah, Muha al-hakim, 1982; L'Ecrivain public, 1983; L'Enfant de sable, 1985, English translation as The Sand Child, 1987; La Nuit sacreé, 1987, English translation as The Sacred Night, 1989; Jour de silence à Tanger, 1990, English translation as Silent Day in Tangier, 1991; Les Yeux baissés, 1991. Poetry: Hommes sous linceul de silence, 1970; Cicatrices du soleil, 1972; Le Discours du chameau, 1974; La Memoire future: Anthologie de la nouvelle poesie du Maroc, 1976; Les Amandiers sont morts de leurs blessures, 1976; A l'insu du souvenir, 1980; Sahara, 1987; La Remontée des cendres, 1991. Plays: Chronique d'une solitude, 1976; Entretien avec Monsieur Said Hammadi, ouvrier algerien, 1982; La Fiancée de l'eau, 1984. Non-Fiction: La Plus Haute des solitudes: Misere sexuelle d'emigres nord-africains, 1977; Haut Atlas: L'Exil de pierres, 1982; Hospitalité francaise: Racisme et immigration maghrebine, 1984; Marseille, comme un matin d'insomnie, 1986; Giacometti, 1991. Honours: Prix de l'Amitie Franco-Arabe, 1976; Chevalier des Arts et des Lettres, 1983; Prix Goncourt, 1987; Chevalier de la Légion d'Honneur, 1988; Prix des Hemispheres, 1991. Address: 27 Rue Jacob, 75 Paris 6, France.

BEN-RAFAEL Eliezer, b. 3 Oct 1938, Brussels, Belgium. Professor of Sociology. m. Miriam Neufeld, 3 Aug 1960, 2 daughters. Education: BA, 1966, MA, 1970, PhD, 1973, Hebrew University, Jerusalem. Appointments: Research Fellow, Harvard University, 1974-75; Professor of Sociology, Tel-Aviv University, 1980-; Directeur d'Etudes Associé, Ecole des Hautes Etudes en Sciences Sociales, 1984-85; Visiting Scholar, Oxford Centre for Postgraduate Hebrew Studies, 1989-90; Co-Editor, Israel Social Sciences Review, 1992-. Publications: The Emergence of Ethnicity: Cultural Groups and Social Conflict in Israel, 1982; Le kibboutz, 1983; Status, Power and Conflict in the Kibbutz Gower, 1988; Ethnicity, Religion and Class in Israeli Society, 1991; Language, Identity and Social Division: The Case of Israel, 1994; Crisis and Transformation: The Kibbutz at Century's End, 1997. Contributions to: International Sociology; Ethnics Racial Relations; European Journal of Sociology; British Journal of Sociology; International Journal of Comparative Sociology. Membership: President, Israel Society of Sociology, 1994-. Address: Department of Sociology, Tel-Aviv University, Tel-Aviv 69978, Israel.

BENCE-JONES Mark, b. 29 May 1930, London, England. Writer. m. Gillian Pretyman, 2 Feb 1965, 1 son, 2 daughters. Education: BA 1952, MA 1958, Pembroke College, Cambridge University; MRAC, Royal Agricultural College, Cirencester, 1954. Publications: Clive of India, 1974; The Viceroys of India, 1982; Twilight of the Ascendancy, 1987; Also: All A Nonsense, 1957; Paradise Escaped, 1958; Nothing in the City, 1965; The Remarkable Irish, 1966; Palaces of the Raj, 1973; The Cavaliers, 1976; Burke's Guide to Irish Country Houses, 1984; The British Aristocracy, co-author, 1979; Ancestral Houses, 1984; A Guide to Irish Country Houses, 1989; The Catholic Families, 1992; Life in an Irish Country House, 1996; Introductory articles, Burke's genealogical publications. Contributions to: Irish Times; Country Life. Memberships: Brooks's; Kildare Street and University Club, Dublin; Royal Irish Automobile Club. Address: Glenville Park, Glenville, County Cork, Ireland.

BENEDICTUS David (Henry), b. 16 Sept 1938, London, England. Writer. Education: BA, Baliol College, Oxford, 1959. Appointments: Book Reviewer and Theatre Director; Drama Director, 1964-65; Story Editor, 1967, BBC Television; Assistant Director, Royal Shakespeare Company, 1970-71; Visiting Fellow, Churchill College, Cambridge, 1981-82; Commissioning Editor, Channel 4 Drama Series, 1984-86; Editor, Readings, BBC Radio, 1989-92, Readings and Radio 3 Drama 1992-93, Senior Producer, Serial Readings 1993-94. Publications: The Fourth of June, 1963; You're a Big Boy Now, 1964; This Animal is Mischievous, 1966; Hump, or Bone by Bone Alive, 1968; The Guru and the Golf Club, 1970; A World of Windows, 1972; The Rabbi's Wife, Junk, 1976; Betjemania, 1977; A Twentieth Century Man, 1978; The Antique Collector's Guide, 1980; Lloyd George, 1981; Whose Life Is It Anyway?, Floating Down to Camelot, 1985; Little Sir Nicholas, 1990; Odyssey of a Scientist, 1991; Sunny Intervals and Showers, 1992; The Stamp Collector, 1994; The Essential Guide to London Entertainment, How to Cope When the Money Runs Out, 1987; Numerous Radio, TV and Stage Credits. Address: 19 Oxford Road, Teddington, Middlesex TW11 0QA, England.

BENEDIKT Michael, b. 26 May 1935, New York, New York, USA. Writer; Poet; Critic; Editor. Education: BA, New York University, 1956; MA, Columbia University, 1961. Appointments: Professorships in Literature and Poetry, Bennington College, 1968-69, Sarah Lawrence College 1969-73, Hampshire College 1973-75, Vassar College 1976-77, Boston University 1977-79; Contributing Editor, American Poetry Review, 1973-; Poetry Editor, Paris Review, 1974-78. Publications: The Body (verse), 1968; Sky (verse), 1970; Mole Notes (prose poems), 1971; Night Cries (prose poems), 1976; The Badminton at Great Barrington or Gustav Mahler and the Chattanooga Choo-Choo, poems, 1980; Anthologies: Modern French Theatre: The Avant-Garde, Dada and Surrealism (with George E Wellwarth), 1964, in UK as Modern French Plays: An Anthology from Jarry to Ionesco, 1965; Post-War German Theatre (with George E Wellwarth), 1967; Modern Spanish Theatre (with George E Wellwarth), 1968; Theatre Experiment, 1968; The Poetry of Surrealism, 1975; The Prose Poem: An International Anthology, 1976. Contributions to: Agni Review; Ambit; Art International; Art News; London Magazine; Massachusetts Review; New York Quarterly; Paris Review; Partisan Review; Poetry. Honours: Guggenheim Fellowship, 1968-69; Bess Hokin Prize, 1969; National Endowment for the Arts Prize, 1970; Benedikt: A Profile (critical monograph/Festschrift), 1978; National Endowment for the Arts Fellowship, 1979-80; Retrospective, Library of Congress, videotape, 1986. Memberships: PEN Club of America; Poetry Society of America. Address: 315 West 98th Street, No 6 A, New York, NY 10025, USA.

BENFIELD Derek, b. 11 Mar 1926, Bradford, Yorkshire, England. Playwright; Actor. m. Susan Elspeth Lyall Grant, 17 July 1953, 1 son, 1 daughter. Education: Bingley Grammar School; Royal Academy of Dramatic Art. Publications: Plays: Wild Goose Chase, 1956; Running Riot, 1958; Post Horn Gallop, 1965; Murder for the Asking, 1967; Off the Hook, 1970; Bird in the Hand, 1973; Panic Stations, 1975; Caught on the Hop, 1979; Beyond a Joke, 1980; In for the Kill, 1981; Look Who's Talking, 1984; Touch & Go, 1985; Fish Out of Water, 1986; Flying Feathers, 1987; Bedside Manners, 1988; A Toe in the Water, 1991; Don't Lose the Place, 1992; Anyone for Breakfast?, 1994; Up and Running, 1995; A Fly in the Ointment, 1996. Membership: Society of Authors. Literary Agent: Lemon Unna & Durbridge Ltd, 24 Pottery Lane, Holland Park, London W11 4LZ, England.

BENFORD Gregory (Albert), b. 30 Jan 1941, Mobile, Alabama, USA. Physicist; Science Fiction Author. m. Joan Abbe, 26 Aug 1967, 1 son, 1 daughter. Education: BA, University of Oklahoma, 1963; MS, 1965, PhD, 1967, University of California at San Diego. Appointments: Fellow, 1967-69, Research Physicist, 1969-71, Lawrence Radiation Laboratory, Livermore, California; Assistant Professor, 1971-73, Associate Professor, 1973-79, Professor of Physics, 1979-, University of California at Irvine. Publications: Deeper Than the Darkness, 1970, revised edition as The Stars in the Shroud, 1979; If the Stars Are Gods (with Gordon Eklund), 1977; In the Ocean of Night, 1977; Find the Changeling (with Gordon Eklund), 1980; Shiva Descending (with William Rotsler), 1980; Timescape, 1980; Against Infinity, 1983; Across the Sea of Suns, 1984; Artifact, 1985; Of Space-Time and the River, 1985; In Alien Flesh, 1986; Heart of the Comet (with David Brin), 1986; Great Sky River, 1987; Under the Wheel (with others), 1987; Hitler Victorious: Eleven Stories of the German Victory in World War II (editor with Martin H Greenberg), 1987; We Could Do Worse, 1988; Tides of Light, 1989; Beyond the Fall of Night (with Arthur C Clarke), 1990; Centigrade 233, 1990; Matter's End (editor), 1991; Chiller, 1993; Furious Gulf, 1994; Far Futures, 1995; Sailing Bright Eternity, 1995; Foundation's Fear, 1997. Honours: Woodrow Wilson Fellowship, 1963-64; Nebula Awards, Science Fiction Writers of America, 1975, 1981; British Science Fiction Association Award, 1981; John W Campbell Award, World Science Fiction Convention, 1981; Ditmar Award, Australia, 1981; Various grants. Memberships: American Physical Society; Phi Beta Kappa; Royal Astronomical Society; Science Fiction Writers of America; Social Science Exploration. Address: 1105 Skyline Drive, Lagune Beach, CA 92651, USA.

BENITEZ Sandra, b. 26 Mar 1941, Washington DC, USA. Author. m. James F Kondrick, 25 May 1980, 2 sons. Education: BS Education 1963, MA Comparative Literature 1974, Northeast Missouri State University.Appointments: University of Minnesota Distinguished Edelstein-Keller Writer-in-Residence, Winter 1997. Publications: A Place Where the Sea Remembers Coffee House Press, 1993; A Place Where the Sea Remembers, 1995. Honours: Minnesota Book Award for Fiction, 1993; Barnes & Noble Fiction Award, 1994. Membership: Authors Guild, Poets and Writers. Literary Agent: Ellen Levine. Address: c/o Ellen Levine Literary Agency, 15 East 26th Street #1801, NY, NY 10010, USA.

BENJAMIN David. See: SLAVITT David Rytman.

BENN Tony (Anthony Neil Wedgwood), b. 3 Apr 1925, London, England. Member of Parliament. m. Caroline Middleton De Camp, 1949, 3 sons, 1 daughter. Education: New College, Oxford, 1941-42, 1946-48, MA Oxon, Hon DPhil, HonDSc, HonDTech, HonDCL, Hon LLD. Appointments: Served RAFVR, 1943-45, RNVR, 1945-46, Joined Labour Party, 1943; Member, NEC 1959-60, 1962-94 (Chairman, 1971-72), MP (Lab) Bristol SE, Nov 1950-60 and Aug 1963-83; Postmaster General, 1964-66, recommended establishment of GPO as public corporation and founded Giro; Minister of Technology, 1966-70, assumed responsibility for Ministry of Aviation, 1967 and Minister of Power, 1969-70; Appointed Privy Councillor, 1964. Publications: The Privy Council as a Second Chamber, 1957; The Regeneration of Britain, 1964; The New Politics, 1970; Speeches, 1974; Arguments for Socialism, 1979; Arguments for Democracy, 1981; Parliament, People and Power, 1982; Writings on the Wall; A Radical and Socialist Anthology 1215-1984 (editor), 1984; Sizewell Syndrome, 1984; Fighting Back, 1988; A Future for Socialism, 1991; Diaries: Out of the Wilderness - 1963-68, 1987; Office Without Power - 1968-72, 1988; Against the Tide - 1973-76, 1989; Conflicts of Interest, 1977-80, 1990; End of an Era - 1980-90, 1992; Common Sense: A New Constitution for Britain, 1993; Speaking up in Parliament: Speeches on Video, 1989-93; Years of Hope, 1940-62, 1994, and as an Audiobook; Benn Tapes Diaries I and II, 1994-95; Benn Diaries

1940-62; Westminster Behind Closed Doors, video, 1995. Contributions to: Various journals in the UK and abroad. Membership: National Union of Journalists. Address: House of Commons, London SW1 0AA, England.

BENNETT Alan, b. 9 May 1934, Leeds, England. Dramatist. Education: BA, Modern History, Oxford, 1957. Publications: Forty Years On, 1968; Getting On, 1971; Habeas Corpus, 1973; The Old Country, 1977; Enjoy, 1980; Objects of Affection, 1983; Writer in Disguise, 1984;Kafka's Dick, 1986; Talking Heads, 1988; Single Spies, 1989; The Lady in the Van, 1990; Poetry in Motion, 1990; The Wind in The Willows (adaptation), 1991; The Madness of George III, 1992; Writing Home (autobiography), 1994; Diaries, 1997; Screenplays: A Private Function, 1984; Prick Up Your Ears, 1987; The Madness of King George, 1995. Contributions to: London Review of Books. Literary Agent: A D Peters. Address: Peter, Fraser and Dunlop, The Chambers, Chelsea Harbour, London, SW10 0XF, England.

BENNETT Bernice Spitz (Thin is In), b. 4 Sept 1923, Boston, MA, USA. Writer. m. Jack Bennett, 5 June 1942, 1 s, 1d. Education: Boston Univ; Brandeis Coll; Simmons Coll; Spec Courses. Career: Journalist, Columnist. Publications: Articles in Boston Globe; Newton Graphic. Memberships: Natl Writers Club; Boston Local - Profl Writers; Fell, Intl Biographical Inst, 1990; Free-Lancers over Fifty Soc, Cambridge, MA. Literary Agent: Mockingbird Press, James Stallings, Needham, MA, USA.

BENNETT Bruce Harry, b. 23 Mar 1941, Perth, Australia. University Professor. m. Patricia Ann Staples, 8 July 1967, 1 son, 1 daughter. Education: BA, Western Australia, 1963; MA, Oxford, 1972; MA Ed, London, 1974; FACE, 1990; FAHA, 1995. Appointments: Lecturer, University of Western Australia, 1968; Senior Lecturer, 1975; Associate Professor, 1985; Professor, Head of English, University College, Australian Defence Force Academy, 1993-; Co-Editor, Westerly, 1975-92. Publications: Crossing Cultures; Spirit in Exile; An Australian Compass; Myths, Heroes and Anti-heroes; Western Australian Writing; A Sense of Exile; Place, Region and Community; Cross Currents; The Literature of Western Australia; Windows Onto Worlds. Contributions to: Antipodes; Australian Literary Studies; Overland. Honours: Officer of the Order of Australia, 1993; Fellow, Australian Academy of the Humanities, 1995; Western Australian Premier's Literary Award, 1992. Memberships: Association for the Study of Australian Literature; Australian Society of Authors; Modern Language Association of America; Association of Commonwealth Literature and Language Societies. Address: School of English, University College, University of New South Wales, Australian Defence Force Academy, Canberra, ACT 2600, Australia.

BENNETT Dwight. See: NEWTON D(wight) B(ennett).

BENNETT John J, b. 8 Aug 1938, Brooklyn, New York, USA. Writer. Education: George Washington University; University of Munich. Publications: Tripping in America, 1984; Crime of the Century, 1986; The New World Order, 1991; Bodo (novel), 1995; Karmic Four-Star Buckaroo, 1997; Others: The Adventures of Achilles Jones; The Night of the Great Butcher. Contributions to: Chicago Review; Exquisite Corpse; Northwest Review; Transatlantic Review; New York Quarterly; Seattle Weekly. Honours: Iron Country, 1st prize fiction, 1978; William Wantling Award, 1987; Darrell Bob Houston Award, 1988; Finalist, Drue Heing Literary Prize, 1991. Address: PO Box 1634, Ellensburg, WA 98926, USA.

BENNETT Louise (Simone), b. 7 Sept 1919, Kingston, Jamaica. Lecturer; Poet. m. Eric Coverley. Education: Royal Academy of Dramatic Art, London. Appointments: Resident Artist with the BBC West Indies section, 1950-53; Lecturer and Radio and Television Commentator in Jamaica. Publications: Dialect Verses, 1940; Jamaican Dialect Verses, 1942; Jamaican Humour in Dialect, 1943; Miss Lulu Sez, 1948; Anancy Stories and Dialect Verses, 1950; Laugh with Louise, 1960; Jamaica Labrish, 1966; Anancy and Miss Lou, 1979; Selected Poems, 1982; Various recordings of Jamaican songs and poems. Honours: Norman Manley Award of Excellence; DLitt, University of the West Indies, 1982; Member of the Order of the British Empire; Order of Jamaica. Address: Enfield House, Gordon Town, St Andrew, Jamaica.

BENNETT Paul (Lewis), b. 10 Jan 1921, Gnadenhutten, Ohio, USA. Professor of English (Retired); Poet; Writer; Gardener; Orchardist. m. Martha Jeanne Leonhart, 31 Dec 1942, dec 1995, 2

sons. Education: BA, Ohio University, 1942; AM, Harvard University, 1947. Appointments: Instructor, Samuel Adams School of Social Studies, Boston, 1945-46; Teaching Assistant, Harvard University, 1945-46; Instructor in English, University of Maine, Orono, 1946-47; Instructor to Professor of English, 1947-86, Poet-in-Residence, 1986-, Denison University; Gardener and Orchardist, 1948-; Consultant, Aerospace Laboratories, Owens-Corning Fiberglass Corp, 1964-67, Ohio Arts Council, 1978-81, Ohio Board of Regents, 1985-86. Publications: Poetry: A Strange Affinity, 1975; The Eye of Reason, 1976; Building a House, 1986; The Sun and What It Says Endlessly, 1995. Novels: Robbery on the Highway, 1961; The Living Things, 1975; Follow the River, 1987. Contributions to: Many periodicals. Honours: National Endowment for the Arts Fellowship, 1973-74; Phi Beta Kappa; Pi Delta Epsilon; Significant Achievement Award, Ohio University, 1992. Address: 1281 Burg Street, Granville, OH 43023, USA.

BENSON Daniel. See: COOPER Colin Symons.

BENSON Eugene, b. 6 July 1928, Larne, Northern Ireland. Professor Emeritus; Writer. m. Renate Niklaus, 30 Apr 1968, 2 sons. Education: BA, National University of Ireland, 1950; MA, University of Western Ontario, 1958; PhD, University of Toronto, 1966. Appointments: Lecturer, Royal Military College, Kingston, Ontario, 1960-61; Assistant Professor of English, Laurentian University, 1961-64; Assistant Professor, 1965-67, Associate Professor, 1967-71, Professor of English, 1971-93, University Professor Emeritus, 1994-, University of Guelph. Publications: Encounter: Canadian Drama in Four Media, anthology (editor), 1973; The Bulls of Ronda (novel), 1976; Power Game, or the Making of a Prime Minister (novel), 1980; J M Synge, critical study, 1982; English-Canadian Theatre, critical study (co-author), 1987; Oxford Companion to Canadian Theatre (co-editor), 1989; Encyclopedia of Post-Colonial Literatures in English (co-editor), 1994. Memberships: Association of Canadian Theatre Historians; Canadian Association of Irish Studies; Writers' Union of Canada, chair, 1983-84; PEN Canada, co-president 1984-85. Address: 55 Palmer Street, Guelph, Ontario N1E 2P9, Canada.

BENSON Mary, b. 9 Dec 1919, Pretoria, South Africa. Writer. Publications: Tshekedi Khama, 1960; The African Patriots, 1963; At the Still Point, 1969; South Africa: The Struggle for a Birthright, 1969; Nelson Mandela: The Man and the Movement, 1986, updated, 1994; A Far Cry (autobiography), 1989, updated, 1995; Editor, Athol Fugard Notebooks, 1983. Contributions to: London Magazine; Observer; Yale Theatre; Granta; Botswana Notes & Records; BBC Radio Drama and Documentaries. Address: 34 Langford Court, London NW8 9DN, England.

BENTLEY Eric (Russell), b. 14 Sept 1916, Bolton, Lancashire, England (US citizen, 1948). m. (1) Maja Tschernjakow, diss, (2) Joanne Davis, 1953, twin sons. Education: BA, 1938, BLitt, 1939, Oxford University; PhD, Yale University, 1941. Appointments: Drama Critic, New Republic, 1952-56; Charles Eliot Norton Professor of Poetry, Harvard University, 1960-61; Fulbright Professor, Belgrade, 1980; Professor of Comparative Literature, University of Maryland, College Park, 1982-89. Publications: Larry Park's Day in Court, 1979; Lord Alfred's Lover, 1979; The Kleist Variations, 1982; Monstrous Martyrdoms, 1985; The Pirandello Commentaries, 1985; The Brecht Memoir, 1986; German Requiem, 1990; Round 2, 1991. Honours: Festschrift: The Critic and the Play, 1986; Florida Theatre Festival named in his honour, 1992; Honorary Doctorate, New School for Social Research, 1992; Robert Lewis Award for Life Achievement in the Theatre, 1992. Memberships: American Academy of Arts and Sciences, 1969-; American Academy of Arts and Letters, 1990-. Address: 194 Riverdale Drive, Apt 4 E, New York, NY 10025, USA.

BERCH Bettina, b. 25 May 1950, Washington DC, USA. Writer. 1 daughter. Education: BA, Barnard College, 1971; MA, 1973, PhD, 1976, University of Wisconsin. Publications: The Endless Day: The Political Economy of Women and Work, 1982; Radical by Design: The Life and Style of Elizabeth Hawes, 1988. Contributions to: Early Feminist Fashion; The Resurrection of Out Work; Belles Letters; Paradise of a Kind. Literary Agent: Malaga Baldi. Address: 878 West End, New York, NY 10025, USA.

BERESFORD Anne. See: HAMBURGER Anne (Ellen).

BERESFORD Elisabeth, b. Paris, France. Writer. 1 son, 1 daughter. Appointments: Founder, Alderney Youth Trust. Publications:

The Television Mystery, 1957; Trouble at Tullington Castle, 1958; Gappy Goes West, 1959; Two Gold Dolphins, 1961; Paradise Island, 1963; Escape to Happiness, 1964; Game, Set and Match, 1965; The Hidden Mill, 1965; The Black Mountain Mystery, 1967; Sea-Green Magic, 1968; Stephen and The Shaggy Dog, 1970; The Wandering Wombles, 1970; Dangerous Magic, 1972; The Secret Railway, 1973; The Wombles at Work, 1973; The Wombles Annual, yearly, 1975-78; Snuffle to the Rescue, 1975; Orinoco Runs Away, 1975; Bungo Knows Best, 1976; Tobermory's Big Surprise, 1976; Wombling Free, 1978; The Happy Ghost, 1979; Curious Magic, 1980; The Four of Us, 1982; The Animals Nobody Wanted, 1982; The Tovers, 1982; The Adventures of Poon, 1984; One of the Family, 1985; The Ghosts of Lupus Street School, 1986; The Secret Room, 1987; Emily and the Haunted Castle, 1987; The Oscar Puffin Book, 1987; Once Upon a Time Stories, 1988; The Island Railway Armada Adventure, 1989; Rose; Charlie's Ark; The Wooden Gun; Tim the Trumpet, 1992; Jamie and the Rola Polar Bear, 1993; Lizzy's War, 1993; Rola Polar Bear and the Heatwave, 1995; Lizzy's War Part II, 1996; The Smallest Whale, 1996. Literary Agent: Juvenilia, Avington, Winchester, Hampshire SO21 1DB, England; Stephen Durbridge, 24 Pottery Lane, Holland Park, London W11 4LZ, England. Address: Little Street, Alderney, Channel Islands.

BERESFORD-HOWE Constance, b. 10 Nov 1922, Montreal, Quebec, Canada. Professor of English; Novelist. m. 31 Dec 1960, 1 son. Education: BA 1945, MA 1946, McGill University; PhD 1950, Brown University. Publications: The Book of Eve, 1973; A Population of One, 1976; The Marriage Bed, 1980; Night Studies, 1984; Prospero's Daughter, 1989; A Serious Widow, 1990. Honours: Dodd Mead Intercollegiate Literary Fellowship, 1948; Canadian Booksellers Award, 1974. Memberships: Canadian Authors Association; International PEN; International PEN, Writers in Prison Committee. Address: c/o McClelland and Stewart, 481 University Avenue, Toronto, Ontario M4V 1E2, Canada.

BERG Hans (Cornelisten), b. 24 Dec 1938, Netherlands. Poet; Writer; Editor. Appointments: Lecturer, Art Academy, Arnhem; Writer-in-Residence, University of Texas; Editor, Raster, Grid, literary journals. Publications: Poetry: Gedichten, 3 volumes, 1969; White Shaman, 1973; Poetry of the Aztecs, 1972; Va-banque, 1977; Semblance of Reality, 1981; Texas Elegies, 1983; Songs of Anxiety and Despair, 1988. Novels: Zelfportret met witte muts, 1985; Het geheim van een oppewekt humeur, 1986. Other: The Defence of Poetry, essays, 1988; Prose books: Books of myths and fables of Arctic peoples; Numerous poetry translations. Contributions to: Periodicals. Honours: Van der Hoogt Prize, 1968; Prose Prize, City of Amsterdam, 1971. Memberships: PEN; Society of Dutch Literature. Address: c/o Meulenhoff Publishers, PO Box 100, 1000 AC Amsterdam, Netherlands.

BERG Leila, b. 12 Nov 1917, Salford, Lancashire, England. Writer; Children's Author. 1 son, 1 daughter. Education: University of London. Publications: Risinghill: Death of a Comprehensive School, 1968; Look at Kids, 1972; Reading and Loving, 1977; Many books and stories for children, including: The Hidden Road, 1958; Folk Tales, 1966; The Nippers Stories, 1968-76; The Snap series, 1977; The Chatterbooks series, 1981; The Small World series, 1983; The Steep Street Stories, 1987; Backwards and Forwards, 1994. Contributions to: Anarchy; Guardian; Times Educational Supplement; Times Literary Supplement. Honour: Eleanor Farjeon Award for Services to Children's Literature, 1973. Address: Alice's Cottage, Brook Street, Wivenhoe, Near Colchester CO7 9DS, England.

BERG Stephen (Walter), b. 2 Aug 1934, Philadelphia, Pennsylvania, USA. Poet; Writer; Editor. m. Millie Lane, 1959, 2 daughters. Education: University of Pennsylvania; Boston University; BA, University of Iowa, 1959; Indiana University. Appointments: Teacher, Temple University, Philadelphia, Princeton University, Haverford College, Pennsylvania; Professor, Philadelphia College of Art; Poetry Editor, Saturday Evening Post, 1961-62; Founding Editor (with Stephen Parker and Rhoda Schwartz), American Poetry Review, 1972-. Publications: Poetry: Berg Goodman Mezey, 1957; Bearing Weapons, 1963; The Queen's Triangle: A Romance, 1970; The Daughtyers, 1971; Nothing in the Word: Versions of Aztec Poetry, 1972; Grief: Poems and Versions of Poems, 1975; With Akmatova at the Black Gates: Variations, 1981; In It, 1986; First Song, Bankei, 1653, 1989; Homage to the Afterlife, 1991; New and Selected Poems, 1992; Oblivion: Poems, 1995. Editor: Naked Poetry: Recent American Poetry in Open Forms (with Robert Mezey), 1969; Between People

(with S J Marks), 1972; About Women (with S J Marks), 1973; The New Naked Poetry (with Robert Mezey), 1976; In Praise of What Persists, 1983; Singular Voices: American Poetry Today, 1985. Other: Sea Ice: Versions of Eskimo Songs, 1988. Contributions to: Periodicals. Honours: Rockefeller-Centro Mexicano de Escritores Grant, 1959-61; National Translation Center Grant, 1969; Frank O'Hara Prize, Poetry magazine, 1970; Guggenheim Fellowship, 1974; National Endowment for the Arts Grant, 1976; Columbia University Translation Center Award, 1976. Address: 2005 Mt Vernon Street, Philadelphia, PA 19130, USA.

BERG Y L. See: ELBERG Yehuda.

BERGÉ Carol, b. 4 Oct 1928, New York, New York, USA. Writer; Poet; Editor; Publisher. m. Jack Henry Bergé, June 1955, 1 son. Education: New York University; New School for Social Research, New York City. Appointments: Editor, 1970-84, Publisher, 1991-, Center Magazine; Distinguished Professor of Literature, Thomas Jefferson College, Allendale, Michigan, 1975-76; Instructor, Goddard College, 1976; Teacher, University of California Extension Program, Berkeley, 1976-77; Associate Professor, University of Southern Mississippi, 1977-78; Editor, Mississippi Review, 1977-78; Visiting Professor, University of New Mexico, 1978-79, 1987; Visiting Lecturer, Wright State University, Dayton, Ohio, 1979, State University of New York at Albany, 1980-81; Proprietor, Blue Gate Gallery of Art and Antiques, 1988-95; Editor-Publisher, Center Press, 1991-93. Publications: Fiction: The Unfolding, 1969; A Couple Called Moebius, 1972; Acts of Love: An American Novel, 1973; Timepieces, 1977; The Doppler Effect, 1979; Fierce Meltronome, 1981; Secrets, Gossip, and Slander, 1984; Zebras, or, Contour Lines, 1991. Poetry: The Vulnerable Island, 1964; Poems Made of Skin, 1968; The Chambers, 1969; Circles, as in the Eye, 1969; An American Romance, 1969; From a Soft Angle: Poems About Women, 1972; The Unexpected, 1976; Rituals and Gargoyles, 1976; A Song, A Chant, 1978; Alba Genesis, 1979; Alba Nemesis, 1979. Editor: The New York City Coffeehouse Poets of the 1960's, 1995. Contributions to: Periodicals. Honours: CAPS Award, New York State Council on the Arts, 1974; National Endowment for the Arts Fellowship, 1979-80. Memberships: Authors League; MacDowell Fellows Association; National Press Women; Poets and Writers. Address: 562 Onate Place, Santa Fe, NM 87501, USA.

BERGEL Hans, b. 26 Jul 1925, Kronstadt, Romania. Author. Education: History of Arts, University of Cluj-Napoca. Publications: Rumanien, Portrait einer Nation, 1969; Ten Southern European Short Stories, 1972; Die Sachsen in Siebenbürgen nach dreissig Jahren Kommunismus, 1976; Der Tanz in Ketten, 1977; Siebenburgen, A Picture Book of Transylvania, 1980; Gestalten und Gewalten, 1982; Hermann Oberth oder Der mythische Traum vom Fliegen, 1984; Der Tod des Hirten, 1985; Literaturgeschichte der Deutschen in Siebenburgen, 1987; Das Venusherz, short novel, 1987; Weihnacht ist uberall, eleven short stories, 1988. Contributions to: Periodicals. Honours: Short Story Prize, Bucharest, 1957, Bonn, 1972; Georg Dehio Prize, Esslingen, 1972; Goethe Foundation Prize, Basel, 1972; Medien Prizes, Bavarian Broadcasting Company, 1983, 1989; Bundesverdienstkreuz, 1987; Saxon of Transylvanians Culture Prize, 1988; Geyphius-Prize, 1990. Memberships: Kunstlergilde e V Esslingen; PEN International. Address: Rabensteinstrasse 28, D 8000 Munich 60, Germany.

BERGER Arthur Asa, b. 3 Jan 1933, Boston, Massachusetts, USA. Professor; Writer. m. Phyllis Wolfson Berger, 1961, 2 children. Education: BA, University of Massachusetts; MA, University of Iowa; PhD, University of Minnesota. Appointments: Instructor, University of Minnesota, 1960-65; Fulbright Lecturer, University of Milan, 1963-64; Instructor to Professor, Broadcast and Electronic Communication Arts Department, San Francisco State University, 1965-; Visiting Professor, University of California, Los Angeles, 1984-85. Publications: Li'l Abner, 1970; Pop Culture, 1973; About Man, 1974; The Comic Stripped American, 1974; The TV-Guided American, 1975; Language in Thought and Action, 1975; Film in Society, 1978; Television as an Instrument of Terror, 1978; Media Analysis Techniques, 1982; Signs in Contemporary Culture, 1984; Television in Society, 1986; Semiotics of Advertising, 1987; Media, USA, 1988, 2nd edition, 1991; Seeing is Believing: An Introduction to Visual Communication, 1989; Political Culture and Public Opinion, 1989; Agitpop: Political Culture and Communication Theory, 1989; Scripts: Writing for Radio and Television, 1990; Media Research Techniques, 1991; Reading Matter, 1992; Popular Culture Genres, 1992; An Anatomy of Humor, 1993;

Improving Writing Skills, 1993; Blindmen and Elephants: Perspectives on Humor, 1995; Narratives in Media: Modern Culture and Everyday Life, 1996; Bloom's Morning, 1997; The Genius of the Jewish Joke, 1997; The Art of Comedy Writing, 1997. Address: c/o Broadcast and Electronic Communication Arts Department CA34, San Francisco State University, San Francisco, CA 94132, USA.

BERGER François, b. 16 May 1950, Neuchâtel, Switzerland. Barrister; Writer. Education: Licence degree in Law, Neuchâtel University, 1977; Barrister, Neuchâtel, 1979. Appointment: President literature committee of the Canton of Neuchâtel. Publications: Mémoire d'anges, poetry, 1981; Gestes du veilleur, poetry, 1984; Le Pré, poetry, 1986, Italian translation, 1996; Les Indiennes, poetry, 1988; Le Repos d'Ariane, poetry, 1990; Le Jour avant, novel, 1995. Contributions to: L'Express Feuille d'Avis de Neuchatel. Honours: Louise Labé Prize, Paris, 1982; Distinction of Schiller Foundation, Zürich, 1985; Auguste Bachelin Prize, Neuchâtel, 1988. Memberships: Association des écrivains de langue française; Société suisse des écrivains; Association des écrivains neuchâtelois et jurassiens. Address: 28, Rebatte, CH-2068 Hauterive (Neuchâtel), Switzerland.

BERGER John (Peter), b. 5 Nov 1926, Stoke Newington, London, England. Novelist; Dramatist. m. twice, 3 children. Education: Central School of Art and the Chelsea School of Art, London. Appointments: Television Narrator, About Time, 1985, and Another Way of Telling, 1989; Artist, exhibitions at Wildenstein, Redfern, and Leicester galleries, London. Publications: A Painter of Our Time, 1958; The Foot of Clive, 1962; Corker's Freedom, 1964; G., 1972; Into Their Labours: Pig Earth, 1979; Once in Europa, 1987; Lilac and Flag: An Old Wives' Tale of a City, 1990; Plays: A Question of Geography, 1984; Boris, 1985; Goya's Last Portrait: The Painter Played Today, 1989. Contributions to: Tribune and New Statesman, both London, 1951-60. Honours: Booker Prize, 1972; Guardian Fiction Prize, 1973; New York's Critics Prize, for screenplay, 1976; George Orwell Memorial Prize, 1977; Barcelona Film Festival Europa Award, 1989. Address: Quincy, Mieussy, 74440 Taninges, France.

BERGER Terry, b. 11 Aug 1933, New York, New York, USA. Writer; Children's Author. Education: BA, Brooklyn College, 1954; Teacher's Degree, Hunter College, 1962. Publications: Black Fairy Tales (adaptation), 1969; I Have Feelings (psychology), 1971; Lucky, 1974; Being Alone, Being Together, 1974; Big Sister, Little Brother, 1974; A Friend Can Help, 1974; A New Baby, 1974; Not Everything Changes, 1975; The Turtles' Picnic, 1977; How Does it Feel When Your Parents Get Divorced?, 1977; Special Friends, 1979; Stepchild, 1980; Friends, 1981; Co-author: The Haunted Dollhouse, 1982; Ben's ABC Day, 1982; Country Inns: The Rocky Mountains, 1983. Address: 130 Hill Park Avenue, Great Neck, NY 11021, USA.

BERGMAN (Ernst) Ingmar, b. 14 July 1918, Uppsala, Sweden. Film Director and Script Writer. m. Ingrid von Rosen, 1971. Education: University of Stockholm, 1938-40. Publications: Plays and Screenplays: The Day Ends Early, 1947; Moralities, 1948; Summer with Monica, 1953; Sawdust and Tinsel, 1953; Journey into Autumn, 1955; Smiles of a Summer Night, 1955; The Seventh Seal, 1957; Wild Strawberries, 1957; So Close to Life, 1958; The Virgin Spring, 1960; Through a Glass Darkly, 1961; Winter Light, 1963; The Silence, 1963; Persona, 1966; Hour of the Wolf, 1968; The Rite, 1969; The Passion, 1969; The Touch, 1971; Cries and Whispers, 1973; Scenes from a Marriage, 1973; Face to Face, 1973; Autumn Sonata, 1978; From the Life of the Marionettes, 1980; Fanny and Alexander, 1982; Best Intentions, 1992; Sunday's Children, 1992; Other: The Magic Lantern: An Autobiography, 1988. Honours: Academy Awards, 1961, 1962, 1984; Goethe Prize, 1976; Honorary Professor, Stockholm University, 1985. Address: c/o Norstedts Forlag, Box 2052, 103 12 Stockholm, Sweden.

BERGONZI Bernard, b. 13 Apr 1929, London, England. Author; Poet; Professor of English Emeritus. Education: BLitt, 1961, MA, 1962, Wadham College, Oxford. Appointments: Senior Lecturer, 1966-71, Professor of English, 1971-92, Professor Emeritus, 1992-, University of Warwick, Coventry. Publications: The Early H G Wells, 1961; Heroes' Twilight, 1965, 2nd edition, 1980; Innovations: Essays on Art and Ideas, 1968; T S Eliot: Four Quartets: A Casebook, 1969; The Situation of the Novel, 1970, 2nd edition, 1979; T S Eliot, 1972, 2nd edition, 1978; The Turn of a Century, 1973; H G Wells: A Collection of Critical Essays, 1975; Gerard Manley Hopkins, 1977; Reading the Thirties, 1978; Years: Sixteen Poems, 1979; Poetry 1870-1914, 1980; The Roman Persuasion, novel, 1981; The Myth of Modernism and

Twentieth Century Literature, 1986; Exploding English, 1990; Wartime and Aftermath, 1993; David Lodge, 1995. Address: 19 St Mary's Crescent, Leamington Spa CV31 1JL, England.

BERGSON Leo. See: STEBEL Sidney Leo.

BERKELEY Humphry John, b. 1 Feb 1926, Marlow, England. Writer; Author; Former MP. Education: (Exhibitioner),BA 1947, MA 1963, Pembroke College, Cambridge. Appointments: Member of Parliament (Conservative) for Lancaster, 1959-66, joined Labour Party 1970; Chairman, United Nations Association of Great Britain and Northern Ireland, 1966-70. Publications: The Power of the Prime Minister, 1968; Crossing the Floor, 1972; The Life and Death of Rochester Sneath, 1974; The Odyssey of Enoch: A Political Memoir, 1977; The Myth That Will Not Die: The Formation of the National Government, 1978; Faces of the Eighties (with Jeffrey Archer), 1987. Contributions to: Times; Sunday Times; Daily Telegraph; Financial Times; Spectator; New Statesman. Membership: Savile Club. Literary Agent: Mark Hamilton, A M Heath, 79 St Martin's Lane, London WC2, England. Address: 3 Pages Yard, Church Street, Chiswick, London W4 2PA, England.

BERKOFF Steven, b. 3 Aug 1937, London, England. Writer; Director; Actor. m. Shelley Lee, 1976, div. Education: Webber-Douglas Academy of Dramatic Art, London, 1958-59; École Jacques Lecoq, Paris, 1965. Appointments: Director of plays and actor in many plays, films and television; Founding Director, London Theatre Group, 1973. Publications: Plays: In the Penal Colony, 1968; Metamorphosis, 1969; The Trial, 1970; East, 1975; Agamemnon, 1977; The Fall of the House of Usher, 1977; Greek, 1980; Decadence, 1981; West, 1983; Harry's Christmas, 1985; Kvetch and Acapulco, 1986; Sink the Belgrano!, 1986; With Massage, 1987; Lunch, Dog, Actor, 1994; Brighton Beach Scumbags, 1994; Dahling you were Marvellous, 1994. Other: Gross Intrusion and Other Stories, 1979, reprinted, 1993; The Theatre of Steven Berkoff: Photographic Record, 1992; Overview, 1994; Steven Berkoff's America, 1988; Free Association, autobiography, 1996. Honours: Los Angeles Drama Critics Circle Award for Directing, 1983; Comedy of the Year Award, Evening Standard, 1991. Address: c/o Joanna Marston, Rosica Colin Ltd, 1 Clareville Grove Mews, London SW7 5AH, England.

BERKSON William Craig, (Bill Berkson), b. 30 Aug 1939, New York, USA. Poet; Critic; Editor; Teacher. m. Lynn O'Hare, 17 July 1975, 1 son, 1 daughter. Education: Brown University, 1957-59; Columbia University, 1959-60; New School for Social Research, New York City, 1959-61; New York University Institute of Fine Arts, 1960-61. Appointments: Instructor, New School for Social Research, 1964-69; Editor and Publisher, Big Sky magazine and books, 1971-78; Adjunct Professor, Southampton College, Long Island University, 1980; Associate Professor, California College of Arts and Crafts, 1983-84; Instructor, Marin Community College, 1983-84; Professor and Coordinator of Public Lectures Program, 1984-, Director, Letters and Science, 1994-, San Francisco Art Institute; Poetry Editor, Video and the Arts, 1985-86; Contributing Editor, Zyzzyva, 1987-92; Corresponding Editor, Art in America, 1988-; Visiting Artist/Scholar, American Academy in Rome, 1991. Publications: Poetry: Saturday Night: Poems 1960-1961, 1961; Shining Leaves, 1969; Two Serious Poems and One Other (with Larry Fagin), 1972; Recent Visitors, 1973; Hymns of St Bridget (with Frank O'Hara), 1975; Enigma Variations, 1975; Ants, 1975; 100 Women, 1975; The World of Leon (with Ron Padgett, Larry Fagin and Michael Brownstein), 1976; Blue is the Hero, 1976; Red Devil, 1983; Lush Life, 1983; Start Over, 1984. Criticism: Ronald Bladen: Early and Late, 1991. Editor: Frank O'Hara: In Memory of My Feelings, 1967; Best & Company, 1969; Alex Katz (with Irving Sandler), 1971; Homage to Frank O'Hara (with Joe LeSueur), 1978; Special De Kooning Issue, Art Journal (with Rackstraw Downes), 1989. Contributions to: Anthologies and periodicals. Honours: Poets Foundation Grant, 1968; Yaddo Fellowship, 1968; National Endowment for the Arts Fellowship, 1980; Briarcombe Fellowship, 1983; Artspace Award for New Writing in Art Criticism, 1990; Fund for Poetry Award, 1994. Memberships: International Art Critics Association; PEN West. Address: 787B Castro Street, San Francisco, CA 94114, USA.

BERLIN Sir Isaiah, b. 6 June 1909, Riga, Latvia. Historian; Philosopher. m. Aline de Gunzbourg, 1956. Education: Corpus Christi College, Oxford. Appointments: Lecturer in Philosophy, New College, Oxford, 1932; Fellow, All Souls College, Oxford, 1932-38, 1950-66, 1975-, New College, Oxford, 1938-50; Served with Ministry of

Information, New York, 1941-42, His Majesty's Embassy, Washington, DC, 1942-46, and Moscow, 1945-46; Visiting Professor, Harvard University, 1949, 1951, 1953, 1962, Bryn Mawr College, 1952, University of Chicago, 1955, Princeton University, 1965, Australian National University, Canberra, 1975; Chichele Professor of Social and Political Theory, Oxford University, 1957-67; Professor of Humanities, City University of New York, 1966-71; President, Wolfson College, Oxford, 1966-75. Publications: Karl Marx, 1939, 4th edtion, 1978; Historical Inevitabilty, 1954; The Age of Enlightenment, 1956; Moses Hess, 1958; Two Concepts of Liberty, 1959; Mr Churchill in 1940, 1964; Four Essays on Liberty, 1969; Fathers and Children (translation of Ivan Turgenev's novel), 1972; Vico and Herder, 1976; Russian Thinkers, 1978; Concepts and Categories, 1978; Against the Current, 1979; Personal Impressions, 1980; A Month in the Country (translation of Ivan Turgenev's novel), 1980; The Crooked Timber of Humanity, 1990; The Magus of the North, 1993; The Sense of Reality, 1996. Honours: Commander of the Order of the British Empire, 1946; Knighted, 1957; Order of Merit, 1971; Honorary Fellow, Wolfson College, Oxford, 1975; Erasmus Prize, 1983; Agnelli International Prize for Ethics, 1987; Many honorary doctorates. Memberships include: Corresponding Member, American Academy of Arts and Sciences; Corresponding Member, American Academy and Institute of Arts and Letters; President, British Academy, 1974-78. Address: All Souls College, Oxford OX1 4AL, England.

BERMAN Claire, b. 4 July 1936, New York, New York, USA. Author; Journalist. Education: AB, Barnard College, 1957. Appointments: Senior Editor, Cosmopolitan, 1958-63; Contributing Editor, New York Magazine, 1972-78; Former Director of Public Education, Permanent Families for Children, Child Welfare League of America. Publications: A Great City for Kids: A Parent's Guide to a Child's New York, 1969; We Take This Child: A Candid Look at Modern Adoption, 1974; Making It as a Stepparent, 1980; "What Am I Doing in a Stepfamily?", 1982; A Hole in My Heart: Adult Children of Divorce Speak Out, 1991; Golden Cradle: How the Adoption Establishment Works, 1991; Caring for Yourself while Caring for Your Aging Parents, 1996. Memberships: Past Secretary, American Society of Journalists and Authors; Authors Guild. Literary Agent: James Levine. Address: 52 Riverside Drive, New York, NY 10024, USA.

BERMAN David, 20 Nov 1942, New York, New York, USA. AssociateProfessor of Philosophy; Writer. m. Aileen Jill Mitchell, 25 Dec 1970, 1 son, 2 daughters. Education: BA, New School for Social Research, New York City, 1965; MA, University of Denver, 1966; PhD, Trinity College, Dublin, 1972; Diploma in Psychoanalytic Psychotherapy, St Vincent's Hospital, Dublin, 1992. Appointments: Senior Lecturer in Philosophy, 1981-94, Fellow, 1984, Associate Professor of Philosophy, 1994-, Trinity College, Dublin. Publications: Images of Berkeley (with Raymond Houghton and Maureen Lapan), 1986; A History of Atheism in Britain: From Hobbes to Russell, 1988; George Berkeley: Eighteenth Century Responses (editor), 2 volumes, 1989; George Berkeley's Alciphron or the Minute Philosopher in Focus (editor), 1993; George Berkeley: Idealism and the Man, 1994; Arthur Schopenauer's World as Will and Idea (editor), 1995. Contributions to: Reference works, books, and numerous scholarly journals. Address: c/o Department of Philosophy, Trinity College, University of Dublin, Dublin 2, Ireland.

BERMANT Chaim Icyk, b. 26 Feb 1929, Poland. Author. m. Judith Weil, 16 Dec 1962, 2 sons, 2 daughters. Education: MA Honours, MLitt. Glasgow University; MSc, London School of Economics. Publications include: Troubled Eden, 1967; The Cousinhood. 1970; Coming Home, 1976; The Jews, 1977; The Patriarch, 1981; House of Women, 1982; Dancing Bear, 1984; What's the Joke. study of Jewish humour, 1986; Titch, 1987; The Companion, 1988; Lord Jakobovits, 1990; Murmurings of a Licenced Heretic, 1990. Contributions to: Innumerable publications. Address: c/o Aitken and Stone Ltd. 29 Fernshaw Road. London SW10 0TG, England.

BERNARD Oliver, b. 6 Dec 1925, Chalfont St Peter, Buckinghamshire, England. Writer. 2 sons, 2 daughters. Education: BA, Goldsmiths' College; ACSD, Central School of Speech and Drama. Publications: Rimbaud: Collected Poems, 1962; Apollinaire Selection, 1965; Country Matters (poems), 1961; Poems, 1983; Five Peace Poems, 1985; The Finger Points at The Moon, 1989; Moons and Tides, 1989; Getting Over It, 1992; Quia Amore Langueo, 1995. Contributions to: Botteghe Oscure; Times Literary Supplement; Listener: Poetry (Chicago); Gemini; Spectator; New Statesman; Only Poetry: New Poetry. Honour: Poetry Society Gold Medal for Verse

Speaking, 1982. Memberships: William Morris Society; British Actors' Equity Association; Committee Member, Speak-a-Poem. Literary Agent: Aitken, Stone and Wylie Ltd, 29 Fernshaw Road, London SW10 0TG, England. Address: 1 East Church Street, Kenninghall, Norwich NR16 2EP, England.

BERNARD Robert. See: **MARTIN Robert Bernard.**

BERNAUW Patrick, b. 15 Apr 1962, Alost, Belgium. Writer. m. Elke Van der Elst, 24 Mar 1984, 1 daughter. Appointments: Scenarist Comic Books, Gucky, 1983-84; Producer and Director of Radio Plays, 1988-; Editor, Historische Verhalen (Historical Studies). Publications: Mijn Lieve Spooklidmaat, 1983; De Stillevens Van De Dood, 1985; Mysteries Van Hetlam Gods, 1991; Dromen Van Een Farao, 1991; Landru Bestaat Niet, 1992; Several plays and radio plays. Contributions to: Vlaamse Filmpjes; Kreatief; Bres; Plot; Crime; Ganymedes; short stories and essays. Honours: John Flanders Awards, 1987, 1991. Address: Brusselbaan 296, 9320 Erembodegem, Belgium.

BERNE Stanley, b. 8 June 1923, Port Richmond, Staten Island, New York, USA. Research Professor. m. Arlene Zekowski, July 1952. Education: BS, Rutgers University, 1947; MA, New York University, 1950; Graduate Fellow, Louisiana State University, Baton Rouge, 1954-59. Appointments: Associate Professor, English, 1960-80, Research Professor, English, 1980-, Eastern New Mexico University, Portales; Host, Co-Producer, TV series, Future Writing Today, KENW-TV, PBS, 1984-85. Publications: A First Book of the Neo-Narrative, 1954; Cardinals and Saints: On the aims and purposes of the arts in our time, criticism, 1958; The Dialogues, 1962; The Multiple Modern Gods and Other Stories, 1969; The New Rubaiyat of Stanley Berne, poetry, 1973; Future Language, criticism, 1976; The Great American Empire, 1981; Every Person's Little Book of P-L-U-T-O-N-I-U-M (with Arlene Zekowski), 1992; Alphabet Soup: A Dictionary of Ideas, 1993; Anthologies: Trace, 1965; New World Writing #11; First Person Intense, 1978; Breakthrough Fictioneers, 1979; American Writing Today, 1992; Santa Fe Arts Directory, 1993; Dictionary of the Avant-Gardes, 1993. Honours: Literary research awards, Eastern New Mexico University, 1966-76. Memberships: PEN; COSMEP; New England Small Press Association; Rio Grande Writers Association; Santa Fe Writers. Address: Box 4595, Santa Fe, NM 87502, USA.

BERNER Urs, b. 17 Apr 1944, Schafisheim, Switzerland. Writer. Div. Education: Teacher's Training; Studies in History, University of Zürich. Appointments: Editor, then Freelance Journalist. Publications: Friedrichs einsame Träume in der Stadt am Fluss, novel, 1977; Fluchtrouten, novel, 1980; Wunschzeiten, novel, 1985; Das Wunder von Dublin, stories, 1987; Die Lottokönige, novel, 1989. Address: Scharerstrasse 9, CH-3014 Bern, Switzerland.

BERNSTEIN Carl, b. 14 Feb 1944, Washington, DC, USA. Journalist; Writer. m. Nora Ephron, 14 Apr 1976, div, 2 sons. Education: University of Maryland, 1961-64. Appointments: Copyboy to Reporter, Washington Star, 1960-65; Reporter, Elizabeth Journal, New Jersey, 1965-66, Washington Post, 1966-76, Washington Bureau Chief, 1979-81, Correspondent, 1981-84, ABC-TV; Correspondent, Contributor, Time magazine, 1990-91; Visiting Professor, New York University, 1992-. Publications: All the President's Men (with Bob Woodward), 1973; The Final Days (with Bob Woodward), 1976; Loyalties: A Son's Memoir, 1989. Honours: Drew Pearson Prize for Investigative Reporting, 1972; Pulitzer Prize Citation, 1972; Honorary LLD, Boston University, 1975. Address: c/o Janklow and Nesbit Associates, 598 Madison Avenue, New York, NY 10022, USA.

BERNSTEIN Charles, b. 4 Apr 1950, New York, New York, USA. Professor of Poetry and Poetics; Poet; Writer; Editor. m. Susan Bee Laufer, 1977, 1 son, 1 daughter. Education: AB, Harvard College, 1972. Appointments: Freelance writer in the medical field, 1976-89; Visiting Lecturer in Literature, University of California at San Diego, 1987; Visiting Professor of English, Queens College of the City University of New York, 1988; Faculty and Series Coordinator, Wolfson Center for National Affairs, New School for Social Research, New York City, 1988; Visiting Butler Professor of English, State University of New York at Buffalo, 1989; Lecturer in Creative Writing, Princeton University, 1989, 1990; David Gray Professor of Poetry and Letters, State University of New York at Buffalo, 1990-. Publications: Poetry: Asylums, 1975; Parsing, 1976; Shade, 1978; Poetic Justice. 1979; Senses of Responsibility, 1979; Legend (with others), 1980; Controlling

Interests, 1980; Disfrutes, 1981; The Occurrence of Tune, 1981; Stigma, 1981; Islets/Irritations, 1983; Resistance, 1983; Veil, 1987; The Sophist, 1987; Four Poems, 1988; The Nude Formalism, 1989; The Absent Father in Dumbo, 1990; Fool's Gold (with Susan Bee), 1991; Rough Trades, 1991; Dark City, 1994; The Subject, 1995; Republics of Reality: Poems 1975-1995, 1997. Essays: Content's Dream: Essays 1975-1984, 1986; A Poetics, 1992. Editor: L=A=N=G=U=A=G=E Book (with Bruce Andrews), 4 volumes, 1978-81; The L=A=N=G=U=A=G=E Book (with Bruce Andrews), 1984; The Politics of Poetic Form: Poetry and Public Policy, 1990; Close Listening: Poetry and the Performed Word, 1997. Contributions to: Numerous anthologies, collections, and periodicals. Honours: Phi Beta Kappa, 1972; William Lyon Mackenzie King Fellow, Simon Fraser University, 1973; National Endowment for the Arts Fellowship, 1980; Guggenheim Fellowship, 1985; University of Auckland Foundation Fellowship, 1986; New York Foundation for the Arts Fellowship, 1990, 1995; ASCAP Standard Award, 1993-95. Address: Poetics Program, Department of English, 438 Clemens Hall, State University of New York at Buffalo, Buffalo, NY 14260, USA.

BERNSTEIN Marcelle. See: CLARK Marcelle Ruth.

BERRIDGE Elizabeth, b. 3 Dec 1919, London, England. Author; Critic. m. Reginald Moore, 1940, 1 son, 1 daughter. Appointments:Reviewer, Critic, BBC, Spectator, Books and Bookmen, Tribune, Country Life, 1952-74; Fiction Reviewer, Daily Telegraph, 1967-88; Evening Standard. Publications: House of Defence, 1945; Story of Stanley Brent, 1945; Be Clean, Be Tidy, 1949; Upon Several Occasions, 1953; Across the Common, 1964; Rose Under Glass, 1967; Sing Me Who You Are, 1972; That Surprising Summer, 1973; The Barretts at Hope End (editor), 1974; Run for Home, 1981; Family Matters, 1981; People at Play, 1982; Touch and Go, 1995. Honour: Novel of the Year, Yorkshire Post, 1964. Memberships: Chase Charity, Trustee; PEN. Address: c/o David Higham Associates, 5-8 Lower John Street, London W1R 4HA, England.

BERRY Adrian M(ichael), b. 15 June 1937, London, England. Writer; Journalist. Education: Christ Church, Oxford, 1959. Appointments: Correspondent, Time Magazine, NY, 1965-67; Science Correspondent, Daily Telegraph, London, 1977-. Publications: The Next Ten Thousand Years: A Vision of Man's Future in the Universe, 1974; The Iron Sun: Crossing the Universe Through Black Holes, 1977; From Apes to Astronauts, 1981; The Super Intelligent Machine, 1983; High Skies and Yellow Rain, 1983; Koyama's Diamond (fiction), 1984; Labryinth of Lies (fiction), 1985; Ice With Your Evolution, 1986; Computer Software: The Kings and Queens of England, 1985; Harrap's Book of Scientific Anecdotes, 1989; The Next 500 Years, 1995; Galileo and the Dolphins, 1996. Honour: Royal Geographic Society, fellow, 1984-. Memberships: Royal Astronomical Society, London, fellow, 1973-; British Interplanetary Society, fellow, 1986-. Address: 11 Cottesmore Gardens, Kensington, London W8, England.

BERRY Francis, b. 23 Mar 1915, Ipoh, Malaysia. Poet; Writer; Professor Emeritus. m. (1) Nancy Melloney Graham, 4 Sept 1947, 1 son, 1 daughter, (2) Eileen Marjorie Lear, 9 Apr 1970. Education: University College of the South West, 1937-39, 1946-47; BA, University of London, 1947; MA, University of Exeter, 1949. Appointments: Professor of English Literature, University of Sheffield, 1967-70; Professor of English, Royal Holloway, University of London, 1970-80. Publications: Gospel of Fire, 1933; Snake in the Moon, 1936; The Iron Christ, 1938; Fall of a Tower, 1943; The Galloping Centaur, 1952; Murdock and Other Poems, 1955; Poets' Grammar, 1958; Morant Bay and Other Poems, 1961; Poetry and the Physical Voice, 1962; Ghosts of Greenland, 1966; The Shakespeare Inset, 1966; I Tell of Greenland, 1977; From the Red Fort, 1984; Collected Poems, 1994. Contributions to: Periodicals; BBC. Membership: Fellow, Royal Society of Literature. Address: 4 Eastgate Street, Winchester, Hampshire SO23 8EB, England.

BERRY Ila, b. 9 June 1922. Poet; Writer. Education: AA, Fullerton College, California; BA, John F Kennedy University, Orinda, California; MA, English and Creative Writing, San Francisco State University, 1985. Publications: Poetry: Come Walk With Me, 1979; Rearranging the Landscape, 1986; Rowing in Eden, 1987; Behold the Bright Demons, 1993. Contributions to: Periodicals. Honours: Jessamyn West Creative Award, 1969; Woman of Distinction, Fullerton College, 1969. Memberships: California Federation of Chaparral Poets, Robert Frost Chapter; California State Poetry Society; California Writers Club; Ina Coolbrith Circle, President, 1977-79; National League

of American Pen Women. Address: 761 Sequoia Woods Place, Concord, CA 94518, USA.

BERRY James, b. 1925, Fair Prospect, Jamaica. Poet; Writer; Editor. Publications: Bluefoot Traveller: An Anthology of West Indian Poets in Britain (editor), 1976; Fractured Circles, 1979; News for Babylon: The Chatto Book of West Indian-British Poetry (editor), 1984; Chain of Days, 1985; The Girls and Yanga Marshall (stories), 1987; A Thief in the Village and Other Stories, 1988; Don't Leave an Elephant to Go and Chase a Bird, 1990; When I Dance (poems), 1991; Ajeema and His Son, 1992. Honours: C Day-Lewis Fellowship; Poetry Society Prize, 1981. Boston Globe/Horn Book Award, 1993. Address: c/o Hamish Hamilton Ltd, 27 Wrights Lane, London W8 5TZ, England.

BERRY Paul, b. 25 Dec 1919, Weston-by-Welland, England. Writer; Lecturer. Publications: Daughters of Cain (with Renee Huggett), 1956; By Royal Appointment: A Biography of Mary Ann Clarke, Mistress of the Duke of York 1803-07, 1970; Joint Editor, The Selected Journalism of Winifred Holtby and Vera Brittain, 1985; Vera Brittain: A Life (with Mark Bostridge), 1995; Winifred Holtby: Selected Short Stories (with Marion Shaw), 1997. Address: 1 Bridgefoot Cottages, Stedham, Midhurst, Sussex, England.

BERRY Wendell, b. 5 Aug 1934, Henry County, Kentucky, USA. Writer; Poet; Professor. m. Tanya Amyx Berry, 29 May 1957, 1 son, 1 daughter. Education: BA, 1956, MA, 1957, University of Kentucky. Appointments: Instructor, Georgetown College, 1957-58; E H Jones Lecturer in Creative Writing, 1959-60, Visiting Professor of Creative Writing, 1968-69, Stanford University; Assistant Professor, New York University, 1962-64; Faculty Member, 1964-77, Professor, 1987-93, University of Kentucky; Elliston Poet, University of Cincinnati, 1974; Writer-in-Residence, Centre College, 1977, Bucknell University, 1987. Publications: Fiction: Nathan Coulter, 1960, revised edition, 1985; A Place on North, 1967, revised edition, 1985; The Memory of Old Jack, 1974; The Wild Birds, 1986; Remembering, 1988; The Discovery of Kentucky, 1991; Fidelity, 1992; A Consent, 1993; Watch With Me, 1994; A World Lost, 1996. Poetry: The Broken Ground, 1964; Openings, 1968; Findings, 1969; Farming: A Handbook, 1970; The Country of Marriage, 1973; Sayings and Doings, 1975; Clearing, 1977; A Part, 1980; The Wheel, 1982; Collected Peoms, 1985; Sabbaths, 1987; Sayings and Doings and an Eastward Look, 1990; Entries, 1994; The Farm, 1995. Non-Fiction: The Long-Legged House, 1969; The Hidden Wound, 1970, revised edition, 1989; The Unforseen Wilderness, 1971, revised edition, 1991; A Continuous Harmony, 1972; The Unsettling of America, 1977; Recollected Essays 1965-1980, 1981; The Gift of Good Land, 1981; Standing by Words, 1983; Home Economics, 1987; What Are People For?, 1990; Harlan Hubbard: Life and Work, 1990; Standing on Earth, 1991; Sex, Economy, Freedom and Community, 1993; Another Turn of the Crank, 1995. Honours: Guggenheim Fellowship, 1962; Rockefeller Fellowship, 1965; National Institute of Arts and Letters Award, 1971; Jean Stein Award, American Academy of Arts and Letters, 1987; Lannan Foundation Award for Non-Fiction, 1989; T S Eliot Award, Ingersoll Foundation, 1994; Award for Excellence in Poetry, The Christian Century, 1994; Harry M Caudill Conservationist Award, Cumberland Chapter, Sierra Club, 1996. Address: Lanes Landing Farm, Port Royal, KY 40058, USA.

BERTHA Zoltan, b. 4 June 1955, Szentes, Hungary. Writer; Professor. m. Hajdu Csilla, 5 July 1985, 1 son. Education: MA, 1978, Doctor's Degree, 1982, PhD, 1994, University of Debrecen. Appointments: Scholar, University of Debrecen, 1978-90; Editorial Board, Holnap, 1990-93; Alföld, 1991-93; Member of Parliament, 1990-94; Professor, Protestant University, Budapest, 1994-. Publications: Hungarian Literature in Romania and Transylvania in the 1970s (with A Görömbei), 1983; A Szellem Jelzöfenyei, 1988; Balint Tibor, 1990; Gond es Mu, 1994; Arcvonalban, 1994; Sütö Andras, 1995. Contributions to: Many journals. Honours: Young Critics Scholarship, 1983; Moricz Zsigmond Literary Scholarship, 1989; Kölcsey Prize, 1996. Memberships: Association of Hungarian Writers; International Association of Hungarian Studies; Protestant Cultural Society; Society of Hungarian Literary History; Union of Hungarian Artists. Address: Böszörmenyi ut 69, IV 15, H-4032 Debrecen, Hungary.

BERTOLINO James, b. 4 Oct 1942, Hurley, Wisconsin, USA. Poet; Writer; University Teacher. m. Lois Behling, 29 Nov 1966. Education: BS, University of Wisconsin, 1970; MFA, Cornell University, 1973. Appointments: Teacher, Washington State University, 1970-71; Cornell University, 1971-74, University of Cincinnati, 1974-84,

Washington Community Colleges, 1984-91, Chapman University, 1989-96, Western Washington University, 1991-96. Publications: Poetry: Employed, 1972; Soft Rock, 1973; The Gestures, 1975; Making Space for Our Living, 1975; The Alleged Conception, 1976; New & Selected Poems, 1978; Precint Kali, 1982; First Credo, 1986; Snail River, 1995. Chapbooks: Drool, 1968; Day of Change, 1968; Stone Marrow, 1969; Becoming Human, 1970; Edging Through, 1972; Terminal Placebos, 1975; Are You Tough Enough for the Eighties?, 1979; Like a Planet, 1993. Contributions to: Poetry in 27 anthologies; Prose in 3 anthologies; Poetry, stories, essays, and reviews in periodicals. Honours: Hart Crane Poetry Award, 1969; Discovery Award, 1972; National Endowment for the Arts Fellowship, 1974; Quarterly Review of Literature International Book Awards, 1986, 1995; Djerassi Foundation Residency, 1987; Bumbershoot Big Book Award, 1994. Address: 533 Section Avenue, Anacortes, WA 98221, USA.

BESS Clayton. See: LOCKE Robert Howard.

BETTELINI Lauro, b. 27 Aug 1938, Lugano, Switzerland. Journalist. 1 son, 1 daughter. Education: Technical Architect, 1957; Journalism Degree, Milan, Italy. Appointments: Gazzetta Ticinese, 1975; Swiss Television, 1979. Publications: Narrative Poetry: Noi Della Piazza, 1987; Lo Zodiaco Del Nonno, 1987; Gli Orti Del Disgelo, 1987; Jl Doppio Allo Specchio, 1988; Television Documentary. Contributions to: Numerous magazines and journals. Honours: Premio Nazionale Narrative, La Spezia, Italy, 1985; Premio Letterario L'Autore Poesia, Firenze, 1986; Premio Nazionale Di Poesia, Pisa, 1987; Premio Ascona Finalista Narrativa, Ascona, 1987; Mondo Letterario Finalista Narrative, Milan, 1987. Memberships: Associazione Scrittori della Svizzera Italiana; PEN; Federation of Swiss Journalist. Literary Agent: Lucchini Cristina. Address: Via Crespera 50B, 6932 Breganzona, Switzerland.

BETTERIDGE Anne. See: POTTER Margaret.

BETTS Raymond F(rederick), b. 23 Dec 1925, Bloomfield, New Jersey, USA. Professor of History; Author. m. Irene Donahue, 25 June 1956, 2 sons, 1 daughter. Education: BA, Rutgers University, 1949; MA, 1950, PhD, 1958, Columbia University; Doctorat d'Université, University of Grenoble, 1955; Certificat d'Études africaines, Institut d'Études Politiques, University of Paris, 1955. Appointments: Instructor to Assistant Professor, Bryn Mawr College, 1956-61; Assistant Professor to Professor, Grinnell College, 1961-71; Professor of History, 1971-, Director, Gaines Center for the Humanities, 1983-, University of Kentucky. Publications: Assimilation and Association in French Colonial Theory, 1890-1914, 1961; The Scramble for Africa (editor), 1966, 2nd edition, revised, 1972; Europe Overseas: Phases of Imperialism, 1968; The Ideology of Blackness (editor), 1971; The False Dawn: European Imperialism in the Nineteenth Century, 1975; Tricouleur: A Brief History of Modern French Colonial Empire, 1978; Europe in Retrospect: A Brief History of the Last Two Hundred Years, 1979; Uncertain Dimensions: Western Overseas Empires in the Twentieth Century, 1985; France and Decolonisation, 1991. Contributions to: Books and scholarly journals. Honours: Hallam Book Awards, University of Kentucky, 1976, 1986; Outstanding Kentucky Humanist Award, Kentucky Humanities Council, 1989; Fellowships; Grants. Memberships: African Studies Association; American Historical Association; French Colonial Historical Society; Society for French Historical Studies. Address: 311 Mariemont Drive, Lexington, KY 40505, USA.

BEVAN Alistair. See: ROBERTS Keith John Kingston.

BEVAN Gloria, b. New Zealand. Author. Publications: The Distant Trap, 1969; The Hills of Maketu, 1969; Beyond the Ranges, 1970; Make Way for Tomorrow, 1971; It Began in Te Rangi, 1971; Vineyard in a Valley, 1972; Flame in Fiji, 1973; The Frost and the Fire, 1973; Connelly's Castle, 1974; High Country Wife, 1974; Always a Rainbow, 1975; Dolphin Bay, 1976; Bachelor Territory, 1977; Plantation Moon, 1977; Fringe of Heaven, 1978; Kowhai Country, 1979; Half a World Away, 1980; Master of Mahia, 1981; Emerald Cave, 1981; The Rouseabout Girl, 1983; Southern Sunshine, 1985; Golden Bay, 1986. Address: c/o Mills and Boon Ltd, 15-16 Brooks Mews, London W1A 1DR, England.

BEWES Richard Thomas, b. 1 Dec 1934, Nairobi, Kenya. Anglican Rector. m. Elisabeth Ingrid Jaques, 18 Apr 1964, 2 sons, 1 daughter. Education: Marlborough School, 1948-53; MA, Emmanuel College, Cambridge, 1954-57; Ridley Hall Theological College,

Cambridge, 1957-59. Publications: Talking About Prayer, 1979; The Pocket Handbook of Christian Truth, 1981; The Church Reaches Out, 1981; John Wesley's England, 1981; The Church Overcomes, 1983; On the Way, 1984; Quest for Life, 1985; The Church Marches On, 1986; When God Suprises, 1986; A New Beginning, 1989; The Resurrection, 1989; Does God Reign?, 1995. Contributions to: The Church of England Newspaper. Membership: Guild of British Songwriters. Address: 2 All Souls Place, London, W1N 3DB, England.

BEYE Holly, b. 27 Feb1922, Iowa City, Iowa, USA. Writer; Librarian. Education: BA, Swarthmore College, 1943; MLS, State University of New York, Albany, 1967; Graduate, Rutgers University, 1981. Appointments: Performance and Workshop Writer and Director, The Heads, Cafe Theatre political improvisation group, 1960's; WESAW Improvisation for Elementary School students, 1975-85; Holly's Comets Improvisation Group, 1985-. Publications: Do Keep Thee in the Stony Bowes, prose poem, 1951; In the City of Sorrowing Clouds, 1952; XVI Poems, 1953; Stairwells and Marriages, 1954; Monsters in World Folklore, filmstrips, 1970; Lives of the Comets, video, 1989; Refractions, video, 1990; Plays: Afternoon of the Spawn, 1961; Thus, 1963; It's All Yours!, 1963; The Banana Thief, 1965; About the Cast, 1989; Chance, 1989; Dilly, Dawn and Dell, 1990; The Bat Girl, 1992; Sisters, 1993. Contributions to: Quarterly Review of Literature; New Directions Annual. Honour: Prize, Quarterly Review of Literature, 1962. Membership: Dramatists Guild. Address: PO Box 1043, Woodstock, NY 12498, USA.

BEYFUS Drusilla, b. 1921, London, England. Writer. Appointments: Women's Editor, Sunday Express, London, 1952-53; Columnist, Daily Express, London, 1953-56; Associate Editor, Queen Magazine, London, 1959-63; Home Editor, The Observer, London, 1962-64; Associate Editor, Weekend Telegraph Magazine, London, 1963-71; Editor, Brides and Setting Up Home Magazine, London, 1971-79; Associate Editor, Vogue Magazine, London, 1980-87; Contributing Editor, Telegraph Magazine, 1991-; Visiting Tutor Central St Martins College of Art, 1989-. Publications: Lady Behave (with Anne Edwards), 1956, 1969; The English Marriage, 1968; The Bride's Book, 1981; The Art of Giving, 1987; Modern Manners, 1992; The Move Thing: Courtship, Parties, 1992; Business, Sex, 1993. Contributions to: Sunday Times; Punch; Sunday Telegraph; New Statesman; Daily Telegraph; The Spectator; Weekly Columnist, You Magazine, Mail on Sunday, 1994-. Address: 51g Eaton Square, London SW1, England.

BHAINSA Kuber Chandra, b. 6 May 1970, Salohi, India. Scientific Officer; Writer. Education: BSc, 1990; MSc, Life Sciences, 1992; BEd, 1993. Contribution to: Article, Development of AIDS Vaccine: A Great Challenge, 1996. Honour: Ainthucharan Award for Best Graduate of the Year, 1990. Address: SO/C, BTD, FIPLY, BARC, Trombay, Mumbai 400 085, India.

BHARGAVA Vishal, (Vicky Bhargava), b. 9 Feb 1967. Allahabad, India. Journalist. Education: Science Intermediate (Commerce), ISC, 12th Standard, 1985; Diploma in Printing Technology, Northern Indian Institute of Printing Technology, 1987; Bachelor of Commerce, 1988. Appointments: Bhargava and Bhargave Printers (P) Ltd, 1991. Publication: First book, 1994. Contributions to: Mainly to magazines of Bhargava and Bhargava Printers (P) Ltd. Address: 119 Swami Vivekanand Marg, Allahabad 210003, India.

BHARTI Dharmvir, b. 1926, India. Novelist; Poet. Education: MA, University of Allahabad, 1947. Appointments: Founder, Editor of Charmayug magazine, Bombay; Editor, Alocha quarterly. Publications: Verse: Cold Iron, 1952; The Beloved of Krishna, 1959; Seven Years of Lyrics, 1959; Fiction: The Village of the Dead, 1946; The God of Sins, 1949; The Seventh Horse of the Sun God, 1952; Immortal Son, 1952; The Moon and Broken People, 1965; Heaven and Earth; Plays, The River was Thirsty, 1954; The Blind Age, 1954; Literature and Human Values, 1960. Address: c/o Dharmayug, Bennett, Coleman & Co, Times Building, Dr D B Road, Bombay 400001, India.

BHATNAGAR Om Prakash, b. 30 May 1932, Agra, India. Professor. m. Parvati Bhatnagar, 21 Oct 1959, 1 son, 1 daughter. Education: MA, 1954; MA, 1956; DLitt, 1959; PhD, 1991. Appointment: Editorial Board, Indian Journal of English Studies, 1979-86. Publications: Poetry, Thought Poems; Angles of Retreat; Oneiric Visions; Shadows in Floodlights; Audible Landscape; Perspectives on Indian Poetry in English; Studies in Indian Drama in English. Contributions to: 69 Literary and Research articles. Honours: Plaque of Honor for Excellence in Poetry; G Ramachandran Award for

International Understanding Through Literature. Memberships: Zonal Representative, Indian Association for English Studies; University EnglishTeachers Association. Address: Rituraj, Camp, Amravati 444, 602 India.

BHATTACHARYYA Birendra Kumar, b. 14 Oct 1924, Suffry Sibsagar, Assam, India. Journalist; Writer. m. Binita Bhattacharyya, 1958, 2 son, 1 daughter. Education: Calcutta University; Gauhati University; BSc, MA, PhD. Appointments: Science Teacher, Manipur; Editor, Ramdhenu 1951-61, Sadiniya Navayung, 1963-67; Lecturer, journalism, Gauhati University, 1974-85. Publications: Novels: Iyaruingam; Rajpathe Ringiai (Call of The Main Street); Ai (Mother); Satagnai (Killer); Mrityunjay; Pratipad; Nastachandra; Ballari; Kabar Aru Phul; Ranga Megh; Daini; Collections, short stories: Kolongahioboi (Still Flows The Kolong); Satsari (Necklace); Aurobindo, biography; Survey of Assamese Modern Culture (in Assamese). Honours: Sahitya Akademi Award for Assamese Literature, 1961; Jnanpith Award, 1979. Memberships: President, Sahitya Academi, New Delhi; Ex-President, Assam Sahitya Sabha. Address: Kharghuli Development Area, Guwahati 4, Assam, India.

BHYRAPPA Santeshivara Lingannaiah, b. 26 July 1934, Santeshivara, Karnataka, India. m. Saraswati, 13 Dec 1958, 2 sons. Education: BA (Hons), 1957; MA Philosophy, 1958, PhD Aesthetics, 1963. Publications: 17 novels and 4 books on Literary Criticism including: Novels: Vamsha Vriksha, 1966; Grihabhanga, 1970; Daatu, 1974; Parva, 1979; Nele, 1983; Sakshi, 1986; Truth and Beauty, 1964; Story and Its Substance, 1969; Why Do I Write and Other Essays, 1982; Tantu, 1993; Autobiography: Bhitti (Canvas), 1996. Contributions to: Numerous journals. Honours: Best Book of the Year Award, 1967, 1975; Central Sahihya Akademi Award, 1975; Karnataka Government Rajyotsava Day Award. Memberships: Karnataka State Sahitya Akademi; Central Sahitya Akademi; Bharatiya Jnaanapeeth Foundation; Indian Philosophical Congress. Address: 1007 Kuvempunagar, Mysore 570023, India.

BIBBY Peter Leonard, b. 21 Dec 1940, London, England. Poet; Playwright; Screenwriter. m. 15 Apr 1967, 2 sons, 2 daughters. Education: BA, University of Western Australia; DipEd, Murdoch University. Literary Appointments: Editor, Fellowship of Australian Writers; Editor, Magabala Books, Broome Publishing Project, Australian Bicentennial Authority. Publications: Island Weekend, 1960; Represented in anthologies: Quarry; Breakaway; Summerland; Inprint W A Story; Poetry Australia; Laughing Cry; Broadcast Verse and Drama, ABC. Contributions to: Professional journals including: Bulletin Australia; Outrider; Overland; Poetry Australia. Honours: Tom Collins Literary Awards, Verse, 1978,1982; Lyndall Hadow National Short Story Award, 1983; Donald Stuart, National Short Story Award, 1985. Memberships: Australian Writers Guild; Fellowship of Australian Writers; Australian Film Institute; Computer Graphics Association. Address: c/o PO Box 668, Broome, WA, Australia.

BIBERGER Erich Ludwig, b. 20 July 1927, Passau, Bavaria, Germany. Editor; Writer. Education: Examination Stadt; Wirtschafsaubauschule Passau, 1944; Volkshochschule Passau. Publications include: Dreiklang der Stille (Poems), 1955; Rundgang über dem Nordlicht (Philosophy, Fairy Tales of Atomic Age), 1958; Die Traumwelle (novel), 1962; Denn im Allsein der Welt (poems), 1966; Duadu oder der Mann im Mond (radio plays), 1967; Gar mancher (satirical verses), 1967; Anthology Quer, 1974; Anthology 3 (in 47 languages), 1979; Andere Wege bis Zitterluft (poems), 1982; Was ist hier Schilf, was Reiher (Haiku), 1984; Nichts als das Meer (Poems), 1984; Zwei Pfund Morgenduft (Feuilletons), 1987. Honours: Recipient several honours. Memberships include: Chairman, Regensburger Schriftsellergruppe International, Joint Association of Authors in 25 Countries of the World, 1960-, Honorary President, 1995-; Founder, Director, Internationale Regensbürger Literaturtage, 1967-94; Internationale Jungautoren-Wettbewerbe, 1972-94; Founder, Editor, Publication series RSG Studio International, 1973-, RSG-Forum 15/25, 1977-; Member of Humboldt-Gesllschaft für Wissenschaft und Kunst, 1993-. Address: Altmühlstrasse 12, D 93059 Regensburg, Germany.

BICKHAM Jack (Miles), (Jeff Clinton, John Miles), b. 2 Sept 1930, Columbus, Ohio, USA. Writer; Professor of Journalism. m. Janie R Wallace, 23 Nov 1952, 3 sons, 1 daughter. Education: BA, Ohio State University, 1952; MA, University of Oklahoma, 1960. Appointments: Managing Editor, The Oklahoma Courier, 1966-69; Professor of Journalism, University of Oklahoma, 1969-. Publications: Wildcat Meets Miss Melody, 1968; Build a Box for Wildcat, 1969;

Wildcat's Claim to Fame, 1970; Bounty on Wildcat, 1971; The Apple Dumpling Gang, 1971; Hang High, O'Shea, 1972; The Night Hunters, 1973; The Silver Bullet Gang, 1974; Showdown at Emerald Canyon, 1975; Twister, 1976; The Excalibur Disaster, 1978; A Question of Ethics, 1980; The Regensburg Legacy, 1980; I Still Dream About Columbus, 1982; Ariel, 1984; Miracleworker, 1987; Breakfast at Wimbledon, 1991; Double Fault, 1993. Address: c/o School of Journalism, University of Oklahoma, Norman, OK 73019, USA.

BIDDISS Michael Denis, b. 15 Apr 1942, Farnborough, Kent, England. University Professor. m. Ruth Margaret Cartwright, 8 Apr 1967, 4 daughters. Education: MA, PhD, Queens' College, Cambridge, 1961-66; Centre des Hautes Etudes Européennes, University of Strasbourg, 1965-66. Appointments: Fellow in History, Downing College, Cambridge, 1966-73; Lecturer/Reader in History, University of Leicester, 1973-79; Professor of History, University of Reading, 1979-. Publications: Father of Racist Ideology, 1970; Gobineau: Selected Political Writings (editor), 1970; Disease and History (co-author), 1972; The Age of the Masses, 1977; Images of Race (editor), 1979; Thatchersim: Personality and Politics (co-editor), 1987; The Nuremberg Trial and the Third Reich, 1992. Memberships: Historical Association, president, 1991-94; Faculty, History and Philosophy of Medicine, Society of Apothecaries, London, president, 1994-; Royal Historical Society, joint vice president, 1995-. Address: Department of History, University of Reading, Whiteknights, Reading RG6 6AA, England.

BIEBER Konrad F, b. 24 Mar 1916, Berlin, Germany. Professor of French and Comparative Literature Emeritus. m. Tamara Siew, 29 Sept 1939, dec 1995, 1 son. Education: Licence-es-Lettres, University of Paris, Sorbonne, PhD in Comparative Literature, Yale University, 1953. Appointments: Prisoner-of-War, June 1940; Affiliated French Resistance, 1944-45; Interpreter, interallied Railroad Commission, Paris. Publications: L'Allemagne vue par les Ecrivains de la Resistance Francaise, 1954; Simone de Beauvoir, 1979; translation of Lucie Aubrac's Outwitting the Gestapo, 1993; Ils Partiront dans l'Ivresse. Contributions to: Revue de Litterature Comparee; Esprit; Culture Francaise; Le Francais Contemporain; French Notes; Comparative Literature Studies; The French Review; Dokumente; Jadavpur Comp Lit, Calcutta, India. Honours: Guggenheim Fellow, 1957-58; Chevalier des Palmes Académiques, 1970. Memberships: Modern Language Association, Chair; Comparative Literature Session-American Association of Teachers of French/Chapter President, Connecticut, 1962-64. Address: 1211 Foulkeways, Gwynedd, PA, 19436, USA.

BIEGEL Paul Johannes, b. 25 Mar 1925, Bussum, Netherlands. Author. Education: University of Amsterdam. Publications: The King of the Copper Mountains, 1969; The Seven Times Search, 1971; The Little Captain, 1971; The Twelve Robbers, 1974; The Gardens of Dorr, 1975; Far Beyond & Back Again, 1977; The Elephant Party, 1977; Letters from the General, 1979; The Looking-Glass Castle, 1979; The Dwarfs of Nosegay, 1978; Robber Hopsika, 1978; The Fattest Dwarf of Nosegay, 1980; The Tin Can Beast, 1980; The Curse of the Werewolf, 1981; Virgil Nosegay and the Cake Hunt, 1981; Crocodile Man, 1982; Virgil Nosegay and the Wellington Boots, 1984. Honours: Best Children's Book of the Year, 1965; Golden Pencil Award, 1972, 1993; Silver Pencil Awards, 1972, 1974, 1981, 1988; Nienke van Hichtum prize for Children's Literature, 1973; State Prize, 1974; Woutertje Pieterse Prize, 1991. Memberships: Vereninging van Letterkudigen; Maatschappij van Letterkunde. Address: Keizersgracht 227, Amsterdam, Netherlands.

BIELINSKA Izabela, b. 21 Jan 1925, Lublin, Poland. Writer. Education: Warsaw University. Publications: Margaret, 1960; The Love Not Will Be, stories, 1963; Don't Beat Your Fathers, 9 short stories, 1976; Le Petit Dejeuner, short story, 1980; Taste of the Wild Strawberry Ice-cream, 1986; Harlequin's Costume, short story, 1990; Polish: Smak lodów poziomkowych, co-author Ewa Otwinowska; Literary, Film and Arts reviews; Radio plays; Film scripts. Contributions to: Literary and Film Magazines; Polish Radio. Memberships: Polish Writers Association; Polish Journalists Association; Film Critics Club. Address: Ul Nowowiejska 4 m 57, 00-649 Warsaw, Poland.

BIELSKI Alison Joy Prosser, b. 24 Nov 1925, Newport, Gwent, Wales. Secretary; Writer; Lecturer. m. (1) D Treverton Jones, 19 June 1948, (2) A E Bielski, 30 Nov 1955, 1 son, 1 daughter. Appointment: Honorary Secretary, Welsh Academy, 10 years. Publications: The Story of the Welsh Dragon, 1969; Across the Burning Sand, 1970;

Flower Legends of the Wye Valley, 1974; The Lovetree, 1974; Eagles, 1983; The Story of St Mellons, 1985; Tales and Traditions of Tenby; Selected Poems: That Crimson Flame, 1996. Contributions to: Anglo-Welsh Review; Poetry Wales; Planet; New Welsh Review; Tribune; Poetry Review; Pembroke Magazine; Acument; Doors; New Poetry; Outposts. Honours: Anglo-Welsh Review Poetry Prize, 1970; Arnold Vincent Bowen Poetry Prize, 1971; Recipient, various other prizes and awards in poetry competitions. Memberships: Society of Women Writers and Journalists; Welsh Union of Writers; Gwent Poetry Society; Welsh Academy. Address: 92 Clifton Road, Paignton, Devon TQ3 3LD, England.

BIERMANN Pieke, b. 22 Mar 1950, Stolzenau, Germany. Writer; Translator. m. Dr Thomas Woertche, 15 Oct 1993. Education: MA, German Literature and Political Sciences, 1976; Hanover and Padua Universities. Appointments: Editor for Foreign Literature, Rowohlt Publishers, 1980-81; Freelance, 1982-. Publications: Author and translator of numerous books; Author of novels and short stories. Contributions to: Magazines and periodicals. Honours: Grant, Ingeborg Bachmann Wettbewerb, Austria, 1990; Best German Crime Novel, for Violetra, 1991, for Herzrasen, 1994. Membership: IG Medien. Literary Agent: M Meller, PO Box 400323, 80703 Munich, Germany. Address: PO Box 15 14 10, 10676 Berlin, Germany.

BIERMANN Wolf, b. 15 Nov 1936, Hamburg, Germany. Poet and Songwriter. m. Christine Bark, 2 sons, 1 daughter. Education: Humboldt University, 1959-63. Appointments: Assistant Director, Berliner Ensemble, 1957-59; Song and guitar performances throughout Germany. Publications: Die Drahtharfe: Balladen, Gedichte, Lieder, 1965; Mit Marx- und Engelszungen, 1968; Für meine Genossen, 1972; Deutschland: Ein Wintermärchen, 1972; Nachlass I, 1977; Wolf Biermann: Poems and Ballads, 1977; Preussicher Ikarus, 1978; Verdrehte welt- das seh' ich gerne, 1982; Und als ich von Deutschland nach Deutschland; Three Contemporary German Poets (with others), 1985; Affenels and Barrikade, 1986; Alle Lieder, 1991; Vier Neue Lieder, 1992; Play, Der Dra-Dra: Die Grosse Drachentoterschau in 8 akten mit Musik, 1970; Ich hatte viele Bekümmernis: Meditation on Cantata Nr 21 by J S Bach, 1991. Honours: Möricke Prize, 1991; Buchner Prize, 1991. Address: c/o Verlag Kiepenheuer und Witsch, Rondorfer Strasse 5, 5000 Cologne-Marienburg, Germany.

BIGGLE Lloyd Jr, b. 17 Apr 1923, Waterloo, Iowa, USA. Author. m. Hedwig T Janiszewski, 1947, 1 son, 1 daughter. Education: AB, with High Distiction, Wayne University, 1947; MM in Music Literature, 1948, PhD in Musicology, 1953, University of Michigan. Publications: The Angry Espers, 1961; All the Colors of Darkness, 1963; The Fury Out of Time, 1965; Watchers of the Dark, 1966; The Rule of the Door and Other Fanciful Regulations (short stories), 1967 (in UK as The Silent Sky), 1979; The Still Small Voice of Trumpets, 1968; The World Menders, 1971; The Light That Never Was, 1972; Nebula Award Stories 7 (editor), 1972; The Metallic Muse (short stories), 1972; Monument, 1974; This Darkening Universe, 1975; A Galaxy of Strangers (short stories), 1976; Silence is Deadly, 1977; The Whirligig of Time, 1979; Alien Main (with T L Sherred), 1985; The Quallsford Inheritance, A Memoir of Sherlock Holmes, 1986; Interface for Murder, 1987; The Glendower Conspiracy, A Memoir of Sherlock Holmes, 1990; A Hazard of Losers, 1991; Where Dead Soldiers Walk (novel), 1994. Memberships: Science Fiction Oral History Association, Founder, 1977, President, 1994-. Address: 569 Dubie Avenue, Ypsilanti, MI 48198, USA.

BIGGS Margaret Annette, (Margaret Key Biggs), b. 26 Oct 1933, Pike County, Alabama, USA. Writer; Poet. m. 1 Mar 1956. Education: BS, Troy State University, 1954; MA, California State University, 1979. Publications: Swampfire, 1980; Sister to the Sun, 1981; Magnolias & Such, 1982; Petals from the Womanflower, 1983; Plumage of the Sun, 1986. Contributions to: Panhandler; Earthwise Poetry Journal; Gryphon; International University Poetry Quarterly; Thoreau Journal Quarterly; Echos; Jump River Review; Pipe Dream; Valhalla; Vega; Modern Images; Encore; Black Jack; Unicorn; Taurus; Poetry Monthly; Anthologies include: Peace is Our Profession; Meltdown; Crow Calls; Poets & Peace International; Macomb Fantasy Factory; Best Poems of 1982; Darkness Screams a Yellow Rose; Anthology I, Florida State Poets Association. Literary Agent: Noel S DeLuca. Address: PO Box 551, Port St Joseph, FL 32456, USA.

BIGSBY Christopher William Edgar, b. 27 June 1941, Dundee, Scotland. University Professor; Broadcaster; Novelist. Education: BA, MA, Sheffield University; PhD, Nottingham University. Publications:

Confrontation & Commitment: A Study of Contemporary American Drama, 1967; Edward Albee, 1969; The Black American Writer (editor), 1969; Three Negro Plays, 1969; Dada & Surrealism, 1972; Approaches to Popular Culture, 1975; Tom Stoppard, 1976; Superculture, 1976; Edward Albee, 1976; The Second Black Renaissance, 1980; Contemporary English Drama, 1981; Joe Orton, 1982; A Critical Introduction to 20th Century American Drama, 3 volumes, 1982, 1984, 1985; The Radical Imagination and the Liberal Tradition, 1982; David Mamet, 1985; Cultural Change in the United States since World War II, 1986; Plays by Susan Glaspell, 1987; File on Miller, 1988; American Drama: 1945-1990, 1992; Hester (novel), 1994; Pearl (novel), 1995; 19th Century American Short Stories (editor), 1995; Portable Arthur Miller (editor), 1995; Still Lives (novel), 1996. Contributions to: Broadcaster, TV and Radio Scriptwriter; Times Literary Supplement; Times Higher Education Supplement; Sunday Independent; American Quarterly; Modern Drama; Theatre Quarterly; Guardian; Sunday Telegraph. Agent: Richard Scott Simon Ltd. Literary Address: 3 Church Farm, Colney, Norwich, England.

BILGRAMI Akeel, b. 28 Feb 1950, Hyderabad, India. Professor. m. Carol Rovane, 25 Aug 1990, 1 daughter. Education: BA, Bombay University, 1970; BA, Oxford University, 1974; PhD, University of Chicago, 1983. Appointments: Professor of Philosophy; Chairman of Philosophy Department, Columbia University. Publications: Belief and Meaning, 1992, 1994, 1995; Self-Knowledge and Intentionality, 1996; Internal Dialectics: The Moral Psychology of Identity. Contributions to: Journal of Philosophy; Philosophical Quarterly; Philosophical Topics. Honours: Whitney Humanities Fellow, 1992; Rhodes Scholarship, 1971. Membership: American Philosophical Society. Address: 110 Morningside Drive, #58, New York,NY 10027, USA.

BILLING Graham John, b. 12 Jan 1936, Dunedin, New Zealand. Author. m. Rowan Innes Cunningham, 29 Aug 1978, 1 son, 1 daughter by previous marriage. Education: Otago University, 1955-58. Appointments: Staff, Dunedin Evening Star, 1958-62; Antarctic Division, DSIR, 1962-64; New Zealand Broadcasting Corporation News Service and TV Service (various appointments), 1964-67; Staff, Dominion Sunday Times, 1967-69; Lecturer, writing, Mitchell College Advanced Education, Bathurst, Australia, 1974-75. Publications: Forbush and the Penguins, 1965; The Alpha Trip, 1969; Statues, 1971; The Slipway, 1973; The Primal Therapy of Tom Purslane, 1980; Changing Countries (poetry), 1980; Non-Fiction: South: Man and Nature in Antarctica, 1965; New Zealand, the Sunlit Land, 1966; The New Zealanders, 1974; Radio Plays: Forbush and the Penguins, 1965; Mervyn Gridfern versus the Babsons, 1965; The Slipway, 1976; The Prince of Therapy of Tom Purslane, 1980; Verse: Changing Countries, 1980. Address: 89 Mersey Street, St Albans, Christchurch 1, New Zealand.

BILLINGTON Michael, b. 16 Nov 1939, Leamington Spa, England. Drama Critic. m. Jeanine Bradlaugh, 1978. Education: BA, St Catherine's College, Oxford. Appointments: Trained, as Journalist with Liverpool Daily Post and Echo, 1961-62; Public Liaison Officer, Director, Lincoln Theatre Co, 1962-64; Reviewed Plays, Films and TV for The Times, 1965-71; Film Critic: Birmingham Post, 1968-78, Illustrated London News, 1968-81; Drama Critic, The Guardian, 1971-; London Arts Correspondent, New York Times, 1978-; Drama Critic, Country Life, 1987-. Publications: The Modern Actor, 1974; How Tickled I Am, 1977; The Performing Arts, 1980; The Guiness Book of Theatre Facts and Feats, 1982; Alan Ayckbourn, 1983; Stoppard: The Playwright, 1987; Peggy Ashcroft, 1989; Twelfth Night, 1990; One Night Stands, 1993. Literary Agent: Curtis Brown. Address: 15 Hearne Road, London W4 3NJ, England.

BILLINGTON Rachel (Mary), b. 11 May 1942, Oxford, England. Writer. m. 16 Dec 1967, 2 sons, 2 daughters. Education: BA, English, London University. Publications: All Things Nice; The Big Dipper; Beautiful; A Woman's Age; Occasion of Sin; The Garish Day; Lilacs out of the Dead Land; Cock Robin; A Painted Devil; Children's Books: Rosanna and the Wizard-Robot; Star-Time; The First Christmas; The First Easter; Loving Attitudes, 1988; Theo and Matilda, 1990; The First Miracles, 1990; Bodily Harm, 1992; The Family Year, 1992; The Great Umbilical, 1994; Magic and Fate, 1996; The Life of Jesus, for children, 1996; Perfect Happiness, 1996. Contributions to: Reviewer, Columnist and short story writer for various publications; 2 plays for BBC TV; 4 plays for Radio. Memberships: PEN; Society of Authors. Literary Agent: David Higham Associates, London. Address: The Court House, Poyntington, Near Sherborne, Dorset DT9 4LF, England.

BINCHY Maeve, b. 28 May 1940, Dublin, Ireland. Writer. m. Gordon Thomas Snell, 29 Jan 1977. Education: BA, University College, Dublin, 1960. Appointments: Columnist, Irish Times, London, 1968-; Writer. Publications: My First Book, 1976; The Central Line: Stories of Big City Life, 1978; Maeve's Diary, 1979; Victoria Line, 1980; Light a Penny Candle, 1982; Maeve Binchy's Dublin Four, 1982; The Lilac Bus, 1984; Echoes, 1985; Firefly Summer, 1987; Silver Wedding, 1988; Circle of Friends, 1991; The Copper Beech, 1992; The Glass Lake, 1995. Other: Plays; Television screenplays. Honours: International Television Festival Golden Prague Award, Czech TV, 1979; Jacobs Award, 1979. Address: c/o Irish Times, 85 Fleet Street, London EC4, England.

BINGHAM Caroline Margery Conyers, b. 7 Feb 1938, London, England. Professional Writer. m. Andrew Bingham, 1958, div 1972, 1 daughter. Education: BA Honours, History, University of Bristol, 1960. Publications: The Making of a King: The Early Years of James VI and I, 1968; James V, King of Scots, 1971; Contributor, The Scottish Nation: A History of the Scots from Independence to Union, 1972; The Life and Times of Edward II, 1973; The Stewart Kingdom of Scotland 1371-1603, 1974; The Kings and Queens of Scotland, 1976; The Crowned Lions: The Early Plantagenant Kings, 1978; James VI of Scotland, 1979; The Voice of the Lion, verse anthology, 1980; James I of England, 1981; Land of the Scots: A Short History, 1983; The History of Royal Holloway College 1886-1986, 1987; Beyond the Highland Line: Highland History and Culture, 1991; Darnley: A Life of Henry Stuart, Lord Darnley, Consort of Mary Queen of Scots, 1995. Address: c/o Sheil Land Associates Ltd, 43 Doughty Street, London WC1N 2LF, England.

BINGHAM Charlotte Marie-Therese, b. 29 June 1942, Sussex, England. Playwright; Novelist. m. 15 Jan 1964, 1 son, 1 daughter. Education: Educated in England and France. Publications: Coronet Among the Weeds; Lucinda; Coronet Among the Grass; Belgravia; Country Life; At Home; Television series (with Terence Brady): Upstairs, Downstairs; Nanny; No Honestly; Yes Honestly; Play for Today; Pig in the Middle; Father Matthew's Daughter; Thomas and Sarah; Novels: To Hear a Nightingale; The Business; In Sunshine or In Shadow; Stardust; Change of Heart. Contributions to: Vogue; Tatler; Woman's Journal; Town and Country. Honour: Romantic Novelists Best Novel Award, 1996. Membership: Society of Authors. Literary Agent: Murray Pollinger, c/o 222 Old Brompton Road, London, SW5 0BZ, England. Address: c/o 10 Buckingham Street, London WC1, England.

BINHAM Philip Frank, b. 19 July 1924. Teacher (retired). m. Marja Sola, 21 June 1952, 1 son, 1 daughter. Education: Magdalen College, Oxford, 1935-41; Wadham College, Oxford, 1946-49; BA (Oxon), 1949; MA (Oxon), 1954. Publications: How To Say It, 1965; UK Edition 1968; Executive English I-III, 1968-70; Speak Up, 1975; Snow in May: An Anthology of Finnish Literature 1945-72, 1978; Service with a Smile: Hotel English, Restaurant English 1979, UK Edition 1982; Team 7, 8, 9, 1983-85; Translations: Tamara (Eeva Kilpi), novel, 1972; Compass Rose (Eka Laine), 1985; In Search of Helsinki (Paavo Haavikko), 1986; Five Decades of Social Security (Paavo Haavikko), 1989; The Northeast Passage from the Vikings to Nordenskiöld, 1992; Mare Balticum: The Baltic - Two Thousand Years, 1996. Contributions to: World Literature Today (formerly Books Abroad), 1972-. Honours: Order of the Finnish Lion, 1972; Finnish State Prize for Foreign Translators, 1990. Memberships: Society of Authors; Finnish Society of Scientific Writers; Honorary Member, Finnish Literature Society. Address: Seunalantie 34A, 04200 Kerava, Finland.

BIRCH Carol, b. 3 Jan 1951, Manchester, England. Writer. m. Martin Lucas Butler, 26 Oct 1990, 2 sons. Education: University of Keele, 1968-72. Publications: Life in the Palace, 1988; The Fog Line, 1989; The Unmaking, 1992; Songs of the West, 1994. Contributions to: Times Literary Supplement; Independent; New Statesman. Honours: David Higham Prize; Geoffrey Faber Memorial Award. Membership: Society of Authors. Address: c/o Mic Cheetham Agency, 138 Buckingham Palace Road, London SW1 W9SA, England.

BIRD Charles, See: **WITTICH John Charles Bird.**

BIRD Kai, b. 2 Sept 1951, Eugene, Oregon, USA. Author. m. Susan Gloria Goldmark, 7 June 1975, 1 son. Education: MS Journalism, Medill School of Journalism, Northwestern University, 1975; BA History, Carleton College, 1973. Appointments: Biographer.

Publications: The Chairman: John J McCloy, The Making of the American Establishment, 1992; Hiroshima's Shadow: Writings on the Denial of History and the Smithsonian Controversy, (editor, with Lawrence Lifeshultz), 1997. Contributions to: New York Times; Los Angeles Times; Washington Post; Boston Globe; Christian Science Monitor; Foreign Policy; Journal of Diplomatic History; Washington Monthly; Foreign Service Journal. Honours: John D & Catherine T MacArthur Fellow; German Marshall Fund Fellow; Alicia Patterson Journalism Fellowship; John Simon Guggenheim Fellow. Address: 1914 Biltmore Street, North West Washington, DC 20009, USA.

BIRDSELL Sandra Louise, b. 22 Apr 1942, Manitoba, Canada. Writer. m. Stanley Vivian Birdsell, 1 July 1959, 1 son, 2 daughter. Appointments: Writer-in-Residence, University of Prince Edward Island; University of Alberta, University of Waterloo, Ontario. Publications: Night Travellers, 1982; Ladies of the House, 1984; The Missing Child, 1989; The Chrome Suite, 1993. Contributions to: Western Living; Canadian Living; Quarry; New Quarterly; Prairie Fire; Event; Border Crossing; Grain. Honours: Nominated for Governor General Award, English Language Fiction, 1992; Joseph P Stauffer Award, Canada Council; W H Smith, Books in Canada, 1st Novel Award; National Magazine Award; Canada Council Grant; Major Arts Award, Manitoba Arts Council. Memberships: Writers Guild of Canada; Writers Union of Canada; PEN International; Founding Member, President, Manitoba Writers Guild. Literary Agent: Lucinda Vardey Agency, Toronto, Ontario, Canada. Address: 755 Westminster Avenue, Winnipeg, Manitoba R3G 1A5, Canada.

BIRLEY Julia (Davies), b. 13 May 1928, London, England. Writer. m. 12 Sept 1954, 1 son, 3 daughters. Education: BA Classics, Oxon. Publications: Novels: The Children on the Shore; The Time of the Cuckoo; When You Were There; A Serpent's Egg; Dr Spicer; Short Stories. Contributions to: Articles in Guardian. Memberships: PEN; Charlotte Yonge Society. Literary Agent: Curtis Brown. Address: Upper Bryn, Longtown, Hereford HR2 0NA, England.

BISCHOFF David F(rederick), b. 15 Dec 1951, Washington, DC, USA. Writer. Appointments: Staff member, NBC-TV, Washington, DC, 1974-; Associate Editor, Amazing Magazine. Publications: The Seeker (with Christopher Lampton), 1976; Quest (juvenile), 1977; Strange Encounters (juvenile), 1977; The Phantom of the Opera (juvenile), 1977; The Woodman (with Dennis R Bailey), 1979; Nightworld, 1979; Star Fall, 1980; The Vampires of the Nightworld, 1981; Tin Woodman (with Dennis Bailey), 1982; Star Spring, 1982; War Games, 1983; Mandala, 1983; Day of the Dragonstar (with Thomas F Monteleone), 1983; The Crunch Bunch, 1985; Destiny Dice, 1985; Galactic Warriors, 1985; The Infinite Battle, 1985; The Macrocosmic Conflict, 1986; Manhattan Project, 1986; The Unicorn Gambit, 1986; Abduction: The UFO Conspiracy, 1990; Revelation: The UFO Conspiracy, 1991; Deception: The UFO Conspiracy, 1991; Aliens Versus Predator: Hunter's Planet, 1994. Address: c/o Henry Morrison Inc, 320 Mclain Street, Bedford Hill, NY 10705, USA.

BISHOP Ian Benjamin, b. 18 Apr 1927, Gillingham, Kent, England. University Teacher. m. Pamela Rosemary Haddacks, 14 Dec 1968, 2 daughters. Education: MA, MLitt, Queen's College, Oxford, 1945-51. Appointment: Reader in English, University of Bristol, 1982. Publications: Pearl in Its Setting, 1968; Chaucer's Troilus and Criseyde: A Critical Study, 1981; The Narrative Art of the Canterbury Tales, 1988. Contributions to: Review of English Studies; Medium Aevum; Times Higher Education Supplement; Notes and Queries. Address: 8 Benville Avenue, Coombe Dingle, Bristol BS9 2RX, England.

BISHOP James Drew, b. 18 June 1929, London, England. Journalist. m. 5 June 1959, 2 sons. Education: BA History, Corpus Christi College, Cambridge, 1953. Appointments: Foreign Correspondent, 1957-64, Foreign News Editor, 1964-66, Features Editor, 1966-70, The Times; Editor, 1971-87, Editor-in-Chief, 1987-94, The Illustrated London News. Publications: Social History of Edwardian Britain, 1977; Social History of the First World War, 1982; The Story of The Times, (with Oliver Woods), 1983; Illustrated Counties of England, editor, 1985. Contributor of: USA Chapter in Annual Register, 1960-1988; Articles in many Newspapers and Magazines. Membership: Association of British Editors, Chairman. Address: 11 Willow Road, London NW3 1TJ, England.

BISHOP Michael (Lawson), b. 12 Nov 1945, Lincoln, Nebraska, USA. Writer. m. Jeri Whitaker, 7 June 1969, 1 son, 1 daughter.

Education: BA, 1967, MA, 1968, University of Georgia. Publications: Novels: A Funeral for the Eyes of Fire, 1975, revised edition as Eyes of Fire, 1980; And Strange at Ecbatan the Trees, 1976; Stolen Faces, 1977; A Little Knowledge, 1977; Transfigurations, 1979; Under Heaven's Bridge (with Ian Watson), 1981; No Enemy but Time, 1982; Who Made Steve Cry?, 1984; Ancient of Days, 1985; The Secret Ascension, or, Philip K Dick Is Dead, Alas, 1987; Unicorn Mountain, 1988; Apartheid, Superstrings and Mordecai Thubana, 1989; Count Geiger's Blues, 1992; Brittle Innings, 1994. Stories: Catacomb Years, 1979; Blooded on Arachne, 1982; One Winter in Eden, 1984; Close Encounters with the Deity, 1986; Emphatically Not SF, Almost, 1990; At the City Limits of Fate, 1996. Poetry: Windows and Mirrors, 1977. Editor: Changes (with Ian Watson), anthology, 1982; Light Years and Dark, anthology, 1984; Nebula Awards: Science Fiction Writers of America's Choices for the Best Science Fiction and Fantasy, volumes 23-25, 1989-91. Contributions to: Anthologies and many periodicals. Honours: Phoenix Award, 1977; Clark Ashton Smith Award, 1978; Rhysling Award, Science Fiction Poetry Association, 1979; Nebula Awards, Science Fiction Writers of America, 1981, 1982; Mythopoeic Fantasy Award, 1988; Locus Award, best fantasy novel, 1994. Memberships: Science Fiction Poetry Association; Science Fiction Fantasy Writers of America. Address: Box 646, Pine Mountain, GA 31822, USA.

BISHOP Pike. See: **OBSTFELD Raymond.**

BISHOP Wendy S, b. 13 Jan 1953, Japan. English Professor. m. Marvin E Pollard Jr, 1 son, 1 daughter. Education: BA, English, 1975, BA, Studio Art, 1975, MA, English, 1976, MA, English, 1979, University of California, Davis; PhD, English (Rhetoric and Linguistics), Indiana University of Pennsylvania, 1988. Appointments: Bayero University, Kano, Nigeria, 1980-81; Northern Arizona University, USA, 1981-82; Navajo Community College, 1982-85; University of Alaska, Fairbanks, 1985-89; Florida State University, Tallahassee, 1989-. Publications: Released into Language: Options for Teaching Creative Writing, 1990; Something Old, Something New: College Writing Teachers and Classroom Change, 1990; Working Words: The Process of Creative Writing, 1992; The Subject is Writing: Essays by Teachers and Students on Writing, 1993; Co-editor and Contributor to: Colors of a Different Horse: Rethinking Creative Writing, Theory and Pedagogy, National Council of Teachers of English (NCTE), 1994. Contributions to: Poems, fiction, essays to: American Poetry Review; College English; High Plains Literary Review; Prairie Schooner; Western Humanities Review; Many other journals. Address: Department of English, Florida State University, Tallahassee, FL 32302, USA.

BISSET Donald, b. 30 Aug 1910, London, England . Writer; Actor. Publications: Anytime Stories, 1954; Sometime Stories, 1957; Next Time Stories, 1959; This Time Stories, 1961; Another Time Stories, 1963; Little Bear's Pony, 1966; Hullo Lucy, 1967; Talks With a Tiger, 1967; Kangaroo Tennis, 1968; Nothing, 1969; Upside Down Land, 1969; Benjie the Circus Dog, 1969; Time and Again Stories, 1970; Barcha the Tiger, 1971; Tiger Wants More, 1971; Yak series, 6 volumes, 1971-78; Father Tingtang's Journey, 1973; Jenny Hopalong, 1973; The Happy Horse, 1974; The Aventures of Mandy Duck, 1974; Hazy Mountain, 1974; Oh Dear, Said the Tiger, 1975; Paws With Shapes, 1976; Paws With Numbers, (with Michael Morris), 1976; The Lost Birthday, 1976; The Story of Smokey Horse, 1977; This is Ridiculous, 1977; Jungle Journey, 1977; What Time Is It, When It Isn't, 1980; Cornelia and Other Stories, 1980; Johnny Here and There, 1981; The Hedgehog Who Rolled Uphill, 1982; Snakey Boo Series, 2 volumes, 1982-85; Please Yourself, 1991. Address: 43 Andrewes House, Barbican, London EC2Y 8AX, England.

BISSETT Bill, b. 23 Nov 1939, Halifax, Nova Scotia, Canada. Poet; Artist. Education: Dalhousie University, 1956-57; University of British Columbia, 1963-65. Appointment: Editor, Printer, Blewointmentpress, Vancouver, 1962-83. Publications: The Jinx Ship and other Trips: Poems-drawings-collage, 1966; We Sleep Inside Each Other All, 1966; Fires in the Temple, 1967; Where Is Miss Florence Riddle, 1967; What Poetiks, 1967; Gossamer Bed Pan, 1967; Lebanon Voices, 1967; Of the Land/Divine Service Poems, 1968; Awake in the Red Desert, 1968; Killer Whale, 1969; Sunday Work?, 1969; Liberating Skies, 1969; The Lost Angel Mining Company, 1969; The Outlaw, 1970; Blew Trewz, 1970; Nobody Owns the Earth, 1971; Air 6, 1971; Dragon Fly, 1971; Four Parts Sand: Concrete Poems, 1972; The Ice Bag, 1972; Poems for Yoshi, 1972; Drifting into War, 1972; Air 10-11-12, 1973; Pass the Food, Release the Spirit Book, 1973; The First Sufi Line, 1973; Vancouver Mainland Ice and Cold Storage, 1973;

Living with the Vishyan, 1974; What, 1974; Drawings, 1974; Medicine My Mouths on Fire, 1974; Space Travel, 1974; You Can Eat it at the Opening, 1974; The Fifth Sun, 1975; The Wind up Tongue, 1975; Stardust, 1975; An Allusyun to Macbeth, 1976; Plutonium Missing, 1976; Sailor, 1978; Beyond Even Faithful Legends, 1979; Soul Arrow, 1980; Northern Birds in Color, 1981; Parlant, 1982; Seagull on Yonge Street, 1983; Canada Gees Mate for Life, 1985; Animal Uproar, 1987; What we Have, 1989; Hard 2 Beleev, 1990; Incorrect Thoughts, 1992; Vocalist with the Luddites, Dreaming of the Night, 1992; The Last Photo of the Human Soul, 1993; th Influenza uv Logik, 1995-. Address: Box 272, Str F, Toronto, Ontario M4K 2L7, Canada.

BISSOONDATH Neil (Devindra), b. 19 Apr 1955, Trinidad, West Indies. Writer. Education: BA, York University, Toronto, Ontario, Canada. Publications: Digging Up the Mountains, 1985; A Shady Brutality, 1988; On the Eve of Uncertain Tomorrows, 1990; The Innocence of Age, 1992. Contributions to: Periodicals. Honour: Canadian Authors Association Literary Award, 1993. Address: Crown Books, c/o Random House Inc, 201 East 50th Street, 22nd Floor, New York, NY 10022, USA.

BISWAS Anil Ranjan (Oneil), b. 1 Feb 1916, Bangladesh. Writer; Former Civil Servant and Teacher. m. Lily Mullick, 15 May 1941, 1 son. Education: BA (Hons), 1937; MA, 1942; LLM, 1968; PhD, 1976. Appointments: Editor, Eastern Law Reports, 1982; Laikhi (writing), 1985. Publications: Footsteps, 1951; Twentieth Century Bengali Literature, 1952; Curly Waters, 1961; Shakespeare's Sonnets, 1966; Asutosh's Thoughts on Education, 1968; At Whose Bid the Bell Rings, 1972; Continuum becomes Calcutta, 1973; On the Shores of Anxiety, 1980; Squaring the Circle, 1985; History of India's Freedom Movement, 1990; Variegated Days, 1991; Bengali Prosody, 1992; Calcutta and Calcuttans, 1992. Address: Gairick, 18 Cooperative Road, Calcutta 700070, India.

BJERG Anne Marie, b. 17 Dec 1937, Copenhagen, Denmark. Translator; Writer. m. Chrenn Bjerg, 29 Dec 1962, div 1 daughter. Education: BA, University of Copenhagen, 1970. Appointments: Regular Reader, Gyldendal's Publishing House, 1971-86. Publications: Love from Signe (novel), 1979; Surviving (short stories), 1985; 65 translations, including: 8 novels by Anita Brookner; Dubliners by James Joyce; The Waves by Virginia Woolf; Live or Die by Anne Sexton; Fear of Flying by Erica Jong; Two Serious Ladies by Jane Bowles; numerous novels by Selma Lagerlöf, Kerstin Ekman, Göran Tunström, Per Wästberg (from Swedish). Contributions to: BLM. Honours: Translators Award of the Danish Academy; Honorary Award, Danish Translators' Association; Life long grant, Danish State Art Foundation. Memberships: James Joyce Society; Danish Writers Association; Danish PEN. Address: Laerdalsgade 6A 1tv, DK-2300 Copenhagen S, Denmark.

BJORKSKOG Doris Margareta, b. 19 Mar 1929, Nykarleby, Finland. m. 15 July 1956. Publications: Minnesgrönskan, poems, 1978; Draken och kärleken, 1982; Lunke och Lina, for children, 1984; På vindens villkor, 1987; Den mörka fågeln, 1989; Sommarens spegel, 1993; Stenharen, 1994. Honour: Karleby Culture Prize, 1994. Membership: Finlands Svenska Författareförening. Address: Björkskog 40, 67410 Karleby, Finland.

BJORNSSON Oddur, b. 25 Oct 1932, W-Skaft, Iceland. Playwright; Director of Plays. m. Borghildur Thors, 1954, div 1976, partner Bergljot Gunnarsdottir, 1983-, 1 son, 1 daughter. Education: Matriculated, The Secondary Grammarschool of Akureyri, 1953-; Theaterwissenscaft, Wienna University, 1954-56. Appointment: Director, Akureyri Theatre Company, 1978-80. Publications: Yolk-Life, 1965; Ten Variations, 1968; A Grand Ball, 1974; The Master, 1977; After the Concert, 1983; The 13th Crusade, 1993. Contributions to: Writing on Classic Music (CD disks) in Morgunbladid or The Morning Newspaper. Honour: Culture Award of DV (an Icelandic Newspaper), 1980. Membership: The Union of Icelandic Writers and Association of Icelandic Playwrights. Address: Njardargata 9, 101 Reykjavik, Iceland.

BLACK David, b. 21 Apr 1945, Boston, Massachusetts, USA. Writer; Producer. m. Deborah Hughes Keehn, 22 Jun 1968, 1 son, 1 daughter. Education: BA Magna cum Laude, Amherst College, 1967; MFA, Columbia University, 1971. Appointments: Contributing Writer, New Times, 1975-76; Writer-in-Residence, Mt Holyoke College, 1982-86; Contributing Editor, Rolling Stone, 1986-89. Publications: Mirrors, 1968; Ekstasy, 1975; Like Father, 1978; The King of Fifth Avenue, 1981; Minds, 1982; Murder at the Met, 1984; Medicine Man,

1985; Peep Show, 1986; The Plague Years, 1986; Feature Scripts: Murder at the Met, 1982; Falling Angel, 1984; Catching It, 1988; Passion, 1990; The Man in the Slouch Hat, 1992; Detectives of the Heart, 1992; Television Scripts: Hill Street Blues, 1987; Send Me, 1987; Alaska, 1988-89; Gideon Oliver, 1988; HELP, 1989; In Your Face, 1989; The Nasty Boys, 1989; Law and Order, 1990; Legacy of Lies, 1992; In the Year 2000, 1992. Contributions to: Over 150 stories and articles to numerous national and international magazines. Honours: National Magazine Award; National Association of Science Writers Award; Best Article of The Year Award, Playboy; National Endowment for the Arts Grant in Fiction; Firsts Award, short story, Atlantic Monthly; Notable Book of the Year, New York Times (2); Edgar Nominations (2); Pulitzer Prize Nomination; Writers Foundation of America Gold Medal for Excellence in Writing, 1992; Golden Globe Nomination; Emmy Nomination. Memberships: PEN; Writers Guild-East; Mystery Writers of America; International Association of Crime Writers; Century Association; Williams Club. Address: c/o Dave Wirtschafter, ICM, 8942 Wilshire Boulevard, Beverly Hills, CA 90211, USA.

BLACK David (Macleod), b. 8 Nov 1941, Cape Town, South Africa (British citizen). Lecturer; Poet. Education: MA, Edinburgh University, 1966; MA in Religious Studies, University of Lancaster, 1971. Appointments: Teacher, Chelsea Art School, London, 1966-70; Lecturer and Supervisor, Westminster Pastoral Foundation, London. Publications: Rocklestrakes, 1960; From the Mountain, 1963; Theory of Diet, 1966; With Decorum, 1967; A Dozen Short Poems, 1968; Penguin Modern Poets 11, 1968; The Educators, 1969; The Old Hag, 1972; The Happy Crow, 1974; Gravitations, 1979; Collected Poems 1964-87, 1991; A Place for Exploration, 1991. Honours: Scottish Arts Council Prize, 1968; Arts Council of Great Britain Bursary, 1968; Scottish Arts Council Publication Award, 1991. Address: 30 Cholmley Gardens, Aldred Road, London NW6 1AG, England.

BLACK Jim. See: **HAINING Peter Alexander.**

BLACKBURN Gaston, (Hugues Auburn), b. 4 March 1927, Kenogami, Canada. Pasteur. Education: BA, 1949; Bacc. pédagogie, 1963; Licence ès lettres, 1964; Bacc. théologie, 1965; Diploma, École Normale supérieure, 1965; Brevet enseignement spécialisé, 1965; Bacc. bibliothéconomie, 1966. Appointments: Ministère paroissial and ministère en milieu hospitalier, 1953-94; Professor, French and Latin, 1960-62, Literature, 1966-67. Publications: La Tourmente, 1965; Sous la tente, 1970; Essai de toponymie saguenéenne, 1970; Petits poèmes des Rocheuses, 1974; Promenades septiliennes, 1979; Rocaille, 1981; Promenades hospitalières, 1987. Honours: Chevalier Ordre de la Croix du Sud Guyane française, 1982; Médaille de bronze du Club Muse de Karukera, 1982. Memberships: Équipiers de St Michel, 1946; Société historique du Saguenay, 1959; Société d'archéologie Saguenay, 1964; Corp bibliothécaires, 1970; Union des écrivains, Québec, 1981. Address: 7640, Chemin Coopérative, Alma, Québec G8B 5V3, Canada.

BLACKIN Malcolm. See: **CHAMBERS Aidan.**

BLAINE James. See: **AVALLONE Michael (Angelo Jr).**

BLAINEY Geoffrey Norman, b. 11 Mar 1930, Melbourne, Victoria, Australia. Writer. Education: Wesley College, Melbourne; Queen's College, University of Melbourne. Publications: The Peaks of Lyell, 1954; A Centenary History of the University of Melbourne, 1957; Gold and Paper, 1958; Mines in the Spinifex, 1960; The Rush That Never Ended, 1963; A History of Camberwell, 1965; If I Remember Rightly: The Memoirs of W S Robinson, 1966; Wesley College: The First Hundred Years (co-author and editor), 1967; The Tyranny of Distance, 1966; Across a Red World, 1968; The Rise of Broken Hill, 1968; The Steel Master, 1971; The Causes of War, 1973; Triumph of the Nomads, 1975; A Land Half Won, 1980; The Blainey View, 1982; Our Side of the Country, 1984; All for Australia, 1984; The Great Seesaw, 1988; A Game of our Own: The Origins of Australian Football, 1990; Odd Fellows, 1991; Eye on Australia, 1991; Jumping Over the Wheel, 1993; The Golden Mile, 1993; A Shorter History of Australia, 1994. Honours: Gold Medal, Australian Literature Society, 1963; Encyclopaedia Award, New York, 1988. Memberships: Chairman, Commonwealth Literary Fund, 1971-73; Chairman, Literature Board, 1973-74, Chairman, Australia Council, 1977-81. Address: PO Box 257, East Melbourne, Victoria 3002, Australia.

BLAIR Claude, b. 22 Nov 1922, Manchester, England. Antiquarian; Art Historian. Education: BA, 1950, MA, 1963, University of Manchester. Appointments: Assistant, Tower of London Armouries, 1951-56; Honorary Editor, Journal of Arms and Armour Society, 1953-77; Assistant Keeper, 1966-72, Deputy Keeper, 1966-72, Keeper, 1972-82, Metalwork, Victoria and Albert Museum, London; Consultant, Christie's London, 1982-. Publications: European Armour, 1958; European and American Arms, 1962; Pistols of the World, 1968; Three Presentation Swords in the Victoria and Albert Museum, 1972; The James A de Rothschild Collection at Waddesdon Manor; Arms, Armour and Base-Metalwork, 1974; Pollard's History of Firearms, 1983; A History of Silver, 1987. Address: 90 Links Road, Ashtead, Surrey KT21 2HW, England.

BLAIR Emma. See: **BLAIR Iain John.**

BLAIR Iain John, (Emma Blair), b. 12 Aug 1942, Glasgow, Scotland. Novelist. m. 26 Apr 1975, 2 sons. Education: Royal Scottish Academy of Music and Dramatic Art. Publications: Where No Man Cries, 1982; Nellie Wildchild, 1983; Hester Dark, 1984; This Side of Heaven, 1985; Jessie Gray, 1985; The Princess of Poor Street, 1986; Street Song, 1986; When Dreams Come True, 1987; A Most Determined Woman, 1988; The Blackbird's Tale, 1989; Maggie Jordan, 1990; Scarlet Ribbons, 1991; The Water Meadows, 1992. Memberships: Romantic Novelists Association; British Actors Equity. Literary Agent: Rogers, Coleridge and White, 20 Powis Mews, London W11 1JN, England. Address: The Old Vicarage, Stoke Canon, Near Exeter, Devon EX5 4AS, England.

BLAIR Jessica. See: **SPENCE William (John Duncan).**

BLAIR Pauline Hunter, (Pauline Clarke, Helen Clare). Author. m. Peter Hunter Blair, Feb 1969. Education: BA Honours, Somerville College, Oxford. Publications: As Pauline Clarke: The Pekinese Princess, 1948; The Great Can, 1952; The White Elephant, 1952; Smith's Hoard, 1955; The Boy with the Erpingham Hood, 1956; Sandy the Sailor, 1956; James, the Policeman, 1957; James and the Robbers, 1959; Torolv the Fatherless, 1959, 2nd edition 1974, re-issued 1991; The Lord of the Castle, 1960; The Robin Hooders, 1960; James and the Smugglers, 1961; Keep the Pot Boiling, 1961; The Twelve and the Genii, 1962; Silver Bells and Cockle Shells, 1962; James and the Black Van, 1963; Crowds of Creatures, 1964; The Bonfire Party, 1966; The Two Faces of Silenus, 1972; As Helen Clare: Five Dolls in a House, 1953; Merlin's Magic, 1953; Bel, the Giant and Other Stories, 1956; Five Dolls and the Monkey, 1956; Five Dolls in the Snow, 1957; Five Dolls and Their Friends, 1959; Seven White Pebbles, 1960; Five Dolls and the Duke, 1963; The Cat and the Fiddle and Other Stories from Bel, the Giant, 1968. Honours: Library Association Carnegie Medal, 1962; Lewis Carroll Shelf Award, 1963; Deutsche Jugend Buchpreis, 1968. Address: Church Farm House, Bottisham, Cambridge CB5 9BA, England.

BLAIS Marie-Claire, b. 5 Oct 1939, Quebec, Canada. Novelist; Playwright. Education: Laval University, Quebec. Publications: Fiction: La Belle Bête, 1960; Tête Blanche, 1961; Le Jour est Noir, 1962; Une Saison dans la vie d'Emmanuel, 1965; Les Voyageurs sacrés, 1966; David Sterne, 1967; The Fugitive, 1967; Manuscrits de Pauline Arhange, 4 volumes, 1969-76; The Wolf, 1972; St Lawrence Blues, 1974; A Literary Affair, 1975; Nights in the Underground, 1978; Deaf to the City, 1979; Anna's World, 1982; Pierre, la guerre du printemps, 1981; The Angel of Solitude, 1989; Plays: The Puppet Caravan, 1962; Eleonor, 1962; The Execution, 1967; A Clash of Symbols, 1976; L'Ocean and Murmures, 1976; Sommeil d'hiver, 1984; The Island, 1989; Un jardin dans la tempête, 1990; Radio and Television plays. Honours: Companion, Order of Canada, 1975; Royal Society of Canada. Address: John C Goodwin and Associates, 839 Sherbrooke Est, Suite 2, Montreal, Quebec H2L 1K6, Canada.

BLAKE Jennifer. See: **MAXWELL Patricia Anne.**

BLAKE Ken, See: **BLUMER Henry Kenneth.**

BLAKE Norman (Francis), b. 19 Apr 1934, Ceara, Brazil. Professor; Writer; Editor; Translator. Education: BA, 1956, BLitt, 1959, MA, 1960, Oxford University. Appointments: Lecturer, 1959-68, Senior Lecturer, 1968-73, Professor, 1973-, University of Sheffield. Publications: The Saga of the Jomsvikings, 1962; The Phoenix, 1964, 2nd edition, 1990; Caxton and His World, 1969; William Caxton's Reynard the Fox, 1970; Middle English Religious Prose, 1972;

Selections from William Caxton, 1973; Caxton's Own Prose, 1975; Caxton's Quattuor Sermiones, 1973; Caxton: England's First Publisher, 1976; The English Language in Medieval Literature, 1977; Non-Standard Language in English Literature, 1981; Shakespeare's Language, 1983; Textual Tradition of the Canterbury Tales, 1985; William Caxton: A Bibliographical Guide, 1985; Traditional English Grammar and Beyond, 1988; Index of Printed Middle English Prose, 1985; The Language of Shakespeare (with R E Lewis and A S G Edwards), 1989, 2nd edition, 1994; An Introduction to the Languages of Literature, 1990; William Caxton and English Literary Culture, 1991; The Cambridge History of the English Language, Vol II: 1066-1476, 1992; Introduction to English Language (with J Moorhead), 1993; William Caxton, 1996; Essays in Shakespeare's Language, 1996; History of the English Language, 1996. Address: Department of English Language and Linguistics, University of Sheffield, Sheffield, S10 2TN, England.

BLAKE Patrick, See: EGLETON Clive Frederick William.

BLAKE Robert (Norman William), (Lord Blake of Braydeston, Norfolk), b. 23 Dec 1916, Norfolk, England. Historian. m. Patricia Mary Waters, 22 Aug 1953, 4 daughters. Education: MA, Magdalen College, 1938. Appointments: Lecturer, 1946-47, Tutor in Politics, 1947-68, Censor, 1950-55, University Lecturer and Senior Proctor, 1959-60, Ford Lecturer in English History, 1967-68, Christ Church, Oxford; Conservative Member,Oxford City Council, 1957-64; Provost, 1968-76, Pro-Vice Chancellor of the University, 1971-87, Queen's College, Oxford University; Member, Royal Commission on Historical Manuscripts, 1975-; Trustee, British Museum, 1978-88. Publications: The Private Papers of Diouglas Haig, editor, 1952; The Unknown Prime Minister: The Life and Times of Andrew Bonar Law, 1858-1923, 1955; Esto Perpetua: The Norwich Union Life Insurance Society, 1958; Disraeli, 1966; Conservatism Today: Four Personal Points of View (with others), 1966; Disraeli and Gladstone, 1970; The Conservative Party from Peel to Churchill: Based on the Ford Lectures, Delivered before the University of Oxford in the Hilary Term of 1968, 1970, revised edition as The Conservative Party from Peel to Thatcher, 1977; Dictionary of National Biography (joint editor), 1980-90; Disraeli's Grand Tour: Benjamin Disraeli and the Holy Land, 1830-31, 1982; The English World: History, Character and People (editor), 1982; The Decline of Power, 1915-1964, 1985; An Incongrous POartnership, Lloyd George and Bonar Law, 1992; Gladstone, Disraeli and Queen Victoria, 1993; Churchill: A Major New Assessment of His Life in Peace and War (editor with Roger Louis), 1993. Contributions to: Periodicals. Honours: Life Peer, 1971; DLitt, Glasgow University, 1972, East Anglia University, 1983, Westminster College, Fulton, Missouri, 1987, Buckingham University, 1988; Fellow, Queen's College, Oxford, 1987, Pembroke College, Cambridge. Memberships: Authors Society; British Academy, Fellow; Literary Society, President. Address: Riverview House, Brundall, Norwich, Norfolk NR13 5LA, England.

BLAMIRES Harry, b. 6 Nov 1916, Bradford, England. Lecturer in Higher Education; Author. m. Nancy Bowles, 26 Dec 1940, 5 sons. Education: BA, 1938, MA, 1945, University College, Oxford. Appointments: Head, English Department, 1948-72, Dean, Arts and Sciences, 1972-76, King Alfred's College, Winchester; Clyde Kilby Visiting Professor of English, Wheaton College, Wheaton, Illinois, 1987. Publications: The Christian Mind, 1963; The Bloomsday Book: Guide to Joyce's Ulysses, 1966, revised edition, 1988; Word Unheard: Guide Through Eliot's Four Quartets, 1969; Milton's Creation, 1971; A Short History of English Literature, 1974, revised edition, 1984; Where Do We Stand?, 1980; Twentieth-Century English Literature, 1982, revised edition, 1986; Guide to 20th Century Literature in English, 1983; On Christian Truth, 1983; Words Made Flesh, 1985 (UK edition as The Marks of the Maker, 1987); The Victorian Age of Literature, 1988; Meat Not Milk, 1988; The Age of Romantic Literature, 1989; A History of Literary Criticism, 1991; The Queen's English, 1994. Honour: Hon DLitt, Southampton University, 1993. Membership: Society of Authors. Address: Pinfold, 3 Glebe Close, Keswick, Cumbria CA12 5QQ, England.

BLANDIANA Ana, (Otila Valeria Rusan), b. 25 Mar 1942, Timisoara, Romania. Poet; Writer; Opinion Leader. m. Romulus Rusan. Education: Graduated, University of Cluj, 1967. Appointments: Columnist, Romania literara magazine, 1974-88; Librarian, Institute of Fine Arts, Bucharest, 1975-77; President, Romanian PEN; President, foundation Civic Academy and Civic Alliance. Publications: First-Person Plural, 1964; The Wounded Heel, 1966; The Third Sacrament, 1969; To be a Witness, 1970; 50 Poems, 1972; October,

November, December, 1972; Poems, 1974; The Sleep Within the Sleep, 1977; Four Seasons, 1977; Poems, 1978; The Most Beautiful of All Possible Worlds, 1978; Events in My Garden, 1980; The Cricket's Eye, 1981; Poems, 1982; Projects for the Past, 1982; Corridor of Mirrors, 1984; Star of Prey, 1985; The Hour of Sand: Selected Poems 1969-89, 1989; The Architecture of the Waves (poetry), 1990; 100 Poems, 1991; The Drawer with Applauses (novel), 1992; Imitation of a Nightmare (short stories), 1995; The Morning After the Death (poetry), 1996. Essays: The Witness Quality, 1970; I Write, You Write, He/She Writes, 1975; The Most Beautiful of the Possible Worlds, 1978; Passage of Mirrors, 1983; Self-Portrait with Palimpsest, 1985;Cities of Syllables, 1987. Honours: Romanian Writers' Union, Prize for Poetry, 1969; Romanian Academy, Prize for Poetry, 1970; Association of Writers in Bucharest, Prize for Prose, 1980; Herder Prize, Austria, 1982. Address: Academia Civica, Piata Amzei 13 et 2, C P 22-216, Bucharest, Romania.

BLASER Robin (Francis), b. 18 May 1925, Denver, Colorado, USA. Professor of English; Poet. Education: MA, 1954, MLS, 1955, University of California at Berkeley. Appointments: Professor of English, Centre for the Arts, Simon Fraser University, Burnaby, British Columbia, Canada, 1972-86. Publications: The Moth Poem, 1964; Les Chimères, 1965; Cups, 1968; The Holy Forest Section, 1970; Image-nations 1-12 and The Stadium of the Mirror, 1974; Image-nations 13-14, 1975; Suddenly, 1976; Syntax, 1983; The Faerie Queene and the Park, 1987; Pell Mell, 1988; The Holy Forest, 1993. Honours: Poetry Society Award, 1965; Canada Council Grant, 1989-90. Address: 1636 Trafalgar Street, Vancouver, British Columbia V6K 3R7, Canada.

BLASHFORD-SNELL John Nicholas, b. 22 Oct 1936, Hereford, England. Soldier; Colonel; Explorer. Education: Victoria College, Jersey, Channel Islands; Royal Military Academy, Sandhurst. Publications: A Taste for Adventure, 1978; Operation Drake, 1981; In the Wake of Drake, (with M Cable), 1982; Mysteries - Encounters with the Unexplained, 1983; Operation Raleigh, The Start of an Adventure, 1985; Operation Raleigh, Adventure Challenge (with Ann Tweedy), 1988; Operation Raleigh, Adventure Unlimited (with Ann Tweedy), 1990; Something Lost Behind the Ranges, 1994; Mammoth Hunt (with Rula Lenska), 1996. Contributions to: Expedition: The Field; British Army Review; Gun Digest; Spectator; Yorkshire Post; Scotsman; Traveller; Royal Business Journal; Daily Telegraph; Surrey Telegraph; Country Life. Address: c/o The Scientific Exploration Society, Expedition Base, Motcombe, Dorset SP7 9PB, England.

BLAYNE Diana, See: KYLE Susan (Eloise Spaeth).

BLEAKLEY David (Wylie), b. 11 Jan 1925, Belfast, Northern Ireland. Educator; President, Church Mission Society; Writer. m. Winifred Wason, 5 Aug 1949, 3 sons. Education: Diploma in Economics and Political Science, Ruskin College, Oxford, 1949; BA, 1951, MA, 1955, Queen's University, Belfast. Appointments: Principal, Belfast Further Education Centre, 1955-58; MP, Labour Party, Victoria, Parliament of Northern Ireland, Belfast, 1958-65; Lecturer in Industrial Relations, Kivukoni College, Dar-es-Salaam, 1967-69; Head, Department of Economics and Political Studies, Methodist College, Belfast, 1969-79; Minister of Community Relations, Government of Northern Ireland, 1971; Member, Northern Ireland Labour Party, East Belfast, Northern Ireland Assembly, 1973-75; Visiting Senior Lecturer in Peace Studies, University of Bradford, 1974-; Chief Executive, Irish Council of Churches, 1980-92; President, Church Mission Society, 1983-. Publications: Ulster Since 1800: Regional History Symposium, 1958; Young Ulster and Religion in the Sixties, 1964; Peace in Ulster, 1972; Faulkner: A Biography, 1974; Saidie Patterson: Irish Peacemaker, 1980; In Place of Work, 1981; The Shadow and Substance, 1983; Beyond Work: Free to Be, 1985; Will the Future Work?, 1986; Europe: A Christian Vision, 1992; Ageing and Ageism in a Technological Society, 1994; Peace in Ireland: Two States, One People, 1995. Contributions to: BBC and Periodicals. Honours: Appointed PC, 1971; Honorary MA, Open University, 1975; Commander of the Order of the British Empire, 1984. Address: 8 Thornhill, Bangor, County Down BT19 1RD, Northern Ireland.

BLEASDALE Alan, b. 23 Mar 1946. Playwright; Novelist. m. Julia Moses, 1970, 2 sons, 1 daughter. Education: Teachers Certificate, Padgate Teachers Training College. Publications: Scully, 1975; Who's Been Sleeping in My Bed, 1977; No More Sitting on the Old School Bench, 1979; Boys From the Blackstuff (televised), 1982; Are You Lonesome Tonight?, 1985; No Surrender, 1986; Having a

Ball, 1986; It's A Madhouse, 1986; The Monocled Mutineer (televised), 1986; GBH (television series), 1992. Honours: BAFTA Writer's Award, 1982; RTS Writer's Award, 1982; Broadcasting Press Guild TV Award for Best Series, 1982; Best Musical, London Standard Drama Awards, 1985. Address: c/o Harvey Unna and Stephen Durbridge Ltd, 24 Pottery Lane, Holland Park, London, W11 4LZ, England.

BLISHEN Edward, b. 29 Apr 1920, Whetstone, Middlesex, England. Author. m. Nancy Smith, 4 Nov 1948, 2 sons. Publications: Roaring Boys, 1955; A Cackhanded War, 1971; Sorry Dad, 1978; A Nest of Teachers, 1979; Lizzie Pye, 1982; The Outside Contributor, 1986; The Disturbance Fee, 1988; Also: This Right Soft Lot, 1969; Uncommon Entrance, 1974; Shaky Relations, 1981; Donkey Work, 1983; A Second Skin, 1984; The Penny World, 1990. Contributions to: Numerous magazines and journals. Honours: Carnegie Medal (with Leon Garfield), 1970; Travelling Scholarship, Society of Authors, 1979; J R Ackerley Prize, autobiography, 1981; Fellow, Royal Society of Literature; Hon Doc, Open University. Memberships: Society of Authors; PEN. Literary Agent: A M Heath. Address: 12 Bartrams Lane, Hadley Wood, Barnet, London EN4 0EH, England.

BLIVEN Bruce, b. 31 Jan 1916, Los Angeles, California, USA. Writer. m. Naomi Horowitz, 26 May 1950, 1 son. Education: AB, Harvard College, 1937. Publications: The Wonderful Writing Machine, 1954; Battle for Manhattan, 1956; The Story of D-Day, 1956, 50th anniversary edition, 1994; The American Revolution, 1958; From Pearl Harbor to Okinawa, 1960; From Casablanca to Berlin, 1965; New York (with Naomi Bliven), 1969; Under the Guns, 1972; Book Traveller, 1975; Volunteers, One and All, 1976; The Finishing Touch, 1978; New York: A History, 1981. Contributions to: New Yorker; Many other national magazines. Memberships: Authors Guild, Council, 1970-; Society of American Historians, Board, 1975-; PEN American Centre; American Society of Journalists and Authors. Address: New Yorker, 20 West 43rd Street, New York, NY 10036, USA.

BLOCH Chana (Florence), b. 15 Mar 1940, New York, USA. Professor of English; Poet; Translator; Critic; Essayist. m. Ariel Bloch, 26 Oct 1969, divorced, 2 sons. Education: BA, Cornell University, 1961; MA, 1963, MA, 1965, Brandeis University; PhD, University of California at Berkeley, 1975. Appointments: Instructor of English, Hebrew University, Jerusalem, 1964-67; Associate in Near Eastern Studies, University of California at Berkeley, 1967-69; Instructor, 1973-75, Assistant Professor, 1975-81, Associate Professor, 1981-87, Chairman, Department of English, 1986-89, Professor of English, 1987-, Director, Creative Writing Program, 1993-, Mills College, Oakland, California. Publications: Poetry: The Secrets of the Tribe, 1981; The Past Keeps Changing, 1992. Other: Spelling the Word: George Herbert and the Bible, 1985. Translator: Dahlia Ravikovitch: A Dress of Fire, 1978; Yehuda Amichai: The Selected Poetry (with Stephen Mitchell), 1986, revised edition, 1996; Dahlia Ravikovitch: The Window: New and Selected Poems (with Ariel Bloch), 1989; The Song of Songs: A New Translation, Introduction and Commentary (with Ariel Bloch), 1995; A Dress of Fire by Dahlia Ravikovitch. Contributions to: Poetry, translations, criticism, and essays in various anthologies and periodicals. Honours: Discovery Award, Poetry Centre, New York, 1974; Translation Award, Columbia University, 1978; National Endowment for the Humanities Fellowship, 1980; Book of the Year Award, Conference on Christianity and Literature, 1986; Writers Exchange Award, Poets and Writers, 1988; Yaddo Residencies, 1988, 1990, 1993, 1994, 1995, 1996; MacDowell Colony Residencies, 1988, 1992, 1993; Djerassi Foundation Residencies, 1989, 1991; National Endowment for the Arts Fellowship, 1989-90. Memberships: PEN; Poetry Society of America; Modern Language Association. Address: c/o Department of English, Mills College, Oakland, CA 94613, USA.

BLOCK Francesca Lia, b. 3 Dec 1962, Hollywood, California, USA. Author; Screenwriter. Education: BA, English Literature, University of California at Berkeley. Publications: Weetzie Bat, 1989; Witch Baby, 1991; Cherokee Bat and the GoatGuys, 1992; Missing Angel Juan, 1993; Baby Be Bop, 1995; The Hanged Man; Ecstasia: Primavera; Girl Goddess #9, 1996. Contributions to: Spin; New York Times book review; Los Angeles Times book review. Honours: Phi Beta Kappa; American Library Association Best Books, 1989, 1992, 1993, 1995; School Library Journal Best Book, 1991, 1993. Publishers Weekly Best Books, 1992, 1995. Address: Artist's Agency, 230 West 55th Street, 55th Street 29D, New York, NY, USA.

BLOCK DE BEHAR Lisa, b. 12 Mar 1937, Montevideo, Uruguay. Professor; Writer. m. Isaac Behar, 25 June 1957, 2 sons. Education:

BA, 1961, MS, 1973, Institute de Profesors, Montevideo; PhD, École de Haute Études en Sciences Sociales, Paris, 1983. Appointments: Professor of Literary Theory, Montevideo, 1976; Professor of Semiotics, Montevideo, 1985. Publications: El Lenguajede la Publicidad, 1974, 1976-92; Una retórica del silencio, 1984-94; Al Margen de Borges, 1987; Jules Laforgue, 1987; Dos medios entre dos medios, 1990; Una palabra propiamente dicha, 1994. Contributions to: Periodicals. Honour: Prize Xavier Villurrutia, 1984. Address: Avenida Rivera 6195, Montevideo, Uruguay.

BLOND Anthony, b. 20 Mar 1928, Sale, England. Author. m. Laura Hesketh, 1 Mar 1981, 1 son. Education: MA, New College, Oxford, 1951. Appointments: Active with Anthony Blond Ltd, 1957-71; Director, Blond and Brigg Ltd, publishers, London, 1971-90. Publications: The Publishing Game, 1971; Family Business, 1978; The Book Book, 1983; Blond's Roman Emperors, 1994. Contributions to: Literary Review; Spectator. Address: 9 Rue Thiers, 87300 Bellac, France.

BLONDEL Jean Fernand Pierre, b. 26 Oct 1929, Toulon, France. University Professor. m. (1) Michele Hadet, 1954, div, (2) Teresa Ashton, 1982, 2 daughters. Education: Diploma, Institut Etudes Politiques, Paris, 1953; BLitt, Oxford, England, 1955. Publications: Voters, Parties and Leaders, 1963; An Introduction to Conservative Government, 1969; Comparative Legislatures, 1973; World Leaders, 1980; The Discipline of Politics, 1982; The Organisation of Governments, 1982; Government Ministers in the Contemporary World, 1985; Political Parties, 1978; Political Leadership, 1987; Governing Together, co-editor, 1993; Comparative Government, 1995; Party and Government (co-editor), 1996. Contributions to: European Journal of Political Research. Honours: Honorary Doctorates, University of Salford, 1990, University of Essex, 1992, Catholic University of Louvain, 1992, University of Turku, 1995. Memberships: Royal Swedish Academy of Sciences; American Political Science Association; British Political Studies Association of the UK; Association Francaise de Science Politique. Address: 15 Marloes Road, London W8 6LQ, England.

BLOOM Harold, b. 11 July 1930, New York, New York, USA. Professor of Humanities; Writer. m. Jeanne Gould, 8 May 1958, 2 sons. Education: BA, Cornell University, 1951; PhD, Yale University, 1955. Appointments: Faculty, 1955-65, Professor of English, 1965-77, DeVane Professor of Humanities, 1974-77, Professor of Humanities, 1977-83, Sterling Professor of Humanities, 1983-, Yale University; Visiting Professor, Hebrew University, Jerusalem, 1959, Breadloaf Summer School, 1965-66, Cornell University, 1968-69; Visiting University Professor, New School for Social Research, New York City, 1982-84; Charles Eliot Norton Professor of Poetry, Harvard University, 1987-88; Berg Professor of English, New York University, 1988-. Publications: Shelley's Mythmaking, 1959; The Visionary Company, 1961; Blake's Apocalypse, 1963; Commentary to Blake, 1965; Yeats, 1970; The Ringers in the Tower, 1971; The Anxiety Influence, 1973; A Map of Misreading, 1975; Kabbalah and Criticism, 1975; Poetry and Repression, 1976; Figures of Capable Imagination, 1976; Wallace Stevens: The Poems of Our Climate, 1977; The Flight of Lucifer: A Gnostic Fantasy, 1979; Agon: Towards a Theory of Revisionism, 1981; The Breaking of the Vessels, 1981; The Strong Light of the Canonical, 1987; Freud: Transference and Authority, 1988; Poetics of Influence: New and Selected Criticism, 1988; Ruin the Sacred Truths, 1988; The Book of J, 1989; The American Religion, 1990; The Western Canon, 1994; Omens of Millennium: The Gnosis of Angels, Dreams and Resurrection, 1996. Contributions to: Scholarly books and journals. Honours: Fulbright Fellowship, 1955; Guggenheim Fellowship, 1962; Newton Arvin Award, 1967; Melville Caine Award, 1970; Zabel Prize, 1982; John D and Catharine T MacArthur Foundation Fellowship, 1985; Christian Gauss Prize, 1989. Membership: American Academy of Arts and Letters. Address: 179 Linden Street, New Haven, CT 06511, USA.

BLUM Richard A, b. 28 July 1943, Brooklyn, New York, USA. Television Programme Development Executive; Writer; Educator. Education: BA, FairleighDickinson University, 1965; MS, Boston University, 1967; PhD, University of Southern California, 1977. Appointments: Professor, Screenwriting, University of Maryland, 1983-; Visiting Professor, Screenwriting, Harvard University Summer School, 1984, 1985, 1986; American Film Institute, 1983, 1984, 1986; The Writers Centre, 1984-88. Publications: Television Writing: From Concept to Contract, 1980; American Film Acting, 1984; Primetime: Network TV Programming (co-author), 1987; Working Actors, 1989;

Inside Television Producing, 1991. Contributions to: Writer; Scriptwriter; Educational Editor; Journal of Performing Arts Review; Television Writer, Producer, PBS, NBC-TV, Universal Studios, Columbia Pictures-TV. Honours: Best Playwright, FDU, 1964, 1965; Creative and Performing Arts Award, University of Maryland, 1987; Judge, Nicholl Screenwriting Fellowships, Academy of Motion Pictures Arts and Sciences, 1987, 1988; Judge, Public Television Awards, Corporation for Public Broadcasting, 1988; Ford Foundation Fellowship, 1988. Memberships: Writers Guild of America; Academy of Television Arts and Sciences; University Film and Video Association; Broadcast Education Association; Washington Independent Writers. Address: 2208 Washington Avenue, Silver Spring, MD 20910, USA.

BLUMBERG Stanley, b. 11 Apr 1912, USA. Writer. m. 2 Aug 1952. Education: University of Maryland, 1931; Johns Hopkins University, 1932. Publications: Energy and Conflict - The Life and Times of Edward Teller, 1976; The Survival Factor, Israeli Intelligence from World War I to the Present, 1981; Edward Teller, Giant of the Golden Age of Physics, 1990. Contributions to: Nation; Baltimore Sun; USA Today; Hopkins Magazine; Human Events. Membership: Literary Guild. Address: 6000 Ivydene Terrace, Baltimore, MD 21209, USA.

BLUME Judy (Sussman), b. 12 Feb 1938, Elizabeth, New Jersey, USA. Writer. 1 son, 1 daughter. Education: BS, New York University, 1961. Publications: Are You There, God?; It's Me Margaret; Blubber; Deenie; Freckle Juice; Iggie's House; It's Not the End of the World; The One in the Middle is the Green Kangaroo; Otherwise Known as Sheila the Great; Starring Sally J Freedman as Herself; Superfudge; Tales of a Fourth Grade Nothing; Then Again, Maybe I Won't; Tiger Eyes; The Pain and the Great One; The Judy Blume Diary; Forever; Wifey; Smart Women; Letters to Judy; What Kids Wish They Could Tell You; Just as Long As We're Together; Here's To You, Rachel Robinson. Honours: Numerous. Memberships: Authors Guild Council; PEN; Board, Society of Children's Book Writers. Address: c/o Claire Smith, Harold Ober Associates Inc, 40 East 49th Street, New York, NY 10017, USA.

BLY Robert (Elwood), b. 23 Dec 1926, Madison, Minnesota, USA. Poet; Translator; Editor; Publisher. m. (1) Carolyn McLean, 1955, div 1979, (2) Ruth Counsell, 1980, 2 sons, 2 daughters. Education: St Olaf College, 1946-47; AB, Harvard University, 1950; MA, University of Iowa, 1956. Appointments: Publisher and Editor, 1958-; Various writing workshops. Publications: Poetry: The Lion's Tail and Eyes: Poems Written Out of Laziness and Silence (with William Duffy and James Wright), 1962; Silence in the Snowy Fields, 1962; The Light Around the Body, 1967; Chrysanthemums, 1967; Ducks, 1968; The Morning Glory: Another Thing That Will Never Be My Friend, 1969, revised edition, 1970; The Teeth Mother Naked at Last, 1971; Poems for Tennessee (with William Stafford and William Matthews), 1971; Christmas Eve Service at Midnight at St Michael's, 1972; Water Under the Earth, 1972; The Dead Seal Near McClure's Beach, 1973; Sleepers Joining Hands, 1973; Jumping Out of Bed, 1973; The Hockey Poem, 1974; Point Reyes Poems, 1974; Old Man Rubbing His Eyes, 1975; The Loon, 1977; This Body is Made of Camphor and Gopherwood, 1977; Visiting Emily Dickinson's Grave and Other Poems, 1979; This Tree Will Be Here for a Thousand Years, 1979; The Man in the Black Coat Turns, 1981; Finding an Old Ant Mansion, 1981; Four Ramages, 1983; The Whole Moisty Night, 1983; Out of the Rolling Ocean, 1984; Mirabai Versions, 1984; In the Month of May, 1985; A Love of Minute Particulars, 1985; Selected Poems, 1986; Loving a Woman in Two Worlds, 1987; The Moon on a Fencepost, 1988; The Apple Found in the Plowing, 1989; What Have I Ever Lost By Dying?: Collected Prose Poems, 1993; Gratitude to Old Teachers, 1993; Meditations on the Insatiable Soul, 1994; Morning Poems, 1997. Editor: The Sea and the Honeycomb, 1966; A Poetry Reading Against the Vietnam War (with David Ray), 1967; Forty Poems Touching Upon Recent History, 1970; News of the Universe: Poems of Twofold Consciousness, 1980; Ten Love Poems, 1981; The Fifties and the Sixties, 10 volumes, 1982; The Winged Life: The Poetic Voice of Henry David Thoreau, 1986; The Rag and Bone Shop of the Heart: Poems for Men, 1992; The Soul Is Here for Its Own Joy, 1995. Translator: Over 35 books. Other: A Broadsheet Against the New York Times Book Review, 1961; Talking All Morning: Collected Conversations and Interviews, 1980; The Eight Stages of Translation, 1983, 2nd edition, 1986; The Pillow and the Key: Commentary on the Fairy Tale Iron John, 1987; A Little Book on the Human Shadow (edited by William Booth), 1988; American Poetry: Wildness and Domesticity, 1990; Iron John: A Book About Men, 1990; Remembering James Wright, 1991;

The Sibling Society, 1996. Honours: Fulbright Grant, 1956-57; Lowell Travelling Fellowship, 1964; Guggenheim Fellowships, 1964, 1972; American Academy of Arts and Letters Grant, 1965; Rockefeller Foundation Fellowship, 1967; National Book Award, 1968. Memberships: American Academy and Institute of Arts and Letters; Association of Literary Magazines of America, Executive Committee. Address: 1904 Girard Avenue South, Minneapolis, MN 54403, USA.

BLYTH Alan, b. 27 July 1929, London, England. Music Critic and Editor. m. Ursula Zumloh. Education: MA, Oxford University. Career: Contributor as Critic, The Times, 1963-76; Associate Editor, Opera, 1967-84; Music Editor, Encyclopaedia Britannica, 1971-76; Critic, Daily Telegraph, 1976-89. Publications: The Enjoyment of Opera, 1969; Colin Davis, A Short Biography, 1972; Opera on Record (editor), 1979; Remembering Britten, 1980; Wagner's Ring: An Introduction, 1980; Opera on Record 2 (editor), 1983; Opera on Record 3 (editor), 1984; Song on Record (editor), Volume 1, 1986, Volume 2, 1988; Choral Music on Record, 1990; Opera on CD, 1992; Opera on Video, 1995. Contributions to: Gramophone; BBC; Memberships: Critics' Circle; Garrick Club. Hobbies: Gardening; Wine; Collecting 78 rpm vocal records. Address: 22 Shilling Street, Lavenham, Suffolk CO10 9RH, England.

BLYTHE Ronald George, b. 6 Nov 1922, Acton, Suffolk, England. Author. Appointments: Eastern Arts Association Literature Panel, 1975-84; Society of Authors Management Committee, 1979-84; Associate Editor, New Wessex Edition of the Works of Thomas Hardy, 1978. Publications: A Treasonable Growth, 1960; Immediate Possession, 1961; The Age of Illusion, 1963; Akenfield, 1969; William Hazlett: Selected Writings, editor, 1970; The View in Winter, 1979; From the Headlands, 1982; The Stories of Ronald Blythe, 1985; Divine Landscapes, 1986; Each Returning Day, 1989; Private Words, 1991; Word from Wormingford, 1997; First Friends, 1997. Critical Studies of Jane Austen, Thomas Hardy, Leo Tolstoy, Literature of the Second World War. Contributions to: Observer; Sunday Times; New York Times; Listener; Atlantic Monthly; London Magazine; Tablet; New Statesman; Bottegue Oscure; Guardian. Honours: Heinemann Award, 1969; Society of Authors Travel Scholarship, 1970; FRSL, 1969; Angel Prize for Literature, 1986; Honorary MA, University of East Anglia, 1991. Memberships: Royal Society of Literature; Society of Authors; President, The John Clare Society; Fabian Society. Literary Agent: Deborah Rogers, London. Address: Bottengoms Farm, Wormingford, Colchester, Essex, England.

BOARDMAN Sir John, b. 20 Aug 1927, Ilford, Essex, England. Professor Emeritus of Classical Art and Archaeology. Education: BA, 1948, MA, 1951, Magdalene College. Appointments: Assistant Keeper, Ashmolean Museum, 1955-59; Reader in Classical Archaeology, 1959-78, Lincoln Professor of Classical Art and Archaeology, 1978-94, University of Oxford; Editor, Journal of Hellenic Studies, 1958-65; Co-Editor, Oxford Monographs in Classical Archaeology; Delegate, OUP, 1979-89. Publications: S Marinatos and M Hirmer: Crete and Mycenae (translator), 1960; The Cretan Collection in Oxford, 1961; Island Gems, 1963; The Date of the Knossos Tablets, 1963; The Greek Overseas, 1964, 3rd edition, 1980; Greek Art, 1964, 4th edition, 1996; Excavations at Tocra (with J Dorig, W Fuchs, M Hirmer), 1966; Architecture of Ancient Greece, (with J Dorig); Greek Emporio, 1967; Pre-Classical Style and Civilisation, 1967; Engraved Gems, the Ionides Collection, 1968; Archaic Greek Gems, 1968; Eros in Greece (with E la Rocca), 1978; Greek Sculpture, Archaic Period, 1978; Catalogue of Gems and Finger Rings (with M L Vollenweider), vol I, 1978; Castle Ashby Corpus Vasorum (with M Robertson), 1979; Greek Sculpture, Classical Period, 1985; The Parthenon and its Sculptures, 1985; Athenian Red Figure Vases: Classical Period, 1989; The Diffusion of Classical Art in Antiquity, 1994; Greek Sculpture, The Late Classical Period, 1995. Honours: Knighted, 1989; Professor of Ancient History, Royal Academy, 1989-; Hon Doctorate, University of Athens, 1990, University of Paris, 1994. Membership: Fellow, British Academy, 1969-. Address: 11 Park Street, Woodstock, Oxford OX20 1SJ, England.

BOAST Philip (James), b. 30 Apr 1952, London, England. Writer. m. Rosalind Thorpe, 20 June 1981, 2 sons, 1 daughter. Education: Mill Hill School, 1965-69. Publications: The Assassinators, 1976; London's Child, 1987; The Millionaire, 1989; Watersmeet, 1990; Pride, 1991; The Londons of London, 1992; Gloria, 1993; London's Daughter, 1994. Contributions to: Science Fiction Monthly. Literary Agent: Carol Smith. Address: Rhydda Bank Cottage, Trentishoe, Barnstaple, North Devon EX31 4PL, England.

BOBER Natalie Susan, b. 27 Dec 1930, New York, New York, USA. Author; Biographer; Historian. m. Lawrence H Bober, 27 Aug 1950, 2 sons, 1 daughter. Education: BA, English, 1951; MS, Reading, Education, 1966; Permanent Certification, Teacher of Reading, 1977. Appointment: Consultant to Ken Burns, Television Documentary, 1995. Publications: William Wordsworth: The Wandering Poet, 1975; A Restless Spirit: The Story of Robert Frost, 1981, new edition, 1991; Breaking Tradition: The Story of Louise Nevelson, 1984; Let's Pretend: Poems of Flight and Fancy, 1986, 2nd edition, 1990; Thomas Jefferson: Man on a Mountain, 1988, 3rd edition, 1997; Marc Chagall: Painter of Dreams, 1991; Abigail Adams: Witness to a Revolution, 1995. Contributions to: Lion and the Unicorn; Horn Book. Honours: Boston Globe-Horn Book Award, Best Non-Fiction, 1995; Boston Globe, Best Books of 1995, Best Books in the field of Social Studies; School Library Journal, Best Books of 1995; Booklist, Editor's Choices, 1995; Hungry Minds Review, Best Non-Fiction, Children's Books of Distinction, 1996; Society of Children's Book Writers Award, 1996; American Library Association, Best Books for Young Adults. Membership: Society of Children's Bookwriters and Illustrators. Address: 7 Westfield Lane, White Plains, NY 10605, USA.

BOCEK Alois. See: **VANICEK Zdenek.**

BOCOCK Robert James, b. 29 Sept 1940, Lincoln, Lincolnshire, England. Sociologist; Writer; Lecturer. Education: Diploma, University of London, 1963; PhD, Brunel University, 1973. Appointments: Lecturer in Sociology, Brunel University, 1966-79; Open University, Buckinghamshire, 1979-. Publications: Ritual in Industrial Society, 1974; Freud and Modern Society, 1976; An Introduction to Sociology, 1980; Sigmund Freud, 1983; Religion and Ideology (editor), 1985; Hegemony, 1986; Consumption, 1993. Contributions to: Journals. Memberships: Association of University Teachers; British Sociological Association. Address: Department of Sociology, Faculty of Social Sciences, Crowther Building, The Open University, Walton Hall, Milton Keynes, Buckinghamshire, England.

BODA Laszlo (Ladislas), b. 23 Nov 1929, Dregelypalank, Hungary. Professor. Education: Doctor of Theology, Budapest, 1955. Appointments: Professor of Philosophy, Esztergom, 1955-73; Professor Ordinarius, Moral Theology, Budapest, 1973-. Publications: Moral Theology (I-IV), 1980; Moral Theology of the Christian Maturity, 1986; Inner Performance, a postmodern epos adapted from Dante, 1986; To Be Human or To Have?, 1990; Your Way To Marriage, for young people, 1990; Give to God What is God's, 1991; Inkulturation, Church, Europe. Contributions to: Many periodicals and journals. Memberships: Conferences of European Moral Theology; Societas Ethica; European Theology; Society of Peace and Human Understanding; Society of St Stephen, Hungary; Society of Johannes Messner, Vienna, 1993. Address: David F u 7, Fsz 3, H 1113 Budapest XI, Hungary.

BODELSEN Anders, b. 11 Feb 1937, Copenhagen, Denmark. Novelist. m. Eva Sindahl-Pedersen, 1975. Education: University of Copenhagen, 1956-60. Appointment: Staff, Politiken, 1967-. Publications: Villa Sunset, 1964; The Greenhouse, 1965; Rama Sama, 1967; The Silent Partner, 1968; Hit and Run, Run, Run, 1968; Freezing Point, 1969; Holiday, 1970; Straus, 1971; Help: Seven Stories, 1971; The Girls on the Bridge, 1972; Opposite Number, 1972; Outside Number, 1972; Consider the Verdict, 1973; Law and Order, 1973; Everything You Wish, 1974; The Wind in the Alley, 1974; Operation Cobra, 1975; Money and the Life, 1976; The Good Times, 1977; Year by Year, 1978; Over the Rainbow, 1982; Domino, 1984; The Shelter, 1984; Revision, 1985; I Must Run, 1987; The Blue Hour, 1987; Blackout, 1988; The Town Without Fires, 1989; Red September, 1991; Radio and Television plays. Honours: Swedish Crime Writers Academy Prize, 1990. Address: Christiansholms Parkvej 12, 2930 Klampenborg, Denmark.

BODIE (Elizabeth) Idella (née Fallaw), b. 2 Dec 1925, Ridge Spring, South Carolina, USA. Teacher; Author. m. James E Bodie Sr, 15 Aug 1947, 2 sons, 2 daughters. Education: Associate Degree, Mars Hill Junior College, 1942-44; BA, Columbia College, 1944-46; Graduate Study, University of South Carolina, 1950-51. Appointment: Annual judge in Superintendents' Celebration of the Arts (state), 1985. Publications: Young readers books: The Secret of Telfair Inn, 1971; Mystery of the Pirates Treasure, 1973; Ghost in the Capitol, 1976; Stranded, 1984, Whopper, 1989; Trouble at Star Fort, 1992; Mystery of Edisto Island, 1994; Ghost Tales for Retelling, 1994. Other: South Carolina Women, 1978; Archibald Rutledge, 1980. Contributions to: Guideposts; Mature Living; Sandlapper; Instruction; Christian Home. Honours: District Teacher, 1971, 1974; Business and Professional Woman of Year, 1980; Toastmasters International Communication Achievement Award, 1985; Idella Bodie Creative Writing Award, 1985; Willou Gray Educator Award, 1988; Youth Prison Volunteer of Year, 1990; 3 books nominated for South Carolina Children's Book Award. Address: 1113 Evans Road, Aiken, SC 29803, USA.

BODSWORTH (Charles) Fred(erick), b. 11 Oct 1918, Port Burwell, Ontario, Canada. Novelist. m. Margaret Neville Banner, 1944, 1 son, 2 daughters. Education: Port Burwell Public and High Schools. Appointments: Staff Writer and Editor, Maclean's Magazine, Toronto, 1947-55; Editor, Natural Science of Canada Series, 1980-81. Publications: Last of the Curlews, 1955; The Strange One, 1959; The Atonement of Ashley Morden, 1965; The Sparrow's Fall, 1967; Other non-fictional works. Honour: Doubleday Canadian Novel Award, 1967. Address: 294 Beech Avenue, Toronto, Ontario M4E 3J2, Canada.

BOECKMAN Charles, b. 9 Nov 1920, San Antonio, Texas, USA. Author. m. Patricia Kennelly, 25 July 1965, 1 daughter. Publications: Maverick Brand, 1961; Unsolved Riddles of the Ages, 1965; Our Regional Industries, 1966; Cool, Hot and Blue, 1968; And the Beat Goes On, 1972; Surviving Your Parent's Divorce, 1980; Remember Our Yesterdays, 1991; House of Secrets, 1992; Author of over 1000 short stories and articles, and many anthologies. Honour: Mr Banjo, selected for Anthology, Best Defective Stories of the Year, 1979. Membership: American Society of Journalists and Authors. Address: 322 Del Mar Boulevard, Corpus Christi, TX 78404, USA.

BOESCH Hans, b. 13 Mar 1926, Frumsen, Sennwald, Switzerland. Traffic Engineer. m. Mathilde Kerler, 1 July 1950, 3 daughters. Education: HTL Winterthur, 1941-46. Appointments: Head, Transport Planning, Baudirektion, Canton, Aargau; Scientific Collaborator, Dozent, ORL-Institut, ETH Zürich. Publications: Der junge Os (novel), 1957; Das Gerust (novel), 1960; Die Fliegenfalle (novel), 1968; Menschen im Bau (stories), 1970; Der Kiosk (novel), 1978; Ein David (poems), 1978; Unternehmen Normkopf (satire), 1985; Der Sog (novel), 1988; Der Bann (novel), 1996. Honours: C F Meyer Prize, 1954; Medal of Honour, City of Zürich, 1970, 1978; Prize for Literature, Canton of Aargau, 1983; Prize, Schillerstiftung, 1988; International Bodensee Prize for Literature, 1989; Prize, Jaeckle-Treadwell-Stiftung, Zürich, 1996; Various, Pro Helvetia and Canton of Zürich. Address: Eichstr 10a, 8712 Stafa, Switzerland.

BOGARDE Sir Dirk, b. 28 March 1921. Education: University College School; Allan Glen's (Scotland). Career: Film and Theatre actor from 1947. Publications: A Postillion Struck by Lightning (autobiography), 1977; Snakes and Ladders, 1978; An Orderly Man, 1983; Backcloth, 1986; A Particular Friendship, 1989; The Great Meadow, 1992; A Short Walk From Harrods, 1993; Cleared for Take Off, 1995; novels: A Gentle Occupation, 1980; Voices in the Garden, 1981; West of Sunset, 1984; Jericho, 1992; A Period of Adjustment, 1994. Honour: Knighted, 1992. Address: c/o JAA, 2 Goodwins Court, London WC2N 4LL, England.

BOGDANOVICH Peter, b. 30 July 1939, Kingston, New York, USA. Film Director; Writer; Producer; Actor. m. (1) Polly Platt, 1962, div 1970, 2 daughters, (2) L B Straten, 1988. Appointments: Film Feature-Writer, Esquire, New York Times, Village Voice, Cahiers du Cinema, Los Angeles Times, New York Magazine, Vogue, Variety and others, 1961-. Publications: The Cinema of Orson Welles, 1961; The Cinema of Howard Hawks, 1962; The Cinema of Alfred Hitchcock, 1963; John Ford, 1968; Fritz Lang in America, 1969; Allan Dwan: The Last Pioneer, 1971; Pieces of Time: Peter Bogdanovich on the Movies (in UK as Picture Shows), 1961, enlarged edition, 1985; The Killing of the Unicorn: Dorothy Stratten (1960-1980), 1984; A Year and a Day Calendar (edited with introduction), 1991; This is Orson Welles, 1992; Films: The Wild Angels, 1966; Targets, 1968; The Last Picture Show, 1971; What's Up Doc?, 1972; Paper Moon, 1973; Daisy Miller, 1974; At Long Last Love, 1975; Nickelodeon, 1976; Saint Jack, 1979; They All Laughed, 1981; Mask, 1985; Illegally Yours, 1988; Texasville, 1990; Noises Off, 1992; The Thing Called Love, 1993. Honours: New York Film Critics' Award for Best Screenplay, British Academy Award for Best Screenplay, 1971; Writer's Guild of America Award for Best Screenplay, 1972; Silver Shell, Mar del Plata, Spain, 1973; Best Director, Brussels Festival, 1974; Pasinetti Award, Critics Prize, Venice Festival, 1979. Memberships: Directors Guild of America; Writer's Guild of America; Academy of Motion Picture Arts and

Sciences. Address: c/o William Peiffer, 2040 Avenue of the Stars, Century City, CA 90067, USA.

BOGERT Carroll. International Correspondent, Newsweek. Education: BA, 1984, MA, 1986, Harvard University; Studied Russian, Harvard University, 1988. Appointments: Stringer in Manila, 1986, Stringer in Beijing, 1986, Reporter in Hong Kong Bureau, 1987-88, covered with others, the Tiananmen Square massacre in 1989, Moscow Correspondent, 1989, Moscow Bureau Chief, 1 year, Acting Senior Editor for International News section, 1993, National Correspondent, 1994, International Correspondent, 1995-, Newsweek. Publication: USSR: The Collapse of An Empire. Address: c/o Newsweek, 251 West 57th Street, New York, NY 10019-1894, USA.

BOHME Gernot, b. 3 Jan 1937, Dessau, Germany. University Professor. m. Dr Farideh Akashe, 15 Apr 1983, 5 daughters. Education: Dr phil, 1965; Habilitation for Philosophy, 1972. Publications: Das Andere der Vernunft, 1983; Anthropologie in Pragmatischer Hinsicht, 1985; Der Typ Sokrates, 1988; Am Ende des Baconschen Zeitalters, 1993; Atmosphäre, 1995; Briefe an meine Töchter, 1995; Idee und Kosmos, 1996; Feuw-Wasser-Erde-Luft, 1996.

BOISDEFFRE Pierre Jules Marie Raoul (Néraud Le Mouton de), b. 11 July 1926, Paris, France. Writer; Diplomatist; Broadcasting Official. m. Beatrice Wiedemann-Goiran, 1957, 3 sons. Education: Ecole Libre des Sciences Politiques; Ecole Nationale d'Administration; Harvard University, USA. Appointments: Director of Sound Broadcasting, Office de Radiodiffusion et Television Francaise (ORTF), 1963-68; Cultural Counsellor, French Embassy, London, 1968-71, Brussels, 1972-77; Ministry of Foreign Affairs, 1977-78; Minister Plenipotentiary, 1979; Ambassador to Uruguay 1981-84, Colombia 1984-88, Council of Europe, Strasbourg 1988-91. Publications: Metamorphose de la litterature, 2 volumes, 1950; Ou va le Roman? 1962; Les ecrivains francais d'aujourd'hui, 1963; Lettre ouverte aux hommes de gauche, 1969; La foi des anciens jours, 1977; Le roman francais depuis 1900, 1979; Les nuits, l'Ile aux livres, Paroles de vie, La Belgique, 1980; Histoire de la litterature, 2 volumes, 1985; Souvenirs: Contre le Vent May'eur, 1994. Honours: Numerous national awards, including Prix de la Critique, 1950; Doctor honoris causa, Universities of Hull (Great Britian) and Bogota (Colombia); Officer de la Legion d'honneur; Commandeur de l'ordre national du Merite. Address: 5 Cité Vaneau, 75007 Paris, France.

BOISVERT France, (Marguerite de Nevers), b. 10 June 1959, Sherbrooke, Quebec, Canada. French Teacher; Writer; Poet. 1 son. Education: Baccalaureat, 1983; Master in Literature, 1986. Appointments: Salon, 1991; York University, Canada, 1991; Speeches, Montreal, Public Lectures, 1991-93. Publications: Les Samourailles, 1987; Li Tsing-tao ou Le grand avoir (prose), 1989; Massawippi (poem), 1992; Comme un vol de gerfauts (poem), 1993; Les Herities de Lord Durham, 1995. Contributions to: Liberté; La Presse. Honours: Bursery, Minister of Culture, Quebec, 1989, 1990, 1991. Memberships: Union des Ecrivains du Québec; Administration éLue au Conseil d'administration de L'UNEQ. Address: A/S UNEQ Maison des Ecrivains, 3492 Avenue Laval, Montreal H2X 3C8, Canada.

BOLAND Michael (John), b. 14 Nov 1950, Kingston, Surrey, England. Poet; Civil Servant. Education: Shene County Grammar School. Appointment: Editor, The Arcadian, poetry magazine. Publication: The Midnight Circus; The Trout... Minus One (co-author), 1993. Contributions to: Envoi; Purple Patch; Weyfarers; Firing Squad; Various Anthologies. Honours: Patricia Chown Sonnet Award. Memberships: PEN; Society of Civil Service Authors; Keats-Shelley Memorial Association; Wordsworth Trust; Friends of Coleridge; MIAP. Address: 11 Boxtree Lane, Harrow Weald, Middlesex HA3 6JU, England.

BOLD Alan (Norman), b. 20 Apr 1943, Edinburgh, Scotland. Writer. m. Alice Howell, 29 June 1963, 1 daughter. Education: Edinburgh University. Publications: To Find the New (verse), 1967; A Perpetual Motion Machine (verse), 1969; In This Corner: Selected Poems, 1983; The Edge of the Wood (stories), 1984; MacDiarmid (biography), 1988; A Burns Companion (criticism), 1991; East is West (novel), 1991; Rhymer Rab: An Anthology of Poems and Prose by Robert Burns, 1993. Contributions to: Glasgow Herald; Sunday Times; Times Literary Supplement. Honours: McVitie's Prize for 1989, Scottish Writer of the Year; Arts Award, Royal Philosophical Society of Glasgow, 1990; Honorary President, Auchinieck Boswell Society, 1992. Memberships: Society of Authors; Royal Society of Literature.

Address: Balbirnie Burns East Cottage, Nr Markinch, Glenrothes, Fife KY7 6NE, Scotland.

BOLITHO Elaine Elizabeth, b. 12 Dec 1940, Christchurch, New Zealand. Researcher; Writer on Religion in New Zealand. m. Ian James Bolitho, 14 Dec 1963, 2 sons, 2 daughters. Education: BA 1988, BA Hons 1989, PhD World Religions 1993, Victoria University of Wellington, New Zealand. Publications: Meet the Baptists - Postwar Personalities and Perspectives, 1993; Meet the Methodists - Postwar Personalities and Perspectives, 1994. Contributions to: Stimulus; Wesley Historical Society Jrnl; Affirm; Baptist Research Journal; Possibilities; Re:search; Evening Post. Honours: Eileen Duggan Prize for New Zealand Literature, 1986; Epworth Book of the Month, 1993. Memberships: Christian Writers Guild; Christian Research Association of Aotearoa, New Zealand. Address: 33 Kandy Crescent, Ngaio, Wellington 6004, New Zealand.

BOLTON, Elizabeth. See: JOHNSTON Norma.

BOND Edward, b. 18 July 1934, London, England. Playwright; Poet; Director. Publications: Saved, 1966; Three Sisters (Chekov), translator, 1967; Narrow Road to the Deep North, 1968; Early Morning, 1968; The Pope's Wedding and Other Plays, 1971; Lear, 1972; The Sea, 1973; Bingo: Scenes of Money and Death, 1974; Spring's Awakening (translator), 1974; The Fool, 1975; We Come to the River, libretto for Henze, 1976; A-A-America - The Swing and Grandma Faust, 1976; A-A-America, and Stone, 1976; Plays, 4 volumes, 1977-92; Theatre Poems & Songs, 1978; The Woman, 1978; The Bundle, 1980; The Cat, libretto, 1980; The Restoration, 1981; Summer, 1982; Human Cannon, 1985; War Plays (Red, Black and Ignorant; The Tin Can Riots; Great Peace), 1985; Collected Poems, 1978-85, 1985; Jackets, 1988; In the Company of Men, 1988; Notes on Post-Modernism, 1988; September, 1988; Olly's Prison (3 TV plays), 1992; Tuesday (TV Play), 1993; Selected Letters, 4 volumes, 1994-95; Coffee, 1995; Lulu: A Monster Tragedy (by Frank Wedekind - Translated). Honour: Hon D Litt, Yale University, 1977. Membership: Theatre Writers Union. Literary Agent: Casarotto Ramsay Ltd, National House, 60-66 Wardour Street, London W1V 3HP. Address: c/o Margaret Ramsay Ltd, 14A Goodwin's Court, London WC2N 4LL, England.

BOND Gillian. See: McEVOY Marjorie.

BOND (Thomas) Michael, b. 13 Jan 1926, Newbury, Berkshire, England. Author. m. (1) Brenda May Johnson, 29 June 1950, div 1981, 1 son, 1 daughter, (2) Susan Marfrey Rogers, 1981. Education: Presentation College, 1934-40. Publications: A Bear Called Paddington, 1958; More About Paddington, 1959; Paddington Helps Out, 1960; Paddington Abroad, 1961; Paddington at Large, 1962; Paddington Marches On, 1964; Paddington at Work, 1966; Here Comes Thursday, 1966; Thursday Rides Again, 1968; Paddington Goes to Town, 1968; Thursday Ahoy, 1969; Parsley's Tail, 1969; Parsley's Good Deed, 1969; Parsley's Problem Present, 1970; Parsley's Last Stand, 1970; Paddington Takes the Air, 1970; Thursday in Paris, 1970; Michael Bond's Book of Bears, 1971; Michael Bond's Book of Mice, 1971; The Day the Animals Went on Strike, 1972; Paddington Bear, 1972; Paddington's Garden, 1972; Parsley Parade, 1972; The Tales of Olga de Polga, 1972; Olga Meets Her Match, 1973; Paddington's Blue Peter Story Book, 1973; Paddington at the Circus, 1973; Paddington Goes Shopping, 1973; Paddington at the Seaside, 1974; Paddington at the Tower, 1974; Paddington on Top, 1974; Windmill, 1975; How to Make Flying Things, 1975; Eight Olga Readers, 1975; Paddington's Cartoon Book, 1979; J D Polson and the Dillogate Affair, 1981; Paddington on Screen, 1981; Olga Takes Charge, 1982; The Caravan Puppets, 1983; Paddington at the Zoo, 1984; Paddington's Painting Exhibition, 1985; Elephant, 1985; Paddington Minds the House, 1986; Paddington at the Palace, 1986; Paddington's Busy Day, 1987; Paddington and the Magical Maze, 1987; (Adult Books) Monsieur Pamplemousse, 1983; Monsieur Pamplemousse and the Secret Mission, 1984; Monsieur Pamplemousse Takes the Cure, 1987; The Pleasures of Paris, Guide Book, 1987; Monsieur Pamplemousse Aloft, 1989; Monsieur Pamplemousse Investigates, 1990; Monsieur Pamplemousse Rests His Case, 1991; Monsieur Pamplemousse Stands Firm, 1992; Monsieur Pamplemousse on Location, 1992; Monsieur Pamplemousse Takes the Train, 1993; Bears and Forebears, autobiography, 1996. Literary Agent: The Agency, London. Address: The Agency, 24 Pottery Lane, Holland Park, London W11 4LZ, England.

BOND Nancy Barbara, b. 8 Jan 1945, Bethesda, Maryland, USA. Librarian; Writer. Education: BA, Mount Holyoke College, 1966; Dip Lib Wales, 1972, College of Librarianship, Wales. Appointment: Instructor, part-time, Simmons College, Centre for the Study of Children's Literature, 1979-. Publications: A String in the Harp, 1976; The Best of Enemies, 1978; Country of Broken Stone, 1980; The Voyage Begun, 1981; A Place to Come Back To, 1984; Another Shore, 1988; Truth to Tell, 1994; The Love of Friends, 1997. Honours: International Reading Association Award, 1976; Newbery Honour, 1976; Welsh Arts Council Tir na n'Og Award, 1976. Address: 109 The Valley Road, Concord, MA 01742, USA.

BOND Ruskin, b. 19 May 1934, Kasauli, India. Author; Journalist; Children's Writer. Education: Bishop Cotton School, Simla, India, 1943-50.Appointment: Managing Editor, Imprint, Bombay, 1975-79. Publications: The Room on the Roof, 1956; Grandfather's Private Zoo, 1967; The Last Tiger, 1971; Angry River, 1972; The Blue Umbrella, 1974; Once Upon a Monsoon Time, memoirs, 1974; Man of Destiny: A Biography of Jawaharlal Nehru, 1976; Night of the Leopard, 1979; Big Business, 1979; The Cherry Tree, 1980; The Road to the Bazaar, 1980; A Flight of Pigeons, 1980; The Young Vagrants, 1981; Flames in the Forest, 1981; The Adventures of Rusty, 1981; Tales and Legends of India, 1982; A Garland of Memories, 1982; To Live in Magic, 1982; Tigers Forever, 1983; Earthquakes, 1984; Getting Granny's Glasses, 1985; The Eyes of the Eagle, 1987; The Night Train at Deoli, short stories, 1988; Times Stops at Shamli, short stories, 1989; Ghost Trouble, 1989; Snake Trouble, 1990; Dust on the Mountain, 1990; Our Trees Still Grow in Dehra, 1992; Rain in the Mountains, 1994. Contributions to: Christian Science Monitor (Boston); Books for Keeps (UK); Cricket (USA); School (Australia); Telegraph (Calcutta);Khaleej Times (Dubai); Weekly Sun (New Delhi). Honours: John Hewellyn Rhys Prize, 1957; Sahitya Akademi Award for English writing in India, 1992. Address: Ivy Cottage, Landour, Mussouri, UP 248179, India.

BONE Jesse F, b. 15 June 1916, Tacoma, Washington, USA. Professor of Veterinary Medicine (Retired); Writer. m. (1) Jayne M Clark, 20 Jan 1942, div 1946, 1 daughter, (2) Felizitas Margarete Endter, 15 June 1950, 2 sons, 1 daughter. Education: BA, 1937, BS, 1949, DVM, 1950, Washington State University; MS, Oregon State University, 1953. Appointments: Instructor through to Professor of Veterinary Medicine, Oregon State University, Corvallis, 1950-79, now retired Professor Emeritus. Publications: Observations of the Ovaries of Infertile and Reportedly Infertile Dairy Cattle, 1954; Animal Anatomy, 1958, revised edition as Animal Anatomy and Physiology, 1975, 3rd edition, revised, 1988; Fisiologia y Anatomia Animal, 1983; Canine Medicine, editor, 1959, 2nd edition, 1962; Equine Medicine and Surgery, co-editor, 1963, 2nd edition, 1972. Fiction: The Lani People, 1962; Legacy, 1976; The Meddlers, 1976; Gift of the Manti (with R Myers), 1977; Confederation Matador, 1978. Honours: Fulbright Lecturer in Egypt, 1965-66; Fulbright Professor, Kenya and Zimbabwe, 1980-82; Postdoctoral Award, US Department of Health, Education and Welfare, 1969-70; Fulbright Lecturer in Kenya, 1980-82. Memberships: American Veterinary Medical Association; Phi Kappa Phi; Sigma Xi; Science Fiction Writers of America. Address: 3017 Brae Burn Street, Sierra Vista, AZ 85635, USA.

BONHAM-CARTER Victor, b. 13 Dec 1913, Bearsted, Kent, England. Author. m. (1) Audrey Stogdon, 22 July 1938, 2 sons, (2) Cynthia Clare Sanford, 9 Feb, 1979. Education: MA, Magdalene College, 1935. Appointments: Historian, Records Officer, Dartington Hall Estate, 1951-65; Secretary, Royal Literary Fund, 1966-82; Joint Secretary, Society of Authors, London, 1971-78. Publications: The English Village, 1952; Dartington Hall (with W B Curry), 1958; Exploring Parish Churches, 1959; Farming the Land, 1959; In a Liberal Tradition, 1960; Soldier True, US edition as The Strategy of Victory, 1965; Surgeon in the Crimea (editor), 1968; The Survival of the English Countryside, US edition as Land and Environment, 1971; Authors by Profession, 2 volumes, 1978-84; The Essence of Exmoor, 1991. Memberships: Fellow, Royal Society of Literature; President, Exmoor Society, 1975-. Literary Agent: Curtis Brown. Address: The Mount, Milverton Road, Taunton, Somerset TA4 1QZ, England.

BONNEFOY Yves Jean, b. 24 Jun 1923, Tours, France. Writer. m. Lucille Vine, 1968, 1 daughter. Education: Faculté des Sciences, Poitiers; Faculte des Lettres, Paris; L es L. Appointments: Professor, Collège de France, 1981-; Lectures, seminars. Publications: Poems: Du mouvement et de l'immobilité de Douve, 1953; Pierre ècrite, 1964; Selected Poems, 1968; Dans le leurre du seuil, 1975; Poems,

1947-1975, 1978; Essays: L'Improbable, 1959; Arthur Rimbaud, 1961; Un rêve fait à Mantoue, 1967; Le nuage rouge, 1977; Rue traversière, 1977; On art: Peintures murales de la France Gothique, 1954; Miró, 1963; Rome 1630, 1970; L'Arrière-Pays, 1972; Entretiens sur la poèsie, 1981; La Prèsence et l'Image, 1983; Ce qui fut sans lumière, 1987; Récits en rêve, 1987; other work: Hier règnant désert, 1958; Co-editor, L'Ephémère; translations of Shakespeare; many books also in English. Contributions to: Mercure de France; Critique; Encounter; L'Ephémère. Honours: Prix Montaigne, 1980; Grand Prix de Poésie, Académie Française, 1981; Grand Prix Société des gens de Lettres, 1987; Prix Balzan, 1995. Address: c/o Collège de France, 11 Place Marcelin-Berthelot, 75005 Paris, France.

BONNER Raymond Thomas, b. 11 Apr 1942, Jefferson City, Missouri USA. Author; Journalist. Education: AB, MacMurray College, 1964; JD, Stanford Law School, 1967. Publications: Weakness and Deceit: US Policy and El Salvador, 1984; Waltzing With a Dictator: The Marcoses and The Making of American Policy, 1987. Contributions to: Numerous professional journals. Honour: Robert F Kennedy Memorial Book Award, 1985. Literary Agent: Gloria Loomis, New York, USA. Address: 110 Riverside Drive, 4C, New York, NY 10024, USA.

BONNER Terry Nelson. See: KRAUZER Steven M.

BONTLY Thomas J(ohn), b. 25 Aug 1939, Madison, Wisconsin, USA. Professor; Coordinator of Creative Writing; Author. m. Marilyn R Mackie, 25 Aug 1963, 1 son. Education: BA, University of Wisconsin at Madison, 1961; Research Student, Corpus Christi College, Cambridge University, 1961-62; PhD, Stanford University, 1966. Appointments: Assistant Professor, 1966-71, Associate Professor, 1971-76, Coordinator of Creative Writing, 1975-77, 1987-90, 1995-, and Chairman, 1979-82, Department of English, Professor, 1976-, University of Wisconsin-Milwaukee; Fulbright Senior Lectureship, West Germany, 1984. Publications: Novels: The Competitor, 1966; The Adventures of a Young Outlaw, 1974; Celestial Chess, 1979; The Giant's Shadow, 1989. Other: Short stories in anthologies and many periodicals; Essays and reviews. Honours: Wallace Stegner Creative Writing Fellowship, 1965-66; Maxwell Perkins Commemorative Award, 1966; 1st Prizes for Short Fiction, Council for Wisconsin Writers, 1975, 1989; Wisconsin Arts Board New Work Award, 1990. Membership: Board of Directors for Wisconsin Writers, 1991-. Address: 9077 North Meadowlark Lane, Bayside, WI 53217, USA.

BOOKER Christopher (John Penrice), b. 7 Oct 1937, Eastbourne, Sussex, England. Journalist; Author. m. Valerie, 1979, 2 sons. Education: Corpus Christi College, Cambridge. Appointments: Liberal News, 1960; Jazz Critic, Sunday Telegraph, 1961; Editor, Private Eye, 1961-63; Regular Contributor, 1965-; Resident Scriptwriter, That Was The Week That Was, 1962-63; Not So Much a Programme, 1963-64. Publications: The Neophiliacs: A Study of the Revolution in English Life in the 50's and 60's, 1969; Goodbye London (with Candida Lycett-Green), 1973; The Booker Quiz, 1976; The Seventies, 1980; The Games War: A Moscow Journal, 1981; The Repatriations from Austria in 1945, 1990; The Mad Officials Know the Bureaucrats Are Strangling Britain (with Richard Norton), 1994. Contributions to: Daily Telegraph, 1959-, (Way of The World column, 1987-90); Spectator, 1962-; Sunday Telegraph Columnist, 1990-; Private Eye; Anthologies. Honours: Campaigning Journalist of the Year, with Bennie Gray, 1973; Aims of Industry Free Enterprise Award, 1992. Address: The Old Rectory, Litton, Bath BA3 4PW, England.

BOORSTIN Daniel J(oseph), b. 1 Oct 1914, Atlanta, Georgia, USA. Historian; Librarian of Congress Emeritus. m. Ruth Carolyn Frankel, 9 Apr 1941, 3 sons. Education: AB, summa cum laude, Harvard University, 1934; BA, 1st class honours, Rhodes Scholar, 1936, BCL, 1st class honours 1937, Balliol College, Oxford, 1937; Postgraduate Studies, Inner Temple, London, 1934-37; JSD, Sterling Fellow, Yale University, 1940. Appointments: Instructor, Tutor in History and Literature, Harvard University and Radcliffe College, 1938-42; Lecturer in Legal History, Harvard Law School, 1939-42; Assistant Professor of History, Swarthmore College, 1942-44; Assistant Professor, 1944-49, Professor, 1949-56, Professor of American History, 1956-64, University of Chicago; Fulbright Visiting Lecturer in American History, University of Rome, 1950-51, Kyoto University, 1957; 1st Incumbent of the Chair in American History, University of Paris, 1961-62; Pitt Professor of American History and Institutions, Cambridge University, 1964-65; Director, 1969-73, Senior Historian, 1973-75, National Museum of History and Technology,

Smithsonian Institution, Washington, DC; Shelby and Kathryn Cullom Davis Lecturer, Graduate Institute of International Studies, Geneva, 1973-74; Librarian of Congress, 1975-87, Librarian of Congress Emeritus, 1987-, Washington, DC. Publications: The Mysterious Science of the Law, 1941; Delaware Cases, 1792-1830, 1943; The Lost World of Thomas Jefferson, 1948; The Genius of American Politics, 1953; The Americans: The Colonial Experience, 1958; America and the Image of Europe, 1960; The Image or What Happened to the American Dream, 1962; The Americans: The National Experience, 1965; The Landmark History of the American People, 1968, new edition, 1987; The Decline of Radicalism, 1969; The Sociology of the Absurd, 1970; The Americans: The Democratic Experience, 1973; Democracy and Its Discontents, 1974; The Exploring Spirit, 1976; The Republic of Technology, 1978; A History of the United States (with Brooks M Kelley), 1980, new edition, 1991; The Discoverers, 1983; Hidden History, 1987; The Creators, 1992; Cleopatra's Nose: Essays on the Unexpected, 1994; The Daniel J Boorstin Reader, 1995. Honours: Bancroft Award, 1959; Francis Parkman Prize, 1966; Pulitzer Prize in History, 1974; Dexter Prize, 1974; Watson-Davis Prize, 1986; Charles Frankel Prize, 1989; National Book Award, 1989; Many other honours, including numerous honorary doctorates. Memberships: American Academy of Arts and Sciences; American Antiquarian Society; American Philosophical Society; American Studies Association, president, 1969-71; Organization of American Historians; Royal Historical Society, corresponding member. Address: 3541 Ordway Street North West, Washington DC 20016, USA.

BOOTH Geoffrey Thornton, (Edward Booth O P), b. 16 Aug 1928, Evesham, Worcestershire, England. Roman Catholic Dominican Priest; Teacher; Writer. Education: BA, 1952, MA, 1970, PhD, 1975, Cambridge University. Appointments: Entered English province, Order of Dominicans, 1952; Ordained, Roman Catholic Priest, 1958; Lecturer, Pontifical Beda College, 1978-80, Pontifical University of St Thomas, 1980-88, Rome. Publications: Aristotelian Aporetic Ontology in Islamic and Christian Thinkers, 1983; Saint Augustine and the Western Tradition of Self Knowing: The Saint Augustine Lecture 1986, 1989. Contributions to: The New Grove Dictionary of Music and Musicians, 1980; La Production du livre universitaire au moyen age: Exemplar et Pecia, 1988; Kategorie un Kategorialität, Historisch-Systematische Untersuchungen zum Begriff der Kategorie im philosophischen Denken, Festschrift für Klaus Hartmann, 1990; Also many articles and book reviews in journals. Address: Priesterseminar, Karmeliterstrasse, D-72108 Rottenburg, Germany.

BOOTH Martin, b. 7 Sept 1944, Lancashire, England. Writer. m. 1 son, 1 daughter. Education: Certificate in Education, University of London, 1968; Fellow Commoner, St Peter's College, Oxford, 1971-72. Publications: Hiroshima Joe (novel), 1985; The Jade Pavilion, 1986; Carpet Sahib: A Life of Jim Corbett, 1986; Black Chameleon (novel), 1988; Dreaming of Samarkand, 1989; The Triads: A History of Chinese Secret Societies, 1990; A Very Private Gentleman, 1991; The Humble Disciple, 1992; Rhino Road: The Evolution, Natural History and Conservation of African Rhinos, 1992; The Iron Tree, 1993; The Dragon and the Pearl, 1994; Toys of Glass, 1995; Adrift in the Oceans of Mercy, 1996; War Dog, 1996. Non-fiction: Opium: A History, 1996; Also verse, criticism and screenplays. Contributions to: Literary criticism and travel writing in various publications. Honour: Fellow, Royal Society of Literature, 1980. Address: c/o David Higham Associates, 5-8 Lower John Street, Golden Square, London W1R 4HA, England.

BOOTH Philip, b. 8 Oct 1925, Hanover, New Hampshire, USA. Professor of English (Retired); Poet. m. Margaret Tillman, 1946, 3 daughters. Education: AB, Dartmouth College, 1948; MA, Columbia University, 1949. Appointments: Assistant Professor, Wellesley College, 1954-61; Associate Professor, 1961-65, Professor of English and Poet-in-Residence, 1965-85, Syracuse University. Publications: Letter from a Distant Land, 1957; The Islanders, 1961; North by East, 1966; Weathers and Edges, 1966; Margins: A Sequence of New and Selected Poems, 1970; Available Light, 1976; Before Sleep, 1980; Relations: Selected Poems, 1950-85, 1986; Selves, 1990; Pairs: New Poems, 1994; Trying to Say It, 1996. Honours: Guggenheim Fellowships, 1958, 1965; Theodore Roethke Prize, 1970; National Endowment for the Arts Fellowship, 1980; Academy of American Poets Fellowship, 1983; Rockefeller Fellowship, 1986; Maurice English Poetry Award, 1987. Address: PO Box 330, Castine, ME 04421, USA.

BOOTH Rosemary, (Frances Murray), b. 10 Feb 1928, Glasgow, Scotland. History Teacher; Author. m. Robert Edward Booth, 28 Aug 1950, 3 daughters. Education: University of Glasgow, 1945-47; MA, 1965, Ed Diploma, 1966, University of St Andrews; Teacher's Certificate, Dundee College of Education, 1966. Appointments: History Teacher; Author. Publications: Ponies on the Heather, 1966, revised edition, 1973; The Dear Colleague, 1972; The Burning Lamp, 1973; The Heroine's Sister, 1975; Ponies and Parachutes, 1975; Red Rowan Berry, 1976; Castaway, 1978; White Hope, 1978; Payment for the Piper, 1983, US edition as Brave Kingdom; The Belchamber Scandal, 1985; Shadow Over the Islands, 1986. Address: c/o David Higham Associates, 5-8 Lower John Street, London W1R 4HA, England.

BORDEN Louise Walker, b. 30 Oct 1949, Cincinnati, Ohio, USA. Writer. m. Peter A Borden, 4 Sept 1971, 1 son, 2 daughters. Education: BA, Denison University, 1971. Publications: Caps, Hats, Socks and Mittens, 1989; The Neighborhood Trucker, 1990; The Watching Game, 1991; Albie the Lifeguard, 1993; Just in Time for Christmas, 1994; Paperboy, 1996; The Little Ships, 1997. Memberships: Society of Children's Book Writers; Authors Guild. Address: 628 Myrtle Avenue, Terrace Park, OH 45174, USA.

BORDEN William (Vickers), b. 27 Jan 1938, Indianapolis, Indiana, USA. Chester Fritz Distinguished Professor of English; Writer; Poet; Dramatist; Editor. m. Nancy Lee Johnson, 17 Dec 1960, 1 son, 2 daughters. Education: AB, Columbia University, 1960; MA, University of California at Berkeley, 1962. Appointments: Instructor, 1962-64, Assistant Professor, 1966-70, Associate Professor, 1970-82, Professor of English, 1982-, University of North Dakota; Fiction Editor, North Dakota Quarterly. Publications: Fiction: Superstoe, novel, 1967, new edition 1996; Many short stories. Poetry: Slow Step and Dance, chapbook, 1991. Other: Numerous plays, including the full-length plays: The Last Prostitute, 1980; Tap Dancing Across the Universe, 1981; Loon Dance, 1982; The Only Woman Awake is the Woman Who Has Heard the Flute, 1983; Makin' It, 1984; The Consolation of Philosophy, 1986; When the Meadowlark Sings, 1988; Meet Again, 1990; Turtle Island Blues, 1991; Don't Dance Me Outside, 1993. Musical Drama: Sakakawea, 1987. Also Screenplays, radio plays, video scripts. Contributions to: Many anthologies and periodicals. Honours: North Dakota Centennial Drama Prize, 1989; ASCAP Awards, 1990, 1991, 1992; Burlington Northern Award, University of North Dakota, 1990; Minnesota Distinguished Artist Award, 1992; Minnesota State Arts Board Career Opportunity Grant, 1996. Memberships: American Society of Composers, Authors and Publishers; Associated Writing Programs; Authors League of America; Dramatists Guild; PEN. Address: Route 6, Box 284, Bemidji, MN 56601, USA.

BORENSTEIN Audrey F(arrell), b. 7 Oct 1930, Chicago, Illinois, USA. Writer. m. Walter Borenstein, 5 Sept 1953, 1 son, 1 daughter. Education: AB, 1953, MA, 1954, University of Illinois; PhD, Louisiana State University, 1958. Publications: Custom: An Essay on Social Codes, 1961; Redeeming the Sin, 1978; Older Women in 20th Century America, 1982; Chimes of Change and Hours, 1983; Through the Years: A Chronicle of Cong Ahavath Achim, 1989; Simurgh, 1991. Contributions to: Journals. Honours: National Endowment for the Arts Fellowship, 1976; Rockefeller Foundation Humanities Fellowship, 1978; New York State Fiction Prize, National League of American Pen Women, 1988. Membership: Poets and Writers. Address: 4 Henry Court, New Paltz, NY 12561, USA.

BORIS Martin, b. 7 Aug 1930, New York, New York, USA. Writer. m. Gloria Shanf, 13 June 1952, 1 son, 2 daughters. Education: BA, New York University, University Heights, 1951; MA, New York University, Washington Square, 1953; BA, Lond Island University, Brooklyn College of Pharmacy, 1957. Publications: Two and Two, 1979; Woodridge 1946, 1980; Brief Candle, 1990. Literary Agent: Arthur Pine Literary Agency. Address: 1019 Northfield Road, Woodmere, NY 11598, USA.

BORN Anne, b. 9 July 1930, Cooden Beach, Sussex, England. Poet; Reviewer; Translator. m. Povl Born, 1 June 1950, 3 sons, 1 daughter. Education: MA, Copenhagen, 1955; MLitt, Oxford, 1976. Appointments: Writer-in-Residence: Barnstaple, 1983-85; Kingsbridge, 1985-87; Buckinghamshire, 1996. Publications: 9 Collections of Poetry; another forthcoming, 1997; 4 History books; 28 translated books. Contributions to: Poems in: Times Literary Supplement; Ambit; Rialto; Green Book; Scratch; Cimarron Review; many published articles and reviews. Memberships: Society of Authors; Translators Association, Chair, 1987, 1993-95. Address: Oversteps, Froude Road, Salcombe, South Devon TQ8 8LH, England.

BORODIN George. See: **MILKOMANE George Alexis Milkomanovich.**

BOSLEY Keith Anthony, b. 16 Sept 1937, Bourne End, Buckinghamshire, England. Poet; Translator. m. Satu Salo, 27 Aug 1982, 3 sons. Education: BA Honours, French, Universities of Reading, Paris, Caen. Publications: Mallarmé: The Poems, 1977; Finnish Folk Poetry: Epic, translations, 1977; Stations, poems, 1979; From the Theorems of Master Jean de a Ceppède, 1983; A Chiltern Hundred, poems, 1987; The Kalevala, translation, 1989; I Will Sing of What I Know, Finnish ballads, 1990; Camoes: Epic & Lyric, translations, 1990; The Kanteletar,translation, 1992; The Great Bear, translations, 1993; Aleksis Kivi: Odes, 1994; A Century Pessoa, 1995; A Trail for Singers (translations), 1995; André Frénaud: Rome the Sorceress (translation), 1996; Eve Blossom has Wheels: German Love Poetry, 1997. Contributions to: Numerous journals and magazines. Honours: Finnish State Prize for Translators, 1978; First Prize, British Comparative Literature Association Translation Competition, 1982; Knighthood First Class, Order of the White Rose of Finland, 1991. Membership: Corresponding Member, Finnish Literature Society, Helsinki. Address: 108 Upton Road, Upton-cum-Chalvey, Slough SL1 2AW, England.

BOSQUET Alain, b. 28 Mar 1919, Odessa, Russia. Writer. Education: Free University of Brussels, 1938-39; MA, Sorbonne, University of Paris. Publications: Poems: Poèmes Un 1945-67, (Les Testaments), 1969; 100 Notes Pour Une Solitude, 1970; Notes Pour Un Amour, 1972; Notes Pour Un pluriel, 1974; Le Livre du Doute et de la Grâce, 1977; Sonnets Pour Une Fin de Siècle, 1980; Poèms Deux 1970-74, 1982; Un Jour après la Vie, 1985; Le Tourment de Dieu, 1987; Bourreaux et acrobates, 1990; Le Gardien des Rosées (Aphorisms), 1991; Demain Sans Moi, 1994; La fable et le fouet (aphorisms), 1995; Je ne suis pas un poète d'eau douce 1945-1994, 1996; Novels: Un Besoin de Malheur, 1963; La Confesion Mexicaine, 1965; Les Bonnes Intentions, 1976; Une Mère Russe, 1978; Jean-Louis Trabart, Medecin, 1980; L'Enfant que tu étais, 1982; Ni Guerre Ni Paix, 1983; Les Fêtes Cruelles, 1984; Lettre à mon Père qui aurait eu 100 Ans, 1987; Les Solitudes (trilogy), 1992; Georges et Arnold, Arnold et Georges, 1995; Short stories: Un homme pour un autre, 1985; Le Métier d'Otage, 1989; Comme un refus de la planète, 1989; Plays: Un détenu à Auschwitz, 1991; Numerous essays and translations; Numerous anthologies of poetry, prefaces and books on art with artists. Contributions to: La Revue Des Deux Mondes; Magazine Littéraire; Le Figaro. Honours include: Bronze Star, 1945; Grand Prix de Poésie of French Academy, 1967; Grand Prix du Roman of French Academy, 1978; Officer of Order of the Crown of Belgium, 1993; Grand Prix de la langue, 1994; Officer of Legion of Honour, 1995; Prix for Poetry, Societe des gens de lettres, 1996. Membership: President, Max Jacob Jury; Renaudot 1971, President, Mallarmé Academy, 1994-; Royal Academy of Belgium; Academy of Letters of Quebec. Literary Agent: Editions Gallimard; Grasset. Address: 32 rue de Laborde, 75008 Paris, France.

BOSTON Ray(mond Jack), b. 24 Dec 1927, Manchester, England. Writer; Researcher. m. Elizabeth Isabella Horsfield, 6 Aug 1955, 2 daughters. Education: BA, New College, Oxford, 1951; MA, 1964; MA, University of Wisconsin, USA, 1969. Appointments: Reporter, Manchester Evening News Ltd, 1950-53; Talks Producer, BBC, London, 1953-56; Lecturer, Central London Polytechnic, 1956-67; Writer, Daily Mirror, 1958-60; Sub Editor, The Times, 1960-65; Professor, University of Wisconsin, USA, 1967-69; Professor, University of Illinois, 1970-75; Director, Cardiff, Wales, 1975-85. Publications: The Essential Fleet Street, Cassell; The Newpaper Press in Britain; British Chartists in America. Contributions to: Journalism Studies Review; British Journalism Review; Journalism Quarterly. Honours: Deakin University Fellow; 1st Visiting Fellow, Australia. Membership: Institute of Historical Research, University of London. Address: 85 Severn Grove, Cardiff CF1 9EQ, Wales.

BOSWORTH David, b. 26 Oct 1936, Richmond, Surrey, England. University Lecturer. m. Jenny Lawton, 9 Sept 1961, 1 son, 1 daughter. Education: BA, 1961, B.Phil, 1963, MA, 1968, St John's College, Oxford University. Publications: Logic & Arithmetic, Vol 1, 1974, Vol II, 1979; Plato's Phaedo, 1986; Plato's Theaetetus, 1988. Contributions to: Various Journals. Address: 5-6 Church Street, Twickenham, Middlesex, TW1 3NJ, England.

BOTT George, b. 21 Sept 1920, Ashbourne, England. Retired Educator; Writer. m. Elizabeth Belshaw, 5 Feb 1944, 2 sons. Education: BA, 1942, Diploma in Education, 1947, Leeds University. Appointments: Senior English Master and Librarian, Cockermouth Grammar School, 1949-79; Editor, Scholastic Publications, 1960-68. Publications: George Orwell: Selected Writings (editor), 1958; Read and Relate (editor), 1960; Shakespeare: Man and Boy (editor), 1961; Sponsored Talk, 1971; Read and Respond, 1984; Read, Relate, Communicate, 1984; The Mary Hewetson Cottage Hospital, Keswick: Brief History, 1892-1992; Keswick: The Story of a Lake District Town, 1994. Address: 16 Penrith Road, Keswick, Cumbria CA12 4HF, England.

BOTTING Douglas (Scott), b. 22 Feb 1934, London, England. Author. m. 27 Aug 1964, 2 daughters. Education: BA, St Edmund Hall, Oxford, 1958. Publications: Island of the Dragon's Blood, 1958; The Knights of Bornu, 1961; One Chilly Siberian Morning, 1965; Wilderness Europe, 1976; Rio de Janeiro, 1977; The Pirates, 1978; The Second Front, 1978; The U-Boats, 1979; The Giant Airships, 1980; The Aftermath in Europe, 1945, 1983; Nazi Gold, 1984; In the Ruins of the Reich, 1985; Wild Britain, 1988; Hitler's Last General: The Case Against Wilhelm Mohnke, 1989; Gavin Maxwell: A Life, 1993; Sex Appeal: The Art and Science of Sexual Attraction (with Kate Botting), 1995; The Life of Gerald Durrell, 1997. Contributions to: BBC TV and Radio; Various periodicals. Memberships: Royal Geographical Society; Royal Institute of International Affairs; Society of Authors. Literary Agent: John Johnson Ltd, London. Address: 21 Park Farm Road, Kingston-on-Thames, Surrey, England.

BOUCHER David Ewart George, b. 15 Oct 1951, Wales. m. Clare Mary French Mullen, 8 Sept 1979, 2 daughters. Education: University College, Swansea, 1973-76; BA 1976, London School of Economics; MSc 1977, PhD, 1983, University of Liverpool. Appointments: Advisor, Oxford University Press, 1989; Member, Editorial Board, Australian Journal of Political Science, 1990-92; Reader, University of Wales, Swansea. Publications: Texts in Context; The Political Philosophy of R G Collingwood; Essays in Political Philosophy; The New Leviathan; A Radical Hegelian; Social Contract from Hobbes to Rawls; British Idealist Political Thought. Contributions to: Journal of the History of Ideas; Interpretation; New Literary History; Idealistic Studies; History & Theory; Polity; Political Studies; History of Political Thought; Storia Antropologia e Scienza del Linguagio; Australian Journal of Political Science; Australian Journal of Politics and History. Honours: Tutorial Fellowship; Research Fellowship; Best Special Issue Award; Fellow, Royal Historical Society, 1992; Editor, Collingwood Studies; Senior Associate, Pembroke College, Oxford, 1996. Memberships: Australian Political Science Association; Editorial Board of Association's Journal; Chairman, Trusteees of the R G Collingwood Society. Address: Department of Political Theory and Government, University of Wales, Singleton Park, Swansea SA2 8PP, Wales.

BOULTON David, b. 3 Oct 1935, Richmond, Surrey, England. Author and TV Producer. m. Anthea Ingham, 14 Feb 1969, 2 daughters. Education: Hampton Grammar School, 1947-52. Publications: Jazz in Britain, 1958; Objection Overruled, 1968; The UVF; Protestant Paramilitary Organizations in Ireland, 1973; The Lockheed Papers (in USA, The Grease Machine), 1980; The Making of Tania Hearst, 1975; Early Friends in Dent, 1986. Contributions to: Tribune; New Statesman; The Listener; Guardian. Honour: Cyril Bennet Awards, Royal Television Society, 1981, for creative services to television. Literary Agent: Curtis Brown. Address: Hobsons Farm, Dent, Cumbria LA10 5RF, England.

BOULTON James Thompson, b. 17 Feb 1924, Pickering, Yorkshire, England. University Professor, retired. m. Margaret Helen Leary, 6 Aug 1949, 1 son, 1 daughter. Education: BA, University College, University of Durham, 1948; BLitt, Lincoln College, University of Oxford, 1952; PhD, University of Nottingham, 1960. Appointments: Lecturer, Senior Lecturer, Reader in English Literature, 1951-63; Professor, 1964-75, Dean of Faculty of Arts, 1970-73, University of Nottingham; Professor of English Studies and Head of Department, 1975-88, Dean of Faculty of Arts, 1981-84, Public Orator, 1984-88; Emeritus Professor, 1989-, University of Birmingham. Publications: Edition of Edmund Burke's Sublime and Beautiful, 1958, 3rd edition, 1987; The Language of Politics in the Age of Wilkes and Burke, 1963; Editor: The Letters of D H Lawrence, volumes 1-7, 1979-93, Selected Letters, 1997; Samuel Johnson: The Critical Heritage, 1971; Edition of Defoe's Memoirs of a Cavalier, 1972. Honours: Hon DLitt, Durham

University, 1991, Nottingham University, 1993; Fellow, British Academy, 1993. Address: Institute for Advanced Research in the Humanities, University of Birmingham, Egbaston, Birmingham B15 2TT, England.

BOUMELHA Penelope (Ann), (Penny Boumelha), b. 10 May 1950, London, England. University Professor. 1 daughter. Education: BA, 1972, MA, 1981, DPhil, 1981. Appointments: Researcher, Compiler, Mansell Publishing, 1981-84; Lecturer, University of Western Australia, 1985-90; Jury Professor, University of Adelaide, 1990; Head, Division of Humanities and Social Sciences, University of Adelaide, 1996. Publications: Thomas Hardy and Women: Sexual Ideology and Narrative Form; Charlotte Brontë; Index of English Literary Manuscripts, Vol 3. Contributions to: Women Reading Women's Writing; Grafts: Feminist Cultural Criticism; Feminist Criticism: Theory & Practice; The Sense of Sex: Feminist Perspectives on Hardy; Realism, 1992; Constructing Gender, 1994; Southern Review; Times Literary Supplement English; Australian Victorian Studies Association Conference Papers; Review of English Studies; English Australian Feminist Studies; London Review of Books. Address: Department of English, University of Adelaide, South Australia 5005, Australia.

BOUNDY Donna, b. 4 Dec 1949, Framingham, Connecticut, USA. Journalist; Author. Education: BA, University of Connecticut, 1971; MSW, Hunter College, New York City, 1981. Publications: Straight Talk About Cocaine and Crack, 1988; Willpower's Not Enough, 1989; When Money is the Drug, 1993. Other: Many video scripts. Contributions to: Periodicals. Address: PO Box 1208, Woodstock, NY 12498, USA.

BOURJAILY Vance (Nye), b. 17 Sept 1922, Cleveland, Ohio, USA. Author; Professor. m. (1) Bettina Yensen, 1946, 2 children, (2) Yasmin Mobul, 1985, 1 child. Education: AB, Bowdoin College, 1947. Appointments: Co-Founder, Editor, Discovery, 1951-53; Faculty, University of Iowa Writers Workshops, 1958-80; Distinguished Visiting Professor, Oregon State University, 1968; Visiting Professor, University of Arizona, 1977-78; Boyd Professor, Louisiana State University, 1985-. Publications: The End of My Life, 1947; The Hound of the Earth, 1953; The Violated, 1958; Confessions of a Spent Youth, 1960; The Unnatural Enemy, 1963; The Man Who Knew Kennedy, 1967; Brill Among the Ruins, 1970; Country Matters, 1973; Now Playing at Canterbury, 1976; A Game Men Play, 1980; The Great Fake Book, 1987; Old Soldier, 1990; Fishing By Mail: The Outdoor Life of a Father and Son, 1993. Honour: American Academy of Arts and Letters Award, 1993. Address: c/o Department of English, Louisiana State University, Baton Rouge, LA 70803, USA.

BOURKE Vernon J(oseph), b. 17 Feb 1907, North Bay, Ontario, Canada (US citizen, 1944). Professor Emeritus of Philosophy; Writer. m. (1) Aileen Baechler, 15 Aug 1931, dec 1945, 1 son, 2 daughters, (2) Janet Leahy, 12 June 1947. Education: BA, 1928, MA, 1929, PhD, 1937, University of Toronto. Appointments: Lecturer in Ancient Philosophy, University of Toronto, 1928-31; Instructor, 1931-46, Professor of Philosophy, 1946-75, Professor Emeritus of Philosophy, 1975-, University of St Louis; Associate Editor, The Modern Schoolman, 1948-, Speculum, 1950-66, American Journal of Jurisprudence, 1956-, Augustinian Studies, 1969-80; Director, Center for Thomistic Studies, 1977-79, Cullen Professor of Philosophy, 1983-85, University of St Thomas, Houston; Research Professor, Center for Thomistic Studies, University of Houston, 1979-85. Publications: Thomistic Bibliography, 1920-1940, 1945; Augustine's Quest of Wisdom: Life and Philosophy of the Bishop of Hippo, 1945; St Thomas and the Greek Moralists, 1948; Ethics: Textbook in Moral Philosophy, 1959; The Pocket Aquinas: Selections, 1960; Augustine's View of Reality, 1964; Will in Western Thought: An Historical-Critical Survey, 1964; The Essential Augustine, 1964; Aquinas' Search for Wisdom, 1965; Ethics in Crisis, 1966; History of Ethics, 1968; Joy in Augustine's Ethics, 1979; Thomistic Bibliography, 1940-78 (with Terry Miethe), 1980; Wisdom from St Augustine, 1984; Augustine's Love of Wisdom: An Introspective Philosophy, 1992. Contributions to: Books, dictionaries, encyclopedias and journals. Honours: Gold Key Award, Loyola University, 1960; Aquinas Medal, American Catholic Philosophical Association, 1963; Honorary LittD, Bellarmine College, Louisville, 1974, University of St Thomas, Houston, 1981; Honorary DLitt, St Michael's College, Toronto, 1988. Memberships: American Catholic Philosophical Association, president, 1949; Mediaeval Academy of America; World Union of Catholic Philosophical Societies; American Philosophical Association; Societé Philosophique de

Louvain, Belgium. Address: 638 Laven Del Lane, St Louis, MO 63122, USA.

BOURNE (Rowland) Richard. Journalist; Author. m. Juliet Mary Attenborough, 1966, 2 sons, 1 daughter. Education: BA, Brasenose College, Oxford. Appointments: Journalist, The Guardian, 1962-72; Assistant Editor, New Society, 1972-77; Deputy Editor, 1977-78, London Columnist, 1978-79, Evening Standard; Founder, Editor, Learn Magazine, 1979; Consultant, International Broadcasting Trust, 1980-81; Advisor Council for Adult and Continuing Education, 1982; Deputy Director, Commonwealth Institute, 1983-89; Director, Commonwealth Human Rights Institute, 1990-92; Director, Commonwealth Non-Governmental Office for South Africa. Publications: Political Leaders of Latin America, 1969; The Struggle for Education (with Brian MacArthur), 1970; Getulio Vargas of Brazil, 1974; Assault on the Amazon, 1978; Londoners, 1981; Self-Sufficiency, 16-25 (with Jessica Gould), 1983; Lords of Fleet Street, 1990; News on a Knife-Edge, 1995. Literary Agent: David Higham Associates. Address: 36 Burney Street, London SE10 8EX, England.

BOURNE-JONES Derek, b. 4 Sept 1928, St Leonards-on-Sea, Sussex, England. Director of Studies, B J Tutorials; Linguist; Writer; Poet. m. Hilary Clare Marsh, 2 Aug 1975. Education: St Edmund Hall, Oxford, 1951-54; BA (Hons) Modern Languages 1954, MA (Oxon) 1958. Publications: Senlac, Epic Poem on the Battle of Hastings, 1978; Floating Reefs (poems), 1981; The Singing Days (poems), 1986; Merrily to Meet (on Sir Thomas More), 1988; Behold the Man poetic sequence, illustrated, on the Stations of the Cross, 1990; Brief Candle, poetic study of The Lady Jane Grey, illustrated, 1991. Contributions to: Various journals over the years. Memberships: Founder, Downland Poets Society of Sussex, 1975-90; Oxford Society. Address: 88 Oxendean Gardens, Lower Willingdon, Eastbourne, East Sussex BN22 0RS, England.

BOURQUIN Irène Hélène Marthe, b. 28 Aug 1950, Zürich, Switzerland. Editor, Daily Paper. 1 son. Education: Matura Typus A, 1969; Dr Phil, University of Zürich, 1976. Publications: Atlasblau, 1991; Im Auge des Taifuns, 1992; Das Meer im Dachstock, 1995; Insektenbrevier, 1995; Literaquarium, 1996. Contributions to: Neue Zürcher Zeitung; Entwürfe. Memberships: Literarische Vereinigung; Winterhur. Address: Am Bach 25, 8352 Räterschen, Switzerland.

BOURRET Annie, b. 22 Jan 1961, Val-d'Or, Québec, Canada. Linguist; Freelance Writer and Copy Editor. Education: BA, French Studies and Linguistics, 1986, MA, French Linguistics, 1989, Laval University. Publications: Regards sur la guerre et la paix (with E Poole), 1989; Guerre, paix et désarmement (with E Poole), 1989; Pour l'amour du français, due 1998. Contributions to: Columns on French Language since 1990; Regular contributor to University Affairs; Articles in such publications as: Le Devoir; Globe; Mail; Peace Magazine. Membership: Association des auteures et des auteurs franco-ontariens. Address: 7205 Hewitt Street, Burnaby, British Columbia V5A 3M1, Canada.

BOUVERIE William. See: **CARPENTER Humphrey.**

BOVA Ben(jamin William), b. 8 Nov 1932, Philadelphia, Pennsylvania, USA. Author; Editor; Lecturer. Education: BA, Temple University, 1954; MA, State University of New York at Albany, 1987. Appointments: Editorial Director, Omni Magazine; Editor, Analog Magazine; Lecturer. Publications: Gremlins, Go Home!, 1974; Notes to a Science Fiction Writer, 1975; Science: Who Needs It?, 1975; Viewpoint, 1977; The Exiles Trilogy, 1980; Vision of Tomorrow, 1982; The Astral Mirror, 1985; Voyager Two: The Alien Within, 1986; As on a Darkling Plain, 1991; Empire Builders, 1993; Orion and the Conqueror, 1994; Orion Among the Stars, 1995. Contributions to: Numerous books and periodicals. Honours: Distinguished Alumnus, 1981, Alumni Fellow, 1982, Temple University. Memberships: British Interplanetary Society, fellow; National Space Society, president emeritus; PEN; Science Fiction Writers of America. Address: 32 Gramercy Park South, New York, NY 10003, USA.

BOVEY John, b. 17 Apr 1913, Minneapolis, Minnesota, USA. Retired Diplomat. m. Marcia Peterson, 31 July 1943, 1 daughter. Education: BA, 1935, MA, 1938, Harvard University. Appointments: Teaching Fellow, Instructor, Harvard University, 1938-42; Instructor, US Naval Academy, 1943-45. Publication: Desirable Aliens: The Silent Meteor. Contributions to: Ploughshares; New England Review; Cornhill

Magazine; New York Times; London Magazine. Honours: Emily Green Balch Fiction Award; Angoff Award; David Bruce Contest, 2nd Prize. Address: 19 Chauncy Street, Cambridge, MA 02138, USA.

BOWDEN Anthony. See: **CUDDON John.**

BOWDEN Jim. See: **SPENCE William (John Duncan).**

BOWDEN Roland Heywood, b. 19 Dec 1916, Lincoln, England. Teacher. m. 2 Jan 1946, 1 son, 1 daughter. Education: School of Architecture, Liverpool University, 1934-39. Publications: Poems From Italy, 1970; Every Season is Another, 1986; Death of Paolini, play produced Edinburgh, 1980; After Neruda, play produced Hammersmith Riverside, 1984; The Fence, play produced Brighton, Gardner Centre, 1985. Contributions to: Arts Review: London Magazine; Panurge: Words International. Honours: Arts Council Drama Bursary, 1978; Cheltenham Festival Poetry Prize, 1982; 1st Prize, All-Sussex Poets, 1983. Membership: National Poetry Secretariat. Address: 2 Roughmere Cottage, Lavant, Chichester, West Sussex PO18 0BG, England.

BOWEN John Griffith, b. 5 Nov 1924, Calcutta, India. Writer; TV Producer. Education: MA, Oxford University. Publications: The Truth Will Not Help Us; After the Rain; The Centre of the Green; Storyboard; The Birdcage; A World Elsewhere; Squeak; The McGuffin; The Girls; Fighting Back; The Precious Gift; No Retreat Plays: I Love You Mrs Patterson; After the Rain; Little Boxes; The Disorderly Women; The Corsican Brothers; Hail Caesar; The Waiting Room; Singles; The Inconstant Couple; Which Way Are You Facing?; The Geordie Gentlemen; The Oak Tree Tea-Room Siege; Uncle Jeremy. Contributions to: London Magazine; Times Literary Supplement; Spectator; Gambit; Journal of Royal Asiatic Society; Times Educational Supplement; Listener. Honour: Tokyo Prize, 1974. Memberships: Executive Committee, PEN; Committee of Management Society of Authors; Executive Committee, Writers Guild of Great Britain; Board of Management, ALCS. Address: Old Lodge Farm, Sugarswell Lane, Edgehill, Banbury, Oxon OX15 6HP, England.

BOWEN Lynne, b. 22 Aug 1940, Indian Head, Saskatchewan, Canada. Author. Education: BSc, University of Alberta, 1963; MA, University of Victoria, 1980. Appointment: Maclean Hunter Lectureship of Creative Non-Fiction Writing, University of British Columbia, 1992-. Publications: Boss Whistle: The Coal Miners of Vancouver Island Remember, 1982; Three Dollar Dreams, 1982; Muddling Through: The Remarkable Story of the Barr Colonists, 1992; Those Lake People: Stories of Cowichan Lake, 1995. Honours: Canadian Historical Association Regional Certificates of Merit, 1984, 1993; Lieutenant Governor's Medal, 1987; Hubert Evans Non-Fiction Prize, 1993. Memberships: Writers' Union of Canada; PEN International. Address: 4982 Fillinger Crescent, Nanaimo, British Columbia V9V 1J1, Canada.

BOWERING George, b. 1 Dec 1936, Keremeos, British Columbia, Canada. Writer. m. Angela Luoma, 14 Dec 1963, 1 daughter. Education: BA, 1960, MA, 1963, University of British Columbia. Publications: Mirror on the Floor, 1967; Flycatcher, 1974; A Short Sad Book, 1977; Burning Water, 1980; A Place to Die, 1983; Caprice, 1987; Harry's Fragments, 1990; Urban Snow, 1992; Likely Stories, 1992; Shoot, 1994; Bowering's BC (history), 1996. Contributions to: Periodicals. Honours: Governor-General's Awards, 1969, 1980. Membership: Association of Canadian Television and Radio Artists. Address: 2499 West 37th Avenue, Vancouver, British Columbia V6M 1P4, Canada.

BOWERING Marilyn (Ruthe), b. 13 Apr 1949, Winnipeg, Ontario, Canada. Poet; Writer. m. Michael S Elcock, 3 Sept 1982, 1 daughter. Education: University of British Columbia, 1968-69; BA, 1971, MA, 1973, University of Victoria; Appointments: Visiting Lecturer, 1978-82, Lecturer in Creative Writing, 1982-86, 1989, Visiting Associate Professor of Creative Writing, 1993-96, University of Victoria, British Columbia; Faculty, 1992, Writer-in-Residence, 1993-94, Banff Centre, Alberta; Writer in Residence, Memorial University of Newfoundland, 1995. Publications: Poetry: The Liberation of Newfoundland, 1973; One Who Became Lost, 1976; The Killing Room, 1977; Third/Child Zian, 1978; The Book of Glass, 1978; Sleeping with Lambs, 1980; Giving Back Diamonds, 1982; The Sunday Before Winter, 1984; Anyone Can See I Love You, 1987; Grandfather was a Soldier, 1987; Calling All the World, 1989; Love As It Is, 1993; Autobiography, 1996. Novels: The Visitors Have All Returned, 1979; To All Appearances a Lady, 1990. Editor: Many Voices: An Anthology

of Contemporary Canadian Indian Poetry (with David A Day), 1977; Guide to the Labor Code of British Columbia, 1980. Contributions to: Anthologies and journals. Honours: Many Canada Council Awards for Poetry; Du Maurier Award for Poetry, 1978; National Magazine Award for Poetry, 1989; Long Poem prize, Malahat Review, 1994. Memberships: League of Canadian Poets; Writers Union of Canada. Address: 3777 Jennifer Road, Victoria, British Columbia V8P 3X1, Canada.

BOWERS Edgar, b. 2 Mar 1924, Rome, Georgia, USA. Poet; Professor of English Emeritus. Education: Erskine College, 1941-42; Princeton University, 1943-44; BA, University of North Carolina, 1947; PhD, Stanford University, 1953. Appointments: Instructor in English, Duke University, 1952-55; Assistant Professor of English, Harpur College, State University of New York at Endicott, 1955-58; Assistant Professor, 1958-61, Associate Professor, 1961-67, Professor of English, 1967-91, Professor Emeritus, 1991-, University of California at Santa Barbara. Publications: The Form of Loss, 1956; The Astronomers, 1965; Living Together, 1973; Witnesses, 1981; Chaco Canyon, 1987; Thirteen Views of Santa Barabra, 1989; For Louis Pasteur, 1990; How We Came from Paris to Blois, 1991. Contributions to: Anthologies and periodicals. Honours: Fulbright Fellowship, 1950-51; Guggenheim Fellowships, 1959, 1969; University of California Creative Arts Award, 1963; Ingram Merrill Award, 1976; Brandeis University Creative Arts Award, 1978; Bollingen Prize, 1989; Harriet Monroe Prize, 1989; American Institute of Arts and Letters Award, 1991. Address: 1201 Greenwich Street, Apt 601, San Francisco, CA 94109, USA.

BOWKER John Westerdale, b. 30 July 1935, London, England. Professor; Writer. Education: BA, Oxford, 1958. Appointments: Fellow, Corpus Christi College, Cambridge, 1962-74; Lecturer, University of Cambridge, 1965-74; Professor of Religious Studies, University of Lancaster, 1974-85; Fellow, Dean, Trinity College, Cambridge, 1984-93; Gresham Professor, Gresham College, London, 1992-; Honorary Canon, Canterbury Cathedral, 1985-. Publications: The Targums and Rabbinic Literature, 1969; Problems of Suffering in Religions of the World, 1970; Jesus and the Pharisees, 1973; The Sense of God: Sociological, Anthropological and Psychological Approaches to the Origin of the Sense of God, 1973; Uncle Bolpenny Tries Things Out, 1973; The Religious Imagination and the Sense of God, 1978; Worlds of Faith, 1983; Violence and Aggression (editor), 1984; The Meaning of Death, 1991; A Year to Live, 1991; Hallowed Ground, 1993. Honour: Harper Collins Biennial Prize, 1993. Address: 14 Bowers Croft, Cambridge CB1 4RP, England.

BOWLER Peter John, b. 8 Oct 1944, Leicester, England. Professor of History and Philosophy of Science; Author. m. Sheila Mary Holt, 24 Sept 1966, 1 son, 1 daughter. Education: BA, University of Cambridge, 1966; MSc, University of Sussex, 1967; PhD, University of Toronto, 1971. Appointments: Assistant Professor, University of Toronto, 1971-72; Lecturer, Science University of Malaysia, Penang, 1972-75; Assistant Professor, University of Winnipeg, 1975-79; Lecturer, 1979-87, Reader, 1987-92, Professor of History and Philosophy of Science, 1992-, Queen's University, Belfast. Publications: Fossils and Progress: Paleontology and the Idea of Progressive Evolution in the Nineteenth Century, 1976; The Eclipse of Darwinism: Anti-Darwinian Evolution Theories in the Decades Around 1900, 1983, new edition, 1992; Evolution: The History of an Idea, 1984, revised edition, 1989; Theories of Human Evolution: A Century of Debate, 1844-1944, 1986; The Non-Darwinian Revolution: Reinterpreting a Historical Myth, 1988; The Mendelian Revolution: The Emergence of Hereditarian Concepts in Modern Science and Society, 1989; The Invention of Progress: The Victorians and the Past, 1990; Darwin: L'origine delle specie, 1990; Charles Darwin: The Man and his Influence, 1990, new edition, 1996; The Fontana History of the Environmental Sciences, 1992, US edition as The Norton History of the Environmental Sciences, 1993; Biology and Social Thought, 1850-1914, 5 lectures, 1993; Darwinism, 1993; E Ray Lankester and the Making of Modern British Biology (editor and co-author with J Lester), 1995; Life's Splendid Drama: Evolutionary Biology and the Reconstruction of Life's Ancestry, 1860-1940, 1996. Contributions to: Journals. Honour: Elected, Royal Irish Academy, 1994. Memberships: British Society for the History of Science; History of Science Society; Royal Irish Academy, 1993-. Address: c/o Department of Social Anthropology, Queen's University of Belfast, Belfast BT7 1NN, Northern Ireland.

BOWLES Paul (Frederic), b. 30 Dec 1910, New York, New York, USA. Author; Poet; Composer. m. Jane Sydney Auer, Feb 1938, dec 1973. Education: Studied music with Aaron Copland and Nadia Boulanger. Publications: Novels: The Sheltering Sky, 1949; Let It Come Down, 1952; The Spider's House, 1955; Up Above the World, 1966. Stories: A Little Stone, 1950; Collected Stories, 1979; A Delicate Episode, 1988; Unwelcome Words, 1989. Poetry: The Thicket of Spring, 1972; Next to Nothing, 1981. Other: Their Heads are Green and Their Hands are Blue, 1963; Without Stopping (autobiography), 1972; Points in Time, 1982; In Touch: The Letters of Paul Bowles, 1994; Paul Bowles: Music (essays, interviews, reviews), 1995. Honours: Guggenheim Fellowship, 1941; Rockefeller Grant, 1959. Address: c/o Ecco Press, 100 West Broad Street, Hopewell, NJ 08525, USA.

BOWLING Harry, b. 30 Sept 1931, Bermondsey, London, England. m. Shirley Burgess, 27 July 1957, 1 son, 2 daughters. Publications: Conner Street's War, 1988; Tuppence to Tooley Street, 1989; Ironmonger's Daughter, 1989; Paragon Place, 1990; Gaslight in Page Street, 1991; The Girl From Cotton Lane, 1992; Backstreet Girl, 1993. Literary Agent: Jennifer Kavanagh. Address: Headline Book Publishing plc, Headline House, 79 Great Tichfield Street, London W1P 7FN, England.

BOWLT John Ellis, b. 6 Dec 1943, London, England (US citizen). Professor; Writer. m. Nicoletta Misler, 25 Dec 1981. Education: BA,Russian, 1965, MA, Russian Literature, 1966, University of Birmingham; PhD, Russian Literature and Art, University of St Andrews, Scotland, 1971. Appointments: Assistant to Associate Professor, 1971-81, Associate Professor to Professor, 1981-88, University of Texas, Austin; Visiting Professor, University of Otago, New Zealand, 1982, Hebrew University, Jerusalem, 1985; Professor, University of Southern California, Los Angeles, 1988-. Publications: The Russian Avant-Garde: Theory and Criticism 1902-1934, 1976, revised edition, 1988; The Silver Age: Russian Art of the Early Twentieth Century, 1979; The Life of Vasilii Kandinsky in Russian Art (with Rose Carol Washton-Long), 1980; Pavel Filonov: A Hero and His Fate (with Nicoletta Misler), 1984; Mikalojus Konstantinas Ciurlionis: Music of the Spheres (with Alfred Senn and Danute Staskevicius), 1986; Russian Samizdat Art (co-author), 1986; Gustav Kluzis, 1988; Aus Vollem Halse: Russische Buchillustration und Typographie 1900-1930 (with B Hernad), 1993; Russian and East European Paintings in the Thyssen-Bornemisza Collection (with Nicolette Misler), 1993; The Salon Album of Vera Sudeikin-Stravinsky, 1995. Contributions to: Books, scholarly journals, periodicals and exhibition catalogues. Honours: British Council Scholarship, 1966-68; Woodrow Wilson National Fellowship, 1971; National Humanities Institute Fellow, Yale University, 1977-78; Fulbright-Hays Award, Paris, 1981; American Council of Learned Societies Award, Italy, 1984; Senior Fellow, Wolfsonian Foundation, Miami, 1995. Memberships: American Association for the Advancement of Slavic Studies; College Art Association, New York. Address: c/o Department of Slavic Languages and Literatures, University of Southern California at Los Angeles, Los Angeles, CA 90089, USA.

BOX Edgar. See: **VIDAL Gore**.

BOYCOTT Geoffrey, b. 21 Oct 1940, Fitzwilliam, Yorkshire, England. Career: First class Cricketer for Yorkshire, 1952-86; Test Cricketer for England, 1964-82; Scored 100th first class 100 vs Australia at Headingley, 1977; Commentator for BBC and Channel 9 Television. Publications: Geoff Boycott's Book for Young Cricketers, 1976; Put to the Test: England in Australia 1978-79, 1979; Geoff Boycott's Cricket Quiz, 1979; On Batting, 1980; Opening Up, 1980; In the Fast Lane, 1981; Master Class, 1982; Boycott, The Autobiography, 1987; Boycott on cricket, 1990. Honour: OBE. Address: c/o Yorkshire County Cricket Club, Headingley Cricket Ground, Leeds, Yorkshire LS6 3BY, England.

BOYD Brian David, b. 30 July 1952, Belfast, Northern Ireland.University Teacher; Writer. m. (1) Janet Bower Eden, 1974, div 1980, (2) Bronwen Mary Nicholson, 1983, 3 stepdaughters. Education: BA 1972, MA Hons 1974, University of Canterbury, Christchurch, New Zealand; PhD, University of Toronto, Canada, 1979; Postdoctoral Fellow, University of Auckland, 1979. Appointments: Lecturer, 1980-85, Senior Lecturer, 1985-92, Associate Professor, 1992-, University of Auckland, New Zealand; Editorial Board, Nabokov Studies; Visiting Professor, University of Nice-Sophia Antipolis, 1994-95. Publications: Nabokov's Ada: The Place of Consciousness,

1985; Vladimir Nabokov: The Russian Years, 1990; Vladimir Nabokov: The American Years, 1991. Editor: Nabokov: Novels and Memoirs 1941-1951, 1996; Nabokov: Novels 1955-1962, 1996; Nabokov: Novels 1969-1974, 1996. Honours: Claude McCarthy Fellowship, 1982; Goodman Fielder Wattie Prize (Third), 1991; Goodman Fielder Wattie Prize (Second), 1992; James Cook Research Fellowship, 1997-99. Literary Agent: Georges Borchardt. Address: Department of English, University of Auckland, Private Bag 92019, Auckland, New Zealand.

BOYD (Charles) Malcolm, b. 24 May 1932, Newcastle upon Tyne, England. Lecturer in Music (Retired); Author. m. Beryl Gowen, 3 Apr 1956, 2 sons. Education: Dame Allan's School, Newcastle upon Tyne, 1943-50; BA, 1953, MA, 1962, Durham University. Appointment: Lecturer, University College, Cardiff, retired, 1992. Publications: Harmonizing Bach Chorales, 1967; Bach's Instrumental Counterpoint, 1967; Palestrina Style, 1973; William Mathias, 1978; Grace Williams, 1980; Bach, 1983; Domenico Scarlatti: Master of Music, 1986; Bach: The Brandenburg Concertos, 1993. Contributions to: Dictionaries; Encyclopaedias; Periodicals. Honour: Yorkshire Post Literary Award for Music. Membership: Royal Musical Association. Address: 211 Fidlas Road, Llanishen, Cardiff CF4 5NA, Wales.

BOYD William, b. 7 Mar 1952, Ghana. Writer. Education: Jesus College, Oxford, 1975-80. Appointments: Lecturer in English Literature, St Hilda's College, Oxford, 1980-83; Television Critic, New Statesman, London, 1982-83. Publications: A Good Man in Africa, novel, 1981; On the Yankee Station, short stories, 1981; An Ice-Cream War, novel, 1982; Stars and Bars, novel, 1984; School Ties, screenplay, 1985; The New Confessions, novel, 1987; Brazzaville Beach, 1990; Television Plays: Good and Bad at Games, 1985; Dutch Girls, 1985; Scoop, 1987. Honours: Whitbread Prize, 1981; Somerset Maugham Award, 1982; James Tait Black Memorial Prize, 1990; McVitie's Prize, 1991. Address: c/o Harvey Unna and Stephen Durbridge Ltd, 24 Pottery Lane, London W11 4LZ, England.

BOYLE T(homas) Coraghessan, b. 2 Dec 1948, Peekskill, New York, USA. Professor of English; Author. m. Karen Kvashay, 25 May 1974, 2 sons, 1 daughter. Education: BA, State University of New York at Potsdam, 1968; MFA, 1974, PhD, 1977, University of Iowa. Appointments: Founder-Director, Creative Writing Program, 1978-86, Assistant Professor, 1978-82, Associate Professor, 1982-86, Professor, 1986-, of English, University of Southern California at Los Angeles. Publications: Descent of Man, 1979; Water Music, 1982; Budding Prospects, 1984; Greasy Lake, 1985; World's End, 1987; If the River Was Whiskey, 1989; East is East, 1990; The Road to Wellville, 1993; Without a Hero, 1994; The Tortilla Curtain, 1995. Contributions to: Numerous anthologies and periodicals. Honours: National Endowment for the Arts Grants, 1977, 1983; Guggenheim Fellowship, 1988; PEN/Faulkner Award, 1988; Commonwealth Club of California Gold Medal for Literature, 1988; O'Henry Short Story Awards, 1988, 1989; Prix Passion Publishers' Prize, France, 1989; Editors' Choice, New York Times Book Review, 1989; Honorary Doctor of Humane Letters, State University of New York, 1991; Howard D Vursell Memorial Award, National Academy of Arts and Letters, 1993. Membership: National Endowment of the Arts Literature Panel, 1986-87. Address: c/o Department of English, University of Southern California, Los Angeles, CA 90089, USA.

BOZEMAN Adda B(ruemmer), b. 17 Dec 1908, Geistershof, Latvia. Retired Teacher; Author. m. (1) Virgil Bozeman, 28 Mar 1937, div, 1 daughter, (2) Arne Barkhaus, 8 Feb 1951. Education: École Libre des Sciences Politiques, 1934; Middle Temple, 1936; JD, Southern Methodist University, Dallas, 1937; Hoover Institution, Stanford University, 1938-40. Publications: Regional Conflicts Around Geneva, 1948; The Future of Law in a Multicultural World, 1971; How to Think About Human Rights, 1978; Politics and Culture in International History, 1994. Contributions to: Various publications. Memberships: American Political Science Association; Consortium for the Study of Civilization; International Studies Association. Address: 24 Beale Circle, Bronxville, NY 10708, USA.

BRACEGIRDLE Brian, b. 31 May 1933, Macclesfield, England. Museum Curator. Education: BSc, 1957, PhD, 1975, University of London. Appointments: Research Consultant in Microscopy, Science Museum. Publications: An Atlas of Embryology (with W H Freeman), 1963; An Atlas of Histology (with W H Freeman), 1966; Photography for Books and Reports, 1970; An Atlas of Invertebrate Structure (with W H Freeman), 1971; An Atlas of Plant Structure (with P H Miles), vol

1, 1971, vol II, 1973; The Archaeology of the Industrial Revolution, 1973; Thomas Telford (with P H Miles), 1973; The Darbys and the Ironbridge Gorge (with P H Miles), 1974; An Advanced Atlas of Histology (with W H Freeman), 1976; An Atlas of Chordate Structure (with P H Miles), 1977; The Evolution of Microtechnique, 1978; Beads of Glass: Leeuwenhoek and the Early Microscope (editor), 1983; The Microscopic Photographs of J S Dancer (with J B McCormick), 1993; Scientific Photomicrography (with S Bradbury), 1995; Modern Microscope Manufacturers, 1996. Address: Cold Aston Lodge, Cold Aston, Cheltenham, Glos GL54 3BN, England.

BRACKENBURY Alison, b. 20 May 1953, Gainsborough, Lincolnshire, England. Poet. Education: BA English, St Hugh's College, Oxford, 1975. Publications: Journey to a Cornish Wedding, 1977; Two Poems, 1979; Dreams of Power and Other Poems, 1981; Breaking Ground and Other Poems, 1984; Christmas Roses and Other Poems, 1988; 1982, 1985. Radio play: The Country of Afternoon, 1985. Honours: Eric Gregory Award, 1982. Address: Carcanet Press, 208-212 Corn Exchange Buildings, Manchester M4 3BQ, England.

BRADBURY Edward P. See: **MOORCOCK Michael (John).**

BRADBURY Malcolm Stanley, b. 7 Sept 1932, Sheffield, England. Author; Writer; Professor of American Studies. Education: Queen Mary College, University of London, 1953-55; Indiana University, 1955-56. Publications: Eating People is Wrong, 1959; All Dressed Up and Nowhere To Go, 1962; Evelyn Waugh, 1964; Two Poets (with A Rodway), 1966; The Social Context of Modern English Literature, 1971; Penguin Companion to Literature: American, 1972; Possibilities: Essays on the State of the Novel, 1973; The History Man, 1975; Who Do You Think You Are?: Stories and Parodies, 1976; The Novel Today, 1977; Introduction to American Studies, 1981; Saul Bellow, 1982; The After Dinner Game: Three Television Plays, 1982; Rates of Exchange, 1983; Cuts, 1987; The Modern American Novel, 1984; Doctor Criminale, 1992; The Modern British Novel, 1993; Dangerous Pilgrimages: Transatlantic Mythologies and the Novel, 1995; Atlas of Literature, 1996. Honour: Commander of the Order of the British Empire, 1991. Address: University of East Anglia, Norwich NR4 7TJ, England.

BRADBURY Ray (Douglas), b. 22 Aug 1920, Waukegan, Illinois, USA. Writer; Poet; Dramatist. m. Marguerite Susan McClure, 27 Sept 1947, 4 daughters. Education: Public Schools. Publications: Novels: The Martian Chronicles, 1950; Dandelion Wine, 1957; Something Wicked This Way Comes, 1962; Death is a Lonely Business, 1985; A Graveyard for Lunatics, 1990; Green Shadows, White Whale, 1992. Short Story Collections: Dark Carnival, 1947; The Illustrated Man, 1951; The Golden Apples of the Sun, 1953; Fahrenheit 451, 1953; The October Country, 1955; A Medicine for Melancholy, 1959; The Ghoul Keepers, 1961; The Small Assassin, 1962; The Machineries of Joy, 1964; The Vintage Bradbury, 1965; Tomorrow Midnight, 1966; Twice Twenty-Two, 1966; I Sing the Body Electric!, 1969; Bloch and Bradbury: Ten Masterpieces of Science Fiction (with Robert Bloch), 1969; Whispers From Beyond (with Robert Bloch), 1972; Harrap, 1975; Long After Midnight, 1976; To Sing Strange Songs, 1979; Dinosaur Tales, 1983; A Memory of Murder, 1984; The Toynbee Convector, 1988; Kaleidoscope, 1994. Short Stories: Quicker Than the Eye, 1996. Poetry: Old Ahab's Friend, and Friend to Noah, Speaks His Piece: A Celebration, 1971; When Elephants Last in the Dooryard Bloomed: Celebrations for Almost Any Day in the Year, 1973; That Son of Richard III: A Birth Announcement, 1974; Where Robot Mice and Robot Men Run Round in Robot Towns, 1977; Twin Hieroglyphs That Swim the River Dust, 1978; The Bike Repairman, 1978; The Author Considers His Resources, 1979; The Aqueduct, 1979; The Attic Where the Meadow Greens, 1979; The Last Circus, 1980; The Ghosts of Forever, 1980; The Haunted Computer and the Android Pope, 1981; The Complete Poems of Ray Bradbury, 1982; The Love Affair, 1983; Forever and the Earth, 1984; Death Has Lost Its Charm for Me, 1987. Plays: The Meadow, 1960; Way in the Middle of the Air, 1962; The Anthem Sprinters and Other Antics, 1963; The World of Ray Bradbury, 1964; Leviathan 99, 1966; The Day it Rained Forever, 1966; The Pedestrian, 1966; Dandelion Wine, 1967; Christus Apollo, 1969; The Wonderful Ice-Cream Suit and Other Plays, 1972; Madrigals for the Space Age, 1972; Pillars of Fire and Other Plays for Today, Tomorrow, and Beyond Tomorrow, 1975; That Ghost, That Bride of Time: Excerpts from a Play-in-Progress, 1976; The Martian Chronicles, 1977; Farenheit 451, 1979; A Device Out of Time, 1986; Falling Upward, 1988. Non-Fiction: Teacher's Guide: Science Fiction, 1968; Zen and the Art of Writing, 1973; Mars and the Mind of

Man, 1973; The Mummies of Guanajuato, 1978; Beyond, 1984: Remembrance of Things Future, 1979; Los Angeles, 1984; Orange County, 1985; The Art of Playboy, 1985; Yestermorrow: Obvious Answers to Impossible Futures, 1991; Ray Bradbury on Stage: A Chrestomathy of His Plays, 1991; Journey to Far Metaphor: Further Essays on Creativity, Writing, Literature, and the Arts, 1994; The First Book of Dichotomy, The Second Book of Symbiosis, 1995. Other: Television and film scripts. Honours: O Henry Prizes, 1947, 1948; National Institute of Arts and Letters Award, 1954; Writers Club Award, 1974; Balrog Award for Best Poet, 1979; PEN Body of Work Award, 1985. Memberships: Science Fantasy Writers of America; Screen Writers Guild of America; Writers Guild of America. Address: 10265 Cheviot Drive, Los Angeles, CA 90064, USA.

BRADDIN George. See: **MILKOMANE George Alexis Milkomanovich.**

BRADFORD Barbara Taylor, b. 10 May 1933, Leeds, Yorkshire, England. Journalist; Novelist. m. Robert Bradford, 1963. Appointments: Editor, Columnist, Periodicals in UK & US. Publications: Complete Encyclopedia of Homemaking Ideas, 1968; How To Be the Perfect Wife, 1969-70; Easy Steps to Successful Decorating, 1971; Making Space Grow, 1979; A Woman of Substance, 1979; Voice of the Heart, 1983; Hold the Dream, 1985; Act of Will, 1986; To Be the Best, 1988; The Women in His Life, 1990; Remember, 1991; Angel, 1993; Everything to Gain, 1994; Dangerous To Know, 1995; Love In Another Town, 1995; Her Own Rules, 1996; A Secret Affair, 1996; Power of a Woman, 1997. Address: c/o Bradford Enterprises, 450 Park Avenue, Suite 1903, New York, NY 10022, USA.

BRADFORD Karleen, b. 16 Dec 1936, Toronto, Ontario, Canada. Writer. m. James Creighton Bradford, 22 Aug 1959, 2 sons, 1 daughter. Education: BA, University of Toronto, 1959. Publications: A Year for Growing, 1977; The Other Elizabeth, 1982; Wrong Again, Robbie, 1983; I Wish There Were Unicorns, 1983; The Stone in the Meadow, 1984; The Haunting at Cliff House, 1985; The Nine Days Queen, 1986; Write Now!, 1988; Windward Island, 1989; There Will be Wolves, 1992; Thirteenth Child, 1994; Animal Heroes, 1995; Shadows on a Sword, 1996; More Animal Heroes, 1996. Address: The Writers' Union of Canada, 24 Ryerson Avenue, Toronto, Ontario MT5 2P3, Canada.

BRADFORD S W. See: **BATTIN B W.**

BRADLEY George, b. 22 Jan 1953, Roslyn, New York, USA. Writer; Poet. m. Spencer Boyd, 8 Sept 1984. Education: BA, Yale University, 1975; University of Virginia, 1977-78. Publications: Terms to Be Met, 1986; Of the Knowledge of Good and Evil, 1991. Other: Screenplays; Criticism. Contributions to: Periodicals. Honours: Academy of American Poets prize, 1978; Yale Younger Poets Prize, 1985; Lavan Younger Poets Award, 1990. Address: 82 West Main Street, Chester, CT 06412, USA.

BRADLEY John (Lewis), b. 5 Aug 1917, London, England. Professor (Retired); Writer. m. Elizabeth Hilton Pettingell, 4 Nov 1943, 1 daughter. Education: BA, 1940, PhD, 1950, Yale University; MA, Harvard University, 1946. Publications: Ruskin's Letters from Venice, 1851-52, 1955; Ruskin's Letters to Lord and Lady Mount Temple, 1964; Selections from Mayhew's London Labour and The London Poor, 1965; Ruskin's Unto This Last and Traffic, 1967; An Introduction to Ruskin, 1971; Ruskin: The Critical Heritage, 1984; Lady Curzon's India: Letters of a Vicereine, 1985; Correspondence of John Ruskin and Charles Eliot Norton (with Ian Ousby), 1987; The Cambridge Guide to Literature in English (with Ian Ousby), 1988; A Shelley Chronology, 1993. Contributions to: Essays in Criticism: Journal of English and Germanic Philology; Modern Language Review; Notes and Queries; Times Literary Supplement; Victorian Studies. Honours: Fellow and Grantee, American Philosophical Society; Guggenheim Fellowship, 1961-62. Address: Church Cottage, Hinton St George, Somerset TA17 8SA, England.

BRADWAY Becky, b. 21 Nov 1957, Phoenix, Arizona, USA. Writer; Editor. m. Jan 1985, 1 daughter. Education: MA, Sangaman State University; Columbia University, 1985. Appointment: Writer, Editor, Illinois Coalition Against Sexual Assault, 1986-. Publications: Eating Our Hearts Out; American Fiction Number One; American Fiction. Contributions to: Green Mountains Review; Beloit Fiction Journal; South Carolina Review; Sojourner; Other Voices; Ascent; Crescent Review; Greensboro Review; Soundings East; Four

Quarters. Honours: 1st Prize, Willow Review; Artist Advancement Awards, American Fiction Competition. Memberships: Illinois Writers; Poets and Writers. Address: 924 Bryn Mawr Boulevard, Springfield, IL 62703, USA.

BRADWELL James. See: **KENT Arthur (William Charles).**

BRADY Anne M (Cannon), b. 23 May 1926, Dublin, Ireland. Writer. m. 2 Feb 1957, 2 sons, 2 daughters. Education: BA, English Literature and Language, University College, Dublin; Diploma in Hospital Administration, College of Commerce. Appointments: University Library Assistant, Dublin and Ottawa; Farm Secretary, County Meath. Publications: The Winds of God, 1985; The Biographical Dictionary of Irish writers (with Brian Cleeve), 1985; Honey Off Thorns, 1988. Memberships: University College Dublin Graduates Association; Royal Dublin Society. Literary Agent: Eleanor Corey. Address: Rosbeg, 12 Ard Mhuire Park, Dalkey, County Dublin, Ireland.

BRADY James Winston, b. 15 Nov 1928, New York, USA. Writer; Broadcaster. m. Florence Kelly, 12 Apr 1958, 2 daughters. Education: AB, Manhattan College, 1950; New York University. Publications: Novels: Paris One, 1977; Nielsen's Children, 1979; Press Lord, 1981; Holy Wars, 1983; Designs, 1986; Non Fiction: The Coldest War, 1990; Fashion Show, 1992. Contributions to: Parade; Esquire; Advertising Age; TV Guide; People; Harper's Bazaar. Honour: Emmy Award, 1973-74. Address: PO Box 1584, East Hampton, NY 11937, USA.

BRADY Joan, b. 4 Dec 1939, San Francisco, California, USA. Writer. m. Dexter Wright Masters, 23 Sept 1963, dec 1989, 1 son. Education: BS, Columbia University, 1965. Publications: The Impostor, 1979; The Unmaking of a Dancer, 1982; Theory of War, 1993; Prologue, 1994; Death Comes for Peter Pan, 1996. Contributions to: Harpers; MS; Telegraph; Sunday Times. Honours: Phi Beta Kappa, 1965; National Endowment for the Arts Grant, 1986; Whitbread Novel, 1993; Whitbread Book of the Year, 1993; Prix du Meilleur Livre Etranger, 1995. Membership: Authors Guild.

BRADY John Mary, b. 10 July 1955, Dublin, Ireland. Teacher. m. Johanna Wagner, 1 Aug 1981, 1 son, 1 daughter. Education: BA, Trinity College, 1980; BEd, 1981, MEd, 1985, University of Toronto. Publications: Kaddish in Dublin; Unholy Ground; A Stone of the Heart; All Souls, 1993; The Good Life, 1995. Honours: Arthur Ellis Award; Best First Novel. Address: c/o MGA Agency, 10 St Mary Street, Suite 510, Toronto, Ontario, Canada.

BRADY Nicholas. See: **LEVINSON Leonard.**

BRADY Patricia, b. 20 Jan 1943, Danville, Illinois, USA. Historian. 1 son, 1 daughter. Education: BA cum laude, with honours, Newcomb College, 1965; MA, History, 1966; PhD, History, 1977, Tulane University. Publications: Nelly Custis Lewis's Housekeeping Book, 1982; Encyclopaedia of New Orleans Artists, 1718-1918, 1987; George Washington's Beautiful Nelly, 1991; Mollie Moore Davis: A Literary Life, 1992; The Cities of the Dead: Free Men of Color as Tomb Builders, 1993. Contributions to: Journals. Honours: Phi Beta Kappa, 1965; Honorary Woodrow Wilson Fellow, 1965; National Defense Foreign Language Fellow, 1965-68; Fulbright-Hays Fellow, 1974. Memberships: Board of Directors, Programme Committee Chair, Tennessee Williams-New Orleans Literary Festival; Association for Documentary Editing; Southern Historical Association. Literary Agent: Susan P Urstadt. Address: 1205 Valence Street, New Orleans, LA 70115, USA.

BRADY Terence Joseph, b. 13 Mar 1939, London, England. Playwright; Novelist; Actor; Columnist. m. Charlotte Mary Therese Bingham, 1 son, 1 daughter. Publications: For radio: Lines From My Grandfather's Forehead, 1972; For TV: Broad and Narrow; TWTWTW; With Charlotte Bingham: Boy Meets Girl; Take Three Girls; Upstairs Downstairs; Away From It All; Play For Today; Plays of Marriage; No-Honestly; Yes-Honestly; Thomas and Sarah; Pig In The Middle; The Complete Lack of Charm of the Bourgeoisie; Nanny; Oh Madeline; Father Matthew's Daughter; A View of Meadows Green; Love With a Perfect Stranger; This Magic Moment; For the stage: The Sloane Ranger Revue (contributor), 1985; I Wish I Wish; Novel: Rehearsal, 1972; The Fight Against Slavery, 1976; With Charlotte Bingham: Victoria, 1972; Rose's Story, 1973; Victoria and Company, 1974; Yes-Honestly, 1977; with Michael Felton: Point To Point, 1990; Riders

(TV film); Polo (TV film); Oh Madeline! (US TV). Contributions to: Daily Mail; Living; Country Homes and Interiors; Punch; Sunday Express; The Field; Mail on Sunday. Address: c/o Peters Fraser & Dunlop, 5th Floor, The Chambers, Chelsea Harbour, Lots Road, London SW10 OXF, England

BRAGG Melvyn, b. 6 Oct 1939, Carlisle, Cumberland, England. Writer; Presenter; Editor. m. (1) Marie-Elizabeth Roche, 1961, dec, 1 daughter, (2) Catherine Mary Haste, 1973, 1 son, 1 daughter. Education: MA, Wadham College, Oxford University. Appointments: Presenter, Editor, The South Bank Show, ITV, 1978-; Head of Arts, LWT, 1982-; Deputy Chairman, Border TV, 1985-. Publications: Plays: Mardi Gras, 1976; Orion, 1977; The Hired Man, 1984. Screenplays: Isadora; Jesus Christ Superstar; Clouds of Glory (with Ken Russell); Speak for England, 1976; Land of the Lakes, 1983; Laurence Olivier, 1984; Novels: For Want of a Nail, 1965; The Second Inheritance, 1966; Without a City Wall, 1968; The Hired Man, 1969; A Place in England, 1970; The Nerve, 1971; Josh Lawton, Autumn Manoevres, 1978; Kingdom Come, 1980; Love and Glory, 1983; The Life of Richard Burton, 1989; A Time to Dance, 1990, televised 1992; Crystal Rooms, 1992. Contributions to: Punch; other journals. Memberships: Arts Council; Chairman, Literature, Panel of Arts Council; President, Cumbrians for Peace, 1962-; Northern Arts. Address: 12 Hampstead Hill Gardens, London NW3, England.

BRAM Christopher, b. 22 Feb 1952, Buffalo, New York, USA. Novelist. Education: BA, College of William & Mary, Williamsburg, Virginia, 1974. Publications: Surprising Myself, 1987; Hold Tight, 1988; In Memory of Angel Clare, 1989; Almost History, 1992; Father of Frankenstein, 1995. Screenplays: George and Al, 1987; Lost Language of Cranes, 1989. Contribution to: New York Times Book Review; Newsday; Lambda Book Report; Christopher Street. Membership: Publishing Triangle. Literary Agent: Donadio & Ashworth Associates. Address: 231 West 22nd Street, New York, NY 10011, USA.

BRANCH Edgar Marquess, b. 21 Mar 1913, Chicago, Illinois, USA. University Professor; Educator; Editor; Author. m. Mary Josephine Emerson, 29 Apr 1939, 1 son, 2 daughters. Education: Beloit College, Beliot, Wisconsin, 1930-32, 1933-34; University College, University of London, England, 1932-33; BA, Beloit College,1934; Brown University, 1934-35; MA, University of Chicago, 1938; PhD, University of Iowa, 1941. Appointments: Instructor, 1941-43, Assistant Professor, 1943-49, Associate Professor, 1949-57, Professor, 1957-64, Chairman, Department of English, 1959-64, Research Professor, 1964-78, Miami University, Oxford, Ohio; Visiting Associate Professor, University of Missouri, 1950; Independent Author and Editor, Mark Twain Project, University of California, Berkeley, 1978-. Publications: The Literary Apprenticeship of Mark Twain, 1950; A Bibliography of the Writings of James T Farrell, 1921-1957, 1959; James T Farrell, 1963; Clemens of the Call, 1969; James T Farrell, 1971; The Great Landslide Case, 1972; The Grangerford-Shepherdson Feud: Life and Death at Compromse (with Robert H Hirst), 1985; Men Call Me Lucky, 1985; Mark Twain's Early Tales and Sketches, volumes 1 and 2 (edited with Robert Hirst); Mark Twain's Letters volume 1 (edited with Michael Frank and Kenneth Sanderson). Contributions to: Numerous articles in magazines and journals; Chapters and sections in books, anthologies. Honours: Beloit College Junior Foreign Fellow, 1932-33; Leaves, Research Grants, Miami University, ACLS; Senior Fellow, National Endowment for the Humanities, 1971-72; Literary Executor for James T Farrell, 1975-; Senior Research Fellow, National Endowmenet for the Humanites, 1976-77; Benjamin Harrison Medallion, Miami University, 1978; Distinguished Service Citation, Beloit College, 1979; Guggenheim Fellowship, 1978-79; First Modern Language Association Prize for Distinguished Scholarly Edition, 1995; Pegasus Award, Ohioana Library Association, 1996. Memberships: Phi Beta Kappa; Phi Kappa Psi; Modern Language Association of America; National Council of Teachers of English; Beta Theta Pi. Address: 4810 Bonham Road, Oxford, OH 45056, USA.

BRANCH Taylor, b. 14 Jan 1947, Atlanta, Georgia, USA. Writer. m. Christina Macy, 1 son, 1 daughter. Education: AB, University of North Carolina, 1968; Postgraduate Studies, Princeton University, 1968-70. Appointments: Staff, Washington (DC) Monthly magazine, 1970-73, Harper's magazine, New York City, 1973-75, Esquire magazine, New York City, 1975-76. Publications: Blowing the Whistle: Dissent in the Public Interest (with Charles Peters), 1972; Second Wind: The Memoirs of an Opinionated Man (with Bill Russell), 1979; The Empire Blues, 1981; Labyrinth (with Eugene M Propper), 1982;

Parting the Waters: America in the King Years, 1954-63, 1988. Honours: Christopher Award, 1988; Pulitzer Prize in History, 1989. Address: c/o Diskant and Associates, 1033 Gayley Avenue, Suite 202, Los Angeles, CA 90024, USA.

BRAND Oscar, b. 7 Feb 1920, Winnipeg, Manitoba, Canada. Folk Singer; Folklorist; Writer. Education: BA, Brooklyn College, 1942. Appointments: President, Harlequin Productions; President, Gypsy Hill Music; Lecturer on Dramatic Writing, Hofstra University, Hempstead, New York; Coordinator of Folk Music, WNYC; Host, numerous TV folk-songs programmes; Curator, Songwriters Hall of Fame, New York City. Publications: Courting Songs, 1952; Folksongs for Fun, 1957; The Ballad Mongers, authobiography, 1957; Bawdy Songs, 1958; The Gold Rush (writer, composer), ballet, 1961; In White America (composer), play 1962; A Joyful Noise (co-writer, composer), musical play, 1966; The Education of Hyman Kaplan (co-writer, composer), musical play, 1967; Celebrate (writer-composer), religious songs, 1968; How to Steal an Election (co-writer, composer), musical play, 1969; Songs of '76, music history, 1973; Thunder Rock (writer, composer), musical play, 1974; Party Songs, 1985. Honours: Laureate, Fairfield University, 1972; PhD, University of Winnipeg, 1989; Radio Pioneers of America, 1991; Friends of Old Time Radio, 1991; Peabody Awards, 1982, 1996. Memberships: American Federation of Television and Radio Artists; Screen Actors Guild; American Federation of Musicians; Dramatists Guild. Address: 141 Baker Hill, Great Neck, NY 11023, USA.

BRANDEWYNE (Mary) Rebecca (Wadsworth), b. 4 Mar 1955, Knoxville, Kentucky, USA. Writer. Education: BA, 1975, MA, 1979, Wichita State University. Publications: No Gentle Love, 1980; Forever My Love, 1982; Love, Cherish Me, 1983; Rose of Rapture, 1984; And Gold Was Ours, 1984; The Outlaw Hearts, 1986; Desire in Disguise, 1987; Passion Moon Rising, 1988; Upon a Moon-Dark Moor, 1988; Heatland, 1990; Across a Starlit Sea, 1991; Rainbow's End, 1991; Desperado, 1992; Swan Road, 1994; The Jacarancta Tree, 1995. Memberships: Mensa; National Writers Club; Romance Writers of America; Society of Professional Journalists. Address: PO Box 780036, Wichita, KS 67206, USA.

BRANDIS Marianne. See: **BRENDER A BRANDIS Marianne.**

BRANDON Joe. See: **DAVIS Robert Prunier.**

BRANDON Sheila. See: **RAYNER Claire Berenice.**

BRANDT Richard B(ooker), b. 17 Oct 1910, Wilmington, Ohio, USA. Professor of Philosophy (retired); Writer. m. Mary Elizabeth Harris, 19 June 1937, div 1968, 1 son, 1 daughter. Education: AB, Denison University, 1930; BA, Cambridge University, 1933; Trinity College, Cambridge, 1933-35; University of Tübingen, 1934-35; PhD, Yale University, 1936. Appointments: Instructor to Associate Professor, 1937-52, Professor, 1952-64, Chairman, Department of Philosophy and Religion, 1957-64, Swarthmore College; Professor of Philosophy and Chairman, Department of Philosophy, 1964-77, Sellars Collegiate Professor, 1978-81, Associate, Center for Philosophy and Public Affairs, 1980-81, University of Maryland; Fellow, Center for Advanced Study in the Behavioral Sciences, 1969-70; John Locke Lecturer, Oxford University, 1973-74; Visiting Professor, Florida State University, 1982, Georgetown University, 1982-83, University of California, Irvine, 1990. Publications: The Philosophy of Schleiermacher, 1941; Hopi Ethics: A Theoretical Analysis, 1954; Ethical Theory, 1959; Value and Obligation, 1961; A Theory of the Good and the Right, 1979; Morality, Utilitarianism and Rights, 1992. Contributions to: Scholarly journals. Honours: Guggenheim Fellowship, 1944-45; Senior Fellow, National Endowment for the Humanities, 1971-72; Honorary LDH, Denison University, 1977. Memberships: American Academy of Arts and Sciences; American Association of University Professors; American Philosophical Association; President, American Society for Political and Legal Philosophy, 1965-66; Phi Beta Kappa; President, Society for Philosophy and Psychology, 1979. Address: c/o Department of Philosophy, University of Michigan, Ann Arbor, MI 48109, USA.

BRANFIELD John Charles, b. 19 Jan 1931, Burrow Bridge, Somerset, England. Writer; Teacher. m. Kathleen Elizabeth Peplow, 2 sons, 2 daughters. Education: MA, Queens' College, Cambridge University; MEd, University of Exeter. Publications: Nancekuke,1972; Sugar Mouse, 1973; The Fox in Winter, 1980; Thin Ice, 1983; The Falklands Summer, 1987; The Day I Shot My Dad, 1989; Lanhydrock

Days, 1991. Literary Agent: A P Watt Ltd, 20 John Street, London WC1N 2DR, England. Address: Mingoose Villa, Mingoose, Mount Hawke, Truro, Cornwall TR4 8BX, England.

BRANIGAN Keith, b. 15 Apr 1940, Slough, England. University Lecturer (Archaeology). m. Kuabrat Sivadith, 20 Jun 1965, 1 son, 2 daughters. Education: BA (Hons) 1st Class Archaeology and Ancient History, 1963; PhD, University of Birmingham, 1966. Publications: The Foundations of Palatial Crete, 1970; The Tombs of Mesara, 1970; Latimer, 1971; Verulamium and the Roman Chilterns, 1973; Aegean Metalwork of the Early and Middle Bronze Age, 1974; Prehistoric Britain, 1975; Gatcome: A Roman Villa Estate, 1977; The Roman Villa in Southwest England, 1977; Hellas, 1980; Roman Britain, 1980; The Catuvellauni, 1986; Archaeology Explained, 1988; Romano-British Cavemen, 1992; Dancing With Death, 1993; Barra: Archaeological Research on Ben Tangaval, 1994. Contributions to: Over 100 papers in journals. Honour: Elected Fellow, Society of Antiquaries, 1970; Memberships: Prehistoric Society, Vice- President, 1984-86; Society for Promotion of Roman Studies. Address: Department of Archaeology and Prehistory, University of Sheffield, Sheffield S10 2TN, England.

BRANTENBERG Gerd, b. 27 Oct 1941, Oslo, Norway. Novelist. Education: Graduated University of Oslo, 1971. Appointments: Teacher until 1982; Founder of Literary Women's Forum, Norway. Publications: What Comes Naturally, 1973; The Daughters of Egalia, 1977; Stop Smoking, 1978; The Song of St Croix, 1978; Embraces, 1983; At the Ferry Crossing, 1985; The Four Winds, 1989, Children's Book; The Ompadora Place, 1992; Play: Egalia, 1982. Honours: Sarpsborg Prize, 1989. Address: Medø gård, Medøvn 72, 3145 Tjøme.

BRASHER Christopher William, b. 21 Aug 1928, Guyana. Journalist. m. Shirley Bloomer, 28 Apr 1959, 1 son, 2 daughters. Education: MA, St John's College, Cambridge. Appointments: Columnist, The Observer, 1961-92; Chairman, Berghaus Ltd, The Brasher Boot Co Ltd; President, The London Marathon Ltd. Publications: The Red Snows with Sir John Hunt, 1960; Sportsman of Our Time, 1962; A Diary of the XVIIIth Olympiad, 1964; Mexico, 1968; Munich, 1972; Editor, The London Marathon: The First Ten Years, 1991. Contributions to: Times, Sunday Times and numerous professional journals and magazines. Honours: Sportswriter of the Year, 1968, 1976; National Medal of Honour, Finland, 1975; Commander of Order of the British Empire, 1996. Address: The Navigator's House, River Lane, Richmond, Surrey TW10 7AG, England.

BRATA Sasthi (Sasthibrata Chakravarti), b. 16 July 1939, Calcutta, India (British). Novelist. m. Pamela Joyce Radcliffe, div. Education: Calcutta University. Appointments: Various part time jobs around Europe; Also worked in New York as a Freelance Journalist, London Columnist, Statesman, 1977-80. Publications: Confessions of an Indian Woman Eater, 1971; She and He, 1973; The Sensuous Guru: The Making of a Mystic President, 1980; Short stories: Encounter, 1978; Verse: Eleven Poems, 1960. Address: 33 Savernake Road, London NW3 2JU, England.

BRATHWAITE Edward Kamau, b. 11 May 1930, Bridgetown, Barbados. Professor in History; Poet. Education: BA, Pembroke College, Cambridge, 1953; DPhil, University of Sussex, at Falmer, 1968. Appointments: Founding Secretary, Caribbean Artists Movement, 1966; Professor of Social and Cultural History of the University of the West Indies at Kingston, 1982-. Publications: Poetry: The Arrivants: A New World Trilogy, 1973; Days and Nights, 1975; Other Exiles, 1975; Black Plus Blues, 1976; Mother Poem, 1976; Soweto, 1979; Sun Poem, 1982; Third World Poems, 1983; X-Self, 1987; Other: Folk Culture of the Slaves in Jamaica, 1970; The Development of Creole Society in Jamaica 1770-1820, 1971; Jamaica Poetry: A Checklist 1686-1978, 1979; Barbados Poetry: A Checklist, Slavery to the Present, 1979; The Colonial Encounter: Language, 1984; Jah Music, 1986; Roots, 1986. Honours: Guggenheim Fellowship, 1972; Musgrave Medal, Institute of Jamaica, 1983; Fulbright Fellowship 1987-88. Address: Department of History, University of the West Indies, Mona, Kingston 7, Jamaica.

BRAUN Volker, b. 7 May 1939, Dresden, Germany. Playwright; Poet. Education: University of Leipzig, 1969-64. Publications: Plays: Kipper Paul Bauch, 1967; Hans Furst, 1968; Hinze und Kunze, 1968; Freunde, 1972; Tinka, 1976; Guevara, oder, Der Sonnenstaat, 1977; Grosser Frieden, 1979; Simplex Deutsch, 1980; Dmitri, 1982; Siegfried, 1986; Übergangsgesellschaft, 1987; Transit Europa, 1988;

Lenins Tod, 1988; Das Denkmal, 1991; Verse: Vorlaufiges, 1966; Kriegesarklärung, 1967; Wir und nicht sie, 1970, 1979; Gedichte, 1972, 1976; Gegen die symmetrische Welt, 1974; Zeit-Gedichte, 1977; Der Stoff zum Leben, 1977; Gedichte, 1979; Training des aufrechten Gangs, 1979; Rimbaud: ein psalm der aktualität, 1985; Langsamer knirschender Morgen, 1987; Annatomie, 1989; Stories: Drei Berichte, 1972, 1979; Unvollendete Gesichte, 1977; Berichte von Hinze und Kunze, 1983; Bodenloser Satz, 1990. Honour: Berliner Prize, 1989. Address: Wolfshagener Strasse 68, 1100 Berlin, Germany.

BRAXTON Joanne M(argaret), b. 25 May 1950, Washington, DC, USA. Poet; Critic; Professor. 1 daughter. Education: BA, Sarah Lawrence College, 1972; MA 1974, PhD 1984, Yale University. Appointments: Lecturer, University of Michigan, 1979; Assistant Professor 1980-86, Associate Professor 1986-89, Professor of English 1989-, College of William and Mary. Publications: Sometimes I Think of Maryland (poems), 1977; Black Women Writing Autobiography: A Tradition Within a Tradition, 1989; Wild Women in the Whirlwind: The Renaissance in Contemporary Afra-American Writing (editor with Andree N McLaughlin), 1990; The Collected Poems of Paul Laurence Dunbar (editor), 1993. Contributions to: Books, anthologies, journals and periodicals. Honours: Outstanding Faculty Award, State Council for Higher Education for Virginia, 1992; Fellowships; grants. Memberships: American Studies Association; College Language Association; Modern Language Association. Address: c/o Department of English, St George Tucker Hall, College of William and Mary, Williamsburg, VA 23185, USA.

BRAY John Jefferson, b. 16 Sept 1912, Adelaide, Australia. Retired Chief Justice. Education; St Peter's College, Adelaide, 1925-28; University of Adelaide, 1929-32; LLB (Ord) 1932, LLB (Hons) 1933, LLD 1937, University of Adelaide. Appointments: Chief Justice of South Australia 1967-78; Chancellor, University of Adelaide, 1968-82. Publications: Poems, 1962; Poems 1961-1971, 1972; Poems 1972-1979, 1979; The Bay of Salamis and Other Poems, 1986; Satura: Selected Poetry and Prose, 1988; The Emperor's Doorkeeper (Occasional Addresses), 1988; Seventy Seven (Poems), 1990. Address: 39 Hurtle Square, Adelaide, South Australia 5000, Australia.

BRAYFIELD Celia Frances, b. 21 Aug 1945, Ealing, England. Writer. 1 daughter. Education: St Paul's Girls' School; Universitaire de Grenoble. Appointments: TV Critic, The Evening Standard, 1974-82, The Times, 1984-89, London Daily News, 1987, The Sunday Telegraph, 1989. Publications: The Body Show Book, 1981; Glitter, The Truth About Fame, 1985; Pearls, 1987; The Prince, 1990; White Ice, 1993; Harvest, 1995; Bestseller, 1996. Contributions to: Various journals, magazines and newspapers. Memberships: Society of Authors; Committee of Management, National Council for One Parent Families, 1989-. Address: c/o John Johnson Agency, Clerkenwell House, Clerkenwell Green, London EC1R OHT, England.

BREARS Peter C(harles) D(avid), b. 30 Aug 1944, Wakefield, Yorkshire, England. Writer; Museum Consultant. Education: Dip AD, Leeds College of Art, 1968. Publications: English Country Pottery, 1971; Yorkshire Probate Inventories, 1972; Collector's Book of English Country Pottery, 1974; Horse Brasses, 1980; Traditional Food in Yorkshire, 1987; North Country Folk Art, 1989; Of Curiosities and Rare Things, 1989; Treasures for the People, 1989; Images of Leeds, 1993; Leeds Desrib'd, 1993; Leeds Waterfront Heritage Trail, 1993; The Country House Kitchen, 1996. Contributions to: Connoisseur; Folk Life; Post Medieval Archaelogy. Memberships: Museums Association, fellow; Society of Antiquities, fellow; Society for Folk Life Studies, past president, 1995. Address: 4 Woodbine Terrace, Headingley, Leeds LS6 4AF, England.

BRECHER Michael, b. 14 Mar 1925, Montreal, Quebec, Canada. Political Science Educator. m. Eva Danon, 7 Dec 1950, 3 children. Education: BA, McGill University, 1946; MA, 1948, PhD, 1953, Yale University. Appointments:Faculty, 1952-63, Professor, 1963-93, R B Angus Professor, 1993-, McGill University; Visiting Professor, University of Chicago, Hebrew University of Jerusalem, University of California at Berkeley; Stanford University. Publications include: The Struggle for Kashmir, 1953; Nehru: A Political Biography , 1959; The New States of Asia, 1963; Succession in India, 1966; India and World Politics, 1968; Political Leadership in India, 1969; The Foreign Policy System of Israel, 1972; Decisions in Israel's Foreign Policy, 1975; Studies in Crisis Behavior, 1979; Decisions in Crisis, 1980; Crises in the Twentieth Century 2 volumes, 1988; Crises, Conflict and Instability, 1989; Crises in World Politics, 1993; A Study of Crisis, 1997.

Contributions to: Professional Journals. Honours: Canada Council and Social Sciences and Humanities Research Council of Canada, Research Grantee; Killam Awards; Watamull Prize, American Historical Association; Woodrow Wilson Foundation Award, American Political Science Association; Fieldhouse Teaching Award, McGill University; Distinguished Scholar Award, International Studies Association. Memberships: Several Professional Organisations. Address: McGill University, 855 Sherbrooke Street W, Montreal, Quebec H3A 2T7, Canada.

BRANDIS Marianne, (Marianne Brender a Brandis), b. 5 Oct 1938, Netherlands. Writer. Education: BA, 1960, MA, 1964, McMaster University. Publications: This Spring's Sowing, 1970; A Sense of Dust, 1972; The Tinderbox, 1982; The Quarter Pie Window, 1985; Elizabeth, Duchess of Somerset, 1989; The Sign of the Scales, 1990. Special Nests, 1990; Fire Ship, 1992;. Honours: Young Adult Canadian Book Award, 1986; National Chapter IODE Book Award, 1986; Bilson Award, 1991. Membership: Writer's Union of Canada. Address: 10 Lamport, Apt 206, Toronto, Ontario M4W 1S6, Canada.

BRENDON Piers George Rundle, b. 21 Dec 1940, Stratton, Cornwall, England. Writer. m. Vyvyen Davis, 1968, 2 sons. Education: MA, PhD, Magdelene College, Cambridge. Publications: Hurrell Froude and the Oxford Movement, 1974; Hawker of Morwenstow, 1975; Eminent Edwardians, 1979; The Life and Death of the Press Barons, 1982; Winston Churchill, A Brief Life, 1984; Our Own Dear Queen, 1985; Ike: The Life and Times of Dwight D Eisenhower, 1986; Thomas Cook: 150 Years of Popular Tourism, 1991; The Windsors (with Phillip Whitehead), 1994. Contributions to: Times; Observer; The Mail on Sunday; New York Times; New Statesman. Literary Agent: Curtis Brown Ltd. Address: 4B Millington Road, Cambridge CB3 9HP, England.

BRENNAN Patricia Winifred, (Patricia Daly, Anne Rodway), b. Shaftesbury, Dorset, England. Writer. m. (1) Denis William Reed, 31 Dec 1947, dec, (2) Peter Brennan, 19 Sept 1960, dec. Education: Bristol University; University of London, 1967. Appointments: Production Editor, Pitman Publishing, 1946-48; British Council, 1956-78. Publications: Penguin Parade; Writing Today; Albion; Poems: PEN; The Iron Dominion; Arts Council New Poetry; Women Writing. Contributions to: Kimber Anthologies of Ghost Stories, After Midnight Stories; In My Father's House; The Day Trip; Hesperios; Narcissus; Night Driver; Institute of Jewish Affairs; Patterns of Prejudice; Art & Sexual Taboo; Encounter; Our Family Doctors; Swedish Veekojournalen. Memberships: Society of Authors; PEN; Royal Society of Arts; British Federation of Graduate Women; Richmond & Hampton Association; Bath Association. Address: Iford House, 30 Newbridge Road, Bath BA1 3JZ England.

BRENNAN Robert. See: BACOCK Robert Joseph (Brennan).

BRENT Iris. See: BANCROFT Iris.

BRENT Madeleine. See: O'DONNELL Peter.

BRENTON Howard, b. 13 Dec 1942, Portsmouth, England. Playwright; Poet. Education: BA, St Catherine's College, Cambridge, 1965. Appointments: Resident Dramatist, Royal Court Theatre, London, 1972-73; Resident Writer, University of Warwick, 1978-79. Publications: Notes from a Psychotic Journal and Other Poems, 1969; Revenge, 1969; Scott of the Antartic (or what God didn't see), 1970; Christie in Love and Other Plays, 1970; Lay By (co-author), 1972; Plays for Public Places, 1972; Hitler Diaries, 1972; Brassneck (with David Hare), 1973; Magnificence, 1973; Weapons of Happiness, 1976; The Paradise Run (television play), 1976; Epsom Downs, 1977; Sore Throats, with Sonnets of Love and Opposition, 1979; The Life of Galileo (adaptor), 1980; The Romans in Britain, 1980; Plays for the Poor Theatre,1980; Thirteenth Night and A Short Sharp Shock, 1981; Danton's Death (adaptor), 1982; The Genius, 1983; Desert of Lies (television play), 1983; Sleeping Policemen (with Tunde Ikoli), 1984; Bloody Poetry, 1984; Pravda (with David Hare),1985; Dead Head (television series), 1987; Greenland, 1988; H.I.D. (Hess is Dead), 1989; Iranian Night (with Tariq Ali), 1989; Diving for Pearls (novel), 1989; Moscow Gold (with Tariq Ali), 1990; Berlin Bertie, 1992; Playing Away (opera libretto), 1994; Hot Irons (Essays and Diaries), 1995. Address: c/o Casarotto Ramsay Ltd,National House, 60-66 Wardour Street, London W1V 3HP.

BRETNOR Reginald, (Grendel Briarton), b. 30 July 1911, Vladivostock, Russia. Writer; Editor. m. (1) Helen Harding, dec 1967, (2) Rosalie Leveille, 1969. Publications: Fiction: A Killing in Swords, 1978; The Schimmelhorn File, 1979; Schimmelhorn's Gold, 1986; Gilpin's Space, 1986. Non-Fiction: Decisive Warfare: A Study on Military Theory, 1969, 2nd edition, 1986. Editor: Modern Science Fiction: Its Meaning and Its Future, 1953, 2nd edition, 1979; Science Fiction, Today and Tomorrow, 1974; The Craft of Science Fiction, 1976; The Future of War, 3 volumes, 1978-80; Of Force and Violence and Other Imponderables, 1992; One Man's BEM: Thoughts on Science Fiction, 1993. Contributions to: Periodicals. Memberships: Military Conflict Institute; National Rifle Association; Science Fiction Writers of America; Writers Guild of America. Address: PO Box 1481, Medford, OR 97501, USA.

BRETT Jan (Churchill), b. 1 Dec 1949, Bryn Mawr, Pennsylvania, USA. Illustrator and Writer of Children's Books. m. Joseph Hearne, 18 Aug 1980, 1 daughter. Education: Colby Junior College, 1968-69; Boston Museum School, 1970. Publications: Illustrator and/or Writer of more than 25 children's books. Honours: Outstanding Science Trade Book for Children, National Science Teachers Association, 1984; Children's Book Award, University of Nebraska, 1984; Top Ten Children's Book Award of the Year, Redbook Magazine, 1985; Booklist Magazine Editor's Choice, American Library Association, 1986. Membership: Society of Children's Book Writers. Address: 132 Pleasant Street, Norwell, MA 02061, USA.

BRETT John Michael. See: TRIPP Miles Barton.

BRETT Mary Elizabeth, (Molly Brett), b. England. Artist; Writer. Publications: Teddy Flies Away, Midget and the Pet Shop, 1969; Jiggy's Treasure Hunt, 1973 The Party That Grew, 1976; Jumble Bears, 1977; The Molly Brett Picture Book, 1978; An Alphabet by Molly Brett, 1980; The Runaway Fairy, 1982; Good-Night Time Tales, 1982; Plush and Tatty on the Beach, 1987; The Magic Spectacles, 1987. Address: Chimes Cottage, Horsell Vale, Woking, Surrey, England.

BRETT Michael. See: TRIPP Miles Barton.

BRETT Raymond (Laurence), b. 10 Jan 1917, Bristol, England. Emeritus Professor of English; Writer. Education: BA, University of Bristol, 1937; BLitt, University College, Oxford, 1940. Appointments: Lecturer in English, University of Bristol, 1946-52; G F Grant Professor of English, 1952-82, Dean, Faculty of Arts, 1960-82, Emeritus Professor, 1982-, Honorary DLitt, University of Hull; General Editor, Writers and Their Background Series. Publications: The Third Earl of Shaftsbury, 1952; George Crabbe, 1956, revised edition, 1968; Reason and Imagination, 1960; An Introduction to English Studies, 1965; Poems of Faith and Doubt, 1965; Lyrical Ballads by Wordsworth and Coleridge, 1798-1805 (with A R Jones), 3rd edition, 1968, 4th edition, 1991; Fancy and Imagination, 1969; S T Coleridge, 1971; William Hazlitt, 1977; Andrew Marvell Tercentenary Essays, 1979; Barclay Fox's Journal, 1979; Coleridge, 1980. Address: 19 Mill Walk, Cottingham, East Yorkshire HU16 4RP, England.

BRETT Simon Anthony Lee, b. 28 Oct 1945, Surrey, England. Writer. m. Lucy Victoria McLaren, 27 Nov 1971, 2 sons, 1 daughter. Education: BA Hons, English (1st Class), Wadham College, Oxford, 1963-67. Appointments: Chairman, Crime Writers' Assocation, 1986-87; Chairman, Society of Authors, 1995-97. Publications: 16 Charles Paris Crime Novels, 1975-95; 5 Mrs Pargeter Crime Novels, 1986-96; Editor, Faber Books of Useful Verse, Parodies, Diaries; A Shock To The System, 1984; Dead Romantic, 1985; The Booker Book, 1989; How to Be A Little Sod, 1992; After Henry (Radio and TV Series), 1985-92; Singled Out, 1995. Honours: Best Radio Feature, Writers' Guild, 1973; Outstanding Radio Programme, Broadcasting Press Guild, 1987. Memberships: Crime Writers' Association; Detection Club; PEN; Writers Guild; Society of Authors. Literary Agent: Michael Motley. Address: Frith House, Burpham, Arundel, West Sussex BN18 9RR, England.

BREW (Osborne Henry) Kwesi, b. 1928, Cape Coast, Ghana. Ambassador; Poet. Education: BA, University College of the Gold Coast, Legon, 1953. Appointments: Former Ambassador for Ghana to Britain, India, France, USSR, Germany and Mexico. Publications: The Shadows of Laughter, 1968; Pergamon Poets 2: Poetry from Africa, 1968; African Panorama, 1981; Screenplay: The Harvest. Honours: British Council Prize. Address: c/o Greenfield Review Press, PO Box 80, Greenfield Center, NY 12833, USA.

BREWER Derek Stanley, b. 13 July 1923, Cardiff, Wales. Acedemic; Emeritus Professor. m. Lucie Elisabeth Hoole, 17 Aug 1951, 3 sons, 2 daughters. Education: Magdalen College, Oxford, 1941-42, 1945-48; BA, MA, (Oxon), 1948; PhD, Birmingham University, 1956; LittD, Cambridge University, 1980. Appointments: Master, Emmanuel College, Cambridge, 1977-90; Editor, The Cambridge Review, 1981-86. Publications: Chaucer, 1953; Proteus, 1958; The Parlement of Foulys, editor, 1960; Chaucer: The Critical Heritage, 1978; Chaucer and his World, 1978, reprinted, 1992; Symbolic Stories, 1980, reprinted, 1988; English Gothic Literature, 1983; Chaucer: An Introduction, 1984; Medieval Comic Tales (editor), 1996; Books and articles on Chaucer, Malory and other authors, mediaeval to nineteenth century. Address: Emmanuel College, Cambridge, England.

BREWSTER Elizabeth (Winifred), b. 26 Aug 1922, Chipman, New Brunswick, Canada. Professor Emeritus of English; Poet; Novelist. Education: BA, University of New Brunswick, 1946; MA, Radcliffe College, Cambridge, Massachusetts, 1947; BLS, University of Toronto, 1953; PhD, Indiana University, 1962. Appointments: Faculty, Department of English, University of Victoria, 1960-61; Reference Librarian, Mt Allison University, 1961-65; Visiting Assistant Professor of English, University of Alberta, 1970-71; Assistant Professor, 1972-75, Associate Professor, 1975-80, Professor, 1980-90, Professor Emeritus, 1990-, of English, University of Saskatchewan. Publications: East Coast, 1951; Lilooet, 1954; Roads, 1957; Passage of Summer: Selected Poems, 1969; Sunrise North, 1972; In Search of Eros, 1974; The Sisters, 1974; It's Easy to Fall on the Ice, 1977; Sometimes I Think of Moving, 1977; Digging In, 1982; Junction, 1982; The Way Home, 1982; A House Full of Women, 1983; Selected Poems of Elizabeth Brewster, 1944-1984, 1985; Entertaining Angels, 1988; Spring Again, 1990; The Invention of Truth, 1991; Wheel of Change, 1993; Footnotes to the Book of Job, 1995; Away from Home (autobiography), 1995. Honours: E J Pratt Award for Poetry, University of Toronto, 1953; President's Medal for Poetry, University of Western Ontario, 1980; Honorary LittD, University of New Brunswick, 1982; Canada Council Award, 1985; Lifetime Award for Excellence in the Arts, Saskatchewan Arts Board, 1995; Shortlisted, Governor General's Award for Poetry, 1996. Memberships: League of Canadian Poets; Writers' Union of Canada; Saskatchewan Writers' Guild; PEN. Address: 206, 910-9th Street East, Saskatoon, Saskatchewan S7H 0N1, Canada.

BREWSTER Robin. See: STAPLES Reginald Thomas.

BREYTENBACH Breyten, b. 16 Sept 1939, Bonnievale, South Africa. Poet. Education: Graduated, University of Cape Town, 1959. Appointments: Founder, Okhela anti-apartheid group. Publications: The Iron Cow Must Sweat, 1964; House of the Deaf, 1967; Gangrene, 1969; Lotus, 1970; To Paint a Sinking Ship Blue, 1972; In Other Words: Fruits From the Dream of Silence, 1973; Flower Writing, 1977; Sinking Ship Blues, 1977; And Death White as Words: Anthology, 1978; In Africa Even the Flies are Happy: Selected Poems 1964-1977; Fingermoon: Drawings from Pretoria; Eclipse, 1983; Lewendood, 1985; Other: Catastrophes, 1980; Memory of Snow and Dust, 1980; Season in Paradise, 1980; Mouroir: Mirrornotes of a Novel, 1984; The True Confession of an Albino Terrorist, 1984; End Papers, 1986; Judas Eye, Self Portrait, Deathwatch, 1988; All One Horse, 1990. Honours: Rapport Prize, 1986. Address: c/o Faber and Faber Ltd, 3 Queen Square, London WC1N 3AU, England.

BREZHNEV Dennis. See: BARNETT Paul le Page.

BRIARTON Grendel. See: BRETNOR Reginald.

BRICKLEBANK Peter Noel, b. 19 Oct 1955, Leeds, England. Writer. Education: BA, Communication Studies (Hons), Sheffield Polytechnic, 1977; MA, Literature, City College of New York, USA, 1985. Contributions to: Fiction: American Voice; Carolina Quarterly; Confrontation; Kansas Quarterly; Mid-American Review; Webster Review; Writers' Forum; Crescent Review; Descant; Alaska Quarterly; Queens' Quarterly, Canada; Non-fiction: American Book Reivew; Another Chicago Magazine; Minnesota Review. Honours: Betram D Wolfe Memorial Creative Writing Award, City University of New York, 1985; Nomination, Pushcart Prize, 1989; Fellowship in Fiction, New York Foundation for the Arts, 1990. Address: 1803 Riverside Drive, 2J, New York, NY 10034, USA.

BRICKNER Richard P(ilpel), b. 14 May 1933, New York, USA. Writer; Teacher. Education: Middlebury College, 1951-53; BA, Columbia College, 1957. Appointments: Adjunct in Writing, City College of the City University of New York, 1967-70; Faculty, Writing Program, New School of Social Research, New York City, 1970-. Publications: Novels: The Broken Year, 1962; Bringing Down the House, 1972; Tickets, 1981; After She Left, 1988. Non-Fiction: My Second Twenty Years, 1976. Contributions to: American Review; Life; New Leader; New York Times Book Review; Time. Honours: National Endowment for the Arts Grant, 1974; Guggenheim Fellowship, 1983. Address: 245 East 72nd Street, New York, NY 10021, USA.

BRIDGEMAN Harriet (Victoria Lucy) (Viscountess), b. 30 Mar 1942. Director, The Bridgeman Art Library, London and New York; Author. Education: MA, Trinity College, Dublin. Publications: The British Eccentric, 1974; An Encyclopaedia of Victoriana, 1975; Society Scandals, 1976; Beside the Seaside, 1976; Needlework: An Illustrated History, 1978; A Guide to Gardens of Europe, 1979; The Last Word, 1983. Address: 19 Chepstow Road, London W2 5BP, England.

BRIDWELL Norman (Ray), b. 15 Feb 1928, Kokomo, Indiana, USA. Children's Writer; Artist. Education: John Herron Art Institute, Indianapolis, 1945-49; Cooper Union Art School, New York, 1953-54. Publications: Clifford the Big Red Dog, 1962; Bird in the Hat, 1964; The Witch Next Door, 1965; The Country Cat, 1969; What Do They Do When It Rains, 1969; The Witch's Christmas, 1970; Clifford the Small Red Puppy, 1972; Monster Holidays, 1974; Clifford's Good Deeds, 1974; Clifford at the Circus, 1977; The Witch Grows Up, 1979; Clifford Goes to Hollywood, 1980; Clifford's Kitten, 1984; Clifford's Birthday Party, 1988; Clifford We Love You, 1991; Clifford's Animal Noises, 1991; Clifford's Thanksgiving Visit, 1993; Clifford's Happy Easter, 1994; Clifford The Firehouse Dog, 1994; Clifford The Puppy's First Christmas, 1994. Honours: Jeremiah Ludington Memorial Award, 1991; Honorary Doctor of Humane Letters, Indiana University, 1994. Address: Box 869, Edgartown, MA 02539, USA.

BRIEN Alan, b. 12 Mar 1925, Sunderland, England. Novelist; Journalist. m. (1) Pamela Mary Jones, 1947, 3 daughters, (2)Nancy Newbold Ryan, 1 son. 1 daughter, 1961, (3)Jill Sheila Tweedie, 1973. Education: BA, English Literature, Jesus College, Oxford. Appointments: Associate Editor, Mini-Cinema, 1950-52; Courier, 1952-53; Film Critic, Columnist, Truth, 1953-54; TV Critic, Observer, 1954-55; Film Critic, 1954-56, New York Correspondent, 1956-58, Evening Standard; Drama Critic, Features Editor, Spectator, 1958-61; Columnist, Sunday Daily Mail, 1958-62; Sunday Dispatch, 1962-63; Political Columnist, Sunday Pictorial, 1963-64; Drama Critic, Sunday Telegraph, 1964-67; Columnist, Spectator, 1963-65; New Statesman, 1966-72; Punch, 1972-84; Diarist, 1967-75; Film Critic, 1976-84, Sunday Times. Publications: Domes of Fortune, 1979; Lenin: the Novel, 1986; Heaven's Will (novel), 1989; And When Rome Falls (novel), 1991. Contributions to: Various professional journals. Address: 14 Falkland Road, London NW5, England.

BRIERLEY David, b. 30 July 1936, Durban, South Africa. Author. m. Caroline Gordon Walker, 23 April 1960, 1 daughter. Education; BA, Honours, Oxon. Publications: Cold War, 1979; Blood Group O, 1980; Big Bear, Little Bear, 1981; Shooting Star, 1983; Czechmate, 1984; Skorpion's Death, 1985; Snowline, 1986; One Lives, One Dies, 1987; On Leaving a Prague Window, 1995; The Horizontal Woman, 1996. Literary Agent: James Hale. Address: La Vieille Ferme, 24170 St-Germain-de Belvès, France.

BRIGGS Asa (Baron), b. 7 May 1921, Keighley, Yorkshire, England. m. Susan Anne Banwell, 1955, 2 sons, 2 daughters. Education: 1st Class History Tripos, Parts I and II, Sidney Sussex College, Cambridge, 1941; BSc, 1st Class (Economics), London, 1941. Publications: Victorian People, 1954; The Age of Improvement, 1959; History of Broadcasting in the United Kingdom, 5 volumes, 1961-95; Victorian Cities, 1963; A Social History of England, 1983, new edition, 1994; Victorian Things, 1988. Honours: Marconi Medal for Communications History, 1975; Life Peerage, 1976; Medaille de Vermeil de la Formation, Foundation de l'Academie d'Architecture, 1979; 20 Honorary Degrees. Memberships: British Academy, fellow; American Academy of Arts and Sciences; Social History Society, president. Address: The Caprons, Keere Street, Lewes BN7 1TY, England.

BRIGGS Raymond Redvers, b. 18 Jan 1934, Wimbledon, London, England. Illustrator; Writer; Cartoonist. m. Jean T Clark, 1963,

dec 1973. Education: Wimbledon School of Art; Slade School of Fine Art, London, NDD; DFA; FSIAD. Appointments: Freelance illustrator, 1957-; Children's author, 1961-. Publications: Midnight Adventure, 1961;Ring-a-Ring o'Roses, 1962; The Strange House, 1963; Sledges to the Rescue, 1963; The White Land, 1963; Fee Fi Fo Fum, 1964; The Mother Goose Treasury, 1966; Jim and the Beanstalk, 1970; The Fairy Tale Treausry, 1975; Fungus the Bogeyman, 1977; The Snowman, 1978; Gentleman Jim, 1980; When the Wind Blows, 1982, stage and radio versions, 1983; The Tinpot Foreign General & the Old Iron Woman, 1984; Unlucky Wally, 1987; Unlucky Wally, Twenty Years On, 1989; The Man, 1992. Honours: Kate Greenaway Medals, 1966, 1973; British Academy of Film and Television Arts Award. Address: Weston, Underhill Lane, Westmeston, Near Hassocks, Sussex BN6 8XG, England.

BRIN David, b. 6 Oct 1950, Glendale, California, USA. Author; Book Reviewer; Science Editor. Education: BS, California Institute of Technology, 1972; MS, 1979, PhD, 1981, University of California at San Diego; Post-doctoral Research Fellow, California Space Institute, La Jolla, 1982-84. Appointment: Book Reviewer and Science Editor, Heritage Press, Los Angeles, 1980-. Publications: Sundiver, 1980; Startide Rising, 1983; The Practice Effect, 1984; The Postman, 1985; Heart of the Comet (with Gregory Benford), 1986; The River of Time (short stories), 1986; The Uplift War, 1987; Earth, 1990; The Glory Season, 1993. Contributions to: Scientific journals and popular periodicals. Honours: Locus Awards, 1984, 1986; Nebula Award, 1984; Hugo Awards, 1984, 1986; John W Campbell Memorial Award, 1986. Address: 5081 Baxter Street, San Diego, CA 92117, USA.

BRINGHURST Robert, b. 16 Oct 1946, Los Angeles, California, USA. Poet. Education: BA, Indiana University, 1973; MFA, University of British Columbia, 1975. Appointments: General Editor, Kanchenjunga Poetry Series, 1973-79; Visiting Lecturer, Creative Writing, 1975-77; Lecturer, University of British Columbia, 1979-80; Reviews Editor, Canadian Fiction Magazine, 1974-75; Adjunct Lecturer, Simon Fraser University, 1983-84; Contributing Editor, Fine Print, A Review for the Arts of the Book, 1985-90; Writer-in-Residence, University of winnipeg, 1986, University of Edinburgh, 1989-90; Ashley Fellow, Trent University, Ontario, 1994. Publications: The Shipwright's Log, 1972; Cadastre, 1973; Bergschrund, 1975; The Stonecutter's Horses, 1979; The Beauty of the Weapons: Selected Poems, 1972-82, 1982; Tending the Fire, 1985; Ocean, Paper, Stone, 1984; The Blue Roofs of Japan, 1986; The Raven Steals the Light, 1986; Pieces of Map, Pieces of Music, 1987; The Black Canoe, 1991, 2nd edition, 1992; The Elements of Typographic Style, 1992, 2nd edition, 1996; The Calling: Selected Poems, 1970-1995, 1995; A Story as Sharp as a Knife: An Introduction to Classical Haida Literature, 1996. Honours: Macmillan Prize, 1975; Canada Council Grants; Ontario Arts Council Literary Grant; Alcuin Society Design Award, 1984, 85; Canadian Broadcasting Corporation Poetry Prize, 1985; Guggenheim Fellowship, 1987-88. Address: Box 357, 1917 West 4th Ave, Vancouver, BC, V6J 1M7, Canada.

BRINK Andre Philippus, b. 29 May 1935, Vrede, South Africa. Professor. Education: DLitt, Rhodes University; DLitt (honoris causa) University of the Witwatersrand. Publications: Lobola vir die Lewe, 1962; File on a diplomat, 1966; Mapmakers (essays), 1973; Looking on Darkness, 1974; An Instant in The Wind, 1976; Rumours of Rain, 1978; A Dry White Season, 1979; A Chain of Voices, 1982; The Wall of the Plague, 1984; The Ambassador, 1985; A Land Apart, 1986; States of Emergency, 1988; An Act of Terror, 1991; The First Life of Adamastor, 1993; On the Contrary, 1993; Imaginings of Sand, 1996; Reinventing a Continent (essays), 1996. Contributions to: World Literature Today; Theatre Quartely; Standpunte. Honours: Reina Prinsen Geerlings Prize, 1964; CNA Awards, Twentieth Century Literature, 1965, 1978, 1982; Academy Prize for Prose Translation, 1970; Martin Luther King Memorial Prize, 1980; Prix Medics Etranger, 1980; Chevalier de la Legion d'Honneur, 1982; Commandeur de l'Ordre des Arts et des Lettres, 1992. Address: Department of English, University of Cape Town, Rondebosch 7700, South Africa.

BRINKLEY Alan, b. 2 June 1949, Washington, District of Columbia, USA. Historian. m. Evangeline Morphos, 3 June 1989. Education: AB, Princeton University, 1971;PhD, Harvard University, 1979. Appointments: Assistant Professor of History, Massachusetts Institute of Technology, 1978-82; Dunwalke Associate Professor of American History, Harvard University, 1982-88; Professor of History, City University of New York Graduate School, 1988-91; Professor of History, Columbia University, 1991-. Publications: The Unfinished

Nation: A Concise History of the American People, 1993; Voices of Protest: Huey Long, Father Coughlin, and the Great Depression, 1982; America in the Twentieth Century, 1982; American History: A Survey, 1990. Honours: National Book Award for History, 1983; Guggenheim Fellowship, 1984-85; Woodrow Wilson Center Fellowship, 1985; National Humanities Center Fellowship, 1988-89. Memberships: Executive Board, Society of American Historians; Executive Board, Organization of American Historians. Address: 15 West 81st Street, New York, NY 10024, USA.

BRINKLEY Douglas (Gregg), b. 14 Dec 1960, Atlanta, Georgia, USA. Professor of History; Author. Education: BA, Ohio State University, 1982; MA, 1983, PhD, 1989, Georgetown University. Appointments: Instructor, US Naval Academy, 1987; Visiting Research Fellow, Woodrow Wilson School of Public Policy and International Affairs, 1987-88; Lecturer, Princeton University, 1988; Assistant Professor of History, Hofstra University, 1989-93; Visiting Associate Director, 1993-94, Director, 1994-, Eisenhower Center for American Studies, Associate Professor of History, 1993-96, Professor of History, 1997-, University of New Orleans. Publications: Jean Monnet: The Path of European Unity (editor with Clifford Hackett), 1991; The Atlantic Charter (editor with D Facey-Crowther), 1992; Dean Acheson: The Cold War Years, 1953-1971, 1992; Driven Patriot: The Life and Times of James Forrestal (with Townsend Hoopes), 1992; Dean Acheson and the Making of US Foreign Policy (editor), 1993; Theodore Roosevelt: The Many-Sided American (editor with Gable and Naylor), 1993; The Majic Bus: An American Odyssey, 1993; Franklin Roosevelt and the Creation of the United Nations (with Townsend Hoopes), 1997; John F Kennedy and Europe (editor), 1997; Strategies pf Enlargement: The Clinton Doctrine and US Foreign Policy, 1997; Jimmy Carter: The Post-Presidential Years, 1997; Hunter S Thompson: The Proud Highway: Saga of a Desperate Southern Gentleman 1955-1967, editor, 1997; American Heritage's The New History of the United States, 1998; Jimmy Carter: From Plains to the White House, 1924-76, 1998. Contributions to: Books and scholarly journals. Honours: New York Times Notable Book of the Year (twice), 1993, 1993; Stessin Award for Distinguished Scholarship, Hofstra University, 1993; Theodore and Franklin Roosevelt Naval History Prize, 1993; Bernath Lecture Prize 1996; Honorary Doctorate in Humanities, Trinity College, Connecticut, 1997. Memberships: Theodore Roosevelt Association; Franklin and Eleanor Roosevelt Institute; Century Association; National D-Day Museum. Literary Agent: International Creative Management. Address: c/o Eisenhower Center for American Studies, University of New Orleans, New Orleans, LA 70148, USA.

BRINTON Alexander. See: **BATTIN B W.**

BRISCO Patty. See: **MATTHEWS Patricia Anne.**

BRISKIN Jacqueline, b. 18 Dec 1927, London, England. Novelist; Short Story Writer. m. Bert Briskin, 2 sons, 1 daughter. Education: University of California at Los Angeles, 1946-47. Publications: California Generation, 1970; Afterlove, 1974; Rich Friends, 1976; Paloverde, 1978; The Onyx, 1982; Everything and More, 1983; Too Much Too Soon, 1985; Dreams Are Not Enough, 1987; The Naked Heart, 1989; The Other Side of Love, 1991. Memberships: PEN; Author's Guild. Address: Los Angeles, California, USA.

BRISKIN Mae Seidman, b. 20 Oct 1924, Brooklyn, New York, USA. Writer. m. Herbert B Briskin, 1 Dec 1946, 2 sons, 1 daughter. Education: BA, Brooklyn College, 1944; MA, Columbia University, 1946. Publications: A Boy Like Astrid's Mother, 1988; The Tree Still Stands, 1991. Contributions to: Numerous. Honours: Best American Short Stories, 1976; PEN, Syndicated Fiction Awards, 1985-88; Award for Collection of Short Fiction, 1989. Membership: PEN. Literary Agent: Ellen Levine. Address: 3604 Arbutus Drive, Palo Alto, CA 94303, USA.

BRISTOW Robert O'Neil, b. 17 Nov 1926, St Louis, Missouri, USA. Author. m. Gaylon Walker, 23 Dec 1950, 2 sons, 2 daughters. Education: BA, 1951, MA, 1965, University of Oklahoma. Appointments: Writer in Residence, Winthrop College, South Carolina, 1961-87. Publications: Time for Glory, 1968; Night Season, 1970; A Faraway Drummer, 1973; Laughter in Darkness, 1974. Contributions to: Approximately 200 Short Stories to Magazines and Journals. Honours: Award for Literary Excellence, 1969; Friends of American Writer's Award, 1974. Address: 613 1/2 Charlotte Avenue, Rock Hill, SC 29730, USA.

BRITTAN Samuel, b. 29 Dec 1933, London, England. Journalist. Education: 1st Class Honours, Economics, Jesus College, Cambridge; Research Fellow, Nuffield College, 1973-74. Appointments: Various posts, 1955-61, Principal Economic Commentator, 1966-, Assistant Editor, 1978-, Financial Times, London; Economics Editor, The Observer, 1961-64. Publications: Steering the Economy, 3rd Edition, 1971; Left or Right - The Bogus Dilemma, 1968; The Price of Economic Freedom: A Guide to Flexible Rates, 1970; Is There an Economic Consensus?, 1973; Capitalism and the Permissive Society, 1973, new edition, 1988; Second Thoughts on Full Employments Policy, 1975; The Delusion of Incomes Policy (with Peter Lilley), 1977; The Economic Consequences of Democracy, 1977; How British is the British Sickness?, 1978; How to End the "Monetarist" Controversy, 1981; Role and Limits of Government: Essays in Political Economy, 1983; Jobs, Pay Unions and the Ownership of Capital, 1984; Two Cheers for Self-Interest, 1985; Capitalism with a Human Face, 1994. Honours: Senior Wincott Award for Financial Journalists, 1971; Elected Visiting Fellow, Nuffield College, 1974; George Orwell Prize for Political Journalism, 1981; Honorary DLitt, Heriot-Watt University, 1985; Peacock Committee on the Finance of the BBC, 1985-86; Legion D'Honneur, 1993; Knighted, 1993; Doctor of Essex University, 1994. Address: The Financial Times, Number One Southwark Bridge, London SE1 9HL, England.

BRITTON David, b. 18 Feb 1945, Manchester, England. Writer; Publisher. Education: Mount Carmel, Corpus Christie, 1950-66. Appointment: Editor, Savoy Books, 1975-. Publications: Lord Horror, 1990; Motherfuckers, 1996; The Adventures of Meng and Ecker, 1996. Contributions to: New Worlds; The Independent; The Times. Honour: Winner, Frank Randel Literary Award, 1991. Literary Agent: Giles Gordon. Address: 615b Wilbraham Road, Chorlton, Manchester M16 8EW, England.

BROCK Edwin, b. 19 Oct 1927, Dulwich, England. Writer; Poet; Editor. Education: Grammar School, Dulwich. Appointments: Advertising Writer, 1959-88; Poetry Editor, Ambit magazine, London, 1960-. Publications: An Attempt at Exorcism, 1959; Night Duty on Eleven Beat, radio play, 1960; A Family Affair: Two Sonnet Sequences, 1960; The Little White God, novel, 1962, televised, 1964; With Love from Judas, 1963; Penguin Modern Poets 8, co-author, 1966; Fred's Primer: A Little Girl's Guide to the World Around Her, 1969; A Cold Day at the Zoo, 1970; Invisibility is the Art of Survival: Selected Poems, 1973; Paroxisms, 1974; I Never Saw it Lit, 1974; The Blocked Heart, 1975; Song of Battery Hen: Selected Poems, 1959-1975, 1977; Here, Now, Always, autobiography, 1977; The River and the Train, 1979; Five Ways to Kill a Man: New and Selected Poems, 1990. Address: The Granary, Lower Tharston, Norfolk NR15 2YN, England.

BROCK Rose. See:**HANSEN Joseph.**

BROCK William Ranulf, b. 16 May 1916, Farnham, Surrey, England. University Teacher (retired). m. Constance Helen Brown, 8 July 1950, 1 son, 1 daughter. Education: BA, 1937, MA, 1945, PhD, 1941, Tinity College, Cambridge. Appointments: Fellow, Selwyn College, Cambridge; Professor of Modern History, University of Glasgow, 1967-81. Publications: Lord Liverpool and Liberal Toryism, 1941; Character of American History, 1960; An American Crisis, 1963; Conflict and Transformation: USA 1944-77, 1973, USA 1739-1870 (Sources of History), 1975; Parties and Political Conscience (USA 1840-52), 1979; Evolution of American Democracy, 1979; Scotus Americanus (Scotland and American, 15th C), 1981; Investigation and Responsibility (State Agencies in USA), 1984; Welfare, Democracy and the New Deal, 1988; Selwyn College: A History (with P H M Cooper), 1994. Memberships: Fellow, British Academy; Fellow, Royal Historical Society; British Association of American Studies (Founder member, Committee, 1954-64); Organization of American Historians. Address: 49 Barton Road, Cambridge CB3 9LG, England.

BROCKHOFF Stefan. See: **PLANT Richard.**

BRODERICK Damien (Francis), b. 22 Apr 1944, Australia. Writer. Education: BA, Monash University, 1966; PhD, Deakin University, 1990. Appointments: Writer-in-Residence, Deakin University, 1986. Publications: A Man Returned (stories), 1965; The Zeitgeist Machine (editor), 1977; The Dreaming Dragons, 1980; The Judas Mandala, 1982, revised edition, 1990; Valencies (with Rory Barnes), 1983; Transmitters, 1984; Strange Attractors (editor), 1985; The Black Grail, 1986; Striped Holes, 1988; Matilda at the Speed of

Light (editor), 1988; The Dark Between the Stars (stories), 1991; The Lotto Effect, 1992; The Sea's Furthest End, 1993; The Architecture of Babel: Discourses of Literature and Science, 1994; Reading by Starlight: Postmodern Science Fiction, 1995; The White Abacus, 1997; Zones (with Rory Barnes), 1997; Theory and its Discontents, 1997; The Spike, 1997. Contributions to periodicals; Regular science book reviewer, Weekend Australian newspaper. Honours: Australian Science Fiction Achievement Awards, 1981, 1985, 1989.

BRODEUR Hélène, b. 13 July 1923, Val Racine, Quebec, Canada. Civil Servant retired; Writer. m. Robert L Nantais, 26 Aug 1947, 3 sons, 2 daughters. Education: 1st Class Teacher's Certificate, Ottawa University Normal School, 1940; BA, Ottawa University, 1946; Diploma in Senior Management, Canadian Government College, 1974. Appointments: Writer-in-Residence, Ottawa University, 1991; Visiting Professor, French Creative Writing, Ottawa University. Publications: Chroniques du Nouvel-Ontario, Volume 1, La quête d'Alexandre, 1981, Volume 2, Entre l'aube et le jour, 1983,Volume 3, Les routes incertaines, 1986, L'Ermitage, 1996; Alexander, 1983; Rose-Delima, 1987; The Honourable Donald, 1990; Miniseries for Television: Les Ontariens, 1983. Contributions to: Extension Magazine, 1968; A serial, Murder in the Monastery. Honours: Champlain Award, 1981; Le Droit Award, 1983; Prix du Nouvel-Ontario, 1984. Memberships: Ontario Authors Association; Union des écrivains; PEN International; Press Club. Address: 1506 160 George Street, Ottawa K1N 9M2, Canada.

BRODEUR Paul (Adrian, Jr), b. 16 May 1931, Boston, Massachusetts, USA. Writer. Div, 1 son, 1 daughter. Education: BA, Harvard College, 1953. Appointments: Lecturer, Columbia University Graduate School of Journalism, 1969-80, Boston University School of Public Communications, 1978-79, University of California at San Diego, 1989; Staff Writer, The New Yorker magazine, 1958-66. Publications: The Sick Fox, 1963; The Stunt Man, 1970; Downstream, 1972; Expendable Americans, 1974; The Zapping of America, 1977; Outrageous Misconduct, 1985; Restitution, 1985; Currents of Death, 1989; The Great Power-Line Coverup, 1993; Secrets, 1997. Contributions to: The New Yorker magazine. Honours: Sidney Hillman Prize, 1973; Columbia University National Magazine Award, 1973; American Association for the Advancement of Science Award, 1976; Guggenheim Fellowship, 1976-77; Alicia Patterson Foundation Fellowship, 1978; American Bar Association Certificate of Merit, 1983; Global 500 Honor Roll, 1989. Address: c/o The New Yorker, 20 West 43rd Street, New York, NY 10036, USA.

BROGGER Suzanne, b. 18 Nov 1944, Copenhagen, Denmark. Novelist. m. Keld Zeruneith, 1991. Education: University of Copenhagen. Appointments: Journalist in the Middle East and former Soviet Union. Publications: Deliver us from Love, 1973; Yes, 1984; The Pepper Whistle: Floating Fragments and Fixations, 1986; My World in a Nutshell, 1991; Play: After the Orgy, 1991; Verse: Tone, Epos, 1981; Edward and Elvira: A Ballad, 1988; Also: The Right and Wrong Ways of Love, 1991; Créme Fraiche, 1978; A Pig that's been Fighting Can't be Roasted, 1979; Brew: 1965-80; A Greenland-Essay and Three Other Poems, 1982; Nitrogen: 1980-1990. Honour: Gabor Prize, 1987. Address: Knudstrup Gl Skole, 4270 Hong, Denmark.

BROME (Herbert) Vincent. British. Author. Publications: Anthology, 1936; Clement Attlee, 1947; H G Wells, 1951; Aneurin Bevan, 1953; The Ist Surrender, 1954; The Way Back, 1956; Six Studies in Quarrelling, 1958; Sometimes at Night, 1959; Frank Harris, 1959; Acquaintance with Grief, 1961; We Have Come a Long Way, 1962; The Problems of Progress, 1963; Love in our Time, 1964; Four Realist Novelists, 1964; The International Brigades, 1965; The World of Luke Jympson, 1966; Freud and His Early Circle, 1967; The Sugeon, 1967; Dairy of a Revolution, 1968; The Revolution, 1969; The Imaginary Crime, 1969; Confessions of a Writer, 1970; The Brain Operators, 1970; Private Prosecutions, 1971; Reverse Your Verdict, 1971; London Consequences, 1972; The Embassy, 1972; The Day of Destruction, 1975; The Happy Hostage, 1976; Jung - Man and Myth, 1978; Havelock Ellis - Philosopher of Sex, 1981; Ernest Jones: Freud's Alter Ego,1983; The Day of the Fifth Moon, 1984; J B Priestly, 1988. Contibutions to: The Times; Sunday Times; Observer; Manchester Guardian; New Statesman; New Society; Encounter; Spectator; Times Literary Supplement. Address: 45 Great Ormond Street, London, WC1. England.

BROMIGE David (Mansfield), b. 22 Oct 1933, London, England(Canadian citizen, 1961). Poet and Storyteller; Professor of English. m. 1 son, 1 daughter. Education: BA, University of British Columbia, 1962; MA, 1964, ABD, 1969, University of California at Berkeley. Appointments: Poetry Editor, Northwest Review, 1962-64; Instructor, University of California at Berkeley, 1965-69; Lecturer, California College of Arts and Crafts, 1969; Professor of English, Sonoma State University, California, 1970-93; Contributing editor, Avec, Penngrove, 1986-, Kaimana, Honolulu, 1989-. Publications: The Gathering, 1965; Please, Like Me, 1968; The Ends of the Earth, 1968; The Quivering Roadway, 1969; Threads, 1970; Ten Years in the Making, 1973; Three Stories, 1973; Birds of the West, 1974; Out of My Hands, 1974; Spells and Blessings, 1974; Tight Corners and What's Around Them, 1974; Credences of Winter, 1976; Living in Advance, 1976; My Poetry, 1980; P-E-A-C-E, 1981; In the Uneven Steps of Hung Chow, 1982; It's the Same Only Different, 1984; The Melancholy Owed Categories, 1984; You See, 1985; Red Hats, 1986; Desire, 1988; Men, Women and Vehicles, 1990; Tiny Courts in a World Without Scales, 1991; They Ate, 1992; The Harbormaster of Hong Kong, 1993; A Cast of Tens, 1994; Romantic Traceries, 1994; From the First Century, 1995. Contributions to anthologies including: In the American Tree, 1985; 49+1, 1991; Likely Stories, 1992; Fifty, 1993. Contributions to many periodicals including: Avec, Partisan Review, Hudson Review, This. Honours: Macmillan Poetry Prize, 1957-59; Poet Laureate, University of California (all campuses), 1965; Discovery Award, 1969; Poetry Fellowship, 1980; National Endowment for the Arts; Canada Council Grant in Poetry, 1976-77; Pushcart Prize in Poetry, 1980; Western States Arts Federation Prize in Poetry, 1988; Gertrude Stein Award in Innovative Writing, 1994. Address: 461 High Street, Sebastopol, CA 95472, USA.

BRONISLAWSKI Jerzy-Stanislaw (Kudas), b. 7 May 1930, Lodz, Poland. Editor; Writer. m. Zebina Sobczynska, 18 Dec 1968, 1 son, 1 daughter. Education: MSc, Faculty of Law, 1970, PhD, Institute of Political Science, 1972, Adam Mickiewicz University. Appointments: Editor, Iskry, Warsaw, 1967-74, Mon, Warsaw, 1969-74, Maw, Warsaw, 1974-84, OPZZ, Warsaw, 1985-86, Pojezzierze, Olsztyn, 1987-. Publications: The Invisible in the Crowd, 1967; Before They Come at Daybreak, 1969; Sabres and Usurers, 1970; Mr Bailey's Mistake, 1970; The Anatomy of Treason, 1971; The Alienated, 1972; Life Without Safeguard, 1975; The Master of the Empty House, 1978; Without Scruples, 1979; Mazurian Saga, 1980; The False Prophets, 1981; The Furtively Observed Land, 1987; Polish Dialogue, 1990. Contributions to: Periodicals. Honours: R Urban Award, 1977; Zycie Literackie Award, 1978; Polityka Awards, 1983, 1992; J Iwaszkiewicz Award, 1990. Memberships: Polish Writers Association; Society of Authors. Address: ul Powsinska 70m, 48, 02-903 Warsaw, Poland.

BRONK William, b. 17 Feb 1918, Ft Edward, New York, USA. Poet; Essayist. Publications: Light & Dark, 1956; The World, The Worldless, 1964; The Empty Hands, 1969; That Tantalus, 1971; To Praise the Music, 1972; Utterances, 1972; Looking at It, 1973; The New World, 1974; A Partial Glossary, 1974; Silence and Metaphor, 1975; The Stance, 1975; My Father Photographed with Friends and Other Pictures, 1976; The Meantime, 1976; Finding Losses, 1976; Twelve Losses Found, 1976; That Beauty Still, 1978; The Force of Desire, 1979; Six Duplicities, 1980; The Brother in Elysium, 1980; Life Supports, 1981; Light in a Dark Sky, 1982; Vectors and Smoothable Curves (collected essays), 1985; Careless Love and its Apostrophes, 1985; Manifest and Furthermore, 1987; Death is The Place, 1989; Living Instead, 1991; Some Words, 1992; The Mild Day, 1993; Our Selves, 1994; Selected Poems, 1995; The Cage of Age, 1996. Address: 57 Pearl Street, Hudson Falls, NY 12830, USA.

BRONNUM Jakob, b. 16 Apr 1959, Copenhagen, Denmark. Writer. m. Anette Bronnum, 12 Aug 1995. Education: MA, Theology, 1992. Publications: Skygge Dage (prose), 1989; Europadigte (poetry), 1991, 2nd edition, 1996; Den Lange Sondag (novel), 1994; Morke (novel), 1996. Contributions to: Literaturnaja Gazetta; Parnasso. Memberships: Vice Chairman, Board of Representatives, Chairman, Prose Section, Danish Writers Association. Address: Draabydalen 30, DK-8400 Ebeltoft, Denmark.

BROOKE. See: JACKMAN Stuart.

BROOKE Michael Zachary, b. 5 Nov 1921, Cambridge, England. Author; Consultant. m. Hilda Gilatt, 25 July 1953, 2 son, 1 daughter. Education: BA, History, 1st Class Honours, 1943, MA, University of Cambridge, 1945; MA, 1964, PhD, 1969, University of Manchester. Publications: Frederic Le Play: Engineer and Social Scientist, 1970; The Strategy of Multinational Enterprise (co-author), 1970, 2nd edition 1978; The Multinational Company in Europe (co-author), 1972; A Bibliogrpahy of International Business (co-author), 1977; The International Firm (co-author), 1977; International Corporate Planning (co-author), 1979; International Financial Management Handbook (co-author), 2 volumes, 1983; Centralization and Autonomy, 1984; Selling Mangement Service Contracts in International Business, 1985; International Travel and Tourism Forecasts (co-author), 1985; International Management, 1986, 2nd edition, 1995; Financial Management Handbook; South Pennine Escort, 1987; Handbook of International Trade (co-author), 1988; Profits from Abroad (co-author), 1988; International Business Studies (co-author), 1991; Licensing (co-author), 1995; Easy Cycling in Britain (co-author), 1995. Contributions to: Numerous professional journals, editor and contributor. Honours: Fellow, Academy of International Business. Memberships: Authors North, Chairman, 1978-80; Independent Publishers' Guild, Chairman, North West Region, 1989-91; The Circumnavigator's Club, 1991. Address: 21 Barnfield, Urmston, Manchester M41 9EW, England.

BROOKE Tal, (Robert Taliaferro Brooke), b. 21 Jan 1945, Washington, DC, USA. Think-Tank President and Chairman; Author; Lecturer. Education: BA, University of Virginia, 1969; MDiv, Princeton University, 1986. Appointments: Vice President of Public Relations, Telecom Inc, 1982-83; President and Chairman, SCP Inc, Conservative Think-Tank, Berkeley, California, 1988-; Lecturer on Eastern Thought and the Occult at colleges, universities, conventions and seminars in the US and abroad; Many radio and television appearances. Publications: Lord of the Air, 1976, new edition, 1990; The Other Side of Death, 1979; Avatar of Night, 1979, new edition, 1984; Riders of the Cosmic Circut, 1986; Harvest (with Chuck Smith), 1988; When the World Will Be As One, 1989; Virtual Gods, Designer Universes, 1997. Honours: Spring Arbor National Bestseller, 1989; 1st Place, Critical Review Category, National EPA Awards, 1991. Membership: Society of the Cincinnati. Address: SCP Inc, Box 4308, Berkeley, CA 94704, USA.

BROOKE-ROSE Christine, b. England. Novelist; Critic. Education: MA, Oxford University, 1953; PhD, London University, 1954. Appointments: Reviewer for various London journals and newspapers, 1956-68; Professor of English Language and Literature, University of Paris, 1975-88. Publications: Novels: The Languages of Love, 1957; The Sycamore Tree, 1958; The Dear Deceit, 1960; The Middleman, 1961; Out, 1964; Such, 1965; Between, 1968; Thru, 1975; Amalgammemnon, 1984; Xorandor, 1986; Verbivore, 1990; Textermination, 1991; criticism: A Grammar of Metaphor, 1958; A ZBC of Ezra Pound, 1971; A Rhetoric of the Unreal, 1981; Stories, Theories and Things, 1991; Short Stories and Essays. Honours: James Tait Black Memorial Prize, 1966; Arts Council Translation Prize, 1969. Address: c/o Cambridge University Press, PO Box 110, Cambridge CB2 3RL, England.

BROOKNER Anita, b. 16 July 1928, London, England. Novelist; Art Historian. Education: BA, King's College, London; PhD, Courtauld Institute of Art, London. Appointments: Visiting Lecturer in Art History, University of Reading, 1959-64; Lecturer, 1964-77, Reader in Art History, 1977-88, Courtauld Institute of Art; Slade Professor of Art, Cambridge University, 1967-68. Publications: Fiction: A Start in Life, 1981; Providence, 1982; Look at Me, 1983; Hotel du Lac, 1984; Family and Friends, 1985; A Misalliance, 1986; A Friend from England, 1987; Latecomers, 1988; Lewis Percy, 1989; Brief Lives, 1990; A Closed Eye, 1991; Fraud, 1992; A Family Romance, 1993; A Private View, 1994; Incidents in the Rue Laugier, 1995. Non-Fiction: An Iconography of Cecil Rhodes, 1956; J A Dominique Ingres, 1965; Watteau, 1968; The Genius of the Future: Studies in French Art Criticism, 1971; Greuze: The Rise and Fall of an Eighteenth-Century Phenomenon, 1972; Jacques-Louis David, a Personal Interpretation: Lecture on Aspects of Art, 1974; Jacques-Louis David, 1980, revised edition, 1987. Editor: The Stories of Edith Wharton, 2 volumes, 1988, 1989. Contributions to: Books and periodicals. Honours: Fellow, Royal Society of Literature, 1983; Booker McConnell Prize, National Book League, 1984; Commander of the Order of the British Empire, 1990. Address: 68 Elm Park Gardens, London SW10 9PB, England.

BROOKS Andree Nicole Aelion, b. 2 Feb 1937, London, England. Journalist; Author; Lecturer; Columnist; Educator. m. Ronald J Brooks, div 19 Aug 1959, 1 son, 1 daughter. Education: Queens College, London, 1952; Journalism Certificate, 1958. Appointments: Adjunct Professor, Fairfield University, 1982-87; Associate Fellow, Yale University, 1989-; President, Founder, Womens Campaign School at Yale University. Contributions to: Over 3000 Articles;

Contributing Columnist, New York Times. Honours: Best Non Fiction Book of Year, National Association of Press Women, USA, 1990; Over 30 other Journalism Awards. Address: 15 Hitchcock Road, Westport, CT 06880, USA.

BROOKS George E(dward), b. 20 Apr 1933, Lynn, Massachusetts, USA. Professor; Historian; Writer. m. Elaine Claire Rivron, 16 Aug 1985, 2 daughters. Education: AB, Dartmouth College, 1957; MA, 1958, PhD, 1962, Boston University. Appointments: Instructor, Boston University, 1960, 1962; Assistant Professor, 1962-68, Associate Professor, 1968-75, Professor, 1975-, Indiana University; Visiting Associate Professor, Tufts University, 1969; Visiting Fulbright Professor, University of Zimbabwe, 1984; Visiting Professor, Shandong University, China, 1985. Publications: New England Merchants in Africa: A History Through Documents, 1802-1865 (editor with Norman R Bennett), 1965; Yankee Traders, Old Coasters and African Middlemen: History of American Legitimate Trade with West Africa in the Nineteenth Century, 1970; The Kru Mariner in the Nineteenth Century: An Historical Compendium, 1972; Themes in African and World History, 1973, revised edition, 1983; Perspectives on Luso-African Commerce and Settlement in The Gambia and Guinea-Bissau Region, 16th-19th Centuries, 1980; Kola Trade and State-Building: Upper Guinea Coast and Senegambia, 15th-17th Centuries, 1980; Western Africa to c.1860 A.D.: A Provisional Historical Scheme Based on Climate Periods, 1985; Landlords and Strangers: Ecology, Society, and Trade in Western Africa, 1000-1630, 1993; The Aspen World History Handbook: An Organizational Framework, Lessons, and Book Reviews for Non-Centric World History (editor with Dik A Daso, Marilyn Hitchens, and Heidi Roupp), 1994. Contributions to: Many scholarly books and journals. Honours: Ford Foundation Training Fellowship, 1960-62; Social Science Research Council Grant, 1971-72; National Endowment for the Humanities Grant, 1976-77; Indiana University President's Council on International Programs Award, 1978; American Council of Learned Societies Grant, 1990; Visiting Fellowship, Africa, Precolonial Achievement Conference, Humanities Research Centre, Australian National University, 1995. Memberships: African Studies Association, fellow; American Historical Association; Liberian Studies Association; MANSA/Mande Studies Association; World History Association, executive council, 1990-93. Address: 1600 South Clifton Avenue, Bloomington, IN 47401, USA.

BROOKS Gwendolyn, b. 7 June 1917, Topeka, Kansas, USA. Poet; Writer. m. Henry L Blakely, 17 Sept 1939, 1 son, 1 daughter. Education: Graduated, Wilson Junior College, Chicago, 1936. Appointments: Teacher, Northeastern Illinois State College, Chicago, Columbia College, Chicago, Elmhurst College, Illinois; Rennebohm Professor of English, University of Wisconsin at Madison; Distinguished Professor of the Arts, City College of the City University of New York, 1971; Consultant in Poetry, Library of Congress, Washington, DC, 1985-86; Jefferson Lecturer, 1994. Publications: Poetry: A Street in Bronzeville, 1945; Annie Allen, 1949; Bronzeville Boys and Girls, 1956; The Bean Eaters, 1960; Selected Poems, 1963; We Real Cool, 1966; The Wall, 1967; In the Mecca, 1968; Riot, 1969; Family Pictures, 1970; Black Steel: Joe Frazier and Muhammad Ali, 1971; Aloneness, 1971; Aurora, 1972; Beckonings, 1975; To Disembark, 1981; Black love, 1982; Mayor Harold Washington, and Chicago, The I Will City, 1983; The Near-Johannesburg Boy and Other Poems, 1986; Blacks, 1987; Winnie, 1988; Gottschalk and the Grande Tarantelle, 1988; Children Coming Home, 1991. Other: Maud Martha, 1953; A Portion of That Field (with others), 1967; The World of Gwedolyn Brooks, 1971; A Broadside Treasury (editor), 1971; Jump Bed: A New Chicago Anthology (editor), 1971; Report from Part One, 1972; The Tiger Who Wore White Gloves, or, What You Are Your Are, 1974; A Capsule Course in Black Poetry Writing (with Don L Lee, Keorapetse Kgositsile and Dudley Randall), 1975; Primer for Blacks, 1980; Young Poets' Primer, 1981; Very Young Poets, 1983; Report from Part Two, 1995. Contributions to: Various publications: Honours: American Academy of Arts and Letters Grant, 1946; Guggenheim Fellowship, 1946-47; Pulitzer Prize in Poetry, 1950; Thormod Monsen Award, 1964; Ferguson Memorial Award, 1964; Poet Laureate of Illinois, 1968; Anisfield-Wolf Award, 1968; Black Academy Award, 1971; Shelley Memorial Award, 1976; Frost Medal, Poetry Society of America, 1988; National Endowment for the Arts Lifetime Achievement Award, 1989; Aiken-Taylor Awardm, 1992; National Book Foundation Medal, 1994. Memberships: National Women's Hall of Fame; Society of Midland Authors. Address: 5530 South Shore Drive, Apt 2A, Chicago, IL 60637, USA.

BROSS Irwin D, b. 13 Nov 1921, Halloway, Ohio, USA. Biostatistician. m. Rida S Singer, 7 Aug 1949, 2 sons, 1 daughter. Education: BA, University of California at Los Angeles, 1942; MA, North Carolina State University, 1949; PhD, University of North Carolina, 1949. Publications: Design for Decision, 1953; Scientific Strategies in Human Affairs: To Tell the Truth Exposition, 1975; Scientific Strategies to Save Your Life, 1981; Crimes of Official Science, 1988; Others: A History of US Science and Medicine in the Cold War, 1996. Contributions to: Author, Co-Author of more than 350 publications; Biostatistics, Cancer Research and Public Health. Address: 109 Maynard Drive, Eggertsville, NY 14226, USA.

BROSSARD Nicole, b. 27 Nov 1943, Montreal, Quebec, Canada. Poet; Novelist. Education: Licence ès Lettres, 1968, Scolarité de maîtrise en lettres, 1972, Université de Montréal; Bacc. spécialisé en pédagogie, Université du Québec à Montréal, 1971. Publications: Poetry: Mécanique jongleuse, 1973, English translation as Daydream Mechanics, 1980; Le centre blanc, 1978; Amantes, 1980, English translation as Lovhers, 1986; Double Impression, 1984; Mauve, 1984; Character/Jeu de lettres, 1986; Sous la langue/Under Tongue, bilingual edition, 1987; A tout regard, 1989; Installations, 1989; Langues obscures, 1991; La Nuit verte du parc labyrinthe, trilingual edition, 1992. Fiction: Un livre, 1970, English translation as A Book, 1976; Sold-Out, 1973, English translation as Turn of a Pang, 1976; French Kiss, 1974, English translation, 1986; L'amèr, 1977, English translation as These Our Mothers, or, the Disintegrating Chapter, 1983; Le Sens apparent, 1980, English translation as Surfaces of Sense, 1989; Picture Theory, 1982, English translation, 1991; Le Désert mauve, 1987, English translation as Mauve Desert, 1990; Baroque d'aube, 1995, English translation as Baroque at Dawn, 1997. Book of Essays: La Lettre aèrienne, 1985, English Translation, The Aerial Letter, 1988. Contributions to: Numerous anthologies. Honours: Governor-General Prizes, 1974, 1984; Chapbook Award, Therafields Foundation, 1986; Grand Prix de Poésie, Foundation Les Forges, 1989; Honorary Doctorate, University of Western Ontario, 1991; Prix Athanase-David, 1991. Membership: l'Académie des Lettres du Québec, 1993-. Address: 34 Avenue Robert, Outrement, Quebec H3S 2P2, Canada.

BROUGHTON John Renata, b. 19 Mar 1947, Hastings, New Zealand. University Lecturer in Maori Health. Education: BSc, Massey University, 1971; Bachelor of Dental Surgery, Otago University, 1977. Publications: A Time Journal for Halley's Comet, children's book, 1985; Te Hokinga Mai (The Return Home), stage play, 1990; Te Hara (The Sin), stage play, 1990; Nga Puke (The Hills), stage play, 1990; Nga Mahi Ora, TV documentary on health career for young Maori people, 1990; Michael James Manaia, stage play, 1991; Maraq, stage play, 1992. Contributions to: Te Hau Ora Sports Journal. Honour: Dominion Sunday Times Bruce Mason Playwright Award, 1990. Memberships: PEN New Zealand; Chairman, Araiteura Marae Council Inc; Foundation Member, Maori Health Workforce Development Group, Department of Health; Otago Branch, New Zealand Dental Association, Committee Member 1979-84. Literary Agent: Playmarket, PO Box 9767, Wellington New Zealand. Address: Te Maraeunui, 176 Queen Street, Dunedin, New Zealand.

BROUMAS Olga, b. 6 May 1949, Hermoupolis, Greece. Poet. m. Stephen Edward Bangs, 1973, div 1979. Education: BA, University of Pennsylvania, 1970; MFA, University of Oregon at Eugene, 1973. Appointments: Instructor, University of Oregon, 1972-76; Visiting Associate Professor, University of Idaho, 1978; Poet-in-Residence, Goddard College, Plainfield, Vermont, 1979-81, Women Writers Center, Cazenovia, New York, 1981-82; Founder-Associate Faculty, Freehand Women Writers and Photographers Community, Provincetown, Massachusetts, 1982-87; Visiting Associate Professor, Boston University, 1988-90; Fanny Hurst Poet-in-Residence, Brandeis University, 1990. Publications: Restlessness, 1967; Caritas, 1976; Beginning with O, 1977; Soie Sauvage, 1980; Pastoral Jazz, 1983; Black Holes, Black Stockings, 1985; Perpetua, 1989; Sappho's Gymnasium, 1994. Honours: Yale Younger Poets Award, 1977; National Endowment for the Arts Grant, 1978; Guggenheim Fellowship, 1981-82. Address: 162 Mill Pond Drive, Brewster, MA 02631, USA.

BROWN Archibald Haworth, b. 10 May 1938, Annan, Scotland. Professor of Politics; Writer. m. Patricia Susan Cornwell, 22 Mar 1963, 1 son, 1 daughter. Education: City of Westminster College, 1958-59; BSc in Economics, 1st Class Honours, London School of Economics and Political Science, 1962; MA, Oxford University, 1972. Appointments: Lecturer in Politics, Glasgow University, 1964-71; British Council Exchange Scholar, Moscow University, 1967-68; Lecturer in Soviet Institutions, 1971-89, Professor of Politics, 1989-, Oxford University; Visiting Professor and Henry L Stimson Lecturer, Yale University, 1980; Visiting Professor, University of Connecticut, 1980, Columbia University, 1985, University of Texas at Austin, 1990-91. Publications: Soviet Politics and Political Science, 1974; The Soviet Union Since the Fall of Khrushchev (editor with Michael Kaser), 1975, 2nd edition, 1978; Political Culture and Political Change in Communist States (editor with Jack Gray), 1977, 2nd edition, 1979; Authority, Power, and Policy in the USSR: Essays Dedicated to Leonard Schapiro (editor with T H Rigby and Peter Reddaway), 1980; The Cambridge Encyclopedia of Russia and the Soviet Union (editor with John Fennell, Michael Kaser, and Harry T Willetts), 1982; Soviet Union Policy for the 1980s (editor), 1984; Political Leadership in the Soviet Union (editor), 1989; The Soviet Union: A Biographical Dictionary (editor), 1990; New Thinking in Soviet Politics (editor), 1992; The Cambridge Encyclopedia of Russia and the Former Soviet Union (editor with Michael Kaser and Gerald S Smith), 1994; The Gorbachev Factor, 1996. Contributions to: Scholarly journals and symposia. Memberships: American Association for the Advancement of Slavic Studies; American Political Science Association; British Academy, fellow; British National Association for Russian and East European Studies; International Political Science Association; Political Studies Association of the United Kingdom. Address: St Antony's College, Oxford University, Oxford OX2 6JF, England.

BROWN Craig (Edward Moncrieff), b. 23 May 1967, England. Journalist; Author. m. Frances Welch, 1987, 1 son, 1 daughter. Education: Eton College; University of Bristol. Appointments: Journalist and Columnist with the New Statesman, Observer, Times Literary Supplement, and Mail on Sunday; Columnist, The Times, 1988-; Restaurant Critic, Sunday Times, 1988-93; Columnist (as Wallace Arnold), The Spectator, 1987-, Private Eye, 1989-, Independent on Sunday, 1991, Evening Standard, 1993-, The Guardian (as Bel Littlejohn), 1995-. Publications: The Marsh Marlowe Letters, 1983; A Year Inside, 1988; The Agreeable World of Wallace Arnold, 1990; Rear Columns, 1992; Welcome to My Worlds, 1993; Craig Brown's Greatest Hits, 1993; The Hounding of John Thenos, 1994; The Private Eye Book of Craig Brown Parodies, 1995. Address: c/o The Evening Standard, Northcliffe House, 2 Derry Street, London, W8 5EE, England.

BROWN Diana, b. 8 Aug 1928, Twickenham, England. Research Librarian; Author. m. Ralph Herman Brown, 31 Dec 1964, dec, 2 daughters. Education: AA, San Jose City College, 1974; BA, 1975, MLS, 1976, MA, 1977, San Jose State University. Appointments: Librarian, Signetics Corp, Sunnyvale, California, 1978-79, NASA/Ames Research Center, Moffett Field, 1979-80; Academic Information Specialist, University of Phoenix, San Jose Division, 1984-86; Research Librarian, San Jose Public Library, 1988-. Publications: The Emerald Necklace, 1980; Come Be My Love, 1981; A Debt of Honour, 1981; St Martin's Summer, 1981; The Sandalwood Fan, 1983; The Hand of a Woman, 1984; The Blue Dragon, 1988. Honour: American Library Association Booklist Outstanding Adult Novel, 1984. Memberships: Authors Guild; Jane Austen Society; Special Libraries Association; Phi Kappa Phi. Address: Gate Tree Cottage, PO 2846, Carmel by the Sea, CA 93921, USA.

BROWN Iain Duncan, b. 3 Sept 1967, Sydney, Australia. Publisher. Education: BA, English Literature, Macquarie University, Sydney, 1994; MA, History of the Book, School of Advanced Study, University of London, England, 1996. Publication: The Young Publishers' Handbook, 1991. Contributions to: The Tony Godwin Legacy, in The Bookseller, 1995. Memberships: Royal Society of Literature; The Paternosters; Society of Young Publishers. Address: 67a Prince of Wales Mansions, Prince of Wales Drive, London, SW11 4BJ, England.

BROWN James Willie Jr. See: **KOMUNYAKAA Yusef**.

BROWN John Russell, b. 15 Sept 1923, Bristol, England. Professor of Theatre; Theatre Director; Writer. m. Hilary Sue Baker, 5 Apr 1961, 1 son, 2 daughters. Education: BA, 1949, BLitt, 1951, Oxford University; PhD, University of Birmingham, 1960. Appointments: Fellow, Shakespeare Institute, Stratford-upon-Avon, 1951-53; Faculty, 1955-63, Head, Department of Drama and Theatre Arts, 1964-71, University of Birmingham; Professor of English, Sussex University, 1971-82; Professor of Theatre Arts, State University of New York at Stony Brook, 1982-85; Artistic Director, Project Theatre, 1985-89, Professor of Theatre, 1985-, University of Michigan; Director of various theatre productions in Europe and North America; Visiting Lecturer or Professor in Europe, North America and New Zealand. Publications: Shakespeare and his Comedies, 1957; Shakespeare: The Tragedy of Macbeth, 1963; Shakespeare's Plays in Performance, 1966; Effective Theatre, 1969; Shakespeare's The Tempest, 1969; Shakespeare's Dramatic Style, 1970; Theatre Language, 1972; Free Shakespeare, 1974; Discovering Shakespeare, 1981; Shakespeare and His Theatre, 1982; A Short Guide to Modern British Drama, 1983; Shakescenes, 1993; William Shakespeare: Writing for Performance, 1996; What Theatre?: An Introductin and Exploration, 1997. Contributions to: General Editor: Stratford-upon-Avon Studies, 1960-67; Stratford-upon-Avon Library, 1964-69; Theatre Production Studies, 1981-; Theatre Concepts, 1992-; Oxford Illustrated History of Theatre, 1995. Editor: Various plays of Shakespeare. Contributions to: Scholarly journals. Memberships: Advisory Council, Theatre Museum, 1974-83, chairman, 1979-83; Arts Council of Great Britain, drama panel chairman, 1980-83. Address: Court Lodge, Hooe, Battle, Sussex TN33 9HJ, England.

BROWN Kevin, b. 3 Sept 1960, Kansas City, Missouri, USA. Essayist; Biographer; Journalist. Education: BA, Columbia University, 1988. Publications: Romare Bearden, 1994; Malcom X: His Life & Legacy, 1995; Countée Cullen, 1996. Contributions to: London Times Literary Supplement; Washington Post Bookworld; Threepenny Review; Kirkus Reviews. Honours: General Studies Scholar, Columbia University; New York Public Library Book Awards, 1995, 1996. Membership: PEN International. Literary Agent: Scott Meredith Literary Agency, c/o Lisa Edwards, 845 Third Avenue, New York, NY 10022, USA. Address: 166 West 75th Street, Apt 920, New York, NY 10023, USA.

BROWN Marc (Tolon), b. 25 Nov 1946, Erie, Pennsylvania, USA. Author and Illustrator of Children's Books. m. (1) Stephanie Marini, 1 Sept 1968, diss 1977, 2 sons, (2) Laurene Krasny, 11 Sept 1983, 1 daughter. Education: BFA, Cleveland Institute of Art, 1969. Appointments: Assistant Professor, Garland Junior College, Boston, 1969-76; Author and Illustrator of children's books, 1976-. Publications: Author of over 40 children's books; Illustrator of other children's books. Honours: Many citations and awards. Memberships: Author's Guild; Author's League of America. Address: Martha's Vineyard, MA, USA.

BROWN Patricia Ann Fortini, b. 16 Nov 1936, Oakland, California, USA. University Professor; Art Historian. m. (1) Peter Claus Meyer, May 1957, div 1978, 2 sons, (2) Peter Robert Lamont Brown, Aug 1980, div 1989. Education: AB, 1959; MA, 1978, PhD, 1983, University of California at Berkeley. Appointments: Assistant Professor, 1983-89, Associate Professor, 1989-, Andrew W Mellon Professor, 1991-95, Princeton University. Publication: Venetian Narrative Painting in the Age of Carpaccio; Venice and Antiquity: The Venetian Sense of the Past. Contributions to: Art History; Christian Science Monitor; Monitor Book Review; Burlington Magazine; Renaissance Quarterly; Biography. Honour: Premio Salotto Veneto, Italy. Memberships: Renaissance Society of America; American Academy in Rome; College Art Association. Address: Department of Art and Archaeology, Princeton University, Princeton, NJ 08544-1018, USA.

BROWN Raymond E(dward), b. 22 May 1928, New York, New York, USA. Professor of Biblical Studies Emeritus; Priest; Writer. Education: BA, 1948, MA, 1949, Catholic University of America; STB, 1951, STD, 1955, St Mary's Seminary, Baltimore; PhD, Johns Hopkins University, 1958; SSB, 1959, SSL, 1963, Pontifical Bible Commission, Rome. Appointments: Joined, Society of St Sulpice, 1951; Ordained, Priest, Roman Catholic Church, 1953; Professor of Sacred Scriptures, St Mary's Seminary, Baltimore, 1959-71; Lecturer, Aquinas Institute of Theology, 1963, Duke University, 1967, University of Sydney, 1969, Lancaster Theological Seminary, 1978, Vanderbilt Divinity School, 1980; Thomas More Lecturer, 1966, Shaffer Lecturer, 1978, Yale University; Joint Theological Commission of the World Council of Churches and the Roman Catholic Church, 1967-68; Faith and Order Commission, World Council of Churches, 1968-93; Auburn Professor of Biblical Studies, 1971-90, Professor Emeritus, 1990-, Union Theological Seminary, New York City; American Member, Roman Pontifical Bible Commission, 1972-78, 1996-. Publications: The Parables of the Gospels, 1963; New Testament Essays, 1965; The Gospel According to John, 1966; Jesus, God, and Man, 1967; The Jerome Biblical Commentary, 1968; Biblical Tendencies Today: An Introduction to the Post-Bultmanians (with P J Cahill), 1969; Priest and Bishop: Biblical Reflections, 1970; Peter in the New Testament, 1973;

The Virginal Conception and the Bodily Resurrection of Jesus, 1973; Biblical Reflections on Crises Facing the Church, 1975; The Birth of the Messiah, 1977, 2nd edition, 1993; The Critical Meaning of the Bible, 1981; The Epistles of John, 1982; Biblical Exegesis and Church Doctrine, 1985; The New Jerome Bible Commentary, 1990; The Death of the Messiah, 1994. Contributions to: Religious journals. Honours: National Catholic Book Awards, 1966, 1968, 1973; National Religious Book Award, 1977; Phi Beta Kappa; Many honorary doctorates. Memberships: American Academy of Arts and Sciences; American Schools of Oriental Research; American Theological Society; Biblical Theologians; British Academy, corresponding fellow; Catholic Bible Association, president, 1971-72; Society for Biblical Literature, president, 1976-77; Society for New Testament Studies, president, 1986-87. Address: 3041 Broadway at Reinhold Niebuhr Place, New York, NY 10027, USA.

BROWN Rita Mae, b. 28 Nov 1944, Hannover, Pennsylvania, USA. Author; Poet. Education: AA, Broward Junior College, 1965; BA, New York University, 1968; Cinematography Degree, School of the Visual Arts, 1968; PhD, Institute for Policy Studies, 1976. Appointments: Writer-in-Residence, Women's Writing Center, Cazenovia College, New York, 1977-78; President, American Artists Inc, 1981-; Visiting Instructor, University of Virginia, 1992. Publications: Hrotsvitha: Six Medieval Latin Plays, 1961; The Hand that Cradles the Rock (poem), 1971; Rubyfruit Jungle (novel), 1973; Songs to a Handsome Woman (poems), 1973; In Her Day (novel), 1976; The Plain Brown Rapper (political articles), 1976; Six of One (novel), 1978; Southern Discomfort (novel), 1982; Sudden Death (novel), 1983; High Hearts (novel), 1986; Bingo (novel), 1988; Starting from Scratch: A Different Kind of Writer's Manual, 1988; Wish You Were Here (novel), 1990; Rest in Pieces (novel), 1992; Venus Envy (novel), 1993; Murder at Monticello (novel), 1994; Pay Dirt, or Adventures at Ash Lawn (novel), 1995; Riding Shotgun (novel), 1996; Murder, She Meowed (novel), 1996; Stars and Bars (novel), 1997; Other: Screenplays; teleplays. Contributions to: Anthologies. Honours: National Endowment for the Arts Grant, 1978; New York Public Library Literary Lion, 1987; Honorary Doctorate, Wilson College, 1992. Memberships: International Academy of Poets; PEN International; Poets and Writers. Address: c/o American Artists Inc, PO Box 4671, Charlottesville, VA 22905, USA.

BROWN Robert Douglas, b. 17 Aug 1919, Trealaw, England. Journalist; Publisher. m. Elsie Mary Warner, 17 Aug 1940, 1 son, 2 daughters. Education: BA, Open University, 1986. Appointments: Political Staff, News Chronicle, 1951-60; Managing Director, Anglia Echo Newspapers, 1964-80. Publications: The Battle of Crichel Down; The Survival of the Printed Word; The Port of London; East Anglia-The War Years, 7 volumes. Membership: Fellow, PEN. Address: Lower Green, Stoke By Clare, Sudbury, Suffolk, England.

BROWN Rosellen, b. 12 May 1939, Philadelphia, Pennsylvania, USA. Writer; Poet; Associate Professor. m. Marvin Hoffman, 16 Mar 1963, 2 daughters. Education: BA, Barnard College, 1960; MA, Brandeis University, 1962. Appointments: Instructor, Tougaloo College, Mississippi, 1965-67; Staff, Bread Loaf Writer's Conference, Middlebury, Vermont, 1974, 1991, 1992; Instructor, Goddard College, Plainfield, Vermont, 1976; Visiting Professor of Creative Writing, Boston University, 1977-78; Associate Professor in Creative Writing, University of Houston, 1982-85, 1989-. Publications: Some Deaths in the Delta and Other Poems, 1970; The Whole World Catalog: Creative Writing Ideas for Elementary and Secondary Schools (with others), 1972; Street Games: A Neighborhood (stories), 1974; The Autobiography of My Mother (novel), 1976; Cora Fry (poems), 1977; Banquet: Five Short Stories, 1978; Tender Mercies (novel), 1978; Civil Wars: A Novel, 1984; A Rosellen Brown Reader: Selected Poetry and Prose, 1992; Before and After (novel), 1992. Contributions to: Books, anthologies, and periodicals. Honours: Woodrow Wilson Fellow, 1960; Howard Foundation Grant, 1971-72; National Endowment for the Humanities Grants, 1973-74, 1981-82; Radcliffe Institute Fellow, 1973-75; Great Lakes Colleges New Writers Award, 1976; Guggenheim Fellowship, 1976-77; American Academy and Institute of Arts and Letters Award, 1988; Ingram-Merrill Grant, 1989-90. Address: c/o Creative Writing Program, University of Houston, Houston, TX 77204, USA.

BROWN Stewart, b. 14 Mar 1951, Lymington, Hampshire, England. University Lecturer in African and Caribbean Literature; Writer; Poet; Editor. m. Priscilla Margaret Brant, 1976, 1 son, 1 daughter. Education: BA, Falmouth School of Art, 1978; MA, University of Sussex, 1979; PhD, University of Wales, 1987. Appointments:

Lecturer in English, Bayero University, Kano, Nigeria, 1980-83; Lecturer in African and Caribbean Literature, University of Birmingham, 1988-. Publications: Mekin Foolishness (poems), 1981; Caribbean Poetry Now, 1984, new edition, 1992; Zinder (poems), 1986; Lugard's Bridge (poems), 1989; Voiceprint: An Anthology of Oral and Related Poetry from the Caribbean (editor with Mervyn Morris and Gordon Rohler), 1989; Writers from Africa: A Readers' Guide, 1989; New Wave: The Contemporary Caribbean Short Story, 1990; The Art of Derek Walcott: A Collection of Critical Essays, 1991; Caribbean Stories Now, 1991; The Art of Edward Kamau Brathwaite: A Collection of Critical Essays, 1992; The Heinemann Book of Caribbean Poetry (with Ian McDonald), 1992; The Pressures of the Text: Orality, Texts and the Telling of Tales, 1995; Caribbean New Voices I, 1996. Contributions to: Anthologies and periodicals. Honours: Eric Gregory Award, 1976; Southwest Arts Literature Award, 1978; Honorary Fellow, Centre for Caribbean Studies, University of Warwick, 1990. Memberships: Welsh Academy; Welsh Union of Writers. Address: Centre of West African Studies, University of Birmingham, Edgbaston, Birmingham B15 2TT, England.

BROWN Terence, b. 17 Jan 1944, Loping, China. Associate Professor of English; Writer; Editor. m. Suzanne Marie Krochalis, 1969, 1 son, 1 daughter. Education: BA, 1966, PhD, 1970, Trinity College, Dublin. Appointments: Lecturer, 1968-82, Director of Modern English, 1976-83, Fellow, 1976-86, Registrar, 1980-81, Associate Professor of English, 1982-93, Trinity College, Dublin; Professor of Anglo-Irish Literature, 1993-. Publications: Time Was Away: The World of Louis MacNeice (editor with Alec Reid), 1974; Louis MacNeice: Sceptical Vision, 1975; Northern Voices: Poets from Northern Ulster, 1975; The Irish Short Story (editor with Patrick Rafroidi), 1979; Ireland: A Social and Cultural History, 1922-1979, 1981, new edition as Ireland: A Social and Cultural History, 1922 to the Present, 1985; The Whole Protestant Community: The Making of a Historical Myth, 1985; Hermathena,(editor with N Grene), 1986; Samuel Ferguson: A Centenary Tribute (editor with B Hayley), 1987; Ireland's Literature: Selected Essays, 1988; Traditions and Influence in Anglo-Irish Literature (editor with N Grene), 1989; The Field Day Anthology of Irish Writing (contributing editor), 1991; James Joyce: Dubliners (editor), 1992; Celticism, (editor), 1996; Journalism: Derek Mahon, Selected Prose, (editor), 1996. Memberships: International Association for the Study of Anglo-Irish Literature; Royal Irish Academy; European Society for the Study of English (board member); Academia Europaea; International Association of Professors of English. Address: Department of English, Trinity College, Dublin 2, Ireland.

BROWNE Michael Dennis, b. 28 May 1940, Walton-on-Thames, England (US citizen, 1978). Professor; Writer; Poet. m. Lisa Furlong McLean, 18 July 1981, 1 son, 2 daughters. Education: BA, Hull University, 1962; Oxford University, 1962-63; Ministry of Education Teacher's Certificate, 1963; MA, University of Iowa, 1967. Appointments: Visiting Lecturer, University of Iowa, 1967-68; Instructor, 1967, 1968, Visiting Adjunct Assistant Professor, 1968, Columbia University; Faculty, Bennington College, Vermont, 1969-71; Visiting Assistant Professor, 1971-72, Assistant Professor, 1972-75, Associate Professor, 1975-83, Professor, 1983-, University of Minnesota. Publications: The Wife of Winter, 1970; Sun Exercises, 1976; The Sun Fetcher, 1978; Smoke From the Fires, 1985; You Won't Remember This, 1992; Selected Poems 1965-1995, 1997. Contributions to: Numerous anthologies and journals. Other: Texts for various musical compositions. Honours: Fulbright Scholarship, 1965-67; Borestone Poetry Prize, 1974; National Endowment for the Arts Fellowships, 1977, 1978; Bush Fellowship, 1981; Loft-McKnight Writers' Award, 1986; Minnesota Book Award for Poetry, 1993. Memberships: The Loft; Poetry Society of America. Address: 2111 East 22nd Street, Minneapolis, MN 55404, USA.

BROWNING Robert, b. 15 Jan 1914, Glasgow, Scotland. Emeritus Professor. Education: MA, University of Glasgow, 1931-35; MA, Balliol College. Appointments: Editorial Board, Past & Present, 1960-78; Reviews Editor, Journal of Hellenic Studies, 1964-74. Publications: Medieval and Modern Greek, 1969, revised edition, 1983; Justinian and Theodora, 1971, revised edition, 1987; The Emperor Julian, 1976; Studies in Byzantine History, Literature and Education, 1977; The Byzantine Empire, 1980, revised edition, 1992; The Greek World: Classical, Byzantine, and Modern, 1985; History, Language, and Literacy in the Byzantine World, 1989; Dated Greek Manuscripts from Cyprus to the Year 1570, 1993. Contributions to: Learned Journals in many Countries. Honours: Fellow, British Academy, 1978; Corresponding Member, Academy of Athens, 1982; Hon DLitt,

Birmingham, 1980; Hon Doctor, University of Athens, 1988, University of Ioannina, 1996; Gold Medal of City of Athens, 1994. Membership: Society for the Promotion of Hellenic Studies, President, 1974-77. Address: 17 Belsize Park Gardens, London NW3 4JG, England.

BROWNING Vivenne, (Elaine Vivenne Browning Baly), b. 1 Dec 1922, Sydney, New South Wales, Australia. Writer; Lecturer; Broadcaster. m. W F Baly, 21 Aug 1954, 1 son, 3 daughter. Education: Mary Datchelor, London, 1942; Hazelhurst College, Melbourne. Appointments: Staff Sergeant Intelligence Corps ATS, 1942-46; Civil Resettlement of Repatriated Prisioners of War, 1945-46; Metropolitan Police, CID, London, 1946-50; Board of Directors, International Browning Society, Baylor University. Publications: My Browning Family Album; The Uncommon Medium; BBC Radio; From Store Detective to Private Eye; Living in Addis Ababa; TV Wednesday Magazine Addis Ababa; Lord Haw Haw; St Ives Summer, 1946; The Leach Pottery, 1995. Contributions to: Magazines; The Real Identity of Pauline; From Russia with Love and Plain Speaking. Memberships: Browning Society; New Barnet Literary and Debating Society; Boston Browning Society; Arthur Machen Society; Intelligence Corps Comrades Association; Metropolitan Police Association; Friend of the Royal Academy of Arts; Australian Film Society; Keats Shelley Association; Royal Society of Literature; Society of Authors; PEN; Browning Society; Metropolitan Women Police Association. Address: c/o SKOOB Pub, 25 Lowman Road, North London, England.

BROWNJOHN Alan (Charles), b. 28 July 1931, London, England. Poet; Writer; Critic. Education: BA, 1953, MA, 1961, Merton College, Oxford. Appointments: Lecturer, Battersea College of Education, 1965-76, Polytechnic of the South Bank, 1976-79, Poetry Critic, New Statesman, 1968-76, Encounter, 1978-82, Sunday Times, 1990-. Publications: Poetry: Travellers Alone, 1954; The Railings, 1961; The Lion's Mouths, 1967; Sandgrains on a Tray, 1969; Penguin Modern Poets 14, 1969; First I Say This: A Selection of Poems for Reading Aloud, 1969; Brownjohn's Beasts, 1970; Warrior's Career, 1972; A Song of Good Life, 1975; The Old Flea-Pit, 1987; The Observation Car, 1990; In the Cruel Arcade, 1994. Fiction: To Clear the River, 1964; The Way You Tell Them, 1990. Other: Philip Larkin, 1975; Meet and Write, 1985-87; The Gregory Anthology, 1990; The Long Shadows, 1996. Translations: Torquato Tasso (play), Goethe, 1985; Horace (play), Corneille, 1996. Memberships: Arts Council of Great Britain Literature Panel, 1968-72; Poetry Society, London; Writers' Guild of Great Britain; Society of Authors. Address: 2 Belsize Park, London NW3, England.

BROWNJOHN J(ohn Nevil) Maxwell, b. 11 Apr 1929, Rickmansworth, Hertfordshire, England. Literary Translator; Screenwriter. Education: MA, Lincoln College, Oxford. Publications: Night of the Generals, 1962; Memories of Teilhard de Chardin, 1964; Klemperer Recollections, 1964; Brothers in Arms, 1965; Goya, 1965; Rodin, 1967; The Interpreter, 1967; Alexander the Great, 1968; The Poisoned Stream, 1969; The Human Animal, 1971; Hero in the Tower, 1972; Strength Through Joy, 1973; Madam Kitty, 1973; A Time for Truth, 1974; The Boat, 1974; A Direct Flight to Allah, 1975; The Manipulation Game, 1976; The Hittites, 1977; Willy Brandt Memoirs, 1978; Canaris, 1979; Life with the Enemy, 1979; A German Love Story, 1980; Richard Wagner, 1983; The Middle Kingdom, 1983; Solo Run, 1984; Momo, 1985; The Last Spring in Paris, 1985; Invisible Walls, 1986; Mirror in the Mirror, 1986; The Battle of Wagram, 1987; Asassin, 1987; Daddy, 1989; The Marquis of Bolibar, 1989; Eunuchs for Heaven, 1990; Little Apple, 1990; Jaguar, 1990; Siberian Transfer, 1992; The Swedish Cavalier, 1992; Infanta, 1992; The Survivor, 1994; Acts, 1994; Love Letters From Cell 92, 1994; Turlupin, 1995; Nostradamus, 1995. Screen Credits: Tess (with Roman Polanski), 1979; The Boat, 1981; Pirates, 1986; The Name of the Rose, 1986; The Bear, 1989; Bitter Moon (with Roman Polanski), 1992. Honours: Schlegel Tieck Special Award, 1979; US Pen Prize, 1981; Schlegel Tieck Prize, 1993. Memberships: Translators Association; Society of Authors. Address: The Vine House, Nether Compton, Sherborne, Dorset DT9 4QA, England.

BROWNLOW Kevin, b. 2 June 1938, Crowborough, Sussex, England. Author; Film Director; Former Film Editor. Publications: The Parade's Gone By, 1968; How It Happened Here, 1968; Adventures with D W Griffith, 1973; Hollywood: The Pioneers, 1979; The War, the West, and the Wilderness, 1979; Napoleon: Abel Gance's Classic Film, 1983; Behind the Mask of Innocence, 1990; David Lean - A Biography, 1996. Address: c/o Photoplay, 21 Princess Road, London, NW1 8JR, England.

BROXHOLME John Franklin, (Duncan Kyle, James Meldrum), b. 11 June 1930, Bradford, England. Former Journalist; Author. m. Alison Millar Hair, 22 Sept 1956, 3 children. Education: Bradford, England. Publications: As Duncan Kyle: A Cage of Ice, 1970; Flight into Fear, 1972; A Raft of Swords, 1973; The Suvarov Adventure, 1974; Terror's Cradle, 1975; White-Out, 1976; In Deep, 1976; Black Camelot, 1978; Green River High, 1979; Stalking Point, 1981; The King's Commissar, 1984; The Dancing Men, 1985; The Honey Ant, 1988; As James Meldrum: The Semonov Impulse, 1975. Address: Oak Lodge, Valley Farm Road, Newton, Sudbury, Suffolk, England.

BRUCE George, b. 10 Mar 1909, Fraserburgh, Aberdeenshire, Scotland. Poet; Writer; Broadcaster; Lecturer. m. Elizabeth Duncan, 25 July 1935, 1 son, 1 daughter. Education: MA, Aberdeen University, 1932. Appointments: English Master, Dundee High School, 1934-46; Producer, BBC, Aberdeen, 1946-56, Edinburgh, 1956-70; First Fellow in Creative Writing, Glasgow University, 1971-73; Lecturer in Scotland and abroad. Publications: Sea Talk, 1944; Landscapes and Figures, 1967; Collected Poems, 1940-1970, 1970; Perspectives: Selected Poems, 1970-1986, 1986; The Land Out There, 1991. Other: Anne Redpath: A Monograph of the Scottish Painter, 1975; Some Practical Good: The Cockburn Association, 1875-1975, 1975; Festival in the North, 1947-1975, 1975. Contributions to: Anthologies, books, and periodicals. Honours: Scottish Arts Council Awards, 1967, 1971; Honorary DLitt, College of Wooster, Ohio, USA, 1977; Officer of the Order of the British Empire, 1984. Memberships: Saltire Society; Scottish Poetry Library; Poetry Society. Address: 25 Warriston Crescent, Edinburgh EH3 5LB, Scotland.

BRUCE Lennart, b. 21 Feb 1919, Stockholm, Sweden. Writer. m. Sonja Wiegandt, 22 July 1960, 1 son, 1 daughter. Education: University Studies. Publications: Agenda (on the works of Wilhelm Ekelund), 1976; Sannsaga, 1982; The Broker, 1983; The Second Light (on the works of Wilhelm Ekelund), 1986; Utan synbar anledning, 1988; Forskingringen, 1989; En Nasares Gang, 1993; Kaffereget, 1995. Contributions to: Over 100 poems, articles to US and Swedish literary magazines. Honours: Swedish Academy Award, 1977, 1988. Memberships: PEN American Centre, New York; Swedish Writers Union, Stockholm. Address: 31 Los Cerros Place, Walnut Creek, CA 94598, USA.

BRUCE Robert V(ance), b. 19 Dec 1923, Malden, Massachusetts, USA. Historian; Professor Emeritus. Education: Massachusetts Institute of Technology, 1941-43; BS, University of New Hampshire, 1945; AM, 1947, PhD, 1953, Boston University. Appointments: Instructor, University of Bridgeport, 1947-48; History Master, Lawrence Academy, Groton, Massachusetts, 1948-51; Research Assistant to Benjamin P Thomas, 1953-54; Instructor to Professor of History, 1955-84, Professor Emeritus, 1984-, Boston University; Visiting Professor, University of Wisconsin at Madison, 1962-63. Publications: Lincoln and the Tools of War, 1956; 1877: Year of Violence, 1959; Bell: Alexander Graham Bell and the Conquest of Solitude, 1973; The Launching of Modern American Science, 1846-1876, 1987. Contributions to: Various publications. Honours: Guggenheim Fellowship, 1957-58; Huntington Library Fellow, 1966; Pulitzer Prize in History, 1988; Distinguished Alumni Award, Boston University, 1991. Memberships: American Association for the Advancement of Science; Phi Beta Kappa, honorary; Society of American Historians, fellow. Address: 28 Evans Road, Madbury, NH 03820, USA.

BRUCHAC Joseph, b. 16 Oct 1942, Saratoga Springs, New York, USA. Author; Poet; Storyteller; Publisher; Editor. m. Carol Worthen, 12 June 1964, 2 sons. Education: AB, Cornell University, 1965; MA, Syracuse University, 1966; Graduate Studies, State University of New York at Albany, 1971-73; PhD, Union Institute, Ohio, 1975. Appointments: Co-Founder, Director, Greenfield Review Press, 1969-; Editor, Greenfield Review literary magazine, 1971-90; Visiting Scholar and Writer-in-Residence at various institutions; Member, Dawnland Singers, 1993-. Publications: Fiction and Poetry: Indian Mountain and Other Poems, 1971; Turkey Brother and Other Iroquois Folk Tales, 1976; The Dreams of Jesse Brown (novel), 1977; Stone Giants and Flying Heads: More Iroquois Folk Tales, 1978; The Wind Eagle and Other Abenaki Stories, 1984; Iroquois Stories, 1985; Walking With My Sons and Other Poems, 1986; Near the Mountains: New and Selected Poems, 1987; Keepers of the Earth (stories), 1988; The Faithful Hunter: Abenaki Stories, 1988; Long Memory and Other Poems, 1989; Return of the Sun: Native American Tales from the

Northeast Woodlands, 1989; Hoop Snakes, Hide-Behinds and Side-Hill Winders: Tall Tales from the Adirondacks, 1991; Keepers of the Animals (with Michael Caduto) (stories), 1991; Thirteen Moons on Turtle's Back (with Jonathan London) (poems and stories), 1992; Dawn Land (novel), 1993; The First Strawberries, 1993; Flying With the Eagle, Racing the Great Bear (stories), 1993; The Girl Who Married the Moon (with Gayle Ross) (stories), 1994; A Boy Called Slow, 1995; The Boy Who Lived With Bears (stories), 1995; Dog People (stories), 1995; Long River (novel), 1995; The Story of the Milky Way (with Gayle Ross), 1995; Beneath Earth and Sky, 1996; Children of the Long House (novel), 1996; Four Ancestors: Stories, Songs and Poems from Native North America, 1996. Other: Survival This Way: Interviews with Native American Poets, 1987; The Native American Sweat Lodge: History and Legends, 1993; Roots of Survival: Native American Storytelling and the Sacred, 1996. Editor: Words from the House of the Dead: An Anthology of Prison Writings from Soledad (with William Witherup), 1971; The Last Stop: Writings from Comstock Prison, 1974; Aftermath: An Anthology of Poems in English from Africa, Asia and the Caribbean, 1977; The Next World: Poems by Thirty-Two Third-World Americans, 1978; Songs from This Earth on Turtle's Back: Contemporary American Indian Poetry, 1983; The Light from Another Country: Poetry from American Prisons, 1984; Breaking Silence: An Anthology of Asian American Poetry, 1984; North Country: An Anthology of Contemporary Writing from the Adirondacks and the Upper Hudson Valley (with others), 1985; New Voices from the Longhouse: An Anthology of Contemporary Iroquois Writing, 1989; Returning the Gift: Poetry and Prose from the First North American Native Writers Festival, 1994; Smoke Rising: The Native North American Literary Companion (with others), 1995. Contributions to: Many anthologies, books and periodicals. Honours: National Endowment for the Arts Fellowship, 1974; Rockefeller Foundation Humanities Fellowship, 1982-83; American Book Award, 1985; Notable Children's Book in the Language Arts Award, 1993; Scientific American Young Readers Book Award, 1995; Parents Choice Award, 1995; American Library Association Notable Book Award, 1996; Knickerbocker Award for Juvenile Literature, New York Library Association, 1996. Memberships: National Association for the Preservation and Perpetuation of Storytelling; PEN; Poetry Society of America. Address: PO Box 308, Greenfield Center, NY 12833, USA.

BRUIN John. See: **BRUTUS Dennis (Vincent).**

BRULOTTE Gaëtan, b. Apr 1945, Lévis, Quebec, Canada. Professor; Writer. Education: BA, 1966, 1969, MA, 1972, Laval University; PhD, École des Hautes Études en Sciences Sociales, Paris, 1977. Appointments: Instructor, Laval University, 1969; Professor of French, Trois-Rivières College, 1970-83; Visiting Professor, Université du Québec a Trois-Rivières, 1973, 1980, 1981, 1989, 1990, University of New Mexico, 1981, 1982, 1983, 1984, 1993-94, University of California at Santa Barbara, 1982, Brevard Community College, 1983-84, University of South Florida, 1984-88, Université Stendahl, 1993, Sorbonne, Paris, 1994; Distinguished Visiting Professor, New Mexico State University, 1988; Professor, University of South Florida, 1988-. Publications: L'Imaginaire et l'écriture: Ghelderode, 1972; Aspects du texte érotique, 1977, revised edition as Oeuvres de chair: Figures du discours érotique, 1997; L'Emprise (novel), 1979, revised edition, 1988, English translation as Double Exposure, 1988; Ecrivains de la Mauricie (editor), 1981; Le Surveillant (short stories), 1982, 3rd edition, revised, 1995, English translation as The Secret Voice, 1990; Le Client (play), 1983; Ce qui nous tient, 1988; L'Univers du peintre Jean Paul Lemieux (critical essay), 1996. Contributions to: Books, anthologies, textbooks, scholarly journals, and periodicals. Honours: Adrienne-Choquette Award, 1981; France-Quebec Award, 1983; 1st Prize, XI CBC Radio Drama Contest, 1983; Literary Grand Prize, Trois-Rivières, 1989; John-Glassco Translation Award, 1990. Memberships: International Comparative Literature Association; International Council on Francophone Studies; Modern Language Association. Address: c/o Division of Modern Language, University of South Florida, Tampa, FL 33620, USA.

BRUNNER Eva, b. 26 Nov 1952, Lucerne, Switzerland. Writer; Playwright; translator. Education: Communications, American College of Rome, c/o University of Charleston, West Virginia, 1979-82. Publications: Plays: Kalt, 1984; Granit, 1985; Alles Wird Gut, 1994; Frieda Flachmann, 1997; Radio: Geist trug die Steine, 1988; Herrischer und Herrscherin, 1989; Der Schweiz dem Rücken, 1991. Honours: Various scholarships. Membership: Swiss Writers' Association. Address: Kuglerstrasse 22, 10439 Berlin, Germany.

BRUNSE Niels (Henning), b. 24 Aug 1949, Silkeborg, Denmark. Editor; Writer; Translator. m. Galina Ivashkina, 18 Mar 1977, div. Education: University of Copenhagen; University of Moscow. Appointments: Co-Editor, Hug magazine, 1974-76, Politisk Revy, bi-weekly, 1978-82; Reviewer, Information newspaper, 1982-94; Editor, Danish Writers Association Journal, 1983-85; Writer, Politiken, 1994-. Publications: Several books; Numerous translations. Contributions to: Many periodicals. Honours: Danish State Art Foundation Lifetime Grant; Danish Translators Association Honorary Award; Thornton Niven Wilder Award, Columbia University. Memberships: Danish Dramatists Association; Danish PEN; Danish Writers Association. Address: Aalandsgade 26, DK-2300 Copenhagen, Denmark.

BRUNSKILL Ronald William, b. 3 Jan 1929, Lowton, England. Retired Architect; Professor; Writer. m. Miriam Allsopp, 1960, 2 daughters. Education: BA, 1951, MA, 1952, PhD, 1963, University of Manchester. Appointments: Commonwealth Fund Fellow in Architecture and Town Planning, Massachusetts Institue of Technology, 1956-57; Architect, Williams Deacon's Bank, 1957-60; Lecturer, 1960-73, Senior Lecturer, 1973-84, Reader in Architecture, 1984-89, Honorary Fellow, School of Architecture, 1989-95, University of Manchester; Partner, 1966-69, Consultant, 1969-73, Carter, Brunskill & Associates, architects; Visiting Professor, University of Florida at Gainesville, 1969-70; President, Vernacular Architect Group, 1974-77; Honorary Visiting Professor, 1994-95, Professor, School of the Built Environment, 1995-, De Montfort University. Publications: Illustrated Handbook of Vernacular Architecture, 1971, 3rd edition, enlarged, 1987; Vernacular Architecture of the Lake Counties, 1974; English Brickwork (with Alec Clifton-Taylor), 1977; Traditional Buildings of Britain, 1981, 2nd edition, enlarged, 1992; Traditional Farm Buildings of Britain, 1982, 2nd edition, enlarged, 1987; Timber Building in Britain, 1985, 2nd edition, enlarged, 1994; Brick Building in Britain, 1990; Houses and Cottages of Britain, 1997. Contributions to: Scholarly journals. Honours: Fellow, Society of Antiquaries, 1975-; President's Award, Manchester Society of Architects, 1977; Officer of the Order of the British Empire, 1990. Memberships: Cumberland and Westmorland Antiquarian and Archaeological Society, Vice President, 1975-90, President, 1990-93; Historic Buildings Council for England, 1978-84; Cathedrals Advisory Committee for England, 1981-91; Cathedrals Fabric Commission, 1991-96; Ancient Monuments Society, honorary architect, 1983-88, Vice Chairman, 1988-90, chairman, 1990-; Royal Commission on the Ancient and Historical Monuments for Wales, 1983-, Vice Chairman 1993-; British Historic Buildings Trust, trustee, 1985-92; Commissioner, Historic Buildings and Monuments Commission, 1989-95; Cathedrals Advisory Commission, 1991-96. Address: De Montford University, Centre for Conservation Studies, School of the Built Environment, 12 Castle View, Leicester LE1 5WH, England.

BRUSEWITZ Gunnar (Kurt), b. 7 Oct 1924, Stockholm, Sweden. Author; Artist. m. Ingrid Andersson, 21 Oct 1946, 2 daughter. Education: Royal Academy of Art. Publications: Hunting - A Cultural History Chronicle of Hunting in Europe, 1967; Bjornjagare och Fjarilsmalare, 1968; Skissbok, 1970; Nature in Gambia, 1971; Skog, 1974; Strandspegling, 1979; Wings and Seasons, 1980; Sveriges Natur, 1984. Contributions to: Stockholms Tidningen; Svenska Dagbladet; Various Other Swedish Magazines and Publications. Honours: Stockholm City Presentation Prize, 1970; Dag Hammarskjold Medal, 1975; Die Golde Blume Von Rheydt Düsseldorf, 1989; Honorary DPhil, 1982. Memberships: PEN; Swedish Section, World Wildlife Fund; Royal Society of Science in Uppsala. Literary Agent: Wahlstrom & Windstrand Forlag, Stockholm. Address: Lisinge, 762 93 Rimbo, Sweden.

BRUTON Eric, (Eric Moore), b. 1915, London, England. Author; Company Director. Appointments: Managing Director, NAG Press Ltd, Colchester, 1963-93; Managing Director, Diamond Boutique Ltd, 1965-80; Chairman, Things & Ideas Ltd, 1970-78. Publications: True Book about Clocks, 1957; Death in Ten Point Bold, 1957; Die Darling Die, 1959; Violent Brothers, 1960; True Book about Diamonds, 1961; The Hold Out, 1961; King Diamond, 1961; The Devil's Pawn, 1962; Automation, 1962; Dictionary of Clocks and Watches, 1962; The Laughing Policeman, 1963; The Longcase Clock, 1964, 2nd edition, 1978; The Finsbury Mob, 1964; The Smithfield Slayer, 1964; The Wicked Saint, 1965; The Fire Bug, 1967; Clocks and Watches 1400-1900, 1967; Clocks and Watches, 1968; Diamonds, 1970, 2nd edition, 1977; Antique Clocks and Clock Collecting, 1974; The History of Clocks, 1978; The Wetherby Collection of Clocks, 1980; Legendary Gems, 1984. Honour: Eric Bruton Medal created for awarding to

outstanding student in annual international diamond exams, 1996. Memberships: Council Member, British Horological Institute, 1955-62; Committee Member, Crime Writers Association, 1959-62; Council Member, Gemmological Association of GB, 1972-91, President, 1994-95; President, National Association of Goldsmiths, 1983-85. Address: Pond House, Great Bentley, Colchester CO7 8QG, England.

BRUTUS Dennis (Vincent), (John Bruin), b. 28 Nov 1924, Zimbabwe. Professor of African Literature. m. May Jaggers, 14 May 1950, 4 sons, 4 daughters. Education: BA; CED; DHL; LLD. Publications: Sirens, Knuckles, Boots; Letters to Martha; A Simple Lust; Stubborn Hope; Still the Sirens; Airs and Tributes; Strains; China Poems; Poems from Algiers; Salutes and Censures; As John Bruin: Thoughts Abroad (Poems). Contributions to: Periodicals. Honours: Paul Robeson Award; Langston Hughes Award. Membership: African Literature Association; Union of Writers of African Peoples; ACLU; Amnesty International; PEN. Address: University of Pittsburgh, Pittsburgh, PA 15260, USA.

BRYAN Lynne, b. 10 May 1961, Leicester, England. Writer. Education: BA, Humanities, Wolverhampton Poly, 1980-83; MA, Creative Writing, University of East Anglia, 1984-85. Publication: Envy at the Cheese Handout, 1995. Contributions to: Director, Scottish Feminist magazine, Harpies & Quines, 1990-93; Stories in various anthologies. Honours: Eastern Arts Grant, 1996; BBC Arts Council Award for Write Out Loud, 1996. Literary Agent: Jane Bradish-Ellames, Curtis Brown. Address: c/o Curtis Brown, Haymarket House, 28-29 Haymarket, London SW1Y 4SP, England.

BRYANS Robin. See: HARBINSON-BRYANS Robert.

BRYANT Dorothy (Mae), b. 8 Feb 1930, San Francisco, California, USA. Writer; Teacher; Publisher. m. (1) 1949-64, 1 son, 1 daughter, (2) Robert Bryant, 18 Oct 1968, 1 stepson, 1 stepdaughter. Education: BA, 1950, MA, 1964, San Francisco State University. Appointments: Teacher, High School, 1953-64, San Francisco State University, San Francisco Mission Adult School, Golden Gate College, 1961-64, Contra Costa College, 1964-76; Publisher, Ata Books, 1978-. Publications: Fiction: Ella Price's Journal, 1972; The Kin of Ata Are Waiting for You, 1976; Miss Giardino, 1978; The Garden of Eros, 1979; Prisoners, 1980; Killing Wonder, 1981; A Day in San Francisco, 1983; Confessions of Madame Psyche, 1986; The Test, 1991; Anita, Anita, 1993. Plays: Dear Master, 1991; Tea With Mrs Hardy, 1992; The Panel, 1996; The Trial of Cornelia Connelly, 1996. Non-Fiction: Writing a Novel, 1979; Myths to Lie By: Essays and Stories, 1984. Honour: American Book Award, 1987. Address: 1928 Stuart Street, Berkeley, CA 94703, USA.

BRYANT J(oseph) A(llen), b. 26 Nov 1919, Glasgow, Kentucky, USA. Professor (retired); Writer. m. (1) Mary Virginia Woodruff, 28 Dec 1946, 2 sons, (2) Sara C Bryant, 9 Mar 1993. Education: AB, Western Kentucky University, 1940; MA, Vanderbilt University, 1941; PhD, Yale University, 1948. Appointments: Instructor to Associate Professor, Vanderbilt University, 1945-56; Associate Professor, University of the South at Sewanee, 1956-59, Duke University, 1959-61; Professor, University of North Carolina, 1961-68, Syracuse University, 1968-71, University of Kentucky, 1973-90. Publications: Hippolyta's View: Some Christian Aspects of Shakespeare's Plays, 1961; The Compassionate Satirist: Ben Jonson and His Imperfect World, 1972; Understanding Randall Jarrell, 1986; Shakespeare and the Uses of Comedy, 1986. Address: 713 Old Dobbin Road, Lexington, KY 40502, USA.

BRYDEN John Herbert, b. 15 July 1943. Member of Parliament. m. Catherine Armstrong, 26 Aug 1967, 1 son, 2 daughters. Education: BA, honours, McMaster University, 1966; MPhil, University of Leeds, 1968. Publications: Deadly Allies: Canada's Secret War 1937-1947, 1989; Best Kept Secret: Canadian Secret Intelligence in the Second World War, 1993. Literary Agent: Marian Hebb, 52 St Patrick Street, Toronto, Ontario M5T 1U1, Canada. Address: 83 Lynden Road, Lynden, Toronto, Ontario L0R 1T0, Canada.

BRZEZINSKI Zbigniew (Kazimierz), b. 28 Mar 1928, Warsaw, Poland (US citizen, 1958). Professor of American Foreign Policy; Author. m. Emilie Anna Benes, 3 children. Education: BA, 1949, MA, 1950, McGill University; PhD, Harvard University, 1953. Appointments: Instructor and Research Fellow, 1953-56, Assistant Professor of Government and Research Associate, 1956-60, Harvard University; Associate Professor, 1960-62, Professor of Public Law and Government and Director of the Research Institute on International

Change, 1962-77, 1981-89, Columbia University; Director, Trilateral Commission, 1973-76; Assistant to President Jimmy Carter for National Security Affairs, 1977-81; Counselor, Center for Strategic and International Studies, 1981-; Robert E Osgood Professor of American Foreign Policy, Paul Nitze School of Advanced International Studies, Johns Hopkins University, 1989-; Guest Lecturer and Advisor to governmental and private institutions in the US and abroad; Public Speaker; Television Commentator. Publications: Political Controls in the Soviet Army (editor), 1954; The Permanent Purge: Politics in Soviet Totalitarianism, 1956; Ideology and Foreign Affairs (with others), 1959; The Soviet Bloc: Unity and Conflict, 1960, revised edition, 1967; Totalitarian Dictatorship and Autocracy (with Carl Joachim Friedrich), 1961, 2nd edition, 1965; Ideology and Power in Soviet Politics, 1962, revised edition, 1967; Africa and the Communist World (editor), 1963; Political Power: USA/USSR (with Samuel P Huntington), 1964, 2nd edition, 1977; Alternative to Partition: For a Broader Conception of America's Role in Europe, 1965; Dilemmas of Change in Soviet Politics (editor), 1969; The Fragile Blossom: Crisis and Change in Japan, 1972; Between Two Ages: America's Role in the Technetronic Era, 1970; Power and Principle: Memoirs of the National Security Advisor, 1977-1981, 1983; Democracy Must Work: A Trilateral Agenda for the Decade: A Task Force Report of the Trilateral Commission (with others), 1984; Game Plan: A Geostrategic Framework for the Conduct of the US-Soviet Contest, 1986; Promise or Peril, the Strategic Defense Initiative: Thirty-Five Essays by Statesmen, Scholars, and Strategic Analysts (with Richard Sincere, Marin Strmecki, and Peter Wehner), 1986; In Quest of National Security, 1988; The Grand Failure: The Birth and Death of Communism in the Twentieth Century, 1989; Out of Control: Global Turmoil on the Eve of the Twenty-First Century, 1993. Contributions to: Many publications, journals, and periodicals. Honours: Guggenheim Fellowship, 1960; Presidential Medal of Freedom, 1981; U Thant Award, 1995; Order of the White Eagle, Poland, 1995. Memberships: American Academy of Arts and Sciences, fellow; Amnesty International; Atlantic Council; Council on Foreign Relations; Freedom House; National Endowment for Democracy; Trilateral Commission. Address: Center for Strategic and International Studies, 1800 K Street North West, Washington DC 20006, USA.

BUCH JENSEN Poul, b. 4 Jan 1937, Copenhagen, Denmark. Mechanical Engineer. m. Anna-Lise, 28 July 1962, 1 son, 1 daughter. Education: Bachelor, Engineering; Bachelor, Economics and Marketing. Publications: ISO 9000: A Guide and Commentary, 1991; ISO 9000: Internal Quality Audits, 1992; Service, 1994; Environmental Management and Environmental Certifications, 1994. Contributions to: Numerous magazines and journals. Memberships: Danish Authors Society; American Society for Quality Control; Rotary Club. Address: Alfarvejen 30 - Osted, DK-4000 Roskilde, Denmark.

BUCHANAN Colin Ogilvie, b. 9 Aug 1934, Croydon, Surrey, England. Church of England Clerk in Holy Orders. Education: BA, 1959, MA, 1962, Lincoln College, Oxford; Tyndale Hall, Bristol, 1959-61; DD, 1993. Appointment: Bishop of Woolwich, Diocese of Southark, 1996-. Publications: Editor, Modern Anglican Liturgies, 1958-68, 1968; Further Anglican Liturgies, 1968-75, 1975; Latest Anglican Liturgies, 1976-84, 1985; Modern Anglican Ordination Rites, 1987; The Bishop in Liturgy, 1988; Open to Others, 1992; Joint Author: Growing into Union, 1970; Anglican Worship Today, 1980; Reforming Infant Baptism, 1990; Infant Baptism and the Gospel, 1993; Cut the Connection: Disestablishment and the Church of England, 1994; Editor, News of Liturgy Monthly, 1975-. Membership: House of Bishops of General Synod of the Church of England; Vice President, Electoral Reform Society. Address: c/o Southwark Diocesan Office, Trinity House, 4 Chapel Court, Borough High Street, London SE1 1HW, England.

BUCHER Werner, b. 19 Aug 1938, Zürich, Switzerland. Author; Editor; Journalist. m. Josiane Fidanza, 2 May 1968. Publications: Nicht Solche Aengste, du..., poems, 1974;Zeitzünder 3: Dank an den Engel, 1987; Was Ist Mit Lazarus? 1989; Einst & Jetzt & Morgen, poems, 1989; Mouchette, poems, 1995; Wegschleudern die Brillen, die Lümgem, poems, 1995; Unruhen, 1997. Contributions to: Entwürfe. Memberships: SSV; Schweiz; Schriftstellerverband; Postfach; PEN, Switzerland. Address: Rest, Kreuz, 9427 Zelg-Wolfhalden, Switzerland.

BUCHWALD Art, b. 20 Oct 1925, Mt Vernon, New York, USA. Columnist; Author. m. Ann McGarry, 11 Oct 1952, 1 son, 2 daughters. Education: University of Southern California, Los Angeles, 1945-48.

Appointments: Syndicated columnist for newspapers around the world. Publications: Paris After Dark, 1950; Art Buchwald's Paris, 1954; The Brave Coward, 1957; More Caviar, 1958; Un Cadeau Pour le Patron, 1958; A Gift From the Boys, 1959; Don't Forget to Write, 1960; How Much is That in Dollars?, 1961; Is it Safe to Drink the Water?, 1962; Art Buchwald's Secret List to Paris, 1963; I Chose Capitol Punishment, 1963; And Then I Told the President, 1965; Son of the Great Society, 1966; Have I Ever Lied to You?, 1968; The Establishment is Alive and Well in Washington, 1969; Counting Sheep, 1970; Getting High in Government Circles, 1971; I Never Danced at the White House, 1973; The Bollo Caper, 1974; I Am Not a Crook, 1974; Irving's Delight, 1975; Washington is Leaking, 1976; Down the Seine and Up the Potomac, 1977; The Buchwald Stops Here, 1978; Laid Back in Washington, 1981; While Reagan Slept, 1983; You CAN Fool All of the People All of the Time, 1985; I Think I Don't Remember, 1987; Whose Rose Garden is it Anyway?, 1989; Lighten Up, George, 1991; Leaving Home: A Memoir, 1994. Honours: Priz de la Bonne Humeur, 1958; Pulitzer Prize in Commentary, 1982. Memberships: American Academy of Arts and Sciences; American Academy of Humor Columnists. Address: 2000 Pennsylvania Avenue North West, Washington DC 20006, USA.

BUCK Lilli Lee, b. 25 Feb 1950, Butler, Pennsylvania, USA. Teacher; Professional Astrologer. Education: BA, Anthropology, 1972, MEd, Special Education, 1984, College of William and Mary. Publications: Poems in following books: A Vagabond's Sketchbook, 1980; A Lyrical Fiesta, 1985; Poetic Symphony, 1987; Golden Voices, Past and Present, 1989; Voices on the Wind, 1989; Special Poets' Series, 1990; The Poet's Domain, Vol III, 1991, Vol V, 1992. Contribution to: Fate magazine, 1984. Honours: 3rd Place, World of Poetry Contest, 1983; Excellence in Poetry Award, Fine Arts Press, 1985; Editors Choice Award, National Library of Poetry, 1994. Memberships: Poetry Society of Virginia; Association for Research and Enlightenment; Kappa Delta Pi. Address: 7000 Reedy Creek Rd, Bristol, VA 24202, USA.

BUCKERIDGE Anthony Malcolm, b. 20 June 1912, London, England. Writer. m (1) Sylvia Brown, 1936, (2) Eileen Norah Selby, 25 Feb 1972, 2 sons, 1 daughter. Education: University College, London, 1932-35. Publications: The Jennings Series of Children's Books, Comprising 25 Titles, 1950-91; The Rex Milligan Series, 4 Titles, 1953-56; A Funny Thing Happened, 1953; Musicals: It Happened in Hamelin, 1980; Jennings Abounding, 1979; The Cardboard Conspiracy, 1985. Memberships: Society of Authors; Writers Guild of Great Britain; British Actors Equity. Address: East Crink, Barcombe Mills, Lewes, Sussex BN8 5BL, England.

BUCKLE (Christopher) Richard (Sandford), b. 6 Aug 1916, England. Education: Balliol College, Oxford. Appointments: Director, Theatre Museum Association, 1978-; Ballet Critic, Observer newspaper, 1948-55, The Sunday Times, 1959-75. Publications: John Innocent at Oxford (novel), 1939; The Adventures of a Ballet Critic, 1953; In Search of Diaghilev, 1955; Modern Ballet Design, 1955; The Prettiest Girl in England, 1958; Jacob Epstein, Sculptor, 1963; Nijinsky, 1969; Diaghilev, 1979; Buckle at the Ballet, 1980. Autobiographies: The Most Upsetting Woman, 1981; In the Wake of Diaghilev, 1982; with John Taras, George Balanchine: Ballet Master, 1988. Honour: Commander of the Order of the British Empire, 1979. Address: Roman Road, Gutch Common, Semley, Shaftesbury, Dorset, England.

BUCKLEY William F(rank), Jr, b. 24 Nov 1925, New York, New York, USA. Editor; Author. m. Patricia Taylor, 6 June 1950, 1 son. Education: University of Mexico, 1943; BA, Yale University, 1950. Appointments: Associate Editor, American Mercury magazine, 1952; Founder, President, Editor-in-Chief, 1955-90, Editor-at-Large, 1991-, National Review magazine; Syndicated columnist, 1962-; Host, Firing Line TV programme, 1966-; Lecturer, New School for Social Research, 1967-68; Froman Distinguished Professor, Russell Sage College, 1973; US Delegate, 28th General Assembly, United Nations, 1973. Publications: God and Man at Yale, 1951; McCarthy and His Enemies (with L Brent Bozell), 1954; Up from Liberalism, 1959; Rumbles Left and Right, 1963; The Unmaking of a Mayor, 1966; The Jeweler's Eye, 1968; The Governor Listeth, 1970; Cruising Speed, 1971; Inveighing We Will Go, 1972; Four Reforms, 1973; United Nations Journal, 1974; Execution Eve, 1975; Saving the Queen, 1976; Airborne, 1976; Stained Glass, 1978; A Hymnal, 1978; Who's On First, 1980; Marco Polo, If You Can, 1982; Atlantic High, 1982; Overdrive, 1983; The Story of Henri Tod, 1984; The Temptation of Wilfred Malachey, 1985; See You Later Alligator, 1985; Right Reason, 1985; High Jinx, 1986;

Racing Through Paradise, 1987; Mongoose, R.I.P., 1988; On the Firing Line, 1989; Gratitude, 1990; Windfall, 1992; In Search of Anti-Semitism, 1992; Happy Days Were Here Again: Reflections of the Libertarian Journalist, 1993; A Very Private Plot, 1994. Editor: The Committee and Its Critics, 1962; Odyssey of a Friend: Whittaker Chamber's Letters to William F. Buckley, Jr., 1954-61, 1970; American Conservative Thought in the Twentieth Century, 1970; Keeping the Tablets (with Charles Kesler), 1988.Contributions to: Books and periodicals. Honours: Best Columnist of the Year Award, 1967; Distinguished Achievement Award in Journalism, University of Southern California, 1968; Emmy Award for Outstanding Program Achievement, National Academy of Television Arts and Sciences, 1969; Bellarime Medal, 1977; Shelby Cullen Davis Award, 1986; Julius Award for Outstanding Public Service, University of Southern California, 1990; Presidential Medal of Freedom, 1991; Gold Medal, National Institute of Social Sciences, 1992. Memberships: Council on Foreign Relations; Fellow, Society of Professional Journalists, Sigma Delta Chi. Address: c/o National Review, 150 East 35th Street, New York, NY 10016, USA.

BUCZACKI Stefan Tadeusz, b. 16 Oct 1945, Derby, England. Writer; Broadcaster. m. Beverley Ann Charman, 8 Aug 1970, 2 sons. Education: BSc, Southampton University; DPhil, Oxford University. Publications include: Collins Guide to Pests, Diseases and Disorders of Garden Plants, 1981; Collins Gem Guide to Mushrooms and Toadstools, 1982; Zoosporic Plant Pathogens, 1983; Beat Garden Pests and Diseases, 1985; Gardener's Questions Answered, 1985; Garden Warfare, 1988; Understanding Your Garden, 1990; The Essential Gardener, 1991; The Plant Care Manual, 1992; Collins Guide to Mushrooms and Toadstools of Britain and Europe, 1993; The Gardener's Handbook, 1993; Stefan Buczacki's Best Gardening Series, 1994. Contributions to: Times; Financial Times; Country; Sunday Mirror; Guardian; The Gardener; Geographical Magazine; Countryman; House and Garden; Numerous Other Journals and Magazines. Memberships: Royal Photographic Society; Fellowships: Institute of Biology; Institute of Horticulture; Linnean Society. Address: c/o Barbara Levy, Literary Agent, 64 Greenhill, Hampstead High Street, London NW3 5TZ, England.

BUDDEE Paul (Edgar), b. 12 Mar 1913, Western Australia. Retired School Principal; Author; Poet. m. Elizabeth Vere Bremner, 1944, 1 son, 1 daughter. Education: Claremont Teachers College. Appointments: School Principal, grade class 7 to class 1A, 1935-72. Publications: Stand to and Other War Poems, 1943; The Oscar and Olga Trilogy, 1943-47; The Unwilling Adventurers, 1967; The Mystery of Moma Island, 1969; The Air Patrol Series, 1972; The Ann Rankin Series, 1972; The Escape of the Fenians, 1972; The Peter Devlin Series, 1972; The Escape of John O'Reilly, 1973; The Call of the Sky, 1978; The Fate of the Artful Dodger, 1984; Poems of the Second World War, 1986. Contributions to: Many periodicals. Honours: Australia Citizen of the Year, 1979; Australia Commonwealth Literary Board Grants, 1977, 1978, 1984; OAM, 1989. Memberships: Australian Society of Authors; Fellowship of Writers; PEN International. Address: 2 Butson Road, Leeming, Western Australia 6149, Australia.

BUDRYS Algis, (Algirdas Jonas Budrys), b. 9 Jan 1931, Königsberg, Germany (Lithuanian citizen from birth, US citizen, 1996). Writer; Editor; Publisher. m. Edna F Duna, 24 July 1954, 4 sons. Education: University of Miami, 1947-49; Columbia University, 1951-52. Appointments: Editor-in-Chief, Regency Books, 1962-63; Playboy Press, 1963-65; Operations Manager, Woodall Publishing Co, 1974-75; President, Unifont Co, 1975-; Editor and Publisher, Tomorrow Speculative Fiction magazine, 1992-. Publications: Novels: False Night, 1954, revised edition as Some Will Not Die, 1962; Man of Earth, 1955; Who?, 1958; The Falling Torch, 1959; Rogue Moon, 1960; The Iron Thorn, 1967; Michaelmas, 1977; Falling Torch, revised edition, 1991; Hard Landing, 1993. Collections: The Unexpected Dimension, 1960; The Furious Future, 1963; Blood and Burning, 1979. Non-Fiction: Truman and the Pendergasts, 1963; Bicycles: How They Work and How to Fix Them, 1976; Writing to the Point, 1994. Contributions to: Numerous magazines. Honours: Many awards. Membership: Science Fiction Hall of Fame. Address: 824 Seward Street, Evanston, IL 60202, USA.

BUERO VALLEJO Antonio, b. 29 Sept 1916, Guadalajara, Spain. Dramatist. m. Victoria Rodriguez, 5 Mar 1959, 2 sons. Education: BA, 1932; San Fernando School of Fine Arts, Madrid, 1934-36. Publications: Plays in English Translation: En la ardiente oscuridad, 1951, In the Burning Darkness, 1975; La tejedora de

suenos, 1952, The Dreamweaver, 1967; Un sonador para un pueblo, 1959, A Dreamer for the People, 1994; Las meninas: Fantasia velazquena, 1961, Las meninas: A Fantasy, 1987; El concierto de San Ovidio, 1963, The Concert at Saint Ovide, 1967; El tragaluz, 1968, The Skylight, 1992; La doble historia del doctor Valmy, 1967, The Double Case History of Doctor Valmy, 1967; El sueno de la razon, 1970, The Sleep of Reason, 1971; La fundacion, 1974, The Foundation, 1985; La detonacion, 1977, The Shot, 1989; Jueces en la noche, 1979, Judges in the Night, 1989; Lazaro en el laberinto, 1986, Lazarus in the Labyrinth, 1992; Musica cercana, 1989, The Music Window, 1994; Many other plays in Spanish only. Honours: Premio Lope de Vega, 1949; Premio Nacional de Teatro, 1957, 1958, 1959, 1980; Medalla de Oro del Espectador y la critica, 1967, 1970, 1974, 1976, 1977, 1981, 1984, 1986; Officier des Palmes Academiques de France, 1980; Premio Pablo Iglesias, 1986; Premio Miguel de Cervantes, 1986; Medalla de Oro al Merite en las Bellas Artes, 1994; Medalla de Oro de la Sociedad General de Autores de Espana, 1994; National Letters Prize, 1996. Memberships: Ateneo de Madrid, honorary fellow; Circulo de Bellas Artes de Madrid, honorary fellow; Deutscher Hispanistenverband, honorary fellow; International Committee of the Theatre of the Nations; Modern Language Association of America, honorary fellow; Real Academia Española; Sociedad General de Autores de Espana. Address: Calle General Diaz Porlier 36, Madrid 28001, Spain.

BUISSERET David Joseph, b. 18 Dec 1934, Isle of Wight, England. History Teacher; Researcher. m. Patricia Connolly, 9 Sept 1961, 3 sons, 2 daughters. Education: BA, 1958, PhD, 1961, Corpus Christi College. Appointments: University of West Indies, 1964-80; The Newberry Library, 1960-95; University of Texas at Arlington, 1995. Publications: Sully; Port Royal, Jamaica; Historic Architecture of the Caribbean; Henry IV; Historic Illinois from the Air. Honours: Premiere Medaille, Institute of France; Centennial Medal, Institute of Jamaica; J B Jackson Prize; Chevalier des Palmes Académiques, 1993. Address: Department of History, University of Texas at Arlington, Box 19529, Arlington, TX 76019-0529, USA.

BULLA Clyde Robert, b. 9 Jan 1914, King City, Missouri, USA. Author. Publications: A Tree is a Plant, 1960; Three-Dollar Mule, 1960; The Sugar Pear Tree, 1961; Benito, 1961; What Makes A Shadow?, 1962; The Ring and The Fire: Stories from Wagner's Niebelung Operas, 1962; Viking Adventure, 1963; Indian Hill, 1963; St Valentine's Day, 1965; More Stories of Favorite Operas, 1965; White Bird, 1966; Lincoln's Birthday, 1967; Washington's Bithday, 1967; Flowerpot Gardens, 1967; Stories of Gilbert and Sullivan Operas, 1968; The Ghost of Windy Hill, 1968; Mika's Apple Tree: A Story of Finland, 1968; The Moon Singer, 1969; New Boy in Dublin: A Story of Ireland, 1969; Jonah and the Great Fish, 1970; Joseph the Dreamer, 1971; Pocahontas and the Strangers, 1971; Open the Door and See All the People, 1972; Dexter, 1973; The Wish at the Top, 1974; Shoeshine Girl, 1975; Marco Moonlight, 1976; The Beast of Lor, 1977; Conquista! (with Michael Syson), 1978; Last Look, 1979; The Stubborn Old Woman, 1980; My Friend the Monster, 1980; Daniel's Duck, 1980; A Lion to Guard Us, 1981; Almost a Hero, 1981; Dandelion Hill, 1982; Poor Boy, Rich Boy, 1982; Charlie's House, 1983; The Cardboard Crown, 1984; A Grain of Wheat, 1985; The Chalk Box Kid, 1987; Singing Sam, 1989; The Christmas Coat, 1989; A Place for Angels, 1995. Memberships: Authors Guild; Society of Children's Book Writers and Illustrators. Literary Agent: Curtis Brown Ltd, 10 Astor Place, New York, NY 10003, USA. Address: 1230 Las Flores Drive, Los Angeles, CA 90041, USA.

BULLINS Ed, b. 2 July 1935, Philadelphia, Pennsylvania, USA. Dramatist; Author; Teacher. Education: BA, Antioch University, 1989; MFA, San Francisco State University, 1994. Appointments: Instructor, City College of San Francisco, 1984-88, Contra Costa College, 1989-; Lecturer, Sonoma State University, 1987-88, San Francisco State University, 1993. Publications: Over 40 published plays, many others unpublished. Other: The Hungered One (stories), 1971; The Reluctant Rapist (novel), 1973. Honours: National Endowment for the Arts Grants; Rockefeller Foundation Grants; Guggenheim Fellowships, 1971, 1976; Obie Award, 1975; New York Drama Critics Circle Award, 1975; Honorary LittD, Columbia College, Chicago, 1975. Address: 3617 San Pablo Avenue, No 118, Emeryville, CA 94608, USA.

BULLOCK Kenneth K(en), b. 26 July 1929, Liverpool, England (Canadian citizen, 1951-66, Australian citizen, 1966-). Writing Consultant. 2 sons, 2 daughters. Education: Dip Comm, 1961, Royal Canadian Naval College, HMCS, Victoria. Appointments: British

Merchant Navy, 1946-49; Service aircrew, RCN, RAN, 1950-72; Papua New Guinea Prime Ministers Department, Office of Information, 1980-83; Writer, Editor, Teacher, Journalist Counsellor/External Tutor, James Cook University, 1984-95. Publications: Emergency, 1979; Family Guide to Beach and Water Safety, 1980; Silly Billy Learns a Lesson, 1981; Papua New Guinea, 1981; Water Proofing Your Child, 1982; Pelandok, 1986; Port Pirie the Friendly City, 1988; Chopstik, 1993; Beyond Peril, 1996. Contributions to: Papua New Guinea; Post Courier; National Times; Australia; Adelaide Advertiser; Sunshine Coast Daily. Honours: CD, Canadian Military Service Decoration, 1963; Citizen of the Year, 1984; Port Pirie, 1984-88. Memberships: Fellowship of Australian Writers; Australian Society of Authors. Address: 63 Buderim Garden Villge, Mooloolaba Road, Buderim, Queensland 4556, Australia.

BULLOCK Michael, b. 19 Apr 1918, London, England. Professor Emeritus; Poet; Dramatist; Writer; Translator. Education: Hornsey College of Art. Appointments: Commonwealth Fellow, 1968, Professor of Creative Writing, 1969-83, Professor Emeritus, 1983-, University of British Columbia, Vancouver, Canada; McGuffey Visiting Professor of English, Ohio University, Athens, Ohio, 1969; New Asia Ming Yu Visiting Scholar, 1989, Writer-in-Residence, 1996, New Asia College, Chinese University of Hong Kong; Adviser, New Poetry Society of China, 1995-. Publications: Poetry: Transmutations, 1938; Sunday is a Day of Incest, 1961; World Without Beginning Amen, 1963, 2nd edition, 1973; Two Voices of My Mouth/Zwei Stimmen in meinem mund, bilingual edition, 1967; A Savage Darkness, 1969; Black Wings White Dead, 1978; Lines in the Dark Wood, 1981; Quadriga for Judy, 1982; Prisoner of the Rain, poems in prose, 1983; Brambled Heart, 1985; Dark Water, 1987; Poems on Green Paper, 1988; The Secret Garden, 1990; Avatars of the Moon, 1990; Labyrinths, 1992; The Walled Garden, 1992; The Sorcerer with Deadly Nightshade Eyes, 1993; The Inflowing River, 1993; Moons and Mirrors, 1994; Dark Roses, 1994; Stone and Shadow, 1996. Fiction: Sixteen Stories as They Happened, 1969; Green Beginning Black Ending, 1971; Randolph Cranstone and the Pursuing River, 1975; Randolph Cranstone and the Glass Thimble, 1977; The Man with Flowers Through His Hands, 1985; The Double Ego, 1985; Randolph Cranstone and the Veil of Maya, 1986; The Story of Noire, 1987; Randolph Cranstone Takes the Inward Path, 1988; The Burning Chapel, 1991; The Invulnerable Ovoid Aura, Stories and Poems, 1995; Voices of the River, 1995. Other: Selected Works (co-editors Peter Loeffler and Jack Stewart), 1997. Contributions to: Many anthologies. Honours: Schlegel-Tieck German Translation Prize, 1966; British New Fiction Society Book of the Month, 1977; Canada Council French Translation Award, 1979; San Francisco Review of Books Best Book List, 1982; San Jose Mercury News Best Booklist, 1984; Okanagan Short Fiction Award, 1986. Address: 103-3626 West 28th Avenue, Vancouver, British Columbia V6S 1S4, Canada.

BULMER Henry Kenneth, (Alan Burt Akers, Ken Blake, Kenneth Bulmer, Ernest Corley, Arthur Frazier, Adam Hardy, Kenneth Johns, Philip Kent, Bruno Kraus, Neil Langholm, Karl Maras, Charles R Pike, Andrew Quiller, Richard Silver, Tully Zetford), b. 14 Jan 1921, London, England. Author. m. Pamela Buckmaster, 7 Mar 1953, 1 son, 2 daughters. Publications: City Under the Sea, 1957; The Ulcer Culture, 1969; Dray Prescot Saga, 1972; Roller Coaster World, 1972; Fox Series, 1972-77; Sea Wolf Series, 1978-82; Strike Force Falklands, 1984-86; Fox and Falklands. Contributions to: Periodicals. Address: 5 Holly Mansions, 20 Frant Road, Tunbridge Wells, Kent TN2 5SN, England.

BULPIN Thomas Victor, b. 31 Mar 1918, Umkomaas, South Africa. Writer; Publisher. Education: St John's College, Johannesburg. Appointments: Writer and Publisher, Books of South Africa (Pty) Ltd and TV Bulpin Ltd, Cape Town, 1946-. Publications: Lost Trails on the Low Veld, 1950; Shaka's Country, 1952; To the Shores of Natal, 1953; The Golden Republic, 1953; The Ivory Trail, 1954; Storm Over the Transvaal, 1955; Lost Trails of the Transvaal, 1956; Islands in a Forgotten Sea, 1958; Trail of the Copper King, 1959; The White Whirlwind, 1961; The Hunter is Death, 1962; To the Banks of the Zambexi, 1965; Natal and the Zulu Country, 1966; Low Veld Trails, 1968; The Great Trek, 1969; Discovering South Africa, 1970; Treasury of Travel Series, 1973-74; Southern Africa: Land of Beauty and Splendour, 1976; Illustrated Guide to Southern Africa, 1978; Scenic Wonders of Southern Africa, 1985. Address: PO Box 1516, Cape Town, South Africa.

BUMGARNER Mary. See: SUBRAMAN Belinda.

BUNCH Charlotte (Anne), b. 13 Oct 1944, West Jefferson, North Carolina, USA. Feminist Author and Organizer; Professor in Urban Studies. m. James L Weeks, 25 Mar 1967, div 1971. Education: University of California at Berkeley, 1965; BA in History and Political Science, Duke University, 1966; Graduate Research, Institute for Policy Studies, Washington, DC, 1967-68. Appointments: Visiting President and Tenured Fellow, Institute for Policy Studies, 1969-77; Adjunct Professor, George Washington University, Washington, DC, 1975-76, University of Maryland, College Park, 1978-79; Founding Director, Public Resource Center, Washington, DC, 1977-79; Director, Interfem Consultants, New York, 1979-87; Visiting Professor, 1987-89, Executive Director, Center for Women's Global Leadership, 1989-, Douglass College, Rutgers University; Professor in Urban Studies, Bloustein School of Planning and Public Policy, Rutgers, The State University of New Jersey, 1991-; Speaker at many universities, conferences, seminars, and rallies. Publications: The New Women: A Motive Anthology on Women's Liberation (editor with Joanne Cooke), 1970; Women Remembered: Short Biographies of Women in History (editor with Nancy Myron), 1974; Class and Feminism (editor with Nancy Myron), 1974; Lesbianism and the Woman's Movement (editor with Nancy Myron), 1975; Building Feminist Theory: Essays from Quest (editor with others), 1981; Learning Our Way: Essays in Feminist Education (editor with Sandra Pollack), 1983; International Feminism: Networking Against Female Sexual Slavery (editor with Barry and Castley), 1984; Passionate Politics: Feminist Theory in Action, 1987; Demanding Accountability: The Global Campaign and Vienna Tribunal for Women's Human Righs (with Niamh Reilly), 1994. Contributions to: Many books, journals and periodicals. Memberships: National Women's Political Caucus, advisory board, 1982-; Ms Foundation, board of directors, 1991-; National Council for Research on Women, board of directors, 1991-; Center for Women's Policy Studies, board of directors, 1992-95; Independent Commission on Human Rights Education, 1994-. Address: 19 Bond Street, No 5A, New York, NY 10012, USA.

BUNCH Richard Alan, b. 1 June 1945, Honolulu, Hawaii, USA. Educatcr; Writer. m. Rita Anne Glazar, 11 Aug 1990, 1 son, 1 daughter. Education: AA, Napa Valley College, 1965; BA, Stanford University, 1967; MA, University of Arizona, 1969; MDiv, 1970, DD, 1971, Graduate Studies, 1972-75, Vanderbilt University; Graduate Studies, Temple University, 1975-76; JD, University of Memphis, 1980; Teaching Credential, Sonoma State University, 1988. Publications: Summer Hawk (poetry), 1991; Night Blooms (prose), 1992; Wading the Russian River (poetry), 1993; A Foggy Morning (poetry), 1996; Santa Rosa Plums (poetry), 1996. Contributions to: Mandrake Poetry Review; Hawaii Review; Poetry Nottingham; Cold Mountain Review; Studio; European Judaism; Coe Review; Plaza; West Wind Review; Roanoke Review; Prairie Winds; Xavier Review; Midwest Poetry Review. Honours: Pushcart Prize Nomination, 1988; Grand Prize, Ina Coolbrith National Poetry Contest, 1989; Jessamyn West Prize, 1990. Memberships: Academy of American Poets; Russian River Writers' Guild. Address: 248 Sandpiper Drive, Davis, CA 95616, USA.

BUNGAY Stephen (Francis), b. 2 Sept 1954, Kent, England. Management Consultant. m. Atalanta Armstrong Beaumont, 31 Oct 1987, 2 sons. Education: MA, 1976, PhD, 1981, Oxford. Publications: Beauty and Truth, 1984; Der Entwurf einer Kategorialen Asthetik bei Hegel, in Kategorie und Kategorialität, 1990. Contributions to: Kategorie und Kategorialität, 1990; Hegel Reconsidered, 1994. Address: The Boston Consulting Group Ltd, London W1X 5FH, England.

BUNSHICHI Niyauchi, b. 1 Dec 1908, Kagoshima, Japan. Professor Emeritus. m. 1 Apr 1935, 3 sons, 2 daughters. Education: Department of English Language and Literature, Hiroshima Normal College, 1930; Litterarum Doctor. Appointments: Professor of English Language and Literature, 1955-74, Professor Emeritus, 1974-, Kagoshima University. Publications: Shakespeare's First Step Abroad, 1972; Immortal Longings: The Structure of Shakespeare's Antony and Cleopatra, 1978; Shakespeare's Structural Poetics, 1979; In and Out of Old Sites, 1985. Contributions to: Tragicality of Dialogue, 1950; Whether an Artificer or Not: a Plea for Shakespeare, 1951; Shakespeare's Drifting Soliloquy, 1953; Desire Named Utopia, 1984. Honour: Decorated, Third Order of Merit with the Sacred Treasure, 1993. Memberships: International John Steinbeck Society; Renaissance Institute of Japan; Japan Society of Shakespeare. Address: 201 Cosmo Kamifukuoka, 57-910 Fujma Kawagoe Shi, Saitama Ken 356, Japan.

BURACK Sylvia Kamerman, b. 16 Dec 1916, Hartford, Connecticut, USA. Editor; Publisher. m. Abraham S Burack, 28 Nov 1940, dec, 3 daughters. Education: BA, Smith College, 1938. Appointments: Editor, Publisher, magazines, 1978-. Publications: Editor: Little Plays for Little Players, 1952; Blue Ribbon Plays for Girls, 1955; Blue Ribbon Plays for Graduation, 1957; Fifty Plays for Junior Actors, 1966; Fifty Plays for Holidays, 1969; On Stage for Christmas, 1978; Holiday Plays Round the Year, 1983; Plays of Black Americans, 1987, 1988; Patriotic and Historical Plays for Young People, 1987; Plays from Favorite Folk Tales, 1987; The Big Book of Comedies, 1989; The Bog Book of Holiday Plays, 1990; The Big Book of Folktale Plays, 1991; Plays of Great Achievers, 1992; The Big Book of Dramatized Classics, 1993; The Big Book of Large-Cast Plays, 1995; The Big Book of Skits, 1996. Adult Books: Writing the Short Short Story, 1942; Book Reviewing, 1978; Writing and Selling Fillers, Light Verse, and Short Humor, 1982; Writing & Selling Romance Novels, 1983; Writing Mystery and Crime Fiction, 1985; How to Write and Sell Mystery Fiction, 1990; The Writers Handbook, 1989-96 (an annual). Honours: Honorary Degree, Doctor of Letters, 1985; Distinguished Service Award, 1973; Brookline High School Library Named in Honour; Freedoms Foundation Award, 1988; Smith College Medal, 1995. Memberships: National Book Critics Circle; Friends of the Libraries of Boston University; Phi Beta Kappa; PEN; Director, 1994 , English Speaking Union, American Branch. Address: 72 Penniman Road, Brookline, MA 02146, USA.

BURCH Claire, b. 19 Feb 1925, New York, New York, USA. Writer; Poet; Filmmaker. m. Bradley Bunch, 14 Apr 1944, 1 son, dec, 3 daughters. Education: BA, Washington Square College, 1947. Publications: Stranger in the Family, 1972; Notes of a Survivor, 1972; Shredded Millions, 1980; Goodbye My Coney Island Baby, 1989; Homeless in the Eighties, 1989; Solid Gold Illusion, 1991; You Be the Mother Follies, 1994; Homeless in the Nineties, 1994; Stranger on the Planet: The Small Book of Laurie, 1996. Contributions to: Periodicals. Honours: Carnegie Awards, 1978, 1979; California Arts Council Grants, 1991, 1992, 1993, 1994; Sera Foundation Award, 1996. Membership: Writer's Guild. Literary Agent: Mark Weimar, Regent Press, 6020A Adeline, Oakland, CA 94608, USA. Address: c/o Regent Press, 6020A Adeline, Oakland, CA 94808, USA.

BURCHFIELD Robert William, b. 27 Jan 1923, Wanganui, New Zealand. Lexicographer; Grammarian. m. (1) Ethel May Yates, 2 July 1949, 1 son, 2 daughters, div, (2) Elizabeth Austen Knight, 5 Nov, 1976. Education: MA, Victoria University of Wellington, 1948; BA, 1951, MA, 1955, Magdalen College, Oxford. Appointments: Lecturer, Christ Church, Oxford, 1953-57; Lecturer, Tutorial Fellow, Still Emeritus Fellow, St Peter's College, 1955-. Publications: A Supplement to the Oxford English Dictionary, 4 volumes, 1972-86; The Spoken Word, 1981; The English Language, 1985; The New Zealand Pocket Oxford Dictionary, 1986; Studies in Lexicography, 1987; Unlocking the English Language, 1989; Points of View, 1992; The Cambridge History of the English Language, Vol 5, 1994. Contributions to: Sunday Times; Encounter; Transactions Philological Society. Honours: Commander of the Order of the British Empire, 1975; Hon DLitt, Liverpool, 1978, Victoria University of Wellington, 1983; Freedom of City of Wanganui, 1986; Shakespeare Prize, 1994. Memberships: Early English Text Society; American Academy of Arts and Sciences. Address: 14 The Green, Sutton Courtenay, Oxon OX14 4AE, England.

BURCHILL Julie, b. 3 July 1959, England. Journalist; Writer. m. (1) Tony Parsons, div, (2) Cosmo Landesman, div. Education: Brislington Comprehensive, Bristol. Appointments: Journalist and Writer, New Musical Express, 1976-79, The Face, 1979-84, The Mail on Sunday, 1984-93, The Sunday Times, 1993-94, Vanity Fair, 1995-. Publications: The Boy Looked at Johnny, 1977; Love It or Shove It, 1983; Girls on Film, 1986; Damaged Goods, 1987; Ambition, 1989; No Exit, 1991; Sex and Sensibility, 1992; Traitor's Gate (novel), 1994. Address: c/o David Higham Associates, 5-8 Lower John Street, Golden Square, London W1R 4HA, England.

BURFIELD Eva. See: **EBBETT Frances Eva.**

BURGESS Michael (Roy), b. 11 Feb 1948, Fukuoka, Japan. Librarian; Publisher; Writer; Editor. m. Mary Alice Wickizer Rogers, 15 Oct 1976, 1 stepson, 1 stepdaughter. Education: AB, Gonzaga University, 1969; MLS, University of Southern California at Los Angeles, 1970. Appointments: Periodicals Librarian, 1970-75, Assistant Librarian, 1975-78, Senior Assistant Librarian, 1978-81, Associate Librarian, 1981-84, Librarian with rank of Professor, 1984-, California State University at San Bernardino; Editor, Newcastle Publishing Co Inc, North Hollywood, California, 1971-92; Co-Founder, Publisher, Editor, Borgo Press, San Bernardino, California, 1975-. Publications: Author or editor of some 40 fiction or non-fiction books, many under various pseudonyms, 1970-96. Honours: Many awards and citations. Memberships: American Association of University Professors; American Civil Liberties Union; American Library Association; Horror Writers of America; International PEN; Science Fiction and Fantasy Writers of America; Science Fiction Research Association; World Science Fiction Society. Address: c/o California State University at San Bernardino, 5500 University Parkway, San Bernardino, CA 92407, USA.

BURGIN Richard (Weston), b. 30 June 1947, Boston, Massachusetts, USA. Associate Professor of Communications and English; Writer; Editor. m. Linda K Harris, 7 September 1991, 1 stepdaughter. Education: BA, Brandeis University, 1968; MA, 1969, MPhil, 1981, Columbia University. Appointments: Instructor, Tufts University, 1970-74; Critic-at-Large, Globe Magazine, 1973-74; Founding Editor and Director, New Arts Journal, 1976-83; Visiting Lecturer, University of California at Santa Barbara, 1981-84; Associate Professor of Humanities, Drexel University, 1984-96; Founder-Editor, Boulevard, literary journal, 1985-; Associate Professor of Communications and English, St Louis University, 1996-. Publications: Conservations with Jorge Luis Borges, 1969; The Man with Missing Parts (novella), 1974; Conversations with Isaac Bashevis Singer, 1985; Man Without Memory (short stories), 1989; Private Fame (short stories), 1991. Contributions to: Many anthologies and periodicals. Honours: Pushcart Prizes, 1983, 1986; Various honorable mentions and listings. Membership: National Book Critics Circle, 1988-. Address: Montclair on the Park, 18 South Kingshighway, Apt 10JK, St Louis, MO 63108, USA.

BURKE Colleen Zeita, b. Sydney, Australia. Poet; Author; Tutor. m. Declan Affley, 11 Dec 1967, dec, 1 son, 1 daughter. Education: BA, Sydney University, 1974. Appointments: Writer, Tutor, in community, 1985-94. Publications: Go Down Singing, 1974; Hags, Rags & Scriptures, 1977; The Incurable Romantic, 1979; She Moves Mountains, 1984; Doherty's Corner, 1985; The Edge of It, 1992; Wildlife in Newtown, 1994. Contributions to: Sydney Morning Herald; Southerly; Westerly; Hecate; Imago; Overland; Blast; NSW School Magazine. Honours: The Edge of It, shortlisted New South Wales Literary Awards, 1993; 3 Grants from Australia Council. Literary Agent, Tim Curnow, Curtis Brown. Address: 126 Lennox Street, Newtown 2042, Australia.

BURKE James, b. 22 Dec 1936, Londonderry, Northern Ireland. Writer; Broadcaster. m. Madeline Hamilton, 27 Jan 1967. Education: MA, English Literature, Jesus College, Oxford, 1961. Publications: Tomorrow's World I, 1971; Tomorrow's World II, 1972; Connections, UK, 1978, USA, 1979; Foreign, 1980; The Day the Universe Changed, UK, 1985, USA, 1986; Foreign, 1987. Editor: Weidenfeld and Nicholason Encylcopaedia of World Art, 1964; Zanichelli Italian-English Dictionary, 1965. Contrinutions to: Daily Mail; Listener; Vogue; Vanity Fair; Punch; TV Times; Radio Times. Honours: Gold Medal, 1971, Silver Medal, 1972, Royal Televison Society; Edgar Dale Award for screenwriting, USA, 1986. Memberships: Royal Institution; Savile Club. Address: c/o Jonathan Clowes Ltd, 22 Prince Albert Road, London NW1 7ST, England.

BURKE James Lee, b. 5 Dec 1936, Houston, Texas, USA. Author. m. Pearl Pai, 22 Jan 1960, 1 son, 3 daughters. Education: University of Southwest Louisiana, 1955-57; BA, 1959, MA, 1960, University of Missouri. Publications: Half of Paradise, 1965; To the Bright and Shining Sun, 1970; Lay Down My Sword and Shield, 1971; Two for Texas, 1983; The Convict and Other Stories, 1985; The Lost Get-Back Boogie, 1986; The Neon Rain, 1987; Heaven's Prisoners, 1988; Black Cherry Blues, 1989; A Morning for Flamingos, 1990; A Stained White Radiance, 1992; Texas City, Nineteen Forty-Seven, 1992; In the Electric Mist with Confederate Dead, 1993; Dixie City Jam, 1994; Burning Angel, 1995. Contributions to: Periodicals. Honours: Breadloaf Fellow, 1970; Southern Federation of State Arts Agencies Grant, 1977; Guggenheim Fellowship, 1989; Edgar Allan Poe Award, Mystery Writers of America, 1989. Membership: Amnesty International. Address: 11100 Grant Creek, Missoula, MT 59802, USA.

BURKE John Frederick, (Jonthan Burke, Harriet Esmond, Jonathan George, Joanna Jones, Robert Miall, Sara Morris, Martin Sands), b. 8 Mar 1922, Rye, England. Author. m. (1) Joan Morris, 13

Sept 1940, 5 daughters, (2) Jean Williams, 29 June 1963, 2 sons. Appointments: Production Manager, Museum Press; Editorial Manager, Paul Hamlyn Books for Pleasure Group: European Story Editor, 20th Century Fox Productions. Publications: Swift Summer, 1949; An Illustrated History of England, 1974; Dr Caspian Trilogy, 1976-78; Musical Landscapes, 1983; Illustrated Dictionary of Music, 1988; A Travellers History of Scotland, 1990; Film and TV Novelisations. Contributions to: The Bookseller; Country Life; Denmark. Honour: Atlantic Award in Literature, 1948-49. Memberships: Society of Authors; Danish Club. Literary Agent: David Higham Associates. Address: 5 Castle Gardens, Kirkcudbright, Dumfries & Galloway DG6 4JE, Scotland.

BURKHOLZ Herbert Laurence, b. 9 Dec 1932, New York, USA. Author. m. Susan Blaine, 1 Nov 1961, 2 sons. Education: BA, New York University, 1951. Appointment: Writer-in-Residence, College of William and Mary, 1975. Publications: Sister Bear, 1969; Spy, 1969; The Spanish Soldier, 1973; Mulligan's Seed, 1975; The Death Freak, 1978; The Sleeping Spy, 1983; The Snow Gods, 1985; The Sensitives, 1987; Strange Bedfellows, 1988; Brain Damage, 1992; Writer in Residence, 1992; The FDA Follies, 1994. Contributions to: New York Times; Town & Country; Playboy; Penthouse; Longevity. Honours: Distinguished Scholar, 1976. Address: c/o Georges Borchardt Inc, 136 East 57th Street, New York, NY 10022, USA.

BURLEY William John, b. 1 Aug 1914, Falmouth, Cornwall, England. Retired Teacher; Writer. m. Muriel Wolsey, 10 Apr 1938, 2 sons. Education: Balliol College, Oxford, 1950-53. Publications: A Taste of Power, 1966; Three Toed Pussey, 1968; Death in Willow Pattern, 1969; Guilt Edged, 1971; Death in a Salubrious Place, 1973; Wycliffe and the Schoolgirls, 1976; The Schoolmaster, 1977; Charles and Elizabeth, 1979; Wycliffe and the Beales, 1983; Wycliffe and the Four Jacks, 1985; Wycliffe and the Quiet Virgin, 1986; Wycliffe and the Windsor Blue, 1987; Wycliffe and the Tangled Web, 1988; Wycliffe and the Cycle of Death, 1989; Wycliffe and a Dead Flautist, 1991; Wycliffe and the Last Rites, 1992; Wycliffe and the Dunes Mystery, 1993; Wycliffe and the House of Fear, 1995. Novels successfully adapted for television, 4th series forthcoming. Memberships: Authors Copyright and Lending Society; Crime Writers Association; South West Writers. Address: St Patricks, Holywell, Newquay, Cornwall TR8 5PT, England.

BURN Gordon, b. 16 Jan 1948, Newcastle upon Tyne, England. Writer. Education: BA, University of London, 1969. Publications: Somebody's Husband, Somebody's Son: The Story of Peter Sutcliffe, 1984; Pocket Money, 1986; Alma Cogan: A Novel, 1991; Fullalove, novel, 1995. Contributions to: Sunday Times Magazine; Telegraph; Face; Independent. Honours: Whitbread First Novel Award, 1991; Honorary DLitt, University of Plymouth, 1992 Address: c/o Gillon Aitken & Stone, 29 Fernshaw Road, London SW10 0TG, England.

BURN Michael Clive, b. 11 Dec 1912, London, England. Writer. m. Mary Walter, 27 Mar 1947. Education: Winchester, 1926-31; Open Scholar, New College, Oxford, 1931; POW, Colditz, 1944. Appointments: Staff, The Times, 1938-39; Correspondent, Vienna, Budapest, Belgrade, 1947-49. Publications: Yes Farewell, 1946; The Modern Everyman, 1947; Childhood at Oriol, 1951; The Midnight Diary, 1952; The Flying Castle, 1954; Mr Lyward's Answer, 1956; The Trouble with Jake, 1957; The Debatable Land, 1970; Out on a Limb, 1973; Open Day & Night, 1978; Mary and Richard, 1988. Contributions to: Articles and Poems to Encounter; Guardian; Times Literary Supplement. Honour: Keats Poetry First Prize, 1973. Membership: Society of Authors. Address: Beudy Gwyn, Minffordd, Gwynedd, North Wales.

BURNET Sir James (William Alexander), (Sir Alastair Burnet), b. 12 July 1928, Sheffield, Yorkshire, England. Journalist. m. Maureen Campbell Sinclair, 1958. Education: Worcester College, Oxford. Appointments: Sub-Editor, Leader Writer, Glasgow Herald, 1951-58; Leader Writer, 1958-62, Editor, 1965-74, The Economist; Political Editor, 1963-64, Broadcaster, 1976-91, Associate Editor, 1982-91, Independent Television News; Editor, Daily Express, 1974-76; Director, Times Newspapers Holdings Ltd, 1985-94. Publications: The Time of Our Lives (with Willie Landels), 1981; The Queen Mother, 1985. Contributions to: Television programmes. Honours: Richard Dimbleby Awards, BAFTA, 1966, 1970, 1979; Judges' Award, RTS, 1981; Knighted, 1984. Membership: Institute of Journalists, honorary vice president, 1990-. Address: 33 Westbourne Gardens, Glasgow G12 9PF, Scotland.

BURNETT Al. See: **BURNETT LEYS Alan Arbuthnott.**

BURNETT John, b. 20 Dec 1925, Nottingham, England. Professor of Social History Emeritus; Author. m. Denise Brayshaw, 2 Aug 1951, 1 son. Education: BA, 1946, MA, 1950, LLB, 1951, Cambridge University; PhD, London University, 1958. Appointments: Lecturer, Guildford Technical College, London, 1948-59; Head, Liberal Studies, South Bank Polytechnic, London, 1959-63, General Studies, Brunel College of Technology, 1963-66; Reader, 1966-73, Professor, 1973-90, in Social History, Pro-Vice Chancellor, 1980-85, Professor Emeritus, 1990-, Brunel University. Publications: Plenty and Want: A Social History of Food in England, 1966; A History of the Cost of Living, 1969; Useful Toil, 1974; A Social History of Housing, 1978; Destiny Obscure, 1982; The Autobiography of the Working Class (editor with David Vincent and David Mayall), 3 volumes, 1984-89; Idle Hands, 1994; The Origins and Development of Food Policies in Europe (editor with D J Oddy), 1994. Contributions to: Scholarly journals. Address: Castle Dene, Burgess Wood Road, Beaconsfield, Bucks HP9 1EQ, England.

BURNETT LEYS Alan Arbuthnott, (Al Burnett), b. 10 Jan 1921, Natal, South Africa. Author; Screenwriter. m. 4 July 1960, 2 daughters. Education: BSc, Glasgow University, 1952; DLitt, University of California, 1969. Appointments: Scenario Writer, MGM, 1954-59; Fox, 1960-63; Freelance Scenario Writer, USA, Australia, 1964-80; Editor, Sphere International, 1981-84; Freelance Screenwriter. Publications: Water Wings, 1953; 8 Feature Films; Over 180 Telefilm Series Episodes. Contributions to: Flight International; Rotor and Wing; Yatching Monthly; Motor Boat; Various Travel and Technical Publications. Honour: Croix de Guerre. Memberships: Aviation, Space Writers Association; Australian Writers Guild; Writers Guild of Great Britain; RNVR Officers Association. Literary Agent: ATP, Western Australia; The Sharland Organisation Ltd, London, England. Address: 8 Seaview Place, Cullen, Banffshire AB56 2WA, Scotland.

BURNHAM Sophy, b. 12 Dec 1936, Baltimore, Maryland, USA. Writer; Dramatist. m. David Bright Burnham, 12 Mar 1960, div 1984, 2 daughters. Education: BA, cum laude Smith College, 1958. Appointments: Acquisitions Editor, David McKay Inc, 1971-73; Contributing Editor, Town & Country, 1975-80, New Art Examiner, 1985-86; Independent Consultant to various organizations, 1975-88; Adjunct Lecturer, George Mason University, 1982-83; Staff Writer, New Woman magazine, 1984-92; Staff Writer and Columnist, Museum & Arts/Washington, 1987-96; Manager, Fund for New American Plays, John F Kennedy Center for the Performing Arts, Washington, DC, 1992-. Publications: The Exhibits Speak, 1964; The Art Crowd, 1973; The Threat to Licensed Nuclear Facilities (editor), 1975; Buccaneer (novel), 1977; The Landed Gentry, 1978; The Dogwalker (novel), 1979; A Book of Angels, 1990; Angel Letters, 1991; Revelations (novel), 1992; The President's Angel (novel), 1993; For Writers Only, 1994; Mystical Ecstasies: Running Toward God, 1997. Plays: Penelope, 1976; The Witch's Tale, 1978; The Study, 1979, revised as Snowstorms, 1993; Beauty and the Beast, 1979; The Nightingale, 1980; The Warrior, 1988. Contributions to: Essays and articles in many periodicals. Honours: Daughter of Mark Twain, Mark Twain Society, 1974; 1st Prize, Women's Theatre Award, Seattle, 1981; Helene Wurlitzer Foundation Grants, 1981, 1983, 1991; Virginia Duvall Mann Award, 1993. Memberships: Authors Guild; Authors League of America; Cosmos Club. Address: 1405 31st Street North West, Washington, DC 20007, USA.

BURNINGHAM John Mackingtosh, b. 27 Apr 1936, Farnham, Surrey, England. Author; Designer. m. Helen Gilliam Oxenbury, 15 Aug 1964, 1 son, 2 daughters. Education: National Diploma in Design, Central School of Art, London, 1959. Publications: Borka: The Adventures of a Goose with No Feathers, 1963; Chitty Chitty Bang Bang, 1964; Humbert, Mister Firkin and the Lord Mayor of London, 1965; Cannonball Simp, 1966; Storyland: Wall Frieze, 1966; Harquin: The Fox Who Went Down to the Valley, 1967; Jungleland: Wall Frieze, 1968; Mr Gumpy's Outing, 1970; Around the World: Two Wall Friezes, 1972; Mr Gumpy's Motor Car, 1974; Little Book Series: The Blanket, The Cupboard, The Dog, The Friend, 1975; Come Away From the Water, Shirley, 1977; Would You Rather, 1978; Avocado Baby, 1982; The Wind in the Willows (illustrator), 1983; Granpa, 1984; First Words, 1984; Play and Learn Book: abc, 123, Opposites, Colours, 1985; Where's Julius, 1986; John Patrick Norman McHennessy - The Boy Who is Always Late, 1987; Rhymetime: A Good Job, The Car Ride, 1988; Rhyme, Animal Chatters, A Grand Band, 1989; Oi Get Off Our

Train, 1989; Aldo, 1991; England, 1992; Harvey Slumfenburger's Christmas Present, 1993; Courtney, 1994; Cloudland, 1996. Films: Cannonball Simp, 1967; Granpa, 1989. Honours: Kate Greenaway Medal for Borka, 1963; Mr Gumpy's Outing, 1972; W H Smith Award for Harvey Slumfenburgers, 1994. Address: c/o Jonathan Cape Ltd, 20 Vauxhall Bridge Road, London SW1V 2FA, England.

BURNS Alan, b. 29 Dec 1929, London, England. Author; Professor. m. (1) Carol Lynn, 1954, (2) Jean Illien, 1980, 1 son, 2 daughters. Education: Merchant Taylors' School, London. Appointments: C Day-Lewis Writing Fellow, Woodberry Down School, 1973; Professor of English, University of Minnesota, 1977-90; Writer-in-Residence, Associated Colleges of the Twin Cities, Minneapolis-St Paul, 1980; Writing Fellow, Bush Foundation of Minnesota, 1984-85; Lecturer, Lancaster University, 1993-96. Publications: Buster, 1961; Europe After the Rain, 1965; Celebrations, 1967; Babel, 1969; Dreamerika, 1972; The Angry Brigade, 1973; The Day Daddy Died, 1981; Revolutions of the Night, 1986; Plays: Palach, 1970; To Deprave and Corrupt, 1972; The Imagination on Trial, 1981. Contributions to: Journals and periodicals. Honours: Arts Council Maintenance Grant, 1967, and Bursaries, 1969, 1973. Address: Creative Writing Department, Lancaster University, Lancaster LA1 4YN, England.

BURNS James MacGregor, b. 3 Aug 1918, Melrose, Massachusetts, USA. Political Scientist; Historian; Professor Emeritus; Writer. m. (1) Janet Rose Dismorr Thompson, 23 May 1942, div 1968, 2 sons, 2 daughters, (2) Joan Simpson Meyers, 7 Sept 1969, div 1991. Education: BA, Williams College, 1939; Postgraduate Studies, National Institute of Public Affairs, 1939-40; MA, 1947, PhD, 1947, Harvard University; Postdoctoral Studies, London School of Economics, 1949. Appointments: Faculty, 1941-47, Assistant Professor, 1947-50, Associate Professor, 1950-53, Professor of Political Science, 1953-88, Professor Emeritus, 1988-, Williams College; Faculty, Salzburg Seminar in American Studies, 1954, 1961; Co-Chairman, Project 87, Interdisciplinary Study of the Constitution during the Bicentennial Era, 1976-87; Senior Scholar, Jepson School of Leadership, University of Richmond, 1990-93; Scholar-in-Residence, Center for Political Leadership and Participation, University of Maryland at College Park, 1993-. Publications: Guam: Operations of the 77th Infantry Division, 1944; Okinawa: The Last Battle (co-author), 1947; Congress on Trial: The Legislative Process and the Administrative State, 1949; Government by the People: The Dynamics of American National Government and Local Government (with Jack Walter Peltason and Thomas E Cronin), 1952, 12th edition, 1985; Roosevelt: The Lion and the Fox, 1956; Functions and Policies of American Government (with Jack Walter Peltason), 1958, 3rd edition, 1967; John Kennedy: A Political Profile, 1960; The Deadlock of Democracy: Four-Party Politics in America, 1963; Presidential Government: The Crucible of Leadership, 1966; Roosevelt: The Soldier of Freedom, 1970; Uncommon Sense, 1972; Edward Kennedy and the Camelot Legacy, 1976; State and Local Politics: Government by the People, 1976; Leadership, 1978; The American Constitutional System Under Strong and Weak Parties (with others), 1981; The American Experiment: Vol I, The Vineyard of Liberty, 1982, Vol II, The Workshop of Democracy, 1985, Vol III, The Crosswinds of Freedom, 1989; The Power to Lead: The Crisis of the American Presidency, 1984; Cobblestone Leadership: Majority Rule, Minority Power (with L Marvin Overby), 1990; A People's Charter: The Pursuit of Rights in America (with Stewart Burns), 1991; The Democrats Must Lead (with others), 1992. Honours: Tamiment Institute Award for Best Biography, 1956; Woodrow Wilson Prize, 1957; Pulitzer Prize in History, 1971; National Book Award, 1971; Francis Parkman Prize, Society of American Historians, 1971; Sarah Josepha Hale Award, 1979; Christopher Award, 1983, 1990; Harold D Lassell Award, 1984; Robert F Kennedy Book Award, 1990; Rollo May Award in Humanistic Services, 1994. Memberships: American Civil Liberties Union; American Historical Association; American Legion; American Philosophical Association; American Political Science Association, president, 1975-76; Delta Sigma Rho; International Society of Political Psychology, president, 1982-83; New England Political Science Association, president, 1960-61; Phi Beta Kappa. Address: Highgate Barn, High Mowing, Bee Hill Road, Williamstown, MA 01267, USA.

BURNS Rex (Sehler), b. 13 June 1935, San Diego, California, USA. Professor of English; Writer. M. Terry Fostvedt, 10 Apr 1987, div 17 June, 1996, 5 sons, 2 daughters. Education: AB, Stanford University, 1958; MA, 1963, PhD, 1965, University of Minnesota. Appointments: Assistant Professor, Central Missouri State College,

1965-68; Associate Professor, 1968-75, Professor of English, 1975-, Chairman, Department of English, 1996-, University of Colorado at Denver; Fulbright Lecturer, Aristotle University, Thessaloniki, 1969-70, Universidad Catolico, Buenos Aires, 1974; Book Reviewer, Rocky Mountain News, 1982-92; Senior Lecturer, University of Kent, Canterbury, 1992-93. Publications: Novels: The Alvarez Journal, 1975; The Farnsworth Score, 1977; Speak for the Dead, 1978; Angle of Attack, 1979; The Avenging Angel, 1983; Strip Search, 1984; Ground Money, 1986; Suicide Season, 1987; The Killing Zone, 1988; Parts Unkown, 1990; When Reason Sleeps, 1991; Body Guard, 1991; Endangered Species, 1993; Blood Line, 1995; The Leaning Land, 1997. Editor: Crime Classics: The Mystery Story from Poe to the Present (with Mary Rose Sullivan), 1990. Non-Fiction: Success in America: The Yeoman Dream and the Industrial Revolution, 1976. Contributions to: Periodicals and anthologies. Honours: Edgar Allan Poe Award, Mystery Writers of America, 1976; Colorado Authors League Awards, 1978, 1979, 1980; President's Teaching Scholar (Lifetime Title), University of Colorado System, 1990. Memberships: International Association of Crime Writers; Mystery Writers of America. Address: c/o Department of English, University of Colorado at Denver, Campus Box 175, PO Box 173364, Denver, CO 80217, USA.

BURNS Richard Gordon, (Dick B), b. 15 May 1925, Stockton, California, USA. Author; Retired Attorney. m. Eloise Beil, 23 June 1951, 2 sons. Education: AA with honours, University of California, Berkeley, 1946; AB, Stanford University, 1949; JD, Stanford University Law School, 1951. Publications: The Oxford Group and Alcoholics Anonymous, 1992; Dr Bob's Library, 1994; Anne Smith's Journal, 1994; The Books Early AAs Read for Spiritual Growth, 1994; New Light on Alcoholism: The AA Legacy from Sam Shoemaker, 1994; The Akron Genesis of Alcoholics Anonymous, 1994; Courage to Change (with Bill Pittman), 1994; The Good Book and the Big Book: AA's Roots in the Bible, 1995; Good Morning: Quiet Time, the Morning Watch, Meditation, and Early AA, 1996; That Amazing Grace: The Role of Clarence and Grace S in Early AA, 1996. Memberships: American Historical Association; Maui Writers Guild; Phi Beta Kappa. Address: 2747 South Kihei Road G102, Kihei, HI 96753, USA.

BURNSHAW Stanley, b. 20 June 1906, New York, New York, USA. Publisher; Poet; Writer. m. Lydia Powsner, 2 Sept 1942, dec, 1 daughter. Education: BA, University of Pittsburgh, 1925; University of Poitiers, France, 1927; University of Paris, 1927; MA, Cornell University, 1933. Appointments: President and Editor-in-Chief, The Dryden Press, 1937-58; Program Director, Graduate Institute of Book Publishing, New York University, 1958-62; Vice President, Holt, Rinehart and Winston, publishers, 1958-67; Regents Visiting Lecturer, University of California, 1980; Visiting Distinguished Professor, Miami University, 1989.Publications: Poems, 1927; The Great Dark Love, 1932; Andre Spire and His Poetry, 1933; The Iron Land, 1936; The Bridge, 1945; The Revolt of the Cats in Paradise, 1945; Early and Late Testament, 1952; Caged in an Animal's Mind, 1963; The Hero of Silence, 1965; In the Terrified Radiance, 1972; Mirages: Travel Notes in the Promised Land, 1977; Robert Frost Himself, 1986; A Stanley Burnshaw Reader, 1990; The Seamless Web, 1991. Contributions to: Many periodicals. Honours: National Institute of Arts and Letters Award, 1971; Honorary Doctorate of Humane Letters, Hebrew Union College, 1983; Honorary Doctorate of Letters, City University of New York, 1996. Address: 250 West 89th Street, No PH2G, New York, NY 10024, USA.

BURROUGHS William (Seward), b. 5 Feb 1914, St Louis, Missouri, USA. Author. m. (1) Ilse Herzfeld Klapper, 1937, div 1946, (2) Joan Vollmer, 1946, dec 1951, 1 son, dec 1981. Education: AB, Harvard University, 1936; Postgraduate Studies in Ethnology and Archeology; Medical Studies, University of Vienna. Publications: Junkie: Confessions of an Unredeemed Drug Addict, 1953, new edition as Junky, 1977; The Naked Lunch, 1959; The Exterminator (with Brion Gysin), 1960; Minutes to Go (with Sinclair Beiles, Gregory Corso, and Brion Gysin), 1960; The Soft Machine, 1961; The Ticket That Exploded, 1962; The Yage Letters (with Allen Ginsberg), 1963; Dead Fingers Talk, 1963; Nova Express, 1964; Roosevelt After Inauguration, 1964; Valentine's Day Reading, 1965; The White Subway, 1965; Health Bulletin: APO:33: A Metabolic Regulator, 1965; Darayt (with Lee Harwood), 1965; Time, 1965; So Who Owns Death TV? (with Claude Pelieu and Carl Weissner), 1967; They Do Not Always Remember, 1968; Ali's Smile, 1969; The Dead Star, 1969; Entretiens avec William Burroughs, 1969; Fernsch-Tuberkulose (with Claude Pelieu and Carl Weissner), 1969; The Braille Film (with Carl Weissner), 1970; Third Mind (with Brion Gysin), 1970; The Last Words of Dutch Schultz: A Fiction in the Form of a Film Script, 1970; The Wild Boys: A Book of the Dead, 1971; Jack Kerouac (with Claude Pelieu), 1971; Electronic Revolution, 1971; Brion Gysin, Let the Mice In (with Brion Gysin and Ian Somerville), 1973; Mayfair Academy Series More or Less, 1973; Exterminator!, 1973; The Book of Breething, 1974; Sidestripping (with Charles Gatewood), 1975; Snack: Two Tape Transcripts (with Eric Mottram), 1975; Port of Saints, 1975; Cobblestone Gardens, 1976; The Retreat Diaries, 1976; Short Novels, 1978; Naked Scientology, 1978; Blade Runner: A Movie, 1979; Doctor Benway: A Variant Passage from "The Naked Lunch", 1979; Ah Pook is Here and Other Texts, 1979; Cities of the Red Night, 1981; Easy Routines, 1981; Letters to Allen Ginsberg, 1953-1957, 1981; A William Burroughs Reader, 1982; The Place of Dead Roads, 1984; The Burroughs File, 1984; The Adding Machine: Collected Essays, 1985; Queer, 1986; The Cat Inside, 1986; The Western Lands, 1987; Interzone, 1988; Ghost of Chance, 1991; Speed & Kentucky Ham: Two Novels, 1993; The Letters of William S Burroughs, 1945-1959, 1993; Seven Deadly Sins, 1994; My Educaton: A Book of Dreams, 1994. Address: c/o William Burroughs Communications, PO Box 147, Lawrence, KS 66044, USA.

BURROW John Anthony, b. 1932, Loughton, England. Professor; Writer. Education: BA, 1953, MA, 1955, Christ Church, Oxford. Appointments: Fellow, Jesus College, Oxford University, 1961-75; Winterstoke Professor, University of Bristol, 1976-. Publications: A Reading of Sir Gawain and the Green Knight, 1965; Geoffrey Chaucer: A Critical Anthology, 1969; Ricardian Poetry: Chaucer, Gower Langland and the Gawain Poet, 1971; Sir Gawain and the Green Knight, 1972; English Verse 1300-1500, 1977; Medieval Writers and Their Work, 1982; Essays on Medieval Literature, 1984; The Ages of Man, 1986; A Book of Middle English, 1992; Langlands Fictions, 1993; Thomas Hoccleve, 1994. Address: 9 The Polygon, Clifton, Bristol, England.

BURROWAY Janet (Gay), b. 21 Sept 1936, Tucson, Arizona, USA. Professor; Writer; Poet. m. (1) Walter Eysselinck, 1961, div 1973, 2 sons, (2) William Dean Humphries, 1978, div 1981, (3) Peter Ruppert, 1993, 1 stepdaughter. Education: University of Arizona, 1954-55; AB, Barnard College, 1958; BA, 1960, MA, 1965, Cambridge University; Yale School of Drama, 1960-61. Appointments: Instructor, Harpur College, Binghamton, New York, 1961-62; Lecturer, University of Sussex, 1965-70; Associate Professor, 1972-77, Professor, 1977-, MacKenzie Professor of English, 1989-95, Robert O Lawton Distinguished Professor, 1995-, Florida State University; Fiction Reviewer, 1991-; Essay-Columnist, New Letters: A Magazine of Writing and Art, 1994-. Publications: Fiction: Descend Again, 1960; The Dancer From the Dance, 1965; Eyes, 1966; The Buzzards, 1969; The Truck on the Track, children's book, 1970; The Giant Jam Sandwich, children's book, 1972; Raw Silk, 1977; Opening Nights, 1985; Cutting Stone, 1992. Poetry: But to the Season, 1961; Material Goods, 1980. Other: Writing Fiction: A Guide to Narrative Craft, 1982, 4th edition, 1995. Contributions to: Numerous journals and periodicals. Honours: National Endowment for the Arts Fellowship, 1976; Yaddo Residency Fellowships, 1985, 1987; Lila Wallace-Reader's Digest Fellow, 1993-94; Carolyn Benton Cockefaire Distinguished Writer-in-Residence, University of Missouri, 1995; Woodrow Wilson Visiting Fellow, Furman University, Greenville, South Carolina, 1995. Memberships: Associated Writing Programs, vice president, 1988-89; Authors Guild. Address: 240 De Soto Street, Tallahassee, FL 32303, USA.

BURTON Anthony George Graham, b. 24 Dec 1934, Thornaby, England. Writer; Broadcaster. m. 28 Mar 1959, 2 sons, 1 daughter. Education: St James Grammar School. Publications: A Programmed Guide to Office Warfare, 1969; The Jones Report, 1970; The Canal Builders, 1972, 1981, 1993; The Reluctant Musketeer, 1973; Canals in Colour, 1974; Remains of a Revolution, 1974; The Miners, 1976; Back Door Britain, 1977; A Place to Stand, 1977; The Green Bag Travellers, 1978; The Past At Work, 1980; The Shell Book of Curious Britain, 1982; The National Trust Guide to Our Industrial Past, 1983; Walking the Line, 1985; The Shell Book of Undiscovered Britain and Ireland, 1986; Opening Time, 1987; Walking Through History, 1988; Cityscapes, 1990; Astonishing Britain, 1990; The Railway Builders, 1992; The Grand Union Canal Walk, 1993; The Railway Empire, 1994; The Rise & Fall of British Shipbuilding, 1994; The Cotswold Way, 1995; The Dales Way, 1995; The West Highland Way, 1996; The Southern Upland Way, 1997; The Wye Valley Walk, 1997. Address: 25 Cowper Road, Redland, Bristol, BS6 6NZ, England.

BURTON Gabrielle, b. 21 Feb 1939, Lansing, Michigan, USA. Writer. m. Roger V Burton, 18 August 1962, 5 daughters. Education: BA, Marygrove College, Michigan, 1960. Appointments: Teacher, Fiction in the Schools, Writers in Education Project, New York, 1985; Fellow, American Film Institute, Los Angeles, 1995-97; Various prose readings and workshops. Publications: I'm Running Away From Home But I'm Not Allowed to Cross the Street (non-fiction), 1972; Heartbreak Hotel (novel), 1986. Contributions to: Articles, essays, poems, and reviews in numerous publications. Honours; MacDowell Colony Fellow, 1982, 1987, 1989; Yaddo Fellow, 1983; Maxwell Perkins Prize, 1986; Great Lakes Colleges Association Award, 1987; Bernard De Voto Fellow in Non-Fiction, Breadloaf Writer's Conference, 1994; Mary Pickford Foundation Award for 1st Year Screenwriter, 1996. Address: 211 LeBrun Road, Eggertsville, NY 14229, USA.

BURTON Gregory Keith, b. 12 Feb 1956, Sydney, Australia. Barrister-at-Law; Arbitrator; Mediator; Author. m. Suzanne Brandstater, 1 son, 1 daughter. Education: BA (Hons), University of Sydney, 1978; LLB (Hons), 1980; Bursary to Oxford University; BCL, 1984. Appointments: Editorial Committee, Sydney Law Review, 1978-79; Foundation Editor, Journal of Banking and Finance Law and Practice, 1990-; Co-editor, Weaver and Craigie's Banker and Customer in Australia; Australia/New Zealand Editor, Commercial Law Practitioner, 1993-; Banking and Finance Editor, Australasian Dispute Resolution, 1995-; Publications: Directions in Finance Law, 1990; Australian Financial Transactions Law, 1991; Trusts, Australian Commentary to Halsbury's Laws of England, 1992; Bills of Exchange and Other Negotiable Instruments, Halsbury's Laws of Australia, 1992; Set-Off, The Laws of Australia, 1993; Arbitration in Australia, 1994. Contributions to: Journal of Banking and Finance Law and Practice; Australian Law Journal; Sydney Law Review; Banking Law Association conference publications. Honour: University Medal in History, 1978. Memberships: New South Wales Bar Association; Business Law Section, Law Council of Australia; Banking Law Association; Commercial Law Association; Australian Institute of Administrative Law; Associate, Institute Arbitrators Australia. Address: 5th Floor, Wentworth Chambers, 180 Phillip Street, Sydney, New South Wales 2000, Australia.

BURTON John Andrew, b. 2 Apr 1944, London, England. Writer; Wildlife Consultant. m. Vivien Gledhill, 1 Nov 1980. Publications: The Naturalist in London, 1975; Nature in the City, 1976; Owls of the World (editor), 1976; Field Guide to Amphibians and Reptiles of Europe, 1978; Gem Guide to Animals, 1980; Gem Guide to Zoo Animals, 1984; Collins Guide to Rare Mammals of the World, 1987. Contributions to: New Scientist; Vole; Oryx. Memberships: Fellow, Linnean Society of London; Executive Secretary, Fauna and Flora Preservation Scoiety, 1975-87; Royal Geographical Society; British Ornithologists Union. Literary Agent: Murray Pollinger. Address: 222 Old Brompton Road, London SW5 0BZ, England.

BUSBEE Shirlee, b. 9 Aug 1941, San Jose, California, USA. Author. m. Howard Leon Busbee, 22 June 1963. Eductation: Burbank Business College. Publications: Gypsy Lady, 1977; Lady Vixen, 1980; White Passion Sleeps,1983; Deceive Not My Heart, 1984; The Tiger Lily, 1985; Spanish Rose, 1986; Midnight Masquerade,1988; Whisper to Me of Love, 1991; Each Time We Love, 1993; Love a Dark Rider, 1994. Address: c/o Avon Books, 105 Madison Avenue, New York, NY 10016, USA.

BUSBY F M, b. 11 Mar 1921, Indianapolis, Indiana, USA. Author. m. Elinor Doub, 28 Apr 1954, 1 daughter. Education: BSc, 1946, BScEE, 1947, Washington State University. Appointments: Trick Chief and Project Supervisor, 1947-53, Telegraph Engineer, 1953-70, Alaska Communication System; Writer, 1970-. Publications: Cage a Man, 1974; The Proud Enemy, 1975; Rissa Kerguelen, 1976; The Long View, 1976; All These Earths, 1978; Zelde M'tana, 1980; The Demu Trilogy, 1980; Star Rebel, 1984; The Alien Debt, 1984; Rebel's Quest, 1985; Rebels' Seed, 1986; Getting Home, 1987; The Breeds of Man, 1988; Slow Freight, 1991; The Singularity Project, 1993; Islands of Tomorrow, 1994; Arrow from Earth, 1995; The Triad Worlds, 1996. Contributions to approximately 45 anthologies and magazines. Memberships: Science Fiction Writers of America, vice president, 1974-76; Spectator Amateur Press Society. Address: 2852 14th Avenue West, Seattle, WA 98119, USA.

BUSBY Roger C(harles), b. 24 July 1941, Leicester, England. Writer; Public Relations Officer. Education: Certificate in Journalism, University of Astor, Birmingham. Appointments: Journalist, Caters New

Agency, Birmingham, 1959-66; Journalist, Birmingham Evening Mail, 1966-73; Head of Public Relations, Devon & Cornwall Police, 1973-. Publications: Main Line Kill, 1968; Robbery Blue, 1969; The Frighteners, 1970; Deadlock, 1971; A Reasonable Man, 1972; Pattern of Violence, 1973; New Face in Hell, 1976; Garvey's Code, 1978; Fading Blue, 1984; The Hunter, 1986; Snow Man, 1987; Crackhot, 1990; High Jump, 1992. Memberships: Crime Writers Association; Institute of Public Relations; National Union of Journalists. Address: Sunnymoor, Bridford, Nr Exeter, Devon, England.

BUSCH Frederick (Matthew), b. 1 Aug 1941, New York, New York, USA. Professor of Literature; Writer. m. Judith Burroughs, 29 Nov 1963, 2 sons. Education: BA, Muhlenberg College, 1962; MA, Columbia University, 1967. Appointments: Magazine Writer; Instructor to Professor, 1966-87, Fairchild Professor of Literature, 1987-, Colgate University; Acting Director, Program in Creative Writing, University of Iowa, 1978-79; Visiting Lecturer, Creative Writing Program, Columbia University, 1979. Publications: I Wanted a Year Without Fall, 1971; Breathing Trouble, 1973; Hawkes, 1973; Manual Labor, 1974; Domestic Particulars, 1976; The Mutual Friend, 1978; Hardwater Country, 1979; Invisible Mending, 1984; Sometimes I Live in the Country, 1986; Absent Friends, 1989; Harry and Catherine, 1990; Closing Arguments, 1991; Long Way From Home, 1993; The Children in the Woods: New and Selected Stories, 1994. Contributions to: Various periodicals. Honours: National Endowment for the Arts Fellowship, 1976; Guggenheim Fellowship, 1981-82; Ingram Merrill Foundation Fellowship, 1981-82; National Jewish Book Award for Fiction, Jewish Book Council, 1985; PEN/Malamud Award, 1991; PEN/Faulkner Award Nomination, 1995. Memberships: Authors Guild of America; PEN; Writers Guild of America. Address: RR 1, Box 31A, Sherburne, NY 13460, USA.

BUSH Duncan (Eric), b. 6 Apr 1946, Cardiff, Wales. Poet; Writer; Teacher. m. Annette Jane Weaver, 4 June 1981, 2 sons. Education: BA, 1st Class Honours, in English and European Literature, Warwick University, 1978; Exchange Scholarship, Duke University, USA, 1976-77; DPhil, Research in English Literature, Wadham College, Oxford, 1978-81. Appointments: European editor, The Kansas Quarterly and Arkansas Review; Writing Tutor with various institutions. Publications: Aquarium, 1983; Salt, 1985; Black Faces, Red Mouths, 1986; The Genre of Silence, 1987; Glass Shot, 1991; Masks, 1994. Editor: On Censorship, 1985. Contributions to: BBC and periodicals. Honours: Eric Gregory Award for Poetry, 1978; Barbara Campion Memorial Award for Poetry, 1982; Welsh Arts Council Prizes for Poetry; Arts Council of Wales Book of the Year, for Masks, 1995. Memberships: Welsh Academy; Welsh Union of Writers, vice chairman, 1982-86. Address: Godre Waun Oleu, Brecon Road, Ynyswen, Penycae, Pows SA9 1YY, Wales.

BUSH Ronald, b. 16 June 1946, Philadelphia, Pennsylvania, USA. Professor of American Literature; Writer. m. Marilyn Wolin, 14 Dec 1969, 1 son. Education: BA, University of Pennsylvania, 1968; BA, Cambridge University, 1970; PhD, Princeton University, 1974. Appointments: Assistant to Associate Professor, Harvard University, 1974-82; Associate Professor, 1982-85, Professor, 1985-97, California Institute of Technology; Visiting Fellow, Exeter College, Oxford, 1994-95; Drue Heinz Professor of American Literature, Oxford University, 1997-. Publications: The Genesis of Ezra Pound's Cantos, 1976; T S Eliot: A Study in Character and Style, 1983; T S Eliot: The Modernist in History (editor), 1991; Prehistories of the Future: The Primitivist Project and the Culture of Modernism (editor with Elazar Barkan), 1995. Contributions to: Scholarly books and journals. Honours: National Endowment for the Humanities fellowships, 1977-78, 1992-93. Address: Oxford University, Oxford, England.

BUTALA Sharon, b. 24 Aug 1940, Saskatchewan, Canada. m. 1976, 1 son. Education: University of Saskatchewan. Publications: Country of the Heart, 1984; Queen of the Headaches, 1985; The Gates of the Sun, 1985; Luna, 1988; Fever, 1990; Upstream, 1991; The Fourth Archangel, 1992; The Perfection of the Morning, 1994. Honours: SWG, Major Drama Awards, 1985, 1989; Annual Contributors Prize, 1988; Silver Award, National Magazine Award, 1991; Author's Award, 1992; 1994 Spirit of Saskatchewan & Non-Fiction Awards, Saskatchewan Book Awards, 1994. Address: c/o The Writer's Union of Canada, 24 Ryerson Avenue, Toronto, Ontario, M5T 2P3, Canada.

BUTLER (Frederick) Guy, b. 21 Jan 1918, Cradock, Cape Province, South Africa. Professor; Author. m. Jean Murray Satchwell,

7 Dec 1940, 3 sons, 1 daughter. Education: BA, 1938, MA, 1939, Rhodes University; BA, 1947, MA, 1951, Oxford University. Publications: Poetry: Stranger to Europe, 1951; South of the Zambezi, 1966; Selected Poems, 1975; Song and Ballads, 1978; Pilgrimage to Dias Cross, 1987. Autobiography: Karoo Morning, 1977; Bursting World, 1936-45; A Local Habitation, 1945-90. Plays: The Dam, 1953; Richard Gush of Salem, 1982; Demea, 1990; The Magic Tree, 1989; Poetry Anthologies: Editor: A Book of South African Verse, 1959; The Magic Tree (with J Opland), 1989; Novel: A Rackety Colt, 1989; Contributions to: Literary and Academic Journals. Honours: Cape Tercentenary Foundation Literature Award, 1953; CNA Prize for Literature, 1976; English Academy of South African Gold Medal, 1989; Honorary Degrees from Universities of Natal, 1970, Witwatersrand, 1984, South Africa, 1989, Rhodes University, 1994; Lady Usher Award, 1992; Freedom of the City of Grahamstown, 1994. Memberships: Shakespeare Society of South Africa; English Academy of South Africa. Address: High Corner, 122 High Street, Grahamstown, South Africa.

BUTLER Gwendoline (Williams), (Jennie Melville). b. 19 Aug 1922, London, England. Author. Education: MA, Lady Margaret Hall, Oxford, 1948. Publications: Receipt for Murder, 1956; Dead in a Row, 1957; The Dull Dead, 1958; The Murdering Kind, 1958; The Interloper, 1959; Death Lives Next Door, US edition as Dine and Be Dead, 1960; Make Me a Murderer, 1961; Coffin on the Water; Coffin in Oxford, 1962; Coffin for Baby, 1963; Coffin Waiting, 1963; Coffin in Malta, 1964; A Nameless Coffin, 1966; Coffin Following, 1968; Coffin's Dark Number, 1969; A Coffin form the Past, 1970; A Coffin for Pandora, 1973, US edition Olivia, 1974; A Coffin for the Canary, US edition as Sarsen Place, 1974; The Vesey Inheritance, 1975; Brides of Friedberg, US edition as Meadowsweet, 1977; The Red Staircase, 1979; Albion Walk, 1982; UK Paperback, Cavalcade, 1984; As Jennie Melville: Come Home and Be Killed, 1962; Burning Is a Substitute for Loving, 1963; Murderers' Houses, 1964; There Lies Your Love, 1965; Nell Alone, 1966; A Different Kind of Summer, 1967; The Hunter in the Shadows, 1969; A New Kind of Killer, An Old Kind of Death, 1970, US edition as A New Kind of Killer, 1971; Ironwood, 1972; Nun's Castle, 1973, Raven's Forge, 1975; Dragon's Eye, 1976; Axwater, US edition as Tarot's Tower, 1978; Murder Has a Pretty Face, 1981; The Painted Castle, 1982; The Hand of Glass, 1983; A Series of Charmian Daniels' novels begining with Windsor Red, 1985. Literary Agent: Vanessa Holt Associates. Address: c/o Vanessa Holt Ltd, 59 Crescent Road, Leigh-on-Sea, Essex SS9 2PF, England.

BUTLER Joseph T(homas), b. 25 Jan 1932, Winchester, Virginia, USA. Museum Operations Director Emeritus; Adjunct Assistant Professor. Education: BS, University of Maryland, 1954; MA, Ohio University, 1955; MA, University of Delaware, 1957. Appointments: Director, Museum Operations, Sleepy Hollow Restorations, later Historic Hudson Valley, Tarrytown, New York, 1957-93; American Editor, The Connoisseur, 1967-77; Adjunct Associate Professor of Architecture, Columbia University, 1970-80; Editorial Board, Art & Antiques, 1978-83; Adjunct Assistant Professor, Graduate Division, Fashion Institute of Technology, New York, 1986-. Publications: Washington Irving's Sunnyside, 1962, 3rd edition, revised, 1974; American Antiques 1800-1900: A Collector's History and Guide, 1965; World Furniture, co-author, 1965; Candleholders in America 1650-1900, 1967; The Family Collections at Van Cortlandt Manor, 1967; The Arts in America: The 19th Century (co-author), 1973; The Story of Boscobel and its Builder: States Morris Dyckman, 1974; Warner House: A Compendium, 1975; Van Cortlandt Manor, 1978; Sleepy Hollow Restorations: A Cross Section of the Collection, 1983; A Field Guide to American Antique Furniture, 1985; Treasures of State (co-author), 1991. Contributions to: Encyclopedias and periodicals. Honour: Winterthur Fellow, University of Delaware, 1957. Address: 222 Martling Avenue, Tarrytown, NY 10591, USA.

BUTLER Marilyn, (Speers), b. 11 Feb 1937, Kingston on Thames, England. Rector; Professor; Author. Education: BA, 1958, PhD, 1966, Oxford University. Appointments: Current Affairs Producer, BBC, 1960-63; Research Fellow, St Hildas College, Oxford, 1970-73; Fellow, Tutor, St Hughs College, Lecturer, Oxford University, 1973-86; King Edward VII Professor, Cambridge University, 1986-93; Professional Fellow, Kings College, Cambridge, 1988-93; Rector, Exeter College, Oxford, 1993-. Publications: Maria Edgeworth: A Literary Biography, 1972; Jane Austen and the War of Ideas, 1975; Peacock Displayed: A Satirist in His Context, 1979; Romantics, Rebels and Reactionaries, 1760-1830, 1981; Burke, Paine, Godwin and the Revolution Controversy, 1984; Collected Works of Mary

Wollstonecraft, 1989; Maria Edgeworth, Castle Rackrent and Ennui, 1992; Frankenstein, the 1818 Edition, editor, 1993; Northanger Abbey, editor, 1995. Address: Exeter College, Oxford, England.

BUTLER (Muriel) Dorothy, b. 24 Apr 1925, Auckland, New Zealand. Teacher; Bookseller; Author. m. Roy Edward Butler, 11 Jan 1947, 2 sons, 6 daughters. Education: BA, University of Auckland, 1940; Diploma in Education, 1976. Publications: Gushla And Her Books; Babies Need books; Five to Eight; Come Back Ginger; A Bundle of Birds; My Brown Bear Barney; Higgledy Piddledy Hobbledy Hoy; Good Morning Mrs Martin; Reading Begins at Home; I Will Build You A House. Honours: Eleanor Farjeon Award; May Hill Arbuthnot Honour Lectureshop, American Library Citation; Childrens Literature Association of New Zealand Honour Award; Margaret Mahy Lecture Award; Officer of the Order of the British Empire, 1993. Memberships: PEN; Childrens Literature Association; Reading Association, Childrens Book Foundation. Literary Agent: Richards Literary Agency. Address: The Old House, Karekare, Auckland West, New Zealand.

BUTLER Octavia E(stelle), b. 22 June 1947, Pasadena, California, USA. Writer. Education: AA, Pasadena City College, 1968; California State University at Los Angeles; University of California at Los Angeles. Publications: Pattermaster, 1976; Mind of My Mind, 1977; Survivor, 1978; Kindred, 1979; Wild Seed, 1980; Clay's Ark, 1984; Dawn: Xenogenesis, 1987; Adulthood Rites, 1988; Imago, 1989; Parable of the Sower, 1993. Address: PO Box 6604, Los Angeles, CA 90055, USA.

BUTLER Richard. See: **ALLBEURY Theodore Edward le Bouthillier.**

BUTLIN Martin (Richard Fletcher), b. 7 June 1929, Birmingham, England. Art Consultant; Writer. m. Frances Caroline Chodzko, 1969. Education: BA, 1952, MA, 1957, Trinity College, Cambridge; BA, Courtauld Institute of Art, 1955, D Lit, 1984. Appointments: Assistant Keeper, 1955-67, Keeper of Historic British Collection, 1967-89, Tate Gallery, London; Art Consultant, Christie's, London, 1989-. Publications: A Catalogue of the Works of William Blake in the Tate Gallery, 1957, 3rd edition, 1990; Samuel Palmer's Sketchbook of 1824, 1962; Turner Watercolours, 1962; Turner (with Sir John Rothenstein), 1964; Tate Gallery Catalogues: The Modern British Paintings, Drawings and Sculpture (with Mary Chamot and Dennis Farr), 1964; The Later Works of J M W Turner, 1965; William Blake, 1966; The Blake-Varley Sketchbook of 1819, 1969; The Paintings of J M W Turner (with E Joll), 1977, 2nd edition, 1984; The Paintings and Drawings of William Blake, 1981; Aspects of British Painting 1550-1800, from the Collection of the Sarah Campbell Blaffer Foundation, 1988; Turner at Petworth (with Mollie Luther and Ian Warrell), 1989; William Blake in the Collection of the National Gallery of Victoria (with Ted Gott and Irena Zdanowicz), 1989. Contributions to: Periodicals. Honours: Mitchell Prize for the History of Art, 1978; Commander of the Order of the British Empire, 1990. Membership: British Academy, fellow, 1984-. Address: 74c Eccleston Square, London SW1V 1PJ, England.

BUTLIN Ron, b. 17 Nov 1949, Edinburgh, Scotland. Writer. m. Regula Staub (the writer Yvonne Claire), 18 June 1993. Education: MA, Dip CDAE, Edinburgh University. Appointments: Writer-in-Residence, Edinburgh University, 1983, 1985; Scottish Canadian Writing Fellow, 1984; Writer-in-Residence, Midlothian Region, 1990-91, Stirling University, 1993. Publications: Creatures Tamed by Cruelty, 1979; The Exquisite Instrument, 1982; The Tilting Room, 1984; Ragtime in Unfamiliar Bars, 1985; Sound of My Voice, 1987; Histories of Desire, 1995; Night Visits, 1997; Mauritian Voices (editor), 1997. Contemporary Writing from Mauritius, editor; Night Visits. Contributions to: Scotsman; Edinburgh Review; Poetry Review; Times Literary Supplement. Honours: Writing Bursary, 1977, 1987, 1990, 1994; Scottish Arts Council Book Awards, 1982, 1984; Poetry Book Society Recommendation, 1985. Membership: Literature Committee, Scottish Arts Council, 1995-96. Address: 7W Newington Place, Edinburgh EH9 1QT, Scotland.

BUTOR Michel (Marie François), b. 14 Sept 1926, Mons-en-Barcoeul, Nord, France. Author; Poet; Professor. m. Marie-Josephe Mas, 22 Aug 1958, 4 daughters. Education: License en philosophie, 1946, Diplome d'études superieures de philosophie, 1947, Sorbonne, University of Paris. Appointments: Associate Professor, University of Vincennes, 1969, University of Nice, 1970-73; Professor of Modern French Language and Literature, University of Geneva,

1975-91; Visiting Professorships in the U.S. Publications: Passage de Milan, 1954; L'Emploi du temps, 1956, English translation as Passing Time, 1960; La Modification, 1957, English translation as Change of Heart, 1959; La Génie du lieu, 4 volumes, 1958, 1971, 1978, 1988; Degrés, 1960, English translation as Degrees, 1961; Répertoire, 5 volumes, 1960, 1964, 1968, 1974, 1982; Une histoire extraordinaire: Essai sur un reve de Baudelaire, 1961, English translation as Histoire extraordinaire: Essay on a Dream of Baudelaire's, 1969; Mobile: Étude pour un representation des Etats-Unis, 1962, English translation as Mobile: Study for a Representation of the United States, 1963; Description de San Marco, 1963, English translation as Description of San Marco, 1983; illustrations, 4 volumes, 1964, 1969, 1973, 1976; 6,810,00 litres d'eau par seconde: Étude stereophonic, 1965, English translation as Niagara, 1969; Essai sur "Les Essais", 1968; La Rose des vents: 32 rhumbs pour Charles Fourier, 1970; Matière de reves, 5 volumes, 1975, 1976, 1977, 1981, 1985; Improvisations sur Flaubert, 1984; Improvisations sur Henri Michaux, 1985; Improvisations sur Rimbaud, 1989; Improvisations sur Michel Butor, 1994; Dozens of other volumes of fiction, poetry, essays, etc. Honours: Chevalier de l'Ordre National du Mérite; Chevalier des Arts et des Lettres; Several literary prizes. Address: a l'Ecart, Lucinges, 74380 Bonne, France.

BUTORA Martin, b. 7 Oct 1944, Bratislava, Czechoslovakia. Sociologist; Writer. m. Zora Butorova, 18 Aug 1978, 3 sons, 1 daughter. Education: Graduated in Philosophy, 1976, PhD, 1980, Comenius University, Bratislava. Appointment: Senior Lecturer in Sociology, Charles University, Prague, 1992. Publications: Non-Fiction: Sociological Chapters on Alcoholism, 1989; Self-help Groups in Health Care, 1991; From the Velvet Revolution to the Velvet Divorce?, 1993. Fiction: Several books. Contributions to: Periodicals. Honour: Slovak Literary Fund Prize, 1991. Memberships: International Sociological Association; PEN Club, Bratislava. Address: Lubinska 6, 811 03 Bratislava, Slovakia.

BUTTER Peter Herbert, b. 7 Apr 1921, Coldstream, Scotland. University Professor. m. Bridget Younger, 30 Aug 1958, 1 son, 2 daughters. Education: MA, Balliol College, Oxford 1948. Publications: Shelley's Idols of the Cave, 1954; Francis Thompson, 1961; Edwin Muir, 1962; Edwin Muir: Man & Poet, 1966; Shelley's Alastor, Prometheus Unbound and Other Poems, 1971; Selected Letters of Edwin Muir, 1974; Selected Poems of William Blake, 1982; The Truth of Imagination: Some Uncollected Essays and Reviews of Edwin Muir, 1988; Complete Poems of Edwin Muir, 1992; William Blake, 1996. Contributions to: Akros; Lines Review; Modern Language Review; North Wind; Review of English Literature; Review of English Studies; Scottish Literary Journal. Membership: International Association of University Professors of English. Address: Ashfield, Prieston Road, Bridge of Weir, Renfrewshire PA11 3AW, Scotland.

BUTTERS Dorothy Gilman. See: **GILMAN Dorothy.**

BUTTERWORTH (David) Neil, b. 4 Sept 1934, London, England. Composer; Conductor; Writer; Broadcaster. m. Anne Mary Barnes, 23 Apr 1960, 3 daughters. Education: BA, Honours, English, 1957, BA, Honours, Music, 1958, London University; Guildhall School of Music, London, 1960-62; MA, Nottingham University, 1965. Appointments: Lecturer, Kingston College of Technology, 1960-68; Conductor, Edinburgh Schools Choir, 1968-72, Glasgow Orchestral Society, 1975-83, 1989-, Edinburgh Chamber Orchestra, 1983-85; Head of Music Department, Napier College, Edinburgh, 1968-87. Publications: 400 Aural Training Exercises, 1970; A Musical Quiz Book, 1974; Haydn, 1976; Dvořák, 1980; A Dictionary of American Composers, 1983; Aaron Copland, 1984; Sight-singing Exercises from the Masters, 1984; 20th Century Sight-singing Exercises, 1984; Vaughan Williams, 1989; Neglected Music, 1991; Samuel Barber, 1996. Contributions to: Periodicals. Honours: Conducting Prize; Fellow, London College of Music; Winston Churchill Travelling Fellowship. Memberships: Incorporated Society of Musicians; Performing Rights Society; Scottish Society of Composers. Address: 1 Roderick Place, West Linton, Peeblesshire EH46 7ES, Scotland.

BUTTREY Douglas N(orton), (Densil Neve Barr), b. Harrogate, Yorkshire, England. Playwright; Author. Education: MSc, University of London. Publications: Radio Plays: The Clapham Lamp-Post Saga, 1967; Gladys on the Wardrobe, 1970; But Petrovsky Goes on Forever, 1971; The Last Tramp, 1972; The Square at Bastogne, 1973; The Battle of Brighton Beach, 1975; With Puffins for Pawns, 1978; Anatomy of an Alibi, 1978; The Speech, 1979; Two Gaps in the Curtain, 1979; Klemp's Diary, 1980; Who Was Karl Raeder?, 1980; The Boy in the

Cellar, 1981; The Glory Hallelujah Microchip, 1981; The Dog That Was Only a Prophet, 1982; St Paul Transferred, 1983; The Mythical Isles, 1983. Novels: The Man with Only One Head, 1955; Death of Four Presidents, 1991. Contributions to: Periodicals. Membership: Fellow, PEN. Address: 15 Churchfields, Broxbourne, Hertfordshire EN10 7JU, England.

BUZO Alexander John, b. 23 July 1944, Sydney, New South Wales, Australia. Playwright. Author. m. Merelyn Johnson, 21 Dec 1968. Education: BA, University of New South Wales, 1966. Appointments: Resident Dramatist, Melbourne Theatre Company, 1972-73; Writer-in-Residence, James Cook University, 1985, University of Wollongong, 1989, University of Central Queensland, 1991, University of Indonesia, 1995. Publications: Tautology, 1980; Meet the New Class, 1981; The Search for Harry Allway, 1985; Glancing Blows, 1987; The Young Person's Guide to the Theatre and Almost Everything Else, 1988; Plays: Coralie Lansdowne Says No, 1974; Martello Towers, 1976; Rooted, 1968; The Front Room Boys, 1969; The Roy Murphy Show, 1970; Big River, 1980; Shellcove Road, 1989; The Longest Game, 1990; Prue Flies North, 1991; Kiwese, 1994; Pacific Union, 1995. Contributions to: Australian Way; Independent Monthly; Readers Digest; Playboy; Sydney Morning Herald; Pacific Islands Monthly; New Straits Times; Australian; Bulletin; Discovery; Heritage. Honour: Gold Medal, Australian Literature Society, 1972. Memberships: Centre for Australian Language and Literature Studies; Australian Writers Guild. Literary Agent: Margaret Connolly & Associates, Sydney, New South Wales. Address: 14 Rawson Avenue, Bondi Junction, Sydney, New South Wales 2022, Australia.

BYARS Betsy (Cromer), b. 7 Aug 1928, Charlotte, North Carolina, USA. Children's Author. m. Edward Ford Byars, 24 June 1950, 1 son, 3 daughters. Education: Furman University, 1946-48; BA, Queen's College, Charlotte, 1950. Publications: Clementine, 1962; The Dancing Camel, 1965; Rama, The Gypsy Cat, 1966; The Groober, 1967; The Midnight Fox, 1968; Trouble River, 1969; The Summer of the Swans, 1970; Go and Hush the Baby, 1971; The House of Wings, 1972; The 18th Emergency, 1973; The Winged Colt of Casa Mia, 1973; After the Goat Man, 1974; The Lace Snail, 1975; The TV Kid, 1976; The Pinballs, 1977; The Cartoonist, 1978; Goodbye, Chicken Little, 1979; Night Swimmers, 1980; The Animal, The Vegetable and John D Jones, 1981; The Two Thousand Pound Goldfish, 1981; The Cybil War, 1982; The Glory Girl, 1983; The Computer Nut, 1984; Cracker Jackson, 1985; Sugar and Other Stories, 1987; McMummy, 1993; Wanted...Mud Blossom, 1993; The Golly Sisters Ride Again, 1994. Address: 4 Riverpoint, Clemson, SC 29631, USA.

BYATT A(ntonia) S(usan), b. 24 Aug 1936, Sheffield, Yorkshire, England. Author. m. (1) Ian Charles Rayner Byatt, 1959, diss. 1969, 1 son, dec, 1 daughter, (2) Peter John Duffy, 1969, 2 daughters. Education: BA, Newnham College, Cambridge; Bryn Mawr College, Pennsylvania; Somerville College, Oxford. Appointments: Extra-Mural Lecturer, University of London, 1962-71; Lecturer in Literature, Central School of Art and Design, 1965-69; Lecturer in English, 1972-81; Senior Lecturer, 1981-83, University College, London; Associate, Newnham College, Cambridge, 1977-82. Publications: Fiction: Shadow of the Sun, 1964; Degrees of Freedom, 1965; The Game, 1967; The Virgin in the Garden, 1978; Still Life, 1985; Sugar and Other Stories, 1987; Possession: A Romance, 1990; Angels and Insects, 1992; The Matisse Stories, 1994; The Djinn in the Nightingale's Eye: Five Fairy Stories, 1995; Babel Tower, 1996. Non-Fiction: Wordsworth and Coleridge in their Time, 1970, reprinted as Unruly Times: Wordsworth and Coleridge, Poetry and Life, 1989; Iris Murdoch, 1976; George Eliot: The Mill on the Floss, editor, 1985; George Eliot: Selected Essays, editor, 1990; Passions of the Mind, 1991; Imagining Characters, with Ignes Sodre, 1995. Honours: Fellow, Royal Society of Literature, 1983; Honorary DLitt, Universities of Bradford, 1987, Durham, 1991, Nottingham, 1992, Liverpool, 1993, Portsmouth, 1994, London 1995; Honorary DLitt, University of York, 1991; Commander of the Order of the British Empire, 1990; Booker Prize, 1990; Irish Times/Aer Lingus International Fiction Prize, 1990; Eurasian Section, Best Book in the Commonwealth Prize, 1991. Address: 37 Rusholme Road, London SW15 3LF, England.

BYLINSKY Gene Michael, b. 30 Dec 1930, Belgrade, Yugoslavia. Science Writer. m. Gwen Gallegos, 14 Aug 1955, 1 son, 1 daughter. Education: BA, Journalism, Louisiana State University, USA, 1955. Appointments: Staff Writer, Wall Street Journal, 1957-61; Science Writer, National Observer, 1961-62; Newhouse Newpapers 1962-66; Editorial Board, Fortune Magazine, 1966-. Publications: The

Innovative Millionaires, 1976; Mood Control, 1978; Life in Darwin's Universe, 1981; High Tech Window on the Future (Story of Silicon Valley), 1985. Contributons to: New York Times Sunday Magazine, Sunday Book Review; New Republic; American Legion Magazine; Saturday Evening Post; Omni; Science Digest; Science Year. Honours: Albert Lasker Award, medical journalism, 1970; Deadline Award, Sigma Delta Chi, 1970; Gold Medal, American Chemical Society, 1973; Science writing award, American Medical Association, 1975; Claude Bernard Award, National Association for Medical Research, 1975; Journalism Award, University of Missouri, 1985. Memberships: National Association of Science Writers. Address: c/o Fortune Magazine, Time & Life Building, Rockefeller Centre, New York, NY 10020, USA.

BYRNE John, b. 6 Jan 1940, Paisley, Renfrewshire, Scotland. Writer. m. Alice Simpson, 1964, 1 son, 1 daughter. Education: St Mirin's Academy and Glasgow School of Art, 1958-63. Appointments: Graphic Designer, Scottish Television, Glasgow, 1964-66; Designer, A F Stoddard, Carpet manufacturers, Elderslie, 1966-68; Writer-in-Residence, Borderline Theatre, Irvine, Ayrshire, 1978-79; Duncan of Jordanstone College, Dundee, 1981; Associate Director, Haymarket Theatre, Leciester, 1984-85; Theatrical set and costume designer. Publications: Plays: The Slab Boys Trilogy (originally called Paisley Patterns): The Slab Boys (produced Edinburgh and London 1978, Louisville, 1979, New York, 1980), Cuttin' a Rug (as The Lovliest Night of the Year, produced Edinburgh, 1979, revised version as Threads, produced London, 1980, as Cuttin' a Rug, produced London, 1982), Still Life (produced Edinburgh 1982) Normal Service (produced London, 1979); Hooray for Hollywood (produced Louisville, 1980); The London Cuckolds, adaptation of the play by Edward Ravenscroft (produced Leicester and London, 1985). Radio and Television plays. Honour: Evening Standard Award, 1978. Litarary Agent: Margaret Ramsey Ltd, London. Address: 3 Castle Brae, Newport-on-Tay, Fife, Scotland.

BYRNE John Keyes. See: **LEONARD Hugh (John, Jr)**.

C

CABRERA INFANTE G(uillermo), b. 22 Apr 1929, Gibara, Cuba (British citizen). Novelist. m. Miriam Gomez, 1961. Education: University of Havana, 1949-54. Appointments: Former Chargé d'Affaires in Brussels, Scriptwriter and Professor. Publications: Asi en la paz como en la guerra: cuentos, 1960; Three Trapped Tigers, 1965; A View of Dawn in the Tropics, 1974; Infante's Inferno, 1979; Screenplays: Vanishing Point, 1970; Holy Smoke, 1985; A Twentieth-Century Job, 1991. Honour: Guggenheim Fellowship, 1970. Address: 53 Gloucester Road, London SW7 4QN, England.

CADDEL Richard Ivo, b. 13 July 1949, Bedford, England. Librarian. m. Ann Barker, 31 Aug 1971, 1 son, dec, 1 daughter. Education: BA, Newcastle University, 1971; Newcastle Polytechnic, 1971-72; ALA, 1974. Appointments: Staff, Durham University Library, 1972-; Director, Pig Press, 1973-; Organiser, Modern Tower Readings, 1974-75; Founder, Colpitts Poetry Readings, 1975; Organiser, Basil Bunting Celebration, Newcastle, 1986; Secretary, Basil Bunting Poetry Achive, 1987; Director, Basil Bunting Poetry Centre, 1989-. Publications: Sweet Cicely, 1983; Uncertain Time, 1990; 26 New British Poets, 1991; Basil Bunting: Uncollected Poems, 1991; Basil Bunting: Three Essays, 1994; Basil Bunting: Complete Poems, 1994; Ground, 1994. Contributions to: Poems and Criticism to numerous Magazines and Periodicals. Honours: Northern Arts Writers Awards, 1985, 1988, 1990; Fund for Poetry Award, 1992. Address: 7 Cross View Terrace, Nevilles Cross, Durham, DH1 4JY, England.

CADE Robin. See: **NICOLE Christopher Robin.**

CADET Maurice, b. Jacmel, Haiti. Professor of Literature. Div, 2 sons, 3 daughters. Education: Diplomas in Letters and Modern Languages, Audio-Visual and BS Law. Publications: Turbulences (poetry), 1989; Chalè Pimen (creole poems), 1990; Haute Dissidence (poetry), 1991; Itinéraires d'un enchantment (poetry), 1992; Réjouissances (poetry), 1994. Contributions to: Text published in a number of Quebec Magazines, including: Focus; Résistances; Estuaire; Brèves Littéraires; Ruptures. Honours: Haute dissidence Finalist, Literary Prize, BCP, 1991; Itinéraires d'un enchantment Finalist; Literary Prize Journal of Montreal, 1994; Réjouissances Finalist Price Gala du Livre of Jonquière, Quebec, Canada. Memberships: National Authors Union of Quebec; Language Plus Arts Gallery, Alma, Quebec. Address: 630 Robert Jean Apartment 2, Alma, Quebec G8B 7H1, Canada.

CADOGAN Mary (Rose), b. 30 May 1928, London, England. Writer. m. Alexander Cadogan, 27 May 1950, 1 daughter. Education: Teaching and Perfornace Diplomas, Margaret Morris School of Dance and Movement, 1954. Appointments: Secretary, Krishnamurti Writing Inc, London, 1958-68; Secretary, The Krishnamurti Foundation, Beckenham, Kent, 1968-; Governor, Brockwood Park Education Centre, Bramdean, Hants, 1968-. Publications: The Greyfriars Characters (with John Wernham), 1976; You're a Brick, Angela: A New Look at Girls' Fiction from 1839 to 1975 (with Patricia Craig), 1976; Women and Children First: The Fiction of Two World Wars (with Patricia Craig), 1978; Charles Hamilton Schoolgirls' Album (with John Wernham), 1978; The Lady Investigates: Women Detectives and Spies in Fiction (with Patricia Craig), 1981; The Morcove Companion (with Tommy Keen), 1981; From Wharton Lodge to Linton Hall; The Charles Hamilton Christmas Companion (with Tommy Keen), 1984; Richmal Crompton: The Woman Behind William, 1986. Address: 46 Overbury Avenue, Beckenham, Kent BR3 2PY, England.

CADY Jack (Andrew), b. 20 Mar 1932, Columbus, Ohio, USA. Writer; Teacher. Education: BS, University of Louisville, 1961. Appointments: Assistant Professor, 1968-73, Associate, Continuing Education, 1981-, University of Washington; Visiting Writer, Knox College, Galesburg, Illinois, 1973-74, Clarion College, Pennsylvania, 1974, Olympic College, Bremerton, Washington, 1984, 1985; Senior Faculty, University of Alaska Southeast, 1977-78; Visiting Writer, 1984, Assistant Professor, 1986, Senior Lecturer, 1986-87, Adjunct Professor, 1987-94, Writer-in-Residence, 1994-, Pacific Lutheran University, Tacoma, Washington. Publications: The Burning and Other Stories, 1972; Tattoo and Other Stories, 1978; The Well, 1981; Singleton, 1981; The Jonah Watch, 1982; McDowell's Ghost, 1982; The Man Who Could Make Things Vanish, 1983; The Sons of Noah,

and Other Stories, 1992; The Night We Buried Road Dog, 1993; Inagehi, 1993; Street, 1994; The Off Season, 1995; Kilroy was Here, 1996. Contributions to: Many anthologies and periodicals. Honours: Atlantic Monthly First Award, 1965; National Literary Anthology Award, 1970; Iowa Prize for Short Fiction, 1972; Washington State Governor's Award, 1972; National Endowment for the Arts Fellowship, 1992. Memberships: Associated Writing Programs; Horror Writers of America; PEN International. Address: 315 Logan Street, PO Box 872, Port Townsend, WA 98368, USA.

CAHILL Mike. See: **NOLAN William F(rancis).**

CAIDIN Martin (Karl von Strasser), b. 14 Sept 1927, New York, New York, USA. Author. m. Dee Dee Autry Caidin. Education: College; Courses with US Army, Air Force, and Coast Guard. Appointments: Commercial Pilot; Lecturer; Broadcaster; Author. Publications: Nearly 200 books. Contributions to: Numerous periodicals. Honours: James Strebig Memorial Awards; Master Aviator and Pioneer Aviator Awards, Silver Wings, 1987. Memberships: Authors Guild; Authors League; Aviation/Space Writers Association; Science Fiction Writers; Silver Wings; Valiant Air Command. Address: 13416 University Station, Gainesville, FL 32604, USA.

CAIRNCROSS Alexander Kirkland, b. 11 Feb 1911, Lesmahagow, Scotland. Economist. m. Mary Frances Glynn, 29 May 1943, 3 sons, 2 daughters. Education: MA, University of Glasgow, 1933; PhD, University of Cambridge, 1936. Publications: Introduction to Economics, 1944, 6th edition, 1982; Home and Foreign Investment, 1870-1913, 1953; Factors in Economic Development, 1962; Essays in Economic Management, 1971; Control of Long-Term International Capital Movements, 1973; Inflation, Growth and International Finance, 1975; Snatches, 1980; Sterling in Decline (with Barry Eichengreen), 1983; Years of Recovery, 1985; Economics and Economic Policy, 1986; The Price of War, 1986; A Country to Play With, 1987; The Economic Section (with Nita Watts), 1989; Planning in Wartime, 1991; Goodbye Great Britain (with Kathleen Burk), 1992; The Legacy of the Golden Age (with Frances Cairncross), 1992; Austin Robinson: The Life of an Economic Adviser, 1993; The British Economy Since 1945, 1992, 2nd edition, 1995; Economic Ideas and Government Policy, 1995; Managing the British Economy in the 1960s, 1996; The Wilson Years 1964-69, 1996; Why No Repeats: The Diaries of Robert Hall, 2 volumes (editor). Contributions to: Numerous Journals. Memberships: British Association for Advancement of Science and Technology; Royal Economic Society; Scottish Economic Society. Address: 14 Staverton Road, Oxford OX2 6XJ, England.

CAIRNCROSS Frances Anne, b. 30 Aug 1944, Otley, Yorkshire, England. Journalist. m. Hamish McRae, 10 Sept 1971, 2 daughters. Education: Honours Degree in Modern History, Oxford University, 1962-65; MA, Economics, Brown University, Providence, Rhode Island, USA, 1965-66. Appointments: Staff, The Times, 1967-69, The Banker, 1969, The Observer, 1969-71; Economics Correspondent, The Guardian, 1971-81; Women's Editor, The Guardian, 1981-84; Britain Editor, The Economist, 1984-. Publications: Capital City (with Hamish McRae), 1971; The Second Great Crash, 1973; The Guardian Guide to the Economy, 1981; Changing Perceptions of Economic Policy, 1981; Second Guardian Guide to the Economy, 1983; Guide to the Economy, 1987; Costing the Earth, 1991; Green, Inc, 1995. Address: 6 Canonbury Lane, London N1 2AP, England.

CAIRNS. See: **DOWLING Basil.**

CAIRO Luiz Roberto Velloso, b. 26 Nov 1944, Salvador, BA, Brazil. Professor. Education: Master in Literary Theory and Comparative Literature, Universidade de Sao Paulo, 1978; PhDr in Literary Theory and Comparative Literature, Universidade de Sao Paulo, 1989; Professor of Brazilian Literature, Universidade Estadual Paulista. Appointment: XIV Congress of ICLA/AILC, 1994; 3rd BRASA Conference, September 1996; 5 Congresso da Associacao Internacional de Lusitanistas, 1996; 5th ISSEI Conference, 1996. Publications: O Salto por cima da propria sombra, 1996; Literatura Comparada: Ensaios, 1996. Contributions to: Revista do Instituto de Estudos Brasileiros; Revista de Letras da UNESP; Revista de Estudos Literarios da FALE/UFMG; Anuario Brasileño de Estudios Hispanicos. Membership: Abralic, 1992-94; GT de Literature Comparada ANPOLL, 1992-94, 1994-96; BRASA, 1996-97. Address: Rua da Assembleia,226 19800-000 Assis-SP Brazil.

CALAIS Jean. See: **RODEFER Stephen.**

CALDECOTT Moyra, b. 1 June 1927, Pretoria, South Africa (British citizen). Author. m. Oliver Zerffi Stratford Caldecott, 5 Apr 1951, 2 sons, 1 daughter. Education: BA, 1949, MA, 1950, University of Natal. Publications: The Weapons of the Wolfhound, 1976; The Sacred Stones, Vol I, The Tall Stones, 1977, Vol II, The Temple of the Sun, 1977, Vol III, Shadow on the Stones, 1978; Adventures by Leaf Light, 1978; The Lily and the Bull, 1979; Child of the Dark Star, 1980; The King of Shadows: A Glastonbury Story, 1981; The Twins of the Tylwyth Teg, 1983; Taliesin and Avagddu, 1983; Bran, Son of Llyr, 1985; The Tower and the Emerald, 1985; Guardians of the Tall Stones, 1986; The Son of the Sun, 1986; The Silver Vortex, 1987; Etheldreda, 1987; Women in Celtic Myth, 1988; Daughter of Amun, 1989; The Green Lady and the King of Shadows, 1989; The Crystal Legends, 1990; Myths of the Sacred Tree, 1993; The Winged Man, 1994; Mythical Journeys: Legendary Quests, 1996. Contributions to: Anthologies and periodicals. Address: 52 Southdown Road, Southdown, Bath BA2 1JQ, England.

CALDER Angus, b. 5 Feb 1942, Sutton, Surrey, England. University Teacher. m. (1) Jennifer Daiches, 1 Oct 1963, 1 son, 2 daughters, (2) Catherine Kyle, 21 Dec 1987, 1 son. Education: MA, Kings College, Cambridge, 1963; D Phil, University of Sussex, 1968. Appointments: Lecturer, University of Nairobi, 1968-71; Staff Tutor and Reader in Cultural Studies, Open University in Scotland, 1979-93; Visiting Professor, University of Zimbabwe, 1992; Convener, Scottish Poetry Library, 1983-88; Commonwealth Writers Conference, Edinburgh, 1986; Writing Together, Glasgow, 1990. Publications: The People's War, 1969; Russia Discovered, 1976; Byron, 1987; T S Eliot, 1987; Revolutionary Empire, 1981; The Myth of the Blitz, 1991; Revolving Culture: Notes from the Scottish Republic, 1994; Walking in Waikato, poems, 1997. Contributions to: Editor, Journal of Commonwealth Literature; Articles and Reviews in Cencrastus, London Review of Books; New Statesman; Scotland on Sunday; Chapman. Honours: John Llewellyn Rhys Memorial Prize, 1970; Scottish Arts Council Book Awards, 1981, 1994. Memberships: Society of Authors; Scottish PEN. Literary Agent: Curtis Brown Ltd. Address: c/o Giles Gordon, 6 Ann Street, Edinburgh EH4 1PJ, Scotland.

CALDER Nigel (David Ritchie), b. 2 Dec 1931, London, England. Writer. m. Elisabeth Palmer, 22 May 1954, 2 sons, 3 daughters. Education: BA, 1954, MA, 1957, Sidney Sussex College, Cambridge. Appointments: Research Physicist, Mullard Research Laboratories, Redhill, Surrey, 1954-56; Staff Writer, 1956-60, Science Editor, 1960-62, Editor, 1962-66, New Scientist; Science Correspondent, New Statesman, 1959-62, 1966-71. Publications: The Environment Game, 1967, US edition as Eden Was No Garden: An Inquiry Into the Environment of Man, 1967; Technopolis: Social Control of the Uses of Science, 1969; Violent Universe: An Eyewitness Account of the New Astronomy, 1970; The Mind of Man: An Investigation into Current Research on the Brain and Human Nature, 1970; Restless Earth: A Report on the New Geology, 1972; The Life Game: Evolution and the New Biology, 1974; The Weather Machine: How Our Weather Works and Why It Is Changing, 1975; The Human Conspiracy, 1976; The Key to the Universe: A Report on the New Physics, 1977; Spaceships of the Mind, 1978; Einstein's Universe, 1979; Nuclear Nightmares: An Investigation into Possible Wars, 1980; The Comet is Coming!: The Feverish Legacy of Mr Halley, 1981; Timescale: An Atlas of the Fourth Dimension, 1984; 1984 and Beyond: Nigel Calder Talks to His Computer About the Future, 1984; The English Channel, 1986; The Green Machines, 1986; Future Earth: Exploring the Frontiers of Science (with John Newell), 1989; Scientific Europe, 1990; Spaceship Earth, 1991; Giotto to the Comets, 1992; Out of this World, 1995; The Manic Sun, 1997. Contributions to: Television documentaries; Numerous periodicals. Honours: UNESCO Kalinga Prize, 1972; AAAS, honorary fellow, 1986. Memberships: Association of British Science Writers; Cruising Association; Royal Astronomical Society; Royal Geographical Society. Address: 26 Boundary Road, Northgate, Crawley, West Sussex RH10 2BT, England.

CALDERWOOD James L(ee), b. 7 Apr 1930, Corvallis, Oregon, USA. Professor Emeritus; Writer. m. Cleo Xeniades Calderwood, 15 Aug 1955, 2 sons. Education: BA, University of Oregon, 1953; PhD, University of Washington, 1963. Appointments: Instructor, Michigan State University, 1961-63; Assistant Professor, University of California at Irvine, 1963-66; Assistant Professor, 1966-68, Associate Professor, 1968-71, Professor, 1971-94, Assoicate Dean of Humanities, 1974-94, Professor Emeritus, 1994-, University of California at Irvine; Editorial Board, Studies in English Literature, 1978-, Shakespeare Criticism,

1989-; Evaluator, national Endowment for the Humanities, 1979-. Publications: Shakespearean Metadrama, 1971; Metadrama in Shakespeare's Henriad, 1979; to Be and Not to Be: Negation and Metadrama in Hamlet, 1983; If It Were Done: Tragic Action in Macbeth, 1986; Shakespeare and the Denial of Death, 1987; The Properties of Othello, 1989; A Midsummer Night's Dream, 1992. Editor: Shakespeare's Love's Labour's Lost, 1970. Editor with H E Toliver: Forms of Poetry, 1968; Perspectives on Drama, 1968; Perspectives on Poetry, 1968; Perspectives on Fiction, 1968; Forms of Drama, 1969; Essays in Shakespearean Criticism, 1969; Forms of Prose Fiction, 1972; Forms of Tragedy, 1972. Contributions to: Scholarly journals. Honour: Alumni Achievement Award, University of Oregon, 1991. Address: 1323 Terrace Way, Laguna Beach, CA 92651, USA.

CALHOUN Craig Jackson, b. 16 June 1952, Watseka, Illinois, USA. Professor of Sociology; Writer; Editor. m. Pamela F DeLargy, 2 children. Education: BA in Anthropology, University of Southern California, 1972; MA in Anthropology, Columbia University, 1974; MA in Social Anthropology, Manchester University, 1975; PhD in Sociology and History, St Antony's College, Oxford, 1980. Appointments: Instructor, 1977-80, Assistant Professor, 1980-85, Associate Professor, 1985-89, Professor of Sociology and History, 1989-96, Director, University Center for International Studies, 1993-96, University of North Carolina at Chapel Hill; Editor, Comparative Social Research, 1988-93, Sociological Theory, 1994-; Professor of Sociology, Chair, Department of Sociology, New York University, 1996-; Visiting Lecturer, 1991, Professor, part-time, 1993-, University of Oslo. Publications: The Anthropological Study of Education (editor with F A J Ianni), 1976; The Question of Class Struggle: Social Foundations of Popular Radicalism During the Industrial Revolution, 1982; Sociology (with Donald Light and Suzanne Keller), 1989, 4th edition, 1997; Structures of Power and Constraint: Essays in Honor of Peter M Blau (editor with W R Scott and M Meyer), 1990; Habermas and the Public Sphere (editor), 1992; Bourdieu: Critical Perspectives (editor with E LiPuma and M Postone), 1993; Social Theory and the Politics of Identity (editor), 1994; Neither Gods Nor Emperors: Students and the Struggle for Democracy in China, 1995; Critical Social Theory: Culture, History and the Challenge of Difference, 1995. Contributions to: Numerous books and scholarly journals. Honours: W K Kellogg National Fellowship, 1982-85; Distinguished Contribution to Scholarship Award, Section on Political Sociology, American Sociological Association, 1995. Memberships: American Anthropological Association; American Historical Association; American Sociological Association; International Sociological Association; International Studies Association; Royal Anthropological Institute; Social Science History Association; Society for the Study of Social Problems; Sociological Research Association. Address: Department of Sociology, New York University, 269 Mercer Street, New York, NY 10003-6687, USA.

CALIFANO Joseph A(nthony), b. 15 May 1931, New York, New York, USA. Lawyer; Professor of Public Health Policy; Writer. m. (1), 2 sons, 1 daughter, (2) Hilary Paley Byers, 1983, 2 stepchildren. Education: AB, Holy Cross College, 1952; LLB, Harvard University, 1955. Appointments: Admitted to the Bar, New York, 1955; Lawyer, Dewey Ballantine firm, New York City, 1958-61; Special Assistant to the General Counsel, US Department of Defense, 1961-62, the Secretary of the Army, 1962-63; General Counsel, Department of the Army, 1963-64; Special Assistant to the Secretary and Deputy Secreatry of Defense, 1964-65, to President Lyndon B Johnson, 1965-69; Partner, Arnold & Porter, Washington, DC, 1969-71; Williams, Connolly & Califano, Washington, DC, 1971-77; Secretary, US Department of Health, Education, and Welfare, 1977-79; Partner, Califano, Ross & Heineman, Washington, DC, 1980-82; Senior Partner, Dewey, Ballantine, Bushby, Palmer, & Wood, Washington, DC, 1983-92; Professor of Public Health Policy, Columbia University, 1992-. Publications: The Student Revolution: A Global Confrontation, 1969; A Presidential Nation, 1975; The Media and the Law (with Howard Simons), 1976; The Media and Business (with Howard Simons), 1978; Governing America: An Insiders Report (from the White House and the Cabinet), 1981; The 1982 Report on Drug Abuse and Alcoholism: America's Health Care Revolution, 1985; The Triumph and Tragedy of Lyndon Johnson, 1991; Radical Surgery: What's Next for America's Health Care, 1994. Honours: Distinguished Public Service Medal, US Department of Defense, 1965; Man of the Year Award, Justinian Society of Lawyers, 1966. Address: c/o Schools of Medicine and Public Health, Columbia University, New York, NY 10027, USA.

CALISHER Hortense, b. 20 Dec 1911, New York, New York, USA. Writer. m. (1) 2 sons, (2) Curtis Harnack, 23 Mar 1959. Education: AB, Barnard College, 1932. Appointments: Adjunct Professor, Barnard College, 1956-57, Columbia University, 1968-70, City College of the City University of New York, 1969; Various visiting professorships and lectureships. Publications: Novels: False Entry, 1961; Textures of Life, 1962; Journal from Ellipsis, 1965; The New Yorkers, 1969; Queenie, 1971; Standard Dreaming, 1972; Eagle Eye, 1973; On Keeping Women, 1977; Mysteries of Motion, 1984; The Bobby-Soxer, 1986; Age, 1987; The Small Bang, 1992; In the Palace of the Movie King, 1994. Other: Collected Stories, 1975. Non-Fiction: Herself (autobiography), 1972; Kissing Cousins (memoir), 1988. Contributions to: Periodicals. Honours: Guggenheim Fellowships, 1952, 1955; American Academy of Arts and Letters Award, 1967; Kafka Prize, University of Rochester, 1987; National Endowment for the Arts Lifetime Achievement Award, 1989. Memberships: American Academy of Arts and Letters, president, 1987-90; PEN, president, 1986-87. Address: c/o Donadio & Associates, 121 West 27th Street, Suite 704, New York, NY 10001, USA.

CALLAGHAN Barry, b. 5 July 1937, Toronto, Ontario, Canada. Publisher; Poet. Education: MA, University of Toronto, 1963. Appointments: Professor, York Universiy, 1965-; Founder, Publisher, Exile Magazine, 1972-, Exile Editions, Toronto, 1976-. Publications: The Hogg Poems and Drawings, 1978; As Close We Came, 1982; Stone Blind Love, 1988; Novel, The Way the Angel Spreads her Wings, 1989; The Black Queen Stories, 1982; Editor, Lords of Winter and Love: A Book of Canadian Love Poems, English and French, 1983. Honours: Presidents' Medal, For Journalism, 1982, 1985, 1988; Ontario Arts Council Award, 1987. Address: 69 Sullivan Street, Toronto, Ontario M5T 1C2, Canada.

CALLAHAN Steven (Patrick), b. 6 Feb 1952, Needham, Massachusetts, USA. Author; Illustrator. Education: BA, Syracuse University, 1974. Appointments: Contributing Editor, Sail Magazine, 1982-84, Sailor Magazine, 1984-85; Associate Editor, Cruising World Magazine, 1994-. Publications: Adrift, 76 Days Lost at Sea, 1986; Capsized, 1993. Contributions to: Sail; Sailor; Cruising World; Sailing; Multihull; NE Offshore; Yankee; New York Times; Ultrasport; International Wildlife; Yachting World; Yachts and Yachting. Honours: Salon Du Libre Maritime, 1986; Best Books for Young Adults, 1986. Address: 804 Newport Green, Newport, RI 02840, USA.

CALLAWAY C Wayne, b. 28 May 1941, Easton, Maryland, USA. Physician. m. Jackie Chalkley, 7 Sept 1996. Education: BA, University of Delaware, 1963; MD, Northwestern University, 1967. Publications: The Callaway Diet: Successful Permanent Weight Loss for Starvers, Stuffers and Skippers, 1990; Surviving with AIDS: A Comprehensive Program of Nutritional Co-Therapy, 1991; Clinical Nutrition for the House Officer, 1992. Contributions to: Periodicals. Literary Agent: Jane Dystel. Address: 2311 M Street North West, #301, Washington, DC 20037, USA.

CALLICOTT J(ohn) Baird, b. 9 May 1941, Memphis, Tennessee, USA. Professor of Philosophy and Natural Resources; Writer. m. (1) Ann Nelson Archer, 7 June 1963, div 15 May 1985, 1 son, (2) Frances Moore Lappe, 25 Nov 1985, div 15 July 1990. Education: BA, Rhodes College, 1963; MA, 1966, PhD, 1971, Syracuse University. Appointments: Lecturer, Syracuse University, 1965-66; Instructor, University of Memphis, 1966-69; Assistant Professor, 1969-74, Associate Professor, 1974-82, Professor of Philosophy, 1982-, Professor of Natural Resources, 1984-, University of Wisconsin at Stevens Point; Visiting Professor of Philosophy, University of Florida, 1983; Visiting Professor of Environmental Studies, University of California at Santa Barbara, 1988; Rose Morgan Visiting Professor, University of Kansas, 1993; Knight Visiting Scholar, Presbyterian College, 1995; Visting Professorial Fellow, James Cook University of North Queensland, Australia, 1995; Associate Professor of Philosophy, University of North Texas, 1995-. Publications: Plato's Aesthetics: An Introduction to the Theory of Forms, 1971; Clothed-in-Fur and Other Tales: An Introduction to An Ojibwa World View, 1982; In Defense of the Land Ethic: Essays in Environmental Philosophy, 1989; Earth's Insights: A Survey of Ecological Ethics from the Mediterranean Basin to the Australian Outback, 1994. Editor: Companion to a Sand County Almanac: Interpretive and Critical Essays, 1987; Nature in Asian Traditions of Thought: Essays in Environmental Philosophy with Roger T Ames), 1989; The River of the Mother of God and Other Essays by Aldo Leopold (with Susan L Flader), 1991; Environmental Philosophy: From Animal Rights to Social Ecology (with Michael Zimmerman, George Sessions, Karen Warren, and John Clark), 1993; Earth Summit Ethics: Toward a Reconstructive Postmodern Environmental Philosophy on the Atlantic Rim (with Fernando J R da Rocha), 1996; The Great New Wilderness Debate (with Michael P Nelson), 1997. Contributions to: Many books and numerous journals. Honours: Woodrow Wilson Fellow, 1963-64; Wisconsin Library Association Outstanding Achievement Awards, 1988, 1992; University Scholar Award, University of Wisconsin at Stevens Point, 1995. Memberships: American Philosophical Association; American Society for Environmental History; International Development Ethics Association; International Society for Environmental Ethics; Society for Asian and Comparative Philosophy; Society for Conservation Biology. Address: c/o Department of Philosophy, University of North Texas, Denton, TX 76205, USA.

CALLISON Brian (Richard), b. 13 July 1934, Manchester, England. Writer. m. Phyllis Joyce Jobson, 12 May 1958, 2 sons. Education: Dundee College of Art, 1954-56. Appointments: Deck Officer, British Merchant Navy, 1951-54; Managing Director, Construction Company, 1956-63; General Manager, Entertainment Centre, 1963-67; Freelance Writer, 1967-. Publications: A Flock of Ships, 1970; A Plague of Sailors, 1971; Dawn Attack, 1972; A Web of Salvage, 1973; Trapp's War, 1974; A Ship is Dying, 1976; A Frenzy of Merchantmen, 1977; The Judas Ship, 1978; Trapp's Peace, 1979; The Auriga Madness, 1980; The Sextant, 1981; Spearfish, 1982; Bone Collectors, 1984; Thunder of Crude, 1986; Trapp and World War Three, 1988; The Trojan Hearse, 1990; Crocodile Trapp, 1993. Memberships: Royal Institute of Nagivation (M.R.I.N); Society of Authors. Address: c/o Harper Collins Publishers, 77-85 Fulham Palace Road, Hammersmith, London W6 8JB, England.

CALLOW Philip (Kenneth), b. 26 Oct 1924, Birmingham, England. Writer. Education: St Luke's College, Exeter, 1968-70. Appointment: Creative Writing Fellow, Open University, 1979. Publications: The Hosanna Man, 1956; Common People, 1958; Native Ground, 1959; Pledge for the Earth, 1960; The Honeymooners, 1960; Turning Point, 1961; Clipped Wings, 1963; The Real Life, 1964; In My Own Land, 1965; Going to the Moon, 1968; The Bliss Body, 1969; Flesh of Morning, The Lamb, 1971; Bare Wires, Yours, 1972; Son and Lover: The Young D H Lawrence, 1975; The Story of My Desire, 1976; Janine, 1977; The Subway to New York, 1979; Cave Light, 1981; Woman with a Poet, 1983; New York Insomnia, 1984; Verse, Icons, 1987; Soliloquires of an Eye, 1990; Some Love, 1991. Address: Little Thatch, Haselbury, Nr Crewkerne, Somerset, England.

CALLWOOD June, b. 2 June 1924, Chatham, Ontario, Canada. Writer. m. Trent Frayne, 13 May 1944, 2 sons, 2 daughters. Appointments: Reporter, Brantford Expositor, 1941; Toronto Globe and Mail, 1942; Freelance Journalist, 1945-; Columnist, Globe and Mail, 1983-89. Publications: Emma, 1984; Twelve Weeks in Spring, 1986; Emotions, 1986; Jim: A Life with AIDS, 1988; The Sleepwalker, 1990; Trial Without End, 1995. Honours: City of Toronto Award of Merit, 1974; Order of Canada, 1978, 1986; Canadian News Hall of Fame, 1984; Windsor Press Club Quill Award, 1987; Order of Ontario, 1989; Udo Award, 1989; Lifetime Achievement Award, 1991; 14 Honorary Degrees; Margaret Lawrence Lecture, 1993. Memberships: Writers Union of Canada; Canadian Centre PEN; Toronto Arts Council; Book and Periodical Chair; Beaver Valley Soaring Club. Address: 21 Hillcroft Drive, Islington, Ontario M9B 4X4, Canada.

CALMENSON Stephanie Lyn, b. 28 Nov 1952, New York, New York, USA. Children's Writer. Education: BA, Brooklyn College, 1973; MA, New York University, 1976. Publications: Never Take a Pig to Lunch (anthology), 1982; One Little Monkey, 1982, 4th edition 1983, produced by BBC TV, 1984; My Book of the Seasons, 1982; Where Will the Animals Stay?, 1983; That's Not Fair!, 1983; Where is Grandma Potamus?, 1983; The Birthday Hat: A Grandma Potamus Story, 1983; The Kindergarten Book, 1983; Barney's Sand Castle, 1983; Bambi and the Butterfly, 1983; Ten Furry Monsters, 1984; The Afterschool Book, 1984; All Aboard the Goodnight Train, 1984; Waggleby of Fraggle Rock, 1985; Ten Items or Less, 1985; Happy Birthday Buddy Blue, 1985; The Laugh Book, anthology (with Joanna Cole), 1986; Gobo and the Prize from Outer Space, 1986; The Sesame Street ABC Book, 1986; The Sesame Street Book of First Times, 1986; Little Duck's Moving Day, 1986; The Little Bunny, 1986; Who Said Moo?, 1987; Beginning Sounds Workbook, 1987; The Read-Aloud Treasury, anthology (with Joanna Cole), 1987; Tiger's Bedtime, 1987; One Red Shoe (The Other One's Blue!), 1987; Spaghetti Manners, 1987; The Giggle Book, 1987; Fido, 1987; Where's

Rufus, 1988; Little Duck and the New Baby, 1988; The Children's Aesop, 1988; The Read-Aloud Treasury (with Joanna Cole), 1988; No Stage Fright for Me, 1988; Where is Grandma Rabbit?, 1988; 101 Turkey Jokes, 1988; Ho! Ho! Ho!: Christmas Jokes and Riddles, 1988; What Am I! Very First Riddles, 1989; The Principal's New Clothes, 1989; Come To My Party; Zip, Whiz, Zoom, 1992; The Little Witch Sisters, 1993; Engine, Engine, Number 1, 1996. Contributions to: Periodicals. Memberships: Mystery Writers of America; Society of Children's Book Writers; Authors Guild. Address: c/o Scholastic Press Inc, 555 Broadway, New York, NY 10012, USA.

CALVERT Patricia Joyce, b. 22 July 1931, Great Falls, Montana, USA. Editor; Proofreader. m. George J Calvert, 27 Jan 1951, 2 daughters. Education: BS, Summa Cum Laude, Winona State University, 1976. Publications: The Snowbird, 1980; The Stone Pony, 1982; The Hour of the Wolf, 1983; Hadder MacColl, 1985; Yesterday's Daughter, 1986; Stranger, You and I, 1987; When Morning Comes, 1989; Picking Up the Pieces, 1993. Contributions to: Highlights for Children; Junior Life; Adventurer; American Farmer; Friend; Capper's Weekly; Grit; Writer Magazine; Farmland News; War Cry. Honours: Society of Children's Book Writers, Work-in-Progress Award, 1978; American Library Society, Best Book Award, 1980; Woman in the Arts Award, YWCA, 1981; Friends of American Writers Award, 1981; Society of Midland Authors, 1981. Memberships: Society of Children's Book Writers; Children's Reading Round Table; Minnesota Reading Association; International Reading Association. Literary Agent: Wendy Schmalz, Harold Ober Agency, 426 Madison Avenue, New York, NY 10017, USA. Address: Foxwood Farm, 6130 County Road No 7 South East, Chatfield, MN 55923, USA.

CALVERT Peter Anthony Richard, b. 19 Nov 1936, Islandmagee, County Antrim, Northern Ireland. Professor. m. Susan Ann Milbank, 1987. Education: Campbell College, Belfast; Queens' College, Cambridge; University of Minnesota. Appointments: Lecturer, 1964-71, Senior Lecturer, 1971-74, Reader, 1974-83, Professor, 1984-, University of Southampton. Publications: The Mexican Revolution 1910-1914, 1968; A Study of Revolution, 1970; The Falklands Crisis, 1982; Guatemala, 1985; The Foreign Policy of New States, 1986; Argentina: Political Culture and Instability, (with Susan Calvert) 1989; Revolution and Counter Revolution, 1990; Latin America in the 20th Century, (with Susan Calvert) 1993; An Introduction to Comparative Politics, 1993; International Politics of Latin America, 1994; Politics and Society in the Third World (with Susan Calvert), 1996; Editor: The Process of Political Succession, 1987; The Central American Security System, 1988; Political and Economic Encyclopedia of South America and the Caribbean, 1991. Contributions to: International Affairs Political Studies; World Today. Membership: Fellow, Royal Historical Society. Address: Department of Politics, University of Southampton, Southampton SO17 1BJ, England.

CALVIN Henry. See: **HANLEY Clifford.**

CALVOCORESSI Peter (John Ambrose), b. 17 Nov 1912, England. Author; Publisher. m. Barbara Dorothy Eden, 1938, 2 sons. Education: King's Scholar, Eton; Balliol College, Oxford. Appointments: Called to the Bar, 1935; Wing Commander, Trial of Major War Criminals, Nuremburg, 1945-46; Staff, 1949-54, Council, 1955-70, Royal Institute of International Affairs; Director, Chatto & Windus Ltd and The Hogarth Press Ltd, 1954-65; Chairman, The Africa Bureau, 1963-71, The London Library, 1970-73, Open University Educational Enterprises, 1979-88; Part-Time Reader in International Relations, University of Sussex, 1965-71; Editorial Director, 1972-76, Publisher and Chief Executive, 1973-76, Penguin Books. Publications: Nuremburg: The Facts, the Law and the Consequences, 1947; Survey of International Affairs, Vol I, 1947-48, 1959, Vol II, 1949-50, 1951, Vol III, 1951, 1952, Vol IV, 1952, 1953, Vol V, 1953, 1954; Middle East Crisis (with Guy Wint), 1957; South Africa and World Opinion, 1961; World Order and New States, 1962; World Politics Since 1945, 1968, 6th edition, 1991; Total War (with Guy Wint), 1972, 2nd edition, 1989; The British Experience, 1945-75, 1978; Top Secret Ultra, 1980; Independent Africa and the World, 1985; A Time for Peace, 1987; Who's Who in the Bible, 1987; Resilient Europe, 1870-2000, 1991; Threading My Way (memoirs), 1994. Memberships: Council, Institute for Strategic Studies, 1961-71; International Executive, Amnesty International, 1969-71. Address: 1 Queen's Parade, Bath BA1 2NJ, England.

CAMERON D Y. See: **COOK Dorothy Mary.**

CAMERON Deborah, b. 10 Nov 1958, Glasgow, Scotland. Lecturer; Writer. Education: BA Hons, University of Newcastle upon Tyne, 1980; MLitt, Oxford University, 1985. Appointments: Lecturer, Roehampton Institute of Higher Education, Digby Stuart College, London, 1983-; Visiting Professor, College of William and Mary, 1988-90; Worked as teacher of English as a foreign language; Active in British women's movement for more than ten years. Publications: Feminism and Linguistic Theory, 1985; Analysing Conversation (with T J Taylor), 1987; The Lust to Kill (with Elizabeth Frazer), 1987. Editor: The Feminist Critique of Language, 1990. Editor with Jennifer Coates: Women in Their Speech Communities, 1989. Contributions to: Articles and reviews to magazines and newspapers, including Language and Communicaiton, City Limits and Cosmopolitan. Address: Digby Stuart College, Roehampton Lane, London SW25 5PH, England.

CAMERON Donald. See: **HARBINSON-BRYANS Robert.**

CAMERON Donald (Allan), (Silver Donald Cameron), b. 21 June 1937, Toronto, Ontario, Canada. Author. m. (1) Catherine Ann Cahoon, 21 Aug 1959, 3 sons, 1 daughter. (2) Lulu Terrio, 17 May 1980, dec 6 Apr 1996, 1 son. Education: BA, University of British Columbia, 1959; MA, University of California, 1962; PhD, University of London, 1967. Appointments: Associate Professor of English, University of New Brunswick, 1968-71; Freelance Writer, 1971-; Writer-in-Residence, University College of Cape Breton, 1978-80; University of Prince Edward Island, 1985-86, Nova Scotia College of Art and Design, 1987-88; Owner, Paper Tiger Enterprises Ltd, editorial and consulting sevices; Dean, School of Community Studies, University College of Cape Breton, Sydney, Nova Scotia, 1994-96; Special Assistant to the President, 1997-. Publications: Faces of Leacock, 1967; Conversations with Canadian Novelists, 1973; The Education of Everett Richardson, 1977; Seasons in the Rain (essays), 1978; Dragon Lady, 1980; The Baitchopper (children's novel), 1982; Schooner: Bluenose and Bluenoe II, 1984; Outhouses of the West, 1988; Wind, Whales and Whisky: A Cape Breton Voyage, 1991; Lifetime: A Treasury of Uncommon Wisdoms (co-author), 1992; Once Upon a Schooner: An Offshore Voyage In Bluenose II, 1992; Iceboats to Super Ferries: An Illustrated History of Marine Atlantic (co-author); Sniffing the Coast: An Acadian Voyage, 1993; Sterling Silver: Rants, Raves and Revelations, 1994. Numerous articles, radio drama, short stories, television scripts and stage plays. Honours: ACTRA Award nominations for radio drama; 4 National Magazine Awards; Best Short Film, Canadian Film Celebration; Nominated, Prix Italia for Radio Drama, 1980; City of Dartmouth Book Award, 1992; Atlantic Provinces Booksellers Choice Award, 1992. Memberships: Writers Union, Canada; ACTRA; Writers Federation, Nova Scotia. Address: D'Escousse, Nova Scotia B0E 1K0, Canada.

CAMERON Ian. See: **PAYNE Donald Gordon.**

CAMERON WATT Donald, b. 17 May 1928, Rugby, England. Professor Emeritus; Writer. Education: BA, 1951, MA, 1954, Oriel College, Oxford. Appointments: Assistant Lecturer, 1954-56, Lecturer, 1956-61, Senior Lecturer, 1962-66, Reader, 1966-72, Titular Professor, 1971-82, Stevenson Professor of International History, 1982-93, Professor Emeritus, 1993-, London School of Economics and Political Science, University of London; Assistant Editor, Documents on German Foreign Policy, 1918-45, 1951-54, 1957-59; Editor, Survey of International Affairs, 1962-71; Chairman, Greenwich Forum, 1974-84; Official Historian, Cabinet Office Historical Section, 1976-95. Publications: Britain and the Suez Canal, 1956; Documents on the Suez Crisis, 1957; Survey of International Affairs, 1961-63, 1965, 1969, 1973; A History of the World in the 20th Century, 1967; Contemporary History in Europe, 1969; Hitler's Ranks Kampf, 1969, new edition 1990; Current British Foreign Policy, 1970-72; Documents on British Foreign Affairs, 1867-1939, 1985-97; Succeeeding John Bull, America in Britain's Place 1900-1975, 1983; How War Came, 1989; Argentina Between the Great Powers, 1990. Honours: Fellow, British Academy, DLitt, Oxon; Foreign Member Polish Academy of Arts and Science, Cracow; Wolfson Prize, 1990. Literary Agent: Michael Sissons, A D Peters and Co, 5th Floor, The Chambers, Chelsea Harbour, Lots Road, London SW10 0XF, England. Address: c/o London School of Economics and Political Science, Houghton Street, London WC2A 2AE, England.

CAMPBELL Alistair Te Ariki, b. 25 June 1925, Rarotonga, Cooks Islands. Writer. m. (1) Fleur Adcock, 1952, (2) Meg Andersen, 1958, 3 sons, 2 daughters. Education: BA, Victoria University of Wellington, 1953; Wellington Teacher's College, 1954. Appointments:

Editor, School Publications, 1955-72; Senior Editor, New Zealand Council for Educational Research, 1972-87. Publications: Mine Eyes Dazzle, 1950; Wild Honey, 1964; Island to Island, 1984; The Frigate Bird, 1989; Sidewinder, 1991; Tia, 1993; Pocket Collected Poems, 1996; Fantasy With Witches, forthcoming. Contributions to: Poetry New Zealand; Poetry Australia. Honours: Gold Medal for TV Documentary, Island of Spirits, 1974; New Zealand Book Award, 1982. Memberships: PEN International; Poetry Society. Address: 4 Rawhiti Road, Pukerua Bay, Wellington, New Zealand.

CAMPBELL Ewing, b. 26 Dec 1940, Alice, Texas, USA. Author; Associate Professor. Education: BBA, North Texas State University, 1968; MA, University of Southern Mississippi, 1972; PhD, Oklahoma State University, 1980. Appointments: Lecturer, University of Texas at Austin, 1981-82, Oklahoma State University, 1982-83, Wharton Community College, 1983-84; Assistant Professor, 1984-90, Associate Professor, 1990-, Texas A & M University. Publications: Novels: Weave It Like Nightfall, 1977; The Way of Sequestered Places, 1982; The Rincon Triptych, 1984; The Tex-Mex Express, 1993; Madonna, Maleva, 1995. Short Fiction: Piranesi's Dream, 1986. Criticism: Raymond Carver: A Study of the Short Fiction, 1992. Contributions to: Stories and articles to many periodicals. Honours: Fulbright Scholar, Argentina, 1989, Spain, 1997; National Endowments for the Arts Fellowship, 1990; Dobie-Paisano Ralph A Johnston Award, 1992. Address: 1003 Magnolia, Hearne, TX 77859, USA.

CAMPBELL Ian, b. 25 Aug 1942, Lausanne, Switzerland. Reader in English. Education: MA, Aberdeen, 1964; PhD, Edinburgh, 1970; Appointments: Member, English Literature Deparment, University of Edinburgh, 1967-; British Council Appointments, France, Germany. Publications: Thomas Carlyle Letters, 15 volumes, 1970-87; Carlyle, 1974, 1975, 1978; Nineteenth Century Scottish Ficton: Critical Esays, 1978; Thomas and Jane, 1980; Kailyard, 1981; Lewis Grassic Gibbon, 1986; Spartacus, 1987. Contributions to: Numerous papers to learned journals. Honour: British Academy Research Fellowship, 1980. Memberships: President, Carlyle Society; Scottish Association for the Speaking of Verse; Council Member, Association for Scottish Literary Studies. Address: Department of English, University of Edinburgh, David Hume Tower, George Square, Edinburgh EH8 9JX, Scotland.

CAMPBELL James, b. 5 June 1951, Glasgow, Scotland. Writer. Education: University of Edinburgh. Appointment: Editor, New Edinburgh Review, 1978-82. Publications: Pains Interzone: Richard Wright and Others On The Left Bank, 1945-60; Talking at the Gates: A Life of James Baldwin; Gate Fever; Invisible Country; The New Edinburgh Review Anthology; The Panther Book of Scottish Short Stories. Literary Agent: Antony Harwood, Curtis Brown. Address: c/o TLS, Priory House, St Johns Lane, London, EC1, England.

CAMPBELL John Malcolm, b. 2 Sept 1947, London, England. Writer. m. Alison McCracken, 5 Aug 1972, 1 son, 1 daughter. Education: Charterhouse, 1960-65; MA, 1970, PhD, 1975, University of Edinburgh. Publications: Lloyd George: The Goat in the Wilderness, 1977; F E Smith, First Earl of Birkenhead, 1983; Roy Jenkins: A Biography, 1983; Nye Bevan and the Mirage of British Socialism, 1987; The Experience of World War II, editor, 1989; Makers of the Twentieth Century, editor, 1990-92; Edward Heath, 1993. Contributions to: Regular Book Reviews, The Times; Times Literary Supplement; The Independent; Sunday Telegraph. Honours: Yorkshire Post, Best First Book Award; NCR Book Award for non-fiction, 1994. Memberships: Society of Authors; Royal Historical Society. Literary Agent: Bruce Hunter, David Higham Associates. Address: 35 Ladbroke Square, London W11 3NB, England.

CAMPBELL Judith. See: **PARES Marion.**

CAMPBELL Karen. See: **BEATY Betty Joan Campbell Smith.**

CAMPBELL Martin Crafts, (Marty Campbell), b. 24 June 1946, Oakland, California, USA. Writer. Education: BS, University of Chicago, 1968; MA, Northwestern University, 1972. Appointments: Featured Performer, Poetry, USA and St Croix, 1976-; Publisher, Mar Crafts, 1981-; Editor, SENYA and Companion of Senya, 1989; Editor, Collage Two, 1991; Editor, Poetry Corner, 1991-. Publications: Chapters of Poems, Mesh Up, 1981; Croix These Tears, 1982; Dreem, 1982; Church, 1985; Saint Sea, 1986; Companion to Senya, 1989; Seed, 1994. Contributions to: Hammers; Collage 1, 2 & 3; Caribbean Writer; Verve. Honours: 1st Place, Caribbean Poetry Contest, London, 1981; Black History Monthly Poetry Contest, 1987. Memberships:

Performance Poet and Writer; Poets & Writers; Finmen Ocean Swimmers; St Croix Basket Ball Association; Courtyard Players; Island Center for the Performing Arts. Address: 5016 Est Boetzberg, C'sted, VI 00820-451641, USA.

CAMPBELL (John) Ramsey, b. 4 Jan 1946, Liverpool, England. Writer; Film Reviewer. m. Jenny Chandler, 1 Jan 1971, 1 son, 1 daughter. Appointments: Film Reviewer, BBC Radio Merseyside, 1969-; Full-time Writer, 1973-. Publications: Novels: The Doll Who Ate His Mother, 1976; The Face That Must Die, 1979; The Parasite, 1980; The Nameless, 1981; Incarnate, 1983; The Claw, 1983, Night of the Claw, USA; Obsession, 1985; The Hungry Moon, 1986; The Influence, 1988; Ancient Images, 1989; Midnight Sun, 1990; The Count of Eleven, 1991; The Long Lost, 1993; The One Safe Place, 1995; The House on Nazareth Hill, 1996 Short stories: The Inhabitant of the Lake and Less Welcome Tenants, 1964; Demons by Daylight, 1973; The Height of the Scream, 1976; Dark Companions, 1982; Cold Print, 1985; Black Wine (with Charles L Grant), 1986; Night Visions 3 (with Clive Barker, Lisa Tuttle), 1986; Scared Stiff, 1987; Dark Feasts: The World of Ramsey Campbell, 1987; Waking Nightmares, 1991; Alone With The Horrors, 1993; Strange Things and Stranger Places, 1993; Novella: Needing Ghosts, 1990. Contributions to: Ramsey Campbell, Probably, regular column in Necrofile, USA; Anthologies including: Superhorror, 1976; New Terrors, 1980; New Tales of the Cthulhu Mythos, 1980; Fine Frights: Stories That Scared Me, 1988; Uncanny Banquet, 1992. Honours: World Fantasy Awards: Best Short Story, 1978, Best Novel, 1980; British Fantasy Award, Best Short Story, 1978; British Fantasy Awards, Best Novel, 1980, 1985, 1988, 1989, 1991; Bram Stoker Award, 1989; British and World Fantasy Awards, Best Anthology or Collection, for Best New Horror (co-edited with Stephen Jones), 1991; Liverpool Daily Post and Echo Award for Literature, 1993. Memberships: President, British Fantasy Society; Society of Fantastic Films. Literary Agents: Carol Smith, UK; Kirby McCauley, USA; Ralph Vicinanza, foreign. Address: 31 Penkett Road, Wallasey L45 7QE, Merseyside, England.

CAMPEDELLI Giancarlo, (Ruby De Cadaval), b. 1 Jan 1933, Verona, Italy. Writer; President. m. Grazia Corsini, 31 Mar 1962, 1 son, 1 daughter. Education: Doctor Degree, Literature, Pro Deo University, 1993; Doctor Degree, Literature, World Academy of Arts and Culture, San Francisco, 1995; PhD, St Petersburg University, Russia, 1995. Publications: Coctail di poesie, 1959; L'ultime clarte du soir, 1976; Dove senza di loro, 1978; Colloquio con la pietra, 1985; L'albero del silenzio, 1988; Viaggio nello specchio della vita, 1994; Contributions to: Alla Bottega, Milan; Silarus, Salerno: La Procellaria, Reggio Calabria; La Procellaria; New York Poetry; MPT London; Tree Trunk, Bluffton. Honours: Oscar, Montecarlo; Gold Medal, Ecole Superieure de Culture, France; Gold Medal, University of Urbino; Sovereign Military Teutonic Order of Levante. Memberships: Internationales Institut für Kunstwissenschaften, Zürich; Free World Academy; Internationale Burckhardt Akademie; Accademia Tiberina; International Writers and Artists Association. Literary Agent: ILTE Torino, Instituto Editoriale, Milan. Address: Via Mascagni 5, 37024 Arbizzano, Verona, Italy.

CAMPS Petrus Henricus Johannes Maria, (Arnulf Camps), b. 1 Feb 1925, Eindhoven, Netherlands. Emeritus Professor. Education: B Th, University of Nijmegen, 1951; DD, University of Fribourg, 1957. Appointments: Professor, Karachi Pakistan, 1957-61; Mission Sec, Netherlands, 1961-63; Ordinary Professor, University of Nijmegen, 1963-90; Consultor, Dialogue Vatican, 1964-79; Board of Directors, World Conf, Religion and Peace, 1979-; Board of Directors, Institute of Missiology and Ecumenics, 1978-91. Publications: Partners in Dialogue; The Sanskrit Grammar and Manuscripts of Father Heinrich Roth; Jerome Xavier S J and the Muslims of the Mogul Empire; Trilogy on Theology of Religions; Het Derde Oog, Van een Theologie in Azie near een Aziatsche Theologie. Contributions to: The Identitity of Europe and Cultural Plurality; Studies in Interreligious Dialogue. Honour: Knight of the Order of the Order of Dutch Lion. Address: Helmkruidstraat 35, NL 6602 CZ Wijchen, Netherlands.

CAMPTON David, b. 5 June 1924, Leicester, England. Playwright; Children's Fiction Writer. Appointments: Clerk: City of Leicester Education Department, 1941-49, East Midlands Gas Board, Leicester, 1949-56; Professional Actor, Director, 1959-. Publications: On Stage: Containing 17 Sketches and 1 Monologue, 1964; Resting Place, 1964; The Manipulator, 1964; Split Down the Middle, 1965; Little Brother, Little Sister and Out of the Flying Pan, 1966; Two Leaves and a Stalk, 1967; Angel Unwilling, 1967; Ladies Night: 4 Plays for Women,

1967; More Sketches, 1967; Laughter and Fear, 9 One-Act Plays, 1969; The Right Place, 1969; On Stage Again: Containing 14 Sketches and 2 Monologues, 1969; Now and Then, 1970; The Life and Death of Almost Everybody, 1970; Timesneeze, 1970; Gulliver in Lilliput (reader), 1970; Gulliver in The Land of Giants (reader), 1970; The Wooden Horse of Troy (reader), 1970; Jonah, 1971; The Cagebirds, 1971; Us and Them, 1972; Carmilla, 1972; In Committee, 1972; Come Back Tomorrow, 1972; In Committee, 1972; Three Gothic Plays, 1973; Modern Aesop (reader), 1976; One Possessed, 1977; What Are You Doing Here?, 1978; The Do-It-Yourself Frankenstein Outfit, 1978; Zodiac, 1978; After Midnight: Before Dawn, 1978; Pieces of Campton, 1979; Parcel, 1979; Everybody's Friend, 1979; Who Calls?, 1980; Attitudes, 1980; Freedom Log, 1980; Dark Wings, 1981; Look-Sea, 1981; Great Whales, 1981; Who's a Hero, Then?, 1981; Dead and Alive, 1983; But Not Here, 1984; Singing in the Wilderness, 1986; Mrs Meadowsweet, 1986; The Vampyre (children's book), 1986; Our Branch in Brussels, 1986; Cards, Cups and Crystal Ball, 1986; Can You Hear the Music, 1988; The Winter of 1917, 1989; Smile, 1990; Becoming a Playwright, 1992; The Evergreens, 1994; Permission to Cry, 1996. Contributions to: Amateur Stage; Writers News; Drama; Whispers. Memberships: Writers Guild of Great Britain; Society of Authors. Address: 35 Liberty Road, Glenfield, Leicester LE3 8JF, England.

CANAWAY W(illiam) H(amilton), (Bill Canaway, William Hamilton Hermes), b. 12 June 1925, Altrincham, Cheshire, England. Writer. Education: BA, 1948, Diploma in Education, 1949, MA, 1951, University of Wales. Appointments: Teacher in various education establishments, 1949-62. Publications: A Creel of Willow, 1957; A Snowdon Stream (The Gwyrfai) and How to Fish It, The Ring-Givers, 1958; The Seal, 1959; Sammy Going South (in US as Find the Boy), House on Fire, 1961; The Hunter and the Horns, 1962; My Feet upon a Rock, 1963; Crows in a Green Tree, The Ipcress File (with J Doran), 1965; The Grey Seas of Jutland, 1966; The Mules of Borgo San Marco, 1967; A Moral Obligation, 1969; A Declaration of Independence, Roll Me Over, 1971; Redezvous in Black,1972; Harry Doing Good, 1973; Glory of the Sea, 1975; The Willow-Pattern War, 1976; The Solid Gold Buddha, 1979; Love of Life, The Race for Number One, 1984; The Helmet and the Cross, 1986. Address 43 Main Street, Repton, Derbyshire, England.

CANNON Curt. See: **LOMBINO Salvatore A.**

CANNON Frank. See: **MAYHAR Ardath.**

CANNON Geoffrey John, b. 12 Apr 1940, Witham, Essex, England.Writer. m. (1)Anthonia Mole, 1961, div, (2)Caroline Walker, 1987, dec, 2 son, 1 daughter. Education: BA, Philosophy and Psychology, Balliol College, Oxford, 1958-61. Publications: Dieting Makes You Fat (co-author), 1983; The Food Scandal (co-author), 1984; Additives: Your Complete Survival Guide (contributor), 1986; Fat To Fit, 1986; The Politics of Food, 1987; The Good Fight, 1988; The Safe Food Handbook (contributor), 1990; Healthy Eating: The Experts Agree, 1990; Superbug (co-author), 1991. Contributions to: Most leading British newspapers. Honour: Cantor Lecturer, Royal Society of Arts, 1988. Memberships: Secretary, Guild of Food Writers, 1988-91; Secretary, Caroline Walker Trust; Secretary, London Road Runners; Nutrition Society. Literary Agent: Deborah Rogers. Address: 6 Aldridge Road Villas, London W11 1BP, England.

CANNON Steve, b. 10 Apr 1935, New Orleans, Louisiana, USA. Writer; Educator; Publisher. 1 son (dec). Education: BA, History, University of Nebraska, 1954. Appointments: Professor of Humanities, Medgar Evers College, 1971-92. Publications: Groove, Bang and Jive Around, 1969; Introduction to Rouzing the Rubble, 1991; Reminicin' in C, Callaloo Journal, 1995; Plays: The Set Up, 1991; Chump Change, 1992; Nothing to Lose, 1993; Now What, What Now?, 1994, En Vogue, 1994; Top of the World, 1995; Marvellous, 1996. Contributions to: Excerpts from novel Looney Tunes under Deep Blue Moon, to Gathering of the Tribes, 1991, Pean Sensible, 1992. Membership: PEN, New York Chapter. Address: 285 East Third Street, New York, NY 10009, USA.

CANTALUPO Charles, b. 17 Oct 1951, Orange, New Jersey, USA. Professor of English; Poet; Writer. m. (1) Catherine Musello, 21 Aug 1976, dec 1983, 1 son, dec, (2) Barbara Dorosh, 29 Oct 1988, 1 son, 3 daughters. Education: University of Kent at Canterbury, 1972; BA, Washington University, St Louis, 1973; MA, 1978, PhD, 1980, Rutgers University. Appointments: Teaching Assistant, 1973-76,

Instructor, 1977-79, Rutgers University; Instructor, 1980-81, Assistant Professor, 1981-89, Associate Professor, 1989-96, Professor of English, 1996-, Penn State University, Schuylkill Haven. Publications: The Art of Hope (poems), 1983; A Literary Leviathan: Thomas Hobbe's Masterpiece of Language, 1991; The World of Ngugi wa Thiong'o (editor), 1995; Poetry, Mysticism, and Feminism: From th' Nave to the Chops, 1995; Ngugi wa Thiong'o: Text and Contexts (editor), 1995; Anima/l Wo/man and Other Spirits (poems), 1996. Contributions to: Books, anthologies, scholarly journals, and periodicals. Honour: American Academy of Poets Prize, 1976. Address: c/o Department of English, Penn State University, 200 University Drive, Schuylkill Haven, PA 17972, USA.

CANTOR Norman F(rank), b. 1929, Winnipeg, Manitoba, Canada (US citizen, 1968). Professor; Writer. m. Mindy M Cantor, 1 son, 1 daughter. Education: BA, University of Manitoba, 1951; MA, 1953, PhD, 1957, Princeton University; Rhodes Scholar, Oxford University, 1954-55. Appointments: Instructor to Assistant Professor of History, Princeton University, 1955-60; Visiting Professor, Johns Hopkins University, 1960, Yeshiva University, 1960-61, Brooklyn College, 1972-74; Associate Professor to Professor, Columbia University, 1960-66; Professor, Brandeis University, 1966-70; Distinguished Professor of History, State University of New York at Binghamton, 1970-76; Professor of History, University of Illinois at Chicago Circle, 1976-78; Professor of History, 1978-80, Professor of History and Sociology, 1980-85, Affiliated Professor of Legal History, 1982-88, Professor of History, Sociology, and Comparative Literature, 1983-, New York University; Fulbright Visiting Professor, University of Tel Aviv, 1987-88; University Distinguished Visiting Scholar, Adelphi University, 1988-89; Lecturer in Jewish History, Institute of Secular Jewish Humanism, Detroit, 1996-. Publications: Church, Kingship and Lay Investiture, 1958; Medieval History: The Life and Death of a Civilization, 1963, revised edition as The Civilization of the Middle Ages, 1993; How to Study History (with R Schneider), 1967; The English, 1968; The Age of Protest, 1969; Western Civilization, 2 volumes, 1969-70; Perspectives on the European Past, 1971; The Meaning of the Middle Ages, 1973; Twentieth Century Culture: Modernism to Deconstruction, 1988, revised edition, 1997; Inventing the Middle Ages, 1991; The Civilization of the Middle Ages, 1993; Medieval Lives, 1994; The Medieval Reader, 1994; The Sacred Chain: The History of the Jews, 1994. Contributions to: Books and scholarly journals. Honours: Awards and fellowships. Address: 9 Washington Mews, New York, NY 10003, USA.

CAPIE Forrest, b. 1 Dec 1940, Glasgow, Scotland. Professor of Economic History. m. 11 Feb 1967. Education: BA, University of Auckland, New Zealand, 1967; MSc 1969, PhD 1973, University of London (London School of Economics). Publications: Depression and Protectionism, Britain Between the Wars, 1983; Monetary History of the United Kingdom, 1870-1982, 1985; Tariffs and Growth, 1994; The Future of Central Banking, 1994. Contributions to: Articles in more than 20 journals; Editor, The Economic History Review. Address: Department of Banking and Finance, City University Business School, Frobisher Crescent, Barbican Centre, London EC2Y 8HB, England.

CAPUTO Philip (Joseph), b. 10 June 1941, Chicago, Illinois, USA. Author; Screenwriter. m. (1) Jill Esther Ongemach, 21 June 1969, div 1982, 2 sons, (2) Marcelle Lynn Besse, 30 Oct 1982, div 1985, (3) Leslie Blanchard Ware, 4 June 1988. Education: Purdue University; BA, Loyola University, 1964. Appointments: Staff, 1969-72, Foreign Correspondent, 1972-77, Chicago Tribune; Freelance Writer, 1977-; Screenwriter, Mercury-Douglas Productions, Paramount Pictures, 1987-. Publications: A Rumor of War, memoir, 1977; Horn of Africa, novel, 1980; Del Corso's Gallery, novel, 1983; Indian Country: A Novel, 1987; Means of Escape, memoir, 1991; Equation for Evil, novel, 1996. Contributions to: Various periodicals. Honours: Pulitzer Prize for Reporting (with George Bliss), 1973; George Polk Award, 1973; Overseas Press Club Award; Sidney Hillman Award. Memberships: Authors Guild; National Writers Union. Address: c/o Aaron Priest Literary Agency, 708 Third Avenue, New York, NY 10017, USA.

CARAS Roger (Andrew), (Roger Sarac), b. 24 May 1928, Methuen, Massachusetts, USA. Author; Radio and Television Broadcaster. m. Jill Langdon Barclay, 5 Sept 1954, 1 son, 1 daughter. Education: Northeastern University, 1948-49; Western Reserve University, 1949-50; AB, University of Southern California at Los Angeles, 1954. Appointments: Vice-President, Polaris Productions Inc, New York City, and Hawk Films Ltd, London, 1965-68; Producer, Ivan

Tors Productions, Los Angeles, 1968-69; Author and Radio and Television Broadcaster, 1969-; President, American Society for the Prevention of Cruelty to Animals, 1991-; Adjunct Professor of English, Southampton College, New York; Adjunct Professor of Animal Ecology and Member of the Board of Overseers, School of Veterinary Medicine, University of Pennsylvania. Publications: Dangerous to Man: Wild Animals: A Definitive Study of Their Reputed Dangers to Man, 1964, revised edition, 1976; Last Chance on Earth: A Requiem for Wildlife, 1966; North American Mammals: Fur-Bearing Animals of the United States and Canada, 1967; Death as a Way of Life, 1971; Venomous Animals of the World, 1974; The Private Lives of Animals, 1974; The Roger Caras Pet Book, 1976; Pet Medicine: Health Care and First Aid for All Household Pets (editor with others), 1977; Dog Owner's Bible (editor), 1978; The Forest: A Dramatic Portrait of Life in the American Wild, 1979; The Roger Caras Dog Book, 1980, revised edition, 1992; The Endless Migrations, 1985; Harper's Illustrated Handbook of Cats (editor), 1985; Harper's Illustrated Handbook of Dogs (editor), 1985; Roger Caras' Treasury of Great Cat Stories (editor), 1987; Roger Caras' Treasury of Great Dog Stories (editor), 1987; Animals in Their Places: Tales from the Natural World, 1987; A Cat Is Watching: A Look at the Way Cats See Us, 1989; That Our Children May Know: Vanishing Wildlife in Zoo Portraits (with Sue Pressman), 1990; Roger Caras' Treasury of Great Horse Stories (editor), 1990; Cats at Work (editor with Rhonda Gray and Stephen T Robinson), 1991; Roger Caras' Treasury of Classic Nature Tales (editor), 1992; A Dog Is Listening: The Way Some of Our Closest Friends View Us, 1992; The Cats of Thistle Hill Farm, 1994; Most Dangerous Journey, 1995; A Perfect Harmony, 1996. Contributions to: Numerous journals. Honours: Joseph Wood Krutch Medal, 1977; Oryx Award, Israel, 1984; Humane Award of the Year, American Veterinary Medical Association, 1985; James Herriot Award, 1988; Emmy Award, 1990. Memberships: Authors Guild; Delta Kappa Alpha; Holy Land Conservation Fund; Humane Society of the United States; Outdoor Writers Association of America; Royal Society of Arts, fellow; Wilderness Society; Wildlife Society; Writers Guild of America; Zero Population Growth. Address: Thistle Hill Farm, 21108 Slab Bridge Road, Freeland, MD 21053, USA.

CARD Orson Scott, (Brian Green, Byron Walley), b. 24 Aug 1951, Richland, Washington, USA. Writer; Dramatist; Editor. m. Kristine Allen, 17 May 1977, 2 sons, 2 daughters. Education: BA, Brigham Young University, 1975; MA, University of Utah, 1981. Appointments: Director, Repertory Theatre, Provo, Utah, 1964-75; Editor, Brigham Young University Press, 1974-76; Assistant Editor, Ensign, Salt Lake City, 1976-78; Freelance Writer and Editor, 1978-; Senior Editor, Compute! Books, Greensboro, North Carolina, 1983; Teacher at universities and workshops. Publications: A Planet Called Treason, 1979; Songmaster, 1980; Hart's Hope, 1983; The Worthing Chronicle, 1983; Ender's Game, 1985; Speaker for the Dead, 1986; Seventh Son, 1987; Red Prophet, 1988; Prentice Alvin, 1989; Xenocide, 1991; Lost Boys, 1992; The Memory of Earth, 1992; The Call of Earth, 1993; The Ships of Earth, 1993; Lovelock (with Kathryn H Kidd), 1994; Earthfall, 1994. Contributions to: Periodicals. Honours: Nebula Awards, 1985, 1986; Hugo Awards, 1986, 1987, 1991; Locus Awards, 1988, 1989. Membership: Science Fiction Writers of America. Address: 546 Lindley Road, Greensboro, NC 27410, USA.

CARDENAL (Martinez) Ernesto, b. 20 Jan 1925, Granada, Nicaragua. Poet. Education: University of Mexico, 1944-48; Columbia University, New York, 1948-49. Appointments: Roman Catholic Priest, 1965-; Minister of Culture, 1979-90. Publications: Proclama del conquistador, 1947; Gethsemani, Ky., 1960; La hora O, 1960; Epigramas: poemas, 1961; Oracion por Marilyn Monroe and other poems, 1965; El estrecho dudoso, 1966; Poemas, 1967; Psalms of Struggle and Liberation, 1967; Mayapan, 1968; Poemas reunidos 1949-69; Homage to the American Indians, 1969; Zero Hour and Other Documentary Poems, 1971; Poemas, 1971; Canto nacional, 1973; Oraculo sobre Managua, 1973; Poesia escogida, 1975; Canto a un pais que nace, 1978; Apocalypse and Other Poems, 1977; Nueva antologia poetica, 1979; Waslala, 1983; Poesia dela nueva Nicaragua, 1983; Flights of Victory, 1984; With Walker in Nicaragua and Other Early Poems 1949-54, 1985; From Nicaragua with Love: Poems 1976-1986; Golden UFOS: The Indian Poems, 1992; Cosmic Canticle, 1993. Honours: Premio de la Paz Grant, 1980. Address: Apartado Postal A-252, Managua, Nicaragua.

CARDINAL Marie, b. 9 Mar 1929, Algiers, Algeria. Novelist. m. Jean-Pierre Ronfard, 1953, 1 son, 2 daughters. Education: University of Algiers and Sorbonne, Paris. Appointments: Teacher of French and

Philosophy in Greece, Portugal, Austria. Publications: Ecoutez la mer, 1962; La Mule de Corbillard, 1963; La Souricière, 1965; La Clé sur la porte, 1972; The Words To Say It, 1975; Une Vie pour Deux, 1978; Le Passé empiété, 1983; Devotion and Disorder, 1987; Commesi de rien n'était, 1990; Also: Mao (co-author), 1970; Les Pieds-Noirs: Algérie 1920-54; Translator of works by Euripides and Ibsen. Honours: Prix Littre, 1976. Address: 831 Viger Est, Montreal, Quebec H2L 2P5, Canada.

CARDOSO PIRES Jose (Augusto Neves), b. 2 Oct 1925, Peso, Castelo, Branco, Portugal. Novelist. Education: University of Lisbon. Appointments: Literary Director of various publishing houses in Lisbon. Publications: Historuas de amor, 1952; Estrada 43, 1955; A ancorado, 1958; Jogos de azar, 1963; O hospede de Job, 1963; O delfin, 1968; Dinossauro excelentissimo, 1972; O burro-em-pe, 1978; Ballad of Dogs' Beach: dossier of a crime, 1982; Alexandra Alpha, 1987; A Republica dos Corvos, 1988; Co-translator of Death of a Salesman, by Arthur Miller, 1963; Plays: O render dos herois, 1960, and Corpo-delito na sala de espelhos, 1980. Honours: Grande Premio do Romance e da Novela, 1983. Address: Rua Sao Joao de Brito 7-1, 1700 Lisbon, Portugal.

CAREW Jan (Rynveld), b. 24 Sept 1925, Agricola, Guyana. Professor Emeritus. Appointments: Lecturer in Race Relations, University of London Extra-Mural Department, 1953-57; Writer and Editor, BBC Overseas Service, London, 1954-65; Editor, African Review, Ghana, 1965-66; CBC Broadcaster, Toronto, 1966-69; Senior Fellow, Council of Humanities and Lecturer, Department of Afro-American Studies, Princeton University, 1969-72; Professor, Department of African-American Studies, Northwestern University, 1972-87; Visiting Clarence J Robinson Professor of Caribbean Literature and History, George Mason University, 1989-91; Visiting Professor of International Studies, Illinois Wesleyan University, 1992-93; Co-Chairman, Third World Energy Institute, 1978-85; Co-founder Africa Network, 1981-; Chairman, Caribbean Society for Culture and Science, 1979-. Publications: Streets of Eternity, 1952; Black Midas (in US as A Touch of Midas), The Wild Coast, 1958; The Last Barbarian, 1961; Green Winter, 1964; University of Hunger, 1966; The Third Gift, 1975; The Origins of Racism and Resistance in the Americas, Rape of the Sun-people, 1976; Children of the Sun, 1980; Sea Drums in My Blood, 1981; Grenada: The Hour Will Stike Again, 1985; Fulcrums of Change, 1987. Membership: Co-Chairman, Africa Network, 1981-. Address: Department of African-American Studies, Northwestern University, Evanston, IL 60208, USA.

CAREY Duncan. See: **GARNETT Richard.**

CAREY John, b. 5 Apr 1934, London, England. University Professor. m. Gillian Booth, 13 Aug 1960, 2 sons. Education: Lambe Open Scholar, 1954-57; BA, 1957; D Phil, 1960, St John's College, Oxford. Publications: Milton, 1969; The Violent Effigy: A Study of Dickens' Imagination, 1973; Thackerary, Prodigal Genius, 1977; John Donne: Life, Mind and Art, 1981; Original Copy: Selected Reviews and Journalism, 1987; The Faber Book of Reportage, 1987; Donne, 1990; The Intellectuals and the Masses, 1992; The Faber Book of Science, 1995. Contributions to: Principal Book Reviewer, Sunday Times. Honour: Fellow, Royal Society of Literature; Fellow, British Academy; Honorary Fellow, St John's College, 1991, Balliol College, 1992. Membership: Royal Society of Literature. Literary Agent: Toby Eady, London. Address: Merton College, Oxford OX1 4SD, England.

CAREY Peter Philip, b. 7 May 1943, Bacchus Marsh, Australia. Novelist. m. Alison Summers, 16 Mar 1985, 2 sons. Education: Dr of Letters, University of Queensland, 1989. Appointment: Writer in Residence, New York University, 1990. Publications: The Fat Man in History, 1974; War Crimes, 1979, 1981; Illywhacker, 1985; Oscar & Lucinda, 1989; Until the End of the World, 1990; The Tax Inspector, 1991; The Unusual Life of Triston Smith, 1994. Honours: New South Wales Premier's Literary Award; Miles Franklin Award; National Book Council Award; The Age Book of Year Award; Victorian Premier's Literary Award; Booker Prize. Membership: Royal Society of Literature. Literary Agent: Deborah Rogers, Rogers, Coleridge & White Ltd. Address: c/o Deborah Rogers, Rogers, Coleridge & White Ltd, 20 Powis Mews, London W11 1JN, England.

CARFAX Catherine. See: **FAIRBURN Eleanor M.**

CARKEET David (Corydon), b. 15 Nov 1946, Sonora, California, USA. Professor; Author. m. Barbara Lubin, 16 Aug 1975, 3

daughters. Education: AB, University of California at Davis, 1968; MA, University of Wisconsin, 1970; PhD, Indiana University, 1973. Appointments: Assistant Professor, 1973-79, Associate Professor, 1979-87, Professor, 1987-, University of Missouri. Publications: Novels: Double Negative, 1980; The Greatest Slump of All Time, 1984; I've Been There Before, 1985; The Full Catastrophe, 1990; The Error of Our Ways, 1997. Young Adult Novels: The Silent Treatment, 1988; Quiver River, 1991. Contributions to: Scholarly journals; Short stories and popular essays in periodicals. Honours: James D Phelan Award in Literature, San Francisco Foundation, 1976; Notable Books of the Year, New York Times Book Review, 1981, 1990; O Henry Award, 1982; National Endowment for the Arts Fellowship, 1983. Address: 23 Ridgemoor Drive, St Louis, MO 63105, USA.

CARLISLE D M. See: **COOK Dorothy Mary.**

CARLS Stephen Douglas, b. 15 Feb 1944, Minneapolis, Minnesota, USA. College Professor. m. Alice-Catherine Maire, 25 June 1977, 2 sons, 1 daughter. Education: BA, Wheaton College, Illinois, 1966; MA History, 1968, PhD History, 1982, University of Minnesota. Publication: Louis Loucheur and the Shaping of Modern France, 1993. Honours: McMillan Travel Grant, University of Minnesota, 1976; Loucheur Manuscript Endorsed by the American Historical Association's First Books Program, 1983; Southern Regional Education Board Grant, 1985. Memberships: American Historical Association; Society for French Historical Studies; Western Society for French History; Economic and Business Historical Society; West Tennessee Historical Society; Council for European Studies. Address: Department of History and Political Science, Union University, Jackson, TN 38305, USA.

CARMI T. See: **CHARNY Carmi.**

CARMICHAEL Jack B(lake), b. 31 Jan 1938, Ravenswood, West Virginia, USA. Writer; Poet; Editor. m. Julie Ann Carmichael, 2 Oct 1981, 4 daughters. Education: BA, Ohio Wesleyan University, 1959; PhD, Michigan State University, 1964; Postdoctoral Studies, University of Oregon, 1966-67. Appointment: Editor and Publisher, Dynamics Press, 1990-. Publications: Novels: A New Slain Knight, 1991; Black Knight, 1991; Tales of the Cousin, 1992; Memoirs of the Great Gorgeous, 1992; The Humpty Boys in Michigan, 1996. Contributions to: Poems in anthologies and journals. Honour: Outstanding Achievement Award, American Poetry Association, 1990. Membership: Academy of American Poets. Address: c/o Dynamic Press, 519 South Rogers Street, Mason, MI 48854, USA.

CARMICHAEL Joel, b. 31 Dec 1915, New York, New York, USA. Author; Editor; Translator. Education: BA, MA, Oxford University, 1940; Sorbonne, Paris; École Nationale des Langues Orientales Vivantes. Appointments: European Correspondent, The Nation magazine, 1946-47; Editor, Midstream magazine, 1975-87, 1990-. Publications: An Illustrated History of Russia, 1960; The Death of Jesus, 1962; A Short History of the Russian Revolution, 1964; The Shaping of the Arabs: A Study in Ethnic Identity, 1967; Karl Marx: The Passionate Logician, 1967; An Open Letter to Moses and Muhammed, 1968; A Cultural History of Russia, 1968; Arabs and Jews, 1969; Trotsky: An Appreciation of His Life, 1976; Stalin's Masterpiece, 1977; Arabs Today, 1977; St Paul and the Jews, 1980; The Birth of Christianity: Reality and Myth, 1989; The Satanizing of the Jews: Origin and Development of Mystical Anti-Semitism, 1992; The Unriddling of Christian Origins: A Secular Account, 1995. Translations from Russian: The Russian Revolution 1917, N N Sukhanov, 1955; Anna Karenina, Leo Tolstoy, 1975. Contributions to: Journals and periodicals. Honour: Fulbright Fellowship, 1949-51. Address: 302 West 86th Street, New York, NY 10024, USA.

CAROL Bill J. See: **KNOTT William Cecil.**

CARPENTER (John) Allan, b. 11 May 1917, Waterloo, Iowa, USA. Author; Editor; Publisher. Education: BA, Iowa State Teachers College, 1938. Appointments: Founder, Publisher, Teacher's Digest, Chicago, 1949-48; Public Relations Director, Popular Mechanics, Chicago, 1943-62; Founder, Editor, Publisher, Carpenter Publishing House, Chicago, 1962-; Founder, Chairman of the Board of Directors, Infordata International Inc, 1974-90. Publications: Home Handyman Encyclopedia and Guide, 16 volumes, 1961, supplement, 1963; Enchantment of America, 52 volumes, 1963-68; Enchantment of South America, 13 volumes, 1968-70; Enchantment of Central America, 7 volumes, 1971; Enchantment of Central Africa, 38 volumes, 1972-78;

The Encyclopedia of the Midwest, 1989; The Encyclopedia of the Central West, 1990; The Encyclopedia of the Far West, 1990; Facts About the Cities, 1992. Contributions to: Many magazines. Honour: Achievement Award, University of Northern Iowa, 1988. Address: 175 East Delaware Place, Suite 4602, Chicago, IL 60611, USA.

CARPENTER Bogdana (Maria Magdalena), b. 2 June 1941, Czestochowa, Poland. Professor. m. John Randell Carpenter, 15 Apr 1963, 1 son, 1 daughter. Education: Warsaw University, 1963; PhD, University of California, 1974. Appointments: Assistant Professor, University of Washington, 1974-83; Assistant Professor, 1983-84, Associate Professor, 1985-91, Professor, 1991-, University of Michigan. Publications: The Poetic Avant Garde in Poland; Monumenta Polonica: The First Four Centuries of Polish Poetry; Translations, Selected Poems of Zbigniew Herbert; Report from the Besieged City and Other Poems; Still Life with a Bridle. Contributions to: Journals. Honours: Witter Bynner Poetry Translation Prize; American Council for Polish Culture 1st Prize. Membership: PEN. Address: Department of Slvic Languages and Literature, University of Michigan, 3040 MLB, Ann Arbor, MI 48109, USA.

CARPENTER Humphrey, b. 29 Apr 1946, Oxford, England. Author; Broadcaster; Musician. Education: MA and Diploma in Education, Keble College, Oxford. Appointments: Staff Producer, BBC, 1968-74; Freelance Boradcaster and reviewer. Publications: A Thames Companion (with M Prichard), 1975; J R R Tolkien, The Joshers, 1977; The Inklings: C S Lewis, J R R Tolkien, Charles Williams and their Friends, 1978; The Captian Hook Affair, 1979; Jesus, 1980; W H Auden, The Letters of J R R Tolkien (editor with C Tolkein), 1981; Mr Majeika, The Oxford Companion to Children's Literature (with M Prichard), 1984; O U D S: A Centenary History of the Oxford University Dramatic Society; Secret Gardens: A Study of the Golden Age of Children's Literature, 1985; Mr Majeika and the Music Teacher, 1986; Mr Majeika and the Haunted Hotel, 1987; A Serious Character: The Life of Ezra Pound, 1988; The Brideshead Generation, 1989; Benjamin Britten, 1992. Address: 6 Fardon Road, Oxford OX2 6RG, England.

CARPENTER Lucas, b. 23 April 1947, Elberton, Georgia, USA. Professor of English; Writer; Poet; Editor. m. Judith Leidner, 2 Sept 1972, 1 daughter. Education: BS, College of Charleston, 1968; MA, University of North Carolina at Chapel Hill, 1973; PhD, State University of New York at Stony Brook, 1982. Appointments: Instructor, State University of New York at Stony Brook, 1973-78; Instructor, 1978-80, Associate Professor of English, 1980-85, Suffolk Community College; Editorial Consultant, Prentice-Hall Inc, 1981-; Associate Professor of English, Oxford College of Emory University, 1985-94; Professor of English, 1994-. Publications: A Year for the Spider (poems), 1972; The Selected Poems of John Gould Fletcher (editor with E Leighton Rudolph), 1988; The Selected Essays of John Gould Fletcher (editor), 1989; John Gould Fletcher and Southern Modernism, 1990; The Selected Correspondence of John Gould Fletcher (editor with E Leighton Rudolph), 1996. Contributions to: Anthologies, scholarly journals, and periodicals. Honours: Resident Fellow in Poetry and Fiction Writing, Hambidge Center for the Creative Arts, 1991; Oxford College Professor of the Year Awards, 1994, 1996. Memberships: National Council of Teachers of English; Poetry Atlanta; Poetry Society of America; Southeast Modern Language Association. Address: c/o Department of English, Oxford College of Emory University, Oxford, GA 30267, USA.

CARR Glyn. See: **STYLES Frank Showell.**

CARR Margaret, (Martin Carroll, Carole Kerr), b. 25 Nov 1935, Salford, England. Writer; Local Government Secretary, Retired. Publications: Begotten Murder, 1967; Spring into Love, 1967; Blood Bengeance, 1968; Goodbye is Forever, 1968; Too Beautiful to Die, 1969; Hear No Evil, 1971; Tread Warily at Midnight, 1971; Sitting Duck, 1972; Who's the Target, 1974; Not for Sale, 1975; Shadow of the Hunter, 1975; A Time to Surrender, 1975; Out of the Past, 1976; Twin Tragedy, 1977; Lamb to the Slaughter, 1978; The Wtich of Wykham, 1978; Daggers Drawn, 1980; Stolen Heart, 1981; Deadly Pursuit, 1991; Dark Intruder, 1991. Address: Waverly, Wavering Lane, Gillingham, Dorset SD8 4Nr, England.

CARR Pat (Moore), b. 13 Mar 1932, Grass Creek, Wyoming, USA. Writer; University Teacher. m. (1) Jack Esslinger, 4 June 1955, div 1970, (2) Duane Carr, 26 Mar 1972, 1 son, 3 daughters. Education: BA, MA, Rice University; PhD, Tulane University. Appointments: Teacher, Texas Southern University, 1956-58, University of New

Orleans, 1961, 1965-69, 1987-88, University of Texas at El Paso, 1969-79, University of Arkansas at Little Rock, 1983, 1986-87, Western Kentucky University, 1988-96. Publications: Novels: The Grass Creek Chronicle, 1976, 3rd edition, 1996; Bluebirds, 1993. Short Story Collections: Beneath the Hill of the Three Crosses, 1969; The Women in the Mirror, 1977; Night of the Luminarias, 1986; Sonahchi, 1988, 2nd edition, 1994; Our Brothers' War, 1993. Criticism: Bernard Shaw, 1976; Mimbres Mythology, 1979; In Fine Spirits, 1986. Contributions to: Articles and short stories in numerous publications. Honours: South and West Fiction Award, 1969; Library of Congress Marc IV Award for Short Fiction, 1970; National Endowment for the Humanities Award, 1973; Arkansas Endowment for the Humanities Award, 1985; Green Mountain Short Fiction Award, 1986; First Stage Drama Award, 1990; Al Smith Fellowship in Fiction, 1995. Address: 10695 Venice Road, Elkins, AR 72727, USA.

CARR Roberta. See: **ROBERTS Irene.**

CARR Terry (Gene), (Norman Edwards), b. 19 Feb 1937, Grants Pass, Oregon, USA. Writer; Editor; Lecturer. Education: AA, City College of San Francisco, 1957; University of California at Berkeley, 1957-59. Appointments: Editor, Ace Books, 1964-71, SFWA Bulletin, 1967-68; Founder, Science Fiction Writers of America Forum, 1967-68. Publications: Warlord of Kor (with Ted White), 1963; World's Best Science Fiction (editor), 7 volumes, 1965-71; Universe (editor), 13 volumes, 1971-83; The Best Science Fiction of the Year (editor), 13 volumes, 1972-84; The Light at the End of the Universe (stories), 1976; Cirque, 1977; Classic Science Fiction: The First Golden Age (editor), 1978; The Year's Finest Fantasy (editor), 1978-84; Between Two Worlds, 1986; Spill! The Story of the Exxon Valdez, 1991. Address: c/o Watts Publishing Company, PO Box 4039, Culver City, CA 90231, USA.

CARRIER Warren (Pendleton), b. 3 July 1918, Cheviot, Ohio, USA. University Chancellor (retired); Writer; Poet. m. (1) Marjorie Jane Regan, 3 Apr 1947, dec, 1 son, (2) Judy Lynn Hall, 14 June 1973, 1 son. Education: Wabash College, 1938-40; AB, Miami University, Oxford, Ohio, 1942; MA, Harvard University, 1948; PhD, Occidental College, 1962. Appointments: Founder-Editor, Quarterly Review of Literature, 1943-44; Associate Editor, Western Review, 1949-51; Assistant Professor, University of Iowa, 1949-52; Associate Professor, Bard College, 1953-57; Faculty, Bennington College, 1955-58; Visiting Professor, Sweet Briar College, 1958-60; Professor, Deep Springs College, California, 1960-62, Portland State University, Oregon, 1962-64; Professor, Chairman, Department of English, University of Montana, 1964-68; Associate Dean, Professor of English and Comparative Literature, Chairman, Department of Comparative Literature, Livingston College, Rutgers University, 1968-69; Dean, College of Arts and Letters, San Diego State University, 1969-72; Vice-President, Academic Affairs, University of Bridgeport, Connecticut, 1972-75; Chancellor, University of Wisconsin at Platteville, 1975-82. Publications: City Stopped in Time, 1949; The Hunt, 1952; The Cost of Love, 1953; Reading Modern Poetry (co-editor), 1955, 2nd edition, 1968; Bay of the Damned, 1957; Toward Montebello, 1966; Leave Your Sugar for the Cold Morning, 1977; Guide to World Literature (editor), 1980; Literature from the World (co-editor), 1981; The Diver, 1986; Death of a Chancellor, 1986; An Honorable Spy, 1992; Murder at the Strawberry Festival, 1993. Contributions to: Periodicals. Honours: Phi Beta Kappa, 1942; Award for Poetry, National Foundation for the Arts, 1971; Collady Prize for Poetry, 1986. Address: 69 Colony Park Circle, Galveston, TX 77551, USA.

CARROLL Martin. See: **CARR Margaret.**

CARROLL Paul (Donnelly Michael), b. 15 July 1927, Chicago, Illinois, USA. Professor of English; Poet; Writer. m. Maryrose Carroll, June 1979, 1 son. Education: MA, University of Chicago, 1952. Appointments: Poetry Editor, Chicago Review, 1957-59; Editor, Big Table Magazine, 1959-61, Big Table Books, Follett Publishing Company, 1966-71; Visiting Poet and Professor, University of Iowa, 1966-67; Professor of English, University of Illinois, 1968-. Publications: Edward Dahlberg Reader (editor), 1966; The Young American Poets, 1968; The Luke Poets, 1971; New and Selected Poems, 1978; The Garden of Earthly Delights, 1986; Poems, 1950-1990, 1990. Contributions to: Periodicals. Address: 1682 North Ada Street, Chicago, IL 60622, USA.

CARRUTH Hayden, b. 3 Aug 1921, Waterbury, Connecticut, USA. Poet; Writer; Professor. m. (1) Sara Anderson, 14 Mar 1943, 1 daughter, (2) Eleanor Ray, 29 Nov 1952, (3) Rose Marie Dorn, 28 Oct 1961, 1 son, (4) Joe-Anne McLaughlin, 29 Dec 1989. Education: AB, University of North Carolina, 1943; MA, University of Chicago, 1948. Appointments: Editor-in-Chief, Poetry magazine, 1949-50; Associate Editor, University of Chicago Press, 1950-51; Project Administrator, Intercultural Publications Inc, New York City, 1952-53; Poet-in-Residence, Johnson State College, Vermont, 1972-74; Adjunct Professor, University of Vermont, 1975-78; Poetry Editor, Harper's magazine, 1977-83; Professor, Syracuse University, 1979-85; Professor, Bucknell University, 1985-86; Professor, 1986-91, Professor Emeritus, 1991-, Syracuse University. Publications: Poetry: The Crow and the Heart, 1946-1959, 1959; In Memoriam: G V C, 1960; Journey to a Known Place, 1961; The Norfolk Poems: 1 June to 1 September 1961, 1962; North Winter, 1964; Nothing for Tigers: Poems, 1959-1964, 1965; Contra Mortem, 1967; For You, 1970; The Clay Hill Anthology, 1970; From Snow and Rock, From Chaos: Poems, 1965-1972, 1973; Dark World, 1974; The Bloomingdale Papers, 1975; Loneliness: An Outburst of Hexasyllables, 1976; Aura, 1977; Brothers, I Loved You All, 1978; Almanach du Printemps Vivarois, 1979; The Mythology of Dark and Light, 1982; The Sleeping Beauty, 1983, revised edition, 1990; If You Call This Cry a Song, 1983; Asphalt Georgics, 1985; Lighter Than Air Craft, 1985; The Oldest Killed Lake in North America, 1985; Mother, 1985; The Selected Poetry of Hayden Carruth, 1986; Sonnets, 1989; Tell Me Again How the White Heron Rises and Flies Across the Nacreous River at Twilight Toward the Distant Islands, 1989; Collected Shorter Poems, 1946-1991, 1992; Collected Longer Poems, 1994; Scrambled Eggs and Whiskey: Poems, 1991-1995, 1995. Other: Appendix A (novel), 1963; After "The Stranger": Imaginary Dialogues with Camus, 1964; Working Papers: Selected Essays and Reviews, 1981; Effluences from the Sacred Caves: More Selected Essays and Reviews, 1984; Sitting In: Selected Writings on Jazz, Blues, and Related Topics, 1986. Editor: A New Directions Reader (with James Laughlin), 1964; The Voice That is Great Within Us: American Poetry of the Twentieth Century, 1970; The Bird/Poem Book: Poem on the Wild Birds of North America, 1970. Contributions to: Various periodicals. Honours: Bess Hokin Prize, 1954; Vachel Lindsey Prize, 1956; Levinson Prize, 1958; Harriet Monroe Poetry Prize, 1960; Bollingen Foundation Fellowship, 1962; Helen Bullis Award, 1962; Carl Sandburg Award, 1963; Emily Clark Balch Prize, 1964; Eunice Tietjens Memorial Prize, 1964; Guggenheim Fellowships, 1965, 1979; Morton Dauwen Zabel Prize, 1967; National Endowment for the Humanities Fellowship, 1967; Governor's Medal, Vermont, 1974; Sheele Memorial Award, 1978; Lenore Marshall Poetry Prize, 1978; Whiting Writers Award, 1986; National Endowment for the Arts Senior Fellowship, 1988; Ruth Lilly Poetry Prize, 1990; National Book Critics Circle Award in Poetry, 1993; National Book Award for Poetry, 1996. Address: RR 1, Box 128, Munnsville, NY 13409, USA.

CARRUTHERS Peter (Michael), b. 16 June 1952, Manila, Philippines. Philosopher; Professor; Writer. m. Susan Levi, 21 Oct 1978, 2 sons. Education: University of Leeds, 1971-77; Balliol College, Oxford, 1977-79. Appointments: Lecturer, University of St Andrews, 1979-81, Queens University of Belfast, 1981-83, University of Essex, 1985-91; Visiting Professor, University of Michigan, 1989-90; Senior Lecturer, 1991-92, Professor, 1992-, University of Sheffield. Publications: The Metaphysics of the Tractatus, 1990; Introducing Persons: Theories and Arguments in the Philosophy of Mind, 1991; Human Knowledge and Human Nature: A New Introduction to the Ancient Debate, 1992; The Animals Issue: Moral Theory in Practice, 1992. Contributions to: Journals. Membership: Aristotelian Society. Address: Department of Philosophy, University of Sheffield, Sheffield S10 2TN, England.

CARSWELL John (Patrick), b. 30 May 1918, England. Civil Servant; Writer. Education: MA, St John's College, Oxford, 1940. Appointments: Served with Treasury, 1960-64; Assistant Under Secretary of State, Department of Education and Science 1964-74; Secretary, University Grants Committee, 1974-78; Secretary, British Academy, 1978-83. Publications: Marvellous Campaigns of Baron Munchausen, 1946; The Prospector: The Life of Rudolf Erich Raspe, 1950; The Old Cause: Four Biographical Studies in Whiggism, 1954; The South Sea Bubble, 1960, new enlarged edition 1993; The Civil Servant and His World, 1966; The Descent on England, 1969; From Revolution to Revolution, 1688-1776, 1973; Lives and Letters, 1978; The Exile, 1983; The State and the Universities in Britain, 1966-78, 1985; The Porcupine: The Life of Algernon Sidney, 1989; The Saving of Kenwood and the Northern Heights, 1992. Literary Agent: MBA

Literary Agents, 45 Fitzroy Street, London W1P 5HR, England. Address: 5 Prince Arthur Road, London NW3, England.

CARTANO Tony, b 27 July 1944, Bayonne, France. Author; Editor. m. Françoise Perrin, 10 Nov 1966, 1 son, 1 daughter. Education: Licence es Lettres, 1964, Diploma d'Études Superieurers, 1965, University of Paris. Appointments: Director, Foreign Department, Editions Albin Michel, Paris. Publications: Le Single Hurteur, 1978; Malcolm Lowry (essay), 1979; Blackbird, 1980; La Sourde Oreille, 1982; Schmutz, 1987; Le Bel Arturo, 1989; Le soufflé de Satan, 1991; American Boulevard (travel book), 1992. Honour: Chevalier, l'ordre des Arts et Lettres. Address: 157 Boulevard Davout, 75020 Paris, France.

CARTENS Jan, b. 25 May 1929, Roosendaal, Netherlands. Writer. Publications: Dat meisje uit Munchen, 1975; De thuiskomst, 1976; Vroege herfst, 1978; Een Roomsche Jeugd, 1980; De verleiding, 1983; Maagdenbruiloft, 1987; Het verraad van Nausikaa, 1989; Een indringer, 1990; De bekentenis, 1993; De roze bisschop, 1994; Oorlogsbruid, 1995. Address: Markenland 15, 4871 AM, Etten-Leur, Netherlands.

CARTER Bruce. See: **HOUGH Richard Alexander.**

CARTER Francis William, b. 4 July 1938, Wednesfield, Staffordshire, England. m. Krystyna Stephania Tomaszewska, 3 June 1977. Education: BA, Sheffield; MA, PhD, London; D Nat Sc, Prague; D Phil, Cracow. Publications: Dubrovnik: A Classic City State; An Historical Geography of the Balkans: Trade and Urban Development in Poland; Environmental Problems in Eastern Europe; The Changing Shape of the Ballions: Central Europe after the Fall of the Iron Curtain. Contributions to: Over 100 Articles. Honour: Croatian Academy of USA; Diploma, Romanian Academy of Science (Geography), Croation Geographical Society, Zagreb. Memberships: Institute of British Geographers; Royal Geographical Society; Royal Asiatic Society; PEN. Address: Department of Social Sciences, School of Slavonic and East European Studies, University of London, Malet Street, London WC1E 7HU, England.

CARTER Harold Burnell, b. 3 Jan 1910, Mosman, Sydney, New South Wales, Australia. Scientific Civil Servant, 1939-70. m. Dr Mary Brandon Jones, 21 Sep 1940, 3 sons. Education: University of Sydney, BVSC, 1933. Appointments: Veterinary Officer, Australian Estates Co Ltd. 1933-36; Walter and Eliza Hall Fellow, University of Sydney, 1936-39; Research Scientist, CSIRO, Australia, 1939-54; Senior Principal Scientific Officer, ARC, UK, 1954-70; Honorary Fellow, University of Leeds, 1962-70; Director, Banks Archive Project, British Museum Natural History, 1989-96. Publications: His Majesty's Spanish Flock; The Sheep and Wool Correspondence of Sir Joseph Banks; Sir Joseph Banks: A Guide to Biographical and Bibliographical Sources; Sir Joseph Banks 1743-1820. Contributions to: Australian and British Scientific Journals; Bulletin; British Museum; Historical Series. Honours: American Philosophical Society History of Science Grants; Royal Society History of Science Grants; British Academy Major Awards; Honorary DVSc, University of Sydney, 1996. Memberships: Royal Society of Edinburgh; FLS; FIBiol. Address: Yeo Bank, Congresbury, Nr Bristol, Avon BS19 5JA, England.

CARTER Martin (Wylde), b. 7 June 1927, Georgetown, British Guiana. Politician; Poet; Senior Research Fellow. Education: Queens College, Georgetown. Appointments: Chief Information Officer, Booker Group of Companies, 1959-66; UN Representative, 1966-67, Minister of Information 1967-71, Republic of Guyana; Lecturer, Essex University, England, 1975-76; Writer-in-Residence 1977-81, Senior Research Fellow 1981-, University of Guyana. Publications: Poetry: The Hill of Fire Glows, 1951; To a Dead Slave, 1951; The Kind Eagle, 1952; The Hidden Man, 1952; Returning, 1953; Poems of Resistance from British Guiana, 1954; Poems of Succession, 1977; Poems of Affinity, 1978-1980, 1980; Selected Poems, 1989. Other: New World: Guyana Independence Issue (editor), 1966; Man and Making-Victim and Vehicle, 1971; Creation: Works of Art, 1977. Contributions to: Anthologies and periodicals. Address: c/o New Beacon Books, 76 Stroud Green Road, London N4 3EN, England.

CARTER Nick. See: **LYNDS Dennis.**

CARTER Nick. See: **AVALLONE Michael (Angelo Jr).**

CARTER Nick. See: **GARSIDE Jack Clifford.**

CARTER Peter, b. 13 Aug 1929, England. Writer. m. Gudrun Willege, 17 Feb 1974. Education: MA, Wadham College, Oxford, 1962. Publications: Novels: The Gates of Paradise, 1974; Madatan, 1974. Books for Young People: The Black Lamp, 1973; Mao, biography, 1976; Under Goliath, 1977; The Sentinels, 1980; Children of the Book, 1984; Bury the Dead, 1986; Borderlands, 1990. Translator: Grimms' Fairy Tales, 1982. Honours: Children's Book of the Year, Child Study Association of America, 1975; Carnegie Medal Commendation, British Library Association, 1978; Guardian Award, 1981; Book for the Teen Age, New York Public Library, 1982; Young Observer/Rank Teenage Fiction Award, 1984. Address: c/o Oxford University Press, Walton Street, Oxford OX2 6DP, England.

CARTER Robert Ayres, b. 16 Sept 1923, Omaha, Nebraska, USA. Writer; Lecturer. m. 17 Dec 1983, 2 sons. Education: AB, New School for Social Research. Publications: Manhattan Primitive, 1972; Written In Blood (in US as Casual Slaughters), 1992; Final Edit, 1994; Three Textbooks. Contributions to: Publishers Weekly; International Journal of Book Publishing. Honour: Fulbright Scholar, 1949. Memberships: Poets and Writers; Mystery Writers of America; International Crime Writers Association; Member, Board of Directors, 1980-88, Asst Secretary, 1984-88, Life Member, The Players. Literary Agent: Regula Noetzli, c/o Charlotte Sheedy Agency. Address: 510 North Meadow Street, Richmond, VA 23220, USA.

CARTER Walter Horace, b. 20 Jan 1921, North Carolina. USA. Newspaper Publisher; Author; Magazine Writer. m. (1)Lucille Miller Carter, dec, (2)Brenda C Strickland, 29 Oct 1983, 1 son, 2 daughters. Education: AB, University of North California. Publications: Land That I love, 1978; Creatures and Chronicles from Cross Creek, 1980; Wild and Wonderful Santee Cooper Country, 1982; Nature's Masterpiece, 1984; Return to Cross Creek, 1985; Virus of Fear, 1991; Nature Coast Tales & Truths, 1993; Headstart Fishing Handbook, 1994; Tremblin Earth, 1995; Coastal Carolina's Tales and Truths, 1996. Contributions to: Various Magazines. Honours: Pulitzer Prize, 1953; Sidney Hillman award, 1954. Memberships: Outdoor Writers Association of America; Florida Outdoor Writers Association; Southwestern Outdoor Press Association. Address: Rt3 Box 139A, Hawthorne, FL 32640, USA.

CARTLAND Barbara (Dame). See: **MCCORQUODALE Barbara Hamilton.**

CARY Jud. See: **TUBB E(dwin) C(harles).**

CARY Lorene (Emily), b. 29 Nov 1956, Philadelphia, Pennsylvania, USA. Writer. m. R C Cary, 27 Aug 1983, 1 daughter, 1 stepson. Education: BA, MA, 1978, University of Pennsylvania; MA, University of Sussex, 1979. Appointments: Associate Editor, TV Guide, 1980-82; Contributing Editor, Newsweek Magazine, 1991; Lecturer, University of Pennsylvania, 1995-. Publications: Black Ice, 1991; The Price of a Child, 1995. Honour: Honorary Doctorate of Letters. Memberships: Poets, Essayists and Novelists (PEN); Authors Guild. Address: 2033 Bainbridge Street, Philadelphia, PA 19146, USA.

CASEY John (Dudley), b. 18 Jan 1939, Worcester, Massachusetts, USA. Writer; Professor. m. Rosamond Pinchot Pittman, 26 June 1982, 4 daughters. Education: BA, Harvard College, 1962; LLB, Harvard Law School, 1965; MFA, University of Iowa, 1967. Appointments: Professor, University of Virginia, 1972-92; Residency, American Academy of Arts and Letters, 1992-97. Publications: An American Romance, 1977; Testimony and Demeanor, 1979; Sparting, 1989. Contributions to: Stories, Articles, Reviews, 1968-. Honours: Runner Up, Ernest Hemingway Award, 1978; Guggenheim Fellowship, 1979-80; Friends of American Writers Award, 1980; National Endowment for the Arts Fellowship, 1983; National Book Award, 1989; Ingram Merril Fellowship, 1990. Membership: PEN. Literary Agent: Michael Carlisle, William Morris Agency. Address: Department of English, University of Virginia, Charlottesville, VA 22903, USA.

CASS Zoe. See: **LOW Lois Dorothea.**

CASSELLS Cyrus Curtis, b. 16 May 1957, Dover, Delaware, USA. Poet; Teacher; Translator. Education: BA, Stanford University, 1979. Publications: The Mud Actor, 1982; Soul Make a Path Through Shouting, 1994; Beautiful Signor, 1997. Contributions to: Southern Review; Callaloo; Translation; Seneca Review; Quilt; Sequoia. Honours: Academy of American Poets Prize, 1979; National Poetry Series Winner, 1982; Bay Area Book Reviewers Association Award Nominee, 1983; Callaloo Creative Writing Award, 1983; Massachusetts

Artists Foundation Fellowship, 1985; National Endowment for the Arts Fellowship, 1986; Lavan Younger Poets Award, 1992; Lannan Literacy Award, 1993; William Carlos Williams Award, 1994; Lenore Marshall Prize, finalist, 1995. Memberships: PEN; Poetry Society of America. Address: c/o Mary Cassells, 2190 Belden Place, Escondido, CA 92029, USA.

CASSIAN Nina, b. 27 Nov 1924, Galati, Romania. Poet. Education: University of Bucharest and Conservatory of Music. Appointments: Visiting Professor, New York University, 1985-86. Publications: Verses: 35 books including: At the Scale 1/1, 1947; Ages of the Year, 1957; The Dialogue of Wind and Sea, 1957; Outdoor Performance, 1961; Everyday Holidays, 1961; Gift Giving, 1963; The Discipline of the Harp, 1965; Blood, 1966; Parallel Destinies, 1967; Ambitus, 1968; Chronophagy 1944-69; The Big Conjugation, 1971; Requiem, 1971; Loto Poems, 1974; 100 Poems, 1974; Suave, 1977; Mercy, 1981; Lady of Miracles, 1982; Countdown, 1983; Call Yourself Alive?, 1988; Life Sentence: Selected Poems, 1990; Cheer Leader for a Funeral, 1993; Arguing with Chaos, 1994; Verses and plays for children; Prose: Confessions, 1976; Translations; Musical Compositions, Chamber and Symphonic. Honours: Writers Union of Romania Awards, 1967, 1984; Writers Association of Bucharest Award, 1981; Fulbright Grant. 1986. Address: 555 Main Street, #502, Roosevelt Island, New York, NY 10044, USA.

CASSILL R(onald) V(erlin), (Owen Aherne, Jesse Webster), b. 17 May 1919, Cedar Falls, Iowa, USA. Author; Professor Emeritus. m. (1) Kathleen Rosecrans, 4 June 1941, div 1952, (2) Karilyn Kay Adams, 23 Nov 1956, 2 sons, 1 daughter. Education: BA, 1939, MA, 1949, University of Iowa. Appointments: Instructor, Monticello College, Godfrey, Illinois, 1946-48; Instructor in Writing Workshop, University of Iowa, 1948-52, 1960-66; Editor, Western Review, Iowa City, 1951-52; Collier's Encyclopedia, New York City, 1953-54; Lecturer, Columbia University and New School for Social Research, New York City, 1957-59; Editor, Dude and Gent magazines, New York City, 1958; Writer-in-Residence, Purdue University, 1965-66; Associate Professor, 1966-71, Professor of English, 1972-83, Professor Emeritus, 1983-, Brown University. Publications: Novels: The Eagle on the Coin, 1950; Dormitory Women, 1954; The General Said "Nuts", 1955; The Left Bank of Desire (with Eric Potter), 1955; The Wound of Love, 1956; A Taste of Sin, 1956; The Hungering Shame, 1956; Naked Morning, 1957; Lustful Summer, 1958; Nurses Quarters, 1958; The Wife Next Door, 1959; My Sister's Keeper, 1961; Night School, 1961; Clem Anderson, 1961; Pretty Leslie, 1963; The President, 1964; La Vie Passionnee of Rodney Buckthorne: A Tale of the Great American's Last Rally and Curious Death, 1968; Doctor Cobb's Game, 1970; The Goss Women, 1974; Hoyt's Child, 1976; Labors of Love, 1980; Flame, 1980; After Goliath, 1985; Two Short Novels (with James White), 1990. Stories: Fifteen by Three: R V Cassill, Herbert Gold, and James B Hall, 1957; The Father and Other Stories, 1965; The Happy Marriage and Other Stories, 1966; Three Stories, 1982; Collected Stories, 1989; Late Stories, 1993. Poetry: Patrimonies, 1988. Other: Writing Fiction, 1962, 2nd edition, 1975; In an Iron Time: Statements and Reiterations, 1969; The Norton Anthology of Short Fiction, 1978, 5th edition, 1994; The Norton Anthology of Contemporary Fiction, 1988. Contributions to: Many anthologies and periodicals. Honours: Atlantic "Firsts" Award, 1947; Fulbright Grant, 1952; Rockefeller Foundation Grant, 1954; Blackhawk Award, 1965; Guggenheim Fellowship, 1968-69. Membership: Phi Beta Kappa. Address: 22 Boylston Avenue, Providence, RI 02906, USA.

CASTANEDA Omar, b. 6 Sept 1954, Guatemala. Professor; Writer. m. (1) 11 Aug 1984, (2) 26 Feb 1992, 1 son, 1 daughter. Education: BA, 1980, MFA, 1983, Indiana University. Appointment: Professor, University of Washington. Publications: Remembering to Say Mouth or Face, 1993; Imagining Isabel, 1994. Contributions to: Many periodicals. Honours: Various awards. Memberships: Modern Language Association; PEN. Address: Department of English, Western Washington University, Bellingham, WA 98225, USA.

CASTEDO Elena, b. 1 Sept 1937, Spain. Writer. m. A Denny Elleman, 15 Apr 1973, 2 sons, 1 daughter. Education: University of Chile, 1966; University of California, 1968; Harvard University, 1976. Appointments: Teacher; Teaching Fellow, Harvard University, 1969-72; Lecturer, American University, 1976-77; Editor, Inter American Review, 1987-80; Visiting Writer at Universities of California, Cornell, Chicago, Illinois, Miami, Washington, Wisconsin and Yale, 1990-94. Publications: El Praiso; Paradise; Iguana Dreams; The Sound of Writing; El Teato Chileno de Mediados de Sigioxx; El Teatro Chileuo

de mediadis siglo XX, 1982; El paraiso, 1990; Paradise, 1990; Anthologies: Iguana Dreams; The Sound of Writing; Out of the Mirrored Garden; New Moment in the Americas. Contributions to: Periodicals. Honours: UCLA Masters Award; Simon Bolivar Medal; Several Fellowships; Phoebe Award; Nominated, National Book Award; El Mercurio Book of the Year. Memberships: PEN; Authors Guild; Modern Language Association; Poets and Writers. Address: c/o Accent Media, 36 Lancaster Street, Cambridge, MA 02140-2840, USA.

CASTEL Albert (Edward), b. 11 Nov 1928, Wichita, Kansas, USA. Historian; Professor (Retired). m. GeorgeAnn Bennett, 25 June 1959, 1 son, 1 daughter. Education: BA, 1950, MA, 1951, Wichita State University; PhD, University of Chicago, 1955. Appointments: Instructor, University of California at Los Angeles, 1957-58; Assistant Professor, Waynesburg College, Pennsylvania, 1958-60; Assistant Professor, 1960-63, Associate Professor, 1963-67, Professor, 1967-91, Western Michigan University. Publications: A Frontier State of War, 1958; William Clarke Quantrill, 1962; Sterling Price and the Civil War in the West, 1968; The Guerrilla War, 1974; Fort Sumter: 1861, 1976; The Presidency of Andrew Johnson, 1979; Decision in the West: The Atlanta Campaign of 1864, 1992; Winning and Losing in the Civil War: Essays and Stories, 1996. Contributions to: Many scholarly journals. Honours: Albert J Beveridge Award, American Historical Association, 1957; Best Author Award, Civil War Times Illustrated, 1979; Peterson Award, Eastern National Park and Monument Association, 1989; Harwell Award, Atlanta Civil War Round Table, 1993; Lincoln Prize, Gettysburg College, 1993; Truman Award, Civil War Round Table of Kansas City, 1994. Address: 66 Westwood Drive, Hillsdale, MI 49242, USA.

CASTELL Megan. See:WILLIAMS Jeanne.

CASTELLIN Philippe, b. 26 June 1948, Isle Sur Sorgnes, Vaucluse, France. Fisherman. 3 s. Education: Arege de Philosophie, ENS; Docteur de Letters, University of Paris, Sorbonne. Appointments: Publisher, Director of Docks. Publications include: Rene Char, Traces, 1988; Paesine, 1989; Livre, 1990; Vers la Poesie Totale, 1992; HPS, 1992. Contributions to: Tam Tam; Lotta Poetica; Texture Press; Others. Honours: Charge de Mission, 1990; Expert Manager, Exhibition of Poetry and Painting. Membership: Societe des Gens de Lettres. Address: c/o Akenaton Docks, 20 Rue Bonaparte, F20000 Ajaccio, France.

CASTLE Barbara Anne, Baroness Castle of Blackburn, b. 6 Oct 1910, Chesterfield, England. Journalist; Author. m. Edward Cyril Castle, 1944. Education: St Hughs College, Oxford. Appointments: Editor, Town and County Councillor, 1936-40; Housing Correspondent and Affairs Advisor, Daily Mirror, 1940-45; Labour Member, Blackburn, 1945-79; Member, National Executive Committee, 1950-79' Vice-Chairman, 1957-58; Chairman, 1958-59, Labour Party; Minister of Overseas Development, 1964-65; Privy Counsellor, 1964; Minister of Transport, 1965-68; First Secretary of State for Employment and Productivity, 1968-70; Secretary of State for Social Services, 1974-76; Member, European Parliament, Greater Manchester North, 1979-84, Greater Manchester West, 1984-89; Leader, British Labour Party, European Parliament, 1979-85; Vice-Chairman, Socialist Group, European Parliament, 1979-86. Publications: Castle Diaries 1964-70, 1984; Sylvia & Christabel Pankhurst, 1987; Castle Diaries 1964-76, 1990; Fighting All the Way, 1993. Honours: Honorary Fellow of: St Hugh's College Oxford, 1966, Bradford & Ilkley Community College, 1985, UMIST, 1991, Humberside Polytechnic, 1991, York University, 1992; Honorary Doctor of: Technology, Bradford University, 1968, Technology, Loughborough, 1969, Laws, Lancaster, 1991; Laws, Manchester University, 1993; Cross of Order of Merit, Germany, 1990; Created Life Peer, 1990. Literary Agent: David Higham Associates Ltd. Address: Hell Corner Farm, Grays Lane, Ibstone, Buckinghamshire HP14 3XX, England.

CASTLEDEN Rodney, b. 23 Mar 1945, Worthing, Sussex, England. Head of Humanities, Roedean School. m. Sarah Dee, 29 July 1987. Education: BA, Geography, Hertford College, 1967, Dip Ed, 1968, MA, 1972, MSc, Geomorphology, 1980, Oxford University. Publications: Classic Landforms of the Sussex Coast, 1982; The Wilmington Giant: the Quest for a Lost Myth, 1983; The Stonehenge People: an Exploration of Life in Neolithic Britain, 1987; The Knossos Labyrinth, 1989; Minoans: Life in Bronze Age Crete, 1990; Book of British Dates, 1991; Neolithic Britain, 1992; The Making of Stonehenge, 1993; World History: a Chronological Dictionary of Dates, 1994; British History: a Chronological Dictionary of Dates, 1994; The

Cerne Giant, 1996; Knossos, Temple of the Goddess, 1996; Classic Landforms Series, editor. Contributions to: The Origin of Chalk Dry Valleys; A General Theory of Fluvial Valley Development. Memberships: FGS; FRGS; Royal Society of Literature; Quaternary Research Association; Society of Authors. Address: 15 Knepp Close, Brighton, Sussex, BN2 4LD, England.

CASTLES Alexander Cuthbert, b. 7 Mar 1933, Australia. Emeritus Professor of Law; Author. m. Florence Amelia Ross, 15 Mar 1958, 1 son, 3 daughters. Education: LLB Hons, Melbourne, 1955; JD, Chicago, 1957. Publications: Introduction to Australian Legal History, 1971; Australia and the United Nations, 1973; Chronology of Australia, 1978; An Australian Legal History, 1982; Law Makers and Wayward Whigs, with M C Harris, 1987; Annotated Bibliography of Australian Law, 1994; Shark Arm Murders, 1995; Source Book of Legal History (with J M Bennett), 1979. Contributions to: Articles in Australian, British, Canadian, Hong Kong and United States Law and History Journals. Address: 2/112 Beulah Road, Norwood, South Australia 5067, Australia.

CAULDWELL Frank. See: KING Francis Henry.

CAUSLEY Charles (Stanley), b. 24 Aug 1917, Launceston, Cornwall, England. Editor; Poet. Education: Launceston Colllege. Appointments: Teacher, Cornwall, 1947-76; Member, Arts Council Poetry Panel, 1962-66. Publications: Survivors Leave, 1953; Union Street, 1957; Johnny Alleluia, 1961; Penguin Modern Poets 3, 1962; Ballard of the Breed Man, 1968; Underneath the Water, 1968; Pergamon Poets 10, 1970; Timothy Winters, 1970; Six Women, 1974; Ward 14, 1974; St Martha and the Dragon, 1978; Collected Poems, 1951-75, 1975; Secret Destinations, 1984; 21 Poems, 1986; A Field of Vision, 1988; Plays: Runaway, 1936; The Conquering Hero, 1937; How Pleasant to Know Mrs Lear, 1948; The Ballard of Aucassin and Nicolette, 1978; Jonah, Libretto for William Mathias, 1990; Editions of Verse for Children. Honours: Queen's Gold Medal for Poetry, 1967; D Litt, University of Exeter, 1977; MA, Open University, 1982; Commander of the Order of the British Empire, 1986. Address: 2 Cyprus Well, Launceston, Cornwall PL15 8BT, England.

CAUTE (John) David, b. 16 Dec 1938 Alexandria, Egypt. Writer. Education: DPhil, Wadham College, Oxford, 1962. Appointments: Fellow, All Souls College, Oxford, 1959-65; Visiting Professor, New York and Columbia Universities, 1966-67; Reader in Social and Political Theory, Brunel University, 1967-70; Regents Lecturer, University of California, 1974; Literary and Arts Editor, New Statesman, London, 1979-80; Co-Chairman, Writers Guild of Great Britain, 1981-82. Publications: At Fever Pitch, 1959; Comrade Jacob, 1961; Communism and the French Intellectuals 1914-1960, 1964; The Decline of the West, The Left in Europe Since 1789, 1966; Essential Writings of Karl Marx (editor), 1967; The Demonstration, 1969; Fanon, 1970; The Occupation, 1971; The Illusion, 1971; The Fellow-Travellers, 1973, revised edition, 1988; Collisions: Essays and Reviews, Cuba Yes?, 1974; The Great Fear: The Anti-Communist Purge Under Truman and Eisenhower, 1978; The K-Factor, Under the Skin: The Death of White Rhodesia, 1983; The Espionage of The Saints, News From Nowhere, 1986; Sixty-Eight: The Year of the Barricades, 1988; Veronica of the Two Nations, 1989; The Women's Hour, 1991; Joseph Losey: A Revenge on Life, 1994; Orwell and Mr Blair, 1994; Radio Plays: The Demonstration, 1971; Fallout, 1972; The Zimbabwe Tapes, 1983; Henry and the Dogs, 1986; Sanctions, 1988; Animal Fun Park, 1995. Address: 41 Westcroft Square, London W6 0TA, England.

CAVE Hugh Barnett, b. 11 July 1910, Chester, England. Writer. m. Margaret long, 11 July 1935, 2 sons. Education: Attended Boston University. Publications: Haiti: Highroad to Adventure, 1952; The Cross on the Drum, 1959; The Mission, 1960; Murgunstrumm and Others, 1977; The Evil, 1981; The Voyage, 1988; Disciples of Dread, 1988; The Corpse Maker, 1988; Conquering Kilmarnie, 1989; The Lower Deep, 1990; Lucifer's Eye, 1991; Death Stalks the Night, 1995; The Door Below (collection of stories), due out 1997. Contributions to: Over 800 stories in 100 magazines in 1930s and 1940s; 350 fiction pieces in magazines, including 43 in Saturday Evening Post, 36 in Good Housekeeping; Short stories in over 30 countries. Honours: World Fantasy Award; Phoenix Award; Horror Writers Association's Lifetime Achievement. Literary Agent: Dorian Literary Agency, England. Address: 437 Thomas Street, Sebastian, FL 32958, USA.

CAWS Mary Ann, b. 10 Sept 1933, Wilmington, North Carolina, USA. Professor of English, French, and Comparative Literature; Writer; Editor; Translator. m. Peter Caws, 2 June 1956, div 1987, 1 son, 1 daughter. Education: BA, Bryn Mawr College, 1954; MA, Yale University, 1956; PhD, University of Kansas, 1962. Appointments: Lecturer, Barnard College, 1962-63; Visiting Faculty, Sarah Lawrence College, 1965-66; Assistant Professor, 1966-68, Associate Professor, 1968-70, Professor, 1970-83, Distinguished Professor, 1983-86, Hunter College of the City University of New York; Distinguished Professor of English, French, and Comparative Literature, Graduate School, City University of New York, 1986-; Faculty, Dartmouth School of Theory and Criticism, 1988; Professeur associé, University of Paris VII, 1993-94. Publications: Surrealism and the Literary Imagination, 1966; The Poetry of Dada and Surrealism, 1971; The Inner Theatre of Recent French Poetry, 1972; André Breton, 1974; The Presence of René Char, 1976; René Char, 1976; The Surrealist Voice of Robert Desnos, 1977; La Main de Pierre Reverdy, 1979; The Eye in the Text: Essays on Perception, Mannerist to Modern, 1981; A Metapoetics of the Passage: Architectures Surrealist and After, 1981; L'Oeuvre Filante de René Char, 1981; Yves Bonnefoy, 1984; Reading Frames in Modern Fiction, 1986; Edmond Jabès, 1988; The Art of Interference: Stressed Readings in Visual and Verbal Texts, 1988; Women of Bloomsbury: Virginia, Vanessa, and Carrington, 1990; Robert Motherwell: What Art Holds, 1995; Carrington and Lytton/Alone Together, 1996; André Breton, Revisited, 1996; The Surrealist Look: An Erotics of Encounter, 1997; Bloomsbury and France (with Sarah Bird Wright), 1997; Editor: About French Poetry from Dada to Tel Quel: Theory and Text, 1984; Writing in a Modern Temper, 1984; The Prose Poem in France (with Hermine Riffaterre), 1985; Textual Analysis: Some Readers Reading, 1986; Perspectives on Perception: Philosophy, Art, and Literature, 1988; Edmond Jabès (with Richard Stamelman), 1989; Reading Proust Now (with Ruedi Kuenzli and Gwen Raaberg), 1991; Selected Poems of René Char (with Tina Jolas), 1992; Contre-Courants: Les femmes s'écrivant à travers les siècles (with Nancy K Miller, Elizabeth Houlding, and Cheryl Morgan), 1994; HarperCollins World Reader, 1994, expanded edition, 1996; Joseph Cornell's Theater of the Mind: Selected Journals, Letters, and Files, 1994; Carto-graphies (with Mary Jean Green, Marianne Hirsch, and Ronnie Scharfman), 1995; The Surrealist Painters and Poets, 1997. Contributions to: Books, scholarly journals, and periodicals. Honours: Guggenheim Fellowship, 1972; Fulbright Fellowship, 1972; National Endowment for the Humanities Senior Fellowship, 1979-80; Getty Scholar, 1989-90; Rockefeller Foundation Residency, Belagio, Italy, 1994. Memberships: Academy of Literary Studies, president, 1989-; Association for the Study of Dada and Surrealism, president, 1982-86; Authors' Guild; International Association for Philosophy and Literature; Modern Language Association, president, 1983-84; PEN. Address: 140 East 81st Street, New York, NY 10018, USA.

CEDERING Siv, b. 5 Feb 1939, Sweden. Writer; Artist. m. David Swickard, 11 Sept 1983, 1 son, 2 daughters. Publications: Mother Is, 1975; The Juggler, 1977; The BLue Horse, 1979; Oxen, 1981; Letters from the Floating Worlds, 1984; Several Translations. Contributions to: Harper's; Ms; New Republic; Paris Review; Partisan Review; New York Times; Goergia Review; Fiction Interntional Shenandoah; Confrontation; Over 80 Anthologies and Textbooks. Honours: Best Books of Year, 1980; NY Foundation Fellowship, 1985, 1992. Memberships: Coordinating Council of Literary Magazines; PEN; Poetrey Society of America; Poets and Writers. Literary Agent: Diana Finch, Ellen Levine Agency. Address: Box 800, Amagansett, NY 11930, USA.

CEGIELKA Francis Anthony, b. 16 Mar 1908, Grabow, Poland. Roman Catholic Priest in the Society of the Catholic Apostolate. Education: Collegium Marianum, 1921-27, Wadowice (Krakow); Pontifical Gregorian University, Rome, Italy, 1927-31; Ordained Priest, 1931; Doctorate in Theology (STD) 1931. Appointments: Teacher, Minor Seminary of the Society of the Catholic Apostolate, Chelmno, Poland, 1932-34; Teacher, Major Seminary, SAC, Wadowice, Poland, 1934-36; Rector, Polish Catholic Mission, Paris, France, 1937-47; Prisoner of German Gestapo, held in 9 prisons and 2 concentration camps, 1940-45; Rector, Polish Catholic Mission, Paris, France, 1945-48; Sent to the USA by his Superior General to conduct retreat work; Professor, Felician College, Lodi, New Jersey, 1967-70; Professor, Holy Family College, Philadelphia, USA, 1970-76. Publications: Reparatory Mysticism of Nazareth, 1951; Holy Mass School of Religious Life, 1953; Life on Rocks (among the Natives of the Union of South Africa), 1957; Spiritual Theology for Novices, 1961; Segregavit nos Dominus, 1963; Three Hearts Meditations, 2 volumes

1963-1964; Nazareth Spirituality, 1966; All Things New: Radical Reform of Religious Life, 1969; Handbook of Ecclesiology and Christology, 1971; Toward a New Spring of Humankind, 1987. Honours: Legion d'Honneur, Chevalier, French Government, 1945; Nominated as an outstanding Educator of America, 1972, 1974. Memberships: American Association of University Professors; Polish Institute of Arts and Sciences in America. Address: 3452 Niagara Falls Boulevard, PO Box 563, North Tonawanda, NY 14120, USA.

CELA Camilo José, b. 11 May 1916, Iria Flavia, La Coruña, Spain. Writer; Poet. m. (1) María del Rosario Conde Picavea, 12 Mar 1944, 1 son, (2) Marine Castano, 1991. Education: University of Madrid, 1933-36, 1939-43. Publications: Fiction: La Familia de Pascual Duarte, 1942, English translation as Pascual Duarte's Family, 1946; Pabellón de reposo, 1943, English translation as Rest Home, 1961; Nuevas andanzas y desventuras de Lazarillo de Tormes, 1944; Caminos inciertos: La colmena, 1951, English translation as The Hive, 1953; Santa Balbina 37: Gas en cada piso, 1952; Timoteo, el incomprendido, 1952; Mrs Caldweel habla con su hijo, 1953, English translation as Mrs Caldwell Speaks to Her Son, 1968; Café de artistas, 1955; Historias de Venezuela: La catira, 1955; Tobogán de hambrientos, 1962; Visperas, festividad y octava de San Camilo del año 1936 en Madrid, 1969; Oficio de tinieblas 5, o, Novela de tesis escrita para ser cantada por un de enfermos, 1973; Mazurca para doe muertos, 1983; Cristo versus Arizona, 1988; Also many volumes of stories. Poetry: Pisando la dudosa luz del día, 1945; Reloj de Sangre, 1989. Non-Fiction: Diccionario Secreto, 2 volumes, 1968, 1971; Enciclopedia del Erotismo, 1976-77; Memorias, entendimientos y voluntades (memoirs), 1993. Other: Volumes of essays, travel books. Honours: Premio de la critica, 1955; Spanish National Prize for Literature, 1984; Nobel Prize for Literature, 1989; Planeta Prize, 1994. Membership: Real Academia Espanola, 1957. Address: c/o Agencia Literaria Carmen Balcells, Diagonal 580, 08021 Barcelona, Spain.

CELATI Gianni, b. 1937, Sondrio, Ferrara, Italy. Novelist. Appointments: Lecturer in Anglo-American Literature, University of Bologna. Publications: Comiche, 1971; Le avventure di Guizzardi, 1971; Il chiodo in testa, 1975; La banda dei sospiri, 1976; Lunario del paradiso, 1978; Narratori delle pianure, 1985; Quattro novelle sulle apparenze, 1987; Verso la foce, 1989; Also: Finzioni occidentali, 1975; La bottega dei mimi, 1977; Parlamenti buffi, 1989; Profili delle nuvole, 1989; Éditions and translations. Honours: Mondello Prize, 1990. Address: c/o Feltrinelli, Via Andegari 6, 20121 Milan, Italy.

CEREDIG. See: REES David Benjamin.

CESAIRE Aimé (Fernand), b. 25 June 1913, Basse-Pointe, Martinique, West Indies. Poet; Playwright. Education: Ecole Normale Supérieure, Paris, 1935-39. Appointments: Mayor of Forte-de-France, 1945-84; President, Conseil Régional Martinique, 1983-86. Publications: Les Armes miraculeuses, 1946; Notebook of a Return to the Native Land, 1947; Soloeil cou-coupe, 1948; Lost Body, 1960; Ferrements, 1960; Cadastre, 1961; State of the Union, 1966; Aimé Cesaire: The Collected Poetry, 1983; Non-Viscious Circle: Twenty Poems, 1984; Lyric and Dramatic Poetry 1946-83, 1990; Plays: Et les Chiens se taisaient, 1956; The Tragedy of King Christophe, 1964; A Season in the Congo, 1966; A Tempest, adaptation of Shakespeare, 1969; Also: Toussaint L'ouverture: la révolution française et le problème colonial, 1960. Honours: National Grand Prize for poetry, 1982. Address: La Mairie, 97200 Fort-de-France, Martinique, West Indies.

CHADWICK Sir (William) Owen, b. 20 May 1916, Bromley, Kent, England. Historian. m. Ruth Hallward, 28 Dec 1949, 2 sons, 2 daughters. Appointments: Dean, Trinity Hall, 1949-56, Master, Selwyn College, 1956-83, Dixie Professor of Ecclesiastical History, 1958-68, Regius Professor of Modern History, 1968-83, Cambridge University. Education: BA, 1939, St John's College, Cambridge. Publications: John Cassian, 1950, revised edition, 1968; The Founding of Cuddesdon, 1954; From Bossuet to Newman, 1957, 2nd edition, 1987; Western Asceticism, 1958; Creighton on Luther, 1959; Mackenzie's Grave, 1959; Victorian Miniature, 1960, 2nd edition, 1991; The Mind of the Oxford Movement, 1960; From Uniformity to Unity 1662-1962 (with G Nuttall), 1962; Westcott and the University, 1962; The Reformation, 1964; The Victorian Church, Vol 1, 1966, 3rd edition, 1972; Vol II, 1970, 2nd edition, 1972; Acton and Gladstone, 1976; The Secularization of the European Mind, 1977; Catholicism and History, 1978; The Popes and European Revolution, 1981; The Oxford History of the Christian Church (editor with Henry Chadwick, brother), 1976-;

Newman, 1983; Hensley Henson: A Study in the Friction Between Church and State, 1983; Britain and the Vatican in the Second World War, 1986; Michael Ramsey, 1990, 2nd edition, 1991; The Spirit of the Oxford Movement: Tractarian Essays, 1990; The Christian Church in the Cold War, 1992; A History of Christianity, 1995. Contributions to: Times (London); New Statesman; Spectator; Guardian; Sunday Times; Observer; History Journals. Honours: Wolfson Prize for History, 1981; Knighted, 1982; Order of Merit, 1983. Memberships: Fellow, British Academy; Fellow, Royal Historical Society. Address: 67 Grantchester Street, Cambridge CB3 9HZ, England.

CHADWICK Geoffrey, (Geoffrey Wall), b. 10 July 1950, Cheshire, England. University Lecturer, 3 sons, 1 daughter. Education: BA, University of Sussex, 1972; BPhil, St Edmund Hall, 1975. Publications: Madame Bovary, 1992; Flaubert: Selected Letters, 1997; Flaubert: Dictionary of Received Ideas. Contributions to: Literature and History; Cambridge Quarterly. Memberships: Society of Authors; Association of University Teachers; Translators Association. Address: Department of English, University of York, Heslington, York YO1 5D, England.

CHADWICK Whitney, b. 28 July 1943, Niagara Falls, New York, USA. Professor of Art; Writer. m. Robert A Bechtle, 6 Nov 1982. Education: BA, Middlebury College, 1965; MA, 1968, PhD, 1975, Penn State University. Appointments: Lecturer, 1972, Assistant Professor, 1973-77, Associate Professor, 1978, Massachusetts Institute of Technology; Visiting Assistant Professor of Art History, University of California at Berkeley, 1977; Associate Professor, 1978-82, Professor of Art, 1982-, San Francisco State University; Visting Professor, Massachusetts College of Art, 1996. Publications: Myth and Surrealist Painting, 1929-1939, 1980; Women Artists and the Surrealist Movement, 1985; Women, Art, and Society, 1990; Signifant Others: Creativity and Intimate Partnership, 1993; Leonora Carrington: La Realidad de la Imaginacion, 1995. Contributions to: Books, scholarly journals, and exhibition catalogues; Oxford Art Journal. Honours: National Endowment for the Humanities Fellowship, 1981-82; Senior Scholar, American Council of Learned Societies Fellowship; British Council Travel Grant, 1994; Eleanor Tufts Distinguished Visiting Lecturer, Southern Methodist University, 1995. Address: 871 De Haro Street, San Francisco, CA 94107, USA.

CHAGALL David, b. 22 Nov 1930, Philadelphia, Pennsylvania, USA. Author; Journalist. m. Juneau Joan Alsin, 15 Nov 1957. Education: Swarthmore College, 1948-49; BA, Penn State University, 1952; Sorbonne, University of Paris. Appointments: Associate Editor, IEE, 1960-61; Investigative Reporter, Nation Magazine, 1975-; Editor, Publisher, Inside Campaigning, 1984; Contributing Editor, Los Angeles Magazine, 1986-89; Host, TV Series, The Last Hour, 1994-. Publications: The Century God Slept, 1963; Diary of a Deaf Mute, 1971; The Spieler for the Holy Spirit, 1972; The New Kingmakers, 1981; Television Today, 1981; The Sunshine Road, 1988; The World's Greatest Comebacks, 1989; Surviving the Media Jungle, 1996. Contributions to: Periodicals. Honours: Carnegie Award, 1964; National Book Award, 1972; Health Journalism Award, 1980; Presidential Achievement Award, 1982. Memberships: Authors Guild; American Academy of Political Science. Address: PO Box 85, Agoura Hills, CA 91376 0085, USA.

CHAKRAVARTI Sasthibrata: See: BRATA Sasthi.

CHALFONT Baron, (Alun Arthur Gwynne Jones), b. 5 Dec 1919, Llantaram, Wales. Member, House of Lords; Writer. m. Mona Mitchell, 6 Nov 1948, 1 daughter dec. Education: West Monmouth, England. Appointments: Regular Officer, British Army, 1940-61; Broadcaster and Consultant on Foreign Affairs, BBC, 1961-64; Minister of State, Foreign and Commonwealth Office, 1964-70; Permanent Representative, Western European Union, 1969-70; Foreign Editor, New Statesman, 1970-71; Chairman, Industrial Cleaning Papers, 1979-86, All Party Defence Group of the House of Lords, 1980-, Peter Hamilton Security Consultants Ltd, 1984-86, VSEL Consortium, later VSEL plc, 1987-95, Radio Authority, 1991-94, Marlborough Stirling Group, 1994-; Director, W S Atkins International, 1979-83, IBM UK Ltd, 1973-90, Lazard Brothers & Company Ltd, 1983-90, Sandwick plc, 1985-95, Triangle Holdings, 1986-90; President, Abington Corporation Ltd, 1981-, Nottingham Building Society, 1983-90. Publications: The Sword and the Spirit, 1963; The Great Commanders, editor, 1973; Montgomery of Alamein, 1976; Waterloo: Battle of Three Armies, editor, 1979; Star Wars: Suicide or Survival, 1985; Defence of the Realm, 1987; By God's Will: A Portrait of the Sultan of Brunei, 1989.

Contributions to: Periodicals and journals. Honours: Officer of the Order of the British Empire, 1961; Created a Life Peer, 1964; Honorary Fellow, University College of Wales, 1974; Liveryman, Worshipful Company of Paviors; Freeman of the City of London. Memberships: International Institute for Strategic Studies; Royal Institute of International Affairs; Royal Society of the Arts, fellow; United Nations Association, chairman, 1972-73. Address: House of Lords, London SW1A 0PW, England.

CHALKER Jack L(aurence), b. 17 Dec 1944, Norfolk, Virginia, USA. Editor; Writer. m. Eva C Whitley, 1978. Education: BA, Towson State College, 1966; MLA, Johns Hopkins University, 1969. Appointments: Founder-Editor, 1960-72, Editorial and Marketing Director, 1961-, Mirage Press Ltd, Baltimore. Publications: Numerous science fiction and fantasy novels, including: A Jungle of Stars, 1976; Dancers in the Afterglow, 1978; The Web of the Chosen, 1978; A War of Shadows, 1979; And the Devil Will Drag You Under, 1979; The Devil's Voyage, 1981; The Identity Matrix, 1982; The Messiah Choice, 1985; Downtiming the Night Side, 1985; The Armlet of the Gods, 1986; The Red Tape War (with Mike Resnick and George Alec Effinger), 1991; Various series. Short Stories: Dance Band on the Titanic, 1988. Other: In Memoriam: Clark Ashton Smith (editor), 1963; Mirage on Lovecraft (editor), 1964; The Necronomicon: A Study (with Mark Owings), 1968; An Informal Biography of Scrooge McDuck, 1974; Jack Chalker, autobiography, 1985. Memberships: Science Fiction Writers of America; World Science Fiction Society. Address: c/o Ace Books, 200 Madison Avenue, New York, NY 10016, USA.

CHALLIS Chris, b. 11 Feb 1952, Essex, England. Writer; Lecturer. Education: BA, Leicester University, 1973; MA, (Dist) 1974; PhD, 1979. Appointments: ACGB Writer in Residence, Northampton, 1982-83; Four BBC Radio Stations, 1985; Doncaster Libraries, 1987; WIR Featherstone Library, 1987; WIR County Durham, 1989-90; WIR West Norfolk, 1991-92; Tutor in Creative Writing. Publications: Quest for Kerouac; Highfields Landscape; William of Cloudeslee; The Wild Thing Went from Side to Side; Four Stout Shoes; Jack Kerouac, Charles Bukowski and Me, 3rd edition, 1993; A Little Earth for Charity; Ten Plays; Common Ground; A Sense of Place; Wordscan; Together in Eternity; The Place Project Series; Meaning Light, 1993. Contributions to: Numerous. Honours: Nanda Award; Ema Travel Bursary; Ema Writers Bursary; Judge for Literary Comps; Heinemann Fiction Award. Membership: Writers Guild. Address: 67 Prospect Hill, Leicester LE5 3RT, England.

CHALMERS Mary Eilleen, b. 16 Mar 1927, Camden, New Jersey, USA. Author; Artist. Education: Diploma, College of Art, 1945-48; Barnes Foundation, 1948-49. Publications: A Christmas Story, 1956; Throw A Kiss, Harry, 1958; Take A Nap, Harry, 1964; Come to the Doctor, Harry, 1981; 6 Dogs, 23 Cats, 45 Mice and 116 Spiders, 1986; Easter Parade, 1988. Address: 4Q Laurel Hill Road, Greenbelt, MD 20770, USA.

CHALON Jon. See: CHALONER John.

CHALONER John (Seymour), (Jon Chalon), . 1924, London, England. Writer. Education: Royal Military College, Sandhurst. Publications: Three for the Road, 1954; Eager Beaver, 1965; The Flying Steamroller; The House Next Door, 1967; Sir Lance A Little and the Knights of the Kitchen Table, 1971; The Green Bus, 1973; Family Hold Back, 1975; The Dustmans Holiday, 1976; To the Manor Born, 1978; The Great Balloon Adventure; Will O The Wheels and Speedy Sue, 1990; Occupational Hazard, 1991. Honour: Bundesverdienstkreuz 1st KI for Services to Anglo-German Relations, 1990. Address: 4 Warwick Square, London SW1, England.

CHAMBERS Aidan, (Malcolm Blackin), b. 27 Dec 1934, Chester-le-Street, County Durham, England. Author; Publisher. m. Nancy Harris Lockwood, 30 Mar 1968. Education: Borough Road College, Isleworth, London University. Publications: The Reluctant Reader, 1969; Introducing Books to Children, 1973; Breaktime, 1978; Seal Secret, 1980; The Dream Cage, 1981; Dance on My Grave, 1982; The Present Takers, 1983; Booktalk, 1985; Now I Know, 1987; The Reading Environment, 1991; The Toll Bridge, 1992; Tell Me: Children, Reading & Talk, 1993. Contributions to: Numerous Magazines and Journals. Honours: Childrens Literature Award for Outstanding Criticism, 1978; Eleanor Farjeon Award, 1982; Silver Pencil, 1985, 1986, 1994. Membership: Society of Authors. Address: Lockwood, Station Road, Woodchester, Stroud, Gloucs GL5 5EQ, England.

CHAMBERS Marjorie Elizabeth, b. 15 May 1938, Northern Ireland. University Lecturer. m. Cyril Weir Chambers, 30 June 1969, 1 son. Education: BA, 1961-62, MA, 1968, Trinity College; Sorbonne, Paris, 1961-62; PGCE Goldsmiths College, London, 1964; University of Thessalonika, 1981. Appointment: Lecturer, Queens University, Belfast. Publications: The Charioteer, 1987-88; My Sisters Song, The March of the Ocean, 1989-90; Poems from Collection, The Big Night and the Window; The Offering; Songs of Resurrection; The Sequel, 1991-92; Gift in Abeyance, Chorus; Modern Greek Studies Yearbook, volume 7: Farewell; Translations: Kalamas and Acheron by Christopher Milionis (short stories), 1996; The Four Legs of the Table by Takovos Kampanellis (play), 1996. Contributions to: Trinity College Dublin Review. Honours: British Council Research Grants, 1987, 1990. Memberships: Translators Association; Society of Authors; ITI; Dictionary of Translators and Interpreters; Northern Ireland Representative, Examiner in Modern Greek. Address: 3 The Esplanade, Holywood, County Down BT18 9JG, Northern Ireland.

CHAMBERS Raymond J(ohn), b. 16 Nov 1917, Newcastle, New South Wales, Australia. Professor Emeritus. m. Margaret Scott Brown, 9 Sept 1939, 2 daughters. Education: BEc, University of Sydney, 1939. Appointments: Senior Lecturer, 1953-55, Associate Professor, 1955-59, Professor of Accounting, 1960-82, Emeritus, University of Sydney; Editor, Abacus, 1964-74. Publications: Financial Management, 1947; Function and Design of Company Annual Reports, 1955; Accounting and Action, 1957; The Accounting Frontier, 1965; Accounting, Evaluation and Economic Behavior, 1966; Accounting Finance and Management, 1969; Securities and Obscurities, 1973; Price Variation and Inflation Accounting, 1980. Address: Department of Accounting, University of Sydney, Sydney, New South Wales 2006, Australia.

CHAMPAGNE Maurice (Joseph Pierre), b. 7 May 1936, Montreal, Quebec, Canada. Philosopher; Human Rights Consultant. m. 1 son, 1 daughter. Education: MA, Montreal, 1956; DES, Nice, 1967; DLitt, Nice, 1968. Appointment: Literature Teaching Coordinator, Quebec Education Department, 1968-69. Publications: La Violewce Au Povwoir, 1971; Lettres D'Amour, 1972; La Famille Et L'Homme A Délivrer Du Pouvoir, 1980; Batir Ou Détruire Le Quebec, 1983; L'Homme-Tetard, 1991. Contributions to: Feature Articles, over one hundred in, Le Devoir and Lapresse. Honour: Governor General of Canada Award, 1980. Memberships: Quebec Writers Union; Quebec Criminology Association; Quebec Human Rights Commission; Past President, Director, Civil Liberties Union, 1970-78. Literary Agent: Louise Myette. Address: 3741 Saint Andre, Montreal, Quebec H2L 3V6, Canada.

CHAMPION Larry Stephen, b. 27 Apr 1932, Shelby, North Carolina, USA. Professor of English; Writer. m. Nancy Ann Blanchard, 22 Dec 1956, 1 son, 2 daughters. Education: BA, Davidson College, 1954; MA, University of Virginia, 1955; PhD, University of North Carolina, 1961. Appointments: Instructor, Davidson College, 1955-56; University of North Carolina, Chapel Hill, 1959-60; Instructor, 1960-61, Assistant Professor, 1961-65, Associate Professor, 1965-68, Professor of English, 1968-, North Carolina State University. Publications: Ben Johnson's "Dotages": A Reconsideration of the Late Plays, 1967; The Evolution of Shakespeare's Comedy: A Study in Dramatic Perspective, 1970; Quick Springs of Sense: Studies in the Eighteenth Century (editor), 1974; Shakespeare's Tragic Perspective: The Development of His Dramatic Technique, 1976; Tragic Patterns in Jacobean and Caroline Drama: A Study in Perspective, 1977; Perspective in Shakespeare's English Histories, 1980; King Lear: An Annotated Bibliography Since 1940, 2 volumes, 1981; Thomas Dekker and the Traditions of English Drama, 1985, 2nd edition, 1987; The Essential Shakespeare: An Annotated Bibliography of Major Modern Studies, 2nd edition, revised, 1993; The Noise of Threatening Drum: Dramatic Strategy and Political Ideology in Shakespeare and the English Chronicle Plays, 1990. Contributions to: Books and scholarly journals. Honours: Academy of Outstanding Teachers Award, 1966; Alumni Distinguished Professor, 1987. Memberships: Modern Language Association; National Council of Teachers of English; Phi Beta Kappa; Phi Kappa Phi; Renaissance English Text Society; Renaissance Society of America. Address: 5320 Sendero Drive. Raleigh, NC 27612, USA.

CHAMPOUX Pierrette, b. 26 Jan 1930, Montréal, Quebec, Canada. Journalist; Radio Reporter; Singer; Composer. Education: Dramatic School. Literary Appointments: Daily News Reporter, Radio Station CKVL-Verdun; Writer for several newspapers and magazines;

Composer, Songs, Music; Numerous public appearances on TV Shows, Radio Programs; Fashion Commentator. Publications: Parle-Moi Du Canada, 1992; Raconte-Moi-Montreal, 1992; Les Pionnieres, 1992; Quebec, en Ballades, 1994; Records: Sur Les Bords Du St-Laurent, 1966, Un Enfant, 1979. Contributions to: Canada Nouveau; Radio-Monde. Honours: Grand Prix, Women's International Year's Contest, 1975; Honorable Mention, Canadian Committee for the International Year of the Handicapped, 1981; 1st Prize, Le Concours International des Arts et Lettres, France, 1993. Memberships: President, Women's Press Club; Director, United Nations Canadian Association, Montreal Branch; Conseillére, La Société des Ecrivains Canadiens; L'Union des Artistes, Socan. Address: 1770 rue Perrot, Ile Perrot, Quebec J7V 7P2, Canada.

CHAN Stephen, b. 11 May 1949, Auckland, New Zealand. Professor in International Relations and Ethics; Writer; Poet. Education: BA, 1972, MA, 1975, University of Auckland; MA, King's College, London, 1977; PhD, University of Kent, Canterbury, 1992. Appointments: International Civil Servant, Commonwealth Secretariat, 1977-83; Lecturer in International Relations, University of Zambia, 1983-85; Visiting Lecturer in International Relations, Victoria University of Wellington, 1986; Faculty, University of Kent, 1987-96; Visiting Professor, Graduate Institute of International Studies, Geneva, 1991, University of Tampere, 1994-95; Visiting Lecturer, University of Natal, 1992; Professor in International Relations and Ethics, Head of International Studies, Dean of Humanities, Nottingham Trent University, 1996-. Publications: Scholarly: The Commonwealth Observer Group in Zimbabwe: A Personal Memoir, 1985; Issues in International Relations: A View from Africa, 1987; The Commonwealth in World Politics: A Study of International Action, 1965-85, 1988; Exporting Apartheid: Foreign Policies in Southern Africa, 1978-1988, 1990; Social Development in Africa Today: Some Radical Proposals, 1991; Kaunda and Southern Africa: Image and Reality in Foreign Policy, 1991; Twelve Years of Commonwealth Diplomatic History: Commonwealth Summit Meetings, 1979-1991, 1992; Mediation in South Africa (editor with Vivienne Jabri), 1993; Renegade States: The Foreign Policies of Revolutionary States (editor with Andrew Williams), 1994; Towards a Multicultural Roshamon Paradigm in International Relations, 1996; Portuguese Foreign Policy in Southern Africa (with Moises Venancio), 1996; Snarling at Each Other: Students and Masters in International Relations (editor with Jarrod Wiener), 1996. Poetry: Postcards from Paradise (with Rupert Glover and Merlene Young), 1971; A Charlatan's Mosaic: New Zealand Universities Literary Yearbook (editor), 1972; Arden's Summer, 1975; Songs of the Maori King, 1986; Crimson Rain, 1991. Honours: Visiting fellowships; Honorary LittD, WAAC, Istanbul; Honorary Professor, University of Sambia, 1993-95. Address: c/o Department of International Studies, Nottingham Trent University, Clifton Lane, Nottingham NG11 8NS, England.

CHANCE Stephen. See: **TURNER Philip.**

CHANCELLOR Alexander Surtees, b. 4 Jan 1940, Ware, Hertfordshire, England. Journalist. m. Susanna Elisabeth Debenham, 1964, 2 daughters. Education: Eton; Trinity Hall, Cambridge. Appointments: Staff, Reuters News Agency, 1964-74, Independent Television News, 1974-75; Editor, The Spectator, 1975-84, Time and Tide, 1984-86, The Independent, 1986-88, The Independent Magazine, 1989-92; Associate Editor, The Sunday Telegraph, 1994-. Address: 1 Souldern Road, London W14 0JE, England.

CHANDLER David (Geoffrey), b. 15 Jan 1934, England. Military Historian. Education: DLitt, Oxford, 1991. Appointments: British Army Officer, 1957-60; Lecturer, 1960-64, Senior Lecturer, 1964-69, Deputy Head, 1969-80, Head, 1980-94, Royal Military Academy, Sandhurst; President, 1967-86, President Emeritus, 1986-, British Military History Commission; Vice President, International Commission of Military History, 1975-94; Editor, David Chandler's Newsletter on the Age of Napoleon, 1987-89; Military Affairs Visiting Professor, Quantico, 1991. Publications: A Traveller's Guide to Battlefields of Europe, 1965; The Campaigns of Napoleon, 1966; Marlborough as Military Commander, 1973; The Art of Warfare on Land, 1975; The Art of Warfare in the Age of Marlborough, 1976; Atlas of Military Strategy, 1980, 2nd edition, 1996; A Journal of Marlborough's Wars, 1984; Napoleon's Military Maxims, 1987; On The Napoleonic Wars, 1994; The Oxford Illustrated History of the British Army, 1994. Contributions to: History Today. Honours: Literary Award, Napoleonic Society of America, 1994; Literary Award, International Napoleonic Society of Canada, 1995. Memberships: European Union of Re-enactment Societies; Napoleonic

Society of Great Britain; Fellow, Royal Historical Society. Address: Hindford, Monteagle Lane, Yateley, Hampshire, England.

CHANDLER Frank. See: **HARKNETT Terry.**

CHANEY Edward P(aul) de G(ruyter), b. 11 Apr 1951, Hayes, Middlesex, England. Historian; Lecturer. m. Lisa Maria Jacka, 15 Sept 1973, 2 daughters. Education: BA, University of Reading, 1975; MPhil, 1977, PhD, 1982, Warburg Institute, University of London; Researcher, European University Institute, Florence, 1978-81. Appointments: Lecturer, University of Pisa, 1979-85; Adjunct Assistant Professor, Charles A Strong Center, Georgetown University Florence Program, Villa Le Balze, Florence, 1982, 1983; Shuffrey Research Fellow in Architectural History, Lincoln College, Oxford, 1985-90; Part-time Lecturer, Oxford Polytechnic, 1991, Oxford Brookes University, 1993-; Historian, London Division, English Heritage, 1991-93. Publications: Oxford, China and Italy: Writings in Honour of Sir Harold Acton on his Eightieth Birthday (editor with N Ritchie), 1984; The Grand Tour and the Great Rebellion: Richard Lassels and 'The Voyage of Italy' in the Seventeenth Century, 1985; Florence: A Travellers' Companion (with Harold Acton), 1986; England and the Continental Renaissance: Essays in Honour of J B Trapp (editor with Peter Mack), 1990; English Architecture: Public and Private: Essays for Kerry Downes (editor with John Bold), 1993; The Evolution of the Grand Tour, 1996; Inigo Jones's 'Roman Sketchbook', 1996. Contributions to: Reference works, books, scholarly journals, periodicals, etc. Honours: Laurea di Dottore in Lingue e Letterature Straniere, University of Pisa, 1983; Honorary Life Member, British Institute of Florence, 1984; Elected Fellow, Society of Antiquaries, 1993. Memberships: Beckford Society; British-Italian Society; Catholic Record Society; Georgian Group; International Berkeley Society; Leonardo da Vinci Society; Renaissance Society; Royal Stuart Society; Society of Architectural Historians; Wyndham Lewis Society. Address: 40 Southfield Road, Oxford OX4 1NZ, England.

CHANG Lee. See: **LEVINSON Leonard.**

CHAPLIN Jenny, (Tracie Telfer, Wendy Wentworth), b. 22 Dec 1928, Glasgow, Scotland. Head Mistress; Editor; Publisher. m. J McDonald Chaplin, 21 Apr 1951, 1 daughter. Education: Jordanhill College of Education, 1946-49. Appointments: Editor, Founder, Publisher, International, The Writers Rostrum, 1984-93; Organiser, Lecturer, Writers Workshop, Rarin to Go, 1991. Publications: A Glasgow Childhood; A Glasgow Fair; A Glasgow Hogmanay; One Editor's Life; The Puzzle of Parkinsons Disease; Thoughts on Writing; Island Connections; Arthritis News; Book: Tales of A Glasgow Childhood, 1994; Writers' Workshop Series; Happy Days in Rothesay, 1995; From Scotland's Past, 1996; Childhood Days in Glasgow, 1996. Contributions to: Various periodicals. Address: Tigh na Mara Cottage, 14 Ardbeg Road, Rothesay, Bute PA20 0NJ, Scotland.

CHAPMAN (Constance) Elizabeth, b. 5 Jan 1919. Writer. m. Frank Chapman, 22 Nov 1941, 3 sons. Education: College of Technology, Barnsley, 1938-39. Publications: Marmaduke the Lorry, 1953; Marmaduke and Joe, 1954; Riding with Marmaduke, 1955; Merry Marmaduke, 1957; Marmaduke and His Friends, 1958; Marmaduke and the Elephant, 1959; Marmaduke and the Lambs, 1960; Marmaduke Goes to France, 1961; Marmaduke Goes to Holland, 1963; Marmaduke Goes to America, 1965; Marmaduke Goes to Italy, 1970; Marmaduke Goes to Spain, 1978; Marmaduke Goes to Switzerland, 1977; Marmaduke Goes to Morocco, 1979; Marmaduke Goes to Wales, 1982; Marmaduke Goes to Scotland 1986; Marmaduke Goes to Ireland, 1987. Contributions to: Sunny Stories; Radio Short Stories, Listen With Mother; TV Short Stories, Rainbow. Address: 88 Grange Gardens, Pinner, Middlesex HA5 5QF, England.

CHAPMAN Ivan Douglas, b. 14 Feb 1919, Werris Creek, New South Wales, Australia. Journalist; Military Historian. m. Moria Helen Menzies, 12 Sept 1953, 3 daughters. Education: Sydney Technical College, 1946-47. Appointments: Journalist, ABC News Radio, 1947-52, TV, 1956-76, BBC News, Radio, 1952-54, TV, 1954-56, 1973-74; SBS News Radio, 1979-80. Publications: Details Enclosed; Iven G Mackay; Private Eddie Leonski; Toyko Calling. Contributions to: Australian Dictionary of Biography; Australian Encylopaedia; Weekend Australian; The Bulletin; British History Illustrated; Time Life Books. Memberships: Australian Society of Authors; National Press Club, Canberra; Journalists Club Sydney; Ex PoW Association of Australia. Address: c/o Australian Society of Authors, PO Box 1566, Strawberry Hills, New South Wales 2012, Australia.

CHAPMAN Jean, b. 30 Oct 1939, England. Writer. m. Lionel Alan Chapman, 24 Mar 1951, 1 son, 2 daughters. Education: BA (Hons), Open University, 1989. Appointments: Creative Writing Tutor for East Midlands Arts and Community Colleges. Publications: The Unreasoning Earth, 1981; Tangled Dynasty, 1984; Forbidden Path, 1986; Savage Legacy, 1987; The Bell Makers, 1990; Fortune's Woman, 1992; A World Apart, 1993; The Red Pavilion, 1995; The Soldier's Girl, 1997; Wide Range of Short Stories. Honours: Romantic Novel of Year, Short Listed, 1982, 1996; Kathleen Fidler Award, Short Listed, 1990. Memberships: Society of Authors; Romantic Novelists Association. Literary Agent: Jane Judd. Address: 3 Arnesby Lane, Peatling Magna, Leicester LE8 3UN, England.

CHAPMAN Richard Arnold, b. 15 Aug 1937, Bexleyheath, Kent, England. University Professor. Education: BA, 1961, PhD, 1966, University of Leicester; MA, Carleton University, 1962; DLitt, University of Leicester, 1989. Appointment: Emeritus Professor of Politics, University of Durham. Publications: Decision Making: The Higher Civil Service in Britain; Leadership in the British Civil Service; Ethics in the British Civil Service; The Art of Darkness. Contributions to: Public Policy and Administration; Review of Politics; International Review of Administrative Sciences; International Review of History and Political Science. Membership: Political Studies Association. Address: University of Durham, Department of Politics, 48 Old Elvet, Durham DH1 3LZ, England.

CHAPMAN Stanley D(avid), b. 31 Jan 1935, Nottingham, England. Professor; Writer. Education: BSc, London School of Economics and Political Science, 1956; MA, University of Nottingham, 1960; PhD, University of London, 1966. Appointments: Lecturer, 1968-73, Pasold Reader in Business History, 1973-, Professor, 1993-, University of Nottingham; Editor, Textile History Bi Annual. Publications: The Early Factory Masters, 1967; The Beginnings of Industrial Britain, 1970; The History of Working Class Housing, 1971; The Cotton Industry in the industrial Revolution, 1972; Jesse Boot of Boots the Chemists, 1974; The Devon Cloth Industry in the 18th Century, 1978; Stanton and Staveley, 1981; The Rise of Merchant Banking, 1984; Merchant Enterprise in Britain from the Industrial Revolution to World War I, 1992. Address: Birchlea, Beetham Close, Bingham, Notts NG13 8ED.

CHAPPELL Fred (Davis), b. 28 May 1936, Canton, North Carolina, USA. University Teacher; Poet; Writer. m. Susan Nicholls, 2 Aug 1959, 1 son. Education: BA 1961, MA 1964, Duke University. Appointment: Teacher, University of North Carolina at Greensboro, 1964-. Publications: Poetry: The World Between the Eyes, 1971; River, 1975; The Man Twiced Married to Fire, 1977; Bloodfire, 1978; Awakening to Music, 1979; Wind Mountain, 1979; Earthsleep, 1980; Driftlake: A Lieder Cycle, 1981; Midquest, 1981; Castle Tzingal, 1984; Source, 1985; First and Last Words, 1989; C: 100 Poems, 1993; Spring Garden: New and Selected Poems, 1995. Novels: It is Time, Lord, 1963; The Inkling, 1965; Dagon, 1968; The Gaudy Place, 1972; I Am One of You Forever, 1985; Brighten the Corner Where You Are, 1989; Farewell, I'm Bound to Leave You, 1996. Short Fiction: Moments of Light, 1980; More Shapes Than One, 1991. Collection: The Fred Chappell Reader, 1987. Other: Plow Naked: Selected Writings on Poetry, 1993. Honours: Rockefeller Grant, 1967-68; National Institute of Arts and Letters Award, 1968; Prix de Meilleur des Livres Etrangers, Académie Française, 1972; Sir Walter Raleigh Prize, 1972; Roanoke-Chowan Poetry Prizes, 1972, 1975, 1979, 1980, 1985, 1989; North Carolina Award in Literature, 1980; Bollingen Prize in Poetry, 1985; World Fantasy Awards, 1992, 1994; T S Eliot Prize, Ingersoll Foundation, 1993; Aiken Taylor Award in Poetry, 1996. Address: 305 Kensington Road, Greensboro, NC 27403, USA.

CHAPPELL Mollie, b. England. Publications: Little Tom Sparrow, 1950; The Gentle Giant, 1951; The Sugar and Spice, 1952; The Fortunes of Frick, 1953; Cat with No Fiddle, 1954; The Widow Jones, 1956; Endearing Young Charms, 1957; Bachelor Heaven, 1958; A Wreath of Holly, 1959; One Little Room, 1960; Come by Chance, 1963; The Wind in the Green Trees, 1969; The Hasting Day, 1970; Summer Story, Valley of Lilacs, 1972; Family Portrait, Cressy, 1972; Loving Heart, Country Air, 1977; Dearest Neighbour, 1981; Cousin Amelia, 1982; The Family at Redburn, 1985. Address: c/o Curtis Brown Ltd, Haymarket House, 28-29 Haymarket,London SW1Y 4SP, England.

CHAPPLE J(ohn) A(lfred) V(ictor), b. 25 Apr 1928, Barnstaple, Devonshire, England. Professor Emeritus; Writer. Education: BA, 1953, MA, 1955, University College, London. Appointments: Assistant, University College, 1953-55; Research Assistant, Yale University, 1955-58; Assistant Lecturer, Aberdeen University, 1958-59; Assistant Lecturer, 1959-61, Lecturer, 1961-67, Senior Lecturer, 1967-71, Manchester University; Professor, 1971-92, Professor Emeritus, 1992-, Hull University; Visiting Fellow, Corpus Christi College, Cambridge, 1991-92. Publications: The Letters of Mrs Gaskell, 1966; Documentary and Imaginative Literature 1800-1920, 1970; Elizabeth Gaskell: A Portrait in Letters, 1980; Science and Literature in the 19th Century, 1986; Private Voices: The Diaries of Elizabeth Gaskell and Sophia Holland, 1996; Elizabeth Gaskell: The Early Years, forthcoming. Memberships: Brontë Society; Gaskell Society; International Association of University Professors of English; Larkin Society. Address: 173 Newland Park, Hull, Yorkshire HU5 2DX, England.

CHARD Dorothy Doreen, (Judy Chard), b. 8 May 1916, Tuffley, Gloucestershire, England. Author: Freelance Journalist: Broadcaster.m. Maurice Noel Chard, 26 July 1941. Appointments: Editor, Devon Life Magazine; Tutor, Creative Writing, Devon County Council and WEA; Director of Studies, David and Charles Correspondence College; Critic, South West Arts, 1991; Course Leader, Writer's News Home Studies Division Correspondence College, 1992. Broadcaster, BBC and Local radio. Publications: Through the Green Woods, 1974; The Weeping and the Laughter, 1975; Encounter in Berlin, 1976; The Uncertain Heart, 1977; The Other Side of Sorrow, 1978; In the Heart of Love, 1979; Out of the Shadow, 1980; All Passion Spent, 1981; Seven Lonely Years, 1982; The Darkening Skies, 1982; When the Journey's Over, 1983; Haunted By the Past, 1984; Sweet Love Remembered, Where the Dream Begins, 1985; Rendevouz With Love, 1986; Hold Me in Your Heart, 1987; Live With Fear, 1987; Wings of the Morning, 1987; A Time to Love, 1987; Encounter in Spain, 1994; The Mysterious Lady of the Moor, 1994; Beatrice Chase, 1994; on audio cassette: For Love's Sake, To Be So Loved, Enchantment, Person Unknown, Appointment With Danger; 7 local books on Devon, The Devon Guide; Traditional Cooking. Contributions to: Columnist, Western Morning News, Plymouth, Heritage Magazine; magazines, national and local newspapers; Regular Broadcaster with BBC and Commercial Radio. Address: Morley Farm, Highweek, Newton Abbot, Devon TQ12 6NA, England.

CHARD Judy. See: **CHARD Dorothy Doreen.**

CHARLES Francis. See: **DE BONO Edward.**

CHARLES Gerda, b. 1930, Liverpool, England. Novelist. Education: Liverpool schools. Appointments: Journalist and Reviewer for New Statesman, Daily Telegraph, New York Times, Jewish Chronicle, and other periodicals; Television Critic, Jewish Observer, London, 1978-79. Publications: The True Voice, 1959; The Crossing Point, 1960; A Slanting Light, 1963; A Logical Girl, 1967; The Destiny Waltz, 1971; Several short stories. Honours: James Tait Black Memorial Prize, 1964; Whitbread Award, 1971. Address: 22 Cunningham Court, London W9 1AE, England.

CHARLES Nicholas. See: **KUSKIN Karla.**

CHARLIER Roger H(enri), b. 10 Nov 1924, Antwerp, Belgium (Belgian and US citizen). Geologist; Geographer; Oceanographer; Professor Emeritus; Writer. m. Patricia Mary Simonet, 17 June 1958, 1 son, 1 daughter. Education: Lic Pol and Ec Sc, 1941, Lic Sc, 1945, Free University of Brussels; PhD, Friedrich Alexander University, Erlangen, 1947; Diploma, Industrial College of the Armed Forces, Washington, DC, 1952; Postdoctoral Diploma, Graduate School of Geography, McGill University, 1953; LittD, 1957, ScD, 1958, University of Paris. Appointments: Professor of Geology, Geography and Oceanography, 1961-87, Professor Emeritus, 1988-, Northeastern University; Visiting Professor, 1970-74, 1983, 1984, Honorary Professor en Associé, 1986-, University of Bordeaux I; Professor Extraordinary, 1971-87, Professor Emeritus, 1988-, Free University of Brussels; Executive Director, Institute for the Development of Riverine and Estuarine Systems, 1974-76; Adjunct Professor, Union Graduate School, 1980-90; Member, European Community, XII General Directorate, Commission on Bioconversion, 1985-92; Scientific Advisor, SOPEX NV, Antwerp, 1988-89, HAECON NV, Ghent, 1984-88, 1989-. Publications: Ocean Resources: An Introduction to Economic Oceanography, 1976; Marine Science and Technology, 1981; Tidal Energy, 1982; Ocean Energies: Environmental, Economic and Social Significance, 1993. Contributions to: Numerous books, scholarly journals, and periodicals. Honours: Great Medal, University of Bordeaux, 1973; Fulbright Scholar, 1975, 1976; Paul-Henri Spaak Memorial Lecture Award, 1992; Various grants and awards. Memberships: Association of American University Professors; Geological Society of America; International Association for the History of Oceanography; Education Committees, Marine Technology Society; National Academy of Sciences, Letters and Arts, France; New Jersey Academy of Science; Royal Belgian Society for Geographical Studies. Address: 4055 North Keystone Avenue, Chicago, IL 60641, USA.

CHARLIP Remy, b. 10 Jan 1929, New York, New York, USA. Actor; Dancer; Choreographer; Director; Writer; Illustrator. Education: BFA, Cooper Union, 1949. Appointments: Choreographer, London Contemporary Dance Theatre, 1972-76, Scottish Theatre Ballet, 1973, Welsh Dance Theatre, 1974; Director, Remy Charlip Dance Co; Guest lecturer at colleges and universities. Publications: Handtalk: An ABC of Finger Spelling and Sign Language (with George Ancona and Mary Beth Miller), 1974; Hooray for Me! (with Lilian Moore), 1975; What Good Luck! What Bad Luck!, 1977; First Remy Charlip Reader, 1986; Handtalk Birthday: A Number and Story Book in Sign Language (with Mary Beth Miller), 1987; Various self-illustrated children's books. Other: Amaterasu (performance piece), 1988; Young Omelet (play), 1991. Honours: Ingram Merrill Awards, 1961, 1963; Obie Awards, 1965, 1966; 1st Prize, Bologna Book Fair, 1971; 2 Gulbenkian Awards, 1972; Boston Globe/Horn Book Award, 1976; Award for Professional Achievement, Cooper Union of Fine Arts, 1988. Address: 521 Precita Avenue, San Francisco, CA 94110, USA.

CHARNAS Suzy McKee, b. 22 Oct 1939, New York, New York, USA. Writer. m. Stephen Charnas, 4 Oct 1968, 1 stepson, 1 stepdaughter. Education: BA, Barnard College, 1961; MA, New York University, 1965. Appointments: Formerly English & History Teacher, Nigeria; Teacher, New Lincoln School; Community Mental Health Organisation Worker; Freelance Writer, 1969-; Judge, James Tiptree Award, 1991.Publications: Walk to the End of the World, 1974; Motherlines, 1979; The Vampire Tapestry, 1980; The Bronze King, 1985; Dorothea Dreams, 1986; The Silver Glove, 1988; The Golden Thread, 1989; The Kingdom of Kevin Malone, 1993; Stage Play, Vampire Dreams, Magic Theatre, 1990; The Furies, 1994. Contributions to: Womens Review of Books. Honours: Nebula Award, 1980; Hugo Award, 1989. Memberships: Authors Guild; Science Fictiopn Writers of America; Dramatists Guild. Literary Agent: Jennifer Lyons, Joan Daves Agency, USA. Address: 212 High Street North East, Albuquerque, NM 87102, USA.

CHARNY Carmi, (T Carmi), b. 31 Dec 1925, New York, New York, USA (Israeli citizen). Poet; Editor; Teacher. m. Lilach Peled, 3 sons. Education: BA, Yeshiva University, 1946; Graduate Studies, Columbia University, 1946, Sorbonne, Paris, 1946-47, Hebrew University, 1947, 1949-51. Appointments: Co-Editor, Massa, bi-weekly, Tel Aviv, 1951-54; Editor, Orot, quarterly, Jerusalem, 1955; Editor, Sifriat Hapoalim Publishers, Tel Aviv, 1957-62, Am Oved Publishers, Tel Aviv, 1963-70; Ziskind Visiting Professor of Humanities, Brandeis University, 1969-70; Adjunct Associate Professor, University of Tel Aviv, 1971-73; Editor-in-Chief, Ariel, quarterly, Jerusalem, 1971-74; Visiting Fellow, Oxford Centre for Postgraduate Hebrew Studies, 1974-76; Visiting Professor, Hebrew Union College, Jerusalem, 1978-; Visiting Professor, Stanford University, 1979, Yale University, 1986, New York University, 1986, University of Texas at Austin, 1987. Publications: Poetry: As T Carmi: Mum Vahalom, 1951; Eyn Prahim Shehorim, 1953; Sheleg Birushalayim, 1955; Hayam Ha'aharon, 1958; Nehash Hanehoshet, 1961, English translation as The Brass Serpent, 1964; Ha'unicorn Mistakel Bamar'ah, 1967; Tevi'ah, 1967; Davar Aher/Selected Poems, 1951-1969, 1970; Somebody Likes You, 1971; Hitnatslut Hamehaber, 1974; T Carmi and Dan Pagis: Selected Poems (with Dan Pagis), 1976; El Erets Aheret, 1977; Leyad Even Hato'im, 1981, English translation as At the Stone of Losses, 1983; Hatsi Ta'avati, 1984; Ahat Hi Li, 1985; Shirim Min Ha'azuva, 1989; Emet Vehova, 1993. Editor: As T Carmi: The Modern Hebrew Poem Itself (with Stanley Burnshaw and Ezra Spicehandler), 1965; The Penguin Book of Hebrew Verse, 1981. Other: Translations of plays into Hebrew. Contributions to: Periodicals. Honours: Brenner Prize for Literature, 1972; Prime Minister's Awards for Creative Writing, 1973, 1994; Jewish Memorial Foundation Grants, 1975, 1990; Kovner Award for Poetry, Jewish Book Council, 1978; Guggenheim Fellowship, 1987-88; Tel Aviv Foundation for Literature and Art Grant, 1988; Bialik Prize, 1990; Honorary Doctor of Humane Letters, Hebrew Union College, Jewish Institute of Religion, 1993. Memberships: Academy for the Hebrew Language; Writers Assocaition of Israel. Address: Hebrew

Union College, Jewish Institute of Religion, 13 King David Street, Jerusalem 94101, Israel.

CHARYN Jerome, b. 13 May 1937, New York, New York, USA. Author; Educator. Education: BA, Columbia College, 1959 Appointments: English Teacher, High School of Music and Art, School of Performing Arts, New York City, 1962-64; Assistant Professor, Stanford University, 1965-68; Professor, Herbert Lehman College, City University of New York, 1968-80; Founding Editor, The Dutton Review, 1970; Lecturer, Princeton University, 1980-86. Publications: Once Upon a Droshky, 1964; On the Darkening Green, 1965; Going to Jerusalem, 1967; American Scrapbook, 1969; The Single Voice: An Anthology of Contemporary Fiction, 1969; The Troubled Vision, 1970; The Tar Baby, 1973; Blue Eyes, 1975; Marilyn the Wild, 1976; The Franklin Scare, 1977; Secret Isaac, 1978; The Seventh Babe, 1979; Darlin Bill, 1980; Panna Maria, 1982; Pinocchio's Nose, 1983; The Isaac Quartet, 1984; Metropolis, 1986; Paradise Man, 1987; Movieland, 1989; The Good Policeman, 1990; Marias Girls, 1992; Montezuma's Man, 1993; Little Angel Street, 1994. Memberships: PEN; Mystery Writers of America; International Association of Crime Writers. Literary Agent: George Borchardt. Address: 302 West 12th Street, Apt 10c, New York, NY 10014, USA.

CHASE Elaine Raco, b. 31 Aug 1949, Schenectady, New York, USA. Author. m. Gary Dale Chase, 26 Oct 1969, 1 son, 1 daughter. Education: AA, Albany Business College, 1968; Union College, 1968; State University of New York, 1977. Publications: Rules of the Game, 1980; Tender Yearnings, 1981; A Dream Come True, 1982; Double Occupancy, 1982; Designing Woman, 1982; No Easy Way Out, 1983; Video Vixen, 1983; Best Laid Plans, 1983; Special Delivery, 1984; Lady Be Bad, 1984; Dare the Devil, 1987; Dark Corners, 1988; Partners in Crime, 1994; Amateur Detective (non-fiction), 1996; Rough Edges, 1997. Contributions to: Loves Leading Ladies and How to Write a Romance; Lovelines; So You Want a TV Career; Fine Art of Murder; Sex and The Mystery Novel; Who Are All These Sister's in Crime. Honours: Walden Book Award, 1985; Top Romantic Supsense Series Award, 1987-88. Memberships: Romance Writers of America; Sisters in Crime, national president, 1995-96. Address: 4333 Majestic Lane, Fairfax, VA 22033, USA.

CHASE Glen. See: **LEVINSON Leonard.**

CHASE Isobel. See: **DE GUISE Elizabeth (Mary Teresa).**

CHATTERTON-NEWMAN Roger, b. 17 Mar 1949, Haslemere, Surrey, England. Author. Appointments: Editorial Staff, Haymarket Publishing, 1970-89. Publications: A Hampshire Parish, 1976; Brian Boru, King of Ireland, 1983; Murtagh and the Vikings, 1986; Betwixt Petersfield and Midhurst, 1991; Edward Bruce: A Medieval Tragedy, 1992; Polo at Cowdray, 1992; Murtagh the Warrior, 1996. Contributions to: Hampshire Magazine; Horse and Hound; Polo Quarterly International; West Sussex History; Downs Country; International Polo Review. Honour: Commendation, Reading Association of Ireland Awards, 1987. Address: Rose Cottage, Rake, West Sussex GU33 7JA, England.

CHAUDHURI Amit, b. 15 May 1962, Calcutta, India. Author. m. Rinka Khastgir, 12 Dec 1991. Education: BA, University College, London, 1986; DPhil, Balliol College, Oxford, 1993. Appointment: Creative Arts Fellow, Wolfson College, Oxford, 1992-95. Publications: A Strange and Sublime Address, 1991; Afternoon Raag, 1993. Contributions to: Numerous publications. Honours: Betty Trask Award, 1991; Commonwealth Writers Prize, 1992; Southern Arts Literature Prize, 1993; Arts Council of Great Britain Writers Award, 1993-94; Encore Prize, Society of Authors, 1994. Address: 6 Sunny Park, Flat 10, 8th Floor, Calcutta 700019, India.

CHAWLA Jasbir, b. 20 June 1953, Etawah, India. Government Servant. m. Ravinder Kaur, 15 Oct 1980, 1 son, 2 daughters. Education: Diploma, Russian, 1974; BTech, 1976; MBA, 1990; Diploma, French, 1991. Appointment: Member, Editorial Panel, Vikas, 1984. Publications: Chernobyl, 1989; Roti Ki Gandh, 1990; Eh Nahin Awaz Khalistan Ki, 1991; Niche Wali Chitkhani, 1992; Punjab: Dararen Aurdalal, 1992; Janta Jaan Gayi, 1992. Contributions to: Various journals and periodicals. Honours: Award, Central Hindi Directorate, 1991; Diploma, Excellence for Poetry. Memberships: Authors Guild of India; PEN; Indian Institute of Metals; Institution of Engineers. Address: 247 Defence Colony, Jalandhar City 144001, India.

CHELEKIS George C, b. 21 Sept 1951, Ithaca, New York, USA. Author; Journalist. m. Gwen Content, 7 July 1979, 1 daughter. Education: BA summa cum laude, English Language and Literature, Ohio University, 1973. Publications: The Complete Guide to US Government Real Estate, 1989; The Action Guide to Government Auctions, 1989; Distress Sale!, 1990; The Magic of Credit, 1991; The Official Government Auction Guide, 1992; The Action Guide to Government Grants, Loans and Give-Aways, 1993. Contributions to: Nation's Business; Sky Magazine; Boardroom Reports; Consumer's Digest; Entrepreneur; Business; Bull and Bear. Honour: Gold Charlie, 1993. Memberships: American Society of Journalists and Authors; WISE; International Association of Scientologists. Literary Agent: Jane Gelfman. Address: PO Box 2401, Clearwater, FL 34617, USA.

CHELES Luciano, b. 7 Sept 1948, Cairo, Egypt. Senior Lecturer. Education: BA, Reading University, 1973; PGCE, Cardiff University, 1974; M Phil, Essex University, 1980; PhD, Lancaster University, 1992. Publications: The Studiolo of Urbino: An Iconographic Investigation; Neo-Fascism in Europe; L'affiche d'utilité publique en Italie 1975-1995, 1995; The Far Right in Western and Eastern Europe, 1995. Contributions to: Women in Italy; Atlante di Schifanoia; Le Muse e il Principe; Mots; Artension. Honour: Premio Frontino Montefeltro, 1992. Memberships: Society for Italian Studies; Society for Renaissance Studies; Istituto di Studi Rinascimentali; Association for the Study of Modern Italy. Address: Department of Italian Studies, Lonsdale College, Lancaster University, Lancaster LA1 4YN, England.

CHELTON John. See: **DURST Paul.**

CHEN Jo-Hsi, b. 15 Nov 1938, Taiwan. Novelist. Education: BA, Taiwan National University, 1961; MA, Johns Hopkins University, 1965. Appointments: Lecturer, University of California at Berkeley, 1983. Publications: Fiction: Mayor Yin, 1976; Selected works by Jo-Hsi Chen, 1976; The Old Man, 1978; Repatriation, 1978; The Execution of Mayor Yin, and Other Stories from the Great Proletarian Cultural Revolution, 1978; Inside and Outside the Wall, 1981; Tu Wei, 1983; Selected Short Stories by Jo-Hsi Chen, 1983; Foresight, 1984; The Two Hus, 1985; Paper Marriage, 1986; The Old Man and Other Stories, 1986; Other: Reminiscences of the Cultural Revolution, 1979; Random Notes, 1981; Democracy Wall and the Unofficial Journals, 1982; Read to Kill Time, 1983; Flower Grown Naturally, 1987; Trip to Tibet, 1988; Trip to Inner Mongolia, 1988; Temptation of the Tibetan Plateau. Honours: Wu Zhuoliu Prize, 1978. Address: 428 Boynton Avenue, Berkeley, CA 94707, USA.

CHENG Tsu-yu, b. 18 Mar 1916, China. Professor; Senior Research Fellow. m. Ting Kwee Choo, 1944, 1 son. Education: Diploma of Rhetoric, Institute of Language Teaching, Waseda University, Tokyo, Japan, 1964-65. Appointments: Visiting Professor, Graduate Division of Literature, Waseda University, Tokyo, Japan, 1964-65; Senior Research Fellow, Institute of Chinese Studies, Chinese University of Hong Kong, 1984-; Professor, Daito Bunka University, 1986-; Visiting Professor, Peking University, 1992-. Publications: Poetry and Poetics of Lu Xun, 1951; Criticism of the Works of Huang Zunxian, 1959; Tokyo Lectures, 1963; Evolution of Chinese Rhetoric, 1965; Sinological Research in Japan, 1972; The History of Chinese Rhetoric, 1984; Rhetorical Criticism of the Works of the Eight Prose Masters of the Tang and Song Dynasties, 1992. Contributions to: Journals. Honours: Advisory Professor at Fudan University, Shanghai, 1986-; Advisor, South China Rhetorical Society, Shanghai, 1986-; Honorary Councillor and Academic Consultant, China Rhetorical Society, Peking, 1987. Memberships: China Society, Singapore; Member, Councillor, Honorary Secretary, Editor, South Seas Society, 1949-62. Address: Institute of Chinese Studies, Chinese University of Hong Kong, Shatin, NT, Hong Kong.

CHERNOW Ron, b. 3 Mar 1949, New York, New York, USA. Author. m. Valerie Stearn, 22 Oct 1979. Education: BA, Yale College, 1970; MA, Pembroke College, Cambridge, 1972. Publications: The House of Morgan: An American Banking Dynasty and the Rise of Modern Finance, 1990; The Warburgs: The Twentieth-Century Odyssey of a Remarkable Jewish Family, 1993. Contributions to: Various periodicals. Honours: Jack London Award, United Steelworkers of America, 1980; National Book Award, 1990; Ambassador Book Award, English-Speaking Union of the United States, 1990. Memberships: Authors Guild; Phi Beta Kappa. Address: c/o Melanie Jackson, 250 West 57th Street, Suite 1119, New York, NY 10107, USA.

CHERRY Carolyn Janice, (C J Cherryh), b. 1 Sept 1942, St Louis, Missouri, USA. Writer. Education: BA, University of Oklahoma, 1964; MA, Johns Hopkins University, 1965. Publications: The Faded Sun, 1978; Downbelow Station, 1981; The Pride of Chanur, 1982; Chanur's Venture, 1984; Forty Thousand in Gehenna, 1984; Cuckoo's Egg, 1985; Chanur's Homecoming, 1986; Visible Light, 1986; Angel with the Sword, 1987; The Paladin, 1988; Rusalka, 1989; Rimrunners, 1990; Chernevog, 1991; Heavy Time, 1991; Chanur's Legacy, 1992; The Goblin Mirror, 1993; Hellburner, 1993; Faery in Shadow, 1994; Tripoint, 1994; Fortress in the Eye of Time, 1995; Invader, 1995; Rider at the Gate, 1995; Cloud's Rider, 1996; Lois and Clark, 1996; Inheritor, 1996. Honours: John Campbell Award, 1977; Hugo Awards, 1979, 1982, 1989. Memberships: National Space Society; Science Fiction Writers of America. Address: c/o Warner Books Inc, 1271 Avenue of the Americas, New York, NY 10020, USA.

CHERRY Kelly, b. Baton Rouge, Louisiana, USA. Professor in the Humanities; Writer; Poet. m. Jonathan B Silver, 23 Dec 1966, div 1969. Education: Du Pont Fellow, University of Virginia, 1962-63; University of North Carolina, MFA, 1967; Assistant Associate Professor, 1977-82, Professor 1982-83, Romnes Professor of English, 1983-88, Evjue-Bascom Professor in the Humanities, 1993-, University of Wisconsin at Madison; Writer-in-Residence, Southwest State University, Marshall, Minnesota, 1974, 1975; Visiting Professor and Distinguished Writer-in-Residence, Western Washington University, 1981; Faculty, MFA Program, Vermont College, 1982, 1983; Distinguished Visiting Professor, Rhodes College, Tennessee, 1985. Publications: Fiction: Sick and Full of Burning, 1974; Augusta Played, 1979; Conversion, 1979; In the Wink of an Eye, 1983; The Lost Traveller's Dream, 1984; My Life and Dr Joyce Brothers, 1990. Poetry: Lovers and Agnostics, 1975, revised edition, 1995; Relativity: A Point of View, 1977; Songs for a Soviet Composer, 1980; Natural Theology, 1988; Benjamin John, 1993; God's Loud Hand, 1993; Time Out of Mind, 1994; Death and Transfiguration, 1997. Other: The Exiled Heart: A Meditative Autobiography, 1991; Writing the World (essays and criticism), 1995. Contributions to: Anthologies and periodicals. Honours: Canaras Award, 1974; Bread Loaf Fellow, 1975; Yaddo Fellow, 1979, 1989; National Endowment for the Arts Fellowship, 1979; Romnes Fellowship, 1983; Wisconsin Arts Board Fellowships, 1984, 1989, 1994; Hanes Prize for Poetry, Fellowship of Southern Writers, 1989; Wisconsin Notable Author, 1991; Hawthornden Fellowship, Scotland, 1994; E B Coker Visiting Writer, Converse, 1996. Membership: Associated Writing Programs, Board of Directors, 1990-93. Address: c/o Department of English, University of Wisconsin at Madison, Madison, WI 53706, USA.

CHERRYH C J. See: **CHERRY Carolyn Janice.**

CHESSEX Jacques, b. 1 Mar 1934, Payerne, France. Novelist; Poet. Education: Graduated, University of Lausanne, 1961. Publications: La Tête ouverte, 1962; La Confession du pasteur Burg, 1967; A Father's Love, 1973; L'Ardent Royaume, 1975; Le Séjour des morts, 1977; Les Yeux jaunes, 1979; Où vont mourir les oiseaux, 1980; Judas le transparent, 1983; Jonas, 1987; Morgane Madrigal, 1990; Verse: Le Jour proche, 1954; Chant du printemps, 1955; Une Voix la nuit, 1957; Batailles dans l'air, 1959; Le Jeûne de huit nuits, 1966; L'Ouvert obscur, 1967; Elégie, soleil du regret, 1976; La Calviniste, 1983; Feux d'orée, 1984; Comme l'os, 1988; Also: Maupassant et les autres, 1981; Mort d'un cimetière, 1989; Flaubert, ou, le désert en abîme, 1991. Honour: Prix Goncourt, 1973. Address: Editions Grasset, 61 Rue des Sts-Pères, 75006 Paris, France.

CHESTER Tessa Rose, b. 19 Oct 1950, Stanmore, Middlesex, England. Museum Curator. m. (1) Richard James Overy, 18 Apr 1969, 1 son, 2 daughters, (2) Ronald Albert Chester, 8 Aug 1980. Education: Harrow Art College, 1968-69; BA (Hons), Polytechnic of North London, 1977-81. Appointment: Curator of Childrens Books, Bethnal Green Museum of Childhood, London, 1982-. Publications: A History of Children's Book Illustration; Childrens' Books Research; Sources of Information About Childrens' Books; Provisions of Light, poetry, 1996. Contributions to: Times Educational Supplement; Phaedrus; International Review of Childrens' Literature and Librarianship; Galleries; The Library; Signal; Country Life. Memberships: Childrens Books History Society; Beatrix Potter Society; Poetry Society; British Haiku Society; Society of Authors. Address: Bethnal Green Museum of Childhood, Cambridge Heath Road, London E2 9PA, England.

CHEYNEY-COKER Syl, b. 28 June 1945, Freetown, Sierra Leone. Professor; Poet. Education: University of California, 1970;

University of Wisconsin, Madison, 1971-72. Appointments: Visiting Professor, University of the Philippines, Quezon City, 1975-77; Senior Lecturer, University of Maiduguri, Nigeria, 1979-. Publications: Concero for an Exile, 1972; The Graveyard Also has Teeth, 1974. Honour: Ford Foundation Grant, 1970. Address: University of Maiduguri, Department of English, PMB 1069, Maiduguri, Nigeria.

CHILDS David Haslam, b. 25 Sept 1933, Bolton, England. University Professor. m. 13 June 1964, 2 sons. Education: BSc (Econ) London University, 1956; British Council Scholarship, Hamburg University, 1956-57; PhD, London University, 1962. Appointments: Former Editor PASGAS - Politics and Society in Germany Austria and Switzerland, 1988-92. Publications: GDR Moscow's German Ally (2nd edition, 1988); Britain since 1945 (3rd edition, 1992); Germany since 1918 (2nd edition, 1980); Marx and the Marxists, 1973; East Germany, 1969; East Germany to the 1990s, 1987; West Germany Politics and Society (2nd edition, 1981); Germany on the Road to Unity, 1990; Germany in the 20th Century, 1991; Britain Since 1939: Progress and Decline, 1995; The Stasi, The East German Intelligence and Security System, 1996. Contributions to: Tablet; Political Studies; Anglo-German Review; Contemporary Review; Current History; Journal of Contemporary History; Times; Independent; International Affairs; Daily Telegraph; World Today; Intelligence and National Security; German Politics. Address: 1 Grange Park, West Bridgford, Nottingham NG2 6HW, England.

CHILDS Elizabeth Catharine, b. 5 July 1954, Denver, Colorado, USA. Professor of Art History. m. John R Klein, 7 June 1987, 1 son. Education: BA, Wake Forest University, 1976; MA, Art History 1980, PhD Art History 1989, Columbia University. Appointment: Florence Gould Fellow, Department of Art History, Princeton University, 1992-93. Publications: Handbook to the Peggy Guggenheim Collection (co-author), 1986; Honore Daumier: A Thematic Guide to the Oeuvre (editor), 1989; Femme d'Esprit: Women in Daumier's Caricature (co-author), 1990; Suspended Licenses: Essays in the History of Art and Censorship (editor), 1997. Contributions to: American Art; Art Journal. Honour: National Endowment for the Humanities University Fellowship, 1996-97; National Gallery of Art, Washington, DC, visiting senior fellow, 1997. Address: Department of Art History, Campus Box 1189, Washington University, St Louis, MO 63130, USA.

CHILVER Peter, b. 18 Nov 1933, Southend, Essex, England. Educator; Writer. Education: BA, 1956, MA, 1964, St Edmund Hall, Oxford; Diploma in Speech and Drama, Royal Academy of Dramatic Art, London, 1963; Postgraduate Certificate of Education, 1965, Academic Diploma in Education, 1969, MPhil, 1973, PhD, 1976, University of London. Appointments: Teacher, Inner London Education Authority, 1964-68; Senior Lecturer, Thomas Hucley College, 1968-77; Head of Department of English, Langdon School, 1977-. Publications: Improvised Drama, 1967; Talking Improvisation, 1969; Producing the Play, 1974; Teaching Improvised Dramas, 1978; Learning and Language in the Classroom, 1982; In the Picture Series, 1985; English Coursework for GCSE, 1987. Contributions to: Perspectives on Small Group Learning, 1990. Address: 27 Cavendish Gardens, Barking, Essex, England.

CHINERY Michael, b. 5 June 1938, London, England. Author. Education: MA, Jesus College, Cambridge, 1960. Publications: Pictorial Dictionary of the Animal World, 1966; with Michael Gabb: Human Kind, 1966, The World of Plants, 1966, The Life of Animals with Backbones, 1966; Patterns of Living (with David Larkin), 1966; Breeding and Growing, 1966; Pictorial Dictionary of the Plant World, 1967; Visual Biology, 1968; Purnell's Concise Encyclopedia of Nature, 1971; Animal Communities, 1972; Animals in the Zoo, 1973; Field Guide to the Insects of Britain and Northern Europe, 1973; Life In the Zoo, 1976; The Natural History of the Garden, 1977; The Family Naturalist, 1977; Nature All Around, 1978; Discovering Animals, 1978; Killers of the Wild, 1979; Garden Birds (with Maurice Pledger), 1979; Collins Gem Guide to Butterflies and Moths, 1981; The Natural History of Britain and Europe, 1982; Collins Guide to the Insects of Britain and Western Europe, 1986; Garden Creepy Crawlies, 1986; The Living Garden, 1986; Collins Gem Guide to Insects, 1986; Exploring the Countryside, 1987; Butterflies and Day-Flying Moths of Britain and Europe, 1989; All About Baby Animals; Countryside Handbook, 1990; Shark; Butterfly; Ant; Spider; Snake; Frog (6 Children's Books), 1991; All About Wild Animals, 1991; Explore the World of Insects, 1991; Wild World of Animals: Rainforests 1991, Oceans 1991, Deserts 1991, Grasslands and Prairies 1991, Seashores 1992, Forests 1992, Polar Lands 1992, Lakes and Rivers 1992; The Kingfisher Natural History of

Britain and Europe, 1992; Spiders, 1993. Address: Mousehole, Mill Road, Hundon, Suffolk C010 8EG, England.

CHINERY William Addo, b. 5 Apr 1934, Ghana. Biomedical Scientist; University Professor. m. Bertha Catherine Laing, 3 Sept 1966, 4 sons. Education: BSc, Hons, 1959; DAP&E, 1961; PhD, 1963, London, England. Appointments: Government Medical Entomologist, Ministry of Health, Ghana, 1959; Research Officer, National Institute of Health and Medical Research, 1964; Lecturer, Senior Lecturer, Associate Professor, Ghana Medical School, 1968-80; Visiting Associate Professor, Harvard School of Public Health, USA, with ranking as Full Professor when participating in teaching at the Harvard Medical School, 1976-77; Professor, Ghana Medical School, 1980-; Head of Microbiology Department, 1986-94; Member, Expert Advisory Panel, Vector Biol and Cont. World Health Organisation, 1976-85; Member, Editorial Board, Ghana Journal of Science, 1973-76. Publications: Author of over 65 scientific communications in Medical Entomology and Parasitology, Tropical Medicine and Public Health; Author of some 8 literary papers. Honours: Distinguished Student, London School of Hygiene and Tropical Medicine, 1974; One of three leading mosquito vector workers in Africa, WHO, 1985; Life Deputy Governor, ABIRA (ABI), 1989; Member, Advisory Council, IBA (IBC), 1990; KCMSS, 1990; Knight of Humanity KH, 1990; International Order of Merit (IBC), 1991; Fellow, Institute of Biology (UK), 1993; Fellow, World Literary Academy (FWLA-IBC), 1993. Memberships: Fellow, Royal Society of Tropical Medicine and Hygiene; Ghana Science Association; Institute of Biology, UK; Member and Executive Council Member, Ghana Institute for Laboratory Medicine, 1994. Address: University of Ghana Medical School, PO Box 4236, Accra, Ghana.

CHISSELL Joan Olive, b. 22 May 1919, Cromer, Norfolk, England. Musicologist. Education: ARCM, GRSM, Royal College of Music, 1937-42. Appointments: Piano Teacher, Royal College of Music Junior Department, 1942-53; Lecturer, Extra-Mural Departments, Oxford and London Universities, 1942-48; Assistant Music Critic, The Times, 1948-79; Reviewer, The Gramophone, 1968-; Broadcaster, BBC, 1943-; Jury Member, International Piano Competitions, Milan, Leeds, Zwickau, Budapest, Sydney and Dublin. Publications: Robert Schumann, 1948; Chopin, 1965; Schumann's Piano Music, 1972; Brahms, 1977; Clara Schumann: A Dedicated Spirit, 1983. Contributions to: A Companion to the Concerto, 1988; Numerous Journals and Magazines. Honour: City of Zwickau Robert Schumann Prize, 1991. Memberships: Critics Circle; Royal College of Music Union; Royal Life Boat Society. Address: Flat D, 7 Abbey Road, St Johns Wood, London NW8 9AA, England.

CHITHAM Edward Harry Gordon, b. 16 May 1932, Harborne, Birmingham, England. Education Consultant. m. Mary Patricia Tilley, 29 Dec 1962, 1 son, 2 daughters. Education: BA, MA (Classics), Jesus College, Cambridge, 1952-55; PGCE, University of Birmingham, 1955-56; MA, English, University of Warwick, 1973-77 part-time; PhD, University of Sheffield, 1978-83. Publications: Ghost in the Water, 1972; The Black Country, 1973; The Poems of Anne Brontë, 1979; Brontë Facts and Brontë Problems (with T J Winnifrith), 1983; Selected Brontë Poems (with T J Winnifrith), 1985; The Brontës' Irish Background, 1986; A Life of Emily Brontë, 1987; Charlotte and Emily Brontë (Macmillans Literary Lives, with T J Winnifrith), 1989; A Life of Anne Brontë, 1991; A Bright Start, 1995; The Poems of Emily Brontë (with Derek Roper), 1996. Contributions to: Byron Journal; Gaskell Society Journal; ISIS Magazine. Memberships: Joint Association of Classics Teachers. Gaskell Society; Brontë Society, Former Honorary Publications Secretary and Editor, Brontë Society Transactions. Address: 11 Victoria Road, Harborne, Birmingham B17 0AG, England.

CHITNIS Anand Chidamber, b. 4 Apr 1942, Birmingham, England. Principal. m. Bernice Anne, 4 July 1970, 2 sons, 1 daughter. Education: Stonyhurst College, Lancashire, 1949-60; University of Birmingham, 1960-63; University of Kansas, 1963-65; University of Edinburgh, 1965-68. Publications: The Scottish Enlightenment: A Social History; The Scottish Enlightenment and Early Victorian English Society. Contributions to: Annals of Science; Enlightenment Essays; Medical History; Studies in Voltaire and the Eighteenth Century. Honour: Fellowship, Royal Historical Society. Memberships: Catholic Union of Great Britain; British Society for 18th Century Studies; 18th Century Scottish Studies Society. Literary Agent: David Higham Associates. Address: LSU College of Higher Education, The Avenue, Southampton SO17 1BG, England.

CHITTOCK John (Dudley), b. 29 May 1928. Editor; Publisher; Writer. m. Joyce Kate Winter, 23 Aug 1947. Education: South West Technical College. Appointments: Executive Editor, Focal Press, 1954-58; Part-Time Editor, Industrial Screen, 1962-63; Film and Video Columnist, Financial Times, 1963-87; Founder/Publisher, 1971-96, Editor, 1971-74, Screen Digest; Inaugural Editor, Vision (British Academy of Film and Television Arts), 1976; Consultant Editor, Television: Journal of the Royal Television Society, 1978-82; Founder/Publisher, Training Digest, 1978-87. Publications: Focal Encyclopedia of Photography, executive editor, 1956; How to Produce Magnetic Sound for Films, 1962; Film and Effect, 1967; An International Directory of Stock Shot Libraries, executive editor, 1969; Images of Britain, 1986. Honours: Hood Medal, Royal Photographic Society, 1973; Queen's Silver Jubilee Medal, 1977; Presidential Award, Incorporated Institute of Professional Photography, 1983; Video Writer of the Year Award, 1983; Officer of the Order of the British Empire; Fellow, British Kinematograph, Sound, and Television Society; Fellow, Royal Photographic Society; Fellow, Royal Television Society. Memberships: Royal Society of Arts; Royal Automobile Club, London. Address: 37 Gower Street, London WC1E 6HH, England.

CHITTY Sir Thomas Willes, (Thomas Hinde), b. 2 Mar 1926, England. Author. m. Susan Elspeth, 1951, 1 son, 3 daughters. Education: University College, Oxford. Appointments: Granada Arts Fellow, University of York, 1964-65; Visiting Lecturer, University of Illinois, 1965-67; Visiting Professor, Boston University, 1969-70. Publications: Fiction: Mr Nicholas, 1952; Happy as Larry, 1957; For the Good of the Company, 1961; A Place Like Home, 1962; The Cage, 1962; Ninety Double Martinis, 1963; The Day the Call Came, 1964; Games of Chance: The Interviewer and the Investigator, 1965; The Village, 1966; High, 1968; Bird, 1970; Generally a Virgin, 1972; Agent, 1974; Our Father, 1975; Daymare, 1980. Non-Fiction: Spain, 1963; On Next to Nothing (with wife), 1976; The Great Donkey Walk (with wife), 1977; The Cottage Book, 1979; Sir Henry and Sons (autobiography), 1980; A Field Guide to the English Country Parson, 1983; Stately Gardens of Britain, 1985; Capability Brown, 1986; The Domesday Book: England's Heritage, Then and Now (editor), 1986; Courtiers: 900 Years of Court Life, 1986; Tales from the Pumproom: An Informal History of Bath, 1988; Imps of Promise: A History of the King's School, Canterbury, 1990; Looking Glass Letters, 1991; Paths of Progress: A History of Marlborough College, 1993; A History of Highgate School, 1993; A History of King's College School, 1994; Carpenter's Children: A History of the City of London School, 1995; An Illustrated History of the University of Greenwich, 1996. Address: Bow Cottage, West Hoathly, Sussex RH19 4QF, England.

CHITTY Susan, b. 18 Aug 1929. Freelance Writer, Lecturer and Journalist. Publications: The Diary of a Fashion Model, 1958; The Intelligent Woman's Guide to Good Taste (editor), 1958; White Huntress, 1963; My Life and Horses, 1966; The Woman Who Wrote Black Beauty, 1971; The Beast and the Monk: A Life of Charles Kingsley, 1975; On Next to Nothing (with Thomas Hinde), 1975; Charles Kingsley's Landscape, 1976; The Great Donkey Walk (with Thomas Hinde), 1977; The Young Rider, 1979; Gwen John, 1981; Now To My Mother, 1985; Edward Lear, 1988; Davies of Antonia White (editor), 1991, 1992. Address: Bow Cottage, West Hoathly, Sussex RH19 4QF, England.

CHIU Hungdah, b. 23 Mar 1936, Shanghai, China. Professor of Law; Author; Editor. m. Yuan-yuan Hsieh, 14 May 1966, 1 son. Education: LLB, National Taiwan University, 1958; MA, Long Island University, 1962; LLM, 1962, SJD, 1965, Harvard University. Appointments: Associate in Research, East Asian Research Center, 1964-65; Research Associate in Law, 1966-70, 1972-74, Harvard University; Associate Professor of International Law, National Chengchi University, 1970-72; Associate Professor of Law, 1974-77, Professor of Law, 1977-, University of Maryland at Baltimore; General Editor, Occasional Papers/Reprints Series in Contemporary Asian Studies, 1977-; Editor-in-Chief, Chinese Yearbook of International Law and Affairs, 1981-; Research Member, 1991-95, Member, 1995-, National Unification Council, Republic of China; Minister without Portfolio (Minister of State), Executive Yuan (Cabinet), Republic of China, 1993-94; Affilate Faculty Member, University of Maryland at College Park, 1995-. Publications: China and the Taiwan Issue (editor and contributor), 1979; The Chinese Connection and Normalization (co-editor), 1980; Agreements of the People's Republic of China, 1966-1980: A Calendar, 1981; Multi-system Nations and International Law: The International Status of Germany, Korea and China (co-editor and contributor), 1981; China: 70 Years After the 1911 Hsin-hai

Revolution (co-editor and contributor), 1984; Criminal Justice in Post-Mao China, Analysis and Documents (co-author), 1985; The Future of Hong Kong, Toward 1997 and Beyond (co-editor and contributor), 1987; Survey of Recent Developments in China (Mainland and Taiwan) in 1985-86 (editor), 1987; The United States Constitution and Constitutionalism in China (co-editor), 1988; The Draft Basic Law of Hong Kong: Analysis and Documents (editor), 1988; The International Law of the Sea: Cases, Documents and Readings (co-author), 1991; Proceedings of the International Law Association (ILA) First Asian-Pacific Regional Conference (with Su Yun Chang, Chun-i Chen, and Chih-Yu Wu), 1996. Contributions to: Many scholarly journals. Honours: Certificate of Merit, American Society of International Law, 1976; Toulmin Medal, Society of American Military Engineers, 1982; Outstanding Achievement Award, Mid-America Chinese Science and Technology Association, 1991; 1st Class Merit Service Award, Executive Yuan (Cabinet), Republic of China, 1994. Memberships: American Association for Chinese Studies, president, 1985-87; Association of Chinese Social Scientists in North America, president, 1984-86; Chinese Society of International Law, president, 1993-. Address: c/o Department of Government and Politics, University of Maryland at College Park, College Park, MD 20742, USA.

CHODES John Jay, b. 23 Feb 1939, New York, New York, USA. Writer. Education: BA, Hunter College, City University of New York, 1963; Commercial Photography Certificate, Germain School of Photography, 1965. Appointments: Technical Advisor to Dustin Hoffman, Paramount Pictures Film Marathon Man. Publications: The Myth of America's Military Power, 1972; Corbitt, 1973; Bruce Jenner, 1977; Plays, Avenue A Anthology, 1969; Molineaux, 1979; Frederick Two, 1985; The Longboat, 1987; Molineaux (as Musical), 1995; A Howling Wilderness, forthcoming. Contributions to: Articles on Education, Politics, Social Issues. Honours: Journalistic Excellence Award, 1974; Outstanding Service Award, 1988. Memberships: Dramatists Guild; Professors World Peace Academy; Road Runners Club of New York; Libertarian Party of New York; Southern League. Literary Agent: Stephan Rosenberg. Address: 411 East 10th Street, 22G, New York, NY 10009, USA.

CHOMSKY (Avram) Noam, b. 7 Dec 1928, Philadelphia, Pennsylvania, USA. Linguist; Philosopher; Professor; Author. m. Carol Doris Schatz, 24 Dec 1949, 1 son, 2 daughters. Education: BA, 1949, MA, 1951, PhD, 1955, University of Pennsylvania. Appointments: Assistant to Professor of Modern Languages, 1955-66, Ferrari P Ward Professor of Modern Languages and Linguistics, 1966-76, Institute Professor, 1976-, Massachusetts Institute of Technology; John Locke Lecturer, Oxford University, 1969; Nehru Memorial Lecturer, University of New Delhi, 1972; Whidden Lecturer, McMaster University, 1975; Huizinga Memorial Lecturer, University of Leiden, 1977; Jeanette K Watson Distinguished Visiting Professor, Syracuse University, 1982. Publications include: Language and Mind, 1968; At War with Asia, 1970; The Backroom Boys, 1973; The Logical Structure of Linguistic Theory, 1975; The Political Economy of Human Rights (with Edward Herman), 2 volumes, 1979; Towards a New Cold War, 1982; Turning the Tide, 1985; Pirates and Emperors, 1986; On Power and Ideology, 1987; The Chomsky Reader, 1987; Deterring Democracy, 1991; Year 501: The Conquest Continues, 1993; Letters From Lexington: Reflections on Propaganda, 1993; Language and Thought, 1994; World Orders, Old and New, 1994. Honours: Lannan Literary Award, 1992; Joel Selden Peace Award, Psychologists for Social Responsibility, 1993; Homer Smith Award, New York University School of Medicine, 1994; Loyola Mellon Humanities Award, Loyola University, Chicago, 1994; Many honorary doctorates. Memberships: American Academy of Arts and Sciences; Fellow, American Association for the Advancement of Science; Corresponding Member, British Academy. Address: 15 Suzanne Road, Lexington, MA 02173, USA.

CHORLTON David, b. 15 Feb 1948, Spittal-an-der-Drau, Austria. Writer; Artist. m. Roberta, 21 June 1976. Education: Burnage Grammar School, Manchester, 1959-64; Stockport College, 1966-69. Publications: The Village Painters, chapbook, 1990; Forget the Country You Came From, 1992; Outposts, 1994. Contributions to: Poems in Poet Lore, the Devil's Millhopper, Cumberland Poetry Review. Memberships: PEN USA West; The Writer's Voice. Address: 118 West Palm Lane, Phoenix, AZ 85003, USA.

CHOROSINSKI Eugene Conrad, b. 1 Jan 1930, Sienno, Poland. Author; Poet. Education: University Studies, 4 years. Publication: Through the Years, 1995; Contributions to: Year's Best Poems of 1995

and 1996, National Library of Poetry. Honours: 4 Editor's Choice Awards, 1994, 1995. Membership: International Society of Poets. Address: 131 Madrona Drive, Eustis, FL 32726, USA.

CHOYCE Lesley, b. 21 Mar 1951, Riverside, New Jersey, USA (Canadian citizen). Professor; Writer; Poet; Editor. m. Terry Paul, 19 Aug 1974, 2 daughters. Education: BA, Rutgers University, 1972; MA, Montclair State College, 1974; MA, City University of New York, 1983. Appointments: Editor, Pottersfield Press, 1979-; Professor, Dalhousie University, 1986-. Publications: Adult Fiction: Eastern Sure, 1981; Billy Botzweiler's Last Dance, 1984; Downwind, 1984; Conventional Emotions, 1985; The Dream Auditor, 1986; Coming Up for Air, 1988; The Second Season of Jonas MacPherson, 1989; Magnificent Obsessions, 1991; Ectasy Conspiracy, 1992; Margin of Error, 1992; The Republic of Nothing, 1994; The Trap Door to Heaven, 1996. Young Adult Fiction: Skateboard Shakedown, 1989; Hungry Lizards, 1990; Wavewatch, 1990; Some Kind of Hero, 1991; Wrong Time, Wrong Place, 1991; Clearcut Danger, 1992; Full Tilt, 1993; Good Idea Gone Bad, 1993; Dark End of Dream Street, 1994; Big Burn, 1995; Falling Through the Cracks, 1996. Poetry: Re-Inventing the Wheel, 1980; Fast Living, 1982; The End of Ice, 1985; The Top of the Heart, 1986; The Man Who Borrowed the Bay of Fundy, 1988; The Coastline of Forgetting, 1995. Non-Fiction: An Avalanche of Ocean, 1987; December Six: The Halifax Solution, 1988; Transcendental Anarchy (autobiography), 1993; Nova Scotia: Shaped by the Sea, 1996. Editor: Chezzetcook, 1977; The Pottersfield Portfolio, 7 volumes, 1979-85; Visions from the Edge (with John Bell), 1981; The Cape Breton Collection, 1984; Ark of Ice: Canadian Futurefiction, 1992. Honours: Event Magazine's Creative Nonfiction Competition Winner, 1990; Dartmouth Book Awards, 1990, 1995; Ann Connor Brimer Award for Children's Literature, 1994; Authors Award, Foundation for the Advancement of Canadian Letters, 1995. Address: 83 Leslie Road, E Lawrencetown, Nova Scotia B2Z 1P8, Canada.

CHRAIBI Driss, b. 15 July 1926, El Jadida, Morocco. Novelist. m. Sheena McCallion, 1978. Education: Studied in Casablanca and Paris. Appointments: Professor, University of Laval, Quebec, 1969-70. Publications: The Simple Past, 1954; The Butts, 1955; L'Ane, 1956; De Tous les Horizons, 1958; La Foule, 1961; Heirs to the Past, 1962; Un ami viendra vous voir, 1966; La Mother Comes of Age, 1982; Mort au Canada, 1974; Une Enquête au Pays, 1981; Mother Spring, 1982; Birth at Dawn, 1986; L'Homme du livre, 1994; Radio plays. Honour: Société des Auteurs Prize, 1990. Address: 15 rue Paul Pons, 26400 Crest, France.

CHRISTIAN Carol Cathay, b. 15 Nov 1923, Peking, China. Freelance Writer and Editor. m. John Christian, 23 June 1945, 3 sons, 1 daughter. Education: BA, magna cum laude, Smith College, Northampton, Massachusetts, USA, 1944. Publications: Into Strange Country, 1958; God and One Redhead, Mary Slessor of Calabar, (biography with G Plummer), 1970; Editor, In the Spirit of Truth, a reader in the work of Frank Lake, 1991; EFL Readers: Great People of Our Time, 1973; Johnny Ring, 1975; More People of Our Time, 1978; Famous Women of the 20th Century (with Diana Christian), 1982; Save the Goldfish, 1988; Macmillan Bible Stories, 12 titles, 1996. Memberships: Society of Authors; Clinical Theology Association. Address: 20 Pitfold Avenue, Shottermill, Haslemere, Surrey GU27 1PN, England.

CHRISTIAN John. See: **DIXON Roger.**

CHRISTIANSEN Rupert, b. 1954, England. Appointments: Editor, Oxford University Press, 1979-82; Freelance writer and editor, 1982; Spectator opera critic, 1990-94; Daily Telegraph, 1996-. Publications: Prima Donna: A History, 1984; Romantic Affinities: Portraits from an Age 1780-1830, 1988; The Grand Obsession: A Collins Anthology of Opera, 1988; Contemporary Music Review (editor with Paul Driver), 1989; Tales from the New Babylon: Paris 1869-1875, 1994; Cambridge Arts Theatre: Celebrating 60 Years (editor), 1997. Address: c/o A D Peters, The Chambers, Chelsea Harbour, Lots Road, London SW10, England.

CHRISTIE Ian Ralph, b. 11 May 1919, Preston, Lancashire, England. Retired University Teacher. Education: BA, 1948, MA, 1948, Magdalen College, Oxford. Appointments: War Service, RAF, Britain, West Africa and India, 1940-46; Assistant Lecturer in History, 1948; Lecturer, 1951; Reader, 1960; Professor of Modern British History, 1966-79; Dean of Arts, 1971-73; Chairman, History Department, 1975-79; Astor Professor of British History, 1979-84; Professor

Emeritus and Honorary Research Fellow, 1984-, University College, London. Publications: The End of North's Ministry 1780-1782, 1958; Wilkes, Wyvill and Reform, 1962; Crisis of Empire, 1966; Myth and Reality in late Eighteenth-Century British Politics; 1970; The Correspondence of Jeremy Bentham (Editor), volume 3, 1971; Empire or Independence 1760-1776 (with B W Labaree), 1976; Bibliography of British History 1789-1851 (with Lucy M Brown), 1977; Wars and Revolutions, Britain 1760-1815, 1982; Stress and Stability in Late 18th Century Britain, 1984; The Benthams in Russia 1780-1791, 1993; British "Non-Elite" MPs 1715-1820, 1995. Contributions to: Various journals. Honour: Elected Fellow, British Academy, 1977. Memberships: Royal Historical Society, Joint Literary Director, 1964-70, Member of Council 1970-74; Editorial Board, History of Parliament Trust, 1973-96; Fellow, British Academy, 1977. Address: 10 Green Lane, Croxley Green, Hertfordshire WD3 3HR, England.

CHRISTIE-MURRAY David Hugh Arthur, b. 12 July 1913, London, England. m. (1) Ena Louise Elisabeth Mumford, 11 July 1942, (2) Sheila Mary Blackmore (Watson), 15 Apr 1972, 1 son, 3 daughters, 2 stepdaughters. Education: Diploma in Journalism, University College, University of London, 1932-34; BA, 1942, MA, 1945, General Ordination Examination 1942, St Peter's Hall, Oxford University and Wyclif Hall, Oxford. Publications: Beckenham Heraldy, 1954; Armorial Bearings of British Schools, series, 1956-66, collected edition, 1966; Illustrated Children's Bible, 1974; A History of Heresy, 1976; Voices From the Gods, 1978; My First Prayer Book, 1981; Reincarnation: Ancient Beliefs and Modern Evidence, Norwegian edition, 1989, Spanish Edition 1991; The Practical Astrologer, 1990. Contributions to: Times Literary and Educational Supplements; The Armorial; Christian Parapsychologist; Journal of the Society for Psychical Research; Light. Literary Agent: Watson Little Ltd. Address: Capo di Monte, Windmill Hill, Hampstead, London NW3 6RJ, England.

CHRISTOPHER Matt(hew F), (Fredric Martin), b. 16 Aug 1917, Bath, Pennsylvania, USA. Writer. m. Catherine M Krupa, 13 July 1940, 2 sons, 1 daughter. Education: Graduated, Ludlowville, New York, High School, 1935. Publications: Look for the Body, 1952; The Return of the Headless Horseman, 1982; Favor for a Ghost, 1983. Other: About 85 books for young people. Contributions to: Numerous short stories and articles in various publications. Honours: Boys Club of America Junior Book Award, 1958; Milner Award, 1993. Membership: Society of Childrens Book Writers. Address: 1830 Townes Court, Rock Hill, SC 29730, USA.

CHRISTOPHER Nicholas, b. 28 Feb 1951, New York, New York, USA. Poet; Writer. m. Constance Barbara Davidson, 20 Nov 1980. Education: AB, Harvard College, 1973. Appointments: Adjunct Professor of English, New York University; Lecturer, Columbia University. Publications: On Tour with Rita (poems), 1982; A Short History of the Island of Butterflies (poems), 1986; The Soloist (novel), 1986; Desperate Characters (poems), 1988; Under 35: The New Generation of American Poets (editor), 1989; In the Year of the Comet (poems), 1992; 5 Degrees and Other Poems, 1994; Walk and Other Poems, 1995. Contributions to: Anthologies and periodicals. Honours: New York Foundation for the Arts Fellowship, 1986; National Endowment for the Arts Fellowship, 1987; Peter I B Lavan Award, Academy of American Poets, 1991; Guggenheim Fellowship, 1993; Melville Cane Award, 1994. Address: c/o Janklow & Nesbit Associates, 598 Madison Avenue, New York, NY 10022, USA.

CHRISTOPHERSEN Paul (Hans), b. 18 Nov 1911, Copenhagen, Denmark. Emeritus Professor. m. Margaret Travers, 1 Aug 1950, 1 son. Education: MA, 1937, PhD, 1939, University of Copenhagen; PhD, Corpus Christi College, Cambridge, 1943. Appointments: Research Assistant, Royal Institute of International Affairs, London, 1944-46; Professor of English, University of Copenhagen, 1946-48; Professor of English, University of Ibadan, Nigeria, 1948-54; Professor of English, University of Oslo, Norway, 1954-68; Reader in English, 1969-74, Professor 1974-77, Emeritus Professor, 1977-, New University of Ulster, Northern Ireland; Professor of English, University of Qatar, 1977-81. Publications: The Articles, 1939; A Modern English Grammar (with O Jespersen), Vol 6, 1942; To Start You Talking (with H Krabbe), 1948; Bilingualism, 1949; The Ballad of Sir Aldingar, 1952; An English Phonetics Course, 1956; Some Thoughts on the Study of English as a Foreign Language, 1957; An Advanced English Grammar (with A Sandved), 1969; Second-Language Learning, 1973; Tina, by Herman Bang, translation, 1984. Contributions to: Oxford Companion to the English Language, 1992. Address: 1 Corfe Close, Cambridge CB2 2QA, England.

CHUN Sook-Hee, b. 15 Mar 1919, Korea. Writer. m. Soon-Ku Kang, 1939, 2 sons, 2 daughters. Education: Graduated, Ewha Women's University, Seoul, 1938. Publications: Apology of the Prodigal Son, 1954; In a Low Voice, 1960; For Our Life, 1978; The Korean PEN - Its Past and Today, 1992; Chun Sook-Hee Essay in Russia, 1993. Contributions to: Magazines and Newspapers. Honours: Cultural Medal, Korea, 1977; Grand Literary Award, POK, 1989; Grand Literary Award, Korean Academy of Arts, 1994; Bundesverdienstkruuz, Germany, 1995. Memberships: President, Korean Women Writer's Association, 1980-82; President, Korean PEN Center, 1983-91; Vice President, International PEN, 1991-. Address: 302 10 Dong Samho, Apt 759-3, Bangbae-Dong, Seoul, Korea.

CHURCH Robert, b. 20 July 1932, London, England. Author. m. Dorothy June Bourton, 15 Apr 1953, 2 daughters. Education: Beaufoy College, London, 1946-48. Appointments: Served Army 1950-52; Metropolitan Police, 1952-78; Probation Service, 1978-88. Publications: Murder in East Anglia, 1987; Accidents of Murder, 1989; More Murder in East Anglia, 1990; Anglian Blood, co-editor, 1995; Well Done Boys, 1996. Contributions to: Criminologist; Journals. Memberships: British Society of Criminology; Society of Authors; Crime Writers Association. Literary Agent: Don Short, Solo Literary Agency, 49-53 Kensington High Street, London W8 5ED, England. Address: Woodside, 7 Crome Walk, Gunton Park, Lowestoft, Suffolk NR32 4NF, England.

CHURCHILL Elizabeth. See: **HOUGH Richard Alexander**.

CIEE Grace. See: **CORNISH Gracie**.

CISNEROS Antonio, b. 27 Dec 1942, Lima, Peru. Poet. Education: Catholic and National Universities, Lima; PhD, 1974. Appointments: Teacher of Literature, University of San Marcos, 1972-. Publications: Destierro, 1961; David, 1962; Comentarios reales, 1964; The Spider Hangs Too Far from the Ground, 1970; Agua que no has de beber, 1971; Como higuera en un campo de golf, 1972; El libro de Dios y los hungaros, 1978; Cuatro poetas (with others), 1979; Helicopters in the Kingdom of Peru, 1981; La cronica del Nino Jesus de Chilca, 1981; At Night the Cats, 1985; Land of Angels, 1985; Monologo de la casta Susana y otros poemas, 1986; Propios como ajenos poesia 1962-88, 1989; El arte de envolver pescado, 1990; Poesia, una historia de locos: 1962-1986, 1990. Honours: Casa de las Americas Prize, 1968. Address: Department of Literature, Universidad Nacional de San Marcos de Lima, Avda Republica de Chile 295, Of 506, Casilla 454, Lima, Peru.

CISSNA William David, b. 27 July 1952, Evanston, Illinois, USA. Freelance Writer. m. Kathy Anne Williams, 14 Oct 1978, 1 son. Education: BA English, Allegheny College, Meadville, Pennsylvania, USA. 1974. Contributions to: Short stories and numerous non-fiction articles, 1984-. Memberships: Executive Committee and Board of Trustees, North Carolina Writers' Network, 1994-. Address: 275 Post Oak Road, Kernersville, NC 27284-8028, USA.

CIVASAQUI Jose (Shibasaki Sosuke), b. 12 Jan 1916, Saitama-ken. Lecturer; Translator; Poet. m. 18 Sept 1940, 2 sons, 1 daughter. Education: HHD, World University, Tucson, USA, 1977. Appointments: Managing Director, Japan League of Poets, 1972; Japan Guild of Authors and Composers, 1973; President, 1983-85, Honorary President, 1985-, United Poets Laureate International, USA; President, Poetry Society of Japan, 1987. Publications: In His Bosom, 1950; In Thy Grace, 1971; Doshin Shien, translation of A Child's Garden of Verses, 1973; Beyond Seeing, 1977; Living Water, 1984; Invitation to the World of Haiku, 1985; Kusa No Tsuyu, translation of Dew of Grass, 1987; Chosuichi Doro No Boken, translation of Reservoir Road Adventure, 1990; Green Pastures, poems, 1993. Contributions to: Japan Times, 1947-48; Mainichi, 1949-50, 1954-55; Study of Current English, 1960-61, 1965-68. Honours: Excellence in Poetry, 3rd World Congress of Poets, 1976; International Poet Laureate, 8th World Congress of Poets, 1985; Premio Speciale, Pelle di Luna, Italy, 1985; Premio Internazional San Valentino d'Oro, Italia, 1989; Michael Madhusudan Academy Award, Calcutta, India, 1992; Fourth Order of Merit, (Kun Yontoh Zuihosho) Japan, 1993; Man of Year, ABI, 1994; Silver Medallion Dove in Peace, Poetry Day Australia, 1995. Memberships: Poetry Society of Japan; United Poets Laureate International; PEN, Tokyo. Address: Honcho 2-12-11, Ikebukuro, Toshima-ku, Tokyo 170, Japan.

CIXOUS Helene, b. 5 June 1937, Oran, Algeria. Professor of English Literature. Writer. 1 son, 1 daughter. Education: Agregation d'Anglais, 1959; Docteur es Lettres, 1968. Appointments: Assistante, University of Bordeaux, France, 1962-65; Maître Assistante, University of Paris (Sorbonne), 1965-67; Maître de Conference, University of Paris X, Nanterre, France, 1967-68; helped found the experimental University of Paris VIII (Vincennes, St Denis), 1968, Professor of English Literature, 1968-, Founder and Director of Centre de Recherches en Etudes Feminines, 1974-; Co-founder, Poetique Revue de Theorie d'Analyse Litteraire, 1969; Visiting Professor and Lecturer to many universities in Europe, North America, Japan, India. Publications: Fiction: Le prénom de Dieu, 1967; Le Troisième corps, 1970; Angst, 1977; Le Livre de Promethea, 1983; Manna, 1994; La fiancée juive, 1995; Plays: Le nom d'Oedipe, 1978; L'Indiade ou l'Inde de leurs rêves, 1987; La Ville Parjure ou le Réveil des Erinyes, 1994; Essays: L'exil de James Joyce, ou l'art du remplacement, 1969; Prénoms de personne, 1974; L'heure de Clarice Lispector, 1989; Readings: The Poetics of Blanchot, Joyce, Kafka, Lispector, Tsvetaeva, 1992. Contributions to: Periodicals. Prix Medicis, 1969; Southern Cross of Brazil, 1989; Légion d'Honneur, 1994; Prix des critiques, best theatrical work of the Year, 1994; numerous Honorary Doctorates. Address: Centre d'Etudes Féminines, Universite de Paris VIII, 2 Rue de la Liberte, 93526 St Denis, France.

CIZMAR Paula, b. 30 Aug 1949, Youngstown, Ohio, USA. Playwright; Screenwriter. Education: BA, Ohio University, 1971; Graduate Studies, San Francisco State University, 1972-74. Publications: Plays: The Girl Room, 1979; The Death of a Miner, 1983; Candy and Shelley to the Desert, 1988; Many other plays produced. Contributions to: Periodicals. Honours: Jerome Foundation Commission Fellowship, 1981; National Endowment for the Arts Fellowship, 1982; Rockefeller Foundation International Residency, 1983. Memberships: Dramatists Guild; League of Professional Theatre Women; Writers Guild of America. Address: 2700 North Beachwood Drive, Los Angeles, CA 90068, USA.

CLADPOLE Jim. See: **RICHARDS Sir James**.

CLANCY Joseph Patrick Thomas, b. 8 Mar 1928, New York, New York, USA. College Teacher. m. Gertrude Wiegand, 31 July 1948, 4 sons, 4 daughters. Education: BA, 1947, MA, 1949, PhD, 1957, Fordham University. Appointments: Faculty, 1948, Professor, 1962, Marymount Manhattan College. Publications: The Odes and Epodes of Horace, 1960; Medieval Welsh Lyrics, 1965; The Earliest Welsh Poems, 1970; 20th Century Welsh Poems, 1982; Gwyn Thomas: Living a Life, 1982; The Significance of Flesh: Poems, 1950-83, 1984; Bobi Jones: Selected Poems, 1987. Contributions to: Poetry Wales; Planet; Anglo Welsh Review; Book News from Wales; Epoch; College English; America. Honours: American Philosophical Society Fellowships, 1963, 1968; National Translation Centre Fellowship, 1968; Welsh Arts Council, Literature Award, 1971; Major Bursary, 1972; National Endowment for the Arts Translation Fellowship, 1983; St Davids Society of New York Annual Award, 1986. Memberships: Am Literary Translators Association; Dramatists Guild; Yr Academi Gymreig; Eastern States Celtic Association; St Davids Society of New York. Address: 1549 Benson Street, New York, NY 10461, USA.

CLANCY Laurence James, b. 2 Dec 1942, Melbourne, Victoria, Australia. Senior Lecturer. Div, 2 s. Education: BA, Melbourne University, 1964; MA, La Trobe University, 1973. Publications: A Collapsible Man, 1975; The Wife Specialist, 1978; Xavier Herber, 1981; Perfect Love, 1983; The Novels of Vladimir Nabokov, 1984; City to City, 1989; A Reader's Guide to Australian Fiction, 1992; The Wild Life Reserve, 1994. Contributions to: Regular Contributor, Reviewer to Many Australian Journals and Newspapers. Honours: Co-Winner, National Book Council Award, 1975; Australian Natives Association Award, 1983. Membership: PEN International. Literary Agent: Curtis Brown Pty Ltd. Address: 227 Westgarth Street, Northcote, VA 3070, Australia.

CLANCY Tom, (Thomas L Clancy Jr), b. 1947, Baltimore, Maryland, USA. Author. m. Wanda Thomas, Aug 1969, 1 son, 3 daughters. Education: BA, Loyola College, Baltimore, 1969. Publications: The Hunt for Red October, 1984; Red Storm Rising, 1986; Patriot Games, 1987; The Cardinal of the Kremlin, 1988; Clear and Present Danger, 1989; The Sum of All Fears, 1992; Without Remorse, 1993; Armored Car, 1994; Debut of Honor, 1994; Submarine, 1994; Reality Check: What's Going on Out There?, 1995; Executive Orders, 1996; Into the Storm: A Study in Command (with

Fred Franks Jr), 1997. Address: PO Box 800, Huntingtown, MD 20639, USA.

CLARE Elizabeth, See: **COOK Dorothy Mary.**

CLARE Ellen. See: **SINCLAIR Olga Ellen.**

CLARE Helen. See: **BLAIR Pauline Hunter.**

CLARK Alan, b. 13 April 1928, England. m. Jane Beuttler, 1958, 2 sons. Education: Eton; MA, Christ Church, Oxford. Appointments: MP for Plymouth, Sutton, 1974-92; Under Secretary of State, Department of Employment, 1983-86; Minister for Trade, 1986-89; Minister of State, MoD, 1989-92; MP for Chelsea, 1997-. Publications: The Donkeys, A History of the BEF in 1915, 1961; The Fall of Crete, 1963; Barbarossa, The Russo-German Conflict 1941-45, 1965; Aces High: The War in the Air Over the Western Front 1914-18, 1973; A Good Innings: the Private Papers of Viscount Lee of Fareham, editor, 1974; Diaries, 1993. Honours: Privy Councillor, 1991. Address: Saltwood Castle, Kent CT21 4QU, England.

CLARK Brian Robert, b. 3 June 1932, Playwright. m. (1)Margaret Paling, 1961, 2 sons, (2)Anita Modak, 1983, 1 stepson, 1 stepdaughter, (3)Cherry Potter, 1990. Education: Central School of Speech and Drama, London: BA, Nottingham University. Appointments: Teacher, 1955-61, 1964-68; Staff Tutor, Drama, University of Hull, 1968-72; Author, 1971-; Founder, Amber Lane Press, 1978. Publications: TV Plays, Whose Life is it Anyway; The Saturday Party; TV Series, Telfords Change; Late Starter; Stage plays, Whose Life is it Anyway; Kipling; The Petition, 1986; Hopping to Byzantum, 1990. Honour: Fellowship, Royal Society of Literature. Address: c/o Judy Daish Associates, 2 St Charles Place, London W1 0EG, England.

CLARK David. See: **HARDCASTLE Michael.**

CLARK David R(idgley), b. 17 Sept 1920, Seymour, Connecticut, USA. Professor (retired); Writer. m. Mary Adele Matthieu, 10 July 1948, 2 sons, 2 daughters. Education: BA, Wesleyan University, 1947; MA, 1950, PhD, 1955, Yale University. Appointments: Instructor, 1951-57, Assistant Professor, 1957-58, Associate Professor, 1958-65, Professor, 1965-85, University of Massachusetts; Visiting Professor, St Mary's College, Notre Dame, Indiana, 1985-87; Visiting Professor, Williams College, Williamstown, Massachusetts, 1989-91. Publications: A Curious Quire, 1962; W B Yeats and the Theatre of Desolate Reality, 1965, new edition with Rosalind Clark, 1993; Irish Renaissance, 1965; Dry Tree, 1966; Riders to the Sea, 1970; A Tower of Polished Black Stones: Early Versions of the Shadowy Waters, 1971; Twentieth Century Interpretations of Murder in the Cathedral, 1971; Druid Craft, 1971; That Black Day: The Manuscripts of Crazy Jane on the Day of Judgement, 1980; W B Yeats: The Writing of Sophocles' King Oedipus (with James McGuire), 1989; W B Yeats: The Winding Stair (1929): Manuscript Materials, 1995; W B Yeats: Words for Music Perhaps and Other Poems (1932): Manuscript Materials, 1997. Memberships: American Conference for Irish Studies; Canadian Association for Irish Studies; International Association for the Support of Anglo-Irish Literature; Modern Language Association of America; Yeats Association. Address: 481 Holgerson Road, Sequim, WA 98382, USA.

CLARK Eric, b. 29 July 1937, Birmingham, England. Author; Journalist. m. Marcelle Bernstein, 12 Apr 1972, 1 son, 2 daughters. Appointments: Staff of various newspapers including, Daily Mail, The Guardian, The Observer until 1972; Full-time Author, 1972-. Publications: Len Deighton's London Dossier (Part-author), 1967; Everybody's Guide to Survival, 1969; Corps Diplomatique, 1973, US edition as Diplomat, 1973; Black Gambit, 1978; The Sleeper, 1979; Send in the Lions, 1981; Chinese Burn, 1984, US edition as China Run, 1984; The Want Makers (Inside the Hidden World of Advertising), 1988; Hide and Seek, 1994. Contributions to: Observer; Sunday Times; Daily Mail; Daily Telegraph; Washington Post; Melbourne Age. Memberships: Society of Authors; Fellow, UK Centre International PEN; Crime Writers Association; Mystery Writers of America. Literary Agent: A M Heath & Co Ltd, 79 St Martin's Lane, London, WC2N 4AA. Address: c/o Child and Company, 1 Fleet Street, London EC4Y 1BD, England.

CLARK Joan, b. 12 Oct 1934, Nova Scotia, Canada. m. Jack, 3 children. Education: Acadia University; University of Alberta.

Publications: The Hand of Robin Squires, 1977, 1986, 1994; From a High Thin Wire, 1982; Wild Man of the Woods, 1985; The Moons of Madeleine, 1987; The Victory of Geraldine Gill, 1988, 1994; Swimming Toward the Light, 1990; Eiriksdottir, 1994; The Dream Carvers, 1995. Address: 6 Dover Place, St Johns, Newfoundland A1B 2P5, Canada.

CLARK John Pepper, (J P Clark Bekederemo), b. 6 Apr 1935, Kiagaboo, Nigeria. Writer. m. Ebun Odutola Clark, 1 son, 3 daughter. Education: Warri Government College, 1948-54; University of Ibadan, 1955-60; BA, 1960; Princeton University. Appointments: Information Officer, Government of Nigeria, 1960-61; Head of Features and Editorial Writer, Lagos Daily Express, 1961-62; Research Fellow, 1964-66, Professor, 1964-85, University of Lagos; Founding Editor, Horn Magazine, Ibadan; Co Editor, Black Orpheus, 1968-. Publications: Plays, The Raft, 1966; Included in Three Plays, 1964; Ozidi, Ibadan, London & New York, 1966; The Bikoroa Plays, The Boat; The Return Home; Screen Play, The Ozidi of Atazi; Radio Play, The Raft, 1966; Verse and Other Publications. Memberships: Society of Nigerian Authors. Address: c/o Andrew Best, Curtis Brown, Haymarket House, 28-29 Haymarket, London SW1Y 4SP, England.

CLARK Jonathan Charles Douglas, b. 28 Feb 1951, London, England. Historian. m. Katherine Redwood Penovich, 1996. Education: BA 1972, PhD 1981, Cambridge University. Appointments: Research Fellow, Peterhouse, Cambridge, 1977; Leverhulme Trust, 1983; Fellow, All Souls College, Oxford, 1986; Visiting Professor, Committee on Social Thought, University of Chicago, 1993; Senior Research Fellow, All Souls College, Oxford, 1995; Joyce and Elizabeth Hall Distinguished Professor of British History, University of Kansas, 1995-. Publications: The Dynamics of Change, 1982; English Society 1688-1832, 1985; Revolution and Rebellion, 1986; The Memoirs of James 2nd Earl Waldegrave, 1988; Ideas and Politics in Modern Britain, 1990; The Language of Liberty, 1993; Samuel Johnson, 1994. Contributions to: Revolution and Counter-Revolution, 1990; Christianity and Conservatism, 1990; Articles in learned journals; Features and book reviews in: Times Literary Supplement; Times; Sunday Times; Sunday Telegraph; Independent on Sunday; Evening Standard; Spectator; Daily Telegraph; Daily Mail. Memberships: Fellow, Royal Historical Society; Ecclesiastical History Society; Church of England Record Society; American Historical Association; North American Conference on British Studies; British Society for Eighteenth Century Studies. Address: Hall Center for the Humanities, University of Kansas, Lawrence, KS 66045-2967, USA.

CLARK LaVerne Harrell, b. 6 June 1929, Smithville, Texas, USA. Writer; Photographer; Lecturer. m. L D Clark, 15 Sept 1951. Education: BA, Texas Woman's University, 1950; Columbia University, 1951-54; MA, 1962, MFA, 1992, University of Arizona. Appointments: Reporter, Librarian, Fort Worth Press, 1950-51; Sales and Advertising Department, Columbia University Press, 1951-53; Assistant, Promotion News Department, Episcopal Diocese, New York, 1958-59; Founding Director, 1962-66, Photographer, 1966-, Poetry Centre, University of Arizona. Publications: They Sang for Horses, 1966; The Face of Poetry, 1976; Focus 101, 1979; Revisiting the Plains Indians Country of Mari Sandoz, 1979; The Deadly Swarm and Other Stories, 1985; Keepers of the Earth, 1997. Contributions to: Periodicals. Honours: American Philosophical Society Grant, 1967-69; Non Fiction Award, Biennial Letters Contest, 1968; Distinguished Alumna Award, 1973; Julian Ocean Literary Prize, 1984; Philip A Danielson Award, Westerners International, 1992. Memberships: PEN; National League of American PEN Women; Western Writers of America; Society of Southwestern Authors; Mari Sandoz Heritage Society; Honorary Board Member, Westerners International; Kappa Alpha Mu. Address: 4690 North Campbell No. C, Tucson, AZ 85718, USA.

CLARK Marcelle Ruth, (Marcelle Bernstein), b. 14 June 1945, Manchester, England. Writer; Journalist. m. Eric Clark, 12 Apr 1972, 1 son, 2 daughters. Appointments: Staff, The Guardian, Daily Mirror, Observer. Publications: Nuns, 1976; Sadie, 1983; Salka, 1986; Lili, 1988; Body and Soul, 1991. Contributions to: Numerous US & UK Magazines. Honours: Arts Council Bursary, 1986; Helene Heroys Award, 1988. Memberships: Society of Authors. Literary Agent: Caradoc King, AP Watt. Address: c/o AP Watt, 20 John Street, London WC1N 2DR, England.

CLARK (Marie) Catherine (Audrey) Clifton, (Audrey Curling), b. London, England. Writer. m. Clifton Clark, 16 Feb 1938. Publications: Novels: The Running Tide, 1963; Sparrow's Yard, 1964; Historical Novels: The Echoing Silence, 1967; Caste for Comedy,

1970; The Sapphire and the Pearl, 1970; Cry of the Heart, 1971; A Quarter of the Moon, 1972; Shadows on the Grass, 1973; Enthusiasts in Love, 1975; The Lamps in the House, as Catherine Clifton Clark, 1990; The Saturday Treat, 1993; The Workroom Girls, 1996. Non-fiction: The Young Thackeray, 1966. Contributions to: Periodicals. Honours: Theordora Roscoe Award, 1978; 1st Prize, Wandsworth All London Literary Competition, 1982. Memberships: Society of Authors; Romantic Novelists Association; Society of Women Writers and Journalists, Council Member. Address: 35 Hadley Gardens, Chiswick, London W4 4NU, England.

CLARK Mary Higgins, b. 24 Dec 1929, New York, New York, USA. Writer. m. Waren F Clark, 26 Dec 1949, 2 sons, 3 daughters. Education: BA, Fordham University; Villanora University, 1983; Rider College, 1986. Publications: Where Are The Children, 1975; A Stranger is Watching, 1978; The Cradle will Fall, 1980; A Cry in the Night, 1982; Weep No More My Lady, 1987; While My Pretty One Sleeps, 1989; All Around the Town, 1991; Loves Music, Loves to Dance, 1991; Remember Me, 1994. Contributions to: Ladies Home Journal; Womens Day; Saturday Evening Post. Honours: Grand Prix de Litteratae Policcere, 1980. Memberships: Mystery Writers of America; PEN; American Society of Journalists and Authors. Address: c/o Eugene Winick, McIntosh and Otis Inc, 475 Fifth Avenue, New York, NY 10017, USA.

CLARK Mavis Thorpe, (M R Clark, Mavis Latham), b. Melbourne, Victoria, Australia. Children's Author; Biographer. Education: Methodist Ladies College, Melbourne. Publications: Dark Pool Island, 1949; . The Twins From the Timber Creek, 1949; Jingarooo, 1951; Missing Gold, 1951; The Brown Land was Green, 1957; Pony From Tarella, 1959; They Came South, 1963; Fishing, 1963; Blue Above the Trees, 1967; The Pack-Tracker, 1968; The Opal Miner, 1969; Nowhere to Hide, 1969; Iron Ore Mining, 1971; New Golden Mountain, 1973; The Hundred Islands, 1976; Spanish Queen, 1977; The Lilly-Pilly, 1979; Solomon's Child, 1981; Soft Shoe, 1988; Biograhies: John Batman, 1962; Pastor Doug, 1965; Strolling Players, 1972; No Mean Destiny, 1986. Honours: Highly Commended, Australian Children's Book Council, 1957; Highly Commended by Book of the Year Award, Australian Children's Book Council, 1967; Notable Book, American Library Association, 1969; AM, 1996. Memberships: General Division, Order of Australia, member; Australian Society of Authors; Fellowship of Australian Writers; International PEN Club; National Book Council. Address: Unit I, 22 Rochester Road, Canterbury, Victoria 3126, Australia.

CLARK Patricia Denise (Claire Lorrimer, Patricia Robins, Susan Patrick), b. 1921. British. Writer; Poet. Publications: As Claire Lorrimer: A Voice in the Dark, 1967; The Shadow Falls, 1974; Relentless Storm, 1975; The Secret of Quarry House, 1976; Mavreen, 1976; Tamarisk, 1978; Chantal, 1980; The Garden (a cameo), 1980; The Chatelaine, 1981; The Wilderling, 1982; Last Year's Nightingale, 1984; Frost in the Sun, 1986; House of Tomorrow (biography), 1987; Ortolans, 1990; The Spinning Wheel, 1991; Variations (short stories), 1991; The Silver Link, 1993; Fool's Curtain, 1994; As Patricia Robins: To the Stars, 1944; See No Evil, 1945; Three Loves, 1949; Awake My Heart, 1950; Beneath the Moon, 1951; Leave My Heart Alone, 1951; The Fair Deal, 1952; Heart's Desire, 1953; So This is Love, 1953; Heaven in Our Hearts, 1954; One Who Cares, 1954; Love Cannot Die, 1955; The Foolish Heart, 1956; Give All to Love, 1956; Where Duty Lies, 1957; He Is Mine, 1957; Love Must Wait, 1958; Lonely Quest, 1959; Lady Chatterley's Daughter, 1961; The Last Chance, 1961; The Long Wait, 1962; The Runaways, 1962; Seven Loves, 1962; With All My Love, 1963; The Constant Heart, 1964; Second Love, 1964; The Night is Thine, 1964; There Is But One, 1965; No More Loving, 1965; Topaz Island, 1965; Love Me Tomorrow, 1966; The Uncertain Joy, 1966; The Man Behind the Mask, 1967; Forbidden, 1967; Sapphire in the Sand, 1968; Return to Love, 1968; Laugh on Friday, 1969; No Stone Unturned, 1969; Cinnabar House, 1970; Under the Sky, 1970; The Crimson Tapestry, 1972; Play Fair with Love, 1972; None But He, 1973; Fulfilment, 1993; Forsaken, 1993; Forever, 1993. Membership: Romantic Novelists Association. Address: Chiswell Barn, Marsh Green, Edenbridge, Kent TN8 5PR, England.

CLARKE Anna, b. 28 Apr 1919, Cape Town, South Africa. Author. Education: Schools in Cape Town, Montreal, Canada; BSc Economics, University of London, 1945; BA, Open University, 1971-75; MA, University of Sussex, 1975. Appointments: Private Secretary, Victor Gollancz Publishers, 1947-50; Eyre and Spottiswoode, Publishers, 1951-53; Administrative Secretary, British Association for

American Studies, London, 1956-63. Publications: The Poisoned Web, 1979; Poison Parsley, 1979; Last Voyage, 1980; Game, Set and Danger, 1981; Desire to Kill, 1982; We the Bereaved, 1982; Soon She Must Die, 1983; Paula Glenning stories: Last Judgement, 1985; Cabin 3033, 1986; The Mystery Lady, 1986; Last Seen in London, 1987; Murder in Writing, 1988; The Whitelands Affair, 1989; The Case of the Paranoid Patient, 1993; The Case of the Ludicrous Letters,1994. Contributions to: Short stories in Ellery Queen Mystery Magazine, New York. Literary Agent: Wendy Lipkind, New York. Address: c/o Wendy Lipkind, 165 East 66 Street, New York, NY 10021, USA.

CLARKE Arthur C(harles), b. 16 Dec 1917, Minehead, Somerset, England. Author. m. Marilyn Mayfield, 1953, diss 1964. Education: Huish Grammar School, Taunton, 1928-36; BSc, King's College, London, 1948. Appointments: Assistant Editor, Science Abstracts, 1949-50; Many appearances on UK and US radio and television; Chancellor, Moratuwa University, Sri Lanka, 1979-; Vikram Sarabhai Professor, Physical Research Laboratory, Ahmedabad, 1980. Publications: Non-Fiction: Interplanetary Flight, 1950; The Exploration of Space, 1951; The Exploration of the Moon (with R A Smith), 1954; The Challenge of the Spaceship, 1960; The Challenge of the Sea, 1960; Man and Space (with others), 1964; The Coming of the Space Age, 1967; First on the Moon (with the astronauts), 1970; Beyond Jupiter (with Chesley Bonestell), 1973; Arthur C Clarke's Mysterious World (with Simon Welfare and John Fairley), 1980; Arthur C Clarke's World of Strange Powers (with Simon Welfare and John Fairley), 1984; Arthur C Clarke's Chronicles of the Strange and Mysterious (with Simon Welfare and John Fairley), 1987; Astounding Days, 1988; How the World was One, 1992; Arthur C Clarke's A-Z of Mysteries (with Simon Welfare and John Fairley), 1993; The Snows of Olympus, 1994. Fiction: Prelude to Space, 1951; Against the Fall of Night, 1953; Reach for Tomorrow, 1956; The Other Side of the Sky, 1958; Tales of Ten Worlds, 1962; 2001: A Space Odyssey (with Stanley Kubrick), 1968; The Lost World of 2001, 1972; Rendezvous with Rama, with G Lee, 1973; The Fountains of Paradise, 1979; 2010: Space Odyssey II, 1982; The Songs of Distant Earth, 1986; 2061: Odyssey III, 1988; Rama II, with G Lee, 1989; The Garden of Rama, with G Lee, 1991; Beyond the Fall of Night (with Gregory Benford), 1991; The Hammer of God, 1993; Rama Revealed (with G Lee), 1993; 3001: The Final Odyssey, 1997. Contributions to: Journals and periodicals. Honours: Kalinga Prize, UNESCO, 1961; Stuart Ballantine Medal, Franklin Institute, 1963; Nebula Awards, Science Fiction Writers of America, 1972, 1974, 1979; John Campbell Award, 1974; Hugo Awards, World Science Fiction Convention, 1974, 1980; Vidya Jyothi Medal, 1986; Grand Master, Science Fiction Writers of America, 1986; Charles Lindberg Award, 1987; Commander of the Order of the British Empire, 1989; Lord Perry Award, 1992; Many honorary doctorates. Memberships: Association for the Advancement of Science; International Writers Association, fellow; Royal Astronomical Society, fellow; Society of Authors. Address: 25 Barnes Place, Colombo 7, Sri Lanka.

CLARKE Austin Ardinel Chesterfield, b. 26 July 1934, Barbados, West Indies. Author. m. 14 Sept 1957, 2 daughters. Education: Trinity College, University of Toronto. Appointments: Hoyt Fellow, Yale University, 1968; Margaret Bundy Scott Professor, 1970; Jacob Ziskind Professor, Brandeis University, 1970. Publications: The Meeting Point, 1967; Storm of Fortune, 1972; The Bigger Light, 1972; When He Was Young and Free He Used to Wear Silks, 1972; The Prime Minister, 1977; Growing Up Stupid Under The Union Jack, 1980; When Women Rule, 1985; Nine Men Who Laughed, 1986; Proud Empires, 1986; In This City, 1992; There Are No Eldors, 1993; A Passage Back Home: A Personal Reminiscence of Samuel Selvon, 1994 . Contributions to: Tamarack Review; Canadian Literature. Honours: Presidents Medal, 1965; Canada Council Awards, 1968, 1972; Casa de las Americas Literary Prize, 1980; Arts Council Awards, 1985, 1994; Toronto Arts Award, 1992. Membership: Arts and Letters CLub. Literary Agent: Harold Ober Associates, David Higham Associates, London. Address: 62 McGill Street, Toronto, Ontario M5B 1H2, Canada.

CLARKE Brenda (Margaret Lilian), (Brenda Honeyman, Kate Sedley), b. 30 July 1926, Bristol, England. Author. m. Ronald John Clarke, 5 Mar 1955, 1 son, 1 daughter. Publications: The Glass Island, 1978; tTe Lofty Banners, 1980; The Far Morning, 1982; All Through the Day, 1983; A Rose in May, 1984; Three Women, 1985; Winter Landscape, 1986; Under Heaven, 1988; An Equal Chance, 1989, US edition as Riches of the Heart, 1989; Sisters and Lovers, 1990; Beyond the World, 1991; A Durable Fire, 1993. As Brenda Honeyman: Richard by Grace of God, 1968; The Kingmaker, 1969; Richmond and

Elizabeth, 1970; Harry the King, 1971; Brother Bedford, 1972; Good Duke Humphrey, 1973; The King's Minions, 1974; The Queen and Mortimer, 1974; Edward the Warrior, 1975; All the King's Sons, 1976; The Golden Griffin, 1976; At the King's Court, 1977; A King's Tale, 1977; Macbeth, King of Scots, 1977; Emma, the Queen, 1978; Harold of the English, 1979. As Kate Sedley: Death and the Chapman, 1991; The Plymouth Cloak, 1992; The Hanged Man, 1993; The Holy Innocents, 1994; The Eve of St Hyacinth, 1995. Literary Agent: David Grossman Literary Agency Ltd, 110/114 Clerkenwell Road, London EC1M 5SA, England. Address: 25 Torridge Road, Keynsham, Bristol, Avon BS18 1QQ, England.

CLARKE Gillian, b. 8 June 1937, Cardiff, Wales. Lecturer; Poet. Education: BA, University College Cardiff, 1958. Appointments: Lecturer, Gwent College of Art and Design, Newport, 1975-84; Editor, Anglo-Welsh Review, 1976-84; President, Ty Newydd, 1993-. Publications: Snow on the Mountain, 1971; The Sundial, 1978; Letter from a Far Country, 1982; Selected Poems, 1985; Letting in the Rumour, 1989; The King of Britain's Daughter, 1993; Editor: The Poetry Book Society Anthology, 1987-88, 1987; I Can Move the Sea (anthology), 1996; The Whispering Room (poetry), 1996. Honours: University of Wales, Cardiff, fellow, 1984; University of Wales, Swansea, honorary fellow, 1996; Department of English, University of Wales, Aberystwyth, honorary fellow, 1995-97. Membership: Welsh Academy, Chair, 1988-93. Address: Blaen Cwrt, Talgarreg, Llandysul, Ceredigion SA44 4EU, Wales.

CLARKE Hugh Vincent, b. 27 Nov 1919, Brisbane, Queensland, Australia. Author; Journalist. m. Mary Patricia Ryan, 6 June 1961, 4 sons, 1 daughter. Education: Teachers Training College, Brisbane, 1937; Melbourne Technical College, 1947-48. Appointments: Senior Survey Computer, Department of the Interior, Australia, 1947-56; Director of Information and Publicity, Department of External Territories, Canberra, Australian Capital Territory, 1966-73; Director of Information and Public Relations, Department of Aboriginal Affairs, Canberra, Australian Capital Territory, 1973-75. Publications: The Tub, novel, 1963; Breakout (with Takeo Yamashita), 1965; To Sydney by Stealth (with Takeo yamashita), 1966; The Long Arm, 1974; Fire One!, 1978; The Broke and the Broken, 1982; Last Stop Nagasaki, 1984; Twilight Liberation, 1985; A Life for Every Sleeper, 1986; Prisoners of War (with Colin Burgess and Russell Braddon), 1988; When the Balloon Went Up, 1990; Barbed Wire and Bamboo (with Colin Burgess), 1992; Escape to Death, 1994. Contributions to: Anthologies and periodicals; Bulletin Australasian Post. Memberships: National Press Club; Australian Journalists Association; Canberra Historical Society; Australian Society of Authors. Address: 14 Chemside Street, Deakin, Canberra 2600, Australia.

CLARKE Joan Lorraine, b. 23 Aug 1920, Sydney, New South Wales, Australia. Author; Freelance Editor. m. R G Clarke, 1946, div, 1 son. Education: Diploma, Secretarial College, 1938. Appointments: Editor, The Australian Author, 1977-81; Editor, Australian Society of Authors, Writers Handbook 2nd edition, 1980. Publications: The Tracks We Travel: Australian Short Stories (contributing author), 1953; Girl Fridays in Revolt (co-author), 1969; Max Herz, Surgeon Extraordinary, 1976; Australian Political Milestone, (contributing author), 1976; Gold (co-author), 1981; The Doctor Who Dared, 1982; Just Us, 1988; Growing Up With Barnardo's (editor), 1990; All on One Good Dancing Leg, 1994. Contributions to: Sydney Morning Herald; Australian Women's Weekly; Flair; Pol; The Australian Author; Overland; Radio talks and features for the Australian Broadcasting Commission and commercial radio. Address: Feros Village, PO Box 585, Byron Bay, New South Wales 2481, Australia.

CLARKE Mary, b. 23 Aug 1923, London, England. Editor; Writer. Appointments: Editor, Dancing Times, London. Publications: The Sadler's Wells Ballet: A History and an Appreciation, 1955; Six Great Dancers, 1957; Dancers of Mercury: The Story of Ballet Rambert, 1962; Ballet: An Illustrated History (with Clement Crisp), 1973, 1992; Recent books with Clement Crisp: Design for Ballet; Making a Ballet; Dancer: Men in Dance; Ballerina; History of Dance. Contributions to: Encyclopaedia Britannica; Guardian; Dance Magazine, New York; Dance News, New York; Observer; Sunday Times. Honours: 2nd Prize, Cafe Royal Literary Prize for Best Book on Theatre, 1955; Queen Elizabeth II Award, Royal Academy of Dancing, 1990; Knight, Order of Dannebrog, 1992; Nijinsky Medal, Polish Ministry of Culture, 1995. Membership: Gautier Club. Address: 54 Ripplevale Grove, London N1 1HT, England.

CLARKE Pauline. See: **BLAIR Pauline Hunter.**

CLARKSON Ewan, b. 23 Jan 1929, England. Education: MA, University of Exeter, 1984. Publications: Break for Freedom, 1967; Halic, The Story of a Grey Seal, 1970; The Running of the Deer, 1972; In the Shadow of the Falcon, 1973; Wolf Country, a Wilderness Pilgrimage, 1975; The Badger of Summercombe, 1977; The Many Forked Branch, 1980; Wolves, 1980; Reindeer, 1981; Eagles, 1981; Beavers, 1981; In the Wake of the Storm, 1984; Ice Trek, 1986; King of the Wild, 1990; The Flight of the Osprey, 1995. Address: Moss Rose Cottage, Preston, Newton Abbot, Devon TQ12 3PP, England.

CLARKSON J F. See: **TUBB E(dwin) C(harles).**

CLARKSON Stephen, m. Christina McCall, 3 daughters. Education: Toronto, Oxford and Sorbonne. Appointments: Professor, Political Economy, University of Toronto, 1964-; Co-Founder, Praxis Corp; Former Member, Editorial Board, The Canadian Forum; President, University League for Social Reform. Publications: Many Academic and General Articles; An Independent Foreign Policy for Canada?, 1968; City Lib: Parties and Reform, 1972; The Soviet Theory of Development, 1978; Canada and the Reagan Challenge, 1985; Trudeau and Our Times: The Magnificent Obsession, 1990; Trudeau and Our Times: The Heroic Delusion, 1994. Honours: Rhodes Scholarship, Woodrow Wilson Fellowship; John Porter Award, 1984; Governor General's Award, 1990; John Dafoe Prize, 1995; Jean Monnet Fellow, European University Institute, 1995-96. Address: 59 Lowther Avenue, Toronto, Ontario, M5R 1CS, Canada.

CLARY Sydney Ann, b. 13 Feb 1948, Auburn, Alabama, USA. Writer. m. Bishop D Clary, 26 Sept 1967, 2 daughters. Education: Palm Beach Community College. Publications: Double Solitaire; Devil and the Duchess; Eye of the Storm; A Touch of Passion; Her Golden Eyes; Fire in the Night; With a Little Spice; Southern Comfort; This Wildlife Magic. Contributions to: Numerous Articles to Romantic Times; Articles to Romance Writers of America Magazine. Honours: Reviewers Choice Finalist, 1983, 1984, 1987, 1990; Gold Medallion Finalist, 1988; Reviewers Choice Best All Around Series Author, 1989-90. Membership: Romance Writers of America. Address: c/o Maureen Walters, Curtis Brown Ltd., 10 Astor Place, New York, NY 10013, USA.

CLAYDON Duer. See: **FINCH Robert.**

CLAYTON John J(acob), b. 5 Jan 1935, New York, New York, USA. Professor of English; Writer. m. (1) Marilyn Hirsch, 31 July 1956, div 1974, 1 son, 1 daughter, (2) Marlynn Krebs, div 1983, 1 son, (3) Sharon Dunn, 26 May 1984, 1 son. Education: AB, Columbia University, 1956; MA, New York University, 1959; PhD, Indiana University, 1966. Appointments: Instructor, University of Victoria, British Columbia, 1962-63; Lecturer, Overseas Division, University of Maryland, 1963-64; Assistant Professor of Humanities, Boston University, 1964-69; Associate Professor, 1969-75, Professor of English, 1975-, University of Massachusetts at Amherst. Publications: Saul Bellow: In Defense of Man, 1968, 2nd edition, 1979; What Are Friends For? (novel), 1979; Bodies of the Rich (short stories), 1984; Gestures of Healing: Anxiety and the Modern Novel, 1991. Editor: The D C Heath Introduction to Fiction. Contributions to: Anthologies and periodicals. Honour: 2nd Prize, O Henry Prize Stories, 1995. Address: 12 Lawton Road, RFD 3, Amherst, MA 01002, USA.

CLAYTON Martin David, b. 30 Dec 1967, Harrogate, England. Art Historian; Writer. Education: BA, History of Art, 1986-90, MA, 1993, Christ's College, Cambridge. Appointment: Assistant Curator, Royal Library, Windsor Castle. Publications: Leonardo da Vinci: The Anatomy of Man, 1992; Poussin: Works on Paper, 1995; Leonardo da Vinci: A Curious Vision, 1996. Literary Agent: John Johnstone Limited. Address: Royal Library, Windsor Castle, Berkshire, England.

CLAYTON Mary. See: **LIDE Mary Ruth.**

CLAYTON Peter Arthur, b. 27 Apr 1937, London, England. Publishing Consultant; Archaeological Lecturer. m. Janet Frances Manning, 5 Sept 1964, 2 sons. Education: School of Librarianship; NW Polytechnic, London, 1958; Institute of Archaeology, London University, 1958-62; University College London University, 1958-62; University College, London, 1968-72. Appointments: Librarian, 1953-67; Archaeological Editor, Thames & Hudson, 1963-73; Humanities Publisher, Longmans, 1973; Managing Editor, British

Museum's Publications, 1974-79; Publications Director, BA Seaby, 1980-87; Writer, Lecturer, 1987-. Publications: The Rediscovery of Ancient Egypt; Archaeological Sites of Britain; Seven Wonders of the Ancient World; Treasures of Ancient Rome; Companion to Roman Britain; Great Figures of Mythology; Gods and Symbols of Ancient Egypt; Chronicle of the Pharaohs, 1994; Family Life in Ancient Egypt; The Valley of the Kings, 1995. Contributions to: Journal of Egyptian Archaeology; Numismatic Chronicle; Coin & Medal Bulletin; Minerva. Memberships: Fellow, Library Association; Fellow, Society of Antiquaries of London; Fellow, Royal Numismatic Society. Address: 41 Cardy Road, Boxmoor, Hemel Hempstead, Hertfordshire HP1 1RL, England.

CLEALL Charles, b. 1 June 1927, Heston, Middlesex, England. Writer. m. Mary Turner, 25 July 1953, 2 daughters. Education: Trinity College of Music, London, GTCL; LRAM; ARCO(CHM); Jordanhill College of Education, BMus; FRCO; MA, University College of North Wales; ADCM; Registered Teacher of Sinus tone. Appointments: Instructor Lieutenant, Command Music Advisor, Royal Navy, Plymouth Command, 1946-48; Professor, Solo-Singing and Voice Production, TCL, 1949-52; Choral Scholar, Westminster Abbey, 1949-52; Conductor, Morley College Orchestra, 1950-52; Conductor, Glasgow Choral Union, 1952-54; BBC Music Assistant, Midland Region, 1954-55; Music Master, Glyn County School, 1955-67; Lecturer in Music, Froebel Institute, Roehampton, 1967-68; Music Adviser, London Borough of Harrow, 1968-72; Northern Divisional Music Specialist, Her Majesty's Inspectorate of Schools in Scotland, 1972-87; Editor, Journal of The Ernest George White Society, 1983-87. Publications: Voice Production in Choral Technique, 1955, revised edition, 1970; The Selection and Training of Mixed Choirs in Churches, 1960; Sixty Songs from Sankey, 1960, revised edition, 1966; John Merbecke's Music for the Congregation at Holy Communion, 1963; Music and Holiness, 1964; Plainsong for Pleasure, 1969; Authentic Chanting, 1969; A Guide to Vanity Fair, 1982; Walking Round the Church of St James the Great, Stonehaven, 1993. Contributions to: Master of the Choir; Musical Opinion; Church of England Newspaper; Musical Times; Diapason; Music in Education; Music Teacher; Church and Organ Guide; Methodist Recorder; Organists' Review; Choir and Organ; Promoting Church Music; English Church Music Annual; English Church Music Quarterly; London Quarterly and Holborn Review; Life of Faith; Crusade Monthly; Burrswood Herald; Child Education; Methodist Magazine; Mosaic; Scottish Educational Review; Psychology of Music.Address: 10 Carronhall, Stonehaven, Aberdeen AB39 2QF, Scotland.

CLEARE John Silvey, b. 2 May 1936, London, England. Photographer; Writer. m. (2) Jo Jackson, 12 May 1980, 1 daughter. Education: Wycliffe College, 1945-54; Guildford School of Photography, 1957-60. Appointments: Joint Editor, Mountain Life magazine, 1973-75; Editorial Board, Climber and Rambler magazine, 1975-85. Publications: Rock Climbers in Action in Snowdonia, 1966; Sea-Cliff Climbing in Britain, 1973;Mountains, 1975; World Guide to Mountains, 1979; Mountaineering, 1980; Scrambles Among the Alps, 1986; John Cleare's Best 50 Hill Walks in Britain, 1988; Trekking: Great Walks in the World, 1988; Walking the Great Views, 1991; Discovering the English Lowlands, 1991; On Foot in the Pennines, 1994; On Foot in the Yorkshire Dales, 1996. Contributions to: Times; Sunday Times; Independent; Observer; World; Country Living; Boat International; Intercontinental; Alpine Journal; High; Climber; Great Outdoors. Honour: 35mm Prize, Trento Film Festival, for film The Climbers (as Cameraman), 1971. MNemberships: Executive Committee, BAPLA; Executive Committee, Outdoor Writers Guild. Literary Agent: Laurel Anderson, Photosynthesis/Offshoot, #219 180 Harbor Drive, Sausalito, CA 94965, USA. Address: Hill Cottage, Fonthill Gifford, Salisbury, Wiltshire SP3 6QW, England.

CLEARY Beverly Atlee, b. 12 Apr 1916, McMinnville, Oregon, USA. Writer. m. Clarence T Cleary, 6 Oct 1940, 1 son, 1 daughter. Education: BA, University of California at Berkeley, 1938; BA, University of Washington, 1939. Publications: Henry Huggins, 1950; Fifteen, 1956; The Mouse and the Motorcycle, 1965; Ramona the Pest, 1968; Dear Mr Henshaw, 1983; A Girl From Yamhill: A Memoir, 1988; Strider, 1991; Muggie Magic, 1992. Contributions to: Horn Book Magazine. Honours: Laura Ingalls Wilder Award, 1975; Newberry Honor Books, 1978, 1982; Newbery Award, 1984; Christopher Award, 1984; Everychild Award, 1985; Doctor of Humane Letters, 1992. Membership: Authors League of America. Address: Morrow Junior Books, 1350 Avenue of the Americas, New York, NY 10019, USA.

CLEARY Jon (Stephen), b. 22 Nov 1917, Sydney, New South Wales, Australia. Writer of Novels/Short Stories/Screenplays. Appointments: Journalist, Australian News and Information Bureau, London, 1948-49 and New York City 1949-51. Publications: The Small Glories (short stories), 1945; You Can't See Round Corners, 1947; The Long Shadow, 1949; Just Let Me Be, 1950; The Sundowners, 1952, screenplay 1961; The Climate of Courage (in US asNaked in the Night), 1954; Justin Bayard, 1955; The Green Helmet, 1957, screenplay 1960; Back of Sunset, 1959; (with H Watt) The Siege of Pinchgut (screenplay), 1959; North from Thursday, 1960; The Country of Marriage, 1961; Forest of the Night, 1962; Pillar of Salt (short stories), 1963; A Flight of Chariots, 1964; The Fall of an Eagle, 1965; The Pulse of Danger, 1966; The High Commissioner, 1967; The Long Pursuit, 1968; Season of Doubt, 1969; Remember Jack Hoxie, 1970; Helga's Webb, 1971; The Liberators (in UK as Mask of the Andes), 1971; The Ninth Marquess (in UK as Man's Estate), 1972; Ransom, 1973; Peter's Pence, 1974; Sidecar Boys (screenplay), 1974; The Safe House, 1975; A Sound of Lightning, 1976; High Road to China, 1977; Vortex, 1977; The Beaufort Sisters, 1979; A Very Pirate War, 1980; The Golden Sabre, 1981; The Faraway Drums, 1981; Spearfield's Daughter, 1982; The Phoenix Tree, 1984; The City of Fading Light, 1985; Dragons at the Party, 1987; Now and Then, Amen, 1988; Babylon South, 1989; Murder Song, 1990; Pride's Harvest, 1991; Dark Summer, 1992; Bleak Spring, 1993; Autumn Maze, 1994; Winter Chill, 1995; Endpeace, 1996. Literary Agent: Vivienne Schuster, Curtis Brown Ltd, Haymarket, London, England. Address: c/o Harper Collins, 77-85 Fulham Palace Road, London W6 8JB, England.

CLEESE John (Marwood), b. 27 Oct 1939, Weston-super-Mare, Somerset, England. Author; Actor. m. (1) Connie Booth, 1968, diss 1978, 1 daughter, (2) Barbara Trentham, 1981, diss 1990, 1 daughter, (3) Alyce Faye Eichelberger, 1993. Education: Clifton Sports Academy; MA, Downing College, Cambridge. Appointments: Many stage, television, and film appearances. Publications: Families and How to Survive Them (with Robin Skynner), 1983; The Golden Skits of Wing Commander Muriel Volestrangler FRHS and Bar, 1984; The Complete Fawlty Towers (with Connie Booth), 1989; Life and How to Survive It (with Robin Skynner), 1993. Honour: Honorary LLD, St Andrews. Address: c/o David Wilkinson, 115 Hazlebury Road, London SW6 2LX, England.

CLEEVE Brian Talbot, b. 22 Nov 1921, Thorpe Bay, Essex, England. Author; Journalist. m. Veronica McAdie, 24 Sept 1945, 2 daughters. Education: BA, University of South Africa, 1954; PhD, University of Ireland, Dublin, 1956. Publications: Cry of Morning, 1970; Sara, 1975; House on the Rock, 1980; The Fourth Mary, 1982; Biographical Dictionary of Irish Writers, 1985; A Woman of Fortune, 1993. Contributions to: Numerous short stories, various magazines. Honours: Award, Mystery Writers of America, 1965 (short story, Foxer); Knight of Mark Twain, 1972-73. Literary Agent: Elaine Markson, 44 Greenwich Avenue, NY, USA. Address: 60 Heytesbury Lane, Ballsbridge, Dublin 4, Ireland.

CLEMENT Francois, b. 21 Feb 1929, Paris, France. Physician. m. Jacqueline Tanner, 18 Sept 1986, 2 sons, 1 daughter. Education: Medicine Diploma, 1953; Privat-docent of Haematology, 1969. Appointment: Head of Haematologic Malignancies Unit, CHUV, 1981. Publication: Feuille de Bouleau, 1994. Contributions to: Medical scientific publications. Honours: Viganello Prize, 1964; Samuel Cruchand Prize, 1990. Membership: Société suisse des écrivains. Address: Ave Leman 39, 1005 Lausanne, Switzerland/

CLIFT Eleanor. Editor; Journalist. m. Tom Brazaitis. Appointments: Secretary to National affairs Editor, New York, first woman to move from Secretary to Reporter, Reporter in Atlanta Bureau, White House Correspondent, Congressional and Political Correspondent, 6 years, Washington Deputy Bureau Chief, 1992-94, Contributing Editor, 1994-, Newsweek; White House Correspondent, Los Angeles Times, 1985; Regular Guest on talk show, The McLaughlin Group and many other television shows including CNN'S Crossfire, Inside Politics, CNN & Co, ABC's Nightline and on BBC Radio and TV. Publication: War without Bloodshed: The Art of Politics (with Tom Brazaitis), 1996. Membership: Board, International Women's Media Foundation. Address: c/o Newsweek, 1750 Pennsylvania Avenue NW, Washington DC 20006, USA.

CLIFTON (Thelma) Lucille, b. 27 June 1956, Depew, New York, USA. Professor of Literature and Creative Writing; Poet. m. Fred J Clifton, 1958, dec, 1984, 2 sons, 4 daughters. Education: Howard

University, Washington, DC, 1953-55; Fredonia State Teachers College, New York, 1955. Appointments: Poet-in-Residence, Coppin State College, Baltimore, 1972-76; Poet Laureate of Maryland, 1976-85; Visiting Writer, George Washington University, Washington DC, 1982-83; Professor of Literature and Creative Writing, University of California at Santa Cruz, 1985-; Distinguished Visiting Professor, St Mary's College, Maryland, 1989-91. Publications: Poetry: Good Times, 1969; Good News about the Earth, 1972; An Ordinary Woman, 1974; Two-Headed Woman, 1980; Good Woman: Poems and a Memoir, 1969-1980, 1987; Next, 1987; Ten Oxherding Pictures, 1989; Quilting: Poems, 1987-1990, 1991; The Book of Light, 1993. Other: Generations, 1976. Children's Books: 14 books, 1970-81. Honours: YM-YWHA Poetry Center Discovery Award, 1969; National Endowment for the Arts Grants,. 1970, 1972; Juniper Prize, 1980; Coretta Scott King Award, 1984. Address: c/o Curtis Brown, 10 Astor Place, New York, NY 10003, USA.

CLINTON Dorothy Louise Randle, b. 6 Apr 1925, Des Moines, Iowa, USA. m. Moses S Clinton, 6 June 1950, 1 son. Education: BA, Drake University, 1949. Publications include: The Only Opaque Light, 1989; Memory Lapse, 1983; Ascending Line, 1978; The Look and the See, 1979; Snobbery in Nuance, 1978; Black Dignity in Marsh and Haunting Could Be Love; Selected Poets of the New Era by American Poetry Association; You Don't Hear the Echo, You Don't Know, 1991; Blind Transfer; Stop the Itch Without a Bitch. Honours: Clover Award, 1974, 1975; Editors Choice Award, 1989; Editors' Preference Award of Excellence, 1995; Winner, A Question of Balance Contest; Several Editors' Choice Awards, National Library of Poetry; Several Accomplishments of Merit, Creative Arts and Science Enterprises. Memberships: International Society of Poets; International Society of Authors and Artist. Address: 1530 Maple, Des Moines, IA 50316, USA.

CLINTON Jeff, See: **BICKHAM Jack (Miles).**

CLIVE William. See: **BASSETT Ronald Leslie.**

CLOUDSLEY-THOMPSON John Leonard, b. 23 May 1921, Murree, India. Professor of Zoology Emeritus; Writer. m. Jessie Anne Cloudsley, 1944, 3 sons. Education: BA, 1946, MA, 1948, PhD, 1950, Pembroke College, Cambridge; DSc, London, 1960; F I Biol; FWAAS. Appointments: Lecturer in Zoology, King's College, 1950-60, Reader in Zoology, 1971-72, Professor of Zoology, 1972-86, Professor of Zoology Emeritus, 1986-, Birkbeck College, University of London; Professor of Zoology, University of Khartoum and Keeper, Sudan Natural History Museum, 1960-71; National Science Foundation Senior Resident Fellow, University of New Mexico, 1969; Visiting Professor, University of Kuwait, 1978, 1983, University of Nigeria, 1981, University of Qatar, 1986, Australian National University, 1987, Sultan Qaboos University, Muscat, 1988, Desert Ecological Research Unit of Namibia, 1989, Leverhulme Emeritus Fellow, University College, London, 1987-89; Consultantships; Various expeditions. Publications: Biology of Deserts (editor), 1954; Spiders, Scorpions, Centipedes and Mites, 1958, 2nd edition, 1968; Animal Behaviour, 1960; Rhythmic Activity in Animal Physiology and Behaviour, 1961; Land Invertebrates (with John Sankey), 1961; Life in Deserts (with M J Chadwick), 1964; Desert Life, 1965; Animal Conflict and Adaptation, 1965; Animal Twilight: Man and Game in Eastern Africa, 1967; Microecology, 1967; Zoology of Tropical Africa, 1969; The Temperature and Water Relations of Reptiles, 1972; Terrestrial Environments, 1975; Insects and History, 1976; Evolutionary Trends in the Mating of Anthropoda, 1976; Environmental Physiology of Animals (co-editor), 1976; Man and the Biology of Arid Zones, 1977; The Desert, 1977; Animal Migration, 1978; Why the Dinosaurs Became Extinct, 1978; Wildlife of the Desert, 1979; Biological Clocks: Their Functions in Nature, 1980; Tooth and Claw: Defensive Strategies in the Animal World, 1980; Sahara Desert (editor), 1984; Guide to Woodlands, 1985; Evolution and Adaptation of Terrestrial Arthropods, 1988; Ecophysiology of Desert Arthropods and Reptiles, 1991; Predation and Defence Amongst Reptiles, 1994; The Nile Quest (novel), 1994; Biotic Interactions in Arid Lands, 1996; Editor-in-Chief, Journal of Arid Environments, Springer-Verlag series, Adaptations of Desert Organisms; Monographs; 11 children's books. Contributions to: Encyclopedias and scholarly journals. Honours: Liveryman, Worshipful Company of Skinners, 1952-; Royal African Society Medal, 1969; Silver Jubilee Gold Medal and Honorary DSc, University of Khartoum, 1981; Institute of Biology KSS Charter Award, 1981; J H Grundy Memorial Medal, Royal Army Medical College, 1987; Foundation for Environmental Conservation Prize, Geneva, 1989; Peter Scott Memorial Award, British Naturalists' Association, 1993. Memberships: British Arachnological Society, president, 1982-85;

British Herpetological Society, president, 1991-96; British Society of Chronobiology, president, 1985-87; Linnean Society, vice-president, 1975-76, 1977-78. Address: 10 Battishill Street, London N1 1TE, England.

CLOUGH Brenda W(ang), b. 13 Nov 1955, Washington, District of Columbia, USA. Writer. m. Lawrence A Clough, 21 May 1977, 1 daughter. Education: BA, Carnegie Mellon University, 1977. Publications: The Crystal Crown, 1984; The Dragon of Mishbil, 1985; The Realm Beneath, 1986; The Name of the Sun, 1988; An Impossible Summer, 1992; How Like a God, 1997. Contributions to: Short stories in anthologies and periodicals. Address: 1941 Barton Hill Road, Reston, VA 20191, USA.

CLUSTER Richard Bruce, (Dick Cluster), b. 17 June 1947, Maryland, USA. Writer, 1 son. Education: BA, Harvard University, 1968; Venceremos Brigade, Cuba, 1970; Auto Mechanics Certificate, Newton Massachusetts High School, 1971. Publications: They Should Have Served That Cup of Coffee, 1979; Shrinking Dollars, Vanishing Jobs, 1980; Return to Sender, 1988; Repulse Monkey, 1989; Obligations of the Bone, 1992. Literary Agent: Gina Maccoby, New York, USA; Gregory & Radice, London, England. Address: 33 Jackson Street, Cambridge, MA 02140, USA.

CLUTTERBUCK Richard Lewis, b. 22 Nov 1917, London, England. Security Consultant. m. Angela Muriel Barford, 15 May 1948, 3 sons. Education: MA, Mechanical Sciences, Cambridge University, 1939; PhD, Politics, London University, 1971. Publications: Living with Terrorism, 1975; Guerrillas and Terrorists, 1980; Britain in Agony, 1980; The Media and Political Violence, 1983; Industrial Conflict and Democracy, 1984; Conflict and Violence in Singapore & Malaysia, 1985; Kidnap Hijack and Extortion, 1987; Terrorism Drugs and Crime in Europe After 1992, 1990; Terrorism and Guerrilla Warfare: Forecasts and Remedies, 1990; International Crisis and Conflict, 1993; Terrorism in an Unstable World, 1994; Drugs, Crime and Corruption: Thinking the Unthinkable, 1995; Public Safety and Civil Liberties, 1997. Contributions to: Magazines and journals in UK and USA. Address: Department of Politics, University of Exeter, Exeter EX4 4RJ, England.

CLUYSENAAR Anne, (Alice Andree), b. 15 Mar 1936, Brussels, Belgium, Irish Citizen. Lecturer; Poet; Song-Writer; Librettist; Painter. m. Walter F Jackson, 1976. Education: BA, Trinity College Dublin, 1957; University of Edinburgh. Appointments: Lecturer, Sheffield Polytechnic, 1976-87; Currently, Part-time Lecturer, University of Wales, Cardiff. Publications: A Fan of Shadows, 1967; Nodes, 1969; Double Helix, 1982; Aspects of Literary Stylistics, 1976; Selected Poems of James Burns Singer (editor), 1977; Poetry Introduction 4, 1978; Time-Slips, New and Selected Poems, 1995. Contributions to: Poetry Wales; Planet; New Welsh Review; Poetry Nation Review. Honours: Chair, Verbal Arts Association, 1983-86; Poetry Society Representative, Gwent, 1994-. Address: Little Wentwood Farm, Llantrisant, Usk, Gwent NP5 1ND, Wales.

COASE Ronald (Harry), b. 29 Dec 1910, Willesden, London, England (US citizen). Professor Emeritus and Senior Fellow in Law and Economics; Writer. m. Marian Ruth Hartung, 7 Aug 1937. Education: BCom, 1932, DScEcon, 1951, London School of Economics. Appointments: Assistant Lecturer, Dundee School of Economics, 1932-34, University of Liverpool, 1934-35; Assistant Lecturer to Reader, London School of Economics, 1935-40, 1946-51; Head, Statistical Division, Forestry Commission, 1940-41; Statistician, later Chief Statistician, Central Statistical Office, Offices of War Cabinet, 1941-46; Professor, University of Buffalo, 1951-58, University of Virginia, 1958-64; Editor, Journal of Law and Economics, 1964-92; Clifford R Musser Professor, 1964-82, Professor Emeritus and Senior Fellow in Law and Economics, 1982-, University of Chicago. Publications: British Broadcasting: A Study in Monopoly, 1950; The Firm, the Market and the Law, 1988; Essays on Economics and Economists, 1994. Honours: Rockefeller Fellow, 1948; Senior Research Fellow, Hoover Institution, Stanford University, 1977; Nobel Prize for Economic Science, 1991; honorary doctorates. Memberships: American Academy of Arts and Sciences, fellow; American Economic Association, distinguished fellow; British Academy, corresponding fellow; European Academy; London School of Economics, honorary fellow; Royal Economic Society. Address: 1515 North Astor Street, Chicago, IL 60610, USA.

COATES Kenneth Sidney, b. 16 Sept 1930, Leek, Staffordshire, England. Member, European Parliament; Special Professor in Adult

Education. m. Tamara Tura, 21 Aug 1969, 3 sons, 3 daughters. Education: Mature State Scholar, 1956, BA, 1959, Nottingham University. Appointments: Assistant Tutor to Senior Tutor, 1960-80, Reader, 1980-89, Special Professor in Adult Education, 1990-, Nottingham University; Member, Labour Party, Nottingham, 1989-94, Nottinghamshire North and Chesterfield, 1994-, European Parliament. Publications: Industrial Democracy in Great Britain (with A J Topham), 1967, 3rd edition, 1976; Poverty: The Forgotten Englishman (with R L Silburn), 1970, 4th edition, 1983; The New Unionism (with A J Topham), 1972, 2nd edition, 1974; Trade Unions in Britain (with A J Topham), 1980, 3rd edition, 1988; Heresies: The Most Dangerous Decade, 1984; Trade Unions and Politics (with A J Topham), 1986; Think Globally, Act Locally, 1988; The Making of the Transport and General Workers' Union (with A J Topham), 1991; A European Recovery Programme, 1993; Full Employment for Europe (with Stuart Holland), 1995; Common Ownership: Clause Four and the Labour Party, 1995; The Right to Work: The Loss of Our First Freedom, 1995. Memberships: Bertrand Russell Peace Foundation; Institute of Workers' Control. Address: Bertrand Russell House, Gamble Street, Nottingham NG7 4ET, England.

COBB Vicki, b. 19 Aug 1938, New York, New York, USA. Writer. m. Edward S Cobb, 31 Jan 1960, div 1983, 2 sons. Education: BA, Barnard College, 1958; MA, Columbia University, 1960. Publications: Science Experiments You Can Eat, 1972; Lots of Rot, 1981; How to Really Fool Yourself, 1981; The Secret Life of School Supplies, 1981; Bet You Can't, Science Impossibilities to Fool You, 1981; Gobs to Goo, 1983; The Monsters Who Died, 1983; Chemically Active, 1985; Inspector Bodyguard, 1986; The Science Safari Series; The Imagine Living Here Series; Inventions Series. Contributions to: Numerous Professional Journals. Honours: Childrens Science Book Award, 1981; Washington Irving Childrens Book Choice Award, 1984; Eva L Gordon Award, 1985; Commended by COPUS and the London Science Museum, 1989. Memberships: Authors Guild; ASJA; Society of Childrens Book Writers; National Writers Union. Address: 302 Pondside Drive, White Plains, NY 10607, USA.

COBBETT Richard. See: **PLUCKROSE Henry Arthur.**

COBBING Bob, b. 30 July 1920, Enfield, Middlesex, England. Poet. Education: Teacher's Certificate, Bognor Training College, 1949. Appointments: Coordinator, Association of Little Presses, 1971-92; Co-editor, Poetry and Little Press Information, 1980-92. Publications include: Bill Jubobe: Selected Poems, 1942-75, 1976; Cygnet Ring: Collected Poems 1, 1977; A Movie Book, 1978; Two-Leaf Book, 1978; Concerning Concrete Poetry (with Peter Mayer) 1978; Found: Sound, 1978; Principles of Movement, 1978; Meet Bournemouth, 1978; Fugitive Poem No X, 1978; Game and Set, 1978; Ginetics, 1978; ABC/Wan do Tree: Collected Poems 2, 1978; Sensations of the Retina, 1978; A Peal in Air: Collected Poems 3, 1978; Fiveways, 1978; Niagara, 1978; Grin, 1979; A Short History of London (with Jeremy Adler), 1979; The Kollekted Kris Kringle: Collected Poems 4, 1979; Pattern of Performance, 1979; The Sacred Mushroom (with Jeremy Adler), 1980; Notes from the Correspondence, 1980; Voicings 1980; (Soma), Light Song, 1981; Serial Ten (Portraits), 1981; Four Letter Poems, 2 series, 1981; Sound of Jade, 1982; In Line, 1982; Baker's Dozen, 1982; Lightsong Two, 1983; Bob Cobbing's Girlie Poems, Collected Poems 5, 1983; Sockless in Sandals: Collected Poems 6, 1985; Vowels and Consequences, Collected Poems 7, 1985; Lame, Limping, Mangled, Marred and Mutilated: Collected Poems 9, 1986; Metamorphosis, 1986; Variations on a Theme, 1986; Astound and Risible: Collected Poems 8, 1987; Processual, Collected Poems 10, 1987; Entitled: Entitled: Collected Poems 11, 1987; Improvisation is a Dirty Word: Collected Poems 12, 1990; Bob Jubile: Selected Poems 1944-90, 1990; Resonanzas, 1991; Grogram, 1991; Fuerteventura, 1992; Voice Prints: Collected Poems 13, 1993; Poems by RWC for RWC, collected Poems 14, 1995; Domestic Ambient Noise (with Lawrence Upton) 1994-96; Gibbering His Wares, Collected Poems 15, 1996. Address: 89A Petherton Road, London N5 2QT, England.

COBURN Andrew, b. 1 May 1932, Exeter, New Hampshire, USA. Writer. Education: Suffolk University, Boston, 1954-58. Publications: Novels: The Trespassers, 1974; The Babysitter, 1979; Off Duty, 1980; Company Secrets, 1982; Widow's Walk, 1984; Sweetheart, 1985; Love Nest, 1987; Goldilocks, 1989; No Way Home, 1992; Voices in the Dark, 1994. Contributions to: Transatlantic Magazine. Honour: Honorary DLitt, Merrimack College, USA, 1986. Literary Agent: Smith/Skolnik, 23 East 10th Street, No 712, New York,

NY 10003, USA. Address: 303 Walnut Street, Westfield, NJ 07090, USA.

COCHRAN Jeff. See: **DURST Paul.**

COCKETT Mary, b. 1915, British. Children's Fiction and Non-Fiction. Appointments: Editor, National Institute of Industrial Psychology, 1943-48, International Congress of Mental Health, 1948-49. Publications: The Marvellous Stick, 1972; The Joppy Stories; Boat Girl, 1972; Bells in Our Lives, 1973; Treasure, 1973; The Rainbow Walk, 1973; Look at the Little One, 1974; Dolls and Puppets, 1974; Walls, 1974; Snake in the Camp, 1975; Tower Raven, 1975; Backyard Bird Hospital, 1975; The Story of Cars, 1976; The Drowning Valley, 1978; The Birthday, 1979; Ladybird at the Zoo, Monster in the River, Pig at the Market, 3 Picture Books, 1979; The Christmas Tree, 1979; Money to Spend, 1980; Shadow at Applegarth, 1981; Hoo Ming's Discovery, 1982; The Cat and the Castle, 1982; The School Donkey, 1982; At the Tower, 1984; Crab Apples, 1984; Strange Hill, 1984; Zoo Ticket, 1985; Rescue at the Zoo, 1986; Winning All the Way, 1987; Kate of Candlewick, 1987; The Day of the Squirrels, 1987; A Place of his Own, 1987; Mystery on the Farm, 1988; Bridesmaids, 1989. Address: 24 Benville Avenue, Bristol BS9 2RX, England.

CODRESCU Andrei, b. 20 Dec 1946, Sibiu, Romania (US citizen, 1981). Professor of English; Author; Poet; Editor; Radio and Television Commentator. m. Alice Henderson, 12 Sept 1969, 2 sons. Education: BA, University of Bucharest, 1965. Appointments: Professor of English, Louisiana State University, 1966-; Commentator, All Things Considered, National Public Radio; Editor, Exquisite Corpse, literary journal. Publications: Novels: The Repentence of Lorraine, 1994; The Blood Countess, 1995. Poetry: Comrade Past and Mister Present, 1991; Belligerence, 1993; Alien Candor: Selected Poems, 1970-1995, 1996. Essays: Raised by Puppets Only to be Killed by Research, 1987; Craving for Swan, 1988; The Disappearance of the Outside: A Manifesto for Escape, 1990; The Hole in the Flag: A Romanian Exile's Story of Return and Revolution, 1991; Road Scholar: Coast to Coast Late in the Century, 1993; The Muse is Always Half-Dressed in New Orleans, 1995; Zombification: Essays from NPR, 1995; The Dog With the Chip in His Neck: Essays from NPR & Elsewhere, 1996. Editor: American Poetry Since 1970: Up Late, 1988; The Stiffest of the Corpse: An Exquisite Corpse Reader, 1983-1990, 1990; American Poets Say Goodbye to the 20th Century, 1996. Film: Road Scholar, Public Broadcasting Service, 1994; The Blood Countess; The Muse is Always Half-Dressed in New Orleans; Zombification. Honours: George Foster Peabody Award, 1995; Freedom of Speech Award, American Civil Liberties Union, 1995; Literature Prize, Romanian Cultural Foundation, 1996. Address: 1114 Peniston, New Orleans, LA 70115, USA.

CODY James. See: **ROHRBACH Peter Thomas.**

COE Jonathan, b. 19 Aug 1961, Birmingham, England. Author. m. Janine McKeown, 28 Jan 1989. Education: BA, Trinity College, Cambridge, 1983; MA, 1984, PhD, 1986, Warwick University. Publications: The Accidental Woman, 1987; A Touch of Love, 1989; The Dwarves of Death, 1990; Humphrey Bogart: Take It and Like It, 1991; James Stewart: Leading Man 1994; Windshaw Legacy, 1994. Contributions to: Periodicals. Address: c/o Peake Associates, 14 Grafton Crescent, London NW1 8LS, England.

COERR Eleanor (Beatrice), (Eleanor B Hicks, Eleanor Page), b. 29 May 1922, Kamsack, Saskatchewan, Canada. Writer. m. Wymberley De Renne Coerr, 10 June 1965. Education: BA, American University, 1969; MLS, University of Maryland, 1971. Appointments: Reporter; Editor; Librarian; Writer. Publications: Many children's books, 1953-93. Address: c/o Harper Collins Childrens Books, Harper Collins Publishers Inc, 10 East 53rd Street, New York, NY 10022, USA.

COERS Donald (Vernon), b. 2 June 1941, San Marcos, Texas, USA. Professor of English; University Administrator; Writer; Editor. m. Mary Jeanne Coers, 30 Dec 1966, 1 son, 1 daughter. Education: BA, 1963, MA, 1969, University of Texas at Austin; PhD, Texas A&M University, 1974. Appointments: Assistant Professor, 1969-79, Associate Professor, 1979-86, Professor of English, 1986-, Coordinator of Graduate Studies, 1992-95, Associate Vice-President for Academic Affairs, 1995-, Sam Houston State University; Associate Editor, The Sam Houston Literary Review, 1976-79; Non-Fiction Editor, 1979-82, Associate Editor, 1979-, The Texas Review. Publications: John Steinbeck as Propagandist: The Moon is Down Goes to War,

1991; After the Grapes of Wrath: Essays on John Steinbeck (co-editor with Paul Ruffin), 1995. Contributions to: Books and journals. Honours: Elizabeth Agee Prize, University of Alabama Press, 1990; Excellence in Service Award, Sam Houston State University, 1991; Paul Harris Fellow, 1993; Burkhardt Award, Ball State University Foundation, 1995. Address: 3799 Summer Lane, Huntsville, TX 77340, USA.

COETZEE John Michael, b. 9 Feb 1940, Cape Town, South Africa. Writer; Professor. 1 son, 1 daughter. Education: BA, 1960, MA, 1963, University of Cape Town; PhD, University of Texas, USA, 1969. Appointments: Assistant Professor, English, State University of New York, Buffalo, 1968-71; Lecturer, English, University of Cape Town, 1972-82; Butler Professor of English, State University of New York, Buffalo, 1984, 1986; Professor of General Literature, University of Cape Town, 1984-; Hinkley Professor of English, Johns Hopkins University, 1986, 1989; Visiting Professor, English, Harvard University, 1991. Publications: Dusklands, 1974; In the Heart of the Country, 1977; Waiting for the Barbarians, 1980; Life and Times of Michael K, 1983; Foe, 1986; White Writing, 1988; Age of Iron, 1990; Doubling the Point, 1992; The Master of Petersburg, 1994; Giving Offence, 1996. Contributions to: Essays in various journals. Honours: CNA Literary Awards, 1977, 1980, 1983; James Tait Black Prize, 1980; Geoffrey Faber Award, 1980; Booker McConnell Prize, 1983; Prix Femina Etranger, 1985; Jerusalem Prize, 1987; Sunday Express Award, 1990; Premio Mondello, 1994; Irish Times International Fiction Prize, 1995. Address: PO Box 92, Rondebosch, 7700, South Africa.

COFFEY Brian. See: **KOONTZ Dean R.**

COFFIN Tristram Potter, b. 13 Feb 1922, San Marino, California, USA. Professor; Consultant. m. Ruth Anne Hendrickson, 15 Feb 1944, 2 sons, 2 daughters. Education: BS, Haverford College, 1943; MA, 1947, 1949, PhD, University of Pennsylvania. Appointments: Secretary-Treasurer, American Folklore Society, 1961-65; Editor, various book series in AFS. Publications: The British Traditional Ballad in North America, 1950, 3rd edition, 1977; The Old Ball Game, 1971; The Book of Christmas Folklore, 1973; The Female Hero, 1975; The Folklore of the American Holidays, 1987; Twelve others written or edited. Contributions to: Seventy articles and numerous reviews. Honours: Book of The Month Club Selection, 1974; American Library Association Outstanding Reference Selection, 1988. Address: Box 509, Wakefield, RI 02880, USA.

COFFMAN Virginia (Edith), (Victor Cross, Virginia Du Vaul, Jeanne Duval, Anne Stanfield), b. 30 July 1914, San Francisco, California, USA. Author. Education: AB, University of California at Berkeley, 1938. Publications: Survivor of Darkness, 1973; The Ice Forest, 1976; Looking Glass, 1979; The Lombard Cavalcade, 1982; Dark Winds, 1985; The Royles, 3 volumes, 1991, 1992, 1994. Address: c/o Severn House Publishers Ltd, 41 East 57th Street, 15th Floor, New York, NY 10022, USA.

COGSWELL Frederick William, b. 8 Nov 1917, East Centreville, New Brunswick, Canada. Professor Emeritus; Author; Poet; Editor; Translator. m. (1) Margaret Hynes, 3 July 1944, dec 2 May 1985, 2 daughters, (2) Gail Fox, 8 Nov 1985. Education: BA, 1949, MA, 1950, University of New Brunswick; PhD, University of Edinburgh, 1952. Appointments: Assistant Professor, 1952-57, Associate Professor, 1957-61, Professor, 1961-83, Professor Emeritus, 1983-, University of New Brunswick; Editor, Fiddlehead Magazine, 1952-66, Humanities Association Bulletin, 1967-72. Publications: The Stunted Strong, 1955; The Haloed Tree, 1956; Testament of Cresseid, 1957; Descent from Eden, 1959; Lost Dimensions, 1960; A Canadian Anthology, 1960; Five New Brunswick Poets, 1962; The Arts in New Brunswick, 1966; Star People, 1968; Immortal Plowman, 1969; In Praise of Chastity, 1970; One Hundred Poems of Modern Quebec, 1971; The Chains of Liliput, 1971; The House Without a Door, 1973; Against Perspective, 1979; A Long Apprenticeship: Collected Poems, 1980; Pearls, 1983; The Edge to Life, 1987; The Best Notes Merge, 1988; Black and White Tapestry, 1989; Unfinished Dreams: Contemporary Poetry of Acadie, 1990; Watching an Eagle, 1991; When the Right Light Shines, 1992; In Praise of Old Music, 1992; In My Own Growing, 1993; As I See It, 1994; In Trouble With Light, 1996. Honours: Order of Canada; Medals; Awards. Memberships: League of Canadian Poets; PEN; Writers Federation of New Brunswick. Address: Comp A6, Site 6, RR4, Fredericton, New Brunswick E3B 4X5, Canada.

COHAN Tony, (Anthony Robert Cohan), b. 28 Dec 1939, New York, New York, USA. Writer. m. 1 June 1974, 1 daughter. Education: BA, University of California, 1961. Publications: Nine Ships, 1975; Canary, 1981; The Flame, 1983; Opium, 1984; Agents of Desire, 1997; Mexicolor, 1997. Honour: Notable Book of the Year, 1981. Memberships: Authors Guild; PEN. Address: PO Box 1170, Venice, CA 90294, USA.

COHEN Daniel, b. 12 Mar 1936, Chicago, Illinois, USA. Author. m. Susan Handler, 2 Feb 1958, 1 daughter dec. Education: Journalism degree, University of Illinois, 1959. Appointments: Assistant Editor, 1960-65, Managing Editor, 1965-69, Science Digest. Publications: About 100 books of young adult non-fiction; 10 children's books; 20 other books; Over 25 books in collaboration with wife. Membership: Authors Guild. Address: 24 Elizabeth Street, Port Jervis, NY 12771, USA.

COHEN Leonard, b. 21 Sept 1934, Montreal, Quebec, Canada. Novelist; Short Story Writer; Playwright/Screenplay Writer; Poet; Songwriter/Lyricist; Professional Composer and Singer. Publications: Let Us Compare Mythologies, 1956; The Spice-Box of Earth, 1961; The Favourite Game (novel), 1963; Flowers for Hitler, 1964; Parasites of Heaven, 1966; Beautiful Losers (novel), 1966; Selected Poems, 1956-68, 1968; Leonard Cohen's Song Book, 1969; The Energy of Slaves, 1972; The Next Step (play), 1972; Death of a Lady's Man, 1979; Book of Mercy (poetry), 1984; Stranger Music: Selected Poems and Songs, 1993. Literary Agent: McClelland and Stewart Ltd, Canada. Address: c/o Kelley Lynch, Stranger Management, Suite 91, 419 North Larchmont Blvd, Los Angeles, CA 90004, USA.

COHEN Matthew, b. 30 Dec 1942, Kingston, Ontario, Canada. Novelist; Short Story Writer; Poet; Translator; Former Teacher. Education: BA, 1964, MA, 1965, University of Toronto. Publications: Korsoniloff, 1969; Johnny Crackle Sings, 1971; Columbus and the Fat Lady and Other Stories, 1972; Too Bad Galahad (short stories), 1972; The Disinherited, 1974; Peach Melba (poetry), 1975; The Colours of War, 1978; Night Flights: Stories New and Selected, 1978; The Sweet Second Summer of Kitty Malone, 1979; Flowers of Darkness, 1981; The Expatriate: Collected Short Stories, 1982; Cafe Le Dog (short stories), 1983; The Spanish Doctor (novel), 1984; Nadine (novel), 1986; Living on Water (stories), 1988; Emotional Arithmetic (novel), 1990. Membership: Chairman, The Writer's Union of Canada, 1985-86. Address: c/o Bella Pomer Agency, 22 Shallmar Boulevard, PH2, Toronto, Ontario M5N 2Z8, Canada.

COHEN Michael Joseph, b. 29 Apr 1940, London, England. Professor of History; Writer. Education: BA, University of London, 1969; PhD, London School of Economics and Political Science, 1971. Appointments: Lecturer, 1972-77, Senior Lecturer, 1977-81, Associate Professor, 1981-86, Professor, 1986-, Lazarus Philips Chair of History, 1990-, Bar Ilan University; Visiting Professor, Stanford University, 1977, 1981, Hebrew University, Jerusalem, 1978-80, 1981-83, Duke University and University of North Carolina, Chapel Hill, 1980-81, University of British Columbia, 1985-86; Bernard and Andre Rapaport Fellow, American Jewish Archives, Cincinnati, 1988-89; Meyerhoff Visiting Professor of Israel Studies, University of Maryland, College Park, 1992. Publications: Palestine: Retreat From the Mandate, 1936-45, 1978; Palestine and the Great Powers, 1982; Churchill and the Jews, 1985; The Origins of the Arab-Zionist Conflict, 1914-1948, 1987; Palestine to Israel: From Mandate to Independence, 1988; Truman and Israel, 1990; Fighting World War Three from the Middle East: Allied Contingency Plans, 1945-1954, 1996, Hebrew edition, 1997. Editor: The Weizmann Letters, Volumes XX, XXI, 1936-1945, 1979; The History of the Founding of Israel, Part III, The Struggle for the State of Israel, 1939-1948, 1988; Bar-Ilan Studies in Modern History, 1991; British Security Problems in the Middle East During the 1930s: The Conquest of Abyssinia to World War Two (with Martin Kolinsky), 1992; The Demise of Empire: Britain's Responses to Nationalist Movements in the Middle East, 1943-1955 (with Martin Kolinsky), 1997. Contributions to: Scholarly journals. Address: c/o General History Department, Bar-Ilan University, 52900 Ramat-Gan, Israel.

COHEN Morton Norton, (John Moreton), b. 27 Feb 1921, Calgary, Alberta, Canada. Professor; Lecturer; Author. Education: AB, Tufts University, 1949; MA, 1950, PhD, 1958, Columbia University. Appointments: Tutor to Professor, City College, 1952-81, Member, Doctoral Faculty, City University, 1964-81, Deputy Executive Officer, PhD Programme in English, 1976-78, 1979-80, Professor Emeritus,

1981-, City University of New York. Publications: Rider Haggard: His Life and Works, 1960, 2nd edition, revised, 1968; A Brief Guide to Better Writing (co-author), 1960; Rudyard Kipling to Rider Haggard: The Record of a Friendship, 1965; Lewis Carroll's Photographs of Nude Children, 1978, republished as Lewis Carroll, Photographer of Children: Four Nude Studies, 1979; The Russian Journal II, 1979; Lewis Carroll and the Kitchins, 1980; Lewis Carroll and Alice 1832-1882, 1982; Lewis Carroll: Interviews and Recollections, 1989; Editor: The Letters of Lewis Carroll, 2 volumes, 1979; The Selected Letters of Lewis Carroll, 1982, 3rd edition, 1995; Lewis Carroll and the House of Macmillan (co-editor), 1987; Lewis Carroll: A Biography, 1995. Contributions to: Many magazines, journals, papers and books. Honours: Fulbright Fellow, 1954-55, 1974-75; Guggenheim Fellowship, 1966-67; Research Grant, National Endowment for the Humanities, 1974-75; Publication Grant, Guggenheim Foundation, 1979; Royal Society of Literature, fellow. Memberships: Lewis Carroll Society; Lewis Carroll Society of North America; Tennyson Society; Century Association, New York. Address: 55 East 9th Street, Apartment 10-D, New York, NY 10003, USA.

COHEN Sharleen Cooper, b. 11 June 1940, Los Angeles, California, USA. Author. m. Martin L Cohen, 27 Aug 1972, 2 daughters. Education: University of California at Berkeley, 1957-58; University of California at Los Angeles, 1958-60; Los Angeles Valley Film School, 1976-78. Publications: The Day after Tomorrow, 1979; Regina's Song, 1980; The Ladies of Beverly Hills, 1983; Marital Affairs, 1985; Love, Sex and Money, 1988; Lives of Value, 1991; Innocent Gestures, 1994; Sheba (musical stage production), 1995-96. Contributions to: Good Housekeeping. Memberships: Authors Guild; PEN; Writers Guild of America. Address: 24858 Malibu Road, Malibu, CA 90265, USA.

COHEN Stephen F(rand), b. 25 Nov 1938, Indianapolis, Indiana, USA. Professor of Politics and Russian Studies; Writer. m. (1) Lynn Blair, 25 Aug 1962, div, 1 son, 1 daughter, (2) Katrina vanden Heuvel, 4 Aug 1988, 1 daughter. Education: BA, 1960, MA, 1962, Indiana University; PhD, 1969, Russian Institute Certificate, 1969, Columbia University. Appointments: Instructor, Columbia College, 1965-68; Junior Fellow, 1965-68, Senior Fellow, 1971-73, 1976-77, 1985, Associate, 1972-85, Visiting Professor, 1973-84, Visiting Scholar, 1980-81, Columbia University; Assistant Professor, 1968-73, Faculty Associate, Center of International Studies, 1969-, Director, Russian Studies Program, 1973-80, 1989-94, Princeton University; Consultant and Commentator, CBS News; Associate Editor, World Politics. Publications: The Great Purge Trial (co-editor), 1965; Bukharin and the Bolshevik Revolution: A Political Biography, 1888-1938, 1973; The Soviet Union Since Stalin (co-editor), 1980; An End to Silence: Uncensored Opinion in the Soviet Union (editor), 1982; Rethinking the Soviet Experience: Politics and History Since 1917, 1985, expanded edition, 1997; Sovieticus: American Perceptions and the Soviet Realities, 1985; Voices of Glasnost: Interviews with Gorbachev's Reformers (co-author and co-editor), 1989. Contributions to: Books, scholarly journals and periodicals. Honours: Guggenheim Fellowships, 1976-77, 1989; Rockefeller Foundation Humanities Fellowship, 1980-81; National Endowment for the Humanities Fellowship, 1984-85; Fulbright-Hays Faculty Research Abroad Fellowship, 1988-89. Memberships: American Association for the Advancement of Slavic Studies; American Historical Association; American Political Science Association; Council on Foreign Relations. Address: c/o Department of Politics, 247 Corwin Hall, Princeton University, Princeton, NJ 08544, USA.

COHEN Susan, b. 27 Mar 1938, Chicago, Illinois, USA. Author. m. Daniel Cohen, 2 Feb 1958, 1 daughter dec. Education: University of Illinois, 1957-59; BA, New School for Social Research, 1960; MSW, Adelphi University, 1962. Publications: 25 books in collaboration with husband; 8 Gothic books; 4 mystery books. Address: 24 Elizabeth Street, Port Jervis, NY 12771, USA.

COHN Samuel Kline Jr, b. 13 Apr 1949, Birmingham, Alabama, USA. Professor of Medieval History; Writer. m. Genevieve A Warwick, 15 July 1994, 1 son. Education: BA, Union College, 1971; MA, University of Wisconsin at Madison, 1973; Dip di Statistica, Universita degli Studi di Firenze, 1976-77; PhD, Harvard University, 1978. Appointments: Assistant Professor, Wesleyan University, 1978-79; Assistant Professor, 1979-85, Associate Professor, 1986-89, Professor of History, 1989-95, Brandeis University; Visiting Professor, Brown University, 1990-91; Professor of Medieval History, University of Glasgow, 1995-. Publications: The Laboring Classes in Renaissance Florence, 1980; Death and Property in Siena 1205-1800: Strategies for the Afterlife, 1988; The Cult of Remembrance and the Black Death: Six Renaissance Cities in Central Italy, 1992; Portraits of Medieval and Renaissance Living: Essays in Memory of David Herlihy (editor), 1996; Women in the Streets: Essays on Sex and Power in the Italian Renaissance, 1996; The Black Death and the Transformation of the West (with David Herlihy), 1996. Contributions to: Scholarly books and journals. Honours: Honorary Krupp Foundation Fellowship, 1976; Fulbright-Hays Fellowship, Italy, 1977; Fellow, Center for European Studies, Harvard University, 1977-; National Endowment for the Humanities Research Fellowship, 1982-83; Guest Fellow, Villa I Tatti, Settignano, Italy, 1988-89; Howard R Marraro Prize, American Catholic Historical Association, 1989; Outstanding Academic Book Selection, Choice magazine, 1993; Villa I Tatti Fellowship, 1993-94; Guggenheim Fellowship, 1994-95. Memberships: American Historical Association; Society for Italian Historical Studies; Royal Historical Society, fellow. Address: 8 Clevedon Crescent, Glasgow G12 0PB, Scotland.

COLBORN Nigel, b. 20 Feb 1944, Nottingham, England. Journalist; TV Presenter; Author; Gardener. m. Rosamund F M Hewlett, 10 Nov 1972, 2 sons, 2 daughters. Education: King's School, Ely, Cambs, England; BSc, Cornell University, USA, 1968. Publications: The Classic Horticulturist, 1987; This Gardening Business (Humour), 1989; Leisurely Gardening, 1989; Family Piles (Humour), 1990; The Container Garden, 1990; Short Cuts to Great Gardens, 1993; The Good Old Fashioned Gardener, 1993; Annuals and Bedding Plants, 1994; The Kirkland Acres (novel), 1994; The Congregation (novel), 1996; A Flower for Every Day, 1996. Contributions to: Gardening and rural press, including New York Times, Country Life, Homes and Gardens, Hortus, The Garden; BBC Gardeners' World Magazine; Sunday Telegraph; Times; Country Homes. Honour: Royal Society of Arts, fellow. Memberships: Society of Authors; Royal Horticultural Society, Member of Standing Committee; Hardy Plant Society; Alpine Garden Society; International PEN. Address: Careby Manor, Careby, Stamford, Lincolnshire PE9 4EA, England.

COLE Adrian Christopher Synnot, b. 22 July 1949, Plymouth, England. Local Government Officer; Author. m. 25 May 1977, 1 son, 1 daughter. Publications: The Dream Lords, 1975; Madness Emerging, 1976; Paths in Darkness, 1977; The Lucifer Experiment, 1981; The Sleep of Giants, 1984; A Place Among the Fallen, 1986; The God in Anger, 1988; Mother of Storms, 1989; Thief of Dreams, 1989; Warlord of Heaven, 1990; Labyrinth of Worlds, 1990. Contributions to: Numerous Magazines and Journals. Membership: British Fantasy Society. Literary Agent: Abner Stein. Address: The Old Forge, 35 Meddon Street, Bideford, Devon Ex39 2EF, England.

COLE Barry, b. 13 Nov 1936, Woking, Surrey, England. Writer. m. Rita Linihan, 1959, 3 daughters. Literary Appointments: Northern Arts Fellow in Literature, Universities of Durham and Newcastle-upon-Tyne, England, 1970-72. Publications: Blood Ties, 1967; Ulysses in the Town of Coloured Glass, 1968; A Run Across the Island, 1968; Moon Search, 1968; Joseph Winter's Patronage, 1969; The Search for Rita, 1970; The Visitors, 1970; The Giver, 1971; Vanessa in the City, 1971; Pathetic Fallacies, 1973; The Rehousing of Scaffardi; Dedications, 1977; The Edge of the Common, 1989; Inside Out: New and Selected Poems, 1997. Contributions to: New Statesman; Spectator; Listener; Times Educational Supplement; Times Higher Educational Supplement; Critical Survey; Atlantic Monthly; Tribune; London Magazine; Transatlantic Review; The Observer; The Guardian. Address: 68 Myddelton Square, London EC1R 1XP, England.

COLE Joanna, (Ann Cooke), b. 11 Aug 1944, Newark, New Jersey, USA. Children's Author. m. Philip A Cole, 8 Oct 1965, 1 daughter. Education: University of Massachusetts at Amherst; Indiana University; BA, City College of New York, 1967. Publications: Over 35 non-fiction books for children; 28 fiction books for children; 9 anthologies for children. Honours: Numerous awards and citations. Memberships: Authors Guild; Authors League of America; Society of Children's Book Writers. Address: 3 Dug Hill, Newton, CT 06470, USA.

COLE John Morrison, b. 23 Nov 1927, Belfast, Northern Ireland. Journalist; Broadcaster. m. Margaret Isobel Williamson, 4 Sept 1956, 4 sons. Eduction: London University, 1952. Publications: The Poor of the Earth, 1976; The Thatcher Years, 1987; As It Seemed to Me: political memoirs, 1995. Contributions to: Guardian; New Statesman. Honours: Granada Television newspaper awards, 1960; Royal Television Society Broadcast Journalist of the Year, 1990;

BAFTA Richard Dimbleby Award, 1992; Honorary Doctorates from Open University, 1992, Queen's University, Belfast, 1992, University of Ulster, 1992 and St Andrews University, 1993. Membership: Athenaeum Club. Address: c/o BBC Office, House of Commons, Westminister, London SW1A 0AA, England.

COLE William (Rossa), b. 20 Nov 1919, Staten Island, New York, USA. Author; Poet; Reviewer. m. (1) Peggy Bennett, May 1947, div, 2 daughters, (2) Galen Williams, 10 July 1967, 2 sons. Appointments: Publicity Director, 1946-58, Publicity Director and Editor, 1958-61, Simon & Schuster Inc, New York City; Columnist, Trade Winds, Saturday Review, 1974-79; Book Reviewer, Endless Vacation, 1990-. Publications: A Cat-Hater's Handbook, or, The Ailurophobe's Delight (with Tomi Ungerer), 1963; Uncoupled Couplets: A Game of Rhymes, 1966. Editor: 8 poetry anthologies and 10 other anthologies; 7 anthologies for children; 35 cartoon anthologies. Contributions to: Periodicals. Honour: American Library Association Notable Books, 1958, 1964, 1965. Memberships: Authors Guild; American PEN; International PEN; Poets and Writers; Poetry Society of America. Address: 201 West 54th Street, New York, NY 10019, USA.

COLEGATE Isabel Diana, b. 10 Sept 1931, London, England. Novelist. m. Michael Briggs, 12 Sept 1953, 2 sons, 1 daughter. Education: Runton Hill School, Norfolk, England. Appointment: Literary Agent, Anthony Blond (London) Ltd, 1952-57. Publications: The Blackmailer, 1958; A Man of Power, 1960; The Great Occasion, 1962; Statues in a Garden, 1964; Orlando King, 1968; Orlando at the Brazen Threshold, 1971; Agatha, 1973; News from the City of the Sun, 1979; The Shooting Party, 1980 (filmed 1985); A Glimpse of Sion's Glory, 1985; Deceits of Time, 1988; The Summer of the Royal Visit, 1991; Winter Journey, 1995. Honours: Fellow, Royal Society of Literature, 1981; W H Smith Literary Award, 1981; Honorary MA, University of Bath, 1988. Memberships: Author's Society. Literary Agent: Peters Fraser & Dunlop. Address: Midford Castle, Bath BA1 7BU, England.

COLEMAN Jane (Winthrop) Candia, b. 9 Jan 1939, Pittsburgh, Pennsylvania, USA. Writer. m. (1) Bernard D Coleman, div 1989, (2) Glenn G Boyer, 1989, 2 sons. Education: BA, University of Pittsburgh, 1961. Appointments: Writer-in-Residence, 1980-85, Director, Women's Creative Writing Center, 1985-86, Carlow College, Pittsburgh; Lecturer, University of Pittsburgh, 1981. Publications: Stories from Mesa Country; No Roof But Sky; Deep in His Heart JR is Laughing at Us; Discovering Eve; Shadows in My Hands, 1993; Doc Holliday's Woman, 1995; Moving On, 1997. Contributions to: Christian Science Monitor; Horseman; Puerto Del Sol; South Dakota Review; Pennsylvania Review; Yankee; Aqassiz Review; Snowy Egret. Honours: Writing Grant, Pennsylvania Council on the Arts; Western Heritage Award, Poetry, Short Fiction; Grant, Arizona Arts Commission, 1993; Spur Award, Western Writers of America, 1993. Memberships: Western Writers of America; Authors Guild; PEN. Literary Agent: Susan Crawford, Box 198 Evans Road, Barnstead, NH 03218, USA. Address: PO Box 40, Rodeo, NM 88056, USA.

COLEMAN Robert Gordon, b. 17 July 1922, Beechworth, Victoria, Australia. Journalist; Author. m. Lilian Gill, 4 June 1949, 1 daughter. Appointments: Working Journalist (reporter, feature writer, cadet counsellor, columnist, leader writer), 1940-86; Freelance Journalist and Author, 1986-. Publications: Reporting for Work (editor), 1970; The Pyjama Girl, 1978; Above Renown, 1988; Seasons in the Sun, 1993. Honours: Australian Automobile Association National Journalism Award, 1967; Highly Commended, Graham Perkin Award for Journalist of the Year, 1980. Memberships: Australian Journalists Association (Honorary); Victorian Fellowship of Australian Writers. Address: 34 Folkestone Crescent, Beaumaris, Victoria 3193, Australia.

COLEMAN Terry, b. 13 Feb 1931, Bournemouth, England. Reporter; Author. Education: LLB, London University, England. Appointments: Reporter, Poole Herald; Editor, Savoir Faire; Sub-editor, Sunday Mercury; Birmingham Post; Reporter, Arts Correspondent and then Chief Feature Writer, Guardian 1961-74; Special Writer, Daily Mail, 1974-76; Special Correspondent, 1976-79, New York Correspondent, 1980-81, Special Correspondent, 1982-89, Guardian; Associate Editor, The Independent, 1989-91; Columnist, Guardian and Mail on Sunday, 1992-. Publications: The Railway Navvies, 1965; Providence and Mr Hardy (with Lois Deacon), 1966; The Only True History, 1969; Passage to America, 1971; The Liners, 1976; Southern Cross, 1979; The Scented Brawl, 1979; Thanksgiving, 1981; Movers and Shakers, 1987; Thatcher's Britain, 1987; Empire,

1994. Contributions to: Sunday Times; Times; Observer; Daily Telegraph; Sunday Telegraph; New Statesman; Queen; Illustrated London News; Night and Day; New York Times; Saturday Evening Post. Honours: Yorkshire Post Prize, Best First Book of Year, 1965; Feature Writer of the Year, British Press Awards, 1982; Journalist of the Year, Granada Awards, 1988. Membership: Society of Authors. Address: 18 North Side, London SW4 0RQ, England.

COLERIDGE Nicholas David, b. 4 Mar 1957, London, England. Journalist; Author. m. Georgia Elizabeth Metcalfe, 22 July 1989, 2 sons, 1 daughter. Education: Trinity College, Cambridge; Eton College. Appointments: Editor, Harpers & Queen Magazine, 1986-89; Editorial Director, 1989-91, Managing Director, 1992-, Conde Nast Publishers. Publications: Tunnel Vision, 1981; Around the World in 78 Days, 1984; Shooting Stars, 1984; The Fashion Conspiracy, 1988; How I Met My Wife and Other Stories, 1991; Paper Tigers, 1993; With Friends Like These, 1997. Contributions to: Harpers & Queen; Spectator; Daily Telegraph; Sunday Telegraph; Tatler; Evening Standard; GQ; Vanity Fair. Honour: Young Journalist of the Year, 1983. Literary Agent: Ed Victor. Address: 39 Kensington Park Gardens, London W11, England.

COLES Donald Langdon, b. 12 Apr 1928, Woodstock, Ontario, Canada. Professor; Poet. m. 28 Dec 1958, 1 son, 1 daughter. Education: BA, Victoria College; MA, University of Toronto; MA (Cantab), 1954.Appointments: Fiction Editor, The Canadian Forum, 1975-76; Director, Creative Writing Programme, York University, 1979-85; Poetry Editor, May Studio, Banff Centre for the Fine Arts, 1984-93. Publications: Sometimes All Over, 1975; Anniversaries, 1979; The Prinzhorn Collection, 1982; Landslides, 1986; K in Love, 1987; Little Bird, 1991; Forests of the Medieval World, 1993; Someone Has Stayed in Stockholm: Selected and New Poems, 1994. Contributions to: Saturday Night; Canadian Forum; London Review of Books; Poetry (Chicago); Globe and Mail; Arc; Ariel. Honours: CBC Literary Competition, 1980; Gold Medal for Poetry, National Magazine Awards, 1986; Governor General's Award for Poetry, Canada, 1993. Membership: PEN International. Address: 122 Glenview Avenue, Toronto, Ontario M4R 1P8, Canada.

COLES Robert (Martin), b. 12 Oct 1929, Boston, Massachusetts, USA. Physician; Teacher; Writer. m. Jane Hallowell, 3 sons. Education: AB, English, Harvard College, 1950; MD, College of Physicians and Surgeons, Columbia University, 1954; Internship, University of Chicago Clinics, 1954-55; Psychiatric Residency, McLean Hospital, 1956-57. Appointments: Contributing Editor: New Republic, 1966-, American Poetry Review, 1972-, Aperture, 1974-, Literature and Medicine, 1981-, New Oxford Review, 1981-. Publications: Children of Crisis, 5 volumes, 1967, 1972, 1978; The Middle Americans, 1970; The Geography of Faith, 1971; The Old Ones of New Mexico, 1973; William Carlos Williams, 1975; Walker Percy, 1978; Flannery O'Connor's South, 1980; The Moral Life of Children, 1986; The Political Life of Children, 1986; Simone Weil, 1987; Dorothy Day, 1987; The Call of Stories: Teaching and the Moral Imagination, 1989. Contributions to: Atlantic Monthly; New Yorker; New York Times Book Review. Honours: Atlantic Grant, 1966; McAlpin Medal, 1972; Weatherford Prize, 1973; Lillian Smith Award, 1973; Pulitzer Prize in General Non-Fiction, 1973; MacArthur Prize, 1981. Address: 81 Carr Road, Concord, MA 01742, USA.

COLLIER Catrin, See: WATKINS Karen Christna.

COLLIER Jane. See: COLLIER Zena.

COLLIER Richard Hughesdon, b. 8 Mar 1924, London, England. Author. m. Patricia Eveline Russell, 24 July 1953. Education: Whitgift School, Croydon, England. Appointments: Associate Editor, Phoenix Magazine for the Forces, SE Asia, 1945-46; Editor, Town and Country Magazine, 1946-48; Features Staff, Daily Mail, 1948-49. Publications: Ten Thousand Eyes, 1958; The Sands of Dunkirk, 1961; The General Next to God, 1965; Eagle Day, 1966; Duce!, 1971; Bridge Across the Sky, 1978; The City That Wouldn't Die, 1979; 1940: The World in Flames, 1979; 1941: Armageddon, 1981; The War That Stalin Won, 1983; The Rainbow People, 1984; The Warcos, 1989; The Few (co-author), 1989; D-Day: 6 June 1944, 1992; The Past is a Foreign Country, 1996. Contributions to: Reader's Digest; Holiday; The Times. Honour: Knight of Mark Twain, 1972. Memberships: Author's Guild of America; Author's League of America; Society of Theatre Research; Society of Authors. Literary Agent: Curtis Brown. Address: c/o Curtis Brown Group Limited, 28-29 Haymarket, London SW1Y 4SP, England.

COLLIER Zena, (Jane Collier, Zena Shumsky), b. 21 Jan 1926, London, England. Writer. m. (1) Louis Shumsky, 2 sons, 1 dec, (2) Thomas M Hampson, 30 Dec 1969. Appointments: Writer-in-Residence, Just Buffalo, 1984-, Southern Tier Library System, Corning, 1985-, Niagara Erie Writers, Buffalo, 1986; Teacher, Writers Workshop, Nazareth College, Rochester. Publications: Novels: A Cooler Climate, 1990; Ghost Note, 1992; Children's books: As Zena Collier: Next Time I'll Know; Seven for the People - Public Interest Groups at Work; as Jane Collier: The Year of the Dream; A Tangled Web; as Zena Shumsky with Lou Shumsky: First Flight; Shutterbug. Contributions to: Southern Humanities Review; Southwest Review; Prairie Schooner; McCalls; Alfred Hitchcock's Mystery Magazine; Literary Review; New Letters; Upstate; Publishers Weekly; Los Angeles Times Book Review. Honours: Hoepfner Prize; Citation on Honour Roll of Best American Short Stories; Nomination for Pushcart Prize; Resident Fellow: Yaddo, Macdowell, Virginia Center for the Creative Arts, Alfred University Summer Place. Memberships: Authors Guild; Writers and Books; Poets and Writers. Address: c/o Harvey Klinger, 301 West 53rd Street, New York, NY 10019, USA.

COLLINS Hunt. See: **LOMBINO Salvatore A.**

COLLINS Jackie, b. England. Novelist; Short Story Writer; Actress. m. Oscar Lerman. Publications: The World is full of Married Men, 1968; The Stud, 1969; Lovehead, 1974; The World is Full of Divorced Women, 1975; The Love Killers, 1977; Lovers and Gamblers, 1977; The Bitch, 1979; Chances, 1981; Sinners, 1981; Hollywood Wives, 1983; Lucky, 1985; Hollywood Husbands, 1986; Rock Star, 1988; Lady Boss, 1990; American Star, 1993; The World is Full of Married Men, 1993. Address: c/o Simon and Schuster, 1230 Avenue of the Americas, New York, NY 10020, USA.

COLLINS Jim, (James Lee Collins), b. 30 Dec 1945, Beloit, Wisconsin, USA. Author; Editor. m. Joan Hertel, 27 Dec 1974, 2 sons. Publications: Comanche Trail, 1984; Gone to Texas, 1984; War Clouds, 1984; Campaigning, 1985; Orphans Preferred, 1985; Riding Shotgun, 1985; Mister Henry, 1986; The Brass Boy, 1987; Spencer's Revenge, 1987; Western Writers Handbook, 1987; Settling the American West, 1993. Contributions to: The Blue and the Gray; Writers Digest Magazine. Memberships: Colorado Authors League; National Writers Club; Western Writers of America. Address: c/o NWC 194500 South Havana Street, Suite 620, Aurora, CO 80014, USA.

COLLINS Joan, b. 23 May 1933, London, England. Education: RADA. Career: Film and television Actress, 1951-. Publications include: Past Imperfect, 1978; Joan Collins's Beauty Book, 1982; Katy - A Fight for Life, 1983; Prime Time, 1988; Love and Desire and Hate, 1990; My Secrets, 1994; Too Damn Famous, 1995. Honours include: Golden Globe Best Actress, 1983; People's Choice Most Popular Actress, 1983, 1984. Address: c/o Stella Wilson Publicity, 130 Calabria Road, Highbury, London N5, England.

COLLINS Larry, (John Laurence Collins Jr.), b. 14 Sept 1929, Hartford, Connecticut, USA. Author. Education: BA, Yale University, 1951. Appointments: Correspondent, United Press International, Paris, Rome and Beirut, 1957-59; Correspondent, Beirut, 1959-61, Bureau Chief, Paris, 1961-65, Newsweek magazine. Publications: Is Paris Burning? (with Dominique Lapierre), 1965; Or I'll Dress You in Mourning, 1968; O Jerusalem, 1972; Freedom at Midnight, 1975; The Fifth Horseman, 1980; Fall from Grace, 1985; Maze, 1989; Black Eagles, 1993. Honours: Deauville Film Festival Literary Award, 1985; Mannesman Talley Literary Prize, 1989. Literary Agent: Alan Nevini, Renaissance, 8325 Sunset Boulevard, Los Angeles, CA, USA. Address: c/o E P Dutton, 340 Hudson Street. New York, NY, USA.

COLLINS Michael. See: **LYNDS Dennis.**

COLLINS Philip (Arthur William), b. 28 May 1923, London, England. Professor of English (retired); Author. Education: MA, Emmanuel College, Cambridge, 1947. Appointments: Warden, Vaughan College, 1954-62; Senior Lecturer 1962-64, Professor of English 1964-82, University of Leicester; Member, Board of Directors, The National Theatre, 1976-82. Publications: James Boswell, 1956; English Christmas (editor), 1956; Dickens and Crime, 1962; Dickens and Education, 1963; The Impress of the Moving Age, 1965; Thomas Cooper the Chartist: Byron and the Poets of the Poor, 1969; A Dickens Bibliography, 1970; Dickens: A Christmas Carol: The Public Reading Version, 1971; Bleak House: A Commentary, 1971; Dickens: The Critical Heritage (editor), 1971; Reading Aloud: A Victorian Metier,

1972; Charles Dickens: The Public Readings (editor), 1975; Charles Dickens: David Copperfield (editor), 1977; Charles Dickens: Hard Times (editor), 1978; Dickens: Interviews and Recollections (editor), 1981; Thackeray: Interviews and Recollections (editor), 1982; Tennyson, Poet of Lincolnshire, 1985; The Annotated Dickens (edited with Edward Giuliano), 1986; Tennyson: Seven Essays (editor), 1992. Contributions to: Encyclopaedia Britannica; Listener; Times Literary Supplement. Address: 26 Knighton Drive, Leicester LE2 3HB, England.

COLLIS Louise Edith, b. 29 Jan 1925, Arakan, Burma. Writer. Education: BA History, Reading University, England, 1945. Publications: Without a Voice, 1951; A Year Passed, 1952; After the Holiday, 1954; The Angel's Name, 1955; Seven in the Tower, 1958; The Apprentice Saint, 1964; Solider in Paradise, 1965; The Great Flood, 1966; A Private View of Stanley Spencer, 1972; Maurice Collis Diaries (editor), 1976; Impetuous Heart, the story of Ethel Smyth, 1984. Contributions to: Books and Bookmen; Connoisseur; Art and Artists; Arts Review; Collectors Guide; Art and Antiques. Memberships: Society of Authors; International Association of Art Critics. Address: 65 Cornwall Gardens, London SW7 4BD, England.

COLLOMS Brenda, (Brenda Cross, Brenda Hughes), b. 1 Jan 1919, London, England. Author; Editor. Education: BA, University of London, 1956; MA, University of Liverpool, 1958. Appointment: Editor, The Film Star Diary, Cramp Publishers, London, 1948-63. Publications: Happy Ever After (as Brenda Cross), 1947; The Film Hamlet (as Brenda Cross), 1948; New Guinea Folk Tales (as Brenda Hughes), 1959; Folk Tales from Chile (as Brenda Hughes), 1962; Certificate History, Books 1-4: Britain and Europe, 1966-70; Israel, 1971; The Mayflower Pilgrims, 1973; Charles Kingsley, 1975; Victorian Country Parsons, 1977; Victorian Visionaries, 1982; The Making of Tottie Fox, (as Brenda Colloms). Address: 123A Gloucester Avenue, London NW1 8LB, England.

COLMAN E(rnest) A(drian) M(ackenzie), b. 8 Dec 1930, Glasgow, Scotland. Professor Emeritus of English; Writer; Editor. Education: MA, University of Glasgow 1952; PhD, University of New South Wales, 1970. Appointments: Lecturer in English 1962-70, Senior Lecturer 1970-74, Associate Professor 1974-78, University of Sydney, New South Wales; Research Associate, Shakespeare Institute, University of Birmingham, England, 1968-69; Professor of English, University of Tasmania, Hobart, 1978-90; Chairman of Board, Australian Theatre for Young People, 1975-78. Publications: Shakespeare's Julius Caesar, 1965; The Structure of Shakespeare's Antony and Cleopatra, 1971; The Dramatic Use of Bawdy in Shakespeare, 1974; Poems of Sir Walter Raleigh (editor), 1977; King Lear (editor), 1982; Henry IV Part I (editor), 1987; Romeo and Juliet (editor), 1993. Address: 250 Churchill Avenue, Sandy Bay, Tasmania, Tas 7005, Australia.

COLOMBO Furio Marco, b. 1 Jan 1931, Chatillon, Italy. Journalist; Writer. m. Alice Oxman, 16 Aug 1969, 1 daughter. Education: Law Degree, University of Turin, 1954. Appointments: Editor, Communicazione Visiva, University of Bologna, 1970-77; Communicazioni di Massa, Milan, 1979-84; Sanpaolo Clair, International Journalism, Graduate School of Journalism, Columbia University, 1991. Publications: Nuovo Teatro Americano, 1963; L'America di Kennedy, 1964; Le Donne Matte, 1964; Il Prigioniero della Torre Velasca, 1965; Cosa Faro da Grande, 1986; Carriera: Vale Una Vita Rizzoli, 1989; Il Destino Del Libro E Altri Destini, 1990; Il Terzo Dopoguerra, 1990; Scene Da Una Vittoria, 1991; Oer Israele, 1991; La Citta Profona, 1991. Contributions to: Books and journals. Honours: Trumball Lecturer, Yale University, USA, 1964; Chair, Italian Culture, University of California, Berkeley, 1975; Tevere Prize for Literature, Rome, 1986; Amalfi Prize for Best TV Documentary; Capri Prize for Journalism. Memberships: Scientific Committee, Pio Manzu International Research Centre; Secretary, Friends of Palazzo Grassi Committee, Venice; Board of Visitors, Columbia University, New York. Address: 444 Madison Avenue, Suite 2109, New York, NY 10022, USA.

COLOMBO John (Robert), b. 24 Mar 1936, Kitchener, Ontario, Canada. Author; Editor; Translator; Communications Consultant. m. Ruth Florence Brown, 11 May 1959, 2 sons, 1 daughter. Education: Waterloo College, 1956-57; BA, 1959, Graduate Studies, 1959-60, University of Toronto. Appointments: Author, editor or translator of over 100 varied titles such as collections of quotations, anthologies. Contributions to: Periodicals and radio programmes. Honours: 1st Writer-in-Residence, Mohawk College, 1979-80; Various prizes and awards. Address: 42 Dell Park Avenue, Toronto, Ontario M6B 2T6, Canada.

COLQUHOUN Keith, b. 5 Aug 1937, London, England. Journalist; Novelist. 3 sons, 3 daughters. Appointments: Reporter, provincial British newspapers, 1955-59; Chief Sub-Editor, London Daily Herald, Sun, 1959-70; Managing Editor, Observer, 1970-77; News Editor, Far Eastern Economic Review, Hong Kong, 1977-80; Asian Affairs Writer, The Economist, 1980-. Publications: The Money Tree, 1958; Point of Stress, 1960; The Sugar Coating, 1973; St Petersburg Rainbow, 1975; Goebbels and Gladys, 1981; Filthy Rich, 1982; Kiss of Life, 1983; Foreign Wars, 1985; Mad Dog, 1992. Address: The Old Rectory, East Mersea, Essex, England.

COLTON James. See: **HANSEN Joseph.**

COLVIN Sir Howard (Montagu), b. 15 Oct 1919, Sidcup, Kent, England. Historian. m. Christina Edgeworth Butler, 16 Aug 1943, 2 sons. Education: BA, University College, London; MA, Oxford University, 1948. Publications: The White Canons in England, 1951; A History of Deddington, 1963; The History of the King's Works (general editor and part author), 6 volumes, 1962-82; Catalogue of Architectural Drawings in Worcester College Library, 1964; A Biographical Dictionary of British Architects 1600-1840, 1978, 3rd edition, 1995; Unbuilt Oxford, 1983; Calke Abbey, Derbyshire, 1985; The Canterbury Quadrangle: St John's College, Oxford, 1988; All Souls: An Oxford College and its Buildings (with J S G Simmons), 1989; Architecture and the After-Life, 1991. Contributions to: among others: Archaeological Journal; Architectural Review; Country Life. Honour: Knighted, 1995. Address: 50 Plantation Road, Oxford OX2 6JE, England.

COLWELL Maxwell Gordon, b. 10 Oct 1926, Brompton, South Australia. Author. m. Betty Joy Holthouse, 27 Nov 1948, 2 sons. Appointment: Journalist, The Young Australian, 1960-62. Publications: Half Days and Patched Pants; Full Days and Pressed Pants; Glorious Days and Khaki Pants; Whaling Around Australia; Voyages of Matthew Flinders; The Journey of Burke and Wills; Others Big Rivers; Lights Vision the City of Adelaide. Contributions to: Bulletin. Honour: Australian Council Literature Board Senior Fellowship; Order of Australia, 1994. Membership: Australian Society of Authors. Address: 102 8th Avenue, Joslin, South Australia 5070, Australia.

COMAROFF John L(ionel), b. 1 Jan 1945, Cape Town, South Africa (US citizen). Professor of Anthropology and Social Sciences; Writer. m. Jean Rakoff, 15 Jan 1967, 1 son, 1 daughter. Education: BA, University of Cape Town, 1966; PhD, University of London, 1973. Appointments: Lecturer in Social Anthropology, University College of Swansea, 1971-72, University of Manchester, 1972-78; Visiting Assistant Professor of Anthropology, 1978, Associate Professor of Anthropology and Sociology, 1981-87, Professor of Anthropology and Social Sciences, 1987-96, Harold H Swift Distinguished Service Professor of Anthropology and Social Sciences, 1996-, University of Chicago; Directeur d'Études, 1988, Directeur d'Études Associé, 1995, École des Hautes Études en Sciences Sociales, Paris. Publications: The Diary of Sol T Plaatje: An African at Mafeking (editor), 1974; The Structure of Agricultural Transformation in Barolong, 1977; The Meaning of Marriage Payments (editor), 1980; Essays on African Marriage in Southern Africa (editor with E J Krige), 1981; Rules and Processes: The Cultural Logic of Dispute in an African Context (with S A Roberts), 1981; Of Revelation and Revolution: Christianity and Colonialism in South Africa (with J Comaroff), 1991; Ethnography and the Historical Imagination (with J Comaroff), 1992; Modernity and its Malcontents: Ritual and Power in Africa (editor with J Comaroff), 1993; Perspectives on Nationalism and War (editor with Paul C Stern), 1993. Contributions to: Scholarly books and journals. Honours: National Endowment for the Humanities Grants, 1984-85, 1986-87; National Science Foundation Grants, 1986-87, 1993; Spencer Foundation Grant, 1991; Laing Prize, University of Chicago, 1993; American Academy of Arts and Sciences, 1995; Spencer Foundation Mentor Award, 1996. Memberships: Royal Anthropological Institute, fellow; African Studies Association; International African Institute, fellow; Association of Social Anthroplogists; American Anthropological Association, fellow; Association of Political and Legal Anthropology, president, 1995-96. Address: c/o Department of Anthropology, University of Chicago, 1126 East 59th Street, Chicago, IL 60637, USA.

COMFORT Alexander, b. 10 Feb 1920, London, England. Physician; Adjunct Professor; Writer; Poet. m. (1) Ruth Muriel Harris,

1943, div 1973, 1 son, (2) Jane Tristam Henderson, 1973, dec 1991. Education: BA, 1943, MB, BCh, 1944, MA, 1945, Cambridge University; MRCS, LRCP, London Hospital, 1944; DCH, 1946, PhD, 1949, DSc, 1963, University of London. Appointments: House Physician, London Hospital, 1944; Resident Medical Officer, Royal Waterloo Hospital, London, 1944-45; Lecturer in Physiology, London Hospital Medical College, 1948-51; Honorary Research Associate, Department of Zoology, 1951-73, and Director of Research, Gerontology, 1966-73, University College, London; Clinical Lecturer, Department of Psychiatry, Stanford University, 1974-83; Professor, Department of Pathology, University of California School of Medicine at Irvine, 1976-78; Consultant Psychiatrist, Brentwood Veterans Administration Hospital, Los Angeles, 1978-81; Adjunct Professor, Neuropsychiatric Institute, University of California at Los Angeles, 1980-91; Consultant, Ventura County Hospital, California, 1981-91. Publications: Non-Fiction: Art and Social Responsibility: Lectures on the Ideology of Romanticism, 1946; The Novel and Our Time, 1948; Barbarism and Sexual Freedom: Lectures on the Sociology of Sex from the Standpoint of Anarchism, 1948; First Year Physiological Technique, 1948; Sexual Behavior in Society, 1950; Authority and Delinquency in the Modern State: A Criminological Approach to the Problem of Power, 1950; The Biology of Senescence, 1956; Darwin and the Naked Lady: Discursive Essays on Biology and Art, 1961; The Process of Ageing, 1964; The Nature of Human Nature, 1966; The Anxiety Makers: Some Curious Preoccupations of the Medical Profession, 1967; The Joy of Sex: A Cordon Bleu Guide to Lovemaking, 1972; More Joy: A Lovemaking Companion to "The Joy of Sex", 1974; A Good Age, 1975; Sexual Consequences of Disability, 1978; I and That: Notes on the Biology of Religion, 1979; The Facts of Love (with Jane Comfort), 1979; A Practice of Geriatric Psychiatry, 1980; What Is a Doctor?, 1980; Reality and Empathy: Physics, Mind, and Science in the 21st Century, 1984; Say Yes to Old Age: Developing a Positive Attitude Toward Aging, 1990; The New Joy of Sex, 1991; Writings Against Power and Death, 1993. Fiction: The Silver River, 1937; No Such Liberty, 1941; The Almond Tree, 1943; The Powerhouse, 1945; On This Side of Nothing, 1948; A Giant's Strength, 1952; Come Out to Play, 1961; Tetrach, 1980; Imperial Patient: The Memoirs of Nero's Doctor, 1987; The Philosophers, 1989. Poetry: France and Other Poems, 1942; A Wreath for the Living, 1942; Three New Poets: Roy McFadden, Alex Comfort, Ian Serrailler, 1942; Elegies, 1944; The Song of Lazarus, 1945; The Signal to Engage, 1946; And All But He Departed, 1951; Haste to the Wedding, 1962; Poems for Jane, 1979; Mikrokosmos, 1994. Honours: Ciba Foundation Prize for Research in Gerontology, 1958; Borestone Poetry Award, 2nd Prize, 1962; Karger Memorial Prize, 1969. Memberships: American Association of Sex Educators, Counselors and Therapists; American Medical Association; American Psychiatric Association; British Society for Research on Aging; Gerontological Society; Peace Pledge Union; Royal Society of Medicine. Address: 2 Fitzwarren House, Hornsey Lane, London N6 5LX, England.

COMFORT Nicholas Alfred Fenner, b. 4 Aug 1946, London, England. Political and Media Consultant. m. (1) 1970, div 1988, 1 son, 1 daughter, (2) Corinne Reed, 1990, 1 son. Education: MA History (Exhibitioner), Trinity College, Cambridge, England, 1968. Appointments: Morning Telegraph, Sheffield, 1968-74; Daily Telegraph, 1974-89 (Washington 1976-78, Political Staff, 1978-87, Leader Writer, 1987-89); Political Editor, The Independent on Sunday, 1989-90, The European, 1990-92, Daily Record, 1992-95; Consultant, Politics International 1996-. Publications: Mid-Suffolk Light Railway, 1986, new edition due 1997; The Tunnel - The Channel and Beyond, Contributor, 1987; Brewer's Politics - a Phase and Fable Dictionary, 1993, revised edition, 1995; The Lost City of Dunwich, 1994. Contributions to: Numerous political, transport and other journals. Membership: Fellow, Royal Geographical Society. Literary Agent: Patrick Walsh (of Christopher Little). Address: The Manor House, Swalcliffe, Banbury, Oxon, OX15 5EH, England.

COMINI Alessandra, b. 24 Nov 1934, Winona, Minnesota, USA. Professor of Art History; Author. Education: BA, Barnard College, 1956; MA, University of California, Berkeley, 1964; PhD, Columbia University, 1969. Appointments: Instructor, 1968-69, Assistant Professor, 1969-74, Columbia University; Visiting Assistant Professor, 1970, 1973, Associate Professor, 1974-75, Professor, 1976-, University Distinguished Professor of Art History, 1983-, Southern Methodist University; Alfred Hodder Fellow, Princeton University, 1972-73; Visiting Assistant Professor, Yale University, 1973; Associate Editor, Arts Magazine, 1977-88; Lansdown Professor, University of Victoria, British Columbia, 1981; Visiting Distinguished Professor,

California State University, Chico, 1990; Distinguished Visiting Fellow, European Humanities Research Centre, Oxford University, 1996. Publications: Schiele in Prison, 1973; Egon Schiele's Portraits, 1974; Gustav Klimt, 1975; Egon Schiele, 1976; The Fantastic Art of Vienna, 1978; The Changing Image of Beethoven: A Study in Mythmaking, 1987; Egon Schiele's Nudes, 1994. Contributions to: Books, journals, magazines, and exhibition catalogues. Honours: Charles Rufus Morey Book Award, College Art Association of America, 1976; Grand Decoration of Honour for Services to the Austrian Republic, 1990; Lifetime Achievement Award, Women's Caucus for Art, 1995. Memberships: College Art Association of America; Texas Institute of Letters; Women's Caucus for Art. Address: 2900 McFarlin, Dallas, TX 75205, USA.

COMMAGER Henry Steele, b. 25 Oct 1902, Pittsburgh, Pennsylvania, USA. Historian; Author. m. (1) Evan Carroll, 3 July 1928, 1 son, 2 daughters, (2) Mary E Powlesland, 14 July 1979. Education: PhB, 1923, MA, 1924, PhD, 1928, University of Chicago; MA, University of Copenhagen, Cambridge University, Oxford University. Appointments: Instructor, 1926-29, Assistant Professor, 1929-30, Associate Professor, 1930-31, Professor, 1931-38, in History, New York University; Professor of American History, 1939-56, Adjunct Professor, 1956-59, Sperenza Lecturer, 1960, Columbia University; Smith Professor of History, 1956-72, Simpson Lecturer, 1972-92, Amherst College; Many visiting lectureships and professorships in the US and abroad; Editor-in-Chief, The Rise of the American Nation series, 50 projected volumes. Publications: The Literature of the Pioneer West, 1927; The Growth of the American Republic (with Samuel Eliot Morison), 1931, 7th edition, 1980; Our Nation's Development, 1934; Theodore Parker, 1936; America: The Story of a Free People (with Allan Nevins), 1942, revised edition, 1982; Majority Rule and Minority Rights, 1943; A Short History of the United States (with Allan Nevins), 1945, 6th edition, 1976; The American Mind: An Interpretation of American Thought and Character Since the 1880's, 1950; Civil Liberties Under Attack (with others), 1951; Europe and America Since 1492 (with Geoffrey Brunn), 1954; Freedom, Loyalty, Dissent, 1954; Federal Centralization and the Press, 1956; Education in a Free Society (with Robert W McEwen and Brand Blanshard), 1961; The Nature and the Study of History, 1965; The Role of Scholarship in an Age of Science, 1965; Freedom and Order: A Commentary on the American Political Scene, 1966; The Study of History, 1966; Was America a Mistake?: An Eighteenth Century Controversy, 1967; The Search for a Usable Past, and Other Essays in Historiography, 1967; Colonies in Transition (with Richard B Morris), 1968; The Commonwealth of Learning, 1968; The Defeat of America: Presidential Power and the National Character, 1974; Britain Through American Eyes, 1974; Jefferson, Nationalism, and the Enlightenment, 1974; The Empire of Reason: How Europe Imagined and America Realized the Enlightenment, 1977; The Study and Teaching of History (with Raymond H Muessig), 1980. Other: Editor of many volumes, including: Documents of American History, 1934, 9th edition, 1973; The Heritage of America (with Allan Nevins), 1939, revised edition, 1949; The Story of the Second World War, 1945; The Blue and the Gray: The Story of the Civil War as Told by Participants, 1950; Living Ideas in America, 1951, revised edition, 1967; The Spirit of "Seventy-Six": The Story of the American Revolution as Told by the Participants (with Richard B Morris), 1958; Official Atlas of the Civil War, 1958; Living Documents of American History, 1960; The Era of Reform, 1830-1860, 1960; The Defeat of the Confederacy: A Documentary Survey, 1964; Fifty Basic Civil War Documents, 1965; The Struggle for Racial Equality: A Documentary Record, 1967; The West: An Illustrated History (with others), 1976; Illustrated History of the American Civil War (with others), 1979. Contributions to: Many books, scholarly journals and periodicals. Honours: Hillman Foundation Special Award, 1954; Knight, Order of Dannebrog, Denmark, 1957; Guggenheim Fellowship, 1960-61; American Academy and Institute of Arts and Letters Gold Medal, 1972; Sarah Josepha Hale Award, 1973; Pepper Medal, 1984; Jefferson Medal, Council for the Advancement and Support of Education, 1987; Gold Medal for Arts, Brandeis University, 1988; Many honorary doctorates. Memberships: American Academy of Arts and Letters; American Antiquarian Society; Massachusetts Historical Society; Phi Beta Kappa. Address: PO Box 2187, Amherst, MA 01004, USA.

COMPTON D(avid) G(uy), (Guy Compton, Frances Lynch), b. 19 Aug 1930, London, England. Writer. Education: Cheltenham College, Gloucester, 1941-50. Appointment: Editor, Reader's Digest Condensed Books, London, 1969-81. Publications: Too Many Murderers, 1962; Medium for Murder, 1963; Dead on Cue, 1964; Disguise for a Dead Gentleman, 1964; High Tide for Hanging, 1965; The Quality of Mercy, 1965; Farewell Earth's Bliss, 1966; The Silent Multitude, 1966; And Murder Came Too, 1966; Synthajoy, 1968; The Palace, 1969; The Electric Crocodile, 1970; Hot Wireless Sets, Aspirin Tablets, the Sandpaper Sides of Used Matchboxes and Something that Might Have Been Castor Oil, 1971; The Missionaries, 1972; The Continuous Katherine Mortenhoe, 1974; Twice Ten Thousand Miles, 1974; The Fine and Handsome Captain, 1975; Stranger at the Wedding, 1977; A Dangerous Magic, 1978; A Usual Lunacy, 1978; Windows, 1979; In the House of Dark Music, 1979; Ascendancies, 1980; Scudder's Game, 1985; Ragnarok (with John Gribbin), 1991; Normansland, 1992; Stammering, 1993; Justice City, 1994; Back of Town Blues, 1996. Address: c/o David Higham Associates, 5-8 Lower John Street, London, W1R 4HA, England.

CONDÉ Maryse, b. 11 Feb 1937, Pointe-à-Pitre, Guadeloupe, West Indies. Author; Playwright. m. (1) Mamadou Condé, 1958, div 1981, 3 children, (2) Richard Philcox, 1982. Education: PhD, Sorbonne, University of Paris, 1976. Appointments: Programme Producer, French Services, BBC, London, 1968-70, Radio France Internationale, 1980-; Assistant, Jussieu, 1970-72, Lecturer, Nantes, 1973-80, University of Paris divisions; Chargé de cours, Sorbonne, University of Paris, 1980-85; Professor of Francophone Literature, Columbia University, New York, 1995. Publications: Fiction: Heremakhonon, 1976, English translation, 1982; Une Saison a Rihata, 1981, English translation as A Season in Rihata, 1988; Ségou: Les murailles de terre, 1984, English translation as Segu, 1987; Ségou II: La terre en miettes, 1985, English translation as The Children of Segu, 1989; Pays Melé, short stories, 1985; Moi, Tituba, sorcière noire de Salem, 1986, English translation, 1992; La Vie scelerate (English translation as Tree of Life, 1992), 1987; Traversée de la mangrove, 1990, English translation, 1995; Les Derniers Rois Mages, 1992; La Migration des Coeurs, novel, 1995. Plays: Dieu nous l'a donne, 1972; Mort d'Oluwemi d'Ajumako, 1973; Pension les Alizes, 1988. Other: Anthologie de la litterature africaine d'expression française (editor), 1966; La Poesie antillaise (editor), 1977; La Roman antillais (editor), 1977; La Civilisation du bossale, 1978; Le profil d'une oeuvre: Cahier d'un retour au pays natal, 1978; La Parole des femmes, 1979. Contributions to: Anthologies and journals. Honours: Fulbright Scholar, 1985-86; Prix litteraire de la Femme, 1986; Prix Alain Boucheron, 1986; Guggenheim Fellowship, 1987-88; Académie Française Prize, 1988. Address: Montebello, 97190 Petit Bourg, Guadeloupe, West Indies.

CONDRY William Moreton, b. 1 Mar 1918, Birmingham, England. Writer. m. Penny Bailey, 17 Apr 1946. Education: BA 1939, DipEd 1940, Birmingham University; BA Hons French, London, 1945; MA, Wales,1951. Publications: Thoreau, 1954; The Snowdonia National Park, 1966; Birds and Wild Africa, 1967; Exploring Wales, 1970; Pathway to the Wild, 1975; Woodlands, 1974; The Natural History of Wales, 1981; Snowdonia, 1987; World of a Mountain, 1977; The National Trust - Wales, 1991. Contributor of the introduction and most of the text in Selborne (Gertrude Hermes Wood-engravings), 1988; A Welsh Country Diary, 1993; Contributor of a chapter in The History of Cardiganshire, Vol I, 1994; Wildlife, My Life, 1995; Welsh Country Essays, 1996. Contributions to: Many articles in Country Life, and other magazines; Author, A Country Diary, in the Manchester Guardian, later The Guardian, 1957-. Honour: MSc (Honoris Causa), University of Wales, 1980. Address: Ynys Edwin, Eglwysfach, Machynlleth, Powys SY20 8TA, Wales.

CONE Molly Zelda, b. 3 Oct 1918, Tacoma, Washington, USA. Writer. m. Gerald J Cone, 9 Sept 1939, 1 son, 2 daughters. Education: University of Washington, 1936-38. Publications: For children: Mishmash; Mishmash and the Substitute Teacher; Mishmash and the Sauerkraut Mystery; Mishmash and the Venus Flytrap; Mishmash and the Big Fat Problem; Come Back, Salmon (with photographs by Sidnee Wheelwright), 1992; Listen to the Trees - Jews and the Earth, 1995; Squishy, Misty, Damp & Muddy - The In-Between World of Wetlands, 1996; Biographies: Hurry Henrietta, 1966; Leonard Bernstein, 1970; The Ringing Brothers, 1971; Non-fiction: Stories of Jewish Symbols, 1963; Who Knows Ten, 1965; The Jewish Sabbath, 1966; The Jewish New Year, 1966; Purim, 1967; The Mystery of Being Jewish, 1989; Play: John Bunyan and His Blue Ox, 1966. Honours: Neveh Shalom Centennial Award for Literary Contribution toward Education of Jewish Children, 1970; Second Place Award, National Federation of Press Women, 1972; Shirley Kravitz Children's Book Award, Association of Jewish Libraries, 1973; Washington Governor's Writers Award, 1993; Horn Book Fanfare, 1993. Memberships: Authors

League of America; Seattle Free Lancers. Literary Agent: McIntosh and Otis Inc, 310 Madison Avenue, New York, NY 10017, USA. Address: 8003 Sand Point Way North East, B-24, Seattle, WA 98115, USA.

CONEY Michael (Greatrex), b. 28 Sept 1932, Birmingham, England. Writer. m. Daphne Coney, 14 May 1957, 1 son, 1 daughter. Publications: King of the Scepter'd Isle; A Judge of Men, 1969; Whatever Became of the McGowans?, 1971; The Snow Princess, 1971; Susanna! Susanna!, 1971; Mirror Image, 1972; The Bridge on the Scraw, 1973; Syzygy, 1973; Friends Come in Boxes, 1973; The Hero of Downways, 1973; The Hook, the Eye and the Whip, 1974; Winter's Children, 1974; Monitor Found in Orbit, 1974; The Jaws That Bite, The Claws That Catch, 1975; Charisma, 1975; The Hollow Where, 1975; Trading Post, 1976; Hello Summer, Goodbye, 1976; Brontomek!, 1976; Just an Old-Fashioned War Story, 1977; Penny on a Skyhorse, 1979; The Ultimate Jungle, 1979; Neptune's Children, 1981; Cat Karina, 1982; The Celestial Steam Locomotive, 1983; The Byrds, 1983; Gods of the Greataway, 1984; Fang, the Gnome, 1988; No Place for a Sealion; A Tomcat Called Sabrina; Sophie's Spyglass, 1993; Die Lorelie, 1993; The Small Penance of Lady Disdain, 1993; Tea and Hamsters, 1994. Honour: Best British Novel Award for Brontomek!, British Science Fiction Association, 1976. Memberships: Science Fiction Writers of America; Institute of Chartered Accountants. Literary Agents: MBA Literary Agents, England; Virginia Kidd, USA. Address: 2082 Neptune Road, Sidney, British Columbia, V8L 5J5, Canada.

CONLON Kathleen. See: **LLOYD Kathleen Annie.**

CONN Stewart, b. 5 Nov 1936, Glasgow, Scotland. Appointments: Radio Producer, BBC, Glasgow, 1962-77; Head of Radio Drama, BBC Edinburgh, 1977-92; Literary Adviser, Edinburgh Royal Lyceum Theatre, 1972-75. Publications: Thunder in the Air: Poems, The Chinese Tower, 1967; Stoats in the Sunlight: Poems (in US as Ambush and Other Poems), 1968; The Burning, 1971; In Transit, An Ear to the Ground (poems), 1972; PEN New Poems, 1973-74 (editor), 1974; Thistlewood, 1975; The Aquarium, The Man in the Green Muffler, I Didn't Always Live Here, 1976; Under the Ice (poems), 1978; Play Donkey, 1980; In the Kibble Palace, New and Selected Poems, 1987; The Luncheon of the Boating Party (poems), 1992; In the Blood (poems), 1995; At the Aviary (poems), 1995. Contributions to: Anthologies, journals and radio programmes. Honours: EC Gregory Award, 1964; Scottish Arts Council Awards and Poetry prize, 1968, 1978, 1992; English-Speaking Union Travel Scholarship, 1984; Scottish Arts Council Playwrights Bursary, 1995; Society of Authors Travel Bursary, 1996; Fellow, Royal Scottish Academy of Music and Drama. Membership: Knight of Mark Twain. Literary Agent: Lemon, Unna & Durbridge, 24 Pottery Lane, London, England. Address: 1 Fettes Row, Edinburgh EH3 6SF, Scotland.

CONNELL Brian (Reginald), b. 12 Apr 1916, London, England. Author; Journalist; Broadcaster. m. Esmee Jean Mackenzie, 27 Nov 1944. Education: University of Madrid, 1933-36; University of Berlin, 1936-37. Appointments: Reuters, 1940-43, Daily Mail, 1946-50, News Chronicle, 1950-55, Independent Television News, 1955-86, Chairman, Connell Literary Enterprises/Partner, Connell Editors, 1960-; Programme Adviser, Anglia Television, 1961-86. Publications: Manifest Destiny, 1953; Knight Errant, 1955; Portrait of a Whig Peer, 1957; Watcher on the Rhine, 1957; The Plains of Abraham, 1959; Return of the Tiger, 1960; Regina v Palmerston, 1962; The War in the Peninsula, 1973; The Siege of Quebec, 1976; America in the Making, 1977; Editor and compiler of 10 autobiographies. Contributions to: Periodicals. Honours: Producers Guild Award, 1963; Cannes Festival International Award, 1965. Membership: National Union of Journalists. Address: B2 Marine Gate, Marine Drive, Brighton, Sussex BN2 5TQ, England.

CONNOLLY Ray, b. 4 Dec 1940, St Helens, Lancashire, England. Writer. Education: BSc, London School of Economics and Political Science, 1963. Appointments: Columnist, London Evening Standard, 1967-73, 1983-84; The Times, 1989-90. Publications and Screenplays: A Girl Who Came to Stay, That'll Be the Day, 1973; Stardust, 1974; Trick or Treat?, 1975; James Dean: The First American Teenager, 1975; Newsdeath, 1978; A Sunday Kind of Woman, 1980; Honky Tonk Heroes, 1980; John Lennon 1940-1980, 1981; The Sun Place, 1981; An Easy Game to Play, 1982; Stardust Memories, 1983; Forever Young, 1984; Lytton's Diary, 1985; Defrosting The Fridge, 1988; Perfect Scoundrels, 1989; Sunday

Morning, 1992; Shadows on a Wall, 1994; In the Sixties (anthology), 1995; Lost Fortnight, 1996. Honour: Stardust, Best Original British Screenplay, 1974, Writers Guild of Great Britain. Literary Agent: Gill Coleridge, Rogers, Coleridge and White, London. Address: c/o Rogers, Coleridge and White, 20 Powis Mews, London W11 1JN, England.

CONNOR Fergus. See: **MILLER Karl.**

CONNORS Bruton. See: **ROHEN Edward.**

CONQUEST (George) Robert (Acworth), b. 15 July 1917, Malvern, Worcestershire, England. Writer. m. (1) Joan Watkins, 2 sons, (4) Elizabeth Neece, 1 Dec 1979. Education: University of Grenoble, France, 1935-36; Magdalen College, Oxford, 1936-39; MA (Oxon), 1972; DLitt (Oxon), 1975. Appointments: Visiting Poet, University of Buffalo, 1959-60; Literary Editor, The Spectator, 1962-63. Publications: Poems, 1955; A World of Difference, 1955; Power and Policy in the USSR, 1961; Between Mars and Venus, 1962; The Egyptologists (with Kingsley Amis), 1965; The Great Terror, 1968, as The Great Terror, A Reassessment, 1990; Arias from a Love Opera, 1969; The Nation Killers, 1970; Lenin, 1972; Kolyma, 1978; Forays, 1979; The Abomination of Moab, 1979; We and They, 1980; Inside Stalin's Secret Police, 1985; The Harvest of Sorrow, 1986; New and Collected Poems, 1988; Tyrants and Typewriters, 1989; Stalin: Breaker of Nations, 1991. Contributions to: London Magazine; Times Literary Supplement; Analog Science Fiction; Soviet Studies; Neva, Leningrad; Novy Mir, Moscow; Poetry, Chicago; New Republic; Spectator. Honours: Officer of the Order of the British Empire, 1955; CMG, 1996. Memberships: Fellow, British Academy; Fellow, Royal Society of Literature; Travellers Club; Fellow, British Interplanetary Society; Society for the Promotion of Roman Studies; American Association for the Advancement of Slavic Studies. Literary Agent: Curtis Brown. Address: 52 Peter Coutts Circle, Stanford, CA 94305, USA.

CONRAD Peter, b. 1948, Australia. Education: Australia and England. Appointments: Freelance Writer; Fellow in English Literature, Christ Church College, Oxford. Publications: The Victorian Treasure House, 1973; Romantic Opera and Literary Form, 1977; Shandyism: The Character of Romantic Irony, 1978; Imagining America, 1980; Television: The Medium and its Manners, 1984; The Art of the City: Views and Versions of New York, 1984; The Everyman History of English Literature, 1985; A Song of Love and Death: The Meaning of Opera, 1987; The History of English Literature: One Indivisible, Unending Book, 1987; Down Home: Revisiting Tasmania, 1988; Where I Fell to Earth: A Life in Four Cities, 1990; Feasting with Panthers, or the Importance of Being Famous, 1994. Address: c/o Christ Church College, Oxford OX1 1DP, England.

CONRAN Anthony, b. 7 Apr 1931, Kharghpur, India. Poet; Writer. Education: BA, 1953, MA, 1956, University of Wales. Appointments: Research Fellow, 1957-66, Tutor in English, 1966-, University of Wales. Publications: Formal Poems, 1960; Icons, Asymptotes, A String o Blethers, Sequence of the Blu Flower, The Mountain, For the Marriage of Gerald and Linda, 1963; Stalae and Other Poems, 1965; Guernica, 1966; The Penguin Book of Welsh Verse, 1967; Claim, Claim, Claim, A Book of Poems, 1969; Life Fund, On to the Fields of Praise: Essays on the English Poets of Wales, 1979; The Cost of Strangeness, 1982; Welsh Verse, 1987. Address: 1 Frondirion, Glanrafon, Bangor, Carnavanshire, Wales.

CONRAN Shirley (Ida), b. 21 Sept 1932, London, England. Writer. m. Terence Conran, 1955, div 1962, 2 sons. Education: Southern College of Art, Portsmouth, England. Appointments: Founder, Co-Owner, Conran Fabrics Ltd, 1957-62; Design Consultant and Design Writer for various periodicals. Publications: Superwoman: Everywoman's Book of Household Management, 2 volumes, 1975, 1977; Superwoman Yearbook, 1976; Superwoman Yearbook, 1977; Superwoman Two, 1977; Future: How to Survive Life After Thirty, 1979, revised edition as Futurewoman: How to Survive Life, 1981; Lace: A Novel, 1982; The Magic Garden, 1983; Lace II, 1985; The Legend, 1985; Savages, 1987; Down with Superwoman, 1990; The Amazing Umbrella Shop, 1990; Crimson, 1992; Tiger Eyes, 1994. Address: 39 Avenue Princess Grace, Monte Carlo, Monaco.

CONROY John, b. 29 Mar 1951, Chicago, Illinois, USA. Writer. m. Colette Davison, May 1986. Education: BA, University of Illinois, 1973. Appointments: Senior Editor, Chicago Magazine, 1974-76; Staff Writer, Chicago Reader, 1978. Publications: Belfast Diary: War as a

Way of Life, 1987, UK edition as War as a Way of Life: A Belfast Diary, 1988. Contributions to: New York Times; Boston Globe; Boston Pheonix; Chicago Daily News; Chicago Tribune; Atlanta Constitution; Dallas Morning News; San Diego Union; Village Voice. Honours: Peter Lisagor Award, 1977, 1991; National Award for Magazine Writing, Society of Professional Journalists, 1978; Alicia Patterson Fellowship, 1980; Society of Midland Authors Award, 1987; Friends of Literature Award,best non-fiction book of 1987; Carl Sandburg Award, best non-fiction book of 1987; Research and Writing Grant, John D and Catherine T MacArthur Foundation, 1990; John Bartlow Martin Award for Public Interest Magazine Journalism, 1991. Address: c/o Chicago Reader, 11 East Illinois Street, Chicago, IL 60611, USA.

CONSTABLE Trevor James, b. 17 Sept 1925, Wellington, New Zealand. Radio Electronics Officer. m. Gloria Garcia, 14 Sept 1983, 1 daughter. Education: Rongotai College, 1936-42. Appointments: Staff Writer, National Commercial Broadcasting Service, 1942-44, International Broadcasting Company, 1950-52; US Correspondent, New Zealand Weekly News, 1958-68; Freelance Magazine Writer, 1960-70. Publications: Fighter Aces, 1966; Horrido, 1968; Blond Knight of Germany, 1970; Hidden Heroes, 1971; Fighter Aces of the USA, 1977; Fighter Aces of the Luftwaffe, 1978; The Cosmic Pulse of Life, 1978; Fighter General, the Life of Adolf Galland, 1988. Contributions to: Numerous Military and Aviation Articles. Honour: Aviation, Space Writers Book of the Year Award, 1978. Memberships: Aviation, Space Writers Association; National Maritime Historical Society; American Radio Association. Address: 3726 Bluff Place, San Pedro, CA 90731, USA.

CONSTANTINE David (John), b. 4 Mar 1944, Salford, Lancashire, England. Fellow in German; Poet; Writer; Translator. m. Helen Frances Best, 9 July 1966, 1 son, 1 daughter. Education: BA, 1966, PhD, 1971, Wadham College, Oxford. Appointments: Lecturer to Senior Lecturer in German, University of Durham, 1969-81; Fellow in German, Queen's College, Oxford, 1981-. Publications: Poetry: A Brightness to Cast Shadows, 1980; Watching for Dolphins, 1983; Mappi Mundi, 1984; Madder, 1987; Selected Poems, 1991; Caspar Hauser, 1994; Sleeper, 1995. Fiction: Davies, 1985; Back at the Spike, 1994. Non-fiction: The Significance of Locality in the Poetry of Friedrich Hölderlin, 1979; Early Greek Travellers and the Hellenic Ideal, 1984; Hölderlin, 1988; Friedrich Hölderlin, 1992. Translator: Hölderlin: Selected Poems, 1990, enlarged edition, 1996; Henri Michaux: Spaced, Displaced (with Helen Constantine), 1992; Philippe Jaccottet: Under Clouded Skies/Beauregard (with Mark Treharne), 1994; Goethe: Elective Affinities, 1994; Kleist: Stories and Plays, 1997. Editor: German Short Stories 2, 1972. Honours: Alice Hunt Bartlett Prize, 1984; Runciman Prize, 1985; Southern Arts Literature Prize, 1987. Membership: Poetry Society. Address: 1 Hilltop Road, Oxford, OX4 1PB, England.

CONTRERAS Joseph. Journalist. m. Caroline Contreras, 1 son, 2 daughters. Education: BA, Social Studies, Harvard University, 1979; MS, International Relations, London School of Economics, 1980. Appointments: Associate Editorial Chairman, The Crimson, campus' daily newspaper; Intern, Los Angeles Bureau, 1978; Summer Intern, Washington Post, 1979; Stringer, Newsweek, London, 1979-80; Correspondent in Los Angeles Bureau, 1980, Mexico Bureau Chief, 1984, Buenos Aries Bureau Chief, 1988, Johannesburg Bureau Chief, 1990-96, Jerusalem Bureau Chief, 1996-, Newsweek. Honours: Co-Winner, Robert Bell Award for Excellence in the Coverage of Aerospace Stories, for cover story, Saturn's Rings, Aviation and Space Writers Association, 1980; Citation for coverage of the international adoption market, Overseas Press Club, 1989. Address: c/o Newsweek, 251 West 57th Street, New York, NY 10019-1894, USA.

CONWAY Peter. See: **MILKOMANE George Alexis Milkomanovich.**

CONWAY Troy. See: **AVALLONE Michael (Angelo Jr).**

COOK Christopher Piers, b. 20 June 1945, Leicester, England. Writer; Historian. Education: BA (1st Class Honours) History 1967, MA 1970, Cambridge University; DPhil, Modern History, Oxford University, 1974. Appointment: Editor, Pears Cyclopedia, 1976-. Publications: Sources in British Political History, 6 volumes, 1975-84; The Slump (with John Stevenson), 1976; Dictionary of Historical Terms, 2nd edition 1989; World Political Almanac, 1989; Longman Handbook of World History Since 1914, 1991; Longman Handbook of Modern European History 1763-1991, 1992; A Short History of the Liberal

Party 1900-92, 1993; Britain Since 1945 (with John Stevenson), 1995; Longman Handbook of Modern British History 1714-1995, 1996; What Happened Where (with Diccon Bewes), 1996. Contributions to: Guardian; Times Literary Supplement; THES. Honour: Fellow, Royal Historical Society, 1977. Literary Agent: Derek Johns, A P Watt & Co, 20 John Street, London WC1. Address: c/o Pears Cyclopedia, Penguin Books, 27 Wrights Lane, Kensington, London W8 5TZ, England.

COOK David, b. 21 Sept 1940, Preston, Lancashire, England. Education: Royal College of Dramatic Art, 1959-61. Appointments: Professional Actor, 1961-; Writer-in-Residence, St Martin's College, Lancaster, England, 1982-83. Publications: Albert's Memorial, 1972; Happy Endings, 1974; Walter, 1978; Winter Doves, 1979; Sunrising, 1983; Missing Persons, 1986; Crying Out Loud, 1988; Walter and June, 1989; Second Best, 1991. Honours: E M Forster Award, 1977; Hawthornden Prize, 1978; Southern Arts Fiction Prize, 1984; Arthur Welton Scholarship, 1991; Oddfellows Social Concern Award, 1992. Membership: Society of Authors. Literary Agent: Deborah Rogers, 20 Powis Mews, London W11 1JN, England. Address: 7 Sydney Place, London SW7 3NL, England.

COOK Dorothy Mary, (D Y Cameron, D M Carlisle, Elizabeth Clare), b. 13 Feb 1907, Gravesend, England. Author. Education: Grammar School, Rochester, England. Publications: 17 novels as D Y Cameron, 1962-81; 4 novels as D M Carlisle, 1974-86; 12 novels as Elizabeth Clare, 1966-81. Memberships: Fellowship of Reconciliation; Romantic Novelists Association. Address: c/o Hale, 45-47 Clerkenwell Green, London EC1R 0HT, England.

COOK Glen (Charles), b. 9 July 1944, New York, New York, USA. Auto Assembler; Writer. m. 14 June 1971, 3 sons. Publications: The Black Company, series, 1984-89; A Matter of Time, 1985; Pasaage At Arms, 1985; The Garrett Files, series, 1987-; The Dragon Never Sleeps, 1988; The Tower of Fear, 1989. Contributions to: Numerous magazines and journals. Literary Agent: Russell Galen, Scouil-Chichak-Galen, 381 Park Avenue South, Suite 1020, New York, NY 10016, USA. Address: c/o Scott Meredith Inc, 845 Third Avenue, New York, NY 10022, USA.

COOK Lila. See: **AFRICANO Lillian.**

COOK Lyn. See: **WADDELL Evelyn Margaret.**

COOK Norman Edgar, b. 4 Mar 1920. Editor; Book Critic. m. Mildred Warburton, 1942, 3 sons. Appointments: Ministry of Information, 1943-45; Editor, Northwich Guardian, 1945-47, Liverpool Daily Post, 1947-49;Information Officer, Air Ministry, 1949-53; Night News Editor, Daily Post, 1953-55; Deputy News Editor, 1955-59, London Editor, 1959-72, Executive News Editor, 1972-77, Editor, 1978-79, 1979, Chief Book Critic, 1980-91, Liverpool Daily Post. Publications: Numerous articles and review. Honour: Commander of the Order of the British Empire, 1980. Address: 7 Trinity Gardens, Southport, Lancashire PR8 1AU, England.

COOK Petronelle Marguerite Mary, (Margot Arnold), b. 16 May 1925, Plymouth, Devon, England. Writer; Teacher. m. Philip R Cook, 20 July 1949, 2 sons, 1 daughter. Education: BA (Hons), 1946, Diploma in Prehistoric Archaeology and Anthropology, 1947, MA, 1950, Oxford University. Publications: The Officers' Woman, 1972; The Villa on the Palatine, 1975; Marie, 1979; Exit Actors, Dying, 1980; The Cape Cod Caper, 1980; Death of a Voodoo Doll, 1981; Zadok's Treasurer, 1981; Affairs of State, 1981; Love Among the Allies, 1982; Lament for a Lady Laird, 1982; Death on the Dragon's Tongue, 1982; Desperate Measures, 1983; Sinister Purposes, 1985; The Menehune Murders, 1989; Toby's Folly, 1990; The Catacomb Conspiracy, 1991; The Cape Cod Conundrum, 1992; Dirge for a Dorset Druid, 1994; The Midas Murders, 1995; As Petronelle Cook: The Queen Consorts of England, 1993. Contributions to: Numerous short stories to magazines. Honours: Elected President, Oxford University Archaeological Society, 1945; Fiction Prize, National Writers Club, 1983. Memberships: New England Historic and Genealogical Society; Mystery Writers of America, Participant, Mentor programme for fledgling writers. Literary Agent: Collier Associates, PO Box 21361, West Palm Beach, FL 33416, USA Address: 11 High School Road, Hyannis, MA 02601-3901, USA.

COOK Stanley, b. 12 Apr 1922, Austerfield, Yorkshire, England. Lecturer; Poet. m. Kathleen Mary Daly, 1 son, 2 daughters. Education: BA, Christ Church, Oxford, 1943. Appointments: Lecturer, Huddersfield

Polytechnic, 1969-81; Editor, Poetry Nottingham, 1981-85. Publications: Form Photograph, 1971; Sign of Life, 1972; Staff Photograph, 1976; Alphabet, 1976; Woods Beyond a Cornfield, 1981; Concrete Poems, 1984; Barnsdale, 1986; Selected Poems, 1972-86, 1986; The Northern Seasons, 1988; Poems for Children. Honour: Cheltenham Festival Competition Prize, 1972. Address: 600 Barnsley Road, Sheffield, South Yorkshire S5 6UA, England.

COOK Thomas, b. 19 Sept 1947, Alabama, USA. m. Susan Terner, 17 Mar 1978, 1 daughter. Education: Georgia State College; MA, Hunter College; MPhil, Columbia University. Publications: Blood Innocents, 1980; The Orchids, 1982; Tabernacle, 1983; Elena, 1986; Sacrificial Ground, 1988; Flesh and Blood, 1989; Streets of Fire, 1989; Night Secrets, 1990; Breakheart Hill, 1994. Contributions to: Atlanta Magazine. Honours: Edgar Allan Poe Awards, 1981, 1988. Address: c/o Russell & Volkening, 50 West 29th Street, New York, NY 10001, USA.

COOKE (Alfred) Alistair, b. 20 Nov 1908, Manchester, England (US citizen, 1941). Writer; Broadcaster. m. (1) Ruth Emerson, 1 son, (2) Jane White Hawkes, 1 daughter. Education: 1st Class English Tripos, 1929, BA, 1930, Jesus College, Cambridge; Commonwealth Fund Fellow, Yale University, 1932-33, Harvard University, 1933-34. Appointments: Film Critic, 1934-37, Commentator on American Affairs, 1938-, BBC; London Correspondent, NBC, 1936-37; Special Correspondent on American Affairs, The Times, 1938-42; American Feature Writer, Daily Herald, 1941-43; United Nations Correspondent, 1945-48, Chief US Correspondent, 1948-72, Manchester Guardian, later The Guardian; Host, Omnibus television programme, 1952-61, Masterpiece Theater, PBS series, 1971-92; Writer, Narrator, America: A Personal History of the US, television series, 1972-73. Publications: Garbo and the Night Watchman (editor), 1937; Douglas Fairbanks, 1940; A Generation on Trial: USA v Alger Hiss, 1950; One Man's America (in UK as Letters from America), 1952; Christmas Eve, 1952; A Commencement Address, 1954; The Vintage Mencken (editor), 1955; Around the World in Fifty Years, 1966; Talk About America, 1968; Alistair Cooke's America, 1973; Six Men, 1977; The Americans: Fifty Letters from America on Our Life and Times, 1979; Above London (with Robert Cameron), 1980; Masterpieces, 1981; The Patient Has the Floor, 1986; America Observed, 1988; Fun and Games with Alistair Cooke, 1994. Honours: George Foster Peabody Awards for International News Reporting, 1952, 1973; 4 Emmy Awards, 1973; Benjamin Franklin Medal, Royal Society of Arts, 1973; Dimbleby Award, 1973; Honorary Knighthood, 1973; Howland Medal, Yale University, 1977; Special George Foster Peabody Award, 1983; Several honorary doctorates. Address: 1150 Fifth Avenue, New York, NY 10128, USA.

COOKE Ann. See: **COLE Joanna.**

COOKSON Dame Catherine (Ann), (Catherine Fawcett, Catherine Marchant), b. 20 June 1906, Tyne Dock, South Shields, England. Writer. Publications: Mary Ann and Bill, 1967; Katie Mulholland, 1967; The Round Tower, 1968; Joe and the Gladiator (juvenile), 1968; The Glass Virgin, 1969; The Nice Bloke, 1969, in US as The Husband, 1976; Our Kate: An Autobiography, 1969, 1982; The Invitation, 1970; The Nipper (juvenile), 1970; The Dwelling Place, 1971; Feathers in the Fire, 1971; Pure as the Lily, 1972; Blue Baccy (juvenile), 1972; The Mallen Girl, 1973; The Mallen Steak, 1973; The Mallen Lot (in UK as The Mallen Litter), 1974; Our John Willy (juvenile), 1974; The Invisible Cord, 1975; The Gambling Man, 1975; Miss Martha Mary Crawford, 1975; The Tide of Life, 1976; The Slow Awakening, 1976; Mrs Flannagan's Trumpet (juvenile), 1976; Go Tell It to Mrs Golightly (juvenile), 1977; The Girl, 1977; The Cinder Path, 1978; The Man Who Cried, 1979; Tilly Trotter (in US as Tilly), 1980; Tilly Trotter Wed (in US as Tilly Wed), 1981; Lanky Jones (juvenile), 1981; Tilly Trotter Widowed (in US as Tilly Alone), 1982; The Whip, 1982; Nancy Nutall and the Mongrel (juvenile), 1982; Hamilton, 1983; The Black Velvet Gown 1984; Goodbye Hamilton, 1984; A Dinner of Herbs, 1985; Harold, 1985; The Moth, 1985; Bill Bailey, 1985; Catherine Cookson Country, 1986; The Parson's Daughter, 1987; Bill Bailey's Lot, 1987; The Cultured Handmaiden, 1988; Bill Bailey's Daughter, 1988; Let Me Make Myself Plain, 1988; The Harrogate Secret, 1989; The Black Candle, 1989; The Wingless Bird, 1990; The Gillivors, 1990; My Beloved Son, 1991; The Rag Nymph, 1991; The House of Women, 1992; The Maltese Angel, 1992; The Year of the Virgins, 1993; The Golden Straw, 1993; Justice is a Woman, 1994; The Upstart, 1996. Honours: Officer of the Order of the British Empire, 1985; Hon DLitt, 1991; Dame Commander of the Order of the British

Empire, 1993. Address: c/o Anthony Sheil, Sheil and Associates, 43 Doughty Street, London WC1N 2LF, England.

COOLIDGE Clark, b. 26 Feb 1939, Providence, Rhode Island, USA. Poet. m. Susan Hopkins, 1 daughter. Education: Brown University, 1956-58. Publications: Flag Flutter and US Electric, 1966; Poems, 1967; Ing, 1969; Space, 1970; The So, 1971; Moroccan Variations, 1971; Suite V, 1973; The Maintains, 1974; Polaroid, 1975; Quartz Hearts, 1978; Own Face, 1978; Smithsonian Depositions, and Subjects to a Film, 1980; American Ones, 1981; A Geology, 1981; Research, 1982; Mine: The One That Enters the Stories, 1982; Solution Passage: Poems, 1978-1981, 1986; The Crystal Text, 1986; Mesh, 1988; At Egypt, 1988; Sound as Thought: Poems, 1982-1984, 1990; The Book of During, 1991; Odes of Roba, 1991; Baffling Means, 1991; On the Slates, 1992; Lowell Connector: Lines and Shots from Kerouac's Town, 1993; Own Face, 1994; Registers: (People in All), 1994; The ROVA Improvisations, 1994. Honours: National Endowment for the Arts Grant, 1966; New York Poets Foundation Award, 1968. Address: c/o The Figures, 5 Castle Hill, Great Barrington, MA 01230, USA.

COOMBS Patricia, b.23 July 1926, Los Angeles, California, USA. Author; Illustrator of Childrens' Books. m. L James Fox, 13 July 1951, 2 daughters. Education: BA 1947, MA 1950, University of Washington. Publications: Dorrie and the Blue Witch, 1964; Dorrie and the Haunted House, 1970; Dorrie and the Goblin, 1972; Mouse Cafe, 1972; Molly Mullett, 1975; The Magic Pot, 1977; Dorrie and the Screebit Ghost, 1979; The Magician McTree, 1984; Dorrie and the Pin Witch, 1989; Dorrie and the Haunted Schoolhouse, 1992. Contributions to: Partisan Review; Hudson Review; Poetry. Honours: Dorries Magic, New York Times Ten Best Books of the Year, 1963; Dorrie and the Haunted House, Child Study Association, Childrens Books of the Year, 1970; Mouse Cafe, New York Times 10 Best Illustrated Books of the Year, 1972. Memberships: Authors Guild. Literary Agent: Dorothy Markinko, McIntosh and Otis, New York, USA; Gerald Pollinger, Laurance Pollinger Ltd, London, England. Address: 178 Oswegatchie Road, Waterford, CT 06385, USA.

COONEY Ray, (Raymond George Alfred Cooney), b. 30 May 1932, London, England. Actor; Writer; Director. m. Linda Dixon, 8 Dec 1962, 2 sons. Publications: Plays, both solo in collaboration with others: One for the Pot, 1961; Chase Me, Conrad, 1964, Charlie Girl, 1965; Stand by Your Bedouin, 1966; Not Now, Darling, 1967; My Giddy Aunt, 1968; Move Over Mrs Markham, 1969; Why Not Stay for Breakfast?, 1970; There Goes the Bridge, 1974; Run For Your Wife, 1984; Two Into One, 1985; Wife Begins at Forty, 1986; It Runs in the Family, 1987; Out of Order, 1990; Funny Money, 1994. Membership: Dramatists Club. Address: Hollowfield Cottage, Littleton, Surrey GU3 1HN, England.

COONTZ Stephanie, b. 31 Aug 1944, Seattle, Washington, USA. Professor of History and Women's Studies; Writer. 1 son. Education: BA, University of California at Berkeley, 1966; MA, University of Washington, Seattle, 1970. Appointments: Faculty, History and Family Studies, Evergreen State College, Olympia, Washington, 1975-; Visiting Faculty, University of Washington, Seattle, 1976; Exchange Professor, Kobe University of Commerce, Japan, 1986; Exchange Professor, 1992, Visiting Associate Professor, 1994, University of Hawaii at Hilo. Publications: Women's Work, Men's Property: On the Origins of Gender and Class (with Peta Henderson), 1986; The Social Origins of Private Life: A History of American Families, 1988; The Way We Never Were: American Families and the Nostalgia Trap, 1992; The Way We Really Are: Coming to Terms with America's Changing Families, 1997. Contributions to: Books, professional journals and general periodicals. Honours: Governor's Writers Award, 1988; National Scholar, The National Faculty, 1994-; Dale Richmond Award, American Academy of Pediatrics, 1995. Memberships: American Historical Association; American Studies Association; Organization of American Historians. Address: 808 North Rogers, Olympia, WA 98502, USA.

COOPER (Brenda) Clare, b. 21 Jan 1935, Falmouth, Cornwall, England. Writer. m. Bill Cooper, 6 Apr 1953, 2 sons, 1 daughter. Publications: David's Ghost; The Black Horn; Earthchange; Ashar of Qarius; The Skyrifters; Andrews and the Gargoyle; A Wizard Called Jones; Kings of the Mountain; Children of the Camps; The Settlement on Planet B; Miracles and Rubies; Timeloft, Marya's Emmets, 1995. Honour: Runner Up, Tir Na Nog Award. Memberships: PEN; Society of Authors; Welsh Academy. Address: Tyrhibin Newydd, Newport, Dyfed SA42 0NT,Wales.

COOPER Bryan, (Robert Wright), b. 6 Feb 1932, Paris, France. Editor; Author. m. (1) Patricia Barnard, 27 Feb 1954, 2 sons, 1 daughter, (2) Judith Williams, 7 Apr 1979. Appointments: Reporter, Kentish Times, 1948-50; Feature Writer, Flying Review magazine, 1950-52; Sub-editor, Exchange Telegraph, 1953-54; Public Relations Executive, British Petroleum, London, 1954-58, New York, 1958-64; Editor and Publisher, Petroleum Economist, the International Energy Journal, 1975-89; Energy Writer and Consultant, Energy Research Ltd, Cyprus, 1990-94. Publications: North Sea Oil - The Great Gamble, 1966; The Ironclads of Cambrai, 1967; Battle of the Torpedo Boats, 1970; The Buccaneers, 1970; PT Boats, 1970; Alaska - The Last Frontier, 1972; Tank Battles of World War 1, 1973; Fighter, 1973; Bomber, 1974; Stones of Evil (novel), 1974; The E Boat Threat, 1976; The Wildcatters (novel), 1976; The Adventure of North Sea Oil, 1982. Contributions to: The Times; Financial Times; Numerous magazines. Scriptwriter, over 100 Radio and TV and Film Scripts. Memberships: Writer's Guild of Great Britain; Garrick; London Press Club. Literary Agent: Watson, Little Ltd, 12 Egbert Street, London NW1 8LJ, England. Address: Woodbine, 11 Victoria Road, Deal, Kent CT14 7AS, England.

COOPER Colin Symons, (Daniel Benson), b. 5 July 1926, Birkenhead, England. Journalist; Editor. m. Maureen Elizabeth Goodwin, 6 Sept 1966, 2 sons. Appointments: Features Editor, Guitar Magazine, 1972-73; News Editor 1982-84, General Editor 1984-, Classical Guitar. Publications: The Thunder and Lightning Man, 1968; Outcrop, 1969; Dargason, 1977; The Epping Pyramid, 1978; The Argyll Killings, 1980. Contributions to: Times Literary Supplement; Times Education Supplement; Guardian; Independent; Gendai Guitar (Tokyo); Asta Journal (USA); European; Raconteur. Membership: Writers' Guild of Great Britain. Address: 24 Blurton Road, London E5 0NL, England.

COOPER Derek Macdonand, b.25 May 1925. Author; Broadcaster; Journalist. m. Janet Marian Feaster, 1953, 1 son, 1 daughter. Education: University College, Cardiff, Wales; Wadham College, Oxford; MA (hons), Oxon. Appointments: Columnist, Listener, Guardian, Observer Magazine, World Listener, Guardian, Observer Magazine, World Medicine, Scottish Field, Sunday Standard, Homes and Gardens, Saga Magazine, Women's Journal. Publications: The Bad Food Guide, 1967; Skye, 1970, 2nd edition, 1977; The Beverage Report, 1970; The Gullibility Gap, 1974; Hebridean Connection, 1977; Guide to the Whiskies of Scotland, 1978; Road to the Isles, 1979; Enjoying Scotch (with Dione Pattullo), 1980; Wines With Food, 1982, 2nd edition, 1986; The Whisky Roads of Scotland (with Fay Goodwin), 1982; The Century Companion to Whiskies, 1983; Skye Remembered, 1983; The World of Cooking, 1983; The Road to Mingulay, 1985; The Gunge File, 1986; A Taste of Scotch, 1989. Contributions to: In Britain: Signature; Taste; A La Carte; The West Highland Free Press; Television programmes. Honours: Glenfiddich Trophy as Wine and Food Writer, 1973, 1980; Scottish Arts Council Award, 1980; Broadcaster of the Year, 1984; House of Fraser Press Award, 1984. Membership: Founder Member, 1st Chairman, Guild of Food Writers. Address: Seafield House, Portree, Isle of Skye, Scotland.

COOPER Helen, b. 6 Feb 1947, Nottingham, England. University Professor. m. M G Cooper, 18 July 1970, 2 daughters. Education: BA, New Hall, Cambridge, 1968; MA, PhD, 1972. Appointments: English Editor, Medium AEvum, 1989. Publications: The Oxford Guides to Chaucer: The Canterbury Tales; The Structure of the Canterbury Tales; Pastoral: Medieval into Renaissance; Great Grand Mother Goose. Contributions to: Numerous. Address: University College, Oxford OX1 4BH, England.

COOPER Jean Campbell, b. 27 Nov 1905, Chefoo, North China. Author; Lecturer. m. Commander V M Cooper DSO, OBE, RN, 21 June 1945. Education: Various boarding schools in China, Australia and England; LLA Hons, 1st Class, Moral Philosophy, St Andrew's University, 1930. Publications: Taoism, the Way of the Mystic, 1972; An Illustrated Encyclopedia of Traditional Symbols, 1978; Yin and Yang, the Harmony of Opposites, 1982; Fairy Tales, Allegories of the Inner Life, 1983; Chinese Alchemy, 1984; Aquarian Dictionary of Festivals, 1990; Symbolic and Mythological Animals, 1993; Brewer's Myth and Legend, 1993; The Cassell Dictionary of Christianity, 1996. Contributions to: Articles, translations, reviews for Studies in Comparative Religion. Memberships: English PEN; Life Member,

Royal Commonwealth Society; Justice of the Peace. Address: Bobbin Mill, Ulpha, Broughton-in-Furness, Cumbria LA20 6DU, England.

COOPER Jilly (Sallitt), b.21 Feb 1937, Hornchurch, Essex, England. Writer; Journalist. Appointments: Reporter, Middlesex Independent Newspaper, Brentford, 1957-59; Columnist, The Sunday Times, 1969-85; Columnist, The Mail on Sunday, 1985-. Publications: How to Stay Married, 1969; How to Survive from Nine to Five, 1970; Jolly Super, 1971; Men and Super Men, 1972; Jolly Super Too, 1973; Women and Super Women, 1974; Jolly Superlative, 1975; Emily (romance novel), 1975; Super Men and Super Women (omnibus), 1976; Bella (romance novel), 1976; Harriet (romance novel), 1976; Octavia (romance novel), 1977; Work and Wedlock (omnibus), 1977; Superjilly, 1977; Imogen (romance novel), 1978; Prudence (romance novel), 1978; Class: A View from Middle England, 1979; Supercooper, 1980; Little Mabel series, juvenile, 4 volumes, 1980-85; Violets and Vinegar: An Anthology of Women's Writings and Sayings (editor with Tom Hartman), 1980; The British in Love (editor), 1980; Love and Other Heartaches, 1981; Jolly Marsupial, 1982; Animals in War, 1983; The Common Years, 1984; Leo and Jilly Cooper on Rugby, 1984; Riders, 1985; Hotfoot to Zabriskie Point, 1985; How to Survive Christmas, 1986; Turn Right at The Spotted Dog, 1987; Rivals, 1988; Angels Rush In, 1990; Polo, 1991; The Man Who Made Husbands Jealous, 1993; Araminta's Wedding, 1993; Appassionata, 1996. Address: c/o Desmond Elliot, 15-17 King Street, St James, London SW1, England.

COOPER Kenneth H(ardy), b. 4 Mar 1931, Oklahoma City, Oklahoma, USA. Physician; Author. m. Mildred Lucille Clark, 7 Aug 1959, 1 son, 1 daughter. Education: BS, 1952, MD, 1956, University of Oklahoma; MPH, Harvard School of Public Health, 1962; Certified Diplomate, American Board of Preventive Medicine, 1966. Appointments: US Air Force, 1957-70, serving as Senior Flight Surgeon and Developer of the 12 minute test and the Aerobics Point System; Founder and Physician, Cooper Aerobics Center, Dallas, 1970-; Consultant and Lecturer on Aerobics. Publications: Aerobics, 1968; The New Aerobics, 1970; Aerobics for Women (with Mildred Cooper), 1972; The Aerobics Way, 1977; The Aerobics Program for Total Well-Being, 1982; Running Without Fear, 1985; Controlling Cholesterol, 1988; The New Aerobics for Women (with Mildred Cooper), 1988; Preventing Osteoporosis, 1989; Overcoming Hypertension, 1990; Kid Fitness, 1991; The Antioxidant Revolution, 1994; It's Better to Believe, 1995. Honours: Daniel Webster Award, International Platform Association, 1977; Nurmi Award for Best Scientific Development or Achievement, Runner's World, 1980; Outstanding Texas Citizen, Exchange Clubs of Texas, 1982; Oklahoma Hall of Fame, Oklahoma Heritage Society, 1983; Distinguished Service Citation, University of Oklahoma, 1984; American Academy of Achievement Honoree, 1986; Lifetime Achievement Award, 1988, and Hall of Fame, 1992, International Dance and Exercise Association; Academy of Dentistry International Humanitarian Award, 1991; Order of Eagle Exemplar, Dwight D Eisenhower Fitness Award, United States Sports Academy, 1992; Kenneth Cooper Middle School named in his honour, Oklahoma City, 1993; Harvard University Presidential Citation, 1995; Several honorary doctorates. Memberships: American College of Preventive Medicine, Fellow; American College of Sports Medicine, Fellow; American Geriatrics Society, Fellow; American Medical Association; American Running and Fitness Association; Texas Medical Association; Texas Medical Foundation. Address: The Cooper Aerobics Center, 12200 Preston Road, Dallas, TX 75230, USA.

COOPER Nancy. Journalist. m., 1 daughter. Education: Graduate, Harvard College. Appointments: Letters Correspondent, 1981, Researcher in National Affairs section, 1983, General Editor, 1987, Senior Writer in International section, 1989, Deputy National Editor, 1989, Senior Editor of International section, 1992-, Newsweek. Honours: Awards for photography and foreign affairs reporting as part of Newsweek's international section. Address: c/o Newsweek, 251 West 57th Street, New York, NY 10019-1894, USA.

COOPER Richard Newell, b. 14 June 1934, Seattle, Washington, USA. Economist; Educator. m. Carolyn Cahalan, 5 June 1956, 1 son, 1 daughter. Education: AB, Oberlin College, 1956; MSc, London School of Economics, England, 1958; PhD, Harvard University, 1962. Publications: The Economics of Interdependence, 1968; A World Re-Ordered, 1973; Economic Policy in an Interdependent World, 1986; The International Monetary System, 1987; Economic Stabilization and Debt in Developing Countries, 1992;

Environmental and Resource Policies for the World Economy, 1994; Co-author: Can Nations Agree?, 1989; Boom, Crisis, and Adjustment, 1993; Macroeconomics Policy and Adjustment in Korea, 1994. Contributions to: New Republic; New York Times; Washington Post; Journal for Political Economy; Quarterly Journal of Ecnomics; Others. Honours: Phi Beta Kappa, 1955; Marshall Scholarship, 1956; LLD, Oberlin College, 1958; Elected Fellow, American Academy of Arts and Sciences, 1974. Memberships: Council on Foreign Relations; American Economic Association; Trilateral Commission. Address: 1737 Cambridge Street, Cambridge, MA 02138, USA.

COOPER Robert Cecil, b. 24 Nov 1917, Wellington, New Zealand. Retired Botanist. m. (1) Jessica Sommerville Scott, 16 Dec 1938, (2) Una Vivienne Cassie, 29 Sept 1984, 1 son, 1 daughter. Education: Accountants' Professional, 1940; BCom, 1948; BA, 1949; MA, 1950; PhD, 1953. Appointment: Botanist; Auckland Museum, 1948-71. Publications: New Zealand Medicinal Plants, 1961-62; Economic Native Plants of New Zealand, 1988, 2nd edition, 1991. Address: 1/117 Cambridge Road, Hillcrest, Hamilton, New Zealand.

COOPER Susan Mary, b. 23 May 1935, Burnham, Buckinghamshire, England. Writer. m. (1) Nicholas J Grant, 1963, div 1982, 1 son, 1 daughter, (2) Hume Cronyn, 1996. Education: MA, Somerville College, Oxford, 1956. Publications: Mandrake, 1964; Over Sea, Under Stone, 1965; Behind the Golden Curtain: A View of the USA, 1968; J B Priestley: Portrait of an Author, 1970; Dawn of Fear, 1970; The Dark is Rising, 1973; Greenwitch, 1974; The Grey King, 1975; Silver on the Tree, 1977; Jethro and the Jumbie, 1979; Seaward, 1983; The Silver Cow, 1983; The Selkie Girl, 1986; Matthew's Dragon, 1990; Danny and the Kings, 1993; The Boggart, 1994; Dreams and Wishes: Essays on Writing for Children, 1996; The Boggart and the Monster, 1997. Contributions to: Periodicals. Honours: Boston Globe-Horn Book Award, 1973; Newbery Medal, 1976; Welsh Arts Council Tir Nan og Awards, 1976, 1978; Hugo Award, 1984; Writers Guild of America Awards, 1984, 1985; Christopher Medal, 1985. Memberships: Authors Guild; Society of Authors; Writers Guild of America. Address: c/o Margaret K McElderry Books, Simon & Schuster, 1230 Sixth Avenue, New York, NY 10020, USA.

COOPER William. See: **HOFF Harry Summerfield.**

COOVER Robert (Lowell), b. 4 Feb 1932, Charles City, Iowa, USA. Writer; Dramatist; Poet; University Teacher. m. Maria del Pilar Sans-Mallagre, 3 June 1959, 1 son, 2 daughters. Education: Southern Illinois University; BA, Indiana University, 1953; MA, University of Chicago, 1965. Appointments: Teacher, Bard College 1966-67, University of Iowa 1967-69, Princeton University 1972-73, Brown University 1980-; Various guest lectureships and professorships. Publications: The Origin of the Brunists, 1966; The Universal Baseball Association, J Henry Waugh, Prop., 1968; Pricksongs & Descants (short fictions), 1969; A Theological Position (plays), 1972; The Public Burning, 1977; A Political Fable (The Cat in the Hat for President), 1980; Spanking the Maid, 1982; Gerald's Party, 1986; A Night at the Movies, 1987; Whatever Happened to Gloomy Gus of the Chicago Bears?, 1987; Pinocchio in Venice, 1991; John's Wife, 1996; Briar Rose, 1997. Contributions to: Plays, poems, fiction, translations, essays and criticism in various publications. Honours: William Faulkner Award for Best First Novel, 1966; Rockefeller Foundation Grant, 1969; Guggenheim Fellowships, 1971, 1974; Obie Awards, 1972-73; American Academy of Arts and Letters Award, 1976; National Endowment for the Arts Grant, 1985; Rhode Island Governor's Arts Award, 1988; Deutscher Akademischer Austauschdienst Fellowship, Berlin, 1990. Memberships: American Academy and Institute of Arts and Letters; PEN International. Address: c/o Department of English, Brown University, Providence, RI 02912, USA.

COPE Robert Knox, (Jack Cope), b. 3 June 1913, Mooi River, Natal, South Africa. Writer; Poet; Editor. m. Lesley de Villiers, 4 June 1942, 2 sons. Appointment: Co-Founder and Editor, Contrast, South African Literary Magazine, 1960-80. Publications: Lyrics and Diatribes, 1948; Selected Poems of Ingrid Jonker (co-translator), 1968, revised edition, 1988; The Rain Maker, 1971; The Student of Zend, 1972; My Son Max, 1977. Editor: Penguin Book of South African Verse. Other: Stage, radio and television adaptations. Contributions to: School textbooks and magazines. Honours: British Council Award, 1960; Carnegie Fellowship, 1966; CNA Prize, Argus Prize, and Gold Medallist for Literature, Veld Trust Prize, 1971; Honorary DLitt, Rhodes. Address: 21 Bearton Road, Hitchin, Herts SG5 1UB, England.

COPE Wendy, b. 21 July 1945, Erith, Kent, England. Teacher; Poet. Education: BA, St Hilda's College, Oxford, 1966. Appointments: Teacher in London primary schools, 1967-86; Freelance Writer, 1986-. Publications: Across the City, 1980; Hope and the 42, 1984; Making Cocoa for Kingsley Amis, 1986; Poem from a Colour Chart of Houspaints, 1986; Men and Their Boring Arguments, 1988; Does She Like Wordgames?, 1988; The River Girl, 1990; Serious Concerns, 1992; Editor: Is That The New Moon?; Poems by Women Poets, 1989; The Orchard Book of Funny Poems, 1993. Honour: Cholmondeley Award, 1987; Fellow, Royal Society of Literature; American Academy of Arts and Letters Michael Braude Award, 1995. Address: c/o Peters Fraser and Dunlop, 5th Floor, The Chambers, Chelsea Harbour, Lots Road, London SW10 0XF, England.

COPELAND Ann. See: **FURTWANGLER Virginia Anne.**

CORBELA-GARDINER Licia Paloma, b. 9 June 1963, Montreal, Quebec, Canada. Journalist. m. James Stephen Gardiner, 25 Apr 1987. Education: Arts and Science Diploma, 1985, Journalism Diploma, Vancouver Community College, 1987. Appointments: Lifestyle/Travel Editor, 1994, Associate Editor, 1996-, Calgary Sun. Publication: For Love and Money, The Tale of the Joudries, 1996. Contributions to: The Province (Vancouver); The Toronto Star (Toronto); The Toronto Sun (Toronto); The Scarborough Mirror (Toronto); The Calgary Sun. Honours: Edward Dunlop Award of Excellence, 1992; Ontario Reporters Association Award, 1992. Address: 2615 12th St NE, Calgary, Alberta T2E 7W9, Canada.

CORBEN Beverly Balkum, b. 6 Aug 1926. Artist/Writer; Educator (retired). m. Dr Herbert Charles Corben, 25 Oct 1957, 1 stepson, 2 stepdaughters. Education: AA, Santa Monica College, 1950; BA with honours, University of California, Los Angeles, 1960; MA, Case Western Reserve University, 1972. Appointments: Editorial Associate, Technical Public Relations, The Ramo-Wooldridge Corporation (now TRC Inc), 1954-57; Teaching Assistant, 1972-73, Director of Writing Laboratory, 1973-82 (on leave 1978-80), Scarborough College, University of Toronto, Canada; Visiting Scholar, 1978-80, Scholar-in-Residence, 1982-88, Harvey Mudd College. Publications: On Death and Other Reasons for Living (poems), 1972, 2nd printing, 1993. Contributions to: Poetic Justice; Texas Review; Voices International; Prophetic Voices; Modern Haiku; Old Hickory Review. Honours: Cleveland State University Honorary Alumna, 1971; More than 60 awards for poetry and fiction nationwide, 1989-. Memberships: Mississippi Poetry Society; Gulf Coast Writers Association; Writers Unlimited, President, 1991, 1992; Academy of American Poets. Address: 4304 O'Leary Avenue, Pascagoula, MS 39581, USA.

CORDELL Alexander. See: **GRABER Alexander.**

COREN Alan, b. 27 June 1938, London, England. Editor. m. Anne Kasriel, 14 Oct 1963, 1 son, 1 daughter. Education: BA, 1st Class Honours, Wadham College, Oxford, 1961; Harkness Fellowship, Yale University, 1961-62, University of California, Berkeley, 1962-63. Appointments: Assistant Editor, 1963-67, Literary Editor, 1967-69, Deputy Editor, 1969-77, Editor, 1978-87, Punch Magazine; Editor, The Listener, 1988-89. Publications: The Dog It Was That Died, 1965; All Except the Bastard, 1969; The Sanity Inspector, 1974; The Collected Bulletins of Idi Amin, 1974; Golfing for Cats, 1975; The Further Bulletin of Idi Amin, 1975; The Rhinestone as Big as the Ritz, 1977; The Peanut Papers, 1978; The Lady from Stalingrad Mansions, 1979; Tissues for Men, 1980; The Cricklewood Diet, 1982; Bumf, 1984; Something for the Weekend, 1986; Bin Ends, 1987; 12 novels for children (The Arthur Books, 1979-82); The Penguin Book of Modern Humour (editor), 1983; Seems Like Old Times (autobiography), 1989; More Like Old Times, 1990; A Year in Cricklewood, 1991; Toujours Cricklewood?, 1993; Sunday Best, 1993; Animal Passions, 1994; A Bit on the Side, 1995; The Alan Coren Omnibus, 1996. Contributions to: Atlantic Monthly; Tatler; Harper's; Playboy; London Review of Books; Listener; Sunday Times; Observer; Daily Mail; Times; Telegraph; Vogue; Nova; Era; New York Times; Evening Standard. Honours: Editor of the Year, British Society of Magazine Editors, 1986; Hon DLitt, University of Nottingham, 1993. Address: c/o Robson Books, 5 Clipstone Street, London WC1, England.

CORK Richard Graham, b. 25 Mar 1947, Eastbourne, England. Art Critic; Writer. m. Vena Jackson, Mar 1970, 2 sons, 2 daughters. Education: Kingswood School, Bath, 1960-64; MA, PhD, Trinity Hall, Cambridge. Appointments: Art Critic, Evening Standard, 1969-77,

1980-83, The Listener, 1984-90; Editor, Studio International, 1975-79; Durning-Lawrence Lecturer, University College, London, 1987; Slade Professor of Fine Art, Cambridge, 1989-90; Chief Art Critic, The Times, 1991-; Henry Moore Foundation Senior Fellow, Courtauld Institute of Art, London, 1992-95. Publications: Vorticism and Abstract Art in the First Machine Age, 2 volumes, 1975, 1976; The Social Role of Art, 1979; Art Beyond the Gallery in Early Twentieth Century England, 1985; David Bomberg, 1987; Architect's Choice, 1992; A Bitter Truth: Avant-Garde Art and the Great War, 1994. Contributions to: Periodicals. Honours: John Llewelyn Rhys Memorial Prize, 1976; Sir Banister Fletcher Award, 1986; National Art Collections Fund Award, 1995. Memberships: Chairman, Arts Council Visual Arts Panel; British Council Visual Arts Advisory Committee; Contemporary Art Society, Committee; South Bank Board Visual Art Advisory Panel. Address: 24 Milman Road, London NW6 6EG, England.

CORKHILL Annette Robyn, (Annette Robyn Vernon), b. 10 Sept 1955, Brisbane, Australia. Translator. m. Alan Corkhill, 18 Mar 1977, 2 sons, 1 daughter. Education: BA(Hon), 1977; DipEd, 1978; MA, 1985; PhD, 1993. Publications: The Jogger, Anthology of Australian Poetry, 1987; Destination, Outrider, 1987; Mangoes Encounter - Queensland Summer, 1987; Age 1, LINQ, 1987; Two Soldiers of Tiananmen, Earth Against Heaven, 1990; Australian Writing: Ethnic Writers 1945-1991, 1994; The Immigrant Experience in Australian Literature, 1995. Contributions to: Outrider; Australian Literary Studies. Honours: Honorary Mention, The Creativity Centre, Harold Kesteven Poetry Prize, 1987. Address: 5 Wattletree Place, The Gap, Queensland 4061, Australia.

CORLETT William, b. 8 Oct 1938, Darlington, Durham, England. Children's Author; Dramatist; Actor. Education: Royal Academy of Dramatic Art, London, 1956-58. Publications: The Gentle Avalanche, 1962; Another Round, 1962; Return Ticket, 1962; The Scallop Shell, 1963; Flight of a Lone Sparrow, 1965; Dead Set at Dream Boy, 1965; The Scourging of Matthew Barrow, 1965; Tinker's Curse, 1968; We Never Went to Cheddar Gorge, 1968; The Story Teller, 1969; The Illusionist, 1969; National Trust, 1970; The Deliverance of Fanny Blaydon, 1971; A Memory of Two Loves, 1972; Conversations in the Dark, 1972; The Gate of Eden, 1974; The Land Beyond, 1975; The Ideal Tale, 1975; The Once and Forever Christmas (with John Moore), 1975; Return to the Gate, 1975; Mr Oddy, 1975; The Orsini Emeralds, 1975; Emmerdale Farm series, 1975-77; Orlando the Marmalade Cat Buys a Cottage, adaptation of story by Kathleen Hale, 1975; The Dark Side of the Moon, 1976; Orlando's Camping Holiday, adaptation of a story by Kathleen Hale, 1976; Paper Lads, 1978-79; Question series (The Question of Religion, The Christ Story, The Hindu Sound, The Judaic Law, The Buddha Way, The Islamic Space), 1978-79; Kids series, 1979; Going Back, 1979; The Gate of Eden, 1980; Barriers series, 1980; Agatha Christie Hour, adaptation of 4 short stories, 1982; The Machine Gunners, adaptation of Robert Westall book, 1982; Dearly Beloved, 1983; Bloxworth Blue, 1984; Return to the Gate, 1986; The Secret Line, 1988; The Steps up the Chimney, 1990; The Door in the Tree, 1991; The Tunnel Behind the Waterfall, 1991; The Bridge in the Clouds, 1992; The Gondolier's Cat, 1993; Now and Then, 1995; Television and Film: The Watchouse, adaptation of Robert Westall book, 1989; Torch, 6 part family adventure series, BBC TV, 1992; Moonacre, 6 part family adventure series, BBC TV, 1994. Honour: Dillons First Fiction Award, 1995. Memberships: Society of Authors; Writers Guild of Great Britain. Literary Agent: Tessa Sayle Agency, 11 Jubilee Place, London SW3 3TE, England. Address: Churchfields, Hope Mansel, Nr Ross-on-Wye, Herefordshire HR9 5TL, England.

CORLEY Ernest. See: BULMER Henry Kenneth.

CORMAN Avery, b.28 Nov 1935, New York, New York, USA. Novelist. m. Judith Lishinsky, 5 Nov 1967, 2 sons. Education: BS, New York University, 1952. Publications: Oh God!, 1971; Kramer Vs Kramer, 1977; The Bust-Out King, 1977; The Old Neighborhood, 1980; Fifty, 1987; Prized Possessions, 1991; The Big Hype, 1992. Memberships: PEN American Center; Writers Guild of America. Address: c/o Janklow & Newbit Associates, 598 Madison Avenue, New York City, NY 10022, USA.

CORMAN Cid (Sidney), b. 29 June 1924, Boston, Massachusetts, USA. Poet; Writer; Editor. m. Shizumi Konishi, 1965. Education: AB, Tufts University, 1945; Graduate Studies, University of Michigan, 1946-47, University of North Carolina, 1947, Sorbonne, University of Paris, 1954-55. Appointments: Poetry broadcaster, WMEX, Boston, 1949-51; Editor, Origin Magazine and Origin Press,

Kyoto, Japan, 1951-71. Publications: Poetry: Sabluna, 1945; Thanksgiving Eclogue, 1954; The Responses, 1956; Stances and Distances, 1957; A Table in Provence, 1958; The Descent from Daimonji, 1959; For Sure, 1959; For Instance, 1959; For Good, 1961; In Good Time, 1964; In No Time, 1964; All in All, 1965; For Granted, 1966; At Bottom, 1966; Words for Each Other, 1967; And Without End, 1968; No Less, 1968; No More, 1969; Nigh, 1969; Livingdying, 1970; Of the Breath of, 1970; For Keeps, 1970; For Now, 1971; Out and Out, 1972; A Language Without Words, 1973; So Far, 1973; Breathing, 1973; O/1, 1974; Once and For All, 1976; Auspices, 1978; Aegis: Selected Poems, 1970-1980, 1983; And the Word, 1987. Other: The Gist of Origin: An Anthology (editor), 1973; At Their Word: Essays on the Arts of Language, 2 volumes, 1977-78; Where We Are Now: Essays and Postscription, 1991. Honours: Fulbright Fellowship, 1954; Lenore Marshall Memorial Poetry Award, 1974; National Endowment for the Arts Award, 1974. Address: c/o Black Sparrow Press, PO Box 3993, Santa Barbara, CA 93130, USA.

CORMIER Robert (Edmund), b. 17 Jan 1925, Leominster, Massachusetts, USA. Writer. m. Constance B Senay, 6 Nov 1948, 1 son, 3 daughters. Education: Fitchburg State College, 1943-44. Appointments: Writer, Radio WTAG, Worcester, Massachusetts, 1946-48; Reporter, Columnist, Worcester Telegram and Gazette, 1948-55, Fitchburg Sentinel and Enterprise, 1955-78. Publications: Now and at the Hour, 1960; A Little Raw on Monday Morning, 1963; Take Me Where the Good Times Are, 1965; The Chocolate War, 1974; I Am the Cheese, 1977; After the First Death, 1979; Eight Plus One, 1980; The Bumblebee Flies Anyway, 1983; Beyond the Chocolate War, 1985; Fade, 1988; Other Bells for Us to Ring, 1990; We All Fall Down, 1991; I Have Words to Spend, 1991; Tunes for Bears to Dance to, 1992; In the Middle of the Night, 1995. Honours: Alan Award, National Council of Teachers of English, 1982; Margaret Edwards Award, American Library Association, School Library Journal, 1981. Address: 1177 Main Street, Leominster, MA 01453, USA.

CORN Alfred, b. 14 Aug 1943, Bainbridge, Georgia, USA. Poet; Writer; Critic; Translator. m. Ann Jones, 1967, div 1971. Education: BA, Emory University, 1965; MA, Columbia University, 1967. Appointments: Poet-in-Residence, George Mason University, 1980, Blaffer Foundation, New Harmony, Indiana, 1989, James Thurber House, 1990; Humanities Lecturer, New School for Social Research, New York City, 1988; Ellison Chair in Poetry, University of Cincinnati, 1989; Bell Distinguished Visiting Professor, University of Tulsa, 1992; Hurst Residency in Poetry, Washington University, St Louis, 1994; Numerous college and university seminars and workshops; Many poetry readings. Publications: Poetry: The Various Light, 1980; Tongues on Trees, 1980; The New Life, 1983; Notes from a Child of Paradise, 1984; An Xmas Murder, 1987; The West Door, 1988; Autobiographies, 1992; Present, 1997. Novel: Part of His Story, 1997. Criticism: The Metamorphoses of Metaphor, 1987. Editor, Incarnation: Contemporary Writers on the New Testament, 1990; The Pith Helmet, 1992; A Manual of Prosody, 1997. Contributions to: Books, anthologies, scholarly journals, and periodicals. Honours: Woodrow Wilson Fellow, 1965-66; Fulbright Fellow, Paris, 1967-68; Ingram Merrill Fellowships, 1974, 1981; National Endowment for the Arts Fellowships for Poetry, 1980, 1991; Gustav Davidson Prize, Poetry Society of America, 1983; American Academy and Institute of Arts and Letters Award, 1983; New York Foundation for the Arts Fellowships, 1986, 1995; Guggenheim Fellowship, 1986-87; Academy of American Poets Prize, 1987; Yaddo Corporation Fellowship in Poetry, 1989; Djerassi Foundation Fellowship in Poetry, 1990; Rockefeller Foundation Fellowship in Poetry, Bellagio, Italy, 1992; MacDowell Colony Fellowships in Poetry, 1994, 1996. Memberships: National Book Critics Circle; PEN; Poetry Society of America. Address: 350 West 14th Street Apt 6A, New York, NY 10014, USA.

CORNWELL Bernard, (Susannah Kells), b. 23 Feb 1944, London, England. Romance/Historical Novelist. m. Judy Acker, 1980. Education: BA, University of London, 1967. Appointments: Producer, BBC Television, London, 1969-76; Head of Current Affairs, BBC Television, Belfast, 1976-79; News Editor, Thames Television, London, 1979-80. Publications: Novels as Bernard Cornwell: Sharpe's Eagle, 1981; Sharpe's Gold, 1981; Sharpe's Company, 1982; Sharpe's Sword, 1983; Sharpe's Enemy, 1984; Sharpe's Honour, 1985; Sharpe's Regiment, 1986; Sharpe's Siege, 1987; Sharpe's Rifles, 1988; Wildtrack, 1988; Sharpe's Revenge, 1989; Sea Lord, 1989; Killer's Wake, 1989; Sharpe's Waterloo, 1990; Crackdown, 1990; Sharpe's Devil, 1991; Stormchild, 1991; Scoundrel, 1992; Rebel, 1993; Copperhead, 1993; The Winter King, 1996. As Susannah King: A

Crowning Mercy, 1983; The Fallen Angels, 1984; Coat of Arms, 1986. Film adaptations: Sharpe, 1993; Sharpe's Rifles, 1993. Literary Agent: Toby Eady. Address: c/o Toby Eady Associates, 7 Gledhow Gardens, London SW5 0BL, England.

CORNWELL David John Moore, (John le Carré), b. 19 Oct 1931. Writer. m. (1) Alison Ann Veronica Sharp, 1954, div 1971, 3 sons, (2) Valerie Jane Eustace, 1972, 1 son. Education: Berne University; Lincoln College, Oxford. Appointments: Teacher, Eton College, 1956-58; Foreign Service, 1959-64. Publications: Call for the Dead, 1961 (filmed as The Deadly Affair, 1967); Murder of Quality, 1962; The Spy Who Came in From the Cold, 1963; The Looking Glass War, 1965; A Small Town in Germany, 1968; The Naive and Sentimental Lover, 1971; Tinker Tailor Soldier Spy, 1974; The Honourable Schoolboy, 1977; Smiley's People, 1979; The Quest for Karla (collected edition of previous 3 titles), 1982; The Little Drummer Girl, 1983; A Perfect Spy, 1986; The Russia House, 1989; The Secret Pilgrim, 1991; The Night Manager, 1993; Our Game, 1995. Honours: Somerset Maugham Award, 1963; Edgar Allan Poe Award, 1965, Grand Master Award, 1986, Mystery Writers of America; James Tait Black Award, 1977; Gold Dagger Award, 1978, Diamond Dagger Award, 1988, Crime Writers Association; Premio Malaparte, 1987; Nikos Kazanzakis Prize, 1991; Honorary Fellow, Lincoln College, Oxford; Honorary Doctorate, Exeter University. Address: David Higham Associates, 5-8 Lower John Street, Golden Square, London W1R 4HA, England.

CORNWELL Patricia Daniels, b. 1956, Miami, Florida, USA. Mystery/Crime Novelist. m. Charles Cornwell, 1980, div 1990. Education: BA, Davidson College, 1979. Appointments: Police Reporter, Charlotte Observer, Charlotte, North Carolina, 1979-81; Computer Analyst, Office of the Chief Medical Examiner, Richmond, Virginia, 1985-; Volunteer Police Officer; Writer, 1983-. Publications: Biography: A Time for Remembering, 1983. Novels: Postmortem, 1990; Body of Evidence, 1991; All That Remains, 1993; Cruel and Unusual, 1993; From Potter's Field, 1995. Honours: Investigative Reporting Award, North Carolina Press Association, 1980; Gold Medallion Book Award, Evangelical Christian Publishers Association, 1985; John Greasy Award, 1990; Edgar Award, 1990; Finalist, Anthony Award, 1990. Memberships: Authors Guild; Mystery Writers of America; International Crime Writers' Association; National Association of Medical Examiners; Virginia Writers' Club. Address: c/o Don Congdon Associates Inc, 156 Fifth Avenue, Suite 625, New York, NY 10010, USA.

CORSO Gregory, b. 26 Mar 1930, New York, New York, USA. Poet; Dramatist; Writer. m. (1) Sally November, 7 Maya 1963, div, 1 daughter, (2) Belle Carpenter, 1968, 1 son, 1 daughter. Education: Elementary school. Publications: Poetry: The Vestal Lady of Brattle, and Other Poems, 1955; Bomb, 1958; Gasoline, 1958, new edition, 1992; A Pulp Magazine for the Dead Generation: Poems (with Henk Marsman), 1959; The Happy Birthday of Death, 1960; Long Live Man, 1962; Selected Poems, 1962; There is Yet Time to Run Back Through Life and Expiate All That's Been Sadly Done, 1965; The Geometric Poem: A Long Experimental Poem, Composite of Many Lines and Angles Selective, 1966; 10 Times a Poem: Collected at Random From 2 Suitcases Filled with Poems: The Gathering of 5 Years, 1967; Elegiac Feelings: American, 1970; Herald of the Autochthonic Spirit, 1981; Wings, Words, Windows, 1982; Mindfield: New and Selected Poems, 1989; Many others. Novel: American Express, 1961; Plays: This Hung-up Age, 1955; Way Out: A Poem in Discord, 1974; Collected Plays, 1980. Non-Fiction: Some of My Beginnings and What I Feel Right Now, 1982. Contributions to: Penguin Modern Poets 5, 1963; A Controversy of Poets, 1965. Honours: Jean Stein Award for Poetry, American Academy and Institute of Arts and Letters, 1986; Longview Award; Poetry Foundation Award. Address: c/o Roger Richards Rare Books, 26 Horatio Street, No 24, New York, NY 10014, USA.

CORTEN Irina H Shapiro, (Renata Starr), b. 15 Feb 1941, Moscow, Russia. Professor of Russian Literature and Culture. m. Barry Corten, 11 Apr 1964, div 1974, 1 daughter. Education: BA, Barnard College, 1962; MA, Harvard University, 1963; PhD, University of California at Berkeley, 1972. Publications: Nicholas Roerich: An Annotated Bibliography, 1984; Flowers of Morya: The Poetry of Nicholas Roerich, 1986; Vocabulary of Soviet Society and Culture, 1992. Contributions to: Periodicals and journals. Honours: Numerous guest lectures and research grants. Memberships: Association of

Literary Scholars and Critics; Literary Translators Association. Address: 3725 South 39th Avenue, Minneapolis, MN 55406, USA.

COSGRAVE Patrick, b. 28 Sept 1941, Dublin, Ireland. Writer. m. (1) Ruth Dudley Edwards, 1965, div, (2) Norma Alice Green, 1974, div, 1 daughter, (3) Shirley Ward, 1981. Education: BA, 1964, MA, 1965, University College, Dublin; PhD, Peterhouse, Cambridge, 1968. Appointments: London Editor, Radio Telefis Eireann, 1968-69; Conservative Research Deptarment, 1969-71; Political Editor, The Spectator, 1971-75; Features Editor, Telegraph Magazine, 1974-76; Special Advisor to Rt Hon Mrs Margaret Thatcher, 1975-79; Managing Editor, Quartet Crime (Quartet Books), 1979-81. Publications: The Public Poetry of Robert Lowell, 1969; Churchill at War: Alone, 1974; Cheyney's Law (novel), 1976; Margaret Thatcher: A Tory and her Party, 1978, 2nd edition as Margaret Thatcher: Prime Minister, 1979; The Three Colonels (novel), 1979; R A Butler: An English Life, 1981; Adventure of State (novel), 1984; Thatcher: The First Term, 1985; Carrington: A Life and a Policy, 1985; The Lives of Enoch Powell, 1989; The Strange Death of Socialist Britain, 1992. Contributions to: Various journals and magazines. Literary Agent: Michael Shaw, Curtis Brown, 162-168 Regent St, London W1R 5TB, England. Address: 21 Thornton Road, London SW12 0JX, England.

ĆOSIĆ Dobrica, b. 29 Dec 1921, Velika Drenova, Yugoslavia. Writer; Politician. Education: University of Belgrade. Appointments: Journalist, then freelance writer; Founder, Committee for Defence of Freedom of Thought and Speech; President, Federal Republic of Yugoslavia, 1992-93. Publications: Far Away is the Sun, 1951; Roots, 1954; Seven Days in Budapest, 1957; Divisions, 1961; Responsibilities, 1964; A Fairy Tale, 1966; Power and Anxieties, 1971; This Land, This Time, 4 volumes, 1972-79; The Real and the Possible, 1982; Sinner, 1985; Renegade, 1986; Serbian Question: Democratic Question, 1987; Believer, 1990; Changes, 1992; A Time of Power, 1996. Membership: Serbian Academy of Arts and Sciences. Address: c/o Serbian Academy of Arts and Sciences, Belgrade, Yugoslavia.

COSSI Olga, b. 28 Jan 1921, St Helena, California, USA. Children's Book Writer. Appointments: Correspondent, columnist, regional newspapers. Publications: Over 15 books. Honours: Several. Membership: Society of Children's Book Writers and Illustrators. Address: 574 Spinnaker Court, Santa Cruz, CA 95062, USA.

COTES Peter, b. 19 Mar 1912, Maidenhead, Berkshire, England. Actor; Director; Producer; Writer. m. Joan Miller, 19 May 1948, dec 1988. Education: Italia Conti Stage School. Appointments: Lecturer in Drama, Rose Bruford College; Adjudicator and Public Speaker. Publications: No Star Nonense, 1949; The Little Fellow (with Thelma Niklaus), 1951; Handbook for the Amateur Theatre, 1957; George Robey, 1972; JP: The Man Called Mitch, 1976; Elvira Barney, 1977; World Circue (with R Croft-Cooke), 1978; Performing (Album of the Arts), 1980; Dickie: The Story of Dickie Henderson, 1988; Sincerely Yours, 1989; Thinking Aloud, 1993. Contributions to: Daily Telegraph; Guardian; Independent; Times; Field; Stage; Plays and Players; Irish Times; Spectator. Honours: Fellow, Royal Society of Arts; Knight of Mark Twain. Memberships: Savage Club; Our Society; Society of Authors. Address: 7 Hill Lawn Court, Chipping Norton, Oxon 0X7 5AF, England.

COTTERILL Kenneth Matthew, b. 17 Sept 1950, Sheffield, England. Playwright. m. Marilyn Bokiagon, 6 Oct 1984, 1 son. Education: BA, University of Queensland, 1980; Queensland University of Technology, 1981. Publications: Re-Electing Roger; Richard the Third's Revenge; Perfect Murder; Rhinocerus Hides. Contributions to: Australian Jewish Democrat; British Soccer Week; Flashing Blade; International Association of Agricultural Information Specialists, Quarterly Bulletin. Honours: Australia Bicentennial Award; Australia Day Award for Culture, 1994. Memberships: Australian Writers Guild; Playlab. Address: 44 Martin Avenue, Mareeba, Queensland, Australia.

COTTINGHAM Valery Jean, Countesse de Casselet, b. 4 Sept 1934, Kingston-Upon-Hull, Yorkshire, England. m. George Cottingham, 28 Dec 1965, dec 1991. Education: Endyke Fifth Avenue High School, Kingston-Upon-Hull. Publications: Memories, A Collection of Poems & Short Stories, Volumes I, II, III. Contributions to: Modern Poetry, Volumes 1-8, 1981, 1982, 1983, 1984; Poetry for Everyone, UK, 1983; Winter Gold, 1991; New Beginnings, 1993; Writers World Anthology, Australia, 1995; New Dimensions, Anthology Special Edition (No5), Australia, 1995. Honours: Certificate of Merit, Writer's World

Publishers, Australia; Certificate of Merit, California, USA. Address: 58 Colliers Close, Horsell, Woking, Surrey GU21 3AW, England.

COTTON John, b.7 Mar 1925, Hackney, London, England. m. Peggy Midson, 27 Dec 1948, 2 sons. Education: BA, Hons, English, London University, 1956. Literary Appointments: Editor, Priapus, a magazine of poetry and art, 1962-72, The Private Library, a book collectors' journal, 1969-79; Advisory Editor, Contemporary Poets of the English Language. Publications: Old Movies and Other Poems, 1971; Kilroy Was Here, 1975; Daybook, 1983; The Storyville Portraits, 1984; The Crystal Zoo, 1984; Oh Those Happy Feet, 1986; The Poetry File, 1989; Two by Two (with Fred Sedgwick), 1990; Here's Looking At You Kid, 1992; Oscar the Dog, 1994; This is the Song, 1996. Contributions to: Sunday Observer; Poetry Chicago; Times Literary Supplement; Encounter; New Review; Outposts; Ambit. Honours: Art Council Publication Award, 1971; Deputy Lieutenant of the County of Hertfordshire, 1989. Memberships: Poetry Society, Chairman 1972-74, 1977, Treasurer, 1986-89; President, Ver Poets; Chairman, Toddington Poetry Society. Address: 37 Lombardy Drive, Berkhamstead, Hertfordshire HP4 2LQ, England.

COTTRELL HOULE Mary, b. 1953. Children's Writer. Publications: One City's Wilderness: Portland's Forest Park, 1988; Wings For My Flight: The Peregrine Falcons of Chimney Rock, 1991. Honour: Christopher Award, 1992. Address: c/o Addison Wesley Publishing-Publicity D, 170 Fifth Avenue, New York, NY 10010, USA.

COTTRET Bernard J, b. 23 Apr 1951, Paris, France. Professor of British Studies. m. Monique Astruc, 22 Sept 1951, 1 son. Education: Ecole Normale Superieure de Saint-Cloud, 1971-76. Appointments: Professor, University of Versailles, University of Charleston, South Carolina, 1994; Consultant, Bibliotheque Nationale, Paris, 1988-91. Publications: Glorieuse Révolution d'Angleterre, 1988; Le Christ des Lumières, 1990; The Huguenots in England, 1991; Cromwell, 1992; Bolingbroke, 1992; Histoire des îles Britanniques, 1994; Bolingbroke's Political Writings, 1994; Calvin, Biographie, 1995; Histoire d'Angleterre, 1996. Honours: Docteur ès Lettres; Prix Monseigneur Marcel, Académie Francaise, Silver Medal, 1993; Consultant, Bibliotheque Nationale de France, 1994-; Chairman, Department of Humanities, University of Versailles. Address: 1 Res du Lac, 94470 Boissy-St-Léger, France.

COULSON Juanita Ruth, b. 12 Feb 1933, Anderson, Indiana, USA. Freelance Writer. m. Robert Stratton Coulson, 21 Aug 1954, 1 son. Education: BS, 1954, MA, 1961, Ball State University. Publications: Crisis on Cheiron, 1967; The Singing Stones, 1968; Door into Terror, 1972; Dark Priestess, 1976; Space Trap, 1976; Web of Wizardry, 1978; The Death God's Citadel, 1980; Tomorrow's Heritage, 1981; Outward Bound, 1982; Legacy of Earth, 1989; The Past of Forever, 1989; Starsister, 1990; Cold, Hard Silver, in anthology Tales of Ravenloft, 1994; A Matter of Faith, in anthology Women At War, 1995. Contributions to: Magazine of Fantasy and Science Fiction; Fantastic Science Fiction and Fantasy Science Stories; Goldman Fantasy Foliant III. Honour: Co-winner, Hugo, Best Amateur Publication, World Science Fiction Convention, London, 1965. Address: 2677 West 500 North, Hartford City, IN 47348, USA.

COULSON Robert Stratton, (Thomas Stratton), b. 12 May 1928, Sullivan, Indiana, USA. Writer. m. Juanita Ruth Coulson, 21 Aug 1954, 1 sons. Publications: The Invisibility Affair, 1967; The Mind-Twisters Affair, 1967; Now You See It/Him/Them, 1975; Gates of the Universe, 1975 But What of Earth?, 1976; To Renew the Ages, 1976; Charles Fort Never Mentioned Wombats, 1977; Nightmare Universe, 1985. Contributions to: Books and periodicals. Address: 2677 West 500 North, Hartford City, IN 47348, USA.

COULTER Harris Livermore, b. 8 Oct 1932, Baltimore, Maryland, USA. Writer; Translator; Interpreter. m. Catherine Nebolsine, 10 Jan 1960, 2 sons, 2 daughters. Education: BA, Yale University, 1954; PhD, Columbia University, 1969. Publications: Divided Legacy: A History of the Schism in Medical Thought, Volume I: The Patterns Emerge, 1975, Volume II: The Origins of Modern Western Medicine, 1977, Volume III: Homeopathy and the American Medical Association, 1981 Volume IV: Twentieth-Century Medicine: The Bacteriological Era, 1994; Homeopathic Science and Modern Medicine, 1981; DPT: A Shot in the Dark (with Barbara Fisher), 1985; Vaccination, Social Violence, and Criminality, 1990; The Controlled Clinical Trial: An Analysis, 1991; Empirical Therapies Inc, Washington, DC, founder, president. Honours: Hahnemann Prize, Société Royale

Belge d'Homéopathie, 1985; La Medalla d'Or del Centenari, Academia Medico-Homepatica de Barcelona, 1990. Membership: American Institute of Homeopathy. Address: Center for Empirical Medicine, 4221 45th Street North West, Washington, DC 20016, USA.

COULTON James. See: **HANSEN Joseph.**

COURLANDER Harold, b. 18 Sept 1908, Indianapolis, Indiana, USA. Author. Education: BA, University of Michigan, 1931; Postgraduate work, Columbia University, 1939-50. Publications: Haiti Singing, 1939; Uncle Bouqui of Haiti, 1942; The Cow-Tail Switch (with George Herzog), 1947; The Fire on the Mountain (with Wolf Leslau), 1950; Ride with the Sun, 1955; Terrapin's Pot of Sense, 1957; The Hat Shaking Dance, 1957; Kantchil's Lime Pit, 1959; The Tiger's Whisker, 1959; On Recognizing the Human Species, 1960; Negro Songs from Alabama, 1960; The Drum and the Hoe, 1960; The King's Drum, 1962; Negro Folk Music USA, 1963; Religion and Politics in Haiti (with Rémy Bastien), 1966; People of the Short Blue Corn, 1970; The Fourth World of the Hopis, 1971; Tales of Yoruba Gods and Heroes, 1973; A Treasury of African Folklore, 1975; A Treasury of Afro-American Folklore, 1976; The Crest and the Hide, 1982; The Heart of the Ngoni, 1982; Hopi Voices, 1982; Novels: The Caballero, 1940; The Big Old World of Richard Creeks, 1962; The African, 1967; The Son of the Leopard, 1974; The Mesa of Flowers, 1977; The Master of the Forge, 1985; The Bordeaux Narrative, 1990; Compiler, Editor, Annotator: Big Falling Snow, 1978. Contributions to:Scholarly journals and periodicals. Honours: Guggenheim Fellowships, 1948, 1955; Various awards and academic grants in aid; Outstanding Achievement Award, University of Michigan, 1984. Address: 5512 Brite Drive, Bethesda, MD 20817, USA.

COURTER Gay, b. 1 Oct 1944, Pittsburgh, Pennsylvania, USA. Writer; Film Maker. m. Philip Courter, 18 Aug 1968, 2 sons. Education: AB, Drama, Film, Antioch College, Ohio, 1966. Publications: The Bean Sprout Book, 1974; The Midwife, 1981; River of Dreams, 1984; Code Ezra, 1986; Flowers in the Blood, 1990; The Midwife's Advice, 1992; I Speak for This Child, 1995. Contributions to: Parents; Women's Day; Publishers Weekly; Others. Memberships: Authors Guild; Writers Guild of America East; Guardian Ad Litem; International Childbirth Association. Literary Agent: Donald Cutler, Bookmark: The Literary Agency. Address: 121 North West Crystal Street, Crystal River, FL 34428, USA.

COURTNEY Nicholas Piers, b.20 Dec 1944, Berkshire, England. Author. m. Vanessa Hardwicke, 30 Oct 1980. Education: ARICS, Nautical College, Berkshire, 1966; MRAC, Royal Agricultural College, Cirencester. Publications: Shopping & Cooking in Europe, 1980; The Tiger, Symbol of Freedom, 1981; Diana, Princess of Wales, 1982; Royal Children, 1982; Prince Andrew, 1983;Sporting Royals, 1983; Diana, Princess of Fashion, 1984; Queen Elizabeth, The Queen Mother, 1984; The Very Best of British, 1985; In Society, The Brideshead Era, 1986; Princess Anne, 1986; Luxury Shopping in London, 1987; Sisters in Law, 1988; A Stratford Kinshall, 1989; The Mall, 1990; Windsor Castle, 1991; A Little History of Antiques, 1995. Contributions to: Times; Redbook; Spectator; Independent; House and Garden. Memberships: Brookes's. Address: 9 Kempson Road, London SW6 4PX, England.

COUSINEAU Philip Robert, b. 26 Nov 1952, Columbia, South Carolina, USA. Writer. Education: BA Journalism, University of Detroit, cum laude, 1974. Publications: The Hero's Journey: Joseph Campbell on His Life and Work, 1990; The Soul of the World, 1991; Deadlines: A Rhapsody on a Theme of Famous Last Words, 1991; Soul: An Archaeology: Readings from Socrates to Ray Charles, 1994; Prayers at 3am, 1995; Design Outlaws (with Christopher Zelov), 1996. Contributions to: Parabola Magazine; Paris Magazine. Address: c/o Harper San Francisco, 1160 Battery Street, San Francisco, CA 94111, USA.

COUZYN Jeni, b. 26 July 1942, South Africa (Canadian citizen). Lecturer; Poet; Psychotherapist. Education: BA, University of Natal, 1963. Appointments: Freelance Poet, Broadcaster, Lecturer, 1968-; Writer in Residence, University of Victoria, British Columbia, 1976. Publications: Flying, 1970; Monkeys' Wedding, 1972; Christmas in Africa, 1975; House of Changes, 1978; The Happiness Bird, 1978; Life by Drowning, 1983; In the Skin House, 1993; Books for Children and Editions of Poetry; Bloodaxe Book of Contemporary Women Poets (editor), 1985; Singing Down the Bones (editor), 1989. Honours: Arts Council of Great Britain Grants, 1971, 1974; Canada Council Grants,

1977, 1983; Fondation Espace Enfants, Geneva. Membership: General Council, Poetry Society, 1968-75; Guild of Psychotherapists. Literary Agent: Andrew Mann, 1 Old Compton Street, London W1V 5PH, England. Address: c/o Bloodaxe Books, PO Box 1SN, Newcastle Upon Tyne, NE99, England.

COVARRUBIAS ORTIZ Miguel, b. 27 Feb 1940, Monterrey, Mexico. Writer; Professor. m. Silvia Mijares, 18 Mar 1967, 2 daughters. Education: Licenciado en letras, 1973, Maestria en letras espanolas, (pasantia), 1987, Universidad Autonoma de Nuevo Leon, Monterrey. Appointments: Coordinator, Department of Literature, Summer School, University of Nuevo Leon, 1970; Director, Centre for Literary and Linguistic Research, 1976-79, Director, Institute of Beauty Arts, 1976-79, Coordinator, Creative Writing Workshop, 1981-, Universidad Autonoma de Nuevo Leon, Monterrey. Publications: Story: La raiz ausente, 1962; Custodia de silencios, 1965, 1982; Minusculario, 1966; Poetry: El poeta, 1969; El segundo poeta, 1977, 1981, 1988; Pandora, 1987; Essays: Papeleria, 1970; Olavide o Sade, 1975; Nueva papeleria, 1978; Papeleria en trámite, 1997; Editor: Antologia de autores contemporáneos (narrative), 1972, 1974, 1975, 1979; Antologia de autores contemporáneos (dramaturgia), 1980; Desde el Cerro de la Silla (arts and literature of Nuevo León), research, 1992; Traduction: El traidor (contemporary French and German poets), 1993; Conversations: Junto a una taza de café, 1994; Director, Deslinde (culture review), 1985-. Contributions to: Various publications. Honours: 2nd Place, Story, Xalapa Arts Festival, 1962; Arts Prize, Literature, Universidad Autónoma de Nuevo Leon, 1989; Medal of Civic Merit in Literature and Arts, Gobierno del Estado du Nuevo León, 1993; Poetry Traduction Prize, National Institute of Beauty Arts, Mexico, 1993. Membership: Sociedad General de Escritores de Mexico. Address: Kant 2801, Contry-La Silla, Guadalupe, N L, Mexico 67170, Mexico.

COVILLE Bruce (Farrington), b. 16 May 1950, Syracuse, New York, USA. Children's Writer; Dramatist. Separated, 2 sons, 1 daughter. Education: Duke University, 1968-69; State University of New York at Binghamton, 1969-72; BA, State University College of Oswego, 1972, 1973. Publications: Fiction: Sarah's Unicorn, 1979; The Monster's Ring, 1982; Sarah and the Dragon, 1984; Operation Sherlock, 1986; Ghost in the Third Row, 1987; My Teacher is an Alien, 1989; Herds of Thunder, Manes of Gold, 1989; Jennifer Murdley's Toad, 1992; Space Brat, 1993; Aliens Ate My Homework, 1993. Plays: The Dragonslayers, 1981; Out of the Blue, 1982; It's Midnight, 1983; Faculty Room, 1988. Honours: 2nd Place, Colorado Children's Book Award, 1984; South Carolina Children's Choice Award, 1984-85; IRA Children's Choice List, 1985, 1987. Memberships: Dramatists Guild; Science Fiction Writers of America; Society of Children's Book Writers. Address: 14 East 11th Street, New York, NY 10003, USA.

COWAN Peter, b. 4 Nov 1914, Perth, Western Australia. Academic Author. Education: BA, University of Western Australia, 1940. Appointments: Senior English Master, Scotch College, Swanbourne, Western Australia, 1950-62; Member of Faculty, 1962-79, Research Fellow, Department of English, 1979-, University of Western Australia, Nedlands. Publications: Drift Stories, 1944; The Unploughed Land: Stories, 1959; Summer, 1964; Short Story Landscape: The Modern Short Story (editor), 1964; The Empty Street: Stories, 1965; Seed, 1966; Spectrum One To Three (co-editor), 1970-79; Today: Contemporary Short Stories (editor), 1971; The Tins and Other Stories, 1973; A Faithful Picture: Letters of Eliza and Thomas Brown, Swan River Colony 1841-1851 (editor), 1977; A Unique Position: A Biography of Edith Dircksey Cowan, 1978; Westerly 21 (editor), 1978; Mobiles (stories), 1979; Perspectives One (editor), short fiction, 1985; A Window in Mrs X's Place (short stories), 1986; The Color of the Sky (novel), 1986; Voices (short fiction), 1988; Maitland Brown: A View of Nineteenth Century Western Australia (biography), 1988; The Hills of Apollo Bay (novel), 1989; Impressions: West Coast Fiction 1829-1988, (editor), 1989; Western Australian Writing: A Bibliography, (co-editor), 1990; The Tenants (novel), 1994. Address: 149 Alfred Road, Mount Claremont, Western Australia 6010, Australia.

COWANNA Betty. See: **HARRISON Elizabeth C.**

COWASJEE Saros, b. 12 July 1931, Secundrabad, India. Professor Emeritus of English; Writer; Editor. Education: BA, St John's College, Agra, 1951; MA, Agra University, 1955; PhD, University of Leeds, 1960. Appointments: Assistant Editor, Times of India Press, Bombay, 1961-63; Teaching, 1963-71, Professor of English, 1971-95,

Professor Emeritus, 1995-, University of Regina, Canada; General Editor, Literature of the Raj series, Arnold Publishers, New Delhi, 1984-. Publications: Sean O'Casey: The Man Behind the Plays, 1963; Sean O'Casey, 1966; Stories and Sketches, 1970; Goodbye to Elsa (novel), 1974; So Many Freedoms: A Study of the Major Fiction of Mulk Raj Anand, 1977; Nude Therapy (short stories), 1978; The Last of the Maharajas (screenplay), 1980; Suffer Little Children (novel), 1982; Studies in Indian and Anglo-Indian Fiction, 1993; The Assistant Professor (novel), 1996. Others: Editor, several fiction anthologies including: Stories from the Raj, 1982; More Stories from the Raj and After, 1986; Women Writers of the Raj, 1990; The Best Short Stories of Flora Annie Steel, 1995; Orphans of the Storm: Short Fiction on the Partitioning of India, 1995. Contributions to: Encounter; A Review of English Literature; Journal of Commonwealth Literature; Literary Criterion; World Literature Written in English; Literature East and West; International Fiction Review; Journal of Canadian Fiction. Honours: J N Tata Scholarship, 1957-69; Canada Council and SSHRC Leave Fellowships, 1968-69, 1974-75, 1978-79, 1986-87. Memberships: Cambridge Society; Writers Union of Canada; Authors Guild of India; Association of Commonwealth Literature and Language Studies. Address: Department of English, University of Regina, Regina, Saskatchewan S4S 0A2, Canada.

COWDREY Herbert Edward John, b. 29 Nov 1926, Basingstoke, Hants, England. University Teacher. m. Judith Watson Davis, 14 July 1959, 1 son, 2 daughters. Education: BA, 1949, MA, 1951, Oxford University, 1949. Appointments: Chaplain and Tutor, St Stephen's House, Oxford, 1952-56; Fellow, 1956-94, Fellow Emeritus, 1994-, St Edmund Hall, Oxford. Publications: The Cluniacs and the Gregorian Reform; The Epistolae Vagantes of Pope Gregory VII; Two Studies in Cluniac History; The Age of Abbot Desiderius; Popes, Monks and Crusaders. Contributions to: Many articles. Honour: Fellow of the British Academy. Memberships: Royal Historical Society; Henry Bradshaw Society. Address: 30 Oxford Road, Old Marston, Oxford OX3 0PQ, England.

COWELL Stephanie, b. 25 July 1943, New York, New York, USA. m. Russell O'Neal Clay, 2 Dec 1995, 2 sons. Education: Self-educated. Publications: Nicholas Cooke (actor, soldier, physician, priest), 1993; The Physician of London, 1995; The Players: a novel of the young Shakespeare, 1997. Honour: American Book Award, 1966. Membership: Author's Guild. Literary Agent: Donald Maass Literary Agents. Address: 585 West End Avenue, New York, NY 10024, USA.

COWEN Athol Ernest, b. 18 Jan 1942, Corbridge, Hexham, England. Writer; Publisher. Publications: Word Pictures (Brain Soup), 1989; Huh!, 1991. Contributions to: Various anthologies. Memberships: Publishers' Association; Poetry Society; Writers' Guild of Great Britain; Musicians' Union; Guild of International Songwriters and Composers. Address: 40 Gibson Street, Wrexham LL13 7TS, Wales.

COWIE Leonard Wallace, b. 10 May 1919, Brighton, England. Clerk in Holy Orders. m. Evelyn Elizabeth Trafford, 9 Aug 1949, 1 son. Education: BA 1941, MA 1946, Pembroke College, Oxford; PhD, University of London, 1954. Publications: Seventeenth-Century Europe, 1960; The March of the Cross, 1962; Eighteenth-Century Europe, 1963; Hanoverian England, 1967; The Reformation, 1968; Martin Luther, 1969; Sixteenth-Century Europe, 1977; Life in Britain, 1980; Years of Nationalism (with R Wolfson), 1985; The French Revolution, 1987; Lord Nelson: A Bibliography, 1990; William Wilberforce: A Bibliography, 1992; Edmund Burke: A Bibliography, 1994; Sir Robert Peel: A Bibliography, 1996. Contributions to: History To-Day; History; Church Times. Memberships: Royal Historical Society, Fellow; The Athenaeum. Address: 38 Stratton Road, Merton Park, London SW19 3JG, England.

COWLES Fleur, b. USA. Painter and Writer. Appointments: Associate Editor, Look Magazine, USA, 1949-55; Founder, Editor, Flair Magazine, USA, 1950-51; Editor, Flairbook, USA, 1952. Publications: Bloody Precedent, 1951; The Case of Salvador Dali, 1959; The Hidden World of Hadhramoutt, 1964; I Can Tell It Now, 1965; Treasures of the British Museum, 1966; Tiger Flower, 1969; Lion and Blue, 1974; Friends and Memories, 1975; Romany Free, 1977; The Love of Tiger Flower, 1980; All Too True, 1980; The Flower Game, 1983; Flowers, 1985; People as Animals, 1985; To Be a Unicorn, An Artist's Journey, 1986; The Life and Times of the Rose, 1991; She Made Friends - And Kept Them, 1996; The Best of FLAIR, 1996. Membership: Royal Society of Arts. Membership: Senior Fellow, Royal College of Art. Address: A5 Albany, Piccadilly, London W1, England.

COWLEY Geoffrey. Journalist. m. Susan Pelzer, 1 son. Education: BA, English, Lewis and Clark College, Portland, Oregon; MA, English, University of Washington. Appointments: Reporter and Feature Writer, Seattle Times, and Writer and Editor, Seattle Weekly, 1980-85; Senior Editor, The Sciences, 1985-88; General Editor, 1988, Senior Writer, 1988-, Newsweek. Honours: Clarion Award for Best Magazine Article, 1993; Award for Excellence for Best Feature Reporting, Society of Professional Journalists, New York, 1992; Second Place, National Headliner Award for Consistently Outstanding Feature Writing, 1994; Consumer Journalism Award, National Press Club, 1995. Address: c/o Newsweek, 251 West 57th Street, New York, NY 10019-1894, USA.

COX Charles Brian, b. 5 Sept 1928, Grimsby, Lincolnshire, England. Professor Emeritus of English Literature; Writer. Education: BA, 1952, MA, 1955, MLitt, 1958, Pembroke College, Cambridge. Appointments: Lecturer, Senior Lecturer, University of Hull, 1954-66; Co-editor, Critical Quarterly, 1959-; Professor of English Literature, 1966-93, Professor Emeritus, 1993-, Pro-Vice Chancellor, 1987-91, University of Manchester; Visiting Professor, King's College, London, 1994; Honorary Fellow, Westminster College, Oxford, 1994. Publications: The Free Spirit, 1963; Modern Poetry (with A E Dyson), 1963; Conrad's Nostromo, 1964; The Practical Criticism of Poetry (with A E Dyson), 1965; Poems of This Century (editor with A E Dyson), 1968; Word in the Desert (editor with A E Dyson), 1968; The Waste Land: A Casebook (editor with A P Hinchliffe), 1968; The Black Papers on Education (editor with A E Dyson), 1971; The Twentieth Century Mind (editor with A E Dyson), 3 volumes, 1972; Conrad: Youth, Heart of Darkness and The End of the Tether (editor), 1974; Joseph Conrad: The Modern Imagination, 1974; Black Paper 1975 (editor with R Boyson), 1975; Black Paper 1977 (editor with R Boyson), 1977; Conrad, 1977; Every Common Sight (verse), 1981; Two Headed Monster (verse), 1985; Cox on Cox: An English Curriculum for the 1990's, 1991; The Great Betrayal: Autobiography, 1992; Collected Poems, 1993; The Battle for the English Curriculum, 1995. Honours: Commander of the Order of the British Empire, 1990; Fellow, Royal Society of Literature, 1993. Address: 20 Park Gates Drive, Cheadle Hulme, Stockport SK8 7DF, England.

COX David Dundas, b. 20June 1933, Goondiwindi, Australia. Graphic Artist; Author. m. Elizabeth Beath, 21 Feb 1976, 1 son, 2 daughters. Education: St Martin's School of Art, London, England. Appointments: Head Artist, The Courier Mail, Brisbane. Publications: Various children's books, several in collaboration with wife. Honours: Walkeley Award (Illustration), 1978; Highly Commended Children's Book of the Year Awards, 1983, 1985. Memberships: Australian Society of Authors; Opera for Youth, USA; Greek Community of St George, Queensland; Playlab, Queensland. Address: 8 St James Street, Highgate Hill, Queensland 4101, Australia.

COX Sir Geoffrey (Sandford), b. 7 Apr 1910, Palmerston North, New Zealand. Writer; Broadcaster; Editor. m. Cecily Barbara Talbot Turner, 25 May 1935, dec 1993, 2 sons, 2 daughters. Education: Otago University, New Zealand, 1931; Rhodes Scholar, BA, Oriel College, Oxford, 1932-35. Appointments: Reporter, Foreign and War Correspondent, News Chronicle, 1935-37; Daily Express, 1937-40; First Secretary and Chargé d'Affaires, New Zealand Legation, Washington, DC, 1943; Political Correspondent, 1945-54, Assistant Editor, 1954-56, News Chronicle; Contributor, BBC Radio and Television, 1945-56; Editor and Chief Executive, Independent Television News, 1956-68; Deputy Chairman, Yorkshire Television, 1968-71; Chairman, Tyne Tees Television, 1971-74; LBC Radio, 1978-81; Independent Director, The Observer, 1981-89. Publications: Defence of Madrid, 1937; The Red Army Moves, 1941; The Road to Trieste, 1946; The Race for Trieste, 1977; See It Happen, 1983; A Tale of Two Battles, 1987; Countdown to War, 1988. Honours: Member of the Order of the British Empire, 1945; Commander of the Order of the British Empire, 1959; Television Producers' Guild Award, 1962; Royal Television Society Silver Medal, 1963, Gold Medal, 1978; Knighted, 1966. Memberships: British Kinematograph and Television Society, Fellow; Royal Television Society, Fellow. Address: c/o Garrick Club, London WC2, England.

COX (John) Madison IV, b. 23 Sept 1958, Bellingham, Washington, USA. Garden Designer; Author. Education: BFA, Parson's School of Design, Paris, 1984. Publications: Private Gardens of Paris, 1989; Gardens of the World (co-author), 1991; Artists' Gardens, 1993. Contributions to: Elle Decor, USA; House and Garden,

USA. Address: c/o Helen Pratt, 1165 Fifth Avenue, New York, NY 10029, USA.

COX Richard, b. 8 Mar 1931, Winchester, Hampshire, England. m. 1963, 2 sons, 1 daughter. Education: Stowe School; Honours degree in English, St Catherine's College, Oxford, 1955. Publications: Operation Sealion, 1974; Sam, 1976; Auction, 1978; KGB Directive, 1981; Ground Zero, 1985; An Agent of Influence, 1988; Park Plaza, 1991; Eclipse, 1996. Contributions to: Daily Telegraph (Staff Correspondent, 1966-72); Travel & Leisure; Traveller; Orient Express Magazine. Honour: Territorial Decoration, 1966. Membership: Army and Navy Club; Board Member, CARE International UK, 1985-; Mystery Writers Association of America. Literary Agent: William Morris Agency, New York. Address: PO Box 88, Alderney, Channel Islands.

COX William Trevor, (William Trevor), b. 24 May 1928, Mitchelstown, County Cork, Ireland. Author. m. Jane Ryan, 26 Aug 1952, 2 sons. Education: St Columba's College, Dublin, 1941-46; BA, Trinity College, Dublin, 1950. Publications: The Old Boys, 1964; The Boarding House, 1965; The Love Department, 1966; The Day We Got Drunk on Cake, 1967; Mrs Eckdorf in O'Neill's Hotel, 1968; Miss Gomez and the Brethren, 1969; The Ballroom of Romance, 1970; Elizabeth Alone, 1972; Angels at the Ritz, 1973; The Children of Dynmouth, 1976; Lovers of Their Time, 1979; Other People's Worlds, 1980; Beyond the Pale, 1981; Fools of Fortune, 1983; A Writer's Ireland: Landscape in Literature, 1984; The News from Ireland, 1986; Nights at the Alexandra, 1987; Family Sins and Other Stories, 1989; The Silence in the Garden, 1989; The Oxford Book of Irish Short Stories (editor), 1989; Two Lives, 1991; Juliet's Story, 1992; Collected Stories, 1992; Felicia's Journey, 1994. Honours: Hawthornden Prize, 1964; Honorary Commander of the Order of the British Empire, 1977; Prize, Royal Society of Literature, 1978; Whitbread Prize for Fiction, 1978, 1983; Allied Irish Banks Award for Services to Literature, 1978; Honorary DLitt: Exeter, 1984, Dublin, 1986, Queen's University, Belfast, 1989, Cork, 1990; Winner, Sunday Express Book of the Year Award, 1994; Whitbread Fiction Awards, 1976, 1983; Whitbread Book of the Year Award, 1994; Whitbread Literary Awards, 1983, 1994. Membership: Irish Academy of Letters. Address: c/o A D Peters, 5th Floor, The Chambers, Chelsea Harbour, London SW10, England.

COX-JOHNSON Ann. See: SAUNDERS Ann Loreille.

COYLE Harold, b. 6 Feb 1952, New Brunswick, New Jersey, USA. Writer. m. Patricia A Bannon, 5 Oct 1974, 2 sons, 1 daughter. Education: BA, History, Virginia Military Institute, 1974. Appointments: Commissioned Officer, US Army, 1974-91. Publications: Team Yankee, 1987; Sword Point, 1988; Bright Star, 1991; Trial by Fire, 1992; The Ten Thousand, 1993; Code of Honor, 1994. Memberships: Association of Civil War Sites; Reserve Officers Association. Address: c/o Robert Gottlieb, William Morris Agency, 1350 Avenue of the Americas, New York, NY 10019, USA.

CRACE Jim, b. 1 Mar 1946, Brocket Hall, Lemsford, Hertfordshire, England. Novelist. m. Pamela Ann Turton, 1975, 1 son, 1 daughter. Education: Birmingham College of Commerce, 1965-68; BA (Hons) in English, University of London (external), 1968. Appointments: Freelance Journalist and Writer, 1972-86; Full-time Novelist, 1986-. Publications: Continent, 1986; The Gift of Stones, 1988; Arcadia, 1992; Signals of Distress, 1994; Uncollected short stories: Refugees, 1977; Annie, California Plates, 1977; Helter Skelter, Hang Sorrow, Care'll Kill a Cat, 1977; Seven Ages, 1980; The Slow Digestion of the Night, 1995; Quarantine, 1997. Radio plays. Honours: David Higham Award, 1986; Whitbread Award, 1986; Guardian Prize for Fiction, 1986; Antico Fattore Prize, Italy, 1988; GAP International Prize for Literature, 1989; Society of Authors Travel Award, 1992; Royal Society of Literature Winifred Holty Memorial Prize, 1995; E M Forster Award, 1996. Literary Agent: David Godwin Associates, 14 Goodwins Court, London WC2N 4LL, England.

CRAFT Robert (Lawson), b. 20 Oct 1923, Kingston, New York, USA. Orchestral Conductor; Author. Education: BA, Juilliard School of Music, New York City, 1946; Berkshire Music Center, Tanglewood, Massachusetts; Studied conducting with Pierre Monteux. Appointments: Conductor, Evenings-on-the-Roof and Monday Evening Concerts, Los Angeles, 1950-68; Assistant to, and later closest associate of Igor Stravinsky, 1948-71. Publications: With Igor Stravinsky: Conversations with Igor Stravinsky, 1959; Memories and Commentaries, 1960; Expositions and Developments, 1962; Dialogues and a Diary, 1963; Themes and Episodes, 1967; Retrospections and

Conclusions, 1969; Other: Chronicle of a Friendship, 1972; Prejudices in Disguise, 1974; Stravinsky in Photographs and Documents (with Vera Stravinsky), 1976; Current Convictions: Views and Reviews, 1977; Present Perspectives, 1984; Stravinsky: Glimpses of a Life, 1992. Contributions to: Many publications. Address: 1390 South Ocean Boulevard, Pompano Beach, FL 33062, USA.

CRAGGS Robert S, (Jack Creek, Luke Lanside), b. 6 Apr 1920, Manitoba, Canada. Freelance Writer. Publications: Trees for Shade and Beauty, 1961; Sir Adams Archibald, 1967; Ghostwriting for the Mail Order Trade, 1968; Writer Without a By-Line, 1968; Organic Gardening for Profit, 1990; Prophet of the Wheat Fields, in The Almanac for Farmers and City Folk, 1994; Canada's Men of Letters, 1995; Classic Comics on Stamps, 1995. Contributions to: Hundreds of articles, short stories, cartoon gags to Canadian and US publications; Columnist for various publications. Memberships: National Writers Association; Friends of Merril Collection. Address: 25 McMillan Avenue, West Hill, Ontario M1E 4B4, Canada.

CRAIG Alisa. See: **MACLEOD Charlotte.**

CRAIG Gordon A(lexander), b. 26 Nov 1913, Glasgow, Scotland. Retired Professor of History; Writer. m. Phyllis Halcomb, 16 June 1939, 1 son, 3 daughters. Education: AB, 1936, MA, 1939, PhD, 1941, Princeton University; BLitt, Balliol College, Oxford, 1938. Appointments: Instructor, Yale University, 1939-41; Instructor to Professor, Princeton University, 1941-61; Member, Institute for Advanced Study, Princeton, New Jersey, 1951; Fellow, Center for Advanced Study in the Behavioral Sciences, 1956-57; Shaw Lecturer, Johns Hopkins University, 1958; Haynes Lecturer, University of California at Riverside, 1961; Professor of History, 1961-85, J E Wallace Sterling Professor of Humanities, 1969-85, Stanford University; Curti Lecturer, University of Wisconsin, 1982. Publications: The Politics of the Prussian Army, 1640-1945, 1955; From Bismarck to Adenauer: Aspects of German Statecraft, 1958; Europe Since 1815, 1961, 5th edition, 1979; The Battle of Königgrätz, 1964, new edition, 1996; War, Politics and Diplomacy: Selected Essays, 1966; Germany, 1866-1945, 1978; The Germans, 1982; Force and Statecraft: Diplomatic Problems of Our Time (with Alexander L George), 1983, 3rd edition, revised, 1995; The End of Prussia, 1984; Geld und Geist: Zürich im Zeitalter des Liberalismus, 1830-1869, 1988, English translation as The Triumph of Liberalism: Zürich in the Golden Age, 1830-1869, 1989; Die Politik der Unpolitischen: Deutsche Schriftsteller und die Macht, 1770-1871, 1993, English translation as The Politics of the Unpolitical: German Writers and the Problem of Power, 1770-1871, 1995; Geneva, Zürich, Basel: History, Culture, National Identity (with Nicolas Bouvier and Lionel Grossman), 1994. Editor: Makers of Modern Strategy: Military Thought from Machiavelli to Hitler (with Edward Mead Earle and Felix Gilbert), 1943; The Diplomats, 1919-1939 (with Felix Gilbert), 1953; Treitschke's History of Modern Germany, 1975; Economic Interest, Militarism and Foreign Policy: Essays of Eckart Kehr, 1977; Makers of Modern Strategy: From Machiavelli to the Nuclear Age (with Pepter Paret and Felix Gilbert), 1986; The Diplomats, 1939-1979 (with Francis L Loewenheim), 1994. Honours: Honorary Professor, Free University of Berlin, 1962-; Guggenheim Fellowships, 1969-70, 1982-83; Commander's Cross of the Legion of Merit, Federal Republic of Germany, 1984; Goethe Medaille, Goethe Gesellschaft, 1987; Honorary Fellow, Balliol College, Oxford, 1989-; Member, Orden Pour le Merité für Wissenschaften und Künste, 1990-. Memberships: American Academy of Arts and Sciences; American Historical Association, president, 1982; American Philosophical Society; British Academy, fellow; Comité International des Sciences Historiques. Address: 451 Oak Grove Avenue, Menlo Park, CA 94025, USA.

CRAIG Jasmine. See: **CRESSWELL Jasmine Rosemary.**

CRAIG Malcolm McDearmid, b. 1 July 1937, South Shields, County Durham, England. Publisher/Writer. m. Jill Christine Hampson, 31 Jan 1965, 1 son, 2 daughters. Education: BSc Econ (Hons), Dip Cam; Sloan Fellow, London Graduate School of Business. Appointments: Editor, Stockmarket Confidential; Editor, Finance Confidential; Editor and Publisher, Craig's Investment Letter; Craig's Confidential Finance Letter. Publications: The Sterling Money Markets, 1975; Successful Investment, 1977; Investing to Survive the 80's, 1979; Invisible Britain, 1981; Making Money Out of Gold, 1982; Making Money Out of Shares, 1983; Successful Investment Strategy, 1984, 2nd edition, 1987. Contributions to: All UK national and leading provincial press, specialist investment and financial publications; BBC

Radio; BBC TV. Literary Agent: Dasha Shankman, Ed Victor Literary Agency. Address: 15 Dukes Ride, Gerrards Cross, Buckinghamshire, England.

CRAIG William. See: **BERKSON Bill.**

CRAIK Elizabeth M(ary), b. 25 Jan 1939, Portmoak, Scotland. University Teacher; Writer; Editor. m. Alexander Craik, 15 July 1964, 1 son, 1 daughter. Education: MA, University of St Andrews, 1960; MLitt, Girton College, Cambridge, 1963. Appointments: Research Fellow in Greek, University of Birmingham, 1963-64; Assistant Lecturer to Senior Lecturer in Greek, University of St Andrews, 1967-. Publications: The Dorian Aegean, 1980; Marriage and Property (editor), 1984; Euripides: Phoenician Women, 1988; Owls to Athens (editor), 1990. Contributions to: Scholarly journals. Honours: British Academy Awards, 1981, 1986; Carnegie Trust Award, 1986. Memberships: Association of University Teachers; Cambridge Philological Society; Hellenic Society. Address: c/o Department of Greek, University of St Andrews, St Andrews KY16 9AL, Scotland.

CRAIK Thomas Wallace, b. 17 Apr 1927, Warrington, England. Professor of English Emeritus; Writer; Editor. m. Wendy Ann Sowter, 25 Aug 1955, div 1975, 1 son. Education: BA, English Tripos, Part 1, 1947, Part 2, 1948, MA, 1952, PhD, 1952, Christ's College, Cambridge. Appointments: Assistant Lecturer, 1953, Lecturer, 1954-65, University of Leicester, 1965-67; Senior Lecturer, 1967-73, University of Aberdeen; Professor of English, University of Dundee, 1973-77; Professor of English, 1977-89, Professor of English Emeritus, 1989-, University of Durham. Publications: The Tudor Interlude, 1958; The Comic Tales of Chaucer, 1964. Editor: Marlowe: The Jew of Malta, 1966; Shakespeare: Twelfth Night, 1975; Beaumont and Fletcher: The Maid's Tragedy, 1988; Shakespeare: The Merry Wives of Windsor, 1989; Shakespeare: King Henry V, 1995. Contributions to: Scholarly journals. Membership: International Shakespeare Association. Address: 58 Albert Street, Western Hill, Durham City DH1 4RJ, England.

CRAMER Richard Ben, b. 12 June 1950, Rochester, New York, USA. Journalist; Writer. Education: BA, Johns Hopkins University, 1971; MS, Columbia University, 1972. Publications: Ted Williams: The Season of the Kid, 1991; What It Takes: The Way to the White House, 1992. Contributions to: Periodicals. Honours: Journalism awards. Address: c/o Sterling Lord Literistic Inc, 65 Bleecker Street, New York, NY 10012-2420, USA.

CRANE Richard Arthur, b. 4 Dec 1944, York, England. Writer. m. Faynia Williams, 5 Sept 1975, 2 sons, 2 step-daughters. Education: BA Hons, Classics/English, 1966; MA, 1971, Jesus College, Cambridge. Appointments: Fellow in Theatre, University of Bradford, 1972-74; Resident Dramatist, National Theatre, 1974-75; Fellow in Creative Writing, University of Leicester, 1976; Literary Manager, Royal Court Theatre, 1978-79; Associate Director, Brighton Theatre, 1980-85; Dramaturg, Tron Theatre, Glasgow, 1983-84; Visiting Writers Fellowship, University of East Anglia, 1988; Writer-in-Residence, Birmingham Polytechnic, 1990-91, HM Prison Bedford, 1993; Lecturer in Creative Writing, University of Sussex, 1994-. Publications: Thunder, 1976; Gunslinger, 1979; Crippen, 1993; Under the Stars, 1994; Stage Plays: The Tenant, 1971; Crippen, 1971; Decent Things, 1972; Secrets, 1973; The Quest, 1974; Clownmaker, 1975; Venus and Superkid, 1975; Bloody Neighbours, 1975; Satan's Ball, 1977; Gogol, 1979; Vanity, 1980; Brothers Karamazov, 1981; The Possessed, 1985; Mutiny! (with David Essex), 1985; Soldier Soldier (with Tony Parker) 1986; Envy (with Donald Swann), 1986; Pushkin, 1987; Red Magic, 1988; Rolling the Stone, 1989; Phaedra (with Michael Glenny), 1990; Baggage and Bombshells, 1991; Under the Stars, 1993; Poems from the Waiting Room (editor), 1993; The Last Minute Book (editor), 1995; TV Plays: Rottingdean, 1980; The Possessed, 1985; Radio Plays: Gogol, 1980; Decent Things, 1984; Optimistic Tragedy, 1986; Anna and Marina, 1991; Understudies, 1992; Vlad the Impaler, 1992; The Sea The Sea (classic serial), 1993; Plutopia (with Donald Swann), 1994. Contributions to: Edinburgh Fringe; Guardian; Index on Censorship, Times Literary Supplement. Honours: Edinburgh Fringe First Awards, 1973, 1974, 1975, 1977, 1980, 1986, 1987, 1988, 1989. Literary Agent: Casarotto-Ramsay Ltd, Address: c/o Casarotto-Ramsay Ltd, National House, 60-66 Wardour Street, London W1V 3HP, England.

CRAWFORD Linda, b. 2 Aug 1938, Detroit, Michigan, USA. Writer. Education: BA, 1960, MA, 1961, University of Michigan.

Publications: In a Class by Herself, 1976; Something to Make Us Happy, 1978; Vanishing Acts, 1981; Ghost of a Chance, 1985. Membership: PEN. Address: 131 Prince Street, New York, NY 10012, USA.

CRAWFORD Robert. See: **RAE Hugh Crauford.**

CRAWFORD Thomas, b. 6 July 1920, Dundee, Scotland. Honorary Reader in English; Author. m. Jean Rennie McBride, 19 Aug 1946, 1 son, 1 daughter. Education: MA, University of Edinburgh, 1944; MA, University of Auckland, 1953. Appointments: Lecturer, 1953-60, Senior Lecturer, 1961-62, Associate Professor of English, 1962-65, University of Auckland; Lecturer in English, University of Edinburgh, 1965; Commonwealth Research Fellow, McMaster University, Hamilton, Ontario, Canada, 1966-67; Reader in English, 1967-85, Honorary Reader in English, 1985-, University of Aberdeen; Editor, Scottish Literary Journal, 1974-84. Publications: Burns: A Study of the Poems, 1960; Scott, 1965, revised edition, 1982; Sir Walter Scott: Selected Poems (editor), 1972; Love, Labour, and Liberty, 1976; Society and the Lyric, 1979; Longer Scottish Poems, 1987; Boswell, Burns and the French Revolution, 1989. Contributions to: Scholarly journals. Memberships: Association for Scottish Literary Studies, president, 1984-88; Saltire Society; Scots Language Society; Scottish Text Society. Address: c/o Department of English, University of Aberdeen, Old Aberdeen AB9 2UB, Scotland.

CRAWLEY Tony, (Anthony Francis Crawley), b. 26 Mar 1938, Farnham, Surrey, England. Journalist; Writer. m. (1) Janet Wild, 30 Sept 1961, div 17 Feb 1970, (2) Nicole Michelet, 26 Feb 1970, 1 son, 1 daughter. Education: Victoria Technical Institute, Trowbridge, Wiltshire. Appointments: Editor, Cinema X, 1967-78; Founder-Editor, Premiere, 1969, and Cinema Blue, 1975-78. Publications: The Films of Sophia Loren, 1974; Bebe: The Films of Brigitte Bardot, 1975, revised edition, 1994; Screen Dreams: The Hollywood Pin-up, 1982; The Steven Spielberg Story, 1983; Entre deux censures (with François Jouffa), 1989; Chambers Film Quotes, 1992. Contributions to: Newspapers and magazines. Membership: National Union of Journalists. Address: 6 Allée Claude Monet, 78160 Marly-le-Roi, France.

CRAY Robert. See: **EMERSON Ru.**

CREASEY Jeanne. See: **WILLIAMS Jeanne.**

CRECY Jeanne. See: **WILLIAMS Jeanne.**

CREE Mary Crowther, b. 19 Mar 1919, Tasmania. Author; Lecturer. m. CEA Cree, 20 Feb 1945, 2 sons, 1 daughter. Education: Toorak College. Appointment: Director, Anglican Newspaper, 1974. Publications: Cumquat May, 1978; Edith May 1895-1974: Life in Early Tasmania, 1983; Looking for Antiques in Tasmania, 1986; Notes of Antiques, 1993; Emily Ida - A Victorian Matriarch in Colonial Tasmania, 1994; Looking for Antiques in Sydney, 1994; Tasmanian & Colonial Furniture in New Zealand, 1996. Honour: Life Governor, Royal Childrens' Hospital, Melbourne, Australia. Membership: Australian Authors. Address: 31 Adelaide St, Armadale, Melbourne 3143, Australia.

CREEK Jack. See: **CRAGGS Robert S.**

CREELEY Robert White, b. 21 May 1926, Arlington, Massachusetts, USA. Writer; Poet; Professor of English. m. (1) Ann McKinnon, 1946, div 1955, 2 sons, 1 daughter, (2) Bobbie Louise Hall, 1957, div 1976, 4 daughters, (3) Penelope Highton, 1977, 1 son, 1 daughter. Education: BA, Black Mountain College, 1954; MA, University of New Mexico, 1960. Appointments: Professor, 1967-78, David Gray Professor, Poetry, Letters, 1978-89; Samuel P Capen Professor, Poetry, Humanities, 1989, Director, Poetics Programme, 1991-92, State University of New York, Buffalo; Advisory Editor, American Book Review, 1983-; Sagetrieb, 1983-; New York Quarterly, 1984-. Publications: Poetry: For Love, Poems 1950-60, 1962; Words, 1967; Pieces, 1969; A Day Book, 1972; Selected Poems, 1976, revised edition, 1991; Hello, 1978; Later, 1979; Mirrors, 1983; Collected Poems 1945-75, 1983; Memory Gardens, 1986; Windows, 1990; Echoes, 1994; Prose: The Island, 1963; The Gold Diggers, 1965; Mabel: A Story, 1976; The Collected Prose, 1984; Tales Out of School, 1993; Criticism: A Quick Graph, 1970; Was That a Real Poem and Other Essays, 1976; Collected Essays, 1989; Autobiography, 1990; Co-editor: New American Story, 1965; The New Writng in the USA,

1967; Editor: Selected Writings of Charles Olson, 1967; Whitman, Selected Poems, 1973; The Essential Burns, 1989; Charles Olson, Selected Poems, 1993. Honours: Guggenheim Fellow, 1964, 1967. Rockefeller Grantee, 1965; Shelley Memorial Award, 1981, Frost Medal, 1987, Poetry Society of America; National Endowment for the Arts Grantee, 1982; Berlin Artists Programme Grants, 1983, 1987; Leone d'Oro Premio Speziale, 1984; Distinguished Fulbright Award, Bicentennial Chair of American Studies, University of Helsinki, 1988; Distinguished Professor, State University of New York, 1989; Walt Whitman Citation, State Poet of New York, 1989-91; Horst Bienek Preis für Lyrik, Munich, 1993; Honorary LittD, University of New Mexico, 1993; America Award in Poetry, 1995; Fulbright Award, University of Auckland, 1995; Lila Wallace-Reader's Digest Writer's Award, 1995 Memberships: American Academy and Institute of Arts and Letters; PEN American Center. Address: 64 Amherst Street, Buffalo, NY 14207, USA.

CREGAN David (Appleton Quartus), b. 30 Sept 1931, Buxton, England. m. Ailsa Mary Wynne Willson, 1960, 3 sons, 1 adopted daughter. Author; Dramatist. Education: BA, English Tripos, Clare College, Cambridge, 1955. Appointments: Worked with Cambridge Footlights, 1953, 1954, The Royal Court Theatre Studio, London, 1964, 1968, Midlands Art Centre, Birmingham, 1971; Head of English Department, Palm Beach Private School, Florida, USA, 1955-57; Assistant English Master, Burnage Boys Grammar School, Manchester, England, 1957; Assistant English Master, Head of Drama Department, 1958-62, Part-time Drama Teacher, 1962-67, Hatfield School, Herts; Conducted 3 week studio, Royal Shakespeare Company Memorial Theatre, Stratford-upon-Avon, 1971; Tutor in Drama, Southampton University Adult Education Panel. Publications: Ronald Rossiter, novel, 1959; Plays: Miniatures, 1965; The Dancers, 1966; Transcending, 1966; Three Men for Colverton, 1966; Houses by the Green, 1968; numerous other plays and pantomimes; Television plays: Pipkins (children's television series); Events in a Museum, 1984; A Still Small Shout, 1985; Goodbye Days, 1986; Goodbye and I Hope We Meet Again, 1989; Radio plays: Numerous plays for national radio broadcast. Contributions to: Guardian, New Socialist. Honours: Charles Henry Foyle New Plays Award, 1966; Sony Award, Best Radio Script, 1987; Giles Cooper Radio Drama Award, 1991. Membership: Drama Panel, West Midlands Art Association, 1972-75; Theatre Writers' Union, founder member; Eastern Arts Drama panel, 1981-85, 1990-. Address: 76 Wood Close, Hatfield, Herts, England.

CREGIER Don M(esick), b. 28 Mar 1930, Schenectady, New York, USA. Professor of History; Writer. m. Sharon Kathleen Ellis, 29 June 1965. Education: BA, Union College, New York, 1951; MA, University of Michigan, 1952. Appointments: Assistant Instructor, Clark University, Worcester, Massachusetts, 1952-54; Instructor, University of Tennessee at Martin, 1956-57; Assistant Professor, Baker University, Baldwin, Kansas, 1958-61; Assistant Professor, Keuka College, Keuka Park, New York, 1962-64; Visiting Assistant Professor, St John's University, Collegeville, Minnesota, 1964-65; Senior Fellow and Tutor, Mark Hopkins College, Brattleboro, Vermont, 1965-66; Associate Professor, St Dunstan's University, Charlottetown, Prince Edward Island, 1966-69; Associate Professor, 1969-85, Professor of History, 1985-, University of Prince Edward Island; Abstractor, ABC/Clio Information Services, 1978-; Foreign Book Review Editor, Canadian Review of Studies in Nationalism, 1996-. Publications: Bounder from Wales: Lloyd George's Career Before the First World War, 1976; Novel Exposures: Victorian Studies Featuring Contemporary Novels, 1979; Chiefs Without Indians: Asquith, Lloyd George, and the Liberal Remnant, 1916-1935, 1982; The Decline of the British Liberal Party: Why and How?, 1985; Freedom and Order: The Growth of British Liberalism Before 1868, 1988; The Rise of the Global Village (co-author), 1988. Contributions to: Encyclopedias. Honours: Mark Hopkins Fellow, 1965; Canada Council Fellow, 1972, Social Sciences and Humanities Research Grant, Research Council of Canada, 1984-86. Memberships: American Historical Association; Canadian Association of University Teachers; Mark Twain Society; North American Conference on British Studies; Phi Beta Kappa; Phi Kappa Phi; Phi Sigma Phi. Address: c/o Department of History, University of Prince Edward Island, 550 University Avenue, Charlottetown, Prince Edward Island C1A 4P3, Canada.

CRERAR. See: **REANEY James.**

CRESSWELL Helen, b. 11 July 1934, Nottinghamshire, England. Author. m. Brian Rowe, 14 Aug 1962, div 1995, 2 daughters. Education: BA, English, Honours, King's College, London.

Publications: TV Series: Lizzie Dripping, 1973-75; Jumbo Spencer, 1976; The Bagthorpe Saga, 1980; The Haunted School, 1987; The Secret World of Polly Flint, 1987; Moondial, 1988; Five Children and It, 1990; The Return of the Psammead, 1993; Numerous TV Plays. Books: Sonya-by-the-Shire, 1961; Jumbo Spencer, 1963; The White Sea Horse, 1964; Pietro and the Mule, 1965; Jumbo Back to Nature, 1965; Where the Wind Blows, 1966; Jumbo Afloat, 1966; The Piemakers, 1967; A Tide for the Captain, 1967; The Signposters, 1968; The Sea Piper, 1968; The Barge Children, 1968; The Nightwatchman, 1969; A Game of Catch, 1969; A Gift from Winklesea, 1969; The Outlanders, 1970; The Wilkses, 1970; The Bird Fancier, 1971; At the Stroke of Midnight, 1971; The Beachcombers, 1972; Lizzie Dripping, 1972; Thee Bongleweed, 1972; Lizzie Dripping Again, 1974; Butterfly Chase, 1975; The Winter of the Birds, 1975; My Aunt Polly, 1979; My Aunt Polly By the Sea, 1980; Dear Shrink, 1982; The Secret World of Polly Flint, 1982; Ellie and the Hagwitch, 1984; The Bagthorpe Saga: pt 1, Ordinary Jack, 1977, pt 2, Absolute Zero, 1978, pt 3, Bagthorpes Unlimited, 1978, pt 4, Bagthorpes v the World, 1979, pt 5, Bagthorpes Abroad, 1984, pt 6, Bagthorpes Haunted, 1985, pt 7, Bagthorpes Liberated, 1988; Time Out, 1987; Whodunnit, 1987; Moondial, 1987; Two Hoots, 1988; The Story of Grace Darling, 1988; Dragon Ride, 1988; Trouble, 1988; Rosie and the Boredom Eater, 1989; Whatever Happened in Winklesea?, 1989; Meet Posy Bates, 1990; Hokey Pokey Did It!, 1990; Posy Bates Again, 1991; Lizzie Dripping and the Witch, 1991; Posy Bates and the Bag Lady, 1992; The Watchers, 1993; Classic Fairy Tales Retold, 1993; the Little Sea More, 1995; Stonestruck, 1995; Mystery at Winklesea, 1995; Polly Thumb, 1995; Giant, 1996; Puffin Book of Funny Stories, editor, 1995; Mystery Stories, editor, 1995; TV Series: The Demon Headmaster, 1996; The Famous Five, 1996; The Demon Headmaster Strikes Again, 1996. Literary Agent: A M Heath, London. Address: Old Church Farm, Eakring, Newark, Notts NG22 0DA, England.

CRESSWELL Jasmine Rosemary, (Jasmine Craig), b. 14 Jan 1941, Dolgelly, Wales (US citizen, 1983). Writer. m. Malcolm Candlish, 15 Apr 1963, 1 son, 3 daughters. Education: BA, Melbourne University, 1972; BA (Honours), Macquarie University, 1973; MA, Case Western Reserve University, 1975. Publications: More than 40 novels including: Romantic Suspense include: House Guest, 1992; Nowhere to Hide, 1992; Keeping Secrets, 1993; Edge of Eternity, 1994; Historical Romances and Regencies include: The Princess, 1982; Lord Rutherford's Affair, 1984; Traitor's Heir, 1984; The Moreton Scandal, 1986; as Jasmine Craig, Empire of the Heart, 1989; The Devil's Envoy, 1988; Contemporary Romances include: Mixed Doubles, 1984; Hunter's Prey, 1986; Love for Hire, 1992; The Perfect Bride, 1993; as Jasmine Craig, Refuge in his Arms, 1984; Suprised by Love, 1984; Under Cover of Night, 1984; Master Touch, 1985; One Step to Paradise, 1986; For Love of Christy, 1987; Knave of Hearts, 1988; Anthology: Marriage on the Run, 1994. Honours: Colorado Romance Writer of the Year, 1986, 1987; Top Hand Award for Best Original Paperback published by Colorado Author. Memberships: President, Colorado Authors League; Editor, Writers of America; Authors Guild of America; Novelists Inc, President, 1993. Address: c/o Maureen Walters, 10 Astor Place, New York, NY 10003, USA.

CREW Gary David, b. 23 Sept 1947, Brisbane, Queensland, Australia. Lecturer; Writer. m. Christine Joy Crew, 4 Apr 1970, 1 son, 2 daughters. Education: Civil Engineering Drafting Diploma, 1970; BA, 1979, MA, 1984, University of Queensland. Appointments: Lecturer, Queensland University of Technology, 1987-. Publications: Inner Circle, 1986; The House of Tomorrow, 1988; Strange Objects, 1991; No Such Country, 1992; Tracks, 1992; Lucy's Bay, 1992; The Angel's Gate, 1993. Honours: Australian Children's Book of the Year, New South Wales Premier's Award and The Alan Marshall Prize, 1991; National Children's Book Award, 1993. Membership: Australian Society of Authors. Literary Agent: Fran Kelly, 23 Main Street, Eastwood, South Australia 5063, Australia. Address: Green Mansions, 66 Picnic Street, Enoggera, Queensland 4051, Australia.

CREWS Frederick (Campbell), b. 20 Feb 1933, Philadelphia, Pennsylvania, USA. Professor Emeritus; Writer. m. Elizabeth Peterson, 9 Sept 1959, 2 daughters. Education: BA, Yale University, 1955; PhD, Princeton University, 1958. Appointments: Instructor, 1958-60, Assistant Professor, 1960-62, Associate Professor, 1962-66, Professor of English, 1966-94, Professor Emeritus, 1994-, University of California at Berkeley; Ward-Phillips Lecturer, University of Notre Dame, 1974-75; Dorothy T Burstein Lecturer, University of California at Los Angeles, 1984; Frederick Ives Carpenter Visiting Professor, University of Chicago, 1985; Nina Mae Kellogg Lecturer, Portland State University, Oregon, 1989; David L Kubal Memorial Lecturer, California State University, Los Angeles, 1994. Publications: The Tragedy of Manners, 1957; E M Forster: The Perils of Humanism, 1962; The Pooh Perplex, 1963; The Sins of the Fathers, 1966; Starting Over, 1970; Psychoanalysis and Literary Process, 1970; The Random House Handbook, 1974, 6th edition, 1992; The Random House Reader, 1981; Out of My System, 1975; The Borzoi Handbook for Writers (co-author), 1985, 3rd edition, 1993; Skeptical Engagements, 1986; The Critics Bear It Away, 1992; The Memory Wars (co-author), 1995. Contributions to: Scholarly journals and to magazines. Honours: Fulbright Lecturer, Turin, 1961-62; American Council of Learned Societies Fellow, 1965-66; Center for Advanced Study in the Behavioral Sciences Fellow, 1965-66; Guggenheim Fellowship, 1970-71; Distinguished Teaching Award, University of California at Berkeley, 1985; Spielvogel Diamonstein PEN Prize, 1992. Membership: American Academy of Arts and Sciences, fellow. Address: 636 Vincente Avenue, Berkeley, CA 94707, USA.

CRICHTON (John) Michael, (John Michael, Jeffrey Hudson, John Lange), b. 23 Oct 1942, Chicago, Illinois, USA. Film Director; Author. Education: AB summa cum laude, 1964, MD, 1969, Harvard University; Cambridge University, England, 1965; Postdoctoral Fellow, Salk Institute for Biological Sciences, California, 1969-70. Publications: The Andromeda Strain, 1969; Five Patients, 1970; The Terminal Man, 1972; The Great Train Robbery, 1975; Eaters of the Dead, 1976; Jasper Johns, 1977; Congo, 1980; Electronic Life, 1983; Sphere, 1987; Travels, 1988; Jurassic Park, 1990; Rising Sun, 1992; Disclosure, 1994. Honours: Edgar Awards, Mystery Writers of America, 1968, 1979. Memberships: Authors Guild; Writers Guild of America; Directors Guild; Academy of Motion Picture Arts & Sciences. Address: c/o Lynn Nesbit, ICM, 40 West 57th Street, New York, NY 10025, USA.

CRICK Bernard, b. 16 Dec 1929, England. Education: University College, London. Appointments: Political writer, biographer and journalist; Literary Editor, Political Quarterly; Professor of Politics, Birbeck College, London, 1971-84; Emeritus Professor, University of London, 1993-. Publications: The American Science of Politics, 1958; In Defence of Politics, 1962, 4th edition, 1992; The Reform of Parliament, 1964; Theory and Practice: Essays in Politics, 1972; Basic Forms of Government, 1973; Crime, Rape and Gin: Reflections on Contemporary Attitudes to Violence, Pornography and Addiction, 1977; Political Education and Political Literacy, 1978; George Orwell: A Life, 1980, 3rd edition 1992; Orwell Remembered (co-editor), 1984; Socialism, 1987; Politics and Literature, 1987; Political Thoughts and Polemics, 1990; National Identities (editor), 1991. Honours: Fellow, Royal Society of Arts; Honorary Doctorates: Queens University, Belfast; Universities of Sheffield, East London, Kingston. Address: 8A Bellevue Terrace, Edinburgh EH7 4DT, Scotland.

CRICK Donald Herbert, b. 16 July 1916, Sydney, Australia. m. 24 Dec 1943, 1 daughter. Publications: Novels: Bikini Girl, 1963; Martin Place, 1964; Period of Adjustment, 1966; A Different Drummer, 1972; The Moon to Play With, 1981; Screenplays: The Veronica, 1983; A Different Drummer, 1985; The Moon to Play With, 1987. Contributions to: Sydney Morning Herald; The Australian; Overland; The Australian Author. Honours: Mary Gilmore Centenary Award, Novel, 1966; Rigby Anniversary Award, Novel, 1980; Awgie Screenplay Award, 1983-85. Membership: Australian Society of Authors, Board of Management. Address: 1/1 Elamang Avenue, Kirribilli, New South Wales 2061, Australia.

CRISCUOLO Anthony Thomas, (Tony Crisp), b. 10 May 1937, Amersham, Buckinghamshire, England. Photographer; Nurse; Driver; Journalist; Plumber; Writer; Therapist. 4 sons, 1 daughter. Publications: Yoga and Relaxation, 1970; Do You Dream?, 1971; Yield, 1974; Yoga and Childbirth, 1975; The Instant Dream Book, 1984; Mind and Movement, 1987; Dream Dictionary, 1989; Liberating the Body, 1992. Contributions to: Dream Columnist for Daily Mail, 1982-84; She; Over 21; Cosmopolitan; 1 to 1; Yoga and Health; Energy and Character; Bio-Energy (Japan); Best; LBC Dream Therapist (Broadcasting Radio); Teletext's Dream Interpreter (TV Channel 4). Address: Ashram, King Street, Combe Martin, Devon EX34 0AG, England.

CRISP Tony. See: **CRISCUOLO Anthony Thomas.**

CRISTOFER Michael See: **PROCASSION Michael.**

CRITCHLEY Sir Julian (Michael Gordon), b. 8 Dec 1930, Chelsea, London, England. Member of Parliament; Writer; Broadcaster; Journalist. m. (1) Paula Joan Baron, 1955, div 1965, 2 daughters, (2) Heather Goodrick, 1965, 1 son, 1 daughter. Education: Sorbonne, University of Paris; MA, Pembroke College, Oxford. Appointments: Member of Parliament, Conservative Party, Rochester and Chatham, 1959-64, Aldershot and North Hants, 1970-74, Aldershot, 1974-; Chairman, Western European Union Defence Committee, 1975-79, Conservative Party Media Committee, 1976-81; Steward, British Boxing Board of Control, 1987-; Judge, Whitbread Book of the Year Competition, 1996. Publications: Collective Security (with O Pick), 1974; Warning and Response, 1978; The North Atlantic Alliance and the Soviet Union in the 1980s, 1982; Nuclear Weapons in Europe (co-author), 1984; Westminster Blues, 1985; Britain: A View from Westminster (editor), 1986; Heseltine: The Unauthorized Biography, 1987, revised edition, 1994; Palace of Varieties: An Insider's View of Westminster, 1989; Hung Parliament, 1991; Floating Voter, 1992; A Bag of Boiled Sweets (autobiography), 1995-96; Borderlands, 1996. Contributions to: Books and periodicals. Honours: Political Journalist of the Year, 1985; Knighted, 1995. Memberships: Various professional organizations. Address: 19 Broad Street, Ludlow SY8 1NG, England.

CROCOMBE Ronald Gordon, b. 8 Oct 1929, Auckland, New Zealand. m. Marjorie Tuainekore Crocombe, 7 Apr 1959, 3 sons, 1 daughter. Education: BA, Victoria University, 1955; PhD, Australian National University, 1961. Appointments: Director, Institute of Pacific Studies, University of the South Pacific, 1976-85; Chairman of Judges, Asia/Pacific Region, Commonwealth Writers Prize, 1987, 1988. Publications: The South Pacific, 1973, 5th edition, revised, 1989; The Pacific Way, 1976; Land Tenure in the Pacific, 1971, revised edition, 1987; Foreign Forces in Pacific Politics, 1983; Pacific Universities, 1988; Pacific Neighbours, 1992; The Pacific Islands and the USA, 1995. Contributions to: Numerous professional and academic journals. Memberships: South Pacific Social Sciences Association, Past President; Pacific History Association, Past President; South Pacific Creative Arts Society. Address: Box 309, Rarotonga, Cook Islands.

CROFT Julian (Charles Basset), b. 31 May 1941, Newcastle, New South Wales, Australia. Professor; Writer. m. (1) Loretta De Plevitz, 23 Oct 1967, 1 son, (2) Caroline Ruming, 12 Dec 1987, 1 son. Education: BA, University of New South Wales, 1961; MA, University of Newcastle, New South Wales, 1966. Appointments: Lecturer, University of Sierra Leone, 1968-70; Associate Professor, 1970-94, Professor, 1994-, University of New England, Armidale, Australia. Publications: T J Jones, 1975; The Collected Poems of T Harri James (editor with Don Dale-Jones), 1976; Breakfasts in Shanghai (poems), 1984; Their Solitary Way (novel), 1985; The Portable Robert D FitzGerald (editor), 1987; Confessions of a Corinthian, 1991; The Life and Opinions of Tom Collins, 1991. Membership: Association for the Study of Australian Literature. Address: Department of English, University of New England, Armidale 2351, Australia.

CROMWELL Rue LeVelle, b. 17 Nov 1928, Linton, Indiana, USA. Professor; Clinical Psychology. m. Ginni H Zhang, 9 July 1987, 2 sons, 1 adopted, 3 daughters. Education: AB Psychology, Indiana University, 1950; MA, Clinical Psychology, 1952, PhD, Clinical Psychology, 1955, Ohio State University. Publications: Stress Factors and Myocardial Infarction: Reaction & Recovering, 1977; The Nature of Schizophrenia, 1978; Sschizophrenia, 1993. Contributions to: Over 100 to scientific refereed journals. Address: 1104 Prescott Drive, Lawrence, KS 66049, USA.

CRONE Alla Marguerite, b. 22 Dec 1923, Harbin, Manchuria. Writer. m. Richard I Crone, 27 Mar 1946, 2 sons. Education: San Francisco Conservatory of Music, 1953-57. Publications: Novels: East Lies the Sun, 1982; Winds Over Manchuria, 1983; North of the Moon, 1984; Legacy of Amber, 1985. Contributions to: Christian Science Monitor; Michigan Quarterly Review. Honours: Gold Medal, West Coast Review of Books, 1982; Finalist, Gold Medallion Romance Writers, 1983; 2nd Prize, National League of American Penwomen, 1984; Best Book on Russia, Romantic Times, New York, 1985. Memberships: Authors Guild; Romance Writers of America; California Writers Club. Address: Santa Rosa, CA 95405, USA.

CRONIN Anthony, b. 23 Dec 1928, Enniscorthy, County Wexford, Ireland. Author; Poet. m. Theresa Campbell, 1955, 1 daughter. Education: BA, University College, Dublin, 1948. Appointments: Visiting Lecturer, University of Montana, 1966-68;

Poet-in-Residence, Drake University, 1968-70; Columnist, Irish Times, 1973-86; Cultural Adviser, Irish Prime Minister. Publications: Poems, 1957; Collected Poesm, 1950-73, 1973; Reductionist Poem, 1980; RMS Titanic, 1981; 41 Sonnet Poems, 1982; New & Selected Poems, 1982; Letter to an Englishman, 1985; The End of the Modern World, 1989; Play: The Shame of It, 1971; Novels: The Life of Riley, 1964; Identity Papers, 1979; No Laughing Matter: The Life and Times of Flann O'Brian, 1989; Memoir: Dead as Doornails, 1976; Essays: Heritage Now, 1983; An Irish Eye, 1985; Biography: Samuel Beckett: The Last Modernist, 1996. Honour: Marten Toonder Award, 1983. Address: Office of the Taoiseach, Government Buildings, Dublin 2, Ireland.

CRONIN Vincent Archibald Patrick, b. 24 May 1924, Tredegar, Wales. Author. m. Chantal De Rolland, 25 Aug 1949, 2 sons, 3 daughters. Education: Harvard University, 1941-43; BA, Trinity College, Oxford, 1947. Publications: The Golden Honeycomb, 1954; The Wise Man from the West, 1955; The Last Migration, 1957; A Pear to India, 1959; The Letter after Z, 1960; Louis XIV, 1964; Four Women in Pursuit of an Ideal, 1965; The Florentine Renaissance, 1967; The Flowering of the Renaissance, 1970; Napoleon, 1971; Louis and Antoinette, 1974; Catherine, Empress of all the Russias, 1978; The View from Planet Earth, 1981; Paris on the Eve, 1989; Paris: City of Light 1919-1939, 1995. Address: Manor de Brion, Dragey Par, 50530 Sartilly, France.

CRONON William (John), b. 11 Sept 1954, New Haven, Connecticut, USA. Professor of History, Geography, and Environmental Studies; Author. m. Nancy Elizabeth Fey, 27 Aug 1977, 1 son, 1 daughter. Education: BA, University of Wisconsin at Madison, 1976, MA, 1979, MPhil, 1980, PhD, 1990, Yale University; DPhil, Oxford University, 1981. Appointments: Assistant Professor, 1981-86, Associate Professor, 1986-91, Professor of History, 1991-92, Yale University; Frederick Jackson Turner Professor of History, Geography, and Environmental Studies, University of Wisconsin at Madison, 1992-. Publications: Changes in the Land: Indians, Colonists, and the Ecology of New England, 1983; Nature's Metropolis: Chicago and the Great West, 1991; Under an Open Sky: Rethinking America's Western Past (co-editor with George Miles and Jay Gitlin), 1992; Uncommon Ground: Toward Reinventing Nature (editor), 1995. Contributions to: Books and scholarly journals. Honours: Rhodes Scholarship, 1976-78; Francis Parkman Prize, 1984; MacArthur Fellowship, 1985-90; Bancroft Prize, 1992; George Perkins Marsh Prize, American Society for Environmental History, 1992; Charles A Weyerhaeuser Award, Forest History Society, 1993; Guggenheim Fellowship, 1995. Memberships: Agricultural History Society; American Anthropological Association; American Antiquarian Society; American Historical Association; American Society for Environmental History; American Society for Ethnohistory; American Studies Association; Association of American Geographers; Ecological Society of America; Economic History Association; Forest History Society; Organization of American Historians; Society of American Historians; Urban History Association. Address: c/o Department of History, 3211 Humanities Building, 455 North Park Street, University of Wisconsin at Madison, Madison, WI 53706, USA.

CROOK Joseph Mordaunt, b. 27 Feb 1937, London, England. Professor of Architectural History; Writer. m. (1) Margaret Mullholland, 1964, (2) Susan Mayor, 9 July 1975. Education: Wimbledon College; BA, 1st Class, Modern History, 1958, DPhil, 1961, MA, 1962, Oxford University. Appointments: Research Fellow, Institute of Historical Research, 1961-62, Bedford College, London, 1962-63; Warburg Institute, London, 1970-71; Assistant Lecturer, University of Leicester, 1963-65; Lecturer, 1965-75, Reader in Architectural History, 1975-81, Bedford College, London; Editor, Architectural History, 1967-75; Slade Professor of Fine Art, Oxford University, 1979-80; Visiting Fellow, Brasenose College, Oxford, 1979-80, Humanities Research Centre, Australian National University, Canberra, 1985, Gonville and Caius College, Cambridge, 1986; Professor of Architectural History, University of London at Royal Holloway and Bedford New College, 1981-; Waynflete Lecturer and Visiting Fellow, Magdalen College, Oxford, 1984-85; Public Orator, University of London, 1988-90; Humanities Fellow, Princeton University, 1990; Director, Victorian Studies, Royal Holloway and Bedford New College, 1990-. Publications: The Greek Revival, 1968; Victorian Architecture: A Visual Anthology, 1971; The British Museum, 1972, 2nd edition, 1973; The Greek Revival: Neo-Classical Attitudes in British Architecture 1760-1870, 1973, 2nd edition, 1995; The History of the King' Works (co-author), Vol VI, 1973, Vol V, 1976; William Burges and the High

Victorian Dream, 1981; Axel Haig and the Victorian Vision of the Middle Ages (co-author), 1984; The Dilemma of Style: Architectural Ideas from the Picturesque to the Post-Modern, 1987, 2nd edition, 1989; John Carter and the Mind of the Gothic Revival, 1995. Editor: Eastlake: A History of the Gothic Revival, 1970, revised edition, 1978; Emmet: Six Essays, 1972; Kerr: The Gentleman's House, 1972; The Strange Genius of William Burges, 1981; Clark: The Gothic Revival, 1995. Contributions to: Books and scholarly journals. Honours: Hitchcock Medallion, 1974; Freeman, 1979, Liveryman, 1984, Worshipful Company of Goldsmiths. Memberships: British Academy, Fellow, 1988-, Council, 1989-92; Historic Buildings Council for England, 1974-80; Society of Architectural Historians of Great Britain, Executive Committee, 1964-77, President, 1980-84; Victorian Society, Executive Committee, 1970-77, Council, 1978-88. Address: 55 Gloucester Avenue, London NW1 7BA, England.

CROSLAND Margaret (McQueen), b. 17 June 1920, Bridgnorth, Shropshire, England. Writer; Translator. m. Max Denis, 1950, div 1959, 1 son. Education: BA, University of London, 1941. Publications: Strange Tempe (poems), 1946; Madame Colette: A Provincial in Paris, 1953; Jean Cocteau, 1955; Ballet Carnival: A Companion to Ballet, 1955, new edition, 1957; Home Book of Opera, 1957; Ballet Lover's Dictionary, 1962; Louise of Stolberg, Countess of Albany, 1962; The Young Ballet Lover's Companion, 1962; Philosophy Pocket Crammer, 1964; Colette-The Difficulty of Loving: A Biography, 1973; Raymond Radiguet: A Biographical Study with Selections from His Work, 1976; Women of Iron and Velvet: French Women Writers after George Sand, 1976; Beyond the Lighthouse: English Women Novelists in the Twentieth Century, 1981; Piaf, 1985; The Passionate Philosopher: A de Sade Reader, 1991; Simone de Beauvoir, The Woman and Her Work, 1992; Sade's Wife, 1995. Editor: Marquis de Sade: Selected Letters, 1965; A Traveller's Guide to Literary Europe, 1965; Jean Cocteau: My Contemporaries, 1967; Cocteau's World: An Anthology of Major Writings by Jean Cocteau, 1972. Translator: Over 30 books. Honours: Prix de Bourgogne, France, 1973-74; Enid McLeod Prize, Franco-British Society, 1992-93. Address: The Long Croft, Upper Hartfield, Sussex TN7 4DT, England.

CROSS (Alan) Beverley, b. 13 Apr 1931, London, England. Dramatist. m. Dame Maggie Smith, 1975. Education: Balliol College, Oxford, 1952-54. Publications: Plays: One More River, 1956; Boeing-Boeing, 1962; Miranda, 1987; Musicals: Half A Sixpence, 1962; Jorrocks, 1965; Hans Andersen, 1972; Opera Libretti: Mines of Sulphur, 1966; The Rising of the Moon, 1972; Screenplays: Jason and the Argonauts; Genghis Khan; Half A Sixpence; Clash of the Titans. Membership: Garrick Club. Address: c/o Curtis Brown, Haymarket House, 28/29 Haymarket, London SW1Y 4SP, England.

CROSS Anthony Glenn, b. 21 Oct 1936, Nottingham, England. Educator. m. Margaret Elson, 11 Aug 1960, 2 daughters. Education: MA 1964, PhD 1966, Cambridge University; MA, Harvard University, USA, 1961; LittD, University of East Anglia, 1981. Appointments: Review Editor, Journal of European Studies, 1971-; Editor, Newsletter, Study Group of 18th Century Russia, 1973-; Chairman, British Academic Committee for Cooperation with Russian Archives, 1981-95; Currently, Professor of Slavonic Studies. Publications: N M Karamzin, 1971; Russia Under Western Eyes, 1971; Russian Literature in the Age of Catherine the Great, 1976; Russians in 18th Century Britain, 1981; The Russian Theme in English Literature, 1985; Anglo-Russica, 1993; Engraved in the Memory, 1993; By the Banks of the Neva: The British in Eighteenth Century Russia, 1996. Contributions to: Professional journals. Honours: Frank Knox Fellow, Harvard University, 1960-61; Visiting Fellow, University of Illinois, Urbana 1969-70, All Souls College, Oxford 1978-79; Fellow, British Academy, 1989. Memberships: British University Association of Slavists, President 1982-84. Address: Department of Slavonic Studies, University of Cambridge, Sidgwick Avenue, Cambridge CB3 9DA, England.

CROSS Brenda. See: **COLLOMS Brenda.**

CROSS Gillian Clare, b. 24 Dec 1945, London, England. Writer. m. Martin Cross, 10 May 1967, 2 sons, 2 daughters. Education: BA (Hons) Class I, Somerville College, Oxford, 1965-69; DPhil, University of Sussex, 1970-73. Publications: The Runaway, 1979; The Iron Way, 1979; Revolt at Ratcliffe's Rags, 1980; Save Our School, 1981; A Whisper of Lace, 1981; The Demon Headmaster, 1982; The Dark Behind the Curtain, 1982; The Mintyglo Kid, 1983; Born of the Sun, 1983; On the Edge, 1984; The Prime Minster's Brain, 1985;

Swimathon, 1986; Chartbreak, 1986; Roscoe's Leap, 1987; A Map of Nowhere, 1988; Rescuing Gloria, 1989; The Monster From Underground, 1990; Twin and Super-Twin, 1990; Wolf, 1990; Gobbo the Great, 1991; Rent-a-Genius, 1991; The Great Elephant Chase, 1992; Beware Olga!, 1993; Furry Maccaloo, 1993; The Tree House, 1993; Hunky Parker is Watching You, 1994; What Will Emily Do? 1994; New World, 1994; The Crazy Shoe Shuffle, 1995; Posh Watson, 1995; The Roman Beanfeast, 1996; Pictures in the Dark, 1996; The Demon Headmaster Strikes Again, 1996. Honours: Carnegie Medal, 1990; Whitbread Children's Novel Award and Smarties Prize, 1992. Membership: Society of Authors. Address: The Gate House, 39 Main Street, Wolston, Coventry CV8 3HH, England.

CROSS Victor. See: **COFFMAN Virginia (Edith).**

CROSSLEY-HOLLAND Kevin (John William), b. 7 Feb 1941, Mursley, Buckinghamshire, England. Professor; Poet; Writer; Editor; Translator. m. (1) Caroline Fendall Thompson, 1963, 2 sons, (2) Ruth Marris, 1972, (3) Gillian Paula Cook, 1982, 2 daughters. Education: MA, St Edmund Hall, Oxford. Appointments: Editor, Macmillan & Co, 1962-69; Lecturer in English, Tufts-in-London Program, 1967-78, University of Regensburg, 1978-80; Gregory Fellow in Poetry, University of Leeds, 1969-71; Talks Producer, BBC, 1972; Editorial Director, Victor Gollancz, 1972-77; Arts Council Fellow in Writing, Winchester School of Arts, 1983, 1984; Visiting Professor of English and Fulbright Scholar-in-Residence, St Olaf College, Minnesota, 1987-90; Professor and Endowed Chair in Humanities and Fine Arts, University of St Thomas, St Paul, Minnesota, 1991-95; Director, American Composers Forum, 1993-. Publications: Poetry: The Rain-Giver, 1972; The Dream-House, 1976; Time's Oriel, 1983; Waterslain, 1986; The Painting-Room, 1988; New and Selected Poems, 1991; The Language of Yes, 1996. For Children: Havelok the Dane, 1964; King Horn, 1965; The Green Children, 1966; The Callow Pit Coffer, 1968; Wordhoard (with Jill Paton Walsh), 1969; Storm and Other Old English Riddles, 1970; The Pedlar of Swaffham, 1971; The Sea Stranger, 1973; The Fire-Brother, 1974; Green Blades Rising, 1975; The Earth-Father, 1976; The Wildman, 1976; The Dead Moon, 1982; Beowulf, 1982; The Mabinogion (with Gwyn Thomas), 1984; Axe-Age Wolf-Age, 1985; Storm, 1985; The Fox and the Cat (with Susanne Lugert), 1985; British Folk Tales, 1987; Wulf, 1988; The Quest for the Olwen (with Gwyn Thomas), 1988; Piper and Pooka, 1988; Small Tooth Dog, 1988; Boo!, 1988; Dathera Dad, 1989; Under the Sun and Over the Moon (with Ian Penney), 1989; Sleeping Nanna, 1989; Sea Tongue, 1991; Tales from Europe, 1991; Long Tom and the Dead Hand, 1992; Taliesin (with Gwyn Thomas), 1992; The Labours of Herakles, 1993; Norse Myths, 1993; The Green Children, 1994; The Dark Horseman, 1995. Non-Fiction: Pieces of Land, 1972; The Norse Myths, 1980; The Stones Remain (with Andrew Rafferty, 1989. Editor: Running to Paradise, 1967; Winter's Tales for Children 3, 1967; Winter's Tales 14, 1968; New Poetry 2 (with Patricia Beer), 1976; The Faber Book of Northern Legends, 1977; The Faber Book of Northern Folk-Tales, 1980; The Anglo-Saxon World, 1982; The Riddle Book, 1982; Folk-Tales of the British Isles, 1985; The Oxford Book of Travel Verse, 1986; Northern Lights, 1987; Medieval Lovers, 1988; Medieval Gardens, 1990; Peter Grimes by George Crabbe, 1990. Translations from Old English: The Battle of Maldon (with Bruce Mitchell), 1965; Beowulf (with Bruce Mitchell), 1968; The Exeter Book Riddles, 1978; The Illustrated Beowulf, 1987; The Anglo-Saxon Elegies, 1988. Opera Libretti: The Green Children (with Nicola LeFanu), 1990; The Wildman (with Nicola LeFanu), 1995. Contributions to: Numerous journals and magazines. Honours: Arts Council Awards, Best Book for Young Children, 1966-68; Poetry Book Society Choice, 1976, and Recommendation, 1986; Carnegie Medal, 1985. Membership: Director, American Composers Forum, 1993-. Literary Agent: Rogers, Coleridge and White, 20 Powis Mews, London W11 1JN, England. Address: c/o Rogers, Coleridge and White, 20 Powis Mews, London W11 1JN, England.

CROWDER Ashby Bland Jr, b. 29 June 1941, Richmond, Virginia, USA. m. Lynn O'Malley, 10 Mar 1973, 1 son. Education: BA, Randolph-Macon College, 1963; MA, University of Tennessee, 1965; PhD, University of London, 1972. Appointments: Instructor, Centre College, Danville, Kentucky, 1965-67; Assistant Professor, Eastern Kentucky University, 1969-74; Professor Hendrix College, 1974-. Publications: Writing in the Southern Tradition, Interviews with Five Contemporary Authors, 1990; Poets and Critics, Their Means and Meanings, 1993; The Complete Works of Robert Browning XIII, 1995. Contributions to: Articles in South Dakota Review; Papers on Language and Literature; Studies in Browning and His Circle; Thomas

Hardy Review; Victorian Studies; Southern Quarterly; Southern Review; Mississippi Quarterly; Browning Institute Studies; Poetry in English; Cumberland Poetry Review; Adena; Cloverdale Review; Slant. Honours: Andrew Mellon Fellowship; National Endowment for Humanities Fellowships. Memberships: Thomas Hardy Society; South Atlantic Modern Language Association; Arkansas Literary Society. Address: 109 Crystal Court, Little Rock, Arkansas 72205, USA.

CROWE John. See: **LYNDS Dennis.**

CROWLEY John, b. 1 Dec 1942, Presque Isle, Maine, USA. Writer. Education: BA, Indiana University, 1964. Publications: The Deep, 1975; Beasts, 1976; Engine Summer, 1979; Little Big, 1981; Aegypt, 1987; Novelty (short stories), 1989; Great Work of Time, 1991; Antiquities: Seven Stories, 1993; Love and Sleep, 1994. Other: Film Scripts; Television scripts, including America Lost and Found, and No Place to Hide. Contributions to: Periodicals. Honours: American Film Festival Award, 1982; American Academy and Institute of Arts and Letters Fellow, 1992. Address: Box 395, Conway, MA 01341, USA.

CROZIER Andrew, b. 1943, England. Lecturer; Poet. Education: MA, Cambridge University; PhD, University of Essex. Appointment: Reader, University of Sussex. Publications: Loved Litter of Time Spent, 1967; Train Rides, 1968; Walking on Grass, 1969; In One Side Out The Other, 1970; Neglected Information, 1973; The Veil Poem, 1974; Printed Circuit, 1974; Seven Contemporary Sun Dials, 1975; Pleats, 1975; Duets, 1976; Residing, 1976; High Zero Were There, 1978; Utamoro Variations, 1982; All Where Each Is, 1985; Selected Poems (with Donald Davie and C H Sisson); Ghosts in the Corridor, 1992. Address: Arts Building, University of Sussex, Brighton, Sussex BN1 9QN, England.

CROZIER Brian Rossiter, (John Rossiter), b. 4 Aug 1918, Kuridala, Queensland, Australia. Journalist; Writer; Consultant. m. Mary Lillian Samuel, 7 Sept 1940, dec 1993, 1 son, 3 daughters. Education: Lycée, Montpellier; Peterborough College, Harrow; Trinity College of Music, London. Appointments: Music and Art Critic, London, 1936-39; Reporter, Sub-Editor, Stoke-on-Trent, Stockport, London, 1940-41; Sub-Editor, Reuters, 1943-44; News Chronicle, 1944-48; Sub-Editor and Writer, Sydney Morning Herald, 1948-51; Correspondent, Reuters-AAP, 1951-52; Features Editor, Straits Times, 1952-53; Leader Writer, Correspondent, and Editor, Foreign Report, The Economist, 1954-64; Commentator, BBC English, French, and Spanish Overseas Services, 1954-66; Chairman, Forum World Features, 1965-74; Co-Founder and Director, Institute for the Study of Conflict, 1970-79; Columnist, National Review, New York, 1978-94; Columnist, Now!, 1979-81, The Times, 1982-83, The Free Nation, later Freedom Today, 1982-89; Adjunct Scholar, Heritage Foundation, Washington, DC, 1984-95; Distinguished Visiting Fellow, Hoover Institution, Stanford, California, 1996-. Publications: The Rebels, 1960; The Morning After, 1963; Neo-Colonialism, 1964; South-East Asia in Turmoil, 1965, 3rd edition, 1968; The Struggle for the Third World, 1966; Franco, 1967; The Masters of Power, 1969; The Future of Communist Power (US edition as Since Stalin), 1970; De Gaulle, 2 volumes, 1973, 1974; A Theory of Conflict, 1974; The Man Who Lost China (Chiang Kai-shek), 1976; Strategy of Survival, 1978; The Minimum State, 1979; Franco: Crepúsculo de un hombre, 1980; The Price of Peace, 1980, new edition, 1983; Socialism Explained (co-author), 1984; This War Called Peace (co-author), 1984; The Andropov Deception (novel published under the name John Rossiter), 1984 (published in the US under own name), 1986; Socialism: Dream and Reality, 1987; The Grenada Documents (editor), 1987; The Gorbachev Phenomenon, 1990; Communism: Why Prolong its Death-Throes?, 1990; Free Agent, 1993; The KGB Lawsuits, 1995; Le Phénix Rouge (Paris) (co-author), 1995. Contributions to: Numerous journals. Address: Flat AA, 1 Carlisle Place, London SW1P 1NP, England.

CROZIER Lorna, b. 24 May 1948, Swift Current, Saskatchewan, Canada. Associate Professor; Poet. Education: BA, University of Saskatchewan, 1969; MA, University of Alberta, 1980. Appointments: Creative Writing Teacher, Saskatchewan Summer School of the Arts, Fort San, 1977-81; Writer-in-Residence, Cypress Hills Community College, Swift Current, 1980-81, Regina Public Library, Saskatchewan, 1984-85, University of Toronto, 1989-90; Broadcaster and Writer, CBC Radio, 1986; Guest Instructor, Banff School of Fine Arts, Alberta, 1986, 1987; Special Lecturer, University of Saskatchewan, 1986-91; Associate Professor, University of Victoria, British Columbia, 1991-. Publications: Inside is the Sky, 1976; Crow's Black Joy, 1978; No

Longer Two People (with Patrick Lane), 1979; Animals of Fall, 1979; Humans and Other Beasts, 1980; The Weather, 1983; The Garden Going On Without Us, 1985; Angels of Flesh, Angels of Silence, 1988; Inventing the Hawk, 1992; Everything Arrives at the Light, 1995; A Saving Grace: The Collected Poems of Mrs Bentley, 1996. Editor: A Sudden Radiance: Saskatchewan Poetry (with Gary Hyland), 1987; Breathing Fire: The New Generation of Canadian Poets (with Patrick Lane), 1995. Honours: CBC Prize, 1987; Governor General's Award for Poetry, 1992; Canadian Author's Award for Poetry, 1992; Pat Lowther Award, League of Canadian Poets, 1992, 1996; National Magazine Award Gold Medal, 1996. Membership: Saskatchewan Writers' Guild. Address: c/o McClelland and Stewart Inc, 481 University Avenue, Suite 900, Toronto, Ontario M5G 2E9, Canada.

CRYSTAL David, b. 6 July 1941, Lisburn, County Antrim, Northern Ireland. Writer; Editor. m. (1) Molly Stack, 1 Apr 1964, dec 1976, 2 sons, 2 daughters, (2) Hilary Norman, 18 Sept 1976, 1 son. Education: BA, 1962, PhD, 1966, FCST, 1983, University College, London. Appointments: Assistant Lecturer, University College of North Wales, 1963-65; Lecturer and Reader, 1965-76, University of Reading; Professor of Linguistic Science, 1976-85, University of Reading; Professorial Fellow, University of Wales, Bangor, 1985-; Editor, Child Language Teaching and Therapy, 1985-96; Linguistics Abstracts, 1985-96; Consultant Editor, English Today, 1986-94. Publications: Child Language, Learning and Linguistics, 1976; Working with LARSP, 1979; Eric Partridge: In His Own Words, 1980; A First Dictionary of Linguistics and Phoentics, 1980; Clinical Linguistics, 1981; Directions in Applied Linguistics, 1981; Linguistic Controversies, 1981; Profiling Linguistic Disability, 1982; Linguistic Encounters with Language Handicap, 1984; Language Handicap in Children, 1984; Who Cares About English Usage?, 1984; Listen to Your Child, 1986; The English Language, 1988; Cambridge Encyclopedia of Language, 1987, 2nd edition, 1997; Rediscover Grammar, 1988; The Cambridge Encyclopedia, 1990, 2nd edition, revised, 1994; Language A-Z, 1991; Nineties Knowledge, 1992; An Encyclopedic Dictionary of Language and Languages, 1992; The Cambridge Encyclopedia of the English Language, 1995. Children's Non-fiction books. Honour: Order of the British Empire, 1995. Address: Akaroa, Gors Avenue, Holyhead, Anglesey, Gwynedd LL65 1PB, Wales.

CSERES Tibor, b. 1 Apr 1915, Gyergyoremete, Tras, Hungary. Writer. m. Nora Ulkey, 15 Nov 1944, 1 daughter. Education: University of Economics, Kolozsvar. Publications: Cold Days, 1964; Players and Lovers, 1970; I, Lajos Kossuth, 1980; Pass of Foksany, 1985; Battles of Vizamua, 1988; Vendeta in Backa, 1991. Honours: Kossuth Prize, 1975; Order of Flag, Hungarian Republic, 1990. Memberships: President, Hungarian Writers Association, 1986-89; President, Hungarian Writers Chamber; Hungarian Academy of Literature and Arts. Address: Orlo 14, 1026 Budapest II, Hungary.

CSOORI Sandor, b. 3 Feb 1930, Zamoly, Transbanubia, Hungary. Poet. Education: Lenin Institute, Papa. Appointment: Dramaturg of the Hungarian Film Studio, 1971-. Publications: The Bird Takes Wing, 1954; Devil's Moth, 1957; Flight from Solitude, 1962; We Live in Harsh Times, 1967; My Second Birth, 1967; Clowns of a Jam Circus, 1969; Dialogue in the Dark, 1973; The Memories of a Visitor, 1977; Predictions About Your Time, 1979; The 10th Evening, 1980; Wings of Knives amd Nails, 1981; Nightmare Postponed, 1982; Waiting in the Spring, 1983; Memory of Snow, 1983; In My Hand a Green Branch, 1985; Bright Sunshine on Foot, 1987; Breviary, 1988; Monuments of the World, 1989; Selected Poems, 1992; Screenplays; Also: Cuban Diary, 1965; The Poet and the Monkey Face, 1966; From Wall to Wall, 1969; Reassurance, 1973; Journey While Half-Asleep, 1974; The Wanderer's Diary, 1979; Mud-Rain, 1981; The Sea and the Walnut Leaf, 1982; Preparation for the Day of Reckoning, 1987. Honour: Herder Prize, Austria, 1981. Address: Magveto Konyvkiado, Vorosmartyr ter 1, 1806 Budapest, Hungary.

CUDDON John, b. 2 June 1928, Southsea, England. Writer; Teacher. m. Anna-Claire Dale, 17 May 1975, 1 son, 2 daughters. Education: MA, BLitt, Brasenose College, Oxford, 1949-55. Publications: Novels: A Multitude of Sins, 1961; Testament of Iscariot, 1962; Acts of Darkness, 1963; The Six Wounds, 1964; The Bride of Battersea, 1967. Other: The Owl's Watchsong (travel), 1960; Jugoslavia (travel), 1968; Dictionary of Literary Terms, 1977; Dictionary of Sports and Games, 1981; Penguin Book of Ghost Stories, 1984; Penguin Book of Horror Stories, 1984; Penguin Dictionary of Literary Terms and Literary Theory, 1996. Contributions to: Periodicals and journals. Address: 43 Alderbrook Road, London SW12, England.

CUMBERLEGE Marcus (Crossley), b. 23 Dec 1938, Antibes, France. Poet; Translator. m. (1) Ava Nicole Paranjoti, 11 Dec 1965, div 1972, (2) Maria Lefever, 9 Nov 1973, 1 daughter. Education: BA, St John's College, Oxford, 1961. Appointments: Lecturer, Universities of Hilversum and Lugano, 1978-83. Publications: Oases, 1968; Poems for Quena and Tabla, 1970; Running Towards a New Life, 1973; Bruges, Bruges (with Owen Davis), 1975; Firelines, 1977; The Poetry Millionaire, 1977; La Nuit Noire, 1977; Twintig Vriendelijke Vragen (with Horst de Blaere), 1977; Northern Lights, 1981; Life is a Flower, 1981; Vlaamse Fables, 1982; Sweet Poor Hobo, 1984; Things I Cannot Change, 1993. Honour: Eric Gregory Award, 1967. Address: Eekhoutstraat 42, 8000 Bruges, Belgium.

CUMMING Peter E, b. 23 Mar 1951, Brampton, Ontario, Canada. Writer; Teacher. m. Mary Shelleen Nelson, 14 Oct 1970. Education: BA, English Literature, 1972; Diploma in Education, 1976; MA, English Literature, 1992. Appointments: Resident Artist in Drama, Wilfrid Laurier University, 1972-73; Executive Director, Atlantic Publishers Association, 1984-85. Publications: Snowdreams, 1982; Ti-Jean, 1983; A Horse Called Farmer, 1984; Mogul and Me, 1989; Out on the Ice in the Middle of the Bay, 1993. Contributions to: Contributing editor, Quill and Quire, 1982-84. Honours: 1st Prize, Children's Prose, 1980, 1st Prize, Adult Fiction, 1981, Writers Federation of Nova Scotia; Toronto Board of Education Canada Day Playwriting Competition, 1981; Our Choice, Children's Book Centre, 1984, 1989, 1993; Hilroy Award for Innovative Teaching, 1990; George Wicken Prize in Canadian Literature, 1994; Tiny Torgi Award, 1995. Memberships: Playwrights Union of Canada; Writers Union of Canada; Canadian Society of Children's Authors, Illustrators, and Performers; Association of Canadian College and University Teachers of English. Address: 201 Front Street, Stratford, Ontario N5A 4H8, Canada.

CUMMINGS David Michael, b. 10 Oct 1942, London, England. Lexicographer. m. Anne Marie Zammit-Tabona, 1970, 2 sons, 1 daughter. Education: Dartington Hall School, 1953-60; BEd, Hons, Sidney Webb College, London, 1971-75. Career: School Teacher, 1975-; Lexicographer, Music Reference Books, 1980-. Contributions to: Baker's Biographical Dictionary of Musicians, New York, 1984; The Oxford Dictionary of Music, Oxford, 1985 and 1994; The Grove Concise Dictionary of Music, London, 1988; Penguin Dictionary of Musical Performers, 1990; Grosses Sängerlexikon (Ergänzungsband) Berne, 1991-93; New Grove Dictionary of Opera, 4 vols, 1992; Concise Oxford Dictionary of Opera, 1996. Publications: New Everyman Dictionary of Music, 6th Edition, London, 1988; Editor, International Who's Who in Music, 12th-15th Editions, 1990-96; Hutchinson Encyclopedia of Music (book and CD versions), 1995. Hobbies: Armchair Cricket; Casaubonology. Address: 7 Gerard Road, Harrow HA1 2ND, England.

CUMMINS Walter (Merrill), b. 6 Feb 1936, Long Branch, New Jersey, USA. Professor of English; Writer; Editor. m. (1) Judith Gruenberg, 14 June 1957, div 1981, (2) Alison Cunningham, 14 Feb 1981, 2 daughters. Education: BA, Rutgers University, 1957; MA, 1962, MFA, 1962, PhD, 1965, University of Iowa. Appointments: Instructor, University of Iowa, 1962-65; Assistant Professor, 1965-69, Associate Professor, 1969-74, Professor of English, 1974-, Fairleigh Dickinson University; Associate Editor, 1978-83, Editor-in-Chief, 1983-, The Literary Review. Publications: A Stranger to the Deed (novel), 1968; Into Temptation (novel), 1968; The Other Sides of Reality: Myths, Visions and Fantasies (co-editor), 1972; Student Writing Guide (co-editor), 1973; Witness (stories), 1975; Managing Management Climate (with George G Gordon), 1979; Where We Live (stories), 1983; Shifting Borders: East European Poetry of the Eighties (editor), 1993. Contributions to: Stories, articles, and reviews in many publications. Honours: New Jersey State Council on the Arts Fellowship, 1982-83; National Endowment for the Arts Grants, 1987-88, 1990-91. Memberships: American Association of University Professors; Association for Business Communication; College English Association. Address: 98 Brandywyne Drive, Florham Park, NJ 07932, USA.

CUNLIFFE Barrington (Windsor), (Barry Cunliffe), b. 10 Dec 1939, Portsmouth, Hampshire, England. Archaeologist; Professor; Writer. m. Margaret Herdman, 5 Jan 1979, 1 son, 1 daughter. Education: BA, 1961, MA, 1963, PhD, 1966, LittD, 1976, St John's College, Cambridge. Appointments: Lecturer in Classics, University of Bristol, 1963-66; Professor of Archaeology, University of Southampton, 1966-72; Professor of European Archaeology and Fellow of Keble College, Oxford, 1972-; Commissioner, Historic Buildings and Monuments Commission for England, 1987-92; Governor, Museum of London, 1995-. Publications: Excavations at Richborough, Vol 5, 1968; Roman Bath (editor), 1969; Excavations at Fishbourne, 1961-69, 2 volumes, 1971, 2nd edition, 1984; Guide to the Roman Remains of Bath, 1971; The Cradle of England, 1972; The Making of the English, 1973; The Regni, 1974; Iron Age Communities in Britain: An Account of England, Scotland, and Wales from the Seventh Century B C until the Roman Conquest, 1974, 3rd edition, 1991; Excavations at Porchester Castle, Hants, 4 volumes, 1975, 1976, 1977, 1985; Rome and the Barbarians, 1975; Oppida: The Beginnings of Urbanisation in Barbican Europe (with Trevor Rowley), 1976; Hengistbury Head, 1978; Rome and Her Empire, 1978, 2nd edition, 1994; The Celtic World, 1979, 2nd edition, 1993; Excavating Bath, 1950-75 (editor), 1979; Coinage and Society in Britain and Gaul: Some Current Problems (editor), 1981; Antiquity and Man (editor), 1982; Danebury: Anatomy of an Iron Age Hillfort, 1983; Aspects of the Iron Age in Central Southern Britain (editor with David Miles), 1984; Danebury: An Iron Age Hillfort in Hampshire, Vols 1 and 2, 1984, Vols 4 and 5, 1991; Heywood Sumner's Wessex, 1985; Temple of Sulis Minerva at Bath (with Peter Davenport), Vol I, 1985; The City of Bath, 1986; Hengistbury Head, Darcet, Vol I, 1987; Origins: The Roots of European Civilisation (editor), 1987; Mount Batten, Plymouth: A Prehistorical and Roman Port, 1988; Greeks, Romans & Barbarians: Spheres of Interaction, 1988; Wessex to AD 1000, 1993; The Oxford Illustrated Prehistory of Europe (editor), 1994. Contributions to: Periodicals and archaeological journals. Honours: Commander of the Order of the British Empire, 1994; Honorary doctorates. Memberships: British Academy, Fellow; Medieval Society; Prehistoric Society; Royal Archaeological Institute; Society of Antiquaries, Fellow, Vice President, 1982-86, President 1994-95. Address: Institute of Archaeology, Oxford University, 36 Beaumont Street, Oxford OX1 2PG, England.

CURL James Stevens, b. 26 Mar 1937, Belfast, Northern Ireland. Professor of Architectural History; Architect; Historian. m. (1) Eileen Elizabeth Blackstock, 1 Jan 1960, div 1986, 2 daughters, (2) Stanisława Dorota Iwaniec 1993. Education: Queen's University School of Architecture, Belfast, 1954-58; DiplArch, Oxford School of Architecture, 1961-63; Dip TP, Oxford Department of Land Use Studies, 1963-67; PhD, University College, London, 1978-81; FSA; RIBA; MRTPI; ARIAS; FSAScot. Appointment: Professor of Architectural History, De Montfort University, Leicester. Publications: The Victorian Celebration of Death, 1972; City of London Pubs, 1973; The Egyptian Revival, 1982; The Life and Work of Henry Roberts (1803-76), Architect, 1983; The Londonderry Plantation 1609-1914, 1986; English Architecture: An Illustrated Glossary, 1987; Victorian Architecture, 1990; The Art and Architecture of Freemasonry, 1991; Classical Architecture, 1992; Encyclopaedia of Architectural Terms, 1993; Georgian Architecture, 1993; A Celebration of Death, 1993; Egyptomania, 1994; Victorian Churches, 1995. Contributions to: Connaissance des Arts; Country Life; Royal Society of Arts Journal; Architects' Journal; Bauwelt; World of Interiors; Literary Review. Honours: Sir Charles Lanyon Prize, 1956, 1958; Ulster Arts Club Prize, 1958; Stevens Prize for Thesis, 1963; Baroque Prize, 1962; British Academy Research Awards, 1982, 1983; Society of Antiquaries of London Research Awards, 1980, 1981; Sir Banister Fletcher Award for Best Book of Year, 1992. Address: 15 Torgrange, Holywood, County Down BT18 0NG, Northern Ireland.

CURLING Audrey. See: **CLARK Marie Catherine Audrey.**

CURNOW Thomas Allen Monro, b. 17 June 1911, Timaru, New Zealand. Poet. m. (1) Elizabeth Jaumaud Le Cren, 1936, 2 sons, 1 daughter, (2) Jenifer Mary Tole, 1965. Education: BA 1934, LittD 1965, Universities of Canterbury and Auckland. Appointments: Staff, The Press, 1935-48, News Chronicle, London, 1949; Associate Professor, University of Auckland, 1967-76. Publications: Poetry: Not in Narrow Seas, 1939; Island and Time, 1941; Sailing or Drowning, 1943; At Dead Low Water, 1949; A Small Room with Large Windows, 1962; Trees, Effigies, Moving Objects, 1972; Collected Poems, 1933-73, 1974; An Incorrigible Music, 1979; You Will Know When You Get There, 1982; The Loop in Lone Kauri Road, 1986; Continuum, New & Later Poems, 1988; Selected Poems, 1940-89, 1990. Critical Writings: Look Back Harder, 1987; Penguin Modern Poets vol 7 (with Donald Davie and Samuel Menashe), 1996. Plays: The Axe, 1949; The Duke's Miracle, 1968. Contributions to: Encounter; London Magazine; London Review of Books; Partisan Review; Times Literary Supplement; Islands; Landfall; Verse; Sport; PN Review. Honours: New Zealand Book Award for Poetry, 5 times, 1958-83; Katherine Mansfield Memorial Fellowship, 1983; LittD, 1975; Commander of the Order of the British Empire 1986; Dillons Commonwealth (overall) Poetry Prize, 1989; The Queen's Gold Medal for Poetry, 1989; Order of New Zealand, 1990; Cholmondeley Award, 1992. Address: 62 Tohunga Crescent, Parnell, Auckland 1, New Zealand.

CURRAN Colleen, b. 23 Aug 1954, Montreal, Quebec, Canada. Dramatist; Writer; Novelist. Education: BA, Loyola College, Concordia University, 1976; Teacher's Certificate, McGill University, 1981. Appointments: Playwright-in-Residence, Centaur Theatre, Montreal, 1984-85; Co-Artistic Director, Triumvirate Theatre Co, Montreal, 1992-. Publications: Cake-Walk, Villa Eden; Something Drastic, novel. Honours: Dorothy White Playwrighting Award, Ottawa, 1983; Best New Play, Quebec Drama Festival, 1984; Gabriel Radio Award, Texas, 1991; Nominee, Prix Parizeau. Memberships: Writers Guild of Canada; ACTRA Performers Guild;Playwrights Union of Canada; Playwrights Workshop, Montreal; Siamsa School of Music and Dance. Address: 4955 West Broadway, Montreal, Quebec H4V 1R5, Canada.

CURREY Ralph Nixon, b. 14 Dec 1907, Mafeking, South Africa. Poet; Writer; Biographer; Broadcaster. Education: BA, Wadham College, Oxford, 1930. Appointments: Senior Master for Arts Subjects, Royal Grammar School, Colchester, 1964-72. Publications: Tiresias and Other Poems, 1940; This Other Planet, 1945; Indian Landscape: A Book of Descriptive Poems, 1947; Formal Spring, 1950; Radio Plays: Between Two Worlds, 1948; Early Morning in Vaaldorp, 1958; The Africa We Knew, 1973; Letters of a Natal Sheriff (Thomas Phipson 1815-65), 1968; Vinncombe's Trek, 1989. Honours: Viceroy's All-India Poetry Prize, 1944; South Africa Poetry Prize, 1959; South African Poetry Prize, 1968; Fellow, Royal Society of Literature, 1970; President, 1967-79, Suffolk Poetry Society. Address: 3 Beverley Road, Colchester, Essex CO3 3NG, England.

CURRIE Edwina, b. 13 Oct 1946, England. m. Raymond Frank Currie, 1972, 2 daughters. Education: MA, St Anne's College, Oxford; MSc, London School of Economics. Appointments: Teacher, Lecturer, 1972-81; Member of Parliament for Derbyshire South, 1983-; Minister of Health, 1986-88; Vice Chairman, European Movement, 1995-. Publications include: Life Lines, 1989; What Women Want, 1990; Three Line Quips, 1992; A Parliamentary Affair (novel), 1994; A Woman's Place (novel), 1996; Fierce Creatures, 1996; She's Leaving Home (novel), 1997. Contributions to: Articles and reviews. Address: c/o Curtis Brown Ltd, 28-29 Haymarket, London SW1Y 4SP, England.

CURRY Jane Louise, b. 24 Sept 1932, East Liverpool, Ohio, USA. Writer. Education: Pennsylvania State University, 1950-51; BA, Indiana University of Pennsylvania, 1954; University of California, Los Angeles, 1957-59; London University, England, 1961-62, 1965-66; AM, 1962, PhD, 1969, Stanford University. Appointments: Teaching Assistant, 1959-61, 1963-65, Acting Instructor, 1967-68, Instructor, 1983-84, Lecturer, 1987, English Department, Stanford University, Stanford, California; Freelance Lecturer, Consultant on Children's Books, 1970-. Publications: Beneath the Hill, 1967; The Sleepers, 1968; The Change-Child, 1969; The Day Breakers, 1970; The Housenapper (also published as Mindy's Mysterious Miniature and The Mysterious Shrinking House), 1970; The Ice Ghosts Mystery, 1972; The Lost Farm, 1974; Poor Tom's Ghost, 1977; The Great Flood Mystery, 1985; The Lotus Cup, 1986; Me, Myself and I, 1986; Little Little Sister, 1989; The Big Smith Snatch, 1989; What the Dickens!, 1991; The Christmas Knight, 1993; The Great Smith House Hustle, 1993; Robin Hood and His Merry Men, 1994; Robin Hood in the Greenwood, 1995; Moon Window, 1996. Contributions to: Medium Aevum. Honours: Fulbright Grant, 1961-62; Stanford Leverhulme Fellowship, 1965-66; Book Award, 1971, Special Award, 1979, Southern California Council on Literature for Children; Ohioana Book Award, 1978, 1987. Memberships: Authors Guild; International Arthurian Society; Southern California Council on Literature for Children and Young People. Address: McElderry Books, Simon & Schuster Children's Publishing Division, 1230 Avenue of the Americas, New York, NY 10020, USA.

CURRY Mary Earle Lowry, b. 13 May 1917, Seneca, South Carolina, USA. Writer. m. Reverend Peden Gene Curry, 25 Dec 1941, 1 son, 1 daughter. Education: Furman University, 1944-45. Publications: Looking Up, 1949; Looking Within, 1961, 1980; Hymn: Church in the Heart of the City, 1973. Contributions to: Numerous anthologies and journals including: Yearbook of Modern Poetry; Poets of America; Poetic Voice of America; We, the People; Poetry Digest; Poetry Anthology of Verse; International Anthology on World Brotherhood and Peace; The Greenville News; Inman Times. Honours:

World Award for Culture, Centro Studi e Ricerche della Nazioni, Italy, 1985. Memberships: Auxiliary Rotary, Charleston, South Carolina, 1972-74; Centro Studi Scambi Internazionali, Rome; United Methodist Church Women's Organizations; United Methodist Church Ministers; Wives Club, President 1973-74, Charleston; Community clubs. Address: 345 Curry Drive, Seneca, SC 29678, USA.

CURRY Richard Orr, b. 26 Jan 1931, USA. Professor of History. m. 11 Feb 1968, 2 sons, 2 daughters. Education: BA, 1952, MA, 1956, Marshall University; PhD, University of Pennsylvania, 1961; Postdoctoral Fellow, Harvard University, 1965-66; Professor Emeritus. Publications: The Shaping of America, 1972; Conspiracy: The Fear of Subversion in American History, 1972; Radicalism, Racism and Party Realignment: The Border States During Reconstruction, 1973; The Abolitionists, 1985; Freedom at Risk: Secrecy, Censorship and Repression in the 1980's, 1988; An Uncertain Future: Thought Control and Repression during the Reagan-Bush Era, 1992. Contributions to: Journal of Southern History; Civil War History; Mid-America; Journal of the Early Republic; Ohio History; Others. Honours: Award of Merit, American Association of State and Local History, 1971; Senior Fulbright Lecturer, 1981; Von Mises Postdoctoral Fellow, 1982-83; Distinguished Alumnus Award, 1986; H L Mencken Award, 1989; Outstanding Book Award, 1989; Outstanding Book Award, Gustavus Myers Center for the Study of Human rights in the United States, 1993. Memberships: Organization of American Historians. Address: 106 Windham Street, Willmantic, CT 06226, USA.

CURTEIS Ian (Bayley), b. 1 May 1935, London, England. Playwright; Actor; Director. m. (1) Joan Macdonald, 1964, diss, 2 sons, (2) Joanna Trollope, 12 Apr 1985, 2 stepdaughters. Appointments: Actor and Director in British Theatres; Playwright. Publications: Numerous television plays and drama series, screenplays, stage plays, and adaptations. Honours: Various nominations. Memberships: Royal Society of Literature; Writers Guild of Great Britain, Chairman, Committee on Censorship, 1981-85. Address: c/o Coutts & Co, Campbell's Office, 440 Strand, London WC2R 0QS, England.

CURTIS Anthony Samuel, b. 12 Mar 1926, London, England. Journalist. m. Sarah, 3 Oct 1960, 3 sons. Education: Midhurst Grammer School, 1940-44; BA (Inter MA) 1st Class Hons, English, Chancellor's Prize for an English Essay, Oxford University, Merton College, 1948-50; US Harkness Fellowship in Journalism, 1958-59. Appointments: Deputy Editor, Times Literary Supplement, 1959-60; Literary Editor, Financial Times, 1970-90. Publications: The Pattern of Maugham, 1974; Somerset Maugham: The Critical Heritage (with John Whitehead), 1987. Contributions to: Times Literary Supplement; Financial Times; BBC Radio 3 and 4. Honour: Fellow, Royal Society of Arts. Memberships: Treasurer, Royal Literary Fund; Trustee, Society of Authors Pension Fund; Garrick Club; Travellers; Beefsteak. Literary Agent: A M Heath. Address: 9 Essex Villas, London W8 7BP, England.

CURTIS Edward. See: **PREBBLE John**.

CURTIS Richard Hale. See: **LEVINSON Leonard**.

CURTIS Tony, b. 26 Dec 1946, Carmathen, Wales. Poet. m. Margaret Blundell, 1970, 1 son, 1 daughter. Education: BA, University College of Swansea, 1968; MFA, Goddard College, Vermont, 1980. Appointment: Professor of Poetry, University of Glamorgan. Publications: Poetry: Walk Down a Welsh Wind, 1972; Home Movies, 1973; Album, 1974; The Deerslayers, 1978; Carnival, 1978; Preparations: Poems, 1974-79, 1980; Letting Go, 1983; Selected Poems, 1970-85, 1986; The Last Candles, 1989; Taken for Pearls, 1993; Other: Islands (radio play), 1975; Out of the Dark Wood: Prose Poems, Stories, 1977; Dannie Abse, 1985; The Art of Seamus Heaney, editor, 1986, 3rd edition, 1994; How to Study Modern Poetry, 1990; How Poets Work, editor, 1996. Honours: National Poetry Competition Winner, 1984; Dylan Thomas Prize, 1993. Address: Pentwyn, 55 Colcot Road, Barry, South Glamorgan CF6 8BQ, Wales.

CUSHMAN Dan, b. 9 June 1909, Marion, Michigan, USA. Writer. m. Elizabeth Louden, 1940, 3 sons, 1 daughter. Education: BS, University of Montana, 1934. Publications: Montana, Here I Be, 1950; Badlands Justice, 1951; Naked Ebony, 1951; Jewel of the Java Sea, 1951; The Ripper from Rawhide, 1952; Savage Interlude, 1952; Stay Away, Joe, 1953; Timberjack, 1953; Jungle She, 1953; The Fabulous Finn, 1954; Tongking, 1954; Port Orient, 1955; The Fastest Gun, 1955; The Old Copper Collar, 1957; The Silver Mountain, 1957; Tall Wyoming, 1957; The Forbidden Land, 1958; Goodbye, Old Dry, 1959,

Paperback Edition as The Con Man, 1960; The Half-Caste, 1960; Brothers in Kickapoo, 1962, UK Edition as Boomtown, US Paperback as On the Make, 1963; 4 for Texas, novelisation of screenplay, 1963; The Grand and the Glorious, 1963; Opium Flower, 1963; North Fork to Hell, 1964; The Long Riders, 1967; The Muskrat Farm, 1977; Rusty Iron, 1984. Non-fiction: The Great North Trail: America's Route of the Ages, 1966; Cow Country Cook Book, 1967; Montana: The Gold Frontier, 1975.Address: 1500 Fourth Avenue North, Great Falls, MT 59401, USA.

CUSSLER Clive (Eric), b. 15 July 1931, Aurora, Illinois, USA. Author; Advertising Executive. m. Barbara Knight, 28 Aug 1955, 3 children. Education: Pasadena City College, 1949-51; Orange Coast College; California State University. Appointments: Advertising Directorships; Author. Publications: The Mediterranean Caper, 1973; Iceberg, 1975; Raise the Titanic, 1976; Vixen O-Three, 1978; Night Probe, 1981; Pacific Vortex, 1982; Deep Six, 1984; Cyclops, 1986; Treasure, 1988; Dragon, 1990; Sahara, 1992; Inca Gold, 1994; Shock Wave, 1996. Honours: Numerous advertising awards. Memberships: Explorers Club, Fellow; Royal Geographical Society. Address: PO Box 635, Golden, CO 80402, USA.

CZIGÁNY Lóránt György, b. 3 June 1935, Sátoraljaújhely, Hungary. m. Magda Salacz, 28 Sept 1957, 1 daughter. Education: University of Szeged, 1954-56; University of Oxford, 1957-58; BA, 1960, PhD, 1964, University of London. Appointments: Szepsi Csombor Literary Circle, 1965-88; Editor, Atelier Hongrois, Paris, 1974; Minister Plenipotentiary for Cultural Affairs, 1990-92. Publications: The Oxford History of Hungarian Literature; The Reception of Hungarian Literature in Victorian England; The Origins of State Control of Hungarian Literature; The Béla Iványi-Grünwald Collection of Hungarica. Contributions to: Times; BBC Overseas Service; Outside Contributor. Honour: Honorary Doctorate, University of Miskolc, Hungary, 1995. Memberships: Szepsi Csombor Literary Circle; International Association of Hungarian Studies. Address: 15 Temple Fortune Lane, London NW11 7UB, England.

D

D'AGUIAR Fred, b. 2 Feb 1960, London, England. Poet; Novelist. Education: BA Hons, University of Kent, 1985. Appointments: Writer-in-Residence, London Borough of Lewisham, 1986-87; Birmingham Polytechnic, 1988-89; Writing Instructor, The Arvon Foundation week-long residential courses on a once-yearly basis, 1986-; Visiting Writer, Amherst College, 1992-94; Assistant Professor of English, Bates College, 1994-95; Professor of English, University of Miami, Florida, USA, 1995-. Publications: Mama Dot, 1985, 2nd edition, 1989; Airy Hall, 1989; British Subjects, 1993. Co-Editor: The New British Poetry, 1988. Novel: The Longest Memory, 1994. Play: A Jamaican Airman Forsees His Death, 1995. Television: Sweet Thames (poem/documentary for BBC), 1992; Rain (poem/documentary for BBC), 1994. Radio: 1492 (long poem for BBC Radio broadcast), 1992. Other: Dear Future, fiction, 1996; Bill of Rights, poetry, 1996. Contributions to: Essays and poems in various journals and magazines in the UK and USA. Honours: T S Eliot Prize for Poetry, University of Kent, 1984; Malcolm X Prize for Poetry, 1986; Guyana Prize for Poetry, 1989; BBC's Race in the Media Award, 1992, and the British Film Institute's Most Innovative Film Award, 1993; David Higham Award and the Whitbread Best First Novel Award. Address: c/o Curtis Brown, The Haymarket, 28 Haymarket, London, England.

DABYDEEN Cyril, b. 15 Oct 1945, Guyana. Poet; Writer. m. 6 June 1989, 1 daughter. Education: BA (Hons), Lakehead University, Thunder Bay, Ontario, 1973; MA, 1974; MPA, Queen's University, Ottawa. Publications: Poetry; Distances, 1977; Goatsong, 1977; Heart's Frame, 1979; This Planet Earth, 1980; Still Close to the Island, 1980; Islands Lovelier Than a Vision, 1988; The Wizard Swami, 1989; Dark Swirl, 1989; Jogging in Havana, 1992; Stoning the Wind, 1994; Discussing Columbus, 1996, 1997. Fiction: Sometimes Hard (novel), 1994; Berbice Crossing (stories), 1996; Black Jesus and Other Stories, 1997. Editor: A Shapely Fire: Changing the Literary Landscape, 1987; Another Way to Dance: Asian-Canadian Poetry, 1990; Another Way to Dance: Contemporary Voices of Asian Poetry in America and Canada, 2nd edition, 1996. Contributions to: Canadian Forum; Canadian Fiction Magazine; Fiddlehead; Dalhousie Review; Antigonish Review; Canadian Author and Bookman; Toronto South Asian Review; Journal of South Asian Literature; Wascana Review; Literary Review; Globe and Mail; Caribbean Quarterly. Honours: Sandbach Parker Gold Medal; A J Seymour Lyric Poetry Prize; Poet Laureate of Ottawa; Okanagan Fiction Award. Memberships: Canadian Association of Commonwealth Language and Literature Studies. Address: 106 Blackburn, Ottawa, Ontario K1N 8A7, Canada.

DABYDEEN David, b. 9 Dec 1955, Guyana. Poet; Writer; Senior Lecturer. Education: BA, Cambridge University, 1978; PhD, London University, 1982. Appointments: Junior Research Fellow, Oxford University, 1983-87; Senior Lecturer, Warwick University, 1987-. Publications: Slave Song, 1984; Coolie Odyssey, 1988; Disappearance, 1993; Turner, 1994; The Counting House, 1996; Across the Dark Waters: Indian Identity in the Caribbean, 1996. Contributions to: Various periodicals. Honours: Commonwealth Poetry Prize, 1984; Guyana Literature Prize, 1992. Memberships: Literature Panel, Arts Council of Great Britain, 1985-89; Fellow, Royal Society of the Arts. Literary Agent: Jane Brandish-Ellames, Curtis Brown Ltd. Address: c/o Warwick University, Coventry, CV4 7AL, England.

DACEY Philip, b. 9 May 1939, St Louis, Missouri, USA. Poet; Teacher. m. Florence Chard, 1963, div 1986, 2 sons, 1 daughter. Education: BA, St Louis University, 1961; MA, Stanford University, 1967; MFA, University of Iowa, 1970. Appointments: Instructor in English, University of Missouri at St Louis, 1967-68; Faculty, Department of English, Southwest State University, Marshall, Minnesota, 1970-; Distinguished Writer-in-Residence, Wichita State University, 1985. Publications: Poetry: The Beast with Two Backs, 1969; Fist, Sweet Giraffe, The Lion, Snake, and Owl, 1970; Four Nudes, 1971; How I Escaped from the Labyrinth and Other Poems, 1977; The Boy Under the Bed, 1979; The Condom Poems, 1979; Gerard Manley Hopkins Meets Walt Whitman in Heaven and Other Poems, 1982; Fives, 1984; The Man with Red Suspenders, 1986; The Condom Poems II, 1989; Night Shift at the Crucifix Factory, 1991. Editor: I Love You All Day: It is That Simple (with Gerald M Knoll), 1970; Strong Measures: Contemporary American Poetry in Traditional Forms (with David Jaus), 1986. Honours: Woodrow Wilson Fellowship,

1961; New York YM-YWHA Discovery Award, 1974; National Endowment for the Arts Fellowships, 1975, 1980; Minnesota State Arts Board Fellowships, 1975, 1983; Bush Foundation Fellowship, 1977; Loft-McKnight Fellowship, 1984; Fulbright Lecturer, 1988. Address: Route 1, Box 89, Lynd, MN 56157, USA.

DAFTARY Farhad, b. 23 Dec 1938, Brussels, Belgium. Academic. m. Fereshteh Kashanchi, Feb 1980, 1 daughter. Education: BA, 1962, MA, 1964, American University; MA, 1966, PhD, 1971, University of California. Appointments: Lecturer, Tehran University, 1972-73, National University, Tehran, 1973-74; Professor, 1988-, Head, Department of Academic Research and Publications, 1992-, Institute of Ismaili Studies, London; Consulting Editor, Encyclopaedia Iranica. Publications: The Ismailis: Their History & Doctrines; The Assassin Legends; A Short History of the Ismailis; Mediaeval Ismaili History & Thought. Contributions to: Islamic Culture; Arabica; Iran; Studia Islamica; Encyclopedia Iranica; Encyclopedia of Islam; Persian Encyclopaedia of Islam; Turkish Encyclopaedia of Islam; Great Encyclopaedia of Islam. Memberships: American Oriental Society; British Institute of Persian Studies; British Society for Middle Eastern Studies; Society for Iranian Studies. Address: 77 Hamilton Terrace, London NW8, England.

DAICHES David, b. 2 Sept 1912, Sunderland, England. Professor Emeritus; Writer. m. Isobel Janet Mackay, 28 July, 1937, 1 son, 2 daughters. Education: MA, Edinburgh University, 1934; DPhil, Oxford University, 1939. Appointments: Fellow, Balliol College, Oxford, 1936-37; Assistant Professor, University of Chicago, 1939-43; Professor, Cornell University, 1946-51, Sussex University, 1961-77; University Lecturer, 1951-61, Fellow, Jesus College, 1957-62, Cambridge; Director, Institute for Advanced Studies, Edinburgh University, 1980-86. Publications: 45 books including: The Novel and the Modern World, 1939; Robert Burns, 1950; Two Worlds, 1956; A Critical History of English Literature, 1960; The Paradox of Scottish Culture, 1964; God and the Poets, 1984; Edinburgh: A Traveller's Companion, 1986; A Weekly Scotsman and Other Poems, 1994. Honours: Royal Society of Literature, fellow, 1957; Scottish Arts Council Book Award, 1973; Scottish Book of the Year Award, 1984; Commander of the Order of the British Empire, 1991; Various honorary doctorates. Memberships: Honorary President, Association for Scottish Literary Studies; Honorary Member, Modern Language Association of America; Honorary President, Saltire Society. Address: 22 Belgrave Crescent, Edinburgh, EH4 3AL, Scotland.

DALE Margaret Jessy, (Margaret J Miller), b. 27 Aug 1911, Edinburgh, Scotland. Writer. m. Clunie Rutherford Dale, 3 Sep 1938, div 1954, 1 son, 2 daughters. Education: 2nd Class Honours BA, English Language and Literature, Lady Margaret Hall, Oxford, 1933. Appointments: Scenario Writer, Associated Screen News, Montreal, Canada, 1935-36; Assistant Editor, Shell Magazine, London, 1937-39. Publications: The Queen's Music, 1961; The Powers of the Sapphire, 1962; Mouse Tails, 1967;Emily, A Life of Emily Brontë, 1969; Knights, Beasts and Wonders, 1969; The Fearsome Road, 1975; The Fearsome Island, 1975; The Fearsome Tide, 1976; The Far Castles, 1978. Contributions to: 200 scripts for Schools Broadcasting; Times; Times Literary Supplement; Scottish Field; Scots Magazine; Scotland's Magazine. Memberships: PEN; National Book League. Address: 26 Grey's Hill, Henley, Oxon RG9 1SJ, England.

DALESKI H(illel) M(atthew), b. 19 July 1926, Johannesburg, South Africa. Professor Emeritus of English; Writer. m. (1) Aviva Prop, 29 June 1950, div, 4 children, (2) Shirley Kaufman, 20 June 1974. Education: BA, 1947, BA, Hons, 1949, MA, 1952, University of the Witwatersrand; PhD, Hebrew University, Jerusalem, 1963. Appointments: Assistant Lecturer to Associate Professor, 1958-76, Professor of English 1976-, Chairman, Department of English, 1968-70, 1984-85, Provost, School of Overseas Students, 1973-76, Hebrew University, Jerusalem. Publications: The Forked Flame: A Study of D H Lawrence, 1965; Dickens and the Art of Analogy, 1970; Joseph Conrad: The Way of Dispossession, 1977; The Divided Heroine: A Recurrent Pattern in Six English Novels, 1984; Unities: Studies in the English Novel, 1985; Thomas Hardy: Catastrophes of Love, forthcoming. Honour: Israel Academy of Sciences and Humanities, 1993. Membership: President, Dickens Society, 1985. Address: Department of English, Hebrew University, Jerusalem, Israel.

DALTON Annie, b . 18 Jan 1948, Weymouth, England. Writer. div. 1 son, 2 daughters. Education: Upper 2nd, English and American Literature, University of Warwick, 1967-70. Publications: Nightmaze:

The After Dark Princess; The Real Tilly Beany; The Alpha Box; Swan Sister; The Witch Rose; Demon Spawn; Out of the Ordinary; Naming the Dark, 1992. Honours: East Midlands Arts Bursary, 1987; Nottingham Oak Children's Book Award, 1991; Commended for Carnegie, 1992. Literary Agent: Elizabeth Stevens, Curtis Brown. Address: 13 Selbourne Street, Loughborough, Leics LE11 1BS, England.

DALTON Priscilla. See: AVALLONE Michael (Angelo Jr).

DALY Maureen, (Maureen Daly McGivern), b. 15 Mar 1921, Castlecaufield, County Tyrone, Ireland. Journalist; Writer. m. William P McGivern, 28 Dec 1946, dec 1983, 1 son, 1 daughter, dec. Education: BA, Rosary College, 1942. Appointments: Reporter and Columnist, Chicago Tribune, 1941-44; Associate Editor, Ladies' Home Journal, 1944-49; Consultant to the editors, Saturday Evening Post, 1960-69; Reporter and Columnist, Desert Sun, Palm Desert, California, 1987-. Publications: The Perfect Hostess: Complete Etiquette and Entertainment for the Home, 1950; Mention My Name in Mombasa: The Unscheduled Adventures of an American Family Abroad (with William P McGivern), 1958; A Matter of Honour (with William P McGivern), 1984. Young adult fiction: Seventeenth Summer, 1942; Sixteen and Other Stories, 1961; Acts of Love, 1986; First A Dream, 1990. Young adult non-fiction: Smarter and Smoother: A Handbook on How To Be That Way, 1944; What's Your P Q (Personality Quotient)?, 1952, revised edition, 1966; Twelve Around the World, 1957; Spanish Roundabout, 1960; Moroccan Roundabout, 1961. Juvenile: Patrick Visits the Library, 1961; Patrick Visits the Zoo, 1963; The Ginger Horse, 1964; Spain: Wonderland of Contrasts, 1965; The Small War of Sergeant Donkey, 1966; Rosie, the Dancing Elephant, 1967. Editor: My Favorite Stories, 1948; My Favorite Mystery Stories, 1966; My Favorite Suspense Stories, 1968. Contributions to: Anthologies and many periodicals. Honours: O Henry Memorial Award, 1938; Dodd, Mead Intercollegiate Literary Fellowship Novel Award, 1942; Freedoms Foundation Award, 1952; Gimble Fashion Award, 1962; Lewis Carroll Shelf Award, 1969; One of 10 great books for teens, Redbook Magazine, 1987. Memberships: Mystery Writers of America; Writers Guild of America. Address: Ironwood Street, Palm Desert, CA 92260, USA.

DALY Niki, (Nicholas Daly), b. 13 June 1946, Cape Town, South Africa. Writer; Illustrator. m. Judith Mary Kenny, 7 July 1973, 2 sons. Education: Diploma, Cape Town Technikon, 1970. Appointments: Graphics Teacher, East Ham Technical College, London, 1976-79; Head, Songololo Books, 1989-. Publications: Children's books: The Little Girl Who Lived Down the Road, 1978; Vim the Rag Mouse, 1979; Joseph's Other Red Sock, 1982; Leo's Christmas Surprise, 1983; Ben's Gingerbread Man, 1985; Teddy's Ear, 1985; Monsters Are Like That, 1985; Just Like Archie, 1986; Look at Me!, 1986; Not So Fast, Songololo, 1985; Thank You Henrietta, 1986; Mama, Papa, and Baby Joe, 1991; Papa Lucky's Shadow, 1991; Mary Mallory and the Baby Who Couldn't Sleep, 1994; One Round Moon, 1995; Why the Sun and the Moon Live in the Sky, 1995; My Dad, 1995; The Dinosaurs are Back and It's Your Fault Edward! (co-author Wendy Hartmann), 1995, UK edition, 1996. Illustrator: Maybe It's a Tiger, by Kathleen Hersom, 1981; Fly Eagle Fly, by Christopher Gregorowski, 1982; I Want to See the Moon, by Louis Baum, 1994; The Day of the Rainbow, by Ruth Craft, 1988; Charlie's House, by Reviva Schermbrucker, 1989; All the Magic in the World, by Wendy Harmann, 1993; Red Light, Green Light, Mama and Me, by Cari Best, 1995. Honours: British Arts Council Illustration Award, 1978; Parents' Choice Book Award for Literature, 1986; Katrine Harries Awards for Illustration, 1986-87; Horn Book Honor List, 1987; New York Times One of the Best Illustrated Books of the Year Award, 1995; Anne Izard Story Teller's Choice Award, 1996; IBBY Honour List Book, 1996. Membership: Association of Illustrators, London. Address: 36 Strubens Road, 7700 Cape Town, South Africa.

DALY Patricia. See: BRENNAN Patricia Winifred.

DALYELL Tam, b. 9 Aug 1932, Edinburgh, Scotland. Member of Parliament. m. Kathleen Wheatley, 26 Dec 1963, 1 son, 1 daughter. Education: Eton, 1945-50; King's College, Cambridge, 1952-56. Appointment: House of Commons, 1962-. Publications: The Case for Ship Schools, 1958; Ship School Dunera, 1961; One Man's Falklands, 1982; A Science Policy for Britain, 1983; Misrule: How Mrs Thatcher Deceived Parliament, 1987; Dick Crossman: A Portrait, 1988. Contributions to: Weekly Columnist, New Scientist, 1967-; Many Obituaries, Independent and Daily Newspapers. Honours: Various

Awards of Science; Honorary Doctor of Science, University of Edinburgh, 1994. Address: House of Commons, London SW1 A0AA, England.

DANA Robert (Patrick), b. 2 June 1929, Allston, Massachusetts, USA. Emeritus Professor of English; Poet. m. (1) Mary Kowalke, 2 June 1951, div 1973, 3 children, (2) Margaret Sellen, 14 Sept 1974. Education: AB, Drake University, 1951; MA, University of Iowa, 1954. Appointments: Assistant Professor, Associate Professor, Professor of English, Cornell College, Mount Vernon, Iowa, 1953-94; Editor, Hillside Press, Mount Vernon, 1957-67; Editor, 1964-68, Contributing Editor, 1991-, North American Review; Contributing Editor, American Poetry Review, 1973-88, New Letters, 1980-83. Publications: My Glass Brother and Other Poems, 1957; The Dark Flags of Waking, 1964; Journeys from the Skin: A Poem in Two Parts, 1966; Some Versions of Silence: Poems, 1967; The Power of the Visible, 1971; In a Fugitive Season, 1980; What the Stones Know, 1984; Blood Harvest, 1986; Against the Grain: Interviews with Maverick American Publishers, 1986; Starting Out for the Difficult World, 1987; What I Think I Know: New and Selected Poems, 1990; Wildebeest, 1993; Yes, Everything, 1994; Hello, Stranger: Beach Poems, 1996. Contributions to: New Yorker; New York Times; Poetry; Georgia Review; Manoa. Honours: Rainer Maria Rilke Prize, 1984; National Endowment for the Arts Fellowships, 1985, 1993; Delmore Schwartz Memorial Poetry Award, 1989; Carl Sandburg Medal for Poetry, 1994; Pushcart Prize, 1996. Memberships: Academy of American Poets; PEN; Associated Writing Programs; Poetry Society of America. Address: 1466 Westview Drive, Coralville, IA 52241, USA.

DANCE Helen Oakley, b. 15 Feb 1913, Toronto, Ontario, Canada. Writer. m. Stanley Dance, 30 Jan 1947, 2 sons, 2 daughters. Education: University of Toronto; Les Fougéres, Switzerland. Publication: Stormy Monday: The T-Bone Walker Story, 1987. Contributions to: Down Beat, Tempo, Swing, Hot Jazz (Paris), Melody News, Saturday Review, Music Journal, Jazz Times, 1934-96. Address: 1745 Bittersweet Hill, Vista, CA 92084-7621, USA.

DANCE Stanley (Frank), b. 15 Sept 1910, Braintree, England. Reviewer; Writer. m. Helen Oakley, 30 Jan 1947, 2 sons, 2 daughters. Education: Framlingham College, 1925-28. Appointments: Reviewer, Jazz Journal, London, 1948-96, Saturday Review, New York City, 1962-72, Music Journal, New York City, 1962-79, Jazz Times, Silver Spring, Maryland, 1980-96. Publications: Jazz Era (editor), 1961; The World of Duke Ellington, 1970; The Night People (with Dicky Wells), 1971; The World of Swing, 1974; The World of Earl Hines, 1977; Duke Ellington in Person (with Mercer Ellington), 1978; The World of Count Basie, 1980; Those Swinging Years (with Charlie Barnet), 1984. Honour: American Society of Composers, Authors, and Publishers, Deems Taylor Award, 1979. Address: 1745 Bittersweet Hill, Vista, CA 92084-7621, USA.

DANE Mark. See: AVALLONE Michael (Angelo Jr).

DANESHVAR Simin, b. 23 Apr 1921, Shiraz, Iran. Novelist. Education: PhD, University of Teheran, 1949. Appointments: Professor, Department of Archaeology, University of Teheran; Emeritus, 1979-. Publications: The Extinguished Fire, 1948; A City Like Paradise, 1961; Savushun, 1969; To Whom Shall I Say Hello?, 1980; Jalal's Sunset, 1981; Daneshvar's Playhouse: A Collection of Stories, 1989; Translations of works by Alan Paton, Hawthorne, Chekhov and Shaw. Address: c/o Mage Books, 1032 29th Street North West, Washington, DC 20007, USA.

DANIEL Colin. See: WINDSOR Patricia.

DANIEL Wayne W(endell), b. 14 Feb 1929, Tallapoosa, Georgia, USA. Professor Emeritus of Decision Sciences; Writer. m. Mary Yarbrough, 2 June 1956, 1 son, 2 daughters. Education: BSEd, University of Georgia, 1951; MPH, University of North Carolina, 1959; PhD, University of Oklahoma, 1965. Appointments: Statistical Research Assistant, 1957-58, Research Statistician, 1959-60, Biostatistical Analyst, 1960-63, Chief, Mental Health Statistics Section, Biostatistics Service, 1965-67, Director, Biostatistics Service, 1967-68, Chief Statistician, 1968, Georgia Department of Public Health; Assistant Professor to Professor of Decision Sciences, 1968-91, Professor Emeritus, 1991-, Georgia State University. Publications: Biostatistics: A Foundation for Analysis in the Health Sciences, 1974, 6th edition, 1994; Business Statistics for Management and Economics (with James C Terrell), 1975, 7th edition, 1994; Introductory Statistics with Applications, 1977; Applied Nonparametric Statistics, 1978, 2nd edition, 1990; Essentials of Business Statistics, 1984, 2nd edition, 1988; Pickin' on Peachtree: A History of Country Music in Atlanta, 1990. Contributions to: Numerous journals and periodicals. Memberships: Alpha Iota Delta; Fellow, American Public Health Association; Delta Sigma Pi; Phi Kappa Phi. Address: 2943 Appling Drive, Chamblee, GA 30341, USA.

DANIELS Dorothy, (Danielle Dorsett, Angela Gray, Cynthia Kavanaugh, Helaine Ross, Suzanne Somers, Geraldine Thayer, Helen Gray Weston), b . 1 July 1915, Waterbury, USA. Writer. m. 7 Oct 1937. Education: Normal School, New Brittain, Connecticut. Publications: The Magic Ring, 1978; Purple and The Gold, 1978; Yesterday's Evil, 1980; Veil of Treachery, 1980; Legend of Death, 1980; Valley of Shadows, 1980; Monte Carlo, 1981; Saratoga, 1981; Sisters of Valcour, 1981; For Love and Valcour, 1983; Crisis at Valcour, 1985; Illusion of Haven's Edge, 1990. Honours: National Honorary Member, National League of American Pen Women. Memberships: Authors Guild; National League of American Pen Women; Ventura County Writers. Address: 6107 Village 6, Camarillo, CA 93010, USA.

DANIELS Lucy. See: **INMAN Lucy Daniels**.

DANIELS Max. See: **GELLIS Roberta Leah**.

DANIELS Molly Ann, (Shouri Daniels), b. 2 July 1932, Kerala, India.Writer; Teacher; Editor. 1 son, 1 daughter. Education: PhD, University of Chicago's Committee on Social Thought, 1986. Appointment: Director, Clothesline School of Writing, Chicago, Illinois, 1984-. Publications: The Yellow Fish, 1966; The Clotheslines Review, 4 issues of anthology of fiction (editor), 1986-90; The Prophetic Novel: A Study of A Passage to India, 1990; Father Gander Rhymes and Other Poems (editor), 1990; The Clothesline Review Manual for Writers, textbook. Contributions to: Indian PEN; Quest; Femina; Chicago Review; Primavera; Carleton Miscellany; Tri-Quarterly; Journal of Literary Studies; Saul Bellow Journal. Honours: Fulbright-Smith Mundt, 1961-62; Illinois Arts Council Fiction, 1978; Illinois Arts Council Criticism, 1982; Syndicated Fiction Award, PEN. Membership: Midwest Authors. Address: Clothesline School of Writing, Department of Continuing Education, University of Chicago, 5835 South Kimbark, Chicago, IL 60637, USA.

DANIELS Olga. See: **SINCLAIR Olga Ellen**.

DANIELS Shouri. See: **DANIELS Molly Ann**.

DANIELSON Carl. See: **KRUMMACHER Johann Henrich Karl Daniel**.

DANIELSSON Jon, b. 5 Mar 1949, Blonduos, Iceland. Writer; Translator. m. Marion McGreevy, 31 Dec 1993, 3 sons, 2 daughters. Education: Icelandic Student Degree, MA Akureyri Iceland, 1970; Studied at University of Iceland and University of Stockholm, Sweden. Honour: Translator of the Year, Children's Books, 1995. Membership: Icelandic Authors Union. Literary Agent: Skyaldborg Publishers Ltd, Armula 23-15108, Iceland. Address: Skulagata, 62-105 Reykjavik, Iceland.

DANKOVA Jana. See: **TANSKA Natalie**.

DANN Colin Michael, b. 10 Mar 1943, Richmond, Surrey, England. Author. m. Janet Elizabeth Stratton, 4 June 1977. Education: Shene County Grammar School. Publications: The Animals of Farthing Wood, 1979; In the Grip of Winter, 1981; Fox's Feud, 1982; The Fox Cub Bold, 1983; The Seige of White Deer Park, 1985; The Ram of Sweetriver, 1986; King of the Vagabonds, 1987; The Beach Dogs, 1988; The Flight from Farthing Wood, 1988; Just Nuffin, 1989; In the Path of the Storm, 1989; A Great Escape, 1990; A Legacy of Ghosts, 1991; The City Cats, 1991; Battle for the Park, 1992; The Adventure Begins, 1994. Honour: Arts Council National Award for Children's Literature, 1980. Membership: Society of Authors. Address: Castle Oast, Ewhurst Green, East Sussex, England.

DANN Jack, b . 15 Feb 1945, Johnson City, USA. Author. m. Jeanne Van Buren Dann. Education: BA, State University of New York, Binghamton, 1968. Publications: Wandering Stars (editor), 1974; Novels: Starhiker, 1977; Time Tipping, 1980; Junction, 1981; The Man Who Melted, 1984; In the Field of Fire (editor with wife), 1987;

Unicorns II, 1992; Dragons, 1993. Contributions to: New Dimensions; Orbit; New Worlds; Asimov's Science Fiction Magazines; Fiction Writers Handbook. Honours: Esteemed Knight, Mark Twain Society, 1975-; Gilgamesh |Award, (co-winner), 1986.Memberships: Science Fiction Writers of America; Authors Guild; World Future Society. Address: 825 Front Street, Binghamton, NY 13905, USA.

DANTO Arthur C(oleman), b. 1 Jan 1924, Ann Arbor, Michigan, USA. Professor Emeritus of Philosophy; Writer; Editor. m. (1) Shirley Rovetch, 9 Aug 1946, dec 1978, 2 daughters, (2) Barbara Westman, 15 Feb 1980. Education: BA, Wayne State University, 1948; MA, 1949, PhD, 1952, Columbia University; Postgraduate Studies, University of Paris, 1949-50. Appointments: Teacher, 1952-72, Johnsonian Professor of Philosophy, 1972-92, Chairman, Philosophy Department, 1979-87, Professor Emeritus, 1992-, Columbia University; Editor, Journal of Philosophy, 1975-; Art Critic, The Nation, 1984-. Publications: Analytical Philosophy of History, 1965; Nietzsche as Philosopher, 1965; Analytical Philosophy of Knowledge, 1968; What Philosophy Is, 1968; Mysticism and Morality, 1972; Analytical Philosophy of Action, 1973; Jean-Paul Sartre, 1975; The Transfiguration of the Commonplace, 1981; Narration and Knowledge, 1985; The Philosophical Disenfranchisement of Art, 1986; The State of the Art, 1987; Connections to the World, 1989; Encounters and Reflections, 1990; Beyond the Brillo Box, 1992; Embodied Meanings, 1994; Playing with the Edge, 1995; After the End of Art, 1996. Contributions to: Articles and reviews in many publications. Honours: Fulbright Scholarship, 1949-50; Guggenheim Fellowships, 1969, 1982; Distinguished Fulbright Professor to Yugoslavia, 1976; Lionel Trilling Book Prize, 1982; George S Polk Award for Criticism, 1985; National Book Critics Circle Award in Criticism, 1990; New York Public Library Literary Lion, 1993; Frank Jewett Mather Prize in Criticism, College Art Association, 1996. Address: 420 Riverside Drive, New York, NY 10025, USA.

DARBY Catherine. See: **PETERS Maureen**.

DARBY John, b . 18 Nov 1940, Belfast, Northern Ireland. University Professor. m. Marie, 13 Apr 1966, 2 sons. Education: BA, Honours, Modern History, 1962; HDipEd, 1970; DPhil, Ulster, 1985. Appointments: Editorial Board, International Journal of Group Tensions; Editorial Committee, Cahier du Centre Irelandaises, Paris, 1982; Director, Centre for the Study of Conflict, 1991-96; Director, INCORE, 1992-; Member, International Advisory Council, Centre for International Understanding, St Louis, 1993-. Publications: Conflict in Northern Ireland, 1976; Violence and Social Services in Northern Ireland, 1978; Northern Ireland: Background to the Conflict, 1983; Dressed to Kill: Cartoonists and Northern Irish Conflict, 1983; Intimidation and the Control of Conflict in Northern Ireland, 1986; Political Violence: Ireland in a Comparative Perspective, 1990. Contributions to: Managing Difference: The Case of Northern Ireland, 1995. Address: 61 Strand Road, Portstewart BT55 7LU, Northern Ireland.

DARCY Clare, b . America. Writer. Publications: Georgia, 1971; Cecily, or A Young Lady of Quality, 1972; Lydia, or Love in Town, 1973; Victoire, 1974; Allegra, 1975; Lady Pamela, 1975; Regina, 1976; Elyza, 1976; Cressida, 1977; Eugenia, 1977; Gwendolen, 1978; Rolande, 1978; Letty, 1980; Caroline and Julia, 1982; Eugenia, 1990;Georgia, 1990; Rolande, 1991; Cressida, 1991. Address: c/o Walker & Co, 720 Fifth Avenue, New York, NY 10019, USA.

DARDIS Thomas A, b . 19 Aug 1926, New York, USA. Writer; Teacher. Education: BA 1949; MA 1952; PhD 1980. Publications: Some Time in the Sun, 1976; Keaton, 1979; Harold Lloyd, 1983; The Thirsty Muse, 1989; Firebrand: The Life of Horace Liveright, 1995. Contributions to: American Film; Journal of Popular Film and Television; Antioch Review. Membership: PEN. Literary Agent: George Borichardt. Address: 2727 Palisade Avenue, New York, NY 10463, USA.

DARKE Marjorie Sheila, b. 25 Jan 1929, Birmingham, England. Writer. m. 1952, 2 sons, 1 daughter. Education: Worcester Grammar School for Girls, 1938-47; Leicester College of Art, 1947-50; Central School of Art, London, 1950-51. Publications: For Young Adults: Ride the Iron Horse, 1973; The Star Trap, 1974; A Question of Courage, 1975; The First of Midnight, 1977; A Long Way to Go, 1978; Comeback, 1981; Tom Post's Private Eye, 1982; Messages and Other Shivery Tales, 1984; A Rose From Blighty, 1990. For Beginner Readers: Mike's Bike, 1974; What Can I Do, 1975; The Big Brass

Band, 1976; My Uncle Charlie, 1977; Carnival Day, 1979. For Young Children: Kipper's Turn, 1976; Kipper Skips, 1979; Imp, 1985; The Rainbow Sandwich, 1989; Night Windows, 1990; Emma's Monster, 1992; Just Bear and Friends, 1996. Memberships: Society of Authors, Committee Member, Children's Writers Group, 1980-83; International PEN. Address: c/o Rogers, Coleridge & White, 20 Powis Mews, London, W11 1JN, England.

DARLIN Sergio. See: **JOSÉ Héctor Oscar.**

DARNTON Robert (Choate), b. 10 May 1939, New York, New York, USA. Professor of European History; Writer. m. Susan Lee Glover, 29 June 1963, 1 son, 2 daughters. Education: BA Magna cum Laude, Harvard College, 1960; Bachelor of Philosophy in History, 1962, Doctorate of Philosophy in History, 1964, Oxford University. Appointments: Reporter, New York Times, 1964-65; Junior Fellow, Society of Fellows, Harvard University, 1965-68; Assistant Professor, 1968-71, Associate Professor, 1971-72, Professor, 1972-, Shelby Cullom Davis Professor of European History, 1985-, Director, Program in European Cultural Studies, 1987-95, Princeton University; Director d'Études, École des Hautes Études en Sciences Sociales, Paris, 1971, 1981, 1985; Fellow, Center for Advanced Study in the Behavioral Sciences, Stanford, 1973-74, Netherlands Institute for Advanced Study, 1976-77, Institute for Advanced Study, Berlin, 1989-90, 1993-94; Member, Institute for Advanced Study, Princeton, New Jersey, 1977-81; George Eastman Visiting Professor, Oxford University, 1986-87; Lecturer, Collège de France, 1987; Member, All Souls College, Oxford, 1996-; Honorary Professor, University of Warwick, 1996-. Publications: Mesmerism and the End of the Enlightenment, 1968; The Business of Enlightenment: A Publishing History of the Encyclopédie, 1979; The Literary Underground of the Old Regime, 1982; The Great Cat Massacre and Other Episodes in French Cultural History, 1984; Revolution in Print: The Press in France 1775-1800 (editor with Daniel Roche), 1989; The Kiss of Lamourette: Reflections in Cultural History, 1989; Edition et sédition: L'univers de la littérature clandestine au XVIIIe siècle, 1991; Berlin Journal, 1989-1990, 1991; Gens de Lettres, Gens du Livre, 1992; The Forbidden Best-Sellers of Prerevolutionary France, 1995; The Corpus of Clandestine Literature in France, 1769-1789, 1995. Honours: Koren Prize, Society for French Historical Studies, 1973; Leo Gershoy Prize, American Historical Association, 1979; John D and Catharine T MacArthur Foundation Fellowship, 1982-87; Los Angeles Times Book Prize, 1984; Behrman Humanities Award, Princeton University, 1987; Chevalier, 1988, Officer, 1993, Ordre des Arts et des Lettres, France; Prix Médicis, 1991; Prix Chateaubriand, 1991; National Book Critics Circle Award, 1996. Memberships: Academia Europaea; Académie Royale de Langue et de Littérature Françaises, Belgium; American Academy of Arts and Sciences, fellow; American Antiquarian Society; American Philosophical Society; American Society for Eighteenth-Century Studies; International Society for Eighteenth-Century Studies, president, 1987-91. Address: c/o Department of History, Princeton University, 129 Dickinson Hall, Princeton, NJ 08544, USA.

DARUWALLA Keki N(asserwanji), b. 24 Jan 1937, Lahore, Pakistan. Poet. Education: MA, University of Punjab, Chandigarh. Publications: Under Orion, 1970; Apparition in April, 1971; Crossing the Rivers, 1976; Winter Poems, 1980; The Keeper of the Dead, 1982; Landscapes, 1987. Stories: Sword and Abyss, 1979; Editor, Two Decades of Indian poetry, 1960-80. Honours: Sahitya Akademi (National Academy of Letters) Award, 1984; Commonwealth Poetry Award (Asia Region), 1987. Address: OUP, PO Box 43, YMCA Library Building, 1st Floor, Jai Singh Road, New Delhi 100 001, India.

DARVI Andrea. See: **PLATE Andrea.**

DARVILL Timothy Charles, b. 22 Dec 1957, Cheltenham, England. Archaeologist. Education: BA, 1979; PhD, 1983. Appointment: Reviews Editor, Transactions of the Bristol and Gloucestershire Archaeological Society, 1985-90. Publications: Prehistoric Britain; Ancient Monuments in the Countryside; The Archaeology of the Uplands; Prehistoric Gloucestershire; Glovebox Guide to Ancient Britain; New Approaches to Our Past; Megalithic Chambered Tombs of the Cotswold Severn Region. Contributions to: 40 articles to journals. Memberships: Institute of Field Archaeologists, Chairman, 1989-91; Fellow of the Society of Antiquaries of London; Society of Antiquaries of Scotland; Council of the National Trust, 1988. Address: Department of Conservation Science, Bournemouth University, Fern Barrow, Poole, Dorset, England.

DARWISH (Ahmed) Adel (Abed El-Moneim), b. 8 Dec 1945, Alexandria, Egypt. Writer; Journalist. m. Elizabeth Catherine Darwish, div, 1 son, 1 daughter. Education: Graduate, University of Alexandria, 1966; University of London, 1975. Appointments: Editor, Ashara Al-Ansal, London, 1984-86; Reporter, The Independent, London, 1986-; Consultant on the Middle East. Publications: Between the Quill and the Sword: The Political Background to the Rushdie Affair, 1989; Unholy Babylon: The Secret History of Saddam's War, 1991; Water Wars: Coming Conflict in the Middle East, 1993; Rafsanjani's Iran: Iran's Foreign Policy in the 1990's, 1993. Contributions to: Books and periodicals. Memberships: National Union of Journalists; Writers Guild. Address: c/o The Independent, 40 City Road, London E4, England.

DAS Kamala, b. 31 Mar 1934, Malabar, South India. Poetry Editor; Poet; Writer. m. K Madhava Das, 1949, 3 sons. Education: Private. Appointments: Poetry Editor, Illustrated Weekly of India, Bombay, 1971-79. Publications: Summer in Calcutta: Fifty Poems, 1965; The Descendants, 1967; The Old Playhouse and Other Poems, 1973; Tonight This Savage Rite: The Love Poetry of Kamala Das and Pritish Nandy, 1979; Collected Poems, 1987. Novels: Alphabet of Lust, 1977; Manomi, 1987; The Sandalwood Tree, 1988. Honours: Kerala Sahitya Academy Award for Fiction, 1969; Asian World Prize for Literature, 1985. Address: Sthanuvilas Bungalow, Sastgamangalam, Trivndrum 10, Kerala, India.

DASSANOWSKY Robert von, b. 28 Jan 1960, New York, New York, USA. Writer; Poet; Dramatist; Editor; University Professor. Education: Graduate, American Academy of Dramatic Arts, Pasadena, California, 1977; American Film Institute Conservatory Program, Los Angeles, 1979-81; BA, 1985, MA, 1988, PhD, 1992, University of California at Los Angeles. Appointments: Editor, New German Review, 1986-91; Founding Editor, Rohwedder: International Magazine of Literature and Art, 1986-93; Teaching Fellow, Department of Germanic Languages, 1989-92, Visiting Professor of German, 1992-93, University of California at Los Angeles; Writer, researcher, Disney Channel, 1990-92; Corresponding Editor, Rampike, 1991-93; German Language Editor, Osiris, 1991-; Assistant Professor of German, Head, German Studies, Development Director of Film Studies, University of Colorado at Colorado Springs, 1993-; Founding President, PEN Colorado, 1993-. Publications: Phantom Empires: The Novels of Alexander Lernet-Holenia and the Question of Postimperial Austrian Identity, 1996; Hans Raimund: Verses of a Marriage (translator), 1996; Telegrams from the Metropole: Selected Poetry 1980-1995, 1997; Verses of a Remarriage, Translation of Poetry by Hans Raimund, 1996; Alexander Lernet-Holenia: Mars in Aries (translator), 1997. Other: Several plays and television scripts. Contributions to: Periodicals and anthologies . Honours: Julie Harris/Beverly Hills Theater Guild Playwrighting Award, 1984; Academico Honoris Causa, Academia Culturale d'Europa, Italy, 1989; University of Colorado President's Fund for the Humanities Grant, 1996. Memberships: Authors League; Dramatists Guild; Paneuropa Union, Austria; Modern Language Association; PEN; Poet and Writers; Society for Cinema Studies. Address: c/o Department of Languages, University of Colorado at Colorado Springs, Colorado Springs, CO 80933, USA.

DASZKOWSKI Eugeniusz Andrzei, b. 4 Feb 1930, Wyszkow, Poland. Master Mariner. m. Danuta Jankowska, 30 May 1958, 1 daughter. Education: Navigation School, Szczecin, 1948-50; Engineering Polytechnical School, Szczecin, 1952-56; Rector, Maritime University, Szczecin, 1972-78. Publications: The Watch, 1972; The Sailor's Sea-Line, 1973; To the Port of Design, 1975; The African Meetings, 1975; The Sea Polutions by Ship, 1977; The Sea Doorsteps, 1978; The Fere, 1981; The Last Trip of Narvik, 1982; The Zahi, 1985; The Blinders From San Pedro, 1986; The Monkey Trip, 1988; My Wyszkow, 1996; The Sailor's Knot, 1996. Contributions to: Periodicals and journals. Honours: Award, Sea Polish Trade Union, 1970; Josef Conrad Award, 1975; Readers Award, 1987. Memberships: Polish Writers Association; Societe des Auteurs. Address: ul Anhellego 13, 834455 Szczecin, Poland.

DATHORNE O(scar) R(onald), b. 19 Nov 1934, Georgetown, Guyana. Professor of English; Writer; Poet. Education: BA, 1958, MA, 1960, PhD, 1966, University of Sheffield; Graduate Certificate in Education, 1959, Diploma in Education, 1967, University of London; MBA, MPA, 1984, University of Miami. Appointments: Associate Professor, Ahmadu Bello University, Zaria, 1959-63; University of Ibadan, 1963-66; UNESCO Consultant to the Government of Sierra Leone, 1967-68; Professor of English, Njala University College,

University of Sierra Leone, 1968-69; Professor of African Literature, Howard University, 1970; Professor of Afro-American Literature, University of Wisconsin, Madison, 1970-71; Professor of English and Black Literature, Ohio State University, 1975-77; Professor of English, University of Miami, Coral Gables, Florida, 1977-. Publications: Dumplings in the Soup (novel), 1963; The Scholar Man (novel), 1964; Carribean Narrative (editor), 1965; Carribean Verse (editor), 1967; Africa in Prose, 1969; The Black Mind, 1975; African Literature in the Twentieth Century, 1976; Dark Ancestor, 1981; Dele's Child, 1985; Imagining the World: Typical Belief vs Reality in Global Encounters, 1994. Address: Department of English, University of Miami, Coral Gables, FL 33124, USA.

DAUNTON Martin James, b. 7 Feb 1949, Cardiff. University Professor. m. Claire Gobbi, 7 Jan 1984. Education: BA, University of Nottingham, 1970; PhD, University of Kent, 1974. Appointments: Lecturer, University of Durham, 1973-79; Lecturer, 1979-85, Reader, 1985-89, Professor, 1989-, University College London; Convenor, Studies in History series, Royal Historical Society, 1995-. Publications: Coal Metropolis: Cardiff; House and Home in the Victorian City, 1850-1914; Royal Mail: The Post office Since 1840; A Property Owning Democracy?; Progress and Poverty. Contributions to: Economic History Review; Past & Present; Business History; Historical Research; Journal of Urban History; Charity, Self-Interest and Welfare in the English Past, 1996; English Historical Review; Twentieth Century British History. Membership: Royal Historical Society. Address: Department of History, University College London, Gower Street, London WC1E 6BT, England.

DAVEY Frank(land Wilmot), b. 19 Apr 1940, Vancouver, British Columbia, Canada. Professor of Canadian Literature; Writer; Poet; Editor. m. 1) Helen Simmons, 1962, div 1969, 2) Linda McCartney, 1969, 1 son, 1 daughter. Education: BA, 1961, MA, 1963, University of British Columbia, Vancouver; PhD, University of Southern California at Los Angeles, 1968. Appointments: Founding Editor, Tish Magazine, Vancouver, 1961-63, Open Letter, Toronto, 1965-; Lecturer, 1963-67, Assistant Professor, 1967-69, Royal Roads Military College, Victoria, British Columbia; Writer-in-Residence, Sir George Williams University, Montreasl, 1969-70; Assistant Professor, 1970-72, Associate Professor, 1972-80, Professor of English, 1980-90, Chair, Department of English, 1985-88, 1989-90, York University, Toronto; General Editor, Quebec Translations Series, 1973-90, New Canadian Criticism Series, 1977-; Visiting Professor, Shastri Indo-Canadian Institute, Karnatak University, India, 1982; Director, Swift Current Literary Database and Magazine Project, 1984-90; Carl F Klinck Professor of Canadian Literature, University of Western Ontario, London, 1990-. Publications: Poetry: D-Day and After, 1962; City of the Gulls and Sea, 1964; Bridge Force, 1965; The Scarred Hill, 1966; Four Myths for Sam Perry, 1970; Weeds, 1970; Griffon, 1972; King of Swords, 1972; L'An Trentiesme: Selected Poems 1961-70, 1972; Arcana, 1973; The Clallam, 1973; War Poems, 1979; The Arches: Selected Poems, 1981; Capitalistic Affection!, 1982; Edward and Patricia, 1984; The Louis Riel Organ and Piano Company, 1985; The Abbotsford Guide to India, 1986; Postcard Translations, 1988; Popular Narratives, 1991; Cultural Mischief: A Practical Guide to Multiculturalism, 1996. Criticism: Five Readings of Olson's "Maximus", 1970; Earle Birney, 1971; From There to Here: A Guide to English-Canadian Literature Since 1960, 1974; Louis Dudek and Raymond Souster, 1981; The Contemporary Canadian Long Poem, 1983; Surviving the Paraphrase: 11 Essays on Canadian Literature, 1983; Margaret Atwood: A Feminist Poetics, 1984; Reading Canadian Reading, 1988; Post-National Arguments: The Politics of the Anglophone-Canadian Novel Since 1967, 1993; Reading "KIM" Right, 1993; Canadian Literary Power: Essays on Anglophone-Canadian Literary Conflict, 1994; Karla's Web: A Cultural Examination of the Mahaffy-French Murders, 1994, revised edition, 1995. Contributions to: Books and journals. Honours: Macmillan Prize, 1962; Department of Defence Arts Research Grants, 1965, 1966, 1968; Canada Council Fellowships, 1966, 1974; Humanities Research Council of Canada Grants, 1974, 1981; Canadian Federation for the Humanities Grants, 1979, 1992; Social Sciences and Humanities Research Council Fellowship, 1981. Membership: Association of Canadian College and University Teachers of English, President, 1994-96. Address: 499 Dufferin Avenue, London, Ontario N6B 2A1, Canada.

DAVEY Thomas A, b. 2 Jan 1954, Philadelphia, Pennsylvania, USA. Adult and Child Psychologist; Writer. Education: BA, Duke University, 1976; EdD, Harvard University, 1984. Appointments: Teaching Fellow, Harvard University; Conducts Private Practice in Adult and Child Psychology, Cambridge. Publication: A Generation

Divided: German Children and the Berlin Wall, 1987. Contributions to: Articles and reviews to magazines and newspapers. Honours: German Academic Exchange Service Grants, 1981-82, 1988; Lyndhurst Foundation Prize, 1985. Memberships: American Psychological Association; Massachusetts Psychological Association. Address: 23 Bigelow Street, No 2, Boston, MA 02135, USA.

DAVIDSON Basil Risbridger, b. 9 Nov 1914, Bristol, England. Writer. m. Marion Young, 7 July 1943, 3 sons. Publications: Old Africa Rediscovered, 1959; The African Slave Trade, 1961; The Africans, 1969; Africa in Modern History, 1978; Special Operations Europe, 1980; The Fortunate Isles, 1989; African Civilisation Revisited, 1991; The Black Man's Burden: Africa and the Curse of the Nation-State, 1992; The Search for Africa, 1994. Honours: Military Cross, British Army; Bronze Star, US Army; Ansfield Woolf Award, 1959; D. Letters (hc), University of Ibadan, 1975; University of Dar-es-Salaam, 1985; DUniv (hc), Open University of Great Britain, 1980; University of Edinburgh, 1981; Agnelli Visiting Professor, University of Turin, 1990. Address: Old Cider Mill, North Wootton, Somerset BA4 4HA, England.

DAVIDSON Donald (Herbert), b. 6 Mar 1917, Springfield, Massachusetts, USA. Philosopher; Professor; Writer. m. (1) 1 daughter, (2) Nancy Hirshberg, 4 Apr 1975, dec 1979, (3) Marcia Cavell, 3 July 1984. Education: BA, 1939, MA, 1941, PhD, 1949, Harvard University. Appointments: Professor, Rockefeller University, New York City, 1970-76, University of Chicago, 1976-81, University of California, Berkeley, 1981-; John Dewey Lecturer, University of Michigan, 1973, Columbia University, 1989; George Eastman Visiting Professor, Balliol College, Oxford, 1984-85; Fulbright Distinguished Lecturer, India, 1985-86; S J Keeling Memorial Lecturer in Greek Philosophy, University College, London, 1986; Thalheimer Lecturer, Johns Hopkins University, 1987; Alfred North Whitehead Lecturer, Harvard University, 1990; Kant Lecturer, University of Munich, 1993. Publications: Decision Making: An Experimental Approach (with Patrick Suppes), 1957; Words and Objections (editor with J Hintikka), 1969; Semantics for Natural Languages (editor with Gilbert Harman), 1970; The Logic of Grammar (co-editor), 1975; Essays on Actions and Events, 1980; Inquiries into Truth and Interpretation, 1983. Honours: Teschemacher Fellow in Classics and Philosophy, 1939-41; Rockefeller Fellowship in the Humanities, 1945-46; American Council of Learned Societies Fellowship, 1958-59; National Science Foundation Research Grants, 1964-65, 1968; Fellow, Center for Advanced Study in the Behavioral Sciences, 1969-70; Guggenheim Fellowship, 1973-74; Fellow, All Souls College, Oxford, 1973-74; Honorary Research Fellow, University College, London, 1978; Sherman Fairchild Distinguished Scholar, California Institute of Technology, 1989; Hegel Prize, City of Stuttgart, 1991; DDL honoris causa, Oxford University, 1995. Memberships: American Academy of Arts and Sciences; Corresponding Member, British Academy. Address: c/o Department of Philosophy, University of California at Berkeley, Berkeley, CA 94720, USA.

DAVIDSON Lionel, (David Line), b. 31 Mar 1922, Hull, Yorkshire, England. Author. m. (1) Fay Jacobs, 1949, dec 1988, 2 sons, (2) Frances Ullman, 1989. Publications: The Night of Wenceslas, 1960; The Rose of Tibet, 1962; A Long Way to Shiloh, 1966; Run for Your Life, 1966; Making Good Again, 1968; Smith's Gazelle, 1971; Mike and Me, 1974; The Sun Chemist, 1976; The Chelsea Murders, 1978; Under Plum Lake, 1980; Screaming High, 1985; Kolymsky Heights, 1994. Honours: Silver Quill Award, Authors Club, 1961; Gold Dagger Awards, Crime Writers Association, 1961, 1967, 1979. Address: c/o Curtis Brown, Haymarket House, 28/29 Haymarket, London SW1Y 4SP, England.

DAVIDSON Michael, b. 18 Dec 1944, Oakland, California, USA. Professor of Literature; Poet; Writer. m. (1) Carol Wikarska, 1970, div 1974, (2) Lois Chamberlain, 1988, 2 children. Education: BA, San Francisco State University, 1967; PhD, State University of New York at Buffalo, 1971; Post-doctoral Fellow, University of California at Berkeley, 1974-75. Appointments: Visiting Lecturer, San Diego State University, 1973-76; Curator, Archive for New Poetry, 1975-85, Professor of Literature, 1977-, University of California at San Diego. Publications: Poetry: Exchanges, 1972; Two Views of Pears, 1973; The Mutabilities, and The Foul Papers, 1976; Summer Letters, 1976; Grillwork, 1980; Discovering Motion, 1980; The Prose of Fact, 1981; The Landing of Rochambeau, 1985; Analogy of the Ion, 1988; Post Hoc, 1990. Other: The San Francisco Renaissance: Poetics and Community at Mid-Century, 1989. Contributions to: Periodicals. Honour: National Endowment for the Arts Grant, 1976. Address: c/o

Department of Literature, University of California at San Diego, La Jolla, CA 92093, USA.

DAVIDSON William H(arley), b. 25 Sept 1951, Albuquerque, New Mexico, USA. Associate Professor; Researcher; Consultant; Writer. m. Anneke Rozendaal, 16 June 1973, 3 sons. Education: AB, Harvard College, 1973; MBA, 1975, DBA, 1979, Harvard Business School. Appointments: Assistant Professor, Amos Tuck School, Dartmouth College, 1978-82; Adjunct Professor, Fletcher School of Law and Diplomacy, Tufts University, 1980; Visiting Professor, INSEAD, Fontainebleau, France, 1981-83, Dalian Institute of Science and Technology, China, 1984, International University of Japan, 1988-90; Associate Professor, Colgate Darden School, University of Virginia, 1982-86; Founder-Chairman, Management Education Services Associates, 1985-; Associate Professor, School of Business Administration, University of Southern California, 1986-; Partner, Deloitte & Touche Management Consulting, 1996-. Publications: Tracing the Multinationals (with J C Curhan and Rajan Suri), 1977; Foreign Production of Technology-Intensive Products by US based Multinational Enterprises (with Raymond Vernon), 1979; Experience Effects in International Investment and Technology Transfer, 1980; Global Strategic Management, 1982; The Amazing Race, 1984; Revitalizing American Industry: Lessons from our Competitors (editor with M S Hochmuth), 1985; US Competiveness: The Case of the Textile Industry (with C Feigenoff and F G Ghadar), 1987; Managing the Global Corporation: Cases in Strategy and Management (with José de la Torre), 1989; 2020 Vision (with Stanley Davis), 1991. Contributions to: Books and journals. Honours: Best Business Book of the Year Selection, Fortune Magazine, 1992. Membership: Academy of International Business. Address: C/o MESA Research, 1611 South Pacific Coast Highway, Suite 303, Redondo Beach, CA 90277, USA.

DAVIE Elspeth, b . 1919, Kilmarnock, Scotland. Teacher; Author. m. George Elder Davie. Education: DA, Edinburgh College of Art. Publications: Novels: Providing, 1965; Creating a Scene, 1971; Climbers on a Stair, 1978. Short Stories: The Spark and Other Stories, 1968; The High Tide Talker and Other Stories, 1976; The Night of the Funny Hats, 1980; A Traveller's Room, 1985; Coming to Light, 1989. Honours: Scottish Arts Council Grants, 1971, 1977, 1979; Katherine Mansfield Prize, English Centre of International PEN, 1978.

DAVIE-MARTIN Hugh. See: **McCUTCHEON Hugh.**

DAVIES (Edward) Hunter, b . 7 Jan 1936, Renfrew, Scotland. Writer. m. 11 June 1960, 1 son, 2 daughters. Education: BA, DipEd, University College, Durham, England. Publications: 40 Books including: Here We Go Round the Mulberry Bush, 1965; The Beaties, 1968, 2nd edition, 1985; The Glory Game, 1972, 2nd edition, 1985; A Walk Along the Wall, 1974, 2nd edition, 1986; A Walk Along the Lakes, 1979; Fit for the Sixth, 1989; In Search of Columbus, 1991. Contributions to: Sunday Times, 1960-84; Punch, 1979-89; Independent, London, 1990-. Literary Agent: Giles Gordon. Address: 11 Boscastle Road, London NW5, England.

DAVIES James Atterbury, b. 25 Feb 1939, Llandeilo, Dyfed, Wales. University Lecturer. m. Jennifer Hicks, 1 Jan 1966, 1 son, 1 daughter. Education: BA, 1965; PhD, 1969. Appointments: Senior Lecturer, University College of Swansea, 1990-; Visiting Professor, Baylor University, Texas, 1981; Mellon Research Fellow, HRHRC, University of Texas, 1993. Publications: John Forster: A Literary Life; The Textual Life of Dickens's Characters; Leslie Norris; Dylan Thomas's Places; The Heart of Wales (editor), 1995. Membership: University of Wales Association for the Study of Welsh Writing in English. Address: Department of English, University College of Swansea, Swansea SA2 8PP, Wales.

DAVIES Pauline. See: **FISK Pauline.**

DAVIES Peter Joseph, b. 15 May 1937, Terang, Victoria, Australia. Physician; Writer. m. Clare Loughnan, 21 Dec 1960, 1 daughter. Education: MB, 1961; MRACP, 1968; FRACP, 1974; MRCP, 1970; MD, 1991. Publications: Mozart in Person: His Character and Health, 1989; Mozart's Health, Illnesses and Death, 1993; The Cause of Beethoven's Deafness, 1996. Contributions to: Journal of Medical Biography, 1995. Memberships: Royal Australian College of Physicians; Gastro-Enterological Society of Australia; Royal Society of Medicine. Address: 14 Hamilton Street, East Kew, Victoria 3102, Australia.

DAVIES Piers (Anthony David), b. 15 June 1941, Sydney, New South Wales, Australia. Barrister; Solicitor; Screenwriter; Poet. m. Margaret Elaine Haswell, 24 Aug 1973, 1 daughter. Education: LLB, University of Auckland, 1964; Diploma in English and Comparative Literature, City of London College, 1967. Appointments: Barrister and Solicitor, Jordan, Smith and Davies, Auckland, New Zealand; Chairperson, Short Film Fund, New Zealand Film Commission, 1987-91. Publications: East and Other Gong songs, 1967; The Life and Flight of Rev Buck Shotte (with Peter Weir), screenplay, 1969; Day Trip from Mount Meru, 1969; Homesdale (with Peter Weir), screenplay, 1971; The Cars That Ate Paris (with Peter Weir), screenplay, 1973; Diaspora, 1974; Bourgeois Homage to Dada, 1974; Central Almanac (editor), 1974; Skin Deep, screenplay, 1978; R V Huckleberry Finn, video documentary, 1979; Olaf's Coast, documentary, 1982; Jetsam, 1984; The Lamb of God, screenplay, 1985. Contributions to: Shipping Law Section, Encyclopedia of New Zealand Forms and Precedents, 1994; Anthologies and periodicals; A Fair Hearing, screenplay, 1995. Address: 16 Crocus Place, Remuera, Auckland 5, New Zealand.

DAVIES William Thomas Pennar, b . 12 Nov 1911, Aberpennar (Mountain Ash), Glamorgan, Wales. m. Rosemarie Wolff, 26 June 1943, 4 sons, 1 daughter. Education: University of Wales, Cardiff, 1929-34; Balliol College, Oxford, 1934-36; Yale University, USA, 1936-38; Mansfield College, Oxford, 1940-43; BA (Wales), 1932; BLitt (Oxon), 1938; PhD (Yale), 1943. Publications: Cudd fy Meiau, diary, 1957; Anadl o'r Uchelder, novel, 1958; Yr Efrydd o lyn Cynon, poems, 1961; Caregl Nwyf, short stories, 1966; Meibion Darogan, novel, 1968; Llais y Durtur, short stories, 1985. Also: Cinio'r Cythraul, poems, 1946; Naw Wftt, poems, 1957; Rhwng Chwedl a Chredo, studies, 1966; Y Tlws yn y Lotws, poems, 1971; Y Brenin Alltud, studies; Yr Awen Almaeneg, anthology, German verse in Welsh translation, 1984; Llef, poems, 1987. Contributions to: Articles, reviews, studies, various periodicals, published separately. Honours: Commonwealth Fund Fellow, 1936-38; Fellow, University of Wales, 1938-40; Welsh Academy Prize, 1968; Fellow Honoris Causa, 1986, Honorary DD, 1987, University of Wales, Cardiff; Honorary Fellow, Yr Academi Gymreig (Welsh Academy), 1989. Memberships: Undeb Awduron Cymru. Address: 10 Heol Grosvenor, Sgeti, Abertawe, Swansea SA2 0SP, Wales.

DAVIS Alan R, b. 30 June 1950, New Orleans, Louisiana, USA. Writer; Professor. m. Catherine Culloden, 4 July 1981, 1 son, 1 daughter. Education: BA, 1973, MA, 1975, University of Louisiana; PhD, University of Denver, 1981. Appointments: Loyola University, 1980-81; University of North Carolina, 1981-85; Chair of English, Director of Creative Writing, Moorhead State University, Minnesota, 1985-; Editor, American Fiction, 1987-. Publications: Rumors From the Lost World; American Fiction. Contributions to: New York Times Book Review; San Francisco Chronicle; Cleveland Plain Dealer; Chicago Sun Times; Hudson Review; Kansas Quarterly. Honours: Breadloaf Scholarship; State Arts Board Fellow; Minnesota Voices Winner; Loft-McKnight Award of Distinction in Creative Prose, 1995. Memberships: National Book Critics Circle; Associated Writing Programs. Address: PO Box 229, Moorhead State University, Moorhead, MN 56563, USA.

DAVIS Andrew (Wynford), b . 1936, England. Lecturer; Writer; Playwright. Appointments: Teacher, St Clement Danes Grammar School, 1958-61 and Woodberry Down School, 1961-63, London; Lecturer, Coventry College of Education and University of Warwick, Coventry College, 1963-. Publications: Plays: Marmalade Atkins in Space, 1982; Also Radio and television plays for children and numerous radio plays for adults. Children's Fiction: The Fantastic Feats of Doctor Box, 1972; Conrad's War, 1978; Marmalade and Rufus, 1979, as Marmalade Atkins Dreadful Deeds, 1982; Marmalade Atkins in Space, 1982; Educating Marmalade, 1983; Danger! Marmalade at Work, 1984; Alfonso Bonzo, 1986; Getting Hurt, 1989; Poonam's Pets, 1990; Dirty Foxes, 1990; B Monkey, 1992. Address: c/o Leinon Unna & Durbridge, 24 Pottery Lane, London W11 4LZ, England.

DAVIS Burke, b . 24 July 1913, Durham, North Carolina, USA. Historian; Biographer. m. (1) Evangeline McLennan, 11 Aug 1940, div 1980, 1 son, 1 daughter, (2) Juliet Halliburton, 6 Feb 1982. Education: Duke University, 1931-32, 1933-34; Guilford College, 1935-36; AB, University of North Carolina, 1937. Appointments: Editor, Feature Writer and Sports Editor, Charlotte News, North Carolina, 1937-47; Reporter, Baltimore Evening Sun, Maryland, 1947 52; Reporter, Greensboro News, North Carolina, 1951-60; Writer and Historian,

Colonial Williamsburg, Virginia, 1960-78. Publications: Whisper My Name, 1949; The Ragged Ones, 1951; Yorktown, 1952; They Called Him Stonewall, 1954; Gray Fox, 1956; Robert E Lee, 1956; Jeb Stuart, The Last Cavalier, 1957; To Appomattox, 1959; Our Incredible Civil War, 1960; Marinel, 1961; The Cowpens-Guilford Courthouse Campaign, 1962; America's First Army, 1962; Appomattox: Closing Struggle of the Civil War, 1963; The Summer Land, 1965; A Rebel Raider, (co-author), 1966; The Billy Mitchell Affair, 1967; A Williamsburg Galaxy, 1967; The World of Currier & Ives, (co-author), 1968; Get Yamamoto, 1969; Yorktown: The Winning of American Independence, 1969; Billy Mitchell Story, 1969; The Campaign that Won America: Yorktown, 1970; Heroes of the American Revolution, 1971; Jamestown, 1971; Thomas Jefferson's Virginia, 1971; Amelia Earhart, 1972; Biography of a Leaf, 1972; Three for Revolution, 1975; Biography of a Kingsnake, 1975; George Washington and the American Revolution, 1975; Newer and Better Organic Gardening, 1976; Biography of a Fish Hawk, 1976; Old Hickory: A Life of Andrew Jackson, 1977; Mr Lincoln's Whiskers, 1978; Sherman's March, 1980; The Long Surrender, 1985; The Southern Railway, 1985; War Bird: The Life and Times of Elliott White Springs, 1986; Civil War: Strange and Fascinating Facts, 1989; Marine: The Life of Chesty Puller, 1991; To Appomattox: 9 April 1865, 1989. Address: Rt 1 Box 66, Meadows of Dan, VA 24120, USA.

DAVIS Christopher, b. 23 Oct 1928, Philadelphia, USA. Writer; Teacher. Education: BA, University of Pennsylvania, 1955. Appointments: Pennsylvania Council on the Arts, 1981-86. Publications: Lost Summer; A Kind of Darkness; A Peep Into the 20th Century; Suicide Note; Waiting For It; The Producer; Dog Horse Rat; First Family; Belmarch; Ishmael; The Sun in Mid Career. Contributions to: Periodicals. Honours: O'Henry Prize Story; American Academy of Arts and Letters Literature Award, 1991. Membership: PEN. Address: Curtis Brown, 10 Aster Place, New York, NY 10003, USA.

DAVIS David Brion, b. 16 Feb 1927, Denver, Colorado, USA. Professor of History; Writer. m. (1) 1 son, 2 daughters, (2) Toni Hahn Davis, 9 Sept 1971, 2 sons. Education: AB, Dartmouth College, 1950; AM, 1953, PhD, 1956, Harvard University. Appointments: Instructor, Dartmouth College, 1953-54; Assistant Professor, 1955-58, Associate Professor, 1958-63, Professor and Ernest I White Professor of History, 1963-69, Cornell University; Fulbright Senior Lecturer, American Studies Research Centre, Hyderabad, India, 1967; Harmsworth Professor, Oxford University, 1969-70; Professor and Farnam Professor of History, 1969-78, Sterling Professor of History, 1978-, Yale University; Fellow, Center for Advanced Study in the Behavioral Sciences, Stanford, 1972-73; Fulbright Lecturer, Universities of Guyana and the West Indies, 1974; French-American Foundation Chair in American Civilization, École des Hautes Études en Sciences Sociales, Paris, 1980-81; Gilder-Lehrman Inaugural Fellow, 1996-97. Publications: Homicide in American Fiction, 1798-1860: A Study in Social Values, 1957; The Problem of Slavery in Western Culture, 1966, revised edition, 1988; Ante-Bellum Reform (editor), 1967; The Slave Power Conspiracy and the Paranoid Style, 1969; Was Thomas Jefferson an Authentic Enemy of Slavery?, 1970; The Fear of Conspiracy: Images of Unamerican Subversion from the Revolution to to the Present (editor), 1971; The Problem of Slavery in the Age of Revolution, 1770-1823, 1975; The Great Republic (with others), 1977, 4th edition, revised, 1992; Antebellum American Culture; An Interpretive Anthology, 1979, new edition, 1997; The Emancipation Moment, 1984; Slavery and Human Progress, 1984; Slavery in the Colonial Chesapeake, 1986; From Homicide to Slavery: Studies in American Culture, 1986; Revolutions: Reflections on American Equality and Foreign Liberations, 1990; The Antislavery Debate: Capitalism and Abolitionism as a Problem in Historical Interpretation (with Thomas Bender), 1992. Contributions to: Scholarly journals. Honours: Guggenheim Fellowship, 1958-59; Pulitzer Prize in General Non-Fiction, 1967; Anisfield-Wolf Award, 1967; Albert J Beveridge Award, American Historical Association, 1975; National Book Award, 1976; Bancroft Prize, Columbia University, 1976; Presidential Medal for Outstanding Leadership and Achievement, Dartmouth College, 1991. Memberships: American Academy of Arts and Sciences; American Antiquarian Society; American Philosophical Society; British Academy, corresponding fellow; Institute of Early American History and Culture; Organization of American Historians. Address: c/o Department of History, PO Box 208324, Yale University, New Haven, CT 06520, USA.

DAVIS Dick, b. 18 Apr 1945, Portsmouth, Hampshire, England. Professor; Poet. m. Afkham Darbandi, 1974, 2 daughters. Education:

BA, King's College, Cambridge, 1966; PhD, University of Manchester, 1988. Appointments: Assistant Professor, 1988-93, Associate Professor of Persian, 1993-, Ohio State University. Publications: Shade Mariners, 1970; In The Distance, 1975; Seeing the World, 1980; The Selected Writings of Thomas Traherne (editor), 1980; The Covenant, 1984; Visitations, 1983; What the Mind Wants, 1984; Lares, 1986; Devices and Desires: New and Selected Poems, 1967-87, 1989; The Rubaiyat of Omar Khayyam, Translated by Edward Fitzgerald (editor), 1989; A Kind of Love, New & Selected Poems, 1991; Epic & Sedition, One Case of Ferdonzi's Shahnameh, 1992. Translations: The Conference of the Birds, 1984; The Legend of Seyavash, 1992. Honour: Royal Society of Literature Heinemann Award, 1981. Address: Department of Near Eastern Languages, Ohio State University, 190 North Oval Mall, Columbus, OH 43210, USA.

DAVIS Dorothy Salisbury, b . 26 Apr 1916, Chicago, Illinois, USA. Writer. m. Harry Davis, 25 Apr 1946. Education: AB, Barat College, Lake Forest, Illinois, 1938. Publications: A Gentle Murderer, 1951; Men of No Property, 1956; The Evening of the Good Samaritan, 1961; Enemy and Brother, 1967; Where the Dark Streets Go, 1969; The Little Brothers, 1974; A Death in the Life, 1976; Scarlet Night, 1980; Lullaby of Murder, 1984; Tales for a Stormy Night, 1985; The Habit of Fear, 1987; A Gentleman Called, 1989; Old Sinners Never Die, 1991; Black Sheep, White Lambs, 1993. Contributions to: New Republic. Honours: Grand Master's Award, Mystery Writers of America, 1985; Lifetime Achievement Award, Bouchereon XX, 1989. Memberships: President, Executive Vice President, Mystery Writers of America; Crime Writers Association, England; Authors Guild. Address: Palisades, New York, NY 10964, USA.

DAVIS Gordon. See: LEVINSON Leonard.

DAVIS Jack (Leonard), b. 11 Mar 1917, Perth, Western Australia. Poet; Dramatist; Writer. m. Madelon Jantine Wilkens, 12 Dec 1987, 1 daughter. Appointment: Writer-in-Residence, Murdoch University, 1982. Publications: The First Born and Other Poems, 1968; Jagardoo Poems from Aboriginal Australia, 1978; The Dreamers (play), 1983; Kullark (play), 1983; John Pat and Other Poems, 1988; Burungin (Smell the Wind) (play), 1989; Plays From Black Australia, 1989. Contributions to: Identity. Honours: Human Rights Award, 1987; BHP Award, 1988; Australian Artists Creative Fellowship, 1989; Honorary doctorates. Memberships: Chairman, Aboriginal Writers Oral Literature and Dramatists Association; Australian Writers Guild; Life Member, PEN International. Address: 3 Little Howard Street, Fremantle, Western Australia, Australia.

DAVIS Jon Edward, b . 28 Oct 1952, New Haven, Connecticut, USA. Author. m. Terry Layton, 8 Jan 1978, 1 daughter. Education: BA, English, 1984, MFA, Creative Writing, 1985, University of Montana. Appointments: Writing Program Co-ordinator, Fine Arts Work Centre, Provincetown, 1987-. Publications: West of New England, 1983; Dangerous Amusements, 1987. Contributions to: Poetry; Georgia Review; Missouri Review; Stand; Malahat Review. Honours: Academy of American Poets Prize, 1985; National Endowment for the Arts Fellowship, 1986; Fine Arts Work Centre, Provincetown Creative Writing Fellowship, 1986-87. Memberships: Academy of American Poets; Poets and Writers; Associated Writing Programs. Address: Fine Arts Work Centre, Box 565, Provincetown, MA 02657, USA.

DAVIS Joy Lynn Edwards, b. 4 Apr 1945, Speedwell, Tennessee, USA. Teacher of English. m. Joe Mac Davis, 22 July 1969. Education: BA, Lincoln Memorial University, 1969; MA, Union College, 1974; Stokely Fellow, University of Tennessee, 1984. Publications: Immigrants and First Families of America, 1982; Old Speedwell Families, 1983; More Speedwell Families, 1988; American Poetry Anthology, 1990; Great Poets of Our Time, 1993; Distinguished Poets of America, 1993. Honours: Lincoln Memorial University Literary Hall of Fame, 1982; Teacher of the Year, 1991; Delta Kappa Gamma. Memberships: American Federation of Teachers; PETA. Address: Route, 2, Box 302, LaFollette, TN 37766, USA.

DAVIS Kenneth (Sidney), b. 29 Sept 1912, Salina, Kansas, USA. Journalist; Writer. m. Florence Marie Olenhouse, 19 Feb 1938, dec. Education: BS, Kansas State University; MA, University of Wisconsin. Appointments: Journalist; Assistant to Milton S Eisenhower, 1947-49; Personal Staff, Adlai Stevenson, 1955-56. Publications: In the Forests of the Night, 1942; Morning in Kansas, 1952; The Experience of War, 1965; Eisenhower: American Hero, 1969; FDR, 4 volumes, 1972-93; Invincible Summer: An Intimate

Portrait of the Roosevelts, 1974; A Sense of History, 1985. Honours: Friend of American Writers Award, 1943; Kansas Centennial Award, 1963; Francis Parkman Prize, 1973; Achievement Award, Kansas Authors Club, 1977. Address: 3330 Arrowhead Drive, Manhattan, KS 66502, USA.

DAVIS Margaret (Thomson), b. 24 May 1926, Bathgate, West Lothian, Scotland. Writer. Div, 1 son. Education: Albert Secondary Modern School, Glasgow. Publications: The Breadmakers, 1972; A Baby Might Be Crying, 1973; A Sort of Peace, 1973; The Prisoner, 1974; The Prince and the Tobacco Lords, 1976; Roots of Bondage, 1977; Scorpion in the Fire, 1977; The Dark Side of Pleasure, 1981; The Making of a Novelist, 1982; A Very Civilized Man, 1982; Light and Dark, 1984; Rag Woman, Rich Woman, 1987; Mothers and Daughters, 1988; Wounds of War, 1989; A Woman of Property, 1991; A Sense of Belonging, 1993; Hold Me Forever, 1994; Kiss Me No More, 1995; A Kind of Immortality, 1996. Contributions to: 200 short stories in various periodicals. Memberships: PEN; Scottish Labour History Society; Society of Authors. Address: c/o Heather Jeeves Literary Agency, 9 Dryden Place, Edinburgh, EH9 1RP, Scotland.

DAVIS Nathaniel, b. 12 Apr 1925, Boston, Massachusetts, USA. Diplomat (retired); Professor of Humanities. m. Elizabeth Kirkbride Creese, 24 Nov 1956, 2 sons, 2 daughters. Education: AB, Brown University, 1944; MA, 1947, PhD, 1960, Fletcher School of Law and Diplomacy: Cornell University, 1953; Russian Institute, Columbia University, 1953-54; Middlebury College, Vermont, 1954; Universidad Central de Venezuela, Caracas, 1961-62. Appointments: US Foreign Service: 3rd Secretary, Prague, 1947-49; Vice Consul, Florence, 1949-52; 2nd Secretary, Rome, 1952-53, Moscow, 1954-56; Soviet Desk Officer and Deputy Officer in Charge, USSR Affairs, 1956-60; 1st Secretary, Caracas, 1960-62; Special Assistant to the Director, 1962-63, Deputy Associate Director for Program Development and Operations, 1963-65, Peace Coprs; US Mᵃnister to Bulgaria, 1965-66; Senior Staff, National Security Council, 1966-68; US Ambassador to Guatemala, 1968-71, Chile, 1971-73, Switzerland, 1975-77; Director General, US Foreign Service, 1973-75; Assistant Secretary of State for African Affairs, 1975; State Department Advisor, US Naval War College, 1977-83; Teacher: Tufts College, 1947, University Branch, Centro Venezolano-Americano, 1961, Howard University, 1962-68, Salve Regina College, Newport, Rhode Island, 1981-82; Chester W Nimitz Chair of National Security and Foreign Affairs, US Naval War College, 1977-83; Alexander and Adelaide Hixon Chair, Harvey Mudd College and the faculty of Claremont Graduate School, California, 1983-. Publications: The Last Two Years of Salvador Allende, 1985, Spanish edition, 1986, Portuguese edition, 1990; A Long Walk to Church: A Contemporary History of Russian Orthodoxy, 1995. Contributions to: Books, newspapers, journals, and magazines. Honours: Honorary LLD, Brown University, 1970; Distinguished Public Service Award, US Navy, 1983. Memberships: American Academy of Diplomacy; American Foreign Service Association; Council on Foreign Relations. Address: c/o Harvey Mudd College, Claremont, CA 91711, USA.

DAVIS Sonia. See: **WILLIAMS Alberta Noring**.

DAVIS William, b . 6 Mar 1933. Author; Publisher; Broadcaster. m. Sylvette Jouclas, 1967. Appointments: Staff, Financial Times, 1954-59; Editor, Investor's Guide, 1959-60; City Editor, Evening Standard, 1960-65 (with one years break as City Editor, Sunday Express); Financial Editor, The Guardian, 1965-68; Editor, Punch, 1968-77; Editor, Publisher, High Life, 1973-; Chairman, Headway Publications, 1977-; Editorial Director, Executive World, 1980-; Moneycare, 1983-; Presenter, Money Programme, BBC TV, 1967-69; English Tourist Board, 1990-. Publications: Three Years Hard Labour: The Road to Devaluation, 1968; Merger Mania, 1970; Money Talks, 1972; Have Expenses Will Travel, 1975; It's No Sin To Be Rich, 1976; The Best of Everything (editor), 1980; Money in the 1980's, 1981; The Rich: A Study of the Species, 1982; Fantasy: A Practical Guide to Escapism, 1984; The Corporate Infighter's Handbook, 1984; The World's Best Business Hotels, (editor), 1985; Children of the Rich, 1989. Address: British Tourist Authority, Thames Tower, Black's Road, London W6 9EL, England.

DAVIS-FLOYD Robbie E(lizabeth), b. 26 Apr 1951, Casper, Wyoming, USA. Anthropologist; Writer. m. Robert N Floyd, 30 June 1978, 1 son, 1 daughter. Education: BA, 1972, MA, 1974, PhD, 1986, University of Texas, Austin. Appointments: Adjunct Assistant Professor, University of Tennessee, Chattanooga, 1980-83, Trinity

University, 1987-89; Lecturer, University of Texas, Austin, 1990-92; Visiting Lecturer, Rice University, 1993, 1996. Publications: Birth as an American Rite of Passage, 1992; Birth in Four Cultures (revised edition of Brigitte Jordan's 1978 book), 1993; Childbirth and Authoritative Knowledge: Cross-Cultural Perspectives (editor with Carolyn Sargent), 1997; Intuition: The Inside Story (editor with Sven Arvidson), 1997; From Doctor to Healer: Physicians in Transition (with Gloria St John), 1997; Cyborg Babies: From Techno-Sex to Techno-Tots (editor with Joseph Dumit), 1997; Intuition: Interdisciplinary Perspectives, (editor with Sven Arvidson), forthcoming. Contributions to: Books and journals. Honours: National Endowment for the Humanities Grant, 1980; Fetzer Institute Award, 1994; Institute of Noetic Sciences Grant, 1995; Wenner-Gren Foundation for Anthropological Research Grant, 1996. Memberships: American Anthropological Association; American Ethnological Society; American Holistic Medical Association; American Public Health Association; Association for Feminist Anthropology; Association for Pre- and Perinatal Psychology and Health; Council on Anthropology and Reproduction; Midwives' Alliance of North America; Social Neuroscience Network; Society for Applied Anthropology; Society for Medical Anthropology; Society for the Social Study of Science. Address: 1301 Capital of Texas Highway, B128, Austin, TX 78746, USA.

DAVIS-GARDNER Angela, b. 21 Apr 1942, Charlotte, North Carolina, USA. Writer; Professor. 1 son. Education: BA, Duke University, 1963; MFA, University of North Carolina at Greensboro, 1965. Publications: Felice, 1982; Forms of Shelter, 1991. Contributions to: Short stories in: Kansas Quarterly, Carolina Quarterly; Crescent Review; Greensboro Review; other literary quarterlies. Honours: Phi Beta Kappa, 1963; Artists Fellowship, North Carolina Arts Council, 1981-82; Sir Walter Raleigh Award, 1991; Best Novel by North Carolinian. Membership: Authors Guild, Poets and Writers. Address: Department of English, North Carolina State University, Box 8105, Raleigh, NC 27695-8105, USA.

DAVIS-GOFF Annabel Claire, b. 19 Feb 1942, Ireland. Writer. m. Mike Nichols, 1976, div 1987, 1 son, 1 daughter. Publications: Night Tennis, 1978; Tail Spin, 1980; Walled Gardens, 1989. Address: 1 West 67th Street, New York, NY 10023, USA.

DAVISON Geoffrey Joseph, b. 10 Aug 1927, Newcastle-upon-Tyne, England. m. Marlene Margaret Wilson, 15 Sept 1956, 2 sons. Education: TD; FRICS. Publications: The Spy Who Swapped Shoes, 1967; Nest of Spies, 1968; The Chessboard Spies, 1969; The Fallen Eagles, 1970; The Honorable Assassins, 1971; Spy Puppets, 1973; The Berlin Spy Trap, 1974; No Names on Their Graves, 1978; The Bloody Legionnaires, 1981. Membership: Pen and Palette Club. Address: 95 Cheviot View, Ponteland, Newcastle-upon-Tyne NE20 9BH, England.

DAWE (Donald) Bruce, b. 15 Feb 1930, Geelong, Victoria, Australia. Associate Professor; Poet; Writer. m. Gloria Desley Blain, 27 Jan 1964, 2 sons, 2 daughters. Education: BA, 1969, MA, 1975, PhD, 1980, University of Queensland. Appointments: Lecturer, 1971-78, Senior Lecturer, 1978-83, DDIAE; Writer-in-Residence, University of Queensland, 1984; Senior Lecturer, 1985-90, Associate Professor, 1990-93, School of Arts, Darling Heights, Toowoomba. Publications: No Fixed Address, 1962; A Need of Similar Name, 1964; Beyond the Subdivisions, 1968; An Eye for a Tooth, 1969; Heat-Wave, 1970; Condolences of the Season: Selected Poems, 1971; Just a Dugong at Twilight, 1974; Sometimes Gladness: Collected Poems, 1978, 4th edition, revised, 1993; Over Here Harv! and Other Stories, 1983; Towards Sunrise, 1986; This Side of Silence, 1990; Bruce Dawe: Essays and Opinions, 1990; Mortal Instruments: Poems 1990-1995, 1995. Contributions to: Various periodicals. Honours: Myer Poetry Prizes, 1966, 1969; Ampol Arts Award for Creative Literature, 1967; Dame Mary Gilmore Medal, Australian Literary Society, 1973; Braille Book of the Year, 1978; Grace Leven Prize for Poetry, 1978; Patrick White Literary Award, 1980; Christopher Brennan Award, 1984; Order of Australia, 1992; Distinguished Alumni Award, UNE, 1996. Memberships: Honorary Life Member, Australian Association for Teaching English; Centre for Australian Studies in Literature; Honorary Life Member, Victorian Association for Teaching of English. Address: 30 Cumming Street, Toowoomba, Queensland 4350, Australia.

DAWKINS (Clinton) Richard, b. 26 Mar 1941, England. Zoologist. m. 1 daughter. Education: MA, DPhil, DSc, Balliol College, Oxford. Assistant Professor of Zoology, University of California at Berkeley, 1967-69; Fellow, New College Oxford 1970-; Lecturer in

Zoology, 1970-89, Reader in Zoology, 1989-, Oxford University. Publications: The Selfish Gene, 1976, 2nd edition, 1989; The Extended Phenotype, 1982; The Blind Watchmaker, 1986; River Out of Eden, 1995. Honours: Michael Faraday Award, Royal Society, 1990; Nakayama Prize, 1994. Address: New College, Oxford OX1 3BN, England.

DAWSEY James Marshall, b. 12 Apr 1947, Spartanburg, SC, USA. Professor. m. Dixie Marie Preuss, 27 Aug 1971, 1 son, 1 daughter. Education: BS, Florida Southern College, 1970; MDiv, Emory University, 1973; PhD, Emory University, 1983. Appointments: Alumni Professor of Religion, Auburn University, 1992-94; Dean of Faculty, Emory & Henry College, 1994-. Publications: The Lukan Voice: Confusion and Irony in the Gospel of Luke, 1986; A Scholar's Guide to Academic Journals in Religion, 1988; Living Waters, 1989; From Wasteland to Promised Land, 1992. Contributions to: Annie Ayres Newman Ranson, 1995. Membership: de Diputadas, Congreso Nacional, Argentina, 1993. Address: Emory & Henry College, Emory, VA 24327, USA.

DAWSON Clay. See: **LEVINSON Leonard.**

DAWSON Jennifer, (Jenny Hinton, Jenny Sargesson), b. 23 Jan 1929, Hertfordshire, England. Writer. m. Michael Hinton, 2 Apr 1964. Education: St Anne's College, Oxford; University College, London. Publications: The Ha-Ha, 1961; Fowlers Snare, 1962; The Queen of Trent (with W Mitchell), 1962; The Cold Country, 1965; Strawberry Boy, 1976; Hospital Wedding, 1978; A Field of Scarlet Poppies, 1979; The Upstairs People, 1988; Judasland, 1989; The Flying Gardens, 1993. Poems in: Ambit. Honours: James Tait Black Award, 1961; Cheltenham Festival Award, 1962; Fawcett Society Fiction Award, 1990. Address: 6 Fisher Lane, Charlbury, Oxon OX7 3RX, England.

DAWSON Jill Dianne, b. 1962. Writer; Editor. 1 son. Education: BA, American Studies, University of Nottingham, 1980-83; MA, Sheffield Hallam University, 1993-95; Literature Development Worker, Eastside, London, 1994-. Appointments: Writer in Residence, Doncaster; Fareham College, Hampshire; Tutor of Creative Writing. Publications: Editor of: School Tales, 1990; How Do I Look? (non-fiction), 1991; Virago Book of Wicked Verse, 1992; The Virago Book of Love Letters, 1994; White Fish With Painted Nails (poetry), 1994; Trick of the Light, 1996. Contributions to: Anthologies; Periodicals. Honours: Major E Gregory Award; 2nd Prize, London Writers Short Story Competition, 1994; Blue Nose Poet of the Year, 1995. Memberships: Society of Authors; Poetry Society; National Association of Writers in Education. Address: 38 Lockhurst Street, London E5 0AP, England.

DAY Sir Robin , b . 24 Oct 1923, London, England. TV and Radio Journalist. m. Katherine Mary Ainslie, 1965, div 1986, 2 sons. Education: Oxford University. Appointments: President, Oxford Union, 1950; Called to the Bar, 1952; BBC Radio Journalist, 1954-55; Independent TV News Newscaster and Political Correspondent, 1955-59; BBC TV Political Interviewer and Reporter, 1959-89; BBC Radio World at One Presenter, 1979-. Publications: Television - A Personal Report, 1961; The Case for Television Parliament, 1968; Troubled Reflections of a TV Journalist, 1970; Day by Day, 1975; Grand Inquisitor (autobiography), 1989; But With Respect (political interviews), 1993. Honours: Richard Dimbleby Award, 1974; Broadcasting Press Guild Award (for Question Time), 1980; Knighted, 1981; RTS Judges Award for 30 years TV Journalism, 1985; Hon LLD, Exeter, 1986 and Keele, 1988; Hon DU, Essex, 1988; Hon Bencher Middle Temple, 1990. Memberships: Phillimore Committee on Law of Contempt, 1971-74; Chairman, Hansard Society for Parliamentary Government, 1981-83. Address: c/o Capron Productions, Gardiner House, Broomhill Road, London SW18 4JQ, England.

DAY Stacey (Biswas), b. 31 Dec 1927, London, England. Physician; Writer; Poet; Editor. m. Ivana Podvalova, 23 Oct 1973, 2 sons. Education: MD, Dublin, 1955; PhD, McGill University, Montreal, 1964; DSc, University of Cincinnati, 1970. Appointments: Editor-in-Chief, Biosciences Communications and Health Communications; Consulting Editor. Publications: Editor of over 30 medical and scientific books; Author of 15 literary books. Contributions to: Numerous journals and magazines. Honours: Various medical distinctions and communications awards. Memberships: Many professional organizations. Address: 6 Lomond Avenue, Spring Valley, NY 10977, USA.

DE ARAUGO Sarah Therese (Tess), b.26 May 1930, Lismore, Victoria, Australia. Writer. m. Maurice De Araugo, 11 Apr 1950, 2 sons, 2 daughters. Education: Notre Dame de Sion College, Warragal, Victoria. Publications: You Are What You Make Yourself To Be, 1980, revised edition, 1989; The Kurnai of Gippsland, 1985; Boonorong on the Mornington Peninsula, 1993. Contributions to: Encyclopaedias and periodicals. Honours: New South Wales Premier's Award for Australian Literature, 1985; Banjo Award, Australian Literature, National Book Council, 1985; Fellowship, 1987, Writer's Grant, 1989, Australian Literature Board; Short Story Award, PEN International, Australia, 1991. Memberships: Australian Society of Authors; Fellowship of Australian Writers; Royal Historical Society of Victoria; Women Writers of Australia; Nepean Historical Society. Address: 19 Grenville Grove, Rosebud West, Victoria 3940, Australia.

DE BELSER Raymond Charles Maria, (Ward Ruyslinck), b. 17 Jun 1929, Antwerp, Belgium. Retired Librarian; Author. m. (1), 1 son, (2) Monika Macken, 18 Dec 1992. Publications: De ontaarde slapers, 1957, as The Deadbeats, 1968; Wierook en tranen, 1958; Het dal van Hinnom, 1961; Het reservaat, 1964 as The Reservation, 1978; Golden Ophelia, 1966; De heksenkring, 1972; Het ganzenbord, 1974; Wurgtechnieken, 1980; Leegstaande huizen, 1983; De uilen van Minerva, 1985; Stille waters, 1987; Ljlings naar nergens, 1989. Contributions to: Periodicals. Honours: Ark Prize for Free Speech, 1960; Flemish Reader Award, 1964; Prize for Literature of the Flemish Provinces, 1967; Europalia Prize for Literature, 1980. Membership: Royal Flemish Academy of Language and Literature, Ex-Chairman. Address: Potaardestraat 25, 1860 Meise, Belgium.

DE BERNIERE-SMART Louis Henry Piers, (Louis de Bernieres), b . 8 Dec 1954, Woolwich, London, England. Novelist. Education: Bradfield College, Berkshire; BA, Manchester University, BA; MA, Leicester Polytechnic and University of London. Publications: The War of Don Emmanuels Nether Parts; Senior Vivo & The Coea Lord; The Troublesome Offspring of Cardinal Guzman; Captain Corelli's Mandolin. Contributions to: Second Thoughts and Granta. Honours: Commonwealth Writers Prizes, 1991, 1992, 1995; Best of Young British Novelists, 1993; Lannan Award, 1995. Memberships: PEN. Address: c/o Secker and Warburg, Michelin House, 81 Fulham Road, London SW3 6RB, England.

DE BERNIERES Louis. See: **DE BERNIERE-SMART Louis Henry Piers.**

DE BLASIS Celeste Ninette, b. 8 May 1946, California, USA. Writer. Education: Wellesley College, 1964-65; Oregon State University, 1965-66; BA cum laude, English, Pomona College, 1968. Publications: The Night Child, 1975; Suffer a Sea Change, 1976; The Proud Breed, 1978; The Tiger's Woman, 1981; Wild Swan, 1984; Swan's Chance, 1985; A Season of Swans, 1989; Graveyard Peaches: A California Memoir, 1991. Contributions to: Writers Digest. Memberships: Authors Guild; Novelists Inc; Nature Conservancy; California State Library Foundation. Address: c/o Witherspoon Associates Inc, 157 West 57th Street, Suite 700, New York, NY 10019, USA.

DE BOISSIERE Ralph (Anthony Charles), b. 6 Oct 1907, Port-of-Spain, Trinidad (Australian citizen, 1970). Novelist. m. Ivy Alcantara, 1935, 2 daughters. Appointments: Freelance Writer, 1955-60. Publications: Crown Jewel, 1952; Rum and Coca-Cola, 1956; No Saddles for Kangaroos, 1964; Uncollected short stories: Booze and the Goberdaw, 1979; The Woman on the Pavement, 1979; Play: Calypso Isle, 1955. Literary Agent: Reinhard Sander, Department of Black Studies, Amherst College, Amherst, MA 01002, USA. Address: 10 Vega Street, North Balwyn, Victoria 3104, Australia.

DE BONO Edward (Francis Charles Publius), b. 19 May 1933, Malta. Author; Physician; Inventor; Lecturer. m. Josephine Hall-White, 1971, 2 sons. Education: St Edward's College, Malta; BSc 1953, MD, 1955, Royal University of Malta; MA, 1957, DPhil, 1961, Oxford University; PhD, Cambridge University, 1963. Appointments: Research Assistant, 1957-60, Lecturer, 1960-61, Oxford University; Assistant Director of Research, 1963-76, Lecturer in Medicine, 1976-83, Cambridge University; Honorary Director and Founding Member, Cognitive Research Trust, 1971-; Secretary-General, Supranational Independent Thinking Organisation, 1983-; Lecturer. Publications: Opportunities: A Handbook of Business Opportunity Search, 1978; The Happiness Purpose, 1978; Future Positive, 1979; Atlas of Management Thinking, 1981; De Bono's Thinking Course, 1982; Learn to Think, 1982; Tactics: The Art and Science of Success, 1984; Conflicts: A Better Way to Resolve Them, 1985; Six Thinking Hats: An Essential Approach to Business Management from the Creator of Lateral Thinking, 1985; CoRT Thinking Program: CoRT 1-Breadth, 1987; Letters to Thinkers: Further Thoughts on Lateral Thinking, 1987; Masterthinker II: Six Thinking Hats, 1988; Masterthinker, 1990; Masterthinker's Handbook, 1990; Thinking Skills for Success, 1990; I Am Right, You Are Wrong: From This to the New Renaissance: From Rock Logic to Water Logic, 1990; Handbook for the Positive Revolution, 1991; Six Action Shoes, 1991; Serious Creativity: Using the Power of Lateral Thinking to Create New Ideas, 1992; Surpetition: Creating Value Monopolies When Everyone Else is Merely Competing, 1992; Teach Your Child How to Think, 1993. Contributions to: Television series, professional journals, and periodicals. Honour: Rhodes Scholar. Membership: Medical Research Society. Address: 12 Albany, Piccadilly, London W1V 9RR, England.

DE BRISSAC. See: **DOBSON Rosemary.**

DE CADAVAL Rudy. See: **CAMPEDELLI Giancarlo.**

DE CAMP L(yon) Sprague, b. 27 Nov 1907, New York, New York, USA. Writer; Poet. m. Catherine Adelaide Crook, 12 Aug 1939, 2 sons. Education: BS, Aeronautical Engineering, California Institute of Technology, 1930; MS, Engineering and Economics, Stevens Institute of Technology, 1933. Publications: Over 130 books, including science fiction, fantasy, historical novels, history, biography, textbooks and juvenile, among others. Contributions to: Numerous stories, articles and poems in anthologies, periodicals and other publications. Honours: International Fantasy Award, 1953; Grandmaster Fantasy Award, 1976; Nebula Award, Science Fiction Writers of America, 1978; World Fantasy Conference Award, 1984. Memberships: Authors Guild; History of Science Society; Science Fiction and Fantasy Writers of America; Society for the History of Technology. Address: 3453 Hearst Castle Way, Plano, TX 75025, USA.

DE CRESPIGNY (Richard) Rafe (Champion), b. 16 Mar 1936, Adelaide, South Australia, Australia. m. Christa Charlotte Boltz, 1 son, 1 daughter. Education: BA, 1957, Ma, 1961, Cambridge University; BA, University of Melbourne, 1961; BA, 1962, MA, 1964, PhD, 1957, Australian National University. Appointments: Lecturer 1964-70, Senior Lecturer, 1970-73, Reader in Chinese 1973-, Australian National University, Canberra; Master, University House, 1991-. Publications: The Biography of Sun Chien, 1966; Official Titles of the Former Han Dynasty (with H H Dubs), 1967; The Last of the Han, 1969; The Records of the Three Kingdoms, 1970; China: The Land and Its People, 1971; China This Century: A History of Modern China, 1975, 2nd edition, 1992; Portents of Protest, 1976; Northern Frontier, 1984; Emperor Huan and Emperor Ling, 1989; Generals of the South, 1990; To Establish Peace, 1996. Membership: Fellow, Australian Academy of the Humanities. Address: 5 Rous Crescent, Forrest, ACT 2603, Australia.

DE GRAZIA Sebastien, b. 11 Aug 1917, Chicago, USA. Political Philosopher. m. (1) Miriam Lund Carlson, 1 son, 2 daughters, (2) Anna Maria d'Annunzio di Montenevoso, 2 sons, (3) Lucia Heffelfinger. Education: AB, University of Chicago, 1939; PhD, 1947; With FCC, 1941-43; OSS, 1943-45. Appointments: Faculty of University Chicago, 1945-50; Consultant, business firms, state and US Government, 1947-; Director, research study time, work and leisure, Twentieth Century Fund, 1957-61; Professor, Political Philosophy, Rutgers University, 1962-88; Visiting Professor, University of Florence, Italy, 1950-52, Princeton University, 1957, 1991-92, University of Madrid, 1963, John Jay College of Criminal Justice, 1967-71, Institute of Advanced Study, Princeton, 1983. Publications: The Political Community, 1948; Errors of Psychotherapy, 1953; Of Time, Work and Leisure, 1962; Masters of Chinese Political Thought, 1973; Machiavelli in Hell, 1989. Honours: Pulitzer Prize for biography, for Machiavelli in Hell, 1990; Grantee, American Philosophy Society. Memberships: Research council, American Council of Learned Societies; Member, American Political Science Association; American Society of Political and Legal Philosophy; Institut International de Philosophie Politique. Address: 914 Great Road, Princeton, NJ 08540-1205, USA.

DE GUISE Elizabeth (Mary Teresa), (Isobel Chase, Elizabeth Hunter), b . 1934, Nairobi, Kenya. Education: Open University. Appointments: Landholder in Kent, England, 1952-58; English Teacher to Arabic Students in Folkestone, England, 1958-62; Writer 1960-. Publications: Romance Novels under the pseudonym Elizabeth Hunter:

Fountains of Paradise, 1983; London Pride, 1983; Shared Destiny, 1983; A Silver Nutmeg, 1983; Kiss of the Rising Sun, 1984; Rain on the Wind, 1984; Song of Surrender, 1984; A Tower of Strength, 1984; A Time to Wed, 1984; Loving Relations, 1984; Eye of the Wind, 1985; Legend of the Sun, 1985; The Painted Veil, 1986; The Tides of Love, 1988. Romance Novels under the pseudonym Isobel Chase: The House of Scissors, 1972; The Dragon's Cave, 1972; The Edge of Beyond, 1973; A Man of Kent, 1973; The Elban Adventure, 1974; The Cornish Hearth, 1975; A Canopy of Rose Leaves, 1976; The Clouded Veil, 1976; The Desert Castle, 1976; Singing in the Wilderness, 1976; The Whistling Thorn, 1977; The Mouth of Truth, 1977; Second Best Wife, 1978; Undesirable Wife, 1978. Historical Novels under the name Elizabeth De Guise: Dance of the Peacocks, 1988; Flight of the Dragonfly, 1990; Came Forth the Sun, 1991; Bridge of Sighs, 1992. Contributions to: Women & Home; Woman's Weekly. Memberships: Campaign for Nuclear Disarmament; Pax Christi; Romantic Novelists Association. Literary Agent: June Hall Literary Agents Ltd, 504 The Chambers, Chelsea Harbour, London SW10 0XF. Address: 113 Nun Street, St Davids, Haverfordwest, Dyfed SA62 6BP, Wales.

DE JONGE Alex, b . 1938, England. University Fellow and Tutor; Writer. Appointments: Fellow and Tutor, New College, Oxford, 1965-. Publications: Nineteenth Century Russian Literature (with others), 1973; Nightmare Culture, Lautreamont and Les Chants de Maldoror, 1973; Dostoevsky and the Age of Intensity, 1975; Prince of Clouds: A Biography of Baudelaire, 1976; The Weimar Chronicle: A Prelude to History, 1977; Napoleon's Last Will and Testament, 1977; Fire and Water: A Life of Peter the Great, 1979; The Life and Times of Grigorii Rasputin, 1982; Stalin and the Shaping of the Soviet Union, 1986. Address: New College, Oxford, England.

DE LANGE Nicholas (Robert Michael), b. 7 Aug 1944, Nottingham, England. Scholar; Translator. Education: MA, 1969, DPhil, 1970, Christ Church, Oxford. Publications: Apocrypha, 1978; Atlas of the Jewish World, 1984; Judaism, 1986. Other: Many translations. Contributions to: Tel Aviv Review. Honour: George Webber Prize for Translation, 1990. Memberships: British Association of Jewish Studies; Society of Authors; Translators Association; Fellow, Wolfson College, Cambridge. Address: The Divinity School, St John's Street, Cambridge,, CB2 1TW, England.

DE LAPLANTE Jean, b. 29 Sept 1919, Montreal, Quebec, Canada. Writer; Journalist; Social Researcher. m. Fernande Lachance, 29 Dec 1941, 1 son, 1 daughter. Publications: La Communauté Montréalaise, 1952; Le Petit Juif (novel), 1962; Les Parcs de Montréal (essay), 1990. Contributions to: Journals and newspapers. Membership: Union des Ecrivains du Quebec. Address: 10360 Tolhurst, Montreal, Quebec H3L 3A3, Canada.

DE LINT Charles (Henri Diederick Hoefsmit), b. 22 Dec 1951, Bussum, Netherlands (Canadian citizen, 1961). Editor; Writer; Poet. m. Mary Ann Harris, 15 Sept 1980. Appointments: Owner-Editor, Triskell Press; Writer-in-Residence, Ottawa and Gloucester Public Libraries, 1995. Publications: Drink Down the Moon: A Novel of Urban Faerie, 1990; Death Leaves an Echo, 1991; Dreaming Place, 1992; From a Whisper to a Scream, 1992; Dreams Underfoot: The Newford Collection, 1993; Memory and Dream, 1994; The Ivory and the Horn, 1995. Contributions to: Anthologies and periodicals. Honours: Various awards. Memberships: Horror Writers of America, vice-president, 1992-93; Science Fiction Writers of America; Small Press Writers and Artists Organization. Literary Agent: Jimmy Vines, The Vines Agency, 409 East 6th Street, No 4, New York, NY 10009, USA. Address: PO Box 9480, Ottawa, Ontario K1G 3V2, Canada.

DE MEDICI Lorenza, b. 17 July 1926, Milan, Italy. Foodwriter. m. Piero Stucchi Prinetti, 18 Apr 1953, 3 sons, 1 daughter. Education: University Degree in Italy, Italian Literature, 1948. Publications: Italy: The Beautiful Cookbook; The Renaissance of Italian Cooking; The Heritage of Italian Cooking; The De'Medici Kitchen; The Villa Table; Others: Great Dessert. Contributions to: Food and Wine; Gardenia; Vogue Italy. Honour: Brillat Savarin, Paris, for the Heritage of Italian Cooking, 1991. Address: Badia A Coltibuono, 53013 Gaiole, Chianti, Siena, Italy.

DE MILLE Nelson. See: **LEVINSON Leonard.**

DE NATALE Francine. See: **MALZBERG Barry.**

DE NEVERS Marguerite. See: **BOISVERT France.**

DE PRE Jean-Anne. See: **AVALLONE Michael (Angelo Jr).**

DE QUIROS Beltran. See: **ROMEU Jorge Luis.**

DE REGNIERS Beatrice (Schenk), (Tamara Kitt), b. 16 Aug 1914, Lafayette, Indiana, USA. Children's Writer, Poet and Playwright. Education: University of Illinois, 1931-33; PhD, 1935, Graduate Studies, 1936-37, University of Chicago; MEd, Winnetka Graduate Teachers College, 1941. Appointments: Director, Educational Materials, American Heart Association, New York City, 1949-61; Editor, Lucky Book Club, Scholastic Inc, New York City, 1961-81. Publications: Over 50 children's books. Memberships: Authors Guild; Dramatists Guild; PEN; Society of Children's Book Writers and Illustrators. Literary Agent: Marian Reiner, 20 Cedar Street, New Rochelle, NY 10801, USA. Address: 4530 Connecticut Avenue North West, Apartment 302, Washington, DC 20008-4311, USA.

DE ROO Anne (Louise), b . 1931, Gore, New Zealand. Children's Fiction Writer. Education: BA, University of Canterbury, Christchurch, 1952. Appointments: Library Assistant, Dunedin Public Library, 1956; Assistant Librarian, Dunedin Teachers College, 1957-59; Governess, Part-time Gardener, Shropshire, England, 1962-68; Part-time Secretary, Hertfordshire, England, 1969-73. Publications: The Gold Dog, 1969; Moa Valley, 1969; Boy and the Sea Beast, 1971; Cinnamon and Nutmeg, 1972; Mick's Country Cousins, 1974; Scrub Fire, 1977; Traveller, 1979; Because of Rosie, 1980; Jack Nobody, 1984; Friend Troll, Friend Taniwha, 1986; The Bat's Nest, 1986. Address: 38 Joseph Street, Palmerston North, New Zealand.

DE SOUZA Eunice, b. 1 Aug 1940, Poona, India. Lecturer; Poet. Education: BA, University of Bombay, 1960; PhD, 1988. Appointments: Lecturer, Head, Department of English, St Xaviers College, Bombay, 1990. Publications: Fix, 1979; Women in Dutch Painting, 1988; Ways of Belonging: Selected Poems, 1990; For Children: All About Birbal, 1969; Himalayan Tales, 1973; More About Birbal; Tales of Birbal; Statements: An Anthology of Indian Prose in English (co-editor); Selected and New Poems, (editor, Keith Fernandes), 1994. Honour: Poetry Book Society Recommendation, 1990. Address: St Xaviers College, Bombay 400 001 India.

DE VRIES-EVANS Susanna Mary, (Susanna Devries), b. 6 Oct 1935. Author; Lecturer in Art History. m. Jake de Vries, 25 July 1982. Education: Cours de Civilisation Francaise, Sorbonne, University of Paris, 1953; Universidad Menendez Pelayo, Santander, Spain, 1954; Complutense University, Madrid. Appointments: Lecturer, Continuing Education Department, University of Queensland, 1991. Publications: Historic Sydney: Its Early Artists, 1982, 2nd edition, 1987; Pioneer Women, Pioneer Land, 1988; The Impressionists Revealed: Masterpieces and Collectors, 1982, 2nd edition 1994; Conrad Martens on the Beagle; Strength of Spirit: Pioneering Women of Achievement from the First Fleet to Federation. Contributions to: The Australian Newspaper (Arts Section) Australian Collector Magazine. Honours: Fellowship, Literary Board, Australia Council, 1990; Winston Churchill Fellowship, Arts History, 1994. Memberships: Lyceum Club, Brisbane; Australian Society of Authors. Literary Agent: Selwa Anthony, 10 Loves Avenue, Oyster Bay, New South Wales 2225, Australia. Address: 10 Matingara Street, Chapel Hill, Brisbane 4069, Australia.

DE WEESE Thomas Eugene "Gene", (Jean DeWeese, Thomas Stratton, Victoria Thomas), b. 31 Jan 1934, Rochester, Indiana, USA. Writer. m. Beverly Amers, 1955. Education: Associate Degree, Electronic Engineering, Valparaiso Technical Institute, Indiana, 1953; Indiana University, Kokomo; University of Wisconsin, Milwaukee; Marquette University, Milwaukee. Appointments: Electronics Technician, Delco Radio, Kokomo, 1954-59; Technical Writer, Delco Electronics, Milwaukee, 1959-74. Publications: Fiction: Jeremy Case, 1976; The Wanting Factor, 1980; A Different Darkness, 1982; Something Answered, 1983; Chain of Attack, 1987; The Peacekeepers, 1988; The Final Nexus, 1988; Renegade, 1991; Into the Nebula, 1995; King of the Dead, 1996; Lord of the Necropolis, 1997. (Wth Robert Coulson): The Invisibility Affair, 1967; The Mind-Twisters Affair, 1967; Gates of the Universe, 1975; Now You See It/Him/Them..., 1976; Charles Fort Never Mentioned Wombats, 1977; Nightmare Universe, 1985.(As Jean DeWeese): The Reimann Curse, 1975; The Moonstone Spirit, 1975; The Carnelian Cat, 1975; Cave of the Moaning Wind, 1976; Web of Guilt, 1976; The Doll With Opal Eyes, 1976; Nightmare in Pewter, 1978; Hour of the Cat, 1980; The Backhoe Gothic, 1981. (As Victoria Thomas): Ginger's Wish (with Connie Kugi), 1987. Other: Black Suits From Outer Space; Several other science

fiction novels for juveniles. Non-fiction: Fundamentals of Space Navigation, 1968; Fundamentals of Digital Computers, 1972; Fundamentals of Integrated Circuits, 1972; Making American Folk Art Dolls (with Gini Rogowski), 1975; Computers in Entertainment and the Arts, 1984. Contributions to: Anthologies and magazines. Honours: Best Novel Awards, 1976, 1982, Best Juvenile Book Award, 1979, Council for Wisconsin Writers; Notable Science Book of the Year, NSTA, 1984. Address: 2718 North Prospect, Milwaukee, WI 53211, USA.

DE'ATH Richard. See: **HAINING Peter Alexander.**

DEANE Dorothy. See: **CATCHAPAW Dorothy Deane Johnson.**

DEANE Seamus Francis, b. 9 Feb 1940, Ireland. Professor of English and American Literature; Writer. m. Marion Treacy, 1963, 3 sons, 1 daughter. Education: Queens University, Belfast; Cambridge University; Fulbright and Woodrow Wilson Scholar. Appointments: Visiting Lecturer, Reed College, Portland, Oregon, 1966-67, University of California at Berkeley, 1967-68, Visiting Professor, 1978; Lecturer, 1968-77, Senior Lecturer, 1978-80, Professor of English and American Literature, 1980, University College, Dublin; Visiting Professor, University of Notre Dame, Indiana, 1977; Director, Field Day Theatre Company, 1980-; Walker Ames Professor, University of Washington, Seattle, 1987; Jules Benedict Distinguished Visiting Professor, Carleton College. Publications: Celtic Revivals, 1985; Short History of Irish Literature, 1986; Selected Poems, 1988; The French Revolution and Enlightenment in England 1789-1832, 1988; Field Day Anthology of Irish Writing 550-1990, 1991; Reading in the Dark, 1996; Strange Country, 1997. Honours: AE Memorial Award for Literature, 1972; Ireland/America Fund Literary Award, 1988; Guardian Fiction Prize, 1996; South Bank Show Award for Literature, 1997. Membership: Royal Irish Academy, 1982. Address: c/o Department of English, University of Notre Dame, Notre Dame, IN 46556, USA.

DEAR Nick, b. 11 June 1955, Portsmouth, England. Playwright. Partner: Penny Downie, 2 sons. Education: BA, Hons, European Literature, University of Essex, 1977. Appointments: Playwright in Residence, Essex University, 1985, Royal Exchange Theatre, 1987-88. Publications: Temptation, 1984; The Art of Success, 1986; Food of Love, 1988; A Family Affair (after Ostrovsky), 1988; In the Ruins, 1989; The Last Days of Don Juan (after Tirso), 1990; Le Bourgeois Gentilhomme (after Molière), 1992; Pure Science, 1994; Zenobia, 1995; Opera Libretti: A Family Affair, 1993; Siren Song, 1994; Several plays for radio; Films: The Monkey Parade, 1983; The Ranter, 1988; Persuasion, 1995. Honours: John Whiting Award, 1987; Olivier Award nominations, 1987, 1988; BAFTA Award, 1996; Broadcasting Press Guild Award, 1996. Membership: Writer's Guild of Great Britain. Address: c/o Rosica Colin Ltd, 1 Clareville Grove Mews, London SW7 5AH, England.

DEARDEN James Shackley, b. 9 Aug 1931, Barrow-in-Furness, England. Curator. Appointment: Curator, Ruskin Galleries, Bembridge School, Isle of Wight, 1957-. Publications: The Professor: Arthur Severn's Memoir of Ruskin, 1967; A Short History of Brantwood, 1967; Iteriad by John Ruskin (editor), 1969; Facets of Ruskin, 1970; Ruskin and Coniston (with K G Thorne), 1971; John Ruskin, 1973, 1981; Turner's Isle of Wight Sketch Book, 1979; John Ruskin and Les Alpi, 1989; John Ruskin's Camberwell, 1990; A Tour to the Lakes in Cumberland, John Ruskin's Diary for 1830 (editor), 1990; John Ruskin and Victorian Art, 1993; Ruskin, Bembridge and Brantwood, 1994; Hare Hunting on the Isle of Wight, 1996. Contributions to: Book Collector; Connoisseur; Apollo; Burlington; Bulletin of John Rylands Library; Country Life; Ruskin Newsletter (editor); Ruskin Research Series (general editor); Journal of Pre-Raphaelite Studies (editorial advisory board); Whitehouse Edition of Ruskin's Works (joint general editor). Memberships: Ruskin Association, Secretary and Treasurer; Turner Society; Companion of the Guild of St George, Director for Ruskin Affairs; Old Bembridgians Association (Past President); Isle of Wight Foot Beagles, Vice President, past Chairman and Master; Friends of Ruskin's Brantwood, Vice President. Address: 4 Woodlands, Foreland Road, Bembridge, Isle of Wight, England.

DEBONIS Steven Larry, b. 10 Jan 1949, Brooklyn, New York, USA. Writer; Teacher. m. Laurie Kuntz, 1 son. Education: BA Psychology, University of Connecticut, 1971. Publication: Children of the Enemy: Oral Histories of Vietnamese Amerasians and their

Mothers, 1995. Address: 1-28, 2 chome Hirahata, Misawa-shi, Aomori-ken 033, Japan.

DeCLEMENTS Barthe, b. 8 Oct 1920, Seattle, Washington, USA. Writer. m. (1) Don Macri, div, (2) Gordon Greimes, div, 4 children. Education: Western Washington College, 1940-42; BA 1944, MEd 1970, University of Washington, Seattle. Appointments: Schoolteacher, 1944-46, 1961-78; High School Counselor, 1978-83. Publications: Nothing's Fair in Fifth Grade, 1981; How Do You Lose Those Ninth Grade Blues?, 1983; Seventeen and In-Between, 1984; Sixth Grade Can Really Kill You, 1985; I Never Asked You to Understand Me, 1986; Double Trouble (with Christopher Greimes), 1987; No Place For Me, 1987; The Fourth Grade Wizards, 1988; Five-Finger Discount, 1989; Monkey See, Monkey Do, 1990; Wake Me At Midnight, 1991; Breaking Out, 1991; The Bite of the Gold Bug, 1992; The Pickle Song, 1993; Tough Loser, 1994. Contributions to: Periodicals. Honours: Over 25 awards. Address: c/o Viking Penguin, 375 Hudson Street, New York, NY 10014, USA.

DEFORD Frank, b. 16 Dec 1938, Baltimore, Maryland, USA. Writer; Editor. m. Carol Penner, 28 Aug 1965, 1 son, 2 daughters. Education: BA, Princeton University, 1962. Appointments: Writer, Sports Illustrated, 1962-89; Commentator, Cable News Network, 1980-86, National Public Radio, 1980-89, 1991-, NBC, 1986-89; ESPN, 1992-; Editor-in-Chief, The National, 1989-91; Writer, Newsweek Magazine, 1991-93, 1996-; Contributing Editor, Vanity Fair, 1993-96. Publications: Five Strides on the Banked Track, 1969; Cut'N'Run, 1971; There She Is, 1972; The Owner, 1974; Big Bill Tilden: The Triumphs and the Tragedy, 1977; Everybody's All-American, 1981; Alex: The Life of a Child, 1982; Spy in the Deuce Court, 1987; World's Tallest Midget, 1988; Casey on the Loose, 1989; Love and Infamy, 1993. Contributions to: Numerous magazines. Honours: Sportswriter of the Year, National Association of Sportswriters and Sportscasters, 1982-88; Emmy, 1988; Cable Ace, 1996. Literary Agent: Sterling Lord, Sterling Lord Literistic, 65 Bleecker Street, New York, NY 10012, USA. Address: Box 1109, Greens Farms, CT 06436, USA.

DEGTJARJEVA Natalia Ivanovna, b. 6 Aug 1949, Krasny Sulin, Rostov Region, Russia. Musicologist. m. Tchumatchenko Georgy Viktorovitch, 21 June 1977, 1 son. Education: St Petersburg State Conservatoire, Graduated 1973; Postgraduate Study, St Petersburg Conservatoire, 1976; Candidate of Science Diploma, 1981; Assistant Professor Certificate, 1991; Assistant Professor, Department of Foreign Music, St Petersburg Conservatoire. Appointment: Associate Professor, Department of Foreign Music, St Petersburg Conservatoire. Publications: Symphonic Conception of Mahler's Later Work, 1977; Mahler's 8th Symphony, 1981; Gustav Mahler's Later Work, Philosophical and Aesthetic Features of Symphonic Conception, 1981; Asafjev B V about Austrian-German Symphonism of XIX-XX Century, 1987; Russian Conception of Mozart and Russian Musical Culture, 1991; Anatoli Nikitin - Musician and Teacher, 1996. Contributions to: Living Document of the Epoch, 1986. Address: Vosnessensky av 37 apt 65, 190068 St Petersburg, Russia.

DEGUY Michel, b. 23 May 1930, Paris, France. Poet. Education: University of Paris. Appointment: President, Maison des Écrivains, Paris; University Professor, Paris. Publications: Les Meurtrières, 1959; Fragments du cadastre, 1960; Poèmes de la Presqu'ile, 1961; Biefs, 1964; Oui-dire, 1966; Figurations, 1969; Poèmes 1960-1970, 1973; Jumelages; Made in USA, 1978; Given Giving: Selected Poems, 1984; Gisants, 1985; Poèmes II: 1970-1980, 1986; Arrêts frequents, 1990; Also: Le Monde de Thomas Mann, 1962; Reliefs, 1975; Brevets, 1986; La poésie n'est pas seule, 1988; Aux Heures d'affluence, 1991; Axiomatique rosace, 1991; Un Poleoscope, 1991; A ce qui n'en finit pas, 1995. Honour: Poetry Prize, 1989. Address: 26 rue Las-Cases, Paris 75007, France.

DEIGHTON Len (Leonard Cyril Deighton), b. 18 Feb 1929, London, England. Writer. Education: Marylebone Grammer School; Royal College of Art, 1952-55. Publications: The Ipcress File, 1962; Horse Under Water, 1963; Funeral in Berlin, 1964; Action Cook Book: Len Deighton's Guide To Eating (in US as Cookstrip Cook Book), 1965; Ou est le Garlic: Len Deighton's French Cook Book, 1965, revised edition as Basic French Cooking, 1978; The Billion Dollar Brain, 1966; An Expensive Place to Die, 1967; London Dossier, (editor), 1967; The Assassination of President Kennedy (co-author) 1967; Only When I Larf, 1968; Len Deighton's Continental Dossier: A Collection of Cultural Culinary, Historical, Spooky, Grim and Preposterous Facts, 1968; Bomber, 1970; Declarations of War (stories), 1971; Close-Up, 1972; Spy Story, 1974; Yesterday's Spy, 1975; Twinkle, Twinkle, Little Spy, 1976; Fighter: The True Story of the Battle of Britain, 1977; SS-GB, 1978; Airshipwreck (with Arnold Schwartsman), 1978; Blitzkrieg: From the Rise of Hitler to the Fall of Dunkirk, 1979; Battle of Britain, 1980; XPD 1981; Goodbye Mickey Mouse, 1982; Berlin Game, 1983; Mexico Set, 1984; London Match, 1985; Spy Hook, 1988; Spy Line, 1989; ABC of French Food, 1989; Spy Sinker, 1990; Basic French Cookery Course, 1990; MAMista, 1991; City of Gold, 1992; Violent Ward, 1993; Blood, Tears and Folly, 1993; Faith, 1994; Hope, 1995; Charity, 1996. Address: c/o Jonathon Clowes Ltd, 10 Iron Bridge House, Bridge Approach, London NW1 8BD, England.

DEIMER Lorena Ruth, b. 11 Jan 1926, Thermopolis, Wyoming, USA. Freelance Writer. m. (1) 1946, (2) Marshall F Deimer, 21 Feb 1959, 1 son, 1 daughter. Education: Casper Junior College; International Aurora Community College. Publications: Magnolia Blossoms; Poetry: Golden Voices Past and Present, 1989; World Treasury of Great Poems, 1989; Great Poems of the Western World, Vol 11, 1989; Today's Poets, 1989; Misty and Me, 1991; The Write Technique, 1991. Contributions to: Periodicals. Honours: Golden Poet Awards, 1987, 1988, 1989. Memberships: National Wirters Club; Fictional Group, Denver Chapter, Genealogical Club; Baptist Youth Fellowship Group, President, 1944. Literary Agent: James Lee Young, National Writers Club. Address: 1164 Macon Street, Aurora, CO 80010, USA.

DEJEVSKY Nikolai James, b. 22 Sep 1945, Hanau, Germany. Publishing Consultant. m. Mary Peake, 13 Sep 1975. Education: BA, Cornell University, USA, 1968; MA, University of Pennsylvania, USA, 1971; DPhil, Christ Church, University of Oxford, 1977. Appointments: Assistant Editor, Clio Press Ltd, Oxford, 1977-80; Publishing Manager, Pergamon Press Ltd, Oxford, 1980-82; Publisher, Professional Publishing Ltd, London, 1982-84; Editorial Director, Gower Publishing Ltd, Aldershot, 1984-85; Publisher, Longman Group Ltd, Harlow, 1985-88; Freelance writer and journalist, 1990-. Publications: Cultural Atlas of Russia and the Soviet Union, 1989; Free-wheeling in Bear Country, 1994. Contributions to: California Slavic Studies; Cambridge Encyclopaedia of Archaeology; Medieval Scandinavia; Solanus; Modern Encyclopaedia of Russian and Soviet History; Year's Work in Modern Language Studies; Business Eastern Europe, 1991; International Automotive Review, 1991-. Address: 37 Ulysses Road, West Hampstead, London NW6 1ED, England.

DEKKER Carl. See: **LYNDS Dennis.**

DELAGE Denys, b. 2 Apr 1942, Montreal, Quebec, Canada. m. (1), 2 sons, (2) Andrée Gendreau, 26 July 1995. Education: MA, Sociology, University of Montréal, 1968; PhD, Social History, Ecole des Hautes Etudes en Sciences Sociales, Paris, 1980. Publication: Bitter Feast, Amerindians and Europeans in Northeastern North America, 1600-64, 1993. Contributions to: Recherche Amerindiennes au Quebec, Anthropologie et Sociétés. Honours: John Porter Award, Canadian Association of Sociology and Anthropology; Lionel Groulx Award, Histoire de l'Ameridue Française. Address: 378 Franciscains Quebec City, Quebec, GIS 2P8, Canada.

DELANEY Shelagh, b. 25 Nov 1939, Salford, Lancashire, England. Playwright. 1 daughter. Education: Broughton Secondary School. Publications: Plays: A Taste of Honey, 1958; The Lion in Love, 1960; Films: A Taste of Honey; The White Bus, 1966; Charlie Bubbles, 1968; Dance with a Stranger, 1985; TV Plays: St Martin's Summer, 1974; Find Me First, 1979; TV Series: The House That Jack Built, 1977 (stage adaptation, New York, 1979); Radio Plays: So Does The Nightingale, 1980; Don't Worry About Matilda, 1983; Sweetly Sings The Donkey, 1963. Honours: Charles Henry Foyle New Play Award; Arts Council Bursary, 1961; New York Drama Critics Award, 1961; British Film Academy Award, Robert Flaherty Award, 1961; Prix Film Jeunesse Etranger, Cannes, 1985. Address: c/o Tessa Sayle, 11 Jubilee Place, London SW3 3TE, England.

DELANY Samuel R(ay), b. 1 Apr 1942, New York, New York, USA. Writer; Professor. m. 24 Aug 1961, div 1980, 1 son, 1 daughter. Education: City College, New York City, 1960, 1962-63. Appointments: Editor, Wuark, 1970-71; Senior Fellow, Center for 20th Century Studies, University of Wisconsin, Milwaukee, 1977; Society for the Humanities, Cornell University, 1987; Professor of Comparative Literature, University of Massachusetts, Amherst, 1988-. Publications:

The Jewels of Aptor, 1962, unabridged edition, 1968; The Fall of the Towers, vol 1, Captives of the Flames, 1963, as Out of the Dead City, 1968, vol 2, The Towers of Toron, 1964, vol 3, City of a Thousand Suns, 1965; The Ballad of Beta-2, 1965; Empire Star, 1966; Babel-17, 1966; The Einstein Intersection, 1967; Nova, 1968; Driftglass: Ten Tales of Speculative Fiction, 1971; Dhalgren, 1975; Triton, 1976; The Jewel-Hinged Jaw: Notes on the Language of Science Fiction, 1977; The American Shore, 1978; Empire, 1978; Nebula Award Winners 13 (editor), 1979; Distant Stars, 1981; Stars in My Pocket Like Grains of Sand, 1984; Starboard Wine: More Notes on the Language of Science Fiction, 1984; The Splendour and Misery of Bodies, 1985; Flight from Neveryon, 1985; They Fly at Ciron, 1992; Neveryon, 1993; Tales of Neveryon, 1993; The Mad Man, 1994. Literary Agent: Henry Morrison, Box 234, Bedford Hills, NY 10507, USA. Address: c/o Bantam Books, 666 Fifth Avenue, New York, NY 10019, USA.

DELBANCO Andrew (Henry), b. 20 Feb 1952, White Plains, New York, USA. Professor in the Humanities; Writer. m. Dawn Ho Delbanco, 1973, 1 son, 1 daughter. Education: AB, 1973, AM, 1976, PhD, 1980, Harvard University. Appointments: Assistant Professor, Harvard University, 1981-85; Associate Professor, 1985-87; Professor, 1987-, Julian Clarence Levi Professor in the Humanities, 1995-, Columbia University; Adjunct Professor, Yale University, 1989. Publications: William Ellery Channing: An Essay on the Liberal Spirit in America, 1981; The Puritan Ordeal, 1989; The Death of Satan: How Americans Have Lost the Sense of Evil, 1995; Required Reading: Why Our American Classics Matter Now, 1997; Editor: The Puritans in America: A Narrative Anthology (with Alan Heimert), 1985; The Sermons of Ralph Waldo Emerson, Vol II (with Teresa Toulouse), 1990; The Portable Abraham Lincoln, 1992. Contributions to: Professional journals and to general periodicals. Honours: Guggenheim Fellowship; American Council of Learned Societies Fellowship; National Endowment for the Humanities Fellowship; National Humanities Center Fellowship. Memberships: Society of American Historians. Address: c/o Department of English and Comparative Literature, Columbia University, 1150 Amsterdam Avenue, New York, NY 10027, USA.

DELBANCO Nicholas Franklin, b . 27 Aug 1942, London, England. Writer. m. Elena Carter Greenhouse, 12 Sept 1970, 2 daughters. Education: BA, History and Literature, Harvard College, 1963; MA, English Comparative Literature, Columbia University, 1966. Appointments: Member, Language and Literature Division, Bennington College, 1966-85; Director, Bennington Writing Workshops, 1977-85; Visiting Professor, Iowa Writers Program, University of Iowa, 1979; Adjunct Professor, School of the Arts, Columbia University, 1979-96; Visiting Artist in Residence, Trinity College, 1980; Visiting Professor, Williams College, 1982; Professor of English, Skidmore College, 1984-85; Professor of English, Director, MFA Program, University of Michigan, 1985-; Director, Hopwood Awards Programme, 1988-. Publications: The Martlet's Tale, 1966; Grasse 3/23/66, 1968; Consider Sappho Burning, 1969; News, 1970; In the Middle Distance, 1971; Fathering, 1973; Small Rain, 1975; Possession, 1977; Sherbrooks, 1978; Stillness, 1980; Group Portrait: Conrad, Crane, Ford, James, and Wells, 1982; About My Table and Other Stories, 1983; The Beaux Arts Trio: A Portrait, 1985; Running in Place: Scenes from the South of France, 1989; The Writers' Trade, and Other Stories, 1990; In the Name of Mercy, 1995. Contributions to: Periodicals. Honours: National Endowment for the Arts Creative Writing Fellowships, 1973, 1982; Guggenheim Fellowship, 1979. Memberships: Authors League; Authors Guild; Signet Society; Phi Beta Kappa; New York State Writers Institute; PEN. Literary Agent: Gail Hochman, Brandt and Brandt. Address: c/o Department of English, University of Michigan, 7601 Haven Hall, Ann Arbor, MI 48109, USA.

DELDERFIELD Eric Raymond, b . 4 May 1909, London, England. Author; Journalist. m. 1934, 1 daughter. Appointments: Director, David & Charles Publishers, 1962-67. Publications: Lynmouth Flood Disaster, 1953, reprinted 14 times; British Inn Signs and Their Stories, 1965, 2nd edition, 1984; West Country Houses and Their Families, 3 volumes, 1968, 1970, 1973; Kings and Queens of England, 1966, 3rd edition, 1981; True Animal Stories, 4 volumes, 1970-73; Cotswold Villages and Churches, 1961, 2nd edition, 1985; Exmoor Wanderings; Kings and Queens Colour, 1990; numerous guides on areas of Britain. Contributions to: Devon Life; This England; and others. Address: 51 Ashleigh Road, Exmouth, Devon EX8 2JY, England.

DELEHANTY Randolph, b. 5 July 1944, Memphis, Tennessee, USA. Writer; Lecturer; Art Curator. Education: BA, Georgetown University, 1966; MA, University of Chicago, 1968; MA, 1969, PhD, 1992, Harvard University. Publications: In the Victorian Style; San Francisco: The Ultimate Guide; Preserving The West; California: A Guidebook; San Francisco: Walks and Tours in the Golden Gate City; New Orleans: Elegance and Decadence; Classic Natchez; New Orleans: The Favor of the Crescent City, forthcoming; Art in the American South. Address: The Roger Houston Ogden Collection of Southern Art, 460 Broadway Street, New Orleans, LA 70118, USA.

DELGADO James P, b . 11 Jan 1958, San Jose, California, USA. Historian; Museum Director. m. Mary Jean Bremmer, 7 Oct 1978, 1 son, 1 daughter. Education: BA magna cum laude, American History, San Francisco State University, 1981; MA, Maritime History, Underwater Research, East Carolina University, Greenville, North Carolina, 1985. Appointments: Assistant to Regional Historian, Western Region (Hawaii, Guam, American Samoa, California, Arizona), 1978-79; Chief Historian, Golden Gate National Recreation Area, San Francisco, 1979-86; Chief Maritime Historian, National Park Service, Washington, 1987-91; Executive Director, Vancouver Maritime Museum, Canada, 1991-. Publications: Alcatraz Island: The Story Behind the Scenery, 1985; The Log of the Apollo: Joseph Perkins Beach's Log of the Voyage of the Ship Apollo from New York to San Francisco 1849 (editor), 1986; Shipwrecks at the Golden Gate (with Stephen A Haller), 1989; To California By Sea: A Maritime History of the California Gold Rush, 1990; National Parks of America, 1990; Pearl Harbor Recalled: New Images of the Day of Infamy (with Tom Freeman), 1991; Great American Ships (with J Candace Clifford), 1991; Great American Ships (with J Candace Clifford). 1991; Alcatraz Island, 1991; Dauntless St Roch: The Mounties Arctic Schooner, 1992; Shipwrecks of the Northern Shore; Ghost Fleet of the Atomic Age: The Sunken Ships of Bikini Atoll. Contributions to: Pacific Historian; Book Club of California Quarterly; Point Reyes Historian; Public Historian; American History Illustrated; CRM Bulletin. Memberships: Society for Historical Archaeology; California Historical Society; Canadian Nautical Research Society; National Maritime Historical Society; Canadian Representative, International Committee on Monuments and Sites; Committee on the International Underwater Heritage; Trustee, Council of American Maritime Museums. Address: 4204 West 10th Avenue, Vancouver, British Columbia V6R 2H4, Canada.

DELIUS Anthony (Ronald Martin), b. 11 June 1916, Simonstown, South Africa. Freelance Writer; Poet. Education: BA, Rhodes University, Grahamstown, 1938. Appointments: Writer, BBC Africa Service, London, 1968-77; Freelance Writer, 1977-. Publications: An Unkown Border, 1954; The Last Division, 1959; A Corner of the World: Thirty Four Poems, 1962; Black South Easter, 1966; Play: The Fall: A Play About Rhodes, 1957; Novels: The Young Traveller in South Africa, 1947; The Long Way Round, 1956; Upsurge in Africa, 1960; Border, 1963; The Day Natal Took Off: A Satire, 1963. Honour: CNA Literary Award, 1977. Address: 30 Graemesdyke Avenue, London SW14 7BJ, England.

DELVIN David George, b. 28 Jan 1939. Doctor; TV Broadcaster; Writer. Education: MB, BS, LRCP, MRCS, King's College Hospital, University of London; D.Obst, RCOG; DCH; Dip Ven; FPA Cert; MRCGP. Appointments: Associate Editor, New English Encyclopaedia; Consultant Editor, General Practitioner; Consulting Editor, SHE. Publications: The Home Doctor; The Book of Love; You and Your Back; A Patient's Guide to Operations; Your Good Health; Common Childhood Illnesses; Taking the Pill; How to Improve Your Sex Life; Dear Doc; Carefree Love; An A-Z of Your Child's Health. Contributions to: Periodicals. Honours: Medical Journalists' Association Award of Special Merit, 1974,jointly 1975; American Medical Writers' Association Best Book Award, 1976; Médaille de la Ville de Paris, Echelon Argent, 1983; Consumer Columnist of the Year, 1986. Memberships: Vice Chairman, Medical Journalists' Association; GMC; Royal Society of Medicine; BMA. Literary Agent: A P Watt. Address: c/o Coutts Ltd, 440 Strand, London WC2R OQS, England.

DEMARIA Robert, b. 28 Sept 1928, New York, New York, USA. Writer; Professor. m. (1) Maddalena Buzeo, (2) Ellen Hope Meyer, 3 sons, 1 daughter. Education: BA, 1948, MA, 1949, PhD, 1959, Columbia University. Appointments: Professor of English, University of Oregon, 1949-52; Professor of English, Hofstra University, 1952-61; Associate Dean, New School for Social Research, New York City, 1961-64; Professor of English, Dowling College, 1965-; Editor, Publisher, The Mediterranean Review, 1969-73. Publications: Carnival of Angels, 1961; Clodia, 1965; Don Juan in Lourdes, 1966; The Satyr, 1972; The Decline and Fall of America, 1973; To Be a King, 1976; Sons and Brothers, 1985. Contributions to: Antaeus; California Quarterly; Southwest Review; Cimarron Review; Beloit Fiction Journal; New Letters; Florida Review. Memberships: Authors Guild; PEN American Center. Literary Agent: Diane Cleaver, 55 Fifth Avenue, New York, NY 10003, USA. Address: 106 Vineyard Place, Port Jefferson, NY 11777, USA.

DEMARIS Ovid. See:DESMARAIS Ovide E.

DEMETILLO Ricaredo, b. 2 June 1920, Dumangas, Philippines. Professor of Humanities; Writer; Poet. Education: AB, Silliman University, 1947; MFA, University of Iowa, 1952. Appointments: Assistant Professor 1959-70, Chairman, Department of Humanities 1961-62, Associate Professor 1970-75, Professor of Humanities, 1975-, University of the Philippines, Diliman, Quezon City. Publications: No Certian Weather: A Collection of Poetry, 1956; La Via: A Spiritual Journey, 1958; Daedalus and Other Poems, 1961; Barter in Panay (poetry), 1961; The Authentic Voice of Poetry, 1962; Masks and Signature (poetry), 1968; The Scare-Crow Christ (poetry), 1973; The Heart of Emptiness is Black (play), 1973; The City and the Thread of Light (poetry), 1974; Lazarus, Troubadour (poetry), 1974; The Genesis of a Troubled Vision (novel), 1976; Major and Monor Keys (criticism), 1986; First and Last Fruits (poetry), 1989. Address: 38 Balacan Street, West Avenue, Quezon City, Philippines.

DEMPSTER Nigel Richard Patton, b. 1 Nov 1941. Editorial Executive. m. (1) Emma de Bendern, 1971, div 1974, (2) Lady Camilla Godolphin Osborne, 1978, 1 daughter. Appointments: Broker, Lloyds of London, 1958-59; Stock Exchange, 1959-60; PR Account Executive, Earl of Kimberley Associates, 1960-63; Journalist, Daily Express, 1963-71; Columnist, Daily Mail, 1971-. Publications: H.R.H. The Princess Margaret - A Life Unfulfilled (biography), 1981; Heiress - The Story of Christina Onassis, 1989; Nigel Dempster's Address Book (biography), 1991; Behind Palace Doors (with Peter Evans), 1993. Contributions to: Queen Magazine; Columnist (Grovel), Private Eye Magazine, 1969-85; Broadcaster with ABC, USA and CBC, Canada, 1976-, and with TV am, 1983-90. Address: c/o Daily Mail, Northcliffe House, 2 Derry Street, London W8 5TT, England.

DENGLER Sandy, b. 8 June 1939, Newark, Ohio, USA. Writer. m. William F Dengler, 11 Jan 1963, 2 daughters. Education: BS, Bowling Green State University, Ohio, 1961; MS, Arizona State University, 1967. Publications: Fanny Crosby, 1985; John Bunyan, 1986; D L Moody, 1987; Susanna Wesley, 1987; Florence Nightingale, 1988; Romance novels, juvenile historical novels including: Barn Social, 1978; Yosemite's Marvellous Creatures, 1979; Summer of the Wild Pig, 1979; Melon Hound, 1980; Horse Who Loved Picnics, 1980; Mystery at McGehan Ranch, 1982; Chain Five Mystery, 1984; Summer Snow, 1984; Winterspring, 1985; This Rolling Land, 1986; Jungle Gold, 1987; Code of Honor, 1988; Power of Pinjarra, 1989; Taste of Victory, 1989; East of Outback, 1990; Death Valley, 1993; Cat Killer, 1993; Dublin Crossing, 1993; Mouse Trapped, 1993; Gila Monster, 1994; Last Dinosaur, 1994; Murder on the Mount, 1994; Shamrock Shore, 1994; Emerald Sea, 1994; The Quick and the Dead, 1995; King of the Stars, 1995. Contributions to: Numerous articles to journals and magazines. Honours: Writer of the Year, Warm Beach, 1986; Golden Medallion, Romance Writers of America, 1987. Address: 2623 Cypress Avenue, Norman, OK 73072, USA.

DENKER Henry, b. 25 Nov 1912, New York, New York, USA. Writer; Playwright. Education: LLB, New York University, 1934. Publications: I'll Be Right Home, Ma, 1947; My Son, the Lawyer, 1949; Salome: Princess of Galilee, 1951; The First Easter, 1951; The Child is Mine, 1955; The Director, 1970; The Kingmaker, 1972; A Place for the Mighty, 1974; The Physicians, 1975; The Experiment, 1976; The Starmaker, 1977; The Scofield Diagnosis, 1977; The Actress, 1978; Error of Judgement, 1979; Horowitz and Mrs Washington, 1979, as play, 1980; The Warfield Syndrome, 1981; Outrage, 1982, as play, 1983, as film, 1985; The Healers, 1983; Kincaid, 1984; Robert, My Son, 1985; Judge Spence Dissents, 1986; The Choice, 1987; The Retreat, 1988; A Gift of Life, 1989; Payment in Full, 1990; Doctor on Trial, 1991; Mrs Washington and Horowitz, too, 1992; Labyrinth, 1994; This Child is Mine, 1995; To Marcy, With Love, 1996; Plays: Time Limit, 1957; A Far Country, 1961; A Case of Libel, 1963; What Did We Do Wrong?, 1967; The Headhunters, 1976; The Second Time Around, 1977. Memberships: Dramatists Guild, Council, 1970-73; Authors Guild; Authors League, Council; Writers Guild of America East.

Literary Agent: Mitch Douglas, ICM, 40 West 57th Street, New York, NY 10019. USA. Address: 241 Central Park West, New York, NY 10024, USA.

DENNING Alfred Thompson, Baron of Whitchurch, b. 23 Jan 1899, Whitchurch, Hampshire, England. Lawyer; Former Master of the Rolls. m. (1) Mary Harvey, 1932, dec 1941, 1 son, (2) Joan, 1945, dec 1992. Education: Magdalen College, Oxford; Eldon Scholar, 1921; Prize Student, Inns of Court. Appointments: Called to the Bar, 1923; King's Counsel, 1938; Judge of the High Court of Justice, 1944; Lord Justice of Appeal, 1948-57; President, Birbeck College, 1952-83; Lord of Appeal in Ordinary, 1957-62; Master of the Rolls, 1962-82. Publications: Smith's Leading Cases (joint editor), 1929; Bullen and Leake's Precedents (joint editor), 1935; Freedom Under the Law (Hamlyn Lectures), 1949; The Changing Law, 1953; The Road to Justice, 1955; The Discipline of the Law, 1979; The Due Process of Law, 1980; The Family Story, 1981; What Next in the Law, 1982; The Closing Chapter, 1983; Landmarks in the Law, 1984; Leaves From My Library, 1986. Honours: Knighted, 1944; Created a Life Peer, 1957; Many honorary doctorates. Address: The Lawn, Whitchurch, Hampshire, RG28 7AS, England.

DENNING Mark. See: STEVENSON John.

DENNIS Everette Eugene Jr, b. 15 Aug 1942, Seattle, Washington, USA. Foundation Executive; Educator; Author. m. Emily J Smith, 15 June 1988. Education: BS, University of Oregon, 1964; MA, Syracuse University, 1966; PhD, University of Minnesota, 1974. Appointments: Assistant Professor, Journalism, Mass Communication, Kansas State University, Manhattan, 1968-72; Instructor, Assistant Professor, Associate Professor, School of Journalism and Mass Communication, University of Minnesota, 1972-81; Visiting Professor, Medill School of Journalism, Northwestern University, 1976-77; Dean, Professor, School of Journalism, University of Oregon, 1981-84; Executive Director, The Freedom Forum Media Studies Center, Columbia University; Senior Vice-President, The Freedom Forum, Arlington, Virginia; Editor-in-Chief, Media Studies Journal. Publications: Other Voices: The New Journalism in America, 1973; The Media Society, 1978; The Economics of Libel, 1986; Understanding Mass Communication (editor), 1988, 6th edition, 1996; Demystifying Media Technology, 1993; America's Schools and the Mass Media, 1993; The Culture of Crime, 1995; Radio, The Forgotten Medium, 1995; American Communication Research, 1996. Contributions to: Hundreds of articles to popular, professional and scholarly periodicals. Honours: 4 Harvard University Fellowships, 1978-79, 1980, 1981; Other fellowships; Various writing prizes and awards. Memberships: Kappa Tau Alpha; International Communication Association; Eastman House International Museum of Photographs; American Antiquarian Society; Association for Education in Journalism and Mass Communication; International Press Institute; Society of Professional Journalists. Address: 420 Riverside Drive, New York, NY 10027, USA.

DENNIS-JONES Harold, (Paul Hamilton, Dennis Hessing), b. 2 Dec 1915, Port-Louis, Mauritius. Journalist; Author; Photographer. 2 daughters. Education: Open Scholar in Classics, St John's College, Oxford, 1934-38; First Class Honours in Classical Honour Moderations; Second Class Lt Hum. Appointments: Kensley Newspapers 1945-47; Travel Correspondent, Geographical Magazine, 1947-56; London Correspondent, Het Geillustreede Pers, Amsterdam, 1947-52; UK Editor, Guide Kleber, Paris, 1963-72. Publications: Fifty-six guide books titles/editions, covering all Europe, Morocco, Israel; verse translations from Greek, French, Spanish, Romanian; three language learning titles, French, Spanish, Italian. Contributions to: Most UK Newspapers; many magazines in UK; newspapers and magazines in Europe, USA, etc; Radio and TV Broadcasts. Memberships: British Society of Authors; British Guild of Travel Writers. Address: 53 Sunhill Court, High Street, Pembury, Tunbridge Wells TN2 4NT, England.

DENNYS Louise, b. 7 Dec 1948, Ismailia, Egypt. Publisher; Editor. m. Eric P Young. Education: BA Hon, MA English Language and Literature, Oxford University. Appointments: Publisher, Alfred A Knopf Canada; Vice-President, Random House of Canada. Publication: The Changing Resource, 1975. Honours: Woman of the Year Award, Toronto Life Annual Award, 1984. Memberships: Harbourfront International Authors Festival, past member, Board of Directors; PEN Canada, past president. Address: Random House of

Canada, 33 Yonge Street, Suite 210, Toronto, Ontario M5E 1G4, Canada.

DENOO Joris, b. 6 July 1953, Torhout, Belgium. Author; Teacher. m. Lut Vandemeulebroecke, 23 July 1976, 1 son, 2 daughters. Education: Graduate, German Philology, Louvain, 1975; Aggregation PHO, 1976. Appointments: Freelance Reporter, Book Reviewer, Flemish Journals, 1986-91. Publications: Repelsteel in Bourgondië, novel, 1986; De Bende van de Beeldenaar, story for children, 1986; Binnenscheepvaart, poetry, 1988; Staat van Medewerking, poetry, 1988; Een Paar Kinderen, Graag, story for children, 1992; Voltooid Verwarmde Tijd, poetry, 1992; Taal is een Aardig Ding, essay, 1993; Verkeerde Lieveheer, novel, 1993; Vallen en Opstaan: Diary of an Epileptic Child, 1996. Contributions to: Many Flemish and Dutch magazines and journals. Honours: Vlaamse Klub Prize, Brussels, 1979; Premies West-Vlaanderen, 1983, 1991; Prijs Tielt Boekenstad, 1992; Essay Prize, Royal Academy for Dutch Language and Literature, 1996. Membership: SABAM, Belgium. Address: Oude Ieperseweg, B-8501 Heule, b elgium.

DEPAOLA Tomie, (Thomas Anthony Depaola), b. 15 Sept 1934, Meriden, Connecticut, USA. Children's Book Artist and Writer. Education: BFA, Pratt Institute, 1956; MFA, California College of Arts and Crafts, 1969; Doctoral Equivalency, Lone Mountain College, 1970. Publications: Over 200 books; Country Angel Christmas, 1995; Strega Nona: Her Story, 1996. Honours: Caldecott Honor Book, American Library Association, 1976; Regina Medal, Catholic Library Association, 1983; Honorary Doctor of Letters, Colby-Sawyer College, 1985; Honorary DHL, Saint Anselm College, 1994. Memberships: Authors Guild; Society of Children's Book Writers. Address: c/o G P Putnam's Sons, 11th Floor, 200 Madison Avenue, New York, NY 10016, USA.

DEPESTRE Réné, b. 29 Aug 1926, Jacmel, Haiti (French citizen). Poet. m. Nelly Campano, 1962. Education: Sorbonne and University of Paris, 1946-51. Appointments: Attaché to the Office of Culture at UNESCO, Paris, 1982-86. Publications: Etincelles, 1945; Gerbe de Sang, 1946; Vegetations of Splendour, 1951; Minerai noir, 1956; Journal d'un animal marin, 1964; A Rainbow for the Christian West, 1967; Poète à Cuba, 1976; En Etat de poésie, 1980; Journal d'un animal marin: choisi de poèmes 1956-1990, 1990; Au Matin de la negritude, 1990; Anthologie personnelle, 1992; Fiction: The Festival of the Greasy Pole, 1979; Alleluia pour une femme-jardin, 1982; Hadriana dans tous mes rêves, 1988; Eros dans un train chinois, 1990; Editor and translator, Poésie Cubaine 1959-1966. Honours: Prix Goncourt, 1982. Address: 31 bis, Route de Roubia, 11200 Lezignan-Corbieres, France.

DERFLER (Arnold) Leslie, b. 11 Jan 1933, New York, New York, USA. Professor of History; Writer. m. Gunilla Derfler, 25 June 1962, 4 daughters. Education: BA, City College of New York, 1954; University of Chicago, 1956; University of Paris, 1960; MA, 1957, PhD, 1962, Columbia University. Appointments: Faculty, City College of New York, 1959-62, Carnegie Mellon University, 1962-68, University of Massachusetts, Amherst, 1968-69; Professor of History, Florida Atlantic University, 1969-; Visiting Professor, London Center, Florida State University, 1985. Publications: The Dreyfus Affair: Tragedy of Errors, 1963; The Third French Republic, 1870-1940, 1966; Socialism Since Marx, 1973; Alexandre Millerand: The Socialist Years, 1977; President and Parliament: A Short History of the French Presidency, 1984; An Age of Conflict: Readings in 20th Century European History, 1990, 2nd edition, 1996; Paul Lafargue and the Founding of French Marxism, 1842-1882, 1991; Paul Lafargue and the Flowering of French Socialism, 1882-1912, forthcoming. Honours: American Philosophical Society Grants, 1967, 1976, 1981, 1991; Distinguished Scholar Award, Florida Atlantic University, 1982; National Endowment for the Humanities Fellowship, 1984-85. Address: c/o Department of History, Florida Atlantic University, Boca Raton, FL 33431, USA.

DERIEX Suzanne. See: **PIGUET-CUENDET Suzanne.**

DERR Mark (Burgess), b. 20 Jan 1950, Baltimore, Maryland, USA. Writer. m. Gina L Maranto, 11 Sept 1982. Education: AB, 1972, MA, 1973, Johns Hopkins University. Publications: Some Kind of Paradise: Over Florida, 1989; The Frontiersman: The Real Life and the Many Legends of Davy Crockett, 1993; Dog's Best Friend: Annals of the Dog-Human Relationship, 1997. Contributions to: The Atlantic; Audubon Society; Natural History; Men's Journal. Address: 4245 Sheridan Avenue, Miami Beach, FL 33140, USA.

DERRIDA Jacques, b. 15 July 1930, El Biar, Algeria. Philosopher; Writer. m. Marguérite Aucouturier, 1957, 2 sons. Education: École Normale Supérieure, Paris, 1952-56; Licence es Lettres, 1953, Licence de Philosophie, 1953, Diplome d'Études Supérieures, 1954, Sorbonne, University of Paris; Certificat d'Ethnologie, 1954, Agregation de Philosophie, 1956, Doctorat en Philosophie, 1967, Doctorat d'Etat es Lettres, 1980; Graduate Studies, Harvard University, 1956-57. Appointments: Professor de lettres supérieures, Lycée du Mans, 1959-60; Professor of Philosophy, Sorbonne, University of Paris, 1960-64, École Normale Supérieure, Paris, 1964-84; Director, École des Hautes Études en Sciences Sociales, Paris, 1984-; Many visiting lectureships and professorships. Publications: La voix et le phénomène: Introduction au probleme du signe dans la phénomènologie de Husserl, 1967, English translation as Speech and Phenomena and Other Essays on Husserl's Theory of Signs, 1973; De la grammatologie, 1967, English translation as Of Grammatology, 1976; L'écriture et la difference, 1967, English translation as Writing and Difference, 1978; La dissémination, 1972, English translation, 1981; Marges de la philosophie, 1972, English translation as Margins of Philosophy, 1982; Glas, 1974, English translation, 1986; L'archeologie du frivole, 1976, English translation as The Archeology of the Frivolous: Reading Condillac, 1980; Eperons: Les styles de Nietzsche, 1976, English translation as Spurs: Nietzsche's Styles, 1979; Limited Inc: abc, 1977; La vérité en peinture, 1978; La carte postale: De Socrate à Freud et au-dela, 1980, English translation as The Post Card: From Socrates to Freud and Beyond, 1987; L'oreille de l'autre: Otobiographies, transferts, traductions: Textes et debats avec Jacques Derrida, 1982, English translation as The Ear of the Other: Otobiography, Transference, Translation, 1985; Signeponge/Signsponge (French and English text), 1984, revised edition, 1988; Mémoires: Lectures for Paul de Man, 1986; De l'esprit: Heidegger et la question, 1987; Psyché: Inventions de l'autre, 1987; Mémoires: Pour Paul de Man, 1988; Du droit à la philosophie, 1990; Mémoires d'aveugle, 1990; Le problème de la genèse dans la philosophie de Husserl, 1990; L'autre cap, 1991; Donner le temps, 1991; Qu'est-ce que la poésie?, 1991; Reader, 1991; Acts of Literature, 1992; Conders, 1992; Spectres de Marx, 1993; Aporias, 1994. Honours: Liste d'aptitude a l'enseignement Supérieur, 1968; Chevalier, 1968, Officier, 1980, des Palmes Academiques; Honorary doctorates, Columbia University, 1980, University of Louvain, 1983, University of Essex, 1987, Cambridge University, 1992; Commandeur des Arts et des Lettres, France, 1983; Prix Nietzsche, Association Internationale de Philosophie, 1988. Address: c/o École des Hautes Études en Sciences Sociales, 54 Bouelvard Raspail, 75006 Paris, France.

DERSHOWITZ Alan (Morton), b. 1 Sept 1938, New York, New York, USA. Lawyer; Professor of Law; Writer. m. Carolyn Cohen, 2 sons, 1 daughter. Education: BA, Brooklyn College, 1959; LLB, Yale University, 1962. Appointments: Called to the Bar, Washington, DC, 1963, Massachusetts, 1968, US Supreme Court, 1968; Law Clerk to Chief Judge David L Bazelon, US Court of Appeals, 1962-63, to Justice Arthur J Golberg, US Supreme Court; Faculty, 1964-, Professor of Law, 1967-, Fellow, Center for Advanced Study of Behavioral Sciences, 1971-72, Felix Frankfurter Professor of Law, 1993-, Harvard University. Publications: Psychoanalysis, Psychiatry and the Law (with others), 1967; Criminal Law: Theory and Process, 1974; The Best Defense, 1982; Reversal of Fortune: Inside the von Bulow Case, 1986; Taking Liberties: A Decade of Hard Cases, Bad Laws and Bum Raps, 1988; Chutzpah, 1991; Contrary to Popular Opinion, 1992; The Abuse Excuse, 1994; The Advocate's Devil, 1994; Reasonable Doubts, 1996. Contributions to: Periodicals. Honours: Guggenheim Fellowship, 1978-79; Honorary doctorates. Memberships: Order of the Coif; Phi Beta Kappa. Address: c/o Harvard University Law School, Cambridge, MA 02138, USA.

DESAI Anita, b. 24 June 1937, Mussoorie, India. Writer. m. Ashvin Desai, 13 Dec 1958, 2 sons, 2 daughters. Education: BA, Honours, Miranda House, University of Delhi. Appointments: Member, Advisory Board for English, Sahitya Akademi, India, 1975-80. Publications: Cry, The Peacock; Voices in the City; Fire on the Mountain; Clear Light of Day; In Custody, (also a film, Merchant Ivory Productions, 1994); Baumgartner's Bombay; Where Shall We Go This Summer?; Bye Bye Blackbird; The Peacock Garden; Cat on a Houseboat; The Village by the Sea, (also BBC TV Serial, 1992); Games at Twilight; Journey to Ithaca, 1995. Contributions to: Periodicals. Honours: Winifred Holtby Award, Royal Society of Literature, 1978; Sahitya Akademi Award for English, 1978; Federation of Indian Publishers Award, 1978; The Padma Shri Award, India, 1989;

Hadassah Magazine Award, 1989; Guardian Prize for Children's Fiction, 1993; Literary Lion, New York Public Library, 1993; Neil Gunn International Writers Fellowship, Scotland, 1994. Memberships: Royal Society of Literature; Sahitya Akademi of India; PEN; Fellow, American Academy of Arts and Letters, 1992; Fellow, Girton College and of Clare Hall, Cambridge. Address: c/o Rogers, Coleridge and White Ltd, 20 Powis Mews, London W11 1JN, England.

DESHPANDE Shashi, b. 19 Aug 1938, Dharwad, India. Novelist. m. D H Deshpande, 1962, 2 sons. Education: BA (Hons) in Economics, 1956, Diploma in Journalism, 1970, MA in English, 1970, University of Bombay; BL, University of Mysore, Karnataka, 1959. Publications: The Dark Holds no Terrors, 1980; If I Die Today, 1982; Roots and Shadows, 1983; Come Up and Be Dead, 1985; That Long Silence, 1988; Short stories: The Legacy and Other Stories, 1978; It Was Dark, 1986; The Miracle and Other Stories, 1986; It Was the Nightingale, 1986; The Binding Vine, novel, 1993; The Intrusion and Other Stories, short story collection, 1994; Also a screenplay and children's works. Honours: Rangammal Prize, 1984; Sahitya Academy Award, 1990; Nanjangud Thirumalamba Award, 1991. Address: 409 41st Cross, Jayanagar V Block, Bangalore 560041, India.

DESMARAIS Ovide E, b. 6 Sept 1919, Biddeford, Maine, USA. Writer; Newspaper Reporter. m. Inez E Frakes, 15 May 1942, 2 daughters. Education: AB, College of Idaho, 1948; Law, Syracuse University; MS, Boston University, 1950. Publications: Mystery novels: Ride the Gold Mare, 1956; The Hoods Take Over, 1957; The Long Night, 1957; The Lusting Drive, 1958; The Slasher, 1959; The Enforcer, 1960; The Extortioners, 1960; The Gold-Plated Sewer, 1960; Candyleg, 1961 (as Machine Gun McCanin, 1970); The Parasite, 1963; The Organization, 1965 (as The Contract 1970); The Overlord, 1972. Other: Lucky Luciano, 1960; The Linbergh Kidnapping Case, 1961; The Dillinger Story, 1961; The Green Felt Jungle (with Edward Reid), 1963; Jack Ruby (with Gary Wills), 1968; Captive City; Chicago in Chains, 1969; America the Violent, 1970; Poso del Mundo: Inside the Mexican-American Border, 1970; Dirty Business: The Corporate-Political Money-Power Game, 1974; The Director: An Oral Biography of J Edgar Hoover, 1975; Brothers in Blood: The International Terrorist Network, 1977; The Last Mafioso: The Treacherous World of Jimmy Fratianno, 1981; The Vegas Legacy, 1983; The Boardwalk Jungle, 1987; J Edgar Hoover: As They Knew Him, 1994. Contributions to: Professional journals and periodicals. Address: PO Box 6071, Santa Barbara, CA 93111, USA.

DESMEE Gilbert Georges, b. 29 Jan 1951, Suresnes, France. Writer; Editor; Educator. m. Maria Desmee, 28 Jan 1982. Education: Diploma of electrotechnic and automatism, University of Cachan, 1973; Diploma of Educator in Social Science, Versailles, 1981. Publications: Le Schiste Métamorphique, 1990; L'Infini pour respirer in Histoire de livres d'artistes, 1991; Un Magdalénien Contemporain in Robert Pérot, 1994; En écho des corps d'écriture, 1995; Je m'en dit tu, 1996; Seul le geste serait fécond, 1997; L'eau s'émeut du feu, 1997. Contributions to: Encres Vives; Sapriphage; Agone; Contre-Vox; L'Estracelle; Textuerre; Présage. Membership: Director of Sapriphage (literary review), 1988-; Emile Snyder Prize, 1991-; 3 Canettes, 1994-; Wallonie Bruxelles, 1996-. Address: 118 Avenue Pablo Picasso, 92000 Nanterre, France.

DEUTSCH André, b. 15 Nov 1917. Publisher. Education: Budapest, Vienna and Zürich. Appointments: Founder, Allan Wingate Ltd, publishers, 1945; Founder, Chairman, and Managing Director, 1951-84, Joint Chairman and Joint Managing Director, 1984-87, Joint Chairman, 1987-89, President, 1989-91, André Deutsch Ltd, publishers; Founder, African Universities Press, Lagos, 1962, East Africa Publishing House, Nairobi, 1964; Director, Libra, Budapest, 1991-; Chairman, Aurum Press. Honour: Commander of the Order of the British Empire, 1989. Address: 5 Selwood Terrace, London, SW7 3QN, England.

DEVALLE Susana Beatriz Cristina, b. 31 May 1945, Buenos Aires, Argentina. Social and Political Anthropologist. Education: MA, Indian Studies, El Colegio de Mexico, 1973; BA Honours in Anthropological Science, Buenos Aires National University, 1967; PhD, Social Anthropology, University of London, England, 1989. Appointments: Consultant, PEMEX, Mexican State Oil Company, 1979-80; Visiting Fellow, Faculty of Asian Studies, The Australian National University, 1983-84; Consultant, Australian Parliamentary Library, Foreign Affairs, 1984-85; National Researcher, Sistema Nacional de Investigadores, Secretaria de Educacion Publica, Mexico,

1987-; Visiting Fellow, Ethnic Studies Programme, University of Hawaii at Manoa, 1990; Director of Research Group, Ethnicity and Nationalisms in Asia, Africa and Latin America, 1994-; Coordinator of Research Group, Culture of Violence, Coexistence and Human Rights, 1994. Publications: Books: La Palabra de la Tierra, Protesta Campesina en India, siglo XIX (The Word of the Land, Peasant Protest in India, Nineteenth Century), 1977; Peasantry and National Integration, co-editor and co-author, 1981; Discourses of Ethnicity, Culture and Protest in Jharkhand, 1992; Power, Violence and Human Rights, editor and co-author, 1996; Documents: Multiethnicity in India, The Adivasi Peasants of Chota Nagpur and Santal Parganas, 1980; Le Problematica Indigena en el Pacifico (The Indigenous Problematique in the Pacific), 1989; Articles: Tribe in India: The Fallacy of a Colonial Category, 1990; Beyond Ecology? Indigenous Territories and Natural Resources, 1993; Territory, Forests and Historical Continuity: Indigenous Rights and Natural Resources in India, 1993. Honours: Research Fellowship, El Colegio de México; Research Grant, University Grants Commission, India; Grant, International Rural Sociology Association; Faculty Enrichment Award. Memberships: Association for Asian Studies; Asociacion Latinoamericana de Asia y Africa; International Union of Anthropological and Ethnological Sciences; American Anthropological Association. Address: Centro de Estudios de Asia y Africa, El Colegio de México, Camino al Ajusco No 20, México DF 01000, México.

DEVERELL Rex Johnson, b. 17 July 1941, Toronto, Ontario, Canada. Playwright. m. Rita Joyce Shelton, 24 May 1967, 1 son. Education: BA, 1963, BD, 1966, McMaster University; STM, Union Theological Seminary, 1967. Appointments: Resident Playwright, Globe Theatre, Regina, 1975-91; President, Playwrights Union of Canada, 1991-93. Publications: Boiler Room Suite, 1978; Superwheel, 1979; Drift, 1981; Black Powder, 1981; 3 Plays for Children; Various other plays, TV and radio scripts; Anthology, Deverell of the Globe, Opera Libretti, Boiler Room Suite, Land. Contributions to: Canadian Theatre Review; Canadian Children's Literature; Canadian Drama; Prairie Fire; Grain; Others. Honours: McMaster University Honour Society, 1963; Ohio State Award, 1974; Canadian Authors Association Medal, 1978; Major Armstrong Award, 1986; Nominee, Chalmers Award, 1994. Memberships: Saskatchewan Writers Guild; Playwrights Union of Canada; Saskatchewan Playwrights Centre; Amnesty International. Address: 36 Oneida Avenue, RR 4, Coldwater, Ontario L0K 1E0, Canada.

DEVERELL William H(erbert), b. 4 Mar 1937, Regina, Saskatchewan, Canada. Author. m. Tekla Melnyk, 1 son, 1 daughter. Education: BA, LLB, University of Saskatchewan, 1962. Appointments: Staff, Saskatoon Star-Phoenix, 1956-60, Canadian Press, Montreal, 1960-62, Vancouver Sun, 1963; Partner in law firm, Vancouver, 1964-79; Writer, 1979-. Publications: Fiction: Needles, 1979; High Crimes, 1979; Mecca, 1983; Dance of Shiva, 1984; Platinum Blues, 1988; Mindfield, 1989; Kill All the Lawyers, 1994. Non-fiction: Fatal Cruise: The Trial of Robert Frisbee, 1991; Street Legal - The Betrayal, 1995. Honours: McClelland and Stewart/Seal First Novel Award, 1979; Book of the Year Award, Periodical Distributors Association of Canada, 1980. Memberships: British Columbia Bar Association; British Columbia Civil Liberties Association; British Crime Writers Association; Crime Writers of Canada; Chairman, Writers Union of Canada, 1994-95. Address: Box 14, Rural Route 1, North Pender Island, British Columbia V0N 2M0, Canada.

DEVEREUX Eve. See: BARNETT Paul le Page.

DEVINE Thomas Martin, b. 30 July 1945, Motherwell, Scotland. m. Catherine Mary Lynas, 6 Jul 1971, 2 sons, 3 daughters. Education:BA, University of Strathclyde, 1968; PhD, 1971; D Litt, 1991; Fellow, Royal Society of Edinburgh, 1992; Fellow of the British Academy, 1994. Appointments: Assistant Lecturer, 1969-71, Lecturer, Senior Lecturer, 1971-83, Reader, 1983-88; Professor, 1988; Dean of Faculty of Arts and Social Studies, 1993; Deputy Principal, University of Strathclyde, 1994-; Adjunct Professor in History, University of Guelph, Canada; Director, Research Centre in Scottish History, University of Strathclyde. Publications: The Tobacco Lords, Ireland and Scotland 1700-1850; The Great Highland Famine; People and Society in Scotland; Farm Servants and Labour in Lowland Scotland; Irish Immigrants and Scottish Society in the Eighteenth and Nineteenth Centuries; Scottish Emigration and Scottish Society; Clanship to Crofters' War: The Social Transformation of the Scottish Highlands; The Transformation of Rural Scotland: Agrarian & Social Change 1680-1815; Glasgow, volume 1, Beginnings to 1930, 1995; Scotland in the Twentieth Century, 1996. Contributions to: Times Literary Supplement; Times Higher Education Supplement; Economic History Review; Social History; Scottish Historical Review; History Today; Scottish Economic & Social History. Honours: Senior Hume Brown Prize; Saltire Prize; Fellow, British Academy, 1994; Henry Duncan Prize Lectureship, Royal Society of Edinburgh, 1995; British Academy/Leverhulme Trust Senior Research Fellowship, 1992-93. Memberships: Economic and Social History Society of Scotland; Scottish Catholic Historical Association; Royal Society; Royal Historical Society; Trustee, National Museums of Scotland. Address: Deputy Principal's Office, Livingstone Tower, University of Strathclyde, 26 Richmond Street, Glasgow G1 1XH, Scotland.

DEVRIES Susanna. See: **DE VRIES-EVANS Susanna Mary.**

DEW Robb (Reavill) Forman, b. 26 Oct 1946, Mount Vernon, Ohio, USA. Writer. m. Charles Burgess Dew, 26 Jan 1968, 2 sons. Education: Louisiana State University. Publications: Dale Loves Sophie to Death, 1982; The Time of Her Life, 1984; Fortunate Lives, 1991; A Southern Thanksgiving: Recipes and Musings for a Manageable Feast, 1992; The Family Heart: A Memoir of When Our Son Came Out, 1994. Honour: American Book Award 1st Novel, 1982. Address: c/o Russell and Volkening, 50 West 29th Street, Apt 7E, New York, NY 10001, USA.

DEWDNEY Christopher, b. 9 May 1951, London, Ontario, Canada. Poet; Writer. m. (1) Suzanne Dennison, 1971, div 1975, 1 daughter, (2) Lise Downe, 1977, 1 son. Education: South and Westminster Collegiate Institutes, London, Ontario; H B Beal Art Annex, London, Ontario. Appointments: Associate Fellow, Winters College, York University, Toronto, 1984; Eminence Verte, Society for the Preservation of Wild Culture, Toronto, 1987; Poetry Editor, Coach House Publishing, Toronto, 1988. Publications: Poetry: Golders Green, 1972; A Paleozoic Geology of London, Ontario, 1973; Fovea Centralis, 1975; Spring Trances in the Control Emerald Night, 1978; Alter Sublime, 1980; The Cenozoic Asylum, 1983; Predators of the Adoration: Selected Poems 1972-1982, 1983; Permugenesis, 1987; The Radiant Inventory, 1988; Demon Pond, 1994. Other: The Immaculate Perception, 1986; Recent Artifacts from the Institute of Applied Fiction, 1990; Concordant Proviso Ascendant: A Natural History of Southwestern Ontario, Book III, 1991; The Secular Grail, 1993. Contributions to: Periodicals. Honours: Design Canada Award, 1974; Canada Council Grants, 1974, 1976, 1981, 1985; CBC Prize, 1986. Address: c/o McClelland and Stewart Inc, 481 University Avenue, Suite 900, Toronto, Ontario M5G 2E9, Canada.

DeWEESE Jean. See: **DE WEESE Thomas Eugene "Gene".**

DEWEY Jennifer Owings, b . 2 Oct 1941, Chicago, Illinois, USA. Writer; Illustrator. Div, 1 daughter. Education: University of New Mexico, 1960-63; Rhode Island School of Design. Publications: CLEM, The Story of a Raven, 1986; At the Edge of the Pond, 1987; Birds of Antarctica, The Adelie Penguin, 1989; Can You Find Me, A Book About Animal Camouflage, 1989; Animal Architecture, 1991; Night & Day in the Desert, 1991; Various illustrated books. Honours: Several awards for book illustrations. Memberships: San Francisco Society of Illustrators; American Society of Scientific Illustrators; President, Founder, The No Poets Society. Address: 607 Old Taos Highway, Santa Fe, NM 87501, USA.

DEWHIRST Ian, b. 17 Oct 1936, Keighley, Yorkshire, England. Librarian; Writer. Education: BA Hons, Victoria University of Manchester, 1958. Appointment: Staff, Keighley Public Library, 1960-91. Publications: Gleanings From Victorian Yorkshire, 1972; A History of Keighley, 1974; Yorkshire Through the Years, 1975; Gleanings from Edwardian Yorkshire, 1975; The Story of a Nobody, 1980; You Don't Remember Bananas, 1985; Keighley in Old Picture Postcards, 1987; In the Reign of the Peacemaker, 1993; Down Memory Lane, 1993. Contributions to: Yorkshire Ridings Magazine; Lancashire Magazine; Dalesman; Cumbria; Pennine Magazine; Transactions of the Yorkshire Dialect Society; Yorkshire Journal. Honour: Honorary Doctor of Letters, University of Bradford, 1996. Memberships: Yorkshire Dialect Society; Brontë Society; Edward Thomas Fellowship; Associate of the Library Association. Address: 14 Raglan Avenue, Fell Lane, Keighley, West Yorkshire BD22 6BJ, England.

DEWHURST Eileen Mary, b. 27 May 1929, Liverpool, England. Author. Div. Education: BA (Hons) English Language and Literature,

St Anne's College, Oxford, 1951. Publications: Crime novels: Death Came Smiling, 1975; After the Ball, 1976; Curtain Fall, 1977; Drink This, 1980; Trio in Three Flats, 1981; Whoever I Am, 1982; The House That Jack Built, 1983; There Was a Little Girl, 1984; Playing Safe, 1985; A Private Prosecution, 1986; A Nice Little Business, 1987; The Sleeper, 1988; Dear Mr Right, 1990; The Innocence of Guilt, 1991; Death in Candie Gardens, 1992; Now You See Her, 1995; The Verdict on Winter; 1996; Alias the Enemy, 1997. Contributions to: Various newspapers and journals. Memberships: Crime Writers Association; Society of Authors. Address: c/o Gregory and Radice, 3 Barb Mews, London W6 7PA, England.

DEWHURST Keith, b. 24 Dec 1931, Oldham, England. Writer. m. (1) Eve Pearce, 14 July 1958, div 1980, 1 son, 2 daughters, (2) Alexandra Cann, 4 Nov 1980. Education: BA, Peterhouse College, Cambridge, 1953. Appointments: Sports Writer, Evening Chronicle, Manchester, 1955-59; Presenter, Granada Television, 1968-69, BBC2 Television, London, 1972; Arts Columnist, The Guardian, London, 1969-72; Writer-in-Residence, Western Australia APA, Perth, 1984. Publications: Lark Rise to Candleford (2 plays), 1980; Captain of the Sands (novel), 1981; Don Quixote (play), 1982; McSullivan's Beach (novel), 1986; Black Snow, 1992. Address: c/o Alexandra Cann Representation, 337 Fulham Road, London, SW10 9TW, England.

DEXTER Colin, b. 29 Sept 1930, Stamford, Lincolnshire, England. Educational Administrator. Education: Christ's College, Cambridge; MA (Cantab): MA (Oxon). Publications: Last Bus to Woodstock, 1975; Last Seen Wearing, 1976; The Silent World of Nicholas Quinn, 1977; Service of All the Dead, 1979; The Dead of Jericho, 1981; The Riddle of the Third Mile, 1983; The Secret of Annexe 3, 1983; The Wench is Dead, 1989; The Jewel That Was Ours, 1991; The Way Through the Woods, 1992; Morse's Greatest Mystery, 1993; The Daughters of Cain, 1994; Death is Now My Neighbour, 1996. Honours: Silver Dagger, 1979, 1981, Gold Dagger, 1989, 1992, Diamond Dagger, 1997, Crime Writers Association; Macavity Award, Best Short Story, 1995; Lotos Club Medal of Merit, New York, 1996. Memberships: Crime Writers Association; Detection Club. Address: 456 Banbury Road, Oxford OX2 7RG, England.

DI CICCO Pier Giorgio, b. 5 July 1949, Arezzo, Italy. Roman Catholic Priest; Poet. Education: BA, 1972, BEd, 1973, Master of Divinity, 1990, University of Toronto; Bachelor of Sacred Theology, St Paul's University, 1990. Appointments: Founder-Poetry Editor, Poetry Toronto Newsletter, 1976-77; Associate Editor, Books in Canada, 1976-79; Co-Editor, 1976-79, Poetry Editor, 1980-82, Waves; Ordained Roman Catholic Priest and Associate Pastor, St Anne's Church, Brampton, Ontario, 1993-. Publications: We Are the Light Turning, 1975; The Sad Facts, 1977; The Circular Dark, 1977; Dancing in the House of Cards, 1977; A Burning Patience, 1978; Roman Candles: An Anthology of 17 Italo-Canadian Poets (editor), 1978; Dolce-Amaro, 1979; The Tough Romance, 1979; A Straw Hat for Everything, 1981; Flying Deeper into the Century, 1982; Dark to Light: Reasons for Humanness: Poems 1976-1979, 1983; Women We Never See Again, 1984; Twenty Poems, 1984; Post-Sixties Nocturne, 1985; Virgin Science: Hunting Holistic Paradignms, 1986. Honours: Canada Council Awards, 1974, 1976, 1980; Carleton University Italo-Canadian Literature Award, 1979. Address: PO Box 344, King City, Ontario L0G 1K0, Canada.

DI PRIMA Diane, b. 6 Aug 1934, New York, New York, USA. Poet; Writer; Dramatist; Artist. m. (1) Alan S Marlow, 1962, div 1969, (2) Grant Fisher, 1972, div 1975, 1 son, 4 daughters. Education: Swarthmore College, 1951-53. Appointments: Co-Founder, New York Poets Theater, 1961-65; Co-Editor (with LeRoi Jones), 1961-63, Editor, 1963-69, Floating Bear magazine; Publisher, Poets Press, 1964-69, Eidolon Editions, 1974-; Faculty, New College of California, San Francisco, 1980-81; Co-Founder, San Francisco Institute of Magical and Healing Arts, 1983-91; Senior Lecturer, California College of Arts and Crafts, Oakland, 1990-92; Visiting Faculty, San Francisco Art Institute, 1992; Adjunct Faculty, California Institute of Integral Studies, 1994. Publications: Poetry: This Kind of Bird Flies Backward, 1958; The Monster, 1961; The New Handbook of Heaven, 1963; Unless You Clock In, 1963; Combination Theatre Poem and Birthday Poem for Ten People, 1965; Haiku, 1967; Earthsong: Poems 1957-59, 1968; Hotel Albert, 1968; New Mexico Poem, June-July 1967, 1968; The Star, the Child, the Light, 1968; LA Odyssey, 1969; New As..., 1969; The Book of Hours, 1970; Kerhonkson Journal 1966, 1971; Prayer to the Mothers, 1971; So Fine, 1971; XV Dedications, 1971; Revolutionary Letters, 1971; The Calculus of Letters, 1972; Loba, Part 1, 1973;

Freddie Poems, 1974; North Country Medicine, 1974; Brass Furnace Going Out: Song, After an Abortion, 1975; Selected Poems 1956-1975, 1975, revised edition, 1977; Loba as Eve, 1975; Loba, Part 2, 1976; Loba, Parts 1-8, 1978; Wyoming Series, 1988; The Mysteries of Vision, 1988; Pieces of a Song: Selected Poems, 1990; Seminary Poems, 1991; The Mask is the Path of the Star, 1993. Fiction: Dinners and Nightmares, 1961, revised edition, 1974; The Calculus of Variation, 1966; Spring and Autumn Annals, 1966; Memoirs of a Beatnik, 1969. Plays: Paideuma, 1960; The Discontentment of the Russian Prince, 1961; Murder Cake, 1963; Like, 1964, Poets Vaudeville, 1964; Monuments, 1968; The Discovery of America, 1972; Whale Honey, 1975; Zip Code: Collected Plays, 1994. Other: Various Fables from Various Places (editor), 1960; War Poems (editor), 1968; Notes on the Summer Solstice, 1969. Contributions to: Various publications. Honours: National Endowment for the Arts Grants, 1966, 1973; Coordinating Council of Little Magazines Grants, 1967, 1970; Lapis Foundation Awards, 1978, 1979; Institute for Aesthetic Development Award, 1986; Lifetime Service Award, National Poetry Association, 1993. Address: 584 Castro Street, Suite 346, San Francisco, CA 94114, USA.

DICKEY Christopher. Paris Bureau Chief, Newsweek. Appointments: Managing Editor, Washington Post Magazine; Assistant Editor, Columnist, Book World section; Metro Reporter; Mexico Bureau Chief, 3 years, Cairo Bureau Chief, Washington Post; Cairo Bureau Chief, 1986-88, Paris Bureau Chief, 1988-93, 1995-, Middle East Regional Editor, 1993, Newsweek. Publications: With the Contras, 1986; Expats: Travels in Arabia from Tripoli to Teheran, 1990; Indolent Blood (novel), 1997. Honours: Edward R Murrow Press Fellow, Council of Foreign Relations; Tom Wallace Award for coverage of El Salvador, Inter-American Press Association, 1980; Mary Hemingway Award for Best Reporting from Abroad, Overseas Press Club, 1983. Address: c/o Newsweek, 251 West 57th Street, New York, NY 10019-1894, USA.

DICKINSON Donald Percy, b. 28 Dec 1947, Prince Albert, Saskatchewan, Canada. Writer; Teacher. m. Chellie Eaton, 1 May 1970, 2 sons, 1 daughter. Education: BA, University of Saskatchewan, 1973; MFA, University of British Columbia, 1979. Appointments: Fiction Editor, Prisim International 1977-79. Publications: Fighting the Upstream; Blue Husbands; The Crew. Contributions to: Best Canadian Short Fiction; Words We Call Home; The New Writers. Honours: Bankson Award; Governor General of Canada Award Nominee; Ethel Wilson Fiction Prize. Membership: Writers Union of Canada. Address: 554 Victoria Street, Lillooet, British Columbia V0K 1V0, Canada.

DICKINSON Margaret. See: **MUGGESON Margaret Elizabeth.**

DICKSON Gordon (Rupert), b. 1 Nov 1923, Edmonton, Alberta, Canada. Writer. Education: BA, 1948, Graduate Studies, 1948-50, University of Minnesota. Publications: Alien From Archturus, Mankind on the Run, 1956; Earthman's Burden (with Poul Anderson), 1957; Secret Under the Sea, Time to Teleport, The Genetic General, Delusion World, 1960; Special Delivery, Naked to the Stars, 1961; Necromancer, 1962; Secret Under Antarctica, 1963; Secret Under the Carribean, Space Winners, The Alien Way, Mission to Universe, 1965; Planet Run, Soldier Ask Not, The Space Swimmers, 1967; None But Man, Spacepaw, Wolfing, 1969; Hour of the Horde, Danger - Human (also known as The Book Of Gordon R Dickson), Mutants, 1970; Sleepwalker's World, The Tactics of Mistake, 1971; The Outposter, The Pritcher Mass, 1972; The Star Road, Alien Art, The R-Master, 1973; Gremlins Go Home! (with Ben Bova), Ancient My Enemy, 1974; Three to Dorsai, Combat SF (editor), Star Prince Charlie (with P Anderson), 1975; The Lifeship (with Harry Harrison), The Dragon and The George, 1976; Time Storm, 1977; Nebula Award Stories Twelve (editor), The Far Call, Home From the Shore, 1978; Spirit of Dorsai, Masters of Everon, Lost Dorsai, 1980; In Iron Years, Love Not Human, 1981; The Soace Swimmers, The Outposter, 1982; The Pitcher Mass, 1983; Dragon at War, Dragon on The Border, 1992; Blood and War, 1993. Address: PO Box 1569, Twin Cities Airport, MN 55111, USA.

DICKSON Mora Agnes, b. 20 Apr 1918, Glasgow, Scotland. Author; Artist. Education: Diploma of Art, Edinburgh College of Art, 1941; Certificate, Byam Shaw School of Drawing and Painting, London, 1950. Publications: New Nigerians, 1960; Baghdad and Beyond, 1961; A Season in Sarawak, 1962; A World Elsewhere, 1964; Israeli Interlude, 1966; Count Us In, 1968; Longhouse in Sarawak, 1971; Beloved Partner, 1974; A Chance to Serve (editor), The

Inseparable Grief, 1977; Assignment in Asia, 1979; The Powerful Bond, 1980; Nannie, 1988. Address: 19 Blenheim Road, London W4, England.

DIDION Joan, b. 5 Dec 1934, Sacramento, California, USA. Novelist; Reporter; Essayist. m. John Gregory Dunn, 30 Jan 1964, 1 daughter. Education: BA, University of California at Berkeley, 1956. Publications: Run River; Slouching Towards Bethleham; Play It as It Lays; A Book of Common Prayer; The White Album; Salvador; Democracy; Miami; After Henry. Contributions to: Best American Essays; New York Review of Books; New Yorker. Address: c/o Janklow & Nesbit Associates, 598 Madison Avenue, New York, NY 10022, USA.

DIECKMANN Friedrich, b. 25 May 1937, Landsberg, Germany. Writer. m. Christine Dieckmann geb Decker, 1976, 1 daughter. Education: University of Leipzig, Germanistics, Philosophy, Physics, 1983; Glockenläuten und Offene Fragen, 1991; Vom Einbringen/Vaterländische Beiträge, 1993; Wege durch Mitte, 1995; Dresdner Ansichten, 1995. Publications: Richard Wagner in Venedig, 1983, 2nd edition, 1994; Hilfsmittel wider die alternde Zeit (essays), 1990; Die Geschichte Don Giovannis, 1991; Temperatursprung/Deutsche Verhältnisse, 1995; Der Irrtum des Verschwindens (essays), 1996. Other: Karl von Appens Bühnenbilder am Berliner Ensemble, 1971; Streifzüge (essays), 1977; Theaterbilder (essays), 1979; Orpheus, eingeweiht, novel. Honours: Heinrich-Mann-Preis, Berlin, 1983; Richard-Wagner-Preis, 1983. Memberships: Sächsische Akademie der Künste, Vice President; Deutsche Akademie für Sprache und Dichtung; Freie Akademie der Künste zu Leipzig; Deutsches PEN-Zentrum (Ost); Schriftstellerverband. Address: Moosdorfstrasse 13, D-12435 Berlin, Germany.

DIGBY Joan (Hildreth), b. 16 Nov 1942, New York, New York, USA. Professor of English; Writer. m. (1) William Howard Owen, 26 Nov 1965, div, (2) John Michael Digby, 3 Mar 1979. Education: BA summa cum laude, 1963, PhD, 1969, New York University; MA, University of Delaware, 1965. Appointments: Assistant Professor, 1969-73, Associate Professor, 1973-77, Professor of English, Director of Honours Program and Merit Fellowship, 1977-, Long Island University, C W Post Campus, Brookville, New York. Publications: A Sound of Feathers, prose poems (with collage illustrations by husband John Digby), 1982; Two Presses, nonfiction, 1988; With John Digby: The Collage Handbook, 1985; The Wood Engraving of John de Pol, 1988; Permutations: Readings in Science and Literature (editor with Bob Brier), 1985; Editor with John Digby: Food for Thought, 1987; Inspired By Drink, 1988. Honour: Excellence in Teaching Award, New York State Council of English Teachers, 1987. Memberships: American Society for Eighteenth Century Studies; National Collegiate Honors Council; Phi Beta Kappa. Address: 30 Kellogg Street, Oyster Bay, NY 11771, USA.

DIGBY John (Michael), b. 18 Jan 1938, London, England. Emigrated, USA, 1978. Poet; Collagist. m. (1) Erica Susan Christine Berwick-Stephens, 1963, div, 1 son, (2) Joan Hildreth Weiss, 3 Mar 1979. Publications: The Structure of Biofocal Distance, poems, 1974; Sailing Away From Night, poems, collages, 1978; To Amuse a Shrinking Sun, poems, collages, 1985; The Collage Handbook (with wife, Joan Digby), 1985; Miss Liberty, collages, 1986; Incantation, poems, collages, 1987; A Parliament of Owls, poems, collages, 1989; Editor with Joan Digby: Inspired by Drink, 1988; The Wood Engravings of John de Pol, 1988. Address: 30 Kellogg Street, Oyster Bay, NY 11771, USA.

DIGREGORIO Charlotte Antonia, b. 30 Aug 1953, Portland, Oregon, USA. Author; Editorial Consultant; Professional Speaker. Education: BA, Pomona College, 1975; MA, University of Chicago, 1979. Appointment: Host, radio programme Poetry Beat, Oregon Public Broadcasting, 1995-. Publications: Beginners' Guide to Writing and Selling Quality Features, 1990; You Can Be a Columnist, 1993; Your Original Personal Ad, 1995. Contributions to: Magazines and Journals. Memberships: International Women's Writing Guild; Northwest Association of Book Publishers; Publishers Marketing Association; International Women's Writing Guild, regional representative, 1995-96. Address: 2770 South West Old Orchard Road, Portland, OR 97201, USA.

DILLARD Annie, b. 30 Apr 1945, Pittsburgh, Pennsylvania, USA. Adjunct Professor; Writer in Residence. m. (1) Richard Dillard,

4 June 1964, (2) Gary Clevidence, 12 Apr 1980, (3) Robert D Richardson Jr, 1988. Education: BA, 1967, MA, 1968, Hollins College. Appointments: Scholar in Residence, Western Washington University, 1975-79; Visiting Professor, 1979-81, Adjunct Professor, 1983-, Writer-in-Residence, 1987-, Wesleyan University. Publications: Pilgrim at Tinker Creek, 1974; Holy the Firm, 1977; Teaching a Stone to Talk, 1983; Encounters with Chinese Writers, 1984; An American Childhood, 1987; The Writing Life, 1989; The Living, 1992; The Annie Dillard Reader, 1994; Tickets for a Prayer Wheel, 1994; Mornings Like This, 1995. Honours: Pulitzer Prize, 1975; New York Press Club Award, 1975; Washington Governor's Award, 1977; National Endowment for the Arts Grant, 1985; Guggenheim Fellowship, 1986; Appalachian Gold Medallion, 1989; Ambassador Book Award, 1990; Campion Award, 1994; Milton Prize, 1994. Memberships: PEN International; Poetry Society of America; Western Writers of America; Century Association; National Association for the Advancement of Colored People; Society of American Historians. Address: c/o Tim Seldes, Russel & Volkening, 50 West 29th, New York 10001, USA.

DILLARD R(ichard) H(enry) W(ilde), b. 11 Oct 1937, Roanoke, Virginia, USA. Professor of English; Writer; Poet; Editor. m. (1) Annie Doak, 1965, div 1972, (2) Cathy Hankla, 1979. Education: BA, Roanoke College, Salem, Virginia, 1958; MA, 1959, PhD, 1965, University of Virginia. Appointments: Instructor, Roanoke College, 1961, University of Virginia, 1961-64; Assistant Professor, 1964-68, Associate Professor, 1968-74, Professor of English, 1974-, Hollins College, Virginia; Contributing Editor, Hollins Critic, 1966-77; Editor-in-Chief, Children's Literature, 1992-. Publications: Fiction: The Book of Changes, 1974; The First Man on the Sun, 1983; Omniphobia, 1995. Poetry: The Day I Stopped Dreaming About Barbara Steele and Other Poems, 1966; News of the Nile, 1971; After Borges, 1972; The Greeting: New and Selected Poems, 1981; Just Here, Just Now, 1994. Non-Fiction: Horror Films, 1976; Understanding George Garrett, 1988. Editor: The Experience of America: A Book of Readings (with Louis D Rubin Jr), 1969; The Sounder Few: Essays from "The Hollins Critic" (with George Garrett and John Rees Moore), 1971. Contributions to: Periodicals. Honours: Academy of American Poets Prize, 1961; Ford Foundation Grant, 1972; O B Hardison, Jr Poetry Award, Folger Shakespeare Library, Washington, DC, 1994. Address: Box 8671, Hollins College, CA 24020, USA.

DILLINGHAM William Byron, b. 7 Mar 1930, Atlanta, Georgia, USA; Writer. m. Elizabeth Joiner, 3 July 1952, 1 son, 2 daughters. Education: BA, 1955, MA, 1956, Emory University; PhD, University of Pennsylvania, 1961. Appointments: Instructor, 1956-58, Assistant Professor, Associate Professor, Professor, Charles Howard Candler Professor of American Literature, 1959-96, Emeritus Professor 1996-; Emory University; Editorial Boards, Nineteenth-Century Literature, South Atlantic Bulletin. Publications: Humor of the Old Southwest, 1965, 3rd edition, 1994; Frank Norris: Instinct and Art, 1969; An Artist in the Rigging: The Early Work of Herman Melville, 1972; Melville's Short Fiction, 1853-1856, 1977; Melville's Later Novels, 1986; Practical English Handbook, 9th Edition, 1992, 10th edition, 1996; Melville and His Circle: The Last Years, 1996. Contributions to: Many articles and reviews to scholarly journals. Address: 1416 Vistaleaf Drive, Decatur, GA 30033, USA.

DILLON Millicent Gerson, b. 24 May 1925. Writer. m. Murray Lesser, 1 June 1948, 2 daughters. Education: BA, Hunter College, 1944; MA, San Francisco State University, 1966. Publications: Baby Perpetua and Other Stories, 1971; The One in the Back is Medea (novel), 1973; A Little Original Sin: The Life and Work of Jane Bowles, 1981; After Egypt, 1990; The Dance of the Mothers (novel), 1991. Contributions to: Southwest Review; Witness; Threepenny Review. Honours: 5 O. Henry Short Story Awards; Best American Short Stories, 1992; Guggenheim Fellowship; National Endowment for the Humanities Fellowship. Memberships: PEN; Authors Guild. Address: 83 6th Avenue, San Francisco, CA 94118, USA.

DIMBLEBY David, b. 28 Oct 1938, London England. Broadcaster; Newspaper Proprietor. m. Josceline Gaskell, 1967, 1 son, 2 daughters, divorced. Education: Christ Church, Oxford; Universities of Paris and Perugia. Appointments: News Reporter, BBC Bristol, 1960-61; Presenter, Interviewer, various scientific, religious and political programmes, BBC TV 1961-87; Managing Director, 1966-86, Chairman, 1986-, Dimbleby Newspaper Group. Publication: An Ocean Apart (with David Reynolds), 1988. Honours: Supreme Documentary Award, 1979; Emmy Award, 1991; Golden Nymph

Award, 1991. Address: c/o BBC, Broadcasting House, Portland Place, London W1 1AA, England.

DIMBLEBY Jonathan, b. 31 July 1944, Aylesbury, Buckinghamshire, England. Freelance Broadcaster; Journalist; Author. m. Bel Mooney, 1968, 1 son, 1 daughter. Education: BA Honours, Philosophy, University College, London. Appointments: TV and Radio Reporter, BBC Bristol, 1969-70; BBC Radio, World at One, 1970-71; for Thames TV: This Week, 1972-78; TV Eye, 1979; Jonathan Dimbleby in South America, 1979; For Yorkshire TV: series, Jonathan Dimbleby in Evidence: The Police, 1980; The Bomb, 1980; The Eagle and the Bear, 1981; The Cold War Games, 1982; The American Dream, 1984; Four Years On - the Bomb, 1984; First Tuesday (Associate Editor, Presenter), 1982-86; TV AM: Jonathan Dimbleby on Sunday (Presenter/Editor), 1985-86; Thames Television: (Presenter/Reporter) This Week, 1986-88, Series Editor, Witness, documentary series, 1986-88; BBC Radio 4, Chairman, Any Questions, 1987-; BBC Radio 4, Chairman, Any Answers, 1987-; BBC, On the Record, 1988-93; BBC 1 and Radio 4, Election Call, 1992; Central TV, Charles: The Private Man, the Public Role, 1994; LWT, Jonathan Dimbleby, 1995-; General Election Coverage, ITV, 1997; The Last Governor, documentary series, BBC, 1997. Publications: Richard Dimbleby, 1975; The Palestinians, 1979; The Prince of Wales, A Biography, 1994; The Last Governor, 1997. Memberships: President, Council for the Protection of Rural England, 1992-97; Member of Boards, Richard Dimbleby Cancer Fund and Voluntary Service Overseas. Address: c/o David Higham Associates, 5 Lower John Street, London W1R 4HA, England.

DIMBLEBY Josceline Rose, b. 1 Feb 1943, Oxford, England. m. 20 Jan 1967, 1 son, 2 daughters. Appointments: Contributor, Daily Mail, 1976-78; Cookery Editor, Sunday Telegraph, 1982-; Regular Contributor to Country Homes and Interiors, 1986-. Publications: A Taste of Dreams, 1976; Party Pieces, 1977; Cooking for Christmas, 1978; Josceline Dimbleby's Book of Puddings, Desserts & Savouries, 1979; Cooking With Herbs and Spices, 1979; Curries and Oriental Cookery, 1980; Salads for All Seasons, 1981; Festive Food, 1982; Marvellous Meals with Mince, 1982; Sweet Dreams, 1983; The Josceline Dimbleby Collection, 1984 First Impressions, 1984; Main Attractions, 1985; A Traveller's Tastes, 1986; The Josceline Dimbleby Christmas Book, 1987; The Josceline Dimbleby Book of Entertaining, 1988; The Essential Josceline Dimbleby, 1989; The Cook's Companion, 1991; The Almost Vegetarian Cookbook, 1994; The Christmas Book, 1994; Josceline Dimbleby's Complete Cookbook. Contributions to: Numerous magazines; various TV programmes. Honours: Andre Simon Memorial Award, 1979; Glenfiddich Cookery Writer of the Year, 1993. Literary Agent: Curtis Brown. Address: 14 King Street, Richmond, Surrey TW9 1NF, England.

DIMITROFF Pashanko, b. 22 Mar 1924, Stanimaka, Bulgaria. Journalist. m. Margaret Greenwood, 18 July 1959, 2 sons. Education: Law, University of Sofia, 1943-46; Music, Cello, Academy of Music, Sofia, 1943; Doctor of Law, Faculte de Droit, Paris, 1959. Publications: Boris III of Bulgaria, 1986; The Silent Bulgarians (in Bulgarian), 1991; King of Mercy, 1993; Princess Clementine, 1994. Address: 20 Old Station Way, Wooburn Green, Bucks, HP10 0HZ.

DIMONT Penelope. See: MORTIMER Penelope (Ruth).

DINNERSTEIN Leonard, b. 5 May 1934, New York, New York, USA. Professor of History; Writer. m. Myra Anne Rosenberg, 20 Aug 1961, 1 son, 1 daughter. Education: BA, City College of New York, 1955; MA, 1960, PhD, 1966, Columbia University. Appointments: Instructor, New York Institute of Technology, 1960-65; Assistant Professor, Fairleigh Dickinson University, 1967-70; Associate Professor, 1970-72, Professor of American History,1972-, University of Arizona, Tucson. Publications: The Leo Frank Case, 1968; The Aliens (with F C Jaher), 1970, as Uncertain Americans, 1977; American Vistas (with K T Jackson), 1971, 7th edition, 1995; Antisemitism in the United States, 1971; Jews in the South (with M D Palsson), 1973; Decisions and Revisions (with J Christie), 1975; Ethnic Americans: A History of Immigration and Assimilation (with D M Reimers), 1975, 3rd edition, 1988; Natives and Strangers (with R L Nichols and D M Reimers), 1979, 2nd edition, 1990; America and the Survivors of the Holocaust, 1982; Uneasy at Home, 1987; Antisemitism in America, 1994. Address: 5821 East 7th Street, Tucson, AZ 85711, USA.

DISCH Thomas M(ichael), (Leonie Hargrave, Dobbin Thorpe), b. 2 Feb 1940, Des Moines, Iowa, USA. Writer; Poet; Dramatist; Librettist; Lecturer. Education: Cooper Union, New York; New York University. Appointments: Lecturer at colleges and universities; Artist-in-Residence, College of William and Mary, 1996. Publications: Novels: The Genocides, 1965; Mankind Under the Leash, 1966; The House That Fear Built (with John Sladek), 1966; Echo Round His Bones, 1967; Black Alice (with John Sladek), 1968; Camp Concentration, 1968; The Prisoner, 1969; 334, 1974; Clara Reeve, 1975; On Wings of Song, 1979; Triplicity, 1980; Neighboring Lives (with Charles Naylor), 1981; The Businessman: A Tale of Terror, 1984; Amnesia 1985; The M.D.: A Horror Story, 1991; The Priest: A Gothic Romance, 1995. Poetry: The Right Way to Figure Plumbing, 1972; ABCDEFG HIJKLM NOPQRST UVWXYZ, 1981; Orders of the Retina, 1982; Burn This, 1982; Here I Am, There You Are, Where Were We, 1984; Yes, Let's: New and Selected Poetry, 1989; Dark Verses and Light, 1991; The Dark Old House, 1995. Criticism: The Castle of Indolence, 1995. Other: Short story collections; plays; opera libretti; juvenile books. Contributions to: Many anthologies and periodicals. Honours: O Henry Prizes, 1975, 1979; John W Campbell Memorial Award, 1980; British Science Fiction Award, 1981. Memberships: National Book Critics Circle; PEN; Writers Guild. Address: Box 226, Barryville, NY 12719, USA.

DITTON James. See: **CLARK Douglas.**

DIVINE Robert A(lexander), b. 10 May 1929, New York, New York, USA. Professor of American History Emeritus; Author. m. (1) Barbara Christine Renick, 6 Aug 1955, 3 sons, 1 daughter, dec 1993, (2) Darlene S Harris, 1 June 1996. Education: BA, 1951, MA, 1952, PhD, 1954, Yale University. Appointments: Instructor, 1954-57, Assistant Professor, 1957-61, Associate Professor, 1961-63, Professor, 1963-80, George W Littlefield Professor of American History, 1981-96, Professor Emeritus, 1996-, University of Texas at Austin; Fellow, Center for Advanced Study in the Behavioural Sciences, Stanford, 1962-63; Albert Shaw Lecturer, Johns Hopkins University, 1968. Publications: American Immigration Policy 1924-1952, 1957; The Illusion of Neutrality, 1962; The Reluctant Belligerent: American Entry into World War II, 1965, 2nd edition, 1979; Second Chance: The Triumph of Internationalism in America During World War II, 1967; Roosevelt and World War II, 1969; Foreign Policy and US Presidential Elections, 1940-1960, 2 volumes, 1974; Since 1945: Politics and Diplomacy in Recent American History, 1975, 3rd edition, 1985; Blowing on the Wind, 1978; Eisenhower and the Cold War, 1981; America: Past and Present (with T H Breen, George Frederickson and R Hal Williams), 1984, 4th edition, 1995; The Sputnik Challenge, 1993. Editor: American Foreign Policy, 1960; The Age of Insecurity: America 1920-1945, 1968; Twentieth-Century America: Contemporary Documents and Opinions (with John A Garraty), 1968; American Foreign Policy Since 1945, 1969; Causes and Consequences of World War II, 1969; The Cuban Missile Crisis, 1971, 2nd edition, 1988; Exploring the Johnson Years, 1981; The Johnson Years: Vol Two, Vietnam, the Environment and Science, 1987; The Johnson Years: Vol Three, LBJ at Home and Abroad, 1994. Contributions to: Scholarly books and journals. Honours: Rockefeller Humanities Fellowship, 1976-77; Graduate Teaching Award, University of Texas, 1986. Memberships: Phi Beta Kappa; Texas Institute of Letters. Address: 10617 Sans Souci Place, Austin, TX 78759, USA.

DIVINSKY Nathan J(oseph), b. 29 Oct 1925, Winnipeg, Manitoba, Canada. Mathematician. 3 daughters. Education: BSc, University of Manitoba, 1946; SM, 1947, PhD, 1950, University of Chicago, USA. Appointments: Editor, Canadian Chess Chat, 1959-74. Publications: Around the Chess World in 80 Years, 1963; Rings and Radicals, 1965; Linear Algebra, 1970; Warriors of the Mind (with R Keene), 1988; Chess Encyclopedia, 1990; Life Maps of the Great Chessmasters, 1994. Memberships: Life Master, ACBL (Bridge League); President, Commonwealth Chess Association, 1988-94; Canada's Representative to FIDE (World Chess Federation), 1987-94. Address: 5689 McMaster Road, Vancouver, British Columbia V6T 1K1, Canada.

DIVOK Mario J, b. 22 Sept 1944, Benus, Czechoslovakia. Real Estate Broker; Investments Executive; Poet; Dramatist. m. Eva Pytlova, 1 son, 2 daughters. Education: MA, Pedagogic Institute, Martin, Czechoslovakia, 1967; MPA, California State University, Long Beach, 1977; Management, University of California, Irvine, 1995. Publications: The Relations, 1975; The Voice, 1975; The Wind of Changes, 1978; Equinox, 1978; The Collection, 1978; I Walk the Earth,

1980; The Blind Man, 1980; Looking for the Road to the Earth, 1983; The Birthday, 1984; Stranger in the Land, 1989; Selected Works, 1992. Contributions to: Various periodicals. Honours: Schlossar Award, Hall Publishers, Switzerland, 1980; American Poetry Association Award, 1988; World of Poetry Award, 1990. Memberships: American Association of Poets; American Playwrights Association. Address: 5 Misty Meadow Drive, Irvine, CA 92612, USA.

DIXON Dougal, b. 3 Mar 1947, Dumfries, Scotland. Writer. m. Jean Mary Young, 3 Apr 1971, 1 son, 1 daughter. Education: BSc, 1970, MSc, 1972, University of St Andrews. Appointments: Researcher, Editor, Mitchell-Beazley Ltd, 1973-78, Blandford Press, 1978-80; Part-time Tutor, Earth Sciences, Open University, 1976-78; Chairman, Bournemouth Science Fiction and Fantasy Group, 1981-82; Freelance Writer, 1980-. Publications: Doomsday Planet (comic strip), 1980; After Man: A Zoology for the Future, 1981; Discovering Earth Sciences, 1982; Science World: Geology, 1982; Science World: Geography, 1983; Picture Atlas: Mountains, 1984; Picture Atlas: Forests, 1984; Picture Atlas: Deserts, 1984; Find Out About Prehistoric Reptiles, 1984; Find Out About Jungles, 1984; The Age of Dinosaurs (with Jane Burton), 1984; Nature Detective Series: Minerals Rocks and Fossils, 1984; Time Machine 7: Ice Age Explorer, 1985; Secrets of the Earth, 1986; Find Out About Dinosaurs, 1986. Address: c/o Hamlyn, 69 London Road, Twickenham, Middlesex TW1 3SB, England.

DIXON Jean Clarence, b. 9 Apr 1915, Sydney, New South Wales, Australia. Author; Editor. m. Douglas Lindsay Dixon, 12 Dec 1936, dec 1995, 2 sons, 1 daughter. Education: Creative Writing Course, Sydney University, 1969; Selected Member, Writers' Retreat New England University, Armidale, New South Wales, 1968; Pilot Group Women Playwrights, 1974. Appointments: Commissioned Novelisation of Filmscript for children's movie "Blue Fire Lady", 1978; Commissioned Researcher Women's prison procedures for TV series "Prisoner", 1978; Editor, "Bushland News", 1974-88; International PEN, Sydney Centre, Editor, Pen Quarterly, 1981-86; Member, Management Committee, 1989-93; Returning Officer, PEN Short Story Award, 1989-93; Editor, Newsletter for Society of Women Writers New South Wales Inc, 1995-96. Publications: First 3 Novels Serialised in magazines: That Way Madness, 1964; The Poison Tree, 1968; Death Takes the Chair, 1973; Books: Blue Fire Lady, 1977; The Riddle of Powder Works Road, 1980, 1990; Hello Mr Melody Man (editor), 1983; The Climber, 1987; Short stories; Commissioned articles "The Australian Author". Memberships: International PEN, Sydney Centre; Australian Society of Authors; New South Wales Society of Women Writers; New South Wales State Library Society; New South Wales Writers' Centre. Address: P O Box 431, Mona Vale, New South Wales 2103, Australia.

DIXON Larry, b. Tulsa, Oklahoma, USA. Writer; Artist. m. Mercedes Lackey, 14 Dec 1990. Publications: Winds of Fate, 1991; Serrated Edge series: Born to Run, 1992; The Mage-Wars; The Black Gryphon; The Mage-Wind books: Winds of Change, 1992; Winds of Fury, 1993. Membership: Science Fiction and Fantasy Writers of America. Address: PO Box 8309, Tulsa, OK 74101, USA.

DIXON Roger, (John Christian, Charles Lewis), b. 6 Jan 1930, Portsmouth, England. Author; Playwright. m. Carolyn Anne Shepheard, 28 June 1966, 2 sons, 4 daughters. Publications: Over 50 radio plays and series; novels: Noah II, 1970; Christ on Trial, 1973; The Messiah, 1974; Five Gates to Armageddon (as John Christian), 1975; The Cain Factor (as Charles Lewis), 1975; Going to Jerusalem, 1977; Georgiana, 1984; Return to Nebo, 1991; Musical: The Commander of New York (with Phil Medley and Basil Bova), 1987. Adddress: Badgers, Warren Lane, Croos-in-Hand, Heathfield, Sussex, England.

DIXON Stephen, b. 6 June 1936, New York, New York, USA. Writer; University Teacher. m. Anne Frydman, 17 Jan 1982, 2 daughters. Education: BA, City College of New York, 1958. Publications: No Relief, 1976; Work, 1977; Too Late, 1978; Quite Contrary, 1979; 14 Stories, 1980; Movies, 1983; Time to Go, 1984; Fall and Rise, 1985; Garbage, 1988; Love and Will, 1989; The Play and Other Stories, 1989; All Gone, 1990; Friends, 1990; Frog, 1991; Long Made Short, 1993; The Stories of Stephen Dixon, 1994; Interstate, 1995; Man on Stage, 1996; Gould, 1997. Contributions to: 400 short stories to magazines and journals including Atlantic; Harper's; Esquire; Playboy; Paris Review; Triquarterly; Western Humanities Review; Ambit; Bananas; Boulevard; Glimmer Train; Partisan Review; O. Henry Prize Stories, 1977, 1982, 1993; Best American Stories, 1993, 1996. Honours: Stegner Fiction Fellowship, Stanford University, 1964-65;

National Endowment of the Arts Grants, 1974-75, 1990-91; American Academy and Institute of Arts and Letters Award, 1983; John Train Prize, Paris Review, 1984; Guggenheim Fellowship, 1985-86. Address: 1315 Boyce Avenue, Baltimore, MD 21204, USA.

DJERASSI Carl, b. 29 Oct 1923, Vienna, Austria. University Professor; Chemist; Writer. m. Diane Wood Middlebrook, 20 June 1985, 1 son. Education: AB summa cum laude, Kenyon College, 1942; PhD, University of Wisconsin, 1945. Appointments: Associate Professor, 1952-53, Professor of Chemistry, 1953-59, Wayne State University; Professor of Chemistry, Stanford University, 1959-. Publications: Optical Rotatory Dispersion, 1959; Steroid Reactions, 1963; Mass Spectrometry of Organic Compounds (with H Budzikiewicz and D H Williams), 1967; The Politics of Contraception, 1979; The Futurist and Other Stories, 1988; Cantor's Dilemma (novel), 1989; Steroids Made It Possible, 1990; The Clock Runs Backward (poetry), 1991; The Pill, Pygmy Chimps, and Degas' Horse (autobiography), 1992; The Bourbaki Gambit (novel), 1994; From the Lab into the World (collected essays), 1994; Marx, Deceased (novel), 1996; Menachem's Seed (novel), 1997. Contributions to: Kenyon Review; Southern Review; Grand Street; New Letters; Exquisite Corpse; Michigan Quarterly Review; South Dakota Review; Frank; Midwest Quarterly. Memberships: National Academy of Sciences; American Academy of Arts and Sciences; Swedish, German, Brazilian and Mexican Academies of Science; Royal Society of Chemistry. Literary Agents: Andrew Nurnberg Associates, 45-47 Clerkenwell Green, London EC1R 0HT, England. Address: Department of Chemistry, Stanford University, Stanford, CA 94305-5080, USA.

DOAN Eleanor Lloyd, (Lloyd E Werth), b. 4 June 1914, Idaho, USA. Journalist; Writer; Publicist. Education: University of Nevada, 1936; Graduate Work, Wheaton College, Illinois, 1937; Marketing Research, University of California, Los Angeles, 1956, 1957. Publications: VBS Courses, 57 books, 1944, 1950; Mother's Day Source Book, 1973; Child's Treasury of Verse, 1977; Complete Speakers Source Book, 1996. Contributions to: Periodicals and journals. Address: 10749 Galvin Street, Ventura, CA 93004, USA.

DOBAI Peter, b. 12 Aug 1944, Budapest, Hungary. Writer. m. (1) Donatella Failoni, 1972, (2) Maria Mate, 1992. Education: Sailor, Mate, 1963-65; Teacher's Diploma, Philosophy, Italian, Faculty of Humanities, Budapest, 1970. Appointments: Scriptwriter, Dramaturgist, Assisstant Director, Mafilm, 1970. Publications: Film scripts: Punitive Expedition, 1971; Csontvary, The Painter, 1979; Mephisto, 1980; Colonel Redl, 1983; Hanussen, the Prophet, 1984; Consciousness, 1987; Rembrandt van Rijn (Life and Works), 1992. Poetry: Kilvoglas egy öszi erödböl, 1973; Egy arc modosulasai, 1976; Lying on the Back, 1978; Pitfalls of Eden, 1985; Selected Poems, 1989. Novels: Csontmolnarok, 1974; Belonging Life, 1975; Avalanche, 1980; Wilderness, 1982; A birodalom ezredese, 1985; Arch, 1988; Fly-Wheel, 1989. Short story collections: Jatek a szobakkal, 1976; Chessboard With Two Figures, 1978; 1964 -Island, diary, 1977; Archaic Torso, scripts, essays, 1983. Contributions to: Essays, articles and reviews to magazines and journals. Honours: Joszef Attila Prize, 1976; Several Awards, Hungarian Literary Foundation and Minister of Culture; Best Filmscript for Mephisto, Cannes Film Festival, 1981; Balazs Bela Prize for scripts, 1990. Memberships: Executive Board, Hungarian Writers Association, Chamber of Writers; Hungarian Academy of Artists; Hungarian PEN Club; Association of Hungarian Film and Television Artists; Professional Feature Film Advisory Board; Hungarian Seaman's Association. Address: Kozraktar u 12 B, 1093 Budapest, Hungary.

DOBSON Andrew Nicholas Howard, b. 15 Apr 1957, Doncaster, England. Politics Lecturer. Education: BA 1st Class, Politics, Reading University, 1979; DPhil Politics, Oxford University, 1983. Appointments: Editorial Board, Environmental Values, 1991-, Environmental Politics, 1991-; Anarchist Studies, 1991-; Chair of Politics, Keele University, 1993-. Publications: Introduction to the Politics and Philosophy of José Ortega y Gasset, 1989; Green Political Thought, 1990, 2nd edition, 1995; The Green Reader, 1991; The Politics of Nature: Explorations in Green Political Theory (edited with Paul Lucardie), 1993; Jean-Paul Sartre and the Politics of Reason: A Theory of History, 1993. Contributions to: Numerous articles and book reviews to magazines and journals. Honours: Spanish Government Scholar, 1983-84; ERSC Postdoctoral Fellow, 1984-87. Address: Politics Department, Keele University, Keele, Staffs ST5 5BG, England.

DOBSON Julia Lissant, (Julia Tugendhat), b. 23 Sept 1941, Tanzania. Writer. m. Christopher Tugendhat, 8 Apr 1967, 2 sons. Education: BA, Lady Margaret Hall, Oxford, 1963. Publications: The Children of Charles I, 1975; The Smallest Man in England, 1977; Mountbatten Sailor Hero, Children of the Tower, 1978; They Were at Waterloo, 1979; The Ivory Poachers: A Crisp Twins Adventure, The Tomb Robbers, 1981; The Wreck Finders, The Animal Rescuers, 1982; Danger in the Magic Kingdom, 1983; The Chinese Puzzle, 1984; As Julia Tugendhat: What Teenagers Can Tell Us About Divorce and Step Families, 1990; The Adoption Triangle, 1992. Address: 35 Westbourne Park Road, London W2, England.

DOBSON Rosemary (de Brissac), b. 18 June 1920, Sydney, New South Wales, Australia. Poet; Editor; Translator. m. A T Bolton, 1951, 2 sons, 1 daughter. Education: Frensham, Mittagong, New South Wales. Publications: In A Convex Mirror, 1944; The Ship of Ice & Other Poems, 1948; Child with a Cockatoo and Other Poems, 1955; Poems, 1963; Cock Crow, 1965; Selected Poems, 1973, revised edition, 1980; Greek Coins: A Sequence of Poems, 1977; Over the Frontier, 1978; The Three Fates and Other Poems, 1984; Collected Poems, 1991; Untold Lives, A Sequence of Poems, 1992. Honours: Patrick White Award, 1984; Officer, Order of Australia, 1987; Honorary DLitt, Sydney University, 1996. Address: 61 Stonehaven Crescent, Deakin, Canberra Australian Capital Territory 2600, Australia.

DOBYNS Stephen, b. 19 Feb 1941, Orange, New Jersey, USA. Professor of Creative Writing; Poet; Writer. m. 2 children. Education: Shimer College, Mount Carroll, Illinois, 1959-60; BA, Wayne State University, 1964; MFA, University of Iowa, 1967. Appointments: Instructor, State University of New York College at Brockport, 1968-69; Reporter, Detroit News, 1969-71; Visiting Writer, University of New Hampshire, 1973-75, University of Iowa, 1977-79, Boston University, 1978-79, 1980-81, Syracuse University, 1986; Faculty, Goddard College, Plainfield, Vermont, 1978-80, Warren Wilson College, Swannanoa, North Carolina, 1982-87; Professor of Creative Writing, Syracuse University, New York, 1987-. Publications: Poetry: Concurring Beasts, 1972; Griffon, 1976; Heat Death, 1980; The Balthus Poems, 1982; Black Dog, Red Dog, 1984; Cemetery Nights, 1987; Body Traffic, 1991; Velocities: New and Selected Poems, 1966-1992, 1994. Fiction: A Man of Little Evils, 1973; Saratoga Longshot, 1976; Saratoga Swimmer, 1981; Dancer with One Leg, 1983; Saratoga Headhunter, 1985; Cold Dog Soup, 1985; Saratoga Snapper, 1986; A Boat Off the Coast, 1987; The Two Deaths of Senora Puccini, 1988; Saratoga Bestiary, 1988; The House of Alexandrine, 1989; Saratoga Hexameter, 1990; After Shocks/Near Escapes, 1991; Saratoga Haunting, 1993; The Wrestler's Cruel Study, 1993; Saratoga Backtalk, 1994; Saratoga Fleshpot, 1995; Saratoga Trifecta, 1995. Honours: Lamont Poetry Selection Award, 1971; MacDowell Colony Fellowships, 1972, 1976; Yaddo Fellowships, 1972, 1973, 1977, 1981, 1982; National Endowment for the Arts Grants, 1974, 1981; Guggenheim Fellowship, 1983; National Poetry Series Prize, 1984. Address: 208 Brattle Road, Syracuse, NY 13203, USA.

DOCHERTY John. See: SILLS-DOCHERTY Jonathon John.

DOCTOROW Edgar Lawrence, b. 6 Sep 1931, New York, New York, USA. Writer. m. Helen Setzer, 20 Aug 1954, 1 son, 2 daughters. Education: AB, Kenyon College, 1952; Graduate Study, Columbia University, 1952-53. Appointments: Script Reader, Columbia Pictures, 1959-59; Senior Editor, New American Library, 1960-64; Editor-in-Chief, Dial Press, 1964-69; Publisher, 1969; Writer-in-Residence, University of California, Irvine, 1969-70; Member of Faculty, Sarah Lawrence College, 1971-78; Creative Writing Fellow, Yale School of Drama, 1974-75; Visiting Senior Fellow, Council on the Humanities, Princeton University, 1980; Glucksman Professor of American and English Letters, New York University, 1987-. Publications: Welcome to Hard Times, 1960; Big as Life, 1966; The Book of Daniel, 1971; Ragtime, 1975; Drinks Before Dinner (play), 1979; Loon Lake, 1980; Lives of the Poets, 1984; World's Fair, 1985; Billy Bathgate, 1989; Jack London, Hemingway and the Constitution, 1993; The Waterworks, 1994. Honours: Guggenheim Fellowship, 1973; Arts and Letters Award, American Academy and National Institute for Arts and Letters, 1976; National Book Critics Circle Awards, 1976, 1989; National Book Award, 1985; PEN/Faulkner Award, 1990; Howells Medal, American Academy and Institute for Arts and Letters for Most Distinguished Work of Fiction in Five Years, 1990. Memberships: PEN, American Center; Writers Guild of America; Authors Guild; Century Association. Literary Agent: Arlene Donovan,

ICM, 40 West 57th Street, New York, NY 10022, USA. Address: c/o Random House, 201 East 50th Street, New York, NY 10019, USA.

DOHERTY Berlie, b. 6 Nov 1943, Liverpool, England. Novelist; Playwright; Poet. m. Gerard Doherty, 17 Dec 1966, 1 son, 2 daughters, div 1996, 1 son, 2 daughters. Education: BA Hons, English, Durham University, 1964; Post-Graduate Certificate in Social Studies, 1965, Liverpool University; Post-Graduate Certificate of Education, Sheffield University, 1976. Appointments: Member, Literature Panel, Yorkshire Arts Association, 1986-87; Chairperson, Arvon Foundation, Lumb Bank, 1988-93; Deputy Chairperson, National Association of Writers in Education, 1988. Publications: Requiem (novel), 1991; The Vinegar Jar (novel), 1994; Children's books: How Green You Are, 1982; The Making of Fingers Finnigan, 1983; White Peak Farm, 1984; Children of Winter, 1985; Granny Was A Buffer Girl, 1986; Tilly Mint Tales, 1986; Tilly Mint and the Dodo, 1988; Paddiwak and Cosy, 1988; Tough Luck, 1988; Spellhorn, 1989; Dear Nobody, 1990; Snowy, 1992; Big, Bulgy Fat Black Slug, 1993; Old Father Christmas, 1993; Street Child, 1993; Walking on Air (poetry), 1993; Willa and Old Miss Annie, 1994; The Snake-Stone, 1995; The Golden Bird, 1995; Dear Nobody (play), 1995; The Magical Bicycle, 1995; Our Field, 1996; Morgan's Field (play), 1996; Daughter of the Sea, 1996. Contributions to: Periodicals. Honours: Carnegie Medals, 1987, 1991; Boston Globe Horn Honor, 1987; Burnley Children's Book of the Year Award, 1987; Bronze Award, International Film and Television, 1988; Children's Award, Picture Book Section, 1993; Writer's Guild of Great Britain Children's Play Award, 1994. Membership: Arvon Foundation. Literary Agent: Jacqueline Korn (David Higham Associates). Address: 222 Old Brompton Road, London, England.

DOKIC Jérôme André, b. 19 Aug 1965, Fribourg, Switzerland. Researcher; Teaching Assistant. Education: Licence Lettres (BA), 1989, DES (MA), 1990, PhD, 1995, University of Geneva. Publications: La Philosophie Du Son (with R Casati); Penser en Contexte (with E Corazza), 1993; The Dynamics of Deistic Thoughts, in Philosophical Studies; La Signification des Expressions Igocentriques, in Journal Proust; Why is Fregi's Puzzle Still Puzzling? (with E Corazza), Sense and Reference 100 Years Later, 1995. Address: Department of Philosophy, University of Geneva, 2 Rue Candolle, CH-1211 Geneva 4, Switzerland.

DOLL Mary Aswell, b. 4 Jun 1940, New York, New York, USA. Professor of English. m. William Elder Doll Jr, 25 June 1966, 1 son, dec. Education: BA, Connecticut College, New London, 1962; MA, Johns Hopkins University, 1970; PhD, Syracuse University, 1980. Appointments: Assistant Professor, State University of New York, Oswego, 1978-84; Lecturer, University of Redlands, California, 1985-88; Assistant Professor, Loyola University, 1988; Visiting Assistant Professor, Tulane University, 1988; Associate Professor, 1989-93, Professor, 1993-, Our Lady of Holy Cross College. Publications: Rites of Story: The Old Man at Play, 1987; Beckett and Myth: An Archetypal Approach, 1988; In the Shadow of the Giant: Thomas Wolfe, 1988; Walking and Rocking, 1989; Joseph Campbell and the Power of the Wilderness, 1992; Stoppard's Theatre of Unknowing, 1993; To the Lighthouse and Back, 1996. Contributions to: Periodicals. Honours: In the Shadow selected as 1 of Choice's Outstanding Books, 1989; Sears-Roebuck Teaching Excellence Award. Memberships: Modern Language Association; Board of Directors, Thomas Wolfe Society; American Academy of Religion. Address: 4154 State Street Drive, New Orleans, LA 70125, USA.

DOMARADZKI Théodore Felix, (Felice), b. 27 Oct 1910, Warsaw, Poland. University Professor (retired); Director General of Institute of Comparative Civilization. m. Maria Dobija, 20 Apr 1954. Education: Diploma, Political Science, Warsaw, 1933; MA, Warsaw University, 1939; LittD, Rome University, 1941. Appointments: Member, Doctoral Examination Commissions, Literature, University of Ottawa, 1950-53, University of Montreal, 1950-76; Editor-in-Chief, Slavic and East European Studies/Etudes Slaves et Est-Européennes, Montreal-Quebec, 1956-76; Director-General, Institute of Comparative Civilization, Montreal. Publications: Le Culte de la Vierge Marie et le Catholicisme de C K Norwid, 1961; La réalité du mal chez C Baudelaire et C Norwid, 1973; Les post-Romantiques polonais, 1973; Le symbolisme et l'universalisme de C K Norwid, 1974; Personalités ethniques au Québec, 1991. Contributions to: as Felice, Journals and encyclopaedias. Honours: Order of Merit, Polish Literature, University of Lublin, 1969; Order of Canada, 1989; Award of Merit, Canadian Multilingual Press Federation, 1991; Order of Polonia Restituta, 1991; Commemorative Medal, Literary Society of Warsaw, 1992.

Memberships: PEN Club International, Quebec Section; Société des Ecrivains Canadiens; Polish Scientific Society, London; Société Historique et Littéraire Polonaise, Paris; Honorary Life Member: Canadian Association of Slavists; Canadian Society for Comparative Study of Civilizations; Quebec Ethnic Press Association; Polish Institute of Arts and Sciences in Canada; Istituto Italiano di Cultura. Address: 6100 Deacon Road 4E, Montreal, Quebec H3S 2V6, Canada.

DONAGHUE Bernard (Baron), b. 1934. Appointments: Editorial Staff, The Economist, London, 1959-60; Senior Research Officer, Political and Economic Planning (PEP), London, 1960-63; Senior Lecturer, Politics, London School of Economics, 1963-74; Senior Policy Adviser to The Prime Minister 1974-79; Director, Economist Intelligence Unit, London, 1979-81; Assisstant Editor, The Times, London, 1981-82; Head of Research, Kleinworth, Grieveson and Company, 1982-. Publications: Oxford poetry, 1956; British Politics and the American Revolution, 1963; The People into Parliament (co-author), 1964; Herbert Morrison, Portrait of a Politician (co-author), 1973; Prime Minister, 1987. Address: 71 Ebury Mews West, London SW1W 9QA, England.

DONAGHUE Denis, b. 1928, Ireland. Writer. Appointments: Henry James Professor of English and American Letters, New York University. Publications: The Third Voice: Modern British and American Verse Drama, 1959; Conoisseurs of Chaos: Ideas of Order in Modern American Literature, 1965; An Honoured Guest: New Essays on W B Yeats (with J R Mulryne), 1965; Swift Revisited, 1968; The Ordinary Universe: Soundings in Modern Literature, 1968; Jonathan Swift: A Critical Introduction, 1969; Emily Dickinson, 1969; William Butler Yeats, 1971; Jonathan Swift: A Critical Anthology, 1971; Memoirs, by W B Yeats, 1973; Thieves of Fire, 1973; The Sovereign Ghost: Studies in Imagination, 1976; Ferocious Alphabets, 1981; The Ants Without Mystery, 1983; Being Modern Together, 1991; The Pure Good of Theory, 1992; The Old Moderns; Warrenpoint, 1993. Contributions to: New York Review of Books. Address: Department of English, New York University, New York, NY 10003, USA.

DONALD David Herbert, b. 1 Oct 1920, Goodman, Mississippi, USA. Professor of History Emeritus; Author. m. Aida DiPace, 1955, 1 son. Education: AB, Millsaps College, Jackson, Mississippi, 1941; Graduate Study in History, University of North Carolina, 1942; MA, 1942, PhD, 1945, in History, University of Illinois. Appointments: Teaching Fellow, University of North Carolina, 1942; Research Assistant, 1943-45, Research Associate, 1946-47, University of Illinois; Fellow, Social Science Rsearch Council, 1945-46; Instructor, 1947-49, Assistant Professor, 1951-52, Associate Professor, 1952-57, Professor of History, 1957-59, Columbia University; Associate Professor of History, Smith College, 1949-51; Visiting Associate Professor, Amherst College, 1950; Fulbright Lecturer in American History, University College of North Wales, 1953-54; Member, Institute for Advanced Study, 1957-58; Harmsworth Professor of American History, Oxford University, 1959-60; Professor of History, Princeton University, 1959-62; Harry C Black Professor of American History and Director of the Institute of Southern History, Johns Hopkins University, 1962-73; Charles Warren Professor of American History and Professor of American Civilization, 1973-91, Professor Emeritus, 1991-, Harvard University; Walter Lynwood Fleming Lecturer, Louisiana State University, 1965; Commonwealth Lecturer, University College of London, 1975; Samuel Paley Lecturer, Hebrew University of Jerusalem, 1991. Publications: Lincoln's Herndon, 1948; Divided We Fought: A Pictorial History of the War, 1961-1865, 1952; Inside Lincoln's Cabinet: The Civil War Diaries of Salmon P Chase, 1954; Lincoln Reconsidered: Essays on the Civil War Era, 1956, revised edition, 1961; Charles Sumner and the Coming of the Civil War, 1960; Why the North Won the Civil War, 1960; The Civil War and Reconstruction (with J G Randall), 2nd edition, 1961, revised edition, 1969; The Divided Union, 1961; The Politics of Reconstruction, 1863-1867, 1965; The Nation in Crisis, 1861-1877, 1969; Charles Sumner and the Rights of Man, 1970; The South Since the War (with Sidney Andrews), 1970; Gone for a Soldier: The Civil War Memoirs of Private Alfred Bellard, 1975; The Great Republic: A History of the American People (with others), 1977, 4th edition, 1992; Liberty and Union: The Crisis of Popular Government, 1830-1890, 1978; Look Homeward: A Life of Thomas Wolfe, 1987; Lincoln, 1995. Contributions to: Scholarly journals. Honours: George A and Eliza G Howard Fellow, 1957-58; Pulitzer Prizes in Biography, 1960, 1988; Guggenheim Fellowships, 1964-65, 1985-86; American Council of Learned Societies Fellow, 1969-70; Center for Advanced Study in the Behavioral Sciences Fellow, 1969-70; National Endowment for the Humanities

Fellow, 1971-72; C Hugh Holman Prize, Modern Language Association, 1988; Distinguished Alumnus Award, University of Illinois, 1988; Benjamin L C Wailes Award, Mississippi Historical Society, 1994; Lincoln Prize, 1996; Christopher Award, 1996; Distinguished Non-Fiction Award, American Library Association, 1996. Memberships: American Antiquarian Society; American Historical Association; Massachusetts Historical Association; Omicron Delta Kappa; Organization of American Historians; Southern Historical Association, president, 1969; Honorary doctorates. Address: 41 Lincoln Road, Po Box 6158, Lincoln, MA 01773, USA.

DONALDSON Ivan MacGregor, b. 28 Aug 1941, Dunedin, New Zealand. Neurologist; Wine Writer; Wine Maker. m. Christine Collett Taylor, 19 Feb 1968, 4 sons. Education: MB ChB 1966, MRACP 1970, MRCP (UK) 1972, FRACP, 1975, MD 1976, FRCP (Lond) 1982. Publications: Wine - A New Zealand Perspective, 1982; Movement Disorders, in press. Contributions to: Wine Columnist, "The Press", Christchurch, New Zealand; Christchurch Star; New Zealand Sunday Times; Regular Neurological Publications. Address: 112 Heaton Street, Christchurch, New Zealand 8005.

DONALDSON Stephen Reeder, (Reed Stephens), b. 13 May 1947, Cleveland, Ohio, USA. Writer. 1 son, 1 daughter. Education: BA, English, Wooster College, 1968; MA, Kent State University, 1971. Appointments: Associate Instructor, Ghost Ranch Writers Workshops, 1973-77; Contributing Editor, Journal of the Fantastic in the Arts. Publications: Lord Foul's Bane, 1977; The Earth War, 1977; The Power That Preserves, 1977; The Wounded Land, 1980; The One Tree, 1982; White Gold Wielder, 1983; Daughter of Regals, 1984; The Mirror of Her Dreams, 1986; A Man Rides Through, 1987; The Real Story, 1991; Forbidden Knowledge, 1991; A Dark and Hungry God Arises, 1992; The Gap Into Madness: Chaos and Order, 1994; As Reed Stephens: The Man Who Killed His Brother, 1980; The Man Who Risked His Partner, 1984; The Man Who Tried to Get Away, 1990. Honours: Best Novel, British Fantasy Society, 1979; Best New Writer, John W Campbell, 1979; Honorary DLitt, College of Wooster, 1993. Address: c/o Howard Morhaim, 175 Fifth Avenue, New York, NY 10010, USA.

DONKIN Nance (CLare), b. 1915, West Maitland, New South Wales, Australia. Children's Fiction Writer; Journalist. m. Victor Donkin, 14 Jan 1939, 1 son, 1 daughter. Appointments: Journalist, Daily Mercury, Maitland, Morning Herald, Newcastle; President, Children's Book Council, Victoria, 1968-76. Publications: Araluen Adeventures, 1946; No Medals For Meg, 1947; Julie Stands By, 1948; Blue Ribbon Beth, 1951; The Australian's Children's Annual, 1963; Sheep, 1967; Sugar, 1967; An Emancipist, 1968; A Currency Lass, 1969; House By the Water, 1969; An Orphan, 1971; Johnny Neptune, 1971; The Cool Man, 1974; A Friend for Petros, 1974; Margaret Catchpole, 1974; Patchwork Grandmother, 1975; Green Christmas, 1976; Yellowgum Girl, 1976; A Handful of Ghosts, 1976; The Best of the Bunch, 1978; The Maidens of Pefka, 1979; Nini, 1979; Stranger and Friend, 1983; We of the Never Retold for Children, 1983; Two at Sullivan Bay, 1985; Blackout, 1987; A Family Affair, 1988; The Women Were There, 1988; Always a Lady, 1990. Honours: Member of the Order of Austalia, 1986; Alice Award for Distinguished Contribution to Australian Literature, Society Women Writers, 1990. Memberships: Fellowship Australian Writers; Australian Society of Authors; Society of Women Writers of Australia; Royal Historical Society; Children's Book Council; Gallery Society; National Trust; Melbourne Theatre Company. Address: 18/26 Rochester Road, Canterbury, Victoria 3126, Australia.

DONLEAVY J(ames) P(atrick), b. 23 Apr 1926, New York, New York, USA (Irish citizen, 1967). Author; Dramatist. m. (1) Valerie Heron, div, 1 son, 1 daughter, (2) Mary Wilson Price, div, 1 son, 1 daughter. Education: Trinity College, Dublin. Publications: Fiction: The Ginger Man, 1955, unexpurgated edition, 1963; A Singular Man, 1963; Meet My Maker the Mad Molecule (short stories), 1964; The Saddest Summer of Samuel S, 1966; The Beastly Beatitudes of Balthazar B, 1968; The Onion Eaters, 1971; A Fairy Tale of New York, 1973; The Destinies of Darcy Dancer, Gentleman, 1977; Schultz, 1979; Leila: Further in the Destinies of Darcy Dancer, Gentleman, 1983; Are You Listening Rabbi Löw, 1987; That Darcy, That Dancer, That Gentleman, 1990; The Lady Who Liked Clean Rest Rooms, 1996. Plays: The Ginger Man, 1961; Fairy Tales of New York, 1961; A Singular Man, 1964; The Plays of J P Donleavy, 1973; The Beastly Beatitudes of Balthazar B, 1981. Other: The Unexpurgated Code: A Complete Manual of Survival and Manners, 1975; De Alfonce Tennis: The Superlative Game of Eccentric Champions, Its History, Accoutrements,

Rules, Conduct, and Regimes, 1984; J P Donleavy's Ireland: In All Her Sins and in Some of Her Graces, 1986; A Singular Country, 1989; The History of the Ginger Man, 1994; The Lady Who Liked Clean Rest Rooms, 1996; Wrong Information Is Being Given Out At Princeton, 1997. Contributions to: Periodicals. Honours: Most Promising Playwright Award, Evening Standard, 1960; Brandeis University Creative Arts Award, 1961-62; American Academy of Arts and Letters Grant, 1975; Worldfest Houston Gold Award, 1992; Cine Golden Eagle Award, 1993. Address: Levington Park, Mullingar, County Westmeath, Ireland.

DONNE Maxim. See: **DUKE Madelaine (Elizabeth).**

DOR Moshe, b. 9 Dec 1932, Tel Aviv, Israel. Poet; Journalist. m. Ziona Dor, 29 Mar 1955, 2 sons. Education: Hebrew University of Jerusalem, 1949-52; BA, Political Science, University of Tel Aviv, 1956. Appointments: Counsellor for Cultural Affairs, Embassy of Israel, London, England, 1975-77; Distinguished Writer-In-Residence, American University, Washington, DC, USA, 1987; President, Israel PEN Centre, 1988-90. Publications: From the Outset, 1984; On Top of the Cliff (in Hebrew),1986; Crossing the River, 1989; From the Outset (selected poems in Dutch translation), 1989; Crossing the River (selected poems in English translation), 1989; Love and Other Calamities (poems in Hebrew), 1993; Khamsin (memoirs and poetry in English translation), 1994; The Silence of the Builder (poems in Hebrew), 1996. Other books of poetry, children's verse, literary essays, interviews with writers. Honours: Honourable Citation, International Hans Christian Andersen Prize for Children's Literature, 1975; Holon Prize for Literature, 1981; Prime Minister's Award for Creative Writing, 1986; Balik Prize for Literature, 1987; Memberships: Association of Hebrew Writers, Israel; National Federation of Israel Journalists; Israel Pen Centre. Address: 11 Brodetsky Street, Tel Aviv 69051, Israel.

DORET Michel, b. 5 Jan 1938, Petion-Ville, Haiti. m. Liselotte Bencze, 30 Nov 1970. Education: BA, Pace University, 1970; BS, State University of New York, 1978; MA, New York University, 1972; MPhil, 1980, PhD, 1982, George Washington University. Appointment: Founder and Director, Les Editions Amon Râ, 1982-97. Publications: Glossary of Basic Technical Terminology for Architects, 1980; La Poésie francophone, 8 volumes, 1980; Panorama de la poésie féminine Suisse Romande, 1982; Panorama de la Poesie feminine francophone, 1984; La negritude dans la poésie haitienne, 1985; Poétesses Genevoises francophones, 1985; Haiti en Poésie, 1990; Leksik Kreyol franse, 1990; Le Style Gingerbread, 1994; History of the Architecture of Ayiti, 2 volumes; Frédéric Doret (1866-1935) La Vie et l'oevre, 1995; Over 300 titles of the Editions Amon Râ Fund. Contributions to: Over 100 poems in reviews and anthologies in many countries including France, Spain and India; Over 100 technical, scientific and literary articles published worldwide. Honours: Medaille de Bronze, 1991; Medaille d'Argent Internationale de la Poésie, 1995. Memberships: SGLF; SACEM; SCAM; Titulaire: Syndicat des Journalistes et Ecrivains; Academician Associé, Accademia International Greci-Marino; Asociación Mundial de Escritores. Literary Agent: Sibel Consult, c/o Philippe Bellerive, PO Box 659, Port-au-Prince, Haiti. Address: 1364 rue de Gex, 01210 Ornex-Maconnex, France.

DORFMAN Ariel, b. 6 May 1942, Buenos Aires, Argentina (Chilean citizen). Novelist; Playwright. Education: Graduated, University of Chile at Santiago, 1967. Appointment: Walter Hines Page Research Professor of Literature and Latin, Centre for International Studies, Duke University, North Carolina, USA, 1984-. Publications: Non-fiction: How to Read Donald Duck (with Armand Mattelart), 1971; The Empire's Old Clothes, 1983; Some Write to the Future, 1991; Films: Death and the Maiden, 1994; Prisoners in Time, BBC teleplay, 1995; My House is on Fire, 1997; Fiction: Hard Rain, 1973; My House is on Fire, 1979; Widows, 1983; Dorando la pildora, 1985; Travesia, 1986; The Last Song of Manuel Sendero, 1986; Mascara, 1988; Konfidenz, 1995; Plays: Widows, 1988; Death and the Maiden, 1991; Reader, 1992; Who's Who (with Rodrigo Dortman), 1997; Poems include Last Waltz in Santiago and Other Poems of Exile and Disappearance, 1988. Honours: Olivier Award, London, 1991; Time Out Award, 1991, Literary Lion, New York Public Library, 1992; Dora Award, 1994; Charity randall Citation of the International Poetry Forum, 1994; Best Play or Film for Television for Prisoners in Time, Writers Guild of Great Britain, 1996. Address: Center for International Studies, Duke University, Durham, NC 27708-0404, USA.

DORJI Chen-Kyo Tshering (City), b. 11 June 1949, Uma, Bhutan. Civil Servant; Academician; Historian. m. Sangay Xam, 4 sons, 5 daughters. Education: MA; PhD, Magadh University, India; Studied, London School of Economics and Political Science. Appointments: Bhutan Civil Service, 1968; Joint Director and Registrar, Royal Institute of Management, Thimphu. Publications: Books: The Development of Road Transport Communication in Bhutan (AMIRT thesis), 1973; A Historical Analysis of Civil Service Training in SAARC Member Countries (MPA dissertation), 1992; The Guarantee of Buddhism in Bhutan, 1993; An Introduction to Modern Bhutanese Administrative System, 1994; History of Bhutan Based on Buddhism, 1994; A Political and Religious History of Bhutan (1651-1907), 1995; An Introduction to Bhutanese Languages, 1996; Blue Annals of Bhutan, 1996; A Brief History of Bhutan, 1996; Research and Conference Papers: A Guide to the Places of Buddhist Pilgrimage in Bhutan, 1985; Palden Drukpi Driglam Namzha, Bhutanese Traditional Etiquette, 1987; Open and Distance Learning in Bhutan, 1988; The Advent and Development of the Drukpa Kagyudpa Sect of Buddhism in Bhutan, 1991; The Chhosi Nyidhen, Dual System of Government in Bhutan, 1992; An Introduction to Bhutanese Culture, 1992; Contemporary Literature of Bhutan, 1992; A Continuing Education in Bhutan, 1993; Education Systems in Bhutan, 1993; Buddhism as Bhutanese Way of Life, 1993; An Introduction to Local Administration in Bhutan, 1993; Dzongkha Language and Its Literature, 1994; Education for the Minorities in Bhutan, 1994; A Historical Development of Dzongkha and Its Impact on Modernisation, 1994; The Role of Dzongkha in the Process of Industrialisation, 1994; Buddhist Literature and Its Perspective in Bhutan, 1994. Address: Post Box No 417, Thimphu, Bhutan.

DORMAN Michael L, b. 9 Oct 1932, New York, New York, USA. Writer. m. Jeanne Darrin O'Brien, 25 June 1955, 2 daughters. Education: BS, Journalism, New York University, 1953. Appointments: Correspondent, New York Times, 1952-53; Reporter, Editor, Houston Press, 1953-58; Newsday, Long Island, New York, 1959-64; Freelance Writer, 1965-. Publications: We Shall Overcome, 1964; The Secret Service Story, 1967; King of the Courtroom, 1969; The Second Man, 1969; Under 21, 1970; Payoff: The Role of Organized Crime in American Politics, 1972; The Making of a Slum, 1972; Confrontation: Politics and Protest, 1974; Vesco: The Infernal Money-Making Machine, 1975; The George Wallace Myth, 1976; Witch Hunt, 1976; Detectives of the Sky, 1976; Dirty Politics, 1979; Blood and Revenge, 1991. Contributions to: Periodicals. Address: 7 Lauren Avenue South, Dix Hills, NY 11746, USA.

DORN Ed(ward Merton), b. 2 Apr 1929, Villa Grove, Illinois, USA. Poet; Writer; Translator; Anthropologist; Ethnologist; Professor. m. Jennifer Dunbar, 1969. Education: University of Illinois at Urbana-Champaign, 1949-50; BA, Black Mountain College, 1954. Appointments: Lecturer, Idaho State University, Pocatello, 1961-65; Co-Editor, Wild Dog, Pocatello, 1964-65; Visiting Professor, University of Kansas, Lawrence, 1968-69; Fulbright Lecturer in American Literature, Member English Department, 1969-70, 1974-75, University of Essex, Colchester, England; Regent's Lecturer, University of California at Riverside, 1973-74; Writer-in-Residence, University of California at San Diego, La Jolla, 1976; Professor, University of Colorado at Boulder, 1977-. Publications: Poetry: The Newly Fallen, 1961; Hands Up!, 1964; From Gloucester Out, 1964; Idaho Out, 1965; Geography, 1965; The North Atlantic Turbine, 1967; Gunslinger I, 1968, II, 1969; The Midwest Is That Space Between the Buffalo Statler and the Lawrence Eldridge, 1969; The Cosmology of Finding Your Spot, 1969; Twenty-Four Love Songs, 1969; Songs: Set Two, A Short Count, 1970; Spectrum Breakdown: A Microbook, 1971; By the Sound, 1971; The Cycle, 1971; A Poem Called Alexander Hamilton, 1971; The Hamadyas Baboon at the Lincoln Park Zoo, 1972; Gunslinger, Book III: The Winterbook, Prologue to the Great Book IV Kornerstone, 1972; Recollections of Gran Apacheria, 1974; with Jennifer Dunbar, Manchester Square, 1975; Collected Poems: 1956-1974, 1975; Hello, La Jolla, 1978; Selected Poems, 1978; Abhorrences, 1989. Fiction: Some Business Recently Transacted in the White World (short stories), 1971; Non-Fiction: What I See in the Maximum Poems, 1960; Prose 1 (with Michail Rumaker and Warren Tallamn), 1964; The Rites of Passage: A Brief History, 1965; The Shoshoneans: The People of the Bsin-Plateau, 1966; Way West: Essays and Verse Accounts 1963-1993, 1993. Translations: Our Word: Guerilla Poems from Latin America (with Gordon Brotherston), 1968; Tree Between Two Walls (with Gordon Brotherston), 1969; Selected Poems of Cesar Vallejo, 1976. Honours: D H Lawrence Fellow, 1969. Address: 1035 Mapleton, Boulder, CO 80302, USA.

DORNER Majorie, b. 21 Jan 1942, Luxembourg, Wisconsin, USA. University Professor; 2 daughters. Education: BA, English, St Norbert College, 1964; MA, English, Marquette University, 1965; PhD, English, Purdue University, 1971. Appointment: Professor of English Literature, Winona State University, Minnesota, 1971-. Publications: Nightmare, 1987; Family Closets, 1989; Freeze Frame, 1990; Winter Roads, Summer Fields, 1992; Blood Kin, 1992. Contributions to: Various publications. Honours: Minnesota Book Awards, 1991, 1993. Address: 777 West Broadway, Winona, MN 55987, USA.

DORSETT Danielle. See:**DANIELS Dorothy**.

DOTY Mark, b. 10 Aug 1953, Maryville, Tennessee, USA. Writer; Poet; Professor. Education: BA, Drake University, 1978; MFA, Goddard College, 1980. Appointments: Faculty, MFA Writing Program, Vermont College, 1981-94, Writing and Literature, Goddard College, 1985-90; Guest Faculty, Sarah Lawrence College, 1990-94, 1996; Fannie Hurst Visiting Professor, Brandeis University, 1994; Visiting Faculty, University of Iowa, 1995, 1996, Columbia University, 1996; Professor, Creative Writing Program, University of Utah, 1997-. Publications: Turtle, Swan, 1987; Bethlehem in Broad Daylight, 1991; My Alexandria, 1993; Atlantis, 1995; Heaven's Coast (memoir), 1996. Contributions to: Many anthologies and journals. Honours: Theodore Roethke Prize, 1986; National Endowment for the Arts Fellowships in Poetry, 1987, 1995; Pushcart Prizes, 1987, 1989; Los Angeles Times Book Prize, 1993; Ingram Merrill Foundation Award, 1994; National Book Critics Circle Award, 1994; Guggenheim Fellowship, 1994; Whiting Writers Award, 1994; Rockefeller Foundation Fellowship, Bellagio, Italy, 1995; New York Times Notable Book of the Year, 1995; American Library Association Notable Book of the Year, 1995; T S Eliot Prize, 1996; Bingham Poetry Prize, 1996; Ambassador Book Award, 1996; Lambda Literary Award, 1996; New York Times No-talk Book of the Year, 1996. Address: c/o Creative Writing Program, University of Utah, Salt Lake City, UT 84112, USA.

DOUBTFIRE Dianne Joan, b. 18 Oct 1918, Leeds, Yorkshire, England. Author. m. Stanley Doubtfire, 1946, 1 son. Education: Diploma, Slade School of Fine Art, 1941; ATD, Institute of Education, University of London, 1947. Appointments: Lecturer, Creative Writing, Isle of Wight County Council Adult Education, 1965-85; Lecturer, Creative Writing, University of Surrey, 1986-. Publications: Lust for Innocence, 1960; Reason for Violence, 1961; Kick a Tin Can, 1964; The Flesh is Strong, 1966; Behind the Screen, 1969; Escape on Monday, 1970; This Jim, 1974; Girl in Cotton Wool, 1975; A Girl Called Rosemary, 1977; Sky Girl, 1978; The Craft of Novel Writing, 1978; Girl in a Gondola, 1980; Sky Lovers, 1981; Teach Yourself Creative Writing, 1983, revised edition, 1996; The Wrong Face, 1985; Overcoming Shyness, 1988; Getting Along With People, 1990. Contributions to: Radio Times; Guardian; Homes and Gardens; Writers' Monthly; Vogue. Memberships: Society of Authors; PEN English Centre. Literary Agent: Curtis Brown Ltd. Address: April Cottage, Beech Hill, Headley Down, Hampshire GU35, 8EQ, England.

DOUGALL Robert Neill, b. 27 Nov 1913, Croydon, England. BBC TV Newscaster, retired; Writer. m. N A Byam, 7 June 1947, 1 son, 1 stepdaughter. Publications: In and Out of the Box, 1973; A Celebration of Birds, 1978; Now for the Good News, 1976; British Birds, 1983; Years Ahead, 1984; Birdwatch Round Britain, 1985. Contributions to: Periodicals. Honour: Member of the Order of the British Empire, 1965. Memberships: Royal Society for Literature, 1975-83; Garrick Club; President, Royal Society for the Protection of Birds, 1970-75. Address: Kendal House, 62 New Street, Woodbridge, Suffolk IP12 1DX, England.

DOVE Rita (Frances), b. 28 Aug 1952, Akron, Ohio, USA. Poet; Writer; Professor. m. Fred Viebahn, 23 Mar 1979, 1 daughter. Education: BA summa cum laude, Miami University, Oxford, Ohio, 1973; Postgraduate studies, University of Tübingen, 1974-75; MFA, University of Iowa, 1977. Appointments: Assistant Professor, 1981-84, Associate Professor, 1984-87, Professor of English, 1987-89, Arizona State University, Tempe; Writer-in-Residence, Tuskagee Institute, 1982; Associate Editor, Callaloo, 1986-; Advisor and Contributing Editor, Gettysburg Review, 1987-, Triquarterly, 1988-, Georgia Review, 1994; Professor of English, 1989-93, Commonwealth Professor, 1993-, University of Virginia; Poet Laureate of the USA, 1993-95. Publications: Poetry: Ten Poems, 1977; The Only Dark Spot in the Sky, 1980; The Yellow House on the Corner, 1980; Mandolin, 1982; Museum, 1983; Thomas and Beulah, 1986; The Other Side of the House, 1988; Grace Notes, 1989; Selected Poems, 1993; Lady

Freedon Among Us, 1994; Mother Love, 1995. Other: The Darker Face of Earth (verse play), 1994; The Poet's World (essays), 1995. Contributions to: Numerous magazines and journals. Honours: Fulbright Fellow, 1974-75; National Endowment for the Arts Grants. 1978, 1989; Portia Pittman Fellow, Tuskegee Institute, 1982; Guggenheim Fellowship, 1983-84; Peter I B Lavan Younger Poets Award, Academy of American Poets, 1986; Pulitzer Prize in Poetry, 1987; General Electric Foundation Award for Younger Writers, 1987; Rockefeller Foundation Residency, Bellagio, Italy, 1988; Ohio Governor's Award, 1988; Mellon Fellow, National Humanities Center, 1988-89; Fellow, Center for Advanced Studies, University of Virginia, 1989-92; NAACP Great American Artist Award, 1993; Renaissance Forum Award, Folger Shakespeare Library, 1994; Phi Beta Kappa; Phi Kappa Phi; Many honorary doctorates. Memberships: Literature Panel, 1984-86, Chair, Poetry Grants, 1985, National Endowment for the Arts; Editorial Board, National Forum, 1984-, Iris, 1989-; Commissioner, Schomburg Center for the Preservation of Black Culture, New York Public Library, 1987; Renaissance Forum, Folger Academy of American Poets; Associate Writing Programs; Poetry Society of America; Poets and Writer. Address: Department of English, Bryan Hall, University of Virginia, Charlottesville, VA 22903, USA.

DOVRING Karin Elsa Ingeborg, b. 5 Dec 1919, Stenstorp, Sweden. Journalist; Author; Communications Analyst. m. Folke Ossiannilsson Dovring, 30 May 1943. Education: Fil.Mag, 1942, Fil.Dr, 1951, Lund University; Fil.Lic, Gothenburg University, 1947. Appointments: Journalist, Swedish Newspapers and Magazines, 1945-60; Foreign Correspondent, Switzerland, France, Germany, Italy, 1953-60; Editor, Journal of Communication, 1965-70; Writer, American Newspapers, 1976-; Writer, Illinois Alliance to Prevent Nuclear War, 1982-; Featured Speaker, Yale Law School, 1992, 1993. Publications: Road of Propaganda, 1959; Songs of Zion, 1-2, 1951; Land Reform as a Propaganda Theme, 3rd edition, 1965; Frontiers of Communication, 1975; Harold Dwight Lasswell: His Communication with a Future, 2nd edition, 1988; If the Bombs Fall: A World of its Own, 1982; Heart in Escrow (novel), 1990; English as Lingua Franca, 1997; Hollywood Songwriter (cassette albums), 1994-; Film and Television Plays: A Lady of the Jury and Open House, 1994; Three Poetry Collections, 1995-97; Represented in several anthologies, 1995-97. Contributions to: Numerous professional journals. Honours: Visiting Professor, Vatican's University for International Studies, Rome, 1956-58; International Poetry Hall of Fame, 1996; Karin Dovring Poetry Exhibit on Internet, 1996. Memberships: President, Scandinavian Linguists, 1945-46; National Society of Communications; Distinguished Member, International Society of Poets, 1996. Literary Agent: Joseph Nicoletti, Hollywood, USA. Address: 613 West Vermont Avenue, Urbana, IL 61801, USA.

DOWLING Basil (Cairns), b. 29 Apr 1910, Southbridge, Canterbury, New Zealand. Poet. m. Margaret Wilson, 1938, 1 son, 2 daughters. Education: Canterbury, Otaga and Cambridge Universities; New Zealand Library School, Wellington. Appointments: Head, Department of English, Raine's Foundation Grammar School, London, 1965-75; Freelance Writer, 1975-. Publications: A Day's Journey, 1941; Signs and Wonders, 1944; Canterbury and Other Poems, 1949; Hatherley: Collective Lyrics, 1968; A Little Gallery of Characters, 1971; Bedlam: A Mid Century Satire, 1972; The Unreturning Native, 1973; The Stream, 1979; Windfalls, 1983. Honour: Jessie Mackay Memorial Prize, 1961. Address: 12 Mill Road, Rye, East Sussex TN31 7NN, England.

DOWNER Lesley Ann, b. 9 May 1949, London, England. Writer; Journalist; Broadcaster. Education: St Anne's College, Oxford, 1968-71; BA (Hons), MA, English Language and Literature, Oxford University; MA, Area Studies, South Asia, School of Oriental and African Studies, University of London, 1974. Publications: Step-by-Step Japanese Cooking, 1986; Japanese Vegetarian Cookery, 1986; Economist Business Traveller's Guide to Japan (consultant editor, co-author), 1986; On the Narrow Road to the Deep North, 1989; A Taste of Japan, 1991; The Brothers: The Saga of the Richest Family in Japan, 1994. Contributions to: Independent; Financial Times; Observer; Sunday Times Magazine; Telegraph Magazine; New York Times Magazine; Wall Street Journal Europe. Honour: Glenfiddich Food Book of the Year, 1986. Memberships: Society of Authors; Groucho Club; PEN. Literay Agent: Gill Coleridge. Address: 40 Beresford Road, London N5 2HZ, England.

DOWNES David Anthony, b. 17 Aug 1927, Victor, Colorado, USA. Professor of English. m. Audrey Romaine Ernst, 7 Sep 1949, 1

son, 3 daughters. Education: BA cum laude, Regis College, 1949; MA, Marquette College, 1950; PhD, University of Washington, 1956. Appointments: Assistant Professor, Professor, Chairman of Department, University of Seattle, 1953-68; Professor of English, Dean of Humanities and Fine Arts, 1968-72, Director of Educational Development Projects, 1972-73, Director of Humanities Programme, 1973-74, Director of Graduate English Studies, 1975-78, Chairman of Department, 1978-84, Emeritus Professorship, 1991, California State University, Chico. Publications: Gerard Manley Hopkins: A Study of His Ignatian Spirit, 1959; Victorian Portraits: Hopkins and Pater, 1965; The Temper of Victorian Belief: Studies in Victorian Religious Fiction; Pater, Kingsley and Newman, 1972; The Great Sacrifice: Studies in Hopkins, 1983; Ruskin's Landscape of Beatitude, 1984; Hopkins' Sanctifying Imagination, 1985; The Ignatian Personality of Gerard Manley Hopkins, 1990; chapters in: Hopkins, the Man and the City, 1988; The Fine Delight: Centenary Essays, 1989; Gerard Manley Hopkins: New Essays, 1989; Critical Essays on Gerard Manley Hopkins, 1990; Gerard Manley Hopkins and Critical Discourse, 1993; Saving Beauty, 1994; Rereading Hopkins: Selected New Essays, 1996; Hopkins Achieved Self, 1996. Contributions to: Thought; Victorian Poetry; Hopkins Quarterly; University Journal, Editor, 1974-77; Nineteenth Century Literature; Ultimate Reality and Meaning. Honours: Andrew Mellon Grant for Summer Seminar, Stanford University, 1982; Senior Scholar, International Hopkins Association; Professional Achievement Award, 1984; Exceptional Merit Award for Scholarship, 1984, 1988, 1990; Exceptional Merit Award for Scholarship, 1992; The Downes Collection placed in the Hopkins Collection, Foley Center, Gonzaga University. Address: 1076 San Ramon Drive, Chico, CA 95973, USA.

DOWNES Mary Raby, b. 31 May 1920, Calcutta, India. Writer. m. (1)Henry May Poade Ashby , 25 Nov 1942, dec, (2) Eric Mytton Downes, 28 Dec 1963, dec, 2 daughters. Education: Oxford and Cambridge School Certificate, 1938; Countryside Conservation 2 year course, Department of Continuing Education, University of Oxford, 1990-91. Appointment: Village Correspondent, Andover Midweek Advertiser. Publications: Loving is Living, 1965; Out of Evil, novel, 1975; Emma's Family Pony Delight, 1992. Contributions to: Two Worlds; Psychic News; London Calling; Resurgence; Light; Prediction: Game Research; Poem to Scottish Forestry and other publications; Poem to Arrival Press Anthology, 1992. Honours: 1st Prize, national newspaper's competition for The Best Day of My Holiday. Memberships: PEN; Society of Authors; College of Psychic Studies; National Federation of Spiritual Healers; BHS, Dressage Group; Danebury Riding Club; Overseas League; Poetry Society; Mike Shields Poetry Society. Address: Wheat Cottage, Barton Stacey, Winchester, Hants SO21 3RS, England.

DOWNIE Leonard, b. 1 May 1942, Cleveland, Ohio, USA. Newpaper Editor; Author. m. (1) Barbara Lindsey, 1960, div 1971, (2) Geraldine Rebach, 1971, 3 sons, 1 daughter. Education: MA, Ohio State University. Appointments: Reporter, Editor, 1964-74, Metropolitan Editor, 1974-79, London Correspondent, 1979-82, National Editor, 1982-84, Managing Editor, 1984-91, Executive Editor, 1991-, Washington Post. Publications: Justice Denied, 1971; Mortgage on America, 1974; The New Muckrakers, 1976. Address: Washington Post, 1150 15th Street North West, Washington DC 20071, USA.

DOWNIE Mary Alice Dawe (nee Hunter), b. 12 Feb 1934, Alton, Illinois, USA. Writer. m. John Downie, 27 June 1959, 3 daughters. Education: BA (Hons), English Language and Literature, Trinity College, University of Toronto. Appointment: Book Review Editor, Kingston Whig-Standard, 1973-78. Publications: The Wind Has Wings: Poems from Canada, (with Barbara Robertson), 1968; Scared Sarah, 1974; Dragon on Parade, 1974; The Last Ship, 1980; Jenny Greenteeth, 1981; A Proper Acadian (with George Rawlyk), 1982; The Wicked Fairy-Wife, 1983; Alison's Ghost (with John Downie), 1984; Stones and Cones (with Jillian Gilliland), 1984; Stories: Four short stories, 1973; La Belle et la Laide, 1978; Chapters From Honour Bound, reprinted in Inside and Outside and Measure Me Sky, 1979; Stories From the Witch of the North, reprinted in Story Tellers Rendevouz, 1980; Crossroads 1, 1979 and Out and About, 1981; The Window of Dreams: New Canadian Writing for Children, 1986; The Well-Filled Cupboard (with Barbara Robertson), 1987; How the Devil Got His Cat, 1988; The Buffalo Boy and the Weaver Girl, 1989; Doctor Dwarf and Other Poems for Children, 1990; Cathal the Giant-Killer and the Dun Shaggy Filly, 1991; Written in Stone: A Kingston Reader (with M A Thompson), 1993; The Cat Park, 1993; Snow Paws, 1996. Contributions to: Hornbook Magazine; Pittsburgh Press; Kingston

Whig-Standard; Ottawa Citizen; Globe and Mail; United Church Observer; OWL Magazine; Chickadee; Crackers. Memberships: Writers Union of Canada; PEN. Address: 190 Union Street, Kingston, Ontario K7L 2P6, Canada.

DOWNING Angela, b. 28 Sep 1933, Liverpool, England. Professor of English. m. Enrique Hidalgo, 22 Aug 1959, 2 sons, 3 daughters. Education: BA, Modern Languages, 1956, MA, 1962, University of Oxford; Licenciatura in English Philology, 1973; PhD, 1976, Universidad Complutense de Madrid. Appointments: Professor of English, Universidad Complutense, Madrid, Spain; editor, Estudios Ingleses de la Universidas Complutense, 1991. Publications: La metáfora gramatical de M A K Halliday y su motivación funcional en el discurso, 1991; An Alternative Approach to Theme: A Systemic Functional Perspective, 1991; A University Course in English Grammer (with Philip Locke), 1992; Thematic layering and focus assignment in Geoffrey Chaucer's General Prologue to the Canterbury Tales (essay), 1995; The semantics of get-passives (essay), 1996; Discourse-pragmatic distinctions of the Past-in-Present in English and Spanish (essay), 1996; Register and/or Genre (essay), 1996; Thematic progression as a functional resource in analysing texts, 1996; Discourse-pragmatic functions of the Theme constituent in spoken European Spanish, 1997. Contributions to: Specialized journals. Honours: Mary Ewart Scholar, Somerville College, Oxford, 1952-55; Duke of Edinburgh's Award, 1992. Memberships: Philological Society. European Society for the Study of English; Sociedad Española de Linguistica; Asociación Espanola de Linguistica Aplicada; Asociación Espanola de Estudios Ingleses Medievales; International Association of University Professors of English. Address: Arascues 43, 28023 Madrid, Spain.

DOWNS Donald Alexander, b. 2 Dec 1948, Toronto, Ontario, Canada. Assistant Professor. m. Susan Yeager Downs, 30 Jan 1971, 1 son, 1 daughter. Education: BA, Cornell University, 1971; MA, University of Illinois, 1974; PhD, University of California, Berkeley, 1983. Appointment: Assistant Professor, Political Science, University of Wisconsin, Madison. Publications: Nazis in Skokie: Freedom Community and the First Amendment, 1985; The New Politics of Pornography and the Forms of Democracy, 1988. Contributions to: Professional journals, newspapers and magazines. Memberships: American Political Science Association; Amnesty International; Southern Poverty Association. Address: 4429 Waite Lane, Madison, WI 53711, USA.

DOYLE Charles (Desmond), b. 18 Oct 1928, Birmingham, Warwickshire, England. Professor Emeritus; Poet; Critic; Biographer. m. (1) Doran Ross Smithells, 1959, div, (2) Rita Jean Brown, 1992; 3 sons, 1 daughter. Education: Diploma of Teaching (New Zealand), 1956; MA (New Zealand), 1958; Ph.D (Auckland), 1968. Appointments: Associate Professor, 1968-76, Professor, 1976-93, University of Vancouver, British Columbia. Publications: A Splinter of Glass, 1956; The Night Shift: Poems on Aspects of Love (with others), 1957; Distances, 1963; Messages for Herod, 1965; Earth Meditations, 1971; Earthshot, 1972; Preparing for the Ark, 1973; Plnes (with P K Irwin), 1975; Stonedancer, 1976; A Steady Hand, 1982; The Urge to Raise Hats, 1989; Separate Fidelities, 1991; Intimate Absences: Selected Poems 1954-92, 1993. Other: James K Baxter, 1976; William Carlos Williams and the American Poem, 1982; William Carlos Williams: The Critical Heritage (editor), 1982; The New Reality (co-editor), 1984; Wallace Stevens: The Critical Heritage (editor), 1985; Richard Aldington: A Biography, 1989; Richard Aldington: Reappraisals (editor), 1990. Address: 641 Oliver Street, Victoria, British Columbia V8S 4W2, Canada.

DOYLE Roddy, b. 1958, Dublin, Ireland. Novelist; Playwright; Screenwriter. m. Belinda, 2 sons. Appointments: Lecturer at universities. Publications: Novels: The Commitments, 1988; The Snapper, 1990; The Van, 1991; Paddy Clarke Ha Ha Ha, 1993. Plays: Brown Bread, 1992; USA, 1992. Screenplays: The Commitments (with Dick Clement and Ian La Frenais), 1991; The Snapper, 1993. Honours: Shortlisted, 1991, Recipient, 1993, Booker Prize; People's Choice Award, Best Film, Toronto Film Festival. Literary Agent: Secker & Warburg. Address: c/o Patti Kelly, Viking Books, 375 Hudson Street, New York, NY 10014, USA.

DOZOIS Gardner R(aymond), b. 23 July 1947, Salam, Massachusetts, USA. Writer; Editor. Appointments: Reader, Dell and Award Publishers, Galaxy, If, Worlds of Fantasy, Worlds of Tomorrow, 1970-73; Co-founder and Associate Editor, 1976-77; Editor, 1985-,

Isaac Asimov's Science Fiction Magazine. Publications: A Day in the Life, 1972; Beyond the Golden Age: Nightmare Blue (with George Alec Effinger), 1975; Future Power (with Jack Dann), 1976; Another World (juvenile), 1977; The Visible Man (short stories), 1977; The Fiction of James Tiptree, Jr, 1977; Best Science Fiction Stories of the Year 6-9, 4 volumes, 1977-80; Strangers, 1978; Aliens! (with Jack Dann), 1980; The Year's Best Science Fiction (with Jim Frankell) 1984; Modern Classics of Science Fiction (editor), 1991; Isaac Asimov's Science Fiction Lite (editor), 1993. Address: 401 Quince Street, Philadelphia, PA 19147, USA.

DRABBLE Margaret, b. 5 June 1939, Sheffield, England. Author; Biographer; Editor. m. (1) Clive Walter Swift, 1960, div 1975, 2 sons, 1 daughter, (2) Michael Holroyd, 1982. Education: BA, Newnham College, Cambridge, 1960. Publications: Novels: A Summer Bird-Cage, 1963; The Garrick Year, 1964; The Millstone, 1965; Jerusalem the Golden, 1967; The Waterfall, 1969; The Needle's Eye, 1972; The Realms of Gold, 1975; The Ice Age, 1977; The Middle Ground, 1980; The Radiant Way, 1987; A Natural Curiosity, 1989; The Gates of Ivory, 1991; The Witch of Exmoor, 1996. Dramatic: Laura (television play), 1964; Isadora (screenplay), 1968; Thank You All Very Much (screenplay), 1969; Bird of Paradise (play), 1969. Non-fiction: Wordsworth, 1966; Arnold Bennett, 1974; Editor, The Genius of Thomas Hardy, 1976; For Queen and Country: Britain in the Victorian Age, 1978; A Writer's Britain: Landscape and Literature, 1979; The Oxford Companion to English Literature (editor), 5th edition 1985, revised edition, 1995; The Concise Oxford Companion to English Literature (editor with Jenny Stringer), 1987; Angus Wilson: A Biography, 1995. Honours: John Llewelyn Rhys Memorial Award, 1966; James Tait Black Memorial Book Prize, 1968; Book of the Year Award, Yorkshire Post, 1972; E M Forster Award, American Academy and Institute of Arts and Literature, 1973; Honorary Doctorates, Universities of Sheffield, 1976, Manchester, 1987, Bradford, 1988, Keele, 1988, Hull, 1992, East Anglia, 1994 and York, 1995; Commander of the Order of the British Empire, 1980. Membership: Chairperson, National Book League, 1980-82. Address: c/o A D Peters, Fifth Floor, The Chambers, Chelsea Harbour, Lots Road, London, SW10 0XF, England.

DRACKETT Phil(ip Arthur), (Paul King), b. 25 Dec 1922, Finchley, Middlesex, England. Writer; Broadcaster. m. Joan Isobel Davies, 19 June 1948. Education: Woodhouse School, 1934-39; Junior County Award, Cambridge University; General Schools, London University. Appointments: News Chronicle; Press Association; Puck Publications: Royal Automobile Club. Publications: You and Your Car, 1957; Great Moments in Motoring, 1958; Automobiles Work Like This, 1958; Like Father like Son, 1969; Rally of the Forests, 1970; The Classic Mercedes-Benz, 1984; Flashing Blades, 1988; They Call it Courage, The Story of the Segrave Trophy, 1990; Benetton and Ford, A Racing Partnership, 1991; Vendetta on Ice, 1992; Just Another Incident, 1994. Contributions to: Newspapers and magazines. Memberships: Sports Writers Association; Guild of Motoring Writers; British Ice Hockey Writers Association; Friends of Mundesley Library. Address: 9 Victoria Road, Mundesley, Norfolk NR11 8RG, England.

DRAGONWAGON Crescent, b. 25 Nov 1952, New York, New York, USA. Freelance Writer. m. Ned Shank, 20 Oct 1978. Publications: Always, Always, 1984; The Year it Rained, 1985; The Dairy Hollow House Cookbook, 1986; Half a Moon and One Whole Star, 1986; Alligator Arrived with Apples: A Thanksgiving Potluck Alphabet, 1987; Margaret Zeigler, 1988; This is the Bread I Baked for Ned, 1988; Home Place, 1990; The Itch Book, 1990; Winter Holding Spring, 1990; Dairy Hollow House Soup and Bread, A Country Inn Cookbook, 1992; Annie Flies the Birthday Bike, 1993; Alligators and Others, All Year Long: A Book of Months, 1993; Brass Button, 1997. Honours: Porter Fund Prize for Literary Excellence, 1991; William Allen White Children's Book Award Master List, 1992-93. Memberships: Author's Guild; Society of Children's Book Writers; IACP. Address: Route 4 Box 1, Eureka Springs, AR 72632, USA.

DRAKE Albert Dee, b. 26 Mar 1935, Portland, Oregon, USA. Professor; Writer. div. 1 son, 2 daughters. Education: Portland State College, 1956-59; BA, Englaish, 1962, MFA, English, 1966, University of Oregon. Appointments: Research Assistant, 1965, Teaching Assistant, 1965-66, University of Oregon; Assistant Professor, 1966-70, Associate Professor, 1970-79, Professor, 1979-, Michigan State University, East Lansing. Publications: Michigan Signatures (editor), 1968; Riding Bike, 1973; Roadsalt, 1975; Returning to Oregon, 1975; The Postcard Mysteries, 1976; Tillamook Burn, 1977; In the

Time of Surveys, 1978; One Summer, 1979; Garage, 1980; Beyond the Pavement, 1981; The Big Little GTO Book, 1982; Street Was Fun in '51, 1982; I Remember the Day That James Dean Died, 1983; Homesick, 1988; Herding Goats, 1989. Contributions to: Numerous periodicals. Honours: 1st Ernest Haycox Fiction Award, 1962; National Endowment for the Arts Grants, 1974-75, 1983-84; 1st Prize, Writer's Digest Fiction Contest, 1979; Michigan Council for the Arts Grant, 1982. Address: Department of English, Michigan State University, East Lansing, MI 48824, USA.

DRAPER Alfred Ernest, b. 26 Oct 1924, London, England. Author. m. Barbara Pilcher, 31 Mar 1951, 2 sons. Education: North West London Polytechnic. Publications: Swansong for a Rare Bird, 1969; The Death Penalty, 1972 (made into a French Film); Smoke Without Fire, 1974; The Prince of Wales, 1975; The Story of the Goons, 1976; Operation Fish, 1978; Amritsar, 1979; Grey Seal, 1981; Grey Seal: The Restless Waves, 1983; The Raging of the Deep, 1985; Storm over Singapore, 1986; The Con Man, 1987; Dawns Like Thunder, 1987; The Great Avenging Day, 1989; A Crimson Splendour, 1991; Operation Midas, 1993. Contributions to: Numerous periodicals. Memberships: Society of Authors; Life Member of NUJ. Address: 31 Oakridge Avenue, Radlett, Herts WD7 8EW, England.

DRAPER Ronald Philip, b. 3 Oct 1928, Nottingham, England. Professor Emeritus of English; Author. m. Irene Margaret Aldridge, 19 June 1950, 3 daughters. Education: BA, 1950, PhD, 1953, University of Nottingham. Appointments: Lecturer in English, University of Adelaide, 1955-56; Lecturer, 1957-68, Senior Lecturer, 1968-73, University of Leicester; Professor, 1973-86, Regius Chalmers Professor of English, 1986-94, Professor Emeritus, 1994-, University of Aberdeen. Publications: D H Lawrence, 1964, 3rd edition, 1984. D H Lawrence: The Critical Heritage (editor), 1970, 3rd edition, 1986; Hardy: The Tragic Novels (editor), 1975, revised edition, 1991; George Eliot, The Mill on the Floss and Silas Marner, 1977, 3rd edition, 1984; Tragedy, Developments in Criticism (editor), 1980; Lyric Tragedy, 1985; The Winter's Tale: Text and Performance, 1985; Hardy: Three Pastoral Novels, 1987; The Literature of Region and Nation, 1989; An Annotated Critical Bibliography of Thomas Hardy (with Martin Ray), 1989; The Epic: Developments in Criticism (editor), 1990; Co-editor: A Spacious Vision: Essays on Hardy, 1994. Contributions to: Books and scholarly journals. Address: Maynestay, Chipping Camden, Gloucestershire, GL55 6DJ, England.

DRECKI Zbigniew Bogdan, b. 20 Nov 1922, Warsaw, Poland. Artist. m. Cynthia Josephine Scott, 22 Feb 1961. Education: Humanistic Gymnasium (High School), Warsaw, 1928-39; Art Diploma, Darmstadt Academy of Art, 1952. Publication: Freedom and Justice Spring From the Ashes of Auschwitz, 1992, Polish version in Auschwitz Museum. Contributions to: Polish medical journals; British and US newspapers. Memberships: Life Member, West Country Writers Association; Association of Little Presses. Address: Winterhaven, 23 Albion Street, Exmouth, Devon EX8 1JJ, England.

DREIER Ole, b. 15 Apr 1946, Nyborg, Denmark. Professor of Social Psychology; Author. m. Dorthe Bukh, 5 Sept 1983, 1 son, 1 daughter. Education: MA, Psychology, 1970; PhD, 1979; DPhil, 1993. Appointment: Professor of Social Psychology, University of Copenhagen. Publications: Society and Psychology, 1978; Critical Psychology, 1979; Familiäres Sein und Jamiliäres Bewusstaein, 1980; Psychosocial Treatment, 1993; Contributions in several collected volumes in German and English. Contributions to: Udkast; Nordisk Psykologi; Philosophia; Forum Kritische Psychologie. Honours: Visiting Professor, Mexico City, Berkeley, Leipzig, 1984-86. Memberships: Danish Authors Association; Boards of several journals; Danish Psychological Association; International Society of Theoretical Psychology. Address: Dr Olgas Vej 37, 2000 Frederiksberg, Denmark.

DREW Bettina, b. 23 Apr 1956, New York, New York, USA. Writer; Teacher. Education: BA, Philosophy, University of California, Berkeley, 1977; MA, Creative Writing, City College of New York, 1983; MA, American Studies, Yale University, 1995. Appointments: Lecturer in English, College of New York; Lecturer in Humanities, New York University, 1990-93; Part-time Acting Instructor, Yale University, 1995-97. Publications: Nelson Algren: A Life on the Wild Side, 1989; The Texas Stories of Nelson Algren (editor), 1995; Travels in Expendable Landscapes, forthcoming. Contributions to: Essays in Boulevard; The Writer; Chicago Tribune; Threepenny Review; Book reviews in Washington Post Book World, Chicago Tribune Book World; Ms; Black American Literature Forum; Michigan Quarterly Review;

Poems to various magazines. Memberships: PEN American Center; Biography Seminar, New York University. Literary Agent: Theresa Park, Sanford J Greenberg Associates, 55 Fifth New York, NY 10003, USA. Address: 87 Olive Street, New Haven, CT 06511, USA.

DREWE Robert (Duncan), b. 9 Jan 1943, Melbourne, Victoria, Australia. Novelist. m. (3) Candida Baker, 4 sons, 2 daughters. Education: Hale School, Perth, Western Australia. Appointments: Writer-in-Residence, University of Western Australia, Nedlands, 1979, La Trobe University, Bundoora, Victoria, 1986; Columnist, Mode, Sydney, and Sydney City Monthly, 1981-83. Publications: The Savage Crows, 1976; A Cry in the Jungle Bar, 1979; Fortune, 1986; Our Sunshine, 1991; Short stories: The Bodysurfers, 1983; The Bay of Contented Men, 1989; Plays: The Bodysurfers, 1989; South American Barbecue, 1991. Honours: National Book Award, 1987; Commonwealth Literary Prize, 1990. Address: Hickson Associates, 128 Queen Street, Wollahra, New South Wales 2025, Australia.

DRISCOLL Peter (John), b. 4 Feb 1942, London, England. Writer; Journalist. m. Angela Hennessy, 14 Jan 1967, 1 son, 1 daughter. Education: BA, University of the Witwatersrand, 1967. Appointments: Reporter, Rand Daily Mail, Johannesburg, South Africa, 1959-67; Sub-editor, Scriptwriter, ITV News, London, 1969-73. Publications: The White Lie Assignment, 1971; The Wilby Conspiracy, 1972; In Connection with Kilshaw, 1974; The Barboza Credentials, 1976; Pangolin, 1979; Heritage, 1982; Spearhead, 1987; Secrets of State, 1991. Address: c/o David Higham Associates, 5-8 Lower John Street, London, W1R 4HA, England.

DRIVER Charles Jonathan, (Jonty), b. 19 Aug 1939, Cape Town, South Africa. Headmaster. m. Ann Elizabeth Hoogewerf, 8 June 1967, 2 sons, 1 daughter. Education: BA, BEd, University of Cape Town, 1958-62; MPhil, Trinity College, Oxford University, England, 1965-67. Appointments: Literature Panel, 1975-77, Chairman, 1977, Lincolnshire and Humberide Arts; Literature Panel, Arts Council, 1975-77; Editor, Conference & Common Room, 1993-. Publications: Elegy for a Revolutionary, 1968; Send War in our Time, O Lord, 1970; Death of Fathers, 1972; A Messiah of the Last Days, 1974; Hong Kong Portraits, 1985; I Live Here Now, 1979; Occasional Light (with Jack Cope), 1979; Patrick Duncan (biography), 1980; In the Water-Margins (poems), 1994. Contributions to: Numerous magazines and journals. Honour: Fellow, Royal Society of Arts. Membership: Headmasters' Conference. Literary Agent: Andrew Hewson, John Johnson Author's Agents. Address: The Master's Lodge, Wellington College, Crowthorne, Berkshire RG45 7PU, England.

DRIVER Paul William, b. 14 Aug 1954, Manchester England. Music Critic; Writer. Education: MA (Hons), Oxford University, 1979. Appointments: Music Critic, The Boston Globe, 1983-84; Sunday Times, 1985-; Member, Editorial Board, Contemporary Music Review. Publications: A Diversity of Creatures (editor), 1987; Music and Text (editor), 1989; Manchester Pieces, 1996. Contributions to: Sunday Times; Financial Times; Tempo; London Review of Books; numerous others. Membership: Critics Circle. Literary Agent: Toby Eady Associates. Address: 15 Victoria Road, London NW6 6SX, England.

DROBOT Eve Joanna, b. 7 Feb 1951, Cracow, Poland. (US citizen, 1968). Journalist; Author. m. Jack Kapica, 9 Apr 1983, 1 daughter. Education: Baccalaureat, Universite d'Aix Marseilles, Aix-en-Provence, France, 1971; BA magna cum laude, Tufts University, Medford, Massachussetts, USA, 1973. Appointments: Columnist, Globe and Mail, 1980-82, 1990-; Contributing Editor, Saturday Night Magazine, 1988-; Toronto Correspondent, L'Actualite Magazine, 1989-. Publications: Words for Sale (co-editor), 1979, 3rd edition, 1989; Class Acts, 1982; Zen and Now, 1985; Amazing Investigations: Money, 1987; Chicken Soup and Other Nostrums, 1987. Contributions to: Hundreds, including book reviews, to magazines and journals. Honours: Gold Medal, Canadian National Magazine Award, 1989; Canadian Authors Award, 1989. Membership: International PEN. Address: 17 Simpson Avenue, Toronto, Ontario M4K 1A1, Canada.

DROWER G(eorge) M(atthew) F(rederick), b. 21 July 1954, London, England. Feature Writer. Education: BA (Hons), Politics and Government, City of London Polytechnic, 1979; MA, Area Studies, University of London, 1980; PhD, London School of Economics, 1989. Publications: Neil Kinnock: The Path To Leadership, 1984; Britain's Dependent Territories: A Fistful of Islands, 1992. Contributions to: The Times; The Sunday Times; Financial Times; Independent Mail on

Sunday; Sun; House and Garden; Traditional Homes. Honours: University of London Central Research Fund Travelling Scholarship to Hong Kong; London School of Economics Director's Fund Scholarship. Membership: Inner Temple Rowing Club. Literay Agent: Serafina Clarke, 98 Tunis Road, London W12, England. Address: 480A Church Road, Northolt, Middlesex UB5 5AU, England.

DRUCKER Henry Matthew, b. 29 Apr 1942, Paterson, New Jersey, USA. Managing Director; Visiting Professor of Government. m. Nancy Livia Neuman, 29 Mar 1975. Education: BA in Philosophy, Allegheny College, Meadville, Pennsylvania, 1964; PhD in Political Science, London School of Economics and Political Science, 1967. Appointments: Lecturer, 1964-76, Senior Lecturer, 1976-86, in Politics, Univesity of Edinburgh; Director, University Development Office, Oxford University, 1987-93, Campaign for Oxford, 1988-93; Managing Director, Oxford Philanthropic, 1994-; Visiting Professor of Government, London School of Economics and Political Science, 1994-. Publications: Political Uses of Ideology, 1974; Our Changing Scotland (editor with M G Clarke), 1977; Breakaway: The Scottish Labour Party, 1978; Scottish Government Yearbook (editor with Nancy Drucker), 1978-82; Doctrine and Ethos in the Labour Party, 1979;Multi-Party Britain (editor), 1979; The Politics of Nationalism and Devolution (with Gordon Brown), 1980; John P Mackintosh on Scotland (editor), 1982; Developments in British Politics (general editor), 1, 1983, 2, 1986, revised edition, 1988. Address: c/o Oxford Philanthropic Ltd, 36 Windmill Road, Oxford OX3 7BX, England.

DRUCKER Peter (Ferdinand), b. 19 Nov 1909, Vienna, Austria. Management Consultant; Professor of Social Science; Writer. m. Doris Schmitz, 1937, 1 son, 3 daughters. Education: Austria, Germany and England. Appointments: Investment Banker, London, 1933-36; Professor of Philosophy and Politics, Bennington College, Vermont, 1942-49; International Management Consultant to businesses and governments, 1943-; Professor of Management, New York University, 1950-72; Clarke Professor of Social Science, Claremont Graduate School, California, 1971-; Professorial Lecturer in Oriental Art, Claremont Colleges, California, 1980-86. Publications: The Practice of Management, 1954, new edition, 1992; America's Next Twenty Years, 1959; Landmarks of Tomorrow, 1960; Managing for Results, 1964, new edition, 1992; The Effective Executive, 1966, new edition, 1992; The Age of Discontinuity, 1969, new edition, 1992; Technology, Management and Society, 1970; Men, Ideas and Politics, 1971; The New Markets ... and Other Essays, 1971; Management: Tasks, Responsibilities, Practices, 1974, new edition, 1992; The Unseen Revolution: How Pension Fund Socialism Came to America, 1976; Adventures of a Bystander, 1979, new edition, 1994; Managing in Turbulent Times, 1980, new edition, 1992; Toward the New Economics, 1981; The Changing World of the Executive, 1982; Innovation and Entrepreneurship, 1985, new edition, 1992; The Frontiers of Management, 1986; The New Realities, 1989; Managing the Non-Profit Organization, 1990; Managing for the Future, 1992; The Ecological Vision, 1993; Post Capitalist Society, 1993; Managing at a Time of Great Change, 1995. Honours: Order of the Sacred Treasure of Japan; Grand Cross of Austria; Several honorary doctorates. Memberships: Fellow, American Academy of Management; Fellow, International Academy of Management. Address: 636 Wellesley Drive, Claremont, CA 91711, USA.

DRUMMOND June, b. 15 Nov 1923, Durban, South Africa. Author. Education: BA, English, University of Cape Town. Publications: Slowly the Poison, 1975; The Patriots, 1979; The Trojan Mule, 1982; The Bluestocking, 1985; Junta, 1989; The Unsuitable Miss Pelham, 1990. Memberships: Soroptimist International; Writers Circle of South Africa. Address: 24 Miller Grove, Durban 4001, South Africa.

DRURY Allen Stuart, b. 2 Sept 1918, Houston, Texas, USA. Writer. Education: BA, Stanford University. Appointments: Editor, Tulare Bee, 1940-41; County Editor, Bakersfield Californian, 1942; Senate Staff, United Press, 1943-45; Freelance Correspondent, Washington DC, 1946-47; National Editor, Pathfinder Magazine, 1947-52; National Staff, Washington Evening Star, 1952-54; Senate Staff, New York Times, 1954-59. Publications: Advise and Consent, 1959; A Shade of Difference, 1962; A Senate Journal, 1963; That Summer, 1965; Three Kids in a Cart, 1965; Capable of Honor, 1966; A Very Strange Society, 1967; Preserve and Protect, 1968; The Throne of Saturn, 1971; Courage and Hesitation, 1972; Come Ninevah, Come Tyre, 1973; The Promise of Joy, 1975; A God Against the Gods, 1976; Return to Thebes, 1977; Anna Hastings, 1977; Mark Coffin, U S S, 1979; Egypt, the Eternal Smile, 1980; The Hill of Summer, 1981;

Decision, 1983; The Roads of Earth, 1984; Pentagon, 1986; Toward What Bright Glory?, 1990; Into What Far Harbour?, 1993. Contributions to: Readers Digest, 1959-62. Honours: National Editorial Award, Sigma Delta Chi, 1942; Pulitzer Prize for Fiction, 1960. Memberships: Authors Guild; Sigma Delta Chi; University and Cosmos, Washington DC; Bohemian, San Francisco. Address: PO Box 941, Tiburon, CA 94920, USA.

DRYDEN Pamela. See: **JOHNSTON Norma.**

DRYSDALE Helena Claire, b. 6 May 1960, London, England. Writer. m. Richard Pomeroy, 21 May 1987, 2 daughters. Education: Charterhouse, 1975-77, Trinity College Cambridge, 1978-82; BA Hons, History, Art History, Cambridge. Publications: Alone Through China and Tibet, 1986; Dancing With the Dead, 1991; Looking for Gheorghe: Love and Death in Romania, 1995; Looking for George, 1996. Contributions to: Vogue; Marie Claire; Independent; Independent on Sunday; Harpers and Queen; Cosmopolitan; World. Honours: Exhibitioner, Trinity College; Shortlisted, Esquire/Waterstones Non-Fiction Award, 1995; PEN/J R Ackerley Award for Autobiograhy, 1995. Membership: Royal Geographical Society. Literary Agent: A P Watt. Address: 22 Stockwell Park Road, London SW9 OAJ, England.

DU VAUL Virginia. See: **COFFMAN Virginia (Edith).**

DUBERMAN Martin (Bauml), b. 6 Aug 1930, New York, New York, USA. Professor of History; Writer. Education: BA, Yale University, 1952; MA, 1953, PhD, 1957, Harvard University. Appointments: Teaching Fellow, Harvard University, 1955-57; Instructor, 1957-61, Morse Fellow, 1961-62, Yale University; Bicentennial Preceptor and Assistant Professor, 1962-65, Associate Professor, 1965-67, Professor, 1967-71, Princeton University; Distinguished Professor of History, Lehman College and the Graduate Center, City University of New York, 1972-; Founder-Director, Center for Lesbian and Gay Studies, Graduate Center, City University of New York, 1991-; Visiting Randolph Distinguished Professor, Vassar College, 1992; Associate Editor, Journal of The History of Sexuality, 1993-, Masculinities: interdisciplinary studies on gender, 1993-. Publications: Charles Francis Adams, 1807-1886, 1960; In White America, 1964; The Antislavery Vanguard: New Essays on the Abolitionists (editor), 1965' James Russell Lowell, 1966; The Uncompleted Past, 1969; The Memory Bank, 1970; Black Mountain: An Exploration in Community, 1972; Male Armor: Selected Plays, 1968-1974, 1975; Visions of Kerouac, 1977; About Time: Exloring the Gay Past, 1986, revised edition, 1991; Hidden from History: Reclaiming the Gay and Lesbian Past (co-editor), 1989; Paul Robeson, 1989; Cures: A Gay Man's Odyssey, 1991; Other Earth: An Epic Play on The Life of Emma Goldman, 1991; Stonewall, 1993; Midlife Queer, 1996; A Queer World: The Center for Lesbian and Gay Studies Reader (editor), 1997; Queer Representations: Reading Lives, Reading Cultures (editor), 1997. Contributions to: Journals and newspapers. Honours: Bancroft Prize, 1961; Vernon Rice/Drama Desk Award, 1965; President's Gold Medal in Literature, Borough of Manhattan, 1988; 2 Lambda Book Awards, 1990; Distinguished Service Award, Association of Gay and Lesbian Psychiatrists, 1996. Address: c/o Graduate School and University Center of the City University of New York, 33 West 42nd Street, Room 404N, NEw York, NY 10036, USA.

DUBERSTEIN Larry, b. 18 May 1944, New York, New York, USA. Writer; Cabinetmaker. 3 daughters. Education: BA, Wesleyan University, 1966; MA, Harvard University, 1971. Publications: Nobody's Jaw, 1979; The Marriage Hearse, 1983; Carnovsky's Retreat, 1988; Postcards From Pinsk, 1991; Eccentric Circles, 1992; The Alibi Breakfast, 1995. Contributions to: Articles, essays, reviews to: Saturday Review; Boston Review; The National; The Phoenix; New York Times Book Review; others. Address: Box 609, Cambridge, MA 02139, USA.

DUBIE Norman (Evans, Jr), b. 10 Apr 1945, Barre, Vermont, USA. Professor of English; Writer; Poet. Education: BA, Goddard College, 1969; MFA, University of Iowa, 1971. Appointments: Teaching Assistant, Goddard College, 1967-69; Teaching Assistant, 1969-70, Writing Fellow, 1970-71, Distinguished Lecturer and Member of the Graduate Faculty, 1971-74, University of Iowa; Poetry Editor, Iowa Review, 1971-72, Now Magazine, 1973-74; Assistant Professor, Ohio University, 1974-75; Lecturer, 1975-76, Director, Creative Writing, 1976-77, Associate Professor, 1978-81, Professor of English, 1982-, Arizona State University. Publications: The Horsehair Sofa, 1969; Alehouse Sonnets, 1971; Indian Summer, 1973; The Prayers of the

North American Martyrs, 1975; Popham of the New Song, 1975; In the Dead of the Night, 1975; The Illustrations, 1977; A Thousand Little Things, 1977; Odalisque in White, 1978; The City of the Olesha Fruit, 1979; Comes Winter, the Sea Hunting, 1979; The Everlastings, 1989; The Window in the Field, 1982; Selected & New Poems, 1983, new edition, 1996; The Springhouse, 1986; Groom Falconer, 1989; Radio Sky, 1991; The Clouds of Magellan, 1991; The Choirs of June and January, 1993. Contributions to: Anthologies and periodicals. Honours: Bess Hokin Prize, 1976; Guggenheim Fellowship, 1977-78; Pushcart Prize, 1978-79; National Endowment for the Arts Grant, 1986; Ingram Merrill Grant, 1987. Memberships: Boston Computer Society; Society for Documentation Professionals; Association of Teachers of Technical Writing. Address: 35B Apple Lane, Hollis, NH 03049, USA.

DUBIE William, b. 24 July 1953, Salem, Massachussetts, USA. Writer; Editor. m. Jo-Ann Trudel, 6 June 1987. Education: BA, English, Salem State College, 1977; AA, Liberal Arts, 1981, AA, General Studies, 1984, North Shore Community College; BS, University of the State of New York, 1989; MA, Media Studies, New School of Social Research. Publications: Closing the Moviehouse (poems), 1981; The Birdhouse Cathedral (poems), 1990. Contributions to: Poems and articles in more than 90 small press and university magazines. Honours: Chapbook Competition winner, 1981; First Prize, Spring Concourse, American Collegiate Press, 1983; Sparrowgrass Poetry Forum, 1990. Membership: Society of Technical Communications. Address: 150A Ayer Road, Shirley, MA 01464, USA.

DUBOIS J E. See: **PARKES Joyce Evelyne.**

DUBOIS M. See: **KENT Arthur (William Charles).**

DUBUS Andre, b. 11 Aug 1936, Lake Charles, Louisiana, USA. Writer. m. (1) Patricia Lowe, 22 Feb 1958, div, 1970, 1 son, 2 daughters, (2) Tommie Gail Cotter, June 1977, div, 1977, (3) Peggy Rambach, 16 Dec 1979, 1 daughter. Education: BA, McNeese State College, Lake Charles, Louisiana, 1958; MFA, University of Iowa, 1966. Appointments: Teacher, Bradford College, Massachusetts, 1966-84; Visiting teacher at various colleges and universities. Publications: The Lieutenant (novel), 1967; Voices From The Moon (with David R Godine) (novella), 1984. Short story collections: Separate Flights, 1975; Adultery and Other Choices, 1977; Finding a Girl in America, 1980; The Times Are Never So Bad, 1983; We Don't Live Here Anymore, 1984; Land Where My Father Died, 1984; The Last Worthless Evening, 1986; Selected Stories, 1988; Dancing After Hours, 1996. Essays: Broken Vessels, 1991. Contributions to: Collections and periodicals. Honours: National Endowmwnt for the Arts Fellowship, 1985; Jean Stern Award, 1986; John D and T MacArthur Fellowship, 1988-93; PEN-Malamud Award, 1991; Rea Award, 1996. Address: 753 East Broadway, Haverhill, MA 01830, USA.

DUCKWORTH Marilyn, b. 10 Nov 1935, Auckland, New Zealand. Writer. m. (1) Harry Duckworth, 28 May 1955, (2) Ian MacFarlane, 2 Oct 1964, (3) Dan Donovan, 9 Dec 1974, (4) John Batstone, 8 June 1985, 4 daughters. Publications: A Gap in the Spectrum, 1959; The Matchbox House, 1960; A Barbarous Tongue, 1963; Over the Fence is Out, 1969; Disorderly Conduct, 1984; Married Alive, 1985; Rest for the Wicked, 1986; Pulling Faces, 1987; A Message From Harpo, 1989; Explosions on the Sun, 1989; Unlawful Entry, 1992; Seeing Red, 1993; Leather Wings, 1995; Cherries on a Plate, editor, 1996. Contributions to: Landfall; New Zealand Listener; Critical Quarterly; Islands; others. Honours: New Zealand Literary Fund Scholarships in Letters, 1961, 1994; Katherine Mansfield Fellowship, 1980; New Zealand Book Award for Fiction, 1985; Shortlisted, Wattie Book of the Year Award, 1985; Officer of the Order of the British Empire, 1987; Fulbright Visiting Writers Fellowship, 1987; Australia-New Zealand Writers Exchange Fellowship, 1989; Victoria University of Wellington Writers Fellowship, 1990; Auckland University Literary Fellowship, 1996; Shortlisted, Commonwealth Writers Prize, 1996. Membership: PEN. Literary Agent: Tim Curnow, Curtis Brown, Australia. Address: 41 Queen Street, Wellington, New Zealand.

DUCORNET Erica Lynn, (Rikki Ducornet), b. 19 Apr 1943, New York, New York, USA. Writer; Artist; Teacher. 1 son. Education: Bard College, 1964. Appointments: Novelist-in-Residence, University of Denver, 1988-; Visiting Professor, University of Trento, Italy, 1994. Publications: The Stain, 1984; Entering Fire, 1986; The Fountains of Neptune, 1989; The Jade Cabinet, 1993; The Butcher's Tales, 1994; Phosphor in Dreamland, 1995. Contributions to: Periodicals. Honours: National Book Critics Circle Award Nomination; Bunting, 1987; Eben

Demarst, 1990; Lannan, 1993. Membership: PEN. Address: c/o Department of English, University of Denver, Denver, CO 80208, USA.

DUDEK Louis, b. 6 Feb 1918, Montreal, Quebec, Canada. Poet; Teacher; Editor. m. (1) Stephanie Zuperko, 1943, div 1965, 1 son, (2) Aileen Collins, 1970. Education: Senior Matriculation, Montreal High School, 1936; BA, McGill University, 1939; MA, History, 1947, PhD, Engish and Comparative Literature, 1955, Columbia University. Appointments include: Lecturer in English to Assistant Professor, 1951-68, Greenshield Professor of English, 1969-84, Profesor Emeritus, 1984-, McGill University; Co-Founder, Contact Press, poetry publishing; Editor, Delta Canada (later DC Books), book publishers. Publications: East of the City (poetry), 1946; The Searching Image, 1952; Twenty-Four Poems, 1952; Europe, 1954, reprint 1991; The Transparent Sea, 1956; Literature and the Press (prose), 1956; Laughing Stalks, 1958; En Mexico, 1958; Poems published in books: Unit of Five, 1944; Other Canadians, 1947; Cerberus, 1952; Editor, Poetry of Our Time (anthology), 1965; Co-Editor, The Making of Modern Poetry in Canada, 1967; Atlantis, 1967; The First Person in Literature, 1967; Collected Poetry, 1971; Selected Essays and Criticism, 1978; Technology and Culture, 1979; Cross Section: Poems 1940-1980, 1980; Poems from Atlantis, 1980; Continuation I, 1981, II, 1990; Louis Dudek: Open Letter Nos 8-9, 1981; In Defence of Art (essays), 1988; Infinite Worlds (poetry), 1988; Small Perfect Things, 1991; Paradise: Essays on Art, Myth and Reality, 1992; Notebooks 1960-1994, 1994; The Birth of Reason, 1994. Contributions to: Various journals. Honours: Order of Canada, 1984; Various honorary doctorates including Doctor of Laws, St Thomas University, Fredericton, 1996, Lakehead Univerity, 1996. Address: 5 Ingleside Avenue, Montreal, Quebec H3Z 1N4, Canada.

DUDLEY Helen. See: **HOPE-SIMPSON Jacynth (Ann).**

DUFF-WARE Freddie. See: **BARNETT Paul (le Page).**

DUFFY Carol Ann, b. 23 Dec 1955, Glasgow, Scotland. Poet. Education: BA, Honours, Philosophy, University of Liverpoool, 1977. Publications: Standing Female Nude, 1985; Selling Manhattan, 1987; also, Fleshweathercock, Fifth Last Song, Thrown Voices (limited edition poetry), 3 stage plays, 2 radio plays. Contributions to: Numerous magazines and journals. Honours: C Day-Lewis Fellowship, 1983; Eric Gregory Award, 1985; Book Award, Scottish Arts Council, 1986. Address: c/o Liz Graham, 4 Camp View, London, SW19, 4VL, England.

DUFFY Maureen Patricia, b. 21 Oct 1933, Worthing, Sussex, England. Author. Education: BA (Hons) English, King's College, University of London, 1956. Appointments: Chairman, Copyright Licencing Agency, 1996; Vice President, European Writers Congress. Publications: That's How it Was, 1962; The Microsm, 1966; Wounds, 1969; Love Child, 1971; The Venus Touch, 1971; The Erotic World of Faery, 1972; I Want to Go to Moscow, 1973; Capital, 1975; The Passionate Shepherdess, 1977; Housespy, 1978; Illuminations, 1991; Ocean's Razor, 1993. Poetry: Lyrics for the Dog Hour, 1968; Evensong, 1975; Memorials for the Quick and the Dead, 1979; Rites, 1969; A Nightingale in Bloomsbury Square, 1974; Visual art: Prop Art Exhibition (with Brigid Brophy), 1969; Gorsaga, 1981; Londoners, 1983; Change, 1987; A Thousand Capricious Chances, 1989. Contributions to: New Statesman. Honour: Fellow, Royal Society of Literature. Memberships: Co-founder, Writer's Action Group; President, Writer's Guild of Great Britain; Chair, Author's Licensing and Collecting Society; British Copywright Council. Literary Agent: Jonathon Clowes Ltd, 88D Iron Bridge House, Bridge Approach, London NW1, England. Address: 18 Fabian Road, London, SW6 7TZ, England.

DUGAN Alan, b. 12 Feb 1923, Brooklyn, New York, USA. Poet. m. Judith Shahn. Education: Queens College; Olivet College; BA, Mexico City College. Appointments: Teacher, Sarah Lawrence College, 1967-71, Fine Arts Work Center, Provincetown, Massachusetts, 1971-. Publications: General Prothalamion in Populous Times, 1961; Poems, 1961; Poems 2, 1963; Poems 3, 1967; Collected Poems, 1969; Poems 4, 1974; Sequence, 1976; Collected Poems, 1961-1983, 1983; Poems 6, 1989. Contributions to: Several magazines. Honours: Yale Series of Younger Poets Award, 1961; National Book Award, 1961; Pulitzer Prizes in Poetry, 1962, 1967; Rome Fellowship, American Academy of Arts and Letters, 1962-63; Guggenheim Fellowship, 1963-64; Rockefeller Foundation Fellowship, 1966-67; Levinson Poetry Prize, 1967. Address: Box 97, Truro, MA 02666, USA.

DUGGER Ronnie, b. 16 Apr 1930, Illinois, USA. Writer; Publisher. m. Patricia Blake Dugger, 29 June 1982, 1 son, 1 daughter. Education: BA, 1950, 1951-52, 1954, University of Texas; Oxford University, 1950-51. Appointments: Owner-Publisher, The Texas Observer, 1965-94; Visiting Professor, Hampshire College, 1976, University of Illinois, 1976, University of Virginia. Publications: Dark Star: Hiroshima Reconsidered, 1967; Three Men in Texas, 1967; Our Invaded Universities, 1974; The Politician: The Life and Times of Lyndon Johnson, 1982; On Reagan: The Man and His Presidency, 1983. Contributions to: Periodicals. Honours: Rockefeller Foundation Fellowship, 1969-70; National Endowment for the Humanities Fellowship, 1978; Woodrow Wilson Center for Scholars Fellow, 1983-84; Alicia Patterson Fellowship, 1994. Memberships: Authors Guild; PEN; Philosophical Society of Texas; Texas Institute of Letters. Address: Box 311, 70A Greenwich Avenue, New York, NY 1011, USA.

DUKE Elizabeth. See: **WALLINGTON Vivienne Elizabeth.**

DUKE Madelaine (Elizabeth), (Maxim Donne, Alex Duncan), b. 21 Aug 1925, Geneva, Switzerland. Author. Education: BSc, University of St Andrews, 1945; MB, ChB, 1955, University of Edinburgh. Publications: Novels: Azael and the Children, 1958; No Margin of Error,1959; A City Built To Music, 1960; Ride the Brooding Wind, 1961; Thirty Pieces of Nickel, 1962; The Sovereign Lords, 1963; Sobaka, 1965; The Lethal Innocents, 1968; Because of Fear in the Night, 1973; Novels as Alex Duncan: It's A Vet's Life, 1961; The Vet Has Nine Lives, 1962; Vets in the Belfrey, 1964; Vet Among the Pigeons, 1977; Vets in Congress, 1978; Vet in the Manger, 1978; Vet in a State, 1979; Vet on Vacation, 1979; To Be a Country Doctor, 1980; God and the Doctor, 1981; The Diary of a Country Doctor, 1982; The Doctor's Affairs All Told, 1983; The Women's Specialist, 1988; Mystery Novels: Claret, Sandwiches and Sin, 1964; This Business of Blumfog, 1967; Death of a Holy Murderer, 1975; Death at the Wedding, 1976; The Bormann Receipt, 1977; Death of a Dandie Dimont, 1978; Flashpoint, 1982; Others: The Secret Mission, 1954; Slipstream: The Story of Anthony Duke, 1955; No Passport: The Story of Jan Felix, 1957; Beyond the Pillars of Hercules: A Spanish Journey, 1957; the Secret People (juvenile), 1989; Once in Austria, 1987. Address: c/o Mondial Books Ltd, Norman Alexander & Co, 5th Floor, Grosvenor Gardens House, 35/37 Grosvenor Gardens, London SW1 OBS, England.

DUKES Carol Muske. See: **MUSKE Carol Anne.**

DUKORE Bernard F(rank), b. 11 July 1931, New York, New York, USA. Professor of Theatre Arts and Humanities Emeritus; Writer. m. Barbara Cromwell, 14 June 1986, 2 sons, 1 daughter. Education: BA, Brooklyn College, 1952; MA, Ohio State University, 1953; PhD, University of Illinois, 1957. Appointments: Instructor, Hunter College in the Bronx, 1957-60; Assistant Professor, University of Southern California, Los Angeles, 1960-62; Assistant to Associate Professor, California State University, Los Angeles, 1962-66; Associate Professor to Professor of Theatre, City University of New York, 1966-72; Professor of Drama and Theatre, University of Hawaii, 1972-86; University Distinguished Professor of Theatre Arts and Humanities, 1986-97, Professor Emeritus, 1997-, Virginia Polytechnic Institute and State University, Blacksburg. Publications: Bernard Shaw, Director, 1971; Bernard Shaw, Playwright, 1973; Dramatic Theory and Criticism, 1974; Where Laughter Stops: Pinter's Tragicomedy, 1976; Collected Screenplays of Bernard Shaw, 1980; Money and Politics in Ibsen, Shaw and Brecht, 1980; The Theatre of Peter Barnes, 1981; Harold Pinter, 1982; Alan Ayckbourn: A Casebook, 1991; The Drama Observed (editor and annotator), 4 volumes, 1993; 1992: Shaw and the Last Hundred Years (editor), 1994; Barnestorm: The Plays of Peter Barnes, 1995; Bernard Shaw and Gabriel Pascal, 1996; Not Bloody Likely: The Columbia Book of Bernard Shaw Quotations, 1997; Shaw on Cinema (editor and annotator), 1997. Honours: Guggenheim Fellowship, 1969-70; National Endowment for the Humanities Fellowships, 1976-77, 1984-85, 1990; Fulbright Research Scholarship, England and Ireland, 1991-92. Memberships: Fellow, American Theatre Association; Pinter Society. Address: 3330 Waterford Drive, Clearwater, FL 34621, USA.

DUMAS Claudine. See: **MALZBERG Barry.**

DUMMETT Michael (Anthony Eardley), b. 27 June 1925, London, England. Professor of Logic Emeritus; Writer. m. Ann Chesney, 1951, 3 sons, 2 daughters. Education: Winchester College; Christ Church, Oxford. Appointments: Fellow, 1950-79, Emeritus

Fellow, 1979-, Senior Research Fellow, 1974-79, All Souls College, Oxford; Commonwealth Fund Fellow, University of California, Berkeley, 1955-56; Reader in the Philosophy of Mathematics, 1962-74, Wykeham Professor of Logic, 1979-92, Professor of Logic Emeritus, 1992-, Oxford University; Fellow, 1979-92, Fellow Emeritus, 1992-, New College, Oxford; Various visiting lectureships and professorships. Publications: Philosophy of Language, 1973, 2nd edition, 1981; The Justification of Deduction, 1973; Elements of Intuitionism, 1977; Truth and Other Enigmas, 1978; Immigration: Where the Debate Goes Wrong, 1978; Catholicism and the World Order, 1979; The Game of Tarot, 1980; Twelve Tarot Games, 1980; The Interpretation of Frege's Philosophy, 1981; Voting Procedures, 1984; The Visconti-Sforza Tarot Cards, 1986; Ursprünge der analytischen Philosophie, 1988, revised edition as Origins of Analytical Philosophy, 1993; Frege and Other Philosophers, 1991; The Logical Basis of Metaphysics, 1991; Frege: Philosophy of Mathematics, 1991; Grammar and Style for Examination Candidates and Others, 1993; The Seas of Language, 1993; Il Mondo e l'Angelo, 1993; I Tarocchi siciliani (with R Dedcer and T Depaulis), 1995; A Wicked Pack of Cards, 1996; Principles of Electoral Reform, 1997. Contributions to: Various books and scholarly journals. Honours: Lakatos Award in the Philosophy of Science, 1994; Roy Schock Prize for Philosophy and Logic, 1995; Honorary DLitt, Oxford, 1989; other honorary doctorates. Memberships: Honorary Member, American Academy of Arts and Sciences; Fellow, British Academy; Academia Europaea. Address: 54 Park Town, Oxford, OX2 6SJ, England.

DUMONT André, b. 12 Apr 1929, Campbellton, New Brunswick, Canada. Steamfitter; Radar Technician; Teacher. m. Germaine Richard, 1958, 2 sons, 2 daughters. Education: BA, 1961; BEd, 1964. Publications: Francais Renouvele I, 1964, II, 1966; Le Parti Acadien (co-author), 1972; Jeunesse Mouvementée, 1979; Quand Je Serai Grand, 1989; Pour un Francais Moderne, 1990; Avancez en Arrière, 1996. Contributions to: Over 100 articles on different topics, mostly political. Address: 3330 rue Maricourt #37, Sainte-Foy, Quebec G1W 2L8, Canada.

DUNANT Peter. See: **DUNANT Sarah.**

DUNANT Sarah, (Peter Dunant), b. 8 Aug 1950, London. England. Writer; Broadcaster. Partner of Ian David Willox, 2 daughters. Education: Newnham College, Cambridge, 1969-72; BA, 2:1 History, Cambridge University, 1972. Publications: as Peter Dunant: Exterminating Angels (co-author), 1983; Intensive Care (co-author), 1986; as Sarah Dunant: Snow Falls in a Hot Climate, 1988; Birth Marks, 1991; Fatlands, 1993; The War of the Words: Essays on Political Correctness (editor), 1994; Under My Skin, 1995; The Age of Anxiety (editor), 1996; Transgressions, 1997. Contributions to: Various London magzines; Listener; Guardian. Honours: Shortlisted for Crime Writers Golden Dagger, 1987, 1991; Silver Dagger Award, 1993. Address: c/o Gillon Aitken, 29 Fernshaw Road, London SW10 OTG, England.

DUNBAR Andrea, b. 22 May 1961, Bradford, Yorkshire, England. Playwright. 1 son, 2 daughter. Education: Buttershaw Comprehensive School, Bradford. Publications: Plays: The Arbor (produced, London 1980, New York, 1983), 1980; Rite, Sue and Bob Too (produced London 1982), 1982; Shirley (produced London 1986); Screenplay, Rite, Sue and Bob Too, 1987. Honour: George Devine Award, 1981. Address: 7 Edge End Gardens, Buttershaw, Bradford, West Yorkshire BD6 2BB, England.

DUNBAR-HALL Peter, b. 15 July 1951, Sydney, Australia. Lecturer. Education: BA, Honours, 1972; MMus, 1989; PhD, 1995. Publications: Music - A Practical Teaching Guide, 1987; A Guide to Rock'n'Pop, 1988; Music in Perspective, 1990; A Guide to Music Around the World, 1991; Teaching Popular Music, 1992; Discography of Aboriginal and Torres Strait Islander Performers, 1995; Strella Wilson: The Career of an Australian Singer, 1997. Contributions to: Many articles in Education Australia; Papers in International Review of Aesthetics and Sociology of Music; British Journal of Music Education; International Journal of Music Education; Research Studies in Music Education; Perfect Beat. Honours: Frank Albert Prize, Sydney University, 1971; Busby Music Scholarship, Sydney University, 1971; Lady Henley Award for Excellence in Teaching, Sydney Conservatorium of Music, 1993. Address: 5/198 Kurraba Road, Neutral Bay, New South Wales 2089, Australia.

DUNCAN Alex. See: **DUKE Madelaine (Elizabeth).**

DUNCAN Lois, b. 28 Apr 1934, Philadelphia, Pennsylvania, USA. Writer. m. Donald W Arquette, 15 July 1965, 2 sons, 3 daughters. Education: Duke University, 1952-53; BA, University of New Mexico, 1977. Publications: Ransom, 1966; A Gift of Magic, 1971; I Know What You Did Last Summer, 1973; Down a Dark Hall, 1974; Summer of Fear, 1976; Killing Mr Griffin, 1978; Daughters of Eve, 1979; Stranger With My Face, 1981; My Growth as a Writer, 1982; The Third Eye, 1984; Locked in Time, 1985; Horses of Dreamland, 1986; The Twisted Window, 1987; Songs From Dreamland, 1989; The Birthday Moon, 1989; Don't Look Behind You, 1989; Who Killed My Daughter?, 1992. Address: c/o 1540 Broadway, New York, NY 10036, USA.

DUNCAN Paul Edwin, b. 20 Aug 1959, Cape Town, South Africa. Writer; Journalist. Education: University of Edinburgh, 1978-84; MA, (Hons), History of Art. Appointments: London Correspondent, Casa Vogue, 1989-92; Writer, Researcher, Royal Fine Art Commission, England, 1991-95; Speech Writer, President's Office, IBM Europe, Middle East, Africa, 1995-. Publications: Scandal, Georgian London in Decay (co-author), 1986; Insight Guide Tuscany (contributor), 1989; Discovering the Hill Towns of Italy, 1991; AA Tour Guide Rome; AA Tour Guide South Africa; AA Tour Guide Italy, 1991; Sicily, A Traveller's Companion, 1991; The Traditional Architecture of Rural Italy, 1993; Nelson Mandela's Illustrated Walk to Freedom (editor), 1996; Italy (contributor), 1996. Contributions to: Italian Vogue; conde Nast Traveler (USA); Vogue Glamour; Casa Vogue; GQ; World of Interiors; Independent; Sunday Times; Evening Standard; Harpers and Queen, Architect's Journal; Elle; Elle Decoration: L'Uomo Vogue; Country Life; Cosmopolitan; Sunday Life (South Africa). Memberships: Architectural Association. Literary Agent: Anne Engel. Address: 13 Primrose Mansions, Prince of Wales Drive, London SW11 4ED, England.

DUNHAM William Wade, b. 8 Dec 1947, Pittsburgh, Pennsylvania, USA. Professor of Mathematics. m. Penelope Higgins, 26 Sept 1970, 2 sons. Education: BS, University of Pittsburgh, 1969; MS, 1970; PhD, 1974, Ohio State University. Appointment: Truman Koehler Professor of Mathematics, Muhlenberg College, 1992-. Publication: Journey Through Genius: The Great Theorems of Mathematics, 1990; The Mathematical Universe, 1994. Contributions to: American Mathematical Monthly; Mathematics Magazine; College Mathematics Journal; Mathematics Teacher. Honours: Phi Beta Kappa, 1968; M M Culver Award, University of Pittsburgh, 1969; Master Teacher Award, Hanover College, 1981; National Endowment for the Humanities Summer Seminars on Great Theorems, 1988-96;, Humanities Achievement Award for Scholarship, Indiana Humanities Council, 1991; George Pólya Award, Mathematical Association of America, 1993. Memberships: Mathematical Association of America; National Council of Teachers of Mathematics Civil War Roundtable. Address: Department of Mathematics, Muhlenberg College, Allentown, PA 18104, USA.

DUNKERLEY James, b. 15 Aug 1953, Wokingham, England. Reader in Politics; Writer. Education: BA, University of York, 1974; BPhil, Hertford College, Oxford, 1977; PhD, Nuffield College, Oxford, 1979. Appointments: Researcher, Latin America Bureau, London, 1979-80, 1983-84; Research Fellow, Institute for Latin American Studies, University of London, 1981-82, Centre for Latin American Studies, University of Liverpool, 1982-83; Fellow, Kellogg Institute, University of Notre Dame, Indiana, 1985; Reader in Politics, Queen Mary and Westfield College, University of London, 1986-. Publications: Unity is Strength: Trade Unions in Latin America (with C Whitehouse), 1980; Bolivia: Coup d'Etat, 1980; The Long War: Dictatorship and Revolution in El Salvador, 1982; Rebellion in the Veins: Political Struggle in Bolivia, 1952-1982, 1984; Granada: Whose Freedom? (with F Amburseley), 1984; Origenes del podermilitair on Bolivia, 1879-1935, 1987; Power in the Isthmus: A Political History of Central America, 1988; Political Suicide in Latin America and Other Essays, 1992; The Pacification of Central America, 1994. Contributions to: Scholarly journals, newspapers, and magazines. Address: c/o Department of Political Studies, Queen Mary and Westfield College, University of London, Mile End Road, London, E1 4NS, England.

DUNKLEY Christopher, b. 22 Jan 1944, Scarborough, Yorkshire, England. Critic; Broadcaster. m. Carolyn Elizabeth Lyons, 18 Feb 1967, 1 son, 1 daughter. Appointments: Mass media correspondent, Television critic, The Times, 1968-73; Television critic, Financial Times, 1973-; Presenter, Feedback, BBC Radio 4, 1986-. Publications: Television Today and Tomorrow: Wall to Wall Dallas?,

1985. Contributions to: Telegraph Magazine; Listener; Sunday Times; Stills; Television World; Electronic Media. Honours: Critic of the Year, British Press Awards, 1976, 1986; Broadcaster Journalist of the Year, 1989 and Judges Award, 1990, TV-AM Awards. Memberships: Commodore, Theta Club. Address: 38 Leverton Street, London NW5 2PG, England.

DUNLAP Leslie W(hittaker), b. 3 Aug 1911, Portland, Oregon, USA. Dean of Library Administration Emeritus; Writer. m. Marie Neese, 15 Apr 1933, 1 son, 1 daughter. Education: BA, University of Oregon, 1933; Graduate Studies, University of Freiburg, 1933-34; AM, 1938, BS, 1939, PhD, 1944, Columbia University. Appointments: Associate Director, University of Illinois Libraries, 1951-58; Director of Libraries, 1958-70, Dean of Library Administration, 1970-82, Dean Emeritus, 1982-, University of Iowa. Publications: The Letters of Willis Gaylord Clark and Lewis Gaylord Clark, 1940; American Historical Societies, 1944; Readings in Library History, 1972; The Wallace Papers: An Index, 1975; The Publication of American Historical Manuscripts, 1976; Your Affectionate Husband, J F Culver, 1978; Our Vice-Presidents and Second Ladies, 1988. Address: 640 Stuart Court, Iowa City, IA 52245, USA.

DUNLOP Richard, b. 20 June 1921, Chicago, Illinois, USA. Writer. Education: BS, Northwestern University, 1945. Publications: The Mississippi River, 1956; St Louis, 1957; Burma, 1958; The Young David (novel), 1959; Doctors of the American Frontier, 1965; Great Trails of the West, 1971; Outdoor Recreation Guide, 1974; Backpacking and Outdoor Guide, 1977; Wheels West, 1977; Behind Japanese Lines: With the OSS in Burma, 1979; Donovan: America's Master Spy, 1982; On the Road in an RV, 1987. Honours: Midland Author's Best Biography Award. Memberships: President, Society of American Travel Writers, 1971; Society of Midland Authors, 1980. Address: 1115 Mayfair Road, Arlington Heights, IL 60004, USA.

DUNMORE John, b. 6 Aug 1923, Trouville, France. University Professor. m. Joyce Megan Langley, 22 April 1946, 1 son, 1 daughter. Education: BA (Hons), London, 1950; PhD, New Zealand, 1962. Publications: French Explorers in the Pacific, 1966-69; The Fateful Voyage of the St Jean Baptiste, 1969; Norman Kirk: A Portrait, 1972; Pacific Explorer, 1985; New Zealand and the French, 1990; The French and the Maoris, 1992; Who's Who in Pacific Navigation, 1992; The Journal of La Perouse, 1994-95. Contributions to: Numerous learned journals and periodicals. Honours: New Zealand Book of the Year, 1970; Legion of Honour, 1976; Academic Palms, 1986; New Zealand Commemation Medal, 1990; Massey Medal, 1993. Membership: Australasian Language and Literature Association, president, 1980-82. Address: 35 Oriwa Street, Waikanae, New Zealand.

DUNN Douglas Eaglesham, b. 23 Oct 1942, Inchinnan, Scotland. Writer; Professor of English. m. Lesley Jane Bathgate, 10 Aug 1985, 1 son, 1 daughter. Education: BA, University of Hull, England. Apointments: Writer-in-Residence: University of Hull, 1974-75; University of Dundee, Scotland, 1981-82; Duncan of Jordanstone College of Art, Dundee District Library, 1986-88; Honorary Visiting Professor, University of Dundee, 1987-89; Fellow in Creative Writing, 1989-91, Professor of English, University of St Andrews, 1991-. Publications: Terry Street, 1969; The Happier Life, 1972; Love or Nothing, 1974; Barbarians, 1979; St Kilda's Parliament, 1981; Elegies,1981; Secret Villages, 1985; Selected Poems, 1986; Northlight, 1988; New and Selected Poems (USA), 1989; Poll Tax: The Fiscal Fake, 1990; Andromache, 1990; Scotland: An Anthology, 1991; Faber Book of 20th Century Scottish Poetry, 1992; Dante's Drum-Kit, 1993; Boyfriends and Girlfriends, 1994; Oxford Book of Scottish Short Stories, 1995. Contributions to: New Yorker; Punch; Times Literary Supplement; Glasgow Herald. Honours: Fellow, Royal Society of Literature, 1981; Whitbread Book of the Year Award, 1985; Honorary Fellow, Humberside College, 1987; Honorary LLD, University of Dundee, 1987; Honorary DLitt, University of Hull, 1995. Membership: Scottish PEN. Address: School of English, The University, St Andrews, Fife KY16 9AL, Scotland.

DUNN Stephen, b. 24 June 1939, New York, New York, USA. Poet; Writer. m. Lois Kelly, 1964, 2 daughters. Education: BA in History, Hofstra University, 1962; New School for Social Research, New York City, 1964-66; MA in Creative Writing, Syracuse University, 1970. Appointments: Assistant Professor, Southwest Minnesota State College, Marshall, 1970-73; Visiting Poet, Syracuse University, 1973-74, University of Washington at Seattle, 1980; Associate

Professor to Professor, 1974-90, Stockton State College, New Jersey; Adjunct Professor of Poetry, Columbia University, 1983-87. Publications: Poetry: Five Impersonations, 1971; Looking for Holes in the Ceiling, 1974; Full of Lust and Good Usage, 1976; A Circus of Needs, 1978; Work and Love, 1981; Not Dancing, 1984; Local Time, 1986; Between Angels, 1989; Landscape at the End of the Century, 1991; New and Selected Poems, 1974-1994, 1994. Other: Walking Light: Essays and Memoirs, 1993. Contributions to: Periodicals. Honours: Academy of American Poets Prize, 1970; National Endowment for the Arts Fellowships, 1973, 1982, 1989; Bread Loaf Writers Conference Robert Frost Fellowship, 1975; Theodore Roethke Prize, 1977; New Jersey Arts Council Fellowships, 1979, 1983; Helen Bullis Prize, 1982; Guggenheim Fellowship, 1984; Levinson Prize, 1988; Oscar Blumenthal Prize, 1991; James Wright Prize, 1993. Address: 445 Chestnut Neck Road, Port Republic, NJ 078241, USA.

DUNNETT Dorothy, (Dorothy Halliday), b. 25 Aug 1925, Dunfermline, Scotland. Novelist; Portrait Painter. m. Sir Alastair M Dunnett, 17 Sept 1946, 2 sons. Publications: The Game of Kings, 1961, 12th edition, 1997; Queen's Play, 1964, 12th edition 1997; The Disorderly Knights, 1966, 12th edition, 1997; Dolly and the Singing Bird (also the Photogenic Soprano), 1968, 5th edition, 1991; Pawn in Frankincense, 1969, 12th edition, 1997; Dolly and the Cookie Bird (also Murder in the Round), 1970, 5th edition 1993; The Ringed Castle, 1971, 12th edition 1997; Dolly and the Doctor Bird (also Match for a Murder), 1971, 5th edition, 1985; Dolly and the Starry Bird, 1973, 5th edition, 1993; Checkmate, 1975, 12th edition, 1997; King Hereafter, 1982, 4th edition, 1992; Dolly and the Bird of Paradise, 1983, 5th edition, 1991; Niccolo Rising, 1986, 5th edition, 1992; The Spring of the Ram, 1987, 6th edition, 1992; The Scottish Highlands (with Alastair M Dunnett and David Paterson), 1988; Race of Scorpions, 1989, 4th edition, 1993; Moroccan Traffic, 1991, 3rd edition, 1993; Scales of Gold, 1991, 1993; The Unicorn Hunt, 1993, 4th edition, 1994; To Lie with Lions, 1995, 4th edition, 1996; Caprice and Rando, 1997. Honours: Scottish Arts Council, 1976; Officer of the Order of the British Empire, 1992. Memberships: Fellow, Royal Society of the Arts; Trustee, National Library of Scotland. Literary Agent: Curtis Brown. Address: 87 Colinton Road, Edinburgh EH10 5DF, Scotland.

DUO Duo. See: LI Shizheng.

DUPONT (Jean) Louis, b. 17 Jan 1924, Shawinigan, Canada. School Principal retired. m. Beaulieu Madeleine, 1 Aug 1953, 2 sons, 3 daughters. Education: Superior Diploma, Primary Teaching, 1948; MA, 1952; Master of Public Administration, 1967. Publications: La Guerre du Castor, 1984; La Légende de Thogoruk, 1993. Contributions to: La Presse; Lettres Québécoises. Memberships: La Société Littéraire de Laval; L'Union des Ecrivains Québécois. Address: 1255 Montpellier, Laval, Quebec H7E 3C8, Canada.

DURANTI Francesca. See: ROSSI Maria Francesca.

DURBAND Alan, b. 3 June 1927, Liverpool, England. Writer. m. Audrey Atherton, 26 July 1952, 1 son, 1 daughter. Education: BA, 1951, MA, 1956, Downing College, Cambridge. Publications: English Workshop, books 1-3, 1959; New Directions: Five One-Act Plays in the Modern Idiom, 1961; Contemporary English Books 1-2, 1962; Shorter Contemporary English, 1964; New English Books, 1-4, 1966; Playbill 1-3, 1969; Second Playbill, 1-3, 1973; Prompt 1-3, 1975; Wordplays 1-2, 1982; Shakespeare Made Easy (12 plays), 1984-89. Address: Ty-Nant, Lansilin, Near Oswestry, Salop, SY10 7QQ, England.

DURBRIDGE Francis Henry, (Paul Temple) b. 25 Nov 1912, Hull, England. Playwright; Author. m. Norah Elizabeth Lawley, 1940, 2 sons. Education: Birmingham University. Publications: Radio plays: Promotion, 1933; created character of Paul Temple: entered TV with The Broken Horseshoe, 1952 (the first adult TV serial), other serials followed: Portrait of Alison, 1954; My Friend Charles, 1955; The Other Man, 1956; The Scarf, 1960; The World of Tim Frazer (executive producer), 1960-61; Melissa, 1962; Bat Out of Hell, 1964; Stupid Like a Fox, 1971; The Doll, 1976; Breakaway, 1980; Films: 2 for Korda and Romulus, 1954-57; Stage plays: Suddenly at Home, 1971; The Gentle Hook, 1974; Murder With Love, 1976; House Guest, 1980; Nightcap, 1983; Murder Diary, 1986; The Small Hours, 1989; Sweet Revenge, 1991; Side Effects. Contributions to: Various journals, newspapers and magazines. Address: c/o Lemon, Unna and Durbridge Ltd, 24 Pottery Lane, Holland Park, London W11 4LZ, England.

DURCAN Paul, b. 16 Oct 1944, Dublin, Ireland. Poet. Education: BA. Publications: Endsville, 1967; O Westport in the Light of Asia Minor, 1975; Teresa's Bar, 1976; Sam's Cross, 1978; Jesus, Break His Fall, 1980; Ark of the North, 1982; The Selected Paul Durcan, 1985; Jumping the Train Tracks With Angela, 1983; The Berlin Wall Cafe, 1985; Going Home to Russia, 1987; In the Land of Punt, 1988; Jesus and Angela, 1988; Daddy, Daddy, 1990; Crazy About Women, 1991; A Snail in My Prime, 1993; Give Me Your Hand, 1994. Contributions to: Irish Press; Irish Times; Hibernia; Magill; Cyphers; Honest Ulsterman; Gorey Detail; Cork Examiner; Aquarius. Honours: Patrick Kavanagh Poetry Award, 1974; Arts Council of Ireland Bursary for Creative Writing, 1976, 1980-81; Poetry Book Society Choice 1985; Irish American Cultural Institute Poetry Award, 1989; Whitbread Poetry Award, 1990; Heinemann Award, 1995. Membership: Aosdána. Address: 14 Cambridge Avenue, Ringsend, Dublin 4, Ireland.

DURGNAT Raymond Eric, (O O Green), b. 1 Sept 1932, London, England. Writer; Lecturer. Education: BA Hons, English Literature, Pembroke College, Cambridge, 1957; MA, 1970. Appointment: Staff Writer, British Picture Corporation, Elstree Studios, 1957-60. Publications: A Mirror for England, 1973; The Strange Case of Alfred Hitchcock, 1973; Durgnat on Film, 1976; Luis Bunuel, 1988; Michael Powell and the English Genius, 1991. Contributions to: British Journal of Aesthetics. Membership: British Society of Aesthetics. Address: 84 Saint Thomas's Road, London N4 2QW, England.

DURKIN Barbara (Rae Wernecke), b. 13 Jan 1944, Baltimore, Maryland, USA. Writer. m. William J Durkin, 20 May 1973, 2 sons. Education: AA, Essex Community College, 1964; BS, Towson State College, 1966; Graduate Studies, Morgan State College, 1968, John Hopkins University, 1968-70. Publications: Oh, You Dundalk Girls, Can't You Dance the Polka?, 1984; Visions and Viewpoints (editor), 1993. Honour: Best of 1984 List, American Library Association, 1984. Memberships: American PEN Women; International Women's Writing Guild. Address: 531 Phillips Road, Webster, NY 14580, USA.

DURST Paul, b. 23 Apr 1921, Archbald, Pennsylvania, USA. Writer. Education: Colorado State College, 1938-40; Northwest Missouri State College, 1940-41. Appointments: Editorial Writer; Newcaster, St Joseph News-Press, 1946-48; Advertising Supervisor, Southwestern Bell Telephone Company, Kansas City and St Louis, 1948-50; Advertising Manager, Crofts Engineering, Bradford, 1958-60; J G Graves, Mail Order Firm, Sheffield, 1960-62. Publications: Die! Damn You, 1952; Bloody River, 1953; Trail Herd North, 1953; Guns of Circle 8 (as Jeff Cochran), 1954; Along the Yermo Rim (as John Shane), 1954; My Deadly Angel (as John Chelton), 1955; Showdown, 1955; Justice, 1956; Kid From Canadian, 1956; Prairie Reckoning, 1956; Sundown in Sundance (as John Shane), 1956; Six-Gun Thursday (as John Shane), 1956; Gunsmoke Dawn (as John Shane), 1957; John Law, Keep Out, 1957; Ambush at North Platte, 1957; The River Flows West, 1957; If They Want Me Dead (as Peter Bannon), 1958; If I Should Die (as Peter Bannon), 1958; Kansas Guns, 1958; Dead Man's Range, 1958; The Gun Doctor, 1959; Johnny Nation, 1960; Whisper Murder Softly (as Peter Bannon), 1963; Backlash, 1967; Badge of Infamy (crime), 1968; Intended Treason: What Really Happened to the Gunpowder Plot, 1970; A Roomful of Shadows (autobiography), 1975; The Florentine Table, 1980; Paradiso Country, 1985. Address: The Keep, West Wall, Presteigne, Powys LD8 2BY, Wales.

DUTHIE Gilbert William Arthur, b. 21 May 1912, Nhill, Victoria, Australia. Uniting Church Minister. m. Jeannette E Blake, 8 Mar 1941, 3 daughters. Publication: The Jesus Tale Words Never Knew. Contributions to: In Parliament with 8 Prime Ministers; How Did They Shape Up? Honours: BA, 1937; LTH, 1936. Memberships: Order of Australia Award, 1986. Address: 03 63442611, Launceston, Tasmania, Australia.

DUTTON Geoffrey Piers Henry, b. 2 Aug 1922, Anlaby, South Australia. Writer. m. (1) Ninette Trott, 1944, 2 sons, 1 daughter, (2) Robin Lucas, 1985. Education: University of Adelaide; BA, Magdalen College, Oxford, 1949. Appointments: Co-Editor, Australian Letters, 1957-68, Australian Book Review, 1961-70; Editorial Director, Sun Books Ltd, 1965-83; Editor, The Bulletin Literary Supplement, 1980-85, The Australian Literary Magazine, 1985-88. Publications: Nightflight and Sunrise, 1945; The Hero as Murderer, 1967; Andy, 1968; Walt Whitman: Patrick White, 1961; Findings and Keepings, 1970; Queen Emma of the South Seas, 1976; Patterns of Australia, 1978; White on Black, 1978; Snow on the Saltbush, 1984; The Innovators, 1986;

Kenneth Slessor, 1991; Flying Low, 1992; New & Selected Poems, 1993; Out in the Open: An Autobiography, 1994. Contributions to: Numerous journals and magazines and broadcasting services. Honour: Officer of the Order of Australia, 1976. Address: c/o Curtis Brown, PO Box 19, Paddington, New South Wales 2021, Australia.

DUTTON Ninette Clarice Bernadette, b. 24 July 1923, Adelaide, South Australia, Australia. Enameller; Artist; Author. m. Geoffrey Dutton, 31 July 1944, 2 sons, 1 daughter. Education: University of Adelaide. Publications: The Beautiful Art of Enamelling, 1966; Portrait of a Year, 1976; An Australian Wildflower Diary, 1982; Wildflower Journeys, 1985; Probabilities, short stories, 1987; A Passionate Gardener, 1990; Firing, a Memoir, 1994. Contributions to: Adelaide Advertiser; Your Garden magazine; Regular broadcasts. Honours: Medal, Order of Australia. Memberships: Australian Society of Authors; Fellowship of Australian Writers. Address: PO Box 342, Williamstown, South Australia 5351, Australia.

DUVAL Jeanne. See: COFFMAN Virginia (Edith).

DWORKIN Ronald (Myles), b. 11 Dec 1931, Worcester, Massachusetts, USA. Professor of Jurisprudence; Writer. m. Betsy Ross, 18 July 1958, 1 son, 1 daughter. Education: BA, 1953, LLB, 1957, Harvard University; BA, Oxford University, 1955. Appointments: Admitted to the Bar, New York, 1959; Faculty, 1962-69, Hohfeld Professor of Jurisprudence, 1968-69, Yale Law School; Visiting Professor of Philosophy, 1963, 1974-75, Gauss Seminarian, 1966, Princeton University; Master, Trumball College, 1966-69; Visiting Professor of Law, Stanford University, 1967; Professor of Jurisprudence, Oxford University, 1969-; Professor of Law, New York University, 1975-; Academic Freedom Lecturer, University of the Witwatersrand, 1976; Professor-at-Large, Cornell University, 1976-; Visiting Professor of Law and Philosophy, 1977, Visiting Professor of Philosophy, 1979, Harvard University. Publications: Taking Rights Seriously, 1977; Philosophy of Law (editor), 1977; A Matter of Principle, 1985; Law's Empire, 1986; A Bill of Rights of Britain, 1990; Life's Dominion, 1993; Freedom's Law, 1996. Contributions to: Professional journals. Memberships: American Academy of Arts and Sciences; British Academy, fellow. Address: c/o School of Law, New York University, 40 Washington Square South, New York, NY 10012, USA.

DWYER K R. See: KOONTZ Dean R.

DYBEK Stuart, b. 10 Apr 1942, Chicago, Illinois, USA. Poet; Writer; Professor of English. m. Caren Bassett, 1966, 1 son, 1 daughter. Education: BS, 1964, MA, 1967, Loyola University; MFA, University of Iowa, 1973. Appointments: Teaching Assistant, 1970-72, Teaching and Writing Fellow, 1972-73, University of Iowa; Professor of English, Western Michigan University, 1973-; Guest Writer and Teacher, Michigan Council for the Arts' Writer in the Schools Program, 1973-92; Faculty, Warren Wilson MFA Program in Creative Writing, 1985-89; Visiting Professor of Creative Writing, Princeton University, 1990, University of California, Irvine, 1995; Numerous readings, lectures and workshops. Publications: Brass Knuckles (poems), 1979; Childhood and Other Neighbourhoods (stories), 1980; The Coast of Chicago (stories), 1990; The Story of Mist (short fiction and prose poems), 1994. Contributions to: Many anthologies and magazines. Honours: Award in Fiction, Society of Midwest Authors, 1981; Cliffdwellers Award for Fiction, Friends of American Literature, 1981; Special Citation, PEN/Hemingway Prize Committee, 1981; Michigan Council for the Arts Grants, 1981, 1992; Guggenheim Fellowship, 1982; National Endowment for the Arts Fellowships, 1982, 1994; Pushcart Prize, 1985; 1st Prize, O Henry Award, 1985; Nelson Algren Prize, 1985; Whiting Writers Award, 1985; Michigan Arts Award, Arts Foundation of Michigan, 1986; American Academy of Arts and Letters Award for Fiction, 1994; PEN/Malamud Award, 1995; Rockefeller Residency, Bellagio, Italy, 1996. Address: 310 Monroe, Kalamazoo, MI 49006, USA.

DYER James Frederick, b. 23 Feb 1934, Luton, England. Archaeological Writer. Education: MA, Leicester University, 1964. Appointment: Editor, Shire Archaeology, 1974-. Publications: Southern England, An Archaeological Guide, 1973; Penguin Guide to Prehistoric England and Wales, 1981; Discovering Archaeology in England and Wales, 1985; Ancient Britain, 1990; Discovering Prehistoric England, 1993. Contributions to: Bedfordshire Magazine; Illustrated London News; Archaeological Journal. Memberships: Society of Authors;

Royal Archaeological Institute; Society of Antiquaries. Address: 6 Rogate Road, Luton, Bedfordshire LU2 8HR, England.

DYMOKE Juliet, b. 28 June 1919, Enfield, England. Writer. m. Hugo de Schanschieff, 9 May 1942, 1 son, 1 daughter. Publications: The Cloisterman, 1969; Norman Triology, 1970-74; The White Cockade, 1979; Plantagenet Series, 6 volumes 1978-80; A King of Warfare, 1981; March to Corunna, 1985; The Queen's Diamond, 1985; Aboard the Mary Rose, 1985; Two Flags for France, 1986; A Border Knight, 1987; Ride to Glencoe, 1989; Portrait of Jenny, 1990; Hollander's House, 1991; Cry of the Peacock, 1992; Winter's Daughter, 1994. Contribution to: The Lady. Membership: Romantic Novelists Association. Literary Agent: Jane Conway-Gordon, 1 Old Compton Street, London, W1, England. Address: Heronswood, Chapel Lane, Forest Row, East Sussex, RH18 5BS, England.

DYSON A(nthony) E(dward), b. 28 Nov 1928, London, England. Writer. Education: MLitt, Pembroke College, Cambridge, 1952. Appointments: Co-Founder, Director, Critical Quarterly Society, 1960-84; Visiting Professor, Concordia University, Montreal, Canada, 1967, 1969; General Editor, Macmillan Casebooks, England, 1968-; Visiting Professor, University of Connecticut, USA, 1976; Director, Norwich Tapes Ltd, England, 1979-; Honorary Fellow, former Reader in English, University of East Anglia, Norwich. Publications: Modern Poetry (with C B Cox), 1963; The Crazy Fabric: Essays in Irony, 1965; The Practical Criticism of Poetry (with C B Cox), 1965; Modern Judgements on Dickens, 1968; Word in the Desert (with C B Cox), 1968; Casebook on Bleak House, 1969; Black Papers on Education, 3 volumes, 1969-70; The Inimitable Dickens, 1970; Between Two Worlds: Aspects of Literary Form, 1972; Twentieth Century Mind, 3 volumes, (with C B Cox), 1972; English Poetry: Select Bibliographical Guides, 1973; English Novel: Select Bibliographical Guides, 1974; Casebook on Paradise Lost (with Julian Lovelock), 1974; Masterful Images: Metaphysicals to Romantics (with Julian Lovelock), 1975; Education and Democracy (with Julian Lovelock), 1975; Yeats, Eliot and R S Thomas: Riding the Echo, 1981; Poetry Criticism and Practice, 1986; Thom Gunn, Ted Hughes and R S Thomas, 1990; The Fifth Dimension, 1996. Contributions to: Over 100 articles in world of English criticism to various, US, UK and European Community journals; 8 teaching tapes. Address: c/o Macmillan Publishers, Hampshire RG21 2XS, England.

DYSON Freeman J(ohn), b. 15 Dec 1923, Crowthorne, England (US citizen, 1957). Professor of Physics Emeritus. m. (1) Verena Haefeli-Huber, 11 Aug 1950, div 1958, 1 son, 1 daughter, (2) Imme Jung, 21 Nov 1958, 4 daughters. Education: BA, Cambridge University, 1945; Graduate Studies, Cornell University, 1947-48, Institute for Advanced Study, Princeton, New Jersey, 1948-49. Appointments: Research Fellow, Trinity College, Cambridge, 1946-49; Warren Research Fellow, University of Birmingham, England, 1949-51; Professor of Physics, Cornell University, 1951-53; Professor of Physics, 1953-94, Professor Emeritus, 1994-, Institute for Advanced Study. Publications: Symmetry Groups in Nuclear and Particle Physics, 1966; Neutron Stars and Pulsars, 1971; Disturbing the Universe, 1979; Values at War, 1983; Weapons and Hope, 1984; Origins of Life, 1986; Infinite in All Directions, 1988; From Eros to Gaia, 1992; Imagined Worlds, 1997. Honours: Heineman Prize, American Institute of Physics, 1966; Lorentz Medal, Royal Netherlands Academy of Sciences, 1966; Hughes Medal, Royal Society, 1968; Max Planck Medal, German Physical Society, 1969; J Robert Oppenheimer Memorial Prize, Center for Theoretical Studies, 1970; Harvey Prize, Israel Institute of Technology, 1977; Wolf Prize, Wolf Foundation, 1981; National Book Critics Circle Award, 1984; Honorary doctorates. Memberships: American Physical Society; National Academy of Sciences; Fellow, Royal Society. Address: 105 Battle Road Circle, Princeton, NJ 08540, USA.

E

EAGLETON Terence Francis, b. 22 February 1943, Salford, England. Professor of English Literature; Author. m. Elizabeth Rosemary Galpin, 1966, 2 daughters. Education: MA, Trinity College, Cambridge, 1964; PhD, Jesus College, Cambridge, 1967. Appointments: Fellow in English, Jesus College, Cambridge, 1964-69; Tutorial Fellow, Wadham College, 1969-89, Lecturer in Critical Theory, 1989-92, Fellow, Linacre College, 1989-92, Thomas Warton Professor of Literature and Fellow of St Catherine's College, Oxford, 1992-. Publications: Criticism and Ideology, 1976; Marxism and Literary Criticism, 1976; Walter Benjamin, 1981; Literary Theory: An Introduction, 1983; The Function of Criticism, 1984; The Rape of Clarissa, 1985; Against the Grain, 1986; William Shakespeare, 1986; The Ideology of the Aesthetic, 1990; Ideology: An Introduction, 1993; Heathcliff and the Great Hunger: Studies in Irish Culture, 1995. Contributions to: Periodicals. Honours: Irish Sunday Tribune Arts Award, 1990; Honorary DLitt, Salford, 1993. Address: St Catherine's College, Oxford, Oxford OX1 3UJ, England.

EARL Maureen J, b. 4 Sept 1944, Cairo, Egypt (British nationality). Writer; Journalist; Screenwriter; Documentary Maker. m. Clifford Irving, 1984, 1 son, 1 daughter. Publications: Gulliver Quick, 1992; Boat of Stone, 1993. Contributions to: Various magazines and journals worldwide. Honours: Best Young Journalist Award, New Zealand, 1967; Exceptional Political Reporting Award, Australia, 1970; Best Independent Documentary, Australia, 1972; Emmy Award, 1975; Emmy Award Nominee, 1976; Jewish Book of the Year, 1993; Runner Up Critics Circle Award, 1993. Memberships: Authors' Guild; New York Writers' Guild; PEN International; Author's League. Literary Agent: Jane Cushman, JCA Literary Agents, New York, USA. Address: Aldama 1, San Miguel de Allende, GTO 37700, Mexico.

EARLY Gerald, b. 21 Apr 1952, Philadelphia, Pennsylvania, USA. Professor of English and Afro-American Studies; Writer; Poet. m. Ida Haynes, 27 Aug 1977, 2 daughters. Education: BA cum laude, English, University of Pennsylvania, 1974; MA, English, 1980, PhD, English, 1982, Cornell University. Publications: Tuxedo Junction: Essays on American Culture, 1990; My Soul's High Song, 1991; Lure and Loathing, 1993; Daughters: One Family and Fatherhood, 1994; Culture of Bruising, 1994; How the War in the Streets is Won, 1995. Contributions to: Essays and reviews to many journals; Poetry: American Poetry Review; Northwest Review; Tar River Poetry; Raccoon; Seneca Review; Obsidian II; Black American Literature Forum. Honours: Whiting Foundation Writer's Award, 1988; CCLM-General Electric Foundation Award for Younger Writers, 1988; Several Fellowships. Address: Washington University, Campus Box 1109, One Brookings Drive, St Louis, MO 63130, USA.

EAST Morris. See: **WEST Morris.**

EASTAUGH Kenneth, b. 30 Jan 1929, Preston, England. Appointments: Television Critic, 1965-67, Show Business Writer, 1967-70, Daily Mirror, London; Chief Show Business Writer, The Sun, London, 1970-73; TV Columnist, The Times, London, 1977; Film Critic, Prima Magazine, Music Critic, Classical Music Weekly, 1976-; Chief Show Business Executive, Daily Star, London, 1978-83. Publications: The Event (television play), 1968; Better Than a Man (televsion play), 1970; Dapple Downs (radio serial), 1973-74; Awkward Cuss (play), 1976; Havergal Brian: The Making of a Composer (biography), 1976; Coronation Street (television series), 1977-78; The Carry On Book (cinema), 1978; Havergal Who? (television documentary), 1980; Mr Love (novel, screenplay), 1986; Dallas (television serial), 1989; Three film contract with David Puttman/Warner Brothers, 1992. Address: David Higham Associates, 5-8 Lower John Street, Golden Square, London W1R 4HA, England.

EASTHOPE Antony Kelynge Revington, b. 14 Apr 1939, Portsmouth, England. Professor. m. Diane Garside, 1 Feb 1972, 1 son, 2 daughters. Education: BA, 1961, MA, 1965, MLitt, 1967, Christ's College, Cambridge. Appointments: Brown University, Rhode Island, USA, 1964-66; Warwick University, England, 1967-68; Manchester Metropolitan University, 1969-. Publications: Poetry as Discourse, 1983; What a Man's Gotta Do, 1986; British Post-Structuralism, 1988; Poetry and Phantasy, 1989; Literary into Cultural Studies, 1991; Wordsworth, Now and Then, 1993. Contributions to: Numerous

magazines and journals. Honours: Charter Fellow, Wolfson College, Oxford, 1985-86; Visiting Fellow, University of Virginia, 1990. Address: 27 Victoria Avenue, Didsbury, Manchester, M20 8QX, England.

EASTON Robert Olney, b. 4 July 1915, San Francisco, California, USA. Writer. m. Jane Faust, 24 Sept 1940, 4 daughters. Education: Stanford University, 1933-34; SB, Harvard University, 1938; MA, University of California, 1960. Publications: The Happy Man, 1943; Lord of Beasts (co-author), 1961; The Book of the American West (co-author), 1963; The Hearing, 1964; Californian Condor (co-author), 1964; Max Brand, 1970; Black Tide, 1972; This Promised Land, 1982; China Caravans, 1982; Life and Work (co-author), 1988; Power and Glory, 1989; Love and War (co-author), 1991. Contributions to: Magazines. Literary Agent: Jon Tuska. Address: 2222 Las Canoas Road, Santa Barbara, CA 93105, USA.

EATON Charles Edward, b. 25 June 1916, Winston-Salem, North Carolina, USA. Poet; Writer. m. Isabel Patterson, 1950. Education: Duke University, 1932-33; BA, University of North Carolina at Chapel Hill, 1936; Princeton University, 1936-37; MA in English, Harvard University, 1940. Appointments: Instructor in Creative Writing, University of Missouri, 1940-42; Vice Consul, American Embassy, Rio de Janeiro, 1942-46; Professor of Creative Writing, University of North Caolina, 1946-52. Publications: Poetry: The Bright Plain, 1942; The Shadow of the Swimmer, 1951; The Greenhouse in the Garden, 1956; Countermoves, 1963; On the Edge of the Knife, 1970; The Man in the Green Chair, 1977; Colophon of the Rover, 1980; The Thing King, 1983; The Work of the Wrench, 1985; New and Selected Poems 1942-1987, 1987; A Guest on Mild Evenings, 1991; The Country of the Blue, 1994; The Fox and I, 1996, Novel: A Lady of Pleasure, 1993. Short Stories: Write Me From Rio, 1959; The Girl From Ipanema, 1972; The Case of the Missing Photographs, 1978; New and Selected Stories 1959-1989, 1989. Honours: Bread Loaf Writers Conference Robert Frost Fellowship, 1941; Ridgely Torrence Memorial Award, 1951; Gertrude Boatwright Harris Award, 1955; Arizona Quarterly Awards, 1956, 1975, 1977, 1979, 1982; Roanoke-Chowan Awards, 1970, 1987, 1991; Oscar Arnold Young Award, 1971; O Henry Award, 1972; Alice Faye di Castagnola Award, 1974; Arvon Foundation Award, 1980; Hollins Critic Award, 1984; Brockman Awards, 1984, 1986; Kansas Quarterly Awards, 1987; North Carolina Literature Award, 1988; Fortner Award, 1993. Contributions to: Periodicals. Memberships: American Academy of Poets. Address: 808 Greenwood Road, Chapel Hill, NC 27514, USA.

EATON Trevor Michael William, b. 26 Mar 1934, Harrow, London, England. Writer; Editor; Professional performer of Chaucer. m. Beryl Elizabeth Rose Conley, 29 Sept 1958, 2 sons, 2 daughters. Education: New College, Oxford University, 1955-58; MA, English Language and Literature, Oxford; MA, Applied Linguistics, University of Kent, Canterbury, 1988. Appointments: Founder-Editor, Journal of Literary Semantics, 1972-; Founder, International Association of Literary Semantics, 1992. Publications: The Semantics of Literature, 1966; Theoretical Semics, 1972; Editor, Essays in Literary Semantics, 1978; Poetries: Their Media and Ends (I A Richards); Commercial recordings: Chaucer's The Canterbury Tales, recited on 18 audio cassettes in Middle English, 1986-93, Sir Gawain and the Green Knight in Middle English, 1995. Contributions to: Linguistics; Cahier Roumains d'Etudes Littéraires; Style; Educational Studies. Memberships: International Association of Literary Semantics; International PEN; Linguistics Association of Great Britain; PALA. Address: Honeywood Cottage, 35 Seaton Avenue, Hythe, Kent CT21 5HH, England.

EBEJER Francis, b. 28 Aug 1925, Malta. Author; Dramatist; Poet. m. Jane Couch, 5 Sept 1947, separated 1957, 2 sons, 1 dec, 1 daughter. Education: Matriculated, Malta Lyceum, 1939; Fulbright Grant, USA, 1961-62. Appointments: Drama and Literature Lecturer. Publications: A Wreath of Maltese Innocents, 1958; Evil of the King Cockroach, 1960; In the Eye of the Sun, 1969; Requiem for a Maltese Fascist, 1980; Come Again in Spring, 1980; Leap of Malta Dolphins, 1982. Plays: Over 40 in Maltese, 7 volumes, 1950-85; 11 in English, 3 volumes, 1950-85. Contributions: Short stories, poems, essays etc. in various Maltese publications; Contributed chapter to book No Longer Silent, 1995. Honours: Cheyney Award for Drama, 1964; 4 Malta Literary Awards, 1972-; Phoenicia Trophy Award for Culture, 1982; Médaille d'Honneur de la Ville d'Avignon, France, 1986. Memberships: English PEN, fellow; French Academy of Vaucluse; Malta Literary Society, honorary president; Maltese Academy of Letters, council member, 1984-88. Address: Nivea Court, Sweigqi Valley, Swieqi STJ05, Malta.

EBEL Suzanne, (Suzanne Goodwin, Cecily Shelbourne), Writer. Publications: Love, The Magician, 1956; Journey from Yesterday, 1963; The Half-Enchanted, 1964; The Love Campaign, 1965; The Dangerous Winter, 1965; A Perfect Stranger, 1966; A Name in Lights, 1968; A Most Auspicious Star, 1968; Somersault, 1971; Portrait of Jill, 1972; Dear Kate, 1972; To Seek a Star, 1973; The Family Feeling, 1973; Girl by the Sea, 1974; Music in Winter, 1975; A Grove of Olives, 1976; River Voices, 1976; The Double Rainbow, 1977; A Rose in Heather, 1978; Julia's Sister, 1982; The Provencal Summer, 1982; House of Nightingales, 1986; The Clover Field, 1987; As Suzanne Goodwin: The Winter Spring, 1978 (USA - Stage of Love, as Cecily Shelbourne, 1978); The Winter Sisters, 1980; Emerald, 1980; Floodtide, 1983; Sisters, 1985; Cousins, 1986; Daughters, 1987; Lovers, 1988; To Love a Hero, 1989; A Change of Season, 1990; The Rising Storm, 1992; While the Music Lasts, 1993; The Difference, 1995; Sheer Chance, 1997. Non-fiction: Explore the Cotswolds by Bicycle (with Doreen Impey), 1973; London's Riverside, From Hampton Court in the West to Greenwich Palace in the East (with Doreen Impey), 1975. Literary Agent: Curtis Brown. Address: 52A Digby Mansions, Hammersmith Bridge Road, London W6 9DF, England.

EBERSOHN Wessel (Schalk), b. 6 Mar 1940, Cape Town, South Africa. Author; Writer. Appointments: Technician, Department of Posts and Telecommunications, Pretoria, 1956-62; Gowlett Alpha, Johannesburg, 1962-69; Department of Posts and Telecommunications, Durban, 1970-79; Freelance Writer, 1979-. Publications: A Lonely Place to Die (mystery novel), 1979; The Centurion (mystery novel), 1979; Store up the Anger (novel), 1981; Divide the Night (mystery novel), 1981; Klara's Visitors (novel), 1987. Address: 491 Long Avenue, Ferndale 2194, Transvaal, South Africa.

EBERT Alan, b. 14 Sep 1935, New York, New York, USA. Author. Education: BA, Brooklyn College, 1957; MA, Fordham University, 1975. Publications: The Homosexuals, 1977; Every Body is Beautiful (with Ron Fletcher), 1978; Intimacies, 1979; Traditions (novel), 1981; The Long Way Home (novel), 1984; Marriages (novel), 1987. Contributions to: Family Circle; Essence; Look; Us; Good Housekeeping. Membership: American Society of Journalists and Authors. Address: 353 West 56th Street, New York, NY 10019, USA.

EBERT Roger (Joseph), b. 18 June 1942, Urbana, Illinois, USA. Film Critic; Writer; Lecturer. m. Chaz Hammelsmith, 18 July 1992. Education: BS, University of Illinois, 1964; University of Cape Town, 1965; University of Chicago, 1966-67. Appointments: Reporter, News Gazette, Champaign-Urbana, Illinois, 1958-66; Instructor, Chicago City College, 1967-68; Film Critic, Chicago Sun-Times, 1967-, US Magazine, 1978-79, WMAQ-TV, Chicago, 1980-83, WLS-TV, Chicago, 1984-, New York Post, 1986-88, New York Daily News, 1988-92, CompuServe, 1991-, Microsoft Cinemania, 1994-; Lecturer, University of Chicago, 1969-; Co-Host, Sneak Previews, WTTW-TV, Chicago, 1977-82; At the Movies, syndicated television programme, 1982-86; Siskel and Ebert, syndicated television programme, 1986-; President, Ebert Co Ltd, 1981-. Publications: An Illini Century, 1967; A Kiss is Still a Kiss, 1984; Roger Ebert's Movie Home Companion (annual volumes), 1986-93, subsequently Roger Ebert's Video Companion, 1994-; The Perfect London Walk (with Daniel Curley), 1986; Two Weeks in the Midday Sun: A Cannes Notebook, 1987; The Future of the Movies: Interviews with Martin Scorses, Steven Spielberg, and George Lucas (with Gene Siskel), 1991; Behind the Phantom's Mask, 1993; Ebert's Little Movie Glossary, 1994; Roger Ebert's Book of the Movies, 1996. Contributions to: Newspapers and magazines. Honours: Overseas Press Club Award, 1963; Rotary Fellow, 1965; Pulitzer Prize for Criticism, 1975; Chicago Emmy Award, 1979; Honorary Doctorate, University of Colorado, 1993; Kluge Fellow in Film Studies, University of Virginia, 1995-96. Memberships: Academy of London; American Newspaper Guild; National Society of Film Critics; Phi Delta Theta; Sigma Delta Chi; Writers Guild of America. Address: c/o ChicagoSun-Times, 401 North Wabash, Chicago, IL 60611, USA.

EBERT Tibor, b. 14 Oct 1926, Bratislava, Czechoslovakia. Writer; Poet; Dramatist. m. Eva Gati, 11 Feb 1968, 1 daughter. Education: BA, Music, Ferenc Liszt Academy of Music, 1952; Law, Philosophy, Literature studies, Department of Law and Philosophy, Eotvos Lorand University, Budapest, 1951-53. Appointments: Dramaturg, Jozsef Attila Theatre, Budapest, Hungary, 1984-85;

Editor-in-Chief, Agora Publishers, Budapest, 1989-92; Editor, Hirvivo Literary Magazine, 1990-92. Publications: Mikrodramak, 1971; Rosarium, 1987; Kobayashi, 1989; Legenda egy fuvoszenekarrol, 1990; Job konyve, 1991; Fagyott Orpheusz, poems, 1993; Eső, 1996; Egy város glóriája, 1997; Bartók, 1997. Several plays performed on stage including: Les Escaliers; Musique de Chambre; Demosthenes; Esterhazy. Contributions to: Numerous short stories, poems, dramas and essays to several leading Hungarian literary journals and magazines. Honours: Honorary Member, Franco-Hungarian Society, 1980-; Bartok Prize, 1987; Commemorative Medal, City of Pozsony-Pressburg-Bratislava, 1991; Esterhazy Prize, 1993; Order of the Hungarian Republic, 1996. Memberships: PEN Club; Association of Hungarian Writers; Literary Association Berzsenyi. Literary Agent: Artisjus Budapest, Hungary. Address: Csevi u 15c, 1025 Budapest, Hungary.

ECHERUO Michael (Joseph Chukwudalu), b. 14 Mar 1937, Umunumo, Mbano Division, Nigeria. Professor of English; Poet. Education: University College, Ibadan, 1955-60; PhD, Cornell University, New York, 1965. Appointments: Professor of English, 1974-80, Vice-Chancellor, 1981-, Imo State University, Owerri. Publications: Mortality, 1968; Joyce Cary and the Novel of Africa, 1973; Distanced: New Poems, 1975; Victorian Lagos, 1977; Poets, Prophets and Professors, 1977; The Conditioned Imagination from Shakespeare to Conrad: Studies in the Exo-Cultural Stereotype, 1978; Editor, Shakespeare's The Tempest, 1980. Honours: All-Africa Poetry Competition Prize, 1963. Address: Vice-Chancellor's Office, Imo State University, Owerri, Nigeria.

ECKARDT A(rthur) Roy, b. 8 Aug 1918, New York, New York, USA. Professor of Religion Emeritus; Senior Associate Fellow; Writer. m. Alice Lyons Eckardt, 2 Sept 1944, 1 son, 1 daughter. Education: BA, Brooklyn College, 1942; MDiv, The Divinity School, Yale University, 1944; PhD, Columbia University, 1947; Union Theological Seminary, New York City. Appointments: Assistant Professor of Philosophy and Religion, Hamline University, 1946-47; Assistant Professor of Religion, Lawrence College, Appleton, Wisconsin, 1947-50, Duke University, 1950-51; Associate Professor, 1951-56, Head, Department of Religion, 1951-80, Professor of Religion, 1956-80, Professor Emeritus, 1980-, Lehigh University; Editor, Journal of the American Academy of Religion, 1961-69; Visiting Scholar, 1982, 1985, Maxwell Fellow, 1989-90, Senior Associate Fellow, 1990-, Resident Fellow, 1994, Oxford Centre for Hebrew and Jewish Studies, Oxford University. Publications: Christianity and the Children of Israel, 1948; The Surge of Piety in America, 1958; Elder and Younger Brothers: The Encounter of Jews and Christians, 1967; The Theologian at Work (editor), 1968; Encounter with Israel (with Alice L Eckhardt), 1970; Your People, My People, 1974; Long Day's Journey Into Day: Life and Faith After the Holocaust (with Alice L Eckhardt), 1982, revised edition as Long Night's Journey Into Day: A Revised Retrospective on the Holocaust, 1988; Jews and Christians, 1986; For Righteous' Sake, 1987; Black-Woman-Jew, 1989; Reclaiming the Jesus of History: Christology Today, 1992; Sitting in the Earth and Laughing: A Handbook of Humor, 1992; Collecting Myself: A Writer's Retrospective, 1993; No Longer Aliens, No Longer Strangers, 1994; How to Tell God From the Devil, 1995; On the Way to Death: Essays Toward a Comic Vision, 1996. Contributions to: Many Journals. Honours: Ford Foundation Fellow, 1955-56; Lilly Foundation Fellow, 1963-64; National Foundation for Jewish Culture Fellow, 1968-69; Honorary LHD, Hebrew Union College, 1969; Rockefeller Fellow, 1975-76; Jabotinsky Centennial Medal, 1980. Memberships: American Academy of Religion; Christian Scholars Group on Judaism and the Jewish People; Consultation on the Church and the Jewish People, World Council of Churches; International Council of Christians and Jews; International Society for Humor Studies; Phi Beta Kappa. Address: 6011 Beverly Hill Road, Coopersburg, PA 18036, USA.

ECO Umberto, b. 5 Jan 1932, Alessandria, Italy. Writer. m. Renate Ramge, 24 Sep 1962, 1 son, 1 daughter. Education: PhD, University of Turin, 1954. Publications: Diario minimo, 1963, revised edition, 1976; Appunti per una semiologia delle communicazioni visive, 1967; La definizione dell'arte, 1968; Le forme del contenuto, 1971; I pampini bugiardi, 1972; Estetica e teoria dell'infomazione (editor), 1972; Storia di una rivoluzione mai esistita l'esperimento Vaduz, 1976; Dalla periferia dell'impero, 1976; Come si fa una tesi di laurea, 1977; Perche continuiamo a fare e a insegnare arte?, 1979; Sette anni di desiderio, 1983; in English: A Theory of Semiotics, 1976; The Role of the Reader: Explorations in the Semotics of Texts, 1979; Semotics and the Philosophy of Language, 1984; Sign of the Three: Dupin, Holmes,

Pierce, 1984; The Name of the Rose; Fouccult's Pendulum, 1989. Contributions to: Numerous encyclopedias including Enciclopedia Filosofica and Encyclopedic Dictionary of Semotics; Essays, Reviews to numerous periodicals including Espresso, Corriere della Sera, Times Literary Supplement, Revue Internationale de Sciences Sociales, Nouvelle Revue Francaise. Honours: Premio Stega and Premio Anghiari, 1981; Honorary Citizen of Monte Cerignon, Italy, 1982; Prize for Best Foreign Novel, 1982; Los Angeles Times Fiction Prize Nomination, 1982. Memberships: Secretary General, 1972-79, Vice President, 1979-, International Association for Semiotic Studies; Honorary Trustee, James Joyce Foundation. Address: Istituto della Comunicazioni, Università de Bologna, Via Guerrazzi 20, 40125 Bologna, Italy.

ECO-LOGIJA. See: **XERRI Raymond Christian.**

EDDINGS David, b. 7 July 1931, Spokane, Washington, USA. Writer. m. Judith Leigh Schall, 27 Oct 1962. Education: Everett Junior College, 1950-52; BA, Reed College, 1954; MA, University of Washington, Seattle, 1961. Publications: High Hunt, 1973; Pawn of Prophecy, 1982; Queen of Sorcery, 1982; Magician's Gambit, 1983; Castle of Wizardry, 1984; Guardians of the West, 1987; King of the Margos, 1988; Demon Lord of Karanda, 1988; The Diamond Throne, 1989; The Sorceress of Darshiva, 1989; The Ruby Knight, 1990; The Seeress of Kell, 1991; The Losers, 1992; The Sapphire Rose, 1992; Domes of Fire, 1993; The Hidden City, 1994; The Shining Ones, 1994. Address: c/o Ballantine Books Inc, 201 East 50th Street, New York, NY 10022, USA.

EDELMAN Bernard, b. 14 Dec 1946, Brooklyn, New York, USA. Editor; Consultant. m. Ellen M Leary, 31 May 1985. Education: BA, Brooklyn College, 1968; MA, John Jay College of Criminal Justice, 1983. Publication: Dear America: Letters Home From Vietnam (editor), 1985. Contributions to: Periodicals. Honours: 2 Emmy Awards and many film citations. Address: Mount Joy Road, Finesville, NJ 08865, USA.

EDGAR David, b. 26 Feb 1948, Birmingham, England. Playwright. Education: BA honours, Drama, Manchester University, 1969. Appointments: Lecturer in Playwriting, 1974-78, Honorary Senior Research Fellow, 1988-, Honorary Professor, 1992-, Birmingham University; Resident Playwright, Birmingham Repertory Theatre, 1985-; Literary Consultant, Royal Shakespeare Company, 1984-88. Publications: The Second Time as Farce, 1988; Edgar Shorts (Blood Sports with Ball Boys, Baby Love, The National Theatre, The Midas Connection), 1990; Plays: Maydays, London, 1983, revised edition, 1984; Entertaining Strangers: A Play for Dorchester, Dorchester, Dorset, 1985, revised version, London, 1987; That Summer, London, 1987; Plays I (includes The Jail Diary of Albie Sachs, Mary Barnes, Saigon Rose, O Fair Jerusalem, Destiny), 1987; Heartlanders (with Stephen Bill and Anne Devlin), 1989; The Shape of The Table, 1990; Dr Jekyll and Mr Hyde, 1991; Screenplay: Lady Jane, 1986; Radio Plays: Ecclesiastes, 1977; A Movie Starring Me, 1991; Television Plays: The Eagle Has Landed, 1973; Sanctuary From His Play Gangsters, 1973; I Know What I Meant, 1974; The Midas Connection, 1975; Censors (with Hugh Whitemore and Robert Muller), 1975; Voe For Them (with Neil Grant), 1989; Buying a Landslide, 1992. Honours: John Whiting Award, 1976; Bicentennial Exchange Fellowship, 1978; Society of West End Theatre Award, 1980; New York Drama Critics Circle Award, 1982; Tony Award, 1982. Literary Agent: Michael Imison. Address: c/o Michael Imison Playwrights, 28 Almeida Street, London, N1 1TD, England.

EDGECOMBE Jean Marjorie, b. 28 Feb 1914, Bathurst, New South Wales, Australia. Author. m. Gordon Henry Edgecombe, 2 Feb 1945, 2 sons, 2 daughters. Education: BA Hons, Sydney University, 1935. Publications: Discovering Lord Howe Island, (with Isobel Bennett), 1978; Discovering Norfolk Island, (with Isobel Bennett), 1983; Flinders Island, the Furneaux Group, 1985; Flinders Island and Eastern Bass Strait, 1986, 2nd edition, 1994; Lord Howe Island, World Heritage Area, 1987; Phillip Island and Western Port, 1989; Norfolk Island, South Pacific: Island of History and Many Delights, 1991; Discovering Flinders Island, 1992; Discovering King Island, Western Bass Strait, 1993. Contributions to: Articles and poems, chiefly to Habitat (Australian Conservation Foundation); Lord Howe Island in Macmillan's "The Book of Australian Islands", 1986. Honour: Medal of the Order of Australia, 1995. Membership: Australian Society of Authors. Address: 7 Oakleigh Avenue, Thornleigh, 2120 New South Wales, Australia.

EDMOND Lauris Dorothy, b. 2 Apr 1924, Dannevirke, New Zealand. Writer; Editor; University Tutor. m. 16 May 1945, 1 son, 5 daughters. Education: Teaching Diploma, 1943; Speech Therapy Diploma, 1944; BA, Waikato University, 1966; MA, Victoria University, 1971. Appointments: Katherine Mansfield Memorial Fellowship, 1981; Writer in Residence, Deakin University, 1985; Writers Fellowship, Victoria University, 1987. Publications: In Middle Air, 1975; The Pear Tree, 1977; Salt from the North, 1980; Wellington Letter, (poems), 1980; Between Night and Morning, (play), 1981; The Mountain Cycle (4 radio plays), 1981; Catching It, (poems), 1983; High Country Weather, (novel), 1983; Selected Poems, 1984; Seasons and Creatures, 1986; Women in Wartime, (editor), 1986; Summer Near the Arctic Circle, (poems), 1988; Hot October, (autobiography), Vol 1, 1989; Bonfires in the Rain, Vol 2, 1991, The Quick World, Vol 3, 1992; New and Selected Poems, 1991; Scenes from a Small City, (poems), 1994; Autobiography (single volume), 1994; Selected Poems, 1975-1994, 1994; A Matter of Timing (poems, New Zealand edition), 1996; In Position (poems, English edition), 1996. Contributions to: Womens Fiction, PB Review; Stand; Planet; The Honest Ulsterman; Verse; Numbers; Poetry Now, UK; Meanjin; Westerly; Overland; Landfall; Poetry New Zealand; The New Zealand Listener; Islands. Honours: Best First book, PEN, 1975; Commonwealth Poetry Prize, 1985; Officer of the Order of the British Empire, 1986; Lilian Ida Smith Award, 1987; Honorary DLitt Massey University, 1988. Memberships: PEN; Wellington Poetry Society. Address: 22 Grass Street, Oriental Bay, Wellington, New Zealand.

EDMOND Murray (Donald), b. 1949, New Zealand. Director; Actor; Poet. Appointments: Director and Actor, Town and Country Players, Wellington; Lecturer in Drama, University of Auckland, 1991. Publications: Entering the Eye, 1973; Patchwork, 1978; End Wall, 1981; Letters and Paragraphs, 1987; The New Poets of the 80's: Initiatives in New Zealand Poetry (co-editor), 1987; From the Word Go, 1992; The Switch, 1994. Address: English Department, University of Auckland, Private Bag 92019, Auckland, New Zealand.

EDRIC Robert. See: **ARMITAGE G E.**

EDSON Russell, b. 9 Apr 1935, USA. Poet; Writer. m. Frances Edson. Education: Art Students League, New York City; New School for Social Research, New York City; Columbia University; Black Mountain College, North Carolina. Publications: Poetry: Appearances: Fables and Drawings, 1961; A Stone is Nobody's: Fables and Drawings, 1964; The Brain Kitchen: Writings and Woodcuts, 1965; What a Man Can See, 1969; The Childhood of an Equestrian, 1973; The Calm Theatre, 1973; A Roof with Some Clouds Behind It, 1975; The Intuitive Journey and Other Works, 1976; The Reason Why the Closet-Man is Never Sad, 1977; Edson's Mentality, 1977; The Traffic, 1978; The Wounded Breakfast: Ten Poems, 1978; With Sincerest Regrets, 1981; Wuck Wuck Wuck!, 1984; The Wounded Breakfast, 1985; Tick Tock, 1992; The Tunnel: Selected Poems, 1994. Fiction: Gulping's Recital, 1984; The Song of Percival Peacock, 1992. Honours: Guggenheim Fellowship, 1974; National Endowment for the Arts Grant, 1976; National Endowment for the Arts Fellowship, 1982; Whiting Foundation Award, 1989. Address: 149 Weed Avenue, Stamford, CT 06902, USA.

EDWARDS Anne, b. 20 Aug 1927, Porchester, New York, USA. Writer. Education: University of California at Los Angeles, 1943-46; Southern Methodist University, 1947-48. Publications: A Child's Bible, (adaptor) 1967; The Survivors, 1968; Miklos Alexandrovitch is Missing, 1969; Shadow of a Lion, 1970; The Hesitant Heart, 1974; Judy Garland: A Biography, 1974; Haunted Summer, 1974; The Inn and Us (with Stephen Citron), 1975; Child of Night, 1975; P T Barnum, 1976; The Great Houdini, 1977; Vivien Leigh: A Biography, 1977; Sonya: The Life of the Countess Tolstoy, 1981; The Road to Tara: The Life of Margaret Mitchell, 1983; Matriarch: Queen Mary and the House of Windsor, 1984; A Remarkable Woman: Katherine Hepburn, 1985; Early Reagan: The Rise to Power, 1986; The Demilles: An American Dynasty, 1987; American Princess: A Biography of Shirley Temple, 1988; Royal Sisters: Queen Elizabeth and Princess Margaret, 1990; Wallis - the Novel, 1991; The Grimaldis of Monaco: Centuries of Scandals, Years of Grace, 1992; La Divina, 1994; Throne of Gold: The Lives of the Aga Khans, 1995; Streisand: It Only Happens Once. Address: c/o International Creative Management Inc, 40 West 57th Street, New York, NY 10019, USA.

EDWARDS Josh. See: **LEVINSON Leonard.**

EDWARDS Norman, See: **CARR Terry (Gene).**

EDWARDS Page Lawrence Jr, b. 15 Jan 1941, Gooding, Idaho, USA. Archivist. m. Diana Selser, 26 Aug 1986, 2 sons, 2 daughters. Education: BA, Stanford University, 1963; MFA, University of Iowa, 1974; MLS, Simmons College, 1982. Appointments: Staff, Breadloaf Writers' Conference, 1982-84; Writer-in-Residence, Flagler College, St Augustine, Florida, 1985-. Publications: Mules That Angels Ride, 1972; Touring, 1974; Staking Claims, 1976; Peggy Salte, 1984; Scarface Joe, 1985; The Lake, 1986; American Girl, 1990. Contributions to: Redbook; Woman's World; Bananas; Iowa Review. Address: c/o Marion Boyars Ltd, 26 East 33rd Street, New York, NY 10016, USA.

EDWARDS Philip Walter, b. 7 Feb 1923, Cumbria, England. Professor. m. Sheila Mary Wilkes, 8 May 1952, 3 sons, 1 daughter. Education: BA, 1942, MA, 1946, PhD, 1960, University of Birmingham. Appointments: Lecturer, University of Birmingham, 1946-60; Professor, Trinity College, Dublin, 1960-66, University of Essex, 1966-74, University of Liverpool, 1974-90. Publications: Sir Walter Ralegh, 1953; Kyd, The Spanish Tragedy, 1959; Shakespeare and the Confines of Art, 1968; Massinger: Plays and Poems, 1976; Shakespeare's Pericles, 1976; Threshold of a Nation, 1979; Hamlet, 1985; Shakespeare: A Writers Progress, 1986; Last Voyages, 1988; The Story of the Voyage, 1994; Sea-Mark, 1997. Membership: British Academy, Fellow, 1986-. Address: High Gillinggrove, Gillinggate, Kendal, Cumbria LA9 4JB, England.

EDWARDS Rowan (Judith), b. 19 Nov 1945, India. Writer; Former A E Teacher. m. Martin Brian Edwards, 18 Dec 1965, 1 son, 1 daughter. Education: BA, King's College, University of London, 1966; RSA Certificate in ESL, 1976. Appointments: Teacher of Adults, Inner London Education Authority; Personal Assistant to MP; Freelance Writer, Novelist, Journalist; Examiner; Creative Writing Tutor. Publications: 16 Romantic Novels, 1983-94, translated into 16 languages in paperback and large print editions. Contributions to: newspapers and magazines. Honours: Bristol Poetry Competition, 1988; ORBIS, 1989; 1st Prize, South West Arts, for Radio Play, 1989. Memberships: Society of Authors; Romantic Novelists Association; Address: 2 Highbury Hall, 22 Highbury Road, Weston Super Mare BS23 2DN, England.

EDWARDS Ted (Brian), b. 25 Apr 1939, Leigh, Lancashire, England. Explorer; Author; Teacher; Song Writer. Education: BEd, Manchester Polytechnic, 1975-79. Publications: A Slutchy Brew, 1971; Beyond the Last Oasis, 1985; Fight the Wild Island, 1986; The Empty Quarter, 1984. Contributions to: Journals and magazines. Address: The Garret, 6 Westminster Road, Eccles, Manchester M30 9HF, England.

EFFINGER George Alec, b. 10 Jan 1947, Cleveland, Ohio, USA. Writer. Education: Yale University, 1965, 1969; New York University, 1968. Appointment: Teacher, Tulane University, New Orleans, 1973-74. Publications: What Entropy Means to Me, 1972; Relatives, 1973; Mixed Feelings (short stories), 1974; Nightmare Blue (with G Dozois), 1975; Irrational Numbers (short stories), 1976; Those Gentle Voices, 1976; Felicia, 1976; Death in Florence, 1978, as Utopia Three, 1980; Dirty Tricks (short stories), 1978; Heroics, 1979; The Wolves of Memory, 1981; Idle Pleasures (short stories), 1983; The Nick of Time, 1986; The Bird of Time, 1986; When Gravity Fails, 1987; Exile Kiss, 1991; Maureen Birnbaum, Barbarian Swordsperson, 1993. Address: Box 15183, New Orleans, LA 70175, USA.

EGEMO Constance Alpha Marie, b. 28 Feb 1933, St Paul, Minnesota, USA. Retired RN; Poet; Fiction Writer. m. Robert Julian Egemo, 29 Dec 1956, 2 sons, 1 daughter. Education: RN, Hamline University, St Paul, Minnesota. Publications: The Poet Dreaming in the Artist's House; Anthologies, Border Crossings. Contributions to: Poetry published in American Scholar; Yankee; Negative Capability; The National Forum; Amicus; Twin Cities Magazine; Midwest Quarterly; Dreamworks; Iowa Woman; The Lyric; Menomonie Review; others. Honour: The Loft (Minneapolis) first Mentor Series, Sri Chinmoy Spiritual Poetry Contest. Address: 1011 Clark Avenue, Ames, IA 50010, USA.

EGGERTSSON Thorsteinn, b. 25 Feb 1942, Keflavik, Iceland. Author; Lyricist; Journalist. Education: Graphic Design, Akademiet for Friog Merkantil Kunst, Copenhagen, 1964. Appointment: Most Prolific Pop-Lyricist in Scandinavian Countries. Publications: The Paper King's Subjects, 1991; Va (Danger), 1993. Contributions to: Short stories and poetry in several magazines in Iceland and Denmark, numerous articles in dailies and magazines in Iceland. Honour: Best Pop Lyricist in Iceland, 1968, 1969. Memberships: The Writers Union of Iceland, 1995-; STEF in Iceland, 1965-; FTT in Iceland, 1983-. Address: Asgardur 20, 108 Reykjavik, Iceland.

EGLETON Clive Frederick William, (Patrick Blake, John Tarrant), b. 25 Nov 1927. Author; Retired Army Officer; Retired Civil Servant. m. Joan Evelyn Lane, 9 Apr 1949, dec 22 Feb 1996, 2 sons. Education: Staff College, Camberley, 1957. Publications: The Winter Touch, 1982; Backfire, 1979; Conflict of Interests, 1984; The October Plot, 1985; Picture of the Year, 1987; Gone Missing, 1988; Seven Days to a Killing, 1988; In the Red, 1990; Last Act, 1991; A Double Deception, 1992; Hostile Intent, 1993; A Killing in Moscow, 1994; Death Throes, 1994; A Lethal Involvement, 1995; Warning Shot, 1996. Memberships: Crime Writers Association; Society of Authors. Literary Agent: Anthony Goff, David Higham Associates Ltd. Address: Dolphin House, Beach House Lane, Bembridge, Isle of Wight PO35 5TA, England.

EHRENBERG Miriam Colbert, b. 6 Mar 1930, New York, New York, USA. Psychologist. m. Otto Ehrenberg, 20 Sept 1956, 2 daughters. Education: BA, Queens College; MA, City University of New York; PhD, New School for Social Research, New York. Publications: The Psychotherapy Maze, 1977, 2nd edition, 1986; Optimum Brain Power, 1985; The Intimate Circle, 1988. Contributions to: Ready Reference: Women's Issues; Transforming the Categories; Gay and Lesbian Mental Health. Membership: American Psychological Association. Address: 118 Riverside Drive, New York, NY 10024, USA.

EHRENREICH Barbara, b. 26 Aug 1941, Butte, Montana, USA. Feminist; Critic; Novelist. m. (1) John Ehrenreich, 6 Aug 1966, 1 son, 1 daughter, (2) Gary Stevenson, 10 Dec 1983. Education: BA, Reed College, 1963, PhD, Rockefeller University, 1968. Appointments: Essayist, Time Magazine, 1990-; Columnist, The Guardian (London), 1991-. Publications: Long March, Short Spring, 1969; For Her Own Good, 1978; The Hearts of Men, 1983; Remaking Love, 1986; The Mean Season, 1987; Fear of Falling, 1989; The Worst Years of Our Lives, 1990; Kipper's Game, 1993. Contributions to: New York Times; Mother Jones; Atlantic; MS; New Republic; Radical America. Honours: National Magazine Award, 1980; Ford Foundation Award for Humanistic Perspectives on Contemporary Issues, 1981; Guggenheim Fellowship, 1987, Long Island NOW Women's Equality Award, 1988; National Book Critics' Award Nominee; National Magazine Award Finalist for essays, 1992. Address: c/o Time, Time-Life Building, Rockefeller Center, New York, NY 10020, USA.

EHRLICH Eugene, b. 21 May 1922, New York, New York, USA. Lexicographer; Writer. Education: BS, City College, 1942; MA, Columbia University, 1948. Appointments: Assistant Professor, Fairleigh Dickinson University, 1946-48; Associate in English, Columbia University, 1949-87. Publications include: How to Study Better, 1960; The Art of Technical Writing (with D Murphy), 1962; Researching and Writing Term Papers and Reports (with D Murphy), 1964; College Developmental Reading (with D Murphy and D Pace), 1966; Basic Grammar for Writing (with D Murphy), 1970; Concise Index to English (with D Murphy), 1974; Basic Vocabulary Builder, 1975; English Grammar, 1976; Punctuation, Capitalization and Spelling, 1977; Oxford American Dictionary (with others), 1980; The Oxford Illustrated Literary Guide to the United States (with Gorton Carruth), 1982; Speak for Success, 1984; Amo, Amas, Amat and More, 1985; The Bantam Concise Handbook of English, 1986; Harper's Dictionary of Foreign Terms, number 3, 1990; Collins Gem Dictionary, 1990; Collins Gem Thesaurus, 1990; Choose the Right Word (with S I Hayakawa), 1994; Veni, Vidi, Vici, 1995; the Highly selective Dictionary for the Extraordinarily Literate, 1997; Les Bons Mots, 1997. Address: c/o HarperCollins, 10 East 53rd Street, New York, NY 10022, USA.

EHRLICH Paul (Ralph), b. 29 May 1932, Philadelphia, Pennsylvania, USA. Biologist; Professor; Writer. m. Anne Fitzhugh Howland, 18 Dec 1954, 1 daughter. Education: AB, University of Pennsylvania, 1953; AM, 1955, PhD, 1957, University of Kansas. Appointments: Research Associate, University of Kansas, 1958-59; Assistant Professor, 1959-62, Associate Professor, 1962-66, Professor, 1966-, Bing Professor of Population Studies, 1976-, Stanford University; President, Center for Conservation Biology, 1988-; Correspondent, NBC News, 1989-92. Publications: How to Know the Butterflies, 1961; Process of Evolution, 1963; Principles of Modern

Biology, 1968; Population Bomb, 1968, 2nd edition, 1971; Population, Resources, Environment: Issues in Human Ecology, 1970, 2nd edition, 1972; How to be a Survivor, 1971; Global Ecology: Readings Toward a Rational Strategy for Man, 1971; Man and the Ecosphere, 1971; Introductory Biology, 1973; Human Ecology: Problems and Solutions, 1973; Ark II: Social Response to Environmental Imperatives, 1974; The End of Affluence: A Blueprint for the Future, 1974; Biology and Society, 1976; Race Bomb, 1977; Ecoscience: Population, Resources, Environment, 1977; Insect Biology, 1978; The Golden Door: International Migration, Mexico, and the US, 1979; Extinction: The Causes and Consequences of the Disappearance of Species, 1981; The Machinery of Nature, 1986; Earth, 1987; The Science of Ecology, 1987; The Birder's Handbook, 1988; New World/New Mind, 1989; The Population Explosion, 1990; Healing the Planet, 1991; Birds in Jeopardy, 1992; The Birdwatchers Handbook, 1994; The Stork and the Plow, 1995. Contributions to: Scholarly journals. Honours: World Wildlife Federation Medal, 1987; Co-winner, Crafoord Prize in Population Biology and Conservation Biology Diversity, 1990; John D and Catherine T MacArthur Foundation Fellowship, 1990-95; Volvo Environmental Prize, 1993; United Nations Sasakawa Environmental Prize, 1994; Heinz Prize for the Environment, 1995. Memberships: American Academy of Arts and Sciences, fellow; American Philosophical Society, fellow; American Society of Naturalists; Entomological Society of America; Lepidopterists Society; National Academy of Sciences; Society for the Study of Evolution; Society of Systematic Zoology. Address: c/o Department of Biological Sciences, Stanford University, Stanford, CA 94305, USA.

EHRLICHMAN John (Daniel), b. 20 Mar 1925, Tacoma, Washington, USA. Lawyer; Writer; Radio and Television Commentator. m. (1) Jeanne Fisher, 21 Aug 1949, div, 5 children, (2) Christy Mclaurine, Nov 1978. Education: AB, University of California at Los Angeles, 1948; LLB, Stanford University, 1951. Appointments: Founder-Partner, Hullin, Erlichman, Roberts, and Hodge law firm, Seattle, Washington, 1952-68; Instructor in Law, University of Washington, 1967; Counsel to Richard Nixon, 1968-69; Assistant to the President for Domestic Affairs, Washington, DC, 1969-73; Convicted of conspiracy, obstruction of justice, and 2 counts of perjury in the wake of the Watergate investigation and served time in the Federal Prison Camp, Safford, Arizona, 1976-78; Radio and Television Commentator, Mutual Broadcasting System, 1978-; Executive, Law Cos Group, Atlanta, Georgia, 1991-. Publications: The Company (also published as Washington Behind Closed Doors), (novel), 1976; The Whole Truth, (novel), 1979; Witness to Power: The Nixon Years, (memoirs), 1982; The China Card, (novel), 1986; Sketches and Notes, 1987; The Rigby File, 1989. Contributions to: Periodicals. Address: c/o Law Cos Group, 1000 Abernathy Road, Atlanta, GA 30328, USA.

EIBEL Deborah, b. 25 June 1940, Montreal, Quebec, Canada. Poet. Education: BA, McGill University, 1960; AM, Radcliffe College, 1962; MA, Johns Hopkins University, 1971. Publications: Kayak Sickness, 1972; Streets Too Narrow for Parades, 1985; Making Fun of Travellers, 1992; Gold Rush and Other Poems (forthcoming). Contributions to: Anthologies and periodicals. Honours: Chester McNaughton Award, 1959; Arthur Davison Ficke Sonnet Award, Poetry Society of America, 1965. Memberships: League of Canadian Poets; Poetry Society of America. Address: 6657 Wilderton Avenue, Montreal, Quebec H3S 2LB, Canada.

EICHENBAUM Luise Ronni, b. 22 July 1952, New York, New York, USA. Psychotherapist; Lecturer; Writer. m. Jeremy Pikser, 1 son, 1 daughter. Education: BA, City College of the City University of New York, 1973; MSW, State University of New York at Stony Brook, 1975. Appointments: Co-founder and Director, Women's Therapy Centre Institute, New York City, 1980-. Publications: Understanding Women: A Feminist Psychoanalytic Approach, 1983; What Do Women Want?: Exploring the Myth of Dependency, 1983; Between Women: Love, Envy, and Competition in Women's Friendships, 1989. Address: 562 West End Avenue, New York, NY 10024, USA.

EINARSSON Sveinn, b. 18 Sept 1934, Reykjavik, Iceland. Writer; Dramatist; Theatre and Television Director. m. Thora Kristjansdottir, 17 Oct 1964, 1 daughter. Education: Stockholm. Appointments: Theatre and Television Director; Vice President, International Theatre Institute, 1979-81; President, Poetry Committee, Council of Europe, 1987-90. Publications: Gabriella in Portugal, 1985; Dordingull, 1994; Amlodi Saca, 1996. Other: Several plays for the stage, radio, and television; Books on the theatre. Contributions to: Periodicals. Honours: Children's Book of the Year Award, 1986; Clara

Lachman Prize, 1990; First Prize, Icelandic Radio Short Story Competition. Memberships: Union of Icelandic Playwrights; Icelandic Writers Union. Address: Tjarnargata 26, 101 Reykavik, Iceland.

EIRIKSSON Asgeir Hannes, b. 19 May 1947, Reykjavik, Iceland. Former Member of Parliament. m. Valgerdur Hjartardottir, 14 Apr 1974, 1 son, 2 daughters. Education: Commercial College, 1967; Hotel and Catering College, 1971; Dane End House College, Herts, England, 1963-65. Publications: Thad Er Allt Haegt Vinvr!, 1989, 1992; Ein Med Ollu, 1990; Sogur Ur Reykjavik, 1992. Contributions to: Newspapers and magazines, 1975-; Columnist, Newspaper Timinn, 1992-. Honour: Icelandic Mission to UN General Assembly, New York, 1990. Memberships: North Atlantic Assembly, NATO, 1989-91; Alternative Member, Reykjavik City Council, 1990-94. Address: Klapparberg 16, 111 Reykjavik, Iceland.

EISELE Robert, b. 9 June 1948, Altadena, California, USA. Playwright. Education: BA, 1971, MFA, 1974, University of California at Los Angeles. Appointments: Playwrighting Fellow and Actor, American Conservatory Theatre, 1975-76; Associate Professor of Theatre Arts, Rio Hondo College, California, 1976-87. Publications: Plays. Other: Many television scripts. Honours: Samuel Goldwyn Writing Award, 1973; Oscar Hammerstein Playwrighting Fellowship, 1973-74; Donald Davis Dramatic Writing Award, 1974; American Conservatory Theatre Playwrighting Fellowship, 1975-76; 1st Prize, Theatre Arts Corporation Contest, 1979; Humanitas Award, 1986; Writers Guild Award Nominations, 1994, 1996. Memberships: Academy of Television Arts and Sciences; Actors Equity Association; Dramatists Guild; Screen Actors Guild; Writers Guild of America. Address: c/o Ken Shearman & Associates, 99507 Santa Monica Boulevard, No 212, Beverly Hills, CA 90210, USA.

EISEN Sydney, b. 5 Feb 1929, Poland. University Professor; Writer. m. Doris Kirschbaum, 22 Jan 1957, 2 sons, 2 daughters. Education: Harbord Collegiate Institute, Toronto, 1946; BA, University of Toronto, 1950; PhD, Johns Hopkins University, 1957. Appointments: Instructor, 1955-58, Assistant Professor, 1958-61, Williams College, Williamstown, Massachusetts; Assistant Professor, City College of the City University of New York, 1961-65; Associate Professor, 1965-68, Professor of History and Humanities, 1968-93, Director, Centre for Jewish Studies, 1989-95, University Professor, 1993-, York University, Ontario. Publications: The Human Adventure: Readings in World History (with M Filler), 2 volumes, 1964; Victorian Science and Religion: A Bibliography with Emphasis on Evolution, Belief, and Unbelief, Comprised of Works Published from c.1900-75 (with Bernard Lightman), 1984. Contributions to: Victorian Faith in Crisis (edited by Richard Helmadter and Bernard Lightman), 1990; Articles and reviews in scholarly journals. Honours: Grant, 1967, Fellowship, 1968-69, Canada Council; Sydney Eisen Prize for General Honors Students established in his honour by York University, 1978; Shem Tov Award, Toronto Jewish Federation, 1988; Sadowski Medal, 1994; Faculty of Arts Teaching Award, 1989; Ben Sadowski Award, Toronto Jewish Federation, 1994. Memberships: American Historical Association; Conference on British Studies; Victorian Studies Association. Address: 5 Renoak Drive, Willowdale, Ontario M2R 3E1, Canada.

EISENBERG Gerson G, b. 5 Mar 1909. Author. m. 15 Sept 1967. Education: AB, George Washington University, 1930; Graduate Student, John Hopkins University, 1937-38; MBA, New York University, 1944; Jewish and Christian Studies at St Mary's Ecumenical Institute. Publications: Learning Vacations, 6 editions, 1977-86; Marylanders Who Served the Nation, 1990. Contributions to: Baltimore Views the Great Depression, to Maryland Historical Society, 1976; Impressionist paintings to Baltimore Museum of Art; Seminar Room to Johns Hopkins University Library (Milton Eisenhower Library). Memberships: Baltimore Writers Association; Authors Guild of America; Board Member of numerous organizations. Address: 11 Slade Avenue 116, Baltimore, MD 21208, USA.

EISENMANN-WESTPHAL Eva Elsa Dorothea, b. 1 May 1910, Beuthen, Silesia. m. Will Eisenmann, 17 June 1948, 5 sons. Education: Matura, 1930. Studied violin, singing and acting. Publications: Die Freunde, 1986; Schach, TV-Spiel, 1994; Zaghafte Hoffnung, 1991; Von Zeit zu Zeit regnet es in der Wüste, 1988. Contributions to: Numerous magazines. Memberships: Swiss Pen-Club; Swiss Writers' Club; German Writers' Club. Address: Rigistrasse 37, CH-6353 Weggis, Switzerland.

EKINS Paul Whitfield, b. 24 July 1950, Djakarta, Indonesia. Economist. m. Susan Anne Lofthouse, 24 Sept 1979, 1 son. Education: BSC, Imperial College, London, 1971; MSC, Birkbeck College, London, 1988; MPhil, University of Bradford, 1990; PhD, Birkbeck College, London, 1996. Publications: The Living Economy: A New Economy in the Making, 1986; A New World Order, 1992; Wealth Beyond Measure, 1992; Real Life Economics, 1992. Contributions to: Ecologist; Journal of Environmental Conservation; Development; International Environmental Affairs; Integrated Environmental Management; Science and Public Policy; Resurgence; Ecological Economics; Environmental and Resource Economics; Medicine and War. Memberships: European Association of Evolutionary Political Economy; International Society for Ecological Economics; Society for the Advancement of Socio Economics; Society for International Development. Address: Department of Economics, Keele University, Staffordshire, ST5 5BG, England.

EKLUND Gordon (Stewart), b. 24 July 1945, Seattle, Washington, USA. Writer. 1 daughter. Education: Contra Costs College, 1973-75. Publications: The Eclipse of Dawn, 1971; A Trace of Dreams, 1972; Beyond the Resurrection, 1973; All Times Possible, 1974; Serving in Time, 1975; Falling Toward Forever, 1975; If the Stars are Gods, 1976; The Dance of the Apocalypse, 1976; The Grayspace Beast, 1976; Find the Changeling, 1980; The Garden of Winter, 1980; Thunder on Neptune, 1989. Contributions to: Analog; Galaxy; If Science Fiction; Fantasy and Science Fiction; Universe; New Dimensions; Amazing Stories; Fantastic. Honour: Nebula Award, 1975. Membership: Science Fiction Writers of America. Address: 6305 East D Street, Tacoma, WA 98404, USA.

EKSTROM (Sigrid) Margareta, b. 23 Apr 1930, Stockholm, Sweden. Writer. 1 son, 1 daughter. Education: BA, University of Stockholm, 1958. Publications: Death's Midwives, 1985; The Day I Begun My Studies in Philosophy, and Other Stories, 1989; Food for Memory, 1993; Olga on Olga, 1994; One Alive for Dead, 1995. Contributions to: Periodicals. Membership: International PEN. Address: Styrmansag 41, 11454 Stockholm, Sweden.

EKWENSI Cyprian, (Odiatu Duaka), b. 26 Sept 1921, Minna, Nigeria. Pharmacist; Author. Education: Government College, Ibadan; Achimota College, Ghana; School of Forestry, Ibadan; Chelsea School of Pharmacy, University of London; University of Iowa. Appointments: Lecturer, Igbobi College, Lagos, 1947-49; Lecturer, Pharmacy, Lagos, 1949-56; Pharmacist, Nigerian Medical Service, 1956; Head, Features, Nigerian Broadcasting Corporation, 1956-61; Director of Information, Federal Ministry of Information, Lagos, 1961-66; Director, Information Services, Enugu, 1966; Managing Director, Star Printing and Publishing Company Ltd, 1975-79, Niger Eagle Press, 1981-. Publications: When Love Whispers, Ikolo The Wrestler, 1947; The Leopard's Claw, 1950; People of the City, 1954; Passport of Mallam Ilia; The Drummer Boy, 1960; Jagua Nana, 1961; Burning Grass; An African Night's Entertainment; Yaba Round About Murder, 1962; Beautiful Feathers, 1963; Great Elephant Bird; Rainmaker, 1965; Lokotown Juju Rock; Trouble in Form VI; Iska; Boa Suitor, 1966; Coal Camp Boy, 1973; Samankwe in the Strange Forest, 1974; Samankwe and the Highway Robbers; Restless City; Christmas Gold, 1975; Survive the Peace, 1976; Divided We Stand, 1980; Motherless Baby, 1980; Jaguanana's Daughter, 1986; For a Roll of Parchment, 1986. Address: 12 Hillview Crescent, Independence Layout, PO Box 317, Enugu, Nigeria.

ELBEE Miss. See: **BAKER Lillian.**

ELBERG Yehuda, (Y Renas, Y L Berg), b. 15 May 1912, Poland. Novelist. 2 sons, 1 daughter. Education: Rabinical Ordination, 1929; Textile Engineering, 1932. Appointments: Author-in-Residence, Bar-Ilan University Israel, 1988; Lecturer in Hebrew Studies, Oxford University, 1990, 1994. Publications: Under Copper Skies, 1951; On the Tip of a Mast, 1974; Scattered Stalks, 1976; Tales, 1980; The Empire of Kalman the Cripple, 1983; In Clay Houses, I and II, 1983; A Man Is But a Man, 1983; Between Morning and Evening, 1983; The Fifteen Powers, 1989. Honours: Feffer Prize, Congress for Jewish Culture, Sao Paulo, Brazil, 1951; J I Segal Prize, Montreal, 1975; Wasjslic-Cymerman Award, Sydney, Australia, 1975; Gonopolsky Prize, Paris, 1977; Manger Prize, Yiddish Literature, Government of Israel, City of Tel Aviv and Manger Prize Foundation, 1977; Prime Minister's Award, Yiddish Literature, Israel, 1984; I M Wisenberg Prize, Congress for Jewish Culture, New York, 1984; J I Segal Award, Yiddish Hebrew Literature, J I Segal Cultural Foundation, Canada,

1988; Membership: PEN International. Address: 1745 Cedar Avenue, Montreal, Quebec H3G 1A7, Canada.

ELDRIDGE Colin Clifford, b. 16 May 1942, Walthamstow, England. University Lecturer. m. Ruth Margaret Evans, 3 Aug 1970, 1 daughter. Education: BA, 1963, PhD, 1966, Nottingham University. Appointments: Lecturer, 1968-75, Senior Lecturer in History, 1975-92, Reader, 1992-, University of Wales. Publications: England's Mission: The Imperial Idea in the Age of Gladstone and Disraeli, 1973; Victorian Imperialism, 1978; Essays in Honour of C D Chandaman, 1980; British Imperialism in the 19th Century, 1984; Empire, Politics and Popular Culture, 1989; From Rebellion to Patriation: Canada & Britain in the Nineteenth & Twentieth Centuries, 1989; Disraeli and the Rise of a New Imperialism, 1996; The Imperial Experience: From Carlyle to Forster, 1996; The Zulu War, 1879, 1996. Contributions to: Various Learned Journals. Honour: Fellow, Royal Historical Society. Memberships: Historical Association; Association of History Teachers in Wales; British Association of Canadian Studies; British Australian Studies Association. Address: Tanerdy, Cilau Aeron, Lampeter, Dyfed SA48 8DL, Wales.

ELEGANT Robert Sampson, b. 7 Mar 1928, New York, New York, USA. Author; Journalist; Novelist. m. Moira Clarissa Brady, 16 Apr 1956, 1 son, 1 daughter. Education: AB, University of Pennsylvania, 1946; Japanese Army Language School, 1947-48; Yale University, 1948; MA, 1950, MS, 1951, Columbia University. Appointments: War, Southeast Asia Correspondent, Various Agencies, 1951-61; Central European Bureau, Newsweek, 1962-64; Others, Los Angeles Times, Washington Post, 1965-70; Foreign Affairs Columnist, 1970-76; Independent Author and Journalist, 1977-. Publications: China's Red Masters, 1951; The Dragon Seed, 1959; The Centre of the World, 1961; The Seeking, 1969; Mao v Chiang: The Battle for China, 1972; The Great Cities, Hong Kong, 1977; Pacific Destiny, 1990. Novels: A Kind of Treason, 1966; The Seeking, 1969; Dynasty, 1977; Manchu, 1980; Mandarin, 1983; White Sun, Red Star, 1987; Bianca, 1992; The Everlasting Sorrow, 1994; Last Year in Hong Kong, 1997. Contributions to: Newspapers and periodicals. Honours: Phi Beta Kappa; Pulitzer Fellow, 1951-52; Ford Foundation, 1954-55; Edgar Allan Poe Award, 1967; Sigma Delta Chi Award, 1967; Fellow, American Institute for Public Policy Research, Washington, DC, 1976-78; Senior Fellow, Institute for Advanced Study, Berlin, 1993-94. Memberships: Authors League of America; Hong Kong Foreign Correspondents Club. Address: The Manor House, Middle Green, Nr Langley, Bucks SL3 6BS, England.

ELIAS Victor Jorge, b. 21 July 1937, Tucuman, Argentina. Economist. m. Ana M Ganum, 21 May 1966, 1 son, 2 daughters. Education: PhD Economics, University of Chicago, Illinois, USA, 1969. Appointments: Full Professor, 1965, Director Magister of Economics, 1988-, University of Tucuman; Director, Institute of Applied Economics, FBET, 1994-. Publications: Estimacion del Capital, Trabajo, Producto de la Industria en Argentina: 1935-1965, 1969; Sources of Growth: A Study of Seven Latin American Economies, 1992. Contributions to: The Role of Total Factor Productivity on Economic Growth, 1993. Honour: Guggenheim Fellowship, 1974. Membership: Full Member, National Academy of Economics Science of Argentina. Address: Balcarce 740, Tucuman 4000, Argentina.

ELISHA Ron, b. 19 Dec 1951, Jerusalem, Israel. Medical Practitioner; Playwright. m. Bertha Rita Rubin, 6 Dec 1981, 1 son, 1 daughter. Education: BMed, BSurg, Melbourne University, 1975. Publications: In Duty Bound, 1983; Two, 1985; Einstein, 1986; The Levine Comedy, 1987; Pax Americana, 1988; Safe House, 1989; Esterhaz, 1990; Impropriety, 1993; Choice, 1994; Unknown Soldier, 1996; Pigtales, 1994; Too Big, 1997. Contributions to: Business Review Weekly; The Age; Vogue Australia; Generation Magazine; Australian Book Review; Centre Stage Magazine; Melbourne Jewish Chronicle; The Westerly. Honours: Best Stage Play, 1982; Major Award, 1982; Best Stage Play, 1984; Gold Award, Best Screenplay, 1990; Best TV Feature, Australian Writers Guild Award, 1992. Memberships: Australian Writers Guild; International PEN; Fellowship of Austrian Writers. Address: 4 Bruce Court, Elsternwick Victoria 3185, Australia.

ELIZABETH Von S. See: **FREEMAN Gillian.**

ELKINS Aaron, b. 24 July 1935, New York, New York, USA. Writer. m. (1) Toby Siev, 1959, div 1972, 2 sons, (2) Charlotte Trangmar, 1972. Education: BA, Hunter College, 1956; Graduate

Studies, University of Wisconsin at Madison, 1957-59; MA, University of Arizona, 1960; MA, California State University at Los Angeles, 1962; EdD, University of California at Berkeley, 1976. Appointments: Director, Management Development, Contra Costa County Government, 1971-76, 1980-83; Lecturer, University of Maryland at College Park, European Division, 1976-78, 1984-85; Management Analyst, US Office of Personnel Management, San Francisco, 1979-80; Member, Clallam County Civil Service Commission, 1987-. Publications: Fellowship of Fear, 1982; The Dark Place, 1983; Murder in the Queen's Armes, 1985; A Deceptive Clarity, 1987; Old Bones, 1987; Dead Men's Hearts, 1994. Honour: Edgar Allan Poe Award, Mystery Writers of America, 1988. Address: c/o Karpfinger Agency, 500 Fifth Avenue, Suite 2800, New York, NY 10110, USA.

ELLEN Margaret. See: **OSBORNE Maggie.**

ELLERBECK Rosemary Anne L'Estrange, (Anna L'Estrange, Nicola Thorne, Katherine Yorke), b. England. Writer. Education: BSc, Sociology, London School of Economics. Publications: Inclination to Murder, 1965; The Girls (as N Thorne), 1967; Bridie Climbing (as N Thorne), 1969; In Love (as N Thorne), 1973; Hammersleigh, 1976; Rose, Rose Where Are You?, 1977; Return to Wuthering Heights (as A L'Estrange), 1978; A Woman Like Us (as N Thorne), 1979; Perfect Wife and Mother (as N Thorne), 1980; Daughters of the House (as N Thorne), 1981; Where the Rivers Meet (as N Thorne), 1982; Affairs of Love (as N Thorne), 1983; A Woman's Place (as K Yorke), 1983; Pair Bond (as K Yorke), 1984; Never Such Innocence (as N Thorne), 1985; Askham Chronicles 1898-1967, 4 titles (as N Thorne), 1985-87; Champagne (as N Thorne), 1988. Membership: PEN. Address: 96 Townshend Court, Mackennal Street, London NW8 6LD, England.

ELLIOT Alistair, b. 13 Oct 1932, Liverpool, Lancashire, England. Librarian; Poet. Education: Fettes College, Edinburgh; BA, Christ Church, Oxford, 1955. Appointment: Special Collections Librarian, Newcastle upon Tyne University Library, 1967-82. Publications: Air in the Wrong Place, 1968; Contentions, 1977; Kisses, 1978; Talking to Bede, 1982; Talking Back, 1982; On the Appian Way, 1984; My Country: Collected Poems, 1989; Turning the Stones, 1993; Facing Things, 1997. Editor: Poems by James I and Others, 1970; The Georgics with John Dryden's Translation, 1981. Editor and Translator: French Love Poems (bilingual), 1991; Italian Landscape Poems (bilingual), 1993. Translator: Alcestis by Euripides, 1965, Peace by Aristophanes, 1965; Translator: Femmes Hombres by Paul Verlaine, 1979; Translator: The Lazarus Poems by Heinrich Heine, 1979; Medea by Euripides, 1993; Translator: La Jeune Parque by Paul Valéry, 1997. Honours: Arts Council Grant, 1979; Ingram Merrill Foundation Fellowship, 1983; Prudence Farmer Awards, New Statesman, 1983, 1991. Address: 27 Hawthorn Road, Newcastle upon Tyne NE3 4DE, England.

ELLIOT Zena Marjorie, b. 13 June 1922, New Zealand. Retired Art Teacher. m. A J Elliot, 10 Aug 1946, div 1958, 2 sons, 1 daughter. Education: Certified Teacher: New Zealand, 1942; New South Wales, 1960; Diploma, Home Economics, 1969; Diploma, Art Education, 1974. Career: Graduate Assistant, New South Wales, Australia, 1974; Teacher of Art; Retired, 1993. Publications: Concise Coppercraft Book, 1975; Creative Weaving with Art to Wear, 1995. Memberships: Telopea Gallery; Craft at the Rocks; Handweavers and Spinners Guild; National Parks and Wild Life; New South Wales Trust Fund; Blue Mountains Creative Art Centre; Textile Fibre Forum. Address: 15 Hopewell Street, Paddington, New South Wales 2021, Australia.

ELLIOTT Dorinda. Hong Kong Bureau Chief, Newsweek. m. Adi Ignatius, 2 children. Education: Studied at National Taiwan Normal University, Mandarin Centre, 1978-79; BA, cum laude, East Asian Studies, Harvard University, 1981. Appointments: Copy Editor, Asian Wall Street Journal, 1983; Reporter covering China, Hong Kong, Taiwan and the Philippines, Businessweek, 1984-86; Correspondent, Hong Kong Bureau, 1986, Bureau Chief in Beijing, 1987, Moscow Correspondent, 1992, Moscow Bureau Chief, 1993, Special Correspondent based in Brussels and later Hong Kong, 1995, Hong Kong Bureau Chief, 1996-, Newsweek. Address: c/o Newsweek, 251 West 57th Street, New York, NY 10019-1894, USA.

ELLIOTT Janice, b. 14 Oct 1931, Derby, England. Novelist. Education: BA, St Anne's College, Oxford, 1953. Publications: Cave With Echoes, 1962; The Somnambulists, 1964; The Godmother, 1966; The Buttercup Chain, 1967; The Singing Head, 1968; Angels Falling, 1969; The Kindling, 1970; A State of Peace, 1971; Private Life, 1972;

Heaven on Earth, 1975; A Loving Eye, 1977; The Honey Tree, 1978; Summer People, 1979; Secret Places, 1981; The Country of Her Dreams, 1982; Magic, 1983; The Italian Lesson, 1985; Dr Gruber's Daughter, 1986; The Sadness of Witches, 1987; Life on the Nile, 1989; Necessary Rites, 1990; The Noise From the Zoo, 1991; City of Gates, 1992; Children's Books: The Birthday Unicorn, 1970; Alexander in the Land of Mog, 1973; The Incompetent Dragon, 1982; The King Awakes, 1987; The Empty Throne, 1988. Contributions to: Numerous magazines and newspapers, short story collections. Honour: Southern Arts Award for Literature, 1981. Memberships: Royal Society of Literature, Fellow; PEN; Society of Authors. Address: c/o Hodder and Stoughton, 47 Bedford Square, London WC1B 3DP, England.

ELLIS (Christopher) Royston (George), (Richard Tresilian), b. 10 Feb 1941, Pinner, Middlesex, England. Author; Travel Writer; Cruise Ship Lecturer. 1 son. Appointments: Assistant Editor, Jersey News and Features Agency, 1961-63; Associate Editor, Canary Islands Sun, Las Palmas, 1963-66; Editor, The Educator, Director, Dominica Broadcasting Services and Reuter, Cana Correspondent, 1974-76; Managing Editor, Wordsman Features Agency, 1977-86; Editorial Consultant, Explore Sri Lanka, 1990-95; Managing Director, Wordsman Inc, 1997-. Publications: Jiving to Gyp, 1959; Rave, 1960; The Big Beat Scene, 1961; The Rainbow Walking Stick, 1961; Rebel, 1962; Burn Up, 1963; The Mattress Flowers, 1963; The Flesh Merchants, 1966; The Rush at the End, 1967; The Bondmaster Series, 1977-83; The Fleshtrader Series, 1984-85; The Bloodheart Series, 1985-87; Giselle, 1987; Guide to Mauritius, 1988; India By Rail, 1989; Sri Lanka By Rail, 1994; Guide to Maldives (with Gemunu Amarasinghe), 1995; A Maldives Celebration (with Gemunu Amarasinghe), 1997; The Book of Ceylon Tea (with Gemunu Amarasinghe), 1997. Contributions to: Newspapers and magazines. Honours: Dominica National Poetry Awards, 1967, 1971. Memberships: Institute of Rail Transport, India; Royal Commonwealth Society. Address: Royal Cottage, Bentota, Sri Lanka.

ELLIS Alice Thomas. See: **HAYCRAFT Anna (Margaret).**

ELLIS Bret Easton, b. 7 Mar 1964, California, USA. Writer. Education: BA, Bennington College, 1986. Publications: Less Than Zero, 1985; The Rules of Attraction, 1987; American Psycho, 1993; The Informers, 1994. Contributions to: Rolling Stone; Vanity Fair; Elle; Wall Street Journal; Bennington Review. Membership: Authors Guild. Address: c/o Amanda Urban, ICM, 40 West 57th Street, New York, NY 10019, USA.

ELLIS Ella Thorp, b. 14 July 1928, Los Angeles, California, USA. Novelist. m. Leo H Ellis, 17 Dec 1949, 3 sons. Education: BA, English, University of California, Los Angeles, 1967; MA, English, San Francisco State University, 1975. Publications: Roam the Wild Country, 1967; Riptide, 1969; Celebrate the Morning, 1972; Hallelujah, 1974; Hugo and the Princess Nina, 1983; Where the Road Ends; Swimming with the Whales. Contributions to: Mademoiselle. Honours: American Library Association Honor Books, 1967, 1969, 1972. Memberships: Author's Guild; Society of Children's Book Writers; California Writers' Club; Sierra Club; American Civil Liberties Union; Opera International. Address: 1438 Grizzly Peak , Berkeley, CA 94708, USA.

ELLIS Mark Karl, b. 1 Aug 1945, Musoorie, India. Training Consultant; Author. m. Printha Jane, 30 Aug 1969, 2 sons. Education: MA, Christ's College, Cambridge, 1967; Postgraduate Diploma, University of Leeds, 1970. Publications: Bannerman; Adoration of the Hanged Man; Fatal Charade; Survivors Beyond Babel; Nelson Counterpoint Series; Nelson Skill of Reading Series; Longman Business Skills Series; Professional English; The Economist: An English Language Guide; Giving Presentations; Teaching Business English; Kiss in the Dark. Address: 39 St Martins, Marlborough, Wiltshire SN8 1AS, England.

ELLIS Richard J, b. 27 Nov 1960, Leicester, England. Associate Professor. m. Juli Takenaka, 18 July 1987. Education: BA, with highest honours, University of California, Santa Cruz, 1982; MA, Political Science, 1984, PhD, Politics, 1989, University of California, Berkeley. Appointments: Assistant Professor, 1990-95, Associate Professor, 1995-, Williamette University, Salem, Oregon. Publications: Dilemmas of Presidential Leadership (co-author), 1989; Cultural Theory (co-author), 1990; American Political Cultures, 1993; Presidential Lightning Rods: The Politics of Blame Avoidance, 1994; Politics Policy and Culture (co-editor), 1994. Contributions to: Comparative Studies in Society and History; Journal of Behavioural Economics; Presidential Studies Quarterly; Journal of Theoretical Politics: Studies in American Political Development; Review of Politics; Polity; Western Political Quarterly; Critical Review. Honours: Regents Fellowship, University of California, 1983-85; I G S Harris Fellowship, 1986-88; Summer Stipend, National Endowment for the Humanities, 1991; Fellowship, George and Eliza Howard Foundation, 1993-94. Memberships: American Political Science Association; Organization of American Historians. Address: Williamette University, Salem, OR 97301, USA.

ELLISON Harlan Jay, b. 27 May 1934, Cleveland, Ohio, USA. Author. m. Susan Toth, Sept 1986. Education: Ohio State University, 1953-55. Appointments: Instructor, Clarion Writer's Workshop, Michigan State University, 1969-77, 1984; Book Critic, Los Angeles Times, 1969-82; Editorial Commentator, Canadian Broadcasting Corporation, 1972-78, Sci-Fi Channel, USA, 1993-; President, Kilimanjaro Corporation, 1979-. Publications: 65 books including: Harlan Ellison's Dream Corridor (comic book), 1995; The City on the Edge of Forever, 1995. Contributions to: Newspapers. Motion Pictures and Television: 40 Screenplays. Honours: Nebula Awards, 1965, 1969, 1977; Various Hugo Awards, 1966-86; Edgar Allan Poe Awards, 1974, 1988; British Fanatasy Award, 1978; American Mystery Award, 1987; Bram Stoker Awards, 1987, 1989, 1994, 1995; Life Achievement Award, World Fantasy Convention, 1993; Only four-times winner, Writers Guild Award. Memberships: Science Fiction Writers of America, vice-president, 1965-66; Writers Guild of America. Address: PO Box 55548, Sherman Oaks, CA 91413, USA.

ELMAN Richard, b. 23 Apr 1934, Brooklyn, New York, USA. Writer. m. Alice Neufeld, 9 Apr 1978, 2 daughters. Education: BA, Honours, Syracuse University, 1955; MA, Stanford University, 1957. Literary Appointments: Lecturer, Literature, Bennington College, 1967-68; Adjunct Professor, Creative Writing, Columbia University, 1968-74; Lecturer, Sarah Lawrence College, 1971; Visiting Professor, University of Pennsylvania, 1980-82, State University of New York at Stony Brook, 1983, University of Arizona, Tucson, 1985, University of Michigan, Ann Arbor, 1988; Abrams Professor, Notre Dame University, 1990; Distinguished Visiting Professor, Creative Writing, Wichita State University, 1994-95. Publications: The Poorhouse State, 1966; The 28th Day of Elul, 1967; Lilo's Diary, 1968; The Reckoning, 1969; An Education in Blood, 1970; Homage to Fats Navarro, 1975; Taxi Driver, 1976; Breadfruit Lotteries, 1980; Cocktails at Somoza's, 1981; The Menu Cypher, 1983; Disco Frito, 1988; Tar Beach, 1991. Forthcoming: The Dancing Master's Diaries; Love Handles. Contributions to: Reviewer; New York Times; Newsday; National Public Radio; Nation; Geo; Atlantic; New Republic; Antaeus; Los Angeles Daily News; Wall Street Journal; Peace News; Midstream; Partisan Review. Memberships: PEN; Author's Guild; National Yiddish Book Centre. Address: c/o William Goodman, 26 Pickman Drive, Bedford, MA 01730, USA.

ELMSLIE Kenward Gray, b. 27 Apr 1929, New York, New York, USA. Poet; Librettist; Talespinner; Performer. Education: BA, Harvard University, 1950. Publications: Motor Disturbance, 1971; Circus Nerves, 1971; The Grass Harp (musical play), 1972; The Orchid Stories, 1973; The Seagull, (libretto), 1974; Tropicalism, 1975; 26 Bars, 1987; City Junket, 1987; Sung Sex, 1989; Pay Dirt, 1992; Postcards on Parade (musical play), 1993; Champ Dust, 1994. Contributions to: Partisan Review; Paris Review; Oxford Literary Review; Art & Literature; Big Sky: New American Writing; Locus Solus; Conjunctions; Oblek. Honour: Frank O'Hara Poetry Award, 1971. Membership: American Society of Composers, Authors and Publishers. Address: Box 38, Calais, VT 05648, USA.

ELPHINSTONE Francis. See: **POWELL-SMITH Vincent.**

ELSOM John Edward, b. 31 Oct 1934, Leigh on Sea, Essex, England. Author; Journalist; Broadcaster; Lecturer. m. Sally Mays, 3 Dec 1956, 2 sons. Education: BA, 1956; PhD, City University, London, 1991. Appointments: Script Advisor, Paramount Pictures, 1960-68; Theatre Critic, London Magazine, 1963-68, The Listener, 1972-82; Correspondent, Contemporary Review, 1978-88; Lecturer, Course Leader, Arts Criticism, City University, London, 1986-96 Consultant, South Bank University, 1996-97, School for Oriental and African Studies, University of London, 1997. Publications: Plays; Plays produced: How I Coped, 1969; Malone Dies, 1984; The Man of the Future is Dead, 1986. Theatre Outside London, 1969; Erotic Theatre, 1972; Post-War British Theatre, 1976, 1979; The History of the National Theatre, 1978; Change and Choice, 1978; Post-War British

Theatre Criticism (editor), 1981; Is Shakespeare Still Our Contemporary? (editor), 1989; Cold War Theatre, 1992. Contributions to: Observer; Mail on Sunday; Encounter; Times Literary Supplement; The World and I; Sunday Telegraph; Plays International; Plays & Players; San Diego Union; Numerous others. Memberships: Liberal Party of Great Britain, Art and Broadcasting Committee; Liberal Democrats, Convenor and Chair, Arts and Broadcasting Committee; International Association of Theatre Critics, 1978-. Address: Stella Maris, Anglesea Road, Kingston Upon Thames, Surrey KT1 2EW, England.

ELSTOB Peter, b. 22 Dec 1915, London, England. Writer. Education: University of Michigan, 1934-35. Appointments: Director, Arts Theatre Club, London, 1946-54, Trade Wind Films, 1958-62, Archive Press Ltd, 1965-; Press Officer, 1970-74, Secretary General, 1974-82, Vice-President, 1982-, International PEN. Publications: Spanish Prisoner, 1938; The Flight of the Small World (co-author), 1959; Warriors for the Working Day, 1960; The Armed Rehearsal, 1964; Bastogne: The Road Block, 1968; The Battle of Reichswald, 1970; Hitler's Last Offensive, 1971; A Register of the Regiments and Corps of the British Army (editor), 1972; Condor Legion, 1973; The Survival of Literature (editor), 1979; Scoundrel, 1986. Memberships: English and International PEN; Society of Authors; Writers Guild. Address: Pond Cottage, Burley Lawn, Hampshire BH24 4DL, England.

ELSY Mary, b. England. Freelance Travel Journalist; Writer. Education: Teaching Diploma, Oakley Training College for Teachers, Cheltenham, 1945. Appointments: Teacher, 1946-51; Realist Film Unit, 1953-55; Editorial Assistant, Childrens Encyclopedia, 1959-62; British Publishing Corporation, 1963; Evans Brothers, 1965-66; Childrens Book Editor, Abelard Schuman, 1967-68. Publications: Travels in Belgium and Luxembourg, 1966; Brittany and Normandy, 1972; Travels in Brittany, 1988; Travels in Normandy, 1988; Travels in Alsace and Lorraine, 1989; Travels in Burgundy, 1989. Contributions to: Daily Telegraph; Sunday Telegraph; Observer; Irish Times; Universe; Womans Journal; In Britain; Illustrated London News; Travel; Ham and High; Camping and Walking; My Family; Voyager; Family Life; Christian Herald; Home and Country. Memberships: PEN International; Society of Authors; Institute of Journalists; British Guild of Travel Writers; R Overseas League; Camden History Society. Address: 519c Finchley Road, London NW3 7BB, England.

ELTIS Walter (Alfred), b. 23 May 1933, Warnsdorf, Czechoslovakia. Economist. m. Shelagh Mary Owen, 5 Sept 1959, 1 son, 2 daughters. Education: Emmanuel College, Cambridge; BA, Cambridge University; MA, Nuffield College, 1960; DLitt, Oxford University, 1990. Appointments: Fellow, Tutor, Economics, 1963-88, Emeritus Fellow, 1988-, Exeter College, Oxford; Director General, National Economic Development Office, London, 1988-92; Chief Economic Adviser to the President of the Board of Trade, 1992-; Visiting Professor, 1992-93, Professor of Commerce, 1993-, University of Reading. Publications: Growth and Distribution, 1973; Britains Economic Problem: Too Few Producers (with Robert Bacon), 1976; The Classical Theory of Economic Growth, 1984; Keynes and Economic Policy (with Peter Sinclair), 1988; Classical Economics, Public Expenditure and Growth, 1993; Britain's Economic Problem Revisited, 1996. Contributions to: Economic Journals and Bank Reviews. Honour: Adam Smith Prize. Memberships: Reform Club (Chairman, 1994-95); Royal Automobile Club; Political Economy Club. Address: Danesway, Jarn Way, Boars Hill, Oxford OX1 5JF, England.

ELTON Ben(jamin Charles), b. 3 May 1959, England. Writer; Comedian. Education: BA in Drama, University of Manchester. Appointments: Writer of television series and for British comedians; Stand-up comedian; Host, Friday Night Live television comedy showcase; Co-writer and presenter, South of Watford documentary television series, 1984-85. Publications: Bachelor Boys, 1984; Stark, 1989; Gridlock, 1992; This Other Eden, 1994; Popcorn, 1996. Plays: Gasping, 1990; Silly Cow, 1991; Popcorn, 1996. Other: Recordings: The Young Ones, 1986; Motovation (album), 1988; Motormouth, 1987; Motorvation, 1989; The Thin Blue Line (sitcom), 1995-96; This Other Eden, 1994; Popcorn, 1996. Videos: The Man From Auntie, 1991; Ben Elton Live, 1989; Ben Elton Live 2, 1993; The Man From Auntie 2, 1994. Honours: Best Comedy Show Awards, British Academy, 1984, 1987; Various other awards. Address: c/o Phil McIntyre, 35 Soho Square, London W1V 50G, England.

EMECHETA (Florence Onye) Buchi, b. 21 July 1944, Lagos, Nigeria. Writer; Visiting Professor; Lecturer. m. S Onwordi, 7 May

1960, 2 sons, 3 daughters. Education: BSc, London University, 1974. Appointments: Professional Senior Research Fellow, University of Calabar, Nigeria; Visiting Professor, Many American Universities, 1982-87; Fellow, University of London, 1986-. Publications: Second Class Citizen, 1975; The Bride Price, 1976; The Slave Girl, 1977; Joys of Motherhood, 1979; Naura Power, 1981; Double Yoke, 1982; Destination Biafra, 1982; A Land of Marriage, 1983; Head Above Water, 1987; Gwendoline, 1989. Contributions to: New Statesman; New Society; New International Sunday Times Magazine. Honours: Jack Campbell Award. New Statesman, 1979; One of Best Young British Writers, 1983. Membership: PEN Internationl. Address: Collins Publishers, 8 Grafton Street, London W1X 3LA, England.

EMENYONU Ernest NNeji, b. Nigeria. Professor of English. Married, 4 children. Education: University of Nigeria, Nsuka; Teachers College, Columbia University, New York; London University, England; University of Wisconsin, Madison, USA; BA, First Class Honours, English and Education; MA, Teaching of English as a Foreign Language; PhD, African Literature. Appointments: Teacher, Knoxville College, Tennessee; Virginia State College, Petersburg; College of William and Mary, Williamsburg, Virginia; University of Colorado, Boulder; University of Montana; Head, Department of English and Literary Studies, Dean, Faculty of Arts, Chairman, Committee of Deans, Deputy Vice-Chancellor of University, University of Calabar, Nigeria, 1988-90. Publications: Cyprian Ekwensi, 1974; The Rise of the Igbo Novel, 1978; African Literature for Schools and Colleges, 1985; The Essential Ekwensi, 1987; Studies on the Nigerian Novel, 1991; Current Trends in Literature and Language Studies in West Africa, 1994; Ideas and Challenges in Nigerian Education, 1994. Children's Books: Bed Time Stories for African Children, Vol I, Stories About Animals, 1989; Vol II: The Adventures of Ebeleako, 1991; UZO Remembers His Father, 1991; General Editor of the critical series, Calabar Studies in African Literature. Memberships: President, Liteary Society of Nigeria; President, West African Association for Commonwealth Literature and Language Studies, 1965-95; Nigerian Academy of Education, 1995-; President, Association for Commonwealth Literature and Language Studies. Address: c/o Department of English Language and Literature, Alvan Ikoku College of Education, P M B 1033, Owerri, Imo State, Nigeria.

EMERSON Ru, (Robert Cray), b. 15 Dec 1944, Monterey, California, USA. Writer. Education: University of Montana, 1963-66. Publications: Princess of Flames, 1986; To the Haunted Mountains, 1987; In the Caves of Exile, 1988; On the Seas of Destiny, 1989; Spell Bound, 1990; Trilogy: Night Threads, 1990, 1991, 1992; The Bard's Tale: Fortress of Frost and Fire (with Mercedes Lackey), 1993; Night Threads: The Craft of Light, 1993. Contributions to: Anthologies and magazines. Membership: Science Fiction Writers of America. Address: 2600 Reuben Boise, Dallas, OR 97338, USA.

EMERSON Tony. General Editor, Newsweek International. Education: BA, Political Science, Cornell University. Appointments: Reporter, Intern, Washington, DC, Bureau, The Blade, Toledo, Ohio, 1982; Staff Writer, Daily Journal, Elizabeth, New Jersey; Stringer, Scarsdale Enquirer; Research Intern, Newsweek, 1987; Associate Editor, various sections of the magazine, 1989-91, General Editor covering politics and current affairs, sport and adventure, 1992-, specializing in coverage of Asian affairs, 1996-, Senir Writer, 1996-, Newsweek International. Address: c/o Newsweek International, 251 West 57th Street, New York, NY 10019-1894, USA.

EN-NEHAS Jamal, b. 11 May 1961, Casablanca, Morocco. m. Sheri En-nehas, 23 Sept 1995, 2 daughters. Education: BA, English Language and Literature, University of Hassan II, Casablanca, Morocco, 1985; Postgraduate Diploma in Comparative Literature, University of Essex, Colchester, England, 1986; MA, 19th and 20th Century English and United States Literature, University of Essex, 1987; PhD, English, University of New Brunswick, Fredericton, Canada. Appointments: Assistant editor, Maknasat, 1991-92; Book reviewer, World Literature Today, 1995-. Publications: The Writing Guide for Students of English in Moroccan Universities (in progress); Laurens Van Der Post's Ventures to the Interior: A Study in Travel, Cultural Quests and Self-Exploration (in progress). Contributions to: Maknasat; International Fiction Review; World Literature Today; Chimo: The News-Journal of the Canadian Association for Commonwealth Literature and Language Studies. Honours: Moroccan Government Scholarship for Higher Education, 1985; Honorary Visiting Fellowship, Rhodes University, 1995; DWL Earl Fellowship, University of New Brunswick, 1995; Honourary Visiting Scholarship, Columbia

University, 1996. Address: Cité Ifriquia Rue 30 No 54, Casablanca 20450, Morocco.

ENG Stephen Richard, b. 31 Oct 1940, San Diego, California, USA. Biographer; Poet; Literary Journalist; Scholar. m. Anne Jeanne Kangas, 15 May 1969, 2 sons, 2 daughters. Education: AB English Literature, George Washington University, Washinton, DC, 1963; MS Education (Counseling) Portland State University, Oregon, 1973. Appointments: Poetry Editor, The Diversifier, 1977-78; Associate Editor, Triads, 1985; Director and Editor, Nashville House, 1991-; Staff book reviewer, Nashville Banner, 1993-. Publications: Elusive Butterfly and Other Lyrics (editor), 1971; The Face of Fear and Other Poems (editor), 1984; The Hunter of Time: Gnomic Verses (editor), 1984; Toreros: Poems (editor), 1990; Poets of the Fantastic (co-editor), 1992; A Satisfied Mind: The Country Music Life of Porter Wagoner, 1992; Jimmy Buffett: The Man From Margaritaville Revealed, 1996. Contributions to: Lyric; Night Cry; Journal of Country Music; Tennessee Historical Quarterly; Bookpage; Nashville Banner; Music City Blues; Space & Time. Honours: Focus Poet, Bachaet, 1971; First Poetry Prize, 1973; American Poets' Fellowship Society Certificate of Merit, 1973; Co-Winner, Rhysling Award for short poem, Science Fiction Poetry Association 1979; Best Writer, 1979, 1983, Special Achievement, 1985, Small Press Writers and Artists Organization. Memberships: Broadcast Music Inc, 1993-; Syndic, F. Marion Crawford Memorial Society, 1978-; Country Music Association, 1990-; Science-Fiction Poetry Association, 1990-; Nashville Songwriters' Association International, 1995. Address: PO Box 111864, Nashville, TN 37222, USA.

ENGEL Matthew (Lewis), b. 11 June 1951, Northampton, England. Journalist. Education: BA, Economics, Manchester University, 1972. Appointments: Staff, Northampton Chronicle and Echo, 1972-75, Reuters, 1977-79; Staff, 1979-, Cricket Correspondent, 1983-87, Feature Writer and Columnist, 1987-, Guardian; Editor, Wisden Cricket Monthly, 1996-. Publications: Ashes '85, 1985; The Guardian Book of Cricket (editor), 1986; Sportswriter's Eye, 1989; Sportspages Almanac, 1989. Honour: Sports Writer of the Year, 1985. Address: 39 York Rise, London NW5, England.

ENGELS John (David), b. 19 Jan 1931, South Bend, Indiana, USA. Professor of English; Poet; Writer. m. Gail Jochimsen, 1957, 4 sons, 2 daughters. Education: AB, University of Notre Dame, 1952; University College, Dublin, 1955; MFA, University of Iowa, 1957. Appointments: Instructor, Norbert College, West De Pere, Wisconsin, 1957-62; Assistant Professor, 1962-70, Professor of English, 1970-, St Michael's College, Winooski Park, Vermont; Visiting Lecturer, University of Vermont, 1974, 1975, 1976; Slaughter Lecturer, Sweet Briar College, 1976; Writer-in-Residence, Randolph Macon Women's College, 1992. Publications: Poetry: The Homer Mitchell Place, 1968; Signals from the Safety Coffin, 1975; Blood Mountain, 1977; Vivaldi in Early Fall, 1981; The Seasons in Vermont, 1982; Weather-Fear: New and Selected Poems 1958-1982, 1983; Cardinals in the Ice Age, 1987; Walking to Cootehill: New and Selected Poems 1958-1992, 1993; Big Water, 1995. Other: Writing Techniques (with Norbert Engels), 1962; Experience and Imagination (with Norbert Engels), 1965; The Merrill Guide to William Carlos Williams (editor), 1969; The Merrill Studies in Paterson (editor), 1971. Honours: Bread Loaf Writers Conference Scholarship, 1960, and Robert Frost Fellowship, 1976; Guggenheim Fellowship, 1979. Address: c/o Department of English, St Michaels' College, Winooski Park, VT 05404, USA.

ENGLISH Sir David, b. 26 May 1931, England. Journalist; Editor; Media Chairman. m. Irene Mainwood, 1954, 1 son, 2 daughters. Education: Bournemouth School. Appointments: Daily Mirror, 1951-53; Feature Editor, 1956, Editor, 1969-71, Daily Sketch; Foreign Correspondent, 1961-63, Chief American Correspondent, 1963-65, Foreign Editor, 1965-67, Associate Editor, 1967-69, Express; Editor, Daily Mail, 1971-92, Mail on Sunday, 1982; Vice-Chairman, 1986-88, Joint Deputy Chairman, 1989-92, Editor-in-Chief, 1989-, Chairman, 1992-, Associated Newspapers; Chairman, Burlington Magazines, 1988-, New Era TV, 1988-, Teletext UK, 1993-, Channel One TV, 1993-. Publication: Divided They Stand (A British View of the 1968 American Presidential Election), 1969. Honour: Knighted, 1982. Memberships: Association of British Editors, board, 1985-; Commonwealth Press Union, president, 1994-. Address: Northcliffe House, 2 Derry Street, London W5 5TT, England.

ENQUIST Per Olov, b. 23 Sept 1934, Bureå, Västerbotten, Sweden. Novelist; Playwright. m. Lone Bastholm. Education: PhD,

University of Uppsala, 1964. Appointments: Critic, Expressen, Stockholm, 1967-. Publications: The Crystal Eye, 1962; The Route, 1963; The Casey Brothers, 1964; The Magnetist's Fifth Winter, 1964; Hess, 1966; The Legionnaires, 1968; The Seconder, 1971; Tales from the Age of Cancelled Rebellions, 1974; The March of the Musicians, 1978; Dr Mabuse's New Will, 1982; Downfall: A Love Story, 1985; Protagora's Theory, 1987; Captain Nemo's Library, 1991. Plays: The Night of the Tribades, 1975; Chez Nous: Pictures from Swedish Community Life, 1976; Man on the Pavement, 1979; To Phaedra, 1980; The Rain Snakes, 1981; The Hour of the Lynx, 1988. Other: Strindberg - A Life, 1984. Honours: Nordic Council Prize, 1969. Address: c/o Norstedts Forlag, Box 2052, 103 12 Stockholm 2, Sweden.

ENRIGHT D(ennis) J(oseph), B. 11 Mar 1920, Leamington, Warwickshire, England. Writer. m. Madeleine Harders, 3 Nov 1949, 1 daughter. Education: BA, Cambridge, 1949; MA, 1946; D Litt, University of Alexandria, Egypt, 1949. Appointments: Teacher of English Literature, 1947-70; Co-Editor, Encounter, 1970-72; Director, Chatto and Windus Publishers, 1974-82. Publications: Academic Year, 1955; Memoirs of a Mendicant Professor, 1969; The Oxford Book of Death, 1983; A Mania for Sentences, 1983; The Alluring Problem, 1986; Collected Poems, 1987; Fields of Vision, 1988; The Faber Book of Fevers and Frets, 1989; The Oxford Book of Friendship (co-editor with David Rawlinson), 1991; The Way of the Cat, 1992; Old Men and Comets, 1993; The Oxford Book of the Supernatural, 1994; The Sayings of Goethe, 1996. Interplay: A Kind of Commonplace Book, 1995. Contributions to: Scrutiny; Times Literary Supplement; Encounter; Observer; Listener; London Magazine; New York Review of Books. Honours: Cholomondeley Award, 1974; Queen's Gold Medal for Poetry, 1981; Honorary DLitt, University of Warwick, 1982; Honorary Doctor, University of Surrey, 1985; Order of the British Empire, 1991. Membership: Fellow, Royal Society of Literature. Address: 35a Viewfield Road, London SW18 5JD, England.

ENSLIN Theodore (Vernon), b. 25 Mar 1925, Chester, Pennsylvania, USA. Poet; Writer. m. (1) Mildred Marie Stout, 1945, div 1961, 1 son, 1 daughter, (2) Alison Jane Jose, 1969, 1 son. Education: Public and Private; Studied composition with Nadia Boulanger. Appointment: Columnist, The Cape Codder, Orleans, Massachusetts, 1949-56. Publications: Poetry: The Work Proposed, 1958; New Sharon's Prospect, 1962; The Place Where I Am Standing, 1964; To Come to Have Become, 1966; The Diabelli Variations and Other Poems, 1967; 2/30-6/31: Poems 1967, 1967; The Poems, 1970; Forms, 5 volumes, 1970-74; The Median Flow: Poems 1943-73, 1974; Ranger, Ranger 2, 2 volumes, 1979, 1980; Music for Several Occasions, 1985; Case Book, 1987; Love and Science, 1990; A Sonare, 1994. Fiction: 2 + 12 (short stories), 1979. Play: Barometric Pressure 29.83 and Steady, 1965. Other: Mahler, 1975; The July Book, 1976. Honours: Nieman Award for Journalism, 1955; National Endowment for the Arts Grant, 1976. Address: RFD Box 289, Kansas Road, Milbridge, MA 04658, USA.

ENSMINGER Audrey Helen, b. 30 Dec 1919. Nutrition Consultant; Author. m. Marion Eugene Ensminger, 11 June 1941, 1 son, 1 daughter (dec). Education: BSc, University of Manitoba, 1940; MSc, Washington State University, 1943; Certified Nutrition Specialist. Publications: Foods & Nutrition Encyclopedia, 2nd edition, 1995; The Concise Encyclopedia of Foods & Nutrition, 1995; China - The Impossible Dream. Honours: American Medical Writers Association; Distinguished Service Award, American Medical Association; Humanitarian Award, Academy of Dentistry International. Address: 648 West Sierra Avenue, Clovis, CA 93612, USA.

ENTMAN Robert Mathew, b. 7 Nov 1949, New York, New York, USA. Professor of Communications; Consultant; Writer. m. Frances Seymour, 1 June 1979, 1 son, 1 daughter. Education: AB, Duke University, 1971; PhD, Yale University, 1977; M in Public Policy, University of California at Berkeley, 1980. Appointments: Assistant Professor, Dickinson College, Carlisle, Pennsylvania, 1975-77; Duke University, 1980-89; Postdoctoral Fellow, University of California, 1978-80; Consultant, US House of Representatives Subcommittee on Telecommunications, 1982, National Telecomunications and Information Administration, Washington, DC, 1984-85, Aspen Institute, 1986-; Guest Scholar, Woodrow Wilson Center, Washington, DC, 1989; Associate Professor of Communication, Northwestern University, 1989-94; Professor of Communication, North Carolina State University, 1994-; Adjunct Professor, University of North Carolina at Chapel Hill, 1995-. Publications: Media Power Politics (co-author),

1981; Democracy Without Citizens, 1989; Blacks in the News, 1991; Privatisation of Broadcast Media, 1997. Contributions to: Journals. Honours: Markle Foundation Research Grants, 1984, 1986, 1988, 1995; Ameritech Research Fellow, 1989-90; McGannon Award for Communications Policy Research, 1993. Memberships; American Political Science Association; International Communication Association. Address: c/o Department of Communication, North Carolina State University, Box 8104, Raleigh, NC 27695, USA.

ENYEART James L(yle), b. 13 Jan 1943, Auburn, Washington, USA. Photographer; Adjunct Professor; Writer. m. Roxanne Malone, 3 children. Education: BFA, Kansas City Art Institute, 1965; MFA, University of Kansas, 1972. Appointments: Director, Albrecht Galley of Art, Instructor, Drawing and Design, Missouri Western University, 1967-68; Curator of Photography, Spencer Museum of Art, Associate Professor, Department Art History, University of Kansas, 1968-76; Director, Center for Creative Photography, Adjunct Professor of Art, University of Arizona, 1977-89; Director, George Eastman House, 1989-. Publications: Kansas Album (editor), 1977; Francis Brugiere, 1977; George Fiske: Yosemite Photographer, 1980; Photography of the Fifties: An American Perspective, 1980; Heineckan (editor), 1980; W Eugene Smith: Master of the Photographic Essay, 1981; Jerry Uelsmann: Twenty-five Years, a Retrospective, 1982; Aaron Siskind: Terrors and Pleasures 1931-80, 1982; Three Classic American Photographs: Texts and Contexts (with R D Monroe and Philip Stoker) 1982; Edward Weston Omnibus (with others), 1984; Edward Weston's California Landscapes, 1984; Judy Dater: Twenty Years, 1986; Andreas Feininger: A Retrospective (editor with Henry Holmes Smith) 1986. Honours: Photokina Obelisk Award, Cologne, Germany, 1982; Guggenheim Fellowship, 1987; Josef Sudek Medal, Ministry of Culture, Prague, Czechoslovakia, 1989. Memberships: American Association of Art Museum Directors; American Association of Art Museums; Oracle (Co-Founder). Address: George Eastman House, 900 East Avenue, Rochester, NY 14607, USA.

ENZENSBERGER Hans Magnus, b. 11 Nov 1929, Kaufbeuren, Germany. Poet; Playwright. m. Katharine Bonitz, 1986. Education: University of Hamburg; PhD, University of Erlangen, 1955. Appointment: Professor of Poetry, University of Frankfurt, 1965-. Publications: Verteidigung der Wolfe, 1957; Landessprache, 1960; Gedichte, 1962; Blindenschrift, 1964; Poems for People Who Don't Read Poems, 1968; Mausoleum, 1975; The Sinking of the Titanic, 1978; Beschreibung eines Dickichts, 1979; Die Furie des Verschwindens: Die Gedichte, 1981; Gedichte 1950-85, 1986; Diderot und das dunkle Ei: Eine Mystifikation, 1990; Zukunftsmusik, 1991; Plays: Das Verhör von Habana, 1970; El Cimarron (music by Hans Werner Henze), 1970; La Cubana (music by Henze), 1975; Der Menschenfeind (after Molière), 1979; Die Tochter der Luft, 1992; Also: Critical Essays, 1982; Dreamers of the Absolute: Essays on Politics, Crime, and Culture, 1988; Requiem für eine romantische Frau, 1988; Der fliegende Robert: Gedichte, Szenen, Essays, 1989. Honour: Bavarian Academy of Fine Arts Award, 1987. Address: c/o Suhrkamp Verlag, Postfach 101945, 6000 Frankfurt, Germany.

EPSTEIN Seymour, (Sy Epstein), b. 2 Dec 1917, New York, New York, USA. Writer; Retired Professor. M. Miriam Kligman, 5 May 1956, 2 sons. Education: College, 2 years. Publications: Pillar of Salt, 1960; Leah, 1964; Caught in That Music, 1967; The Dream Museum, 1971; Looking for Fred Schmidt, 1973; A Special Destiny, 1986; September Faces, 1987; Light, 1989. Contributions to: periodicals. Honour: Edward Lewis Wallant Memorial Award, 1965; Guggenheim Fellowship, 1965. Memberships: Author's Guild; PEN. Address: 750 Kappock Street, Apt 608, Riverdale, Bronx, NY 10463, USA.

ERBA Luciano, b. 18 Sept 1922, Milan, Italy. Poet; Translator; Professor. Education: PhD, Catholic University, Milan, 1947. Appointments: Professor of French Literature, University of Padua, 1973-82, University of Verona, 1982-87, Catholic University of Milan, 1987-97. Publications: Linea K, 1951; Il bel paese, 1956; Il prete di Ratana, 1959; Il male minore, 1960; Il prato più verde, 1977; Il nastro di Moebius, 1981; Il cerchio aperto, 1983; L'ippopotamo, 1989; L'ipotesi circense, 1995. Radio and Television plays. Novel: Françoise, 1982. Translator of works by Thom Gunn, Cyrano de Bergerac, and others. Honours: Viareggio Prize, 1980; Bagutta Prize, 1988; Librex-Guggenheim E. Montale Prize, 1989; Italian Pen Club Prize, 1995. Address: Via Giason del Maino 16, 20146 Milan, Italy.

ERDRICH (Karen) Louise, b. 7 June 1954, Little Falls, Minnesota, USA. Writer; Poet. m. Michael Anthony Dorris, 10 Oct

1981, dec 1997, 6 children. Education: BA, Dartmouth College, 1976; MA, Johns Hopkins University, 1979. Appointments: Visiting Poet and Teacher, North Dakota State Arts Council, 1977-78; Writing Instructor, Johns Hopkins University, 1978-79; Communications Director and Editor of Circle of the Boston Indian Council, 1979-80. Publications: Fiction: Love Medicine, 1984, augumented edition, 1993; The Beet Queen, 1986; Tracks, 1988; The Crown of Columbus (with Michael Anthony Dorris), 1991; The Bingo Palace, 1994. Poetry: Jacklight, 1984; Baptism of Desire, 1989. Other: Imagination, textbook, 1980. Contributions to: Anthologies: American Indian Quarterly; Atlantic; Frontiers; Kenyon Review; Ms; New England Review; New York Times Book Review; New Yorker; North American Review; Redbook; Others. Honours: MacDowell Colony Fellowship, 1980; Yaddo Colony Fellowship, 1981; Dartmouth College Visiting Fellow, 1981; National Magazine Fiction Awards, 1983, 1987; National Book Critics Circle Award for Best Work of Fiction, 1984; Virginia McCormick Scully Prize for Best Book of the Year, 1984; Best First Fiction Award, American Academy and Institute of Arts and Letters, 1985; Guggenheim Fellowship, 1985-86; First Prize, O Henry Awards, 1987. Address: Hanover, NH, USA.

ERICKSON Peter Brown, b. 11 Aug 1945, Worcester, Massachusetts, USA. Literary Critic; Librarian. m. Tay Gavin, 30 June 1968, 2 sons, 1 daughter. Education: BA, Amherst College, 1967; Centre for Contemporary Cultural Studies, University of Birmingham, England, 1967-68; PhD, University of California, Santa Cruz, 1975; MSLS, Simmons College, 1984. Appointments: Assistant Professor, Williams College, 1976-81; Visiting Assistant Professor, Wesleyan University, 1982-83; Research Librarian, Clark Art Institute, 1985-. Publications: Patriarchal Structures in Shakespeare's Drama, 1985; Shakespeare's Rough Magic, Renaissance Essays in Honor of C L Barber, 1985; Rewriting Shakespeare, Rewriting Ourselves, 1991; Shakespeare's Comedies, 1998. Contributions to: Books and journals. Honours: Phi Beta Kappa, 1967; Amherst Memorial Fellowship, 1967-68; Kent Fellowship, Wesleyan University, 1981-82. Memberships: Shakespeare Association of America; Renaissance Society of America; Modern Language Association. Address: Clark Art Institute, PO Box 8, Williamstown, MA 01267, USA.

ERICKSON Stephen (Michael), (Steve Erickson) b. 20 Apr 1950, Santa Monica, California, USA. Novelist. Education: BA, 1972, Master of Journalism, 1973, University of California, Los Angeles. Appointments: Arts Editor, 1989-91; Film Editor, 1992-93, Los Angeles Weekly. Publications: Days Between Stations, 1985; Rubicon Beach, 1986; Tours of the Black Clock, 1989; Leap Year, 1989; Arc d'X, 1993; Amnesiascope, 1996; American Nomad, 1997. Contributions to: New York Times; Esquire; Rolling Stone; Details; Elle; Los Angeles Times; Los Angeles Style; Los Angeles Weekly. Honours: Samuel Goldwyn Award, 1972; National Endowment for the Arts Fellowship, 1987. Address: c/o Melanie Jackson, 250 West 57th Street, Suite 1119, New York 10107, USA.

ERLINGSSON Fridrik, b. Reykjavik, Iceland. Writer; Scriptwriter. Education: BA, Graphic Design, 1983. Publications: Benjamin Dove, novella for young people, 1992; A Winter's Fire, novel, 1995; Behind Schedule, screenplay, 1993; The Virgin Boy, screenplay for TV, 1994; Benjamin Dove, screenplay based on book, 1995; My Grandpa in the Country, 1987, Volume 2, 1993. Honours: Icelandic Children Books Award, 1992, 1993; IBBY Award, 1993; EBU Special prix du Jury, 1994. Literary AgentL Lichtblicht, Copenhagen, Denmark. Address: PO Box 5144, 125-Reykjavik, Iceland.

ERSKINE Barbara, b. 10 Aug 1944, Nottingham, England. Writer. m. 2 sons. Education: MA Honours, Edinburgh University, 1967. Publications: Lady of Hay, 1986; Kingdom of Shadows, 1988; Encounters, 1990; Child of the Phoenix, 1992; Midnight is a Lonely Place, 1994; House of Echoes, 1996; Distant Voices, 1996. Contributions to: Numerous short stories to magazines and journals. Membership: Society of Authors. Address: c/o Blake Friedmann, 37-41 Gower Street, London WC1E 6HH, England.

ERTUGHRUL Jeff, b. 2 Aug 1936, Avtepe, Cyprus. Telecommunications Engineer. m. Sheila Mary, 31 Dec 1963, 2 sons. Education: Turkish Lyceé, Nicosia, 1951-55; Northern Polytechnic, London, England, 1960-62. Appointment: Editor, Opal Magazine, 1986. Publications: The Postal Services of Unicyp, 1980; The Postal Services of the Turkish Forces in Cyprus, 1980; The Postal Services of Military Forces in Cyprus, 1984; The Postal Services of Kibris, 1984; Kibris 1 and 2, 1984, reprint 1985. Contributions to: British, American

and European Philatelic Journals; London Correspondent of Sabah Newspaper, 1974-76. Honour: Albert Harris Publication literature trophy, 1986. Memberships: Philatelic Writers Society; Association Internationale des Journalistes Philateliques.

ERZHEMSKY George, b. 24 Dec 1918, Petrograd, Russia. Conductor; Psychologist; Investigator. m. Tatiana Lavrova, 12 May 1953, 1 daughter. Education: Leningrad Conservatoire, Piano Faculty, Diploma, 1941; Leningrad Conservatoire, External Exams for Conducting Faculty Course, 1955. Publications: Psychology of Conducting Practice, (in Russian), 1983; Regularities and Paradoxes of Conducting Practice, (in Russian), 1993; Culture as a Factor of Transformation of Russia, 1995; Psychological Paradoxes of Conducting, 1996; Psychological Structure of Conductor's Language, (in Russian), 1996. Contributions to: Psychological Mechanisms of Performing Actions of a Conductor in: Psychological Journal, 1983, no 2, in Russian. Honours: 8 government medals, 1945, 1955, 1957, 1965, 1975, 1985, 1995; Title of Honoured Art Worker, 1953. Address: 28/11 Novgorodskaya str, fl 14, 193124 Saint Petersburg, Russia.

ESCANDELL Noemi, b. 27 Sept 1936, Havana, Cuba. Poet; Educator. Education: Bachiller en Letras, Instituto de la Víbora, 1955; BA, Queens College, NY, 1968; MA, 1971, PhD, 1976, Harvard University, USA. Publications: Cuadros; Ciclos; Palabras. Contributions to: Letras Feminas; Third Woman; Dialogue; Peregrine; El Gato Tuerto; Plaza; El Comercio; Verbena; Stone County, CPU Review; Horizontes 2000; San Fernando Poetry Journal. Honours: Residencies, Millay Colony for the Arts, 1983, 1990; Special Mention, Federico Garcia Lorca Poetry Competition, 1995. Membership: Feministas Unidas; Iberoamerican Poetry Academy, Washington DC Chapter. Address: 7 Holland Avenue, Westfield, MA 01085, USA.

ESHLEMAN Clayton, b. 1 June 1935, Indianpolis, Indiana, USA. Professor of English; Poet; Writer; Translator. m. Barbra Novak, 1961, div 1967, 1 son (2) Caryl Reiter, 1969. Education: BA in Philosophy, 1958, MA in Creative Writing, 1961, Indiana University. Appointments: Editor, Folio, 1959-60; Instructor, University of Maryland Eastern Overseas Division, 1961-62, New York University American Language Institute, 1966-68; Publisher, Caterpillar Books, 1966-68, Editor, Caterpillar magazine, 1967-73; Faculty, School of Critical Studies, California Institute of the Arts, Valencia, 1970-72; Teacher, University of California at Los Angeles, 1975-77; Dreyfuss Poet-in-Residence and Lecturer, California Institute of Technology, Pasadena, 1979-84; Visiting Lecturer in Creative Writing, University of California at San Diego, Riverside, Los Angeles, and Santa Barbara, 1979-86; Reviewer, Los Angles Times Book Review, 1979-86; Founder-Editor, Sulfur magazine, 1981-; Professor of English, Eastern Michigan University, 1986-. Publications: Poetry: Mexico and North, 1962; The Chavin Illumination, 1965; Lachrymae Mateo: 3 Poems for Christmas 1966, 1966; Walks, 1967; The Crocus Bud, 1967; Brother Stones, 1968; Cantaloups and Splendour, 1968; T'ai, 1969; The House of Okumura, 1969; Indiana, 1969; The House of Ibuki: A Poem, New York City, 14 March-30 Sept 1967, 1969; Yellow River Record, 1969; A Pitchblende, 1969; The Wand, 1971; Bearings, 1971; Altars, 1971; The Sandjo Bridge, 1972; Coils, 1973; Human Wedding, 1973; The Lst Judgement: For Caryl Her Thirty-First Birthday, the End of Her Pain, 1973; Aux Morts, 1974; Realignment, 1974; Portrait of Francis Bacon, 1975; The Cull Wall: Poems and Essays, 1975; Cogollo, 1976; The Woman Who Saw Through Paradise, 1976; Grotesca, 1977; On Mules Sent From Chavin: A Journal and Poems 1965-66, 1977; Core Meander, 1977; The Name Encanyoned River, 1977; The Gospel of Celine Arnauld, 1978; What She Means, 1978; A Note on Apprenticeship, 1979; The Lich Gate, 1980; Nights We Put the Rock Together, 1980; Our Lady of the Three-Pronged Devil, 1981; Hades in Mangagnese, 1981; Foetus Graffiti, 1981; Fracture, 1983; Visions of the Fathers of Lascaux, 1983; The Name Encanyoned River: Selected Poems 1960-1985, 1986; Hotel Cro-Magnon, 1989. Other: A Caterpillar Anthology: A Selection of Poetry and Prose from Caterpillar Magazine (editor), 1971; Antiphonal Swing: Selected Prose 1962-1987, 1989; Novices: A Study of Poetic Apprenticeship, 1989. Translations: 19 books, 1962-90. Honours: National Endowment for the Arts Grant, 1969, Fellowships, 1979, 1981; Guggenheim Fellowship, 1978; National Book Award for Translation, 1979; National Endowment for the Humanities Grant, 1980, and Fellowship, 1981; Michigan Arts Council Grant, 1988. Address: 210 Washtenaw Avenue, Ypsilanti, MI 48197, USA.

ESMOND Harriet. See: **BURKE John Frederick.**

ESSLIN Martin, b. 8 June 1918, Hungary (British citizen). m. Renate Gerstenberg, 1947, 1 daughter. Education: Vienna University. Appointments: Head of Drama, BBC Radio, 1963-77; Professor of Drama, Stanford University, California, 1977-88; now Professor Emeritus. Publications: Brecht: A Choice of Evils: A Critical Study of the Man, His Work and His Opinions, 1959; The Theatre of the Absurd, 1961, 1968; Samuel Beckett: A Collection of Critical Essays (editor), 1965; Harold Pinter, 1967; The Genius of the German Theatre (editor), 1968; Berthold Brecht, 1969; Brief Chronicles: Essays on Modern Theatre, 1970; The Peopled Wound: The Work of Harold Pinter, 1970; The New Theatre of Europe, Vol 4 (editor), 1970; An Anatomy of a Drama, 1976; Artaud, 1976; Mediation, 1980; The Age of Television, 1982; The Field of Drama, 1987; Antonin Artaud, 1992. Address: 64 Loudoun Road, London NW8, England.

ESSOP Ahmed, b. 1 Sept 1931, Dabhel, India. m. 17 Apr 1960, 1 son, 3 daughters. Education: BA Honours, English, University of South Africa, 1964. Publications: The Hajii and Other Stories, 1978; The Visitation, 1980; The Emperor, 1984; Noorjehan and Other Stories, 1990. Honour: Olive Schyeiner Award, English Academy of Southern Africa, 1979. Address: PO Box 1747, Lenasia 1820, Johannesburg, South Africa.

ESTERHAZY Péter, b. 14 Apr 1950, Budapest, Hungary. Novelist. m. Gitta Reen. Education: Graduated, University of Budapest and Eotvos Lorand University, 1974. Publications: Fancsiko and Pinta, 1976; Don't Be a Pirate on Papal Waters, 1977; Production Novel, 1979; Indirect, 1981; Who Can Guarantee the Lady's Safety?, 1982; Hauliers, 1983; Little Hungarian Pornography, 1984; Helping Verbs of the Heart, 1985; Seventeen Swans, 1987; The Stuffed Swan, 1988; Certain Adventure, 1989; Hrabal's Book, 1990; The Glance of Countess Hahn-Hahn, 1991; The Wonderful Life of the Little Fish, 1991; From the Ivory Tower, 1991; Notes of a Blue Stocking, 1994; Farewell Symphony, 1994; She Loves Me, 1995. Honour: Attila József Prize; Lajis Kossuth Prize. Address: c/o Hungarian Writers' Federation, Bajza-utca 18, 1962 Budapest, Hungary.

ESTLEMAN Loren D, b. 15 Sept 1952, Ann Arbor, Michigan, USA. Writer. Education: BA, English Literature/Journalism, Eastern Michigan University, 1974. Publications: Novels: The Oklahoma Punk, 1976; The Hider, 1978; Sherlock Holmes vs Dracula, 1978; The High Rocks, 1979; Dr Jekyll and Mr Holmes, 1979; Stamping Ground, 1980; Motor City Blue, 1980; Aces and Eights, 1981; Angel Eyes, 1981; The Wolfer, 1981; Murdock's Law, 1982; The Midnight Man, 1982; Mister St John, 1983; This Old Bill, 1984; Kill Zone, 1984; Sugartown, 1984; Roses are Dead, 1985; Gun Man, 1985; Every Brilliant Eye, 1986; Any Man's Death, 1986; Lady Yesterday, 1987; Downriver, 1988; Bloody Season, 1988; Silent Thunder, 1989; Peeper, 1989; Sweet Women Lie, 1990; Whiskey River, 1990; Sudden Country, 1991; Motown, 1991; King of the Corner, 1992; City of Widows, 1994; Edsel, 1995; Stress, 1996; Billy Gashade, 1997; Never Street, 1997. Non-fiction: The Wister Trace, 1987. Contributions to: Journals. Honours: Golden Spur Awards, 1981, 1987, Stirrup Award, 1983, Western Writers of America; Shamus Awards, 1984, 1985, 1988, Private Eye Writers of America; Michigan Arts Foundation Award, 1987; American Mystery Award, 1988, 1990. Address: 5552 Walsh Road, Whitmore Lake, MI 48189, USA.

ESTORIL Jean. See: ALLAN Mabel Esther.

ETCHEMENDY Nancy Howell, b. 19 Feb 1952, Reno, Nevada, USA. Writer; Graphic Designer. m. 14 Apr 1973, 1 son. Education: BA, University of Nevada, Reno, 1974. Publications: The Watchers of Space, 1980; Stranger From the Stars, 1983; The Crystal City, 1985. Contributions to: Anthologies and magazines. Memberships: Science Fiction Writers of America; Society of Children's Book Writers; Horror Writers Association, Treasurer, 1996-97. Address: 410 French Court, Menlo Park, CA 94025, USA.

ETTER Dave (David) Pearson, b. 18 Mar 1928, Huntington Park, California, USA. Poet; Author. m. Margaret Ann Cochran, 8 Aug 1959, 1 son, 1 daughter. Education: BA, University of Iowa. Publications: Go Read the River, 1966; The Last Train to Prophetstown, 1968; West of Chicago, 1981; Alliance, Illinois, 1983; Selected Poems, 1987; Sunflower County, 1994; How High the Moon, 1996. Contributions to: Slow Dancer (England); El Corno Emplumado (Mexico); The Far Point (Canada); The Nation; Saturday Review; Massachusetts Review. Honours: Midland Authors Poetry Prize, 1967;

Theodore Roethke Prize, 1972; Carl Sandburg Poetry Prize, 1982. Address: PO Box 413, Elburn, IL 60119, USA.

ETZIONI HALEVY Eva, b. 21 Mar 1934, Vienna, Austria. Political Sociologist; Professor. m. Zvi Halevy, 2 sons, 1 daughter. Education: PhD, Tel Aviv University, 1971. Appointment: Professor, Bar Ilan University, Ramat Gan, Israel. Publications: Social Change, 1981; Bureaucracy and Democracy, 1985; The Knowledge Elite and the Failure of Prophecy, 1985; National Broadcasting Under Siege, 1987; Fragile Democracy, 1989; The Elite Connection, 1992; The Elite Connection and Democracy in Israel, 1993. Contributions to: Numerous magazines and journals. Honour: Fellow, Academy of Social Sciences in Australia. Address: Department of Sociology, Bar Ilan University, Ramat Gan 52900, Israel.

EULO Ken, b. 17 Nov 1939, Newark, New Jersey, USA. Playwright; Director; Novelist. m. 1 son. Education: University of Heidelberg, 1961-64. Appointments: Artistic Director, Courtyard Playhouse, New York; Staff Writer, Paramount. Publications: Plays: Bang?, 1969; Zarf, I Love You, 1969; SRO, 1970; Puritan Night, 1971; Billy Hofer and the Quarterback Sneak, 1971; Black Jesus, 1972; The Elevator, 1972; 48 Spring Street, 1973; Final Exams, 1975; The Frankenstein Affair, 1979; Say Hello to Daddy, 1979. Novels: Bloodstone, 1982; The Brownstone, 1982; The Deathstone, 1982; Nocturnal, 1983; The Ghost of Veronica, 1985; House of Caine, 1988. Other: Television scripts. Contributions to: Magazines and newspapers. Memberships: Dramatists Guild; Italian Playwrights of America; Writers Guild of America. Address: 14633 Valley Vista Boulevard, Sherman Oaks, CA 91403, USA.

EVANS Alan. See: STOKER Alan.

EVANS Aled Lewis, b. 9 Aug 1961, Machynlleth, Wales. Teacher; Broadcaster. Education: Joint Honours Degree, Welsh, English, University College of North Wales, Bangor. Publications: Border Town, 1983; Whispers, 1986; Waves, 1989; Can I Have A Patch of Blue Sky, 1991; Between Two September Tides, 1994. Contributions to: Welsh Language Periodicals, Golwg; Barn; Tu Chwith; English Language, Chester Poets Anthologies. Honour: National Eisteddfodof Wales Award for Poetry, 1991. Memberships: Gorsedd Bards; Chester Poets. Address: 28 Jubilee Road, Pentrefelin, Wrexham, Clwyd LL13 7NN, Wales.

EVANS Donald, (Onwy), b. 12 June 1940, Cardiganshire, Wales. Welsh Master. m. Pat Thomas, 29 Dec 1972, 1 son. Education: Honours degree in Welsh, 1962, Diploma in Education, 1963, University College of Wales, Aberystwyth. Publications: Y Flodeugerodd O Gywyddau (The Anthology of Cywyddau) (editor), 1981; Machlud Canrif (Century's Sunset), 1983; Iasau (Sensations), 1988; Seren Poets 2 (with others), 1990; Life and Work of Rhydwen Williams (Writers of Wales series), 1991; Wrth Reddf (By Instinct), 1994. Contributions to: Welsh Society's Poetry Magazine; Poetry Wales; Modern Poetry in Translation. Honours: Welsh Arts Council Prizes, 1977, 1983, 1989; Welsh Academy Literary Award, 1989. Memberships: Welsh Poetry Society; Welsh Academy. Address: Y Plas, Talgarreg, Llandysul, County of Ceredigion, SA44 4XA, Wales.

EVANS Harold Matthew, b. 28 June 1928, England. Editor; Publisher; Writer. m. (1) Enid Muriel Evans, 15 Aug 1953, div 1979, 1 son, 2 daughters, (2) Cristina Hamley Brown, 20 Aug 1982, 1 son, 1 daughter. Education: BA, Durham University, 1952; MA, Dunelm, 1966. Appointments: Ashton-under-Lyne, Reporter Newspapers, 1944-46, 1949; Manchester Evening News, 1952; Commonwealth Fund Fellow in Journalism, University of Chicago and Stanford University, 1956-57; Assistant Editor, Manchester Evening News, 1958-61; Editor, Northern Echo, 1961-66; Editor-in-Chief, North of England Newspaper Co, 1963-66; Managing Editor, 1966-67, Editor, 1967-81, Sunday Times; Editor, The Times, 1981-82; Editor-in-Chief, Atlantic Monthly Press, 1984-86; Editorial Director, 1984-86, Contributing Editor, 1986-, US News & World Report; Vice-President and Senior Editor, Weidenfeld & Nicolson, 1986-87; Founder-Editor, Condé-Nast Traveler Magazine, 1986-90; President and Publisher, Random House Trade Group, 1990-. Publications: The Active Newsroom, 1961; Editing and Design, 5 volumes, 1972-77; We Learned to Ski, 1974; The Story of Thalidomide, 1978; Eye Witness (editor), 1981; How We Learned to Ski, 1983; Good Times, Bad Times (autobiography), 1983; Front Page History, 1984. Contributions to: Periodicals. Honours: International Editor of the Year, 1975; Gold Medal Award, Institute of Journalists, 1979; Hood Medal, Royal

Photographic Society, 1981; Honorary Doctorate, University of Stirling, 1981; Editor of the Year, 1982; Lotos Club Medal, New York, 1993. Membership: Society of American Historians. Address: c/o Random House, 201 East 50th Street, New York, New York, NY 10022, USA.

EVANS Jonathan. See: **FREEMANTLE Brian.**

EVANS Mari, b. 16 July 1923, Toledo, Ohio, USA. Poet; Writer. Div, 2 sons. Education: University of Toledo. Appointments: Writer, producer and director, The Black Experience television programme, Indianapolis, 1969-70; Assistant Professor of Black Literature and Writer-in-Residence, Indiana University, 1970-78, Purdue University, 1978-80; Writer-in-Residence and Visiting Assistant Pofessor, Northwestern University, 1972-73; Visiting Professor, Washington University, 1980, Cornell University, 1981-84, University of Miami at Coral Gables, 1989; Associate Professor, State University of New York at Albany, 1985-86; Writer-in-Residence, Spelman College, Atlanta, 1989-90. Publications: Poetry: Where Is All the Music?, 1968; I Am A Black Woman, 1970; Whisper, 1979; Nightstar, 1981; A Dark and Splendid Mass, 1992. Other: Rap Stories, 1973; J D, 1973; I Look at Me, 1974; Singing Black, 1976; Jim Flying High, 1979; Black Woman Writers 1950-1980; A Critical Evaluation (editor), 1984. Honours: John Hay Whitney Fellowship, 1965; Woodrow Wilson Foundation Grant, 1968; Black Academy of Arts and Letters Award, 1971; MacDowell Fellowship, 1975; Copeland Fellowship, 1980; National Endowment for the Arts Award, 1981; Yaddo Fellowship, 1984. Address: PO Box 483, Indianapolis, IN 4606, USA.

EVANS Max, b. 29 Aug 1925, USA. Writer; Painter Publications: Southwest Wind (short stories), 1958; Long John Dunn of Taos, 1959; The Rounders, 1960; The Hi Lo Country, 1961; Three Short Novels: The Great Wedding, The One-Eyed Sky, My Pardner, 1963; The Mountain of Gold, 1965; Shadow of Thunder, 1969; Three West: Conversations with Vardis Fisher, Max Evans, Michael Straight, 1970; Sam Peckinpah, Master of Violence, 1972; Bobby Jack Smith, You Dirty Coward!, 1974; The White Shadow, 1977; Xavier's Folly and Other Stories, 1984; Super Bull and Other True Escapades, 1985. Address: 1111 Ridgecrest Drive South East, Albuquerque, NM 87108, USA.

EVANS Richard Rowland, b. 26 May 1936, Tabor, Dolgellau, Wales. Retired Headteacher. m. Bronwen Edwards, 21 Aug 1965, 1 daughter. Education: Teacher's Certificate, 1958; Diploma in Bilingual Education, 1964; BEd, University College of Wales, 1980. Appointment: Welsh Editor, The Normalite/Y Normalydd, 1957-58. Publication: Mynd i'r Lleuad, 1973. Contributions to: Articles and poetry to Dalen, Godre'r Gader; The Normalite/Y Normalydd; Y Cyfnod; Y Dydd. Honour: Winner of Book Writing Competition, 1970, and Bardic Chair, 1988. Memberships: Barddas; Cymdeithas Bob Owen; Undeb Awduron Cymru. Address: Rhandir Mwyn, Cae Deintur, Dolgellau, Gwynedd, North Wales.

EVANS Tabor. See: **KNOTT William Cecil.**

EVERS Lawrence Joseph, (Larry Evans), b. 15 Aug 1946, Grand Island, Nebraska, USA. Professor of English. m. Barbara Zion Grygutis, 20 Dec 1982, 1 son, 1 daughter. Education: BA, 1968, MA, 1969, PhD, 1972, University of Nebraska, Lincoln; Postdoctoral Fellow, University of Chicago, 1973-74. Appointments: Assistant to Full Professor, 1974-86, Full Professor, 1986-, of English, University of Arizona, Tucson. Publications: Words and Place: Native Literature from the American Southwest, 1979; The South Corner of Time, 1980; With Felipe S Molina: Yaqui Deer Songs - Maso Bwrikam, 1987; Woi Bwikam - Coyote Songs, 1990; Hiakim: The Yaqui Homeland, 1992; Homeplaces, 1995. Honours: National Endowment for the Humanities Fellowship, 1972-73; 1st Place, Chicago Folklore Prize, 1987; Burlington Foundation Award, 1992. Membership: Modern Language Association. Address: 273 North Main Avenue, Tucson, AZ 85701, USA.

EXTON Clive (Jack Montague), b. 11 Apr 1930, London, England. Scriptwriter; Playwright. m. (1) Patricia Fletcher Ferguson, 1951, div, Dec 1983, 2 daughters, (2) Margaret Josephine Reid, 1 son, 2 daughters. Education: Christ's Hospital. Publications: Over 15 television plays: Somthing's Got to Give, 1996; Several screenplays: The Boundary (with Tom Stoppard). Address: c/o Rochell Stevens & Co, 2 Terrets Place, London N1 1QZ, England.

EYSENCK Hans J(urgen), b. 4 Mar 1916, Berlin, Germany. Professor of Psychology Emeritus; Writer. m (1) Margaret Malcolm Davies, 1938, 1 son, (2) Sybil Bianca Giuletta Rostal, 1950, 3 sons, 1 daughter. Education: BA, 1938, PHD, 1940, University of London. Appointments: Reader in Psychology and Director of Psychology Department, 1950-55, Professor of Psychology, 1955-83; Professor Emeritus, 1983-, Institute of Psychiatry, University of London. Publications: Dimensions of Personality: A Record of Research, 1947; The Scientific Study of Personality, 1952; The Structures of Personality, 1952, 3rd edition, 1970; Uses and Abuses of Psychology, 1953; The Psychology of Politics, 1954; Psychology and the Foundations of Psychiatry, 1955; Sense and Nonsense in Psychology, 1957; The Dynamics of Anxiety and Hysteria: An Experimental Application of Modern Learning Theory to Psychiatry, 1957; Perceptual Processes and Mental Illness (with G Granger and J C Brengelmann), 1957; Crime and Personality, 1964, 3rd edition, revised, 1977; The Causes and Cures of Neurosis: An Introduction to the Modern Behaviour Therapy Based on Learning Theory and the Principles of Conditioning (with Stanley Rachman), 1965; Fact and Fiction in Psychology, 1965; The Effects of Psychotherapy, 1966; The Biologcal Basis of Personality, 1967; Personality Structure and Measurement (with S B Eysenck), 1969; Race, Intelligence and Education, 1971; Sex and Personality, 1972; The Experimental Study of Freudian Theories (wth Glenn D Wilson), 1973; Eysenck on Extraversion, 1973; The Inequality of Man, 1973; Psychotism as a Dimension of Personality (with S B Eysenck), 1976; Reminiscence, Motivation, and Personality: A Case Study in Experimental Psychology (with C D Frith), 1977; Sex, Violence, and the Media (with D K B Nias), 1978; The Structure and the Measurement of Intelligence (with David W Fulker), 1979; The Psychology of Sex (with Glenn D Wilson), 1979; Mindwatching (with Michael Eysenck), 1981; The Battle for the Mind (with Michael Eysenck), 1985; Decline and Fall of the Freudian Empire, 1985; Rebel with a Cause (autobiography), 1990; Genius: The Natural History of Creativity, 1995. Editor: Handbook of Abnormal Psychology: An Experimental Approach, 1960, 2nd edition, 1973; Experiments in Psychology, 2 volumes, 1960; Behaviour Therapy and Neuroses: Readings in Modern Methods of Treatment Derived from Learning Theory, 1960; Experiments with Drugs: Studies in the Relation between Personality, Learning Theory and Drug Action, 1963; Experiments in Motivation, 1964; Experiments in Behaviour Therapy: Readings in Modern Methods of Treatment of Mental Disorders Derived from Learning Theory, 1964; Readings in Extraversion-Introversion, 3 volumes, 1970; Encyclopedia of Psychology, 3 volumes, 1972, 2nd edition, 1979; The Measurement of Intelligence, 1973; Case Studies in Behaviour Therapy, 1976; The Measure of Personality, 1976; A Textbook of Human Psychology (with Glenn D Wilson), 1976; Advances in Behaviour Research and Therapy (with Stanley Rachman), 2 volumes, 1977, 1979; A Model for Personality, 1981; A Model for Intelligence, 1982; Personality, Genetics, and Behaviour, 1982; Personality Dimensions and Arousal (with Jan Strelau), 1987; Theoretical Foundation of Behaviour Therapy (with Irene Martin), 1987; Suggestion and Suggestibilty (with V A Gheroghiu, P Netter, and R Rosenthal), 1989. Honours: Distinguished Scientist Award, 1988; Presidential Citation, 1993, American Psychological Association; William James Fellow, American Psychological Society, 1994. Memberships: American Psychological Association, fellow; British Psychological Society; International Society for the Study of Individual Differences, president. Address: 10 Dorchester Drive, London SE24 ODQ, England.

EYTHORSDOTTIR Sigridur, b. 21 Aug 1940, Selvogur, Iceland. Teacher. m. Jon Laxdalarnalds, 24 Aug 1963, 1 son, 1 daughter. Education: Diploma in Drama, 1968; Professional Skills in Special Education, 1988; Graduated as a Teacher, University of Teaching. Publications: Gunnar Eignast Systur, 1979; Lena Sol, 1983; 3 Radio Dramas; 4 Short Stories; 4 Plays and Forty Poems. Contributions to: Short Stories in Aeskan and Morgunbladid; Poems in Morgunbladid. Honours: Award: Malog Menning, 1982; Kramhusio, 1992; Ibbx, 1996. Membership: Writer's Association of Iceland. Address: Asvallagata 26, 101 Reykjavik, Iceland.

EZEKIEL Nissim, b. 16 Dec 1924, Bombay, India. Professor; Poet. m. Daisy Jacob, 1952, 1 son, 2 daughters. Education: M, University of Bombay, 1947. Appointments: Reader, 1972-81, Professor, 1981-85, University of Bombay; Writer in Residence, National University of Singapore, 1988-89. Publications: A Time to Change and Other Poems, 1952; Sixty Poems, 1953; The Third, 1958; The Unfinished Man: 1959, 1960; The Exact Name, 1960-64, 1965; A Martin Luther King Reader (editor), 1969; Pergamon Poets 9, 1970;

Hymns in Darkness, 1976; Collected Poems, 1952-88, 1990. Honours: National Academy Award, 1983; Padma Shree, 1988. Address: 18 Kala Niketan, 6th Floor, 47C, Bhulabhai Desai Road, Bombay 400 026, India.

F

FABEND Firth Haring, (Firth Haring), b. 12 Aug 1937, Tappan, New York, USA. Writer; Historian. m. Carl Fabend, 12 Feb 1966, 2 daughters. Education: BA, Barnard College, 1959; PhD, New York University, 1988. Publications: As Firth Haring: The Best of Intentions, 1968; Three Women, 1972; A Perfect Stranger, 1973; The Woman Who Went Away, 1981; Greek Revival, 1985; As Firth Haring Fabend: A Dutch Family in the Middle Colonies, 1660-1800. Contributions to: de Halve Maen; New York History. Honours: Ms Award, New York State Historical Association, 1989; Hendricks Prize, 1989; Fellow, Holland Society of New York, 1993; Fellow, New Netherland Project, 1996. Address: Upper Montclair, NJ 07043, USA.

FABRI Peter, b. 21 Dec 1953, Budapest, Hungary. Writer; Poet; Librettist. m. (1) 1 son, (2) Krista Kovats, 7 June 1986, 1 daughter. Education: Eotvos Lorand University, Budapest, 1973-78. Publications: Folytatsos Regeny, 1981; Napfordulo, 1987; Bameszkodasaim Konyve, 1991; Kolumbusz, Az Orult Spanyol, 1992. Other: Librettos for musicals; Lyrics for songs. Contributions to: Periodicals. Honour: Emerton Prize, Best Lyricist of the Year, 1990. Membership: Hungarian PEN. Address: Rippl Ronai u 27, 1068 Budapest, Hungary.

FAGAN Brian Murray, b. 1 Aug 1936, Birmingham, England. Professor of Anthropology; Writer. m. Lesley Ann Newhart, 16 Mar 1985, 2 children. Education: BA, 1959, MA, 1962, PhD, 1963, Pembroke College, Cambridge. Appointments: Keeper of Prehistory, Livingstone Museum, Zambia, 1959-65; Former Director, Bantu Studies Project, British Institute in Eastern Africa; Visiting Associate Professor, University of Illinois, 1965-66; Associate Professor, 1967-69, Professor of Anthropology, 1969-, University of California, Santa Barbara. Publications: Victoria Falls Handbook, 1964; Southern Africa During the Iron Age (editor), 1966; Iron Age Cultures in Zambia (with S G H Daniels and D W Phillipson), volume 1, 1967, volume II, 1969; A Short History of Zambia, 1968; The Hunter-Gatherers of Gwisho (with F Van Noten), 1971; In the Beginning, 1972, 7th edition, 1991; People of the Earth, 1974, 7th edition, 1992; The Rape of the Nile, 1975; Elusive Treasure, 1977; Quest for the Past, Archaeology: A Brief Introduction, 1978, 4th edition, 1991; Return to Babylon, 1979; The Aztecs, Clash of Cultures, 1984; Adventures in Archaeology, Bareboating, Anchoring, 1985; The Great Journey, 1987; The Journey From Eden, 1990; Ancient North America, 1991; Kingdoms of Jade, Kingdoms of Gold, 1991; Time Detectives, 1995; Oxford Companion to Archaeology, 1997. Address: Department of Anthropology, University of California, Santa Barbara, CA 93106, USA.

FAINLIGHT Ruth (Esther), b. 2 May 1931, New York, New York, USA. Writer; Poet; Translator; Librettist. m. Alan Sillitoe, 19 Nov 1959, 1 son, 1 daughter. Education: Colleges of Arts and Crafts, Birmingham, Brighton. Appointment: Poet-in-Residence, Vanderbilt University, USA. Publications: Poems: Cages, 1966; To See the Matter Clearly, 1968; The Region's Violence, 1973; Another Full Moon, 1976; Sibyls and Others, 1980; Climates, 1983; Fifteen to Infinity, 1983; Selected Poems, 1987; The Knot, 1990; Sibyls, 1991; This Time of Year, 1994; Selected Poems, 1995; Sugar-Paper Blue, forthcoming. Translations: Play, All Citizens Are Soldiers, from Lope de Vega, 1969; Navigations, 1983; Marine Rose, Selected Poems of Sophia de Mello Breyner, 1988; Visitacao, 1995. Libretti: The Dancer Hotoke, 1991; The European Story, 1993; Bedlam Britannica, 1995. Contributions to: Atlantic Monthly; Critical Quarterly; English; Hudson Review; Lettre Internationale; London Magazine; London Review of Books; New Yorker; Threepenny Review; Times Literary Supplement; Yale Review. Honours: Hawthornden Award for Poetry, 1994. Memberships: PEN; Writers in Prison Committee. Address: 14 Ladbroke Terrace, London W11 3PG, England.

FAIRBAIRNS Zoe Ann, b. 20 Dec 1948, United Kingdom. Writer. Education: MA, Honours, University of St Andrews, Scotland, 1972. Appointments: C Day-Lewis Fellowship, Rutherford School, London, 1977-78; Writer-in-Residence, Deakin University, Australia, 1983, Sunderland Polytechnic, 1983-85. Publications: Live as Family, 1968; Down, 1969; Benefits, 1979; Stand We at Last, 1983; Here Today, 1984; Closing, 1987; Daddy's Girls, 1991. Contributions to: New Scientist; Guardian; Women's Studies International Quarterly; Spare Rib; Arts Express. Honour: Fawcett Book Prize, 1985. Membership:

Writer's Guild. Address: c/o A M Heath, 79 St Martins Road, London, WC2N 4AA, England.

FAIRBURN Eleanor M, (Catherine Carfax, Emma Gayle, Elena Lyons), b. 23 Feb 1928, Ireland. Author. m. Brian Fairburn, 1 daughter. Appointments: Past Member, Literary Panel for Northern Arts; Tutor, Practical Writing, University of Leeds Adult Education Centre. Publications: The Green Popinjays, 1962; The White Seahorse, 1964, 3rd edition, 1996; The Golden Hive, 1966; Crowned Ermine, 1968; The Rose in Spring, 1971; White Rose, Dark Summer, 1972; The Sleeping Salamander, 1973, 3rd edition, 1986; The Rose at Harvest End, 1975; Winter's Rose, 1976. As Catherine Carfax: A Silence with Voices, 1969; The Semper Inheritance, 1972; To Die A Little, 1972. As Emma Gayle: Cousin Caroline, 1980; Frenchman's Harvest, 1980. As Elena Lyons: The Haunting of Abbotsgarth, 1980; A Scent of Lilacs, 1982. Biographies (as Eleanor Fairburn): Edith Cavell, 1985; Mary Hornbeck Glyn, 1987; Grace Darling, 1988. Honour:Winner, Mail on Sunday novel-opening competition, 1989. Membership: Middlesbrough Writers Group, president, 1988. Address: 27 Minsterley Drive, Acklam, Middlesbrough, Cleveland, TS5 8QU, England.

FAIRFAX John, b. 9 Nov 1930, London, England. Writer, 2 sons. Publications: The Fifth Horseman of the Apocalypse, 1969; Double Image, 1971; Adrift on the Star Brow of Taliesin, 1974; Bone Harvest Done, 1980; Wild Children, 1985; The Way to Write, 1981; Creative Writing, 1989; Spindrift Lp, 1981; 100 Poems, 1992; The Art of Space CD, 1996; Zuihitsu, 1996. Contributions to: Most major literary magazines. Literary Agent: A D Peters. Address: The Thatched Cottage, Eling, Hermitage, Newbury, Berkshire, RG16 9XR, England.

FAIRFIELD Darrell. See: LARKIN Rochelle.

FAIRLEY John Alexander, b. 15 April 1939, Liverpool, England. Broadcasting Executive; Writer. 3 daughters. Education: MA, Queen's College, Oxford. Appointments: Journalist, Bristol Evening Post, 1963, London Evening Standard, 1964; Producer, BBC Radio, 1965-68; Producer, 1968-78, Director of Programmes, 1984-92, Managing Director, 1992-95, Yorkshire TV; Chairman, ITV Broadcast Board, 1995-. Publications: The Coup, 1975; The Monocled Mutineer (with W Allison), 1975; Arthur C Clarke's Mysterious World, 1980; Great Racehorses in Art, 1984; Chronicles of the Strange and Mysterious, 1987; Racing in Art, 1990; The Cabinet of Curiosities, 1991; A Century of Mysteries, 1993; The Art of the Horse, 1995. Address: 539 Willoughby House, Barbican, London EC2Y 8BN, England.

FALCK (Adrian) Colin, b. 14 July 1934, London, England. University Teacher; Writer. 1 daughter. Education: BA, 1957, MA, 1986, University of Oxford; PhD, 1988, University of London. Appointments: Associate Editor, The Review, 1962-72; Poetry Editor, The New Review, 1974-78; Associate Professor, York College, 1989-. Publications: Backwards into the Smoke, 1973; Poems Since 1900 (with Ian Hamilton), 1975; In This Dark Light, 1978; Robinson Jeffers, Selected Poems, 1987; Myth Truth and Literature, 1989, 2nd edition, 1994; Edna St Vincent Millay, Selected Poems, 1991; Memorabilia, 1992. Contributions to: Many ILiterary and philosophical journals in UK and USA. Address: 20 Thurlow Road, London NW3 5PP, England.

FALDBAKKEN Knut (Robert), b. 31 Aug 1941, Oslo, Norway. Novelist; Playwright. Appointment: Literary Reviewer, Dagbladet, Oslo, 1972-. Publications: The Grey Rainbow, 1967; His Mother's House, 1969; Fairytales, 1970; The Sleeping Prince, 1971; E 18, 1980; The Honeymoon, 1982; Glahn, 1985; Bad Boy, 1988; Forever Yours, 1990; To the End of the World, 1991; Plays: The Bull and the Virgin, 1976; Life with Marilyn, 1987. Honour: Riksmal Prize, 1978. Address: Gyldendal Norsk Forlag, Postboks 6860, St Olavs Plass, 0130 Oslo 1, Norway.

FALKIRK Richard. See: LAMBERT Derek (William).

FALLACI Oriana, b. 29 June 1930, Florence, Italy. Writer; Journalist. Education: Liceo Classico Galileo Galilei; Faculty Medicine, University of Florence, 1946-48. Appointments: Editor, Special Correspondent, Europeo Magazine, Milan, 1958-77; Special Correspondent, Corriere della Sera, Milan. Publications: The Seven Sins of Hollywood, 1958; The Useless Sex (Voyage Around the Woman), 1962; The Egotists, 1965; Penelope at War, (novel), 1966; If the Sun Dies, 1967; Nothing and So Be It, 1972; Interview With History, 1976; Letter to a Child Never Born, (novel), 1977; A Man, (novel), 1979; Inshallah, 1990. Contributions to: Look; Life; Washington Post; New York Times; London Times; Corriere della Sera; Europeo; Der Spiegel; L'Express. Honours: St Vincent Awards for Journalism, 1971, 1973; Bancarella Award, 1972; Honorary LittD, Columbia College, Chicago, 1977; 2 Varieggio Prize Awards, 1979; Hemingway Prize for Literature, 1991; Super Bancarella Prize, 1991; Prix d'Antibes, 1993. Address: c/o RCS Rizzoli Corp, 31 West 57th Street, New York, NY 10019, USA

FALLON Ivan Gregory, b. 26 June 1944, Wexford, Ireland. Deputy Editor. m. Susan Mary Lurring, 1 son, 2 daughters. Education: St Peter's College, Wexford, 1952-62; BBS, Trinity College, Dublin, 1966. Appointments: Irish Times, 1964-66; Thomson Provincial Newspapers, 1966-67; Daily Mirror, 1967-68; Sunday Telegraph, 1968-70; Deputy City Editor, Sunday Express, 1970-71; Sunday Telegraph, 1971-84; Deputy Editor, Sunday Times, 1984-94; Editorial Director, Argus Group, 1994-95; Deputy Chief Executive, Editorial Director, Independent Newspapers Holdings Ltd, 1995-; Director, N Brown Holdings, 1994-, Independent Newspapers Plc, 1995-, Independent Newspapers of South Africa,1996-. Publications: Delorean: The Rise and Fall of a Dream Maker (with James L Strodes), 1983; Takeovers (with James L Strodes), 1987; The Brothers - The Rise of Saatchi and Saatchi, 1988; Billionaire: The Life and Times of Sir James Goldsmith, 1991; Paperchase, 1993; The Player, the Life of Tony O'Reilly, 1994. Memberships: Council of Governors, United Medical and Dental Schools of Guy's and St Thomas' Hospitals, 1985-94, Trustee, Project Trust, 1984-94, Generation Trust, Guy's Hospital, 1985-94; President, Trinity College, Dublin, Business Alumni, London Chapter; Fellow, Royal Society of Arts, 1989; Beefsteak; Political Economy; Rand Club, Johannesburg. Literary Agent: Vivienne Schuster, Curtis Brown. Address: c/o Independent Newspapers Holdings Ltd, PO Box 1014, 47 Saver Street, Johannesburg 2000, South Africa.

FALLON Martin. See: PATTERSON Harry.

FALLON Peter, b. 26 Feb 1951, Osnabruck, Germany (Irish citizen). Editor; Poet. 2 children. Education: BA, 1975, H Dip Ed, 1976, MA, 1979, Trinity College, Dublin. Appointments: Founder, Editor, Gallery Press, Dublin, 1970-; Poet-in-Residence, Deerfield Academy, Massachusetts, 1976-77; International Writer-in-Residence at various Indiana Schools, 1979; Fiction Editor, O'Brien Press, Dublin, 1980-85; Teacher, Contemporary Irish Poetry, School of Irish Studies, Dublin, 1985-89; Writer Fellow, Poet-in-Residence, Trinity College, Dublin, 1994. Publications: Among the Walls, 1971; Co-incidence of Flesh, 1972; The First Affair, 1974; Finding the Dead, 1978; The Speaking Stones, 1978; Winter Work, 1983; The News and Weather, 1987; Penguin Book of Contemporary Irish Poetry (editor, with Derek Mahon), 1990; Editor of prose and poems by Irish writers. Contributions to: Poetry anthologies, periodicals and journals. Honours: Irish Arts Council Bursary, 1981; National Poetry Competition, England, 1982; Meath Merit Award, Arts and Culture, 1987; O'Shaughnessy Poetry Award, 1993. Address: Gallery Press, Loughcrew, Oldcastle, County Meath, Ireland.

FANTHORPE Robert Lionel, b. 9 Feb 1935, Dereham, Norfolk, England. Priest; Author; Broadcaster; Consultant; Lecturer; Tutor. m. Patricia Alice Tooke, 7 Sept 1957, 2 daughters. Education: BA; FIMgt; FCP; Anglican Ordination Certificate. Appointments: Consultant and Festival Co-ordinator, UK Year of Literature and Writing, 1995; Presenter, Fortean TV, Channel 4, 1997. Publications: The Black Lion, 1979; The Holy Grail Revealed, 1982; Life of St Francis, 1988; God in All Things, 1988; Thoughts and Prayers for Troubled Times, 1989; Birds and Animals of the Bible, 1990; Thoughts and Prayers for Lonely Times, 1990; The First Christmas, 1990; Rennes-le-Château, 1992; The Oak Island Mystery, 1995; The Abbot's Kitchen, 1995. Contributions to: Purnells History of World War 1; Las Enigmas, Madrid; The X-Factor. Honours: Electrical Development Association Diploma, 1958; Holder of Four World Championships for Professional Authors: Prose, Drama, Poetry and Autobiography; Finalist, Bard of the Year, Poetry Digest. Memberships: MENSA; Society of Authors; Welsh Academy. Address: Rivendell, 48 Claude Road, Roath Cardiff, Wales.

FANTHORPE Ursula Askham, b. 22 July 1929, Kent, England. Writer; Poet. Education: BA, MA, Oxford University. Appointments: Writer in Residence, St Martin's College, Lancaster, 1983-85; Northern Arts Literary Fellow, Universities of Durham and Newcastle, 1987. Publications: Side Effects, 1978; Standing To, 1982; Voices Off, 1984; Selected Poems, 1986; A Watching Brief, 1987; Neck Verse, 1992;

Safe as Houses, 1995; Penguin Modern Poets 6, 1996. Contributions to: Times Literary Supplement; Encounter; Outposts; Firebird; Bananas; South West Review; Quarto; Tribune; Country LIfe; Use of English; Poetry Review; Poetry Book Society Supplement; Writing Women; Spectator; BBC. Honours: Travelling Scholarship, Society of Authors, 1983; Hawthornden Scholarship, 1987; Fellow, Royal Society of Literature; Arts Council Writers Award, 1994; Chomondeley Award, Society of Authors, 1995; Honorary DLitt, UWE; National Poetry Competition, judge, 1996. Membership: PEN. Address: Culverhay House, Wotton-under-Edge, Gloucestershire GL12 7LS, England.

FARAH Nuruddin, b. 24 Nov 1945, Baidoa, Somalia. Writer. m. (1), 1 son, 1 daughter, (2) Amina Mama, 24 July 1992. Education: Panjab University, 1966-70; University of London, 1974-75; Essex University, 1975-76. Appointments: Writer-in-Residence, University of Jos, Nigeria, 1981-83, University of Minnesota, 1989, Brown University, 1991; Professor, Makerere University, Uganda, 1989-91. Publications: From a Crooked Rib, 1970; A Naked Needle, 1976; Sardines, 1981; Close Sesame, 1983; Maps, 1986; Gifts, 1992. Contributions to: Guardian; New African; Transition Magazine; New York Times; Observer; Times Literary Supplement. Honours: English Speaking Literary Award, 1980; Deutscher Akademischer Austauschdienst Residency, 1990; Tycholsky Award, 1991; Premio Cavour Award, 1992; Zimbabwe Annual Award, 1993. Membership: Union of Writers of the African People. Address: c/o Rogers, Coleridge & White, 20 Powis Mews, London W11 1JN, England.

FARELY Alison. See: POLAND Dorothy Elisabeth Hayward.

FARIAS Victor, b. 4 May 1940, Santiago, Chile. Philosopher; Writer. m. Teresa Zurita, 31 Dec 1960, 1 son, 2 daughters. Education: Catholic University, Santiago, 1957-60; Dr Phil, University of Freiburg, 1967; Dr Hab, Free University, Berlin, 1985. Appointment: Free University, Berlin. Publications: Sein und Gegenstand, 1967; Los Manuscriptos de Melquiades, 1981; La Estetica de la Agresion: Doálogo de J L Borges e Jünger, 1986; Heidegger et le Nazisme, 1987; Logica, Lecciones de Verano de Martin en el legado de Helene Weiss, 1991; La Metaficicia del Arrabel: El tamaño de mi Esperanza, un Libro Desconocido de Jorge Luis Borges, 1992; Las Actas Secretas, 1994. Address: c/o Free University, Rudesheimerstrasse 54-56, 14197 Berlin, Germany.

FARICY Robert, b. 29 Aug 1926, St Paul, Minnesota, USA. Professor. Education: BS, USNA, 1949; PhL, 1954, MA, 1955, St Louis University; STL, Lyon-Fourvière University, 1963; STD, Catholic University of America, 1966. Publications: The Spirituality of Teilhard de Chardin, 1981; Wind and Sea Obey Him, 1983; Seeking Jesus in Contemplation and Discernment, 1983; The Lord's Dealing: The Primacy of the Feminine, 1988; Lord Jesus, Teach Me To Pray (with L Rooney), 1989. Contributions to: Over 100 to many theological and philosophical journals. Address: Gregorian University, Piazza della Pilotta 4, 00187 Rome, Italy.

FARLEY Carol, b. 20 Dec 1936, Ludington, Michigan, USA. Children's Book Writer. m. 21 Jun 1954, 1 son, 3 daughters. Education: Western Michigan University, 1956; BA, Michigan State University, 1980; MA, Children's Literature, Central Michigan University, 1983. Publications: Mystery of the Fog Man, 1974; The Garden is Doing Fine, 1976; Mystery in the Ravine, 1976; Mystery of the Melted Diamonds, 1985; Case of the Vanishing Villain, 1986; Case of the Lost Look Alike, 1988; Korea, Land of the Morning Calm, 1991; King Sejong's Secret, 1996; A Very Good Story, 1997. Contributions to: The Writer; Society of Children's Book Writer's Bulletin; Cricket; Disney Adventures; Challenge; Spider; Pockets. Honours: Best Book of Year, Child Study Association, 1976; Best Juvenile Book by Mid-West Writer, Friends of the Writer, 1978; IRA/CBC Children's Choice Book, 1987. Memberships: Mystery Writers of America; Authors Guild: Children's Book Guild; Society of Children's Book Writers; Chicago Childrens Reading Round Table. Address: 8574 West Higgins Lake Road, Roscommon, MI 48653, USA.

FARMER Beverley, b. 1941, Australia. Novelist. Publications: Alone, 1980; Short stories: Milk, 1983; Home Time, 1985; A Body of Water: A Year's Notebook, 1990; Place of Birth, 1990; The Seal Woman, 1992; The House in the Light, 1995; Collected Stories, 1996. Address: c/o University of Queensland Press, PO Box 42, St Lucia, Queensland 4067, Australia.

FARMER David Hugh, b. 30 Jan 1923, Ealing, London, England. Lecturer; Reader; Writer. m. Pauline Ann Widgery, 1966, 2 sons. Education: Linacre College, Oxford. Appointments: Lecturer, 1967-77, Reader, 1977-88, Reading University. Publications: Life of St Hugh of Lincoln, 1961, 2nd edition, 1985; The Monk of Farne, 1962; The Rule of St Benedict, 1968; The Oxford Dictionary of Saints, 1978, 2nd edition, 1992; Dizionario dei Santi, 1989; Benedict's Disciples, 1980, 2nd edition, 1995; The Age of Bede, 1983, 4th edition, 1997; St Hugh of Lincoln, 1985, 2nd edition, 1987; Bede's Ecclesiastical History, 1990; Christ Crucified and Other Meditations, 1994. Contributions to: Dictionnaire D'Histoire Ecclesiastique; New Catholic Encyclopedia; Bibliotheca Sanctorum; Lexikon der Christlichen Ikonographie; Studia Monastica; Studia Anselmiana; Journal of Ecclesiastical History; The Tablet. Honours: FSA, 1962; FRHistS, 1967. Address: 26 Swanston Field, Whitchurch, Reading, Berks RG8 7HP, England.

FARMER James, b. 12 Jan 1920, Marshall, Texas, USA. Civil Rights Leader; Professor; Writer. m. Lula Peterson, 21 May 1949, dec May 1977, 2 daughters. Education: BS, Wiley College, Marshall, Texas, 1938; BD, Howard University, 1941. Appointments: Founder-National Chairman, 1942-44, 1950, National Director, 1961-66, Congress of Racial Equality; Race Relations Secretary, Fellowship of Reconciliation, 1941-45; Organizer, Upholsterer's International Union of North America, 1945-47; Student Field Secretary, League of Industrial Democracy, 1950-54; International Representative, State, County, and Municipal Employees Union, 1954-59; Program Director, National Association for the Advancement of Colored People, 1959-61; Leader, Congress of Racial Equality Freedom Ride, 1961; Professor of Social Welfare, Lincoln University, Pennsylvania, 1966-67; Adjunct professor, New York University, 1969; Assistant Secretary for Administration, US Department of Health, Education, and Welfare, Washington, DC, 1969-70; Executive Director, Coalition of American Public Employees, 1977-82; Visiting Professor, Antioch University, 1983-84; Distinguished Visiting Professor, 1985-94, Distinguished College Professor, 1994-, Mary Washington College, Fredericksburg, Virginia. Publications: Freedom-When, 1965; Lay Bare the Heart: An Autobiography, 1985. Contributions to: Many publications. Honours: Omega Psi Phi Awards, 1961, 1963; John Dewey Award, League of Industrial Democarcy, 1962; Distinguished Postgraduate Achievement Alumni Award, Howard Unversity, 1964. Memberships: American Civil Liberties Union; Americans for Democratic Action; Black World Foundation; Friends of the Earth; League of Industrial Democracy. Address: c/o Mary Washington College, Frdericksburg, VA 22401, USA.

FARMER Penelope (Jane), b. 14 June 1939, Westerham, Kent, England. Writer. m. (1) Michael John Mockridge, 16 Aug 1962, div 1977, 1 son, 1 daughter, (2) Simon Shorvon, 20 Jan 1984. Education: Degree in History, St Anne's College, Oxford, 1960; Diploma in Social Studies, Bedford College, London, 1962. Publications: Novels: Standing in the Shadow, 1984; Eve: Her Story, 1985; Away from Home, 1987; Glasshouses, 1988; Snakes and Ladders, 1993. Children's Books: The China People, 1960; The Summer Birds, 1962, revised edition, 1985; The Magic Stone, 1964; The Saturday Shillings, 1965; The Seagull, 1965; Emma in Winter, 1966; Charlotte Sometimes, 1969, revised edition, 1985; Dragonfly Summer, 1971; A Castle of Bone, 1972; William and Mary, 1974; Heracles, 1975; August the Fourth, 1975; Year King, 1977; The Coal Train, 1977; Beginnings: Creation Myths of the World (editor), 1979; The Runaway Train, 1980; Thicker Than Water, 1989; Stone Croc, 1991; Penelope, 1994; Twin Trouble, 1996. Other: Anthology: Two: The Book of Twins and Doubles, 1996; Short stories; Radio and television scripts. Contributions to: Periodicals. Honours: American Library Association Notable Book, 1962; Carnegie Medal Commendation, 1963. Memberships: PEN; Society of Authors. Address: 12 Dalling Road, London W6 0JB, England.

FARRELL M J. See: **KEANE Molly.**

FARRELL Pamela Barnard, b. 11 Oct 1943, Mt Holly, New Jersey, USA. Writer; Poet; Teacher. m. Joseph Donald Farrell, 1 Sept 1968. Education: BA, English, Radford College, 1965; MS, English, Radford University, 1975; MA, Writing, Northeastern University, 1988. Appointments: Editor, The Grapevine, Northeastern University Writing Progam Newsletter, 1986-90; Poetry Teacher/Consultant, Geraldine R Dodge Foundation, 1986-; Editorial Board, Computers and Composition, 1987-90; The Writing Center Journal, 1988-; Caldwell Chair of Composition, The McCallie School, 1991- Publications: Waking Dreams, poems, 1989; The High School Writing Center:

Establishing and Maintaining One, 1989; Waking Dreams II (poems), 1990; National Directory of Writing Centres, 1992. Contributions to: Anthologies, books, and journals. Honours: Woodrow Wilson National Fellowship Foundation Fellow, 1985; Golden Poet Award, 1986. Memberships: Modern Language Association; National Writing Center Association, President; Assembly of Computer in English, treasurer. Address: The McCallie School, 2850 McCallie Avenue, Chattanooga, TN 37404, USA.

FARRINGTON David Philip, b. 7 Mar 1944, Ormskirk, Lancashire, England. Psychologist; Criminologist. m. Sally Chamberlain, 30 July 1966, 3 daughters. Education: BA, 1966, MA, 1970, PhD, 1970, Cambridge University. Publications: Who Becomes Delinquent, 1973; The Delinquent Way of Life, 1977; Psychology, Law and Legal Processes, 1979; Behaviour Modification with Offenders, 1979; Abnormal Offenders, Delinquency and the Criminal Justice System, 1982; Prediction in Criminology, 1985; Reactions to Crime, 1985; Aggression and Dangerousness, 1985; Understanding and Controlling Crime, 1986; Human Development and Criminal Behaviour, 1991; Offenders and Victims, 1992; Integrating Individual and Ecological Aspects of Crime, 1993; Psychological Explanations of Crime, 1994; Building A Safer Society, 1995; Understanding and Preventing Youth Crime, 1996. Contributions to: Over 180 Articles to Journals. Honours: Sellin Glueck Award for International Contributions to Criminology, 1984. Memberships: British Society of Criminology; British Psychological Society; European Association of Psychology and Law; American Society of Criminology; American Psychological Association; Association for Child Psychology and Psychiatry. Address: Institute of Criminology, 7 West Road, Cambridge CB3 9DT, England.

FARROW James S. See: **TUBB E(dwin) C(harles).**

FARSON Daniel Negley, b. 8 Jan 1927, London, England. Writer; Journalist; Photographer. Education: BA, Pembroke College, Cambridge. Appointments: Founder-Editor, Panorama; Youngest Lobby Correspondent, House of Commons Central Press; Television Interviewer; Photographer. Publications: Jack the Ripper, 1972; The Man Who Wrote Dracula, 1975; Henry, Biography of Henry Williamson, 1982; Soho in the Fifties, 1987; Sacred Monsters, 1988; Escapades, 1989; Gallery, 1990; With Gilbert & George in Moscow, 1991; Limehouse Days, 1991; The Gilded Gutter Life of Francis Bacon, 1993; A Dry Ship to the Mountains, 1993; Never a Normal Man, (autobiography), 1997; Not Before Time, (major photographic exhibition), 1997. Contributions to: Mail on Sunday; Sunday Today; Daily Telegraph. Membership: London Library. Literary Agent: Bill Hamilton, A M Heath, 79 St Martin's Lane, London WC2, England. Address: 129 Irsha Street, Appledore, North Devon, England.

FATCHEN Maxwell Edgar, b. 3 Aug 1920, Adelaide, South Australia. Author. m. Jean Wohlers, 15 May 1942, 2 sons, 1 daughter. Appointments: Journalist, Feature Writer, Adelaide News, 1946-55; Special Writer, 1955, 1981-84, Literary Editor, 1971-81, The Advertiser. Publications: The River Kings, 1966; Conquest of the River, 1970; The Spirit Wind, 1973; Chase Through the Night, 1977; Closer to the Stars, 1981; Wry Rhymes, 1987; A Country Christmas, 1990; Tea for Three, 1994. Contributions to: Denver Post; Sydney Sun; Regional South Australian Histories. Honours: Commendation, 1967; Runner Up, 1974, Australian Childrens Book of Year; Member of the Order of Australia, 1980; Honour Award, 1988; Advance Australia Award for Literature, 1991; AMP-Walkley Award for Journalism, 1996. Memberships: Australian Society of Authors; Australian Fellowship of Writers; South Australian Writers Centre; Australian Journalists Association. Literary Agent: John Johnson, London, EC1R 0HT. Address: 15 Jane Street Box 6, Smithfield, South Australia 5114, Australia.

FAULK Odie, b. 26 Aug 1933, Winnsboro, Texas, USA. Professor of History Emeritus; Writer. m. Laura Ella Whalen, 22 Aug 1959, 1 son, 1 daughter. Education: BS, 1958, MA, 1960, PhD, 1962, Texas Tech University. Appointments: Professor Texas A & M University, 1962, University of Arizona, 1963; Professor of History, 1968-88, Professor Emeritus, 1988-, Oklahoma State University. Publications: Author, co-author, or editor of over 50 books. Contributions to: Over 100 scholarly history journals. Honour: Best Non-Fiction Book of the Year, Southwestern Border Library Association, 1973. Memberships: Oklahoma Historical Society; Texas State Historical Association, fellow; Westerners International. Address: 5008 Sturbridge, Temple, TX 76502, USA.

FAUST Naomi, b. Salisbury, North Carolina, USA. Educator; Author; Poet. m. Roy M Faust. Education: AB, Bennett College; MA, University of Michigan; PhD, New York University. Career: Elementary Teacher, Public School System, Gaffney, South Carolina; English Teacher, Atkins High School, Winston-Salem, North Carolina; Instructor of English, Bennett College and Southern University, Scotlandville, Louisiana; Professor of English, Morgan State University, Baltimore, Maryland; Teacher, Greensboro Public Schools and New York City Public Schools; Professor of English/Education, Queens College of the City University of New York. Publications: Discipline and the Classroom Teacher, 1977. Books of Poems: Poetry: Speaking in Verse, 1974; All Beautiful Things, 1983; And I Travel by Rhythms and Words, 1990. Contributions to: Anthologies and magazines. Honours: Alpha Epsilon; Teacher-Author of Year by Teacher-Writer; International Eminent Poet Award, International Poets Academy, 1987. Memberships: New York Poetry Forum; World Poetry Society Intercontinental; National Women's Book Association; National Council of Teachers of English; American Association of University Professors. Address: 112-01 175th Street, Jamaica, NY 11433, USA.

FAWCETT Catherine. See: COOKSON Catherine (Ann).

FAWKES Richard Brian, b. 31 July 1944, Camberley, Surrey, England. Writer; Film Director. m. Cherry Elizabeth Cole, 17 Apr 1971, 2 sons. Education: BA, Honours, St David's University College, 1967. Publications: The Last Corner of Arabia (with Michael Darlow), 1976; Fighting for a Laugh, 1978; Dion Boucicault - A Biography, 1979; Notes from a Low Singer (with Michael Langdon), 1982; Welsh National Opera, 1986; Plays for TV, Radio and Stage; Documentary Film Scripts; Book and Lyrics for Musical, The Misfortunes of Elphin, 1988. Contributions to: Classical Music; Sunday Times; Observer; She; Music and Musicians; Various other journals and magazines. Honour: West Midlands Arts Association Bursary, 1978. Memberships: Society of Authors; ACTT; Society for Theatre Research. Address: 5-8 Lower John Street, Golden Square, London W1R 4HA, England.

FAYER Steve, b. 11 Mar 1935, Brooklyn, New York, USA. Writer. Education: BA honours in English Literature, University of Pennsylvania, 1956. Appointments: Series Writer, Eyes on the Prize I, 6 1-hour documentaries for Public Broadcasting Service, 1987; Series Writer, Eyes on the Prize II, 8 1-hour documentaries for Public Broadcasting Service, 1990; Series Writer, The Great Depression, 7 1-hour documentaries for Public Broadcasting Service, 1993; Also Writer, Frederick Douglass - When The Lion Wrote History, 1994; Co-Writer, Malcolm X: Make It Plain, 1994. Publications: Voices of Freedom, 1990. Honours: Emmy Award, National Academy of Television Arts and Sciences, 1987. Membership: Writers Guild of America. Address: 189A Bay State Road, Boston, MA 02215, USA.

FEDERMAN Raymond, b. 15 May 1928, Paris, France. Novelist; Poet. m. Erica Hubscher, 14 Sept 1960, 1 daughter. Education: BA, Columbia University, USA, 1957; MA, 1958, PhD, 1963, University of California, Los Angeles. Publications: Novels: Double or Nothing, 1971; Amer Eldorado, 1974; Take It or Leave It, 1976; The Voice in the Closet, 1979; The Twofold Vibration, 1982; Smiles on Washington Square, 1985; To Whom It May Concern, 1990. Criticism: Journey to Chaos, 1965; Samuel Beckett, 1970; Surfiction, (essays), 1976. Poetry: Among the Beasts, 1967. Contributions to: Paris Review; Partisan Review; Chicago Review; The Quarterly; Mississippi Review; Fiction International Caliban. Honours: Guggenheim Fellowship, 1967; Frances Steloff Fiction Prize, 1971; American Book Award, 1986; Distinguished Faculty Professor, State University of New York, 1990. Memberships: PEN American Center; Board of Editors, Fiction Collective. Address: 46 Four Seasons West, Eggertsville, NY 14226, USA.

FEIFFER Jules (Ralph), b. 26 Jan 1929, New York, New York, USA. Cartoonist; Writer. m. Judith Sheftel, 1961, 1 daughter. Education: Art Students League; Pratt Institute. Appointments: Contributing cartoonist, Village Voice, New York City, 1956-; Cartoons nationally syndicated in USA, 1959-. Publications: Sick, Sick, Sick, 1959; Passionella and Other Stories, 1960; The Explainers, 1961; Boy, Girl, Boy, Girl, 1962; Hold Me!, 1962; Harry, The Rat With Women (novel), 1963; Feiffer's Album, 1963; The Unexpurgated Memoirs of Bernard Mergendeiler, 1965; The Great Comic Book Heroes, 1967; Feiffer's Marriage Manual, 1967; Pictures at a Prosecution, 1971; Ackroyd (novel), 1978; Tantrum, 1980; Jules Feiffer's America: From Eisenhower to Reagan, 1982; Marriage is an Invasion of Privacy, 1984; Feiffer's Children, 1986. Other: Plays and screenplays. Honours:

Academy Award for Animated Cartoon, Munro, 1961; Special George Polk Memorial Award, 1962. Address: c/o Universal Press Syndicate, 4400 Johnson Drive, Fairway, KS 66205, USA.

FEIKEMA Feike. See: MANFRED Frederick Feikema.

FEINBERG Joan Miriam, (Joan Schuchman), b. 13 Oct 1934, Far Rockaway, New York, USA. Freelance Writer. m. Arnold I Feinberg, 4 Oct 1986, 2 sons. Education: Brooklyn College, 1952-54; BA, 1970, University of Minnesota. Publications: Astrology: Science or Hoax?, 1978; Help for Your Hyperactive Child, 1978; Two Places to Sleep, 1979; Broken Dreams, 1992. Contributions to: Today's Family; Conquest Magazine; Horoscope Guide; World Book and Travel; New York Times Syndicate; International Travel News. Memberships: Conservatory of American Letters; Women in Communication; Florida Freelance Writers Association; International Women's Writer's Guild. Address: 4725 Excelsior Boulevard, Suite 300, Minneapolis, MN 55416, USA.

FEINBERG Joel, b. 19 Oct 1926, Detroit, Michigan, USA. Professor of Philosophy and Law; Writer. m. Betty Grey Sowers, 29 May 1955, 1 son, 1 daughter. Education: BA, 1949, MA, 1951, PhD, 1957, University of Michigan. Appointments: Instructor, 1955-57, Assistant Professor, 1957-62, Brown University; Assistant Professor, 1962-64, Associate Professor, 1964-66, Princeton University; Professor, University of California at Los Angeles, 1966-67; Professor, 1967-77, Chairman, Department of Philosophy, 1971-77, Rockefeller University; Professor, 1977-, Head, 1978-81, Acting Head, 1983-84, Department of Philosophy, Professor of Philosophy and Law, 1985-, Regents Professor of Philosophy and Law, 1988-94, Regents Professor Emeritus, 1994-, University of Arizona; Numerous visiting appointments. Publications: Reason and Responsibilty (editor), 1965, 9th edition, 1995; Moral Concepts (editor), 1970; Doing and Deserving: Essays in the Theory of Responsibilty, 1970, revised edition, 1974; Social Philosophy, 1973; The Problem of Abortion (editor), 1973, 2nd edition, 1983; Philosophy of Law (editor with Hyman Gross), 1975, 5th edition, 1994; Moral Philosophy: Classic Texts and Contemporary Problems (editor with Henry West), 1977; Philosophy and the Human Condition (editor with Tom L Beauchamp and William T Blackstone), 1980, 2nd edition, 1988; Rights, Justice, and the Bounds of Liberty, 1980; The Moral Limits of the Criminal Law, Vol I, Harm to others, 1984, Vol II, Offense to Others, 1985, Vol III, Harm to Self, 1986, Vol IV, Harmless Wrongdoing, 1988; Freedom and Fulfilment, 1992. Contributions to: Reference works, books, and professional journals. Honours: Fellow, Center for Advanced Study in the Behavioral Sciences, Stanford, 1960-61; Liberal Arts Fellow, Harvard Law School, 1963-64; Guggenheim Fellowship, 1974-75; National Endowment for the Humanities Fellowship, 1977; Rockefeller Foundation Fellowship, 1981-82; Romanell-Phi Beta Kappa Professorship in Philosophy, 1989-90. Memberships: American Academy of Arts and Sciences, Fellow; American Philosophical Association; American Society for Political and Legal Philosophy, president, 1989-92; Council for Philosophical Studies. Address: 5322 North Via Entrada, Tucson, AZ 85718, USA.

FEINSTEIN (Allan) David, b. 22 Dec 1946, Brooklyn, New York, USA. Psychologist. m. Donna Eden, 7 Oct 1984. Education: BA, Whittier College, 1968; MA, US International University, 1970; PhD, Union Institute, 1973. Publications: Personal Mythology, 1988; Rituals for Living and Dying, 1990; The Mythic Path, 1997; Serenade at the Doorway, (album), 1991. Contributions to: Common Boundary; Magical Blend; Psychotherapy; American Journal of Orthopsychiatry; American Journal of Hypnosis. Honour: William James Award, 1968. Memberships: American Psychological Association; Association for Humanistic Psychology. Address: 777 East Main Street, Ashland, OR 97520, USA.

FEINSTEIN Elaine, b. 24 Oct 1930, Bootle, Lancashire, England. Education: Newnham College, Cambridge, 1952. Appointments: Editorial Staff, Cambridge University Press, 1960-62; Lecturer, Bishops Stortford College, 1963-66; Assistant Lecturer, University of Essex, 1967-70. Publications: In a Green Eye, 1966; The Circle, 1970; The Magic Apple Tree, 1971; At the Edge, 1972; The Celebrants and Other Poems, The Glass Alembic, 1973; The Children of the Rose, 1974; The Ecstasy of Miriam Garner, 1976; Some Unease and Angles, 1977; The Shadow Master, Three Russian Poets, 1978; The Silent Areas, The Feast of Euridice, 1980; The Survivors, 1982; The Border, 1984; Bessie Smith, 1985; A Captive Lion: The Life of Marina Tsvetayeva, 1987; Mother's Girl, 1988; All You Need, 1989; Verse,

City Music, 1990. Address: c/o Hutchinson Publishing Group Ltd, 62-65 Chandos Place, London WC2N 4NW, England.

FEKETE John, b. 7 Aug 1946, Budapest, Hungary. Professor of English and Cultural Studies. Education: BA with Honours, English Literature, 1968, MA, English Literature, 1969, McGill University; PhD, Cambridge University, 1973. Appointments: Visiting Assistant Professor, English, McGill University, Montreal, Quebec, 1973-74; Associate Editor, Telos, 1974-84; Visiting Assistant Professor, Humanities, York University, Toronto, Ontario, 1975-76; Assistant Professor, 1976-78, Associate Professor, 1978-84, Professor, English, Cultural Studies, 1984-, Trent University, Peterborough, Ontario. Publications: The Critical Twilight: Explorations in the Ideology of Anglo-American Literary Theory from Eliot to McLuhan, 1978; The Structural Allegory: Reconstructive Encounters With the New French Thought, 1984; Life After Postmodernism: Essays on Culture and Value, 1987; Moral Panic: Biopolitics Rising, 1994. Contributions to: Editorial contributor to Canadian Journal of Political and Social Theory; Canadian Journal of Communications; Science-Fiction Studies. Address: 181 Wallis Drive, Peterborough, Ontario K9J 6C4, Canada.

FELDMAN Alan Grad, b. 16 Mar 1945, New York, New York, USA. Writer; Poet; Teacher. m. Nanette Hass, 22 Oct 1972, 1 son, 1 daughter. Education: AB, Columbia College, 1966; MA, Columbia University, 1969; PhD, State University of New York, Buffalo, 1973. Publications: The Household, 1966; The Happy Genius, 1978; Frank O'Hara, 1978; The Personals, 1982; Lucy Mastermind, 1985; Anniversary, 1992. Contributions to: New Yorker; Atlantic; Kenyon Review; Mississippi Review; Ploughshares; North American Review; Threepenny Review; Boston Review; Tendril; College English. Honours: Award for Best Short Story in a College Literary Magazine, Saturday Review-National Student Association, 1965; Elliston Book Award for Best Book of Poems by a Small Press in US, for The Happy Genius, 1978. Address: 399 Belknap Road, Framingham, MA 01701, USA.

FELDMAN Gerald D(onald), b. 24 April 1937, New York, New York, USA. Professor of History; Writer. m. (1), 1 son, 1 daughter, (2) Norma von Ragenfeld, 30 Nov 1983. Education: BA, Columbia College, 1958; MA, 1959, PhD, 1964, Harvard University. Appointments: Assistant Professor, 1963-68, Associate Professor, 1968-70, Professor of History, 1970-, Director, Center for German and European Studies, 1994-, University of California at Berkeley. Publications: Army, Industry and Labor in Germany, 1914-1918, 1966; Iron and Steel in the German Inflation, 1916-1923, 1977; Industrie und Inflation: Studien und Dokumente zur Politik der deutschen Unternehmer 1916 bis 1923 (with Heidrun Homburg), 1977; Vom Weltkrieg zur Weltwirtschaftskrise: Studien zur deutschen Wirtschafts-und Sozialgeschichte 1914-1932, 1984; Industrie und Gewerkschaften 1918-1924 Die überforderte Zentralarbeitsgmeinscahft (with Irmgard Steinisch), 1985; The Great Disorder: Politics, Economics, and Society in the German Inflation, 1914-1924, 1993. Editor: German Imperialism, 1914-1918, 1972; A Documentary History of Modern Europe (with Thomas G Barnes), 4 volumes, 1972; Historische Prozesse der deutschen Inflation 1914-1924 (with Otto Büsch), 1978; The German Inflation Reconsidered: A Preliminary Balance (with Carl-Ludwig Holtfrerich, Gerhard A Ritter, and Peter-Christian Witt), 1984; Die Nachwirkungen der Inflation auf die deutsche Geschichte 1924-1933 (with Elizabeth Müller-Luckner), 1985; Die Anpassung and die Inflation/The Adaption to Inflation (with Carl-Ludwig Holtfrerich, Gerhard A Ritter, and Peter-Christian Witt), 1986; Konsequenzen des Inflation/Consequences of Inflation (with Carl-Ludwig Holtfrerich Gerhard A Ritter and Peter-Christian Witt), 1989; Arbeiter, Unternehmer und Staat im Bergbau: Industrielle Beziehungen im internationalen Vergleich (with Klaus Tenfelde), 1989, English translation as Workers, Owners and Politics in Coal Mining: An International Comparison of Industrial Relations, 1990; The Evolution of Modern Financial Institutions in the Twentieth Century: Proceedings: Eleventh International Economic History congress: Milan, September 1994 (with Ulf Olsson, Michael D Bordo, and Youssef Cassis), 1994; The Evolution of Financial Institutions and Markets in Twentieth-Century Europe (with Youssef Cassis and Ulf Olsson), 1995; How to Write the History of a Bank (with Martin M G Fase and Manfred Pohl), 1995. Contributions to: Many scholarly books and journals. Honours: American Council of Learned Societies Fellowships 1966-67, 1970-71; Guggenheim Fellowship, 1973-74; National Endowment for the Humanities Fellowship, 1977-78; German Marshall Fund Fellow, 1981-82; Rockefeller Foundation Center Residency, Bellagio, Italy,

1987; Wisenschaftskolleg, Berlin, 1987-88; Woodrow Wilson Center Fellow, 1991-92; Book Prize, Conference Group for Central European History, American Historical Association, 1995; DAAD Book Prize, German Studies Association, 1995; Co-Winner, Financial Times/Booz-Allen & Hamilton Business-Award, 1995. Address: c/o University of California at Berkeley, Department of History, Berkeley, CA 94720, USA. .

FELDMAN Irving (Mordecai), b. 22 Sept 1928, Brooklyn, New York, USA. Professor of English; Poet. m. Carmen Alvarez del Olmo, 1955, 1 son. Education: BS, City College, New York City, 1950; MA, Columbia University, 1953. Appointments: Teacher, University of Puerto Rico, Rio Piedras, 1954-56, University of Lyons, France, 1957-58, Kenyon College, Gambier, Ohio, 1958-64; Professor of English, State University of New York at Buffalo, 1964-. Publications: Poetry: Work and Days and Other Poems, 1961; The Pripet Marshes and Other Poems, 1965; Magic Papers and Other Poems, 1970; Lost Originals, 1972; Leaping Clear, 1976; New and Selected Poems, 1979; Teach Me, Dear Sister, and Other Poems, 1983; All of us Here and Other Poems, 1986. Other: The Life and Letters, 1994. Honours: Kovner Award, Jewish Book Council of America, 1962; Ingram Merrill Foundation Grant, 1963; American Academy of Arts and Letters Grant, 1973; Guggenheim Fellowship, 1973; Creative Artists Public Service Grant, 1980; Academy of American Poets Fellowship, 1986; John D and Catherine T MacArthur Foundation Fellowship, 1992. Address: c/o Department of English, State University of New York at Buffalo, Buffalo, NY 14260, USA.

FELDMAN Paula R, b. 4 July 1948, Washington, District of Columbia, USA. University Professor; Writer. Education: BA, Bucknell University, 1970; MA 1971, PhD 1974, Northwestern University. Appointments: Assistant Professor, English, 1974-79, Associate Professor, English, 1979-89, Professor, English, 1989-, Director, Graduate Studies in English, 1991-93, University of South Carolina, Columbia. Publications: The Microcomputer and Business Writing (with David Byrd and Phyllis Fleishel), 1986; The Journals of Mary Shelley (editor with Diana Scott-Kilvert), 2 volumes, 1987; The Wordworthy Computer: Classroom and Research Applications in Language and Literature (with Buford Norman), 1987; Romantic Women Writers: Voices and Countervoices, (editor with Theresa Kelley), 1995; British Women Poets of the Romantic Era: 1770-1840, 1996. Contributions to: Studies in English Literature; Papers of the Bibliographical Society of America; Approaches to Teaching Shelley's Frankenstein, 1990; Blake: An Illustrated Quarterly, 1994. Address: Department of English, University of South Carolina, Columbia, SC 29208, USA.

FELICE. See: DOMARADZKI Théodore Felix.

FELICE Cynthia, b. 10 Oct 1942, Chicago, Illinois, USA. Writer. m. Robert E Felice Sr, 23 Dec 1961, 2 sons. Publications: Godsfire, 1978; The Sunbound, 1981; Water Witch (with Connie Willis), 1982; Eclipses, 1983; Downtime, 1985; Double Nocturne, 1986; Light Raid (with Connie Willis), 1988. Contributions to: Anthologies and periodicals. Membership: Science Fiction Writers Association. Address: 5025 Park Vista Boulevard, Colorado Springs, CO 80918, USA.

FELINTO Marilene Barbosa de Lima, b. 5 Dec 1957, Recife, Brazil. Writer; Journalist. Education: Bachelor in Portuguese and English Language, Brazilian, American and English Literatures, University of Sao Paulo, 1981. Appointments: Visiting Writer in the USA, by University of California in Berkeley, 1992; Haus der Kulturen der Welt, 1994. Publications: As Mulheres de Tijucopapo (novel), 1982, English translation as The Women of Tijucopapo, 1992, Dutch translation as De Vrouwen van Tijucopapo, 1997; O Lago Encantado de Grongonzo (novel), 1987; Postcard, (short stories), 1991; Others: Outros Herois e Esse Graciliano (essay), 1983. Honour: Jabuti prize in literature, Brazil, 1983. Address: Av Afonso Mariano Fagundes, 472/32 04054-000 Sao Paulo SP Brazil.

FENG Jicai, b. 9 Feb 1942, Tianjin, China. Novelist. Education: Graduate of High School, Tanggu, Tianjin. Publications: The Boxers, 1977; Flowering Branch Road, 1979; A Letter, 1980; The Magic Lantern, 1981; The Carved Pipe, 1981; Man in the Fog, 1983; Into the Storm, 1983; The Miraculous Pigtail, 1984; The Tall Woman and her Short Husband, 1984; Chrysanthemums, 1985; Thanks to Life, 1985; Three-Inch Golden Lotus, 1986; The Eight Diagrams of Yin and Yang,

1988; Voices from the Whirlwind, 1991. Other: Radio and television plays. Address: 801 Yun-Feng-Lou A, Nanjing Road, Tianjin, China.

FENNARIO David, b. 26 April 1947, Verdun, Quebec, Canada. Playwright. m. Elizabeth Fennario, 1976, 1 child. Education: Dawson College, Montreal, 1969-71. Appointments: Playwright-in-Residence, Centaur Theatre, Montreal, 1973-; Co-Founder, Cultural Workers Association. Publications: Plays: On The Job, 1976; Nothing to Lose, 1977; Without a Parachute, 1978; Balconville, 1980; Changes, 1980; Moving, 1983; Joe Beef, 1991; Doctor Thomas Weill Cream, 1994; Placeville Marie, 1996. Honours: Canada Council Grant, 1973; Chalmers Award, 1976, 1979; Prix Pauline Julien, 1986. Membership: International Socialist. Address: 627 Beatty, Verdun, Quebec H4H 1X9, Canada.

FENNELLY Tony (Antonia), b. 25 Nov 1945, Orange, New Jersey, USA. Author. m. James Richard Catoire, 24 Dec 1972. Education: BA, Drama and Communications, University of New Orleans, 1976. Publications: The Glory Hole Murders, 1985; The Closet Hanging, 1987; Kiss Yourself Goodbye, 1989; Der Hippie in Der Wand, 1992; Hurenglanz, 1993; 1(900) D-E-A-D, 1997. Honour: Edgar Allan Poe Special Award, Mystery Writers of America, 1986. Memberships: Mystery Writers of America; Authors Guild; International Association of Crime Writers; Sisters in Crime. Address: 921 Clouet Street, New Orleans, LA 70117, USA.

FENNER Carol Elizabeth, b. 1929, USA. Children's Fiction Writer; Lecturer; Instructor. m. Jiles B Williams. Publications: Tigers in the Cellar, 1963; Christmas Tree on the Mountain, 1966; Lagalag the Wanderer, 1968; Gorilla Gorilla, 1973; The Skates of Uncle Richard, 1978; Saving Amelia Earhart, 1982; Deer Flight, 1986; A Summer of Horses, 1989; Randall's Wall, 1991; Yolonda's Genius, 1995. Honours: Library of Congress Book of the Year Award, 1973; Christopher Award; Newbery Honor Book for Yoland's Genius, 1996. Address: 190 Rebecca Road, Battle Creek, MI 49015, USA.

FENNER James R. See: **TUBB E(dwin) C(harles).**

FENNO Jack. See: **CALISHER Hortense.**

FENTON James Martin, b. 25 Apr 1949, Lincoln, England. Writer. Education: MA, Magdalen College, Oxford, 1970. Appointments: Assistant Literary Editor, 1971, Editorial Assistant, 1972, New Statesman; Freelance Correspondent, Indo-China, 1973-75; Political Columnist, New Statesman, 1976-78; German Correspondent, The Guardian, 1978-79; Theatre Critic, Sunday Times, 1979-84; Far East Correspondent, The Independent, 1986-88. Publications: Our Western Furniture, 1968; Terminal Moraine, 1972; A Vacant Possession, 1978; A German Requiem, 1980; Dead Soldiers, 1981; The Memory of War, 1982; You Were Marvellous, 1983; The Original Michael Frayn (editor), 1983; Children in Exile, 1984; Poems 1968-83, 1985; Partingtime Hall (with John Fuller), 1987; All the Wrong Places, Adrift in the Poltics of Asia, 1989. Address: c/o A D Peters & Co Ltd, 10 Buckingham Street, London WC2N 6BU, England.

FERDINANDY György (Georges), b. 11 Oct 1935, Budapest, Hungary. Professor. m. (1) Colette Peyrethon, 27 May 1958, (2) Maria Teresa Reyes-Cortes, 3 Jan 1981, 3 sons, 1 daughter. Education: Doctorate in Literature, University of Strasbourg, France, 1969. Appointments: Freelance Literary Critic, Radio Free Europe, 1977-86; Professor, University of Puerto Rico, Cayey, Puerto Rico. Publications: In French: L'ile sous l'eau, 1960; Famine au Paradis, 1962; Le seul jour de l'année, 1967; Itinéraires, 1973; Chica, Claudine, Cali, 1973; L'oeuvre hispanoaméricaine de Zs Remenyik, 1975; Fantomes magnétiques, 1979; Youri, 1983; Hors jeu, 1986; Mémoires d'un exil terminé, 1992; In Hungarian: Latoszemueknek, 1962; Tizenharom Töredék, 1964; Futoszalagon, 1965; Nemezio Gonzalex, 1970; Valenciana a tenger, 1975; Mammuttemető, 1982; A Mosoly Albuma, 1982; Az elveszett gyermek, 1984; A Vadak Utjan, 1986; Szerecsenségem Története, 1988; Furcsa, idegen szerelem, 1990; Uzenőfüzet, 1991; Szomorú Szigetek, 1992; À Francia Völegény, 1993.Contributions to: Le Monde; NRF; Europe; Elet és Irodalom; Kortars; Uj Hold; Magyar Naplo. Honours: Del Duca Prix, 1961; St Exupéry Literary Award, 1964; Book of the Year, 1993. Memberships: Société des Gens de Lettres, France; Hungarian Writers Association; International PEN. Address: Joaquin Lopez Lopez 1056, Sta Rita, Rio Piedras, PR 00925, USA.

FERGUSON Joseph Francis, b. 11 Feb 1952, Yonkers, New York, USA. Public Relations; Journalist; Critic; Author. m. Janice Robinson, 30 July 1986, 1 son. Education: BA, State University of New York at New Paltz, 1979; MS, Pace University (not completed). Publications: Night Image; Duecy and Detour; Priorities; Autumn Road Kill; Autumn Poem; Sky and Stream at Sunset; End of Daylight in a Car Mirror; The Atlar; Jazz; New Orleans; The Glory; Another Damn Dream Poem; Grave Dreams; View From the Graveyard Shift. Contributions to: Numerous publications. Honour: Golden Poet Award, World of Poetry, 1990. Address: 26 Bank Street, Cold Spring, NY 10516, USA.

FERGUSON Robert Thomas, b. 2 June 1948, Stoke On Trent, England. Writer. m. 3 Apr 1987. Education: BA, University College, London, 1980. Publications: Enigma, The Life of Knut Hamsun, 1987; Henry Miller, A Life, 1991; Henrik Ibsen: a new biography, 1996; As Contributor, Best Radio Drama, 1984; Best Radio Drama, 1986. Honours: BBC Methuen Giles Cooper Awards, 1984, 1986; J G Robertson Prize, 1985-87. Address: Steinspranget 7, 1156 Oslo 11, Norway.

FERGUSON William (Rotch), b. 14 Feb 1943, Fall River, Massachusetts, USA. Associate Professor of Spanish; Writer; Poet. m. Nancy King, 26 Nov 1983. Education: BA, 1965, MA, 1970, PhD, 1975, Harvard University. Appointments: Instructor, 1971-75, Assistant Professor, 1975-77, Boston University; Visiting Professor, 1977-79, Assistant Professor, 1979-83, Associate Professor of Spanish, 1983-, Adjunct Professor of English, 1989-, Chairman, Foreign Languages, 1990-, Clark University, Worcester, Massachusetts; Visiting Lecturer in Spanish Renaissance Literature, University of Pennsylvania, 1986-87; Associate Editor, Hispanic Review, 1986-87. Publications: Dream Reader (poems), 1973; Light of Paradise (poems), 1973; La versificación imitativa en Fernanado de Herrera, 1981; Freedom and Other Fictions (stories), 1984. Contributions to: Scholarly journals, anthologies, periodicals andmagazines. Memberships: American Association of University Professors; International Institute in Spain; Modern Language Association; Phi Beta Kappa; Sigma Delta Pi. Address: 1 Tahanto Road, Worcester, MA 01602, USA.

FERLINGHETTI Lawrence (Monsanto), b. 24 Mar 1920, Yonkers, New York, USA. Poet; Writer; Dramatist; Publisher; Editor; Painter. m. Selden Kirby-Smith, Apr 1951, div, 1 son, 1 daughter. Education: AB, University of North Carolina, 1941; MA, Columbia University, 1948; Doctorat (with honours), Sorbonne, University of Paris, 1951. Appointments: Co-Owner, City Lights Pocket Bookshop, later City Lights Books, San Francisco, 1953-; Founder-Editor, City Lights Books, publishing, San Francisco, 1955-; Many poetry readings; Participation in many national and international literary conferences; Retrospective exhibition of paintings, Palazzo delle Esposizione, Rome, Italy, 1996. Publications: Poetry: Pictures of the Gone World, 1955; A Coney Island of the Mind, 1958; Berlin, 1961; Starting from San Francisco, 1961, revised edition, 1967; Where is Vietnam?, 1965; An Eye on the World: Selected Poems, 1967; After the Cries of the Birds, 1967; The Secret Meaning of Things, 1969; Tyrannus Nix?, 1969; Back Roads to Far Places, 1971; Open Eye, Open Heart, 1973; Who Are We Now?, 1976; Landscapes of Living and Dying, 1979; A Trip to Italy and France, 1980; Endless Life: Selected Poems, 1984; Over All the Obscene Boundaries: European Poems and Transitions, 1985; Inside the Trojan Horse, 1987; When I Look at Pictures, 1990; These Are My Rivers: New and Selected Poems, 1955-1993, 1993; Novels: Her, 1960; Love in the Days of Rage, 1988. Other Writings: Dear Ferlinghetti (with Jack Spicer), 1962; The Mexican Night: Travel Journal, 1970; Northwest Ecolog, 1978; Literary San Francisco: A Pictorial History from the Beginning to the Present (with Nancy J Peters), 1980; The Populist Manifestos, 1983; Seven Days in Nicaragua Libre, journal, 1985. Editor: Beatitude Anthology, 1960; City Lights Anthology, 1974; City Lights Review, No 1, 1987, and No 2, 1988. Plays: Unfair Arguments with Existence: Seven Plays for a New Theatre, 1963; Routines, collection of 13 short plays, 1964. Contributions to: Numerous books and periodicals and periodicals. Honours: National Book Award Nomination, 1970; Notable Book of 1979 Citation, Library Journal, 1980; Silver Medal for Poetry, Commonwealth Club of California, 1986; Poetry Prize, City of Rome, 1993. Address: c/o City Lights Books, 261 Columbus Avenue, San Francisco, CA 94133, USA.

FERLITA Ernest Charles, b. 1 Dec 1927, Tampa, Florida, USA. Jesuit Priest; Educator; Playwright. Education: BS, Spring Hill College, 1950; STL, St Louis University, 1964; DFA, Yale University, 1969.

Publications: The Theatre of Pilgrimage, 1971; Film Odyssey (co-author), 1976; The Way of the River, 1977; The Parables of Lina Wertmuller (co-author), 1977; Religion in Film (contributor), 1982; Gospel Journey, 1983; The Mask of Hiroshima in Best Short Plays, 1989; The Uttermost Mark, 1990; The Paths of Life: Cycle A, B, C, 1992, 1993, 1994; The Paths of Life: Cycles A, B,C, 1992, 1993, 1994. Honours: 1st Prize, Christian Theatre Artists Guild, 1971; American Radio Scriptwriting Contest, 1985; Miller Award, 1986. Memberships: Dramatists Guild; International Hopkins Society. Address: Loyola University, New Orleans, LA 70118, USA.

FERNANDEZ DIAZ Natalia, b. 12 Mar 1967, Súria, Barcelona, Spain. Researcher; Teacher. m. Maximo R Mewe, 28 Feb 1994. Education: BA, Germanic Languages and Linguistics, University of Barcelona, 1985-90; Master in Human Sexuality, UNED University, Madrid, Spain, 1992-94; PhD in Critical Discourse Analysis, University of Amsterdam and Universidad Autónoma of Madrid, in progress. Appointment: Literary Contributions for Cultural Programmes in Radio Nederland International. Publications: Preludios de Juventud, 1983; La Profesión del Espejo o el Tierno Oasis, 1989; El Árbol que mira nacia la Luz, 1992; Quaderns de Poesia (with others), 1993; Poemas de la Luz (with others), 1994; Several articles in newspapers and magazines. Contributions to: Anthropos and Fempress. Honour: El Taller, Ex-Equo, Poetry, Barcelona, 1995. Memberships: Pen Club, Nederland, Amsterdam; International Writers and Artists Association, Bluffton College, Ohio, USA. Address: Lepelaarlaan 17, 1241 EE Kortenhoef, The Netherlands.

FERNANDEZ-ARMESTO Felipe Fermin Ricardo, b. 6 Dec 1950, London, England. Historian. m. Lesley Patricia Hook, 16 July 1977, 2 sons. Education: Magdalen College, Oxford, 1969-72; 1st Class Hons, Modern History, 1972, MA 1976, DPhil, 1977, Oxford University. Appointment: Journalist, The Diplomatist, 1972-74. Publications: The Canary Islands after the Conquest, 1982; Before Columbus, 1987; The Spanish Armada, 1988; Barcelona, 1991; The Times Atlas of World Exploration (general editor), 1991; Columbus, 1991; Edward Gibbon's Atlas of the World, 1992; Millennium, 1995; The Times Guide to the People of Europe, 1995; The Times Illustrated History of Europe, 1995; Reformation (with Derek Wilson), 1996. Contributions to: English Historical Review; History; History Today; Anuarto de Estudios Atlanticos; Sunday Times Magazines. Honours: Arnold Modern History Prize, 1971; Leverhulme Research Fellowship, 1981; Commendation, Library Association, 1992. Fellow, Royal Historical Society. Memberships: Council, Hakluyt Society; Society of Authors; PEN; General Library Committee, Athenaeum; Historical Association; Association of Hispanists; Society of Antiquaries. Literary Agent: Serafina Clarke. Address: High Gables, Oxford, OX3 0DW, England.

FERRARI Ronald Leslie, b. 3 Feb 1930, Romford, Essex, England. Electrical Engineer. m. Judith Wainwright, 5 Sept 1959, 1 son, 3 daughters. Education: BSc, DIC, Imperial College, London; MA, ScD. Appointments: Lecturer, Cambridge University, 1965; Fellow, Trinity College, Cambridge, 1966. Publications: Problems in Physical Electronics, 1973; Introduction to Electromagnetic Fields, 1975; Finite Elements for Electrical Engineers, 1983, 3rd edition, 1996. Contributions to: Special Issue of IEE Proceedings. Membership: Institute of Electrical Engineers. Address: Trinity College, Cambridge CB2 1T, England.

FERRIS Paul (Frederick), b. 15 Feb 1929, Swansea, Wales. Writer. Publications: A Changed Man, 1958; The City, 1960; Then We Fall, 1960; The Church of England, 1962; A Family Affair, 1963; The Doctors, 1965; The Destroyer, 1965; The Nameless Abortion in Britain Today, 1966; The Dam, 1967; Men and Money: Financial Europe Today, 1968; The House of Northcliffe, 1971; The New Militants, 1972; The Detectives, 1976; Dylan Thomas, 1977; Talk to Me about England, 1979; Richard Burton, 1981; A Distant Country, 1983; Gentlemen of Fortune, 1984; Collected Letters of Dylan Thomas, 1985; Children of Dust, 1988; Sex and the British, 1993; Caitlin, 1993; The Divining Heart, 1995. TV Plays: The Revivalist, 1975; Dylan, 1978; Nye, 1982; The Extremist, 1983; The Fasting Girl, 1984. Address: c/o Curtis Brown Limited, Haymarket House, 28/29 Haymarket, London SW14 4SP, England.

FERRON Madeleine, b. 24 July 1922, Louiseville, Quebec, Canada. Writer. m. Robert Cliche, 22 Sept 1945, 2 sons, 1 daughter. Publications: Short Stories: Coeur de Sucre, 1966; Le Chemin des Dames, 1977; Histoires Edifiantes, 1981; Un Singulier Amour, 1987;

Le Grand Theatre, 1989. Novels: La Fin des Loups-Garous, 1966; Le Baron Ecarlate, 1971; Sur le Chemin Craig, 1982. Essays: Quand le Peuple fait la loi, 1972; Les Beaucerons, ces insoumis, 1974; Adrienne, une saga familiale, 1993. Honour: Ordre National du Quebec, Chevalier, 1992. Address: 1130 de la Tour, Quebec G1R 2W7, Canada.

FESTA Georges, b. 17 Apr 1956, Algeria. Professor. Education: DLitt, Universite Blaise, 1991. Publications: L'image de la femme dans l'oeuvre de Gabriele d'Annunzio, 1979; Les Etudes sur le Prince de Ligne du XVIIIe siecle a nos jours, 1979; Les Etudes sur le marquis de Sade: Contribution a une bibliographie analytique, 1981; Le Voyage d'Italie de Sade 1775-1776: Genese d'un immoralisme visionnaire, 1991. Contributions to: Professional journals. Address: 75 bd Gambetta, F-93130 Noisy-Le-Sec, France.

FICKERT Kurt (Jon), b. 19 Dec 1920, Pausa, Germany. Professor Emeritus; Writer. m. Madlyn Barbara Janda, 6 Aug 1946, 2 sons, 1 daughter. Education: BA, Hofstra University, 1941; MA, 1947, PHD, 1952, New York University. Appointments: Instructor, Assistant Professor, Hofstra University, 1947-53; Assistant Professor, Florida State University, 1953-54, Kansas State University at Fort Hays, 1954-56; Assistant to Professor, 1956-86, Professor Emeritus, 1986-, Wittenberg University, Springfield, Ohio. Publications: To Heaven and Back: The New Morality in the Plays of Friedrich Dürrenmatt, 1972; Herman Hesse's Quest, 1978; Kafka's Doubles, 1979; Signs and Portents: Myth in the Work of Wolfgang Borchert, 1980; Franz Kafka: Life, Work, Criticism, 1984; Neither Left and Right: The Politics of Individualism in Uwe Johnson's Work, 1987; End of a Mission: Kafka's Search for Truth in His Last Stories, 1993; Dialogue With the Reader: The Narrative Stance in Uwe Johnson's Fiction, 1996. Contributions to: Books and journals. Memberships: American Association of Teachers of German; Phi Beta Kappa; Wolfgang Borchert Gesellschaft. Address: 33 South Kensington Place, Springfield, OH 45504, USA.

FIELD D M. See: GRANT Neil.

FIELD Edward, b. 7 June 1924, Brooklyn, New York, USA. Writer. Education: New York University (no degree), 1946-48. Appointments: Guggenheim Fellow, 1963; Fellow, American Academy of Rome, 1980. Publications: Stand Up, Friend, With Me, 1963; Variety Photoplays, 1967; Eskimo Songs and Stories, 1973; A Full Heart, 1977; A Geography of Poets(editor), 1979; New and Selected Poems, 1987; Counting Myself Lucky, 1992. Contributions to: New Yorker; New York Review of Books; Partisan Review; Evergreen Review; Botteghe Oscure; Harper's; Kenyon Review; Listener. Honours: Lamont Award, 1963; Shelley Memorial Award, 1978; Lambda Award, 1993. Membership: Authors Guild. Address: 463 West Street, A323, New York, NY 10014, USA.

FIELDER Mildred (Craig), b. 14 Jan 1913, Quinn, South Dakota, USA. Author; Poet. m. Ronald G Fielder, 17 Sept 1932, 2 sons. Education: Huron College, 1930-31; University of Colorado, 1946. Publications: Wandering Foot in the West, 1955; Railroads of the Black Hills, 1960; Wild Bill and Deadwood, 1965; Treasure of Homestake Gold, 1970; Guide to Black Hills Ghost Mines, 1972; Chinese in the Black Hills, 1972; Potato Creek Johnny, 1973; Hiking Trails in the Black Hills, 1973; Wild Bill Hickok Gun Man, 1974; Theodore Roosevelt in Dakota Territory, 1974; Deadwood Dick and the Dime Novels, 1974; Sioux Indian Leaders, 1975; Plant Medicine and Folklore, 1975; Lost Gold, 1978; Poker Alice, 1978; Silver is the Fortune, 1978; Preacher Smith of Deadwood, 1981; Fielder's Herbal Helper, 1982; The Legend of Lame Johnny Creek, 1982; Wild Fruits, 1983; Captain Jack Crawford, 1983; Invitation to Fans, 1988. Contributions to: Anthologies and periodicals. Honours: Numerous. Memberships: Life Member, Society of American Historians; South Dakota Historical Society; National League of American Pen Women. Address: 264 San Jacinto Drive, Los Osos, CA 93402, USA.

FIENNES Ranulph (Twisleton-Wykeham), b. 7 Mar 1944, Windsor, England. Explorer; Writer. m. Virginia Pepper, 9 Sept 1970. Education: Eton College. Appointments: British Army, 1965-70; Special Air Service, 1966; Sultan of Muscat's Armed Forces, 1968-70; Led British Expeditions to White Nile, 1969, Jostedalsbre Glacier, 1970, Headless Valley, British Columbia, 1970; Transglobal expedition, circumpolar journey round the world, 1979-82, North Pole (5 expeditions), 1985-90, Ubar Expedition (discovered the lost city of Ubar, Oman), 1992, Pentland unsupported crossing of Atlantic, 1993; Lectures; Television and film documentary appearances. Publications:

A Talent for Trouble, 1970; Ice Fall on Norway, 1972; The Headless Valley, 1973; Where Soldiers Fear to Tread, 1975; Hell on Ice, 1979; To the Ends of the Earth: The Transglobe Expedition - The First Pole-to-Pole Circumnavigation of the Globe, 1983; Bothie the Polar Dog (with Virginia Fiennes), 1984; Living Dangerously (autobiography), 1988; The Feather Men, 1991; Atlantis of the Sands, 1992; Mind Over Matter: The Epic Crossing of the Antarctic Continent, 1994; The Sett, 1996. Honours: Dhofar Campaign Medal, 1969; Sultan of Muscat Bravery Medal, 1970; Krug Award for Excellence, 1980; Gold Medal and Honorary Life Membership, Explorer's Club of New York, 1983; Livingstone's Gold Medal, Royal Scottish Geographic Society, 1983; Founder's Medal, Royal Geographic Society, 1984; Guiness Hall of Fame, 1987; Polar Medal and bar, 1987; ITN Award, 1990; Officer of the Order of the British Empire, 1993; Polar Medal and bar, 1994. Address: Greenlands, Exford, Somerset TA24 7NU, England.

FIFIELD Christopher (George), b. 4 Sept 1945, Croydon, England. Musician. m. Judith Weyman, 28 Oct 1972. Education: ARCO, 1967; MusB, 1968; GRSM, 1969; ARMCM, 1969. Publications: Max Bruch: His Life and Works, 1988; Wagner in Performance, 1992; Hans Richter, 1993. Contributions to: Musical Times; Strad; Classical Music; Music and Letters; BBC Music Magazine. Address: Coach House, 38 Wrights Road, London SE25 6RY, England.

FIGES Eva, b. 15 April 1932, Berlin, Germany. Writer. 1 son, 1 daughter. Education: BA, Honours, English Language and Literature, University of London, 1953. Publications: Winter Journey, 1967; Patriarchal Attitudes, 1970; B, 1972; Nelly's Version, 1977; Little Eden, 1978; Waking, 1981; Sex and Subterfuge, 1982; Light, 1983; The Seven Ages, 1986; Ghosts, 1988; The Tree of Knowledge, 1990; The Tenancy, 1993; The Knot, 1996. Honour: Guardian Fiction Prize, 1967. Membership: Writers Guild of Great Britain, chairperson, 1986-87. Address: 24 Fitzjohns Avenue, London NW3 5NB, England.

FIGUEROA John (Joseph Maria), b. 4 Aug 1920, Kingston, Jamaica. Professor (retired); Writer; Poet. m. Dorothy Grace Murray Alexander, 3 Aug 1944, 4 sons, 3 daughters. Education: AB, College of the Holy Cross, 1942; Teachers Diploma, 1947, MA, 1950, University of London; Graduate Studies, Indiana University, 1964. Appointments: Lecturer, University of London, 1948-53; Senior Lecturer, 1953-57, Professor of Education, 1957-73, Dean of the Faculty of Education, 1966-69, University College of the West Indies, Kingston; Professor of English and Consultant to the President, University of Puerto Rico, 1971-73; Professor of Humanities, El Centro Caribeno de Estudios Postgraduados, Puerto Rico, 1973-76; Professor of Education, University of Jos, Nigeria, 1976-80; Visiting Professor of Humanities, Bradford College, Yorkshire, England, 1980; Fellow, Centre of Caribbean Studies, Warwick University, 1988. Publications: Blue Mountain Peak (poems and prose), 1944; Love Leaps Here (poems), 1962; Editor, Caribbean Voices: An Anthology of West Indian Poetry, 2 volumes, 1966, 1970; Society, Schools and Progress in the West Indies, 1971; Ignoring Hurts: Poems, 1976; Dreams and Realities: Six One-Act Comedies (editor), 1978; Caribbean Writers (editor with others), 1979; An Anthology of African and Caribbean Writing in English (editor) 1982; Third World Studies: Caribbean Sampler (editor), 1983. Contributions to: Journals and periodicals. Honours: British Council Fellowship, 1946-47; Carnegie Fellowship, 1960; Guggenheim Fellowship, 1964; Lilly Foundation Grant, 1973; Institute of Jamaica Medal, 1980. Address: 77 Station Road, Woburn Sands, Buckinghamshire, MK17 8SH, England.

FILATOV Artiom. See: **KLIMOV Jouri Moiseevitch.**

FINALE Frank Louis, b. 10 Mar 1942, Brooklyn, New York, USA. Editor; Poet. m. Barbra Long, 20 Oct 1973, 3 sons. Education: BA, Ohio State University, 1964; MA, Fairleigh Dickinson University, 1976. Appointment: Founding Editor, 1983, Editor-in-Chief, Without Halos, 1995-95; Founder member, Ocean County Peots Collective, 1983; Poetry Editor, The New Renaissance magazine, 1996. Publication: Under a Gull's Wing: Poems and Photographs of the Jersey Shore (co-editor), 1996. Contributions to: Poems in various anthologies and many periodicals including: New Jersey Outdoors; LIPS; Xanadu. Memberships: New Jersey Education Association; National Education Association. Address: 19 Quail Run, Bayville, NJ 08721, USA.

FINCH Matthew. See: **FINK Merton.**

FINCH Merton. See: **FINK Merton.**

FINCH Peter, b. 6 Mar 1947, Cardiff, Wales. Poet; Writer; Bookshop Manager at HMSO Oriel. 2 sons, 1 daughter. Education: Glamorgan Polytechnic. Appointment: Editor, Second Aeon, 1966-75. Publications: Wanted, 1967; Pieces of the Universe, 1968; How to Learn Welsh, 1977; Between 35 and 42 (short stories), 1982; Some Music and a Little War, 1984; How to Publish Your Poetry, 1985; Reds in the Bed, 1986; Selected Poems, 1987; How to Publish Yourself, 1988; Make, 1990; Poems for Ghosts, 1991; Five Hundred Cobbings, 1994; The Spe Ell, 1995; The Poetry Business, 1995; Antibodies, 1997. Contributions to: Magazines and journals. Memberships: Welsh Academy; Welsh Union of Writers. Address: 19 Southminster Road, Roath, Cardiff CF2 5AT, Wales.

FINCH Robert (Duer Claydon), b. 14 May 1900, Freeport, Long Island, New York, USA. Emeritus Professor; Poet. Education: University of Toronto and Sorbonne, Paris. Appointments: Professor of French, University College, Toronto, Canada, 1952-68. Publications: Poems, 1946; The Strength of the Hills, 1948; Acis in Oxford and Other Poems, 1959; Dover Beach Revisited and Other Poems, 1961; Silverthorn Bush and Other Poems, 1966; Variations and Theme, 1980; Has and Is, 1981; Twelve for Christmas, 1982; The Grand Duke of Moscow's Favourite Solo, 1983; Double Tuning, 1984; For the Back of a Likeness, 1986; Sail-boat and Lake and Other Poems, 1988; Miracle at the Jetty, 1991; 31 Impromptus, 1994. Honours: Fellow, Royal Society of Canada, 1963; LLD, University of Winnipeg, 1984. Address: Massey College, 4 Devonshire Place, Toronto, Ontario M5S 2E1, Canada.

FINCKE Gary (William), b. 7 July 1945, Pittsburgh, Pennsylvania, USA. College Educator; Writer. m. Elizabeth Locker, 17 Aug 1968, 2 sons, 1 daughter. Education: BA, Thiel College, 1967; MA, Miami University, 1969; PhD, Kent State University, 1974. Appointment: Writing Program Director, Susquehanna University, 1980-. Publications: Inventing Angels; For Keepsies; The Double Negatives of the Living; Plant Voices; The Public Talk of Death; The Days of Uncertain Health; Handing the Self Back; The Coat in the Heart; Breath; The Inadvertent Scofflaw; Emergency Calls; The Technology of Paradise. Contributions to: Harper's; Paris Review; Poetry; Yankee; Georgia Review; Quarterly; Kenyon Review; Missouri Review; Gettysburg Review; Poetry Northwest. Honours: Poetry/Fiction Fellowships; PEN Syndicated Fiction Prize; Bess Hokin Prize. Memberships: Poetry Society of America; Associated Writers Program; Poets and Writers. Address: 3 Melody Lane, Selinsgrove, PA 17870, USA.

FINDLEY Timothy (Irving Frederick), b. 30 Oct 1930, Toronto, Ontario, Canada. Author; Dramatist. Education: Mainly audiodidact. Appointments: Playwright-in-Residence, National Arts Centre, Ottawa, 1974-75; Writer-in-Residence, University of Toronto, 1978-79, Trent University, 1984, University of Winnipeg, 1985. Publications: The Last of the Crazy People, 1967; The Butterfly Plague, 1969; Can You See Me Yet? (play), 1977; The Wars, 1977; John A...Himself (play), 1979; Famous Last Words, 1981; Not Wanted on the Voyage, 1984; Dinner Along the Amazon (stories), 1984; The Telling of Lies, 1986; Stones (stories), 1988; Inside Memory: Pages From a Writer's Workbook, 1990; Headhunter, 1993; The Stillborn Lover (play), 1993; The Piano Man's Daughter, 1995; The Trials of Ezra Pound, 1995; You Went Away, 1996. Other: Screenplays; Radio, film and television documentaries. Contributions to: Newspapers and periodicals. Honours: Major Armstrong Award, 1970; Association of Canadian Television and Radio Artists Award, 1975; Governor-General's Award for Fiction, 1977; City of Toronto Book Award, 1977; Canada Council Senior Arts Award, 1978; Canadian Authors Association Literary Awards, 1985, 1991, 1994; Officer of the Order of Canada, 1986; Order of Ontario, 1991; Chevalier de l'Ordre des Arts et des Lettres, 1996. Memberships: Association of Canadian Television and Radio Artists; Authors Guild; Authors League of America; Chairman, Writers' Union of Canada, 1977-78; President, English-Canadian Centre, International PEN, 1986-87. Address: c/o W Whitehead, PO Box 419, Cannington, Ontario L0E 1E0, Canada.

FINE Anne, b. 7 Dec 1947, Leicester, England. Writer. m. Kit Fine, 3 Aug 1968, 2 daughters. Education: BA Hons, University of Warwick. Publications: Novels: The Killjoy, 1986; Taking the Devil's Advice, 1990; In Cold Domain, 1994. For Older Children: The Summer House Loon, 1978; The Other Darker Ned, 1979; The Stone Menagerie, 1980; Round Behind the Ice House, 1981; The Granny Project, 1983; Madame Doubtfire, 1987; Goggle Eyes, 1989; The Book of the Banshee, 1991; Flour Babies, 1992; Step by Wicked Step, 1995.

Honours: Guardian Children's Award, 1989; Carnegie Medals, 1989, 1993; Smarties Prize, 1990; Guardian Children's Literature Award, 1990; Publishing News, Children's Author of Year, 1990, 1993; Whitbread Children's Novel Award, 1993. Memberships: Society of Authors. Address: 222 Old Brompton Road, London SW5 0BZ, England.

FINEGAN Jack, b. 11 July 1908, Des Moines, Iowa, USA. Professor; Reverend. m. Mildred Catherine Meader, 4 Sept 1934, 1 son. Education: BA, 1928, MA, 1929, BD, 1930, Drake University; BD, 1931, MTh, 1932, Colgate Rochester Divinity School; Licensed Theol, magna cum laude, Friedrich Wilhelms Universität, Berlin, 1934; LLD, Drake University, 1953; LittD, Chapman College, 1964. Appointment: Emeritus Professor, New Testament History and Archaeology, Pacific School of Religion, Berkeley, California. Publications: Archaeological History of the Ancient Middle East, 1979; The Archaeology of the New Testament, The Mediterranean World of the Early Christian Apostles, 1981; Discovering Israel: A Popular Guide to The Holy Land, 1981; Tibet: A Dreamt of Image, 1986; Myth and Mystery: An Introduction to the Pagan Religions of the Biblical World, 1989; An Archaeological History of Religions of Indian Asia, 1989; The Archaeology of the New Testament, The Life of Jesus and the Beginning of the Early Church, 1992; Handbook of Biblical Chronology, Principles of Time Reckoning in the Ancient World and Problems of Chronology in the Bible. Honour: Phi Beta Kappa. Membership: Former Member, Studiorum Novi Testament Societas. Address: Pacific School of Religion, 1798 Scenic Avenue, Berkeley, CA 94709, USA.

FINK Merton, (Matthew Finch, Merton Finch), b. 17 Nov 1921, Liverpool, England. Author. m. (1) 15 Mar 1953, 1 son, 1 daughter, (2) 24 Nov 1981. Education: School of Military Engineers, 1942; School of Military Intelligence, 1943; LDS, Liverpool University, 1947-52; Police interpreter, 1956-. Publications: Dentist in the Chair, 1953; Teething Troubles, 1954; The Third Set, 1955; Hang Your Hat on a Pension, 1956; The Empire Builder, 1957; Solo Fiddle, 1959; Matchbreakers, 1961; Five Are the Symbols, 1962; Chew this Over, 1965; Eye with Mascara, 1966; Eye Spy, 1967; Simon Bar Cochba, 1971; A Fox Called Flavius, 1973; Open Wide, 1976. Contributions to: Dental Practice, 1956-; Bath Chronicle, 1995. Honour: Richard Edwards Scholar, 1950. Memberships: Civil Service Writers; Deputy Chairman, Bath Literary Society; British Dental Association; Chairman, Service Committee, Bath British Legion. Address: 27 Harbutts, Bathampton, Bath BA2 6TA, England.

FINKEL Donald, b. 21 Oct 1929, New York, New York, USA. Poet; University Teacher (retired). m. Constance Urdang, 1956, 1 son, 2 daughters. Education: BA, 1952, MA 1953, Columbia University. Appointments: Teacher, University of Iowa, 1957-58, Bard College, 1958-60; Faculty, 1960-92, Poet-in-Residence, 1965-92, Poet-in-Residence Emeritus, 1992-, Washington University, St Louis; Visiting Lecturer, Bennington College, 1966-67, Princeton University, 1985. Publications: The Clothing's New Emperor and Other Poems, 1959; Simeon, 1964; A Joyful Noise, 1966; Answer Back, 1968; The Garbage Wars, 1970; Adequate Earth, 1972; A Mote in Heaven's Eye, 1975; Going Under, and Endurance: An Arctic Idyll: Two Poems, 1978; What Manner of Beast, 1981; The Detachable Man, 1984; Selected Shorter Poems, 1987; The Wake of the Electron, 1987; Beyond Despair, 1994. Honours: Helen Bullis Prize, 1964; Guggenheim Fellowship, 1967; National Endowment for the Arts Grants, 1969, 1973; Ingram Merrill Foundation Grant, 1972; Theodore Roethke Memorial Prize, 1974; Morton Dauwen Zabel Award, American Academy of Arts and Letters, 1980. Membership: Phi Beta Kappa. Address: 2051 Park Avenue, Apt D, St Louis, MO 63104, USA.

FINLAY William. See: **MACKAY James Alexander.**

FINNIGAN Joan, b. 23 Nov 1925, Ottawa, Ontario, Canada. Writer. m. Charles Grant Mackenzie, 23 May 1949, 2 sons, 1 daughter. Education: BA, Queens University, 1967. Publications: Through the Glass, Darkly, 1963; A Dream of Lilies, 1965; Entrance to the Greenhouse, 1968; It Was Warm and Sunny When We Set Out, 1970; In the Brown Cottage on Loughborough Lake, 1970; Living Together, 1976; A Reminder of Familiar Faces, 1978; This Series Has Been Discontinued, 1980; The Watershed Collection, 1988; Wintering Over, 1992; Other Genres: Old Scores: New Goals, History of Ottawa Senators 1891-1992, 1992; Lisgar Collegiate Institute 1843-1993, 1993; Withes, Ghosts and Soups-Garous, 1994; Dancing at the Crossroads, 1995. Screenplay: The Best Damn Fiddler from Calabogie to Kaladar, 1967; CBC Radio Scripts, Songs for the Bible Belt, May

Day Rounds, Children of the Shadows, There's No Good Time Left - None at All. Address: Hartington, Ontario K0H 1W0, Canada.

FINNIS John (Mitchell), b. 28 July 1940, Adelaide, South Australia. Professor of Law and Legal Philosophy; Writer. m. Marie Carmel McNally, 1964, 3 sons, 4 daughters. Education: St Peter's College, Adelaide; LLB, St Mark's College, University of Adelaide, 1961; Rhodes Scholar, 1962, DPhil, 1965, University College, Oxford. Appointments: Associate in Law, University of California, Berkeley, 1965-66; Fellow and Praelector in Jurisprudence, 1966-, Stowell Civil Law Fellow, 1973-, University College, Oxford; Called to the Bar, Gray's Inn, 1970; Rhodes Reader in the Laws of the British Commonwealth and the United States, 1972-89, Professor of Law and Legal Philosophy, 1989-, Oxford University; Professor and Head, Department of Law, University of Malawi, 1976-78; Consultor, Pontifical Commission, Iustitia et Pax, 1977-89; Huber Distinguished Visiting Professor, Boston College, 1993-94; Biolchini Professor of Law, University of Notre Dame, Indiana, 1995-. Publications: Commonwealth and Dependencies (Halsbury's Laws of England), Vol 6, 4th edition, 1974, revised edition, 1991; Natural Law and Natural Rights, 1980; Fundamentals of Ethics, 1983; Nuclear Deterrence, Morality and Realism (with Joseph Boyle and Germain Grisez), 1987; Moral Absolutes, 1991. Memberships: Catholic Bishops' Joint Committee on Bio-Ethical Issues, 1981-88; International Theological Commission, Vatican, 1986-92; Pontifical Council de Iustitia et Pace, 1990-96. Address: University College, Oxford, OX1 4BH, England.

FINSTAD Suzanne, b. 14 Sept 1955, Minneapolis, Minnesota, USA. Author; Attorney (non-practising). Education: University of Texas, Austin, 1973-74; BA, French, University of Houston, 1976; University of Grenoble, France, 1979; JD, Bates College of Law, 1980; London School of Economics, 1980. Publications: Heir Not Apparent, 1984; Ulterior Motives, 1987; Sleeping with the Devil, 1991. Contributions to: Magazines. Honours: American Jurisprudence Award in Criminal Law, Bancroft-Whitney Publishing Co, 1979; Order of the Barons, 1980; Frank Wardlaw Award, 1985. Address: c/o Joel Gotler, 152 North La Peer Drive, Beverly Hills, CA 90048, USA.

FIRTH Anne Catherine, (Anne Valery), b. 24 Feb 1926, London, England. Scriptwriter; Autobiographer; Novelist; Theatre Playwright. Education: Matriculation (Hons), Badminton Public School. Publications: The Edge of a Smile, 1974; Baron Von Kodak, Shirley Temple and Me, 1973; The Passing Out Parade (theatre), 1979; Tenko Reunion, 1984; Talking About the War... (non-fiction), 1991. Other: Over 50 TV plays. Contributions to: Articles in Radio Times. Honours: Book of the Month, Telegraph; BAFTA Award, Tenko (TV Series), 1984. Memberships: PEN International; Fawcett Society. Literary Agent: Linda Seifut (plays), Jacintha Alexander (books). Address: 5 Abbot's Place, London NW6 4NP, England.

FISCHER Lynn Helen, b. 2 June 1943, Red Wing, Minnesota, USA. Author; Inventor. Education: Approximately 4 years college, Doctor of Genius Degree, 1986. Literary Appointment: Author, Editor, Publisher, Genius NewsLetter, 1990-. Publications include: The 1, 2, 4, Theory: A Synthesis, 1971; Sexual Equations of Electricity, Magnetism, & Gravitation, 1971; Human Sexual Evolution, 1971; Middle Concept Theory, 1972; A Revised Meaning of Paradox, 1972; Unitary Theory, 1973; An Introduction To Circular or Fischerian Geometry, 1976; Two Four, Eight Theory, 1976; Fischer's Brief Dictionary of Sound Meanings, 1977; Introducing the Magnetic Sleeve: A Novel Sexual Organ, 1983; The Expansion of Duality, 1984; The Inger Poems, 1985; Letters of the Poet Lynn, on cassette, 1987; Country Wit/The Inger Poems & Early Poems (cassette spoken by Lynn - Country Wit is by Lynn's father, R H "Bud" Fischer (1909-1985), poetry from Fischer Frolics in Poetry (privately published; Mathematical Philosophy of the Poet Lynn/The Mathematics of Poetry on one cassette, 1987; The Inventions and Essays, on cassette, 1988; Cave Man Talk and Other Essays, on cassette, 1989; Circular Geometry, 1990; The Four Inventions, 1990; The Expansion of Dualism *A 2 4 8 System, 1990; The Early Poems by Musical Lynn, 1990; The Musical Lynn Song Lyrics, 1991; The Musical Lynn Essays, Vol 1, 1992; Caveman Talk, 1992; The Three in One Ring (And) The Magnetic Woman, 1992; Apple Skies, 1993; Music That Sings or In Memory of Alice; Also, A Welcome Neighbor newsletter, 1995-; A Triversal Woman, 1997 Membership: National Association for Female Executives (NAFE). Address: Norwegian Lutheran Memorial Church, Lynn of the Twin Cities, 1415 East 22nd St, Apt 1108, Minneapolis, MN 55404 3016, USA.

FISH Stanley (Eugene), b. 19 Apr 1938, Providence, Rhode Island, USA. Professor of English and Law. m. 7 Aug 1982, 1 daughter. Education: BA, University of Pennsylvania, 1959; MA 1960, PhD 1963, Yale University. Appointments: Full Professor, English, University of California, Berkeley, 1962-74; William Kenan Jr Professor, Humanities, Johns Hopkins University, 1974-85; Arts and Science Distinguished Professor of English, Professor of Law, Duke University; Executive Director, Duke University Press, 1994. Publications: John Skelton's Poetry, 1965; Surprised by Sin: The Reader in Paradise Lost, 1967; Self-Consuming Artifacts, 1972; Living Temple: George Herbert and Catechizing, 1978; Is There a Text in This Class?, 1980; Doing What Comes Naturally, 1989; There's No Such Thing as Free Speech and It's a Good Thing Too, 1994; Professional Correctness: Literary Studies and Political Change, 1995. Contributions to: Various scholarly journals. Honours: American Council of Learned Societies Fellowship, 1966; Guggenheim Fellowship, 1969-70; Honoured Scholar, Milton Society of America, 1991; PEN/Spielvogel-Diamonstein Award, 1994. Memberships: Past President, Milton Society of America; American Academy of Arts and Sciences. Address: Department of English, 314 Allen Building, Duke University, Box 90015, Durham, NC 27708, USA.

FISHER Allen, b. 1 Nov 1944, Norbury, Surrey, England. Painter; Poet; Art Historian. Education: BA, University of London; MA, University of Essex. Publications: Over 100 Books including: Place Book One, 1974; Brixton Fractals, 1985; Unpolished Mirrors, 1985; Stepping Out, 1989; Future Exiles, 1991; Fizz, 1994; Civic Crime, 1994; Breadboard, 1994; Now's the Time, 1995. Contributions to: Various Magazines and Journals. Honour: Co-Winner, Alice Hunt Bartlett Award, 1975. Address: 14 Hopton Road, Hereford HR1 1BE, England.

FISHER Leonard Everett, b. 24 June 1924, New York, New York, USA. Artist; Author. m. Margery Meskin, 21 Dec 1952, 1 son, 2 daughters. Education: BFA 1949, MFA 1950, Yale University. Appointment: President of Westport (CT) Public Library Board of Trustees, 1986-89. Publications: 80 books written and illustrated including: Non Fiction: Colonial Americans, 19 volumes, 1964-76; Ellis Island, 1986; Look Around, 1987; The Tower of London, 1987; Galileo, 1992; Tracks Across America, 1992; Stars and Stripes, 1993; Marie Curie, 1994; Moses, 1995; Gandhi, 1995; Niagara Falls, 1996; Anasazi, 1997. Fiction: Death of Evening Star, 1972; Across the Sea from Galway, 1975; Sailboat Lost, 1991; Cyclops, 1991; Kinderdike, 1994; William Tell, 1996. Illustrator of more than 250 books for young readers. Honours: Premio Grafico Fiera di Bologno, Italy, 1968; Medallion of the University of Southern Mississippi, USA, 1979; Christopher Medal, USA, 1980; National Jewish Book Award for Children's Literature, USA, 1981; Children's Book Guild, Washington Post Non-Fiction Award, USA, 1989; Regina Medal of the Catholic Library Association, USA, 1991; Kerlan Award of the University of Minnesota, USa, 1991; Arbuthnot House Lecture Citation of the American Library Association, USA, 1994. Memberships: PEN; Authors Guild. Address: 7 Twin Bridge Acres Road, Westport, CT 06880, USA.

FISHER Roy, b. 11 June 1930, Birmingham, England. Poet; Musician. Education: BA, 1951, MA, 1970, Birmingham University. Publications: City, 1961; Interiors, 1966; The Ship's Orchestra, 1967; The Memorial Fountain, 1968; Collected Poems 1968, 1968; Matrix, 1971; Cut Pages, 1971; Metamorphoses, 1971; The Thing About Joe Sullivan, 1978; Poems 1955-1980; A Furnace, 1986; The Left-Handed Punch, 1987; Poems 1955-1987, 1988; Birmingham River, 1994; The Dow Low Drop: New and Selected Poems, 1996. Contributions to: Numerous journals and magazines. Honours: Andrew Kelus Prize, 1979; Cholmondeley Award, 1981. Memberships: Musicians Union; Society of Authors. Address: Four Ways, Earl Sterndale, Buxton, Derbyshire SK17 0EP, England.

FISHLOCK Trevor, b. 21 Feb 1941, Hereford, England. Journalist; Author. m. Penelope Symon, 1978. Appointments: Portsmouth Evening News, 1957-62; Freelance News Agency Reporter, 1962-68; Staff Correspondent, Wales and West England, 1968-77, South Asia Correspondent, 1980-83, New York Correspondent, 1983-86, Times; Roving Foreign Correspondent, 1986-89 and 1993-, Moscow Correspondent, 1989-91, Daily Telegraph; Roving Foreign Correspondent, Sunday Telegraph, 1991-93; Roving Correspondent, Daily Telegraph, 1993-96. Publications: Wales and the Welsh, 1972; Discovering Britain - Wales, 1975; Talking of Wales, 1975; Americans and Nothing Else, 1980; India File, 1983; The State of America, 1986; Indira Gandhi (children's

book), 1986; Out of Red Darkness, 1992; My Foreign Country, 1997. Honours: David Holden Award for Foreign Reporting, 1983, International Reporter of the Year, 1986, British Press Awards. Memberships: Society of Authors; World Press Institute. Address: 56 Dovercourt Road, London SE22 8ST, England.

FISHMAN Charles (Munro), b. 10 July 1942, Oceanside, New York, USA. Educator; Writer. m. Ellen Marci Haselkorn, 25 June 1967. Education: BA, MA, Hofstra University; Doctor of Arts, State University of New York, Albany, 1982. Appointments: Poet-in-Residence, 1970, Director, Visiting Writers Program, 1979, Director, Programs in the Arts, 1987, State University of New York, Farmingdale. Publications: Aurora, 1974; Mortal Companions, 1977; Warm-Blooded Animals, 1977; Index to Women's Magazines & Presses, 1977; The Death Mazurka, 1987; Zoom, 1990; Blood to Remember: American Poets on the Holocaust, 1991; Catlives (with Marina Roscher), 1991; As the Sun Goes Down in Fire, 1992; Nineteenth Century Rain, 1994; The Firewalkers, 1996; An Aztec Memory, 1997. Contributions to: Prism International; Poetry Canada Review; Cyphers, Ireland; Abiko Quarterly, Japan; Tel Aviv Review, Israel; Boulevard, US; Georgia Review, USA; Jewish Chronical, NZ; European Judaism, England; Jewish Chronicle, New Zealand; Contemporary Poetics, Korea; Georgia Review, USA; New Letters, USA; Numerous others. Honours: Firman Houghton Award, New England Poetry Club, 1995; Fellowship in Poetry, New York Foundation for the Arts, 1995. Membership: Associated Writing Programs. Address: Knapp Hall, State University of New York at Farmingdale, Farmingdale, NY 11735, USA.

FISK Pauline, (Pauline Davies), b. 27 Sept 1948, London, England. Writer. m. David Davies, 12 Feb 1972, 2 sons, 3 daughters. Publications: Midnight Blue, 1990; Telling the Sea, 1992; Tyger Pool, 1994; Beast of Whixall Moss, 1997. Contributions to: Homes and Gardens, 1989; Something to Do With Love (anthology), 1996. Honours: Smarties Grand Prix Prize, 1990; Shortlisted, Whitbread Award. Address: c/o Laura Cecil, 17 Alwyne Villas, London N1 2HG, England.

FISKE Sharon. See: **HILL Pamela**.

FISKE Tarleton. See: **BLOCH Robert**.

FITTER Richard (Sidney Richmond), b. 1 Mar 1913, London, England. Naturalist; Writer; Editor. m. Alice Mary Stewart Park, 1938, deceased, 2 sons, 1 daughter. Education: Eastbourne College; BSc, London School of Economics and Political Science, 1933. Appointments: Editor, London Naturalist, 1942-46, Kingfisher, 1965-72; Assistant Editor, Countryman, 1946-59; Open Air Correspondent, Observer, 1958-66. Publications: Fitter's Rural Rides: The Observer Illustrated Map-Guide to the Countryside, 1963; Wildlife in Britain, 1963; Wildlife and Death, 1964; British Wildlife: Rarities and Introductions, 1966; The Penguin Dictionary of British Natural History (with Alice Fitter), 1967; Vanishing Wild Animals of the World, 1968; The Birds of Britain and Europe with North Africa and the Middle East (with Hermann Heinzel and J L F Parslow), 1972; Finding Wild Flowers, 1972; The Wild Flowers of Britain and Northern Europe (with Alastair Fitter), 1974; The Penitent Butchers (with Sir Peter Scott), 1978; Handguide to the Wild Flowers of Britain and Europe (with Marjorie Blamey), 1979; Wild Flowers, 1980; The Complete Guide to British Wildlife (with Alastair Fitter), 1981; John Clare's Birds (editor with Eric Robinson), 1982; Collins Guide to the Countryside (with Alastair Fitter), 1984; The Grasses, Sedges, Rushes and Fens of Britain and Northern Europe (with Alastair Fitter), 1984; Wildlife for Men: How and Why We Should Conserve Our Species, 1986; Field Guide to the Freshwater Life of Britain and Northwest Europe (with R Manuel), 1986; The Road to Extinction: Problems of Categorizing the Status of Taxa Threatened with Extinction, (editor with Maisie Fitter), 1987; Guide to the Countryside in Winter (with Alastair Fitter), 1988. Honour: Officer, Order of the Golden Ark, Netherlands, 1978. Memberships: Former Honorary Secretary, British Trust for Ornithology; Chairman, Fauna and Flora Preservation Society, 1983-88; International Union for Conservation of Nature, former Chairman; Royal Society for the Protection of Birds, Former Chairman, Finance and General Purpose Committee; World Wildlife Fund, former Trustee; Fellow, Zoological Society of London; Society of Authors. Address: Drifts, Chinnor Hill, Oxford, OX9 4BS, England.

FITZGERALD Frances, b. 21 Oct 1940, New York, New York, USA. Education: BA, Radcliffe College, 1962. Publications: Fire in the Lake: The Vietnamese & Americans in Vietnam, 1972; America

Revised: History Schoolbooks in the Twentieth Century, 1979; Cities on a Hill: A Journey Through Contemporary American Culture, 1986. Contributions to: New Yorker; Atlantic Monthly; New York Review of Books; Harper's; Vogue; Look; Nation; New Times. Honours: Pulitzer Prize for General Non-Fiction, 1973; National Book Award, 1973; Bancroft Prize, 1973; Christopher Award, 1973; American Academy of Arts and Letters Award, 1973; National Institute of Arts and Letters Award, 1973. Address: c/o Lescher & Lescher Ltd, 67 Irving Place, New York, NY 10003, USA.

FITZGERALD Maureen Elizabeth, b. 24 Dec 1920, Mumbles, Glamorgan, Wales. Journalist. Education: Pensionnat des Servites, Brussels, Belgium; BSc, Economics, University College, London, 1946-49. Appointments: Associate Editor, 1952-62, Editor, Local Government Chronicle, 1963-73, Director, 1968-77, Managing Editor, 1973-77, Editorial Adviser, 1978-80, Consultant and Profile Writer, 1981-85, Profile Writer, 1985-88, Local Government Chronicle. Publication: The Story of a Parish, 1990. Contributions to: Local Government Chronicle; District Council Review; Rating and Valuation; Chamber's Encyclopaedia, Review of the Year; Local Government Review. Honour: Member of the Order of the British Empire, 1979. Memberships: Society of Women Writers and Journalists; Chartered Institute of Journalists; New Cavendish Club. Address: 5 Buckingham Court, Chestnut Lane, Amersham, Buckinghamshire HP6 6EL, England.

FITZGERALD Penelope Mary, b. 17 Dec 1916, Lincoln, England. Teacher; Writer. m. Desmond Fitzgerald, 1942, 1 son, 2 daughters. Education: BA, Somerville College, Oxford. Appointment: English Tutor, Westerminster Tutors, London, 1965-. Publications: The Knox Brothers, 1977; The Bookship, 1978; The Golden Child, 1978; Offshore, 1979; Human Voices, 1980; At Freddies, 1982; Charlotte New and Her Friends, 1984; Innocence, 1986; The Beginning of Spring, 1989; The Gate of Angels, 1990; The Blue Flower, 1995. Honour: Booker McConnell Prize, 1979; Heywood Hill Award for Literary Achievement. Membership: Fellow, Royal Society of Literature; International PEN. Address: c/o Harper-Collins Publishers, 77-85 Fulham Palace Road, London, W6 8BJ, England.

FITZHARDINGE Joan Margaret, (Joan Phipson), b. 16 Nov 1912, Warrawee, New South Wales, Australia. Freelance Writer; Grazier. Publications: Good Luck to the Rider, 1953; Six and Silver, 1954; It Happened One Summer, 1957; The Boundary Riders, 1962; The Family Conspiracy, 1962; Threat to the Barkers, 1963; Birkin, 1965; The Crew of the Merlin, 1966; A Lamb in the Family, 1966; Peter and Butch, 1969; The Haunted Night, 1970; The Way Home, 1973; Polly's Tiger, 1973; Helping Horse, 1974; Bennelong, 1975; The Cats, 1976; Fly into Danger, 1977 (Australian edition as The Bird Smugglers, 1979); Hide Till Daytime, 1977; Keep Calm, 1978; No Escape, 1979; Mr Pringle and the Prince, 1979; A Tide Flowing, 1981; The Watcher in the Garden, 1982; Beryl the Rainmaker, 1984; The Grannie Season, 1985; Dinko, 1985; Hit and Run, 1985; Bianca, 1988. Address: Wongalong, Mandurama, New South Wales 2792, Australia.

FITZSIMMONS Thomas, b. 21 Oct 1926, Lowell, Massachusetts, USA. Poet; Educator. m. Karen Hargreaves, 2 sons. Education: Fresno State College, 1947-49; Sorbonne, Institut de Science Politique, Paris, 1949-50; BA, Stanford University, 1951; MA Honours, Columbia University, 1952. Appointments: Writer, Editor, New Republic magazine, Washington DC, 1952-55; Faculty 1961-, Professor of English 1966-, Oakland University, Michigan; Visiting Lecturer/Professor, various Japanese Universities; Editor/Publisher, Katydid Books, University of Hawaii Press. Publications: This Time This Place, 1969; Morningdew, 1970; Downinside, 1970; Meditation Seeds, 1970; Mooning, 1971; With the Water: Selected Poems, 1969-70, 1972; Playseeds, 1973; Big Huge, 1975; House of My Friend, 1977; Trip Poems, 1978; Great Hawaiian Conquest, 1979; Nine Seas & Eight Mountains, 1981; Rocking Mirror Daybreak, 1983; Japan Personally, 1985. Translations: Ghazals of Ghalib, 1971; Japanese Poetry Now, 1972; A String Around Autumn, 1982; Editor: A Play of Mirrors: Eight Major Poets of Modern Japan, 1986; Muscle and Machine Dream, 1986; The New Poetry of Japan, the 70s and 80s, 1993; The Dream Machine, 1994. Honours: Fulbright Lecturer, 1962-64, 1967-68, 1988-89; National Endowment for the Arts Awards, 1967, 1982, 1990. Memberships: Poetry Center of New Mexico, Board of Directors; PEN. Address: c/o Department of English, Oakland University, Rochester, MI 48063, USA.

FLAM Jack (Donald), b. 2 Apr 1940, Paterson, New Jersey, USA. Professor of Art History; Writer. m. Bonnie Burnham, 7 Oct 1972, 1 daughter. Education: BA, Rutgers University, 1961; MA, Columbia University, 1963; PhD, New York University, 1969. Appointments: Instructor in Art, Newark College of Arts and Sciences, Rutgers University, 1962-66; Assistant Professor of Art, 1966-69, Associate Professor of Art, 1969-72, University of Florida; Associate Professor of Art, 1975-79, Professor of Art, 1980-91, Distinguished Professor of Art, 1991-, Brooklyn College of the City University of New York; Associate Professor of Art History, 1979-80, Professor of Art History, 1980-91, Distinguished Professor of Art History, 1991-, Graduate School and University Center of the City University of New York; Art Critic, The Wall Street Journal, 1984-92. Publications: Matisse on Art, 1973, revised edition, 1995; Zoltan Gorency, 1974; Bread and Butter, 1977; Henri Matisse Paper Cut-Outs (co-author), 1977; Robert Motherwell (co-author), 1983; Matisse: The Man and His Art 1869-1918, 1986; Fernand Léger, 1987; Matisse: A Retrospective, 1988; Motherwell, 1991; Richard Diebenkorn: Ocean Park, 1992; Matisse: The Dance, 1993; Western Artists/African Art, 1994; The Paine Webber Art Collection (co-author), 1995; The Collected Writings (editor), 1996. Contributions to: Apollo. Honours: Guggenheim Fellowship, 1979-80; National Endowment for the Humanities Fellowship, 1987-88. Memberships: International Association of Art Critics; PEN. Address: 35 West 81st Street, New York, NY 10024, USA.

FLEET Kenneth George, b. 12 Sept 1929, Cheshire, England. Journalist. m. (Alice) Brenda Wilkinson, 28 Mar 1953, 3 sons, 1 daughter. Education: BSc, Economics, London School of Economics. Appointments: Journal of Commerce, Liverpool, 1950-52; Sunday Times, 1955-56; Deputy City Editor, Birmingham Post, 1956-58; Deputy Financial Editor, Guardian, 1958-63; Deputy City Editor, 1963, City Editor 1966-77, Daily Telegraph; City Editor, Sunday Telegraph, 1963-66; Editor, Business News, Sunday Times, 1977-78; City Editor, Sunday Express, 1978-82; City Editor-in-Chief, Express Newspapers plc, 1982-85; Executive Editor, Finance and Industry, The Times, 1983-87; Chairman, Chichester Festival Theatre, 1985-; Governor, London Schools of Economics, 1989-; Director, TUS Entertainment plc, 1990-93. Honour: Wincott Award, 1974. Address: c/o 20 Farrington Road, London EC1M 3NH, England.

FLEISCHMAN Paul, b. 5 Sept 1952, Monterey, California, USA. Children's Book Writer. m. Becky Mojica, 15 Dec 1978, 2 sons. Education: University of California at Berkeley, USA; BA, University of New Mexico, USA. Publications: The Birthday Tree, 1979; The Half-a-Moon Inn, 1980; Graven Images, 1982; Path of the Pale Horse, 1983; Finzel the Farsighted, 1983; Coming-and-Going Men, 1985; I Am Phoenix: Poems for Two Voices, 1985; Rondo in C, 1988; Joyful Noise: Poems for Two Voices, 1989; Saturnalia, 1990; Shadow Play, 1990; The Borning Room, 1991; Time Train, 1991. Honours: Silver Medal, Commonwealth Club of California, 1980; Newberry Medals, American Library Association, 1983, 1989; Parents Choice Award, 1983; Numerous citations by Society of Children's Book Writers, American Library Association, New York Times. Memberships: Authors Guild; Society of Children's Book Writers. Address: 855 Marin Pines, Pacific Grove, CA 93950, USA.

FLEISCHMAN (Albert) Sid(ney), b. 16 Mar 1920, New York, New York, USA. Writer. Education: BA, San Diego State College, 1949. Publications: 10 adult novels, 1948-63; Over 40 juvenile books, 1962-95. Address: 305 Tenth Street, Santa Monica, CA 90402, USA.

FLEMING Laurence William Howie, b. 8 Sept 1929, Shillong, Assam, India. Author; Artist; Landscape Designer. Education: The New School, Darjeeling, India, 1941-44; Repton School, Derbyshire, 1945-47; Royal Air Force, 1947-49; St Catharine's College, Cambridge, 1949-52. Publications include: A Diet of Crumbs, 1959; The English Garden, 1979; The One Hour Garden, 1985; Old English Villages, 1986; Roberto Burle Marx, A Portrait, 1996. Contributions to: Journals. Memberships: International PEN; Writers Guild; Anglo Brazilian Society. Address: c/o Lloyds Bank Plc, 112 Kensington High Street, London W8 4SN, England.

FLETCHER John Walter James, (Jonathan Fune), b. 23 June 1937, Barking, England. University Teacher. m. Beryl Sibley Connop, 14 Sept 1961, 2 sons, 1 daughter. Education: BA, University of Cambridge, 1959; MA, 1963, M Phil, University of Toulouse, 1961; PhD, 1964. Appointment: University of East Anglia. Publications: The Novels of Samuel Beckett; Samuel Beckett's Art; Claude Simon and

Fiction Now; Novel and Reader; Alain Robbe-Grillet; New Directions in Literature; Samuel Beckett: His Works and His Critics. Contributions to: Spectator; New Statesman; Numerous Academic Journals. Honours: Scott Moncrieff Translation Prize. Memberships: Society of Authors; Translators Association; Society for the Study of French History; Association for the Study of Modern and Contemporary France; Association of University Teachers. Address: School of Modern Languages and European Studies, University of East Anglia, Norwich NR4 7TJ, England.

FLETCHER Richard. See: **BUTLIN Martin.**

FLEXNER James Thomas, b. 13 Jan 1908, New York, New York, USA. Historian; Biographer. m. Beatrice Hundson, 1 Aug 1950, 1 daughter. Education: BS, Harvard University, 1929. Publications: Doctors on Horseback: Pioneers of American Medicine, 1937; America's Old Masters, 1939, 2nd edition, revised, 1980; William Henry Welch and the Heroic Age of American Medicine (with Simon Flexner), 1941; Steamboats Come True, 1944; History of American Painting, 3 volumes, 1947, 1954, 1962; John Singleton Copley, 1947; A Short History of American Painting, 1950; The Traitor and the Spy: Benedict Arnold and John André, 1953, revised edition, 1975; Gilbert Stuart, 1955; Mohawk Baronet: Sir William Johnson of New York, 1959, revised edition as Lord of the Mohawks: A Biography of Sir William Johnson, 1979; George Washington: A Biography, 4 volumes, 1965, 1968, 1970, 1972; The World of Winslow Homer, 1836-1910, 1966; The Double Adventure of John Singleton Copley, 1969; Nineteenth Century Painting, 1970; Washington: The Indispensable Man, 1974; The Face of Liberty, 1975; The Young Hamilton, 1978; States Dyckman: American Loyalist, 1980; Asher B Durand: An Engraver's and a Farmer's Art, 1983; An American Saga: The Story of Helen Thomas and Simon Flexner, 1984; Poems of the Nineteen Twenties, 1991; On Desperate Seas: Biography of Gilbert Stuart, 1995. Contributions to: Many publications. Honours: Life in America Prize, 1946; Guggenheim Fellowships, 1953, 1979; Francis Parkman Prize, 1963; National Book Award, 1972; Special Pulitzer Prize Citation, 1972; Christopher Award, 1974; Archives of American Art Award, Smithsonian Institution, 1979; Peabody Award, 1984; Gold Medal for Eminence in Biography, American Academy and Institute of Arts and Letters, 1988. Memberships: American Academy and Institute of Arts and Letters; Authors League of America; PEN; Societyof American Historicans, President, 1976-77. Address: 530 86th Street, New York, NY 10028, USA.

FLINT John. See: **WELLS Peter Frederick.**

FLOGSTAD Kjartan, b. 7 June 1944, Sauda, Norway. Novelist. m. Kathrine Norre, 1977. Education: MA, University of Oslo, 1971. Publications: Mooring Lines, 1972; Rasmus, 1974; Not Even Death, 1975; One for All, 1976; Dollar Road, 1977; Fire and Flame, 1980; U3, 1983; The Seventh Climate: Salim Mahmood in Media Thule, 1986; The Knife at the Throat, 1991; Verse: Pilgrimage, 1968; Ceremonies, 1969; Also: The Secret Cheering, 1970; The Law West of Pecos and Other Essays on Popular Art and the Culture Industry, 1981; Wording, 1983; Tyrannosaurus Text, 1988; Portrait of a Magic Life: The Poet Claes Gill, 1988; The Light of Work, 1990. Honours: Melsom Prize, 1980. Address: Gyldendal Norsk Forlag, Postboks 6860, St Olave Plass, 0130 Oslo 1, Norway.

FLORA Joseph Martin, b. 9 Feb 1934, Toledo, Ohio, USA. Educator; Professor. m. 30 Jan 1959, 4 sons. Education: BA, 1956, MA, 1957, PhD, 1962, University of Michigan. Publications: Vardis Fisher, 1965; William Ernest Henley, 1970; Frederick Manfred, 1974; Hemingway's Nick Adams, 1982; Ernest Hemingway: The Art of the Short Fiction, 1989; The English Short Story 1880-1945 (editor), 1985; Co-editor: Southern Writers: A Biographical Dictionary; Fifty Southern Writers Before 1900, 1987; Fifty Southern Writers After 1900, 1987; Contemporary Fiction Writers of the South, 1993; Contemporary Poetry, Dramatists, Essayists, and Novelists of the South, 1994. Contributions to: Studies in Short Fiction; Dialogue; South Atlantic Review; Hemingway Review. Membership: President, Thomas Wolfe Society, 1995-97. Address: 505 Caswell Road, Chapel Hill, NC 27514, USA.

FLOREN Lee, (Brett Austin, Lisa Franchon, Claudia Hall, Wade Hamilton, Matt Harding, Matthew Whitman Harding, Felix Lee Horton, Stuart Jason, Grace Lang, Marguerite Nelson, Lew Smith, Maria Sandra Sterling, Lee Thomas, Len Turner, Will Watson, Dave Wilson), b. 22 Mar 1910, Hinsdale, Montana, USA.

Author. Education: BA, Santa Barbara State College; Teacher's Certificate, Occidental College; MA, Texas Western College, 1964. Publications: Over 300 novels, 1944-. Address: c/o Hale, 45-47 Clerkenwell Green, London EC1R 0HT, England.

FLYNN Robert (Lopez), b. 12 Apr 1932, Chillicothe, Texas, USA. Professor; Writer. m. Jean Sorrels, 1 June 1953, 2 daughters. Appointments: Assistant Professor, Baylor University, Waco, Texas, 1959-63; Professor, Novelist-in-Residence, Trinity University, San Antonio, Texas, 1963-. Publications: North to Yesterday, 1967; In the House of the Lord, 1969; The Sounds of Rescue, The Signs of Hope, 1970; Seasonal Rain and Other Stories, 1986; Wanderer Springs, 1987; A Personal War in Vietnam, 1989; When I Was Just Your Age, 1992; The Last Klick, 1994; Living with the Hyenas, 1996. Address: 101 Cliffside Drive, San Antonio, TX 78231, USA.

FLYNT Candace, b. 12 Mar 1947, Greensboro, North Carolina, USA. Author. m. John Franklin Kime, 29 Jan 1992, 1 son. Education: BA, Greensboro College, 1969; MFA, University of North Carolina, 1974. Publications: Mother Love; Chasing Dad. Memberships: Authors Guild; PEN. Address: c/o Rhoda A Weyr, 151 Bergen Street, Brooklyn, NY 11217, USA.

FO Dario, b. 24 Mar 1926, San Giano, Lombardy, Italy. Playwright. Education: Academy of Fine Arts, Milan. Appointment: Founder, La Comune Theatre Collective, Milan, 1970. Publications: The Virtuous Burglars, One Was Nude and One Wore Tails, Women Undresses and Bodies Ready to be Dispatched, all 1957; Archangels Don't Play Pinball, 1959; Two Pistols, 1960; He Who Steals a Foot is Lucky in Love, 1961; Teatro Comico, 1963; Le Commedie I-IX, 1966-91; The Boss's Funeral, 1969; Accidental Death of an Anarchist, 1970; Basta con i fascisti, 1973; We Can't Pay We Won't Pay, 1974; Female Parts: One Woman Plays, 1977; The Fourth Wall, Waking Up, A Woman and The Same Old Story, all 1984; The Tale of a Tiger, 1978; Betty, 1980; About Face, 1981; Adaptations of Stravinsky's The Soldier's Tale and Gay's The Beggar's Opera, 1979; The Mother, 1982; Obscene Fables, 1982; The Open Couple, 1983; Elizabeth: Almost by Chance a Woman, 1984; The History of Masks, 1984; Eve's Diary, 1984; The Whore in the Madhouse and I'm Ulrike, Screaming, 1985; An Ordinary Day, 1986; Il ratto della Francesca, 1986; The Pope and the Witch, 1989; Plays One, 1992; Television plays. Honour: Soning Award, 1981. Address: c/o CTFR, Viale Piave 11, 20129 Milan, Italy.

FOGEL Robert William, b. 1 July 1926, New York, New York, USA. Economic Historian; Professor. m. Enid Cassandra Morgan, 2 Apr 1949, 2 sons. Education: AB, Cornell University, 1948; AM, Columbia University, 1960; PhD, Johns Hopkins University, 1963; MA, University of Cambridge, 1975, Harvard University, 1976; DSc, University of Rochester, 1987, University of Palermo, 1994. Appointments: Ford Foundation Visiting Research Professor, 1963-64, Associate Professor, 1964-65, Professor of Economics, 1965-69, Professor of Economics and History, 1970-75, Charles R Walgreen Distinguished Service Professor of American Institutions, 1981-, University of Chicago; Research Associate, 1978-, Director, DAE Program, 1978-91, National Bureau of Economic Research. Publications: The Dimensions of Quantitative Research in History (with others), 1972; Time on the Cross: The Economics of American Negro Slavery (with S L Engerman), 1974; Ten Lectures on the New Economic History, 1977; Which Road to the Past?: Two Views of History (with G R Elton), 1983; Long-Term Changes in Nutrition and the Standard of Living (editor), 1986; Without Consent or Contract: The Rise and Fall of American Slavery (with others), 4 volumes, 1989, 1992; Egalitarianism: The Economic Revolution of the 20th Century, 1994; The Escape from Hunger and Premature Death: Europe, America and the Third World: 1700-2100, 1995; The Political Realignment of the 1850s: A Socioeconomic Analysis, 1996. Contributions to: Numerous books and scholarly journals. Honours: Gilman Fellowship, 1957-60; Arthur H Cole Prize, 1968; Schumpeter Prize, 1971; Bancroft Prize, 1975; Gustavus Myers Prize, 1990; Nobel Prize in Economic Science, 1993. Memberships: American Academy of Arts and Sciences; American Economic Society; American Historical Association; Corresponding Fellow, British Academy; Fellow, Econometric Society. Address: c/o Graduate School of Business, University of Chicago, 1101 East 58th Street, Chicago, IL 60637, USA.

FOLEY (Mary) Louise Munro, b. 22 Oct 1933, Toronto, Ontario, Canada. (US citizen). Author. m. Donald J Foley, 9 Aug 1957, 2 sons. Education: University of Western Ontario, 1951-52; Ryerson Institute of Technology, 1952-53; BA, California State University, Sacramento, 1976. Appointments: Columnist, News-Argus, Goldsboro, North Carolina, USA, 1971-73; Editor of Publications, Institute for Human Service Management, California State University, Sacramento, 1975-80. Publications: The Caper Club, 1969; No Talking, Sammy's Sister, A Job for Joey, 1970; Somebody Stole Second, 1972; Stand Close to the Door (editor), 1976; Tackle 22, 1978; Women in Skilled Labor (editor), 1980; The Train of Terror, 1982; The Sinister Studies of KESP-TV, 1983; The Lost Tribe, 1983; The Mystery of the Highland Crest, 1984; The Mystery of Echo Lodge, Danger at Anchor Mine, 1985; The Mardi Gras Mystery, 1987; Mystery of the Sacred Stones, 1988; Australia! Find the Flying Foxes, 1988; The Cobra Connection, 1990; Ghost Train, 1991; Poison! Said the Cat, 1992; Blood! Said the Cat, 1992; Thief! Said the Cat, 1992; In Search of the Hidden Statue, 1993; Moving Target, 1993; Stolen Affections, 1995; Running Into Trouble, 1996; The Vampire Cat Series: My Substitute Teacher's Gone Baity, 1996, The Bird-Brained Fiasco, 1996, The Phoney Baloney Professor, 1996, The Cat-Nap Cat-Astrophe, 1997. Memberships: Authors Guild; California Writers Club; National League of American Pen Women; Society of Children's Book Writers and Illustrators; Novelists Inc. Address: 5010 Jennings Way, Sacramento, CA 95819, USA.

FOLKE Will. See: **BLOCH Robert.**

FOLLETT Ken(neth Martin), b. 5 June 1949, Cardiff, Wales. Author. m. (1) 5 Jan 1968, 1 son, 1 daughter, (2) 8 Nov 1985. Education: BA Honours, University College, London; Apprenticeship in Journalism. Publications: The Shakeout, 1975; The Bear Raid, 1976; The Modigliani Scandal, 1976; The Power Twins and the Worm Puzzle, 1976; The Secret of Kellerman's Studio, 1976; Paper Money, 1977; Eye of the Needle, 1978; Triple, 1979; The Key to Rebecca, 1980; The Man from St Petersburg, 1982; On Wings of Eagles, 1983; Lie Down with Lions, 1986; The Pillars of the Earth, 1989; Night Over Water, 1991; A Dangerous Fortune, 1993; A Place Called Freedom, 1995; The Third Twin, 1996; Other: Various Screenplays. Contributions to: Book reviews and essays among others, in many publications. Honour: Edgar Award for Best Novel, Mystery Writers of America, 1979. Memberships: National Union of Journalists, UK; Writers Guild, USA. Address: PO Box 708, London, SW10 0DH, England.

FONER Eric, b. 7 Feb 1943, New York, New York, USA. Professor of History; Writer. m. Lynn Garafola, 1 May 1980, 1 daughter. Education: BA, Columbia College, 1963; BA, Oriel College, Oxford, 1965; PhD, Columbia University, 1969. Appointments: Professor, City College and Graduate Center, City University of New York, 1973-82; Pitt Professor of American History and Institutions, Cambridge University, 1980-81; Professor, 1982-88, DeWitt Clinton Professor of History, 1988-, Columbia University; Fulbright Professor of American History, Moscow State University, 1990; Harmsworth Professor of American History, Oxford University, 1993-94. Publications: Nothing But Freedom: Emancipation and Its Legacy, 1983; Reconstruction: America's Unfinished Revolution 1863-1877, 1988; A Short History of Reconstruction, 1990; A House Divided: America in the Age of Lincoln (with Olivia Mahoney), 1990; The New American History (editor), 1990; Reader's Companion to American History (editor with John A Garraty), 1991; Freedom's Lawmakers: A Directory of Black Officeholders During Reconstruction, 1993, revised edition, 1996; Thomas Paine, 1995; America's Reconstruction: People and Politics After the Civil War (with Olivia Mahoney), 1995. Contributions to: Scholarly journals and periodicals. Honours: American Council of Learned Societies Fellowship, 1972-73; Guggenheim Fellowship, 1975-76; National Endowment for the Humanities Senior Fellowship, 1982-83, 1996-97; Los Angeles Times Book Award for History, 1989; Bancroft Prize, 1989; Parkman Prize, 1989; Lionel Trilling Award, 1989; Owsley Prize, 1989; James Harvey Robinson Prize, American Historical Association, 1991; Literary Lion, New York Public Library, 1994; Scholar of the Year Award, New York Council for the Humanities, 1995. Memberships: American Academy of Arts and Sciences; Corresponding Fellow, British Academy. Address: 606 West 116th Street, New York, NY 10027, USA.

FONSECA James William, b. 13 Oct 1947, Fall River, Massachusetts, USA. College Professor and Administrator. m. Elaine Rae Hart, 20 Nov 1971, 1 son. Education: BA Geography, Bridgewater State College, Massachusetts, 1969; PhD Geography, Clark University, 1974. Publications: Urban Rank Size Hierarchy, 1988; Atlas of American Higher Education, (with Alice Andrews), 1993; Atlas of American Society, (with Alice Andrews), 1995. Membership: Manassas

Area Writer's Roundtable. Address: George Mason University, 7946 Donegan Drive, Manassas, VA 20109-2870, USA.

FOOT Michael, b. 23 July 1913, Plymouth, England. Journalist; Politician. m. Jill Craigie, 1949. Education: Wadham College, Oxford. Appointments: Assistant Editor, 1937-38, Joint Editor, 1948-52, Editor, 1952-59, Managing Editor, 1952-74, Tribune; Staff, 1938, Acting Editor, 1942-44, Evening Standard; Political Colunist, Daily Herald, 1944-64; Member of Parliament, Labour Party, Devonport Division of Plymouth, 1945-55, Ebbw Vale, 1960-83, Blaenau Gwent, 1983-92; Secretary of State for Employment, 1974-76; Lord President of the Council and Leader of the House of Commons, 1976-79; Deputy Leader, 1976-80, Leader, 1980-83, Labour Party. Publications: Guilty Men (with Frank Owen and Peter Howard), 1940; Armistice 1918-1939, 1940; Trial of Mussolini, 1943; Brendan and Beverley, 1944; Who Are the Patriots?, 1949; Still at Large, 1950; Full Speed Ahead, 1950; The Pen and the Sword, 1957; Parliament in Danger, 1959; Aneurin Bevan, 2 volumes, 1962, 1973; Harold Wilson: A Political Biography, 1964; Debts of Honour, 1980; Another Heart and Other Pulses, 1984; Loyalists and Loners, 1986; The Politics of Paradise, 1988; H G, The History of Mr Wells, 1995. Honours: Honorary Fellow, Wadham College, 1969; Honorary DLitt, University of Wales, 1985. Address: 308 Gray's Inn Road, London WC1X 8DY, England.

FOOT Michael (Richard Daniel), b. 14 Dec 1919, London, England. Professor of Modern History; Writer. Education: New College, Oxford. Appointments: Teacher, Oxford, 1947-59; Professor of Modern History, University of Manchester, 1967-73; Director of Studies, European Discussion Centre, 1973-75. Publications: Gladstone and Liberalism (with J L Hammond), 1952; British Foreign Policy Since 1898, 1952; Men in Uniform, 1961; SOE in France, 1966; The Gladstone Diaries (editor), 4 volumes, 1968, 1974; War and Society, 1973; Resistance, 1976; Six Faces of Courage, 1978; M19 (with J M Langley), 1979; SOE: An Outline History, 1984; Art and War, 1990; Holland at War Against Hitler (editor), 1990; The Oxford Companion to the Second World War (joint editor), 1995. Honours: French Croix de Guerre, 1945; Officer of the Order of Orange Nassau, Netherlands, 1989. Address: Martins Cottage, Bell Lane, Nuthampstead, Hertfordshire, SG8 8ND, England.

FOOT Paul (Mackintosh), b. 8 Nov 1937, Haifa, Palestine. Writer; Journalist. m. 3 sons, 1 daughter. Education: BA, University College, Oxford, 1961. Appointments: Editor, Isis, 1961, Socialist Worker, 1974-75; President, Oxford Union, 1961; TUC Delegate, National Union of Journalists, 1967, 1971; Staff, Daily Mirror, 1979-93, Private Eye, 1993-. Publications: Immigration and Race in British Politics, 1965; The Politics of Harold Wilson, 1968; The Rise of Enoch Powell, 1969; Who Killed Hanratty?, 1971; Why You Should Be a Socialist, 1977; Red Shelley, 1981; The Helen Smith Story, 1983; Murder at the Farm: Who Killed Carl Bridgewater?, 1986; Who Framed Colin Wallace?, 1989; Words as Weapons, 1990. Honours: Journalist of the Year Awards, 1972, 1989; Campaigning Journalist of the Year, British Press Awards, 1980; George Orwell Prize for Journalism, 1994. Address: c/o Private Eye, 6 Carlisle Street, London W1V 5RG, England.

FOOT Philippa Ruth, b. 3 Oct 1920. Philosopher; Professor; Writer. m. M R D Foot, 1945, div 1960. Education: BA, 1942, MA, 1946, Somerville College, Oxford. Appointments: Lecturer in Philosophy, 1947, Fellow and Tutor, 1950-69, Vice Principal, 1967-69, Senior Research Fellow, 1970-88, Somerville College, Oxford; Professor of Philosophy, 1974-91, Griffin Professor, 1988-91, Professor Emeritus, 1991-, University of California, Los Angeles; Fellow, Center for Advanced Studies in the Behavioral Sciences, Stanford, California, 1981-82; Various visiting professorships. Publications: Theories of Ethics (editor), 1967; Virtues and Vices, 1978. Contributions to: Scholarly journals and periodicals. Memberships: Fellow, American Academy of Arts and Sciences; American Philosophical Association. Address: 15 Walton Street, Oxford, OX1 2HG, England.

FOOTE (Albert) Horton (Jr), b. 14 Mar 1916, Wharton, Texas, USA. Dramatist; Scriptwriter. m. Lillian Vallish, 4 June 1945, 2 sons, 2 daughters. Education: Pasadena Playhouse School Theatre, California, 1933-35; Tamara Daykarhanova School Theatre, New York City, 1937-39. Appointments: Actor, American Actors Theatre, New York City, 1939-42; Theatre Workshop Director and Producer, King-Smith School of Creative Arts, Washington, DC, 1944-45;

Manager, Productions Inc, Washington, DC, 1945-48. Publications: Novel: The Chase, 1956. Plays: Texas Town, 1942; Out of My House, 1942; Only the Heart, 1944; Celebration, 1948; The Chase, 1952; The Trip to Bountiful, 1953; The Midnight Caller, 1953; A Young Lady of Property, 1954; The Traveling Lady, 1955; The Roads to Home, 1955; Tomorrow, 1960; Roots in a Parched Ground, 1962; The Road to the Graveyard, 1985; Blind Date, 1986; Habitation of Dragons, 1988; Dividing the Estate, 1989; Talking Pictures, 1990; The Young Man from Atlanta, 1994; Night Seasons, 1994; Laura Dennis, 1994. Screenplays: Storm Fear, 1956; To Kill a Mockingbird, 1962; Baby, The Rain Must Fall, 1965; Hurry Sundown, 1966; Tomorrow, 1971; Tender Mercies, 1983; 1918, 1984; On Valentine's Day, 1985; The Trip to Bountiful, 1985; Spring Moon, 1987; Convicts, 1991; Of Mice and Men, 1992. Other: Many television scripts. Honours: Academy Awards, 1962, 1983; Writers Guild of America Awards, 1962, 1989; Pulitzer Prize in Drama, 1995. Address: c/o Lucy Kroll Agency, 390 West End Avenue, New York, NY 10024, USA.

FOOTE Shelby, b. 17 Nov 1916, Greenville, Mississippi, USA. Author; Historian; Dramatist. m. Gwyn Rainer, 5 Sept 1956, 1 son, 1 daughter. Education: University of North Carolina, 1935-37. Appointments: Guest Lecturer, University of Virginia, 1963; Playwright-in-Residence, Arena Stage, Washington, DC, 1963-64; Writer-in-Residence, Hollins College, Virginia, 1968; Academic Advisory Board, US Naval Academy, 1988-89. Publications: Fiction: Tournament, 1949; Follow Me Down, 1950; Love in a Dry Season, 1951; Shiloh, 1952; Jordan County: A Landscape in Narrative, 1954; September September, 1977. Non-fiction: The Civil War: A Narrative: Vol I: Fort Sumter to Perryville, 1958, Vol II: Fredericksburg to Meridian, 1963, Vol III: Red River to Appomattox, 1974; The Novelist's View of History, 1981; Stars in Their Courses, 1994; The Beleaguered City, 1995; Play: Jordan County: A Landscape in the Round, 1964. Editor: The Night Before Chancellorsville and Other Civil War Stories, 1957; Chickamauga and Other Civil War Stories, 1993. Other: The Civil War, adapted for PBS telecast, 1990. Honours: Guggenheim Fellowships, 1955-57; Ford Foundation Grant, 1963; Fletcher Pratt Awards, 1963, 1974; Distinguished Alumnus, University of North Carolina, 1975; Dos Passos Prize for Literature, 1988; Charles Frankel Award, 1992; St Louis Literary Award, 1992; Nevins-Freeman Award, 1992; Several honorary doctorates. Memberships: American Academy of Arts and Letters; Fellowship of Southern Writers; Society of American Historians. Address: 542 East Parkway South, Memphis, TN 38104, USA.

FORBES Bryan, b. 22 July 1926, Stratford, London, England. Film Executive; Director; Screenwriter. m. Nanette Newman, 1955, 2 daughters. Education: West Ham Secondary School; Royal Academy Dramatic of Art. Publications: Truth Lies Sleeping, 1951; The Distant Laughter, 1972; Notes for a Life, 1974; The Slipper and the Rose, 1976; Ned's Girl, 1977; Familiar Strangers, 1979; The Despicable Race, 1980; The Rewrite Man, 1983; The Endless Game, 1986; A Song at Twilight, 1989; A Divided Life, 1992; The Twisted Playground, 1993; Partly Cloudy, 1995. Honours: Best Screenplay Awards; UN Award; Many Film Festival Prizes; Honorary DL, London, 1987. Memberships: Beatrix Potter Society; National Youth Theatre of Great Britain; Writers Guild of Great Britain. Address: c/o The Bookshop, Virginia Water, Surrey, England.

FORBES Colin. See: **SAWKINS Raymond H(arold).**

FORBES John, b. 1 Sept 1950, Melbourne, Victoria, Australia. Poet; Writer. Education: BA, University of Sydney, 1973. Appointment: Editor, Surfer's Paradise, 1974-83. Publications: Tropical Skiing, 1976; On the Beach, 1977; Drugs, 1980; Stalin's Holidays, 1981; The Stunned Mullet and Other Poems, 1988; New and Selected Poems, 1992. Contributions to: Newspapers and magazines. Honours: New Poetry Prize, 1973; Southerly Prize, 1976; Grace Leverson Prize, 1993. Membership: Australian Society of Authors. Address: 54 Morris Street, Summerhill, New South Wales, Australia.

FORBES (DeLoris Florine) Stanton, (Forbes Rydell, Tobias Wells), b. 29 July 1923, Kansas City, Missouri, USA. Writer. m. William James Forbes, 29 Oct 1948, 2 sons, 1 daughter. Appointment: Associate Editor, Wellesley Townsmen, Massachusetts, 1960-72. Publications: Over 40 mystery novels. Contributions to: Magazines. Honour: Best Mystery of the Year, 1963. Membership: Mystery Writers of America. Address: Sanford, FL 32771, USA.

FORCHE Carolyn (Louise), b. 28 Apr 1950, Detroit, Michigan, USA. Poet; Writer; Associate Professor. m. Henry E Mattison, 27 Dec 1984, 1 son. Education BA, Michigan State University, 1972; MFA, Bowling Green State University, 1975. Appointments: Visiting Lecturer in Poetry, Michigan State University, Justin Morrill College, East Lansing, 1974; Visiting Lecturer, 1975, Assistant Professor, 1976-78, San Diego State University; Journalist and Human Rights Activist, El Salvador, 1978-80; Visiting Lecturer, 1979, Visiting Associate Professor, 1982-83, University of Virginia; Assistant Professor, 1980, Associate Professor, 1981, Universityof Arkansas at Fayetteville; Visiting Writer, New York University, 1983, 1985, Vassar College, 1984; Adjunct Associate Professor, Columbia University, 1984-85; Visiting Associate Professor, University of Minnesota, 1985; Writer-in-Residence, State University of New York at Albany, 1985; Associate Professor, George Mason University, 1994-. Publications: Poetry: Gathering the Tribes, 1976; The Country Between Us, 1981; The Angel of History, 1994. Non-fiction: Women in the Labor Movement, 1835-1925: An Annotated Bibliography (with Martha Jane Soltow), 1972; Women and War in El Salvador (editor), 1980; El Salvador: The Work of Thirty Photographers (with others), 1983. Other: Claribel Alegria: Flowers from the Volcano (translator), 1982; Against Forgetting: Twentieth-Century Poetry of Witness (editor), 1993. Contributions tio: Anthologies and periodicals. Honours: Devine Memeorial fellowship in Poetry, 1975; Yale Series of Younger Poets Award, 1975; Tennessee Williams Fellowship in Poetry, Bread Loaf Writers Conference, 1976; National Endowment for the Arts Fellowships, 1977, 1984; Guggenheim Fellowship, 1978; Emily Clark Balch prize, Virginia Quarterly Review, 1979; Alice Fay di Castagnola Award, Poetry Society of America, 1981; Lamont Poetry Selection Award, Academy of American Poets, 1981; Los Angeles Times Book Award for Poetry, 1994. Memberships: Academy of American Poets; Amnesty International; Associated Writing Programs, president, 1994-; PEN American Centre; Poetry Society of America; Theta Sigma Phi. Address: c/o Department of English, George Mason University, 4400 University Drive, Fairfax, VA 22030, USA.

FORD David. See: **HARKNETT Terry.**

FORD Kirk. See: **SPENCE William (John Duncan).**

FORD Peter, b. 3 June 1936, Harpenden, Hertfordshire, England. Author; Editorial Consultant, div, 2 sons, 1 daughter. Education: St Georges School, 1948-52. Appointments: Editor, Cassell, 1958-61; Senior Copy Editor, Penguin Books, 1961-64; Senior Editor, Thomas Nelson, 1964-70. Publications: The Fool on the Hill, 1975; Scientists and Inventors, 1979; The True History of the Elephant Man, 1980; Medical Mysteries, 1985; The Picture Buyer's Handbook, 1988; A Collector's Guide to Teddy Bears, 1990; Rings and Curtains: Family and Personal Memoirs, 1992; The Monkey's Paw and Other Stories by W W Jacobs, 1994. Memberships: Society of Authors; New York Academy of Sciences; Folklore Society. Address: The Storehouse, Longhope, Orkney, KW16 3PQ, Scotland.

FORD Richard, b. 16 Feb 1944, Jackson, Mississippi, USA. Writer. m. Kristina Hensley, 1968. Education: BA, Michigan State University, 1966; MFA, University of California, Irvine, 1970. Appointments: Lecturer, University of Michigan, Ann Arbor, 1974-76; Assistant Professor of English, Williams College, Williamstown, Massachusetts, 1978-79; Lecturer, Princeton University, 1979-80. Publications: Fiction: A Piece of My Heart, 1976; The Ultimate Good Luck, 1981; The Sportswriter, 1986; Rock Springs: Stories, 1987; Wildlife, 1990; Independence Day, 1995. Play: American Tropical, 1983; Screenplay: Bright Angel, 1991. Editor: The Best American Short Stories (with Shannon Ravenal), 1990; The Granta Book of the American Short Story, 1992. Contributions to: Various periodicals. Honours: Guggenheim Fellowship, 1977-78; National Endowment for the Arts Fellowships, 1979-80, 1985-86; Mississippi Academy of Arts and Letters Literature Award, 1987; American Academy and Institute of Arts and Letters Award, 1989; Echoing Green Foundation Award, 1991; Pulitzer Prize in Fiction, 1996; PEN-Faulkner Award, 1996. Memberships: PEN; Writers Guild. Address: c/o Amanda Urban, International Creative Management, 40 West 57th Street, New York, NY 10019, USA.

FORD R(obert) A(rthur) D(ouglass), b. 8 Jan 1915, Ottawa, Ontario, Canada. Former Ambassador; Poet. Education: MA, Cornell University, New York. Appointments: Ambassador to the Soviet Union, 1964-80. Publications: A Window on the North, 1956; The Solitary City, 1969; Holes in Space, 1979; Needle in the Eye, 1983; Doors, Words and Silence, 1985; Dostoevsky and Other Poems, 1988; Coming From Afar: Selected Poems, 1990; Our Man in Moscow: A Diplomat's Reflection on the Soviet Union from Stalin to Brezhnev, 1989; A Moscow Literary Memoir, 1993. Honours: Governor-General's Medal, 1956; Companion of Canada, 1971; LLD, University of Toronto, 1987. Address: La Poivrière, Saint Sylvestre Pragoulin, 63310 Randan, France.

FORDHAM William. See: SEARLE Ronald.

FOREMAN Richard, b. 10 June 1937, New York, New York, USA. Dramatist; Director. m. Amy Taubin, 1961, div 1972. Education: BA, Brown University, 1959; MFA, Yale University, 1962. Appointments: Artistic Director, Ontological-Hysteric Theatre, New York City, 1968-, Theatre O H, Paris, 1973-85; Director-in-Residence, New York Shakespeare Festival, 1975-76; Director, Broadway and Off-Broadway plays. Publications: Dr Selavy's Magic Theater, 1972; Rhoda in Potatoland, 1976; Theatre of Images, 1977; Reverberation Machines, 1985; Film is Evil: Radio is Good, 1987; Unbalancing Acts: Foundations for a Theater, 1992; My Head Was a Sledgehammer, 1995. Honours: Creative Artists Public Service Fellow, New York State Arts Council, 1971, 1974; Guggenheim Fellowship, 1972; Rockefeller Foundation Fellow, 1974; Lifetime Achievement Award, National Endowment for the Arts, 1990; American Academy of Arts and Letters Prize in Literature, 1992; Honorary DArts, Brown University, 1993; MacArthur Fellow, 1995-2000. Memberships: Dramatists Guild; PEN; Society of Stage Directors. Address: 152 Wooster Street, New York, NY 10012, USA.

FORGAS Joseph Paul, b. 16 May 1947, Budapest, Hungary. University Professor. m. Letitia Jane Carr, 16 Mar 1974, 2 sons. Education: BA Hons, Macquarie, 1974; DPhil, 1977; DSc, 1990, Oxford. Publications: Social Episodes, 1979; Social Cognition, 1981; Interpersonal Behavior, 1985; Affect, Cognition - Social Behaviour (with K Fiedler), 1988; Emotion and Social Judgement, 1991; Soziale Kognition und Kommunikation, 1993. Contributions to: Over 100 articles - chapters published. Honours: APS Early Career Award, 1983; Alexander von Humboldt Prize, 1994. Address: Psychology, University of New South Wales, Sydney 2052, Australia.

FORKER Charles R(ush), b. 11 Mar 1927, Pittsburgh, Pennsylvania, USA. Professor Emeritus; Writer. Education: AB, Bowdoin College, 1951; BA, 1953, MA, 1955, Merton College, Oxford; PhD, Harvard University, 1957. Appointments: Instructor, University of Wisconsin, 1957-59; Instructor, 1959-61, Assistant Professor, 1961-65, Associate Professor, 1965-68, Professor, 1968-92, Professor Emeritus, 1992-, Indiana University; Visiting Professor, University of Michigan, 1969-70, Dartmouth College, 1982-83, Concordia University, Montreal, 1989. Publications: James Shirley: The Cardinal (editor), 1964; William Shakespeare: Henry V (editor), 1971; Edward Phillips's "History of the Literature of England and Scotland": A Translation from the "Compendiosa Enumeratio Poetarum" with an Introduction and Commentary (with Daniel G Calder), 1973; Visions and Voices of the New Midwest (associate editor), 1978; Henry V: An Annotated Bibliography (with Joseph Candido), 1983; Skull Beneath the Skin: The Achievement of John Webster, 1986; Fancy's Images: Contexts, Settings, and Perspectives in Shakespeare and His Contemporaries, 1990; Christopher Marlowe: Edward the Second (editor), 1994; Richard II: The Critical Tradition, 1997. Contributions to: Scholarly books and journals. Honours: Fulbright Fellowship, England, 1951-53; Folger Fellow, 1963; Huntington Library Fellow, 1969; National Endowment for the Humanities Senior Research Fellow, 1980-81. Memberships: American Association of University Professors; Guild of Anglican Scholars, president; International Shakespeare Association; Malone Society; Marlowe Society; Modern Language Association; Renaissance Society of America; Shakespeare Society of America; World Centre for Shakespeare Studies, advisory board. Address: 1219 East Maxwell Lane, Bloomington, IN 47401, USA.

FORREST Leon, b. 8 Jan 1937, Chicago, Illinois, USA. Professor; Writer. Education: Wilson Junior College, 1955-56; Roosevelt University, 1957-58; University of Chicago, 1958-60, 1962-64. Appointments: Associate Editor, 1969-72, Managing Editor, 1972-73, Muhammad Speaks newspaper; Associate Professor, 1973-84, Professor, 1984-, Chairman, Department of African-American Studies, 1985-, Northwestern University. Publications: There is a Tree More Ancient Than Eden, 1973; The Bloodworth Orphans, 1977; Two Wings to Veil My Face, 1984; Relocations of the Spirit: Essays, 1994. Address: c/o Department of African-American Studies, Northwestern

University, Arthur Anderson Hall, 2003 Sheridan Road, Evanston, IL 60201, USA.

FORREST Richard (Stockton), (Stockton Woods), b. 8 May 1932, Orange, New Jersey, USA. Writer. m. (1) Frances Anne Reese, 20 Dec 1952, div 1955, 1 son, (2) Mary Bolan Brumby, 11 May 1955, dec 1996, 5 children. Education: New York Dramatic Workshop, 1950; University of South Carolina, 1953-55. Publications: Who Killed Mr Garland's Mistress?, 1974; A Child's Garden of Death, 1975; The Wizard of Death, 1977; Death Through the Looking Glass, 1978; The Death in the Willows, 1979; The Killing Edge, 1980; The Laughing Man, 1980; Death at Yew Corner, 1981; Game Bet, 1981; The Man Who Heard Too Much, 1983; Death Under the Lilacs, 1985; Lark, 1986; Death on the Mississippi, 1989; The Complete Nursing Home Guide (with Mary Forrest), 1990; Retirement Living (with Mary Forrest), 1991; Pied Piper of Death, 1997. Contributions to: Periodicals. Honour: Edgar Allan Poe Award, Mystery Writers of America, 1975. Memberships: Mystery Writers of America. Address: 3501 St Paul Street, Apt 312, Baltimore, MD 21218, USA.

FORREST Studley. See: HUGHES Robert.

FORSTER Margaret, b. 25 May 1938, Carlisle, Cumberland, England. Writer. m. Hunter Davies, 11 June 1960, 1 son, 2 daughters. Education: BA, Sommerville College, Oxford, 1960. Appointments: Teacher, Barnbury Girls School, London, 1961-63; Chief Non Fiction Reviewer, London Evening Standard, 1977-80. Publications: Georgy Girl, 1963; The Bogeyman, 1966; The Park, 1968; Mr Bone's Retreat, 1971; Mother, Can You Hear Me?, 1979; Marital Rites, 1981; Private Papers, 1986; Lady's Maid, 1989; The Battle for Christobel, 1991. Membership: Royal Society of Literature. Address: 11 Boscastle Road, London, NW5, England.

FORSYTH Frederick, b. 1938, Ashford, Kent, England. Writer. m. Carole, Sept 1973, 2 sons. Education: University of Granada. Appointments: Reporter, Eastern Daily Press, 1958-61, Reuters News Agency, 1961-65; Reporter, 1965-67, Assistant Diplomatic Correspondent, 1967-68, BBC. Publications: Novels: The Day of the Jackal, 1971; The Odessa File, 1972; The Dogs of War, 1974; The Shepherd, 1975; The Devil's Alternative, 1979; The Fourth Protocol, 1984; The Negotiator, 1989; The Deceiver, 1991. Other: The Biafra Story, 1969, revised edition as The Making of an African Legend: The Biafra Story, 1977; Emeka, 1982; No Comebacks: Collected Short Stories, 1982; The Fourth Protocol (screenplay), 1987. Honour: Edgar Allan Poe Award, Mystery Writers of America, 1971. Address: St John's Wood, London, England.

FOSTER David (Manning), b. 15 May 1944, Sydney, New South Wales, Australia. Novelist. Education: BSc in Chemistry, University of Sydney, 1967; PhD, Australian National University, Canberra, 1970. Publications: The Pure Land, 1974; The Empathy Experiment, 1977; Moonlite, 1981; Plumbum, 1983; Dog Rock: A Postal Pastoral, 1985; The Adventures of Christian Rosy Cross, 1986; Testostero, 1987; The Pale Blue Crochet Coathanger Cover, 1988; Mates of Mars, 1991; Self Portraits (editor), 1991; A Slab of Fosters, 1994; The Glade Within the Grove, 1996; The Ballad of Erinungarah, 1997. Short stories: North South West: Three Novellas, 1973; Escape to Reality, 1977; Hitting the Wall: Two Novellas, 1989. Honours: Australian National Book Council Award, 1981; New South Wales Premier's Fellowship, 1986; Australian Artists Creative Fellowship, 1991; Keating Fellowship, 1991-94; James Joyce Foundation Award, 1996. Address: PO Box 57, Bundanoon, New South Wales 2578, Australia.

FOSTER Donald Wayne, b. 22 June 1950, Chicago, Illinois, USA. m. Gwen Bell Foster, 29 Dec 1974, 2 sons. Education: BA, Wheaton College, 1972; MA, 1983, PhD, 1985, University of California. Appointments: Visiting Lecturer, University of California, Santa Barbara, 1984-85; Assistant Professor, 1986-90, Associate Professor, 1990-, Jean Webster Chair of Dramatic Literature, 1991-, Vassar College. Publications: Eleg, by W S: A Study in Attribution; Women's Works: An Anthology of British Literature; SHAXICON: A lexical database for Shakespeare studies, 1995. Contributions to: Books and scholarly journals. Honours: William Riley Parker Prize; Delaware Shakespeare Prize. Memberships: Modern Language Association; Shakespeare Association of America; Renaissance English Text Society; American Association of University Professors. Address: Box 388, Vassar College, Poughkeepsie, NY 12601, USA.

FOSTER James Anthony, (Tony Foster), b. 2 Aug 1932, Winnipeg, Manitoba, Canada. Writer. m. 10 Oct 1964, 1 son, 2 daughters. Education: University of Brunswick, 1950. Appointments: Royal Canadian Air Force, 1950; US Army 10th Special Forces Group, 1952-53; Itinerant Crop Duster Pilot, 1954; Bush Pilot for Saskatchewan, 1957-58; Chief Pilot, 1959; Real Estate Development in Caribbean, 1968; MGm & Wm, 1976. Publications: Zig Zag to Armageddon; The Bush Pilots; By Pass; The Money Burn; Heart of Oak; Sea Wings; Meeting of Generals; Muskets to Missiles; Rue Du Bac; For Love and Glory; Ransom for a God; The Sound and the Silence; Swan Song. Contributions to: Numerous TV movies, documentaries and series scripts. Memberships: Writers Union of Canada; Canadian Authors Association; PEN; Writers Guild of America. Address: 67 Briarwood Crescent, Halifax, Nova Scotia B3M 1P2, Canada.

FOSTER Jeanne. See: **WILLIAMS Jeanne.**

FOSTER John Bellamy, b. 19 Aug 1953, Seattle, Washington, USA. m. Laura Tamkin, 30 Aug 1987, 1 son, 1 daughter. Education: BA, The Evergreen State College, 1975; MA, York University, 1977; PhD, York University, 1984. Publications: The Faltering Economy (co-edited with Henryk Szlaifer), 1984; The Theory of Monopoly Capitalism, 1986; The Limits of Environmentalism Without Class (pamphlet), 1993; The Vulnerable Planet, 1994. Contributions to: Monthly Review; Quarterly Journal of Economics; Capitalism, Nature, Socialism; Review of Radical Political Economy; Science and Society; Dollars & Sense. Address: Dept of Sociology, University of Oregon, Eugene, OR 97403, USA.

FOSTER Linda Nemec, b. 29 May 1950, Garfield Heights, Ohio, USA. Poet; Writer; Teacher. m. Anthony Jesse Foster, 26 Oct 1974, 1 son, 1 daughter. Education: BA, Aquinas College, Grand Rapids, 1972; MFA, Goddard College, Plainfield, Vermont, 1979. Appointments: Teacher of Creative Writing and Poetry, Michigan Council for the Arts, 1980-93; Instructor of English Composition, Ferris State University, 1983-84; Guest Lecturer at many schools, colleges and conferences. Publications: A History of the Body, 1987; A Modern Fairy Tale: The Baba Yaga Poems, 1992; Trying to Balance the Heart, 1993; Living in the Fire Nest, 1996. Contributions to: Periodicals. Honour: Grand Prize, American Poetry Association, 1986. Memberships: Academy of American Poets; Poetry Society of America. Address: 2024 Wilshire Drive South East, Grand Rapids, MI 49506, USA.

FOSTER Paul, b. 15 Oct 1931, Pennsgrove, New Jersey, USA. Writer. Education: BA, Rutgers University; LLB, New York University Law School. Publications: 25 books of plays including: Tom Paine, 1971; Madonna in the Orchard, 1971; Satyricon, 1972; Elizabeth I, 1972; Marcus Brutus, 1976; Silver Queen Saloon, 1976; Mellon and the National Art Gallery, 1980; A Kiss is Just a Kiss, 1984; 3 Mystery Comedies, 1985; The Dark and Mr Stone, 1985; Odon von Horvath's Faith, Hope and Charity, translation, 1987; Make Believe (with music by Solt Dome), musical book and lyrics, 1994; Films: Smile, 1980; Cop and the Anthem, 1982; When You're Smiling, 1983; Cinderella, 1984; Home Port, 1984. Contributions to: Off-Off Broadway Book, 1972; Best American Plays of the Modern Theatre, 1975; New Stages magazine. Honours: Rockefeller Foundation Fellowship, 1967; British Arts Council Award, 1973; J S Guggenheim Fellowship, 1974; Theater Heute Award, 1977. Memberships: Dramatists Guild; Society of Composers and Dramatic Authors, France; Players Club, New York City. Address: 44 West 10th Street, New York, NY 10011, USA.

FOURNIS Kate. See: **MURRAY Terry.**

FOWLER Alastair (David Shaw), b. 17 Aug 1930, Glasgow, Scotland. Professor of English; Writer. m. Jenny Catherine Simpson, 23 Dec 1950, 1 son, 1 daughter. Education: MA, University of Edinburgh, 1952; MA, 1955, DPhil, 1957, Oxford University. Appointments: Member, Institute for Advanced Study, Princeton, New Jersey, 1966, 1980; Regius Professor of Rhetoric and English Literature, 1972-84, Professor Emeritus, 1984-, University Fellow, 1985-87, University of Edinburgh; Advisory Editor, New Literary History, 1972-; Visiting Fellow, Council of the Humanities, Princeton University, 1974, Humanities Research Centre, Canberra, 1980, All Souls College, Oxford, 1984; General Editor, Longman Annotated Anthologies of English Verse, 1977-80; Member, Editorial Board, English Literary Renaissance, 1978-, Word and Image, 1984-91, The Seventeenth Century, 1986-, Connotations, 1990-, English Review,

1990-, Translation and Literature, 1990-; Professor of English, University of Virginia, 1990-. Publications: Richard Wills: De re poetica (editor and translator), 1958; Spenser and the Numbers of Time, 1964; C S Lewis: Spenser's Images of Life (editor) 1967; The Poems of John Milton (editor with John Carey), 1968; Triumphal Forms, 1970; Silent Poetry (editor), 1970; Topics in Criticism (editor with Christopher Butler), 1971; Seventeen, 1971; Conceitful Thought, 1975; Catacomb Suburb, 1976; Edmund Spenser, 1977; From the Domain of Arnheim, 1982; Kinds of Literature, 1982; A History of English Literature, 1987; The New Oxford Book of Seventeenth Century Verse, 1991; The Country House Poem, 1994; Time's Purpled Masquers, 1996. Contributions to: Books and scholarly journals. Membership: Fellow, British Academy, 1974. Literary Agent: Christopher Busby. Address: c/o Department of English, University of Edinburgh, David Hume Tower, George Square, Edinburgh, EH8 9JX, Scotland.

FOWLER Don D, b. 24 Apr 1936, Torrey, Utah, USA. Professor of Anthropology; Writer. m. Catherine Sweeney, 14 June 1963. Education: Weber State College, 1954-55; BA, 1959, Graduate Studies, 1959-62, University of Utah; PhD, University of Pittsburgh, 1965. Appointments: Instructor, 1964-65, Assistant Professor, 1965-67, Associate Professor of Anthropology and Executive Director of Human Systems Center of the Desert Research Institute, 1968-71, Research Professor and Executive Director of the Social Sciences Center of the Desert Research Institute, 1971-78, Mamie Kelberg Professor of Historic Preservation and Anthropology, 1978-, Chairperson, Department of Anthropology, 1990-, University of Nevada, Reno; Visiting Postdoctoral Fellow, 1967-68, Research Associate, 1970-, Smithsonian Institution, Washington, DC. Publications: In a Sacred Manner We Live: Edward S Curtis' Indian Photographs, 1972; Material Culture of the Numa: The John Wesley Powell Collection, 1867-1880 (with J F Matley), 1979; American Archaeology Past and Future: A Celebration of the Society for American Archaeology, 1935-1985 (editor with D J Metzger and J A Sabloff), 1986; Anthropology of the Desert West: Essays in Honor of Jesse D Jennings (editor with Carol J Condie), 1986; Regional Conferences: Summary Report, Society for American Archaeology (editor with Cynthia Irwin-Williams), 1986; The Western Photographs of Jack Hillers, "Myself in the Water", 1989; Others Knowing Others: Perspectives on Ethnographic Careers (editor with Donald L Hardesty), 1994. Contributions to: Many scholarly journals. Honours: Many private and government grants; Distinguished Graduate Medal, University of Pittsburgh, 1986. Memberships: Fellow, American Anthropological Association; American Society for Ethnohistory; Current Anthropology; President, Society for American Archaeology, 1985-87; Southwestern Anthropological Association. Honours: Distinguished Graduate Medal, University of Pittsburgh, 1986. Address: 1010 Foothill Road, Reno, NV 89511, USA.

FOWLER Marian Elizabeth, b. 15 Oct 1929, Newmarket, Ontario, Canada. Writer. m. Dr Rodney Singleton Fowler, 19 Sept 1953, div 1977, 1 son, 1 daughter. Education: BA Hons, English, 1951, MA, English, 1965, PhD, English, 1970, University of Toronto, Canada. Publications: The Embroidered Tent, Five Gentlewomen in Early Canada, 1982; Redney: A Life of Sara Jeannette Duncan, 1983; Below the Peacock Fan: First Ladies of the Raj, 1987; Blenhein: Biography of a Palace, 1989; In a Gilded Cage: From Heiress to Duchess, 1993; The Way She Looks Tonight: Five Women of Style, 1996. Contributions to: English Studies in Canada; University of Toronto Quarterly; Dalhousie Review; Ontario History; Dictionary of Canadian Biography; Oxford Companion to Canadian Literature; New Canadian Encyclopaedia. Honours: Governor-General's Gold Medal in English, 1951; Canadian Biography Award, 1979. Memberships: International PEN; Writers' Union of Canada. Address: Apt 503, 77 St Clair Avenue East, Toronto M4T 1M5, Canada.

FOWLES John (Robert), b. 31 Mar 1926, Leigh-on-Sea, Essex, England. Novelist. m. Elizabeth Whitton, 1956, dec 1990. Education: Edinburgh University, 1944; BA (Hons) in French, New College, Oxford, 1950. Appointments: Lecturer in English, University of Poitiers, France, 1959-51; Teacher at Anargyrios College, Spetsai, Greece, 1951-52, and in London, 1953-63. Publications: The Collector, 1963; The Magus, 1965; The French Lieutenant's Woman, 1969; Daniel Martin, 1977; Mantissa, 1982; A Maggot, 1985; Short story: The Ebony Tower; Collected Novellas, 1974; Also several plays, verse and non-fiction work. Honours: W H Smith Literary Award, 1970; Christopher Award, 1981. Address: Sheil and Associates, 43 Doughty Street, London WC1N 2LF, England.

FOX Geoffrey Edmund, b. 3 Apr 1941, Chicago, Illinois, USA. Writer; Sociologist; Translator. m. (1) Sylvia Herrera, 8 Aug 1966, (2) Mirtha Quintanales, 15 June 1975, (3) Susana Torre, 5 Oct 1979, 2 sons. Education: BA, Harvard University, 1963; PhD, Northwestern University, 1975. Appointments: Editor, Hispanic Monitor, 1983-84; Guest Editor, NACLA Report on the Americas, 1989; Publications Director, New York City Commission on Human Rights, 1994-95; Publications Consultant, College of Urban, Labor and Metropolitan Affairs, Wayne State University, 1996-. Publications: Welcome to My Contry; The Land and People of Argentina; The Land and People of Venezuela; Working Class Emigres from Cuba; Hispanic Nation; Culture, Politics and the Constructing of Ideality, 1996. Contributions to: New York Times; Nation: Village Voice; Yellow Silk; Fiction International; Central Park; Newsday; Solidarity. Memberships: Authors Guild; National Writers Union; Latin American Studies Association. Literary Agent: Colleen Mohyde. Address: 8120 E Jefferson, Apt 4E, Detroit, MI 48214, USA.

FOX Levi, b. 28 Aug 1914, Leicestershire, England. Author. m. Jane Richards, 1 son, 2 daughters. Education: BA, 1936, MA, 1938, Oriel College, Oxford; MA, University of Manitoba, 1938. Appointments: General Editor, Dugdale Society, 1945-80; Director and Secretary, 1945-89, Director Emeritus, 1990-, Shakespeare Birthplace Trust. Publications: Leicester Abbey, 1938; Administration of the Honor of Leicester in the Fourteenth Century, 1940; Leicester Castle, 1943; Leicester Forest (with P Russell), 1945; Coventry's Heritage, 1946; Stratford-upon-Avon, 1949; Shakespeare's Town, 1949; Oxford, 1951; Shakespeare's Stratford-upon-Avon, 1951; Shakespeare's Country, 1953; The Borough Town of Stratford-upon-Avon, 1953; English Historical Scholarship in the 16th and 17th Centuries (editor), 1956; Shakespeare's Town and Country, 1959, 3rd edition, 1990; Stratford-upon-Avon: An Appreciation, 1963, 2nd edition 1976; The 1964 Shakespeare Anniversary Book, 1964; Celebrating Shakespeare, 1965; Correspondence of the Reverend Joseph Greene, 1965; A Country Grammar School, 1967; The Shakespeare Book, 1969; Shakespeare's Sonnets (editor), 1970; Shakespeare's England, 1972; In Honour of Shakespeare, 1972, 2nd edition, 1982; The Shakespeare Treasury, compiler, 1972; The Stratford-upon-Avon Shakespeare Anthology, compiler, 1975; Stratford: Past and Present, 1975; Shakespeare's Flowers, 1978, 2nd edition, 1990; Shakespeare's Birds, 1978; The Shakespeare Centre, 1982; Shakespeare in Medallic Art, 1982; Shakespeare's Magic, 1982; The Early History of King Edward VI School, Stratford-upon-Avon, 1984; Coventry Constables' Presentments, 1986; Historic Stratford-upon-Avon, 1986; Shakespeare's Town and Country, 1986; Minutes and Accounts of the Corporation of Stratford-upon-Avon (1592-96), 1990. Address: The Shakespeare Centre, Stratford-upon Avon CV37 6QW, England.

FOX Mem, (Merrion Frances Fox), b. 5 Mar 1946, Melbourne, Victoria, Australia. Associate Professor. m. Malcolm, 2 Jan 1969, 1 daughter. Education: BA, Flinders University, 1978; B Ed, Sturt College, 1979; Graduate Diploma, Underdale College, 1981. Publications: Children's books: Possum Magic, 1983; Wilfrid Gordon McDonald Partridge, 1984; How to Teach Drama to Infants, 1984; A Cat Called Kite, 1985; Zoo-Looking, 1986; Hattie and the Fox, 1986; Sail Away, 1986; Arabella, 1986; Just Like That, 1986; A Bedtime Story, 1987; The Straight Line Wonder, 1987; Goodnight Sleep Tight, 1988; Guess What?, 1988; Koala Lou, 1988; Night Noises, 1989; Shoes for Grandpa, 1989; Sophie, 1989; Memories, 1992; Tough Boris, 1994; Wombat Divine, 1995; Boo to a Goose, 1996; Feathers and Fools, 1996; Books for adults: Mem's the Word, 1990; Dear Mem Fox, I Have Read All Your Books, Even the Pathetic Ones, 1992; Co-author: English Essentials: The Wouldn't-be-without-it Handbook on Writing Well, 1993; Radical Reflections: Passionate Opinions on Teaching, Learning and Living, 1993. Contributions to: Language Arts; The Horn Book; Australian Journal of Language and Literacy; The Reading Teacher; The Reading and Writing Quarterly; The Dragon Lode. Honours: New South Wales Premier's Literary Award, Best Children's Book, 1984; KOALA First Prize, 1987; The Dromkeen Medal for Outstanding Services to Children's Literature, 1990; Advance Australia Award, 1990; Order of Australia (AM), 1994; The Alice Award, Fellowship of Australian Women Writers, 1994; Honorary Doctorate, University of Wollongong, 1996. Memberships: Australian Society of Authors; Australian Children's Book Council. Literary Agent: Australian Literary Management.

FOX Paula, b. 22 Apr 1923, New York, New York, USA. Author. m. (1) Richard Sigerson, 1948, div 1954, 2 sons, 1 daughter, (2) Martin Greenberg, 9 June 1962. Education: Columbia University, 1955-58.

Appointments: State University of New York, 1974; University of Pennsylvania, 1980-85; New York University, 1989. Publications: How Many Miles to Babylon?, 1967; Desparate Characters, 1970; The Western Coast, 1972; The Slave Dancer, 1974; The Widow's Children, 1976; A Servant's Tale, 1983; One-Eyed Cat, 1984; The Village by the Sea, 1989; The God of Nightmares, 1990. Honours: Guggenheim Fellowship, 1972; American Academy of Arts and Letters Award, 1972; National Endowment for the Arts Award, 1973; Newbery Medals, 1974, 1986; American Book Award, 1980; Hans Christian Andersen Medal, 1983; Brandeis Fiction Citation, 1984; Rockefeller Foundation Residency Fellow, 1985; Boston Globe-Horn Book Award, 1989. Membership: PEN. Address: c/o Robert Lescher, 67 Irving Place, New York, NY 10003, USA.

FOX-GENOVESE Elizabeth, b. 28 May 1941, Boston, Massachusetts, USA. Professor of History. m. Eugene D Genovese, 6 June 1969. Education: BA, Bryn Mawr College, 1963; Institut d'Etudes Politiques, Paris, France, 1961-62; MA, 1966, PhD, 1974, Harvard University; Special Candidate, Center for Psychoanalytic Training and Research, Columbia University, 1977-79; Newberry Library, Institute in Quantitative Methods, 1979. Appointment: Professor of History, Emory University. Publications: The Origins of Physiocracy: Economic Revolution and Social Order in 18th Century France, 1976; Fruits of Merchant Capital: Slavery and Bourgeois Property in the Rise and Expansion of Capitalism (with Eugene Genovese), 1983; Within the Plantation Household: Black and White Women of the Old South, 1988; Feminism without Illusions: A Critique of Individualism, 1991; Feminism is Not the Story of My Life: How Today's Feminist Elite Has Lost Touch with the Real Concerns of Women, 1996. Contributions to: Washington Post; Boston Globe; First Things; Common Knowledge; New York Times Book Review; Times Literary Supplement; The New Republic; National Review; London Review of Books; Commonweal; Regeneration; Washington Times; Tikkun. Honours: Doctor of Letters, Millsaps College; C Hugh Holman Prize, Society for Southern Literature; Julia Cherry Spruill Prize, Southern Association of Women Historians. Memberships: Modern Language Association; Society for Study of Southern Literature; South Atlantic Modern Language Association; American Comparative Literature Association; American Antiquarian Society; Society of American Historians; American Political Science Association; American Academy of Religion; Organization of American Historians; Southern Political Science Association. Address: History Department, Emory University, Atlanta, GA 30322, USA.

FRAILE Medardo, b. 21 Mar 1925, Madrid, Spain. Writer; Emeritus Professor in Spanish. Education: DPh, DLitt, University of Madrid, 1968. Publications: Cuentos con Algun Amor, 1954; A La Luz Cambian las Cosas, 1959; Cuentos de Verdad, 1964; Descubridor de Nada y Otros Cuentos, 1970; Con Los Dias Contados, 1972; Samuel Ros Hacia una Generacion Sin Critica, 1972; La Penultima Inglaterra, 1973; Poesia y Teatro Espanoles Contemporaneos, 1974; Ejemplario, 1979; Autobiografia, 1986; Cuento Espanol de Posguerra, 1986; El gallo puesto en hora, 1987; Entre parentesis, 1988; Santa Engracia, numero dos o tres, 1989; Teatro Espanol en un Acto, 1989; El rey y el pais con granos, 1991; Cuentos Completos, 1991; Claudina y los, cacos, 1992; La Familia irreal inglesa, 1993; Los brazos invisibles, 1994; Documento Nacional, 1996. Translation: El Weir de Hermiston by R L Stevenson, 1995. Contributions to: Many publications. Honours: Sesamo Prize, 1956; Literary Grant, Fundacion Juan March, 1960; Critics Book of the Year, 1965; La Estafeta literaria Prize, 1970; Hucha de Oro Prize, 1971; Research Grant, Carnegie Trust for Universities of Scotland, 1975; Colegiado de Honor del Colegio heraldico de España y de las Indias, 1995. Memberships: General Society of Spanish Authors; Working Community of Book Writers, Spain; Association of University Teachers. Address: 24 Etive Crescent, Bishopbriggs, Glasgow G64 1ES, Scotland.

FRAJLICH-ZAJAC Anna, b. 10 Mar 1942, Osz, Kyrgyzstan. Writer; Academic Teacher; Scholar. m. Wladyslaw Zajac, 31 July 1965, 1 son. Education: Masters of Polish Literature, Warsaw University, 1965; PhD Slavic Literatures, New York University, 1991. Appointment: Adjunct Assistant Professor, Department of Slavic Languages, Columbia University. Publications: Indian Summer, 1982; Ktory las, 1986; Between Dawn and the Wind, 1991; Ogrodem i ogrodzeniem (The Garden and the Fence), 1993; Jeszcze w drodze (Still on its Way), 1994; Others: Tylko ziemia (Just Earth); Aby wiatr namalowac (To Paint the Wind). Contributions to: Terra Poetica; Artful Dodge; The Polish Review; Wisconsin Review; Mr Cogito; The Jewish Quarterly; Poésie Premiére. Honour: Koscielski Foundation Award,

Switzerland, 1981. Memberships: Executive Board of Intern, PEN Club Centre for Writers in Exile; Association of Polish Writers. Address: 345 East 81 Street, Apt 11J, New York, NY 10028-4018, USA.

FRAME Janet (Paterson), (surname legally changed to Clutha), b. 28 Aug 1924, Dunedin, New Zealand. Author. Education: University of Otago Teachers Training College. Publications: The Lagoon and Other Stories, 1951; Faces in the Water, 1961; The Edge of the Alphabet, 1961; Scented Gardens for the Blind, 1963; The Reservoir Stories and Sketches, Snowman, 1963; The Adaptable Man, 1965; A State of Siege, 1966; The Reservoir and Other Stories, 1966; The Pocket Mirror, 1967; The Rainbirds, 1968; Mona Minim and the Small of the Sun, 1969; Daughter Buffalo, 1972; Living in the Maniototo, 1979; To the Island, 1982; You Are Now Entering the Human Heart, 1984; The Envoy from the Mirror City, 1985; The Carpathians, 1988. Address: 276 Glenfield Road, Auckland 10, New Zealand.

FRANCE (Evelyn) Christine, b. 23 Dec 1939, Sydney, New South Wales, Australia. Art Historian. m. Stephen Robert Bruce France, 22 Dec 1962, 1 daughter. Education: BA, University of Sydney. Publications: Justin O'Brien: Image and Icon, 1987; Margaret Olley, 1990; Marea Gazzard, Form and Clay, 1994. Contributions to: Art and Australia; Australian newspapers. Address: Old Baerami, Baerami, Wales 2333, Australia.

FRANCHON Lisa. See: **FLOREN Lee.**

FRANCIS Alexander. See: **HEATH-STUBBS John.**

FRANCIS Clare, b. 17 Apr 1946, Surrey, England. Writer. 1 son. Education: Economics Degree, University College, London. Publications: Come Hell or High Water, 1977; Come Wind or Weather, 1978; The Commanding Sea, 1981; Night Sky, 1983; Red Crystal, 1985; Wolf Winter, 1987; Requiem, 1991; Deceit, 1993; Betrayal, 1995. Honours: Member of the Order of the British Empire; University College, London, honorary fellow; University of Manchester Institute of Technology, honorary fellow. Membership: Society of Authors. Literary Agent: John Johnson Agency. Address: c/o John Johnson, Clerkenwell House, 45-47 Clerkenwell Green, London EC1R 0HT, England.

FRANCIS Dick, (Richard Stanley Francis), b. 31 Oct 1920, Pembrokeshire, South Wales. Ex Steeplechase Jockey; Author. m. Mary Margaret Brenchley, 21 June 1947, 2 sons. Appointments: Racing Correspondent, London Sunday Express, 1957-63. Publications: Dead Cert, 1962; Nerve, 1964; For Kicks, 1965; Odds Against, 1965; Flying Finish, 1966; Blood Sport, 1967; Forfeit, 1968; Enquiry, 1969; Rat Race, 1970; Bonecrack, 1971; Smokescreen, 1972; Slay-Ride, 1973; Knock Down, 1974; High Stakes, 1975; In the Frame, 1976; Risk, 1977; Trial Run, 1978; Whip Hand, 1979; Reflex, 1980; Twice Shy, 1981; Banker, 1982; The Danger, 1983; Proof, 1984; Break In, 1985; Bolt, 1986; Hot Money, 1987; The Edge, 1988; Straight, 1989; Longshot, 1990; Comeback, 1991; Driving Force, 1992; Decider, 1993; Wild Horses, 1994; Come to Grief, 1995; To The Hilt; 1996. Autobiography: The Sport of Queens, 1957. Biography: Lester, 1986. Contributions to: Sunday Express; Daily Express; Sunday Times; Daily Mail; New York Times; Washington Post; The Age, Melbourne; Horse & Hound; Sports Illustrated; Classic. Honours: Officer of the Order of the British Empire, 1954; Gold Dagger Awards, Crime Writers Association, 1966, 1980; Edgar Allan Poe Best Novel Awards, Mystery Writers of America, 1970, 1981; Honorary LHD, Tufts University, 1991. Memberships: Crime Writers Association, Chairman, 1965-66; Mystery Writers of America; Society of Authors; Racecourse Association. Literary Agent: John Johnson. Address: c/o John Johnson Agency, 45/47 Clerkenwell Green, London EC1R 0HT, England.

FRANCK Thomas M(artin), b. 14 July 1931, Berlin, Germany (US citizen, 1977). Professor of Law; Writer. Education: BA, 1952, LLB, 1953, University of British Columbia; LLM, 1954, SJD, 1959, Harvard Law School; Hon LLD, University of British Columbia, 1995. Appointments: Assistant Professor, University of Nebraska College of Law, 1954-56; Associate Professor, 1960-62, Professor of Law, 1962-, Director, Center for International Studies, 1965-, New York University School of Law; Visiting Professor, Stanford Law School, 1963, University of East Africa Law School, Dar es Salaam, 1963-66, Osgood Hall Law School, York University, Toronto, 1972-76, Woodrow Wilson School, Princeton University, 1979; Director, International Law Program, Cargenie Endowment for International Peace, 1973-79; Director of Research, United Nations Institute for Training and Research, 1980-82; Lecturer, The Hague Academy of International Law, 1993; Visiting Fellow, Trinity College, Cambridge, 1996-97. Publications: Race and Nationalism, 1960; The Role of the United States in the Congo (co-author), 1963; African Law (co-author), 1963; East African Unity Through Law, 1964; Comparative Constitutional Process: Cases and Materials in the Comparative Constitutional Process of Nation Building, 1968; The Structure of Impartiality, 1968; A Free Trade Association (with others), 1968; Why Federations Fail (co-author), 1968; Word Politics: Verbal Strategy Among the Superpowers (co-author), 1971; Secrecy and Foreign Policy (co-author), 1974; Resignation in Protest: Political and Ethical Choices Between Loyalty to Team and Loyalty to Conscience in American Public Life (co-author), 1975; Control of Sea Resources by Semi-Autonomous States: Prevailing Legal Relationships Between Metropolitan Governments and Their Overseas Commonwealths, Associated States, and Self-Governing Dependencies, 1978; Foreign Policy by Congress (co-author), 1979; United States Foreign Relations Law: Documents and Sources (co-author), 5 volumes, 1980-84; The Tethered Presidency, 1981; Human Rights in Third World Perspective, 3 volumes, 1982; Nation Against Nation: What Happened to the U.N. Dream and What the U.S. Can Do About It, 1985; Judging the World Court, 1986; Foreign Relations and National Security Law, 1987; The Power of Legitimacy Among Nations, 1990; Political Questions/Judicial Answers: Does the Rule of Law Apply to Foreign Affairs?, 1992; Fairness in the International Legal and Institutional System, 1993; Fairness in International Law and Institutions, 1995; International Law Decisions in National Courts (co-editor), 1996. Contributions to: Scholarly journals and periodicals. Honours: Guggenheim Fellowships, 1973-74, 1982-83; Christopher Medal, 1976; Certificates of Merit, American Society of International Law, 1981, 1986, 1994, 1996; John E Read Medal, Canadian Council on International Law, 1994. Memberships: Africa Watch; American Society of International Law; Canadian Council on International Law; Council on Foreign Relations; French Society of International Law; German Society of International Law; Institut du Droit International; International Law Association, vice-president, 1973-94, honorary vice-president, 1994-; International Peace Academy. Address: c/o New York University School of Law, 40 Washington Square South, New York, NY 10012, USA.

FRANCO Tomaso, b. 23 May 1933, Bologna, Italy. Writer; Poet. Div, 2 sons. Education: Liceo, Classical Studies, 1952; Doctorate in Law, 1959; Art studies. Publications: Uno Scatto dell'Evoluzione (poems), 1984; Parole d'Archivio (poems), 1986; Il Libro dei Torti (poems), 1988; Lettere a un Fuoruscito (essay), 1988; Casa di Frontiera (poems), 1990; Il Soldato dei Sogni (novel), 1995. Contributions to: Cenobio, 1961; Prove, 1951-62; Kalos, 1971; L'Ozio Letterario, 1985; Human Space, 1987-92; Schema, 1988-93; Zeitschrift für Kunstgeschichte, 1984; Poesia 90 (anthology), 1993; Annali, 1994; Vernice; Astolfo; Various newspapers, journals and anthologies. Honours: First Award, Clemente Rèbora, Milan, 1986; Gold Medal, Citta di Como, 1990; First Award, National, Associazione Promozione Cultura in Toscana, 1992. Literary Agent: Techniche Editoriali, Via Crescenzio 82, I-00193 Rome, Italy. Address: Via San Domenico 2, I-36100 Vicenza, Italy.

FRANÇOIS Marie. See: **BUTOR Michel.**

FRANK Elizabeth, b. 14 Sept 1945, Los Angeles, California, USA. Writer; Professor. m. Howard Buchwald, 3 Aug 1984, 1 daughter. Education: Bennington College; BA, MA, PhD, University of California at Berkeley, USA. Appointment: Professor, Bard College. Publications: Jackson Pollock, 1984; Louise Brogan: A Portrait, 1985. Honour: Pulitzer Prize, 1986. Address: Department of Language and Literature, Bard College, Annandale on Hudson, NY 12504, USA.

FRANK Joseph Nathaniel, b. 6 Oct 1918, New York, New York, USA. Professor Emeritus of Comparative Literature and Slavic Languages and Literatures. m. Marguerite J Straus, 11 May 1953, 2 daughters. Education: New York University, 1937-38, University of Wisconsin 1941-42, University of Paris, 1950-51; PhD University of Chicago, 1960. Appointments: Editor, Bureau of National Affairs, Washington, 1942-50; Assistant Professor, Department of English, University of Minnesota, 1958-61; Associate Professor, Rutgers University, 1961-66; Professor of Comparative Literature, 1966-85, University of East Africa Law School, Dar es Salaam, 1963-66, Director of Christian Gauss Seminars, 1966-83, Princeton University; Visiting Member, Institute for Advanced Study, 1984-87; Professor of Comparative Literature and Slavic Languages and Literatures, 1985-89, Professor Emeritus, 1989-, Stanford University. Publications: The Widening Gyre, Crisis and Mastery in Modern Literature, 1963; F

M Dostoevsky: The Seeds of Revolt, 1821-1849, 1976; A Primer of Ignorance (editor), 1967; F M Dostoevsky: The Years of Ordeal, 1850-1859, 1983; Dostoevsky: The Stir of Liberation, 1860-1865, 1986; Selected Letters of Fyodor Dostoevsky (co-editor), 1987; Through the Russian Prism, 1989; The Idea of Spatial Form, 1991; Dostoevsky: The Miraculous Years, 1865-1871, 1995. Contributions to: Southern Review; Sewanee Review; Hudson Review; Partisan Review; Art News; Critique; Chicago Review; Minnesota Review; Russian Review; Le Contrat Social; Commentary; Encounter; New York Review. Various books, numerous book reviews, and translations. Honours: Fulbright Scholar, 1950-51; Rockefeller Fellow, 1952-53, 1953-54; Guggenheim Fellow, 1956-57, 1975-76; Award, National Institute of Arts and Letters, 1958; Fellow, American Academy of Arts and Sciences, 1969; Research Grants; American Council of Learned Societies, 1964-65, 1967-68, 1970-71; James Russell Lowell Prize, 1977; Christian Gauss Award, 1977; Rockefeller Foundation, 1979-80, 1983-84; National Book Critics Circle Award, 1984; Christian Gauss Award, 1996. Address: Slavic Languages and Literature, Stanford University, Stanford, CT 99305, USA.

FRANKEL Ellen, b. 22 May 1951, New York, New York, USA. Editor; Writer; Story Teller. m. Herbert Levine, 3 Aug 1975, 1 son, 1 daughter. Education: BA, University of Michigan, 1973; PhD, Princeton University, 1978. Appointment: Editor-in-Chief, Jewish Publication Society, 1991-. Publications: Choosing to Be Chosen, Ktav; The Classic Tales: 4000 Years of Jewish Lore; The Encyclopedia of Jewish Symbols, with Betsy Teutsch; George Washington and the Constitution; Tell It Like It Is: Tough Choices for Today's Teens, with Sarah Levine; The Five Books of Miriam: A Woman's Commentary on the Torah. Contributions to: Judaism; Jewish Spectator; Moment; Jewish Monthly; Shofar Magazine. Memberships: Association of Jewish Studies; Phi Beta Kappa. Address: 6670 Lincoln Drive, Philadelphia, PA 19119, USA.

FRANKFURT Harry, b. 29 May 1929, Langhorne, Pennsylvania, USA. Professor of Philosophy; Writer. m. Joan Gilbert. Education: BA, 1949, MA, 1953, PhD, 1954, Johns Hopkins University; Cornell University, 1949-51. Appointments: Instructor, 1956-59, Assistant Professor, 1959-62, Ohio State University; Associate Professor, State University of New York at Binghamton, 1962-63; Research Associate, 1963-64, Associate Professor, 1964-71, Professor of Philosophy, 1971-76, Rockefeller University, New York City; Visiting Fellow, All Souls College, Oxford, 1971-72; Visiting Professor, Vassar College, 1973-74, University of Pittsburgh, 1975-76, University of California at Los Angeles, 1990; Professor of Philosophy, 1976-89, Chairman, Department of Philosophy, 1978-87, John M Schiff Professor, 1989, Yale University; Professor of Philosophy, Princeton University, 1990-. Publications: Demons, Dreamers, and Madmen: The Defense of Reason in Descartes's Meditations, 1970; Leibniz: A Collection of Critical Essays (editor), 1972; The Importance of What We Care About, 1988. Contributions to: Many scholarly books and journals. Honours: National Endowment for the Humanities Fellowships, 1981-82, 1994; Guggenheim Fellowship, 1993. Memberships: American Academy of Arts and Sciences, fellow; American Philosophical Association. Address: c/o Department of Philosophy, 1879 Hall, Princeton University, Princeton, NJ 08544, USA.

FRANKLAND (Anthony) Noble, b. 4 July 1922, Ravenstonedale, England. Historian; Biographer. m. (1) Diana Madeline Fovargue Tavernor, 28 Feb 1944, dec 1981, 1 son, 1 daughter, (2) Sarah Katharine Davies, 7 May 1982. Education: Open Scholar, MA, 1948, DPhil, 1951, Trinity College, Oxford. Appointments: Official British Military Historian, 1951-60; Deputy Director of Studies, Royal Institute of International Affairs, 1956-60; Director, Imperial War Museum, 1960-82. Publications: Crown of Tragedy: Nicholas II, 1960; The Strategic Air Offensive Against Germany (co-author), 4 volumes, 1961; The Bombing Offensive Against Germany: Outlines and Perspectives, 1965; Bomber Offensive: The Devastation of Europe, 1970; Prince Henry, Duke of Gloucester, 1980; Witness of a Century, Prince Arthur, Duke of Connaught, 1850-1942, 1993; Encyclopedia of Twentieth Century Warfare (general editor and contributor), 1989; The Politics and Strategy of the Second World War (joint editor), 9 volumes. Contributions to: Encyclopaedia Britannica; Times Literary Supplement; The Times; Daily Telegraph; Observer; Military Journals. Honours: Companion of the Order of the Bath; Commander of the Order of the British Empire; Holder of the Distinguished Flying Cross. Address: Thames House, Eynsham, Witney, Oxon OX8 1DA, England.

FRANKLIN John Hope, b. 2 Jan 1915, Rentiesville, Oklahoma, USA. Historian; Professor; Author. m. Aurelia E Whittington, 11 June 1940, 1 son. Education: AB, Fisk University, 1935; AM, 1936, PhD, 1941, Harvard University. Appointments: Instructor, Fisk University, 1936-37; Professor of History, St Augustine's College, 1939-43, North Carolina College at Durham, 1943-47, Howard University, 1947-56; Chairman, Department of History, Brooklyn College, 1956-64; Professor of American History, 1964-82, Chairman, Department of History, 1967-70, John Matthews Manly Distinguished Service Professor, 1969-82, University of Chicago; James B Duke Professor of History, 1982-85, Professor of Legal History, 1985-92, Duke University; Various visiting professorships. Publications: Free Negro in North Carolina, 1943; From Slavery to Freedom: A History of American Negroes, 1947, 7th edition, 1994; Militant South, 1956; Reconstruction After the Civil War, 1961; The Emancipation Proclamation, 1963; Land of the Free (with others), 1966; Illustrated History of Black Americans (with others), 1970; A Southern Odyssey, 1976; Racial Equality in America, 1976; George Washington Williams: A Biography, 1985; The Color Line: Legacy for the 21st Century, 1993. Editor: Civil War Diary of James T Ayres, 1947; A Fool's Errand by Albion Tourgee, 1961; Army Life in a Black Regiment by Thomas Higginson, 1962; Color and Race, 1968; Reminiscences of an Active Life by John R Lynch, 1970; Black Leaders in the Twentieth Century (with August Meier), 1982. Contributions to: Scholarly journals. Honours: Edward Austin Fellow, 1937-39; Guggenheim Fellowships, 1950-51, 1973-74; President's Fellow, Brown University, 1952-53; Center for Advanced Study in the Behavioral Sciences Fellow, 1973-74; Senior Mellon Fellow, National Humanities Center, 1980-82; Cleanth Brooks Medal, Fellowship of Southern Writers, 1989; Gold Medal, Encyclopaedia Britannica, 1990; North Carolina Medals, 1992, 1993; Charles Frankel Medal, 1993; Bruce Catton Award, Society of American Historians, 1994; Sidney Hook Award, Phi Beta Kappa Society, 1994; Over 100 honorary doctorates. Memberships: American Academy of Arts and Sciences, fellow; American Association of University Professors; American Historical Association, president, 1978-79; American Philosophical Society; American Studies Association; Association for the Study of Negro Life and History; Phi Alpha Theta; Phi Beta Kappa, president, 1973-76; Organization of American Historians, president, 1974-75; Southern Historical Association, president, 1970-71. Address: c/o Department of History, Duke University, Durham, NC 27707, USA.

FRAPPELL Ruth Meredith, (Ruth Teale), b. 8 Mar 1942, Bathurst, New South Wales, Australia. Academic; Freelance Writer. m. Leighton Frappell, 15 Aug 1970, 1 son, 2 daughters. Education: BA, 1963, L.Mus.A, Australian Music Exam Board, 1964; MA, 1968, PhD, University of Sydney, 1992. Appointments: Writer, Australian Dictionary of Biography, 1968-; Journal Royal Australian Historical Society, 1994-; Editor, Journal of Religious History, 1995-. Publications: Thomas Brisbane, 1971; Colonial Eve, 1979. Contributions to: Australian Dictionary of Biography; Journal of Religious History; Journal of Ecclesiastical History; Journal of Royal Australian Historical Society. Honour: Australia Council Literature Board, 1980. Memberships: Life Member, Senior Vice President, Royal Australian Historical Society; Association for Journal of Religious History; President, Macquarie University Library Friends; Australian Historical Association. Address: 22 Ingalara Avenue, Wahroonga 2076, Australia.

FRASER Lady Antonia, (Lady Antonia Pinter), b. 27 Aug 1932, London, England. Author. m. (1) Sir Hugh Fraser, 1956, diss 1977, 3 sons, 3 daughters, (2) Harold Pinter, 1980. Education: MA, Lady Margaret Hall, Oxford. Appointment: General Editor, Kings and Queens of England series. Publications: King Arthur and the Knights of the Round Table, 1954; Robin Hood, 1955; Dolls, 1963; A History of Toys, 1966; Mary Queen of Scots, 1969; Cromwell, Our Chief of Men, 1973; King James: VI of Scotland, I of England, 1974; Kings and Queens of England (editor), 1975; Scottish Love Poems: A Personal Anthology (editor) 1975; Love Letters: An Anthology, (editor) 1976, revised edition, 1989; Quiet as a Nun, 1977; The Wild Island, 1978; King Charles II, 1979; Heroes and Heroines (editor) 1980; A Splash of Red, 1981; Mary Queen of Scots: Poetry Anthology (editor), 1981; Oxford and Oxfordshire in Verse: An Anthology (editor), 1982; Cool Repentance, 1982; The Weaker Vessel: Woman's Lot in Seventeenth Century England, 1984; Oxford Blood, 1985; Jemima Shore's First Case, 1986; Your Royal Hostage, 1987; Boadicea's Chariot: The Warrior Queens, 1988; The Cavalier Case, 1990; Jemima Shore at the Sunny Grave, 1991; The Six Wives of Henry VIII, 1992; Editor, The Pleasure of Reading, 1992; Political Death, 1994; Gunpowder Plot,

1996. Other: Several books adapted for television. Contributions to: Anthologies. Honours: James Tait Black Memorial Prize, 1969; Wolfson History Award, 1984; Prix Caumont-La Force, 1985; Honorary DLitt, Universities of Hull, 1986, Sussex, 1990, Nottingham, 1993 and St Andrews, 1994. Memberships: Chairman, Society of Authors, 1974-75; Chairman, Crimewriters' Association, 1985-86; Chairman, 1985-88, 1990, Writers in Prison Committee; Vice President, English PEN, 1990-. Address: c/o Curtis Brown Ltd, Haymarket House, 28-29 Haymarket, London SW1Y 4SP, England.

FRASER Conon, b. 8 Mar 1930, Cambridge, England. Retired Documentary Film Producer and Director; Writer. m. Jacqueline Stearns, 17 Mar 1955, 5 sons. Education: Marlborough College, 1943-47; Royal Military Academy, Sandhurst, 1948-50. Publications include: The Underground Explorers, 1957; Oystercatcher Bay, 1962; Looking at New Zealand, 1969; Beyond the Roaring Forties, 1986. Contributions to: New Zealand's Heritage; Argosy (UK); New Zealand Listener. Honours: Silver Medal for documentary film, Coal Valley, Festival of the Americas, 1979; Silver Screen Award, United States Industrial Film Festival, 1980; Mitra Award of Honour, 26th Asian Film Festival, 1980. Address: Matapuna Road, RD6 Raetihi, New Zealand.

FRASER George MacDonald, b. 2 Apr 1925, Carlisle, England. Author; Journalist. m. Kathleen Margarette, 1949, 2 sons, 1 daughter. Education: Glasgow Academy. Appointments: Deputy Editor, Glasgow Herald newspaper, 1964-69. Publications: Flashman, 1969; Royal Flash, 1970, screenplay, 1975; The General Danced at Dawn, 1970; Flash for Freedom, 1971; Steel Bonnets, 1971; Flashman at the Charge, 1973; The Three Musketeers, screenplay, 1973; The Four Musketeers, screenplay, 1974; McAuslan in the Rough, 1974; Flashman in the Great Game, 1975; The Prince and the Pauper, screenplay, 1976; Flashman's Lady, 1977; Mr American, 1980; Flashman and the Redskins, 1982; Octopussy, screenplay, 1983; The Pyrates, 1983; Flashman and the Dragon, 1985; Casanova, TV screenplay, 1987; The Hollywood History of the World, 1988; The Sheikh and the Dustbin, 1988; The Return of the Musketeers, screenplay, 1989; Flashman and the Mountain of the Light, 1990; Quartered Safe Out Here, 1992; The Candlemass Road, 1993; Flashman and the Angel of the Lord, 1994; Black Ajax, 1997. Address: Baldrine, Isle of Man, Great Britain.

FRASER Jane. See: **PILCHER Rosamunde.**

FRASER Kathleen, b. 22 Mar 1937, Tulsa, Oklahoma, USA. Professor; Poet. m. Jack Marshall, 1961, div 1970, 1 son. Education: BA, Occidental College, Los Angles, 1959; Columbia University, 1960-61; New School for Social Research, New York City, 1960-61; Doctoral Equivalency in Creative Writing, San Francisco State University, 1976-77. Appointments: Visiting Professor, University of Iowa, 1969-71; Writer-in-Residence, Reed College, Portland, Oregon, 1971-72; Director, Poetry Center, 1972-75, Associate Professor, 1975-78, Professor, 1978-, San Francisco State University. Publications: Poetry: Change of Address and Other Poems, 1966; In Defiance of the Rains, 1969; Little Notes to You from Lucas Street, 1972; What I Want, 1974; Magritte Series, 1978; New Shoes, 1978; Each Next, 1980; Something (Even Human Voices) in the Foreground, A Lake, 1984; Noted Preceding Trust, 1987; Boundary, 1988; Giotto, Arena, 1991; When New Time Folds Up, 1993. Editor: Feminist Poetics; A Consideration of Female Construction of Language, 1984. Honours: YMM-YWHA Discovery Award, 1964; National Endowment for the Arts Grant, 1969, and Fellowship, 1978. Address: 1936 Leavenworth Street, San Francisco, CA 94133, USA.

FRASER Sylvia Lois, b. 8 Mar 1935, Hamilton, Ontario, Canada. Author; Novelist; Journalist. Education: BA, University of Western Ontario, 1957. Appointments: Guest Lecturer, Banff Centre, 1973-79, 1985, 1987, 1988; Arts Advisory Panel to Canada Council, 1978-81; Writer in Residence, University of Western Ontario, 1980; Member, Canadian Cultural Delegation to China, 1985; Instructor, University of New Brunswick, 1986. Publications: The Ancestral Suitcase; The Book of Strange; My Father's House; Berlin Solstice; The Candy Factory; Pandora; A Casual Affair; The Emperor's Virgin; The Ancestral Suitcase, 1996. Contributions to: Feature writer, Toronto Star Weekly Magazine. Honours: Women's Press Club Award; President's Medal for Canadian Journalism; Non-Fiction Book Award, Canadian Authors Association; National Magazine Award; Gold Medal for Essays, National Magazine, 1994; American Literary Association Medal, 1994. Memberships: Writers Development Trust; PEN; ACTRA. Literary Agent: Sterling Lord Literistic, 1 Madison Avenue, New York, NY

10010, USA. Address: 701 King Street West 302, Toronto, Ontario M5V 2W7, Canada.

FRATTI Mario, b. 5 July 1927, L'Aquila, Italy. (US Citizen, 1974). Playwright; Educator. 3 children. Education: PhD, Ca Foscari University, 1951. Appointments: Teacher, Adelphi College, 1964-65; Faculty, Columbia University, 1965-66; Professor of Literature, New School, Hunter College, 1967-; Faculty, Hofstra University, 1973-74; Drama Critic: Paese, 1963-; Progresso, 1963-; Ridotto, 1963-; Ora Zero, 1963-. Publications: Plays: Cage-Suicide, 1964; Academy-Return, 1967; Mafia, 1971; Bridge, 1971; Races, 1972; Eleven Plays in Spanish, 1977; Refrigerators, 1977; Eleonora Duse-Victim, 1981; Nine, 1982; Biography of Fratti, 1982; AIDS, 1987;Porno, 1988, Encounter, musical, 1989; Family, 1990; Friends, 1991; Lovers, 1992; Leningrad Euthanasia, 1993; Holy Father, 1994; Sacrifices, 1995; Jurors, 1996. Honours: Tony Award, 1982; Other awards for plays and musicals. Memberships: Drama Desk; American Theatre Critics; Outer Critics Circle, Vice-President. Literary Agent: Susan Schulman, 454 West 44th Street, New York, NY 10036, USA. Address: 145 West 55th Street, Apt 15D, New York, NY 10019-5355, USA.

FRAYN Michael, b. 3 Sept 1933, London, England. Author; Journalist. Education: BA, Emmanuel College, Cambridge University. Publications: Novels: The Tin Men, 1966; The Russian Interpreter, 1967; A Very Private Life, 1968; Towards the End of the Morning, 1969; Sweet Dreams, 1973; The Trick of It, 1989; A Landing on the Sun, 1991; Now You Know, 1992; Here, 1993. Philosophy: Constructions, 1974; Plays: The Two of Us, 1970; Alphabetical Order and Donkeys Years, 1977; Clouds, 1977; Make and Break, 1980; Noises Off, 1982; Benefactors, 1984; Translations: Chekhov: The Cherry Orchard, 1978; Tolstoy: The Fruits of Enlightenment, 1979; Chekhov: Three Sisters, 1983, Wild Honey, 1984; The Seagull, 1987; Balmoral, 1987; Uncle Vanya, 1989; The Sneeze, 1989. Honours: Somerset Maugham Award, 1966; Hawthornden Prize, 1967; National Press Award, 1970; 3 SWET/Olivier Awards; 4 Evening Standard Drama Awards; Sunday Express Book of the Year Award, 1991. Memberships: Felloe, Royal Society of Literature; Hon Fellow, Emmanuel College, Cambridge. Address: c/o Elaine Greene Limited, 31 Newington Green, London N16 9PU, England.

FRAZER Fred. See: **AVALLONE Michael (Angelo Jr).**

FRAZIER Arthur. See: **BULMER Henry Kenneth.**

FREEBORN Richard Harry, b. 19 Oct 1926, South Wales. University Professor (Retired). m. Anne Davis, 14 Feb 1954, 1 son, 3 daughters. Education: MA, PhD, Brasenose College, Oxford University. Appointments: Emeritus Professor of Russian Literature, University of London. Publications: Turgenev, The Novelist's Novelist: A Study, 1960; Two Ways of Life, 1962; The Emigration of Sergev Ivanovich, 1962; A Short History of Modern Russia, 1966; Turgenev: Sketches from a Hunter's Album, 1967; Turgenev: Home of the Gentry, 1970; The Rise of the Russian Novel, 1973; Turgenev: Rudin, 1975; Russian Roulette, 1979; The Russian Revolutionary, (novel), 1982; Turgenev: Love and Death, 1983; The Russian Crucifix, 1987; Turgenev: First Love and Other Stories, 1989; Ideology in Russian Literature, 1990; Turgenev: Sketches from a Hunter's Album, 1990; Turgenev: Fathers and Sons, 1991; Turgenev: A Month in the Country, 1991; Chekhov: The Steppe and Other Stories, 1991; Goncharov: Oblomov, 1992; Dostoevsky, An Accidental Family, 1994. Honour: DLit, University of London, 1984. Membership: BASEES. Address: 24 Park Road, Surbiton, Surrey KT5 8QD, England.

FREEDMAN David N(oel), b. 12 May 1922, New York, New York, USA. Professor of Biblical Studies; Writer; Editor. m. Cornelia Anne Pryor, 16 May 1944, 2 sons, 2 daughters. Education: City College of New York, 1935-38; AB, University of California at Los Angeles, 1938-39; ThB, Old Testament, Princeton Theological Seminary, 1944; PhD, Semitic Languages and Literature, Johns Hopkins University, 1948. Appointments: Ordained Minister, Presbyterian Church USA, 1944; Stated Supply Minister, Acme and Deming, Washington, Presbyterian Churches, 1944-45; Teaching Fellow, 1946-47, Assistant Instructor, 1947-48, Johns Hopkins University; Assistant Professor of Old Testament, 1948-51, Professor of Hebrew and Old Testament, 1951-60, Western Theological Seminary, Pittsburgh; Associate Editor, 1952-54, Editor, 1955-59, Journal of Biblical Literature; Professor of Hebrew and Old Testament, 1960-61, James A Kelso Professor of Hebrew and Old Testament,

1961-64, Pittsburgh Theological Seminary; Professor of Old Testament, 1964-70, Dean of Faculty, 1966-70, Gray Professor of Old Testament Exegesis, 1970-71, San Francisco Theological Seminary; Professor of Old Testament, Graduate Theological Union, 1964-71; Vice President 1970-82, Director of Publications, 1974-82, American Schools of Oriental Research; Editor, Biblical Archaeologist, 1976-82; Professor of Biblical Studies, 1971-92, Director, Program on Studies in Religion, 1971-91, Arthur F Thurnau Professor in Old Testament Studies, 1984-92, University of Michigan; Visiting Professor in Old Testament Studies, 1985-86, Professor in Hebrew Biblical Studies, 1987, Endowed Chair in Hebrew Biblical Studies, 1987-, University of California at San Diego; Numerous visiting lectureships and professorships. Publications: God Has Spoken (with J D Smart), 1949, Studies in Ancient Yahwistic Poetry (with Frank M Cross), 1950; Early Hebrew Orthography (with Frank M Cross), 1952; The People of the Dead Sea Scrolls (with J M Allegro), 1958; The Secret Saying of Jesus (with R M Grant), 1960; Ashdod I (with M Dothan), 1967; The Published Works of W F Albright (with R B MacDonald and D L Mattson), 1975; William Foxwell Albright: Twentieth Century Genius (with L G Running), 1975, 2nd edition, 1991; The Mountain of the Lord (with B Mazar and G Cornfeld), 1975; An Explorer's Life of Jesus (with W Phillips), 1975; Hosea (Anchor Bible Series; with F I Andersen), 1980; Pottery, Poetry, and Prophecy, 1981; The Paleo-Hebrew Leviticus Scroll (with K A Mathews), 1985; Amos (Anchor Bible Series; with F I Andersen), 1989; The Unity of the Hebrew Bible, 1991; Studies in Hebrew and Aramaic Orthography (with D Forbes and F I Andersen), 1992; The Relationship Between Herodotus' History and Primary History (with Sara Mandell), 1993. Other: The Biblical Archaeologist Reader (co-editor), 4 volumes, 1961, 1964, 1970, 1982; Anchor Bible Series (co-editor), 18 volumes, 1964-72; 50 volumes (general editor), 1972-; Computer Bible Series (co-editor), 18 volumes, 1971-80; Anchor Bible Reference Library (general editor), 16 volumes, 1988-96; Anchor Bible Dictionary (editor-in-chief), 6 volumes, 1992. Honours: Guggenheim Fellowship, 1958-59; AATS Fellowship, 1965; Honorary Doctorates. Memberships: American Academy of Religion; American Archaeological Institute; American Oriental Society; American Schools of Oriental Research; Explorers Club; Society of Biblical Literature. Address: c/o Department of History, No 0104, University of California at San Diego, La Jolla, CA 92093, USA.

FREEDMAN Lawrence. Publications: Arms Production in the United Kingdom, 1978; The West & the Modernization of China, 1979; Britain & Nuclear Weapons, 1980; Evolution of Nuclear Strategy, 1981; Atlas of Global Strategy, 1985; Price of Peace: Living with the Nuclear Dilemma, 1986; Britain & the Falklands War, 1988; Europe Transformed, 1990; Signals of War: The Falklands Conflict of 1982, 1991; Population Change & International Strategy, 1992; War, Strategy & International Politics, 1992; The Gulf Conflict 1990-91, 1993; Military Intervention in Europe, 1994; War, 1994. Membership: Fellow, British Academy, 1995. Address: c/o Department of War Studies, King's College London, The Strand, London, WC2R 2LS, England.

FREEDMAN (Bruce), Russell, b. 11 Oct 1929, San Francisco, California, USA. Children's Book Writer. Education: San Jose State University; BA, University of California at Berkeley. Publications: Thomas Alva Edison, 1961; 2000 Years of Space Travel, 1963; Scouting with Baden Powell, 1967; The First Days of Life, 1974; How Animals Defend Their Young, 1978; Immigrant Kids, 1980; When Winter Comes, 1981; Dinosaurs & Their Young, 1983; Children of the Wild West, 1984; Lincoln: A Photobiography, 1985; Cowboys of the Wild West, 1985; Sharks, 1985; The First Fifty Years, 1985; Indian Chiefs, 1987; The Wright Brothers, 1991; Eleanor Roosevelt, 1993. Contributions to: Reference books and periodicals. Honours: Notable Book of the Year Citation, American Library Association, 1980, 1983, 1985; Western Heritage Award, 1984; Newberry Medal, 1988; Newberry Honour Citation, American Library Association, 1992; Boston Globe/Horn Book Award, 1994. Memberships: Authors League of America; American Civil Liberties Union. Address: 280 Riverside Drive, New York, NY 10025, USA.

FREELING Nicolas, b. 3 Mar 1927, London, England. Writer. m. Cornelia Termes, 1954, 4 sons, 1 daughter. Education: University of Dublin. Publications: Fiction: Love in Amsterdam, 1961; Because of the Cats, 1962; Gun Before Butter, 1963; Valparaiso, 1964; Double Barrel, 1964; Criminal Conversation, 1965; The King of the Rainy Country, 1966; The Dresden Green, 1966; Strike Out Where Not Applicable, 1967; This is the Castle, 1968; Tsing-Boum, 1969; Over the High Side, 1970; A Long Silence, 1971; Dressing of Diamond, 1974; What Are the Bugles Blowing For?, 1975; Lake Isle, 1976;

Gadget, 1977; The Night Lords, 1978; The Widow, 1979; Castang's City, 1980; One Damned Thing After Another, 1981; Wolfnight, 1982; The Back of the North Wind, 1983; No Part in Your Death, 1984; A City Solitary, 1985; Cold Iron, 1986; Not as Far as Velma, 1989; Sand Castles, 1989; Those in Peril, 1990; Flanders Sky, 1992; You Know Who, 1994; The Seacoast of Bohemia, 1995; A Dwarf Kingdom, 1996. Other: The Kitchen: A Delicious Account of the Author's Years as a Grand Hotel Cook, 1970; Criminal Convictions: Errant Essays on Perpetrators of Literary License, 1994. Honours: Crime Writers Award, 1963; Grand Prix de Roman Policier, 1965; Edgar Allan Poe Award, Mystery Writers of America, 1966. Address: Grandfontaine, 67130 Schirmeck, Bas Rhin, France.

FREEMAN Anne Hobson, b. 19 Mar 1934, Richmond, Virginia, USA. Fiction Writer; Essayist. m. George Clemon Freeman Jr, 6 Dec 1958, 2 sons, 1 daughter. Education: AB, Bryn Mawr College, 1956; MA, University of Virginia, 1973. Appointments: Reporter, International News Service, Russia and Eastern Europe, 1957; Editor, Member's Bulletin, Virginia Museum of Fine Arts, 1958-63; Lecturer, English, University of Virginia, 1973-88. Publication: The Style of a Law Firm: Eight Gentlemen from Virginia, 1990; A Hand Well Played, The Life of Jim Wheat, Jr, 1994. Contributions to: Anthologies and periodicals. Address: Oyster Shell Point Farm, Callao, VA 22435-0686, USA.

FREEMAN Gillian (Elizabeth Von S), b. 5 Dec 1929, London, England. Writer. m. Edward Thorpe, 12 Sept 1955, 2 daughters. Education: BA, Honours, University of Reading, 1951. Publications: The Liberty Man, 1955; Fall of Innocence, 1956; Jack Would be a Gentleman, 1959; The Story of Albert Einstein, 1960; The Leather Boys, 1961; The Campaign, 1963; The Leader, 1965; The Undergrowth of Literature, 1969; The Alabaster Egg, 1970; The Marriage Machine, 1975; The Schoolgirl Ethic: The Life and Work of Angela Brazil, 1976; Nazi Lady, 1979, (1st edition as Elizabeth von S); An Easter Egg Hunt, 1981; Lovechild, 1984; Ballet Genius (with Edward Thorpe), 1988; Termination Rock, 1989. Other: Screenplays and adaptations; Ballet scenarios. Contributions to: Periodicals. Memberships: Arts Council; Writers Guild of Great Britain. Address: c/o Richard Scott Simon, 48 Doughty Street, London WC1N 2LP, England.

FREEMAN James M(ontague), b. 1 Dec 1936, Chicago, Illinois, USA. Professor of Anthropology; Writer. Education: BA, Northwestern University, 1958; MA, 1964, PhD, 1968, Harvard University. Appointments: Assistant Professor to Professor of Anthropology, San Jose State University, 1966-. Publications: Scarcity and Opportunity in an Indian Village, 1977; Untouchable: An Indian Life History, 1979; Hearts of Sorrow: Vietnamese-American Lives, 1989; Changing Identities: Vietnamese Americans 1975-1995, 1996. Contributions to: Scholarly books and journals. Honours: Choice Outstanding Academic Book, 1979; Phi Kappa Phi Distinguished Academic Achievement Award, 1982; National Endowment for the Humanities Fellowship, 1983-84; President's Scholar, San Jose State University, 1984; Before Columbus Foundation American Book Award, 1990; Association for Asian-American Studies Outstanding Book Award, 1990; Austin D Warburton Award for Outstanding Scholarship, 1991. Memberships: Aid to Refugee Children Without Parents, 1988-95, and its successor, Aid to Children Without Parents, Inc, chairman of the board, 1995-; Southwestern Anthropological Association, president, 1991-92. Address: c/o Department of Anthropology, San Jose State University, San Jose, CA 95192, USA.

FREEMAN-GRENVILLE Greville Stewart Parker, b. 29 June 1918, Hook Norton, Oxfordshire, England. Historian; Writer. Education: BLitt, 1940, MA, 1943, DPhil, 1957, Worcester College, Oxford. Publications: The Medieval History of the Coast of Tanganyika, 1962; The East African Coast: Select Documents (editor and translator), 1962, 2nd edition 1975; The Muslim and Christian Calendars, 1963, 2nd edition, 1977, 3rd edition; French at Kilwa Island, 1965; Chronology of African History, 1973; Chronology of World History, 1975; A Modern Atlas of African History, 1976; The Queen's Lineage, 1977; Atlas of British History, 1979; The Mombasa Rising Against the Portuguese 1631, 1980; The Beauty of Cairo, 1981; Buzurg ibn Shahriyar: The Book of Wonders of India (c 953) (editor and translator), 1982; Emily Said-Ruete: Memoirs of an Arabian Princess (1888) (editor), 1982, 2nd edition, 1994; The Beauty of Jerusalem and the Holy Places of the Gospels, 1982, 2nd edition, 1987; The Stations of the Cross, 1982; The Beauty of Rome, 1988; The Swahili Coast: Islam, Christianity and Commerce in Eastern Africa, 1988; A New Atlas for African History, 1991; Historical Atlas of the Middle East,

1993; The Basilica of the Nativity at Bethlehem, 1993; The Basilica of the Holy Sepulchre in Jerusalem, 1993; The Basilica of the Annunciation at Nazareth and other nearby shrines, 1993; The Holy Land: A Pilgrim's Guide to Israel, Jordan and the Sinai, 1995; Islamic and Christian Calendars, AD 622-2222, 1995; Wordsworth's Kings and Queens of Great Britain, 1997. Contributions to: Numerous journals, reviews and encyclopaedias including Journal of the Royal Asiatic Society; Numismatic Chronocle; Encyclopaedia of Islam; Encyclopaedia Britannica. Memberships: Fellow, Society of Antiquaries; Fellow, Royal Asiatic Society; Palestine Exploration Fund. Address: North View House, Sheriff Hutton, York Y06 1PT, England.

FREEMANTLE Brian (Harry), (Jonathan Evans, Richard Gant, John Maxwell, Jack Winchester), b. 10 June 1936, Southampton, England. Author. m. Maureen Hazel Tipney, 8 Dec 1957, 3 daughters. Education: Secondary school, Southampton. Appointments: Reporter, New Milton Advertiser, 1953-58, Bristol Evening News, 1958, Evening News, London, 1959-61; Reporter, 1961-63, Assistant Foreign Editor, 1963-69, Daily Express; Foreign Editor, Daily Sketch, London, 1969-70, Daily Mail, London, 1971-75. Publications: Novels: The Touchables, 1968; Goodbye to an Old Friend, 1973; Face Me When You Walk Away, 1974; The Man Who Wanted Tomorrow, 1975; The November Man, 1976; Deaken's War, 1982; Rules of Engagement, 1984; Vietnam Legacy, 1984; The Lost American, 1984; The Laundryman, 1986; The Kremlin Kiss, 1986; The Bearpit, 1988; O'Farrell's Law, 1990; The Factory, 1990; The Choice of Eddie Franks, 1990; Betrayals, 1991; Little Grey Mice, 1992; The Button Man, 1993; No Time for Heroes, 1995. Other: 11 books in the Charlie Muffin mystery series. Non-fiction: KGB, 1982; CIA, 1983; The Fix: Inside the World Drug Trade, 1985; The Steal: Counterfeiting and Industrial Espionage, 1987; The Octopus: Europe in the Grip of Organised Crime, 1996. Contributions to: Periodicals. Address: c/o Jonathan Clowes, 10 Iron Bridge House, Bridge Approach, London, NW1 8BD, England.

FRENCH David, b. 18 Jan 1939, Coleys Point, Newfoundland, Canada. m. Leslie Gray, 5 Jan 1978. Playwright. Education: Studied Acting, Pasadena Playhouse, Toronto, Canada; Roy Lawler Acting School, Toronto, Canada. Publications: A Company of Strangers (novel), 1968; Leaving Home, 1972; Of the Fields, Lately, 1973; One Crack Out, 1976; The Seagull, by Anton Chekov, translation, 1978; Jitters, 1980; Salt-Water Moon, 1985; "1949", 1989. Contributions to: Montrealer; Canadian Boy. Honours: Chalmers Award, Best Canadian Play, Ontario Arts Council, 1973; Lieutenant Governors Award, 1974; Canada Council Grants, 1974, 1975. Address: c/o Tarragon Theatre, 30 Bridgman Avenue, Toronto, Ontario M5R 1X3, Canada.

FRENCH Fiona, b. 27 June 1944, Bath, Somerset, England. Children's Writer; Illustrator. Education: NDD, Croydon College of Art, Surrey, 1966. Publications: Jack of Hearts, 1970; Huni, 1971; The Blue Bird, 1972; King Tree, 1973; City of Gold, 1975; Aio the Rainmaker, 1975; Matteo, 1976; Hunt the Thimble, 1978; Oscar Wilde's Star Child, 1979; The Princess and the Musician, 1981; John Barley Corn, 1982; Future Story, 1983; Fat Cat, 1984; Going to Squintums, 1985; Maid of the Wood, 1985; Snow White in New York, 1986; Song of the Nightingale, 1986; Cinderella, 1987; Rise Shine!, 1989; The Magic Vase, 1990. Address: Flat B, 70 Colney Hatch Lane, London N10 1EA, England.

FRENCH Linda. See: **MARIZ Linda Catherine French.**

FRENCH Philip (Neville), b. 28 Aug 1933, Liverpool, England. Writer; Broadcaster; Film Critic. m. Kersti Elisabet Molin, 1957, 3 sons. Education: BA, Exeter College, Oxford; Indiana University. Appointments: Reporter, Bristol Evening Post, 1958-59; Producer, North American Service, 1959-61; Talks Producer, 1961-67, Senior Producer, 1968-90, BBC Radio; Theatre Critic, 1967-68, Arts Columnist 1967-72, New Statesman; Film Critic, The Observer, 1978-. Publications: The Age of Austerity, 1945-51 (editor with Michael Sissons), 1963; The Novelist as Innovator (Editor), 1966; The Movie Moguls, 1969; Westerns: Aspects of a Movie Genre, 1974, revised edition, 1977; Three Honest Men: Portraits of Edmund Wilson, F R Leavis, Lionel Trilling, 1980; The Third Dimension: Voices from Radio Three (editor), 1983; The Press: Observed and Projected (editor with Deac Rossell), 1991; Editor, Malle on Malle, 1992; The Faber Book of Movie Verse (editor with Ken Wlaschin), 1993; Wild Strawberries (with Kersti French), 1995. Contributions to: Many anthologies and periodicals. Address: 62 Dartmouth Park Road, London, NW5 1SN, England.

FRENCH Warren Graham, b. 26 Jan 1922, Philadelphia, Pennsylvania, USA. Retired College Professor. Education: BA, University of Pennsylvania, 1943; MA 1948, PhD, American Literature 1954, University of Texas. Publications: John Steinbeck, 1961, revised edition, 1974; Frank Norris, 1962; J D Salinger, 1963; The Social Novel at the End of an Era, 1966; Jack Kerouac, 1986; J D Salinger, Revisited, 1988; The San Francisco Poetry Renaissance, 1955-1960, 1991; Editor: The South in Film, 1981; The Thirties, 1967; The Forties, 1969; The Fifties, 1971; The Twenties, 1975. Contributions to: Numerous American Academic Journals. Honour: DHL, Ohio University, 1985. Memberships: President, International John Steinbeck Society; Editorial Board, American Literature; Modern Language Association of America; American Studies Association; Western American Literature Association. Address: 23 Beechwood Road, Uplands, Swansea, West Glamorgan SA2 0HL, Wales.

FREWER Glyn Mervyn Louis, (Mervyn Lewis), b. 4 Sept 1931, Oxford, England. m. Lorna Townsend, 11 Aug 1956, 2 sons, 1 daughter. Education: MA, English Language and Literature, St Catherine's College, Oxford, 1955. Appointments: Advertising Agency Associate Director, 1974-85; Proprietor antiquarian/secondhand bookshop, 1985; Author, scriptwriter. Publications: The Hitch-Hikers (BBC Radio Play), 1957; Adventure in Forgotten Valley, 1962; Adventure in the Barren Lands, 1964; The Last of the Wispies, 1965; Death of Gold (as Mervyn Lewis), 1970; The Token of Elkin, 1970; Crossroad, 1970; The Square Peg, 1972; The Raid, 1976; The Trackers, 1976; Tyto: The Odyssey of an Owl, 1978; Bryn of Brockle Hanger, 1980; Fox, 1984; The Call of the Raven, 1987; also scripts for children's TV series, industrial films etc. Contributions to: Birds; Imagery. Honour: Made a Freeman of the City of Oxford, 1967. Literary Agent: Watson, Little Ltd. Address: Cottage Farm, Taston, Oxford, OX7 3JN.

FRIDRIKSSON Gudjon, b. 9 Mar 1945, Reykjavik, Iceland. Historian; Writer; Journalist. m. Hildur Kjartanspottir, 26 Mar 1983, 2 daughters. Education: BA, University of Iceland, 1970. Appointments: Teacher in Litterature, 1972-75; Journalist, Daily Newspaper Thjodvilsinn, 1976-80; Editor, Sunday Edition of Thjodvilsinn, 1980-84; Editor, Offical History of Reykjavik, 1985-91; Freelance Writer. Publications: Togarasaga Magnusar Runólfssonar, 1983; Baerin Vaknar Saga Reykjavikur 1870-1940 (Awakening of a Town: History of Reykjavik 1870-1940), 2 volumes, 1991-94; Saga Jonasar Jonssonar Fra Hriflu (The Biography of the Politician Jonas Jonsson from Hrifla), 1991-93; Indaela Reykjavik (Wonderful Reykjavik), 1995. Contributions to: Heimsmynd, 1989-94. Honours: Mother Tongue Prize for Journalists, 1985; Icelandic Literature Prize, 1991. Membership: Icelandic Writers Union, Board of Directors, 1994-. Address: Tjarnargata 44, 101 Reykjavik, Iceland.

FRIEDBERG Maurice, b. 3 Dec 1929, Rzeszow, Poland. Professor of Slavic Languages and Literatures. m. Barbara Bisguier, 1956, 2 daughters. Education: BA, Brooklyn College, 1951; AM, 1953, PhD, 1958, Columbia University. Appointments: Associate Professor of Russian, Chairman of Russian Division, Hunter College, City University of New York, 1955-65; Fulbright Professor of Russian Literature, Hebrew University, Jerusalem, Israel, 1965-66; Professor of Slavic Languages and Literatures, 1966-75, Director, Russian and East European Institute, 1967-71, Indiana University; Professor of Slavic Languages and Literatures, Department Head, University of Illinois, Urbana, 1975-95; Directeur d'Etudes Associés, Ecole des Hautes Etudes en Sciences Sociales, Paris, 1984-85; Center for Advanced Study Professor of Russian Literature, University of Illinois, 1995-. Publications: Russian Classics in Soviet Jackets, 1962; A Bilingual Edition of Russian Short Stories, volume II (editor and translator with R A Maguire), 1965; The Jew in Post Stalin Soviet Literature, 1970; Encyclopedia Judaica (editor and co-author), 16 volumes, 1971-72; The Young Lenin, by Leon Trotsky (editor), 1972; A Decade of Euphoria: Western Literature in Post-Stalin Russia, 1977; Russian Culture in the 1980's, 1986; Soviet Society under Gorbachev (editor with Heyward Isham), 1987; The Red Pencil (editor with Marianna Tax Choldin), 1989; How Things Were Done in Odessa, 1991. Honours: Two Guggenheim Fellowships; National Endowment for the Humanities Fellowship. Address: 3001 Meadowbrook Court, Champaign, IL 61821, USA.

FRIEDEN Bernard J(oel), b. 11 Aug 1930, New York, New York, USA. Professor of Urban Development; Writer. m. Elaine Leibowitz, 23 Nov 1958, 1 daughter. Education: BA, Cornell University, 1951; MA, Penn State University, 1953; MCP, 1957, PhD, 1962, Massachusetts

Institute of Technology. Appointments: Assistant Professor, 1961-65, Associate Professor, 1965-69, Professor of Urban Studies and Planning, 1969-; Chairman, Faculty, 1987-89, Ford Professor of Urban Development, 1989-, Associate Dean, Architecture and Planning, 1993-, Massachusetts Institute of Technology; Research Fellow, 1978-89, Senior Fellow, 1989-, Urban Land Institute; Visiting Scholar, University of California, Berkeley, 1990-91. Publications: The Future of Old Neighborhoods, 1964; Metropolitan America, 1966; Urban Planning and Social Policy (with Robert Morris), 1968; Shaping an Urban Future (with William W Nash), 1969; The Politics of Neglect (with Marshall Kaplan), 1975, 2nd edition, 1977; Managing Human Services (with Wayne E Anderson and Michael J Murphy), 1977; The Environmental Protection Hustle, 1979; Downtown, Inc (with Lynne B Sagalyn), 1989. Contributions to: Books and encyclopaedias. Honour: Guggenheim Fellowship, 1975-76. Memberships: American Institute of Certified Planners; American Planning Association. Address: 245 Highland Avenue, Newton, MA 02165, USA.

FRIEDMAN Alan Howard, b. 4 Jan 1928, New York, New York, USA. Writer. m. 1) Lenore Ann Helman, 1 Aug 1950, div, 1 son, (2) Kate Miler Gilbert, 30 Oct 1977, 1 son. Education: BA, Harvard College, 1949; MA, Columbia University, 1950; PhD, University of California, Berkeley, 1964. Publications: The Turn of the Novel, 1966; Hermaphrodeity: The Autobiography of a Poet, 1972. Contributions to: Books, journals and magazines. Honours: D H Lawrence Fellowship, 1974; National Endowment for the Arts Award, 1975; PEN Syndicated Fiction Award, 1987; Illinois Arts Council Award, 1992. Memberships: American PEN; Executive Board, PEN Midwest. Address: 2406 Park Place, Evanston, IL 60201, USA.

FRIEDMAN Bruce Jay, b. 26 Apr 1930, New York, New York, USA. Writer; Dramatist; Screenwriter. m. (1) Ginger Howard, 13 June 1954, div 1978, 3 sons, (2) Patricia O'Donohue, 3 July 1983, 1 daughter. Education: BJ, University of Missouri, 1951. Appointment: Editorial Director, Magazine Management Co, New York City, 1953-64. Publications: Stern, 1962; Far From the City of Class, and Other Stories, 1963; A Mother's Kisses, 1964; Black Humour (editor), 1965; Black Angels, 1966; Pardon Me, Sir, But Is My Eye Hurting Your Elbow? (with others), 1968; The Dick, 1970; About Harry Towns, 1974; The Lonely Guys Book of Life, 1978; Let's Hear It for a Beautiful Guy, and Other Works of Short Fiction, 1984; Tokyo Woes, 1985; Violencia, 1988; The Current Climate, 1990; Collected Short Fiction of Bruce Jay Friedman, 1995; The Slightly Older Guy, 1995. Plays and screenplays including Have You Spoken to Any Jews Lately, 1995; A Father's Kisses, 1996. Memberships: PEN; Sigma Delta Chi. Literary Agent: Candida Denadio, 121 W 27th Street, New York, NY 10001, USA. Address: PO Box 746, Water Mill, NY 11976, USA.

FRIEDMAN Dennis, b. 23 Feb 1924, London, England. Psychiatrist. m. Rosemary Tibber, 2 Feb 1949, 4 daughters. Education: MRCS, LRCP, London, 1948; MRCPsych, 1972; FRCPsych, 1978. Publications: Chapter in Progress in Behaviour Therapy, 1968; Chapters in Handbook of Sexology, 1977; Chapter in Sex Therapy, 1988; Inheritance: A Psychological History of the Royal Family, 1993. Contributions to:Professional journals. Membership: Royal Society of Medicine. Address: 2 St Katharine's Precinct, Regent's Park, London NW1 4HH, England.

FRIEDMAN Lawrence J, b. 8 Oct 1940, Cleveland, Ohio, USA. Professor of History; Writer. m. Sharon Bloom, 3 Apr 1966, 1 daughter. Education: BA, University of California at Riverside, 1962; MA, 1965, PhD, 1967, University of California at Los Angeles; Post-doctoral Fellow, Menninger Foundation Interdisciplinary Studies Program, 1981. Appointments: Assistant Professor, Arizona State University, 1967-71; Associate Professor, 1971-77, Professor of History and American Studies, 1977-91, Distinguished University Professor, 1991-93, Bowling Green State University; Visiting Scholar, Harvard University, 1991; Professor of History, Indiana University, 1993-. Publications: The White Savage: Racial Fantasies in the Postbellum South, 1970; Inventors of the Promised Land, 1975; Gregarious Saints: Self and Community in American Abolitionism, 1830-1870, 1982; Menninger: The Family and the Clinic, 1990. Contributions to: Books and professional journals. Honours: National Endowment for the Humanities Fellowships, 1979-80, 1986-87, 1994-95; Ohioana Library Association Book Award in History, 1983; Paul and Ruth Olscamp Distinguished Research Award, 1989-92. Memberships: American Association of University Professors; American Historical Association; Cheiron; Group for the Use of Psychology in History; Organization of American Historians; Society of American Historians. Address:

Department of History, Indiana University, Bloomington, IN 47405, USA.

FRIEDMAN Lawrence Meir, b. 2 Apr 1930, Chicago, Illinois, USA. Professor of Law; Writer. m. Leah Feigenbaum, 27 Mar 1955, 2 daughters. Education: AB, 1948, JD, 1951, MLL, 1953, University of Chicago. Appointments: Assistant to Associate Professor, St Louis University, 1957-61; Associate Professor to Professor of Law, University of Wisconsin, Madison, 1961-68; Professor of Law, 1968-76, Marion Rice Kirkwood Professor of Law, 1976-, Stanford University; David Stouffer Memorial Lecturer, Rutgers University, 1969; Fellow, Center for Advanced Study in the Behavioral Sciences, 1973-74; Sibley Lecturer, University of Georgia, 1976; Wayne Morse Lecturer, University of Oregon, 1985; Fellow, Institute for Advanced Study, Berlin, 1985; Childress Memorial Lecturer, St Louis University, 1987. Publications: Contract Law in America, 1965; Government and Slum Housing: A Century of Frustration, 1968; Law and the Behavioral Sciences (with Stewart Macaulay), 1969, 2nd edition, 1977; A History of American Law, 1973, 2nd edition, 1985; The Legal System: A Social Science Perspective, 1975; Law and Society: An Introduction, 1978; The Roots of Justice: Crime and Punishment in Alameda County, California, 1870-1910, 1981; Fundamentals of Clinical Trials (with Curt D Furberg and David L DeMets), 1982; American Law, 1984; Total Justice: What Americans Want from the Legal System and Why, 1985; Your Time Will Come: The Law of Age Discrimination and Mandatory Retirement, 1985; American Law and the Constitutional Order Historical Perspectives (editor with Harry N Schrieber), 1988; The Republic of Choice: Law, Authority and Culture, 1990; Crime and Punishment in American History, 1993. Honours: Scribes Award, 1974; Triennial Award, Order of Coif, 1976; Willard Hurst Prize, 1982; Harry Kalven Prize, 1992. Memberships: American Academy of Arts and Sciences; President, Law and Society Association, 1979-81; President, American Society for Legal History, 1990-91. Address: c/o School of Law, Stanford University, Stanford, CA 94305, USA.

FRIEDMAN Milton, b. 31 July 1912, New York, New York, USA. Professor of Economics Emeritus; Senior Research Fellow; Writer. m. Rose Director, 25 June 1938, 1 son, 1 daughter. Education: BA, Rutgers University, 1932; AM, University of Chicago, 1933; PhD, Columbia University, 1946. Appointments: Associate Economist, Natural Resources Committee, Washington, DC, 1935-37, National Bureau of Economic Research, New York, 1937-40; Principal Economist, Tax Research Division, US Treasury Department, Washington, DC, 1941-43; Associate Director, Statistical Research Group, Division of War Research, Columbia University, 1943-45; Professor of Economics, 1948-82, Professor Emeritus, 1982-, University of Chicago; Member, Research Staff, National Bureau of Economic Research, 1948-81; Fulbright Lecturer, Cambridge University, 1953-54; Columnist, 1966-84, Contributing Editor, 1974-84, Newsweek magazine; Senior Research Fellow, Hoover Institution, Stanford University, 1976-. Publications: Income from Independent Professional Practice (with Simon Kuznets), 1946; Sampling Inspection (with others), 1948; Essays in Positive Economics, 1953; Studies in the Quantity Theory of Money (editor), 1956; A Theory of the Consumption Function, 1957; A Program for Monetary Stability, 1960; Capitalism and Freedom, 1962; Price Theory: A Provisional Text, 1962; A Monetary History of the United States 1867-1960 (with Anna J Schwartz), 1963; Inflation: Causes and Consequences, 1963; The Balance of Payments: Free Versus Flexible Exchange Rates (with Robert V Roosa), 1967; Dollars and Deficits, 1968; Optimum Quantity of Money and Other Essays, 1969; Monetary Policy Versus Fiscal Policy (with Walter W Heller), 1969; Monetary Statistics of the United States (with Anna J Schwartz), 1970; A Theoretical Framework for Monetary Analysis, 1971; Social Security: Universal or Selective? (with Wilbur J Cohen), 1972; An Economist's Protest, 1972; Money and Economic Development, 1973; There's No Such Thing as a Free Lunch, 1975; Price Theory, 1976; Free to Choose (with Rose Friedman), 1980; Monetary Trends in the United States and the United Kingdom (with Anna J Schwartz), 1982; Bright Promises, Dismal Performance, 1983; Tyranny of the Status Quo (with Rose Friedman), 1984; Money Mischief, 1992. Honours: John Bates Clark Medal, American Economic Association, 1951; Nobel Prize for Economic Science, 1976; Grand Cordon, Sacred Treasure, Japan, 1986; US Presidential Medal of Freedom, 1988; National Medal of Science, 1988; Various fellowships, awards and honorary doctorates. Memberships: American Economic Association, president, 1967; Mont Pelerin Society, president, 1970-72; Royal Economic Society. Address: c/o Hoover Institution, Stanford, CA 94305, USA.

FRIEDMAN (Eve) Rosemary, (Robert Tibber, Rosemary Tibber), b. 5 Feb 1929, London, England. Writer. m. Dennis Friedman, 2 Feb 1949, 4 daughters. Education: Queen's College, Harley Street, London; Law Faculty, University College, London University. Publications: The Life Situation, 1977; The Long Hot Summer, 1980; Proofs of Affection, 1982; A Loving Mistress, 1983; Rose of Jericho, 1984; A Second Wife, 1986; To Live in Peace, 1987; An Eligible Man, 1989; Golden Boy, 1994; Vintage, 1996; As Robert Tibber: No White Coat, 1957; Love on My List, 1959; We All Fall Down, 1960; Patients of a Saint, 1961; The Fraternity, 1963; The Commonplace Day, 1964; The General Practice, 1967; Practice Makes Perfect, 1969; Vintage, 1996. Confrontations with Judaism (contributor), 1967; For Euston Films: Shrinks. Others: Several screenplays and television dramas. Contributions to: Reviewer; Sunday Times; Times Literary Supplement; Guardian; Sunday Times; Jewish Quarterly. Memberships: Fellow, PEN; Royal Society of Literature; Society of Authors; Writers' Guild of Great Britain; Judge: Authors Club First Novel Award, 1989, Betty Trask Fiction Award, 1991, Jewish Quarterly Literary Prizes, 1993, Macmillan Silver Pen Award, 1995. Memberships: Fellow, PEN; BAFTA; Writers' Guild; Royal Society of Literature; Society of Authors. Literary Agent: Sonia Land, Sheil Land, 43 Doughty Street, London WC1 2LF, England. Address: 2 St Katherine's Precinct, Regents Park, London NW1 4HH, England.

FRIEDMAN Thomas (Loren), b. 20 July 1953, Minneapolis, Minnesota, USA. Journalist. m. Ann Louise Bucksbaum, 23 Nov 1978, 2 daughters. Education: BA, Brandeis University, 1975; MPhil, St Anthony's College, Oxford, 1978. Appointments: Correspondent, London and Beirut, United Press International, 1978-81; Business Reporter, 1981-82, Beirut Bureau Chief, 1982-84, Jerusalem Bureau Chief, 1984-89, Chief Diplomatic Correspondent, Washington, DC, Bureau, 1989-, New York Times. Publications: War Torn, 1984; From Beirut to Jerusalem, 1989. Contributions to: New York Times Magazine. Honours: Overseas Press Club Award, 1980; George Polk Award, 1982; Livingston Award for Young Journalists, 1983; Pulitzer Prize for Journalism, 1983, 1988; Page One Award, New York Newspaper Guild, 1984; Colonel Robert D Heinl Jr, Memorial Award in Marine Corps History, Marine Corps Historical Foundation, 1985; National Book Award, National Book Foundation, 1989. Membership: Phi Beta Kappa. Address: c/o New York Times, Washington, DC, Bureau, 1627 I Street North West, Washington, DC 20006, USA.

FRIEL Brian, b. 9 Jan 1929, Killyclogher, County Tyrone, Ireland. Writer. m. Anne Morrison, 1954, 1 son, 4 daughters. Education: St Columb's College, Derry; St Patrick's College, Maynooth; St Joseph's Training College, Belfast. Appointments: Taught in various schools, 1950-60; Writer, 1960-. Publications: Collected Stories: The Saucer of Larks, 1962; The Gold in the Sea, 1966; Plays: Philadelphia Here I Come!, 1965; The Loves of Cass McGuire, 1967; Lovers, 1968; The Mundy Scheme, 1969; Crystal and Fox, 1970; The Gentle Island, 1971; The Freedom of the City, 1973; Volunteers, 1975; Living Quarters, 1976; Aristocrats, 1979; Faith Healer, 1979; Three Sisters, translation, 1981; The Communication Cord, 1983; Fathers and Sons, translation, 1987; Making History, 1988; Dancing at Lughnara, 1990; The London Vertigo, adaptation of a play by Charles Macklin, 1992; A Month in the Country, adaptation of Turgenev, 1992. Honours: Honorary DLitt, NUI, 1983; Ewart Biggs Memorial Prize, Belfast Theatre Association Award. Address: Drumaweir House, Greencastle, County Donegal, Ireland.

FRITH David (Edward John), b. 16 Mar 1937, London, England. Cricket Writer. m. 11 May 1957, 2 sons, 1 daughter. Education: Canterbury High School, Sydney, 1949-53. Appointments: Editor, The Cricketer, 1973-78, Wisden Cricket Monthly, 1979-96. Publications: Runs in the Family, 1969; A E Stoddart: Biography, 1970; The Archie Jackson Story, 1974; The Fast Men, 1975; Cricket Gallery (editor), 1976; England v Australia Pictorial History, 1977; The Ashes '77, 1977; The Golden Age of Cricket 1890-1914, 1978; Ashes '79, 1979; Jeff Thomson: Biography, 1980; The Slow Men, 1984; Cricket's Golden Summer, 1985; England v Australia Test Match Records, 1986; Pageant of Cricket, 1987; By His Own Hand, 1991; Stoddy's Mission, 1994. Contributions to: Periodicals. Honours: Cricket Society Jubilee Literary Awards, 1970, 1987; Cricket Writer of the Year, Wombwell Cricket-Lovers Society, 1984; British Magazine Sportswriter of the Year, 1988. Memberships: Association of Cricket Statisticians; Cricket Society; Committee Member, Cricket Writers Club, 1977-. Address: 6 Beech Lane, Guildford, Surrey, GU2 5ES, England.

FRITZ Jean, b. 16 Nov 1915, Hankow, China. Writer. m. Michael Fritz, 1 Nov 1941, 1 son, 1 daughter. Education: BA, Wheaton College, Norton, Massachusetts. 1937. Publications: The Cabin Faced West, 1957; And Then What Happened, Paul Revere, 1973; Stonewall, 1979; Homesick: My Own Story, 1982; The Double Life of Pocahontas, 1983; The Great Little Madison, 1989; Bully for You, Teddy Roosevelt, 1991; Around the World in a Hundred Years, 1994; Harriet Beecher Stowe and the Beecher Preachers, 1994; You Want Women to Vote, Lizzie Stanton?, 1995. Contributions to: New Yorker; Redbook; New York Times; Washington Post; Seventeen; Horn Book; Children's Literature in Education. Honours: National Book Award, 1982; Laura Ingalls Wilder Award, 1986. Literary Agent: Gina MacCaby. Address: 50 Bellewood Avenue, Dobbs Ferry, NY 10522, USA.

FRITZ Walter Helmut, b. 26 Aug 1929. Writer. Education: Literature and Philosophy, University of Heidelberg. Publications: Achtsam sein, 1956; Veranderte Jahre, 1963; Umwege, 1964; Zwischenbemerkungen, 1965; Abweichung, 1965; Die Zuverlassigkeit der Unruhe, 1966; Bemerkungen zu einer Gegend, 1969; Die Verwechslung, 1970; Aus der Nahe, 1972; Die Beschaffenheit solcher Tage, 1972; Bevor uns Horen und Sehen Vergeht, 1975; Schwierige Uberfahrt, 1976; Auch jetzt und morgen, 1979; Gesammelte Gedichte, 1979; Wunschtraum alptraum, 1981; Werkzeuge der Freiheit, 1983; Cornelias Traum und andere Aufzeichnungen, 1985; Immer einfacher, immer schwieriger, 1987; Zeit des Sehens, 1989; Die Schlüssel sind vertauscht, 1992; Gesammelte Gedichte 1979-1994, 1994. Contributions to: Neue Rundschau; Neue Deutsche Hefte; Frankfurter Hefte; Jahresring; Ensemble. Honours: Literature Prize, City of Karlsruhe, 1960; Prize, Bavarian Academy of Fine Arts, 1962; Heine-Taler, Lyrik Prize, 1966; Prize, Culture Circle, Federation of German Industry, 1971; Stuttgarter Literaturpreis, 1986; Georg-Trakl-Preis, 1992. Memberships: German Academy for Speech and Poetry; Academy for Sciences and Literature; Bavarian Academy of Fine Arts; PEN; Union of German Writers. Address: Kolbergerstrasse 2a, 76139 Karlsruhe 1, Germany.

FROMMER Harvey, b. 10 Oct 1937, Brooklyn, New York, USA. Professor; Author. m. Myrna Katz, 23 Jan 1960, 2 sons, 1 daughter. Education: BS, Journalism, MA, English, PhD, Communications, New York University. Appointments: Professor, Writing, Speech, New York City Technical College, City University of New York, 1970-96; Professor Emeritus, City University, New York; Professor, Liberal Studies, Dartmouth College, 1992, 1994, Graduate Liberal Studies, Wesleyan University, 1994; Reviewer, Yankees Magazine, Library Journal, Choice, Kliatt Paperback Book Guide, Dodger Blue; Frequent Lecturer. Publications: Growing Up At Bat: 50 Years of Little League Baseball, 1989; Running Tough: The Autobiography of Tony Dorsett, 1989; Throwing Heat: The Autobiography of Nolan Ryan, 1989; It Happened in the Catskills: An Oral history of the Catskill Resorts (with Myrna Katz Frommer), 1990; Behind the Lines: The Autobiography of Don Strock, 1991; Holzman on Hoops, 1991; Shoeless Joe and Ragtime Baseball, 1992, It Happened in Brooklyn: An oral history of growing up in the borough in the 1940s, 1950s and 1960s, 1993; Big Apple Baseball, 1995; Growing Up Jewish in America (with Myrna Katz Frommer), 1995; It Happened On Broadway (with Myrna Katz Frommer), 1997; New York Yankees Encyclopaedia, 1997. Contributions to: New York Times; Red Book Magazine. Address: 83 Franklin Hill Road, Lyme, NH 03768, USA.

FROST Sir David (Paradine), b. 7 Apr 1939, Beccles, Suffolk, England. Television Personality; Author. m. (1) Lynn Frederick, 1981, div 1982, (2) Lady Carina Fitzlan-Howard, 1983, 3 sons. Education: MA, Gonville and Caius College, Cambridge. Appointments: Various BBC TV series, 1962-; Many ITV series, 1966-; Chairman and Chief Executive, David Paradine Ltd, 1966-; Joint Founder and Director, TV-am, 1981-93; Regular appearances on US television. Publications: That Was the Week That Was, 1963; How to Live Under Labour, 1964; Talking with Frost, 1967; To England With Love, 1967; The Presidential Debate 1968, 1968; The Americans, 1970; Whitlam and Frost, 1974; I Gave Them a Sword, 1978; I Could Have Kicked Myself, 1982; Who Wants to be a Millionaire?, 1983; The Mid-Atlantic Companion (jointly), 1986; The Rich Tide (jointly), 1986; The World's Shortest Books, 1987; David Frost: An Autobiography, Part I: From Congregations to Audiences, 1993. Honours: Golden Rose Award, Montreux, 1967; Richard Dimbleby Award, 1967; Silver Medal, Royal Television Society, 1967; Officer of the Order of the British Empire, 1970; Religious Heritage of America Award, 1970; Emmy Awards, 1970, 1971; Albert Einstein Award, 1971; Knighted, 1993. Address: c/o

David Paradine Ltd, 5 St Mary Abbots Place, London, W8 6LS, England.

FROST Jason. See: OBSTFELD Raymond.

FRUMKIN Gene, b. 29 Jan 1928, New York, New York, USA. Poet; Professor. m. Lydia Samuels, 3 July 1955, 1 son, 1 daughter. Education: BA, English, University of California, Los Angeles. Appointments: Professor, University of New Mexico; Editor, Coastlines Literary Magazine, 1958-62; Guest Editor, New Mexico Quarterly, 1969; Visiting Professor, Modern Literature, State University of New York, Buffalo, 1975; Co-Editor, San Marcos Review, 1978-83; Exchange Professor, 1980-81, 1984-85, Writer-in-Residence, 1989, University of Hawaii. Publications: Hawk and the Lizard, 1963; Orange Tree, 1965; Rainbow-Walker, 1969; Dostoyevsky and Other Nature Poems, 1972; Locust Cry: Poems 1958-65, 1973; Mystic Writing-Pad, 1977; Indian Rio Grande: Recent Poems from 3 Cultures (co-editor), anthology, 1977; Clouds and Red Earth, 1982; Lover's Quarrel With America, 1985; Sweetness in the Air, 1987; Comma in the Ear, 1991; Saturn Is Mostly Weather, 1992. Contributions to: Paris Review; Prairie Schooner; Yankee; Conjunctions; Sulfur; Poetry; Saturday Review; Nation; Evergreen Review; Dacotah Territory; Malahat Review; Minnesota Review. Honour: 1st Prize for Poetry, Yankee magazine, 1979. Memberships: Past President, Rio Grande Writers Association; Hawaii Literary Arts Council; PEN West. Address: 3721 Mesa Verde North East, Albuquerque, NM 87110, USA.

FRY Christopher, b. 18 Dec 1907, Bristol, England. Dramatist. m. Phyllis Marjorie Hart, 1936, dec 1987, 1 son. Education: Bedford Modern School; Actor at Citizen House, Bath, 1927. Publications: The Boy with a Cart, 1939; The Firstborn, 1946; A Phoenix too Frequent, 1946; The Lady's Not for Burning, 1949; Thor, with Angels, 1949; Venus Observed, 1950, revised, 1992; A Sleep of Prisoners, 1951; The Dark is Light Enough, 1954; The Lark, 1955; Tiger at the Gates, 1955; Duel of Angels, 1958; Curtmantle, 1961; Judith, 1962; A Yard of Sun, 1970; Peer Gynt, 1970; Television Plays: The Brontes at Haworth, 1973; Sister Dora, 1977; The Best of Enemies, 1977; Can You Find Me: A Family History, 1978; Editor and Introduction Charlie Hammond's Sketch Book, 1980; Selected Plays, 1985; Genius, Talent and Failure, 1986 (Adam Lecture); One Thing More of Caedmon Construed, 1987; A Journey into the Light, 1992; Films: The Queen is Crowned, 1953; The Beggar's Opera, 1953; Ben Hur, 1958; Barabbas, 1960; The Bible: In the Beginning, 1962. Honours: Fellow, Royal Society of Literature; Queen's Gold Medal for Poetry, 1962; Honorary Fellow, Manchester Metropolitan University, 1988; DLitt, Lambeth, 1988; Hon DLitt, Sussex University, 1994; Hon DLitt, De Montfort University, 1994. Membership: Garrick Club. Address: The Toft, East Dean, Chichester, West Sussex PO18 0JA, England.

FRYE Roland Mushat, b. 3 July 1921, Birmingham, Alabama, USA. Literary and Theological Scholar. m. Jean Elbert Steiner, 11 Jan 1947, 1 son. Education: AB, 1943, PhD, 1952, Princeton University; Special Student, Theology, Princeton Theological Seminary, 1950-52. Appointments: Emory University , 1952-61; Reverend Professor, Folger Shakespeare Library, 1961-65; Faculty, 1965-83, Emeritus Professor, 1983-, National Phi Beta Kappa Visiting Scholar, 1985-86, University of Pennsylvania; L P Stone Foundation Lecturer, Princeton Theological Seminary, 1959; Chairman, 1989-91, Chairman Emeritus, 1991-, Center of Theological Inquiry, Princeton, New Jersey. Publications: God, Man and Satan: Patterns of Christian Thought and Life, 1960; Shakespeare and Christian Doctrine, 1963; Shakespeare's Life and Times: A Pictorial Record, 1967; Milton's Imagery and the Visual Arts Iconographic Tradition in the Epic Poems, 1978; Is God a Creationist? The Religious Case Against Creation-Science, 1983; The Renaissance Hamlet Issues and Responses in 1600, 1984. Contributions to: The Dissidence of Dissent and the Origins of Religious Freedom in America: John Milton and the Puritans, to Proceedings of the American Philosophical Society, 1989; Numerous other articles in learned journals, literary and theological. Address: 226 West Valley Road, Strafford-Wayne, PA 19087, USA.

FRYER Jonathan, (G L Morton), b. 5 June 1950, Manchester, England. Writer; Broadcaster; University Lecturer. Education: Diplome D'Etudes Françaises, Université de Poitiers (France), 1967; BA Hons (Chinese with Japanese), 1973, MA, St Edmund Hall, University of Oxford, 1980. Appointments: Visiting Lecturer, School of Journalism, University of Nairobi, Kenya, 1976; Subject Teacher, School of Oriental and African Studies, University of London, 1993. Publications: The Great Wall of China, 1975; Isherwood, 1977 (updated and

reissued as Eye of the Camera, 1993); Brussels as Seen by Naif Artists (with Rona Dobson), 1979; Food for Thought, 1981; George Fox and the Children of the Light, 1991; Dylan, 1993; The Sitwells (with Sarah Bradford and John Pearson), 1994; André and Oscar, 1997; Numerous political pamphlets, mainly on Third World themes. Contributions to: Economist; Tablet; Geographical Magazine; Guardian; Independent; Times; Observer; European. Membership: Executive Committee, English PEN; Executive Committee, Association fo Foreign Affairs Journalists, president, 1997-; Royal Society of Literature; Society of Authors. Literary Agent: Jennifer Kavanagh, 44 Langham Street, London W1N 5RG, England. Address: 140 Bow Common Lane, London E3 4BH, England.

FUCHS Sir Vivian (Ernest), b. 11 Feb 1908, Freshwater, Isle of Wight. Geologist; Explorer. m. (1) Joyce Connell, 6 Sept 1933, dec 1990, 1 son, 2 daughters, (2) Eleanor Honnywill, 8 Aug 1991. Education: BA, 1929, MA, 1935, PhD, 1936, Cambridge University. Appointments: Geologist, Cambridge East Greenland Expedition, 1929, Cambridge East African Lakes Expedition, 1930-31, East African Archaeological Expedition, 1931-32; Leader, Lake Rudolf Rift Valley Expedition, 1933-34, Lake Rukwa Expedition, 1937-38; Military Service, 1939-46; Leader, Falkland Islands Dependence Survey, Antarctica, 1947-50, Commonwealth Trans-Antarctic Expedition, 1955-58; Director, British Antarctic Survey, 1958-73. Publications: The Crossing of Antarctica (with Sir Edmund Hillary), 1958; Antarctic Adventure, 1959; Forces of Nature (editor), 1977; Of Ice and Men, 1982; A Time to Speak (autobiography), 1990. Contributions to: Scientific journals. Honours: Knighted, 1958; Many UK and foreign medals and awards; Honorary doctorates. Memberships: Vice President, 1961-64, President, 1982-84, Honorary Vice President, 1985-, Royal Geographical Society; President, International Glaciological Society, 1963-66; British Association for the Advancement of Science, 1972; Fellow, Royal Society, 1974. Address: 106 Barton Road, Cambridge CB3 9LH, England.

FUENTES Carlos, b. 11 Nov 1928, Panama City, Panama. Professor of Latin American Studies; Writer. m. (1) Rita Macedo, 1957, 1 daughter, (2) Sylvia Lemus, 24 Jan 1973, 1 son, 1 daughter. Education: Law School, National University of Mexico; Institute de Hautes Études Internationales, Geneva. Appointments: Head, Cultural Relations Department, Ministry of Foreign Affairs, Mexico, 1955-58; Mexican Ambassador to France, 1975-77; Professor of English and Romance Languages, University of Pennsylvania, 1978-83; Professor of Comparative Literature, 1984-86, Robert F Kennedy Professor of Latin American Studies, 1987-, Harvard University; Simon Bolivar Professor, Cambridge University, 1986-87. Publications: La Region Mas Transparente, 1958; Las Buenas Conciencias, 1959; Aura, 1962; La Muerte de Artemio Cruz, 1962; Cantar de Ciegos, 1964; Cambio de Piel, 1967; Zona Sagrada, 1967; Terra Nostra, 1975; Una Familia Lejana, 1980; Agua Quemada, 1983; Gringo Viejo, 1985; Cristóbal Nonato, 1987; Myself with Others (essays), 1987; Orchids in the Moonlight (play), 1987; The Campaign, 1991; The Buried Mirror, 1992; El Naranjo, 1993; Geography of the Novel: Essays, 1993. Contributions to: Periodicals. Honours: Biblioteca Breva Prize, Barcelona, 1967; Rómulo Gallegos Prize, Caracas, 1975; National Prize for Literature, Mexico, 1984; Miguel de Cervantes Prize for Literature, Madrid, 1988; Légion d'Honneur, France, 1992; Honorary doctorates. Memberships: American Academy and Institute of Arts and Letters; El Colegio Nacional, Mexico; Mexican National Commission on Human Rights. Address: c/o Harvard University, 401 Boylston Hall, Cambridge, MA 02138, USA.

FUGARD (Harold) Athol, b. 11 June 1932, Middelburg Cape, South Africa. Playwright. m. Sheila Meiring, 22 Sept 1956, 1 daughter. Appointments: Playwright; Director; Actor. Publications: Three Port Elizabeth Plays, 1974; Statements: Three Plays (co-author), 1974; Sizwi Banzzi is Dead, and The Island (co-author), 1976; Dimetos and Two Early Plays, 1977; Boesman and Lena and Other Plays, 1978; Tsotsi (novel), 1980; A Lesson from Aloes, 1981; Master Harold and the Boys, 1982; The Road to Mecca, 1985; Notebooks 1960-1977, 1983. Film Scripts: The Guest, 1977; Marigolds in August, 1981; My Children! My Africa! 1990; Playland, 1991. Honours: New York Drama Critics Circle Award for Best Play, 1980-81 Season; Evening Standard Award, Best Play of the Year, 1984. Memberships: Fellow. Royal Society of Literature; American Academy of Arts and Sciences. Address: PO Box 5090 Walmer, Port Elizabeth 6065, South Africa.

FULLER Jean Violet Overton, b. 7 Mar 1915, Iver Heath, Bucks, England. Author. Education: Brighton High School, 1927-31;

Royal Academy of Dramatic Art, 1931-32; BA, University of London, 1944; University College of London, 1948-50. Publications: The Comte de Saint Germain, 1988; Blavatsky and Her Teachers, 1988; Dericourt and the Chequered Spy, 1989; Sickert and the Ripper Crimes, 1990; Cats and other Immortals, 1992. Honour: Writers Manifold Poems of the Decade, 1968. Membership: Society of Authors. Address: Fuller D'Arch Smith Ltd, 37B New Cavendish Street, London, England.

FULLER John Leopold, b. 1 Jan 1937, Ashford, Kent, England. Poet; Writer. Cicely Prudence Martin, 20 July 1960, 3 daughters. Education: New College, Oxford, 1957-62; BA, BLitt, MA. Publications: The Illusionists, 1980; Flying to Nowhere, 1983; Selected Poems 1954-82, 1985; Adventures of Speedfall, 1985; Partingtime Hall (with James Fenton), 1987; The Burning Boys, 1989; Took Twice, 1991; The Mechanical Body, 1991; The Worm and Star, 1993. Honours: Geoffrey Faber Memorial Prize, 1974; Southern Arts Prize, 1980; Whitbread Prize, 1983; Shortlisted, Booker Prize, 1983; Fellow, Royal Society of Literature; Fellow, Magdalen College, Oxford. Literary Agent: Peters, Fraser & Dunlop. Address: 4 Benson Place, Oxford OX2 6QH, England.

FULLERTON Alexander Fergus, b. 20 Sept 1924, Saxmundham, Suffolk, England. Writer. m. Priscilla Mary Edelston, 10 May 1956, 3 sons. Education: Royal Naval College, Dartmouth, 1938-41; School of Slavonic Studies, Cambridge University, 1947. Appointments: Editorial Director, Peter Davies Ltd, 1961-64; General Manager, Arrow Books, 1964-67. Publications: Surface!, 1953; A Wren Called Smith, 1957; The White Men Sang, 1958; The Everard Series of Naval Novels: The Blooding of the Guns, 1976; Sixty Minutes for St George, 1977; Patrol to the Golden Horn, 1978; Storm Force to Narvik, 1979; Last Lift from Crete, 1980; All the Drowning Seas, 1981; A Share of Honour, 1982; The Torch Bearers, 1983; The Gatecrashers, 1984; Special Deliverance, 1986; Special Dynamic, 1987; Special Deception, 1988; Bloody Sunset, 1991; Look to the Wolves, 1992; Love for an Enemy, 1993; Not Thinking of Death, 1994; Into the Fire, 1995; Band of Brothers, 1996; Return to the Field, 1997. Literary Agent: John Johnson Limited. Address: c/o John Johnson Ltd, 45 Clerkenwell Green, London EC1R 0HT, England.

FULTON Alice, b. 25 Jan 1952, Troy, New York, USA. Professor of English; Poet. m. Hank De Leo, 1980. Education: BA, Empire State College, Albany, New York, 1978; MFA, Cornell University, 1982; Appointments: Assistant Professor, 1983-86, Willam Willhartz Professor, 1986-89, Associate Professor, 1989-92, Professor of English, 1992-, University of Michigan; Visiting Professor of Creative Writing, Vermont College, 1987, University of California at Los Angeles, 1991. Publications: Anchors of Light, 1979; Dance Script with Electric Ballerina, 1983; Palladium, 1986; Powers of Congress, 1990; Sensual Math, 1995. Honours: Macdowell Colony Fellowships, 1978, 1979; Millay Colony Fellowship, 1980; Emily Dickinson Award, 1980; Academy of American Poets Prize, 1982; Consuelo Ford Award, 1984; Rainer Maria Rilke Award, 1984; Michigan Council for the Arts Grants, 1986, 1991; Guggenheim Fellowship, 1986-87; Yaddo Colony Fellowship, 1987; Bess Hokin Prize, 1989; Ingram Merrill Foundation Award, 1990; John D and Catherine T MacArthur Fellowship, 1991-96; Elizabeth Matchett Stover Award, 1994. Address: 2370 Le Forge Road, RR2, Ypsilanti, MI 48198, USA.

FULTON Robin, b. 6 May 1937, Arran, Scotland. Writer. Education: MA, Hons, 1959, PhD, 1972, Edinburgh; LittD. Appointment: Editor, Lines Review, 1967-76. Publications: Poetry: Instances, 1967; Inventories, 1969; The Spaces Between the Stones, 1971; The Man with the Surbahar, 1971; Tree-Lines, 1974; Music and Flight, 1975; Between Flights, 1976; Places to Stay In, 1978; Following a Mirror, 1980; Selected Poems, 1963-78, 1980; Fields of Focus, 1982; Coming Down to Earth and Spring is Soon, 1990. Criticism: Contemporary Scottish Poetry: Individuals and Contexts, 1974; The Way the Words are Taken, Selected Essays, 1989. New Poets from Edinburgh (editor), 1971; Iain Crichton Smith: Selected Poems, 1955-80, 1982; Robert Garioch: The Complete Poetical Works with Notes, 1983; Robert Garioch: A Garioch Miscellany, Selected Prose and Letters, 1986. Translations: An Italian Quartet, 1966; Blok's Twelve, 1968; Five Swedish Poets, 1972; Lars Gustafsson, Selected Poems, 1972; Gunnar Harding: They Killed Sitting Bull and Other Poems, 1973; Tomas Tranströmer: Citoyens, 1974; Tomas Tranströmer: Selected Poems, 1974, editor, 1980; Osten Sjöstrand: The Hidden Music & Other Poems, 1975; Toward the Solitary Star: Selected Poetry and Prose, 1988; Werner Aspenström: 37 Poems, 1976; Tomas Tranströmer: Baltics, 1980; Johannes Edfelt: Family

Tree, 1981; Werner Aspenström: The Blue Whale and Other Prose Pieces, 1981; Kjell Espmark: Béla Bartók Against the Third Reich and Other Poems, 1985; Olva Hauge: Don't Give Me the Whole Truth and Other Poems, 1985; Tomas Tranströmer: Collected Poems, 1987; Stig Dagerman: German Autumn, 1988; Par Lagervist: Guest of Reality, 1989; Preparations for Clight, and other Swedish Stories, 1990; Four Swedish Poets (Kjell Espmark, Lennart Sjögren, Eva Ström & Tomas Transtromer), 1990; Olva Hauge: Selected Poems, 1990; Hermann Starheimstaeter: Stone-Shadows, 1991. Contributions to: Various journals and magazines. Honours: Gregory Award, 1967; Writers Fellowship, Edinburgh University, 1969; Scottish Arts Council Writers Bursary, 1972; Arthur Lundquist Award for translations from Swedish, 1977; Swedish Academy Award, 1978. Address: Postboks 467, N 4001, Stavanger, Norway.

FUNE Jonathan. See: **FLETCHER John Walter James.**

FURTWÄNGLER Virginia Anne, (Ann Copeland), b. 16 Dec 1932, Hartford, Connecticut, USA. Fiction Writer; Teacher. m. Albert Furtwangler, 17 Aug 1968, 2 sons. Education: BA, College of New Rochelle, 1954; MA, Catholic University of America, 1959; PhD, Cornell University, Kent, 1970. Appointments: Writer-in-Residence, College of Idaho, 1980, Linfield College, 1980-81, University of Idaho, 1982, 1986, Wichita State University, 1988, Mt Allison University, 1990, St Mary's University, 1993; Hallie Brown Ford Chair of English, Willamette University, 1996. Publications: At Peace; The Back room; Earthen Vessels; The Golden Thread; The Back Room; The ABC's of Writing Fiction, 1996; The Season of Apples, 1996. Contributions to: Anthologies and magazines.. Honours: Kent Fellowship; Canada Council Grant; 2nd National Endowment for the Arts Writing Fellowship, 1994; Ingram Merrill Award. Memberships: Authors Guild; Writers Union of Canada; International Womens Writing Guild. Literary Agent: Barbara Kouts, PO Box 558, Bellport, NY 11713-0560, USA. Address: 235 Oak Way NE, Salem, OR 97301, USA.

G

GAAN Margaret, b. 18 Aug 1914, Shanghai, China. Writer. Appointments: Executive Secretary, China Mercantile Co, Shanghai, 1949-49; Programme Officer, 1950-65, Chief, Asia Desk, 1966-68, Deputy Regional Director for East Asia and Pakistan, 1969-74, United Nations Children's Fund. Publications: Last Moments of a World, autobiography, 1978; Novels: Little Sister, 1983; Red Barbarian, 1984; White Poppy, 1985; Blue Mountain, 1987. Address: 967 Commons Drive, Sacramento, CA 95825, USA.

GADGIL Gangadhar, b. Bombay, India. Writer; Economic Adviser. m. Vasanta Gadgil, 12 Dec 1948, 1 son, 2 daughters. Education: MA, Bombay University, 1944. Appointments: Honorary Professor, University of Bombay;Director: Ravalagaon Sugar Farm Ltd, Walchand Hindustan Ltd, Deposit Insurance and Credit Guarantee Corporation; President, Marathi Sahitya Mahamandal, 1987; Vice President, Sahitya Akademi, 1988-93; President, Mumbai Marathi Sahitya Sangh; Vice President, Mumbai Marathi Granth Sangrahalay; President, Mumbai Grahak Panchayat. Publications: Durdamya; Bandoo; Crazy Bombay; Women and Other Stories; Kadu and God, Eka Mungiche Mahabharat, 1992; The Throttled Street and Other Stories, 1994; Indian Literature - Issues and Explorations; Issues and Explorations. Contributions to: Satyakatha; Hans; Kirloskar; Yugawani; Illustrated Weekly of India; Times of India; Indian Express; Economic Times; Quest; Marg; Evergreen; Review; American Review; Western Humanities Review; Quadrant. Honours: R S Jog Award; N C Kelkar Award; State Award, Sata Samudra Palikade; State Award, Ole Unha; State Award, Talavatale Chandana; Abhiruchi Award; President, All India Marathi Literary Conference, Raipur, 1981-82; Invited to preside over conference of Maharashtrians, Houston, USA, 1995; Invited to inaugurate Kokan Marathi Sahitya Sammelan, 1996; Sahitya Akademi Award; Invited to inaugurate Marathi Drama Conference; Numerous Presidential addresses and lectures. Memberships: Mumbai Marathi Sahitya Sangh; Mumbai Marathi Grantha Sangrahalay; Asiatic Society of Bombay; Vidarbha Sahitya Sangh; Marathwada Sahitya Parishad; Maharashtra Sahitya Parishad; Indian PEN. Address: 4 Abhang, Sahitya Sahawas, Bandra, Bombay 400051, India.

GAGLIANO Frank, b. 18 Nov 1931, New York, New York, USA. Playwright; Screenwriter; Novelist; Professor of Playwriting. Education: Queens College, New York City, 1949-53; BA, University of Iowa, 1954; MFA, Columbia University, 1957. Appointments: Playwright-in-Residence, Royal Shakespeare Company, London, 1967-69; Assistant Professor of Drama, Playwright-in-Residence, Director of Contemporary Playwrights Center, Florida State University, Tallahassee, 1969-73; Lecturer in Playwriting, Director of Conkie Workshop for Playwrights, University of Texas, Austin, 1973-75; Distinguished Visiting Professor, University of Rhode Island, 1975; Benedum Professor of Theatre, West Virginia University, 1976-; Artistic Director, Carnegie Mellon, Showcase of New Plays, 1986-. Publications: The City Scene (2 plays), 1966; Night of the Dunce, 1967; Father Uxbridge Wants to Marry, 1968; The Hide-and-Seek Odyssey of Madeleine Gimple, 1970; Big Sur, 1970; The Prince of Peasantmania, 1970; The Private Eye of Hiram Bodoni (TV play), 1971; Quasimodo (musical), 1971; Anywhere the Wind Blows (musical), 1972; In the Voodoo Parlour of Marie Laveau, 1974; The Comedia World of Lafcadio Beau, 1974; The Resurrection of Jackie Cramer (musical), 1974; Congo Square (musical), 1975, revised, 1989; The Total Immersion of Madelaine Favorini, 1981; San Ysidro (dramatic cantata), 1985; From the Bodoni County Songbook Anthology, Book I, 1986, musical version, 1989; Anton's Leap (novel), 1987. Address: c/o Gilbert Parker, William Morris Agency, 1350 Avenue of the Americas, New York, NY 10019, USA.

GAIL. See: **KATZ Bobbi.**

GAINES Ernest J(ames), b. 15 Jan 1933, River Lake Plantation, Pointe Coupee Parish, Louisiana, USA. Professor of English; Writer. Education: BA, San Francisco State College, 1957; Graduate Studies, Stanford University, 1958-59. Appointments: Writer-in-Residence, Denison University, 1971, Stanford University, 1981; Visiting Professor, 1983, Writer-in-Residence, 1983-, University of Southwestern Louisiana. Publications: Catherine Carmier, 1964; Of Love and Dust, 1967; Bloodline (short stories), 1968; The Autobiography of Miss Jane Pittman, 1971; In My Father's House,

1978; A Gathering of Old Men, 1983; A Lesson Before Dying, 1993. Contributions to: Anthologies and periodicals. Honours: National Endowment for the Arts Award, 1967; Rockefeller Grant, 1970; Guggenheim Fellowship, 1971; Black Academy of Arts and Letters Award, 1972; Fiction Gold Medals, Commonwealth Club of California, 1972, 1984; 9 Emmy Awards, 1975; American Academy and Institute of Arts and Letters Award, 1987; John D and Catherine T MacArthur Foundation Fellowship, 1993; National Book Critics Circle Award, 1994; Honorary doctorates. Address: 932 Divosadero Street, San Francisco, CA 94115, USA.

GAINHAM Sarah, b. 1 Oct 1922, London, England. Writer. m. Kenneth Robert Ames, 14 Apr 1964, dec 1975. Publications: Time Right Deadly, 1956; Cold Dark Night, 1957; The Mythmaker, 1957; Stone Roses, 1959; Silent Hostage, 1960; Night Falls on the City, 1967; A Place in the Country, 1968; Takeover Bid, 1970; Private Worlds, 1971; Maculan's Daughter, 1973; To the Opera Ball, 1975; The Habsburg Twlight, 1979; The Tiger, Life, 1983. Contributions to: Encounter; Atlantic; BBC. Address: Altes Forsthaus,Schlosspark, A2404 Petronell, Austria.

GALBRAITH James Kenneth, b. 29 Jan 1952, Boston, Massachusetts, USA. Professor. m. (1) Lucy Ferguson, 28 July 1979, div, 1 son, 1 daughter, (2) Ying Tang, 17 July 1993. Education: AB, Harvard College, 1974; University of Cambridge, 1974-75; MA, 1976, MPhil, 1977, PhD, 1981, Yale University. Appointments: Professor, LBJ School of Public Affairs, University of Texas at Austin, 1985-. Publications: Balancing Acts; The Economic Problem; Macroeconomics. Contributions to: Numerous. Honours: Marshall Scholar, University of Cambridge. Memberships: American Economic Association; Association for Public Policy Analysis and Management. Address: LBJ School of Public Affairs, University of Texas at Austin, Austin, TX 78713, USA.

GALBRAITH John Kenneth, b. 15 Oct 1908, Iona Station, Ontario, Canada (US citizen, 1937). Professor of Economics Emeritus; Author. m. Catherine Atwater, 17 Sept 1937, 3 sons. Education: BS, University of Guelph, 1931; MS, 1933, PhD, 1934, University of California; Postgraduate Studies, Cambridge University, 1937-38. Appointments: Research Fellow, University of California, 1931-34; Instructor and Tutor, 1934-39, Lecturer 1948-49, Professor of Economics 1949-75, Paul M Warburg Professor of Economics 1959-75, Professor Emeritus 1975-, Harvard University; Assistant Professor of Economics, Princeton University, 1939-42; Economic Adviser, National Defense Advisory Commission, Washington, DC, 1940-41; Assistant Administrator, Price Division, 1941-42, Deputy Administrator, 1942-43, Office of Price Administration, Washington, DC; Director, US Strategic Bombing Survey, 1945; Office of Economic Security Policy, US State Department, Washington, DC, 1946; US Ambassador to India, 1961-63; Adviser to Presidents John F Kennedy and Lyndon B Johnson. Publications: Modern Competition and Business Policy (with Henry Sturgis Dennison), 1938; American Capitalism: The Concept of Countervailing Power, 1952; A Theory of Price Control, 1952; The Great Crash, 1929, 1955; Marketing Efficiency in Puerto Rico (with others), 1955; Journey to Poland and Yugoslavia, 1958; The Affluent Society, 1958, 4th edition, 1984; The Liberal Hour, 1960; Economic Development in Perspective, 1962, revised edition as Economic Development, 1964; The McLandress Dimension (satire published under the name Mark Epernay), 1963, revised edition, 1968; The Scotch (memoir), 1964, 2nd edition, 1985; The New Industrial State, 1967, 4th edition, 1985; How to Get Out of Vietnam: A Workable Solution to the Worst Problem of Our Time, 1967; The Triumph: A Novel of Modern Diplomacy, 1968; Indian Painting: The Scene, Themes and Legends (with Mohinder Singh Randhawa), 1968; How to Control the Military, 1969; Ambassador's Journal: A Personal Account of the Kennedy Years, 1969; Who Needs the Democrats, and What It Takes to Be Needed, 1970; A Contemporary Guide to Economics, Peace, and Laughter (essays), 1971; A China Passage, 1973; Economics and the Public Purpose, 1973; Money: Whence It Came, Where It Went, 1975; The Age of Uncertainty, 1977; Almost Everyone's Guide to Economics (with Nicole Salinger), 1978; Annals of an Abiding Liberal, 1979; The Nature of Mass Poverty, 1979; A Life in Our Times: Memoirs, 1981; The Anatomy of Power, 1983; The Voice of the Poor: Essays in Economic and Political Persuasion, 1983; A View from the Stands: Of People, Politics, Military Power, and the Arts, 1986; Economics in Perspective: A Critical History, 1987; Capitalism, Communism and Coexistence: From the Bitter Past to the Bitter Present (with Stanislav Menshikov), 1988; A Tenured Professor (novel), 1990; The Culture of Contentment,

1992; A Short History of Financial Euphoria, 1993; A Journey Through Economic Time, 1994. Contributions to: Books and scholarly journals. Honours: Social Science Research Council Fellow, 1937-38; US Medal of Freedom, 1964; Many honorary doctorates. Memberships: American Academy of Arts and Sciences, Fellow; American Academy and Institute of Arts and Letters, President, 1984-87; American Economic Association, President, 1972; American Agricultural Economics Association; Americans for Democratic Action, Chairman, 1967-68. Address: 30 Francis Avenue, Cambridge, MA 02138, USA.

GALIOTO Salvatore, b. 6 June 1925, Italy. Professor of Humanities (retired). m. Nancy Morris, 8 July 1978, 1 son. Education: BA, University of New Mexico, 1952; MA, University of Denver, 1955; John Hay Fellow, Yale University, 1959-60; Catskill Area Project Fellow, Columbia University, 1961-62; Mediaeval and Renaissance Doctoral Programme, University of New Haven. Publications: The Humanities: Classical Athens, Renaissance Florence and Contemporary New York, 1970; Bibliographic Materials on Indian Culture, 1972; Let Us Be Modern (poems), English, Italian, 1985; INAGO Newsletter (poems), 1988; Many poems in Snow Summits in the Sun, poetry anthology, 1989; Is Anybody Listening (poems), English, 1990; Flap Your Wings (poems), English, 1992; Rosebushes and the Poor (poems), Italian, 1993. Contributions to: Periodicals. Honours: Purple Heart, Bronze Star, 1944; John Hay Fellowship, 1958-59; Asian Studies Fellow, 1965-66; Mole of Turin, 1st Prize, Foreign Writer, 1984; 1st Prize, Chapbook Competition, The Poet, 1985, 1986; 1st Prize, Poetry, Gli Etrusci, Italy, 1985; Trofeo delle Nazioni, Poetry, Italy; Gold Medal, Istituto Carlo Capodieci, 1987; Poet for 1989, INAGO newspaper. Memberships: Long Island Historians Society; Asian Society; ASLA, Sicily; California State Poetry Society, Poets and Writers of America; Representative in Italy, International Society of Poets. Address: Via Bruno Buozzi 15, Montecatini Terme 51016 (Pistoia), Italy.

GALL Henderson Alexander (Sandy), b. 1 Oct 1927, Penang, Malaysia. Television Journalist. m. Aug 1958, 1 son, 3 daughters. Education: MA, Aberdeen University, Scotland, 1952. Publications: Gold Scoop, 1977; Chasing the Dragon, 1981; Don't Worry about the Money Now, 1983; Behind Russian Lines: An Afghan Journal, 1983; Afghanistan: Agony of a Nation, 1988; Salang, 1989; George Adamson: Lord of the Lions, 1991; News From the Front: The Life of a Television Reporter, 1994. Honours: Rector, 1978-81, Honorary LLD, 1981, Aberdeen University; Sitara-i-Pakistan, 1986; Lawrence of Arabia Medal, 1987; Commander of the Order of the British Empire, 1988. Address: Peters, Fraser and Dunlop, 503/4 The Chambers, Chelsea Harbour, London SW10 0XF, England.

GALL Sally Moore, b. 28 July 1941, New York, New York, USA. Librettist. m. William Einar Gall, 8 Dec 1967. Education: BA cum laude, Harvard University, 1963; MA, 1971, PhD, 1976, New York University. Appointments: Poetry Editor, Free Inquiry, 1981-84; Founding Editor, Eidos, The International Prosody Bulletin, 1984-88. Publications: The Modern Poetic Sequence: The Genius of Modern Poetry (co-author), 1983; Ramon Guthrie's Maximum Security Ward: An American Classic, 1984; Maximum Security Ward and Other Poems (editor), 1984; Poetry in English: An Anthology (versification editor), 1987; Kill Bear Comes Home, 1994; Eleanor Roosevelt, 1996. Contributions to: Reference books, professional journals and literary magazines. Honours: Penfield Fellow, New York University, 1973-74; Academy of American Poets Award, New York University, 1975; Key Pin and Scroll Award, New York University, 1976; Co-winner, Explicator Literary Foundation Award, 1984. Memberships: American Music Center; ASCAP; Dramatists Guild; National Opera Association; Opera For Youth; Opera America; International Alliance for Women in Music; Poets and Writers; Various wildlife societies and community music groups. Address: 5820 Folsom Drive, La Jolla, CA 92037, USA.

GALLAGHER Richard. See: **LEVINSON Leonard.**

GALLAHER John G(erard), b. 28 Dec 1928, St Louis, Missouri, USA. Professor of History Emeritus. m. C Maia Hofacker, 2 June 1956, 1 son, 2 daughters. Education: University of Paris, 1950-51; University of Grenoble, 1951-52; BA, Washington University, 1954; MA, 1957, PhD, 1960, St Louis University. Appointments: Professor to Professor of History Emeritus, Southern Illinois University at Edwardsville. Publications: The Iron Marshal: A Biography of Louis N Davout, 1976; The Students of Paris and the Revolution of 1848, 1980; Napoleon's Irish Legion, 1993; General Alexandre Dumas: Soldier of the French Revolution, 1997. Contributions to: Reference works, books and scholarly journals. Honours: Fulbright Research Scholar, France, 1959-60; University Research Fellow, Southern Illinois University at Edwardsville, 1978-79. Address: c/o College of Arts and Sciences, Department of History, Southern Illinois University at Edwardsville, Edwardsville, IL 62026, USA.

GALLANT Mavis, b. 11 Aug 1922, Montreal, Quebec, Canada. Novelist. Education: Schools in Montreal and New York. Appointment: Writer-in-Residence, University of Toronto, 1983-84. Publications: Green Water, Green Sky, 1959; A Fairly Good Time, 1970; Short Stories, The Other Paris, 1956; My Heart is Broken: Eight Short Stories and a Short Novel, 1964; From the Fifteenth District: A Novel and Eight Short Stories, 1979; Home Truths: Selected Canadian Stories, 1981; In Transit, Twenty Stories, 1988; Numerous Uncollected Short Stories and a Play. Honours: Officer, Order of Canada, 1981; Governor General's Award, 1982; Canada-Australia Literary Prize, 1984; Honorary Degree, University Sainte Anne, Pointe de Eglise, Nova Scotia, 1984. Address: 14 Ruse Jean Ferrandi, 75006 Paris, France.

GALLANT Roy Arthur, b. 17 Apr 1924, Portland, Maine, USA. Author; Teacher. m. Kathryn Dale, 1952, 2 sons. Education: BA, 1948, MS, 1949, Bowdoin College; Doctoral work, 1953-59, Columbia University. Appointments: Managing Editor, Scholastic Teachers Magazine, 1954-57; Author-in-Residence, Doubleday, 1957-59; Editorial Director, Aldus Books, London, 1959-62; Editor-in-Chief, The Natural History Press, 1962-65; Consultant, The Edison Project, Israel Arts and Sciences Academy. Publications: Our Universe, 1986; Private Lives of the Stars, 1986; Rainbows, Mirages and Sundogs, 1987; Before the Sun Dies, 1989; Ancient Indians, 1989; The Peopling of Planet Earth, 1990; Earth's Vanishing Forests, 1991; A Young Person's Guide to Science, 1993; The Day the Sky Split Apart, 1995; Geysers, 1997; Sand Dunes, 1997; Limestone Caves, 1997; Glaciers, 1997; Planet Earth, 1997. Address: PO Box 228, Beaver Mountain Lake, Rengeley, ME 04990, USA.

GALLINER Peter, b. 19 Sept 1920, Berlin, Germany. Publisher. m. (1) Edith Marguerite Goldsmidt, 1948, 1 daughter, (2) Helga Stenschke, 1990. Education: Berlin and London. Appointments: Worked for Reuters, London, England, 1944-47; Foreign Man, Financial Times, London, 1947-60; Chairman of Board, Managing Director, Illstein Publishing Group, Berlin, Germany, 1969-64; Vice-Chairman, Managing Director, British Printing Corporation, 1965-70; International Publishing Consultant, 1965-67, 1970-75; Chairman, Peter Galliner Associates, 1970-; Director, International Press Institute, 1975-93; Director Emeritus, International Press Institute, 1993-; Chairman, International Encounters, 1995-. Honours: Order of Merit, 1st Class, Germany, 1965; Ecomienda, Orden de Isabel la Catolica, Spain, 1982; Commander's Cross, Order of Merit, Germany, 1990. Address: 27 Walsingham, Queensmead, St John's Wood Park, London NW8 6RY, England.

GALLOWAY David Darryl, b. 5 May 1937, Memphis, Tennessee, USA. Journalist; Novelist; Professor; Art Consultant. m. Sally Lee Gantt, dec, 1 son. Education: BA, Harvard College, 1959; PhD, State University of New York, 1962. Appointments: Lecturer, State University of New York, 1962-64, University of Sussex, 1964-67; Chair of American Studies, University of Hamburg, 1967-68; Associate Professor, Case Western Reserve University, 1968-72; Chair of American Studies, Ruhr University, Germany, 1972-; Editor-in-Chief, German-American Cultural Review, 1993-. Publications: The Absurd Hero; Lamaar Ransom; Calamus; Artware; A Family Album; Tamsen; The Selected Writings of Edgar Allan Poe; Melody Jones. Contributions to: International Herald Tribune; Art in America; Art News. Memberships: Royal Society of Arts; The Harvard Club. Address: Band Strasse 13, 42105 Wuppertal, Germany.

GALLUN Raymond Zinke, b. 22 Mar 1911, Beaver Dam, Wisconsin, USA. Technical Writer. m. (1) Frieda Talmey, 26 Dec 1959, dec 1974, (2) Bertha Erickson, 25 Feb 1977, dec 1989, 1 stepdaughter. Education: University of Wisconsin-Madison, 1929-30. Publications: People Minus X, 1957; The Eden Cycle, 1974; The Best of Raymond Z Gallun, 1977; Sky Climber, 1982; Bioblast, 1985; Star Climber, autobiography, 1990. Contributions to: Science Wonder Stories; Air Wonder Stories; Astounding Stories; Colliers Magazine; The Best of Science Fiction; Adventures in Time and Space. Honours: Hall of Fame Award, Sealon 37th World Science Fiction Convention, Brighton, England, 1979; Lifetime Achievement Award, I-CON IV, New York

State University Campus, Stony Brook, 1985. Address: 110-20 The Avenue, Forest Hills, NY 11375, USA.

GALTON Herbert, b. 1 Oct 1917, Vienna, Austro-Hungary. University Professor; Writer. m. 28 Jan 1992. Education: High School, Vienna, 1935; University of Vienna, 1935-38; PhD, Russian Philology, University of London, 1951. Appointment: Professor, University of Kansas, 1962-88. Publications: Aorist und Aspekt im Slavischen, 1962; The Main Functions of the Slavic Verbal Aspect, 1976; Reisetagebuch, 1990. Contributions to: The Equality Principle, in anthology, 1974; Freedom - from Illusions, 1984; Lyrische Annalen, 1995. Honour: Gold Medal, Macedonian Academy of Sciences, 1987. Memberships: Austrian Writers' Union; Austrian PEN Club; Societas Linguistica Europaea. Address: Kaiserstrasse 12/18, Vienna 1070, Austria.

GALTON Raymond Percy, b. 17 July 1930. Author; Scriptwriter. m. Tonia Phillips, 1956, 1 son, 2 daughters. Publications: TV - With Alan Simpson: Hancock's Half House, 1954-61; Comedy Playhouse, 1962-63; Steptoe and Son, 1962-74; Galton-Simpson Comedy, 1969; Clochermerle, 1971; Casanova, '74, 1974; Dawson's Weekly, 1975; The Galton and Simpson Playhouse, 1976-77; With Johnny Speight: Tea Ladies, 1979; Spooner's Patch, 1979-80; With John Antrobus: Room at the Bottom, 1986; Films with Alan Simpson: The Rebel, 1960; The Bargee, 1963; The Wrong Arm of the Law, 1963; The Spy with a Cold Nose, 1966; Loot, 1969; Steptoe and Son, 1971; Steptoe and Son Ride Again, 1973; Den Siste Fleksnes, 1974; Die Skraphandlerne, 1975; Theatre with Alan Simpson: Way Out in Piccadilly, 1969; The Wind in the Sassfras Trees, 1968; Albert och Herbert, 1981; Fleksnes, 1983; Mordet pa Skolgatan 15, 1984; With John Antrobus: When Did You Last See Your Trousers?, 1986; Books: With Alan Simpson Hancock, 1961; Steptoe and Son, 1963; The Reunion and Other Plays, 1966; Hancock Scripts, 1974; The Best of Hancock, 1986. Address: The Ivy House, Hampton Court, Middlesex, England.

GALVIN Brendan, b. 20 Oct 1938, Everett, Massachusetts, USA. Professor of English; Poet. m. Ellen Baer, 1968, 1 son, 1 daughter. Education: BS, Boston College, 1960; MA, Northeastern University, 1964; MFA, 1967, PhD, 1970, University of Massachusetts. Appointments: Instructor, Northeastern University, 1964-65; Assistant Professor, Slippery Rock State College, 1968-69; Assistant Professor, 1969-74, Associate Professor, 1974-80, Professor of English, 1980-, Central Connecticut State University; Visiting Professor, Connecticut College, 1975-76; Editor (with George Garrett), Poultry: A Magazine of Voice, 1981-; Coal Royalty Chairholder in Creative Writing, University of Alabama, 1993. Publications: The Narrow Land, 1971; The Salt Farm, 1972; No Time for Good Reasons, 1974; The Minutes No One Owns, 1977; Atlantic Flyway, 1980; Winter Oysters, 1983; A Birder's Dozen, 1984; Seals in the Inner Harbour, 1985; Wampanoag Traveler, 1989; Raising Irish Walls, 1989; Great Blue: New and Selected Poems, 1990; Early Returns, 1992; Saints in Their Ox-Hide Boat, 1992; Islands, 1993. Honours: National Endowment for the Arts Fellowships, 1974, 1988; Connecticut Commission on the Arts Fellowships, 1981, 1984; Guggenheim Fellowship, 1988; Sotheby Prize, Arvon International Foundation, 1988; Levinson Prize, Poetry magazine, 1989; O B Hardison Jr Poetry Prize, Folger Shakespeare Library, 1991; Charity Randall Citation, International Poetry Forum, 1994. Address: PO Box 54, Durham, CT 06422, USA.

GALVIN James, b. 8 May 1951, Chicago, Illinois, USA. Poet. Education: BA, Antioch College; MFA, University of Iowa. Appointments: Professor; Editor, Crazyhorse, 1979-81. Publications: Imagining Timber, 1980; God's Mistress, 1984; Elements, 1988. Contributions to: New Yorker; Nation; Antioch Review; Poetry Now; Antaeus; Sewanee Review. Honours: Discovery Award, Nation/Young Men's Hebrew Association, 1977; National Poetry Series Open Competition, Co-winner, 1984. Address: Iowa Writers Workshop, Univerity of Iowa, 436 EPB, Iowa City, IA 52242, USA.

GALVIN Patrick, b. 1927, Cork, Ireland. Dramatist; Poet. m. Diana Ferrier, 2 sons. Appointments: Resident Dramatist, Lyric Theatre, Belfast, 1974-77; Writer-in-Residence, West Midlands Arts Association, 1979-80. Publications: Heart of Grace, 1957; Christ in London, 1960; Two Summers, Parts 1-3, 1970; By Nature Diffident, 1971; Lon Chaney, 1971; The Woodburners, 1973; Man on the Porch, 1980; Collected Poems and Letters, 1985; Let the Seahorse Take Me Home and Other Poems, 1986; Plays: And His Stretched, 1960; Cry the Believers, 1961; Nightfall to Belfast, 1973; The Last Burning, 1974; We Do It For Love, 1976; The Devil's Own People, 1976; Collected Plays and Letters, 1986. Honours: Leverhulme Fellowship, 1974-76.

Address: c/o Martin, Brian and O'Keefe, 78 Coleraine Road, Blackheath, London SE3, England.

GALWAY Robert Conington. See: McCUTCHAN Philip Donald.

GAMBARO Griselda, b. 28 July 1928, Buenos Aires, Argentina. Playwright; Novelist. m. Juan Carlos Distefano. Appointments: Drama Teacher; Lecturer. Publications: Matrimonio, 1965; El desatino, 1966; Las paredes, 1966; Los siameses, 1967; The Camp, 1968; Nada que ver, 1972; Solo un aspecto, 1974; El viaje a Bahia Blanca, 1975; El hombre, 1976; Putting Two and Two Together, 1976; Decir si, 1981; La malasangre, 1982; Real envido, 1983; Del sol naciente, 1984; Teatro, 4 volumes, 1984-90; Information for Foreigners, 1986; The Impenetrable Madam X, 1991; Fiction: Cuentos, 1953; Madrigal en ciudad, 1963; Un Felicidad con menos pena, 1968; Nada que ver con ora historia, 1972; Ganarse la muertel, 1976; Lo impenetrable, 1984. Honour: Guggenheim Fellowship, 1982. Address: c/o Argentores, Virrey Pacheo De Melo, 1126 Buenos Aires, Argentina.

GAMBONE Philip Arthur, b. 21 July 1948, Melrose, Massachusetts, USA. Teacher; Writer. Education: AB, Harvard University, 1970; MA, Episcopal Divinity School, 1976. Publications: The Language We Use Up Here and Other Stories; Men on Men VI, 1996; Flash Point; Boys Like Us; Fuori. Contributing author: Hometowns: Gay Men Write About Where They Belong; A Member of the Family; Men on Men III, 1990; Sister and Brother, 1994. Contributions to: Book reviews to New York Times, Lambda Book Report, Bay Windows. Honours: MacDowell Colony Fellow; Nominee, Lambda Literary Award; Helene Wurlitzer Foundation Award, 1996. Membership: PEN. Literary Agent: Edward Hibbert. Address: 47 Waldeck Street, Dorchester, MA 02124, USA.

GAMST Frederick Charles, b. 24 May 1936, New York, New York, USA. Professor of Anthropology. m. Marilou Swanson, 28 Jan 1961, 1 daughter. Education: AB, University of California, Los Angeles, 1961; PhD, University of California, Berkeley, 1967. Appointments: Instructor, Anthropology, 1966-67, Assistant Professor, Anthropology, 1967-71, Associate Professor, Anthropology, 1971-75, Rice University; Professor of Anthropology, University of Massachusetts, Boston, 1975-. Publications: Travel and Research in Northwestern Ethiopia, 1965; The Qemant: A Pagan-Hebraic Peasantry of Ethiopia, 1969; Peasants in Complex Society, 1974; Studies in Cultural Anthropology, 1975; Ideas of Culture: Sources and Uses, 1976; The Hoghead: An Industrial Ethnology of the Locomotive Engineer, 1980; Highballing with Flimsies: Working under Train Orders on the Espee's Coast Line, 1990; Meanings of Work: Considerations for the Twenty-first Century, 1995; Early American Railroads: Franze Anton Ritter von Gerstner's Die innern Communicationen 1842-1843, 2 volumes, 1997. Contributions to: Magazines and journals. Honour: Conrad Arensberg Award, 1995. Memberships: Society for the Anthropology of Work of the American Anthropological Association; Railroad and Locomotive Historical Society; Society for Applied Anthropology; Royal Anthropology Institute. Address: 73 Forest Avenue, Cohasset, MA 02025, USA.

GANDLEY Kenneth Royce, (Oliver Jacks, Kenneth Royce), b. 11 Dec 1920, Croydon, Surrey, England. Novelist. m. Stella Parker, 16 Mar 1946. Publications: My Turn to Die, 1958; The Soft Footed Moor, 1959; The Long Corridor, 1960; No Paradise, 1961; The Night Seekers, 1962; The Angry Island, 1963; The Day the Wind Dropped, 1964; Bones in the Sand, 1967; A Peck of Salt, 1968; A Single to Hong Kong, 1969; The XYY Man (also adapted for TV), 1970; The Concrete Boot (also adapted for TV), 1971; The Miniatures Frame (also adapted for TV), 1972; Spider Underground, 1973; Trapspider, 1974; Man on a Short Leash, 1974; The Woodcutter Operation (also adapted for TV), 1975; Bustillo, 1976; Assassination Day, 1976; Autumn Heroes, 1977; The Satan Touch (also adapted for TV), 1978; The Third Arm, 1980; 10,000 Days, 1981; Channel Assault, 1982; The Stalin Account, 1983; The Crypto Man, 1984; The Mosley Receipt, 1985; Breakout, 1986; No Way Back, 1987; The President is Dead, 1988; Fall-Out, 1989; Exchange of Doves, 1990; Limbo, 1992; Remote Control, 1993; The Ambassador's Son, 1994; Shadows, 1995; The Judas Trail, 1996. Memberships: Society of Authors; Crime Writers Association. Literary Agent: David Higham Associates. Address: 3 Abbotts Close, Abbotts Ann, Andover, Hants SP11 7NP, England.

GANNETT Ruth Stiles, b. 12 Aug 1923, New York, New York, USA. Author. m. Hans Peter Kahn, 21 Mar 1947, 7 daughters.

Education: AB, Vasser College, 1944. Publications: My Father's Dragon, 1948; The Wonderful House-Boat-Train, 1949; Elmer and the Dragon, 1950; The Dragons of Blueland, 1951; Katie and the Sad Noise, 1961. Honours: Herald Tribune Spring Book Award, 1948; Honour Book, Newberry, 1948; Junior Literary Guild Selections. Address: 8315 Route 227, Trumansburg, NY 14886, USA.

GANO Lila Lee, b. 25 Sept 1949, Ft Benning, Georgia, USA. Public Relations; Writer; Editor. Education: BA Sociology, Psychology, Anthropology, 1971; MA Counseling and Psychology, Writing Courses, Public Relations Courses, TV Production Courses, Scripting, 1975. Publications: Smoking, 1989; Television - Electronic Pictures, 1990; Hazardous Waste, 1994. Contributions to: San Diego Women's Magazine; Housewife Writer's Forum; San Diego Homes and Gardens. Honours: Society for Technical Communication Achievement Awards, 1994-96. Memberships: Society for Technical Communications; Tallahassee Writer's Association. Address: 2528 Pretty Bayou Island, Panama City, FL 32405, USA.

GANT Jonathon. See: **ADAMS Clifton.**

GANT Richard. See: **FREEMANTLE Brian.**

GARAFOLA Lynn, b. 12 Dec 1946, New York, New York, USA. Dance Critic; Historian. m. Eric Foner, 1 May 1980, 1 daughter. Education: AB, Barnard College, 1968; PhD, City University of New York, 1985. Appointment: Editor, Studies in Dance History, 1990-. Publications: Diaghilev's Ballets Russes; André Levinson on Dance: Writings from Paris in the Twenties; The Diaries of Marius Petipa. Contributions to: Dance Magazine; Ballet Review; Dancing Times; Dance Research Journal; Raritan; The Nation; Women's Review of Books; Times Literary Supplement; New York Times Book Review. Honour: Torre de lo Bueno Prize. Memberships: Society of Dance History Scholars; Dance Critics Association; Association Européenne des Historiens de la Danse. Address: 606 West 116th Street, New York, NY 10027, USA.

GARCÍA MARQUEZ Gabriel (José), b. 6 Mar 1928, Aracataca, Colombia. Author. m. Mercedes Barch, Mar 1958, 2 sons. Education: Universidad Nacional de Colombia, 1947-48; Universidad de Cartagena, 1948-49. Appointments: Journalist, 1947-65; Founder-President, Fundacion Habeas, 1979-. Publications: Fiction: La hojarasca, 1955; El coronel no tiene quien le escriba, 1961, English translation as No One Writes to the Colonel and Other Stories, 1968; La mala hora, 1961, English translation as In Evil Hour, 1979; Los funerales de la Mama Grande, 1962; Cien anos de soledad, 1967, English translation as One Hundred Years of Solitude, 1970; Isabel viendo llover en Macondo, 1967; La incredible y triste historia de la candida Erendira y su abuela desalmada, 1972; El negro que hizo esperar a los angeles, 1972; Ojos de perro azul, 1972; Leaf Storm and Other Stories, 1972; El otono del patriarca, 1975, English translation as The Autumn of the Patriarch, 1976; Todos los cuentos de Gabriel García Marquez: 1947-1972, 1975; Cronica de una muerte anunciada, 1981, English translation as Chronicle of a Death Foretold, 1982; El rastro de tu sangre en la nieve: El verano feliz de la senora Forbes, 1982; Collected Stories, 1984; El amor en los tiempos del colera, 1985, English translation as Love in the Time of Cholera, 1988; El general en su labertino, 1989, English translation as The General in His Laybyrinth, 1990; Collected Novellas, 1990; Doce cuentos peregrinos, 1992, English translation as Strange Pilgrims: Twelve Stories, 1993; Del amor y otros demonios, 1994, English translation as Of Love and Other Demons, 1995. Non-Fiction: La novela en America Latina: Dialogo (with Mario Vargas), 1968; Relato de un naufrago, 1970, English translation as The Story of a Shipwrecked Sailor, 1986; Cuando era feliz e indocumentado, 1973; Cronicas y reportajes, 1978; Periodismo militante, 1978; De viaje por los paises socialistas: 90 dias en la "Cortina de hierro", 1978; Obra periodistica, 4 volumes, 1981-83; El olor de la guayaba: Conversaciones con Plinio Apuleyo Mendoza, 1982, English translation as The Fragrance of Guava, 1983; Persecucion y muerte de minorias: Dos perspectivas, 1984; La aventura de Miguel Littin, clandestino en Chile: Un reportaje, 1986, English translation as Clandestine in Chile: The Adventures of Miguel Littin, 1987; Primeros reportajes, 1990; Notas de prensa, 1980-1984, 1991; Elogio de la utopia: Una entrevista de Nahuel Maciel, 1992. Honours: Colombian Association of Writers and Artists Award, 1954; Premio Literario Esso, Colombia, 1961; Chianciano Award, Italy, 1969; Prix de Meilleur Livre Etranger, France, 1969; Ròmulo Gallegos Prize, Venezuela, 1971; Honorary LLD, Columbia University, New York City, 1971; Books Abroad/Neustadt International Prize for Literature, 1972;

Nobel Prize for Literature, 1982; Los Angeles Times Book Prize for Fiction, 1988; Serfin Prize, 1989. Membership: American Academy of Arts and Letters, honorary fellow. Address: PO Box 20736, Mexico City DF, Mexico.

GARDAM Jane Mary, b. 11 July 1928, Yorkshire, England. Writer. m. David Hill Gardam, 20 Apr 1954, 2 sons, 1 daughter. Education: BA, Bedford College, London University, 1949. Appointments: Sub-Editor, Weldon's Ladies Journal, 1952; Assistant Literary Editor, Time and Tide, 1952-54. Publications: Fiction: A Long Way From Verona, 1971; The Summer After the Funeral, 1973; Bilgewater, 1977; God on the Rocks, 1978; The Hollow Land, 1981; Bridget and William, 1981; Horse, 1982; Kit, 1983; Crusoe's Daughter, 1985; Kit in Boots, 1986; Swan, 1987; Through the Doll's House Door, 1987; The Queen of the Tambourine, 1991; Earth Fox, 1995. Short Stories: A Few Fair Days, 1971; Black Faces, White Faces, 1975; The Sidmouth Letters, 1980; The Pangs of Love, 1983; Showing the Flag, 1989; Going Into a Dark House, 1994. Non-Fiction: The Iron Coast, 1994. Contributions to: Newspapers and magazines. Honours: David Higham's Award, 1978; Winifred Holtby Award, 1978; Whitbread Literary Award, 1983; Katherine Mansfield Award, 1984; Whitbread Novel Award, 1991; Whitbread Award for Fiction, 1992; Silver Pen Award, PEN, 1995. Memberships: PEN; Royal Society of Literature, fellow. Address: Haven House, Sandwich, Kent CT13 9ES, England.

GARDAPHE Fred Louis, b. 7 Sept 1952, Chicago, Illinois, USA. Writer; Professor. m. Susan Rose Stolder, 18 Sept 1982, 1 son, 1 daughter. Education: BS, Education, University of Wisconsin-Madison, 1976; AM, English, University of Chicago, 1982; PhD, English, University of Illinois at Chicago, 1993. Appointments: Columbia College, Chicago, 1979-; Editor, FràNoi, 1984-, Voices in Italian Anericana, 1990-. Publications: Italian American Ways, 1989; New Chicago Stories (editor), 1991; The Italian American Writer, 1995; Italian Signs, American Streets, 1996; Dagos Read, 1996; From the Margin (contributing editor). Contributions to: Voices in Italian America; MELUS; Borderlines; FràNoi; Altre Italie; Italian American Review; Forkroads. Honours: UNICO National Prize, 1987; Illinois Arts Council, 1988. Memberships: Modern Language Association; American Italian Historical Association, President, 1997-99. Address: Department of English, Columbia College, 600 South Michigan Avenue, Chicago, IL 60605-1996, USA.

GARDEN Bruce. See: **MACKAY James Alexander.**

GARDEN Nancy, b. 15 May 1938, Boston, Massachusetts, USA. Writer; Editor; Teacher. Education: BFA, Columbia University School of Dramatic Arts, 1961; MA, Teachers College, Columbia University, 1962. Appointments: Actress, Lighting Designer, 1954-64; Teacher of Speech and Dramatics, 1961-64; Editor, educational materials, textbooks, 1964-76; Teacher of Writing, Adult Education, 1974; Correspondence School, 1974-. Publications: What Happened in Marston, 1971; The Loners, 1972; Maria's Mountain, 1981; Fours Crossing, 1981; Annie on My Mind, 1982; Favourite Tales from Grimm, 1982; Watersmeet, 1983; Prisoner of Vampires, 1984; Peace, O River, 1986; The Door Between, 1987; Lark in the Morning, 1991; My Sister, the Vampire, 1992; Dove and Sword, 1995; My Brother, the Werewolf, 1995; Good Moon Rising, 1996. The Monster Hunter series: Case No 1, Mystery of the Night Raiders, 1987; Case No 2: Mystery of the Midnight Menace, 1988; Case No 3: Mystery of the Secret Marks, 1989; Case No 4: Mystery of the Kidnapped Kidnapper, 1994; Case No 5: Mystery of the Watchful Witches, 1995. Non-Fiction: Berlin: City Split in Two, 1971; Vampires, 1973; Werewolves, 1973; Witches, 1975; Devils and Demons, 1976; Fun with Forecasting Weather, 1977; The Kids' Code and Cipher Book, 1981. Contributions to: Lambda Book Report. Membership: Society of Children's Book Writers and Illustrators. Address: c/o McIntosh and Otis Inc, 310 Madison Avenue, New York, NY 10017, USA.

GARDNER Herb(ert), b. 1934, New York, New York, USA. Dramatist; Writer. Education: Carnegie Institute of Technology; Antioch College. Publications: Plays: The Elevator, 1952; A Thousand Clowns, 1962; The Goodbye People, 1974; Thieves, 1977; I'm Not Rappaport, 1986; Conversations with My Father, 1993. Other: A Piece of the Action (novel), 1958; One Night Stand (book and lyrics for the Jules Styne musical), 1980. Contributions to: Magazines. Honour: Screenwriters Guild Award, 1965. Membership: Dramatists Guild. Address: c/o International Creative Management, 40 West 57th Street, New York, NY 10019, USA.

GARDNER Sandra, b. 22 May 1940, Everett, Massachusetts, USA. Author of Young/Adult Books. m. Lewis Gardner, 16 Feb 1969, 1 son, 2 daughters. Education: BA, magna cum laude, English Literature, Hunter College, New York, 1979. Publications: Six Who Dared, 1981; Street Gangs, 1983; Street Gangs in America, 1992; Teenage Suicide, 1985, 2nd edition, 1990. Contributions to: New York Times New Jersey Weekly Section, 1981-86, 1991-93. Honours: Honourable Mention, Poetry Award, Hunter College, 1979; Juvenile Book Award, National Federation of Press Women, 1993. Literary Agent: Claudia Menza, New York, New York. Address: 16 Cedar Way, Woodstock, NY 12498, USA.

GARDONS S S. See: **SNODGRASS W D.**

GARFINKEL Patricia Gail, b. 15 Feb 1938, New York, New York, USA. Writer. 2 sons. Education: BA, New York University. Publications: Ram's Horn, poems, 1980; From the Red Eye of Jupiter (poems), 1990. Contributions to: Numerous publications and anthologies. Honours: Poetry in Public Places Award for New York State, 1977; 1st Prize, Lip Service Poetry Competition, 1990; Book Competition, Washington Writers Publishing House, 1990. Membership: Poets and Writers. Address: 2031 Approach Lane, Reston, VA 22091, USA.

GARFITT Roger, b. 12 Apr 1944, Wiltshire, England. Poet; Writer. Education: BA, Hons, Merton College, Oxford, 1968. Appointments: Arts Council Poet in Residence, University College of North Wales, Bangor, 1975-77; Editor, Poetry Review 1978-81; Arts Council Poet in Residence, Sunderland Polytechnic, 1978-80; Member, Literature Panel of Arts Council of Great Britain, 1986-90. Publications: Poetry: Caught on Blue, 1970; West of Elm, 1974; The Broken Road, 1982; Rowlstone Haiku, 1982; Given Ground, 1989; Border Songs, 1996. Contributions to: Prose in Granta 27 and 29, 1989; Travelling on Sunshine. Honours: Guinness International Poetry Prize, 1973; Gregory Award, 1974. Address: c/o Jane Turnbull, 13 Wendell Road, London W12 9RS, England.

GARLICK Helen Patricia, b. 21 Apr 1958, Doncaster, England. Writer; Solicitor. m. Richard Howard, 1 daughter. Education: LLB Class 2i (Hons), University of Bristol, 1979; Solicitor of Supreme Court, 1983. Appointments: TV and radio appearances. Publications: The Separation Survival Handbook, 1989; The Good Marriage, 1990; The Which? Good Divorce Guide, 1992; Penguin Guide to the Law, 1992. Contributions to: Independent; Guardian; Various magazines. Memberships: Chair, National Council for One Parent Families; Family Law Adviser to Consumers Association. Address: c/o Carolyn Brunton, Studio 8, 125 Moore Park Road, London SW6 4PS, England.

GARLICK Raymond, b. 21 Sept 1926. Lecturer; Poet. m. Elin Jane Hughes, 1948, 1 son, 1 daughter. Education: BA, University College of North Wales, Bangor, 1948. Appointment: Principal Lecturer, Trinity College, Carmarthen, 1972-86. Publications: Poetry: Poems from the Mountain-House, 1950; Requiem for a Poet, 1954; Poems from Pembrokeshire, 1954; The Welsh-Speaking Sea, 1954; Blaenau Observed, 1957; Landscapes and Figures: Selected Poems, 1949-63, 1964; A Sense of Europe: Collected Poems 1954-68, 1968; A Sense of Time: Poems and Antipoems, 1969-72, 1972; Incense: Poems 1972-75; Collected Poems 1946-86, 1987; Travel Notes: New Poems, 1992. Other: An Introduction to Anglo-Welsh Literature, 1970; Anglo-Welsh Poetry 1480-1900 (editor), 1982. Honours: Welsh Arts Council Prizes; Honorary Fellow, Trinity College, Carmarthen; Fellow, Welsh Academy. Address: 26 Glannant House, College Road, Carmarthen SA31 3EF, Wales.

GARLINSKI Jozef, b. 14 Oct 1913, Poland. Writer. Education: MA, University of Warsaw, 1942; PhD, London School of Economics and Political Science, 1973. Appointments: Chairman, Executive Committee, Polish Home Army Circle, London, England, 1954-65; Cultural Vice-Chairman, Polish Cultural and Social Centre, London, 1970-79; Chairman, Union of Polish Writers Abroad, 1975-. Publications: Dramat i Opatrznosc, 1961; Matki i zony, 1962; Ziemia, novel, 1964; Miedzy Londynem i Warszawa, 1966; Polish SOE and the Allies, 1969; Fighting Auschwitz, 1975; Hitler's Last Weapons, 1978; Intercept: Secrets of the Enigma War, 1979; The Swiss Corridor, 1981; Polska w Drugiej Wojnie Swiatowej, 1982; Poland in the Second World War, 1985; Szwajcarski Kryterz, 1987; Niezapomniane lata, 1987. Address: 94 Ramillies Road, London W4 1JA, England.

GARNER Alan, b. 17 Oct 1934, Cheshire, England. Author. m. (1) Ann Cook, 1956, div, 1 son, 2 daughters, (2) Griselda Greaves, 1972, 1 son, 1 daughter. Education: Magdalen College, Oxford, 1955-56. Appointments: Member of International Editorial Board, Detskaya Literatura Publishers, Moscow, 1991-. Publications: The Weirdstone of Brisingamen, 1960; The Moon of Gomrath, 1963; Elidor, 1965; Holly from the Bongs, 1966; The Owl Service, 1967; The Book of Goblins, 1969; Red Shift, 1973; The Guizer, 1975; The Stone Book Quartet, 1976-78; Fairy Tales of Gold, 1979; The Lad of the Gad, 1980; British Fairy Tales, 1984; A Bag of Moonshine, 1986; Jack and the Beanstalk, 1992; Once Upon a Time, 1993; Strandloper, 1996. Honours: Carnegie Medal, 1967; Guardian Award, 1968; Lewis Carroll Shelf Award, USA, 1970; Gold Plaque, Chicago International Film Festival, 1981; Children's Literature Association International Phoenix Award, 1996. Membership: Portico Library, Manchester. Literary Agent: Sheil Land Associates Limited. Address: Blackden, Holmes Chapel, Crewe, Cheshire CW4 8BY, England.

GARNER Helen, b. 7 Nov 1942, Geelong, Victoria, Australia. Novelist; Journalist. m. (3) Murray Bail, 1992. Education: BA, Melbourne University, 1965. Publications: Monkey Grip, 1977; Honour, and Other People's Children, 1980; The Children's Bach, 1984; Postcards from Surfers, 1985; Cosmo Cosmolino, 1992; The Last Days of Chez Nous, 1993; The First Stone, 1995; True Stories, 1996. Honours: Australia Council Fellowships; National Book Council Award, 1978; New South Wales Premiers Award, 1986. Address: c/o Barbara Mobbs, PO Box 126, Edgecliff, NSW 2027, Australia.

GARNER William, b. 1920, Grimsby, Lincolnshire, England. Writer. Publications: 14 novels, 1965-96, including Overkill; The Deep Deep Freeze; The Us or Them Way; The Andra Fiasco; Ditto, Brother Rat; A Big Enough Wreath; The Mobius Trip; Think Big, Think Dirty; Rats' Alley; Zones of Silence; Paper Chase; Sleeping Dogs. Contributions to: Numerous newspapers and magazines. Address: c/o Heaton Green Ltd, 37 Goldhawk Road, London W12 8QQ, England.

GARNETT Michael Pearson, b. 24 Nov 1938, Essex, England. m. 2 sons. Education: Framlingham College, Suffolk; Diploma, Business Management, British Institute of Careers, New South Wales, Australia. Appointments: Flight Lieutenant, Royal Air Force in Far East during Malaya emergency, RAAF Reserve; Executive, Australian Real Tennis Association. Publications: A History of Royal Tennis in Australia, 1983; The Garnett Family: A History, 1985; Tennis, Rackets and Other Ball Games, 1986; Royal Tennis - For the Record, 1991. Contributions to: Periodicals. Membership: Melbourne Press Club. Literary Agent: Historical Publications, Melbourne. Address: The Chase, Romsey, Victoria 3434, Australia.

GARNETT Richard (Duncan Carey), b. 8 Jan 1923, London, England. Writer; Publisher; Translator. Education: BA, King's College, Cambridge, 1949; MA, 1987. Appointments: Production Manager, 1951-59, Director, 1954-66, Rupert Hart-Davis Ltd; Director, Adlard Coles Ltd, 1963-66; Editor, 1966-82, Director, 1972-82, Macmillan, London; Director, Macmillan Publishers, 1982-87. Publications: Goldsmith: Selected Works (editor), 1950; Robert Gruss: The Art of the Aqualung (translator), 1955; The Silver Kingdom (in US as The Undersea Treasure), 1956; Bernard Heuvelmans: On the Track of Unknown Animals (translator), 1958; The White Dragon, 1963; Jack of Dover, 1966; Bernard Heuvelmans: In the Wake of the Sea-Serpents (translator), 1968; Joyce, (editor with Reggie Grenfell), 1980; Constance Garnett, A Heroic Life, 1991; Sylvia and David, The Townsend Warner/Garnett Letters (editor), 1994. Address: Hilton Hall, Hilton, Huntingdon, Cambridgeshire PE18 9NE, England.

GARRETT George (Palmer Jr), b. 11 June 1929, Orlando, Florida, USA. Professor of English; Writer; Poet; Editor. m. Susan Parrish Jackson, 1952, 2 sons, 1 daughter. Education: BA, 1952, MA, 1956, PhD, 1985, Princeton University. Appointments: Assistant Professor, Wesleyan University, 1957-60; US Poetry Editor, Transatlantic Review, 1958-71; Visiting Lecturer, Rice University, 1961-62; Associate Professor, 1962-67, Hoyns Professor of English, 1984-, University of Virginia; Writer-in-Residence, Princeton University, 1964-65; Bennington College, Vermont, 1979, University of Michigan, 1979-80, 1983-84; Co-Editor, Hollins Critic, 1965-71; Worksheet, 1972-; Poultry: A Magazine of Voice, 1981-; Professor of English, Hollins College, Virginia, 1967-71; Professor of English and Writer-in-Residence, University of South Carolina, 1971-73; Senior Fellow, Council of the Humanities, Princeton University, 1974-78; Adjunct Professor, Columbia University, 1977-78. Publications:

Novels: The Finished Man, 1959; Which Ones Are the Enemy?, 1961; Do, Lord, Remember Me, 1965; Death of the Fox, 1971; The Succession: A Novel of Elizabeth and James, 1983; Poison Pen, or, Live Now and Pay Later, 1986; Entered from the Sun, 1990; The Old Army Game, 1994. Short Stories: King of the Mountain, 1958; In the Briar Patch, 1961; Cold Ground Was My Bed Last Night, 1964; A Wreath for Garibaldi and Other Stories, 1969; The Magic Striptease, 1973; To Recollect a Cloud of Ghosts: Christmas in England, 1979; An Evening Performance: New and Selected Short Stories, 1985. Poetry: The Reverend Ghost, 1957; The Sleeping Gypsy and Other Poems, 1958; Abraham's Knife and Other Poems, 1961; For a Bitter Season: New and Selected Poems, 1967; Welcome to the Medicine Show: Postcards, Flashcards, Snapshots, 1978; Luck's Shining Child: A Miscellany of Poems and Verses, 1981; The Collected Poems of George Garrett, 1984. Other: James Jones, 1984; Understanding Mary Lee Settle, 1988; The Sorrows of Fat City, 1992; Whistling in the Dark, 1992; My Silk Purse and Yours, 1993. Editor: 18 books, 1963-93. Honours: Sewanee Review Fellowship, 1958; American Academy in Rome Fellowship, 1958; Ford Foundation Grant, 1960; National Endowment for the Arts Grant, 1967; Contempora Award, 1971; Guggenheim Fellowship, 1974; American Academy of Arts and Letters Award, 1985; Cultural Laureate of Virginia, 1986; T S Eliot Award, 1989. Membership: Fellowship of Southern Letters, vice-chancellor, 1987-93, chancellor, 1993-. Address: 1845 Wayside Place, Charlottesville, VA 22903, USA.

GARRETT Richard, b. 15 Jan 1920, London, England. Author; Journalist. m. Margaret Anne Selves, 20 Aug 1945, 2 sons, 1 daughter. Education: Bradfield College. Publications: Fast and Furious - The Story of the World Championship of Drivers, 1968; Cross Channel, 1972; Scharnhorst and Gneisenau - The Elusive Sisters, 1978; The Raiders, 1980; POW, 1981; Atlantic Disaster - The Titanic and Other Victims, 1986; Flight Into Mystery, 1986; Voyage Into Mystery, 1987; Great Escapes of World War II, 1989; The Final Betrayal - The Armistice, 1918 ... And Afterwards, 1990; Sky High, 1991; Biographies of Generals Gordon Wolfe and Clive, and a number of children's books. Contributions to: Magazines and radio. Membership: Society of Authors. Address: c/o Watson, Little Ltd, Capo di Monte, Windmill Hill, London, NW3 6RJ, England.

GARRISON Omar V, b. 2 June 1913, LaJunta, Colorado, USA. Author. m. Virginia Leah Herrick, 11 Sept 1952. Education: PhD, 1938. Publications: Tantra, philosophy, 1964; Spy Government, 1967; Howard Hughes in Las Vegas, 1970; Balboa Conquistador, biography, 1971; Lost Gems of Secret Knowledge, 1973; Hidden Story of Scientology, 1974; Secret World of Interpol, 1977; Playing Dirty, 1980; The Baby That Laughed All Night (novel), 1989. Membership: Authors Guild. Address: 26812 Cherry Hills Blvd, #224, Sun City, CA 92586-2505, USA.

GARROW David J(effries), b. 11 May 1953, New Bedford, Massachusetts, USA. Author/Professor. m. Susan Foster Newcomer, 18 Dec 1984. Education: BA magna cum laude, Wesleyan University, 1975; MA, 1978, PhD, 1981, Duke University. Appointments: Senior Fellow, The Twentieth Century Fund, 1991-93; Visiting Distinguished Professor, The Cooper Union, 1992-93; James Pinckney Harrison Professor of History, College of William and Mary, 1994-95; Distinguished Historian-in-Residence, The America University, Washington, DC, 1995-96; Presidential Visiting Distinguished Professor, Emory University, 1997-. Publications: Protest at Selma, 1978; The FBI and Martin Luther King Jr, 1981; Bearing the Cross, 1986; The Montgomery Bus Boycott and the Women Who Started It (editor), 1987; Liberty and Sexuality, 1994. Contributions to: New York Times; Washington Post; Newsweek; Dissent; Journal of American History; Constitutional Commentary. Honours: Pulitzer Prize in Biography, 1987; Robert F Kennedy Book Award, 1987; Gustavus Myers Human Rights Book Award, 1987. Memberships: Authors Guild; Phi Beta Kappa. Address: Emory University Law School, Atlanta, GA 30322-2770, USA.

GARTNER Chloe Maria, b. 21 Mar 1916, Troy, Kansas, USA. Writer. m. Peter Godfrey Trimble, 22 Jan 1942, div 1957, 1 daughter. Education: University of California; Mesa College, Grand Junction, Colorado; College Marin, Kentfield, California. Publications: The Infidels, 1960; Drums of Khartoum, 1967; Die Lange Sommer, 1970; Woman From the Glen, 1973; Mistress of the Highlands, 1976; Anne Bonney, 1977; The Image and the Dream, 1980; Still Falls the Rain, 1983; Greenleaf, 1987; Lower Than the Angels, 1989. Contributions to: Cosmopolitan; Good Housekeeping; Others. Honour: Silver Medal,

Commonwealth Club of California, 1960. Memberships: Authors Guild. Address: c/o Kidde, Hoyt and Picard, 355 East 51st Street, New York, NY 10022, USA.

GARTON ASH Timothy John, b. 12 July 1955, England. Writer; Fellow of St Antony's College, Oxford. m. Danuta Maria, 1982, 2 sons. Education: Sherborne, Oxford. Appointments: Editorial Writer, The Times, 1984-86; Foreign Editor, The Spectator, 1984-90; Columnist, The Independent, 1988-91; Fellow, St Antony's College, Oxford, 1990-. Publications: The File; In Europe's Name; We the People; The Uses of Adversity; The Polish Revolution. Contributions to: New York Review of Books; Spectator; Independent; Times; Granta. Honours: Somerset Maugham Award; David Watt Memorial Prize; Prix Européen de Essai; Order of Merit, Poland; Bundesverdienstkreuz, Germany. Literary Agent: Gill Coleridge. Address: St Antony's College, Oxford OX2 6JF, England.

GASCOIGNE Bamber, b. 24 Jan 1935, London, England. Author; Broadcaster. m. Christina Ditchburn, 1965. Education: Scholar, Eton; Scholar, Magdalene College, Cambridge; Commonwealth Fund Fellow, Yale University, 1958-59. Appointments: Theatre Critic, Spectator, 1961-63, Observer, 1963-64; Co-editor, Theatre Notebook, 1968-74; Founder, Saint Helena Press, 1977; Chairman, Ackermann Publishing, 1981-85. Publications: Twentieth Century Drama, 1962; World Theatre, 1968; The Great Moghuls, 1971; Murgatreud's Empire, 1972; The Heyday, 1973; The Treasures and Dynasties of China, 1973; Ticker Khan, 1974; The Christians, 1977; Images of Richmond, 1978; Images of Twickenham, 1981; Why the Rope went Tight, 1981; Fearless Freddy's Magic Wish, 1982; Fearless Freddy's Sunken Treasure, 1982; Quest for the Golden Hare, 1983; Cod Streuth, 1986; How to Identify Prints, 1986; Encyclopedia of Britain, 1993; Milestones in Colour Printing, 1997. TV Presenter: University Challenge, 1962-87; Connoisseur, 1988-89; Presenter and author of documentary series: The Christians, 1977; Victorian Values, 1987; Man and Music, 1987-89; The Great Moghuls, 1990; Brother Felix and the Virgin Saint, 1992. Address: Saint Helena Terrace, Richmond, Surrey TW9 1NR, England.

GASCOIGNE John, b. 20 Jan 1951, Liverpool, England. Historian. m. Kathleen May Bock, 6 Apr 1980, 1 son, 1 daughter. Education: BA, Sydney University, 1969-72; MA, Princeton University, 1973-74; PhD, Cambridge University, 1974-80. Appointments: Lecturer, Department of History, University of Papua, 1977-78; Tutor, 1980-84, Lecturer, 1984-89, Senior Lecturer, 1989-, Associate professor, 1997-, University of New South Wales. Publications: Cambridge in the Age of the Enlightenment; Joseph Banks and the English Enlightenment; Useful Knowledge and Polite Culture, 1994. Contributions to: Historical Journal; Social Studies of Science; History; Science in Context. Honour: Joint Winner, Australian Historical Association Hancock Prize. Address: School of History, University of New South Wales, Sydney, New South Wales 2052, Australia.

GASCOIGNE Marguerite. See: LAZARUS Marguerite.

GASCOYNE David Emery, b. 10 Oct 1916, Harrow, Middlesex, England. Writer; Poet. m. Judy Tyler Lewis, May 1975, 4 stepchildren. Education: Regent Street Polytechnic Secondary, London, 1930-32. Publications: A Short Survey of Surrealism, 1936, USA; Night Thoughts, 1956; Collected Poems, 1965; Collected Verse Translations, 1970; Paris Journal 1937-39, 1978; Journal 1936-37, 1980; Collected Poems, 1988; The Collected Journals 1936-42, 1990. Contributions to: New Verse; Criterion; Partisan Review; New Writing; Adam International; Horizon; Poetry Nation Review; Cahiers du Sud; Nouvelle Revue Française; Europe; Botteghe Oscure; Temenos; Times Literary Supplement; The Independent. Honours: Atlantic Award, 1946-47; Primo Biella-Poesia Europea, 1982. Memberships: Fellow, Royal Literary Society; Committee Member, World Organization of Poets, Luxembourg; Committee Member, Biennales Internationales de Poésie, Belgium. Literary Agent: Alan Clodd, 22 Huntington Road, London N2 9DU, England. Address: 48 Oxford Street, Northwood, Cowes, Isle of Wight PO31 8PT, England.

GASH Jonathan See: GRANT John.

GASKELL Jane, b. 7 July 1941, Lancashire, England. Writer. Appointments: Feature Writer, Daily Express, 1961-65, Daily Sketch, 1965-71, Daily Mail, 1971-84. Publications: Atlan Books, including The Serpent (fantasy books), 1961 onwards; Strange Evil, 1957; King's Daughter, 1958; All Neat in Black Stockings, 1964 (filmed 1966); A

Sweet Sweet Summer, 1970; Attic Summer; The Shiny Narrow Grin; The Fabulous Heroine; Summer Coming; Some Summer Lands, 1977; Sun Bubble, 1990. Honour: Somerset Maugham Award, 1970. Address: Sharland Organisation, 9 Marlborough Crescent, Bedford Park, London W4 1HE, England.

GASKIN Catherine Marjella, b. 2 Apr 1929, County Louth, Dundalk, Ireland. Novelist. m. Sol Cornberg, 1 Dec 1955. Education: Holy Cross College, Sydney, Australia; Conservatorium of Music, Sydney. Publications: This Other Eden, 1946; With Every Year, 1947; Dust in Sunlight, 1950; All Else is Folly, 1951; Daughter of the House, 1952; Sara Dane, 1955; Blake's Reach, 1958; Corporation Wife, 1960; I Know My Love, 1962; The Tilsit Inheritance, 1963; The File on Devlin, 1965; Edge of Glass, 1967; Fiona, 1970; A Falcon for a Queen, 1972; The Property of a Gentleman, 1974; The Lynmara Legacy, 1975; The Summer of the Spanish Woman, 1977; Family Affairs, 1980; Promises, 1982; The Ambassador's Women, 1985; The Charmed Circle, 1988. Memberships: Society of Authors; Author's Guild of America. Address: White Rigg, East Ballaterson, Maughold IM7 1AR, Isle of Man.

GASKIN J(ohn) C(harles) A(ddison), b. 4 Apr 1936, Hitchin, Hertfordshire, England. Professor of Philosophy; Writer. m. Diana Dobbin, 20 May 1972, 1 son, 1 daughter. Education: MA, 1963, BLitt, 1965, St Peter's College, Oxford; MA, Trinity College, Dublin, 1967. Appointments: Lecturer, 1965-78, Fellow, 1978-, Professor of Philosophy, 1982-, Trinity College, Dublin. Publications: Hume's Philosophy of Religion, 1978, revised edition, 1988; The Quest for Eternity: An Outline of the Philosophy of Religion, 1984; Varieties of Unbelief From Epicurus to Sarte, 1989; David Hume: Dialogues Concerning Natural Religion and the Natural History of Religion (editor), 1993; The Epicurean Philosophers (editor), 1994; Thomas Hobbes: Human Nature and the De Corpore (editor), 1994. Contributions to: Scholarly journals and periodicals. Membership: Royal Institute of Philosophy. Address: Trinity College, University of Dublin, Dublin 2, Ireland.

GASS William Howard, b. 30 July 1924, Fargo, North Dakota, USA. Professor. m. (1) Mary Pat O'Kelly, 1952, 2 sons, 1 daughter, (2) Mary Henderson, 1969, 2 daughters. Education: AB, Kenyon College, 1947; PhD, Cornell University, 1954; DLitt, Purdue University, 1985. Appointments: Director, International Writers Center, Washington University, St Louis, Missouri, 1991-. Publications: Omensetters Luck; In the Heart of the Heart of the Country; Fiction and the Figures of Life; On Being Blue; Habitations of the Word; Willie Masters' Lonesome Wife; The World Within the Word; The Tunnel; Finding a Form. Contributions to: New York Review of Books; New York Times Book Review; Times Literary Supplement; New Republic; Harper's; The Nation; Esquire; Yale Review; Salmagundi; Iowa Review; River Styx; New Yorker; New American Review. Address: International Writers Center, Washington University, Campus Box 1071, St Louis, MO 63130, USA.

GASTON Patricia M Sullivan, b. 8 Aug 1946, Philadelphia, Pennsylvania, USA. Associate Professor of English. 1 son, 2 daughters. Education: PhD, University of Florida, USA, 1986; BA, MA, Western Michigan University, USA. Publication: Preparing the Waverley Prefaces, 1991. Contributions to: Periodicals. Honours: National Endowment to the Humanities Seminars, 1990, 1994. Memberships: South Atlantic Modern Language Association; Modern Language Association; National Council of Teachers of English. Address: Humanities Division, West Virginia University, Parkersburg, WV 26101, USA.

GATENBY Greg, b. 5 May 1950, Toronto, Ontario, Canada. Artistic Director; Poet. Education: BA, English Literature, York University, 1972. Appointments: Editor, McClelland and Stewart, Toronto, 1973-75; Artistic Director, Harbourfront Reading Series and concomitant festivals, 1975-. Publications: Imaginative Work: Rondeaus for Erica, 1976; Adrienne's Blessing, 1976; The Brown Stealer, 1977; The Salmon Country, 1978; Growing Still, 1981. Anthologies: 52 Pickup, 1977; Whale Sound, 1977; Whales: A Celebration, 1983; The Definitive Notes, 1991; The Wild Is Always There, 1993. Translator: Selected Poems, by Giorgio Bassani, 1980; The Wild Is Always There, Vol 2, 1995; The Very Richness of that Past, 1995. Honours: City of Toronto Arts Award (Literature), 1989; League of Canadian Poets Honorary Lifetime Member, 1991; Jack Award (honouring Lifetime Promotion of Canadian Books), 1994; E J Pratt Lifetime Fellow, 1995. Memberships: PEN, Canadian Centre;

Writers Union of Canada. Address: c/o Harbourfront Reading Series, 410 Queen's Quay West, Toronto, Ontario M5V 2Z3, Canada.

GATES Henry Louis Jr, b. 16 Sept 1950, Keyser, West Virginia, USA. Professor of Humanities and Afro-American Studies; Writer. Education: BA summa cum laude, History, Yale University, 1973; MA, English Language and Literature, 1974, PhD, English Language and Literature, 1979, Clare College, University of Cambridge. Appointments: Lecturer, Director of Undergraduate Studies, 1976-79, Assistant Professor, 1979-84, Associate Professor, 1984-85, English, Afro-American Studies, Yale University; Professor, English, Comparative Literature, Africana Studies, 1985-88, W E B DuBois Professor of Literature, 1988-90, Cornell University; John Spencer Bassett Professor of English, Duke University, 1990; Currently Chairman, Afro-American Studies Department, Harvard University; Numerous editorial appointments. Publications: Figures in Black: Words, Signs and the Racial Self, 1987; The Signifying Monkey: Towards A Theory of Afro-American Literary Criticism, 1988; Colored People, 1994; Thirteen Ways of Looking at a Black Man; Editor, many books including: Their Eyes Were Watching God, 1989; Jonah's Gourd Vine, 1990; Tell My Horse, 1990; Mules and Men, 1990; Voodoo Gods of Haiti, 1990; Reading Black, Reading Feminist, 1990; Frederick Douglass: Autobiographies, 1994; Norton Anthology of African American Literature. Contributions to: Numerous essays, articles, book reviews, to magazines and journals. Honours: Yale Afro-American Cultural Center Faculty Prize, 1983; Award for Cultural Scholarship, Zora Neal Hurston Society, 1986; Honourable Mention, John Hope Franklin Prize, American Studies Association, 1988; Candle Award, Morehouse College, 1989; American Book Award, 1989. Memberships: Council on Foreign Relations; Union of Writers of the African Peoples; African Roundtable; African Literature Association. Address: Afro-American Studies Department, Harvard University, Cambridge, MA 02138, USA.

GATHORNE-HARDY Jonathan, b. 15 May 1933, Edinburgh, Scotland. Author. m. (1) Sabrina Tennant, 1962, 1 son, 1 daughter, (2) Nicolette Sinclair Loutit, 12 Sept 1985. Education: BA Arts, Trinity College, Cambridge, 1954-57. Publications: One Foot in the Clouds (novel), 1961; Chameleon (novel), 1967; The Office (novel), 1970; The Rise & Fall of the British Nanny, 1972 (new editions), 1985-93; The Public School Phenomenon, 1977; Love, Sex, Marriage & Divorce, 1981; Doctors, 1983; The Centre of the Universe is 18 Baedeker Strasse (short stories), 1985; The City Beneath the Skin (novel), 1986; The Interior Castle - A Life of Gerald Brenan (biography), 1992; Particle Theory (novel), 1996; 11 novels for children. Contributions to: Numerous magazines and journals. Literary Agents: Sinclair Stevenson; For Children's books: Laura Cecil. Address: 31 Blacksmith's Yard, Binham, Fakenham, Norfolk NR21 0AL, England.

GATTEY Charles Neilson, b. 3 Sept 1921, London, England. Author; Playwright; Lecturer. Education: London University. Publications: Books: The Incredible Mrs Van Der Eist, 1972; They Saw Tomorrow, 1977; Queens of Song, 1979; The Elephant that Swallowed a Nightingale, 1981; Peacocks on the Podium, 1982; Foie Gras and Trumpets, 1984; Excess in Food, Drink and Sex, 1987; Prophecy and Prediction in the 20th Century, 1989; Luisa Tetrazzini, 1995; TV Play: The White Falcon, 1955; Film: The Love Lottery, 1954. Memberships: Society of Civil Service Authors, president, 1980; The Garrick. Address: 15 St Lawrence Drive, Pinner, Middlesex HA5 2RL, England.

GATTI Armand, b. 26 Jan 1924, Monaco (French citizen). Playwright. Education: Seminary of Saint Paul, near Cannes. Appointment: Former Journalist. Publications: Le Poisson noir, 1958; La Crapaud buffle, 1959; Theatre, 3 volumes, 1960-64; L'Enfant - rat, 1961; Le Voyage de Grand Tchou, 1960; Public Performance Before Two Electric Chairs, 1966; Un Homme Seul, 1966; V comme Vietnam, 1967; Le Passion du Général Franco, 1967; La Cigogne, 1968; La Naissance, 1968; Rosa Collective, 1971; La Colonne Durruti, 1972; Le Joint, 1974; Four Schizophrenics in Search of an Unknown Country, 1974; Le Labyrinthe, 1982; Opéra avec titre long, 1986; Le Train, 1987; Oeuvres Théâtrales, 3 volumes, 1991; Screenplays and television plays. Honour: Fenon Prize, 1959. Address: La Parole Errante, 3 rue François Debergue, 931000 Montreuil, France.

GAUNT Graham See: **GRANT John.**

GAVIN Catherine, b. Aberdeen, Scotland. Author. m. John Ashcraft, 1948. Education: MA, PhD, University of Aberdeen; Sorbonne, Paris, France. Publications: Liberated France, 1955;

Madeleine, 1957; The Cactus and the Crown, 1962; The Fortress, 1964; The Moon Into Blood, 1966; The Devil in Harbour, 1968; The House of War, 1970; Give Me the Daggers, 1972; The Snow Mountain, 1973; Traitors' Gate, 1976; None Dare Call It Treason, 1978; How Sleep the Brave, 1980; The Sunset Dream, 1983; The Glory Road, 1987; A Dawn of Splendour, 1989; The French Fortune, 1991. Contributions to: Time magazine; Kemsley newspapers; Daily Express. Honours: University Medal of Honour, Helsinki, 1970; Honorary DLitt, University of Aberdeen, 1986. Literary Agent: Scott Ferris Associates, London, England. Address: 1201 California Street, San Francisco, CA 94109, USA.

GAVIN Thomas Michael, b. 1 Feb 1941, Newport News, Virginia, USA. Professor. m. Susan Holahan, 5 July 1991, 2 daughters. Education: BA, MA, University of Toledo. Appointments: Delta College, University Center, Michigan, 1972-75; Middlebury College, Vermont, 1975-80; University of Rochester, New York, 1980-. Publications: Breathing Water; Kingkill; The Last Film of Emile Vico; "The Truth Beyond Facts". Contributions to: Georgia Review; TriQuarterly. Honours: National Endowment for the Arts Fellowship; Andrew W Mellon Fellowship; Lillian Fairchild Award. Literary Agent: Georges Borchardt. Address: English Department, University of Rochester, Rochester, NY 14627, USA.

GAY Peter (Jack), b. 20 June 1923, Berlin, Germany. Writer. m. Ruth Slotkin, 30 May 1959, 3 stepdaughters. Education: AB, University of Denver, 1946; MA, 1947, PhD, 1951, Columbia University; Psychoanalytic training, Western New England Institute for Psychoanalysis, 1976-83. Publications: The Dilemma of Democratic Socialism: Eduard Bernstein's Challenge to Marx, 1952; The Question of Jean Jacques Rousseau (editor), 1954; Voltaire's Politics: The Poet as Realist, 1959; Voltaire: Philosophical Dictionary (translator), 1962; Voltaire: Candide (translator) 1963; The Party of Humanity: Essays in the French Enlightenment, 1964; John Locke on Education (editor) 1964; The Enlightenment: An Interpretation, Vol I: The Rise of Modern Paganism, 1966, Vol II: The Science of Freedom, 1969; A Loss of Mastery: Puritan Historians in Colonial America, 1966; Weimar Culture: The Outsider as Insider, 1968; Deism: An Anthology, 1968; Columbia History of the World (with John A Garraty), 1972; Modern Europe (with R K Webb), 2 volumes, 1973; The Enlightenment: A Comprehensive Anthology, 1973, revised edition, 1985; Style in History, 1974; Art and Act: On Causes in History - Manet, Gropius, Mondrian, 1976; The Bourgeois Experience, Victoria to Freud, Vol I, Education of the Senses, 1984, Vol II, The Tender Passion, 1986, Vol III, The Cultivation of Hatred, 1993, Vol IV, The Naked Heart; Freud: A Life for Our Time, 1989; Reading Freud, 1990. Honours: Frederic G Melcher Book Award and National Book Award, 1967; Guggenheim Fellowships, 1967-68, 1977-78; Gold Medal, American Academy of Arts and Letters. Membership: Phi Beta Kappa. Address: 105 Blue Trail, Hamden, CT 06518, USA.

GAYLE Emma. See: **FAIRBURN Eleanor M.**

GEDDES Gary, b. 9 June 1940, Vancouver, British Columbia, Canada, Professor of English; Writer; Poet. m. (1) Norma Joan Fugler, 1963, div 1969, 1 daughter, (2) Jan Macht, 2 May 1973, 2 daughters. Education: BA, University of British Columbia, 1962; Diploma in Education, 1964, University of Reading, 1964; MA, 1966, PhD, 1975, University of Toronto. Appointments: Visiting Assistant Professor, Trent University, Peterborough, Ontario, Canada, 1968-69; Lecturer, Carleton University, Ottawa, Ontario, 1971-72; Lecturer, University of Victoria, British Columbia, 1972-74; Writer-in-Residence, 1976-77, Visiting Associate Professor, 1977-78, University of Alberta, Edmonton; Visiting Associate Professor, 1978-79, Professor of English, 1979-, Concordia University, Montreal, Quebec; General Editor, Studies in Canadian Literature series. Publications: 20th Century Poetry and Poets, 1969, 3rd edition, 1985; 15 Canadian Poets (editor with Phyllis Bruce), 1970, 3rd edition, 1988; Poems, 1970; Rivers Inlet (verse), 1972; Snakeroot (verse), 1973; Letter of the Master of Horse (verse), 1973; Skookum Wawa: Writings of the Canadian Northwest (editor), 1975; The Inner Ear: An Anthology of New Canadian Poets (editor), 1983; The Terracotta Army (verse), 1984; I Didn't Notice the Mountain Growing Dark (co-translator), 1985; Changes of State (verse), 1986; Vancouver: Soul of a City (editor), 1986; The Unsettling of the West (stories), 1986; Hong Kong (verse), 1987; Letters from Managua, 1990; Light of Burning Towers (verse), 1990; The Art of Short Fiction: An International Anthology, 1992; Girl By The Water, 1994; The Perfect Cold Warrior, 1995; Active Trading: Selected Poems, 1996. Honours: E J Pratt Medal; National Poetry

Prize, Canadian Authors Association; America's Best Book Award; Writers Choice Award; National Magazine Award; Archibald Lampman Prize; Milton Acorn Competition; Gabriela Mistral Prize, 1996. Address: RR 1, Dunvegan, Ontario K0C 1J0, Canada.

GEE Maggie (Mary), b. 2 Nov 1948, Poole, Dorset, England. Novelist. m. Nicholas Rankin, 1983. Education: BA, 1969, B Litt, 1972, PhD, 1980, Somerville College, Oxford. Appointments: Research Assistant, Wolverhampton Polytechnic, 1975-79; Eastern Arts Writing Fellow, University of East Anglia, 1982; Honorary Visiting Fellow, Sussex University, 1986-; Hawthornden Fellow and Booker Prize Judge, 1989; Member, Management Committee, Society of Authors, 1991-94; Fellow, Royal Society of Literature, 1994; Northern Arts Writer-in-Residence, University of Northumbria, 1996. Publications: Dying, In Other Words, 1981; The Burning Book, 1983; Light Years, 1985; Grace, 1988; Where Are the Snows, 1991; Lost Children, 1994. Address: c/o Gillon Aitken, Aitken & Stone, 29 Fernshaw Road, London SW10 0TG, England.

GEE Maurice Gough, b. 22 Aug 1931, Whakatane, New Zealand. Writer. Education: MA, University of Auckland, 1954. Appointments: Robert Burns Fellow, University of Otago, 1964; Writing Fellow, Victoria University of Wellington, 1989; Katherine Mansfield Fellow, Menton, France, 1992. Publications: Plumb, 1978; Meg, 1981; Sole Survivor, 1983; Collected Stories, 1986; Prowlers, 1987; The Burning Boy, 1990; Going West, 1993; Crime Story, 1994;Loving Ways, 1996; Eight novels for children. Honours: New Zealand Book Awards, 1976, 1979, 1981, 1991, 1993; James Tait Black Memorial Prize, 1979; Hon DLitt, Victoria University of Wellington, 1987. Membership: PEN (New Zealand Centre), National Vice-President, 1990-91. Address: 41 Chelmsford Street, Ngaio, Wellington, New Zealand.

GEE Shirley, b. 25 Apr 1932, London, England. Dramatist. m. Donald Gee, 30 Jan 1965, 2 sons. Education: Webber-Douglas Academy of Music and Drama. Publications: Stones, 1974; Moonshine, 1977; Typhoid Mary, 1979; Bedrock, 1982; Never in My Lifetime, 1983; Flights, 1984; Long Live the Babe, 1985; Ask for the Moon, 1986; Against the Wind, 1988; Warrior, 1989. Other: Stage adaptations, including The Forsyte Saga (co-adapter); Children's poems, stories and songs. Honours: Radio Times Drama Bursary Award, 1974; Pye Award, 1979; Jury's Special Commendation, Prix Italia, 1979; Giles Cooper Awards, 1979, 1983; Sony Award, 1983; Samuel Beckett Award, 1984; Susan Smith Blackburn Prize, 1985. Memberships: Society of Authors; Writers Guild. Address: c/o Shiel Lane Associates Ltd, 43 Doughty Street, London WC1N 2LF, England.

GEERTZ Clifford (James), b. 23 Aug 1926, San Francisco, California, USA. Professor of Social Science; Writer. m. (1) Hildred Storey, 30 Oct 1948, div 1982, 1 son, 1 daughter, (2) Karen Blu, 1987. Education: AB, Antioch College, 1950; PhD, Harvard University, 1956. Appointments: Research Assistant, 1952-56, Research Associate, 1957-58, Massachusetts Institute of Technology; Instructor and Research Associate, Harvard University, 1956-57; Fellow, Center for Advanced Study in the Behavioral Sciences, Stanford, 1958-59; Assistant Professor of Anthropology, University of California at Berkeley, 1958-60; Assistant Professor, 1960-61, Associate Professor, 1962-64, Professor, 1964-68, Divisional Professor, 1968-70, University of Chicago; Senior Research Career Fellow, National Institute for Mental Health, 1964-70; Professor of Social Science, 1970-, Harold F Linder Professor of Social Science, 1982-, Institute for Advanced Study, Princeton, New Jersey; Visiting Lecturer with Rank of Professor, Princeton University, 1975-; Various guest lectureships. Publications: The Religion of Java, 1960; Old Societies and New States (editor), 1963; Agricultural Involution, the Processes of Ecological Change in Indonesia, 1963; Peddlers and Princes, 1963; The Social History of an Indonesian Town, 1965; Person, Time and Conduct in Bali: An Essay in Cultural Analysis, 1966; Islam Observed: Religious Development in Morocco and Indonesia, 1968; The Interpretation of Cultures: Selected Essays, 1973; Myth, Symbol and Culture (editor), 1974; Kinship in Bali (with Hildred Geertz), 1975; Meaning and Order in Moroccan Society (with Hildred Geertz and Lawrence Rosen), 1979; Negara: The Theatre State in Nineteenth Century Bali, 1980; Local Knowledge: Further Essays in Interpretive Anthropology, 1983; Bali, interprétation d'une culture, 1983; Works and Lives: The Anthropologist as Author, 1988; After the Fact: Two Countries, Four Decades, One Anthropologist, 1995. Contributions to: Scholarly books and journals. Honours: Talcott Parsons Prize, American Academy of Arts and Sciences, 1974; Sorokin Prize,

American Sociological Association, 1974; Distinguished Lecturer, American Anthropological Association, 1983; Huxley Memorial Lecturer and Medalist, Royal Anthropological Institute, 1983; Distinguished Scholar Award, Association for Asian Studies, 1987; National Book Critics Circle Prize in Criticism, 1988; Horace Mann Distinguished Alumnus Award, Antioch College, 1992; Fukuoka Asian Cultural Prize, 1992. Memberships: American Academy of Arts and Sciences, fellow; American Association for the Advancement of Science, fellow; American Philosophical Society, fellow; British Academy, corresponding fellow; Council on Foreign Relations, fellow; National Academy of Sciences, fellow; Royal Anthropological Institute, honorary fellow. Address: c/o School of Social Science, Institute for Advanced Study, Princeton, NJ 08540, USA.

GEISMAR L(udwig) L(eo), b. 25 Feb 1921, Mannheim, Germany. Professor of Social Work and Sociology; Writer. m. Shirley Ann Cooperman, 18 Sept 1948, 3 daughters. Education: BA, 1947, MA, 1950, University of Minnesota; PhD, Hebrew University, Jerusalem, 1956. Appointments: Coordinator of Social Research, Ministry of Social Welfare, Israel, 1954-56; Research Director, Family Centred Project, St Paul, Minnesota, USA, 1956-59; Associate Professor, 1959-62, Professor, Social Work and Sociology, Director, Social Work Research Center, Graduate School of Social Work and Department of Sociology, 1963-91, Rutgers University. Publications: Understanding the Multi-Problem Family: A Conceptual Analysis and Exploration in Early Identification (with M A LaSorte), 1964; The Forgotten Neighborhood: Site of an Early Skirmish in the War on Poverty (with J Krisberg), 1967; Preventive Intervention in Social Work, 1969; Family and Community Functioning, 1971; Early Supports for Family Life, 1972; 555 Families: A Social Psychological Study of Young Families in Transition, 1973; Families in an Urban Mold (with S Geismar), 1979; A Quarter Century of Social Work Education (editor with M Dinerman), 1984; Family and Delinquency: Resocializing the Young Offender (with K Wood), 1986; Families at Risk (with K Wood), 1989; The Family Functioning Scale: A Guide to Research and Practice (with M Camasso), 1993. Address: 347 Valentine Street, Highland Park, NJ 08904, USA.

GELBART Larry (Simon), b. 25 Feb 1928, Chicago, Illinois, USA. Writer. m. Pat Marshall, 25 Nov 1956, 3 sons, 2 daughters. Publications: Co-author: A Funny Thing Happened on the Way to the Forum (musical comedy), 1963; Tootsie (screenplay), 1984; Mastergate (play), 1989; Author: City of Angels (musical), 1989; The Wrong Box (screenplay); Oh, God (screenplay); Movie, Movie (screenplay). Developed and wrote for TV: MASH series; Barbarians at the Gate, 1993. Contributions to: Harper's Bazaar, 1993-94. Address: 9255 Sunset Boulevard, Suite 404, Los Angeles, CA 90069, USA.

GÉLINAS Gratien, b. 8 Dec 1909, Saint-Tite, Quebec, Canada. Dramatist; Actor; Director. m. (1) Simone Lalonde, 1935, dec 1967, 4 sons, 1 daughter, (2) Huguette Oligny, 1973. Education: Graduated, Collège de Montréal, 1929. Appointments: Actor, creator of the character Fridolin in 9 revues, 1938-46; Founder, Comédie-Canadienne, Montreal, 1957. Publications: Tit-Coq, 1950, English translation, 1967; Bousille et les justes, 1960, English translation as Bousille and the Just, 1961; Yesterday the Children Were Dancing, 1967; Les Fridolinades, 1945 et 1946, 1980; Les Fridolinades, 1943 et 1944, 1981; Les Fridolinades, 1941 et 1942, 1981; La Passion de Narcisse Mondoux, 1987, English translation as The Passion of Narcisse Mondoux, 1992; Les Fridolinades, 1938, 1939, 1940, 1988. Honours: Grand Prix, Dramatists Society, 1949; Film of the Year Award, 1953; Honorary LLD, University of Saskatchewan, 1966, McGill University, 1968, University of New Brunswick, 1969, Trent University, 1970, Mount Allison University, 1973; Victor Morin Prize, 1967. Memberships: Canada Film Development Corporation, chairman, 1969-78; Canada Theatre Institute, president, 1959-60; National Theatre School of Canada, founding member, 1960; Royal Society of Canada. Address: 316 Girouard Street, Box 207, Oka, Quebec J0N 1E0, Canada.

GELLIS Roberta Leah, (Max Daniels, Priscilla Hamilton, Leah Jacobs), b. 27 Sept 1927, Brooklyn, New York, USA. Author. m. Charles Gellis, 14 Apr 1947, 1 son. Education: BA, Hunter College, 1947; MS, Brooklyn Polytechnic Institute, 1952. Appointments: Copy Editor, McGraw Hill Book Company, 1953-55; Freelance Editor, 1955-. Publications: Knight's Honor, 1964; Bonds of Blood, 1965; The Dragon and the Rose, 1977; The Sword and the Swan, 1977; The Space Guardian (as Max Daniels), 1978; The Roselynde Chronicles series:

Roselynde, 1978, Alinor, 1978, Joanna, 1979, Gilliane, 1980, Rhiannon, 1982, Sybelle, 1983; Offworld (as Max Daniels), 1979; The Love Token (as Priscilla Hamilton), 1979; The Royal Dynasty series: Siren Song, 1980, Winter Song, 1982, Fire Song, 1984, A Silver Mirror, 1989; The Napoleonic Era series: The English Heiress, 1980, The Cornish Heiress, 1981, The Kent Heiress, 1982, Fortune's Bride, 1983, A Woman's Estate, 1984; Tales of Jernaeve series: Tapestry of Dreams, 1985, Fires of Winter, 1986, Irish Magic, 1995, Shimmering Splendor, 1995, Enchanted Fire, 1996, Irish Magic II, 1997. Address: PO Box 483, Roslyn Heights, NY 11577, USA.

GENOVESE Eugene D(ominick), b. 19 May 1930, New York, New York, USA. Historian. m. Elizabeth Ann Fox, 6 June 1969. Education: BA, Brooklyn College, 1953; MA, 1955, PhD, 1959, Columbia University. Publications: The Political Economy of Slavery, 1965; The World the Slaveholders Made, 1969; From Rebellion to Revolution, 1979; The Slaveholders Dilemma, 1991; The Southern Tradition, 1994; The Southern Front, 1995. Honours: American Academy of the Arts Award, 1975; Bancroft Prize, 1994. Membership: American Academy of Arts and Science. Address: 1482 Sheridan Walk, Atlanta, GA 30324, USA.

GENSLER Kinereth Dushkin, b. 17 Sept 1922, New York, New York, USA. Poet; Teacher. Widow, 2 sons, 1 daughter. Education: BA, University of Chicago, 1943; MA, Columbia University, 1946. Appointment: Editor, Alice James Books, 1976-90. Publications: Threesome Poems, 1976; The Poetry Connection (co-author), 1978; Without Roof, 1981; Journey Fruit, 1997; Book chapters: Dream Poems in Broad Daylight, 1975; Poetry and the Impossible, 1988; Poems in anthologies: Best Poems of 1975. Contributions to: Journals and periodicals. Honours: Members Award, Poetry Society of America, 1969; Power Dalton Award, New England Poetry Club, 1971; Borestone Mountain Award, 1973; Residency, Ragdale, 1981; Residency, MacDowell Colony, 1982, 1983. Memberships: Academy of American Poets; Alice James Cooperative Society; New England Poetry Club; Poetry Society of America. Address: 221 Mt Auburn Street, Cambridge, MA 02138, USA.

GENTLE Mary Rosalyn, b. 29 Mar 1956, Sussex, England. Writer. Education: BA, English, Politics, Geography, 1985, MA, 17th Century Studies, 1988; MA, War Studies, 1995. Publications: A Hawk in Silver, 1977; Golden Witchbreed, 1983; Ancient Light, 1987; Scholars and Soldiers, 1989; Rats and Gargoyles, 1990; The Architecture of Desire, 1991; Grunts!, 1992; Left to His Own Devices, 1994; Co-editor, Midnight Rose/Penguin Books anthologies: The Weerde Book 1, 1992; Villains!, 1992; The Weerde Book 2, The Book of the Ancients, 1993. Contributions to: Review Column, Interzone, Washington Post book reviews. Memberships: Society of Authors; British Science Fiction Association. Literary Agent: Maggie Noach, The Maggie Noach Literary Agency, 21 Redan Street, London W14 0AB, England. Address: 29 Sish Lane, Stevenage, Herts, England.

GENTRY Robert Bryan, b. 21 July 1936, Knoxville, Tennessee, USA. Writer; Educator. m. Mary Sue Koeppel, 31 May 1980, 2 sons. Education: BS, 1958, MA, 1966, University of Tennessee; US Army Language School, 1959; Graduate work: University of Georgia, 1968-72; University of New Hampshire, 1977. Appointments: Professor of Humanities, Florida Community College, 1972-; Editor, Riverside-Avondale Historic Preservation Publication, 1975-76; College Historian, Florida Community College, 1988-91. Publications: The Rise of the Hump House, novel, 1976; A College Tells Its Story: An Oral History of Florida Community College at Jacksonville, 1963-1991, 1991. Contributions to: A Diarist's Journal; Kalliope: A Journal of Women's Art; Teaching English in the Two-Year College. Honours: Professor of the Year, Florida Community College, 1985; Prize Winner, Quest for Peace Writing Contest, University of California, 1988; Nominated for National Pushcart Award, 1989; Award, National Endowment in the Humanities, 1993. Memberships: Community College Humanities Association; US English. Address: 3879 Oldfield Trail, Jacksonville, FL 32223, USA.

GEORGE Barbara. See: KATZ Bobbi.

GEORGE Elizabeth, b. 26 Feb 1949, Warren, Ohio, USA. Author. m. Jay Toibin, 28 May 1971, div 11 Nov 1995. Education: AA, Foothill Community College, 1969; BA, University of California at Riverside, 1970; MS, California State University, 1979. Appointment: Teacher of Creative Writing, Coastline College, Costa Mesa, California, 1988-. Publications: A Great Deliverance, 1988; Payment in Blood, 1989; Well-Schooled in Murder, 1990; A Suitable Vengeance, 1991; For the Sake of Elena, 1992; Missing Joseph, 1993; Playing for the Ashes, 1994; In the Presence of the Enemy, 1996. Honours: Anthony Award, 1989; Agatha Award, 1989; Grand Prix de Littérature Policière, 1990. Address: c/o Deborah Schneider, 250 West 57th Street, New York, NY 10107, USA.

GEORGE Emily. See: **KATZ Bobbi.**

GEORGE Jean Craighead, b. 21 July 1919, Washington, District of Columbia, USA. Author; Illustrator. m. John L George, 28 Jan 1944, div 1963, 2 sons, 1 daughter. Education: BA, Pennsylvania State University. Appointments: Reporter, Washington Post, 1943-46; Roving Editor, Reader's Digest, 1965-84. Publications: My Side of the Mountain, 1959; Summer of the Falcon, 1962; The Thirteen Moons, 1967-69; Julie of the Wolves, 1972; Going to the Sun, 1976; Wounded Wolf, 1978; The American Walk Book, 1978; River Rats, 1979; The Grizzly Bear with the Golden Ears, 1982; The Cry of the Crow, 1982; Journey Inward, 1982; Talking Earth, 1983; How to Talk to Your Animals, 1985; Water Sky, 1987; One Day in the Woods, 1988, as musical, 1989; Shark Beneath the Reef, 1989; On the Far Side of the Mountain, 1990; One Day in a Tropical Rain Forest, 1990; Missing 'Gator of Gumbo Limbo, 1992; The Fire Bug Connection, 1993; Dear Rebecca Winter is Here, 1993; The First Thanksgiving, 1993; Julie, 1994; Animals Who Have Won Our Love, 1994; The Tarantula in My Purse, 1996; Look to the North, 1997; Julie's Wolf Pack, 1997. Address: 20 William Street, Chappaqua, NY 10514, USA.

GEORGE Jonathan. See: **BURKE John Frederick.**

GEORGE Kathleen Elizabeth, b. 7 July 1943, Johnstown, Pennsylvania, USA. Associate Professor. Education: BA, 1964; MA, 1966; PhD, 1975, MFA, 1988. Appointment: Associate Professor, University of Pittsburgh Theatre Department. Publications: Rhythm in Drama; Playwriting: The First Workshop, 1994. Contributions to: Mademoiselle Magazine; Cimarron Review; Great Stream; Gulf Stream; Alaska Quarterly; West Branch; North American Review; Other Voices. Honours: Louise Laetitia Miele Writing Award; Best American Short Stories: Honours List; Finalist, Pirates Alley Contest. Memberships: Poets and Writers; Association for Theater in Higher Education; Associated Writing Programs; Theater Communication Group; Dramatists Guild. Literary Agent: Kit Ward. Address: 1617 CL, University of Pittsburgh, Pittsburgh, PA 15260, USA.

GEORGEOGLOU Nitsa-Athina, b. 4 Sept 1922, Athens, Greece. Author. m. 9 Nov 1947, 2 sons. Education: Graduate: Greek Gymasium, 1938; Superior Studies, French Institute of Athens. Publications: Once in Missolonghi, 1971; The Secret Society, 1973; A Ship Called Hope, 1975; Enterprise Archemides, 1977; Toto is My Guest, 1977; Waves and Islands, 1978; The Wrath of the Earth, 1978; Up the Hill, 1979; Vravron, before the Christian Era, 1980; Chronicle of Thyateira, 1981; The Horse Farm, 1981; The Golden Coin, 1982; Saturn Calling, 1984; On Foreign Land, 1985; The Will of Youth, 1987; Uranus Calling, 1987; Walking Through the Centuries, 1987; Difficult Steps, 1988; The Gods of Olympus, 1988; The Three S's, 1989; Adventure in Athens, 1990; Soldiers for Fun, 1991; Sealed Envelopes, 1992; Sunrise, 1993; On the Wings of Youth, 1993; Written on the Waves, 1994; Storm and Lull, 1994. Contributions to: Numerous journals and magazines. Honours: Woman's Literary Committee of Athens Award, 1969, 1970, 1971, 1979, 1980, 1981, 1985, 1992; Circle of Greek Children's Book Authors Award, 1970, 1977, 1978; Hans Christian Anderson Honour List, 1982; National Award for the best book for Youth for the year 1989, awarded in 1992. Memberships: National Society of Greek Authors; Greek IBBY; Vice President, Greek Union, International Soroptimist; Hestia Cultural Club. Address: 83 Plastira Street, 171 21 Nea Smirni, Athens, Greece.

GERDES Eckhard, b. 17 Nov 1959, Atlanta, Georgia, USA. Novelist; Playwright; Educator. m. Persis Alisa Wilhelm, 30 Jan 1988, 3 sons. Education: BA, hons, English, University of Dubuque, Iowa, 1988; MA, English, Roosevelt University, Chicago, 1994. Appointments: Instructor, University of Alaska, Anchorage, 1988-90; Co-Director, Dreamer's Fiction Reading Series, Chicago, 1991-92; Lecturer, Roosevelt University, 1994-; Editor, Journal of Experimental Fiction, 1994-. Publications: Projections, 1986; Truly Fine Citizen, 1989; Ring in a River, 1994. Contributions to: Rampike; Oyez Review; Coe Review; Tomorrow Magazine; Planet Roc; Strong Coffee; No Magazine; Random Weirdness. Honours: Richard Pike Bissell

Creative Writing Awards, 1987, 1988. Membership: COSMEP. Address: 2909 Colfax Street, Evanston, IL 60201, USA.

GERRISH Brian Albert, b. 14 Aug 1931, London, England. University Professor. m. (1) 1 son, 1 daughter, (2) Dawn Ann De Vries, 3 Aug 1990, 1 daughter. Education: BA, 1952, MA, 1956, Queens' College, Cambridge; STM, Union Theological Seminary, New York City, 1956; PhD, Columbia University, 1958. Appointments: Associate Professor, Historical, Theology, 1965-68, Professor, 1968-85, John Nuveen Professor, 1985-, Divinity School, University of Chicago; Co-Editor, Journal of Religion, 1972-85; john Nuveen Professor Emeritus, 1996-; Distinguished Service Professor of Theology, Union Theological Seminary, Virginia, 1996-. Publications: Grace and Reason: A Study in the Theology of Luther, 1962, Japanese translation, 1974, reprint, 1979; Tradition and the Modern World: Reformed Theology in the Nineteenth Century, 1978; The Old Protestantism and the New: Essays on the Reformation Heritage, 1982; A Prince of the Church: Schleiermacher and the Beginnings of Modern Theology, 1984, Korean translation, 1988; Grace and Gratitude: The Eucharistic Theology of John Calvin, 1993; Continuing the Reformation: Essays on Modern Religious Thought, 1993. Editor: The Faith of Christendom: A Source Book of Creeds and Confessions, 1963; Reformers in Profile, 1967; Reformatio Perennis: Essays on Calvin and the Reformation in Honor of Ford Lewis Battles, 1981. Address: 9142 Sycamaore Hill Place, Mechanicsville, VA 23116, USA.

GERROLD David, (born Jarrold David Friedman), b. 24 Jan 1944, Chicago, Illinois, USA. Author; Computer Columnist. Education: University of Southern California at Los Angeles; BA, California State University at Northridge. Appointments: Story Editor, TV series Land of the Lost, 1974; Computer Columnist, CIT Profiles, 1984-; Columnist, Starlos and Galileo magazines; Freelance Writer, science fiction, short stories, screenplays, TV plays. Publications: The Flying Sorcerers (with Larry Niven), 1971; Generation (editor), 1972; Space Skimmer, 1972; Yesterday's Children, 1972; When Harlie Was One, 1972; With a Finger in My I (short stories), 1972; Battle for the Planet of the Apes (novelisation of screenplay), 1973; The Man Who Folded Himself, 1973; The Trouble with Tribbles, 1973; The World of Star Trek, 1973; Deathbeast, 1978; The Galactic Whirlpool, 1980; The War Against the Chtorr: A Matter for Man, 1983; A Day for Damnation, 1984; When Harlie Was One, 1987; When Harlie Was Two, 1987. Editor with Stephen Goldin: Protostars, 1971; Science Fiction Emphasis I, 1974; Alternities, 1974; Ascents of Wonder, 1977. Address: Box 1190, Hollywood, CA 90028, USA.

GERSTLER Amy, b. 24 Oct 1956, San Diego, California, USA. Poet; Writer. Education: BA, Pitzer College. Publications: Poetry: Yonder, 1981; Christy's Alpine Inn, 1982; White Marriage/Recovery, 1984; Early Heavens, 1984; The True Bride, 1986; Bitter Angel, 1990; Nerve Storm, 1993. Fiction: Martine's Mouth, 1985; Primitive Man, 1987. Other: Past Lives (with Alexis Smith), 1989. Contributions to: Magazines. Honour: National Book Critics Circle Award, 1991. Address: c/o Viking Penguin, 375 Hudson Street, New York, NY 10014, USA.

GERVAIS C(harles) H(enry), b. 20 Oct 1946, Windsor, Ontario, Canada. Poet; Writer; Editor. m. Donna Wright, 1968, 2 sons, 1 daughter. Education: BA, University of Guelph, 1971; MA, University of Windsor, 1972. Appointments: Staff, Toronto Globe and Mail, 1966; Canadian Press, Toronto, 1967; Reporter, Daily Commercial News, Toronto, 1967; Chatham Daily News, 1972-73; Teacher of Creative Writing, St Clair College, Windsor, 1969-71; Publisher, Black Moss Press, Windsor, 1969-; Editor, Sunday Standard, Windsor, 1972; General News Reporter, 1973-74, 1976-81, Bureau Chief, 1974-76, Religion Editor, 1979-80, Book Editor, 1980-, Entertainment Writer, 1990-, Windsor Star. Publications: Poetry: Sister Saint Anne, 1968; Something, 1969; Other Marriage Vows, 1969; A Sympathy Orchestra, 1970; Bittersweet, 1972; Poems for American Daughters, 1976; The Believable Body, 1979; Up Country Lines, 1979; Silence Comes with Lake Voices, 1980; Into a Blue Morning: Selected Poems, 1982; Public Fanatasy: The Maggie T Poems, 1983; Letters From the Equator, 1986; Autobiographies, 1989; Playing God: New Poems, 1994. Other: The Rumrunners: A Prohibition Scrapbook, 1980; Voices Like Thunder, 1984; The Border Police: One Hundred and Twenty-Five Years of Policing in Windsor, 1992; Seeds in the Wilderness: Profiles of World Religious Leaders, 1994; From America Sent: Letters to Henry Miller, 1995. Editor: The Writing Life: Historical and Critical Views of the Tish Movement, 1976; Children's Books: How Bruises Lost His Secret, 1975; Doctor Troyer and the Secret in the Moonstone,

1976; If I Had a Birthday Everyday, 1983. Honours: Western Ontario Newspaper Awards, 1983, 1984, 1987. Address: 1939 Alsace Avenue, Windsor, Ontario N8W 1M5, Canada.

GEVE Thomas, 1929, Germany. Engineer. m. 1963, 1 son, 2 daughters. Education: National Diploma of Building, 1950; BSc, 1957. Publications: Youth in Chains, 1958, enlarged edition, 1981; Guns and Barbed Wire, 1987; There Are No Children Here, 1997; Aufbrueche, 1997 (English version forthcoming); Thomas Geve: Nichts als das Leben (film), 1997. Literary Agent: M J Wald, New York, USA. Address: PO Box 4727, Haifa, Israel.

GEYER Georgie Anne, b. 2 Apr 1935, Chicago, Illinois, USA. Syndicated Columnist; Author; Foreign Correspondent; Speaker; Educator. Education: BS, Journalism, Northwestern University, 1956; Fulbright Scholar, University of Vienna, 1956-57. Appointments: Reporter, 1959-64, Foreign Correspondent, 1964-75, Chicago Daily News; Syndicated Columnist: Los Angeles Times, 1975-80, Universal Press, 1980-. Publications: New Latins, 1970; The New 100 Years' War, 1972; The Young Russians, 1976; Buying the Night Flight, 1983, new edition, 1996; Guerrilla Prince, 1991; Waiting for Winter to End, 1994; Americans No More: The Death of Citizenship, 1996. Chapters in: The Responsibilities of Journalism, 1984; Beyond Reagan: The Politics of Upheaval, 1986; The Conceit of Innocence, 1997. Contributions to: Numerous journals, including: Reader's Digest, People, Kiwanis. Honours: Numerous honorary degrees and doctorates; More than 12 other honours including: Chicago Journalism Hall of Fame, 1991; Northwestern University Alumni Association Award, 1991; Society of Professional Journalists, fellow, 1992. Memberships: Chicago Council of Foreign Relations, board member, 1972-75; Center for Strategic and International Studies, Advisory Board member; Washington Institute on Foreign Affairs. Address: The Plaza, 800 25th Street North West, Washington, DC 20037, USA.

GHOSE Zulfikar, b. 1935, Sialkot, Pakistan. Author; Poet. Appointments: Cricket Correspondent, The Observer, London, England, 1960-65; Teacher, London, 1963-69. Publications: Statement Against Corpes (with B S Johnson), 1964; The Loss of India, (verse), 1964; Confessions of a Native-Alien, 1965; Jets from Orange (verse), 1967; The Violent West (verse), 1972; Penguin Modern Poets 25 (with Gavin Ewart and B S Johnson), 1974; Hamlet, Prufrock and Language, 1978; The Fiction of Reality (criticism), 1983; A Memory of Asia (poetry), 1984; Selected Poems, 1991; The Art of Creating Fiction (criticism), 1991; Shakespeare's Mortal Knowledge (criticism), 1993; Novels: The Contradictions, 1966; The Murder of Aziz Khan, 1967; The Incredible Brazilian Book 1, 1972; Crump's Terms, 1975; The Beautiful Empire, 1975; A Different World, 1978; Hulme's Investigations into the Bogart Script, 1981; A New History of Torments, 1982; Don Bueno, 1983; Figures of Enchantment, 1986; The Triple Mirror of the Self, 1992. Address: Department of English, University of Texas, Austin, TX 78712, USA.

GHOSH Ajit Kumar, b. 1 Jan 1919, Shaistanager, Noakhali, India. Professor. m. Belarani Ghosh, 20 Apr 1940, 2 sons. Education: Matriculation, 1st Division, 1934; BA, Honours in English, 2nd class, 1938; MA, Bengali, 2nd class, 1940; PhD, 1959; DLitt, 1969. Appointments: Lecturer in Bengali, M M College, Jessore, 1941-47, Surendranath College, Calcutta, 1947-63; Lecturer, Reader, then Professor, 1963-91, Dean, Faculty of Arts, Head, Department of Bengali, 1970-83, Rabindra Bharati University; Editor, Encyclopaedia of Indian Literature, 1987, Modern Indian Literature, 1987, 2nd edition, 1992, Masterpieces of Indian Literature, 1993. Publications: Many books in Bengali. Contributions to: Over 50 scholarly articles to various magazines and journals. Honours: Dwijendralal Roy Reader, Rammohan Roy Lecturer, Dineschandra Sen Lecturer, Calcutta University. Memberships: President, Bangiya Sahitya Parishad; Bangla Akademi; Natya Akademi; Senate, Calcutta University; Court, Rabindra Bharati University; President, Calcutta Film Circle; President, Natya Vicharak Samiti. Address: AE 510, Salt Lake, Calcutta 700064, India.

GHOSH Oroon Kumar, b. 22 Aug 1917, Calcutta, India. Civil Servant. m. Rekha Majurndar, 29 June 1943. 1 daughter. Education: Bachelor of Science, Rangoon University, 1938; Delhi University, 1953. Appointment: Editorial Director, Minerva Associates, 1976-90. Publications: Tales from the Indian Classics; The Dance of Shiva and Other Tales From India; Science, Society and Philosophy; Convergence of Civilizations; How India Won Freedom. Contributions to: Radical Humanist; World History Bulletin; Jijnasa. Memberships:

PEN; Royal Asiatic Society; International Society for the Comparative Study of Civilizations; World History Association. Address: CD 6 Sector I, Salt Lake, Calcutta 700064, India.

GIBSON Charles E(dmund), b. 16 Dec 1916, England. Children's Writer. Education: Wandsworth Training College, London. Publications: The Story of the Ship, 1948; The Secret Tunnel, 1948; Wandering Beauties, 1960; The Clash of Fleets, 1961; Knots and Splices, 1962; Plain Sailing, 1963; Daring Prows, 1963; Be Your Own Weatherman, 1963; The Two Olafs of Norway, 1964; With a Cross on Their Shields, 1964; The Ship with Five Names, 1965; Knots and Splices, 1979; Death of a Phantom Raider, 1987. Literary Agent: A M Heath & Co Ltd. Address: 59 Victoria Road, Shoreham-by-Sea, Sussex BN43 5WR, England.

GIBSON Graeme C, b. 9 Aug 1934, London, Ontario, Canada. Author. m. (1) Shirley Mann, div, 2 sons, (2) Margaret Atwood, 1 daughter. Education: University of Edinburgh, 1955-56; BA, 1957, Graduate Studies, 1957-58, University of Western Ontario. Appointments: Writer-in-Residence, University of Waterloo, 1982, University of Ottawa, 1985. Publications: Five Legs, 1969; Communion, 1971; Eleven Canadian Novelists, 1973; Perpetual Motion, 1983; Gentleman Death, 1993. Contributions to: Various. Honours: Toronto Arts Award, 1990; Order of Canada, 1992; Harbour Front Festival Prize, 1993. Memberships: Writers Union of Canada, Chairman 1974-75; PEN, President 1987-89. Literary Agent: Charlotte Sheedy Agency, 611 Broadway, #428, New York, NY 10012, USA. Address: c/o Writers Union, 24 Ryerson Avenue, Toronto, Ontario M5T 2P3, Canada.

GIBSON Helen Alice, b. 9 Oct 1910, Forbes, Nne South Wales, Australia. Kindergarten Teacher (Retired). Education: Pre-school Playleaders Certificate. Publications: An Australian Christmas, 1961; Buster the Fire Truck, 1962; Woorayl, The Lyrebird, 1987; Story in the Breakfast Bird (an anthology), 1987; Discovery, 1989. Contributions to: Puffinalia, New South Wales School Magazine; Short Story International, Student 1984, 1986; Seedling, 1984, 1993. Honours: 1st, 2nd and 4th prizes for children's stories in various competitions. Memberships: Society of Women Writers, Victoria; Fellowship of Australian Writers. Address: Meringo, 20 Mt Morton Road, Belgrave South 3160, Australia.

GIBSON Josephine. See: JOSLIN Sesyle.

GIBSON Margaret, b. 4 June 1948, Toronto, Ontario, Canada. Poet; Writer. m. S Silboord, separated, 1 son. Education: High School, Toronto. Publications: Lunes: Poems, 1973; On the Cutting Edge, 1976; The Butterfly Ward, 1977; Considering the Condition, 1978; Signs: Poems, 1979; Long Walks in the Afternoon, 1982; Memories of the Future: The Daybooks of Tina Modotti, 1986; Out in the Open, 1989; The Vigil: A Poem in 4 Voices, 1993. Honours: Literary Award, City of Toronto, 1976; Melville Cane Award, 1988. Address: c/o Louisiana State University Press, PO Box 25053, Baton Rouge, LA 70894, USA.

GIBSON Morgan, b. 6 June 1929, Cleveland, Ohio, USA. Poet; Writer; Professor. m. (1) Barbara Gibson, 1950, div 1972, 2 daughters, (2) Keiko Matsui, 1978, 1 son. Education: BA, Oberlin College, 1950; MA, 1952, PhD, 1959, University of Iowa. Appointment: Professor of English, Kanda University of International Studies. Publications: Revolutionary Rexroth: Poet of East West Wisdom; Tantric Poetry of Kukai; Among Buddhas in Japan; The Great Brook Book; Speaking of Light. Address: 5-202 Flat Fukuju, 1-2 Hongo-cho, Naka-ku, Yokohama 231, Japan.

GIBSON Walter Samuel, b. 31 Mar 1932, Columbus, Ohio, USA. Professor of the Humanities; Writer. Education: BFA, 1957, MA, 1960, Ohio State University; PhD, Harvard University, 1969. Appointments: Assistant Professor, 1966-71, Associate Professor, 1971-78, Acting Chairman, 1970-71, Chairman, 1971-79, Department of Art, Andrew W Mellon Professor of the Humanities, 1978-, Case Western Reserve University; Murphy Lecturer, University of Kansas and the Nelson-Atkins Museum of Art, 1988; Clark Visiting Professor of Art History, Williams College, 1989, 1992. Publications: Hieronymus Bosch, 1973; The Paintings of Cornelis Engebrechtsz, 1977; Bruegel, 1977; Hieronymus Bosch: An Annotated Bibliography, 1983; "Mirror of the Earth": The World Landscape in Sixteenth-Century Flemish Painting, 1989; Peter Bruegel the Elder: Two Studies, 1991. Contributions to: Scholarly books and journals. Honours: Fulbright

Scholarship, 1960-61, 1984; Guggenheim Fellowship, 1978-79; Fellow-in-Residence, Netherlands Institute for Advanced Study, Wasenaar, 1995-96. Memberships: American Association of Netherlandic Studies; College Art Association; Historians of Netherlandish Art; Midwest Art History Society; Renaissance Society of America; Society for Emblem Studies; Société Internationale pour l'Etude du Théâtre Medieval; Vereeniging van Nederlandse Kunsthistorici. Address: c/o Department of Art, Case Western Reserve University, Cleveland OH 44106, USA.

GIBSON William (Ford), b. 1948, Conway, South Carolina, USA. Author. m. Deborah Thompson, June 1972, 1 son, 1 daughter. Education: BA, University of British Columbia, 1977. Publications: Neuromancer, 1984; Count Zero, 1985; Burning Chrome, 1986; Mona Lisa Overdrive, 1987; Dream Jumbo, 1989; The Difference Engine, 1990; Virtual Light, 1993. Contributions to: Omni; Rolling Stone; Science Fiction Review. Honours: Hugo Award, 1983; Nebula Awards, 1984; Philip K Dick Award, 1984; Porgie Award, 1985; Ditmer Award, Australia. Address: c/o Martha Millard Literary Agency, 204 Park Avenue, Madison, NJ 07940, USA.

GIFFORD Barry Colby, b. 18 Oct 1946, Chicago, Illinois, USA. Writer. m. Mary Lou Nelson, 23 Oct 1970, 1 son, 1 daughter. Education: University of Missouri, 1964-65; Cambridge University, 1966. Publications: Jack's Book (co-author), biography, 1978; Port Tropique, 1980; Landscape with Traveler, 1980; The Neighborhood of Baseball, 1981; Devil Thumbs A Ride, 1988; Ghosts No Horse Can Carry, 1989; Wild at Heart, 1990; Sailor's Holiday, 1991; New Mysteries of Paris, 1991; A Good Man to Know, 1992; Night People, 1992; Arise and Walk, 1994; Hotel Room Trilogy, 1995; Baby Cat-Face, 1995; The Phantom Father, 1997; Lost Highway (co-author), 1997; Flaubert at Key West, 1997. Contributions to: Punch; Esquire; Rolling Stone. Honours: Notable Book Awards, American Library Association, 1978, 1988; National Endowment for the Arts Fellowship, 1982; Maxwell Perkins Award, PEN, 1983; Syndicated Fiction Award, PEN, 1987; Premio Brancati, Italy, 1993. Literary Agent: Peter Ginsberg, President, Curtis Brown Ltd, 10 Astor Place, New York, NY 10003, USA. Address: 1814 Sonoma Avenue, Berkeley, CA 94707, USA.

GIFFORD Denis, b. 26 Dec 1927, London, England. Author; Cartoonist. div., 1 daughter. Appointment: Art Assistant, Reynolds News, 1944-45. Publications: Pictorial History of Horror Movies, 1973; British Comic Catalogue 1874-1974, 1974; British Film Catalogue 1895-1980, 1980; International Book of Comics, 1984; Golden Age of Radio, 1985; Encyclopaedia of Comic Characters, 1987; Best of Eagle Annual 1951-59, 1989; Comic Art of Charlie Chaplin, 1989; The American Comic Book Catalogue, 1990; Books and Plays in Films, 1991. Contributions to: TV Times; Radio Times; Guardian; Times; Observer; Sunday Times; Independent; Collectors Fayre; Book Collector. Memberships: Founder, Association of Comics Enthusiasts; Co-Founder, Society of Strip Illustration; Edgar Wallace Society; Old Bill Society; Founder, Savers of Television and Radio Shows; 1940 Society. Address: 80 Silverdale, Sydenham, London SE26 4SJ, England.

GIGGAL Kenneth, (Henry Marlin, Angus Ross), b. 19 Mar 1927, Dewsbury, Yorkshire, England. Publications: The Manchester Thing, 1970; The Huddersfield Job, 1971; The London Assignment, 1972; The Dunfermline Affair, 1973; The Bradford Business, 1974; The Amsterdam Diversion, 1974; The Leeds Fiasco, 1975; The Edinburgh Exercise, 1975; The Ampurias Exchange, 1976; The Aberdeen Conundrum, 1977; The Congleton Lark, 1979; The Hamburg Switch, 1980; A Bad April, 1980; The Menwith Tangle, 1982; The Darlington Jaunt, 1983; The Luxembourg Run, 1985; Doom Indigo, 1986; The Tyneside Ultimatum, 1988; Classic Sailing Ships, 1988; The Greenham Plot, 1989; The Leipzig Manuscript, 1990; The Last One, 1992; John Worsley's War, 1992; Scripts and Films for TV. Contributions to: Many magazines, national and international. Honour: Truth Prize for Fiction, 1954. Memberships: Savage Club; Arms and Armour Society. Literary Agent: Andrew Mann Ltd. Address: The Old Granary, Bishop Monkton, Near Harrogate, North Yorkshire, England.

GIGUERE Diane Liliane, b. 6 Dec 1937, Montreal, Quebec, Canada. Author. Education: College Marie de France, 1941; Conservatory of Dramatic Arts, 1954-56. Publications: Le Temps des Jeux, 1961; L'eau est Profonde, 1965; Dans Les Ailes du vent, 1976; L'Abandon, 1993. Honours: Pri du Cercle du Livre de France, 1961; Guggenheim Fellowship Award, 1969; France Quebec Prize, 1977.

Memberships: Writers' Union, Quebec; Association of French Speaking Writers at Home and Overseas. Address: 60 rue William Paul 304, Ile des Soeurs, Quebec H3E 1M6, Canada.

GIL David Georg, b. 16 Mar 1924, Vienna, Austria. Professor of Social Policy; Director, Center for Social Change; Author. m. Eva Breslauer, 2 Aug 1947, 2 sons. Education: Certificate in Psychotherapy with Children, Israeli Society for Child Psychiatry, 1952; Diploma in Social Work, School of Social Work, 1953, BA, 1957, Hebrew University, Jerusalem, Israel; MSW, 1958, DSW, 1963, University of Pennsylvania. Appointment: Professor of Social Policy, Brandeis University. Publications: Violence Against Children, 1970; Unraveling Social Policy, 1973, 5th edition, 1992; The Challenge of Social Equality, 1976; Beyond the Jungle, 1979; Child Abuse and Violence (editor), 1979; Toward Social and Economic Justice (editor with Eva Gil), 1985; The Future of Work (editor, with Eva Gil), 1987. Contributions to: Over 50 articles to professional journals, book chapters, book reviews. Address: Heller Graduate School, Brandeis University, Waltham, MA 02254, USA.

GILB Dagoberto G, b. 31 July 1950, Los Angeles, California, USA. Writer. m. Rebeca Santos, 1978, 2 sons. Education: BA, MA, University of California. Appointments: Visiting Writer, University of Texas, 1988-89; Visiting Writer, University of Arizona, 1992-93, University of Wyoming, 1994. Publications: Winners on the Pass Line, 1985; The Magic of Blood, 1993; The Last Known Residence of Mickey Acuña, 1994. Honours: James D Phelan Award; Dobie Paisano Fellowship; Creative Writing Fellowship, National Endowment for the Arts; Whiting Writers Award, 1993; Best Book of Fiction Award, Texas Institute of Letters, 1993; Ernest Hemingway Foundation Award, 1994. Memberships: Texas Institute of Letters; PEN. Literary Agent: Kim Witherspoon. Address: PO Box 31001, El Paso, TX 79931, USA.

GILBERT Anna. See: LAZARUS Marguerite.

GILBERT Bentley Brinkerhoff, b. 5 Apr 1924, Mansfield, Ohio, USA. Professor of History; Writer. Education: AB, Honours in History, Miami University, Oxford, Ohio, 1949; MA, University of Cincinnati, 1950; PhD, University of Wisconsin, 1954. Appointments: Faculty, University of Cincinnati, Colorado College, 1955-67; Faculty, Professor of History, 1967-, University of Illinois at Chicago; Editor, Journal of British Studies, 1978-83. Publications: The Evolution of National Insurance in Great Britain: The Origins of the Welfare State, 1966; Britain Since 1918, 1967, revised edition, 1980; British Social Policy, 1970; David Lloyd George: A Political Life, Vol I, The Architect of Change 1863-1912, 1987, Vol II, The Organiser of Victory, 1912-1916, 1992; Britain, 1914-1945: The Aftermath of Power, 1996. Contributions to: Reference works and professional journals. Honours: Guggenheim Fellowship, 1973-74; Society of Midland Authors Biography Prize, 1993; Various grants. Memberships: North American Conference on British Studies; Royal Historical Society, fellow. Address: c/o Department of History University of Illinois at Chicago, Chicago, IL 60607, USA.

GILBERT Harriett Sarah, b. 25 Aug 1948, London, England. Writer. Education: Diploma, Rose Bruford College of Speech and Drama, 1966-69. Appointments: Co-Books Editor, City Limits magazine, 1981-83; Deputy Literary Editor, 1983-86, Literary Editor, 1986-88, New Statesman; Lecturer in Journalism, City University, London, 1992-. Publications: I Know Where I've Been, 1972; Hotels with Empty Rooms, 1973; An Offence Against the Persons, 1974; Tide Race, 1977; Running Away, 1979; The Riding Mistress, 1983; A Women's History of Sex, 1987; The Sexual Imagination (editor), 1993. Contributions to: Time Out; City Limits; New Statesman; Guardian; BBC; Australian Broadcasting Corporation; Washington Post; BBC World Service Radio. Memberships: Writers Guild of Great Britain. Literary Agent: Richard Scott Simon. Address: 2 Oaktree Court, Valmar Road, London SE5 9NH, England.

GILBERT Ilsa, b. 27 Apr 1933, Brooklyn, New York, USA. Poet; Playwright; Librettist; Lyricist. Education: University of Michigan, 1951-52; BA, Brooklyn College, 1955. Appointments: Editor, Copywriter, Creative Director, various companies, 1955-68; Freelance Copywriter, Vantage Press, 1962-79. Publications: Pardon the Prisoner, mini-play, 1976; Survivors and Other New York Poems, 1985; Rooms to Let Live; 45 productions, staged readings, various 1-act plays, verse plays, musicals, concert pieces for theatre, mainly Off-Off Broadway, New York City, including: The Bundle Man, 1967; The Dead Dentist, 1968; A Dialogue Between Didey Warbucks and

Mama Vaseline, 1969; Little Onion Annie, 1971; The Black Carousel (later called Berlin Blues), 1977; Travellers, 1977; Watering Holes and Garden Paths, 1983; The First Word, 1987; The Bundle Man (opera), 1993. Contributions to: Numerous magazines. Honours: Honourable Mention, Atlantic Monthly Nationwide College Poetry Contest, 1955; Best Subjective Poem published in Poet Lore, 1968; Guest Poet and Playwright, Proscenium, Cable TV, 1973; Writers Colony Residencies, Dorset, Vermont, 1982, 1986, 1987. Memberships: Pentangle Literary Society; Women's Salon; PEN American Center; Poets and Writers; Dramatists Guild; Authors League of America. Literary Agent: Claudia Menza. Address: 203 Bleecker Street, Apt 9, New York, NY 10012, USA.

GILBERT Jack, b. 17 Feb 1925, Pittsburgh, Pennsylvania, USA. Writer. Education: BA, University of Pittsburgh, 1954; MA, San Francisco State University, 1962. Appointments: University of California, Berkeley, 1958-59; Faculty, San Francisco State University, 1962-63, 1965-67, 1971; Syracuse University, 1982-83, University of San Francisco, 1985; Professor, Kyoto University, Tokyo, Japan, 1974-75; Chair, Creative Writing, University of Alabama, Tuscaloosa, 1986. Publications: Poems: Views of Jeopardy, 1962; Monolithos, 1982; Kochan, 1984. Contributions to: New Yorker; American Poetry Review; Kenyon; Poetry, Chicago; The Atlantic Monthly; The Nation; Ironwood; Iowa Review; Encounter, England; The Quarterly. Honours: Winner, Yale Younger Poets Award, 1962; Guggenheim Fellowship, 1964; National Endowment of the Arts Award, 1974; 1st Prize, American Poetry Review, 1983; Stanley Kunitz Prize, 1983. Address: 136 Montana Street, San Francisco, CA 94112, USA.

GILBERT John (Raphael), b. 8 Apr 1926, London, England. Writer. m. 3 sons. Education: Columbia University, 1941-42; BA, King's College, London, 1945. Publications: Modern World Book of Animals, 1947; Cats, Cats, Cats, 1961; Famous Jewish Lives, 1970; Myths of Ancient Rome, 1970; Pirates and Buccaneers, 1971; Highwaymen and Outlaws, 1971; Charting the Vast Pacific, 1971; National Costumes of the World, 1972; World of Wildlife, 1972-74; Miracles of Nature, 1975; Knights of the Crusades, 1978; Vikings, 1978; Prehistoric Man, 1978; Leonardo da Vinci, 1978; La Scala, 1979; Dinosaurs Discovered, 1980; Macdonald Guide to Trees, 1983; Macdonald Encyclopedia of House Plants, 1986; Theory and Use of Colour, 1986; Macdonald Encyclopedia of Roses, 1987; Gardens of Britain, 1987; Macdonald Encyclopedia of Butterflies and Moths, 1988; Trekking in the USA, 1989; Macdonald Encyclopedia of Orchids, 1989; Macdonald Encyclopedia of Bulbs, 1989; Trekking in Europe, 1990; Macdonald Encyclopedia of Herbs and Spices, 1990; Macdonald Encyclopedia of Bonsai, 1990; Macdonald Encyclopedia of Amphibians and Reptiles, 1990; Macdonald Encyclopedia of Saltwater Fishes, 1992; Decorating Chinese Porcelain, 1994. Address: 28 Lyndale Avenue, London NW2, England.

GILBERT Sir Martin (John), b. 25 Oct 1936, London, England. Historian. m. (1) Helen Constance, 1963, 1 daughter, (2) Susan Sacher, 2 sons. Education: Magdalen College, Oxford. Appointments: Senior Research Scholar, St Antony's College, Oxford, 1960-62; Visiting Lecturer, University of Budapest, 1961; Research Assistant to Senior Research Assistant to Randolph S Churchill, 1962-67; Fellow, 1962-94, Honorary Fellow, 1994-, Merton College, Oxford; Visiting Professor, University of South Carolina, 1965, University of Tel Aviv, 1979, Hebrew University of Jerusalem, 1980-, University College, London, 1995-96; Official Biographer of Sir Winston Churchill, 1968-. Publications: The Appeasers (with Richard Gott), 1963; Britain and Germany Between the Wars, 1964; The European Powers, 1900-1945, 1965; Plough My Own Furrow: The Life of Lord Allen of Hurtwood, 1965; Servant of India: A Study of Imperial Rule, 1905-1910, 1966; The Roots of Appeasement, 1966; Recent History Atlas 1860-1960, 1966; Winston Churchill, 1966; British History Atlas, 1968, 2nd edition, 1993; American History Atlas, 1968, 3rd edition, 1993; Jewish History Atlas, 1969, 5th edition, 1993; First World War Atlas, 1970, 2nd edition, 1994; Winston S Churchill, Vol III, 1914-1916, 1971, companion volume, 1973, Vol IV, 1917-1922, 1975, companion volume, 1977, Vol V, 1922-1939, 1976, companion volume, 1980, 1981, 1982, Vol VI, Finest Hour, 1939-1941, 1983, Vol VII, Road to Victory, 1986, Vol VIII, "Never Despair", 1945-1965, 1988; Russian History Atlas, 1972, 2nd edition, 1993; Sir Horace Rumbold: Portrait of a Diplomat, 1973; Churchill: A Photographic Portrait, 1974, 2nd edition, 1988; The Arab-Israeli Conflict: Its History in Maps, 1974, 6th edition, 1993; The Jews in Arab Lands: Their History in Maps, 1975; The Jews of Russia: Illustrated History Atlas, 1976; Jerusalem Illustrated History Atlas, 1977, 2nd edition, 1994; Exile and Return: The Emergence of Jewish

Statehood, 1978; Children's Illustrated Bible Atlas, 1979; Final Journey, the Fate of the Jews of Nazi Europe, 1979; Auschwitz and the Allies, 1981; Churchill's Political Philosophy, 1981; Atlas of the Holocaust, 1982, 2nd edition, 1993; The Jews of Hope: The Plight of Soviet Jewry Today, 1984; Jerusalem: Rebirth of a City, 1985; The Holocaust: The Jewish Tragedy, 1986; Shcharansky: Hero of Our Time, 1986; Second World War, 1989; Churchill: A Life, 1991; Atlas of British Charities, 1993; The Churchill War Papers, 3 volumes, 1993, 1995, 1996; In Search of Churchill, 1994; First World War, a History, 1994; The Day the War Ended: VE Day, 1945, 1995; Jerusalem in the 20th Century, 1996; The Boys: Triumph Over Adversity, 1996. Editor: A Century of Conflict: Essays Presented to A J P Taylor, 1966; Churchill, 1967; Lloyd George, 1968; Jackdaws: Winston Churchill, 1970; The Coming of War in 1939, 1973. Other: Script designer and co-author of the film Genocide, 1981; Writer and narrator, Churchill, BBC TV, 1989-91; The Day the War Ended (VE Day, 1995; Jerusalem in the Twentieth Century, 1996. Contributions to: Periodicals. Honours: Academy Award, 1981; Wolfson Award, 1983; Commander of the Order of the British Empire, 1990; Knighted, 1995. Membership: Royal Society of Literature, fellow. Address: Merton College, Oxford OX1 4JD, England.

GILBERT Michael (Francis), b. 17 July 1912, Billinghay, Lincolnshire, England. Author; Solicitor. m. Roberta Mary Marsden, 26 July 1947, 2 sons, 5 daughters. Publications: Close Quarters, 1947; They Never Looked Inside, 1948; The Doors Open, 1949; Smallbone Deceased, 1950; Death has Deep Roots, 1951; Death in Captivity, 1952; Fear to Tread, 1953; Sky High, 1955; Be Shot for Sixpence, 1956; The Tichborn Claimant, 1957; Blood and Judgement, 1958; After the Fine Weather, 1963; The Crack in the Teacup, 1965; The Dust and the Heat, 1967; Game Without Rules (stories), 1967; The Etruscan Net, 1969; The Body of a Girl, 1972; The Ninety Second Tiger, 1973; Amateur in Violence (stories), 1973; Flash Point, 1975; The Night of the Twelfth, 1976; Petrella at Q (stories), 1977; The Empty House, 1978; Death of a Favourite Girl (in US as The Killing of Katie Steelstock), 1980; Mr Calder and Mr Behrens (stories), 1982; The Final Throw (in US as End-Game), 1982; The Black Seraphim, 1983; The Long Journey Home, 1985; The Oxford Book of Legal Anecdotes, 1986; Trouble, 1987; Paint Gold & Blood, 1989; Anything for a Quiet Life, 1991; Prep School (anthology), 1991; Roller-Coaster, 1993. Honours: Lauréat de Grand Prix de Littérature Policière, 1957; Grand Master, Swedish DeKarademins, 1981; Grand Master, Mystery Writers of America, 1987; Crime Writers Association Cartier Diamond Dagger, 1994. Memberships: Garrick Club; HAC, Crime Writers Association. Address: Luddesdown Old Rectory, Gravesend, Kent DA13 0XE, England.

GILBERT Robert Andrew, b. 6 Oct 1942, Bristol, England. Antiquarian Bookseller. m. Patricia Kathleen Linnell, 20 June 1970, 3 sons, 2 daughters. Education: BA (Hons), Philosophy, Psychology, University of Bristol, 1964. Appointment: Editor, Ars Quatuor Coronatorum, 1994-. Publications: The Golden Dawn: Twilight of the Magicians, 1983; A E Waite: a Bibliography, 1983; The Golden Dawn Companion, 1986; A E Waite: Magician of Many Parts, 1987; The Treasure of Montsegur (with W N Birks), 1987; Elements of Mysticism, 1991; World Freemasonry: An Illustrated History, 1992; World Freemasonry: A Celebration of the Craft, 1992; Casting the First Stone (with J M Hamill), 1993. Editor with M A Cox: The Oxford Book of English Ghost Stories, 1986; Victorian Ghost Stories, an Oxford Anthology, 1991; The Golden Dawn Scrapbook, 1997. Contributions to: Ars Quatuor Coronatorum; Avallaunius; Christian Parapsychologist; Gnosis; Hermetic Journal; Cauda Pavonis; Yeats Annual. Memberships: Advisor, Arthur Machen Society; Society of Authors; Antiquarian Booksellers Association; Librarian, Societas Rosicruciana in Anglia. Address: 4 Julius Road, Bishopston, Bristol BS7 8EU, England.

GILCHRIST Ellen, b. 20 Feb 1935, Vicksburg, Mississippi, USA. Author; Poet. Education: BA, Millsaps College, Jackson, Mississippi, 1967; Postgraduate Studies, University of Arkansas, 1976. Publications: The Land Surveyor's Daughter (poems) 1979; The Land of Dreamy Dreams (stories), 1981; The Annunciation (novel), 1983; Victory Over Japan: A Book of Stories, 1984; Drunk With Love (stories), 1986; Riding Out the Tropical Depression (poems), 1986; Falling Through Space: The Journals of Ellen Gilchrist, 1987; The Anna Papers (novel), 1988; Light Can Be Both Wave and Particle: A Book of Stories, 1989; I Cannot Get You Close Enough (3 novellas), 1990; Net of Jewels (novel), 1992; Anabasis: A Journey to the Interior, 1994; Starcarbon: A Meditation on Love, 1994; An Age of Miracles (stories), 1995; Rhoda: A Life in Stories, 1995. Contributions to: Many journals and periodicals. Honours: National Endowment for the Arts Grant in Fiction, 1979; Pucshcart Prizes, 1979-80, 1983; Louisiana Library Association Honor Book, 1981; Mississippi Academy of Arts and Sciences Awards, 1982, 1985; Saxifrage Award, 1983; American Book Award for Fiction, 1984; J William Fulbright Award for Literature, University of Arkansas, 1985; Mississippi Institute of Arts and Letters Literature Award, 1985. Memberships: Authors Guild; Authors League of America. Address: 834 Eastwood Drive, Fayetteville, AR 72701, USA.

GILES Frank (Thomas Robertson), b. 31 July 1919, London, England. Journalist (retired); Writer. m. Lady Katharine Sackville, 29 June 1946, 1 son, 2 daughters. Education: Wellington College; MA, Open Scholar in History, Brasenose College, Oxford, 1946. Appointments: Assistant Correspondent, Paris Bureau, 1947-50, Chief Correspondent, Rome Bureau, 1950-53, and Paris Bureau, 1953-61, The Times, London; Foreign Editor, 1961-77, Deputy Editor, 1967-81, Editor, 1981-83, The Sunday Times, London; Director, The Times Newspapers, 1981-85. Publications: A Prince of Journalists: The Life and Times of Henri de Blowitz, 1962; Sunday Times, autobiography, 1986; Years On, editor, 1990; The Locust Years, History of the 4th French Republic, 1991; Corfu: The Garden Isle, editor, 1994. Contributions to: Books, newspapers and periodicals. Honour: Franco-British Society Prize. Address: 42 Blomfield Road, London W9 2PF, England.

GILES Richard Lawrence, b. 24 May 1937, Petersham, New South Wales, Australia. Teacher. m. Faye Laurel, 3 May 1969. Education: BA, 1957; DipEd, 1969; ATCL, 1971; AMusA, 1973. Literary Appointments: Editor, Good Government, 1980. Publications: Technology, Employment and the Industrial Revolution, 1984; For and Against, 1989, 2nd edition, 1993; Debating, 1992; Understanding Our Economy. 1995. Contributions to: Good Government; Progress; The Individual; Australian Land Economics Review. Membership: Director, Australian School for Social Science. Literary Agent: Jacaranda Press. Address: PO Box 443, Enfield, New South Wales 2136, Australia.

GILL Anton, b. 22 Oct 1948, Essex, England. Writer. m. Nicola Susan Browne, 6 Nov 1982. Education: Clare College, Cambridge, 1967-70. Publications: The Journey Back From Hell; Berlin to Bucharest; City of the Horizon; City of Dreams; A Dance Between Flames; City of the Dead; An Honourable Defeat. Honour: HH Wingate Award. Address: c/o Sarah Leigh, PFD Group Ltd, 5 The Chambers, Chelsea Harbour SW10 0XF, England.

GILL Bartholomew. See: McGARRITY Mark.

GILL Jerry Henry, b. 7 Feb 1933, Lynden, Washington, USA. College Teacher. m. M Sorri, 3 Sept 1982. Education: BA, Westmont College, 1956; MA, University of Washington, 1957; MDiv, New York Theological Seminary, 1960; PhD, Duke University, 1966. Publications: Philosophy Today, 3 volumes, 1968-70; Essays on Kierkegaard, 1969; Possibility of Religious Knowledge, 1971; Wittgenstein and Metaphor, 1980, revised edition, 1996; On Knowing God, 1981; Faith in Dialogue, 1985; Mediated Transcendence, 1989; Post-Modern Epistemology (with M Sorri), 1989; Enduring Questions (with M Rader), 1990; Merleau-Ponty and Metaphor, 1991, Learning to Learn, 1992; At the Threshold of Language, 1996. Contributions to: Theology Today; Soundings; International Philosophical Quarterly; Mind; Philosophy and Phenomenological Research; Journal of Aesthetics. Honour: Danforth Teacher Grant, 1964-66. Address: 521 West Shadow Place, Tucson, AZ 85737, USA.

GILL Stephen Matthew, b. 25 June 1932, Sialkot, Panjab, India. Writer. m. Sarala Gill, 1 son, 2 daughters. Education: BA, Panjab University, 1956; MA, Agra University, 1963; University of Ottawa, 1967-70; Oxford University, 1971. Appointments: Teacher, India, Ethiopia, Canada; Editor, Canadian World Federalist, 1971-73, 1977-79; President, Vesta Publications Ltd, 1974-90; Editor, Writers Lifeline, 1982-; Chief Delegate. World University for Canada. Publications: Simon and the Snow King; The Blessing of a Bird; Tales From Canada for Children Everywhere; English Grammar for Beginners; Six Symbolist Plays of Yeats; Anti War Poems, 2 volumes; Seaway Valley Poets; Poets of the Capital; Songs for Harmony (poems); Shrine; The Flowers of Thirst (love poems); Life's Vagaries (short stories); The Loyalist City (novel); Immigrant (novel); Scientific Romances of H G Wells (critical study); Discovery of Bangladesh (history); Sketches of India, illustrated essays about India; The Dove

of Peace (poems), 1993; Political Convictions of G B Shaw (critical studies), 1993; Green Show (editor), 1993; Divergent Shades (poems), 1995; Aman Di Kughi (poems in Panjabi), 1995; Aman Kajazira (poems in Urdu), 1996. Honours: Ontario Graduate Fellowship; Two Honorary Doctorates in Literature; Volunteer Service Award; Honorary Life Membership, Texas State Poetry Society, 1991; Pegasus International Poetry for Peace Award, 1991; Certificate of Appreciation, Asian Canada Biological Centre, 1992; Laureate Man of Letters, United Poets Laureate International, 1992; Honourable Mention, 3rd Place, 53rd Annual International Poetry Contest, 1993; Award of Appreciation in Literature, Municipal Corporation of Cornwall, Ontario, 1994; Best Poet of Peace in the World for 1993, Roger Cable 11, 1994; Trophy by Al-Mohajev, 1995; Pact of Peace Award, Pakistan Association of Ottawa, 1995; Global NRI Award, Indian European Union Friendship Society, 1996; Maan Patter by International Panjabi Sahit Sabha UK, 1996; Poet of Peace Award, Pakistan Association of Ottawa, Canada, 1995. Memberships: PEN; The Writers Union of Canada; World Federalists of Canada. Address: PO Box 32, Cornwall, Ontario K6H 5R9, Canada.

GILLESPIE Robert B(yrne), b. 31 Dec 1917, Brooklyn, New York, USA. Writer. m. Marianna Albert, 26 June 1957, dec, 1 daughter. Education: Brooklyn College, 1935-37; LLB, St John's Law School, 1937-40. Publications: The Crossword Mystery, 1979; Little Sally Does It Again, 1982; Print-Out, 1983; Heads You Lose, 1985; Empress of Coney Island, 1986; The Hell's Kitchen Connections, 1987; The Last of the Honeywells, 1988; Deathstorm, 1990; Many crossword books. Contributions to: St John's Law Review; Discovery 6. Memberships: Authors Guild; Mystery Writers of America. Address: 226 Bay Street, Douglaston, NY 11363, USA.

GILLIE Christopher, b. 22 Jan 1914, London, England. Writer; Teacher. m. Margery Beaumont, 8 July 1947, 1 son, 3 daughters. Education: MA, Trinity Hall, Cambridge, 1935. Appointments: Lecturer in English Literature, Trinity Hall, Cambridge, 1967-80; Tutor, Open University. Publications: Character in English Literature, 1964; Longman's Companion to English Literature, 1972; Jane Austin: A Preface Book, 1974; Movements in English Literature, 1900-1939, 1975; E M Forster: A Preface Book, 1983. Address: 1 Barton Close, Cambridge CB3 9LQ, England.

GILLIES Valerie, b. 4 June 1948, Edmonton, Alberta, Canada (British citizen). Writer. m. William Gillies, 1972, 1 son, 2 daughters. Education: MA, 1970, MLitt, 1974, University of Edinburgh; FSA Scot, 1991. Appointment: Writer-in-Residence, University of Edinburgh, 1995-97. Publications: Trio: New Poets From Edinburgh, 1971; Each Bright Eye: Selected Poems, 1977; Bed of Stone, 1984; Tweed Journey, 1989; The Chanter's Tune, 1990; The Ringing Rock, 1995. Radio plays: Stories of the Mountains, 1979; Ballad of Tam Lin, 1979. Television: BBC2, Caledonians and Romans. Honours: Scottish Arts Council Bursary, 1976; Eric Gregory Award, 1976; Scottish Arts Council Book Award, 1996. Address: c/o Scottish Cultural Press, Unit 14, Leith Walk Business Centre, 130 Leith Walk, Edinburgh, EH6 5DT, Scotland.

GILLIS Launa. See: PARTLETT Launa.

GILLON Adam, b. 17 July 1921. Author; Emeritus Professor. Appointments: Professor, English, Department Head, Acadia University, Nova Scotia, Canada, 1957-62; Faculty, 1962-, currently Emeritus Professor, English, Comparative Literature, State University of New York, New Paltz, USA; Editor, Polish Series, Twayne Publishers Inc, 1963-72; Regional Editor, Conradiana, 1968-72; Editor, Joseph Conrad Today, 1975; Editorial Board, Institute for Textual Studies, Texas Technical University, Lubbock. Publications: The Eternal Solitary: A Study of Joseph Conrad, 1960; Selected Poems and Translations, 1962; Introduction to Modern Polish Literature (editor, translator, contributor), 1964; In the Manner of Haiku: Seven Aspects of Man, 1967; Julian Tuwim's The Dancing Socrates and Other Poems (editor, translator), 1968; Poems of the Ghetto: A Testament of Lost Men (editor, translator, contributor), 1969; Daily New and Old: Poems in the Manner of Haiku, 1971; Strange Mutations in the Manner of Haiku, 1973; Joseph Conrad: Commemorative Essays (editor), 1975; Summer Morn...Winter Weather: Poems 'Twixt Haiku and Senryu, 1975; Conrad and Shakespeare and Other Essays, 1976; Joseph Conrad, 1982; The Withered Leaf: A Medley of Haiku and Senryu, 1982; Joseph Conrad: Comparative Essays, 1994; Novels: A Cup of Fury, 1962; Jared, 1986; Radio plays: Joseph Conrad, 1959; The Bet, 1969; The Solitary, 1969; Screenplays: The

Conspirators (co-author), 1985; Dark Country, 1989; Under Western Eyes, 1989; The Bet, 1990; From Russia with Hope, 1990. Film: The Bet, 1995. Literary Agent: Bertha Klausner, International Literary Agency, 71 Park Avenue, New York, NY 10016, USA. Address: Lake Illyria, 490 Rt 299 West, New Paltz, NY 12561, USA.

GILMAN Dorothy, (Dorothy Gilman Butters), b. 25 June 1923, New Brunswick, New Jersey, USA. Author; Children's Writer. m. Edgar A Butters, 15 Sept 1945, div 1965, 2 sons. Education: Pennsylvania Academy of Fine Arts, 1940-45; University of Pennsylvania and Art Students League, 1963-64. Publications: Novels: The Unexpected Mrs Pollifax, 1966, in UK as Mrs Pollifax, Spy, 1971; Uncertain Voyage, 1967; The Amazing Mrs Pollifax, 1970; The Elusive Mrs Pollifax, 1971; A Palm for Mrs Pollifax, 1973; A Nun in the Closet, 1975, in UK as A Nun in the Cupboard, 1976; The Clairvoyant Countess, 1975; Mrs Pollifax on Safari, 1977; A New Kind of Country, non-mystery novel, 1978; The Tightrope Walker, 1979; Mrs Pollifax on the China Station, 1983; The Maze in the Heart of the Castle, 1983; Mrs Pollifax and the Hong Kong Buddha, 1985; Mrs Pollifax and the Golden Triangle, 1988; Incident at Badamya, 1989; Mrs Pollifax and the Whirling Dervish, 1990; Mrs Pollifax and the Second Thief, 1993; Mrs Pollifax Pursued, 1995. For children: Enchanted Caravan, 1949; Carnival Gypsy, 1950; Ragamuffin Alley, 1951; The Calico Year, 1953; Four-Party Line, 1954; Papa Dolphin's Table, 1955; Girl in Buckskin, 1956; Heartbreak Street, 1958; Witch's Silver, 1959; Masquerade, 1961; Ten Leagues to Boston Town, 1962; The Bells of Freedom, 1963. Contributions to: Magazines. Honour: Catholic Book Award, 1975. Membership: Authors Guild. Address: c/o Howard Morhaim Agency, 175 Fifth Avenue, New York, NY 10010, USA.

GILMAN George G. See: **HARKNETT Terry.**

GILMAN Sander L(awrence), b. 21 Feb 1944, Buffalo, New York, USA. Professor; Writer. m. Marina von Eckardt, 28 Dec 1969. Education: BA, PhD, Tulane University; University of Munich, Germany; Free University of Berlin. Appointments: Professor of German Language and Literature; Professor of Psychiatry. Publications: Nietzchean Parody, 1976; The Face of Madness: Hugh W Diamond and the Origin of Psychiatric Photography, 1976; Bertold Brecht's Berlin, 1976; Seeing the Insane, 1981; Sexuality: An Illustrated History, 1989; The Jew's Body, 1991; Freud, Race and Gender, 1993; The Case of Sigmund Freud: Medicine and Identity at Fin de Siècle, 1994; Re-emerging Jewish Culture in Today's Germany, 1994; Franz Kafka, The Jewish Patient, 1995; Jews in Today's German Culture, 1995; Also scholarly editions of German texts and monographs. Address: Goldwin Smith Pro of Human Studies, Department of Modern Languages, Cornell University 203 Merrill Hall, Ithaca, NY 14853-0001, USA.

GILMOUR Robin, b. 17 June 1943, Hamilton, Scotland. Reader in Literature; Writer. m. Elizabeth Simpson, 29 Dec 1969, 2 sons, 2 daughters. Education: MA, St John's College, Cambridge, 1964; PhD, Edinburgh University, 1969. Appointments: Lecturer, University of Ulster, 1969-73; Lecturer, 1973-84, Senior Lecturer, 1984-90, Reader in Literature, 1990-, University of Aberdeen. Publications: The Idea of the Gentleman in the Victorian Novel; The Novel in the Victorian Age. Contributions to: Journals. Address: 9 Brighton Place, Aberdeen, AB1 6RT, Scotland.

GILROY Frank D(aniel), b. 13 Oct 1925, New York, New York, USA. Writer. m. Ruth Dorothy Gaydos, 1954, 3 sons. Education: BA magna cum laude, Dartmouth College, 1950; Yale University School of Drama, 1950-51. Publications: Plays: Who'll Save the Plowboy?, 1962; The Subject Was Roses, 1964; That Summer - That Fall, 1966; The Only Game in Town, 1969; The Next Contestant, 1978; Dreams of Glory, 1979; Last Licks, 1979, produced as The Housekeeper, Brighton and London, 1982; Real to Reel, 1987; Match Point, 1990; A Way with Words, 1991; Any Given Day, 1993. Screenplays: The Fastest Gun Alive, 1956; The Gallant Hours (with Bierne Lay), 1960; The Subject Was Roses, 1978; The Only Game in Town, 1969; Desperate Characters, 1971; From Noon till Three, 1976; Once in Paris, 1978; The Gig, 1985; The Luckiest Man in the World, 1989. Television plays: Plays for US Steel Hour, Omnibus, Kraft Theater, Studio One, Lux Video Theatre and Playhgouse 90, 1952-; Nero Wolfe, from Rex Stout's novel The Doorbell Rang, 1979; Money Plays, 1997; Burke's Law series. Other: Private (novel), 1970; Little Ego (with Ruth Gilroy) (children's book), 1970; From Noon till Three: The Possibly True and Certainly Tragic Story of an Outlaw and a Lady Whose Love Knew No Bounds (novel), 1973, as For Want of a Horse, 1975; I Wake

Up Screening, Everything You Need To Know About Making Independent Films Including a Thousand Reasons Not To (non-fiction), 1993. Address: c/o Dramatists Guild, 1501 Broadway, New York, NY 10036, USA.

GILSON Estelle, b. 16 June 1926, New York, New York, USA. Author; Translator. m. Saul B Gilson, 21 Dec 1950, 2 sons. Education: AB, Brooklyn College, 1946; MSSW, Columbia University, 1949. Appointment: Teacher, College of Mt St Vincent Seton Seminars. Publications: Gabriel Preil: To Be Recorded (translator), 1992; Umberto Saba: The Stories and Recollections of Umberto Saba (translator), 1993. Contributions to: Anthologies. Honours: Italo Calvino Award, Translation Center, 1991; Renato Poggioli Award, PEN, 1992; Aldo and Jeanne Scaglione Award, Modern Language Association, 1994; National Endowment for the Arts Grant, 1995. Memberships: American Society of Journalists and Authors; PEN. Address: 7 Sigma Place, Riverside, NY 10471, USA.

GINSBURG Mark Barry, b. 9 Dec 1949, Los Angles, California, USA. University Professor. m. Barbara Iris Chasin, 5 Sept 1971, 1 son, 2 daughters. Education: BA, Sociology, Dartmouth College, 1972; MA, Sociology, 1974, PhD, Education, 1976, University of Los Angeles at Los Angeles. Publications: Contradictions in Teacher Education and Society, 1988; Understanding Educational Reform in Global Context, 1991; The Politics of Educators' Work and Lives, 1995; The Political Dimension in Teacher Education, 1995. Contributions to: Comparative Education Review; Educational Foundations; Journal of Education; Oxford Review of Education, Honours: AESA Critics Choice (Book Award), 1990. Memberships: Board of Directors, American Educational Studies Association, 1990-93; President, Comparative and International Education Society, 1991-92. Address: 1125 Wightman Street, Pittsburgh, PA 15217, USA.

GIOSEFFI Daniela, b. 12 Feb 1941, Orange, New Jersey, USA. Poet; Singer; Novelist; Actress; Lyricist; Dancer. m. (1) Richard J Kearney, 5 Sept 1965, div 1982, 1 daughter, (2) Lionel B Luttinger, 1986. Education: BA, Montclair State College; MFA, Drama, Catholic University of America. Career: Singer and vocalist with River Run: Duo. Publications: The Great American Belly Dance, 1977; Earth Dancing: Mother Nature's Oldest Rite, 1980; Women on War, 1989; On Prejudice: A Global Perspective, 1993; Words, Wounds and Flowers, 1995; Dust Disappears: Translations of Spanish Poems written by Corilda Oliver Labra, 1995; In Bed With the Exotic Enemy: Stories and Novella, 1997. Contributions to: Nation; Chelsea; Ambit; Poetry Review; Modern Poetry Studies. Honour: American Book Award, 1990. Address: P O Box 15, Andover, New Jersey, NJ 07821-1015, USA.

GIOVANNI Nikki, (Yolande Cornelia Giovanni), b. 7 June 1943, Knoxville, Tennessee, USA. Poet; Writer; Professor of Creative Writing. 1 son. Education: BA, Fisk University, 1967; School of Social Work, University of Pennsylvania, 1967; Columbia University, 1968. Appointments: Assistant Professor, Queens College of the City University of New York, 1968; Associate Professor, Livingston College, Rutgers University, 1968-72; Founder-Publisher, Niktom Publishers, 1970-74; Visiting Professor, Ohio State University, 1984; Professor of Creative Writing, Mount St Joseph on the Ohio, 1985-. Publications: Poetry: Black Judgement, 1968; Black Feeling, Black Talk, 1968; Re: Creation, 1970; Poem for Angela Yvonne Davis, 1970; My House, 1972; The Women and the Men, 1975; Cotton Candy on a Rainy Day, 1978; Those Who Ride the Night Winds, 1983. Children's Poetry: Spin a Soft Black Dog, 1971, revised edition, 1985; Ego Tripping and Otyher Poems for Young Readers, 1973; Vacation Time, 1980; Knoxville, Tennessee, 1994. Non-Fiction: Gemini: An Extended Autobiographical Statement on My First Twenty-Five Years of Being a Black Poet, 1971; A Dialogue: James Baldwin and Nikki Giovanni, 1973; A Poetic Equation: Conversations Between Nikki Giovanni and Margaret Walker, 1974; Sacred Cows ... and Other Edibles, 1988; Conversations with Nikki Giovanni, 1992; Racism 101, 1994. Editor: Night Comes Softly: An Anthology of Black Female Voices, 1970; Appalachian Elders: A Warm Hearth Sampler (with Cathee Dennison), 1991; Grandmothes: Poems, Reminiscences, and Short Stories About the Keepers of Our Traditions, 1994. Honours: Ford Foundation Grant, 1968; National Endowment for the Arts Grant, 1969; Honorary doctorates. Address: c/o William Morrow Inc, 105 Madison Avenue, New York, NY 10016, USA.

GLADSTONE William, See: **WICKHAM Glynne.**

GLAISTER Lesley Gillian, b. 4 Oct 1956, Wellinborough, Northamptonshire, England. Writer. 3 sons. Education: MA, University of Sheffield. Publications: Honour Thy Father; Trick or Treat; Digging to Australia; Limestone and Clay, 1993; Partial Eclipse, 1994; The Private Parts of Women, 1996; Easy Peasy, 1997. Honours: Somerset Maugham Award; Betty Trask Award; Yorkshire Author of Year Award, 1993. Membership: Fellow, Royal Society of Literature. Address: 43 Walton Road, Sheffield S11 8RE, England.

GLANVILLE Brian Lester, b. 24 Sept 1931, London, England. Author; Journalist. m. Elizabeth Pamela De Boer, 19 Mar 1959, 2 sons, 2 daughters. Education: Charterhouse, England, 1945-49. Appointment: Literary Adviser to the Bodley Head, 1958-62. Publications: The Reluctant Dictator, 1952; Henry Sows the Wind, 1954; Along the Arno, 1956; The Bankrupts, 1958; After Rome Africa, 1959; A Bad Streak, 1961; Diamond, 1962; The Director's Wife, 1963; The King of Hackney Marshes, 1965; The Olympian, 1969; A Cry of Crickets, 1970; Goalkeepers are Different, children's novel, 1971; The Thing He Loves, 1973; Never Look Back, 1980; Kissing America, 1985; Love is not Love, 1985; The Catacomb, 1988. Sporting Books: Soccer Nemesis, 1955; Footballer's Companion (editor), 1962; The Joy of Football (editor), 1986; Champions of Europe, 1991; Story of the World Cup (passim), 1993. Contributions to: Sunday Times (as Football correspondent and sports columnist), 1958-92; Sports Columnist, The People, 1992-96; The Times, 1996. New Statesman; Spectator. Honour: Thomas Y Coward Award, New York, 1969. Address: 160 Holland Park Avenue, London W11 4UH, England.

GLAZEBROOK Philip Kirkland, b. 3 Apr 1937, London, England. Writer. m. Clare Rosemary Gemmell, 5 Oct 1968, 2 sons, 2 daughters. Education: MA, Trinity College, Cambridge. Publications: Try Pleasure, 1968; The Eye of the Beholder, 1975; Byzantine Honeymoon, 1978; Journey to Kars, 1985; Captain Vinegar's Commission, 1988; The Walled Garden, 1989; The Gate at the End of the World, 1989; Journey to Khiva, 1992. Contributions to: Spectator; Sunday Times; New York Times; Washington Post; Daily Telegraph. Literary Agent: Richard Scott Simon. Address: Strode Manor, Bridport, Dorset, England.

GLEASNER Diana (Cottle), b. 26 Apr 1936, New Brunswick, New Jersey, USA. Writer. m. G William Gleasner, 12 July 1958, 1 son, 1 daughter. Education: BA cum laude, Ohio Wesleyan University, 1958; MA, University of Buffalo, 1964. Publications: The Plaid Mouse, 1966; Pete Polar Bear's Trip Down the Erie Canal, 1970; Women in Swimming, 1975; Women in Track and Field, 1977; Hawaiian Gardens, 1978; Kauai Traveler's Guide, 1978; Oahu Traveler's Guide, 1978; Big Island Traveler's Guide, 1978; Maui Traveler's Guide, 1978; Breakthrough: Women in Writing, 1980; Illustrated Dictionary of Surfing, Swimming and Diving, 1980; Sea Islands of the South, 1980; Rock Climbing, 1980; Callaway Gardens, 1981; Inventions That Changed Our Lives: Dynamite, 1982; Inventions That Changed Our Lives: The Movies, 1983; Breakthrough: Women in Science, 1983; Charlotte: A Touch of Gold, 1983; Woodloch Pines - An American Dream, 1984; Windsurfing, 1985; Lake Norman - Our Inland Sea, 1986; Florida Off the Beaten Path, 1996; Governor's Island - From the Beginning, 1988; Driving America's Backroads - Florida, 1989; Touring by Bus at Home and Abroad, 1989. Contributions to: Numerous magazines and newspapers. Memberships: American Society of Journalists and Authors; Society of American Travel Writers; Travel Journalists Guild. Address: 7994 Holly Court, Denver, NC 28037, USA.

GLECKNER Robert F(rancis), b. 1925, Rahway, New Jersey, USA. Professor of English; Writer. m. Glenda Jean Karr, 7 Feb 1946, 1 son, 1 daughter. Education: BA, Williams College, 1948; PhD, Johns Hopkins University, 1954. Appointments: Editor, Research Studies Institute, Maxwell Air Force Base, Alabama, 1951-52; Instructor in English, University of cincinnati and University of Wisconsin, 1952-57; Assistant Professor, Associate Professor, Wayne State University, Detroit, 1957-62; Professor, English, 1962-78, Chairman, Department of English, 1962-66, Dean, College of Humanities, 1968-75, University of California, Riverside; Advisory Editor: Criticism, 1959-1962, Blake Studies, 1970-, Studies in Romanticism, 1977-; Professor, English, 1978-, Acting Department Chairman, 1983, Duke University; Advisory Editor: Romanticism Past and Present (now Nineteenth Century Contexts), 1980-, The Byron Journal, 1990-; South Atlantic Review, 1997-. Publications: The Piper and the Bard: A Study of William Blake, 1957; Byron and the Ruins of Paradise, 1967, 2nd edition, 1982; Blake's Prelude: Poetical Sketches, 1982; Blake and Spenser, 1985; Gray Minutes: Thomas Gray and Masculine Friendship, 1996;

Romanticism: Points of View (with G E Enscoe), 1962, revised edition (sole editor), 1970, 3rd edition, 1974. Editor: Selected Writings of William Blake, 1967, 2nd Edition, 1970; Complete Poetical Works of Lord Byron, 1975; Approaches to Teaching Blake's Songs (with M L Greenberg), 1989; Critical Essays on Lord Byron, 1991; Byron's Plays: Critical Essays (with Bernard Beatty), 1997. Contributions to: A James Joyce Miscellany, 1962; Essays on the 25th Anniversary of Finnegan's Wake, 1966; William Blake: Essays for S Foster Damon, 1969; William Blake and the Moderns, 1982; Speak Silence: Blake's Poetical Sketches, 1996; Bibliographer, Reviewer, Romantic Movement Bibliography, 1989-. Honours: Poetry Society of America Award; Elected Faculty Research Lecturer, University of California, Riverside, 1973; Mellon Research Fellow, Huntington Library, San Marino, California, 1987, 1991; Distinguished Scholar Award, Keats-Shelley Association of America, 1991. Memberships: Keats-Shelley Association of America; North American Society for the Study of Romanticism; Byron Society. Address: Department of English, Duke University, Box 90015, Durham, NC 27708, USA.

GLEN Duncan Munro, (Ronald Eadie Munro), b. 11 Jan 1933, Lanarkshire, Scotland. Retired Professor; Writer. m. Margaret Eadie, 4 Jan 1958, 1 son, 1 daughter. Publications: Hugh MacDiarmid and the Scottish Renaissance, 1964; Selected Essays of Hugh MacDiarmid (editor), 1969; In Appearances: A Sequence of Poems, 1971; The Individual and the Twentieth Century Scottish Literary Tradition, 1971; Mr & Mrs J L Stoddard at Home (poems), 1975; Buits and Wellies: A Sequence of Poems, 1976; Gaitherings (poems), 1977; Realities, (poems), 1980; On Midsummer Eve in Merriest of Nichts? 1981; The Turn of the Earth: Sequence of Poems, 1985; The Autobiography of a Poet, 1986; Tales to Be Told, 1987; European Poetry in Scotland (editor), 1990; The Poetry of the Scots, 1991; Selected Poems, 1965-1990, 1991; Hugh MacDiarmid: Out of Langholm and Into the World, 1992; The Bright Writers' Guides to Scottish Culture (editor), 1995; A Nation in a Parish: A New Historical Prospect of Scotland, 1995; Splendid Lanarkshire, 1997. Contributions to: Numerous journals and magazines. Honours: Special Prize, Services to Scottish Literature, Scottish Arts Council, 1975. Membership: Fellow, Chartered Society of Designers. Address: 33 Lady Nairn Avenue, Kirkaldy, Fife KY1 2AW, Scotland.

GLENDINNING Victoria, b. 23 Apr 1937, Sheffield, England. Author; Journalist. m. (1) O N V Glendinning, 1958, 4 sons, (2) Terence de Vere White, 1981, (3) K P O'Sullivan, 1996. Education: BA, Honours, Modern Languages, Somerville College, Oxford, 1959; Diploma, Social Administration, 1969. Appointment: Editorial Assistant, Times Literary Supplement, 1970-74. Publications: A Suppressed Cry, Life & Death of a Quaker Daughter, 1969; Elizabeth Bowen: Portrait of a Writer, 1977; Edith Sitwell: A Unicorn Among Lions, 1981; Vita: The Life of V Sackville West, 1983; Rebecca West: A Life, 1987; The Grown-ups, (novel), 1989; Hertfordshire, 1989; Trollope, 1992; Electricity (novel), 1995; Sons and Mothers (co-editor), 1996. Contributions to: Various journals, newspapers and magazines. Honours: Duff Cooper Memorial Award and James Tait Black Prize, 1981; Whitbread Awards, 1983, 1992; Whitbread Award, Trollope, 1992; Hon DLitt, Southampton University, 1994, University of Ulster, 1995, Trinity College, Dublin, 1995. Memberships: Fellow, Royal Society of Literature; PEN. Address: David Higham Associates, 5/8 Lower John Street, Golden Square, London W1, England.

GLENDOWER Rose. See: **HARRIS Marion Rose.**

GLISSANT Édouard, b. 21 Sept 1928, Sainte-Marie, Martinique. Writer; Dramatist; Poet. Education: DPhil, 1953, State Doctorate, 1977, Sorbonne, Université de Paris; Musée de l'homme, Paris. Appointments: Instructor in Philosophy, Lycée des Jeunes Filles, Fort-de-France, Martinique, 1965; Founder, 1967, Director, 1967-78, Institut Martiniquais d'Etudes, Fort-de-France; Co-founder, ACOMA Review, 1970; Editor, UNESCO, Paris, France, 1981-88; Distinguished Professor and Director of Center for French and Francophone Studies, Louisiana State University, Baton Rouge, USA, 1988-. Publications: Poetry: Un champ d'îles, 1953; La terre inquiète, 1954; Les Indes: Poèmes de l'une et l'autre terre, 1955; Le sel noir, 1959; Le sang rivé, 1960; Poèmes, 1963; Boises, 1979; Pays rêvé, pays réel, 1985; Fastes, 1992. Non-fiction: Soleil de la conscience, 1956; L'intention poétique, 1969; Le discours antillais, 1981, in English as Caribbean Discourse: Selected Essays, 1989; Poétique de la relation, 1990. Fiction: La Lézarde, 1958; Le quatrième siècle, 1964; Malemort, 1975; La case du commandeur, 1981; Mahagony, 1987; Tout-monde, 1993. Play: Monsiuer Toussaint, 1961, revised version, 1978. Honours:

Ordre des Francophones d'Amérique, Quebec; Prix Rénaudot, 1958; Prix Charles Veillon, 1965; Award, 12th Putterbaugh Conference, Norman, Oklahoma, 1989; Honorary LittD, York University, 1989; Honorary Doctorate, Glendon College, York University, 1989; Roger Callois International Prize, 1991. Address: 213 Prescott, Baton Rouge, LA 70803-5309, USA.

GLOAG Julian, b. 2 July 1930, London, England. Novelist. 1 son, 1 daughter. Education: Exhibitioner, BA, 1953, MA, 1959, Magdalene College, Cambridge. Publications: Our Mother's House, 1963; A Sentence of Life, 1966; Maundy, 1969; A Woman of Character, 1973; Sleeping Dogs Lie, 1980; Lost and Found, 1981; Blood for Blood, 1985; Only Yesterday, 1986; Love as a Foreign Language, 1991; Le passeur de la nuit, 1996; Chambre d'ombre, 1996; Teleplays: Only Yesterday, 1986; The Dark Room, 1988. Memberships: Fellow, Royal Society of Literature; Authors Guild. Address: c/o Michelle Lapautre, 6 rue Jean Carriès, 75007 Paris, France.

GLOVER Judith, b. 31 Mar 1943, Wolverhampton, England. Author. 2 daughters. Education: Wolverhampton High School for Girls, 1954-59; Aston Polytechnic, 1960. Publications: Drink Your Own Garden (non-fiction), 1979; The Sussex Quartet: The Stallion Man, 1982, Sisters and Brothers, 1984, To Everything a Season, 1986 and Birds in a Gilded Cage, 1987; The Imagination of the Heart, 1989; Tiger Lilies, 1991; Mirabelle, 1992; Minerva Lane, 1994; Pride of Place, 1995. Literary Agent: Artellus. Address: c/o Artellus Ltd, 30 Dorset House, Gloucester Place, London NW1 5AD, England.

GLÜCK Louise, b. 22 Apr 1943, New York, New York, USA. Author; Poet. (1) Charles Hertz, div, 1 son; (2) John Dranow, 1 Jan 1977, 1 son. Education: Sarah Lawrence College, 1962; Columbia University, 1963-66, 1967-68. Appointments: Artist-in-Residence, 1971-72, Faculty Member, 1973-74, Goddard College, Plainfield, Vermont; Poet-in-Residence, University of North Carolina at Greensboro, 1973; Visiting Professor, University of Iowa, 1976-77; Columbia University, 1979; University of California at Davis, 1983; Faculty Member, Board Member, MFA Writing Program, 1976-80; Ellison Professor of Poetry, University of Cincinnati, 1978; Faculty Member, Board Member, MFA Writing Program, Warren Wilson College, Swannoa, North Carolina, 1980-84; Holloway Lecturer, University of California at Berkeley, 1982; Scott Professor of Poetry, 1983, Senior Lecturer in English, part-time, 1984-, Williams College, Williamstown, Massachusetts; Regents Professor of Poetry, University of California at Los Angeles, 1985-88; Phi Beta Kappa Poet, 1990, Visiting Professor, 1995, Harvard University. Publications: Poetry: Firstborn, 1968; The House on the Marshland, 1975; The Garden, 1976; Descending Figure, 1980; The Triumph of Achilles, 1985; Ararat, 1990; The Wild Iris, 1992; The First Four Book of Poems, 1995; Meadowlands, 1996. Other: Proofs and Theories: Essays on Poetry, 1994. Contributions to: Many anthologies and periodicals. Honours: Academy of American Poets Prize, 1967; Rockefeller Foundation Grant, 1968-69; National Endowment for the Arts Fellowships, 1969-70, 1979-80, 1988-89; Eunice Tietjens Memorial Prize, 1971; Guggenheim Fellowships, 1975-76, 1987-88; Vermont Council for the Arts Grant, 1978-79; American Academy and Institute of Arts and Letters Award, 1981; National Book Critics Circle Award, Poetry Society of America, 1985; Sara Teasdale Memorial Prize, Wellesley College, 1986; Co-recipient, Bobbitt National Prize, 1992; Pulitzer Prize in Poetry, 1993; William Carlos Williams Award, 1993; LLD, Williams College, 1993; Poet Laureate of Vermont, 1994; PEN/Martha Altrand Award, 1995; LLD, Skidmore College, 1995; Phi Beta Kappa. Memberships: Fellow, American Academy of Arts and Sciences; PEN. Address: Creamery Road, Plainfield, VT 05667, USA.

GOAD Johnny. See: PHILANDERSON Flavian Titus.

GODBER John (Harry), b. 15 May 1956, Upton, Yorkshire, England. Writer. Education: Bretton Hall College, West Bretton, Yorkshire, 1974-78; Certificate of Education, 1977; BEd (Honours), 1978; MA, Theatre, Leeds University, 1979; Graduate studies, 1979-83. Appointments: Teacher, Minsthorpe High School, 1981-83; Artistic Director, Hull Truck Theatre Company, 1984-; Director: Own plays; Imagine (Stephen Jeffreys), Hedda Gabler (Ibsen), The Dock (Phil Woods), Hull, 1987. Publications: Plays include: A Clockwork Orange, adaptation of novel by Anthony Burgess produced Edinburgh, 1980, London, 1984; Cry Wolf, produced Rotherham, Yorkshire, 1981; Blood, Sweat and Tears, produced Hull and London, 1986; The Ritz, televised, 1987, produced as Putting on the Ritz, Leicester, 1987;

Teechers, produced Edinburgh and London, 1987; TV plays: Series scripts for Grange Hill, 1981-83, Brookside, 1983-84, Crown Court, 1983; The Rainbow Coloured Disco Dancer, from work by C P Taylor, 1984; The Ritz series, 1987; The Continental, 1987. Honours: Edinburgh Festival Awards, 1981, 1982, 1984; Olivier Award, 1984; Los Angeles Drama Critics Circle Award, 1986. Address: Hull Truck, Spring Street Theatre, Spring Street, Hull, Yorkshire HU2 8RW, England.

GODDEN Rumer, b. 10 Dec 1907, Sussex, England. Author; Poet; Translator. m. (1) Laurence S Foster, 1934, dec, 2 daughters, (2) James Haynes Dixson, 11 Nov 1949, dec 1973. Education: Moira House, Eastbourne. Publications: Fiction: The Greenage Summer, 1958; China Court: The Hours of a Country House, 1961; The Battle of the Villa Fiorta, 1963; Swans and Turtles: Stories, 1968; In This House of Brede, 1969; The Peacock Spring, 1975; Five for Sorrow, Ten for Joy, 1979; The Dark Horse, 1981; Thursday's Children, 1984; A House with Four Rooms, 1989; Pippa Passes, 1994. Non-Fiction: Two Under the Indian Sun, 1966; Shiva's Pigeons: An Experience of India, 1972. Editor: Round the Day, Round the Year, the World Around: Poetry Programmes for Classroom or Library, 6 volumes, 1966-67; The Raphael Bible, 1970; Premlate and the Festival of Lights (juvenile), 1996; A Pocket Book of Spiritual Poems, 1996. Other: Books for young readers, translations. Honour: Officer of the Order of the British Empire. Address: c/o Curtis Brown Ltd, Haymarket House, 28-29 Haymarket, London SW1Y 4SP, England.

GODFREY (William) Dave, b. 9 Aug 1938, Winnipeg, Manitoba, Canada. Novelist. m. Ellen Swartz, 1963, 2 sons, 1 daughter. Education: BA, 1960, MFA, 1963, PhD, 1966, University of Iowa; MA, Stanford University, 1963; University of Chicago, 1965. Appointments: General Editor, Canadian Writers Series, McClelland and Stewart, 1968-72; Co Founding Editor, News Press, Toronto, 1969-73; Editor, Press Porcepic, Erin, Ontario, 1972-; Vice President, Inter Provincial Association for Telematcis and Telidon, 1982-. Publications: The New Ancestors, 1970; Short Stories: Death Goes Better with Coca Cola, 1967; New Canadian Writing, 1968, 1969; Dark Must Yield, 1978; Other Non Fiction Works. Honours: University of Western Ontario Presidents Medal, 1965; Canada Council Award, 1969; Governor-General's Award, 1971. Address: Porcepic Books, 4252 Commerce Circle, Vancouver, British Columbia V87 4M2, Canada.

GODFREY Ellen Rachel, b. 15 Sept 1942, Chicago, Illinois, USA. Company President; Author. m. William David Godfrey, 25 Aug 1963, 1 son, 1 daughter. Publications: Georgia Disappeared; Murder Behind Locked Doors; By Reason of Doubt; Murder Among the Well to Do; The Case of the Cold Murderer; Common or Garden Murderer. Honours: Special Award; Edgar Allan Poe Award. Memberships: Canadian Crime Writers Association; Women in Crime Association; Working Opportunities Fund, advisory board; Vancouver Island Advanced Technology Centre; University of Victoria Coop Council; Premier Advisory Council on Science and Technology. Literary Agent: Bruce Westwood Creative Artists. Address: 4355 Gordon Head Road, Victoria, British Columbia V8N 3Y4, Canada.

GODFREY John M, b. 7 July 1945, Massena, New York, USA. Poet. Education: AB, Princeton University, 1967. Publications: 26 Poems, Adventures in Poetry, 1971; Three Poems, Bouwerie Editions, 1973; Music of the Curbs, Adventures in Poetry, 1976; Dabble: Poems 1966-1980, 1982; Where the Weather Suits My Clothes, 1984; Midnight on Your Left, The Figures, 1988. Contributions to: Mother; Paris Review; United Artists; MagCity; Big Sky; ZZZZZ; The World; Oink!; Broadway; An Anthology of Poets and Painters. Honours: Poetry Fellow, General Electric Foundation/Coordinating Council of Literary Magazines, 1984. Address: 437 East 12th Street, Apt 32, New York, NY 10009, USA.

GODFREY Martyn N, b. 17 Apr 1949, Birmingham, England. (Naturalised Canadian Citizen). Writer. m. Carolyn Boswell, 1973, div 1985, 2 children. Education: BA (Hons), 1973, BEd, 1974, University of Toronto. Appointments: Teacher, elementary schools in Kitchener and Waterloo, Ontario, Canada, 1974-77; Mississauga, Ontario, 1977-80, Assumption, Alberta, 1980-82; Junior High School Teacher, Edson, Alberta, 1983-85; Writer, 1985-. Publications: For children: The Last War, 1986; It Isn't Easy Being Ms Teeny-Wonderful, 1987; Wild Night, 1987; More Than Weird, 1987; Rebel Yell, 1987; It Seemed Like a Good Idea at the Time, 1987; Baseball Crazy, 1987; Sweat Hog, 1988; Send in Ms Teeny-Wonderful, 1988; In the Time of the Monsters, 1988; The Day the Sky Exploded, 1991; Don't Worry About Me, I'm

Just Crazy, 1992; Wally Stutzgummer, 1992. Honours: Award for Best Children's Short Story, Canadian Authors Association, 1985; Award for Best Children's Book, University of Lethbridge, 1987. Memberships: Writers Union of Canada; Canadian Authors Association; Canadian Society of Children's Authors, Illustrators and Performers; Writers Guild of Alberta, Vice-President, 1986, President, 1987. Literary Agent: Joanne Killock, Edmonton, Canada. Address: c/o Killock and Associates, 11017-80 Avenue, Edmonton, Alberta T6G 0R2, Canada.

GODKIN Celia Marilyn, b. 15 Apr 1948, London, England, Teacher; Illustrator; Children's Author; Biologist. Education: BSc, London University, 1969; MSc, University of Toronto, 1983; AOCA, Ontario College of Art, 1983. Publications: Wolf Island; Ladybug Garden. Contributions to: Bulletin of Marine Science; Environmental Biology of Fishes; Guild of Natural Science Illustrators Newsletter. Honours: Best Information Book Award. Memberships: Guild of Natural Science Illustrators; Canadian Society of Children's Authors, Illustrators and Performers; Writer's Union of Canada. Address: Division of Biomedical Communications, University of Toronto, Medical Sciences Building, 1 King's College Circle, Toronto, Ontario M5S 1A8, Canada.

GODMAN Arthur, b. 10 Oct 1916, Hereford, England. Educationalist. m. Jean Barr Morton, 24 June 1950, 2 sons, 1 daughter. Education: BSc, 1937, BSc Hons, Chemistry, 1938, University College, London; Dip Ed, Institute of Education, London, 1939; Malay Government Exam Standard III, 1948; CChem; MRSC; FRAS. Appointments: Colonial Education Service, 1946-63; Educational Consultant, Longman Group, 1966-77; Honorary Fellow, University of Kent, 1978-; Research Fellow, Department of South East Asian Studies, 1978-. Publications: Chemistry: A New Certificate Approach (with S T Bajah), 1969; Human and Social Biology, 1973; Dictionary of Scientific Usage (with E M F Payne), 1979; Illustrated Science Dictionary, 1981; Illustrated Dictionary of Chemistry, 1981; Illustrated Thesaurus of Computer Sciences, 1984; Energy Supply, 1990. Contributions to: Babel, 1990. Memberships: Society of Authors; Royal Society of Chemistry; Royal Asiatic Society. Address: Sondes House, Patrixbourne, Canterbury, Kent CT4 5DD, England.

GODWIN Peter (Christopher), b. 4 Dec 1957, Rhodesia. Journalist; Writer. Education: MA, Cambridge University. Appointments: East European Correspondent, 1984-86, Africa Correspondent, 1986-, The Sunday Times, London. Publication: Rhodesians Never Die: The Impact of War and Political Change on White Rhodesia, 1970-1980 (with Ian Hancock), 1993. Contributions to: Newspapers and periodicals. Honour: Commended, British Press Awards, 1984. Membership: Foreign Correspondents Association. Address: c/o The Sunday Times, Foreign Department, 1 Pennington Street, London E1, England.

GODWIN Rebecca Thompson, b. 9 July 1950, Charleston, South Carolina, USA. Writer. m. (1) 2 daughters, (2) Deane Bogardus, 24 Aug 1988. Education: BA, Coastal Carolina College, 1977; MA, Middlebury College, 1988. Appointments: Teacher, Bennington Writing Workshops, 1995; Teacher, Wildacres Writing Workshops, 1996. Publications: Keeper of the House, 1994; Private Parts, 1992. Contributions to: South Carolina Review; Paris Review; Iris; Crescent Review; First Magazine. Honours: Winner, S C Fiction Project, 1988; National Endowment for the Arts, 1994-95. Membership: AWP. Literary Agent: Colleen Mohyde, The Doe Coover Agency, Winchester, MA, USA. Address: PO Box 211, Poestenkill, NY 12140, USA.

GOEDICKE Patricia, b. 21 June 1931, Boston, Massachusetts, USA. Poet. m. Leonard Wallace Robinson, 3 June 1971. Education: BA, Middlebury College, 1953; MA, Ohio University, 1965. Appointments: Editorial Secretary, Harcourt, Brace & World Inc, 1953-54, T Y Crowell Co, 1955-56; Lecturer, English, Ohio University, 1963-68, Hunter College, 1969-71; Associate Professor, Creative Writing, Instituto Allende, 1972-79; Visiting Writer-in-Residence, Kalamazoo College, 1977; Guest Faculty, Writing Programme, Sarah Lawrence College, 1980; Visiting Poet in Residence, 1981-82, 1982-83, Associate Professor, 1983-90, Professor, Creative Writing, 1990-, University of Montana, Missoula. Publications: Between Oceans, 1968; For the Four Corners, 1976; The Trail That Turns On Itself, 1978; The Dog That Was Barking Yesterday, 1980; Crossing the Same River, 1980; The King of Childhood, 1984; The Wind of Our Going, 1985; Listen Love, 1986; The Tongues We Speak, 1989; Paul Bunyan's Bearskin, 1992; Invisible Horses, 1996. Contributions to: Periodicals. Honours: Pushcart Prize, 1977-78; National Endowment

for the Arts Fellowship, 1976; Several distinguished scholarly awards. Memberships: Associated Writing Programs, Academy of American Poets; PEN USA; PEN America; Poetry Society of America. Address: 310 McLeod, Missoula, MT 59801, USA.

GOELDLIN Michel, b. 3 Aug 1934, Lausanne, Switzerland. Writer. m. Yucki Zur Muhlen, 23 May 1959, 1 son, 1 daughter. Education: Baccalaureate es lettres classiques, 1955. Publications: Novels: Les Sentiers Obliques, 1972; Le Vent meurt à Midi, 1976; Juliette Crucifée, 1977; A l'ouest de Lake Placid, 1979; Les Désemparés, 1983; Les Moissons du Désert, 1984; L'Espace d'un Homme, essay, 1989; La Planète des Victimes, war report, 1990; Panne de Cerveau, novel, 1996; Michel Goeldlin, Espaces du Réel, Cheminements de Création by M Jacqnot, 1995. Honours: prix Alpes Jura de l'Association des Ecrivains de Langue Française, Adelf, Paris, 1992. Membership: Honorary Member, Association pour le Rayonnement des Langues Européennes, Paris; Parlement international des Ecrivains, Strasbourg. Address: 2 rue Honoré Labande, MC-98000 Monaco.

GOFF James Rudolph Jr, b. 9 Jan 1957, Goldsboro, North Carolina, USA. Historian; Writer. m. Connie Goff, 22 Dec 1978, 1 son, 1 daughter. Education: BA, Wake Forest University, 1978; MDiv, Duke University, 1981; PhD, University of Arkansas, 1987. Appointments: Teaching Assistant, University of Arkansas, 1982-86; Lecturer, 1986-87, 1988-89, Instructor, 1987-88, Assistant Professor, 1989-94, Associate Professor, 1994-. Appalachian State University, Boone, North Carolina. Publication: Fields White Unto Harvest. Contributions to: Christianity Today; Kansas History; Ozark Historical Review; Pentecostals From The Inside Out. Honours: Faculty Award; Phi Theta Kappa; Gordon H McNeil Award; Charles Oxford Scholar. Memberships: Organization of American Church Historians; Organization of American Historians; Society for Pentecostal Studies; Southern Historical Association. Address: Department of History, Appalachian State University, Boone, NC 28608, USA.

GOLD Ivan, b. 12 May 1932, New York, New York, USA. Writer. m. Vera Cochran, 22 Oct 1968, 1 son. Education: BA, Columbia College, New York City, 1953; MA, University of London. Appointments: Writer-in-Residence, Austin Peay State University, 1991, University of Massachusetts, Boston, 1992. Publications: Nickel Miseries; Sick Friends; Sams in a Dry Season. Address: c/o Many Yost Associates, 59 East 54th Street, New York, NY 10022, USA.

GOLDBARTH Albert, b. 31 Jan 1948, Chicago, Illinois, USA. Poet; Writer; Assistant Professor of Creative Writing. Education: BA, University of Illinois, 1969; MFA, University of Iowa, 1971; University of Utah, 1973-74. Appointments: Instructor, Elgin Community College, Illinois, 1971-72, Central YMCA Community College, Chicago, 1971-73, University of Utah, 1973-74; Assistant Professor, Cornell University, 1974-76; Visiting Professor, Syracuse University, 1976; Assistant Professor of Creative Writing, University of Texas at Austin, 1977-. Publications: Poetry: Under Cover, 1973; Coprolites, 1973; Opticks: A Poem in Seven Sections, 1974; Jan 31, 1974; Keeping, 1975; A Year of Happy, 1976; Comings Back: A Sequence of Poems, 1976; Curve: Overlapping Narratives, 1977; Different Flashes, 1979; Eurekas, 1980; Ink Blood Semen, 1980; The Smugglers Handbook, 1980; Faith, 1981; Who Gathered and Whispered Behind Me, 1981; Goldbarth's Book of Occult Phenomena, 1982; Original Light: New and Selected Poems 1973-1983, 1983; Albert's Horoscope Alamanac, 1986; Arts and Sciences, 1986; Popular Culture, 1989; Delft: An Essay Poem, 1990; Heaven and Earth: A Cosmology, 1991; Across the Layers: Poems Old and New, 1993; The Gods, 1993. Fiction: Marriage and Other Science Fiction, 1994. Essays: A Sympathy of Souls, 1990; Great Topics of the World: Essays, 1994. Editor: Every Pleasure: The "Seneca Review" Long Poem Anthology, 1979. Honours: Theodore Roethke Prize, 1972; Ark River Review Prizes, 1973, 1975; National Endowment for the Arts Grants, 1974, 1979; Guggenheim Fellowship, 1983. Address: c/o Department of English, University of Texas at Austin, Austin, TX 78712, USA.

GOLDBERG Barbara June, b. 26 Apr 1943, Wilmington, Delaware, USA. Writer; Poet; Editor. m. (1) J Peter Kiers, 1963, div 1970, (2) Charles Goldberg, 1971, div 1990, 2 sons. Education: BA, Mount Holyoke College, 1963; MA, Yeshiva University, 1969; MEd, Columbia University, 1971; MFA, American University, 1985. Appointments: Director, Editorial Board, The World Works publishers, 1987-; Executive Editor, Poet Lore, 1990-. Publications: Berta Broad Foot and Pepin the Short; Cautionary Tales; The Stones Remember.

Contributions to: American Scholar; Antioch Review; New England Review; Bread Loaf Quarterly. Honours: Work in Progress Grant; National Endowment for the Arts Fellowship; Armand G Erpf Award; Writter Bynner Foundation Award. Memberships: Poetry Society of America; Poets and Writers; Poetry Committee, Greater Washington Area. Address: 6623 Fairfax Road, Chevy Chase, MD 20815, USA.

GOLDBERG Hillel, b. 10 Jan 1946, Denver, Colorado, USA. Writer; Rabbi. m. Elaine Silberstein, 19 May 1969, 2 son, 4 daughter. Education: BA, Yeshiva University, 1969; MA, 1972, PhD, 1978, Brandeis University; Rabbinical Ordination, Chief Rabbi of Israel, 1976. Appointments: Co-Publisher, Co-Editor, Tempo, 1964; Executive Editor, Editor of Literary Supplement, Intermountain Jewish News, 1966-; Editor, Pulse, 1968-69; Member, Editorial Board, Tradition, 1978-; Associate Editor, Tradition, 1988-; Contributing Editor, Jewish Action, 1987-. Publications: Israel Salanter: Text, Structure, Idea, The Ethics and Theology of an Early Psychologist of the Unconscious, 1982; The Fire Within: The Living Heritage of the Musar Movement, 1987; Between Berlin and Slobadka: Jewish Transition Figures from Eastern Europe, 1989. Contributions to: Various journals and newspapers. Honours: Academic Book of the Year Citation, Choice, 1982; Rockower Awards for Distinguished Editorial Writing, 1983, 1984, 1986, 1987, for Distinguished News Reportage, 1988; Joseph Polakoff Award, 1994. Memberships: Literary Guild; Corresponding Secretary, American Jewish Press Association. Address: 1275 Sherman Street, Denver, CO 80203, USA.

GOLDBERG Lester, b. 3 Feb 1924, Brooklyn, New York, USA. Real Estate Official; Writer. m. Dorothy Weinstein, June 1947, 1 son, 3 daughters. Education: BS, City College, 1946. Appointments: Worked in Real Estate, affiliated with State Division of Housing, 1988-. Publications: One More River, stories, 1978; In Siberia It Is Very Cold, (novel), 1987. Contributions to: Anthologies and periodicals. Honours: Fellow, National Endowment for the Arts, 1979; Grants, New Jersey Arts Council, 1982, 1986; Award for short story, International PEN Syndicated Fiction Project, 1984. Memberships: Poets and Writers; Metropolitan Association of Housing and Redevelopment Officials. Address: 18 Woods Hole Road, Cranford, NJ 07016, USA.

GOLDEN Mark, b. 6 Aug 1948, Winnipeg, Manitoba, Canada. Associate Professor of Classics. m. Monica Becker, 1 son. Education: BA, 1970, MA, 1976, PhD, 1981, University of Toronto. Appointment: Professor of Classics, University of Winnipeg, 1982-. Publications: Children and Childhood in Classical Athens; Inventing Ancient Culture (editor with Peter Toohey). Address: Department of Classics, University of Winnipeg, Winnipeg, Manitoba R3B 2E9, Canada.

GOLDIN Barbara Diamond, b. 4 Oct 1946, New York, New York, USA. Teacher; Writer. m. Alan Goldin, Mar 1968, div 1991, 1 son, 1 daughter. Education: BA, University of Chicago. Publications: Just Enough Is Plenty; The World's Birthday; A Family Book of Midrash; Cakes and Miracles; Fire; The Magician's Visit; Red Means Good Fortune; The Passover Journey: A Seder Companion; Night Lights: A Sukkot Story; Creating Angels: Stories of Tzedakah; Bat Mitzvah: A Jewish Girl's Coming of Age; Coyote and the Fire Stick; The Girl Who Lived with the Bears; While the Candles Burn: Eight Stories for Hanukkah. Contributions to: Cricket Highlights; Jack and Jill; Childlife; Shofan Magazine. Honours: National Jewish Book Award; Anne Izand Storytellers Choice Award; Sydney Taylor Picture Book Award. Membership: Society of Children's Book Writers. Literary Agent: Virginia Knowlton. Address: PO Box 981, Northampton, MA 01061, USA.

GOLDIN Stephen, b. 28 Feb 1947, Philadelphia, Pennsylvania, USA. Writer. Education: BA, University of California at Los Angeles, 1968. Appointments: Editor: Jaundice Press, Van Nuys, California, 1973-74; San Francisco Ball, 1973-74; Science Fiction Writers of America Bulletin, 1975-77; Director, Merrimont House Creative Consultations. Publications: The Alien Condition (editor), 1973; Herds, 1975; Caravan, 1975; Scavenger Hunt, 1975; Finish Line, 1976; Imperial Stars, 1976; Strangler's Moon, 1976; The Clockwork Traitor, 1976; Assault on the Gods, 1977; Getaway World, 1977; Mindflight, 1978; Appointments at Bloodstar, UK edition as The Bloodstar Conspiracy, 1978; The Purity Plot, 1978; Trek to Madworld, 1979; The Eternity Brigade, 1980; A World Called Solitude, 1981; And Not Make Dreams Your Master, 1981; Planet of Treachery, 1982; The Business of Being a Writer (with Kathleen Sky), non-fiction, 1982; Eclipsing Binaries, 1984; The Omicron Invasion, 1984; Revolt of the Galaxy, 1985; Editor with David Gerrold: Protostars, 1971; Science Fiction

Emphasis 1, 1974; Alternities, 1974; Ascents of Wonder, 1977. Address: 389 Florin Road, No 22, Sacramento, CA 95831, USA.

GOLDMAN James, b. 30 June 1927, Chicago, Illinois, USA. Playwright; Novelist. Education: PhB, 1947, MA, 1950, University of Chicago; Postgraduate study, Musicology, Columbia University, 1950-52. Publications: Plays: They Might be Giants, 1960; Blood, Sweat and Stanley Poole, (with William Goldman), 1961; The Lion in Winter, 1966; Tolstox, 1996; Musicals: A Family Affair (with William Goldman), 1962; Follies (music by Stephen Sondheim), 1972, new book, 1987; Novels: Waldorf, 1965, Penguin, 1968; The Man From Greek and Roman, 1974; Myself As Witness, 1980, Penguin, 1981; Fulton County, 1989; Screenplays: The Lion in Winter, 1968; They Might Be Giants, 1970; Nicholas and Alexandra, 1971; Robin and Marian, 1976; White Nights (with Eric Hughes), 1985; Television: Evening Primrose (music by Stephen Sondheim), 1967; Oliver Twist, 1982; Anna Karenina, 1985; Anastasia: The Mystery of Anna, 1986. Address: c/o William Morris Agency, 1350 Avenue of the Americas, New York, NY 10019, USA.

GOLDMAN Paul H(enry) J(oseph), b. 3 Apr 1950, London, England. Museum Curator; Art Historian. m. Corinna Maroulis, 11 July 1987. Education: BA Hons, English, London University, 1971; Postgraduate Diploma in Art Gallery and Museum Studies (Dip AGMS) University of Manchester, 1972; Diploma of the Museums Association in Art (AMA), 1978. Publications: Sporting Life, An Anthology of British Sporting Prints, 1983; Looking at Prints, Drawings and Watercolours, 1988; Victorian Illustrated Books 1850-1870 - The Heyday of Wood-Engraving, 1994; Victorian Illustration - The Pre-Raphaelites, The Idyllic School and the High Victorians, 1996. Contributions to: Connoisseur; Antique Collector; British Library Journal; Antique and New Art; Antiquarian Book Monthly Review; Print Quarterly; Art Bulletin of Tasmania; International Journal of Heritage Studies; Book Dealer; Book Collector. Honours: Elected Fellow of the Royal Society of Arts, 1989 (FRSA); Elected Fellow of the Museums Association (FMA), 1990. Memberships: Society of Authors; Museums Association; Trustee, Cartoon Art Trust, 1993; Imaginative Book Illustration Society, committee member. Address: c/o Department of Prints and Drawings, The British Museum, Great Russell Street, London WC1, England.

GOLDREIN Iain Saville, b. 10 Aug 1952, Crosby, Liverpool, England. Barrister. m. Margaret de Haas, 18 May 1980, 1 son, 1 daughter. Education: Pembroke College, Cambridge. Appointment: Visiting Professor, Sir Jack Jacob Chair of Litigation, Nottingham Law School. Publications: Personal Injury Litigation Practice and Precedents, 1985; Ship Sale and Purchase Law and Technique, 1985; Commerical Litigation Pre-Emptive Remedies, 1987, 2nd edition 1991; Butterworths Personal Injury Litigation Service, 1988; Pleadings: Principles and Practice (with Sir Jack Jacob), 1990; Bullen, Leake & Jacob, Precedents of Pleadings, 1990. Contributions to: Law Society Gazette; New Law Journal; Solicitors Journal, Insurance at Re-insurance Research Group. Memberships: Middle Temple; Inner Temple; Northern Circuit; Associate of the Chartered Institute of Arbitrators; British Academy of Experts; Britith Insurance Law Association; Committee of the International Litigation Practitioners Forum; International Union of Lawyers. Address: J Harcourt Buildings, Temple, London EC4Y 9DA, England.

GOLDSCHEIDER Gabriele Maria, b. 7 Mar 1929, Vienna, Austria. Bookseller; Author; Publisher. Education: Convent of Our Lady of Sion, Acton, Burnell, 1940-47; Blunt House, Oxted, 1947-49; Ruskin School of Art, Oxford, 1949-53; Dip French, Neuchatel University, 1953. Appointments: Editor, Hamlyn Publications, Feltham, Middlesex, England, 1967-74; General Editor, Medallion Collectors' Series, 1979-83. Publications: A Bibliography of Sir Arthur Conan Doyle, 1977; Dolls, 1979; Ed & Publr, Richard Jeffries: A Modern Appraisal, 1984; A Sheaf of Verses by Radclyffe Hall (Editor and Publisher), 1985; A Bibliography of Eleanor Farjeon. Contributions to: Journals. Address: Deep Dene, Baring Road, Cowes, Isle of Wight PO31 8DB, England.

GOLDSMITH Edward Rene David, b. 8 Nov 1928. Author; Publisher; Editor. m. (1) Gillian Marion Pretty, 1953, 1 son, 2 daughters, (2) Katherine Victoria James, 1981, 2 sons. Education: MA, Magdalen College, Oxford. Appointments: Publisher, Editor, The Ecologist, 1970-; Adjunct Associate Professor, University of Michigan, 1975; Visiting Professor, Sangamon State Univesity, 1984. Publications: Can Britain Survive? (editor), 1971; A Blueprint for Survival (with R Allen), 1972; The Future of an Affluent Society: The Case of Canada, 1976; The Stable Society(editor with J M Brunett),

1977; La Medecine a la Question (editor with J M Brunett), 1981; The Social and Environmental Effects of Large Dams, vol 1 (with N Hildyard), 1984, vol II (editor with N Hildyard), 1986; Green Britain or Industrial Wasteland? (with N Hildyard), 1986; The Earth Report (editor with N Hildyard), 1988; The Great U-Turn, 1988. Address: Whitehay, Witiel, Bodmin, Cornwall, England.

GOLDSTEIN Rebecca, b. 23 Feb 1950, New York, New York, USA. Novelist; Philosopher. m. Sheldon Goldstein, 25 June 1969, 2 daughters. Education: BA, Barnard College, Columbia University, 1972; PhD, Princeton University, 1976. Publications: The Mind Body Problem, 1983; The Late Summer Passion of a Woman of Mind, 1989; The Dark Sister, 1991; Strange Attractors: Stories, 1993; Mazel, 1995. Honours: Whiting Writers Award, 1991; MacArthur Fellow, 1996. Membership: PEN. Address: 15th N 7th Avenue, Highland Park, NJ 08904, USA.

GOLDSTEIN Robert Justin, b. 28 Mar 1947, Albany, New York, USA. College Professor. Education: BA, University of Illinois, 1969; MA, 1971, PhD, 1976, University of Chicago. Appointments: Research and Administrative Assistant, University of Illinois, 1972-73; Lecturer, San Diego State University, 1974-76; Assistant Professor, Associate Professor, Full Professor, Oakland University, Rochester, Michigan, 1976-. Publications: Political Repression in Modern America, 1978; Political Repression in Nineteenth Century Europe, 1983; Political Censorship of the Press and the Arts in Nineteenth Century Europe, 1989; Censorship of Political Caricature in Nineteenth Century France, 1989; Saving "Old Glory": The History of the American Flag Desecration Controversy, 1995; Burning the Flag: The Great 1989-90 American Flag Desecration Controversy, 1996; Descrating the American Flag: Key Documents form the Controversy from the Civil War to 1995, 1996. Address: Department of Political Science, Oakland University, Rochester, MI 48309, USA.

GOLDSWORTHY Peter, b. 12 Oct 1951, Minlaton, South Australia, Australia. Poet. m. Helen Louise Wharldall, 1972, 1 son, 2 daughters. Education: BMed and BSurg, University of Adelaide. Appointment: Medical Practitioner, Adelaide, 1974-. Publications: Readings from Ecclesiastes, 1982; This Goes With This, 1988; Novel: Maestro, 1989; Short stories: Archipelagoes, 1982; Zooing, 1986; Bleak Rooms, 1988. Co-editor: Number Three Friendly Street: Poetry Reader, 1979. Honours: Commonwealth Poetry Prize, 1982; Australia Council Fellowships. Address: 8 Rose Street, Prospect, South Australia 5082, Australia.

GOMERY Douglas, b. 5 Apr 1945, New York, New York, USA. Professor; Writer. m. Marilyn Moon, 1973. Education: BS, Lehigh University, 1967; MA, 1970, PhD, 1975, University of Wisconsin at Madison. Appointments: Instructor to Associate Professor, University of Wisconsin at Milwaukee, 1974-81; Visiting Professor, University of Wisconsin at Madison, 1977, Northwestern University, 1981, University of Iowa, 1982, University of Utrecht, 1990, 1992; Associate Professor, 1981-86, Professor, Department of Radio-Television-Film, 1987-92, then College of Journalism, 1992-, University of Maryland; Senior Researcher, Woodrow Wilson Center for International Scholars, Washington, DC, 1988-92. Publications: High Sierra: Screenplay and Analysis, 1979; Film History: Theory and Practice (with Robert C Allen), 1985; The Hollywood Studio System, 1986; The Will Hays Papers, 1987; American Media (with Philip Cook and Lawrence W Lichty), 1989; The Art of Moving Shadows (with Annette Michelson and Patrick Loughney), 1989; Movie History: A Survey, 1991; Shared Pleasures, 1992; The Future of News (with Philip Cook and Lawrence W Lichty), 1992; A Media Studies Primer (with Michael Cornfield and Lawrence W Lichty), 1997. Contributions to: Books and scholarly journals. Honours: Jeffrey Weiss Literary Prize, Theatre Historical Society, 1988; Prize, Theatre Library Association, 1992. Address: 4817 Drummond Avenue, Chevy Chase, MD 20815, USA.

GOMEZ Christine, b. 24 Apr 1947, Madras, India. Teacher. m. Patrick Gomez, 21 Oct 1970, 1 son. Education: BSc, 1966; MA, 1968; PhD, 1982. Appointments: Board of Studies, Bharathidasan University, 1982-84; Ad Hoc Committee, Mother Theresa Womens University, 1984-85; Board of Studies, Bharathi Dasan University, 1984-87. Publications: The Alienated Figure in Drama; Fire Blossoms; The Treasure Hunt; Favourite Stories; Lamplight and Shadows; Love's Triumph; Deiva Dharisanam; Stations of the Cross; Yatra. Contributions to: Hamlet Studies; Indian Journal of Shakespeare Studies. Honour: First Prize, All India Play Writing Competition. Memberships: PEN; Indian Society for Commonwealth Studies; Indian

Association of Literary Critics and Theorists; ASRC. Address: Vilma, C91 North East Extension, Thillainagar, Tiruchy 620018, India.

GONCZ Arpad, b. 10 Feb 1922, Budapest, Hungary. President, Republic of Hungary. Writer. m. Zsuzsanna Maria Gonter, 2 sons, 2 daughters. Education: Pazmany Peter University, 1938-44; University of Agricultural Sciences, 1952-56. Appointment: President, Republic of Hungary, 1990-, Re-elected, 1995. Publications: Hungarian Medea; Men of God; Iron Bars; Balance; A Pessimistic Comedy; Persephone; Encounters; Homecoming. Contributions to: Regularly in Hungarian Literary Magazines. Honours: Jozsef Attila Award; Wheatland Prize; Premio Mediterraneo. Memberships: Hungarian Writers Association; Hungarian Writers Union; Hungarian PEN Club. Literary Agent: Artisjus, Agency for Literature and Theatre. Address: Parliament, Kossuth ter 1-3, Budapest V, 1055, Hungary.

GONZALEZ Luis Daniel, b. 5 Apr 1955, El Rosal, Pontevedra, Spain. Education: Graduate, Physical Sciences, Valladolid, Spain, 1977. Publications: Deporte y Educación, 1993; Los Mejores - La Ambición y el Liderazgo en el Deporte, 1993; Islas Llenas de Tesoros - Elogio de Los Clásicos Juveniles (co-author and editor), 1994; Guía de Clásicos de Literatura Infantil y Juvenil, 1997. Address: Gamazo 12 30, 47004 Valladolid, Spain.

GONZALEZ-CRUSSI Frank, b. 4 Oct 1936, Mexico City, Mexico. Professor; Writer. m. (1) Ana Luz, div, 2 sons, 1 daughters, (2) Wei Hsueh, 7 Oct 1978. Education: BA, 1954, MD, 1961, Universidad Nacional Autonoma de Mexico. Appointments: Intern, Penrose Hospital, Colorado Springs, 1962; Resident in Pathology, St Lawrence Hospital, Lansing; Shands Teaching Hospital, University of Florida, Gainesville; 1963-67; Assistant Professor of Pathology, Queens University, Kingston, 1967-73; Associate Professor of Pathology, Indiana University-Purdue University at Indianapolis, 1973-78; Professor of Pathology, Northwestern University, Chicago, 1978-; Head of Laboratories, Children's Memorial Hospital,, Chicago. Publications: Notes of an Anatomist, 1985; Three Forms of Sudden Death; Other Reflections on the Grandeur and Misery of the Body, 1986; On the Nature of Things Erotic, 1988; Extragonadal Teratomas; Wilm's Tumor and Related Renal Neoplasms of Childhood. Contributions to: Numerous specialized medial journals. Honour: Best Nonfiction Award for the Society of Midland Authors, 1985. Memberships: International Academy of Pathology; Society for Pediatric Patholgy; American Society of Clinical Pathologists; Royal College of Physicians and Surgeons of Canada; Chicago Pathology Society; Authors Guild; Society of Midland Authors. Address: 2626 North Lakeview Avenue, Chicago, IL 60614, USA.

GOOCH John, b. 25 Aug 1945, Weston Favell. Professor. m. Catherine Ann Staley. Education: BA (First Class Honours), 1966, PhD 1969, King's College, London. Appointments: Secretary of the Navy Senior Research Fellow, US Naval War College, Newport, Rhode Island, USA, 1985-86; Reader in History, University of Lancaster, England, 1986-87; Visiting Professor, Yale University, USA, 1988; Professor of History, University of Lancaster, 1987-91; Professor, International History, University of Leeds, England, 1992-. Publications: The Plans of War: The General Staff and British Military Strategy c. 1900-1916, 1974; Armies in Europe, 1980; The Prospect of War: Studies in British Defence Policy 1847-1942, 1981; Strategy and the Social Sciences, 1981; Politicians and Defence: Studies in the Formulation of British Defence Policy (with Ian F W Beckett), Military Deception and Strategic Suprise, 1982; Army State and Society in Italy 1870-1915, 1989; Military Misfortunes (with Eliot A Cohen), 1990; Decisive Campaignes of the Second World War, 1990; Air Power: Theory and Practice, 1995. Contributions to: History Journals. Memberships: Fellow, Royal Historical Society; Chairman, Army Records Society; Vice President, Royal Historical Society. Honours: Premio internazionale di cultura, Citta di Anghiari, 1983; Knight of the Royal Military Order of Vila Viçosa, Portugal, 1991. Address: c/o School of History, University of Leeds, Leeds LS2 9JT, England.

GOOCH Stanley Alfred, b. 13 June 1932, London, England. m. Ruth Senior, 1 Apr 1961. Education: BA (Hons), Modern Languages, King's College, 1955; Diploma in Education, Institute of Education, London, 1957; BSc (Hons), Psychology, Birkbeck College, 1962, London. Publications: Four Years On, 1966; Total Man, 1972; Personality and Evolution, 1973; The Neanderthal Question, 1977; The Paranormal, 1978; Guardians of the Ancient Wisdom, 1979; The Double Helix of the Mind, 1980; The Secret Life of Humans, 1981; Creatures from Inner Space, 1984; The Child with Asthma, 1986;

Cities of Dreams, 1989, revised, 1995. Contributions to: New Scientist; New Society; British Journal of Psychology; British Journal of Social and Clinical Psychology; British Journal of Educational Psychology; International Journal of Human Development. Honours: Royal Literary Fund Awards, 1984, 1987, 1994. Address: c/o David Percy, 25 Belsize Park, Hampstead, London NW3 4DU, England.

GOOCH Steve, b. 22 July 1945, Surrey, England. Dramatist. Education: BA, Trinity College, 1967; Graduate Studies, St John's College, Cambridge, 1967-68, University of Birmingham, 1968-69. Appointments: Assistant Editor, Plays and Players magazines, London, 1972-73; Resident Dramatist, Half Moon Theatre, London, 1973-74, Greenwich Theatre, London, 1974-75, Solent People's Theatre, Southampton, 1982, Theatre Venture, London, 1983-84, Warehouse Theatre, Croydon, 1986-87, Gate Theatre, Notting Hill, 1990-91. Publications: Big Wolf(translation), 1972; The Mother (translation), 1973; Female Transport, 1974; The Motor Show (with Paul Thompson), 1974; Will Wat, If Not, What Will, 1975; Wolf Biermann's Poems and Ballads (translation), 1977; The Women Pirates, 1978; Wallraff: The Undesirable Journalist (translation), 1978; Fast One, 1982; Landmark, 1982; All Together Now, 1984; Taking Liberties, 1984; Mr Fun, 1986; Writing A Play, 1988, new edition 1995; Lulu and the Marquis of Keith (translation), 1990; Stages of Translation (essay), 1996. Contributions to: Time Out; Theatre Quarterly; Drama. Honours: Harper-Wood Scholarship, 1968; Arts Council of Great Britain Bursaries: 1980, 1987, 1992. Address: c/o Micheline Steinberg Playwrights, 409 Triumph House, 187-191 Regent Street, London W1R 7WF, England.

GOODFIELD June (Gwyneth), b. 1 June 1927, Stratford-on-Avon, England. Author; Clarence J Robinson Professor. Education: BSc (Honours) Zoology, University of London, England, 1949; PhD, History and Philosophy of Science, University of Leeds, 1959. Publications: From the Face of the Earth; An Imagined World; Play God; The Siege of Cancer; Courier to Peking (novel); A Chance to Live; The Planned Miracle, 1991. Contributions to: London Review of Books; Nature; Scientific American; American Scholar; Science. Memberships: PEN Club; English Speaking Union; President, United Nations Association (London), 1986-87. Literary Agent: Hilary Rubinstein, A P Watt Ltd, London. Address: The Manor House, Alfriston, East Sussex BN26 5SY, England.

GOODHEART Eugene, b. 26 June 1931, New York, New York, USA. Professor of Humanities; Writer. m. Joan Bamberger, 1 son, 1 daughter. Education: BA in English, Columbia College, 1953; MA in English, University of Virginia, 1954; Sorbonne, University of Paris, 1956-57; PhD in English and Comparative Literature, Columbia University, 1961. Appointments: Instructor, 1958-60, Assistant Professor, 1960-62, Bard College; Assistant Professor, University of Chicago, 1962-66; Associate Professor, Mount Holyoke College, 1966-67; Associate Professor, Professor, 1970-74, Massachusetts Institute of Technology; Visiting Professor, Wellesley College, 1968; Professor, Boston University, 1974-83; Corresponding Editor, Partisan Review, 1978-; Edytha Macy Gross Professor of Humanities, 1983-, Director, Center for the Humanities, 1986-, Brandeis University; Adjunct Professor of English, Columbia Unversity, 1986. Publications: The Utopian Vision of D H Lawrence, 1963; The Cult of the Ego: The Self in Modern Literature, 1968; Culture and the Radical Conscience, 1978; The Failure of Criticism, 1978; The Skeptic Disposition in Contemporary Criticism, 1984, new edition, 1991; Pieces of Resistance, 1987; Desire and Its Discontents, 1991; The Reign of Ideology, 1996. Contributions to: Journals and periodicals. Honours: Fulbright Scholarship, Paris, 1956-57; American Council of Learned Societies Fellowship, 1965-66; Guggenheim Felowship, 1970-71; National Endowment for the Humanities Senior Fellowship, 1981; National Humanities Center Fellow, 1987-88; Rockefeller Foundation Fellowship, Bellagio, Italy, 1989; Phi Beta Kappa. Memberships: PEN. Address: c/o Department of English, Brandeis University, Waltham, MA 02254, USA.

GOODISON Lorna (Gaye), b. 1 Aug 1947, Kingston, Jamaica. Poet; Painter; Freelance Writer. Education: Art schools in Kingston and New York, 1967-69. Appointments: Teacher of Creative Writing, various schools in the USA and Canada. Publications: Poetry: Tamarind Season, 1980; I Am Becoming My Mother, 1986; Heartease, 1988; To Us All Flowers Are Roses, 1992; Selected Poems, 1992; Short stories: Baby Mother and the King of Swords, 1989. Honours: Institute of Jamaica Centenary Prize, 1981; Commonwealth Poetry Prize, 1986. Address: 8 Marley Close, Kingston 6, Jamaica, West Indies.

GOODMAN Jonathan, b. 17 Jan 1931, London, England. Author; Publisher; Editor. Appointments: Theatre Director and Television Producer, various companies, United Kingdom, 1951-64; Director, Anmbar Publications Ltd, London, 1967-; General Editor, Celebrated Trials Series, David & Charles (Publishers) Ltd, Newton Abbott, Devon, 1972-. Publications: Martinee Idylls (poetry), 1954; Instead of Murder (novel), 1961; Criminal Tendencies (novel), 1964; Hello Cruel World Goodbye (novel), 1964; The Killing of Julia Wallace, 1969; Bloody Versicles, 1971; Posts-Mortem, 1971; Trial of Ian Brady and Myra Hindley (editor), 1973; Trial of Ian Ruth Ellis (editor), 1975; The Burning of Evelyn Foster, 1977; The Last Sentence (novel), 1978; The Stabbing of George Harry Storrs, 1982; Pleasure of Murder, 1983; Railway Murders, 1984; Who-He, 1984; Seaside Murders, 1985; The Crippen File (editor) 1985; The Underworld (with I Will), 1985; Christmas Murders (editor) 1986; The Moors Murders, 1986; Acts of Murder, 1986; Murder in High Places, 1986; The Slaying of Joseph Bowne Elwell, 1987. Address: 43 Ealing Village, London W5 2LZ, England.

GOODRICH Norma Lorre, b. 10 May 1917, Huntington, Vermont, USA. Professor. m. (1) Captain J M A Lorre, 1944, (2) Captain J H Howard, 1964.1 son. Education: BS, University of Vermont, 1938; Université de Grenoble, 1939; Université de Paris, 1946-53; PhD, Columbia University, 1965; Litt D, University of Vermont, 1995. Appointments: Writer, newspaper articles throughout USA, 1938-59; Encyclopaedia articles: Grolier Corporation and Princeton University Press, 1953-70; Princeton University Press, 1965-70; Author, Franklin Watts Publishers, 1982-, Harper Collins, 1986-. Publications: The Doctor and Maria Theresa, 1962; Charles, Duke of Orleans, 1963; Ways of Love, Medieval Romances, 1965; Charles of Orleans, 1967; Medieval Myths, republished in hardcover, 1994, paperback, 1997. Ancient Myths, republished in hardcover, 1994, paperback, 1997. King Arthur; Merlin; Guinevere; Priestesses; Jean Giono, A Study of Themes; The Holy Grail. Contributions to: Etudes Rabelaisiennes; Romantic Review; Revue de Littérature Comparée; French Review. Address: 620 Diablo Drive, Claremont, CA 91711, USA.

GOODRICK-CLARKE Nicholas, b. 15 Jan 1953, Lincoln, England. Author; Historian. m. Clare Radene Badham, 11 May 1985. Education: Lancing College, 1966-70; Jagdschloss Glienicke, Berlin, 1971; University of Bristol, 1971-74; University of Oxford, 1975-78. Appointments: Editor, Essential Readings, 1983-; Director, IKON Productions Ltd, 1988-. Publications: The Occult Roots of Nazism; Paracelsus; The Enchanted City; Hitler's Priestess, The International Nazi Underground. Contributions to: Durham University Journal; Theosophical History; Images of War; Decadence and Innovation; Ambix; Politica Hermetica; Le Nouvel Observateur. The Times. Memberships: Society of Authors; Scientific & Medical Network; Keston College. Address: Manor Farm House, Manor Road, Wantage OX12 8NE, England.

GOODWIN SUZANNE. See: EBEL Suzanne.

GOODWIN (Trevor) Noël, b. 25 Dec 1927, Fowey, Cornwall, England. Writer; Critic. m. Anne Mason Myers, 23 Nov 1963, 1 stepson. Education: BA, London. Appointments: Assistant Music Critic, News Chronicle, 1952-54; Manchester Guardian, 1954-55; Music & Dance Critic, Daily Express, 1956-78; Associate Editor, Dance & Dancers, 1958-; Executive Editor, Music & Musicians, 1963-71; London Dance Critic, International Herald Tribune, Paris, 1978-83; London Correspondent, Opera News, New York, 1980-91; Overseas News Editor, Opera, 1985-91, now member of Editorial Board; planned and presented numerous radio programmes. Publications: London Symphony, Portrait of an Orchestra; A Ballet for Scotland; A Knight at the Opera; Royal Opera and Royal Ballet Yearbooks; Area Editor, Writer, New Grove Dictionary of Music and Musicians; A Portrait of the Royal Ballet. Contributions to: Encyclopaedia Britannica; Encyclopaedia of Opera; Britannica Books of the Year; Cambridge Encyclopaedia of Russia and the Former Soviet Union; New Oxford Companion to Music; Pipers Enzyklopädie des Musiktheaters; New Grove Dictionary of Opera; Viking Opera Guide; International Dictionary of Ballet; Metropolitan Opera Guide to Recorded Opera. Membership: Critics' Circle of Great Britain, president 1977. Address: 76 Skeena Hill, London SW18 5PN, England.

GOONERATNE Malini Yasmine, b. 22 Dec 1935, Colombo, Sri Lanka. Writer; Poet; Editor; Professor. m. Brendon Gooneratne, 31 Dec 1962, 1 son, 1 daughter. Education: BA, 1st Class Honours, Ceylon, 1959; PhD, English Literature, Cambridge University, 1962; DLitt, English and Commonwealth Literature, Macquarie University, Australia, 1981. Appointments: Editor, New Ceylon Writing, 1971-; Director, Post-Colonial Literature and Language Research Centre, 1988-93, Personal Chair in English Literature, 1991, Macquarie University; Visiting Professor of English, University of Michigan, USA, Edith Cowan University, Western Australia, 1991; External Advisor, Department of English, University of the South Pacific, 1993, 1995. Publications: English Literature in Ceylon 1815-1878: The Development of an Anglo-Ceylonese Literature, 1968; Jane Austen, 1970; Word Bird, Motif, 53 Poems, 1971; The Lizard's Cry and Other Poems, 1972; Alexander Pope, 1976; Poems from India, Sri Lanka, Malaysia and Singapore (editor), 1979; Stories from Sri Lanka (editor), 1979; Diverse Inheritance: A Personal Perspective on Commonwealth Literature, 1980; 6000 Foot Death Dive, poems, 1981; Silence, Exile, and Cunning: The Fiction of Ruth Prawer Jhabvala, 1983; Relative Merits, 1986; Celebrations and Departures, poems, 1991; A Change of Skies, novel, 1991; The Pleasures of Conquest, 1995; Raredom House Australia, 1996. Contributions to: Various publications. Honours: Order of Australia, 1990; Eleanor Dark Writers Fellowship, 1991; Marjorie Barnard Literary Award for Fiction, 1992; Several research and travel grants. Memberships: Australian Society of Authors; Fédération Internationales des Langues et Littératures Modernes, vice-president, 1990-96; International Association of University Professors of English; Jane Austen Society of Australia, patron; Friends of Macquarie University Library, vice-president; New South Wales Writers Centre; South Asian Studies Association of Australia; South Pacific Branch of the Association for Commonwealth Literature and Language Studies. Address: c/o School of English, Linguistics and Media, Macquarie University, North Ryde, New South Wales 2109, Australia.

GOONETILLEKE Devapriya Chitra Ranjan Alwis, b. 9 Oct 1938, Colombo, Sir Lanka. Professor of English. m. Chitranganie Lalitha Dalpatadu, 23 Nov 1967, 2 sons. Education: BA, 1961; PhD, 1970. Appointments: Regional Representative, The Journal of Commonwealth Literature, 1978; Associate Editor, Journal of South Asian Literature, 1980; National Editor, The Routledge Encyclopaedia of Commonwealth Literature, 1990; Advisor, Contemporary Novelists, 1990; Advisor, Reference Guide to Short Fiction, 1992. Publications: Developing Countries in British Fiction; Images of the Raj; Joseph Conrad: Beyond Culture and Background; The Penguin New Writing in Sri Lanka; Between Cultures: Essays on Literature, Language and Education; Joseph Conrad: Heart of Darkness, 1995. Contributions to: 60 articles. Honours: Commonwealth Scholar; Foundation Visiting Fellow, Clare Hall; Henry Charles Chapman Visiting Fellow, University of London. Memberships: International Chairperson, the Association for Commonwealth Literature and Language Studies; American Studies Association. Address: No 1 Kandewatta Road, Nugegoda, Sri Lanka.

GOPALACHAR Aalavandar, b. 1 July 1929, Nanjangud, Kamataka, India. Author; Poet. m. 3 sons, 2 daughters. Publications: Over 30 novels; Numerous short stories; Poems. Contributions to: Various publications. Honours: Several awards. Membership: Poets International. Address: Sahitya Kuteera, No 261/1, Byrappa Block, 2nd Main, Thyagarajanagar Post, Banglore 560 028, Kamataka, South India.

GOPU. See: **GOKANI Pushkar Haridas.**

GORAK Jan, b. 12 Oct 1952, Blackburn, Lancashire, England. Professor of English; Writer. m. Irene Elizabeth Mannion, 12 Dec 1983. Education: BA, University of Warwick, 1975; MA, 1981, PhD, 1983, University of Southern California, Los Angeles. Appointments: Lecturer, 1984-87, Senior Lecturer, 1988, University of the Witwatersrand; Associate Professor, 1988-92, Professor of English, 1992-, University of Denver. Publications: God the Artist: American Novelists in a Post-Realist Age, 1987; Frank Kermode: Critic of Crisis, 1987; The Alien Mind of Raymond Williams, 1988; The Making of the Modern Canon: Genesis and Crisis of a Literary Idea, 1991; "Canons, 1660-1800", in the Cambridge History of Literary Criticism, Vol I, 1996. Contributions to: Books and scholarly journals. Honours: Thomas Pringle Award for Literary Articles, English Academy of Southern Africa, 1986; Andrew W Mellon/ Eighteenth-Century Society Fellowship, University of Texas at Austin, 1994; External Fellowship,

Oregon State University, 1994-95. Memberships: American Society for Eighteenth-Century Studies; T S Eliot Society. Address: c/o Department of English, University of Denver, Denver, CO 80208, USA.

GORDIMER Nadine, b. 20 Nov 1923, Springs, South Africa. Author. m. (1) Gerald Gavronsky, 4 Mar 1949, div 1952, 1 daughter, (2) Reinhold Cassirer, 29 Jan 1954, 1 son. Publications: The Soft Voice of the Serpent; The Lying Days, 1953; Six Feet of the Country, 1956; A World of Strangers, 1958; Friday's Footprint, 1960; Occasion for Loving, 1963; Not for Publication, 1965; The Late Bourgeois World, 1966; A Guest of Honour, 1970; Livingstone's Companions, 1972; The Black Interpreters (literary criticism), 1973; The Conservationist, 1974; Selected Stories, 1975; Some Monday for Sure, 1976; Burger's Daughter, 1979; A Soldier's Embrace, 1980; July's People, 1981; Something Out There, 1984; Six Feet of Country, 1986; A Sport of Nature, 1987; The Essential Gesture (essays), 1988; My Sons' Story (novel), 1991; Jump (story collection), 1992; None to Accompany Me (novel), 1994; Writing and Being, 1995. Contributions to: Co-editor, South African Writing Today, 1967. Honours: W H Smith Literary Award, 1961; Thomas Pringle Award, 1969; James Tait Black Memorial Prize, 1971; Booker Prize (co-winner), 1974; Grand Aigle d'Or Prize, France, 1975; Scottish Arts Council Neil M Gun Fellowship, 1981; Modern Language Association Award, USA, 1981; Memberships: American Academy of Art and Sciences, honorary fellow; American Academy and Institute of Arts and Letters, honorary member; Congress of South African Writers; International PEN; Modern Language Association of America, honorary fellow; Royal Society of Literature, fellow. Address: 7 Frere Road, Parktown, Johannesburg 2193, South Africa.

GORDON Diana. See: **ANDREWS Lucilla Matthew.**

GORDON Donald. See: **PAYNE Donald Gordon.**

GORDON Donald Ramsay, b. 14 Sept 1929, Toronto, Ontario, Canada. Writer. m. Helen E Currie, 21 Dec 1952, 3 sons. Education: BA (Hons), Political Science, Economics, Queen's University, Kingston, 1953; MA, Political Economy, University of Toronto, 1955; Predoctoral studies, Political Science, London School of Economics and Political Science, England, 1956-63. Appointments: Writer, Filing Editor, The Canadian Press, Toronto, Montreal, Edmonton, 1955; Assistant Editor, The Financial Post, Toronto, 1955-57; European Correspondent, Canadian Broadcasting Corporation, London, 1957-63; Assistant Professor, Associate Professor, Political Science, University of Calgary, Alberta, 1963-66, University of Waterloo, Ontario, 1966-75; Self-employed Writer, Consultant, 1975-81; Chief Writer, The Image Corporation, Waterloo, 1983-92; Instructor, Conestoga College, Kitchener, Ontario, 1991-, Long Ridge Writers Group, West Redding, Connecticut, USA, 1992-. Publications: Language, Logic and the Mass Media, 1966; The New Literacy, 1971; The Media, 1972; Fineswine, 1984; The Rock Candy Bandits, 1984; S.P.E.E.D. 1984; The Prosperian Papers, 1989; The Choice, 1990; The Sex Shoppe, 1991. Address: 134 Iroquois Place, Waterloo, Ontario N2L 2S5, Canada.

GORDON Giles b. 23 May 1940, Edinburgh, Scotland. Writer; Literary Agent; Editor; Lecturer. m. (1) Margaret Eastoe, dec, 2 sons, 1 dec, 1 daughter, (2) Maggie McKernan, 2 daughters. Education: Edinburgh Academy. Appointments: Editor, Hutchinson & Co, and Penguin Books; Editorial Director, Victor Gollancz Ltd; Lecturer, Tufts and Hollins Universities; Editor, Short Story Collections, Bloomsbury Classics, 1995-, Clarion Tales, 1996-. Publications: Two and Two Makes One, 1966; Two Elegies, 1968; Pictures from an Exhibition, 1970; The Umbrella Man, 1971; Twelve Poems for Callum, 1972; About a Marriage, 1972; Girl with Red Hair, 1974; Farewell Fond Dreams, 1975; Beyond the Words (editor), 1975; 100 Scenes from Married Life, 1976; Members of the Jury (editor with Dulan Barber), 1976; Enemies, 1977; Ambrose's Vision, 1980; Modern Short Stories, 1940-1980 (editor); 1982; Best Short Stories (editor with David Hughes), 10 volumes, 1986-95; The Twentieth Century Short Story in English, 1989; Aren't We Due a Royalty Statement?, 1993. Contributions to: Times, Scotsman, Spectator, London Daily News, Observer. Memberships: Royal Society of Literature, fellow; Society of Authors; PEN. Address: 6 Ann Street, Edinburgh EH4 1JP, Scotland.

GORDON Jaimy, b. 4 July 1944, Baltimore, Maryland, USA. Professor of English; Writer. m. Peter Blickle, 1988. Education: BA, Antioch College, 1966; MA, 1972, DA, 1975, Brown University. Appointments: Writer-in-Residence, Rhode Island State Council on the Arts, 1975-77; Director, Creative Writing Program, Stephens College,

Columbia, Missouri, 1980-81; Assistant Professor, 1981-87, Associate Professor, 1987-92, Professor of English, 1992-, Western Michigan University, Kalamazoo. Publications: Shamp of the City-Solo, 1974; The Bend, the Lip, the Kid (narrative poem), 1978; Circumspection from an Equestrian Statue, 1979; Maria Beig: Lost Weddings (translator with Peter Blickle), 1990; She Drove Without Stopping, 1990. Contributions to: Magazines. Honours: National Endowment for the Arts Fellowships, 1979, 1991; American Academy and Institute of Arts and Letters Award, 1991. Address: 1803 Hazel Street, Kalamazoo, MI 49008, USA.

GORDON John Fraser, b. 18 Feb 1916, London, England. Writer. Education: City of London College. Appointments: Managing Director, Dongora Mill Co Ltd, London and J F Gordon (London) Ltd, 1963-. Publications: Staffordshire Bull Terrier Handbook, Bull Terrier Handbook, Bulldog Handbook, Dandie Dinmont Terrier Handbook, 1952-59; Staffordshire Bull Terriers, 1964; Miniature Schnauzers, 1966; Spaniel Owner's Encyclopaedia, 1967; Staffordshire Bull Terrier Owner's Encyclopaedia, 1967; The Beagle Guide, 1968; The Miniature Schnauzer Guide, 1968; All About the Boxer, 1970; The Staffordshire Bull Terrier, 11 editions, 1970; All About the Cocker Spaniel, 1971; The Pug, 1973; The German Shepherd, 1978; World of Dogs Atlas Pictorials, 1978; The Pyrenean Mountain Dog, 1978; The Alaskan Malamute, 1979; Schnauzers, 1982; All About the Staffordshire Bull Terrier, 1984; All About The Cairn Terrier, 1987; Lecturer, Canine Matters. Honours: Freeman of the City of London and Member of the Guild of Freemen, 1938; Horticultural Hybridist of Fuchsia Gordon's China Rose, 1953. Membership: Society of Authors, 1969; Life Vice-President, Southern Counties Staffordshire Terrier Society of London; Antiquarian Horological Society. Address: The Moat House, 4 St Martins Mews, Chipping Ongar, Essex CM5 9HY, England.

GORDON John William, b. 19 Nov 1925, Jarrow-on-Tyne, England. Writer. m. Sylvia Young, 9 Jan 1954, 1 son, 1 daughter. Publications: The Giant Under the Snow, 1968, sequel, Ride the Wind, 1989; The House on the Brink, 1970; The Ghost on the Hill, 1976; The Waterfall Box, 1978; The Spitfire Grave, 1979; The Edge of the World, 1983; Catch Your Death, 1984; The Quelling Eye, 1986; The Grasshopper, 1987; Secret Corridor, 1990; Blood Brothers, 1991; Ordinary Seaman (autobiography), 1992; The Burning Baby, 1992; Gilray's Ghost, 1995; The Flesh Eater, forthcoming. Contributions to: Beginnings (Signal 1989); Ghosts & Scholars 21. Membership: Society of Authors. Address: 99 George Borrow Road, Norwich, NR4 7HU, England.

GORDON Lois, b. 13 Nov 1938, USA. Professor. m. Alan Gordon, MD, 26 Nov 1961, 1 son. Education: BA, University of Michigan, 1960; MA, 1962, PhD, 1966, University of Wisconsin. Appointments: Lecturer, City College of the City University of New Yoak, 1964-66; Univ of Missouri, Kansas City, 1966-68, Fairleigh Dickenson University, 1968-; Visiting Exchange Professor, Rutgers University, 1994. Publications: Donald Barthelme, 1980; Robert Coover: The Universal Fiction Making Process, 1982; American Chronicle: Six Decades in American Life 1920-1979, 1987; Harold Pinter: A Casebook, 1990; American Chronicle, 7 Decades in American Life, 1920-1989, 1990; The Columbia Chronicles of American Life, 1910-1992, 1995; The World of Samuel Beckett, 1996. Contributions to: Numerous scholarly essays on contemporary authors and American culture; book reviews for journals such as Modern Drama, and newspapers such as The New York Times. Honours: National Merit Supplementary Scholarship, 1960-62; Barber Scholarship, 1960-62; Research Scholarships at University of Wisconsin, University of Missouri, Fairleigh Dickenson University. Memberships: PEN; Modern Language Association; Academy of American Poets; Harold Pinter Society; Samuel Beckett Society. Address: 300 Central Park West, New York, NY 10024, USA.

GORDON Michael. See: **CRITCHLEY Sir Julian.**

GORDON Rex. See: **HOUGH Stanley Bennett.**

GORES Joseph (Nicholas), b. 25 Dec 1931, Rochester, Minnesota, USA. Writer; Novelist; Screenwriter. m. Dori Corfitzen, 16 May 1976, 1 son, 1 daughter. Education: BA, University of Notre Dame, 1953; MA, Stanford University, 1961. Appointment: Story Editor, B L Stryker Mystery Movie Series, ABC-TV, 1988-89. Publications: A Time of Predators, 1969; Marine Salvage (non-fiction), 1971; Dead Skip, 1972; Final Notice, 1973; Interface, 1974; Hammett, 1975; Gone, No Forwarding, 1978; Come Morning, 1986; Wolf Time,

1989; Mostly Murder (short story collection), 1992; 32 Cadillacs, 1992; Dead Man, 1993; Menaced Assassin, 1994; Contract Null and Void, 1996. Contributions to: Numerous magazines and anthologies; 8 film scripts; 25 hours of television drama. Honours: Edgar, Mystery Writers of America: Best First Novel, 1969, Best Short Story, 1969, Edgar, Best Episodic TV Drama, 1975; Falcon, The Maltese Falcon Society of Japan, 1986. Memberships: Mystery Writers of America, President, 1986; International Association of Crime Writers; Crime Writers Association; Private Eye Writers of America. Address: PO Box 446, Fairfax, CA 94978, USA.

GORMAN Ed, b. 29 Nov 1941, Cedar Rapids, Iowa, USA. Writer. m. Carol Maxwell, 2 Jan 1982, 1 son. Education: Coe College, 1962-66. Appointment: Editor, Mystery Scene Magazine. Publications: Night Kills; The Autumn Dead; The Night Remembers; Prisoners Collection of Short Stories; A Cry of Shadows; Blood Moon, 1994. Contributions to: Redbook; Ellery Queen; Mayayne of Poetry. Address: 3601 Skylark Lane, Cedar Rapids, IA 52403, USA.

GORZELSKI Roman, b. 12 Apr 1934, Luck, Poland. Journalist; Writer. Education: University of Warsaw, 1962. Appointments: Staff, weekly papers in Lodz, 1964-69, Warsaw, 1970-. Publications: The Town and the Poem, 1975; Pronunciation of Words, 1977; The Bitter Man, 1982; Silver Thoughts, 1986; The Thoughts in Section, 1995; The Fears of Cupido, 1996; Other: Author of 5 plays; Translator of 10 books into Polish; Author, 10 books of poems, 2 books of aphorism, 5 books of prose; Several of his books translated into other languages. Honours: Nike Warszawska Award, 1969; Merit of Polish Culture Award, 1977. Membership: Union of Polish Writers. Literary Agent: Festinus, ul Nawrot 72m 25, Lodz, Poland. Address: ul Chodkiewicza 6, 94-028 Lodz, Poland.

GOSLING Paula Louise, b. 12 Oct 1939, Detroit, Michigan, USA. Author. m. (1) Christopher Gosling, 20 July 1968, 2 daughters, div, (2) John Anthony Hare, 17 Sept 1981. Education: BA, Wayne State University. Publications: Running Duck, 1978; Zero Trap, 1979; Loser's Blues, 1980; Minds Eye, 1980; Woman in Red, 1983; Monkey Puzzle, 1985; The Wychford Murders, 1986; Hoodwink, 1988; Backlash, 1989; Death Penalties, 1991; The Body in Blackwater Bay, 1992; A Few Dying Words, 1993; The Dead of Winter, 1995. Contributions to: Various Womens Magazines. Honours: John Creasey Award, 1978; Gold Dagger Award, 1986; Arts Achievement Award, Wayne State University, 1994. Membership: Society of Authors; Crime Writers' Association, Deputy Chairman, 1987, Chairman, 1988. Address: c/o Greene & Heaton, 37 Goldhawk Road, London W12 8QQ, England.

GOULD James L, b. 31 July 1945, Tulsa, Oklahoma, USA. Professor. m. Carol Holly Grant, 6 June 1970, 1 son, 1 daughter. Education: BS, California Institute of Technology, 1970; PhD, Rockefeller University, 1975. Appointment: Professor, Princeton University. Publications: Ethology, 1982; Biological Science, 6th edition, 1996; Honey Bee, 1988, 2nd edition, 1995; Life at the Edge, 1988; Sexual Selection, 1989, 2nd edition, 1996; The Animal Mind, 1994. Contributions to: More than 100 articles to journals and magazines. Honours: Guggenheim Fellowship, 1987; Fellow, American Association for the Advancement of Science, 1989; Fellow, Animal Behavior Society, 1991; NJ Professor of the Year, 1996. Address: Department of Ecology and Evolutionary Biology, Princeton University, Princeton, NJ 08544, USA.

GOULD Stephen Jay, b. 10 Sept 1941, New York, New York, USA. Professor of Geology and Zoology; Curator; Writer. m. Deborah Ann Lee, 3 Oct 1965, 2 sons. Education: AB, Antioch College, 1963; PhD, Columbia University, 1967. Appointments: Assistant Professor, 1967-71, Associate Professor, 1971-73, Professor of Geology, 1973-, Alexander Agassiz Professor of Zoology, 1982-, Assistant Curator, 1967-71, Associate Curator, 1971-73, Curator, 1973-, Invertebrate Paleontology, Museum of Comparative Zoology, Harvard University; Lecturer, Cambridge University, 1984, Yale University, 1986, Stanford University, 1989. Publications: Ontogeny and Phylogeny, 1977; Ever Since Darwin, 1977; The Panda's Thumb, 1980; The Mismeasure of Man, 1981; Hen's Teeth and Horse's Toes, 1983; The Flamingo's Smile, 1985; Time's Arrow, Time's Cycle, 1987; An Urchin in the Storm, 1987; Wonderful Life, 1989; Bully for Brontosaurus, 1991; Finders, Keepers (with R W Purcell), 1992; Eight Little Piggies, 1993. Contributions to: Journals. Honours: American Book Award, 1981; National Book Award, 1981; John D and Catharine T MacArthur Foundation Fellowship, 1981-86; National Book Critics Circle Award,

1982; Outstanding Book Award, American Educational Research Association, 1983; Phi Beta Kappa Book Awards, 1983, 1990; Brandeis University Creative Arts Award, 1986; Medal, City of Edinburgh, 1990; Forkosch Award, 1990; Rhone-Poulenc Prize, 1991; Silver Medal, Linnean Society, 1992; Over 35 honorary doctorates; Numerous other awards, medals, etc. Memberships: American Academy of Arts and Sciences, fellow; American Society of Naturalists, president, 1977-80; History of Science Association; National Academy of Sciences; Paleontological Society, president, 1985-; Sigma Xi; Society for the Study of Evolution, president, 1990; Society for the Systematic Study of Zoology. Address: c/o Museum of Comparative Zoology, Department of Earth Sciences, Harvard University, Cambridge, MA 02138, USA.

GOULDEN Joseph C, (Henry S A Becket), b. 23 May 1934, Marshall, Texas, USA. Writer. m. (1), 2 sons, (2) Leslie Cantrell Smith, 23 June 1979. Education: University of Texas, 1952-56. Appointments: Staff Writer, Dallas Morning News, Philadelphia Inquirer, 1958-68. Publications: The Curtis Caper, 1965; Monopoly, 1968; Truth is the First Casualty, 1969; The Money Givers, 1971; The Superlawyers, 1972; Meany: The Unchallenged Strong Man of American Labor, 1972; The Benchwarmers, 1974; Mencken's Last Campaign (editor), 1976; The Best Years, 1976; The Million Dollar Lawyers, 1978; Korea: Untold Story of War, 1982; Myth-Informed (with Paul Dickson), 1983; The News Manipulators (with Reed Irvine and Cliff Kincaid), 1983; Jerry Wurf: Labor's Last Angry Man, 1982; The Death Merchant, 1984; There Are Alligators in Our Sewers (with Paul Dickson), 1984; Dictionary of Espionage (as Henry S A Becket), 1987; Fit to Print: A M Rosenthal and His Times, 1988. Contributions to: Over 200 articles to magazines. Address: 1534 29th Street NW, Washington, DC 20007, USA.

GOYTISOLO Juan, b. 5 Jan 1931, Barcelona, Spain. Novelist. Education: Universities of Madrid and Barcelona, 1948-52. Appointments: Visiting Professor at universities in the USA. Publications: The Young Assassins, 1954; Children of Chaos, 1955; El Circo, 1957; La resaca, 1958; Fiestas, 1958; Para vivir aquí, 1960; Island of Women, 1961; The Party's Over: Four Attempts to Define a Love Story, 1962; Marks of Identity, 1966; Count Julian, 1970; Juan the Landless, 1975; Complete Works, 1977; Makbara, 1980; Landscapes after the Battle, 1982; The Virtues of the Solitary Bird, 1988; La Cuarentena, 1991; Also: The Countryside of Najir, 1960; Forbidden Territory (autobiography), 1985; Realms of Strife, 1986; Space in Motion, 1987. Honour: Europalia International Prize, 1985. Address: c/o Balcells, Diagonal 580, 08021, Barcelona, Spain.

GRABBE Crockett Lane, b. 3 Dec 1951, Silverton, Texas, USA. Research Scientist (Physics). Education: BSc, Physics, University of Texas, Austin, 1972; MA, Physics and Math, University of Texas, 1973; PhD, Applied Physics, Caltech (Pasadena College, 1978. Appointments: Visiting Assistant Professor, University of Tennessee, 1978-79; Research Scientist, Naval Research Labs, Washington, DC, 1979-81; Research Scientist, University of Iowa, 1981-. Publications: Advances in Space Research (co-author), 1985; Author, Editor, Plasma Waves and Instabilities, 1986; Space Weapons and the Strategic Defense Initiating, 1991; Trends in Geophysical Research 2 (co-author), 1993. Contributions to: Scientific journals. Honour: National Science Foundation Postdoctoral Fellowship, 1977-78. Memberships: American Physical Society; American Association of Physics Teachers; International Union of Radio Science; American Geophysical Union; Federation of American Scientists. Address: Department of Physics and Astronomy, University of Iowa, Iowa City, IA 52242, USA.

GRABER Alexander, (Alexander Cordell), b. 9 Sept 1914, Colombo, Ceylon. Author; Poet. m. Rosina Wells, 1937, 1 daughter. Education: Private tutoring, partly at Marist Brothers College, Tientsin, China. Publications: A Thought of Honour, 1954; The Rape of the Fair Country, 1959; The Hosts of Rebecca, US edition as Robe of Honour, 1960; The Race of the Tiger, 1963; The Sinews of Love, 1965; The Bright Cantonese, 1967; Song of the Earth, 1969; The Traitor Within, 1971; The Fire People, 1972; If You Believe the Soldiers, 1973; The Dream and the Destiny, 1975; This Sweet and Bitter Earth, 1978; Sea Urchin, 1979; Rogue's March, 1980; To Slay the Dreamer, 1981; Land of My Fathers, 1982; Peerless Jim, 1984; Tunnel Tigers, 1986; This Proud and Savage Land, 1987; Tales from Tiger Bay, 1987; Requiem for a Patriot, 1988; Moll, 1989. Contributions to: Periodicals. Address: The Conifers, Railway Road, Rhosddu, Wrexham, Clwyd, LLII 2DU, Wales.

GRABES Herbert, b. 8 June 1936. Professor. m. Hannelore Koch, 2 Mar 1962, 2 sons, 1 daughter. Education: University of Cologne, 1963; University of Mannheim, 1969. Publications: Der Begriff Des a Priori in Nicolai Hartmann; Fictitious Biographies: The Mutable Glass; Fiktion, Imitation, Ästhetik; Das englische Pamphlet I; Elizabethan Sonnet Sequences, editor; Das Amerikanische Drama der Gegenwart; Text, Leser, Bedeutung; Literatur in Film und Fernsehen; Anglistentag, 1980; Wissenschaft und Neues Weltbild; REAL, volumes 1-12. Contributions to: 70 longer articles in various German and international journals. Memberships: Nabokov Society; Deutsche Shakespeare-Gesellschaft; Gesellschaft für Amerikastudien; Deutsche Gesellschaft für das Englischsprachige Theater; IAUPE; ESSE; Angistentag. Address: Sonnenstrasse 37, 35444 Biebertal, Germany.

GRACE Julien. See: POIRIER Louis.

GRACE Patricia (Frances), b. 1937, Wellington, New Zealand. Novelist. m. 7 children. Education: St Marys College; Wellington Teachers College. Appointments: Teacher, Primary and Secondary Schools, King Country, Northland and Porirua; Writing Fellow, Victoria University, Wellington, 1985. Publications: Mutuwhenua: The Moon Sleeps, 1978; Potiki, 1986; Cousins, 1992; Short Stories: Waiariki, 1975; The Dream Sleepers and Other Stories, 1980; Electric City and Other Stories, 1980; Selected Stories, 1991; The Sky People, 1994; Collected Stories, 1994; Several Publications for Children including Areta and the Kahawai (picture book in English), 1994; Ko Areta me Nga Kahawai (picture book in Maori), 1994. Honours: New Zealand Fiction Award, 1987; HLD, Victoria University, 1989. Address: c/o Longman Paul Ltd, Private Bag, Takapuna, Auckland 9, New Zealand.

GRAEF Roger Arthur, b. 18 Apr 1936, New York, New York, USA. Writer; Television Producer; Filmmaker. m. Susan Mary Richards, 20 Nov 1985, 1 son, 1 daughter. Education: BA, Honours, Harvard University; Actors Studio, New York City. Appointments: Consultant, Collins Publishers, 1982-88; Chairman, Signals International Trust: Book Aid (1 million books to Russia); Over 80 films and television programmes for British and International television. Publications: Talking Blues, 1989; Living Dangerously, 1993. Contributions to: Media columnist: Times, 1993-95; Telegraph; Sunday Telegraph; Observer; Guardian; Independent; Independent on Sunday; Sunday Times; Evening Standard; Mail on Sunday. Honours: Winner, Royal Televison Society Award, 1979; British Academy of Televison and Film Arts, 1982; European Television Magazine Award. Membership: Writers' Guild; Fellow, Mannheim Centre of Criminology; Fellow, Royal Television Society; European Analytical College of Crime Prevention. Address: 72 Westbourne Park Villas, London, W2, England.

GRAFF Henry F(ranklin), b. 11 Aug 1921, New York, New York, USA. Professor of History Emeritus; Writer. m. Edith Krantz, 16 June 1946, 2 daughters. Education: BSS, City College, New York City, 1941; MA, 1942, PhD, 1949, Columbia Unversity. Appointments: Fellow in History, 1941-42, Tutor in History, 1946, City College, New York City; Lecturer, 1946-47, Instructor to Associate Professor, 1946-61, Chairman, Department of History, 1961-64, Professor of History, 1961-91, Professor Emeritus, 1991-, Columbia University; Lecturer, Vassar College, 1953, Yale School of Medicine, 1993; Presidential appointee, National Historical Publications Commission, 1965, 1971, President John F Kennedy Assassination Records Review Board, 1993-; Senior Fellow, Freedom Foundation Media Studies Center, New York City, 1991-92; Dean's Distinguished Lecturer in the Humanities, Columbia University College of Physicians and Surgeons, 1992. Publications: Bluejackets with Perry in Japan, 1952; The Modern Researcher (with Jacques Barzun), 1962, 5th edition 1992; American Themes (with Clifford Lord), 1963; Thomas Jefferson, 1968; American Imperialism and the Philippine Insurrection, 1969; The Tuesday Cabinet: Deliberation and Decision on Peace and War under Lyndon B Johnson, 1970; The Call of Freedom (with Paul J Bohannan), 1978; The Promise of Democracy, 1978; This Great Nation, 1983; The Presidents: A Reference History, 1984, 2nd edition, 1996; America: The Glorious Republic, 1985, revised edition, 1990. Contributions to: Scholarly journals and to general periodicals. Honours: Townsend Harris Medal, City College of the City University of New York, 1966; Mark Van Doren Award, New England History Teachers Association, 1990; Phi Beta Kappa. Memberships: American Historical Association; Author's Guild; Council on Foreign Relations; Organization of American Historians; PEN; Society of American Historians. Address: 47 Andrea Lane, Scarsdale, NY 10583, USA.

GRAHAM Ada, b. 22 Aug 1931, Dayton, Ohio, USA. Writer. m. Frank Graham Jr, 31 Oct 1953. Education: Bowling Green State University, 1949-52; AB, Hunter College, New York City, 1957. Appointments: Vice-Chairman, Maine State Commissionon the Arts, 1975-80; Board Memebr, New England Foundation for the Arts, 1977-80; Developer, Writer, Audobon Adventures, National Audobon Society, 1984-. Publications: The Great American Shopping Cart (with F Graham), 1969; Wildlife Rescue (with F Graham) 1970; Puffin Island (with F Graham), 1971; The Mystery of the Everglades, 1972; Dooryard Garden, 1974; Let's Discover the Winter Woods, 1974; Discover Changes Everywhere, 1974; Let's Discover Birds in Our World, 1974; The Careless Animal, 1974; The Milkweed and Its World of Animals (wth F Graham), 1976; Foxtails, Ferns and Fishscales: A Handbook of Art and Nature Projects, 1976; Whale Watch, 1978; Bug Hunters, 1978; Coyote Song, 1978; Falcon Flight, 1978; Audobon Readers (with F Graham) 6 volumes, 1978-81; Alligators (with F Graham), 1979; Careers in Conservation (with F Graham), 1980; Birds of the Northern Seas (with F Graham), 1980; Bears, 1981; The Changing Desert (with F Graham), 1981; Jacob and the Owl (with F Graham) 1981; Three Million Mice (with F Graham), 1981; Six Little Chicadees, 1982; Busy Bugs (with F Graham), 1983; The Big Stretch (with F Graham) 1985; We Watch Squirrels (with F Graham), 1985. Honours: First Prize, Annual Children's Science Book Award, New York Academy of Sciences, 1986; Eva L Gordon Award, American Nature Study Society, 1989. Address: Milbridge, ME 04658, USA.

GRAHAM Charles S. See: **TUBB E(dwin) C(harles).**

GRAHAM Frank Jr, b. 31 Mar 1925, New York, New York, USA. Writer. m. Ada Graham, 31 Oct 1953. Education: AB, Columbia University, 1950. Appointments: Field Editor, Audubon magazine, 1968-. Publications: It Takes Heart (with M Allen), 1959; Disaster by Default, 1966; The Great American Shopping Cart (with A Graham), 1969; Since Silent Spring, 1970; Wildlife Rescue, (with A Graham), 1970; Puffin Island (with A Graham), 1971; Man's Dominion, 1971; The Mystery of the Everglades (with A Graham), 1972; Where the Place Called Morning Lies, 1973; Audubon Primers (with A Graham, 4 volumes, 1974; The Careless Animal (with A Graham), 1975; Gulls: A Social History, 1975; Potomac: The Nation's River, 1976; The Milkweed and its Wrold of Animals (with A Graham), 1976; The Adirondack Park: A Political History, 1978; Audubon Readers (with A Graham), 6 volumes, 1978-81; Careers in Conservation (with A Graham) 1980; Birds of the Northern Seas (with A Graham), 1981; A Farewell to Heroes, 1981; The Changing Desert (with A Graham), 1981; Jacob and Owl (with A Graham), 1981; Three Million Mice (with A Graham) 1981; Busy Bugs (with A Graham) 1983; The Dragon Hunters, 1984; The Big Stretch (with A Graham), 1985; We Watch Squirrels (with A Graham), 1985; The Audubon Ark, 1990. Address: Milbridge, ME 04658, USA.

GRAHAM Henry, b. 1 Dec 1930, Liverpool, England. Lecturer. Education: Liverpool College of Art, 1950-52. Appointment: Poetry Editor, Ambit, London, 1969-90. Publications: Good Luck to You Kafka/You'll Need It Boss, 1969; Soup City Zoo, 1969; Passport to Earth, 1971; Poker in Paradise Lost, 1977; Europe After Rain, 1981; Bomb, 1985; The Very Fragrant Death of Paul Gauguin, 1987; Jardin Gobe Avions, 1991. Contributions to: Ambit; Transatlantic Review; Prism International Review; Evergreen Review; Numerous anthrologies worldwide. Honours: Arts Council Literature Awards, 1969, 1971, 1975. Address: Flat 5, 23 Marmion Road, Liverpool L17 8TT, England.

GRAHAM James. See: **PATTERSON Harry.**

GRAHAM Jorie, b. 9 May 1951, New York, New York, USA. Poet; Teacher. m. James Galvin. Education: BFA, New York University, 1973; MFA, University of Iowa, 1978. Appointments: Poetry Editor, Crazy Horse, 1978-81; Assistant Professor, Murray State University, Kentucky, 1978-79, Humboldt State University, Arcata, California, 1979-81; Instructor, Columbia University, 1981-83; Staff, University of Iowa, 1983-. Publications: Hybrids of Plants and of Ghosts, 1980; Erosion, 1983; The End of Beauty, 1987; The Best American Poetry (editor with David Lehman, 1990; Region of Unlikeness, 1991; Materialism, 1993; The Dream of the Unified Field, 1995. Honours: American Academy of Poets Award, 1977; Young Poets Prize, Poetry Northwest, 1980; Pushcart Prizes, 1980, 1982; Ingram Merrill Foundation Grant, 1981; Great Lakes Colleges Association Award, 1981; American Poetry Review Prize, 1982; Bunting Fellow, Radcliffe Institute, 1982; Guggenheim Fellowship,

1983-84; MacArthur Foundation Fellowship, 1990; Pulitzer Prize in Poetry, 1996. Address: c/o Department of Creative Writing, University of Iowa, Iowa City, IA 52242, USA.

GRAHAM Leonard. See: **BALFOUR Michael.**

GRAHAM Sonia. See: **SINCLAIR Sonia Elizabeth.**

GRAHAM Winston Mawdsley, b. 30 June 1910, Victoria Park, Manchester, England. m. Jean Mary Williamson, 1939, dec 1992, 1 son, 1 daughter. Publications: Night Journey, 1941, revised edition, 1966; The Merciless Ladies, 1944, revised edition, 1979; The Forgotten Story, 1945 (ITV production, 1983); Ross Poldark, 1945; Demelza, 1946; Take My Life, 1947 (filmed, 1947); Cordelia, 1949; Night Without Stars, 1950 (filmed, 1950); Jeremy Poldark, 1950; Fortune is a Woman, 1953 (filmed 1958); Greek Fire, 1957; The Tumbled House, 1959; Marnie, 1961 (filmed 1963); The Grove of Eagles, 1963; After the Act, 1965; The Walking Stick, 1967 (filmed 1970); The Spanish Armadas, 1972; The Black Moon, 1973; Woman in the Morror, 1975; The Four Swans, 1976; The Angry Tide, 1977; The Stranger from the Sea, 1981; The Millers Dance, 1982; Poldark's Cornwall, 1983; The Loving Cup, 1984; The Green Flash, 1986; Cameo, 1988; The Twisted Sword, 1990; Stephanie, 1992; Tremor, 1995; BBC TV Series Poldark (the first 4 Poldark novels), 1975-76, second series (the next 3 Poldark novels), 1977; Circumstantial Evidence, play, 1979. Honours: Officer of the Order of the British Empire, 1983; Fellow, Royal Society of Literature. Address: Abbotswood House, Buxted, East Sussex TN22 4PB, England.

GRAHAM-YOOLL Andrew Michael, b. 5 Jan 1944, Buenos Aires, Argentina. Journalist; Writer. m. 17 Jan 1966, 1 son, 2 daughters. Appointments: News Editor and Political Columnist, Buenos Aires Herald, 1966-76; Freelance Writer, San Francisco Chronicle, 1967-70, 1976, Baltimore Sun, 1967-69, 1976, Miami Herald, 1969, Kansas City Star, 1969-73, New York Times, 1970, Newsweek, 1970; Broadcaster, BBC World Service, London, 1976; Occasional News Commentary, London Broadcasting Company; Sub Editor, Foreign News, Daily Telegraph, London, 1976-77; Foreign Correspondent, The Guardian, London, 1977-84; Editor, Writers News, London, 1983-85; Deputy Editor, 1984-85, Editor, 1985-88, South Magazine, London; Editor, Index on Censorship, 1989-93; Senior Visiting Fellow, Queen Mary and Westfield College, London, 1990-; Press Fellow, Wolfson College, University of Cambridge, 1994; Editor-in-Chief, Buenos Aires Herald, 1994-. Publications: The Press in Argentina, 1973-78, 1979; Portrait of an Exile, 1981; The Forgotten Colony, 1981; Small Wars You May Have Missed (in South America), 1983; A State of Fear, 1986; Argentina, Peron to Videla 1955-1976, 1989; After the Despots, 1991; Point of Arrival, 1992; Committed Observer, 1995. Short Stories: The Date Might Be Forgotten, 1967; The Premonition, 1968; Twenty Pages of Garcia, 1974; Money Cures Melancholy, 1974; Sirens, 1980; Poetry in Spanish. Honours: Poetry Prize, El Vidente Ciego Magazine Rosario, Argentina, 1975; British Council Visitorship to Britain, 1976; Nicholas Tomalin Memorial Award for Journalists, 1977. Memberships: PEN, Press Officer, 1979-87; Writers Guild of Great Britain, Executive Council, 1983; Argentine Writers Society; Anglo-Argentine Society, Committee Member, 1989-90; Royal Literary Fund, Life Member, 1987; Association of British Editors, Member of the Board, 1990-93; Arts Council Literature Touring Panel, 1992-. Address: c/o Buenos Aires Herald, Azopardo 455, 1107 Buenos Aires, Argentina.

GRAMLEY Judith, b. 22 Oct 1941, Mansfield, Ohio, USA. Professor of Spanish. m. Harold Dean Gramley, 18 Jan 1969, 2 sons. Education: BS, 1963, MA, 1966, Kent State University, Ohio; AS, 1984, BS, 1986, Edinboro University of Pennsylvania; ABD, University of Pittsburgh. Publications: The Americas Reviewed: Review of 200 años de gringos by Carlos Montaner, 1977; Revolución: Idea y acción, Review of Los diez días que estremecieron al mundo, 1979; El realismo y el racismo: Review of A Kind of Dying by Angus Richmond, 1980; Human Sacrifice and Cannibalism Among the Aztecs: A Moral or Barbaric Act?, 1993; Clémence Ravaçon Mershon: A Life-long Commitment, 1994; Adapting the Novel to Film: The Case of Galdós's Doña Perfecta, 1995; Crossing Borders Through Language, 1995. Contributions to: Periodicals and journals. Honours: Sigma Delta Pi; Phi Sigma Iota; Alpha Chi. Address: 126B Biggers House, Edinboro University of Pennsylvania, Edinboro, PA 16444, USA.

GRAMPP William D, b. 22 Aug 1914, Columbus, Ohio, USA. Education: PhD, Economics, University of Chicago, 1944. Publications: The Manchester School of Economics, 1960; Economic Liberalism,

1965; Pricing the Priceless: Art, Artists and Economics, 1989. Contributions to: Professional journals in economics, history and philosophy; General periodicals in politics, art and literature. Address: 5426 Ridgewood Court, Chicago, IL 60615, USA.

GRANADOS Paul. See: **KENT Arthur (William Charles).**

GRANDOWER Elissa. See: **WAUGH Hillary Baldwin.**

GRANGE Peter. See: **NICOLE Christopher Robin.**

GRANT Anthony. See: **PARES Marion.**

GRANT Charles, b. 12 Sept 1942, Newark, New Jersey, USA. Writer. Education: BA, Trinity College, Hartford, Connecticut, 1964. Publications: The Shadow of Alpha, 1976; The Curse, 1976; The Hour of the Oxrum Dead, 1977; Writing and Selling Science Fiction (editor), 1977; The Ravens of the Moon, 1978; The Sound of Midnight, 1978; Shadows (editor), 9 volumes, 1978-86; Nightmares (editor), 1979; The Last Call of Mourning, 1979; Legion, 1979; Tales from the Nightside, 1981; Glow of Candles and Other Stories, 1981; Nightmare Seasons, 1982; Night Songs, 1984; The Tea Party, 1985; The Pet, 1986; The Orchards, 1987; Something Stirs, 1992. Address: c/o Tor Books, 175 Fifth Avenue, New York, NY 10010, USA.

GRANT Ellen Catherine Gardner, b. 29 Sept 1934, Scotland. Medical Practitioner. m. David Norman Grant, 12 Sept 1959, 1 son, 2 daughters. Education: MB ChB (Commend), St Andrews University, 1958; DRCOG, London, England, 1959. Appointments: Member, International Editorial Board, Journal of Nutritional and Environmental Medicine, 1995; Honorary Secretary, Doctors Against Abuse from Steroid Sex Hormones (DASH). Publications: The Bitter Pill, 1985; Sexual Chemistry, 1994; Chapters in: Smoking and Migraine, 1981; Biological Aspects of Schizophrenia and Addiction, 1982. Contributions to: Lancet; British Medical Journal; Clinical Oncology; The Ecologist; Journal of Obstetrics and Gynaecology of the British Commonwealth; Headache; International Journal of Environmental Studies; Nutrition and Health; Journal of Nutritional Medicine. Memberships: British Society for Nutritional Medicine; British Society for Allergy and Environmental Medicine; Foresight (Association for the Promotion of Preconception Care); Dyslexia Institute. Address: 20 Coombe Ridings, Kingston-upon-Thames, Surrey KT2 7JU, England.

GRANT John, (Jonathan Gash, Graham Gaunt), b. 30 Sept 1933, Bolton, Lancashire, England. Physician; Author. m. Pamela Richard, 19 Feb 1955, 3 daughters. Education: MB, 1958, BS, 1958, University of London; MRCS, 1958, LRCP, 1958, Royal College of Surgeons and Physicians. Appointments: General Practitioner, London, 1958-59; Pathologist, London and Essex, 1959-62; Clinical Pathologist, Hannover and Berlin, 1962-65; Lecturer in Clinical Pathology and Head of the Pathology Division, University of Hong Kong, 1965-68; Microbiologist in Hong Kong and London, 1968-71; Head of the Bacteriology Unit, School of Hygiene and Tropical Medicine, University of London, 1971-88. Publications: As Jonathan Gash: The Judas Pair, 1977; Gold by Gemini, 1978; The Grail Tree, 1979; Spend Game, 1981; The Vatican Rip, 1981; The Sleepers of Erin, 1983; Firefly Gadroom, 1984; The Gondola Scam, 1984; Pearlhanger, 1985; The Tartan Ringers, 1986; Moonspender, 1987; Jade Woman, 1989; The Very Last Gambado, 1990; The Great California Game, 1991; The Lies of Fair Ladies, 1992; Paid and Loving Eyes, 1993. As Graham Gaunt: The Incomer, 1982. Honour: Crime Writers' Association Award, 1977. Memberships: International College of Surgeons, fellow; Royal Society of Tropical Medicine, fellow. Address: Silver Willows, Chapel Lane, West Bergholt, Colchester, Essex CO6 3EF, England.

GRANT John. See: **BARNETT Paul le Page.**

GRANT Maxwell. See: **LYNDS Dennis.**

GRANT Michael, b. 21 Nov 1914, London, England. Academic (retired); Writer. m. Anne Sophie Beskow, 2 Aug 1944, 2 sons. Education: BA, 1936, MA, 1940, Trinity College, Cambridge. Appointments: Fellow, Trinity College, Cambridge, 1938-49; Professor of Latin Literature, University of Edinburgh, 1948-59; Vice-Chancellor, University of Khartoum, 1956-58; President and Vice-Chancellor, Queen's University, Belfast, 1959-66; Chairperson, Advisory Council for Education in Northern Ireland, 1959-66, and Commonwealth Conference on English as a Second Language, 1960. Publications:

From Imperium to Auctoritas: A Historical Study of Aes Coinage in the Roman Empire, 49 BC-AD 14, 1946; Aspects of the Principate of Tiberius: Historical Comments on the Colonial Coinage Issued Outside Spain, 1950; Roman Anniversary Issues: An Exploratory Study of the Numismatic and Medallic Commemoration and Anniversary Years, 49 BC-AD 375, 1950; Ancient History, 1952; The Six Main Aes Coinage of Augustus, 1953; Roman Imperial Money, 1954; Roman Literature, 1954, revised edition, 1964; Roman Readings (editor), 1958; Roman History from Coins, 1958; Greeks (with Don Pottinger), 1958; Romans (with Don Pottinger), 1960; The World of Rome, 1960; Myths of the Greeks and Romans, 1962; The Birth of Western Civilization: Greece and Rome, 1964; The Civilizations of Europe, 1966, revised edition, 1971; Cambridge, 1966; Gladiators, 1967, revised edition, 1971; The Climax of Rome: The Final Achievements of the Ancient World, AD 161-337, 1968; The Ancient Mediterranean, 1969; Julius Caesar, 1969; The Ancient Historians, 1970; The Rome Forum, 1970; Nero: Emperor in Revolt, 1970; Cities of Vesuvius: Pompeii and Herculaneum, 1971; Herod the Great, 1971; Roman Myths, 1971; Cleopatra, 1972; Ancient History Atlas, 1972; The Jews in the Roman World, 1973; Gods and Mortals in Classical Mythology (with John Hazel), 1973; Greek Literature in Translation (editor), 1973; Who's Who in Classical Mythology (with John Hazel), 1973; Caesar, 1974; The Army of the Caesars, 1974; The Twelve Caesars, 1975; Eros in Pompeii: The Secret Rooms of the National Museum of Naples, 1975; The Fall of the Roman Empire: A Reappraisal, 1976; Saint Paul, 1976; Jesus: An Historian's Review of the Gospels, 1977; The History of Rome, 1978; The Art and Life of Pompeii and Herculaneum, 1979; Latin Literature: An Anthology (editor), 1979; The Etruscans, 1980; Greek and Latin Authors, 800 BC-AD 1000, 1980; Dawn of the Middle Ages, 1981; From Alexander to Cleopatra: The Hellenistic World, 1980; History of Ancient Israel, 1984; The Roman Emperors: A Biographical Guide to the Rulers of Ancient Rome, 31 BC-AD 476, 1985; Guide to the Classical World: A Dictionary of Place-Names, 1986; The Rise and Fall of the Greeks, 1988; The Classical Greeks, 1988; The Founders of the Western World, 1991; A Social History of Greece and Rome, 1992; Saint Peter, 1994; My First Eighty Years, 1994; The Antonines, 1994; The Sayings of the Bible, 1994; Art in the Roman Empire, 1995; Greek and Roman Historians: Information and Misinformation, 1995; The Severans, 1996. Other: Editor and translator of various Roman writers. Honours: Officer of the Order of the British Empire, 1946; Commander of the Order of the British Empire, 1958; Leverhulme Research Fellow, 1958; Premio Latina, 1981; Several honorary doctorates. Memberships: British Institute of Archaeology at Ankara, vice-president, 1961-; Classical Association, president, 1977-78; Roman Society, vice-president, 1961-; Royal Numismatic Society, president, 1953-56; Virgil Society, president, 1963-66. Address: Le Pitturacce, Gattaiola, 55050 Lucca, Italy.

GRANT Neil (David Mountfield, D M Field, Gail Trenton), b. 9 June 1938, England. Writer. m. Vera Steiner, 23 Sept 1979, 2 daughters. Education: MA (Hons), St John's College, Cambridge, 1961. Publications: A History of Polar Exploration, 1974; Neil Grant's Book of Spies and Spying, 1975; A History of African Exploration, 1976; Children's History of Britain, 1977; Greek and Roman Erotica, 1982; The White Bear, fiction, 1983; American Folktales and Legends, 1988; London's Villages, 1990. Membership: Royal Geographical Society. Address: 2 Avenue Road, Teddington, Middlesex TW11 0BT, England.

GRANT Nicholas. See: **NICOLE Christopher Robin.**

GRANT Roderick, b. 16 Jan 1941, Forres, Morayshire, Scotland. Author. Appointment: Sub Editor, Weekly Scotsman, 1965-67. Publications: Adventure in My Veins, 1968; Seek Out the Guilty, 1969; Where No Angels Dwell, 1969; Gorbals Doctor, 1970; The Dark Horizon (with Alexander Highlands), 1971; The Lone Voyage of Betty Mouat, 1973; The Stalking of Adrian Lawford, 1974; The Clutch of Caution, 1975, 2nd edition, 1985; The 51st Highland Division at War, 1976; Strathalder: A Highland Estate, 1978, 2nd edition, 1989; A Savage Freedom, 1978; The Great Canal,1978; A Private Vendetta, 1978; But Not in Anger (with C Cole), 1979; Clap Hands for the Singing Molecatcher, 1989. Address: 3 Back Lane Cottages, Bucks Horn Oak, Farmham, Surrey, England.

GRASSBY Albert Jaime, b. 12 July 1926, Brisbane, Queensland, Australia. Author. m. Ellnor Judith Louez, 3 Feb 1962, 1 daughter. Education: Special Studies, University of California, Berkeley; PhD, University of Munich, Germany. Publications: Griffith of the Four Faces, 1960; Morning After, 1979; The Spanish

Contribution to Australia, 1983; Six Australian Battlefields, 1988; Oodgeroo Noonuccal, 1990; The Australian Republic, 1992; The Tyranny of Prejudice, 1994. Contributions to: Australia's Italians; Republican Australia; Pacific Islander Migration; many journals. Honours: Knight Commander of Order of Solidarity, Italy, 1971; Special Citation, University of Santo Tomas, Manila, 1974; Honorary Citizenship of Plati and Sinopoli, Italy, 1974; Honorary Citizenship, Akrata and Platynos, Greece, 1977; Knight Commander, Order of Santa Agata, Malta, 1979; Doctor of Philosophy (HC), Munich, 1979; Order of Australia, 1985; UN Peace Medal, 1986; Knight Commander of the Order of Isabella La Catolica, Spain, 1986. Address: GPO Box 1611, Canberra 2601, Australia.

GRAU Shirley Ann, b. 8 July 1929, New Orleans, Louisiana, USA. Writer. m. James Feibleman, 4 Aug 1955, 2 sons, 2 daughters. Education: BA, Tulane University. Publications: The Black Prince, 1955; The Hard Blue Sky, 1958; The House on Coleseum Street, 1961; The Keepers of the House, 1964; The Condor Passes, 1971; The Wind Shifting West, 1973; Evidence of Love, 1977; Nine Women, 1985; Roadwalkers, 1994. Contributions to: New Yorker; Saturday Evening Post; Others. Honour: Pulitzer Prize for Fiction, 1965. Literary Agent: Brandt and Brandt, New York City, USA. Address: 210 Baronne Street, Suite 1120, New Orleans, LA 70112, USA.

GRAVER Elizabeth, b. 2 July 1964, Los Angeles, California, USA. Writer; Teacher. Education: BA, Wesleyan University, 1986; MFA, Washington University, 1990. Appointments: Visiting Professor of English and Creative Writing, Boston College, 1993-95; Assistant Professor of Creative Writing and English, Boston College, 1995-. Publication: Have You Seen Me? Contributions to: Best American Short Stories; Story; Southern Review; Antaeus; Seventeen; Southwest Review; O Henry Prize Stories, 1994, 1996; Louder Than Words; Ploughshares. Honours: Fulbright Fellowship; Drue Heinz Literature Prize; National Endowment for the Arts Fellowship; Writers Exchange Winner. Membership: Phi Beta Kappa. Address: c/o Richard Parks Agency, 138 East 16th Street 58, New York, NY 10003, USA.

GRAVER Lawrence Stanley, b. 6 Dec 1931, New York, New York, USA. Professor of English. m. Suzanne Levy Graver, 28 Jan 1960, 2 daughters. Education: BA, City College of New York, 1954; PhD, University of California, Berkeley, 1961. Appointments: Assistant Professor, University of California, Los Angeles, 1961-64; Associate Professor, 1964-71, Professor, 1971-, Williams College, 1964-. Publications: Conrad's Short Fiction, 1968; Carson McCullers, 1969; Mastering the Film, 1974; Beckett: The Critical Heritage, 1979; Beckett: Waiting for Godot, 1989; An Obsession with Anne Frank: Meyer Levin and The Diary, 1995. Contributions to: New York Times Book Review; Saturday Review; New Republic; New Leader; 19th Century Fiction. Membership: Modern Language Association. Address: Department of English, Williams College, Williamstown, MA 01267, USA.

GRAY Alasdair (James), b. 28 Dec 1934, Glasgow, Scotland. 1 son. Education: Diploma, Glasgow Art School, 1957. Awarded Bellahouston Travelling Scholarship. Appointments: Part time art teacher 1958-62; Theatrical scene painter 1962-63; Free-lance playwright and painter, 8 one-man exhibitions, one retrospective, 17 TV and radio plays broadcast, 4 plays professionally staged, 1964-76; Artist-recorder, People's Palace (local history museum) 1977; Writer-in-Residence, University of Glasgow, 1977-79; Free-lance painter and maker of books 1979-. Publications: Lanark, 1981, revised edition, 1985; Unlikely Stories, 1983, revised edition, 1984; Janine, 1984, revised edition, 1985; The Fall of Kelvin Walker: A Fable of the Sixties, 1985; Lean Tales (with James Kelman and Agnes Owens), 1985; Saltire Self-Portrait 4, 1988; McGrotty and Ludmilla, or The Harbinger Report: A Romance of the Eighties, 1989; Something Leather, 1990; Why Scots Should Rule Scotland 1997, 1997; Poor Things, 1992; Ten Tales Tall and True, 1993; A History Maker, 1994. Contributions to: Periodicals. Honours: Saltire Society, 1982; Whitbread Award, 1992. Memberships: Society of Authors; Scottish Society of Playwrights; Glasgow Print Workshop; Various organizations supporting coal miners and nuclear disarmament. Address: 2 Marchmont Terrace, Glasgow G12 9LT, Scotland.

GRAY Alfred Orren, b. 8 Sept 1914, Sun Prairie, Wisconsin, USA. Retired College Professor of Journalism; Professor Emeritus. m. Nicolin Jane Plank, 5 Sept 1947, 2 sons. Education: BA, 1939, MA, 1941, University of Wisconsin. Appointments: Historian, Chief Writer, US Ordnance ETO, 1944-45; Head, Department of Journalism,

Whitworth College, 1946-80; Diamond Anniversary Historian, Whitworth College, 1963-65; Centennial Historian, First Presbyterian Church, Spokane, 1981-83. Publications: History of the US Ordnance Service, 1946; Publicity and Public Relations for the Church, 1958; Not By Might: The Story of Whitworth College, 1965; Eight Generations from Gondelsheim, 1980; Many Lamps, One Light: A Centennial History, 1984; Contributions to: Articles on religious, educational and general subjects to national and regional magazines, journals and newspapers. Honours: University High Honours; Phi Beta Kappa; Bronze Star Medal; Army Commendation Medal; Whitworth College Alumni Citation for Outstanding Teaching of Journalism; Distinguished Newspaper Adviser among Colleges and Universities, 1979. Membership: Phi Beta Kappa, president, Inland Empire Professional Chapter, 3 terms. Address: W304 Hoerner Avenue, Spokane, WA 99218, USA.

GRAY Alice Wirth, b. 29 Apr 1934, Chicago, Illinois, USA. Writer. m. Ralph Gareth Gray, 16 July 1954, 2 daughters. Education: BA, 1958, MA, 1960, University of California. Publication: What the Poor Eat, 1993. Contributions to: Atlantic; American Scholar; Poetry; Breakfast Without Meat; Little Magazine; Helicon Nine; Primavera; Sequoia. Honours: Illinois Arts Council Literary Award; Gordon Barber Memorial Award; Duncan Lawrie Award. Memberships: Poetry Society of America; PEN Center USA West. Address: 1001 Merced Street, Berkeley, CA 94707, USA.

GRAY Angela. See: DANIELS Dorothy.

GRAY Anne, b. 26 Oct 1941, Vienna, Austria (US citizen, 1948). Author; Professor of Music, Speech, and Drama; Musicologist. m. Charles R Bubb III, 7 Aug 1966, 2 sons. Education: BA cum laude in Music, Speech, and Drama, Hunter College of the City of University of New York, 1963; MA with Honours in English and Education, San Diego State University, 1968; PhD summa cum laude in Humanities, University of California at San Diego, 1982. Appointments: Teacher, San Diego Public Schools, 1963-68; Professor of English, Mesa College, California, 1968-71. Publications: The Wonderful World of San Diego, 1971, 2nd edition, 1976; Where Have You Been All Your Life?, 1990; How to Hang Onto Your Husband!, 1990; The Popular Guide to Classical Music, 1993; The Popular Guide to Women in Classical Music, forthcoming. Contributions to: Reference books, journals, periodicals, and newspapers. Honours: Music Award, San Diego Public Schools, 1968; Award of Merit, San Diego Historical Society, 1976; Outstanding Leadership Award, Toastmasters of America, 1981; Certificates of Appreciation, San Diego Symphony Orchestra, 1983, 1985, 1987; Achievement Award, San Diego Writers Guild, 1989; Literary Medals, San Diego Public Library, 1990, 1993, 1995; Outstanding Author of the Year Award, National League of American Penwomen, 1996. Memberships: American Association of University Women; National League of Penwomen; International Platform Speakers Association; International Alliance of Women in Music; College Music Society. Address: c/o WordWorld, 2222 Bahia Drive, La Jolla, CA 92037, USA.

GRAY Caroline. See: NICOLE Christopher Robin.

GRAY Douglas, b. 17 Feb 1930, Melbourne, Victoria, Australia. University Teacher; Writer. m. 3 Sept 1959, 1 son. Education: MA, Victoria University of Wellington, New Zealand, 1952; BA, 1956, MA, 1960, Merton College, Oxford. Appointment: J R R Tolkien Professor of English, Oxford, 1980-. Publications: Themes and Images in the Medieval English Religious Lyric, 1972; Robert Henryson, 1979; The Oxford Book of Late Medieval Verse and Prose (editor), 1985. Contributions to: Scholarly journals. Honours: British Academy, fellow, 1989; Honorary LitD, Victorian University of Wellington, 1995. Memberships: Early English Text Society; Society for the Study of Medieval Languages and Literatures, president, 1982-86. Address: Lady Margaret Hall, Oxford OX2 6QA, England.

GRAY Dulcie Winifred, b. 20 Nov 1920. Writer. m. Michael Denison 29 Apr 1939. Publications: Murder on the Stairs, 1957; Baby Face, 1959; For Richer for Richer, 1970; Ride on Tiger, 1975; Butterflies on my Mind, 1978; Dark Calypso, 1979; The Glanvill Women, 1982; Mirror Image, 1987; Looking Forward, Looking Back (autobiography), 1991. Contributions to: Daily Express; Evening Standard; Womans Own; Vogue. Honours: Queen's Silver Jubilee Medal, 1977; Times Educational Supplement Senior Information Award, 1978; Commander of the Order of the British Empire, 1983. Memberships: Society of Authors; Royal Society of Arts, Fellow;

Linnean Society; British Actors Equity. Address: 28 Charring Cross Road, London, WC2, England.

GRAY Francine du Plessix, b. 25 Sept 1930, Warsaw, Poland. Author. m. Clive Gray, 23 Apr 1957, 2 sons. Education: Bryn Mawr College, 1948-50; Black Mountain College, 1951, 1952; BA, Barnard College, 1952. Appointments: Reporter, United Press International, New York City, 1952-54; Assistant Editor, Realites Magazine, Paris, 1954-55; Book Editor, Art in America, New York City, 1962-64; Visiting Professor, City University of New York, 1975; Yale University, 1981, Columbia University, 1983; Ferris Professor, Princeton University, 1986. Publications: Divine Disobedience: Profiles in Catholic Radicalism, 1970; Hawai: The Sugar-Coated Fortress, 1972; Lovers and Tyrants, 1976; World Without End, 1981; October Blood, 1985; Adam and Eve and the City, 1987; Soviet Women: Walking the Tightrope, 1991; Rage and Fire: A Life of Louise Colet, 1994. Membership: American Academy of Arts and Letters. Address: c/o Georges Borchardt Inc, 145 East 57th Street, New York, NY 10022, USA.

GRAY Marianne Claire, b. 21 Sept 1947, Cape Town, South Africa. Journalist; Biographer. Education: Certificat d'Assiduite, University of Aix-Marseille, 1966; Cambridge Polytechnic, 1967; BA, UNISA, 1972. Appointments: Reporter, Argus Group, South Africa, 1968-70; Cape Times, 1970-73; Editor, Athens News, 1974; Syndication Assistant, South African National Magazines, London, 1975-77; Freelance Journalist, 1977-. Publications: Depardieu; La Moreau; Freelance Alternative; The Other 'Arf; Working from Home; Thoughts About Architecture. Contributions to: Sky; Cosmopolitan; Arena; Options; Empire; Company; The Face; You; New Woman; Woman's Journal; Premiere. Memberships: Women in Publishing; Critics Circle; Lawrence Durrell Research Centre; Women in Film International; Women in Journalism. Literary Agent: Blake Friedmann. Address: 32 Eburne Road, London N7 6AU, England; 20 Rue du Caminol, St Jean de Fos, 34150 France.

GRAY (John) Richard, b. 1929, United Kingdom. Professor Emeritus; Writer. Appointments: Professor Emeritus of African History, University of London; Editor, Journal of African History, 1968-71. Publications: The Two Nations: Aspects of the Development of Race Relations in the Rhodesias and Nyasaland, 1960; A History of the Southern Sudan, 1839-1889, 1961; Materials for West African History in Italian Archives (with D Chambers), 1965; Pre-Colonial African Trade (editor with D Birmingham), 1970; Cambridge History of Africa, Vol IV (editor), 1975; Christianity in Independent Africa (editor with E Fasholé-Luke and others), 1978; Black Christians and White Missionaries, 1990. Membership: Britain-Zimbabwe Society, chairman, 1981-85. Address: 39 Rotherwick Road, London NW11 7DD, England.

GRAY Robert, b. 23 Feb 1945, Australia. Poet. Appointment: Writer-in-Residence, Tokyo, 1985. Publications: Introspect, Retrospect, 1970; Creekwater Journal, 1974; Grass Script, 1978; The Skylight, 1983; Selected Poems 1963-83, 1985; Piano, 1988; Co-editor: The Young Australian Poets, 1983; Co-author: Alun Leach-Jones, 1988. Honours: Adelaide Arts Festival National Poetry Award, 1985; New South Wales Premier's Award, 1986. Address: c/o Angus and Robertson, PO Box 290, North Ryde, New South Wales 2113, Australia.

GRAY Simon (James Holliday), (Hamish Reade), b. 21 Oct 1936, Hayling Island, Hants, England. Playwright; Writer. m. Beryl Mary Keven, 1965, 1 son, 1 daughter. Education: Dalhousie University; MA, Trinity College, Cambridge. Appointments: Senior Instructor in English, University of British Columbia, 1963-64; Lecturer in English, London University, 1965-85; Co-Director, The Common Pursuit, Promenade Theatre, New York, 1986; Director, Phoenix Theatre, 1988. Publications: Novels: Colmain, 1963; Simple People, 1965; Little Portia, 1967; A Comeback for Stark, 1968. Plays: Wise Child, 1968; Sleeping Dog, 1968; Dutch Uncle, 1969; The Idiot, 1971; Spoiled, 1971; Butley, 1971; Otherwise Engaged, 1975; Plaintiffs and Defendants, 1975; Two Sundays, 1975; Dog Days, 1976; Molly, 1977; The Rear Column, 1978; Close of Play, 1979; Stage Struck, 1979; Quartermaine's Terms, 1981 (televised, 1987); The Common Pursuit, 1984 (televised, 1992); Plays One, 1986; Melon, 1987; Hidden Laughter, 1990; Cell Mates, 1995. Television Plays: After Pilkington, 1987; Old Flames, 1990; They Never Slept, 1991; Running Late, 1992; Unnatural Pursuits, 1993; Femme Fatale, 1993. Screenplay: A Month in the Country, 1987. Radio Plays: The Rector's Daughter, 1992; Suffer the Little Children, 1993; With a Nod and a Bow, 1993; Cell Mates,

1995. Non-Fiction: An Unnatural Pursuit and Other Pieces, 1985; How's That for Telling 'Em, Fat Lady?, 1988; Fat Chance, 1995. Honours: Several drama awards in the UK and US. Address: c/o Judy Daish Associates, 2 St Charles Place, London W10 6EG, England.

GRAY Tony (George Hugh), b. 23 Aug 1922, Dublin, Ireland. Writer. m. Patricia Mary Walters, 1 Oct 1946, 1 son, 1 daughter. Education: St Andrews College, Dublin, 1935-39. Appointment: Features Editor, Daily Mirror, London, 1959-62. Publications: Starting from Tomorrow, 1965; The Real Professionals, 1966; Gone the Time, 1967; The Irish Answer, 1967; The Record Breakers (with L Villa), 1970; The Last Laugh, 1972; The Orange Order, 1972; Psalms and Slaughter, 1972; The White Lions of Timbavati (with C McBride), 1977; Some of My Best Friends Are Animals (with T Murphy), 1979; Operation White Lion (with C McBride), 1981; The Irish Times Book of the 20th Century, 1985; The Road to Success: Alfred McAlpine, 1935-85, 1987; Fleet Street Remembered, 1990; Mr Smyllie, Sir, 1991; Ireland This Century, 1994; Saint Patrick's People, 1996; A Peculiar Man: A Life of George Moore. Address: 3 Broomfield Road, Kew Gardens, Richmond, Surrey, England.

GREAVES Margaret, b. 13 June 1914, Birmingham, England. Lecturer in English (retired); Children's Writer. Education: BA, 1936, BLitt, 1938, MA, 1947, St Hugh's College, Oxford. Appointments: Lecturer in English, 1946-61, Principal Lecturer and Head of English Department, 1961-70, St Mary's College, Cheltenham. Publications: The Blazon of Honour, 1964; Regency Patron, 1966; Gallery, 1968; Gallimaufry, 1971; The Dagger and the Bird, 1971; The Grandmother Stone, 1972; Little Jacko, 1973; The Gryphon Quest, 1974; Curfew, 1975; Nothing Even Happens on Sundays, 1976; The Night of the Goat, 1976; A Net to Catch the Wind, 1979; The Abbottsbury Ring, 1979; Charlie and Emma Series, 4 volumes, 1980-87; Cat's Magic, 1980; The Snake Whistle, 1980; Once There Were No Pandas, 1985; Nicky's Knitting Granny, 1986; The Mouse of Nibbling Village, 1986; Hetty Pegler, 1987; Mouse Mischief, 1989; Juniper's Journey, 1990; Magic from the Ground, 1990; Henry's Wild Morning, 1990. Address: 8 Greenways, Winchcombe GL54 5LG, England.

GREELEY Andrew (Moran), b. 5 Feb 1928, Oak Park, Illinois, USA. Professor; Author. Education: AB, 1950, STB, 1952, STL, 1954, St Mary of the Lake Seminary; MA, 1961, PhD, 1962, University of Chicago. Appointments: Ordained, Roman Catholic Priest, 1954; Assistant Pastor, Church of Christ the King, Chicago, 1954-64; Senior Study Director, 1961-68, Program Director for Higher Education, 1968-70, Director of Center for the Study of American Pluralism, 1971-85, Research Associate, 1985-, Professor of Social Science, 1991-, University of Chicago; Professor of Sociology, University of Arizona at Tucson, 1978-. Publications: Non-Fiction: Letters to a Young Man, 1964; Letters to Nancy, from Andrew M Greeley, 1964; And Young Men Shall See Visions: Letters from Andrew M Greeley, 1964; The Hesitant Pilgrim: American Catholicism after the Council, 1966; The Catholic Experience: An Interpretation of the History of American Catholicism, 1967; Uncertain Trumpet: The Priest in Modern America, 1968; What Do We Believe? The Stance of Religion in America (with Martin E Marty and Stuart E Rosenberg), 1968; Life for a Wanderer: A New Look at Christian Spirituality, 1969; Come Blow Your Mind with Me (essays), 1971; The Jesus Myth, 1971; What a Modern Catholic Believes about God, 1971; The Denominational Society: A Sociological Approach to Religion in America, 1972; The Sinai Myth, 1972; The Unsecular Man: The Persistence of Religion, 1972; The Devil, You Say! Man and His Personal Devils and Angels, 1974; The Sociology of the Paranormal: A Reconnaissance, 1975; Death and Beyond, 1976; The Great Mysteries: An Essential Catechism, 1976; The Mary Myth: On the Femininity of God, 1977; No Bigger Than Necessary: An Alternative to Socialism, Capitalism, and Anarchism, 1977; The Best of Times, The Worst of Times (with J N Kotre), 1978; Religion: A Secular Theory, 1982; How to Save the Catholic Church, 1984; Confessions of a Parish Priest: An Autobiography, 1986; Patience of a Saint, 1986; God in Popular Culture, 1989; Myths of Religion, 1989; Complaints Against God, 1989; Andrew Greeley (autobiography), 1990; The Bible and Us: A Priest and a Rabbi Read Scripture Together (with Jacob Neusner), 1990; Faithful Attraction: Discovering Intimacy, Love and Fidelity in American Marriage, 1991; Love Affair: A Prayer Journal, 1992; The Sense of Love, 1992. Fiction: Nora Maeve and Sebi, 1976; The Magic Cup: An Irish Legend, 1979; Death in April, 1980; The Cardinal Sins, 1981; Thy Brother's Wife, 1982; Ascent into Hell, 1984; Virgin and Martyr, 1985; Happy Are the Meek, 1985; Angels of September, 1986; God Game, 1986; The Final Planet, 1987; Happy Are Those Who Thirst For

Justice, 1987; Lord of the Dance, 1987; Rite of Spring, 1987; Angel Fire, 1988; Happy Are the Clean of Heart, 1988; Love Song, 1988; All About Women, 1989; St Valentine's Night, 1989; The Search for Maggie Ward, 1991; The Cardinal Virtues, 1991; An Occasion of Sin, 1992; Happy Are the Merciful, 1992; Wages of Sin, 1992; Fall from Grace, 1993; Happy Are the Peacemakers, 1993; Happy Are the Poor in Spirit, 1994. Honours: C Albert Kobb Award, National Catholic Education Association, 1977; Mark Twain Award, Society for the Study of Midwestern Literature, 1987; Several honorary doctorates. Memberships: American Catholic Sociological Society; American Sociological Association; Religious Research Association; Society for the Scientific Study of Religion. Address: 1012 East 47th Street, Chicago, IL 60653, USA.

GREEN O O. See: **DURGNAT Raymond Eric.**

GREEN Benjamin, b. 17 July 1956, San Bernardino, California, USA. Writer. Education: BA, Humboldt State University, Arcata, 1985. Publications: The Field Notes of a Madman; The Lost Coast; From a Greyhound Bus; Monologs from the Realm of Silence; Green Grace, 1993; This Coast of Many Colors, 1993. Honours: Ucross Fellow. Address: 3415 Patricks Point Drive 3, Trinidad, CA 95570, USA.

GREEN Benny (Bernard), b. 9 Dec 1927, Leeds, Yorkshire, England. Freelance Writer. m. Antoinette Kanal, 1962, 3 sons, 1 daughter. Appointments: Saxophonist, 1947-60; Jazz Critic, Observer, 1958-77; Literary Critic, Spectator, 1970-; Film Critic, Punch, 1972-77; TV Critic, 1977-. Publications: Books and Lyrics: Boots with Strawberry Jam 1968; Co-Deviser, Cole, 1974; Oh Mr Porter, 1977; D D Lambeth, 1985. Books: The Reluctant Art, 1962; Blame it on My Youth, 1967; 58 Minutes to London, 1969; Drums in my Ears, 1973; I've Lost My Little Willie, 1976; Swingtime in Tottenham 1976; Cricket Addict's Archive, 1977; Shaw's Champions, 1978; Fred Astaire, 1979; Wisden Anthology, vol 1 1864-1900, 1979, vol II, 1900-1940, 1983; P G Woodhouse: A literary Biography, 1981; Wisden Book of Obituaries, 1986; A Histroy of Cricket, 1988; Let's Pace the Music,1989. Address: c/o BBC Broadcasting House, Portland Place, London, W1, England.

GREEN Brian. See: **CARD Orson Scott.**

GREEN Clifford, b. 6 Dec 1934, Melbourne, Victoria, Australia. Author; Screenwriter. m. Judith Irene Painter, 16 May 1959, 1 son, 3 daughters. Education: Primary Teachers Certificate, Toorak Teachers' College, 1959. Publications: Marion, 1974; The Incredible Steam-Driven Adventures of Riverboat Bill, 1975; Picnic at Hanging Rock: A Film, 1975; Break of Day, 1976; The Sun is Up, 1978; Four Scripts, 1978; Burn the Butterflies, 1979; Lawson's Mates, 1980; The Further Adventures of Riverboat Bill, 1981; Plays for Kids, 1981; Cop Out! Riverboat Bill Steams Again, 1985; Boy Soldiers, 1990. Honours: Australian Writers Guild Awards, 1973, 1974, 1976, 1978, 1979, 1990, 1992; Television Society of Australia Awards, 1974, 1976, 1978, 1980; Variety Club of Australia Award, 1978. Membership: Australian Writers Guild. Address: c/o Rick Raftos Management, PO Box 445, Paddington, New South Wales 2021, Australia.

GREEN Hannah. See: **GREENBERG Joanne.**

GREEN John F, b. 5 June 1943, Saskatoon, Saskatchewan, Canada. Teacher. m. Maureen Anne Horne, 1 Feb 1969, 3 sons, 1 daughter. Education: Ryerson Institute, 1964-67; Teachers Certificate, Red River Community College, 1976. Appointments: Professor, Arts and Sciences, Durham College, Oshawa, Ontario, 1976-; Writer and producer for western Canadian broadcasting companies. Publications: There are Trolls, The Bargain, 1974; The House on Geoffrey Street, 1981; The Gadfly, 1983; There's a Dragon in My Closet, 1986; Alice and The Birthday Giant, 1989; Junk-Pile Jennifer, 1991; The House that Max Built, 1991. Honour: Canadian Children's Book Centre Gold Seal Award, 1990. Address: 966 Adelaide Street East, No 70 Oshawa, Ontario L1K 1L2, Canada.

GREEN Jonathon, b. 20 Apr 1948, Kidderminster, Worcs, England. Writer; Broadcaster. 2 sons. Education: BA, Brasenose College, Oxford, 1969. Publications: Dictionary of Contemporary Slang; Dictionary of Contemporary Quotations; Dictionary of Jargon; Days in the Life; Them; Famous Last Words, Slang Down the Ages; Chasing the Sun. Address: c/o Jacintha Alexander Assoc, 47 Emperor's Gate, London SW7 4HJ, England.

GREEN Martin (Burgess), b. 21 Sept 1927, London, England. Professor of English; Writer. m. Carol Elizabeth Hurd, 1967, 1 son, 2 daughters. Education: BA, 1948, MA, 1952, St John's College, Cambridge; Teachers Diploma, King's College, London, 1951; Certificat d'Etudes Françaises, Sorbonne, Paris, 1952; PhD, University of Michigan, 1957. Apppointments: Instructor, Wellesley College, Massachussetts, USA, 1957-61; Lecturer, Birmingham University, England, 1965-68; Professor of English, Tufts University, Medford, Massachusetts, 1968-. Publications: Mirror for Anglo-Saxons, 1960; Reappraisals, 1965; Science and the Shabby Curate of Poetry, 1965; Yeat's Blessings on von Hugel, 1968; Cities of Light and Sons of the Morning, 1972; The von Richthofen Sisters, 1974; Children of the Sun, 1975; The Earth Again Redeemed (novel), 1976; Transatlantic Patterns, 1977; The Challenge of the Mahatmas,1978; Dreams of Adventure, Deeds of Empire, 1980; The Old English Elegies, 1983; Tolstoy and Gandhi, 1983; The Great American Adventure, 1984; Montains of Truth, 1986; The Triumph of Pierrot (with J Swan), 1986. Address: 8 Boylston Terrace, Medford, MA 02144, USA.

GREEN Michael Frederick, b. 2 Jan 1927, Leicester, England. Writer. Education: BA, Honours, Open University. Publications: The Art of Coarse Rugby, 1960; The Art of Coarse Sailing, 1962; Even Coarser Rugby, 1963; The Art of Coarse Acting, 1964; The Art of Coarse Golf, 1967; The Art of Coarse Moving, 1969 (TV serial, 1977); The Art of Coarse Drinking, 1973; Squire Haggard's Journal, 1976 (TV serial, 1990 and 1992); Four Plays For Coarse Actors, 1978; The Coarse Acting Show Two, 1980; Tonight Josephine, 1981; The Art of Coarse Sex, 1981; Don't Swing from the Balcony Romeo, 1983; The Art of Coarse Office Life, 1985; The Third Great Coarse Acting Show, 1985; The Boy Who Shot Down an Airship, 1988; Nobody Hurt in Small Earthquake, 1990. Memberships: Society of Authors; Equity; National Union of Journalists. Literary Agent: Anthony Sheil Associates. Address: 78 Sandall Road, Ealing, London W5 1JB, England.

GREEN Sharon, b. 6 July 1942, New York, New York, USA. Writer. div, 3 sons. Education: BA, New York University, 1963. Publications: The Crystals of Mida, 1982; The Warrior Within, 1982; The Warrior Enchained, 1983; An Oath to Mida, 1983; Chosen of Mida, 1984; The Warrior Rearmed, 1984; Mind Guest, 1984; Gateway to Xanadu, 1985; The Will of the Gods, 1985; To Battle the Gods, 1986; The Warrior Challenged, 1986; Rebel Prince, 1986; The Far Side of Forever, 1987; The Warrior Victorious, 1987; Lady Blade, Lord Fighter, 1987; Mists of the Ages, 1988; Hellhound Magic, 1989; Dawn Song, 1990; Haunted House, 1990; Silver Princess, Golden Knight, 1993; The Hidden Realms, 1993; Werewolfmoon, 1993; Fantasy Man, 1993; Flame of Fury, 1993; Dark Mirror, Dark Dreams, 1994; Silken Dreams, 1994; Enchanting, 1994; Wind Whispers, Shadow Shouts, 1995. Contributions to: Anthologies and magazines. Membership: Science Fiction Writers of America. Address: 110 Bellevue Road, No 28, Nashville, TN 37221, USA.

GREEN Timothy (Seton), b. 29 May 1936, Beccles, England. Writer. m. Maureen Snowbald, Oct 1959, 1 daughter. Education: BA, Christ's College, Cambridge, 1957; Graduate Diploma in Journalism, University of Western Ontario, 1958. Appointments: London Correspondent, Horizon, and American Heritage, 1959-62; Life, 1962-64; Editor, Illustrated London News, 1964-66. Publications: The World of Gold, 1968; The Smugglers, 1969; Restless Spirit, UK edition as The Adventurers, 1970; The Universal Eye, 1972; World of Gold Today, 1973; How to Buy Gold, 1975; The Smuggling Business, 1977; The World of Diamonds, 1981; The New World of Gold, 1982, 2nd edition, 1985; The Prospect for Gold, 1987; The World of Gold, 1993; The Good Water Guide, 1994; New Frontiers in Diamonds: The Mining Revolution, 1996. Address: Premier House, 10 Greycoat Place, London SW1P 1SB, England.

GREEN Vivian Hubert Howard, b. 18 Nov 1915, Wembley, Middlesex, England. Honorary Fellow, Lincoln College, Oxford. Education: BA, 1937, BD, 1941, Cambridge University; DD, (Oxford and Cambridge) 1957. Publications: Renaissance and Reformation, 1952; Oxford Common Room, 1957; The Young Mr Wesley, 1961; Religion at Oxford and Cambridge, 1964; The Commonwealth of Lincoln College 1427-1977, 1979; Love in a Cool Climate: The Letters of Mark Pattison and Meta Bradley, 1985; The Madness of Kings, 1993; A New History of Christianity, 1996. Honours: Thirlwall Prize and Medal, Cambridge University, 1940. Membership: Fellow of the Royal Historical Society. Address: Calendars, Sheep Street, Burford, Oxford OX8 4LS, England.

GREENBERG Alvin David, b. 10 May 1932, Cincinnati, Ohio, USA. Author; Teacher. Education: BA, MA, University of Cincinnati, USA; PhD, University of Washington. Appointments: University of Kentucky, 1963-65; Professor, English, Macalester College, St Paul, 1965-. Publications: The Metaphysical Giraffe, 1968; Going Nowhere, 1971; House of the Would-Be Gardener, 1972; Dark Lands, 1973; Metaform, 1975; The Invention of the West, 1976; In Direction, 1978; The Discovery of America and Other Tales, 1980; And Yet, 1981; Delta Q, 1983; The Man in the Cardboard Mask, 1985; Heavy Wings (poetry), 1988; Why We Live With Animals (poetry), 1990. Contributions to: American Review; Antioch Review; Ploughshares; Poetry North-West; American Poetry Review; Mississippi Review; Georgia Review; Gettysburg Review; Ohio Review. Honours: National Endowment for the Arts Fellowships, 1972, 1992; Bush Foundation Artist Fellowships, 1976, 1980; Short Fiction Award, Associated Writing Programes, 1982; Pablo Neruda Poetry Prize, 1988; Chelsea Poetry Award, 1994; Loft McKnight Award of Distinction in Poetry, 1994. Address: Department of English, Macalester College, St Paul, MN 55105, USA.

GREENBERG Joanne, (Hannah Green), b. 24 Sep 1932, Brooklyn, New York, USA. Author; Teacher. m. Albert Greenberg, 4 Sept 1955, 2 sons. Education: BA, American University. Publications: The King's Persons, 1963; I Never Promised You a Rose Garden, 1964; The Monday Voices, 1965; Summering: A Book of Short Stories, 1966; In This Sign, 1970; Rites of Passage, 1972; Founder's Praise, 1976; High Crimes and Misdemeanors, 1979; A Season of Delight, 1981; The Far Side of Victory, 1983; Simple Gifts, 1986; Age of Consent, 1987; Of Such Small Differences, 1988; With the Snow Queen (short stories), 1991; No Reck'ning Made, 1993. Contributions to: Articles, reviews, short stories to numerous periodicals. Honours: Harry and Ethel Daroff Memorial Fiction Award, 1963; William and Janice Epstein Fiction Award, 1964; Marcus L Kenner Awards, 1971; Christopher Book Award, 1971; Freida Fromm Reichman Memorial Award, 1971; Rocky Mountain Women's Institute Award, 1983; Denver Public Library Bookplate Award, 1990; Colorado Author of the Year. Memberships: Authors Guild; PEN: Colorado Authors League; National Association of the Deaf. Address: 29221 Rainbow Hill Road, Golden, CO 80401, USA.

GREENBERG Martin, b. 3 Feb 1918, Norfolk, Virginia, USA. Writer; Translator. m. Paula Fox, 9 June 1962, 1 son. Education: BA, University of Michigan. Appointments: Editor; Professor. Publications: The Terror of Art: Kafka and Modern Literature, 1968; The Hamlet Vocation of Coleridge and Wordsworth, 1986; Translations: The Diaries of Franz Kafka 1914-23, 1948-49; The Marquise of O & Other Stories, 1960; Five Plays (von Kleist), 1988; Faust, Part One, 1992; Faust, Part Two, 1996. Honours: Literature Award, American Academy and Institute of Arts and Letters, 1989; Harold Morton Lansdon Translation Award, 1989. Membership: Academy of American Poets. Address: 306 Clinton Street, Brooklyn, NY 11201, USA.

GREENBLATT Stephen (Jay), b. 7 Nov 1943, Cambridge, Massachusetts, USA. Professor of English; Writer. m. Ellen Schmidt, 27 Apr 1969, 2 sons. Education: BA, 1964, MPhil, 1968, PhD, 1969, Yale University; BA, 1966, MA, 1969, Pembroke College, Cambridge. Appointments: Assistant Professor, 1969-74, Associate Professor, 1974-79, Professor of English, 1979-84, Class of 1932 Professor, 1984-, University of California at Berkeley; Visiting Professor, University of California at Santa Cruz, 1981, University of Beijing, 1982, Northwestern University, 1984, University of Bologna, 1988, University of Chicago, 1989, École des Hautes en Sciences Sociales, Paris, 1989, Harvard University, 1990, 1991, 1993, 1994, University of Trieste, 1991, Dartmouth College, 1992, University of Florence, 1992; Clarendon Lecturer, Oxford University, 1988; Wissenschaftskolleg zu Berlin, 1996-97; University of Torino, 1997. Publications: Three Modern Satirists: Waugh, Orwell and Huxley, 1965; Sir Walter Raleigh: The Renaissance Man and His Roles, 1973; Renaissance Self-Fashioning: From More to Shakespeare, 1980; Shakespearean Negotiations: The Circulation of Social Energy in Renaissance England, 1988; Learning to Curse: Essays in Early Modern Culture, 1990; Marvelous Possessions: The Wonder of the New World, 1991. Editor: Allegory and Representation, 1981; The Power of Forms in the English Renaissance, 1982; Representing the English Renaissance, 1988; Essays in Memory of Joel Fineman, 1989; Redrawing the Boundaries: The Transformation of English and American Literary Studies (with Giles Gunn), 1992; New World Encounters, 1992; Norton Shakespeare, 1997. Contributions to: Scholarly journals. Honours: Fulbright Scholarship, Cambridge, 1964-66; National Endowment for

the Humanities Fellowship, 1971-72; Guggenheim Fellowships, 1975, 1983; British Council Prize in the Humanities, 1981; James Russell Lowell Prize, Modern Language Association, 1989. Memberships: American Academy of Arts and Sciences, fellow; International Association of University Professor of English; Modern Language Association; Renaissance Society of America; Wissenschaftskolleg zu Berlin, fellow. Address: 1004 Oxford Street, Berkeley, CA 94707, USA.

GREENE A(lvin) C(arl), b. 4 Nov 1923, Abilene, Texas, USA. Professor; Historian; Author. m. (1) Betty Jo Dozier, 1 May 1950, 3 sons, 1 daughter, (2) Judy Dalton, 20 Jan 1990. Education: Phillips University, 1942; Kansas State College, 1943; BA, Abilene Christian College, 1948; Graduate Studies, Hardin-Simmons University, 1951, University of Texas at Austin, 1968-70. Appointment: Co-Director, Centre for Texas Studies, University of North Texas. Publications: A Personal Country, 1969; The Santa Claus Bank Robbery, 1972; The Last Captive, 1972; Dallas: The Deciding Years, 1972; The Highland Park Woman, 1984; Taking Heart, 1990. Contributions to: Atlantic; McCalls; Southwestern History Quarterly; New York Times Book Review. Honours: National Conference of Christians and Jews, 1964; Dobie-Paisano Fellow, 1968; Fellow, Texas State History Association, 1990. Memberships: Texas Institute of Letters, president, 1969-71, fellow 1981-; Writers Guild of America, West; PEN International. Address: 4359 Shirley Drive, Dallas, TX 75229, USA.

GREENE Constance C(larke), b. 27 Oct 1924, New York, New York, USA. Writer. m. Philip M Greene, 8 June 1946, 2 sons, 3 daughters. Education: Skidmore College, 1942-44. Publications: A Girl Called Al, 1969; Leo the Lioness, 1970; The Good-Luck Bogie Hat, 1971; Unmaking of Rabbit, 1972; Isabelle the Itch, 1973; The Ears of Louis, 1974; I Know You, Al, 1975; Beat the Turtle Drum, 1976; Getting Nowhere, 1977; I and Sproggy, 1978; Your Old Pal, Al, 1979; Dotty's Suitcase, 1980; Double-Dare O'Toole, 1981; Al(exandra) the Great, 1982; Ask Anybody, 1983; Isabelle Shows Her Stuff, 1984; Star Shine, 1985; Other Plans, 1985; The Love Letters of J Timothy Owen, 1986; Just Plain Al, 1986; Isabelle and Little Orphan Frannie, 1988; Monday I Love You, 1988; Al's Blind Date, 1989; Funny You Should Ask, 1992; Odds on Oliver, 1992. Contributions to: Magazines and newspapers. Honours: American Library Association Notable Books, 1970, 1977, 1987. Address: c/o Viking Press Inc, 40 West 23rd Street, New York, NY 10010, USA.

GREENE James, b. 12 Mar 1915, Elmwood, Nebraska, USA. Educator; Consultant; Author. m. Barbara Holt, 18 Aug 1943, 1 son, 1 daughter. Education: BS, Mechanical Engineering, 1947, MS, Industrial Engineering, 1948, PhD, University of Iowa. Publications: Operation Planning and Control, English and Japanese editions, 1967; Production and Inventory Control Handbook, 2nd edition, 1967, 3rd edition, 1997. Contributions to: Over 50 articles in various journals. Honours: Fulbright Award; Presidential Award for American Production and Inventory Control Society; Pi Tau Sigma; Alpha Pi Mu; Tau Beta Pi Outstanding Teacher Award. Address: School of Industrial Engineering, Purdue University, West Lafayette, IN 42906, USA.

GREENE Jonathon (Edward), b. 19 Apr 1943, New York, New York, USA. Editor; Poet. m. (1) Alice-Anne Kingston, 5 June 1963, div, 1 daughter, (2) Dobree Adams, 23 May 1974, 2 sons. Education: BA, Bard College, 1965. Appointments: Founding Editor, Director, Gnomon Press, Frankfort, Kentucky, 1965-; Editor, Kentucky Renaissance, 1976. Publications: The Reckoning, 1966; Instance, 1968; The Lapidary, 1969; A 17th Century Garner, 1969; An Unspoken Complaint, 1970; The Poor in Church, by Arthur Rimbaud (translation), 1973; Scaling the Walls, 1974; Glossary of the Everyday, 1974; Peripatetics, 1978; Jonathan Williams: A 50th Birthday Celebration (editor), 1979; Once a Kingdom Again, 1979; Quiet Goods, 1980; Idylls, 1983, revised edition, 1990; Small Change for the Long Haul, 1984; Trickster Tales, 1985; Les Chambre des Poètes, 1990; The Man Came to Haul Stone, 1995. Address: PO Box 475, Frankfort, KY 40602, USA.

GREENER Michael John, b. 28 Nov 1931, Barry, Wales. Chartered Accountant Company Director. m. May 1964, div 1972, 1 son. Education: BA, University of South Wales and Monmouthshire, 1949-53; Articled, Deloitte Plender Griffiths, Cardiff, Wales, 1949-57; Qualified as Chartered Accountant, 1957; FCA, 1967; BA, Open University, 1991. Publications: Between the Lines of the Balance Sheet, 1968, revised, 1980; Penguin Dictionary of Commerce, 1970, revised, 1980, revised and reissued as Penguin Business Dictionary, 1987, revised, 1994; Problems for Discussion in Mercantile Law, 1970;

The Red Bus, 1973. Contributions to: Many articles in business and professional journals. Membership: Fellow, Institute of Chartered Accountants, 1967. Address: 33 Glan Hafren, Maes-y-Coed, Barry, South Glamorgan, CF62 6TA, Wales.

GREENFIELD Jeanette, b. Melbourne, Australia. International Lawyer; Author. Education: LLB, University of Melbourne, 1968; Called to the Bar, Supreme Court of Victoria, 1969; LLB, 1973, PhD, 1976, Wolfson College, Cambridge University. Publications: China and the Law of the Sea, Air and Environment, 1979; The Return of Cultural Treasures, 1989, 2nd edition, 1996; China's Practice in the Law of the Sea, 1991. Contributions to: Chambers Biographical Dictionary; Antiquity; Apollo; Australian Outlook. Honour: British Academy Grant, 1986. Address: 59 River Court, Upper Ground, London SE1 9PB, England.

GREENHILL Basil Jack, b. 26 Feb 1920, Weston-Super-Mare, Somerset, England. Author. m. (1) Gillian Stratton, 1950, dec 1959, 1 son, (2) Anne Giffard, 1961, 1 son. Education: BA, 1946, PhD, 1981,Bristol University. Appointments: Diplomatic Service, 1946-66; Director, 1967-83, Caird Research Fellow, 1983-86, National Maritime Museum, Greenwich; Chairman, 1982-92, Vice-President, 1992-, SS Great Britain Project; Consultant, Conway Maritime Press, 1990-96; Chairman, Centre for Maritime Historical Studies, University of Exeter, 1991-; Chatham Publishing, 1996-. Publications: The Merchant Schooners, Vol I, 1951, Vol II, 1957, 4th edition, revised, 1988; Sailing for a Living, 1962; Westcountrymen in Prince Edward's Isle (with Ann Giffard), 1967, 3rd edition, 1990; The Merchant Sailing Ship: A Photographic History (with Ann Giffard), 1970; Women Under Sail (with Ann Giffard), 1970; Captain Cook, 1970; Boats and Boatmen of Pakistan, 1971; Travelling by Sea in the Nineteenth Century (with Ann Giffard), 1972; Sail and Steam (with P W Brock), 1973; West Country Coasting Ketches (with W J Slade), 1974; A Victorian Maritime Album, 1974; A Quayside Camera, 1975; The Coastal Trade: Sailing Craft of British Waters 900-1900 (with L Willis), 1975; Archaeology of the Boat, 1976; Victorian and Edwardian Ships and Harbours (with Ann Giffard), 1978; Victorian and Edwardian Merchant Steamships (with Ann Giffard), 1979; Schooners, 1980; The Life and Death of the Sailing Ship, 1980; The British Seafarer (with Michael Mason), 1980; Seafaring Under Sail (with Denis Stonham), 1981; Karlsson, 1982; The Woodshipbuilders, 1986; The Grain Races, 1986; The British Assault on Finland, 1854-55 (with Ann Giffard), 1988; The Evolution of the Wooden Ship, 1988; The Herzogin Cecilie (with John Hackman), 1991; The New Maritime History of Devon (co-editor), 2 volumes, 1993, 1994; The Advent of Steam (editor), 1993; The Last Century of Sail (editor), 1993; The Arby Boat (with Owain Roberts), 1993; Steam, Politics and Patronage (with Ann Giffard), 1994; The Bertha L Downs, 1995; The New Archaeology of the Boat, 1995; The Schooner, 1995; The Archaeology of Boats and Ships, 1995; The Evolution of the Sailing Ship, 1995; Paddle Wheels, Sail and Screw (with Peter Allington), 1997. Contributions to: Many publications. Honours: Companion of the Order of St Michael and St George, 1967; Knight Commander of the Order of the White Rose, Finland, 1980; Companion of the Order of the Bath, 1981; Honorary Fellow, University of Exeter, 1985; Honorary D Litt, University of Plymouth, 1996. Memberships: Ancient Monuments Board for England, 1972-84; Devon Historical Society, president, 1993-; Maritime Trust, council, 1977-83, honorary vice-president, 1984-; Royal Historical Society, fellow; Society for Nautical Research, vice-president, 1975-; Society of Authors, fellow. Address: West Boetheric Farmhouse, St Dominic, Saltash, Cornwall PL12 6SZ, England.

GREENLAND Colin, b. 17 May 1954, Dover, Kent, England. Writer. Education: MA, 1978, DPhil, 1981, Pembroke College, Oxford. Appointments: Writer-in-Residence, North East London Polytechnic, 1980-82. Publications: The Entropy Exhibition, 1983; Daybreak on a Different Mountain, 1984; Magnetic Storm (with Roger and Martyn Dean), 1984; Interzone: The First Anthology (editor), 1985; The Freelance Writer's Handbook (with Paul Kerton), 1986; The Hour of the Thin Ox, 1987; Storm Warnings (co-editor), 1987; Other Voices, 1988; Take Back Plenty, 1990; Michael Moorcock: Death is No Obstacle, 1992; Harm's Way, 1993; Seasons of Plenty, 1995. Contributions to: Many anthologies and periodicals. Honours: Eaton Award for Science Fiction Criticism, 1985; Arthur C Clarke Award, 1992; British Science Fiction Association Award, 1992; Eastercon Award, 1992; Guest of Honour, Evolution, National Science Fiction Easter Convention, 1996. Memberships: Science Fiction Foundation; Science Fiction Writers' Conference, Milford. Address: 98 Sturton Street, Cambridge CB1 2QA, England.

GREENLEAF Stephen (Howell), b. 17 July 1942, Washington, DC, USA. Attorney; Writer. m. Ann Garrison, 20 July 1968, 1 son. Education: BA, Carleton College, 1964; JD, University of California, at Berkeley, 1967; Creative Writing, University of Iowa, 1978-79. Appointments: Admitted to the Bar, California, 1968, Iowa, 1977. Publications: Grave Error, 1979; Death Bed, 1980; State's Evidence, 1982; Fatal Obsession, 1983; The Ditto List, 1985; Beyond Blame, 1986; Toll Call, 1987; Impact, 1989; Book Case, 1991; Blood Type, 1992; Southern Cross, 1993; False Conception, 1994. Honour: Maltese Falcon Award, Japan, 1993. Address: c/o Esther Newberg, ICM, 40 West 57th Street, New York, NY 10019, USA.

GREENVILLE John A(shley) S(Oames), b. 11 Jan 1928, Berlin, Germany. Historian; Professor. m. (1) Betty Anne Rosenberg, 1960, dec 1974, 3 sons, (2) Patricia Carnie, 1975, 1 daughter, 1 stepdaughter. Education: Correspondence course, Birbeck College, and London School of Economics and Political Science; BA, Yale University; PhD, London University. Appointments: Postgraduate Scholar, London University, 1951-53; Assistant Lecturer to Lecturer, 1953-64, Reader in Modern History, 1964-66, Nottingham University; Commonwealth Fund Fellow, 1958-59; Postdoctoral Fellow, Yale University, 1960-63; Professor of International History, Leeds University, 1966-69; Editor, Fontana History of War and Society, 1969-78, Leo Baeck Year Book, 1992-; Professor of Modern History, 1969-94, Professorial Research Fellow, Institute of German Studies, 1994-, University of Birmingham. Publications: The Coming of the Europeans (with J G Fuller), 1962; Lord Salisbury and Foreign Policy, 1964, 2nd edition, 1970; Politics, Strategy and American Diplomacy: Studies in Foreign Policy 1873-1917 (with G B Young), 1966, 2nd edition, 1971; The Major International Treaties 1914-1973: A History and Guide, 1974, enlarged edition, 2 volumes, 1987; Europe Reshaped 1848-1878, 1975; World History of the Twentieth Century, Vol I, 1900-1945, 1980; Collins World History of the Twentieth Century, 1994. Other: Films with N Pronay: The Munich Crisis, 1968; The End of Illusion: From Munich to Dunkirk, 1970; Nazi Germany, 1976. Contributions to: Scholarly journals. Address: c/o Institute of German Studies, University of Birmingham, Birmingham B15 2TT, England.

GREENWOOD Ted, (Edward Alister Greenwood), b. 4 Dec 1930, Melbourne, Victoria, Australia. Children's Writer. m. Florence Lorraine Peart, 15 Jan 1954, 4 daughters. Education: Primary Teacher's Certificate, Melbourne Teacher's College, 1949; Diploma of Art, Royal Melbourne Institute of Technology, 1959. Publications: Obstreperous, 1969; Alfred, 1970; Curious Eddie, 1970; VIP: Very Important Plant, 1971; Joseph and Lulu and the Prindiville House Pigeons, 1972; Terry's Brrrmmm GT, 1974; The Pochetto Coat, 1978; Ginnie, 1979; The Boy Who Saw God, 1980; Everlasting Circle, 1981; Flora's Treasurers, 1982; Marley and Friends, 1983; Warts and All (with S Fennessy), 1984; Ship Rock, 1985; I Don't Want to Know (with S Fennessy), 1986; Windows, 1989; Uncle Theo is a Number Nine, 1990; Spooner or Later, 1992; Duck for Cover, 1994, Freeze a Crowd, 1996, with Paul Jennings and Terry Denton; What Do We Do With Dawson?, with Terry Denton, 1996. Address: 50 Hilton Road, Ferny Creek, Victoria 3786, Australia.

GREER Germaine b. 29 Jan 1939, Melbourne, Victoria, Australia. Writer; Broadcaster. Education: BA Hons, Melbourne University, 1959; MA Hons, Sydney University, 1962; PhD, Cambridge University, 1967. Appointments: Senior English Tutor, Sydney University, 1963-64; Assistant Lecturer and Lecturer, English, University of Warwick, 1967-72; Lecturer, American Program Bureau, 1973-78; Visiting Professor, Graduate Faculty of Modern Letters, 1979, Professor of Modern Letters, 1980-83, University of Tulsa; Founder-Director, Tulsa Centre for Studies in Women's Literature, 1981; Director, Stump Cross Books, 1988-; Special Lecturer and Unofficial Fellow, Newnham College, Cambridge, 1989-. Publications: The Female Eunuch, 1969; The Obstacle Race: The Fortunes of Women Painters and Their Work, 1979; Sex and Destiny: The Politics of Human Fertility, 1984; Shakespeare (editor), 1986; The Madwoman's Underclothes (selected journalism), 1986; Kissing the Rod: An Anthology of Seventeenth Century Verse, 1988; Daddy, We Hardly Knew You, 1989; The Uncollected Verse of Aphra Benn, 1989; The Change: Women, Ageing and the Menopause, 1991; Slip-Shod Sibyls: Recognition and the Woman Poet, 1995. Contributions to: Journalist, columnist, reviewer, 1972-79. Honours: Scholarships, 1952, 1956; Commonwealth Scholarship, 1964; J R Ackerly Prize and Premio Internazionale Mondello, 1989. Address: c/o Aitken and Stone Ltd, 29 Fernshaw Road, London SW10 0TG, England.

GREGORIOU Gregory, b. 20 May 1929, Athens, Greece. Physician; Psychiatrist. Education: Diploma, Psychiatry, McGill University, 1965; Specialist Certificate, Royal College of Physicians and Surgeons of Canada, 1965; Specialist Certificate, College of Physicians and Surgeons of the Province of Quebec, 1968. Appointments: Faculty Lecturer, Department of Psychiatry, McGill University, 1968-; Psychiatrist, Queen Elizabeth Hospital, Montreal; Co-ordinator, Continuing Medical Education Program, Department of Psychiatry, Queen Elizabeth Hospital, Montreal; Director, Creativity Clinic, Department of Psychiatry, Queen Elizabeth Hospital, Montreal. Publications: Le Devin du Village - Un coté peu connu de l'oeuvre de Jean-Jacques Rousseau, 1984; Le livret de l'opéra de Jean-Jacques Rousseau, Le Devin du Village une expression lyrique de sa philosophie, 1989; Musicothérapie, 1992; La Renaissance de la Psychiatrie, 1992; Le Danger des Paranoiaques et des Sociopathes Pour La Société, 1993; Le Passé et L'Avenir de L'Humanisme Medical, 1994; Actes du Colloque International J J Rousseau de Montmorency, 1989; Nostalgies, poetry, 1990; La Moisson Litteraire, 1993. Contributions to: Le Rôle de la Litterature Consacrée aux Yeunes dans la Promotion de Leur Santé Psychique, Le Medecin du Quebec, 1994. Honours: Cesare Pavese Prize, 1990; International Man of Year, IBC, 1995-96. Memberships: Fellow, Royal College of Physicians and Surgeons of Canada; Professional Corporation of Physicians of Quebec; Quebec Medical Association; Quebec Psychiatric Association; Federation of Medical Specialists of Quebec; Medical Association of Athens, Greece; Association of Doctors Writers of France; Hellenic Doctors Writers Association; World Association of Doctors Writers; American Physicians Poetry Association; Canadian Writers Association; International Hippocratic Foundation of Kos, Greece; American Association of French Philosophy; North American Association for the Study of J J Rousseau; Charter member of Société Américaine de Philosophie de Langue Française, founding member; World Literary Academy. Address: 5025 Rue Sherbrooke 0, Westmount Quebec H4A 1S9, Canada.

GREGORY Richard (Langton), b. 24 July 1923, London, England. Professor of Neuropsychology Emeritus; Writer. m. (1) Margaret Hope Pattison Muir, 1953, div 1966, 1 son, 1 daughter, (2) Freja Mary Balchin, div 1976. Education: Downing College, Cambridge, 1947-50; DSc, University of Bristol, 1983. Appointments: Research, MRC Applied Psychology Research Unit, Cambridge, 1950-53; University Demonstrator, later Lecturer, Department of Psychology, Cambridge, 1953-67; Fellow, Corpus Christi College, Cambridge, 1962-67; Professor of Bionics, University of Edinburgh, 1967-70; Professor of Neuropsychology and Director of the Brain and Perception Laboratory, 1970-88, Professor Emeritus, 1988-, University of Bristol; Founder and Chairman of the Trustees, 1983-91, President, 1991-, Exploratory Hands-on Science Centre; Advisory Committee, Royal Society Representative, The British Library, 1996-97. Publications: Recovery from Early Blindness (with Jean Wallace), 1963; Eye and Brain, 1966, 5th edition, 1997; The Intelligent Eye, 1970; Illusion in Nature and Art (co-editor), 1973; Concepts and Mechanisms of Perception, 1974; Mind in Science, 1981; Odd Perceptions (essays), 1986; The Oxford Companion to the Mind (editor), 1987; Evolution of the Eye and Visual System (co-editor), Vol II of Vision and Visual Dysfunction, 1991; Even Odder Perceptions (essays), 1994; Mirrors in Mind, 1997. The Artful Eye, 1995; Mirrors in Mind, 1996. Contributions to: Scientific journals. Honours: Commander of the Order of the British Empire, 1989; Michael Faraday Medal, Royal Society, 1993; Corpus Christi College, Cambridge, honorary fellowship; Honorary doctorates. Memberships: Royal Institution; Royal Society, fellow. Address: 23 Royal York Crescent,Clifton, Bristol BS8 4JX, England.

GRENDEL Lajos, b. 6 Apr 1948, Levice, Czechoslovakia. Writer. m. Agota Sebok, 6 July 1974, 1 son, 1 daughter. Education: University Komens Keho. Appointments: Editor, Publishing House, Medech Brehsleva; Editor in Chief, Literary Monthly, Kalligram; Chairman, Publishing House, Kalligram, 1992. Publications: Elesloveszet; Attetelil; Borondok Tartalma; Theszevz es a Pekete ozvegy; Einstien harangjai; Galeir; Hutleneck. Contributions to: Hungarian and Slovak magazines. Honours: Dery Prize; Jozsef Attila Prize; Cryslal Vilenica; Füst Milan Award, 1995. Membership: Union of Hungarian Writers. Address: Vazovova 15, 81107 Bratislava, Czech Republic.

GRENNAN Eamon, b. 13 Nov 1941, Dublin, Ireland. Professor; Poet. 1 son, 2 daughters. Education: BA, 1963, MA, 1964, University College, Dublin; PhD, Harvard University, 1973. Appointments: Lecturer in English, University College, Dublin, 1966-67; Assistant Professor, Herbert Lehman College, City University of New York, 1971-74; Assistant Professor, 1974-83, Associate Professor, 1983-89, Professor, 1989-. Vassar College. Publications: Wildly for Days, 1983; What Light There Is, 1987; Twelve Poems, 1988; What Light There Is and Other Poems, 1989; As If It Matters, 1991; So It Goes, 1995; Selected Poems of Giacomo Leopardi (translator), 1995. Contributions to: Anthologies and periodicals. Honours: National Endowment for the Humanities Grant, 1986; National Endowment for the Arts Grant, 1991; Guggenheim Fellowship, 1995. Address: c/o Department of English, Vassar College, Poughkeepsie, NY 12604-0352, USA.

GRENVILLE John A(shley) S(oames), b. 11 Jan 1928, Berlin, Germany. Historian; Professor. m. (1) Betty Anne Rosenberg, 1960, dec 1974, 3 sons, (2) Patricia Carnie, 1975, 1 daughter, 1 stepdaughter. Education: Correspondence courses, Birbeck College, and London School of Economics and Political Science; BA, Yale University; PhD, London University. Appointments: Postgraduate Scholar, London University, 1951-53; Assistant Lecturer to Lecturer, 1953-64, Reader in Modern History, 1964-65, Nottingham University; Commonwealth Fund Fellow, 1958-59; Postdoctoral Fellow, Yale University, 1960-63; Professor of International History, Leeds University, 1965-69; Editor, Fontana History of War and Society, 1969-78, Leo Baeck Year Book, 1992-; Professor of Modern History, 1969-94, Professorial Research Fellow, Institute of German Studies, 1994-, University of Birmingham. Publications: The Coming of the Europeans (with J G Fuller), 1962; Lord Salisbury and Foreign Policy, 1964, 2nd edition, 1970; Politics, Strategy and American Diplomacy: Studies in Foreign Policy 1873-1917 (with G B Young), 1966, 2nd edition, 1971; The Major International Treaties 1914-1973: A History and Guide, 1974, enlarged edition, 2 volumes, 1987; Europe Reshaped 1848-1878, 1975; Nazi Germany, 1976; World History of the Twentieth Century, Vol I, 1900-1945, 1980; Collins World History of the Twentieth Century, 1994. Other: Films with N Pronay: The Munich Crisis, 1968; The End of Illusion: From Munich to Dunkirk, 1970. Contributions to: Scholarly journals. Address: c/o Institute of German Studies, University of Birmingham, Birmingham B15 2TT, England.

GREY Anthony (Keith), b. 5 July 1938, Norwich, England. Author; Television and Radio reporter; Presenter. m. Shirley McGuinn, 4 Apr 1970, 2 daughters. Appointments: Journalist, Eastern Daily Press, 1960-64; Foreign Correspondent, Reuters, East Berlin and Prague, 1965-67, Beijing, 1967-69. Publications: Hostage in Peking, 1970; A Man Alone, 1971; Some Put Their Trust in Chariots, 1973; Crossroads from Peking, 1975; The Bulgarian Exclusive, 1976; Himself (radio play), 1976; The Chinese Assassin, 1978; Saigon, 1982; The Prime Minister was a Spy, 1983; Peking, 1988; The Naked Angels, 1990; The Bangkok Secret, 1990; Tokyo Bay, 1996. Contributions to: Radio, television and various publications. Honours: Officer of the Order of the British Empire, 1969; UK Journalist of the Year, 1970. Memberships: MCC; RAC Pall Mall; PEN International; Royal Institute of International Affairs; Society of Authors. Address: c/o A D Peters & Co Ltd, The Chambers, 5th Floor, Chelsea Harbour, Lots Road, London SW10 0XF, England.

GREY Belinda. See: **PETERS Maureen.**

GREY Charles. See: **TUBB E(dwin) C(harles).**

GRIDBAN Volsted. See: **TUBB E(dwin) C(harles).**

GRIFFIN Keith B(roadwell), b. 6 Nov 1938, Panama. Economist; Professor. m. Dixie Beth Griffin, 2 Apr 1956, 2 daughters. Education: BA, Williams College, 1960; BPhil, 1962, DPhil, 1965, Balliol College, Oxford. Appointment: Professor, University of California at Riverside. Publications: Underdevelopment in Spanish America, 1969; Planning Development (with John Enos), 1970; Financing Development in Latin America (editor), 1971; Growth and Inequality in Pakistan (editor with A R Khan), 1972; The Political Economy of Agrarian Change, 1974; Land Concentration and Rural Poverty, 1976; International Inequality and National Poverty, 1978; The Transition to Egalitarian Development (with J James), 1981; Growth and Equality in Rural China, (with A Saith), 1981; Institutional Reform and Economic Development in the Chinese Countryside (editor), 1984; World Hunger and the World Economy, 1987; Alternative Strategies for Economic Development, 1989; Human Development and the International Development Strategy for the 1990s (editor with J Knight), 1990; The Economy of Ethiopia, (editor), 1992; Globalisation and the Developing World (with A R Khan), 1992; The Distribution of Income in China (editor with Zhao Renwei), 1993; Implementing a Human

Development Strategy (with Terry McKinley), 1994; Poverty and the Transition to a Market Economy in Mongolia, editor, 1995; Social Policy and Economic Transformation in Uzbekistan, editor, 1996; Studies in Globalization and Economic Transitions, 1996. Address: Department of Economics, University of California, Riverside, CA 92521, USA.

GRIFFITH A(rthur) Leonard, b. 19 Mar 1920, Lancashire, England. Retired Minister of Religion. m. Anne Merelie Cayford, 17 June 1947, 2 daughters. Education: BA, McGill University, 1942; BD, Queen's University, Kingston, Ontario, 1958. Publications: The Roman Letter Today, 1959; God and His People, 1960; Beneath the Cross of Jesus, 1961; What is a Christian, 1962; Barriers to Christian Belief, 1962; A Pilgrimage to the Holy Land, 1962; The Eternal Legacy, 1963; Pathways to Happiness, 1964; God's Time and Ours, 1964; The Crucial Encounter, 1965; This is Living, 1966; God is Man's Experience, 1968; Illusions of Our Culture, 1969; The Need to Preach, 1971; Hang on to the Lord's Prayer, 1973; We Have This Ministry, 1973; Ephesians: A Positive Affirmation, 1975; Gospel Characters, 1976; Reactions to God, 1979; Take Hold of the Treasure, 1981; From Sunday to Sunday, 1987. Address: 71 Old Mill Road, 105 Etobicoke, Ontario M8X 1G9, Canada.

GRIFFITHS Helen, (Helen Santos), b. 8 May 1939, London, England. Writer. Publications: Horse in the Clouds, 1957; Wild and Free, 1958; Moonlight, 1959; Africano, 1960; The Wild Heart, 1962; The Greyhound, 1963; Wild Horse of Santander, 1965; Dark Swallows, 1965; Leon, 1966; Stallion of the Sands, 1967; Monshie Cat, 1968; Patch, 1969; Federico, 1970; Russian Blue, 1973; Just a Dog, 1974; Witch Fear, 1975; Pablo, 1976; Kershaw Dogs, 1978; The Last Summer, 1979; Blackface Stallion, 1980; Dancing Horses, 1981; Hari's Pigeon, 1982; Rafa's Fog, 1983; Jesus, As Told By Mark, 1983; Dog at the Window, 1984; Also, as Helen Santos: Caleb's Lamb, 1984; If Only, 1987; Pepe's Dog, 1996. Scripture Union. Honours: Daughter of Mark Twain, 1966; Highly Commended, Carnegie Medal Award, 1966; Silver Pencil Award, best children's book, Netherlands, 1978. Address: 9 Ashley Terrace, Bath, Avon, BA1 3OP, England.

GRIFFITHS Paul (Anthony), b. 24 Nov 1947, Bridgend, Glamorgan, Wales. m. Sally Mclaughlin, 1979. Education: BA, MSc, Lincoln College, Oxford. Appointments: Area Editor for Grove's Dictionary of Music and Musicians, 1973-76; Music Critic, The Times, 1982-92, The New Yorker, 1992-. Publications: A Concise History of Modern Music, 1978; Boulez, 1978; A Guide to Electronic Music, 1979; Modern Music, 1980; Cage, 1981; Peter Maxwell Davies, 1982; The String Quartet, 1983; György Ligeti, 1983; Bartók, 1984; Olivier Messiaen, 1985; New Sounds, New Personalities, 1985; The Thames & Hudson Encyclopedia of 20th Century Music, 1986; Myself and Marco Polo (novel), 1987; The Life of Sir Tristram (novel), 1991; The Jewel Box (opera libretto), 1991; Stravinsky, 1992; Modern Music and After, 1995. Address: The Old Bakery, Lower Heyford, Oxford OX6 3NS, England.

GRIFFITHS Trevor, b. 4 Apr 1935, Manchester, Lancashire, England. Playwright. m. (1) Janice Elaine Stansfield, 1960, dec 1977, 1 son, 2 daughters, (2) Gillian Cliff, 1992. Education: St Bede's College, Manchester, 1945-52; BA, English, Manchester University, 1955. Appointments: Lecturer in Liberal Studies, Stockport Technical College, Cheshire, 1962-65; Co-Editor, Labour's Northern Voice, 1962-65; Series Editor, Workers Northern Publishing Society; Further Education Officer, BBC, Leeds, 1965-72. Publication: Collected Plays for Television, 1988. Other: Various plays produced in London and other UK cities, 1972-96. Honour: BAFTA Writer's Award, 1982. Address: c/o Peters, Fraser & Dunlop Group Ltd, The Chambers, 503-4 Chelsea Harbour, Lots Road, London SW10 0XF, England.

GRIFO Lionello. See: VAGGE Ornello.

GRIGG John (Edward Poynder), b. 15 Apr 1924, London, England. Writer. m. Marion Patricia Campbell, 3 Dec 1958, 2 sons. Education: MA, New College, Oxford, 1948. Appointments: Grenadier Guards, 1943-45; Editor, National and English Review, 1954-60; Columnist, The Guardian, 1960-70. Publications: Two Anglican Essays, 1958; The Young Lloyd George, 1973; Lloyd George: The People's Champion, 1978; The Victory That Never Was, 1980; Nancy Astor: Portrait of a Pioneer, 1980; Lloyd George: From Peace to War 1912-1916, 1985; The Thomson Years (vol VI in The History of the Times), 1993. Contributions to: Various books of essays, magazines and journals. Honours: Whitbread Award, 1978; Wolfson Literary Prize,

1985. Memberships: Blackheath Society, president; London Library, chairman, 1985-91, president, 1996-; Royal Society of Literature, fellow. Address: 32 Dartmouth Row, London SE10, England.

GRIMM Barbara Lockett, (Cherry Wilder), b. 3 Sept 1930, Auckland, New Zealand. Writer. m. Horst Grimm, 1963, 2 daughters. Education: BA, Canterbury University College, Christchurch, 1952. Publications: The Luck of Brin's Five, 1977; The Nearest Fire, 1979; The Tapestry Warriors, 1982; Second Nature, 1982; A Princess of the Chameln, 1983; Yorath the Wolf, 1984; The Summer's King, 1985; Cruel Designs, 1988; Dealings in Light and Darkness, 1994. Contributions to: Anthologies, magazines and newspapers. Honours: Australia Council Literary Grants, 1973, 1975; Dimar, Australian Science Fiction Award, 1978. Memberships: British Science Fiction Association; Science Fiction Club of Germany; Science Fiction Writers of America; Women Writers of Australia. Address: Kurt Schumacher Strasse 36, D-6070 Langen/Hessen, Germany.

GRINSELL Leslie Valentine, b. 14 Feb 1907, Hornsey, North London, England. Museum Curator (retired). Education: Highgate School, 1921-23. Appointments: Clerk, Barclays Bank, 1925-49; Staff, Victoria County History of Wiltshire, 1949-52; Curator in Archaeology, Bristol City Museum, 1952-72. Publications: Ancient Burial Mounds of England, 1936, 3rd edition, 1975; Egyptian Pyramids, 1947; Archaeology of Wessex, 1958; Archaeology of Exmoor, 1970; Barrow, Pyramid and Tomb, 1975. Contributions to: Proceedings of various societies. Honours: MA, Bristol University, 1971; Officer of the Order of the British Empire, 1972. Memberships: County Archaeological Societies in Southern England; Society of Antiquaries, London; Prehistoric Society, treasurer, 1947-70. Address: 32 Queens Court, Clifton, Bristol BS8 1ND, England.

GRISEZ Germain, b. 30 Sept 1929, University Heights, Ohio, USA. Professor of Christian Ethics; Writer. m. Jeannette Selby, 9 June 1951, 4 sons. Education: BA, John Carroll University, University Heights, Ohio, 1951; MA and PhL, Dominican College of St Thomas Aquinas, River Forest, Illinois, 1951; PhD, University of Chicago, 1959. Appointments: Assistant Professor to Professor, Georgetown University, 1957-72; Lecturer in Medieval Philosophy, University of Virginia at Charlottesville, 1961-62; Special Assistant to Patrick Cardinal O'Boyle, Archbishop of Washington, DC, 1968-69; Consultant, Archdiocese of Washington, DC, 1969-72; Professor of Philosophy, Campion College, University of Regina, Saskatchewan, Canada, 1972-79; Archbishop Harry J Flynn Professor of Christian Ethics, Mount Saint Mary's College, Emmitsburg, Maryland, 1979-. Publications: Contraception and the Natural Law, 1964; Abortion: The Myths, the Realities, and the Arguments, 1970; Beyond the New Morality: The Responsibilities of Freedom (with Russell Shaw), 1974, 3rd edition, 1988; Beyond the New Theism: A Philosophy of Religion, 1975; Free Choice: A Self-Referential Argument (with Joseph M Boyle Jr and Olaf Tollefsen), 1976; Life and Death with Liberty and Justice: A Contribution to the Euthanasia Debate (with Joseph M Boyle Jr), 1979; The Way of the Lord Jesus, Vol I, Christian Moral Principles (with others), 1983, Vol II, Living a Christian Life (with others), 1993; Nuclear Deterrence, Morality and Realism (with John Finnis and Joseph M Boyle Jr), 1987; Fulfilment in Christ: A Summary of Christian Moral Principles (with Russell Shaw), 1991. Contributions to: Many scholarly journals. Honours: Pro ecclesia et pontifice Medal, 1972; Special Award for Scholarly Work, 1981, Cardinal Wright Award for Service to the Church, 1983, Fellowship of Catholic Scholars; Various other fellowships and grants. Memberships: American Catholic Philosophical Association, president, 1983-84; Catholic Theological Society of America; Fellowship of Catholic Scholars, founding member. Address: Mount Saint Mary's College, Emmitsburg, MD 21727, USA.

GRISHAM John, b. 8 Feb 1955, Jonesboro, Arkansas, USA. Writer. m. Renee Jones, 1 son, 1 daughter. Education: BS, Mississippi State University; JD, University of Mississippi. Appointments: Admitted to the Bar, Mississippi, 1981; Attorney, Southaven, Mississippi, 1981-90; Member, Mississippi House of Representatives, 1984-90. Publications: A Time to Kill, 1989; The Firm, 1991; The Pelican Brief, 1992; The Client, 1993; The Chamber, 1994; Rainmaker, 1995; The Runaway Jury, 1996; The Partner, 1997. Address: c/o Jay Garon-Brooke Associates Inc, 101 West 55th Street, Suite 5K, New York, NY 10019, USA.

GROSS John (Jacob), b. 12 Mar 1935, London, England. Writer; Critic; Editor. m. Miriam May, 1965, div 1988, 1 son, 1

daughter. Education: MA, Wadham College, Oxford, 1955; Graduate Studies, Princeton University, 1958-59. Appointments: Editor, Victor Gollancz Ltd, 1956-58, Times Literary Supplement, 1974-81; Assistant Lecturer, Queen Mary College, University of London, 1959-62; Fellow, King's College, Cambridge, 1962-65; Literary Editor, New Statesman, 1973; Director, Times Newspapers Holdings, 1982; Staff, New York Times, 1983-89; Theatre Critic, Sunday Telegraph, 1989-. Publications: Dickens and the Twentieth Century (editor with Gabriel Pearson), 1962; John P Marquand, 1963; The Rise and Fall of the Man of Letters: Aspects of English Literary Life since 1800, 1969; James Joyce, 1970; Rudyard Kipling: The Man, His Work, and His World (editor), 1972; The Oxford Book of Aphorisms (editor), 1983; The Oxford Book of Essays (editor), 1991; Shylock, 1992; The Modern Movement (editor), 1992; The Oxford Book of Comic Verse (editor), 1994. Contributions to: Periodicals and newspapers. Honours: Harkness Fellow, Princeton University, 1958-59; Duff Cooper Memorial Prize, 1969; Honorary DHL, Adelphi University, 1995. Address: 74 Princess Court, Queensway, London W2 4RE, England.

GROSS Miriam (Marianna) (Lady Owen), b. 12 May 1939, England. m. (1) John Gross, 1965, div 1988, (2) Sir Geoffrey Owen, 1993. Education: Dartington Hall School; MA, St Anne's College, Oxford. Appointments: Deputy Literary Editor, The Observer, 1969-81; Arts Editor, The Daily Telegraph, 1986-91; Editor, Book Choice, Channel 4 Television, 1986-91; Literary Editor, Sunday Telegraph, 1991-. Publications: The World of George Orwell (editor), 1971; The World of Raymond Chandler (editor), 1976. Address: 24 St Peterborough Place, London W2 4LB, England.

GROSS Natan, b. 16 Nov 1919, Poland. Film Director; Poet; Translator; Journalist. m. Shulamit Lifszyc, 1 son, 1 daughter. Education: Diploma Film Directing, Polish Film Institute, 1946. Appointments: Editor, Youth Monthly Stowo Mtodych (Youth's Word), 1946-49; Film Critic, Daily Al Hamishmar, 1962-82. Publications: Selection of New Hebrew Poetry, 1947; Song of Israel, 1948; What is Left of it All, 1971; Holocaust in Hebrew Poetry (anthology with J Kest and R Klinow), 1974); Songs of Holocaust and Rebellion, 1975; Crumbs of Youth, 1976; Children in the Ghetto (with Sarah Nishmith), 1978; Palukst (art monography), 1982; Homage to Janusz Korczak (poetry anthology, co-editor), 1986; Who Are You Mr Grymek?, 1989; History of Jewish Film in Poland, 1989; History of Hebrew Film (with Jacob Gross), 1991; Meir Bossak - Historian - Writer - Poet (editor), 1993; Poets and Holocaust, 1994; Gebirtig's Fife (editor), 1997. Contributions to: Journals and magazines. Honours: Ben-Dor Prize, Davar Newspaper, 1960; Jugendpreis, Film Festival Berlin, 1964; Israeli and International Film Festival Awards; Leon Lustig Prize, 1986; IUPA Award, 1988; Israel, Film Academy Award, 1991. Memberships: Israeli Film Union, Secretary 1951-71; Film and TV Directors Guild of Israel; Israel Journalists Association; Israel Federation of Writers Union. Address: 14 Herzog Street, Givatayim 53586, Israel.

GROSSKURTH Phyllis, b. 16 Mar 1924, Toronto, Ontario, Canada. Professor; Author. m. (1) Robert A Grosskurth, 2 sons, 1 daughter, (2) Mavor Moore, 1968, div 1980, (3) Robert McMullan, 1986. Education: BA, University of Toronto, 1946; MA, University of Ottawa, 1960; PhD, University of London, 1962. Appointments: Lecturer, Carleton University, 1964-65; Professor of English, 1965-87, Faculty, Humanities and Psychoanalysis Programme, 1987-, University of Toronto. Publications: John Addington Symonds: A Biography, 1964; Notes on Browning's Works, 1967; Leslie Stephen, 1968; Gabrielle Roy, 1969; Havelock Ellis: A Biography, 1980; The Memoirs of John Addington Symonds (editor), 1984; Melanie Klein: Her World and Her Work, 1986; Margaret Mead: A Life of Controversy, 1988; The Secret Ring: Freud's Inner Circle and the Politics of Psychoanalysis, 1991. Contributions to: Periodicals. Honours: Governor-General's Award for Non-Fiction, 1965; University of British Columbia Award for Biography, 1965. Memebership: PEN. Address: 147 Spruce Street, Toronto, Ontario M5A 2EJ, Canada.

GROSSMAN David, b. 25 Jan 1954, Jerusalem, Israel. Writer. m. Michal Grossman, 2 sons, 1 daughter. Education: BA, Hebrew University, Jerusalem, 1979. Publications: Hiyukh ha-gedi, 1983, English translation as The Smile of the Lamb, 1991; 'Ayen 'erekh--ahavah, 1986, English translation as See Under: Love, 1989; Ha-Zeman ha-tsahov, 1987, English translation as The Yellow Wind, 1988; Gan Riki: Mahazeh bi-shete ma'arakhot (play), 1988, English translation as Rikki's Kindergarten, 1988; Sefer hakikduk hapnimi, 1991, English translation as Book of Internal Grammar, 1993; Hanochachim hanifkadim, 1992, English translation as Sleeping on a

Wire, 1992. Other: Short stories; children's books. Contributions to: Periodicals. Honours: Children's Literature Prize, Ministry of Education, 1983; Prime Minister's Hebrew Literature Prize, 1984; Israeli Publisher's Association Prize for Best Novel, 1985; Vallombrosa Prize, Italy, 1989; Nelly Sachs Prize, Germany, 1992; Premio Mondelo, Italy. Address: c/o Deborah Harris, The Harris/Elon Agency, PO Box 4143, Jerusalem 91041, Israel.

GROVE Fred(erick Herridge), b. 4 July 1913, Hominy, Oklahoma, USA. Writer; Former Journalist. Education: BA, University of Oklahoma, 1937 Appointments: Reporter, Sports Editor, Daily Citizen, Cushing, Oklahoma, 1937-40; Reporter, Morningin News, Shawnee, Oklahoma, 1940-42; Sports Editor, Star, Harlingen, Texas, 1942; Reporter, 1943-44, Managing Editor, 1944-45, Morning News and Star, Shawneee; On copy desk, Times and Daily Oklahoma, Oklahoma City, 1946-47; Senior Assistant, University of Oklahoma Public Relations Officer, 1947-53; Part-time Instructor of Journalism, University of Oklahoma, 1964-68; Director of Public Information, Oklahoma Educational Television Authority, Norman, 1969-74. Publications: Flame of the Osage, 1958; Sun Dance, 1958; No Bugles, No Glory, 1959; Comanche Captives, 1961; The Land Seekers, 1963; Buffalo Spring, 1967; The Buffalo Runners, 1968; War Journey, 1971; The Child Stealers, 1973; Warrior Road, 1974; Drums Without Warriors, 1976; The Great Horse Race, 1977; Bush Track, 1978; The Running Hoses, 1980; Phantom Warrior, 1981; Match Race, 1982; A Far Trumpet, 1985; Search for the Breed, 1986; Deception Trail, 1988; Bitter Trumpet, 1989; Trail of Rogues, 1993. Address: PO Box 1248, Silver City, NM 88062, USA.

GRUFFYDD Peter, b. 12 Apr 1935, Liverpool, England. Writer; Poet; Translator (German, fluent Welsh); Actor. m. (1), 1 son, 1 daughter, (2) Susan Soar, 28 Dec 1974, 2 sons. Education: BA, Honours, University of Wales, Bangor, 1960. Publications: Triad, 1963; Welsh Voices, 1967; Poems, 1969; The Lilting House, 1970; Poems, 1972; The Shivering Seed, 1972; On Censorship, 1985; Environmental Teletex, 1989; Damned Braces, 1993. Contributions to: Anthologies and periodicals. Honours: Eric Gregory Trust, 1963; 2nd Prize, Young Poets Competition, Welsh Arts Council, 1969; 1st Prize, 1984, 1994, 3rd Prizes, 1986, 1991, 1993, Aberystwyth Open Poetry Competitions; Duncan Lawrie Prize, Arvon-Observer International Poetry Competition, 1993. Memberships: Equity; PEN International, founder-member, Welsh Branch, 1993; Welsh Union of Writers; Yr Academi Gymraeg. Address: 21 Beech Road, Norton, Stourbridge, West Midlands DY8 2AS, England.

GRUMBACH Doris (Isaac), b. 12 July 1918, New York, New York, USA. Author; Critic; Former Professor of English. m. Leonard Grumbach, 15 Oct 1941, div 1972, 4 daughters. Education:AB, Washington Square College, 1939; MA, Cornell University, 1940. Appointments: Associate Editor, Architectural Forum, 1942-43; Teacher of English, Albany Academy for Girls, New York, 1952-55; Instructor, 1955-58, Assistant Professor, 1958-60, Associate Professor, 1960-69, Professor of English, 1969-73, College of Saint Rose, Albany; Visiting University Fellow, Empire State College, 1972-73; Literary Editor, New Republic, 1973-75; Adjunct Professor of English, University of Maryland, 1974-75; Professor of American Literature, American University, Washington, DC, 1975-85; Columnist and reviewer for various publications, radio, and television. Publications: The Spoil of the Flowers, 1962; The Short Throat, the Tender Mouth, 1964; The Company She Kept (biography of Mary McCarthy), 1967; Chamber Music, 1979; The Missing Person, 1981; The Ladies, 1984; The Magician's Girl, 1987; Coming Into the End Zone, 1992; Extra Innings: A Memoir, 1993; Fifty Days of Solitude, 1994; The Book of Knowledge: A Novel, 1995. Contributions to: Books and periodicals. Memberships: PEN; Phi Beta Kappa. Address: c/o Maxine Groffsky, 2 Fifth Avenue, New York, NY 10011, USA.

GRÜNBAUM Adolf, b. 15 May 1923, Cologne, Germany (US citizen, 1944). Professor of Philosophy; Research Professor of Psychiatry; Writer. m. Thelma Braverman, 26 June 1949, 1 daughter. Education: BA, Wesleyan University, 1943; MS, Physics, 1948, PhD, Philosophy, 1951, Yale University. Appointments:Faculty, 1950-55, Professor of Philosophy, 1955-56, Selfridge Professor of Philosophy, 1956-60, Lehigh University; Visiting Research Professor, Minnesota Center for the Philosophy of Science, 1956, 1959; Andrew Mellon Professor of Philosophy, 1960-, Director, 1960-78, later Chairman, Center for the Philosophy of Science, Research Professor of Psychiatry, 1979-, University of Pittsburgh; Werner Heisenberg Lecturer, Bavarian Academy of Sciences, 1985; Gifford Lecturer,

University of Edinburgh, 1985; Visiting Mellon Professor, California Institute of Technology, 1990. Publications: Philosophical Problems of Space and Time, 1963, 2nd edition, 1973; Modern Science and Zeno's Paradoxes, 2nd edition, 1968; Geometry and Chronometry in Philosophical Perspective, 1968; The Foundations of Psychoanalysis: A Philosophical Critique, 1984; Psicoanalisi: Obiezioni e Risposte, 1988; Validation in the Clinical Theory of Psychoanalysis, 1993; La Psychanalyse à l'Épreuve, 1993. Contributions to: Books and scholarly journals. Honours: J Walker Tomb Prize, Princeton University, 1958; Honour Citation, Wesleyan University, 1959; Festschriften published in his honour, 1983, 1993; Senior US Scientist Prize, Alexander von Humboldt Foundation, 1985; Fregene Prize for Science, Italian Parliament, 1989; Master Scholar and Professor Award, University of Pittsburgh, 1989; Wilbur Lucius Cross Medal, Yale University, 1990; Honorary Doctorate, University of Konstanz, Germany, 1995. Memberships: American Academy of Arts and Sciences; American Philosophical Association; Academie Internationale de Philosophie des Sciences; International Academy of Humanism; Philosophy of Science Association, president, 1965-70; American Association for the Advancement of Science. Address: 7141 Roycrest Place, Pittsburgh, PA 15208, USA.

GRYNBERG Henryk, b. 4 July 1936, Warsaw, Poland. m. Krystyna Walczak, 30 July 1967, 1 son, 1 daughter. Education: Master's in Journalism, Warsaw University, 1959; MA Slavic Languages and Literatures, University of California, Los Angeles, 1971. Appointment: Literary workshop, Warsaw University, 1993-94. Publications: Zydowska wojna, 1965, 2nd edition, 1989; Zwyciestwo, 1969, 2nd edition, 1990; Kadisz, 1987, 1992; Prawda Nieartystyczna, 1984, second edition, 1994; Rysuje w Pamieci, 1995; Zycie Ideologiczne; Zycie Osobiste; Dzieci Syjonu, Pomnik nad Potomakiem. Contributions to: Commentary; Midstream; Tygodnik Powszechny; Odra; Kresy; Tel-Aviv Review. Honours: Various awards. Memberships: ZLP; ZPPO; Pen American Center; SPP. Address: 6251 N Kensington Street, McLean, VA 22101-4902, USA.

GUARE John, b. 5 Feb 1938, New York, New York, USA. Dramatist. m. Adele Chatfield-Taylor, 20 May 1981. Education: AB, Georgetown University, 1961; MFA, Yale University, 1963. Appointments: Co-Founder, Eugene O'Neill Theater Center, Waterford, Connecticut, 1965; Resident Playwright, New York Shakespeare Festival, 1976; Seminar-in-Writing Fellow, 1977-78, Adjunct Professor, 1978-81, Yale University; Co-Editor, Lincoln Center New Theatre Review, 1977-; Visiting Artist, Harvard University, 1990-91; Fellow, Juilliard School, 1993-94. Publications: Plays: Theatre Girl, 1959; The Toadstool Boy, 1960; The Golden Cherub, 1962; Did You Write My Name in the Snow?, 1962; To Wally Pantoni, We Leave a Credenza, 1964; The Loveliest Afternoon of the Year, 1966; Something I'll Tell You Tuesday, 1966; Muzeeka, 1967; Cop-Out, 1968; A Play by Brecht, 1969; Home Fires, 1969; Kissing Sweet, 1969; The House of Blue Leaves, 1971, as a musical, 1986; Two Gentlemen of Verona, 1971; A Day for Surprises, 1971; Un Pape a New York, 1972; Marco Polo Sings a Solo, 1973; Optimism, or the Adventures of Candide, 1973; Rich and Famous, 1974; Landscape of the Body, 1977; Take a Dream, 1978; Bosoms and Neglect, 1979; In Fireworks Lie Secret Codes, 1981; Lydie Breeze, 1982; Gardenia, 1982; Stay a While, 1984; Women and Water, 1984; Gluttony, 1985; The Talking Dog, 1985; Moon Over Miami, 1989, revised version as Moon Under Miami, 1995; Six Degrees of Separation, 1990; Four Baboons Adoring the Sun, 1992; Chuck Close, 1995; The War Against the Kitchen Sink (volume of plays), 1996. Honours: Obie Awards, 1968, 1971, 1990; New York Drama Critics Circle Awards, 1969, 1971, 1972, 1990; Drama Desk Awards, 1972; Tony Awards, 1972, 1986; Joseph Jefferson Award, 1977; Award of Merit, American Academy of Arts and Letters, 1981; Los Angeles Film Critics Award, 1981; National Society of Film Critics Circle Award, 1981; New York Film Critics Award, 1981; Venice Film Festival Grand Prize, 1981; Olivier Best Play Award, 1993; New York State Governor's Award, 1996. Memberships: American Academy of Arts and Letters; Dramatists Guild. Address: c/o R Andrew Boose, 1 Dag Hammarskjöld Plaza, New York, NY 10017, USA.

GUARNIERI Patrizia, b. 16 June 1954, Florence, Italy. Historian; Lecturer in Italian and History of Science; Narrative Translator. m. Franco Cardini, 2 Aug 1991, 1 son, 1 daughter. Education: MA, Philosophy, University of Florence, 1977; PhD, University of Urbino, 1979; Fulbright Visiting Scholar, Harvard University, Massachusetts, 1981. Appointments: Lecturer in Italian Culture and Language, University of Florence, 1978-81, Stanford University Programme in Italy, 1982-93; Professor, History of Science, University of Trieste,

1988-91. Publications: Introduzione a James, 1985; Individualita' Difformi, 1986; L'Ammazzabambini, 1988, English edition as A Case of Child Murder, 1992; Between Soma and Psyche, 1988; Theatre and Laboratory, 1988; The Psyche in Trance, 1990; Carta Penna e Psiche, 1990; La Storia della Psichiatria, 1991; Per Una Storia delle Scienze del Bambino, 1996. Contributions to: Kos; Physis; Nuncius; Belfagor. Honours: CNR-NATO Fellow, 1983; Jean Monnet Fellow, 1989. Membership: Scientific Council, European Association of the History of Psychiatry. Address: Via Faentina 231, 50133 Florence, Italy.

GUDMUNDSDOTTIR Kristjana Emilia, b. 23 Apr 1939, Stykkishólmur, Iceland. m. 10 June 1957, 3 sons, 3 daughters. Education: Journeymans Certificate Bookbinding, 1985. Publications: Ljóðnálar, 1982; Ljóðspeglar, 1989; Ljóðblik, 1993; Ljóðgeislar, 1995; Ljóð Dagsins, 1995; Gluggi, 1996; Lifid Sjálft, 1996; The Iclandic art Festival Book of Poems, 1996. Contributions to: Poems and articles in newspapers. Membership: Fithöfundasamband Islands. Address: Borgarholtsbraut 27, 200 Kópavogur, Iceland.

GUEST Henry Bayly (Harry), b. 6 Oct 1932, Penarth, Glamorgan, Wales. Schoolmaster; Poet; Writer. m. Lynn Doremus Dunbar, 28 Dec 1963, 1 son, 1 daughter. Education: BA, Trinity Hall, Cambridge, 1951-54; DES, Sorbonne, 1954-55. Publications: Arrangements, 1968; The Cutting-Room, 1970; Post-War Japanese Poetry (editor and translator), 1972; A House Against the Night, 1976; Days, 1978; The Distance, The Shadows, 1981; Lost and Found, 1983; The Emperor of Outer Space (radio play), broadcast 1976, published 1983; Lost Pictures, 1991; Coming to Terms, 1994; Traveller's Literary Companion to Japan, 1994. Contributions to: Agenda; Ambit; Atlantic Review; Outposts; Pacific Quarterly; Poetry Australia; Poetry Review; Times Educational Supplement. Honour: Honorary Research Fellow, Exeter University, 1994-. Memberships: General Council, Poetry Society, 1972-75. Address: 1 Alexandra Terrace, Exeter, Devon EX4 6SY, England.

GUNN James Edwin, b. 12 July 1923, Kansas City, Kansas, USA. Professor Emeritus; Writer. m. Jane Frances Anderson, 6 Feb 1947, 2 sons. Education: BS, Journalism, 1947, MA, English, 1951, University of Kansas. Appointments: Assistant Instructor, 1950-51, 1955, Instructor, 1958-70, Lecturer, 1970-74, Professor, 1974-93, Professor Emeritus, 1993-, University of Kansas. Publications: This Fortress World, 1955; Star Bridge (with Jack Williamson), 1955; Station in Space, 1958; The Joy Makers, 1961; The Immortals, 1962; Future Imperfect, 1964; The Witching Hour, 1970; The Burning, 1972; Breaking Point, 1972; The Listeners, 1972; The Magicians, 1976; Kampus, 1977; The Dreamers, 1981. Editor: Alternate Worlds: The Illustrated History of Science Fiction, 1975; Isaac Asimov: The Foundations of Science Fiction, 1982; The Road to Science Fiction, 4 volumes, 1977, 1979, 1979, 1982; Crisis, 1986; The New Encyclopedia of Science Fiction, 1988; The Best of Astounding: Classic Short Novels from the Golden Age of Science Fiction, 1992; Inside Science Fiction, 1992; The Unpublished Gunn, Part 1, 1992, Part 2, 1996; The Joy Machine, 1996. Contributions to: Many magazines and journals. Honours: Byron Caldwell Smith Prize, 1971; Pilgrim Award, Science Fiction Research Association, 1976; Hugo Awards, 1976, 1983; Edward Grier Award, 1989; Eaton Award for Lifetime Achievement, 1992. Memberships: Authors Guild; Science Fiction Research Association, president, 1980-82; Science Fiction Writers of America, president, 1971-72. Address: 2215 Orchard lane, Lawrence, KS 66049, USA.

GUNN Robin Jones, b. 18 Apr 1955, Wisconsin, USA. m. Ross Gunn III, 13 Aug 1977, 1 son, 1 daughter. Education: Biola University, 1973-75. Appointment: Host, Kids Korner program, KNIS, Carson City, Nevada, 1993-94. Publications: 37 books; 14 picture books. Honours: First Place, Article Writing Contest, Biola Writer's Conference, 1988; Sherwood E Wirt Award, 1989; Mount Hermon Christian Writer's Conference Poetry Award, 1993; EPA Article of the Year, 1994; Bookstore Journal Best Seller's List, 9 titles on list, 1995, 8 titles, 1996; Mount Hermon Pacesetter Award, 1996. Address: 8002 NE Highway 99, Suite 52, Vancouver, WA 98665, USA.

GUNN Thom(son William), b. 29 Aug 1929, Gravesend, England. Poet. Education: Trinity College, Cambridge. Appointments: Taught English, 1958-66; Lecturer, English, 1977-, Senior Lecturer, 1988-, University of California, Berkeley, USA. Publications: Fighting Terms, 1954; The Sense of Movement, 1957; My Sad Captains, 1961; Positives (with Ander Gunn), 1966; Touch, 1967; Moly, 1971; Jack Straw's Castle, 1976; Selected Poems, 1979; The Passages of Joy,

1982; The Occasions of Poetry (prose), 1982, expanded edition, 1985; The Man with Night Sweats, 1992; Collected Poems, 1993; Shelf Life (prose), 1993. Honours: Levinson Prize, 1955; Somerset Maugham Prize, 1959; National Institute of Arts and Letters Grant, 1964; Rockefeller Foundation, 1966; Guggenheim Fellowship, 1972; Lila Wallace/ Reader's Digest Fund Award, 1991; Forward Poetry Prize, 1992; MacArthur Fellowship, 1993; Lenore Marshall Prize, 1993. Address: 1216 Cole Street, San Francisco, CA 94117, USA.

GUNNARSSON Baldur, b. 22 Dec 1953, Reykjavik, Iceland. University Lecturer. 1 son, 1 daughter. Education: BA, University of Iceland, 1981; Cand mag, 1984; MA, State Univeristy of New York at Stony Brook, 1987. Publications: The Labyrinth (novel), 1990; Seaside-Cafe (novel), 1992; Full Fathom Five (novel), 1993; Perpetuum Mobile (novel), 1994. Membership: Writers' Union of Iceland. Literary Agent: Fjölvi, Njörvasundi 15a, 104 Reykjavik, Iceland. Address: Neshagi 9, 107 Reykjavik, Iceland.

GUNNARSSON Kristjan J, b. 29 Nov 1919, Marteinstunga, Rangarvallasysla, south coast of Iceland. Administration in Education. m. Thordis Kristjansdóttir, 9 Sept 1944, 2 sons, 3 daughters. Education: Graduated, Icelandic Teachers College, 1944. Appointments: Superintendent of schools in Reyjavik; In Rangárvallasysla on South Coast of Iceland. Appointments: Editor of Lesbok Barnanna, 1957-71; Skolaljod, 1964. Publications: Refska, 1986; Leirkarlsvisur, 1989; Graglettnar Stundir, 1993; Okkar A milli sagt, 1995. Membership: Writers' Union of Iceland.

GUNSTON Bill, (William Tudor Gunston), b. 1 Mar 1927, London, England. Author. m. Margaret Anne, 10 Oct 1964, 2 daughters. Education: University College, Durham, 1945-46; RAF Pilot, 1946-48; City University, London, 1948-51. Appointments: Editorial Staff, 1951-55, Technical Editor, Flight, 1955-64; Technology Editor, Science Journal, 1964-70; Freelance author, 1970-; Director, So Few Ltd. Publications: Sole author of over 330 publications including: Aircraft of The Soviet Union, 1983; Jane's Aerospace Dictionary, 1980, 3rd edition, 1988; Encyclopaedia of World Aero Engines, 1986, 3rd edition, 1995; Encyclopaedia of Aircraft Armament, 1987; Giants of The Sky, 1991; Faster Than Sound, 1992; World Encyclopaedia of Aircraft Manufacturers, 1993; Jet Bombers, 1993; Piston Areo Engines, 1994; Encyclopaedia of Russian Aircraft, 1995; Jet and Turbine Aero Engines, 1995. Contributions to: 188 periodicals; 18 partworks; 75 video scripts. Honours: Fellow, Royal Aeronautical Society; Officer of the Order of the British Empire. Address: High Beech, Kingsley Green, Haslemere, Surrey GU27 3LL, England.

GUNTER Pete A Y, b. 20 Oct 1936, Hammond, Indiana, USA. College Professor. m. Elizabeth Ellington Gunter, 2 Apr 1969, 1 daughter. Education: BA, University of Texas, Austin, 1958; BA, Cambridge University, 1960; PhD, Yale University, 1963. Appointments: Auburn University, Alabama, 1962-65; University of Tenessee at Knoxville, 1965-69; University of North Texas, 1969-. Publications: Bergsen and the Evolution of Physics, 1969; Henri Bergson: A Bibliography, 1974, 2nd edition, 1986; The Big Thicket: A Challenge for Conservation, 1972; River in Dry Grass, 1984; The Big Thicket: An Ecological Reconsideration, 1997; Creativity in George Herbert Mead. Contributions to: Journal of the History of Ideas; Process Studies; Revue Internationale de Philosophie; Texas Observer. Honours: Marshall Scholar, 1958-60; Dallas area Phi Beta Kappa, 1984. Memberships: Texas Institute of Letters, 1974; Southwestern Philosophical Society, president, 1978-79; Foundation for Philosophy of Creativity, executive director, 1983-91. Address: Department of Philosophy and Religion Studies, University of North Texas, Denton, TX 76203, USA.

GUNTRUM Suzanne Simmons, (Suzanne Simmons), b. 29 Aug 1946, Storm Lake, Iowa, USA. Writer. m. Robert Ray Guntrum, 9 Sept 1967, 1 son. Education: BA, English Literature, Penn State University, 1967. Publications: Moment in Time, 1982; Of Passion Born, 1982; A Wild Sweet Magic, 1983; All the Night Long, 1983; Dream Within a Dream, 1984; Only This Night, 1984; Moment of Truth, 1986; Nothing Ventured, 1986; Christmas in April, 1986; The Genuine Article, 1987; Made in Heaven, 1988. Contributions to: Magazines. Memberships: Authors Guild; Romance Writers of America. Address: 5245 Willowview Road, Racine, WI 53402, USA.

GURGANUS Allan, b. 11 June 1947, Rocky Mount, North Carolina, USA. Writer; Artist. Education: Monterey Language School, 1966; Radioman and Cryptography School, 1966; University of

Pennsylvania, 1966-67; Pennsylvania Academy of Fine Arts, 1966-67; Harvard University, 1969-70; BA, Sarah Lawrence College, 1972; MFA, University of Iowa Writers' Workshop, 1974; Stanford University, 1974-76. Appointments: Professor of Fiction Writing, 1972-74, Writer's Workshop, 1989-90, University of Iowa, Stanford University, 1974-76, Duke University, 1976-78, Sarah Lawrence College, 1978-86; Artist. Publications: Oldest Living Confederate Widow Tells All, 1989; White People: Stories and Novellas, 1991; Practical Heart, 1993. Contributions to: Periodicals. Honours: National Endowment for the Arts Grants, 1976-77, 1987-88; Ingram Merrill Grant, 1986; Sue Kaufman Prize for First Fiction, American Academy and Institute of Arts and Letters, 1990; Books Across the Sea Ambassador Book Award, English-Speaking Union of the United States, 1990; Los Angeles Times Book Prize, 1991. Address: c/o Amanda Urban, International Creative Management, 40 West 57th Street, New York, NY 10019, USA.

GURI Haim, b. 9 Oct 1923, Tel Aviv, Palestine. Poet. Education: Hebrew University, Jerusalem, and Sorbonne, Paris. Publications: Flowers of Fire, 1949; Till Dawn Rises, 1950; Seal Poems, 1954; Rose of the Winds, 1960; Movement to Contact, 1968; Visions of Gebazi, 1974; Pages from the Cycle of the Eagle, 1974; To the Eagle Line, 1975; Selected Poems, 1975; Terrible, 1979; And Still He Wants Her, 1987; Notebooks of Elul, 1988; Selected Poems 1945-1987, 1988; Stories: The Chocolate Deal, 1968; The Crazy Book, 1971; Who Knows Joseph G.?, 1980; The Interrogation: Reuel's Story, 1981; Also: Facing the Glass Cell, 1963; Jerusalem Years, 1968; The Family of the Palmach: A Collection of Songs and Deeds, 1976. Honours: Israel Prize, 1987. Address: c/o Hakibuts Publishing House, PO Box 16040, 34 Hayetzirah Street, Tel Aviv 61160, Israel.

GURNEY A(lbert) R(amsdell), b. 1 Nov 1930, Buffalo, New York, USA. Professor of Literature; Dramatist; Writer. m. Mary Goodyear, 1957, 2 sons, 2 daughters. Education: BA, Williams College, 1952; MFA, Yale University School of Drama, 1958. Appointments: Faculty, 1960-, Professor of Literature, 1970-, Massachusetts Institute of Technology. Publications: Plays: Children, 1974; The Dining Room, 1982; The Perfect Party, 1986; Another Antigone, 1986; Sweet Sue, 1986; The Cocktail Hour, 1988; Love Letters, 1989; The Old Boy, 1991; The Fourth Wall, 1992; Later Life, 1993; A Cheever Evening, 1994; Sylvia, 1995; Overtime, 1995. Novels: The Gospel According to Joe, 1974; The Snow Ball, 1985. Screenplay: The House of Mirth, 1972. Television Play: O Youth and Beauty (from a story by John Cheever), 1979. Honours: Drama Desk Award, 1971; Rockefeller Foundation Grant, 1977; National Endowment for the Arts Award, 1982; Theatre Award, American Academy of Arts and Sciences, 1990; Honorary doctorates. Address: 40 Wellers Bridge Road, Roxbury, CT 06783, USA.

GURR Andrew (John), b. 23 Dec 1936, Leicester, England. University Teacher. m. Elizabeth Gordon, 1 July 1961, 3 sons. Education: BA, 1957, MA 1958, University of Auckland, New Zealand; PhD, University of Cambridge, 1963. Appointments: Lecturer, Leeds University, 1962; Professor, University of Nairobi, 1969; Professor, University of Reading, 1976-. Publications: The Shakespeare Stage 1574-1642, 1970, 3rd edition, 1992; Writers In Exile, 1982; Katherine Mansfield, 1982; Playgoing in Shakespeare's London, 1987, 2nd edition, 1996; Studying Shakespeare, 1988; Rebuilding Shakespeare's Globe, 1989; The Shakespearian Playing Companies, 1996. Editor: Plays of Shakespeare and Beaumont and Fletcher. Contributions to: Scholarly journals and periodicals. Memberships: International Shakespeare Association; Association of Commonwealth Literature and Language Studies; Society for Theatre Research; Malone Society. Address: English Department, University of Reading, PO Box 218, Reading, Berkshire RG6 2AA, England.

GURR David, b. 5 Feb 1936, London, England. Writer. m. Judith Deverell, 30 Aug 1958, 2 sons, 1 daughter. Education: Canadian Naval College, 1954-56; BSc, University of Victoria, British Columbia, 1965. Appointments: Career Officer, Royal Canadian Navy, 1954-70; House Designer and Builder, 1972-81. Publications: Troika, 1979; A Woman Called Scylla, 1981; An American Spy Story, 1984; The Action of the Tiger, 1984; On the Endangered List, 1985; The Ring Master, 1987; The Voice of the Crane, 1989; Arcadia West: The Novel, 1994. Memberships: Crime Writers of Canada; Writers' Guild of America; Writers' Union of Canada. Address: c/o Henry Morrison, Henry Morrison Inc, Box 235, Bedford Hills, NY 10507, USA.

GUSTAFSON David A(rthur), b. 2 Sept 1946, Superior, Wisconsin, USA. Executive; Writer. m. Aleta Gustafson, 1969, div 1973. Education: University of Wisconsin at Madison, 1964-67; BS, University of San Francisco, 1984. Appointments: Computer Programmer and Systems Analyst, Anaheim, 1970-78; Computer Scientist, Tustin, California, 1978-81; Founder and Chief Executive Officer, Personal Computer Corporation of America, 1981-82; President, Management Associates, Hidden Meadows, California, 1982-. Publications: Points: The Most Practical Program Ever to Improve Your Self-Image, 1992; Choices, 1993; Race, 1993. Address: 28405 Faircrest Way, Escondido, CA 92026, USA.

GUSTAFSSON Lars, b. 17 May 1936, Västerås, Sweden. Novelist; Poet. m. Dena Chasnoff, 1982. Education: Graduated, 1961, PhD, 1978, University of Uppsala. Appointments: Adjunct Professor, University of Texas at Austin, 1983-. Publications: The Last Days and Death of the Poet Brumberg, 1959; The Brothers: An Allegorical Story, 1960; The Travel Company, 1962; The Essential Story of Mr Arenander, 1966; Preparations for Flight and Other Tales, 1967; Cracks in the Wall, 5 volumes, 1971-78; Summer Stories: Six Swedish Novellas, 1973; The Tennis Players, 1977; The Small World, 1977; Stories of Happy People, 1981; Funeral Music for Freemasons; Bernard Foy's Third Castling, 1986; Collected Stories, 1987; The Strange Animal from the North and Other Science-Fiction Stories, 1989. Verse: The Balloonists, 1962; A Morning in Sweden, 1963; A Journey to the Centre of the Earth and Other Poems, 1966; The Poems of a Private Man, 1967; Declaration of Love to a Sephardic Lady, 1970; Selected Poems, 1972; Warm Rooms and Cold, 1972; The Native Country Under the Earth, 1973; Sonnets, 1977; Artesian Wells Cartesian Dreams, 1980; Out of the Picture, in the Picture: Collected Poems 1950-80; The Stillness of the World Before Bach, 1982, 1988; The Creative Impulse, 1989; Preparations for the Winter Season: Elegies and Other Poems, 1990; Plays and broadcast plays; Essays and political texts. Address: 2312 Tower Drive, Austin, TX 78703, USA.

GUT-RUSSENBERGER Margrit, (Greta Rosenberg, Gret Stamm), b. 29 Apr 1938, CH, Switzerland. Secondary Teacher. m. Robert Gut, 5 Aug 1966, 3 sons, 3 daughters. Education: Secondary Teacher, University of Zürich, Switzerland. Publications: Jakob, 1976; Ich Glaube, 1978; Ein Wort für CHB, 1993; Bilder, text German/English), 1996. Memberships: Innerschweizer Schriftstellerverein; Schweizerischer Schriftstellerverband. Address: Mattweid 12, 6204 Sempach, Switzerland.

GUTHRIE Alan. See: TUBB E(dwin) C(harles).

GUTIERREZ José Ismael, b. 7 Aug 1964, Tenerife, Islas Canarias, Spain. Teacher, Spanish Language and Literature. Education: Doctor, Hispanic Philology, 1996. Publication: De La Cronica al Relato. Contributions to: Articles about Spanish-American literature in several professional journals. Memberships: Instituto Literario y Cultural Hispánico; CELCIRP, Paris; Instituto Internacional de Literatura Iberoamericana. Address: Calle Los Bajos, No 36, 38380 La Victoria, Tenerife, Islas Canarias, Spain.

GUTTERIDGE Don(ald George), b. 30 Sept 1937, Sarnia, Ontario, Canada. Professor of English; Poet. m. Anne Barnett, 1961, 1 son, 1 daughter. Appointment: Professor of English Methods, University of Western Ontario, 1977; Professor Emeritus. Publications: The Brooding Sky, 1960; New Poems, 1964; Intimations of Winter, 1967; Riel: A Poem for Voices, 1968; The Village Within: Poems Towards a Biography, 1970; Death at Quebec and Other Poems, 1971; Perspectives, 1971; Saying Grace: An Elegy, 1972; Coppermine: The Quest for North, 1973; Borderlands, 1975; Tecumseh, 1976; A True History of Lambton County, 1977; God's Geography, 1982; The Exiled Heart: Selected Narratives 1968-82, 1986; Love in the Wintertime, 1990; Flute Music in the Cello's Belly, 1996. Novels: Bus-Ride, 1974; All in Good Time, 1980; St Vitus Dance, 1987; Shaman's Ground, 1988; How the World Began, 1991; Summer's Idyll, 1993. Editor: Rites of Passage, 1979; Winter's Descent (novel), 1996. Honour: President's Medal, University of Western Ontario, 1971. Address: 114 Victoria Street, London, Ontario N6A 2B5, Canada.

GUTTMAN Allen, b. 13 Oct 1932, Chicago, Illinois, USA. Professor of English and American Studies; Writer. m. (1) Martha Britt Ellis, 1955, div 1972, 1 son, 1 daughter, (2) Doris Bargen, 1974. Education: BA, University of Florida, 1953; MA, Columbia University, 1956; PhD, University of Minnesota, 1961. Appointments: Instructor,

1959-62, Assistant Professor, 1962-66, Associate Professor, 1966-71, Professor of English and American Studies, 1971-, Amherst College. Publications: The Wound in the Heart: America and the Spanish Civil War (edito), 1963; Communism, the Constitution, and the Courts (editor with Benjamin Ziegler), 1964; The Conservative Tradition in America, 1967; Jewish Writer in America: Assimilation and the Crisis of Identity, 1971; Korea: Cold War and Limited War (editor), 1972; From Ritual to Record: The Nature of Modern Sport, 1978; The Games Must Go On: Avery Brundage and the Olympic Movement, 1984; Sports Spectators, 1986; A Whole New Ball Game, 1988; Women's Sports, 1991; The Olympics: A History of the Modern Games, 1992. Honours: Carnegie Fellowship; Guggenheim Fellowship. Memberships: American Studies Association; British Association for Sport History; International Committee for Sport Sociology; North American Association for Sport Sociology. Address: c/o Department of English, Amherst College, Amherst, MA 01002, USA.

GUY Rosa (Cuthbert), b. 9 Jan 1928, Trinidad, West Indies. Professor; Writer-in Residence. Appointment: Writer-in-Residence, Michigan Technical University. Publications: My Love My Love, 1996; The Friends, 1973; Edith Jackson, 1978; Ruby, 1976; The Disappearance, 1979; A Measure of Time, 1983; New Guys Around the Block, 1983; Pee Wee and Big Dog, 1984; I Heard a Bird Sing, 1986; Music of Summer, 1992. Play: Once on This Island (adaptation of My Love My Love), 1990. Contributions to: New York Times Sunday Magazine; Red Book; Cosmopolitan. Honours: The Other Award, England; Best of the Best, New York Times. Memberships: Harlem Writers Guild, president; PEN. Literary Agent: Ellen Levine. Address: 20 West 72nd Street, New York, NY 10023, USA.

GYARFAS Endre, b. 6 May 1936, Szeged, Hungary. Poet; Novelist; Playwright. m. Edit Kincses, 7 Dec 1963, 1 son. Education: Hungarian and English Literature, Elte University of Budapest, 1961. Appointments: Editor, Publisher Europa, 1960-63; Hungarian Television, 1964-66. Publications: Partkozelben (poems), 1964; Pazarlo Skotok (travel book), 1970; Apaczai (novel), 1978; Varazslasok (poems), 1984; Hosszu Utnak Pora (novel), 1988; Zsuzsanna Kertje (novel), 1989; Zoldag-Parittya (poems), 1990; Cowboyok, Aranyasok, Csavargok, Folk Poetry of North America, 1992; Szölöhegyi varazslat, 1995. Honours: Gold Medal for Children's Literature, 1976; Fulbright Grant, 1988. Memberships: PEN Club of Hungary; Union of Hungarian Writers. Address: I Attila ut 133, Budapest 1012, Hungary.

GYLLENSTEN Lars Johan Wictor, b. 12 Nov 1921, Stockholm, Sweden. Former Professor of Histology; Author. Education: MD. Publications: Barnabok, 1952; Senilia, 1956; Sokratod, 1960; Desparados (short stories), 1962; Juvenilia, 1965; Palatset i parken, 1970; Ur min offentliga sektor (essays), 1971; Grottan i oknen, 1973; I skuggan av Don Juan, 1975; Baklangesminnen, 1978; Skuggans aterkomst, 1985; Sju vise mastare om kanlek (short stories), 1986; Just sa elle kahske det (short stories), 1989; Det himmelska gästabudet, 1991; Anteckningar fån en vindskupa, 1993. Memberships: Royal Swedish Academy of Sciences; Royal Swedish Academy of Letters, History and Antiquities. Address: Karlavagen 121, 115 26 Stockholm, Sweden.

GYORE Balazs, b. 8 May 1951, Hungary. Writer. m. Adrienn Scheer, 25 Sept 1980, 1 daughter. Education: Eotvos Lorand University in Budapest, 1971-76. Publications: The Hand of Humble Abbot Paphnutius (poems), 1982; I Can Safely Sleep on the 91 Bus (novel), 1989; One Has to Search For His Own Death (short novels), 1993; To Call Somebody is Illusion (short stories), 1994; If He Doesn't Live, Please Burn It Without Reading, 1996; It Is In Reality Too, novel, 1997. Contributions to: Ujhold; Liget; Elet es Irodalom. Memberships: Association of Hungarian Writers; Hungarian PEN Club. Address: Bartok B 52, 1111 Budapest, Hungary.

H

HAAKANA Anna-Liisa, b. 20 Jan 1937, Rovaniemi, Finland. Author. m. Veikko Olavi Haakana, 24 Feb 1963, 1 son, 1 daughter. Education: Literature studies, University of Tapere. Publications: Ykä All Alone, 1980; Top Girl, 1981; A Flower, Nevertheless, 1983; The Black Sheep of the Family, 1986; The Love of an Ugly Girl, 1989; Bird, Little Bird, 1991; Sticks in the Heart, 1993. Honours: National Award for Literature, 1981; Anni Swan Medal, 1982; H C Andersen's Certificate of Honour, 1982; Church's Award for Literature, 1982; Arvid Lydecken Award, 1984. Memberships: Association of Finnish Writers for Children and Youth; Finnish Society of Authors. Address: 99600 Sodankylä, Finland.

HAAVIKKO Paavo (Juhani), b. 25 Jan 1931, Helsinki, Finland. Poet; Playwright. Education: University of Helsinki, 1951. Appointment: Director, Arthouse Publishing Group, Helsinki, 1983-. Publications: Verse: Roads to Far Away, 1951; On Windy Nights, 1953; Land of Birth, 1955; Leaves, Leaves, 1958; Winter Palace, 1959; Poems 1951-61; The Trees, All their Green, 1966; Selected Poems, 1968; Poems from a Voyage Across the Sound, 1973; Poems 1949-74; Longer Poems, 1975; May, Eternal, 1975; Kullervo's Story, 1975; Wine, Writing, 1976; Bridges: Selected Poems, 1984; Five Sequences from Fast-Flowing Life, 1987; Of Love and Death, 1989; Winter Poems, 1990; Poems, Poems, 1992. Plays: Munchhausen, 1958; The Dolls, 1960; Agricola and the Fox, 1968; The Brotterus Family, 1969; The Feather, 1973; The Horseman (libretto for opera by Aulis Sallinen), 1975; The Strongest Men Don't Remain Unscathed, 1976; Kaisa and Otto, 1977. Radio and Television plays. Stories: Private Affairs, 1960; Another Heaven and Earth, 1961; Years, 1962; A Man Named Barr, 1976; Fleur's Autumn Term, 1993. Honours: Knight First Class of the White Rose of Finland, 1978. Address: c/o Arthouse Group, Bulevardi 19C, 00120 Helsinki, Finland.

HABGOOD John Stapylton, b. 23 June 1927, England. Former Archbishop of York; Writer. m. Rosalie Mary Ann Boston, 7 June 1961, 2 sons, 2 daughters. Education: MA, PhD, King's College, Cambridge. Cuddesdon College, Oxford. Publications: Religion and Science, 1964; A Working Faith: Essays and Addresses on science, Medicine and Ethics, 1980; Church and Nation in a Secular Age, 1983; Confessions of a Conservative Liberal, 1988; Making Sense, 1993; Faith and Uncertainty, 1997. Contributions to: Various publications. Honours: Hon.DD, Durham, 1975, Cambridge, 1984, Hon.DD, Aberdeen, 1988, Huron 1990, Hull, 1991; Hon Fellow, King's College, Cambridge, 1985; Life Peer, 1995; Hon DD, Oxford, Manchester, York, 1996. Address: 18 The Mount, Malton, N Yorkshire, YO17 0ND, England.

HACKER Marilyn, b. 27 Nov 1942, New York, New York, USA. Poet; Writer; Critic; Editor; Teacher. 1 daughter. Education: BA in Romance Languages, New York University, 1964. Appointments: Editor, Quark: A Quarterly of Speculative Fiction, 1969-71, The Kenyon Review, 1990-94; Jenny McKean Moore Chair in Writing, George Washington University, 1976-77; Member, Editorial Collective, 1977-80, Editor-in-Chief, 1979, The Little Magazine; Teacher, School of General Studies, Columbia University, 1979-81; Visiting Artist, Fine Arts Work Center, Provincetown, Massachusetts, 1981; Visiting Professor, University of Idaho, 1982; Editor-in-Chief, Thirteenth Moon: A Feminist Literary Magazine, 1982-86; Writer-in-Residence, State University of New York at Albany, 1988; Columbia University, 1988; George Elliston Poet-in-Residence, University of Cincinnati, 1988; Distinguished Writer-in-Residence, American University, Washington, DC, 1989; Visiting Professor of Creative Writing, State University of New York at Binghamton, 1990, University of Utah, 1995, Barnard College, 1995, Princeton University, 1997; Fannie Hurst Poet-in-Residence, Brandeis University, 1996. Publications: Presentation Piece, 1974; Separations, 1976; Taking Notice, 1980; Assumptions, 1985; Love, Death and the Changing of the Seasons, 1986; The Hang-Glider's Daughter: New and Selected Poems, 1990; Going Back to the River, 1990; Selected Poems: 1965-1990, 1994; Winter Numbers, 1994; Edge (translator of poems by Claire Malroux), 1996. Contributions to: Numerous anthologies and other publications. Honours: National Endowment for the Arts Grants, 1973-74, 1985-86, 1995; National Book Award in Poetry, 1975; Guggenheim Fellowship, 1980-81; Ingram Merrill Foundation Grant, 1984-85; Robert F Winner Awards, 1987, 1989, John Masefield Memorial Award, 1994, Poetry Society of America; Lambda Literary Awards, 1991, 1995; Lenore Marshall Award, Academy of American Poets, 1995; Poets' Prize, 1995. Address: 230 West 105th Street, New York, NY 10025, USA.

HACKETT George, b. Boston, Massachusetts, USA. Senior Editor, Newsweek. Education: BA, Literature, Yale University, 1975; MA, Journalism, University of California, Berkeley, 1980. Appointments: Editorial Assistant researching television industry, 1980, Senior Editorial Assistant, 1981, Reporting Intern in San Francisco Bureau, 1982, Assistant Editor, 1983, Associate Editor, 1984, General Editor, 1985, Writer on sports, television and newsmakers, Back of the Book section, Editor for Periscope, Perspectives and My Turn sections, 1991, Senior Editor, 1992-, Technology Editor, 1995-, Newsweek. Address: c/o Newsweek, 251 West 57th Street, New York, NY 10019-1894, USA.

HACKETT General Sir John Winthrop, b. 5 Nov 1910, Perth, Australia. Soldier; Academic; Author. m. Margaret Frena, 21 Mar 1942, 1 daughter, dec, 2 adopted stepdaughters. Education: MA, BLitt, New College, Oxford, 1929-33. Appointments: Regular Army, Commissioned 8th King's Royal Hussars, 1931; Service before, during, and after World War II, wounded, 1941, 1942; Commandant, Royal Military College of Science, 1958-61; Deputy Chief, Imperial General Staff, 1963-64, and Ministry of Defence, 1964-66; Commander-in-Chief, British Army of the Rhine, and Commander, Northern Army Group in NATO, 1966-68; Principal, 1968-75, Visiting Professor in Classics, 1977-, King's College, London. Publications: I Was a Stranger, 1977; The Third World War (co-author), 1978; The Untold Story (co-author), 1982; The Profession of Arms, 1983; Warfare in the Ancient World (editor), 1989. Contributions to: Books and periodicals. Honours: Member of the Order of the British Empire, 1938; Commander of the Order of the British Empire, 1953; Knighted, 1962; Honorary Liveryman, Worshipful Company of Dyers, 1975; Freeman of the City of London, 1976; Honorary doctorates. Memberships: English Association, president, 1973; Royal Society of Literature, fellow; UK Classical Association, president, 1971. Address: Coberley Mill, Cheltenham, Glos GL53 9NH, England.

HADAS Rachel, b. 8 Nov 1948, New York, New York, USA. Professor of English; Poet; Writer. m. (1) Stavros Kondilis, 7 Nov 1970, div 1978, (2) George Edwards, 22 July 1978, 1 son. Education: BA Classics, Radcliffe College, 1969; MA, Poetry, Johns Hopkins University, 1977; PhD, Comparative Literature, Princeton University, 1982. Appointments: Assistant Professor, 1982-87, Associate Professor, 1987-92, Professor of English, 1992-, Rutgers University; Adjunct Professor, Columbia University, 1992-93; Visiting Professor, Princeton University, 1995, 1996. Publications: Starting From Troy, 1975; Slow Transparency, 1983; A Son from Sleep, 1987; Pass It On, 1989; Living in Time, 1990; Unending Dialogue, 1991; Mirrors of Astonishment, 1992; Other Worlds Than This, 1994; The Empty Bed, 1995; The Double Legacy, 1995. Contributions to: Periodicals. Honours: Ingram Merrill Foundation Fellowship, 1976-77; Guggenheim Fellowship, 1988-89; American Academy and Institute of Arts and Letters Award, 1990. Memberships: American Academy of Arts and Sciences, Fellow; Modern Greek Studies Association; Modern Language Association; PEN; Poetry Society of America. Address: 838 West End Avenue, No 3A, New York, NY 10025, USA.

HAFNER Katie. Technology Correspondent, Newsweek. Appointments: Staff Editor, Business Week; Writer, New York Times, New Republic, and Wired; Contributing Editor, 1994-, San Francisco Bay Area, 1996-, Newsweek. Publications: Cyberpunk: Outlaws and Hackers on the Computer Frontier (co-author), 1991; The House at the Bridge: A Story of Modern Germany, 1995; Where Wizards Stay Up Late: The Origins of the Internet (co-author), 1996. Address: 251 West 57th Street, New York, NY 10019-1894, USA.

HAGELIN Aiban L, b. 24 Dec 1934. MD. m. Nora Stigol, 1 son, 1 daughter. Education: MD, 1961; Psychoanalyst; Member, 1971; Full Member, 1974; Training Analyst, 1975; Training Professor, 1977; Child Analyst, 1978. Publications: Infantile Psichosis, 1980; Narcissism, 1985; Autism, 1995. Contributions to: 20 papers. Address: Ayacucho 2030 70, 1112 Buenos Aires, Argentina.

HAGGER Alfred James, b. 16 Nov 1922, Melbourne, Australia. Economist. m. Elsie Rona Clark, 13 Aug 1950, 1 son, 1 daughter. Education: BCom (Melb), 1942; PhD (Lond), 1952. Publications: Books include: Inflation, in Surveys of Australian Economics, 1978; The Objectives of Macro-Economic Policy, London, 1970; Price Stability, Growth and Balance, Cheshire, Melbourne, 1968; Economics: An

Australian Introduction, Cheshire, Melbourne, 1964; The Theory of Inflation, Melbourne, 1964; Articles include: The Role of Excess Demand in the Australian Price Equation, 1978; The Demand for Money and Aggregation Over Time, in Economic Analysis and Policy, Vol 9 No.1, 1979; Demand for Labour Functions: The Wrong Track?, Oxford University Institute of Statistics, Vol 49, 1982. Membership: Academy of the Social Sciences in Australia, elected in 1980. Address: Centre for Regional Economic Analysis, GPO Box 252-90, Hobart, Tasmania 7005, Australia.

HAGGER Nicholas Osborne, b. 22 May 1939, London, England. British Poet; Verse Dramatist; Short Story Writer; Lecturer; Author. m. Madeline Ann Johnson, 22 Feb 1974, 2 sons, 1 daughter. Education: MA English Literature, Worcester College, Oxford, 1958-61. Appointments: Lecturer in English, University of Baghdad, 1961-62; Professor of English Literature, Tokyo University of Education and Keio University, Tokyo, 1963-67; Lecturer in English, University of Libya, Tripoli, 1968-70; Freelance Features for Times, 1970-72. Publications: The Fire and the Stones: A Grand Unified Theory of World History and Religion, 1991; Selected Poems: A Metaphysical's Way of Fire, 1991; The Universe and the Light: A New View of the Universe and Reality, 1993; A White Radiance: The Collected Poems 1958-93, 1994; A Mystic Way: A Spiritual Autobiography, 1994; Awakening to the Light: Diaries, Vol 1, 1958-67, 1994; A Spade Fresh with Mud: Collected Stories, Vol 1, 1995; The Warlords: From D-Day to Berlin, A Verse Drama, 1995; A Smell of Leaves and Summer: Collected Stories, Vol 2, 1995; Overlord, The Triumph of Light 1944-1945: An Epic Poem, Books 1 & 2, 1995, Books 3-6, 1996, Books 7-9, 10-12, 1997. Address: c/o Orchard Cottage, Coopersale Hall, Epping, Essex, CM16 7PE, England.

HAGON Priscilla. See: ALLAN Mabel Esther.

HAIBLUM Isidore, b. 23 May 1935, New York, New York, USA. Writer. Education: BA, City College, New York City, 1958. Publications: The Tsaddik of the Seven Wonders, 1971; The Return, 1973; Transfer to Yesterday, 1973, revised edition, 1981; The Wilk Are Among Us, 1975, revised edition, 1979; Interworld, 1977; Interworld, 1977; Outerworld, 1979; Nightmare Express, 1979; Faster Than a Speeding Bullet: An Informal History of Radio's Golden Age (with Stuart Silver), 1980; The Mutants Are Coming, 1984; The Identity Plunderers, 1984; The Hand of Gantz, 1985; Murder in Yiddish, 1988; Bad Neighbors, 1990; Out of Sync, 1990; Specterworld, 1991; Crystalword, 1992. Contributions to: Periodicals. Address: 160 West 77th Street, New York, NY 10024, USA.

HAIDA. See: NAGARAJA RAO C K.

HAIDAR Qurratulain, b. 1927, Aligarh, India. Novelist. Education: MA, Lucknow University, 1947. Appointments: Visiting Professor, New Delhi University, Aligarh Muslim University, 1979. Publications: Before the Stars, 1947; My Temples Too, 1949; Safina's Woeful Heart, 1952; Houses of Glass, 1952; The Exiles: A Novelette, 1955; River of Fire, 1959; Autumn's Voice, 1967; An Instrument, 1976; The Task of Life is Long, 2 volumes, 1977-79; Last Night's Travellers, 1979; Four Novellettes, 1981; The Light's Speed, 1982; Circling the Colours of the Garden, 1987; Candi Begum, 1990; The Fireflies' World, 1990. Also: Ghalib and His Poetry, 1970; Picture Gallery, 1983. Honours: Jnanpith Award, 1989. Address: c/o Sterling Publishers, L-10 Green Park Extension, New Delhi 110016, India.

HAIGH Christopher, b. 28 Aug 1944, Birkenhead, England. Lecturer. 2 daughters. Education: BA, Cambridge University, 1966; PhD, Victoria University of Manchester, 1969. Appointments: Lecturer in History, Victoria University of Manchester, 1969-79; Lecturer in Modern History, Christ Church, Oxford, 1979-. Publications: The Last Days of the Lancashire Monasteries, 1969; Reformation and Resistance in Tudor Lancashire, 1975; The Cambridge Historical Encyclopaedia of Great Britain and Ireland, 1984; The Reign of Elizabeth I, 1985; The English Reformation, 1987; Elizabeth I: A Profile in Power, 1988; English Reformations: Religion, Politics and Society Under the Tudors, 1993; The Church of England and Its People, 1559-1642, forthcoming. Membership: Fellow, Royal Historical Society. Address: c/o Christ Church, Oxford, OX1 1DP, England.

HAIGH Jack, b. 21 Feb 1910, West Hartlepool, England. Journalist. m. Josephine Agnes Mary McLoughlin, 7 July 1949. Appointments: Editor, Jerusalem Services Magazine, 1941-42; Staff, The Racing Calendar, 1956-68; Sport Sub Editor, Daily Mail, 1972-84;

Proprietor, Greenfriar Press. Publications: Theory of Genius, 1972; Constellation of Genius, 1982; Phillimore: The Postcard Art of R P Phillimore, 1985; Psychology of Genius, 1991. Membership: Honorary Secretary, Freelance Specialist Panel, Institute of Journalists, 1951-53, 1964-72. Address: 28 Manville Road, London, SW17 8JN, England.

HAILEY Arthur, b. 5 Apr 1920, Luton, England (British and Canadian citizen). Author; Screenwriter. m. (1) Joan Fishwick, 1944, div 1950, 3 sons, (2) Sheila Dunlop, 1951, 1 son, 2 daughters. Education: British elementary schools. Appointments: Pilot, Flight Lieutenant, Royal Air Force, 1939-47; Flight Lieutenant, Royal Canadian Air Force Reserve, 1951; Industry and sales positions; Writer, 1956-. Publications: Runway-Zero Eight (with John Castle), 1958; The Final Diagnosis, 1959; Close-up (collected plays), 1960; In High Places, 1962; Hotel, 1965; Airport, 1968; Wheels, 1971; The Moneychangers, 1975; Overload, 1979; Strong Medicine, 1984; The Evening News, 1990; Detective, 1997. Novels published in 39 languages, approximately 160 million copies in print worldwide. Films: Zero Hour, 1956; Time Lock, 1957; The Young Doctors, 1961; Hotel, 1966; Airport, 1970; The Moneychangers, 1976; Wheels, 1978; Strong Medicine, 1986. Honours: Canadian Council of Artists and Authors Award, 1956; Best Canadian TV Playwright Awards, 1957, 1959; Doubleday Prize Novel Award, 1962. Memberships: Alliance of Canadian Cinema, Television and Radio Artists,Honorary Life Member; Authors League of America; Writers Guild of America, Life Member. Address: Lyford Cay, PO Box N7776, Nassau, Bahamas.

HAILEY Elizabeth Forsythe, b. 31 Aug 1938, Dallas, Texas, USA. Writer; Dramatist. m. Oliver Daffan Hailey, 25 June 1960, dec 1993, 2 daughters. Education: Diploma, Sorbonne, University of Paris, 1959; BA, Hollins College, Virginia, 1960. Publications: Fiction: A Woman of Independent Means, 1978; Life Sentences, 1982; Joanna's Husband and David's Wife, 1986; Home Free, 1991. Plays: A Woman of Independent Means, 1984; Joanna's Husband and David's Wife, 1989. Contributions to: Books and periodicals. Honours: Siver Medal for Best First Novel, Commonwealth Club of California, 1978; PEN; Writers Guild of America West. Address: 11747 Canton Place, Studio City, CA 91604, USA.

HAILSHAM OF SAINT MARYLEBONE, Baron of Herstmonceux, Quintin McGarel Hogg, b. 9 Oct 1907, London, England. Lawyer; Politician. m. (1) Mary Evelyn Martin, 18 Apr 1944, dec 1978, 2 sons, 3 daughters, (2) Deirdre Shannon, 1986. Education: 1st Class Honour Moderatous, 1928, 1st Class Literae Humanicores, 1930, Christ Church, Oxford. Appointments: Fellow, All Souls College, Oxford, 1931-38, 1961-; Barrister, 1932, Bencher, 1956, Treasurer, 1975, Lincoln's Inn; Member of Parliament, Conservative Party, Oxford City, 1938-50, Saint Marylebone, 1963-70; Military service, World War II, 1939-45, wounded, 1941; First Lord of the Admiralty, 1956-57; Minister of Education, 1957; Lord President of the Council, 1957-59, 1960-64; Deputy Leader, 1957-60, Leader, 1960-63, House of Lords; Lord Privy Seal, 1959-60; Rector, Glasgow University, 1959-62; Minister for Science and Technology, 1959-60; Lord High Chancellor of Great Britain, 1970-74, 1979-87; Chancellor, University of Buckingham, 1983-92. Publications: The Law of Arbitration, 1935; One Year's Work, 1944; The Law and Employers' Liabilty, 1944; The Times We Live In, 1944; Making Peace, 1945; The Left Was Never Right, 1945; The Purpose of Parliament, 1946; The Case for Conservatism, 1947; The Law of Monopolies, Restrictive Practices and Resale Price Maintenance, 1956; The Conservative Case, 1959; Interdependence, 1961; Science and Politics, 1963; The Devil's Own Song, 1968; Halsbury's Laws of England (editor), 4th edition, 1972; The Door Wherein I Went, 1975; Elective Dictatorship, 1976; The Dilemma of Democracy, 1978; Hamlyn Revisited: The British Legal System, 1983; A Sparrow's Flight (autobiography), 1990; On the Constitution, 1992; Values: Collapse and Cure, 1994. Honours: Companion of Honour, 1974; Knight of the Garter, 1988; Honorary doctorates. Memberships: Classical Association, president, 1960-61; Royal Society, fellow. Address: House of Lords, London SW1A OPW, England.

HAINES John (Meade), b. 29 June 1924, Norfolk, Virginia, USA. Poet; Writer; Teacher. m. (1) Jo Ella Hussey, 10 Oct 1960, (2) Jane McWhorter, 23 Nov 1970, div 1974, (3) Leslie Senntee, Oct 1978, div 4, children. Education: National Art School, Washington, DC, 1946-47; American University, 1948-49; Hans Hoffman School of Fine Art, New York City, 1950-52; University of Washington, 1974. Appointments: Poet-in-Residence, University of Alaska, 1972-73; Visiting Porfessor in English, University of Washington, 1974; Visting Lecturer in English, University of Montana, 1974; Writer-in-Residence, Sheldon Jackson

College, 1982-83; Ucross Foundation, 1987; Montalvo Center for the Arts, 1988, Djerassi Foundation, 1988; Visting Lecturer, University of California at Santa Cruz, 1986; Visting Writer, The Loft Mentor Series, 1987; Visiting Professor, Ohio University, 1989-90; Visiting Writer, George Washington University, Washington, DC, 1991-92; Elliston Fellow in Poetry, University of Cincinnati, 1992. Publications: Poetry: Winter News, 1966, revised edition, 1983; Suite for the Pied Piper, 1968; The Legend of Paper Plates, 1970; The Mirror, 1970; The Stone Harp, 1971; Twenty Poems, 1971, 3rd edition, 1982; Leaves and Ashes, 1975; In Five Years, 1976; Cicada, 1977; In a Dusty Light, 1977; The Sun on Your Shoulder, 1977; News From the Glacier: Selected Poems, 1960-80, 1982; New Poems: 1980-1988, 1990; Rain Country, 1990; The Owl in the Mask of a Dreamer, 1993. Non-Fiction: Minus Thirty-One and the Wind Blowing: Nine Reflections About Living on the Land (with others), 1980; Living Off the Country: Essays on Poetry and Place, 1981; Other Days, 1982; Of Traps and Snares, 1982; Stories We Listened To, 1986; You and I and the World, 1988; The Stars, the Snow, the Fire, 1989; Fables and Distances: New and Selected Essays, 1996. Contributions to: Gettysburg Review; Graywolf Annual; Harper's; Hudson Review; Michigan Quarterly Review; Nation; New Criterion; New England Review; Northwest Review; Ohio Review; Triquarterly; Manoa. Honours: Guggenheim Fellowships, 1965-66, 1984-85; National Endowment for the Arts Grant, 1967-68; Amy Lowell Scholarship, 1976-77; Alaska State Council on the Arts Grant, 1979, and Fellowship, 1987; Governor's Award for lifetime contributions to the arts in Alaska, 1982; Honorary LD, University of Alaska, 1983; Ingram Merrill Foundation Grant, 1987; Western States Federation Award, 1990; Lenore Marshall Nation Award, 1991; Chair of Excellence in the Arts, Austin Peay State University, Clarksville, Tennessee, 1993; Literary Award, American Academy of Arts and Letters, 1995. Memberships: Academy of American Poets; Alaska Conservation Society; Natural Resources Defense Council; PEN American Center; Poetry Society of America; Sierra Club; Wilderness Society. Address: PO Box 103431, Anchorage, AL 99510, USA.

HAINES Pamela Mary, b. 4 Nov 1929, Harrogate, England. Writer. m. Anthony Haines, 24 June 1955, 2 sons, 3 daughters. Education: Honours degree, English Literature, Newnham College, Cambridge University, 1949-52. Publications: Tea at Gunters, 1974; A Kind of War, 1976; Men on White Horses, 1978; The Kissing Gate, 1981; The Diamond Waterfall, 1984; The Golden Lion, 1986; Daughter of the Northern Fields, 1987. Honours: Spectator New Writing Prize, 1971; Yorkshire Arts Young Writers Award, 1975. Memberships: Society of Authors; PEN; Royal Commonwealth Institute; Academy Club. Address: 57 Middle Lane, London, N8 8PE, England.

HAINING Peter (Alexander), (Peter Alex, Jim Black, Richard De'ath, William Pattrick, Richard Peters, Richard Peyton, Sean Richards), b. 2 Apr 1940, Enfield, Middlesex, England. Writer. Publications: The Ghost Ship, 1985; Tune in for Fear, 1985; Vampire, 1985; Stories of the Walking Dead, 1986; Supernatural Sleuths, 1986; Tales of Dungeons and Dragons, 1986; Poltergeist, 1987; Werewolf, 1987; Irish Tales of Terror, 1988; The Mummy, 1988; The Scarecrow: Fact and Fable, 1988; Bob Hope: Thanks for the Memory, 1989; The Day War Broke Out, 1989; Hook Line and Laughter, 1989; The Legend of Garbo, 1990; The Legend That is Buddy Holly, 1990; Spitfire Summer, 1990; The English Highwayman, 1991; Sinister Gambits, 1991; Great Irish Stories of the Supernatural, 1992; The Supernatural Coast, 1992; The Television Detectives Omnibus, 1992; The Armchair Detectives, 1993; Great Irish Detective Stories, 1993; The MG Log, 1993; Masters of the Macabre, 1993; Tombstone Humour, 1993; The Complete Maigret, 1994; London After Midnight, 1995; Murder at the Races, 1995; Agatha Christie's Poirot, 1996. Membership: PEN International. Address: Peyton House, Boxford, Suffolk, England.

HAKIM Seymour (Sy), b. 23 Jan 1933, New York, New York, USA. Poet; Writer; Artist; Educator. m. Odetta Roverso, 18 Aug 1970. Education: AB, Eastern New Mexico University, 1954; MA, New York University, 1960; Postgraduate work, various universities. Appointments: Consultant Editor, Poet Gallery Press, New York, 1970; Editor, Overseas Teacher, 1977. Publications: The Sacred Family, 1970; Manhattan Goodbye, poems, 1970; Under Moon, 1971; Museum of the Mind, 1971; Wine Theorem, 1972; Substituting Memories, 1976; Iris Elegy, 1979; Balancing Act, 1981; Birth of a Poet, 1985; Eleanor, Goodbye, 1988. Contributions to: Overseas Educator; California State Poetry Quarterly; American Writing; Dan River Anthology; It's On My Wall; Older Eyes. Honours: Exhibits with accompanying writings: 1970, 1973, 1982-83, 1985; Art works in public collections in various countries including prints in collections in Taiwan, Korea and Japan.

Memberships: Association of Poets and Writers; National Photo Instructors Association; Italo-Brittanica Association, 1972-80. Address: Via Chiesanuova No 1, 36023 Longare, VI 36023, Itlay.

HAKIMZADEH. See: **ZAND Roxane.**

HALBERSTAM David, b. 10 Apr 1934, New York, New York, USA. m. (1) Elizabeth Tchizerska, 13 June 1965, div, (2) Jean Sanders, 29 June 1979, 1 daughter. Education: AB, Harvard University. Career: Journalist; Writer, 1971-. Publications: The Noblest Roman, 1961; The Making of Quaguire, 1965; The Unfinished Odyssey of Robert Kennedy, 1969; The Best & The Brightest, 1972; The Powers That Be, 1979; The Breaks of the Game, 1981; The Amateurs, 1986; The Reckoning, 1986; Summer of '49, 1989; The Next Century, 1991; The Fifties, 1993; October 1964, 1994. Contributions to: Esquire; Atlantic Monthly; McCall's; Harpers. Honours: Page One Award, Newspaper Guild of America, 1962; George Polk Award, 1964; Louis M Lyons Award, 1964; Pulitzer Prize for Vietnam Reporting, 1964; Overseas Press Club Award, 1973; National Book Award, nominee (twice). Address: c/o Random House, 201 East 50th Street, 12th Floor Reception, New York, NY 10022, USA.

HALDEMAN Joe William, b. 9 June 1943, Oklahoma City, Oklahoma, USA. Novelist. m. Mary Gay Potter, 21 Aug 1965. Education: BS, Physics and Astronomy, University of Maryland, 1967; MFA, English, University of Iowa, 1975. Appointment: Associate Professor, writing programme, Massachusetts Institute of Technology, 1983-. Publications: War Year, 1972; Cosmic Laughter (editor), 1974; The Forever Year, 1975; Mindbridge, 1976; Planet of Judgement, 1977; All My Sins Remembered, 1977; Study War No More (editor), 1977; Infinite Dreams, 1978; World Without End, 1979; Worlds, 1981; There is No Darkness (co-author), 1983; Worlds Apart, 1983; Nebula Awards 17, 1983; Dealing in Futures, 1985; Body Armour 2000, 1986; Tool of the Trade, 1987; Supertanks (co-editor), 1987; Starfighters (co-editor), 1988; The Long Habit of Living, 1989; The Hemingway Hoax, 1990; Worlds Enough and Time, 1992; 1968, 1995; None So Blind, 1996. Honours: Purple Heart, US Army, 1969; Nebula Awards, 1975, 1990, 1993; Hugo Awards, 1976, 1977, 1991, 1995; Rhysling Award, 1984, 1990; World Fantasy Award, 1993. Memberships: President, Science Fiction and Fantasy Writers of America; Author's Guild; Poets and Writers National Space Institute; Writers Guild. Literary Agent: Ralph Vicinanza. Address: 5412 North West 14th Avenue, Gainesville, FL 32605, USA.

HALEY Kenneth Harold Dobson, b. 19 Apr 1920, Southport, England. Historian. m. Iris Houghton, 22 Mar 1948, 1 son, 2 daughters. Education: MA; BLitt, Balliol College, 1938-40, 1945-47. Appointments: Professor of Modern History, 1962-82, Professor Emeritus, 1982, Sheffield University. Publications: William of Orange and The English Opposition 1672-74, 1953; The First Earl of Shaftesbury, 1968; The Dutch in the Seventeenth Century, 1972; Politics in the Reign of Charles II, 1985; An English Diplomat in the Low Countries: Sir William Temple and John de Witt, 1986; The British and The Dutch, 1988. Contributions to: Articles to various historical journals. Honour: Fellow, British Academy, 1987. Membership: Honorary Vice-President, Historical Association, 1994. Address: 15 Haugh Lane, Sheffield S11 9SA, England.

HALL Angus, b. 24 Mar 1932, Newcastle uopn Tyne, England. Author; Editor. Appointments: Editor, IPC Publishers, London, 1971-, BPC Publishers, London, 1972-. Publications: London in Smoky Region, 1962, High-Bouncing Lover, 1966; Live Like a Hero, 1967; Comeuppance of Arthur Hearne, 1967; Qualtrough, 1968; Late Boy Wonder, 1969; Devilday, 1970; To Play the Devil, 1971; Scars of Dracula, 1971; Long Way to Fall, 1971; On the Run, 1974; Signs of Things to Come: A History of Divination, 1975; Monsters and Mythic Beasts, 1976; Strange Cults, 1977; The Rigoletto Murder, 1978; Self-Destruct, 1985. Address: 96 High Street, Old Town, Hastings, Sussex, England.

HALL Claudia. See: **FLOREN Lee.**

HALL Donald (Andrew Jr), b. 20 Sept 1928, New Haven, Connecticut, USA. Poet; Writer; Professor of English (retired). m. (1) Kirby Thompson, 1952, div 1969, 1 son, 1 daughter, (2) Jane Kenyon, 1972, dec 1995. Education: BA, Harvard University, 1951; BLitt, Oxford University, 1953; Stanford University, 1953-54. Appointments: Poetry Editor, Paris Review, 1953-62; Junior Fellow, Society of Fellows, Harvard University, 1954-57; Assistant Professor, 1957-61, Associate

Professor, 1961-66, Professor of English, 1966-75, University of Michigan. Publications: Poetry: Poems, 1952; Exile, 1952; To the Loud Wind and Other Poems, 1955; Exiles and Marriages, 1955; The Dark Houses, 1958; A Roof of Tiger Lilies, 1964; The Alligator Bride: Poems New and Selected, 1969; The Yellow Room: Love Poems, 1971; A Blue Tit Tilts at the Edge of the Sea: Selected Poems 1964-1974, 1975; The Town of Hill, 1975; Kicking the Leaves, 1978; The Toy Bone, 1979; The Twelve Seasons, 1983; Brief Lives, 1983; Great Day at the Cows' House, 1984; The Happy Man, 1986; The One Day: A Poem in Three Parts, 1988; Old and New Poems, 1990; The One Day and Poems (1947-1990), 1991; The Museum of Clear Ideas, 1993. Short Stories: The Ideal Bakery, 1987. Other: String Too Short to Be Saved, 1961; Henry Moore: The Life and Work of a Great Sculptor, 1966; Marianne Moore: The Cage and the Animal, 1970; As the Eye Moves: A Sculpture by Henry Moore, 1970; The Gentlemen's Alphabet Book, 1972; Writing Well, 1973, 7th edition, revised, 1991; Playing Around: The Million-Dollar Infield Goes to Florida (with others), 1974; Dock Ellis in the Country of Baseball (with Dock Ellis), 1976; Remembering Poets: Reminiscences and Opinions--Dylan Thomas, Robert Frost, T S Eliot, Ezra Pound, 1978; Goatfoot Milktongue Twinbird: Interviews, Essays and Notes on Poetry 1970-76, 1978; To Keep Moving, 1980; To Read Literature: Fiction, Poetry, Drama, 1981, 3rd edition, revised, 1987; The Weather for Poetry: Essays, Reviews and Notes on Poetry 1977-81, 1982; Fathers Playing Catch with Sons: Essays on Sports (Mostly Baseball), 1985; Winter, 1986; Seasons at Eagle Pond, 1987; Poetry and Ambition: Essays 1982-1988, 1988; Anecdotes of Modern Art (with Pat Corrigan Wykes), 1990; Here at Eagle Pond, 1990; Their Ancient Glittering Eyes, 1992; Life Work, 1993; Death to Death of Poetry, 1994; Principal Products of Portugal, 1995. Editor: The Harvard Advocate Anthology, 1950; New Poets of England and America (with Robert Pack and Louis Simpson), 1957; Whittier, 1961; Contemporary American Poetry, 1962, revised edition, 1971; A Poetry Sampler, 1962; The Concise Encyclopedia of English and American Poets and Poetry (with Stephen Spender), 1963, revised edition, 1970; Poetry in English (with Warren Taylor), 1963, revised edition, 1970; The Faber Book of Modern Verse, 1965; A Choice of Whitman's Verse, 1968; The Modern Stylists: Writers on the Art of Writing, 1968; Man and Boy: An Anthology, 1968; American Poetry An Introductory Anthology, 1969; The Pleasures of Poetry, 1971; A Writer's Reader (with D L EMblem), 1976, 5th edition, revised, 1988; To Read Literature, 1980; To Read Poetry, 1981; The Oxford Book of American Literary Anecdotes, 1981; Claims for Poetry, 1982; The Contemporary Essay, 1984; The Oxford Book of Children's Verse in America, 1985; To Read Fiction, 1987; The Best American Poetry (with David Lehman), 1989; The Essential Andrew Marvell, 1991; The Essential E A Robinson, 1993. Honours: Edna St Vincent Millay Memorial Prize, 1956; Longview Foundation Award, 1960; Guggenheim Fellowships, 1963, 1972; Sarah Josepha Hale Award, 1983; Poet Laureate of New Hampshire, 1984-89; Lenore Marshall Award, 1987; National Book Critics Circle Award, 1989; Los Angeles Times Book Award, 1989; Robert Frost Silver Medal, Poetry Society of America, 1991; Lifetime Achievement Award, New Hampshire Writers and Publishers Project, 1992; New England Book Award for Non-Fiction, 1993; Ruth Lilly Prize for Poetry, 1994; Honorary Doctorates. Address: Eagle Pond Farm, Danbury, NH 03230, USA.

HALL Hugh Gaston, b. 7 Nov 1931, Jackson, Mississippi, USA. Reader Emeritus; Writer. m. Gillian Gladys Lund, 16 July 1955, 1 son, 2 daughters. Education: BA, Millsaps College, 1952; Diplome pour l'Enseignement, University of Toulouse, 1953; MA, Oxon, 1959; PhD, Yale University, 1959. Appointments: Faculty, Yale University, 1958-60; Lecturer, University of Glasgow, 1960-64; Assistant Professor, University of California at Berkeley, 1965; Senior Lecturer, 1966-74, Reader, 1974-89, Reader Emeritus, 1989-, University of Warwick; Professor of Romance Languages, City University of New York, 1970-72; Fellow, Humanities Research Centre, Canberra, 1984; Camargo Foundation, Cassis, 1987, 1990. Publications: Molière: Tartuffe, 1960; Quadruped Octaves, 1983; Comedy in Context, 1984; Alphabet Aviary, 1987; Richelieu's Desmarets and the Century of Louis XIV, 1990; Molière's Le Bourgeois Gentilhomme, 1990. Contributions to: Reference books and scholarly journals. Address: 18 Abbey End, Kenilworth, Warwickshire, England.

HALL James Byron, b. 21 July 1918, Midland, Ohio, USA. Writer. Professor. m. Elizabeth Cushman, 14 Feb 1946, (dec), 1 son, 4 daughters. Education: Miami University, Oxford, Ohio, 1938-39; University of Hawaii, 1938-40; BA 1947; MA, 1948, PhD, 1953, University of Iowa. Appointments: Writer-in-Residence, various universities; Faculty 1958-68, Professor, 1960-68, Director, Writing Centre, 1965-68, University of California, Irvine; Provost, 1968-75, Porter, Sesnon College, 1970-78, Emeritus, 1983-, University of California, Santa Cruz. Publications: Not By The Door, 1954; The Short Story, 1955; Racers to the Sun, 1960; Us He Devours, 1964; Realm of Fiction, 1965; Moern Culture and Arts, 1967; Mayo Sergeant, 1967; The Hunt Within, 1973; Short Hall, stories, 1981; Squall Line, 1989; Bereavements (poems), 1991; I Like it Better Now (stories), 1992; Art and Craft of the Short Story, 1995. Contributions to: Stories, poetry, various anthologies. Honours: Numerous prizes and awards, poetry and fiction; Rockefeller Foundation Grant, 1955; James B Hall Gallery named, University of California Regents, 1985; Jams B Hall Travelling Fellowships founded, University of California, Santa Cruz, 1985. Memberships: American Association of University Professors; National Writers Union. Address: 4926 SW Corbett #404, Portland, OR 97201, USA.

HALL J(ohn) C(live), b. 12 Sept 1920, London, England. Poet. Education: Oriel College, Oxford. Appointments: Editor, Literary Executor of Keith Douglas. Publications: Poetry: Selected Poems, 1943; The Summer Dance and Other Poems, 1951; The Burning Hare, 1966; A House of Voices, 1973; Selected and New Poems 1939-84, 1985; Other: Collected Poems of Edwin Muir, 1921-51 (editor), 1952; New Poems (co-editor), 1955; Edwin Muir, 1956. Address: 9 Warwick Road, Mount Sion, Tunbridge Wells, Kent TN1 1YL, England.

HALL Oakley Maxwell (Jason Manor), b. 1 July 1920, San Diego, California, USA. Author. m. Barbara Erdinger, 28 Jun 1945, 1 son, 3 daughters. Education: BA, University of California, Berkeley, 1943; MFA, University of Iowa, 1950. Appointments: Director, Programs in Writing, University of California, Irvine, 1969-89; Squaw Valley Community of Writers, 1969-. Publications: So Many Doors, 1950; Corpus of Joe Bailey, 1953; Mardios Beach, 1955; Warlock, 1958; The Downhill Racers, 1962; The Pleasure Garden, 1962; A Game for Eagles, 1970; Report from Beau Harbor, 1971; The Adelita, 1975; The Badlands, 1978; Lullaby, 1982; The Children of the Sun, 1983; The Coming of the Kid, 1985; Apaches, 1986; The Art and Craft of Novel Writing, 1989; (as O M Hall) Murder City, 1949; (as Jason Manor) Too Dead to Run, 1953; The Red Jaguar, 1954; The Pawns of Fear, 1955; The Tramplers, 1956. Honours: Nomination for Pulitzer Prize, 1953; Commonwealth Club of California Silver Medal, 1954; Western Writers of America Golden Spur Award, 1984; Cowboy Hall of Fame Wrangler Award, 1989. Address: Department of English, University of California, Irvine, CA 92717, USA.

HALL Peter (Geoffrey), b. 19 Mar 1932, London, England. Professor of Planning; Writer. m. (1) Carla Maria Wartenberg, 1962, div 1966, (2) Magdalena Mróz, 1967. Education: MA, PhD, St Catherine's College, Cambridge. Appointments: Assistant Lecturer, 1957-60, Lecturer, 1960-66, Birbeck College, University of London; Reader in Geography, London School of Economics and Political Science, 1966-68; Professor of Geography, 1968-89, Professor of Emeritus, 1989-, University of Reading; Editor, Built Environment, 1977-; Professor of City and Regional Planning, 1980-92, Professor Emeritus, 1992-, University of California at Berkeley; Professor of Planning, University College, London, 1992-. Publications: The Industries of London, 1962; London 2000, 1963, revised edition, 1969; Labour's New Frontiers, 1964; Von Thunen's Isolated State (editor), 1966; An Advanced Geography of North West Europe (co-author), 1967; Theory and Practice of Regional Planning, 1970; Containment of Urban England: Urban and Metropolitan Growth Processes or Megapolis Denied (co-author), 1973; Containment of Urban England: The Planning System: Objectives, Operations, Impacts (co-author), 1973; Planning and Urban Growth: An Anglo-American Comparison (with M Clawson), 1973; Urban and Regional Planning: An Introduction, 1974, 2nd edition, 1982; Europe 2000, 1977; Great Planning Disasters, 1980; Growth Centres in the European Urban System, 1980; Transport and Public Policy Planning (editor with D Banister), 1980; The Inner City in Context (editor), 1981; Silicon Landscapes (editor), 1985; Can Rail Save the City? (co-author), 1985; High-Tech America (co-author), 1986; Western Surprise (co-author), 1987; The Carrier Wave (co-author), 1988; Cities of Tomorrow, 1988; London 2001, 1989; The Rise of the Gunbelt, 1991; Technoples of the World, 1994. Honour: Honouary Fellow, St Catharine's College, Cambridge, 1988. Memberships: British Academy, fellow: Fabian Society, chairman, 1971-72; Tawney Society, chairman, 1983-85. Address: c/o Bartlett School, University College, London, Wates House, 22 Gordon Street, London WC1H oQB, England.

HALL Sir Peter (Reginald Frederick), b. 22 Nov 1930, Bury St Edmunds, Suffolk, England. m. (4) Nicola Frei, 1990. Education: MA (Hons), St Catherine's College, Cambridge. Appointments: Director, Aldwych Theatre, 1960-68; Director, 1961-68, Co-director, 1968-73, Royal Shakespeare Theatre, Stratford; Director, National Theatre, London, 1973-88; Artistic Director, Glyndebourne Festival, 1984-90; Artistic Director, Peter Hall Company at The Old Vic, 1996-. Publications: Shakespeare adaptation, The Wars of the Roses (with John Barton), 1970; co-translator, Ibsen's John Gabriel Borkman, 1975; Peter Hall's Diaries, The Story of a Dramatic Battle, 1983; co-author, adaptation of George Orwell's Animal Farm, as a musical, 1985; co-adaptor, Ibsen's the Wild Duck, 1990, Ibsen's The Master Builder, 1995; autobiography, Making an Exhibition of Myself, with Nicki Frei, 1993; Translator: Feydeau's An Absolute Turkey, 1994; Feydeau's L'Occupe toi d'Amelie, 1996. Honours: Commander of the British Empire, 1963; Knighted, 1977. Address: c/o The Old Vic, Waterloo Road, London SE1 8NB, England.

HALL Rodney, b. 18 Nov 1935, Solihull, England. Writer. m. Bet MacPhail, 3 daughters. Education: BA, Queensland University, Australia. Appointments: Poetry Editor, The Australian, 1967-78; Creative Arts Fellow, Australian National University, 1968-69; Chairman, The Australia Council, 1991-1994. Publications: Poetry: Penniless Till Doomsday, 1962; Selected Poems, 1975; Black Bagatelles, 1978; Novels: The Ship on The Coin, 1972; A Place Among People, 1975, 2nd edition 1984; Just Relations, 1982, 4th edition 1985; Kisses of The Enemy, 1987; Captivity Captive, 1988; The Second Bridegroom, 1991; The Grisly Wife, 1993. Contributions to: Hundreds of poems and several short stories in Australian Literary Magazines, Newspapers, Journals; Book Reviews, The Australian; Sydney Morning Herald; The Bulletin. Honours: Grace Leven Prize for Poetry, 1973; Australia Council, Senior Fellowships, 1973, 1976, 1983, 1985; Miles Franklin Awards, 1982, 1994. Memberships: The Order of Australia, 1990. Address: PO Box 7, Bermagui South New South Wales 2546, Australia.

HALL Roger Leighton, b. 17 Jan 1939, Woodford, Wells, Essex, England. Writer. m. Dianne Sturm, 20 Jan 1968, 1 son, 1 daughter. Education: BA, 1966; MA, 1968, Victoria University, Wellington, New Zealand; Diploma of Teaching. Publications: Plays: Glide Time, 1976; Middle Age Spread, 1977; State of the Play, 1978; Prisoners of Mother England, 1979; The Rose, 1981; Hot Water, 1982; Fifty-Fifty, 1982; Multiple Choice, 1984; Dream of Sussex Downs, 1986; The Hansard Show, 1986; The Share Club, 1987; After the Crash, 1988; Conjugal Rites, 1990; By Degrees, 1993; Musicals with Philip Norman and A K Grant; many plays for TV, Radio and for children. Honours: Robert Burns Fellow, Otago University, 1977, 1978; Fulbright Travel Award, 1982; QSO, 1987; Turnovsky Award, Outstanding Contribution to the Arts, 1987. Memberships: PEN; New Zealand; Scriptwriters Guild. Address: c/o Playmarket, PO Box 9767, Wellington, New Zealand.

HALL Willis, b. 6 Apr 1929, Leeds, England. Writer. m. Valerie Shute, 1973, 1 son, (3 sons by previous marriages). Publications: The Villa Maroc; They Don't Open Men's Boutiques; Song at Twilight; The Road to 1984; TV series: Stan's Last Game, 1983; The Bright Side, 1985; The Return of The Antelope, 1986; Books: (with Michael Parkinson) Football Classified, 1974; My Sporting Life, Football Final, 1975; Children's Books: The Last Vampire, 1982; The Inflatable Shop, 1984; The Return of the Antelope, 1985; Dragon Days, 1986; The Antelope Company Ashore, Spooky Rhymes, The Antelope Company at Large, 1987; Doctor Jekyll and Mr Hollins, 1988; The Vampire's Holiday, 1992; The Vampire's Christmas, 1994; The Vampire Vanishes, 1995; Vampire Park, 1996. Plays: England Our England, 1962; Squat Betty and the Sponge Room, 1963; Say Who You Are, 1965; Whoops a Daisy, 1968; Children's Day, 1969; Who's Who, 1972; Saturday, Sunday, Monday (adapation from de Filippo), 1973; Filumena (adaptation from de Filippo), 1977; Jane Eyre (adaptation from Charlotte Bronte), 1992; Mansfield Park (adaptation from Jane Austen), 1993; The Three Musketeers (adaptation from Alexandre Dumas), 1994; Musicals: (with Keith Waterhouse) The Card, 1973; (with Denis King): Treasure Island, 1985; The Wind in The Willows (adaptation from A A Milne), 1985; (with John Cooper) The Water Babies (adaptation from Charles Kingsley), 1987. Address: c/o Alexander Cann Representation, 337 Fulham Road, London SW10 9TW, England.

HALLIDAY Dorothy. See: **DUNNETT Dorothy.**

HALLMUNDSSON Hallberg, b. 29 Oct 1930, Iceland. Poet; Translator; Editor. m. May Newman, 29 July 1960. Education: BA, University of Iceland, 1954; University of Barcelona, 1955-56; New York University, 1961. Appointments: Columnist, Frjals Thjod, 1954-60; Stringer, Newsweek 1960; Assistant, Associate Senior Editor, Encyclopedia International, 1961-76; Senior Editor, Americana Annual, 1977-78; Senior Editor, Funk & Wagnalls New Encyclopedia, 1979-82; Production Copy Editor, Business Week, 1984-. Publications: Anthology of Scandinavian Literature, 1966. Poetry, Haustmal, 1968; Neikvaeda 1977; Spjaldvisur, 1985; Thraetubók, 1990; Spjaldvisur II, 1991; Skyggnur, 1993. Short Stories: Eg kalla mig Ofeig, 1970; Icelandic Folk and Fairy Tales (with May Hallmundsson), 1987. Poetry: Vandraedur, 1995. Translator various books. Contributions to: Americana Annual; Icelandic Canadian; Georgia Review; Beacons; Metamorphoses; Iceland Review; Visions International; Grand Street 1993. Honours include: 1st Prize, short story contest, Reykjavik, 1953; 1st prize, Translation of Norwegian Poetry, Minneapolis, 1966; Grant, Translation Centre, New York, 1975; Grant, government of Iceland, 1976-79; Award, Iceland Writers Fund, 1985; Grant, American Scandinavian Society, 1991; Grants, Translation Fund (Iceland), 1994, 1996. Memberships: Writers Union of Iceland; American Literary Translators Association; Reykjavik Drama Critics' Society, treasurer 1957-59. Address: 30 5th Avenue, New York, NY 10011, USA.

HALLS Geraldine. See: **JAY Geraldine Mary.**

HALLWORTH Grace Norma Leonie, b. 4 Jan 1928, Trinidad, West Indies. Ex-Librarian; Author; Storyteller. m. Trevor David Hallworth, 31 Oct 1964. Education: Exemptions from Matriculation, 1946; Associate of Library Association, 1956; Diploma in Education, London University, 1976; Editorial Board Member, Institute of Education, University of London, 1995. Publications: Listen to this Story, 1977; Mouth Open Story Jump Out, 1984; Web of Stories, 1990; Cric Crac, 1990; Buy a Penny Ginger, 1994; Pour Me One, 1995; Rythm & Rhyme, 1995. Contributions to: Books and journals. Membership: Society for Storytelling, chairperson, 1993-94. Address: 18 Mayflower Avenue, Hemel Hempstead, Hertfordshire HP2 4AE, England.

HALPERN Daniel, b. 11 Sept 1945, Syracuse, New York, USA. Associate Professor; Poet; Editor. m. Jeanne Catherine Carter, 1982. Education: San Francisco State College, 1963-64; BA, California State University at Northridge, 1969; MFA, Columbia University, 1972. Appointments: Editor, Antaeus magazine, 1969-; Instructor, New School for Social Research, New York City, 1971-76; Editor-in-Chief, Ecco Press, 1971-; Visiting Professor, Princeton University, 1975-76, 1987-88; Associate Professor, 1976-, Chairman, School of the Arts, 1978-, Columbia University; Founder-Director, National Poetry Series, 1978-. Publications: Poetry: Traveling on Credit, 1972; The Keeper of Height, 1974; The Lady Knife-Thrower, 1975; Treble Poets 2 (with Gerda Mayer and Florence Elon), 1975; Street Fire, 1975; Life Among Others, 1978; Seasonal Rights, 1982; Tango, 1987; Foreign Neon, 1991; Selected Poems, 1994. Non-Fiction: The Good Food: Soups, Stews and Pasta (with Julie Strand), 1985; Halpern's Guide to the Essential Restaurants of Italy, 1990. Editor: Borges on Writing (with Norman Thomas di Giovanni and Frank MacShane), 1973; The American Poetry Anthology, 1975; The Art of the Tale: An International Anthology of Short Stories 1945-1985, 1986, UK edition as the Penguin Book of International Short Stories 1945-1985, 1989; The Antaeus Anthology, 1986; On Nature: Nature, Landscape and Natural History, 1987; On Reading, 1987; Literature as Pleasure, 1987; Reading the Fights (with Joyce Carol Oates), 1988; Writers on Artists, 1988; Our Private Lives: Journals, Notebooks and Diaries, 1989; Plays in One Act, 1991; Sophisticated Cat: A Gathering of Stories, Poems and Miscellaneous Writings about Cats (with Joyce Carol Oates), 1992; The Autobiographical Eye, 1993; Too Far From Home: The Selected Writings of Paul Bowles, 1993; Dante's Inferno: Translations by Twenty Contemporary Poets, 1993; Not for Bread Alone: Writers on Food, Wine and the Art of Eating, 1993; Nine Visionary Poets and the Quest for Enlightenment, 1994; On Music (with Jeanne Wilmot Carter), 1994; Who's Writing This?: Notations on the Authorial I, with Self Portraits, 1994. Honours: Rehder Award, Southern Poetry Review, 1971; YM-YWHA Discovery Award, 1971; Bread Loaf Writers Conference Robert Frost Fellowship, 1974; National Endowment for the Arts Fellowships, 1974, 1975, 1987; Creative Arts Public Service Grant, 1978; Guggenheim Fellowship, 1988-89. Address: c/o Ecco Press Ltd, 100 West Broad Street, Hopewell, NJ 08525, USA.

HAM Debra Lynn Newman, b. 27 Aug 1948, York, Pennsylvania, USA. Professor; Black History Specialist. m. Lester James Ham, 29 Apr 1989, 1 son, 1 daughter. Education: BA, 1970, PhD, 1984, Howard University; MA, Boston University, 1971. Appointments: Professor of History; Morgan State University, 1994. Publications: Black History: A Guide to Civilian Records in the National Archives, 1984; The African-American Mosaic: A Library of Congress Resource Guide for the Study of Black History and Culture, 1993; Jesus and Justice: Nannie Helen Burroughs and Her Struggle for Civil Rights, Society and Humanity. Contributions to: They Left With the British: Black Women in the Evacuation of Philadelphia, Pennsylvania Heritage, 1978. Honour: Coker Prize, Society of American Archivists, 1985. Membership: Association for the Study of Afro-American Life and History, Member of Executive Council, 1989. Address: Morgan State University, Cold Spring Lane and Hillen Road, Baltimore, MD 21239, USA.

HAMBRICK-STOWE Charles Edwin, b. 4 Feb 1948, Worcester, Massachusetts, USA. m. Elizabeth Anne Hambrick-Stowe, 11 Sept 1971, 2 sons, 1 daughter. Education: BA, Hamilton College, 1970; MA and MDiv, Pacific School of Religion, 1973; PhD, Boston University Graduate School, 1980. Appointment: Religion Columnist, Evening Sun Newspaper, Carrol County, MD, 1982-85. Publications: Massachusetts Militia Companies and The Officers of the Lexington Alarm, 1976; Practice of Piety: Puritan Devotional Disciplines in 17th Century New England, 1982; Early New England Meditative Poetry: Anne Bradstreet and Edward Taylor, 1988; Theology and Identity: Traditions Movements and Issues in the United Church of Christ, 1990; A Living Theological Heritage: American Beginnings, 1995; Charles G Finney and the Spirit of American Evangelicalism. Contributions to: Reference works, books and journals. Honour: Jamestown Prize for Early American History, 1980. Memberships: American Historical Association; American Society of Church History; American Academy of Religion; Cliosophic Society. Address: 1101 Davis Drive, Lancaster, PA 17603, USA.

HAMBURGER Anne (Ellen), (Anne Beresford), b. 10 Sept 1928, Redhill, Surrey, England. Poet; Writer; Actress; Teacher. m. Michael Hamburger, 28 July 1951, 1 son, 2 daughters. Education: Central School of Dramatic Art, London, 1944-46. Appointments: Actress, various repertory companies, 1946-48, BBC Radio, 1960-78; Teacher; General Council, Poetry Society, 1976-78; Committee Member, 1989, Advisor on Agenda, Editorial Board, 1993-, Aldeburgh Poetry Festival. Publications: Poetry: Walking Without Moving, 1967; The Lair, 1968; The Courtship, 1972; Footsteps on Snow, 1972; The Curving Shore, 1975; Songs a Thracian Taught Me, 1980; The Songs of Almut, 1980; The Sele of the Morning, 1988; Landscape With Figures, 1994. Other: Struck by Apollo, radio play (with Michael Hamburger), 1965; The Villa, radio short story, 1968; Alexandros Poems of Vera Lungu, translator, 1974; Duet for Three Voices, dramatised poems for Anglia TV, 1982; Snapshots from an Album, 1884-1895, 1992. Contributions to: Periodicals. Address: Marsh Acres, Middleton, Saxmundham, Suffolk IP17 3NH, England.

HAMBURGER Michael (Peter Leopold), b. 22 Mar 1924, Berlin, Germany (British citizen). Poet. Education: MA, Christ Church, Oxford, 1948. Appointments: Visiting Professor at American Universities, 1969, University of Essex at Wivenhoe, 1978-. Publications: Later Hogarth, 1945; Flowering Cactus: Poems 1942-49, 1950; Poems 1950-51, 1952; The Dual Site, 1957; Weather and Seasons: New Poems, 1963; In Flashlight, 1965; In Massachusetts, 1967; Feeding the Chickadees, 1968; Travelling; Poems 1963-68, 1969; Penguin Modern Poets 14, 1969; Home, 1969; In Memoriam: Friedrich Hölderlin, 1970; Travelling I-V, 1972; Ownerless Earth: New and Selected Poems 1950-72, 1973; Conversations with Charwomen, 1973; Babes in the Wood, 1974; Real Estate, 1977; Palinode: A Poet's Progress, 1977; Moralities, 1977; Variations in Suffolk IV, 1980; Variations, 1981; In Suffolk, 1982; Collected Poems 1941-83, 1987; Selected Poems, 1988; Trees, 1988; Roots in the Air, 1991; Collected Poems 1941-1994, 1994; Editions, translations and studies of German literature. Honours: Institute of Linguists Gold Medal, 1977; DLitt, University of East Anglia at Norwich, 1988; Officer of the Order of the British Empire, 1992. Address: c/o John Johnson Ltd, Clerkenwell House, 45-47 Clerkenwell Green, London EC1R 0HT, England.

HAMBURGER Philip (Paul), b. 2 July 1914, Wheeling, Virginia, USA. Writer. m. (1) Edith Iglauer, 24 Dec 1942, (2) Anna Walling Matson, 27 Oct 1968, 2 sons. Education: BA, Johns Hopkins University, 1935; MS, Graduate School of Journalism, Columbia University, 1938. Appointment: Staff Writer, The New Yorker, 1939-. Publications: The Oblong Blur and Other Odysseys, 1949; J P Marquand, Esquire, 1952; Mayor Watching and Other Pleasures, 1958; Our Man Stanley, 1963; An American Notebook, 1965; Curious World, A New Yorker at Large, 1987. Contributions to: The New Yorker. Honours: New York Public Library Literary Lion Award, 1986; George Polk Career Award, 1994. Memberships: Authors League of America; PEN USA; Board of Directors, Authors League Fund and National Press Club, Washington. Literary Agent: Sterling Lord Literistic. Address: c/o The New Yorker, 20 West 43rd Street, New York, NY 10036, USA.

HAMELIN Claude, b. 25 Aug 1943, Montreal, Quebec, Canada. Poet; Scientist. m. Renée Artinian, 11 Sept 1970, 1 son, 1 daughter. Education: BPed, 1965; BSc, 1970; MSc, 1972; PhD, 1975. Appointments: 40 Recitals done inside and outside Quebec. Publications: Fables des quatre-temps (poetry), 1990; Lueurs froides (poetry), 1991; Nef des fous (poetry), 1992; Roman d'un quartier (novel), 1993; Néant bleu/Nada azul/Blue Nothingness (poetry), 1994; Contributions to: Anthologies and journals. Honour: Jaycee's Five Outstanding Young Canadians, 1983. Address: 4630 ave Lacombe, Montreal, Quebec, H3W 1R3, Canada.

HAMILL (William) Pete, b. 24 June 1934, New York, New York, USA. Journalist; Columnist; Writer. m. (1) Ramona Negron, 3 Feb 1962, div 1970, 2 daughters, (2) Fukiko Aoki, 23 May 1987. Education: Pratt Institute, 1952; Mexico City College, 1956-57. Appointments: Reporter, later columnist, 1960-74, 1988-93, New York Post; Contributing Editor, Saturday Evening Post, 1963-64; Contributor, Village Voice and New York Magazine, 1974-; Columnist, New York Daily News, 1975-79, 1982-84, Esquire Magazine, 1989-91; Editor, Mexico City News, 1986-87. Publications: Fiction: A Killing for Christ, 1968; The Gift, 1973; Flesh and Blood, 1977; Loving Women, 1990; Tokyo Sketches, 1993. Non-Fiction: Irrational Ravings, 1972; The Invisible City: A New York Sketchbook, 1980; A Drinking Life: A Memoir, 1994. Contributions to: Many periodicals. Honours: Meyer Berger Award, Columbia School of Journalism, 1962; Newspaper Reporters Association Award, 1962; 25 Year Achievement Award, Society of Silurians, 1989; Peter Kihss Award, 1992. Membership: Writers Guild of America. Address: c/o New York Magazine, 755 Second Avenue, New York, NY 10017, USA.

HAMILTON Donald B(engtsson), b. 24 Mar 1916, Uppsala, Sweden. Writer. m. Kathleen Stick, 12 Sep 1941, dec Oct 1989, 2 sons, 2 daughters. Education: BS, University of Chicago, 1938. Publications: 25 novels featuring agent Matt Helm, 1960-93; The Big Country, 1958; 4 western novels, 1954-60; 5 mystery novels, 1947-56; On Guns and Hunting, 1970; Cruises with Kathleen, 1980. Contributions to: Periodicals. Honour: Western Writers of America; Spur, 1967. Memberships: Author's Guild; Mystery Writers of America; Western Writers of America; Outdoor Writer's Association of America. Address: PO Box 1141, Old Saybrook, CT 06475, USA.

HAMILTON (Robert) Ian, b. 24 Mar 1938, King's Lynn, Norfolk, England. Lecturer; Poet. Education: BA, Keble College, Oxford, 1962. Appointments: Poetry and Fiction Editor, Times Literary Supplement, 1965-73; Presenter, Bookmark, BBC TV, 1984-87. Publications: Pretending Not to Sleep, 1964; The Visit, 1970; Anniversary and Vigil, 1971; Returning, 1976; Fifty Poems, 1988. Other: A Poetry Chronicle: Essays and Reviews, 1973; The Little Magazines: A Study of Six Editors, 1976; Robert Lowell: A Biography, 1983; In Search of J D Salinger, 1988; Editions of contemporary poetry. Honours: Eric Gregory Award, 1963; English-Speaking Union Award, 1984. Address: 54 Queen's Road, London SW19, England.

HAMILTON John Maxwell, b. 28 Mar 1947, Evanston, Illinois, USA. Journalist; Lecturer. m. Regina N, 19 Aug 1975, 1 s. Education: BA, Journalism, Marquette University, 1969; MS, Journalism, Boston University, 1974; PhD, American Civilization, George Washington University, 1983. Appointments: The Milwaukee Journal, 1967-69; Marine Corps, 1969-73; Freelance Writer, ABC Radio correspondent, 1973-78; Agency for International Development (political appointee) 1979-81; House Foreign Affairs Committee, 1981-83; World Bank, 1983-84, 1982-92; Visiting Professor, Journalism, Northwestern University, 1985-87; Dean, Manship School of Mass Communication, Louisiana State University. Publications: Main Street America and the Third World, 1986, revised, enlarged edition, 1988; Edgar Snow: A Biography, 1988; Entangling Alliances, 1990; Hold The Press: The Inside Story on Newspapers (co-author), 1996. Contributions to:

Numerous books and periodicals. Honours: Ford Fondation, German Marshall Fund, Carnegie Corporation and Benton Foundation Grants, 1985-88; Frank Luther Mott Journalism Research Award, 1989; By-line Award, Marguette University, 1993. Memberships: Society of Professional Journalists; Society of International Development; Director, Board of Directors, International Centre for Journalists. Address: 567 LSU Avenue, Baton Rouge, LA 70808, USA.

HAMILTON Mollie. See: **KAY Mary Margaret.**

HAMILTON Morse, b. 16 Aug 1943, Detroit, Michigan, USA. Teacher. m. Sharon Saros, 20 Aug 1966, 3 daughters. Education: BA, University of Michigan, 1967; MA, 1968; PhD, Columbia University, 1974. Publications: Children's books: My Name is Emily, 1979; Big Sisters are Bad Witches, 1980; Who's Afraid of the Dark?, 1983; How do You Do Mr Birdsteps?, 1983; Effie's House (novel), 1990; Little Sister for Sale, 1992; The Black Hen, 1994; Yellow Blue Bus Means I Love You (novel), 1994. Honours: Hopwood Award, 1967; Woodrow Wilson Dissertation Fellow, 1971; George Bennet Memorial Fellow, 1973. Address: c/o English Department, Tufts University, Medford, MA 02155, USA.

HAMILTON Paul. See: **DENNIS-JONES Harold.**

HAMILTON Priscilla. See: **GELLIS Roberta Leah.**

HAMILTON Virginia, b. 12 Mar 1936, Yellow Springs, Ohio, USA. Writer. m. Arnold Adoff, 19 Mar 1960, 2 sons. Education: Antioch College, 1952-55; Ohio State University, 1957-58; New School for Social Research, New York City. Publications: Zeely, 1967; The House of Dies Drear, 1968; The Time-Ago Tales of Jadhu, 1969; The Planet of Junior Brown, 1971; W E B DuBois: A Biography, 1972; Time-Ago Lost: More Tales of Jadhu, 1973; M C Higgins, the Great, 1974; Paul Robeson: The Life and Times of a Free Black Man, 1974; The Writings of W E B DuBois (editor), 1975; Arilla Sun Down, 1976; Illusion and Reality, 1976; Justice and Her Brothers, 1978; Jahdu, 1980; Dustland, 1980; The Gathering, 1981; Sweet Whispers, Brother Rush, 1982; The Magical Adventures of Pretty Pearl, 1983; Willie Bea and the Time the Martians Landed, 1983; A Little Love, 1984; Junius Over Far, 1985; The People Could Fly: American Black Folktales, 1985; The Mystery of Drear House, 1987; A White Romance, 1987; In The Beginning: Creation Stories from Around the World, 1988; Anthony Burns: The Defeat and Triumph of a Fugitive Slave, 1988; The Bells of Christmas, 1989; The Dark Way: Stories from the Spirit World, 1990; Cousins, 1990; The All Jahdu Storybook, 1991; Many Thousands Gone, 1992; Plain City, 1993; Jaguarundi, 1994; Her Story: African American Folktales, 1995. Honours: Edgar Allan Poe Award, 1969; Newbery Honor Books Awards, 1971, 1983, 1989; Boston Globe/Horn Book Awards, 1974, 1983, 1988; John Newbery Medal, 1975; National Book Award, 1975; Coretta Scott King Awards, 1983, 1986, 1989; Horn Book Fanfare Award, 1985; Regina Medal, Catholic Library Association, 1990; Laura Ingalls Wilder Award, American Library Association, 1995. Address: c/o Arnold Adoff Agency, PO Box 293, Yellow Springs, OH 45387, USA.

HAMILTON Wade. See: **FLOREN Lee.**

HAMMICK Georgina, b. 24 May 1939, Hampshire, England. Writer; Poet. m. 24 Oct 1961, 1 son, 2 daughters. Education: Academie Julian, Paris, 1956-57; Salisbury Art School, 1957-59. Publications: A Poetry Quintet (poems), 1976; People for Lunch, 1987; Spoilt (short stories), 1992; The Virago Book of Love and Loss (editor), 1992; The Arizona Game, 1996. Contributions to: Journals and periodicals. Membership: Writers Guild. Address: Bridgewalk House, Brixton, Deverill, Warminster, Wiltshire BA12 7EJ, England.

HAMMOND Jane. See: **POLAND Dorothy Elizabeth Hayward.**

HAMMOND Ralph. See: **HAMMOND INNES Ralph.**

HAMMOND INNES Ralph, (Ralph Hammond, Hammond Innes), b. 15 July 1913, Horsham, Sussex, England. Author. m. Dorothy Mary Lang, 21 Aug 1937, dec 3 Feb 1989. Education: Feltonfleet and Cranbrook School. Publications: Wreckers Must Breathe, 1940; The Trojan Horse, 1940; Attack Alarm, 1941; Dead and Alive, 1946; The Lonely Skier, 1947; The Killer Mine, 1947; Maddon's Rock, 1948; The Blue Ice, 1948; The White South, 1949; The Angry Mountain, 1950; Air Bridge, 1951; Campbell's Kingdom, 1952; The Strange Land, 1954; The Mary Deare (Book Society Choice), 1956;

The Land God Gave to Cain, 1958; Harvest of Journeys, 1959; The Doomed Oasis, 1960; Atlantic Fury, 1962; Scandinavia, 1963; The Strode Venturer, 1965; Sea and Islands, 1967; The Conquistadors, 1969; Levkas Man, 1971; Golden Soak, 1973; North Star, 1974; The Big Footprints, 1977; The Last Voyage (Cook), 1978; Solomon's Seal, 1980; The Black Tide, 1982; High Stand, 1985; Hammond Innes' East Anglia, 1986; Medusa, 1988; Isvik, 1991; Target Antarctica, 1993; Delta Connection, 1996. Contributions to: Fiction and travel articles in numerous journals. Honours: Commander of the Order of the British Empire, 1978; Hon DLitt, Bristol University, 1985. Memberships: PEN; Society of Authors; Garrick Club; RORC; RCC. Address: Ayres End, Kersey, Suffolk, IP7 6EB, England.

HAMPSHIRE Sir Stuart (Newton), b. 1 Oct 1914, Healing, Lincolnshire, England. Professor of Philosophy (retired); Writer. m. (1) Renee Ayer, 1961, dec 1980, 2 daughters, (2) Nancy Cartwright, 1985. Education: Balliol College, Oxford. Appointments: Fellow and Lecturer in Philosophy, 1936-40, Domestic Bursar and Research Fellow, 1955-60, All Souls College, Oxford; Service in the British Army, 1940-45; Personal Assistant to the Minister of State, British Foreign Office, 1945; Lecturer in Philosophy, University College, London, 1947-50; Fellow, New College, Oxford, 1950-55; Grote Professor of Philosophy of Mind and Logic, University of London, 1960-63; Professor of Philosophy, Princeton University, 1963-70; Warden, Wadham College, Oxford, 1970-84; Professor, Stanford University, 1985-91. Publications: Spinoza, 1951; Thought and Action, 1959; Freedom of the Individual, 1965; Modern Writers and Other Essays, 1969; Freedom of Mind and Other Essays, 1971; The Socialist Idea (co-editor), 1975; Two Theories of Morality, 1977; Public and Private Morality (editor), 1978; Morality and Conflict, 1983; Innocence and Experience, 1989. Contributions to: Philosophical journals. Honours: Honorary DLitt, University of Glasgow, 1973; Knighted, 1979. Memberships: Fellow, American Academy of Arts and Sciences; Fellow, British Academy. Address: 7 Beaumont Road, The Quarry, Headington, Oxford, OX3 8JN, England.

HAMPSHIRE Susan, b. 12 May 1942, London, England. Actress; Writer. m. (1) Pierre Granier-Deferre, div 1974, 1 son, (2) Eddie Kulukundis, 1980. Education: Knightsbridge, England. Appointments: Actress on the London stage, 1959-; Film and television appearances; Writer. Publications: Susan's Story: An Autobiographical Account of My Struggle with Dyslexia, 1982; The Maternal Instinct, 1985; Lucy Jane at the Ballet, 1987; Trouble Free Gardening, 1989; Lucy Jane on Television, 1989; Every Letter Counts, 1990; Lucy Jane and the Dancing Competition, 1990; Easy Gardening, 1992; Lucy Jane and the Russian Ballet, 1993; Rosie's First Ballet Lesson, 1995. Honours: Emmy Awards, 1970, 1971, 1973; Honorary doctorates, London University, 1984, St Andrew's University, 1986, Kingston University, 1994, Pine Manor College, Boston, USA; Officer of the Order of the British Empire, 1995. Memberships: President, British Dyslexia Association; Royal Society of Authors. Address: c/o Chatto and Linnit Ltd, Prince of Wales Theatre, Coventry Street, London W1V 7FE, England.

HAMPSON Norman, b. 8 Apr 1922, Leyland, Lancashire, England. Retired University Professor. m. Jacqueline Gardin, 22 Apr 1948, 2 daughters. Education: University College Oxford, 1940-41, 1945-47. Publications: La Marine de l'An II, 1959; A Social History of The French Revolution, 1963; The First European Revolution, 1963; The Enlightenment, 1968; The Life and Opinions of Maximilien Robespierre, 1974; A Concise History of the French Revolution, 1975; Danton, 1978; Will and Circumstance: Montesquieu, Rousseau and The French Revolution, 1983; Prelude to Terror, 1988; Saint-Just, 1991. Contributions to: Numerous magazines and journals. Honour: D Litt (Edinburgh), 1989. Memberships: Fellow, British Academy; Fellow, Royal Historical Society. Address: 305 Hull Road, York, YO1 3LB, England.

HAMPTON Angeline Agnes, (A A Kelly), b. 28 Feb 1924, London, England. Writer. m. George Hughan Hampton, 31 Dec 1944, 1 son, 3 daughters. Education: BA (Ext) English Honours, University of London, 1965; L Es- L, 1969, D Es- L, 1973, University of Geneva, Switzerland. Publications: Liam O'Flaherty the Storyteller, 1976; Mary Lavin: Quiet Rebel, 1980; Joseph Campbell, 1879-1944, Poet and Nationalist, 1988; The Pillars of The House (editor), 1987; Wandering Women, 1994; The Letters of Liam O'Flaherty (editor), 1996. Contributions to: English Studies; Comparative Education; Eire, Ireland; Hibernia; Linen Hall Review; Geneva News and International Report; Christian. Honours: British Academy Grant, 1987.

Memberships: International Association for The Study of Anglo-Irish Literature; Society of Authors; PEN International. Address: Gate Cottage, Pilley Green, Lymington, Hampshire SO41 5QQ, England.

HAMPTON Christopher (James), b. 26 Jan 1946, Fayal, The Azores. Playwright. m. Laura de Holesch, 1971, 2 daughters. Education: Lancing College, Sussex, 1959-63; BA, Modern Languages, 1968, MA, New College, Oxford. Appointment: Resident Dramatist, Royal Court Theatre, London, 1968-70. Publications: Tales from Hollywood, 1983; Tartuffe or The Imposter (adaptation of Moliére's play), 1984; Les Liaisons Dangereuses (adaptation of C de Laclos's novel), 1985; Hedda Gabler and a Doll's House (translations of Ibsen's plays), 1989; Faith, Hope and Charity (translator), 1989; The Ginger Tree (adaptation of Oscar Wynd's novel), 1989; White Chameleon, 1991; The Philanthropist and Other Plays, 1991; Other: Screenplays, radio and television plays. Membership: Fellow, Royal Society of Literature. Address: National House, 60-66 Wardour Street, London, W1V 3HP, England.

HAMRE Ida, b. 16 Mar 1941, Denmark. Teacher; Researcher; Writer. 1 son. Education: BEd; Drama Teacher, 1987; PhD, 1993. Appointments: Lecturer, Textiles Disciplines, Teachers College, 1969; Teacher, Royal Danish School of Educational Studies, 1985-93; Freelance, 1993- Publications: With Hanne Meedom: Making Simple Clothes - The Structure and Development of Clothes from Other Cultures, 1978; The Theatre of Animation as an art and as an element of aesthetic development and education, PhD, thesis, 1993; With Anne Maj Nielsen, Billeder, Stoffer, Mad og Musik, 1994; Marionet og Menneske, Animationsteater-Billedteater, 1997. Contributions to: Books, magazines and journals. Membership: Dansk Forfatterforening, Copenhagen. Address: Biskop Monrads vej 29, DK 2830 Virum, Denmark.

HAMLYN Pul Bertrand, b. 12 Feb 1926, Berlin, Germany. Publisher. m. (1)Eileen Margaret Watson, 1952, divorced 1969, (2)Helen Guest, 1970, 1 s, 1 d. Appointments: Founder, Hamlyn Publishing Group; Formed Books for Pleasure, 1949; Prints for Pleasure, 1960; Records for Pleasure; Golden Pleasure Books, 1961; Music for Pleasure (EMI) 1965; Paul Hamlyn Group acquired by IPC, 1964; joined IPC Board with speical responsibility for all book publishing activities, acquired Butterworth and Co, 1968; Director IPC 1965-70, Chairman, IPC Books, 1965-70; Joint Managing Director, News International Ltd, 1970-71; Founder, Chairman, Octopus Publishing Group, 1971-; Chairman, Octopus Books Ltd 1971-, Mandarin Publishers, Hong Kong, 1971-; Co-founder (with David Frost), and Dirctor, Sundial Publications, 1973-; Co-founder (with Doubleday and Co, New York), and Director, Octopus Books International BV, Netherlands, 1973-; Director, News America, Tigerpring Ltd, News International etc, TV AM, 1981-83; Co-Chairman Conran Octopus Ltd, 1983-; Chairman, Heinemann Group of Publishers Lltd, 1985-; Hamlyn Publishing Group, 1986-; Borad Director, International Plc, Chairman, Reed International Books, 1987-; Chancellor of Thames Valley University, 1993-; Chairman, Book Club Associates, 1993; Director, Reed Elsevier PLC, 1993-. Honours: University of Keele, 1988; University of Warwick, 1991. Address: Michelin House, 81 Fulham Road, London, SW3 56RB, England.

HAN Suyin, b. 12 Sept 1917, Sinyang, China. Novelist; Medical Doctor. Education: Yenching University, Beijing, China; Brussels University, Belgium; London University, Royal Free Hospital, London. Publications: A Many Splendoured Thing, 1952; The Mountain is Young, 1958; The Crippled Tree, 1965; Lhassa, the Open City, 1977; My House Has Two Doors,1980; Till Morning Comes, 1982; The Enchantress, 1985; A Share of Loving, 1987; Han Suyin's China, 1987. Contributions to: Periodicals. Honours: Bancaralla Prize, Italy, 1956; McGill Beatty Prize, Canada, 1968; Nutting Prize, Canada, 1980; Woman Reader Prize, Italy, 1983. Address: c/o Jonathan Cape, 32 Bedford Square, London WC1, England.

HANBURY-TENISON (Airling) Robin, b. 7 May 1936, London, England. Writer; Farmer. Education: BA, MA, Magdalen College, Oxford. Appointment: Chief Executive, British Field Sports Society, 1995. Publications: The Rough and the Smooth, 1969; A Question of Survival for the Indians of Brazil, 1973; A Pattern of Peoples: A Journey Among the Tribes of the Outer Indonesian Islands, 1975; Mulu: The Rain Forest, 1980; The Aborigines of the Amazon Rain Forest: The Yanomami, 1982; Worlds Apart (autobiography), 1984; White Horses Over France, 1985; A Ride Along the Great Wall, 1987; Fragile Eden: A Ride Through New Zealand, 1989; Spanish

Pilgrimage: A Canter to St James, 1990; The Oxford Book of Exploration, 1993; Jakes Escape, 1996. Contributions to:Frontiers Column in Geographical Magazine, 1995-. Honours: Royal Geographical Society Gold Medal, 1979; Officer of the Order of the British Empire, 1981; Thomas Cook Travel Book Award, 1984. Memberships: Council Member, 1968-82, 1995- Vice President, 1982-86, Royal Geographical Society; President, Survival International, 1969-. Address: Cabilla Manor, Cardinham, Bodmin, Cornwall PL30 4DW, England.

HANCOCK Geoffrey White, b. 14 Apr 1946, New Westminster, New Brunswick, Canada. Writer; Literary Journalist. m. Gay Allison, 6 Aug 1983, 1 daughter. Education: BFA, 1973, MFA, University of British Columbia, 1975. Appointments: Editor in Chief, Canadian Fiction Magazine, 1975; Consulting editor, Canadian Author and Bookman, 1978; Fiction editor, Cross-Canada Writers Quarterly, 1980; Literary consultant, CBC Radio, 1980. Publications: Magic Realism, 1980; Illusion: Fables Fantasies and Metafictions, 1983; Metavisions, 1983; Shoes and Shit: Stories for Pedestrians, 1984; Moving Off the Map: From Story to Fiction, 1986; Invisible Fictions: Contemporary Stories from Quebec, 1987; Canadian Writers at Work: Interviews, 1987; Singularities, 1990; Fast Travelling, 1995. Contributions to: Toronto Star; Writer's Quarterly; Canadian Author and Bookman; Books In Canada; Canadian Forum. Honour: Fiona Mee Award for Literary Journalism, 1979. Membership: Periodical Writers of Canada; Address: c/o Canadian Fiction Magazine, Box No 1061, Kingston, Ontario K7L 4Y5, Canada.

HANCOCK Lyn, b. 5 Jan 1938, Fremantle, West Australia. Writer; Photographer; Lecturer. Education: Teaching Diploma, 1955, 1977; ASDA, 1955; LTCL, 1959; LSDA, 1957; LRAM (mime), 1961; LRAM (Speech), 1961; BEduc, Simon Fraser University, 1977; MA, Communications, 1981. Appointments: Twelve years teaching in three countries (Grade 3 to university level); Principal of a privately-owned Academy of Speech and Drama in Western Australia, 1954-59. Publications: There's a Seal in My Sleeping Bag, 1972; There's a Raccoon in My Parka, 1977; Looking for the Wild, 1986; Northwest Territories, 1993; Nunavut, 1995; Winging It in the North, 1996; Yukon, 1996; Destination Vancouver, 1997. Contributions to: Frequent Contributor to Above and Beyond; Globe and Mail; numerous other magazines. Honours: Pacific Northwest Booksellers Award, 1973; Francis H Kortnight Conservation Award, 1978, 1987; American Express Travel Writing Awards, 1981, 1983. Address: 8270 Sabre Road, Lantzville, British Columbia VOR 2HO, Canada.

HANDLIN Oscar, b. 29 Sept 1915, New York, New York, USA. Professor of History; Writer. m. (1) Mary Flug, 18 Sept 1937, 1 son, 2 daughters, (2) Lilian Bombach, 17 June 1977. Education: AB, Brooklyn College, 1934; AM, 1935, LLD, 1940, Harvard University. Appointments: Instructor, Brooklyn College, 1936-38; Instructor, 1939-44, Assistant Professor, 1944-48, Associate Professor, 1948-54, Professor, 1954- , of History, Director, Center for the Study of Liberty in America,1958-66, Winthrop Professor of History, 1962-65, Charles Warren Professor of History, 1965-72, Director, Charles Warren Center for Studies in American History, 1965-72, Carl H Pforzheimer University Professor, 1972-84, Director, University Library, 1979-84, Carl M Loeb University Professor, 1984-86, Harvard University; Harmsworth Professor, Oxford University, 1972-73. Publications: Boston's Immigrants, 1941; Commonwealth, 1947; This Was America, 1949; The Uprooted, 1951, 2nd edition, 1973; The American People in the Twentieth Century, 1954; Adventure in Freedom, 1954; Chance or Destiny, 1955; Race and Nationality in American Life, 1956; Readings in American History, 1957, revised edition, 1970; Al Smith and His America, 1958; Immigration as a Factor in American History, 1959; The Newcomers: Negroes and Puerto Ricans in a Changing Metropolis, 1959; American Principles and Issues, 1961; The Dimensions of Liberty, 1961; The Americans, 1963; Fire-Bell in the Night, 1964; Children of the Uprooted, 1966; Popular Sources of Political Authority, 1967; History of the United States, 1967; America: A History, 1968; The American College and American Culture, 1970; Statue of Liberty, 1971; Facing Life: Youth and the Family in American History, 1971; A Pictorial History of Immigration, 1972; The Wealth of the American People, 1975; Truth in History, 1979, revised edition, 1997; Abraham Lincoln and the Union, 1980; The Distortion of America, 1981, revised edition, 1996; Liberty and Power, 1986; Liberty in Expansion, 1989; Liberty in Peril, 1992; Liberty and Equality, 1994. Contributions to: Scholarly journals. Honours: J H Dunning Prize, American History Association, 1941; Award of Honor, Brooklyn College, 1945; Pulitzer Prize in History, 1952; Guggenheim Fellowship,

1954; Christopher Award, 1958; Robert H Lord Award, 1972; Many honorary doctorates. Memberships: American Academy of Arts and Sciences, Fellow; American Jewish Historical Society; Colonial Society of Massachusetts; Massachusetts Historical Society. Address: 18 Agassiz Street, Cambridge, MA 02140, USA.

HANKIN Cherry Anne, b. 30 Sept 1937, Nelson, New Zealand. University Professor. m. John Charles Garrett, 18 May 1981. Education: MA, University of New Zealand, 1959; PhD, University of California, Berkeley, 1971. Appointments: The University of Canterbury, Christchurch, New Zealand, 1971-; Chief Fiction Judge, New Zealand Department of Internal Affairs Literary Awards, 1975; Judge, Katherine Mansfield Centennial Award, 1988; Fiction Judge, New Zealand Book Awards, 1995. Publications: Katherine Mansfield and Her Confessional Stories; The Letters of John Middleton Murray to Katherine Mansfield; Letters Between John Middleton Murray and Katherine Mansfield; Critical Essays on The New Zealand Novel; Life in A Young Colony: Selections from Early New Zealand Writing; Critical Essays on The New Zealand Short Story. Contributions to: Books and journals. Honours: Advanced Graduate Travelling Fellowship in English, University of California, Berkeley, 1969. Memberships: Board of Trustees, Christchurch Theatre Trust. Address: 22 West Tamaki Road, St Heliers, Auckland, New Zealand.

HANKINSON Alan, b. 25 May 1926, Gatley, Cheshire, England. Freelance Writer. m. Roberta Lorna Gibson, 15 Dec 1951, div 1985, 1 son. Education: MA, History, Magdalen College, Oxford, 1949. Publications: The First Tigers, 1972; Camera on the Crags, 1975; The Mountain Men, 1977; Man of Wars, 1982; The Blue Box, 1983; The Regatta Men, 1988; A Century on the Crags, 1988; Coleridge Walks the Fells, 1991; Geoffrey Winthrop Young, 1995. Contributions to: Cumbria Life. Honours: BP Arts Journalism, runner up, 1991; Portico Prize, 1991; Cumbria Book of the Year, 1992; Boardman Tasker Award, 1995. Address: 30 Skiddaw Street, Keswick, Cumbria CA12 4BY, England.

HANLEY Clifford (Henry Calvin), b. 28 Oct 1922, Glasgow, Scotland. Writer. m. Anna Clark, 10 Jan 1948, 1 son, 2 daughters. Education: Eastbank Academy, Glasgow. Appointments: Professor of Creative Writing, York University, Toronto, 1979. Publications: Dancing in the Streets, 1958; The Taste of Too Much, 1960; Nothing But the Best, 1964; Prissy, 1978; The Scots, 1980; Another Street Another Dance, 1983; Plays: The Durable Element, 1961; Oh For an Island, 1966; Dick McWhittie, 1967; Jack O'The Cudgel, 1969; Oh Glorious Jubilee, 1970; The Clyde Moralities, 1972. Contributions to: Numerous articles in magazines and journals. Honour: Oscar for Best Foriegn Documentary, 1960. Memberships: Ours Club, Glasgow, President; PEN, Scottish president, 1975. Address: 35 Hamilton Drive, Glasgow, Scotland.

HANNAH Barry, b. 23 Apr 1942, Meridian, Mississippi, USA. Author. Div, 3 sons. Education: BA, Mississippi College, Clinton, 1964; MA, 1966, MFA, 1967, University of Arkansas. Appointments: Teacher, Clemson University, 1967-73, University of Alabama, Tuscaloosa, 1975-80; Writer-in-Residence, Middlebury College, Vermont, 1974-75, University of Iowa, 1981, University of Mississippi, University, 1982, 1984-85, University of Montana, Missoula, 1982-83. Publications: Geronimo Rex, 1972; Nightwatchmen, 1973; Airships, 1978; Ray, 1981; Two Stories, 1982; Black Butterfly, 1982; Power and Light, 1983; The Tennis Handsome, 1983; Captain Maximus, 1985; Hey Jack!, 1987; Boomerang, 1989; Never Die, 1991; Bats Out of Hell, 1993. Contributions to: Magazines. Honours: Bellaman Foundation Award, 1970; Atherton Fellowship, Bread Loaf Writers Conference, 1971; Arnold Gingrich Award, Esquire Magazine, 1978; American Academy of Arts and Letters Award, 1978. Address: c/o NAL/Dutton, 375 Hudson Street, New York, NY 10014, USA.

HANNON Ezra. See: **LOMBINO Salvatore A.**

HANSEN Joseph, (Rose Brock, James Colton, James Coulton), b. 19 July 1923, Aberdeen, South Dakota, USA. Author. m. Jane Bancroft, 4 Aug 1943, 1 daughter. Education: Public Schools. Publications: Lost on Twilight Road, 1964; Strange Marriage, 1965; The Corruptor and Other Stories, 1968; Known Homosexual, 1968, revised edition as Stranger to Himself, 1977, republished as Pretty Boy Dead, 1984; Cocksure, 1969; Gard, 1969; Hang-Up, 1969; Fadeout, 1970; The Outward Side, 1971; Tarn House, 1971; Todd, 1971; Death Claims, 1973; Longleaf, 1974; Troublemaker, 1975; One Foot in the Boat (poems), 1977; The Man Everybody Was Afraid Of, 1978;

Skinflick, 1979; The Dog and Other Stories, 1979; A Smile in His Lifetime, 1981; Gravedigger, 1982; Backtrack, 1982; Job's Year, 1983; Nightwork, 1984; Brandsetter and Others: Five Fictions, 1984; Steps Going Down, 1985; The Little Dog Laughed, 1986; Early Graves, 1987; Bohannon's Book: Five Mysteries, 1988; Obedience, 1988; The Boy Who Was Buried This Morning, 1990; A Country of Old Men, 1991; Living Upstairs, 1993; Bohannon's Country (short stories), 1993. Contributions to: Anthologies and periodicals. Honours: National Endowment for the Arts Grant, 1974; Outstanding Literary Contribution to the Lesbian and Gay Communities Citation, Out/Look Foundation, San Francisco, 1991. Memberships: Mystery Writers of America; PEN; Private Eye Writers of America. Address: 2638 Cullen Street, Los Angeles, CA 90034, USA.

HANSEN Poul Einer, b. 24 Mar 1939, Hœve, Denmark. Associate Professor (Mathematics). m. Jette Cassias, 29 May 1993. Education: Cand Mag et Mag Scient, 1962. Publications: The Count of Monte Cristo (translation), 1991; Various books for children and adolescents (in translation), 1992-95; Af Gammel Jehannes hans Bivelskistarri, modern part, 1993; Politisk Korrekt (with Roald Als), 1995. Contributions to: Periodicals. Address: Vester Sœgade 18, 2 th, DK-1601 Copenhagen V, Denmark.

HANSON William Stewart, b. 22 Jan 1950, Doncaster, Yorkshire, England. University Lecturer; Archaeologist. m. Lesley Macinnes. Education: BA Ancient History/Archaeology, 1972, PhD Archaeology, 1982, Manchester. Publications: Rome's North-West Frontier: The Antonine Wall, 1983; Agricola and the Conquest of the North, 1987; Scottish Archaeology: New Perceptions (co-editor), 1991. Contributions to: Major academic archaeological and antiquarian journals. Memberships: Fellow, Societies of Antiquaries of London and Scotland; Vice President, Council for British Archaeology. Address: 4 Victoria Road, Stirling, Scotland.

HARBINSON Robert. See: **HARBINSON-BRYANS Robert.**

HARBINSON William Allen, b. 9 Sept 1941, Belfast, Northern Ireland. Writer. m. Ursula Elizabeth Mayer, 3 Nov 1969, 1 son, 1 daughter. Education: Belfast College of Technology, 1956-57; Liverpool College of Building, 1958-61. Publications: Genesis; Inception; Revelation; Otherworld; The Lodestone; Dream Maker; The Light of Eden; None But the Damned; Knock; Strykers Kingdom; Elvis Presley: An Illustrated Biography; Charles Bronson; George C Scott; Evita Peron; Fiction: Projekt Saucer: Book 1, Inception, Book 2, Phoenix, Book 3, Genesis, Book 4, Millennium; Biography: Growing Up With the Memphis Flash. Contributions to: Books and Bookmen; The Lady; 19; Lookout; The Unexplained; Disc; Goldmine; Club International; Mayfair. Memberships: PEN; Society of Authors; Institute of Journalists; British Film Institute. Address: 44 Rosebery Road, Muswell Hill, London, N10 2LJ, England.

HARBINSON-BRYANS Robert (Robin Bryans) b. 24 Apr 1928, Belfast, Northern Ireland. Author. Publications: Gateway to the Khyber, 1959; Madeira, 1959; Summer Saga, 1960; No Surrender, 1960; Song of Erne, 1960; Up Spake the Cabin Boy, 1961; Danish Episode, 1961; Tattoo Lily, 1962; Fanfare for Brazil, 1962; The Protégé, 1963; The Azores, 1963; Ulster, 1964; Lucio, 1964; Malta and Gozo, 1966; The Field of Sighing, 1966; Trinidad and Tobago, 1967; Faber Best True Adventure Stories (editor), 1967; Sons of El Dorado, 1968; Crete, 1969; Songs Out of Oriel; The Dust Has Never Settled, 1992; Let the Petals Fall, 1993; Checkmate, 1994. Address: 58 Argyle Road, London W13 8AA, England.

HARBOTTLE Michael Neale, b. 7 Feb 1917, Littlehampton, Sussex, England. Army. m. (1), 1 Aug 1940, div, 1 son, 1 daughter, (2) Eirwen Helen Simonds, 5 Aug 1972. Publications: The Impartial Soldier, 1970; Blue Berets, 1971; Knaves of Diamonds, 1976; The Thin Blue Line (co-author), 1974; The Peace Keepers Handbook (compiler), 1978; Ten Questions Answered, 1983; Reflections on Security in The Nuclear Age, 1988; What is Proper Soldiering, 1991. Contributions to: Various publications. Honours: Officer of the Order of the British Empire, 1960; Doctor of Philosophy, The Open International University for Complementary Medicines, 1994. Memberships: Royal Institute for International Affairs, United Kingdom; International Council, Center for Conflict Analysis and Resolution, George Mason University, Washington DC, USA. Address: 9 West Street, Chipping Norton, Oxon, OX7 5LH, England.

HARCOURT Geoffrey (Colin), b. 27 June 1931, Melbourne, Australia. Academic; Professor Emeritus; Economist; Writer. m. Joan Margaret Bartrop, 30 July 1955, 2 sons, 2 daughters. Education: BCom, Honours, 1954, MCom, 1956, University of Melbourne; PhD, 1960, LittD, 1988, Cambridge University. Appointments: Professor Emeritus, University of Adelaide, 1988; President, Jesus College, Cambridge, 1988-89, 1990-92; Reader in the History of Economic Theory, Cambridge University, 1990. Publications: Economic Activity, 1967; Readings in the Concept and Measurement of Income, 1969; Capital and Growth: Selected Readings, 1971; Some Cambridge Controversies in the Theory of Capital, 1972; The Social Science Imperialists (selected essays), 1982; Controversies in Political Economy (selected essays), 1986; Readings in the Concept and Measurement of Income (editor with R H Parker and G Whittington), 2nd edition, 1986; Keynes and His Contemporaries: The Sixth and Centennial Keynes Seminar Held in the University of Kent at Canterbury (editor), 1983; On Political Economists and Modern Political Economy (selected essays), 1992; Post-Keynesian Essays in Biography: Portraits of Twentieth Century Political Economists, 1993; The Dynamics of the Wealth of Nations: Essays in Honour of Luigi Pasinetti (editor with others), 1993; Income and Employment in Theory and Practice (editor with Alessandro Ronlaglia and Robin Rowley), 1994; Capitalism, Socialism and Post-Keynesianism: Selected Essays, 1995; A Second Edition of The General Theory (editor, with P A Riach), 2 volumes, 1997. Contributions to: Many books and scholarly journals. Honours: Economic Society of Australia, distinguished fellow, 1996; Honorary DLitt, De Montfort University, 1997. Memberships: Fellow, Academy of the Social Sciences in Australia; President, Economic Society of Australia and New Zealand, 1974-77; Officer in the General Division of the Order of Australia, 1994; Royal Economic Society. Address: Jesus College, Cambridge CB5 8BL, England.

HARCOURT Palma, Author. Publications: Climate for Conspiracy, 1974; A Fair Exchange, 1975; Dance for Diplomats, 1976; At High Risk, 1977; Agents of Influence, 1978; A Sleep of Spies, 1979; Tomorrow's Treason, 1980; A Turn of Traitors, 1981; The Twisted Tree, 1982; Shadows of Doubt, 1983; The Distant Stranger, 1984; A Cloud of Doves, 1985; A Matter of Conscience, 1986; Limited Options, 1987; Clash of Loyalties, 1988; Cover for A Traitor, 1989; Double Deceit, 1990; The Reluctant Defector, 1991; Cue For Conspiracy, 1992; Bitter Betrayal, 1993; The Vermont Myth, 1994; Shadows of the Past, 1996. Address: c/o Murray Pollinger, Literary Agent, 222 Old Brompton Road, London, SW5 0BZ, England.

HARDCASTLE Michael (David Clark), b. 6 Feb 1933, Huddersfield, England. Author. m. Barbara Ellis Shepherd, 30 Aug 1979, 4 daughters. Appointment: Literary Editor, Bristol Evening Post, 1960-65. Publications: Author of over 100 children's books, 1966-; One Kick, 1986; James and the TV Star, 1986; Mascot, 1987; Quake, 1988; The Green Machine, 1989; Walking the Goldfish, 1990; Penalty, 1990; Advantage Miss Jackson, 1991; Dog Bites Goalie, 1993; One Good Horse, 1993; Soccer Captain, 1994; Puzzle, 1995; Please Come Home, 1995. Contributions to: Numerous articles in magazines and journals. Honour: MBE, 1988. Memberships: Federation of Children's Book Groups, National Chair, 1989-90; Society of Authors. Address: 17 Molescroft Park, Beverley, East Yorkshire HU17 7EB, England.

HARDEN Blaine (Charles), b. 4 Apr 1952, Moses Lake, Washington, USA. Journalist. Education: BA, Philosophy and Political Science, Gonzaga University, 1974; MA, Journalism, Syracuse University, 1976. Appointments: Africa Correspondent, 1985-89, East European Correspondent, 1989-93, Reporter, 1995-, Washington Post. Publication: Africa: Dispatches From a Fragile Continent, 1990. Contributions to: Washington Post. Honours: Livingston Award for Young Journalists, 1986; Martha Albrand Citation for First Book of Non-Fiction, PEN, 1991; Ernie Pyle Award for Human Interest Reporting, 1993. Address: c/o Washington Post, 1150 15th Street North West, Washington, DC 20071, USA.

HARDIE (Katherine) Melissa, b. 20 Apr 1939, Houston, Texas, USA. Writer; Publisher; Collector. m. (1) J W Woelfel, 1958, 2 daughters, (2) M C Hardie, 1974, (3) Philip Graham Budden, 8 Jan 1986. Education: BA, English Language and Literature, Boston University, 1961; SRN, St Thomas Hospital, England, 1969; PhD, Social Science, Edinburgh University, 1980. Appointments: Publisher, Patten Press, 1981-; Director, Jamieson Library of Women's History, 1986-. Publications: Understanding Ageing, Facing Common Family Problems, 1978; Nursing Auxiliaries in Health Care, 1978; In Time & Place, Lamorna, Life of E Lamorna Kerr, 1990; A Mere Interlude,

Some Literary Visitors to Lyonnesse (editor), 1992; One Hundred Years at Newlyn, Diary of a Gallery (editor), 1995. Contributions to: Nursing Times; International Hospitals; Social Work Today; Health & Society Service Journal. Honours: Winston Churchill Travelling Fellow, 1975; YWCA Woman of the West, 1994. Memberships: Thomas Hardy Society; West Country Writers Association; Private Libraries Association. Address: The Old Post Office, New Mill, Penzance TR29 4XN, England.

HARDIN Clement. See: **NEWTON D(wight) B(ennett)**.

HARDING Cole. See: **KRAUZER Steven M**.

HARDING James, b. 1929, England. Appointments: Senior Lecturer in French, University of Greenwich, 1966-94. Publications: Saint-Saëns and His Circle, 1965; The Duke of Wellington, 1968; Massenet, 1970; Rossini, 1971; The Ox on the Roof, 1972; Lord Chesterfield's Letters to his Son, 1973; Erik Satie, 1975; Poulenc: My Friends and Myself (translator), 1978; Folies de Paris: The Rise and Fall of the French Operetta, 1979; Offenbach, 1980; Maurice Chevalier, 1982; Jacques Tati: Frame by Frame, 1984; James Agate, 1986; Ivor Novello, 1987; The Rocky Horror Show Book, 1987; Gerald du Maurier, 1989; George Robey and the Music Hall, 1991; Emlyn Williams, A Life, 1993. Address: 100 Ridgemount Gardens, Torrington Place, London WC1E 7AZ, England.

HARDING Karl Gunnar, b. 11 June 1940, Sundsvalla, Sweden. Poet; Translator; Critic; Editor. m. Ann Charlotte Jending, Sept 1966, 1 son, 3 daughters. Education: BA, University of Uppsala, 1967. Appointments: Editor, FIB: Lyrikklabb and Magazine, Lyrikvannen, 1971-74; Poetry Critic, Expressen, Daily Paper, 1970-88; Editor, Artes Magazine, 1989. Publications: Blommortil James Dean, 1969; Ballander, 1975; Starnberger See, 1977; Stjarndykarens, 1987; Mitt Vinterland, 1991; Vortex, 1990; Kreol, 1991. Contributions to: Evergreen Review; Ambit. Honours: Lifetime Scholarship, Swedish Writer's Union; Several Poetry Prizes. Memberships: Vice President, Swedish PEN, 1975-78; Swedish Writer's Union; Swedish Bunk Johnson Society. Address: Vasterled 206, S-16142, Bromma, Sweden.

HARDING Matt. See: **FLOREN Lee**.

HARDWICK Elizabeth, b. 27 July 1916, Lexington, Kentucky, USA. Writer; Critic; Teacher. m. Robert Lowell, 28 July 1949, div 1972, 1 daughter. Education: AB, 1938, MA, 1939, University of Kentucky; Columbia University. Appointments: Co-Founder and Advisory Editor, New York Review of Books, 1963-; Adjunct Associate Professor of English, Barnard College. Publications: Fiction: The Ghostly Lover, 1945; The Simple Truth, 1955; Sleepless Nights, 1979. Non-fiction: The Selected Letters of William James (editor), 1960; A View of My Own: Essays on Literature and Society, 1962; Seduction and Betrayal: Women and Literature, 1974; Rediscovered Fiction by American Women: A Personal Selection (editor), 18 volumes, 1977; Bartleby in Manhattan (essays), 1984; The Best American Essays 1986 (editor), 1986. Contributions to: Periodicals. Honour: Gold Medal, American Academy and Institute of Arts and Letters, 1993. Address: 15 West 67th Street, New York, NY 10023, USA.

HARDY Barbara (Gladys),Writer; Lecturer. Appointments: Emeritus Professor, University of London, Birbeck College; Honorary Professor, University College of Wales, Swansea. Publications: The Novels of George Eliot: A Study in Form, 1959; Wuthering Heights, 1963; The Appropriate Form: An Essay on the Novel, 1964; Jane Eyre, 1964; Middlemarch: Critical Approaches to the Novel, 1967; Charles Dickens: The Later Novels, 1968; Critical Essays on George Eliot, 1970; The Moral Art of Dickens, 1970; The Exposure of Luxury: Radical Themes in Thackeray, 1972; Tellers and Listeners: The Narrative Imagination, 1975; A Reading of Jane Austen, 1976; The Advantage of Lyric: Essays on Feeling in Poetry, 1976; Particularities: Readings in George Eliot, 1983; Forms of Feeling in Victorian Fiction, 1985; Narrators and Novelists, 1989; Swansea Girl, 1994; London Lovers, 1996; Henry James: The Later Writing, 1996. Memberships: Honorary Member, Modern Language Association; Fellow, Welsh Academy; Vice President, George Eliot Fellowship, Thomas Hardy Society. Address: Birkbeck College, Malet Street, London WC1E 7HX, England.

HARDY Frank, b. 21 Mar 1917, Southern Cross, Victoria, Australia. Novelist. Appointments: President, Realist Writers Group, Melbourne, Sydney, 1954-74; Co Founder, Australian Society of

Authors, Sydney, 1968-74; President, Carringbush Writers, Melbourne, 1980-83. Publications: The Four Legged Lottery, 1958; Power Without Glory, 1962; The Outcasts of Follgarah, 1971; Who Shot George Kirkland? 1981; Warrant of Distress, 1983; The Obsession of Oscar Oswald, 1983. Short Stories: The Loser Now Will be Later to Win, 1985; Hardys People, 1986. Plays: Black Diamonds, 1956; The Ringbolter, 1964; Who Was Harry Larse1985; Faces in the Street: An Epic Drama, 1990. Address: 9/76 Elizabeth Bay Road, Elizabeth Bay, New South Wales 2011, Australia.

HARE David, b. 5 June 1947, St Leonards, Sussex, England. Dramatist; Director. m. (1) Margaret Matheson, 1970, div 1980, 2 sons, 1 daughter, (2) Nicole Farhi, 1992. Education: Lancing College; MA with Honours, Jesus College, Cambridge. Appointments: Founder, Portable Theatre, 1968, Joint Stock Theatre Group, 1975, Greenpoint Films, 1982; Literary Manager and Resident Dramatist, Royal Court, 1969-71; Resident Dramatist, Nottingham Playhouse, 1973; Associate Director, National Theatre, 1984-88, 1989-. Publications: Slag, 1970; The Great Exhibition, 1972; Knuckle, 1974; Brassneck, 1974; Teeth 'n' Smiles, 1976; Plenty, 1978; Licking Hitler, 1978; Dreams of Leaving, 1980; A Map of the World, 1982; Saigon, 1983; The History Plays, 1984; Pravda, 1985; Wetherby, 1985; The Asian Plays, 1986; The Bay at Nice and Wrecked Eggs, 1986; The Secret Rapture, 1988; Paris by Night, 1989; Straples, 1990; Racing Demon, 1990; Writing Lefthanded, 1991; Heading Home, 1991; The Early Plays, 1991; Murmuring Judges, 1991; The Absence of War, 1993; Asking Around, 1993; Skylight, 1995; Mother Courage, 1995. Honours: John Llewellyn Rhys Award, 1974; BAFTA Award, 1978; New York Drama Critics' Circle Award, 1983; London Standard Award, 1985; Plays and Players Awards, 1985, 1990; Drama Award, 1988; Olivier Award, 1990; Critic's Circle Best Play of the Year, 1990; Time Out Award, 1990. Membership: Fellow, Royal Society of Literature. Address: c/o Margaret Ramsay Ltd, 14a Goodwins Court, St Martins Lane, London WC2, England.

HARFIELD Alan, b. 12 Dec 1926, Gosport, Hampshire, England. Freelance Author. m. June Bowler, 6 June 1966, 1 daughter. Publications include: A History of the Village of Chilmark, 1961; The Royal Brunei Malay Regiment, English and Malay, 1977; Headdress and Badges of the Royal Signals, 1982; British & Indian Armies in the East Indies, 1984; Blandford and the Military, 1984; Fort Canning Cemetery, 1981; Christian Cemeteries and Memorials in Malacca, 1984; Bencoolen, the Christian Cemetery and the Fort Marlborough Monuments, 1986; Early Signalling Equipment, 1986; Christian Cemeteries of Penang and Perak, 1987; Early Cemeteries in Singapore, 1988; Pigeon to Packhorse, 1989; British and Indian Armies on the China Coast 1785-1985, 1990; Indian Army of the Empress 1861-1903, 1990; Meerut, The First Sixty Years 1815-1875, 1992; Bencoolen, A History of the East India Company's Garrison on the West Coast of Sumatra 1685-1825, 1994. Contributions to: Crown Imperial; Hamilton's Medal Journal Despatch; The Military Chest; Military Historical Society Journal; Journal of the Society for Army Research; Orders & Medals Research Society Journal; Journal of the Company of Military Historians; Durbar, The Journal of Indian Military Historical Society; Special Publications of the Gosport Society. Honours: Fellow, Royal Historical Society; Fellow, Company of Military Historians (of USA, Class of 89); Military, British Empire Medal, 1953; Most Blessed Order of the Setia Negara Brunei 3rd Class. Memberships: Royal Asiatic Society; Company of Military Historians; The Military Historical Society, Hon Editor, 1978-90; Society for Army Historical Research, Hon Treasurer, 1990-93; Hon Editor & Membership Secretary, 1994-; Orders & Medals Research Society; Indian Military Historical Society, Hon Auditor. Address: Plum Tree Cottage, Royston Place, Barton-on-Sea, Hampshire BH25 7AJ, England.

HARGITAI Peter, b. 28 Jan 1947, Budapest, Hungary. Writer. m. Dianne Kress, 24 July 1967, 1 son, 1 daughter. Education: MFA, University of Massachusetts, 1988. Appointments: Lecturer in English, University of Miami, 1980-85, University of Massachusetts, 1987-88; Professor and Writing Specialist, Florida International University, 1990-. Publications: Forum: Ten Poets of the Western Reserve, 1976; Perched on Nothings Branch, 1986; Magyar Tales, 1989; Budapest to Bellevue, 1989; Budapesttöl New Yorkig és tovább..., 1991; Fodois Budget Zion, 1991; The Traveler, 1994; Attila: A Barbarian's Bedtime Story, 1994. Contributions to: North Atlantic Review; Colorado Quarterly; Nimrod; College English; California Quarterly; Spirit; Prairie Schooner; Poetry East; Cornfield Review; Blue Unicorn. Honours: Academy of American Poets Translation Award, 1988; Fulbright Grant,

1988; Florida Arts Council Fellowship, 1990; Fust Milan Award from Hungarian Academy of Sciences, 1994. Memberships: PEN International; Literary Network, New York. Address: Katalin Katai, Artisjus, Budapest, Hungary.

HARGRAVE Leonie. See: **DISCH Thomas M(ichael).**

HARING Firth. See: **FABEND Firth Haring.**

HARITAS. See: **NAGARAJA RAO C K.**

HARKEY Ira Brown, Jr, b. 15 Jan 1918, New Orleans, Louisiana, USA. Journalist; Executive; Writer. m. (1) Marie Ella Gore, 1939, div 1962, 3 sons, 3 daughters, (2) Marion Marks Drake, 10 Dec 1963, div 1976, 1 daughter, (3) Virgia Quin Mioton, 24 Feb 1977. Education: BA, Tulane University, 1941; MA, Journalism, PhD, Political Science, Ohio State University. Appointments: Staff, Times-Picayune, New Orleans, 1939-42, 1946-49; Editor, Publisher, and President, The Chronicle, Pascagoula, Mississippi, 1949-63; President, Gulf Coast Times, Ocean Springs, Mississippi, and Advertiser Printing Inc, Pascagoula, 1949-63; Faculty, Ohio State University, 1965-66; Secretary, Vice President, and Director, Oklahoma Coca-Cola Bottling Co Inc, Oklahoma City, 1965-80, and Great Plains Industries, 1979-80; Carnegie Visiting Professor, University of Alaska, 1968-69; Lecturer, University of Montana, 1970, University of Oregon, 1972; President, Indian Creek Co Inc, 1981-83. Publications: Dedicated to the Proposition..., 1963; The Smell of Burning Crosses, 1967; Pioneer Bush Pilot: The Story of Noel Wien, 1974; Alton Ochsner: Surgeon to the South (co-author), 1990. Contributions to: Periodicals. Honours: Pulitzer Prize for Distinguished Editorial Writing, 1963; Sidney Hillman Foundation Award, 1963; Sigma Delta Chi National Award for Distinguished Public Service in Newspaper Journalism, 1963; Civil Libertarian of the Year Award, Mississippi Civil Liberties Union, 1992; Hall of Fame, Mississippi Press Association, 1993. Memberships: American Political Science Association; Authors Guild; Delta Kappa Epsilon; Kappa Tau Alpha; Phi Beta Kappa; Pi Sigma Alpha. Address: HCR 5, Box 574-540, Kerrville, TX 78028, USA.

HARKNETT Terry, (Frank Chandler, David Ford, William M James, Charles R Pike, James Russell, William Terry), b. 14 Dec 1936, Rainham, Essex, England. Writer. Appointments: Editor, Newspaper Features Ltd, 1958-61; Reporter and Features Editor, National Newsagent, 1961-72. Publications: Edge series: The Godforsaken, 1982; Arapaho Revenge, 1983; The Blind Side, 1983; House of the Range, 1983; Edge Meets Steele No 3 Double Action, 1984; The Moving Cage, 1984; School for Slaughter, 1985; Revenge Ride, 1985; Shadow of the Gallows, 1985; A Time for Killing, 1986; Brutal Border, 1986; Hitting Paydirt, 1986; Backshort, 1987; Uneasy Riders, 1987. Adam Steele series: Canyon of Death, 1985; High Stakes, 1985; Rough Justice, 1985; The Sunset Ride, 1986; The Killing Strain, 1986; The Big Gunfight, 1987; The Hunted, 1987; Code of the West, 1987. The Undertaker series: Three Graves to a Showdown, 1982; Back from the Dead, 1982; Death in the Desert, 1982. As William Terry: Red Sun (novelization of screenplay), 1972. As Frank Chandler: A Fistful of Dollars (novelization of screenplay), 1972. As Charles R Pike: Jubal Cade series, The Killing Trail, 1974; Double Cross, 1974; The Hungary Gun, 1975. As William M James: Apache series - The First Death, 1974; Duel to the Death, 1974; Fort Treachery, 1975. As Terry Harknett: The Caribbean, 1972. As James Russell: The Balearic Islands, 1972. As David Ford: Cyprus, 1973; Address: Spring Acre, Springhead Road, Uplyme, Lyme Regis, Dorset DT7 3RS, England.

HARLAN Louis R(udolph), b. 13 July 1922, West Point, Mississippi, USA. Professor Emeritus; Historian. m. Sadie Morton, 6 Sept 1947, 2 sons. Education: BA, Emory University, 1943; MA, Vanderbilt University, 1948; PhD, Johns Hopkins University, 1955. Appointments: Assistant to Associate Professor, East Texas State College, 1950-59; Associate Professor to Professor, University of Cincinnati, 1959-66; Professor of History, 1966-84, Distinguished Professor of History, 1984-92, Professor Emeritus, 1992-, University of Maryland, College Park. Publications: Separate and Unequal, 1958; The Booker T Washington Papers (Editor), 14 volumes, 1972-89; Booker T Washington: Volume I, The Making of a Black Leader, 1972, Volume II, The Wizard of Tuskegee, 1983; Booker T Washington in Perspective, 1988. Contributions to: Periodicals. Honours: Bancroft Prizes, 1973, 1984; Guggenheim Fellowship, 1975; Pulitzer Prize in Biography, 1984; Albert J Beveridge Award, 1984; Julian P Boyd Award, 1989; National Historical Publications and Records

Commission Award, 1991. Memberships: President, American Historical Association, 1989; Association for the Study of Afro-American Life and History; National Historical Publications and Records Commission; President, Organization of American Historians, 1989-90; Phi Beta Kappa; Phi Kappa Phi; Fellow, Society of American Historians. Address: 6924 Pineway, Hyattsville, MD 20782, USA.

HARLE Elizabeth. See: **ROBERTS Irene.**

HARLEMAN Ann, b. 28 Oct 1945, Youngstown, Ohio, USA. Writer; Educator. m. Bruce A Rosenberg, 20 June 1981, 1 daughter. Education: BA, English Literature, Rutgers University, 1967; PhD, Linguistics, Princeton University, 1972; MFA, Creative Writing, Brown University, 1988. Appointments: Assistant Professor of English, Rutgers University, 1973-74; Assistant Professor of English, 1974-79, Associate Professor,1979-84, University of Washington; Visiting Professor of Rhetoric, Massachusetts Institute of Technology, 1984-86; Visiting Scholar, Programme in American Civilisation, Brown University, 1986-; Cole Distinguished Professor of English, Wheaton College, 1992. Publications: Graphic Representation of Models in Linguistic Theory, 1976; Ian Fleming: A Critical Biography (with Bruce A Rosenberg), 1989; Mute Phone Calls, (translation of fiction by Ruth Zernova), 1992; Happiness, 1994; Bitter Lake, 1996. Honours: Guggenheim Fellowship, 1976; Fulbright Fellowship, 1980; Raymond Carver Contest, 1986; MacDowell Colony Fellow, 1988; National Endowment for the Humanities Fellowship, 1989; Rhode Island State Council on the Arts Fellowship, 1990; PEN Syndicated Fiction Award, 1991; Iowa Short Fiction Prize, 1993; Senior Fellow, American Council of Learned Societies, 1993. Memberships: Modern Language Association, Chair, General Linguistics Executive Committee; Poets and Writers; PEN American Center. Address: 55 Summit Avenue, Providence, RI 02906, USA.

HARMON Maurice, b. 21 June 1930, Dublin, Ireland. Professor Emeritus; Writer; Editor. Education: BA, 1951, HDE, 1953, MA, 1955, PhD, 1961, University College, Dublin; AM, Harvard University, 1957. Appointments: Lecturer in English, 1964-76, Associate Professor of Anglo-Irish Literature and Drama, 1976-90, Professor Emeritus, 1990-, University College, Dublin; Editor, University Review, 1964-68, Irish University Review, 1970-. Publications: Romeo and Juliet, by Shakespeare (editor), 1970; J M Synge Centenary Papers 1971 (editor), 1971; King Richard II, by Shakespeare (editor), 1971; Coriolanus, by Shakespeare (editor), 1972; The Poetry of Thomas Kinsella, 1974; The Irish Novel in Our Time (editor with Patrick Rafroidi), 1976; Select Bibliography for the Study of Anglo-Irish Literature and Its Backgrounds, 1976; Richard Murphy: Poet of Two Traditions (editor), 1978; Irish Poetry After Yeats: Seven Poets (editor), 1979; Image and Illusion: Anglo-Irish Literature and Its Contexts (editor), 1979; A Short History of Anglo-Irish Literature From Its Origins to the Present (with Roger McHugh), 1982; The Irish Writer and the City (editor), 1985; James Joyce: The Centennial Symposium (with Morris Beja et al), 1986; Austin Clarke: A Critical Introduction, 1989; The Book of Precedence (poems), 1994; Sean O'Faolan, A Life, 1994. Address: 20 Sycamore Road, Mount Merrion, Blackrock, County Dublin, Ireland.

HARPER Daniel, See: **BROSSARD Chandler.**

HARPER Marjory-Ann Denoon, Dr, b. 6 Apr 1956, Blackpool, Lancashire, England. University Lecturer. m. Andrew J Shere, 22 Aug 1991. Education: MA Hons History, 1978, PhD, 1984, University of Aberdeen. Publications: Emigration from North East Scotland: Willing Exiles, 1988; Emigration from North East Scotland: Beyond the Broad Atlantic, 1988. Contributions to: History Today; British Journal of Canadian Studies; Northern Scotland; Southwestern Historical Quarterly; Aberdeen Leopard; The Weekend Scotsman; Glasgow Herald; The Highlander. Memberships: Fellow, Royal Historical Society; British Association of Canadian Studies. Address: Department of History, University of Aberdeen, Old Aberdeen AB9 2UB, Scotland.

HARPER Michael S(teven), b. 18 Mar 1938, New York, New York, USA. Professor of English; Poet. m. 3 children. Education: BA, 1961, MA, 1963, California State University at Los Angeles; MA, University of Iowa Writers Workshop, 1963; ad eundem, Brown University, 1972. Appointments: Visiting Professor, Lewis and Clark College, 1968-69; Reed College, 1968-69; Harvard University, 1974-77, Yale University, 1976; Professor of English, Brown University, 1970-; Benedict Distinguished Professor, Carleton College, 1979; Elliston Poet and Distinguished Professor, University of

Cincinnati, 1979; National Endowment for the Humanities Professor, Colgate University, 1985; Distinguished Minority Professor, University of Delaware, 1988, Macalester College, 1989; 1st Poet Laureate of the State of Rhode Island, 1988-93; Phi Beta Kappa Visiting Scholar, 1991; Berg Distinguished Visiting Professor, New York University, 1992. Publications: Dear John, Dear Coltrane, 1970; History is Your Own Heartbeat, 1971; History as Apple Tree, 1972; Song: I Want a Witness, 1972; Debridement, 1973; Nightmare Begins Responsibility, 1975; Images of Kin, 1977; Chant of Saints (co-editor), 1979; Healing Song for the Inner Ear, 1985; Songlines: Mosaics, 1991; Every Shut Eye Ain't Asleep, 1994; Honorable Admendments, 1995; Collected Poems, 1996. Honours: Black Academy of Arts and Letters Award, 1972; National Institute of Arts and Letters Grants, 1975, 1976, 1985; Guggenheim Fellowship, 1976; Melville Cane Award, Poetry Society of America, 1978; Governor's Poetry Award, Rhode Island Council of the Arts, 1987; Robert Hayden Memorial Poetry Award, United Negro College Fund, 1990; Literary Lion, New York Public Library, 1992; Honorary doctorates. Membership: American Academy of Arts and Sciences. Address: c/o Department of English, Brown University, Providence, RI 02912, USA.

HARPER Stephen (Dennis), b. 15 Sep 1924, Newport, Monmouthshire, England. Journalist. Publications: Novels: A Necessary End, 1975; Mirror Image, 1976; Live Till Tomorrow, 1977. Non-Fiction: Last Sunset, 1978; Miracle of Deliverance, 1985. Membership: Society of Authors. Address: Green Dene Lodge, Greene Dene, East Horsley, Surrey, England.

HARRINGTON Alan Stewart, b. 16 Jan 1919, Newton, Massachusetts, USA. Writer. m. (1) Virginia Hannah Luba Petrova, 28 Nov 1941, (2) Margaret Young, 18 Jan 1968, 2 sons, 1 daughter. Education: AB, English Literature, Harvard University, 1939. Appointments: Adjunct Lecturer, Creative Writing Programme, University of Arizona, 1983-92; Lecturer in Creative Writing, University of Arizona Extended University, 1990-92. Publications: The Revelations of Dr Modesto: Life in the Crystal Palace, 1959; The Secret Swinger, 1966; The Immortalist, 1969; Psychopaths... 1972; Love and Evil: From a Probation Officer's Casebook, 1974; Paradise I, 1978; The White Rainbow, 1981. Contributions to: Harper's; Atlantic; Saturday Review; Nation; New Republic; Playboy; Penthouse; Chicago Review. Memberships: PEN; Author's Guild. Address: 2831 North Orlando Avenue, Tucson, AZ 85712, USA.

HARRIS Francis C, b. 25 Sept 1957, Brooklyn, New York, USA. Author; Historian. Education: Masters of Education/Management, Cambridge College, Massachusetts, 1992-. Appointments: Senior Researcher, A Hard Road to Glory, A History of the African American Athlete by Arthur R Ashe Jr, 1983-86, 1987, 1992-93. Publication: The Amistad Pictorial History of the African American Athlete, 1997. Address: 140-35 Burden Crescent, #207, Briarwood, New York 11435, USA.

HARRIS Jana N, b. 21 Sep 1947, San Francisco, California, USA. Writer. m. Mark Allen Bothwell. Education: BS, University of Oregon, 1969; MA, San Francisco State University, 1972. Appointments: Instructor, Creative Writing, New York University, 1980; University of Washington, 1986-, Pacific Lutheran University, 1988. Publications: This House That Rocks with Every Truck on the Road, 1976; Pin Money, 1977; The Clackamas, 1980; Alaska (novel), 1980; Who's That Pushy Bitch, 1981; Running Scared, 1981; Manhattan as a Second Language, 1982; The Sourlands, Poems by Jana Harris, 1989; Oh How Can I Keep on Singing, Voices of Pioneer Women (Poems), 1993. Contributions to: Periodicals. Honours: Berkeley Civic Arts Commemoration Grant 1974; Washington State Arts Council Fellowship, 1993. Memberships: Feminist Writers Guild; Associated Writing Programs; Women's Salon; PEN; Poetry Society of America; National Book Critics Club. Address: 32814 120th Street South East, Sultan, WA 98294, USA.

HARRIS Jocelyn Margaret, b. 10 Sept 1939, Dunedin, New Zealand. University Teacher; Writer. 1 son, 1 daughter. Education: MA, University of Otago; PhD, University of London. Appointments: Faculty, Department of English, University of Otago. Publications: Samuel Richardson: Sir Charles Grandison (editor), 1972; Samuel Richardson, 1989; Jane Austen's Art of Memory, 1989. Contributions to: Scholarly journals. Membership: Australian and South Pacific 18th Century Society. Address: c/o Department of English, University of Otago, Box 56, Dunedin, New Zealand.

HARRIS Kenneth, b . 11 Nov 1919. Journalist; Author; Business Executive. m. (1) Doris Young-Smith, 1949, dec 1970, (2) Jocelyn Rymer, 1987. Education: Wadham College, Oxford. Appointments: War Service, R.A, 1940-45; Washington Correspondent, 1950-53, Associate Editor, 1976-, Director, 1978, The Observer; Radio and TV work (mainly for BBC), 1957-; Chairman, George Outram Ltd, The Observer Group, 1981-. Publications: Travelling Tongues: Debating Across America, 1949; About Britain, 1967; Conversations, 1968; Life of Attlee, 1982; The Wildcatter: The Life of Robert O Anderson; David Owen, 1987; Thatcher, 1988. Address: The Observer, Chelsea Bridge House, Queenstown Road, London SW8, England.

HARRIS Lavinia. See: **JOHNSTON Norma.**

HARRIS Marion Rose, (Rose Glendower, Rose Young), b. 12 July 1925, Cardiff, South Wales. Author. m. Kenneth Mackenzie Harris, 18 Aug 1943, 2 sons, 1 daughter. Appointments: Freelance, 1953-63; Editor/Owner, Regional Feature Service, 1964-74; Editorial Controller, W Foulsham and Company Ltd, 1974-82; Authorship, 1982-. Publications: Captain of Her Heart, 1976; Just a Handsome Stranger, 1983; The Queen's Windsor, 1985; Soldiers' Wives, 1986; Officers' Ladies, 1987; Nesta, 1988; Amelda, 1989; Sighing for The Moon (as Rose Glendower), 1991; To Love and Love Again (as Rose Young), 1993. Memberships: Society of Authors; Romantic Novelists Association; The Welsh Academy. Literary Agent: International Scripts, 1 Norland Square, Holland Park, London, W1 4PX, England. Address: Walpole Cottage, Long Drive, Burnham, Slough, SL1 8AJ, England.

HARRIS Philip Robert, b. 22 Jan 1926, New York, New York, USA. Management Consultant; Writer; Editor. m. Dorothy Lipp, 3 July 1965. Education: BBA, St John's University, 1949; New York University, 1948-49; MS in Psychology, 1952, PhD, 1956, Fordham University; Syracuse University, 1961. Appointments: Director of Guidance, St Francis Preparatory School, New York City, 1952-56; Director of Student Personnel and Vice-President, St Francis College, New York City, 1956-63; Fulbright Professor to India, 1962-63; Visiting Professor, Penn State University, 1965-66; Senior Associate, Leadership Resources Inc, 1966-69; Vice-President, Copley International Corp, 1970-71; President, Management and Organizational Development Inc, and its successor, Harris International Ltd, La Jolla, California, 1971-; Research Associate, California Space Institute, University of California at San Diego, 1984-90; Senior Scientist, Netrologic Inc, La Jolla, 1990-93; Executive Editor, Space Governance Journal, 1993-95; Executive Vice President, United Societies in Space Inc, 1994-; Founding Editor Emeritus, 1996-. Publications: Organizational Dynamics, 1973; Effective Management of Change, 1976; Improving Management Communication Skills (with D Harris), 1978; Managing Cultural Differences (with R Moran), 1979, 4th edition, 1996; Innovations in Global Consultation (with G Malin), 1980; Managing Cultural Synergy (with R Moran), 1982; New Worlds, New Ways, New Management, 1983; Global Strategies for Human Resource Development, 1984; Management in Transition, 1985; Living and Working in Space, 1992, 2nd edition, 1996; Transcultural Leadership (with G M Simmons and C Vaquez), 1993; Multicultural Management (with F Elashmarie), 1993, 2nd edition, 1997; Developing Global Organizations (with R Moran and W Stripp), 1993; Multicultural Law Enforcement (co-author), 1994; High Performance Leadership, 1989, 2nd edition, 1994; The New Work Culture Series, 3 volumes, 1994-97. Contributions to: 200 articles published in numerous professional journals. Honours: 4 Journalism Awards, Aviation Space Writers Association, 1986, 1988, 1989, 1993. Membership: American Institute of Aeronautics and Astronautics, associate fellow; Editorial Advisory Board, European Business Review, 1990-. Address: 2702 Costebelle Drive, La Jolla, CA 93037, USA.

HARRIS Randy Allen, b. 6 Sept 1956, Kitimat, British Columbia,Canada. Professor; Author. m. Indira Naidoo-Harris, 4 Aug 1984. Education: BA, honours, English Literature, Queen's University, 1980; MA, English Literature, Dalhousie University, 1982; MSc, Linguistics, University of Alberta, 1985; MS, Technical Communication, 1986; PhD, Communication and Rhetoric, 1990, Rensselaer Polytechnic Institute. Publications: Acoustic Dimensions of Functor Comprehension in Broca's Aphasia, 1988; Linguistics Wars, 1993; Landmark Essays in Rhetoric of Science, 1995. Contributions to: College English; Perspectives on Science; Rhetoric Review; Historiographia Linguistica; Rhetoric Society Quarterly; Neuropsychologia. Honours: Heritage Scholar; Rensselaer Scholar; Killam Scholar; Killam Fellow. Memberships: Authors Guild; Linguistic

Society of America. Address: Department of English, University of Waterloo, Waterloo, Ontario N2L 3G1, Canada.

HARRIS Robert (Dennis), b. 7 Mar 1957, Nottingham, England. Writer. m. Gillian Hornby, 1988, 1 son, 1 daughter. Education: BA, honours, Selwyn College, Cambridge, 1978. Appointments: Researcher and Film Director for Tonight, Nationwide and Panorama, 1978-81, Reporter for Newsnight, 1981-85, and for Panorama, BBC, 1985-87; Political Editor, Observer, London, 1987-89; Political Reporter for This Week, Thames Television, 1988-89; Political Columnist, Sunday Times, London, 1989-92. Publications: A Higher Form of Killing: The Secret of Gas and Germ Warfare (with Jeremy Paxman), 1982; Form of Killing: The Secret Story of Chemical and Biological Warfare, 1982; Gotcha!: The Media, the Government, and the Falklands Crisis, 1983; The Making of Neil Kinnock, 1984; Selling Hitler, 1987; Good and Faithful Servant: The Unauthorized Biography of Bernard Ingham, 1990; Fatherland (novel), 1992; Enigma (novel), 1996. Address: The Old Vicarage, Kintbury, Berkshire R915 0TR, England.

HARRIS Rosemary (Jeanne), b. 12 July 1925, Cardiff, Wales. Author. Appointments: Formerly picture restorer, Reader for Metro-Goldwyn-Mayer, 1951-52; Children's Book Reviewer, The Times, London, 1970-73. Publications: The Summer-House, 1956; Voyage to Cythera, 1958; Venus with Sparrows, 1961; All My Enemies, 1967; The Nice Girl's Story, 1968 (in USA as Nor Evil Dreams, 1974); The Moon in The Cloud, 1968; A Wicked Pack of Cards, 1969; The Shadow on the Sun, 1970; The Seal-Singing, 1971; The Child in the Bamboo Grove, 1972; The Bright and Morning Star, 1972; The King's White Elephant, 1973; The Double Snare, 1974; The Lotus and the Grail: Legends from East to West (abridged edition in USA as Sea Magic and Other Stories of Enchantment), 1974; The Flying Ship, 1975; The Little Dog of Fo, 1976; Three Candles for the Dark, 1976; I Want to Be a Fish, 1977; A Quest for Orion, 1978; Beauty and the Beast (folklore), 1979; Green Finger House, 1980; Tower of the Stars, 1980; The Enchanted Horse, 1981; Janni's Stork, 1981; Zed, 1982; Summers of the Wild Rose, 1987; Love and The Merry-Go-Round, 1988; Ticket to Freedom, 1991. Honour: Library Association Carnegie Medal, 1967. Membership: Society of Authors. Address: c/o A P Watt Ltd, 20 John Street, London, WC1N 2DR, England.

HARRIS Thomas, b. 1940, USA. Writer. Publications: Black Sunday, 1975; Red Dragon, 1981; Silence of the Lambs, 1988. Address: c/o St Martin's Press, 175 5th Avenue, New York, NY 10010, USA.

HARRIS William M(cKinley) Sr, b. 29 Oct 1941, Richmond, Virginia, USA. Professor of City Planning; Writer. 3 daughters. Education: BS in Physics, Howard University, 1964; Master of Urban Planning, 1972, PhD, 1974, University of Washington, Seattle. Appointments: Director, Center for Urban Studies, Western Washington State University, Seattle, 1974; Assistant Professor, Portland State University, 1974-76; Associate Professor, 1976-82, Professor of City Planning, 1982-, University of Virginia; Adjunct Professor of Urban Planning, Virginia State University, 1979-85; Visiting Professor, Cornell University, 1986. Publications: A Design for Desegregation Evaluation, 1976; Black Community Development, 1976; Perspectives on Black Studies (with Darrell Millner), 1977. Contributions to: The Ethics of Social Intervention, 1978; Lectures: Black Scholars on Black Issues, 1979; The Housing Status of Black Americans, 1992; Confronting Environmental Racism: Voices from the Grassroots, 1993; Journal of Black Studies; Journal of Environmental Management; Also articles in professional journals. Honour: NDEA Fellow, University of Washington, 1992-94. Memberships: American Planning Association; American Institute of Certified Planners; Association for the Study of Afro-American Life and History; International Association of Community Development; Team Leader, APA Community Planning Team, 1995-96; Urban Affairs Association. Address: 485 14th Street North West, Charlottesville, VA 22903, USA.

HARRIS (Theodore) Wilson, b. 24 Mar 1921, New Amsterdam, British Guiana. Poet; Novelist. m. (1) Cecily Carew, 1945, (2) Margaret Whitaker, 1959. Education: Queen's College, Georgetown. Appointments: Visiting Lecturer, State University of New York, Buffalo, 1970; Writer-in-Residence, University of West Indies, Kingston, Jamaica, Scarborough College, University of Toronto, 1970, University of Newcastle, New South Wales, 1979; Commonwealth Fellow in Caribbean Literature, Leeds University, Yorkshire, 1971; Visiting

Professor, University of Texas, Austin, 1972, 1981-82, University of Mysore, 1978; Yale University, New Haven, Connecticut, 1979; Regents Lecturer, University of California, Santa Cruz, 1983. Publications: Verse: Fetish, 1951; The Well and the Land, 1952; Eternity to Season, 1954, revised edition, 1979. Novels: The Guyana Quartet, 1960-63; Tumatumari, 1968; Black Marsden, 1972; Companions of the Day and Night, 1975; Da Silva's Cultivated Wilderness, 1977; Genesis of the Clowns, 1977; The Tree of the Sun, 1978; The Angel at the Gate, 1982; The Carnival Trilogy, 1985-90; Resurrection at Sorrow Hill, 1993-. Other: Short stories and other publications. Address: c/o Faber and Faber Ltd, 3 Queen Square, London WC1N 3AU, England.

HARRISON Edward Hardy, (Ted Harrison), b. 28 Aug 1926, Wingate, County Durham, England. Artist; Writer. m. Robina McNicol, 12 Nov 1960, 1 son. Education: Hartlepool College of Art, 1943-45, 1948-50; National Diploma, Design, Kings College, Newcastle-upon-Tyne, 1951; BEd, University of Alberta, Canada, 1977. Publications: Children of the Yukon, 1977; The Last Horizon, 1980; A Northern Alphabet, 1982; The Blue Raven (television story), 1987, Canada, 1992. Honours: Best Childrens Book, A Child Study Association of Canada, 1977; Choice Book, Childrens Book Centre, Toronto, 1978; Ibby - Certificate of Honour for Illustration, 1984. Memberships: Writers Union of Canada; Order of Canada; PEN, Canada; Honorary Doctorate, Athabasca University, 1991. Address: 2029 Romney Place, Victoria, British Columbia V8S 4J6, Canada.

HARRISON Elizabeth Fancourt, b. 12 Jan 1921, Watford, Hertfordshire, England. Author. Publications: Coffee at Dobree's, 1965; The Physicians, 1966; The Ravelston Affair, 1967; Corridors of Healing, 1968; Emergency Call, 1970; Accident Call, 1971; Ambulance Call, 1972; Surgeon's Call, 1973; On Call, 1974; Hospital Call, 1975; Dangerous Call, 1976; To Mend a Heart, 1977; Young Dr Goddard, 1978; A Doctor Called Caroline, 1979; A Surgeon Called Amanda, 1982; A Surgeon's Life, 1983; Marrying a Doctor, 1984; Surgeon's Affair, 1985; A Surgeon at St Mark's, 1986; The Surgeon She Married, 1988; The Faithful Type, 1993; The Senior Partner's Daughter, 1994; Made for Each Other, 1995. Honours: Runner-up, 1970, shortlisted, 1971, 1972, 1973, major award, Romantics Novelists Association. Memberships: Society of Authors; Romantic Novelists Association. Address: 71 Wingfield Road, Kingston on Thames, Surrey, KT2 5LR, England.

HARRISON James (Thomas), (Jim Harrison), b. 11 Dec 1937, Grayling, Michigan. Author; Poet. m. Linda May King, 10 Oct 1959, 2 daughters. Education: BA, 1960, MA, 1964, Michigan State University. Appointment: Instructor, State University of New York at Stony Brook, 1965-66. Publications: Fiction: Wolf: A False Memoir, 1971; A Good Day to Die, 1973; Farmer, 1976; Legends of the Fall, 1979; Warlock, 1981; Sundog, 1984; Dalva, 1988; The Woman Lit by Fireflies, 1990; Sunset Limited, 1990; Julip, 1994. Poetry: Plain Song, 1965; Locations, 1968; Walking, 1969; Outlyer and Ghazals, 1971; Letters to Yesinin, 1973; Returning to Earth, 1977; New and Selected Poems, 1961-81, 1982; The Theory and Practice of Rivers, 1986; Country Stores, 1993. Screenplays: Cold Feet (with Tom McGuane), 1989; Revenge (with Jeffrey Fishkin), 1990; Wolf (with Wesley Strick), 1994. Non-Fiction: Just Before Dark, 1991. Honours: National Endowment for the Arts Grant, 1967-69; Guggenheim Fellowship, 1968-69. Address: PO Box 135, Lake Leelanau, MI 49653, USA.

HARRISON Raymond Vincent, b. 28 Oct 1928, Chorley, Lancashire, England. Inspector of Taxes; Financial Consultant. m. 7 Apr 1977. Education: BA Hons, 1952; MA, 1954, Magdalene College, Cambridge. Publications: French Ordinary Murder, 1983; Death of An Honourable Member, 1984; Deathwatch, 1985; Death of a Dancing Lady, 1985; Counterfeit of Murder, 1986; A Season for Death, 1987; Harvest of Death, 1988; Tincture of Death, 1989; Sphere of Death, 1990; Patently Murder, 1991; Akin to Murder, 1992; Murder in Petticoat Square, 1993; Murder by Design, 1996. Address: Forthill, Kinsale, County Cork, Eire.

HARRISON Sarah, b. 7 Aug 1946, Exeter, England. Author. Education: BA, University of London, 1967. Appointment: Journalist, IPC Magazines, London, 1967-71. Publications: The Flowers of the Field, 1980; In Granny's Garden (children's book), 1980; A Flower That's Free, 1984; Hot Breath, 1985; Laura From Lark Rise, series (children's books), 4 volumes, 1986; An Imperfect Lady, 1987; Cold Feet, 1989; Foreign Parts, 1991; The Forests of the Night, 1992; Be An Angel, 1993; Both Your Houses, 1995; Life After Lunch, 1996.

Non-Fiction: How to Write a Blockbuster, 1995. Address: 17 Station Road, Steeple Morden, Royston, Hertfordshire, England.

HARRISON Sue (Ann McHaney), b. 29 Aug 1950, Lansing, Michigan, USA. Novelist. m. Neil Douglas Harrison, 22 Aug 1969, 1 son, 2 daughters, 1 dec. Education: BA, English, 1971. Publications: Mother Earth, Father Sky, 1990; My Sister the Moon, 1992; Brother Wind, 1994. Address: PO Box 6, 18 Mile Road, Pickford, MI 49774, USA.

HARRISON Tony, b. 30 Apr 1937, Leeds, England. Poet; Translator. m. (1) Rosemarie Crossfield, 1960, 1 son, 1 daughter, (2) Teresa Stratas, 1984. Education: BA, University of Leeds. Appointments: Lecturer in English, Ahmadu Bello University, Zaria, Nigeria, 1962-66, Charles University, Prague, 1966-67; Northern Arts Fellow in Poetry, University of Newcastle and University of Durham, 1967-68, 1976-77; UNESCO Fellow in Poetry, Cuba, Brazil, Senegal, The Gambia, 1969; Gregynog Arts Fellow, University of Wales, 1973-74; Resident Dramatist, National Theatre, 1977-79; UK/US Bicentennial Fellow, New York, 1979-80. Publications: Earthworks, 1964; Aitkin Mata (play with J Simmons), 1965; Newcastle is Peru, 1969; The Loiners, 1970; Voortrekker, 1972; The Misanthrope (translation of Molière's play), 1973; Poems of Palladas of Alexandria (editor and translator), 1973; Phaedra Britannica (translation of Racine's Phèdre), 1975; Bow Down (music theatre), 1977; The Passion (play), 1977; The Bartered Bridge (libretto), 1978; From the "School of Eloquence" and Other Poems, 1978; Continuous, 1981; A Kumquat for John Keats, 1981; The Oresteia (translation), 1981; US Martial, 1981; Selected Poems, 1984, revised edition, 1987; Dramatic Verse, 1973-1985, 1985; The Fire-Gap, 1985; The Mysteries, 1985; V, 1985; Theatre Works, 1973-1985, 1986; Loving Memory, 1987; The Blasphemers' Banquet, 1989; The Trackers of Oxyrhynchus, 1990; V and Other Poems, 1990; A Cold Coming: Gulf War Poems, 1991; The Common Chorus, 1992; The Gaze of the Gorgon, 1992; Square Rounds, 1992; Black Daisies for the Bride, 1993; Poetry or Bust, 1993; A Maybe Day in Kazakhstan, 1994; The Shadow of Hiroshima, 1995; Permanently Bard, 1995; The Prince's Ray, 1996; The Labourers of Herakles (plays) 1996. Honours: Cholmondley Award for Poetry, 1969; Geoffrey Faber Memorial Prize, 1972; European Poetry Translation Prize, 1983; Whitbread Award for Poetry, 1992; Prix d'Italia, 1994. Memberships: Classical Association, President, 1987-88; Royal Society of Literature, Fellow. Address: c/o Peters, Fraser & Dunlop, 5th Floor, The Chambers, Chelsea Harbour, Lots Road, London SW10 0XF, England.

HARRY J S, b. 1939, Adelaide, South Australia, Australia. Poet. Appointments: Writer-in-Residence, Australian National University, Canberra, 1989, Narrabundah College, Canberra, 1995. Publications: The Deer Under the Skin, 1970; Hold for a Little While, and Turn Gently, 1979; A Dandelion for Van Gogh, 1985; Life on Water and the Life Beneath, 1995; Selected Poems, 1995. Honours: Harri Jones Memorial Prize, 1971; PEN International Lynne Phillips Prize, 1987. Address: PO Box 184, Randwick, New South Wales 2031, Australia.

HARSENT David, b. 9 Dec 1942, Devonshire, England. Poet; Writer. m. (1), div, 2 sons, 1 daughter, (2), 1 daughter. Appointments: Fiction Critic, Times Literary Supplement, London, 1965-73; Poetry Critic, Spectator, London, 1970-73. Publications: Poetry: Tonight's Lover, 1968; A Violent Country, 1969; Ashridge, 1970; After Dark, 1973; Truce, 1973; Dreams of the Dead, 1977; Mister Punch, 1984; Selected Poems, 1989; News From the Front, 1993. Novel: From an Inland Sea, 1985. Libretto: Gawain (for Harrison Birtwistle's Opera), 1991. Editor: New Poetry 7, 1981; Poetry Book Society Supplement, 1983; Savremena Britanska Poezija, 1988. Honours: Eric Gregory Award, 1967; Cheltenham Festival Prize, 1968; Arts Council Bursaries, 1969, 1984; Geoffrey Faber Memorial Prize, 1978; Society of Authors Travel Fellowship, 1989. Address: c/o Oxford University Press, Walton Street, Oxford OX2 6DP, England.

HART Jonathan Locke, b. 30 June 1956, Halifax, Nova Scotia, Canada. Professor. m. Mary Alice Marshall, 15 Aug 1981, 1 son, 1 daughter. Education: BA, 1978; MA, 1979; PhD, 1984. Publications: Theater and World, 1992; Northrop Five, 1994; Explorations in Difference, 1996; Reading the Renaissance, 1996; Imagining Culture, 1996; Breath and Dust, 1996. Contributions to: Harvard Review; Quarry; Antigonish Review; Mattoid; Grain; Dalhousie Review. Honours: Senior Fellow, Toronto, 1986; Visiting Scholar, Harvard University, 1986-87; Visiting Fellow, Cambridge, 1993-94; Fulbright

Fellow, Harvard University, 1996-97. Address: Department of English, University of Alberta, Edmonton, Alberta T6G 2E5, Canada.

HART Kevin, b. 5 July 1954, London, England (Australian citizen). Professor of English; Poet. Education: Stanford University, California, and University of Melbourne; PhD, 1987. Appointments: Lecturer in English, Melbourne University, Australia, 1986-87; Lecturer in Literary Studies, Deakin University, Victoria, 1987-91; Senior Lecturer, 1991-95, Associate Professor, 1991-95, Professor of English, 1995-, Monash University. Publications: Nebuchadnezzar, 1976; The Departure, 1978; The Lines of the Hand: Poems 1976-79; Your Shadow, 1984; Peniel, 1990; The Buried Harbour, 1990; A D Hope, 1992; The Oxford Book of Australian Religious Verse (editor), 1994; New and Selected Poems, 1995; Dark Angel, 1996. Honours: Australian Literature Board Fellowship, 1977; New South Wales Premier's Award, 1985; Grace Levin Award for Poetry, 1991. Memberships: Editor, Johnson Society of Australia; Fellow, Australian Academy of the Humanities. Address: 247 Richardson Street, North Carlton, Victoria 3054, Australia.

HART Veronica. See: **KELLEHER Victor.**

HART-DAVIS Duff, b. 3 June 1936, London, England. Author. Education: Eton College, 1949-54; BA, Oxford University, 1960. Appointments: Feature Writer, 1972-76, Literary Editor, 1976-77, Assistant Editor, 1977-78, Sunday Telegraph, London; Country Columnist, Independent, 1986-. Publications: The Megacull, 1968; The Gold of St Matthew (in USA as The Gold Trackers), 1968; Spider in the Morning, 1972; Ascension: The Story of a South Atlantic Island, 1972; Peter Fleming (biography), 1974; Monarchs of the Glen, 1978; The Heights of Rimring, 1980; Fighter Pilot (with C Strong), 1981; Level Five, 1982; Fire Falcon, 1984; The Man-Eater of Jassapur, 1985; Hitler's Games, 1986; Armada, 1988; The House the Berrys Built, 1990; Horses at War, 1991; Country Matters, 1991; Wildings: The Secret Garden of Eileen Soper, 1992; Further Country Matters, 1993. Address: Owlpen Farm, Uley, Dursley, Gloucestershire, England.

HART-DAVIS Sir Rupert (Charles), b. 28 Aug 1907, London, England. Author; Editor; Former Publisher. m. (1) Peggy Ashcroft, 1929, div, (2) Catherine Comfort Borden-Turner, 1933, 2 sons, 1 daughter, div, (3) Winifred Ruth Simon, 1964, dec 1967, (4) June Clifford, 1968. Education: Eton; Balliol College, Oxford; Student, Old Vic, 1927-28; DLitt, Reading University, 1964; DLitt, Durham University, 1981. Appointments: Actor, Lyric Theatre, Hammersmith, 1928-29; Office Boy, William Heinemann Ltd., 1929-31; Manager, Book Society, 1932; Director, Jonathan Cape Ltd., 1933-40; Served in Coldstream Guards, 1940-45; Founder, 1946, Director, 1946-64, Rupert Hart-Davis Ltd. Publications: Hugh Walpole, a Biography, 1952; The Arms of Time, a memoir, 1979; The Power of Chance, 1991. Editor: The Essential Neville Cardus, 1949; E.V. Lucas: Cricket all his Life, 1950; George Moore: Letters to Lady Cunard, 1957; The Letters of Oscar Wilde, 1962; Max Beerbohm: Letters to Reggie Turner, 1964; Max Beerbohm: More Theatres, 1969; Max Beerbohm: Last Theatres, 1970; Max Beerbohm: A Peep into the Past, 1972; A Catalogue of the Caricatures of Max Beerbohm, 1972; The Autobiography of Arthur Ransome, 1976; William Plomer: Electric Delights, 1978; The Lyttelton Hart-Davis Letters, volume I, 1978, vol II, 1979, vol III, 1981, vol IV, 1982, vol V, 1983, vol VI, 1984; Selected Letters of Oscar Wilde, 1979; Two Men of Letters, 1979; Siegfried Sassoon Diaries: 1920-1922, 1981, 1915-1918, 1983, 1923-1925, 1985; The War Poems of Siegfried Sassoon, 1983; A Beggar in Purple: A Commonplace Book, 1983; More Letters of Oscar Wilde, 1985; Siegfried Sassoon: Letters to Max Beerbohm, 1988; Letters of Max Beerbohm 1892-1956, 1989; The Power of Chance, 1991. Address: The Old Rectory, Marske-in-Swaledale, Richmond, North Yorkshire DL11 7NA, England.

HARTCUP Adeline, b. 26 Apr 1918, Isle of Wight, England. Writer. m. John Hartcup, 11 Feb 1950, 2 sons. Education: MA, Oxon, Classics and English Literature. Appointments: Editorial Staff, Times Educational Supplement; Honorary Press Officer, Kent Voluntary Service Council. Publications: Angelica, 1954; Morning Faces, 1963; Below Stairs in the Great Country Houses, 1980; Children of the Great Country Houses, 1982; Love and Marriage in the Great Country Houses, 1984; Spello: Life Today in Ancient Umbria, 1985. Contributions to: Times Educational Supplement; Harper's; Queen; Times Higher Educational Supplement. Address: Swanton Court, Sevington, Ashford, Kent, TN24 0LL, England.

HARTE Marjorie. See: **McEVOY Marjorie.**

HARTILL Rosemary Jane, b. 11 Aug 1949, Oswestry, England. Writer; Broadcaster. Education: BA Hons, English, University of Bristol, 1970. Appointments: BBC Religious Affairs Correspondent, 1982-88; Presenter of BBC World Service's Meridian Books Programme, 1990-92, 1994; Presenter of Writers Revealed (Radio 4, 18 part, BBC Series); and Immortal Diamonds (Radio 4, 12 part, Series on Poets). Publications: Emily Brontë: Poems (editor), 1973; Wild Animals, 1976; In Perspective, 1988; Writers Revealed, 1989; Were You There?, 1995. Honours: Nominated for Sony Award for Radio Reporter of the Year, 1988 and Best Arts Radio Feature, 1990; Sandford St Martin Trust Personal Award, 1994. Address: Old Post Office, 24 Eglingham Village, Alnwick, Northumberland NE66 2TX, England.

HARTLAND Michael, b. 1941, Cornwall, England. Writer. m. 1975, 2 daughters. Education: MA, Christ's College, Cambridge, 1963. Appointments: British Diplomatic and Civil Service, 1963-78; United Nations, 1978-83; Full-time Writer, 1983-; Regular Book Reviewer and Feature Writer, The Sunday Times, The Times, Guardian and Daily Telegraph; Resident Thriller Critic, The Times, 1989-90; Daily Telegraph, 1993-; Chairman, Wade Hartland Films Ltd. Publications: Down Among the Dead Men; Seven Steps to Treason (dramatized for BBC Radio 4, 1990); The Third Betrayal; Frontier of Fear; The Year of the Scorpion (adapted as feature film, 1996). Honours: Fellow, Royal Society of Arts; Honorary Fellow, University of Exeter; South West Arts Literary Award. Memberships: Crime Writers Association; Mystery Writers of America; Society of Authors. Address: Cotte Barton, Branscombe, Devon, EX12 3BH, England.

HARTMAN Geoffrey H, b. 11 Aug 1929, Frankfurt am Main, Germany (US citizen, 1946). Professor of English and Comparative Literature; Writer. m. Renee Gross, 21 Oct 1956, 1 son, 1 daughter. Education: BA, Queens College, New York City, 1949; PhD, Yale University, 1953. Appointments: Fulbright Fellow, University of Dijon, 1951-52; Faculty, Yale University, 1955-62; Associate Professor, 1962-64, Professor of English, 1964-65, University of Iowa; Professor of English, 1965-67, Sterling Professor, 1994-, Cornell University; Professor of English and Comparative Literature, 1967-, Karl Young Professor, 1974-94, Yale University; Gauss Seminarist, Princeton University, 1968; Director, School of Theory and Criticism, Dartmouth College, 1982-87; Associate Fellow, Center for Research in Philosophy and Literature, University of Warwick, 1993; Fellow, Woodrow Wilson International Center, 1995; Various guest lectureships and professorships. Publications: The Unmediated Vision, 1954; André Malraux, 1960; Wordsworth's Poetry, 1964; Beyond Formalism, 1970; The Fate of Reading, 1975; Akiba's Children, 1978; Criticism in the Wilderness, 1980; Saving the Text, 1981; Easy Pieces, 1985; The Unremarkable Wordsworth, 1987; Minor Prophecies, 1991. Editor: Hopkins: A Collection of Critical Essays, 1966; Selected Poetry and Prose of William Wordsworth, 1970; Romanticism: Vistas, Instances, Continuities, 1973; Psychoanalysis and the Question of the Text, 1978; Shakespeare and the Question of Theory, 1985; Bitburg in Moral and Political Perspective, 1986; Midrash and Literature, 1986; Holocaust Remembrance: The Shapes of Memory, 1993. Honours: Christian Gauss Award, Phi Beta Kappa, 1965; Guggenheim Fellowships, 1969, 1986; Honorary LHD, Queens College, New York City, 1990. Memberships: American Academy of Arts and Sciences; Modern Language Association. Address: 260 Everit Street, New Haven, CT 06511, USA.

HARTMAN Jan, b. 23 May 1936, Stockholm, Sweden. Writer-Dramatist. m. 9 June 1960, 2 daughters. Education: Phillips Andover Academy, 1956; BA, Harvard College, 1960. Appointments: Resident Playwright, The Theatre of The Living Arts, Philadelphia, 1964-65; Director, Founder, Playwrights Theatre Project Circle in the Square, 1967-69, and Eleventh Hour Productions, 1977; Resident Playwright, Theatre St Clements, 1977-78; Visiting Professor, Syracuse University, 1985-86; Professor of Dramatic Writing and Shakespeare, New York University, 1981-. Publications: Numerous television plays. Stage Plays: Samuel Hoopes Reading From His Own Works, 1963; The Shadow of the Valley, 1964; Legend of Daniel Boone, 1966; Antique Masks, 1966; Final Solutions, 1967; Fragment of a Last Judgment, 1967; The American War Crimes Trial, 1973; Flight 981, 1977; To the Ninth Circle, 1983; K, 1987. Contributions to: Dramatists Guild Quarterly. Honours: Many Awards and Fellowships given in recognition of work commissioned. Memberships: PEN; Writers Guild of America; Eugene O'Neill Memorial Theatre Foundation; American National Theatre and Academy; Dramatists Guild. Address: c/o Robert A Freeman Dramatic Agency Inc, 1501 Broadway, Suite 2310, NY 10036, USA.

HARTNETT David William, b. 4 Sept 1952, London, England. Writer; Poet. m. Margaret R N Thomas, 26 Aug 1976, 1 son, 1 daughter. Education: Scholarship to read English Language and Literature, 1971, First Class Honour Moderations, 1973, First Class BA in English Language and Literature, 1975, MA, 1981, D Phil, 1987, Oxford University. Appointment: Editor (with Michael O'Neill and Gareth Reeves) of the literary magazine Poetry Durham (founded 1982). Publications: Poetry: A Signalled Love, 1985; House of Moon, 1988; Dark Ages, 1992. Novel: Black Milk, 1994. Contributions to: Times Literary Supplement. Honour: Times Literary Supplement/Cheltenham Festival Poetry Competition, 1989. Address: c/o Jonathan Cape, 20 Vauxhall Bridge Road, London SW1V 2SA, England.

HARTNETT Michael, b. 18 Sept 1941, County Limerick, Ireland. Poet. Education: University and Trinity College, Dublin. Appointment: Teacher of Physical Education, National College, Limerick. Publications: Anatomy of a Cliche, 1968; Selected Poems, 1971; Culuide, The Retreat of Ita Cagney, 1975; A Farewell to English and Other Poems, 1975; Poems in English, 1977; Prisoners, 1978; Collected Poems, 2 Volumes, 1985, 1987; A Necklace of Wrens: Poems in English and Irish, 1987; House of Moon, 1989. Address: c/o Gallery Press, Loughcrew, Oldcastle, County Meath, Ireland.

HARTSTON W(illiam) R(oland), b . 12 Aug 1947, London, England. Writer. Education: MA, Jesus College, 1972. Appointment: Chess Columnist, The Mail on Sunday. Publications: The King's Indian Defence (with L Barden and R Keene), 1969; The Benoni, 1969; The Grunfeld Defence, 1971; Karpov-Korchnoi (with R Keene), 1974; The Best Games of C H O'D Alexander (with H Golombek), 1975; How to Cheat at Chess, 1976; The Battle of Baguio City, 1978; Soft Pawn, 1979; The Penguin Book of Chess Openings, 1980; Play Chess 1 and 2, 2 volumes, 1980-81; London (with S Reuben), 1980; The Master Game Book Two (with J James), 1981; Karpov v Korchnoi, 1981; The Psychology of Chess (with P C Wason), 1983; The Ultimate Irrelevant Encyclopaedia (with J Dawson), 1984; Teach Yourself Chess, 1985; Kings of Chess, 1985; Chess: The Making of a Musical, 1986. Address: 48 Sotheby Road, London N5 2UR, England.

HARUKI Murakami, b. 1949, Kyôto, Japan. Writer. Publications: Novels: Kaze no Uta o Kike/Hear the Wind Sing, 1979; Hitsuji o Meguru Bôken/A Wild Sheep Chase, 1982; Sekai no Owari to Haado-Boirudo Wandaarando/Hard-Boiled Wonderland and the End of the World, 1985; Noriwei no Mori/Norwegian Wood, 1987; Dansu, Dansu, Dansu/Dance Dance Dance, 1988; Kokkyô no Minami, Taiyô no Nishi/South of the Border, West of the Sun, 1992; Nejimakidori kuronikuru/The Chronicle of the Wind-Up Bird, 3 Volumes, 1994-95. Short Stories: Elephant Vanishes, 1986; Kreta Kanô, 1989. Honours: New Writer Award, Gunzô Magazine, 1979; Nome Award for New Writers, 1982; Tanizaki Jun'ichiro Award, 1985; Yomiuri Literary Award, 1996. Address: 4-17-35-6E, Minami-Aoyama, Minato-ku, Tokyo 107, Japan.

HARVEY Anne (Berenice), b. 27 Apr 1933, London, England. Actress; Writer; Editor. m. Alan Harvey, 13 Apr 1957, 1 son, 1 daughter. Education: Guildhall School of Music and Drama, 1950-54. Publications: A Present for Nellie, 1981; Poets in Hand, 1985; Of Caterpillars, Cats and Cattle, 1987; In Time of War: War Poetry, 1987; Something I Remember (selected poetry of Eleanor Farjeon), 1987; A Picnic of Poetry, 1988; The Language of Love, 1989; Six of the Best, 1989; Faces in the Crowd, 1990; Headlines from the Jungle (with Virginia McKenna), 1990; Occasions, 1990; Flora's Red Socks, 1991; Shades of Green, 1991; Elected Friends (poems for and about Edward Thomas), 1991; He Said, She Said, They Said (conversation poems, editor), 1993; Solo Audition Speeches for Young Actors, 1993; Criminal Records: Poetry of Crime (editor), 1994; Methuen Book of Duologues, 1995; Starlight, Starbright: Poems of Night, 1995; Swings and Shadows: Poems of Times Past and Present, 1996. Series editor: Poetry Originals 1992-95. Contributions to: Radio, journals, and magazines. Honour: Signal Poetry Award, 1992. Memberships: Poetry Society; Friends of the Dymock Poets; Eighteen Nineties Society; Imaginative Book Illustration Society. Address: 37 St Stephen's Road, Ealing, London W13 8HJ, England.

HARVEY Brett, b. 28 Apr 1936, New York, New York, USA. Writer; Critic. 1 son, 1 daughter. Appointments: Drama and Literature Director, WBAI-FM, 1971-74; Publicity and Promotion Director, The Feminist Press, Old Westbury, 1974-80, New York; Freelance journalist, book critic and children's book author, 1980-. Publications:

My Prairie Year, 1986; Immigrant Girl, 1987; Cassie's Journey, Various Gifts: Brooklyn Fiction, 1988; My Prairie Christmas, 1990; The Fifties: A Women's Oral History, 1993. Contributions to: Village Voice, New York Times Book Review, Psychology Today, Voice Literary Supplement, Mirabella, Mother Jones, Mademoiselle. Address: 305 8th Avenue, Brooklyn, NY 11215, USA.

HARVEY Caroline. See: TROLLOPE Joanna.

HARVEY John Barton, b. 21 Dec 1938, London, England. Writer. Education: Goldsmith College, University of London; Hatfield Polytechnic; University of Nottingham. Publications: What about it, Sharon, 1979; Lonely Hearts, 1989; Rough Treatment, 1990; Cutting Edge, 1991; Off Minor, 1992; Ghosts of a Chance (collected poems), 1992; Wasted Years, 1993; Cold Light, 1994; Living Proof, 1995; Numerous Scripts for Radio and Television. Address: 37-41 Gower Street, London, WC1E 6HH, England.

HARVEY John Robert, b. 25 June 1942, Bishops Stortford, Hertfordshire, England. University Lecturer. m. Julietta Chloe Papadopoulou, 1968, 1 daughter. Education: BA, Honours Class 1, English, 1964, MA, 1967, PhD, 1969, University of Cambridge. Appointments: English Faculty, Emmanuel College, Cambridge; Editor, Cambridge Quarterly, 1978-86. Publications: Victorian Novelists and Their Illustrators, 1970; Novels: The Plate Shop, 1979; Coup d'Etat, 1985; The Legend of Captain Space, 1990; Men in Black, 1995. Contributions to: London Review of Books; Sunday Times; Sunday Telegraph; Listener; Encounter; Cambridge Quarterley; Essays in Criticism. Honour: David Higham Prize, 1979. Literary Agent: Curtis Brown. Address: Emmanuel College, Cambridge, England.

HARWOOD Lee, b . 6 June 1939, Leicester, England. Poet; Translator; Writer. Education: BA, Queen Mary College, London, 1961. Publications: Verse: Title Illegible, 1965; The Man With Blue Eyes, 1966; The White Room, 1968; The Beautiful Atlas, 1969; Landscapes, 1969; The Sinking Colony, 1970; Penguin Modern Poets 19 (with John Ashbery and Tom Raworth), 1971; The First Poem, 1971; New Year, 1971; Captain Harwood's Log of Stern Statements and Stout Sayings, 1973; Freighters, 1975; H.M.S Little Fox, 1976; Boston - Brighton, 1977; Old Bosham Bird Watch and Other Stories, 1977; Wish You Were Here (with A Lopez), 1979; All the Wrong Notes, 1981; Faded Ribbons, 1982; Wine Tales (with Richard Caddel), 1984; Crossing the Frozen River: Selected Poems 1965-1980, 1984, revised edition, 1994; Monster Masks, 1986; Translations of the works of Tristan Tzara: A Poem Sequence, 1969, revised edition as Cosmic Realities Vanilla Tobacco Drawings, 1975; Destroyed Days, 1971; Selected Poems, 1975. Address: c/o 9 Highfield Road, Chertsey, Surrey, England.

HARWOOD Ronald, b. 9 Nov 1934, Cape Town, South Africa. Dramatist; Writer. m. Natasha Riehle, 1959, 1 son, 2 daughters. Education: Royal Academy of Dramatic Art. Appointments: Actor, 1953-60; Presenter, Kaleidoscope, BBC, 1973, Read All About It, BBC TV, 1978-79; Artistic Director, Cheltenham Festival of Literature, 1975; Visitor in Theatre, Balliol College, Oxford, 1986. Publications: Stage Plays: Country Matters, 1969; The Ordeal of Gilbert Pinfold (after Evelyn Waugh), 1977; A Family, 1978; The Dresser, 1980; After the Lions, 1982; Tramway Road, 1984; The Deliberate Death of a Polish Priest, 1985; Interpreters, 1985; J J Farr, 1987; Ivanov (after Anton Chekov), 1989; Another Time, 1989; Reflected Glory, 1992; Poison Pen, 1993; Taking Sides, 1995. Television Plays: The Barber of Stamford Hill, 1960; Private Potter (with Casper Wrede), 1961; The Guests, 1972; Breakthrough at Reykjavik, 1987; Screenplays: A High Wind in Jamaica, 1965; One Day in the Life of Ivan Denisovich, 1971; Evita Perón, 1981; The Dresser, 1983; Mandela, 1987; The Browning Version, 1994; Cry, Beloved Country, 1995. Novels: All the Same Shadows, 1961; The Guilt Merchants, 1963; The Girl in Melanie Klein, 1969; Articles of Faith, 1973; The Genoa Ferry, 1976; Cesar and Augusta, 1978; Home, 1993. Non-Fiction: Sir Donald Wolfit, CBE: His Life and Work in the Unfashionable Theatre, 1971. Editor: A Night at the Theatre, 1983; The Ages of Gielgud, 1984; Dear Alec: Guinness at Seventy-Five, 1989; The Faber Book of Theatre, 1993. Honours: New Standard Drama Award, 1981; Drama Critics Award, 1981; Molière Award for Best Play, Paris, 1993. Memberships: Arts Council of Great Britain, Literature Panel, 1978-79; English PEN, President, 1989-93; International PEN, President, 1993-; Royal Society of Literature, Fellow; Writers Guild of Great Britain, Chairman, 1969. Address: c/o Judy Daish Associates, 2 St Charles Place, London W10 6EG, England.

HASHMI (Aurangzeb) Alamgir, b. 15 Nov 1951, Lahore, Pakistan. Professor; Poet; Writer; Editor; Broadcaster. m. Beatrice Stoerk, 15 Dec 1978, 2 sons, 1 daughter. Education: MA, University of Louisville, 1977. Appointments: Broadcaster, Pakistan Broadcasting Corp, Lahore, 1968-74, 1988-; Staff, Government College, Lahore, 1971-73; Lecturer, Forman Christian College, Lahore, 1973-74; Davidson International Visiting Scholar from Pakistan, University of North Carolina, 1974-75; Lecturer in English, University of Louisville, 1975-78, University of Zürich and Volkshochschule, Zurich, 1980-85; Assistant Professor of English, University of Bahawalpur, Pakistan, 1979-80; Lecturer, University of Bern, University of Basel, 1982; Visiting Lecturer in English, University of Zürich, 1982-; Associate Professor of Englsh, International Islamic University, Islamabad, 1985-86; Visiting Professor of English, University of Fribourg, Switzerland, 1985-; Course Director, Foreign Service Training Institute, Pakistan Ministry of Foreign Affairs, Islamabad, 1988-; Professor of English and Comparative Literature, Pakistan Futuristics Institute, Islamabad, 1990. Publications: Poetry: The Oak and Amen: Love Poems, 1976; America is a Punjabi Word, 1979; An Old Chair, 1979; My Second in Kentucky, 1981; This Time in Lahore, 1983; Neither This Time/Nor That Place, 1984; Inland and Other Poems, 1988; The Poems of Alamgir Hashmi, 1992; Sun and Moon and Other Poems, 1992; Others to Sport with Amaryllis in the Shade, 1992. Other: Pakistani Literature (editor), 2 volumes, 1978, 2nd edition as Pakistani Literature: The Contemporary English Writers, 1987; Commonwealth Literature, 1983; Ezra Pound in Melbourne (editor with others), 1983; The Worlds of Muslim Imagination (editor), 1986; The Commonwealth, Comparative Literature and the World, 1988; Pakistani Short Stories in English (editor), 1992; Studies in Pakistani Literature (editor), 1992; Encyclopedia of Post-Colonial Literatures (co-editor), 1994; Where Coyotes Howl and Wind Blows Free (editor with Alexandra Haslam), 1995; The Great Tejon Club Jubilee, 1996. Contributions to: Many books, journals, and periodicals. Honours: Honorary D.Litt, Centre Universitaire de Luxembourg, 1984, San Francisco State University, 1984; Patras Bokhari Award, Pakistan Academy of Letters, 1985. Memberships: Associated Writing Programs; Association for Asian Studies; Commonwealth Club, 1996-; Association for Commonwealth Literature and Language Studies; International Association of University Professors of English; International Centre for Asian Studies, fellow; International PEN, fellow; Modern Language Association of America. Address: House 162, Street 64, Ramna 8/1, Islamabad, Pakistan.

HASKINS James, b. 19 Sept 1941, Demopolis, Alabama, USA. Professor of English; Writer. Education: BA in Psychology, Georgetown University, 1960; BS in History, Alabama State University, 1962; MA in Social Psychology, University of New Mexico, 1963. Appointments: Teacher, Board of Education, New York City, 1966-69; Visiting Lecturer, New School for Social Research, New York City, 1966-69, State University of New York at New Paltz, 1970-72, Manhattanville College, Purchase, New York, 1972-76; Indiana University-Purdue University at Indianapolis, 1973-76; Associate Professor, S I Community College, New York City, 1972-76; Visiting Professor, College of New Rochelle, New York, 1977; Professor of English, University of Florida at Gainesville, 1977-. Publications: Diary of a Harlem Schoolteacher, 1969; The War and the Protest, 1970; Resistance: Profiles in Nonviolence, 1970; Revolutionaries: Agents of Change, 1971; Profiles in Black Power, 1972; Religions, 1973; Ralph Bunche: A Most Reluctant Hero, 1974; Adam Clayton Powell: Portrait of a Marching Black, 1974; Witchcraft, Mysticism and Magic in the Black World, 1974; Babe Ruth and Hank Aaron: The Home Run Kings, 1974; The Creoles of Color of New Orleans, 1975; Fighting Shirley Chisholm, 1975; Dr J: A Biography of Julius Erving, 1975; The Story of Stevie Wonder, 1976; Always Movin' On: A Biography of Langston Hughes, 1976; A Long Struggle: American Labor, 1976; Pele: A Biography, 1976; The Life and Death of Martin Luther King, Jr, 1977; Barbara Jordan, 1977; Voodoo and Hoodoo, 1978; James Van DerZee: The Picture Takin' Man, 1979; Andrew Young: Man with a Mission, 1979; I'm Gonna Make You Love Me: The Story of Diana Ross, 1980; Werewolves, 1981; Sugar Ray Leonard, 1982; Black Theater in America, 1982; Lena Horne, 1983; Diana Ross: Star Supreme, 1985; Black Music in America: A History Through its People, 1987; Queen of the Blues: The Story of Dinah Washington, 1987; Mabel Mercer: A Life, 1988; Corazon Aquino: Leader of the Philippines, 1988; India Under Indira and Rajiv Gandhi, 1989; Outward Dreams: Black Inventors and Their Inventions, 1991; The Day That Martin Luther King Jr was Shot, 1992; Amazing Grace: The Story Behind the Song, 1992; Jesse Jackson, 1992; Against All Opposition: Black Explorers in America, 1992; Colin Powell, 1992; Thurgood

Marshall: A Life for Justice, 1992; Get on Board: The Story of the Underground Railroad, 1992; I Have a Dream: The Life of Martin Luther King Jr, 1992; The Methodist Church, 1992; The March on Washington, 1993; Freedom Rides, 1994; The Headless Haunt and Other African-American Ghost Stories, 1994; Black Eagles: African Americans in Aviation, 1995; The Day They Fired on Fort Sumter, 1995. With Others: Scott Joplin, 1978; Nat King Cole, 1984; Mr Bojangles: Biography of Bill Robinson, 1988; The Sixties Reader, 1988; Scatman, 1991; Hippocrene Guide to the Historic Black South, 1993. Honours: Coretta Scott King Award, 1976; ASCAP-Deems Taylor Award, 1979; Washington Post/Children's Book Guild Award, 1979; Washington Post/Children's Book Guild Award, 1994. Address: 325 West End Avenue, No 7D, New York, NY 10023, USA.

HASLAM Gerald William, b. 18 Mar 1937, Bakersfield, California, USA. Writer; Educator. m. Janice E Pettichord, 1 July 1961, 3 sons, 2 daughters. Education: BA, 1963; MA, 1965, San Francisco State University; PhD, Union Graduate School, 1980. Appointments: Associate Editor, ETC; A Review of General Semantics, 1967-69; Editor, Ecolit, 1971-73; General Editor, Western American, 1973-76; Columnist, California English, 1987-93; Columnist, San Francisco Chronicle, 1992-93. Publications: Okies, 1973; Masks, 1976; The Wages of Sin, 1980; Snapshots, 1985; The Man Who Cultivated Fire, 1987; Voices of a Place, 1987; Coming of Age in California, 1990; That Constant Coyote, 1990; The Other California, 1990, revised edition, 1994; The Great Central Valley: California's Heartland, 1993; Condor Dreams and Other Fictions, 1994. Editor: Forgotten Pages of American Literature, 1970; Western Writing, 1974; California Heartland (with James D Houston), 1978; Many Californias, 1992. Address: Box 969, Penngrove, CA 94951, USA.

HASLUCK Nicholas (Paul), b. 17 Oct 1942, Canberra, Australia. Novelist. Education: University of Western Australia, 1960-63; Oxford University, 1964-66. Appointments: Barrister, Solicitor, Supreme Court of Western Australia, 1968; Deputy Chairman, Australia Council, 1978-82. Publications: Fiction: Quarantine, 1978; The Blue Guitar, 1980; The Hand that Feeds You: A Satiric Nightmare, 1982; The Bellarmine Jug, 1984; The Country without Music, 1990; The Blosseville File, 1992; Offcuts From a Legal Literary Life, 1993; A Grain of Truth, 1994. Stories: The Hat on the Letter O and Other Stories, 1978; Verse, Anchor and Other Poems, 1976; On the Edge, 1980; Chinese Journey, 1985. Honours: The Age Book of Year Award, 1984; Member of the Order of Australia, 1986. Address: 14 Reserve Street, Claremont, Western Australia 6010, Australia.

HASS Robert (Louis), b. 1 Mar 1941, San Francisco, California, USA. Poet; Writer; Translator; Editor; Professor. m. Earlene Joan Leif, 1 Sep 1962, div 1986, 2 sons, 1 daughter. Education: BA, St Mary's College of California, 1963; MA, 1965, PhD, 1971, Stanford University. Appointments: Assistant Professor, State University of New York, Buffalo, 1967-71; Professor of English, St Mary's College of California, 1971-89, and University of California, Berkeley, 1989-; Visiting Lecturer, University of Virginia, 1974, Goddard College, 1976, Columbia University, 1982, and University of California, Berkeley, 1983; Poet-in-Residence, The Frost Place, Franconia, New Hampshire, 1978; Poet Laureate of the USA, 1995-97. Publications: Poetry: Field Guide, 1973; Winter Morning in Charlottesville, 1977; Praise, 1979; The Apple Tree at Olema, 1989; Human Wishes, 1989. Other: Twentieth Century Pleasures: Prose on Poetry, 1984; Into the Garden - A Wedding Anthology: Poetry and Prose on Love and Marriage, 1993; Translations: Czeslaw Milosz's The Separate Notebooks (with Robert Pinsteyli), 1983; Czeslaw Milosz's Unattainable Earth (with Czeslaw Milosz), 1986; Czeslaw Milosz's Collected Poems, 1931-1987 (with Louis Iribane and Peter Scott), 1988. Editor: Rock and Hawk: A Selection of Shorter Poems by Robinson Jeffers, 1987; The Pushcart Prize XII (with Bill Henderson and Jorie Graham), 1987; Tomaz Salamun: Selected Poems (with Charles Simic), 1988; Selected Poems of Tomas Transtromer, 1954-1986 (with others), 1989; The Essential Haiku: Versions of Basho, Buson and Issa, 1994. Contributions to: Anthologies and other publications. Honours: Woodrow Wilson Fellowship, 1963-64; Danforth Fellowship, 1963-67; Yale Series of Younger Poets Award, Yale University Press, 1972; US-Great Britain Bicentennial Exchange Fellow in the Arts, 1976-77; William Carlos Williams Award, 1979; National Book Critics Circle Award, 1984; Award of Merit, American Academy of Arts and Letters, 1984; MacArthur Foundation Grant, 1984. Address: PO Box 807, Inverness, CA 94937, USA.

HASTINGS March. See: **LEVINSON Leonard.**

HASTINGS Max Macdonald, b. 28 Dec 1945, London, England. Author; Broadcaster; Journalist. m. Patricia Edmondson, 27 May 1972, 2 sons, 1 daughter. Education: Exhibitioner, University College, Oxford, 1964-65; Fellow, World Press Institute, St Paul, Minnesota, USA, 1967-68. Appointments: Researcher, BBC TV, 1963-64; Reporter, London Evening Standard, 1965-67, BBC TV Current Affairs, 1970-73; Editor, Evening Standard Londoner's Diary, 1976-77; Columnist, Daily Express, 1981-83, Sunday Times, 1985-86; Editor, Daily Telegraph, 1986-95, Evening Standard, 1996-; Editor-in-Chief and a Director, Daily Telegraph Plc, 1949-. Publications: The Fire This Time, 1968; Ulster, 1969; The Struggle for Civil Rights in Northern Ireland, 1970; Montrose: The King's Champion, 1977; Yoni: The Hero of Entebbe, 1979; Bomber Command, 1979; The Battle of Britain (with Lee Deighton), 1980; Das Reich, 1981; Battle for the Falklands, with Simon Jenkins, 1983; Overlord: D-Day & the Battle for Normandy, 1984; Oxford Book of Military Anecdotes, editor, 1985; Victory in Europe, 1985; The Korean War, 1987; Outside Days, 1989. Honours: Somerset Maugham Prize, non-fiction, 1979; British Press Awards, Journalist of the Year, 1982 (cited 1973, 1980); Granada TV Reporter of the Year, 1982; Yorkshire Post Book of the Year Awards, 1983, 1984; Editor of the Year, 1988. Literary Agent: The Peters, Fraser and Dunlop Group Ltd. Address: Northcliffe House, 2 Derry Street, London W8 5EE, England.

HASTINGS Michael (Gerald), b. 2 Sept 1938, London, England. Dramatist; Author. m. (1), 2 sons, 1 daughter, (2) Victoria Hardie, 1975. Education: London schools. Publications: Plays: Don't Destroy Me, Yes and After, and The World's Baby, 1966; The Silence of Saint-Just, 1970; Tom and Viv, 1985; Three Political Plays (The Silence of Lee Harvey Oswald, For the West, and the Emperor), 1990; A Dream of People, 1992; Unfinished Business and Other Plays, 1994. Fiction: The Game, 1957; The Frauds, 1960; Tussy Is Me: A Romance, 1970; The Nightcomers, 1972; And in the Forest the Indians, 1975; Bart's Mornings and Other Tales from Modern Brazil, 1975; A Spy in Winter, 1984. Poetry: Love Me Lambeth and Other Poems, 1961. Non-Fiction: The Handsomest Young Man in England: Rupert Brooke, 1967; Sir Richard Burton: A Biography, 1978. Contributions to: Films and television. Honours: Arts Council Award, 1956; Emmy Award, 1972; Writers Guild Award, 1972; Somerset Maugham Award, 1972; Comedy of the Year Award, Evening Standard, 1978. Address: 2 Helix Gardens, Brixton Hill, London SW2, England.

HASWELL Chetwynd John Drake, b. 18 July 1919, Penn Buckinghamshire, England. Soldier; Author. m. Charlotte Annette Petter, 25 Oct 1947, 2 sons, 1 daughter. Education: Winchester College, 1933-37; Royal Military College, Sandhurst, 1938-39. Appointments: Soldier, 1939-60; Author, Service Intelligence, Intelligence Centre, Ashford, 1966-84. Publications: (Under the name George Foster) Indian File, 1960; Soldier on Loan, 1961; (Under the name Jock Haswell) The Queen's Royal Regiment, 1967; The First Respectable Spy, 1969; James II, Soldier and Sailor, 1972; British Military Intelligence, 1973; Citizen Armies, 1973; The British Army, 1975; The Ardent Queen, Margaret of Anjou, 1976; The Battle for Empire, 1976; Spies and Spymasters, 1977; The Intelligence and Deception of the D Day Landings, 1979; The Tangled Web, 1985; The Queen's Regiment, 1986; Spies and Spying, 1986. Membership: Regimental Historian for the Queen's Regiment. Address: The Grey House, Lyminge, Folkestone, Kent, CT18 8ED, England.

HATCHER Robin Lee, b. 10 May 1951, Payette, Idaho, USA. Novelist. m. Jerrold W Neu, 6 May 1989, 2 daughters. Education: General High School Diploma, 1969. Publications: Stormy Surrender, 1984; Heart's Landing, 1984; Thorn of Love, 1985; Passion's Gamble, 1986; Heart Storm, 1986; Pirate's Lady, 1987; Gemfire, 1988; The Wager, 1989; Dream Tide, 1990; Promised Sunrise, 1990; Promise Me Spring, 1991; Rugged Splendor, 1991; The Hawk and the Heather, 1992; Devlin's Promise, 1992; Midnight Rose, 1992; A Frontier Christmas, 1992; The Magic, 1993; Where The Heart Is, 1993; Forever, Rose, 1994; Remember When, 1994. Contributions to: Various publications. Address: PO Box 4722, Boise, ID 83711, USA.

HATTENDORF John Brewster, b. 22 Dec 1941, Hinsdale, Illinois, USA. Naval and Maritime Historian. m. Berit Sundell, 15 Apr 1978, 3 daughters. Education: AB Kenyon College, 1964; AM Brown University, 1971; DPhil, University of Oxford, 1979. Appointments: Serving Officer, US Navy, 1964-73; Professor, Military History, National University of Singapore, 1981-83; Ernest J King Professor of Maritime History, US Naval War College, 1984-. Publications: The Writings of Stephen B Luce, 1975; On His Majesty's Service, 1983;

Sailors and Scholars, 1984; England in the War of the Spanish Succession, 1987; Maritime Strategy and the Balance of Power, 1989; The Limitations of Military Power, 1990; Mahan on Naval Strategy, 1990; Mahan is Not Enough, 1993; British Naval Documents (co-editor), 1993; A Bibliography of the Works of A T Mahan, 1986; Ubi Sumnus: The State of Maritime and Naval History, 1994; Doing Naval History, 1995; Sea of Words (with Dean King), 1995; Maritime History: The Age of Discovery, 1996; Maritime History: The Eighteenth Century, 1996. Contributions to: Naval War College Review; International History Review. Memberships: Navy Records Society; Hakluyt Society; Academie du Var; Fellow, Royal Historical Society; Royal Swedish Academy of Naval Science; Society for Nautical Research. Address: 28 John Street, Newport, RI 02840-3106, USA.

HATTERSLEY Roy (Sydney George), b. 28 Dec 1932, Sheffield, England. Politician; Writer. Education: BSc, University of Hull. Appointments: Journalist and Health Service Executive, 1956-64; Member of City Council, Sheffield, 1957-65; Labour Member of Parliament (UK) for Sparkbrook Division of Birmingham, 1964-, Parliamentary Private Secretary, Minister of Pensions and National Insurance, 1964-67, Parliamentary Secretary, Ministry of Labour, 1967-68, Department of Employment and Productivity, 1968-69, Minister of Defence for Administration, 1969-70, Labour Party Spokesman on Defence, 1972 and on Education, 1972-74, Minister of State, Foreign and Commonwealth Office, 1974-76, Secretary of State for Prices and Consumer Protection, 1976-79, Opposition Spokesman on Home Affairs, 1980-83, on Treasury Affairs, 1983-, Deputy Leader of the Labour Party, 1983-; Director, Campaign for a European Political Community, 1966-67; Columnist for the Guardian, 1981-, Punch, 1982-87. Publications: Nelson: A Biography, 1974; Goodbye to Yorkshire, 1976; Politics Apart, 1982; A Yorkshire Boyhood, Press Gang, 1983; Endpiece Revisited, 1984; Choose Freedom, 1987; Economic Priorities for a Labour Government, 1987; The Maker's Mark (novel), 1991; In That Quiet Earth, 1991; Skylark's Story, 1994; Between Ourselves (essays), 1994; Who Goes Home?, 1995. Address: House of Commons, London SW1A DAA, England.

HAUCK Dennis William, b . 8 Apr 1945, Hammond, Indiana, USA. Writer. Education: Indiana University, 1963-66; University of Vienna, Austria, 1969-72. Appointments: Editor, Infor Services Inc, 1973-76; Countrywide Publications, New York, 1976-79; Writer, Oldenberg Group Inc, Sacramento, 1983-91; Columnist, Today's Supervisor, Sacramento, 1991-. Publications: The UFO Handbook, 1974; Ufology, 1975; The Secret of the Emerald Tablet, 1991; The Haunted Places Guidebook, 1991; William Shatner: A Biography, 1992; Jewish Alchemy, 1992. Contributions to: Magazines and periodicals. Honour: Appeared in and wrote script for theatrical release, Mysteries of the Gods, 1976. Memberships: Authors Guild; National Writers Union; Society for Technical Communication; California Writers Club. Address: PO 22201, Sacremento, CA 95822, USA.

HAUGAARD Erik Christian, b . 13 Apr 1923, Copenhagen, Denmark. Author. m. (1) Myra Seld, 23 Dec 1949, dec 1981, (2) Masako Taira, 27 July 1986, 1 son, 1 daughter. Publications: The Little Fishes, 1967; Orphas of the Wind, 1969; The Untold Tale, 1972; Translated all Hans Christian Andersen's Fairy Tales, 1973; Chase Me Catch Nobody, 1980; Leif the Unlucky, 1982; The Samurai's Tale, 1984; Princess Horrid, 1990; The Boy and the Samurai, 1991; The Death of Mr Angel, 1992; Under the Black Flag, 1993; The Revenge of the Forty Seven Samurai, 1995. Honours: Herald Tribune Award; Boston Globe-Horn Book Award; Jane Addams Award; Danish Cultural Ministry Award; 1988 Phoenix Award. Memberships: Authors Guild; Society of Authors; British PEN; Danish Authors Union. Address: Toad Hall, Ballydehob, West Cork, Ireland.

HAUGEN Paal-Helge, b. 26 Apr 1945, Valle, Norway. Poet; Writer; Dramatist. Education: Medicine, film and theatre, Norway and the USA. Appointments: Chairman, Norwegian State Film Production Board, 1980-85; Chairman, Board of Literary Advisors, Association of Norwegian Authors, 1984-88, International Pegasus Prize Committee, 1988. Publications: 28 books including: Anne (novel), 1968; Stone Fences, 1986; A (libretto for monodrama by Iannis Xenakis), 1993; Poesi: Collected Poems, 1965-1995, 1995. Other: Plays for stage, radio and television; Opera libretti. Contributions to: Professional journals; work translated into 20 languages. Honours: Dobloug Prize, 1986; Norwegian Literary Critics Prize, 1993; Norwegian National Brage Prize, 1994. Address: Skrefjellv 5, 4645 Nodeland, Norway.

HAUPTMAN William (Thornton), b. 26 Nov 1942, Wichita Falls, Texas, USA. Dramatist; Writer. m. (1) Barbara Barbat, 1968, div 1977, 1 daughter, (2) Marjorie Endreich, 1985, 1 son. Education: BFA in Drama, University of Texas at Austin, 1966; MFA in Playwrighting, Yale University School of Drama, 1973. Publications: Plays: Hear, 1977; Domino Courts/Comanche Cafe, 1977; Big River (with Roger Miller), 1986; Gillette, 1989. Television Drama: A House Divided (series), 1981. Fiction: Good Rockin' Tonight and Other Stories, 1988; The Storm Season, 1992. Honours: National Endowment for the Arts Grant, 1977; Boston Theatre Critics Circle Award, 1984; Tony Award, 1985; Drama-Lounge Award, 1986; Jesse Jones Award, Texas Institute of Letters, 1989. Address: 240 Warren Street, Apt E, Brooklyn, NY 11201, USA.

HAUTZIG Esther Rudomin, b. 18 Oct 1930, Vilna, Poland. American. Publications: Let's Cook Without Cooking (as E Rudomin), 1955; Let's Make Presents, 1961; Redecorating Your Room for Practically Nothing, 1967; The Endless Steppe, In the Park, 1968; At Home 1969; In School, 1971; Let's Make More Presents, 1973; Cool Cooking, 1974; I L Peretz: The Case Against the Wind and Other Stories (translator and adaptor), 1975; Life with Working Parents, 1976; A Gift for Mama, 1981; Holiday Treats, 1983; I L Peretz: The Seven Good Years and Other Stories (translator and adaptor), 1984; Make It Special, 1986; Christmas Goodies, 1989; Remember Who You Are, 1990; On the Air, 1991; Riches, 1992; New Introduction to a fascimile edition of Vilna by Israel Cohen, 1992. Contributions to: Publishers Weekly, 1969; Horn Book, 1970; The Five Owls, 1986; Something About the Author Autobiographical Series, 1992. Memberships: Authors Guild; Authors League of America. Address: 505 West End Avenue, New York, NY 10024, USA.

HAVEL Václav, b. 5 Oct 1936, Prague, Czechoslovakia. President of the Czech Republic; Writer. m. Olga Splichová, 1964, dec 27 Jan 1996. Education: Faculty of Economy, 1955-57; Drama Department, Academy of Arts, Prague, 1966. Appointments: ABC Theatre Prague, 1959-68, Editorial board Tvár, 1965, Lidové noviny, 1987-89; Co-founder, Charter 77, 1977, VONS, 1978, Civic Forum, 1989; President, Czech Republic, 1993-. Publications: 13 Plays; 10 Books: Many Essays; English translations include: The Garden Party, 1969; The Increased Difficulty of Concentration, 1972; Václav Havel or Living in Truth, 1986; Letters to Olga, 1988; Disturbing the Peace, 1990; Open Letters: Selected Writings 1965-90, 1991; Selected Plays by Václav Havel, 1991; Summer Meditations, 1992; Toward a Civil Society, 1994. Honours: Many awards for writing, and work for human rights, including: The Olof Palme Prize, 1989; Simon Bolívar Prize, UNESCO, 1990; Political Book of the Year, 1990. Memberships: Czech PEN, 1989; Honorary member, PEN-Centre, Germany; PEN, Sweden; Hamburg Academy of Liberal Arts; Austrian PEN club committee; Royal British Legion, 1991; Associé entranger Académie des sciences morales et politiques Institut de France, 1992. Literary Agent: Aura Pont Agency, Prague. Address: Kancelár prezidenta republiky, 119 08 Praha-Hrad, Czech Republic.

HAVIARAS Stratis, b. 28 June 1935, Nea Kios, Greece. Author; Librarian. m. Heather E Cole, 30 Mar 1990, 1 daughter. Education: BA, 1973, MFA, 1976, Goddard College. Appointments: Served on grants panels for National Education Association and Massachusetts Arts Council. Publications: 4 Books of poetry written in Greek and published in Greece, 1963, 1965, 1967, 1972; Crossing the River Twice (poetry), 1976; When the Tree Sings (novel), 1979; The Heroic Age (novel), 1984. Other: Editor: Seamus Heaney at Harvard (audio cassettes), 1987; Harvard Review, 1992-; Seamus Heaney, A Celebration (book), 1996. Contributions to: Sunday Telegraph Magazine and several American, Greek and Italian magazines and newspapers including: Iowa Review; To Vima; Stilb. Honour: National Book Critics Circle Awards. Memberships: Phi Beta Kappa and Signet, Harvard University; PEN New England; Société Imaginaire. Literary Agents: Sterling Lord, USA; A D Peters, UK. Address: Poetry Room, Harvard University Library, Cambridge, MA 02138, USA.

HAWKES John (Clendennin Burne Jr), b. 17 Aug 1925, Stanford, Connecticut, USA. Author; Professor Emeritus. m. Sophie Goode Tazewell, 5 Sept 1947, 3 sons, 1 daughter. Education: AB, Harvard University, 1949. Appointments: Visiting Lecturer, 1955-56, Instructor in English, 1956-58, Harvard University; Assistant Professor, 1958-62, Associate Professor, 1962-67, Professor of English, 1967-88, T B Stowe University Professor, 1973-88, Professor Emeritus, 1988-, Brown University; Writer-in-Residence, University of Virginia, 1965; Visiting Professor of Creative Writing, Stanford University, 1966-67;

Visiting Distinguished Professor of Creative Writing, City College of the City University of New York, 1971-72. Publications: Novels: The Cannibal, 1949; The Beetle Leg, 1951; The Goose on the Grave, 1954; The Owl, 1954; The Lime Twig, 1961; Second Skin, 1964; The Blood Oranges, 1971; Death, Sleep and the Traveler, 1974; Travesty, 1976; The Passion Artist, 1979; Virginie: Her Two Lives, 1982; Adventures in the Alaskan Skin Trade, 1985; Whistlejacket, 1988; Sweet William: A Memoir of Old Horse, 1993; The Frog, 1996. Other: Fiasco Hall (poems), 1949; The Personal Voice: Four Short Plays, 1967; The American Literary Anthology I: The First Annual Collection of the Best from the Literary Magazines (editor with others), 1968; Lunar Landscapes: Stories and Short Novels, 1949-63; Humors of Blood & Skin: A John Hawkes Reader, 1984. Contributions to: Anthologies and other publications. Honours: American Academy and Institute of Arts and Letters Award, 1962; Guggenheim Fellowship, 1962-63; Ford Foundation Fellowship, 1964-65; Rockefeller Foundation Grant, 1966; Prix du Meilleur Livre Etranger, 1973; Prix Medicis Etranger, 1986; Prix Medicis etranger, 1986. Membership: American Academy of Arts and Letters. Address: 18 Everett Avenue, Providence, RI 02906, USA.

HAWKESWORTH John (Stanley), b. 7 Dec 1920, London, England. Film and Television Producer; Dramatist. m. Hyacinthe Gregson-Ellis, 1943, 1 son. Education: BA, Oxford University. Appointments: Film Industry Designer; Film and Television Producer: Painter with one-man show, The Studio, Glebe Place, London, 1989, 1995, exhibition, Pembrokeshire, Newport, 1994. Publications: Upstairs, Downstairs, 1972; In My Lady's Chamber, 1973. Honour: Numerous television awards. Address: Fishponds House, Knossington, Oakham, Rutland LE15 8LX, England.

HAWKING Stephen (William), b. 8 Jan 1942, Oxford, England. Professor of Mathematics; Writer. m. Jane Wilde, 1965, div, 2 sons, 1 daughter. Education: BA, University College, Oxford, PhD, Trinity Hall, Cambridge. Appointments: Research Fellow, 1965-69, Fellow for Distinction in Science, 1969-, Gonville and Caius College, Cambridge; Member, Institute of Theoretical Astronomy, Cambridge, 1968-72; Research Assistant, Institute of Astronomy, Cambridge, 1972-73; Research Assistant, Department of Applied Mathematics and Theoretical Physics, 1973-75, Reader in Gravitational Physics, 1975-77, Professor, 1977-79, Lucasian Professor of Mathematics, 1979-, Cambridge University. Publications: The Large Scale Structure of Space-Time (with G F R Ellis), 1973; General Relativity: An Einstein Centenary Survey (editor with W W Israel), 1979; Is the End in Sight for Theoretical Physics?: An Inaugural Lecture, 1980; Superspace and Supergravity: Proceedings of the Nuffield Workshop (editor with M Rocek), 1981; The Very Early Universe: Proceedings of the Nuffield Workshop (co-editor), 1983; Three Hundred Years of Gravitation (with W W Israel), 1987; A Brief History of Time: From the Big Bang to Black Holes, 1988; Black Holes and Baby Universes and Other Essays, 1993. Contributions to: Scholarly journals. Honours: Eddington Medal, 1975, Gold Medal, 1985, Royal Academy of Science; Pius XI Gold Medal, Pontifical Academy of Sciences, 1975; William Hopkins Prize, Cambridge Philosophical Society, 1976; Maxwell Medal, Institute of Physics, 1976; Dannie Heinemann Prize for Mathematical Physics, American Physical Society and American Institute of Physics, 1976; Honorary Fellow, University College, Oxford, 1977; Trinity Hall, Cambridge, 1984; Commander of the Order of the British Empire, 1982; Paul Dirac Medal and Prize, Institute of Physics, 1987; Wolf Foundation Prize for Physics, 1988; Companion of Honour, 1989; Honorary doctorates. Memberships: American Academy of Arts and Sciences; American Philosophical Society; Pontifical Academy of Sciences; Royal Society, Fellow. Address: c/o Department of Applied Mathematics and Theoretical Physics, Cambridge University, Silver Street, Cambridge CB3 9EW, England.

HAWKINS Angus Brian, b. 12 Apr 1953, Portsmouth, England. Historian. m. Esther Armstrong, 20 May 1980, 2 daughters. Education: BA Hons, Reading University, 1975; PhD, London School of Economics, 1980. Publications: Parliament, Party and the Art of Politics in Britain, 1987; Victorian Britain: An Encyclopaedia, 1989. Contributions to: English Historical Review, Parliamentary History, Journal of British Studies, Victorian Studies; Nineteenth Century Prose, Archive. Honours: McCann Award, 1972; Gladstone Memorial Prize, 1978. Memberships: Reform Club. Address: Rewley House, University of Oxford, 1 Wellington Square, Oxford, England.

HAWORTH-BOOTH Mark, b. 20 Aug 1944, Westow, Yorks, England. m. Rosemary Joanna Miles, 19 July 1979, 2 daughters. Education: English Tripos, parts I & II, Cambridge University, 1963-66;

Postgraduate Diploma in Fine Art, Edinburgh University, 1967-69. Publications: E McKnight Kauffer: A Designer and his Public, 1979; The Golden Age of British Photography 1839-1900, 1983; Bill Brandt's Literary Britain, 1984; Photography Now, 1989; Camille Silvy: River Scene, France, 1992. Contributions to: Times Literary Supplement; London Magazine; The Spectator; New Statesman; Aperture. Honours: Hood Medal, 1988; Sudek Medal, 1989. Address: Victoria & Albert Museum, London, SW7 2RL, England.

HAWTHORNE Susan, b. 30 Nov 1951, Wagga Wagga, New South Wales, Australia. Writer; Editor; Publisher. Education: DipT, 1972, MA (Prelim), 1981, University of Melbourne; BA with Honours, La Trobe University, 1976. Appointments: Editor, Commissioning Editor, Penguin Books, Australia, 1987-91; Publisher, Spinifex Press, 1991-. Publications: Difference (editor), 1985; Moments of Desire, 1989; The Exploring Frangipani, 1990; Angels of Power, 1991; The Spinifex Book of Women's Answers, 1991; The Falling Women, 1992; The Language in My Tongue, 1993; The Spinifex Quiz Book, 1993; Australia for Women (co-editor), 1994; Car Maintenance, Explosives and Love (co-editor), 1997; Cyberfeminism, 1997. Address: c/o Spinifex Press, 504 Queensbury Street, North Melbourne, Victoria 3051, Australia.

HAYCRAFT Anna (Margaret), (Alice Thomas Ellis, Brenda O'Casey), Writer. Appointment: Director, Duckworth, publishers, London; Columnist (Home life), The Spectator, 1984-90, The Universe, 1989-90, The Catholic Herald, 1990-. Publications: Natural Baby Food: A Cookery Book (as Brenda O'Casey), 1977; The Sin Eater (novel), 1977; Darling You Shouldn't Have Gone to So Much Trouble (cookery) (as Anna Haycraft with Caroline Blackwood), 1980; The Birds of the Air (novel), 1980; The 27th Kingdom (novel), 1982; The Other Side of the Fire (novel), 1983; Unexplained Laughter (novel), 1985; Home Life (collected columns from the Spectator), 1986; Secrets of Strangers (with Tom Pitt Aikens) (psychiatry), 1986; The Clothes in the Wardrobe (novel), 1987; More Home Life (collection), 1987; The Skeleton in the Cupboard (novel), 1988; Home Life III (collection), 1988; The Loss of the Good Authority (with Tom Pitt Aikens), (psychiatry), 1989; Wales: An Anthology, 1989; The Fly in the Ointment (novel), 1989; Home Life IV (collection), 1989; The Inn at the Edge of the World (novel), 1990; A Welsh Childhood (autobiography), 1990; Pillars of Gold, 1992; The Serpent on the Rocks, 1994; The Evening of Adam, 1994. Address: 22 Gloucester Crescent, London, NW1 7DS, England.

HAYDEN Dolores, b. 15 Mar 1945, New York, USA. Professor; Author. m. Peter Marris, 18 May 1975, 1 daughter. Education: BA, Mount Holyoke College, 1966; Diploma, English Studies, Girton College, Cambridge, 1967; M.Arch, Harvard Graduate School of Design, 1972. Publications: Seven American Utopias, 1976; The Grand Domestic Revolution, 1981; Redesigning the American Dream, 1984; The Power of Place, 1995. Contributions to: Numerous journals. Honours: National Endowment for the Humanities Fellowship, 1976; National Endowment for the Arts Fellowship, 1980; Guggenheim Fellowship, 1981; Rockefeller Foundation Fellowship, 1981; American Council of Learned Societies/Ford Foundation Fellowship, 1988. Memberships: American Studies Association; Organization of American Historians. Address: School of Architecture, Yale University, PO Box 208242, New Haven, CT 06520, USA.

HAYES Charles Langley. See: HOLMES Bryan John.

HAYES Minnie M Mitchell, b. 30 Nov 1948, USA. Writer. m. James E Hayes, 2 sons. Education: BAS, Universityof Illinois; MFA, Vermont College, 1991. Appointments: Journalist; Teacher, Columbia College, Illinois; Fellow, Ragdale Artist Colony, Illinois, 1992. Contributions to: Magazines. Honours: Screenwriting fellowships; Katherine Anne Porter Prize, 1994; In Selected New Stories of the South: Best of 1995. Memberships: PEN Midwest; Art Institute of Chicago. Address: 431 Sheridan Road, Kenilworth, IL 60043, USA.

HAYFLICK Leonard, b. 20 May 1928, Philadelphia, Pennsylvania, USA. Professor. m. Ruth Heckler, 2 Oct 1955, 1 son, 4 daughters. Education: BA, 1951, MS, 1953, PhD, 1956, University of Pennsylvania. Appointments: Editor-in-Chief, Experimental Gerontology. Publications: The Mycoplasmatales and the L-Phase of Bacteria, 1969; Handbook of the Biology of Aging, 1977; How and Why We Age, 1994. Contributions to: Science; Nature; Scientific American; American History Magazine. Honours: Sandoz Award; Kleemeier Award; Brookdale. Address: 36991 Greencroft Close, PO Box No 89, The Sea Ranch, CA 95497, USA.

HAYLOCK John Mervyn, b. 22 Sept 1918, Bournemouth, England. Writer. Education: Diploma francais, Institut de Touraine, Tours, France, 1937; Certificat d'Immatriculation, Grenoble University, France, 1938; BA Hons, 1940, MA Hons, 1946, Pembroke College, Cambridge. Publications: New Babylon, A Portrait of Iraq (with Desmond Stewart), 1956; See You Again, 1963; It's All Your Fault, 1964; Choice and Other Stories, 1979; One Hot Summer in Kyoto, 1980; Tokyo Sketch Book, 1980; Japanese Exercises 1981; Japanese Memories, 1987; Romance Trip and Other Stories, 1988; A Touch of the Orient, 1990; Uneasy Relations, 1993; Translation from French of Philippe Jullian's Flight into Egypt, 1970. Contributions to: Magazines and periodicals. Memberships: Fellow, Royal Society of Literature; Orient Club, London. Literary Agent: Rivens Scott, 15 Gledhow Gardens, London SW5 0AY, England. Address: 5 Powis Grove, Brighton BN1 3HF, England.

HAYMAN David, b . 7 Jan 1927, New York, USA. University Professor. m. Loni Goldschmidt, 28 June 1951, 2 daughters. Education: BA, New York University, 1948; Doctorat d'Universite de Paris, 1955. Appointments: Instructor of English, 1955-57, Assistant Professor, 1957-58, Associate Professor, 1958-65, University of Texas; Professor of English and Comparative Literature, University of Iowa, 1965-73; Professor of Comparative Literature, 1973-, Evjue-Baslom Professor, 1990-, University of Wisconsin. Publications: Joyce et Mallarme, 1956; A First Draft Version of Finnegans Wake, 1963; Configuration Critique de James Joyce (editor), 1965; Ulysses: The Mechanics of Meaning, 1970; Form in Fiction (with Eric Rabkin), 1974; The James Joyce Archive (editor), 1978; Philippe Sollers: Writing and the Experience of Limits (editor and co-translator), 1980; Re-forming the Narrative, 1987; The Wake in Transit, 1990. Contributions to: Many scholarly books and journals. Honours: Guggenheim Fellowship 1958-59; National Endowment for the Humanities 1979-80; Harry Levin Prize (American Comparative Literature Association), 1989. Address: 2913 Columbia Road, Madison, WI 53705, USA.

HAYMAN Ronald, b. 4 May 1932, Bournemouth, England. Writer. Education: BA, 1954, MA, 1963, Trinity Hall, Cambridge. Publications: Harold Pinter, 1968; Samuel Beckett, 1968; John Osborne, 1968; John Arden, 1968; Robert Bolt, 1969; John Whiting, 1969; Collected Plays of John Whiting (editor), 2 volumes, 1969; Techniques of Acting, 1969; The Art of the Dramatist and Other Pieces (editor), 1970; Arthur Miller, 1970; Tolstoy, 1970; Arnold Wesker, 1970; John Gielgud, 1971; Edward Albee, 1971; Eugène Ionesco, 1972; Playback, 1973; The Set-Up, 1974; Playback 2, 1974; The First Thrust, 1975; The German Theatre (editor), 1975; How to Read a Play, 1977; Artaud and After, 1977; De Sade, 1978; Theatre and Anti-Theatre, 1979; British Theatre Since 1955: A Reassessment, 1979; Nietzsche: A Critical Life, 1980; K: A Biography of Kafka, 1981; Brecht: A Biography, 1983; Fassbinder: Film Maker, 1984; Brecht: The Plays, 1984; Günter Grass, 1985; Secrets: Boyhood in a Jewish Hotel, 1932-54, 1985; Writing Against: A Biography of Sartre, 1986; Proust: A Biography, 1990; The Death and Life of Sylvia Plath, 1991; Tennessee Williams: Everyone Else is an Audience, 1994; Thomas Mann, 1995; Hitler and Geli, 1997. Membership: Society of Authors. Address: 3 Chesterford Gardens, London NW3, England.

HAYTER Alethea Catharine, b. 1911, Cairo, Egypt. Former British Council Representative and Cultural Attache; Writer. Education: MA, University of Oxford. Publications: Mrs Browning: A Poet's Work and Its Setting, 1962; A Sultry Month: Scenes of London Literary Life in 1846, 1965; Elizabeth Barrett Browning, 1965; Opium and the Romantic Imagination, 1968; Horatio's Version, 1972; A Voyage in Vain, 1973; Fitzgerald to His Friends: Selected Letters of Edward Fitzgerald, 1979; Portrait of a Friendship, Drawn From New Letters of James Russell Lonell to Sybella Lady Lyttelton 1881-1891, 1990; The Backbone: Diaries of a Military Family in The Napoleonic Wars, 1993; Charlotte Yonge, 1996. Contributions to: Oxford Companion to English Literature; Sunday Times; Times Literary Supplement; New Statesman; History Today; Ariel; London Review of Books; Longman Encyclopedia. Honours: W.H. Heinemann Prize, Royal Society of Literature, 1963; Rose Mary Crawshay Prize, British Academy, for Opium and the Romantic Imagination; Officer of the Order of the British Empire. Memberships: Royal Society of Literature, fellow; Society of Authors, Committee of Management, 1975-79; PEN. Address: 22 Aldebert Terrace, London, SW8 1BJ, England.

HAYWARD Lana James, b. 9 Oct 1943, Ft Worth, Texas, USA. Writer. m. John Edward Hayward, 1 Dec 1961, 1 daughter. Education:

University of Texas at San Antonio, 1981-86. Publications: Nickels and Dimes, 1985; Ink on the Trees, 1987; Son of Man, 1987; Clean, 1992; House Cleaning, 1992; Of Hobos and Rainbows, 1992; Cat's in Cradle, 1993. Contributions to: Journals and Periodicals. Honours: Denver Woman's Press Club Award, 1990; 3rd Place, National League of American PEN Women, 1992; National Writers Club Award, 1992. Membership: National Writers Club. Address: Aurora, CO 80013, USA.

HAZEN Robert M(iller), b. 1 Nov 1948, Rockville Centre, New York, USA. Scientist; Musician; Writer. m. Margaret Hindle, 9 Aug 1969, 1 son, 1 daughter. Education: BS, SM, Massachusetts Institute of Technology, 1971; PhD, Harvard University, 1975. Appointments: NATO Fellow, Cambridge University, 1975-76; Research Scientist, Geophysical Laboratory, Carnegie Institution, Washington, DC, 1976-; Clarence Robinson Professor, George Mason University; Trumpeter with many orchestras. Publications: Comparative Crystal Chemistry, 1982; Poetry of Geology, 1982; Music Men, 1987; The Breakthrough, 1988; Science Matters, 1990; Keepers of the Flame, 1991; The New Alchemist, 1993; The Sciences, 1995; Why Aren't Black Holes Black?, 1997. Contributions to: Many scientific journals and to periodicals. Honours: Mineralogical Society of America Award, 1981; Ipatief Prize, 1984; ASCAP-Deems Taylor Award, 1988; Education Press Association Award, 1992. Memberships: American Chemistry Society; American Geophysical Union; History of Science Society; International Guild of Trumpeters; Mineralogical Society of America; Phi Lambda Upsilon; Sigma Xi; Education Press Award. Literary Agent: Artellus Ltd, London. Address: c/o Geophysical Laboratory, Carnegie Institution, 5251 Broad Branch Road North West, Washington, DC 20015, USA.

HAZLETON Lesley, b. 20 Sept 1945, Reading, England. Writer. Education: BA with Honours in Psychology, Manchester University, 1966; MA in Psychology, Hebrew University of Jerusalem, 1972. Appointments: Automotive Columnist, Detroit Free Press. Publications: Israeli Women, 1978; Where Mountains Roar, 1980; In Defence of Depression, 1984; Jerusalem, Jerusalem, 1986; England, Bloody England, 1989; Confessions of a Fast Woman, 1992; Everything Women Always Wanted to Know About Cars, 1995; Driving to Detroit, 1998. Contributions to: Many periodicals and magazines. Memberships: International Motor Press Association; PEN American Center. Address: c/o Watkins-Loomis Inc, 133 East 35th Street, New York, NY 10016, USA.

HAZO Samuel (John), b. 19 July 1928, Pittsburgh, Pennsylvania, USA. Professor of English; Writer; Poet. Education: BA, University of Pittsburgh, 1957. Appointments: Faculty, 1955-65, Dean, College of Arts and Sciences, 1961-66, Professor of English, 1965-, Duquesne University; Director, International Forum, 1966-. Publications: Discovery and Other Poems, 1959; The Quiet Wars, 1962; Hart Crane: An Introduction and Interpretation, 1963, new edition as Smithereened Apart: A Critique of Hart Crane, 1978; The Christian Intellectual Studies in the Relation of Catholicism to the Human Sciences (editor), 1963; A Selection of Contemporary Religious Poetry (editor), 1963; Listen With the Eye, 1964; My Sons in God: Selected and New Poems, 1965; Blood Rights, 1968; The Blood of Adonis (with Ali Ahmed Said), 1971; Twelve Poems (with George Nama), 1972; Seascript: A Mediterranean Logbook, 1972; Once for the Last Bandit: New and Previous Poems, 1972; Quartered, 1974; Inscripts, 1975; The Very Fall of the Sun, 1978; To Paris, 1981; The Wanton Summer Air, 1982; Thank a Bored Angel, 1983; The Feast of Icarus, 1984; The Color of Reluctance, 1986; The Pittsburgh That Starts Within You, 1986; Silence Spoken Here, 1988; Stills, 1989; The Rest is Prose, 1989; Lebanon, 1990; Picks, 1990; The Past Won't Stay Behind You, 1993. Address: 785 Somerville Drive, Pittsburgh, PA 15243, USA.

HAZZARD Shirley, b. 30 Jan 1931, Sydney, New South Wales, Australia. Writer. m. Francis Steegmuller, 22 Dec 1963, dec 1994. Education: Queenwood School, Sydney. Appointments: Member, Combined Services Intelligence, Hong Kong, 1947-48, UK High Commissioner's Officer, Wellington, New Zealand, 1949-50; General Service Post, United Nations, New York City, 1952-62; Boyer Lecturer, Australia, 1984, 1988. Publications: Fiction: The Evening of the Holiday, 1966; The Bay of Noon, 1970; The Transit of Venus, 1980. Stories: Cliffs of Falls and Other Stories, 1963; People in Glass Houses, 1967. Non-Fiction: Defeat of an Ideal: A Study of the Self-Destruction of the United Nations, 1973; Countenance of Truth, 1990. Contributions to: Magazines. Honours: National Institute of Arts and Letters Award, 1966; Guggenheim Fellowship, 1974; 1st Prize, O Henry Short Story Awards, 1976; National Book Critics Award for

Fiction, 1981. Membership: American Academy and National Institute of Arts and Letters. Address: 200 East 66th Street, New York, NY 10021, USA.

HEADLEY Elizabeth. See: HARRISON Elizabeth C.

HEADLEY John Miles, b. 23 Oct 1929, New York, USA. Educator; Historian. m. Anne Renouf, 27 July 1965, div. Education: BA, Princeton University, 1951; MA, 1952; PhD, 1960, Yale University. Appointment: Faculty, Department of History, University of New Carolina at Chapel Hill. Publications: Luther's View of Church History, 1963; The Emperor and his Chancellor, 1983. Co-author: San Carlo Borromeo: Catholic Reform and Ecclesiastical Politics, 1988. Editor: Responsio ad Lutherum, Complete works of St Thomas More, 1969. Contributions to: Several journals including, Journal of the History of Ideas. Honours: Guggenheim Fellow, 1974; Selma V Forkosch Prize, 1988. Memberships: American Society for Reformation Research, President, 1978-80; Renaissance Society of America. Address: Deptartment of History, University of North Carolina, Chapel Hll, NC 27599, USA.

HEALD Timothy Villiers, (David Lancaster), b. 28 Jan 1944, Dorset, England. Writer. m. Alison Martina Leslie, 30 Mar 1968, 2 sons, 2 daughters. Education: MA, Honours, Balliol College, Oxford, 1962-65. Publications: Unbecoming Habits; HRH: The Man Who Would Be King; The Character of Cricket; Networks; Class Distinctions; Murder at Moosejaw; Blue Blood Will Out: Deadline; Let Sleeping Dogs Die; Masterstroke; Red Herrings; Brought to Book; Business Unusual; The Rigby File (editor); Its a Dog's Life; Making of Space 1999; John Steed (The Authorised Biography) vol 1; The Newest London Spy (editor); By Appointments: 150 Years of the Royal Warrant and Its Holders; My Lord's (editor); A Classic English Crime (editor), 1990; The Duke: A Portrait of Prince Philip, 1991; Honourable Estates, 1992; Barbara Cartland: A Life of Love, 1994; Denis: The Authorised Biography of the Incomparable Compton, 1994. Memberships: Crime Writers Association, chairman, 1987-88; PEN; Society of Authors. Address: 305 Sheen Road, Richmond, Surrey, TW10 5AW, England.

HEALEY, Baron of Riddlesden in the County of West Yorkshire, Denis (Winston), b. 30 Aug 1917, Nottingham, England. Politican; Writer. Education: Balliol College, Oxford; First Class Hons Mods, 1938; Jenkyns Exhib, 1939; Harmsworth Senior Scholar, First Class Hum, BA, 1940, MA, 1945. Appointments: Secretary, International Department, Labour Party, 1945-52; Member of Parliament, Labour Party, South East Leeds, 1951-55, Leeds East, 1955-92; Shadow Cabinet, 1959-64, 1970-74, 1979-87; Secretary of State for Defence, 1964-70; Chancellor of the Exchequer, 1974-79; Deputy Leader, Labour Party, 1980-83; President, Birkbeck College, 1993. Publications: The Curtain Falls, 1951; New Fabian Essays, 1952; Neutralism, 1955; Fabian International Essays, 1956; A Neutral Belt in Europe, 1958; NATO and American Security, 1959; The Race Against the H Bomb, 1960; Labour, Britain and the World, 1963; Healey's Eye, 1980; Labour and a World Society, 1985; Beyond Nuclear Deterrence, 1986; The Time of My Life (autobiography), 1989; When Shrimps Learn to Whistle (essays), 1990; My Secret Planet, 1992; Dennis Healey's Yorkshire Dales, 1996. Honours: Member of the Order of the British Empire, 1945; Companion of Honour, 1979; Grand Cross of the Order of Merit, Federal of Germany, 1979; Created Baron Healey of Riddlesden, 1992; Freeman, City of Leeds, 1992; Honorary doctorates. Membership: Royal Society of Literature, Fellow. Address: Pingles Place, Alfriston, East Sussex BN26 5TT, England.

HEANEY Seamus (Justin), b. 13 Apr 1939, County Londonderry, Northern Ireland. Poet; Writer; Professor. m. Marie Devlin, 1965, 2 sons, 1 daughter. Education: St Columb's College, Derry; BA 1st Class, Queen's University, Belfast, 1961. Appointments: Teacher, St Thomas's Secondary School, Belfast, 1962-63; Lecturer, St Joseph's College of Education, Belfast, 1963-66; Queen's University, Belfast, 1966-72; Carysfort College, 1975-81; Senior Visting Lecturer, 1982-85, Boylston Professor of Rhetoric and Oratory, Harvard University, 1985-; Professor of Poetry, Oxford University, 1989-94. Publications: Eleven Poems, 1965; Death of a Naturalist, 1966; Door Into the Dark, 1969; Wintering Out, 1972; North, 1975; Field Work, 1979; Selected Poems, 1965-1975, 1980; Sweeney Astray, 1984, revised edition as Sweeney's Flight, 1992; Station Island, 1984; The Haw Lantern, 1987; New Selected Poems, 1966-1987, 1990; Seeing Things, 1991. Prose: Preoccupations: Selected Prose, 1968-1978, 1980; The Government of the Tongue, 1988; The Place of

Writing, 1989; The Redress of Poetry: Oxford Lectures, 1995; The Spirit Level, 1996. Editor: The May Anthology of Oxford and Cambridge Poetry, 1993. Other: The Cure at Troy, version of Sophocles's Philiocrites, 1990. Honours: Somerset Maugham Award, 1967; Cholmondeley Award, 1968; W H Smith Award, 1975; Duff Cooper Prize, 1975; Whitbread Awards, 1987, 1996; Nobel Prize for Literature, 1995. Membership: Irish Academy of Letters. Address: c/o Faber & Faber, 3 Queen Square, London WC1N 3RU, England.

HEARD Anthony Hazlitt, b. 20 Nov 1937, Johannesburg, South Africa. Journalist. m. (1) Valerie Joy Hermanson, 1959, (2) Mary Ann Barker, 1988, 1 son, 3 daughters. Education: BA, University of Cape Town; BA (Hons), 1st Class, in Political Philosophy, 1964. Appointments: Editor, The Cape Times, 1971-87; Freelance writer for international newspapers, 1987-94. Publication: The Cape of Storms: A Personal History of the Crisis in South Africa, 1990. Contributions to: Many newspapers. Honour: Golden Pen of Freedom from World Association of Newspapers (formerly FIEJ), 1986. Address: PO Box 12189, Mill Street, Gardens 8010, South Africa.

HEARDEN Patrick Joseph, b. 17 Sept 1942, Green Bay, Wisconsin, USA. Historian. m. Carol J Morgan, 27 July 1991. Education: BS 1965, MS 1966, PhD 1971, University of Wisconsin, Madison. Appointments: Case Western Reserve University, 1971-72; University of South Dakota, 1973-75; University of Missouri, 1975-78; University of Arizona, 1979-80; University of Wisconsin, 1981-82; Purdue University, 1983-. Publications: Independence and Empire, 1982; Roosevelt Confronts Hitler, 1987; Vietnam: Four American Perspectives (editor), 1990; The Tragedy of Vietnam, 1991. Contributions to: American Historical Review; Journal of Southern History; Journal of Interdisciplinary History; South Atlantic Quarterly. Memberships: Organization of American Historians; Society for Historians of American Foreign Relations. Address: 2107 Fairway Lane, West Lafayette, IN 47906, USA.

HEARNE Vicki, b. 13 Feb 1946, Austin, Texas, USA. Assistant Professor of English; Writer; Poet. m. (1), div, 1 daughter, (2) Robert Tragesser, 1980. Education: BA, University of California at Riverside, 1981-84; Assistant Professor of English, Yale University, 1984-. Publications: Nervous Horses, poems, 1980; In the Absence of Horses, poems, 1983; Adam's Task: Calling Animals by Name, 1986; The White German Shepherd (novel), 1988; Bandit: Dossier of a Dangerous Dog, 1991; Animal Happiness, 1993; The Parts of Light, poems, 1994. Honours: Peter Lavan Younger Poets Award, Academy of American Poets, 1984; American Academy and Institute of Arts and Letters Award, 1992. Memberships: American Working Dog Association; PEN; Endangered Breeds Association. Address: c/o Yale Institution for Social and Policy Studies, Yale University, New Haven, CT 16520, USA.

HEARON Shelby, b. 18 Jan 1931, Kentucky, USA. Writer. m. (1) Robert Hearon Jr, 15 June 1953, (2) Billy Joe Lucas, 19 Apr 1981, 1 son, 1 daughter. Education: BA, University of Texas at Austin, 1953. Appointments: Visiting Lecturer, University of Texas at Austin, 1978-80; Visiting Writer, Associate Professor, University of Houston, 1981; Writer-in-Residence, Wichita State University, 1984, Clark University, 1985, University of california at Irvine, 1987, Ohio Wesleyan University, 1989; Professor, University of Illinois at Chicago, 1993, Colgate University, 1993. Publications: Armadillo in the Grass, 1968; The Second Dune, 1973; Hannah's House, 1975; Now and Another Time, 1976; A Prince of a Fellow, 1978; Painted Dresses, 1981; Afternoon of a Faun, 1983; Group Therapy, 1984; A Small Town, 1985; Five Hundred Scorpions, 1987; Owning Jolene, 1989; Hug Dancing, 1991; Friends for Life, 1993. Honours: Guggenheim Fellowship, 1982; National Endowment for the Arts Fellowship, 1983; Ingram Merrill Grant, 1987; American Academy and Institute of Arts and Letters Prize, 1990. Memberships: PEN American Centre; Authors League and Authors Guild; Associated Writing Program; Poets and Writers; Women in Communications; Texas Institute of Letters. Literary Agent: Wendy Weil; Lecture Agent: Bill Thomson. Address: 5 Church Street, North White Plains, NY 10603, USA.

HEATER Derek Benjamin, b. 28 Nov 1931, Sydenham, England. Writer. m. Gwyneth Mary Owen, 12 Mar 1982, 1 son, 1 daughter. Education: BA, Honours, History, University College, London, 1950-53; Postgraduate Certificate in Education, Institute of Education, University of London, 1953-54. Appointments: Editor, Teaching Politics, 1973-79; Co-editor, with Bernard Crick, Political Realities Series, 1974-93. Publications: Political Ideas in the Modern

World, 1960; Order and Rebellion, 1964; World Affairs (with Gwyneth Owen), 1972; Contemporary Political Ideas, 1974; Britain and the Outside World, 1976; Essays in Political Education (with Bernard Crick), 1977; World Studies, 1980; Our World This Century, 1982; Peace Through Education, 1984; Reform and Revolution, 1987; Refugees, 1988; Case Studies in Twentieth-Century World History, 1988; Citizenship: The Civic Ideal in World History, Politics and Education, 1990; The Idea of European Unity, 1992; The Remarkable History of Rottingdean, 1993; Introduction to International Politics (with G.R. Berridge), 1993; Foundations of Citizenship (with Dawn Oliver), 1994; National Self-Determination, 1994; World Citizenship and Government, 1996. Contributions to: Articles in learned journals, educational press and contributions to symposia; entries for encyclopaedias. Honours: Children's Book of the Year Award for Refugees, 1988; Fellow of the Politics Association, 1994. Memberships: Founder-Chairman, The Politics Association, 1969-73; Honorary Life Member, Council for Education in World Citizenship. Address: 3 The Rotyngs, Rottingdean, Brighton, BN2 7DX, England.

HEATH Roy A(ubrey) K(elvin), b. 13 Aug 1926, Georgetown, British Guiana. Author. m. Aemilia Oberli, 3 children. Education: BA, University of London, 1956. Appointments: Teacher, London, 1959-; Called to the Bar, Lincoln's Inn, 1964. Publications: Fiction: A Man Come Home, 1974; The Murderer, 1978; From the Heat of the Day, 1979; One Generation, 1980; Genetha, 1981; Kwaku, or, The Man Who Could Not Keep His Mouth Shut, 1982; Orealla, 1984; The Shadow Bridge, 1988. Non-Fiction: Art and History, 1983; Shadows Round the Moon (memoirs), 1990. Play: Inez Combray, 1972. Honours: Drama Award, Theatre Guild of Guyana, 1971; Fiction Prize, The Guardian, London, 1978; Guyana Award for Literature, 1989. Address: c/o Harper/Collins, 77 Fulham Palace Road, London W6 8J, England.

HEATH-STUBBS John (Francis Alexander), b. 9 July 1918, London, England. Education. Worcester College for the Blind; Queen's College, Oxford. Appointments: English Tutor, 1944-45; Editorial Assistant, Hutchinsons, 1945-46; Gregory Fellow, Poetry, University of Leeds, 1952-55; Visiting Professor English, University of Alexandria, 1955-58, University of Michigan, 1960-61; Lecturer, English Literature, College of St Mark and St John, Chelsea, 1963-73; President, Poetry Society, 1992-. Publications: Poetry: Wounded Thammuz, 1942; Beauty and the Beast, 1943; The Divided Ways, 1946; The Swarming of the Bees, 1950; A Charm Against the Toothache, 1954; The Triumph of the Muse, 1958; The Blue Fly in his Head, 1962; Selected Poems, 1965; Satires and Epigrams, 1968; Artorius, 1973; A Parliament of Birds, 1975; The Watchman's Flute, 1978; Birds Reconvened, 1980; Buzz Buzz, 1981; Naming of the Best, 1982; The Immolation of Aleph, 1985; Cats Parnassus, 1987; Time Pieces, 1988; Partridge in a Pear Tree, 1988; Ninefold of Charms, 1989; The Parson's Cat, 1991; Collected Poems, 1990; Sweet Earth, 1993; Chimeras, 1994. Drama: Helen in Egypt, 1958. Criticism: The Darkling Plain, 1950; Charles Williams, 1955; The Pastoral, 1969; The Ode, 1969; The Verse Satire, 1969. Autobiography: Hindsights, 1993. Other: Translations; editions.. Honours: Queen's Gold Medal for Poetry, 1973; Officer of the Order of the British Empire, 1989. Address: 22 Artesian Road, London W2, England.

HEATHCOTT Mary. See: **KEEGAN Mary Constance.**

HEATON Tom, (Thomas Peter Starke), b. 16 Nov 1928, Celle, Germany. BBC Editor and Arabic Monitor. m. Jackie Noble, 20 Dec 1972, 1 son. Education: BA Honours, 1955, MA Distinction, 1960, School of Oriental and African Studies, London; Postgraduate Certificate in Education, London, 1957. Publication: In Teleki's Footsteps: A Walk Across East Africa, 1990. Contributions to: Regular contributor to the World Tax Report of the Financial Times. Address: PO Box 24945, Nairobi, Kenya.

HEBALD Carol, b. 6 July 1934, New York, New York, USA. Writer. Education: MFA, University of Iowa, 1971; BA, City College of City University of New York, 1969. Publications: Three Blind Mice, 1989; Clara Kleinschmidt, 1989; Martha (play), 1991. Contributions to: Antioch Review; Kansas Quarterly; Texas Quarterly; Massachusetts Review; The Humanist; New Letters; Confrontation; North American Review; New York Tribune. Honours: Pushcart Prizes, 1987, 1994. Memberships: PEN American Centre; Authors Guild of America; Poet and Writers. Address: 463 West Street, No 353, New York, NY 10014, USA.

HEBERT Anne, b. 1 Aug 1916, Sainte-Catherine-de-Fossambault, Quebec, Canada. Novelist; Poet. Education: Collège Notre Dame, Bellevue, Quebec. Publications: The Torrent: Novellas and Short Stories, 1950; The Silent Rooms, 1958, 2nd edition, 1974; Kamouraska, 1970; Children of the Black Sabbath, 1975; Heloise, 1980; In the Shadow of the Wind, 1982; The First Garden, 1988; The Dreaming Child, 1992; Verse: Les Songes en équilibre, 1942; The Tomb of the Kings, 1953; Poems, 1960; Selected Poetry, (in translation), 1978; Eve: Poems, 1980; Selected Poems, 1987; Plays: Le Temps sauvage, La Mercière assassinée and Les Invités au procès, all 1966; La Cage and L'Ile de la demoiselle, 1990. Honours: Académie Française Award, 1975; DLitt, Universities of Toronto and Quebec. Address: 24 rue de Pontoise, 75005 Paris, France.

HECHT Anthony (Evan), b. 16 Jan 1923, New York, New York, USA. Poet; Professor. m. (1) Patricia Harris, 27 Feb 1954, div 1961, 2 sons, (2) Helen D'Alessandro, 12 June 1971, 1 son. Education: BA, Bard College, 1944; MA, Columbia University, 1950. Appointments: Teacher, Kenyon College, 1947-48; State University of Iowa, 1948-49; New York University, 1949-56; Smith College, 1956-59; Associate Professor of English, Bard College, 1961-67; Faculty, 1967-68, John D Deane Professor of English of Rhetoric and Poetry, 1968-85, University of Rochester, New York; Hurst Professor, Washington University, St Louis, 1971; Visiting Professor, Harvard University, 1973; Yale University, 1977; Faculty, Salzburg Seminar in American Studies, 1977; Professor, Georgetown University, 1985-93; Consultant in Poetry, Library of Congress, Washington, DC, 1982-84; Andrew Mellon Lecturer in Fine Arts, National Gallery of Art, Washington, DC, 1992. Publications: A Summoning of Stones, 1954; The Seven Deadly Sins, 1958; A Bestiary, 1960; The Hard Hours, 1968; Millions of Strange Shadows, 1977; The Venetian Vespers, 1977; Obligati: Essays in Criticism, 1986; The Transparent Man, 1990; Collected Earlier Poems, 1990; The Hidden Law: The Poetry of W H Auden, 1993; On the Laws of the Poetic Art, 1995; The Presumption of Death, 1995; Flight Among the Tombs, 1996. Co-Author and Co-Editor: Jiggery-Pokery: A Compendium of Double Dactyls (with John Hollander), 1967. Editor: The Essential Herbert, 1987. Translator: Seven Against Thebes (with Helen Bacon), 1973. Contributions to: Many anthologies; Hudson Review; New York Review of Books; Quarterly Review of Literature; Transatlantic Review; Voices. Honours: Prix de Rome Fellowship, 1950; Guggenheim Fellowships, 1954, 1959; Hudson Review Fellowship, 1958; Ford Foundation Fellowships, 1960, 1968; Academy of American Poets Fellowship, 1969; Bollingen Prize, 1983; Eugenio Montale Award, 1983; Harriet Monroe Award, 1987; Ruth Lilly Award, 1988; Aiken Taylor Award of the Sewanee Review, 1988; National Endowment for the Arts Grant, 1989; Phi Beta Kappa. Memberships: Academy of American Poets, honorary chancellor, 1971-95; American Academy of Arts and Sciences; American Academy of Arts and Letters; Phi Beta Kappa. Address: 4256 Nebraska Avenue North West, Washington, DC 20016, USA.

HECKLER Jonellen, b . 28 Oct 1943, Pittsburgh, Pennsylvania, USA. Writer. m. Lou Heckler, 17 Aug 1968, 1 son. Education: BA, English Literature, University of Pittsburgh, 1965. Publications: Safekeeping, 1983; A Fragile Peace, 1986; White Lies, 1989; Circumstances Unknown, 1993; Final Tour, 1994. Contributions to: Numerous poems and short stories in Ladies Home Journal Magazine, 1975-83. Membership: Authors Guild. Address: 5562 Pernod Drive South West, Ft Myers, FL 33919, USA.

HEDIN Mary Ann, b . 3 Aug 1929, Minneapolis, Minnesota, USA. Writer; Poet. m. Roger Willard Hedin, 3 sons, 1 daughter. Education: BS, University of Minnesota; MA, University of California. Appointments: Fellow, Yaddo, 1974; Writer-in-Residence, Robinson Jeffers Town House Foundation, 1984-85. Publications: Fly Away Home, 1980; Direction, 1983. Contributions to: Anthologies and journals. Honours: John H McGinnis Memorial Award, 1979; Iowa School of Letters Award for Short Fiction, 1979. Memberships: Authors Guild; PEN; American Poetry Society. Address: 182 Oak Avenue, San Anselmo, CA 94960, USA.

HEDLEY Annie. See: **HUNT Fay Ann.**

HEDMAN Dag Sven Gustav, (Julius Mosca), b. 11 June 1953, Lahäll, Sweden. Professor of Literature. m. Eva Ingrid Sabler, 1 Sept 1990, 1 son. Education: PhD, 1985. Publications: Eleganta eskapader. Frank Hellers författarskap till och med Kejsarens gamla klåder, dissertation, 1985; Gunnar Serner (Frank Heller), bibliography, 1987;

Stanislaw Ignacy Witkiewicz: Fem dramer (with A N Uggla), 1988; Brott, kärlek, äventyr, 1995; Två polska dramatiker: S Wyspianski, S I Witkiewicz (with A N Uggla), 1996. Contributions to: Various periodicals. Address: University of Linköping, Department of Literature, 581 83 Linköping, Sweden.

HEFFERNAN Thomas (Patric Carroll), b. 19 Aug 1939, Hyannis, Massachusetts, USA. American and English Studies Educator; Writer; Poet. m. Nancy E Iler, 15 July 1972, div 1978. Education: AB, Boston College, 1961; MA, English Literature, University of Manchester, England, 1963; Universita per-Stranieri, Perugia, Italy, 1965; PhD English Literature, Sophia University, Tokyo, 1990. Appointments: Poet in Schools, North Carolina Department of Public Instruction, Raleigh, 1973-77; Visiting Artist, Poetry, North Carolina Department of Community Colleges, 1977-81; Visiting Artist, Poetry, South Carolina Arts Commission, 1981-82; Co-editor, The Plover (Chidori), bilingual haiku journal, Japan, 1989-; Professor of English, Kagoshima Prefectura 1 University, Japan. Publications: Mobiles, 1973; A Poem is A Smile You Can Hear (Editor), 1976; A Narrative of Jeremy Bentham, 1978; The Liam Poems, 1981; City Renewing Itself, 1983; Art and Emblem: Early Seventeenth Century English Poetry of Devotion, 1991. Contributions to: Anthologies and other publications. Honours: National Endowment for the Arts Literary Fellowship, 1977; Gordon Barber Memorial Award, 1979; Portfolio Award, 1983; Roanoke Chowan Prize, 1982. Memberships: Modern Language Association; Japan English Literary Society; Japan American Literary Society. Address: Kagoshima Prefectural University, 1-52-1 Shimo-ishiki-cho, Kagoshima-shi, Japan 890.

HEFFRON Dorris, b. 18 Oct 1944, Noranda, Quebec, Canada. Writer. m. (1) William Newton-Smith, 29 June 1968, div, 2 daughters, (2) D L Gauer, 29 Oct 1980, 1 son, 1 daughter. Education: BA, 1967, MA, 1969, Queen's University, Kingston, Ontario. Appointments: Tutor, Oxford University, 1972-80, The Open University, 1975-78, University of Malaysia, 1978; Writer-in-Residence, Wainfleet Public Library, 1989-90. Publications: A Nice Fire and Some Moonpennies, 1971; Crusty Crossed, 1976; Rain and I, 1982; A Shark in the House, 1996. Contributions to: Various publications. Honours: Canada Council Arts Grant, 1974. Memberships: Authors Society; PEN; Writers Union of Canada. Address: 202 Riverside Drive, Toronto, Ontario M6S 4A9, Canada.

HEGELER Sten, b. 28 Apr 1923, Copenhagen, Denmark. Psychoanalyst; Psychologist. Education: Candidate for Psychology, University of Copenhagen, 1953. Publications: Peter & Caroline; Men Only; Choosing Toys for Children; What Everybody Should Know About AIDS; On Selenium; An ABZ of Love (with I Hegeler); Ask Inge & Sten; World's Best Slimming Diet; On Being Lonesome; XYZ of Love; Living is Loving. Contributions to: Aktuelt; Info; Editor, Taenk magazine. Honour: Co-recipient, PH-Fund, 1970. Memberships: Danish Psychological Association; Danish Journalist Association; Danish Authors Association. Address: Frederiksberg Alle 25, DK-1820 Fredenksberg, Denmark.

HEGI Ursula (Johanna), b. 23 May 1946, Büderich, Germany. Professor of English; Writer; Poet; Critic. 2 sons. Education: BA, 1978, MA, 1979, University of New Hampshire. Appointments: Instructor, University of New Hampshire, 1980-84; Book Critic, Los Angeles Times, New York Times, Washington Post, 1982-; Assistant Professor, 1984-89, Associate Professor, 1989-95, Professor of English, 1995-, Eastern Washington University; Visiting Writer, various universities. Publications: Fiction: Intrusions, 1981; Unearned Pleasures and Other Stories, 1988; Floating in My Mother's Palm, 1990; Stones from the River, 1994; Salt Dancers, 1995. Non-Fiction: Tearing the Silence: On Being German in America, 1997. Contributions to: Anthologies, newspapers, journals and magazines. Honours: Indiana Fiction Award, 1988; National Endowment for the Arts Fellowship, 1990; New York Times Best Books Selections, 1990, 1994; Pacific Northwest Booksellers Association Award, 1991; Governor's Writers Awards, 1991, 1994. Memberships: Associated Writing Programs; National Book Critics Circle, board of directors, 1992-94. Address: c/o Department of English, Eastern Washington University, Cheney, WA 99004, USA.

HEIDELBERGER Michael (Johannes), b. 9 Aug 1947, Karlsruhe, Germany. Professor of Philosophy; Writer. m. Nicole Jeannet, 16 Sept 1978, 1 son, 1 daughter. Education: PhD in Philosophy and the History of Science, University of Munich, 1978; Habilitation in the Philosophy of Science, University of Göttingen,

1989. Appointment: Professor of Philosophy, Humboldt-University of Berlin. Publications: Natur und Erfahrung, 1981; The Probabilistic Revolution, 1987; Die innere Seite der Natur: Gustav Fechners wissenschaftlich-philosophische Weltauffassung, 1993. Contributions to: Many anthologies, journals, and other publications. Address: Hümboldt-Universität zu Berlin, Institut für Philosophie, Unter den Linden 6, D-10099 Berlin, Germany.

HEIGERT Hans A, b. 21 Mar 1925, Mainz, Germany. Journalist. m. Hildegard Straub, 1951, 3 sons, 2 daughters. Education: PhD, Universities of Stuttgart, Heidelberg and Oklahoma. Appointments: Journalist, Newspapers, Radio and TV, 1950-; Chief Editor, Süddeutsche Zeitung, 1970-85. Publications: Statten der Jugend, 1958; Sehnsucht nach der Nation, 1966; Deutschlands falsche Traume, 1968. Honours: Theodor Heuss Preis, 1969; Bayersicher Verdienstorden, 1974; Bundesverdienstrkreuz, 1979. Membership: Goethe Institute, Munich, 1984-93, President, 1989-93. Address: Eichenstr. 12, 82110 Germering, Germany.

HEILBRONER Robert L(ouis), b. 24 Mar 1919, New York, New York, USA. Professor of Economics; Writer. m. (1) Joan Knapp, div, 2 sons, (2) Shirley E T Davis. Education: BA, Harvard University, 1940; PhD, New School for Social Research, New York City. Appointments: Economist in government and business; Norman Thomas Professor of Economics, New School for Social Research, New York City, 1972-; Lecturer to various organizations. Publications: The Worldly Philosophers, 1953, 6th edition, 1986; The Quest for Wealth, 1956; The Future as History, 1960; The Making of Economic Society, 1962, 9th edition, 1993; The Great Ascent, 1963; A Primer on Government Spending (with P L Bernstein), 1963, 2nd edition, 1971; Understanding Macroeconomics (with James Galbraith), 1965, 9th edition, 1990; The Limits of American Capitalism, 1966; The Economic Problem (with James Galbraith), 1968, 9th edition, 1990; Understanding Microeconomics (with James Galbraith), 1968, 9th edition, 1990; Economic Means and Social Ends (editor with others), 1969; Between Capitalism and Socialism: Essays in Political Economics, 1970; Is Economics Relevant? (editor with A M Ford), 1971; In the Name of Profit (with others), 1972; Corporate Social Policy (editor with Paul London), 1975; An Inquiry into the Human Prospect, 1975, 3rd edition, 1991; Business Civilization in Decline, 1976; Economic Relevance: A Second Look (with A M Ford), 1976; The Economic Transformation of America (with Aaron Singer), 1977, 3rd edition, 1994; Beyond Boom and Crash, 1978; Marxism: For and Against, 1980; Five Economic Challenges (with Lester C Thurow), 1981; Economics Explained (with Lester C Thurow), 1982, 3rd edition, 1994; The Nature and Logic of Capitalism, 1985; The Essential Adam Smith (editor), 1986; Beyond the Veil of Economics, 1988; Twenty-First Century Capitalism, 1993; The Crisis of Unsion in Modern Economic Thought; Visions of the Future, 1995; The Crisis of Vision in Modern Economic Thought (with William Milberg), 1995; Teachings from the Worldly Philosophy (editor), 1996. Contributions to: Many periodicals. Honours: Guggenheim Fellowship, 1983; Honorary Doctorates; Scholar of the Year, 1995. Memberships: American Economic Association; Council on Economic Priorities; Phi Beta Kappa. Address: 830 Park Avenue, New York, NY 10021, USA.

HEILBRUN Carolyn (Gold), b. 13 Jan 1926, East Orange, New Jersey, USA. Professor of English Literature Emerita; Writer. m. James Heilbrun, 20 Feb 1945, 1 son, 2 daughters. Education: BA, Wellesley College, 1947; MA, 1951, PhD, 1959, Columbia University. Appointments: Instructor, Brooklyn College, 1959-60; Instructor, 1960-62, Assistant Professor, 1962-67, Associate Professor, 1967-72, Professor of English Literature, 1972-86, Avalon Foundation Professor of Humanities, 1986-93, Professor Emerita, 1993-, Columbia University; Visiting Professor, University of California at Santa Cruz, 1979, Princeton University, 1981, Yale Law School, 1989. Publications: The Garrett Family, 1961; In the Last Analysis, 1964; Christopher Isherwood, 1970; Toward a Recognition of Androgyny, 1973; Lady Ottoline's Album, 1976; Reinventing Womanhood, 1979; Representation of Women in Fiction (editor), 1983; Writing a Woman's Life, 1988; Hamlet's Mother and Other Women, 1990; The Education of a Woman: The Life of Gloria Steinem, 1995. Honours: Guggenheim Fellowship, 1966; Rockefeller Foundation Fellowship, 1976; Senior Research Fellow, National Endowment for the Humanities, 1983; Alumnae Achievement Award, Wellesley College, 1984; Award of Excellence, Graduate Faculty of Columbia University Alumni, 1984; Many honorary doctorates. Memberships: Modern Language Association, President, 1984; Mystery Writers of America; Phi Beta

Kappa. Address: c/o Department of English, Columbia University, New York, NY 10027, USA.

HEIN Christoph, b. 8 Apr 1944, Heinzendorf/Schlesien, Germany. Novelist; Playwright. Education: University of Leipzig and Humboldt University, Berlin. Appointments: Dramaturg and Playwright, Deutsches Theater, East Berlin, 1971-79. Publications: Nachfahrt und früher Morgen, 1980; The Distant Lover, 1982; Horns Ende, 1985; Der Tangospieler, 1989. Plays: Cromwell, 1977; Lassalle fragt Herrn Herbert nach Sonja, 1981; Der neue Mendoza, 1981; Schlotel, oder was solls, 1981; The True Story of Ah Q, 1983; Passage, 1987; Die Ritter der Tafelrunde, 1989. Also: Jamie and his Friends (for children), 1984; I Saw Stalin as a Child, 1990. Honours: City of Hamburg Prize, 1986; Lessing Prize, 1989. Address: c/o Aufbau-Verlag, Postfach 1217, 1086 Berlin, Germany.

HEINESEN Jens Pauli, b. 12 Nov 1932, Torshavn, Faroe Islands. Novelist. Education: University of Copenhagen, 1953-54. Appointment: Teacher, Torshavn, 1957-70. Publications: The Dawn Shower, 1953; The Beautiful Calm, 1959; You, World of Origin, 3 volumes, 1962-64; The Waves Play on the Shore, 1969; In the Garden of Eden, 1971; The Serpent's Name is Fraenir, 1973; The Beachcomber, 1977; Drops in the Ocean of Life, 1978; They Carve Their Idols, 1979; Now You are a Child of Man on Earth, 1980; The World Now Shines Before You, 1981; Your Playing is Like the Bright Day, 1982; The World Now Stretches Boundless Before You, 1983; A Depth of Precious Time, 1984; The Mysteries of Love, 1986; Exposed to the Wind, 1986; Blue Mountain, 1992; Stories, Gestur, and Little Frants Vilhelm, 1972. Honours: Nordic Council Prize, 1987. Address: Stoffalag 18, Torshavn, The Faroe Islands, via Denmark.

HELIANOS Orestis. See: STYLIANOPOULOS Orestis.

HELLER Joseph, b. 1 May 1923, New York, New York, USA. Author. m. (1) Shirley Held, 3 Sept 1945, div 1984, 1 son, 1 daughter, (2) Valerie Humphries, 1987. Education: University of Southern California, Los Angeles; BA, New York University, 1948; MA, Columbia University, 1949; Graduate Studies, Oxford University, 1949-50. Appointments: Teacher, Penn State University, Yale University, University of Pennsylvania; Distinguished Professor of English, City College of the City University of New York; Full-time Author, 1975- . Publications: Fiction: Catch-22, 1961; Something Happened, 1974; Good as Gold, 1979; God Knows, 1984; Picture This, 1988; Closing Time, 1994. Plays: We Bombed in New Haven, 1968; Catch-22: A Dramatization, 1971; Clevinger's Trial, 1971. Screenplays: Sex and the Single Girl (with David R Schwartz), 1964; Casino Royale, 1967; Dirty Dingus Magee (with Tom Waldman and Frank Waldman), 1970; Of Men and Women (with others), 1972. Non-Fiction: No Laughing Matter (with Speed Vogel), 1986. Contributions to: Magazines. Honours: Fulbright Scholar, 1949-50; National Institute of Arts and Letters Grant, 1963; Prix Interallie, France, 1985; Prix Medicis Etranger, France, 1985. Memberships: National Institute of Arts and Letters; Phi Beta Kappa. Address: c/o Simon and Schuster, 1230 Avenue of the Americas, New York, NY 10020, USA.

HELPRIN Mark, b. 28 June 1947, New York, New York, USA. Writer. m. Lisa Kennedy, 28 June 1980, 2 daughters. Education: AB, 1969, AM, 1972, Harvard University; Postgraduate Studies, Magdalen College, Oxford, 1976-77. Appointments: Contributing Editor, The Wall Street Journal; Speechwriter for Senator Robert J Dole, 1996. Publications: A Dove of the East and Other Stories, 1975; Refiner's Fire, 1977; Ellis Island and Other Stories, 1981; Winter's Tale, 1983; Swan Lake, 1989; A Soldier of the Great War, 1991; Memoir from Antproof Case, 1995; A City in Winter, 1996. Honours: Prix de Rome, American Academy and Institute of Arts and Letters, 1982; National Jewish Book Award, 1982. Membership: Council on Foreign Relations. Address: c/o The Wall Street Journal, 200 Liberty Street, New York, NY 10281, USA.

HELWIG David (Gordon), b. 5 Apr 1938, Toronto, Ontario, Canada. Poet; Writer; Editor. m. Nancy Keeling, 1959, 2 daughters. Education: Graduated, Stamford Collegiate Institute, 1956; BA, University of Toronto, 1960; MA, University of Liverpool, 1962. Appointments: Faculty, Department of English, Queen's Unversity, Kingston, Ontario, 1962-80; Co-Editor, Quarry magazine. Publications: Poetry: Figures in a Landscape, 1967; The Sign of the Gunman, 1969; The Best Name of Silence, 1972; Atlantic Crossings, 1974; A Book of the Hours, 1979; The Rain Falls Like Rain, 1982; Catchpenny Poems, 1983; The Hundred Old Names, 1988; The Beloved, 1992. Fiction: The

Day Before Tomorrow, 1971; The Glass Knight, 1976; Jennifer, 1979; The King's Evil, 1981; It Is Always Summer, 1982; A Sound Like Laughter, 1983; The Only Son, 1984; The Bishop, 1986; A Postcard From Rome, 1988; Old Wars, 1989; Of Desire, 1990; Blueberry Cliffs, 1993; Just Say the Words, 1994. Editor: Fourteen Stories High: Best Canadian Stories of 71 (with Tom Marshall), 1971; 72, 73, 74 and 75: New Canadian Stories (with Joan Harcourt), 4 volumes, 1972-75; Words From Inside, 1972; The Human Elements: Critical Essays, 2 volumes, 1978, 1981; Love and Money: The Politics of Culture, 1980; 83, 84, 85 and 86: Best Canadian Stories (with Sandra Martin), 4 volumes, 1983-86; Coming Attractions 1987 and 1988 (with Maggie Helwig), 4 volumes, 1987-91. Honour: CBC Literary Prize, 1983. Address: c/o Viking Penguin, 375 Hudson Street, New York, NY 10014, USA.

HELYAR Jane Penelope Josephine, (Josephine Poole), b. 12 Feb 1933, London, England. Writer. m. (1) T R Poole, 1956, (2) V J H Helyar, 1975, 1 son, 5 daughters. Publications: A Dream in the House, 1961; Moon Eyes, 1965; The Lilywhite Boys, 1967; Catch as Catch Can, 1969; Yokeham, 1970; Billy Buck, 1972; Touch and Go, 1976; When Fishes Flew, 1978; The Open Grave, The Forbidden Room (remedial readers), 1979; Hannah Chance, 1980; Diamond Jack, 1983; The Country Dairy Companion (to accompany Central TV series), 1983; Three For Luck, 1985; Wildlife Tales, 1986; The Loving Ghosts, 1988; Angel, 1989; This is Me Speaking, 1990; Paul Loves Amy Loves Christo, 1992. TV scripts: The Harbourer, 1975; The Sabbatical, 1981; The Breakdown, 1981; Miss Constantine, 1981; Ring a Ring a Rosie, 1983; With Love, Belinda, 1983; The Wit to Woo, 1983. Stories: Fox, 1984; Buzzard, 1984; Dartmoor Pony, 1984; Pinocchio (re-written), 1994; Scared to Death, 1994; Deadly Inheritance, 1995. Address: Poundisford Lodge, Poundisford, Taunton, Somerset TA3 7AE, England.

HEMLEY Robin, b. 28 May 1958, New York, New York, USA. Assistant Professor of English; Writer. m. Beverly Bertling Hemley, 18 July 1987, 2 daughters. Education: BA, Indiana University, 1980; MFA, University of Iowa, 1982. Appointments: Associate Professor of English, University of North Carolina at Charlotte, 1986-94; Assistant Professor of English, Western Washington University, Bellingham, 1994-. Publications: The Mouse Town, 1987; All You Can Eat, 1988; The Last Studebaker, 1992; Turning Life into Fiction, 1994. Address: c/o Elizabeth Grossman, Sterling Lord Literistic, 1 Madison Avenue, New York, NY 10010, USA.

HEMMING John Henry, b. 5 Jan 1935, Vancouver, British Columbia, Canada. Author; Publisher. m. Sukie Babington-Smith, 1979, 1 son, 1 daughter. Education: McGill and Oxford Universities; MA; D.Litt. Appointments: Director, Secretary, Royal Geographical Society, 1975-; Joint Chairman, Hemming Publishing Ltd, 1976-; Chair, Brintex Ltd., Newman Books Ltd; Explorations in Peru and Brazil, 1960, 1961, 1971, 1972, 1986-87. Publications: The Conquest of the Incas, 1970; Tribes of the Amazon Basin in Brazil (with others), 1973; Red Gold: The Conquest of the Brazilian Indians, 1978; The Search for El Dorado, 1978; Machu Picchu, 1982; Monuments of the Incas, 1983; Change in the Amazon Basin, 2 volumes (editor), 1985; Amazon Frontier: The Defeat of the Brazilian Indians, 1987; Maracá, 1988; Roraima: Brazil's Northernmost Frontier, 1990; The Rainforest Edge (editor), 1994. Honour: CMG. Address: Hemming Publishing Ltd, 32 Vauxhall Bridge Road, London SW1V 2SS, England.

HENDERSON Graeme John, b. 8 Feb 1947, Perth, Western Australia. Museum Director. m. Kandy-Jane Hodgson, 15 Apr 1977, 1 son. Education: BA, 1968; Diploma of Education, 1970; MA, 1975; Diploma of Public Sector Management, 1992. Publications: Last Voyage of the James Matthews, 1979; Western Australians and the Sea, 1981; Maritime Archaeology in Australia, 1986. Contributions to: over 100 articles in journals and magazines. Honour: Australian Heritage Award, 1988. Memberships: President, ICOMOS International Committees on the Underwater Cultural Heritage Inc. Address: 3B Braunton St Bicton, Western Australia 6157, Australia.

HENDERSON Hamish, b. 11 Nov 1919, Blairgowrie, Perthshire, Scotland. Poet; Lecturer. Education: MA, Downing College, Cambridge. Appointments: Senior Lecturer and Research Fellow, School of Scottish Studies, University of Edinburgh, 1951-. Publications: Elegies for the Dead in Cyrenaica, 1948; Freedom Come-All-Ye, 1967; Alias MacAlias, 1990; Collected Essays, 1990. Contributions to: Ballads of World War II. Honours: Somerset Maugham Award, 1949. Address: 27 George Square, Edinburgh EH8

9LD, Scotland.

HENDERSON Kathy Caecilia, b. 22 Apr 1949, Oxford, England. Writer; Illustrator; Editor. 2 sons, 1 daughter. Education: BA Hons, English Language and Literature, Oxford, 1969. Publications: My Song is My Own, 1979; Sam and the Big Machines, 1985; 15 Ways to go to Bed, 1986; Series, Where does it come from? Water, 1986, Sweater, 1986, Lego, 1986, Banana, 1986, Bread, 1987, Letter, 1987; Sam and the Box, 1987; The Babysitter, 1988; Don't Interrupt, 1988; The Baby's Book of Babies, 1988; 15 Ways to get Dressed, 1989; Sam, Lizzie and the Bonfire, 1989; Baby Knows Best, 1991; Annie and the Birds, 1991; Second Time Charley, 1991; In the Middle of the Night, 1992; Pappy Mashy, 1992; Annie and the Tiger, 1992; Jim's Winter, 1992. Honours: Book Trust's Childrens Book of the Year, 1987, 1989, 1990, 1993. Address: Muswell Hill, London N10 3UN, England.

HENDERSON Kent William, b. 29 Jan 1954, Geelong, Victoria, Australia. Author; Teacher. m. Marise de Quadros, 19 Dec 1993, 1 daughter. Education: Deakin University and Victoria University of Technology; Diploma of Teaching; BEd; Graduate Certificate of Education; Graduate Diploma of Education; MEd. Publications: Masonic World Guide, 1984; Naracoorte Caves - South Australia, 1986; Masonic Grand Masters of Australia, 1989; Jenolan Caves, 1989; Buchan and Murrindal Caves, 1992. Contributions to: Australasian Cave and Karst Management Association Journal (editor); Transactions, Victorian Lodge of Masonic Research Annual Book; Numerous to journals and magazines. Membership: Fellowship of Australian Writers. Address: PO Box 332, Williamstown, Victoria 3016, Australia.

HENDERSON-HOWAT Gerald. See: HOWAT Gerald Malcolm David.

HENDRIKS A(rthur) L(emiere), b . 7 Apr 1922, Kingston, Jamaica. Poet; Freelance Writer. Education: Open University. Publications: The Independence Anthology of Jamaican Literature (with C Lindo), 1962; On This Mountain and Other Poems, 1965; These Green Islands, 1971; Muet, 1971; Madonna of the Unknown Nation, 1974; The Islanders and Other Poems, 1983; Archie and the Princess and the Everythingest Horse (for children), 1983; The Naked Ghost and Other Poems, 1984; Great Families of Jamaica, 1984; To Speak Slowly: Selected Poems, 1986. Address: Box 265, Constant Spring, Kingston 8, Jamaica.

HENDRY Diana (Lois), b. 2 Oct 1941, Meols, Wirral, England. Teacher; Poet; Children's Writer. m. George Hendry, 9 Oct 1965, div 1981, 1 son, 1 daughter. Education: BA with Honours, 1984, MLitt, 1986, University of Bristol. Appointments: Assistant Literature Editor, Sunday Times, London, 1958-60; Reporter and Feature Writer, Western Mail, Cardiff, 1960-65; Freelance journalist, 1965-80; Part-time English Teacher, Clifton College, 1984-87; Part-time Lecturer, Bristol Polytechnic, 1987; WEA, Modern Poets Course, 1987-; Tutor, Open University, 1991-92; Part-time Tutor, Creative Writing, University of Bristol, 1993-. Publications: Midnight Pirate, 1984; Fiona Finds Her Tongue, 1985; Hetty's First Fling, 1985; The Not Anywhere House, 1989; The Rainbow Watchers, 1989; The Carey Street Cat, 1989; Christmas on Exeter Street, 1989; Sam Sticks and Delilah, 1990; A Camel Called April, 1990; Double Vision, 1990; Harvey Angell, 1991; Kid Kibble, 1992; The Thing-in-a-Box, 1992; Wonderful Robert and Sweetie-Pie Nell, 1992; Back Soon, 1993; Making Blue, 1995; Strange Goings-on, 1995; The Awesome Bird, 1995; The Thing on Two Legs, 1995. Contributions to: Anthologies and periodicals. Honours: Stoud Festival International Poetry Competition, 1976; Peterloo Poetry Competition, 3rd Prize, 1991, 2nd Prize, 1993; Whitbread Award, 1991; Housman Poetry Society, 1st Prize, 1996. Address: 52 York Road, Montpelier, Bristol BS6 5QF, England.

HENDRY Joy McLaggan, b. 3 Feb 1953, Perth, Scotland. Writer; Broadcaster. m. Ian Montgomery, 25 July 1986. Education: MA, Honours, 1976, Diploma in Education, 1977, University of Edinburgh. Appointments: Editor, Chapman Magazine; General Editor, Scottish Critics Series, Edinburgh University Press; Director, Chapman Publications; Radio critic, Scotsman newspaper; Chair, Scottish Actors Studio, 1994-. Publications: Poems and Pictures by Wendy Wood (editor), 1985; Critical Essays on Sorley MacLean (editor with Raymond J Ross), 1986; Critical Essays on Norman MacCaig (editor with Raymond Ross), 1991. Plays: Gang down wi' a Sang, 1990; The Wa' at the World's End, 1993. Contributions to: Cencrastus; Oxford Poetry; Agenda; Lallans; Scottish Literary Journal; Scots Magazine;

Scotsman; Glasgow Herald; Scotland on Sunday; Guardian; Der Spiegel; Poetry Ireland; BBC Scotland, Radio 3, Radio 4 and STV; Temenos. Address: 4 Broughton Place, Edinburgh, EH1 3RX, Scotland.

HENLEY Elizabeth Becker, b. 8 May 1952, Jackson, Mississippi, USA. Playwright. Education: BFA, Southern Methodist University. Publications: Crimes of the Heart, 1981; The Wake of Jamey Foster, 1982; Am I Blue, 1982; The Miss Firecracker Contest, 1984; The Lucky Spot, 1987; The Debutante Ball, 1988; Abundance, 1990; Control Freaks, 1993. Honours: Pulitzer Prize for Drama, 1981; New York Drama Critics Circle Best Play Award, 1981; George Oppenheimer/Newsday Playwriting Award, 1981. Address: c/o Gilbert Parker, The William Morris Agency, 1350 Avenue of the Americas, New York, NY 10019,USA.

HENNESSY Helen. See: **VENDLER Helen.**

HENNESSY Peter John, b. 28 Mar 1947, London, England. Author; Professor; Journalist; Broadcaster. m. Enid Mary Candler, 14 June 1969, 2 daughters. Education: BA, 1969, PhD, 1990, Cambridge; London School of Economics, 1969-71; Kennedy Memorial Scholar, Harvard University, 1971-72. Appointments: Times Higher Educational Supplement, 1972-74; The Times, 1974-76; Lobby Correspondent, Financial Times, 1976; Whitehall Correspondent, The Times, 1976-82; The Economist, 1982; Leader Writer, The Times, 1982-84; Columnist, New Statesman, 1986-87, The Independent, 1987-91; Professor of Contemporary History, Queen Mary and Westfield College, University of London, 1992-; Professor of Rhetoric, Gresham College, 1994-97; Chairman, Kennedy Memorial Trust, 1995-. Publications: States of Emergency, 1983; Sources Close to the Prime Minister, 1984; What the Papers Never Said, 1985; Cabinet, 1986; Whitehall, 1989; Never Again: Britain, 1945-51, 1993; The Hidden Writing: Unearthing the British Constitution, 1995; Muddling Through: Power, Politics and the Quality of Government in Postwar Britain, 1996. Contributions to: Columnist, Director Magazine, 1990-94. Membership: Fellow, Royal Historical Society, 1993. Literary Agent: Curtis Brown. Address: Department of History, Queen Mary and Westfield College, Mile End Road, London, E1 9NS, England.

HENNING Ann Margareta Maria (Countess of Roden), b. 5 Aug 1948, Göteborg, Sweden. Author; Playwright; Translator. m. Earl of Roden, 13 Feb 1986, 1 son. Education: BA, Lund University, Sweden, 1975. Appointments: Artistic Director, 4th International Women Playwrights' Conference; Artistic Director of the Connemara Theatre Company. Publications: The Connemara Whirlwind, 1990; The Connemara Stallion, 1991; The Connemara Champion, 1994; Honeylove the Bearcub, 1995; The Cosmos and You, 1995. Contributions to: Vogue Magazine. Memberships: Translators Association; Society of Authors; Irish Writer's Union. Address: 4 The Boltons, London SW10 9TB, England.

HENRI Adrian (Maurice), b. 10 Apr 1932, Birkenhead, Cheshire, England. Painter; Poet. Education: BA Fine Art, King's College, Newcastle, 1955. Appointments: Lecturer, Manchester College of Art, 1961-64; Liverpool College of Art, 1964-1967; Liverpool Scene, poetry-rock group, 1967-70; Visiting Lecturer, Bradford College, 1973-76, Trent Polytechnic, 1989. Publications: The Mersey Sound: Penguin Modern Poets 10 (with McGough and Patten), 1967; Tonight at at Noon, 1968; City, 1969; Talking After Christmas Blues, 1969; Poems for Wales and Six Landscapes for Susan, 1970; Autobiography, 1971; America, 1972; The Best of Henri: Selected Poems 1968-70, 1976; One Year, 1976; City Hedges: Poems 1970-76; Words without a Story, 1979; From the Loveless Motel: Poems 1976-79, 1980; Harbour, 1982; Penny Arcade 1978-82; New Volume, (with Roger McGough and Brian Patten), 1983; Holiday Snaps 1967-85; Wish You Were Here, 1990; Not Fade Away, 1994; Liverpool Accents: Seven Poets and a City, 1996; Verse for children; Plays; Novel: I Want, with Nell Dunn, 1972. Honours: DLitt, Liverpool Polytechnic, 1990. Literary Agent: Rogers, Coleridge & White, 20 Powis Mews, London W11 1JN, England. Address: 21 Mount Street, Liverpool L1 9HD, England.

HENRY Desmond Paul, b. 5 July 1921, Almondbury, Yorks, England. Philosopher; Artist. m. Louise H J Bayen, 19 May 1945, 3 daughters. Education: BA Hons, Philosophy, University of Leeds, 1949; PhD, University of Manchester, 1960. Appointments: Philosophy Teacher, University of Manchester, 1949-82; Visiting Professor, Brown University, 1966, University of Pennsylvania, 1970. Publications: The

Logic of St Anselm, 1967; Medieval Logic and Metaphysics, 1972; Commentary on De Grammatico, 1974; That Most Subtle Question, 1984; Medieval Meréology, 1991; Contributions to: Various publications. Memberships: Manchester Medieval Society. Address: 4 Burford Drive, Whalley Range, Manchester M16 8FJ, England.

HENRY Stuart, b. 18 Oct 1949, London, England. Professor of Criminology. m. Lee Doric, 5 Mar 1988. Education: BA Hons, Sociology, 1972; PhD, Sociology of Deviance, 1976. Appointment: Professor, Eastern Michigan University. Publications: The Hidden Economy, 1978; Private Justice, 1983; The Deviance Process, 1993; Criminological Theory, 1995; Constitutive Criminology, 1996. Others: Self-Help & Health, 1977; Informal Institutions, 1981; The Informal Economy, 1987; Degrees of Deviance, 1990; Employee Dismissal, 1994; Inside Jobs, 1994; Social Control, 1994. Contributions to: New Society; Criminology; Sociology; Law & Society. Honours: State of Michigan Teaching Excellence Awards, 1990, 1994; Research and Creativity Award, 1995. Literary Agent: John Pawsey. Address: Department of Sociology, Eastern Michigan University, Ypsilanti, MI 48197, USA.

HENSEL Klaus, b. 14 May 1954, Brasov, Transylvania, Romania. Writer; Journalist; Filmmaker. Education: Lic Phil, German and English Literature, University of Bucharest. Publications: Das Letzte Fruehstueck mit Gertrude, 1980; Oktober Lichtspiel, 1988; Stradivarius Geigenstein, 1990; Summen im Falsett, 1995. Honours: Kranichsteiner Literaturpreis, Germany, 1988; Villa-Massimo-Grant, Rome, Italy, 1994-95. Address: Humboldstrasse 56, D-60318 Frankfurt, Germany.

HEPBURN Ronald William, b. 16 Mar 1927, Scotland. Retired Professor of Moral Philosophy; Writer. m. Agnes Forbes Anderson, 1953, 2 sons, 1 daughter. Education: MA, 1951, PhD, 1955, University of Aberdeen. Appointments: Assistant, 1952-55, Lecturer, 1955-60, Department of Moral Philosophy, University of Aberdeen; Visiting Associate Professor, New York University, 1959-60; Professor of Philosophy, University of Nottingham, 1960-64; Professor of Philosophy, 1964-75, Professor of Moral Philosophy, 1975-96, University of Edinburgh; Stanton Lecturer in the Philosophy of Religion, Cambridge University, 1965-68. Publications: Metaphysical Beliefs (jointly), 1957; Christianity and Paradox: Critical Studies in Twentieth-Century Theology, 1958; Wonder and Other Essays: Eight Studies in Aesthetics and Neighbouring Fields, 1984. Contributions to: Scholarly books and journals. Address: 8 Albert Terrace, Edinburgh EH10 5EA, Scotland.

HERALD Kathleen. See: **PEYTON Kathleen Wendy.**

HERBERT Brian Patrick, b. 29 June 1947, Seattle, Washington, USA. Author. Education: BA in Sociology, University of California at Berkeley, 1968. Publications: Classic Comebacks, 1981; Incredible Insurance Claims, 1982; Sidney's Comet, 1983; The Garbage Chronicles, 1984; Sudanna, 1985; Man of Two Worlds (with Frank Herbert), 1986; Prisoners of Arionn, 1987; The Notebooks of Dune (editor), 1988; Memorymakers (with Marie Landis), 1990; The Race for God, 1990; Never As It Seems (editor), 1992; Songs of Maud' Dib (editor), 1992; The Notebooks of Frank Herbert's Dune (editor), 1993; Blood on the Sun (with Marie Landis), 1996. Short Stories: The Bone Lady (with Marie Landis in Dark Destiny I Anthology), 1994; Blood Month (with Marie Landis in Dark Destiny II Anthology), 1995; Dropoff (with Marie Landis in Dante's Disciples Anthology), 1995; The Contract (with Marie Landis in Forbidden Acts Anthology), 1995; Raiders from the Ghost World (with Marie Landis in Pawn of Chaos Anthology); Legends of Dune (editor with Ed Kramer), forthcoming. Contributions to: Several publications including In Celebration of Sidney, 1987; Things Happen, 1993. Memberships: L-5 Society; National Writers Club; Science Fiction Writers of America; Horror Writers Association. Address: PO Box 10164, Bainbridge Island, WA 98110, USA.

HERBERT (Edward) Ivor (Montgomery), b. 20 Aug 1925, Johannesburg, South Africa. Author; Journalist; Scriptwriter. Education: MA, Trinity College, Cambridge, 1949. Appointments: Travel Editor, Racing Editor, The Mail on Sunday, 1982-. Publications: Eastern Windows, 1953; Point to Point, 1964; Arkel: The Story of a Champion, 1966, 2nd edition, 1975; The Great St Trinian's Train Robbery (screenplay), 1966; The Queen Mother's Horses, 1967; The Winter Kings (co- author), 1968, enlarged, 1989; The Way to the Top, 1969; Night of the Blue Demands, play (co-author), 1971; Over Our Dead Bodies, 1972; The Diamond Diggers, 1972; Scarlet Fever (co-author), 1972; Winter's Tale, 1974; Red Rum: Story of a Horse of Courage, 1974; The Filly (novel), 1977; Six at the Top, 1977; Classic Touch (TV documentary), 1985; Spot the Winner, 1978, updated, 1990; Longacre, 1978; Horse Racing, 1980; Vincent O'Brien's Great Horses, 1984; Revolting Behaviour, 1987; Herbert's Travels, 1987; Reflections on Racing (co-author), 1990; Riding Through My Life (with HRH The Princess Royal), 1991. Address: The Old Rectory, Bradenham, Buckinghamshire HP14 4HD, England.

HERBERT James (John), b. 8 Apr 1943, London, England. Author. Education: Hornsey College of Art, 1959. Publications: The Rats, 1974; The Fog, 1975; The Survivor, 1976; Fluke, 1977; The Spear, 1978; Lair, 1979; The Dark, 1980; The Jonah, 1981; Shrine, 1983; Domain, 1984; Moon, 1985; The Magic Cottage, 1986; Sepulchre, 1987; Haunted, 1988; Creed, 1990; Portent, 1992; James Herbert: By Horror Haunted, 1992; James Herbert's Dark Places, 1993; The City, 1994; The Ghosts of Sleath, 1994; '48, 1996. Films: The Rats, 1982; The Survivor, 1986; Fluke, 1995; Haunted, 1995. Address: c/o Bruce Hunter, David Higham Associates, 5-8 Lower John Street, London W1R 4HA, England.

HERBST Philip H, b. 1 June 1944, Peoria, Illinois, USA. Editor; Writer; Researcher. Education: BA, University of Illinois, 1966; PhD, Cornell University, 1976. Appointments: Instructor in Anthropology, State University of New York at Potsdam, 1971-74; Visiting Scholar, Northwestern University, 1989-92. Publications: A Multicultural Dictionary: A Guide to Ethnic and Racial Words, 1993; The Color of Words: An Encyclopedic Dictionary of Ethnic Bias in the United States, 1997. Contributions to: Several publications. Address: 2415 Central Street, Evanston, IL 60201, USA.

HERMODSSON Elisabet, b . 20 Sept 1927, Göteborg, Sweden. Writer; Artist; Songwriter. m. (1) Ingemar Olsson, 1951; (2) Olof Hellstrom, 1956, 2 daughters. Publications: Poem-things, 1966; Human Landscape Unfairly, 1968; Rite and Revolution, 1968; Swedish Soul-life, 1970; Culture at the Bottom, 1971; Voices in the Human Landscape, 1971; What Shall We Do With The Summer, Comrades? (songs), 1973; Disa Nilsons Songs, 1974; Through the Red Waist Coat of the Ground 75; Visional Turning Point, 1975; Words in Woman's Time, 1979; Wake Up With a Summer Soul, 1979; Make Yourself Visible, 1980; Discources Meanwhile, 1983; Stones, Shards, Layers of Earth, 1985; Creation Betrayed, 1986; Streams of Mist, 1990; Cloud Steps, 1994. Contributions to: Journals, Magazines and the Editor of Several Anthologies. Honour: Royal Medal, Litteris et Artibus, 1994. Memberships: PEN Club. Address: Ostra Agatan 67, 75322 Uppsala, Sweden.

HERNANDEZ de Mendoza Cecilia de, b. 15 Mar 1915, Bogota, Colombia. Critic. m. Carlos de Mendoza, 23 Dec 1940. Education: PhD Philosophy, Colegio Mayor de Nuestra Senora del Rosario; Profesor Emerito, Instituto Caro y Cuervo. Publications: El Estilo Literario de Bolivar, 1943; Introduccion a la Estilistica - Instituto Caro y Cuervo, 1961; El Significado y Su Expresion, 1990; El Poeta Jorge Rojas, 1993; Obra Poetica de Leon de Greiff, 1993; Others: Antologia de Gerardo; Valencia. Contributions to: El Tiempo; El Espectador; Revista de Indias; Bolivar; Revista de Los Andes; Thesaurus; Noticias Culturales; Boletin de la Academia Colombiana. Honours: Sociedad Bolivariana, Medal; Ministry of Education, Medal. Memberships: Real Academia Espanola; Academia Colombiana. Address: Calle 92, #16-68, Apt 201, Santafe Bogota, Colombia.

HERR Pamela (Staley), b. 24 July 1939, Cambridge, Massachusetts, USA. Writer. 2 daughters. Education: BA, magna cum laude, Harvard University, 1961; MA, George Washington University, 1971. Appointments: Writer and Editor, Field Educational Publications, 1973; Editor, Sullivan Associates, 1973-74; Project Manager, Sanford Associates, Education Development Corporation, Menlo Park, 1974-76; Managing Editor, American West, Cupertino, California, 1976-79; Historian and Writer, 1980-. Publications: Jessie Benton Fremont: A Biography, 1987; Letters of Jessie Benton Fremont (with Mary Lee Spence), 1993. Honour: Phi Beta Kappa. Address: 559 Seale Avenue, Palo Alto, CA 94301, USA.

HERRA Maurice. See: ASSELINEAU Roger Maurice.

HERSEY April (Maeve), b. 4 Apr 1924. Writer; Editor. Appointments: Consultant Scriptwriter, Pilgrim International; Editor: Craft Australia, 1974-81, POL, 1976, Oz Arts Magazine, 1990-. Publications: Australian Style, 1968; New Zealand, 1969; Hooked On

God, 1970; The Insulted Heart - Recovery from Bypass Surgery, 1996; 4 novels in progress. Contributions to: Bulletin; Sun Herald; Women's Day; Home and Family; Home; House and Garden; Life; Sunday Times; Reader's Digest. Memberships: Australian Society of Authors; Fellowship of Australian Writers. Address: 12 Wright Street, Glenbrook, New South Wales 2773, Australia.

HERSH Burton David, b . 18 Sept 1933, Chicago, Illinois, USA. Author; Biographer. m. Ellen Eiseman, 3 Aug 1957, 1 son, 1 daughter. Education: BA magna cum laude, Harvard College, 1955; Fulbright Scholar, 1955-56. Publications: The Ski People, 1968; The Education of Edward Kennedy, 1972; The Mellon Family, 1978; The Old Boys, 1992. Contributions to: Many magazines. Honours: Book Find Selection, 1972; Book-of-the-Month Club, 1978. Memberships: Authors Guild; American Society of Journalists and Authors; PEN. Address: PO Box 433, Bradford, NH 03221, USA.

HERZBERG Judith, b. 4 Nov 1934, Amsterdam, Netherlands. Poet; Playwright. Education: Graduated Montessori Lyceum, 1952. Appointments: Teacher at film schools in Netherlands and Israel. Publications: Slow Boat, 1964; Meadow Grass, 1968; Flies, 1970; Grazing Light, 1971; 27 Love Songs, 1973; Botshol, 1980; Remains of the Day, 1984; Twenty Poems, 1984; But What: Selected Poems, 1988; Plays: Near Archangel, 1971; It Is Not A Dog, 1973; That Day May Dawn, 1974; Lea's Wedding, 1982; The Fall of Icarus, 1983; And/Or, 1984; The Little Mermaid, 1986; Scratch, 1989; Lulu, adaptation of Wedekind, 1989; A Good Head, 1991. Other: Texts for the Stage and Film, 1972-88; Screenplays and Television plays; Translations, including The Trojan Women, by Euripides, and Ghosts, by Ibsen. Honour: Netherlands-Vlaamse drama prize, 1989. Address: c/o De Harmonie, Postbus 3547, 1001 AH Amsterdam, Netherlands.

HESKETH Phoebe, b. 29 Jan 1909, Preston, Lancashire, England. Lecturer (Emeritus); Poet. Education: Cheltenham Ladies' College, 1924-26. Appointments: Lecturer, Bolton Women's College, 1967-69; Teacher of Creative Writing, Bolton School, 1977-79. Publications: Poems: Lean Forward, Spring, 1948; No Time for Cowards, 1952; Out of the Dark, 1954; Between Wheels and Stars, 1956; The Buttercup Children, 1958; Prayer for Sun, 1966; A Song of Sunlight, 1974; Preparing to Leave, 1977; The Eighth Day, 1980; A Ring of Leaves, 1985; Over the Brook, 1985; Netting the Sun: New and Collected Poems, 1989; Sundowner, 1992; The Leave Train, New and Selected Poems, 1994; A Box of Silver Birch, poems, 1997. Prose: My Aunt Edith, 1966; Rivington: The Story of a Village, 1972; What Can the Matter Be?, 1985; Rivington: Village of the Mountain Ash, 1989. Honour: Honorary Fellow, University of Central Lancashire, 1992. Address: 10 The Green, Heath Charnock, Chorley, Lancashire PR6 9JH, England.

HESSAYON David Gerald, b. 13 Feb 1928, Manchester, England. Author. m. Joan Parker Gray, 2 Apr 1951, 2 daughters. Education: BSC, Leeds University, 1950; PhD, Manchester University, 1954. Publications: The House Plant Expert, 1980; The Armchair Book of the Garden, 1983; The Tree Shrub Expert, 1983; The Flower Expert, 1984; The Indoor Plant Spotter, 1985; The Garden Expert, 1986; The Home Expert, 1987; The Fruit Expert, 1990; Be Your Own Greenhouse Expert, 1990; The New House Plant Expert, 1991; The Garden DIY Expert, 1992; The Rock and Water Garden Expert, 1993; The Flowering Shrub Expert, 1994; The Greenhouse Expert, 1994; The Flower Arranging Expert, 1994; The Container Expert, 1995; The Bulb Expert, 1995; The Easy-Care Gardening Expert, 1996; The New Bedding Plant Expert, 1996; The New Rose Expert, 1996; The New Vegetable and Herb Expert, 1997; The New Lawn Expert, 1997. Honours: Lifetime Achievement Trophy, National British Book Awards, 1992; Gold Veitch Memorial Medal, Royal Horticultural Society, 1992; Gardening Book of the Year Award, 1993. Membership: Society of Authors. Address: Sloe House, Halstead, Essex CO9 1PA, England.

HESSAYON Joan Parker, b. 21 Jan 1932, Louisville, Kentucky, USA. Author. m. David Hessayon, 2 Apr 1951, 2 daughters. Publications: All Kinds of Courage, 1983; For All Good Men, 1984; Little Maid All Unwary, 1985; Sybilla, 1986; Thorsby, 1987; Lady from St Louis, 1989; Belle's Daughter, 1990; Roxanne's War, 1991; House on Pine Street, 1992; Capel Bells, 1995; Helmingham Rose, 1997. Memberships: Romantic Novelists Association; Society of Authors. Address: Sloe House, Halstead, Essex CO9 1PA, England.

HESSING Dennis. See: DENNIS-JONES Harold.

HESTER William, b . 6 June 1933, Detroit, Michigan, USA. Author; Lyricist. Div, 1 daughter. Education: Brown University, 1951-52; University of Detroit, 1956; BA, Mesa College, 1970; MA, Special Studies, University of California at Los Angeles, New York University. Appointments: Staff, Warner Brothers Pictures, 1961-62; Creative Staff, Sierra Productions, 1962-65; Staff, Playboy Magazine, 1966-68; Associate Director, Vance Publications, 1970-73. Publications: Please Don't Die In My House, 1965; Selections, 1967; Running Off, 1970; Not the Right Season, 1984; Another Town, 1984; Still Not the Right Season, 1985; Our Place, 1986; Sleeping Neighbours, 1986; Tyranny/2000, 1988. Also music. Contributions to: Pulpsmith; Confrontation; Amelia; Easy Riders; The Poet; Playboy; Witness; Golf Magazine; Fortune News; Wind. Honours: Eisner Fellowship, 1984; 1st & 2nd Awards, fiction and non-fiction, PEN American Centre, 1985, 1986; Various awards, American Song Festival. Memberships: Authors Guild; Conservatory of American Letters; Broadcast Music Inc. Address: c/o James McDonald Inc, 1130-20th Street, 5 Santa Monica, CA 90403, USA.

HESTNES Stefan, b. Denmark. Author; Journalist; Publisher. Publications: RAV - Find det selv!; Norsk Fjeldhåndbog; Succes med hons: haven; Nyt Dansk komma; Others. Contributions to: Numerous ar5ticles. Memberships: Dansk Forfatter Forening; Danish Union of Journalists. Address: Stenloseves 108, DK-5260 Odense-S, Denmark.

HETHERINGTON (Hector) Alastair, b. 31 Oct 1919, Llanishen, Glamorganshire, Wales. Journalist; Writer. m. (1) Helen Miranda Oliver, 1957, div 1978, 2 sons, 2 daughters, (2) Sheila Cameron, 1979. Education: MA, Corpus Christi College, Oxford. Appointments: Staff, Glasgow Herald, 1946-50; Staff, 1950-53, Foreign Editor, 1953-56, Editor, 1956-75, Manchester Guardian; Director, Guardian Newspapers Ltd, 1967-75; Staff, BBC, 1975-80; Controller, BBC Scotland, 1975-78; Manager, BBC Highland, 1979-80; Research Professor, 1982-88, Professor Emeritus, 1988-, Stirling University. Publications: Guardian Years, 1981; News, Newspapers and Television, 1985; Perthshire in Trust, 1988; News in the Regions, 1989; Highlands and Islands, a Generation of Progress, 1990; Cameras in the Commons, 1990; Inside BBC Scotland, 1975-1980, 1992; A Walker's Guide to Arran, 1994. Address: High Corrie, Isle of Arran KA27 8GB, Scotland.

HETHERINGTON Norriss Swigart, b. 30 Jan 1942, Berkeley, California, USA. Professor. m. Edith Wiley White, 10 Dec 1966, 1 son, 1 daughter. Education: BA, 1963, MA, 1965, MA, 1967, University of California, Berkeley; PhD, Indiana University, 1970. Appointments: Lecturer in Physics and Astronomy, Agnes Scott College, Decatur, Gorgia 1967-68; Assistant Professor of Mathematics and Science, York University, Toronto, Ontario, 1970-72; Administrative Specialist, National Aeronautics and Space Aministration, 1972; Assistant Professor of History, University of Kansas, 1972-76; Assistant Professor of Science, Technology and Society, Razi University, Sanandaj, Iran, 1976-77; Visiting Scholar, Cambridge University, England, 1977-78; Research Associate, Office for History of Science and Technology, University of Calfornia, Berkeley, 1978-; Associate Professor of the History of Science, University of Oklahoma at Norman, 1981; Director, Institute for the History of Astronomy, 1988-. Publications: Ancient Astronomy and Civilization, 1987; Science and Objectivity: Episodes in the History of Astronomy, 1988; The Edwin Hubble Papers, 1990; Encyclopedia of Cosmology, 1993; Cosmology: Historical, Literary, Philosophical, Religious and Scientific Perspectives, 1993; Hubble's Cosmology: A Guided Study of Selected Texts, 1996. Honour: Goddard Historical Essay Award, 1974. Address: Office for History of Science and Technology, 543 Stephens Hall, University of California at Berkeley, Berkeley, CA 94720, USA.

HEWETT Dorothy (Coade), b . 21 May 1923, Perth, Western Australia. Author; Playwright; Poet. Education: BA, 1961, MA, 1963, University of Western Australia. Appointments: Advertising Copywriter, Sydney, 1956-58; Poetry Editor, Westerly Magazine, Perth, 1972-73; Editorial Committee, Overland Magazine, Melbourne, 1970-; Poetry Editor, Westerly Magazine, Perth, 1972-73; Writer-in-Residence, Monash University, Melbourne, 1975; Editor, Director, Big Smoke Books, Review Editor, Poetry, Sydney, 1975-. Publications: Bobbin Up (novel), 1959; What about the People (poetry with Merv Lilly), 1962; The Australians have a Word for It (stories), 1964; The Old Man Comes Rolling Home, 1968; Windmill Country (poetry), 1968; The Hidden Journey (poetry), 1969; Late Night Bulletin (poetry), 1970; The Chapel Perilous, or The Perilous Adventures of Sally Bonner, 1971; Sandgropers: A Western Australian Anthology, 1973; Rapunzel in

Surburbia (poetry), 1975; Miss Hewett's Shenanigans, 1975; Bon-Bons and Roses for Dolly, and The Tatty Hollow Story, 1976; Greenhouse (poetry), 1979; The Man from Mukinupin (play), 1979; Susannah's Dreaming, and The Golden Oldies (plays), 1981; Joan, 1984; Golden Valley, Song of the Seals, 1985. Address: 49 Jersey Road, Woollahra, NSW 2025, Australia.

HEYEN William (Helmuth), b. 1 Nov 1940, Brooklyn, New York, USA. Professor of English; Poet; Writer. m. Hannelore Greiner, 7 July 1962, 1 son, 1 daughter. Education: BS in Education, State University of New York College at Brockport, 1961; MA in English, 1963, PhD in English, 1967, Ohio University. Appointments: Instructor, State University of New York College at Cortland, 1963-65; Assistant Professor to Professor of English and Poet-in-Residence, State University of New York College at Brockport, 1967-; Teacher, University of Hannover, Germany, 1971-72; Visiting Creative Writer, University of Wisconsin at Milwaukee, 1980; Visiting Writer, Hofstra University, 1981, 1983, Southampton College, 1984, 1985; Visiting Professor of English, University of Hawaii, 1985. Publications: Depth of Field, 1970; A Profile of Theodore Roethke (editor), 1971; Noise in the Trees: Poems and a Memoir, 1974; American Poets in 1976 (editor), 1976; The Swastika Poems, 1977; Long Island Light: Poems and a Memoir, 1979; The City Parables, 1980; Lord Dragonfly: Five Sequences, 1981; Erika: Poems of the Holocaust, 1984; The Generation of 2000: Contemporary American Poets (editor), 1984; Vic Holyfield and the Class of 1957: A Romance, 1986; The Chestnut Rain: A Poem, 1986; Brockport, New York: Beginning with "And", 1988; Falling From Heaven (co-author), 1991; Pterodactyl Rose: Poems of Ecology, 1991; Ribbons: The Gulf War, 1991; The Host: Selected Poems 1965-1990, 1994; With Me Far Away: A Memoir, 1994; Crazy Horse in Stillness: Poems, 1996. Contributions to: Many books, chapbooks, journals and magazines. Honours: Borestone Mountain Poetry Prize, 1965; National Endowment for the Arts Fellowships, 1973-74, 1984-85; American Library Association Notable American Book, 1974; Ontario Review Poetry Prize, 1977; Guggenheim Fellowship, 1977-78; Eunice Tietjens Memorial Award, 1978; Witter Bynner Prize for Poetry, 1982; New York Foundation for the Arts Poetry Fellowship, 1984-85; Lillian Fairchild Award, 1996. Address: c/o Department of English, State University of New York College at Brockport, Brockport, NY 14420, USA.

HEYERDAHL Thor, b . 6 Oct 1914, Laskit, Norway. Author; Anthropologist. m. (1) Liv Coucheron Torp, 1936, dec 1969, 2 sons, (2) Yvonne Dedekam-Simonsen, 1949, 3 daughters. Education: University of Oslo, 1933-36. Appointments: Organised and Led, Kon-Tiki Expedition, 1947; Made Crossing from Safi, Morocco to West Indies in Papyrus Boat, RAII, 1970. Publications: Paa Jakt efter Paradiset, 1938; The Kon-Tiki Expedition, 1948; American Indians in the Pacific: The Theory Behind the Kon-Tiki Expedition, 1952; Archaeological Evidence of Pre-Spanish Visits to the Galapagos Islands (with A Skjolsvold), 1956; Aku-Aku: The Secrets of Easter Island, 1961, Vol II, Miscellaneous Papers, 1965; Indianer und Alt-Asiaten im Pazifik: Das Abenteuer einer heorie, 1965; Sea Routes to Polynesia, 1968; The Ra Expeditions, 1970; Chapters in Quest for America, 1971; Fatu-Hiva Back to Nature, 1974; Art of Easter Island, 1975; Zwischen den Kontinenten, 1975; Early Man and the Ocean, 1978; The Tigris Expedition, 1980; The Mystery of the Maldives, 1986; Easter Island, 1990. Contributions to: Numerous professional journals. Honours: Gold Medal, Royal Geographical Society, London, 1964; Commander with Star, Order of St Olav, Norway, 1970; Order of Merit, Egypt, 1971; Grand Officer, Royal Alaouites Order, Morocco, 1971; Honorary Citizen, Larvik, Norway, 1971; International Pahlavi Environment Prize, UN, 1978; Order of Golden Ark, Netherlands, 1980. Address: Kan-Tiki Museum, Oslo, Norway.

HEYM Stefan, b. 10 Apr 1913, Chemnitz, Germany. Novelist. Education: Universities of Berlin and Chicago; MA, 1935. Publications: Hostages, 1942; Of Smiling Peace, 1944; The Crusaders, 1948; The Eye of Reason, 1951; Goldsborough, 1953; The Cannibals and Other Stories, 1953; Shadows and Light: Eight Short Stories, 1960; The Lenz Papers, 1964; Uncertain Friend, 1969; The Queen Against Defoe and Other Stories, 1972; The King David Report (novel), 1972; Five Days in June, 1974; Collin, 1980; The Wandering Jew, 1984; Schwarzenberg, 1984; Collected Stories, 1984; Built on Sand, 1990; Filz (essays), 1991; Radek, 1995; Play: Tom Sawyer's Great Adventure, 1952. Other: Nazis in USA: An Exposé of Hitler's Aims and Agents in the USA, 1938; A Visit to Soviet Science, 1959; Nachruf (autobiography), 1988; Selected Prose, 1990. Honours: DLitt, University of Cambridge, 1991; Dr Theol.h.c, University of Berne;

Jerusalem Prize, 1993. Memberships: German Academy of Arts; PEN.

HIBBERD Jean, (J O McDonald), b. 11 Oct 1931, London, England. Coordinator; Creative Writing Teacher. m. Reginald George Hibberd, 8 Mar 1952, 2 sons, 2 daughters. Education: Diploma, Short Story Writing, 1980. Appointments: Coordinator, Nepean Community College; Editor, Compiler, Nepean Community College Annual Anthology, 1985-; Holiday and Travel Writer, Western Weekender, 1991-93. Publications: The Adventures of Peter Possum and His Friends, 1985; Further Adventures of Peter Possum and His Friends, 1987; Duty to My God, 1989; On the Sea of the Moon, romance; Ordeal by Love; The Artist and the Gypsy; Poetry of the Sun; Short Stories from Aound the World. Contributions to: Periodicals. Honours: Medal of Merit, Scout Association, 1971; Order of Australia Medal, 1994. Memberships: Fellowship of Australian Writers; Australian Society of Authors; Order of Australia. Address: 7 Rusden Road, Blaxland, New South Wales 2774, Australia.

HIBBERT Christopher, b. 5 Mar 1924, Enderby, Leicestershire, England. Author. m. Susan Piggford, 1948, 2 sons, 1 daughter. Education: MA, Oriel College, Oxford. Appointments: Served in Italy, 1944-45; Captain, London Irish Rifles; Partner, firm of land agents, auctioneers and surveyors, 1948-59. Publications: The Road to Tyburn, 1957; King Mob, 1958; Wolfe at Quebec, 1959; The Destruction of Lord Raglan, 1961; Corunna, 1961; Benito Mussolini 1962; The Battle of Arnhem, 1962; The Roots of Evil, 1963; The Court at Windsor, 1964; Agincourt, 1964; The Wheatley Diary (editor), 1964; Garibaldi and His Enemies, 1965; The Making of Charles Dickens, 1967; Waterloo: Napoleon's Last Campaign (editor), 1967; An American in Regency England: The Journal of Louis Simond (editor), 1968; Charles I, 1968; The Grand Tour, 1969; London: Biography of a City, 1969; The Search for King Arthur, 1970; Anzio: The Bid for Rome, 1970; The Dragon Wakes: China and the West, 1793-1911, 1970; The Personal History of Samuel Johnson, 1971; George IV, Prince of Wales 1762-1811, 1972; George IV, Regent and King 1812-1830, 1973; The Rise and Fall of the House of Medici, 1974; Edward VII: A Portrait, 1976; The Great Mutiny: India, 1857, 1978; The French Revolution, 1981; Africa Explored: Europeans in the Dark Continent, 1796-1889, 1982; The London Encyclopaedia (editor), 1983; Queen Victoria in Her Letters and Journals, 1984; Rome: The Biography of a City, 1985; Critics and Civilizations, 1985; The English: A Social History, 1987; Venice: Biography of a City, 1988; The Encyclopaedia of Oxford (editor), 1988; Redcoats and Rebels: The War for America 1760-1781, 1990; The Virgin Queen: The Personal History of Elizabeth I, 1990; Captain Gronow: His Reminiscences of Regency and Victorian Life (editor), 1991; Cavaliers and Roundheads: The English at War 1642-1649, 1993; Florence: Biography of a City, 1993; Nelson: A Personal History, 1994; Wellington: A Personal History, 1997. Honours: Heinemann Award for Literature, 1962; McColvin Medal, 1989; Hon DLitt, Leicester University, 1996. Address: c/o David Higham Associates, 5-8 Lower John Street, Golden Square, London W1R 4HA, England.

HICK John (Harwood), b. 20 Jan 1922, Scarborough, Yorkshire, England. Professor of the Philosophy of Religion (retired); Writer. m. Joan Hazel Bowers, 30 Aug 1953, 3 sons, 1 daughter. Education: MA, 1948, DLitt, 1975, University of Edinburgh; DPhil, Oxford University, 1950; Postgraduate Studies, Westminster Theological College, 1950-53; PhD, Cambridge University, 1964. Appointments: Ordained to the Ministry, United Reformed Church, England, 1953; Minister, Belford Presbyterian Church, Northumberland, England, 1953-56; Assistant Professor of Philosophy, Cornell University, 1956-59; Stuart Professor of Christian Philosophy, Princeton Theological Seminary, 1959-64; Lecturer, 1964-67, Arthur Stanley Eddington Memorial Lecturer, 1972, Stanton Lecturer, 1974-77, Cambridge University; H G Wood Professor of Theology, Birmingham University, 1967-82; Ingersoll Lecturer, Harvard University, 1977; Danforth Professor of the Philosophy of Religion, Claremont Graduate School, California, 1979-92; Gifford Lecturer, University of Edinburgh, 1986-87; Resler Lecturer, Ohio State University, 1991. Publications: Faith and Knowledge, 1957, 2nd edition, 1966; The Philosophy of Religion, 1963, 4th edition, 1990; Evil and the God of Love, 1966, 2nd edition, 1977; God and the Universe of Faiths, 1973; Death and Eternal Life, 1976; God Has Many Names, 1980; Problems of Religious Pluralism, 1985; An Interpretation of Religion, 1989. Honours: Guggenheim Fellowships, 1963-64, 1985-86; Leverhulme Research Fellowships, 1976, 1990; Grawemeyer Award in Religion, 1991. Memberships: American Academy of Religion; American Philosophical Association. Address: c/o Claremont Graduate School, Claremont, CA 91711, USA.

HICKOK Gloria Vando, b. 21 May 1934, New York, New York, USA. Poet; Publisher; Editor. m. (1) Maurice Peress, 2 July 1955, 1 son, 2 daughters, (2) William Harrison Hickok, 4 Oct 1980. Education: BA, Texas A & I College, Corpus Christi, 1975; Graduate Studies, Southampton College, Long Island University, New York. Publications: Caprichos (A Chapbook), 1987; Promesas: Geography of the Impossible, 1993. Contributions to: Cottonwood Magazine, Gloria Vando Issue, Summer 1994; Kenyon Review; Western Humanities Review; Seattle Review. Honours: Billee Murray Denny Prize, 1991; Thorpe Menn Book Award, 1994. Memberships: PEN International; Poetry Society of America; The Writers Place, Kansas City, Missouri, co-founder; The Cockefair Chair, Universty of Missouri-Kansas City, board; Clearing House for Midcontinent Foundations, art chair, 1988-90; Midwest Center for the Literary Arts Inc, president of board. Address: c/o Helicon Nine Editions, PO Box 22412, Kansas City, MO 64113, USA.

HICKS Eleanor B. See: **COERR Eleanor (Beatrice)**.

HIGDON Hal, b. 17 June 1931, Chicago, Illinois, USA. Writer. Education: BA, Carleton College, 1953. Appointment: Assistant Editor, The Kiwanis Magazine, 1957-59. Publications: The Union vs Dr Mudd, 1964; Heroes of the Olympics, 1965; Pro Football USA, 1967; The Horse That Played Center Field, 1967; The Business Healers, 1968; Stars of the Tennis Courts, 1969; 30 Days in May, 1969; The Electronic Olympics, 1969; On The Run from Dogs and People, 1969; Finding the Groove, 1973; Find the Key Man, 1974; The Last Series, 1974; Six Seconds to Glory, 1974; The Crime of the Century, 1976; Summer of Triumph, 1977; Fitness after Forty, 1977; Beginner's Running Guide, 1978; Runner's Cookbook, 1979; Johnny Rutherford, 1980; The Marathoners, 1980; The Team That Played in the Space Bowl, 1981; The Masters Running Guide, 1990; Run Fast, 1992; Marathon: The Ultimate Training and Racing Guide, 1993; Falconara: A Family Odyssey, 1993; Ideas For Rent, The VOP Story, 1994; Boston: A Century of Running, 1995. Memberships: American Society of Journalists and Authors; The Authors Guild; North American Ski Journalists Association. Address: Box 1034, Michigan City, IN 46360, USA.

HIGGINBOTHAM (Prieur) Jay, b. 16 July 1937, Pascagoula, Mississippi, USA. Archivist; Writer. m. Alice Louisa Martin, 27 June 1970, 2 sons, 1 daughter. Education: BA, University of Mississippi, 1960; Graduate Studies, Hunter College of the City University of New York, American University, Washington, DC. Appointments: Head, Local History Department, Mobile Municipal library, 1973-83; Director, Mobile Municipal Archives, 1983-. Publications: The Mobile Indians, 1966; The World Around, 1966; Family Biographies, 1967; The Pascagoula Indians, 1967; Pascagoula: Singing River City, 1968; Mobile: City by the Bay, 1968; The Journal of Sauvole, 1969; Fort Maurepas: The Birth of Louisiana, 1969; Brother Holyfield, 1972; A Voyage to Dauphin Island, 1974; Old Mobile: Fort Louis de la Louisiane, 1702-1711, 1977; Autumn in Petrishchevo, 1986; Discovering Russia, 1989; Mauvila, 1990; Kazula (play), 1991. Contributions to: Periodicals. Honours: General L Kemper Williams Prize, Louisiana Historical Association, 1977; Award of Merit, Mississippi Historical Society, 1978; Non-Fiction Award, Alabama Library Association, 1978; Gilbert Chinard Prize, Institute Français de Washington and Society for French Historical Studies, 1978. Memberships: Authors League of America; Franklin Society; Smithsonian Associates. Address: c/o Mobile Municipal Archives, 457 Church Street, Mobile, AL 36602, USA.

HIGGINS Aidan, b. 3 Mar 1927, Celbridge, County Kildare, Ireland. Novelist. Education: Clongowes Wood College, County Kildare. Publications: Stories Felo De Se, 1960; Langrishe, Go Down, 1966; Balcony of Europe, 1972; Scenes from a Receding Past, 1977; Bornholm Night Ferry, 1983; Helsingor Station & Other Departures, 1989; Ronda Gorge & Other Precipices: Travel Writings, 1959-89; Lions of The Grunewald, (novel), 1993; Donkey's Years (Memories of a Life as Story Told), 1995; Secker, Flotsam and Jetsam, Collected Stories, 1997. Honours: British Arts Council Grant; James Tait Black Memorial Prize, 1967; Irish Academy of Letters Award, 1970; American Ireland Fund, 1977. Address: c/o Secker and Warburg, Michelin House, 91 Fulham Road, London SW3 6RB, England.

HIGGINS George V(incent), b . 13 Nov 1939, Brockton, Massachussets, USA. Writer; Journalist. m. (1) Elizabeth Mulkerin, 4 Sept 1965, div, 1 son, 1 daughter, (2) Loretta Lucas Cubberley, 23 Aug 1979. Education: BA, 1961, JD, 1967, Boston College; MA, Stanford

University, 1965. Appointments: Reporter, Journal and Evening Bulletin, Providence, Rhode Island, 1962-63; Newsman, Boston, Massachussets, 1964; Writer, Instructor in Law Enforcement Programs, Northeastern University, Boston, 1969-71; Consultant, National Institute of Law Enforcement and Criminal Justice, Washington DC, 1970-71; Columnist, Boston Herald American, 1977-79, Boston Globe, 1979-85, Wall Street Journal, 1984-. Publications: The Friends of Eddie Coyle, 1972; The Digger's Game, 1973; Cogan's Trade, 1974; A City on a Hill, 1975; The Judgement of Deke Hunter, 1976; Dreamland, 1977; A Year or So with Edgar, 1979; Kennedy for the Defense, 1980; The Rat on Fire, 1981; The Patriot Game, 1982; A Choice of Enemies, 1984; Penance for Jerry Kennedy, 1985; Imposters, 1986; Wonderful Years, Wonderful Years, 1989; Trust, 1989. Contributions to: Journals and magazines. Honour: The Friends of Eddie Coyle, chosen as one of the top twenty postwar American novels by Book Marketing Council, 1985. Membership: Writers Guild of America. Address: 15 Brush Hill Lane, Milton, MA 02186, USA.

HIGGINS Jack. See: **PATTERSON Harry.**

HIGGINS John Dalby, b . 7 Jan 1934, Hong Kong. Editorial Executive. m. Linda Christmas, 3 Sept 1977. Education: MA, Worcester College, Oxford, 1957. Appointments: Literary/Arts Editor, Financial Times, 1966-69; Arts Editor, 1970-88, Chief Opera Critic/Obituaries Editor, The Times, 1988-. Publications: Design, 1978-88; Don Giovanni - The Making of an Opera, 1977; Glyndebourne - A Celebration (editor), 1984. Honours: Chevalier des Arts et des Lettres; Ehrenkreuz für Kunst und Wissenschaft, Austria; Goldenes Verdienstzeichnis. Memberships: Royal Literary Fund, Committee, 1970-. Address: The Times, London, England.

HIGGINS Richard Carter, (Dick Higgins), b. 15 Mar 1938, Cambridge, England. Composer; Performer; Music Publisher; Writer; Poet. m. (1) 1960, div 1970, (2) 1984, 2 daughters. Education: BS, Columbia University, 1960; MA, New York University, 1977. Appointments: Co-Founder, Fluxus, 1961; Founder-Director, A Something Else Press, 1964-73, Unpublished Editions, 1972-78, Printed Editions, 1978-85; Teacher, California Institute of the Arts, 1970-71; Research Associate in Visual Arts, State University of New York at Purchase, 1983-89; Professor in Art, Williams College, 1987. Publications: Over 40 books, from poetry to criticism, 1960-96. Contributions to: Numerous anthologies, group books, magazines, and museum catalogues. Honours: Bill C Davis Drama Award, 1986-87; Pollock-Krasner Foundation Grant, 1993; Various other grants. Address: PO Box 27, Barrytown, NY 12507, USA.

HIGH Peter Brown, b. 6 Sept 1944, New York, New York, USA. Professor; Writer. m. 21 Oct 1972, 1 son. Education: BA, The American University, 1966; MA, California State University, 1982; PhD, Nagoya University, 1985. Appointments: Columnist, Asahi Shimbun, Japanese Language, 1987-92; Professor of Film and Literature, Nagoya University, 1987-. Publications: An Outline of American Literature, 1985; Read All About It, 1986; A Journalist Looks At Popular Culture, 1991; The Imperial Screen: Japanese Cinema and the 15 Year War, 1995; A History of Cinema, 1997; Assorted language textbooks in the ESL field. Contributions to: Journals. Address: 43 Meidai Shukusha, Kogawa-cho, Chikusa-ku, Nagoya, Japan.

HIGHAM Charles, b. 18 Feb 1931, London, England. Author. Appointments: Regents Professor, University of California, Santa Cruz, California. Publications include: Kate: The Life of Katharine Hepburn, 1975; The Adventures of Conan Doyle, 1976; Marlene: The Life of Marlene Dietrich, 1978; Orson Welles: The Rise and Fall of an American Genius, 1985; The Duchess of Windsor, 1987; Rose: The Life of Rose Fitzgerald Kennedy, 1994. Contributions to: The Times Literary Supplement; The London Magazine; The Hudson Review; The New York Times; Yale Review. Honours: Prix des Createurs; Academie Française, 1976; Cesar Award, Pan-American Theatrical Association. Membership: Dramatists Guild. Address: c/o Jay Harris, 909 Third Avenue, New York, NY 10022, USA.

HIGHAM Robin (David Stewart), b . 20 June 1925, London, England. Historian. m. Barbara Jane Davies, 5 Aug 1950, 3 daughters. Education: AB cum laude, 1950, PhD, 1957, Harvard University; MA, Claremont Graduate School, 1953. Appointments: Editor, Military Affairs, 1968-88; Bibliographical Military Advisory Editor, 1974-; Aerospace Historian, 1976-88; Journal of the West and President, Sunflower University Press, 1977-. Publications: Britain's Imperial Air

Routes, 1960; The British Rigid Airship, 1961; Armed Forces in Peacetime, 1963; The Military Intellectuals in Britain, 1966; Air Power: A Concise History, 1973, 3rd edition, 1988; The Diary of a Disaster, 1986. Contributions to: American Neptune; Balkan Studies; Business History Review; Airpower Historian; Military Affairs; Naval War College Review; Dictionary of Business Biography; New Dictionary of Business Biography; ACTA, International Commission for Comparative Military History. Honours: Aviation and Space Writers Award, 1973; History Book Club Selection, 1973; Samuel Eliot Morison Prize, American Military Institute, 1985. Memberships: Publications Committee, Conference on British Studies; Editorial Advisory Board, Technology and Culture. Literary Agent: Henry Dunow, Harold Ober. Address: 2961 Nevada Street, Manhattan, KS 66502, USA.

HIGHLAND Dora. See: **AVALLONE Michael (Angelo Jr).**

HIGHLAND Monica. See: **SEE Carolyn.**

HIGHWATER Jamake, b. 14 Feb 1942, Montana, USA. Writer; Poet; Lecturer. Appointments: Senior Editor, Fodor Travel Guides, 1970-75; Classical Music Editor, Soho Weekly News, 1975-79; Graduate Lecturer, School of Continuing Education, New York University, 1979-83; Assistant Adjunct Professor, Graduate School of Architecture, Columbia University, 1983-84; Contributing Arts Critic, Christian Science Monitor, 1988-92; Contributing Editor to several periodicals; Guest Lecturer in colleges and universities in North America. Publications: Indian America: A Cultural and Travel Guide, 1975; Song from the Earth: American Indian Painting, 1976; Ritual of the Wind: North American Indian Ceremonies, Music and Dances, 1977; Anpao: An American Indian Odyssey, 1977; Journey to the Sky, 1978; Many Smokes, Many Moons, 1978; Dance: Rituals of Experience, 1978; Masterpieces of American Indian Painting, 2 volumes, 1978, 1980; The Sun, He Dies, 1980; The Sweet Grass Lives On: Fifty Contemporary North American Indian Artists, 1980; The Primal Mind: Vision and Reality in Indian America, 1981; Moonsong Lullaby (poems), 1981; Eyes of Darkness, 1983; Leaves From the Sacred Tree: Arts of the Indian Americas, 1983; Words in the Blood: Contemporary Indian Writers of North and South America, 1984; Legend Days, 1984; I Wear the Morning Star, 1986; Native Land: Sagas of American Civilizations, 1986; Shadow Show: An Autobiographical Insinuation, 1987; Kill Hole, 1988; Myth and Sexuality, 1990; The World of 1492, 1992; Dark Legend, 1994; The Language of Vision, 1994; Rama, 1994; Songs for the Seasons (poems), 1995. Other: Writer, Host and Narrator, PBS TV series, Native Land, 1986. Honours: Newbery Honor Award, 1978; Best Book for Young Adults Awards, American Library Association, 1978, 1986; Virginia McCormick Scully Literary Award, 1982; National Educational Film Festival Best Film of the Year Award, 1986; Ace Award, Discovery Channel, 1991; Best Book for Young Adults Award, New York Public Library, 1994. Memberships: American Federation of Television and Radio Artists; American Poetry Center, board member, 1991-; Authors Guild; Authors League; Dramatists Guild; Indian Art Foundation, founder-member, 1980-87; Native American Rights Fund, national advisory board member, 1980-87; PEN. Address: Native Lands Foundation, 1201 Larrabee Street, Suite 202, Los Angeles, CA 90069, USA.

HIGSON Philip John Willoughby, b. 21 Feb 1933, Newcastle-under-Lyme, England. Poet; Translator; Editor; Historian; Art Historian. Education: BA, honours, 1956, MA, 1959, PhD, 1971, Liverpool University; PGCE, Keele University, 1972. Appointments: Lecturer, Senior Lecturer, History, 1972-89, Visiting Lecturer, 1989-90, University College, Chester; Chairman, President, Anthology Editor, Chester Poets, 1974-92; President, La Société Baudelaire, Paris, 1992-. Publications: The Riposte and Other Poems, 1971; Chester Poets Anthology Series (editor and contributor), 1974-92; Baudelaire: Flowers of Evil (editor and co-translator), 1974; Sonnets to my Goddess, 1983; Rollinat: Les Névroses, selected English versions, 1986; Baudelaire: The Complete Poems with Illustrations by Limouse (editor and main translator), 1992; A Warning to Europe: The Testimony of Limouse (co-author), 1992; Limouse: The Nudes, 1994; Childhood in Wartime Keele: Poems of Reminiscence, 1995; Sonnets to my Goddess in this Life and the Next, 1995. Contributions to: Historical and literary journals. Honours: FSA, 1975; Brian O'Connor Trophy for Poetry, 1981, 1982, 1983; 1st Prize, Eclectic Muse Competition, Vancouver, 1990; David St John Thomas Poetry Publication Prize, 1996; Lexikon Poetry Competition Prizewinner, 1996. Address: 1 Westlands Avenue, Newcastle-under-Lyme, Staffordshire ST5 2PU, England.

HIGUCHI Yoichi, b. 10 Sept 1934, Sendai, Japan. Law Professor Emeritus. Education: Dr honoris causa, University of Paris, Rouen. Publications: Le constitutionnalisme et ses problemes au Japon, 1984; L'Etat et l'individu au Japon, 1990. Contributions to: Pouvoirs; Revue Internationale de Droit Comparé. Memberships: International Association of Constitutional Law, 1st Vice-president; International Academy of Comparative Law, associate member. Address: Akasaka 7-5-48-401, Minato-ku, Tokyo 107, Japan.

HILD Jack. See: GARSIDE Jack Clifford.

HILDICK (Edmund) Wallace, (E W Hildick), b. 29 Dec 1925, Bradford, England. Author. m. Doris Clayton, 9 Dec 1950. Education: Teacher's Certificate, City of Leeds Training College, 1950. Appointment: Visiting Critic and Associate Editor, The Kenyon Review, Gambier, Ohio, 1966-67. Publications: Fiction: Bed and Work, 1962; A Town on the Never, 1963; Lunch with Ashurbanipal, 1965; Bracknell's Law, 1975; The Weirdown Experiment, 1976; Vandals, 1977; The Loop, 1977. Non-Fiction: Word for Word: A Study of Authors' Alterations, with Exercises, 1965; Writing with Care: Two Hundred Problems in the Use of English, 1967; Thirteen Types of Narrative, 1968; Children and Fiction: A Critical Study in Depth of the Artistic and Psychological Factors Involved in Writing Fiction for and about Children, 1971, revised edition, 1974; Storypacks: A New Concept in English Teaching, 1971; Only the Best: Six Qualities of Excellence, 1973. Other: Many books for juvenile readers, including the Jim Starling series, 7 books, 1958-63, the Birdy Jones series, 6 books, 1963-74, the Lemon Kelly series, 3 books, 1963-68, the Louie series, 4 books, 1965-78, the Questers series, 3 books, 1966-67, the McGurk Mystery series, 26 books, 1973-96, the Ghost Squad series, 6 books, 1984-88. Contributions to: Numerous periodicals. Honours: Tom-Gallon Trust Award, 1957; Honour Book Citation, International Hans Christian Andersen Award, 1968; American Ambassador Books Booklist Selection, 1970; Honour Book Citation, Austrian Children and Youth Book Prize Award, 1976; Edgar Allan Poe Special Awards, Mystery Writers of America, 1979, 1995. Memberships: Authors Guild; Mystery Writers of America; Society of Authors. Address: c/o Coutts & Co, 440 Strand, London WC2R 0QS.

HILL Anthony Robert, b. 24 May 1942, Melbourne, Australia. Writer; Journalist. m. Gillian Mann, 15 Oct 1965, 1 daughter. Publications: The Bunburyists, 1985; Antique Furniture in Australia, 1985; Bird Song, 1988; The Burnt Stick, 1994; Spindrift, 1996; The Grandfather Clock, 1996. Honour: Children's Book Council of Australia Honour Book, 1995. Membership: Australian Society of Authors. Address: PO Box 85, Yarralumla, ACT 2600, Australia.

HILL (John Edward) Christopher, (K E Holme), b. 6 Feb 1912, York, England. Historian. Education: BA, 1934, MA, 1938, Balliol College, Oxford. Publications: The English Revolution 1640, 1940; As K.E. Holme: Two Commonwealths, 1945; Lenin and the Russian Revolution, 1947; The Good Old Cause (with E Dell), 1949; Economic Problems of the Church, 1956; Puritanism and Revolution, 1958; The Century of Revolution, 1961; Society and Puritanism, 1964; Intellectual Origins of the English Revolution, 1965; Reformation to Industrial Revolution, 1967; God's Englishman, 1970; Antichrist in Seventeenth Century England, 1971; The World Turned Upside Down, 1972; The Law of Freedom and Other Writings by Gerrard Winstanley, 1973; Change and Continuity in Seventeenth Century England, 1975; Milton and the English Revolution, 1978; Some Intellectual Consequences of the English Revolution, 1980; The Experience of Defeat, 1983; Writing and Revolution, 1985; Religion and Politics in 17th Century England, 1986; People and Ideas in 17th Century England, 1986; A Turbulent 5 Editions & Factives People: John Bunyan and his Church, 1988; A Nation of Change and Novelty, 1990; The English Bible and the 17th Century Revolution, 1993. Address: Woodway House, Sibford Ferris, Oxon, England.

HILL Douglas Arthur, (Martin Hillman), b. 6 Apr 1935, Brandon, Manitoba, Canada. Author. m. Gail Robinson, 8 Apr 1958, div, 1 son. Education: BA, University of Saskatchewan, 1957. Appointment: Literary Editor, Tribune, London, 1971-84. Publications: The Supernatural, 1965; The Opening of the Canadian West, 1967; John Keats, 1969; The Scots to Canada, 1972; Galactic Warlord, 1980; The Huntsman, 1982; The Last Legionary Quartet, 1985; Penelope's Pendant, 1990; The Unicorn Dream, 1992; The Lightless Dome, 1993; The Voyage of Mudjack, 1993; World of the Stiks, 1994; The Leafless Forest, 1994; CADE: Galaxy's Edge, 1996; The Dragon Charmer,

1997. Memberships: Society of Authors; Children's Book Circle. Address: 3 Hillfield Avenue, London N8 7DU, England.

HILL Elizabeth Starr, b. 4 Nov 1925, Lynn Haven, Florida, USA. Writer. m. Russell Gibson Hill, 28 May 1949, 1 son, 1 daughter. Education: Finch Junior College; Columbia University. Publications: The Wonderful Visit to Miss Liberty, 1961; The Window Tulip, 1964; Evan's Corner, 1967; Pardon My Fangs, 1969; Bells: A Book to Begin On, 1970; Ever-After Island, 1977; Fangs Aren't Everything, 1985; When Christmas Comes, 1989; The Street Dancers, 1991; Broadway Chances, 1992; The Banjo Player, 1993; Curtain Going Up!, 1995. Contributions to: Magazines. Honours: Notable Book for Children Citation, American Library Association, 1967; Junior Literary Guild Selections, 1977, 1989; Pick of the Lists Citation, American Book Association, 1992. Memberships: Authors Guild; Authors League. Address: Langford Apartments, PO Box 940, Winter Park, FL 32790, USA.

HILL Errol Gaston, b . 5 Aug 1921, Trinidad, West Indies. College Professor Emeritus. m. Grace Lucille Eunice Hope, 11 Aug 1956, 1 son, 3 daughters. Education: Graduate Diploma, Royal Academy of Dramatic Art, London, England, 1951; Diploma in Dramatic Art with distinction, London University, 1951; BA summa cum laude, 1962, MFA, Playwriting, 1962, DFA, Theatre History, 1966, Yale University, USA. Publications: Man Better Man: A Musical Comedy, 1964, reprinted, 1985; The Trinidad Carnival, 1972; The Theatre of Black Americans, 1980, reprinted, 1987; Shakespeare in Sable: A History of Black Shakespearean Actors, 1984; The Jamaican Stage, 1655-1900, 1992. Editor: Caribbean Plays, Vol 1, 1958, Vol 2, 1965; A Time and a Season: 8 Caribbean Plays, 1976; Plays for Today, 1985; Black Heroes: Seven Plays, 1989; The Cambridge Guide to African and Caribbean Theatre (co-author), 1994. Contributions to: McGraw Encyclopaedia of World Drama, 1984; Theatre Journal; Theatre History Studies; American Literature Forum; Caribbean Quarterly; Cambridge Guide to World Theatre. Honours: British Council Scholarship, 1949-51; Rockefeller Foundation Fellowships, 1958-60, 1965; Theatre Guild of America Fellowship, 1961; Guggenheim Fellowship, 1985-86; Barnard Hewitt Award for Theatre History, 1985; Fulbright Fellowship, 1988. Memberships: American Society for Theatre Research; American Theatre and Drama Society; Association of Commonwealth Language and Literature Studies; Phi Beta Kappa; International Federation for Theatre Research. Address: 3 Haskins Road, Hanover, NH 03755, USA.

HILL Geoffrey (William), b. 18 June 1932, Bromsgrove, Worcestershire, England. Professor of Literature and Religion; Poet; Writer. m. (1) Nancy Whittaker, 1956, div 1983, 3 sons, 1 daughter, (2) Alice Goodman, 1987, 1 daughter. Education: BA, 1953, MA, Keble College, Oxford. Appointments: Staff, 1954-76, Professor of English Literature, 1976-80, University of Leeds; Churchill Fellow, University of Bristol, 1980; University Lecturer in English and Fellow, Emmanuel College, Cambridge, 1981-88; Clark Lecturer, Trinity College, Cambridge, 1986; University Professor and Professor of Literature and Religion, Boston University, 1988-. Publications: Poetry: Poems, 1952; For the Unfallen: Poems, 1952-58, 1959; Preghiere, 1964; King Log, 1968; Mercian Hymns, 1971; Somewhere is Such a Kingdom: Poems 1952-72, 1975; Tenebrae, 1978; The Mystery of the Charity of Charles Péguy, 1983; New and Collected Poems 1952-92, 1994; Canaan, 1996. Other: Brand (adaptation of Henrik Ibsen's play), 1978. Honours: Gregory Award, 1961; Hawthornden Prize, 1969; Alice Hunt Bartlett Award, 1971; Geoffrey Faber Memorial Prize, 1971; Whitbread Award, 1971; Duff Cooper Memorial Prize, 1979; Honorary Fellow, Keble College, Oxford, 1981, Emmanuel College, Cambridge, 1990; Loines Award, American Academy and Institute of Arts and Letters, 1983; Ingram-Merrill Foundation Award, 1988; Honorary DLitt, University of Leeds, 1988; Fellow, Royal Society of Literature; Fellow, American Academy of Arts and Sciences, elected 1996. Address: The University Professors, Boston University, 745 Commonwealth Avenue, Boston, MA 02215, USA.

HILL Jane (Bowers), b. 17 Oct 1950, Seneca, South Carolina, USA. Teacher; Editor; Writer. m. Robert W Hill, 16 Aug 1980, 1 daughter. Education: BA 1972, MA 1978, Clemson University; PhD, University of Illinois, 1986. Appointments: Associate Editor, Peachtree Publishers, 1986-88; Senior Editor, Longstreet Press, 1988-91; Director, Kennesaw Summer Writers Workshop, 1988-92; Assistant Professor, West Georgia College, 1992-. Publications: Gail Godwin, 1992. Editor: An American Christmas: A Sampler of Contemporary Stories and Poems, 1986; Our Mutual Room: Modern Literary Portraits of the Opposite Sex, 1987; Songs: New Voices in Fiction, 1990; Cobb County: At the Heart of Change, 1991. Contributions to: Numerous stories, poems, essays and reviews. Honours: Frank O'Connor Prize for Fiction, 1989; Syvenna Foundation Fellow, 1991; Monticello Fellowship for Female Writers, 1992. Membership: Modern Language Association. Address: 1419 Arden Drive, Marietta, GA 30060, USA.

HILL Pamela, (Sharon Fiske), b. 26 Nov 1920, Nairobi, Kenya. Writer. Education: DA, Glasgow School of Art, 1943; BSc, Equivalent, University of Glasgow, 1952. Publications: Flaming Janet, 1954; The Devil of Aske, 1972; The Malvie Inheritance, 1973; Homage to a Rose, 1979; Fire Opal, 1980; This Rough Beginning, 1981; My Lady Glamis, 1981; Summer Cypress, 1981; The House of Cray, 1982; The Governess, 1985; Venables, 1988; The Sutburys, 1987; The Brocken, 1991; The Sword and the Flame, 1991; Mercer, 1992; The Silver Runaways, 1992; O Madcap Duchess, 1993; The Parson's Children, 1993; The Man for the North, 1994; Journey Beyond Innocence, 1994; The Charmed Descent, 1995; The Inadvisable Marriages, 1995; Saints' Names for Confirmation, 1995; Alice the Palace, 1996; Murder in Store, 1996. Contributions to: Argosy; Chambers Journal. Memberships: Royal Society of Literature; Society of Authors. Literary Agent: Robert Hale Limited. Address: c/o Robert Hale Limited, Clerkenwell House, Clerkenwell Green, London EC1R 0HT, England.

HILL Reginald (Charles), (Dick Morland, Patrick Ruell, Charles Underhill), b. 3 Apr 1936, West Hartlepool, England. Author; Playwright. Education: BA, St Catherine's College, Oxford, 1960. Publications: As Reginald Hill: A Clubbable Woman, 1970; Fell of Dark, 1971; An Advancement of Learning, 1972; A Fairly Dangerous Thing, 1972; An Affair of Honour (play), 1972; Ruling Passion, 1973; A Very Good Hater, 1974; An April Shroud, 1975; Another Death in Venice, 1976; A Pinch of Snuff, 1978; Pascoe's Ghost (stories), 1979; A Killing Kindness, 1980; The Spy's Wife, 1980; Who Guards a Prince, 1981; Traitor's Blood, 1983; Deadheads, 1983; Exit Lines, 1984; No Man's Land, 1984; Child's Play, 1987; The Collaborators, 1987; There Are No Ghosts in the Soviet Union, 1987; Under World, 1988; Bones and Silence, 1990; One Small Step (novella), 1990; Recalled to Life, 1992; Blood Sympathy, 1993; Pictures of Perfection, 1994; Born Guilty, 1995; The Wood Beyond, 1996; Killing the Lawyers, 1997. As Dick Morland: Heart Clock, 1973; Albion! Albion!, 1974. As Patrick Ruell: The Castle of Demon, 1971; Red Christmas, 1972; Death Takes the Low Road, 1974; Urn Burial, 1976; The Long Kill, 1986; Death of a Dormouse, 1987; Dream of Darkness, 1989; The Only Game, 1991. As Charles Underhill: Captain Fantom, 1978; The Forging of Fantom, 1979. Honours: Gold Dagger Award, 1990; Diamond Dagger Award, 1995. Address: c/o A P Watt Ltd, 20 John Street, London WC1N 2DR, England.

HILL Selima (Wood), b. 13 Oct 1945, London. Poet. 2 sons, 2 daughters. Education: New Hall College, Cambridge. Literary Appointments: Writing Fellow, University of East Anglia, 1991; Writer-in-Residence, Exeter and Devon Arts Centre, 1996. Publications: Saying Hello at the Station, 1984; My Darling Camel, 1988; The Accumulation of Small Acts of Kindness, 1989; A Little Book of Meat, 1993; Trembling Hearts in the Bodies of Dogs, 1994; My Sister's Horse, 1996; Violet, 1997. Honours: Cholmondeley Prize, 1986; Arvon Observer Poetry Competition Prize, 1988; Arts Council Writers Bursary, 1993; H K Travel Scholarship to Mongolia, 1994; Judge: Kent, Exeter, 1995, Bournemouth, 1996. Address: c/o Bloodaxe Books, PO Box 1SN, Newcastle Upon Tyne, NE99 1SN, England.

HILL Susan Elizabeth, b. 5 Feb 1942, Scarborough, Yorkshire, England. Novelist; Playwright. m. Stanley W Wells, 3 daughters, 1 dec. Education: BA, University of London, 1963. Appointments: Literary Critic, Various Journals, 1963; Numerous Plays for BBC, 1970-. Publications: The Enclosure, 1961; Do Me a Favour, 1963; Gentleman and Ladies, 1969; A Change for the Better, 1969; I'm the King of the Castle, 1970; Strange Meeting, 1971; The Bird of Night, 1972; The Cold Country and Other Plays for Radio, 1975; The Magic Apple Tree, 1982; The Woman in Black, 1983; Through the Garden Gate, 1986; Mothers Magic, 1986; Lanterns Across the Snow, 1987; Can It Be True?, 1988. Membership: Royal Society of Literature, fellow. Address: Midsummer Cottage, Church Lane, Beckley, Oxon, England.

HILLERMAN Tony, b. 27 May 1925, USA. Professor of Journalism Emeritus; Author. m. Mary Unzner, 16 Aug 1948, 3 sons, 3 daughters. Education: Oklahoma State University, 1943; BA, University of Oklahoma, 1946; MA, University of New Mexico, 1966. Appointments: Reporter, Borger News Herald, Texas, 1948; City

Editor, Morning Press-Constitution, Lawton, Oklahoma, 1948-50; Political Reporter, Oklahoma City, 1950-52, Bureau Manager, Santa Fe, 1952-54, United Press International; Political Reporter and Executive Editor, New Mexican, Santa Fe, 1954-63; Associate Professor, 1965-66, Professor of Journalism, 1966-85, Professor Emeritus, 1985-, University of New Mexico. Publications: Fiction: The Blessing Way, 1970; The Fly on the Wall, 1971; Dance Hall of the Wind, 1981; Ghostway, 1984; A Thief of Time, 1985; Skinwalkers, 1986; The Joe Leaphorn Mysteries (collection), 1989; Talking God, 1989; Coyote Waits, 1990; Best of the West: An Anthology of Classic Writing from the American West (editor), 1991; The Jim Chee Mysteries (collection), 1992; Sacred Clowns, 1993; Finding Moon, 1994; The Fallen Man, 1996. Non-Fiction: The Spell of New Mexico (editor), 1984; Indian Country: America's Sacred Land, 1987; Hillerman Country: A Journey through the Southwest with Tony Hillerman, 1991; Talking Mysteries: A Conversation with Tony Hillerman (with Ernie Bulow), 1991; New Mexico, Rio Grande, and Other Essays, 1992. Other: The Oxford Book of the American Detective Story, 1996. Contributions to: Magazines. Honour: Edgar Allan Poe Award, Mystery Writers of America, 1974. Memberships: Phi Kappa Phi; Sigma Delta Chi. Address: 1632 Francisca North, Albuquerque, NM 87107, USA.

HILLIS Rick, b. 3 Feb 1956, Nipawin, Sakatchewan, Canada. Writer; Poet; Teacher. m. Patricia Appelgren, 29 Aug, 1 son, 1 daughter. Education: University of Victoria, 1977-78; BEd, University of Saskatchewan, 1979; Graduate Studies, Concordia University, 1983; MFA, University of Iowa, 1984; Stanford University, 1988-90. Appointments: Stegner Fellow, Stanford University, 1988-90; Lecturer, California State University at Hayward, 1990; Jones Lecturer, Stanford University, 1990-92; Chesterfield Film Writer's Fellowship, 1991-92; Visiting Assistant Professor of English, Reed College, 1992-96. Publications: The Blue Machines of Night (poems), 1988; Coming Attractions (co-author), 1988; Canadian Brash (co-author), 1990; Limbo Stories, 1990. Contributions to: Anthologies and periodicals. Honours: Canada Council Grants, 1985, 1987, 1989; Drue Heinz Literature Prize, 1990. Address: c/o Department of English, Lewis and Clark College, Portland, OR 97202, USA.

HILLMAN Ellis Simon, b. 17 nov 1928, London, England. Lecturer in Environmental Studies; Writer. m. Louise Hillman, 10 Dec 1967, 1 son. Education: University College School, 1942-46; BSc, Chelsea College of Science and Technology. Appointments: Chairman, London Subterranean Survey Association, 1968-; Governor, Imperial College of Science and Technology, later Imperial College of Science, Technology and Medicine, 1969-91, Queen Mary College, 1973-82; Principal Lecturer in Environmental Studies, North East London Polytechnic, later Polytechnic of East London, and finally University of East London, 1972-; Councillor, Labour Party, Colindale, 1986-, Mayor, London Borough of Barnet, 1994-95. Publications: Essays in Local Government Enterprise, 1964-67; Towards a Wider Use (editor), 1976; Space for the Living or Space for the Dead (editor), 1977; Novellae on the Scroll of Esther, 1982; London Under London, 1985. Contributions to: Professional journals. Honour: National Book League Prize, 1986. Memberships: Green Alliance; Lewis Carroll Society, founder-honorary president, 1969-; Royal Society of Architects, fellow; Society of Educational Consultants. Address: 29 Haslemere Avenue, London NW4 2PU, England.

HILLMAN Martin. See: HILL Douglas Arthur.

HILLS Charles Albert Reis, b. 21 Aug 1955, London, England. Report Writer, BBC Monitoring. Publications: The Facist Dictatorships, 1979; The Hitler File, 1980; World Trade, 1981; Modern Industry, 1982; Growing Up in The 1950s, 1983; The Second World War, 1985; The Destruction of Pompeii and Herculaneum, 1987. Contributions to: Guardian; Daily Telegraph; Encounter; Books; Jennings Magazine; Lady. Memberships: English Centre PEN. Address: 3 Lucas House, Albion Avenue, London SW8 2AD, England.

HILLS Geraldine. See: JAY Geraldine Mary.

HILTON Margot Pamela, b . 18 Aug 1947, London, England. Arts Administrator; Writer; Journalist. m. Graeme Blundell, 3 Oct 1979, 1 son, 1 daughter. Education: BA, English, Honours, 1971, MA, Drama and Theatre Arts, 1972, Leeds University. Appointments: Drama Adviser, Victorian Ministry for the Arts, 1974-79; Executive Officer, Australian Society of Authors, 1981-84; Playwright-in-Residence, Australian National Playwrights Conference, 1983; Executive Secretary, Victorian Premier's Inaugural Literary Awards, 1984-85;

Publicity Manager, Angus & Robertson Publishers, 1985-87. Publications: Women on Men, 1987; Potiphar's Wife, 1987. Contributions to: Theatre Australia; Playboy; New Review; Australian Author; Bulletin; Architecture Australia; National Times; Times on Sunday; Sydney Morning Herald; Sun-Herald. Address: 84 Surrey Street, Potts Point, New South Wales 2011, Australia.

HILTON Suzanne McLean, b. 3 Sept 1922, Pittsburgh, Pennslyvania, USA. Writer. m. Warren Mitchell Hilton, 15 June 1946, 1 son, 1 daughter. Education: BA, Beaver College, 1946. Appointments: Editor, Bulletin of Old York Road Historical Society, 1976-92; Associate Editor, Montgomery County History, 1983; Editor, Bulletin of Historical Society of Montomery County, 1987-89. Publications: How Do They Get Rid of It?, 1970; How Do They Cope with It?, 1970; Beat It, Burn It and Drown It, 1974; Who Do You Think You Are?, 1976; Yesterday's People, 1976; Here Today and Gone Tomorrow, 1978; Faster than a Horse: Moving West with Engine Power, 1983; Montomery County, The Second Hundred Years, 1983; The World of Young Tom Jefferson, 1986; The World of Young George Washsington, 1986; The World of Young Herbert Hoover, 1987; The World of Young Andrew Jackson, 1988; A Capital Capitol City, 1991; Miners, Merchants and Maids, 1995. Contributions to: Historical journals. Honours: Legion of Honour, Chapel of the Four Chaplains, 1978; Award for Excellence in Non Fiction, Drexel University, 1979; Golden Spur, Western Writers of America, 1980; Gold Disc, Beaver College, 1981. Memberships: Society of Children's Book Writers and Illustrators; Philadelphia Childrens Reading Round Table. Address: 3320 108th St NW, Gig Harbour, WA 98332, USA.

HIMMELFARB Gertrude, b. 8 Aug 1922, New York, New York, USA. Professor of History Emerita; Writer. m. Irving Kristol, 18 Jan 1942, 1 son, 1 daughter. Education: Jewish Theological Seminrary, 1939-42; BA, Brooklyn College, 1942; MA, 1944, PhD, 1950, University of Chicago; Girton College, Cambridge, 1946-47. Appointments: Professor, 1965-78, Distinguished Professor of History, 1978-88, Professor Emerita, 1988-, Brooklyn College and Graduate School of the City University of New York. Publications: Lord Acton: A Study in Conscience and Politics, 1952; Darwin and the Darwinian Revolution, 1959, revised edition, 1968; Victorian Minds: Essays on Nineteenth Century Intellectuals, 1968; On Liberty and Liberalism: The Case of John Stuart Mill, 1974; The Idea of Poverty: England in the Industrial Age, 1984; Marriage and Morals Among the Victorians and Other Essays, 1986; The New History and the Old, 1987; Poverty and Compassion: The Moral Imagination of the Late Victorians, 1991; On Looking Into the Abyss: Untimely Thoughts on Culture and Society, 1994; The De-Moralization of Society, 1995. Contributions to: Scholarly books and journals. Honours: American Association of University Women Fellowship, 1951-52; American Philosophical Society Fellowship, 1953-54; Guggenheim Fellowships, 1955-56, 1957-58; National Endowment for the Humanities Senior Fellowship, 1968-69; American Council of Learned Societies Fellowship, 1972-73; Phi Beta Kappa Visiting Scholarship, 1972-73; Woodrow Wilson Center Fellowship, 1976-77; Rockefeller Humanities Fellowship, 1980-81. Memberships: American Academy of Arts and Sciences; American Historical Association; American Philosophical Society; British Academy, Fellow; Royal Historical Society, Fellow; Society of American Historians. Address: 2510 Virginia Avenue, NW, Washignton, DC 20037, USA.

HINDE Thomas. See: CHITTY Sir Thomas Willes.

HINDIN Nathan. See: BLOCH Robert.

HINE (William) Daryl, b. 24 Feb 1936, Burnaby, British Columbia, Canada. Poet; Writer; Translator. Education: McGill University, 1954-58; MA, 1965, PhD, 1967, University of Chicago. Appointments: Assistant Professor of English, University of Chicago, 1967-69; Editor, Poetry magazine, Chicago, 1968-78. Publications: Poetry: Five Poems, 1954, 1955; The Carnal and the Crane, 1957; The Devil's Picture Book, 1960; Heroics, 1961; The Wooden Horse, 1965; Minutes, 1968; Resident Alien, 1975; In and Out: A Confessional Poem, 1975; Daylight Saving, 1978; Selected Poems, 1980; Academic Festival Overtures, 1985; Arrondissments, 1988; Postscripts, 1992. Novel: The Prince of Darkness & Co, 1961. Other: Polish Subtitles: Impressions from a Journey, 1962; The "Poetry" Anthology 1912-1977 (editor with Joseph Parisi), 1978; Theocritus: Idylls and Epigrams, 1982; Ovid's Heroines: A Verse Translation from the Heroides, 1991. Honours: Canada Foundation-Rockefeller Fellowship, 1958; Canada Council Grants 1959, 1979; Ingram Merrill Foundation Grants, 1962,

1963, 1983; Guggenheim Fellowship, 1980; American Academy of Arts and Letters Award, 1982; John D and Catherine T McArthur Foundation Fellowship, 1986. Address: 2740 Ridge Avenue, Evanston, IL 60201, USA.

HINES Barry Melvin, b. 30 June 1939, Barnsley, Yorkshire, England. Writer. Div, 1 son, 1 daughter. Education: Loughborough College of Education, 1958-60, 1962-63. Appointments: Yorkshire Arts Association Fellow, Sheffield University, 1972-74; East Midlands Art Association Fellow, Matlock College of Higher Education, 1975-77; Arts Council of Great Britain Fellow, Sheffield City Polytechnic, 1982-84. Publications: The Blinder, 1966; A Kestrel for a Knave, 1968; First Signs, 1972; The TheGamekeeper, 1975; The Price of Coal, 1979; Unfinished Business, 1983; A Question of Leadership, 1981; Looks and Smiles, 1981; The Heart of It,1994. TV and Film: Two Men from Derby, 1967; Kes, 1969; The Price of Coal, 2 films, 1975; The Gamekeeper, 1976; Looks and Smiles, 1979; A Question of Leadership, 1981; Threads, 1984; Shooting Stars, 1990; Born Kicking, 1992. Address: 323 Fulwood Road, Sheffield, S10 3BJ, England.

HINES Donald (Merrill), b. 23 Jan 1931, St Paul, Minnesota, USA. Writer; Teacher. m. Linda Marie Arnold, 10 June 1961, 3 sons. Education: BS, Lewis and Clark College, Portland, Oregon, 1953; MAT, Reed College, Portland, Oregon, 1960; PhD, Indiana University, 1969. Appointments: Faculty, Washington State University, 1968-77, King Saud University, Abha, Saudi Arabia, 1982-90, Blue Mountain Community College, Pendleton, Oregon, 1990-91. Publications: Cultural History of the Inland Pacific Northwest Frontier, 1976; Tales of the Okanogans, 1976; Tales of the Nez Perce, 1984; The Forgotten Tribes: Oral Tales of the Tenino and Adjacent Mid-Columbia River Indian Nations, 1991; Ghost Voices: Yakima Indian Myths, Legends, Humour and Hunting Stories, 1992; Celilo Tales: Waseo Myths, Legends, Tales of Magic and the Marvelous, 1996. Contributions to: Journals. Honours: Ford Foundation Fellowship, 1965; 3rd Prize, Chicago Folklore Contest, University of Chicago, 1970. Membership: American Folklore Society. Address: 3623 219th Place South East, Issaquah, WA 98029, USA.

HINOJOSA-SMITH Rolando, b. 21 Jan 1929, Mercedes, Texas, USA. English Professor; Writer. m. Patricia Sorensen, 1 Sept 1963, 1 son, 2 daughters. Education: BS University of Texas at Austin, 1953; Highlands University, New Mexico, 1963; PhD, University of Illinois, 1969. Appointments: University of Minnesota, 1977-81; University of Texas, 1981-. Publications: Korean Love Songs, 1978; The Valley, 1983; Dear Rafe, 1985; Rites and Witnesses, 1984; Klail City, 1986; Partners in Crime, 1987; Becky and her Friends, 1989; The Useless Servants, 1993. Contributions to: Texas Monthly; Southwest Airlines Spirit; Latin American Review Magazine; Southwest Review. Honours: Best Novel, 1973, 1976, 1981; Qinto Sol Prize, Case de Las Americas Prize; Best Writing in the Humanities Prize, 1981; Alumnus of the University of Illinois, 1989. Memberships: Modern Language Association; Board of Directors, Texas Committee on the Humanities. Address: Department of English, University of Texas at Austin, TX 78712, USA.

HINRIKSSON Larus, b. 28 feb 1956, Reykjavik, Iceland. Writer. m. Freyja Baldursdottir, Aug 1982, 1 son, 1 daughter. Education: Industrial School of Iceland, 1980. PuBlications: Enigma Well, 1993; The Lupin, 1994; Echo of Time Broken Glass, poems, 1995. Membership: Writers' Union of Iceland. Address: Box 410, 602 Akureyri, Iceland.

HINSON Edward Glenn, b. 27 July 1931, St Louis, Missouri, USA. m. Martha Anne Burks, 1 Sept 1956, 1 son, 1 daughter. Education: BA, Washington University, St Louis, 1954; BD, 1957, ThD, 1962, Southern Baptist Theological Seminary, Louisville; DPhil, Oxford University, 1973. Publications: Seekers After Mature Faith, 1967; A Serious Call to a Contemplative Lifestyle, 1974, new edition, 1993; The Integrity of the Church, 1978; The Evangelization of the Roman Empire, 1981; The Early Church, 1995; Glossolalia; Doubleday Devotional Classics; The Church Triumphant. Contributions to: Revue de Quran; Christian Century; Church History; Review and Expositor; One in Christ; Weavings; Sojurners; Cistercian Standards. Honours: Fellowship, Association of Theological Schools, 1966, 1975. Address: 1204 Palmyra Avenue, Rchmond, VA 23227, USA.

HINTON Jenny. See: DAWSON Jennifer.

HIPPOPOTAMUS Eugene H. See: KRAUS Robert.

HIRO Dilip. Writer. Education: MS, State University of Virginia, USA, 1962. Publications: A Triangular View, 1969; Black British, White British, 1971, revised edition, 1992; To Anchor a Cloud, 1972; The Untouchables of India, 1975; Inside India Today, 1976; Clean Break (play), 1978; Apply, Apply, No Reply (play), 1978; Interior, Exchange, Exterior, 1980; Inside the Middle East, 1982; Iran Under the Ayatollahs, 1985; Three Plays, 1987; Iran: The Revolution Within, 1988; Islamic Fundamentalism, 1988; The Longest War: The Iran-Iraq Military Conflict, 1989; Desert Shield to Desert Storm: The Second Gulf War, 1992; Lebanon, Fire and Embers: A History of the Lebanese Civil War, 1993; Between Marx and Muhammed: The Changing Face of Central Asia, 1994; Dictionary of the Middle East, 1996; The Middle East, 1996; Sharing the Promised Land: An Interwoven Tale of Israelis and Palestinians, 1996. Contributions to: Newspapers and journals. Honour: Silver Hugo, Chicago Film Festival, 1975. Memberships: Middle East Studies Association of North America; Centre for Iranian Research and Analysis. Address: 31 Waldegrave Road, Ealing, London W5 3HT, England.

HIROKO Takenishi, b. 1929, Hiroshima, Japan. Writer. Education: Graduated in Japanese Literature, Waseda University, Tokyo. Appointments: Worked in publishing company; Writer, 1963-. Publications: Essays: Oukan no ki - Nihon no Koten ni omou; Yamakawa Tomiko - Myoujô no kajin. Novels: Tsuru, 1976; Kangen sai, 1978; Heitai yado, 1981; Gishiki; Mizu-umi; Aisatsu; Choujô no kaze. Honours: Tamura Tishiko Literary Prize, 1964; Hirabayashi Prize of Literature, 1973; Minister of Education Prize for Young Writers, 1976; Women's Literary Award, 1978; Kawabata Yasunari Literary Award, 1981; Mainichi Art Award, 1986; Japan Art Academy Prize, 1994. Memberships: Japan Art Academy; Japan PEN Club; Board of Directors, Japan Writers' Association. Address: c/o Japan Writers' Association, Bungei Shunjyu Building, 9th Floor, 3-23 Kioi-cho, Chiyoda-ku, Tokyo 102, Japan.

HIRSCH Edward (Mark), b. 20 Jan 1950, Chicago, Illinois, USA. Professor of English; Poet; Writer. m. Janet Landay, 29 May 1977, 1 son. Education: BA, Grinnell College, 1972; PhD, University of Pennsylvania, 1979. Apointments: Assistant Professor, 1979-82, Associate Professor of English, 1982-85, Wayne State University; Associate Professor, 1985-88, Professor of English, 1988-, University of Houston. Publications: For the Sleepwalkers, 1981; Wild Gratitude, 1986; The Night Parade, 1989; Earthly Measures, 1994; Transforming Vision: Writers on Art (editor), 1994. Contributions to: Periodicals. Honours: Awards, 1975-77, Peter I B Lavan Younger Poets Award, 1983, Academy of American Poets; Ingram Merrill Foundation Award, 1978-79; American Council of Learned Societies Fellow, 1981; National Endowment for the Arts Fellowship, 1982; Delmore Scwartz Memorial Poetry Award, New York University, 1985; Guggenheim Fellowship, 1985-86; National Book Critics Circle Award, 1987; Rome Prize, American Academy and Institute of Arts and Letters, 1988; William Riley Parker Prize, Modern Language Association, 1992; Phi Beta Kappa. Memberships: Authors Guild; Authors League of America; Modern Language Association; PEN; Poetry Society of America. Address: c/o Department of English, University of Houston, Houston, TX 77204, USA.

HIRSCHFELD Vizhar, b. 6 Feb 1950, Jerusalem, Israel. Archaeologist. m. Hannah, 4 Jan 1983, 3 daughters. Education: PhD, Classical Archaeology, Hebrew University of Jerusalem. Publications: The Judean Desert Monasteries in the Byzantine Period,1992; The Palestinian Dwelling in the Roman-Byzantine Period, 1995. Address: Institute of Archaeology, Hebrew University, Jersualem, Israel.

HIRSCHHORN Clive Errol, b . 20 Feb 1940, Johannesburg, South Africa. Critic. Education: BA, University of the Witwatersrand, Johannesburg. Appointment: Film and Theatre Critic, London Sunday Express, 1966-. Publications: Gene Kelly - A Biography, 1974; Films of James Mason, 1976; The Warner Brothers' Story, 1978; The Hollywood Musical, 1981; The Universal Story, 1983; The Columbia Story, 1989. Address: 42a South Audley Street, Mayfair, London W1, England.

HIRSCHMAN Jack, b. 13 Dec 1933, New York, New York, USA. Poet; Translator. m. Ruth Epstein, 1954, 1 son, 1 daughter. Education: BA, City College of New York, 1955; AM, 1957, PhD, 1961, Indiana University. Publications: Poetry: Fragments, 1952; Correspondence of Americans, 1960; Two, 1963; Interchange, 1964; Kline Sky, 1965; Yod, 1966; London Seen Directly, 1967; Wasn't Like This in the Woodcut, 1967; William Blake, 1967; A Word in Your Season (with Asa

Benveniste), 1967; Ltd Interchangeable in Eternity: Poems of Jackruthdavidcelia Hirschman, 1967; Jerusalem, 1968; Aleph, Benoni and Zaddik, 1968; Jerusalem Ltd, 1968; Shekinah, 1969; Broadside Golem, 1969; Black Alephs: Poems 1960-68, 1969; NHR, 1970; Scintilla, 1970; Soledeth, 1971; DT, 1971; The Burning of Los Angeles, 1971; HNYC, 1971; Les Vidanges, 1972; The R of the Ari's Raziel, 1972; Adamnan, 1972; K'wai Sing: The Origin of the Dragon, 1973; Cantillations, 1973; Aur Sea, 1974; Djackson, 1974; Cockroach Street, 1975; The Cool Boyetz Cycle, 1975; Kashtaniyah Segodnyah, 1976; Lyripol, 1976; The Arcanes of Le Comte de St Germain, 1977; The Proletarian Arcane, 1978; The Jonestown Arcane, 1979; The Caliostro Arcane, 1981; The David Arcane, 1982; Class Questions, 1982; Kallatumba, 1984; The Necessary Is, 1984; The Bottom Line, 1988; Sunsong, 1988; The Tirana Arcane, 1991; The Satin Arcane, 1991; Endless Threshold, 1992; The Back of a Spoon, 1992; The Heartbeat Arcane, 1993; The Xibalba Arcane, 1994; Editor: Artaud Anthology, 1965; Would You Wear My Eyes: A Tribute to Bob Kaufman, 1989; Translator: Over 25 volumes, 1970-95. Address: PO Box 26517, San Francisco, CA 94126, USA.

HIRSH Michael. Journalist. Education: BA magna cum laude, Philosophy, Tufts University, 1979; Graduate Degree, International and Public Affairs, Columbia University. Appointments: Tokyo Correspondent, National Editor, New York, Associated Press; Tokyo-based Asia Bureau Chief, Institutional Investor, 1992-94; New York-based Senior Writer, 1994, currently Senior Editor responsible for coverage of business and economics, Newsweek International. Address: c/o Newsweek International, 251 West 57th Street, New York, NY 10019-1894, USA.

HISLOP Ian (David), b. 13 July 1960, England. m. Victoria Hanson, 1988, 1 son, 1 daughter. Education: BA Hons, Magdalen College, Oxford. Appointments: Writer, 1981-, Deputy Editor, 1985-86, Editor, 1986-, Private Eye; Columnist, The Listener, 1985-89; Radio work includes Fourth Column, Newsquiz, 1985-; Team Captain, TV Quiz, Have I Got News For You, 1990-. Publications: Secret Diary of Lord Gnome (editor), 1985; Gnome of the Rose (editor), 1987; Satiric Verses, 1989; Fib and Lie Diet (editor), 1991; Secret Diary of John Major, 1992; Second Secret Diary of John Major, 1993; Gnome in Provence (editor), 1993; Absolutely Libellous, 1994; Third and Last Secret Diary of John Major, 1994. Other: Script writer: Spitting Image (satirical TV series), Harry Enfield's Television Programme. Television Plays: The Stone Age (for Trevor Eve); Briefcase Encounter (for Maureen Lipman); The Case of the Missing, He Died a Death, Mangez Merveillac (for Dawn French). Honours: Editor's Editor, British Society of Magazine Editor's highest award, 1991; Private Eye awarded Magazine of the Year, What The Papers Say (current affairs review), 1991; Have I Got News For You awarded best light entertainment, British Academy of Film and Television Arts, 1992. Address: c/o Private Eye, 6 Carlisle Street, London W1V 5RG, England.

HISSEY Jane Elizabeth, b. 1 Sept 1952, Norwich, Norfolk, England. Author; Illustrator. m. Ivan James Hissey, 1 Aug 1979, 2 sons, 1 daughter. Education: Art Foundation Course, Great Yarmouth College of Art and Design, 1970; BA, 1974, Art Teachers Certificate, Brighton Polytechnic, 1975. Publications: Old Bear, 1986; Little Bears Trousers, 1987; Little Bear Lost, 1989; Jolly Tall, 1990; Jolly Snow, 1991; Old Bear Tales, 1991; Little Bear's Day, Little Bear's Bedtime, 1992; Ruff, 1994. Honours: BAFTA, 1993. Address: c/o Hutchinson Childrens Books, Random House, 20 Vauxhall Bridge Road, London SW1V 2SA, England.

HJORTSBERG William Reinhold, b. 23 Feb 1941, New York, New York, USA. Author. Education: BA, Dartmouth College, 1962; Postgraduate Studies, Yale Drama School, 1962-63; Stanford University, 1967-68. Publications: Alp, 1969; Gray Matters, 1971; Symbiography, 1973; Torol Torol Torol, 1974; Falling Angel, 1978; Tales and Fables, 1985; Nevermore, 1994. Films: Thunder and Lightning, 1977; Georgia Peaches (co-author), 1980; Legend, 1986. Contributions to: various journals, magazines and newspapers. Address: Main Boulder Route, McLeod, MT 59052, USA.

HOAGLAND Edward, b. 21 Dec 1932, New York, New York, USA. Author; Teacher. m. (1) Amy J Ferrara, 1960l, div 1964, (2) Marion Magid, 28 Mar 1968, 1 daughter. Education: AB, Harvard University, 1954. Appointments: Faculty, New School for Social Research, New York City, 1963-64, Rutgers University, 1966, Sarah Lawrence College, 1967, 1971, City University of New York, 1967, 1968, University of Iowa, 1978, 1982, Columbia University, 1980, 1981,

Bennington College, 1987-97, Brown University, 1988, University of California at Davis, 1990, 1992. Publications: Cat Man, 1956; The Circle Home, 1960; The Peacock's Tail, 1965; Notes from the Century Before: A Journal from British Columbia, 1969; The Courage of Turtles, 1971; Walking the Dead Diamond River, 1973; The Moose on the Wall: Field Notes from the Vermont Wilderness, 1974; Red Wolves and Black Bears, 1976; African Calliope: A Journey to the Sudan, 1979; The Edward Hoagland Reader, 1979; The Tugman's Passage, 1982; City Tales, 1986; Seven Rivers West, 1986; Heart's Desire, 1988; The Final Fate of the Alligators, 1992; Balancing Acts, 1992. Contributions to: Periodicals. Honours: Houghton Mifflin Literary Fellowship, 1954; Longview Foundation Award, 1961; Prix de Rome, 1964; Guggenheim Fellowships, 1964, 1975; O Henry Award, 1971; New York State Council on the Arts Award, 1972; National Book Critics Circle Award, 1980; Harold D Vursell Award, 1981; National Endowment for the Arts Award, 1982; Literary Lion Award, New York Public Library, 1988; National Magazine Award, 1989; Lannon Foundation Literary Award, 1993; Literary Lights Award, Boston Public Library, 1995. Address: c/o Simon and Schuster, 1230 Avenue of the Americas, New York, NY 10020, USA.

HOBAN Russell (Conwell), b. 4 Feb 1925, Lansdale, Pennsylvania, USA. Writer. m. (1) Lillian Aberman, 31 Jan 1944, div, 1 son, 3 daughters, (2) Gundula Ahl, 14 Aug 1975, 3 sons. Education: High School, Philadelphia. Appointments: General Illustrator, Wexton Company, New York City, 1950-52; Television Art Director, Batten, Barton, Durstine & Osborne, New York City, 1952-57; Copywriter, Doyle Dane Bernbach, New York City, 1965-67. Publications: The Lion of Boaz-Jachin and Jachin-Boaz, 1973; Kleinzeit, 1974; Turtle Diary, 1975; Riddley Walker, 1980, 2nd edition, 1986; Pilgermann, 1983; The Medusa Frequency, 1987; The Moment Under the Moment, 1992; The Court of the Winged Serpent, 1994. Libretto: The Second Mrs Kong (for Harrison Birtwistle's Opera), 1994. Children's Books: Over 55 books, 1959-94. Honours: Whitbread Children's Book Award, 1974; John W Campbell Memorial Award for Best Science Fiction Novel, 1981; Science Fiction Achievement Award, 1981. Memberships: PEN; Royal Society of Literature, Fellow; Society of Authors. Address: c/o David Higham Associates Ltd, Golden Square, 5-8 Lower John Street, London W1R 4HA, England.

HOBFALL Stevan E(arl), b. 25 Sept 1951, Chicago, Illinois, USA. Psychologist; Writer; Editor. m. Ivonne Heras, 18 May 1977, 2 sons, 1 daughter. Education: King's College, London, 1971-72; BS, Psychology, University of Illinois, 1973; MA, 1975, PhD, 1977, Psychology, University of South Florida. Appointments: Senior Lecturer, Ben Gurion University, Beersheba, Israel, 1980-83; Fellow Professor in Psychology, Tel Aviv University, 1983-87; Director, Applied Psychology Center, Kent State University, Ohio, 1987-; Editor, Anxiety, Stress and Coping: An International Journal, 1992-. Publications: Stress, Social Support, and Women, 1986; The Ecology of Stress, 1988; Conservation of Resources, 1989; War-Related Stress, 1991; Work Won't Love You Back: The Dual Career Couple's Survival Guide (with Ivonne Hobfall), 1994. Contributions to: Many books and journals. Honour: Peer recognition award for work in the HIV/AIDS Ohio racial and ethnic communities, 1990. Memberships: American Psychological Association, Fellow; International Society for the Study of Personal Relationships; Stress and Test Anxiety Research Society. Address: c/o Applied Psychology Centre, 106 Kent Hall, Kent State University, Kent, OH 44242, USA.

HOBHOUSE (Mary) Hermione, b. 1934, Somerset, England. Conservationist; Writer. m. Henry Trevenen Davidson Graham, 1958, div 1988, 1 son, 1 daughter. Education: Ladies' College, Cheltenham; Hons Modern History, Lady Margaret Hall, Oxford. Appointments: Researcher/Writer, Associated-Rediffusion Television, 1956-58; Granada Television, 1958-63; General Editor, Survey of London RCHME, 1983-94. Publications: The Ward of Cheap in the City of London, 1963; Thomas Cubitt: Master Builder, 1971, 2nd edition, 1995; Lost London, 1971; History of Regent Street, 1975; Oxford and Cambridge, 1980; Prince Albert: His Life and Work, 1983; County Hall, 1991; Poplar, Blackwall and the Isle of Dogs, 1994; London Survey'd: The Work of the Survey of London 1894-1994, 1994. Contributions to: Journals. Honours: Hitchcock Medallion, 1972; Member of the Order of the British Empire, 1981. Memberships: National Trust, Council, 1983-; Society of Antiquaries, Council, 1984-87. Address: 61 St Dunstan's Road, London W6 8RE, England.

HOBHOUSE Penelope. See: **MALINS Penelope.**

HOBSBAUM Philip Dennis, b. 29 June 1932, London, England. Writer. University Professor. m. Rosemary Phillips, 20 July 1976. Education: BA, 1955, MA, 1961, Downing College, Cambridge; LRAM, Royal Academy of Music, 1956; PhD, University of Sheffield, 1968. Appointments: Lecturer in English, Queen's University, Belfast, Northern Ireland, 1962-66; Lecturer in English Literature, 1966-72, Senior Lecturer, 1972-79, Reader, 1979-85, Titular Professor, 1985-, Glasgow University, Scotland. Publications: The Place's Fault and Other Poems, 1964; In Retreat and Other Poems, 1966; Coming Out Fighting: Poems, 1969; A Theory of Communication, 1970; Women and Animals: Poems, 1972; A Reader's Guide to Charles Dickens, 1972, 1982; Tradition and Experiment in English Poetry, 1979; A Reader's Guide to D H Lawrence, 1981; Essentials of Literary Criticism, 1982. Contributions to: Times Literary Supplement; Spectator; Listener; Poetry Review; Outposts; Hudson Review; Encounter; Modern Language Review. Memberships: Chairman, Sheffield University Arts Society, 1960-61; Scottish Association for Literary Studies; BBC Club; Association of University Teachers. Address: c/o Department of English Literature, University of Glasgow, Glasgow G20 6BS, Scotland.

HOBSBAWN Eric, b. 9 June 1917. Professor (retired). m. Marlene Schwarz, 1962, 1 son, 1 daughter. Education: BA, PhD, University of Cambridge. Appointments: Fellow, King's College, Cambridge, 1949-55; Professor of Economics and Social History, University of London, 1970-82. Publications: Labour's Turning Point, 1948; Primitive Rebels, 1959; The Jazz Scene, 1959; The Age of Revolution, 1962; Labouring Man, 1964; Karl Marx, Precapitalist Formations (editor), 1964; Industry and Empire, 1968; Bandits, 1969; Revolutionaries, 1973; The Age of Capital, 1975; The Invention of Tradition (co-author), 1983; Worlds of Labour, 1984; The Age of Empire, 1987; Politics for a Rational Left, 1989; Nations and Nationalism Since 1780, 1990; Echos of the Marseillaise, 1990; Age of Extremes: The Short Twentieth Century, 1994. Honour: Fellow, British Academy, 1976. Address: c/o Birbeck College, University of London, Malet Street, London WC1, England.

HOBSON Fred Colby Jr, b. 23 Apr 1943, Winston-Salem, North Carolina, USA. Professor of Literature; Writer. m. 17 June 1967, div, 1 daughter. Education: AB, English, University of North Carolina, 1965; MA, History, Duke University, 1967; PhD, English, University of North Carolina, 1972. Appointments: Professor of English, University of Alabama, 1972-86; Professor of English and Co-Editor, Southern Review, Louisiana State University, 1986-89; Professor of English and Co-Editor, Southern Literary Journal, University of North Carolina, 1989-. Publications: Serpent in Eden: H L Mencken and the South, 1974; Literature at the Barricades: The American Writer in the 1930's (co-editor), 1983; Tell About the South: The Southern Rage to Explain, 1984; South-Watching: Selected Essays of Gerald W Johnson (editor), 1984; The Southern Writer in the Post-Modern World, 1990; Mencken: A Life, 1994; Thirty-Five Years of Newspaper Work by H L Mencken (co-editor), 1994. Contributions to: Virginia Quarterly Review; Sewanee Review; Kenyon Review; New York Times Book Review; American Literature; Times Literary Supplement. Address: Department of English, University of North Carolina, Chapel Hill, NC 27514, USA.

HOBSON Polly. See: **EVANS Julia.**

HOCH Edward D(entinger), b. 22 Feb 1930, Rochester, New York, USA. Writer. m. Patricia A McMahon, 5 June 1957. Education: University of Rochester, 1947-49. Publications: The Shattered Raven, 1969; The Spy and the Thief, 1971; The Transvection Machine, 1971; The Thefts of Nick Velvet, 1978; The Quests of Simon Ark, 1984; Leopold's Way, 1985; The Night My Friend, 1991; Diagnosis: Impossible, 1996. Editor: Best Detective Stories of the Year, 6 volumes, 1976-81; All But Impossible, 1981; Year's Best Mystery and Suspense Stories, 14 volumes, 1982-95. Contributions to: Numerous anthologies and magazines. Memberships: Author's Guild; Crime Writers Association, England; Mustery Writers of America, President, 1982-83; Science Fiction Writers of America. Address: 2941 Lake Avenue, Rochester, NY 14612, USA.

HOCHHUTH Rolf, b. 1 Apr 1931, Eschwege, Germany. Dramatist; Author. m. Marianne Heinneman, 29 June 1957, div 1972, 2 sons. Education: University of Marburg; University of Munich; University of Heidelberg. Publications: Plays: Der Stellvertreter, 1963, English translation as The Deputy, 1964; Soldaten: Nekrolog auf Genf, 1967, English translation as Soldiers: An Obituary for Geneva, 1968; Guerillas, 1970; Die Hebamme, 1971; Lysistrate und die NATO, 1973;

Tod eines Jaegers, 1976; Juristen, 1979; Judith, 1984; The Immaculate Conception, 1989. Fiction: Die Berliner Antigone, 1975; Eine Liebe in Deutschland, 1978; A German Love Story, 1980. Non-Fiction: Krieg und Klassenkrieg (essays), 1971. Honours: Gerhart Hauptmann Prize, 1964; Kunstpreis, Berlin, 1964; Basel Art Prize, 1976. Membership: PEN. Address: PO Box 661, 4002 Basel, Switzerland.

HOCHSCHILD Adam, b. 5 Oct 1942, New York, New York, USA. Writer. m. Arlie Russell, 26 June 1965, 2 sons. Education: AB cum laude, Harvard University, 1963. Appointments: Reporter, San Francisco Chronicle, 1965-66; Editor and Writer, Ramparts Magazine, 1966-68, 1973-74; Commentator, National Public Radio, 1982-83;Co-Founder, Editor, Writer, Mother Jones Magazine, 1974-81, 1986-87; Public Interest Radio, 1987-88; Regents Lecturer, University of California at Santa Cruz, 1987; Lecturer, Graduate School of Journalism, University of California at Berkeley, 1992, 1995, 1997. Publications: Half the Way Home: A Memoir of Father and Son, 1986; The Mirror at Midnight: A South African Journey, 1990; The Unquiet Ghost: Russians Remember Stalin, 1994; Finding the Trapdoor: Essays, Portraits, Travels, 1997. Contributions to: New Yorker; Harper's; New York Times; Los Angeles Times; Washington Post; Progressive; Village Voice; New York Review of Books; Mother Jones. Honours: Thomas Storke Award, World Affairs Council, 1987; Madeleine Dane Ross Award, Overseas Press Club of America, 1995; Lowell Thomas Award, Society of American Travel Writers, 1995. Memberships: PEN; National Writers Union; National Book Critics Circle. Literary Agent: Georges Borchardt Inc, NYC. Address: 84 Seward St, San Francisco, CA 94114, USA.

HOCKING Mary (Eunice), b. 8 Apr 1921, Acton, London, England. Writer. Appointment: Local government officer, 1946-70. Publications: The Winter City, 1961; Visitors to the Crescent, 1962; The Sparrow, 1964; The Young Spaniard, 1965; Ask No Question, 1967; A Time of War, 1968; Checkmate, 1969; The Hopeful Traveller, 1970; The Climbing Frame, 1971; Family Circle, 1972; Daniel Come to Judgement, 1974; The Bright Day, 1975; The Mind Has Mountains, 1976; Look, Stranger!, 1978; He Who Plays the King, 1980; March House, 1981; Trilogy: Good Daughters, 1984; Indifferent Heroes, 1985; Welcome Strangers, 1986; An Irrelevant Woman, 1987; A Particular Place, 1989; Letters from Constance, 1991; The Very Dead of Winter, 1993; The Meeting Place, 1996. Memberships: Royal Society of Literature, fellow; Society of Authors. Address: 3 Church Row, Lewes, Sussex, England.

HODGE Jane Aiken, b. 4 Dec 1917, Watertown, Massachusetts, USA. Author. m. Alan Hodge, 3 Jan 1948, dec 1979, 2 daughters. Education: BA, Somerville College, Oxford, 1938; AM, Radcliffe College, 1939. Publications: Fiction: Maulever Hall, 1964; The Adventurers, 1965; Watch the Wall, My Darling, 1966; Here Comes a Candle, 1967; The Winding Stair, 1968; Marry in Haste, 1970; Greek Wedding, 1970; Savannah Purchase, 1971; Strangers in Company, 1973; Shadow of a Lady, 1974; One Way to Venice, 1975; Rebel Heiress, 1975; Runaway Bridge, 1976; Judas Flowering, 1976; Red Sky at Night: Lover's Delight?, 1978; Last Act, 1979; Wide is the Water, 1981; The Lost Garden, 1981; Secret Island, 1985; Polonaise, 1987; First Night, 1989; Leading Lady, 1990; Windover, 1992; Escapade, 1993; Whispering, 1995. Non-Fiction: The Double Life of Jane Austen, 1972; The Private World of Georgette Heyer, 1984; Passion and Principle: The Loves and Lives of Regency Women, 1996. Contributions to: Newspapers and journals. Membership: Society of Authors. Address: 23 Eastport Lane, Lewes, East Sussex BN7 1TL, England.

HODGE Paul William, b. 8 Nov 1934, Seattle, Washington, USA. Professor of Astronomy; Writer. m. Ann Uran, 14 June 1962, 2 sons, 1 daughter. Education: BS, Yale University, 1956; PhD, Harvard University, 1960. Appointments: Physicist, Smithsonian Astrophysical Observatory, Cambridge, Massachusetts, 1956-74; Lecturer, Harvard University, 1960-61; Fellow, Mount Wilson Palomar Observatory, California Institute of Technology, Pasadena, 1960-61; Assistant Professor of Astronomy, University of California at Berkeley, 1961-65; Associate Professor, 1965-69, Professor of Astronomy, 1969-, Chairman, Department of Astronomy, 1987-91, University of Washington; Editor, The Astronomical Journal, 1984-. Publications: Solar System Astrophysics, 1964; Galaxies and Cosmology, 1966; The Large Magellanic Cloud, 1967; Concepts of the Universe, 1969; Revolution in Astronomy, 1970; Galaxies, 1972; Concepts of Contemporary Astronomy, 1974; The Small Magellanic Cloud, 1977;

An Atlas of the Andromeda Galaxy, 1981; Interplanetary Dust, 1982; The Universe of Galaxies, 1985; Galaxies, 1986; The Andromeda Galaxy, 1992; Meteorite Craters and Impact Structures of the World, 1994. Contributions to: Astronomical journals. Honours: Beckwith Prize in Astronomy, 1956; Bart Bok Prize in Astronomy, 1962; Best Physical Science Book Award, 1986. Memberships: American Astronomical Society, Vice President, 1990-93; Astronomical Society of the Pacific, Vice-President, 1974-75; International Astronomical Union. Address: c/o Department of Astronomy, Box 351580, University of Washington, Seattle, WA 98195, USA.

HODGINS Jack Stanley, b. 3 Oct 1938, Vancouver Island, British Columbia, Canada. Novelist; Teacher. m. Dianne Child, 17 Dec 1960, 2 sons, 1 daughter. Education: BEd, University of British Columbia. Publications: Spit Delaney's Island, 1976; The Invention of the World, 1977; The Resurrection of Joseph Bourne, 1979; The Honorary Patron, 1987; Innocent Cities, 1990; Over Forty in Broken Hill, 1992; A Passion for Narrative, 1993; The Macken Charm, 1995. Honours: Gibson First Novel Award, 1978; Governor General's Award for Fiction, 1980; Canada-Australia Literature Prize, 1986; Commonwealth Literature Prize, 1988; DLitt, University of British Columbia, 1995. Memberships: PEN; Writers Union of Canada. Address: Department of Writing, University of Victoria, PO Box 1700, Victoria, British Columbia V8W 2Y2, Canada.

HOEFSMIT Henri Diederick. See: DE LINT Charles.

HOEG Peter, b. 1957, Denmark. Writer. 2 daughters. Appointments: Former Drama Teacher and Sailor; Writer. Publications: Forestilling om det tyvende arhundrede (novel), 1988, English translation as The History of Danish Dreams, 1995; Fortaellinger om natten, 1990, English translation as Borderliners by Barbara Haveland, 1994; De Maske Egnede, 1993; Frøken Smillas fornemmelse for sne (novel), 1992, English translation as Smilla's Sense of Snow by Tiina Nunnally, 1993; Kvinden og Aben, 1996, English translation as The Woman and The Ape by Barbara Haveland, 1996. Address: c/o Merete Ries, Munksgaard Rosinante, Norre Sogad 35, DK-1016 Copenhagen K, Denmark.

HOERR John Peter III, b . 12 Dec 1930, McKeesport, Pennsylvania, USA. Writer. m. Joanne Lillig, 24 Nov 1960, 2 sons. Education: AB, Penn State University, 1953. Appointments: Reporter, United Press International, 1956-57, 1958-60; The Daily Tribune, Royal Oak, Mich, 1957-58, Business Week, 1960-63, 1964-69; Reporter and Commentator, WQED-TV, Pittsburgh, 1969-74; Labour Editor, Senior Writer, Business Week, 1975-91. Publications: The Reindustrialization of America (co-author), 1981; And The Wolf Finally Came: The Decline of the American Steel Industry, 1988. Contributions to: Atlantic; American Prospect; Pittsburgh Magazine; Harvard Business Review. Honours: Page One Awards, New York Newspaper Guild, 1985, 1988; Richard A Lester Award, Princeton University, 1988. Memberships: National Writers Union; Industrial Relations Research Association. Address: 12 Parker Lane, Teaneck, NJ 07666, USA.

HOFF Harry Summerfield, (Willim Cooper), b. 4 Aug 1910, Crewe, England. Novelist. m. Joyce Barbara Harris, 1951, 2 daughters. Education: MA, Christ's College, Cambridge, 1933. Appointments: Assistant Commissioner, Civil Service Commission, 1945-56; Personnel Consultant to UKAEA, 1958-72; CEGB, 1958-72; Commission of European Communities, 1972-73; Assistant Director, Civil Service Selection Board, 1973-76; Member, Board of Crown Agents, 1975-77; Personnel Advisor, Millbank Technical Services, 1975-77; Adjunct Professor, Syracuse University, 1977-90. Publications: Rhea, 1935; Three Marriages, 1946; Scenes from Provincial Life, 1950; The Struggles of Albert Woods, 1952; Young People, 1958; Scenes from Married Life, 1961; Memoirs of a New Man, 1966; Shall We Ever Know?, 1971; Love on the Coast, 1973; Scences From Metropolitan Life, 1982; Scences From Later Life, 1983; From Early Life, 1990; Immortality At Any Price, 1991. Memberships: Royal Society of Literature; International PEN. Address: 22 Kenilworth Court, Lower Richmond Road, London SW15 1EW, England.

HOFFMAN Alice, b . 16 Mar 1952, New York, USA. Freelance Writer. m. Tom Martin, 2 sons. Education: BA, Adelphi University, 1973; MA, Stanford University, 1975. Publications: Property Of, 1977; The Drowning Season, 1979; Angel Landing, 1980; White Horses, 1982; Fortune's Daughter, 1985; Illumination Night, 1987; At Risk, 1988; Seventh Heaven, 1990; Second Nature, 1993; Also various screenplays. Contributions to: Redbook; American Review; Playgirl.

Address: c/o Putnam, 200 Madison Avenue, New York, NY 10016, USA.

HOFFMAN Daniel (Gerard), b. 3 Apr 1923, New York, New York, USA. Professor of English Emeritus; Poet; Writer. m. Elizabeth McFarland, 1948, 2 children. Education: AB, 1947, MA, 1949, PhD, 1956, Columbia University. Appointments: Instructor, Columbia University, 1952-56; Visiting Professor, University of Dijon, 1956-57; Assistant Professor, 1957-60, Associate Professor, 1960-65, Professor of English, 1965-66, Swarthmore College; Fellow, School of Letters, Indiana University, 1959; Elliston Lecturer, University of Cincinnati, 1964; Lecturer, International School of Yeats Studies, Sligo, Ireland, 1965; Professor of English, 1966-83, Poet-in-Residence, 1978-, Felix E Schelling Professor of English, 1983-93, Professor Emeritus, 1993-, University of Pennsylvania; Consultant in Poetry, 1973-74, Honorary Consultant in American Letters, 1974-77, Library of Congress, Washington, DC; Poet-in-Residence, Cathedral of St John the Divine, New York City, 1988-; Visiting Professor of English, King's College, London, 1991-92. Publications: Poetry: An Armada of Thirty Whales, 1954; A Little Geste and Other Poems, 1960; The City of Satisfactions, 1963; Striking the Stones, 1968; Broken Laws, 1970; Corgi Modern Poets in Focus 4 (with others), 1971; The Center of Attention, 1974; Able Was I Ere I Saw Elba: Selected Poems 1954-1974, 1977; Brotherly Love, 1981; Hang-Gliding from Helicon: New and Selected Poems 1948-1988, 1988; Middens of the Tribe, 1995. Other: Paul Bunyan: Last of the Frontier Demigods, 1952; The Poetry of Stephen Crane, 1957; Form and Fable in American Fiction, 1961; Barbarous Knowledge: Myth in the Poetry of Yeats, Graves and Muir, 1967; Poe Poe Poe Poe Poe Poe Poe, 1972; Faulkner's Country Matters: Folklore and Fable in Yoknapatawpha, 1989; Words to Create a World: Interviews, Essays and Reviews of Contemporary Poetry, 1993. Editor: American Poetry and Poetics: Poems and Critical Documents from the Puritans to Robert Frost, 1962; English Literary Criticism: Romantic and Victorian (with Samuel Hynes), 1966; Harvard Guide to Contemporary American Writing, 1979; Ezra Pound and William Carlos Williams: The University of Pennsylvania Conference Papers, 1983. Honours: Yale Series of Younger Poets Award, 1954; Ansley Prize, 1957; American Council of Learned Societies Fellowships, 1961-62, 1966-67; Columbia University Medal for Excellence, 1964; American Academy of Arts and Letters Grant, 1967; Ingram Merrill Foundation Grant, 1971; National Endowment for the Humanities Fellowship, 1975-76; Hungarian PEN Medal, 1980; Guggenheim Fellowship, 1983; Hazlett Memorial Award, 1984; Paterson Poetry Prize, 1989. Membership: Academy of American Poets. Address: c/o Department of English, University of Pennsylvania, Philadelphia, PA 19104, USA.

HOFFMAN Eva Alfreda, b. 1 July 1945, Cracow, Poland. Writer. Appointment: Editor, The New York Times Book Review, 1987-90. Publications: Lost in Translation: A Life in a New Language, 1989; Exit Into History: A Journey Through the New Eastern Europe, 1993. Contributions to: Newspapers and periodicals. Honours: American Academy of Arts and Letters Award, 1990; Whiting Award, 1992; Guggenheim Fellowship, 1993. Memberships: PEN; New York University Institute for the Humanities. Address: c/o Georges Barchardt, 136 East 57th Str, New York, NY 10022, USA.

HOFFMAN Mary Margaret Lassiter, b. 20 Apr 1945, Eastleigh, Hants, Englnd. Writer; Journalist. m. Stephen James Barber, 22 Dec 1972, 3 daughters. Education: BA, 1967, MA, 1973, Newnham College, Cambridge; University College, London, 1970. Publications: 60 Children's Books including, My Grandma Has Black Hair, 1989; Amazing Grace, 1991; Henry's Baby, 1993; Grace and Family, 1995; Song of the Earth, 1995. Contributions to: Daily Telegraph; Guardian; Independent; Sunday Times; Specialist Children's Book Press. Honours: Waldenbooks Best Children's Book Honor Award, 1991. Memberships: Society of Authors; CENTRAL; IBBY. Address: c/o Rogers, Coleridge & White, 20 Powis Mews, London W11 1JN, England.

HOFFMAN William, b. 12 Apr 1939, New York, New York, USA. Writer. Education: BA, City College of the City University of New York. Publications: As Is, 1985; The Ghosts of Versailles (libretto for opera by John Corigliano), 1991. Editor: New American Plays 2, 3, 4, 1968, 1970, 1971; Gay Plays, 1977. Contributions to: Journals and magazines. Honours: Drama Desk Award, 1985; Obie, 1985; International Classical Music Award, 1991; Emmy, 1992; WGA Award, 1992; Erwin Piscator, 1994. Memberships: American Society of Composers, Authors, and Publishers; Dramatists Guild; PEN; Writers

Guild of America. Address: c/o Mitch Douglas, ICM, 40 West 57th Street, New York, NY 10019, USA.

HOFFMANN Ann Marie, b. 6 May 1930, Abingdon, Berks, England. Author; Researcher. Education: Tunbridge Wells County Grammar School, 1940-46; St Godrics College, London, 1947-48. Appointments: Various, Publishing, International Conference Organising, London, 1948-51, 1962-66; United Nations, Geneva, Paris, The Hague, 1952-58; Personal Assistant to Author, Robert Henriques, 1959-61; Principal, Author's Research Services, 1966-87. Publications: Research for Writers, 1975, 4th edition, 1992; Majorca, 1978; Lives of the Tudors, 1977; Bocking Deanery, 1976; The Dutch: How They Live and Work, 1971, 1973. Memberships: Society of Authors; PEN; Society of Women Writers and Journalists; Society of Sussex Authors.

HOFFMANN Donald, b. 24 June 1933, Illinois, USA. Architectural Critic; Historian. m. Theresa McGrath, 12 Apr 1958, 4 sons, 1 daughter. Education: University of Chicago, University of Kansas City. Appointments: General Assignment Reporter, 1956-65, Art Critic, 1965-90, Kansas City Star; Assistant Editor, Journal of the Society of Architectural Historians, 1970-72. Publications: The Meanings of Architecture: Buildings and Writings by John Wellborn Root (editor), 1967; The Architecture of John Wellborn Root, 1973; Frank Lloyd Wright's Fallingwater, 1978, 2nd edition, 1993; Frank Lloyd Wright's Robie House, 1984; Frank Lloyd Wright's Hollyhock House, 1992. Honours: Fellow, National Endowment for the Humanities, 1970-71; Fellow, National Endowment for the Arts, 1974; Graham Foundation Grant, 1981. Memberships: Life Member, The Art Institute of Chicago. Address: 6441 Holmes Street, Kansas City, MO 64131-1110, USA.

HOFFMANN Margaret May Jones, (Peggy Hoffmann), b. 25 Aug 1910, Delaware, Ohio, USA. Writer; Church organist; Teacher. m. Arnold E Hoffmann, 23 June 1935, 2 sons, 1 daughter. Education: BA, Miami University, Oxford, Ohio, 1934; Study at Chicago Theological Seminary, 1934-35; Intermittent study at other colleges. Appointments: Poetry in the Schools, North Carolina public schools; Teacher, Creatve Writing, Meredith College, Raleigh. Publications: Miss B's First Cookbook, 1950; Sew Easy!, 1954; Sew Far, Sew Good, 1958; The Wild Rocket, 1960; Shift to High, 1965; A Forest of Feathers, 1966; The Money Hat, 1969; My Dear Cousin, 1970; The Sea Wedding; Been There and Back, 1976; Editor: 15 books of choral and organ music, 1954-80s, 2 books of organ music, 1963, 1991. Honours: National Award, Friends of American Writers, 1971; Raleigh Medal of the Arts, 1987. Memberships: North Carolina Writers Conference, 1953-, chairman, 1971; Longview Writers, 1967, chairman, 1974-. Address: 501 East Whitaker Mill Road, Apt 203 C, Raleigh, NC 27608, USA.

HOFMAN David, b. 26 Sept 1908, Poona, India. Author; Editor; Publisher. 1 son, 1 daughter. Appointments: Editor, New World Order, 1937-39, The Baha'i World, 1963-88; Founder, George Ronald Publishers, 1984. Publications: The Renewal of Civilization, 1946; A Commentary on the Will and Testament of Abdul Baha, 1950; George Townshend, 1983; Baha u'i Ilah: The Prince of Peace, a Portrait, 1992. Membership: Publishers Association. Address: 28 Kirk Close, North Oxford OX2 8JN, England.

HOFMANN Michael, b. 25 Aug 1957, Freiburg, Germany. Poet. Education: BA, Magadalene College, Cambridge, 1979. Appointments: Teacher in Creative Writing, University of Florida, Gainesville, 1990-94; University of Michigan, Ann Arbor, 1994. Publications: Nights in the Iron Hotel, 1983; Acrimony, 1986; K S in Lakeland: New and Selected Poems, 1990; Corona, Corona, 1993; Plays: The Double Bass (adaptation of a play by Patrick Suskind), 1987; The Good Person of Sichuan (adaptation of a play by Brecht), 1989; Translations. Honours: Cholmondeley Award, 1984; Geoffrey Faber Memorial Rrize, 1988; Schlegel Tieck Prize, 1988. Address: c/o Faber and Faber, 3 Queen Square, London WC1N 3AU, England.

HOGAN Desmond, b. 10 Dec 1950, Ballinasloe, Ireland. Writer; Teacher. Education: BA, 1972, MA, 1973, University College, Dublin. Appointment: Strode Fellow, University of Alabama, 1989. Publications: The Ikon Maker, 1976; The Leaves on Grey, 1980; A Curious Street, 1984; A New Shirt, 1984; A Link with the River, 1989; The Edge of the City, 1993. Honours: John Llewellyn Memorial Prize, 1980; Irish Post Award, 1985; Deutscher Akademischer Austauschdienst Fellowship, Berlin, 1991. Address: Basement, 6 Stanstead Grove, London SE6 4UD, England.

HOGAN James P(atrick), b. 27 June 1941, London, England. Writer. m. (1) Iris Crossley, 1961, div 1977, 3 daughters, (3) Lynda Shirley Dockerty, div 1980, (3) Jackie Price, 1983, 3 sons. Education: Certificates, Royal Aircraft Establishment Technical College, 1963, Reading Technical College, 1965. Publications: Inherit the Stars, 1977; The Genesis Machine, 1978; The Gentle Giants of Ganymede, 1978; The Two Faces of Tomorrow, 1979; Thrice Upon a Time, 1980; Giants' Star, 1981; Voyage from Yesteryear, 1982; Code of the Lifemaker, 1983; The Proteus Operation, 1985; Minds, Machines and Evolution (short stories), 1986; Entoverse, 1992; Realtime Interrupt, 1995. Contributions to: Anthologies and magazines. Address: c/o Eleanor Wood, Spectrum Literary Agency, 111 Eighth Avenue, Suite 1501, New York, NY 10016, USA.

HOGAN Kathleen Margaret, (Kay Hogan), b. 13 Feb 1935, Bronx, New York, USA. Writer; Lab Technician; Housewife. m. James P Hogan, 4 sons, 1 daughter. Education: High School Graduate, 1952. Publications: The El Train, 1882; The Silent Men, 1984; Widow Women, 1985; Little Green Girl, 1986; Of Saints and Other Things, 1992; The Women Wore Black, 1993. Contributions to: Descant; Long Pond Review; Journal of Irish Literature; North Country Anthology; Catholic Girls Anthologoy; Glens Falls Review. Address: 154 East Avenue, Saratoga Springs, NY 12866, USA.

HOGAN Robert (Goode), b . 29 May 1930, Boonville, Missouri, USA. Professor of English; Writer. m. (1) Betty Mathews, 1 Dec 1950, div 1978, 2 sons, 3 daughters, (2) Mary Rose Callaghan, 21 Dec 1979. Education: BA, 1953, MA, 1954, PhD, 1956, University of Missouri. Appointments: Publisher, Proscenium Press, 1964-; Professor of English, University of Delaware, 1970-; Editor, Journal of Irish Literature, 1972-, George Spelvin's Theatre Book, 1978-85. Publications: Experiments of Sean O'Casey, 1960; Feathers from the Green Crow, 1962; Drama: The Major Genres (editor with S Molin), 1962; Arthur Miller, 1964; Independence of Elmer Rice, 1965; Joseph Holloway's Abbey Theatre (editor with M J O'Neill), 1967; The Plain Style (with H Bogart), 1967; After the Irish Renaissance, 1967; Seven Irish Plays (editor), 1967; Joseph Holloway's Irish Theatre (editor with M J O'Neill), 3 volumes, 1968-70; Dion Boucicault, 1969; The Fan Club, 1969; Betty and the Beast, 1969; Lost Plays of the Irish Renaissance (with J Kilroy), 1970; Crows of Mephistopheles (editor), 1970; Towards a National Theatre (editor), 1970; Eimar O'Duffy, 1972; Mervyn Wall, 1972; Conor Cruise O'Brien (with E Young-Bruehl), 1974; A History of the Modern Irish Drama, Vol 1, The Irish Literary Theatre (with J Kilroy), 1975, Vol II, Laying the Foundation (with J Kilroy), 1976, Vol III, The Abbey Theatre 1905-09 (with J Kilroy), 1978, Vol IV, The Rise of the Realists, 1910-1915 (with R Burnham and D P Poteet), 1979, Vol V, The Art of the Amateur 1916-1920 (with R Burnham), 1984, Vol V1, The Years of O'Casey (with R Burnham), 1992; The Dictionary of Irish Literature (editor), 1979; Since O'Casey, 1983; The Plays of Frances Sheridan (edited with J C Beasley), 1984; Guarini's The Faithful Shepherd, translated by Thomas Sheridan (edited and completed with E Nickerson), 1990; Murder at the Abbey (with J Douglas), 1993. Address: PO Box 361, Newark, DE 19711, USA.

HOGGART Richard, b. 24 Sept 1918, England. Writer. m. Mary Holt France, 1942, 2 sons, 1 daughter. Education: MA Litt, Leeds University, 1978. Appointments: Senior Lecturer, University of Leicester, 1959-62; Professor of English, Birmingham University, 1962-73; Director, Centre for Contemporary Cultural Studies, 1964-73; Assistant Director General, UNESCO, 1970-75; Warden, Goldsmiths' College, London, 1976-84; Chairman, National Advisory Council for Adult and Continuing Education; Chairman, Book Trust, 1995-. Publications: Auden, 1951; The Uses of Literacy, 1957; W H Auden, 1957; Teaching Literature, 1963; Speaking to Each Other, 2 volumes, 1970; Only Connect (Reith Lectures), 1972; An Idea and Its Servants, 1978; An English Temper, 1982; An Idea of Europe (co-author), 1987; Autobiography, 3 Volumes: A Local Habitation, 1988, A Sort of Clowning, 1990, An Imagined Life, 1992; Townscape with Figures, 1994; The Way We Live Now, 1995. Honours: Honorary Doctorates from Universities in France, Canada and England. Address: Mortonsfield, Beavers Hill, Farnham, Surrey, GU9 7DF, England.

HOGGART Simon (David), b. 26 May 1946, England. Journalist. m. Alyson Clare Corner, 1983, 1 son, 1 daughter. Education: MA, King's College, Cambridge. Appointments: Reporter, 1968-71; Northern Ireland Correspondent, 1971-73, Political Correspondent, 1973-81, The Guardian; Political Columnist, Punch, 1979-85; Feature Writer, 1981-85, US Correspondent, 1985-89, Political Editor, 1992-93, The Observer; Parliamentary sketch-writer, The Guardian, 1993-.

Publications: The Pact (with Alistair Michie), 1978; Michael Foot: A Portrait (with David Leigh), 1981; On the House, 1981; Back on the House, 1982; House of Ill Fame, 1985; America: A Users Guide, 1990; House of Correction, 1994; Bizarre Beliefs (with Michael Hutchinson), 1995; Live Briefs (with Steve Bell), 1996. Contributions to: Spectator; Times Literary Supplement; New Statesman; Literary Review; Presenter, News Quiz. Honour: David Holden Award for Resident Foreign Correspondent, British Press Awards, 1987. Address: c/o The Guardian, 119 Farringdon Road, London EC1R 3ER, England.

HOGNAS Kurt Carl Alexander, b. 2 Feb 1931, Jakobstad, Finland. Writer. m. Siv Gunnel, 30 Dec 1956, 4 sons. Education: BA, 1955, MA, 1960, Helsinki University, 1960. Publications: Glashus, 1972; Överskridningar, 1978; Italiensk Svit (prose poems), 1979; En handfull Ljus, 1981; Nattens lökar, 1985; Tunnelbana, 1987; Monvass, 1992; Röster fran en gräns, 1995.Contributions to: Vasabladet; Hufvudstadsbladet; Horisont; Café Existens. Honours: Prizes from Svenska Litteratursällskapet, 1983, 1995; Svenska Akademin, 1988. Membership: Finland's Svenska Författarförening. Literary Agent: Söderströms Förlag, Helsinki, Finland. Address: Sibeliusgatan 3, 67100 Kristinestad, Finland.

HOGWOOD Christopher (Jarvis Haley), b. 10 Sept 1941, Nottingham, England. Harpischordist; Conductor; Musicologist; Writer; Editor; Broadcaster. Education: BA, Pembroke College, Cambridge, 1964; Charles University, Prague; Academy of Music, Prague. Appointments: Founder-Member, Early Music Consort of London, 1967-76; Founder-Director, Academy of Ancient Music, 1973-; Faculty, Cambridge University, 1975-; Artistic Director, Handel and Haydn Society, Boston, 1986-; Honorary Professor of Music, University of Keele, 1986-89; Music Director, 1988-92, Principal Guest Conductor, 1992-, St Paul Chamber Orchestra, Minnesota; International Professor of Early Music Performance, Royal Academy of Music, London, 1992-; Visiting Professor, King's College, London, 1992-. Publications: Music at Court, 1977; The Trio Sonata, 1979; Haydn's Visits to England, 1980; Music in Eighteenth-Century England (editor), 1983; Handel, 1984; Holme's Life of Mozart (editor), 1991. Contributions to: The New Grove Dictionary of Music and Musicians, 1980. Honours: Walter Wilson Cobbett Medal, 1986; Commander of the Order of the British Empire, 1989; Honorary Fellow, Jesus College, Cambridge, 1989, Pembroke College, Cambridge, 1992; Freeman, Worshipful Company of Musicians, 1989. Membership: Royal Society of Authors, Fellow. Address: 10 Brookside, Cambridge CB2 1JE, England.

HOLBROOK David (Kenneth), b. 9 Jan 1923, Norwich, England. Author. m. 23 Apr 1949, 2 sons, 2 daughters. Education: MA, Downing College, Cambridge, 1945. Appointments: Fellow, Kings College, Cambridge, 1961-65; Senior Leverhulme Research Fellow, 1965, Leverhulme Emeritus Research Fellow, 1988-90; Writer-in-Residence, Dartington Hall, 1972-73; Fellow and Director of English Studies, 1981-88, Emeritus Fellow, 1988, Downing College; Publications: English for Maturity, 1961; Imaginings, 1961; Against the Cruel Frost, 1963; English for the Rejected, 1964; The Secret Places, 1964; Flesh Wounds, 1966; Children's Writing, 1967; The Exploring World, 1967; Object Relations, 1967; Old World New World, 1969; English in Australia Now, 1972; Chance of a Lifetime, 1978; A Play of Passion, 1978; English for Meaning, 1980; Nothing Larger than Life, 1987; The Novel and Authenticity, 1987; A Little Athens, 1990; Edith Wharton and the Unsatisfactory Man, 1991; Jennifer, 1991; The Gold in Father's Heart, 1992; Where D H Lawrence Was Wrong About Women, 1992; Creativity and Popular Culture, 1994; Even If They Fail, 1994; Tolstoy, Women and Death, 1996. Contributions to: Numerous professional journals. Honour: Festschrift, 1996 Membership: Society of Authors. Literary Agent: M C Martinez Literary Agency, 60 Oakwood Avenue, Southgate, London N14 6QL, England. Address: Denmore Lodge, Brunswick Gardens, Cambridge CB6 8DQ, England.

HOLDEN Anthony, b. 22 May 1947, England. Journalist; Author. m. (1) Amanda Warren, 1971, div 1988; (2) Cynthia Blake, 1990. Education: MA, Merton College, Oxford. Appointments: Correspondent, Sunday Times, 1973-77; Columnist (Atticus), 1977-79, Chief US Correspondent, The Observer, 1979-81; Features Editor and Assistant Editor, The Times, 1981-82; Freelance journalist and author; Broadcaster on Radio and TV. Publications: Agememnon of Aeschylus, 1969; The Greek Anthology, 1973; The St Albans Poisoner, 1974; Charles, Prince of Wales, 1979; Their Royal Highnesses, 1981; Of Presidents, Prime Ministers and Princes, 1984; The Queen Mother, 1985; Charles, 1988; Olivier, 1988; Big Deal, 1990; The Last Paragraph (editor), 1990; A Princely Marriage, 1991; The Oscars,

1993; The Tarnished Crown, 1993; Power and the Throne (contributor), 1994; Tchaikovsky, 1995. Honour: Columnist of the Year, British Press Awards, 1977. Address: c/o Rogers Coleridge White, 20 Powis Mews, London W11 1JN, England.

HOLDEN Joan, b. 18 Jan 1939, Berkeley, California, USA. Playwright. m. (1) Arthur Holden, 1958, div, (2) Daniel Chumley, 1968, 3 daughters. Education: BA, Reed College, Portland Oregon, 1960; MA, University of California, Berkeley, 1964; Appointments: Copywriter, Librairie Larousse, Paris, 1964-66; Research Aassistant, University of California, Berkeley, 1966-67; Playwright, 1967-; Editor, Pacific News Service, 1973-75; Instructor in Playwriting, University of California, Davis, 1975, 1977, 1979, 1983, 1985, 1987. Publications: Americans; or, Last Tango in Huahuatenango, with Daniel Chumley (produced Dayton, Ohio and London, 1981, New York, 1982); Factwino Meets the Moral Majority, with others (produced San Francisco, 1981, New York, 1982), Published in West Coast Plays 15-16, 1983; Factwino vs Armaggedonman (produced San Fransicso, 1982), Published in West Coast Plays 15-16, 1983; Steeltown, music by Bruce Barthol (produced San Francisco, 1984, New York, 1985), 1985 with others (produced San Francisco, 1985, Spain /36, music by Bruce Barthol, produced Los Angeles, 1986); The Mozamgola Caper, with others (produced San Fancicso, 1986); Seeing Double, 1989; Back to Normal, 1990; Offshore, 1993. Contributions to: Melodrama, 1990; Collaborating Offshore, 1994. Honours: Obie Award, 1973, 1990; Rockefeller Grant, 1985; Edward G Robbins Playwriting Award, 1992. Address: San Francisco Mime Troupe, 855 Treat Street, San Francisco, CA 94110, USA.

HOLDSTOCK Robert, b. 2 Aug 1948, Hythe, Kent. England. Writer. Education: BSc, University College of North Wales, 1970; MSc, London School of Hygiene and Tropical Medicine, 1971. Publications include: Eye Among the Blind, 1976; Earthwind, 1977; Octopus Encyclopaedia of Science Fiction, 1978; Stars of Albion, 1979; Alien Landscapes, 1979; Tour of the Universe, 1980; Where Time Winds Blow, 1981; Mythago Wood, Emerald Forest, 1985; The Labyrinth, 1987; Other Edens, 1987; Lavondyss, 1988; The Fetch, 1991; The Bone Forest, 1992; The Hollowing, 1993; Merlin's Wood, 1994. Honours: World Fantasy Awards, 1985, 1993. Address: 54 Raleigh Road, London N8, England.

HOLLAND Cecelia (Anastasia), b . 31 Dec 1943, Henderson, Nevada, USA. Author. Education: Pennsylvania State University; BA, Connecticut College, 1965. Publications: The Firedrake, 1966; Rakosy, 1967; Kings in Winter, 1968; Until the Sun Falls, 1969; Ghost on the Steppe, 1969; The King's Road, 1970; Cold Iron, 1970; Antichrist, 1970; Wonder of the World, 1970; The Earl, 1971; The Death of Attila, 1973; The Great Maria, 1975; Floating Worlds, 1976; Two Ravens, 1977; The Earl, 1979; Home Ground, 1981; The Sea Beggars, 1982; The Belt of Gold, 1984; Pillar of the Sky, 1985; The Bear Flag, 1992; Jerusalem, 1996. Honour: Guggenheim Fellowship, 1981-82. Address: c/o Alfred A Knopf, 201 East 50th Street, New York, NY 10022, USA.

HOLLAND Isabelle, b. 16 June 1920, Basel, Switzerland (US citizen). Writer. Education: University of Liverpool; BA, Tulane University, 1942. Appointments: Publicity Director, Crown Publishers, New York City, 1956-60, J B Lippincott Company, New York City, 1960-66, G P Putnam's Sons, New York City, 1968-69; Assistant to the Publisher, Harper's, New York City, 1967-68. Publications: Kilgaren, 1974; Trelawny, 1974; Moncrieff, 1975; Darcourt, 1976; Grenelle, 1976; The deMaury Papers, 1977; Tower Abbey, 1978; The Marchington Papers, 1980; Counterpoint, 1980; The Lost Madonna, 1981; A Death at St Anselm's, 1984; Flight of the Archangel, 1985; A Lover Scorned, 1986; Bump in the Night, 1988; A Fatal Advent, 1989; The Long Search, 1990; Love and Inheritance, 1991; Family Trust, 1994. Other: About 35 books for children and young adults, 1967-96. Honour: Ott Award, Church and Synagogue Library Association, 1983. Memberships: Authors Guild; Authors League of America; PEN. Address: 1199 Park Avenue, New York, NY 10028, USA.

HOLLAND Norman N(orwood), b. 29 Sept 1927, New York, New York, USA. Scholar; Writer. m. Jane Kelley, 17 Dec 1954, 1 son, 1 daughter. Education: BS, Massachusetts Institute of Technology, 1947; LLB, 1950, PhD, 1956, Harvard University. Appointments: Instructor to Associate Professor, Massachusetts Institute of Technlogy, 1955-66; McNulty Professor of English, State University of New York at Buffalo, 1966-83; Associate Professor, University of Paris, 1971-72, 1985; Marston-Milbauer Eminent Scholar, University of Florida at Gainesville, 1983-. Publications: The First Modern

Comedies, 1959, 2nd edition, 1967; The Shakespearean Imagination, 1964, 2nd edition, 1968; Psychoanalysis and Shakespeare, 1966, 2nd edition, 1975; The Dynamics of Literary Response, 1968, 2nd edition, 1989; Poems in Persons: An Introduction to Psychoanalysis of Literature, 1973; 5 Readers Reading, 1975; Laughing: A Psychology of Humor, 1982; The I, 1985; The Brain of Robert Frost: A Cognitive Approach to Literature, 1988; Holland's Guide to Psychoanalytic Psychology and Literature-and-Psychology, 1990; The Critical I, 1992; Death in a Delphi Seminar, 1995. Honours: American Council of Learned Societies Fellow, 1974-75; Guggenheim Fellowship, 1979-80. Memberships: American Academy of Psychoanalysis; Boston Psychoanalytic Society; Modern Language Association. Address: c/o Department of English, University of Florida at Gainesville, Gainseville, FL 32611, USA.

HOLLANDER John, b. 28 Oct 1929, New York, New York, USA. Professor of English; Poet; Critic; Editor. m. (1) Anne Loesser, 15 June 1953, div, 2 daughters, (2) Natalie Charkow, 17 Dec 1982. Education: AB, 1950, MA, 1952, Columbia University; PhD, Indiana University, 1959. Appointments: Junior Fellow, Society of Fellows, Harvard University, 1954-57; Lecturer, Connecticut College, 1957-59; Poetry Editor, Partisan Review, 1959-65; Instructor to Associate Professor, 1959-66, Professor of English, 1977-86, A Bartlett Giametti Professor of English, 1986-95, Sterling Professor of English, 1995-, Yale University; Christian Gauss Seminarian, Princeton University, 1962; Visiting Professor, 1964, Patten Lecturer, 1986, Fellow, Institute for Advanced Study, 1986, Indiana University; Faculty, Salzburg Seminar in American Studies, 1965; Professor of English, Hunter College and the Graduate Center of the City University of New York, 1966-77; Overseas Fellow, Churchill College, Cambridge, 1967-68; Elliston Professor of Poetry, University of Cincinnati, 1969; Resident Guest Writer, City of Jerusalem, 1980; Phi Beta Kappa Lecturer, 1981-82; Glasgow Lecturer, Washington and Lee University, 1984. Publications: Poetry: A Crackling of Thorns, 1958; Movie-Going and Other Poems, 1962; Visions from the Ramble, 1965; Types of Shape, 1968, expanded edition, 1991; The Night Mirror, 1971; Town and Country Matters, 1972; Selected Poems, 1972; Tales Told of the Fathers, 1975; Reflections on Espionage, 1976; Spectral Emanations: New and Selected Poems, 1978; Blue Wine, 1979; Flowers of Thirteen, 1983; In Time and Place, 1986; Harp Lake, 1988; Selected Poetry, 1993; Tesserae, 1993. Criticism: The Untuning of the Sky, 1960; Images of Voice, 1970; Vision and Resonance, 1975, 2nd edition, 1985; The Figure of Echo, 1981; Rhyme's Reason, 1981, 2nd edition, revised and expanded, 1989; Melodious Guile, 1988; William Bailey, 1990; The Gazer's Spirit, 1995; The Work of Poetry, 1997. Editor: The Wind and the Rain (with Harold Bloom), 1961; Jiggery-Pokery (with Anthony Hecht), 1966, 2nd edition, 1984; Poems of Our Moment, 1968; Modern Poetry: Essays in Criticism, 1968; American Short Stories Since 1945, 1968; The Oxford Anthology of English Literature (with Frank Kermode, Harold Bloom, J B Trapp, Martin Price and Lionel Trilling), 1973; I A Richards: Essays in His Honor (with R A Brower and Helen Vendler), 1973; Literature as Experience (with David Bromwich and Irving Howe), 1979; The Poetics of Influence (selected essays of Harold Bloom), 1988; The Essential Rossetti (selected poetry of Dante Gabriel Rossetti), 1990; Nineteenth-Century American Poetry, 2 volumes, 1993; Animal Poems, 1994; Garden Poems, 1996. Other: The Death of Moses (libretto for Alexander Goehr's opera), 1992. Honours: Poetry Chapbook Award, 1962, Melville Cane Award, 1990, Poetry Society of America; National Institute of Arts and Letters Award, 1963; National Endowment for the Humanities Senior Fellowship, 1973-74; Levinson Prize, 1974; Washington Monthly Prize, 1976; Guggenheim Fellowship, 1979-80; Mina P Shaughnessy Award, Modern Language Association, 1982; Bollingen Prize, 1983; Shenandoah Prize, 1985; John D and Catharine T MacArthur Foundation Fellowship 1990-95. Memberships: Academy of American Poets; American Academy of Arts and Letters; American Academy of Arts and Sciences, Fellow. Address: c/o Department of English, Yale University, PO Box 208302, New Haven, CT 06520, USA.

HOLLANDER Paul, b. 3 Oct 1932, Budapest, Hungary. Professor. m. Mina Harrison, 1976, 1 daughter. Education: BA LSE, 1959; MA, University of Illinois, 1960; MA, 1962, PhD, 1963, Princeton University, all in Sociology. Publications: Editor, American and Soviet Society, 1969; Soviet and American Society: A Comparison, 1973, 2nd edition, 1978; Many Faces of Socialism, 1984; Survivial of the Adversary Culture, 1988; Political Pilgrims, 1981, 3rd edition, 1990; Anti-Americanism, 1992, 2nd edition, 1995; Decline and Discontent, 1992. Contributions to: Commentary; Encounter; Partisan; Review; Policy Review; American Sociological Review; Problems of

Communism; Society; Wall Street Journal; New York Times; National Review; Academic Questions; Orbis. Honours: Ford Foundation Fellow, 1963; Guggenheim Fellowship, 1973-74; Visiting Scholar, Hoover Institution, 1985, 1986, 1993. Membership: National Association of Scholars, Advisory Panel. Address: University of Massachusetts, Amherst, MA 01003, USA.

HOLLANDS Roy Derrick, b. 20 July 1924, Canterbury, Kent, England. Author of Mathematics Books. m. Sarah Carroll, 14 Apr 1945, 1 daughter. Education: BSc, Southampton, 1951; Certificate in Education, 1952; Advanced Certificate in Education, 1969; MA, Exeter University, 1969; MSc, Newcastle University, 1980. Appointment: Adviser to Longman, Ginn, Blackwell, MacMillan and others, 1969-. Publications: SMP 7-13, 1973; Headway Maths, 1979; Ginn Mathematics, 1983; Let's Solve Problems, 1986; National Curriculum Ginn Mathematics, 1995; Author, Co-author, of over 200 books; Primary maths series for Nigeria, Egypt, Cameroon, Caribbean, UK, Lesotho, Uganda; Secondary maths series for UK, Egypt, Tanzania. Contributions to: Over 100 articles published in main mathematical journals; also numerous book reviews. Honours: Fellow, College of Preceptors, 1979; Mensa Chess Champion, 1992. Membership: Past Chairman, Society of Authors Educational Writer Group. Address: Flat 62, Berkeley Court, Wilmington Square, East Bourne, East Sussex BN21 4DX, England.

HOLLAR David Wason, b. 17 July 1960, Yadkinville, North Carolina, USA. Biologist; Educator. m. Virginia Paige Dean, 28 Nov 1992, 1 daughter. Education: BS, Biology, University of North Carolina, Chapel Hill, USA, 1982; MS Molecular Biology, Vanderbilt University, 1984; PhD Dissertation in Progress, University of North Carolina-Greensboro. Publication: The Origin and Evolution of Life on Earth, 1992. Address: 911 South Elm Street, Eden, NC 27288, USA.

HOLLES Robert Owen, b. 11 Oct 1926, London, England. Author; Playwright. m. Philippa Elmer, 12 July 1952, 2 sons, 1 daughter. Appointment: Artist-in-Residence, Central State University of Oklahoma, 1981-82. Publications: Now Thrive the Armourers, 1952; The Bribe Scorners, 1956; Captain Cat, 1960; The Siege of Battersea, 1962; Religion and Davey Peach, 1962; The Nature of the Beast, 1965; Spawn, 1978; I'll Walk Beside You, 1979; Sunblight, 1981; The Guide to Real Village Cricket, 1983; The Guide to Real Subversive Soldiering, 1985. Other: 30 Plays in Television Series. Contributions to: Magazines and journals. Honour: Best Novel of the Year Citation, Time magazine, 1960. Address: Crown Cottage, 14 Crown Street, Castle Hedingham, Essex, England.

HOLLEY Irving Brinton Jr, b. 8 Feb 1919, Hartford, Connecticut, USA. Historian. m. Janet Carlson, 9 Oct 1945, 3 daughters. Education: BA, Amherst College, 1940; MA, 1942, PhD, 1947, Yale University. Publications: Ideas & Weapons, 1953, 3rd edition, 1983; Buying Aircraft, 1964, 1989; General John M Palmer, Citizen Soldiers and the Army of a Democracy, 1982. Contributions to: Aerospace Historian; Military Review; Technology and Culture; Defense Analysis; Air Force Journal of Logistics. Honours: USAF DSM, Legion of Merit; Civilian Service Medal, US Army and USAF. Memberships: American Historical Society; Society for the History of Technology; Society for Military History. Address: 2701 Pickett Road, Apt 3028, Durham, NC 27705, USA.

HOLLINGDALE Reginald John, b. 20 Oct 1930, London, England. Writer. Appointment: Sub Editor, The Guardian Newspaper, 1968-91. Publications: Thus Spoke Zarathustra, 1961; One Summer on Majorca, 1961; The Voyage to Africa, 1964; Nietzsche, The Man and His Philosophy, 1965; Western Philosophy, An Introduction, 1966, 2nd edition, 1979; Essays and Aphorisms of Schopenhauer, 1970; Thomas Mann, 1971; A Nietzsche Reader, 1977; Aphorisms of Lichtenberg, 1990. Other: Editions of Nietzsche's Writings. Contributions to: Three Essays by Wolfgang Müller-Lauter, 1993; Nietzsche: A Critical Reader, 1995; The Cambridge Companion to Nietzsche, 1996. Honour: Visiting Fellow, Trinity College, Melbourne, 1991. Memberships: Honorary President, B Nietzsche Society; National Union of Journalists. Address: 32 Warrington Crescent, London W9 1EL, England.

HOLLINGHURST Alan, b. 26 May 1954, Stroud, Gloucestershire. Novelist. Education: BA, 1975, M.Litt, 1979, Magdalen College, Oxford. Appointments: Assistant Editor, 1982-84, Deputy Editor, 1985-90, Poetry Editor, 1991-, Times Literary Supplement, London. Publications: Novels, The Swimming-Pool

Library, 1988; The Folding Star, 1994. Verse: Confidential Chats with Boys, 1982; Translator: Bajazet, by Jean Racine, 1991. Address: c/o Times Literary Supplement, Admiral House, 66-68 East Smithfield, London E1 9XY, England.

HOLLINS Amy, b. Birkenhead, England. Poet; Novelist. m. Professor T H B Hollins, 2 sons, 2 daughters. Education: BA with Honours, Modern Languages, Diploma in Education, Liverpool University. Appointments: Former Tutor on Critical Service Panel, National Poetry Society; Assistant Editor, New Poetry. Publications: Axe and Tree, 1973; Many People, Many Voices (co-editor), 1978, reprinting in part, 1997; The Quality, 1985; Centrepiece, 1994; Special Number, in International Poets, Madras, to feature her work, 1997; Works included in international and national anthologies; Various BBC broadcasts. Contributions to: Observer; Spectator; New Statesman; Use of English; Ally (USA); Quest (India); Poet (India); International Poets (India); Poetry Auraq (Pakistan). Memberships: Royal Society of Literature; Society of Authors; National Poetry Society; Women Writers Network. Address: 2 Lidgett Park Avenue, Leeds, West Yorkshire LS8 1DP, England.

HOLLO Anselm, (Paul Alexis), b. 12 Apr 1934, Helsinki, Finland. Poet; Translator; Associate Professor. Education: University of Helsinki; University of Tübingen. Appointments: Programme Assistant and Co-ordinator, BBC, London, 1958-66; Visiting Lecuter, 1968-69; Lecturer in English and Music, 1970-71; Head, Translation Workship, 1971-72, University of Iowa; Poetry Editor, Iowa Review, Iowa City, 1971-72; Associate and Visiting Professor, Bowling Green University, Ohio, 1972-73; Poet-in-Residence, Hobart and William Smith College, Geneva, New York, 1973-74; Writer-in-Residence, Sweet Briar College, Virginia, 1978-80; Associate Professor, Writing and Poetics, The Naropa Institute, Boulder, CO, 1989-. Publications: The Twelve and Other Poems by Aleksandr Blok, 1971; Surviving in America, (with Jack Marshall and Sam Hamod), 1972; Sensation 27, 1972; Some Worlds, 1974; Lingering Tangos, 1976; Sojourner Microcosms: New and Selected Poems, 1959-1977, 1977; Heavy Jars, 1977; Curious Data, 1978; Recent Swedish Poetry in Translation, 1979; With Ruth in Mind, 1979; Finite Continued, 1980; No Complaints, 1983; Pentti Saarikoski, Poems 1958-80 (editor and translator), 1983; Pick Up the House, 1986; Egon Schiele: The Poems, 1988; Peter Stephan Jungk: Franz Werfel: The Story of a Life, 1990; Outlying Districts: New Poems, 1990; Near Miss Haiku, 1990; Space Baltic: The science fiction poems, 1962-1987, 1991; Paavo Haavikko: Selected Poems, 1949-1989, 1991; Blue Ceiling (poem), 1992; Jaan Kross: The Czar's Madman (novel), 1993; High Beam: 12 Poems, 1993; West Is Left on the Map (poem sequence), 1993; Corvus (poems), 1995. Address: 3336 14th Street, Boulder, CO 80304, USA.

HOLLOWAY (Percival) Geoffrey, b. 23 May 1918, Birmingham Warwickshire, England. Poet. Education: University of Southampton, 1946-48. Publications: To Have Eyes, 1972; Rhine Jump, 1974; All I Can Say, 1979; The Crones of Aphrodite, 1985; Salt, Roses, Vinegar, 1986; Precepts Without Deference, 1987; My Ghost in Your Eye, 1988; The Strangest Thing, 1990; The Leaping Pool, 1993; A Sheaf of Flowers, 1994. Membership: Brewery Poets. Address: 4 Gowan Crescent, Staveley, Nr Kendal, Cumbria LA8 9NF, England.

HOLLOWAY John, b. 1 Aug 1920, Croydon, Surrey, England. Professor of Modern English (retired); Writer; Poet. m. (1) Audrey Gooding, 1946, 1 son, 1 daughter, (2) Joan Black, 1978. Education: 1st Class Modern Greats, New College, Oxford, 1941; DPhil, Oxon, 1947. Appointments: Temporary Lecturer in Philosophy, New College, Oxford, 1945; Fellow, All Souls College, Oxford, 1946-60; Lecturer in English, University of Aberdeen, 1949-54, University of Cambridge, 1954-66; Fellow, 1955-82, Life Fellow, 1982-, Queens' College, Cambridge; Reader, 1966-72, Professor of Modern English, 1972-82, University of Cambridge; Various visiting lectureships and professorships. Publications: Language and Intelligence, 1951; The Victorian Sage, 1953; Poems of the Mid-Century (editor), 1957; The Charted Mirror (essays), 1960; Selections from Shelley (editor), 1960; Shakespeare's Tragedies, 1961; The Colours of Clarity (essays), 1964; The Lion Hunt, 1964; Widening Horizons in English Verse, 1966; A London Childhood, 1966; Blake: The Lyric Poetry, 1968; The Establishment of English, 1972; Later English Broadside Ballads (editor with J Black), 2 volumes, 1975, 1979; The Proud Knowledge, 1977; Narrative and Structure, 1979; The Slumber of Apollo, 1983; The Oxford Book of Local Verses (editor), 1987. Poetry: The Minute, 1956; The Fugue, 1960; The Landfallers, 1962; Wood and Windfall, 1965; New Poems, 1970; Planet of Winds, 1977; Civitatula: Cambridge, the

Little City, 1994. Contributions to: Professional journals. Membership: Royal Society of Literature, fellow, 1956. Address: c/o Queens' College, Cambridge CB3 9ET, England.

HOLLY David C, b. 17 Oct 1915, Baltimore, Maryland, USA. Retired Naval Officer; University Professor. m. Carolyn King, 15 June 1949, 3 sons. Education: BS, John Hopkins University, 1938; MA, University of Maryland, 1939; PhD, American University, 1964. Publications: Exodus 1947, 2nd edition, 1969; Steamboat on the Chesapeake, 1987; Tidewater by Steamboat, 1991; Chesapeake Steamboats: Vanished Fleet, 1994. Contributions to: Numerous articles to professional journals and periodicals. Honours: Phi Kappa Phi; Pi Sigma Alpha; Pi Gamma Mu; Legion of Merit; Bronze Star; Order of Merit. Address: 918 Schooner Circle, Annapolis, MD 21401, USA.

HOLME K E. See: **HILL (John Edward) Christopher.**

HOLMES Bryan John,(Charles Langley Hayes, Ethan Wall), b. 18 May 1939, Birmingham, England. Lecturer. m. 1962, 2 sons. Education: BA, University of Keele, 1968. Publications: The Avenging Four, 1978; Hazard, 1979; Blood, Sweat and Gold, 1980; Gunfall, 1980; A Noose for Yanqui, 1981; Shard, 1982; Bad Times at Backwheel, 1982; Guns of the Reaper, 1983; On the Spin of a Dollar, 1983; Another Day, Another Dollar, 1984; Dark Rider, 1987; I Rode with Wyatt, 1989; Dollars for the Reaper, 1990; A Legend Called Shatterhand, 1990; Loco, 1991; Shatterhand and the People, 1992; The Last Days of Billy Patch, 1992; Blood on the Reaper, 1992; All Trails Leads to Dodge, 1993; Montana Hit, 1993; A Coffin for the Reaper, 1994; Comes the Reaper, 1995; Utah Hit, 1995; Dakota Hit, 1995; Viva Reaper, 1996; The Shard Brand, 1996. Contributions to: Professional journals, periodicals and general magazines. Address: c/o Robert Hale Ltd, Clerkenwell Green, London EC1R 0HT, England.

HOLMES Charlotte (Amalie), b. 26 Apr 1956, Georgia, USA. Assistant Professor; Writer. m. James Brasfield, 7 Mar 1983, 1 son. Education: MFA, Columbia University, 1977; BA, Louisiana State University, 1980. Appointments: Editorial Assistant, Paris Review, 1979-80; Associate and Managing Editor, The Ecco Press, 1980-82; Instructor, Western Carolina University, 1984-87; Assistant Professor, Penn State University, 1987-. Publication: Gifts and Other Stories, 1994. Contributions to: Periodicals. Honours: Stegner Fellowship, Stanford University, 1982; North Carolina Arts Council Grant, 1986; Pennsylvania Council on the Arts Fellowships, 1988, 1993; Bread Loaf Writer's Conference National Arts Club Scholarship, 1990; Poets and Writers Award, 1993. Membership: Associated Writing Programs. Address: c/o Department of English, Penn State University, University Park, PA 16802, USA.

HOLMES John. See: **SOUSTER Raymond (Holmes).**

HOLMES John, b. 12 May 1913, Bishopton, Renfrewshire, Scotland. Farmer; Dog Breeder/Trainer. m. Kathleen Mary Trevethick, 6 Dec 1955. Education: Edinburgh and East of Scotland College of Agriculture, 1929-30. Publications: The Family Dog, 1957, 13 editions; The Farmers Dog, 1960, 13 editions; The Obedient Dog, 1975, 6 editions; Looking After Your Dog (with Mary Holmes), 1985; The Complete Australian Cattle Dog (with Mary Holmes), 1993; The Pet Owners Guide to Puppy Care and Training (with Mary Holmes), 1995. Contributions to: The Kennel Gazette; Dog World; Our Dogs; The Field; Carriage Driving; Horse and Hound; Pedigree Digest. Honour: Maxwell Award for Short Books, Dog Writers Association of America, 1995. Memberships: Society of Authors; British Actors Equity Association; UK Registry of Canine Behaviourists. Address: Formakin Farm, Cranborne, Dorset BH21 5QY, England.

HOLMES Leslie Templeman, b. 5 Oct 1948, London, England. Professor of Political Science. m. Susan Mary Bleasby, 4 Sept 1971, divorced Oct 1989. Education: BA Hons Russian Studies and German, Hull University, 1971; MA, Soviet Government and Politics, 1974, PhD, Comparative Government, 1979, Essex University. Appointment: Professor of Political Science, University of Melbourne. Publications: The Policy Progress in Communist States, 1981; The Withering Away of the State? (editor), 1981; Politics in the Communist World, 1986; The End of Communist Power, 1993; Post-Communism, 1996. Honour: Fellow, Academy of the Social Sciences in Australia, 1995. Address: Department of Political Science, University of Melbourne, Parkville, Victoria 3052, Australia.

HOLMES Marjorie Rose, b. 22 Sept 1910, Storm Lake, Iowa, USA. Author. m. (1) Lynn Mighell, 9 Apr 1932, 1 son, 2 daughters, (2) George Schmieler, 4 July 1981. Education: Buena Vista College, 1922-29; BA, Cornell College, 1931. Publications: World by the Tail, 1943; Ten O'Clock Scholar, 1946; Saturday Night, 1959; Cherry Blossom Princess,1960; Follow Your Dream, 1961; Love is a Hopscotch thing; 1963; Senior Trip, 1962; Love and Laughter, 1967; I've got to talk to Somebody, God, 1969; Writing the Creative Article, 1969; Who Am I, God?, 1969; To Treasure our Days, 1971; Two from Galilee, 1972; Nobody Else Will Listen, 1973; You and I and Yesterday, 1973; As Tall as My Heart, 1974; How Can I Find You God: 1975; Beauty in Your Own Back Yard, 1976; Hold Me Up a Little Longer, Lord, 1977; Lord, Let Me Love, 1978; God and Vitamins, 1980; To Help You Through the Hurting, 1983; Three from Galilee, 1985; Secrets of Health, Energy and Staying Young, 1987; The Messiah, 1987; At Christmas the Heart Goes Home, 1991; The Inspriational Writings of Marjorie Holmes, 1991; Gifts Freely Given, 1992; Second Wife, Second Life, 1993; Writing Articles from the Heart, 1993; Still By Your Side: How I Know a Great Love Never Dies, 1996. Contributions to: Numerous journals and magazines. Address: 8681 Cobb Road, Lake Jackson Hills, Manassas, VA 20112, USA.

HOLMES Raymond. See: **SOUSTER Raymond (Holmes).**

HOLMES Richard (Gordon Heath), b. 5 Nov 1945, London, England. Writer; Poet. Education: BA, Churchill College, Cambridge. Appointments: Reviewer and Historical Features Writer, The Times, London, 1967-92; Earnest Jones Memorial Lecturer, British Institute of Psycho-Analysis, 1990; John Keats Memorial Lecturer, Royal College of Surgeons, 1995. Publications: Thomas Chatterton: The Case Re-Opened, 1970; One for Sorrows (poems), 1970; Shelley: The Pursuit, 1974; Shelley on Love (editor), 1980; Coleridge, 1982; Nerval: The Chimeras (with Peter Jay), 1985; Footsteps: Adventures of a Romantic Biographer, 1985; Mary Wollenscraft and William Godwin (editor), 1987; Kipling: Something Myself (editor with Robert Hampson), 1987; Coleridge: Early Visions, 1989; Dr Johnson and Mr Savage, 1993; Coleridge: Selected Poems (editor), 1996. Honours: Somerset Maugham Award, 1977; Whitbread Book of the Year Prize, 1989; Officer of the Order of the British Empire, 1992; James Tait Black Memorial Prize, 1994. Membership: Royal Society of Literature, fellow. Address: c/o HarperCollins, 77 Fulham Palace Road, London W6 8JB, England.

HOLROYD Michael (de Courcy Fraser), b. 27 Aug 1935, London, England. Biographer; Writer. m. Margaret Drabble, 17 Sept 1982. Education: Eton College. Appointment: Visiting Fellow, Penn State University, 1979. Publications: Hugh Kingsmill: A Critical Biography, 1964; Lytton Strachey: A Critical Biography, 2 volumes, 1967, 1968, revised edition, 1994; A Dog's Life (novel), 1969; The Best of Hugh Kingsmill (editor), 1970; Lytton Strachey by Himself: A Self-Portrait (editor), 1971, new edition, 1994; Unreceived Opinions (essays), 1973; Augustus John, 2 volumes, 1974, 1975, revised edition, 1996; The Art of Augustus John (with Malcolm Easton), 1974; The Genius of Shaw (editor), 1979; The Shorter Strachey (editor with Paul Levy), 1980; William Gerhardie's God Fifth Column (editor with Robert Skidelsky), 1981; Essays by Diverse Hands (editor), Vol XLII, 1982; Peterley Harvest; The Private Diary of David Peterley (editor), 1985; Bernard Shaw: Vol I, The Search for Love 1856-1898, 1988, Vol II, The Pursuit of Power 1898-1918, 1989, Vol III, The Lure of Fantasy 1918-1950, 1991, Vol IV, The Last Laugh 1950-1991, 1992, Vol V, The Shaw Companion, 1992, one-volume abridged edition, 1997. Contributions to: Radio, television, and periodicals. Honours: Saxton Memorial Fellowship, 1964; Bollingen Fellowship, 1966; Winston Churchill Fellowship, 1971; Commander of the Order of the British Empire, 1989; Hon DLitts: Ulster, 1992, Sheffield, 1993, Warwick, 1994, and East Anglia, 1994. Memberships: Arts Council, Chairman, Literature Panel, 1992-95; National Book League, Chairman, 1976-78; PEN, President, British Branch, 1985-88; Royal Historical Society, Fellow; Royal Society of Literature, Fellow; Society of Authors, Chairman, 1973-74; Fellow, Royal Society of Arts; Strachey Trust, Chairman, 1990-95. Address: c/o A P Watt Ltd, 20 John Street, London WC1N 2DR, England.

HOLT George. See: **TUBB E(dwin) C(harles).**

HOLUB Miroslav, b. 13 Sept 1923, Pilsen, Czechoslovakia. Scientific Worker; Writer. m. Jitka Langrova, 6 July 1969, 2 sons, 1 daughter. Education: MD, Charles University, Prague, 1953; PhD, Czechoslovak Academy of Science, 1958. Appointments: Scientist;

Member, Editorial and Scientific Boards of Literary Magazines, Oberlin, Ohio, 1985. Publications: Selected Poems, 1967; Notes of a Clay Pigeon, 1977; Vanishing Lung Syndrome, 1990; The Dimension of the Present Moment, 1990; Jingle Bell Principle, 1992; Supposed to Fly, 1996; Intensive Care, 1996. Contributions to: Magazines and newspapers. Honours: Honorary DHL degree, Oberlin College; J E Purkynje Medal, 1988; G Theiner Award, 1991. Memberships: Czech PEN; European Society for the Promotion of Poetry; Czech Writers Union; Bavarian Academy of Arts; British Poetry Society. Literary Agent: Irene Skolnick, New York, USA. Address: Svepomocna 107 Hrncire, CS 149 00 Prague 4, Czech Republic.

HOMBERGER Eric (Ross), b. 30 May 1942, Philadelphia, Pennsylvania, USA. Reader in American Literature; Writer. m. Judy Jones, 2 June 1967, 2 sons, 1 daughter. Education: BA, University of California at Berkeley, 1964; MA, University of Chicago, 1965; PhD, Cambridge University, 1972. Appointments: Temporary Lecturer in American Literature, University of Exeter, 1969-70; Lecturer, 1970-88, Reader in American Literature, 1988-, University of East Anglia; Visiting Faculty, University of Minnesota, 1977-78; Visiting Professor of American Literature, University of New Hampshire, 1991-92. Publications: The Cambridge Mind: Ninety Years of the "Cambridge Review", 1879-1969 (editor with William Janeway and Simon Schama), 1970; Ezra Pound: The Critical Heritage (editor), 1972; The Art of the Real: Poetry in England and America since 1939, 1977; The Second World War in Fiction (editor with Holger Klein and John Flower), 1984; Scenes from the Life of a City: Corruption and Conscience in Old New York, 1984; John le Carre, 1986; American Writers and Radical Politics, 1900-1939: Equivocal Commitments, 1987; The Troubled Face of Biography (editor with John Charmley), 1987; John Reed, 1990; John Reed and the Russian Revolution: Uncollected Articles, Letters and Speeches in Russia, 1917-1920 (editor with John Biggart), 1992. Contributions to: Periodicals. Honour: Leverhulme Fellowship, 1978-79. Membership: British Association for American Studies. Address: 74 Clarendon Road, Norwich NR2 2PN, England.

HONAN Park, b. 17 Sept 1928, Utica, New York, USA. Professor of English and American Literature; Writer; Editor. Education: MA, University of Chicago, 1951; PhD, University of Leeds, 1959. Appointments: Dumptruck Driver, Oregon Lumber Mills, 1950's; Professor of English and American Literature, University of Leeds, 1984-; British Editor, Novel: A Forum on Fiction; Co-Editor, Ohio and Baylor Presses Browning Edition. Publications: Browning's Characters: A Study in Poetic Technique, 1961; Shelley (editor), 1963; Bulwer Lytton's Falkland (editor), 1967; The Complete Works of Robert Browning (co-editor), 9 volumes, 1969-; The Book, The Ring and The Poet: A Biography of Robert Browning (co-author), 1975; Matthew Arnold: A Life, 1981; Jane Austen: Her Life, 1987; The Beats: An Anthology of "Beat" Writing (editor), 1987; Authors' Lives: On Literary Biography and the Arts of Language, 1990. Address: School of English, University of Leeds, Leeds LS2 9JT, England.

HONAN William Holmes, b. 11 May 1930, New York, New York, USA. Journalist. m. Nancy Burton, 22 June 1975, 2 sons, 1 daughter. Education: BA, Oberlin College, 1952; MA, University of Virginia, 1955. Appointments: Editor, The Villager, New York, 1957-60; Assistant Editor, New Yorker Magazine, 1960-64; Associate Editor, Newsweek, New York City, 1969; Assistant Editor, New York Times Magazine, 1969-70; Travel Editor, 1970-72, 1973-74; Arts and Leisure Editor, 1974-82; Culture Editor, 1982-88; Chief Cultural Correspondent, 1988-93, National Higher Education Correspondent, 1993-; New York Times; Managing Editor, Saturday Review, 1972-73. Publications; Greenwich Village Guide, 1959; Ted Kennedy: Profile of a Survivor, 1972; Bywater: The Man Who Invented the Pacific War, 1990; Visions of Infamy: The Untold Story of How Journalist Hector C Bywater Devised the Plans that Led to Pearl Harbour, 1991; Fire When Ready, Gridley! - Great Naval Stories from Manila Bay to Vietnam (editor), 1992; Treasure Hunt: A New York Times Reporter Tracks the Quedlinburg Treasures, 1997. Contributions to: Periodicals. Address: c/o New York Times, 229 West 43rd St, New York, NY 10036. USA.

HONE Joseph, b. 25 Feb 1937, London, England. Writer; Broadcaster. m. Jacqueline Mary Yeend, 5 Mar 1963, 1 son, 1 daughter. Education: Kilkenny College, Sandford Park School, Dublin; St Columba's College, Dublin. Publications: The Flowers of the Forest, 1982; Children of the Country, 1986; Duck Soup in the Black Sea, 1988; Summer Hill, 1990; Firesong, 1997. Contributions to: Periodicals. Membership: Upton House Cricket Club. Address: c/o

Aitken & Stone Ltd, 29 Fernshaw Road, London SW10, England.

HONEYCOMBE Gordon, b. 27 Sept 1936, Karachi, India. Writer; TV Presenter; Actor. Education: Edinburgh Academy, 1946-55; University College, Oxford, 1957-61. Publications: The Redemption, 1964; Neither the Sea Nor the Sand, 1969; Dragon under the Hill, 1972; Red Watch, 1976; The Edge of Heaven, 1981; Royal Wedding, 1981; The Murders of the Black Museum, 1982; The Year of the Princess, 1982; TV-AM's Official Celebration of the Royal Wedding, 1986; Siren Song, 1992; More Murders of the Black Museum, 1993; TV Plays, Stage Plays. Address: c/o Martyn Smith, Stephenson & Co, 43 Poole Road, Bournemouth BH4 9DN, England.

HONEYMAN Brenda. See: CLARK Brenda (Margaret Lilian).

HONIG Edwin, b. 3 Sept 1919, New York, New York, USA. Poet; Playwright; Author. m. (1) Charlotte Gilchrist, 1940, dec 1963, (2) Margot S Dennes, 1963, div 1978, 2 sons. Education: BA, 1941, MA, 1947, University of Wisconsin, Madison. Appointments: Library Assistant, Library of Congress, Washington DC, 1941-42; Instructor in English, Purdue University, 1942-43, New York University and Illinois Institute of Technology, Chicago, 1946-47, University of New Mexico, Albuquerque, 1947-48; Poetry Editor, New Mexico Quarterly, 1948-52; Instructor, 1949-52, Assistant Professor, 1952-57, Harvard University; Professor of Comparative Literature, Brown University, 1957-82; Visiting Professor, University of California, Davis, 1964-65; Mellon Professor, Boston University, 1977; Director, Rhode Island Poetry in the Schools Program, 1968-72. Publications: Poetry: Survival, 1964; Spring Journal, 1968; Four Springs, 1972; At Sixes, 1974; Selected Poems 1955-1976, 1979; Interrupted Praise: New and Selected Poems, 1983; Gifts of Light, 1983; The Imminence of Love: Poems 1963-1993. Plays: Cervantes: Eight Interludes, 1964; Calisto and Melibea, 1966, published, 1972; Ends of the World and Other Plays, 1983; Calderon, Six Plays, 1993. Honours: Guggenheim Fellowships, 1948, 1962; Saturday Review Prize 1957; New England Poetry Club Golden Rose, 1961; Bollingen Grant for translation, 1962; American Academy and Institute of Arts and Letters Grant, 1966; Amy Lowell Travelling Poetry Fellowship, 1968; National Endowment for the Arts Grants, 1975, 1977. Address: Box 1852, Brown University, Providence, RI 02912, USA.

HOOD Hugh (John Blagdon), b. 30 Apr 1928, Toronto, Ontario, Canada. Writer;Teacher. m. Noreen Mallory, 22 Apr 1957, 2 sons. Education: BA 1952, MA 1952, PhD 1955, University of Toronto. Appointment: Professor Titulaire, Department of English Studies, University of Montreal, 1961-. Publications: Flying a Red Kite, 1962; The Swing in the Garden, 1975; Black and White Keys, 1982; You'll Catch Your Death, 1992; Be Sure to Close Your Eyes, 1993; Dead Men's Watches, 1995. Honours: City of Toronto Literary Award, 1975; SQPELL Literary Award, 1988; Officer of the Order of Canada, 1988. Membership: Arts and Letters Club of Toronto. Address: 4242 Hampton Avenue, Montreal, Quebec H4A 2K9, Canada.

HOOKER Jeremy (Peter), b. 23 Mar 1941, Warsash, Hampshire, England. College Professor. Education: BA 1963, MA 1965,Southampton University. Appointments: Arts Council Creative Writing Fellow, Winchester School of Art, 1981-83. Publications: Soliloquies of a Chalk Giant, 1974; Solent Shore, 1978; Poetry of Place, 1982;A View from the Source: Selected Poems, 1982; The Presence of the Past, 1987; Master of the Leaping Figures, 1987; Their Silence a Language (with Lee Grandjean), 1994. Contributions to: Anglo-Welsh Review; New Welsh Review; PN Review; Planet; The Green Book; Poetry Wales; Agenda: Modern Painters. Honour: Welsh Arts Council Literature Prize, 1975. Memberships: Academi Gymreig, English Language Section; Powys Society; Richard Jefferies Society; Honorary President, Salisbury Poetry Circle. Address: Old School House, 7 Sunnyside Frome, Somerset, BA11 1LD, England.

HOOVER Helen Mary, (Jennifer Price), b . 5 Apr 1935, Stark County, Ohio, USA. Writer. Publications: Children of Morrow, 1973; The Lion Cub, 1974; Treasures of Morrow, 1976; The Delikon, 1977; The Rains of Eridan, 1977; The Lost Star, 1979; Return to Earth, 1980; The Time of Darkness, 1980; Another Heaven, Another Earth, 1981; The Bell Tree, 1982; The Shepherd Moon, 1984; Orvis, 1987; The Dawn Palace, 1988; Away Is A Strange Place To Be, 1989. Contributions to: Language Arts; Top of the News; Journal of American Library Association. Honours: Ohioana Award, 1982; Award, Outstanding Contribution to Children's Literature, Central Missouri State University, 1984; Parents Choice Award, 1987, 1988; Library of

Congress Best Book of 1988; American Library Association, Best Young Adult Book of 1988. Memberships: Authors Guild. Address: c/o Viking Penguin Children's Books, 40 West 23rd Street, New York City, NY 10010, USA.

HOOVER Paul, b. 30 Apr 1946, Harrisonburg, Virginia, USA. Writer; Poet; Teacher. m. Maxine Chernoff, 5 Oct 1974, 2 sons, 1 daughter. Education: BA cum Laude, Manchester College, 1968; MA, University of Illinois, 1973. Appointments: Poet-in-Residence, Columbia College, Chicago, 1974-; Editor, New American Writing, journal. Publications: Idea, 1987; The Novel, 1990; Postmodern American Poetry (editor), 1993. Contributions to: Periodicals. Honours: National Endowment for the Arts Fellowship in Poetry, 1980; General Electric Foundation Award for Younger Writers, 1984; Carl Sandburg Award for Poetry, 1987. Memberships: Associated Writing Programs; Modern Language Association. Address: 2920 West Pratt, Chicago, IL 60645, USA.

HOPCRAFT Arthur Edward, b. 29 Nov 1932, Essex, England. Writer. Appointments: Staff, The Daily Mirror, 1956-59; The Guardian, 1959-64. Publications: The Football Man, 1968; The Great Apple Raid, 1970; Mid-Century Men, 1982; TV Dramatisations and Screenplays, 1971-92: Hard Times; Bleak House; The Nearly Man; The Reporters; Baa Baa Blacksheep; A Tale of Two Cities; Hostage; Tinker, Tailor, Soldier, Spy; A Perfect Spy. Contributions to: Observer; Sunday Times; Nova; New Statesman; Listener. Honours: Broadcasting Press Guild TV Award; Best Single Play; Best Drama Series; British Academy of Film and TV Arts Writers Award. Membership: Writers Guild of Great Britain. Address: c/o 20 John Street, London WC1N 2DL, England.

HOPE Catherine (Cathy) Jane Margaret, b. 15 Sept 1945, Waikari, South Island, New Zealand. Primary School Teacher; Educational Author. m. Terry Hope, 30 Dec 1966, 2 daughters. Education: Trained Infant School Teacher, Coburg Teachers College, Victoria, 1965. Publications: Thematic Approach to Tadpoles 'N' Things, 1978; Themes through the Year, 1980; Ideas for Excursions, 1981; Everyone's Different, 1981; Seasons-Themes through the Year, 1982; Everyone Ages, 1983; Themes from the Playground, 1984; All Australian Themes, 1987; Ideas for Multicultural Education, 1992; Fundraising for Schools, 1994. Membership: Fellowship of Australian Writers. Address: c/- Thomas Nelson, 102 Dodds Street, South Melbourne, Victoria 3205, Australia.

HOPE Christopher David Tully, b. 26 Feb 1944, Johannesburg, South Africa. Writer. m. Eleanor Marilyn Margaret Klein, 1967, 2 sons. Education: BA, Natal University, 1969; MA, University of Witwatersrand, 1972. Publications: Cape Drives, 1974; A Separate Development, 1981; The Country of the Black Pig, 1981; The King, the Cat and the Fiddle, 1983; Kruger's Alp, 1984; The Dragon Wore Pink, 1985; White Boy Running, 1988; My Chocolate Redeemer, 1989; Serenity House, 1992; The Love Songs of Nathan J Swirsky, 1993; Darkest England, 1996. Contributions to: Times Literary Supplement; London Magazine; Les Temps Modernes. Honours: Cholmondeley Award, 1974; David Higham Prize, 1981; International PEN Award, 1983; Whitbread Prize, 1985. Memberships: Royal Society of Literature, fellow; Society of Authors. Address: c/o Rogers, Coleridge & White Ltd, 20 Powis Mews, London W11 1JN, England.

HOPE Ronald (Sidney), b. 4 Apr 1921, London, England. Writer. Education: BA, 1941, MA, 1946, DPhil, New College, Oxford. Appointments: Fellow, Brasenose College, Oxford, 1945-47, Seafarer's Education Service, London, 1947-76; Director, The Marine Society, 1976-86. Publications: Spare Time at Sea, 1954; Economic Geography, 1956; Dick Small in the Half Deck, Ships, 1958; The British Shipping Industry, 1959; The Shoregoer's Guide to World ports, 1963; Seamen and the Sea, 1965; Introduction to the Merchant Navy, 1965; Retirement from the Sea, 1967; In Cabined Ships at Sea, 1969; Twenty Singing Seamen, 1979; The Seamen's World, 1982; A New History of British Shipping, 1990. Address: 2 Park Place, Dollar, FK14 7AA.

HOPE-SIMPSON Jacynth (Ann), (Helen Dudley), b. 10 Nov 1930, Birmingham, England. Writer. Education: University of Lausanne, 1949; MA and Diploma in Education, Oxford University, 1953. Publications: The Stranger in the Train, 1960; The Bishop of Kenelminster, 1961; The Man Who Came Back, 1962; The Bishop's Picture, 1962; The Unravished Bridge, 1963; The Witch's Cave, 1964; The Hamish Hamilton Book of Myths and Legends, 1965; The Hamish

Hamilton Book of Witches, 1966; Escape to the Castle, 1967; The Unknown Island, 1968; They Sailed from Plymouth, 1970; Elizabeth I, 1971; Tales in School, 1971; The Gunner's Boy, 1973; Save Tarranmoor!, 1974; Always on the Move, 1975; The Hijacked Hovercraft, 1975; Black Madonna, 1976; Vote for Victoria, 1976; The Making of the Machine Age, 1978; The Hooded Falcon, 1979; Island of Perfumes, 1985; Cottage Dreams, 1986. Address: Franchise Cottage, Newtown, Milborne, Port Sherborne, Dorset, England.

HOPKINS Antony, b. 21 Mar 1921, London, England. Composer; Conductor; Lecturer; Writer. m. Alison Purves, 1947, dec 1991. Education: Royal College of Music, London. Appointments: Director, Intimate Opera Company, 1952-64; Presenter, Talking About Music, BBC, 1954-92; Lecturer, Royal College of Music, London. Publications: Talking About Symphonies, 1961, reprinted 1996; Talking About Concertos, 1964; Music All Around Me, 1967; Music Face to Face, 1971; Talking About Sonatas, 1971; Downbeat Guide, 1977; Understanding Music, 1979; The Nine Symphonies of Beethoven, 1980; Songs for Swinging Golfers, 1981; Sounds of Music, 1982; Beating Time, 1982; Pathway to Music, 1983; The Concertgoer's Companion, 2 volumes, 1984, 1986, reprinted as single volume, 1994; The Seven Concertos of Beethoven, 1996. Honours: Gold Medal, Royal College of Music, 1943; Italia Prizes, 1951, 1957; Medal for Services to Music, City of Tokyo, 1973; Commander of the Order of the British Empire, 1976. Address: Woodyard, Ashridge, Berkhamsted, Hertfordshire HP4 1PS, England.

HOPKINS Bruce R, b. 25 Apr 1941, Sault Ste Marie, Michigan, USA. Lawyer. 1 son. Education: BA, University of Michigan, 1964; JD, 1967, LLM, 1971, George Washington University. Publications: The Law of Tax-Exempt Organizations, 6th edition, 1992; A Legal Guide to Starting and Managing a Nonprofit Organization, 2nd edition, 1993; The Legal Answer Book for Nonprofit Organizations, 1996; The Law of Fund-Raising, 2nd edition, 1996; Nonprofit Law Dictionary, 1994; The Law of Tax-Exempt Healthcare Organizations, 1995; Intermediate Sanctions: Curbing Nonprofits' Abuse, 1997; Private Foundations: Tax Law and Compliance, 1997. Contributions to: Over 100 articles in law, management, and fund raising journals. Honour: First National Society of Fund Raising Executives/Staley/Robeson/Ryan/St Lawrence Research Award. Literary Agent: Martha Cooley, John Wiley & Sons Inc, New York, NY, USA. Address: 700 West 47th Street, Suite 1000, Kansas City, MO 64112-1802, USA.

HOPKINS Harry, b. 26 Mar 1913, Preston, Lancashire, England. Journalist; Author. m. Endla Kustlov, 26 Jan 1948. Education: BA, Merton College, 1935. Appointments: Assistant Editor, Birmingham Gazette, 1936-38; Diplomatic Correspondent, Manchester Evening News, 1946-47; Feature Writer, John Bull Magazine, 1947-60. Publications: New World Arising: A Journey Through the New Nations of South East Asia, 1952; England is Rich, 1957; The New Look: A Social History, 1963; Egypt the Crucible, 1969; The Numbers Game, 1972; The Strange Death of Private White, 1977; The Long Affray, 1985. Memberships: National Union of Journalists; Society of Authors. Address: 61 Clifton Hill, St Johns Wood, London NW8 0JN, England.

HOPKINS Lee Bennett, b. 13 Apr 1938, Scranton, Pennsylvania, USA. Writer; Editor; Educational Consultant. Education: BA, Kean College, 1960; MS, Bank St College, 1964; Diploma, Hunter College of the City University of New York, 1966. Appointments: Curriculum Specialist, Scholastic Inc, 1968-75; Educational Consultant, 1975-. Publications: Author and/or editor of numerous children's books. Contributions to: Professional journals and to magazines. Honours: Educational Leadership Award, Phi Delta Kappa, 1980; Award, International Reading Association, 1983; Children's Literature Award, University of Southern Mississippi, 1989. Address: Kemeys Cove, 307, Scarborough, NY 10510, USA.

HOPPE Matthias, b. 5 Dec 1952, Schluechtern, Germany. Editor. 1 daughter. Education: Studies, German Language and Literature, History and Politics. Publications: Muenchen, 1982; Was macht Arno im Sommer, 1989; Mouse and Elephant, 1991; Muenchen, Fit and Fun, 1995; Exploring Germany, 1996; Verrueckt ist ganz normal, 1996. Contributions to: Abendzeitung Muenchen; Stern; Die Zeit; Frankfurter Rundschau; TV Stations. Memberships: IG Medien; Verband Deutscher Schriftsteller VS. Address: Post Box 900526, 81505 Munich, Germany.

HORNBY Nick, b. 1957, London, England. Freelance Journalist; Novelist. Publications: Contemporary American Fiction (essays), 1992;

Fever Pitch (memoirs), 1992; My Favourite Year: A Collection of New Football Writing (editor), 1993; High Fidelity (novel), 1995; Script for film version of Fever Pitch, 1997. Contributions to: Sunday Times; Times Literary Supplement; Literary Review. Address: c/o Victor Gollancz Ltd, Villiers House, 41-47 The Strand, London WC2N 5JE, England.

HORNE Alister Allan, b. 9 Nov 1925, London, England. Author; Journalist; Lecturer. m. (1) Renira Margaret Hawkins, 3 daughters, (2) The Hon Mrs Sheelin Eccles, 1987. Education: MA, Jesus College, Cambridge. Appointments: Foreign Correspondent, Daily Telegraph, 1952-55; Official Biographer, Prime Minister Harold MacMillan, 1979. Publications: Back into Power, 1955; The Land is Bright, 1958; Canada and the Canadians, 1961; The Fall of Paris 1870-1871, 1965; To Lose a Battle: France 1940, 1969; Death of a Generation, 1970; The Paris Commune, 1971; Small Earthquake in Chile, 1972; Napoleon, Master of Europe 1805-1807, 1979; The French Army and Politics 1870-1970, 1984; MacMillan, Vol I, 1894-1956, 198,; Vol II, 1957-1986, 1989; A Bundle from Britain, 1993; The Lonely Leader: Monty 1944-45, 1994. Contributions to: Various Periodicals. Honours: Hawthorden Prize, 1963; Yorkshire Post Book of Year Prize, 1978; Wolfson Literary Award, 1978; Enid Macleod Prize, 1985; Officer of the Order of the British Empire, 1992; Chevalier, Legion d'Honneur, 1993; LittD. Memberships: Society of Authors; Royal Society of Literature. Address: The Old Vicarage, Turville, Nr Henley on Thames, Oxon RG9 6QU, England.

HORNE Donald Richmond, b. 26 Dec 1921, Sydney, Australia. Author; Lecturer; Professor Emeritus. m. 22 Mar 1960, 1 son, 1 daughter. Education: Sydney University, Canberra University College, 1944-45. Appointments: Editor, The Observer, 1958-61, The Bulletin, 1961-62, 1967-72, Quadrant, 1963-66; Contributing Editor, Newsweek International, 1973-76; Chancellor, University of Canberra, 1992-. Publications: The Lucky Country, 1964; The Permit, 1965; The Education of Young Donald, 1967; God is an Englishman, 1969; The Next Australia, 1970; But What If There Are No Pelicans?, 1971; Money Made Us, 1976; The Death of the Lucky Country, 1976; His Excellency's Pleasure, 1977; Right Way Don't Go Back, 1978; In Search of Billy Hughes, 1979; Time of Hope, 1980; Winner Take All, 1981; The Great Museum, 1984; Confessions of New Boy, 1985; The Story of the Australian People, 1985; The Public Culture, 1986, 1994; The Lucky Country Revisited, 1987; Portrait of an Optimist, 1988; Ideas for a Nation, 1989; The Intelligent Tourist, 1993. Contributions to: Numerous Professional Journals. Honours: AO, 1982; Honorary doctorates; Fellow, Australian Academy of Humanities. Memberships: Australian Society of Authors; Copyright Agency Ltd. Address: 53 Grosvenor Street, Woollahra, Sydney, New South Wales 2025, Australia.

HOROVITZ Michael, b. 4 Apr 1935, Frankfurt am Main, Germany. Writer; Poet; Editor; Publisher. Education: BA, 1959, MA, 1964, Brasenose, College, Oxford. Appointments: Editor and Publisher, New Departures International Review, 1959-; Founder, Co-ordinator and Torchbearer, Poetry Olympics Festivals, 1980-. Publications: Europa (translator), 1961; Alan Davie, 1963; Declaration, 1963; Strangers: Poems, 1965; Poetry for the People: An Essay in Bop Prosody, 1966; Bank Holiday: A New Testament for the Love Generation, 1967; Children of Albion (editor), 1969; The Wolverhampton Wanderer: An Epic of Football, Fate and Fun, 1970; Love Poems, 1971; A Contemplation, 1978; Growing Up: Selected Poems and Pictures 1951-1979, 1979; The Egghead Republic (translator), 1983; A Celebration of and for Frances Horovitz, 1984; Midsummer Morning Jog Log, 1986; Bop Paintings, Collages and Drawings, 1989; Grandchildren of Albion (editor), 1992; Wordsounds & Sightlines: New and Selected Poems, 1994; Grandchildren of Albion Live (editor), 1996; The POW! Anthology, 1996. Address: New Departures, Mullions, Bisley, Stroud, Gloucestershire GL6 7BU, England.

HOROWITZ Donald (Leonard), b. 27 June 1939, New York, New York, USA. Professor of Law and Political Science; Writer. m. Judith Anne Present, 4 Sept 1960, 2 sons, 1 daughter. Education: AB, 1959, LLB, 1961, Syracuse University; LLM, 1962, AM, 1965, PhD, 1967, Harvard University. Appointments: Admitted to the Bar, New York, 1962; Research Associate, Center for International Affairs, Harvard University, 1967-69, Brookings Institution, Washington, DC, 1972-75; Attorney, US Department of Justice, Washington, DC, 1969-71; Fellow, Council on Foreign Relations and Woodrow Wilson International Center for Scholars, Washington, DC, 1971-72; Senior

Fellow, Research Institute on Immigration and Ethnic Studies, Smithsonian Institution, Washington, DC, 1975-81; McDonald-Currie Memorial Lecturer, McGill University, Montreal, 1980; Professor of Law and Political Science, 1980-, Charles S Murphy Professor, 1988-93, James B Duke Professor, 1994-, Duke University; Visiting Professor and Charles J Merriam Scholar, University of Chicago, 1988; Visiting Fellow, Cambridge University, 1988; Visiting Scholar, Universiti Kebangsaan, Malaysia, 1991. Publications: The Courts and Social Policy, 1977; The Jurocracy: Government Lawyers, Agency Programs and Judicial Decisions, 1977; Coup Theories and Officers' Motives, 1980; Ethnic Groups in Conflict, 1985; A Democratic South Africa?: Constitutional Engineering in a Divided Society, 1991. Contributions to: Professional journals, newspapers, and periodicals. Honours: Louis Brownlow Prize, National Academy of Public Administration, 1977; Guggenheim Fellowship, 1980-81; Ralph J Bunche Award, American Political Science Association, 1992. Membership: American Academy of Arts and Sciences, Fellow. Address: School of Law, Duke University, Durham, NC 27706, USA.

HOROWITZ Irving (Louis), b. 25 Sept 1929, New York, New York, USA. Professor of Social and Political Theory; Writer; Editor; Publisher. m. (1) Ruth Lenore Horowitz, 1950, div 1964, 2 sons, (2) Mary Curtis Horowitz, 9 Oct 1979. Education: BSS, City College, New York City, 1951; MA, Columbia University, 1952; PhD, University of Buenos Aires, 1957; Postgraduate Fellow, Brandeis University, 1958-59. Appointments: Associate Professor, University of Buenos Aires, 1955-58; Visiting Professor of Sociology, University of Caracas, 1957, University of Buenos Aires, 1959, 1961, 1963, State University of New York at Buffalo, 1960, Syracuse University, 1961, University of Rochester, 1962, University of California at Davis, 1966, University of Wisconsin at Madison, 1967, Stanford University, 1968-69, American University, 1972, Queen's University, Canada, 1973, Princeton University, 1976, University of Miami, 1992; Assistant Professor, Bard College, 1960; Chairman, Department of Sociology, Hobart and William Smith Colleges, 1960-63; Visiting Lecturer, London School of Economics and Political Science, 1962; Editor-in-Chief, Transaction Society, 1962-94; Associate Professor to Professor of Sociology, Washington University, St Louis, 1963-69; President, Transaction Books, 1966-94; Chairman, Department of Sociology, Livingston College, Rutgers University, 1969-73; Professor of Sociology, Graduate Faculty, 1969-, Hannah Arendt Professor of Social and Political Theory, 1979-, Rutgers University; Bacardi Chair of Cuban Studies, Miami University, 1992-93; Editorial Chairman and President Emeritus, Transaction/USA and Transaction/UK. Publications: Idea of War and Peace in Contemporary Philosophy, 1957; Philosophy, Science and the Sociology of Knowledge, 1960; Radicalism and the Revolt Against Reason: The Social Theories of Georges Sorel, 1962, 2nd edition, 1968; The War Game: Studies of the New Civilian Militarists, 1963; Professing Sociology: The Life Cycle of a Social Science, 1963; The New Sociology: Essays in Social Science and Social Values in Honor of C Wright Mills (editor), 1964; Revolution in Brazil: Politics and Society in a Developing Nation, 1964; The Rise and Fall of Project Camelot, 1967, revised edition, 1976; Three Worlds of Development: The Theory and Practice of International Stratification, 1967, revised edition, 1972; Latin American Radicalism: A Documentary Report on Nationalist and Left Movements, 1969; Sociological Self-Images, 1969; The Knowledge Factory: Masses in Latin America, 1970; Cuban Communism, 1970, 7th edition, 1990; Foundations of Political Sociology, 1972; Social Science and Public Policy in the United States, 1975; Ideology and Utopia in the United States, 1977; Dialogues on American Politics, 1979; Taking Lives: Genocide and State Power, 1979, 4th edition, 1997; Beyond Empire and Revolution, 1982; C Wright Mills: An American Utopian, 1983; Winners and Losers, 1985; Communicating Ideas, 1987; Daydreams and Nightmares: Reflections of a Harlem Childhood, 1990; The Decomposition of Sociology, 1993. Contributions to: Professional journals. Honours: Harold D Lasswell Award; Festschrift, 1994; National Jewish Book Award in Biography/Autobiography. Memberships: American Academy of Arts and Sciences; American Association of University Professors; American Political Science Association; Authors Guild; Council on Foreign Relations; International Society of Political Psychology, Founder; National Association of Scholars. Literary Agent: Brandt and Brandt. Address: 1247 State Road, Route 206, Blanwenberg Road, Rocky Hill Intersection, Princeton, NJ 08540, USA.

HORSFORD Howard C(larke), b. 26 Nov 1921, Montezuma, Iowa, USA. Professor (retired); Writer. Education: BA magna cum laude, Ripon Collge, 1943; University of Iowa, 1947; MA, 1951, PhD,

1952, Princeton University. Appointments: Instructor, Assistant Professor, Princeton University, 1951-60; Assistant to Full Professor, University of Rochester, 1960-87; Bread Loaf School of English, 1980, 1961, 1963, 1964. Publications: Melville's Journal of a Voyage to Europe and the Levant, 1956-57, 1955; An Oxford Anthology of English Poetry (editor), 1956; The Southern Mandarins: Letters of Caroline Gordon to Sally Wood, 1984; Melville's Journals, 1989. Honours: Phi Beta Kappa, 1955; Bicentennial Preceptor, Princeton University, 1957-60. Memberships: Melville Society, president 1957. Address: Department of English, University of Rochester, NY 14627, USA.

HORTON Felix Lee. See: **FLOREN Lee.**

HORWOOD Harold Andrew, b. 2 Nov 1923, St John's Newfoundland, Canada. Writer. Appointments: Creative Writing Teacher, Memorial University, 1974; Writer in Residence, University of Western Ontario, 1976, University of Waterloo, 1980, 1982. Publications: Tomorrow will be Sunday, 1966; The Foxes of Beachy Cove, 1967; Newfoundland, 1969; White Eskimo, 1972; Death on Ice, 1972; Voices Underground, 1972; Beyond the Road, 1976; Bartlett, 1977; Only the Gods Speak, 1979; Tales of the Labrador Indians, 1981; The Colonial Dream, 1981; A History of Canada, 1983; Pirates and Outlaws of Canada, 1984; Corner Brook, 1986; A History of Newfoundland Ranger Force, 1986; Bandits and Privateers, 1987; Dancing on the Shore, 1987; Joey: The Life and Political Times of Joey Smallwood, 1989; The Power of the Pen, 1989; The Magic Ground, 1996; Evening Light, 1997; Walking in the Dreamtime, 1997. Contributions to: Numerous publications. Honours: Beta Sigma Phi first Novel, 1966; Best Scientific Book of the Year, 1967; Canada Council Senior Arts Award, 1975; Order of Canada, 1980. Memberships: Writers Union of Canada. Address: PO Box 489, Annapolis Royal, Nova Scotia, BOS 1A0, Canada.

HOSAKA Kazushi, b. 1956, Yamanashi Prefecture, Japan. Writer. Education: Graduated, Political Science, Waseda University, Tokyo, 1981. Publications: Plainsong, 1990; Breakfast on the Grass, 1993; Time Passes on Cats, 1994; A Person's Limit, 1995; Memories of Seasons, 1996. Honours: Noma Literary Award for New Writers, 1993; Akutagawa Literary Prize, 1995. Address: c/o Japan PEN Club, 265 Akasaka Residential Hotel, 9-1-7 Akasaka, Minato-ku, Tokyo 107, Japan.

HOSIER Peter. See: **CLARK Douglas.**

HOSILLO Lucila V, b. 29 June 1931, Tanza, Iloilo City, Philippines. Education: AB, English, Far Eastern University, Manila, 1958; AM, Comparative Literature, 1962, PhD 1964, Indiana University, USA. Appointments: Instructor, State University of New York at Buffalo, 1963-64; Assistant Professor, Full Professor of Comparative Literature, University of the Philippines, 1966-85; Visiting Professor, National University of Singapore, 1983-84; Cultural Consultant, Freelance, 1985-. Publications: The Concentric Sphere and Other Essays in Comparative Literature, 1968; Philippine American Literary Relations 1898-1942, 1969; Philippine Literature and Contemporary Events, 1970; Anthology of Third World Poetry, 1978; Originality as Vengeance in Philippine Literature, 1984; Perempuam (Woman), editor, 1987; Hiligaynon Literature: Texts and Contexts, 1992. Contributions to: Books. Honours: 1st Prize, Hiligaynon Short Story Writing Contest, Liwayway Publications, 1969; 1st Prize, ASEAN Literary Contest, Manila, 1977; Grand Prize, Literary Criticism in English, Cultural Centre of the Philippines 10th Anniversary Literary Contest, 1979; 2nd Prize, UNESCO Contest on Least Developed Countries, 1981. Memberships: Federation Internationale des Langues et Literatures Modernes; Association Internationale de Litterature Comparée; American Comparative Literature Association; ASEAN Writers Association; Founder, Chairman and President, Illonggo Language and Literature Foundation Inc. Address: 5 Peace Street, East Fairview 1121, Quezon City, Philippines.

HOSPITAL Janette Turner, b. 12 Nov 1942, Melbourne, Victoria, Australia. Novelist. Education: BA, University of Queensland, Brisbane, 1965; MA, Queen's University, Canada, 1973. Appointments: Lecturer, Queens University, St Lawrence College, Kingston, Ontario, 1971-82; Writer-in-Residence, Massachusetts Institute of Technology, 1985-89; Adjunct Professor, La Trobe University, 1991-93; Visiting Fellow and Writer-In-Residence, University of East Anglia, Norwich, 1996. Publications: The Ivory Swing, 1982; The Tiger in the Tiger Pit, 1983; Borderline, 1985; Charades, 1988; A Very Proper Death, 1990;

The Last Magician, 1992; Oyster, 1996. Contributions to: Times Literary Supplement; London Review of Books; Independent; New York Times; Boston Globe. Honours: Seal Award, 1982; Fellowship of Australian Writers Award, 1988. Address: c/o Mic Cheetham, 138 Buckingham Palace Road, London SW1W 9SA, England.

HOSTE Pol, b. 25 Mar 1947, Lokeren, Belgium. Writer. Education: Licentiate Germanic Philology, State University of Ghent, 1970. Publications: De Veranderingen, 1979; Vrouwelijk Enkelvoud, 1987; Een Schoon Bestaan, 1989; Brieven aan Mozart, 1991; Ontroeringen van een Forens, 1993; High Key, 1995. Address: Kortedagsteeg 31, B-9000 Gent, Belgium.

HOTCHNER Aaron Edward, b. 28 June 1920, St Louis, Missouri, USA. Author; Dramatist. Education: LLB, Washington University, St Louis, 1941. Publications: The Dangerous American, 1958; The White House (play), 1964; Papa Hemingway: A Personal Memoir, 1966; The Hemingway Hero (play), 1967; Treasure, 1970; Do You Take This Man? (play), 1970; King of the Hill, 1972; Looking for Miracles, 1974; Doris Day: Her Own Story, 1976; Sophia: Living and Loving, 1979; Sweet Prince (play), 1980; The Man Who Lived at the Ritz, 1982; Choice People, 1984; Hemingway and His World, 1988; Welcome to the Club (musical), 1989; Blown Away, 1990. Contributions to: Magazines. Honours: Honorary DHL, Washington University, 1992; Distinguished Alumni Award, Washington University Law School, 1992. Memberships: Authors League; Dramatists Guild; PEN. Address: 14 Hillandale Road, Westport, CT 06880, USA.

HOUGH (Helen) Charlotte, b. 24 May 1924, Hampshire, England. Writer. m. Richard Hough, 17 July 1941, div 1973, 4 daughters. Publications: Jim Tiger, 1956; Morton's Pony, 1957; The Hampshire Pig, 1958; The Story of Mr Pinks, 1958; The Animal Game, 1959; The Homemakers, 1959; The Trackers, 1960; Algernon, 1962; Three Little Funny Ones, 1962; The Owl in the Barn, 1964; More Funny Ones, 1965; Red Biddy, 1966; Anna Minnie, 1967; Sir Frog, 1968; My Aunt's Alphabet, 1969; A Bad Child's Book of Moral Verse, 1970; The Bassington Murder, 1980. Memberships: Crime Writers Association; PEN; Society of Authors. Address: 1A Ivor Street, London NW1 9PL, England.

HOUGH Julia Marie. See: **TAYLOR Judy.**

HOUGH Richard Alexander, (Bruce Carter, Elizabeth Churchill, Pat Strong), b. 15 May 1922, Brighton, Sussex, England. Writer. m. (1) Helen Charlotte, 1943, div, 4 daughters. (2) Judy Taylor, 1980. Appointments: Publisher, 1947-70; Bodley Head, 1955; Director, Managing Director, Hamish Hamilton Childrens Books, 1955-70. Publications: The Fleet that Had to Die, 1958; Admirals in Collinson, 1959; The Potemkin Mutiny, 1960; The Big Battleship, 1966; First Sea Lord: An Authorised Life of Admiral Lord Fisher, 1969; The Pursuit of Admiral von Spee, 1969; The Blind Horns Hate, 1971; Captain Bligh and Mr Christian, 1972; One Boy's War, 1975; Advice to a Grand Daughter, 1975; The Great Admirals, 1977; The Murder of Captain James Cook, 1979; Man O War, 1979; Fight to the Finish, 1979; Nelson, 1980; Mountbatten, 1980; Bullers Guns, 1981; Razor Eyes, 1981; Bullers Dreadnought, 1982; Bless Our Ship: Mountbatten and the Kelly, 1982; The Great War at Sea, 1914-1918, 1983; Bullers Victory, 1984; Former Naval Person: Churchill and the Wars at Sea, 1985; The Longest Battle: The War at Sea, 1986; Born Royal: The Lives and Loves of the Young Windsors, 1988; Other Days Around Me (memoirs), 1992; Edward and Alexandra, 1992; Captain James Cook, 1994; Victoria and Albert, 1996. Address: 31 Meadowbank, Primrose Hill, London NW3, England.

HOUGH Stanley Bennett, (Rex Gordon, Bennett Stanley), b . 25 Feb 1917, Preston, Lancashire, England. Author. m. Justa E C Wodschow, 1938. Appointments: Radio Operator, Marconi Company, 1936-38; Radio Officer, International Marine Radio, 1939-45; Professional Yachtsman, 1946-51. Publications: Frontier Incident, 1951; Moment of Decision, 1952; Mission in Guemo, 1953; The Seas South, 1953; The Primitives, 1954; Sea to Eden, 1954; Extinction Bomber, 1956; A Pound a Day Inclusive, 1957; Expedition Everyman, 1959; Beyond the Eleventh Hour, 1961; The Tender Killer, 1962; Where?, 1965; Dear Daughter Dead, 1965; Sweet Sister Seduced, 1968; Fear Fortune Father, 1974; Honour: Infinity Award for Science Fiction, 1957. Membership: Royal Cornwall Polytechnic Society, 1985-88. Address: 21 St Michael's Road, Ponsanooth, Truro TR3 7ED, England.

HOUGHTON Eric, b. 4 Jan 1930, West Yorkshire, England. Teacher; Author. m. Cecile Wolffe, 4 June 1954, 1 son, 1 daughter. Education: Sheffield City College of Education, 1952. Publications include: The White Wall, 1961; Summer Silver, 1963; They Marched with Spartacus, 1963; A Giant Can Do Anything, 1975; The Mouse and the Magician, 1976; The Remarkable Feat of King Caboodle, 1978; Steps Out of Time, 1979; Gates of Glass, 1987; Walter's Wand, 1989; The Magic Cheese, 1991; The Backwards Watch, 1991; Vincent the Invisible, 1993; Rosie and the Robbers, 1997. Contribution to: Review. Honour: American Junior Book Award, 1964. Memberships: Society of Authors; Childrens Writers Group. Address: The Crest, 42 Collier Road, Hastings, East Sussex TN34 3JR, England.

HOUSKOVA Anna, b. 22 Oct 1948, Prague, Czechoslovakia. Professor of Spanish-American Literature. 1 daughter. Education: Charles University, 1966-71; PhD, 1976. Publications: The Novel and The "Genius Loci" (co-author), 1993; Dictionary of Spanish-American Writers, 1996; Utopias of the World (editor), 1992. Contributions to: Ibero-Americana Pragensia, Rumbos (Neuchâtel); Revista Unversidad del Valle (Bogotá); RCLL (Lima). Memberships: Instituto Internacional de Literatura; Iberoamericana (Pittsburgh). Address: Faculty of Philosophy, Charles University, nám Jana Palacha, 116 38 Prague, Czech Republic.

HOUSTON James A(rchibald), b. 12 June 1921, Toronto, Ontario, Canada. Author. m. (1) Alma G Bardon, 1950, div 1966, (2) Alice Daggett Watson, 9 Dec 1967, 2 sons. Education: Ontario College of Art, 1938-40; Academie la Grande Chaumiere, Paris, 1947-48; Unichi-Hiratsuka, Tokyo, 1958-59; Atelier 17, Paris, 1961. Appointments: Arctic Adviser, Canadian Guild of Crafts, 1949-52; Civil Administrator, West Baffin, Northwest Territories, Canada, 1952-62; Associate Director, 1962-72, Master Designer, 1972-, Steuben Glass, New York City; President, Indian and Eskimo Art of the Americas. Publications: Fiction: The White Dawn: An Eskimo Saga, 1971; Ghost Fox, 1977; Spirit Wrestler, 1980; Eagle Song, 1983; Running West, 1989. Children's Books: Over 15 books, 1965-92. Non-Fiction: Canadian Eskimo Art, 1955; Eskimo Graphic Art, 1960; Eskimo Prints, 1967, 2nd edition, 1971; Songs of the Dream People: Chants and Images from the Indians and Eskimos of North America, 1972; Ojibwa Summer, 1972; Confessions of an Igloo Dweller, 1995. Screenplays: The White Dawn, 1973; The Mask and the Drum, 1975; So Sings the Wolf, 1976; Kalvak, 1976. Contributions to: Magazines; Canadian Encyclopedia. Honours: American Indian and Eskimo Cultural Foundation Award, 1966; Canadian Library Association of the Year Awards, 1966, 1968, 1980; American Library Association Notable Books Awards, 1967, 1968, 1971; Officer of the Order of Canada, 1972; Inuit Kuavati Award of Merit, 1979; Citation of Merit Award, Royal Canadian Academy of Arts, 1987; Max and Gretta Ebel Award, Canadian Society of Children's Authors, Illustrators, and Performers, 1989; Honorary doctorates. Memberships: American Indian Arts Center; Canadian Arctic Producers; Canadian Eskimo Arts Center; Explorers Club; Producers Guild of America; Royal Society of the Arts, Fellow; Writers Union of Canada; Writers Guild of Canada. Address: 24 Main Street, Stonington, CT 06378, USA.

HOUSTON R B. See: **RAE Hugh Crauford.**

HOWARD Anthony Michell, b. 12 Feb 1934, London, England. Editor; Writer. m. 26 May 1965. Education: BA, Oxford University, 1955; Called to Bar, Inner Temple, 1956. Appointments: Editor, New Statesman, 1972-78, Listener, 1979-81; Deputy Editor, Observer, 1981-88; Obituaries Editor, The Times. Publications: The Making of the Prime Minister, 1965; The Crossman Diaries: Selections from the Diaries of a Cabinet Minister, 1979; Rab: The Life of R A Butler, 1987; Crossman: The Pursuit of Power, 1990; Lives Remembered, 1993. Contributions to: The Baldwin Age, 1960; The Age of Austerity, 1963; Sunday Times; Times Literary Supplement; New York Times Book Review; Independent; London Review of Books; Spectator. Literary Agent: Peters, Fraser and Dunlop. Address: 11 Campden House Court, 42 Gloucester Walk, London, W8 4HU, England.

HOWARD Clark, b. 1934, USA. Author. Publications: The Arm, 1967; A Movement Toward Eden, 1969; The Doomsday Squad, 1970; The Killings, 1973; Last Contract, 1973; Summit Kill, 1975; Mark the Sparrow, 1975; The Hunters, 1976; The Last Great Death Stunt, 1976; Six Against the Rock, 1977; The Wardens, 1979; Zebra: The True Account of the 179 Days of Terror in San Francisco, 1979, UK edition as The Zebra Killings, 1980; American Saturday, 1981; Brothers in Blood, 1983; Dirt Rich, 1986; Hard City, 1990; Love's Blood, 1993; City

Blood, 1994. Honours: Edgar Allan Poe Award, 1980; Ellery Queen Awards, 1985, 1986, 1988, 1990. Memberships: Mystery Writers of America. Address: The Roslyn Targ Agency, 105 West 13th Street, Suite 15-E, New York, NY 10011, USA.

HOWARD Deborah (Janet), b. 26 Feb 1946, London, England. Architectural Historian; Writer. m. Malcolm S Longair, 26 Sept 1975, 1 son, 1 daughter. Education: BA, Hons, 1968, MA, 1972, Newnham College, Cambridge; MA, 1969, PhD, 1973, University of London. Appointment: Reader in Architectural History, University of Cambridge; Fellow, St John's College, Cambridge. Publications: Jacopo Sansovino: Architecture and Patronage in Renaissance Venice, 1975, 2nd edition, 1987; The Architectural History of Venice, 1980, 3rd edition, 1987; Scottish Architecture from the Reformation to the Restoration, 1560-1660, 1995. Contributions to: Professional journals. Honour: Hon Fellow, Royal Incorporation of Architects of Scotland. Memberships: Commissioner, Royal Commission on the Ancient and Historical Monuments of Scotland; Society of Antiquarians of Scotland; Society of Antiquaries, Fellow; Fellow, Royal Incorporation of Architects in Scotland. Address: St John's College, Cambridge CB2 1TP, England.

HOWARD Elizabeth Jane, b. 26 Mar 1923, London, England. Author. m. (1) Peter Scott, 1941, 1 daughter, (2) Kingsley Amis, 1965, div 1983. Education: Trained as Actress, London Mask Theatre School, Scott Thorndike Student Repertory. Appointments: Honorary Director, Cheltenham Literary Festival, 1962; Co-Director, Salisbury Festival, 1973. Publications: The Beautiful Visit, 1950; The Long View, 1956; The Sea Change, 1959; After Julius, 1965; Odd Girl Out, 1972; The Lovers Companion; Howard and Maschler on Food, 1987; Bettina, 1953; Mr Wrong, 1975; Getting It Right, 1982; The Light Years, 1990; Making Time, 1991; Confusion, 1993; Casting Off, 1995; 14 TV Plays; 3 Film Scripts. Contributions to: The Times; Sunday Times; Telegraph; Encounter; Vogue; Harper's; Queen. Honours: Yorkshire Post Novel of the Year, 1982. Memberships: Fellow, Royal Society of Literature; Authors Lending and Copyright Society. Address: c/o Jonathan Clowes, Ivan Bridge house, Bridge Approach, London NW1 8BD, England.

HOWARD Ellen, b. 8 May 1943, New Bern, North Carolina, USA. Writer. m. Charles Howard Jr, 29 June 1975, 4 daughters. Education: University of Oregon, 1961-63; BA Honors in English, Portland State University, 1979. Publications: Circle of Giving, 1984; Gillyflower, 1986; Edith Herself, 1987; Her Own Song, 1988; The Log Cabin Quilt, 1996. Others: When Daylight Comes, 1985; The Chickenhouse House, 1991; The Cellar, 1992; The Tower Room, 1993; The Big Seed, 1993; Murphy and Kate, 1995; A Different Kind of Courage, 1996. Honours: Golden Kite Honor Book, 1984; International PEN USA Center West, 1989; Children's Middle Grade Award; Christopher Robin Award, 1997. Memberships: Authors Guild; Society of Children's Book Writers and Illustrators, Regional Advisor, Oregon, 1985-88, Michigan, 1992-95. Literary Agent: Emilie Jacobson, Curtis Brown Ltd. Address: 1811 Montview Boulevard, Greeley, CO 80631, USA.

HOWARD Lynette Desley (Lynsey Stevens), b. 28 Sept 1947, Sherwood, Queensland, Australia. Writer; Ex-Librarian. Publications: Ryan's Return, 1981; Terebori's Gold, 1981; Race for Revenge, 1981; Play Our Song Again, 1981; Tropical Knight, 1982; Starting Over, 1982; Man of Vengeance, 1982; Closest Place to Heaven, 1983; Forbidden Wine, 1983; The Ashby Affair, 1983; Lingering Embers, 1984; Leave Yesterday Behind, 1986; But Never Love, 1988; A Rising Passion, 1990; Touched by Desire, 1993; A Physical Affair, 1994. Honour: Arty, Romantic Times, Worldwide Romance, 1984. Memberships: Romantic Novelists Association, UK; Queensland Writers Centre; Australian Society of Authors; Romance Writers of America; Romance Writers of Australia. Address: PO Box 264, Runaway Bay, Queensland 4216, Australia.

HOWARD Maureen, b. 28 June 1930, Bridgeport, Connecticut, USA. Lecturer; Writer. m. (1) Daniel F Howard, 28 Aug 1954, div 1967, 1 daughter, (2) David J Gordon, 2 Apr 1968, div, (3) Mark Probst, 1981. Education: BA, Smith College, 1952. Appointments: Lecturer, New School for Social Research, New York City, 1967-68, 1970-71, 1974-, University of California at Santa Barbara, 1968-69, Amherst College, Brooklyn College of the City University of New York, Columbia University. Publications: Fiction: Not a Word About Nightingales, 1961; Bridgeport Bus, 1966; Before My Time, 1975; Grace Abounding, 1982; Expensive Habits, 1986; Natural History,

1992. Non-Fiction: Facts of Life (autobiography), 1978. Editor: Seven American Women Writers of the Twentieth Century, 1977; Contemporary American Essays, 1984. Honours: Guggenheim Fellowship, 1967-68; Radcliffe Institute Fellow, 1967-68; National Book Critics Circle Award, 1980; Ingram Merrill Foundation Fellow, 1988; Literary Lion Award, New York Public Library, 1993. Address: c/o Simon and Schuster, 1230 Avenue of the Americas, New York, NY 10020, USA.

HOWARD Philip Nicholas Charles, b . 2 Nov 1933, London, England. Writer; Literary Editor. m. Myrtle Janet Mary Houldsworth, 17 Oct 1959, 2 sons, 1 daughter. Education: MA, Major Scholar, Trinity College, Oxford, 1953-57. Appointments: Reporter, Feature Writer, Leader Writer, Parliamentary Correspondent, The Glasgow Herald, 1960-64; Reporter, Feature Writer, Columnist, Leader Writer, 1964-, Literary Editor, 1978-, The Times. Publications: The State of the Language, 1984; We Thundered Out, 200 Years of The Times, 1985; Winged Words, 1988; A Word in Time, 1990. Contributions to: Diverse magazines and journals. Honours: Fellow, Royal Society of Literature, 1985; IPC Press Awards. Memberships: Literary Society; Society of Bookmen; Council, Classical Association; International PEN; Society of Authors; National Union of Journalists. Address: Flat 1, 47 Ladbroke Grove, London W11 3AR, England.

HOWARD Richard (Joseph), b. 13 Oct 1929, Cleveland, Ohio, USA. Poet; Critic; Editor; Translator. Educaton: BA, 1951, MA, 1952, Columbia University; Postgraduate Studies, Sorbonne, University of Paris, 1952-53. Appointments: Lexicographer, World Publishing Company, 1954-58; Poetry Editor, New American Review, New Republic, Paris Review, Shenandoah; Rhodes Professor of Comparative Literature, University of Cincinnati. Publications: Poetry: Quantities, 1962; The Damages, 1967; Untitled Subjects, 1969; Findings, 1971; Two-Part Inventions, 1974; Fellow Feelings, 1976; Misgivings, 1979; Lining Up, 1984; Quantities/Damages, 1984; No Traveller, 1989; Like Most Revelations: New Poems, 1994. Criticism: Alone With America, 1969; Passengers Must Not Ride on Fenders, 1974. Editor: Preferences: Fifty-One American Poets Choose Poems from Their Own Work and from the Past, 1974; The War in Algeria, 1975. Translator: Over 65 books. Contributions to: Magazines and journals. Honours: Guggenheim Fellowship, 1966-67; Harriet Monroe Memorial Prize, 1969; Pulitzer Prize in Poetry, 1970; Levinson Prize, 1973; Cleveland Arts Prize, 1974; American Academy and Institute of Arts and Letters Medal for Poetry, 1980; American Book Award for Translation, 1984; PEN American Center Medal for Translation, 1986; France-American Foundation Award for Translation, 1987; National Endowment for the Arts Fellowship, 1987. Address: c/o Alfred A Knopf Inc, 201 East 50th Street, New York, NY 10022, USA.

HOWARD Roger, b. 19 June 1938, Warwick, England. Theatre Writer; Poet; Lecturer. Education: MA, Drama. Appointments: Writing Fellow, York University, 1976-78, East Anglia University, 1978-79; Lecturer, then, Senior Lecturer, University of Essex, 1979-. Publications: Slaughter Night and Other Plays, 1971; Contemporary Chinese Theatre, 1978; A Break in Berlin, 1979; The Siege, 1981; Senile Poems, 1988; The Tragedy of Mao, 1989; Britannia & Other Plays, 1990; Selected Poems 1966-96, 1997. Contributions to: Transatlantic Review; Stand; Bananas; Times Literary Supplement; Double Space; New Society; Times Education Supplement; Minnesota Review; New Comparison; History of European Ideas; Theatre Quarterly; Plays & Players; Theatre Research International; Journal of American Studies. Address: c/o Theatre Underground, Department of Literature, University of Essex, Wivenhoe Park, Colchester, Essex CO4 3SQ, England.

HOWATCH Susan, b. 14 July 1940, Leatherhead, Surrey, England. Writer. Education: LLB, Kings College, University of London, 1958-61. Publications: The Dark Shore, 1965; The Waiting Sands, 1966; Call in the Night, 1967; The Shrouded Walls, 1968; April's Grave, 1969; The Devil on Lammas Night, 1970; Penmarric, 1971; Cashelmara, 1974; The Rich are Different, 1977; Sins of the Fathers, 1980; The Wheel of Fortune, 1984; Glittering Images, 1987; Glamorous Powers, 1988; Ultimate Prizes, 1989; Scandalous Risks, 1991; Mystical Paths, 1992; Absolute Truths, 1994. Contributions to: Writer; Church Times; Tablet. Honour: Winifred Mary Stanford Memorial Prize, 1992. Memberships: PEN; Society of Authors; Royal Overseas League. Address: c/o Aitken & Stone, 29 Fernshaw Road, London SW10 0TG, England.

HOWCROFT Wilbur Gordon, b. 28 Aug 1917, Kerang, Australia. Writer. m. Barbara Innes McLennan, 17 Aug 1942. Publications: Outback Observations, 1970; This Side of the Rabbit Proof Fence, 1971; The Clancy That Overflowed, 1971; Random Ramblings, 1972; The Farm that Blew Away, 1973; Facts, Fables and Foolery, 1973; Sand in the Stew, 1974; The Old Working Hat, 1975; The Eucalypt Trail, 1975; Black with White Cockatoos, 1977; Dungarees and Dust, 1978; Nonsery Rhymes, 1978; Bush Ballads & Buffoonery, 1979; Bush Ballads and Buldust, 1982; Hello Cocky, 1982; The Bushman Who Laughed, 1982; The Bushman Who Laughed Again, 1983; The Wilbur Howcroft Omnibus, 1985; Bush Characters, 1986; Aussie Odes, 1988; Billabongs and Billy Tea, 1989; Mopokes and Mallee Roots, 1989; Whimsical Wanderings. Contributions to: Frequent Radio and TV appearances; Professional journals, newspapers and magazines. Memberships: Australian Society of Authors. Address: PO Box 36, Culgoa, Vic 3530, Australia.

HOWE James, b. 2 Aug 1946, Oneida, New York, USA. Children's Writer. m. Betsy Imershein, 5 Apr 1981, 1 daughter. Education: BFA, Boston University, 1968; MA, Hunter College, 1977. Publications: Bunnicula, 1979; Teddy Bear's Scrapbook, 1980; The Hospital Book, 1981; Howliday Inn, 1982; A Night Without Stars, 1983; The Celery Stalks at Midnight, 1983; Morgan's Zoo, 1984; The Day the Teacher Went Bananas, 1984; What Eric Knew, 1985; Stage Fright, 1986; When You Go to the Kindergarten, 1986; There's a Monster Under My Bed, 1986; Babes in Toyland, 1986; Eat Your Poison, Dear, 1987; Nighty-Nightmare, 1987; I Wish I Were a Butterfly, 1987; The Fright Before Christmas, 1988; Scared Silly, 1989; Hot Fudge, 1990; Dew Drop Dead, 1990; Pinky and Rex, 1990; Pinky and Rex Get Married, 1990; Pinky and Rex and the Spelling Bee, 1991; Pinky and Red and the Mean Old Witch, 1991; Greepy-Crawly Birthday, 1991; Dances With Wolves: A Story for Children, 1991; Return to Howliday Inn, 1992; Pinky and Rex Go To Camp, 1992; Pinky and Rex and the New Baby, 1993; Rabbit-Cadabral, 1993; Bunnicula Fun Book, 1993; Bunnicula Escapes! A Pop-up Adventure, 1994; There's a Dragon in My Sleeping Bag, 1994; Playing With Words, 1994; Pinky and Rex and the Double-Dad Weekend, 1995. Contributions to: Writing for the Hidden Child in The Horn Book Magazine, 1985; School Library Journal; Writing Mysteries for Children - The Horn Book Magazine, 1990. Address: Writers House, 21 West 26th Street, New York, NY 10010, USA.

HOWE Susan, b. 1937, USA. Poet. Education: BFA in Painting, Museum of Fine Arts, Boston, 1961. Appointments: Butler Fellow in English, 1988, Professor of English, 1989, State University of New York at Buffalo; Visiting Scholar and Professor of English, Temple University, Philadelphia, 1990, 1991; Visiting Poet and Leo Block Professor, University of Denver, 1993-94; Visiting Brittingham Scholar, University of Wisconsin at Madison, 1994; Visiting Poet, University of Arizona, 1994. Publications: Poetry: Hinge Picture, 1974; The Western Borders, 1976; Secret History of the Dividing Line, 1978; Cabbage Gardens, 1979; The Liberties, 1980; Pythagorean Silence, 1982; Defenestration of Prague, 1983; Articulation of Sound Forms in Time, 1987; A Bibliography of the King's Book, or Eikon Basilike, 1989; The Europe of Trusts: Selected Poems, 1990; Singularities, 1990; The Nonconformist's Memorial, 1993. Frame Structures: Early Poems 1974-1979, 1996; Other: My Emily Dickinson, 1985; Incloser, 1990; The Birthmark: Unsettling the Wilderness in American Literary History, 1993. Honours: Before Columbus Foundation American Book Awards, 1980, 1986; New York City Fund for Poetry Grant, 1988; Guggenheim Fellowship for Poetry, 1996; Roy Harvey Pearce Award for the Birth-Mark, 1996. Address: 115 New Quarry Road, Guilford, CT 06437, USA.

HOWE Tina, b. 21 Nov 1937, New York, New York, USA. Playwright; Professor. m. Norman Levy, 1961, 1 son, 1 daughter. Education: BA, Sarah Lawrence College, Bronxville, New York, 1959. Appointments: Adjunct Professor, New York University, 1983-; Visiting Professor, Hunter College, New York, 1990-. Publications: The Nest, 1969; Museum, 1979; The Art of Dining, 1980; Painting Churches, 1984; Coastal Disturbances, 1987. Productions: One Shoe Off, New York, 1993; Approaching Zanzibar and Other Plays, Theatre Communications Group, 1995; Birth and After Birth, Philadelphia and Washington DC, 1995-96. Honours: Obie for Distinguished Playwriting, 1983; Outer Critics Circle Award, 1983; Rockefeller Grant, 1984; Two NEA Fellowships, 1985, 1995; Guggenheim Fellowship, 1990; American Academy of Arts and Letters Award in Literature, 1993. Memberships: Council of the Dramatists Guild, 1990-; PEN. Address: Flora Roberts Inc, 157 West 57th Street, New York, NY 10019, USA.

HOWELL Virginia Tier. See: **ELLISON Virginia Howell.**

HOWELL Anthony, b. 20 Apr 1945, London. Poet; Writer. Education: Leighton Park School; Royal Ballet School, London. Appointments: Lecturer, Grenoble University, 1969-70; Editor, Softly Loudly Books, London; Lecturer (Time based studies), Cardiff School of Art; Editor, Grey Suit, video for Art and Literature. Publications: Poetry: Inside the Castle, 1969; Femina Deserta, 1971; Oslo: A Tantric Ode, 1975; The Mekon, 1976; Notions of a Mirror: Poems, 1964-82, 1983; Winter's Not Gone, 1984; Why I May Never See the Walls of China, 1986; Howell's Law, 1990. Fiction: In the Company of Others, 1986; First Time in Japan, 1995. Honour: Welsh Arts Council Bursary, 1989. Address: 21 Augusta Street, Adamsdown, Cardiff CF2 1EN, Wales.

HOWELLS Coral Ann, b. 22 Oct 1939, Maryborough, Australia. Academic. m. Robin Jonathan Howells, 17 Dec 1963, 2 daughters. Education: BA, 1962, MA, 1965, University of Queensland; PhD, University of London, 1969. Appointment: Professor of English and Canadian Literature, University of Reading, 1990-. Publications: Love, Mystery and Misery: Feeling in Gothic Fiction, 1978, 2nd edition, 1995; Private and Fictional Words: Canadian Women Novelists of the 1970s and 80s, 1987; Jean Rhys, 1991; Margaret Atwood, 1996. Contributions to: Many academic journals. Membership: President, British Association for Canadian Studies, 1992-94. Address: Department of English, University of Reading, Whiternights, Reading RG6 6AA, Berkshire, England.

HOWLAND Bette, b. 28 Jan 1937, Chicago, Illinois, USA. Writer. 2 sons. Education: AB, University of Chicago, 1955. Appointment: Visiting Professor, University of Chicago, 1993. Publications: W3, 1974; Blue in Chicago, 1978; Things to Come and Go, 1983; German Lessons, 1993. Contributions to: Newspapers, journals, and magazines. Honours: Rockefeller Foundation Grant, 1969; Marsden Foundation Grant, 1973; Guggenheim Fellowship, 1978; John D and Catherine T MacArthur Foundation Fellowship, 1984-89. Address: 102 Mulbarger Lane, Bellefonte, PA 16823, USA.

HOYLAND Michael (David), b. 1 Apr 1925, Nagpur, India. Retired Art Lecturer; Author. m. Marette Nicol Fraser, 21 July 1948, 2 sons, 2 daughters. Appointments: School Teacher, 1951-63; Lecturer, 1963-65, Senior Lecturer in Art, 1963-80, Kesteven College of Education. Publications: Introduction Three, 1967; Art for Children, 1970; Variations: An Integrated Approach to Art, 1975; A Love Affair with War, 1981; The Bright Way In, 1984; Dominus-Domina (play); Poems in journals and a collection; 6 Short Stories. Contributions to: Reviewing for Ore; Jade. Memberships: Stamford Writers Group; PEN; Welland Valley Art Society; East Anglian Potters Association. Address: Foxfoot House, South Luffenham, Nr Oakham Rutland, Leics LE15 8NP, England.

HOYLE Sir Fred, b. 24 June 1915, Bingley, Yorkshire, England. Scientist; Honorary Research Professor; Author. m. Barbara Clark, 1939, 1 son, 1 daughter. Education: Emmanuel College, Cambridge. Appointments: Fellow, St John's College, Cambridge, 1939-72; University Lecturer in Mathematics, 1945-58, Plumian Professor of Astronomy and Experimental Philosophy, 1958-72, Director, Institute of Theoretical Astronomy, 1967-73, Cambridge; Staff, Mount Wilson and Palomar Observatories, 1957-62; Visiting Associate in Physics, California Institute of Technology, 1963-; Andrew D White Professor-at-Large, Cornell University, 1972-78; Honorary Research Professor, University of Manchester, 1972-, University College, Cardiff, 1975-. Publications: Non-Fiction: Some Recent Researches in Solar Physics, 1949; The Nature of the Universe, 1951; A Decade of Decision, 1953; Frontiers of Astronomy, 1955; Man and Materialism, 1956; Astronomy, 1962; Star Formation, 1963; Of Men and Galaxies, 1964; Encounter with the Future, 1965; Galaxies, Nuclei and Quasars, 1965; Man in the Universe, 1966; From Stonehenge to Modern Cosmology, 1972; Nicolaus Copernicus, 1973; The Relation of Physics and Cosmology, 1973; Action-at-a-Distance in Physics and Cosmology (with J V Narlikar), 1974; Astronomy and Cosmology, 1975; Astronomy Today, 1975; Ten Faces of the Universe, 1977; On Stonehenge, 1977; Energy or Extinction, 1977; Lifecloud (with N C Wickramasinghe), 1978; The Cosmogony of the Solar System, 1978; Diseases From Space (with N C Wickramasinghe), 1979; Commonsense and Nuclear Energy (with G Hoyle), 1979; The Physics-Astronomy Frontier (with J V Narlikar), 1980; Space Travellers: The Bringers of Life (with N C Wickramasinghe), 1981; Ice, 1981; Evolution from Space (with N C Wickramasinghe), 1981; The Intelligent Universe, 1983; The Small

World of Fred Hoyle, 1986; Archaeopteryx, the Primordial Bird: A Case of Fossil Forgery (with N C Wickramasinghe), 1986; Cosmic Life Force (with N C Wickramasinghe), 1988; The Theory of Cosmic Grains (with N C Wickramasinghe), 1991; Our Place in the Cosmos (with N C Wickramasinghe), 1993; Home is Where the Wind Blows, 1994. Fiction: The Black Cloud, 1957; Ossian's Ride, 1959; A for Andromeda (with J Elliot), 1962; Fifth Planet (with G Hoyle), 1963; Andromeda Breakthrough (with J Elliot), 1964; October the First is Too Late, 1966; Element 79, 1967; Rockets in Ursa Major (with G Hoyle), 1969; Seven Steps to the Sun (with G Hoyle), 1970; The Molecule Men (with G Hoyle), 1971; The Inferno (with G Hoyle), 1973; Into Deepest Space (with G Hoyle), 1973; The Incandescent Ones (with G Hoyle), 1977; The Westminster Disaster (with G Hoyle), 1978. Other: Children's stories. Contributions to: Professional journals. Honours: Gold Medal, Royal Astronomical Society, 1968; Knighted, 1972; Royal Medal, Royal Society, 1974; Dag Hammarskjöld Gold Medal, Académie Diplomatique de la Paix, 1986; Honorary doctorates. Memberships: American Academy of Arts and Sciences, honorary member; American Philosophical Society; Royal Astronomical Society, President, 1971-73; Royal Society, Fellow. Address: c/o The Royal Society, 6 Carlton House Terrace, London SW1Y 5AG, England.

HOYLE Geoffrey, b. 12 Jan 1942, Scunthorpe, Lancashire, England. Author. Education: St John's College, Cambridge, 1961-62. Publications: (with Fred Hoyle): Fifth Planet, 1963; Rockets in Ursa Major, 1969; Seven Steps to the Sun, 1970; The Molecule Men, 1971; The Inferno, 1973; Into Deepest Space, 1974; The Incandescent Ones, 1977; The Westminster Disaster, 1978; Commonsense and Nuclear Energy, 1979. Other: The Energy Pirate, 1982; The Giants of Universal Park, 1982; The Frozen of Azuron, 1982; The Planet of Death, 1982; Flight, 1984. Address: RMYC, RMYCS Enchantress, Sandbanks, Poole, Dorset BH13 7RE, England.

HOYT Erich, b. 28 Sept 1950, Akron, Ohio, USA. Writer. m. Sarah Elizabeth Wedden, 4 Mar 1989, 1 son, 2 daughters. Education: Vannevar Bush Fellow in Science Journalism, Massachusetts Institute of Technology, 1985-86. Appointments: Contributing Editor, Equinox Magazine, Canada, 1982-87; Field Correspondent, Defenders Magazine, USA, 1985-; Visiting Lecturer, Massachusetts Institute of Technology, Cambridge, 1986-87, Ohio State University, 1992-, University of Edinburgh, Medical School, 1994-95; Consultant for science and botanical museums and conservation organizations, 1987-. Publications: Orca: The Whale Called Killer, 1981, 3rd edition, 1990; The Whale Watcher's Handbook, 1984, German edition, 1987; Conserving the Wild Relatives of Crops, 1988, French, Chinese, Portuguese and Spanish editions, 1992; Seasons of the Whale, 1990, French edition, 1993; Extinction A-Z, 1991; Meeting the Whales, 1991; Riding with the Dolphins, 1992; The Earth Dwellers, 1996. Contributions to: Anthologies and textbooks; National Geographic; New York Times; Globe and Mail, Toronto; Discover; Guardian; Over 100 other journals. Honours: Francis H Kortwright Award, 1st place, Magazines, 1983; Environment Canada Award for Best Magazine Article, 1986; BBC Wildlife Award for Nature Writing, 2nd place for Essay, 1988; James Thurber Writer-in-Residence, Thurber House, 1992; 1st Place, Magazines, Outdoor Writers of Canada, 1994; Finalist, ASJA Outstanding Article Award, American Society of Journalists and Authors Inc, 1994; Animal Rights Writing Award, Best Book 1994. Memberships: The Writers Guild; American Society of Journalists and Authors; International Science Writers Association; National Association of Science Writers; Outdoor Writers of Canada; Society for Marine Mammalogy; Association of British Science Writers; Society for Economic Botany; Xerces Society. Address: The Gannetry, 11 Bramerton Court, North Berwick EH39 4BE, Scotland.

HUCKER Hazel Zoë, (Hazel Hucker), b. 7 Aug 1937, London, England. Writer; Novelist; Justice of the Peace. m. His Honour Judge Michael Hucker, 7 Jan 1961, 2 sons (1 deceased), 1 daughter. Education: BSc (Econ) Hons, LSE, 1960. Publications: The Aftermath of Oliver, 1993; La Herencia del Recuerdo, 1994; A Dangerous Happiness, 1994; Cousin Susannah, 1995; Trials of Friendship, 1996. Membership: Society of Authors. Literary Agent: Jennifer Kavanagh, 44 Langham Street, London W1N 5RG, England.

HUDDLE David, b. 11 July, 1942, Ivanhoe, Virginia, USA. Professor of English; Writer; Poet. m. Lindsey M Huddle, 2 daughters. Education: BA, Foreign Affairs, University of Virginia, 1968; MA, English, Hollins College, 1969; MFA, Writing, Columbia University, 1971. Appointments: Faculty, Warren Wilson College, 1981-85; Professor of English, University of Vermont, 1982-; Editor, New

England Review, 1993-94. Publications: A Dream With No Stump Roots In It, 1975; Paper Boy, 1979; Only the Little Bone, 1986; Stopping by Home, 1988; The High Spirits, 1992; The Writing Habit: Essays on Writing, 1992; The Nature of Yearning, 1992; Intimates, 1993; Tenormen, 1995. Contributions to: Esquire; Harper's; New York Times Book Review; Kentucky Poetry Review; Texas Quarterly; Poetry; Shenandoah; American Poetry Review. Honours: Honorary Doctorate of Humanities, Shenandoah College and Conservatory, Virginia, 1989; Bread Loaf School of English Commencement Speaker, 1989; Robert Frost Professor of American Literature, 1991. Address: Department of English, University of Vermont, Burlington, VT 05405, USA.

HUDSON Christopher, b. 29 Sept 1946, England. Writer. m. Kirsty McLeod, 10 Mar 1978, 1 son. Education: Scholar, Jesus College, Cambridge. Appointments: Editor, Faber & Faber, 1968; Literary Editor, The Spectator, 1971, The Standard, 1981; Editorial Page Editor, The Daily Telegraph, 1992. Publications: Overlord, 1975; The Final Act, 1980; Insider Out, 1982; The Killing Fields, 1984; Colombo Heat, 1986; Playing in the Sand, 1989; Spring Street Summer, 1993. Address: Little Dame, Biddendem, Kent TN27 8JT, England.

HUDSON Helen. See: **LANE Helen.**

HUDSON Jeffrey. See: **CRICHTON Michael.**

HUDSON Liam, b. 20 July 1933, London, England. Psychologist; Writer. m. Bernadine Jacot de Boinod, 2 July 1965, 3 sons, 1 daughter. Education: MA, Exeter College, 1954-57; PhD, Cambridge University, 1957-61. Publications: Contrary Imaginations, 1966; Frames of Mind, 1968; The Ecology of Human Intelligence, 1970; The Cult of the Fact, 1972; Human Beings, 1975; The Nympholepts, 1978; Bodies of Knowledge, 1982; Night Life, 1985; The Way Men Think, 1991; Intimate Relations, 1995. Contributions to: Times Literary Supplement. Honour: Tanner Lectures, Yale University, 1997. Membership: British Psychological Society. Address: Balas Copartnership, 34 North Park, Gerrards Cross, Bucks, England.

HUDSON Michael. See: **KUBE-MCDOWELL Michael Paul.**

HUFANA Alejandrino G, b. 22 Oct 1926, San Fernando, La Union, Philippines. Editor; Writer. Education: AB, 1952, MA, 1961, University of the Philippines; University of California at Berkely, 1957-58; MS, Columbia University, 1969. Appointments: Research Assistant, 1954-56; English Department, 1956, Principle Research, Iloko Literature, 1972, Professor, 1975, University of Philippines; Co-Founding Editor, Signatures Magazine, 1955, Comment Magazine, 1956-67, Heritage Magazine, 1967-68, University College, 1961-72; Editor, Panorama Magazine, 1959-61; Managing Editor, University of the Philippines Press, 1965-66; Director, 1970, Editor, 1971, Pamana Magazine, Cultural Centre of the Philippines; Associate, University of Philippines, 1979-82; Literary Editor, Heritage Magazine, 1987-. Publications: 13 Kalisud, 1955; Man in the Moon, 1956; Sickle Season, 1948-58, 1959; Poro Print, 1955-1960, 1961; Curtain Raisers: First Five Plays, 1964; A Philippine Cultural Miscellany, 1970; The Wife of Lot and Other New Poems, 1971; Notes on Poetry, 1973; Philippine Writing, 1977; Shining On, 1985; Dumanon, 1994; No Facetious Claim: Notes on Writers and Writing, 1995. Address: c/o Heritage, 20218 Tajauta Avenue, Carson, CA 90746, USA.

HUGGETT Joyce, b. 16 Sept 1937, Exeter, England. Teacher. m. David John Huggett, 16 July 1960, 1 son, 1 daughter. Appointments: Teacher, Nuffield Priory School, 1960-62; Peripatetic Teacher, Health Centre, Croydon, 1963-65, Cambridge, 1971-73; Director of Pastoral Care and Counselor, St Nicholas Church, 1973-; Regular Broadcaster on TV and Radio. Publications: Two into One: Relating in Christian Marriage, 1981; Growing into Love; We Believe in Marriage, 1982; Growing into Freedom, 1984; Conflict: Friend or Foe, 1984; Just Good Friends, 1985; The Joy of Listening to God, 1986; Writer of Scripture Notes: Open to God, 1989; The Smile of Love: Scripture Notes for Scripture Union and Bible Reading Fellowship. Contributions to: Magazines and newspapers. Address: 18 Lenton Road, The Park, Nottingham NG7 1DU, England.

HUGHES Brenda. See: **COLLOMS Brenda.**

HUGHES David (John), b. 27 July 1930, Alton, Hampshire, England. Writer; Critic; Editor. m. (1) Mai Zetterling, 1957, (2) Elizabeth

Westoll, 1980, 1 son, 1 daughter. Education: MA, Christ Church, Oxford. Appointments: Editorial Assistant, London Magazine, 1960-61, New Fiction Society, 1975-78, 1981-82, Letters, journal of the Royal Society of Literature, 1992-96; Assistant Visiting Professor, University of Iowa, 1978-79, 1987, University of Alabama, 1979; Film Critic, Sunday Times, 1982-83; Fiction Critic, Mail on Sunday, 1982-; Visiting Associate Professor, University of Houston, 1986; Editor, Letters, 1992-96, Theatre Critic, 1996, Mail on Sunday. Publications: Fiction: A Feeling in the Air, 1957; Sealed with a Loving Kiss, 1958; The Horsehair Sofa, 1961; The Major, 1964; The Man Who Invented Tomorrow, 1968; Memories of Dying, 1976; A Genoese Fancy, 1979; The Imperial German Dinner Service, 1983; The Pork Butcher, 1984, film version as Souvenir, 1989; But for Bunter, 1985; The Little Book, 1996. Non-Fiction: J B Priestley: An Informal Study, 1958; The Road to Stockholm, 1964; The Seven Ages of England, 1967; The Rosewater Revolution, 1971; Evergreens, 1976; Himself and Other Animals, 1997. Editor: Winter's Tales: New Series I, 1985; Best Short Stories (with Giles Gordon), 10 volumes, 1986-95; The Best of Best Short Stories 1986-1995, 1995. Honours: Welsh Arts Council Fiction Prize, 1984; W H Smith Literary Award, 1985. Membership: Fellow, Royal Society of Literature. Literary Agent: Giles Gordon, Curtis Brown. Address: 163 Kennington Road, London SE11 6SF, England.

HUGHES Glyn, b. 25 May 1935, Middlewich, Cheshire, England. Author; Poet. m. Jane Mackay, 5 Mar 1990, 1 son. Education: College of Art, Manchester, 1952-56. Appointments: Teacher, Lancaster and Yorkshire, 1956-72; Art Council Fellow, Bishop Grosseteste College, Lincoln, 1979-81; Southern Arts Writer-in-Residence, Farnborough, 1982-84; Arts Council Writer-in-Residence, D H Lawrence Centenary Festival, 1985. Publications: Novels: Where I Used to Play on the Green, 1982; The Hawthorn Goddess, 1984; The Antique Collector, 1990; Roth, 1992; Bronte, 1996. Autobiography: Millstone Grit, 1975; Fair Prospects, 1976. Verse: Neighbours, 1970; Rest the Poor Straggler, 1972; Best of Neighbours, 1979. Plays, Mary Hepton's Heaven, 1984; Various Plays for BBC School Broadcasts on TV and Radio. Honours: Welsh Arts Council Poets Prize, 1970; Guardian Fiction Prize, 1982; David Higham Fiction Prize, 1982. Literary Agent: Mic Cheetham. Address: Mors House, 1 Mill Bank Road, Mill Bank, Sowerby Bridge, West Yorkshire HX6 3DY, England.

HUGHES Ian. See: **PATERSON Alistair.**

HUGHES Matilda. See: **MACLEOD Charlotte.**

HUGHES Monica (Ince), b. 3 Nov 1925, Liverpool, England. Writer. m. Glen Hughes, 22 Apr 1957, 2 sons, 2 daughters. Publications: Crisis on Conshelf Ten, 1975; The Keeper of the Isis Light, 1980; Hunter in the Dark, 1982; Ring-Rise, Ring-Set, 1982; Invitation to the Game, 1991; The Crystal Drop, 1992; The Golden Aquarians, 1994; Castle Tourmandyne, 1995; Where Have You Been, Billy Boy?, 1995; The Seven Magpies, 1996. Contributions to: Various publications. Literary Agent: Pamela Paul, 253 High Park Avenue, Toronto, Ontario M6P 2S5, Canada. Address: 13816-110A Avenue, Edmonton, Alberta T5M 2M9, Canada.

HUGHES Richard Joseph, b. 8 July 1931, Melbourne, Australia. Journalist; Jazz Pianist. m. Fay Parsons, 5 June 1962, 3 daughters. Education: BA Hons, University of Melbourne, 1951. Publications: Daddy's Practising Again, 1977; Don't You Sing!, 1994. Contributions to: Quadrant; The Bulletin; Australian Jazz Quarterly; Australian Blues and Jazz Journal. Literary Agent: Curtis Brown. Address: Conga Brava, 11 Girilang Avenue, Vaucluse, New South Wales 2030, Australia.

HUGHES Robert (Studley Forrest), b. 28 July 1938, New South Wales, Australia. Writer; Art Critic; Maker of Television Documentaries. m. 1 son. Education: University of Sydney. Publications: Many books, essays, and exhibition catalogues. Other: Various television documentaries. Address: c/o Time Magazine, Time-Life Building, Rockefeller Center, New York, NY 10020, USA.

HUGHES Shirley, b. 16 July 1927, Hoylake, England. Children's Fiction Writer, Illustrator. Education: Liverpool Art School; Ruskin School of Drawing and Fine Arts, Oxford. Appointments: Public Lending Right Registrars Advisory Committee, 1984-88; Library and Information Services Council, 1989-92. Publications: Lucy & Tom Series, 6 volumes, 1960-87; The Trouble with Jack, 1970; Sallys Secret, 1973; It's too Frightening for Me, 1977; Moving Molly, 1978; Up and Up, 1979; Charlie Moon and the Big Bonanza Bust Up, 1982; An

Evening at Alfies, 1984; The Nursery Collection, 6 volumes, 1985-86; Another Helping of Chips, 1986; The Big Alfie and Annie Rose Story Book, 1988; Out and About, 1989; The Big Alfie Out of Doors Story Book, 1992. Honours: Kate Greenaway Medal for Dogger, 1977; Eleanor Farjeon Award, 1984. Membership: Society of Authors.

HUGHES Ted, (Edward James Hughes), b. 17 Aug 1930, Mytholmroyd, West Yorkshire, England. Poet; Dramatist; Author; Poet; Poet Laureate of England. m. (1) Sylvia Plath, 1956, dec 1963, 1 son, 1 daughter, (2) Carol Orchard, 1970. Education: BA, 1954, MA, 1959, Pembroke College, Cambridge. Appointments: Founding Editor (with Daniel Weissbort), Modern Poetry in Translation magazine, London, 1964-71; Poet Laureate of England, 1984-. Publications: Poetry: The Hawk in the Rain, 1957, new edition, 1968; Pike, 1959; Lupercal, 1960; Meet My Folks (children's verse), 1961; Selected Poems (with Thom Gunn), 1962; How the Whale Became (children's stories), 1963; The Burning of the Brothel, 1966; Recklings, 1967; Scapegoats and Rabies, 1967; Wodwo, 1967; Poetry in the Making (prose), 1967; Animal Poems, 1967; Gravestones, 1967; The Iron Man (children's story), 1968; I Said Goodbye to Earth, 1969; Seneca's Oedipus (adaptation), 1969; A Crow Hymn, 1970; The Martyrdom of Bishop Farrar, 1970; The Coming of the Kings (children's plays), 1970; A Few Crows, 1970; Four Crow Poems, 1970; Crow: From the Life and Songs of the Crow, 1970, revised edition, 1972; Fighting for Jerusalem, 1970; Amulet, 1970; Crow Wakes, 1971; Poems (with Ruth Fainlight and Alan Sillitoe), 1971; In the Little Girl's Angel Gaze, 1972; Selected Poems 1957-1967, 1972; Prometheus on His Crag, 1973; The Interrogator: A Titled Vulturess, 1975; Cave Birds, 1975, revised edition as Cave Birds: An Alchemical Cave Drama, 1978; The New World, 1975; Eclipse, 1976; Gaudete, 1977; Chiasmadon, 1977; Sunstruck, 1977; A Solstice, 1978; Orts, 1978; Moortown Elegies, 1978; Adam and the Sacred Nine, 1979; Remains of Elmet: A Pennine Sequence, 1979, 3rd edition, revised, as Elmet: Poems, 1994; Four Tales Told by an Idiot, 1979; Moortown, 1979, revised edition as Moortown Diary, 1989; Sky-Furnace, 1981; A Primer of Birds, 1981; Selected Poems 1957-1981, 1982; River, 1983; What is the Truth? (children's verse), 1984; Flowers and Insects: Some Birds and a Pair of Spiders, 1986; Tales of the Early World, 1988; Wolfwatching, 1989; Capriccio, 1990; The Unicorn, 1992; Nessie and the Mannerless Monster (children's), new edition, 1992; The Iron Woman (children's), 1993; Rain-Charm for the Duchy and Other Laureate Poems, 1993; Earth Dances, 1994; The Dreamfighter and other Creation Tales (children's, 1995; New Selected Poems 1957-1994, 1995. Plays: The House of Aries, 1960; The Calm, 1961; The Wound, 1962, revised edition, 1972; Epithalamium, 1963; The House of Donkeys, 1965; Oedipus (adaptation of Seneca's play), 1968; Orghast, 1971; Eat Crow, 1971. Plays for Children: Several. Stories: The Threshold, 1979; The Dreamfighter and Other Creation Tales, 1995; Difficulties of a Bridegroom, 1996. Other: Henry Williamson: A Tribute, 1979; Shakespeare and the Goddess of Complete Being, 1992; A Dancer to God: Tributes to T S Eliot, 1992; Winter Pollen: Occasional Prose, 1995. Editor: New Poems 1962 (with Patricia Beer and Vernon Scannell), 1962; Here Today, 1963; Five American Poets (with Thom Gunn), 1963; A Choice of Emily Dickinson's Verse, 1968; With Fairest Flowers While Summer Last: Poems from Shakespeare, 1971; New Poetry 6, 1980; The Collected Poems of Sylvia Plath, 1981; The Journals of Sylvia Plath (with Frances McCullough), 1982; 1980 Anthology: Arvon Foundation Poetry Competition (with Seamus Heaney), 1982; The Rattle Bag: An Anthology (with Seamus Heaney), 1982; Sylvia Plath's Selected Poems, 1985. Honours: First Publication Award, New York Poetry Center, 1957; 1st Prize, Guinness Poetry Awards, 1958; Guggenheim Fellowship, 1959-60; Somerset Maugham Award, 1960; Hawthornden Prize, 1961; International Poetry Prize, 1969; Premio Internazionale Taormina, 1973; Queen's Gold Medal for Poetry, 1974; Officer of the Order of the British Empire, 1977; Signed Poetry Awards, 1979, 1983, 1985; Heinemann Award, Royal Society of Literature, 1980; Poet Laureate of England, 1984-; Guardian Children's Fiction Award, 1985; Maschler Award, 1985; Honorary Fellow, Pembroke College, Cambridge, 1986. Address: c/o Faber and Faber Ltd., 3 Queen Square, London WC1N 3AU, England.

HUHNE Christopher Murray Paul, b. 2 July 1954, London, England. Economist. m. Vasiliki Courmouzis, 19 May 1984, 2 sons, 1 daughter. Education: Sorbonne, University of Paris, 1972; BA, Oxford University, 1975. Publications: Debt and Danger, 1985, 1987; Real World Economics, 1990; The ECU Report, 1991. Honours: Wincott Awards for Financial Journalism, 1981, 1990. Membership: Royal Economics Society. Address: 8 Crescent Grove, London SW4 7AH, England.

HULME Keri, b. 9 Mar 1947, Christchurch, New Zealand. Writer. Education: Canterbury University, Christchurch. Publications: The Silences Between, 1982; The Bone People, 1984; Lost Possessions, 1986; Te Kaihau, the Windeater, 1986; Homeplaces, 1989; Strands, 1992; Bait, 1996. Contributions to: Various publications. Honours: New Zealand Writing Bursary, 1983; New Zealand Book of the Year, 1984; Mobil Pegasus Prize, 1984; Booker McConnell Award, 1985; Special Scholarship in Letters, 1990. Memberships: New Zealand Society of Authors; Nga Puna Wailhanga. Address: PO Box 1, Whataroa, South Westland, Aotearoa, New Zealand.

HULSE Michael William, b. 12 June 1955, Stoke on Trent, England. Freelance Translator; Critic; Poet. Education: MA, University of St Andrews, 1977. Appointment: English Editor, Benedikt Taschen Verlag, 1988. Publications: Monochrome Blood, 1980; Dole Queue, 1981; Knowing and Forgetting, 1981; Propaganda, 1985.Contributions to: About 200 Essays and Reviews. Honours: 1st Prize, National Poetry Competition, 1979; Eric Gregory Award, 1980; 3rd Prize, Tate Gallery Poetry Competition, 1985; 2nd Prize, Times Literary Supplement, Cheltenham Literature Festival Poetry Competition, 1987. Address: c/o Secker & Warburg Ltd, 54 Poland Street, London W1V 3DF, England.

HUME George Hailburton, (Basil Hume), b. 2 Mar 1923, Newcastle upon Tyne, England. Education: M, St Benets Hall, 1947; STL, University of Fribourg, 1951. Appointments: Entered Ordo Sancti Benedicti, 1941; Ordained Priest, Ampleforth, 1950; Senior Master in Modern Languages, 1952-63; Housemaster, St Bede's, 1955-63; Professor of Dogmatic Theology, 1955-63; Magister Scholarum, English Benedictine Congregation, 1957-63; Abbot of Ampleforth, 1963-76; Chairman, Benedictine Ecumenical Commission, 1972-76; Installed as Archbishop of Westminster, 1976; Created Cardinal-Priest of the Title San Silvestro in Capite, 1976; President, Council of Christians and Jews. Publications: Searching for God, 1977; In Praise of Benedict, 1981; To BE a Pilgrim: A Spiritual Notebook, 1984; Towards a Civilisation of Love, 1988; Light in the Lord, 1991; Remaking Europe, 1994; Footprints of the Northern Saints, 1996; The Mystery of Love, 1996. Contributions to: Periodicals. Honours: Hon DD: Cambridge, 1979, Newcastle upon Tyne, 1979, London, 1980, Oxon, 1981, York, 1982, Kent, 1983, Durham, 1987, Collegio S Anselm, Rome, 1987, Hull, 1989, Keele, 1990; Hon DHL: Manhattan College, New York, 1980, Catholic University of America, 1980; Hon Doctor of Law: University of Northumbria at Newcastle, 1992; Hon D, University of Surrey, 1992; Member of Athenaeum Club; Hon Freeman, Worshipful Company of Skinners, 1994; Honorary Bencher of Inner Temple, 1976; Hon Freeman of London and Newcastle upon Tyne, 1980. Memberships: President, Bishops' Conference of England and Wales, 1979; President, Council of European Bishops' Conferences, 1978-87; Joint President, Churches Together in England, 1990-; Congregation for the Sacraments and Divine Worship; Congregation for Religious and Secular Institutes; Congregation for Eastern Churches; Pontifical Council for the Promotion of Christian Unity; Pontifical Council for Pastoral Assistance to Health Care Workers; Relator for the Synod on Consecrated Life, 1994. Address: Archbishops House, Ambrosden Avenue, Westminster, London SW1P 1QJ, England.

HUME John Robert, b. 26 Feb 1939, Glasgow, Scotland. Lecturer; Writer. Education: BSc, University of Glasgow, 1961. Appointments: Lecturer, 1964-82, Senior Lecturer, University of Strathclyde, 1982-; Treasurer, 1968-71, Editor, 1971-79, Scottish Society for Industrial Archaeology; Director, Scottish Industrial Archaeology Survey, 1978-85; Seconded to Historic Scotland as Principal Inspector of Ancient Monuments, 1984-91, Principal Inspector of Historic Buildings, 1991-93, Chief Inspector of Historic Buildings, 1993-. Publications: Industrial History in Pictures: Scotland, 1968; Glasgow as it Was, 3 volumes, 1975-76; A Plumbers Pastime, 1975; The Workshop of the British Empire, The Industrial Archaeology of Scotland: The Lowlands and Borders, 1976; The Highlands and the Islands, 1977; Beardmore: History of a Scottish Industrial Giant, 1979; A Bed of Nails, 1983; Shipbuilders to the World: A History of Harland Wolff, Belfast, 1986; Various Guidebooks to Historic Scotland Monuments in Care. Honour: Andre Simon Prize, 1981. Memberships: Society of Antiquaries: Society of Antiquarie of Scotland. Address: Historic Scotland, Longmire House, Salisbury Place, Edinburgh EN9 15Y, Scotland.

HUMPHREYS Emyr Owen, b. 15 Apr 1919, Clwyd, Wales. Author. m. Elinor Myfanwy, 1946, 3 sons, 1 daughter. Education:

University College, Aberystwyth; University College, Bangor. Publications: The Little Kingdom, 1945; The Voice of a Stranger, 1949; A Change of Heart, 1951; Hear and Forgive, 1952; A Mans Estate, 1955; The Italian Wife, 1957; A Toy Epic, 1958; The Gift, 1963; Outside the House of Baal, 1965; Natives, 1968; Ancestor Worship, 1970; National Winner, 1971; Flesh and Blood, 1974; Landscapes, 1976; The Best of Friends, 1978; The Kingdom of Bran, 1979; The Anchor Tree, 1980; Pwyll a Riannon, 1980; Miscellany Two, 1981; The Taliesin Tradition, 1983; Salt of the Earth, 1985; An Absolute Hero, 1986; Open Secrets, 1988; The Triple Net, 1988; Bonds of Attachment, 1990; Outside Time, 1991. Honours: Somerset Maugham Award, 1953; Hawthornden Prize, 1959; Society of Authors Travel Award, 1978; Welsh Arts Council Prize, 1983; Honorary DLitt, University of Wales, 1990 L1; Welsh Book of the Year, 1992; Honorary Professor of English, University College of North Wales, Bagnor. Literary Agent: Richard Scott Simon. Address: Llinon, Penyberth, Llanfairpwll, Ynys Môn, Gwynedd LL61 5YT, Wales.

HUMPHRYES Josephine, b. 2 Feb 1945, Charleston, South Carolina, USA. Novelist. m. Thomas A Hutcheson, 30 Nov 1968, 2 sons. Education: AB, Duke University, 1967; MA, Yale University, 1968. Publications: Dreams of Sleep, 1984; Rich in Love, 1987; The Fireman's Fair, 1991. Contributions to: Newspapers and periodicals. Honours: PEN, Ernest Hemingway Foundation, 1985; Guggenheim Fellowship, 1985; Lyndhurst Prize, 1986. Address: c/o Harriet Wasserman, 137 East 36th Street, New York, NY 10016, USA.

HUMPHRY Derek John, b. 29 Apr 1930, Bath, England. Journalist; Author; Broadcaster. Appointments: Messenger Boy, Yorkshire Post, London, 1945-56; Cub Reporter, Evening World, Bristol, 1946-51; Junior Reporter, Evening News, Manchester, 1951-55; Reporter, Daily Mail, 1955-61; Deputy Editor, The Luton News, 1961-63; Editor, Havering Recorder, 1963-67, Hemlock Quarterly, 1983-92, Euthanasia Review, 1986-88, World Right to Die Newsletter, 1992-94; Home Affairs Correspondent, Special Writer, Los Angeles Times, 1978-79. Publications: Because They're Black, 1971; Police Power and Black People, 1972; Passports and Politics, 1974; False Messiah, 1977; The Cricket Conpiracy, 1976; Jean's Way, 1978; Let Me Die Before I Wake, 1982; The Right to Die!: Understanding Euthanasia, 1986; Final Exit, 1991; Dying with Dignity, 1992; Lawful Exit, 1993. Contributions to: New Statesman; Independent, London; USA Today; Joint Editor, The Euthanasia Review, New York. Literary Agent: Robert I Ducas, 350 Hudson St, New York, NY 10014, Address: 24829 Norris Lane, Junction City, OR 97448-9559, USA.

HUNT Bruce J(ames), b. 23 June 1956, Walla Walla, Washington, USA. Associate Professor of History; Writer. m. Elizabeth Hedrick, 17 July 1992, 1 son. Education: BA in History and BS in Physics, University of Washington, Seattle, 1979; PhD in the History of Science, Johns Hopkins University, 1984. Appointments: Assistant Professor, 1985-92, Associate Professor of History, 1992-, University of Texas at Austin; Visiting Fellow, Clare Hall, Cambridge, 1989-90. Publication: The Maxwellians, 1991. Contributions to: Scholarly books and journals, 1983-97. Honours: Fulbright Fellowship, England, 1981-82; Smithsonian Institution Postdoctoral Fellowship, 1984; National Science Foundation Grant, 1989. Memberships: British Society for the History of Science; History of Science Society; Society for the History of Technology. Address: c/o Department of History, University of Texas at Austin, Austin, TX 78712, USA.

HUNT Fay Ann, (Annie Hedley), b. 18 July 1935, Cornwall, England. Farmer; Teacher; Writer. div, 3 sons. Education: Redland College of Education. Publications: Listen: Let's Make Music, 1980; Look at Home Before you Look Away, 1983; Creative Activities for the Mentally Handicapped, 1986; Motherin' Sunday, 1990. Contributions to: TES; Lancet; Special Education; Cornish Scene; Observer; Correspondent; Western Morning News; Cornish Times. Honours: 1st Prize, Ian S James Award, 1990. Memberships: West Country Writers Association. Literary Agent: Gill Coleridge, Coleridge, White & Taylor. Address: Clift Farmhouse, Anthony, Torpoint, Cornwall PL11 2PH, England.

HUNT Francesca. See: **HOLLAND Isabelle.**

HUNT Gill. See: **TUBB E(dwin) C(harles).**

HUNT Morton M(agill), b. 20 Feb 1920, Philadelphia, Pennsylvania, USA. Writer. m. (3)Bernice Weinick, 10 Sept 1951. Education: AB, Temple University, 1941. Publications: The Natural

History of Love, 1959; Her Infinite Variety: The American Woman as Lover, Mate and Rival, 1962; The Affair: A Portrait of Extramarital Love in Contemporary America, 1969; The Mugging, 1972; Sexual Behaviour in the 1970's, 1974; Prime Time: A Guide to the Pleasures and Opportunities of the New Middle Age, 1975; The Divorce Experience, 1977; Profiles of Social Research: The Scientific Study of Human Interaction, 1985; The Compassionate Beast: What Science is Discovering About the Humane Side of Humankind, 1990; The Story of Psychology, 1993. Contributions to: Newspapers and periodicals. Honours: American Association for the Advancement of Science Westinghouse Award, 1952; Claude Bernard Award, 1971; American Society of Journalists and Authors, 1983. Address: 15 Kingstown Avenue, East Hampton, NY 11937, USA.

HUNT Sam, b. 4 July 1946, Auckland, New Zealand. Poet. Publications: Between Islands, 1964; A Fat Flat Blues, 1969; Selected Poems, 1965-69, 1970; A Song About Her, 1970; Postcard of a Cabbage Tree, 1970; Bracken Country, 1971; Letter to Jerusalem, 1971; Bottle Creek Blues, 1971; Bottle Creek, 1972; Beware the Man, 1972; Birth on Bottle Creek, 1972; South into Winter, 1973; Roadsong Paekakariki, 1973; Time to Ride, 1976; Drunkards Garden, 1978; Collected Poems, 1963-80, 1980; Three Poems of Separation, 1981; Running Scared, 1982; Approaches to Paremata, 1985; Selected Poems, 1987. Address: PO Box 1, Mana, Wellington, New Zealand.

HUNT Tim(othy Arthur), b. 22 Dec 1949, Calistoga, California, USA. College Teacher. m. Susan D Spurlock, 1 son, 1 daughter. Education: AB cum laude, 1970; MA, 1974; PhD, 1975, Cornell University. Appointments: Assistant, Associate Professor, English Department, Indiana-Purdue University, Fort Wayne, 1985-87; Academic Dean, Deep Springs College, California, 1987-90; Associate Professor of English, Coordinator for Humanities, Washington State University, Vancouver, 1990-. Publications: Kerouac's Crooked Road: Development of a Fiction, 1981; The Collected Poetry of Robinson Jeffers: Vol 1, 1920-28; 1988; Vol II, 1928-38, 1989; Vol III, 1938-62, 1991. Contributions to: Various publications, Address 323 North West 74th Street, Vancouver, WA 98665, USA.

HUNTER Alan James Herbert, b. 25 June 1922, Hoveton St John, Norwich, England. Author. m. Adelaide Elizabeth Cecily Cubitt, 6 Mar 1944, 1 daughter. Education: RAF, 1940-46. Appointments: Crime Reviewer, Eastern Daily Press, 1955-71. Publications: Gently Go Man, 1961; Vivienne: Gently Where She Lay, 1972; The Honfleur Decision, 1980; Gabrielles Way, 1981; The Unhung Man, 1984; Traitors End, 1988; Bomber's Moon, 1994; The Norwich Poems, 1945; Author of 43 crime novels to 1996. Contributions to: Magazines and journals. Memberships: Society of Authors; Crime Writers Association; Authors Licensing and Collecting Society. Address: 3 St Laurence Avenue, Brundall, Norwich NR13 5QH, England.

HUNTER Elizabeth. See: **DE GUISE Elizabeth (Mary Teresa).**

HUNTER Evan. See: **LOMBINO Salvatore A.**

HUNTINGTON Samuel (Phillips), b. 18 Apr 1927, New York, New York, USA. Political Scientist; Writer. m. Nancy Alice Arkelyan, 8 Sept 1957, 2 sons. Education: BA, Yale University, 1946; MA, University of Chicago, 1948; PhD, Harvard University, 1951. Appointments: Instructor, 1950-53, Assistant Professor, 1953-58, Professor of Government, 1962-, Research Associate, 1963-64, Faculty, 1964-, Associate Director, 1973-78, Acting Director, 1975-76, Director, 1978-89, Center for International Affairs, Thomson Professor of Government, 1967-81, Clarence Dillon Professor of International Affairs, 1981-82, Eaton Professor of the Science of Government, 1982-, Director, John M Olin Institute for Strategic Studies, 1989-, Harvard University; Research Associate, Brookings Institution, Washington, DC, 1952-53; Research Fellow, Social Science Research Council, New York City, 1954-57; Assistant Director, 1958-59, Research Associate, 1958-63, Associate Director, 1959-62, Associate Professor of Government, 1959-62, Institute of War and Peace Studies, Columbia University; Fellow, Center for Advanced Study in the Behavioral Sciences, Stanford, California, 1969-70; Co-Editor, Foreign Policy Quarterly, 1970-77; Visiting Fellow, All Souls College, Oxford, 1973; Coordinator, Security Planning, National Security Council, 1977-78. Publications: The Soldier and the State: The Theory and Politics of Civil-Military Relations, 1957; The Common Defense: Strategic Programs in National Politics, 1961; Changing Patterns of Military Politics (co-editor), 1962; Political Power: USA/USSR (co-author), 1964; Political Order in Changing Societies, 1968;

Authoritarian Politics in Modern Society: The Dynamics of Established One-Party Systems (co-editor), 1970; The Crisis of Democracy (co-author), 1975; No Easy Choice: Political Participation in Developing Countries (with J M Nelson), 1976; American Politics: The Promise of Disharmony, 1981; The Strategic Imperative: New Policies for American Security, 1982; Living with Nuclear Weapons (co-author), 1983; Global Dilemmas (co-editor), 1985; Reorganizing America's Defense (co-editor), 1985; Understanding Political Development (co-editor), 1987; The Third Wave: Democratization in the Late Twentieth Century, 1991; The Clash of Civilizations and the Remaking of the World Order, 1996. Contributions to: Professional journals. Honours: Silver Pen Award, 1960; Grawemayer World Order Award, 1992. Memberships: American Academy of Arts and Sciences, Fellow; American Political Science Association, President, 1986-87; Council on Foreign Relations; International Institute for Strategic Studies; International Political Science Association. Address: c/o John M Olin Institute for Strategic Studies, Harvard University, 1737 Cambridge Street, Cambridge, MA 02138, USA.

HUOT Cécile, b. 2 May 1919, Boischatel, Quebec, Canada. Teacher. Education: BA, 1958, Licence, 1965, Laval University; B Pedogogie, Licence, Montreal University, 1959-61; Doctorat, Lettres, Toulouse, France, 1973. Publications: Une Symphonie inachevée, Wilfrid Pelletier's Mémoirs, 1972; Entretiens avec Omer Létourneau, 1979; More than 70 items for The Encyclopédie de la Musique au Canaca Fides, 1983, new edition, 1993; Dictionnaire des Genres, 1983, new edition, 1991; Simon Violon m'etait conté, 1988. Contributions to: Les Cahiers Canadiens de la Musique. Memberships: L'Union des Ecrivains Québécois; Conseil International d'Etudes Francophones. Address: 5025 ave Notre Dame de Grace, Montreal, Quebec H4A 1K2, Canada.

HURBON Laennec, b. 21 June 1940, France. Sociologist; Director. m. 17 Mar 1994, 1 son, 1 daughter. Education: DTh, 1972, Diploma, Social Sciences, 1973, Doctor in Sociology, 1976, Paris. Publications: Dieu daus le roodon haithen, 1972; Culture et dictatune en Haiti L'imaginaire ams controle, 1979; Le Phénomene uligieur daus la Caraibe, 1989; Le Barbane imaginaine, 1988. Contributions to: Periodicals and journals. Address: Universite Quisqueya, BP 796, Port-au-Prince, Haiti.

HURD Douglas (Richard), b. 8 Mar 1930, Marlborough, England. Politician; Diplomat; Writer. m. (1) Tatiana Elizabeth Michelle, 1960, div, 3 sons, (2) Judy Smart, 1982, 1 son, 1 daughter. Education: Eton; Trinity College, Cambridge. Appointments: HM Diplomatic Service, 1952-66; Joined Conservative Research Department, 1966, Head, Foreign Affairs Section, 1968; Private Secretary to the Leader of the Opposition, 1968-70; Political Secretary to the Prime Minister, 1970-74; Member of Parliament, Conservative Party, Mid-Oxon, 1974-83, Witney, 1983-97; Opposition Spokesman on European Affairs, 1976-79; Visiting Fellow, Nuffield College, 1978-86; Minister of State, Foreign and Commonwealth Office, 1979-83, Home Office, 1983-84; Secretary of State for Northern Ireland, 1984-85, Home Secretary, 1985-89, Foreign Secretary, 1989-95; Deputy Chairman, NatWest Markets, 1995-. Publications: The Arrow War, 1967; Send Him Victorious (with Andrew Osmond), 1968; The Smile on the Face of the Tiger (with Andrew Osmond), 1969; Scotch on the Rocks (with Andrew Osmond), 1971; Truth Game, 1972; Vote to Kill, 1975; An End to Promises, 1979; War Without Frontiers (with Andrew Osmond), 1982; Palace of Enchantments (with Stephen Lamport), 1985. Honours: Commander of the Order of the British Empire, 1974; Privy Counsellor, 1982; Companion of Honour, 1995. Address: c/o NatWest Markets, 135B Bishopsgate, London EC2M 3UR, England.

HURD Michael John, b. 19 Dec 1928, Gloucester, England. Composer; Author. Education: BA, 1953, MA, 1957, Pembroke College, Oxford. Appointment: Professor of Theory, Royal Marines School of Music, 1953-59. Publications: Immortal Hour: The Life and Period of Rutland Boughton, 1962, revised edition as Rutland Boughton and the Glastonbury Festivals, 1993; The Composer, 1968; An Outline History of European Music, 1968, revised edition, 1988; Elgar, 1969; Vaughan Williams, 1970; Mendelssohn, 1970; The Ordeal of Ivor Gurney, 1978; The Oxford Junior Companion to Music, 1979; Vincent Novello and Company, 1981; The Orchestra, 1981. Contributions to: Reference books. Address: 4 Church Street, West Liss, Hampshire GU33 6JX, England.

HURST Frances. See: **MAYHAR Ardath.**

HUSTON Nancy Louise, b. 16 Sept 1953, Alberta, Canada. Writer. m. Tzvetan Todorov, 18 May 1981, 1 son, 1 daughter. Education: BA, Sarah Lawrence College, 1975; Diploma, École des Hautes Études, 1977. Appointments: Writer-in-Residence, American University, Paris, 1989; Facilitator, South African Writers Workshop, 1994; Visiting Professor, Harvard University, 1994. Publications: Journal de la Création, 1990; Les Variations Goldberg, 1991; Cantique des Plaines, 1993; La Virevolte, 1994; Instruments des ténèbres, 1996; The Story of Omaya; Plainsong. Honours: Prix, Binet Sangle de l'Acaderue, 1980; Prix Contrepoint, 1981; Prix du Gouverneur-Général, 1993; Prix Suisse Canada; Prix Louis Hémon, 1995. Address: c/o Mary Kling, La Nouvelle Agence, 7 Rue Corneille, 75006 Paris, France.

HUTCHEON Linda Ann Marie, b. 24 Aug 1947, Toronto, Ontario, Canada. Professor; Writer. m. Michael Alexander Hutcheon, 30 May 1970. Education: BA, Modern Language and Literature, 1969, PhD, Comparative Literature, 1975, University of Toronto; MA, Romance Studies, Cornell University, 1971. Appointments: Assistant, Associate and full Professor of English, McMaster University, 1976-88; Professor of English and Comparative Literature, University of Toronto, 1988-96; University Professor, University of Toronto, 1996-. Publications: Narcissistic Narrative, 1980; Formalism and the Freudian Aesthetic, 1984; A Theory of Parody, 1985; A Poetics of Postmodernism, 1988; The Canadian Postmodern 1988; The Politics of Postmodernisms, 1989; Splitting Images, 1991; Irony's Edge, 1995. Opera: Desire, Disease, Death (with Michael Hutcheon), 1996. Editor: Other Solitudes, 1990; Double-Talking, 1992; Likely Stories, 1992; A Postmodern Reader, 1993. Contributions to: Diacritics; Textual Practice; Cultural Critique and other journals. Honours: FRSC, 1990; LLD, 1995. Address: University of Toronto, Ontario M5S 1A1, Canada.

HUTCHINS Pat, b. 18 June 1942, Yorkshire, England. Writer; Illustrator. m. 20 Aug 1966, 2 sons. Education: Darlington School of Art, 1958-61; Leeds College of Art, 1961-63; National Diploma in Design. Publications: Rosie's Walk, 1968; Tom and Sam, 1968; The Surprise Party, 1969; Clocks and More Clocks, 1970; Changes, Changes, 1971; Titch, 1971; Goodnight Owl, 1972; The Wind Blew, 1974; The Very Worst Monster, 1985; The House That Sailed Away, 1975; The Tale of Thomas Mead, 1980; King Henry's Palace, 1983; One Hunter, 1982; You'll Soon Grow into Them Titch, 1983; The Curse of the Egyptian Mummy, 1983; The Doorbell Rang, 1986; Where's the Baby?, 1988; Which Witch is Which?, 1989; Rats, 1989; What Game Shall We Play?, 1990; Tidy Titch, 1991; Silly Billy, 1992; My Best Friend, 1992; Little Pink Pig, 1993; Three Star Billy, 1994; Titch and Daisy, 1996. Honour: Kate Greenaway Medal, 1975.

HUTCHINSON Gregory Owen, b. 5 Dec 1957, London, England. m. Yvonne Downing, 4 Aug 1979, 1 daughter. Education: City of London School, 1968-74; BA, MA, DPhil, Oxford University (Balliol and Christ Church), 1975-83. Publications: Aeschylus, Septem Contra Thebas (edited with introduction and commentary), 1985; Hellenistic Poetry, 1988; Latin Literature from Seneca to Juvenal: A Critical Study, 1993. Address: Exeter College, Oxford OX1 3DP, England.

HUTCHINSON Ron, b. Northern Ireland. Appointments: Resident Writer, Royal Shakespeare Company, 1978-79. Publications: Plays: The Dillen, 1983; Rat in the Skull, 1984; Mary, After the Queen, 1985; Curse of the Baskervilles, 1987. Novel: Connie, 1985. Radio Plays: Murphy Unchained, 1978; The Winkler, 1979; Bull Week, 1980; The Marksman, 1987. Honours: George Devine Award, 1978; John Whiting Award, 1984. Address: c/o Judy Daish Associates, Eastbourne Mews, London, W2 6LQ, England.

HUTTON Ronald Edmund, b. 19 Dec 1953, Ootacamund, India. Historian. m. Lisa Radulovic, 5 Aug 1988. Education: BA, Cantab, 1976; MA, 1980; DPhil, 1980. Appointments: Professor of British History, Bristol University, 1996-. Publications: The Royalist War Effort, 1981; The Restoration, 1985; Charles II, 1989; The British Republic, 1990; The Pagan Religions of the Ancient British Isles, 1991; The Rise and Fall of Merry England, 1994; The Stations of the Sun, 1996. Contributions to: Journals. Honour: Benjamin Franklin Prize, 1993. Memberships: Royal Historical Society; Folklore Society. Address: 13 Woodland Road, Bristol BS8 1TB, England.

HUXLEY Elspeth Josceline, b. 23 July 1907, London, England. Writer. m. Gervas Huxley, 12 Dec 1931, 1 son. Education: Reading University, 1925-27; Cornell University, 1927-28. Appointments: Assistant Press Officer, Empire Marketing Board, 1929-32; News Department, BBC, 1941-43. Publications: White Man's Country, 1935;

Murder on Safari, 1937; The African Poison Murders, 1938The Flame Trees of Thika, 1959; The Mottled Lizard, 1961; Out in the Midday Sun, 1985; Nine Faces of Kenya, 1990; Peter Scott, Painter and Naturalist, 1993. Contributions to: New York Times Magazine; Daily Telegraph; Encounter; Times and Tide. Honour: Commander of the Order of the British Empire, 1962. Membership: Society of Authors. Address: Green End, Oaksey, Malmesbury, Wilts SW16 9TL, England.

HUYLER Jean Wiley, b. 30 Mar 1935, Seattle, Washington, USA. Communications Management Consultant; Author-Writer; Editor; Photojournalist. Div, 1 son, 1 daughter. Education: Business Administration, University of Washington, 1953-55; BA, Maryhurst College, 1979; MA, Pacific Lutheran University, 1979; D Litt, Fairfax University, 1989. Appointments: Various newspaper and magazine editorships, 1963-96; Editor, books for Education System Managers, Washington School Directors Association, 1977-81; Designer and Editor, For the Record, A History of Tacoma Public Schools, Tacoma School District 1985-. Publications: Demystifying the Media, 1980; Campaign Savvy - School Support, 2nd edition, 1981; Communications is a People Process, 1981; Crisis Communications, 1983; How to Get Competent Communications Help, 1983; Sharing a Vision for Gifted Education with Business and Education Leaders, 1988; Lifespan Learning on Centerstage of the Future, 1988; Learning to Learn - New Techniques for Corporate Education, 1989. Address: 5407 64th Street, Gig Harbor, WA 98335-7449, USA.

HWANG David Henry, b. 11 Aug 1957, Los Angeles, California, USA. Playwright; Director. m. Ophelia Y M Chong, 1985. Education: AB, Stanford University, 1979; Yale University, School of Drama, 1980-81. Publications: Family Devotions, 1981; Sound and Beauty, 1983; Broken Promises, 1983; The Sound of a Voice, 1984; Rich Relations, 1986; As the Crow Flies, 1986; The House of Sleeping Beauties, 1987. Honours: Drama Logue Award, 1980-86; Obie Award, 1981; Rockefeller Fellowship, 1983; Guggenheim Fellowship, 1984; National Endowment for the Arts Fellowship, 1985. Address: c/o Pual Yamamoto and William Craver, Writers and Artists Agency, 70 West 36th Street, New York, NY 10018, USA.

HYLAND Paul, b. 15 Sept 1947, Poole, England. Author. Education: BSc, Bristol University, 1968. Publications: Purbeck: The Ingrained Island, 1978; Poems of Z, 1982; Wight: Biography of an Island, 1984; The Stubborn Forest, 1984; The Black Heart: A Voyage into Central Africa, 1988; Getting into Poetry, 1992; Indian Balm: Travels in the Southern Subcontinent, 1994; Kicking Sawdust, 1995; Babel Guide to the Fiction of Portugal, Brazil and Africa (co-author), 1995; Backwards Out of the Big World, 1996. Contributions to: Many periodical and anthologies. Honours: Eric Gregory Award, 1976; Alice Hunt Bartlett Award, 1985; Authors' Foundation Award, 1995. Memberships: Poetry Society; Society of Authors; Orchard Theatre Company; Dorset Natural History and Archaeological Society. Address: 3 The Maltings, Cerne Abbas, Dorchester, Dorset DT2 7JX, England.

HYMAN Harold M(elvin), b. 24 July 1924, New York, New York, USA. Professor of History; Author. m. Ferne Beverly Handelsman, 11 Mar 1946, 2 sons, 1 daughter. Education: BA, University of California at Los Angeles, 1948; MA, 1950, PhD, 1952, Columbia University. Appointments: Instructor, City College, New York City, 1950-52; Columbia University, 1953, University of Washington, 1960, Brooklyn College, 1962, University of Chicago, 1965; Assistant Professor, Earlham College, 1952-55; Visiting Assistant Professor, 1955-56, Professor, 1963-68, University of California at Los Angeles; Associate Professor, Arizona State University, Tempe, 1956-57; Professor of History, University of Illinois, 1963-68; William P Hobby Professor of History, 1968-96, Professor Emeritus, 1997-, Rice University; Graduate Faculty in Political Science, University of Tokyo, 1973; Faculty of Law, Keio University, 1973; Adjunct Professor of Legal History, Bates College of Law, University of Houston, 1977, and of American Legal History, School of Law, University of Texas, 1986; Meyer Visiting Distinguished Professor of Legal History, School of Law, New York University, 1982-83. Publications: Era of the Oath: Northern Loyalty Tests During the Civil War and Reconstruction, 1954; To Try Men's Souls: Loyalty Tests in American History, 1959; Stanton: The Life and Times of Lincoln's Secretary of War (with Benjamin P Thomas), 1962; Soldiers and Spruce: The Loyal Legion of Loggers and Lumbermen, the Army's Labor Union of World War I, 1963; A More Perfect Union: The Impact of the Civil War and Reconstruction on the Constitution, 1973; Union and Confidence: The 1860s, 1976; Equal Justice Under Law: Constitutional History, 1835-1875 (with William

Wiecek), 1982; Quiet Past and Stormy Present?: War Powers in American History, 1986; American Singularity: The 1787 Northwest Ordinance, the 1862 Homestead-Morrill Acts, and the 1944 G I Bill, 1986; Oleander Odyssey: The Kempners of Galveston, 1870-1980, 1990; The Reconstruction Justice of Salmon P Chase: In Re Turner and Texas v White, 1997; Craftsmanship and Character: A History of the Vinson & Elkins Law Firm of Houston, 1917-1990s, forthcoming. Editor: Several books and reprint editions. Contributions to: Scholarly journals. Honours: Albert J Beveridge Award, American Historical Association, 1952; Coral H Tullis Memorial Prize, Texas A & M University Press, 1990; T R Fehrenbach Book Award, Texas Historical Commission, 1990; Ottis Lock Endowment Award, East Texas Historical Association, 1991. Memberships: American Historical Association; American Society of Legal History, president, 1994-95; Organization of American Historians; Southern Historical Association. Address: c/o Department of History - M5 42, Rice University, 6100 Main Street, Houston, TX 77005-1892, USA.

I

IGGERS Georg Gerson, b. 7 Dec 1926, Hamburg, Germany. Historian; Writer. m. Wilma Abeles, 23 Dec 1948, 3 sons. Education: BA, University of Richmond, Virginia, 1944; AM 1945, PhD 1951, University of Chicago; Graduate Studies, New School for Social Research, New York City, 1945-46. Appointments: Instructor, University of Akron, 1948-50; Associate Professor, Philander Smith College, 1950-56; Visiting Professor, University of Arkansas, 1956-57, 1964, University of Rochester, New York, 1970-71, University of Leipzig, 1992; Associate Professor, Dillard University, New Orleans, 1957-63; Visiting Associate Professor, Tulane University, 1957-60, 1962-63; Associate Professor, Roosevelt University, Chicago, 1963-65; Professor, 1965-; Distinguished Professor, 1978-, State University of New York at Buffalo; Visiting Scholar, Technische Hochschule, Darmstadt, 1971; Forschungsschwerpunkt Zeithistorische Studien, Potsdam, 1993. Publications: Cult of Authority, Political Philosophy of the Saint Simonians, 1958; German Conception of History, 1968; Leopold von Ranke, the Theory and Practice of History (co-editor), 1973; New Directions in European Historiography, 1975; International Handbook of Historical Studies (co-editor), 1979; Social History of Politics (editor), 1985; Aufklarung und Geschichte (co-editor), 1986; Leopold von Ranke and the Shaping of the Historical Discipline (co-editor), 1990; Marxist Historiography in Transition: Historical Writings in East Germany in the 1980's (editor), 1991; Geschichtswissenschaft 20 Jahrhundert, 1993; Historiography in the Twentieth Century: From Scientific Objectivity to the Postmodern Challenge, 1997. Contributions to: Scholarly journals. Honour: Recipient of Research Prize, Alexander von Humboldt Foundation, 1995-96; President, International Commission for the History and Theory of Historiography, 1995-. Address: c/o Department of History, State University of New York at Buffalo, Buffalo, NY 14260, USA.

IGGULDEN John Manners, (Jack), b. 12 Feb 1917, Brighton, Victoria, Australia. Author; Industrialist. m. Helen Carroll Schapper, 1 son dec, 2 daughters. Appointments: Manager, family-owned manufacturing companies, 1940-59; Writer, 1959-70; Businessman, 1970-; Part-time writer, 1980-; Currently, Chief Executive, Planet Lighting, Lucinda Glassworks, Bellingen, New South Wales, Australia. Publications: Breakthrough, 1960; The Storms of Summer, 1960; The Clouded Sky, 1964; Dark Stranger, 1965; Summer's Tales 3, 1966; Manual of Standard Procedures, Gliding Federation of Australia, 1964; Gliding Instructor's Handbook, 1968; The Promised Land Papers Vol 1, The Revolution of the Good, 1986, Vol 2, How Things Are Wrong and How to Fix Them, 1988; Vol 3, The Modification of Freedom, 1993. Address: The Fox Chase Agency Inc, The Public Ledger Building, Independence Square, Philadelphia, PA 19106, USA.

IHIMAERA Witi, b. 7 Feb 1944, Gisborne, New Zealand. Author. Education: University of Auckland, 1963-66; Victoria University, 1968-72. Publications: Pounamu, Pounamy, 1972; Tangi, 1973; Whanau, 1974; Maori, 1975; The New Net Goes Fishing, 1977; Into the World of Light, 1980; The Matriarch, 1986; The Whale Rider, 1987; Dear Miss Mansfield, 1989. Address: c/o Ministry of Foreign Affairs, Private Bag, Wellington 1, New Zealand.

IKEDA Daisaku, b. 2 Jan 1928, Tokyo, Japan. Buddhist Philospher; Poet; Peace Activist. Education: Fuji College. Publications: Human Revolution, volumes 1-5, 1972-84; Choose Life: a Dialogue with Arnold Toynbee, 1976; The Living Buddha: An Interpretative Biography, 1976, 1995; Buddhism, the First Millenium, 1977; Songs From my Heart, 1978; Glass Children and Other Essays, 1979, 1983; Life: An Enigma, a Precious Jewel, 1982; Buddhism and the Cosmos, 1985; The Flower of Chinese Buddhism, 1986; Human Values in a Changing World (with Bryan Wilson), 1987; Unlocking the Mysteries of Birth and Death: Buddhism in the Contemporary World, 1988, 1995; The Snow Country Prince, 1900; A Lifelong Quest for Peace (with Linus Pauling), 1992; Choose Peace (with Johan Galtung), 1995; A New Humanism: The University Addresses of Daisaku Ikeda, 1996; Kenko no Chie (A New Century of Health: Buddhism and the Art of Medicine), 1997. Contributions to: Seikyo, Nihon-Keizai and Yomiuri newspapers; Ushio and Poet (World Poetry Society) magazines. Honours: Poet Laureate, World Academy of Arts and Culture, 1981; Kenya Oral Literature Award, 1986; Honorary Doctorate from University of Glasgow, 1994. Memberships: Non-resident Member, Brazilian Academy of Letters; Honorary Member, The Club of Rome;

Honorary Senator, European Academy of Sciences and Arts. Address: c/o Soka Gakkai International, 15-3 Samon-cho, Shinjuku-ku, Tokyo 160, Japan.

IMPEY Rose(mary June), b. 7 June 1947, Northwich, Cheshire, England. 2 daughters. Education: Teachers Certificate, 1970. Publications: Who's a Clever Girl, Then, 1985; The Baked Bean Queen, 1986; Desperate for a Dog, 1988; The Flat Man, 1988; The Girls Gang, 1986; Letter to Father Christmas, 1988; Joe's Cafe, 1990; First Class, 1992; Trouble with the Tucker Twins, 1992; Revenge of the Rabbit, 1990; Instant Sisters, 1989; Orchard Book of Fairytales, 1992; Animal Crackers, 1993. Honours: 100 Most Borrowed Library Books award; Shortlisted, Smarties Childrens Books Prize. Address: 6 The Homestead, Mountsorrel, Loughborough, Leicestershire LE12 7HS, England.

INDICK Benjamin Philip, b. 11 Aug 1923, New Jersey, USA. Pharmacist; Writer. m. 23 Aug 1953, 1 son, 1 daughter. Education: BS, Biology, Rutgers University, 1947; BS, Pharmacy, Ohio State University, 1951; New School for Social Research, New York, 1960-61, no degree. Publications: Plays: Incident at Cross Plains, 1976; He, She and the End of the World, 1982; The Children of King, 1989; Books: A Gentleman from Providence Pens a Letter, 1975; The Drama of Ray Bradbury, 1976; Ray Bradbury: Dramatist, 1989. Non Fiction: Exploring Fantasy Worlds, 1985; Discovering Modern Horror Fiction, 1, 1985, II, 1988; Kingdon of Fear, 1986; Discovering H P Lovecraft, 1987; Reign of Fear, 1988; Penguin Encyclopaedia of Horror and the Supernatural, 1986; George Alec Effinger: From Entropy to Budayeen, 1993. Contributions to: Books and magazines. Honours: First Prizes, Playwright Contests, 1962, 1964, 1965. Memberships: Dramatists Guild; Horror Writers of America; Rho Chi; Phi Lambada Epsilon. Address: 428 Sagamore Avenue, Teaneck, NJ 07666, USA.

INGALLS Jeremy, b. 2 Apr 1911, Gloucester, Massachusetts, USA. Poet; Translator; Professor (retired). Education: AB, 1932, AM, 1933, Tufts University; Student, 1938, 1939, Research Fellow, Classical Chinese, 1945-46, University of Chicago. Appointments: Assistant Professor, Western College, Oxford, Ohio, 1941-43; Resident Poet, 1947, Assistant Professor, 1948-50, Associate Professor, 1953-55, Professor of English and Asian Studies, 1955-60, Rockford College, Illinois; Visiting Lecturer at numerous colleges and universities. Publications: A Book of Legends (stories), 1941; The Metaphysical Sword (poems), 1941; Tahl (narrative poem), 1945; The Galilean Way, 1953; The Woman from the Island (poems), 1958; These Islands Also (poems), 1959; This Stubborn Quantum: Sixty Poems, 1983; Summer Liturgy (verse play), 1985; The Epic Tradition and Related Essays, 1988. Contributions to: Various publications. Honours: Yale Series of Younger Poets Prize, 1941; Guggenheim Fellowship, 1943-44; American Academy of Arts and Letters Grant, 1944-45; Shelley Memorial Award for Poetry, 1950; Lola Ridge Memorial Awards for Poetry, 1951, 1962; Ford Foundation Faculty Fellow, 1952-53; Fulbright Lecturer, Kobe, Japan, 1957-58; Rockefeller Foundation Lecturer, Kyoto, Japan, 1960; Honorary Epic Poet Laureate, United Poets Laureate International, 1965; Honorary doctorates. Memberships: Dante Society; Modern Language Association; Phi Beta Kappa; Poetry Society of America. Address: 6269 East Rosewood, Tucson, AZ 85711, USA.

INGALLS Rachel (Holmes), b. 13 May 1940, Boston, Massachusetts, USA. Author. Education: BA, Radcliffe College, 1964. Publications: Theft, 1970; The Man Who Was Left Behind, 1974; Mediterranean Cruise, 1973, 1990; Mrs Caliban, 1982; Binstead's Safari, 1983; I See a Long Journey, 1985; The Pearlkillers, 1986; The End of the Tragedy, 1987; Something to Write Home About, 1990; Black Diamond, 1992; Be My Guest, 1992. Honours: First Novel Award, Author's Club, England, 1971; British Book Marketing Council; Best Book Award, 1986. Membership: American Academy and Institute of Arts and Letters, fellow. Address: c/o Georges Borchardt Inc, 136 East 57th Street, New York, NY 10022, USA.

INGHAM Daniel. See: **LAMBOT Isobel Mary.**

INGHAM Kenneth, b. 9 Aug 1921, Harden, England. Professor of History Emeritus; Writer. m. Elizabeth Mary Southall, 18 June 1949, 1 son, 1 daughter. Education: Exhibitioner, Keble College, Oxford, 1940; Frere Exhibitioner in Indian Studies, 1947, DPhil, 1950, Oxford University. Appointments: Lecturer, 1950-56, Professor, 1956-62, Makerere College, Uganda; Director of Studies, Royal Military Academy, Sandhurst, 1962-67; Professor of History, 1967-84, Head,

Department of History, 1970-84, Part-time Professor of History, 1984-86, Professor Emeritus, 1986-, University of Bristol. Publications: Reformers in India, 1956; The Making of Modern Uganda, 1958; A History of East Africa, 1962; The Kingdom of Toro in Uganda, 1975; Jan Christian Smuts: The Conscience of a South African, 1986; Politics in Modern Africa, 1990; Obote: A Political Biography, 1994. Contributions to: Reference books and professional journals. Honours: Military Cross, 1946; Officer of the Order of the British Empire, 1961. Memberships: British Institute in Eastern Africa; Royal African Society; Royal Historical Society. Address: The Woodlands, 94 West Town Lane, Bristol BS4 5DZ, England.

INGLE Stephen James, b. 6 Nov 1940, Ripon, Yorkshire, England.University Professor. m. Margaret Anne Farmer, 5 Aug 1964, 2 sons, 1 daughter. Education: BA, 1962, DipEd, 1963, MA, 1965, University of Sheffield; PhD, Victoria University, New Zealand, 1967. Appointment: Professor, University of Stirling. Publications: Socialist Thought in Imaginative Literature, 1979; Parliament and Health Policy, 1981; British Party System, 1989; George Orwell: A Political Life, 1993. Contributions to: Many in Fields of Politics and Literature. Honours: Commonwealth Scholar, 1964-67; Erasmus Scholar, 1989; Visiting Research Fellow, Victoria University, New Zealand, 1993. Memberships: Political Studies Association. Address: Department of Politics, University of Stirling, Stirling FK9 4LA, Scotland.

INGRAMS Richard Reid, (Philip Reid), b. 11 Aug 1937, London, England. Journalist. m. 1962, 2 sons, 1 dec, 1 daughter. Education: University College, Oxford. Appointments: Editor, 1963-86, Chairman, 1974-, Private Eye; TV Critic, The Spectator, 1976-84; Editor, The Oldie, 1993-94. Publications: Private Eye on London, 1962; Private Eye's Romantic England, 1963; Mrs Wilson's Diary, 1966; The Tale of Driver Grope, 1968; The Life and Times of Private Eye, 1971; Harris in Wonderland, 1973; Cobbets's Country Book, 1974; The Best of Private Eye, 1974; God's Apology, 1977; Goldenballs, 1979; The Other Hald, 1981; Piper's Places, 1983; Down the Hatch, 1985; Just the One, 1986; John Stewart Collis: A Memoir, 1986; The Best of Dear Bill, 1986; Mud in Your Eye, 1987; You Might as Well Be Dead, 1988; Number 10, 1989; On and On, 1990. Address: c/o Private Eye, 6 Carlisle Street, London W1, England.

INMAN Lucy Daniels, (Lucy Daniels), b. 24 Mar 1934, Durham, North Carolina, USA. Clinical Psychologist. 3 sons, 1 daughter. Education: AB, Psychology, 1972, PhD, Clinical Psychology, 1977, University of North Carolina. Publications: Caleb, My Son, 1956; High on a Hill, 1961; A Room of One's Own Revisited; Socarides, 1995. Contributions to: Journals and magazines. Honour: Guggenheim Fellowship, 1957. Literary Agent: Carl D Brandt, 1501 Broadway, New York, NY 10036, USA. Address: 2636 Tatton Drive, Raleigh, NC 27608, USA.

INNAURATO Albert (Francis), b. 2 June 1947, Philadelphia, Pennsylvania, USA. Playwright; Director. Education: BA, Temple University; BFA, California Institute of the Arts, 1972; MFA, Yale University, 1975. Appointments: Playwright-in-Residence, Public Theatre, New York City, 1977, Circle Repertory Theatre, New York City, 1979, Playwright's Horizons, New York City, 1983; Adjunct Professor, Columbia University, Princeton University, 1987-89; Instructor, Yale School of Drama, 1993. Publications: Plays: Earthworms, 1974; Gemini, 1977; The Transfiguration of Bennon Blimpie, 1977; Verna the USO Girl, 1980; Gus and Al, 1988; Magda and Callas, 1988. Other: Coming of Age in Soho, 1985. Contributions to: Newspapers and journals. Honours: Guggenheim Fellowship, 1976; Rockefeller Foundation Grant, 1977; Obie Awards, 1977, 1978; Emmy Award, 1981; National Endowment for the Arts Grants, 1986, 1989; Drama League Award, 1987. Memberships: Dramatists Guild; Writers Guild of America. Address: 325 West 22nd Street, New York, NY 10011, USA.

INNES Brian, b. 4 May 1928, Croydon, Surrey, England. Writer; Publisher. m. (1) Felicity McNair Wilson, 5 Oct 1956, (2) Eunice Lynch, 2 Apr 1971, 3 sons. Education: Whitgift School, Croydon, 1938-46; BSc, Kings College, London, 1946-49. Appointments: Assistant Editor, Chemical Age, 1953-55; Associate Editor, The British Printer, 1955-60; Art Director, Hamlyn Group, 1960-62; Director, Temperance Seven Ltd, 1961-; Proprietor, Brian Innes Agency, 1964-66; Immediate Books, 1966-70, FOT Library, 1970-; Creative Director, Deputy Chairman, Orbis Publishing Ltd, 1970-86; Editorial Director, Mirror Publishing, 1986-88. Publications: Book of Pirates, 1966; Book of Spies, 1967; Book of Revolutions, 1967; Book of Outlaws, 1968; Flight, 1970; Saga

of the Railways, 1972; Horoscopes, 1976; The Tarot, 1977; Book of Change, 1979; The Red Baron Lives, 1981; Red Red Baron, 1983; The Havana Cigar, 1983; Crooks and Conmen, 1993; Catalogue of Ghost Sightings, 1996. Contributions to: Man, Myth & Magic; Take Off; Real Life Crimes; Fire Power; The Story of Scotland; Discover Scotland; Numerous recordings, films, radio and TV broadcasts; Many photographs published. Honour: Royal Variety Command Performance, 1961. Memberships: Chartered Society of Designers; Royal Society of Arts; Institute of Printing; Crime Writers Association; British Actors' Equity. Address: Les Forges de Montgaillard, 11330 Mouthoumet, France.

INNES Hammond. See: HAMMOND INNES Ralph.

INOGUCHI Takashi, b. 17 Jan 1944, Niigata, Japan. Professor; Writer. m. Kuniko Yokota, 8 Aug 1974, 2 daughters. Education: BA, MA, University of Tokyo; PhD, Massachusetts Institute of Technology, USA. Publications: The Framework of Contemporary Japan's Political Economy, 1985; The Political Economy of Japan, Vol 2, 1988; Japan's International Relations, 1991; Japan: The Governing of a Great Economic Power, 1993; Global Change, 1994; US-Japanese Relations after the Cold War and the Role of International Institutions; Northeast Asian Regional Security. Others: Contemporary Political Science; East Asian States and Societies. Contributions to: International Organization, Government and Opposition; Behavioral Science; Current History; Journal of Japanese Studies; Asian Journal of Political Science; Die Zeit; Le Monde; Far Eastern Economic Review. Honour: Suntory Award for Best Social Science Book for International Political Economy, 1982. Address: University of Tokyo, Institute of Oriental Culture, 7-3-1 Hongo, Bunkyoku, Tokyo 113, Japan.

IOANNOU Noris, b. 22 Feb 1947, Larnaca, Cyprus. Cultural Historian; Critic; Writer. Education: BSc (Hons), 1969, DipEd, 1973, University of Adelaide; PhD, Visual Arts, Archaeology, Flinders University, South Australia, 1989. Publications: Ceramics in South Australia 1836-1986, 1986; The Culture Brokers, 1989; Craft in Society (editor), 1992; Australian Studio Glass, 1995; The Barossa Folk: The Story of Germanic Furniture and Other Traditions in Australia, 1995; Masters of their Craft. Contributions to: Books and journals. Honours: Australian Heritage Award, 1987; Writing Fellowship, Australian Council, 1989; Churchill Fellow, 1996. Memberships: President, Association of Professional Historians; Australiana Society; Australian Society of Authors; Independent Scholars Association of Australia. Address: 28 Osmond Terrace, Norwood, Adelaide, South Australia 5067, Australia.

IOANNOU Susan, b. 4 Oct 1944, Toronto, Ontario, Canada. Writer; Editor. m. Lazaros Ioannou, 28 Aug 1967, 1 son, 1 daughter. Education: BA, 1966; MA, 1967, University of Toronto. Appointments: Managing Editor, Coiffure du Canada, 1979-80; Associate Editor, Cross-Canada Writers' Magazine, 1980-89; Poetry Editor, Arts Scarborough Newsletter, 1980-85; Poetry Instructor, Toronto Board of Education, 1982-94, University of Toronto, 1989-90; Director, Wordwrights Canada, 1985-. Publications: Spare Words, 1984; Motherpoems, 1985; The Crafted Poem, 1985; Familiar Faces, Private Griefs, 1986; Ten Ways To Tighten Your Prose, 1988; Writing Reader-Friendly Poems, 1989; Clarity Between Clouds, 1991; Read-Aloud Poems: For Students from Elementary through Senior High School, 1993; Polly's Punctuation Primer, 1994; Where the Light Waits, 1996. Address: PO Box 456, Station O, Toronto, Ontario M4A 2P1, Canada.

IPSEN David Carl, b. 15 Feb 1921, Schenectady, New York, USA. Freelance Writer. m. Heather Marian Zoccola, 28 Aug 1949, 2 sons. Education: BS, Engineering, University of Michigan, 1942; PhD, Mechanical Engineering, University of California, 1953. Publications: Units, Dimensions and Dimensionless Numbers, 1960; The Riddle of the Stegosaurus, 1969; Rattlesnakes and Scientists, 1970; What Does a Bee See?, 1971; The Elusive Zebra, 1971; Eye of the Whirlwind: The Story of John Scopes, 1973; Isaac Newton: Reluctant Genius, 1985; Archimedes: Greatest Scientist of the Ancient World, 1988. Membership: Authors Guild. Address: 655 Vistamont Avenue, Berkeley, CA 94708, USA.

IRBY Kenneth (Lee), b. 18 Nov 1936, Bowie, Texas, USA. Writer; Teacher. Education: BA, Univerity of Kansas; MA, 1960, PhD Studies, 1962-63, Harvard University; MLS, University of California, 1968. Publications: The Roadrunner Poem, 1964; Kansas-New Mexico, 1965; Movements/Sequences,1965; The Flower of Having

Passed Through Paradise in a Dream, 1968; Relation,1970; T Max Douglas, 1971; Archipelago, 1976; Catalpa, 1977; Orexis, 1981; Riding the Dog, 1982; A Set, 1983; Call Steps, 1992. Contributions to: Anthologies and magazines. Address: N-311 Regency Place, Lawrence, KS 66049, USA.

IRELAND David, b. 24 Aug 1927, Lakemba, New South Wales, Australia. Novelist. Education: State Schools, New South Wales. Publications: The Chantic Bird, 1968; The Unknown Industrial Prisoner, 1971; The Flesheaters, 1972; Burn, 1974; The Glass Canoe, 1976; A Woman of the Future, 1979; City of Women, 1981; Archimedes and the Eagle, 1984; Bloodfather, 1987. Short Story: The Wild Colonial Boy, 1979; Play, Image in the Clay, 1962. Honours: Adelaide Advertiser Award, 1966; Age Book of Year Award, 1980; Member, Order of Australia, 1981.Address: c/o Curtis Brown Ltd, 27 Union Street, Paddington, NSW 2021, Australia.

IRELAND Kevin Mark, b. 18 July 1933, Auckland, New Zealand. Writer. m. Phoebe Caroline Dalwood, 2 sons. Appointments: Writer in Residence, Canterbury University, 1986; Sargeson Fellow, 1987, Literary Fellow, 1989, Auckland University. Publications: Poetry, Face to Face, 1964; Educating the Body, 1967; A Letter From Amsterdam, 1972; A Grammar of Dreams, 1975; Literary Cartoons, 1978; The Dangers of Art, 1980; Practice Night in the Drill Hall, 1984; The Year of the Comet, 1986; Selected Poems, 1987; Tiberius at the Beehive, 1990; Skinning a Fish, 1994; Sleeping with the Angels (stories), 1995; Blowing My Top (novel), 1996. Honours: New Zealand National Book Award, 1979; Commonwealth Medal, 1990; Officer of the Order of the British Empire, 1992. Membership: PEN. Address: 8 Domain Street, Devonport, Auckland 9, New Zealand.

IRVING Clifford (Michael), (John Luckless), b. 5 Nov 1930, New York, New York, USA. Author; Screenwriter. Education: BA, Cornell University, 1951. Publications: On a Darkling Plain, 1956; The Losers, 1957; The Valley, 1962; The 38th Floor, 1965; Spy, 1969; The Battle of Jerusalem, 1970; Fake, 1970; Global Village Idiot, 1973; Project Octavio, 1978; The Death Freak, 1979; The Hoax, 1981; Tom Mix and Pancho Villa, 1982; The Sleeping Spy, 1983; The Angel of Zin, 1984; Daddy's Girl, 1988; Trial, 1990; Final Argument, 1993. Address: c/o Frank Cooper, 10100 Santa Monica Boulevard, Los Angeles, CA 90067, USA.

IRVING John Winslow, b. 2 Mar 1942, New Hampshire, USA. Novelist. m. (1) Shyla Leary, 1964, div 1981, 2 sons, (2) Janet Turnbull, 1987, 1 son. Education: BA, University of New Hampshire; MFA, University of Iowa, 1967. Publications: Setting Free the Bears, 1969; The Water-Method Man, 1972; The 158 Pound Marriage, 1974; The World According to Garp, 1978; The Hotel New Hampshire, 1981; The Cider House Rules, 1985; A Prayer for Owen Meany, 1989; A Son of the Circus, 1994; Trying to Save Piggy Sneed, 1996. Contributions to: New York Times Book Review; New Yorker; Rolling Stone; Esquire; Playboy. Honours: Pushcart Prize, Best of the Small Presses, 1978; American Book Award, 1979; O'Henry Prize, 1981. Membership: Executive Board, PEN American Centre. Address: c/o The Turnbull Agency, PO Box 757, Dorset, VT 05251, USA.

ISAACS Alan, (Alec Valentine), b. 14 Jan 1925, London, England. Writer; Lexicographer. m. Alison Coster, 1 son, 3 daughters. Education: St Pauls School, 1938-42; Imperial College, 1942-50. Publications: Penguin Dictionary of Science, 1964; Introducing Science, 1965; Survival of God in the Scientific Age, 1967; Longman Dictionary of Physics, 1975; Collins English Dictionary, 1978; Macmillan Encyclopedia, 1981; Brewer's Twentieth Century Phrase and Fable, 1991; Sex and Sexuality: A Thematic Dictionary of Quotations, 1993. Contributions to: Nature; New Scientist. Address: 74 West Street, Harrow on the Hill HA1 3ER, England.

ISAACS Susan, b. 7 Dec 1943, New York, New York, USA. Novelist; Screenwriter. m. 11 Aug 1968, 1 son, 1 daughter. Education: Queens College of the City University of New York. Publications: Compromising Positions, 1978; Close Relations, 1980; Almost Paradise, 1984; Shining Through, 1988; Magic Hour, 1991; After All These Years, 1993. Contributions to: Newspapers and magazines. Memberships: Authors Guild; International Crime Writers Association; Mystery Writers of America; National Book Critics Circle; PEN; Poets and Writers. Address: c/o Harper Collins, 10 East 53rd Street, New York, NY 10022, USA.

ISHIGURO Kazuo, b. 8 Nov 1954, Nagasaki, Japan. Writer; Resettlement Worker. Education: BA, University of Kent, 1978; MA, University of East Anglia. Appointment: Residential Social Worker, London, 1970-. Publications: A Pale View of Hills, 1982; A Profile of Arthur J Mason, 1985; An Artist of the Floating World, 1986; The Gourmet, 1987; The Remains of the Day, 1989; The Unconsoled Heart, 1995. Honours: Winifred Holtby Prize; Whitbread Book of Year Award; Booker Prize, 1989; Fellow, Royal Society of Literature, 1989; Honorary Doctor of Letters, 1990; Officer of the Order of the British Empire, Services to Literature, 1995; Cheltenham Prize, 1995. Membership: Royal Society of Arts, fellow, 1990. Address: c/o Faber & Faber Ltd, 3 Queen Square, London WC1N 3AU, England.

ISIKOFF Michael. Journalist. m. Lisa Stein, 1 daughter. Education: BA, Washington University, 1974. Appointments: Reporter, Washington Star; Reporter, Washington Post, 1991-94; Investigative Correspondent, Newsweek, 1994-; Frequent guest on radio and television shows. Honours: Story of the Year Award, Baltimore-Washington Newspaper Guild, 1984; Finalist, Pulitzer Prize, 1991. Address: c/o Newsweek, 251 West 57th Street, New York, NY 10019-1894, USA.

ISLER Ursula, b. 26 Mar 1923, Zürich, Switzerland. Writer; Doctor; Critic. Education: Gymnasium and University of Zürich. Publications: Nadine - eine Reise, 1967; Landschaft mit Regenbogen, 1975; Madame Schweizer, 1982; Die Ruinen von Zürich, 1985; Frauen aus Zürich, 1991; Der Künstler und sein Fälscher, 1992. Contributions to: Staff, Neue Zürcher Zeitung, 1950-. Honours: Numerous literary awards. Address: Hornweg 14, 8700 Küsnacht, Switzerland.

IVANOVA Larisa Pavlovna, b. 3 Jan 1945, Leningrad, Russia. Musicologist. Education: Musical College, 1961-65; St PetersburgConservatoire, 1965-70; Diploma of Musicology, 1970; Postgraduate Studentship, 1970-73; Degree of the Candidate of Musicology, 1980. Publications: On the Intonation and Functional Integrity of the Cycle of the 9th Symphony of Beethoven, 1977; Contrast and Composite Form in the Instrumental Cycles of Soviet Composers, 1977; Problems of the Cycle Form as an Integral Structure Based on Works of Beethoven, 1980; Concerto Form in First Movements of Brandenburo Concertos of I S Bach, 1990; On the Integrity of the Cycle Form in First Three Symphonies of Tchaikovsky, 1995. Address: Prayskaja st 23, Apt 41, St Petersburg 192238, Russia.

IVIMY May. See: **BADMAN May Edith.**

IYAYI Festus, b. 1947, Nigeria. Novelist. Education: PhD, University of Bradford, Yorkshire, 1980. Appointment: Lecturer, University of Benin. Publications: Violence, 1979; The Contract, 1982; Heroes, 1986; Awaiting Court Martial, 1996. Honours: Association of Nigerian Authors Prize, 1987; Commonwealth Writers Prize, 1988; Pius Okigbo Africa Prize for Literature, 1996; Nigerian Author of the Year, 1996. Address: Department of Business Administration, University of Benin, PMB 1145, Ugbowo Campus, Benin City, Nigeria.

IZAWA Motohiko, b. 1 Feb 1954, Nagoya City, Japan. Author. m. 1980. Education: Graduate, Law Department, Waseda University, 1961. Publications: Sarumaru Genshiko, 1980; The Hidden Mikado, 1990; The Court of Hatred, 1991; Soul of Language, 1991; The Paradox of Japanese History I-V, 1993-97. Honour: Edogawa Ranpo Award for Sarumaru Genshiko, 1980. Memberships: Japan Writers Association; Japan Pen Club; Mystery Writers of Japan; Mystery Writers of America; Science Fiction Writers Club of Japan. Literary Agent: Woodbell Co Ltd. Address: 437-29 Nanabayashi-cho, Funabashi, Chiba, Japan.

J

J J. See: **JUNOR Sir John Donald Brown.**

JACCOTTET Philippe, b. 30 June 1925, Moudon, Switzerland. Poet. Education: Graduated, University of Lausanne, 1946. Publications: Poetry: Requiem, 1947; L'Effraie et autres poésies, 1953; L'ignorant: Poèmes 1952-56. Airs: Poèmes 1961-64; Poésie 1946-67; Leçons, 1969; Chants d'en bas, 1974; Breathings, 1974; Pensées sous les nuages, 1983; Selected Poems, 1987; Cahier de verdure, 1990; Libretto, 1990; Other: Through the Orchard, 1975; Des Histoires de passage: Prose 1948-78; Autres Journées, 1987; Translator of works by Robert Musil, Thomas Mann, Leopardi, Homer and Hölderlin. Honour: Larbaud Prize, 1978. Address: c/o Editions Gallimard, 5 rue Sebastien-Bottin, 75007 Paris, France.

JACK Dana Crowley, b. 19 Mar 1945, Texas, USA. Professor; Psychologist. m. Rand Jack, 16 Mar 1968, 1 son, 1 daughter. Education: BA, Mount Holyoke College, 1963-67; MSW, University of Washington, 1970-72; EdD, Harvard University, 1979-84. Publications: Moral Vision & Professional Decisions: The Changing Values of Women and Men Lawyers (with Rand Jack), 1989; Silencing The Self: Women and Depression, 1991; The Silencing the Self Scale (with D Dill), 1992. Contributions to: 5 chapters in various edited books. Address: 5790 Schornbush Road, Deming, WA 98244, USA.

JACK Ian, (Robert James), b. 5 Dec 1923, Edinburgh, Scotland. Professor of English Literature Emeritus; Writer. m. (1) Jane Henderson MacDonald, 1948, div, 2 sons, 1 daughter, (2) Margaret Elizabeth Crone, 1972, 1 son. Education: George Watson's College; MA, University of Edinburgh, 1947; DPhil, Merton College, Oxford, 1950. Appointments: Lecturer in English Literature, 1950-55, Senior Research Fellow, 1955-61, Brasenose College, Oxford; Visiting Professor, University of Alexandria, 1960, University of Chicago, 1968-69, University of California at Berkeley, 1968-69, University of British Columbia, 1975, University of Virginia, 1980-81, Tsuda College, Tokyo, 1981, New York University, 1989; Lecturer in English Literature, 1961-73, Reader in English Poetry, 1973-76, Professor of English Literature, 1976-89, Professor Emeritus, 1989-, University of Cambridge; Fellow, 1961-89, Librarian, 1965-75, Fellow Emeritus, 1989-, Pembroke College, Cambridge; de Carle Lecturer, University of Otago, 1964; Warton Lecturer in English Poetry, British Academy, 1967. Publications: Augustan Satire, 1952; English Literature 1815-1832, Vol X of The Oxford History of English Literature, 1963; Keats and the Mirror of Art, 1967; Browning's Major Poetry, 1973; The Poet and His Audience, 1984. General Editor: Brontë novels, Clarendon edition, 7 volumes, 1969-72; The Poetical Works of Browning, 1983, Vols I-V, 1983-95. Contributions to: Scholarly books and professional journals. Honour: Leverhulme Emeritus Fellow, 1990, 1991. Memberships: British Academy, Fellow; Brontë Society, vice-president, 1973-; Browning Society, President, 1980-83; Charles Lamb Society, President, 1970-80; Johnson Society, Lichfield, President, 1986-87. Address: Highfield House, High Street, Fen Ditton, Cambridgeshire CB5 8ST, England.

JACKMAN Brian, b. 25 Apr 1935, Epsom, Surrey, England. Freelance Journalist. m. (1) 14 Feb 1964, div Dec 1992, 1 daughter, m (2) Jan 1993. Education: Grammar School. Appointment: Staff, Sunday Times, 1970-90. Publications: We Learned to Ski, 1974; Dorset Coast Path, 1977; The Marsh Lions, 1982; The Countryside in Winter, 1986; My Serengeti Years, 1987; A Roaring at Dawn, 1996; The Big Cat Diary, 1996. Contributions to: Sunday Times; The Times; Daily Telegraph; Daily Mail; Country Living; Country Life; BBC Wildlife. Honours: TTG Travel Writer of Year, 1982; Wildscreen Award, 1982. Memberships: Royal Geographical Society; Fauna and Flora Preservation Society. Address: Spick Hatch, West Milton, Nr Bridport, Dorset DT6 3SH, England.

JACKMAN Stuart (Brooke), b. 1922, England. Appointments: Congregational Minister, Barnstaple, Devon, 1948-52, Pretoria, 1952-55, Caterham, Surrey, 1955-61, Auckland, 1961-65, Upminster, Essex, 1965-67, Oxford, Surrey, 1969-; Editor, Council for World Mission, 1967-71, Oxted, Surrey, 1969-81, Melbourne, Cambridgeshire, 1981-87. Publications: Portrait in Two Colours, 1948; But They Won't Lie Down, 1954; The Numbered Days, 1954; Angels Unawares, 1956; One Finger for God, 1957; The Waters of Dinyanti,

1959; The Daybreak Boys, 1961; The Desiable Property, 1966; The Davidson Affair, 1966; The Golden Orphans, 1968; Guns Covered with Flowers, 1973; Slingshot, 1975; The Burning Men, 1976; Operation Catcher, 1980; A Game of Soldiers, The Davidson File, 1981. Address: c/o Curtis Brown Ltd, Haymarket House, 28-29 Haymarket, London SW1Y 4SP, England.

JACKONT Amnon, b. 3 Oct 1948, Israel. Insurance Underwriter; Broker; Analyst; Editor. m. Varda Rasiel Jackont, 30 Sep 1990, 1 son. Education: Hebrew University of Jerusalem; Israel Insurance Academy; Bar Ilan University. Appointment: Editor, Keter Publishing House, Jerusalem. Publications: Borrowed Time, 1982; The Rainy Day Man, 1987; The Last of the Wise Lovers, 1991; Honey Trap, 1994. Contributions to: Magazines and journals. Memberships: Israel Authors Association; Israel's Chamber of Insurance Brokers. Address: 20 Manne Street, Tel Aviv 64363, Israel.

JACKOWSKA Nicolette (Susan), (Nicki Jackowska), b. 6 Aug 1942, Brighton, Sussex, England. Poet; Novelist; Writer; Teacher. m. Andrzej Jackowski, 1 May 1970, div, 1 daughter. Education: ANEA Acting Diploma, 1965; BA, 1977, MA, 1978, University of Sussex. Appointments: Founder-Tutor, Brighton Writing School; Writer-in-Residence at various venues; Readings; Radio and television appearances. Publications: The House That Manda Built, 1981; Doctor Marbles and Marianne, 1982; Earthwalks, 1982; Letters to Superman, 1984; Gates to the City, 1985; The Road to Orc, 1985; The Islanders, 1987; News from the Brighton Front, 1993; Write for Life, 1997; Lighting a Slow Fuse, Selected Poems, forthcoming. Contributions to: Various publications. Honours: Winner, Stroud Festival Poetry Competition, 1972; Continental Bursary, South East Arts, 1978; C Day-Lewis Fellowship, 1982; Writer's Fellowship, 1984-85; Writer's Bursary, 1994; Arts Council. Membership: Poetry Society. Address: 98 Ewart Street, Brighton, Sussex BN2 2UQ, England.

JACKS Oliver. See: **GANDLEY Kenneth Royce.**

JACKSON Alan, b. 6 Sept 1938, Liverpool, Lancashire, England. Poet. m. Margaret Dickson, 1963, 2 sons. Education: Edinburgh University, 1956-59, 1964-65. Appointments: Founding Director, Kevin Press, Edinburgh; Director, Live Readings, Scotland, 1967-. Publications: Under Water Wedding, 1961; Sixpenny Poems, 1962; Well Ye Ken Noo, 1963; All Fall Down, 1965; The Worstest Beast, 1967; Penguin Modern Poets, 1968; The Grim Wayfarer, 1969; Idiots are Freelance, 1973; Heart of the Sun, 1986; Salutations: Collected Poems, 1960-89, 1990. Honours: Scottish Arts Council Bursaries. Address: c/o Polygon, 22 George Square, Edinburgh EH8 9LF, Scotland.

JACKSON E F. See: **TUBB E(dwin) C(harles).**

JACKSON Everatt. See: **MUGGESON Margaret Elizabeth.**

JACKSON Guida. See: **JACKSON-LAUFER Guida Myrl Miller.**

JACKSON (William) Keith, b. 5 Sept 1928, Colchester, Essex, England. Emeritus Professor. m. (1), 3 children, (2) Jennifer Mary Louch, 21 Dec 1990. Education: London University Teaching Certificate, 1947; BA Honours, University of Nottingham, 1953; PhD, University of Otago, New Zealand, 1967. Publications: New Zealand Politics in Action (with A V Mitchell and R M Chapman), 1962; New Zealand (with J Harré), 1969; New Zealand Legislative Council, 1972; Politics of Change, 1972; The Dilemma of Parliament, 1987; Historical Dictionary of New Zealand (with A D McRobie), 1996; Editor, Fight for Life, New Zealand, Britain and the EEC. Contributions to: Numerous professional journals. Honours: Mobil Award for Best Spoken Current Affairs Programme, Radio New Zealand, 1979; Henry Chapman Fellow, Institute of Commonwealth Studies, London, 1963; Canterbury Fellowship, 1987; Asia 2000 Fellowship, 1996. Address: 92A, Hinau Street, Christchurch 4, New Zealand.

JACKSON Keith. See: **KELLY Tim.**

JACKSON Kenneth T(erry), b. 27 July 1939, Memphis, Tennessee, USA. Professor of History; Writer. m. Barbara Ann Bruce, 25 Aug 1962, 2 sons, 1 dec. Education: BA, University of Memphis, 1961; MA, 1963, PhD, 1966, University of Chicago. Appointments: Assistant Professor, 1968-71, Associate Professor, 1971-76, Professor, 1976-87, Mellon Professor, 1987-90, Barzun Professor of History and Social Sciences, 1990-, Chairman, Department of History,

1994-, Columbia University; Visiting Professor, Princeton University, 1973-74, George Washington University, 1982-83, University of California at Los Angeles, 1986-87; Chairman, Bradley Commission on History in the Schools, 1987-90, National Council for History Education, 1990-92. Publications: The Ku Klux Klan in the City 1915-1930, 1967; American Vistas (editor with L Dinnerstein), 2 volumes, 1971, 7th edition, 1995; Cities in American History (editor with S K Schultz), 1972; Atlas of American History, 1978; Columbia History of Urban Life (general editor), 1980-; Crabgrass Frontier: The Suburbanization of the United States, 1985; Silent Cities: The Evolution of the American Cemetery (with Camilo Verqara), 1989; Dictionary of American Biography (editor-in-chief), 1991-95. Contributions to: Scholarly books and professional journals. Honours: Woodrow Wilson Foundation Fellow, 1961-62; National Endowment for the Humanities Senior Fellow, 1979-80; Guggenheim Fellowship, 1983-84; Bancroft Prize, 1986; Francis Parkman Prize, 1986; Mark Van Doren Grant Teaching Award, Columbia University, 1989; Outstanding Alumni Award, University of Memphis, 1989. Memberships: American Historical Association; Organization of American Historians; Society of American Historians, Vice President, 1992-; Urban History Association, president, 1994-. Address: c/o Department of History, 603 Fayerweather Hall, Columbia University, New York, NY 10027, USA.

JACKSON MacDonald Pairman, b. 13 Oct 1938, Auckland, New Zealand. University Professor. m. Nicole Philippa Lovett, 2 Sept 1964, 1 son, 2 daughters. Education: MA, University of New Zealand, 1960; BLitt, Oxford, 1964. Appointments: Lecturer, 1964-89, Professor, 1989-, University of Auckland. Publications: Studies in Attribution: Middleton and Shakespeare, 1979; The Revenger's Tragedy, 1983; The Oxford Book of New Zealand Writing Since 1945, 1983; The Selected Plays of John Marston, 1986; A R D Fairburn: Selected Poems, 1995. Contributions to: Chapters in Cambridge Companion to Shakespeare Studies, 1986; The Oxford History of New Zealand Literature in English, 1991; Academic and literary journals. Honours: Folger Shakespeare Library Fellowship, 1989; Huntington Library Fellowship, 1993. Membership: International Shakespeare Association. Address: 21 Te Kowhai Place, Remuera, Auckland 5, New Zealand.

JACKSON Malcolm. See: **CLARK Douglas.**

JACKSON Richard Paul, b. 17 Nov 1946, Lawrence, Massachusetts, USA. Writer; College Professor; Editor. m. Margaret McCarthy, 28 June 1970, 1 daughter. Education: BA, Merrimack College, 1969; MA, Middlebury College, 1972; PhD, Yale University, 1976. Appointments: Journal Editor, University of Tennessee at Chattanooga Faculty; Journal Editor, Mala Revija. Publications: Part of the Story, 1983; Acts of Mind, 1983; Worlds Apart, 1987; Dismantling Time in Contemporary Poetry, 1989; Alive All Day, 1993. Contributions to: Georgia Review; Antioch Review; North American Review; New England Review. Honours: National Endowment for the Humanities Fellowship, 1980; National Endowment for the Arts Fellowship, 1985; Fulbright Exchange Fellowship, 1986, 1987; Agee Prize, 1989; CSU Poetry Award, 1992. Memberships: Sarajevo Committee of Slovene; PEN; Associated Writers Programs. Address: 3413 Alta Vista Drive, Chattanooga, TN 37411, USA.

JACKSON Robert Howard, b. 31 Dec 1955, Alameda, California, USA. History Professor. m. Ana Solorio Rodriguez, 17 Dec 1977, 2 sons, 1 daughter. Education: BA History, University of California, Santa Cruz, 1980; MA History, University of Arizona, 1982; PhD History, University of California, Berkeley, 1988. Appointment: Assistant Professor of History, Texas Southern University, 1990. Publications: Indian Population Decline: The Missions of Northwestern New Spain 1687-1840, 1994; Regional Markets and Agrarian Transformation in Bolivia: Cochabamba 1539-1960, 1995; Indians, Franciscans and Spanish Colonization: The Impact of the Mission System on California Indians (with Ed Castillo), 1995; The New Latin American Mission History (editor with Erick Langer), 1995. Contributions to: Numerous journals. Membership: Conference on Latin American History. Address: 22830 Thadds Trail, Spring, TX 77373, USA.

JACKSON Robert L(ouis), b. 10 Nov 1923, New York, New York, USA. Professor of Slavic Languages and Literatures; Writer; Editor. m. Elizabeth Mann Gillette, 18 July 1951, 2 daughters. Education: BA, Cornell University, 1944; MA, 1949, Certificate, Russian Institute, 1949, Columbia University; PhD, University of

California at Berkeley, 1956. Appointments: Instructor, 1954-58, Assistant Professor, 1958-67, Professor of Russian Literature, 1967-91, B E Bensinger Professor of Slavic Languages and Literatures, 1991-, Yale University. Publications: Dostoevsky's Underground Man in Russian Literature, 1958; Dostoevsky's Quest for Form: A Study of His Philosophy of Art, 1966; The Art of Dostoevsky, 1981; Dialogues with Dostoevsky: The Overwhelming Questions, 1993. Editor: Chekov: Collected Critical Essays, 1967; Crime and Punishment: Collected Critical Essays, 1974; Dostoevsky: Collected Critical Essays, 1984; Reading Chekov's Text, 1993. Contributions to: Professional journals. Address: c/o Department of Slavic Languages and Literatures, Yale University, New Haven, CT 06520, USA.

JACKSON Sir William Godfrey Fothergill, b. 28 Aug 1917, Lancashire, England. Retired, British Army; Historian. m. Joan Mary Buesden, 7 Sept 1946, 1 son, 1 daughter. Education: Shrewsbury School; King's College, Cambridge; Staff College, Camberley; Imperial Defence College. Appointments: British Army; Governor and Commander-in-Chief of Gibraltar, 1978-82. Publications: Attack in the West, 1953; Seven Roads to Moscow, 1957; Battle for Italy, 1967; Battle for Rome, 1968; North African Campaigns, 1975; Overlord: Normandy, 1944, 1978; Rock of the Gibraltarians, 1986; Withdrawal from Empire, 1986; British Official History of the Mediterranean and Middle East Campaigns, 1940-45, Vol VI, 1986-88; The Alternative Third World War, 1987; Britain's Defence Dilemmas, 1990; The Chiefs, 1992; The Pomp of Yesterday, 1994; As Ninevah and Tyre, 1995; Fortress to Democracy: A Political Biography of Sir Joshua Hassan, 1996. Honours: King's Medal, 1937; Military Cross, 1940, Bar, 1944; Officer of the Order of the British Empire, 1958; Knight Commander of the Order of the Bath, 1971; Knight, Grand Cross of the British Empire, 1975. Address: West Stowell, Marlborough, Wiltshire SN8 4JU, England.

JACKSON-LAUFER Guida Myrl Miller, (Guida Jackson), b. Clarendon, Texas, USA. Author; University Lecturer; Editor. m. (1) Prentice Lamar Jackson, 3 sons, 1 daughter, 1954, (2) William Hervey Laufer, 1986. Education: BA, Texas Tech University, 1954; MA, California State University, 1986; PhD, Greenwich University International Institute of Advanced Studies, 1989. Appointments: Managing Editor, Touchstone Literary Journal, 1976-; Lecturer in Writing, 1986-. Publications: Passing Through, 1979; The Lamentable Affair of the Vicar's Wife, 1981; The Three Ingredients (co-author), 1981; Heart to Heart, 1988; Women Who Ruled, 1990; African Women Write (compiler), 1990; Virginia Diaspora, 1992; Encyclopaedia of Traditional Epic, 1994; Legacy of the Texas Plains, 1994. Contributions to: Books and periodicals. Address: c/o Touchstone, PO Box 8308, Spring, TX 77387-8308, USA.

JACOB John, b. 27 Aug 1950, Chicago, Illinois, USA. 1 son, 1 daughter. Education: AB, University of Michigan, 1972; MA, 1973, PhD, 1989, University of Illinois. Appointments: Instructor, 1974-79, 1984-, Northwestern University; Lecturer, Roosevelt University, 1975-; Assistant Professor, North Central College, 1987-. Publications: Scatter: Selected Poems, 1979; Hawk Spin, 1983; Wooden Indian, 1987; Long Ride Back, The Light Fandango, 1988. Contributions to: Margins; ALB Booklist. Honours: Carl Sandburg Award, 1980; Illinois Arts Council Grants, 1985, 1987. Memberships: International PEN; Modern Language Association; Associated Writing Programs; Authors Guild; Multi Ethnic Literature Society of the US. Address: 527 Lyman Street, Oak Park, IL 60304, USA.

JACOBS Barbara, b. 6 Feb 1945, St Helens, England. Journalist; Writer. m. Mark Jacobs, 26 Feb 1968, div, 1 son. Education: BA, 1966, PGCE, 1967, Leicester University. Appointment: Freelance journalist, 1978-. Publications: Ridby Graham, 1982; Two Times Two, 1984; The Fire Proof Hero, 1986; Desperadoes, 1987; Listen to My Heartbeat, 1988; Stick, 1988; Goodbye My Love, 1989; Just How Far, 1989; Loves a Pain, 1990; Not Really Working, 1990. Contributions to: Periodicals. Address: 29 Gotham Street, Leicester LE2 0NA, England.

JACOBS Leah. See: **GELLIS Roberta Leah.**

JACOBSON Dan, b. 7 Mar 1929, Johannesburg, South Africa. Professor Emeritus; Writer. m. Margaret Pye, 3 sons, 1 daughter. Education: BA, University of the Witwatersrand. Appointments: Professor, Syracuse University, New York, 1965-66; Lecturer, 1975-80, Reader, 1980-87, Professor, 1988-94, Professor Emeritus, 1994-, University College, London. Publications: The Trap, 1955; A Dance in the Sun, 1956; The Prize of Diamonds, 1957; The Evidence of Love, 1960; The Beginners, 1965; The Rape of Tamar, 1970; The Confessions of Josef Baisz, 1979; The Story of the Stories, 1982; Time and Time Again, 1985; Adult Pleasures, 1988; Hidden in the Heart, 1991; The God Fearer, 1992; The Electronic Elephant, 1994. Contributions to: Periodicals and newspapers. Honours: John Llewelyn Rhys Memorial Award, 1958; W Somerset Maugham Award, 1964; H H Wingate Award, 1979; J R Ackerley Award, 1986; Mary Elinore Smith Prize, 1992. Membership: Royal Society of Literature, fellow. Address: c/o A M Heath & Co Ltd, 79 St Martins Lane, London WC2, England.

JACOBSON Howard, b. 25 Aug 1942, Manchester, England. Novelist. m. Rosalin Sadler, 1978, 1 son. Education: BA, Downing College, Cambridge. Appointments: Lecturer, University of Sydney, 1965-68; Supervisor, Selwyn College, Cambridge, 1969-72; Senior Lecturer, Wolverhampton Polytechnic, 1974-80; TV Critic, The Sunday Correspondent, 1989-90; Writer/Presenter, Yo, Mrs Askew! (BBC2), 1991, Roots Schmoots (Channel 4 TV), 1993, Sorry, Judas (Channel 4 TV), 1993; Seriously Funny: An Argument for Comedy (Channel 4 TV), 1997. Publications: Shakespeare's Magnanimity: Four Tragic Heroes, Their Friends and Families, 1978; Coming From Behind, 1983; Peeping Tom, 1984; Redback, 1986; Travel in the Land of Oz, 1987; The Very Model of a Man, 1992; Roots Schmoots, 1993; Seeing With the Eye: The Peter Fuller Memorial Lecture, 1993; Seriously Funny, 1997. Membership: Editorial Board, Modern Painters. Address: Peter Fraser & Dunlop, 503-4 The Chambers, Chelsea Harbour, Lots Road, London SW10 0XF, England.

JACOBUS Lee A, b. 20 Aug 1935, Orange, New Jersey, USA. Professor of English. m. Joanna Jacobus, 1958, 2 children. Education: BA, 1957, MA, 1959, Brown University; PhD, Claremont Graduate School, 1968. Appointments: Faculty, Western Connecticut State University, 1960-68; Assistant Professor, 1968-71, Associate Professor, 1971-76, Professor, English, 1976-, University of Connecticut; Visiting Professor, Brown University, 1981; Visiting Fellow, Yale University, 1983. Publications: Improving College Reading, 1967, 6th edition, 1993; Issues and Responses, 1968, revised edition, 1972; Developing College Reading, 1970, 5th edition, 1995; Humanities Through the Arts (with F David Martin), 1974, 4th edition, 1990; John Cleveland: A Critical Study, 1975; Sudden Apprehension: Aspects of Knowledge in Paradise Lost, 1976; The Paragraph and Essay Book, 1977; The Sentence Book, 1980; Humanities: The Evolution of Values, 1986; Writing as Thinking, 1989; Shakespeare and the Dialectic of Certainty, 1993. Editor: Aesthetics and the Arts, 1968; 17 From Everywhere: Short Stories from Around the World, 1971; Poems in Context (William T Moynihan), 1974; Longman Anthology of American Drama, 1982; The Bedford Introduction to Drama, 2nd edition, 1992; A World of Ideas, 4th edition, 1994; Enjoying Literature, 1995. Contributions to: Scholarly books, journals, and other publications. Address: Department of English U-25, University of Connecticut, Storrs, CT 06269, USA.

JACOBUS Mary, b. 4 May 1944, Cheltenham, Gloucestershire, England. Professor of English; Writer. Education: BA, 1965, MA, 1970, DPhil, 1970, Oxford University. Appointments: Lecturer, Department of English, Manchester University, 1970-71; Fellow, Tutor in English, Lady Margaret Hall, Oxford, 1971-80; Lecturer in English, Oxford University, 1971-80; Associate Professor, 1980-82, Professor, 1982-, John Wendell Anderson Professor of English, 1989, Department of English, Cornell University, Ithaca, New York, USA. Publications: Tradition and Experiment in Wordsworth's Lyrical Ballads (1798), 1976; Women Writing and Women about Women (editor), 1979; Reading Women, 1986; Romanticism, Writing, and Sexual Difference: Essays on The Prelude, 1989; Body/Politics: Women and the Discourses of Science (co-editor), 1989; First Things: Thinking the Maternal Body, 1995. Contributions to: Numerous magazines and journals. Honour: Guggenheim Fellowship, 1988-89. Membership: Modern Language Association. Address: Department of English, Cornell University, Ithaca, NY 14853, USA.

JADAV Kishore, b. 15 Apr 1938, Gujarat, India. Government Service. m. Smt Kumsangkola Ao, 4 Mar 1967, 2 sons, 3 daughters. Education: BCom, 1960, MCom, 1963. Appointments: General Secretary, 1976, Vice President, 1986, North Eastern Writers Academy. Publications: Suryarohan, 1972; Nishachakra, 1979; Chhadmavesh, 1982; Kishore Jadavni Vartao, 1984; Riktaraag, 1989; Aatash, 1993; Novels, Critical Essays, Contemporary Gujarati Short Stories. Contributions to: Kishore Jadav Sathe Vartalap; Kishore Jadavni; Sahityik Goshthi; Kishore Jadav Sathe Cartakala Vishe

Vartalap. Honours: Awards from Gujarat Goverment, 1972; Gujarati Sahitya Parishad Award, 1988; Critics Sandham Award, 1988. Memberships: Gujarati Sahitya Parishad; Indian PEN; Lions Club. Address: PO Box 19 Nagaland, PO Kohima 797 001, India.

JAFFEE Annette Williams, b. 10 Jan 1945, Abilene, Texas, USA. Novelist. Div, 1 son, 1 daughter. Education: BS, Boston University, 1966. Publications: Adult Education, 1981; Recent History, 1988. Contributions to: Ploughshares; Missouri Review; Ontario Review. Honours: New Jersey Arts Council Grant, 1986; Dodge Fellow at Yaddo, 1991. Memberships: Authors Guild; PEN. Address: PO Box 26, River Road, Lumberville, PA 18933, USA.

JAGLOM Henry David, b. 26 Jan 1943, London, England. Film Writer; Film Director; Actor. m. Victoria Foyt Jaglom, 22 Oct 1991, 1 son, 1 daughter. Education: University of Pennsylvania; Actors Studio. Publications: Writer, Director, films: A Safe Place, 1971; Tracks, 1976; Sitting Ducks, 1980; Can She Bake a Cherry Pie, 1983; Always But Not Forever, 1985; Someone to Love, 1987; New Year's Day, 1989; Eating, 1990; Venice/Venice, 1992; Babyfever, 1994; Last Summer in the Hamptons, 1996. Books: Eating (A Very Serious Comedy about Women and Food), 1992; Babyfever (For Those Who Hear Their Clock Ticking), 1994. Address: Rainbow Film Company, 9165 Sunset Boulevard, The Penthouse, Los Angeles, CA 90069, USA.

JAKES John (William), b. 31 Mar 1932, Chicago, Illinois, USA. Author. m. Rachel Ann Payne, 15 June 1951, 1 son, 3 daughters. Education: AB, DePauw University, 1953; MA, Ohio State University, 1954. Appointment: Research Fellow, University of South Carolina, 1989. Publications: Brak the Barbarian, 1968; Brak the Barbarian Versus the Sorceress, 1969; Brak Versus the Mark of the Demons, 1969; Six Gun Planet, 1970; On Wheels, 1973; The Bastard, 1974; The Rebels, 1975; The Seekers, 1975; The Titans, 1976; The Furies, 1976; The Best of John Jakes, 1977; The Warriors, 1977; Brak: When the Idols Walked, 1978; The Lawless, 1978; The Americans, 1980; Fortunes of Brak, 1980; North and South, 1982; Love and War, 1984; Heaven and Hell, 1988; California Gold, 1989; The Best Western Stories of John Jakes, 1991; Homeland, 1993; New Trails (co-editor), 1994. Contributions to: Magazines. Honours: Honorary LLD, Wright State University, 1976; Honorary LittD, DePauw University, 1977; Porgie Award, 1977; Ohioana Book Award, 1978; Honorary LDH, Winthrop College, 1985, University of South Carolina, 1993; Distinguished Alumni Award, Ohio State University, 1995; Western Heritage Literature Award, Cowboy Hall of Fame, 1995; Honorary Doctor of Humanities, Ohio State University, 1996. Memberships: Authors Guild; Authors League of America; Dramatists Guild; PEN; Western Writers of America. Address: c/o Rembar and Curtis, 19 West 44th Street, New York, NY 10036, USA.

JAMES Alan, b. 22 Aug 1943, Guilford, England. Educator; Writer. Education: St John's College, York; BSc (Econ), London University; MEd, PhD, Newcastle University. Appointments: Master, Junior School, Royal Grammar School, Newcastle upon Tyne, 1968-78; Deputy Head, Runnymede First School, Ponteland, 1979-. Publications: Animals, Hospital, 1969; Buses and Coaches, 1971; Tunnels, Sir Rowland Hilland the Post Office, Living Light Book Two, 1972; Clock and Watches, Zoos, 1974; Keeping Pets, Newspapers, Buildings, Living Light Book Five, 1975; Spiders and Scorpions, The Telephone Operator, The Vet, 1976; Stocks and Shares, 1977; Circuses, 1978; Let's Visit Finland, 1979; Let's Visit Austria, Let's Visit Denmark, 1984; Homes in Hot Places, 1987; Homes in Cold Places, 1987; Castles and Mansions, 1988; Homes on Water, 1988; Gilbert and Sullivan: Their Lives and Time, 1990. Address: The Stable, Market Square, Holy Island, Northumberland TD15 2RU, England.

JAMES Anthony Stephen, b. 27 Oct 1956, Penllergaer, South Wales. Writer; Poet. m. Penny Windsor, 24 May 1987, div 1994, 1 daughter. Education: BA, University College of Swansea, 1991. Publications: Novel: A House with Blunt Knives. Poetry: All That the City Has to Offer; Introducing Kivi; As Antonia James: The Serpent in April. Contributions to: Numerous publications. Honour: Eileen Illtyd David Award, 1983. Membership: Literature for More than One Year Group. Address: 16 Buckingham Road, Bonymaen, Swansea SA1 7AL, Wales.

JAMES Clive (Vivian Leopold), b. 7 Oct 1939, Kogarah, New South Wales, Australia. Writer; Poet; Broadcaster; Journalist. Education: BA, Sydney University, 1960; MA, Pembroke College, Cambridge, 1967. Appointments: Assistant Editor, Morning Herald,

Sydney, 1961; Television Critic, 1972-82, Feature Editor, 1972-, Observer, London; Various television series and documentaries. Publications: Poetry: Peregrine Prykke's Pilgramage Through the London Literary World, 1974, revised edition, 1976; The Fate of Felicity Fark in the Land of the Media, 1975; Britannia Bright's Bewilderment in the Wilderness of Westminster, 1976; Fan-Mail, 1977; Charles Charming's Challenges on the Pathway to the Throne, 1981; Poem of the Year, 1983; Other Passports: Poems, 1958-1985, 1986. Fiction: Brilliant Creatures, 1983; The Remake, 1987; Brrm! Brrm!, 1991. Non-Fiction: The Metropolitan Critic, 1974; Visions Before Midnight, 1977; At the Pillars of Hercules, 1979; Unreliable Memoirs, 1980; The Crystal Bucket, 1981; From the Land of Shadows, 1982; Glued to the Box, 1983; Flying Visits, 1984; Falling Towards England (Unreliable Memoirs Continued), 1985; Snakecharmers in Texas, 1988; May Week Was in June: Unreliable Memoirs III, 1990; Fame in the 20th Century, 1993. Contributions to: Commentary; Encounter; Listener; London Review of Books; Nation; New Review; New Statesman; New York Review of Books; New Yorker; Times Literary Supplement; Others. Address: c/o Observer, 8 St Andrew's Hill, London EC4V 5JA, England.

JAMES Dana. See: **POLLARD Jane.**

JAMES Irene. See: **JAMES Robin.**

JAMES Noel David Glaves, b. 16 Sept 1911, Author; Retired Land Agent. m. Laura Cecilia Livingstone, 29 Dec 1949, dec, 3 sons, 1 dec. Education: Haileybury College, 1925-28; Diploma, Royal Agricultural College, Cirencester, 1932. Publications: Before the Echoes Die Away, 1980; A History of English Forestry, 1981; The Foresters Companion, 1989; The Arboriculturist, 1990; An Historical Dictionary of Forestry and Woodland Terms, 1991. Honours: Military Cross, 1945; Territorial Decoration, 1946; Officer of the Order of the British Empire, 1964; Gold Medal for Distinguished Service to Foresty; Bledisloe Gold Medal. Memberships: Chartered Land Agents Society; Royal Forestry Society of England, Wales and Northern Ireland. Address: Blackemore House, Kersbrook, Budleigh Salterton, Devon EX9 7AB, England.

JAMES P(hyllis) D(orothy), (Baroness of Holland Park), b. 3 Aug 1920, Oxford, England. Writer (as P D James); Former Civil Servant. 2 daughters. Appointments: Member, BBC General Advisory Council, 1987-88, Arts Council, 1988-92, British Council, 1988-93; Chairman, Booker Prize Panel of Judges, 1987; Governor, BBC, 1988-93. Publications: Cover Her Face, 1962; A Mind to Murder, 1963; Unnatural Causes, 1967; Shroud for a Nightingale, 1971; The Maul and the Pear Tree (with T A Critchley), 1971; An Unsuitable Job for a Woman, 1972; Innocent Blood, 1980; The Skull Beneath the Skin, 1982; A Taste for Death, 1986; Devices and Desires, 1989; The Children of Men, 1992; Original Sin, 1994. Honours: Officer of the Order of the British Empire; Honorary Doctor of Letters, University of Buckingham, 1992, University of Glasgow, 1995; Honorary Doctor of Literature, University of London, 1993, University of Hertfordshire, 1994; Honorary Doctor, University of Essex, 1996. Memberships: Royal Society of Literature, fellow; Royal Society of Arts, fellow. Address: c/o Greene & Heaton Ltd, 37 Goldhawk Road, London W12 8QQ, England.

JAMES Robert. See: **JACK Ian.**

JAMES Sir R(obert) V(idal) Rhodes, b. 10 Apr 1933, Murree, India. Politician; Writer. m. Angela Margaret Robertson, 1956, 4 daughters. Education: Private schools, India; Sedbergh School; Worcester College, Oxford. Appointments: Assistant Clerk, 1955-61, Senior Clerk, 1961-64, House of Commons; Fellow, All Souls College, Oxford, 1965-68, 1979-81, Wolfson College, Cambridge, 1991-; Kratter Professor of European History, Stanford University, 1968; Director, Institute for the Study of International Organisation, University of Sussex, 1968-73; Principal Officer, Executive Office of the Secretary-General of the United Nations, 1973-76; Member of Parliament, Conservative Party, Cambridge, 1976-92; Parliamentary Private Secretary, Foreign and Commonwealth Office, 1979-82; Chairman, History of Parliament Trust, 1983-92. Publications: Lord Randolph Churchill, 1959; An Introduction to the House of Commons, 1961; Rosebery, 1963; Gallipoli, 1965; Standardization and Production of Military Equipment in NATO, 1967; Churchill: A Study in Failure, 1900-1939, 1970; Ambitions and Realities: British Politics 1964-70, 1972; Victor Cazalet: A Portrait, 1976; Albert, Prince Consort, 1983; Anthony Eden, 1986; Bob Boothby: A Portrait, 1991; Henry Wellcome,

1994. Editor: Chips: The Diaries of Sir Henry Channon, 1967; The Czechoslovak Crisis 1968, 1969; The Complete Speeches of Sir Winston Churchill 1897-1963, 1974. Contributions to: Books and periodicals. Honours: John Llewelyn Rhys Memorial Prize, 1962; Royal Society of Literature Award, 1964; Knighted, 1991; Angel Literature Award, 1992. Memberships: Anglo-Israel Association, vice-president, 1990-; Conservative Friends of Israel, chairman, 1989-; Royal Historical Society, fellow; Royal Society of Literature, fellow. Address: The Stone House, Great Gransden, near Sandy, Bedfordshire SG19 3AF, England.

JAMES Tegan. See: **ODGERS Sally Farrell.**

JAMES William M. See: **HARKNETT Terry.**

JANDL Ernst, b. 1 Aug 1925, Vienna, Austria. Writer. Education: Teachers Diploma, 1949, PhD, 1950, University of Vienna. Publications: Laut und Luise, 1966; Fünf Mann Menschen, 1968; Der künstliche Baum, 1970; Aus der Fremde, 1980; Gesammelte Werke, 3 volumes, 1985; Idyllen, 1989; Stanzen, 1992; Peter und die Kuh, 1996. Honours: Hörspielpreis der Kriegsblinden, 1968; Georg Trakl Prize, 1974; Prize of the City of Vienna, 1976; Austrian State Prize, 1984; Georg Büchner Preis, 1984; Medal of Honour in Gold of the City of Vienna, 1986; Peter Huchel Preis, 1990; Heinrich von Kleist Preis, 1993. Memberships: Academy of Arts, Berlin; Deutsche Akademie für Sprache und Dichtung, Darmstadt; Academy of Fine Arts, Munich; Forum Stadtpark, Graz; Grazer Autorenversammlung. Address: PO Box 227, A-1041 Vienna, Austria.

JANES Joseph Robert, b. 23 May 1935, Toronto, Ontario, Canada. Writer. m. Gracia Joyce Lind, 16 May 1958, 2 sons, 2 daughters. Education: BSc, Mining Engineering, 1958, MEng, Geology, 1967, University of Toronto. Publications: Children's books: The Tree-Fort War, 1976; Theft of Gold, 1980; Danger on the River, 1982; Spies for Dinner, 1984; Murder in the Market, 1985. Adult books: The Toy Shop, 1981; The Watcher, 1982; The Third Story, 1983; The Hiding Place, 1984; The Alice Factor, 1991; Mayhem, 1992; Carousel, 1992; Kaleidoscope, 1993; Salamander, 1994; Mannequin, 1994; Dollmaker, 1995; Stonekiller, 1995; Sandman, 1996; Gypsy, 1997. Non-Fiction: The Great Canadian Outback, 1978. Textbooks: Hot Geophoto Resource Kits, 1972; Rocks, Minerals and Fossils, 1973; Earth Science, 1974; Geology and the New Global Tectonics, 1976; Searching for Structure (co-author), 1977. Teachers Guide: Searching for Structure (co-author), 1977; Airphoto Interpretation and the Canadian Landscape (with J D Mollard), 1984. Contributions to: Toronto Star; Toronto Globe and Mail; The Canadian; Winnipeg Free Press; Canadian Children's Annual. Honours: Grants: Canada Council; Ontario Arts Council; J P Bickell Foundation; Thesis Award, Canadian Institute of Mining and Metallurgy; Works-in-progress Grant, Ontario Arts Council, 1991. Memberships: Crime Writers of Canada. Literary Agent: Acacia House, 51 Acacia Road, Toronto, Ontario M4S 2K6, Canada. Address: PO Box 1590, Niagara-on-the-Lake, Ontario L0S 1J0, Canada.

JANET Lillian. See: **O'DANIEL Janet.**

JANIFER Laurence M. See: **HARRIS Laurence Mark.**

JANOV Jill E, b. Los Angeles, California, USA. Consultant to Organizations. 1 son. Education: Master of Organisation Development (MSOD), 1983. Publication: The Inventive Organization: Hope and Daring at Work. Contributions to: Vision/Action; R & D Innovator; At Work; Training and Development Journal, 1995. Address: 745 Grand View Avenue, San Francisco, CA 94114, USA.

JANOWITZ Phyllis, b. 3 Mar 1940, New York, New York, USA. Poet. Div, 1 son, 1 daughter. Education: BA, Queens College; MFA, University of Massachusetts, Amherst, 1970; Appointments: Hodder Fellow in Poetry, Princeton University, 1979-80; Associate Professor in English, then Professor, Cornell University, 1980-. Publications: Rites of Strangers, 1978; Visiting Rites, 1982; Temporary Dwellings, 1988. Contributions to: Poems to New Yorker; Atlantic; Nation; New Republic; Paris Review; Ploughshares; Radcliffe Quarterly; Prairie Schooner; Esquire; Andover Review; Harvard Magazine Backbone; Literary Review; Mid-Atlantic Review. Honour: National Endowment for the Arts Fellowship, 1989. Honour: National Endowment for the Arts Fellowship, 1989. Address: Department of English, Cornell University, Ithaca, NY 14853, USA.

JANSEN Garfield Auburn Mariano, (Mariananda), b. 15 Aug 1967, Coimbatore, South Africa. Writer; Model; Counsellor; Lecturer; Social Worker. Education: BA (Psychology), 1989; Courses in counselling, philosophy, theology; DLitt, Harmony College of Applied Sciences, USA; Receiving PhD in Mariology from International University of California, USA. Appointments: Ashama Aikya, 1989; Divyodaya, 1990; Oblate of St Benedict, 1991; Bharatiya Vidya Parishad, 1993; United Writers Association, 1996. Publications: Assumption of Our Lady Mary, 1994; Mary Mother and Queen, 1995; Hail Mary Full of Grace, 1996; Mystic Woman, 1997; Fragrance of Modelling, 1997; Catholic Restoration; Becoming Saints; Book of Poor Christ. Contributions to: New Leader; St Philomenas Messenger; Messenger of Cross Examiner; SAR News, Delhi; Herald-Calcutta Indian Journal of Spirituality; Malabar Herald; Proclaim; Voice of Delhi ICP; Coastal Observer; Indian Currents. Honours: May Ash Prize, 1985; Best Model Awards, 1992, 1993, 1994; Prince Charming, 1993; Best Look of the Year, 1992, 1993; Most Handsome Male Model, 1992; Winged World Award, 1996. Memberships: Stop the Killing, president; United Writers Association; International Socio-Literary Foundation. Address: 1275 Trichy Road, Near Sreepathy Theatre, Coimbatore 641018, South India.

JANSSENS Jessica Rolande Julienne, b. 8 July 1962, Deurne, Belgium. Publisher; Literary Agent. Education: Degree in Theory of Music, 1976, Degree in Chamber Music, Academy of Music; Library Management Graduate, STLBW, 1980-83; Degree in Recorder Playing (Flute), Academy of Music, 1981; Degree in Public Library Management, STLBW, 1981. Appointments: Publisher; Literary Agent, Toneelfonds J Janssens. Address: Toneelfonds J Janssens BVBA, Te Boelaerlei 107, 2140 Antwerp, Belgium.

JANUS Ludwig, b. 21 Aug 1939, Essen, Germany. Psychoanalyst; Psychotherapist. m. Brigitte Janus-Stanek, 17 Nov 1972, 3 sons, 3 daughters. Education: Dr Med, 1969, Psychoanalyst, 1974. Publications: Die Psychoanalyse der vorgeburtlichen Lebenszeit und der Geburt, 1991; Wie die Seele, 1993; Ungewollte Kinder (with Helga Haesing), 1994; Editor of several books on prenatal psychology. Contributions to: Professional journals. Memberships: German Psychoanalytical Society; International Society of Prenatal and Perinatal Psychology and Medicine. Address: 69118 Heidelberg, Koepfelweg 52, Germany.

JAQUES Elliott, b. 18 Jan 1917, Toronto, Ontario, Canada. Social Analyst; Professor Emeritus. Education: BA Honours in Science, 1936, MA, Psychology, 1937, University of Toronto; MD, Johns Hopkins Medical School, 1940; PhS, Social Relations, Harvard University, 1950; FRCP (England), 1972. Appointments: Social Analyst, Professor Emeritus, Brunel University; Visiting Research Professor, Management Science, George Washington University. Publications: Changing Culture of a Factory, 1951; Time-Span Handbook, 1964; General Theory of Bureaucracy, 1976; Form of Time, 1982; Requisite Organization, 1989, revised, 1996; Creativity & Work, 1990; Executive Leadership, 1991; Human Capability, 1994. Contributions to: Harvard Business Review; Quality and Participation; The World and I; Human Relations. Address: c/o Rebecca Cason, Cason Hall & Co Ltd., 51 Monroe Street, Suite 608, Rockville, MD 20850, USA.

JARMAN Mark Foster, b. 5 June 1952, Mt Sterling, Kentucky, USA. Poet; Teacher. m. Amy Kane Jarman, 28 Dec 1974, 2 daughters. Education: BA, University of California, Santa Cruz; MFA, University of Iowa. Appointment: Faculty, Vanderbilt University. Publications: Tonight is the Night of the Prom, a Chapbook of Verse, 1974; North Sea, 1978; The Rote Walker, 1981; Far and Away, 1985; The Black Riviera 1990; Iris, 1992; Questions for Ecclesiastes, 1997. Contributions to: American Poetry Review; Hudson Review; New Yorker; Ohio Review; Partisan Review; Poetry; Prairie Schooner; Reaper. Address: Department of English, Vanderbilt University, Nashville, TN 37235, USA.

JAROS Peter, b. 22 Jan 1940, Hybe, Slovakia. Writer. m. Maria Zuzana Kristova, 5 July 1980. 2 sons, 1 daughter. Education: Philosophical Faculty, Komensky University, Bratislava, 1962. Appointments: Editor, Kulturny Zivot, 1964-66; Literary Department, Slovak Radio, 1967-71, Slovak Film, 1972-91. Publications: Popoludnie na Terase (Afternoon of the Terrace), 1963; Zdesenie (Anxiety), 1965; Menuet, 1967; Krvaviny (Stories of Blood), 1970; Orechy (Nuts), 1972; Tisicrocna Vcela (1000 year old Bee), 1979; Nerne Ucho, Hluche Oko (Dumb Ear, Deaf Eye), 1984; Lasky Hmat (A

Clutch of Love), 1988. Contributions to: Various publications. Honours: Ivan Krasko's Award, 1963; Award, Publishing House Smena, 1967; Award, Publishing House Slovensky spisovatel, 1968; Award, Slovak Union of Writers, 1979. Memberships: Slovak Union of Writers; Slovak PEN Club. Literary Agent: LITA, Slovak Literary Agency, Bratislava. Address: Klzava 11, 83101 Bratislava, Slovakia.

JARRETT Amanda Jean. See: AVALLONE Michael (Angelo Jr).

JARVIS Martin, b. 4 Aug 1941, Cheltenham, Gloucestershire, England. Actor; Writer. m. (1), div, 2 sons, (2) Rosalind Ayres, 23 Nov 1974. Education: Diploma (Hons), Royal Academy of Dramatic Art, 1962. Appointments: Numerous appearances as an actor on stage and in films, radio, and television; Founder-Director, Jarvis and Ayres Productions, 1986-; Active as a producer and director; Co-star in the film Buster, 1988, and as Monsieur de Renal in the BBC-TV production Scarlet and Black, 1993. Publications: Play: Bright Boy, 1977. Short Stories: Name Out of a Hat, 1967; Alphonse, 1972; Late Burst, 1976. Other: Spoken Word Cassettes. Honours: Vanbrugh Award, Silver Medal, Royal Academy of Dramatic Art, 1968; Emmy Award, 1991; Sony Silver Award, 1992. Memberships: National Youth Theatre, council member; Children's Film Unit, board member. Address: 76 Oxford Street, London W1, England.

JARVIS Sharon, b. 1 Oct 1943, Brooklyn, New York, USA. Literary Agent; Editor; Writer. Education: BFA, Hunter College, 1964. Appointments: Copy Editor, Ace Books, 1969; Assistant Managing Editor, Popular Library, 1971; Editor, Ballantine Books, 1972, Doubleday and Co, 1975; Senior Editor, Playboy Books, 1978. Publications: The Alien Trace (with K Buckley), 1984; Time Twister, 1984; Inside Outer Space, 1985; True Tales of the Unknown, 1985; True Tales of the Unknown: The Uninvited, 1989; True Tales of the Unknown: Beyond Reality, 1991; Dead Zones, 1992; Dark Zones, 1992. Memberships: International Fortean Organization; Association of Authors Representatives; American Booksellers Association; Endless Mountains Council of the Arts. Address: RR2 Box 16B, Laceyville, PA 18623, USA.

JASON Kathrine, b. 9 Feb 1953, New York, New York, USA. Instructor; Writer. m. Peter Rondinone, 23 Apr 1984. Education: AB, Bard College, 1975; MF, Columbia University, 1978; Doctoral Study, Graduate Center of the City University of New York, 1980-81. Appointment: Instructor, Hunter College, City University of New York, 1981-. Publications: Racers, What People, 1984; Words in Commotion and Other Stories, 1986; Name and Tears: Forty Years of Italian Fiction, 1990. Contributions to: Anthologies and periodicals. Honour: Fulbright Fellowship, 1978-79; Finalist for Renato Poggioli Award, 1984; Finalist, Nation Award for Unstringing, 1985. Address: 348 West 11th Street, No. 38, New York, NY 10014, USA.

JASON Stuart. See: AVALLONE Michael (Angelo Jr).

JASON Stuart. See: FLOREN Lee.

JASPER David, b. 1 Aug 1951, Stockton on Tees, England. University Teacher; Clergyman. m. Alison Elizabeth Collins, 29 Oct 1976, 3 daughters. Education: Dulwich College, 1959-69; Jesus College, Cambridge, 1969-72; BA, MA, 1976, BD, Keble College, Oxford, 1976-80; PhD, Hatfield College, Durham, 1979-83. Appointments: Director, Centre for the Study of Literature and Theology, Durham University, 1986-91, Glasgow University, 1991-; Editor, Literature and Theology. Publications: Coleridge as Poet and Religious Thinker, 1985; The New Testament and the Literary Imagination, 1987; The Study of Literature and Religion, 1989; General Editor of Macmillan Series, Studies in Literature and Translation. Contributions to: Rhetoric Power and Community, 1992. Honours: Dana Fellow, Emory University, Atlanta, 1991; Honorary Fellow, Research Foundation, Durham University, 1991. Memberships: European Society for Literature and Religion, secretary; American Academy of Religion; Modern Language Association. Address: Netherwood, 124 Old Manse Road, Wishaw, Lanarkshire ML2 0EP, Scotland.

JAY Sir Anthony (Rupert), b. 20 Apr 1930, London, England. Writer; Producer. m. Rosemary Jill Watkins, 15 June 1957, 2 sons, 2 daughters. Education: BA (1st Class Honours) in Classics and Comparative Philology, 1952, MA, 1955, Magdalene College, Cambridge. Appointments: Staff, BBC, 1955-64; Chairman, Video Arts

Ltd, 1972-89; Writer (with Jonathon Lynn), Yes, Minister and Yes, Prime Minister, BBC-TV series, 1980-88. Publications: Management and Machiavelli, 1967, 2nd edition, 1987; To England With Love (with David Frost), 1967; Effective Presentation, 1970; Corporation Man, 1972; The Householder's Guide to Community Defence Against Bureaucratic Aggression, 1972; Yes, Minister (with Jonathan Lynn), 3 volumes, 1981-83; The Complete Yes, Minister (with Jonathan Lynn), 1984; Yes, Prime Minister (with Jonathon Lynn), 2 volumes, 1986-87; The Complete Yes, Prime Minister (with Jonathan Lynn), 1989; Elizabeth R, 1992; Oxford Dictionary of Political Quotations (editor), 1996; How to Beat Sir Humphrey, 1997. Honours: Knighted, 1988; Honorary MA, Sheffield, 1987; Doctor of Business Administration, International Management Centre from Buckingham, 1988; Royal Society of Arts, Fellow, 1992; Companion, Institute of Management, 1992; Commander of the Royal Victorian Order, 1993. Address: c/o Video Arts Ltd, 68 Oxford Street, London W1N 9LA, England.

JAY Charlotte. See: JAY Geraldine Mary.

JAY Geraldine Mary, (Geraldine Hills, Charlotte Jay), b. 1919, Australia. Appointments: Oriental Antiques Business, Somerset, England, 1958-71, Adelaide, 1971-. Publications: The Knife is Feminine, 1951; Beat Not the Bones, The Fugitive Eye, 1953; The Yellow Turbn, 1955; The Feast of the Dead, 1956; The Silk Project, 1956; The Man Who Walked Away, 1958; Arms for Adonis, 1960; A Hank of Hair, 1964; The Cats of Benares, 1967; The Cobra Kite, 1971; The Voice of the Crab, 1974; The Last of the Men Shortage, 1976; The Felling of Thawle, 1979; The Last Inheritor, 1980; Talking to Strangers, 1982. Address: 21 Commercial Road, Hyde Park, South Australia 5061, Australia.

JAY Martin (Evan), b. 4 May 1944, New York, New York, USA. Professor of History; Writer. m. Catherine Gallagher, 6 July 1974, 2 daughters. Education: BA, Union College, 1965; PhD, Harvard University, 1971. Appointments: Assistant Professor, 1971-76, Associate Professor 1976-82, Professor of History, 1982-, University of California at Berkeley. Publications: The Dialectical Imagination: A History of the Frankfurt School and the Institute of Social Research, 1923-1950, 1973, 1996; Adorno, 1984; Marxism and Totality, 1984; Permanent Exiles, 1985; Fin de Siècle Socialism, 1989; Downcast Eyes, 1993; Force Fields, 1993; Cultural Semantics, 1997. Contributions to: Salmagundi. Honour: Herbert Baxter Adams Award, American Academy of Arts and Sciences, 1973. Memberships: American Historical Association; Society for Exile Studies. Address: 718 Contra Costa Avenue, Berkeley, CA 94707, USA.

JEAL Tim, b. 27 Jan 1945, London, England. Author. m. Joyce Timewell, 11 Oct 1969, 3 daughters. Education: MA, Christ Church, Oxford. Publications: For Love of Money, 1967; Livingstone, 1973; Cushing's Crusade, 1974; Until the Colours Fade, 1976; A Marriage of Convenience, 1979; Baden Powell, 1989; The Missionary's Wife, 1997. Honours: Joint Winner, Llewellyn Rhys Memorial Prize, 1974; Writers Guild Laurel Award. Memberships: Writers Guild of Great Britain; Society of Authors. Address: 29 Willow Road, London NW3 1TL, England.

JEFFERSON Alan (Rigby), b. 20 Mar 1921, Ashstead, Surrey, England. Writer. m. (1), 1 son, (2) 2 sons, 1 daughter (3) Antonia Dora Raeburn, 24 Sept 1976, 2 sons. Education: Rydal School, Colwyn Bay, 1935-37; Old Vic Theatre School, 1947-48. Appointments: Administrator, London Symphony Orchestra, 1968-69; Visiting Professor of Vocal Interpretation, Guildhall School of Music and Drama, London, 1968-74; Manager, BBC Concert Orchestra, London, 1969-73; Editor, The Monthly Guide to Recorded Music, 1980-82. Publications: The Operas of Richard Strauss in Great Britain 1910-1963, 1964; The Lieder of Richard Strauss, 1971; Delius, 1972; The Life of Richard Strauss, 1973; Inside the Orchestra, 1974; Strauss, 1975; The Glory of Opera, 1976, 2nd edition, 1983; Discography of Richard Strauss's Operas, 1977; Strauss, 1978; Sir Thomas Beecham, 1979; The Complete Gilbert and Sullivan Opera Guide, 1984; Der Rosenkavalier, 1986; Lotte Lehmann: A Centenary Biography, 1989; CD ROM: An Introduction to Classical Music, 1996; Elisabeth Schwarzkopf, 1996. Contributions to: Periodicals. Memberships: Royal Society of Musicians; Society of Authors; Savile Club. Address: c/o Society of Authors, 84 Drayton Gardens, London SW10 9SB, England.

JELLICOE (Patricia) Ann, b. 15 July 1927, Middlesborough, Yorkshire, England. Dramatist; Director. m. (1) C E Knight-Clarke, 1950, div 1961, (2) Roger Mayne, 1962, 1 son, 1 daughter. Education:

Polam Hall, Darlington; Queen Margaret's, York; Central School of Speech and Drama. Appointments: Actress, stage manager, and director, 1947-51; Founder-Manager, Cockpit Theatre Club, 1952-54; Teacher and Director of Plays, Central School of Speech and Drama, 1954-56; Literary Manager, Royal Court Theatre, 1973-75; Founder-Director, 1979-85, President, 1986, Colway Theatre Trust. Publications: Plays: The Sport of My Mad Mother, 1958; The Knack, 1962; Shelley or The Idealist, 1966; The Rising Generation, 1969; The Giveaway, 1970; 3 Jelliplays, 1975. Other: Some Unconscious Influences in the Theatre, 1967; Shell Guide to Devon (with Roger Mayne), 1975; Community Plays: How to Put Them On, 1987. Honour: Officer of the Order of the British Empire, 1984. Address: Colway Manor, Lyme Regis, Dorset DT7 3HD, England.

JENCKS Charles Alexander, b. 21 June 1939, Baltimore, Maryland, USA. Writer; Architect; Professor. m. Margaret Keswick, 3 sons, 1 daughter. Education: BA, 1961, BA, MA, 1965, Harvrd University; PHP, London University. Appointment: Editorial Advisor, Architectural Design, London, 1979. Publications: Ad Hocism, 1972; Modern Movemnets in Architecture, 1973, 2nd edition, 1984; Le Corbusier and the Tragic View of Architecture, 1974; The Language of Post Modern Architecture, 1977; Daydream Houses of Los Angeles, 1978; Late Modern Architecture, 1980; Architecture Today, 1982, 2nd edition, 1988. Contributions to: Architectural Design; Times Literary Supplement; Encounter. Honours: Melbourne Oration, 1974; Boston Lectures, Royal Society of Arts. Literary Agent: Ed Victor. Address: Architectural Association, 36 Bedford Square, London WC1, England.

JENKINS John (Geraint), b. 4 Jan 1929, Llangrannog, Dyfed, Wales. Museum Curator; Writer. m. 8 Jan 1954, 3 sons. Education: BA, 1952, MA, 1953, DSc, 1980, University of Wales, Swansea and Aberystwyth. Appointments: Museum Curator; Editor, Folk Life, 1963-78. Publications: The English Farm Wagon, 1963; Traditional Country Craftsment, 1965; Agricultural Transport in Wales, 1966; The Welsh Woollen Industry, 1969; Life and Tradition in Rural Wales, 1973; Nets and Coracles, 1974; The Coracle, 1985; Exploring Museums, Wales, 1990; Interpreting the Heritage of Wales, 1990; Getting Yesterday Right, 1993; The In-Shore Fishermen of Wales, 1993. Contributions to: Journals and magazines. Honour: Druid Eoredd of Bards, National Eisteddfod of Wales, 1969. Memberships: Society for Folk Life Studies, president, 1983-86; Society for the Interpretation of Britain's Heritage, chairman, 1975-81; Coracle Society, 1990-; Wales Arts Council, West Wales Region, chairman, 1996-; Ceredigion County Council, councillor. Address: Cilhaul, Sarnau, Ceredigion SA44 6QT, Wales.

JENKINS (John) Robin, b. 11 Sept 1912, Cambusland, Lanarkshire, England. Teacher (retired); Writer. Education: BA, Glasgow University, 1935. Appointments: Teacher, Gjazi College, Khabul, 1957-59; British Institute, Barcelona, 1959-61, Gaya School, Sabah, 1963-68. Publications: Go Gaily Sings the Lark, 1951; Happy for the Child, 1953; The Thistle and the Grail, 1954; The Cone-Gatherers, 1955; Guests of War, 1956; The Missionaries, 1957; The Changeling, 1958; Love is a Fervent Fire, 1959; Some Kind of Grace, 1960; Dust on the Paw, 1961; The Tiger of Gold, 1962; A Love of Innocence, 1963; The Sardana Dancers, 1964; A Very Scotch Affair, 1968; The Holly Tree, 1969; The Expatriates, 1971; A Toast to the Lord, 1972; A Figure of Fun, 1974; A Would-Be-Saint, 1978; Fergus Lamont, 1979; The Awakening of George Darroch, 1985; Poverty Castle, 1991. Address: Fairhaven, Toward by Dunoon, Argyll PA23 7UE, Scotland.

JENKINS Roy (Harris), Lord Jenkins of Hillhead, b. 11 Nov 1920, Abersychan, Monmouthshire, Wales. Politician; Writer. m. Jennifer Morris, 2 sons, 1 daughter. Education: BA, Balliol College, Oxford, 1941. Appointments: Member of Parliament, Labour Party, Central Southward, London, 1948-50, Strechford, Birmingham, 1950-77; Home Secretary, 1965-67, 1974-76; Chancellor of the Exchequer, 1967-70; President, European Commission, 1977-81; Co-Founder, 1981, Leader, 1982-83, Member of Parliament, Hillhead, Glasgow, 1982-87, Social Democratic Party; Chancellor, Oxford University, 1987-. Publications: Purpose and Policy (editor), 1947; Mr Attlee: An Interim Biography, 1948; New Fabian Essays (contributor), 1952; Pursuit of Progress, 1953; Mr Balfour's Poodle, 1954; Sir Charles Dilke: A Victorian Tragedy, 1958; The Labour Chase, 1959; Asquith, 1964; Essays and Speeches, 1967; Afternoon on the Potomac?, 1972; What Matters Now, 1973; Nine Men of Power, 1974; Partnership of Principle, 1985; Truman, 1986; Baldwin, 1987; Twentieth Century Portraits, 1988; European Diary, 1989; A Life at the

Centre, 1991; Portraits and Miniatures, 1993; Gladstone, 1995. Honours: Privy Councillor, 1964; Life Peer, 1987-; Order of Merit, 1993; Numerous honorary doctorates, awards and prizes. Address: 2 Kensington Park Gardens, London W11, England.

JENKINS Simon David, b. 10 June 1943, Birmingham, England. Journalist; Editor. m. Gayle Hunnicutt, 1978. Education: BA, St John's College, Oxford. Appointments: Staff, Country Life Magazine, 1965; News Editor, Times Educational Supplement, 1966-68; Leader Writer, Columnist, Features Editor, 1968-74, Editor, 1977-78, Evening Standard; Insight Editor, Sunday Times, 1974-76; Political Editor, The Economist, 1979-86; Director, Faber and Faber (Publishers) Ltd., 1981-90. Publications: A City at Risk, 1971; Landlords to London, 1974; Newspapers: The Power and the Money, 1979; The Companion Guide to Outer London, 1981; Images of Hampstead, 1982; The Battle for the Falklands, 1983; With Respect, Ambassador, 1985; Market for Glory, 1986; The Selling of Mary Davies, 1993. Memberships: Board, Old Vic Co., 1979-81; Part-time Member, British Rail Board, 1979-90; London Regional Transport Board, 1984-86; Museum of London, 1984-88; Vice Chairman, Thirties Society, 1979-90; Director, The Municipal Journal, 1980-90; Historic Buildings and Monuments Commission, 1985-90; South Bank Board, 1985-90. Address: 174 Regents Park Road, London NW1, England.

JENSEN De Lamar, b. 22 Apr 1925, Roseworth, Idaho, USA. Professor of History; Writer. Education: BA, Brigham Young University, 1952; MA, 1953, PhD, 1957, Columbia University. Appointments: Instructor in History, New York University, 1954-57; Professor of History, Brigham Young University, 1957-. Publications: Machiavelli: Cynic, Patriot or Political Scientist? (compiler, editor), 1960; Diplomacy and Dogmatism: Bernardino de Mendoza and the French Catholic League, 1964; The Expansion of Europe: Motives, Methods and Meanings (compiler, editor), 1967; The World of Europe: The Sixteenth Century; Confrontation at Worms: Martin Luther and the Diet of Worms, 1973; Renaissance Europe, 1980, 2nd edition, 1991; Reformation Europe, 1981, 2nd edition, 1991. Address: 1079 Briar Avenue, Provo, UT 84604, USA.

JENSEN Laura Linnea, b. 16 Nov 1948, Tacoma, Washington, USA. Poet. Education: BA, University of Washington, 1972; MFA, University of Iowa, 1974. Appointments: Occasional Teacher; Visiting Poet, Oklahoma State University, 1978. Publications: After I Have Voted, 1972; Anxiety and Ashes, 1976; Bad Boats, 1977; Tapwater, 1978; The Story Makes Them Whole, 1979; Memory, 1982; Shelter, 1985; A Sky Empty of Orion, 1985. Contributions to: Periodicals. Honours: National Endowment for the Arts Fellowship, 1980-81; Ingram Merrill Foundation Grant, 1983; Theodore Roethke Award, 1986; Guggenheim Fellowship, 1989-90; Lila Wallace-Reader's Digest Writers Award, 1993. Memberships: Academy of American Poets; Associated Writing Programs; Poets and Writers. Address: 302 North Yakima, No C3, Tacoma, WA 98403, USA.

JENSEN Ruby Jean, b. 1 Mar 1930, USA. Author. m. Vaughn Jensen, 1 daughter. Publications: The House That Samuel Built, 1974; The Seventh All Hallows Eve, 1974; Dark Angel, 1978; Hear the Children Cry, 1981; Such a Good Baby, 1982; Mama, 1983; Home Sweet Home, 1985; Annabelle, 1987; Chain Letter, 1987; House of Illusions, 1988; Jump Rope, 1988; Death Stone, 1989; Baby Dolly, 1991; Celia, 1991; The Reckoning, 1992; The Living Exile, 1993; The Haunting, 1994. Address: 41 West 82nd Street, New York, NY 10024, USA.

JERSILD Per Christian, b. 14 Mar 1935, Katrineholm, Sweden. Writer. m. Ulla Jersild, 1960, 2 sons. Education: MD. Publications: The Animal Doctor, 1975, 2nd edition, 1988; After the Flood, 1986; Childrens Island, 1987; The House of Babel, 1987; A Living Soul, 1988; also 29 books published in Sweden. Honours: Swedish Grand Novel Prize, 1981; Swedish Academy Award, 1982. Membership: Swedish PEN, Board. Address: Rosensdalsv. 20, 5-19454 Uppl. Vasby, Sweden.

JESSUP Frances, b. 29 July 1936, England. Author. m. Clive Turner, 2 Jan 1960, 1 son, 3 daughters. Education: BA Hons Philosophy, King's College, London University, 1955-58. Appointment: Organiser of Theatre Writing in Halesmere, UNA, 1992. Publication: The Fifth Child's Conception, 1970. Contributions to: New Poetry, 1980; New Stories, 1981; Hard Lines, 1987; Words Etcetera; Words Broadsheet; Pen Broadsheet, 1986; Weyfarers; Overspill; MTD Journal. Honours: First Prize for Fiction and Poetry, Moor Park

College, 1972; UNA Trust Award (for Peace Play Festival), 1988; University of Surrey Arts Committee Literary Festival Award, 1991. Memberships: PEN; TWU. Literary Agent: Patricia Robertson. Address: Strone Grove Road, Hindhead, Surrey GU26 6QP, England.

JHABVALA Ruth Prawer, b. 7 May 1927, Cologne, Germany. Writer. m. 16 June 1951, 3 daughters. Education: BA, 1948, MA, 1951, DLitt, London. Publications: The Householder, 1960; A New Dominion, 1971; Heat and Dust, 1975; Out of India, 1986; Three Continents, 1987; Poet and Dancer, 1993; Shards of Memory, 1995. Honours: Booker Prize, 1975; Neil Gunn International Fellowship, 1979; MacArthur Foundation Fellowship, 1984-89; Academy Awards, 1987, 1993; American Academy of Arts and Letters Literature Award, 1992. Memberships: Royal Society of Literature, fellow; Authors Guild; Writers Guild of America. Address: 400 East 52nd Street, New York, NY 10022, USA.

JOB Stefania, b. 7 May 1909, Pozega, Croatia. Lecturer; Writer. Education: Real Gymnasium-Matura, Zagreb, 1928; Literature Studies, Zürich, Switzerland. Appointment: C J Jung Institute, Zürich. Publications: Ja Vorhof; Die Vernachläsigte Muse; Frau sein im Alter; Das Geschenk. Contributions to: Numerous magazines and journals. Memberships: PEN, Germany and Switzerland. Address: CH-8702 Zollikon, Switzerland.

JOHANSEN Birgit Dagmar Johansen, b. 14 Sept 1942, Viborg, Denmark. Psychiatrist; Sexologist; Writer. 1 son, 1 daughter. Education: MD, 1973; Psychiatrist, Teacher in Sexology, Advanced Level, University of Gôtteborg, Sweden, 1984. Publications: Den Skjulte Lyst, 1988; Incest, 1989; Dit Seksuelle Indre, 1990; Smertens Lyst, 1990; Love Has No Age, 1997; Co-author of several books in field. Contributions to: Helse, monthly columnist; Alt for Damerne, weekly columnisdt. Memberships: National Press Club of Denmark; Danish Writers' Union. Address: Ved Stranden 16, DK-1061 Copenhagen, Denmark.

JOHANSSON-BACKE Karl Erik, b. 24 Nov 1914, Stockholm, Sweden. Teacher (Retired 1963); Author; Playwright. m. Kerstin Gunhild Bergquist, (childrens author), 21 Nov 1943, 1 son, 3 daughters. Education: Degree, High School Teacher. Publications: A Pole in the River (novel), 1950; Daybreak (novel), 1954; Lust and Flame (poetry), 1981; The Mountain of Temptation (novel), 1983; The Ghost Aviator (documentary), 1985; The Tree and the Bread (novel), 1987; King of Mountains (novel), 1993. Honours: Many literary awards, 1961-93. Memberships: Swedish Authors Federation; Honorary Member, Swedish Playwrights Federation, 1986. Literary Agent: Arbetarkultur, Stockholm; Bonniers, Stockholm; Proprius, Stockholm. Address: Kopmangstan 56, 83133 Ostersund, Sweden.

JOHN Katherine. See: **WATKINS Karen Christna**.

JOHN Nicholas. See: **VIDOR Miklos Janos**.

JOHNS Kenneth. See: **BULMER Henry Kenneth**.

JOHNS Richard Alton Jr, b. 17 July 1929, Tyler, Texas, USA. Commerical Artist; Writer. m. Joan Turner, 8 Nov 1958, 1 son, 1 daughter. Education: AA, Tyler Junior College, 1948; BA, North Texas University, 1950. Publications: The Legacy, 1963; Thirteenth Apostle, 1966; Garden of the Okapi, 1968; Return to Heroism, 1969; The Andrews Center (history), 1992; Jarvis College (history), 1994. Contributions to: Chronicles; Cable Guide. Honour: Grand Prize, Short Story, 1994. Address: 3324 Teakwood Drive, Tyler, TX 75701, USA.

JOHNSON Alison Findlay, b. 19 Nov 1947, Stafford, England. Author. m. Andrew J D Johnson, 1973, 1 daughter. Education: MA, Aberdeen University, 1968; BPhil, Oxford, 1970. Publications: A House by the Shore, 1986; Scarista Style, 1987; Children of Disobedience, 1989; Islands in the Sound, 1989; The Wicked Generation, 1992. Contributions to: West Highland Press; The Times. Address: c/o Vivien Green, 43 Doughty Street, London WC1N 2LF, England.

JOHNSON Carlos Alberto, b. 26 June 1943, Lima, Peru. Writer. Education: BS, Education and Spanish, Buffalo State College, 1971-72; MA, Spanish, Brooklyn College, 1972-74; Completed 60 Credits Toward PhD, Spanish, City University of New York Graduate Centre, 1974-76. Appointments: Correspondent and Reporter for El Dominical of the Peruvian Newspaper El Diario el Comercio, 1981-88. Publications: Adivina quien es?, 1976; El Ojo-Cara del Professor,

1983; El monologo del vendedor ambulante, 1984; Cuando me muera que me arrojen al Rimac en un cajon blanco, 1990. Contributions to: Newspapers and journals. Honour: National Endowment for the Arts Fellowship, 1989. Address: 30-98 Crescent Street, Apt 1C, Astoria, NY 11102, USA.

JOHNSON Charles, b. 1 Jan 1942, Erdington, Birmingham, England. m. Rosalind Mora MacInnes, 15 July 1977, 1 daughter. Education: Newcastle upon Tyne College of Commerce (Associate of the Library Association), 1964-65; Editorial Partner, Flarestock Publishing. Publication: A Box of Professional Secrets: Poems, 1995. Contributions to: Anthologies: Above the Salt, 1992; One for Jimmy, 1992; Along the Line, 1996. Contributions to: Wide Skirt; Blade; Headlock; Southfields; Open Access; Fatchance; Orbis; Iota; Exile; Staple; Envoi; Frogmore Papers; Other Poetry; Seam; Tandem; Smiths Knoll; Writing in Education; Fire; People to People; Journal of Contemporary Anglo-Scandinavian Poetry. Memberships: St Johns Poetry Workshop; Droitwich Poetry Group; Redditch Poets Workshop (founder). Address: 41 Buckleys Green, Alvechurch, Birmingham B48 7NG, England.

JOHNSON Colin, b. 23 July 1939, Beverley, Western Australia. Novelist. Appointment: Lecturer, University of Queensland, St Lucia. Publications: Wild Cat Falling, 1965; Long Live Sandawara, 1979; Before the Invasion: Aboriginal Life to 1788, 1980; Doctor Wooreddy's Prescription for Enduring the End of the World, 1983; Doin' Wildcat, 1988; Dalwurra: The Black Bittern, 1988; Writing from the Fringe, 1990. Honours: Wieckhard Prize, 1979; Western Australia Literary Award, 1989. Address: c/o Department of English, University of Queensland, St Lucia, Queensland 4067, Australia.

JOHNSON David, b. 26 Aug 1927, Meir, Staffs, England. Historian. Education: Repton; Sandhurst. Publications: Sabre General, 1959; Promenade in Champagne, 1960; Lanterns in Gascony, 1965; A Candle in Aragon, 1970; Regency Revolution, 1974; Napoleon's Cavalry and its Leaders, 1978; The French Cavalry 1792-1815, 1989. Contributions to: Military History, USA. Address: 16 Belgrave Gardens, London NW8 0RB, England.

JOHNSON Denis, b. 1949, Munich, Germany. Writer. Publications: The Man Among the Seals, 1969; Inner Weather, 1976; The Incognito Lounge and Other Poems, 1982; Angels, 1983; Fiskadoro, 1985; The Stars at Noon, 1986; Jesus' Son, 1993. Honour: American Academy of Arts and Letters Literature Award, 1993. Address: Alfred A Knopf Inc, 201 East 50th Street, New York, NY 10022, USA.

JOHNSON Diane Lain, b. 28 Apr 1934, Moline, Illinois, USA. Writer. m. John Frederick Murray, 9 Nov 1969, 4 children. Education: AA, Stephens College, 1953; BA, University of Utah, 1957; MA, PhD, 1968, University of California at Los Angeles. Appointment: Faculty, Department of English, University of California, 1968-87. Publications: Fair Game, 1965; Loving Hands at Home, 1968; Lesser Lives, 1972; The Shadow Knows, 1975; Terrorists and Novelists, 1982; Dashiell Hammett, 1983; Perian Nights, 1987; Health and Happiness, 1990; Natural Opium, 1993. Contributions to: Newspapers and magazines. Honours: Several awards. Memberships: PEN; Writers Guild of America. Address: Attorney Lizbeth Hasse, 2000 Center Street, Suite 300, Berkeley, CA 94704, USA.

JOHNSON George (Laclede), b. 20 Jan 1952, Fayetteville, Arkansas, USA. Writer. Education: BA, University of New Mexico, 1975; MA, American University, 1979. Publications: Architects of Fear, 1984; Machinery of the Mind, 1986; In the Places of Memory, 1991. Contributions to: Newspapers and magazines. Honour: Alicia Patterson Journalism Fellow, 1984. Address: c/o Esther Newbery, ICM, 40 West 57th Street, New York, NY 10019, USA.

JOHNSON Hugh Eric Allan, b. 10 Mar 1939, London, England. Author; Editor. m. Judith Eve Grinling, 1965, 1 son, 2 daughters. Education: MA, King's College, Cambridge. Appointments: Feature Writer, Condé Nast Magazines, 1960-63; Editor, Wine and Food Magazine, 1963-65; Wine Correspondent, Sunday Times, 1965-67; Travel Editor, 1967; Editor, Queen Magazine, 1968-70; Wine Editor, Cuisine Magazine, New York, 1983-84; Editorial Consultant, The Garden, 1975-. Publications: Wine, 1966; The World Atlas of Wine, 1971, 4th edition, 1994; The International Book of Trees, 1973, 2nd edition, 1994; The California Wine Book (with Bob Thompson), 1975; Hugh Johnson's Pocket Wine Book, annually, 1977-; The Principles of

Gardening, 1979, revised edition, 1996; Hugh Johnson's Wine Companion, 1983, latest edition, 1997; Hugh Johnson's Cellar Book, 1986; The Atlas of German Wines, 1986; Understanding Wine (A Sainsbury Guide), 1986; Atlas of the Wines of France (with Hubrecht Duijker), 1987; The Story of Wine, 1989; The Art and Science of Wine (with James Halliday), 1992; Hugh Johnson on Gardening, 1993. Other: How to Handle a Wine (video), 1984; A History of Wine (Channel 4 TV series), 1989. Address: Saling Hall, Great Saling, Essex CM7 5DT, England.

JOHNSON James (Henry), b. 19 Nov 1930, Coleraine, Northern Ireland. Professor of Geography; Writer. m. Jean McKane, 31 Mar 1956, 2 sons, 2 daughters. Education: BA, Queen's University of Belfast, 1953; MA, University of Wisconsin, 1954; PhD, University of London, 1962. Appointments: Professor of Geography; Editor, Aspects of Geography series, 1980-96. Publications: Urban Geography: An Introductory Analysis, 1967; Trends in Geography (editor), 1969; Geographical Mobility of Labour in England and Wales (co-author), 1974; Suburban Growth (editor), 1974; Urbanisation, 1980; The Structure of Nineteenth Century Cities (co-editor), 1982; Labour Migration (co-editor), 1990; Population Migration (co-author), 1990; The Human Geography of Ireland, 1994. Contributions to: Geographical journals. Address: The Coach-house, Wyreside Hall, Dolphinholme, Lancaster LA2 9DH, England.

JOHNSON James Ralph, b. 20 May 1922, Fort Payne, Alabama, USA. Writer; Artist. m. (1) 2 sons, 1 daughter, (2) Burdetta F Beebe, 11 Oct 1961. Education: BS, Economics, Howard College, Birmingham, Alabama; US Navy Intelligence School, Anacostia, Maryland, 1951; Armed Forces Staff College, Norfolk, Virginia, 1960. Publications: Mountain Bobcat, 1953; Lost on Hawk Mountain, 1954; The Last Passenger, 1956; Big Cypress Buck, 1957; Horsemen Blue and Gray, 1960; Anyone Can Live Off the Land, 1961; Best Photos of the Civil War, 1961; Wild Venture, 1961; Utah Lion, 1962; Anyone Can Camp in Comfort, 1964; American Wild Horses, 1964; Camels West, 1964; Anyone Can Backpack in Comfort, 1965; The Wolf Cub, 1966; Advanced Camping Techniques, 1967; Pepper, 1967; Ringtail, 1968; Blackie the Gorilla, 1968; Animal Paradise, 1969; Moses Band of Chimpanzees, 1969; Everglades Adventure, 1970; Southern Swamps of America, 1970; Zoos of Today, 1971; Photography for Young People, 1971; Animals and Their Food, 1972. Contributions to: Marine Corps Gazette; Leatherneck; Saga; Boys' Life; Field and Stream. Memberships: Western Writers of America; Outdoor Writers of America; Santa Fe Society of Artists. Address: Box 5295, Santa Fe, NM 87502, USA.

JOHNSON Mel. See: **MALZBERG Barry.**

JOHNSON Nora, b. 31 Jan 1933, Hollywood, California, USA. Author. m. (1) Leonard Siwek, 1955, (2) John A Milici, 1965, 2 sons, 2 daughters. Education: BA, Smith College, 1954. Publications: The World of Henry Orient, 1958; A Step Beyond Innocence, 1961; Love Letter in the Dead Letter Office, 1966; Flashback, 1979; You Can Go Home Again, 1982; The Two of Us, 1984; Tender Offer, 1985; Uncharted Places, 1988; Perfect Together, 1991. Contributions to: Newspapers and magazines. Honours: McCall's Short Story Prize, 1962; O Henry Award Story, 1982; New York Times Best Book Citations, 1982, 1984. Memberships: Author's Guild; PEN. Address: 1385 York Avenue, 8G, New York, NY 10021, USA.

JOHNSON Owen Verne, b. 22 Feb 1946, Madison, Wisconsin, USA. Historian; Associate Professor. m. Marta Kucerova, 17 July 1969, 2 daughters. Education: BA, Washington State University, 1968; MA, 1970, Certificate, 1978, PhD, 1978, University of Michigan. Appointments: Sports Editor, General Assignment Reporter, Pullman Washington Herald, 1961-67; Reporter, Editor, Producer, WUOM, Ann Arbor, Michigan, 1969-77; Administrative Assistant, Russian and East European Center, University of Michigan, 1978-79; Assistant Professor, Journalism, Southern Illinois University, 1979-80; Assistant Professor, Journalism, 1980-87, Associate Professor, Journalism, 1987-, Acting Director, Polish Studies Center, 1989-90, Director, Russian and East European Institute, 1991-, Indiana University, Bloomington. Publications: Slovakia 1918-1938: Education and the Making of a Nation, 1985. Editor: Czech Marks, 1982-84; Clio Among the Media, 1983-84. Address: School of Journalism, Indiana University, Bloomington, IN 47405, USA.

JOHNSON Paul (Bede), b. 2 Nov 1928, Barton, England. Historian; Journalist; Broadcaster. m. Marigold Hunt, 1957, 3 sons, 1

daughter. Education: BA, Magdalen College, Oxford. Appointments: Assistant Executive Editor, Realites, Paris, 1952-55; Assistant Editor, 1955-60, Deputy Editor, 1960-64, Editor, 1965-70, Director, 1965-75, New Statesman; DeWitt Wallace Professor of Communications, American Enterprise Institute, Washington, DC, 1980; Freelance Writer; Daily Mail Columnist. Publications: The Offshore Islanders, 1972; Elizabeth I: A Study in Power and Intellect, 1974; Pope John XXIII, 1975; A History of Christianity, 1976; Enemies of Society, 1977; The National Trust Book of British Castles, 1978; The Civilization of Ancient Egypt, 1978; Civilizations of the Holy Land, 1979; British Cathedrals, 1980; Ireland: Land of Troubles, 1980; The Recovery of Freedom, 1980; Pope John Paul II and the Catholic Restoration, 1982; History of the Modern World: From 1917 to the 1980s, 1984; The Pick of Paul Johnson, 1985; A History of the Jews, 1986; The Oxford Book of Political Anecdotes (editor), 1986; The Intellectuals, 1989; The Birth of the Modern World Society, 1815-30, 1991. Honours: Book of the Year Prize, Yorkshire Post, 1975; Francis Boyer Award for Services to Public Policy, 1979; Krag Award for Excellence, Literature, 1980. Memberships: Royal Commission on the Press, 1974-77; Cable Authority, 1984-. Address: 29 Newton Road, London W2, England.

JOHNSON (John) Stephen, b. 3 June 1947, Mansfield, England. Writer. Education: MA, 1976, DPhil, 1976, Oxford University. Publications: The Roman Fort of the Saxon Shore, 1976; Later Roman Britain, 1980; Late Roman Fortifications, 1983; Hadrian's Wall, 1989; Rome and its Empire, 1989. Address: 50 Holmdere Avenue, London SE24 9LF, England.

JOHNSON Stowers, British. Appointments: Principal, Dagenham Literary Institute, 1936-39; Headmaster, Aveley School, 1939-68; Editor, Anglo-Soviet Journal, 1966-68; Art Curator, National Liberal Club, London, 1974-79. Publications: Branches Green and Branches Black, 1944; London Saga, 1946; The Mundane Tree, 1947; Mountains and No Mules, Sonntes They Say, 1949; Before and After Puck, 1953; When Fountains Fall, 1961; Gay Bulgaria, 1964; Yugoslav Summer, 1967; Collector's Luck, 1968; Turkish Panorama, The Two Faces of Russia, 1969; Agents Extraordinary, 1975; Headmastering Man, 1986; Hearthstones in the Hills, 1987; Collector's World, 1989. Address: Corbiere, 45 Rayleigh Road, Hutton, Brentwood, Essex, England.

JOHNSON Terry, b. 20 Dec 1955. Playwright. Education: Queens School, Bushey, Hertfordshire; BA, Drama, University of Birmingham, 1976. Publications: Plays: Amabel (produced London, 1979); Days Here so Dark (produced London, Edinburgh, 1981); Insignificance (produced London, 1982, New York, 1986); Bellevue (toured 1982); The Idea (produced Bristol, 1983); Unsuitable for Adults (produced London, 1984, Costa Mesa, California, 1986); Cries From the Mammal House (produced London and Leicester, 1984); Tuesdays Child, with Kate Lock (televised 1985, produced, London 1986). Screenplays: Insignificance, 1985; Killing Time, 1985; Way Upstream, 1987. TV plays: Time Trouble, 1985; Tuesdays Child, with Kate Lock, 1985. Honour: Evening Standard Award, 1983. Address: c/o Phil Kelvin, Goodwin Associates, 12 Rabbit Row, London W8 4DX, England.

JOHNSTON George Benson, b. 7 Oct 1913, Hamilton, Ontario, Canada. Poet; Translator. m. Jeanne McRae, 1944, 3 sons, 3 daughters. Education: BA, 1936, MA, 1945, University of Toronto; LLD, Queen's University, Kingston, Ontario, 1971; LitD, Carleton University, 1979. Appointments: Assistant Professor of English, Mount Allison University, Sackville, 1946-48; Staff, English Department, Carleton University, Ottawa, 1950-79. Publications: Verse: The Cruising Auk, 1959; Home Free, 1966; Happy Enough, 1972; Between, 1976; Taking a Grip, 1979; Auk Redivivus: Selected Poems, 1981; Ask Again, 1984; Endeared by Dark (collected poems), 1990. Editor-Translator: Rocky Shores: An Anthology of Faroese Poetry, 1981; George Whalley: Collected Poems, 1986. Translator: The Saga of Gisli, 1963; The Faroe Islanders' Saga, 1975; The Greenlanders' Saga; Wind over Romsdal: Selected Poems (Odegard), 1982; Bee-Buzz, Salmon-Leap (Odegard), verse, 1986; Seeing and Remembering (Matras), verse, 1988; Barbara, novel in translation, 1993; Thrand of Gotu, sagas in translation; Endeared By Dark: Collected Poems, 1990; What is to Come (verse), 1996. Address: PO Box 1706, Huntingdon, Quebec J0S 1H0, Canada.

JOHNSTON Jennifer, b. 12 Jan 1930. Author; Dramatist. m. (1) Ian Smyth, 1951, 2 sons, 2 daughters, (2) David Gilliland, 1976. Publications: Fiction: The Captains and the Kings, 1972; The Gates,

1973; How Many Miles to Babylon?, 1974; Shadows on our Skin, 1978 (dramatised for TV, 1979); The Old Jest, 1979; The Invisible Worm, 1991. Plays: Nightingale and Not the Lark, 1980; Indian Summer, 1983; The Porch, 1986; The Invisible Man, 1986. Contributions to: BBC Radio. Honours: Honorary doctorates. Address: Brook Hall, Culmore Road, Derry BT48 8JE, Northern Ireland.

JOHNSTON Julia (Ann), b. 21 Jan 1941, Smith Falls, Ontario, Canada. Writer. m. Basil W Johnston, 12 Oct 1963, 4 daughters. Education: University of Toronto, 1963; Trent University, 1984. Publications: There's Going to be a Frost, 1979; Don't Give Up the Ghosts, 1981; Tasting the Alternative, 1982; After 30 Years of Law, Ken Starvis Sculpts New Career, 1990; Hero of Lesser Causes, 1992; The Interiors of Pots, 1992; Adam and Eve and Pinch Me, 1994. Honours: Governor-General's Literary Award, 1992; School Library Best Book, 1993; Joan Fassler Memorial Award, 1994. Memberships: Canadian Society of Childrens Authors; Writers Union of Canada. Address: 463 Hunter Street West, Peterborough, Ontario K9H 2M7, Canada.

JOHNSTON Ronald John, b. 30 Mar 1941, Swindon, Wiltshire, England. Professor of Geography; Writer. m. Rita Brennan, 16 Apr 1963, 1 son, 1 daughter. Education: BA, 1962, MA, 1964, University of Manchester; PhD, Monash University, 1967. Appointments: Teaching Fellow, 1964, Senior Teaching Fellow, 1965, Lecturer, 1966, Monash University; Lecturer, 1967-68, Senior Lecturer, 1969-72, Reader, 1973-74, University of Canterbury, New Zealand; Professor of Geography, 1974-92, Pro-Vice Chancellor for Academic Affairs, 1989-92, University of Sheffield; Vice-Chancellor, Essex University, 1992-95; Professor of Geography, Bristol University, 1995-. Publications: Retailing in Melbourne (with P J Rimmer), 1970; Urban Residential Patterns: An Introductory Review, 1971; Spatial Structures: An Introduction to the Study of Spatial Systems in Human Geography, 1973; The New Zealanders: How They Live and Work, 1976; The World Trade System: Some Enquiries Into Its Spatial Structure, 1976; Geography and Inequality (with B E Coates and P L Knox), 1977; Multivariate Statistical Analysis in Geography: A Primer on the General Linear Model, 1978; Political, Electoral and Spatial Systems, 1979; Geography of Elections (with P J Taylor), 1979; Geography and Geographers: Anglo-American Human Geography Since 1945, 1979, 5th edition, 1997; City and Society: An Outline for Urban Geography, 1980; The Geography of Federal Spending in the United States of America, 1980; The American Urban System: A Geographical Perspective, 1982; Geography and the State, 1982; Philosophy and Human Geography: An Introduction to Contemporary Approaches, 1983, 2nd edition, 1986; Residential Segregation, the State and Constitutional Conflict in American Urban Areas, 1984; The Geography of English Politics: The 1983 General Election, 1985; On Human Geography, 1986; Bell-Ringing: The English Art of Change-Ringing, 1986; Money and Votes: Constituency Campaign Spending and Election Results, 1987; The United States: A Contemporary Human Geography (co-author), 1988; A Nation Dividing?: The Electoral Map of Great Britain, 1979-1987 (with C J Pattie and J G Allsopp), 1988; Environmental Problems: Nature, Economy and State, 1989, 2nd edition, 1996; The Dictionary of Human Geography (editor), 1989, 3rd edition, 1993; An Atlas of Bells (co-author), 1990; A Question of Place: Exploring the Practice of Human Geography, 1991. Contributions to: Various books and professional journals. Honours: Murchison Award, 1985; Victoria Medal, Royal Geographical Society, 1990; Honors Award for Distinction in Research, Association of American Geographers, 1991. Memberships: Institute of British Geographers, secretary, 1982-85, president, 1990. Address: c/o Department of Geography, Bristol University, Bristol BS8 1SS, England.

JOHNSTON William, b. 30 July 1925, Belfast, Northern Ireland. Jesuit Roman Catholic Priest; Professor of Theology; Writer. Education: Theological studies. Appointments: Ordained a Roman Catholic Priest, 1957; Professor of Theology, Sophia University, Tokyo, 1960-. Publications: The Mysticism of the Cloud of Unknowing, 1967, 2nd edition, 1975; S Endo: Silence (translator), 1969; The Still Point: On Zen and Christian Mysticism, 1970; Christian Zen, 1971; The Cloud of Unknowing and the Book of Privy Counselling (editor), 1973; Silent Music, 1974; The Inner Eye of Love, 1978; The Mirror Mind, 1981; T Nagai, The Bells of Nagasaki (translator), 1984; The Wounded Stag, 1985; Being in Love: The Practice of Christian Prayer, 1988; Letters to Contemplatives, 1991; Mystical Zheology, 1995. Address: c/o Sophia University, 7 Kioi-Cho, Chiyodaku, Tokyo 102, Japan.

JOHNSTONE Iain Gilmour, b. 8 Apr 1943, Reading, England. Film Critic. m. Maureen Hammond, 1957, 1 son, 2 daughters. Education: LLB Honours; Distinction, Solicitor's finals. Appointment: Film Critic, The Sunday Times. Publications: The Arnhem Report, 1977; The Men With No Name, 1980; Dustin Hoffman, 1984; Cannes: The Novel, 1990; Wimbledon 2000, 1992. Address: 16 Tournay Road, London SW6, England.

JOLLEY (Monica) Elizabeth, b. 4 June 1923, Birmingham, England. Writer; Tutor. m. Leonard Jolley, 1 son, 2 daughters. Education: Nursing Training, 1940-46. Appointment: Writer-in-Residence, Western Australia Institute of Technology, later Curtin University of Technology, Perth, 1980-. Publications: Five Acre Virgin and Other Stories, 1976; The Travelling Entertainer, 1979; Palomino, 1980; The Newspaper of Claremont Street, 1981; Mr Scobie's Riddle, 1983; Woman in a Lampshade, 1983; Miss Peabody's Inheritance, 1983; Milk and Honey, 1984; The Well, 1986; The Sugar Mother, 1988; My Father's Moon, 1989; Cabin Fever, 1990; Central Mischief, 1992; The Georges' Wife, 1993; Diary of a Weekend Farmer (poems), 1993; The Orchard Thieves, 1995. Honours: Honorary Doctorate, Western Australia Institute of Technology, 1986; Officer of the Order of Australia, 1988; Honorary Doctor of Literature, Macquarie University, Sydney, 1995. Address: 28 Agett Road, Claremont, Western Australia 6010, Australia.

JONAS Manfred, b. 9 Apr 1927, Mannheim, Germany. Historian. m. Mancy Jane Greene, 19 July 1952, 2 sons, 2 daughters. Education: BS, City College of New York, 1949; AM, 1951, PhD, 1959, Harvard University. Appointments: Visiting Professor for North American History, Free University of Berlin, 1959-62; Assistant Professor to Professor of History, 1963-81, Washington Irving Professor in Modern Literary and Historical Studies, 1981-86, John Bigelow Professor of History, 1986-, Union College, Schenectady, New York, USA; Dr Otto Salgo Visiting Professor of American Studies, Eötvös Lorand University, Budapest, Hungary, 1983-84. Publications: Die Unabhängigkeitserklärung der Vereingten Staaten, 1964; Isolationism in America 1935-1941, 1966, 2nd edition, 1990; American Foreign Relations in the 20th Century, 1967; Roosevelt and Churchill: Their Secret Wartime Correspondence, 1975, 2nd edition, 1990; New Opportunities in the New Nation, 1982; The United States and Germany: A Diplomatic History, 1984. Contributions to: The Historian; Mid-America; American Studies; Maryland Historical Magazine; Essex County Historical Collections; Jahrbuch für Amerikastudien. Address: Department of History, Union College, Schenectady, NY 12308, USA.

JONES Alun Arthur Gwynne. See: CHALFONT Baron.

JONES Ann Maret, b. 3 Sept 1937, USA. Author; Teacher. Education: MA, University of Michigan, 1961; PhD, University of Wisconsin, 1970. Appointment: Writing Faculty, Mount Holyoke College, 1986-97. Publications: Uncle Tom's Campus, 1973; Women Who Kill, 1980; Everyday Death: Case of Bernadette Powell, 1985; When Love Goes Wrong (with Susan Schechter), 1992; Next Time, She'll Be Dead, 1994. Contributions to: Nation; Ms; Vogue; American Heritage; New York Times; Newsday; Women's Rights Law Reporter; National Geographic; Condé Nast Traveler; Women's Sports. Honour: Author/Journalist of the Year, National Prisoners Rights Union, 1986. Memberships: PEN American Center; Authors Guild; National Writers Union; National Book Critics Circle. Address: c/o Charlotte Sheedy Agency, 65 Bleecker Street, New York, NY 10012, USA.

JONES Brian, b. 1938, England. Writer; Poet. Publications: The Lady With the Little Dog, 1962; Poems, 1966; A Family Album, 1968; Interior, 1969; The Mantis Hand and Other Poems, 1970; For Mad Mary, 1974; The Spitfire on the Northern Line, 1975; The Island Normal, 1980; Children of Separation, 1985; Freeborn John, 1990. Address: c/o Caranet Press, 208 Corn Exchange Buildings, Manchester M4 3BQ, England.

JONES Brian Kinsey. See: BALL Brian Neville.

JONES Christopher Dennis, b. 13 Dec 1949, New York, USA. Playwright. m. Gwendoline Shirley Rose, 18 Aug 1979. Education: BA, English Literature, University of Pittsburgh. Appointments: Resident Playwright, Carnaby Street Theatre, London, 1975-76; Resident Playwright, New Hope Theatre Company, London, 1977- 78. Publications: Plays: Passing Strangers, 1975; Nasty Corners, 1977; New Signals, 1978; In Flight Reunion, 1979; Sterile Landscape, 1982; Ralph Bird's River Race, 1985; Dying Hairless With a Rash, 1985;

Bitter Chalice, 1987; Begging the Ring, 1989; Burning Youth, 1989. Contributions to: Country Life; Arts Review. Membership: Writer's Guild of Great Britain. Address: c/o Richard Wakeley, Fraser and Dunlop, 91 Regent Street, London W1R 8RU, England.

JONES Diana Wynne b. 16 Aug 1934, London, England. Writer. m. J A Burrow, 23 Dec 1956, 3 sons. Education: BA, Oxford University, 1956. Publications: Wilkin's Tooth, 1973; The Ogre Downstairs, 1974; Witch Week, 1974; Cart and Cwidder, 1975; Dogsbody, 1975; Eight Days of Luke, 1975; Power of Three, 1976; Charmed Life, 1977; Drowned Ammet, 1977; Who Got Rid of Angus Flint?, 1978; The Magicians of Caprona, 1979; The Four Grannies, 1980; The Spellcoats, 1980; The Homeward Bounders, 1981; Archer's Goon, 1984; Warlock at the Wheel, 1984; Fire and Hemlock, 1985; Howl's Moving Castle, 1986; A Tale of Time City, 1987; The Lives of Christopher Chant, 1988; Chair Person, 1989; Wild Robert, 1989; Castle in the Air, 1990; Black Maria, 1991; Yes Dear, 1992; A Sudden Wild Magic, 1992; The Crown of Dalemark, 1993; Hexwood, 1993; Fantasy Stories (editor), 1994; Guerard's Ride, 1995; The Tough Guide to Fantasyland, 1996; Minor Arcana, 1996. Contributions to: Newspapers. Honours: Guardian Award for Children's Books, 1978; Honour Book, Boston Globe, 1984; Horn Book Award, 1986. Membership: Society of Authors. Address: 9 The Polygon, Bristol BS8 4PW, England.

JONES Douglas Gordon, b. 1 Jan 1929, Bancroft, Ontario, Canada. Professor; Poet. Education: MA, Queens University, Kingston, Ontario, 1954. Appointment: Professor, University of Sherbrooke, Quebec, 1963-94. Publications: Poetry: Frost on the Sun, 1957; The Is Axeman, 1961; Phrases from Orpheus, 1967; Under the Thunder the Flowers Light Up the Earth, 1977; A Throw of Particles: Selected and New Poems, 1983; Balthazar and Other Poems, 1988; The Floating Garden, 1995. Other: Butterfly on Rock: A Study of Themes and Images in Canadian Literature, 1970. Honours: President's Medal, University of Western Ontario, 1976; Governor General's Award for Poetry, 1977; Honorary DLitt, Guelph University, 1982; Governor General's Award for Translation, 1993. Address: PO Box 356, North Hatley, Quebec JOB 2CO, Canada.

JONES Elwyn Ashford, b. 7 Mar 1941, Cynwyd, Wales. Teacher; Writer. Education: BEd, University of Wales, Bangor. Publications: Y Baal Barfog, 1971; Picell Mewn Cefn, 1978; Nain Ar Goll, 1986; Cicio Nyth Cacwn, 1987; Straeon Hanner Nos, 1989; Heb El Fai, 1992. Contributions to: Various magazines. Address: Pen y Ddol, Cynwyd, Corwen, Clwyd LL21 0ET, Wales.

JONES Evan (Lloyd), b. 20 Nov 1931, Melbourne, Victoria, Australia. Lecturer; Poet. m. Margot Jones, 1966, 4 children. Education: MA, University of Melbourne, 1957; MA, Stanford University, CA. Appointments: Senior Lecturer, University of Melbourne, 1965-89. Publications: Inside the Whale, 1960; Understandings, 1967; Kenneth MacKenzie, 1969; The Poems of Kenneth MacKenzie (co-editor), 1972; Recognitions, 1978; Left at the Post, 1984. Address: c/o Department of English, University of Melbourne, Parkville, VA 3052, Australia.

JONES (Morgan) Glyn, b. 28 Feb 1905, Merthyr Tydfill, Glamorgan, Wales. Teacher of English (retired); Poet; Writer; Translator. m. Phyllis Doreen Jones, 19 Aug 1935. Education: St Paul's College, Cheltenham. Appointment: Teacher of English, South Wales Schools. Publications: Poetry: Poems, 1939; The Dream of Jake Hopkins, 1954; Selected Poems, 1975; Selected Poems, Fragments and Fictions, 1988. Fiction: The Blue Red, 1937; The Water Music, 1944; The Valley, the City, the Village, 1956; The Learning Lark, 1960; The Island of Apples, 1965; Selected Short Stories, 1977. Other: Books of criticism; Translations. Contributions to: Journals and periodicals. Honours: Honorary DLitt, University of Wales, 1974; Honorary Fellow, Trinity College, Carmarthen, Wales, 1993. Membership: Welsh Academy, Fellow. Address: 158 Manor Way, Whitchurch, Cardiff CF4 1RN, Wales.

JONES Gwyn, b. 24 May 1907, Wales. Author. m. (1) Alice Rees, 1928, dec 1979, (2) Mair Sivell, 1979. Education: University of Wales. Appointments: Schoolmaster, 1929-35; Lecturer, University College of South Wales and Monmouthshire, 1935-40; Director, Penmark Press, 1939-; Professor of English Language and Literature, 1940-64, Fellow, 1987, University College of Wales, Aberystwyth; Professor of English Language and Literature, 1965 75, Fellow, 1980, University College, Cardiff; Visiting Professor, University of Iowa, 1982.

Publications: Novels: Richard Savage, 1935; Times Like These, 1936, reprint, 1979; Garland of Bays, 1938; The Green Island, 1946; The Flowers Beneath the Scythe, 1952; The Walk Home, 1962. Short stories: The Buttercup Field, 1945; The Still Waters, 1948; Shepherd's Hey, 1953; Selected Short Stories, 1974. Non-fiction: A Prospect of Wales, 1948; Welsh Legends and Folk-Tales, 1955; Scandinavian Legends and Folk-Tales, 1956; The Norse Atlantic Saga, 1964, new edition, 1986; A History of the Vikings, 1968, revised and enlarged, 1984; Being and Belonging, 1977; Kings, Beasts and Heroes, 1982; Background to Dylan Thomas and Other Explorations, 1992. Translations: The Vatndalers' Saga, 1942; The Mabinogion (with Thomas Jones), 1948; Egil's Saga, 1960; Eirik the Red, 1961. Editor: Welsh Review, 1939-48; Short Stories, 1956; Twenty-Five Welsh Short Stories (with I Ff Elis), 1971; The Oxford Book of Welsh Verse in English, 1977; Fountains of Praise, 1983. Contributions to: Learned and literary journals. Honours: Commander o Orfder of the British Empire, 1965; Christian Gauss Award, Institut International des Arts et des Lettres, 1973; Honorary DLitt, Wales, 1977, Nottingham, 1978, Southampton, 1983; Commander's Cross, Order of the Falcon, Iceland, 1987; Honorary Freeman of Islwyn, 1988. Memberships: Learned societies; Viking Society for Northern Research, President, 1950-52. Address: Castle Cottage, Sea View, Aberystwyth, Dyfed SW23 1DZ, Wales.

JONES Hettie, b. 16 July 1934, Brooklyn, New York, USA. Writer. Div, 2 daughters. Education: BA, Washington College, University of Virginia, 1955; Graduate Studies, Columbia University. Appointments: Faculty, Hunter College of the City University of New York, 1984, State University of New York, 1989-91, New School for Social Research, 1991, University of Wyoming, 1993. Publications: Longhouse Winter, 1974; Big Star Fallin' Mama, 1975; Coyote Tales, 1976; How to Eat Your ABCs, 1978; I Hate to Talk About Your Mother, 1980; How I Became Hettie Jones, 1991. Contributions to: Periodicals. Honours: Best Book for Young Adults Award, New York Public Library, 1975; Best Book of the Year Selection, New York Times, 1991. Memberships: PEN (Prison Writing Committee); Phi Beta Kappa. Address: c/o Berenice Hoffman Literary Agency, 215 West 75th Street, New York, NY 10022, USA.

JONES Ivor Wynne, b. 28 Mar 1927, Liverpool, England. Journalist; Author; Company Director; Book Designer. m. Marion-Jeannette Wrighton, 19 July 1958, 1 son, 1 daughter. Education: BBC Engineering Training School. Appointment: Research Editor, Llechwedd Slate Caverns, Blaenau Ffestiniog, 1972-. Publications: Money for All, 1969; Shipwrecks of North Wales, 1973; Betws-y-coed and the Conway Valley, 1974; Llandudno, Queen of the Welsh Resorts, 1975; Wales and Israel, 1988; The Order of St John in Wales, 1993; Colwyn Bay: A Brief History, 1995. Contributions to: Liverpool Daily Post, Columnist, 1955-; Various historical journals. Honour: European Architectural Year Book Design Award, 1975. Memberships: Undeb Awduron Cymru, Union of Welsh Authors; Lewis Carroll Society. Address: Pegasus, 71 Llandudno Road, Penrhyn Bay, Llandudno LL30 3HN, North Wales.

JONES J Farragut. See: **LEVINSON Leonard.**

JONES Joanna. See: **BURKE John Frederick.**

JONES John R(obert), (John Dalmas), b. 3 Sept 1926, Chicago, Illinois, USA. Author. m. Gail Hill, 15 Sept 1954, 1 son, 1 daughter. Education: BSc, Michigan State College, 1954; Master of Forestry, University of Minnesota, 1955; PhD, Colorado State University, 1967. Publications: The Yngling, 1969; The Varkaus Conspiracy, 1983; Touch the Stars: Emergence (with Carl Martin), 1983; Homecoming, 1984; The Scroll of Man, 1985; Fanglith, 1985; The Reality Mix, 1986; The Walkaway Clause, 1986; The Regiment, 1987; The Playmasters (with Rodney Martin), 1987; Return to Fanglith, 1987; The Lantern of God, 1987; The General's President, 1988; The Lizard War, 1989; The White Regiment, 1990; The Kalif's War, 1991; Yngling and the Circle of Power, 1992; The Orc Wars (collection), 1992; The Regiment's War, 1993; The Yngling in Yamato, 1994; The Lion of Farside, 1995. Contributions to: Journals and magazines. Honours: Xi Sigma Pi Forestry Honorary Society, 1953; Phi Kappa Phi Scholastic Honorary Society, 1954; Sigma Xi Scientific Research Society, 1963. Memberships: Science Fiction Writers of America; Vasa Order of America. Address: 1425 Glass Street, Spokane, WA 99206, USA.

JONES Julia, b. 27 Mar 1923, Liverpool, England. Writer. m. Edmund Bennett, 10 Oct 1950, 1 son, 1 daughter. Education: Royal Academy of Dramatic Art, 1946-48. Publications: The Navigators, 1986; over 50 plays for theatre, television and radio, films; numerous dramatisations. Honour: The Golden Prague, 1st Prize Drama, Prague TV Festival, 1970. Memberships: Dramatists Club; Green Room Club; TV Committee, Writers Guild of Great Britain. Address: c/o Jill Foster Ltd, 35 Brompton Road, London SW3 1DE, England.

JONES Kenneth Westcott, b. 11 Nov 1921, London, England. Editor; Writer. Appointments: Travel Editor, East Anglian Daily Times, 1951-93; Group Travel Correspondent, United Newspapers, 1960-83. Publications: To the Polar Sunrise, 1957; New York, 1958; America Beyond the Bronx, 1961; Great Railway Journeys of the World, 1964; Exciting Railway Journeys of the World, 1967; By Rail to the Ends of the Earth, 1970; Business Air Travellers Guide, 1970; Romantic Railways, 1971; Steam in the Landscape, 1972; Railways for Pleasure, 1981; Scenic America, 1984; Where to Go in America, 1991; Rail Tales of the Unexpected, 1992. Contributions to: Magazines. Honours: Canton of Valais Award, 1964; Thomson Travel Award Travel Writer of the Year, 1971. Memberships: British Guild of Travel Writers, chairman, 1975-76; Royal Geographical Society, fellow. Address: Hillswick, Michael Road, London SE25 6RN, England.

JONES (Everett) LeRoi, (adopted the name Amiri Baraka, 1968), b. 7 Oct 1934, Newark, New Jersey, USA. Professor of Africana Studies; Poet; Dramatist; Writer. m. (1)Hettie Roberta Cohen, 1958, div 1965, 2 daughters, (2) Sylvia Robinson, 1967, 6 children and 2 stepdaughters. Education: Rutgers University, 1951-52; BA in English, Howard University, 1954. Appointments: Founder-Director, Yugen magazine and Totem Press, New York, 1958-62; Co-Editor, Floating Bear magazine, New York, 1961-63; Teacher, New School for Social Research, New York City, 1961-64, 1977-79, State University of New York at Buffalo, 1964, Columbia University, 1964, 1980; Founder-Director, Black Arts Repertory Theatre, Harlem, New York, 1964-66, Spirit House, Newark, 1966-; Visiting Professor, San Francisco State College, 1966-67, Yale University, 1977-78, George Washington University, 1978-79; Chair, Congress of Afrikan People, 1972-75; Assistant Professor, 1980-82, Associate Professor, 1983-84, Professor of Africana Studies, 1985-, State University of New York at Stony Brook. Publications: Poetry: April 13, 1959; Spring and Soforth, 1960; Preface to a Twenty Volume Suicide Note, 1961; The Disguise, 1961; The Dead Lecturer, 1964; Black Art, 1966; A Poem for Black Hearts, 1967; Black Magic: Collected Poetry 1961-1967, 1970; It's Nation Time, 1970; In Our Terribleness: Some Elements and Meaning in Black Style (with Billy Abernathy), 1970; Spirit Reach, 1972; African Revolution, 1973; Hard Facts, 1976; Selected Poetry, 1979; AM/TRAK, 1979; Spring Song, 1979; Reggae or Not!, 1982; Thoughts for You!, 1984; The LeRoi Jones/Amiri Baraka Reader, 1993. Plays: A Good Girl is Hard to Find, 1958; Dante, 1961; The Toilet, 1964; Dutchman, 1964; The Slave, 1964; The Baptism, 1964; Jello, 1965; Experimental Death Unit #1, 1965; A Black Mass, 1966; Arm Yourself or Harm Yourself, 1967; Slave Ship: A Historical Pageant, 1967; Madheart, 1967; Great Goodness of Life (A Coon Show), 1967; Home on the Range, 1968; Police, 1968; The Death of Malcolm X, 1969; Rockgroup, 1969; Insurrection, 1969; Junkies Are Full of (SHHH...), 1970; BA-RA-KA, 1972; Black Power Chant, 1972; Columbia the Gem of the Ocean, 1973; A Recent Killing, 1973; The New Ark's a Moverin, 1974; The Sidnee Poet Heroical, 1975; S-1, 1976; The Motion of History, 1977; What Was the Relationship of the Lone Ranger to the Means of Production?, 1979; At the Dim'cracker Convention, 1980; Boy and Tarzan Appear in a Clearing, 1981; Weimar 2, 1981; Money: A Jazz Opera (with George Gruntz), 1982; Primitive World, 1984; General Hag's Skeezag, 1992. Fiction: The System of Dante's Hell (novel), 1965; Tales (short stories), 1967. Other: Cuba Libre, 1961; Blues People: Negro Music in White America, 1963; Home: Social Essays, 1966; Black Music, 1968; Trippin': A Need for Change with Larry Neal and A B Spellman), 1969; A Black Value System, 1970; Gary and Miami: Before and After, 1970; Raise Race Rays Raze: Essays Since 1965, 1971; Strategy and Tactics of a Pan African Nationalist Party, 1971; Beginning of National Movement, 1972; Kawaida Studies: The New Nationalism, 1972; National Liberation and Politics, 1974; Crisis in Boston!!!!, 1974; African Free School, 1974; Toward Ideological Clarity, 1974; The Creation of the New Ark, 1975; Selected Plays and Prose, 1979; Daggers and Javelins: Essays 1974-1979, 1984; The Autobiography of LeRoi Jones/Amiri Baraka, 1984; The Artist and Social Responsibility, 1986; The Music: Reflections on Jazz and Blues (with Amina Baraka), 1987; A Race Divided, 1991; Conversations with Amiri Baraka, 1994. Editor: Four Young Lady Poets, 1962; The

Moderns: New Fiction in America, 1963; Black Fire: An Anthology of Afro-American Writing (with Larry Neal), 1968; African Congress: A Documentary of the First Modern Pan-African Congress, 1972; Confirmation: An Anthology of African American Women (with Amina Baraka), 1983. Honours: Obie Award, 1964; Guggenheim Fellowship, 1965; Yoruba Academy Fellowship, 1965; Dakar Festival Prize, 1966; Grant, 1966, Award, 1981, National Endowment for the Arts; DHL, Malcolm X College, Chicago, 1972; Rockefeller Foundation Grant, 1981; American Book Award, Before Columbus Foundation, 1984. Membership: Black Academy of Arts and Letters. Address: c/o Department of Africana Studies, State University of New York at Stony Brook, Stony Brook, NY 11794, USA.

JONES Madison Percy, b. 21 Mar 1925, Nashville, Tennessee, USA. Author; Professor of English (retired). m. Shailah McEvilley, 5 Feb 1951, 3 sons, 2 daughters. Education: BA, Vanderbilt University, 1949; MA, University of Florida, 1953. Appointments: Instructor, Miami University of Ohio, 1953-54, University of Tennessee, 1955-56; Professor of English and Writer-in-Residence, Auburn University, 1956-67. Publications: The Innocent, 1957; Forest of the Night, 1960; A Buried Land, 1963; An Exile, 1967; A Cry of Absence, 1971; Passage Through Gehenna, 1978; Season of the Stranger, 1983; Last Things, 1989; To the Winds, 1996; Nashville 1864 – the Dying of the Light, 1997. Contributions to: Journals and magazines. Honours: Sewanee Review Writing Fellowship, 1954-55; Rockefeller Foundation Fellowship, 1968; Alabama Library Association Book Award, 1968; Guggenheim Fellowship, 1973-74. Memberships: Alabama Academy of Distinguished Authors; Fellowship of Southern Writers. Address: 800 Kudena Acres, Auburn, AL 36830, USA.

JONES Malcolm Vince, b. 7 Jan 1940, Stoke-sub-Hamdon, England. Professor of Slavonic Studies; Writer. m. Jennifer Rosemary Durrant, 27 July 1963, 1 son, 1 daughter. Education: Graduate, 1962, Postgraduate Studies, 1962-65, University of Nottingham. Appointment: Emeritus Professor of Slavonic Studies, University of Nottingham. Publications: Dostoyevsky: The Novel of Discord, 1976; New Essays on Tolstoy (editor), 1978; New Essays on Dostoyevsky (editor with Garth M Terry), 1983; Dostoyevsky After Bakhin, 1990. Contributions to: Scholarly journals. Memberships: British Association for Soviet Slavonic and East European Studies, vice-president, 1988-91; British Universities' Association of Slavists, president, 1986-88; International Dostoyevsky Society, president, 1995-98. Address: c/o Department of Slavonic Studies, University of Nottingham, University Park, Nottingham NG7 2RD, England.

JONES Mervyn, b. 27 Feb 1922, London, England. Writer. Education: New York University, 1939-41. Appointments: Assistant Editor, 1955-60, Drama Critic 1958-66, Tribune; Assistant Editor, New Statesman, 1966-68, London. Publications: No Time to Be Young, 1952; The New Town, The Last Barricade, 1953; Helen Blake, 1955; Guilty Men (with Michael Foot), Suez and Cyprus, 1957; On the Last Day, 1958; Potbank, 1961; Big Two (in US as The Antagonists), 1962; Two Ears of Corn: Oxfam in Action (in US as In Famine's Shadow: A Private War on Hunger), A Set of Wives, 1965; John and Mary, 1966; A Survivor, 1968; Joseph, 1970; Mr Armitage Isn't Back Yet, 1971; Life on the Dole, 1972; Holding On (in US as Twilight of the Day), The Revolving Door, 1973; Lord Richard's Passion, Strangers, K S Karol: The Second Chinese Revolution (translator), 1974; The Pursuit of Happiness, 1975; The Oil Rush (with Fay Godwin), Scenes from Bourgeois Life, 1976; Nobody's Fault, 1977; Today the Struggle, 1978; The Beautiful Words, 1979; A Short Time to Live, 1980; Two Women and Their Men, 1982; Joanna's Luck, 1985; Coming Home, 1986; Chances, 1987; That Year in Paris, 1988; A Radical Life, 1991; Michael Foot, 1994. Address: 1 Evelyn Mansions, Carlisle Place, London SW1P 1NH, England.

JONES Owen Marshall, b. 17 Aug 1941, Te Kuiti, New Zealand. Writer. m. Jacqueline Hill, Dec 1965, 2 daughters. Education: MA Hons, University of Canterbury, 1964; Diploma in Teaching, Christchurch Teachers College, 1965. Publications: Supper Waltz Wilson, 1979; The Master of Big Jingles, 1982; The Day Hemingway Died, 1984; The Lynx Hunter, 1987; The Divided World, 1989; Tomorrow We Save the Orphans, 1991. Contributions to: Numerous magazines and journals. Honour: New Zealand Literary Fund Scholarship in Letters, 1988. Address: 10 Morgans Road, Timaru, New Zealand.

JONES Rhydderch Thomas, b. 25 Dec 1935, North Wales. Television Producer. m. 3 Mar 1980. Education: Diploma Education,

Normal College, Bangor. Appointments: Teacher, English Literature and Dramatic Art, Croydon and Llanrwst; BBC, Light Entertainment Department, 1973-. Publications: Roedd Catarinao Gwmpas Ddoe, 1974; Mewn Tri Chyfrwng, 1979; Cofiant Ryan, 1979; Ryan, 1980. Other: Many television and radio dramas. Honours: Pye Award, Best Regional Drama, 1987; Royal TV Society Award for Outstanding Contribution to Creative Writing, 1987. Membership: Yr Academi Gymraeg. Address: 39 Heol Hir, Llanishen, Cardiff, Wales.

JONES Richard Andrew III, b. 8 Aug 1953, London, England. Poet. Education: BA, 1975, MA, 1976, University of Virginia, USA. Publications: Country of Air, 1986; At Last We Enter Pradise, 1991; A Perfect Time, 1994. Contributions to: American Poetry Review; Poetry; Tri Quarterly. Honours: Posner Prize, 1986; Illinois Arts Council Award, 1991; Literary Award, 1991; Literary Award, 1996. Address: Department of English, DePaul University, Chicago, IL 60614, USA.

JONES Robert Gerallt Hamlet, b. 11 Sept 1934, Nefyn, Gwynedd, Wales. University Administrator; Writer; Poet; Editor. m. Susan Lloyd Griffith, 15 Sept 1962, 2 sons, 1 daughter. Education: BA, 1954; MA, 1956, University College of North Wales. Appointments: Creative Writing Fellow, University of Wales, 1976-78; Senior Lecturer in Welsh Studies, University College, Aberystwyth, 1979-89; Editor, Taliesin, Welsh Academy Quarterly, 1988-; Editor, Books From Wales, 1992-. Publications: Over 35 books, including novels, poetry and criticism, many in Welsh. Honours: Prose Medals, National Eisteddfod of Wales, 1977, 1979; Hugh McDiarmid Award, 1984; Welsh Arts Council Poetry Award, 1990. Memberships: Wales Film Council, chairman, 1992-; Welsh Academy, chairman, 1982-87.

JONES Rodney, b. 11 Feb 1950, Hartselle, Alabama, USA. Poet; Writer. m. (1) Virginia Kremza, 1972, div 1979, (2) Gloria Nixon de Zepeda, 21 June 1981, 2 children. Education: BA, University of Alabama, 1971; MFA, University of North Carolina at Greensboro, 1973. Publications: Going Ahead, Looking Back, 1977; The Story They Told Us of Light, 1980; The Unborn, 1985; Transparent Gestures, 1989; Apocalyptic Narrative and Other Poems, 1993. Contributions to: Periodicals. Honours: Lavan Younger Poets Award, Academy of American Poets, 1986; Younger Writers Award, General Electric Foundation, 1986; Jean Stein Prize, American Academy and Institute of Arts and Letters, 1989; National Book Critics Circle Award, 1989. Memberships: Associated Writing Programs; Modern Language Association. Address: c/o Houghton Mifflin Co, 222 Berkeley Street, Boston, MA 02116, USA.

JONES Sally Roberts, b. 30 Nov 1935, London, England. Author; Publisher. Education: BA, University College of North Wales, 1957; ALA, North-Western Polytechnic, 1964. Appointments: Senior Assistant, Reference Library, London Borough of Havering, 1964-67; Reference Librarian, Borough of Port Talbot, Wales, 1967-70; Publisher, Alun Books, 1977-. Publications: Turning Away, 1969; Elen and the Goblin, 1977; The Forgotten Country, 1977; Books of Welsh Interest, 1977; Allen Raine (Writers of Wales), 1979; Relative Values, 1985; The History of Port Talbot, 1991; Pendaruis, 1992. Honour: Welsh Arts Council Literature Prize, 1970. Memberships: Welsh Academy, chairman, 1994-; Afan Poetry Society; Welsh Union of Writers; Library Association; Port Talbot Historical Society. Address: 3 Crown Street, Port Talbot SA13 1BG, Wales.

JONG Erica (Mann), b. 26 Mar 1942, New York, New York, USA. Author; Poet. m. (1) Michael Werthman, 1963, div 1965, (2) Allan Jong, 1966, div 1975, (3) Jonathon Fast, 1977, div 1983, 1 daughter, (4) Kenneth David Burrows, 5 Aug 1989. Education: BA, Barnard College, 1963; MA, Columbia University, 1965. Appointments: Lecturer in English, City College of the City University of New York, 1964-66, 1969-70, University of Maryland Overseas Division, 1967-69; Faculty, Breadloaf Writers Conference, Middlebury, Vermont, 1982, Salzburg Seminar, Austria, 1993. Publications: Fear of Flying, 1973; How to Save Your Own Life, 1977; Fanny, Being the True History of the Adventures of Fanny Hackabout-Jones, 1980; Parachutes and Kisses, 1984; Serenissima: A Novel of Venice, 1987; Any Woman's Blues, 1990; Fear of Fifty: A Midlife Memoir, 1994. Poetry: Fruits and Vegetables, 1971; Half-Lives, 1973; Here Comes and Other Poems, 1975; Loveroot, 1975; The Poetry of Erica Jong, 1976; At the Edge of the Body, 1979; Ordinary Miracles: New Poems, 1983; Becoming Light: Poems, New and Selected, 1991. Other: Four Visions of America (with others), 1977; Witches, 1981; Megan's Book of Divorce: A Kid's Book for Adults, 1984; Erica Jong on Henry Miller: The Devil at Large, 1994. Contributions to: Various publications. Honours:

Academy of American Poets Award, 1963; Bess Hokin Prize, 1971; New York State Council on the Arts Grant, 1971; Alice Faye di Castagnola Award, 1972; National Endowment for the Arts Grant, 1973. Memberships: Authors Guild; Phi Beta Kappa; Poetry Society of America; Poets and Writers; Writers Guild of America. Address: 425 Park Avenue, New York, NY 10022, USA.

JORDAN June, b. 9 July 1936, New York, New York, USA. Professor of African-American Studies; Poet; Writer. m. Michael Meyer, 5 Apr 1955, div 1966, 1 son. Education: Barnard College, 1953-55, 1956-57; University of Chicago, 1955-56. Appointments: Faculty, City College of the City University of New York, 1967-69, Sarah Lawrence College, 1969-70, 1973-74; Professor of English, State University of New York at Stony Brook, 1978-79; Visiting Poet-in-Residence, MacAlester College, 1980; Chancellor's Distinguished Lecturer, 1986, Professor of Afro-American Studies and Women's Studies, 1989-93, Professor of African-American Studies, 1994-, University of California at Berkeley; Playwright-in-Residence, 1987-88, New Dramatists, New York City; Visiting Professor, University of Wisconsin at Madison, 1988; Poet-in-Residence, Walt Whitman Birthplace Association, 1988. Publications: Who Look at Me, 1969; Soulscript, 1970; The Voice of the Children, 1970; Fannie Lou Hamer, 1971; His Own Where, 1971; Dry Victories, 1972; New Days: Poems of Exile and Return, 1974; New Life: New Room, 1975; Passion: New Poems 1977-80, 1980; Civil Wars: Selected Essays 1963-80, 1981; Kimako's Story, 1981; Things I Do in the Dark: Selected Poems 1954-77, 1981; Living Room: New Poems 1980-84, 1985; On Call: New Political Essays, 1981-85, 1985; Lyrical Campaigns: Selected Poems, 1989; Moving Towards Home: Selected Political Essays, 1989; Naming Our Destiny: New and Selected Poems, 1989; Technical Difficulties: New Political Essays, 1992; The Haruko/Love Poetry of June Jordan, 1993. Other: I Was Looking at the Ceiling and Then I Saw the Sky, libretto and lyrics for the Opera, music composed by John Adams, 1995. Contributions to: Professional journals and magazines. Honours: Rockefeller Foundation Grant, 1969; Prix de Rome, 1970; CAPS Grant in Poetry, 1978; Yaddo Fellow, 1979, 1980; National Endowment for the Arts Fellowship, 1982; Achievement Award for International Reporting, National Association of Black Journalists, 1984; New York Foundation for the Arts Fellowship, 1985; MADRE Award for Leadership, 1989; Freedom to Write Award, PEN West, 1991; Lila Wallace-Reader's Digest Writers Award, 1995. Memberships: American Writers Congress; PEN American Center; Poets and Writers. Address: c/o University of California at Berkeley, Berkeley, CA 94720, USA.

JORDAN Leonard. See: **LEVINSON Leonard.**

JORDAN Neil Patrick, b. 25 Feb 1950, Sligo, Ireland. Author; Director. 3 sons, 2 daughters. Education: BA, 1st Class Honours, History/English Literature, University College, Dublin, 1969-72. Appointment: Co-Founder, Irish Writers Cooperative, Dublin, 1974. Publications: Night in Tunisia, 1976; The Dream of a Beast, 1983; The Past, 1979; Sunrise with Sea Monster, 1995. Films as a Director: Angel, 1982; Company of Wolves, 1984; Mona Lisa, 1986; High Spirits, 1988; We're No Angels, 1989; The Miracle, 1990; The Crying Game, 1992; Interview With the Vampire, 1994. Honours: Guardian Fiction Prize, 1979; Los Angeles Film Critics Award; New York Film Critics Award, 1986; London Critics Circle Award, 1986; Oscar, 1992. Address: c/o Jenne Casarotto Co Ltd, National House, 60-66 Wardour Street, London W1V 3HP, England.

JOSÉ Héctor Oscar (Sergio Darlin), b. 14 Feb 1936, Córdoba, Argentina. Writer; Poet. m. Soltero José, 1 daughter. Appointment: One of the creators and theorists of signist (typewriter signi) poetry, international movement of poetry and advanced narrative, 1961. Publications: After Hiroshima, 1965; Reports for an Operating Theater History, 1980; Growth of the Apocalypsis, 1987; New Reports for an Operating Theater History, 1991; The Madness Starts at the Steps, 1991; After Hiroshima III, 1993. Contributions to: Magazines and journals. Honours: Ribbon of Honour, SADE, 1976; Statue of Victory for Personality of 1984; Italian Word Award for Culture, ALPI Biennale Award; Honorary Member, Argentine Writers Association. Address: Pringles 3230, 1605 Florida, Prov Buenos Aires, Argentina.

JOSEPH Jenny, b. 7 May 1932, Birmingham, England. Writer; Lecturer. m. C A Coles, 29 Apr 1961, dec 1985, 1 son, 2 daughters. Education: BA, Honours, English, St Hilda's College, Oxford University, 1950-53. Publications: The Unlooked-for Season, 1960; Warning (poem), 1961; Boots, 1966; Rose in the Afternoon, 1974; The

Thinking Heart, 1978; Beyond Descartes, 1983; Persephone, 1986; The Inland Sea, 1989; Beached Boats, 1991; Selected Poems, 1992; Ghosts and Other Company, 1995; Extended Similes, 1997; Author of 6 books for children. Contributions to: Magazines and anthologies. Honours: Gregory Award, 1962; Cholmondeley Award, 1974; Arts Council of Great Britain Award, 1975; James Tait Black Award for Fiction, 1986; Society of Authors' Travelling Scholarship, 1995; Forward prize, 1995. Membership: National Poetry Society of Great Britain, Council, 1975-78; Patron, Centre for the Spoken Word. Literary Agent: John Johnson Ltd, London. Address: 17 Windwill Road, Minchinhampton, Gloucestershire GL6 9DX, England.

JOSEPHS Ray, b. 1912, USA. Public Relations Consultant; Author; Lecturer. Education: University of Pennsylvania. m. Juanita W Wegner, 1941. Appointments: Chairman of Board, Ray Josephs-David E Levy Inc; Chairman, International Public Relations Co Ltd, New York City; Lecturer, business organisations and universities; General Correspondent, Philadelphia Evening News Bulletin, 1929-40; Columnist, Buenos Aires Herald, 1940-44; Correspondent, Washington Post, Chicago Sun, Time and Variety. Publications: Spies & Saboteurs in Argentina, 1943; Argentine Diary, 1944; Those Perplexing Argentines (with James Bruce), 1952; How to Make Money from Your Ideas, 1954; How to Gain an Extra Hour Every Day, 1955, new version, 1992; Our Housing Jungle and Your Pocketbook, 1960; Streamlining Your Executive Workload, 1960; The Magic Power of Putting Yourself Over with People, 1962. Memberships: Public Relations Society of America; Writers Guild of America; Founders Committee, Tobé Lecture Series; Harvard Graduate School of Business Administration; Founder member, International Public Relations Group of Companies; Counsel to leading US, British, Japanese, Latin American companies and organisations; American (Buenos-Aires); Overseas Press (New York City); Society of Magazine Writers. Address: 860 United Nations Plaza, New York, NY 10017-1815, USA.

JOSEPHY Alvin M Jr, b. 18 May 1915, Woodmere, New York, USA. Author; Editor. m. Elizabeth C Peet, 13 Mar 1948, 1 son, 3 daughters. Education: Harvard University, 1932-34. Appointments: Reporter and Correspondent, New York Herald-Tribune, 1937-38; Staff, WOR-Mutual Radio, New York City, 1938-42, Radio Bureau, Office of War Information, Washington, DC, 1942-43; Screenwriter, Metro-Goldwyn-Mayer Studios, Culver City, California, 1945-51; Associate Editor, Time magazine, 1951-60; Vice-President and Senior Editor, American Heritage Books, 1960-76; Editor, 1976-78, Editor-in-Chief, 1978-79, American Heritage magazine. Publications: The US Marines on Iwo Jima (co-author), 1945; The Long, the Short and the Tall: The Story of a Marine Combat Unit in the Pacific, 1946; Uncommon Valor (co-author), 1946; The American Heritage Book of the Pioneer Spirit (co-author), 1959; The Patriot Chiefs: A Chronicle of American Indian Leadership, 1961; Chief Joseph's People and Their War, 1964; The Nez Perce Indians and the Opening of the Northwest, 1965; The American Heritage Pictorial Atlas of United States History (co-author), 1966; The Artist Was a Young Man, 1970; Red Power: The American Indians' Fight for Freedom, 1971; The Pictorial History of the American Indian (revised edition of the book by Oliver La Farge), 1974; History of the Congress of the United States, 1975; Black Hills, White Sky, 1979; On the Hill, 1979; Now That the Buffalo's Gone: A Study of Today's American Indians, 1982; The Civil War in the American West, 1991; 500 Nations, 1994. Editor: The American Heritage Book of Indians, 1961; The American Heritage History of Flight, 1962; The American Heritage Book of Natural Wonders, 1962; The American Heritage History of World War I, 1964; The American Heritage History of the Great West, 1965; RFK: His Life and Death, 1968; The Horizon History of Africa, 1971; The American Heritage History of Business and Industry, 1972; The Horizon History of Vanishing Primitive Man, 1973; The Law in America, 1974; The Cold War, 1982; America in 1492, 1992. Contributions to: Many books, newspapers and magazines. Honours: National Cowboy Hall of Fame and Western Heritage Center Awards, 1961, 1965; Gold Spur and Golden Saddleman Awards, Western Writers of America, 1965; New York Westerners Buffalo Awards, 1965, 1968; National Award of Merit, American Association for State and Local History, 1966; Guggenheim Fellowship, 1966-67; National Magazine Award for Excellence in Reporting, 1976; Charles E S Wood Award, Oregon Institute of Literary Arts, 1993; Wallace Stegner Award, Century of the American West, Colorado, 1995; Governor's Arts Award, Oregon, 1996. Memberships: American Antiquarian Society; Association on American Indian Affairs; Institute of the American West; Institute of the North American West; New York Westerners; US Capitol Historical Association; Western

History Association, President, 1993-94. Address: 4 Klinsman Lane, Greenwich, CT 06930, USA.

JOSIPOVICI Gabriel David, b. 8 Oct 1940, Nice, France. Professor of English; Writer; Dramatist. Education: BA, Hons 1st Class, St Edmund Hall, Oxford, 1958-61. Publications: Novels: The Inventory, 1968; Migrations, 1977; The Air We Breath, 1981; Contre-Jour, 1986; The Big Glass, 1990; In a Hotel Garden, 1993; Moo Pak, 1994. Stories: Mobius the Striper, 1974; In the Fertile Land. Essays: The World and the Book, 1971; The Book of God: A Response to the Bible, 1988; Text and Voice, 1992; Touch, 1996. Contributions to: Encounter; New York Review of Books; London Review of Books; Times Literary Supplement. Honours: BBC nominations for Italia Prize, 1977, 1989; 1981 Lord Northcliffe Lectures, University of London; Lord Weidenfeld Visiting Professor of Comparative Literature, University of Oxford, 1996-97. Address: 60 Prince Edwards Road, Lewes, Sussex, England.

JOY David (Anthony Welton), b. 14 June 1942, Ilkley, England. Writer; Editor. Education: Leeds College of Commerce, 1961-62. Appointments: General Reporter, Yorkshire Post Newspapers, 1962-65; Editorial Assistant, 1965-70, Books Editor, 1970-88, Editor, 1988-93, Dalesman Publishing Co Ltd; Managing Editor, Atlantic Transport Publishers, 1995-. Publications: Settle-Carlisle Railway (with W R Mitchell), 1966; Main Line Over Shap, 1967; Cumbrain Coast Railways, 1968; Whitby-Pickering Railway, 1969; Railways in the North, Traction Engines in the North, 1970; George Hudson of York (with A J Peacock), 1971; Railways of the Lake Countries, 1973; Regional History of the Railways of Great Britain: South and West Yorkshire, Railways in Lancashire, Settle-Carlisle Centenary, 1975; Railways of Yorkshire, The West Riding, 1976; North Yorkshire Moors Railway (with P Williams), 1977; Steam on the North York Moors, 1978; Yorkshire Railways (with A Haigh), 1979; Steam on the Settle and Carlisle, 1981; Yorkshire Dales Railway, Settle-Carlisle in Colour, 1983; Regional History of the Railways of Great Britain: The Lake Countries, 1984; Portrait of the Settle: Carlisle, 1984; Yorkshire Dales in Colour, 1985; The Dalesman - A Celebration of 50 Years, 1989; Life in the Yorkshire Coalfield, 1989; Settle-Carlisle Celebration, 1990; Best Yorkshire Tales, 1991; Uphill to Paradise, 1991; Yorkshire's Christmas, 1992; The Dalesman Bedside Book, 1993; Yorkshire's Farm Life, 1994; Railways in Your Garden, 1995. Address: Hole Bottom, Hebden, Skipton, North Yorkshire BD23 5D1, England.

JUDD Denis (O'Nan), b. 28 Oct 1938, Byfield, Northamptonshire, England. Historian; Writer. m. Dorothy Woolf, 10 July 1964, 3 sons, 1 daughter. Education: BA Hons, Modern History, Oxford University, 1961; PGCEd, 1962, PhD, 1967, London University. Publications: Balfour and the British Empire, 1968; The Boer War, 1977; Radical Joe: Joseph Chamberlain, 1977; Prince Philip, 1981; Lord Reading, 1982; Alison Uttley, 1986; Jawaharlal Nehru, 1993; Empire: the British Imperial Experience, 1996; 2 novels/books and stories for children; Other history books and biographies. Contributions to: History Today; History; Journal of Imperial and Commonwealth History; Literary Review; Daily Telegraph; New Statesman. Honours: Fellow, Royal Historical Society, 1977; Awarded Professorship, 1990. Address: 20 Mount Pleasant Road, London NW10 3EL, England.

JUDSON John, b. 9 Sept 1930, Stratford, Connecticut, USA. Educator; Editor; Writer. Education: AB, Colby College, 1958; University of Maine, 1962-63; MFA, University of Iowa, 1965. Appointments: Editor, Juniper Press, Northeast/Juniper Books, literary magazine and chapbook series, 1961-; Professor of English, University of Wisconsin, La Crosse, 1965-93. Publications: Two from Where It Snows (co-author), 1963; Surreal Songs, 1968; Within Seasons, 1970; Voyages to the Inland Sea, 6 volumes, 1971-76; Finding Worlds in Winter; West of Burnam South of Troy, 1973; Ash Is the Candle's Wick, 1974; Roots from the Onion's Dark, A Purple Tale, 1978; North of Athens, Letters to Jirac II, 1980; Reasons Why I Am Not Perfect, 1982; The Carrabassett Sweet William Was My River, 1982; Suite for Drury Pond, 1989; Muse(sic), 1992; The Inardo Poems, 1996. Address: 1310 Shorewood Drive, La Crosse, WI 54601, USA.

JUERGENSEN Hans, b. 17 Dec 1919, Myslowitz, Germany (now Poland). Professor Emeritus. m. Ilse Dina Loebenberg, 27 Oct 1945, 1 daughter. Education: BA, Upsala College, New Jersey, USA, 1942; PhD, Johns Hopkins University, 1951. Appointments: Associate Professor, English, Chairman, Quinnipiac College, Hamden, Connecticut, 1953-61; Assistant Professor, Associate Professor, 1961-68, Professor, Humanities, 1968-92, Professor Emeritus, 1992-,

University of South Florida, Tampa; Poetry in Schools Coordinator, Hillsborough County, Florida, 1972-76; Nominating Committee, Nobel Prize in Literature, 1975-. Publications: Poetry: I Feed You From My Cup, 1958; In Need for Names, 1961; Existential Cannon and Other Poems, 1965; Florida Montage, 1966; Sermons from the Ammunition Hatch of the Ship of Fools, 1968; From the Divide, 1970; Hebraic Modes, 1972; Journey toward the Roots, 1976; The Broken Jug, 1977; California Frescoes, 1980; General George H Thomas: A Summary in Perspective, 1980; The Record of a Green Planet, 1982; Fire Tested, 1983; Beachheads and Mountains, 1984; The Ambivalent Journey, 1986; Roma, 1987; Testimony, 1989. Editor: Gryphon, 1974-89; Ipso Facto, 1975; For Neruda, For Chile, 1975; Children's Poetry Anthology, 1975; The Anthology of American Magazine Verse, 1981. Co-editor: Orange Street Poetry Journal, 1958-62; University of South Florida Language Quarterly, 1961-74. Contributions to: Many publications. Address: 7815 Pine Hill Drive, Tampa, FL 33617, USA.

JULIAN Jane. See: WISEMAN David.

JUNKINS Donald (Arthur), b. 19 Dec 1931, Saugus, Massachusetts, USA. Poet; Writer; Professor. m. Marthe Luppold, 28 June 1958, 3 sons. Education: BA, University of Massachusetts, 1953; STB, 1956, STM, 1957, AM, 1959, PhD, 1963, Boston University. Appointments: Instructor, 1961-62, Assistant Professor of English, 1962-63, Emerson College, Boston; Assistant Professor of English, Chico State College, California, 1963-66; Assistant Professor, 1966-69, Associate Professor, 1969-74, Director, Master of Fine Arts Program in English, 1970-78, 1989-90, Professor of English, 1974-, University of Massachusetts, Amherst. Publications: Poetry: The Sunfish and the Partridge, 1965; The Graves of Scotland Parish, 1969; Walden, One Hundred Years After Thoreau, 1969; And Sandpipers She Said, 1970; The Contemporary World of Poets (editor), 1976; The Uncle Harry Poems and Other Maine Reminiscences, 1977; Crossing By Ferry: Poems New and Selected, 1978; The Agamenticus Poems, 1984; Playing for Keeps: Poems, 1978-1988, 1989. Contributions to: Anthologies, including Classic Short Fiction, 1972; Themes in American Literature, 1972; The New Yorker Book of Poems, 1974; American Literature; Antioch Review; Atlantic; Critique; Early American Literature; Harper's; New Yorker; Northwest Review; Poetry; Sewanee Review; Studies in Short Fiction; Various others. Honours: Breadloaf Writers Conference Poetry Scholarship, 1959; Jennie Tane Award for Poetry, 1968; John Masefield Memorial Award, 1973; National Endowment for the Arts Fellowships, 1974, 1979. Address: 63 Hawks Road, Deerfield, MA 01342, USA.

JUSSAWALLA Adil (Jehangir), b. 8 Apr 1940, Bombay, India. Lecturer; Poet. Education: MA, University College, Oxford, 1964. Appointment: Lecturer, St Xavier's College, Bombay, 1972-75; Editor, Debonair, Bombay, 1989. Publications: Lands End, 1962; Missing Person, 1976. Television Plays: Train to Calcutta, 1970; War, 1989. Editor: New Writing in India, 1974. Co-Editor: Statements: An Anthology of Indian Prose in English, 1976. Address: Palm Springs, Flat R2, Cuffe Parade, Bombay 400 005, India.

JUST Ward (Swift), b. 5 Sept 1935, Michigan City, Indiana, USA. Writer. Education: Lake Forest Academy, Illinois, 1949-51; Cranbrook School, Michigan, 1951-53; Trinity College, Hartford, Connecticut, 1953-57. Appointments: Reporter, Waukegan News-Sun, Illinois, 1957-59; Reporter, 1962-63, Correspondent, 1963-65, Newsweek magazine; Correspondent, Washington Post, 1965-70. Publications: To What End: Report from Vietnam, 1968; A Soldier of the Revolution, 1970; Military Men, 1970; The Congressmen Who L:oved Flaubert and Other Washington Stories, 1973; Stringer, 1974; Nicholson at Large, 1975; A Fmily Trust, 1978; Honor, Power, Riches, Fame and the Love of Women, 1979; In the City of Fear, 1982; The American Blues, 1984; The American Ambassador, 1987; Jack Glance, 1989; Twenty-One Selected Stories, 1990; The Translator, 1991; Ambition and Love, 1994. Contributions to: Anthologies and periodicals. Honours: O Henry Awards, 1985, 1986. Address: Vineyard Haven, MA 02568, USA.

JUSTICE Donald (Rodney), b. 12 Aug 1925, Miami, Florida, USA. Professor (retired); Poet; Writer. m. Jean Catherine Ross, 22 Aug 1947, 1 son. Education: BA, University of Miami, 1945; MA, University of North Carolina, 1947; Postgraduate Studies, Stanford University, 1948-49; PhD, University of Iowa, 1954. Appointments: Instructor, University of Miami, 1947-51; Assistant Professor, Hamline University, 1956-57; Lecturer, 1957-60, Assistant Professor 1960 63, Associate Professor, 1963-66, Professor, 1971-82, University of Iowa;

Professor, Syracuse University, 1966-70, University of Florida at Gainesville, 1982-92. Publications: Poetry: The Summer Anniversaries, 1960; Night Light, 1967; Departures, 1973; Selected Poems, 1979; The Sunset Maker, 1987; A Donald Justice Reader, 1992; New and Selected Poems, 1995. Other: The Collected Poems of Weldon Kees (editor), 1962; Platonic Scripts (essays), 1984. Contributions to: Journals and magazines. Honours: Rockefeller Foundation Fellowship, 1954; Lamont Award, 1959; Ford Foundation Fellowship, 1964; National Endowment for the Arts Grants, 1967, 1973, 1980, 1989; Guggenheim Fellowship, 1976; Pulitzer Prize in Poetry, 1980; Academy of American Poets Fellowship, 1988; Co-Winner, Bollingen Prize, 1991. Memberships: American Academy and Institute of Arts and Letters; Academy of American Poets, board of chancellors, 1997-. Address: 338 Rocky Shore Drive, Iowa City, IA 52246, USA.

JUSTICIAR. See: **POWELL-SMITH Vincent.**

JUTEAU Monique, b. 8 Jan 1949, Montreal, Quebec, Canada. Education: MA, French Literature, 1987. Appointment: Teacher, University of Quebec, Trois-Rivieres, 1987-. Publications: Poetry: La Lune Aussi, 1975; Regard Calligraphes, 1986; Trop Plein D'Angles, 1990; Des jours de chemins perdus et retrouvés, 1997. Novels: En Moins de Deux, 1990; L'Emporte-Clé, 1994. Contributions to: Le Sabord, Trois-Rivières; Arcade, Montreal; Estuaire, Montreal; Le Moule A Gaufres (Paris). Honour: Prix Littéraire de la Societé des Ecrivains de la Mauricie. Memberships: Société des Écrivains de la Mauricie; Union des Ecrivains du Québec. Address: 19200, Forest, Saint-Gregoire, Quebec, Canada.

K

KADOHATA Cynthia Lynn, b. 7 Feb 1956, Chicago, Illinois, USA. Writer. m. 30 Aug 1992. Education: Los Angeles City College; University of South Carolina; University of Pittsburgh; Columbia University. Publications: The Floating World, 1989; In the Heart of the Valley of Love, 1992. Contributions to: Newspapers and magazines. Honours: National Endowment for the Arts Grant, 1991; Whiting Writers Award, 1991. Address: c/o Wylie, Aitken and Stone Inc, 250 West 57th Street, Suite 2106, New York, NY 10107, USA.

KADOTA Paul Akira, b. 15 Mar 1930, Kobe, Japan. Retired. m. Theresa Yoko Ishikawa, 27 Dec 1961, 3 sons, 1 daughter. Education: Kobe University, 1949; BEcons, 1955; BEduc, 1957; Visiting Scholar, St Edmond College, Cambridge, England, 1975; Sonoma State University, California, 1988. Appointments: Hyugagakuin Salesian College, 1957; Kagoshima Prefectural College, 1966-95. Publications: The Bombardment of Kagoshima (editor); Diaries of Kanaye Nagasawa (editor); Kariforunia No Shikon (Samurai Spirit in California), 1983; Kanaye Nagasawa: A Biography of a Satsuma Student, 1990; Wakaki Satsuma No Gunzo (Young Satsuma Students), 1991. Contributions to: Reports of the Regional Institute of Kagoshima Prefectural College. Honours: Minami Nippon Broadcasting Co Prize, 1987; The Toyota Minoru Prize, 1992. Membership: Nihon Eigakushi Gakkai, Historical Society of English Studies in Japan. Address: 37-6 Shimoishiki 3-chome, Kagoshima-shi 890, Japan.

KAEL Pauline, b. 19 June 1919, Sonoma County, California, USA. Movie Critic. Education: University of California, Berkeley, 1936-40. Appointment: Movie Critic, The New Yorker, 1968-91. Publications: I Lost it at the Movies, 1965; Kiss Kiss Bang Bang, 1968; Going Steady, 1970; Raising Kane in The Citizen Kane Book, 1971; Deeper into Movies, 1973; Reeling, 1976; When the Lights Go Down, 1980; 5001 Nights at the Movies, 1982; Taking It All In, 1984; State of the Art, 1985; Hooked, 1989; Move Love, 1991; For Keeps, 1994. Contributions to: Partisan Review; Vogue; New Republic; McCall's; Atlantic; Harper's. Honours: Guggenheim Fellowship, 1964; George Polk Memorial Award for Criticism, 1970; National Book Award, 1974; Front Page Awards, Newswomen's Club of New York, Best Magazine Column, 1974, Distinguished Journalism, 1983; 8 honorary degrees. Address: c/o The New Yorker, 20 West 43rd Street, New York, NY 10036, USA.

KAGAN Andrew Aaron, b. 22 Sept 1947, St Louis, Missouri, USA. Art Historian; Art Adviser. m. Jayne Wilner, 17 May 1987. Education: BA, Washington University; MA, 1971, PhD, 1977, Harvard University. Appointments: Advisory Editor, Arts Magazine, 1975-89; Critic of Art, Music, Architecture, St Louis Globe Democrat, 1978-81. Publications: Paul Klee/Art and Music, 1983; Rothko, 1987; Trova, 1988; Marc Chagall, 1989; Paul Klee at the Guggenheim, 1993; Absolute Art, 1995. Contributions to: McMillan Dictionary of Art; Arts Magazine; Burlington Magazine; Others. Honours: Phi Beta Kappa, 1969; Harvard Prize Fellowship, 1970-77; Kingsbury Fellowship, 1977-78; Goldman Prize, 1985. Membership: Founder, Director, Wednesday Night Society. Address: 232 North Kingshighway, No 1709, St Louis, MO 63108, USA.

KAHN James, b. 1947, Englewood, New Jersey, USA. Physician; Writer. Appointments: Resident, Los Angeles County Hospital, 1976-77; University of California at Los Angeles, 1978-79; Physician, Emergency Room, Rancho Encino Hospital, Los Angeles, 1978-. Publications: Diagnosis Murder, Nerves in Patterns (with Jerome McGann), 1978; World Enough and Time, Time's Dark Laughter, Poltergeist, 1982; Return of the Jedi, 1983; Indiana Jones and the Temple of Doom, 1984; Goonies, 1985; Timefall, Poltergeist II, 1986. Address: c/o Jane Jordan Browne, 410 South Michigan Avenue, Suite 724, Chicago, IL 60605, USA.

KAHN Michele Anne, b. 1 Dec 1940, Nice, France. Writer. m. Pierre-Michel Kahn, 8 Jan 1961, 1 son. Education: Diploma In Social Sciences, University of Paris, 1976. Publications: Contes du jardin d'Eden, 1983; Un Ordinateur pas Ordinaire, 1983; Juges et Rois, 1984; de l'autre cote de brouillard, 1985; Hotel Riviera, 1986; Rue du Roi-dore, 1989; La vague noire, 1990; Boucles d'Or et Bebe Ours, 1990; Contes et légendes de la Bible, 2 volumes, 1994, 1995;

Shanghaï-la-juive, 1997. Honours: Diplomes Loisirs Jeunes, 1971; Diplome Loisirs Jeunes, 1983; Liste d'Honneur, Österreichen Kinder-und Jugendbuchpreisen, 1977. Memberships: International PEN Club; Société des Gens des Lettres de France; Société Civile des Auteurs Multimedia. Address: Residence Belloni, 192A Rue de Vaugirard, Paris 75015, France.

KAHN Peggy. See: **KATZ Bobbi.**

KALB Jonathan, b. 30 Oct 1959, New Jersey, USA. Theatre Critic; Associate Professor of Theatre. m. Julie Heffernan, 18 June 1988, 2 sons. Education: BA, English, Wesleyan University; MFA, Dramaturgy, Dramatic Criticism, 1985, DFA, Dramaturgy, Dramatic Criticism, 1987, Yale School of Drama. Appointments: Theatre Critic, The Village Voice, 1987-; Assistant Professor of Performance Studies, 1990-92, Assistant Professor of Theatre, 1992-95, Associate Professor of Theatre, 1996-, Hunter College, City University of New York. Publications: Beckett in Performance, 1989; Free Admissions: Collected Theater Writings, 1993. Contributions to: Newspapers and journals. Honours: Fulbright Hays Grant, 1988-89; T C G Jerome Fellowship, 1989-90; George Jean Nathan Award for Dramatic Criticism, 1990-91. Memberships: Modern Language Association; PEN American Centre. Address: c/o Department of Theatre, Hunter College of the City University of New York, 695 Park Avenue, New York, NY 10021, USA.

KALECHOFSKY Roberta, b. 11 May 1931, New York, New York, USA. Writer; Publisher. m. Robert Kalechofsky, 7 June 1953, 2 sons. Education: BA, Brooklyn College, 1952; MA, 1957, PhD, 1970, English, New York University. Appointments: Literary Editor, Branching Out, Canada, 1973-74; Contributing Editor, Margins, 1974-77, On the Issues, 1987-94. Publications: Stephen's Passion, 1975; La Hoya, 1976; Orestes in Progress, 1976; Solomon's Wisdom, 1978; Rejected Essays and Other Matters, 1980; The 6th Day of Creation, 1986; Bodmin 1349, 1988; Haggadah for the Liberated Lamb, 1988; Autobiography of a Revolutionary: Essays on Animals and Human Rights, 1991; Justice, My Brother, reissued, 1993; Haggadah for the Vegetarian Family, 1993; K'tia: A Savior of the Jewish People, 1995; A Boy, a Chicken and the Lion of Judah: How Ari Became a Vegetarian (children's book), 1995. Contributions to: Confrontation; Works; Ball State University Forum; Western Humanities Review; Rocky Mountain Review; Between the Species; So'western; Response; Reconstructionist. Address: 255 Humphrey Street, Marblehead, MA 01945, USA.

KAMINSKI Ireneusz Gwidon, b. 1 Mar 1925, Gniezno, Poland. Writer. m. Alicja Gardocka, 26 Aug 1960, 2 sons, 2 daughters. Education: MA, Liberal Arts, Mickiewicz University, Poznan, 1952. Appointments: Journalist, Teacher, Librarian, 1950-70; War Correspondent, Vietnam, 1968, 1972; 2nd Editor-in-Chief, Morze (Sea), monthly, 1971-85. Publications: 10 novels, 25 short stories, 1 reportage, 3 radio plays, numerous essays, etc; First published (poetry), 1950; Titles include: Wegierska opowiesc, 1954; Czerwony sokol, 1957; Msciciel przyplywa z Rugii, 1958; Czas slonca, 1960; Biale wrony, 1963; Anastazja, 1969; Paszcza smoka, 1970; Krystyna i rapier, 1971; Odro, rzeko poganska, 1975; Swiety Ateusz, 1987; Kontredans, 1988; Retrospekcja, 1990; Diabelska ballada, 1992; Dziesiata planeta, 1994; Powracajaca fala, 1994. Honours: Literary Awards, City of Szczecin, 1958, 1975, 1985. Memberships: Executive, Polish Writers Union; Sea Yacht Club, Szczecin. Address: 70-791 Szczecin, ul Kozia 16, Poland.

KAMINSKY Stuart M(elvin), b. 29 Sept 1934, Chicago, Illinois, USA. Professor of Radio, Television and Film; Writer. Education: BS, 1957, MA, 1959, University of Illinois; PhD, Northwestern University, 1972. Appointments: Director of Public Relations and Assistant to the Vice President for Public Affairs, University of Chicago, 1969-72; Faculty, later Professor of Radio, Television, and Film, Northwestern University, 1972-. Publications: Non-Fiction: Don Siegal: Director, 1973; Clint Eastwood, 1974; American Film Genres: Approaches to a Critical Theory of Popular Film, 1974; Ingmar Bergman: Essays in Criticism (editor with Joseph Hill), 1975; John Huston: Maker of Magic, 1978; Basic Filmmaking (with Dana Hodgdon), 1981; American Television Genres (with Jeffrey Mahan), 1984. Fiction: Bullet for a Star, 1977; Murder on the Yellow Brick Road, 1978; You Bet Your Life, 1979; The Howard Hughes Affair, 1979; Never Cross a Vampire, 1980; Death of a Dissident, 1981; High Midnight, 1981; Catch a Falling Clown, 1981; He Done Her Wrong, 1983; When the Dark Man Calls, 1983; Black Knight on Red Square, 1983; Down for the Count, 1985;

Red Chameleon, 1985; Exercise in Terror, 1985; Smart Moves, 1987; A Fine Red Rain, 1987; Lieberman's Day, 1994. **Address:** c/o School of Speech, Northwestern University, Evanston, IL 60201, USA.

KAN Sergei, b. 31 Mar 1953, Moscow, Russia (US citizen). Associate Professor of Anthropology and of Native American Studies; Writer. m. Alla Glazman, 19 Dec 1976, 1 daughter. Education: Moscow State University, 1970-73; BA, Boston University, 1976; MA, 1978, PhD, 1982, University of Chicago. Appointments: Lecturer, Sheldon Jackson College, Sitka, Alaska, 1979-80, University of Massachusetts, Boston, 1982-83; Part-time Assistant Professor, Northeastern University, 1981-83; Assistant Professor, University of Michigan, 1983-89; Assistant Professor, 1989-92, Associate Professor of Anthropology and of Native American Studies, 1992-, Dartmouth College. Publications: Symbolic Immortality: The Tlingit Potlatch of the Nineteenth Century, 1989; Memory Eternal: Tlingit Culture and Russian Orthodox Christianity, 1794-1994, 1997. Contributions to: Books and scholarly journals. Honours: Robert F Heizer Prize, American Society for Ethnohistory, 1987; American Book Award, Before Columbus Foundation, 1990; American Council of Learned Societies Fellowship, 1993-94; National Endowment for the Humanities Fellowship, 1993-94. Memberships: Alaska Anthropological Association; American Association for the Advancement of Slavic Studies; American Ethnological Society; American Society for Ethnohistory; International Arctic Social Science Association. Address: 18 Wellington Circle, Lebanon, NH 03766, USA.

KANAME Hiroshi, b. 15 Dec 1940, Osaka, Japan. Professor. m. Motoko Nakata, 29 Apr 1976, 1 son. Education: BA, Kobe City University of Foreign Studies, 1964; MA, Osaka City University, 1969. Appointments: Lecturer, 1973-76, Associate Professor, 1976-91, Professor, 1991-, University of Osaka Prefecture. Publications: American Novels: Study and Appreciation, 1977; Alienation and American Novels, 1982; The Dream and Its Collapse in American Literature, 1988. Memberships: American Literature Society of Japan; International John Steinbeck Society; John Steinbeck Society of Japan. Address: 1-10-14-741, Imafuku-Higashi, Joto-Ku, Osaka-shi, Japan 536.

KANE Penny. See: **RUZICKA Penelope Susan.**

KANE Wilson. See: **BLOCH Robert.**

KANIGEL Robert, b. 28 May 1946, Brooklyn, New York, USA. Writer. m. Judith Schiff Pearl, 28 June 1981, 1 son. Education: BS, Rensselaer Polytechnic Institute, Troy, New York. Appointments: Freelance Writer, 1970-; Instructor, Johns Hopkins University School of Continuing Studies, 1985-91; Visiting Professor of English, University of Baltimore, Maryland, and Senior Fellow, Institute of Publications Design, 1991-. Publications: Apprentice to Genius: The Making of a Scientific Dynasty, 1986, 2nd edition, 1993; The Man Who Knew Infinity: A Life of the Genius Ramanujan, 1991, 2nd edition, 1992; The One Best Way: Frederick Winslow Taylor and the Enigma of Efficency, 1997. Contributions to: New York Times Magazine; The Sciences; Health; Psychology Today; Science 85; Johns Hopkins Magazine; Washington Post; Civilization. Honours: Grady-Stack Award, 1989; Alfred P Sloan Foundation Grant, 1991; Elizabeth Eisenstein Prize, 1994. Memberships: Authors Guild; American Society of Journalists and Authors. Literary Agent: Vicky Bijur. Address: 202 Dunkirk Road,Baltimore, MD 21212, USA.

KANN Mark E, b. 24 Feb 1947, Chicago, Illinois, USA. Professor of Political Science. m. Kathy Michael, 13 Feb 1969, 1 son. Education: BA, 1968, MA, 1972, PhD, 1975, University of Wisconsin, Madison, USA. Appointments: Assistant Professor, 1975-81, Associate Professor, 1981-88, Professor of Political Science, 1988-, University of Southern California at Los Angeles. Publications: Thinking About Politics: Two Political Sciences, 1980; The American Left: Failures and Fortunes, 1983; Middle Class Radicals in Santa Monica, 1986; On the Man in Question: Gender and Civic Virtue in America, 1991. Contributions to: Numerous newspapers, journals and magazines. Honours: Various research and teaching awards. Address: Department of Political Science, University of Southern California, Los Angeles, CA 90089, USA.

KANNAN Lakshmi (Kaaveri), b. 13 Aug 1947, Mysore, India. Writer. m. L V Kannan, 2 sons. Education: BA Hons, MA, PhD, all in English. Appointment: Writer-in-Residence, University of Kent at Canterbury, 1993. Publications: Glow and the Grey, 1976; Exiled

Gods, 1985; Rhythms, 1986; India Gate, 1993; other books in Hindi and Tamil. Address: B-11/8193, Vasant Kunj, New Delhi 110030, India.

KANTARIS Sylvia, b. 9 Jan 1936, Grindleford, Derbyshire, England. Poet; Writer; Teacher. m. Emmanuel Kantaris, 11 Jan 1958, 1 son, 1 daughter. Education: Diplome d'Etudes Civilisation Française, Sorbonne, University of Paris, 1955; BA Hons, 1957, CertEd, 1958, Bristol University, 1958; MA, 1967, PhD, 1972, University of Queensland, Australia. Appointments: Tutor, University of Queensland, Australia, 1963-66, Open University, England, 1974-84; Extra-Mural Lecturer, Exeter University, 1974-. Publications: Time and Motion, 1975; Stocking Up, 1981; The Tenth Muse, 1983; News From the Front (with D M Thomas), 1983; The Sea at the Door, 1985; The Air Mines of Mistila (with Philip Gross), 1988; Dirty Washing: New and Selected Poems, 1989; Lad's Love, 1993. Contributions to: Many anthologies, newspapers, and magazines. Honours: National Poetry Competition Award, 1982; Honorary Doctor of Letters, Exeter University, 1989; Major Arts Council Literature Award, 1991; Society of Authors Award, 1992. Memberships: Poetry Society of Great Britain; South West Arts, literature panel, 1983-87, literary consultant, 1990-. Address: 14 Osborne Parc, Helston, Cornwall TR13 8PB, England.

KANTOR Peter, b. 5 Nov 1949, Budapest, Hungary. Poet. Education: MA in English and Russian Literature, 1973, MA in Hungarian Literature, 1980, Budapest ELTE University. Appointment: Literary Editor, Kortars magazine, 1984-86; Poetry Editor, Élet és Irodalom, magazine, 1997. Publications: Kavics, 1976; Halmadar, 1981; Sebbel Lobbal, 1982; Gradicsok, 1985; Hogy no az eg, 1988; Naplo, 1987-89, 1991; Font lomb, lent avar, 1994; Mentafü (selected poems), 1994. Contributions to: Various publications. Honours: George Soros Fellowship, 1988-89; Wessely Laszlo Award, 1990; Dery Tibor Award, 1991; Fulbright Fellowship, 1991-92; Fust Milan Award, 1992; Jozsef Attila Award, 1994. Memberships: Hungarian Writers Union; International PEN Club. Address: Stollar Bela u 3/a, Budapest 1055, Hungary.

KAPLAN Harold, b. 3 Jan 1916, Chicago, Illinois, USA. Professor Emeritus. m. Isabelle M Ollier, 29 July 1962, 1 son, 2 daughters. Education: BA, 1937, MA, 1938, University of Chicago. Appointments: Instructor of English, Rutgers University, 1946-49; Professor of English, Bennington College, 1950-72; Professor of English, 1972-86, Professor Emeritus, 1986-, Northwestern University. Publications: The Passive Voice, 1966; Democratic Humanism and American Literature, 1972; Power and Order, 1981; Conscience and Memory: Meditations in a Museum of the Holocaust, 1994. Honours: Fulbright Lecturer, 1967, 1981; Rockefeller Foundation Humanities Fellowship, 1982. Address: Turnabout Lane, Bennington, VT 05201, USA.

KAPLAN Morton A, b. 9 May 1921, Philadelphia, Pennsylvania, USA. Political Scientist; Distinguished Service Professor Emeritus; Writer; Editor; Publisher. m. Azie Mortimer, 22 July 1967. Education: BS, Temple University, 1943; PhD, Columbia University, 1951. Appointments: Instructor, Ohio State University, 1951-52; Fellow, 1952-53, Research Associate, 1958-62, Center of International Studies, Princeton, New Jersey; Assistant Professor, Haverford College, 1953-54; Staff, Brookings Institution, Washington, DC, 1954-55; Fellow, Center for Advanced Study in the Behavorial Sciences, Stanford, California, 1955-56; Assistant Professor, 1956-61, Associate Professor, 1961-65, Professor of Political Science, 1965-89, Distinguished Service Professor, 1989-91, Professor Emeritus, 1991-, University of Chicago; Visiting Associate Professor, Yale University, 1961-62; Associate Editor (with others), Journal of Conflict Resolution, 1961-79; Staff, 1961-78, Consultant, 1978-80, Hudson Institute; Director, Center for Strategic and Foreign Policy Studies, 1976-85; Editor and Publisher, The World and I, 1985-. Publications: System and Process in International Politics, 1957; Some Problems in the Strategic Analysis of International Politics, 1959; The Communist Coup in Czechoslovakia (co-author), 1960; The Political Foundations of International Law, 1961; Macropolitics: Essays on the Philosophy and Science of Politics, 1969; On Historical and Political Knowing: An Enquiry into Some Problems of Universal Law and Human Freedom, 1971; On Freedom and Human Dignity: The Importance of the Sacred in Politics, 1973; The Rationale for NATO: Past and Present, 1973; Alienation and Identification, 1976; Justice, Human Nature and Political Obligation (co-author), 1976; Science, Professionalism in International Theory: Macrosystem Analysis, 1979; Science, Language and the Human Condition, 1984, revised edition, 1989; Consolidating Peace in Europe (editor), 1987; The Soviet Union and the Challenge of the

Future (co-editor), 4 volumes, 1988-89; Morality and Religion (co-editor), 1992; Law in a Democratic Society, 1993; The World of 2044: Technological Development and the Future of Society (co-editor), 1994. Contributions to: Many books and professional journals. Memberships: American Academy of Arts and Sciences; American Political Science Association; Institute of Strategic Studies, London. Address: 5446 South Ridgewood Court, Chicago, IL 60615, USA.

KAPLAN Robert David, b. 23 June 1952, New York, New York, USA. Author; Journalist. m. Maria Cabral, 26 Aug 1983, 1 son. Education: BA, University of Connecticut, 1973. Publications: Surrender or Starve: The Wars Behind the Famine, 1988; Soldiers of God: With the Mujahidin in Afghanistan, 1990; Balkan Ghosts: A Journey Through History, 1993; The Arabists: The Romance of an American Elite, 1993; The Ends of the Earth, 1996. Contributions to: Newspapers and magazines. Memberships: Authors Guild; Authors League of America.

KAPUSCINSKI Ryszard, b. 4 Mar 1932, Pinsk, Poland. Journalist; Writer. m. Alicija Mielczarek, 6 Oct 1952, 1 daughter. Education: MA Faculty of History, Warsaw University. Appointments: Sztander Mlodych, daily, 1951; Polityka, weekly, 1957-61; Correspondent, Polish Press Agency (PAP) in Africa, Latin America, 1962-72; Kutura, weekly, 1974-81. Publications: The Emperor; The Soccer War; Another Day of Life; The Shah of Shahs; Bush Polish Style; Lapidarium; Notes; Imperium, 1993. Contributions to: Vanity Fair; Tempo; Independent; Guardian. Honours: Gold Cross of Merit; Knight's Cross, Order Polonia Restituta; Prize of International Journalists Organisation, 1976; State Prize. Memberships: PEN; Polish Centre Club; Board of Advisors, NPQ; Polish Association of Artistic Photographers; Natural Council of Culture. Literary Agent: Ms Eva Koranile, Liepman Agency, Meienburgweg 32, CH-8044, Zürich, Switzerland. Address: ul Prokuratorska 11 m2, 02-074 Warsaw, Poland.

KARAVIA Lia Headzopoulou, b. 27 June 1932, Athens, Greece. Writer; Poet; Dramatist. m. Vassillis, Karavias, 20 Sept 1953, 2 sons. Education: Diploma in English Literature, Pierce College, Athens, 1953; Diploma in French Literature, Institute of France, Athens, 1954; Diploma, Acting School, Athens, 1962; Classical Literature, University of Athens, 1972; Doctorat Nouveau Regime, Comparative Literature, Paris, 1991. Appointments: Actress; Teacher of Acting and the History of the Theatre, Public Schools, 1984-94. Publications: 10 novels; 10 poetry collections; stage and radio plays; television scripts. Contributions to: Anthologies, journals, and magazines; Numerous translations of novels and plays. Honours: Menelaos Loudemis Prize, 1980; Michaela Averof Prize, 1981; Prize for 2 plays for the young, 1986; National Prize for Best Play for the Young, 1989; National Playwrights Prizes, 1990, 1991. Memberships: Actors League of Greece; International Theatre Centre; Maison International de Poesie, Liège; Society of Greek Writers; Union of Greek Playwrights. Address: 51 Aghiou Polycarpou Street, Nea Smyrni 17124, Athens, Greece.

KARL Frederick Robert, b. 10 Apr 1927, Brooklyn, New York, USA. Professor; Writer. m. Dolores Mary Oristaglio, 8 June 1951, 3 daughters. Education: BA, 1948, Columbia College, 1948; MA, Stanford University, 1949; PhD, Columbia University, 1957. Appointments: Professor, City College of New York, 1957-80, New York University, 1981-. Publications: Joseph Conrad: The Three Lives, biography; American Fictions: 1940-1980; Modern and Modernism; Sovereignty of the Artist 1885-1925; The Quest, novel; The Adversary Literary; Collected Letters of Joseph Conrad, Volumes I, II, III, IV (editor); William Faulkner: American Writer; Franz Kafka: Representative Man; Reader's Guide to Joseph Conrad; An Age of Fiction; The Contemporary English Novel; George Eliot: Voice of a Century. Contributions to: Many books and journals. Address: 2 Settlers Landing Lane, East Hampton, NY 11937, USA.

KARLIN Wayne Stephen, b. 13 June 1945, Los Angeles, California, USA. Writer; Teacher. m. Ohnmar Thein, 27 Oct 1977, 1 son. Education: BA, American College, Jerusalem, 1972; MA, Goddard College, 1976. Appointments: President, Co-Editor, First Casualty Press, 1972-73; Visiting Writer, William Joiner Center for the Study of War and Social Consequences, University of Massachusetts, Boston, 1989-93; Director, Fiction, Literary Festival, St Mary's College, 1994-; Editor, Curbstone Press, Vietnamese Writers Series, 1996-. Publications: Free Fire Zone (co-editor, contributor), 1973; Crossover, 1984; Lost Armies, 1988; The Extras, 1989; US, 1993; The Other Side

of Heaven: Postwar Fiction by Vietnamese and American Writers (co-editor with Le Minh Khve, contributor); Rumors and Stones: A Journey, 1996. Contributions to: Prairie Schooner; Glimmer Train; Indiana Review; Swords and Ploughshares: An Anthology; Antietam Review; New Outlook; New Fiction from the South; The Best of 1993, anthology; The Vietnam War in American Songs, Stories and Poems, anthology; Writing Between the Lines, anthology. Honours: Fellowship in Fiction and Individual Artist Award, Maryland State Arts Council, 1988, 1991, 1993; National Endowment for the Arts Fellowship, 1993. Membership: Associated Writing Programs. Address: PO Box 239, St Mary's City, MD 20686, USA.

KARNOW Stanley, b. 4 Feb 1925, New York, New York, USA. Writer. m. Annette Kline, 21 Apr 1959, 2 sons, 1 daughter. Education: BA, Harvard University; Sorbonne, Paris; École des Sciences Politiques, Paris; Nieman Fellow; Fellow, Kennedy School of Government and East Asia Research Center, Harvard University. Publications: Southeast Asia, 1963; Mao and China: From Revolution to Revolution, 1972; Vietnam: A History, 1983; In Our Image: America's Empire in the Philippines, 1989. Contributions to: New York Times; GEO; Atlantic; Foreign Affairs; Foreign Policy; Esquire. Honours: Overseas Press Club Awards, 1967, 1978, 1983; Dupont Polk Award, 1984; Emmy Award, 1984; Pulitzer Prize in History, 1990. Memberships: Century Association; Authors Guild; Council on Foreign Relations; PEN; Society of American Historians. Address: 10850 Springknoll Drive, Potomac, MD 20854, USA.

KAROL Alexander. See: **KENT Arthur (William Charles).**

KARP David, (Adam Singer, Wallace Ware), b. 5 May 1922, New York New York, USA. Writer. m. (1) Lillan Klass, 25 Dec 1944, dec 1987, 2 sons, (2) Claire Leighton, 23 June 1988, 1 son, 1 daughter. Education: BS, Social Sciences, City College of New York, 1948. Publications: Fiction: Hardman, 1952; The Brotherhood of Velvet, 1952; The Girl on Crown Street, 1952; Day of the Monkey, 1955; The Charka Memorial, 1956; All Honorable Men, 1956; Leave Me Alone, 1957; Enter, Sleeping, 1960; Non-fiction:nt in Charge of Revolution (with M D Lincoln), 1960; The Last Believers, 1964. Contributions to: New York Times; National Saturday Review; Los Angeles Times; Others. Honours: Guggenheim Fellowship, 1956; Look Magazine Award for Best TV Play, 1958; Edgar Award, 1959; Emmy Award, 1965. Memberships: PEN; Writers Guild of America. Address: 300 East 56th Street, Apt 3C, New York, NY 10022, USA.

KARSEN Sonja Petra, b. 11 Apr 1919, Berlin, Germany (US citizen). Professor of Spanish Emerita. Education: BA, Carleton College, USA, 1939; MA, Bryn Mawr College, 1941; PhD, Columbia University, 1950. Appointments: Reviewer, Books Abroad, 1959-76, World Literature Today, 1977-92; Editor, Language Association Bulletin, 1980-82. Publications: Guillermo Valencia, Colombian Poet, 1873-1943, 1951; Educational Development in Costa Rica with UNESCO's Technical Assistance, 1951-54, 1954; Jaime Torres Bodet: A Poet in a Changing World, 1963; Selected Poems of Jaime Torres Bodet, 1964; Versos y prosas de Jaime Torres Bodet, 1966; Jaime Torres Bodet, 1971; Essays on Iberoamerican Literature and History, 1988; Bericht über den Vater: Fritz Karsen (1885-1951), 1993. Contributions to: Over 100 articles and book reviews to professional journals. Honours: Faculty Research Lecturer, Skidmore College, 1963; Chevalier dans l'Ordre des Palmes Académiques, Ministere de l'Education Nationale, Paris, 1964; Fulbright Lecturer, Free University, Berlin, 1968; Alumni Achievement Award, Carleton College, 1982; International Women of the Year, IBC, 1991-92. Memberships: Asociación Internacional de Hispanestas; Hispanic Institute, Columbia University; Modern Language Association; AATSP; National Geographic Society. Address: 1755 York Avenue, #37-A, New York, NY 10128-6875, USA.

KARVAS Peter, b. 25 Apr 1920, Banska Bystrica, Czechoslovakia. Writer; Professor. m. Eva Ruhmnn, 15 May 1969, 1 son. Education: PhD, 1946. Publications: 15 books, 1969-93. Contributions to: Various books and journals. Honours: Czechoslovak State Prize, 1960; Czechoslovak Writers Union Prize, 1991. Memberships: Czechoslovak Writers Union; Slovak Writers Union. Address: Vickova 7, 81106 Bratislava, Czech Republic.

KASSEM Lou(ise Sutton Morrell), b. 10 Nov 1931, Elizabethton, Tennessee, USA. Author. m. Shakeep Kassem, 17 June 1951, 4 daughters. Education: East Tennessee State University, 1949-51; Short courses: University of Virginia, 1982, Vassar College,

1985. Publications: Dance of Death, 1984; Middle School Blues, 1986; Listen for Rachel, 1986; Secret Wishes, 1989; A Summer for Secrets, 1989; A Haunting in Williamsburg, 1990; The Treasures of Witch Hat Mountain, 1992; Odd One Out, 1994; The Druid Curse, 1994; The Innkeeper's Daughter, 1996; Sneeze on Monday, 1997. Contributions to: Alan Review; Signal. Honours: Notable Book in Social Studies, American Library Association, 1986; Best Book for Young Readers, Virginia State Reading Association. Memberships: Society of Children's Book Writers; Writers in Virginia; Appalachian Writers; National League of American Pen Women. Address: 715 Burruss Drive North West, Blacksburg, VA 24060, USA.

KATO Shuichi, b. 19 Sept 1919, Tokyo, Japan. Writer; Professor. Education: Graduate, Faculty of Medicine 1943, MD 1950, Tokyo University. Publications: Form, Style, Tradition: Reflexions on Japanese Art and Society, 1969; Japan-China Phenomenon, 1973; Six Lives/Six Deaths, Portraits from Modern Japan (with Robert Lifton and Michael Reich), 1979; Chosakushu (Collected Works), 15 volumes, 1978-80; A History of Japanese Literature, 3 volumes, 1979-83; Japan, Spirit and Form, 1995. Contributions to: Asahi Shimbun; Many Japanese, French and American periodicals. Honours: Osaragi Jiro Prize, 1980; Ordre des Arts et des Lettres, 1985. Membership: PEN Club, Japanese Branch. Address: Kaminage 1-8-16, Setagaya-ku, Tokyo 158, Japan.

KATTAN Naim, b. 26 Aug 1928, Baghdad, Iraq. Writer. m. 21 July 1961, 1 son. Education: Law College, Baghdad, 1945-47; Sorbonne, Paris, 1947-52. Appointments: Head of Writing and Publishing, Associate Director, Canada Council, Ottawa, Canada, 1990-91; Writer-in-Residence, 1991-93, Associate Professor, 1993-, University of Quebec, Montreal. Publications: Reality and Theatre, 1970; Farewell Babylon, 1974; La Memoire de la Promesse, 1980; Le Père, 1988; Farida, 1989; La Réconciliation, 1993; Portraits d'un Pays, 1994; A M Klein, 1994; La distraction, 1994; Culture: Alibi ou liberté, 1996; Idoles et images, 1996; La Célébration, 1997; Figures bibliques, 1997. Contributions to: Critique; Quaizaire; Nouvelle Revue Française; Passages; Le Devoir; Canadian Literature. Honours: Prix France, Canada, 1971; Segal Awards, 1975; Order of Canada, 1987; Order of Arts and Letters, France, 1989; Order of Quebec, 1990. Memberships: Royal Society of Canada; Académie des Lettres, Montreal; Union des Ecrivains du Quebec. Address: 3463 Rue Ste Famille 2114, Montreal, Quebec H2X 2K7, Canada.

KATZ Bobbi, (Gail, Barbara George, Emily George, Peggy Kahn, Don E Plumme, Ali Reich), b. 2 May 1933, Newburgh, New York, USA. Writer; Editor. m. H D Katz, 1956, div, 1979, 1 son, deceased, 1 daughter. Education: BA, Goucher College, 1954. Appointment: Editor, Books for Young Readers, Random House, New York City, 1982-. Publications: Over 90 books for children; Over 700 poems. Contributions to: Cousteau Almanac; First Teacher; Highlights for Children; Ladybug Magazine; Various textbooks. Membership: Authors Guild, PEN. Address: 65 West 96th Street, 21H, New York, NY 10025, USA.

KATZ Steve, b. 14 May 1935, New York, New York, USA. Novelist; Short Story Writer; Poet; Screenwriter; Professor. m. Patricia Bell, 10 June 1956, div. 3 sons. Education: BA, Cornell University, 1956; MA, University of Oregon, 1959. Appointments: English Language Institute, Lecce, Italy, 1960; Overseas Faculty, University of Maryland, Lecce, Italy, 1961-62; Assistant Professor of English, Cornell University, 1962-67; Lecturer in Fiction, University of Iowa, 1969-70; Writer-in-Residence, 1970-71, Co-Director, Projects in Innovative Fiction, 1971-73, Brooklyn College, City University of New York; Adjunct Assistant Professor, Queens College, City University of New York, 1973-75; Associate Professor of English, University of Notre Dame, 1976-78; Associate Professor of English, 1978-82, Professor of English, 1982-, University of Colorado at Boulder. Publications: Novels: The Lestriad, 1962; The Exagggerations of Peter Prince, 1968; Posh, 1971; Saw, 1972; Moving Parts, 1977; Wier and Pouce, 1984; Florry of Washington Heights, 1987; Swanny's Ways, 1995. Short Stories: Creamy and Delicious: Eat my Words (in Other Words), 1970; Stolen Stories, 1985; 43 Fictions, 1991. Poetry: The Weight of Antony, 1964; Cheyenne River Wild Track, 1973; Journalism, 1990. Screenplay: Grassland, 1974. Honours: PEN Grant, 1972; Creative Artists Public Service Grant, 1976; National Educational AssociationGrants, 1976, 1982; GCAH Book of the Year, 1991; America Award in Fiction, for Swanny's Ways, 1995. Memberships; Authors League of America; PEN International; Writers

Guild. Address: 669 Washington Street, No 602, Denver, CO 80203, USA.

KAUFMAN Amy Rebecca, b. 8 Oct 1951, Long Beach, California, USA. Editor; Publisher. Education: BA, University of California, Berkeley. Publications: Founder, Editor, Publisher, Stories Magazine, 1982-. Honours: Selections from stories in Best American Short Stories, 1984, and Prize Stories, 1985: O'Henry Awards. Membership: Magazine Publishers of America. Address: 14 Beacon Street, Boston, MA 02108, USA.

KAUFMAN Gerald (Rt Hon), b. 21 June 1930, England. Politician; Writer. Education: Queen's College, Oxford. Appointments: MP for Manchester, Ardwick, 1970-83, Manchester, Gorton, 1983-; Minister of State, Department of Industry, 1975-79; Shadow Home Secretary, 1983-87; Shadow Foreign Secretary, 1987-92; Chairman, Select Committee on the National Heritage, 1992-. Publications: The Left (editor), 1966; To Build the Promised Land, 1973; How to be a Minister, 1980, updated and revised edition, 1997; Renewal: Labour's Britain in the 1980s (editor), 1983; My Life in the Silver Screen, 1985; Inside the Promised Land, 1986; Meet Me in St Louis, 1994. Honour: Privy Councillor, 1978. Address: House of Commons, London WC1, England.

KAUFMANN Myron S, b. 27 Aug 1921, Boston, Massachusetts, USA. Novelist. m. Paula Goldberg, 6 Feb 1960, div 1980, 1 son, 2 daughters. Education: AB, Harvard University, 1943. Publications: Novels: Remember Me To God, 1957; Thy Daughter's Nakedness, 1968; The Love of Elspeth Baker, 1982. Address: 111 Pond Street, Sharon, MA 02067, USA.

KAUFMANN Thomas DaCosta, b. 7 May 1948, New York, New York, USA. Professor of Art History; Writer. m. Virginia Burns Roehrig, 1 June 1974, 1 daughter. Education: BA, MA, 1970, Yale University, 1970; MPhil, Warburg Institute, University of London, 1972; PhD, Harvard University, 1977. Appointments: Assistant Professor, 1977-83, Associate Professor, 1983-89, Professor of Art, 1989-, Princeton University; Visiting professorships and curatorships. Publications: Variations on the Imperial Theme, 1978; Drawings From the Holy Roman Empire 1540-1650, 1982; L'Ecole de Prague, 1985; Art and Architecture in Central Europe 1550-1620, 1985; The School of Prague: Painting at the Court of Rudolf II, 1988; Central European Drawings 1680-1800, 1989; The Mastery of Nature, 1993; Court, Cloister and City, 1995. Contributions to: Books and professional journals. Honours: Marshall-Allison Fellow, 1970; David E Finley Fellow, National Gallery of Art, Washington, DC, 1974-77; American Council of Learned Societies Award, 1977-78, and Fellowship, 1982; Senior Fellow, Alexander von Humboldt Stiftung, Berlin and Munich, 1985-86, 1989-90; Guggenheim Fellowship, 1993-94; Herzog August Bibliothek Fellow, Wolfenbüttel, 1994. Memberships: College Art Association of America; Renaissance Society of America; Verband Deutscher Kunsthistorien. Address: c/o Department of Art and Archeology, McCormick Hall, Princeton University, Princeton, NJ 08544, USA.

KAVALER Lucy Estrin, b. 29 Aug 1930, New York, New York, USA. Author. m. 9 Nov 1948, 1 son, 1 daughter. Education: BA magna cum laude, Oberlin College, Ohio; Fellowship, Advanced Science Writing, Columbia University Graduate School. Publications: Private World of High Society, 1960; Mushrooms, Molds and Miracles, 1965; The Astors, 1966; Freezing Point, 1970; Noise the New Menace, 1975; A Matter of Degree, 1981; The Secret Lives of the Edmonts, 1989; Heroes and Lovers, 1995. Contributions to: Smithsonian; Natural History; McCall's; Reader's Digest; Redbook; Primary Cardiology; Woman's Day (encyclopaedia); Skin Cancer Foundation Journal; Memories; Female Patient. Address: c/o Phyllis Westberg, Harold Ober Associates, 425 Madison Avenue, New York, NY 10017, USA.

KAVALER Rebecca, b. 26 July 1930, Atlanta, Georgia, USA. Writer. m. Frederic Kavaler, 1955, 2 sons. Education: AB, University of Georgia. Publications: Further Adventures of Brunhild, 1978; Doubting Castle, 1984; Tigers in the Woods, 1986. Honours: Short stories included in Best of Nimrod, 1957-69; Best American Short Stories, 1972; Award for Short Fiction, Association of Writers and Poets, 1978; National Endowment for the Arts Fellowships, 1979, 1985. Membership: PEN. Address: 425 Riverside Drive, New York, NY 10025, USA.

KAVANAGH Dan. See: BARNES Julian Patrick.

KAVANAGH P(atrick) J(oseph), b. 6 Jan 1931, Worthing, Sussex, England. Poet; Writer; Editor. m. (1) Sally Philipps, 1956, dec, (2) Catherine Ward, 1965, 2 sons. Education: MA, Merton College, Oxford. Appointment: Columnist, The Spectator, 1983-96; Times Literary Supplement, 1996-. Publications: Poetry: One and One, 1960; On the Way to the Depot, 1967; About Time, 1970; Edward Thomas in Heaven, 1974; Life Before Death, 1979; Selected Poems, 1982; Presences: New and Selected Poems, 1987; An Enchantment, 1991; Collected Poems, 1992. Fiction: A Song and Dance, 1968; A Happy Man, 1972; People and Weather, 1978; Scarf Jack: The Irish Captain, 1978; Rebel for Good, 1980; Only By Mistake, 1980. Non-Fiction: The Perfect Stranger, 1966; People and Places, 1988; Finding Connections, 1990; Voices in Ireland: A Traveller's Literary Companion, 1994. Editor: The Collected Poems of Ivor Gurney, 1982; The Oxford Book of Short Poems (with James Michie), 1985; The Bodley Head G K Chesterton, 1985; Selected Poems of Ivor Gurney, 1990; A Book of Consolations, 1992. Honours: Richard Hillary Prize, 1966; Guardian Fiction Prize, 1968; Cholmondeley Poetry Prize, 1993. Membership: Royal Society of Literature, fellow. Address: c/o A D Peters, The Chamber, Chelsea Harbour, London SW10 0XF, England.

KAVANAUGH Cynthia. See: DANIELS Dorothy.

KAWALEC Julian, b. 11 Oct 1916, Wrzawy, Poland. Writer. m. Irene Wierzbanowska, 2 June 1948, 1 daughter. Education: Graduate, Jagellonian University, Kraków. Publications: Paths Among Streets, 1957; Scars, 1960; Bound to the Land, 1962; Overthrown Elms, 1963; The Dancing Hawk, 1964; Black Light, 1965; Wedding March, 1966; Appeal, 1968; Searching for Home, 1968; Praise of Hands, 1969; To Cross the River, 1973; Gray-Aureole, 1974; Great Feast, 1974; To Steal the Brother, 1982; Among the Gates, 1989; Dear Sadness (poems), 1992. Contributions to: Literary Life, Kraków; Literary Monthly, Warsaw. Honours: Prize of Polish Editors, 1962; Prizes of Minister of Culture and Art, 1967, 1985; Prize of State, 1975. Memberships: Polish Pen Club; Polish Writers Association; Society European Culture. Address: 39 Zaleskiego, 31-525 Kraków, Poland.

KAWINSKI Wojciech, b. 22 May 1939, Poland. Poet. m. Helena Lorenz, 17 Apr 1964, 1 son, 1 daughter. Education: MA, 1964. Appointments: Sub-Director, Pismo Literacko-Artystyczne, 1985-90. Publications: Odleglosci Posluzne, 1964; Narysowane We Wnetrzu, 1965; Ziarno Rzeki, 1967; Pole Widzewnia, 1970; Spiew Bezimienny, 1978; Pod Okiem Slonca, 1980; Listy Do Ciebie, 1982; Milosc Nienawistna, 1985; Ciemna strona jasnosci, 1989; Wieczorne sniegi, 1989; Czysty zmierzch, 1990; Pamiec zywa, 1990; Zwierciadlo sekund, 1991; Powrity Stów, 1991; Srebro Liści, 1993; Zelazna Rosa, 1995; Planeta Ognia, 1997. Contributions to: Numerous journals and magazines. Honours: Prize, City of Kraków, 1985; Red Rose for Poetry, Gdansk, 1985; Prize of Klemens Jornicki, 1995. Membership: Polish Writers Association. Address: ul Stachiewicza 22a, 31-303 Kraków, Poland.

KAY Guy Gavriel, b. 7 Nov 1954, Weyburn, Saskatchewan, Canada. Author. m. Laura Beth Cohen, 15 July 1984, 2 sons. Education: BA, University of Manitoba, 1975; LLB, University of Toronto, 1978. Appointment: Principal Writer and Associate Producer, The Scales of Justice, CBC Radio Drama, 1981-90. Publications: The Summer Tree, 1984; The Darkest Road, 1986; The Wandering Fire, 1986; Tigana, 1990; A Song for Arbonne, 1992; The Lions of Al-Rassan, 1995. Contributions to: Journals. Honours: Aurora Prizes, 1986, 1990. Memberships: Association of Canadian Radio and TV Artists; Law Society of Upper Canada. Address: c/o Curtis Brown Agency, Haymarket House, 28/29 Haymarket, London SW1Y 4SP, England.

KAYE Geraldine (Hughesdon), b. 14 Jan 1925, Watford, Herts, England. Writer. m. 1948, div 1975, 1 son, 2 daughters. Education: BSc Economics, London School of Economics, 1946-49. Publications: Comfort Herself, 1985; A Breath of Fresh Air, 1986; Summer in Small Street, 1989; Someone Else's Baby, 1990; A Piece of Cake, 1991; Snowgirl, 1991; Stone Boy, 1991; Hands Off My Sister, 1993; Night at the Zoo, 1996; Forests of the Night, 1995; Late in the Day, 1997. Honour: The Other Award, 1986. Memberships: PEN; West Country Writers; Society of Authors. Address: 39 High Kingsdown, Bristol BS2 8EW, England.

KAYE Marvin Nathan, b. 10 Mar 1938, Philadelphia, Pennsylvania, USA. Writer. m. Saralee Bransdorf, 4 Aug 1963, 1 daughter. Education: BA, MA, Pennsylvania State University; Graduate study, University of Denver, Colorado. Appointments: Senior Editor, Harcourt Brace Jovanovich; Adjunct Professor of Creative Writing, New York University, 1994-. Publications: The Histrionic Holmes, 1971; A Lively Game of Death, 1972; A Toy is Born, The Stein and Day Handbook of Magic, 1973; The Grand Ole Opry Murders, The Handbook of Mental Magic, 1974; Bullets for Macbeth, 1976; Catalog of Magic, My Son the Druggist, The Laurel and Hardy Murders, 1977; The Incredible Umbrella, My Brother the Druggist, 1979; The Amorous Umbrella, The Possession of Immanuel Wolf, 1981; The Soap Opera Slaughters, 1982; Fantastique, 1993. With Parke Godwin: The Masters of Solitude, 1978; Wintermind, 1982; A Cold Blue Light, 1983. Editor: Fiends and Creatures, 1975; Brother Theodore's Chamber of Horrors, 1975; Ghosts, 1981; Masterpieces of Terror and the Supernatural, 1985; Ghosts of Night and Morning, Devils and Demons, 1987; Weird Tales, the Magazine That Never Dies, 1988; Witches and Warlocks, 1989; 13 Plays of Ghosts and the Supernatural, 1990; Haunted America, 1991; Lovers and Other Monsters, 1991; Sweet Revenge, 1992; Masterpieces of Terror and the Unknown, 1993; Frantic Comedy, 1993; The Game is Afoot, 1994; Angels of Darkness, 1995; Readers Theatre: How to Stage It, 1995; The Resurrected Holmes, 1996; Play to Stage, 1996. Contributions to: Amazing; Fantastic; Galileo; Family Digest; Columnist, Science Fiction Chronicle. Honour: 1st runner-up, Best Novella, British Fantasy Awards, 1978. Memberships: Several professional organisations. Address: c/o Donald C Maass, 157 West 57th Street, Suite 703, New York, NY 10019, USA.

KAYE Mary Margaret, b. 1909, England. Author. Publications: Six Bars at Seven, 1940; Death Walks in Kashmir, 1954; Death Walks in Berlin, 1955; Death Walks in Cyprus, 1956, as Death in Cyprus, 1984; Shadow of the Moon, revised edition 1979; Later Than You Think, 1958, as Death in Kenya, 1983; House of Shade, 1959, as Death in Zanzibar, 1983; Night on the Island, 1960; Trade Wind, 1963, revised edition, 1981; The Far Pavilions, 1978; The Ordinary Princess, 1980; The Golden Calm (editor), 1980; Thistledown, 1981; Autobiography: Vol 1, The Sun in the Morning, 1990. Address: c/o St Martin's Press, 175 Fifth Avenue, New York, NY 10010, USA.

KAZAN Elia, b. 7 Sept 1909, Constantinople, Turkey (US citizen). Writer; Director. m. (1) Moly Day Thacher, 12 Dec 1983, dec, 2 sons, 2 daughters, (2) Barbara Loden, 5 June 1967, dec, 1 son, (3) Frances Rudge, 28 June 1982. Education: Williams College, 1930; Postgraduate School of Drama, 1932. Publications: America, America, 1962; The Arrangement, 1967; The Assassins, 1972; The Understudy, 1975; Acts of Love, 1978; The Anatolian, 1982; Elia Kazan: A Life, 1988; Beyond the Aegean, 1994. Contributions to: Periodicals. Honours: Honorary doctorates. Address: c/o Alfred A Knopf, 201 East 50th Street, New York, NY 10022, USA.

KAZANTZIS Judith, b. 14 Aug 1940, Oxford, England. Poet. 1 son, 1 daughter. Education: BA, Somerville College, Oxford. Appointments: Poetry Reviewer, Spare Rib Magazine; Poetry Editor, PEN Broadsheet. Publications: Poetry: Minefield, 1977; The Wicked Queen, 1980; Touch Papers, 1982; Let's Pretend, 1984; A Poem from Guatemala, 1988; Flame Tree, 1988; The Rabbit Magician Plate, 1992; Selected Poems, 1977-1992, 1995. Editor: The Gordon Riots: A Collection of Contemporary Documents, 1966; Women in Revolt: The Fight for Emancipation, 1968. Address: 9 Avondale Park Gardens, London W11, England.

KAZHDAN Alexander P, b. 3 Sept 1922, Moscow, Russia. Historian. m. Rimma A Iuhjanskaja, 7 July 1944, 1 son. Education: PhD, Institute for Universal History, Moscow, 1946; Habilitatio, Institute for Slavic and Balkan Studies, Moscow, 1961. Publications: People & Power in Byzantium, (with G Constable), 1982, reprinted, 1991; Studies on Byzantine Literature, (with S Franklin), 1984; Change in Byzantine Culture, (with A Wharton Epstein), 1985, paperback, 1990; Authors & Texts in Byzantium, 1993. Other: Vizantijskaja kul'tura, 1968. Contributions to: Byzantinische Zeitschrift; Byzantion; Byzantinoslavica; Rivista di studi bizantini; Dumbarton Oaks Papers. Honours: Professional & Scholarly Publishing Excellence, 1991; Literati: Award for Excellence Reference Reviews, 1991. Address: 1703 32nd Street North West, Washington, DC 20007-2961, USA.

KEA Pua. See: CIANCIOLO Ingrid Mohn.

KEANE John B(rendan), b. 21 July 1928, Listowel, County Kerry, Ireland. Author. Education: Graduated, St Michael's College, Listowel, 1946. Publications: Sive, 1959; Sharon's Grave, 1960; The Highest House on the Mountain, 1961; Many Young Men of Twenty,

1961; The Street and Other Poems, 1961; Hut 42, 1963; The Man From Clare, 1963; Strong Tea, 1963; The Year of the Hiker, 1964; Self-Portrait, 1964; The Field, 1965; The Rain at the End of the Summer, 1967; Letters of a Successful T D, 1967; Big Maggie, 1969; The Change in Mame Fadden, 1971; Moll, 1971; Letters of an Irish Parish Priest, 1972; Letters of an Irish Publican, 1973; Values, 1973; The Crazy Wall, 1973; The Gentle Art of Matchmaking, 1973; Letters of a Love-Hungry Farmer, 1974; Letters of a Matchmaker, 1975; Death Be Not Proud, 1976; Letters of a Civic Guard, 1976; Is the Holy Ghost Really a Kerryman, 1976; The Good Thing (play), 1976; Letters of a Country Postman, 1977; Unlawful Sex and Other Testy Matters, 1978; The Buds of Ballybunion, 1979; Stories From a Kerry Fireside, 1980; The Chastitute, 1981; More Irish Short Stories, 1981; Letters of Irish Minister of State, 1982; Man of the Triple Name, 1984; Owl Sandwiches, 1985; The Bodhran Makers, 1986; Love Bites, 1991; Duraneo, 1992; The Ram of God, 1992; Christmas Short Stories, 1996. Honours: Hon D Litt, Trinity College, Dublin, 1984; Hon Doc of Fine Arts, Marymount Manhatten College, 1984; Independent Irish Life Award, 1986; Sunday Tribune Award, 1986; Irish American Literary Award, 1988; Person of the Year Award, 1991. Memberships: Irish PEN, President, 1973-74; Hon Life Membership, Royal Dublin Society, 1991. Address: 37 William Street, Listowel, County Kerry, Ireland.

KEATING Frank, b. 4 Oct 1937, Hereford, England. Journalist. m. Jane Anne Sinclair, 8 Aug 1987. Appointments: Editor, Outside Broadcasts, ITV, 1964-70; Columnist, The Guardian, 1975-; Punch, 1980-. Publications: Bowled Over, 1979; Up and Under, 1980; Another Bloody Day in Paradise, 1981; High, Wide, and Handsome, 1985; Long Days, Late Nights, 1986; Gents and Players; Half-Time Whistle, 1992; Band of Brothers, 1996. Contributions to: Punch; New Statesman; Listener; Cricketer. Honours: Sportswriter of the Year, 1978, 1980, 1989; Magazine Writer of the Year, 1987; Sports Journalist of the Year, British Press Awards, 1988. Address: Church House Marden, Hereford HR1 3EN, England.

KEATING Henry Reymond Fitzwalter, b. 31 Oct 1926, St Leonards-on-Sea, Sussex, England. Author. m. 1953, 3 sons, 1 daughter. Education: BA, Trinity College, Dublin. Publications: The Perfect Murder, 1964; Inspector Ghote Trusts the Heart, 1972; The Lucky Alphonse, 1982; Under a Monsoon Cloud, 1986; Dead on Time, 1989; The Iciest Sin, 1990; Cheating Death, 1992; The Man Who (editor), 1992; The Rich Detective, 1993; Doing Wrong, 1994; The Good Detective, 1995; The Bad Detective, 1996. Contributions to: Crime books reviews, The Times, 1967-83. Honours: Gold Dagger, Crime Writers Association, 1964, 1980; Diamond Dagger, 1996. Memberships: Crime Writers Association, chairman, 1970-71; Detection Club, president, 1986; Royal Society of Literature, fellow; Society of Authors, chairman, 1982-84. Address: 35 Northumberland Place, London W2 5AS, England.

KEAY John (Stanley Melville), b. 18 Sept 1941, Devon, England. Author. Education: BA, Magdalen College, Oxford, 1963. Publications: Into India, 1973; When Men and Mountains Meet, 1977; The Gilgit Game, 1979; India Discovered, 1981; Eccentric Travellers, 1982; Highland Drove, 1984; Explorers Extraordinary, 1985; The Royal Geographical Society's History of World Exploration, 1991; The Honourable Company, 1991; Collins Encyclopaedia of Scotland, 1994; Indonesia: From Sabang to Meranke, 1995; The Explorers of the Western Himalayas, 1996; Last Post, 1997. Address: Succoth, Dalmally, Argyll, Scotland.

KEEBLE Neil Howard, b. 7 Aug 1944, London, England. University Reader in English Literature. m. Jenny Bowers, 20 July 1968, 2 sons, 1 daughter. Education: BA Lampeter, 1966; DPhil, Oxford, 1974; D Litt, Stirling, 1994. Publications: Richard Baxter: Puritan Man of Letters, 1982; The Literary Culture of Nonconformity, 1987; Calendar of the Correspondence of Richard Baxter (co-author), 1991. Editor: The Autobiography of Richard Baxter, 1974; The Pilgrim's Progress, 1984; John Bunyan: Conventicle and Parnassus, 1988; The Cultural Identity of Seventeenth-Century Women (a reader), 1994; Lucy Hutchinson, Memoirs of the Life of Colonel Hutchinson, 1995. Contributions to: Numerous articles on cultural history 1500-1700, in academic journals. Honour: Fellow, Royal Historical Society, 1990. Address: Duncraggan House, Airthrey Road, Stirling FK9 5JS, Scotland.

KEEFFE Barrie (Colin), b. 31 Oct 1945, London, England. Playwright. m. (1) Dee Truman, 1969, div 1979, (2) Verity Bargate, 1981, dec 1981, 2 stepsons, (3) Julia Linday, 1983, div 1993.

Appointments: Actor; Reporter, Stratford and Newham Express; Dramatist-in-Residence, Shaw Theatre, London, 1977, Royal Shakespeare Company, 1978; Associate Writer, Theatre Royal Stratford East, London, 1986-91. Publications: Plays: A Mad World, My Masters, 1977, revised version, 1984; Eyre Methuen, 1977; Gimme Shelter, 1977; Frozen Assets, 1978, revised version, 1987; Sus, 1979; Heaven Scent, 1979; Bastard Angel, 1980; Black Lear, 1980; She's So Modern, 1980; Chorus Girls, 1981; A Gentle Spirit (with Jules Croiset), 1981; The Long Good Friday (screenplay), 1984; Better Times, 1985; King of England, 1986; My Girl, 1989; Not Fade Away, 1990; Wild Justice, 1990; I Only Want to Be With You, 1996. Radio Plays: Good Old Uncle Jack, 1975; Pigeon Skyline, 1975; Self-Portrait, 1977; Paradise, 1990. Television Plays: Gotcha, 1977; Champions, 1978; Hanging Around, 1978; Waterloo Sunset, 1979; No Excuses Series, 1983; King, 1984. Honours: French Critics Prix Revelation, 1978; Giles Cooper Award, Best Radio Plays, 1978; Edgar Allan Poe Award, Mystery Writers of America, 1982; Ambassador for United Nations 50th Anniversary, 1995. Address: 110 Annandale Road, London SE10 0JZ, England.

KEEGAN John (Desmond Patrick), b. 15 May 1934, England. Editor. Writer; Defence Correspondent. m. Susanne Everett, 1960, 2 sons, 2 daughters. Education: BA, 1957, MA, 1962, Balliol College, Oxford. Appointments: Senior Lecturer in Military History, Royal Military Academy, Sandhurst, 1960-68; Defence Editor, Daily Telegraph, 1986-. Publications: The Face of Battle, 1976; Who's Who in Military History (co-author), 1976; World Armies (editor), 1979, new edition, 1982; Six Armies in Normandy, 1982; Zones of Conflict (co-author), 1986; The Mask of Command, 1987; The Price of Admiralty, 1988, reissued as Battle at Sea, 1993; The Times Atlas of the Second World War, 1989; Churchill's Generals (editor), 1991; A History of Warfare, 1993; Warpaths: Travels of a Military Historian in North America, 1995. Honours: Officer of the Order of the British Empire, 1991; Duff Cooper Prize, 1994. Address: The Manor House, Kilmington, near Warminster, Wilts BA12 6RD, England.

KEEGAN Mary Constance, (Mary Heathcott, Mary Raymond), b. 30 Sept 1914, Manchester, England. Author. Appointments: Editorial positions, London Evening News, 1934-40, Straits Times and Singapore Free Press, 1940-42, MOI All-India Radio, 1944, Time and Tide, 1945, John Herling's Labor Letter, 1951-54. Publications: As Mary Keegan, Mary Heathcott or Mary Raymond: If Today Be Sweet, 1956; Island of the Heart, 1957; Love Be Wary, 1958; Her Part of the House, 1960; Hide My Heart, 1961; Thief of My Heart, 1962; Never Doubt Me, 1963; Shadow of a Star, 1963; Take-Over, 1965; Girl in a Mask, 1965; The Divided House, 1966; The Long Journey Home, 1967; I Have Three Sons, 1968; That Summer, 1970; Surety for a Stranger, 1971; The Pimpernel Project, 1972; The Silver Girl, 1973; Villa of Flowers, 1976; April Promise, 1980; Grandma Tyson's Legacy, 1982. Address: Cockenskell, Blawith, Ulverston, Cumbria, England.

KEEGAN William James, b. 3 July 1938, London, England. Journalist. m. (1) Tessa Ashton, 7 Feb 1967, div 1982, 2 sons, 2 daughters, (2) Hilary Stonefrost, 1992. Education: Economics Editor, 1977, Associate Editor, 1983-, The Observer; Visiting Professor of Journalism, Sheffield University, 1989-. Publications: Consulting Father Wintergreen (novel), 1974; A Real Killing (novel), 1976; Who Runs the Economy?, 1979; Mrs Thatcher's Economic Experiment, 1984; Britain Without Oil, 1985; Mr Lawson's Gamble, 1989; The Spectre of Capitalism, 1992. Contributions to: The Tablet; Frequent Broadcaster. Membership: Advisory Board, Department of Applied Economics, Cambridge, 1988-93. Address: c/o Garrick Club, London WC2, England.

KEEN Geraldine. See: NORMAN Geraldine.

KEENAN Brian, b. 28 Sept 1950, Belfast, Northern Ireland. Author. m. Audrey Doyle, 20 May 1993. Education: BA, 1974, MA, 1984, Ulster University; PhD, Queen's University, Belfast, 1993. Appointments: Instructor in English, American University, Beirut, Lebanon, 1985-86; Writer-in-Residence, Trinity College, Dublin, 1993-94. Publications: An Evil Cradling: The Five-Year Ordeal of a Hostage, 1992; Blind Fight (screenplay), 1995. Address: c/o Elaine Steel, 110 Gloucester Avenue, London NW1 8JA, England.

KEENE Dennis, b. 10 July 1934, London, England. University Professor; Poet; Translator. m. Keiko Keene, 5 May 1962, 1 daughter. Education: BA, 1957, MA, 1961, DPhil, 1973, St John's College, Oxford. Publications: Yokomitsu Riichi, Modernist, 1980; The Modern

Japanese Prose Poem, 1980; Surviving (poems), 1980; Universe and Other Poems, 1983. Translations: The House of Nire (Kita Morio), 1984; Rain in the Wind (Saiichi Maruya), 1989; Ghosts (Kita Morio), 1991. Contributions to: Various publications. Honours: Independent Foreign Fiction Special Award, 1990; Noma Translation Prize, 1992. Address: 77 Staunton Road, Headington, Oxford OX3 7TL, England.

KEENE Donald, b. 18 June 1922, New York, New York USA. Professor of Japanese Emeritus; Writer; Translator. Education: BA, 1942, MA, 1947, PhD, 1951, Columbia University; MA, 1949, DLitt, 1978, Cambridge University. Appointments: Lecturer, Cambridge University, England, 1948-53; Guest Editor, Asahi Shimbun, Tokyo, Japan; Shincho Professor Emeritus of Japanese, Columbia University. Publications: The Battles of Coxinga, 1951; The Japanese Discovery of Europe, 1952, 2nd edition, 1969; Japanese Literature: An Introduction for Western Readers, 1953; Living Japan, 1957; Bunraku, the Puppet Theater of Japan, 1965; No: The Classical Theatre of Japan, 1966; Landscapes and Portraits, 1971; Some Japanese Portraits, 1978; World Within Walls, 1978; Meeting with Japan, 1978; Travels in Japan, 1981; Dawn to the West, 1984; Travellers of a Hundred Ages, 1990; Seeds in the Heart, 1993; On Familiar Terms, 1994. Editor: Modern Japanese Literature, 1956; Sources of Japanese Tradition, 1958; Twenty Plays of the No Theater, 1970. Translations: The Setting Sun, 1956; Five Modern No Plays, 1957; No Longer Human, 1958; Major Plays of Chikamatsu, 1961; The Old Woman, the Wife and the Archer, 1961; After the Banquet, 1965; Essays in Idleness, 1967; Madame de Sade, 1967; Friends, 1969; The Man Who Turned into a Stick, 1972; Three Plays of Kobo Abe, 1993; The Narrow Road to Oku, 1997. Memberships: Japan Society, New York, director, 1979-82; American Academy of Arts and Letters; Japan Academy, foreign member. Address: 407 Kent Hall, Columbia University, New York, NY 10027, USA.

KEIGER John Frederick Victor, b. 7 Dec 1952, Wembley, England. University Reader. Education: Institut d'etudes Politiques d'Aix-en Provence, University of Aix Marseille III, France, 1971-74; PhD, University of Cambridge, 1975-78. Appointments: Professor, Salford University, Manchester. Publications: France and the Origins of the First World War; Europe 1848-1914 (19 volumes in British Documents on Foreign Affairs, Reports and Papers from the Foreign Office Confidential Print), 1988-92. Contributions to: Times Higher Education Supplement; History; International History Review. Address: Department of Modern Languages, Salford University, Manchester M5 4WT, England.

KEILLOR Garrison, (born Gary Edward Keillor), b. 7 Aug 1942, Anoka, Minnesota, USA. Writer; Radio Host. Education: BA, University of Minnesota, 1966. Appointments: Creator-Host, national public radio programmes, A Prairie Home Companion and American Radio Company. Publications: Happy to Be Here, 1982; Lake Wobegon Days, 1985; Leaving Home, 1987; We Are Still Married: Stories and Letters, 1989; WLT: A Radio Romance, 1991; The Book of Guys, 1993. Children's books: Cat, You Better Come Home, 1995; The Old Man Who Loved Cheese, 1996; Sandy Bottom Orchestra, 1997. Contributions to: Newspapers and magazines. Honours: George Foster Peabody Award, 1980; Grammy Award, 1987; Ace Award, 1988; Best Music and Entertainment Host Awards, 1988, 1989; American Academy and Institute of Arts and Letters Medal, 1990; Music Broadcast Communications Radio Hall of Fame, 1994. Address: c/o Minnesota Public Radio, 45 East 7th Street, St Paul, MN 55101, USA.

KEITH William John, b. 9 May 1934, London, England. University Teacher; Critic. m. Hiroko Teresa Sato, 26 Dec 1965. Education: BA (Cantab), 1958; MA, 1959, PhD, 1961, University of Toronto. Appointments: Faculty, University of Toronto; Editor, University of Toronto Quarterly, 1976-85. Publications: Richard Jefferies: A Critical Study, 1965; The Rural Tradition, 1974; The Poetry of Nature, 1980; Epic Fiction: The Art of Rudy Wiebe, 1981; Canadian Literature in English, 1985; Regions of the Imagination, 1988; A Sense of Style, 1989; An Independent Stance, 1991; Echoes in Silence (poems), 1992; Literary Images of Ontario, 1992. Contributions to: Canadian Literature; Essays on Canadian Writing. Membership: Royal Society of Canada, fellow. Address: University College, University of Toronto, Toronto, Ontario M5S 3H7, Canada.

KELL Richard (Alexander), b. 1 Nov 1927, Youghal, County Cork, Ireland. Lecturer; Poet. Education: BA, Trinity College, Dublin, 1952. Appointments: Senior Lecturer, Newcastle upon Tyne

Polytechnic, 1970-83. Publications: Poems, 1957; Control Tower, 1962; Six Irish Poets, 1962; Differences, 1969; Humours, 1978; Heartwood, 1978; The Broken Circle, 1981; Wall (with others), 1981; In Praise of Warmth, 1987; Rock and Water, 1993. Address: 18 Rectory Grove, Gosforth, Newcastle upon Tyne NE3 1AL, England.

KELLEHER Victor, (Veronica Hart), b. 19 July 1939, London, England. Writer. m. Alison Lyle, 2 Jan 1962, 1 son, 1 daughter. Education: BA, University of Natal, 1961; Diploma in Education, University of St Andrews, 1963; BA (with Honours), University of the Witwatersrand, 1969; MA 1970, DLitt et Phil 1973, University of South Africa. Appointments: Junior Lecturer in English, University of Witwatersrand, Johannesburg, 1969; Lecturer 1970-71, Senior Lecturer in English 1972-73, University of South Africa, Pretoria; Lecturer in English, Massey University, Palmerston North, New Zealand, 1973-76; Lecturer 1976-79, Senior Lecturer 1980-83, Associate Professor of English 1984-87, University of New England, Armidale, Australia. Publications: Voices from the River, Forbidden Paths of Thual, 1979; The Hunting of Shadroth, 1981; Master of the Grove, 1982; Africa and After, 1983; The Beast of Heaven, Papio; The Green Piper, 1984; Taronga, 1986; The Makers, 1987; Em's Story, 1988; Baily's Bones, 1988; The Red King, 1989; Wintering, 1990; Brother Night, 1990; Del-Del, 1991; To the Dark Tower, 1992; Micky Darlin, 1992; Where the Whales Sing, 1994; Parkland, 1994; Double God (as Veronica Hart), 1994; The House That Jack Built (as Veronica Hart), 1994. Contributions to: Anthologies and magazines. Address: 1 Avenue Road, Glebe, New South Wales 2037, Australia.

KELLER Evelyn Fox, b. 20 Mar 1936. Professor of History and Philosophy of Science. 1 son, 1 daughter. Education: BA, Brandeis University, 1957; MA, Radcliffe College, 1959; PhD, Department of Physics, Harvard University, 1963. Appointment: Professor of History and Philosophy of Science, Massachusetts Institute of Technology. Publications: A Feeling for the Organism: The Life and Work of Barbara McClintock, 1983; Reflections on Gender and Science, 1985; Secrets of Life, Secrets of Death: Essays on Language, Gender and Science, 1992; Refiguring Life, 1995. Editor: Body/Politics, 1989; Conflicts in Feminism, 1990; Keywords in Evolutionary Biology, 1992; Feminist Philosophy of Science, 1995. Contributions to: Animals, Humans, Machines; Models of Scientific Practice; History of the Human Sciences; Journal of History of Biology; Social Studies of Science; Great Ideas Today; Perspective in Biology and Medicine; The Human Genome Initiative; The Annals of Scholarship. Address: Program in Science Technology and Society, Massachusetts Institute of Technology, Cambridge, MA 02139, USA.

KELLERMAN Jonathan Seth, b. 9 Aug 1949, New York, New York, USA. Clincial Child Psychologist; Medical School Professor; Author. m. Fate Marder, 23 July 1972, 1 son, 3 daughters. Education: AB, University of California at Los Angeles, 1971; AM, 1973, PhD, 1974, University of Southern California at Los Angeles. Appointments: Freelance Illustrator, 1966-72, Director, Psychsocial Program, 1976-81, Staff Psychologist, 1975-81, Children's Hospital of Los Angeles; Clinical Associate Professor, University of Southern California School of Medicine, Los Angeles, 1979-; Head, Jonathan Kellerman PhD and Associates, Los Angeles, 1981-88. Publications: Psychological Aspects of Childhood Cancer, 1980; Helping the Fearful Child: A Parents' Guide to Everyday Problem Anxieties, 1981; When the Bough Breaks, 1985; Blood Test, 1986; Over the Edge, 1987; The Butcher's Theatre, 1988; Silent Partner, 1989; Time Bomb, 1990; Private Eyes, 1992; Devil's Waltz, 1993; Bad Love, 1994; Daddy, Daddy Can You Touch the Sky?, 1994; Self-Defense, 1995; The Web, 1996. Honours: Edgar Allen Poe Award, Mystery Writers of America, 1985; Anthony Boucher Award, 1986. Address: c/o Barney Karpfinger, 500 Fifth Avenue, New York, NY 10110, USA.

KELLEY Leo P(atrick), b. 10 Sept 1928, Wilkes Barre, Pennsylvania, USA. Author. Education: BA, New School for Social Research, New York City, 1957. Publications: The Counterfeits, 1967; Odyssey to Earthdeath, 1968; Time Rogue, 1970; The Coins of Murph, 1971; Brother John, 1971; Mindmix, 1972; Time: 110100, 1972, UK edition as The Man From Maybe, 1974; Themes in Science Fiction: A Journey Into Wonder (editor), 1972; The Supernatural in Fiction (editor), 1972; Deadlocked (novel), 1973; The Earth Tripper, 1973; Fantasy: The Literature of the Marvellous (editor), 1974. Science fiction novels for children: The Time Trap, 1977; Backward in Time, 1979; Death Sentence, 1979; Earth Two, 1979; Prison Satellite, 1979; Sunworld, 1979; Worlds Apart, 1979; Dead Moon, 1979; King of the Stars, 1979; On the Red World, 1979; Night of Fire and Blood, 1979;

Where No Star Shines, 1979; Vacation in Space, 1979; Star Gold, 1979; Goodbye to Earth, 1979. Western novels: Luke Sutton series, 9 volumes, 1981-90; Cimarron series, 20 volumes, 1983-86; Morgan, 1986; A Man Named Dundee, 1988; Thunder Gods Gold, 1988. Address: 702 Long Boulevard, Long Beach, NY 11561, USA.

KELLMAN Steven G, b. 15 Nov 1947, Brooklyn, New York, USA. Critic; Professor. Education: BA, State University of New York, 1967; MA, 1969, PhD, 1972, University of California, Berkeley. Appointments: Editor- in-Chief, Occident, 1969-70; Assistant Professor, Bemidji State University, Minnesota, 1972-73; Lecturer, Tel-Aviv University, Israel, 1973-75; Visiting Lecturer, University of California, Irvine, 1975-76; Assistant Professor, 1976-80, Associate Professor, 1980-85, Professor, 1985-, Ashbel Smith Professor of Comparative Literature, 1995-, University of Texas, San Antonio; Fulbright Senior Lecturer, USSR, 1980; Visiting Associate Professor, University of California, Berkeley, 1982; Literary Scene Editor, USA Today; Partners of the Americas Lecturer, Peru, 1988; Fulbright Travel Grant, China, 1995; National Endowment for the Humanities Summer Seminar, Natal, South Africa, 1996; John E Sawyer Fellow, Longfellow Institute, Harvard, 1997. Publications: The Self-Begetting Novel, 1980; Approaches to Teaching Camus's The Plague (editor), 1985; Loving Reading: Erotics of the Text, 1985; The Modern American Novel, 1991; The Plague: Fiction and Resistance, 1993; Perspectives on Raging Bull, 1994. Contributions to: San Antonio Light; Village Voice; Nation; Georgia Review; Moment; Newsweek; Modern Fiction Studies; Midstream; New York Times Book Review; Washington Post Book World; Gettysburg Review; Film Critic, Texas Observer. Honour: H L Mencken Award, 1986. Membership: National Book Critics Circle, board of directors, 1996-99. Address: 302 Fawn Drive, San Antonio, TX 78231, USA.

KELLOGG Steven, b. 1941, USA. Children's Fiction Writer. Publications: The Wicked Kings of Bloon, 1970; Can I Keep Him?, 1971; The Mystery Beast of Ostergeest, 1971; The Orchard Cat, 1972; Won't Somebody Play With Me, 1972; The Island of the Skog, 1973; The Mystery of the Missing Red Mitten, 1974; There was an Old Woman, 1974; Much Bigger Than Martin, 1976; Steven Kellogg's Yankee Doodle, 1976; The Mysterious Tadpole, 1977; The Mystery of the Magic Green Ball, 1978; Pinkerton Behave, 1979; The Mystery of the Flying Orange Pumpkin, 1980; A Rose for Pinkerton, 1981; The Mystery of the Stolen Blue Paint, 1982; Tallyho Pinkerton, 1982; Ralph's Secret Weapon, 1983; Paul Bunyan, 1984; Chicken Little, 1985; Best Friends, 1986; Pecos Bill, 1986; Aster Aardvark's Alphabet Adventure, 1987; Prehistoric Pinkerton, 1987; Johnny Appleseed, 1990; Mike Fink, 1992; The Christmas Witch, 1992. Address: Bennett's Bridge Road, Sandy Hook, CT 06482, USA.

KELLS Susannah. See: **CORNWELL Bernard.**

KELLY A A. See: **HAMPTON Angeline Agnes.**

KELLY James Plunkett, b. 21 May 1920, Dublin, Ireland. Author. m. Valerie Koblitz, 4 Sept 1945, 3 sons, 1 daughter. Education: Synge Street Christian Brothers' School, Dublin; Municipal College of Music, Dublin. Appointments: Assistant Head, Drama, Radio Eireann, 1955-61; Head, Features, Telefis Eireann, 1969-72. Publications: The Risen People, 1958; The Trusting and the Maimed, 1959; Strumpet City, 1969; The Gems She Wore, 1972; Collected Short Stories, 1977; Farewell Companions, 1977; The Boy in the Back Wall and Other Essays, 1987; The Circus Animals, 1990. Contributions to: The Bell; Irish Writing; Bookman; Writing Today. Agent: The Peters Fraser and Dunlop Group Ltd, London. Address: 29 Parnell Road, Bray, Co Wicklow, Ireland.

KELLY M(ilton) T(erry), b. 30 Nov 1947, Toronto, Ontario, Canada. Writer; Dramatist. Education: BA, York University, 1970; BEd, University of Toronto, 1976. Appointments: Business Journalist, Maclean-Hunter Ltd, Toronto, 1970-71; Staff, International Press, Toronto, 1972-73; Reporter, Scotsman, Edinburgh, Scotland, 1973-74; Reporter, Moose Jaw Times Herald, Saskatchewan, 1974-75; Columnist, Globe & Mail, Toronto, 1979-81; Contributing Interviewer, Imprint, TV Ontario, 1989-95. Publications: I Do Remember the Fall (novel), 1978; Country You Can't Walk In (poems), 1979; The More Loving One (novel and stories), 1980; The Ruined Season (novel), 1982; The Green Dolphin (play), 1982; Wildfire: The Legend of Tom Longboat (screenplay), 1983; A Dream Like Mine (novel), 1987; Walter Kenyon: Arctic Argonauts (editor), 1990; Breath Dances Between Them (short stories), 1991; Out of the Whirlwind (novel), 1995.

Contributions to: Anthologies and magazines. Honours: Award for Poetry, Toronto Arts Council, 1986; Governor-General's Award for Literature, 1987; President's Prizes for Fiction, York University, 1989, 1990; Various grants. Memberships: Champlain Society; International PEN; Playwrights Canada; Writers Union of Canada. Address: 60 Kendal Avenue, Toronto, Ontario M5R 1L9, Canada.

KELLY Patrick. See: **ALLBEURY Theodore Edward le Bouthilliers.**

KELLY Robert, b. 24 Sept 1935, Brooklyn, New York, USA. Professor of Literature; Poet; Writer. Education: AB, City College, New York City, 1955; Columbia University, 1955-58. Appointments: Editor, Chelsea Review, 1957-60, Matter magazine and Matter publishing, 1964-, Los 1, 1977; Lecturer, Wagner College, 1960-61; Founding Editor (with George Economou), Trobar magazine, 1960-64, Trobar Books, 1962-65; Instructor, 1961-64, Assistant Professor, 1964-69, Associate Professor, 1969-74, Porfessor of English, 1974-86, Director, Writing Programme, 1980-93, Asher B Edelman Professor of Literature, 1986-, Bard College; Assistant Professor, State University of New York at Buffalo, 1964; Visiting Lecturer, Tufts University, 1966-67; Poet-in-Residence, California Institute of Technology, Pasadena, 1971-72, University of Kansas, 1975, Dickinson College, 1976. Publications: Poetry: Armed Descent, 1961; Her Body Against Time, 1963; Round Dances, 1964; Tabula, 1964; Entasy, 1964; Matter/Fact/Sheet/1, 1964; Matter/Fact/Sheet/2, 1964; Lunes, 1964; Lectiones, 1965; Words in Service, 1966; Weeks, 1966; Songs XXIV, 1967; Twenty Poems, 1967; Devotions, 1967; Axon Dendron Tree, 1967; Crooked Bridge Love Society, 1967; A Joining: A Sequence for H D, 1967; Alpha, 1968; Finding the Measure, 1968; From the Common Shore, Book 5, 1968; Songs I-XXX, 1969; Sonnets, 1969; We Are the Arbiters of Beast Desire, 1969; A California Journal, 1969; The Common Shore, Books I-V: A Long Poem About America in Time, 1969; Kali Yuga, 1971; Flesh: Dream; Book, 1971; Ralegh, 1972; The Pastorals, 1972; Reading Her Notes, 1972; The Tears of Edmund Burke, 1973; Whaler Frigate Clippership, 1973; The Bill of Particulars, 1973; The Belt, 1974; The Loom, 1975; Sixteen Odes, 1976; The Lady of, 1977; The Convections, 1978; The Book of Persephone, 1978, revised edition, 1983; The Cruise of the Pnyx, 1979; Kill the Messenger Who Brings the Bad News, 1979; Sentence, 1980; The Alchemist to Mercury, 1981; Spiritual Exercises, 1981; Mulberry Women, 1982; Under Words, 1983; Thor's Thrush, 1984; Not This Island Music, 1987; The Flowers of Unceasing Coincidence, 1988; Oahu, 1988; A Strange Market, 1992; Mont Blanc, 1994. Fiction: The Scorpions, 1967; Cities, 1971; Wheres, 1978; A Transparent Tree: Ren Fictions, 1985; Doctor of Silence, 1988; Cat Scratch Fever: Fictions, 1990; Queen of Terrors: Fictions, 1994. Other: A Controversy of Poets: An Anthology of Contemporary American Poetry (editor with Paris Leary), 1965; Statement, 1968; In Time, 1971; Sulphur, 1972; A Line of Sight, 1974. Honours: Los Angeles Times Book Prize, 1980; American Academy of Arts and Letters Award, 1986. Address: c/o Department of English, Bard College, Annadale-on-Hudson, NY 12504, USA.

KELLY Tim, (Keith Jackson, J Moriarty, Vera Morris, Robert Swift), b. 2 Oct 1937, Saugus, Massachusetts, USA. Playwright; Screenwriter. Education: BA, 1956, MA, 1957, Emerson College; American Broadcasting Fellow, Yale University, 1965. Publications: Over 300 plays. Honours: Numerous awards and grants. Memberships: Authors League; Dramatists Guild; Writers Guild of America; College of Fellows of the American Theatre. Address: 8730 Lookout Mountain Avenue, Hollywood, CA 90046, USA.

KELMAN James, b. 9 June 1946, Glasgow, Scotland. Novelist. m. Marie Connors, 2 daughters. Education: University of Strathclyde, 1975-78, 1981-82. Publications: The Busconductor Hines, 1984; A Chancer, 1985; A Disaffection, 1989. Short Stories: An Old Pub Near the Angel, 1973; Short Tales from the Nightshift, 1978; Not Not While the Giro and Other Stories, 1983; Lran Tales, 1985; Greyhound for Breakfast, 1987; The Burn, 1991; How Late it Was, How Late, 1994. Plays: The Busker, 1985; Le Rodeur, 1987; In the Night, 1988; Hardie and Baird, The Last, 1990. Screenplay: The Return, 1990. Honours: Scottish Arts Council Fellowships; Scottish Arts Council Bursaries, Book Awards, 1983, 1987, 1989; Cheltenham Prize, 1987; James Tait Black Memorial Prize, 1989; Booker Prize, 1994. Address: 244 West Princess Street, Glasgow G4 9DP, Scotland.

KELTON Elmer Stephen, (Lee McElroy), b. 29 Apr 1926, Andrews, Texas, USA. Novelist; Agricultural Journalist. m. Anna Lipp,

3 July 1947, 2 sons, 1 daughter. Education: BA, Journalism, University of Texas, 1948. Publications: The Day the Cowboys Quit, 1971; The Time It Never Rained, 1973; The Good Old Boys, 1978; The Wolf and the Buffalo, 1980; Stand Proud, 1984; The Man Who Rode Midnight, 1987; Honour at Daybreak, 1991; Slaughter, 1992; The Far Canyon, 1994; The Pumpkin Rollers, 1996; Cloudy in the West, 1997. Contributions to: Numerous articles to magazines and newspapers. Honours: 6 Spur Awards, Western Writers of America; 4 Western Heritage Awards, National Cowboy Hall of Fame; Tinkle-McCombs Achievement Award, Texas Institute of Letters; Lifetime Achievement, Western Literature Association. Memberships: Western Writers of America, president, 1963-64; Texas Institute of Letters; Sigma Delta Chi. Address: 2460 Oxford, San Angelo, TX 76904, USA.

KEMAL Yashar, b. 1923, Adana, Turkey. Writer; Journalist. m. Thilda Serrero, 1952, 1 son. Education: Self-educated. Publications: (in English) Memed, My Hawk, 1961; The Wind From the Plain, 1963; Anatolian Tales, 1968; They Burn the Thistles, 1973; Iron Earth, Copper Sky, 1974; The Legend of Ararat, 1975; The Legend of a Thousand Bulls, 1976; The Undying Grass, 1977; The Lords of Akchasaz, Part I, Murder in the Ironsmiths Market, 1979; The Saga of a Seagull, 1981; The Sea-Crossed Fisherman, 1985; The Birds Have Also Gone, 1987; To Crush the Serpent, 1991; novels, short stories, plays and essays in Turkish. Honours: Commander, Legion d'honneur, 1984; Doctor Honoris Causa, Universite de Sciences Humaines, Strasbourg, 1991. Address: PK 14, Basinkoy, Istanbul, Turkey.

KEMP Gene, b. 27 Dec 1926, Wigginton, England. Children's Author; Educator. Education: Graduated, University of Exeter, 1945. Appointments: Teacher, St Sidwell's School, Exeter, 1962-74; Lecturer, Rolle College, 1963-79. Publications: Tamworth Pig series, 4 volumes, 1972-78; The Turbulent Term of Tyke Tiler, 1977; Gowie Corby Plays Chicken, 1979; Ducks and Dragons (editor), 1980; Dog Days and Cat Naps, 1980; The Clock Tower Ghost, 1981; No Place Like, 1983; Charlie Lewis Plays for Time, 1984; The Well, 1984; Jason Bodger and the Priory Ghost, 1985; McMagus is Waiting for You, 1986; Juniper, 1986; I Can't Stand Losing, 1987. Honours: Children's Awards, 1977; Carnegie Medal, 1978; Hon MA, Exeter University, 1984; Runner-up Whitbread, 1985. Address: c/o Laurence Pollinger Ltd, 18 Maddox Street, London W1R OEU, England.

KEMP (Patricia) Penn, b. c.1944, Canada. Writer. 1 son, 1 daughter. Education: Honours in English Language and Literature, 1966, MEduc, 1988, University of Toronto. Appointments: Various Writer-in-Residencies. Publications: Bearing Down, 1972; Binding Twine, 1984; Some Talk Magic, 1986; Eidolons, 1990; Throo, 1990; The Universe is One Poem, 1990; What the Ear Hears Last, 1994. Contributions to: Magazines. Honours: Canada Council Arts Grants, 1979-80, 1981-82, 1991-92; Ontario's Graduate Scholarship, 1987-88. Memberships: League of Canadian Poets; Playwright's Union; Writer's Union. Address: C-7 2163 Queen Street E, Toronto, Ontario M4L 1J1, Canada.

KEMPER Troxey, b. 29 Apr 1915, Oklahoma, USA. Editor; Novelist; Poet. m. Jeanne Doty, 31 July 1954, div. 1964, 2 daughters. Education: BA, University of New Mexico, Albuquerque, 1951. Appointments: Newspaper Reporter, Albuquerque Journal, 1951-69; Editor, Tucumcari Literary Review, 1988-. Publications: Mainly on the Plain, 1982; Whence and Whither, 1983; Folio and Signature, 1983; Part Comanche, 1991; Comanche Warbonnet, 1991; Under a Sky of Azure, 1993. Contributions to: Poets and Writers Magazine; Small Press Review; Amarillo News Globe; Los Angeles Daily News; Los Angeles Times; American Film Magazine. Honour: Honourable Mention, National Writers Club, 1990. Memberships: National Writers Union; Sigma Delta Chi. Address: 3108 West Bellevue Avenue, Los Angeles, CA 90026, USA.

KEMSKE Floyd, b. 11 Mar 1947, Wilmington, Delaware, USA. Writer. m. Alice Geraldine Morse, 21 Dec 1968. Education: BA, University of Delaware, 1970; MA, Michigan State University, 1971. Publications: Novels: Lifetime Employment, 1992; The Virtual Boss, 1993. Membership: National Writers Union. Address: PO Box 841, Melrose, MA 02176, USA.

KENDALL Carol (Seeger), b. 13 Sept 1917, Bucyrus, Ohio, USA. Writer. m. Paul Murray Kendall, 15 June 1939, 2 daughters. Education: AB, Ohio University, 1939. Publications: The Black Seven, 1946; The Baby Snatcher, 1952; The Other Side of the Tunnel, 1956; The Gammage Cup, 1959, as The Minnipins, 1960; The Big Splash,

1960; The Whisper of Glocken, 1965; Sweet and Sour Tales, retold by Carol Kendall and Yao-Wen Li, 1978; The Firelings, 1981; Haunting Tales from Japan, 1985; The Wedding of the Rat Family, 1988. Honours: Ohioana Award, 1960; Newbery Honour Book, 1960; American Library Association Notable Book, 1960; Parents Choice Award, 1982; Aslan Award, Mythopoeic Society, 1983. Memberships: PEN American Center; Authors League of America; Authors Guild. Address: 928 Holiday Drive, Lawrence, KS 66049, USA.

KENEALLY Thomas Michael, b. 7 Oct 1935, Sydney, Australia. Author. m. Judith Mary Martin, 1965, 2 daughters. Education: St Patrick's College, Strathfield, New South Wales, Australia. Appointments: Lecturer, Drama, University of New England, 1968-70; Visiting Professor, University California, Irvine, 1985; Berg Professor, New York University, 1988; Professor, Department of English, University California, Irvine, 1991-. Publications: Bring Larks and Heroes, 1967; Three Cheers for the Paraclete, 1968; The Survivor, 1969; A Dutiful Daughter, 1970; The Chant of Jimmie Blacksmith, 1972; Blood Read, Sister Rose, 1974; Gossip from the Forest, 1975; Season in Purgatory, 1976; A Victim of the Aurora, 1977; Passenger, 1978; Confederates, 1979; Schindler's Ark, 1982; Outback, 1983; The Cut-Rate Kingdom, 1984; A Family Madness, 1985; The Playmaker, 1987; Towards Asmara, 1989; Flying Hero Class, 1991; The Place, Where Souls are Born, 1992; Now and in Time to be Woman of the Inner Sea, 1992; Our Republic, 1993; Jacko, 1993. Honours: Booker Prize, 1983; Royal Society of Literature, 1983; Los Angeles Times Fiction Prize, 1983. Memberships: Australia-China Council; Australian Society of Authors; National Book Council of Australia. Address: c/o Deborah Rogers, 20 Powis Mews, London W11 1JN, England.

KENNAN George (Frost), b. 16 Feb 1904, Milwaukee, Wisconsin, USA. Retired Diplomat; Professor Emeritus; Author. m. Annelise Sorenson, 1 son, 3 daughters. Education: AB, Princeton University, 1925. Appointments: Various diplomatic posts, 1926-45; Deputy for Foreign Affairs, National War College, Washington, DC, 1946; Director, Policy Planning Staff, US Department of State, 1947; Deputy Counselor and Chief Long Range Adviser to the US Secretary of State, 1949-50; Member, 1950-53, Professor, 1956-74, Professor Emeritus, 1974-, Institute for Advanced Study, Princeton, New Jersey; US Ambassador to the USSR, 1952, Yugoslavia, 161-63; George Eastman Visiting Professor, Oxford University, 1957-58; Fellow, Harvard University, 1965-70, All Souls College, Oxford, 1969. Publications: American Diplomacy 1900-1950, 1951; Realities of American Foreign Policy, 1954; Soviet-American Relations 1917-1920, 2 volumes, 1956, 1958; Russia, the Atom and the West, 1958; Soviet Foreign Policy 1917-1945, 1960; Russia and the West Under Lenin and Stalin, 1961; On Dealing with the Communist World, 1963; Memoirs 1925-1950, 1967; Democracy and the Student Left, 1968; From Prague After Munich: Diplomatic Papers 1938-1940, 1968; The Marquis de Custine and His Russia in 1839, 1971; Memoirs 1950-1963, 1972; The Cloud of Danger: Current Realities of American Foreign Policy, 1977; The Decline of Bismarck's European Order: Franco-Russian Relations 1875-1890, 1979; The Nuclear Delusion: Soviet-American Relations in the Atomic Age, 1982; The State Department Policy Planning Staff Papers, 1983; The Fateful Alliance: France, Russia and the Coming of the First World War, 1984; Sketches from a Life, 1989; Around the Cragged Hill, 1993. Contributions to: Scholarly journals. Honours: Freedom House Award, 1951; Bancroft Prize, 1956; National Book Awards, 1957, 1968; Francis Parkman Prize, 1957; Pulitzer Prizes, 1957, 1968; Albert Einstein Peace Prize, 1981; Gold Medal in History, American Academy and Institute of Arts and Letters, 1984; Literary Lion Award, New York Public Library, 1985; Creative Arts Award, Brandeis University, 1986; Toynbee Prize, 1988; Presidential Medal of Freedom, 1989; Ambassador Book Award, 1993; Distinguished Service Award, US Department of State, 1994; Numerous honorary doctorates. Memberships: American Academy of Arts and Letters, president, 1967-71; American Philosophical Society; National Institute of Arts and Letters, president, 1964-67; Royal Society of Arts. Address: 146 Hodge Road, Princeton, NJ 08540, USA.

KENNEDY Adrienne (Lita), b. 13 Sept 1931, Pittsburgh, Pennsylvania, USA. Dramatist. m. Joseph C Kennedy, 15 May 1953, div 1966, 2 sons. Education: BS, Ohio State University, 1953; Columbia University, 1954-56; New School for Social Research, American Theatre Wing, Circle in the Square Theatre School, New York City, 1957-58, 1962. Appointments: Playwright, Actors Studio, New York City, 1962-65; Lecturer, Yale University, 1972-74, Princeton University, 1977; CBS Fellow, School of Drama, New York City, 1973;

Visiting Associate Professor, Brown University, 1979-80; Distinguished Lecturer, University of California, Berkeley, 1980, 1986; Visiting Lecturer, Harvard University, 1990, 1991. Publications: Plays: Funnyhouse of a Negro, 1964; Cities in Bezique, 1965; A Rat's Mass, 1966; A Lesson in Dead Language, 1966; The Lennon Plays, 1968; Sun, 1969; A Movie Star Has to Star in Black and White, 1976; She Talks to Beethoven, 1990; The Alexander Plays, 1992. Other: People Who Led to My Plays, 1987; Letter to My Students, 1992. Contributions to: Anthologies. Honours: Obie Award, 1964; Guggenheim Fellowship, 1968; Rockefeller Foundation Fellowships, 1968, 1974; National Endowment for the Arts Fellowships, 1973, 1993; Manhattan Borough President's Award, 1988; American Academy of Arts and Letters Award, 1994; Lila Wallace-Reader's Digest Award, 1994; Pierre Lecomte du Novy Award, Lincoln Center for the Performing Arts, New York City, 1994. Membership: PEN. Address: c/o University of Minnesota Press, 111 Third Avenue South, Suite 290, Minneapolis, MN 55401, USA.

KENNEDY Beryl, b. 2 Feb 1917, Tamworth, New South Wales, Australia. Physiotherapist; Feldenkrais Practitioner. m. Kenneth Robert Kennedy, 15 Feb 1949, 3 sons. Education: Diploma in Physiotherapy, Sydney, 1937; Continuing postgraduate education, Feldenkrais Training, Sydney, 1986-90. Publications: Dynamic Back Care Through Body Awareness, 1982; Dynamic Back Care Training Program, 1987. Contributions to: Australian Journal of Physiotherapy; Proceedings of the World Confederation for Physical Therapy; New Zealand Journal of Physiotherapy; Physiotherapy Journal, UK. Memberships: Australian Physiotherapy Association; Australian Society of Authors; Australian Feldenkrais Guild; Australian Feldenkrais Interest Group; Australian War Widows Guild. Address: 110 Belmont Road, Mosman, New South Wales 2088, Australia.

KENNEDY John Hines b. 1 Nov 1925, Washington, DC, USA. Cardiothoracic Surgeon (retired); Physiologist; Poet. m. (1), 2 sons, 2 daughters, (2) Shirley Angela Josephine Watson. Education: Princeton University, 1943-45; MD, Harvard Medical School, 1945-49; FACS, 1957; MPhil, Imperial College, London, 1990. Publications: Carnet Parisien, 1987; Vieux Colombier, 1987-88; Les Images, 1991. Contributions to: Books and journals. Honours: Medal of Vishnevsky, Moscow, 1962; Medal, Un Liège, Belgium, 1978. Memberships: PEN club; Cercle de l'Union Intersliée, Paris. Address: Old Court, Clare, Sudbury, Suffolk CO10 8NP, England.

KENNEDY Joseph Charles, (X J Kennedy), b. 21 Aug 1929, Dover, New Jersey, USA. Poet; Writer. m. Dorothy Mintzlaff, 31 Jan 1962, 4 sons, 1 daughter. Education: BSc, Seton Hall University, 1950; MA, Columbia University, 1951; University of Paris, 1956. Appointments: Teaching Fellow, 1956-60, Instructor, 1960-62, University of Michigan; Poetry Editor, The Paris Review, 1961-64; Lecturer, Womens College of the University of North Carolina, 1962-63; Assistant Professor to Professor, Tufts University, 1963-79. Publications: Nude Descending a Staircase, 1961; An Introduction to Poetry (with Dana Gioia), 1968, 8th edition, 1994; The Bedford Reader, 1982 (with Dorothy Kennedy and Jane Aarron),1982, 5th edition, 1994; Cross Ties, 1985; Dark Horses, 1992; 14 children's books. Contributions to: Newspapers and journals. Honours: Lamont Award, 1961; Los Angeles Times Book Award, 1985. Memberships: Authors Guild, John Barton Wolgamot Society; Modern Language Association; PEN. Address: 4 Fern Way, Bedford, MA 01730, USA.

KENNEDY Sir Ludovic Henry Coverley, b. 3 Nov 1919, Edinburgh, Scotland. Writer; Broadcaster. m. Moira Shearer King, 1950, 1 son, 3 daughters. Education: Christ Church, Oxford. Appointments: Editor, Feature, First Reading, BBC Third Programme, 1953-54; Lecturer, British Council, Sweden, Finland, Denmark, 1955, Belgium, Luxembourg, 1956; Introduced Profile, ATV 1955-56; Newscaster, ITV 1956-58; Introducer on Stage, Associated Rediffusion, 1957, This Week, 1958-59; Chairman, BBC Features: Your Verdict, 1962, Your Witness, 1967-70; Commentator, BBC Panorama, 1960-63; Election TV Broadcasts, 1966; Presenter, 24 Hours, BBC 1969-72, AD Lib, BBC 1970-72, Midweek, BBC 1973-75, Newsday, BBC 1975-76; Interviewer, Tonight, BBC 1976-80; Presenter, Lord Mountbatten Remembers, 1980, Changes of Direction, 1980, Did You See, 1980-, Great Railway Journeys of the World, 1980. Publications: Sub-Lieutenant, 1942; Nelson's Band of Brothers, 1951; One Man's Meat, 1953; Murder Story, 1956; Ten Rillington Place, 1961; The Trial of Stephen Ward, 1964; Very Lovely People, 1969; Pursuit: The Chase and Sinking of the Bismarck, 1974; A Presumption of Innocence: The Amazing Case of Patrick Meehan, 1975; The

Portland Spy Case, 1978; Menace: The Life and Death of the Tirpitz, 1979; Wicked Beyond Belief: The Luton Post Office Murder Case, 1980; A Book of Railway Journeys, 1980; A Book of Sea Journeys, 1981; A Book of Air Journeys, 1982; The Airman and the Carpenter: The Lindbergh Case and the Framing of Richard Hauptmann, 1985; On My Way to the Club (autobiography), 1989; Euthanasia, 1990; Truth to Tell (collected writings), 1991; In Bed with an Elephant: A Journey Through Scotland's Past and Present, 1995. Honours: Various honours and awards; Knighted. 1994. Address: c/o Deborah Rogers, Coleridge and White, 20 Powis Mews, London W11 1JN, England.

KENNEDY (George) Michael (Sinclair), b. 19 Feb 1926, Manchester, England. Music Critic; Author. m. Eslyn Durdle, 16 May 1947. Education: Berkhamsted School. Appointments: Staff, 1941-, Northern Music Critic, 1950-, Northern Editor, 1960-86, Joint Chief Music Critic, 1986-89, The Daily Telegraph; Music Critic, The Sunday Telegraph, 1989-. Publications: The Hallé Tradition: A Century of Music, 1960; The Works of Ralph Vaughan Williams, 1964, revised edition, 1980; Portrait of Elgar, 1968, 3rd edition, 1987; Elgar: Orchestral Music, 1969; Portrait of Manchester, 1970; A History of the Royal Manchester College of Music, 1971; Barbirolli: Conductor Laureate, 1971; Mahler, 1974, revised edition, 1990; The Autobiography of Charles Hallé, with Correspondence and Diaries (editor), 1976; Richard Strauss, 1976, revised edition, 1995; The Concise Oxford Dictionary of Music (editor), 1980, revised edition, 1995; Britten, 1981, revised edition, 1993; The Hallé 1858-1983, 1983; Strauss: Tone Poems, 1984; The Oxford Dictionary of Music (editor), 1985, 2nd edition, revised, 1994; Adrian Boult, 1987; Portrait of Walton, 1989; Music Enriches All: The First 21 Years of the Royal Northern College of Music, Manchester, 1994. Contributions to: Newspapers and magazines. Honours: Fellow, Institute of Journalists, 1967; Officer of the Order of the British Empire, 1981; Fellow, Royal Northern College of Music, 1981. Address: 3 Moorwood Drive, Sale, Cheshire, M33 4QB, England.

KENNEDY Moorhead, b. 5 Nov 1930, New York, New York, USA. Foundation Administrator; Writer. m. Louisa Livingston, 8 June 1955, 4 sons. Education: AB, Princeton University, 1952; JD, Harvard University, 1959; National War College, 1974-75. Appointments: Foreign Service Officer, 1961-69, 1975-78, Director, Office of Investment Affairs, 1971-74, US Department of State; Executive Director, Cathedral Peace Institute, New York City, 1981-83, Council for International Understanding, New York City, 1983-90; President, Moorhead Kennedy Institute, New York City, 1990-. Publications: The Ayatollah in the Cathedral, 1986; Terrorism: The New Warfare, 1988; Hostage Crisis, 1989; Death of a Dissident, 1990; Fire in the Forest, 1990; Metalfabriken, 1993; Grocery Store, 1993; Nat-Tel, 1995. Contributions to: Books and professional journals. Honours: Medal for Valor, US Department of State, 1981; Gold Medal, National Institute of Social Sciences, 1991; Many honorary doctorates. Memberships: American Foreign Service Association; Americans for Middle East Understanding; Episcopalian; Freemason. Address: 55 Liberty Street, Apt 7A, New York, NY 10005, USA.

KENNEDY Paul M(ichael), b. 17 June 1945, Wallsend, Northumberland, England. Professor of History; Writer. m. Catherine Urwin, 2 Sept 1967, 3 sons. Education: BA, University of Newcastle, 1966; PhD, Oxford University, 1970. Appointments: Research Assistant to Sir Basil Liddell Hart, 1966-70; Lecturer, 1970-75, Reader, 1975-82, Professor, 1982-83, University of East Anglia; Visiting Fellow, Institute for Advanced Study, Princeton, New Jersey, 1978-79; J Richardson Dilworth Professor of History, 1983-, Director, International Security Studies, 1990-, Yale University; Various guest lectureships including the first Nobel Peace Foundation Lecture, Oslo, 1992. Publications: Pacific Onslaught 1941-43, 1972; Conquest: The Pacific War 1943-1945, 1973; The Samoan Tangle: A Study in Anglo-German-American Relations 1878-1900, 1974; The Rise and Fall of British Naval Mastery, 1976; The Rise of the Anglo-German Antagonism 1860-1914, 1980; The Realities Behind Diplomacy: Background Influences on British External Policy 1865-1980, 1981; Strategy and Diplomacy 1870-1945: Eight Essays, 1983; The Rise and Fall of the Great Powers: Economic Change and Military Conflict from 1500-2000, 1988; Preparing for the Twenty-First Century, 1993. Editor: Germany in the Pacific and Far East 1870-1914 (with John A Moses), 1977; The War Plans of the Great Powers 1880-1914, 1979; Appeasement (with Jack Spence), 1980; Nationalist and Racialist Movements in Britain and Germany Before 1914 (with A J Nicholls), 1981; Grand Strategies in War and Peace, 1991; Global Trends: The World Almanac of Development and Peace (with Ingomar Hauchler),

1994. Contributions to: Professional journals and to general magazines and newspapers. Honours: Various research awards, fellowships, and honorary doctorates. Memberships: American Academy of Arts and Sciences; American Philosophical Society; Fellow, Royal Historical Society; Society of American Historians. Address: 409 Humphrey Street, New Haven, CT 06511, USA.

KENNEDY Thomas Eugene, b. 9 Mar 1944, New York, USA. Writer; Editor; Translator; Teacher; Administrator. m. Monique M Brun, 28 Dec 1974, div 1997, 1 son, 1 daughter. Education: BA (summa cum laude), Fordham University, New York, 1974; MFA, Vermont College, Norwich University, USA, 1985; PhD, Copenhagen University, 1988. Appointments: Guest Editor, Nordic Section, Frank magazine, 1987; European Editor, Rohwedder, 1988-89; International Editor, Cimarron Review, 1989-; Contributing Editor, Pushcart Prize, 1990-; Advisory Editor, Short Story, 1990-; International Editor, Potpourri, 1993-; Editorial Board, International Review, 1994; Advisory Editor, The Literary Review, 1996-. Publications: Andre Dubus: A Study, 1988; Crossing Borders (novel), 1990; The American Short Story Today, 1991; Robert Coover: A Study, 1992; Index, American Award Stories, 1993; A Weather of the Eye (novel), 1996; Unreal City (stories) 1995; New Danish Fiction (editor), 1995; The Book of Angels, novel, 1997; Drove, Dive, Dance and Fight, stories, 1997; New Irish Writing, editor, 1997. Address: Oster Sogade 52, I, DK 2100 Copenhagen, Denmark.

KENNEDY William (Joseph), b. 16 Jan 1928, Albany, New York, USA. Novelist; Professor of English. m. Ana Daisy Dana Segarra, 31 Jan 1957, 1 son, 2 daughters. Education: BA, Siena College, Loudonville, New York, 1949. Appointments: Assistant Sports Editor and Columnist, Glens Falls Post Star, 1949-50; Reporter, 1952-56, Special Writer, 1963-70, Albany Times-Union; Assistant Managing Editor and Columnist, Puerto Rico World Journal, San Juan, 1956; Reporter, Miami Herald, 1957; Correspondent, Time-Life Publishers in Puerto Rico, 1957-59; Reporter, Knight Newspapers, 1957-59; Founding Managing Editor, San Juan Star, 1959-61; Lecturer, 1974-82, Professor of English, 1983-, State University of New York at Albany; Visiting Professor, Cornell University, 1982-83; Founder, New York State Writers Institute, 1983. Publications: The Ink Truck, 1969; Legs, 1975; Billy Phelan's Greatest Game, 1978; O Albany!, 1983; Ironweed, 1983; The Cotton Club (with Francis Ford Coppola), film script, 1984; Charlie Malarkey and the Belly Button Machine (with Brenden Christopher Kennedy), 1986; Quinn's Book, 1988; Very Old Bones, 1992; Riding the Yellow Trolley Car, 1993; Charlie Malarkey and the Singing Moose (with Brenden Christopher Kennedy), 1994; The Flaming Corsage, 1996. Contributions to: Numerous periodicals. Honours: National Endowment for the Arts Fellowship, 1981; MacArthur Foundation Fellowship, 1983; Pulitzer Prize in Fiction, 1984; National Book Critics Circle Award in Fiction, 1984; Creative Arts Award, Brandeis University, 1986; Commander of the Order of Arts and Letters, France, 1993. Memberships: American Academy of Arts and Letters; PEN Club; Writers Guild of America. Address: New York State Writers Institute, 1400 Washington Avenue, Albany, NY 12222, USA.

KENNEDY William S, b. 23 Jan 1926, South Norfolk, Virginia, USA. Journal Editor and Publisher; Short Fiction Genre Founder and Promoter. Career: Founder, Editor, Publisher, Reflect literary journal; Founder, The Spiral Mode (spiral fiction), 1982. Publications: Johnny Mowbrough, spiral novel, published as serial in Puck and Pluck, 1994-; Manuals: Paranormal Writing; Music Writing. Contributions to: Spiral fiction to Reflect and other literary journals. Honours: Reflect included in Top 60 Poetry Magazines in USA and Canada, Writer's Digest, June 1993. Memberships: Norfolk Musicians Union; American Federation of Musicians. Address: 3306 Argonne Avenue, Norfolk, VA 23509, USA.

KENNEDY X J. See: **KENNEDY Joseph Charles**.

KENNELLY Brendan, b. 17 Apr 1936, Ballylongfoed, County Kerry, Ireland. Professor of Modern Literature. Education: BA (1st Class Honours, English and French), 1961, MA 1963, PhD (Trinity College and Leeds University, Yorkshire England), 1966, Trinity College, Dublin. Appointment: Professor of Modern Literature, Trinity College, Dublin. Publications: Poetry: Good Souls to Survive, 1967; Dream of a Black Fox, 1968; Selected Poems, 1969, enlarged edition, 1971; A Drinking Cup: Poems from the Irish, 1970; Bread, 1971; Love Cry, 1972; Salvation, the Stranger, 1972; The Voices, 1973; Shelley in Dublin, 1974, 2nd edition, 1982; A Kind of Trust, 1975; New and Selected Poems, 1976; Islandman, 1977; The Visitor, 1978; A Small

Light, 1979; The Boats Are Home, 1980; The House That Jack Didn't Build, 1982; Cromwell, 1983, reprinted 1984, 1986; Moloney Up and At It, 1984, reprinted 1987; Selected Poems, 1985; Mary, 1987; Love of Ireland, 1989. Novels: The Crooked Cross, 1963; The Florentines, 1967. Editor: The Penguin Book of Irish Verse, 1970, enlarged edition, 1988. Contributions to: International magazines. Honours: AE Memorial Prize for Poetry, 1967; Fellow, Trinity College, 1967; Critics' Special Harveys Award, 1988. Address: Department of English, Arts Building, Trinity College, Dublin 2, Ireland.

KENNER (William) Hugh, b. 7 Jan 1923, Peterborough, Ontario, Canada. Professor of English; Writer. m. (1) Mary J Waite, 30 Aug 1947, dec 1964, 2 sons, 3 daughters, (2) Mary A Bittner, 13 Aug 1965, 1 son, 1 daughter. Education: Peterborough Collegiate Institute, 1936-41; BA, 1945, MA, 1946, University of Toronto; PhD, Yale University, 1950. Appointments: Instructor, 1950-51, Assistant Professor, 1951-56, Associate Professor, 1956-58, Chairman, Department of English, 1956-63, Professor of English, 1958-73, University of California, Santa Barbara; Professor of English, 1973-75, Andrew W Mellon Professor of the Humanities, 1975-91, Chairman, Department of English, 1980-83, Johns Hopkins University; Franklin and Callaway Professor of English, University of Georgia, 1992-; Several visiting appointments. Publications: Seventeenth Century Poetry: The Schools of Donne and Jonson (editor), 1965; Samuel Beckett: A Critical Study, 1961; The Stoic Comedians, 1963; The Counterfeiters, 1968; The Pound Era, 1971; Bucky: A Guided Tour of Buckminster Fuller, 1973; A Reader's Guide to Samuel Beckett, 1973; A Homemade World: The American Modernist Writers, 1975; Geodesic Math and How to Use It, 1976; Joyce's Voices, 1978; Ulysses, 1982; A Colder Eye: The Modern Irish Writers, 1983; The Mechanic Muse, 1987; A Sinking Island: The Modern Irish Writers, 1988; Mazes (essays), 1989; Historical Fictions (essays), 1990; Chuck Jones: A Flurry of Drawings, 1994. Contributions to: About 600 articles and reviews in many periodicals. Honours: American Council of Learned Societies Fellow, 1956; Guggenheim Fellowships, 1956, 1964; Royal Society of Literature Fellow, 1957; National Institute of Arts and Letters Award, 1969; Christian Gauss Prize, 1972; A D Emmart Award, 1977; Several honorary doctorates. Address: 203 Plum Nelly Road, Athens, GA 30606, USA.

KENNET Wayland Hilton Young, (2nd Baron, created 1935), (Wayland Young), b. 2 Aug 1923. Author; Politician. m. Elizabeth Ann, 1948, 1 son, 5 daughters. Education: Stowe, Trinity College, Cambridge. Publications: As Wayland Young: The Italian Left, 1949; The Deadweight, 1952; Now or Never, 1953; Old London Churches (with Elizabeth Young), 1956; The Montesi Scandal, 1957; Still Alive Tomorrow, 1958; Strategy for Survival, 1959; The Profumo Affair, 1963; Eros Denied, 1965; Thirty Four Articles, 1965; Existing Mechanisms of Arms Control, 1965.; As Wayland Kennet: Preservation, 1972; The Futures of Europe, 1976. Editor, The Rebirth of Britain, 1982; London's Churches (with Elizabeth Young), 1986; Northern Lazio, 1990; Fabian and Social Democratic Party pamphlets on defence, disarmament, environment, multinational companies, etc. Address: House of Lords, London SW1A 0PW, England.

KENNEY Catherine, b. 3 Oct 1948, Memphis, Tennessee, USA. Writer; Professor. m. John Patrick Kenney, 1 June 1968, 1 son. Education: BA, English, Siena College, 1968; MA, English, 1970, PhD, English, 1974, Loyola University, Chicago. Publications: Thurber's Anatomy of Confusion, 1984; The Remarkable Case of Dorothy L Sayers, 1990; Dorothy L (play), 1993. Contributions to: Dorothy L Sayers: A Centenary Celebration; Old Maids to Radical Women; 100 Great Detectives; Scholarly journals; Chicago Tribune; Christian Century; Chicago Sun Times; Arkansas Times. Address: 228 Stanley Avenue, Park Ridge, IL 60068, USA.

KENNEY Susan McIlvaine, b. Summit, New Jersey, USA. Novelist; Professor of English and Creative Writing. Education: BA with distinction, honours in English, Northwestern University, 1963; MA, 1965, PhD, English and American Literature, 1968, Cornell University. Appointment: Dana Professor of Creative Writing, Colby College, Waterville, Maine, 1992-. Publications: Garden of Malice, 1983; In Another Country, 1984; Graves in Academe, 1985; Sailing, 1988; One Fell Step, 1990. Honours: Phi Beta Kappa, 1962; O Henry Prize Stories, 1982; QPB New Voices Award, 1985. Memberships: Authors Guild. Address: Department of English, Colby College, Waterville, ME 04901, USA.

KENNY Adele, b. 28 Nov 1948, Perth Amboy, New Jersey, USA. Poet; Writer; Editor; Consultant. Education: BA in English, Newark State College, 1970; MS in Education, College of New Rochelle, 1982. Appointments: Artist-in-Residence, Middlesex County Arts Council, 1979-80; Poetry Editor, New Jersey Art Forum, 1981-83; Associate Editor, Muse-Pie Press, 1988-. Publications: An Archaeology of Ruins, 1982; Illegal Entries, 1984; The Roses Open, 1984; Between Hail Marys, 1986; Migrating Geese, 1987; The Crystal Keepers Handbook, 1988; Counseling Gifted, Creative and Talented Youth Through the Arts, 1989; Castles and Dragons, 1990; Questi Momenti, 1990; Starship Earth, 1990. Contributions to: Periodicals. Honours: Writer's Digest Award, 1981; New Jersey State Council on the Arts Fellowships, 1982, 1987; Merit Book Awards, 1983, 1987; Roselip Award, 1988; Haiku Quarterly Award, 1989. Memberships: Haiku Society of America, president, 1987-88, 1990; Poetry Society of America. Address: 207 Coriell Avenue, Fanwood, NJ 07023, USA.

KENRICK Tony, b. 23 Aug 1935, Sydney, New South Wales, Australia, Author. Appointments: Advertising Copywriter, Sydney, Toronto, San Francisco, New York, London, 1953-72. Publications: The Only Good Body's a Dead One, 1970; A Tough One to Lose, 1972; Two for the Price of One, 1974; Stealing Lillian, 1975; The Seven Day Soldiers, 1976; The Chicago Girl, 1976; Two Lucky People, 1978; The Nighttime Guy, 1979; The 81st Site, 1980; Blast, 1983; Faraday's Flowers, 1985; China White, 1986; Neon Tough, 1988; Glitterbug, 1991; Round Trip, 1996. Address: c/o 216 East 75th Street, New York, NY 10021, USA.

KENT Alexander. See: **REEMAN Douglas Edward.**

KENT Arthur (William Charles), (James Bradwell, M DuBois, Paul Granados, Alexander Karol, Alex Stamper, Brett Vane), b. 31 Jan 1925, London, England. Author. Education: City Literary Institute, London. Appointments: Journalist: News Chronicle, London, 1943-46, Australian Daily Mirror, 1947-53, Beaverbook Newspapers, UK, 1957-69, BBC, London, 1970-71. Publications: Sunny (as Bret Vane), 1953; Gardenia (as Bret Vane), 1953; Broadway Contraband (as Paul Granados), 1954; El Tafile (as M DuBois), 1954; Legion Etrangere (as M DuBois), 1954; March and Die (as M DuBois), 1954; Revolt at Zaluig (as Alex Stamper), 1954; Inclining to Crime, 1957; Special Edition Murder, 1957; Kansas Fast Gun, 1958; Stairway to Murder, 1958; Wake Up Screaming, 1958; The Camp on Blood Island (with G Thomas), 1958; Last Action, 1959; Broken Doll, 1961; Action of the Tiger, 1961; The Weak and the Strong, 1962; The Counterfeiters, 1962; Long Horn, Long Grass, 1964; Black Sunday, 1965; Plant Poppies on My Grave, 1966; Red Red Red, 1966; Fall of Singapore (with I Simon), 1970; The Mean City (as James Bradwell), 1971; A Life in the Wind (with Z de Tyras), 1971; Sword of Vengeance (as Alexander Karol), 1973; Dark Lady (as Alexander Karol), 1974; The King's Witchfinder (as Alexander Karol), 1975; Maverick Squadron, 1975; The Nowhere War, 1975. Address: 26 Verulam Avenue, London E17, England.

KENT Helen. See: **POLLEY Judith Anne.**

KENT Philip. See: **BULMER Henry Kenneth.**

KENYON Bruce (Guy), b. 16 Aug 1929, Cadillac, Michigan, USA. Writer. m. Marian Long, 1950, div 1954. Publications: Rose White, Rose Red, 1983; The Forrester Inheritance, 1985; Fair Game, 1986; A Marriage of Inconvenience, 1986; Wild Rose, 1986; The Counterfeit Lady, 1987; An Elegant Education, 1987; A Lady of Qualities, 1987; Return to Cheyne Spa, 1988; A Certain Reputation, 1990. Contributions to: Periodicals. Memberships: Authors Guild; Authors League. Address: c/o Kearns and Orr, 686 Lexington Avenue, New York, NY 10022, USA.

KENYON Kate. See: **ADORJAN Carol.**

KENYON Michael, b. 26 June 1931, Huddersfield, Yorkshire, England. Author. 3 daughters. Education: Wadham College, Oxford, 1951-54; MA (Oxon), History. Publications: May You Die in Ireland, 1965; The 100,000 Welcomes, 1970; Mr Big, 1973; The Rapist, 1976; A Healthy Way to Die, 1986; Peckover Holds the Baby, 1988; Kill the Butler!, 1991; Peckover Joins the Choir, 1992; A French Affair, 1992; Peckover and the Bog Man, 1994. Contributions to: 35 articles to Gourmet Magazine. Membership: Detection Club. Address: 164 Halsey Street, Southampton, NY 11968, USA.

KEOGH Dermot Francis, b. 12 May 1945, Dublin, Ireland. Academic. m. Ann, 22 Aug 1973, 2 sons, 2 daughters. Education: BA, 1970, MA, 1974, University College, Dublin; PhD, 1980, European University Institute, Florence. Appointments: Lecturer, Department of Modern History, 1970-90, Jean Monnet Professor of Modern Integration, 1990-, University College, Cork. Publications: The Vatican, the Bishops and Irish Politics 1919-1939, 1985; The Rise of the Irish Working Class 1890-1914, 1983; Ireland and Europe 1919-1989, 1989; Church and Politics in Latin America, 1990; Ireland, 1922-1993, 1993. Contributions to: Academic journals and national press. Honour: Fellow, Woodrow Wilson Centre for Scholars, Washington DC, 1988. Address: Department of Modern History, University College, Cork, Ireland.

KERMODE Sir (John) Frank, b. 29 Nov 1919, Douglas, Isle of Man. Literary Critic. Education: BA 1940, MA 1947, Liverpool University; MA, Cambridge, 1974. Publications: Romantic Image, 1957; The Sense of an Ending, 1967; The Classic, 1975; The Genesis of Secrecy, 1979; History and Value, 1988; An Appetite for Poetry, 1989; The Uses of Error, 1991; Not Entitled, 1996. Contributions to: Guardian; New York Times; London Review of Books; New York Review of Books; New Republic. Honours: Honorary Doctorates, University of Chicago, 1975, Liverpool University, 1981, Amsterdam University, 1987, Newcastle University, 1993; Knighted, 1991. Memberships: Royal Society of Literature, fellow; British Academy, fellow; American Academy of Arts and Sciences. Address: 9 The Oast House, Grange Road, Cambridge, CB3 9AP, England.

KERN E R. See: **KERNER Fred.**

KERN Gregory. See: **TUBB E(dwin) C(harles).**

KERNAGHAN Eileen (Shirley), b. 6 Jan 1939, Enderby, British Columbia, Canada. Writer. m. Patrick Walter Kernaghan, 22 Aug 1959, 2 sons, 1 daughter. Education: Elementary Teaching Certificate, University of British Columbia. Publications: The Upper Left-Hand Corner: A Writer's Guide for the Northwest (co-author), 1975, revised edition, 1986; Journey to Aprilioth, 1980; Songs for the Drowned Lands, 1983; Sarsen Witch, 1988; Walking After Midnight, 1991. Contributions to: Journals and periodicals. Honours: Silver Porgy Award, West Coast Review of Books, 1981; Canadian Science Fiction and Fantasy Award, 1985. Memberships: Burnaby Writers Society; Federation of British Columbian Writers; Writers Union of Canada. Address: 5512 Neville Street, Burnaby, British Columbia V5J 2H7, Canada.

KERNER Fred, (E R Kern, Frederick Kerr, M N Thaler), b. 15 Feb 1921, Montreal, Quebec, Canada. Publisher. m. Sally Dee Stouten, 18 May 1959, 2 sons, 1 daughter. Education: BA, Sir George Williams University (Concordia University), Montreal, 1942. Publications: Eat, Think and Be Slender (with L Kotkin), 1954; The Magic Power of Your Mind (with W Germain), 1956; Ten Days to a Successful Memory (with J Brothers), 1957; Love is a Man's Affair, 1958; Stress and Your Heart, 1961; Watch Your Weight Go Down (as Frederick Kerr), 1962; A Treasury of Lincoln Quotations, 1965; Secrets of Your Supraconscious, 1965; What's Best For Your Child... and You (with D Goodman), 1966; Buy Higher, Sell Higher (with J Reid), 1966; It's Fun to Fondue (as M N Thaler), 1968; Nadia (with I Grumeza), 1977; Mad About Fondue, 1986; Folles, folles les fondues, 1987; Prospering Through the Coming Depression (with Andrew Willman), 1988; Home Emergency Handbook, 1990; Lifetime: A Treasury of Uncommon Wisdoms, 1992; Ideas and Tendencies, 1993; The Writer's Essential Desk Reference, 1991, 1996. Contributions to: Numerous magazines and journals. Honours: American Heritage Foundation Award, 1952; Queen's Silver Jubilee Medal, 1977; Allen Sangster Award, 1982; Canadian Book Publishers Council Award, 1984; Air Canada Award, 1984; International Mercury Award, 1990. Memberships: President, Canadian Authors Association; Chairman, Academy of Canadian Writers. Address: 1405-1555 Finch Avenue East, Willowdale, Ontario M2J 4X9, Canada.

KERR Carole. See: **CARR Margaret.**

KERR Frederick. See: **KERNER Fred.**

KERR (Anne) Judith, b. 14 June 1923, Berlin, Germany. Children's Fiction Writer. Appointments: Secretary, Red Cross, London, England, 1941-45; Teacher and Textile Designer, 1948-53; Script Editor, Script Writer, BBC-TV, London, 1953-58. Publications:

The Tiger Who Came to Tea, 1968; Mog the Forgetful Cat, 1970; When Hitler Stole Pink Rabbit, 1971; When Willy Went to the Wedding, 1972; The Other Way Round, 1975; Mog's Christmas, 1976; A Small Person Far Away, 1978; Mog and the Baby, 1980; Mog in the Dark, 1983; Mog and Me, 1984; Mog's Family of Cats, 1985; Mog's Amazing Birthday Caper, 1986; Mog and Bunny, 1988; Mog and Barnaby, 1990; How Mrs Monkey Missed the Ark, 1992; The Adventures of Mog, 1993; Mog on Fox Night, 1993; Mog in the Garden, 1994; Mog's Kittens, 1994. Address: c/o Harper Collins Publishers, 77-85 Fulham Palace Road, London W6 8JB, England.

KERSHAW Peter. See: **LUCIE-SMITH John Edward McKenzie.**

KESSLER Jascha (Frederick), b. 27 Nov 1929, New York, USA. Professor; Poet; Writer; Dramatist. m. 17 July 1950,2 sons, 1 daughter. Education: BA, University of Heights College of NTU, 1950; MA, 1951, PhD, 1955, University of Michigan. Appointments: Faculty, University of Michigan, 1951-54, New York University, 1954-55, Hunter College, 1955-56, Hamilton College, 1957-61; Professor, University of California at Los Angeles, 1961-. Publications: Poetry: Whatever Love Declares, 1969; After the Armies Have Passed, 1970; In Memory of the Future, 1976. Fiction: An Egyptian Bondage, 1967; Death Comes for the Behaviorist, 1983; Classical Illusions: 28 stories, 1985; Transmigrations: 18 Mythologies, 1985; Siren Songs and Classical Illusions (50 stories), 1992. Other: Plays: The Cave (opera libretto); Translations. Honours: National Endowment for the Arts Fellowship, 1974; Rockefeller Foundation Fellowship, 1979; Hungarian PEN Club Memorial Medal. 1979. Memberships: American Literary Translators Association; American Society of Composers, Authors, and Publishers; Poetry Society of America. Address: c/o Department of English, University of California at Los Angeles, Los Angeles, CA 90095, USA.

KESSLER Lauren Jeanne, b. 4 Apr 1951, New York, New York, USA. Author; Professor. m. Thomas Hager, 7 July 1984, 2 sons, 1 daughter. Education: BS, Northwestern University, 1971; MS, University of Oregon, 1975; PhD, University of Washington, 1980. Appointment: Faculty, School of Communications, University of Oregon. Publications: The Dissident Press: Alternative Journalism in American History, 1984; When Worlds Collide, 1984, 4th edition, 1996; Aging Well, 1987; Mastering the Message, 1989; After All These Years: Sixties Ideals in a Different World, 1990; The Search, 1991; The Stubborn Twig: A Japanese Family in America, 1993; Full Court Press, 1997. Contributions to: Scholarly journals. Honours: Excellence in Periodical Writing Award, Council for the Advancement of Secondary Education, 1987; Excellence in Journalism Award, Sigma Delta Chi, 1987; Frances Fuller Victor Award for literary non-fiction, 1994. Memberships: American Journalism Historians Association; Association for Education in Journalism and Mass Communications; Union for Democratic Communication. Address: c/o School of Communications, Allen Hall, University of Oregon, Eugene, OR 97405, USA.

KEYES Daniel, b. 9 Aug 1927, New York, New York, USA. Author. m. Aurea Georgina Vazquez, 14 Oct 1952, 2 daughters. Education: BA, 1950; MA, 1962. Appointments: Lecturer, Wayne State University, 1962-66; Professor, English, Ohio University, 1966-. Publications: Flowers for Algernon, 1966, filmed as Charly; The Touch, 1968; The Fifth Sally, 1980; The Minds of Billy Milligan (non-fiction), 1986; Daniel Keyes Short Stories, 1993; Daniel Keyes Reader, 1994; The Milligan Wars, 1995. Address: c/o William Morris Agency, 1350 Avenue of the Americas, New York, NY 10019, USA.

KHALVATI Mimi, b. 28 Apr 1944, Tehran, Iran. Poet. 1 son, 1 daughter. Education: Drama Centre, London, England. Appointment: Lecturer, Goldsmith's College, University of London, England, 1995. Publications: Persian Miniatures, 1990; In White Ink, 1991; Mirrorwork, 1995; Selections in: New Women Poets, 1990; 60 Women Poets, Forward Book of Poetry, 1996. Contributions to: Poetry Review; PN Review; The Independent; Bete Noire; Critical Quarterly; Pivot, USA. Honour: Arts Council of England Writers Award, 1994. Membership: Poetry Society. Address: 130c Evering Road, London N16 7BD, England.

KHAN Ismith, b. 16 Mar 1925, Trinidad, West Indies. Writer; University Lecturer. m. M Ghose, 14 Feb 1949, 1 son, 1 daughter. Education: BA, New School for Social Research, New York City, 1960; MA, Johns Hopkins University, Baltimore, Maryland, 1970.

Appointments: Freelance Manuscript Consultant; Senior Lecturer, California State University, Long Beach, 1978-83; Adjunct Professor, Humanities Division, Medgar Evers College, Brooklyn, New York, 1986-. Publications: Novels: The Jumbie Bird, UK edition, 1961, American edition, 1962, 2nd UK edition, 1985; The Obeah Man, 1964, radio adaptation, BBC London, 1970; The Crucifixion, 1987; A Day in the Country (collection of short stories), 1994. Contributions to: Journals and magazines. Honour: National Endowment for the Humanities Fellowship, 1972. Membership: PEN.

KHATCHADOURIAN Haig, b. 22 July 1925, Old City, Jerusalem, Palestine. Professor of Philosophy. m. Arpine Yaghlian, 10 Sept 1950, 2 sons, 1 daughter. Education: BA, MA, American University of Beirut, Lebanon; PhD, Duke University, USA. Appointments: American University of Beirut, Lebanon, 1948-49, 1951-67; Professor of Philosophy, University of Southern California, USA, 1968-69; Professor of Philosophy, University of Wisconsin-Milwaukee, 1969-. Publications: The Coherence Theory of Truth: A Critical Evaluation, 1961; Traffic with Time (co-author), poetry, 1963; A Critical Study in Method, 1967; The Concept of Art, 1971; Shadows of Time, poetry, 1983; Music, Film and Art, 1985; Philosophy of Language and Logical Theory: Collected Papers, 1996. Contributions to: Numerous professional and literary journals. Address: Department of Philosophy, University of Wisconsin, Milwaukee, WI 53201, USA.

KHAYAM Massoud, b. 5 May 1947, Tehran, Iran. Consultant Engineer. 2 sons, 1 daughter. Education: BSc, Engineering, 1971; MSc, Engineering, 1975. Appointment: Lecturer, Tehran University of Science, 1990. Publications: Black Hole, 1982; Universal Construction of Knowledge, 1984; Earthly, 1988; The Chess Cage (novel), 1991; Future Line, the Future of Full Automatic Persian Writing, 1993; Omar Khayam and His Songs, 1996; Cry Over the Green, in press; On War, short stories; The Truth and It's Measurement; Mana and Nima; Narrow Stream; 5 other books. Contributions to: Most private journals in Iran. Honour: Best Lecturer Award. Address: PO Box 15875, Tehran 3168, Iran.

KHEIRABADI Masoud, b. 28 Feb 1951, Sabzevar, Iran. Lecturer; Researcher. Education: BS, Geography, University of Tehran, 1973; MS, Agricultural Mechanization, Texas A & M University, 1978; MA, 1983, PhD, Geography, 1987, University of Oregon. Appointments: Lecturer, University of Oregon, 1987-89, Lewis and Clark College, 1989-, Portland State University, 1989-, Clackamas Community College, 1990-. Publication: Iranian Cities: Formation and Development, 1991, 2nd edition, 1993. Contributions to: Books, scholarly journals, newspapers, and magazines. Memberships: Association of American Geographers; Middle East Association of North America; National Geographic Society. Address: 67 South West Oswego Summit, Lake Oswego, OR 97035, USA.

KHERDIAN David, b. 17 Dec 1931, Racine, Wisconsin, USA. Author; Poet. m. (1) Kato Rozeboom, 1968, 1970, (2) Nonny Hogrogian, 17 Mar 1971. Education: BS, University of Wisconsin, 1965. Appointments: Literary Consultant, Northwestern University, 1965; Founder-Editor, Giligia Press, 1966-72; Rare Book Consultant, 1968-69, Lecturer, 1969-70, Fresno State College; Poet-in-the-Schools, State of New Hampshire, 1971; Editor, Ararat magazine, 1971-72; Director, Two Rivers Press, 1978-86; Founder-Editor, The Press at Butternut Creek, 1987-88; Founder, Editor, Fork-Roads: Journal of Ethnic American Literature, 1995-96. Publications: On the Death of My Father and Other Poems, 1970; Homage to Adana, 1970; Looking Over Hills, 1972; The Nonny Poems, 1974; Any Day of Your Life, 1975; Country Cat, City Cat, 1978; I Remember Root River, 1978; The Road from Home: The Story of an Armenian Girl, 1979; The Farm, 1979; It Started With Old Man Bean, 1980; Finding Home, 1981; Taking the Soundings on Third Avenue, 1981; The Farm Book Two, 1981; Beyond Two Rivers, 1981; The Song of the Walnut Grove, 1982; Place of Birth, 1983; Right Now, 1983; The Mystery of the Diamond in the Wood, 1983; Root River Run, 1984; The Animal, 1984; Threads of Light: The Farm Poems Books III and IV, 1985; Bridger: The Story of a Mountain Man, 1987; Poems to an Essence Friend, 1987; A Song for Uncle Harry, 1989; The Cat's Midsummer Jamboree, 1990; The Dividing River/The Meeting Shore, 1990; On a Spaceship with Beelzebub: By a Grandson of Gurdjieff, 1990; The Great Fishing Contest, 1991; Junas's Journey, 1993; Asking the River, 1993; By Myself, 1993; Friends: A Memoir, 1993; My Racine, 1994; Lullaby for Emily, 1995. Editor: Visions of America by the Poets of Our Time, 1973; Settling America: The Ethnic Expression of 14 Contemporary Poets, 1974; Poems Here and Now, 1976;

Traveling America with Today's Poets, 1976; The Dog Writes on the Window with His Nose and Other Poems, 1977; If Dragon Flies Made Honey, 1977; I Sing the Song of Myself, 1978; Beat Voices: An Anthology of Beat Poetry, 1995. Co-Editor: Down at the Santa Fe Depot: 20 Fresno Poets, 1970. Other: Various translations. Honours: Jane Addams Peace Award, 1980; Banta Award, 1980; Boston Globe/Horn Book Award, 1980; Lewis Carroll Shelf Award, 1980; Newbery Honor Book Award, 1980; Friends of American Writers Award, 1982. Membership: PEN. Address: Box 150, Spencertown, NY 12165, USA.

KHOSLA Gurdial Singh, b. 15 Jan 1912, Lahore, India. Writer; Dramatist. m. Manorama Khosla, 16 Oct 1941, 1 son, 1 daughter. Education: BA, Honours, 1931, MA, 1933, in English, Punjab University, Lahore. Appointments: Lecturer in English, Khalsa College, Amritsar, 1934-35; General Manager, Western Railway, 1967-70; Adviser and Head, Department of Dramatic Arts, Punjab University, 1970-72. Publications: The Auction of a City: Literary and Other Essays, 1951; Railway Management in India, 1972; A History of Indian Railways, 1988; Road to Nowhere (novel), 1993. Contributions to: Newspapers and journals. Honours: Eminent Theatreman Citation, Delhi Natya Sangh, 1980, and World Punjabi Conference, 1983; Drama Award, Punjabi Academy, Delhi, 1988, and Sahitya Academy, Punjab, 1989. Memberships: Authors Guild of India; President, Conservation Society, Delhi, 1983-86; Honorary President, General Indian Heritage Society, 1987-93; PEN International. Address: D103 Defence Colony, New Delhi 110-024, India.

KHRAPLIVY Anatoly Petrovich, b. 20 Oct 1939, Ukraine. Engineer; Electromechanic. m. Tchyrsina Ludmila Andreevna, 6 July 1968, 2 daughters. Education: Odessa Technological Institute, 1966; Candidate Degree, 1974; Associate Professor, 1976; Doctor's Degree, 1991; Professor, 1991. Publications: The Use of Circular Scanning for Defect Detection in the Moving Fabric, 1979; Defect Detection of the Moving Fabric in Using Circular Scanning, 1980; Television Transducer for the Control of Fabric Quality, 1983; Mathematical Description of Fabric Scanning in Optical Range, 1985; The Device for Automatic Sorting of Fabric, 1992; Control of Fabric Quality, 1993; The Device for Defect Detection of the Moving Fabric with Printing Pattern, 1993. Address: Zala Egersegf Street 5, Floor 29, Kherson 325005, Ukraine.

KHRUSHCHEV Sergei Nikitich, b. 2 July 1935, Moscow, Russia. Control Systems Engineer. m. Valentina N Golenko, 3 Aug 1985, 3 sons. Education: Moscow Electrical Power Institute, 1952-68; PhD, Engineering, 1967, Assistant Professor, 1968, Moscow Technical University; Doctorate, Ukrainian Academy of Sciences, 1988. Appointments: Professor, Control Computer Institute, 1989; Senior Fellow, Thomas J Watson Jr Institute for International Studies, Brown University, Providence, Rhode Island, 1991; Columnist, Asia Times, 1995-; Columnist, Asia Inc, business magazine for Pacific region, 1992-97. Publications: Khrushchev on Khrushchev, 1990; Pensioner Sousnogo Znachenia, 1991; Nikita Khrushchev: Crises and Missiles, 1994. Contributions to: Publications worldwide. Honours: Lenin Prize for Engineering, 1959; Hero of Soviet Labour, 1963; Council of Ministers Prize, USSR, 1985. Memberships: International Informatization Academy; Russian Computer Society. Address: 3 Laurelhurst Road, Cranston, RI 02920, USA.

KHUE Danh. See: LUU Van Lang.

KHUSRO. See: SHAHRYAR Faridoon.

KIDDER Tracy, b. 12 Nov 1945, New York, New York, USA. Writer. m. Frances T Toland, 2 Jan 1971. Education: AB, Harvard University; MFA, University of Iowa. Publications: The Road to Yuba City: A Journey into the Juan Corona Murders, 1974; The Soul of a New Medicine, 1981; Old Friends, 1994. Contributions: Atlantic Monthly; Science 1983; Country Journal. Honours: Pulitzer Prize, 1982; Altantic First Award (short story); Sidney Hillerman Foundation Prize; American Book Award, 1982. Address: c/o George Borchardt Inc, 136 East 47th Street, New York, NY 10019, USA.

KIDMAN Fiona Judith, b. 26 Mar 1940, Hawera, New Zealand. Writer. m. Ian R Kidman, 20 Aug 1960, 1 son, 1 daughter. Publications: A Breed of Women, 1979; Mandarin Summer, 1981; Mrs Dixon and Friends, 1982; Paddy's Puzzle, 1983; Going to the Chathams, 1985; The Book of Secrets, 1987; Unsuitable Friends, 1988; True Stars, 1990; Wakeful Nights (poems), 1991; The Foreign Woman (short

stories), 1993; Palm Prints (autobiographical essays), 1994; Ricochet Baby, 1996. Contributions to: Numerous. Honours: Scholarship in Letters, 1981, 1985, 1991, 1995; Queen Elizabeth II Arts Council Award for Achievement, 1988; Officer of the Order of the British Empire, 1988; New Zealand Book Award for Fiction, 1988. Memberships: New Zealand Book Council, secretary-organiser, 1972-75, president, 1992-; PEN International New Zealand Centre, president, 1980-82. Address: 28 Rakau Road, Hataitai, Wellington 3, New Zealand.

KIELY Benedict, b. 15 Aug 1919, Dromore, County Tyrone, Ireland. Journalist; Writer. Education: National University of Ireland. Appointments: Journalist, Dublin, 1940-65; Visiting Professor and Writer-in-Residence, several US universities. Publications: Land Without Stars, 1946; In a Harbour Green, 1949; Call for a Miracle, 1950; Honey Seems Bitter, 1952; The Cards of the Gambler: A Folktale, 1953; There Was an Ancient House, 1955; The Captain With the Whiskers, 1960; Dogs Enjoy the Morning, 1968; Proxopera: A Novella, 1977; Nothing Happens in Carmincross, 1985; Drink to the Bird (memoir), 1991; Selected Stories, 1993; As I Rode By Granard Moat: A Personal Anthology, 1997. Honours: American Irish Foundation Award, 1980; Irish Academy of Letters Award, 1980; Irish Independent Literary Award, 1985; Honorary DLitt, National University of Ireland and Queen's University, Belfast. Address: 119 Morehampton Road, Donnybrook, Dublin 4, Ireland.

KIENZLE William X(avier), b. 11 Sept 1928, Detroit, Michigan, USA. Author. m. Javan Herman Andrews, Nov 1974. Education: BA, Sacred Heart Seminary College, 1950; St John's Seminary, 1950-54. Appointments: Editor, The Michigan Catholic, 1962-74, MPLS Magazine, 1974-76. Publications: The Rosary Murders, 1979; Death Wears a Red Hat, 1980; Mind Over Murder, 1981; Assault with Intent, 1982; Shadow of Death, 1983; Kill and Tell, 1984; Sudden Death, 1985; Deathbed, 1986; Deadline for a Critic, 1987; Marked for Murder, 1988; Eminence, 1989; Masquerade, 1990; Chameleon, 1991; Body Count, 1992; Dead Wrong, 1993; Bishop as Pawn, 1994; Call No Man Father, 1995; Requiem for Moses, 1996; The Man Who Loved God, 1997. Honours: Journalism Award for General Excellence, Michigan Knights of Columbus, 1963; Honourable Mention for Editorial Writing, Catholic Press Association, 1974. Membership: Authors Guild. Address: PO Box 645, Keego Harbor, MI 48320, USA.

KIHLMAN Christer Alfred, b. 14 June 1930, Helsingfors. Writer. m. Selinda Enckell, 7 Jan 1956, 1 son, 1 daughter. Education: Studies, University of Helsingfors, 1948-53. Appointment: Artist Professor, 1975. Publications: Sweet Prince, 1983; All My Sons, 1984; The Downfall of Gerdt Bladh, 1989; The Blue Mother, 1990; Several plays for several theaters in Finland, Sweden and Denmark. Contributions to: Columnist at several newspapers in Finland and Sweden. Address: Diktarhemmet, Borga, Finland.

KILBRACKEN John (Raymond Godley), Lord, b. 17 Oct 1920, London, England. Writer; Journalist; Labour Back-Bencher, House of Lords. m. (1) Penelope Reyne, 22 May 1943, div, 2 sons, (2) Susan Heazlewood, 15 May 1981, div, 1 son. Education: Eton; BA, MA, 1948, Balliol College, Oxford. Appointments: Reporter, Daily Mirror, 1947-49, Sunday Express, 1949-51; Foreign Correspondent, Evening Standard, 1960-65; Editorial Director, Worldwatch, 1984-85. Publications: Even For an Hour (poems), 1940; Tell Me the Next One, 1951; Letters from Early New Zealand (editor), 1951; Living Like a Lord, 1955; A Peer Behind the Curtain, 1959; Shamrocks and Unicorns, 1962; Van Meegeren, 1967; Bring Back My Stringbag, 1979; The Easy Way to Bird Recognition, 1982; The Easy Way to Tree Recognition, 1983; The Easy Way to Wild Flower Recognition, 1984. Contributions to: Newspapers and magazines. Honours: Distinguished Service Cross, Royal Navy, 1945; Times Educational Supplement Senior Information Book Award, 1982. Address: Killegar, County Leitrim, Ireland.

KILJUNEN Kimmo Roobert, b. 13 June 1951, Rauha, Finland. Member of Parliament; Development Researcher and Director. m. Marja Liisa Kiljunen, 17 Jan 1972, 2 sons, 2 daughters. Education: MA, Helsinki University, 1973; MPhil, 1977, DPhil, 1985, Sussex University, England. Appointment: Member of Parliament, Finland. Publications: Nambia, The Last Colony (editor), 1981; Kampuchea: Decade of the Genocide, 1984; Region to Region Cooperation Between Developed and Developing Countries, 1990; Finland and the New International Division of Labour, 1992; Finns in the United Nations, 1996; Other: 7 Books in Finnish, 1976-95. Honour: President, Urho Kekkonen Foundation Literary Award, 1992. Membership: Executive Committee,

European Association of Development Research and Training Institutes, 1987-95. Address: Linnoittajanpolku 3 g 15, 01280 Vantaa, Finland.

KILLANIN Michael Morris, Lord, b. 30 July 1914, London, England. Writer; Film Producer; Company Director. m. Mary Sheila Dunlop, 17 Dec 1945, 3 sons, 1 daughter. Education: Eton, 1928-31; Sorbonne, University of Paris, 1931-32; BA, 1935, MA, 1939, Magdalene College, Cambridge. Publications: Four Days, 1938; Sir Godfrey Kneller, 1947; Shell Guide to Ireland (with M V Duigan), 1956; The Olympic Games (with John Rodda), 1976, 3rd edition, 1984; My Ireland: A Personal Impression, 1987. Honours: Various UK and foreign honours. Memberships: French Academy of Sports; President, International Olympic Committee, 1972-80; President, 1950-73, Honorary Life President, 1981-, Olympic Council of Ireland; Fellow, Royal Society of Antiquaries of Ireland; Fellow, Royal Society of Arts; President, National Heritage Council, 1988-. Address: 9 Lower Mount Pleasant Avenue, Dublin 6, Ireland.

KILLDEER John. See: **MAYHAR Ardath.**

KILLOUGH (Karen) Lee, b. 5 May 1942, Syracuse, Kansas, USA. Science Fiction Writer; Radiological Technologist. Publications: A Voice Out of Ramah, 1979; The Doppelganger Gambit, 1979; The Monitor, the Miners, and the Shree, 1980; Aventine, 1981; Deadly Silents, 1982; Liberty's World, 1985; Spider Play, 1986; Blood Hunt, 1987; The Leopard's Daughter, 1987; Bloodlinks, 1988; Dragon's Teeth, 1990. Address: Box 1821, Manhattan, KS 66505-1821, USA.

KILROY Thomas, b. 23 Sept 1934, Callan, Ireland. Writer; University Teacher. m. (1) 3 sons, (2) Julia Lowell Carlson, 9 Dec 1981, 1 daughter. Education: BA, 1956, MA, 1959, University College, Dublin, Ireland. Publications: Death and Resurrection of Mr Roche (play), 1968 The Big Chapel (novel), 1971; Talbots' Box (play), 1977; The Seagull (play adaptation), 1981; Double Cross (play), 1986; Ghosts, 1989; The Madame McAdam Travelling Theatre (play), 1990; Gold in the Streets (television), 1993. Contributions to: Radio, television, journals, and magazines. Honours: Guardian Fiction Prize, 1971; Heinnmann Award for Literature, 1971; Irish Academy of Letters Prize, 1972; American-Irish Foundation Award for Literature, 1974. Memberships: Fellow, Royal Society of Literature, 1971; Irish Academy of Letters, 1973. Literary Agent: Casarotto Ramsay Ltd, National House, 60-66 Wardour Street, London W1V 3HP, England. Address: Kilmaine, County Mayo, Ireland.

KILWORTH Garry, b. 5 July 1941, York, England. Writer. m. Annette Jill Bailey, 30 June 1962, 1 son, 1 daughter. Education: Business Studies, 1974; Honours Degree in English, 1985. Publications: Songbirds of Pain, 1984; Spiral Winds, 1987; Hunter's Moon, 1989; In the Hollow of the Deep-Sea Wave, 1989; Standing on Samshan, 1992. Contributions to: Magazines and newspapers. Honours: Gollancz Short Story Award, Sunday Times, 1974; Carnegie Medal Commendation, Librarian Association, 1991. Membership: PEN. Address: Wychwater, The Chase, Ashington, Essex, England.

KIM Yong-ik, b. 15 May 1920, Korea. Writer. m. 11 Feb 1972, 3 daughters. Education: BA, Aoyama Jakuin College, Tokyo, 1942; BA, Florida Southern College, 1951; MA, University of Kentucky, 1952. Publications: Moons of Korea, 1959; The Happy Days, 1960; The Diving Gourd, 1962; Blue in the Seed, 1964; The Wedding Shoes, 1964; Love in Winter, 1970; The Shoes From Yang San Valley, 1981. Contributions to: Magazines. Honours: First Overseas Korean Literature Prize, Korean Literary and Writers Association, 1990; Main Stream America Award for Excellence in Literature, Asian Pacific Council, 1991. Membership: Korean American Literature Society. Address: 1030 Macon Avenue, Pittsburgh, PA 15218, USA.

KIMBALL Roger, b. 13 Aug 1953, Ohio, USA. Writer; Editor. m. Alexandra Mullen, 1993. Education: BA, Bennington College, 1975; MA, 1977, MPhil, 1978, Yale University. Publication: Tenured Radicals: How Politics has Corrupted our Higher Education, 1990. Contributions to: New Criterion; Wall Street Journal; Times Literary Supplement; Commentary; American Scholar; Architectural Record. Address: 850 7th Avenue, New York, NY 10019, USA.

KIMBROUGH Robert (Alexander III), b. 26 June 1929, Philadelphia, Pennsylvania, USA. Professor of English; Writer. Education: BA, Williams College, 1951; MA, Stanford University, 1955; PhD, Harvard University, 1959. Appointments: Instructor to Associate Professor, 1959-68, Professor of English, 1968-, Chair, Integrated Liberal Studies Department, 1970-75, University of Wisconsin, Madison. Publications: Joseph Conrad: Heart of Darkness: An Authoritative Text, Backgrounds and Sources (editor), 1963, 3rd edition, 1987; Shakespeare's Troilus and Cressida and Its Setting, 1964; Henry James: The Turn of the Screw: An Authoritative Text, Backgrounds and Sources (editor), 1966; Troilus and Cressida: A Scene by Scene Analysis with Critical Commentary, 1966; Sir Philip Sidney: Selected Prose and Poetry (editor), 1969, 2nd edition, 1982; Sir Philip Sidney, 1971; Joseph Conrad: The Nigger of the Narcissus (editor), 1984; Shakespeare and the Art of Human Kindness: The Essay Toward Androgyny, 1990. Contributions to: Professional journals. Address: 3206 Gregory Street, Madison, WI 53711, USA.

KIMMEL Eric Alan, b. 30 Oct 1946, Brooklyn, New York, USA. Author of children's books. m. Doris Ann Dunlap, 16 June 1978, 1 daughter. Education: BA, Lafayette College, 1967; MA, New York University, 1970; PhD, University of Illinois, 1973. Publications: Anansi and Moss-Covered Rock, 1988; Hershel and the Hanukkah Goblins, 1989; I Took My Frog to the Library, 1990; Four Dollars and Fifty Cents, 1990; Anansi and the Talking Melon, 1994; The Adventures of Hershel of Ostropol, 1995; Bar Mitzvah, 1995; The Magic Dreidels, 1996; Billy Lazroe and the King of the Sea, 1996; One Eye, Two Eyes and Three Eyes, 1996; Ali Baba and the Forty Thieves, 1996; Squash It!, 1997. Contributions to: Cricket, Spider, Ladybug, stories and articles. Honours: Caldecott Honor, 1990; Washington State Children's Choices. Memberships: Authors Guild; PEN Northwest; Society of Childrens Book Writers. Literary Agent: Sharon Friedman, Ralph M Vicinauza Ltd, 111 8th Avenue, New York, NY 10011, USA.

KINCAID Jamaica, b. 25 May 1949, St John's, Antigua, West Indies. Writer. Appointment: Contributor, later Staff Writer, The New Yorker magazine, 1974-. Publications: At the Bottom of the River (short stories), 1984; Annie John (novel), 1985; A Small Place (non-fiction), 1988; Lucy (novel), 1990. Contributions to: Periodicals. Honours: Morton Dauwen Zabel Award, 1983; Lila Wallace-Reader's Digest Fund Annual Writers Award, 1992. Address: c/o The New Yorker, 25 West 43rd Street, New York, NY 10036, USA.

KING Betty Alice, b. 17 June 1919, Historical Novelist. m. D James King, 14 June 1941, 2 sons, 1 daughter. Education: Queenswood School, Hertfordshire; Open University. Publications: The Lady Margaret, 1965; The Lord Jasper, 1967; The King's Mother, 1969; Margaret of Anjou, 1974; Emma Hamilton, 1976; Nell Gwyn, 1979; Claybourn, 1980; The French Countess, 1982; We Are Tomorrow's Past, 1984. Contributions to: Hertfordshire Countryside; Enfield Gazette. Memberships: Society of Authors; Samuel Pepys Association. Address: Crescent House, 31 North Road, Hertford, Herts SG14 1LN, England.

KING (David) Clive, b. 28 Apr 1924, Richmond, Surrey, England. Author. m. (1) Jane Tuke, 1948, 1 son, 1 daughter, (2) Penny Timmins, 1974, 1 daughter. Education: Downing College, 1947. Publications: The Town That Went South, 1959; Stig of the Dump, 1963; The Twenty-Two Letters, 1966; The Night the Water Came, 1973; Snakes and Snakes, 1975; Me and My Million, 1976; Ninny's Boat, 1980; The Sound of Propellers, 1986; The Seashore People, 1987; 7 other books. Honour: Boston Globe-Horn Book Award, Honour Book, 1980. Membership: Society of Authors. Address: Pond Cottage, Low Road, Thurlton, Norwich NR14 6PZ, England.

KING Cynthia, b. 27 Aug 1925, New York, New York, USA. Writer. m. Jonathan King, 26 July 1944, 3 sons. Education: Bryn Mawr College, 1943-44; University of Chicago, 1944-45; New York University Writers Workshop, 1964-67. Appointments: Associate Editor, Hillman Periodicals, 1945-50; Managing Editor, Fawcett Publications, 1950-55. Publications: In the Morning of Time, 1970; The Year of Mr Nobody, 1978; Beggars and Choosers, 1980; Sailing Home, 1982. Contributions to: Newspapers and magazines. Honour: Michigan Council for the Arts Grant, 1986. Memberships: Authors Guild; Poets and Writers; Detroit Women Writers. Address: 5306 Institute Lane, Houston, TX 77005, USA.

KING Francis Henry, (Frank Cauldwell), b. 4 Mar 1923, Adelboden, Switzerland. Author; Drama Critic. Education: BA, 1949, MA, 1951, Balliol College, Oxford. Appointment: Drama Critic, Sunday Telegraph, 1978-88. Publications: Novels: To the Dark Tower, 1946; Never Again, 1947; An Air That Kills, 1948; The Dividing Stream, 1951; The Dark Glasses, 1954; The Firewalkers, 1956; The Widow, 1957;

The Man on the Rock, 1957; The Custom House, 1961; The Last of the Pleasure Gardens, 1965; The Waves Behind the Boat, 1967; A Domestic Animal, 1970; Flights, 1973; A Game of Patience, 1974; The Needle, 1975; Danny Hill, 1977; The Action, 1978; Act of Darkness, 1983; Voices in an Empty Room, 1984; Frozen Music, 1987; The Woman Who Was God, 1988; Punishments, 1989; Visiting Cards, 1990; The Ant Colony, 1991; Secret Lives (with Tom Wakefield and Patrick Gale), 1991; The One and Only, 1994; Ash on an Old Man's Sleeve, 1996; Dead Letters, 1997. Short Stories: So Hurt and Humiliated, 1959; The Japanese Umbrella, 1964; The Brighton Belle, 1968; Hard Feelings, 1976; Indirect Method, 1980; One is a Wanderer, 1985; A Hand on the Shutter, 1996. Other: E M Forster and His World, 1978; A Literary Companion to Florence, 1991; Autobiography: Yesterday Came Suddenly, 1993. Honours: Somerset Maugham Award, 1952; Katherine Mansfield Short Story Prize, 1965; Officer, 1979, Commander, 1985, of the Order of the British Empire. Memberships: English PEN, president, 1976-86; International PEN, president, 1986-89, vice-president, 1989-; Royal Society of Literature, fellow. Address: 19 Gordon Place, London W8 4JE, England.

KING Janey. See: THOMAS Rosie.

KING Larry L, b. 1 Jan 1929, Putnam, Texas, USA. Playwright; Author; Actor. m. Barbara S Blaine, 2 sons, 3 daughters. Education: Texas Technical University, 1949-50; Nieman Fellow, Harvard University, 1969-70; Duke Fellow of Communications, Duke University, 1975-76. Appointments: Visiting Ferris Professor of Journalism and Political Science, Princeton University, 1973-74; Poet Laureate (life), Monahans (Texas) Sandhills Literary Society, 1977-. Publications: Plays: The Kingfish, 1979; The Best Little Whorehouse in Texas, 1978; Christmas: 1933, 1986; The Night Hank Williams Died, 1988; The Golden Shadows Old West Museum, 1989; The Best Little Whorehouse Goes Public, 1994; Books: The One-Eyed Man, novel, 1966; ...And Other Dirty Stories, 1968; Confessions of a White Racist, 1971; The Old Man and Lesser Mortals, 1974; Of Outlaws, Whores, Conmen, Politicians and Other Artists, 1980; Warning: Writer at Work, 1985; None But a Blockhead, 1986; Because of Lozo Brown, 1988. Contributions to: Harper's; Atlantic Monthly; Life; New Republic; Texas Monthly; Texas Observer; New York; Playboy; Parade; Esquire; Saturday Evening Post; National Geographic. Address: 3025 Woodland Drive, North West, Washington, DC 20008, USA.

KING Laurie R, b. 19 Sept 1952, Oakland, California, USA. Writer. m. Noel Q King, Nov 1977, 1 son, 1 daughter. Education: BA, University of California, Santa Cruz, 1977; MA, Graduate Theological Union, Berkeley, 1984. Publications: A Grave Talent, 1993; The Beekeeper's Apprentice, 1994; To Play the Fool, 1995; A Monstrous Regiment of Women, 1995; With Child, 1996; A Letter of Mary, 1997. Honours: Edgar Award for Best First Novel, 1993; Creasey Award for Best First Novel, 1995; Nero Wolfe Award, Best Novel, 1996. Memberships: Mystery Writers of America; Sisters in Crime; International Association o f Crime Writers; Crime Writers Association. Address: PO Box 1152, Freedom, CA 95019, USA.

KING Michael, b. 15 Dec 1945, Wellington, New Zealand. Writer. m. 17 Oct 1987, 1 son, 1 daughter. Education: BA, Victoria University, 1967; MA, 1968, DPhil, 1978, Waikato University. Appointments: Katherine Mansfield Fellow, 1976; Writing Fellow, Victoria University, 1983; National Library Fellow, 1990; Fellowship in Humanities, Waikato University, 1991-; Senior Research Fellow, Arts Faculty, University of Auckland, 1996-97. Publications: Te Puea, 1977; Maori, 1983; Being Pakeha, 1985; Death of the Rainbow Warrior, 1986; Moriori, 1989; Frank Sargeson, A Life, 1995. Contributions to: Columnist, and feature writer for variety of newspapers and magazines including New Zealand Listener, New Zealand Sunday Times, Metro. Honours: Feltex Award, 1975; Cowan Prize, 1976; New Zealand Book Award, 1978; Wattie Book of the Year Prizes, 1984, 1990; Officer of the Order of the British Empire, 1988; Literary Fund Achievement Award, 1989. Memberships: PEN, New Zealand, president, 1979-80; New Zealand Authors Fund Advisory Committee, 1980-92; Frank Sargeson Trust, 1982-; Auckland Institute Museum Council, 1986-91; Chatham Islands Conservation Board, 1990-; Hon DLitt, Victoria Univ, 1997. Address: PO Box 109, Whangamata, New Zealand.

KING Paul. See: DRACKETT Phil(ip Arthur).

KING Stephen Edwin, (Richard Bachman), b. 21 Sept 1947, Portland, Maine, USA. Author. m. Tabitha J Spruce, 1971, 2 sons, 1 daughter. Education: University of Maine. Appointments: Teacher of

English, Hampden Academy, Maine, 1971-73; Writer-in-Residence, University of Maine, Orono, 1978-79. Publications: Carrie, 1974; Salem's Lot, 1975; The Shining, 1977; The Stand, 1978; The Dead Zone, 1979; Firestarter, 1980; Danse Macabre, 1981; Cujo, 1981; Christine, 1983; Pet Sematery, 1983; The Talisman (with Peter Straub), 1984; Cycle of the Werewolf, 1985; It, 1986; The Eyes of the Dragon, 1987; Misery, 1987; The Tommyknockers, 1987; The Dark Half, 1989; Four Past Midnight, 1990; Needful Things, 1991; Gerald's Game, 1992; Dolores Claiborne, 1993; Insomnia, 1994; Desperation, 1996; The Green Mile, 1996. Stories: The Dark Tower Stories: Vol 1: The Gunslinger, 1982, Vol 2: The Drawing of the Three, 1984. Short story collections: Night Shift, 1978; Different Seasons, 1982; Skeleton Crew, 1985; Nightmares & Dreamscapes, 1993. As Richard Bachman: Thinner, 1984; The Bachman Books: Rage, The Long Walk, Roadwork, The Running Man, 1985; The Regulators, 1996. Memberships: Authors Guild of America; Screen Artists Guild; Screen Writers of America; Writers Guild. Address: c/o Press Relations, Viking Press, 625 Madison Avenue, New York, NY 10022, USA.

KING-HELE Desmond George, b. 3 Nov 1927, Seaford, England. Author. Education: BA (Hons), 1948, MA, 1952, Trinity College, Cambridge. Appointment: Editor, Notes and Records of the Royal Society, 1989-96. Publications: Shelley: His Thought and Work, 1960, 3rd edition, 1984; Satellites and Scientific Research, 1960, 2nd edition, 1962; Erasmus Darwin, 1963; Satellite Orbits in an Atmosphere, 1964, new edition, 1987; Observing Earth Satellites, 1966, new edition, 1983; Essential Writings of Erasmus Darwin, 1968; The End of the Twentieth Century?, 1970; Poems and Trixies, 1972; Doctor of Revolution, 1977; The Letters of Erasmus Darwin, 1981; Animal Spirits, 1983; Erasmus Darwin and the Romantic Poets, 1986; A Tapestry of Orbits, 1992. Contributions to: Over 400 papers to various journals. Honours: Honorary Degrees: DSc, University of Aston, 1979, D Univ, University of Surrey, 1986; Several Scientific awards. Memberships: Institute of Mathematics and Its Applications, fellow; Royal Astronomical Society, fellow; Royal Society, fellow. Address: 7 Hilltops Court, 65 North Lane, Buriton, Hampshire GU31 5RS, England.

KING-SMITH Dick, b. 27 Mar 1922, Bitton, Gloucestershire, England. Writer. Education: Marlborough College, 1936-40; BEd, Bristol University, 1975. Publications: The Fox Busters, 1978; Daggie Dogfoot, 1980; The Mouse Butcher, 1981; Magnus Powermouse, 1982; The Queen's Nose, 1983; The Sheep-Pig, 1985; Lighnting Fred, 1985; Noah's Brother, 1986; Yob, 1986; E S P, 1986; The Hodgeheg, 1987; Friends and Brothers, 1987; Dodos Are Forever, 1987; Sophie's Snail, 1988; The Trouble With Edward, 1988; Martin's Mice, 1988; The Water Horse, 1990; Paddy's Pot of Gold, 1990; Alphabets, 1992; The Hodgeheg, 1992; numerous others. Address: Diamond's Cottage, Queen Charlton, Near Keynsham, Somerset, BS18 2SJ, England.

KINGDON Robert McCune, b. 29 Dec 1927, Chicago, Illinois, USA. Professor of History; Writer. Education: AB, Oberlin College, 1949; MA, 1950, PhD, 1955, Columbia University; Postgraduate Studies, University of Geneva, 1951-52. Appointments: Assistant Professor to Professor of History, University of Iowa, 1957-65; Visiting Professor, Stanford University, 1964, 1980; Professor of History, 1965-, Hilldale Professor of History, 1988-, University of Wisconsin at Madison; Editor, Sixteenth Century Journal, 1973-; Member, 1974-, Director, 1975-87, Institute for Research in the Humanities. Publications: Geneva and the Coming of the Wars of Religion in France 1555-1563, 1956; Co-Editor (with J-F Bergier) Registres de la Compagnie des Pasteurs de Genévè au Temps de Calvin (co-editor with J-F Bergier), 2 volumes, 1962, 1964; Execution of Justice in England (editor), 1965; William Allen: A True, Sincere and Modest Defence of English Catholics (editor), 1965; Geneva and the Consolidation of the French Protestant Movement 1564-1572, 1967; Calvin and Calvinism: Sources of Democracy (co-editor with R D Linder), 1970; Theodore de Béze: Du Droit des magistrats (editor), 1971; Transition and Revolution: Problems and Issues of European Renaissance and Reformation History (editor), 1974; The Political Thought of Peter Martyr Vermigli, 1980; Church and Society in Reformation Europe, 1985; Myths About the St Bartholomew's Day Massacres 1572-1576, 1988; A Bibliography of the Works of Peter Martyr Vermigli (co-editor with J P Donnelly), 1990; Adultery and Divorce in Calvin's Geneva, 1995. Contributions to: Scholarly journals. Memberships: President, American Society of Reformation Research, 1971; International Federation of Societies and Institutions for the Study of the Renaissance; Executive Board, Renaissance Society of

America, 1972-92; President, American Society of Church History, 1980. Address: 4 Rosewood Court, Madison, WI 53711, USA.

KINGMAN Lee, b. 1919, USA. Freelance Writer and Editor. Publications: Pierre Pidgeon, 1943; Ilenka, 1945; The Rocky Summer, 1948; The Best Christmas, 1949; Philippe's Hill, 1950; The Quarry Adventure, 1951, UK edition as Lauri's Surprising Summer; Kathy and the Mysterious Statue, 1953; Peter's Long Walk, 1953; Mikko's Fortune, 1955; The Magic Christmas Tree, 1956; The Village Band Mystery, 1956; Flivver, the Heroic Horse, 1958; The House of the Blue Horse, 1960; The Saturday Gang, 1961; Peter's Pony, 1963; Sheep Ahoy, 1963; Private Eyes, 1964; Newbery and Caldecott Medal Books: 1956-1965 (editor), 1965; The Year of the Raccoon, 1966; The Secret of the Silver Reindeer, 1968; Illustrators of Children's Books: 1957-1966 (editor with J Foster and R G Lontoft), 1968; The Peter Pan Bag, 1970; Georgina and the Dragon, 1971; The Meeting Post: A Story of Lapland, 1972; Escape from the Evil Prophecy, 1973; Newbery and Caldecott Medal Books: 1966-1975 (editor), 1975; Break a Leg, Betsy Maybe, 1976; The Illustrator's Notebook, 1978; Head over Wheels, 1978; Illustrators of Children's Books: 1967-1976 (editor with G Hogarth and H Quimby), 1978; The Refiner's Fire, 1981; The Luck of the Miss L, 1986; Newbery and Caldecott Medal Books: 1976-1985 (editor), 1986; Catch the Baby!, 1990. Address: 105 High Street, Gloucester, MA 01930, USA.

KINGSTON Maxine Hong, b. 27 Oct 1940, Stockton, California, USA. Writer; Teacher. m. 23 Nov 1962, 1 son. Education: AB, 1962, Secondary Teaching Credential, 1965, University of California, Berkeley. Appointment: Teacher, University of California, Berkeley, 1990-. Publications: The Woman Warrior, 1976; China Men, 1980; Hawaii One Summer, 1987; Tripmaster Monkey: His Fake Book, 1989. Contributions to: Many publications. Honours: National Book Critics Circle Award, 1977; Anisfield-Wolf Race Relations Book Award, 1978; National Endowment for the Arts Fellowship, 1980; National Book Award, 1981; Guggenheim Fellowship, 1981; Hawaii Award for Literature, 1982; California Council for the Humanities Award, 1985; Governor's Award for the Arts, California, 1989; PEN West Award in Fiction, 1990; American Academy and Institute of Arts and Letters Award, 1990; Brandeis University National Women's Committee Major Book Collection Award, 1992; Honorary doctorates. Memberships: American Academy of Arts and Sciences; Authors Guild; PEN American Centre; PEN West. Address: c/o Department of English, University of California, Berkeley, CA 94720, USA.

KINGTON Miles (Beresford), b. 13 May 1941, Downpatrick, Northern Ireland. Writer. m. (1) Sarah Paine, 1964, div 1987, 1 son, 1 daughter, (2) Caroline Maynard, 1987, 1 son. Education: BA, Modern Languages, Trinity College, Oxford, 1963. Appointments: Jazz Reviewer, 1965, Columnist, 1980-87, The Times; Staff, 1967-73, Literary Editor, 1973-80, Columnist, 1980-87, Punch; Columnist, The Independent, 1987-. Publications: The World of Alphonse Allais, 1977, reprinted as A Wolf in Frog's Clothing, 1983; 4 Franglais books, 1979-82; Moreover, Too..., 1985; Welcome to Kington, 1985; The Franglais Lieutenant's Woman, 1986; Steaming Through Britain, 1990; Anthology of Jazz (editor), 1992. Address: Lower Hayze, Limpley Stoke, Bath, BA3 6HR, England.

KINKAID Matt. See: **ADAMS Clifton.**

KINNELL Galway, b. 1 Feb 1927, Providence, Rhode Island, USA. Poet; Writer. 1 son, 1 daughter. Education: Princeton University. Publications: Poetry: What a Kingdom It Was, 1960; Flower Herding on Mount Monadnock, 1963; Body Rags, 1966; The Book of Nightmares, 1971; The Avenue Bearing the Initial of Christ into the New World, 1974; Mortal Acts, Mortal Words, 1980; Selected Poems, 1982; The Past, 1985; When One Has Lived a Long Time Alone, 1990; Imperfect Thirst, 1994. Other: The Poems of François Villon (translation), 1965; Black Light (novel), 1966; On the Motion and Immobility of Douve, 1968; The Lackawanna Elegy, 1970; Interviews: Walking Down the Stairs, 1977; How the Alligator Missed His Breakfast (children's story), 1982; The Essential Whitman (editor), 1987. Honours: National Institute of Arts and Letters Award, 1962; Cecil Hemley Poetry Prize, 1969; Medal of Merit, 1975; Pulitzer Prize in Poetry, 1983; National Book Award, 1983; John D and Catharine T MacArthur Foundation Fellowship, 1984. Memberships: PEN; Poetry Society of America; Modern Language Association. Address: AR 2 Box 138, Sheffield, VT 05866, USA.

KINNEY Arthur F(rederick), b. 5 Sept 1933, Cortland, New York, USA. Author; Editor; Teacher. Education: AB magna cum laude, Syracuse University, 1955; MA, Columbia University, 1956; PhD, University of Michigan, 1963. Appointments: Editor, English Literary Renaissance, 1971-; Twayne English Authors Series in the Renaissance, 1973-; Massachusetts Studies in Early Modern Culture; Thomas W Copeland Professor of Literary History, University of Massachusetts, Amherst. Publications: Humanist Poetics, 1986; John Skelton, Priest as Poet, 1987; Continental Humanist Poetics, 1989; Renaissance Historicism, 1989; Elizabethan Backgrounds, 1990; Rogues, Vagabonds, and Sturdy Beggars, 1990. Contributions to: Renaissance Quarterly; Huntington Library Quarterly; Shakespeare Quarterly; Southern Review; Southern Quarterly; English Literary History; Modern Philology, Journal of English and Germanic Philology; Shakespeare Studies; Shakespeare Survey; Others. Honours: Avery and Jules Hopwood Major Award in Criticism; Bread Loaf Scholar in Fiction and Criticism; Fulbright-Hays Scholar; Senior Fellow: National Endowment for the Humanities, twice; Huntington Library, 3 times; Folger Shakespeare Library, twice. Memberships: Renaissance English Text Society, president, 1985-; Conference of Editors of Learned Journals, president, 1971-73, 1980-82; Board Member and Consultant to many journals and publishers. Address: 25 Hunter Hill Drive, Amherst, MA 01002, USA.

KINSELLA Thomas, b. 4 May 1928, Dublin, Ireland. Professor; Poet. Appointments: Professor, Temple University, Pennsylvania, 1970; Artistic Director, Lyric Players Theatre, Belfast. Publications: The Starlit Eye, 1952; Three Legendary Sonnets, 1952; Another September, 1958; Downstream, 1962; Wormwood, 1966; Nightwalker, 1967; Tear, 1969; A Selected Life, 1972; Notes from the Land of the Dead and Other Poems, 1972; New Poems, 1973; Vertical Man, 1973; The Good Fight, 1973; The Messenger, 1978; Fifteen Dead, 1979; Peppercanister Poems, 1972-78, 1979; One Fond Embrace, 1981; Her Vertical Smile, 1985; Out of Ireland, 1987; St Catherine's Clock, 1987; Blood and Family, 1988; Personal Places, 1990; Madonna and Other Poems, 1991; Open Court, 1991; From Centre City, Poems, 1990-1994, 1994; Editor and Translator. Honour: DLitt, National University of Ireland, Dublin, 1984. Address: Killalane, Laragh, County Wicklow, Ireland.

KINZIE Mary, b. 30 Sept 1944, Montgomery, Alabama, USA. Professor of English; Poet; Writer. Education: BA, Northwestern University, 1967; MA, 1970, MA, 1972, PhD, 1980, Johns Hopkins University. Appointments: Executive Editor, Triquarterly magazine, 1975-78; Instructor, 1975-78, Lecturer, 1978-85, Associate Professor, 1985-90, Professor of English, 1990-, Northwestern University. Publications: Poetry: The Threshold of the Year, 1982; Masked Women and Summers of Vietnam, 1990; Qutumn Eros, 1992. Contributions to: Many periodicals. Honours: Fulbright Scholarship, 1967-68; Illinois Arts Council Award in Poetry, 1981; Guggenheim Fellowship, 1986. Memberships: PEN; Poetry Society of America; Society of Midland Authors. Address: c/o Department of English, Northwestern University, Evanston, IL 60201, USA.

KIRK Geoffrey Stephen, b. 3 Dec 1921, Nottingham, England. Regius Professor of Greek Emeritus; Writer. Education: BA, 1946, MA, 1948, DLitt, 1965, Clare College, Cambridge. Appointments: Fellow, Trinity Hall, 1947-73, Trinity College, 1973-82; Lecturer, 1950-61, Reader, 1961-65, Regius Professor of Greek, 1973-82, Cambridge University; Professor of Classics, Yale University, 1965-71; Bristol University, 1971-73. Publications: Heraclitus: The Cosmic Fragments (editor), 1952; The Presocratic Philosophers (with J E Raven), 1956; The Songs of Homer, 1962; The Language and Background of Homer (editor), 1964; Euripides: Bacchae (editor and translator), 1970; Myth, 1970; The Nature of Greek Myths, 1974; Homer and the Oral Tradition, 1977; The Iliad: A Commentary, 2 volumes, 1985, 1990. Contributions to: Professional journals. Honour: British Academy, fellow, 1959; Academy of Athens, corresponding fellow, 1993-. Address: 12 Sion Hill, Bath, Somerset, BA1 2UH, England.

KIRK Michael. See: **KNOX William.**

KIRK Philip. See: **LEVINSON Leonard.**

KIRK-GREENE Anthony (Hamilton Millard), b. 16 May 1925, Tunbridge Wells, England. University Lecturer in Modern African History; Fellow, St Antony's College, Oxford. Education: BA, 1949, MA, 1954, Clare College, Cambridge; MA, Oxford University, 1964. Appointments: Editorial Advisor, Journal of African Administration,

1960-70, Cultures & Development, 1970-80, African Affairs, 1980-; Series Editor, Africana (Holmes & Meier), 1970-80; Academic Consultant, Radcliffe Press, 1990-; General Editor, Studies in African History, 1970-75, Africana Revivals, 1990-95; Co-Editor, Hoover Colonial Series, 1975-80; Director, Foreign Service Programme, Oxford University, 1986-90; Assistant Editor, New Dictionary of National Biography, 1996-. Publications: Adamawa Past and Present, 1958; The Cattle People of Nigeria (with Caroline Sassoon), 1959; The River Niger (with Caroline Sassoon), 1961; Barth's Travels in Nigeria, 1962; Principles of Native Administration in Nigeria, 1965; The Making of Northern Nigeria (editor), 1965; The Emirates of Northern Nigeria (with S J Hogben), 1966; Hausa Proverbs, 1966; A Modern Hausa Reader (with Y Aliyu), 1967; Lugard and the Amalgamation of Nigeria, 1968; Language and People of Bornu (editor), 1968; Crisis and Conflict in Nigeria, 1971; West African Narratives (with P Newman), 1972; Gazetteers of Northern Nigeria (editor), 1972; Teach Yourself Hausa (with C H Kraft), 1973; The Concept of the Good Man in Hausa, 1974; Nigeria Faces North (with Pauline Ryan), 1975; The Transfer of Power in Africa (editor), 1978; Stand by Your Radios: The Military in Tropical Africa, 1980; Biographical Dictionary of the British Colonial Governor, 1981; Nigeria since 1970 (with D Rimmer), 1981; The Sudan Political Service: A Profile, 1982; Margery Perham: West African Passage (editor), 1983; Pastoralists of the Western Savanna (with Mahdi Adamu), 1986; Margery Perham: Pacific Prelude (editor), 1988; The Sudan Political Service: A Preliminary Register of Second Careers (with Sir Gawain Bell), 1989; A Biographical Dictionary of the British Colonial Service, 1939-66, 1991. Contributions to: Dictionary of National Biography; Encyclopaedia Britannica; Numerous journals; The Emergence of Afircan History at British Universities, editor, 1995; The Diary of a West African Chief (with J Vaughan), 1995. Honours: Member of the Order of the British Empire, 1963; Hans Wolff Memorial Lecturer, 1973; Fellow, Royal Historical Society, 1985. Memberships: Royal African Society; International African Institute; African Studies Association of UK, president, 1989-91; Festschrift: Essays in Honour of Anthony Kirk-Greene, 1993. Address: c/o St Antony's College, Oxford OX2 6JF, England.

KIRKPATRICK Sidney Dale, b. 4 Oct 1955, New York, New York, USA. Writer; Film Maker. m. 26 Nov 1983, 2 sons. Education: BA, Hampshire College, Amherst, 1978; MFA, New York University, 1982. Appointment: Reader, Huntington Library, 1992. Publications: A Cast of Killers, 1986; Turning the Tide, 1991; Lords of Sipan, 1992. Contributions to: Los Angeles Times; American Film. Honours: Winner, American Film Festival, 1982. Membership: PEN Center West, board of directors, 1991-92. Address: c/o Tim Seldes, Russell and Volkening, 50 West 29th Street, New York, NY 10001, USA.

KIRKUP James, b. 23 Apr 1918, South Shields, England. Writer; Playwright; Broadcaster. Education: BA, Durham University; Gregory Fellow, Poetry, Leeds University, 1950-52. Publications: The Cosmic Shape, 1947; The Drowned Sailor, 1948; The Creation, 1950; The Submerged Village, 1951; A Correct Compassion, 1952; A Spring Journey, 1954; Upon This Rock, The Dark Child, The Trump of Harmony, 1955; The True Mystery of the Nativity, Ancestral Voices, The Radiance of the King, 1956; The Descent Into The Cave, The Only Child (autobiography), 1957; Sorrows, Passions and Alarms (autobiography), 1960; The Love of Others (novel), 1962; Tropic Temper (travel), 1963; Refusal to Conform, Last and First Poems, 1963; The Heavenly Mandate, 1964; Japan Industrial Volumes 1 and II, 1964-65; Tokyo, 1966; Bangkok, 1967; Filipinescas, 1968; One Man's Russia, 1968; Streets of Asia, 1969; Hong Kong, 1969; Japan Behind the Fan, 1970; Insect Summer (novel), 1971; Play Strindberg, 1974; The Conformer, 1975; Scenes From Sutcliffe, 1981; Ecce Homo: My Pasolini, 1981; To The Unknown God, 1982; The Bush Toads, 1982; Folktales Japanesque, 1982; The Glory That Was Greece, 1984; Hear in My Heart, 1984; The Sense of the Visit: New Poems, 1984; Trends and Traditions, 1985; Dictionary of Body Language, 1985; English With a Smile, 1986; Fellow Feelings (poems), 1986; Portraits and Souvenirs, 1987; The Mystery and the Magic of Symbols, 1987; The Cry of the Owl: Native American Folktales and Legends, 1987; I of All People: An Autobiography of Youth, 1988; The Best of Britain: Essays, 1989; First Fireworks, 1991; A Room in the Woods, 1991; Shooting Stars, 1992; Notes for an Autobiography, 1992; A Poet Could Not But Be Gay (autobiography), 1992; Gaijin on the Ginza (novel), 1992; Queens Have Died Young and Fair (novel), 1993; Me All Over: Memoirs of a Misfit (autobiography), 1993; Words for Contemplation; Mantras, Poems, 1993; Utsusemi: Original tanka, 1996. Honours: Scott Moncrieff Prize for Translation, 1994; Numerous others. Memberships:

Numerous professional organisations. Address: c/o British Monomarks, Box 2780, London WC1N 3XX, England.

KISS Iren, b. 25 Sept 1947, Budapest, Hungary. Writer; University Professor. m. Laszlo Tabori, 10 June 1988. Education: PhD, History of Literature, Budapest University, 1992. Publications: Szelcsend (poems), 1977; Allokep (novel), 1978; Arkadiat Tatarozxzak (poems), 1979; Maganrecept (cycle), 1982; Kemopera (plays), 1988. Contributions to: Various publications. Honours: Yeats Club Award, 1987; Golden Medal of the Brianza World Competition of Poetry, Italy, 1988. Memberships: Association of the Hungarian Writers; Hungarian PEN. Address: Somloi ut 60/B, Budapest 1118, Hungary.

KISSANE Sharon Florence, b. 2 July 1940, Chicago, Illinois, USA. Writer; Educator. m. James Q Kissane, dec, 2 July 1966, 2 daughters. Education: BA, English and Speech, DePaul University, 1962; MA, Communications, Northwestern University, Evanston, Illinois, 1963; PhD, English Education, Loyola University's School of Education, Chicago, 1970. Appointments: Technical Writer, Editor, Commerce Clearing House, Chicago, 1962-63; Night Editor, Daily Herald newspapers, Des Plains and Park Ridge Editions, 1964-66; Columnist, Daily Herald, Barrington and Palatine Editions, 1982-; Business and Financial Correspondent, Chicago Tribune, 1983-85; Fiction Instructor, Harper College, Palatine, Illinois, 1985-88. Publications: Career Success for People with Physical Disabilities, 1966; Polish Biographical Dictionary (co-author), 1993; What is Child Abuse?, 1994; Gang Awareness, 1995. Contributions to: Journals and magazines. Memberships: Founding Member, Barrington Area Arts Council; Founder, Creative Writing Sub-Group. Address: 15 Turning Shores, South Barrington, IL 60010, USA.

KISSINGER Henry (Alfred), b. 27 May 1923, Furth, Germany (US citizen, 1943). Company Executive; Author. m. (1) Ann Fleischer, 6 Feb 1949, div 1974, 1 son, 1 daughter, (2) Nancy Maginnes, 30 Mar 1974. Education: AB, 1950, MA, 1952, PhD, 1954, Harvard University. Appointments: Associate Professor, 1959-62, Professor of Government, 1962-69, Harvard University; Assistant to the President of the US for National Security Affairs, 1969-75; US Secretary of State, 1973-77; Founder-Chairman, Kissinger Associates Inc, New York City; Consultant, Advisor, and Member of various boards and commissions. Publications: Nuclear Weapons and Foreign Policy, 1957; A World Restored: Castlereagh, Metternich and the Restoration of Peace 1812-1822, 1957; The Necessity for Choice: Prospects of American Foreign Policy, 1961; The Troubled Partnership: A Reappraisal of the Atlantic Alliance, 1965; Problems of National Strategy: A Book of Readings (editor), 1965; American Foreign Policy: Three Essays, 1969; White House Years, 1979; For the Record: Selected Statements 1977-1980, 1981; Years of Upheaval, 1982; Observations: Selected Speeches and Essays 1982-1984, 1985; Diplomacy, 1994. Contributions to: Professional journals. Honours: Woodrow Wilson Prize, 1958; Guggenheim Fellowship, 1965-66; Nobel Prize for Peace, 1973; Distinguished Public Service Award, American Institute of Public Service, 1973; Presidential Medal of Freedom, 1977; Medal of Liberty, 1986. Memberships: American Academy of Arts and Sciences; American Political Science Association; Council on Foreign Relations; Phi Beta Kappa. Address: c/o International Creative Management, 40 West 57th Street, New York, NY 10019, USA.

KITCHEN (Her)Bert (Thomas), b. 24 Apr 1940, Liverpool, England. Artist; Illustrator; Author. m. Muriel Chown, 2 Apr 1960, 2 daughters. Education: London Central School of Arts and Crafts, 1958-61. Publications: Mythical Creatures; Tenrecs Twigs; Somewhere Today; Animal Alphabet; Animal Numbers; Gorilla/Chinchilla; Pig in a Barrow; And So They Build, 1993; When Hunger Calls, 1994. Membership: Society of Authors. Address: 5-8 Lower John Street, Golden Square, London. W1R 4HA, England.

KITCHEN Martin, b. 21 Dec 1936, Nottingham, England. Professor of History; Writer. Education: BA, 1963, PhD, 1966, University of London. Appointment: Professor of History, Simon Fraser University, Burnaby, British Columbia. Publications: The German Officer Corps 1890-1914, 1968; A Military History of Germany, 1975; The Silent Dictatorship, 1976; Fascism, 1976; The Political Economy of Germany 1815-1914, 1978; The Coming of Austrian Fascism, 1980; Germany in the Age of Total War, 1981; British Policy Towards the Soviet Union During the Second World War, 1986; Europe Between the Wars, 1988; The Origins of the Cold War in Comparative Perspective, 1988; The British Empire and Commonwealth, 1996; The Cambridge Illustrated History of Germany, 1996. Contributions to:

Professional journals. Honour: Moncado Prize, American Military Academy, 1978. Memberships: Fellow, Royal Historical Society; Fellow, Royal Society of Canada. Address: c/o Department of History, Simon Fraser University, Burnaby, British Columbia V5A 1S6, Canada.

KITT Tamara. See: **DE REGNIERS Beatrice (Schenk).**

KITTEREDGE William Alfred, b. 14 Aug 1932, Portland, Oregon, USA. Retired Professor of English; Writer. 1 son, 1 daughter. Education: BS Agriculture, Oregon State University, 1953; MFA, University of Iowa, 1969. Appointment: Professor of English, University of Montana, 1969-. Publications: The Van Gogh Field, 1979; We Are Not in This Together, 1984; Owning It All, 1984; Hole in the Sky, 1992; Portable Western Reader, editor, 1997. Contributions to: Harper's; Atlantic; Esquire; Paris Review; Triquarterly. Honours: Governor's Award for Literature, Montana, 1987; Humanist of the Year, Montana, 1988. Address: 143 S 5th E, Missoula, MT 59801, USA.

KIZER Carolyn Ashley, b. 10 Dec 1925, Spokane, Washington, USA. Poet; Professor. Education: BA, Sarah Lawrence College, 1945; Postgraduate studies, Columbia University, 1946-47; Studied poetry with Theodore Roethke, University of Washington, 1953-54. Appointments: Founder-Editor, Poetry North West, 1959-65; Specialist in Literature, US Department of State, Pakistan, 1964-65; 1st Director, Literature Programs, National Endowment for the Arts, 1966-70; Poet-in-Residence, University of North Carolina at Chapel Hill, 1970-74; Hurst Professor of Literature, Washington University, St Louis, 1971; Lecturer, Barnard College, 1972; Acting Director, Graduate Writing Program, Columbia University, 1971; Poet-in-Residence, Ohio University, 1974; Visiting Poet, Iowa Writer's Workshop, 1975; Professor, University of Maryland, 1976-77; Poet-in-Residence, Distinguished Visiting Lecturer, Centre College, Kentucky, 1979; Distinguished Visiting Poet, East Washington University, 1980; Elliston Professor of Poetry, University of Cincinnati, 1981; Bingham Distinguished Professor, University of Louisville, 1982; Distinguished Visiting Poet, Bucknell University, 1982; Visiting Poet, State University of New York at Albany, 1982; Professor, School of Arts, Columbia University, 1982; Professor of Poetry, Stanford University, 1986; Senior Fellow, Humanities Council, Princeton University, 1986. Publications; The Ungrateful Garden, 1961; Knock Upon Silence, 1965; Midnight Was My Cry, 1971; Mermaids in the Basement: Poems for Women, 1984; Yin: New Poems, 1984; Carrying Over, 1988; Prozes, 1993; The Essential John Clare (editor), 1993. Contributions to: Poems and Articles in various American and British Journals. Honours: Governor's Awards, State of Washington, 1965, 1985; Pulitzer Prize in Poetry, 1985; American Academy and Institute of Arts and Letters, 1985; San Francisco Arts Commission Award in Literature, 1986. Memberships: American Civil Liberties Union; American Poets; Amnesty International; PEN. Address: 19772 8th Street East, Sonoma, CA 95476, USA.

KLAPPERT Peter, b. 14 Nov 1942, Rockville Center, New York, USA. Poet; Educator. Education: BA, Cornell University, 1964; MA, 1967, MFA, 1968, University of Iowa. Appointments: Instructor, Rollins College, 1968-71; Briggs-Copeland Lecturer, Harvard University, 1971-74; Visiting Lecturer, New College, Florida, 1972; Writer-in-Residence, 1976-77, Assistant Professor, 1977-81, Director, Graduate Writing Programme, 1979-80, College of William and Mary; Associate Professor, 1981-91, Director, Graduate Writing Programme, 1985-88, Professor, 1991-, George Mason University, Fairfax, Virginia. Publications: Lugging Vegetables to Nantucket, 1971; Circular Stairs, Distress in the Mirrors, 1975; Non Sequitur O'Connor, 1977; The Idiot Princess of the Last Dynasty, 1984; 52 Pick-up; Scenes from The Conspiracy, A Documentary, 1984; Internal Foreigner (audio-cassette), 1984. Contributions to: Antaeus; Atlantic Monthly; Harper's; American Poetry Review; Agni Review; Ploughshares; Missouri Review; Paris Review; Parnassus; Poetry in Review. Address: MS 3E4, Department of English, George Mason University, Fairfax, VA 22030, USA.

KLASS Perri Elizabeth, b. 29 Apr 1958, Trinidad. Pediatrician; Writer. 2 sons, 1 daughter. Education: AB, magna cum laude, Biology, Radcliffe College, Harvard University, 1979; MD, Harvard Medical School, 1986. Publications: Recombinations (novel), 1985; I Am Having An Adventure (short stories), 1986; A Not Entirely Benign Procedure (essays), 1987; Other Women's Children (novel), 1990; Baby Doctor (essays), 1992. Contributions to: New York Times Magazine; Massachusetts Medicine; Discover; Vogue; Glamour; Esquire; Boston Globe Magazine; Mademoiselle; Triquarterly; North American Review. Honours: O Henry Awards, 1983, 1984, 1991, 1992,

1995; Honors Award, New England chapter, American Medical Writers Association, 1995. Memberships: PEN New England, executive board; Media Spokesperson, American Academy of Pediatrics; American Medical Women's Association; Massachusetts Medical Society; Tilling Society. Address: c/o Maxine Groffskiy, 853 Broadway Suite 708, New York, NY 10003, USA.

KLEIN Joe. Journalist. m. Education: BA, American Civilization, University of Pennsylvania. Appointments: Reporter, Essex County Newspapers, Massachusetts, 1969; WGBH-TV, Boston, 1972; News Editor, The Real Paper, Boston, 1972-74; Contributing Editor, 1975-80, Washington Bureau Chief, 1975-77, Rolling Stone; Political Columnist, New York Magazine, 1987-92; Senior Editor, 1992, Contributing Editor, Newsweek, 1996-. Publications: Woody Guthrie: A Life, 1980; Payback: Five Marines After Vietnam, 1984; Primary Colors (political novel), 1996. Contributions to: Newspapers and magazines. Honours: Guggenheim Fellow; Peter Khiss Award; Journalism Award, Washington Monthly, 1989; Honorary DLit, Franklin and Marshall College, Lancaster, Pennsylvania, 1990; National Headliner Award, 1994. Memberships: Council on Foreign Relations. Address: c/o Newsweek, 251 West 57th Street, New York, NY 10019-1894, USA.

KLEIN Theodore Eibon Donald, b. 15 July 1947, New York, New York, USA. Writer; Editor. Education: AB, Brown University, 1969; MFA, Columbia University, 1972. Appointments: Editor-in-chief: Brown Daily Herald, 1968, Twilight Zone magazine, 1981-85, Crime Beat magazine, 1991-93. Publications: The Ceremonies (novel), 1984; Dark Gods (story collection), 1985. Contributions to: New York Times; New York Daily News; Washington Post Book World; Film column, Night Cry Magazine; Writer's Digest. Honours: Phi Beta Kappa, 1969; Award for Best Novel, British Fantasy Society, 1985; Award for Best Novella, World Fantasy, 1986. Membership: Arthur Machen Society. Address: 210 West 89th Street, New York, NY 10024, USA.

KLEIN Zachary, b. 6 July 1948, New Brunswick, New Jersey, USA. Writer. 2 sons. Education: Hillel Academy, Jewish Educational Centre, Mirrer Yeshia; University of Wisconsin. Publications: Still Among the Living, 1990; Two Way Toll, 1991; No Saving Grace, 1994. Honours: Notable Book of 1990, New York Times; Editors Choice, Drood Review. Address: 5 Oakview Terace, Boston, MA 02130, USA.

KLIMA Ivan, b. 14 Sept 1931, Prague, Czechoslovakia. Dramatist; Writer. m. Helena Mala-Klimova, 24 Sept 1958, 1 son, 1 daughter. Education: MA, Charles University, Prague, 1956. Appointments: Editor, publishing, 1958-63, literary weeklies, 1963-69; Visiting Professor, University of Michigan, 1969-70. Publications: The Castle, 1964; Bridegroom for Marcela, 1969; Klara and the Two Men, 1969; The Sweetshop Myriam, 1969; The Master, 1970; The President and the Angel, 1975; The Games, 1985; Kafka and Felice, 1986; The Judge on Trial, 1987; Love and Garbage, 1990; My Golden Trades, 1992. Contributions to: Publications worldwide. Honour: Hostovsky Award, New York, 1985. Memberships: Executive President, Czech PEN Centre, 1990-; Council Member, Czech Writers, 1989-. Address: c/o Adam Bromberg Literary Agency, Stockholm, Sweden.

KLIMOV Jouri Moiseevitch, (Artiom Filatov), b. 15 Oct 1927, Moscow, Russia. Musician. m. Zola Iourievna Bourova, 18 Feb 1958, 2 sons. Education: Diploma, L'Institut Musical d'Etat Gnessina, 1957. Publications: L'Art sur les timbres, Russia & URSS, 1975-77; Catalogue encyklopédique, 1984. Honours: Several medals. Membership: AIJP (Association International Journalist Philatelique). Address: Box 85, Moscow Poste Central , Russia 101000.

KLINE Suzy Weaver, b. 27 Aug 1943, Berkeley, California, USA. Teacher; Children's Author. m. Rufus Kline, 12 Oct 1968, 2 daughters. Education: BA, University of California, Berkeley; Standard Teachers Credential, California State University. Publications: Shhhh!, 1984; Don't Touch, 1985; Herbie Jones, 1985; What's the Matter with Herbie Jones, 1986; Herbie Jones and the Monster Ball, 1988; Horrible Harry in Room 2B, 1988; Ooops, 1988; The Hole Book, 1989; Horrible Harry and the Green Slime, 1989; Horrible Harry and the Ant Invasion, 1989; Herbie Jones and the Hamburger Head, 1989; Orp, 1989; Orp and the Chop Suey Burgers, 1990; Horrible Harry's Secret, 1990; Horrible Harry's Christmas Surprise, 1991; Orp Goes to the Hoop, 1991; Herbie Jones and the Dark Attic, 1992; Herbie Jones Reader's Theater, 1992; Horrible Harry and the Kickball Wedding, 1992; Mary Marony and the Snake, 1992; Mary Marony Hides Out, 1993; Herbie Jones and the Birthday Showdown, 1993; Song Lee in Room 2B, 1993; Who's Orp's

Girlfriend?, 1993; Mary Marony, Mummy Girl, 1994. Address: 124 Hoffman Street, Torrington, CT 06790, USA.

KLINKOWITZ Jerome, b. 24 Dec 1943, Milwaukee, Wisconsin, USA. Author; Professor of English. m. (1) Elaine Plaszynski, 29 Jan 1966, (2) Julie Huffman, 27 May 1978, 1 son, 1 daughter. Education: BA, 1966, MA, 1967, Marquette University; University Fellow, 1968-69, PhD, 1970, University of Wisconsin. Appointments: Assistant Professor, Northern Illinois University, 1969-70; Associate Professor, 1972-75, Professor of English, 1975-, University Distinguished Scholar, 1985-, University of Northern Iowa. Publications: Literary Disruptions, 1975; The Life of Fiction, 1977; The American 1960s, 1980; The Practice of Fiction in America, 1980; Kurt Vonnegut, 1982; Peter Handke and the Postmodern Transformation, 1983; The Self Apparent Word, 1984; Literary Subversions, 1985; The New American Novel of Manners, 1986; Rosenberg/Barthes/Hassan: The Postmodern Habit of Thought, 1988; Short Season and Other Stories, 1988; Their Finest Hours: Narratives of the RAF and Luftwaffe in World War II, 1989; Slaughterhouse-Five: Reinventing the Novel and the World, 1990; Listen: Gerry Mulligan/An Aural Narrative in Jazz, 1991; Donald Barthelme: An Exhibition, 1991; Writing Baseball, 1991; Structuring the Void, 1992; Basepaths, 1995; Yanks Over Europe, 1996; Here at Ogallala State U..,1997; Ahead of the Game, 1997; Vonnegut in Fact, 1997. Contributions to: Over 250 essays to Partisan Review, New Republic, Nation, American Literature; Short stories to North American Review, Chicago Tribune, San Francisco Chronicle. Honours: PEN Syndicated Fiction Prizes, 1984, 1985. Memberships: PEN American Center; Modern Language Association. Address: 1904 Clay Street, Cedar Falls, IA 50613, USA.

KLUBACK William, b. 6 Nov 1927, Brooklyn, New York, USA. Professor of Philosophy. Education: AB, George Washington University; AM, Columbia University; PhD, Hebrew University, Jerusalem. Publications: Paul Valéry, 5 volumes, Vol I, 1987, Vol II, 1993, Vol III, Vol IV, 1996, volume V, 1997; Benjamin Fondane, 1996; Emil Cioran, 1997; Léopold Sédar Senghor, 1997; Juan Ramón Jiménez, 1995.. Contributions to: Midstream; Shofar; Archives de Philosophie. Address: 65 Oriental Boulevard, Apt 8D, Brooklyn, NY 11235, USA.

KLUGER Steve, b. 24 June 1952, Baltimore, Maryland, USA. Writer. Education: University of Southern California, 1971. Publications: Changing Pitches, 1984, 2nd edition, 1990; Lawyers Say the Darndest Things, 1990. Stage Plays: Cafe 50's, 1988-89; James Dean Slept Here, 1989; Pilots of the Purple Twilight, 1989; Jukebox Saturday Night, 1990; Yank: World War II From The Guys Who Brought You Victory, 1990; Bullpen, 1990; Bye Bye Brooklyn, 1997. Films: Once Upon a Crime, 1992; Yankee Doodle Boys, 1996; Bye Bye Brooklyn, 1997; Almost Like Being in Love, 1997. Contributions to: Chicago Tribune; Los Angeles Times; Sports Illustrated; Inside Sports; Diversion; Playboy; Science Digest. Literary Agent: Gail Hochman. Address: c/o Gail Hochman, Brandt & Brandt, 1501 Broadway, Suite 2310, New York, NY 10036, USA.

KNAAK Richard Allen, b. 28 May 1961, Chicago, Illinois, USA. Author. Education: Bachelor's degree (LAS), Rhetoric, University of Illinois. Publications: The Legend of Huma, 1988; Firedrake, 1989; Ice Dragon, 1989; Kaz the Minotaur, 1990; Wolfhelm, 1990; Shadow Steed, 1990; The Shrouded Realm, 1991; Children of the Drake, 1991; Dragon Tome, 1992; The Crystal Dragon, 1993; King of the Grey, 1993; The Dragon Crown, 1994; Frostwing, 1995. Membership: Science Fiction and Fantasy Writers of America. Address: PO Box 8158, Bartlett, IL 60103, USA.

KNASTER Mirka, b. 11 May 1947, Bari, Italy. Writer. Publications: Women in Spanish America From Pre-Conquest to Contemporary Times, 1976; Discovering the Body's Wisdom, 1996. Contributions to: Washington Post; Ladies' Home Journal; East West; Natural Health; Yoga Journal; Massage Therapy Journal; Better Health and Living; Shape; D & B Reports; Honolulu; The Main News; Pleasant Hawaii; Main Inc; America West. Honours: Phi Beta Kappa, 1968; 1st Place, Non-Fiction, Hawaii National Writers Group, 1991; NDEA Title IV Fellowship, 1968-69; Ford Foundation Fellow, 1973-76. Memberships: North Carolina Writers Network. Address: PO Box 7464, Asheville, NC 28802, USA.

KNECHT Robert Jean, b. 20 Sept 1926, London, England. Professor of French History Emeritus. m. (1) Sonia Hodge, 8 Aug 1956, (2) Maureen White, 28 July 1986. Education: BA, 1948, MA,

1953, DLitt, 1984, King's College, London. Publications: The Voyage of Sir Nicholas Carewe, 1959; Francis I and Absolute Monarchy, 1969; The Fronde, 1975; Francis I, 1982; French Renaissance Monarchy, 1984; The French Wars of Religion, 1989; Richelieu, 1991; Renaissance Warrior and Patron, 1994; The Rise and Fall of Renaissance France, 1996. Contributions to: Professional journals and to periodicals. Memberships: Fellow, Royal Historical Society; Chairman, Society of Renaissance Studies, 1989-92; Society for the Study of French History, 1995-; Société de l'Histoire de France. Address: 79 Reddings Road, Moseley, Birmingham B13 8LP, England.

KNEVITT Charles (Philip Paul), b. 10 Aug 1952, Dayton, Ohio, USA (British citizen). Journalist. m. Lucy Joan Isaacs, 4 June 1981, 1 daughter. Education: BA, Honours, School of Architecture, University of Manchester. Appointments: Editor, What's New in Building, 1978-80; Architecture Correspondent, Sunday Telegraph, 1980-84, The Times, 1984-; Architecture and Planning Consultant, Thames News, Thames Television, 1983-86. Publications: Manikata, 1980; Connections, 1984; Monstrous Carbuncles (editor), 1985; Space on Earth, 1985; Perspectives, 1986; Community Architecture (with Nick Wates), 1987; Architectural Anecdotes (editor), 1988. Contributions to: Journals and newspapers. Honours: Commendation, Young Writer of the Year, 1978, Architectural Journalist of the Year, 1984, International Building Press. Memberships: Architecture Club; International Building Press; Fellow, Royal Society of Arts. Address: Crest House, 102-104 Church Road, Teddington, Middlesex, TW11 8PY, England.

KNIGHT Alanna, b. South Shields, Tyne and Wear, England. Novelist; Biographer. m. Alexander Harrow Knight, 2 sons. Appointments: Founder, Chairman, Aberdeen Writers Workshop, 1967; Lecturer, Creative Writing, Workers Educational Association, and Andrews' University Summer School, 1971-75; Tutor, Arvon Foundation, 1982; Secretary, Society of Authors, 1991. Publications: Legend of the Loch, 1969; This Outward Angel, 1971; October Witch, 1971; Castle Clodha, 1972; Lament for Lost Lovers, 1972; White Rose, 1974; A Stranger Came By, 1974; Passionate Kindness, 1974; A Drink for the Bridge, 1976; Black Duchess, 1980; Castle of Foxes, 1981; Colla's Children, 1982; Robert Louis Stevenson Treasury, 1985; The Clan, 1985; Robert Louis Stevenson in the South Seas, 1986; Estella, 1986; Deadly Beloved, 1989; Killing Cousins, 1990; A Quiet Death, 1991; The Bull Slayers, 1995; Murder By Appointment, 1996. Others: Sweet Cheat Gone, 1993; The Outward Angel, 1994; Inspector Faro and the Edinburgh Mysteries, 1994. Non-Fiction: Bright Ring of Words (with E S Warfel), 1994; Inspector Faro's Casebook, 1996. Contributions to: Various publications. Honour: 1st Novel Award, Romantic Novelists Association, 1969. Memberships: Scottish PEN; Committee Member, Crime Writers Association, 1992-95; Radiowriters Association; Romantic Novelists Association; Fellow, Royal Society of Antiquaries, Scotland. Literary Agent: Giles Gordon, Curtis Brown, Haymarket House, 28/29 Haymarket, London SW1Y 4SP, England. Address: 24 March Hall Crescent, Edinburgh EH16 5HL, Scotland.

KNIGHT Arthur Winfield, b. 29 Dec 1937, San Francisco, California, USA. Writer. m. 25 Aug 1976, 1 daughter. Education: AA, Santa Rosa Junior College, 1958; BA, English, 1960, MA, Creative Writing, 1962, San Francisco State University. Appointments: Professor of English, California University of Pennsylvania, 1966-93; Film Critic, Russian River News, Guerneville, 1991-92, Anderson Valley Advertiser, Boonville, California, 1992-, Potpourri, Prairie Village, Kansas, 1993-. Publications: A Marriage of Poets, 1984; King of the Beatniks, 1986; The Beat Vision (co-editor), 1987; Wanted!, 1988; Basically Tender, 1991; Cowboy Poems, 1993, retitled Outlaws, Lawmen and Bad Women; The Darkness Starts Up Where You Stand, 1996; The Secret Life of Jesse James, 1996. Contributions to: New York Quarterly; Poet Lore; Oui; Cape Rock; College English; Massachusetts Review; Redneck Review of Literature; New Frontiers, Vol II. Honour: Winner, 1st Place, 3rd Annual Poetry Competition, Joycean Lively Arts Guild, 1982. Membership: Western Writers of America. Address: PO Box 2580, Petaluma, CA 94953, USA.

KNIGHT Bernard, (Bernard Picton), b. 3 May 1931, Cardiff, Wales. Emeritus Professor of Forensic Pathology; Writer. Education: BMed, BSurg, 1954, Diploma in Medical Jurisprudence, 1966, MD, 1966, FRC, Pathology, 1976, University of Wales. Appointments: Lecturer in Forensic Medicine, University of London, 1959-65; Medical Editor, Medicine, Science and the Law, 1960-63; Lecturer, 1962-65, Senior Lecturer, 1965-76, Reader to Professor and Consultant in Forensic Pathology, College of Medicine, University of Wales, 1976-96; Senior Lecturer in Forensic Pathology, University of

Newcastle, 1965-68; Managing Editor, 1980-92, Pathology Editor, 1992-96, Forensic Science International. Publications: The Lately Deceased, 1963; Thread of Evidence, 1965; Mistress Murder, 1968; Policeman's Progress, 1969; Tiger at Bay, 1970; Murder, Suicide or Accident, 1971; Deg Y Dragwyddoldeb, 1972; Legal Aspects of Medical Practise, 1972, 3rd edition, 1982; In the Dead, 1973; Discovering the Human Body, 1980; Forensic Radiology, 1981; Lawyer's Guide to Forensic Medicine, 1982; Sudden Death in Infancy, 1983; Post-Modern Technicians Handbook, 1984; Pocket Guide to Forensic Medicine, 1985; Simpson's Forensic Medicine, 11th edition, 1996; Forensic Pathology, 1991, 1996; The Estimation of the Time Since Death (editor), 1995. Honour: Commander of the Order of the British Empire, 1993. Memberships: Academi Gymraeg; Crime Writers Association; Welsh Union of Writers. Address: 26 Millwood, Cardiff, CF4 5TL, Wales.

KNIGHT Cranston Sedrick, b. 10 Sept 1950, Chicago, Illinois, USA. Poet. m. Dolores Anderson, 5 Aug 1978, 2 sons, 1 daughter. Education: BA, History, Southern Illinois University, 1977; MA, East Asian and American History, Northeastern Illinois University, 1990. Appointments: Poetry Editor, Eclipses magazine, University of Illinois, 1971; Literary Consultant, Mystic Voyage, 1978-79, B.O.L.T., Southern Illinois University, 1979-80; Editor, C'est la Vie magazine, Northwestern University, 1983-86. Publications: Tour of Duty, 1986; Cadence Magazine, 1986; Samisdat Literary Anthology, 1987; Freedom Song, 1988; Garden of the Beast, 1989; Pearl Magazine Spring, 1989; Wide Open Magazine, 1989. Contributions to: Otherwise Room Anthology; American Poetry Association; Walking Point; Black American Literature Forum; Deros Poetry Magazine; AIM Magazine; Prospective column, Chicago Daily Defender newspaper. Address: 55935 North Magnolia, Apt 1, Chicago, IL 60660, USA.

KNIGHT David. See: PRATHER Richard Scott.

KNIGHT David Marcus, b. 30 Nov 1936, Exeter, England. University Professor. m. Sarah Prideaux, 21 July 1962, 2 sons, 4 daughters. Education: BA Chemistry, 1960, Keble College; Diploma, History and Philosophy of Science, 1962; DPhil, 1964, Oxford University. Appointments: Professor of Philosophy, Durham University; Editor, British Journal of History of Science, 1982-88; General Editor, Cambridge Science Biographies, 1996-. Publications: Zoological Illustration, 1977; The Transcendental Part of Chemistry, 1978; Ordering the World, 1981; Sources for the History of Science, 1984; The Age of Science, 1988; Natural Science Books in English 1600-1900, 1989; A Companion to the Physical Sciences, 1989; Humphry Davy, 1992; Ideas in Chemistry, 1992. Contributions to: Isis; British Journal for the History of Science; Annals of Science; Ambix; Studies in Romanticism. Address: Department of Philosophy, Durham University, 50 Old Elvet, Durham DH1 3HN, England.

KNIGHT Gareth. See: WILBY Basil Leslie.

KNIGHT William Edwards, b. 1 Feb 1922, Tarrytown, New York, USA. US Foreign Service Officer. m. Ruth L Lee, 14 Aug 1946, 2 sons. Education: BA, Yale College, 1942; Pilot Training, US Army Air Force, 1943-44; MA, Yale University, 1946; Industrial College of the Armed Forces, 1961-62; State Department Senior Seminar in Foreign Policy, 1971-72. Appointments:B-24 Co-Pilot, 1944-45; Foreign Service Officer, US Department of State, 1946-75; President and Chief Executive Officer, The Araluen Press, 1992-. Publications: The Tiger Game, 1986; The Bamboo Game, 1993; Footprints in the Sand (light verse), 1995. Contributions to: Various journals and periodicals. Memberships: Washington Independent Writers; Diplomatic and Consular Officers Retired; American Foreign Services Association. Address: Araluen Press, 5000 Park Place, Suite 300, Bethesda, MD 20816, USA.

KNIGHT William Nicholas, b. 18 Apr 1939, Mount Vernon, New York, USA. Professor of English. m. 2 Sep 1961, 1 son, 3 daughters. Education: BA, cum laude, Amherst College, 1961; MA, University of California, Berkeley, 1963; PhD, Indiana University, 1968; Postdoctoral, Institute of Advanced Legal Studies, University of London, 1969-70. Appointments: Wesleyan University, 1966-75; Chairman, Humanities, University of Missouri, Rolla, 1975-. Publications: Death of J K (play), 1969; Shakespeare's Hidden Life, 1974; Law in Spenser, in Spenser Encyclopaedia, Toronto, 1988. Contributions to: Christian Science Monitor; USA Today; Avalon to Camelot; Shakespeare Translation; Review of English Studies; Shakespeare Survey; Erasmus Review; Costerus Essays; American

Legal Studies Association; Reviews, poems, short stories, various small magazines and periodicals. Honours: Scholar, Warburg Institute, University of London, 1969-70; Fellow, Wesleyan Centre for Humanities, 1971; Ford Foundation Fellow, 1972; Newberry Fellow, 1983; Numerous Teaching Awards, Research Grants. Memberships: International Shakespeare Association; Shakespeare Association of America; Spenser Society; Modern Language Association; Missouri Philogical Association. Address: 1313 Whitney Lane, Rolla, MO 65401, USA.

KNIGHTLEY Phillip George, b. 23 Jan 1929, Sydney, Australia. Author; Journalist. m. Yvonne Fernandes, 13 July 1964, 1 son, 2 daughters. Publications: The First Casualty, 1975; The Vestey Affair, 1980; The Second Oldest Profession, 1986; An Affair of State, 1988; Philby: KGB Masterspy, 1989. Honours: British Journalist of the Year, 1980, 1988. Memberships: Society of Authors; National Union of Journalists. Address: 4 Northumberland Place, London W2 5BS, England.

KNOTT Bill. See: KNOTT Will(iam) C(ecil).

KNOTT Will(iam) C(ecil), (Bill Knott), b. 7 Aug 1927, Boston, Massachusetts, USA. Professor of English. Education: AA, 1949; BA, 1951, Boston University; MA, State University of New York, Oswego, 1966. Publications: Circus Catch, 1963; Scatback, 1964; Long Pass, 1966; Night Pursuit, 1966; Junk Pitcher, 1967; Lefty's Long Throw, 1967; High Fly to Center, 1972; Fullback Fury, 1974; The Craft of Fiction, 1974; Taste of Vengeance, 1975; Lyncher's Moon, 1980; Longarm and the Railroaders, 1980; Longarm on the Yellowstone, 1980; Mission Code: King's Pawn, 1981; The Trailsman Series (15 books), 1984-86; The Golden Hawk Series (9 books), 1986-88; The Texan, 1987; Longarm and the Outlaws of Skull Canyon, 1990; Longarm and the Tattoed Lady, 1990. Membership: Western Writers of America, president, 1980-81. Address: 216 Falls of Venice, South Venice, FL 34292, USA.

KNOWLING Michael John, b. 26 Apr 1953, Edinburgh, Scotland. College Principal; Journalist; Editor. Education: MA, with honours, University of Glasgow, 1975; Master of Letters, University of New England, 1987. Appointments: Editor, Northern Newspapers Ltd, New South Wales, 1981-88; College Principal. Publications: Collins Concise Encyclopaedia, 1977; Race Relations in Australia: A History, 1982; University of New England Gazette, 1990-92. Honour: Association of Rhodes Scholars in Australia Scholarship, England-Australia, 1977. Memberships: Media, Entertainment and Arts Alliance; International Federation of Journalists; Australian and New Zealand Communication Association; Australian Rhodes Scholars Association. Address: PO Box 503, Armidale, New South Wales 2350, Australia.

KNOX Elizabeth, b. 15 Feb 1959, Wellington, New Zealand. Novelist. m. Fergus Barrowman, 1989. Education: BA, Victoria University, Wellington, 1986. Appointment: Lecturer, Film Studies, Victoria University, 1989. Publications: After Z Hour, 1987; Paremata, 1989. Short Stories: The Sword, 1990; After Images, 1990; Post Mortem, 1990; Afraid, 1991; Take as Prescribed, 1991. Honours: ICI Bursary, 1988; Pen Award, 1988, Fellowship, 1991. Address: PO Box 11-806 Wellington, New Zealand.

KNOX William, (Michael Kirk, Bill Knox, Robert MacLeod, Noah Webster), b. 20 Feb 1928, Glasgow, Scotland. Author; Journalist. m. Myra Ann Mackill, 31 Mar 1950, 1 son, 2 daughters. Appointments: Deputy News Editor, Evening News, 1957; Scottish Editor, Kemsley Newspapers, 1957-60; News Editor, Scottish Television, 1960-62; Freelance author and broadcaster 1962-; Presenter, STV Crimedesk, 1977-89; Editor, RNLI Scottish Lifeboat, 1984-. Publications: Over 60 novels of crime, sea and adventure; also radio and television adaptations of own work. Honours: William Knox Collection established, Boston University, 1969; Police Review Award, 1986; Paul Harris Fellow, Rotary International, 1989. Memberships: Association of Scottish Motoring Writers; Society of Authors; Crime Writers Association; Mystery Writers Association. Address: 55 Newtonlea Avenue, Newton Mearns, Glasgow G77 5QF, Scotland.

KNOX-JOHNSTON Robin, b. 17 Mar 1939, Putney, London, England. Master Mariner; Author. m. 6 Jan 1962, 1 daughter. Education: Master's Certificate, 1965. Publications: A World of My Own, 1969; Sailing, 1974; Twilight of Sail, 1978; Last But Not Least, 1978; Seamanship, 1986; The BOC Challenge 1986-87, 1987; The

Cape of Good Hope, 1989; The History of Yachting, 1990; The Colombus Venture, 1991; Sea Ice Rock (with Chris Bonington), 1992; Cape Horn, 1994; Beyond Jules Verne, 1995. Contributions to: Yachting Monthly; Cruising World; Guardian. Honours: Commander of the Order of the British Empire 1969; Honorary DSc, Maine Maritime Academy; Honorary Doctor of Technology, Nottingham Trent University, 1993; Knight Bachelor, 1995. Memberships: Younger Brother, Trinity House; Honourable Company of Master Mariners; Royal Geographical Society, fellow; National Maritime Museum, Greenwich; Sail Training Association. Address: St Francis Cottage, Torbryan, Newton Abbot, Devon TQ12 5UR.

KNOX-MAWER June Ellis, b. 10 May 1930, Wrexham, North Wales. Writer; Broadcaster. m. Ronald Knox-Mawer, 30 June 1951, 1 son, 1 daughter. Education: Grove Park Girls Grammar School, Wrexham, 1941-47. Appointments: Trained as Journalist, Chester Chronicle, 1948-50; Aden Correspondent, Daily Express, 1952-56; Presenter and Author, various literary and feature programmes, Womans Hour (BBC Radio 4), 1970-. Publications: The Sultans Came to Tea, 1961; A Gift of Islands, 1965; A World of Islands, 1968; Marama, 1972; A South Sea Spell, 1975; Tales from Paradise, 1986; Marama of the Islands, 1986; Sandstorm, 1991; The Shadow of Wings, 1995. Contributions to: Guardian; Various women's magazines. Honour: Romantic Novel of the Year Award, 1992. Memberships: Royal Commonwealth Society; Commonwealth Trust. Address: c/o David Higham Associates, 5-8 Lower John Street, Golden Square, London W1, England.

KNUDSON R(ozanne) R, b. 1 June 1932, Washington, DC, USA. Writer. Education: BA, Brigham Young University, 1954; MA, University of Georgia, 1958; PhD, Stanford University, 1967. Publications: Selected Objectives in the English Language Arts (with Arnold Lazarus), 1967; Sports Poems (editor with P K Ebert), 1971; Zanballer, 1972; Jesus Song, 1973; You Are the Rain, 1974; Fox Running, 1974; Zanbanger, 1977; Zanboomer, 1978; Weight Training for the Young Athlete (with F Colombo), 1978; Starbodies (with F Colombo), 1978; Rinehart Lifts, 1980; Just Another Love Story, 1982; Speed, 1982; Muscles, 1982; Punch, 1982; Zan Hagen's Marathon, 1984; Babe Didrikson, 1985; Frankenstein's 10 K, 1985; Martina Navratilova, 1986; Rinehart Shouts, 1986; Julie Brown, 1987; American Sports Poems (editor with May Swenson), 1987; The Wonderful Pen of May Swenson, 1993. Address: 73 Boulevard, Sea Cliff, NY 11579, USA.

KOCH Christopher John, b. 16 July 1932, Hobart, Tasmania, Australia. Author. m. Irene Vilnonis, 23 Apr 1960, 1 son. Education: BA Hons; DLitt, University of Tasmania. Publications: The Boys in the Island, 1958; Across the Sea Wall, 1965; The Doubleman, 1965; The Year of Living Dangerously, 1978. Essays: Crossing the Gap, 1987. Honours: National Book Council Award for Australian Literature, 1979; Miles Franklin Prize, 1985. Address: PO Box 19, Paddington, New South Wales 2021, Australia.

KOCH Joanne (Barbara), (Joanna Z Adams), b. 28 Mar 1941, Chicago, Illinois, USA. Author; Dramatist. m. Lewis Z Koch, 30 May 1964, 1 son, 2 daughters. Education: BA, Honours, Cornell University; MA, Columbia University. Appointments: Guest Lecturer, Loyola University, DePaul University; Writer-in-Residence, Lake Forest College, Southern Illinois University; Syndicated Columnist, Newspaper Enterprise Association. Publications: The Marriage Savers (with Lewis Z Koch), 1976; Makeovers (novel), 1987; Rushes (novel), 1988. Other: Various plays. Contributions to: Newspapers and magazines. Honours: Various awards. Memberships: Dramatists Guild; Phi Beta Kappa; Phi Kappa Phi; Society of Midland Authors; Women in film; Women in Theatre. Address: 343 Dodge Avenue, Evanston, IL 60202, USA.

KOCH Kenneth (Jay), b. 27 Feb 1925, Cincinnati, Ohio, USA. Professor of English; Poet; Dramatist; Writer. m. (1) Mary Janice Elwood, 1955, 1 daughter, (2) Karen Steinbrink, 1994. Education: AB, Harvard University, 1948; MA, 1953, PhD, 1959, Columbia University. Appointments: Lecturer, Rutgers University, 1953-54, 1955-56, 1957-58, Brooklyn College, 1957-59; Director, Poetry Workshop, New School for Social Research, New York City, 1958-66; Lecturer, 1959-61, Assistant Professor, 1962-66, Associate Professor, 1966-71, Professor of English, 1971-, Columbia University; Associated with Locus Solus magazine, Lansen-Vercours, France, 1960-62. Publications: Poetry; Poems, 1953; Ko, or, A Season on Earth, 1960; Permanently, 1960; Thank You and Other Poems, 1962; Poems from

1952 and 1953, 1968; When the Sun Tries to Go On, 1969; Sleeping with Women, 1969; The Pleasures of Peace and Other Poems, 1969; Penguin Modern Poets 24 (with Kenward Elmslie and James Schuyler), 1973; The Art of Love, 1975; The Duplications, 1977; The Burning Mystery of Anna in 1951, 1979; From the Air, 1979; Days and Nights, 1982; Selected Poems 1950-1982, 1985; On the Edge, 1986; Seasons on Earth, 1987; One Train, 1994; On the Great Atlantic Rainway: Selected Poems 1950-1988, 1994. Plays: Bertha and Other Plays, 1966; A Change of Hearts: Plays, Films, and Other Dramatic Works 1951-1971, 1973; One Thousand Avant-Garde Plays, 1988. Fiction: Interlocking Lives (with Alex Katz), 1970; The Red Robins, 1975; Hotel Lambosa, 1993. Editor: Sleeping on the Wing: An Anthology of Modern Poetry, with Essays on Reading and Writing (with Kate Farrell), 1981; Talking to the Sun: An Illustrated Anthology of Poems for Young People (with Kate Farrell), 1985. Honours: Fulbright Fellowships, 1950, 1978; Guggenheim Fellowship, 1961; National Endowment for the Arts Grant, 1966; Ingram Merrill Foundation Fellowship, 1969; Harbison Award for Teaching, 1970; Frank O'Hara Prize, 1973; National Institute of Arts and Letters Award, 1976; Award of Merit for Poetry, American Academy of Arts and Letters, 1986; Bollingen Prize for Poetry, 1995; Rebekah Johnson Bobbitt National Prize for Poetry, 1996. Address: 25 Claremont Avenue, Apt 2-B, New York, NY 10027, USA.

KOCH Klaus, b. 4 Oct 1926, Sulzbach, Thüringen, Germany. University Professor. m. Eva-Maria Koch, 28 Mar 1978. Education: Universities of Heidelberg, Mainz and Tübingen, 1945-50; Dr theol, University of Heidelberg, 1953; Habilitation, University of Erlangen, 1956; Dr Theol hc, University of Rostock, 1996. Appointments: Assistant, University of Heidelberg, 1950; Pastor, Lutheran Church, Jena, 1954; Dozent, Old Testament, University of Erlangen, 1956; Dozent, University of Hamburg, 1957; Professor, Old Testament, Kirchliche Hochschule, Wuppertal, 1960; Professor, Old Testament, History of Ancient Near Eastern Religions, University of Hamburg, 1962-; Professor Emeritus, 1991. Publications: Was ist Formgeschichte?, 1964, 5th edition, 1989; Ratlos vor der Apokalyptik, 1970, English translation as The Rediscovery of Apocalyptic, 1972; Die Profeten I, Assyrische Zeit, 1978, 3rd edition, 1995, English translation as The Prophets I, 1982; Die Profeten II, Babylonisch-Persische Zeit, 1980, 2nd edition 1988, English translation as The Prophets II, 1984; Spuren des hebraeischen Denkens, Gesammelte Aufsaetze I, 1991; Geschichte der aegyptischen Religion, 1993. Contributions to: 80 scholarly journals. Memberships: Joachim-Jurgius Gesellschaft der Wissenchaften, Hamburg; Wissenschaftliche Gesellschaft für Theologie. Address: Diekbarg 13 A, D-22397 Hamburg, Germany.

KOELB Clayton, b. 12 Nov 1942, New York, New York, USA. Educator. m. Susan J Noakes, 1 Jan 1979, 1 son, 1 daughter. Education: BA, 1964, MA, 1966, PhD, 1970, Harvard University. Appointments: Assistant Professor, Associate Professor, Professor of German and Comparative Literature, 1969-91, Chairman, Department of Germanic Languages, 1978-82, University of Chicago; Visiting Professor, Purdue University, 1984-85, Princeton University, 1985-86; Visiting Eugene Falk Professor, 1990, Guy B Johnson Professor, 1991-, Chairman, Department of Germanic Languages, 1997-, University of North Carolina, Chapel Hill. Publications: The Incredulous Reader, 1984; Thomas Mann's Goethe and Tolstoy, 1984; The Current in Criticism, 1987; Inventions of Reading, 1988; The Comparative Perspective on Literature, 1988; Kafka's Rhetoric, 1989; Nietzsche as Postmodernist, 1990; Thomas Mann's Death in Venice: A Critical Edition, 1994. Contributions to: Professional journals. Honours: Germanistic Society of America, Fellow, 1964-65; Danforth Foundation Fellow, 1965-69; Woodrow Wilson Foundation Fellow, 1965; Susan Anthony Potter Prize, Harvard University, 1970; Guggenheim Foundation Fellow, 1993-94. Memberships: Modern Language Association of America; International Association for Philosophy and Literature; Semiotics Society of America; Kafka Society of America. Address: University of North Carolina, 414 Dey Hall, Chapel Hill, NC 27599, USA.

KOESTENBAUM Wayne, b. 20 Sept 1958, San Jose, California, USA. Teacher; Poet. Education: BA, Harvard University, 1980; MA, Johns Hopkins University, 1981; PhD, Princeton University, 1988. Appointment: Faculty, Yale University, 1988-. Publications: Double Talk, 1990; Ode to Anna Moffo and Other Poems, 1990; The Queen's Throat, 1993; Rhapsodies of a Repeat Offender, 1994. Address: c/o Department of English, Yale University, New Haven, CT 06520, USA.

KOGAN Norman, b. 15 June 1919, Chicago, Illinois, USA. Professor Emeritus of Political Science. m. Meryl Reich, 18 May 1946, 2 sons. Education: BA, 1940, PhD, 1949, University of Chicago. Appointments: University of Connecticut, 1949-88; Visiting Professorships, University of Rome, Italy, 1973, 1979, 1987. Publications: Italy and the Allies, 1956; The Government of Italy, 1962; The Politics of Italian Foreign Policy, 1963; A Political History of Postwar Italy, 1966; Storia Politica dell' Italia Repubblicana, 1982, 2nd edition, revised and expanded, 1990; A Political History of Italy: The Postwar Years, 1983. Contributions to: Yale Law Journal; Il Ponte; Western Political Quarterly; Journal of Politics; Comparative Politics; Indiana Law Journal. Address: 7 Eastwood Road, Storrs, CT 06268, USA.

KOGAWA Joy (Nozomi), b. 6 June 1935, Vancouver, British Columbia, Canada. Writer; Poet. m. David Kogawa, 2 May 1957, div 1968, 1 son, 1 daughter. Education: University of Alberta, 1954; Anglican Women's Training College, 1956; University of Saskatchewan, 1968. Appointment: Writer-in-Residence, University of Ottawa, 1978. Publications: Poetry: The Splintered Moon, 1967; A Choice of Dreams, 1974; Jericho Road, 1977; Woman in the Woods, 1985; The Rain Ascends, 1995. Fiction: Obasan, 1981; Naomi's Road, 1986; Itsuka, 1992. Contributions to: Canadian Forum; Chicago Review; Prism International; Quarry; Queen's Quarterly; West Coast Review; Others. Honours: First Novel Award, Books in Canada, 1982; Book of the Year Award, Canadian Authors Association, 1982; American Book Award, Before Columbus Foundation, 1982; Best Paperback Award, Periodical Distributors, 1982; Notable Book Citation, American Library Association, 1982; Order of Canada. Memberships: Director, Canadian Civil Liberties Association; Patron, Canadian Tribute to Human Rights; PEN International; Writers Union of Canada. Literary Agent: Lee Davis. Address: c/o Writers Union of Canada, 24 Ryerson, Toronto, Ontario M5T 2P3, Canada.

KOHUT Thomas August, b. 11 Mar 1950, Chicago, Illinois, USA. Professor of History. m. Susan Neeld Kohut, 21 June 1975, 1 son, 1 daughter. Education: BA, Oberlin College, 1972; PhD History, University of Minnesota, 1983; Graduate, Cincinnati Psychoanalytic Institute, 1984. Appointments: Assistant Professor 1989-90, Associate Professor of History 1990-95, Full Professor of History 1995-, Sue and Edgar Wachenheim III Professor of History 1995-, Williams College, Williamstown, MA. Publications: Wilhelm II and the Germans: A Study in Leadership, 1991. Contributions to: Professional journals. Memberships: American Historical Association; Suman Studies Association. Address: Department of History, Williams College, Williamstown, MA 01267, USA.

KOLAKOWSKI Leszek, b. 23 Oct 1927, Radom, Poland. Academic. m. Tamera Dynenson, 19 Nov 1949, 1 daughter. Education: MA, Lodz University, 1950; PhD, Warsaw University, 1953. Publications: Individual and Infinity, 1959; Chrietieus sans eglise, 1969; Main Currents of Marxism, 1978; Religion, 1982; Metaphysical Horror, 1988. Contributions to: Many magazines, newspapers and journals in Britain, Poland, France, Germany and Italy. Honours: Friedenpreis des Deutschen Bouchhandels, 1977; Erasmus Prize, 1982; Prix Europa d'Essai; Jefferson Award, 1985; McArthur Fellowship, 1985. Memberships: Polish Writers Association; PEN Club; British Academy; International Institute of Philosophy; American Academy of Arts and Sciences; Philosophical Societies in Oxford and in Poland. Address: 77 Hamilton Road, Oxford OX2 7QA, England.

KOLLER James, b. 30 May 1936, Oak Park, Illinois, USA. Writer; Artist. div, 2 sons, 4 daughters. Education: BA, North Central College, Naperville, Illinois, 1958. Publications: Poetry: Two Hands, 1965; Brainard and Washington Street Poems, 1965; The Dogs and Other Dark Woods, 1966; Some Cows, 1966; I Went To See My True Love, 1967; California Poems, 1971; Bureau Creek, 1975; Poems for the Blue Sky, 1976; Messages-Botschaften, 1977; Andiamo, 1978; O Didn't He Ramble-O ware er nicht unhergezogen, 1981; Back River, 1981; One Day at a Time, 1981; Great Things Are Happening-Grossartoge Dige passieren, 1984; Give the Dog a Bone, 1986; Graffiti Lyriques (with Franco Beltrametti), graphics and texts, 1987; Openings, 1987; Fortune, 1987; Roses Love Sunshine, 1989; This Is What He Said, graphics and texts, 1991. Prose: Messages, 1972; Working Notes 1960-82, 1985; Gebt dem alten Hund'nen Knochen (Essays, Gedichte and Prosa 1959-85), 1986; The Natural Order, essay and graphics, 1990. Fiction: If You Don't Like Me You Can Leave Me Alone, UK edition, 1974, US edition, 1976; Shannon

Who Was Lost Before, 1975. Address: PO Box 629, Brunswick, ME 04011, USA.

KOLM Ronald Akerson, b. 21 May 1947, Pittsburgh, Pennsylvania, USA. Writer; Editor; Publisher. m. Donna Sterling, 5 Sept 1984, 2 sons. Education: BA, Albright College, 1970. Publications: Plastic Factory, 1989; Welcome to the Barbecue, 1990; Suburban Ambush, 1991; Rank Cologne, 1991. Contributions to: Cover Magazine; Appearances Magazine; New Observations; Semiotext(e); Red Tape. Address: 30-73 47th Street, Long Island City, NY 11103, USA.

KOMUNYAKAA Yusef, (James Willie Brown Jr), b. 29 Apr 1947, Bogalusa, Louisiana, USA. Professor of Creative Writing; Poet. m. Mandy Sayer, 1985. Education: BA, University of Colorado, 1975; MA, Colorado State University, 1979; MFA, University of California at Irvine, 1980. Appointments: Visiting Professor 1985, Associate Professor of Afro-American Studies 1987-96, Indiana University; Professor of Creative Writing, Princeton University, 1997-; Many poetry readings. Publications: Dedications and Other Darkhorses, 1977; Lost in the Bonewheel Factory, 1979; Copacetic, 1984; I Apologize for the Eyes in My Head, 1986; Dien Cai Dau, 1988; The Jazz Poetry Anthology (editor with Sascha Feinstein), 1991; Magic City, 1992; Neon Vernacular: New and Selected Poems, 1993. Contributions to: Anthologies and periodicals. Honours: Pulitzer Prize in Poetry, 1994; Kingsley Tufts Poetry Award, 1994. Address: c/o Department of English, Princeton University, Princeton, NJ 08544, USA.

KONER Pauline, b. 26 June 1912, New York, New York, USA. Choreographer; Writer; Lecturer; Teacher. m. 23 May 1939. Education: Columbia University, 1928; Professional Training with Michel Fokine, Michio Ito and Angel Cansino. Publications: Solitary Song: An Autobiography, 1989; Elements of Performance, 1993. Essays: The Truth about The Moor's Pavane, 1966; Intrinsic Dance, 1966; Pauline Koner Speaking, 1966. Contributions to: Dance Magazine; Ballet Review; Dance Chronicle. Honours: Dance Magazine Award, 1963; Honorary Doctorate of Fine Arts, Rhode Island College, 1985; Special Citation, De La Torre Bueno Award, 1989. Membership: American Dance Guild. Address: 263 West End Avenue, 9F, New York, NY 10023, USA.

KONING Hans, b. 12 Jul 1924, Amsterdam, Netherlands. Writer. m. Kathleen Scanlon, 1 son, 3 daughters. Education: Universities of Amsterdam, Zurich and Paris-Sorbonne. Publications: The Affair, 1958; A Walk With Love and Death, 1960; The Revolutionary, 1967; Death of a Schoolboy, 1974; A New Yorker in Egypt, 1976; The Kleber Flight, 1981; America Made Me, 1983; DeWitt's War, 1983; Acts of Faith, 1986; Nineteen Sixty-Eight, A Report, 1987. Contributions to: New Yorker; Nation; Atlantic Monthly. Honours: National Endowment for the Arts Award, 1978; Connecticut Arts Award, 1980. Address: c/o The Lantz Office, 888 Seventh Avenue, New York, NY 10106, USA.

KONOPINSKI Lech (Kazimierz), b. 16 Mar 1931, Poznan, Poland. Writer; Journalist; Composer. m. Hanna Zapytowska, 26 July 1956, 1 son, 1 daughter. Education: MA, Higher School of Economics, 1955; PhD, University of Lodz, 1973. Appointment: Columnist for various journals, 1954-. Publications: Many books for adults and children, plays, and songs. Honours: Golden Book Award, 1971; Golden Ring Awards, 1973, 1980. Memberships: Association International des Journalistes Philateliques; Polish Authors and Composers Association; Polish Philatelists Association; Polish Writers Association. Address: ul Michalowska 18 m 3, PL 60 645, Poznan, Poland.

KOONTZ Dean R, (David Axton, Brian Coffey, K R Dwyer), b. 9 July 1945, Everett, Pennsylvania, USA. Novelist; Screenwriter. m. Gerda Ann Cerra, 15 Oct 1966. Education: BS, Shippensburg University, 1966. Publications: Whispers, 1980; Phantoms, 1983; Darkness Comes, (in USA as Darkfall), 1984; Strangers, 1986; Watchers, 1987; Twilight Eyes, 1987; Lightning, 1988; Midnight, 1989; The Bad Place, 1990; Mr Murder, 1993; Dark Rivers of the Heart, 1994; Strange Highways, 1995; Intensity, 1996. Contributions to: Numerous journals and magazines. Honours: Daedalus Award, 1988; Honorary Doctor of Letters, Shippenburg University, 1989. Address: PO Box 9529, Newport Beach, CA 92658, USA.

KOOSER Ted, (Theodore Kooser), b. 25 Apr 1939, Ames, Iowa, USA. Poet; Teacher; Company Vice-President. m. (1) Diana Tresslar, 1962, div 1969, 1 son, (2) Kathleen Rutledge, 1977.

Education: BS, Iowa State University, 1962; MA, University of Nebraska, 1968. Appointments: Underwriter, Bankers Life Nebraska, 1965-73; Part-Time Instructor in Creative Writing, University of Nebraska, 1970-; Senior Underwriter, 1973-84, Vice-President, 1984-, Lincoln Benefit Life. Publications: Poetry: Official entry Blank, 1969; Grass County, 1971; Twenty Poems, 1973; A Local Habitation, and a Name, 1974; Shooting a Farmhouse: So This is Nebraska, 1975; Not Coming to be Barked At, 1976; Hatcher, 1978; Old Marriage and New, 1978; Cottonwood County (with William Kloefkorn), 1979; Sure Signs: New and Selected Poems, 1980; One World at a Time, 1985; The Blizzard Voices, 1986; Weather Central, 1994. Editor: The Windflower Home Almanac of Poetry, 1980; As Far as I Can See: Contemporary Writers of the Middle Plains, 1989. Honours: Prairie Schooner Prizes, 1975, 1978; National Endowment for the Arts Fellowships, 1976, 1984; Poetry Award, Society of Midland Authors, 1980; Stanley Kunitz Prize, 1984; Governor's Art Award, Nebraska, 1988; Richard Hugo Prize, 1994. Address: Route 1, Box 10, Garland, NE 68360, USA.

KOPS Bernard, b. 28 Nov 1926, London, England. Novelist. m. Erica Gordon, 1956. Appointments: Lecturer, Spiro Institute, 1985-86, Surrey, Ealing, Inner London Education Authorities, 1989-90, City Literary Institute, London, 1991. Publications: Awake for Mourning, 1958; Motorbike, 1962; Yes From No Man's Land, 1965; By the Waters of Whitechapel, 1970; The Passionate Past of Gloria Gaye, 1971; Settle Down Simon Katz, 1973; Partners, 1975; On Margate Sands, 1978. Plays: The Hamlet of Stepney Green, 1958; Goodbye World, 1959; Change for the Angel, 1960; Stray Cats and Empty Bottles, 1961; Enter Solly Gold, 1962; The Boy Who Wouldn't Play Jesus, 1965; More Out than In, 1980; Ezra, 1981; Simon at Midnight, 1982; Some of these Days, 1990; Sophie, Last of the Red Hot Mamas, 1990; Playing Sinatra, 1991; Androcles and the Lion, 1992; Dreams of Anne Frank, 1992; Who Shall I be Tomorrow?, 1992; Call in the Night, 1995; Green Rabbi, 1997. Other: Radio and Television plays; Verse Collections. Honours: Arts Council Bursaries; C Day-Lewis Fellowship, 1981-83; Writers Guild Award, Best Radio Play, 1995. Address: 35 Canfield Gardens, Flat 1, London NW6, England.

KORDA Michael (Vincent), b. 8 Oct 1933, London, England. Writer; Editor. m. (1) Carolyn Keese, 16 Apr 1958, div, 1 son, (2) Margaret Mogford. Education: BA, Magdalene College, Cambridge, 1958. Appointments: Editorial Assistant to Editor-in-Chief, Simon & Schuster Inc, New York City, 1958-. Publications: Male Chauvinism! How it Works, 1973; Power! How to Get It, How to Use It, 1975; Success!, 1977; Charmed Lives: A Family Romance, 1979; Worldly Goods, 1982; Queenie, 1985; The Fortune, 1988; Curtain, 1991. Contributions to: Periodicals. Address: c/o Simon & Schuster Inc, 1230 Avenue of the Americas, New York, NY 10020, USA.

KORFIS Tasos. See: ROMBOTIS Anastasios.

KORG Jacob, b. 21 Nov 1922, New York, New York, USA. Professor of English Emeritus; Writer. Education: BA, City College of New York, 1943; MA, 1947, PhD, 1952, Columbia University. Appointments: Bard College, 1948-50; City College, 1950-55; Assistant to Associate Professor, 1955-65, Professor of English, 1965-91, Professor Emeritus, 1991-, University of Washington, Seattle. Publications: Westward to Oregon (editor with S F Anderson), 1958; Thought in Prose (editor with R S Beal), 1958, 3rd edition, 1966; An Introduction to Poetry, 1959; London in Dickens's Day (editor), 1960; The Complete Reader (editor with R S Beal), 1961; George Gissing's Commonplace Book (editor), 1962; George Gissing: A Critical Biography, 1963; Dylan Thomas, 1965, updated edition, 1991; The Force of Few Words, 1966; Twentieth Century Interpretations of Bleak House (editor), 1968; The Poetry of Robert Browning (editor), 1971; George Gissing: Thyrza (editor), 1974; George Gissing: The Unclassed (editor), 1978; Language in Modern Literature, 1979, updated edition, 1992; Browning and Italy, 1983; Ritual and Experiment in Modern Poetry, 1995. Contributions to: Professional journals. Memberships: International Association of University Professors of English; Modern Language Association; Association of Literary Scholars and Critics. Address: 6530 51st Street North East, Seattle, WA 98115, USA.

KORMONDY Edward (John), b. 10 June 1926, Beacon, New York, USA. Professor of Biology (retired); Writer. Education: BA, Tusculum College, 1950; MS, 1951, PhD, 1955, University of Michigan. Appointments: Assistant Professor to Professor of Biology, Oberlin College, 1957-68; Director, Commission on Undergraduate Education in the Biological Sciences and the Office of Biological Education, American Institute of Biological Sciences, 1968-71; Faculty, 1971-79, Interim Acting Dean, 1972-73, Vice-President and Provost, 1973-78, Evergreen State College, Olympia, Washington; Senior Professional Associate, National Science Foundation, 1979; Provost and Professor of Biology, University of Southern Maine, Portland, 1979-82; Vice-President for Academic Affairs and Professor of Biology, California State University, Los Angeles, 1982-86; Senior Vice-President, Chancellor, and Professor of Biology, University of Hawaii at Hilo and at West Oahu, 1986-93; President, University of West Los Angeles, 1995-97. Publications: Introduction to Genetics, 1964; Readings in Ecology (editor), 1965; Readings in General Biology (editor), 2 volumes, 1966; Concepts of Ecology, 1969, 4th edition, 1996; Population and Food (editor with Robert Leisner), 1971; Pollution (editor with Robert Leisner), 1971; Ecology (editor with Robert Leisner), 1971; General Biology: The Natural History and Integrity of Organisms (with others), 1977; Handbook of Contemporary Developments in World Ecology (with F McCormick), 1981; Environmental Sciences: The Way the World Works (with B Nebell), 1981, 2nd edition, 1987; Biology (with B Essenfield), 1984, 2nd edition, 1988; International Handbook of Pollution Control, 1989; Fundamentals of Human Ecology (with D Brown), 1998. Contributions to: Professional journals. Address: 1388 Lucile Avenue, Los Angeles, CA 90026, USA.

KORNFELD Robert Jonathan, b. 3 Mar 1919, Newtonville, Massaachusetts, USA. Author; Playwright. m. Celia Seiferth, 23 Aug 1945, 1 son. Education: AB, Harvard University, 1941; Also attended Columbia University, Tulane University, New York University, New School, Circle-in-the-Square School of Theatre, Playwrights Horizons Theatre School and Laboratory. Appointments: Co-chair, Literary Committee, National Arts Club; Member, Freedom-to-Write Committee, PEN; Board Member, Bronx Arts Ensemble. Publications: Plays: Great Southern Mansions, 1977; A Dream Within a Dream, 1987; Landmarks of the Bronx, 1990; Music for Saint Nicholas, 1992; Hot Wind from the South, 1995; The Hanged Man, 1996; Works performed at Lincoln Center, New York, Theater for the New City, New York; Southern repertory Theatre, New Orleans; Playwrights Center of San Francisco; University of Wisconsin Theater, Milwaukee; Numerous others. Honours: Numerous awards and Prizes; Visiting Artist, American in Rome, 1996. Memberships: Dramatists Guild; New York Drama League. Address: 5286 Sycamore Avenue, Riverdale, NY 10471, USA.

KORZENIK Diana, b. 15 Mar 1941, New York, New York, USA. College Educator. Education: Oberlin College; BA, Vassar College; Master's Programme, Columbia University; EdD, Graduate School of Education, Harvard University. Appointments: Professor Emerita, Massachusetts College of Art, Boston. Publications: Art and Cognition, 1977; Drawn to Art, 1986; Art Making and Education (with Maurice Brown), 1993. Contributions to: Professional journals and to magazines. Membership: Friends of Longfellow House, president. Address: 7 Norman Road, Newton Highlands, MA 02161, USA.

KOSTELANETZ Richard (Cory), b. 14 May 1940, New York, New York, USA. Writer; Poet; Critic; Artist; Composer. Education: AB (honours), Brown University, 1962; Graduate Studies, King's College, London, 1964-65; MA, Columbia University, 1966; Study in music and theatre, Morley College, London, and New School for Social Research, New York. Appointments: Co-Founder-President, Assembling Press, New York, 1970-82; Literary Director, Future Press, New York, 1976-; Co-Editor-Publisher, Precisely: A Critical Magazine, 1977-84; Sole Proprietor, R K Editions, New York, 1978-; Coordinator-Interviewer, American Writing Today: Voice of America Forum Series, 1979-81; Contributing Editor to various journals; Guest lecturer and reader at many colleges and universities; Numerous exhibitions as an artist. Publications: Poetry: Visual Language, 1970; I Articulations/Short Fictions, 1974; Portraits From Memory, 1975; Numbers: Poems and Stories, 1976; Rain Rains Rain, 1976; Illuminations, 1977; Numbers Two, 1977; Richard Kostelanetz, 1980; Turfs/Arenas/Fields/Pitches, 1980; Arenas/Fields/Pitches/Turfs, 1982; Fields/Pitches/Turfs/Arenas, 1990; Solos, Duets, Trios, and Choruses, 1991; Wordworks: Poems Selected and New, 1993. Fiction: In the Beginning, novel, 1971; Constructs I, 1975; II, 1978, III, 1991, IV, 1991, V, 1991, VI, 1991; One Night Stood, novel, 1977; Tabula Rasa: A Constructivist Novel, 1978; Exhaustive Parallel Intervals, novel, 1979; Fifty Untitled Constructivist Fictions, 1991; Many others. Non-Fiction: Recyclings: A Literary Autobiogrphy, 2 volumes, 1974, 1984; The End of Intelligent Writing: Literary Politics in America, 1974; Metamorphosis in the Arts, 1980; The Old Poetries and the New, 1981; The Grants-Fix: Publicly Funded Literary Granting in America, 1987; The Old Fictions and the New,

1987; On Innovative Music(ians), 1989; Unfinished Business: An Intellectual Nonhistory, 1990; The New Poetries and Some Old, 1991; Published Encomia, 1967-91, 1991; On Innovative Art(ist)s, 1992; On Innovative Performance(s), 1994; The Fillmore East: 25 Years After: Recollections of Rock Theatre, 1995; Many others. Editor: American Writing Today, 2 vols, 1981, revised edition, 1991; The Avant-Garde Tradition in Literature, 1982; Gertrude Stein Advanced: An Anthology of Criticism, 1990; The Dictionary of the Avant-Gardes, 1993; Many others; Other: Films; Videotapes; Radio Scripts; Recordings. Contributions to: Many anthologies; Numerous poems, articles, essays, reviews, in journals and other publications. Honours: Woodrow Wilson Fellowship, 1962-63; Fulbright Fellowship, 1964-65; Pulitzer Fellowship, 1965-66; Guggenheim Fellowship, 1967; 1 of Best Books, American Institute of Graphic Arts, 1976; Many National Endowment for the Arts Grants; Pushcart Prize, 1977; Deutscher Akademischer Austauschdienst Stipend, Berlin, 1981-83; American Society of Composers, Authors, and Publishers Awards, 1983-91; Phi Beta Kappa; Many others. Memberships: American PEN; American Society of Composers, Authors, and Publishers; Artist Equity; International Association of Art Critics; National Writers Union; Others. Address: PO Box 444, Prince Street Station, New York, NY 10012, USA.

KOTZ Nathan K, (Nick), b. 16 Sept 1932, San Antonio, Texas, USA. Journalist; Author; Educator. m. Mary Lynn Booth, 7 Aug 1960, 1 son. Education: BA magna cum laude, International Relations, Dartmouth College, 1955; London School of Economics, England, 1955-56. Appointments: Reporter, Des Moines Register, 1958-64; Washington Correspondent, Des Moines Register and Minneapolis Tribune, 1964-70; National Correspondent, The Washington Post, 1970-73; Author, Freelance Journalist, 1973-; Adjunct Professor, American University School of Communication, 1978-87; Senior Journalist in Residence, Duke University, 1983. Publications: Let Them Eat Promises: The Politics of Hunger in America, 1970; The Unions (co-author), 1972; A Passion for Equality: George Wiley and the Movement (co-author), 1977; Wild Blue Yonder: Money, Politics and the B-1 Bomber, 1988. Address: Galemont Farm, Broad Run, VA 22014, USA.

KOTZWINKLE William, b. 22 Nov 1938, Scranton, Pennsylvania, USA. Writer. m. Elizabeth Gundy, 1970. Education: Rider College; Penn State University. Publications: Elephant Bangs Train, 1971; Hermes 3000, 1971; The Fat Man, 1974; Night-Book, 1974; Swimmer in the Secret Sea, 1975; Doctor Rat, 1976; Fata Morgana, 1977; Herr Nightingale and the Satin Woman, 1978; Jack in the Box, 1980; Christmas at Fontaine's, 1982; E T, the Extra-Terrestrial: A Novel, 1982; Superman III, 1983; Queen of Swords, 1983; E T, the Book of the Green Planet: A New Novel, 1985; Seduction in Berlin, 1985; Jewell of the Moon, 1985; The Exile, 1987; The Midnight Examiner, 1989; Hot Jazz Trio, 1989; The Game of Thirty, 1994. Other: Many children's books. Honours: National Magazine Award for Fiction, 1972, 1975; O'Henry Prize, 1975; World Fantasy Award for Best Novel, 1977; North Dakota Children's Choice Award, 1983, and Buckeye Award, 1984. Address: c/o Houghton Mifflin Company, 1 Beacon Street, Boston, MA 02108, USA.

KOURVETARIS George A, b. 21 Nov 1933, Eleochorion, Arcadia, Greece. Professor of Sociology; Author; Editor. m. Toula Savas, 22 Nov 1966, div 1987, 2 sons, 1 daughter. Education: Teacher's Diploma, Tripolis, Greece, 1955; BS, Loyola University, Chicago, USA, 1963; MA with honours, Roosevelt University, Chicago, 1965; PhD, Northwestern University, Evanston, Illinois, 1969. Publications: First and Second Generation Greeks in Chicago: An Inquiry Into Their Stratification and Mobility Patterns, 1971. Co-Author: Social Origins and Political Orientations of Officer Corps in a World Perspective, 1973; Society and Politics: An Overview and Reappraisal of Political Sociology, 1980; A Profile of Modern Greece: In Search of Identity, 1987. Co-Editor: World Perspectives in the Sociology of the Military, 1977; Political Sociology: Readings in Research and Theory, 1980; A Book of Poetry in Greek and in part English, 1992; Social Thought, 1994; The Impact of European Integration (co-editor); Political, Sociological and Economic Changes, 1996; Political Sociology, 1997. Memberships: Delta Tau Kappa, International Social Science Honor Society; American Sociological Association; Modern Greek Studies Association; American Humanist Association; American Association of European Union. Address: 109 Andresen Court, DeKalb, IL 60115, USA.

KOVEL Ralph. Author; Company President. m. 1 son, 1 daughter. Publications: Kovels' Dictionary of Marks, Pottery and Porcelain, 1953, updated 1995; A Directory of American Silver, Pewter and Silver Plate, 1958; American Country Furniture 1780-1875, 1963; Kovels' Know Your Antiques, 1967, 4th edition, 1990; Kovels' Antiques and Collectibles Price List, annually since 1968-; Kovels' Bottles Price List, biennially, 1971-; Kovels' Collector's Guide for Collector Plates, Figurines, Paperweights and Other Limited Edition Items, 1978; Kovels' Collectors' guide to Limited Editions, 1974; Kovels' Collector's Guide to American Art Pottery, 1974; Kovels' Organizer for Collectors, 1978, 2nd edition, 1983; Kovels' Illustrated Price Guide to Royal Doulton, 1980, 2nd edition, 1984; Kovels' Depression, Glass and American Dinnerware, Price List, 5th Edition, 1995; Kovels' Know Your Collectibles, 1981; Kovels' Book of Antique Labels, 1982; Kovels' Collectors Source Book, 1983; Kovels' New Dictionary of Marks, Pottery and Porcelain, 1850-Present, 1985; Kovel's Advertising Collectibles Price List, 1986; Kovels' Guide to Selling Your Antiques and Collectibles, 1987, updated, 1990; Kovels' American Silver Marks, 1650 to the Present, 1989; Kovels' Quick Tios: 799 Helpful Hints on How to Care for Your Collectibles, 1995. Contributions to: Monthly column, House Beautiful, 1979-; Newspaper column, Kovels' Antiques and Collecting; Editor, Publisher, Kovels on Antiques and Collectibles, Newsletter, 1974-. Honours: Recipient of numerous honours and awards. Address: 9090 Bank Street, Valley View, OH 44125, USA.

KOWALCZYK David Theodore, b. 22 Nov 1952, New York, USA. Teacher. Education: BA, 1974, MA, English and Creative Writing, 1988, State University of New York, USA. Appointments: English Instructor, Arizona State University, 1983-84, Genesee Community College, 1987-93. Publications: A Gentle Metamorphosis, 1993; Sinner, short story in anthology, Bless Me, Father, 1994. Contributions to: Albany Review; Maryland Review; Oxalis; Entelechy. Honours: First Prize, Poetry Competition, City Magazine, 1984; First Prize, Fiction, Chatauqua Council on Arts Awards, 1990. Membership: Phi Beta Kappa. Address: 73-72 Yong-Ho Dong, Changwon City, Kylingnam-Do, 641-041, South Korea.

KOWALSKI Kazimierz (Maria), b. 18 Aug 1926, Chelmno, Poland. Writer. m. Stanislawa Novak, 12 June 1948, 1 son, 1 daughter. Education: University of Wroclaw. Appointment: Polish Radio, Opole, 1954-92. Publications: Some 30 books; Many radio plays; Various translations. Contributions to: Many publications. Honours: Voivodship Literary Awards, 1959, 1984, 1991; Jan Langowski Award, 1981; Main Award, President of Polish Radio and Television, 1982; Opole City Manager's Literary Award, 1996. Memberships: National Council of Culture; Society of Polish Writers. Address: ul Strzelcow Bytomskich 5 m 6, 45 084 Opole, Poland.

KOWALSKI Marian, b. 8 Sept 1936, Szymonki, Poland. Writer. m. Jadwiga Abrahamow, 13 Jan 1961, 1 daughter. Education: MA, University of Wroclaw. Publications: Many novels, short stories, plays and screenplays. Contributions to: Various publications. Honours: Several awards. Memberships: Polish Marine Writers Association; Polish Writers Union. Address: ul Szafera 130 m 12, 71-245 Szczecin, Poland.

KOZAK Henryk (Jozef), b. 15 July 1945, Krasna, Poland. Writer; Poet. m. Maria Tomasiewicz, 1 July 1967, 2 sons. Education: MA in History, University of Marie Curie-Sklodowskiej, 1969. Publications: Various novels and books of poetry. Contributions to: Numerous journals and magazines. Honours: Josef Czechowicz Literary Awards, 1980, 1987. Membership: Society of Polish Writers. Address: ul Paryska 7 m 6, 20 854 Lublin, Poland.

KOZBELT Laurie, b. 11 Nov 1963, Greensburg, Pennsylvania, USA. Writer; Editor; Designer. Education: BA magna cum laude, Journalism, Indiana University of Pennsylvania, Indiana, Pennsylvania, 1985; MA summa cum laude, Journalism, Communications, Point Park College, Pittsburgh, 1991. Appointments: Editor, Designer, Allegheny Ludlum Corporation, 1988-; Contributing Editor, Out Publishing Company, Pittsburgh, Pennsylvania, 1991. Publication: Book of short stories in progress. Contributions to: Hundreds of news and feature articles in various publications, 1983-; News and features articles, Out monthly magazine, 1988-. Honours: Winner's Circle Award for Best Newsletter, International Association of Business Communicators, 1985; Best in the East Award for Best Internal Publication, Virginia Society for Hospital Public Relations and Marketing, 1985; Gold Quill, International Association of Business Communicators, 1986; 3 Effie Awards, 1986, 4 Effie Awards, 1987, Editors Forum; Honourable Mention, 1987, Award of Excellence, 1991, Matrix Award, Women in Communications; Design Finalist, International Mercury Award,

MerComm Inc, 1990; Honourable Mention, 1992, 1993, Best of Category, 1992, 26th Annual Exhibition, Printing Industry of Western Pennsylvania. Memberships: International Association of Business Communicators; Women in Communications Inc. Address: 3004 Greenridge Drive, Verona, PA 15147-2222, USA.

KOZOL Jonathan, b. 5 Sep 1936, Boston, Massachusetts, USA. Author. Education: Harvard College; Magdalen College, Oxford, England. Appointments: Teacher and Education Director, Boston area, 1964-74; Lecturer, numerous universities, 1973-97. Publications: Death At An Early Age, 1967; Free Schools, 1972; The Night is Dark, 1975; Children of the Revolution, 1978; On Being a Teacher, 1979; Prisoners of Silence, 1980; Illiterate America, 1985; Rachel and Her Children, 1988; Savage Inequalities, 1991; Amazing Grace, 1995. Honours: Rhodes Scholar, 1954; National Book Award, 1968; Guggenheim Fellowships, 1972, 1984, 1985; Field Foundation Fellow, 1973, 1974; Rockefeller Fellow, 1978; Robert F Kennedy Memorial Book Award, 1989; Lannan Book Award, 1994; Anisfield-Wolf Book Award, 1996. Address: PO Box 145, Byfield, MA 01922, USA.

KRAEUTER David Warren, b. 21 Apr 1941, Homestead, Pennsylvania, USA. Librarian. Education: BA, Geneva College, 1963; MLS, University of Pittsburgh, 1968. Appointment: Editor, Pittsburgh Oscillator, 1986-95. Publications: Radio and Television Pioneers, 1992; British Radio and Television Pioneers, 1993; Radio and Electronics Pioneers, 1994; Index to Radio and Electronics Patents, 1995; Numerical Index to Radio and Electronic Patents, 1997. Other: Edited 7 radio monographs for the Pittsburgh Antique Radio Society, 1990-95. Honour: Antique Wireless Association, Ace Author Award, 1992. Address: 506 East Wheeling Street, Washington, PA 15301, USA.

KRAMER Dale (Vernon), b. 13 July 1936, Mitchell, South Dakota, USA. Professor Emeritus of English; Writer. m. Cheris Gamble Kramarae, 21 Dec 1960, 2 children. Education: BS, South Dakota State University, 1958; MA, 1960, PhD, 1963, Case Western Reserve University. Appointments: Instructor, 1962-63, Assistant Professor, 1963-65, Ohio University; Assistant Professor, 1965-67, Associate Professor, 1967-71, Professor of English, 1971-96, Acting Head, Department of English, 1982, 1986-87, Associate Dean, College of Arts and Sciences, 1992-95, University of Illinois; Associate Member, Center for Advanced Study, Urbana, Illinois, 1971; Associate Vice-Provost, University of Oregon, 1990. Publications: Charles Robert Maturin, 1973; Thomas Hardy: The Forms of Tragedy, 1975; Critical Approaches to the Fiction of Thomas Hardy (editor), 1979; Thomas Hardy: The Woodlanders (editor), 1981, 2nd edition, 1985; Thomas Hardy: The Mayor of Casterbridge (editor), 1987; Critical Essays on Thomas Hardy: The Novels (editor), 1990; Thomas Hardy: Tess of the d'Urbervilles, 1991. Contributions to: Professional journals. Honours: American Philosophical Society Grants, 1969, 1986; National Endowment for the Humanities Grant, 1986. Memberships: Association of American University Professors; Association for Documentary Editing; Modern Language Association; Society for Textual Scholarship; Victorian Periodicals Society. Address: c/o Department of English, University of Illinois at Urbana-Champaign, Champaign, IL 61820, USA.

KRAMER Dame Leonie Judith, b. 1 Oct 1924, Melbourne, Victoria, Australia. University Professor and Chancellor; Writer. m. Harold Kramer, 2 Apr 1952, dec, 2 daughters. Education: BA, University of Melbourne, 1946; DPhil, University of Oxford, 1953. Appointments: University Professor; Chair, Board of Directors, National Institute of Dramatic Art, 1987-92; Deputy Chairman and Senior Fellow, Institute of Public Affairs, 1988-; Deputy Chancellor, 1989-91, Chancellor, 1991-, University of Sydney. Publications: Henry Handel Richardson and Some of Her Sources, 1954; Companion to Australia Felix, 1962; Coast to Coast, 1963-64, 1965; Myself When Laura: Fact and Fiction in Henry Handel Richardson's School Career, 1966; Henry Handel Richardson, 1967; Language and Literature: A Synthesis (with R D Eagleson), 1976; A D Hope (co-editor), 1979; Oxford History of Australian Literature, 1981; Oxford Anthology of Australian Literature, 1985; My Country: Australian Poetry and Short Stories, 2 volumes, 1985; James McAuley: Poetry, Essays and Personal Commentary (editor), 1988; David Campbell: Collected Poems (editor), 1989. Contributions to: Numerous journals. Honours: Dame of the Order of the British Empire, 1982; AC, 1993; Honorary doctorates. Membership: Australian Academy of Humanities, fellow. Address: 12 Vaucluse Road, Vaucluse, New South Wales 2030, Australia.

KRAMER Lotte Karoline, b. 22 Oct 1923, Mainz, Germany. Poet; Painter. m. Frederic Kramer, 20 Feb 1943, 1 son. Education: Mainz, 1930-38; Evening classes, Richmond, England, 1958-68. Publications: Poetry: Scrolls, 1979; Ice Break, 1980; Family Arrivals, 1981; A Lifelong House, 1983; The Shoemaker's Wife, 1987; The Desecration of Trees, 1994; Earthquake and Other Poems, 1994; Selected and New Poems 1980-87, 1997. Contributions to: Anthologies, newspapers, and magazines. Honour: 2nd Prize, York Poetry Competition, 1972. Memberships: PEN; Ver Poets; Writers in Schools; Poetry Society, Peterborough Museum Society; Decorative and Fine Arts Society. Address: 4 Apsley Way, Longthorpe, Peterborough PE3 9NE, England.

KRANTZ Judith (Tarcher), b. 9 Jan 1928, New York, New York, USA. Writer. m. Stephen Falk Krantz, 19 Feb 1954, 2 sons. Education: BA, Wellesley College, 1948. Appointments: Fashion Editor, Good Housekeeping, 1949-56; Contributor, McCalls, 1956-59, Ladies Home Journal, 1959-71; Contributing West Coast Editor, Cosmopolitan, 1971-79. Publications: Scruples, 1978; Princess Daisy, 1980; Mistral's Daughter, 1982; I'll Take Manhattan, 1986; Till We Meet Again, 1989; Dazzle, 1990; Scruples Two, 1992; Lovers, 1994; Spring Collection, 1996. Membership: PEN. Address: c/o Morton Janklow, Lyn Nesbitt Associates, 598 Madison Avenue, New York, NY 10022, USA.

KRAPF Norbert, b. 14 Nov 1943, Jasper, Indiana, USA. Professor of English; Writer. m. 13 June 1970, 1 son, 1 daughter. Education: BA in English, St Joseph's College, Indiana, 1965; MA in English, 1966, PhD in English and American Literature, 1971, University of Notre Dame. Appointments: Faculty, 1970-84, Professor of English, 1984-, Long Island University. Publications: Arriving on Paumanok, 1979; Lines Drawn from Durer, 1981; Circus Songs, 1983; A Dream of Plum Blossoms, 1985; Under Open Sky: Poets on William Cullen Bryant (editor), 1986; Beneath the Cherry Sapling: Legends from Franconia (editor and translator), 1988; Shadows on the Sundial: Selected Early Poems of Rainer Maria Rilke (editor and translator), 1990; Somewhere in Southern Indiana: Poems of Midwestern Origins, 1993; Finding the Grain: Pioneer Journals and Letters from Dubois County, Indiana, 1996; Blue-eyed Grass: Poems of Germany, 1997. Contributions to: Professional journals. Address: c/o Department of English, Long Island University, Brookville, NY 11548, USA.

KRAUSS Bruno. See: BULMER Henry Kenneth.

KRAUSS Clifford, b. 30 July 1953, New York, New York, USA. Journalist. Education: BA, Vassar College, 1975; MA, History, University of Chicago, 1976; MS, Journalism, Columbia University, 1977. Publication: Inside Central America: Its People, Politics and History, 1991. Contributions to: Nation; Foreign Affairs; Wilson Quarterly; Times Literary Supplement. Address: 1305 Corcoran Street North West, Washington DC 20009, USA.

KRAUSS Rosalind, b. 30 Nov 1940, Washington, DC, USA. m. Richard I Krauss, 17 Sept 1962, div. Education: AB, Wellesley College; MA, PhD, Harvard University. Appointments: Professor of Art History, Columbia University; Guest Curator. Publications: Terminal Iron Works: The Sculpture of David Smith, 1971; Joan Miro: Magnetic Fields, 1972; Line as Language, 1974; Passages in Modern Sculpture, 1977; Cindy Sherman: 1975-1993, 1993. Contributions to: Art in America; October; Partisan Review; Artforum (editor). Honour: Mather Award for Criticism, College Art Association, 1973. Address: Department of Art History, Columbia University, 2960 Columbia University, New York, NY 10027, USA.

KRAUZER Steven M(ark), (Terry Nelson Bonner), b. 9 June 1948, Jersey City, New Jersey, USA. Writer. m. Dorri T Karasek, 2 Nov 1992, 2 daughters. Education: BA, Yale University, 1970; MA, English Literature, University of New Hampshire, 1974. Publications: The Cord Series, 1982-86; The Executioner Series, 1982-83; Blaze, 1983; The Diggers, 1983; The Dennison's War Series, 1984-86; Framework, 1989; Brainstorm, 1991; Rojak's Rule, 1992. Anthologies: Great Action Stories, 1977; The Great American Detective, 1978; Stories into Film, 1979; Triquarterly 48: Western Stories, 1980. Contributions to: Magazines. Memberships: Writers Guild of America West; Authors Guild; Authors League; Mystery Writers of America. Address: c/o Virginia Barber Literary Agency, 101 5th Avenue, New York, NY 10003, USA.

KRESS Nancy, b. 20 Jan 1948, Buffalo, New York, USA. Teacher. m. (1) Michael Kress, div, 2 sons, (2) Mark P Donnelly, 19

Aug 1988. Education: BS, State University of New York College, Plattsburgh, 1969; MS, Education, 1978, MA, English, 1979, State University of New York College, Brockport. Appointments: Elementary School Teacher, Penn Yan, 1970-73; Adjunct Instructor, State University of New York College, Brockport, 1980-; Senior Copywriter, Stanton and Hucko, Rochester, 1984-. Publications: The Prince of Morning Bells, 1981; The Golden Grove, 1984; The White Pipes, 1985; Trinity and Other Stories, 1985; An Alien Light, 1988; Brain Rose, 1990. Contributions to: Anthologies and periodicals. Honour: Nebula Award, Science Fiction Writers of America, 1985. Membership: Science Fiction Writers of America. Address: 50 Sweden Hill Road, Brockport, NY 14420, USA.

KRESSEL Neil Jeffrey, b. 28 Aug 1957, Newark, New Jersey, USA. Writer; College Professor; Psychologist. m. Dorit Fuchs Kressel JD, 11 Aug 1991, 1 son. Education: BA, Magna Cum Laude, 1978, MA, 1978, Brandeis University; MA, 1981, PhD, 1983, Harvard University. Appointment: Associate Professor of Psychology; William Paterson College of New Jersey, Wayne, New Jersey, 1984-. Publications: Political Psychology, 1993; Mass Hate: The Global Rise of Genocide and Terror, 1996. Contributions to: American Journal of Sociology; Political Psychology; Contemporary Psychology; Midstream; Judaism; New York Daily News; Boston Globe; Boston Herald. Literary Agent: Susan Ann Protter, New York. Address: Department of Psychology, William Paterson College of New Jersey, Wayne, NJ 07470, USA.

KRICHMAR Sava J, b. 11 Dec 1928, Odessa, Russia. Physico-Chemist. 1 daughter. Education: Physico-Chemist, Dniepropetrovsk University, 1950, Physico-Chemist; Doctor of Chemical Sciences, Electrochemist, 1969. Appointment: Professor of the Chair of Chemistry, 1979. Publications: Polarization Mechanism of the Smoothing by Electrochemical Burnishing of the Metals, 1955; Coulometric Detector for Gas Chromatography, 1969; Polarographic Analysis with Polymierdelectrode, 1979; Passage of Gas Across Convectional Barrier, 1989; Preparation of Calibrational Limiting Diluting of Gas Mixtures, 1996. Contributions to: 160 articles. Honours: Medal, Inventor of USSR, 1976, SOCOS, Grant, 1993. Memberships: New York Academy of Sciences, member, 1994; Academy of Sciences of Higher School of Ukraine, 1993. Address: Bereslavskoe Str 6/16, Kherson 325008, Ukraine.

KRIEGER Murray, b. 27 Nov 1923, Newark, New Jersey, USA. Professor; Literary Critic. m. Joan Alice Stone, 15 June 1947, 1 son, 1 daughter. Education: MA, University of Chicago, 1948; PhD, Ohio State University, 1952. Appointments: Assistant, Associate Professor, English, University of Minnesota, 1952-58; Professor, English, University of Illinois, 1958-63; Carpenter Professor, Literary Criticism, University of Iowa, 1963-66; Professor, English, University of California, Irvine, 1966-; Los Angeles, 1973-82; University Professor, University of California, 1974-; Director, 1987-89, School of Criticism and Theory, University of California at Irvine and Northwestern University, 1976-81; Honorary Senior Fellow, 1982-; Director, University of California Humanities Research Institute. Publications: New Apologists for Poetry, 1956; The Tragic Vision, 1960; A Window to Criticism: Shakespeare's Sonnets and Modern Poetics, 1964; The Play and Place of Criticism, 1967; The Classic Vision, 1971; Theory of Criticism, 1976; Poetic Presence and Illusion, 1979; Arts on the Level: The Fall of the Elite Object, 1981; Words About Words About Words: Theory, Criticism and the Literary Text, 1988; A Reopening of Closure: Organicism Against Itself, 1989; Ekphrasis: The Illusion of the Natural Sign, 1992; The Ideological Imperative: Repression and Resistance in Recent American Theory, 1993; The Institution of Theory, 1994. Address: Department of English and Comparative Literature, University of California, Irvine, CA 92697-2650, USA.

KRIEGLER-ELLIOTT Carolyn Patricia, b. 14 Apr 1949, Niagara Falls, New York, USA. Author and Illustrator of Children's Books. m. Tom Elliott, 8 Apr 1983. Education: BFA Honours, Illustration, Virginia Commonwealth University; Early Childhood Education, St Petersburg Junior College, Tarpon Springs, Florida, 1987.Appointments: Children's Book Agent, Richards Literary Agency, 1990; Guest, Aim Children's Book Week, National Library Service, Whangarei, New Zealand, 1992. Publications: Rosie Moonshine (with Anthony Holcroft), 1989; A Lollipop, Please, 1989; Good Night, Little Brother, 1989; Pins and Needles, 1989; Rain, 1990; Chen Li and the River Spirit (with Anthony Holcroft), 1990; Lulu, 1990; Lucky for Some, 1990; Cat Concert, 1990; A Present for Anna, 1990; Higgledy Piggledy Hobbledy Hoy, 1991; Woodsmoke, 1991; The Cave, 1991; Googer in Space, 1991; Night Cat, 1991; By Jingo!, 1992; What Peculiar People, 1992;

Good Night, Alice, 1992; Island in the Lagoon (with Anthony Holcroft), 1992; A Dog for Keeps (with Pauline Cartwright), 1992. Contributions to: Magazines. Memberships: New Zealand Book Council; PEN; Writers in Schools, New Zealand Book Council; Sathya Sai Organization of New Zealand. Address: c/o Richards Literary Agency, PO Box 31240, Milford, Auckland 9, New Zealand.

KRISTENSEN Lise Lotte, b. 13 May 1961, Frederiksberg, Denmark. Writer; Poet. Education: University of Copenhagen, for 5 years. Publications: Immediately but Flowing, 1989; The Time it Takes Being God, 1991; Southern Balm, 1994. Contributions to: Studiekamraten; Ildfisken; Hojskolebladet. Honour: Madam Hollatz Grant. Memberships: Danish Writers Union; Committee for World Peace; Buddhist Forum. Address: Toldbodgade 14B 1 Tv, 1253 Copenhagen, Denmark.

KRISTOF Nicholas, b. 27 April 1959, USA. Journalist. m. 1988, 2 sons. Education: BA, Harvard University, 1981; First degree Honours, Law, Oxford, Rhodes Scholar, 1983. Publication: China Wakes: The Struggle for the Soul of a Rising Power (with Sheryl WuDunn). Honours: Pulitzer Prize, 1990; Polk Award, 1990; Phi Beta Kappa. Literary Agent: Mort Janklow and Anne Sibbald. Address: New York Times Foreign Desk, 229 West 43rd Street, New York, NY 10036, USA.

KRISTOL Irving, b. 22 Jan 1920, New York, New York, USA. Editor; Writer; Professor of Social Thought (retired). m. Gertrude Himmelfarb, 18 June 1942, 1 son, 1 daughter. Education: City College, New York City, 1940. Appointments: Managing Editor, Commentary Magazine, 1947-52; Co-Founder and Co-Editor, Encounter magazine, 1953-58; Editor, The Reporter magazine, 1959-60; Executive Vice-President, Basic Books Inc, 1961-69; Co-Editor, The Public Interest magazine, 1965-; Faculty, 1969-88; New York University; John M Olin Senior Fellow, American Enterprise Institute, 1987-. Publications: On the Democratic Idea in America, 1972; Two Cheers for Capitalism, 1978; Reflections of a Neoconservative, 1983; Neoconservatism: The Autobiography of an Idea, 1995. Editor: Encounters (with Stephen Spender and Melvin Lasky), 1963; Confrontation: The Student Rebellion and the University (with Daniel Bell), 1969; Capitalism Today, 1971; The American Commonwealth (with Nathan Glazer), 1976; The Americans (with Paul Weaver), 1976; The Crisis in Economic Theory, 1981; Third World Instability (with others), 1985. Contributions to: Various publications. Memberships: American Academy of Arts and Sciences, Fellow; Council on Foreign Relations. Address: c/o The Public Interest, 1112 16th Street North West, Suite 530, Washington, DC 20036, USA.

KROETSCH Robert, b. 26 June 1927, Heisler, Alberta, Canada. Professor of English; Writer. Education: BA, University of Alberta, 1948; MA, Middlebury College, Vermont, 1956; PhD, University of Iowa, 1961. Appointments: Assistant Professor, 1961-65, Associate Professor, 1965-68, Professor of English, 1968-78, State University of New York at Binghamton; Professor of English, 1978-85, Distinguished Professor, 1985-, University of Manitoba. Publications: The Studhorse Man, 1969; Badlands, 1975; What the Cow Said, 1978; Alibi, 1983; Completed Field Notes (poems), 1989; The Lovely Treachery of Words, 1989; The Puppeteer, 1992. Address: 4081 Cedar Hill Road, Victoria, British Columbia V8N 3C2, Canada.

KRUKOWSKI Lucian Wladyslaw, b. 22 Nov 1929, New York, New York, USA. Professor of Philosophy; Artist; Writer. m. Marilyn Denmark, 17 Jan 1955, 1 daughter. Education: BA, Brooklyn College, 1952; BFA, Yale University, 1955; MS, Pratt Institute, 1958; PhD, Washington University, St Louis, 1977. Appointments: Faculty, Pratt Institute, 1955-69; Dean, School of Fine Arts, 1969-77, Professor of Philosophy, 1977-, Chairman, Department of Philosophy, 1986-89, Washington University, St Louis. Publications: Art and Concept, 1987; Aesthetic Legacies, 1992. Anthologies: The Arts, Society, and Literature, 1984; The Reasons of Art, 1985; Cultural Literacy and Arts Education, 1990; Ethics and Architecture, 1990; The Future of Art, 1990; Schopenhauer, Philosophy and the Arts, 1996. Contributions to: Professional journals. Memberships: American Philosophical Association; Society for Aesthetics. Address: 24 Washington Terrace, St Louis, MO 63112, USA.

KRUMMACHER Jo(hann Henrich Karl Daniel), (Carl Danielson), b. 27 Dec 1946, Heidelberg, Germany. Writer; Minister. m. Ingrid Elisabeth Weng, 17 July 1986, 6 sons. Education: University Heidelberg; University Tübingen, 1972; Ordained to Ministry, Lutheran

Church, 1972. Publications: Frieden im Klartext, 1980; Motivationen, 1982; Ratgeber für Kriegsdienstverweigerer, 1987; Übergänge, 1987; Wachzweige, 1991; Für jeden Sonn-und Feiertag, 1996. Contributions to: Deutsches Allgemeines Sonntagsblatt; Junge Kirche; Das Plateau. Memberships: Verein für Kirche und Kunst, president, 1993; Executive Director, Protestant Academy, Bad Boll, 1996. Address: Akademieweg 11, D-73087 Bad Boll, Germany.

KRUPAT Arnold, b. 22 Oct 1941, New York, New York, USA. Professor. 1 son, 1 daughter. Education: BA, New York University, 1962; MA, 1965, PhD, 1967, Columbia University. Appointment: Professor, Sarah Lawrence College. Publications: For Those Who Come After, 1985; I Tell You Now (editor with Brian Swann), 1987; Recovering the Word (editor with Brian Swann), 1987; The Voice in the Margin, 1989; Ethnocriticism: Ethnography, History, Literature, 1992; New Voices: Essays on Native American Literature (editor), 1993; Native American Autobiography (editor), 1993; The Turn to the Native: Studies in Culture and Criticism, 1996; Everything Matters: Autobiographical Essays by Native American Writers (editor with Brian Swann), 1997. Contributions to: Numerous critical journals. Address: Sarah Lawrence College, Bronxville, NY 10708, USA.

KUBE-MCDOWELL Michael Paul, (Michael Hudson), b. 29 Aug 1954, Pennsylvania, USA. Writer. m. Karla Jane Kube, 12 Dec 1975, div 7 Oct 1987, 1 son. Education: BA Honours, Michigan State University, 1976; MS Education, Indiana University, 1981. Appointments: Writing Instructor, Miles Laboratories, 1978-80, Goshen College, 1984-85; Correspondent, Elkhart Truth, 1982-84; Jurist, Nebula Award, 1989; Instructor, Clarion Workshop, 1990. Publications: Emprise, 1985; After the Flames, 1985; Enigma, 1986; Empery, 1987; Thieves of Light (as Michael Hudson), 1987; Odyssey (Isaac Asimov's Robot City), 1987; Alternities, 1988; The Quiet Pools, 1990. Teleplays for Tales From the Darkside: Lifebomb; Effect and Cause; The Bitterest Pill, 1985-86. Contributions to: Numerous fiction and non-fiction in various magazines. Honours: National Merit Scholar, 1972; Courier-Post Journalism Award, 1972; Hoosier State Press Association Honourable Mention, 1983; Presidential Scholar Distinguished Teacher, 1985; Philip K Dick Award Finalist, 1986. Memberships: Science Fiction Writers of America; Writers Guild of America; National Space Society; Planetary Society. Address: PO Box 706, Okemos, MI 48805, USA.

KUBRICK Stanley, b. 26 July 1928, New York, New York, USA. Film Writer; Producer; Director. m. Suzanne Harlan, 1958, 3 daughters. Education: City College of New York. Appointments: Staff Photographer, Look, 1946-50; Produced, directed and photographed documentaries for RKO, 1951; Produced, wrote and directed feature films, 1952-. Publications: Paths of Glory (co-writer), 1948; Fear and Desire, 1953; Killer's Kiss, 1955; Dr Strangelove, 1963; The Killing, 1965; 2001: A Space Odyssey (co-author), 1968; A Clockwork Orange, 1971; Barry Lyndon, 1975; The Shining, 1978; Full Metal Jacket, 1987. Honours: New York Critics' Best Film Award, 1964; Oscar, 1968; Best Director Award, 1971. Address: c/o Loeb and Loeb, 10100 Santa Monica Boulevard, Suite 2200, Los Angeles, CA 90067, USA.

KUEI-HSIANG HWANG Hu-Yen, b. 13 Jan 1951, Taipei, Taiwan, China. Columnist. m. 3 Jan 1974, 2 sons, 1 daughter. Education: MD, United Nations Open International University, 1993; Doctor of Philosophy in Natural Medicine, American Pacific Coast University, 1993-94. Publications: The Study of the Psychic World; The Psychic Therapy That Creates Medical Miracles; Getting into the World of Psychic Power; Recovering from the Psychic Disorder; The Wisdom of Living with the Psychic Power; Unveiling the Myth of the Psychic World; The Relationship Between Illness and Parapsychology; The Message from the Psychic World; Life, Death and Reincarnation; Early Detection of Diseases; Affection, Education and Parenthood; Exploring the Spiritual Life from Within. Contributions to: Taiwan Sin-San Newspaper. Honours: Deputy Director General, International Biographical Center, Cambridge, England; Deputy Governor of the American Biographical Institute Research Association. Memberships: Society of Urban Plan, China; Society of Public Policy, China; Society of Surpass Psychology, China; Society of Land Economics, China; American Association of Parapsychology; World Association of Women Journalists and Writers, Chinese Chapter; International Biographical Association of England; American Biographical Institute Research Association. Address: 6F No 26 Lane 50, I-Hsien Road, Taipei, Taiwan, China.

KUHN Laura (Diane), b. 19 Jan 1953, San Francisco, California, USA. Musicologist; Former Assistant Professor. Education: Vocal and piano training, San Francisco, 1975-82; BA, Dominican College, San Rafael, California, 1981; MA, 1986, PhD, 1992, University of California at Los Angeles. Apointments: Member, San Francisco Symphony Chorus, 1980, Oakland Symphony Chorus, 1980-82; Music Critic, Independent Journal, Marin County, California, 1980-82; Reviewer, Los Angeles Times, 1982-87, New York Times, 1986-89; Vocalist, Daniel Lentz Group, 1983-85; Editorial Associate, Nicolas Slinimsky, 1984-95; Associate, John Cage, 1986-92; Assistant Professor, Arizona State University West, Phoenix, 1991-96; Founder-Director, John Cage Trust, New York City, 1993-; Secretary, American Music Center, New York City, 1995-. Publications: Baker's Biographical Dictionary of Musicians (contributing editor), 7th edition, 1984, 8th edition, 1992; A Pronouncing Pocket Manual of Musical Terms (editor), 5th edition, 1995; Baker's Biographical Dictionary of 20th Century Classical Musicians (editor), 1997. Contributions to: Supplement to Music Since 1900, 1986; Music Since 1900, 5th edition, 1994; Music Today; Musical Quarterly; Perspectives of New Music. Membership: American Musicological Society. Address: 10410 North Cave Creek Road, No 2115, Phoenix, AZ 85020, USA.

KULTERMANN Udo, b. 14 Oct 1927, Stettin, Germany (US citizen, 1981). Professor of Architecture Emeritus; Writer. Education: University of Greifswald, 1946-50; PhD, University of Münster, 1953. Appointments: Curatorial Assistant, Kunsthalle, Bremen, 1954-55; Art Editor, Bertelsmann Publishers, 1955-56; Programme Director, America House, Bremen, 1956-59; Director, City Art Museum, Leverkusen, 1959-64; Professor of Architecture 1967-94, Professor Emeritus, 1994-, Washington University, St Louis; International Correspondent, MIMAR, Singapore/London, 1981-92; Member, National Faculty of Humanities, Arts, and Sciences, Atlanta, 1986-; Corresponding Member, Croation Academy of Sciences and Arts, Zagreb, 1997. Publications: Architecture of Today, 1958; Hans und Wassili Luckhardt: Bauten und Projekte, 1958; Dynamische Architektur, 1959; New Japanese Architecture, 1960; Junge Deutsche Bildhauer, 1963; Der Schluessel zur Architektur von heute, 1963; New Architecture in Africa, 1963; New Architecture in the World, 1965, 2nd edition, 1976; Geschichte der Kunstgeschichte: Der Weg einer Wissenschaft, 1966, 3rd edition, revised, 1996; Architektur der Gegenwart, 1967; The New Sculpture, 1967, 2nd edition, 1972; The New Painting, 1969, revised edition, 1978; New Directions in African Architecture, 1969; Kenzo Tange: Architecture and Urban Design, 1970; Modern Architecture in Color (with Werner Hofmann), 1970; Art and Life: The Function of Intermedia, 1970; New Realism, 1972; Ernest Trova, 1977; Die Architektur im 20. Jahrhundert, 1977, 5th edition, 1987; I Contemporanei: Storia della scultura nel mondo, 1979; Architecture in the Seventies, 1980; Architekten der Dritten Welt, 1980; Contemporary Architecture in Eastern Europe, 1985; Kleine Geschichte der Kunsttheorie, 1987; Visible Cities-Invisible Cities: Urban Symbolism and Historical Continuity, 1988; Art and Reality: From Fiedler to Derrida: Ten Approaches, 1991; Architecture in the 20th Century, 1993; History of Art History, 1993; Die Maxentius Basilika - Ein Schluesselwerk spaetantiker Arkitektuur, Weimar, 1996. Contributions to: Books, encyclopedias, and periodicals. Honour: Distinguished Faculty Award, Washington University, St Louis, 1985. Address: 300 Mercer Street, 17B, New York, NY 10003, USA.

KUMAR Satish, b. 27 May 1933, Moga, India. University Professor. m. Manjari, 7 May 1963, 2 daughters. Education: MA, Political Science, Delhi University; PhD, Indian School of International Studies, Delhi University, 1962. Appointments: Assistant Professor, South Asian Studies, Indian School of International Studies, 1961-67, Senior Research Officer (Pakistan), Ministry of External Affairs, 1967-72; Associate Professor, 1972-83, Professor of Diplomacy, School of International Studies, Jawaharlal Nehru University, 1983-; Visiting Professor, University of Turin, Italy, 1990. Publications: Rana Polity in Napal, 1967; The New Pakistan, 1978; CIA and the Third World: A Study in Crypto Diplomacy, 1981; Bangladesh Documents, 2 volumes, 1971, 1972; Documents on India's Foreign Policy, 3 volumes, 1975, 1976, 1977; Yearbook on India's Foreign Policy, 1982-83, 1983-84, 1984-85, 1985-86, 1987-88, 1989, 1990-91. Contributions to: Indian and foreign journals. Address: 66 Dakshinapuram, New Campus, Jawaharlal, Nehru University, New Dehli 110067, India.

KUMIN Maxine, b. 6 June 1925, Philadelphia, Pennsylvania, USA. Poet; Writer; Teacher. m. Victor M Kumin, 29 June 1946, 1 son, 2 daughters. Education: AB, 1946, MA, 1948, Radcliffe College.

Appointments: Instructor, 1958-61, Lecturer in English, 1965-68, Tufts University; Staff, Bread Loaf Writers Conference, 1969-71, 1973, 1975, 1977; Lecturer, Newton College of the Sacred Heart, Massachusetts, 1971; Visiting Lecturer, Professor, and Writer, University of Massachusetts, Amherst, 1972, Columbia University, 1975, Brandeis University, 1975, Washington University, St Louis, 1977, Princeton University, 1977, 1979, 1982, Randolph-Macon Women's College, Lynchburg, Virginia, 1978, Bucknall University, 1983, Atlantic Center for the Arts, New Smyrna Beach, Florida, 1984, University of Miami, 1995; Staff, Sewanee Writers Conference, 1993, 1994. Publications: Poetry: Halfway, 1961; The Privilege, 1965; The Nightmare Factory, 1970; Up Country: Poems of New England, New and Selected, 1972; House, Bridge, Fountain, Gate, 1975; The Retrieval System, 1978; Our Ground Time Here Will Be Brief, 1982; Closing the Ring, 1984; The Long Approach, 1985; Nurture, 1989; Looking for Luck, 1992; Connecting the Dots, 1996. Fiction: Through Dooms of Love, 1965; The Passions of Uxport, 1968; The Abduction, 1971; The Designated Heir, 1974; Why Can't We Live Together Like Civilised Human Beings?, 1982. Other: In Deep: Country Essays, 1987; To Make a Prairie: Essays on Poets, Poetry, and Country Living, 1989; Women, Animals, and Vegetables: Essays and Stories, 1994. For Children: Various books. Contributions to: Numerous magazines and journals. Honours: Lowell Mason Palmer Award, 1960; National Endowment for the Arts Grant, 1966; national Council on the Arts Fellowship, 1967; William Marion Reedy Award, 1968; Eunice Tietjens Memorial Prize, 1972; Pulitzer Prize in Poetry, 1973; American Academy of Arts and Letters Award, 1980; Academy of American Poets Fellowship, 1985; Levinson Award, 1987; Poet Laureate, State of New Hampshire, 1989; Sarah Joseph Hale Award, 1992; Poet's Prize, 1994; Aiken Taylor Poetry Award, 1995; Centennial Award, Harvard Graduate School, 1996; Various honorary doctorates. Memberships: PEN; Poetry Society of America; Writers Union. Address: Joppa Road, Warner, NH 03278, USA.

KUNDERA Milan, b. 1 Apr 1929, Brno, Czechoslovakia. Professor; Writer. m. Vera Hrabankova, 1967. Education: Film Faculty, Academy of Music and Dramatic Arts, Prague. Appointments: Assistant to Assistant Professor, Film Faculty, Academy of Music and Dramatic Arts, Prague, 1958-69; Professor, University of Rennes, 1975-80, École des hautes études en sciences sociales, Paris, 1980-. Publications: Plays: The Owners of the Keys, 1962; Jacques and his Master, 1971-81. Short Stories: Laughable Loves, 1970. Fiction: The Joke, 1967; Life is Elsewhere, 1973; The Farewell Party, 1976; The Book of Laughter and Forgetting, 1979; The Unbearable Lightness of Being, 1984. Other: The Art of the Novel, 1987; Immortality, 1990; Slowness (Essay on the Right to Privacy), 1995; Testaments Betrayed: Essay in 9 Parts, 1995, Slowness, 1996. Honours: Union of Czechoslovak Writer's Prize, 1968; Czechoslovak Writers' Publishing House Prize, 1969; Prix Medicis, 1973; Premio Letterario Mondello, 1978; Commonwealth Award, 1981; Prix Europa-Litterature, 1982; Los Angeles Times Prize, 1984; Jerusalem Prize, 1985; Prix de la critique de l'Academie Française, 1987; Prix Nelly Sachs, 1987; Osterreichischere staatspreis fur europaische litterateur, 1987; Officier, Légion d'honneur, 1990; Prize, The Independent, 1991; Prize, Aujourd'hui, France, 1993; Medal of Merit, Czech Republic, 1995. Address: c/o Ecole des hautes etudes en sciences sociales, 54 boulevard Raspail, Paris 75006, France.

KÜNG Hans, b. 19 Mar 1928, Lucerne, Switzerland. Professor of Ecumenical Theology; Author. Education: Gregorian University, Rome; Institut Catholique, Paris; Sorbonne, University of Paris. Appointments: Ordained Roman Catholic Priest, 1954; Practical Ministry, Lucerne Cathedral, 1957-59; Scientific Assistant for Dogmatic Catholic Theology, University of Münster/Westfalen , 1959-60; Professor of Fundamental Theology, 1960-63, Professor of Dogmatic and Ecumenical Theology, 1963-80, Director, Institute of Ecumenical Research, 1963-96, Professor of Ecumenical Theology, 1980-96, Emeritus, 1996- University of Tübingen; Various guest professorships and lectureships throughout the world. Publications: The Council: Reform and Reunion, 1961; That the World May Believe, 1963; The Council in Action, 1963; Justification: The Doctrine of Karl Barth and a Catholic Reflection, 1964, new edition, 1981; Structures of the Church, 1964, new edition, 1982; Freedom Today, 1966; The Church, 1967; Truthfulness, 1968; Infallible?: An Inquiry, 1971; Why Priests?, 1972; On Being a Christian, 1976; Signposts for the Future, 1978; The Christian Challenge, 1979; Freud and the Problem of God, 1979; Does God Exist?, 1980; The Church Maintained in Truth, 1980; Eternal Life?, 1984; Christianity and the World Religions: Paths to Dialogue with Islam, Hindus and Buddhism (with others), 1986; The Incarnation of

God, 1986; Church and Change: The Irish Experience, 1986; Why I Am Still A Christian, 1987; Theology for a Third Millennium: An Ecumenical View, 1988; Christianity and Chinese Religions (with Julia Ching), 1989; Paradigm Change in Theology: A Symposium for the Future, 1989; Reforming the Church Today, 1990; Global Responsibility: In Search of a New World Ethic, 1991; Judaism, 1992; Credo: The Apostles' Creed Explained for Today, 1993; Great Christian Thinkers, 1994; Christianity, 1995; Islam; A Global Ethic for Global Politics and Economics, 1997. Honours: Oskar Pfister Award, American Psychiatric Association, 1986; Many honorary doctorates. Address: Waldhäuserstrasse 23, 72076 Tübingen, Germany.

KUNITZ Stanley J(asspon), b. 29 July 1905, Worcester, Massachusetts, USA. Poet; Editor; Essayist; Educator. m. (1) Helen Pearce, 1930, div 1937, (2) Eleanor Evans, 21 Nov 1939, div 1958, 1 daughter, (3) Elise Asher, 21 June 1958. Education: AB (summa cum laude), 1926, MA, 1927, Harvard University. Appointments: Editor, Wilson Library Bulletin, 1928-43; Teacher, Bennington College, 1946-49; Professor of English, Potsdam State Teachers College, New York, 1949-50; Director, Potsdam Summer Workshop in Creative Arts, 1949-53; Lecturer, New School for Social Research, New York City, 1950-57; Visiting Professor of English, Queens College, New York City, 1956-57, Brandeis University, 1958-59; Director, Poetry Workshop, Poetry Center, Young Men's Hebrew Association, New York City, 1958-62; Lecturer, 1963-66, Adjunct Professor in Writing, Graduate School of the Arts, 1967-85, Columbia University; Visiting Professor of Poetry, Yale University, 1970, Rutgers University at Camden, New Jersey, 1974; Visiting Professor, Senior Fellow in Humanities, Princeton University, 1978, Vassar College, 1981; Consultant on Poetry, 1974-76, Honorary Consultant in American Letters, 1979-83, Library of Congress, Washington, DC; Numerous poetry readings and lectures. Publications: Poetry: Intellectual Things, 1930; Passport to the War: A Selection of Poems, 1944; Selected Poems, 1928-1958, 1958; The Testing Tree: Poems, 1971; The Terrible Threshold: Selected Poems, 1940-70, 1974; The Coat Without a Seam: Sixty Poems, 1930-72, 1974; The Lincoln Relics, 1978; Poems of Stanley Kunitz: 1928-78, 1979; The Wellfleet Whale and Companion Poems, 1983; Next-to-Last Things: New Poems and Essays, 1985; Passing Through: The Later Poems, 1995. Non-Fiction: Robert Lowell: Poet of Terribilita, 1974; A Kind of Order, a Kind of Folly: Essays and Converstions, 1975; Interviews and Encounters, 1993; Editor: Living Authors: A Book of Biographies, 1931; Authors Today and Yesterday: A Companion Volume to "Living Authors" (with Howard Haycraft), 1933; The Junior Book of Authors: An Introduction to the Lives of Writers and Illustrators for Younger Readers (with Howard Haycraft), 1934, 2nd edition, revised, 1951; British Authors of the Nineteenth Century (with Howard Haycraft), 1936; American Authors, 1600-1900: A Biographical Dictionary of American Literature (with Howard Haycraft), 1938, 8th edition, 1971; Twentieth Century Authors: A Bographical Dictionary (with Howard Haycraft), 1942, first supplement, 1955; British Authors before 1800: A Biographical Dictionary (with Howard Haycraft), 1952; Poems of John Keats, 1964; European Authors, 1000-1900: A Biographical Dictionary of European Literature (with Vineta Colby), 1967; Selections: University and College Poetry Prizes, 1973-78, 1980; Translator: Poems of Anna Akhmatova (with Max Hayward), 1973; Andrei Voznesensky: Story Under Full Sail, 1974. Contributions to: Many anthologies, books, periodicals. Honours: Garrison Medal for Poetry, Harvard University, 1926; Oscar Blumenthal Prize, 1941; Guggenheim Fellowship, 1945-46; Amy Lowell Travelling Fellow for Poetry, 1953-54; Levinson Prize for Poetry, 1956; Harriet Monroe Award, University of Chicago, 1958; Ford Foundation Grant, 1958-59; National Institute of Arts and Letters Grant, 1959; Pulitzer Prize in Poetry, 1959; Brandeis Creative Arts Award, 1964; Lenore Marshall Award for Poetry, 1980; National Endowment for the Arts Senior Fellow, 1984; Bollingen Prize, 1987; Walt Whitman Award, 1987; State Poet of New York, 1987-88; Montgomery Fellow, Dartmouth College, 1991; Centennial Medal, Harvard University, 1992; National Medal of Arts, 1993; National Book Award for Poetry, 1995; Phi Beta Kappa. Memberships: Academy of American Poets, Chancellor, 1970-; American Academy and Institute of Arts and Letters, secretary, 1985-88; Poets House, New York, founding president, 1985-90. Address: 37 West 12th Street, New York, New York 1011, USA.

KUNZE Reiner Alexander, b. 16 Aug 1933, Oelsnitz, Germany. Writer. Education: Philosophy, journalism, literary history, art history, music history, University of Leipzig, 1951-55; MA; DPhil. Publications: Poetry, Prose, Translations, Films: Sensible Wege, 1969; Der Löwe Leopold, 1970; Zimmerlautstärke, 1972; Brief mit blauem Siegel, 1973;

Die wunderbaren Jahre, 1976; Auf eigene Hoffnung, 1981; Eine stadtbekannte Geschichte, 1982; Gespräch mit der Amsel, 1984; Eines jeden einziges Leben, 1986; Das weisse Gedicht, 1989; Deckname Lyrik, 1990; Wohin der Schlaf sich schlafen legt, 1991; Mensch ohne Macht, 1991; Am Sonnenhang, 1993; Steine und Lieder, 1996; Der Dichter Jan Skácel, 1996; Wo Freiheit ist..., 1994; Steine und Lieder, 1996; Der Dichter Jan Skácel, 1996. Honours: Translation Prize, Czech Writers Association, 1968; German Young People's Book Prize, 1970; Moelle Literary Prize, Sweden, 1973; Literary Prize, Bavarian Academy of Fine Arts, 1973; Georg Trakl Prize, Austria, 1977; Andreas Gryphius Prize, 1977; Georg Büchner Prize, 1977; Bavarian Film Prize, 1979; Geschwister Scholl Prize, 1981; Eichendorff Prize, 1984; Bundesverdienstkreuz 1 Klasse, 1984; Bayerischer Verdienstorden, 1988; Kulturpreis Ostbayern, 1989; Herbert und Elsbeth Weichmann Preis, 1990; Hanns Martin Schleyer Preis, 1990; Grosses Verdienstkreuz der Bundesrepublik Deutschland, 1993; Ehrendoktorwürde der Technischen Universität Dresden, 1993; Kulturpreis deutscher Freimaurer, 1993; Ehrenbürgerschaft der Stadt Greiz, 1995; Weilheimer Littraturpreis, 1997. Memberships: Bavarian Academy of Fine Arts; Academy of Arts, Berlin, 1975-92; German Academy for Language and Literature, Darmstadt; Freie Akademie der Künste Mannheim; Sächsische Akademie der Künste; Honorary member, Collegium europaeum Jenense der Friedrich Schiller Universität Jena; Des Ungarischen Schriftstellerverbandes und des Tschechichen PEN-Zentrums. Address: Am Sonnenhang 19, D-94130 Obernzell-Erlau, Germany.

KUO Gloria Liang-Hui, b. 10 July 1926, Kaifeng, Henan, China. Author. m. 1949, 2 sons. Education: BA, National Szechuan University, Chengtu, 1948. Publications: 34 novels, 20 novelettes, 2 non-fiction books, some in English including: Debt of Emotion, 1959; The Lock of a Heart, 1962; Far Far Way to Go, 1962; Stranger in Calcutta, 1973; Taipei Women, 1980; Appreciating Chinese Art, 1985; Untold Tales of Chinese Art, 1987. Contributions to: Newspapers and magazines. Membership: Chinese Literature Association, Taiwan. Address: 11F, 126-23 Chung Hsiao East Road, Sec 4, Taipei, China.

KUPFERBERG Herbert, b. 20 Jan 1918, New York, New York, USA. Journalist; Music Critic. Education: BA, Cornell University, 1939; MA, 1940, MS, 1941, Columbia University. Appointments: Staff, New York Herald Tribune, 1942-66; Music Critic, Atlantic Monthly, 1962-69, National Observer, 1967-77; Senior Editor, Parade magazine, 1967-. Publications: Those Fabulous Philadelphians: The Life and Times of a Great Orchestra, 1969; The Mendelssohns: Three Generations of Genius, 1972; Opera, 1975; Tanglewood, 1976; The Book of Classical Music Lists, 1985; Basically Bach, 1986; Amadeus: A Mozart Mosaic, 1986. For Young People: Felix Mendelssohn: His Life, His Family, His Music, 1972; A Rainbow of Sound: The Instruments of the Orchestra and Their Music, 1973. Contributions to: Newspapers and magazines. Address: 113-114 72 Road, Forest Hills, NY 11375, USA.

KUPPNER Frank, b. 1951, Glasgow, Scotland. Poet; Writer. Education: University of Glasgow. Publications: Poetry: A Bad Day for the Sung Dynasty, 1984; The Intelligent Observation of Naked Women, 1987; Ridiculous! Absurd! Disgusting!, 1989; Everything is Strange; Prose: A Very Quiet Street; A Concussed History of Scotland. Address: c/o Carcanet Press Ltd, 208-212 Corn Exchange Buildings, Manchester M4 3BQ, England.

KURAPEL Alberto, b. 5 Feb 1946, Santiago, Chile. Playwright; Poet; Essayist; Performer. m. Susana Cáceres, 5 Jan 1968. Education: Graduate, School of Theatre, University of Chile, 1969. Appointment: Artistic Director, Compagnie des Arts Exilio, 1981-94. Publications: Correo de Exilio/Courrier de'exil, 1986; 3 Performances, Theatrales de Alberto Kurapel, 1987; Promethée Enchainé selon Alberto Kurapel, 1988; Carta de Ajuste ou Nous N'avons Plus Besoin de Calendrier, 1991; Pasarelas/Passerelles, 1991; Berri-UQAM, 1992; Des marches sur le dos de la neige/Peldaños en la espalda de la nieve, 1993. Contributions to: Canadian Theatre Review; Revue Possibles; La Escena Latinoamericana; Revue Humanitas; Ellipse. Honours: Gold Medal, International Competition, Verso il Futuro, Italy, 1976; Special Prize, F de Santis per la Poesia, Italy, 1976; Honorary Mention, contribution for knowledge and diffussion of Latin American Theatre, University of Santiago and Instituto Internacional de Teoría y Crítica de Teatro Latinoamericano, 1992. Memberships: PEN Club; Playwrights Union of Canada; Union des écrivains et écrivaines québécois; Association des poètes du Québec. Address: La Compagnie des Arts Exilio, 6865 Christophe Colomb 313, Montréal, Québec H2S 2H3, Canada.

KUREISHI Hanif, b. 5 Dec 1954, London, England. Education: BA Philosophy, King's College, University of London. Appointment: Writer-in-Residence, Royal Court Theatre, London, 1981, 1985-86. Publications: Plays: Soaking the Heat (produced London), 1976; The Mother Country (produced London), 1980; The King and Me (produced London), 1980; Outskirts (produced London), 1981; Cinders, from a play by Janusz Glowacki (produced London), 1981; Borderline (produced London), 1981; Artists and Admirers, with David Leveaux, from a play by Alexander Ostrovsky (produced London), 1981; Birds of Passage, 1983; Included in Outskirts, The King and Me, Tomorrow-Today!, London and New York, 1983; Mother Courage, adaptation of a play by Brecht (produced London), 1984; The Buddha of Suburbia. Other varied publications include: My Beautiful Launderette (screenplay) includes essay The Rainbow Sign, London, 1986; Sammy and Rosie Get Laid (screenplay), London, 1988; London Kills Me (feature film), 1991; The Black Album (novel), 1995; Love in a Blue Time (short stories), 1997. Radio Plays: You Can't Go Home, 1980; The Trial, from a novel by Kafka, 1982. Honours: George Devine Award, 1981; Evening Standard Award for Screenplay, 1985, New York Critics Best Screenplay Award, Oscar nomination, 1986, (My Beautiful Launderette);Whitbread Award, Best First Novel (for Buddha of Suburbia), 1990. Address: Stephen Durbridge, The Agency, 24 Pottery Lane, Holland Park, London, W11 4lZ, England.

KURTZ Katherine Irene, b. 18 Oct 1944, Coral Gables, Florida, USA. Author. m. Scott Roderick MacMillan, 9 Apr 1983, 1 son. Education: BS, University of Miami, 1966; MA, University of California, Los Angeles, 1971. Publications: Deryni Rising, 1970; Deryni Checkmate, 1972; High Deryni, 1973; Camber of Culdi, 1976; Saint Camber, 1978; Camber the Heretic, 1981; Lammas Night, 1983; The Bishop's Heir, 1984; The King's Justice, 1985; The Quest for Saint Camber, 1986; The Legacy of Lehr, 1986; The Deryni Archives, 1986; The Harrowing of Gwynedd, 1989; Deryni Magic: A Grimoire, 1990; King Javan's Year, 1992; The Bastard Prince, 1994; Two Crowns for America, 1996; King Kelson's Bride, 1997. With Deborah Turner Harris: The Adept, 1991; Lodge of the Lynx, 1992; The Templar Treasure, 1993; Dagger Magic, 1994; Death of an Adept, 1996. Editor: Tales of The Knights Templar, 1995; Various short stories. Honours: Edmund Hamilton Memorial Award, 1977; Balrog Award, 1982. Memberships: Authors Guild; Science Fiction Writers of America. Address: Holybrooke Hall, Kilmacanogue, Bray, Co Wicklow, Ireland.

KURZMAN Dan, b. 27 Mar 1929, San Francisco, California, USA. m. Florence Knopf. Education: BA, University of California at Berkeley, 1946; Certificate, Sorbonne, University of Paris, 1947. Appointments: Correspondent, International News Service, 1948; Feature Writer, Marshall Plan Information Office, Paris, 1948-49; Correspondent, National Broadcasting Company, Middle East, 1950-53, Washington Post, 1962-69; Bureau Chief, McGraw Hill World News Service, Tokyo, 1954-59; Contributor, Washington Star, 1975-80, Independent News Alliance, 1979-84, San Francisco Chronicle, 1991-92. Publications: Kishi and Japan: The Search for the Sun, 1960; Subversion of the Innocents, 1963; Santo Domingo: Revolt of the Damned, 1965; Genesis 1948: The First Arab-Israeli War, 1970; The Race for Rome, 1975; The Bravest Battle: The Twenty-Eight Days of the Warsaw Ghetto Uprising, 1976; Miracle of November: Madrid's Epic Stand 1936, 1980; Ben-Gurion: Prophet of Fire, 1983; Day of the Bomb: Countdown to Hiroshima, 1985; A Killing Wind: Inside Union Carbide and The Bhopal Catastrophe, 1987; Fatal Voyage: The Sinking of the USS Indianapolis, 1990; Left to Die: The Tragedy of the USS Juneau, 1994; Blood and Water: Sabotaging Hitler's Bomb, 1995. Contributions to: New York Times Op-Ed Page, 1988-; Washington Post (Book Reviewer), 1988-; Los Angeles Times (Book Reviewer), 1988-. Address: The Parker Imperial, 7855-Boulevard East, North Bergen, NJ 07047, USA.

KUSHNER Aleksandr Semyonovich, b. 14 Sep 1936, Leningrad, Russia. Poet. m. Elena Vsevolodovna Nevzgliadova, 21 July 1984, 1 son. Education: Graduate, Leningrad Pedagogical Institute, 1959. Appointments: Editor-in- Chief, Publishing House, Biblioteka Poeta. Publications: First Impression, 1962; Omens, 1969; Letter, 1974; Voice, 1978; The Tavrichesky Garden, 1984; The Hedgerow, 1988; A Night Melody, 1991; Apollo in the Snow, essays on Russian Poetry and personal memoirs, 1991; On a Clouded Star, 1994. Contributions to: Novii Mir; Znamya; Zvezda; Unost; Voprosi Literaturi. Honours: Severnaya Palmira Award, 1995; Russia's State Award, 1996. Memberships: Union of Writers; PEN Club. Address: Kaluzhsky Pereulok 9, Apt 48, St Petersburg 193015, Russia.

KUSHNER Donn Jean, b. 29 Mar 1927, Lake Charles, Louisiana, USA. Professor Emeritus; Writer. m. Eva Milada Dubska, 15 Sept 1949, 3 sons. Education: BSc, Chemistry, Harvard University, 1948; MSc, Biochemistry, 1950, PhD, Biochemistry, 1952, McGill University. Appointments: Editor, Canadian Journal of Microbiology, 1980-84; Editor, Archives of Microbiology, 1986-94. Publications: Books for children and young adults: The Violin Maker's Gift, 1980; The Witnesses and Other Stories, 1980; Uncle Jacob's Ghost Story, 1984; A Book Dragon, 1987; The House of the Good Spirits, 1990; The Dinosaur Duster, 1992; A Thief Among Statues, 1993; The Night Voyagers, 1995. Contributions to: 160 Scentific research articles and book chapters; Editor, Microbial Life in Extreme Environments (book), 1978. Honours: Book of the Year Award for Children, Canadian Library Association, 1981; Ottawa Biological and Biochemical Society Award, 1986; IODE Canada Chapter Award, 1988; Canadian Society of Microbiologists Award, 1992. Memberships: Writers' Union of Canada; Children's Authors, Illustrators and Performers; Canadian Society of Microbiologists (president 1980-81); American Society for Microbiology; American Society for Biological Chemistry and Molecular Biology. Literary Agent: Transatlantic Literary Agency, 72 Glengowan Road, Toronto, Ontario M4N 1G4, Canada. Address: 63 Albany Avenue, Toronto, Ontario M5R 3C2, Canada.

KUSHNER Tony, b. 16 July 1956, New York, New York, USA. Dramatist. Education: BA, Columbia University, 1978; MFA, New York University, 1984. Appointment: Playwright-in-Residence, Juilliard School, New York City, 1990-92. Publications: Yes, Yes, No, No, 1985; Stella, 1987; A Bright Room Called Day, 1987; Hydriotaphia, 1987; The Illusion, 1988, revised version, 1990; Widows (with Ariel Dorfman), 1991; Angels in America: A Gay Fantasia on National Themes, Part One: Millenium Approaches, 1991, and Part Two: Perestroika, 1992. Honours: National Endowment for the Arts Grants, 1985, 1987, 1993; Princess Grace Award, 1986; New York State Council for the Arts Fellowship, 1987; John Whiting Award, Arts Council of Great Britain, 1990; Kennedy Center/American Express Fund for New American Plays Awards, 1990, 1992; Kesselring Award, National Arts Club, 1992; Will Glickman Prize, 1992; Evening Standard Award, 1992; Pulitzer Prize in Drama, 1993; Antoinette Perry Award, 1993; American Academy of Arts and Letters Award, 1994. Address: c/o Joyce Ket, 334 West 89th Street, New York, NY 10024, USA.

KUSKIN Karla (Seidman), (Nicholas J Charles), b. 17 July 1932, New York, New York, USA. Writer and Illustrator of Children's Fiction and Verse. m. (1) Charles M Kuskin, 4 Dec 1955, div Aug 1987, 1 son, 1 daughter, (2) William L Bell, 24 July 1989. Education: Antioch College, 1950-53; BFA, Yale University, 1955. Appointments: Illustrator for several publishers; Conductor of poetry and writing workshops. Publications: Roar and More, 1956, revised edition, 1990; James and the Rain, 1957; In the Moddle of the Trees, 1958; The Animals and the Ark, 1958; Just Like Everyone Else, 1959; Which Horse is William?, 1959; Square As a House, 1960; The Bear Who Saw the Spring, 1961; All Sizes of Noises, 1962; Alexander Soames: His Poems, 1962; How Do You Get From Here to There?, 1962; ABCDEFGHIJKLMNOPQRSTUVWXYZ, 1963; The Rose on My Cake, 1964; Sand and Snow, 1965; Jane Anne June Spoon and Her Very Adventurous Search for the Moon, 1966; The Walk the Mouse Girls Took, 1967; Watson, The Smartest Dog in the USA, 1968; In the Flaky Frosty Morning, 1969; Any Me I Want To Be: Poems, 1972; What Did You Bring Me?, 1973; Near the Window Tree: Poems and Notes, 1975; A Boy Had a Mother Who Brought Him a Hat, 1976; A Space Story, 1978; Herbert Hated Being Small, 1979; Dogs and Dragons, Trees and Dreams: A Collection of Poems, 1980; Night Again, 1981; The Philharmonic Gets Dressed, 1982; Something Sleeping in the Hall, 1985; The Dallas Titans Get Ready for Bed, 1986; Jerusalem, Shining Still, 1987; Soap Soup, 1992; A Great Miracle Happened Here: A Chanukah Story, 1993; Patchwork Island, 1994; The City Dog, 1994; City Noise, 1994. Contributions to: Choice; House and Garden; New York Magazine; New York Times; Parents; Saturday Review; Village Voice; Wilson Library Bulletin. Honours: Book Show Awards, American Institute of Graphic Arts, 1955-60; Children's Book Award, International Reading Association, 1976; Children's Book Council Showcase Selections, 1976-77; National Council of Teachers of English Award, 1979; Children's Science Book Award, New York Academy of Sciences, 1980; American Library Association Awards, 1980, 1982, 1993; Best Book of 1987, School Library Journal; Others. Address: 96 Joralemon Street, Brooklyn, NY 11201, USA.

KUSTOW Michael (David), b. 18 Nov 1939, London, England. Writer. Appointments: Director, Institute of Contemporary Arts, 1967-71; Associate Director, National Theatre of Great Britain, 1973-81; Lecturer in Dramatic Arts, Harvard University, Cambridge, MA, 1980-82; Commissioning Editor, Channel 4 TV, 1981-. Publications: Night of the Assassins (translation), 1968; Tank, Roger Planchon and People's Theatre, 1975; Stravinsky: The Soldier's Story, 1980; Charles Wood's Has Washington Legs, Harold Pinter's Family Voices, 1981; The Manhabbaraten, 1989; The War That Never Ends, 1991. Address: c/o Tom Corrie, The Peters Fraser and Dunlop Group Ltd, The Chambers, Chelsea Harbour, Lots Road, London SW10 0XF, England.

KWITNY Jonathon, b. 23 Mar 1941, Indianapolis, Indiana, USA. Journalist; Writer. Education: BJ, University of Missouri, 1962; MA, New York University, 1964. Publications: The Fountain Pen Conspiracy, 1973; The Mullendove Murder Case, 1974; Shakedown, 1977; Vicious Circles: The Mafia in the Marketplace, 1979; Endless Enemies, 1984; The Crimes of Patriots, 1987; Acceptable Risks, 1992. Address: Box 7333, James A Farley Station, New York, NY 10116, USA.

KYLE Duncan. See: BROXHOLME John Franklin.

KYLE Susan (Eloise Spaeth), (Diana Blayne, Diana Palmer), b. 12 Dec 1946, Cuthbert, Georgio, USA. Author. m. James Edward Kyle, 9 Oct 1972, 1 son. Education: BA, Piedmont College, 1995. Publications: Heather's Song, 1982; Diamond Spur, 1988; Amelia, 1993; Nora, 1994; All That Glitters, 1995; many other books. Contributions to: Journals and Magazines. Honours: Many awards. Membership: Authors Guild. Address: PO Box 844, Cornelia, GA 30531, USA.

L

L'ESTRANGE Anna. See: **ELLERBECK Rosemary Anne L'Estrange.**

L'HEUREUX John (Clarke), b. 26 Oct 1934, South Hadley, Massachusetts, USA. Professor of English; Writer. m. Joan Ann Polston, 26 June 1971. Education: AB, 1959, Licentiate in Philosophy, 1960, Weston College; MA, Boston College, 1963; Licentiate in Sacred Theology, Woodstock College, 1967; Postgraduate Studies, Harvard University, 1967-68. Appointments: Writer-in-Residence, Georgetown University, 1964-65, Regis College, 1968-69; Ordained Roman Catholic Priest, 1966, laicized, 1971; Staff Editor, 1968-19, Contributing Editor, 1969-83, The Atlantic; Visiting Professor, Hamline University, 1971, Tufts College, 1971-72; Visiting Assistant Professor, Harvard University, 1973; Assistant Professor, 1973-79, Director, Creative Writing Programme, 1976-89, Associate Professor, 1979-81, Professor, 1981-, Lane Professor of the Humanities, 1985-90, Stanford University. Publications: Quick as Dandelions, 1964; Rubrics for a Revolution, 1967; Picnic in Babylon, 1967; One Eye and a Measuring Rod, 1968; No Place for Hiding, 1971; Tight White Collar, 1972; The Clang Birds, 1972; Family Affairs, 1974; Jessica Fayer, 1976; Desires, 1981; A Woman Run Mad, 1988; Comedians, 1990; An Honorable Profession, 1991; The Shrine at Altamira, 1992; The Handmaid of Desire, 1996; The Sleep of Reason, 1997. Address: c/o Department of English, Stanford University, Stanford, CA 94305, USA.

LA TOURETTE Jacqueline, b. 5 May 1926, Denver, Colorado, USA. Writer. Education: San Jose State College, 1948-51. Publications: The Joseph Stone, 1971; A Matter of Sixpence, 1972; The Madonna Creek Witch, 1973; The Previous Lady, 1974; The Pompeii Scroll, 1975; Shadows in Umbria, 1979; The Wild Harp, 1981; Patarran, 1983; The House on Octavia Street, 1984; The Incense Tree, 1986. Address: c/o Raines and Raines, 71 Park Avenue, New York, NY 10016, USA.

LABRUSSE Hughes (Henri), b. 21 June 1938, Melun, France. Professor. m. Paris, 1966, 4 sons, 1 daughter. Education: Licence de Philosophie, 1963; Diplome d'Etudes Supérieures de Philosophie, 1965; Agrégation de Philosophie, 1967. Publications: Equerre embarcation, 1976; Rome, ou quand on a un coeur et une chemise, 1978; La Dame du Désert, 1986; Terrena l'arbre excessif, 1986; Le donateur, 1991; Michel Mousseau, le temps de peindre, 1993. Contributions to: Magazines and journals. Honour: Prix Louis Guillaume du poème en prose, 1980. Memberships: Membre de la commission du Livre au Centre Régional des Lettres de Basse-Normandie, France; Conseil de Rédaction de la revue SUD. Address: Le Bourg, 14260 Saint Georges d'Aunay, France.

LACEY Robert, b. 3 Jan 1944, Guildford, Surrey, England. Author. Education: BA, 1966, Diploma in Education, 1967, MA, 1970, Selwyn College, Cambridge. Appointments: Assistant Editor, Sunday Times Magazine, 1969-73; Editor, Look! pages, Sunday Times, 1973-74. Publications: The French Revolution, 2 volumes, 1968; The Rise of Napoleon, 1969; The Peninsular War, 1969; 1812: The Retreat From Moscow, 1969; Robert, Earl of Essex: An Elizabethan Icarus, 1971; The Life and Times of Henry VIII, 1972; The Queens of the North Atlantic, 1973; Sir Walter Raleigh, 1973; Sir Francis Drake and the Golden Hinde, 1975; Heritage of Britain (editor, contributor), 1975; Majesty: Elizabeth II and the House of Windsor, 1977; The Kingdom: Arabia and the House of Saud, 1981; Princess, 1982; Aristocrats, 1983; Ford: The Men and the Machine, 1986; God Bless Her: Her Majesty Queen Elizabeth the Queen Mother, 1987; Little Man: Meyer Lansky and the Gangster Life, 1991; Grace, 1994. Address: 12783 East West Forest Hill Boulevard, Suite 105, West Palm Beach, FL 33414, USA.

LACKEY Mercedes, b. 1950, South Bend, Indiana, USA. Writer. m. 14 Dec 1990. Education: BSci Biology, Purdue University, 1972. Appointments: Computer Programmer, Associates Data Processing, 1979-82; Surveyor, Layout Designer, Analyst, CAIRS, South Bend, 1981-82; Computer Programmer, American Airlines, Tulsa, 1982-. Publications: Arrows of the Queen, 1987; Arrow's Flight, 1987; Arrow's Fall, 1988; Oathbound, 1988; Oathbreakers, 1989; Reap the Whirlwind, 1989; Magic's Pawn, 1989; Burning Water, 1989; Magic's Promise, 1990; The Magic-Winds Books: Winds of Change, 1992; Winds of

Fury, 1993; The Bard's Tale Series: Fortress of Frost and Fire, 1993; Prison of Souls, 1993; Written lyrics for and recorded nearly 50 songs for Off-Centaur. Honour: Best Books, American Library Association, 1987. Membership: Science Fiction and Fantasy Writers of America. Address: PO Box 8309, Tulsa, OK 74101 8309, USA.

LADD Veronica. See: **MINER Jane Claypool.**

LADERO QUESADA Miguel-Angel, b. 14 Jan 1943, Valladolid, Spain. Professor of Mediaeval History. m. Isabel Galan Parra, 22 June 1968, 2 sons, 1 daughter. Education: Doctorate in History, University of Valladolid, 1967. Appointments: Professor of Mediaeval History, La Laguna University, Canary Islands, 1970; Professor of Mediaeval History, University of Seville, 1974; Professor of Mediaeval History, 1978-, Director, Mediaeval History Department, 1980-97, University Vice-Rector, 1986-87, Complutensian University, Madrid. Publications: Castilla y la conquista del reino de Granada, 1967, 3rd edition 1993; Granada Historia de un pais islamico, 1969, 3rd edition, 1988; La Hacienda Real de Castilla en el siglo XV, 1973; Historia de Sevilla La ciudad Medieval, 1976, 3rd edition 1988; Historia Universal Edad Media, 1987, 2nd edition 1992; Los mudejares de Castilla y otros estudios, 1988; Los Reyes Catolicos, La Corona y la unidad de Espana, 1989; Andalusia en torno a 1492, 1992; Fiscalidad y Poder Real en Castilla (1252-1369), Madrid, 1993. Contributions to: Hispania; Anuario de Estudios Medievales; En la Espana Medieval, Madrid; Historia Instituciones, Documentos, Sevilla; Annales ESC, Paris; Sefarad, Madrid; Cuadernos de Historia de Espana, Buenos Aires. Honours: Officer, Ordre des Palmes Academiques, 1987; National Prize for History, 1994. Memberships: Full Member, Royal Historical Academy of Spain; International Commission of Urban History; International Commission of Representative and Parliamentary Institutions; Society for Spanish and Portuguese Historical Studies, USA. Address: Departamento de Historia Medieval, Facultad de Geografia e Historia, Universidad Complutense, 28040 Madrid, Spain.

LADIA Eleni, b. 13 Aug 1945, Athens, Greece. Writer. Education: Graduated, Archaeology, University of Athens, 1970. Publications: Figures on a Krater (short stories), 1973; The Fragmentary Relationship (novel), 1974, 3rd edition, 1983; The Black Hermes (short stories), 1977; The Copper Sleep (short stories), 1980; The Schizophrenic God (short stories), 1983; X, The Lion-Faced (novel), 1986; Horography (short stories), 1990; Frederic and John (narrative), 1991; Physiognomies of places (travelling texts), 1992; Theteia (novel), 1994; Saints of Copts (biographies of saints), 1995. Contributions to: Short stories, essays and archaeological articles to various journals and magazines, Athens and abroad. Honours: 2nd State Prize, 1981; Prize, Academy of Athens-Uranis Foundation, 1991. Memberships: National Greek Literary Society; PEN Club. Address: 44 Kavatha Street, 157 73 Athens, Greece.

LAFFIN John (Alfred Charles), b. 21 Sept 1922, Sydney, New South Wales, Australia. Author; Journalist; Lecturer. m. Hazelle Stonham, 6 Oct 1943, 1 son, 2 daughters. Education: MA; DLitt. Appointments: Battlefield Archaeologist; Advisor/Consultant, War, Military History and Islam. Publications: The Hunger to Come, 1966; Devil's Goad, 1970; The Arab Mind, 1974; Dagger of Islam, 1979; Damn the Dardanelles!, 1980, 2nd edition, 1985; Fight for the Falklands, 1982; The Man the Nazis Couldn't Catch, 1984; On the Western Front, 1985; Know the Middle East, 1985; Brassey's Battles, 1986; War Annual 1, 1986; War Annual 2, 1987; Battlefield Archaeology, 1987; War Annual 3, 1987; Western Front, 1916-17: The Price of Honour, 1988; Western Front, 1917-18: The Cost of Victory, 1988; Holy War - Islam Fights, 1988; War Annual 4, 1988; British Butchers and Bunglers of World War I, 1989; War Annual 5, 1991; The Western Front Illustrated, 1991; Dictionary of Africa Since 1960, 1991; Guidebook to Australian Battlefields of France and Flanders 1916-18, 1992; Digging up the Digger's War, 1993; Panorama of the Western Front, 1993; A Western Front Companion, 1994; Forever Forward, 1994; War Annual 6, 1994; Aussie Guide to Britain, 1995; Hitler Warned Us, 1995. Contributions to: Newspapers, magazines and journals. Memberships: Society of Authors, UK; Australian Society of Authors; Founder, 1988, John Laffin Australian Battlefield Museum. Address: Oxford House, Church St, Knighton, Powys LD7 1AG, Wales; Oxford House, Sundown Village, Narrabundah, ACT 2604, Australia.

LAIRD Elizabeth Mary Risk, b. 21 Oct 1943, New Zealand. Writer. m. David Buchanan McDowall, 19 Apr 1975, 2 sons. Education: BA, Bristol University; MLitt, Edinburgh University. Publications: The Miracle Child, 1985; The Road to Bethlehem, 1987; Red Sky in the

Morning, 1988; Crackers, 1989; Arcadia, 1990; Kiss the Dust, 1991; Toucan Tecs, 1992. Honour: Children's Book Award, The Burnley Express. Membership: Society of Authors. Address: 31 Cambrian Road, Richmond, Surrey TW10 6JQ, England.

LAIRD Nancy, b. 26 Sept 1957, Chico, California, USA. Administrative Assistant. 1 son, 1 daughter. Education: AA, Christian Arts, San Jose Bible College, 1977; Floral Design Diploma, ICS, Scranton, Pennsylvania, 1994. Publications: Heat Wave, 1993; Futility, 1995. Address: 97 Montgomery Drive, Harleyville, PA 19438, USA.

LAKE David John, b. 26 Mar 1929, Bangalore, India. University Professor. m. Marguerite Ivy Ferris, 30 Dec 1964, 1 daughter, 3 stepchildren. Education: BA, MA, DipEd, Trinity College, Cambridge, 1949-53; Diploma of Linguistics, University of Wales (Bangor), 1964-65; PhD, University of Queensland, Australia, 1974. Publications: Hornpipes and Funerals (poems), 1973; The Canon of Thomas Middleton's Plays, 1975; Walkers on the Sky, 1976; The Right Hand of Dextra, 1977; The Wildings of Westron, 1977; The Gods of Xuma, 1978; The Man who Loved Morlocks, 1981; The Changelings of Chaan, 1985. Contributions to: Extrapolation; Science Fiction Studies; Foundation; Notes and Queries; The Explicator; The Ring Bearer. Honours: Ditmar Awards for best Australian Science Fiction Novel, 1977, 1982. Address: 7 8th Avenue, St Lucia, Queensland 4067, Australia.

LAKEHURST Diana. See: **AYRES Philip James.**

LAKER Rosalind. See: **OVSTEDAL Barbara Kathleen.**

LAMANTIA Philip, b. 23 Oct 1927, San Francisco, California, USA. Poet. Education: University of California, Berkeley, 1947-49. Publications: Erotic Poems, 1946; Narcotica: I Demand Extinction of Laws Prohibiting Narcotic Drugs, 1959; Ekstasis, 1959; Destroyed Works, 1962; Touch of the Marvelous, 1966; Selected Poems 1943-1966, 1967; Penguin Modern Poets 13 (with Charles Bukowski and Harold Norse), 1969; The Blood of the Air, 1970; Becoming Visible, 1981; Meadowland West, 1986. Address: c/o City Lights Books, 261 Columbus Avenue, San Francisco, CA 94133, USA.

LAMB Andrew (Martin), b. 23 Sept 1942, England. Writer on Music. m. Wendy Ann Davies, 1 Apr 1970, 1 son, 2 daughters. Education: Corpus Christi College, Oxford, England, 1960-63; MA (Hons), Oxford. Publications: Jerome Kern in Edwardian London, 1985; Ganzl's Book of the Musical Theatre (with Kurt Ganzl), 1988; Skaters' Waltz: The Story of the Waldteufels, 1995. Editor: The Moulin Rouge, 1990; Light Music from Austria, 1992. Contributions to: The New Grove Dictionary of Music and Musicians; The New Grove Dictionary of American Music; The New Grove Dictionary of Opera; Gramophone; Musical Times; Classic CD; American Music; Music and Letters; Wisden Cricket Monthly; Cricketer; Listener. Memberships: Fellow, Institute of Actuaries; Associate Member, Institute of Investment Management and Research; Lancashire County Cricket Club. Address: 12 Fullers Wood, Croydon CR0 8HZ, England.

LAMB Elizabeth Searle, b. 22 Jan 1917, Topeka, Kansas, USA. Writer; Editor. m. F Bruce Lamb, 11 Dec 1941, dec 1992, 1 daughter. Education: BA 1939, BMus 1940, University of Kansas. Appointments: Editor, Frogpond, Haiku Quarterly, 1984-90, 1994; Co-Editor, Haiku Southwest, 1993-94. Publications: Pelican Tree and Other Panama Adventures, 1953; Today and Every Day, 1970; Inside Me, Outside Me, 1974; In This Blaze of Sun, 1975; Picasso's Bust of Sylvette, 1977; 39 Blossoms, 1982; Casting Into a Cloud, 1985; Lines For My Mother, Dying, 1988; The Light of Elizabeth Lamb: 100 American Haiku (in Chinese), 1993. Contributions to: Journals and magazines. Honours: Ruth Mason Rice Awards, 8 times; National League of American Pen Women Awards, 7 times; Cicada Awards, Canada, 1977, 1980; Henderson Awards, 1978, 1981, 1982, 1991, 1993; HSA Merit Book Awards, 1979, 1983, 1987; Dellbrook Poetry Award, 1979; Yuki Teikei, 1981, 1982, 1989, 1994; Poetry Society of Japan, 1987; World Haiku Contest, Japan, 1989; HSA Renku Contest, 1993; Haiku Society of America Certificate of Achievement, 1995; Honorary Curator, American Haiku Archive, California State Library, Sacramento, 1996-97. Memberships: Haiku Society of America; New York Women Poets; National League of American Pen Women; Poetry Society of America; Haiku International Association, Japan; Haiku Canada; Association of International Renku, Japan; Address: 970 Acequia Madre, Sante Fe, NM 87501, USA.

LAMB Sir Larry, b. 15 July 1929, Fitzwilliam, Yorkshire, England. Editor. m. Joan Mary Denise Grogan, 2 sons, 1 daughter. Appointments: Journalist, Brighouse Echo, Shields Gazette, Newcastle Journal, London Evening Standard; Sub-Editor, Daily Mirror; Editor, Daily Mail, Manchester, 1968-69; The Sun, 1969-72, 1975-81; Director, 1970-81, Editorial Director, 1971-81, News International Ltd; Deputy Chairman, News Group, 1979-81; Director, The News Corporation (Australia) Ltd, 1980-81; Deputy Chairman, Editor-in-Chief, Western Mail Ltd, Perth, Australia, 1981-82; Editor-in-Chief, The Australian, 1982-83; Editor, Daily Express, 1983-86; Chairman, Larry Lamb Associates, 1986-. Publication: Sunrise, 1989. Address: 42 Malvern Court, Onslow Square, London SW7 3HY, England.

LAMBDIN Dewey Whitley II, b. 21 Jan 1945, San Diego, California, USA. Formerly TV Producer; Director; Writer; Production Manager; Full-time Writer. m. (1) Melinda Alice Phillips, 17 July 1971, (2) Julie Dawn Pascoe, 27 Oct 1984. Education: BS, Film and Television, Montana State University, 1969. Publications: The King's Coat, 1989; The French Admiral, 1990; King's Commission, 1991; King's Privateer, 1992, 2nd edition, 1996; The Gun Ketch, 1993, 2nd edition, 1996; For King and Country, 1994; HMS Cockerel, 1995, 2nd edition, 1997; King's Commander, 1997. Contributions to: Book Reviewer for the Nashville Banner Daily, Southern Book Trade monthly; Reviews and articles. Honour: Theme Vault, University of Tennessee, 1963. Membership: Sisters in Crime. Literary Agent: Jake Elwell, Wieser & Wieser Inc, 118 East 25th St, New York, NY 10010, USA.

LAMBERT Derek (William), (Richard Falkirk), b. 10 Oct 1929, London, England. Journalist; Author. Appointments: Journalist for Devon, Norfolk, Yorkshire and National newspapers, 1950-68. Publications: Novels: For Infamous Conduct, 1970; Grans Slam, 1971; The Great Land, 1977; The Lottery, 1983. Mystery Novels: Angels in the Snow, 1969; The Kites of War, 1970; The Red House, 1972; The Yermakov Transfer, 1974; Touch the Lion's Paw, 1975; The Saint Peter's Plot, 1978; The Memory Man, 1979; I, Said the Spy, 1980; Trance, 1981; The Red Dove, 1982; The Judas Code, 1983; The Golden Express, 1984; The Man Who Was Saturday, 1985; Chase, 1987; Triad, 1988. Mystery Novels as Richard Falkirk: The Chill Factor, 1971; The Twisted Wire, 1971; Blackstone, 1972; Beau Blackstone, 1973; Blackstone's Fancy, 1973; Blackstone and the Scourge of Europe, 1974; Blackstone Underground, 1976; Blackstone on Broadway, 1977. Other: The Sheltered Days: Growing Up in the War, 1965; Don't Quote Me - But, 1979; And I Quote, 1980; Unquote, 1981; Just Like the Blitz: A Reporter's Notebook, 1987; The Night and the City, 1989; The Gate of the Sun, 1990. Address: 350 Hudson Street, New York, NY 10014, USA.

LAMBOT Isobel Mary, (Daniel Ingham, Mary Turner), b. 21 July 1926, Birmingham, England. Novelist. m. Maurice Edouard Lambot, 19 Dec 1959, dec. Education: BA, Liverpool University; Teaching Certificate, Birmingham University. Appointment: Tutor in Creative Writing, Lichfield Evening Institute, 1973-80. Publications: Under Isobel Lambot: Taste of Murder, 1966; Deadly Return, 1966; Shroud of Canvas, 1967; Dangerous Refuge, 1967; Danger Merchant, 1968; The Queen Dies First, 1968; Killer's Laughter, 1968; Let the Witness Die, 1969; Point of Death, 1969; Watcher on the Shore, 1971; Come Back and Die, 1972; Grip of Fear, 1974; The Identity Trap, 1978; Past Tense, 1979; Rooney's Gold, 1984; Still Waters Run Deadly, 1987; Blood Ties, 1987; Bloody Festival, 1991; The Flower of Violence, 1992; The Craft of Writing Crime Novels, 1992. Under Daniel Ingham: Contract for Death, 1972. Under Mary Turner: The Justice Hunt, 1975; So Bright a Lady, 1977; Runaway Lady, 1980. Contributions to: Women's journals. Memberships: Crime Writers' Association; Society of Authors; Writers' Guild of Great Britain; Mystery Writers of America. Address: 45 Bridge Street, Kington, Herefordshire NR5 3DW, England.

LAMMING George (Eric), b. 8 June 1927, Carrington Village, Barbados. Novelist. Appointments: Writer-in-Residence, University of the West Indies, Kingston, 1967-68. Publications: In the Castle of My Skin, 1953; The Emigrants, 1955; Of Age and Innocence, 1958; Water with Berries, 1971; Natives of My Person, 1972. Short Stories: David's Walk, 1948; A Wedding in Spring, 1960; Birthday Weather, 1966; Birds of a Feather, 1970. Honours: Guggenheim Fellowship, 1954; Maugham Award, 1957; Canada Council Fellowship, 1962; D Litt, University of West Indies, 1980. Address: 14a Highbury Place, London N5, England.

LAMONT Marianne. See: **RUNDLE Anne.**

LAMONT-BROWN Raymond, b. 20 Sept 1939, Horsforth, England. Author; Broadcaster. m. (2) Dr Elizabeth Moira McGregor, 6 Sept 1985. Education: MA; AMIET; FSA (Scot). Appointment: Managing Editor, Writers Monthly, 1984-86. Publications: Over 50 books including: Discovering Fife, 1988; The Life and Times of Berwick-upon-Tweed, 1988; The Life and Times of St Andrews, 1989; Royal Murder Mysteries, 1990; Scottish Epitaphs, 1990; Scottish Superstitions, 1990; Scottish Witchcraft, 1994; Scottish Folklore, 1996. Contributions to: Magazines and newspapers. Memberships: Society of Authors, secretary in Scotland, 1982-89; Rotary International, president, St Andrews Branch, 1984-85. Address: 11 Seabourne Gardens, Broughty Ferry, Dundee DD5 2RT, Scotland.

LAMPARD Dulcie Irene, b. 30 May 1923, Albany, Western Australia. Writer. Publications: Ride!, 1985, Saddle Up!, 1994. Honours: Bookshop of the Year Awards, 1980, 1984, 1988. Address: Lot 4, Mayo Road, Wooroloo, West Australia 6558, Australia.

LAMPITT Dinah, b. 6 Mar 1937, Essex, England. Author. m. L F Lampitt, 28 Nov 1959, dec, 1 son, 1 daughter. Education: Regent Street Polytechnic, London, England, 1950s. Appointments: Worked on Fleet Street for the Times, The Evening News and various magazines, 1950s. Publications: Sutton Place Trilogy: Sutton Place, 1983; The Silver Swan, 1984; Fortune's Soldier, 1985; To Sleep No More, 1987; Pour the Dark Wine, 1989; The King's Women, 1992; As Shadows Haunting, 1993; Banishment, 1994; Writing to Deryn Lake: Death in the Dark Walk, 1995; Death at the Beggars Opera, 1996; Death at the Devil's Tavern, 1997. Serials: The Moonlit Door; The Gemini Syndrome; The Staircase; The Anklets; The Wardrobe. Contributions to: Numerous short stories to women's magazines. Memberships: Society of Authors; Crime Writers Association. Address: c/o Darley Anderson, Estelle House, 11 Eustace Road, London SW6 1JB, England.

LAMPLUGH Lois Violet, b. 9 Jun 1921, Barnstaple, Devon, England. Author. m. Lawrence Carlile Davis, 24 Sep 1955, 1 son, 1 daughter. Education: BA Honours, Open University, 1980. Appointments: Editorial Staff, Jonathan Cape Publishers, 1946-56. Publications: The Pigeongram Puzzle, 1955; Nine Bright Shiners, 1955; Vagabond's Castle, 1957; Rockets in the Dunes, 1958; Sixpenny Runner, 1960; Midsummer Mountains, 1961; Rifle House Friends, 1965; Linhay on Hunter's Hill, 1966; Fur Princess and Fir Prince, 1969; Mandog, 1972; Sean's Leap, 1979; Winter Donkey, 1980; Falcon's Tor, 1984; Barnstaple: Town on the Taw, 1983; History of Ilfracombe, 1984; Minehead and Dunster, 1987; A Shadowed Man: Henry Williamson, 1990; Take Off From Chivenor, 1990; Sandrabbit, 1991; Lundy: Island Without Equal, 1993; A Book of Georgeham and the North West Corner of Devon, 1995; Ilfracombe in Old Photographs, 1996. Contributions to: Western Morning News. Memberships: Society of Authors; West Country Writers Association. Address: Springside, Bydown, Swimbridge, Devon EX32 0QB, England.

LAN David Mark, b. 1 June 1952, Cape Town, South Africa. Writer; Social Anthropologist. Education: BA, University of Cape Town, 1972; BSc 1976, PhD 1983, London School of Economics, UK. Publications: Guns and Rain, Guerrillas and Spirit Mediums in Zimbabwe, 1985. Plays: Painting a Wall, 1974; Bird Child, 1974; Homage to Been Soup, 1975; Paradise, 1975; The Winter Dancers, 1977; Not in Norwich, 1977; Red Earth, 1977; Sergeant Ola and His Followers, 1979; Flight, 1986; A Mouthful of Birds (with Caryl Churchill), 1986; Desire, 1990. Television films: The Sunday Judge, 1985; The Crossing, 1988; Welcome Home Comrades, 1990; Dark City, 1990. Radio Plays: Charley Tango, 1995. Adaptations: Ghetto, 1989; Hippolytos, 1991; Ion, 1993. Honours: John Whiting Award, 1977; George Orwell Memorial Award, 1983; Zürich International Television Prize, 1990. Address: c/o Judy Daish Associates, 83 Eastbourne Mews, London W2, England.

LANCASTER David. See: HEALD Timothy Villiers.

LANCASTER-BROWN Peter, b. 13 Apr 1927, Cue, Western Australia. Author. m. Johanne Nyrerod, 15 Aug 1953, 1 son. Education: Astronomy; Surveying; Mining Engineering; Civil Engineering. Publications: Twelve Came Back, 1957; Call of the Outback, 1970; What Star is That?, 1971; Astronomy in Colour, 1972; Australia's Coast of Coral and Pearl, 1972; Comets, Meteorites, and Men, 1973; Megaliths, Myths, and Men, 1976; Planet Earth in Colour, 1976; Megaliths and Masterminds, 1979; Fjord of Silent Men, 1983; Astronomy, 1984; Halley and His Comet, 1985; Halley's Comet and the

Principia, 1986; Skywatch, 1993. Contributions to: Blackwood's Nature; New Scientist; Sky and Telescope. Membership: Society of Authors. Address: 10A St Peter's Road, Aldeburgh, Suffolk, IP1 5BG, England.

LANDERT Walter, b. 3 Jan 1929, Zürich, Switzerland. Merchant. Education: Higher School of Commerce, Neuchâtel; Merchant Apprentice with diploma; Diploma, Swiss Mercantile School, London; Student Trainee, Westminster Bank, London. Publications: Manager auf Zeit (novel), 1968; Selbstbefragung (poems), 1969; Entwurf Schweiz (literary essay), 1970; Koitzsch (novel), 1971; Traum einer besseren Welt (short stories and poems), 1980; UnKraut im helvetischen Kulturgartchen (literary essays), 1981; Meine Frau baut einen Bahnhof (short stories), 1982; Klemms Memorabilien - Ein Vorspiel (novel), 1989; Umwerfende Zeiten: Ein Prozess (novel), 1990; Treffpunkt: Fondue Bourguignonne (novel), 1993. Contributions to: Various newspapers. Honours: Artemis Jubilee Prize, 1969; Poetry Prize, Literary Union, Saarbrücken, 1977. Memberships: Swiss Authors; Olten Group. Address: Lendikonerstrasse 54, CH 8484 Weisslingen/ZH, Switzerland.

LANDESMAN Jay (Irving), b. 15 July 1919, St Louis, Missouri, USA. Author; Dramatist; Producer; Publisher. m. Frances Deitsch, 15 July 1950, 2 sons. Education: University of Missouri, 1938-40; Rice Institute, Houston, 1940-42. Publications: The Nervous Set (novel), 1954, as a Broadway musical, 1959, A Walk on the Wild Side (musical), 1960; Molly Darling (musical), 1963; The Babies (play), 1969; Bad Nipple (novel), 1970; Rebel Without Applause (memoir), 1987; Small Day Tomorrow (screenplay), 1990; Jaywalking, memoirs vol 2, 1992. Memberships: American Federation of Television and Radio Artists; Dramatists Guild. Address: 8 Duncan Terrace, London N1 8BZ, England.

LANDIS J(ames) D(avid), b. 30 June, 1942, Springfield, Massachusetts, USA. Publisher; Author. m. (1) Patricia Lawrence Straus, 15 Aug 1964, div, 1 daughter, (2) Denise Evelyn Tillar, 20 July 1982, 2 sons. Education: BA, magna cum laude, Yale College, 1964. Appointments: Assitant Editor, Abelard Schuman, 1966-67; Editor to Senior Editor, 1967-80, Senior Vice-President, and Publisher, Quill Trade paperbacks, 1980-85. Publications: The Sisters Impossible, 1979; Love's Detective, 1984; Daddy's Girl, 1984; Joey and the Girls, 1987; The Band Never Dances, 1989; Looks Aren't Everything, 1990; Lying in Bed, 1995. Contibutions to: Periodicals. Honours: Roger Klein Award for Editing, 1973; Advocate Humanitarian Award, 1977; Morton Dauwen Zabel Award for fiction, American Academy of Arts and Letters, 1996. Memberships: PEN; Phi Beta Kappa. Address: 19 Gill Street, Exeter, NH 03833, USA.

LANDON H(oward) C(handler) Robbins, b. 6 Mar 1926, Boston, Massachusetts, USA. Musicologist; Writer. m. (1) Christa Landon, (2) Else Radant. Education: Swarthmore College; BMus, Boston University, 1947. Appointments: Guest Lecturer, various US and European colleges and universities; Many radio and television talks. Publications: The Symphonies of Joseph Haydn, 1955; The Mozart Companion (editor with Donald Mitchell), 1956, 2nd edition, revised, 1965; The Collected Correspondence and London Notebooks of Joseph Haydn, 1959; Beethoven: A Documentary Study, 1970; Essays on the Viennese Classical Style: Gluck, Haydn, Mozart, Beethoven, 1970; Haydn: Chronicle and Works, 5 volumes, 1976-80; Haydn: A Documentary Study, 1981; Mozart and the Masons, 1983; Handel and His World, 1984; 1791: Mozart's Last Year, 1988; Haydn: His Life and Music (with D Jones), 1988; Mozart: The Golden Years, 1989; The Mozart Compendium (editor), 1990; Mozart and Vienna, 1991; Five Centuries of Music in Venice, 1991; Une Journée Particulière de Mozart, 1993; Vivaldi: Voice of the Baroque, 1993; The Mozart Essays, 1995. Other: Editor of complete editions of Haydn's symphonies, 1965-68, string quartets (co-editor), 1968-83, and piano trios, 1970-78. Contributions to: Scholarly books and professional journals. Honours: Various. Memberships: Musicological societies. Address: Chateau de Foncoussières, 81800 Rabastens, Tarn, France.

LANDRY Yves, b. 23 Dec 1952, St Jean sur Richelieu, Quebec, Canada. Historian; Demographer. m. Manon Pomerleau, 17 Aug 1974, 2 sons. Education: BA, History, 1974, MA, History, Université de Montreal, 1977; Doctorate, Historical Demography, Ecole des hautes études en sciences sociales, Paris, 1990. Appointment: Professor of History, Université de Montreal. Publications: Inventaire des registres paroissiaux catholiques du Quebec 1621-1876 (co-author), 1990; Pour le Christ et le Roi La vie au temps des premiers Montréalais (editor), 1992; Orphelines en France, pionnières au Canada: les Filles du roi au

XVII siècle, 1992; The First French Canadians, Pioneers in the St Lawrence Valley (co-author), 1993. Contributions to: Revue d'histoire de l'Amérique française; Histoire sociale-Social History; Annales de Démographie Historique; Journal of Family History; Social Science History; Cahiers Québécois de Démographie; Histoire, Economie et Société. Honours: Queen's Fellowship, Canada Council, 1975; Jean Charles Falardeau Prize, 1993; Percy W Foy Prize, 1993. Memberships: International Union for the Scientific Study of Population, 1985-; Institut d'histoire de l'Amérique Française, treasurer, 1993-95; Société de Démographie Historique; Union des écrivains du Quebec. Address: Départment d'Histoire, Université de Montreal, CP 6128, Succursale Centreville, Montreal, Quebec H3C 3J7, Canada.

LANE Helen, (Helen Hudson), b. 31 Jan 1920, New York, New York, USA. Writer. m. Robert Lane, 15 Nov 1944, 2 sons. Education: BA, Bryn Mawr College, 1941; MA, 1943, PhD, 1950, Columbia University. Publications: Tell the Time to None, 1966; Meyer Meyer, 1967; The Listener, 1968; Farnsbee South, 1971; Criminal Trespass, 1986; A Temporary Residence, 1987. Contributions to: Antioch Review; Sewannee Review; Virginia Quarterly; Northwest Review; Mademoiselle; Quarterly Review of Literature; Red Book; Ellery Queen; Mid-Stream; Best American Short Stories; O Henry Prize Stories. Honour: Virginia Quarterly Prize Story, 1963. Memberships: Authors Guild; Authors League; American PEN. Address: 558 Chapel Street, New Haven, CT 06511, USA.

LANE M Travis, (Millicent Elizabeth Travis), b. 23 Sept 1934, San Antonio, Texas, USA (Canadian citizen, 1973). Writer. m. Lauriat Lane, 26 Aug 1957, 1 son, 1 daughter. Education: BA, Vassar College, 1956; MA, 1957, PhD, 1967, Cornell University. Appointments: Assistantships, Cornell University, University of New Brunswick; Honorary Research Associate, University of New Brunswick. Publications: Five Poets: Cornell, 1960; An Inch or So of Garden, 1969; Poems 1968-72, 1973; Homecomings, 1977; Divinations and Shorter Poems 1973-78, 1980; Reckonings, Poems 1979-85, 1988; Solid Things: Poems New and Selected, 1989; Temporary Shelter, 1993; Night Physics, 1994. Contributions to: Canadian Literature; Dalhousie Review; Ariel; Essays on Canadian Writing; University of Toronto Quarterly; Fiddlehead Magazine. Honour: Pat Lowther Prize, League of Canadian Poets, 1980. Address: 807 Windsor Street, Fredericton, New Brunswick, E3B 4G7, Canada.

LANE Patrick, b. 26 Mar 1939, Nelson, Canada. Writer; Poet. 4 sons, 1 daughter. Appointments: Editor, Very Stone House, Publishers, Vancouver, 1966-72; Writer-in-Residence, University of Manitoba, Winnipeg, 1978-79, University of Ottawa, 1980, University of Alberta, Edmonton, 1981-82, Saskatoon Public Library, 1982-83, Concordia University, 1985, Globe Theatre Company, Regina, Saskatchewan, 1985-. Publications: Letters From the Savage Mind, 1966; For Rita: In Asylum, 1969; Calgary City Jail, 1969; Separations, 1969; Sunflower Seeds, 1969; On the Street, 1970; Mountain Oysters, 1971; Hiway 401 Rhapsody, 1972; The Sun Has Begun to Eat the Mountain, 1972; Passing into Storm, 1973; Beware the Months of Fire, 1974; Certs, 1974; Unborn Things: South American Poems, 1975; For Riel in That Gawdam Prison, 1975; Albino Pheasants, 1977; If, 1977; Poems, New and Selected, 1978; No Longer Two People (with Lorna Uher), 1979; The Measure, 1980; Old Mother, 1982; Woman in the Dust, 1983; A Linen Crow, a Caftan Magpie, 1985; Selected Poems, 1987; Milford and Me, 1989; Winter, 1990; Mortal Remains, 1992; How Do You Spell Beautiful, 1992. Contributions to: Most major Canadian magazines, American and English journals. Honour: Governor-General's Award for Poetry, 1979. Memberships: League of Canadian Poets; Writer's Union of Canada. Address: c/o Writer's Union of Canada, 24 Ryerson Avenue, Toronto, Ontario M5T 2P3, Canada.

LANE Roumelia, b. 31 Dec 1927, Bradford, West Yorkshire, England. Writer.m. Gavin Green, 1 Oct 1949, 1 son, 1 daughter. Appointment: Writer, Bournemouth Echo, mid 1950's. Publications: Numerous books, including: Sea of Zanj; Rose of the Desert; Cafe Mimosa; Harbour of Deceit; Desert Haven; Bamboo Wedding; Night of the Beguine; The Chasm; The Nawindi Flier. Television and film scripts: Stardust; The Chasm; Tender Saboteur; Chantico; Turn of the Tide; Gilligan's Last Gamble; Where Are The Clowns?; Death From the Past. Contributions to: Various journals and magazines. Memberships: Society of Authors of Great Britain; Writers Guild of Great Britain; Affiliate Member, Writers Guild of America (East and West). Address: Casa Mimosa, Santa Eugenia, Majorca, Beleares, Spain.

LANG Grace. See: **FLOREN Lee.**

LANG King. See: **TUBB E(dwin) C(harles).**

LANGDALE Cecily, b. 27 July 1939, New York, New York, USA. Art Dealer; Art Historian. m. Roy Davis, 24 July 1972. Education: BA, Swarthmore College, 1961. Publications: Gwen John: Paintings and Drawings from the Collection of John Quinn and Others (with Betsy G Fryberger), 1982; Monotypes by Maurice Prendergast in the Terra Museum of Art, 1984; Gwen John: An Interior Life (with David Fraser Jenkins), 1985; Gwen John: With a Catalogue of the Paintings and a Selection of the Drawings, 1987. Contributions to: Books and journals; Maurice Brazil Prendergast, Charles Prendergast: A Catalogue Raisonné, 1990. Address: 231 East 60th Street, New York, NY 10022, USA.

LANGE John. See: **CRICHTON Michael.**

LANGER Lawrence L(ee), b. 20 June 1929, New York, New York, USA. Professor Emeritus; Author. m. Sondra Weinstein, 21 Feb 1951, 1 son, 1 daughter. Education: BA, City College, New York City, 1951; MA, 1952, PhD, 1961, Harvard University. Appointments: Instructor, 1956-61, Assistant Professor, 1961-66, Associate Professor, 1966-72, Professor, 1972-76, Alumnae Chair Professor, 1976-92, Professor Emeritus, 1992-, Simmons College. Publications: The Holocaust and the Literary Imagination, 1975; The Age of Artocity: Death in Modern Literature, 1978; Versions of Survival: The Holocaust and the Human Spirit, 1982; Holocaust Testimonies: The Ruins of Memory, 1991; Admitting the Holocaust: Collected Essays, 1994; Art from the Ashes: A Holocaust Anthology, 1994. Contributions to: Journals. Honour: National Book Critics Circle Award, 1991. Membership: PEN. Address: 249 Adams Avenue, West Newton, MA 02165, USA.

LANGFORD Gary (Raymond), b. 21 Aug 1947, Christchurch, New Zealand. Writer; Senior Lecturer. 1 daughter. Education: BA, 1969, MA (Hons), History, 1971, MA (Hons), English, 1973, University of Canterbury; Diploma of Teaching Drama, Christchurch Secondary Teachers College, 1973. Appointments: Senior Lecturer, Creative Writing, University of Western Sydney, 1986; Writer-in-Residence, University of Canterbury, 1989. Publications: 21 Books, including 9 novels such as Death of the Early Morning Hero, 1975; Players in the Ballgame, 1979; Vanities, 1984; Pillbox, 1986; Newlands, 1990 and 7 books of poetry such as Four Ships, 1982; The Pest Exterminator's Shakespeare, 1984; Bushido, 1987; Love at the Traffic Lights, 1990; Poetry and Anthologies; 150-200 performances of scripts and plays on stage, television and radio. Honours: Young Writers Fellowship, Australia Council, 1976; Alan Marshall Award, 1983. Address: c/o Curtis Brown Pty Ltd, Box 19, Paddington, New South Wales 2021, Australia.

LANGFORD GINIBI Ruby, b. 26 Jan 1934, Box Ridge Mission, Coraki, New South Wales, Australia. Author. div, 4 sons, 5 daughters. Appointments: Over 200 lectures in schools, universities and colleges; Lecturer in Aboriginal History, Culture and Politics, last three years. Publications: Don't Take Your Love to Town, 1988; Real Deadly, 1992; My Bundjalung People, 1994; Koori Voices, poetry; Haunted By the Past, The Story of Nobby and Others, due 1997; Only Gammon, book of Koori humour, forthcoming. Contributions to: Women's Weekly. Honours: Human Rights Literature Award, 1988; Inaugural History Fellowship, Ministry of Arts, 1990; Inaugural Honorary Fellow, National Australian Museum, Canberra, 1995. Membership: Australian Society of Authors. Literary Agent: Rose Crestwell, Cameron and Crestwell Agency, Suite 5, Edgecliff Court, 2 New McLean Street, Edgecliff, New South Wales 2027, Australia. Address: 18 Hewlett Street, Granville, New South Wales 2142, Australia.

LANGHOLM Neil. See: **BULMER Henry Kenneth.**

LANGTON Jane (Gillson), b. 30 Dec 1922, Boston, Massachusetts, USA. Writer. m. William Langton, 10 June 1943, 3 sons. Education: BA, 1944, MA, 1945, University of Michigan; MA, Radcliffe College, 1948. Publications: For Adults: The Transcendental Murder, 1964; Dark Nantucket Noon, 1975; The Memorial Hall Murder, 1978; Natural Enemy, 1982; Emily Dickinson is Dead, 1984; Good and Dead, 1986; Murder at the Gardner, 1988; The Dante Game, 1991; God in Concord, 1992; Divine Inspiration, 1993; The Shortest Day, 1995; Dead as a Dodo, 1996. For Children: Her Majesty, Grace Jones, 1961; Diamond in the Window, 1962; The Swing in the Summerhouse, 1967; The Astonishing Stereoscope, 1971; The Boyhood of Grace Jones, 1972; Paper Chains, 1977; The Fledgling, 1980; The Fragile

Flag, 1984. Honours: Newbery Honor Book, 1981; Nero Wolfe Award, 1984. Address: Baker Farm Road, Lincoln, MA 01773, USA.

LANIER Sterling E(dmund), b. 18 Dec 1927, New York, New York, USA. Writer; Sculptor. Appointments: Research Historian, Winterthur Museum, Switzerland, 1958-60; Editor, John C Winston Company, 1961, Chilton Books, 1961-62, 1965-67, Macrae-Smith Company, 1963-64; Full-time Writer and Sculptor, 1967-. Publications: The War for the Lot (juvenile), 1969; The Peculiar Exploits of Brigadier Ffellowes (short stories), 1972; Hiero's Journey, 1973; The Unforsaken Hiero, 1983; Menace Under Marwood, 1983; The Curious Quest of Brig Ffellowes, 1986. Address: c/o Curtis Brown Ltd, 10 Astor Place, New York, NY 10003, USA.

LANSIDE Luke. See: **CRAGGS Robert S.**

LANTRY Mike. See: **TUBB E(dwin) C(harles).**

LAPHAM Lewis H, b. 8 Jan 1935, San Francisco, California, USA. Writer. married, 3 children. Education: BA, Yale University, 1956; Cambridge University. Appointments: Reporter, San Francisco Examiner, 1957-59, New York Herald Tribune, 1960-62; Managing Editor, Harper's Magazine, 1976-81, 1983-; Syndicated newspaper columnist, 1981-87; Lecturer in universities including Yale, Stanford, Michigan, Virginia and Oregon; Appearances on American and British television, National Public Radio and Canadian Public Radio. Publications: Fortune's Child (essays), 1980; Money and Class in America, 1988; Imperial Masquerade, 1990; Hotel America: Scenes in the Lobby of the Fin-de-Siècle, 1995. Host, author of six-part documentary series, America's Century, 1989; Host, editor, Bookmark, a weekly public television series. Contributions to: Monthly essay for Harper's magazine as "Notebook"; Commentary; National Review; The Yale Literary Magazine; Elle; Fortune; Forbes; American Spectator; Vanity Fair; Parade; Channels; Maclean's; London Observer; New York Times; Wall Street Journal. Honour: National Magazine Award, 1995. Address: c/o Harper's Magazine, 666 Broadway, New York, NY 10012, USA.

LAPPE Frances Moore, b. 10 Feb 1944, Pendleton, Oregon, USA. Educator. m. Paul Martin Du Bois, 19 Aug 1991, 1 son, 1 daughter. Education: BA, Earlham College, Indiana. Publications: Diet for a Small Planet, 1971; Food First: Beyond the Myth of Scarcity (co-author), 1977; World Hunger, Ten Myths (co-author), 1979; Aid as Obstacle, 1980; Mozambique and Tanzania: Asking the Big Questions and Casting New Molds: First Steps Toward Worker Control in a Mozambique Factory (co-author), 1980; What to Do After You Turn Off the TV: Fresh Ideas for Enjoying Family Time, 1985; World hunger: Twelve Myths, 1986; Betraying the National Interest (co-author), 1987; Rediscovering America's Values, 1989; Taking Population Seriously (co-author), 1989; The Quickening of America (co-author), 1994. Contributions to: New York Times; Harper's; Reader's Digest; Journal of Nutrition Education; War on Hunger. Address: Center for Living Democracy, Black Fox Road, Brattleboro, VT 05301, USA.

LAPPING Brian (Michael), b. 13 Sept 1937, London, England. Television Producer; Journalist; Editor. Education: BA, Pembroke College, Cambridge, 1959. Appointments: Reporter, Daily Mirror, London, England, 1959-61; Reporter and Deputy Commonwealth Correspondent, The Guardian, London, 1961-67; Editor, Venture, Fabian Society monthly journal, 1965-69; Feature Writer, Financial Times, London, 1967-68; Deputy Editor, New Society, London, 1968-70; Television Producer, Granada Television Ltd, 1970-88; Executive Producer, World in Action 1976-78, The State of the Nation 1978-80, End of Empire 1980-85; Chief Executive, Brian Lapping Associates, 1988-; Executive Producer, Countdown to War, 1989; Hypotheticals (three programmes annually for BBC2); The Second Russian Revolution (8 programmes for BBC2), 1991; Question Time (weekly for BBC1), 1991-94; The Washington Version (for BBC2), 1992; Watergate (for BBC2), 1994; Fall of the Wall (for BBC2), 1994; The Death of Yugoslavia, 1995. Publications: More Power to the People (co-editor), 1968; The Labour Government 1964-70, 1970; The State of the Nation: Parliament (editor), 1973; The State of the Nation: The Bounds of Freedom, 1980; End of Empire, 1985; Apartheid: A History, 1986. Honours: Royal Television Society Award, Broadcasting Press Guild Award, 1991; Emmy Award, DuPont Award; 12 international awards, 1995. Address: 61 Eton Avenue, London NW3, England.

LAQUEUR Walter (Ze'ev), b. 26 May 1921, Breslau, Germany. History Educator. m. Barbara Koch, 29 May 1941, dec, 2 daughters, m. Susi Wichmann, 1995. Appointments: Journalist, Freelance Author, 1944-55; Editor, Survey, 1955-65; Co-Editor, Journal of Contemporary History, 1966-; Member, Center for Strategic and International Studies, Washington, DC. Publications: Communism and Nationalism in the Middle East, 1956; Young Germany, 1961; Russia and Germany, 1965; The Road to War, 1968; Europe since Hitler, 1970; Out of the Ruins of Europe, 1971; Zionism, a History, 1972; Confrontation: The Middle East and World Politics, 1974; Weimar: A Cultural History 1918-1933, 1974; Guerrilla, 1976; Terrorism, 1977; The Missing Years, 1980; A Reader's Guide to Contemporary History (joint editor), 1972; Fascism: A Reader's Guide (editor), 1978; The Terrible Secret, 1980; Farewell to Europe, 1981; Germany Today: A Personal Report, 1985; World of Secrets: The Uses and Limits of Intelligence, 1986; The Long Road to Freedom: Russia and Glasnost, 1989; Thursday's Child Has Far to Go, 1993. Honours: Recipient, 1st Distinguished Writer's Award, Center for Strategic and International Studies, 1969; Inter Nations Award, 1985. Address: Center for Strategic and International Studies, 1800 K Street North West, Washington, DC 20006, USA.

LARDNER Ring(gold Wilmer), Jr, b. 19 Aug 1915, Chicago, Illinois, USA. Screenwriter; Author. m. Frances Chaney, 28 Sept 1946. Education: Phillips Academy, Andover, Massachusetts; Princeton University. Publications: The Ectasy of Owen Muir, 1954; The Lardners: My Family Remembered, 1976; All for Love, 1985. Other: Various screenplays. Honours: Best Original Screenplay, 1942, Best Screenplay Based on Material from Another Medium, 1970, Academy of Motion Picture Arts and Sciences; Best Comedy Award, Writers Guild of America, 1970; Laurel Award for Lifetime Achievement in Screenwriting, Writers Guild of America, 1989. Memberships: PEN; Screen Writers Guild; Writers Guild of America. Address: c/o Jim Preminger Agency, 1650 Westwood Boulevard, Los Angeles, CA 90024, USA.

LARKIN Rochelle, b. 6 May 1935, New York, New York, USA. Writer. Appointments: Editor, Countrywide Publications, 1963; Kanrom Inc, 1964-70, Pinnacle Books, 1970; Editor-in-Chief, Lancer Books, 1973-74, Female Bodybuilding Magazine, 1986-89, Bodybuilding Lifestyles Magazine, 1990-91; Editor, Walman Publishing, 1992-. Publications: Soul Music, 1970; Supermarket Superman, 1970; Teen Scene (with Milburn Smith), 1971; The Godmother, 1971; Honour Thy Godmother, 1972; For Godmother and Country, 1972; 365 Ways to Say I Want To Be Your Friend (with Milburn Smith), 1973; Black Magic, 1974; The Beatles: Yesterday, Today, Tomorrow, 1974; The Greek Goddess, 1975; Call Me Anytime, 1975; International Joke Book, 1975; The Raging Flood, 1976; Hail Columbia, 1976; The First One, 1976; Valency Girl (with Robin Moore), 1976; Pusher, 1976; Sexual Superstars, 1976; Harvest of Desire, 1976; Kitty, 1977; Mafia Wife (with Robin Moore), 1977; Mistress of Desire, 1978; Instant Beauty (with Pablo Manzoni), 1978; Tri (with Robin Moore), 1978; Torches of Desire, 1979; Glitterball, 1980; Beverly Johnson's Guide to a Life of Health and Beauty (with Julie Davis), 1981; Only Perfect, 1981; Golden Days, Silver Nights, 1982; Amber series (as Darrell Fairfield), 6 volumes, 1982; The Crystal Heart, 1983; Angels Never Sleep, 1984. Address: 351 East 84th Street, New York, NY 10028, USA.

LARSEN Eric Everett, b. 29 Nov 1941, Northfield, Minnesota, USA. College Educator; Writer. m. Anne Schnare, 5 June 1965, 2 daughters. Education: BA, Carleton College, 1963; MA, 1964, PhD, 1971, University of Iowa. Appointment: Professor of English, John Jay College of Criminal Justice, City University of New York, 1971-. Publications: Novels: An American Memory, 1988; I Am Zoe Handke, 1992. Contributions to: Harper's; New Republic; Nation; Los Angeles Times Book Review; North American Review; New England Review. Honour: Heartland Prize, Chicago Tribune, 1988. Address: c/o Brandt and Brandt, Literary Agents Inc, 1501 Broadway, New York, NY 10036, USA.

LASKA Vera, b. 21 July 1923, Kosice, Czechoslovakia. Professor; Lecturer; Columnist; Author. m. Andrew J Laska, 5 Nov 1949, 2 sons. Education: MA, History, 1946, MA, Philosophy, 1946, Charles University, Prague; PhD History, University of Chicago, 1959. Appointments: Professor of History, Regis College, Weston, Massachusetts, USA, 1966-; Fulbright Professor, Charles University, Prague, 1993. Publications: Remember the Ladies, Outstanding Women of the American Revolution, 1976; Franklin and Women, 1978; Czechs in America 1633-1977, 1978; Benjamin Franklin the Diplomat,

1982; Women in the Resistance and in the Holocaust, 1983, 2nd edition, 1988; Nazism, Resistance and Holocaust: A Bibliography, 1985. Contributions to: Over 200 articles and book reviews in newspapers and professional journals. Address: 50 Woodchester Drive, Weston, MA 02193, USA.

LASKOWSKI Jacek Andrzej, b. 4 June 1946, Edinburgh, Scotland. Dramatist; Translator. m. Anne Grant Howieson, 8 July 1978, 2 daughters. Education: MagPhil, Jagiellonian Universiy, Krakow, Poland, 1973. Appointment: Literary Manager, Haymarket Theatre, Leicester, 1984-87. Publications: Plays produced: Dreams to Damnation, BBC Radio 3, 1977; Pawn Takes Pawn, BBC Radio 4, 1978; The Secret Agent, BBC Radio 4, 1980; Nostromo, BBC Radio 4, 1985; Phoney Physician (after Molière), 1986; Orestes/Electra (with Nancy Meckler), 1987; Wiseguy Scapino (after Molière), 1993. Memberships: Theatre Writers Union, General Secretary, 1981-82; Society of Authors, Vice-Chairman, Broadcasting Committee, 1983-83. Address: c/o Michael Imison Playwrights, 28 Almeida Street, London N1 1TD, England.

LASSITER Adam. See: **KRAUZER Steven M.**

LATHAM Mavis. See: **CLARK Marvis Thorpe.**

LAU Evelyn, b. 1971, Canada. Poet; Writer. Publications: You Are Not Who You Claim, 1990; Oedipal Dreams, 1992; In the House of Slaves, 1994; Fresh Girls and Other Stories, 1995; Other Women, 1995. Address: c/o Coach House Press, 50 Prince Arthur Avenue, Suite 107, Toronto, Ontario M5R 1B5, Canada.

LAURIDSEN Soren K, b. 12 May 1945, Esbjerg, Denmark. Writer; Director. m. Liselotte, 26 Sept 1992, 2 daughters. Education: MAsters Degree, Royal Academy of Educational Studies, Copenhagen, 1985. Publications: A Place in the Reservate, 1974; Landscape with Windmill, 1982; Against a Sinking Globe, 1988; The Dream of Boca del Cielo, 1993. Membership: Danish Writers Union. Address: Brombaervej 10, 8410 Ronde, Denmark.

LAURIE Rona, b. 16 Sept 1916, Derby, England. Actress; Writer; Drama Lecturer; Professor of Speech and Drama. m. Edward Lewis Neilson, 1961. Education: Penrhos College; University of Birmingham; Royal Academy of Dramatic Art. Appointments: Tutors, Actors Centre; Dramatic Critic Teachers' World; Dramatic Critic, On Stage (Australia); Professor of Speech and Drama, Guildhall School of Music. Publications: A Hundred Speeches from the Theatre, 1966; Adventures in Group Speaking, 1967; Speaking Together I & II, 1966; Scenes and Ideas, 1967; Festivals and Ajudication, 1975; Children's Plays from Beatrix Potter, 1980; Auditioning, 1985; Mrs Tiggywinkle and Friends, 1986; The Actors' Art and Craft, 1994. Contributions to: Speaking Shakespeare Today (Speech and Drama); Speaking the Sonnet (Speech and Drama). Memberships: Guild of Drama Adjudicators; Society of Teachers of Speech and Drama; Royal Society of arts, fellow. Address: 21 New Quebec Street, London W1H 7DE, England.

LAURO Shirley (Shapiro), b. 18 Nov 1933, Des Moines, Iowa, USA. Actress; Playwright; Teacher. m. (1) Norton Mezvinsky, div, (2) Louis Paul Lauro, 18 Aug 1973. Education: BS, Northwestern University, 1955; MS, University of Wisconsin at Madison, 1957. Appointments: Actress, stage, films, and television; Instructor, City College of the City University of New York, 1967-71, Yeshiva University, 1971-76, Manhattan Community College, 1978, Marymount Manhattan College, 1978-79; Literary Consultant, 1975-80, Resident Playwright, 1976-, Ensemble Studio Theatre, New York City; Resident Playwright, Alley Theatre, Houston, 1987; Adjunct Professor of Playwrighting, Tisch School of the Arts, New York University, 1989-. Publications: The Edge, 1965; The Contest, 1975; Open Admissions, Nothing Immediate, I Don't Know Where You're Coming From At All!, The Coal Diamond, Margaret and Kit, 1979; In the Garden of Eden, 1982; Sunday Go to Meetin', 1986; Pearls on the Moon, 1987; A Piece of My Heart, 1992; A Moment in Time, 1994; The Last Trial of Clarence Darrow, 1997; Railing it Uptown, 1997. Contributions to: Periodicals. Honours: Numerous. Memberships: Authors Guild; Authors League; Dramatists Guild; Council and Steering Committee; League of Professional Theatre Women; PEN; Writers Guild of America. Address: 275 Central Park West, New York, NY 10024, USA.

LAVERS Norman, b. 21 Apr 1935, Berkeley, California, USA. Teacher; Writer. m. Cheryl Dicks, 20 July 1967, 1 son. Education: BA,

1960, MA, 1963, San Francisco State University; PhD, University of Iowa, 1969. Publications: Mark Harris (criticism) 1978; Selected Short Stories, 1979; Jerzy Kosinski (criticism) 1982; The Northwest Passage (novel), 1984; Pop Culture Into Art: The Novels of Manuel Puig (criticism), 1988. Contributions to: Editor, Arkansas Review; Contributing Editor, Bird Watcher's Digest. Honours: National Endowment for the Arts Fellowships, 1982, 1991; Editor's Choice Award, 1986; Hohenberg Award, 1986; O Henry Award, 1987; Pushcart Award, 1992; William Peden Prize, 1992; The Porter Fund Award, 1995. Address: 3968 CR 901, Jonesboro, AR 72401, USA.

LAWRENCE Clifford Hugh, b. 28 Dec 1921, London, England. Professor of Mediaeval History. m. Helen Maud Curran, 11 July 1953, 1 son, 5 daughters. Education: Lincoln College, Oxford, 1946-51; BA Hons, Class I, History, 1948; MA, 1953; DPhil (Oxon), 1955. Publications: St Edmund of Abingdon: A Study of Hagiography and History, 1960; The English Church and the Papacy, 1965; Medieval Monasticism, Forms of Religious Life in Western Europe in the Middle Ages, 1984, 2nd edition, 1989; The University in State and Church, History of the University of Oxford, Vol I, 1984; The Friars: The Impact of the Early Mendicant Movement on Medieval Society, 1994; The Life of St Edmund by Matthew Paris, 1996. Contributions to: English Historical Review; History; Journal of Ecclesiastical History; The Month; The Tablet; Times Literary Supplement; Times Higher Education Supplement; Spectator. Memberships: Fellow, Royal Historical Society; Society of Antiquaries; Reform Club. Address: 11 Durham Road, London SW20 0QH, England.

LAWRENCE Jerome, b. 14 July 1915, Cleveland, Ohio, USA. Playwright; Lyricist; Biographer. Education: BA, Ohio State University, 1937; Graduate Studies, University of California at Los Angeles, 1939-40. Appointments: Partner, 1942-, President, 1955, Lawrence and Lee Inc, New York City and Los Angeles; Professor of Playwriting, University of Southern California, New York University, Baylor University, Ohio State University. Publications: Look, Ma, I'm Dancin' (co-author), musical, 1948; Inherit the Wind (with Robert E Lee), 1955; Auntie Mame (with Lee), 1957; The Gang's All Here (with Lee), 1960; Only in America (with Lee), 1960; Checkmate (with Lee), 1961; Mame (co-author), musical, 1967; Dear World, musical, 1969; Sparks Fly Upward (co-author), 1969; The Night Thoreau Spent in Jail (with Lee), 1970; Live Spelled Backwards, 1970; The Incomparable Max (with Lee), 1972; The Crocodile Smile (with Lee), 1972; Actor: The Life and Times of Paul Muni, 1974; Jabberwock (with Lee), 1974; First Monday in October (with Lee), 1975; Whisper in the Mind (with Lee and Norman Cousins), 1987. Memberships: Dramatists Guild; Authors League. Address: 21056 Las Flores Mesa Drive, Malibu, CA 90265, USA.

LAWRENCE Karen Ann, b. 5 Feb 1951, Windsor, Ontario, Canada. Writer. m. Robert Gabhart, 18 Dec 1982, 1 son. Education: BA (Hons), University of Windsor, 1973; MA, University of Alberta, 1977. Publications: Nekuia: The Inanna Poems, 1980; The Life of Helen Alone, 1986; Springs of Living Water, 1990. Honours: W H Smith/Books in Canada First Novel Award, 1987; Best First Novel Award, PEN, Los Angeles Center, 1987. Memberships: Writers' Union of Canada; Association of Canadian Radio and Television Artists. Address: 2153 Pine Street, San Diego, CA 92103, USA.

LAWRENCE Louise, b. 5 June 1943, Surrey, England. Novelist. m. Graham Mace, 28 Aug 1987, 1 son, 2 daughters. Publications: Andra, 1971; Power of Stars, 1972; Wyndcliffe, 1974; Sing and Scatter Daisies, 1977; Star Lord, 1978; Cat Call, 1980; Earth Witch, 1981; Calling B for Butterfly, 1982; Dram Road, 1983; Children of the Dust, 1985; Moonwind, 1986; Warriors of Taan, 1986; Extinction is Forever, 1990; Ben-Harran's Castle, 1992; The Disinherited, 1994. Address: 22 Church Road, Cinderford, Gloucestershire GL14 2EA, England.

LAWRENCE P. See: **TUBB E(dwin) C(harles).**

LAWRENCE Steven C. See: **MURPHY Lawrence Agustus.**

LAWSON Chet. See: **TUBB E(dwin) C(harles).**

LAWSON James, b. 8 Dec 1938, New York, New York, USA. Author; Company Executive. Education: Sorbonne, University of Paris, 1959-60; BA, Boston University, 1961. Appointments: Copywriter, McCann-Marschalk Advertising, 1961-62, Thompson Advertising, 1963-64, Al Paul Lefton Advertising, 1964-66; Reporter, Aspen Times, Colorado, 1962; Vice-President, Copy Supervisor, Doyle Bernbach

Advertising, 1966-78; Senior Vice-President, Director, Creative Services, Doremus and Company, 1978-80, Senior Vice-President, Creative Director, DDB Needham Worldwide, 1982-93. Publications: XXX, 1963; Disconnections, 1968; The American Book of the Dead, 1972; Crimes of the Unconscious, 1974; The Girl Watcher, 1976; The Copley Chronicles, 1980; The Fanatic, 1980; Forgeries of the Heart, 1982; The Madman's Kiss, 1988; Frederick Law Olmsted (teleplay), 1990; The Reluctant God, 1993; Andris in Isolation (play), 1993. Address: 756 Greenwich Street, New York, NY 10014, USA.

LAYTON Andrea. See: **BANCROFT Iris.**

LAYTON Irving (Peter), b. 12 Mar 1912, Neamts, Romania. Poet; Professor of English Literature. m., 2 sons, 3 daughters. Education: BSc, Macdonald College, 1939; MA, McGill University, 1946. Appointments: Part-Time Lecturer, 1949-68, Poet-in-Residence, 1965-69, Sir George Williams University, Montreal; Professor of English Literature, York University, Toronto, 1968-78; Writer-in-Residence, University of Guelph, Ontario, 1969-70, University of Toronto, 1981; Adjunct Professor of Writer-in-Residence, Concordia University, 1988-89. Publications: Periods of the Moon: Poems, 1967; The Shattered Plinths, 1968; The Whole Bloody Bird, 1969; Selected Poems, 1969; Poems to Colour: A Selection of Workshop Poems (editor), 1970; Collected Poems, 1971; Nail Polish, 1971; Engagements: The Prose of Irving Layton, 1972; Lovers and Lesser Men, 1973; Anvil Blood: A Selection of Workshop Poems (editor), 1973; The Pole-Vaulter, 1974; Seventy-Five Greek Poems, 1974; Selected Poems, 2 volumes, 1975; For My Brother Jesus, 1976; The Uncollected Poems, 1936-59, 1976; The Poems of Irving Layton, 1977; The Covenant, 1977; Taking Sides: The Collected Social and Political Writings, 1977; The Tightrope Dancer, 1978; Droppings From Heaven, 1979; The Love Poems of Irving Layton, 1979; There Were No Signs, 1979; An Unlikely Affair: The Correspondence of Irving Layton and Dorothy Rath, 1979; For My Neighbours in Hell, 1980; Europe and Other Bad News, 1981; A Wild Peculiar Joy, 1982; The Gucci Bag, 1983; With Reverence and Delight: The Love Poems, 1984; A Spider Danced a Cozy Jig, 1984; Fortunate Exile, 1987; The Complete Correspondence 1953-78 (with Robert Creeley), 1990; The Improved Binoculars, 1991; Fornalutx, Selected Poems, 1928-1990, 1992. Address: 6879 Monkland Avenue, Montreal, Quebec H4B 1J5, Canada.

LAZARUS Arnold (Leslie), b. 20 Feb 1914, Revere, Massachusetts, USA. Writer; Poet. m. Keo Felker, 24 July 1938, 2 sons, 2 daughters. Education: BA, University of Michigan, 1935; BS, Middlesex Medical School, 1937; MA, 1939, PhD, 1957, University of California, Los Angeles. Publications: Entertainments and Valedictions, 1970; Harbrace Adventures in Literature (co-editor with R Lowell and E Hardwick), 1970; Modern English (co-editor), 1970; A Suit of Four, 1973; The Indiana Experience, 1977; Beyond Graustark (with Victor H Jones), 1981; Glossary of Literature and Composition (editor with H Wendell Smith), 1983; Best of George Ade (editor), 1985; Some Light: New and Selected Verse, 1988; A George Jean Nathan Reader (editor), 1990. Contributions to: Numerous periodicals. Honours: Ford Foundation Fellow, 1954; Kemper McComb Award, 1976. Memberships: Academy of American Poets; American Society for Theatre Research; Comparative Literature Association; Modern Language Association; Poetry Society of America. Address: 709 Chopin Drive, Sunnyvale, CA 94087, USA.

LAZARUS Henry. See: **SLAVITT David Rytman.**

LAZARUS Marguerite, (Marguerite Gascoigne, Anna Gilbert), b. 1 May 1916, Durham, England. Author. m. Jack Lazarus, 3 Apr 1956. Education: BA, Honours, English Language and Literature, 1937, MA, 1945, Durham University. Publications: Images of Rose, 1973; The Look of Innocence, 1975; A Family Likeness, 1977; Remembering Louise, 1978; The Leavetaking, 1979; Flowers for Lilian, 1980; Miss Bede is Staying, 1982; The Long Shadow, 1984; A Walk in the Wood, 1989; The Wedding Guest, 1993; The Treachery of Time, 1995. Contributions to: Magazines and BBC. Honour: Romantic Novelists' Major Award, 1976; Catherine Cookson Award, 1994. Address: c/o Watson Little Ltd, Capo di Monte, Windmill Hill, London NW3 6RJ, England.

LE CARRÉ John. See: **CORNWELL David John Moore.**

LE GUIN Ursula K(roeber), b. 21 Oct 1929, Berkeley, California, USA. Writer; Poet. Education: AB, Radcliffe College, 1951; AM,

Columbia University, 1952. Publications: Wild Angels (poems), 1975; A Very Long Way From Anywhere Else, 1976; The Word for World is Forest, 1976; Orsinian Tales (short stories), 1976; Nebula Award Stories 11 (editor), 1977; The Language of the Night (essays), 1978; Leese Webster, 1979; Malafrena, 1979; The Beginning Place (UK edition as Threshold), 1980; Interfaces (editor with Virginia Kidd), 1980; Edges (editor with Virginia Kidd), 1981; Hard Words and Other Poems (poems), 1981; The Compass Rose (short stories), 1982; The Eye of the Heron, 1983; In The Red Zone (poems), 1983; The Visionary, 1984; Always Coming Home, 1985; Buffalo Gals and Other Animal Presences (short stories), 1987; Solomon Leviathan's 931st Trip Around the World, 1988; A Visit From Dr Katz, 1988; Wild Oats and Fireweed (poems), 1988; Catwings, 1988; Catwings Return, 1989; Fire and Stone, 1989; Dancing at the Edge of the World (essays), 1989; Tehanu: The Last Book to Earthsea, 1990; Searoad, 1991; A Ride on the Red Mare's Back, 1992; Fish Soup, 1992. Honours: Boston Globe-Horn Book Award, 1968; Hugo Awards, 1969, 1972, 1973, 1975, 1988; Nebula Awards, 1969, 1975, 1991; Newbery Honor Medal, 1972; National Book Award, 1972; Gandalf Award, 1979; Janet Heidinger Kafka Award, 1986; Prix Lectures-Jeunesse, 1987; International Fantasy Award, 1988; Pushcart Prize Story, 1991; Harold D Vursell Award, American Academy and Institute of Arts and Letters, 1991; Writers of Distinction Award, National Council for Research on Women, 1992. Address: c/o Virginia Kidd, Box 278, Milford, PA 18337, USA.

LE PLASTRIER Robert. See: **WARNER Francis.**

LEA-JONES Julian, b. 2 Dec 1940, Bristol, England. Avionics Researcher; Writer; Presenter. m. Diane Susan Parsons, 22 Dec 1962, 1 son, 1 daughter. Education: College Certificates; Diplomas for Telecommunications and Business Management Studies. Appointments: Contributing Author, Editor, The Templar, 1980-; Past Joint Editor, Alha Journal, Avon Past, 1986. Publications: St John's Conduit: An Account of Bristol's Medieval Water Supply, 1985; Survey of Parish Boundary Markers and Stones for Eleven of the Ancient Bristol Parishes, 1986; Yesterday's Temple, 1987; Bristol Past Revisited, 1989; Bristol Faces and Places, 1992. Contributions to: AvoIndustrial Archeological Trust, Journal; Newspapers, Radio and TV; Trust, Journal; Also short pieces on Local History. Memberships: West of England Writers Association; Founder, Life Member, Temple Local History Group; Archivist, Bristol History Research Exchange. Address: 33 Springfield Grove, Henleaze, Bristol BS6 7XE, England.

LEACH Penelope (Jane), b. 19 Nov 1937, London, England. Psychologist. m. Gerald Leach, 23 Mar 1963, 1 son, 1 daughter. Education: BA, Cantab, 1959; Graduate Diploma in Social Sciences, London School of Economics and Political Science, 1961; PhD, Psychology, London University, 1964. Publications: Baby and Child (in US as Your Baby and Child), 1977, 2nd edition, 1989, new edition, 1997; The Parents' A-Z (in US as Your Growing Child), 1985; Babyhood, revised edition, 1983; The First Six Months: Coming to Terms With Your Baby, 1986; The Babypack (in US as The Babykit), 1990; Children First: What Society Must Do - And Is Not Doing - for Children Today, 1994. Contributions to: Numerous magazines and journals. Honours: Fellow, British Psychological Society, 1989; Cable Ace Award, Best Informational Television Presentation, 1993; Honorary Doctorate of Education, 1996. Membership: Society of Authors. Address: 3 Tanza Road, London NW3 2UA, England.

LEAKEY Richard (Erskine Frere), b. 19 Dec 1944, Nairobi, Kenya. m. Maeve Gillian Epps, 1970, 3 daughters. Education: Duke of York School, Nairobi. Career includes: Leader, Koobi Fora Research Project, Kenya, 1968-; West Turkana Project, 1990-; Administrative Director, 1968-74, Director, 1974-81, National Museums of Kenya; Managing Director, Richard Leakey and Associates, wildlife consultancy, 1994-. Publications include: Origins, (with R Lewin), 1978; People of the Lake (with R Lewin), 1979; Koobi Fora Research Project, vol 1, (with Mary Leakey), 1979; The Making of Mankind, (with Mary Leakey), 1981; Human Origins, 1982; One Life, autobiography, 1984; Origins Reconsidered, (with R Lewin), 1992; The Origin of Humankind, 1994; The Sixth Extinction (with Roger Leuni), 1995. Address: PO Box 204926, Nairobi, Kenya.

LEALE B(arry) C(avendish), b. 1 Sept 1930, Ashford, Middlesex, England. Poet. Publications: Under a Glass Sky, 1975; Preludes, 1977; Leviathan and Other Poems, 1984; The Colours of Ancient Dreams, 1984. Contributions to: Anthologies and periodicals.

Address: Flat E10, Peabody Estate, Wild Street, London WC2B 4AH, England.

LEAPMAN Michael Henry, b. 24 Apr 1938, London, England. Writer; Journalist. m. Olga Mason, 15 July 1965, 1 son. Appointment: Journalist, The Times, 1969-81. Publications: One Man and His Plot, 1976; Yankee Doodles, 1982; Companion Guide to New York, 1983; Barefaced Cheek, 1983; Treachery, 1984; The Last Days of the Beeb, 1986; Kinnock, 1987; The Book of London (editor), 1989; London's River, 1991; Treacherous Estate, 1992; Eyewitness Guide to London, 1993; Master Race (with Catrine Clay), 1995. Contributions to: Numerous magazines and journals. Honours: Campaigning Journalist of the Year, British Press Award, 1968; Thomas Cook Travel Book Award, Best Guide Book of 1983; Garden Writers Guild Award, 1995 Memberships: Society of Authors; National Union of Journalists. Address: 13 Aldebert Terrace, London SW8 1BH, England.

LEAR Peter. See: **LOVESEY Peter.**

LEASOR (Thomas) James (Andrew MacAllan), b. 20 Dec 1923, Erith, Kent, England. Author. m. Joan Margaret Bevan, 1 Dec 1951, 3 sons. Education: City of London School; BA, 1948, MA, 1952, Oriel College, Oxford. Appointments: Feature Writer, Foreign Correspondent, Daily Express, London, 1948-55; Editorial Advisor, Newness and Pearson, later IPC, publishing, 1955-69; Director, Elm Tree Books, 1970-73. Publications: Novels and non-fiction books. Honours: Order of St John; Fellow, Royal Society of Arts. Address: Swallowcliffe Manor, Salisbury, Wiltshire SP3 5PB, England.

LEBOW Jeanne, b. 29 Jan 1951, Richmond, Virginia, USA. Writer; Poet; Teacher. m. (1) Howard Lebow, (2) Steve Shepard, 5 July 1985. Education: AB, College of William and Mary, 1973; MA, Hollins College, 1982; PhD, University of Southern Mississippi, 1989. Appointments: Instructor, Memphis State University, 1982-84; Graduate Teaching Assistant, University of Southern Mississippi, 1984-87; Fulbright Professor, University of Ouagadougou, West Africa, 1987-88; Assistant Professor, Northeast Missouri State University, 1988-92; Adjunct Professor, University of Southern Mississippi, Gulf Coast. Publication: The Outlaw James Copeland and the Champion-Belted Empress, 1991. Contributions to: Anthologies and magazines. Honours: National Award, Georgia State Poetry Society, 1983; Fulbright Grant to West Africa, 1987-88; Runner-up, Norma Farber First Book Award, 1991. Memberships: Associated Writing Programs; Modern Language Association. Address: PO Box 290, Gautier, MS 39553, USA.

LEBRUN HOLMES Sandra, b. 24 Apr 1924, Bulcoomatta Station, New South Wales, Australia. Writer; Filmmaker; Researcher. m. Cecil William Holmes, 1956, 2 sons, 1 daughter. Education: Anthropology, Sydney University, 2 years. Publications: Yirawala Artist and Man, 1972; Yirawala Painter of the Dreaming, 1992. Contributions to: Various publications. Memberships: Australian Society of Authors; Film Directors Guild. Address: Box 439 PO, Potts Pt, New South Wales 2011, Australia.

LEDOUX Paul Martin, b. 4 Nov 1949, Halifax, Nova Scotia, Canada. Dramatist. m. Ferne Downey. Education: BA, Dalhousie University, Halifax; Postgraduate work, NSCAD, Halifax. Publications: Love is Strange, 1985; Children of the Night, 1986; Fire, 1987; The Secret Garden, 1993; Also numerous teleplays & radio dramas. Honours: Best play, Quebec Drama Festival, 1975; Outstanding Drama, Chalmer Award, 1989; Dora Manor Moore Award, Best Canadian Drama, Toronto, 1990. Memberships: Association of Canadian Television and Radio Artists; Dramatists Cooperative of Nova Scotia; Playwrights Union of Canada, chairman, 1985-87; Society of Composers, Authors, and Music Publishers of Canada. Address: 41 Cowan Avenue, Toronto, Ontario M6K 2N1, Canada.

LEE Dennis Beynon, b. 31 Aug 1939, Toronto, Ontario, Canada. Writer. m. (1) 1 son, 1 daughter, (2) Susan Perly, 1985. Education: Editor, House of Anansi Press, 1967-72; Consulting Editor, Macmillan of Canada, 1972-78; Poetry Editor, McClelland and Stewart, 1981-84. Publications: Children's Poetry: Wiggle to the Laundromat, 1970; Alligator Pie, 1974; Nicholas Knock, 1974; Garbage Delight, 1977; Jelly Belly, 1983; Lizzy's Lion, 1984; The Ice Cream Store, 1991. Children's Tale: The Ordinary Bath, 1979. Adult Poetry: Kingdom of Absence, 1967; Civil Elegies, 1972; The Gods, 1979; The Difficulty of Living on Other Planets, 1988; Riffs, 1993. Adult Non-Fiction: Savage Fields, 1977. Contributions to: Magazines and journals. Honour:

Governor-General's Award for Poetry, 1972. Memberships: Writers' Union of Canada; PEN, Canada. Address: c/o Sterling Lord Associates (Canada), 10 St Mary Street, No 510, Toronto, Ontario M4Y 1P9, Canada.

LEE Hamilton, b. 10 Oct 1921, Zhouxian, Shandong, China. Emeritus Professor of Education. m. Jean C Chang, 24 Aug 1945, 1 son, 3 daughters. Education: BS, Beijing Normal University, 1948; MA, University of Minnesota, Minneapolis, 1958; EdD, Wayne State University, Detroit, Michigan, 1964. Appointments: English Teacher, Taiwan High Schools, China, 1948-56; Research Associate, Wayne State University, Detroit, Michigan, 1958-64; Visiting Professor of Chinese Literature, Seton Hall University, summer 1964; Assistant Professor, Moorhead State University, 1964-65; Associate Professor, University of Wisconsin, 1965-66; Professor, 1966-84, Professor Emeritus, 1984-, East Stroudsburg University, Pennsylvania; Visiting Scholar, Harvard University, summers 1965, 1966; Visiting Fellow, Princeton University, 1976-78. Publications: Readings in Instructional Technology, 1970; Reflection (chap book), 1989; Revelation (chap book), 1989. Other: Works in numerous anthologies, 1974-. Contributions to: Education Tomorrow, 1974-76; World Future Society; Byline; Poetry Norwest; Today Poetry; Poets at Work; Various small literary magazines, 1974-. Honours: Numerous honourable mentions and awards in poetry contests, 1974-; Accomplishment of Merit Award; Fellow, World Literary Academy. Memberships: Poetry Society of America; Advisory Panel, International Society of Poets; Academy of American Poets; Honorary Member, International Biographical Centre; Research Board of Advisors, American Biographical Institute. Address: PO Box 980, Los Altos, CA 94023, USA.

LEE John (Darrell), b. 12 Mar 1931, Indiahoma, Oklahoma, USA. Writer; Former Professor. Education: BA, Texas Technological College, 1952; MSJ, West Virginia University, 1965. Appointment: Former Professor of Journalism. Publications: Caught in the Act, 1968; Diplomatic Persuaders, 1968; Assignation in Algeria, 1971; The Ninth Man, 1976; The Thirteenth Hour, 1978; Lago, 1980; Stalag Texas, 1990. Address: c/o Don Congdon Associates Inc, 156 Fifth Avenue, Suite 625, New York, NY 10010, USA.

LEE Joyce Isabel, b. 19 June 1913, Murtoa, Australia. Pharmacist; Lecturer; Poet. m. Norman Edward, 18 Dec 1937, 2 sons. Education: Methodist Ladies' College; Registered Pharmacist, Victorian College of Pharmacy, Melbourne. Appointments: Lecturer/Tutor (Poetry Writing), Victoria College of Advanced Education, Toorak Campus, 1981-. Publications: Sisters Poets 1, 1979; Abruptly from the Flatlands, 1984; Plain Dreaming, 1991. Contributions to: Various anthologies and journals. Address: 13/205 Burke Road, Glen Iris, Victoria 3146, Australia.

LEE Kuei-shien, b. 19 June 1937, Taipei, Taiwan, China. Patent Agent; Chemical Engineer; Corporation President; Poet; Writer. m. Huei-uei Wang, 1965, 1 son, 1 daughter. Education: Chemical Engineering, Taipei Institute of Technology, 1958; German Literature, European Language Center of the Educational Ministry, 1964. Publications: Various volumes of poems, essays and translations. Address: Asia Enterprise Center, No 142 Minchuan East Road, Sec 3, Taipei, Taiwan, China.

LEE Lance, b. 25 Aug 1942, New York, USA. Writer; Poet; Playwright. m. Jeanne Barbara Hutchings, 30 Aug 1962, 2 daughters. Education: Boston University; BA, Brandeis University, 1964; MFA, Yale School of Drama, 1967. Appointments: Lecturer, Bridgeport University, 1967-68; Instructor, Southern Connecticut State College, 1968; Assistant Professor, Senior Lecturer, University of Southern California, 1968-71; Lecturer, University of California, Los Angeles, 1971-73, California State University, 1981-. Publications: Plays: Fox, Hounds and Huntress, 1973; Time's Up, 1979. Textbook: The Understructure of Writing for Film and Television, 1988. Poetry: Wrestling with the Angel, 1990. Contributions to: Numerous magazines and journals. Honours: Arts of the Theatre Foundation Fellowship, 1967; University of Southern California Research and Publication Grants, 1970-71; Rockefeller Foundation Fellowship, 1971; National Endowment for the Arts Fellowship, 1976. Memberships: Dramatists Guild; Authors League; American Academy of Poets; Poetry Society of America. Address: 1127 Galloway Street, Pacific Palisades, CA 90272, USA.

LEE Laurie, b. 26 June 1914, Stroud, Gloucestershire, England. Author; Poet. Appointments: Scriptwriter, Crown Film Unit, 1942-44;

Publications Editor, Ministry of Information, 1944-46; Member, Green Park Film Unit, 1946-47; Caption Writer-in-Chief, Festival of Britain, 1950-51. Publications: The Sun My Monument, 1944; Land at War, 1945; The Voyage of Magellan: A Dramatic Chronicle for Radio, 1946; The Bloom of Candles, 1947; Peasants' Priest (play), 1947; We Make a Film In Cyprus (with R Keene), 1947; New Poems (editor with C Hassall and Rex Warner), 1954; My Many-Coated Man, 1955; A Rose for Winter: Travels in Andalusia, 1956; Cider With Rosie (US edition as The Edge of Day), 1959; Poems, 1960; The Firstborn (essay on childhood), 1964; As I Walked Out One Midsummer Morning (autobiography), 1969; Pergamon Poets 10 (with Charles Causley), 1970; I Can't Stay Long, 1975; Innocence in the Mirror, 1978; Two Women, 1983; Selected Poems, 1983; A Moment of War, 1991. Address: c/o Andre Deutsch Ltd, 105 Great Russell Street, London WC1B 3LU, England.

LEE Tanith, b. 19 Sept 1947, London, England. Writer; Playwright. Publications: The Betrothed (short stories), 1968; The Dragon Hoard (juvenile), 1971; Princess Hynchatti and Some Other Surprises (juvenile), 1972; Animal Castle (juvenile), 1972; Companions on the Road (juvenile), 1975; The Birthgrave, 1975; Don't Bite the Sun, 1976; The Storm Lord, 1976; The Winter Players (juvenile), 1976; East of Midnight (juvenile), 1977; Drinking Sapphire Wine, 1977; Volkhavaar, 1977; Vazkor, Son of Vazkor, 1978; Quest for the White Witch, 1978; Night's Master, 1978; The Castle of Dark (juvenile), 1978; Shon the Taken (juvenile), 1979; Death's Master, 1979; Electric Forest, 1979; Sabella: or, The Blood Stone, 1980; Kill the Dead, 1980; Day by Night, 1980; Delusion's Master, 1981; The Silver Metal Lover, 1982; Cyrion (short stories), 1982; Prince on a White Horse (juvenile), 1982; Sung in Shadow, 1983; Anackire, 1983; Red as Blood: or, Tales from the Sisters Grimmer, 1983; The Dragon Hoard, 1984; The Beautiful Biting Machine (short stories), 1984; Tamastara, or, the Indian Nights (short stories), 1984; Days of Grass, 1985; The Gorgon and Other Beastly Tales, 1985; Dreams of Dark and Light, 1986. Address: c/o Macmillan London Ltd, 4 Little Essex Street, London WC2R 3LF, England.

LEE Warner. See: **BATTIN B W.**

LEE Wayne C, (Lee Sheldon), b. 2 July 1917, Lamar, Nebraska, USA. Author. Publications: Prairie Vengeance, 1954; Broken Wheel Ranch, 1956; Slugging Backstop, 1957; His Brother's Guns, 1958; Killer's Range, 1958; Bat Masterson, 1960; Gun Brand, 1961; Blood on the Prairie, 1962; Thunder in the Backfield, 1962; Stranger in Stirrup, 1962; The Gun Tamer, 1963; Devil Wire, 1963; The Hostile Land, 1964; Gun in His Hand, 1964; Warpath West, 1965; Fast Gun, 1965; Brand of a Man, 1966; Mystery of Scorpion Creek, 1966; Trail of the Skulls, 1966; Showdown at Julesburg Station, 1967; Return to Gunpoint, 1967; Only the Brave, 1967; Doomed Planet (as Lee Sheldon), 1967; Sudden Guns, 1968; Trouble at Flying H, 1969; Stage to Lonesome Butte, 1969; Showdown at Sunrise, 1971; The Buffalo Hunters, 1972; Suicide Trail, 1972; Wind Over Rimfire, 1973; Son of a Gunman, 1973; Scotty Philip: The Man Who Saved the Buffalo, 1975; Law of the Prairie, 1975; Die Hard, 1975; Law of the Lawless, 1977; Skirmish at Fort Phil Kearney, 1977; Gun Country, 1978; Petticoat Wagon Train, 1978; The Violent Man, 1978; Ghost of a Gunfighter, 1980; McQuaid's Gun, 1980; Trails of the Smoky Hill (non-fiction), 1980; Shadow of the Gun, 1981; Guns at Genesis, 1981; Putnam's Ranch War, 1982; Barbed Wire War, 1983; The Violent Trail, 1984; White Butte Guns, 1984; War at Nugget Creek, 1985; Massacre Creek, 1985; The Waiting Gun, 1986; Hawks of Autumn, 1986; Wild Towns of Nebraska, 1988; Arikaree War Cry, 1992. Memberships: Western Writers of America, president, 1970-71; Nebraska Writers Guild, president, 1974-76. Address: PO Box 906, Imperial, NE 69033, USA.

LEE William. See: **BURROUGHS William Steward.**

LEECH Geoffrey Neil, b. 16 Jan 1936, Gloucester, England. University Professor. m. Frances Anne Berman, 29 July 1961, 1 son, 1 daughter. Education: BA, English Language and Literature, 1959, MA, 1963, PhD, 1968, University College London. Publications: English in Advertising, 1966; A Linguistic Guide to English Poetry, 1969; Towards a Semantic Description of English, 1969; Meaning and the English Verb, 1971, 2nd edition, 1987; A Grammar of Contemporary English (with R Quirk, S Greenbaum, and J Svartvik), 1972; Semantics, 1974, 2nd edition, 1981; A Communicative Grammar of English (with J Svartvik), 1975, 2nd edition, 1994; Explorations in Semantics and Pragmatics, 1980; Style in Fiction (with Michael H

Short), 1981; English Grammar for Today (with R Hoogenraad and M Deuchar), 1982; Principles of Pragmatics, 1983; A Comprehensive Grammar of the English Language (with R Quirk, S Greenbaum, and J Svartvik), 1985; The Computational Analysis of English (editor with R Garside and G Sampson), 1987; An A-Z of English Grammar and Usage, 1989; Introducing English Grammar, 1992; Spoken English on Computer (editor with G Myers and J Thomas), 1995. Contributions to: A Review of English Literature; Lingua; New Society; Linguistics; Dutch Quarterly Review of Anglo-American Letters; Times Literary Supplement; Prose Studies; The Rising Generation; Transactions of the Philological Society. Honours: FilDr, University of Lund, 1987; British Academy, fellow, 1987. Membership: Academia Europea. Address: c/o Peters, Fraser and Dunlop Group Ltd, 503-4 The Chambers, Chelsea Harbour, London SW10 0XF, England.

LEEDOM-ACKERMAN Joanne, b. 7 Feb 1947, Dallas, Texas, USA. Writer; Novelist. m. Peter Ackerman, 3 June 1972, 2 sons. Education: BA, Principia College, 1968; MA, Johns Hopkins University, 1969; MA, Brown University, 1974. Publications: No Marble Angels, 1985; The Dark Path to the River, 1988; Women for All Seasons (editor), 1989. Contributions to: Anthologies, newspapers, and magazines. Membership: International PEN, chair, Writers in Prison Committee, 1993-97; Vice President, International PEN. Address: 48 Phillimore Gardens, London W8 7QG, England.

LEEDY Paul Dellinger, b. 4 Mar 1908, Harrisburg, Pennsylvania, USA. University Professor; Author; Consultant on Format and Readability. m. Irene Brandt Force, 30 Nov 1933, 1 son. Education: AB, Dickinson College, 1930; LLB, American School of Law (Extension), 1933; MA, University of Pennsylvania, 1938; PhD, New York University, 1958. Appointments: Book Reviewer, David C Cook, Publishers, 1935-38; Newark College, Rutgers University, 1938-42; School of Education, New York University, 1943-45; Assistant Editor, Abingdon-Cokesbury Press, New York, 1945-47; Chief Consultant and Senior Specialist in College and Adult Reading, The Reading Institute, New York University, 1950-61; School of Education, The American University, 1961-76; Editorial Consultant, Chilton Publishing Company, 1955-56; James Henry Morgan Lecturer, Dickinson College, 1958; Adjunct Professor, Fairleigh Dickinson University, George Mason Universityand University of Colorado; Abstractor, Psychological Abstracts, Washington, DC, 1959-66. Publications: The Wonderful World of Books (co-author), 1952; Reading Improvement for Adults, 1956; A History of the Origin and Development of Instruction in Reading Improvement at the College Level (microfilm), 1959; Improve Your Reading, 1962; Read with Speed and Precision, 1963; Perspectives in Reading: Adult Reading Instruction (editor), 1963; A Key to Better Reading, 1967; How to Read and Understand Research, 1980; Practical Research: Planning and Design, 1974, 6th edition, 1997. Contributions to: Various journals. Honours: New York University Founder's Day Award, 1958; Outstanding Educators of America Citation, 1972; Men of Achievement Award for Distinguished Achievement in Education and Authorship. Memberships: International Reading Association; Board of Directors, College Reading Association, 1965-68; American Association of University Professors. Address: La Maison des Gros Piliers, 239 North 25th Street, Camp Hill, PA 17011, USA.

LEES-MILNE James, b. 6 Aug 1908, Worcestershire, England. Author. Education: Eton College, 1921-26; Grenoble University, 1927-28; MA, Magdalen College, Oxford, 1931. Appointments: Private Secretary to Baron Lloyd, 1931-35; Staff Member, Reuters, 1935-36. Publications: The National Trust (editor), 1945; The Age of Adam, 1947; National Trust (editor), 1945; The Age of Adam, 1947; National Trust Guide: Buildings, 1948; Tudor Renaissance, 1951; The Age of Inigo Jones, 1953; Roman Mornings, 1956; Baroque in Italy, 1959; Baroque in Spain and Portugal, 1960; Earls of Creation, 1962; Worcestershire: A Shell Guide, 1964; St Peter's 1967; English Country Houses: Baroque, 1970; Another Self, 1970; Heretics in Love (novel), 1973; Ancestral Voices, 1975; William Beckford, 1976; Prophesying Peace, 1977; Round the Clock (novel), 1978; Harold Nicolson, 2 volumes, 1980-81; The Country House (anthology), 1982; The Last Stuarts, 1983; Enigmatic Edwardian, 1986; Some Cotswold Country Houses, 1987; The Fool of Love, 1987; Venetian Evenings, 1988; Bachelor Duke, 1991; People and Places, 1992; A Mingled Measure, 1994; Fourteen Friends, 1996. Honours: Royal Society of Literature, fellow; Society of Arts, fellow. Address: Essex House, Badminton, Avon GL9 1DD, England.

LEESON Robert (Arthur), b. 31 Mar 1928, Barnton, Cheshire, England. Journalist; Writer. m. Gunvor Hagen, 25 May 1954, 1 son, 1 daughter. Education: External Degree in English (Hons), London University, 1972. Appointment: Literary Editor, Morning Star, London, 1960-80. Publications: Third Class Genie, 1975; Silver's Revenge, 1978; Travelling Brothers, 1979; It's My Life, 1980; Candy for King, 1983; Reading and Righting, 1985; Slambash Wangs of a Compo Gorner, 1987; Coming Home, 1991; Zarnia Experiment 1-6, 1993; Robin Hood, 1994; Red, White and Blue, 1996. Contributions to: Newspapers and journals. Honour: Eleanor Farjeon Award for Services to Children and Literature, 1985. Memberships: International Board of Books for Young People, British Section, treasurer, 1972-91; Writers' Guild of Great Britain, chairman, 1985-86. Address: 18 McKenzie Road, Broxbourne, Hertfordshire EN10 7JH, England.

LEFEBURE Molly, b. United Kingdom. Author. Publications: Evidence for the Crown, 1955; Murder with a Difference, 1958; The Lake District, 1963; Scratch and Co, 1968; The Hunting of Wilberforce Pike, 1970; Cumberland Heritage, 1971; The Loona Balloona, 1974; Samuel Taylor Coleridge: A Bondage of Opium, 1974; Cumbrian Discovery, 1977; The Bondage of Love: A Life of Mrs Samuel Taylor Coleridge, 1986; The Illustrated Lake Poets, 1987; Blitz: A Novel of Love and War, 1988; The Coleridge Connection (editor with Richard Gravil), 1990; Thunder in the Sky (novel), 1991; Thomas Hardy's World, 1997. Address: c/o Watson Little Ltd, Capo di Monte, Windmill Hill, London NW3 6RJ, England.

LEFF Leonard J, b. 23 Jan 1942, Houston, Texas, USA. Professor of English. m. Linda Ringer, 26 Jan 1969, 1 son. Education: BBA, University of Texas, Austin, 1963; MA, University of Houston, 1965; PhD, Northern Illinois University, 1971. Appointments: Instructor, English, McNeese State University, 1965-68, University of Illinois, Urbana-Champaign, 1971-72; Northern Illinois University, 1972-73; Assistant Professor, Associate Professor, Head of English, Bellevue College, 1973-79; Assistant Professor, 1979-82, Associate Professor, 1983-91, Interim Head of English, 1989-90, Professor, 1991-, Oklahoma State University, Stillwater. Publications: Film Plots, 2 volumes, 1983, 1988; Hitchcock and Selznick: The Rich and Strange Collaboration of Alfred Hitchcock and David O Selznick in Hollywood, 1987; The Dame in the Kimono: Hollywood, Censorship, and the Production Code from the 1920s to the 1960s (with Jerold Simmons), 1990. Address: 3002 Loma Verde Lane, Stillwater, OK 74074, USA.

LEFFLAND Ella Julia, b. 25 Nov 1931, Martinez, California. Writer. Education: BA, Fine Arts, San Jose State College, 1953. Publications: Mrs Munck, 1970; Love out of Season, 1974; Last Courtesies, 1979; Rumors of Peace, 1980; Death of the Devil, 1990. Contributions to: New Yorker; Harper's; Atlantic Monthly; Mademoiselle; New York Magazine; New York Times. Honours: Gold Medals for Fiction, 1974, 1979, Silver Medal, 1991, Commonwealth Club of California; O Henry First Prize, 1977; Bay Area Book Reviewers Award for Fiction, 1990. Address: Wallace Literary Agency, 177 East 70th Street, New York, NY 10021, USA.

LEGAT Michael Ronald, b. 24 Mar 1923, London, England. Writer. m. Rosetta Clark, 20 Aug 1949, 2 sons. Appointments: Editorial Director, Transworld Publishers Ltd, 1956-78. Publications: Dear Author..., 1972, revised edition, 1989; Mario's Vineyard, 1980; The Silver Fountain, 1982; An Author's Guide to Publishing, 1983, revised edition, 1991; Putting on a Play, 1984; The Shapiro Diamond, 1984; The Silk Maker, 1985; Writing for Pleasure and Profit, 1986, revised edition, 1993; The Cast Iron Man, 1987; The Illustrated Dictionary of Western Literature, 1987; We Beheld His Glory, 1988; The Nuts and Bolts of Writing, 1989; How to Write Historical Novels, 1990; Plotting the Novel, 1992; Understanding Publishers' Contracts, 1992; Non-Fiction: A Writer's Guide, 1993; The Writer's Rights, 1995; An Author's Guide to Literary Agents, 1995. Contributions to: Author; Writers News; Writers' Monthly. Memberships: Weald of Sussex Writers; Society of Authors; Society of Sussex Authors; Uckfield & District Writers Club. Address: Bookends, Lewes Road, Horsted Keynes, Haywards Heath, West Sussex RH17 7DP, England.

LEGGATT Alexander Maxwell, b. 18 Aug 1940, Trafalgar Township, Ontario, Canada. University Teacher. m. Margaret Anna Leggatt, 4 daughters. Education: BA, University of Toronto, 1962; MA, 1963; PhD, 1965, University of Birmingham. Appointments: Professor, University College, University of Toronto; Associate Editor, Modern Drama, 1972-75; Editorial Board, English Studies in Canada, 1984-91; Editorial Board, University of Toronto Quarterly, 1996-. Publications:

Citizen Comedy in The Age of Shakespeare, 1973; Shakespeare's Comedy of Love, 1974; Ben Jonson: His Vision and His Art, 1981; English Drama: Shakespeare to the Restoration, 1988; Harvester-Twayne New Critical Introductions to Shakespeare: King Lear, 1988; Shakespeare's Political Drama, 1988; Shakespeare in Perfomance: King Lear, 1991; Jacobean Public Theatre, 1992. Contributions to: Many scholarly journals. Honour: Guggenheim Fellowship, 1985-86. Memberships: Shakespeare Association of America, trustee, 1986-89; International Shakespeare Association, executive committee, 1987-96; International Association of University Professors of English; Association of Canadian University Teachers of English; PEN Canada. Address: University College, University of Toronto, Toronto, Ontario M5S 3H7, Canada.

LEGUEY-FEILLEUX Jean-Robert, b. 28 Mar 1928, Marseilles, France. University Professor. m. Virginia Hartwell, 19 Sep 1953, 4 daughters. Education: Diplôme Supérieur, École Supérieure de Commerce, Marseilles, 1949; Diplôme Supérieur d'Enseignement Colonial, University d'Aix, 1949; MA, University of Florida, 1951; Certificate, English Life and Institutions, Cambridge, 1952; PhD, Georgetown University, 1965. Appointments: Director of Research, Institute of World Polity, Georgetown University, 1960-66; National Panel of Judges for Fulbright Awards, 1973-75; Visiting Scholar, Harvard Law School, 1974-75. Publications: World Polity, Vol 2, 1960; The Law of Limited International Conflict, 1965; The Implications of Disarmament, 1977; Democracy in a High-Technology Society, 1988; The External Environment, 1991; Great Events from History: Human Rights (contributor), 1992; Science and Politics of Food (contributor), 1995. Contributions to: Peace Research Abstracts Journal (Canada); Respond; Prioritas; Bulletin of Peace Proposals (Norway); Chronicle of the UN Association. Honours: Fulbright Scholar, 1950; Distinguished Service, IIE, New York, 1976; Outstanding Educator, Nutshell Magazine, 1982; Pi Sigma Alpha; Pi Delta Phi; Phi Alpha Theta. Memberships: Academic Council on the UN System; Gold Key Honor Society, Georgetown University; Political Science Honor Society; French Language Honor Society; Advisory Board, World News Report, St Louis. Address: 6139 Kingsbury Avenue, St Louis, MO 63112, USA.

LEHMAN David (Cary), b. 11 June 1948, New York, New York, USA. Writer; Poet. m. Stefanie Green, 2 Dec 1978, 1 son. Education: BA, 1970, PhD, 1978, Columbia University; BA, MA, 1972, Cambridge University. Appointments: Instructor, Brooklyn College of the City University of New York, 1975-76; Assistant Professor, Hamilton College, Clinton, New York, 1976-80; Fellow, Society for the Humanities, Cornell University, 1980-81; Lecturer, Wells College, Aurora, New York, 1981-82; Book Critic and Writer, Newsweek, 1983-89; Series Editor, The Best American Poetry, 1988-; Editorial Adviser in Poetry, W W Norton & Co, 1990-. Publications: Some Nerve, 1973; Day One, 1979; Beyond Amazement: New Essays on John Ashbery (editor), 1980; James Merrill: Essays in Criticism (editor), 1983; An Alternative to Speech, 1986; Ecstatic Occasions, Expedient Forms: 65 Leading Contemporary Poets Select and Comment on Their Poems (editor), 1987; Twenty Questions, 1988; Operation Memory, 1990; The Line Forms Here, 1992; The Best American Poetry (editor with Charles Simic), 1992; The Best American Poetry (editor with Louise Glück), 1993; The Big Question, 1995. Contributions to: Anthologies, journals and newspapers. Honours: Academy of American Poets Prize, 1974; Ingram Merrill Foundation Grants, 1976, 1982, 1984; National Endowment for the Humanities Grant, 1979; National Endowment for the Arts Fellowship, 1987; American Academy of Arts and Letters Fellowship, 1990. Address: 900 West End Avenue, No 14E, New York, NY 10025, USA.

LEHMANN Geoffrey, b. 28 June 1940, Sydney, New South Wales, Australia. Tax Lawyer; Poet. m. 1981, 3 sons, 2 daughters. Education: BA, LLM, University of Sydney. Appointment: Partner, Price Waterhouse. Publications: Ilex Tree (with Les A Murray), 1967; A Voyage of Lions, 1970; Conversation With a Rider, 1972; Spring Day in Autumn, 1974; Selected Poems, 1975; Ross' Poems, 1978; Nero's Poems, 1981; Children's Games, 1990; Spring Forest, 1992; Editor and co-editor of anthologies. Honour: Grace Levin Prize, 1967, 1981. Membership: Literature Board of Australia Council, 1982-85. Address: c/o Curtis Brown (Australia) Pty Ltd, 27 Union Street, Paddington, New South Wales 2021, Australia.

LEHRER Keith (Edward), b. 10 Jan 1936, Minneapolis, Minnesota, USA. Philosopher; Professor; Writer. Education: BA, University of Minnesota, 1957; AM, 1959, PhD, 1960, Brown University. Appointments: Instructor and Assistant Professor, Wayne

State University, 1960-63; Assistant Professor to Professor, University of Rochester, 1963-73; Visiting Associate Professor, University of Calgary, 1966; Visiting Professor, Vanderbilt University, 1970, University of Illinois at Chicago Circle, 1979, University of the Witwatersrand, 1994; Professor, 1974-90, Regents Professor, 1990-, University of Arizona; Director, Summer Seminars, Center for Advanced Study in the Behavioral Sciences, Stanford, 1977; Guest Professor, University of Salzburg, 1982; Honorary Professor, Karl-Franzens-University, Graz, 1985-; Associate, CREA, École Polytechnique, Paris, 1993-94. Publications: Philosophical Problems and Arguments: An Introduction (with James Cornman), 1968, 4th edition, 1992; Knowledge, 1978; Rational Consensus in Science and Society: A Philosophical and Mathematical Study (with Carl Wagner), 1981; Thomas Reid, 1989; Metamind, 1990; Theory of Knowledge, 1990. Editor: Freedom and Determinism, 1966; Theories of Meanings (with Adrienne Lehrer), 1970; New Readings in Philosophical Analysis (with Herbert Feigl and Wilfrid Sellars), 1972; Reid's Inquiry and Essays (with Ronald Beanblossom), 1975, new edition, 1984; Analysis and Metaphysics: Essays in Honor of R M Chisholm, 1975; Science and Morality, 1988; Knowledge and Skepticism (with M Clay), 1989; The Opened Curtain: A US-Soviet Philosophy Summit (with Ernest Sosa), 1991; Knowledge, Teaching and Wisdom (with Jeannie Lum, Beverly Slichta, and Nicholas Smith), 1996. Contributions to: Numerous books and journals. Honours: American Council of Learned Societies Fellowship, 1973-74; National Endowment for the Humanities Fellowship, 1980; Guggenheim Fellowship, 1983-84; Visiting Fellow, University of London, 1996, and Australian National University, 1997. Memberships: American Philosophical Association, president, 1989, chair, national board of officers, 1992-95; Council for Philosophical Studies; Institute International de Philosophie, Paris and Lund; Philosophy of Science Association; Vereinigung für Wissenschaftliche Grundlagen-forschung, Austria, honorary member. Address: c/o Department of Philosophy, University of Arizona, Tuczon, AZ 85721, USA.

LEIGH Meredith. See: **KENYON Bruce Guy.**

LEIGH Mike, b. 20 Feb 1943, Salford, Lancashire, England. Dramatist; Film and Theatre Director. m. Alison Steadman, 1973, 2 sons. Education: Royal Academy of Dramatic Arts; Camberwell School of Arts and Crafts; Central School of Art and Design; London Film School. Publications: Plays: The Box Play, 1965; My Parents Have Gone to Carlisle, The Last Crusade of the Five Little Nuns, 1966; Nenaa, 1967; Individual Fruit Pies, Down Here and Up There, Big Basil, 1968; Epilogue, Glum Victoria and the Lad with Specs, 1969; Bleak Moments, 1970; A Rancid Pong, 1971; Wholesome Glory, The Jaws of Death, Dick Whittington and His Cat, 1973; Babies Grow Old, The Silent Majority, 1974; Abigail's Party, 1977 (also TV play); Ecstasy, 1979; Goose-Pimples, 1981; Smelling a Rat, 1988; Greek Tragedy, 1989; It's a Great Big Shame!, 1993. TV Films: A Mug's Game, Hard Labour, 1973; The Permissive Society, The Bath of the 2001 F A Cup, Final Goalie, Old Chums, Probation, A Light Snack, Afternoon, 1975; Nuts in May, Knock for Knock, 1976; The Kiss of Death, 1977; Who's Who, 1978; Grown Ups, 1980; Home Sweet Home, 1981; Meantime, 1983; Four Days in July, 1984. Feature Films: Bleak Moments, 1971; The Short and Curlies, 1987; High Hopes, 1988; Life is Sweet, 1990; Naked, 1993. Radio Play: Too Much of a Good Thing, 1979. Honours: Golden Leopard, Locarno Film Festival, 1972; Golden Hugo, Chicago Film Festival, 1972; George Devine Award, 1973; Evening Standard Award, 1981; Drama Critics Choice, London, 1981; Critics prize, Venice Film Festival, 1988; Honorary MA, Salford University, 1991; Officer of the Order of the British Empire, 1993; Best Director Award, Cannes Film Festival, 1993; Palme D'Or, Cannes Film Festival, 1996. Address: The Peters, Fraser and Dunlop Group Ltd, 503/4 The Chambers, Chelsea Harbour, London SW10 0XF, England.

LEIGH Richard Harris, b. 16 Aug 1943, New Jersey, USA. Writer. Education: BA, Tufts University, 1965; MA, University of Chicago, 1967; PhD, State University of New York at Stony Brook, 1970. Publications: The Holy Blood and the Holy Grail (with Michael Baigent and Henry Lincoln), 1982; The Messianic Legacy (with Michael Baigent and Henry Lincoln), 1986; The Temple and the Lodge (with Michael Baigent), 1989; The Dead Sea Scrolls Deception (with Michael Baigent), 1991. Contributions to: Anthologies and journals. Address: 21 Kelly Street, London NW1 8PG, England.

LEIGH FERMOR Patrick (Michael), b. 11 Feb 1915, London, England. Author. Education: King's School, Canterbury. Publications:

The Traveller's Tree, 1950; Julie de Carneilhan and Chance Acquaintances, by Colette, translation, 1951; A Time to Keep Silence, 1953; The Violins of Saint-Jacques, 1953; Mani, 1958; Roumeli, 1966; A Time of Gifts, 1977; Between the Woods and the Water, 1986; Three Letters from the Woods, 1991. Honours: DSO; OBE; CLitt. Address: c/o Messrs John Murray Ltd, 50 Albemarle Street, London W1, England.

LEITH Linda, b. 13 Dec 1949, Belfast, Northern Ireland. Writer; Editor. m. András Barnabás Göllner, 19 July 1974, 3 sons. Education: BA, 1st Class Honours, Philosophy, McGill University, 1970; PhD, Queen Mary College, London, 1976. Publications: Telling Differences: New English Fiction From Quebec (anthology), 1989; Introducing Hugh MacLennan's "Two Solitudes" (essay), 1990; Birds of Passage (novel), 1993; The Tragedy Queen (novel), 1995. Contributions to: Many magazines and journals. Address: Department of English, PO Box 2000, Ste Anne de Bellevue, Quebec H9X 3L9, Canada.

LEITHAUSER Brad, b. 27 Feb 1953, Detroit, Michigan, USA. Poet; Writer. m Mary Jo Salter, 1980, 1 daughter. Education: BA, 1975, JD, 1980, Harvard University. Appointment: Research Fellow, Kyoto Comparative Law Center, 1980-83; Visiting Writer, Amherst College, 1984-85; Lecturer, Mount Holyoke College, 1987-88. Publications: Poetry: Hundreds of Fireflies, 1982; A Seaside Mountain: Eight Poems from Japan, 1985; Cats of the Temple, 1986; Between Leaps: Poems 1972-1985, 1987; The Mail from Anywhere: Poems, 1990; Fiction: The Line Of Ladies, 1975; Equal Distance, 1985; Hence, 1989; Seaward, 1993. Non-fiction: Penchants & Places: Essays and Criticism, 1995. Editor: The Norton Book of Ghost Stories, 1994. Honours: Harvard University-Academy of American Poets Prizes, 1973, 1975; Harvard University McKim Garrison Prizes, 1974, 1975; Amy Lowell Traveling Scholarship, 1981-82; Guggenheim Fellowship, 1982-83; Lavan Younger Poets Award, 1983; John D and Catherine T MacArthur Foundation Fellowship, 1983-87. Address: c/o Alfred A Knopf Inc, 201 East 50th Street, New York, NY 10022, USA.

LELAND Christopher Towne, b. 17 Oct 1951. Writer; Professor. Education: BA English, Pomona College, 1973; MA, Spanish, 1980, PhD, Comparative Literature, University of California, San Diego, 1982. Appointment: Professor of English, Wayne State University, 1990-. Publications: Mean Time, 1982; Fiction and the Argentine Reality, 1986; Mrs Randall, 1987; The Book of Marvels, 1990; The Last Happy Men: The Generation of 1922, 1992; The Professor of Aesthetics, 1994. Contributions to: Principal Translator, Open Door by Luise Valengnela, 1988. Honours: Finalist, PEN Hemingway Award, 1982; Fellow, Massachusetts Artists Foundation, 1985. Memberships: Poets and Writers; Modern Language Association. Address: c/o Department of English, Wayne State University, Detroit, MI 48202, USA.

LELCHUK Alan, b. 15 Sept 1938, New York, New York, USA. Writer. m. Barbara Kreiger, 7 Oct 1979, 2 sons. Education: BA, Brooklyn College, 1960; MA, 1963, PhD, English Literature, 1965, Stanford University. Appointments: Brandeis University, 1966-81; Associate Editor, Modern Occasions, 1980-82; Amherst College, 1982-84; Dartmouth College, 1985-; Fulbright Writer-in-Residence, Haifa University, Israel, 1986-87; Visiting Writer, City College of New York, 1991; Editor, Publisher, Steerforth Press, South Royalton, Vermont, 1993-. Publications: American Mischief, 1973; Miriam at Thirty-Four, 1974; Shrinking: The Beginning of My Own Ending, 1978; 8 Great Hebrew Short Novels (co-editor), 1983; Miriam in Her Forties, 1985; On Home Ground, 1987; Brooklyn Boy, 1989; Playing the Game, 1995. Contributions to: New York Times Book Review; Sewanee Review; Atlantic; New Republic; Dissent; New York Review of Books. Honours: Guggenheim Fellowship, 1976-77; Mishkenot Sha'Ananim Resident Fellow, 1976-77; Fulbright Award, 1986-87; Manuscript Collection, Mugar Memorial Library, Boston University. Memberships: PEN; Authors Guild. Address: RFD 2, Canaan, NH 03741, USA.

LELYVELD Joseph (Salem), b. 5 Apr 1937, Cincinnati, Ohio, USA. Journalist; Editor. m. Carolyn Fox, 14 June 1958, 2 daughters. Education: BA, 1958, MA, 1959, Harvard University; MS, Columbia University, 1960. Appointments: Staff, 1963-, Foreign Correspondent, 1965-86, Foreign Editor, 1987-89, Managing Editor, 1990-94, Executive Editor, 1994-, New York Times. Publication: Move Your Shadow: South Africa Black and White, 1985. Contributions to: Periodicals. Honours: George Polk Memorial Awards, 1972, 1984; Guggenheim Fellowship, 1984; Pulitzer Prize in General Non-Fiction, 1986; Los Angeles Times Book Prize, 1986; Sidney Hillman Award,

1986; Cornelius P Ryan Award, 1986. Membership: Century Association. Address: c/o The New York Times, 229 West 43rd Street, New York, NY 10036, USA.

LEM Stanislaw, b. 12 Sep 1921, Lvov, Russia. Author. m. Barbara Lesnik, 11 Aug 1953, 1 son. Education: Studied Medicine in Lvov, 1939-41, and Krakow, Poland, 1944-45. Appointments: Lecturer, University of Krakow, part-time, 1973-. Publications: 40 books translated into 35 languages including: The Star Diaries, 1957; Eden, 1959; Solaris, 1961; Memoirs Found in a Bathtub, 1961; The Invincible, 1964; The Cyberiad, 1965; His Master's Voice, 1968; Tales of Pirx the Pilot, 1968; A Perfect Vacuum, 1971; The Futurological Congress, 1971; The Chain of Chance, 1976; Fiasco, 1986. Contributions to: New Yorker; Encounter; Penthouse; Omni. Honours: Awards of Polish Ministry of Culture, 1965, 1973; Polish State Prize for Literature, 1976; Austrian State Award for European Literature, 1985; Prize of The Alfred Jurzykowski Foundation for Literature, 1987; Honorary PhD, University of Wroclaw. Membership: International Association of Poets, Playwrights, Editors, Essayists and Authors. Address: c/o Franz Rottensteiner, Marchettigasse 9 17, A 1060 Vienna, Austria.

LEMAIRE Michael, b. 6 Aug 1936, Bordeaux, France. Writer. Education: BS in Civil Engineering, 1957; Minors in Literature and Journalism, 1958. Publications: Love Me or at Least Le Me Love You, 1988; A Romantic Interlude, 1990; Poems Published, 1990-91; Vindicated Episode at Salton Sea (novel), 1993; Tracks Through Time and Space (fantasy novel), 1993. Contributions to: Newspapers and journals. Memberships: International Writers and Artists Association, honorary member; Jazz Journalists Association; National Writers Club; Writers Guild. Address: 6030 Shady Creek Road, Agoura, CA 92549, USA.

LEMANN Nancy Elise, b. 4 Feb 1956, New Orleans, Louisiana, USA. Writer. m. Mark Paul Clein, 5 Oct 1991. Education: BA, Brown University, 1978; MFA, Columbia University, 1984. Publications: Lives of the Saints; The Ritz of the Bayou; Sportsmans Paradise. Contributions to: Chicago Tribune; Los Angeles Times; New Republic; New York Review of Books; New York Times; People; Washington Post. Memberships: PEN; Authors Guild. Address: 254 West 73rd Street, No 5, New York, NY 10023, USA.

LEMMON David Hector, b. 4 Apr 1931, London, England. Writer. m. (Jean) Valerie Fletcher, 16 Aug 1958, 2 sons. Education: Teachers Certificate, College of St Mark and John, 1953; BA Honours, English, 1968, London University; Associate, College of Preceptors, 1967; Final Certificate, English Speaking Board, 1967. Appointments: Head of English, Torells Girls School, Thurrock, 1963-68, Nicholas Comprehensive School, Basildon, 1973-83; Examiner, A Level Theatre Studies, 1980-; Editor, TCCB's Official Tour Guide, Compiler, Test Match and Texaco Trophy programmes, 1984-89. Publications: Benson and Hedges Cricket Year, 1982-; Summer of Success, Great One Day Cricket Matches, Tich Freeman, 1982; Wisden Book of Cricket Quotations I, 1982, II, 1990; Johnny Won't Hit Today and The Book of One-Day Internationals, 1983; The Great Wicket-Keepers, A Walk to the Wicket (with Ted Dexter), Cricket Heroes, 1984; Ken McEwan, Percy Chapman, Cricket Reflections (with Ken Kelly), Cricket Mercenaries, 1985; The Great All-Rounder, 1987; The Official History of Essex CCC (with Mike Marshall), 1987, of Middlesex CCC, 1988, of Worcestershire CCC, 1989, of Surrey CCC, 1989; One-Day Cricket, The Crisis of Captaincy, 1988; Know Your Sport - Cricket (with Chris Cowdrey), 1989; British Theatre Yearbook, 1989, 1990; Len Hutton, a Pictorial Biography, 1990; Cricket's Champion Counties, The Cricketing Greigs, 1991; Guinness Book of Test Cricket Captains, Benson and Hedges British Theatre Yearbook, 1992; The Book of Essex Cricketers, 1995; A Vision Achieved, 1996. Contributions to: Cricket World; Guardian. Membership: Cricket Writers Club; MCC. Address: 26 Leigh Road, Leigh-on-Sea, Essex SS9 1LD, England.

LENGYEL Balazs, b. 21 Aug 1918, Budapest, Hungary. Writer. m. (1) Agnes Nemes Nagy, 1944, (2) Veronika Kerek. Education: Doctor of Law. Publications: Collections of essays: Green and Gold, 1988; Returning, 1990; Rome Revisited, 1995. Editor: Ujhold (New Moon), Literary yearbook. Honours: Literary Award, Hungarian Writers' Union; National Széchenyi Award, 1995. Memberships: Presidium, Hungarian Writers' Union; Founding Member, Hungarian Academy of Arts, 1992; Deputy Chairman, Hungarian PEN, 1995. Address: 4 Apat Utca, Budapest 1033, Hungary.

LENTRICCIA Frank, b. 23 May 1940, Utica, New York, USA. Professor; Writer. m. (1) Karen Young, 24 June 1967, div 1973, (2) Melissa Christensen, 1973, 2 children. Education: BA, Utica College of Syracuse University, 1962; MA, 1963, PhD, 1966, Duke University. Appointments: Assistant Professor, University of California at Los Angeles, 1966-68; Assistant Professor, 1968-70, Associate Professor, 1970-76, Professor, 1976-82, University of California at Irvine; Autrey Professor of Humanities, Rice University, 1982-84; Professor, Duke University, 1984-. Publications: The Gaeity of Language: An Essay on the Radical Poetics of W B Yeats and Wallace Stevens, 1968; Robert Frost: Modern Poetics and the Landscapes of Self, 1975; Robert Frost: A Bibliography, 1913-1974 (editor with Melissa Christensen Lentriccia), 1976; After the New Criticism, 1980; Criticism and Social Change, 1983; Ariel and the Police, 1988; Critical Terms for Literary Study, 1990, 2nd edition, 1995; New Essays on White Noise, 1991; Introducing Don DeLillo, 1991; The Edge of Night: A Confession, 1994. Contributions to: Professional journals. Membership: Modern Language Association. Address: c/o Department of English, Duke University, Durham, NC 27706, USA.

LENZ Siegfried, b. 17 Mar 1926, Lyck, East Prussia, Germany. Novelist; Playwright. Education: University of Hamburg, 1945-48. Publications: Hawks were in the Air, 1951; Duel with Shadows, 1955; So Tender was Suleyken, 1955; The Man in the River, 1957; Jager des Spotts, 1958; The Lightship, 1960; Impressions of the Sea, 1962; The Survivor, 1963; Der Spielverderber, 1965; Begegnung mit Tieren, 1966; Das Wrack, and Other Stories, 1967; The German Lesson, 1968; Collected Stories, 1970; An Exemplary Life, 1973; Einstein Crosses the Elbe at Hamburg, 1975; The Heritage, 1978; The Beginning of Something, 1981; The End of a War, 1984; Training Ground, 1985; The Selected Stories of Siegfried Lenz, 1989; The Rehearsal, 1990; Radio plays; Essays; Political texts. Honours: Honorary Doctorate, University of Hamburg, 1976. Address: Preusserstrasse 4, 2000 Hamburg 52, Germany.

LEONARD Dick, (Richard Leonard), b. 12 Dec 1930, Ealing, Middlesex, England. Journalist; Former Member of Parliament. m. Irene Heidelberger, 29 Mar 1963, 1 son, 1 daughter. Education: MA, Essex University, 1969. Appointments: Assistant Editor, The Economist, 1974-85; Brussels Correspondent, The Observer, 1989-96; Editor, CEPS Review, 1996-; Various other editorial posts in magazines and broadcasting. Publications: Elections in Britain, 1968, 3rd edition, 1996, 4th edition, 1997; The Backbencher and Parliament (co-author), 1972; Paying for Party Politics, 1975; The Socialist Agenda (co-author), 1981; World Atlas of Elections (co-author), 1986; The Economist Guide to the EU, 1988, 3rd edition, 1994. Contributions to: Newspapers and periodicals worldwide. Memberships: Fabian Society (Former Chairman); Reform Club. Address: 32 rue des Bégonias, 1170 Brussels, Belgium.

LEONARD Elmore (John, Jr), b. 11 Oct 1925, New Orleans, Louisiana, USA. Novelist. m. (1) Beverly Cline, 30 Aug 1949, 3 sons, 2 daughters, div 7 Oct 1977, (2) Joan Shepard, 15 Sep 1979, dec, 13 Jan 1993, (3) Christine Kent, 15 Aug 1993. Education: BA, University of Detroit, 1950. Publications: 33 novels including: Hombre, 1961; City Primeval, 1980; Split Images, 1981; Cat Chaser, 1982; Stick, 1983; Labrava, 1983; Glitz, 1985; Bandits, 1986; Touch, 1987; Freaky Deaky, 1988; Killshot, 1989; Get Shorty, 1990; Maximum Bob, 1991; Rum Punch, 1992; Pronto, 1993; Riding the Rap, 1995; Out of Sight, 1996. Honours: Edgar Allan Poe Award, 1984, and Grand Master Award, 1992, Mystery Writers of America; Michigan Foundation for the Arts Award for Literature, 1985; Honorary degrees in Letters from Florida Atlantic University, 1995, University of Detroit Mercy, 1997. Memberships: Writers Guild of America; PEN; Authors Guild; Western Writers of America; Mystery Writers of America. Address: c/o Michael Siegel, Brillstein-Grey Entertainment, 9150 Wilshire Blvd, Beverly Hills, CA 90212, USA.

LEONARD Hugh, (John Keyes Byrne), b. 9 Nov 1926, Dublin, Ireland. Playwright. m. Paule Jacquet, 1955, 1 daughter. Publications: Plays: The Big Birthday, 1957; A Leap in the Dark, 1957; Madigan's Lock, 1958; A Walk on the Water, 1960; The Passion of Peter Ginty, 1961; Stephen D, 1962; The Poker Session, 1963; Dublin 1, 1963; The Saints Go Cycling In, 1965; Mick and Mick, 1966; The Quick and the Dead, 1967; The Au Pair Man, 1968; The Barracks, 1969; The Patrick Pearse Motel, 1971; Da, 1973; Thieves, 1973; Summer, 1974; Times of Wolves and Tigers, 1974; Irishmen, 1975; Time Was, 1976; A Life, 1977; Moving Days, 1981; The Mask of Moriarty, 1984. Television: Silent Song, 1967; Nicholas Nickleby, 1977; London Belongs to Me,

1977; The Last Campaign, 1978; The Ring and the Rose, 1978; Strumpet City, 1979; The Little World of Don Camillo, 1980; Kill, 1982; Good Behaviour, 1982; O'Neill, 1983; Beyond the Pale, 1984; The Irish RM, 1985; A Life, 1986; Troubles, 1987. Films: Herself Surprised, 1977; Da, 1984; Widows' Peak, 1984; Troubles, 1984. Autobiography: Home Before Night, 1979; Out After Dark, 1988. Honours: Honorary DHL (RI); Writers Guild Award, 1966; Tony Award; Critics Circle Award; Drama Desk Award; Outer Critics Award, 1978; Doctor of Literature, Trinity College, Dublin, 1988. Address: 6 Rossaun Pilot View, Dalkey, County Dublin, Ireland.

LEONARD Tom, (Thomas Charles Leonard), b. 22 Aug 1944, Glasgow, Scotland. Writer. m. Sonya Maria O'Brien, 24 Dec 1971, 2 sons. Education: MA, Glasgow University, 1976. Appointments: Writer-in-Residence, Renfrew District Libraries, 1986-89, Glasgow University/Strathclyde University, 1991-92, Bell College of Technology, 1993-94. Publications: Intimate Voices (writing 1965-83), 1984; Situations Theoretical and Contemporary, 1986; Radical Renfrew (editor), 1990; Nora's Place, 1990; Places of the Mind: The Life and Work of James Thomson 'BV' Cafe, 1993; Reports From the Present: Selected Work 1982-94, 1995. Contributions to: Edinburgh Review. Honour: Joint Winner, Saltire Scottish Book of the Year Award, 1984. Address: 56 Eldon Street, Glasgow G3 6NJ, Scotland.

LEONG GOR YUN. See: **ELLISON Virginia Howell.**

LEPAN Douglas (Valentine), b. 25 May 1914, Toronto, Ontario, Canada. Professor Emeritus; Poet; Writer. 2 sons. Education: BA, University of Toronto, 1935; BA, 1937, MA, 1948, Oxford University. Appointments: Counsellor, later Minister Counsellor, Canadian Embassy, Washington, DC, 1951-55; Secretary and Director of Research, Royal Commission on Canada's Economic Prospects, 1955-58; Assistant Under Secretary of State for External Affairs, 1958-59; Professor of English Literature, Queen's University, Kingston, 1959-64; Principal, 1964-70, Principal Emeritus, 1970-, University College, University of Toronto; University Professor, 1970-79, University Professor Emeritus, 1979-, University of Toronto; Senior Fellow, 1970-75, Senior Fellow Emeritus, 1985-, Massey College. Publications: The Wounded Prince and Other Poems, 1948; The Net and the Sword, 1953; The Deserter, 1964; Bright Glass of Memory, 1979; Something Still to Find: New Poems, 1982; Weathering It: Complete Poems 1948-87, 1987; Far Voyages: Poems, 1990; Macalister, or Dying in the Work. Honours: Guggenheim Fellowship, 1948-49; Governor-General's Award for Poetry, 1953, and for Fiction, 1964; Lorne Pierce Medal, Royal Society of Canada, 1976. Address: c/o Massey College, 4 Devonshire Place, Toronto, Ontario M5S 2E1, Canada.

LEPSCHY Anna Laura, b. 30 Nov 1933, Turin, Italy. University Professor. m. 20 Dec 1962. Education: BLitt, MA, Somerville College, Oxford, 1952-57. Publications: Viaggio in Terrasanta 1480, 1966; The Italian Language Today (co-author), 1977, new edition, 1991; Tintoretto Observed, 1983; Narrativa e Teatro fra due Secoli, 1984; Varieta linguistiche e pluralità di codici nel Rinascimento, 1996. Contributions to: Italian Studies; Romance Studies; Studi Francesi; Studi sul Boccaccio; Studi Novecenteschi; Yearbook of the Pirandello Society; Modern Languages Notes; Lettere Italiane. Memberships: Pirandello Society, president, 1988-92; Society for Italian Studies, chair, 1988-95; Association for the Study of Modern Italy; Associazione Internazionale di Lingua e Letteratura Italiana. Address: Department of Italian, University College, Gower Street, London WC1E 6BT, England.

LERMAN Rhoda, b. 18 Jan 1936, New York, USA. Writer. m. Robert Lerman, 15 Sept 1957, 1 son, 2 daughters. Education: BA, University of Miami, 1957. Appointments: National Endowment for the Arts Distinguished Professor of Creative Writing, Hartwick College, Oneonta, New York, 1985; Visiting Professor of Creative Writing, 1988, 1990, Chair, English Literature, 1990, State University of New York at Buffalo. Publications: Call Me Ishtar, 1973; Girl That He Marries, 1976; Eleanor, a Novel, 1979; Book of the Night, 1984; God's Ear, 1989; Animal Acts, 1994. Address: c/o Henry Holt & Co, 115 West 18th Street, New York, NY 10011, USA.

LERNER Laurence (David), b. 12 Dec 1925, Cape Town, South Africa. (British citizen). Professor; Poet; Author. Education: MA, University of Cape Town, 1945; BA, Pembroke College, Cambridge. Appointments: Professor of English, University of Sussex, 1962-84; Kenan Professor, Vanderbilt University, Nashville, 1985-95; Visiting Professor, Universities in USA, Europe. Publications: Poems, 1955;

Domestic Interior and Other Poems, 1959; The Directions of Memory: Poems, 1958-63; Selves, 1969; A.R.T.H.U.R: The Life and Opinions of a Digital computer, 1974; The Man I Killed, 1980; A.R.T.H.U.R & M.A.R.T.H.A: Or, The Loves of the Computers, 1980; Chapter and Verse: Bible Poems, 1984; Selected Poems, 1984; Rembrandt's Mirror, 1987. Play: The Experiment, 1980. Novels: The Englishmen, 1959; A Free Man, 1968; My Grandfather's Grandfather, 1985. Criticism includes: Love & Marriage: Literature in its Social Context, 1979; The Frontiers of Literature, 1988; Angels and Absences, 1997. Contributions to: Sunday Times; The Spectator; London Review of Books. Honours: South-East Arts Literature Prize, for Love and Marriage; Royal Society of Literature, fellow, 1986. Address: Abinger, 1-B Gundreda Road, Lewes, East Sussex BN7 1PT, England.

LERNER Michael P(hillip), b. 7 Feb 1943, Newark, New Jersey, USA. Writer. Education: AB, Columbia University, 1964; MA, 1968, PhD, 1972, University of California at Berkeley. Publications: Surplus Powerlessness, 1986; Jewish Renewal, 1994; Blacks and Jews, 1995; The Politics of Meaning, 1995. Contributions to: Newspapers and magazines. Address: c/o Tikkun Magazine, 26 Fell Street, San Francisco, CA 94102, USA.

LERNER Robert E(arl), b. 8 Feb 1940, New York , New York, USA. Professor of History; Writer. m. Erdmut Krumnack, 25 Oct 1963, 2 daughters. Education: BA, University of Chicago, 1960; MA, 1962, PhD, 1964, Princeton University; University of Münster, 1962-63. Appointments: Instructor, Princeton University, 1963-64; Assistant Professor, Western Reserve University, 1964-67; Assistant Professor, 1967-71, Associate Professor, 1971-76, Professor, 1976-, Peter B Ritzma Professor in the Humanities, 1993-, Northwestern University. Publications: The Age of Adversity: The Fourteenth Century, 1968; The Heresy of the Free Spirit in the Later Middle Ages, 1972, revised edition, 1991; The Powers of Prophecy: The Cedar of Lebanon Vision from the Mongol Onslaught to the Dawn of the Enlightenment, 1983; Weissagungen über die Päpste (with Robert Moynihan), 1985; World Civilizations (with P Ralph, S Meacham and E Burns), 9th edition, 1997; Western Civilizations (with Standish Meacham and E M Burns), 12th edition, 1993; Johannes de Rupescissa, Liber secretorum eventuum: Edition critique, traduction et introduction historique (with C Morerod-Fattebert), 1994; Propaganda Miniata: Le origini delle profezie papali 'Ascende Calve' (with Orit Schwartz), 1994; Neue Richtungen in der hoch - und spätmittelalterlichen Bibelexegese (editor), 1995. Contributions to: Professional journals. Honours: Fulbright Senior Fellowship, 1967-68; National Endowment for the Humanities Research Grant, 1972-73; American Academy in Rome Fellowship, 1983-84; Guggenheim Fellowship, 1984-85; Rockefeller Foundation Study Center Residency, Bellagio, Italy, 1989; Historisches Kolleg, Munich, Forschungspreis, 1992, Stipendiat, 1992-93; Woodrow Wilson Center for Scholars Fellow, 1996-97. Address: c/o Department of History, Northwestern University, Evanston, IL 60208, USA.

LESCHAK Peter, b. 11 May 1951, Chisholm, Minnesota, USA. Writer. m. Pamela Cope, May 1974. Appointments: Contributing Editor, Twin Cities magazine, 1984-86, Minnesota Monthly, 1984-. Publications: Letters from Side Lake, 1987; The Bear Guardian, 1990. Honour: Minnesota Book Award, 1991. Membership: Authors Guild. Address: Box 51, Side Lake, MN 55781, USA.

LESSING Doris May, b. 22 Oct 1919, Kermanshah, Persia. Writer. m. (1) Frank Charles Wisdom, 1939, div 1943, 1 son, 1 daughter, (2) Gottfried Anton Nicholas Lessing, 1945, div 1949, 1 son. Publications: The Grass Is Singing 1950; The Golden Notebook, 1962; African Stories, 1964; Briefing for a Descent into Hell, 1971; Canopus in Argos: Archives, 1979-1983; The Good Terrorist, 1985; Prisons We Choose To Live Inside, 1986; The Wind Blows Away Our Words - And Other Documents Relating to the Afghan Resistance, 1987; The Making of the Representative for Planet 8 (Opera libretto for Philip Glass), 1988; The Fifth Child, 1988; Doris Lessing Reader, 1990; London Observed (short stories), 1992; African Laughter: Four Visits to Zimbabwe, 1992; Under My Skin (autobiography), Vol I, 1994; Love, Again, 1996. Address: c/o Jonathon Clowes Ltd, Iron Bridge House, Bridge Approach, London NW1 8BD, England.

LESTER Andrew D(ouglas), b. 8 Aug 1939, Coral Gables, Florida, USA. Professor of Pastoral Theology and Pastoral Counselling. m. Judith L Laesser, 8 Sept 1960, 1 son, 1 daughter. Education: BA, Mississippi College, Clinton, 1961; BD 1964, PhD 1968, Southern Baptist Theological Seminary, Louisville, Kentucky; Clinical Pastoral Education, Central State, Louisville General, Jewish and Children's Hospitals, Louisville, 1964-68; Clinical Training in Pastoral Counselling Service, Clarksville, Indiana, 1964-69; Diplomate, Association of Pastoral Counselors, 1979. Appointments: General Editor, Resources for Living series, 1989-90; Editor, series on Pastoral Counselling, Westminster-John Knox Press, 1992-. Publications: Pastoral Care in Crucial Human Situations (editor with Wayne Oates), 1969; Sex Is More Than a Word, 1973; It Hurts So Bad, Lord!: The Christian Encounters Crisis, 1976; Coping with Your Anger: A Christian Guide, 1983; Pastoral Care with Children in Crisis, 1985; Spiritual Dimensions of Pastoral Care: Witness to the Ministry of Wayne E Oates (editor with Gerald L Borchert), 1985; Hope in Pastoral Care and Counselling, 1995. Address: Brite Divinity School, Texas Christian University, Fort Worth, TX 76129, USA.

LESTER Julius, b. 27 Jan 1939, St Louis, Missouri, USA. Professor of Judaic Studies; Writer; Musician; Singer. 2 sons, 2 daughters. Education: BA, Fisk University, 1960. Appointment: Professor of Judiac Studies, University of Massachusetts, 1971-. Publications: The 12-String Guitar as Played by Leadbelly: An Instructional Manual (with Pete Seeger), 1965; To Praise Our Bridges: An Autobiography by Fanny Lou Hamer (editor with Mary Varela), 1967; Our Folk Tales: High John, The Conqueror, and Other Afro-American Tales (editor with Mary Varela), 1967; The Mud of Vietnam: Photographs and Poems, 1967; Revolutionary Notes, 1969; Ain't No Ambulances for No Nigguhs Tonight, by Stanley Couch (editor), 1969; Look Out Whitey, Black Power's Gon' Get Your Mama, 1968; To Be a Slave, 1968; Black Folktales, 1969; Search for the New Land: History as Subjective Experience, 1969; The Seventh Son: The Thought and Writings of W E B Du Bois (editor), 2 volumes, 1971; The Knee-High Man and Other Tales, 1972; Long Journey Home: Stories from Black History, 1972; Two Love Stories, 1972; Who I Am?, 1974; All Is Well (autobiography), 1976; This Strange New Feeling (short stories), 1982; Do Lord Remember Me, 1984; The Tales of Uncle Remus: The Adventures of Brer Rabbit, 1987; More Tales of Uncle Remus: Further Adventures of Brer Rabbit, His Friends, Enemies and Others, 1988; How Many Spots Does a Leopard Have? and Other Tales, 1989; Further Tales of Uncle Remus: The Misadventure of Brer Rabbit, Brer Fox, Brer Wolf, The Dooding and Other Creatures, 1990; Falling Pieces of the Broken Sky, 1990; Last Tales of Uncle Remus, 1994; And All Our Wounds Forgiven, 1994; The Man Who Knew Too Much, 1994; John Henry, 1994; Othello: A Novel, 1995. Address: PO Box 9634, North Amherst, MA 01059, USA.

LETTE Kathy, b. 11 Nov 1958, Sydney, New South Wales, Australia. Writer; Screenwriter; Playwright. m. Geoffrey Robertson, 1 May 1990, 1 son, 1 daughter. Publications: Plays: Wet Dreams, 1985; Perfect Mismatch, 1985; Grommitts, 1986; I'm So Happy for You, I Really Am, 1991. Books: Puberty Blues, 1979; Hits and Ms, 1984; Girls' Night Out, 1988; The Llama Parlour, 1991; Foetal Attraction, 1993; Mad Cows, 1996. Contributions to: Satirical columnist for the Sydney Morning Herald; The Bulletin; Cleo Magazine; Irregular contributor to the Guardian; She magazine; Women's Journal; New Woman. Honour: Australian Literature Board Grant, 1982. Address: c/o Ed Victor, 6 Bayley Street, Bedford Square, London WC1B 3HB, England.

LEVANT Victor Avrom, b. 26 Nov 1947, Winnipeg, Manitoba, Canada. Professor; Film Consultant; Practising Gestalt Therapist. Education: BA Honours, Economics, Political Science, 1968, MA, Political Science 1975, PhD, Political Philosophy and International Relations, 1981, McGill University; Institut des Sciences Politiques, Sorbonne, Paris, 1968-69. Appointments: Film Consultant: The World Challenge, TV series, 1984; Studio B, Office National du Film, 1984-86; Maximage Productions, 1987; Communications for the Making of an Etching: P Buckley Moss, 1988. Publications: How to Make a Killing: Canadian Military Involvement in the Indo-China War, 1972; How to Buy a Country: Monograph on Global Pentagon Contracts (co-editor), 1973; Capital and Labor: Partners?, 1976; Capital et Travail, 1977; Quiet Complicity: Canada and the Vietnam War, 1987; The Neighborhood Gourmet, 1989; Secrète Alliance, 1990. Address: 2243 Oxford, Montreal, H4A 2X7, Canada.

LEVENDOSKY Charles (Leonard), b. 4 July 1936, New York, New York, USA. Journalist; Poet. Education: BS, Physics, 1958, BA, Mathematics, 1960, University of Oklahoma; MA, Secondary Education, New York University, 1963. Appointments: Assistant Professor, English, New York University, 1967-71; Visiting Poet (Poetry in the Schools), New York State, Georgia, New Jersey, 1971-72; Poet-in-Residence, Wyoming Council on the Arts, 1972-82;

Editorial Page Editor, Casper Star-Tribune, Wyoming, USA; Columnist, New York Times; Poet Laureate of Wyoming, 1988. Publications: Perimeters, 1970; Small Town America, 1974; Words and Fonts, 1975; Aspects of the Vertical, 1978; Distances, 1980; Wyoming Fragments, 1981; Nocturnes, 1982; Hands and Other Poems, 1986; Circle of Light, 1995. Contributions to: Numerous magazines and journals. Address: PO Box 3033, Casper, WY 82602, USA.

LEVENSON Christopher, b. 13 Feb 1934, England (Canadian citizen, 1973). Educator; Poet; Translator. Education: MA, University of Iowa, 1970. Appointments: Teacher, International Quaker School, Eerde, Netherlands, 1957-58, University of Münster, 1958-61, Rodway Technical High School, Mangotsfield, Gloucestershire, 1962-64; Member, English Department, Carleton University, Ottawa, Canada, 1968-; Editor, Arc, 1978-88. Publications: Poetry from Cambridge (editor), 1958; New Poets 1959 (with I Crichton Smith and K Gershon), 1959; Van Gogh, by Abraham M W J Hammacher (translator), 1961; The Golden Casket: Chinese Novels of Two Millennia (translator), 1965; The Leavetaking and Vanishing Point, by Peter Weiss (translator), 1966; Learns, 1969; Stills, 1972; Into the Open, 1977; The Journey Back, 1978; No-Man's Land, 1980; Seeking Hearts Solace (translator), 1981; Light of the World (translator), 1982; Arriving at Night, 1986; The Return, 1986; Half Truths, 1991; Duplicities: New and Selected Poems, 1992. Honours: Eric Gregory Award; Archibald Lampman Award. Address: Department of English, Carleton University, Ottawa, Ontario K1S 5B6, Canada.

LEVER Sir Tresham Christopher Arthur Lindsay (3rd Baronet), b. 9 Jan 1932, London, England. Naturalist. m. Linda Weightman McDowell Goulden, 6 Nov 1975. Education: Eton College, 1945-49; BA, 1954, MA, 1957, Trinity College, Cambridge. Publications: Goldsmiths and Silversmiths of England, 1975; The Naturalized Animals of the British Isles, 1977; Naturalized Mammals of the World, 1985; Naturalized Birds of the World, 1987; The Mandarin Duck, 1990; They Dined on Eland: The Story of the Acclimatisation Societies, 1992; Naturalized Animals: The Ecology of Successfully Introduced Species, 1994; Naturalized Fishes of the World, 1996. Contributions to: Books. Membership: Fellow, Linnean Society of London. Address: Newell House, Winkfield, Berkshire SL4 4SE, England.

LEVERTOV Denise, b. 24 Oct 1923, Ilford, Essex, England (US citizen, 1955). Professor; Writer. m. Mitchell Goodman, 1947, 1 son. Education: Private education. Appointments: Teacher, YM-YMCA Poetry Center, New York, 1964, City College of New York, 1965, Vassar College, Poughkeepsie, New York, 1966-67; Visiting Lecturer, Drew University, Madison, New Jersey, 1965, University of California at Berkeley, 1969; Visiting Professor: Massachusetts Institute of Technology, 1969-70, University of Cincinnati, 1973; Professor, Tufts University, 1973-79, Stanford University, 1981-; Fannie Hurst Professor (Poet in Residence), Brandeis University, 1981-83. Publications: Verse: Life in the Forest, 1978; Collected Earlier Poems 1940-60, 1979; Candles in Babylon, 1982; Poems 1960-67, 1983; Oblique Prayers, 1984; Selected Poems, 1986; Poems 1968-72, 1987; Breathing the Water, 1987; A Door in the Hive, 1989; Evening Train (new poems), 1992; New and Selected Essays, 1992; Recordings, essays and edited works. Honours: Honorary Scholar, Radcliffe Institute for Independent Study, Cambridge, Massachusetts, 1964-66; Longview Award, 1961; Guggenheim Fellowship, 1962; National Institute of Arts and Letters Grant, 1966; National Endowment for the Arts Senior Fellowship, 1991; Lannan Award, 1993; Honorary Doctorate, University of Santa Clara, 1993. Memberships: American Academy and Institute of Arts and Letters, 1980; Elmer Bobst Award, 1983; Academie Mallarmé, corresponding member. Address: New Directions, 80 Eighth Avenue, New York, NY 10011, USA.

LEVESQUE Anne-Michèle, b. 29 May 1939, Val d'Or, Québec, Canada. Div, 2 daughters. Education: BS, University of Montreal, 1957; Outremont Business College, 1958. Publications: Persil Frisé, 1992; A La Recherche d'un Salaud, 1994; Fleurs de Corail, 1994; La Maison du Puits Sacré, 1997. Contributions to: Lumière d'Encre magazine of the Regroupement des Ecrivains de l'Abitibi-TemisCamingue. Honour: First Prize, Concours Litteraire, 1991. Memberships: Regroupement des Ecrivains de l'Abitibi-TemisCamingue; Union des Ecrivains (UNEQ). Address: 184 Williston Street, Val d'Or, Quebec J9P 4S7, Canada.

LEVEY Sir Michael (Vincent), b. 8 June 1927, London, England. Writer. m. Brigid Brophy, 1 daughter. Education: Exeter College,

Oxford. Appointments: Assistant Keeper, 1951-66, Deputy Keeper, 1966-68, Keeper, 1968-73, Deputy Director, 1970-73, Director, 1973-87, National Gallery, London; Slade Professor of Fine Art, Cambridge, 1963-64, and Oxford, 1994-95. Publications: Six Great Painters, 1956; National Gallery Catalogues: 18th Century Italian Schools, 1956; The German School, 1959; Painting in 18th Century Venice, 1959, 3rd edition, 1994; From Giotto to Cézanne, 1962; Dürer, 1964; The Later Italian Paintings in the Collection of HM The Queen, 1964, revised edition, 1991; Canaletto Paintings in the Royal Collection, 1964; Tiepolo's Banquet of Cleopatra, 1966; Rococo to Revolution, 1966; Bronzino, 1967; Early Renaissance, 1967; Fifty Works of English Literature We Could Do Without (co-author), 1967; Holbein's Christina of Denmark, Duchess of Milan, 1968; A History of Western Art, 1968; Painting at Court, 1971; The Life and Death of Mozart, 1971, 2nd edition, 1988; The Nude: Themes and Painters in the National Gallery, 1972; Art and Architecture in 18th Century France (co-author), 1972; The Venetian Scene, 1973; Botticelli, 1974; High Renaissance, 1975; The World of the Ottoman Art, 1976; Jacob van Ruisdael, 1977; The Case of Walter Pater, 1978; The Painter Depicted, 1981; Tempting Fate, 1982; An Affair on the Appian Way, 1984; Pater's Marius the Epicurean (editor), 1985; Giambattista Tiepolo, 1986; The National Gallery Collection: A Selection, 1987; Men at Work, 1989; The Soul of the Eye: Anthology of Painters and Painting (editor), 1990; Painting and Sculpture in France 1700-1789, 1992; Florence: A Portrait, 1995. Contributions to: Periodicals. Honours: Hawthornden Prize, 1968; Knighted, 1981; Honorary Fellow, Royal Academy, 1986; Banister Fletcher Prize, 1987. Memberships: Ateneo Veneto, foreign member; British Academy, fellow; Royal Society of Literature, fellow. Address: 36 Little Lane, Louth, Lincs LN11 9DU, England.

LEVI Peter (Chad Tigar), b. 16 May 1931, Ruislip, Middlesex, England. Poet; Writer; Translator; Professor. m. Deirdre Connolly, 1977, 1 stepson. Education: Beaumont College, 1946-48; Pass degree, Campion Hall, Oxford, 1958; British School of Archaeology, Athens, 1965-68. Appointments: Member, Society of Jesus, 1948-77; Roman Catholic Priest, 1964-77; Tutor and Lecturer in Classics, Campion Hall, Oxford, 1965-77; Fellow, 1977-91, Emeritus Fellow, 1993-, St Catherine's College, Oxford; Lecturer in Classics, Christ Church, Oxford, 1979-82; Professor of Poetry, Oxford University, 1984-89. Publications: Poetry: Earthly Paradise, 1958; The Gravel Ponds, 1958; Beaumont, 1981-1961, 1961; Orpheus Head, 1962; Water, Rock, and Sand, 1962; The Shearwaters, 1965; Fresh Water, Sea Water, 1966; Pancakes for the Queen of Babylon: Ten Poems for Nikos Gatsos, 1968; Ruined Abbeys, 1968; Life is a Platform, 1971; Death is a Pulpit, 1971; Penguin Modern Poets 22 (with John Fuller and Adrian Mitchell), 1973; Collected Poems, 1955-1975, 1976; Five Ages, 1977; Private Ground, 1981; The Echoing Green: Three Elegies, 1983; Shakespeare's Birthday, 1985; Shadow and Bone: Poems 1981-1988, 1989; Goodbye to the Art of Poetry, 1989; The Marches (with Alan Powers), 1989; Rags of Time, 1994. Fiction: The Head in the Soup, novel, 1979; Grave Witness (mystery), 1985; Knit One, Drop One (mystery), 1986; To the Goat, novella, 1988; Shade Those Laurels (with Cyril Connolly), mystery, 1990. Non-Fiction: The Light Garden of the Angel King: Journeys in Afghanistan, 1972; The Noise Made by Poems, 1977; The Hill of Kronos, 1980; The Flutes of Autumn, 1983; The Lamentation of the Dead, 1984; A History of Greek Literature, 1985; The Frontiers of Paradise: A Study of Monks and Monasteries, 1987; The Life and Times of William Shakespeare, 1988; The Art of Poetry, 1990; Boris Pasternak, 1990; Life of Lord Tennyson, 1993; Edward Lear, 1994. Editor: Richard Selig: Poems, 1963; The English Bible, 1534-1859, 1974; Pope, 1974; Atlas of the Greek World, 1980; The Penguin Book of English Christian Verse, 1984; New Verses by Shakespeare, 1988; Translator: Yevgeny Yevtushenko: Selected Poems (with Robin Milner-Gulland), 1962; Pausanias: Guide to Greece, 2 volumes, 1971, revised edition, 1984; The Psalms, 1977; George Pavlopoulos: The Cellar, 1977; Alexandros Papadiamantis: The Murderess, 1982; Marco the Prince: Serbo-Croat Heroic Songs (with Anne Pennington), 1983; The Holy Gospel of John, 1985; Revelation, 1992. Memberships: Corresponding Member, Society of Greek Writers, 1983; Kingman Committee on English, 1987-88; President, Virgil Society, 1993-95. Address: Prospect Cottage, The Green, Frampton on Severn, Glos GL2 7DY, England.

LEVIN (Henry) Bernard, b. 19 Aug 1928. Journalist; Author. Education: BSc Economics, London School of Economics, University of London, England. Appointments: Writer, regular and occasional, many newspapers and magazines, UK and abroad including: The Times, London; Sunday Times; Observer; Manchester Guardian; Truth; Spectator; Daily Express; Daily Mail; Newsweek; International Herald Tribune; Writer, Broadcaster Radio and TV, 1952-. Publications: The Pendulum Years, 1971; Taking Sides, 1979; Conducted Tour, 1981; Speaking Up, 1982; Enthusiasms, 1983; The Way We Live Now, 1984; Hannibal's Footsteps, 1985; In These Times, 1986; To the End of the Rhine, 1987; All Things Considered, 1988; A Walk Up Fifth Avenue, 1989; Now Read On, 1990; If You Want My Opinion, 1992; A World Elsewhere, 1994. Honours: Numerous awards for journalism; Honorary Fellow, London School of Economics, 1977; Commander of the Order of the British Empire, 1990. Membership: Member, Order of Polonia Restituta (by Polish Government in Exile). Address: c/o The Times, 1 Pennington Street, London E1 9XN, England.

LEVIN Michael Graubart, b. 8 Aug 1958, New York, New York, USA. Novelist. Education: BA, Amherst College, 1980; JD, Columbia University Law School, 1985. Appointments: Writers Programme, University of California, Los Angeles, 1990-; Visiting Professor of English, Stonehill College, 1993-94. Publications: Journey to Tradition, 1986; The Socratic Method, 1987; Settling the Score, 1989; Alive and Kicking, 1993; What Every Jew Needs To Know About. Contributions to: New York Times; Jerusalem Post. Honours: John Woodruff Simpson Fellowships, 1982, 1983. Memberships: PEN; Authors Guild; Writers Guild of America. Address: Box 181, Boston, MA 02101, USA.

LEVIN Torres, (Tereska Torres), b. 3 Sept 1920, Paris, France. Writer. m. Meyer Levin, 25 Mar 1948, 3 sons, 1 daughter. Education: French Baccalaureat. Publications: Le Sable et l'ecume, 1945; Women's Barracks, 1951; Not Yet, 1952; The Dangerous Games, 1953; The Golden Cage, 1954; By Colette, 1955; The Only Reason, 1961; The Open Doors, 1968; The Converts, 1971; Les Annees Anglaises, 1980; Le Pays des Chuchotements, 1983; Les Poupees de Cendre, 1978; Les Maisons Hantees de Meyer Levin, 1990. Address: 65 Boulevard Arago, Studio 13, Paris 75013, France.

LEVINE Norman, b. 22 Oct 1923, Ottawa, Ontario, Canada. Writer. m. (1) Margaret Emily Payne, 2 Jan 1952, dec 1978, 3 daughters, (2) Anne Sarginson, 10 Aug 1983. Education: BA, 1948, MA, 1949, McGill University, Montreal; Trinity College, Cambridge, England, 1945; King's College, London, 1949-50. Publications: Canada Made Me (travel), 1958; From a Seaside Town (novel), 1970; I Don't Want to Know Anyone Too Well (stories), 1971; Something Happened Here (stories), 1991-92. Contributions to: Atlantic Monthly; Sunday Times; New Statesman; Spectator; Vogue; Harper's Bazaar; Encounter; Times Literary Supplement; Saturday Night. Address: c/o Liepman AG, Maienburgweg, CH-8044, Zürich, Switzerland.

LEVINE Paul, b. 9 Jan 1948, Williamsport, Pennsylvania, USA. Writer; Lawyer. m. Alice Holmstrom, 22 Aug 1975, div, 27 July 1992, 1 son, 1 daughter. Education: BA, Penn State University, 1969; JD, University of Miami, 1973. Appointments: Admitted to the Bar, State of Florida, 1973; US Supreme Court, 1977; District of Columbia, 1978, Commonwealth of Pennsylvania, 1989; Attorney and/or Partner, various law firms, 1973-91. Publications: What's Your Verdict?, 1980; To Speak for the Dead, 1990; Night Vision, 1992; False Dawn, 1994; Mortal Sin, 1994; Slashback, 1995; Fool Me Twice, 1996. Memberships: American Bar Association; American Trial Lawyers Association; Authors Guild; Kappa Tau Alpha; Omicron Delta Kappa; Phi Eta Sigma; Phi Kappa Phi; Sigma Delta Chi Journalism Society. Address: c/o International Creative Management, 40 West 57th Street, New York, NY 10019, USA.

LEVINE Philip, b. 10 Jan 1928, Detroit, Michigan, USA. Poet; Writer; Professor. m. Frances Artley, 12 July 1954, 3 sons. Education: BA, 1950, AM, 1955, Wayne University; MFA, University of Iowa, 1957; Studies with John Berryman, 1954. Appointments: Instructor, University of Iowa, 1955-57; Instructor, 1958-69, Professor of English, 1969-92, California State University at Fresno; Elliston Professor of Poetry, University of Cincinnati, 1976; Poet-in-Residence, National University of Australia, Canberra, 1978; Visiting Professor of Poetry, Columbia University, 1978, 1981, 1984; New York University, 1984, 1991; Brown University, 1985; Chairman, Literature Panel, National Endowment for the Arts, 1985; Various poetry readings. Publications: Poetry: On the Edge, 1961, 2nd edition, 1963; Silent in America: Vivas for Those Who Failed, 1965; Not This Pig, 1968; 5 Detroits, 1970; Thistles: A Poem of Sequence, 1970; Pili's Wall, 1971, revised edition, 1980; Red Dust, 1971; They Feed, They Lion, 1972; 1933, 1974; New Season, 1975; On the Edge and Over: Poems Old, Lost, and New, 1976; The Names of the Lost, 1976; 7 Years from Somewhere, 1979; Ashes: Poems New and Old, 1979; One For the Rose, 1981; Selected

Poems, 1984; Sweet Will, 1985; A Walk with Tom Jefferson, 1988; New Selected Poems, 1991; What Work Is, 1991; The Simple Truth: Poems, 1994. Non-Fiction: Don't Ask, interviews, 1979; Earth, Stars, and Writers (with others), lectures, 1992; The Bread of Time: Toward an Autobiography, 1994. Editor: Character and Crisis: A Contemporary Reader (with Henri Coulette), 1966; Tarumba: The Selected Poems of Jaime Sabines (with Ernesto Trejo), 1979; Gloria Fuertes: Off the Map: Selected Poems (with Ada Long), 1984; The Pushcart Prize XI (with D Wojahn and B Henderson), 1986; The Essential Keats, 1987. Contributions to: Many anthologies; Atlantic; Harper's; Hudson Review; New York Review of Books; New Yorker; Paris Review; Poetry. Honours: Joseph Henry Jackson Award, San Francisco Foundation, 1961; National Endowment for the Arts Grants, 1969, 1976, 1981, 1987; Frank O'Hara Prizes, 1973, 1974; Award of Merit, American Academy of Arts and Letters, 1974; Levinson Prize, 1974; Guggenheim Fellowships, 1974, 1981; Harriet Monroe Memorial Prizefor Poetry, University of Chicago, 1976; Lenore Marshall Award for Best American Book of Poems, 1976; American Book Award for Poetry, 1979; National Book Critics Circle Prize, 1979; Notable Book Award, American Library Association, 1979; Golden Rose Award, New England Poetry Society, 1985; Ruth Lilly Award, 1987; Elmer Holmes Bobst Award, New York University, 1990; National Book Award for Poetry, 1991; Pulitzer Prize in Poetry, 1995. Address: 4549 North Van Ness Boulevard, Fresno, CA 93704, USA.

LEVINE Stuart (George), (Esteban O'Brien Córdoba, Stephen O'Brien), b. 25 May 1932, New York, USA. College Professor; Editor; Professional Musician. m. Susan Fleming Matthews, 6 June 1963, 2 sons, 1 daughter. Education: AB, Harvard University, 1954; MA 1956, PhD 1958, Brown University. Appointments: Founding Editor, American Studies, 1959-89; Exchange Professor, University of the West Indies, 1988; Professor Emeritus, University of Kansas, 1992-; Naples Chair, Fulbright Distinguished Lecturer, 1994-95; Fiction Author, 1990-. Publications: Materials for Technical Writing, 1963; The American Indian Today (with N O Lurie), 2nd edition 1970; Charles Caffin: The Story of American Painting (editor), 1972; Edgar Poe: Seer and Craftsman, 1972; The Short Fiction of Edgar Allan Poe (with Susan Levine), 1976, 2nd edition, 1989; The Monday-Wednesday-Friday Girl and Other Stories, 1994. Honours: Fulbright Lectureships to Argentina, Costa Rica and Mexico, Address: 1644 University Drive, Lawrence, KS 66044, USA.

LEVINSON Harry, b. 16 Jan 1922, Port Jervis, New York, USA. Clinical Psychologist; Management Consultant. m. Roberta Freiman, 11 Jan 1946, div June 1972, 2 sons, 2 daughters. Education: BSEd, 1943, MSEd, 1947, Psychology, Emporia State University; PhD, Clinical Psychology, University of Kansas, 1952. Appointments: Editorial Advisory Board, Consultation, 1981-83; Editorial Review Board, Academy of Management Executives, 1986-89; Editorial Board, Family Business Review, 1987-; Panel of Editorial Advisors, Human Relations, 1990-. Publications: Men, Management, and Mental Health, 1962; Organizational Diagnosis, 1972; The Great Jackass Fallacy, 1973; Executive Stress, 1975; Psychological Man, 1976; Emotional Health in the World of Work, 1980; Executive, 1981; Ready, Fire, Aim: Avoiding Management by Impulse, 1986; Designing and Managing Your Career (editor), 1989; Career Mastery, 1992. Contributions to: Numerous professional journals and magazines. Address: The Levinson Institute, 404 Wyman Street, Suite 400, Waltham, MA 02154, USA.

LEVINSON Leonard, (Nicholas Brady, Lee Chang, Glen Chase, Richard Hale Curtis, Gordon Davis, Clay Dawson, Nelson De Mille, Josh Edwards, Richard Gallagher, March Hastings, J Farragut Jones, Leonard Jordan, Philip Kirk, John Mackie, Robert Novak, Philip Rawls, Bruno Rossi, Jonathon Scofield, Jonathon Trask, Cynthia Wilkerson). b. 1935, New Bedford, Massachussets, USA. m. (1) div, 1 daughter, (2) dec. Education: BA, Michigan State University, 1961. Publications: (as Bruno Rossi) Worst Way To Die, 1974; Headcrusher, 1974; (as Nicholas Brady) Shark Fighter, 1975; (as Leonard Jordan) Operation Perfida, 1975; Without Mercy, 1981; (as Cynthia Wilkerson) Sweeter Than Candy, 1978; The Fast Life, 1979; (as Philip King) Hydra Conspiracy, 1979; (as Gordon Davis) The Battle of the Bulge, 1981; (as John Mackie) Hit the Beach, 1983; Nightmare Alley, 1985; (as Clay Dawson) Gold Town, 1989; (as J Farragut Jones) 40 Fathoms Down, 1990; (as Josh Edwards) Searcher, 1990; Warpath, 1991, (as Nelson De Mille) The General's Daughter, 1993; Spencerville, 1994. Address: c/o Lowenstein Associates Inc, Suite I6, 121 West 27th Street, New York NY 10001, USA.

LEVIS Larry, b. 30 Sept 1946, Fresno, California, USA. Associate Professor of English; Poet. Education: BA, California State University, 1968; MA, Syracuse University, 1970; PhD, University of Iowa, 1974. Appointments: Instructor, California State University, Fresno, 1970; Lecturer, California State University, Los Angeles, 1970-72; Visiting Lecturer, University of Iowa, Iowa City, 1972; Assistant Professor, University of Missouri, Columbia, 1974-80; Associate Professor of English, University of Utah, Salt Lake City, 1980-. Publications: Wrecking Crew, 1972; The Rain's Witness, 1975; The Afterlife, 1977; The Dollmaker's Ghost, 1981; Winter Stars, 1985. Address: Department of English, University of Utah, Salt Lake City, UT 84112, USA.

LEVY Alan, b. 10 Feb 1932, New York, New York, USA. Journalist; Editor; Author. Education: AB, Brown University, 1952; MS, Columbia University, 1953. Appointments: Reporter, Courier-Journal, Louisville, 1953-60; Foreign Correspondent, Life Magazine and Good Housekeeping Magazine, Prague, 1967-71, New York Times and International Herald Tribune, Vienna, 1971-91; Dramaturg, English Theatre Ltd, Vienna, 1977-82; Founding Editor-in-Chief, Prague Post, 1991-. Publications: Draftee Confidential Guide (with B Krisher and J Cox), 1957, revised edition (with R Flaste), 1966; Operation Elvis, 1960; The Elizabeth Taylor Story, 1961; Wanted: Nazi Criminals at Large, 1962; Interpret Your Dreams, 1962, 2nd edition, 1975; Kind-Hearted Tiger (with G Stuart), 1964; The Culture Vultures, 1968; God Bless You Real Good: My Crusade with Billy Graham, 1969; Rowboat to Prague, 1972; Good Men Still Live, 1974; The Bluebird of Happiness, 1976; Forever, Sophia, 1979, 2nd edition, 1986; So Many Heroes, 1980; The World of Ruth Draper (play), 1982; Just an Accident (libretto for requiem), 1983; Ezra Pound: The Voice of Silence, 1983; W H Auden: In the Autumn of the Age of Anxiety, 1983; Treasures of the Vatican Collections, 1983; Vladimir Nabokov: The Velvet Butterfly, 1984; Ezra Pound: A Jewish View, 1988; The Wiesenthal File, 1993. Contributions to: Newspapers and magazines. Honours: Bernard De Voto Fellowship, 1963; Golden Johann Strauss Medal, Vienna, 1981; Ernst Krenek Prize, Vienna, 1986. Memberships: American PEN; American Society of Journalists and Authors; Authors Guild; Czech Union of Journalists; Dramatists Guild; Foreign Correspondents Association of Prague; Foreign Press Association of Vienna; Overseas Press Club. Address: c/o Serafina Clarke, 96 Tunis Road, London W12 7EY, England.

LEVY Faye, b. 23 May 1951, Washington, District of Columbia, USA. Syndicated Columnist; Cooking Teacher. m. Yakir Levy, 28 Sept 1970. Education: BA, Sociology, Anthropology, Tel Aviv University, 1973; Grand Diplome, École de Cuisine la Varenne, Paris, 1979. Appointments: Cookery Editor, La Varenne, Paris, 1977-81; Columnist, Bon Appetit Magazine, 1982-88, At Magazine, Israel, 1988-, Jerusalem Post, 1990-; Syndicated Columnist, Los Angeles Times, 1990-. Publications: La Cuisine du Poisson, 1984; Faye Levy's Chocolate Sensations, 1986; Fresh from France: Vegetable Creations, 1987; Fresh from France: Dinner Inspirations, 1989; Sensational Pasta, 1989; Fresh from France: Dessert Sensations, 1990; Faye Levy's International Jewish Cookbook, 1991; Faye Levy's International Chicken Cookbook, 1992; Faye Levy's International Vegetable Cookbook, 1993. Address: 5116 Marmol Drive, Woodland Hills, CA 91364, USA.

LEVY Steven. Editor. m. Teresa Carpenter, 1 son. Education: Central High School, Pennsylvania; Temple University, Pennsylvania; MA, Literature, Penn State University. Appointments: Regular Columnist, Rolling Stone, and Macworld; Original Contributing Writer, Wired; Contributing Editor and Columnist, 1995, Senior Editor, 1996-, Newsweek. Publications: Whole Earth Software Catalog (editor); 4 books including: Hackers, 1984; Insanely Great, 1994.Contributions to: Harper's; Premiere; New Yorker; Sunday New York Times Magazine. Honour: Column of the Year Award, Computer Press Association, 1996. Address: 251 West 57th Street, New York, NY 10019-1894, USA.

LEWIN Michael Zinn, b. 21 July 1942, Cambridge, Massachusetts, USA. Writer. 1 son, 1 daughter. Education: AB, Harvard University, 1964; Churchill College, Cambridge, England. Appointment: Co-Editor, Crime Writers Association Annual Anthology, 1992-94. Publications: Author of 15 novels including: Called by a Panther, 1991; Underdog, 1993; Family Business, 1995; Various radio plays, stage plays and short stories. Honours: Maltese Falcon Society Best Novel, 1987; Raymond Chandler Society of Germany, Best Novel, 1992; Mystery Masters Award, 1994. Memberships: Detection

Club; Crime Writers Association; Mystery Writers of America; Private Eye Writers Association; Authors Guild. Address: 5 Welshmill Road, Frome, Somerset BA11 2LA, England.

LEWINS Frank William, b. 18 July 1941, Melbourne, Victoria, Australia. Academic. m. Margaret Houghton, 6 Feb 1964, 2 daughters. Education: Diploma in Physiotherapy, 1961; Bachelor of Arts (Hons), 1972; PhD, 1976. Publications: The Myth of the Universal Church, 1978; Why Ethnic Schools, 1981; The First Wave, 1985; Writing a Thesis, 1987; Recasting the Concept of Ideology, 1989; Social Science Methodology, 1992; Transexualism in Society, 1995; Bioethics for Health Professionals, 1996. Address: 12 Granville Close, Queanbeyan, New South Wales 2620, Australia.

LEWIS Anthony, b. 27 Mar 1927, New York, New York, USA. Journalist; Visiting Professor. m. (1) Linda Rannells, 8 July 1951, div, 1 son, 2 daughters, (2) Margaret H Marshall, 23 Sept 1984. Education: AB, Harvard University, 1948. Appointments: Deskman, Sunday Department, 1948-52, Reporter, Washington Bureau, 1955-64, Chief, London Bureau, 1965-72, Editorial Columnist, 1969-, New York Times; Reporter, Washington Daily News, 1952-55; Lecturer on Law, Harvard University, 1974-89; James Madison Visiting Professor, Columbia University, 1983-. Publications: Gideon's Trumpet, 1964; Portrait of a Decade: The Second American Revolution, 1964; Make No Law: The Sullivan Case and the First Admendment, 1991. Contributions to: Professional journals. Honours: Heywood Broun Award, 1955; Pulitzer Prizes for National Reporting, 1955, 1963; Nieman Fellow, 1956-57; Best Fact-Crime Book Award, Mystery Writers of America, 1964; Honorary DLitt, Adelphi University, 1964, Rutgers University, 1973, Williams College, 1978, Clark University, 1982; Honorary LLD, Syracuse University, 1979, Colby College, 1983, Northeastern University, 1987. Membership: American Academy of Arts and Sciences. Address: c/o New York Times, 2 Faneuil Hall Marketplace, Boston, MA 02109, USA.

LEWIS Bernard, b. 31 May 1916, London, England (US citizen, 1982). Professor of Near Eastern Studies Emeritus; Writer. m. Ruth Helene Oppenhejm, 1947, div 1974, 1 son, 1 daughter. Education: BA, 1936, PhD, 1939, University of London; Diplome des études semitiques, University of Paris, 1937. Appointments: Professor of History of the Near and Middle East, University of London, 1949-74; Visiting Professor, University of California at Los Angeles, 1955-56, Columbia University, 1960, Indiana University, 1963, University of California at Berkeley, 1965, Collège de France, 1980, École des Hautes Études en Sciences Sociales, Paris, 1983, University of Chicago, 1985; Class of 1932 Lecturer, Princeton University, 1964; Visiting Member, 1969, Member, 1974-86, Institute for Advanced Study, Princeton, New Jersey; Gottesman Lecturer, Yeshiva University, 1974; Cleveland E Dodge Professor of Near Eastern Studies, 1974-86, Professor Emeritus, 1986-, Princeton University; Douglas Robb Foundation Lecturer, University of Auckland, 1982; Director, Annenberg Research Institute, Philadelphia, 1986-90; Tanner Lecturer, Brasenose College, Oxford, 1990; Merle Curti Lecturer, University of Wisconsin, 1993. Publications: The Origins of Ismailism: A Study of the Historical Background of the Fatimid Caliphate, 1940; Turkey Today, 1940; A Handbook of Diplomatic and Political Arabic, 1947; Land of Enchanters: Egyptian Short Stories from the Earliest Times to the Present Day (editor), 1948; The Arabs in History, 1950, revised edition, 1993; Notes and Documents from the Turkish Archives: A Contribution to the History of the Jews in the Ottoman Empire, 1952; Encyclopedia of Islam (co-editor), 1956-86; The Emergence of Modern Turkey, 1961, revised edition, 1968; Historians of the Middle East (editor with P M Holt), 1962; Istanbul and the Civilization of the Ottoman Empire, 1963; The Middle East and the West, 1964; The Assassins: A Radical Sect in Islam, 1967; The Cambridge History of Islam (editor with P M Holt and Ann K S Lambton), 2 volumes, 1970; Race and Color in Islam, 1971; Islam in History: Ideas, Men and Events in the Middle East, 1973, revised edition, 1993; Islam, from the Prophet Muhammad to the Capture of Constantinople (editor and translator), 2 volumes, 1974; History--Remembered, Recovered, Invented, 1975; Studies in Classical and Ottoman Islam: Seventh to Sixteenth Centuries, 1976; Islam and the Arab World: Faith, People, Culture, 1976; Population and Revenue in the Towns of Palestine in the Sixteenth Century (with Amnon Cohen), 1978; The Muslim Discovery of Europe, 1982; Christians and Jews in the Ottoman Empire: The Functioning of a Plural Society, 2 volumes, 1982; The Jews of Islam, 1985; Semites and Anti-Semites: An Inquiry into Conflict and Prejudice, 1986; The Political Language of Islam, 1988; Race and Slavery in the Middle

East: A Historical Enquiry, 1990; Islam and the West, 1993; The Shaping of the Modern Middle East, 1994; Cultures in Conflict: Christians, Muslims, and Jews in the Age of Discovery, 1995. Contributions to: Professional journals. Honours: Citation of Honour, Turkish Ministry of Culture, 1973; Fellow, University College, London, 1976; Harvey Prize, Technion-Israel Institute of Technology, 1978; Many honorary doctorates. Memberships: American Academy of Arts and Sciences; American Historical Society; American Oriental Society; American Philosophical Society; British Academy, fellow; Council on Foreign Relations; Royal Asiatic Society; Royal Historical Society; Royal Institute of International Affairs. Address: c/o Department of Near Eastern Studies, 110 Jones Hall, Princeton University, Princeton, NJ 08544, USA.

LEWIS Charles. See: **DIXON Roger.**

LEWIS David K(ellogg), b. 28 Sept 1941, Oberlin, Ohio, USA. Professor of Philosophy; Writer. m. Stephanie Robinson, 5 Sept 1965. Education: BA, Swarthmore College, 1962; MA, 1964, PhD, 1967, Harvard University. Appointments: Assistant Professor of Philosophy, University of California, Los Angeles, 1966-70; Faculty, 1970-73, Professor of Philosophy, 1973-, Princeton University; Fulbright Lecturer, Australia, 1971; John Locke Lecturer, Oxford University, 1984; Kant Lecturer, Stanford University, 1988. Publications: Convention: A Philosophical Study, 1969; Counterfactuals, 1973; Philosophical Papers, 2 volumes, 1983, 1986; On the Plurality of Worlds, 1986; Parts of Classes, 1991. Honours: Matchette Prize for Philosophical Writing, 1972; Fulbright Research Fellow, New Zealand, 1976; Santayana Fellow, Harvard University, 1988. Memberships: American Association of University Professors; Australian Academy of the Humanities; British Academy; National Association of Scholars. Address: c/o Department of Philosophy, Princeton University, Princeton, NJ 08544, USA.

LEWIS David L(evering), b. 25 May 1936, Little Rock, Arkansas, USA. Professor of History; Writer. m. (1) Sharon Siskind, 15 Apr 1966, div Oct 1988, 2 sons, 1 daughter, (2) Ruth Ann Stewart, 15 Apr 1994, 1 daughter. Education: BA, Fisk University, 1956; MA, Columbia University, 1958; PhD, London School of Economics and Political Science, 1962. Appointments: Lecturer, University of Ghana, 1963-64, Howard University, Washington, DC, 1964-65; Assistant Professor, University of Notre Dame, 1965-66; Associate Professor, Morgar, State College, Baltimore, 1966-70, Federal City College, Washington, DC, 1970-74; Professor of History, University of the District of Columbia, 1974-80; University of California at San Diego, La Jolla, 1981-85; Martin Luther King Jr Professor of History, Rutgers University, 1985-. Publications: Martin Luther King: A Critical Biography, 1971, 2nd edition, 1978; Prisoners of Honor: The Dreyfus Affair, 1973; District of Columbia: A Bicentennial History, 1977; When Harlem Was in Vogue: The Politics of the Arts in the Twenties and the Thirties, 1981; Harlem Renaissance: Art of Black America (with others), 1987; The Race to Fashoda: European Colonialism and African Resistance in the Scramble for Africa, 1988; W E B Du Bois: Biography of a Race, 1868-1919, 1994; The Portable Harlem Renaissance Reader (editor), 1994; W E B Du Bois: A Reader (editor), 1995. Honours: American Philosophical Society Grant, 1967; Social Science Research Council Grant, 1971; National Endowment for the Humanities Grant, 1975; Woodrow Wilson International Center for Scholars Fellow, 1977-78; Guggenheim Fellowship, 1986; Bancroft Prize, 1994; Ralph Waldo Emerson Prize, 1994; Pulitzer Prize for Biography, 1994; Francis Parkman Prize, 1994. Memberships: African Studies Association; American Association of University Professors; American Historical Association; Authors Guild; Organization of American Historians; Phi Beta Kappa; Society for French Historical Studies; Southern Historical Association. Address: c/o Department of History, Van Dyck Hall, Rutgers University, New Brunswick, NJ 08903, USA.

LEWIS F(rances) R, b. 30 Apr 1939, USA. Writer. m. Howard D Lewis, 16 Apr 1961, 2 sons, 1 daughter. Education: BA, State University of New York at Albany, 1960. Publications: Various short stories. Contributions to: Anthologies and periodicals. Honours: PEN-National Endowment for the Arts Syndicated Fiction Project Awards, 1986, 1988; Millay Colony Fellow, 1991; MacDowell Colony Fellow, 1993. Memberships: Associated Writing Programs; International Women's Writing Guild; Poets and Writers. Address: PO Box 12093, Albany, NY 12212, USA.

LEWIS Jeremy Morley, b. 15 Mar 1942, Salisbury, Wilts, England. Writer. m. Petra, 28 July 1968, 2 daughters. Education: BA, Trinity College, Dublin, 1965; MA, Sussex University, 1967. Appointments: Publicity Assistant, Collins, 1967-69; Editor, André Deutsch, 1969-70; Literary Agent, AP Watt, 1970-76; Editor, Oxford University Press, 1977-79; Director, Chatto & Windus, 1979-89; Deputy Editor, London Magazine, 1991-94; Editorial Consultant, Peters, Fraser & Dunlop Ltd. Publications: Playing for Time, 1987; Chatto Book of Office Life, 1992; Kindred Spirits, 1995; Cyril Connolly: A Life, forthcoming. Memberships: Fellow, Royal Society of Literature; Secretary, R S Surtees Society. Literary Agent: Gillon Aitken, Aitken & Stone Ltd.

LEWIS Linda Joy, b. 20 June 1946, New York, New York, USA. Writer. m. 31 Mar 1965, 1 son, 1 daughter. Education: BA, City College of New York, 1972; MEd, Florida Atlantic University, 1976. Publications: We Hate Everything But Boys, 1985; Is There Life After Boys?, 1987; We Love Only Older Boys, 1988; 2 Young 2 Go 4 Boys, 1988; My Heart Belongs to That Boy, 1989; All for the Love of That Boy, 1989; Want to Trade 2 Brothers for a Cat?, 1989; Dedicated to That Boy I Love, 1991; Preteen Means in Between, 1992. Membership: Authors Guild. Address: 2872 North East 26 Place, Ft Lauderdale, FL 33306, USA.

LEWIS-SMITH Anne Elizabeth, b. 14 Apr 1925, London, England. Writer; Poet. m. Peter Lewis-Smith, 17 May 1944, 1 son, 2 daughters. Appointments: Editor, 1st WRNS Magazine, Aerostat International Balloon and Airship, 1973-78; Editor, WWNT Bulletin, BAFM Newsletter, 1967-83; Assistant Editor, 1967-83; Editor, 1983-91, Envoi; Editor, British Association of Friends of Museums Yearbook, 1985-91; Publisher, Envoi Poets Publications, 1986-. Publications: Poetry: Seventh Bridge, 1963; The Beginning, 1964; Flesh and Flowers, 1967; Dandelion Flavour, 1971; Dina's Head, 1980; Places and Passions, 1986; In the Dawn, 1987; Circling Sound, 1996. Contributions to: Newspapers and magazines. Honours: Tissadier Diploma, services to International Aviation; Debbie Warley Award, services to International Aviation; Dorothy Tutin Award, services to poetry. Membership: Fellow, PEN. Address: Pen Ffordd, Newport, Pembrokeshire, Dyfed SA42 0QT, Wales.

LEWISOHN Leonard C, b. 28 Aug 1953, New York, USA. Translator; Editor. m. Jane Ferril, 1973. Education: BA, International Relations, Pahlavi University, 1978; PhD, Persian Literature, University of London, 1988. Publications: Beyond Faith and Infidelity: The Sufi Poetry and Teachings of Mahmud Shabistari, 1995; Editor: The Legacy of Mediaeval Persian Sufism, 1992; Persian Sufism from its Origins to Rumi, 1993; A Critical Edition of the Divan of Maghribi, 1993. Translator: Several books. Address: The Old Chapel, High Street, Eydon, Daventry, Northamptonshire NN11 3PP, England.

LEY Alice Chetwynd, b. 12 Oct 1913, Halifax, Yorkshire, England. Novelist; Teacher. m. Kenneth James Ley, 3 Feb 1945, 2 sons. Education: Diploma in Sociology, London University. Appointments: Tutor in Creative Writing, 1962-84, Lecturer in Sociology and Social History, 1968-71, Harrow College of Further Education. Publications: 19 novels. Contributions to: Numerous journals. Memberships: Jane Austen Society; Romantic Novelists Association, chairman, 1970, honorary life member, 1987-; Society of Women Writers and Journalists. Address: 42 Cannonbury Avenue, Pinner, Middlesex HA5 1TS, England.

LEYTON Sophie. See: **WALSH Sheila.**

LEZENSKI Cezary Jerzy, b. 6 Jan 1930, Poznan, Poland. Journalist; Novelist. m. Antonina Czebatul, 1958, 1 son, 1 daughter. Education: Journalism, 1951; MA, Polish Philology, 1952, Jagiellonian University, Kracow. Appointments: Editor-in-Chief, Kurier Polski, 1969-81; Editor-in-Chief, Epoka Literacke, 1981-90; Editor-in-Chief, Poland Today, edited monthly in 7 languages in 104 countries, 1991-93; Editor-in-Chief, Computer Press Agency, Micro Way, 1994-. Publications: 21 books including: Powrot (novel), 1963; Zolnierskie Drogi (story), 1971; Pozostaly ston, 1971; Pozostaly Tylko Slady Podkow (essay), 1978, 1984; Kwatera 139, biography, 1989; Kawaleria Polska XX Wieku (essay), 1991; Za jeden usmiech, 1996; 6 novels for young people. Contributions to: Nowe Ksiaski literary and science magazine, 1978-89. Honours: Polish Military Cross, 1944; Commander, Polonia Restituta, 1978; Order of Smile for young people's novels, 1979. Memberships: Society of Polish Writers, Vice-chairman, Mazurek Dabrowski Society; Chancellor, Chapter of

the Order of Smile (international); UNICEF. Address: ul Frascati 8/10A, 00-483 Warsaw, Poland.

LI Leslie, b. 21 November 1945, New York, USA. Author; Writer; Playwright. Education: BA, University of Michigan, 1967; Alliance Française, 5ème dégré, 1970. Publications: Bittersweet, 1992; The Magic Whip (children's play), 1995; Contributions to: American Identities: Contemporary Multicultural Voices, 1994; New York Times; International Herald Tribune; Health; Gourmet; Modern Maturity; Condé Nast's Traveler. Honour: Leo Maitland Fellowship, 1992. Literary Agent: Kimberly Witherspoon. Address: Witherspoon Associates, 157 West 57 Street, New York, NY 10019, USA.

LI Oleg, b. 28 Apr 1956, Uzbekistan, Yangi-Bazarvil. m. 3 May 1980, 1 son, 2 daughters. Education: 8 Leningrad Medical College, 1973-76; St Petersburg Medical University, 1979-85. Appointments: Professor, Su-jok AC, 1993; Member, International Su-jok Association; President, Baltiskaja Association. Publications: The Connection of Mental and Cosmic from the Point of View of Oriental Philosophy, 1996; The Use of SU YOK Therapy by the Sportsmen for the Sake of Improvement og Their Sports Results, 1996. Contributions to: Economic Effectiveness of Pain and Tension Massage, 1990; Detailed Instruction for Korean Medical Remedy Indan; Application of Su-jok AC. Honour: Member, International Acmeological Academy. Address: Sousa Pechatnicov Str 29 apt 6, St Petersburg, Russia.

LI Shizheng, (Duo Duo), b. 28 Aug 1951, Beijing, China. Writer. Publications: Looking out from Death, 1989; Statements, 1989; Der Mann im Käfig, 1990; Bang dat ik verloren raak, 1991; Een schrijftafel tussen de velden, 1991. Contributions to: Today magazine, regularly; Manhattan Review; American Poetry Review; Lettre, Germany; NRC newspaper, Netherlands. Honours: Poetry Award, Peking University, 1987. Membership: International PEN. Literary Agent: Jennifer Kavanagh, 44 Langham Street, London W1N 5RG, England. Address: Storkwinkel 12, 10711 Berlin, Germany.

LIBBY Ronald Theodore, b. 20 Nov 1941, Los Angeles, California, USA. Professor. m. Kathleen Christina Jacobson, 6 June 1982, 2 daughters. Education: BA, Political Science, Washington State University, 1965; MA, Political Science, 1966, PhD, Political Science, 1975, University of Washington. Appointment: Professor of Political Science, Southwest State University, Marshall, Minnesota. Publications: Toward an Africanized US Policy for Southern Africa, 1980; The Politics of Economic Power in Southern Africa, 1987; Hawke's Law: The Politics of Mining and Aboriginal Land Rights in Australia, 2nd edition, 1992; Protecting Markets: US Policy and the World Grain Trade, 1992. Contributions to: Professional journals. Address: Department of Political Science, Southwest State University, Marshall, MN 56258, USA.

LICKONA Thomas (Edward), b. 4 Apr 1943, Poughkeepsie, New York, USA. Professor of Psychology and Education; Counsellor. m. Judith Barker, 2 sons. Education: BA; MA, Ohio University; PhD, State University of New York at Albany. Appointment: Professor, State University of New York College at Cortland. Publications: Open Education: Increasing Alternatives for Teachers and Children, 1973; Foundations of Interpersonal Attraction, 1974; Moral Development and Behaviour, 1976; Raising Good Children: Helping Your Child Through the Stages of Moral Development, 1983; Education for Character: How Our Schools Can Teach Respect and Responsibility, 1991. Contributions to: Journal of Moral Education, Ethics in Education. Honours: Distinguished Achievement Award, American Association of Colleges of Teacher Education, 1973; Christopher Award, 1992. Memberships: Association of Moral Education; Ethics in Education. Address: Education Department, State University of New York College at Cortland, Cortland, NY 13045, USA.

LIDDLE Peter (Hammond), b. 26 Dec 1934, Sunderland, England. Writer on History; Keeper of the Liddle Collection, University of Leeds. Education: BA, University of Sheffield, 1956; Teacher's Certificate, University of Nottingham, 1957; Diploma in Physical Education, Loughborough University of Technology, 1958. Appointments: History Teacher, Havelock School, Sunderland, 1957; Head, History Department, Gateacre Comprehensive School, Liverpool, 1958-67; Lecturer, Notre Dame College of Education, 1967; Lecturer, 1967-70, Senior Lecturer in History, 1970-, Sunderland Polytechnic; Keeper of the Liddle Collection, University of Leeds, 1988-. Publications: Men of Gallipoli, 1976; World War One: Personal Experience Material for Use in Schools, 1977; Testimony of War

1914-18, 1979; The Sailor's War 1914-18, 1985; Gallipoli: Pens, Pencils and Cameras at War, 1985; 1916: Aspects of Conflict, 1985 (editor and contributor); Home Fires and Foreign Fields, 1985; The Airman's War 1914-18, 1987; The Soldier's War 1914-18, 1988; Voices of War, 1988; The Battle of the Somme, 1992; The Worst Ordeal: Britons at Home and Abroad 1914-18, 1994; Facing Armageddon: The First World War Experienced, Joint Editor and Contributor, 1996; Passchendaele in Perspective: The Third Battle of Ypres, 1997. Contributions to: Journals. Memberships: British Audio Visual Trust; Royal Historical Society, Fellow. Address: Prospect House, 39 Leeds Road, Rawdon, Leeds LS19 6NW, England.

LIDE Mary Ruth, (Mary Lomer, Mary Clayton), b. Cornwall, England. Writer. 3 sons, 1 daughter. Education: MA, History, St Hugh's, Oxford University. Publications: As Mary Lide: The Bait, 1961; Ann of Cambray (Trilogy), 1985, 1986, 1987; Gifts of the Queen, 1985; Diary of Isobelle, 1985; Hawks of Sedgemont, 1987; Tregaran, 1989; Command of the King, 1990; The Legacy, 1991; The Homecoming, 1992; Polmena Cove, 1994. As Mary Lomer: Robert of Normandy, 1991; Fortune's Knave, 1993. As Mary Clayton: Pearls Before Swine, 1995; Deadmen's Bones, 1996; The Prodigal's Return, 1997. Contributions to: Short stories; Poetry; Book reviews. Honours: Avery Hopwood Award for Poetry, 1955; Best Historical Novel, 1984. Address: c/o Goodman Associates, 500 West End Avenue, New York, NY 10024, USA.

LIEBER Robert J(ames), b. 29 Sept 1941, Chicago, Illinois, USA. Professor of Government; Writer. m. Nancy Lee Isaksen, 20 June 1964, 2 sons. Education: BA, University of Wisconsin, 1963; University of Chicago, 1963-64; PhD, Harvard University, 1968; Postdoctoral Studies, Oxford University, 1969-70. Appointments: Assistant Professor, 1968-72, Associate Professor, 1972-77, Professor, 1977-81, University of California at Davis; Visiting Fellow, 1969-70, Senior Associate Member, 1972-73, St Antony's College, Oxford; Research Associate, Center for International Affairs, Harvard University, 1974-75; Visiting Fellow, Atlantic Institute for International Affairs, Paris, 1978-79; Fellow, Wilson Center, Smithsonian Institution, 1980-81; Guest Scholar, Brookings Institution, 1981; Professor of Government, 1982-, Chairman, Department of Government, 1990-96, Georgetown University; Visiting Professor, Fudan University, Shanghai, 1988. Publications: British Politics and European Unity: Parties, Elites and Pressure Groups, 1970; Theory and World Politics, 1972; Contemporary Politics: Europe (with Alexander Groth and Nancy I Lieber), 1976; Oil and the Middle East War: Europe in the Energy Crisis, 1976; Eagle Entangled: US Foreign Policy in a Complex World (editor with Kenneth Oye and Donald Rothchild), 1979; The Oil Decade: Conflict and Cooperation in the West, 1983; Will Europe Fight for Oil?: Energy Relations in the Atlantic Area (editor), 1983; Eagle Defiant: US Foreign Policy in the 1980s (editor with Kenneth Oye and Donald Rothchild), 1983; Eagle Resurgent?: the Reagan Era in American Foreign Policy (editor with Kenneth Oye and Donald Rothchild), 1987; No Common Power: Understanding International Relations, 1988, 3rd edition, 1995; Eagle in a New World: American Grand Strategy in the Post-Cold War Era (editor with Kenneth Oye and Donald Rothchild), 1992; Eagle Adrift: American Foreign Policy at the End of the Century (editor), 1997. Contributions to: Books and professional journals. Honours: Woodrow Wilson Fellowship, 1963; Council on Foreign Relations International Affairs Fellowship, 1972-73; Guggenheim Fellowship, 1973-74; Rockefeller Foundation Fellowship, 1978-79; Ford Foundation Grant, 1981. Memberships: Council on Foreign Relations; International institute for Strategic Studies. Address: c/o Department of Government, Georgetown University, Washington DC 20057, USA.

LIEBERMAN Herbert Henry, b. 22 Sept 1933, New Rochelle, New York, USA. Novelist; Playwright; Editor. m. Judith Barsky, 9 June 1963, 1 daughter. Education: AB, City College of New York, 1955; AM, Columbia University, 1957. Publications: The Adventures of Dolphin Green, 1967; Crawlspace, 1971; The Eighth Square, 1973; Brilliant Kids, 1975; City of the Dead, 1976; The Climate of Hell, 1978; Nightcall from a Distant Time Zone, 1982; Night Bloom, 1984; The Green Train, 1986; Shadow Dancers, 1989; Sandman Sleep, 1993; The Girl with the Botticelli Eyes, 1996. Honours: Charles Sergel, 1st Prize for Playwriting, University of Chicago, 1963; Guggenheim Fellowship, 1964; Grand Prix de Litterature Policiere, Paris, France, 1978. Memberships: Mystery Writers of America; International Association of Crime Writers. Address: c/o Georges Borchardt, 136 East 57th Street, New York, NY 10022, USA.

LIEBERMAN Shari, b. 24 June 1958, New York, USA. Nutrition Scientist. Education: MS, Clinical Nutrition, New York University, 1982; PhD, Clinical Nutrition and Exercise Physiology, 1993. Appointments: Former Officer and present Board Member, American Preventive Medical Association; Professor, University of Bridgeport, School of Human Nutrition; Nutrition Consultant to various companies; Private Practice Clinical Nutritionist. Publication: The Real Vitamin and Mineral Book, 1992, 2nd edition, 1997. Contributions to: Better Nutrition for Todays Living, New Life. Address: 100 Lehigh Drive, Fairfield, NJ 07006, USA.

LIEBERTHAL Kenneth Guy, b. 9 Sept 1943, Asheville, North Carolina, USA. Professor of Political Science. m. Jane Lindsay, 15 June 1968, 2 sons. Education: BA with distinction, Dartmouth College, 1965; MA, 1968, Certificate for East Asian Institute, 1968, PhD, Political Science, 1972, Columbia University. Appointments: Instructor, 1972, Assistant Professor, 1972-75, Associate Professor, 1976-82, Professor, 1982-83, Political Science Department, Swarthmore College; Visiting Professor, 1983, Professor, 1983-, University of Michigan, Ann Arbor; Editorial Boards, China Economic Review, China Quarterly, Journal of Contemporary China. Publications: Policy Making in China: Leaders, Structures and Processes (with Michel Oksenberg), 1988; Research Guide to Central Party and Government Meetings in China 1949-86 (with Bruce Dixon), 1989; Perspectives on Modern China: Four Anniversaries (co-editor), 1991; Bureaucracy, Politics and Policy Making in Post-Mao China (co-editor), 1991; Governing China, 1995. Contributions to: Journals including: Foreign Affairs, China Quarterly; Book reviews to American Political Science Review; China Economic Review; China Quarterly. Address: Center for Chinese Studies, 104 Lane Hall, 204 South State Street, University of Michigan, Ann Arbor, MI 48109, USA.

LIEBESCHUETZ John Hugo Wolfgang Gideon, b. 22 June 1927, Hamburg, Germany. University Teacher (retired). m. Margaret Rosa Taylor, 9 Apr 1955, 1 son, 3 daughters. Education: BA, 1951, PhD, 1957, London. Appointments: Professor and Head of Department of Classical and Archaeological Studies, University of Nottingham, 1979-92. Publications: Antioch, 1972; Continuity and Change in Roman Religion, 1979; Barbarians and Bishops, 1992; From Diocletian to the Arab Conquest, 1992. Honours: Fellow, British Academy, 1992; Corresponding Fellow, German Archaeological Institute, 1994. Address: 1 Clare Valley, The Park, Nottingham NG7 1BU, England.

LIFSHIN Lyn (Diane), b. 12 July 1944, Burlington, Vermont, USA. Poet; Teacher. Education: BA, Syracuse University, 1960; MA, University of Vermont, 1963. Appointments: Instructor, State University of New York at Cobleskill, 1968, 1970; Writing Consultant, New York State Mental Health Department, Albany, 1969, Empire State College of the State University of New York at Saratoga Springs, 1973; Poet-in-Residence, Mansfield State College, Pennsylvania, 1974, University of Rochester, New York, 1986, Antioch's Writers' Conference, Ohio, 1987. Publications: Poetry: Over 75 collections, including: Upstate Madonna: Poems, 1970-74, 1975; Shaker House Poems, 1976; Some Madonna Poems, 1976; Leaning South, 1977; Madonna Who Shifts for Herself, 1983; Kiss the Skin Off, 1985; Many Madonnas, 1988; The Doctor Poems, 1990; Apple Blossoms, 1993; Blue Tattoo, 1995; The Mad Girl Drives in a Daze, 1995. Editor: Tangled Vines: A Collection of Mother and Daughter Poems, 1978; Ariadne's Thread: A Collection of Contemporary Women's Journals, 1982; Unsealed Lips, 1988. Contributions to: Many books and numerous other publications, including journals. Honours: Hart Crane Award; Bread Loaf Scholarship; Yaddo Fellowships, 1970, 1971, 1975, 1979, 1980; MacDowell Fellowship, 1973; Millay Colony Fellowships, 1975, 1979; Jack Kerouac Award, 1984; Centennial Review Poetry Prize, 1985; Madeline Sadin Award, New York Quarterly, 1986; Footwork Award, 1987; Estersceffler Award, 1987. Address: 2142 Appletree Lane, Niskayuna, NY 12309, USA.

LIFTON Betty Jean, American. Writer. Education: PhD (UMM Inst), 1992. Publications: Joji and the Dragon, 1957; Mogo the Mynah, 1958; Joji and the Fog, 1959; Kap the Kappa (play), 1960; The Dwarf Pine Tree, 1963; Joji and the Amanojaku, 1965; The Cock and the Ghost Cat, 1965; The Rice-Cake Rabbit, 1966; The Many Lives of Chio and Goro, 1966; Taka-Chan and I: A Dog's Journey to Japan, 1967; Kap and the Wicked Monkey, 1968; The Secret Seller, 1968; The One-Legged Ghost, 1968; A Dog's Guide to Tokyo, 1969; Return to Hiroshima, 1970; The Silver Crane, 1971; The Mud Snail Son, 1971; Good Night, Orange Monster, 1972; Children of Vietnam (with Thomas C Fox), 1972; Contemporary Children's Theater (editor), 1974; Jaguar,

My Twin, 1976; Lost and Found: The Adoption Experience, 1979; I'm Still Me, 1981; A Place Called Hiroshima, 1985; The King of Children: A Biography of Janusz Korczak, 1988; Tell Me a Real Adoption Story, 1991; The Adoptee's Journey. Address: 300 Central Park West, New York, NY 10024, USA.

LIFTON Robert Jay, b. 16 May 1926, New York, New York, USA. Psychiatrist; Professor; Writer. m. Betty Kirschner, 1 Mar 1952, 2 daughters. Education: Cornell University, 1942-44; MD, New York Medical College, 1948. Appointments: Intern, Jewish Hospital, Brooklyn, 1948-49; Resident, State University of New York Downstate Medical Center, 1949-51; Faculty, Washington School of Psychiatry, 1954-55; Research Associate in Psychiatry, Harvard University, 1955-61; Foundation's Fund for Research Psychiatry Associate Professor of Psychiatry and Psychology, 1961-67, Research Professor, 1967-, Yale Medical School; Distinguished Professor of Psychiatry and Psychology, Director, Center on Violence and Human Survival, John Jay College of Criminal Justice, the Graduate School and University Center, and Mount Sinai School of Medicine, City University of New York, 1985-; Several guest lectureships. Publications: Thought Reform and the Psychology of Totalism: A Study of Brainwashing in China, 1961, new edition, 1989; Revolutionary Immorality: Mao Tse-Tung and the Chinese Cultural Revolution, 1968; Death in Life: Survivors of Hiroshima, 1969, new edition, 1991; History and Human Survival, 1970; Boundaries: Psychological Man in Revolution, 1970; Home from the War: Vietnam Veterans--Neither Victims Nor Executioners, 1973; Living and Dying (with Eric Olson), 1974; The Life of the Self, 1976; Six Lives, Six Deaths: Portraits from Modern Japan (with Shuichi Kato and Michael Reich), 1979; The Broken Connection: On Death and the Continuity of Life, 1979; Indefensible Weapons: The Political and Psychological Case Against Nuclearism (with Richard A Falk), 1982, new edition, 1991; In a Dark Time, 1984; The Nazi Doctors: Medical Killing and Psychology of Genocide, 1986; The Future of Immortality and Other Essays for a Nuclear Age, 1987; The Genocidal Mentality: Nazi Holocaust and Nuclear Threat (with Eric Markusen), 1990; The Protean Self: Human Resilience in an Age of Fragmentation, 1993; Hiroshima in America: Fifty Years of Denial, 1995. Editor: Woman in America, 1965; America and the Asian Revolutions, 1970; Crimes of War (with Richard A Falk and G Kolko), 1971; Explorations in Psychohistry: The Wellfleet Papers (with Eric Olson), 1975; Last Aid: Medical Dimensions of Nuclear War (with Eric Chivian, Suzanna Chivian, and John E Mack), 1982; The Genocidal Mentality: Nazi Doctor and Nuclear Threat, 1990. Contributions to: Professional journals. Honours: National Book Award, 1970; Van Wyck Brooks Award, 1971; Hiroshima Gold Medal, 1975; Gandhi Peace Award, 1984; Bertrand Russell Society Award, 1985; Holocaust Memorial Award, 1986; National Jewish Book Award, 1987; Los Angeles Times Book Prize for History, 1987; Lisl and Leo Eitinger Award, Oslo, 1988; Max A Hayman Award, American Orthopsychiatrists Association, 1992; National Living Treasure Award, Psychiatric Institute, 1994. Memberships: American Academy of Arts and Sciences, fellow; American Psychiatric Association; Association of Asian Studies; Federation of American Scientists; Society for Psychological Study of Social Issues. Address: c/o John Jay College of Criminal Justice, 899 10th Avenue, New York, NY 10019, USA.

LIGHTMAN Alan (Paige), b. 28 Nov 1948, Memphis, Tennessee, USA. Physicist; Professor; Author. m. Jean Greenblatt, 28 Nov 1976, 2 daughters. Education: AB, Princeton University, 1970; PhD in Physics, California Institute of Technology, 1974. Appointments: Postdoctoral Fellow, Cornell University, 1974-76; Assistant Professor, Harvard University, 1976-79; Staff Scientist, Smithsonian Astrophysical Observatory, Cambridge, 1979-88; Professor of Science and Writing, 1988-, John E Burchard Chair, 1995-, Massachusetts Institute of Technology. Publications: Problem Book in Relativity and Gravitation, 1974; Radiative Processes in Astrophysics, 1976; Time Travel and Papa Joe's Pipe, 1984; A Modern Day Yankee in a Connecticut Court, 1986; Origins: The Lives and Worlds of Modern Cosmologists, 1990; Ancient Light, 1992; Great Ideas in Physics, 1992; Time for the Stars, 1992; Einstein's Dreams, 1993; Good Benito, 1995; Dance for Two, 1996. Contributions to: Professional journals and to general publications. Honours: Most Outstanding Science Book in the Physical Sciences Award, Association of American Publishers, 1990; Boston Globe Winship Book Prize, 1993; Andrew Gemant Prize, 1996. Memberships: American Academy of Arts and Sciences, fellow; American Astronomical Society; American Physical Society, fellow. Address: Massachusetts Institute of Technology, 77 Massachusetts Avenue, Cambridge, MA 02139, USA.

LILIAN Margaret. See: **CLARKE Brenda.**

LILIENTHAL Alfred M(orton), b. 25 Dec 1913, New York, New York, USA. Author; Historian; Attorney; Lecturer. Education: BA, Cornell University, 1934; LLD, Columbia University School of Law, 1938. Appointment: Editor, Middle East Perspective, 1968-85. Publications: What Price Israel?, 1953; There Goes the Middle East, 1958; The Other Side of the Coin, 1965; The Zionist Connection I, 1978; The Zionist Connection II, 1982. Contributions to: Numerous journals. Honour: National Press Club Book Honours, 1982. Memberships: University Club; Cornell Club; National Press Club; Capital Hill Club. Address: 800 25 North West, Washington, DC 20037, USA.

LILLINGTON Kenneth (James), b. 7 Sept 1916, London, England. Author; Dramatist; Lecturer in English Literature (retired). Education: St Dunstan's College; Wandsworth Training College. Appointment: Lecturer in English Literature, Brooklands Technical College, Weybridge, Surrey (retired). Publications: The Devil's Grandson, 1954; Soapy and the Pharoah's Curse, 1957; Conjuror's Alibi, 1960; The Secret Arrow, 1960; Blue Murder, 1960; A Man Called Hughes, 1962; My Proud Beauty, 1963; First (and Second) Book of Classroom Plays, 1967-68; Fourth (and Seventh) Windmill Book of One-Act Plays, 1967-72; Cantaloup Crescent, 1970; Olaf and the Ogre, 1972; Nine Lives (editor), 1977; For Better for Worse, 1979; Young Map of Morning, 1979; What Beckoning Ghost, 1983; Selkie, 1985; Full Moon, 1986. Address: 90 Wodeland Avenue, Guildford, Surrey GU2 5LD, England.

LIM Shirley Geok-Lin, b. 27 Dec 1944, Malacca, Malaysia. Author. m. Dr Charles Bazerman, 27 Nov 1972, 1 son. Education: BA, 1st Class Honours, 1967, MA, English and American Literature, 1971, PhD, 1973, Brandeis University. Appointment: Writer-in-Residence, National University of Singapore, 1985. Publications: Crossing the Peninsula, 1980; Another Country, 1982; No Man's Grove, 1985; Modern Secrets, 1988; The Forbidden Stitch, 1989; Nationalism and Literature, 1993; Writing South East Asia in English, 1994; Monsoon History, 1995; Among the White Moon Faces, 1996; Two Dreams, 1997. Contributions to: Periodicals and journals. Honours: Commonwealth Poetry Prize, 1980; Mellon Fellowships, 1983, 1987; American Book Award, 1990; Fulbright, 1996. Memberships American Studies Association: Modern Language Association. Address: Dept of English, University of California, Santa Barbara, CA 93106, USA.

LIMA Robert, b. 7 Nov 1935, Havana, Cuba. University Professor; Writer. m. Sally Murphy, 27 June 1964, 2 sons, 2 daughters. Education: BA, English and Philosophy 1957, MA, Theatre and Drama, 1961, Villanova University; PhD, Romance Literatures, New York University, 1968. Appointments: Professor of Spanish and Comparative Literature, 1965-; Poet-in-Residence, Pontificia Universidad Catolica del Peru, 1976-77; Writer-in-Residence, USIA, 1986. Publications: Criticism: The Theatre of Garcia Lorca, 1963; Ramon del Valle-Inclan, 1972; An Annotated Bibliography of Valle-Inclan, 1972; Dos Ensayos sobre Teatro Espanol de Los 20, 1984; The Lamp of Marvels by Valle-Inclan (translator), 1986; Valle-Inclan: The Theatre of His Life, 1988; Dark Prisms: Occultism in Hispanic Drama, 1995; Valle-Inclan: El teatro de su vida, 1995. Poetry: Fathoms, 1981; The Olde Ground, 1985; Mayaland Poetry, 1992. Contributions to: Anthologies, newspapers, and journals. Address: Pennsylvania State University, N346 Burrowes Building, University Park, PA 16802, USA.

LIMAN Horia, b. 12 Oct 1912, Bucharest, Romania. Writer; Journalist. m. Isabelle Fallet-Liman, 27 Jan 1994. Education: License es Letter, University of Bucharest, 1920-24. Appointments: Director of literary reviews; Critic. Publications: La Foire aux Jeunes Filles, 1987; L'Echeance, 1992; Les Bottes. Contributions to: Discobol, director, 1932-34; Lumea Romaneasca; Contemporanul, Editor, 1947-57; Literary Correspondent in Prague for Romania, 1959-65; Literary Correspondent in Switzerland for Romania, 1965-70. Honour: Prix Schiller, 1993. Memberships: ADELF; SSEE; AENJ. Address: Port-Roulant, 30-2003 Neuchatel, Switzerland.

LIMBAUGH Rush (Hudson), b. 12 Jan 1951, Cape Girardeau, Missouri, USA. Radio and Television Personality. m. Marta Fitzgerald, 27 May 1994. Appointments: Various radio disc jockey posts, 1960-88; Host, The Rush Limbaugh Show, radio, 1988-, television, 1992-96; Editor-Publisher, The Limbaugh Letter, 1995-. Publications: The Way

Things Ought to Be, 1992; See, I Told You So, 1993. Address: c/o WABC, 125 West End Avenue, No 6, New York, NY 10023, USA.

LIMBURG Peter R(ichard), b 14 Nov 1929, New York, New York, USA. Writer; Editor. Education: BA, Yale University, 1950; BSFA, Georgetown University, 1951; MA, Columbia University, 1957. Appointments: Special Editor, Harper Encyclopaedia of Science, 1960-61; Senior Technology Editor, The New Book of Knowledge, 1961-66; Editor, School Department, Harcourt, Brace and World, publishers, 1966-69; Coordinating Editor, Collier's Encyclopaedia, 1969-70; President, Forum Writers for Young People, 1975-76, 1980-81. Publications: The First Book of Engines, 1969; The Story of Corn, 1971; What's in the Names of Fruit, 1972; What's in the Names of Antique Weapons, 1973; Vessels for Underwater Exploration: A Pictorial History (with James B Sweeney), 1973; Watch Out, It's Poison Ivy!, 1973; What's in the Names of Flowers, 1974; 102 Questions and Answers about the Sea (with James B Sweeney), 1975; What's in the Names of Birds, 1975; Chickens, Chickens, Chickens, 1975; What's in the Names of Stars and Constellations, 1976; Poisonous Plants, 1976; What's in the Names of Wild Animals, 1977; Oceanographic Institutions, 1979; The Story of Your Heart, 1979; Farming the Waters, 1980; Stories Behind Words, 1986. Memberships: American Society of Journalists and Authors; National Association of Science Writers. Address: RR 4, Banksville Road, Bedford, NY 10506, USA.

LINCOLN Bruce (Kenneth), b. 5 Mar 1948, Philadelphia, Pennsylvania, USA. Professor; Writer. m. Louise Gibson Hassett, 17 Apr 1971, 2 daughters. Education: BA, Haverford College, 1970; PhD, University of Chicago, 1976. Appointments: Assistant Professor, 1976-79, Associate Professor, 1979-84, Professor of Humanities, Religious Studies and South Asian Studies, and Chair, Religious Studies Programme, 1979-86, Professor of Comparative Studies in Discourse and Society, 1986-93, University of Minnesota; Visiting Professor, Università degli Studi di Siena, 1984-85, University of Uppsala, 1985, Novosibirsk State Pedagogical Institute, 1991; Professor of History of Religions and Anthropology, University of Chicago, 1993-. Publications: Priests, Warriors, and Cattle: A Study in the Ecology of Religions, 1981; Emerging from the Chrysalis: Studies in Rituals of Women's Initiation, 1981, revised edition, 1991; Religion, Rebellion, Revolution: An Interdisciplinary and Crosscultural Collection of Essays (editor), 1985; Myth, Cosmos, and Society: Indo-European Themes of Creation and Destruction, 1986; Discourse and the Construction of Society: Comparative Studies of Myth, Ritual, and Classification, 1989; Death, War, and Sacrifice: Studies in Ideology and Practice, 1991; Authority: Construction and Corrosion, 1994. Contributions to: Professional journals. Honours: American Council of Learned Societies Grant, 1979; Rockefeller Foundation Grant, 1981; Best New Book in History of Religion Citation, American Council of Learned Societies, 1981; Guggenheim Fellowship, 1982-83; National Endowment for the Humanities Grant, 1986; Outstanding Academic Book Citation, Choice, 1989; Scholar of the College, University of Minnesota, 1990-93. Address: 3232 Bryant Avenue South, Minneapolis, MN 55408, USA.

LINCOLN Geoffrey. See: **MORTIMER John Clifford.**

LINCOLN W(illiam) Bruce, b. 6 Sept 1938, Stafford Springs, Connecticut, USA. Professor; Author. m. Mary Lynda Eagle Livingston, 27 Mar 1984. Education: AB, College of William and Mary, 1960; MA, 1962, PhD, 1966, University of Chicago. Appointments: Assistant Professor, Memphis State University, 1966-67; Assistant Professor, 1967-70, Associate Professor, 1970-78, Professor of History, 1978-82, Presidential Research Professor, 1982-86, University Research Professor, 1986-, Northern Illinois University, DeKalb; Visiting Fellow, St Antony's College, Oxford, 1983. Publications: Documents in World History, 1945-67 (editor), 1968; Nikolai Miliutin: An Enlightened Russian Bureaucrat, 1977; Nicholas I: Emperor and Autocrat of All the Russias, 1978; Petr Petrovich Semenov-Tian-Shanskii: The Life of a Russian Geographer, 1980; The Romanovs: Autocrats of All the Russias, 1981; In the Vanguard of Reform: Russia's Enlightened Bureaucrats, 1825-1861, 1982; In War's Dark Shadow: Russians Before the Great War, 1983; Passage through Armageddon: Russia in the Great War, 1914-1918, 1986; Red Against White: Civil War Among the Russians, 1987; The Great Reforms: Autocracy, Bureaucracy, and the Politics of Change in Imperial Russia, 1990; Moscow: Treasures and Traditions (editor), 1990. Contributions to: Numerous professional journals. Honours: Fulbright-Hays Fellowships, 1970-71, 1974, 1978-79, 1982-83; American Council of Learned Societies Grants,

1973, 1978, 1978-79; Guggenheim Fellowship, 1982-83. Memberships: American Association for the Advancement of Slavic Studies; Mid-West Slavic Association; Phi Beta Kappa. Address: c/o Department of History, Northern Illinois University, DeKalb, IL 60115, USA.

LIND William Sturgiss, b. 9 July 1947, Lakewood, Ohio, USA. Writer. Education: AB, Dartmouth College, 1969; MA, Princeton University, 1971. Appointment: Associate Publisher, The New Electric Railway Journal. Publications: Maneuver Warfare Handbook, 1985; America Can Win: The Case for Military Reform (with Gary Hart), 1986; Cultural Conservatism: Toward a New National Agenda (with William H Marshner), 1987; Cultural Conservatism: Theory and Practice (editor with William H Marshner), 1991. Contributions to: Marine Corps Gazette; US Naval Institute Proceedings; Military Review; Parameters; Washington Post; Harper's. Address: Free Congress Foundation, 717 2nd Street North East, Washington, DC 20002, USA.

LINDBLOM Charles Edward, b. 21 Mar 1917, Turlock, California, USA. Professor; Writer. m. Rose K Winther, 4 June 1942, 2 sons, 1 daughter. Education: BA, Stanford University, 1937; PhD, University of Chicago, 1945. Appointments: Instructor, University of Minnesota, 1939-46; Assistant Professor to Professor, Yale University, 1946-. Publications: Unions and Capitalism, 1949; Politics, Economics and Welfare, 1953; The Intelligence of Democracy, 1965; The Policy Making Process, 1968; Politics and Markets, 1977; Usable Knowledge, 1979; Democracy and the Market System, 1988; Inquiry and Change, 1990. Contributions to: Professional journals. Honours: Various. Membership: American Political Science Association. Address: 9 Cooper Road, North Haven, CT 06473, USA.

LINDEY Christine, b. 26 Aug 1947. Art Historian. Education: BA Hons, History of European Art, Courtauld Institute, University of London, England. Publications: Superrealist Painting and Sculpture, 1980; 20th Century Painting: Bonnard to Rothko, 1981; Art in the Cold War, 1990. Address: c/o West Herts College, The Art School, Ridge Street, Watford, Herts WD2 5BY, England.

LINDGREN Gustav Torgny, b. 16 June 1938, Raggsjo, Sweden. Author. m. Stina Andersson, 19 June 1959, 1 son, 2 daughters. Education: DPhil. Publications: Ovriga tragor, 1973; Brannvinsfursten, 1979; Skrammer dig minuten, 1981; Merabs skonhet, 1983; Ormens vag pa halleberget, 1983; Batseba, 1984; Legender, 1986; Ljuset, 1987; Karleksguden Fro, 1988; Till Sanningens lov, 1991; Hummelhonung, 1995. Honours: Prix Fomina, 1986; Guralid Prize, 1990. Memberships: PEN; Swedish Academy. Address: Tjärstad prästgård, S-59041, Rimforsa, Sweden.

LINDMAN-STRAFFORD Kerstin Margareta, b. 30 May 1939, Abo, Finland. Writer; Critic. 2 children. Education: BA, Hum Kand, 1961; MA, 1962. Appointments: Critic, UK Editor, Hufvudstadsbladet, Helsinki, 1964-; Cultural Presenter, OBS Kulturkvarten, Swedish Radio, 1975-. Publications: Sandhogen and Other Essays, 1974; Tancred Borenius, 1976; Landet med manga ansikten, 1979; English Writers in Literaturhandboken, 1984; Faeder och Dottrar, 1986; Moedrar och soener, 1990; Foeraendringen, 1994. Contributions to: Numerous journals and magazines. Honour: Finland's Swedish Literary Society Prize, 1976. Memberships: PEN; Finlands Svenska Litteraturforening. Address: 16 Church Path, Merton Park, London SW19 3HJ, England.

LINDSAY Hilarie Elizabeth, b. 18 Apr 1922, Sydney, New South Wales, Australia. Writer; Museum Curator; Company Director. m. Philip Singleton Lindsay, 19 Feb 1944, 1 son, 2 daughters. Education: Graduate, William's Business College, 1938; BA (Deakin), 1985. Publications: 101 Toys to Make, 1972; So You Want to Be a Writer, 1977; You're On Your Own - Teenage Survival Kit, 1977; One for the Road (short stories), 1978; Midget Mouse Finds a House, 1978; Culinary Capers, 1978; The Short Story, 1979; Learn to Write, 1979; The Naked Gourmet, 1979; The Society of Women Writers Handbook, 1980; The Withered Tree, 1980; One Woman's World, 1980; Echoes of Henry Lawson, 1981; The Gravy Train, 1981; Mr Poppleberry and the Dog's Own Daily, 1983; Mr Poppleberry and the Milk Thieves, 1983; Murder at the Belle Vue, 1983; Mr Poppleberry's Birthday Pie, 1989; Midget Mouse Goes to Sea, 1989; Beyond the Black Stump of My Pencil, 1993; When I Was Ten (with Len Fox), 1993; Sydney Life (with P McGowan), 1994; Mrs Poppleberry's Cuckoo-Clock, 1995.

Address: 19-25 Beeson Street, Leichhardt, New South Wales 2020, Australia.

LINDSAY (John) Maurice, b. 21 July 1918, Glasgow, Scotland. Editor; Poet. Education: Glasgow Academy; Royal Scottish Academy of Music. Appointments: Editor, Scottish Review, 1975-85. Publications: The Advancing Day, 1940; Predicament, 1942; No Crown for Laughter, 1943; The Enemies of Love: Poems, 1941-45, 1946; Selected Poems, 1947; At the Woods Edge, 1950; Ode for St Andrew's Night and Other Poems, 1951; The Exiled Heart: Poems, 1941-56, 1957; Snow Warning and Other Poems, 1962; One Later Day and Other Poems, 1964; This Business of Living, 1971; Comings and Goings, 1971; Selected Poems, 1942-72, 1973; The Run from Life: More Poems, 1942-72, 1975; Walking Without an Overcoat: Poems, 1972-76, 1977; Collected Poems, 1979; A Net to Catch the Wind and Other Poems, 1981; The French Mosquitoe's Woman and Other Diversions, 1985; Requiem for a Sexual Athlete and Other Poems and Diversions, 1988; The Scottish Dog (with Joyce Lindsay), 1989; Collected Poems, 1940-1990, 1991; On the Face of It: Collected Poems, Vol 2, 1993; News of the World: Last Poems, 1995; The Theatre and Opera Lover's Quotation Book (with Joyce Lindsay), 1993. Plays: Fingal and Comala, 1953; The Abbot of Drimock, 1958; The Decision, 1967; Guides to Scotland: Editions of Poetry. Honours: Commander of the Order of the British Empire, 1979; D Litt, University of Glasgow, 1982; Hon Fellow, Royal Incorporation of Architects in Scotland. Address: 7 Milton Hill, Milton, Dumbarton, Dumbartonshire GB2 2TS, Scotland.

LINE David. See: **DAVIDSON Lionel.**

LINETT Deena, b. 30 Aug 1938, Boston, Massachusetts, USA. Professor of English; Writer. 2 sons, 1 daughter. Education: EdD, Rutgers University, 1982. Appointment: Professor of English, Montclair State University. Publications: On Common Ground, 1983; The Translator's Wife, 1986; Visit, 1990. Contributions to: Journals. Honours: Yaddo Fellowships, 1981, 1985; PEN-Syndicated Fiction Project, 1990. Memberships: Modern Language Association; National Council of Teachers of English; PEN; Poets and Writers. Address: c/o Department of English, Montclair State University, Upper Montclair, NJ 07043, USA.

LINGARD Joan Amelia, b. 8 Apr 1932, Edinburgh, Scotland. Author. 3 daughters. Education: Bloomfield Collegiate School, Belfast, 1943-48; General Teaching Diploma, Moray House Training College, Edinburgh. Publications: Children's Books: The Twelfth Day of July, 1970; Frying as Usual, 1971; Across the Barricades, 1972; Into Exile, 1973; The Clearance, 1974; A Proper Place, 1975; The Resettling, 1975; Hostages to Fortune, 1976; The Pilgrimage, 1976; The Reunion, 1977; The Gooseberry, 1978; The File on Fraulein Berg, 1980; Strangers in the House, 1981; The Winter Visitor, 1983; The Freedom Machine, 1986; The Guilty Party, 1987; Rags and Riches, 1988; Tug of War, 1989; Glad Rags, 1990; Between Two Worlds, 1991; Hands Off Our School!, 1992; Night Fires, 1993. Novels: Liam's Daughter, 1963; The Prevailing Wind, 1964; The Tide Comes In, 1966; The Headmaster, 1967; A Sort of Freedom, 1968; The Lord on Our Side, 1970; The Second Flowering of Emily Mountjoy, 1979; Greenyards, 1981; Sisters by Rite, 1984; Reasonable Doubts, 1986; The Women's House, 1989; After Colette, 1993; Lizzie's Leaving, 1995; Dreams of Love and Modest Glory, 1995. Honours: Scottish Arts Council Bursary, 1967-68; Preis der Leseratten ZDF, Germany, 1986; Buxtehuder Bulle, Germany, 1987. Memberships: Society of Authors in Scotland, chairman, 1982-86; Scottish PEN; Director, Edinburgh Book Festival. Address: David Higham Associates Ltd, 5-8 Lower John St, Golden Square, London W1R 4HA, England.

LINGEMAN Richard (Roberts), b. 2 Jan 1931, Crawfordsville, Indiana, USA. Editor; Writer. m. Anthea Judy Nicholson, 3 Apr 1965, 1 daughter. Education: BA, Haverford College, 1953; Postgraduate Studies, Yale Law School, 1956-58, Columbia University Graduate School, 1958-60. Appointments: Executive Editor, Monocle magazine, 1960-69, The Nation, 1978-; Associate Editor, Columnist, The New York Times Book Review, 1969-78. Publications: Drugs from A to Z, 1969; Don't You Know There's a War On?, 1971; Small Town America, 1980; Theodore Dreiser: At the Gates of the City, 1871-1907, 1986; Theodore Dreiser: An American Journey, 1908-1945, 1990. Honour: Chicago Sun-Times Book of the Year Award, 1990. Memberships: Authors Guild; National Book Critics Circle; New York Historical Society; PEN; Phi Beta Kappa; Society of American Historians. Address: c/o The Nation, 72 Fifth Avenue, New York, NY 10011, USA.

LINK Arthur S(tanley), b. 8 Aug 1920, New Market, Virginia, USA. Professor of American History Emeritus; Writer; Editor. m. Margaret McDowell Douglas, 2 June 1945, 3 sons, 1 daughter. Education: AB, 1941, PhD, 1945, University of North Carolina; Postgraduate Studies, Columbia University, 1944-45. Appointments: Instructor, North Carolina State College, 1943-44; Instructor, 1945-48, Assistant Professor, 1948-49, Professor, 1960-65, Edwards Professor of American History, 1965-76, George H Davis '86 Professor of American History, 1976-91, Professor Emeritus, 1991-, Princeton University; Member, Institute for Advanced Study, Princeton, New Jersey, 1949, 1954-55; Associate Professor, 1949-54, Professor, 1954-60, Northwestern University; Albert Shaw Lecturer, Johns Hopkins University, 1956; Harmsworth Professor of American History, Oxford University, 1958-59; Commonwealth Fund Lecturer, University of London, 1977; President, National Commission on Social Studies in the Schools, 1987-90; Distinguished Adjunct Professor of American History, University of North Carolina at Greensboro, 1992-. Publications: Wilson: The Road to the White House, 1947; Woodrow Wilson and the Progressive Era, 1954, 3rd edition, 1988; Wilson: The New Freedom, 1956; Wilson the Diplomatist, 1957; Wilson: The Struggle for Neutrality, 1914-15, 1960; Our American Republic (with D S Muzzey), 1963; Woodrow Wilson: A Brief Biography, 1963; Our Country's History, 1964; Wilson: Confusions and Crises, 1915-16, 1964; Wilson: Campaigns for Progressivism and Peace, 1916-17, 1965; Problems in American History (with R W Leopold and Stanley Cohen), 1972; American Epoch (with William B Catton and William A Link), 2 volumes, 1986. Editor: The Papers of Woodrow Wilson, 69 volumes, 1966-94; Writing Southern History (with R W Patrick), 1967; The Growth of American Democracy, 1968; Woodrow Wilson: A Profile, 1968; The Impact of World War I, 1969; The Diplomacy of World Power: The United States, 1889-1920 (with W M Leary Jr), 1970; The Higher Realism of Woodrow Wilson and Other Essays, 1970; The Democratic Heritage: A History of the United States (with Stanley Cohen), 1971; The Progressive Era and the Great War (with William M Leary Jr), 1978; Woodrow Wilson: Revolution, War, and Peace, 1979; Woodrow Wilson and a Revolutionary World, 1913-21, 1982; Progressivism (with Richard L McCormick), 1983; A Concise History of the American People (with others), 1984; The American People: A History, 1987; The Twentieth Century: An American History (with William A Link), 1991; Brother Woodrow: A Memoir of Woodrow Wilson, by Stockton Axson, 1993. Contributions to: Professional and general journals. Honours: Guggenheim Fellowship, 1950-51; Bancroft Prizes, 1957, 1961; Thomas Jefferson Medal, American Philosophical Society, 1994; Various honorary doctorates. Memberships: American Academy of Arts and Sciences, fellow; American Historical Association, president, 1984; American Philosophical Society; Association of Documentary Editors, president, 1978-79; National Council of Churches, vice-president, 1963-66; Organization of American Historians, president, 1984-85; Phi Beta Kappa; Southern Historical Association, president, 1968-69. Address: 5322 Bermuda Village, Advance, NC 27006, USA.

LINKLATER Magnus (Duncan), b. 21 Feb 1942, Scotland. Journalist; Writer. m. Veronica Lyle, 1967, 2 sons, 1 daughter. Education: Freiburg University; Sorbonne, Paris; Trinity Hall, Cambridge. Appointments: Editor and reporter, Evening Standard, 1966-69, Sunday Times, 1967, Features Editor, 1979-83; Managing Editor, Observer, 1983-86; Editor, The Scotsman, 1988-94. Publications: (all as co-author) Hoax: The Inside Story of the Howard Hughes-Clifford Irving Affair, 1972; Jeremy Thorpe: A Secret Life, 1979; Massacre: The Story of Glencoe, 1982; War in the Falklands, 1982; The Nazi Legacy: Klaus Barbie and the International Fascist Connection, 1984; The Fourth Reich: Klaus Barbie and the Neo-Fascist Connection, 1984; Scotland, 1984; Not with Honour: The Inside Story of the Westland Scandal, 1986; Anatomy of Scotland, 1992; Highland Wilderness, 1993. Honours: Chairman, Scottish Arts Council; Hon DArts, Napier. Address: 5 Drummond Place, Edinburgh EH3 6PH, Scotland.

LINKLETTER Art(hur Gordon), b. 17 July 1912, Moose Jaw, Saskatchewan, Canada. Radio and Television Broadcaster; Businessman; Writer. m. Lois Foerster, 25 Nov 1935, 2 sons, 3 daughters. Education: AB, San Diego State College, 1934. Appointments: Former Host and Writer, People Are Funny, NBC Radio and TV, Art Linkletter's House Party, CBS Radio and TV; President, Linkletter Productions; Chairman of the Board, Linkletter Enterprises; Owner, Art Linkletter Oil Enterprises. Publications: People Are Funny, 1953; Kids Say the Darndest Things, 1957; The Secret World of Kids, 1959; Confessions of a Happy Man, 1961; Kids Still Say the Darndest

Things, 1961; A Child's Garden of Misinformation, 1965; I Wish I'd Said That, 1968; Linkletter Down Under, 1969; Oops, 1969; Drugs at My Door Step, 1973; Women Are My Favorite People, 1974; How to be a Super Salesman, 1974; Yes, You Can!, 1979; I Didn't Do It Alone, 1979; Public Speaking for Private People, 1980; Linkletter on Dynamic Selling, 1982; Old Age is Not for Sissies, 1988. Honours: Many awards. Address: 8484 Wilshire Boulevard, Suite 205, Beverly Hills, CA 90211, USA.

LINNEY Romulus, b. 21 Sept 1930, Philadelphia, Pennsylvania, USA. Dramatist; Writer. m. (1) Ann Leggett Sims, 14 Apr 1963, div 1966, 1 daughter, (2) Jane Andrews, 14 Sept 1967, 1 daughter. Education: AB, Oberlin College, 1953; MFA, Yale School of Drama, 1958; New School for Social Research, New York City, 1960. Appointments: Visiting Associate Professor of Dramatic Arts, University of North Carolina at Chapel Hill, 1961; Director of Fine Arts, North Carolina State College, Raleigh, 1962-64; Faculty, Manhattan School of Music, New York City, 1964-72; Visiting Professor, Columbia University, 1972-74, Connecticut College, 1979, University of Pennsylvania, 1979-86, Princeton University, 1982-85. Publications: Plays: The Sorrows of Frederick, 1966; Democracy and Esther, 1973; The Love Suicide at Schofield Barracks, 1973; Holy Ghosts, 1977; Old Man Joseph and His Family, 1978; El Hermano, 1981; The Captivity of Pixie Shedman, 1981; Childe Byron, 1981; F.M., 1984; The Death of King Philip, 1984; Sand Mountain, 1985; A Woman Without a Name, 1986; Pops, 1987; Heathen Valley, 1990; Three Poets, 1990; Unchanging Love, 1990; Juliet--Yancey--April Snow, 1990; Spain, 1993. Novels: Heathen Valley, 1962; Slowly, by Thy Hand Unfurled, 1965; Jesus Tales, 1980. Honours: National Endowment for the Arts Grant, 1974; Guggenheim Fellowship, 1980; Obie Awards, 1980, 1990; Mishma Prize, 1981; American Academy and Institute of Arts and Letters Award, 1984; Rockefeller Foundation Fellowship, 1986. Memberships: Actor's Equity Association; Authors Guild; Authors League of America; Directors Guild; PEN. Address: 35 Claremont Avenue, 9N, New York, NY 10027, USA.

LINSCOTT Gillian, b. 27 Sept 1944, Windsor, England. Journalist; Writer. m. Tony Geraghty, 18 June 1988. Education: Somerville College, Oxford, 1963-66; Honours Degree, English Language and Literature, Oxford University, 1966. Publications: A Healthy Body, 1984; Murder Makes Tracks, 1985; Knightfall, 1986; A Whiff of Sulphur, 1987; Unknown Hand, 1988; Murder, I Presume, 1990; Sister Beneath the Sheet, 1991; Hanging on the Wire, 1992; Stage Fright, 1993; Widow's Peak, 1994; Crown Witness, 1995; Dead Man's Music, 1996. Memberships: Society of Authors; Crime Writers Association; Mystery Writers of America. Address: c/o David Higham Associates, 5-8 Lower John Street, Golden Square, London W1R 4HA, England.

LIPMAN Elinor, b. 16 Oct 1950, Lowell, Massachusetts, USA. Writer. m. Robert M Austin, 29 July 1975, 1 son. Education: AB, Simmons College, Boston, 1972. Appointments: Lecturer, Smith College, 1997-. Publications: Into Love and Out Again (stories), 1987; Then She Found Me, 1990; The Way Men Act, 1992; Isabel's Bed, 1995; The Inn at Lake Devine (novel), forthcoming. Contributions to: Yankee; Playgirl; Ascent; Ladies Home Journal; Cosmopolitan; Self; New England; Living; Redstart; Wigwag. Honours: Distinguished Story Citations, Best American Short Stories, 1984, 1985. Membership: Author's Guild. Address: 67 Winterberry Lane, Northampton, MA 01060, USA.

LIPSEY David Lawrence, b. 21 Apr 1948, Cheltenham, Gloucestershire, England. Journalist; Writer. m. Margaret Robson, 1982, 1 daughter. Education: Magdalen College, Oxford. Appointments: Research Assistant, General and Municipal Workers' Union, 1970-72; Special Advisor to Anthony Crossland, Member of Parliament, 1972-77; Staff, Prime Minister, 1977-79; Journalist, 1979-80, Editor, 1986-88, New Society; Political Staff, 1980-82, Economics Editor, 1982-86, The Sunday Times; Co-Founder and Deputy Editor, The Sunday Correspondent, 1988-90; Associate Editor, The Times, 1990-92; Journalist, 1992-, Political Editor, 1994-, The Economist. Publications: Labour and Land, 1972; The Socialist Agenda: Crosland's Legacy (editor with Dick Leonard), 1981; Making Government Work, 1982; The Name of the Rose, 1992. Membership: Fabian Society, chairman, 1981-82. Address: 44 Drakefield Road, London SW17 8RP, England.

LIS Ketty Alejandrina de, b. 15 Oct 1946, Santa Fe, Argentina. Writer. m. Dr Abraham Lis, 13 Aug 1971. Education: Advanced Studies

of Psychology, Psychology School of National University of Rosario. Career: Part in publication poetry readings in Rosario & Buenos Aires; Member, Panel Discussions, International Conventions & Festivals in Argentina, and Literary Avant-Garde in Spanish-America: Centennial of Manuel Navarro Luna Meeting, Manzanillo, Cuba; Interviewed through Radio, TV & Literary & General Magazines; Co-Founder Mozart Fund; Member, Executive Committee, Argentine Mozarteum, Rosario Branch. Publications: Imaginaciones, book of poetry, 1987; Poesia Contemporánea: Conflicto y Contenido, article, 1990; Un Genio llamado Wolfgang Amadeus Mozart, opuscule, 1991; Adiós al Poeta Alfredo Veiravé, article, 1991; Cartas para Adriana, book of Poetry, 1992; Quiénes leen poesia hoy?, opuscule, 1994; Alejandra Pizarnik, una muñeca de huesos de pájaro, opuscule, 1994; Juan L Ortiz Localismo y Universalidad, opuscule, 1995; Poems translated into English, French & Italian. Honours: Award for story, La Mami, 1991; Ribbon for Letters to Adriana, 1993; Hector I Astengo Fund Honours the Argentine Mozarteum, Rosario Branch, 1993; Finalist, Literary Contest, Casa de las Americas, 1994; Dr Carlos J Corbella Plate, 1994; Second Award, shared with painter Marilor Statsch, Illustrated Poem Contest, 1994. Memberships: Argentine Writers Society; Argentine Mozarteum, Rosario Branch. Hobbies: Reading of Classics, both in prose and verse; Listening of Classical Music, Lyrical and Choral. Address: Italia 873, 2000 Rosario, Argentina.

LIST Anneliese, (Alice Pervin), b. 6 Jan 1922, Heroldsberg, Germany. Soubrette; Author. m. Huldreich List, 28 Feb 1947, dec. Education: Opera-House Nuremberg Ballet School, 1926-38; Ballet School, Munich, 1939; State Examination as Dancer. Appointments: Dancer, Municipal Theatre Guben; Dance Soubrette, Municipal Theatre of Landsberg/Warthe, Torn and Elbing; Clerk, US European Exchange System; Secretary, Refugee and Migration Section, Nuremberg Field Office, American Consulate General US Embassy's Escapee Programme; Clerk in Charge at Foreign Office, City of Nuremberg. Publications: The Tree, 1973; The Work was in Vain, 1974; Miracles Happen Always Again, 1974; Over and Over Again I Saw the Cross, 1975; What I'll Never Be Able to Forget in All My Life, 1975; My Long Way From the War Until Today, 1975; Not Before Today I Understood Why Mother Left Me, 1975; How I Earned My First Money, 1977; The First Dance, 1977; The Little Witch, 1977; The Luck Behind the Mountains, 1978; A Fairy Tale, 1986; Ten Promises, 1987; First Love, 1987; Realization, 1988; Prayer in the Sunshine and Our Lumpi, 1989; Dedicated to My Little Cat, 1990; Jubilate, 1991; The Heroine, 1992; The Rainbow and the Window, 1992; Thank You, 1993; The Fireplace, 1993; The Revenge is Mine Says Our Lord, 1994; Just a Poor Devil, 1994; Unbelievable Stories, 1995. Contributions to: Stories, poems and articles in various publications including: Main-Echo; Frau Aktuell; 7 Tage; Welt am Sonnabend; True Stories; Zenit. Honours: 2nd Prize, Contest for Best Story in True Stories magazine, 1975; Cultural Doctorate in Literature, Certificate of Merit, World Literary Academy; Woman of the Year, IBC, 1990; International Order of Merit, IBC, 1991; Most Admired Woman of the Decade, 1992; 20th Century Award for Achievement, IBC, 1993. Memberships: World Literary Academy; IBA; Schoenbuch-Verlag, present editor. Address: Ritter-von-Schuh-Platz 15, Nuremberg 90459, Germany.

LISTER Raymond George, b. 28 Mar 1919, Cambridge, England. Writer. Appointments: Managing Director and Editor, Golden Head Press, Cambridge, 1952-72; Senior Research Fellow, 1975-85, Fellow 1985-86, Fellow Emeritus, 1986-, Wolfson College, Cambridge. Publications: The British Miniature, 1951; Silhouettes, 1953; Thomas Gosse, 1953; The Muscovite Peacock: A Study of the Art of Leon Bakst, 1954; Decorated Porcelains of Simon Lissim, 1955; Decorative Wrought Ironwork in Great Britain, 1957; The Loyal Blacksmith, 1957; Decorative Cast Ironwork in Great Britain, 1960; The Craftsman Engineer, 1960; Edward Calvert, 1962; Great Craftsmen, 1962; The Miniature Defined, 1963; Beulah to Byzantium, 1965; How to Identify Old Maps and Globes, 1965; Victorian Narrative Paintings, 1966; The Craftsman in Metal, 1966; Great Works of Craftmanship, 1967; William Blake, 1968; Samuel Palmer and His Etchings, 1969; Hammer and Hand: An Essay on the Ironwork of Cambridge, 1969; British Romantic Art, 1973; Samuel Palmer, 1974; The Letters of Samuel Palmer (editor), 2 volumes, 1974; Infernal Methods: A Study of William Blake's Art Techniques, 1975; Apollo's Bird, 1975; For Love of Leda, 1977; Great Images of British Printmaking, 1978; Samuel Palmer: A Vision Recaptured, 1978; Samuel Palmer in Palmer Country, 1980; George Richmond, 1981; Bergomask, 1982; There Was a Star Danced, 1983; Prints and Printmaking, 1984; Samuel Palmer and the Ancients, 1984; The Paintings of Samuel Palmer, 1985; The Paintings of William Blake, 1986; Catalogue Raisonné of the Works of Samuel Palmer,

1988; British Romantic Painting, 1989; A M St Léon's Stenochoreography (translation), 1992; With My Own Wings (memoirs), 1994. Address: 9 Sylvester Road, Cambridge CB3 9AF, England.

LISTER Richard Percival, b. 23 Nov 1914, Nottingham, England. Author; Painter. m. Ione Mary Wynniatt-Husey, 24 June 1985. Education: BSc, Manchester University. Publications: Novels: The Way Backwards, 1950; The Oyster and the Torpedo, 1951; Rebecca Redfern, 1953; The Rhyme and the Reason, 1963; The Questing Beast, 1965; One Short Summer, 1974. Poems: The Idle Demon, 1958; The Albatross, 1986. Travel: A Journey in Lapland, 1965; Turkey Observed, 1967. Biography: The Secret History of Genghis Khan, 1969; Marco Polo's Travels, 1976; The Travels of Herodotus, 1979; Short Stories: Nine Legends, 1991; Two Northern Stories, 1996. Contributions to: Punch; New Yorker; Atlantic Monthly. Honour: Royal Society of Literature, fellow, 1970. Membership: International PEN. Address: Flat H, 81 Ledbury Road, London W11 2AG, England.

LITOWINSKY Olga Jean, b. 9 Feb 1936, Newark, New Jersey, USA. Writer; Editor. Education: BS Hons History, Columbia University, 1965. Publications: The High Voyage, 1977; The New York Kids Book, 1978; Writing and Publishing Books for Children in the 1990s, 1992. Contributions to: Atlas; Publishers Weekly; The Writer; Writers' Digest; SCBW Bulletin. Honour: Christopher Award, 1979. Membership: Society of Children's Book Writers and Illustrators. Address: c/o Simon and Schuster, 15 Columbus Circle, New York, NY 10023, USA.

LITTELL Robert, b. 1935, USA. Writer. Publications: If Israel Lost the War (with Richard Z Cheznoff and Edward Klein), 1969; The Czech Black Book, 1969; The Defection of A J Lewinter, 1973; Sweet Reason, 1974; The October Circle, 1976; Mother Russia, 1978; The Debriefing, 1979; The Amateur, 1981; The Sisters, 1985; The Revolutionist; The Visiting Professor, 1994. Address: c/o Simon and Schuster, 1230 Sixth Avenue, New York, NY 10020, USA.

LITTLE Charles Eugene, b. 1 Mar 1931, Los Angeles, California, USA. Writer. m. Ila Dawson. Education: BA with distinction in Creative Writing, Wesleyan University, 1955. Appointments: Editorial Director, Open Space Action Magazine, 1968-69; Editor-in-Chief, American Land Forum, 1980-86; Books Editor, Wilderness Magazine, 1987-97; Consulting Editor, Johns Hopkins University Press, 1989-. Publications: Challenge of the Land, 1969; Space for Survival (with J G Mitchell), 1971; A Town is Saved ... (with photos by M Mort), 1973; The American Cropland Crisis (with W Fletcher), 1980; Green Fields Forever, 1987; Louis Bromfield at Malabar (editor), 1988; Greenways for America, 1990; Hope for the Land, 1992; Discover America: The Smithsonian Book of the National Parks, 1995; The Dying of the Trees, 1995. Contributions to: Magazines and journals. Address: 33 Calle del Norte, Placitas, NM 87043, USA.

LITTLE Geraldine Clinton, b. 20 Sept 1925, Portstewart, Ireland. Poet; Writer. m. Robert Knox Little, 26 Sept 1953, 3 sons. Education: BA, Goddard College, 1971; MA, Trenton State College, 1976. Appointment: Adjunct Professor of English. Publications: Hakugai: Poem from a Concentration Camp, 1983; Seasons in Space, 1983; A Well-Tuned Harp, 1988; Beyond the Boxwood Comb, 1988; Heloise and Abelard: A Verse Play, 1989; Star-Mapped, 1989. Contributions to: Journals. Honours: Associated Writing Program Anniversary Award, 1986; Pablo Neruda Award, 1989; Grants. Memberships: Haiku Society of America; PEN; Poetry Society of America. Address: 519 Jacksonville Road, Mt Holly, NJ 08060, USA.

LITTLE (Flora) Jean, b. 2 Jan 1932, Taiwan. Children's Writer. Education: BA, Victoria College, University of Toronto, Canada, 1955. Publications: Mine for Keeps, 1962; Home From Far, 1965; Spring Begins in March, 1966; When the Pie was Opened, 1968; Take Wing, 1968; One to Grow On, 1969; Look Through My Window, 1970; Kate, 1971; From Anna, 1972; Stand In the Wind, 1975; Listen for the Singing, 1977; Mama's Going to Buy You a Mockingbird, 1984; Lost and Found, 1985; Different Dragons, 1986; Hey, World, Here I Am, 1986; Little By Little, 1987; Stars Came Out Within, 1990; Jess was the Brave One, 1991; Revenge of the Small Small, 1992. Honours: Little, Brown Canadian Children's Book Award, 1961; Vicky Metcalf Award, 1974; Canada Council Children's Book Award, 1977; Canadian Library Association Children's Book of the Year Award, 1984; Ruth Schwartz Award, 1984; Boston Globe Horn Book Honor Book, 1988; Shortlisted

for the 1988 Governor General's Children's Literature Award, 1989. Memberships: Writers' Union of Canada; CANSCAIP (Canadian Society for Children's Authors, Illustrators & Performers); Canadian Authors' Association; PEN; IBBY. Address: 198 Glasgow North, Guelph, Ontario N1H 4X2, Canada.

LITVINOFF Emanuel, b. 30 June 1915, London, England. Writer; Dramatist; Director, Contemporary Jewish Library, London, 1958-88; Founder, Jews in Eastern Europe, journal, London. Publications: Conscripts: A Symphonic Declaration, 1941; The Untried Soldier, 1942; A Crown for Cain, 1948; The Lost Europeans, 1959; The Man Next Door, 1968; Journey Through a Small Planet, 1972; Notes for a Survivor, 1973; A Death Out of Season, 1974; Soviet Anti-Semitism: The Paris Trial (editor), 1974; Blood on the Snow, 1975; The Face of Terror, 1978; The Penguin Book of Jewish Short Stories (editor), 1979; Falls the Shadow, 1983. Address: c/o David Higham Associates, 5-8 Lower John Street, London W1R 4HA, England.

LIU Shaotang, b. 29 Feb 1936, Beijing, China. Writer; Poet. m. Zeng Caimei, 1 May 1955, 1 son, 2 daughters. Education: Beijing University, 1954-55. Publications: Many novels, novelettes, short stories, prose collections and poetry volumes. Contributions to: Numerous periodicals. Honours: Several awards. Memberships: Chinese Writers Association; PEN, China Centre. Address: c/o Beijing Writers Association, Beijing, China.

LIVAS Harriet (Haris) Parker, b. 1 Apr 1936, USA. Journalist; Author; Professor. m. John Livas, 18 June 1962, dec 1976, 3 sons, 3 daughters. Education: BS, Syracuse University, 1958; MLitt, University of Pittsburgh, 1960; PhD, Pacific Western University, 1990. Appointments: English Department, University of Maryland Overseas Faculty, 1966-78; Foreign Correspondent, 1978-82; Director, Feature Service, Athens News Agency, Greece, 1982-88; Director, Hellenic Features International, Ministry of the National Economy, Greece, 1988-90; Humberside Council, UK, 1991; Beverley College, 1991-94; University of Hull, 1993-95; University of Lincolnshire and Humberside, 1995-96. Publication: Contemporary Greek Artists, 1992. Contributions to: Periodicals; Book Reviewer, International PEN. Address: 19 Thurlow Avenue, Beverley HU17 7QJ, England.

LIVELY Penelope Margaret, b. 17 Mar 1933, Cairo, Egypt. Writer. m. 27 June 1957, 1 son, 1 daughter. Education: Honours Degree, Modern History, Oxford University, England. Publications: Fiction: The Road to Lichfield, 1977; Nothing Missing But the Samovar, and Other Stories, 1978; Treasures of Time, 1979; Judgement Day, 1980; Next to Nature, Art, 1982; Perfect Happiness, 1983; Corruption and Other Stories, 1984; According to Mark, 1984; Moon Tiger, 1986; Pack of Cards: Stories 1978-86, 1987; Passing On, 1989; City of the Mind, 1991; Cleopatra's Sister, 1993. Non-fiction: The Presence of the Past: An Introduction to Landscape History, 1976. Children's Books: Astercote, 1970; The Whispering Knights, 1971; The Driftway, 1972; Going Back, 1973; The Ghost of Thomas Kempe, 1974; Boy Without a Name, 1975; Fanny's Sister, 1976; The Stained Glass Window, 1976; A Stitch in Time, 1976; Fanny and the Monsters, 1978; The Voyage of QV66, 1978; Fanny and the Battle of Potter's Piece, 1980; The Revenge of Samuel Stokes, 1981; Uninvited Ghosts and Other Stories, 1984; Dragon Trouble, Debbie and the Little Devil, 1984; A House Inside Out, 1987; Passing On, 1989; City of the Mind, 1991. Contributions to: Numerous journals and magazines. Honours: Officer of the Order of the British Empire, 1989; Several literary awards. Address: c/o Murray Pollinger, 222 Old Brompton Road, London SW5 0B2, England.

LIVERSAGE Toni, b. 31 Jan 1935, Hellerup, Denmark. Writer. m. 19 May 1962, 1 son, 1 daughter. Education: MA in Slavonic Languages, University of Copenhagen, 1965. Publications: 10 books. Contributions to: Various newspapers and magazines. Honour: Thit Jensen Award for Women's Literature, 1989. Membership: Danish Writers Union. Address: Morlenesvej 26, 2840 Holte, Denmark.

LIVERSIDGE (Henry) Douglas, b. 12 Mar 1913, Swinton, Yorkshire, England. Journalist; Author. m. Cosmina Pistola, 25 Sept 1954, 1 daughter. Publications: White Horizon, 1951; The Last Continent, 1958; The Third Front, 1960; The Whale Killers, 1963; Saint Francis of Assisi, 1968; Peter the Great, 1968; Lenin, 1969; Joseph Stalin, 1969; Saint Ignatius of Loyola, 1970; The White World, 1972; Queen Elizabeth II, 1974; Prince Charles, 1975; Prince Phillip, 1976; Queen Elizabeth the Queen Mother, 1977; The Mountbattens, 1978.

Contributions to: Numerous journals and newspapers. Address: 56 Love Lane, Pinner, Middlesex HA5 3EX, England.

LIVINGS Henry, b. 20 Sept 1929, Prestwich, Lancashire, England. Writer; Playwright. Education: Liverpool University, 1945-47. Publications: Stop it Whoever You Are, 1961; Nil Caborundum, 1963; Kelly's Eye and Other Plays, 1965; Eh?, 1965; The Little Mrs Foster Show, 1967; Good Grief!, 1968; Honour and Offer, 1969; The Ffinest Ffamily in the Land, 1970; Pongo Plays 1-6, 1971; The Jockey Drives Late Nights, 1972; Six More Pongo Plays, 1974; Jonah, 1975; That the Medals and the Baton Be Put in View: The Story of a Village Band 1875-1975, 1975; Cinderella, 1976; Pennine Tales, 1983; Flying Eggs and Things: More Pennine Tales, 1986; The Rough Side of the Boards, 1994. Address: 49 Grains Road, Delph, Oldham OL3 5DS, England.

LIVINGSTONE Douglas (James), b. 5 May 1932, Kuala Lumpur, Malaya. (South African citizen). Poet. Education: Kearney College, Natal; University of Natal. Publications: The Skull in the Mud, 1960; Sjambok and Other Poems from Africa, 1964; Poems, 1968; Eyes Closed Against the Sun, 1970; The Sea My Winding Sheet and Other Poems, 1971; A Rosary of Bone, 1975-83; The Anvil's Undertone, 1978; Selected Poems, 1984; A Littoral Zone, 1991. Plays: A Rhino for the Boardroom, 1974; The Semblance of the Real, 1976. Honours: D Litt, University of Natal, 1982; Rhodes University, 1990. Address: c/o Council of Scientific and Industrial Research, PO Box 17001, Congella, 4013 Natal, South Africa.

LLEWELLEN John. See: **JONES-EVANS Eric.**

LLEWELLYN Sam, b. 2 Aug 1948, Isles of Scilly. Author. m. Karen Wallace, 15 Feb 1975, 2 sons. Education: St Catherine's College, Oxford; BA (Hons), Oxford University. Appointments: Editor, Picador, 1973-76; Senior Editor, McClelland and Stewart, 1976-79; President, Publisher, Arch Books, 1982-; Captain, SY Lucille, 1993-. Publications: Hell Bay, 1980; The Worst Journey in the Midlands, 1983; Dead Reckoning, 1987; Blood Orange, 1988; Death Roll, 1989; Pig in the Middle, 1989; Deadeye, 1990; Blood Knot, 1991; Riptide, 1992; Clawhammer, 1993; Maelstrom, 1994; The Rope School, 1994; The Magic Boathouse, 1994; The Iron Hotel, 1996; Storm Force from Navarone, 1996. Contributions to: Periodicals. Memberships: Society of Authors; CPRE. Address: c/o John Johnson, Clerkenwell House, Clerkenwell Green, London EC1, England.

LLOYD Geoffrey (Ernest Richard), b. 25 Jan 1933, London, England. Professor of Ancient Philosophy and Science; Writer. m. Janet Elizabeth Lloyd, 1956, 3 sons. Education: BA, 1954, MA, 1958, PhD, 1958, King's College, Cambridge. Appointments: Fellow, 1957, Senior Tutor, 1969-73, King's College, Cambridge; Assistant Lecturer in Classics, 1965-67, Lecturer in Classics, 1967-74, Reader in Ancient Philosophy and Science, 1974-83, Professor of Ancient Philosophy and Science, 1983-, Cambridge University; Bonsall Professor, Stanford University, 1981; Sather Professor, University of California at Berkeley, 1984; Visiting Professor, Beijing University and Academy of Sciences, 1987; Master, Darwin College, 1989-; Professor at Large, Cornell University, 1990. Publications: Polarity and Analogy, 1966; Early Greek Science: Thales to Aristotle, 1970; Greek Science After Aristotle, 1973; Magic, Reason and Experience, 1979; Science, Folklore and Ideology, 1983; Science and Morality in Greco-Roman Antiquity, 1985; The Revolution of Wisdom, 1987; Demystifying Mentalities, 1990; Methods and Problems in Greek Science, 1991; Adversaries and Authorities, 1996; Aristotelian Explorations, 1996. Editor: Hippocratic Writings, 1978; Aristotle on Mind and Senses (with G E L Owen), 1978; Le Savoir Grec (with Jacques Brunschwig), 1996. Contributions to: Books and journals. Honours: Sarton Medal, 1987; Honorary Fellow, King's College, Cambridge, 1990. Memberships: British Academy, fellow; East Asian History of Science Trust, chairman, 1992-. Address: 2 Prospect Row, Cambridge CB1 1DU, England.

LLOYD Kathleen Annie, (Kathleen Conlon), b. 4 Jan 1943, Southport, England. Writer. m. Frank Lloyd, 3 Aug 1962, div, 1 son. Education: BA (Hons), King's College, Durham University. Publications: Apollo's Summer Look, 1968; Tomorrow's Fortune, 1971; My Father's House, 1972; A Twisted Skein, 1975; A Move in the Game, 1979; A Forgotten Season, 1980; Consequences, 1981; The Best of Friends, 1984; Face Values, 1985; Distant Relations, 1989; Unfinished Business, 1990. Contributions to: Atlantic Review; Cosmopolitan; Woman's Journal; Woman; Woman's Own. Membership: Society of Authors. Address: 26A Brighton Road,

Birkdale, Southport PR8 4DD, England.

LLOYD Levannah. See: **PETERS Maureen.**

LLOYD Trevor Owen, b. 30 July 1934, London, England. Professor of History; Writer. Education: BA, Merton College, Oxford, 1956; MA, DPhil, Nuffield College, Oxford, 1959. Appointments: Lecturer, 1959-73, Professor, 1973-, Department of History, University of Toronto. Publications: Canada in World Affairs 1957-59, 1968; The General Election of 1880, 1968; Suffragettes International, 1971; The Growth of Parliamentary Democracy in Britain, 1973; Empire, Welfare State, Europe: English History 1906-1992, 1993; The British Empire 1558-1995, 1996. Contributions to: Various journals. Honour: Guggenheim Fellowship, 1978-79. Memberships: William Morris Society; Victorian Studies Association of Ontario. Address: Department of History, University of Toronto, Toronto M5S 1A1, Canada.

LLOYD-JONES Sir (Peter) Hugh (Jefford), b. 21 Sept 1922, St Peter Port, Jersey, Channel Islands. Classical Scholar. m. (1) Frances Hedley, 1953, div 1981, 2 sons, 1 daughter, (2) Mary R Lefkowitz, 1982. Education: Westminister School; Christ Church, Oxford; MA (Oxon), 1947. Publications: The Justice of Zeus, 1971, 2nd edition, 1983; Blood for the Ghosts, 1982; Supplementum Hellenisticum (with P J Parsons), 1983; Sophoclis Fabulae (with N G Wilson), 1990; Sophoclea (with N G Wilson), 1990; Academic Papers, 2 volumes, 1990; Greek in a Cold Climate, 1991; Sophocles (editor and translator), 3 volumes, 1994-96; Contributions to: Numerous. Honours: Honorary DHL, University of Chicago, 1970; Honorary PhD, University of Tel Aviv, 1984; Knight Bachelor, 1989. Memberships: British Academy, fellow; Academy of Athens, corresponding member; American Academy of Arts and Sciences; American Philosophical Society; Rheinisch-Westfälische Akademie; Bayerische Akademie der Wissenschaften; Accademia di Lettere, Archeologia e Belle Arti, Naples. Address: 15 West Riding, Wellesley, MA 02181, USA.

LOADES David Michael, b. 19 Jan 1934, Cambridge, England. Academic. m. Judith Anne Atkins, 18 Apr 1987. Education: Perse School for Boys, Cambridge, England, 1945-53; Emmanuel College, Cambridge, 1955-61, BA, 1958, MA, PhD, 1961, LittD, 1981. Appointments: Lecturer in Political Science, University of St Andrews, 1961-63; Lecturer in History, University of Durham, 1963-70; Senior Lecturer, 1970-77, Reader, 1977-80, Professor of History, 1980-96, University College of North Wales, Bangor. Publications: Two Tudor Conspiracies, 1965; The Oxford Martyrs, 1970; The Reign of Mary Tudor, 1979; The Tudor Court, 1986; Mary Tudor: A Life, 1989; The Tudor Navy, 1992; John Dudley: Duke of Northumberland, 1996. Editor: The Papers of George Wyatt, 1968; The End of Strife, 1984; Faith and Identity, 1990; John Foxe and the English Reformation, 1997. Contributions to: Journals. Memberships: Royal Historical Society, fellow; Society of Antiquaries of London, fellow. Address: Four Seasons House, 102B, Woodstock Road, Witney, Oxfordshire, OX8 6DH, England.

LOCHHEAD Douglas Grant, b. 25 Mar 1922, Guelph, Ontario, Canada. Writer. Education: BA, 1943, BLS, 1951, McGill University; MA, University of Toronto, 1947. Appointments: Writer-in-Residence, Mount Allison University, 1987-90; President, Goose Lane Editions, 1989-. Publications: The Heart is Fire, 1959; It is All Around, 1960; Poet Talking, 1964; A & B & C &, poems, 1969; Millwood Road Poems, 1970; Prayers in a Field, 1974; The Full Furnace, 1976; High Marsh Road, 1980; Tiger in the Skull, selected poems, 1986; Dykelands, 1989; Upper Cape Poems, 1989; Black Festival, poems, 1992; Homage to Henry Alline and Other Poems, 1992. Contributions to: Canadian literary journals. Honours: Golden Dog Award, 1974; Fellow, Royal Society of Canada, 1976; DLitt, St Mary's University, 1987; LLD, Dalhousie University, 1987. Memberships: League of Canadian Poets; Bibliographical Society of Canada. Address: PO Box 1108, Sackville, New Brunswick E0A 3CO, Canada.

LOCHEAD Liz, b. 26 Dec 1947, Motherwell, Scotland. Poet; Writer of Plays and Screenplays; Teacher. Education: Dilpoma, Glasgow School of Art, 1970. Appointments: Art teacher in Glasgow and Bristol schools; Lecturer, University of Glasgow. Publications: Poetry: Memo for Spring, 1972; The Grimm Sisters, 1981; Dreaming Frankenstein and Collected Poems, 1984; True Confessions and New Clichés, 1985. Screenplay: Now and Then, 1972. Plays: Blood and Ice, 1982; Silver Service, 1984; Dracula, and Mary Queen of Scots Got Her Head Chopped Off, 1989. Honours: BBC Scotland Prize, 1971;

Scottish Arts Council Award, 1972. Address: 11 Kersland Street, Glasgow G12 8BW, Scotland.

LOCKE Elsie Violet, b. 17 Aug 1912, Hamilton, New Zealand. Writer. m. John Gibson Locke, 7 Nov 1941, 2 sons, 2 daughters. Education: BA, Auckland University, 1933. Publications: The Runaway Settlers, 1965; The End of the Harbour, 1968; The Boy with the Snowgrass Hair, 1976; Student at the Gates, 1981; The Kauri and the Willow, 1984; Journey under Warning, 1984; A Canoe in the Mist, 1984; Two Peoples One Land, 1988; Peace People, 1992. Contributions to: Journals. Honours: Katherine Mansfield Award for Non-Fiction, 1959; Honorary DLitt, University of Canterbury, Christchurch, New Zealand, 1987; Children's Literature Association of New Zealand award for distinguished services to children's literature, 1992; Joe's Ruby, 1995. Memberships: Childrens Literature Association; Children's Book Foundation; New Zealand Society of Authors (incorporating PEN). Address: 392 Oxford Tce, Christchurch 1, New Zealand.

LOCKE Hubert G(aylord), b. 30 Apr 1934, Detroit, Michigan, USA. Professor of Public Service; Writer. 2 daughters. Education: BA, Latin and Greek, Wayne State University, 1955; BD, New Testament Studies, University of Chicago, 1959; MA, Comparative Literature, University of Michigan, 1961. Appointments: Assistant Director, 1957-62, Director, 1967-70, Office of Religious Affairs, Adjunct Assistant Professor of Urban Education, 1970-72, Wayne State University; Associate Professor of Urban Studies and Dean, College of Public Affairs and Community Service, University of Nebraska, 1972-75; Professor, 1976-, Associate Dean, College of Arts and Sciences, 1976-77, Vice Provost for Academic Affairs, 1977-82, Dean, Graduate School of Public Affairs, 1982-87, John and Marguerite Corbally Professor of Public Service, 1996-, University of Washington, Seattle. Publications: The Detroit Riot of 1967, 1969; The Care and Feeding of White Liberals, 1970; The German Church Struggle and the Holocaust (editor with Franklin H Littell), 1974; The Church Confronts the Nazis (editor), 1984; Exile in the Fatherland: The Prison Letters of Martin Niemöller (editor), 1986; The Barmen Confession: Papers from the Seattle Assembly (editor), 1986; The Black Antisemitism Controversy: Views of Black Protestants (editor), 1992. Contributions to: Books and professional journals. Honours: Michigan Bar Association Liberty Bell Award, 1967; Honorary Doctor of Divinity, Payne Theological Seminary, 1968, Chicago Theological Seminary, 1971; Honorary Doctor of Humane Letters, University of Akron, 1971, University of Nebraska, 1992; Distinguished Alumni Award, Wayne State University, 1979. Memberships: Commission on State Trial Courts, State of Washington; Institute of European/Asian Studies, board of governors; Interfaith Housing Inc, board of directors; National Academy of Public Administration, board of trustees. Address: c/o Graduate School of Public Affairs, University of Washington, Box 353055, Seattle, WA 98195, USA.

LOCKE Ralph P(aul), b. 9 Mar 1949, Boston, Massachusetts, USA. Musicologist; Teacher; Writer. m. Lona M Farhi, 26 May 1979, 2 daughters. Education: BA, cum laude, in Music, Harvard University, 1970; MA, 1974, PhD, 1980, in History and Theory of Music, University of Chicago. Appointments: Faculty, Eastman School of Music, Rochester, New York, 1975-; Senior Editor, Eastman Studies in Music; Co-Editor, Journal of Musicological Research. Publication: Music, Musicians, and the Saint-Simonians, 1986. Contributions to: Reference books and professional journals. Honours: Best Article Citation, Music Library Association, 1980; Galler Dissertation Prize, 1981; ASCAP-Deems Taylor Awards, 1992, 1996. Memberships: American Musicological Society; International Musicological Society; Institute for Gounod Studies. Address: c/o Department of Musicology, Eastman School of Music, 26 Gibbs Street, Rochester, NY 14604-2599, USA.

LOCKE Robert Howard, (Clayton Bess), b. 30 Dec 1944, Vallejo, California, USA. Librarian; Playwright; Author. Education: BA, Speech Arts, California State University, Chico, 1965; MA, Drama, San Francisco State University, 1967; MS, Library Science, Simmons College, Boston, 1973. Publications: As Clayton Bess: Story for a Black Night, 1982; The Truth About the Moon, 1984; Big Man and the Burn-Out, 1985; Tracks, 1986; The Mayday Rampage, 1993. Plays: The Dolly; Play; Rose Jewel and Harmony; On Daddy's Birthday; Murder and Edna Redrum; Premiere. Honours: Best First Novel, Commonwealth Club of California, 1982; Best Book for Young Adults, American Library Association, 1987. Address: c/o Lookout Press, PO Box 19131, Sacramento, CA 95819, USA.

LOCKERBIE D(onald) Bruce, b. 25 Aug 1935, Capreol, Ontario, Canada. Scholar; Writer. Education: AB, 1956, MA, 1963, New York University. Appointments: Scholar-in-Residence, Stony Brook School, New York, 1957-91; Visiting Consultant at American Schools in Asia and Africa, 1974; Visiting Lecturer/Consultant to American universities. Publications: Billy Sunday, 1965; Patriarchs and Prophets, 1969; Hawthorne, 1970; Melville, 1970; Twain, 1970; Major American Authors, 1970; Success in Writing (with L Westdahl), 1970; Purposeful Writing, 1972; The Way They Should Go, 1972; The Liberating Word, 1974; The Cosmic Center: The Apostles' Creed, 1977; A Man under Orders: Lt Gen William K Harrison, 1979; Who Educates Your Child?, 1980; The Timeless Moment, 1980; Asking Questions, 1980; Fatherlove, 1981; In Peril on the Sea, 1984; The Christian, the Arts and Truth, 1985; Thinking and Acting Like a Christian, 1989; Take Heart (with L Lockerbie), 1990; College: Getting In and Staying In (with D Fonseca), 1990. Address: PO Box 26, Stony Brook, NY 11790, USA.

LOCKLIN Gerald (Ivan), b. 17 Feb 1941, Rochester, New York, USA. Poet; Writer; Professor. m. (1) Mary Alice Keefe, 3 children, (2) Maureen McNicholas, 2 children, (3) Barbara Curry, 2 children. Education: BA, St John Fisher College, 1961; MA, 1963, PhD 1964, University of Arizona. Appointments: Instructor, California State College at Los Angeles, 1964-65; Associate Professor, Professor of English, California State University at Long Beach, 1965-. Publications: Poetry: The Toad Poems, 1970; Poop, and Other Poems, 1973; Tarzan and Shane Meet the Toad (with Ronald Koertge and Charles Stetler), 1975; The Criminal Mentality, 1976; Toad's Sabbatical, 1978; The Last of Toad, 1980; By Land, Sea, and Air, 1982; The Ensenada Poems (with Ray Zepada), 1984; Gringo and Other Poems, 1987; The Death of Jean-Paul Satre and Other Poems, 1988; Lost and Found, 1989; The Firebird Poems, 1992; The Old Mongoose and Other Poems, 1993; Toad Turns Fifty: Selected Poems by Gerald Locklin, 1993. Fiction: Locked In, short stories, 1973; The Chase, novel, 1976; The Four-Day Work Week and Other Stories, 1977; The Cure, novel, 1979; A Weekend in Canada, short stories, 1979; The Case of the Missing Blue Volkswagen, novella, 1984; The Gold Rush and Other Stories, 1989. Contributions to: Many periodicals. Membership: Phi Beta Kappa. Address: Department of English, California State University at Long Beach, CA 90840, USA.

LOCKRIDGE Ernest Hugh, b. 28 Nov 1938, Bloomington, Indiana, USA. Professor; Novelist. m. Laurel Richardson, 12 Dec 1981, 2 sons, 3 daughters. Education: BA, Indiana University, 1960; MA, 1961, PhD, 1964, Yale University. Appointments: Professor, Yale University, 1963-71, Ohio State University, 1971-. Publications: Novels: Hartspring Blows His Mind, 1968; Prince Elmo's Fire, 1974; Flying Elbows, 1975. Non-Fiction: 20th Century Studies of the Great Gatsby, 1968. Contributions to: Professional journals. Honours: Book-of-the-Month Club Selection, 1974; Distinguished Teaching Award, Ohio State University, 1985. Membership: Phi Beta Kappa. Address: 143 West South Street, Washington, OH 43085, USA.

LODGE David John, b. 28 Jan 1935. Honorary Professor of Modern English Literature. m. Mary Frances Jacob, 1959, 2 sons, 1 daughter. Education: BA Honours, MA (London); PhD, Birmingham; National Service, RAC, 1955-57. Appointments: British Council, London, 1959-60; Assistant Lecturer, 1960-62, Lecturer, 1963-71, Senior Lecturer, 1971-73, Reader, English, 1973-76, University of Birmingham; Harkness Commonwealth Fellow, 1964-65; Visiting Associate Professor, University of California, Berkeley, 1969; Henfield Writing Fellow, University of East Anglia, 1977. Publications: Novels: The Picturegoers, 1960; Ginger, You're Barmy, 1962; The British Museum is Falling Down, 1965; Out of the Shelter, 1970, revised edition, 1985; Changing Places, 1975; How Far Can You Go?, 1980; Small World, 1984; Nice Work, 1988; Paradise News, 1991; Therapy, 1995. Criticism: Language of Fiction, 1966; The Novelist at the Crossroads, 1971; The Modes of Modern Writing, 1977; Working with Structuralism, 1981; Write On, 1986; After Bakhtin (essays), 1990; The Art of Fiction, 1992; The Practice of Writing, 1996. Honours: Yorkshire Post Fiction Prize, 1975; Hawthornden Prize, 1976; Whitbread Book of the Year Award, 1980; Sunday Express Book of the Year Award, 1988. Address: Department of English, University of Birmingham, Birmingham B15 2TT, England.

LOEWE Michael Arthur Nathan, b. 2 Nov 1922, Oxford, England. University Lecturer (retired). Education: Magdalen College, Oxford, 1941; BA Hons (London), 1951, PhD, 1962, University of London; MA (Cambridge), 1963. Publications: Records of Han Administration, 1967; Everyday Life in Early Imperial China, 1968, 2nd edition, 1988; Crisis and Conflict in Han China, 1974; Ways to Paradise: The Chinese Quest for Immortality, 1979; Chinese Ideas of Life and Death, 1982; The Cambridge History of China, vol 1 1986; The Pride that was China, 1990; Early Chinese Texts, a Bibliograpical Guide, 1993; Divination Mythology and Monarchy in Han China, 1994. Contributions to: Toung Pao; Bulletin of Museum of Far Eastern Antiquities; Asia Major; Bulletin of School of Oriental and African Studies. Membership: Society of Antiquaries, fellow, 1972; Clare Hall, fellow, 1963-90. Address: Willow House, Grantchester, Cambridge CB3 9NF, England.

LOGAN Ford. See: **NEWTON D(wight) B(ennett).**

LOGAN Jake. See: **RIFKIN Shepard.**

LOGAN Mark. See: **NICOLE Christopher Robin.**

LOGUE Christopher (John), b. 23 Nov 1926, Portsmouth, Hampshire, England. Poet; Writer; Dramatist. m. Rosemary Hill, 1985. Education: Prior College, Bath. Publications: Poetry: Wand and Quadrant, 1953; Devil, Maggot and Son, 1954; The Weakdream Sonnets, 1955; The Man Who Told His Love: 20 Poems Based on P Neruda's "Los Cantos d'amores", 1958, 2nd edition, 1959; Songs, 1960; Songs from "The Lily-White Boys", 1960; The Establishment Songs, 1966; The Girls, 1969; New Numbers, 1970; Abecedary, 1977; Ode to the Dodo, 1981; War Music: An Account of Books 16 to 19 of Homer's Iliad, 1981; Fluff, 1984; Kings: An Account of Books 1 and 2 of Homer's Iliad, 1991, revised edition, 1992; The Husbands: An Account of Books 3 and 4 of Homer's Iliad, 1994; Selected Poems of Christopher Reid, 1996. Plays: The Lily-White Boys (with Harry Cookson), 1959; The Trial of Cob and Leach, 1959; Antigone, 1961; War Music, 1978; Kings, 1993. Screenplay: Savage Messiah, 1972. Other: Lust, by Count Plamiro Vicarion, 1955; The Arrival of the Poet in the City: A Treatment for a Film, 1964; True Stories, 1966; The Bumper Book of True Stories, 1980. Editor: Count Palmiro Vicarion's Book of Limericks, 1959; The Children's Book of Comic Verse, 1979; London in Verse, 1982; Sweet & Sour: An Anthology of Comic Verse, 1983; The Children's Book of Children's Rhymes, 1986. Address: 41 Camberwell Grove, London SE5 8JA, England.

LOMAX Alan, b. 31 Jan 1915, Austin, Texas, USA. Ethnomusicologist; Writer. m. E Harold, 1937, 1 daughter. Education: Harvard University, 1932-33; BA, University of Texas at Austin, 1936; Graduate Studies in Anthropology, Columbia University, 1939. Appointments: Folk Song Collector, US and Europe; Director, Bureau of Applied Social Research, 1963, Cantometrics Project, Columbia University, 1963. Publications: American Folk Song and Folk Lore: A Regional Bibliography (with S Cowell), 1942; Mr Jelly Roll, 1950, 2nd edition, 1973; Harriett and Her Harmonium, 1955; The Rainbow Sign, 1959; Cantometrics: A Handbook and Training Method, 1976; Index of World Song, 1977; The Land Where the Blues Began, 1993. Editor: American Ballads and Folksongs (with John Lomax), 1934; Negro Folk Songs as Sung by Leadbelly (with John Lomax), 1936; Our Singing Country (with John Lomax), 1941; Folk Song: USA (with John Lomax), 1947, 4th edition, 1954; Leadbelly: A Collection of World Famous Songs (with John Lomax), 1959, 2nd edition, 1965; The Folk Songs of North America in the English Language, 1960; The Penguin Book of American Folk Songs, 1966; Hard-Hitting Songs for Hard-Hit People, 1967; Folk song Style and Culture, 1968. Honours: National Medal of Arts, 1986; National Book Critics Circle Award, 1993. Memberships: American Association for the Advancement of Science; American Folklore Society, fellow; American Anthropological Association. Address: c/o Association for Cultural Equity, 450 West 41st Street, 6th Floor, New York, NY 10036, USA.

LOMAX Marion, b. 20 Oct 1953, Newcastle-upon-Tyne, England. Poet; Lecturer. m. Michael Lomax, 29 Aug 1974. Education: BA (Hons), University of Kent, England, 1979; DPhil, University of York, England, 1983. Appointments: Creative Writing Fellow, University of Reading, 1987-88; Lecturer, Senior Lecturer in English, St Mary's University College, Strawberry Hill, Middlesex, 1987-; Writer-in-Residence, Cheltenham Festival of Literature, 1990; Professor of Literature, 1995-. Publications: Stage Images and Traditions: Shakespeare to Ford, 1987; The Peepshow Girl, poems, 1989; Raiding the Borders, poems, 1996. Editor: Time Present and Time Past: Poets at the University of Kent 1965-1985, 1985; Four Plays by John Ford, 1995; The Rover, by Alpha Behn, 1995. Contributions to: Anthologies and periodicals. Honours: E C Gregory Award, Society of Authors, 1981; 1st Prize, Cheltenham Festival

Poetry Competition, 1981; 3rd Place, Southern Arts Literature Award, 1992; Hawthornden Fellowship, 1993. Membership: Poetry Society. Address: c/o Bloodaxe Books, PO Box 1SN, Newcastle upon Tyne NE99 1SN, England.

LOMBINO Salvatore A, (Curt Cannon, Hunt Collins, Ezra Hannon, Evan Hunter, Richard Marsten, Ed McBain), b. 15 Oct 1916, New York, USA. Writer. m. (1) Anita Melnick, 1949, 3 sons, (2) Mary Vann Finley, 1973, 1 stepdaughter. Education: Cooper Union; Hunter College. Publications: The Blackboard Jungle, 1954; Second Ending,1956; Strangers When We Meet, 1958 (screenplay 1959); A Matter of Conviction, 1959; Mother and Daughters, 1961; The Birds (screenplay), 1962; Happy New Year Herbie, 1963; Buddwing, 1964; The Easter Man (play), 1964; The Paper Dragon, 1966; A Horse's Head, 1967; Last Summer, 1968; Sons, 1969; The Conjurer (play), 1969; Nobody Knew They Were There, 1971; Every Little Crook and Nanny, 1972; The Easter Man, 1972; Come Winter, 1973; Streets of Gold, 1974; The Chisholms, 1976; Me and Mr Stenner, 1976; Love, Dad, 1981; 87th Precinct Mysteries, Far From the Sea, 1983; Lizzie, 1984. As Ed McBain: Cop Hater, 1956; The Mugger, 1956; The Pusher, 1956; The Con Man, 1957; Killer's Choice, 1957; Killer's Payoff, 1958; Lady Killer, 1958; Killer's Wedge, 1959; 'Til Death, 1959; King's Ransom, 1959; Give the Boys a Great Big Hand, 1960; The Heckler, 1960; See Them Die, 1960; Lady, Lady, I Did It, 1961; Like Love, 1962; The Empty Hours (3 novelettes), 1962; Ten Plus One, 1963; Ax, 1964; He Who Hesitates, 1965; Doll,1965; The Sentries, 1965; Eighty Million Eyes, 1966; Fuzz, 1968 (screenplay 1972); Shotgun, 1969; Jigsaw, 1970; Hail, Hail, The Gang's All Here, 1971; Sadie When She Died, 1972; Let's Hear It for the Deaf Man, 1972; Hail to the Chief, 1973; Bread, 1974; Where There's Smoke, 1975; Blood Relatives, 1975; So Long as You Both Shall Live, 1976; Long Time No See, 1977; Goldilocks, 1977; Calypso, 1979; Ghosts, 1980; Rumpelstiltskin, 1981; Heat, 1981; Ice, 1983; Beauty and the Beast, 1983; Jack and the Beanstalk, 1984; Lightening, 1984; Snow White and Rose Red, 1985; Eight Black Horses, 1985; Cinderella, 1986; Another Part of the City, 1986; Poison, 1987; Puss in Boots, 1987; Tricks, 1987; McBain's Ladies, 1988; The House That Jack Built, 1988; Lullaby, 1989; McBain's Ladies Too, 1989; Downtown, 1989; Vespers, 1990; Three Blind Mice, 1990. Address: c/o John Farquharson Ltd, 250 West 57th Street, New York, NY 10019, USA.

LOMER Mary. See: **LIDE Mary Ruth.**

LOMPERIS Timothy John, b. 6 Mar 1947, Guntur, A P, India. University Professor. m. Ana Maria Turner, 15 May 1976, 1 son, 1 daughter. Education: AB magna cum laude, Augustana College, Rock Island, Illinois, 1969; MA, Johns Hopkins School of Advanced International Studies, Washington, DC, 1975; MA, Political Science, 1978, PhD, Political Science, 1981, Duke University; Olin Postdoctoral Fellow, Harvard University, 1985-86. Appointments: Assistant Professor, Political Science, Louisiana State University, Baton Rouge, 1980-83; Assistant Professor, Political Science, Duke University, 1983-; Fellow, Woodrow Wilson Center, Smithsonian Institution, 1988-89. Publications: The War Everyone Lost - And Won, 1984, revised edition, 1992; The Hindu Influence on Greek Philosophy, 1984; Reading the Wind, 1987; From People's War to People's Rule: Insurgency, Intervention, and the Lessons of Vietnam. Contributions to: Books and journals. Honours: Bronze Star, 1973; Vietnamese Army Staff Medal, First Class, 1973; Helen Dwight Reid Award for Best Dissertation in International Relations, American Political Science Association, 1981; Finalist, Furniss Award for Best First Book in National Security, 1984. Membership: American Political Science Association. Address: Department of Political Science, Duke University, Durham, NC 27706, USA.

LONDON Herbert Ira, b. 6 Mar 1939, New York, New York, USA. Professor; Writer. m. (1) Joy Weinman, 13 Oct 1962, div 1974, 2 daughters, (2) Vicki Pops, 18 Nov 1980, 1 daughter. Education: BA, 1960, MA, 1961, Columbia University; PhD, New York University, 1966. Appointments: Instructor, New School for Social Research, New York City, 1964-65; Instructor, 1964-65, Assistant Professor, 1967-68, University Ombudsman, 1968-69, Associate Professor, 1969-73, Professor, 1973-, Dean, Gallatin Division, 1972-92, John M Olin University Professor of Humanities, 1992-, New York University; Research Scholar, Australian National University, Canberra, 1966-67; Research Fellow, 1974-, Trustee, 1979-, Hudson Institute, Indianapolis. Publications: Education in the Twenty-First Century (editor), 1969; Non-White Immigration and the White Australia Policy, 1970; Fitting In: Crosswise at Generation Gap, 1974; Social Science

Theory, Structure and Applications (editor), 1975; The Overheated Decade, 1976; The Seventies: Counterfeit Decade, 1979; Myths That Rule America, 1981; Closing the Circle: A Cultural History of the Rock Revolution, 1984; Why Are They Lying to Our Children?, 1984; Military Doctrine and the American Character, 1984; Armageddon in the Classroom, 1986; A Strategy for Victory Without War, 1989; The Broken Apple: Notes on New York in the 1980s, 1989; From the Empire State to the Vampire State: New York in a Downtown Transition, 1994. Contributions to: Professional journals. Honours: Fulbright Award, 1966-67; Defence Science Journal Award, 1985. Memberships: American Historical Association; Education Excellence Center; Ethics and Public Policy Center; Freedom House; Heritage Foundation. Address: 2 Washington Square Village, New York, NY 10012, USA.

LONG Robert Emmet, b. 7 June 1934, New York, USA. Literary Critic; Freelance Writer. Education: BA, 1956, PhD, 1968, Columbia University; MA, Syracuse University, 1964. Appointments: Instructor, State University of New York, 1962-64; Assistant Professor, Queens College, City University of New York, 1968-71. Publications: The Achieving of the Great Gatsby: F Scott Fitgerald 1920-25, 1979; The Great Succession: Henry James and the Legacy of Hawthorne, 1979; Henry James: The Early Novels, 1983; John O'Hara, 1983; Nathanael West, 1985; Barbara Pym, 1986; James Thurber, 1988; James Fenimore Cooper, 1990; The Films of Merchant Ivory, 1991; Ingmar Bergman: Film and Stage, 1994. Editor: American Education, 1985; Drugs and American Society, 1985; Vietnam, Ten Years After, 1986; Mexico, 1986; The Farm Crisis, 1987; The Problem of Waste Disposal, 1988; AIDS, 1989; The Welfare Debate, 1989; Energy and Conservation, 1989; Japan and the USA, 1990; Censorship, 1990; The Crisis in Health Care, 1991; The State of US Education, 1991; The Reunification of Germany, 1992; Immigration to the United States, 1992; Drugs in America, 1993; Banking Scandals: The S&L and BCCI, 1993; Religious Cults in America, 1994; Criminal Sentencing, 1995; Suicide, 1995; Immigration, 1996; Affirmative Action, 1996; Multiculturalism, 1997; Right to Privacy, 1997. Contributions to: Several hundred articles in magazines, journals and newspapers. Address: 254 South Third Street, Fulton, NY 13069, USA.

LONGFORD Countess of (Elizabeth Pakenham), b. 30 Aug 1906, England. m. Hon F A Pakenham, 1931, 4 sons, 3 daughters. Education: MA, Lady Margaret Hall, Oxford. Appointments: Member, Advisory Council, Victoria & Albert Museum, 1969-75; Trustee, National Portrait Gallery, 1968-78; Advisory Board, British Library, 1976-80. Publications: Jameson's Raid, 1960; Victoria RI, 1964; Wellington: The Years of the Sword, 1969; Wellington: Pillar of State, 1972; Churchill, 1974; The Royal House of Windsor, 1974; Byron's Greece, 1975; Byron, 1976; A Pilgramage of Passion: The Life of Wilfred Scawen Blunt, 1979; Louisa: Lady in Waiting, 1979; Images of Chelsea, 1980; The Queen Mother, 1981; Eminent Victorian Women, 1981; Elizabeth R, 1983; The Pebbled Shore: Memoir, 1983; The Oxford Book of Royal Anecdotes, 1989; Darling Loosey: Letters to Princess Louise; Poet's Corner: An Anthology, 1992; Royal Throne: The Future of the Monarchy, 1993. Honours: Honorary Life President, Women Writers and Journalists, 1979. Address: 18 Chesil Court, Chelsea Manor Street, SW3 5QP, England.

LONGLEY Michael, b. 27 July 1939, Belfast, Northern Ireland. Poet; Arts Administrator. m. Edna Broderick, 1964, 1 son, 2 daughters. Education: BA, Trinity College, Dublin, 1963. Appointments: Assistant Master, Avoca School, Blackrock, 1962-63; Belfast High School and Erith Secondary School, 1963-64; Royal Belfast Academical Institution, 1964-69; Director, Literature and the Traditional Arts, Arts Council of Northern Ireland, Belfast, 1970-. Publications: Poetry: Ten Poems, 1965; Room To Rhyme (with Seamus Heaney and David Hammond), 1968; Secret Marriages: Nine Short Poems, 1968; Three Regional Voices (with Barry Tebb and Ian Chrichton Smith), 1968; No Continuing City: Poems, 1963-1968, 1969; Lares, 1972; An Exploded View: Poems, 1968-72, 1973; Fishing in the Sky, 1975; Man Lying on a Wall, 1976; The Echo Gate: Poems 1975-1978, 1979; Selected Poems, 1963-1980, 1980; Patchwork, 1981; Poems 1963-1983, 1985; Gorse Fires, 1991; Editor: Causeway: The Arts in Ulster, 1971; Selected Poems by Louis MacNeice, 1988. Contributions to: Periodicals. Honours: Eric Gregory Award, Society of Authors, 1965; Commonwealth Poetry Prize, 1985. Address: 32 Osborne Gardens, Malone, Belfast 9, Northern Ireland.

LONGMATE Norman Richard, b. 15 Dec 1925, Newbury, Berkshire, England. Freelance Writer. Education: BA, Modern History,

1950, MA 1952, Worcester College, Oxford. Appointments: Leader Writer, Evening Standard, 1952; Feature Writer, Daily Mirror, 1953-56; Administrative Officer, Electricity Council, 1957-63; Schools Radio Producer, 1963-65, Senior, subsequently Chief Assistant, BBC Secretariat, 1965-83, BBC; Freelance Writer, 1983-. Publications: A Socialist Anthology (editor), 1953; Oxford Triumphant, 1955; King Cholera, 1966; The Waterdrinkers, 1968; Alive and Well, 1970; How We Lived Then, 1971; If Britain had Fallen, 1972; The Workhouse, 1974; The Real Dad's Army, 1974; The GI's, 1975; Milestones in Working Class History, 1975; Air Raid, 1976; When We Won the War, 1977; The Hungry Mills, 1978; The Doodlebugs, 1981; The Bombers, 1982; The Breadstealers, 1984; Hitler's Rockets, 1985; Defending the Island from Caeser to the Armada, 1989. Memberships: Oxford Society; Society of Authors; Fortress Study Group; United Kingdom Fortification Club; Historical Association; Ramblers Association; Society of Sussex Downsmen; Prayer Book Society; Royal Historical Society, fellow. Address: c/o Century Hutchison, 62-65 Chandos Place, London WC2 4NW, England.

LONGWORTH Phillip, b. 17 Feb 1933, London, England. Professor of History; Writer. Education: BA, 1956, MA, 1960, Balliol College, Oxford. Appointment: Professor of History, McGill University, Montreal, 1984-. Publications: A Hero of Our Time, by Lermontov (translator), 1962; The Art of Victory, 1965; The Unending Vigil, 1967, new edition, 1985; The Cossacks, 1969; The Three Empresses, 1971; The Rise and Fall of Venice, 1974; Alexis, Tsar of All the Russias, 1984; The Making of Eastern Europe, 1992, new edition, 1997. Contributions to: Periodicals. Address: c/o Heath and Co, 79 St Martin's Lane, London WC2N 4AA, England.

LONGYEAR Barry (Brookes), b. 12 May 1942, Harrisburg, Pennsylvania, USA. Writer. Appointment: Publisher, Sol III Publications, Philadelphia, 1968-72, and Farmington, Maine, 1972-77. Publications: City of Baraboo, 1980; Manifest Destiny (stories), 1980; Circus World (stories), 1980; Elephant Song, 1981; The Tomorrow Testament, 1983; It Came from Schenectady, 1984; Sea of Glass, 1986; Enemy Mine, 1988; Saint MaryBlue, 1988; Naked Came the Robot, 1988; The God Box, 1989; Infinity Hold, 1989; The Homecoming, 1989; Slag Like Me, 1994. Address: PO Box 100, Vienna Road Rt 41, New Shanon, ME 04955, USA.

LOOMIE Albert (Joseph), b. 29 July 1922, New York, New York, USA. Professor of History Emeritus; Writer. Education: BA, Loyola University, 1944; PhL, West Baden College, 1946; MA, Fordham University, 1949; STL, Woodstock College, 1953; PhD, University of London, 1957. Appointments: Member, Jesuit Order, 1939-; Faculty, 1958-68, Professor of History, 1968-93, Professor Emeritus, 1993-, Fordham University. Publications: The Spanish Jesuit Mission in Virginia 1570-72 (with C M Lewis), 1953; Toleration and Diplomacy: The Religious Issue in Anglo-Spanish Relations 1603-05, 1963; The Spanish Elizabethans: The English Exiles at the Court of Philip II, 1964; Guy Fawkes in Spain, 1971; Spain and the Jacobean Catholics, 2 volumes, 1973, 1978; Ceremonies of Charles I: The Notebooks of John Finet 1628-41, 1987; English Polemics at the Spanish Court: Joseph Creswell's Letter to the Ambassador from England, the English and Spanish Texts of 1606, 1993. Contributions to: Professional journals. Address: c/o Loyola-Faber Hall, Fordham University, New York, NY 10458, USA.

LOPATE Phillip, b. 16 Nov 1943, Jamaica, New York, USA. Professor of English; Writer. m. Cheryl Cipriani, 31 Dec 1990. Education: BA, Columbia College, 1964; PhD, Union Institute, 1979. Appointments: Associate Professor of English, University of Houston, 1980-88; Associate Professor of Creative Writing, Columbia University, 1988-91; Professor of English, Bennington College, 1992, then Hofstra University. Publications: The Eyes Don't Always Want to Stay Open, 1972; Being With Children, 1975; The Daily Round, 1976; Confessions of Summer, 1979; Bachelorhood, 1981; The Rug Merchant, 1987; Against Joie de Vivre, 1989; The Art of the Personal Essay, 1994; Portrait of My Body, 1996. Contributions to: Periodicals. Address: 402 Sackett Street, Brooklyn, NY 11231, USA.

LOPES Henri (Marie-Joseph), b. 12 Sept 1937, Leopoldville, Belgian Congo. Novelist. m. Nirva Pasbeau, 13 May 1961, 1 son, 3 daughters. Education: Licence es Lettres, 1962, Diplome d'Etudes Superieures, History, 1963, Sorbonne, University of Paris. Publications: Tribaliques, 1971, English translation as Tribaliks, 1989; La Nouvelle Romance, 1976; Sans Tam-Tam, 1977; The Laughing Cry, 1988; Le Chercheur d'Afriques, 1990; Sur L'Autre Rive, 1992; Le

Lys et le Flamboyant, 1997. Honours: Grand Prix de la Litterature d'Afrique Noire, 1972; Prix Jules Verne, 1990; Doctor Honoris Causa, University Paris-Val de Marne, France; Grand Prix de Littérature de La Francophonie de L'Académie Française, 1993; Homme de Lettres 1993, 1994. Address: UNESCO, 7 Place de Fontenoy, 75352 Paris, France.

LOPEZ Barry (Holstun), b. 6 Jan 1945, Port Chester, New York, USA. Author. m. Sandra Jean Landers, 10 June 1967. Education: BA, 1966, MA, 1968, University of Notre Dame. Publications: Desert Notes, 1976; Giving Birth to Thunder, 1978; Rivert Notes, 1978; Of Wolves and Men, 1978; Winter Count, 1981; Arctic Dreams, 1986; Crossing Open Ground, 1988; The Rediscovery of North America, 1991; Field Notes, 1994. Contributions to: Periodicals. Honours: John Burroughs Medal, 1979; Christopher Medals, 1979, 1987; American Academy of Arts and Letters Award, 1986; Guggenheim Fellowship, 1987; National Book Award, 1987; Honorary LDH, Whittier College, 1988; Lannan Foundation Award, 1990. Membership: PEN American Center. Address: c/o Sterling Lord Listeristic, 1 Madison Avenue, New York, NY 10010, USA.

LOPEZ SAAVEDRA Josefina Del C, b. 21 Oct 1964, Caracas, Venezuela. Poet; Translator; Writer. m. Mauricio Machuca, 7 Apr 1990. Education: Medicine, Universidad Central de Venezuela, 1991; Writing Creative Poetry, School of Continuing Studies, Rice University, Houston, Texas, USA, 1993; Licentiate Degree in Letters, Universidad Catolica Andres Bello. Appointments: Coordinator, 1993, President (since 1994), Founder, Director, Editor, Literary Magazine, 1997, La Casa Del Poeta. Publication: Poems and Friendship, 1991. Contributions to: Periodicals and journals. Memberships: Instituto Internacional de Literatura Iberoamericans; Instituto Literario y Cultural Hispanico; Academia Iberoamericans de Poets; La Casa Del Poeta. Address: Apartado Postal #66908, Caracas 1061-A, Venezuela.

LORD Graham John, b. 16 Feb 1943, Mutare, Zimbabwe. Journalist. m. Jane Carruthers, 12 Sept 1962, 2 daughters. Education: BA Honours, Cambridge University, 1965. Appointments: Literary Editor, Sunday Express, London, 1969-; Originator of Sunday Express Book of the Year Award, 1987, Judge, 1987, 1988, 1989. Publications: Novels: Marshmallow Pie, 1970; A Roof Under Your Feet, 1973; The Spider and the Fly, 1974; God and All His Angels, 1976; The Nostradamus Horoscope, 1981; Time Out of Mind, 1986. Address: Sunday Express, 245 Blackfriars Road, London SE1, England.

LORD Robert Needham, b. 18 July 1945, Rotorua, New Zealand. Playwright. Education: BA, Victoria University of Wellington; Diploma of Teaching, Wellington Teachers' College. Appointment: Burns Fellow, Otago University, 1987. Publications: Heroes and Butterflies, 1973; Well Hung, 1974; Bert and Maisy, 1987; The Travelling Squirrel, 1987; The Affair, 1987; Country Cops, 1988; China Wars, 1988; Glorious Ruins, 1990. Honours: Katherine Mansfield Young Writers Award, 1969; CAPS Grant, New York State, 1984; Burns Fellowship, 1987. Memberships: PEN; Dramatists Guild. Address: 250 West 85th Street, Apt 145, New York, NY 10024, USA.

LORD Walter, b. 8 Oct 1917, Baltimore, Maryland, USA. Author. Education: BA, Princeton University, 1939; LLB, Yale University, 1946. Publications: The Fremantle Diary, 1954; A Night to Remember, 1955, illustrated edition, 1976; Day of Infamy, 1957; The Good Years, 1960; A Time to Stand, 1961; Peary to the Pole, 1963; The Past That Would Not Die, 1965; Incredible Victory, 1967; Dawn's Early Light, 1972; Lonely Vigil, 1977; Miracle of Dunkirk, 1982; The Night Lives On, 1986. Contributions to: Periodicals. Address: 116 East 68th Street, New York, NY 10021, USA.

LORENC Kito, b. 4 Mar 1938, Schleife, Germany (Lusatia). Freelance writer. Education: Sorbian/Russian pedagogical exam, Leipzig University, 1961. Publications: Struga (poems in parallel Serbian and German version, 1967; Flurberinigung (poems), 1973; Serbska citanka/Sorbisches Lesebuch (anthology of Serbian literature), 1981; Die Rasselbande im Schlamassellande (poems for children), 1983; Wortland (poems), 1984; Rymarej a dyrdomej (poems for children), 1985; Gegen den grossen Popanz (poems), 1990; Die wendische Schiffahrt (piece), 1994; Kim Broiler (piece), 1996. Editor: Serbska poezija (series of Serbian poetry), 1973-. Honours: Award Heinrich-Heine-Preis, 1974; Heinrich-Mann-Preis, 1991. Membership: Sächsische Akademie der Künste. Address: D-02627 Wuischke bei Hochirch, Nr 4, Germany.

LORENZ Sarah E. See:**WINSTON Sarah.**

LORRIMER Claire. See: **CLARK Patricia Denise.**

LOTT Bret, b. 8 Oct 1958, Los Angeles, California, USA. Assistant Professor of English; Writer. m. Melanie Kai Swank, 28 June 1980, 2 sons. Education: BA, California State University at Long Beach, 1981; MFA, University of Massachusetts, 1984. Appointments: Reporter, Daily Commercial News, Los Angeles, 1980-81; Instructor in Remedial English, Ohio State University, Columbus, 1984-86; Assistant Professor of English, College of Charleston, 1986-. Publications: The Man Who Owned Vermont, 1987; A Stranger's House, 1988; A Dream of Old Leaves, 1989. Contributions to: Anthologies and periodicals. Honours: Awards and fellowships. Memberships: Associated Writing Programs; Poets and Writers. Address: c/o Department of English, College of Charleston, Charleston, SC 29424, USA.

LOVAT Terence John, b. 29 Mar 1949, Sydney, New South Wales, Australia. Professor of Education. m. Tracey Majella Dennis, 4 Jan 1986, 1 son, 2 daughters. Education: BEd, 1982, MTh, 1983, MA (hons), 1984, PhD, 1988, Sydney University. Appointment: Professor of Education, University of Newcastle, New South Wales, Australia. Publications: Understanding Religion, 1987; What Is This Thing Called Religious Education?, 1989; Studies in Australian Society, 1989; Curriculum: Action on Reflection (with D Smith), 1990, 1995; Bioethics for Medical and Health Professionals (with K Mitchell and I Kerridge), 1991, 1996; Teaching and Learning Religion, 1995. Editor: Sociology for Teachers, 1992; Studies in Religion, 1993. Contributions to: Professional journals. Memberships: Australian College of Education; European Association for Research on Learning and Instruction. Address: Faculty of Education, University of Newcastle, New South Wales 2308, Australia.

LOVE William F, b. 20 Dec 1932, Oklahoma City, Oklahoma, USA. Writer. m. Joyce Mary Athman, 30 May 1970, 2 daughters. Education: BA, St John's University, Collegeville, Minnesota, 1955; MBA, University of Chicago, 1972. Publications: The Chartreuse Clue, 1990; The Fundamentals of Murder, 1991; Bloody Ten, 1992. Memberships: Authors Guild; International Association of Crime Writers; Mystery Writers of America; PEN Midwest; Private Eye Writers of America; Society of Midland Authors. Address: 940 Cleveland, Hinsdale, IL 60521, USA.

LOVELL Sir (Alfred Charles) Bernard, b. 31 Aug 1913, Oldland Common, Gloucestershire, England. Professor of Radio Astronomy Emeritus; Writer. m. Mary Joyce Chesterman, 1937, dec 1993, 2 sons, 3 daughters. Education: University of Bristol. Appointments: Professor of Radio Astronomy, 1951-80, Professor Emeritus, 1980-, University of Manchester; Director, Jodrell Bank Experimental Station, later Nuffield Radio Astronomy Laboratories, 1951-81; Various visiting lectureships. Publications: Science and Civilisation, 1939; World Power Resources and Social Development, 1945; Radio Astronomy, 1951; Meteor Astronomy, 1954; The Exploration of Space by Radio, 1957; The Individual and the Universe, 1958; The Exploration of Outer Space, 1961; Discovering the Universe, 1963; Our Present Knowledge of the Universe, 1967; The Explosion of Science: The Physical Universe (editor with T Margerison), 1967; The Story of Jodrell Bank, 1968; The Origins and International Economics of Space Exploration, 1973; Out of the Zenith, 1973; Man's Relation to the Universe, 1975; P M S Blackett: A Biographical Memoir, 1976; In the Centre of Immensities, 1978; Emerging Cosmology, 1981; The Jodrell Bank Telescopes, 1985; Voice of the Universe, 1987; Pathways to the Universe (with Sir Francis Graham Smith), 1988; Astronomer By Chance (autobiography), 1990; Echoes of War, 1991. Contributions to: Professional journals. Honours: Officer of the Order of the British Empire, 1946; Duddell Medal, 1954; Royal Medal, 1960; Knighted, 1961; Ordre du Mérite pour la Recherche et l'Invention, 1962; Churchill Gold Medal, 1964; Gold Medal, Royal Astronomical Society, 1981; Many honorary doctorates. Memberships: American Academy of Arts and Sciences, honorary foreign member; American Philosophical Society; International Astronomical Union, vice-president, 1970-76; New York Academy; Royal Astronomical Society, president, 1969-71; Royal Society, fellow; Royal Swedish Academy, honorary member. Address: The Quinta, Swettenham, Cheshire CW12 2LD, England.

LOVELL Mary Sybilla, b. 23 Oct 1941, Prestatyn, North Wales, UK. Writer. m. (2) Geoffrey A H Watts, 11 July 1991, 1 son, 2 stepsons, 2 stepdaughters. Publications: Hunting Pageant, 1980; Cats as Pets, 1982; Boys Book of Boats, 1983; Straight on till Morning, 1987; The Splendid Outcast, 1988; The Sound of Wings, 1989; Cast No Shadow, 1991; A Scandalous Life, 1995; The Rebel Heart, 1996. Contributions to: Many technical articles on the subjects of accounting and software. Memberships: Society of Authors; MFHA, 1987-88; New Forest Hunt Club; Vice President, R S Surtees Society, 1980-; Fellow, Royal Geographic Society. Address: Stroat House, Stroat, Gloucs NP6 7LR, England.

LOVELOCK Yann Rufus, b. 11 Feb 1939, Birmingham, England. Writer; Poet; Translator. m. Ann Riddell, 28 Sept 1961. Education: BA, English Literature, St Edmund Hall, Oxford, 1963. Appointments: Various Writer-in-Residencies. Publications: The Vegetable Book, 1972; The Colour of the Weather (editor and translator), 1980; The Line Forward, 1984; A Vanishing Emptiness (editor and part translator), 1989; A Townscape of Flanders, Versions of Grace (translation of Anton van Wilderode), 1990; Landscape with Voices, Poems 1980-95, 1995. Some 25 other books of poems, experimental prose, anthologies and translations. Contributions to: Periodicals and Anthologies. Honour: Silver Medal, Haute Academie d'Art et de Litterature de France, 1986. Memberships: Freundkreis Poesie Europe, assistant director; Corresponding member of La Société de Langue et de la Litterature Wallonnes. Address: 80 Doris Road, Birmingham, West Midlands B11 4NF, England.

LOVESEY Peter, (Peter Lear), b. 10 Sept 1936, Whitton, Middlesex, England. Writer. m. Jacqueline Ruth Lewis, 30 May 1959, 1 son, 1 daughter. Education: BA Honours, English, University of Reading, England, 1958. Publications: The Kings of Distance (non-fiction sports), 1968; Wobble to Death (crime fiction), 1970; The Detective Wore Silk Drawers, 1971; Abracadaver, 1972; Mad Hatters Holiday, 1973; Invitation to a Dynamite Party, 1974; A Case of Spirits, 1975; Swing, Swing Together, 1976; Goldengirl, 1977; Waxwork, 1978; Official Centenary History of the Amateur Athletic Association, 1979; Spider Girl, 1980; The False Inspector Dew, 1982; Keystone, 1983; Butchers (short stories), 1985; The Secret of Spandau, 1986; Rough Cider, 1986; Bertie and the Tinman, 1987; On the Edge, 1989; Bertie and the Seven Bodies, 1990; The Last Detective, 1991; Diamond Solitaire, 1992; Bertie and the Crime of Passion, 1993; The Crime of Miss Oyster Brown (short stories), 1994; The Summons, 1995; Bloodhounds, 1996; Upon a Dark Night, 1997. Honours: Macmillan/Panther 1st Crime Novel Award, 1970; Crime Writers Association Silver Dagger, 1978, 1995, 1996; Gold Dagger, 1982; Grand Prix de Littérature Policière, 1985; Prix du Roman D'Aventures, 1987; Anthony Award, 1992. Memberships: Crime Writers Association, chairman, 1991-92; Detection Club; Society of Authors. Address: 59 Crescent Road, Leigh-on-Sea, Essex SS9 2PF, England.

LOVETT Albert Winston, b. 16 Dec 1944, Abingdon, England. Academic. Education: BA, 1965, PhD, 1969, Cambridge, England. Publications: Philip II and Mateo Vazquez, 1977; Modern Europe 1453-1610, 1979; Early Habsburg Spain 1516-1598, 1986. Contributions to: Historical Journal (Cambridge); European History Quarterly; English Historical Review; Others. Membership: Royal Historical Society, Fellow. Address: Flat 14, Foxleas Court, 4 Spencer Road, Bromley, Kent BR1 3WB, England.

LOW Dorothy Mackie. See: LOW Lois Dorothea.

LOW Lois Dorothea, (Zoe Cass, Dorothy Mackie Low, Lois Paxton), b. 15 July 1916, Edinburgh, Scotland. Writer. Education: Edinburgh Ladies' College. Publications: Isle for a Stranger, 1962; Dear Liar, 1963; A Ripple on the Water, 1964; The Intruder, 1965; A House in the Country, 1968; The Man Who Died Twice, 1969; To Burgundy and Back, 1970; The Quiet Sound of Fear, 1971; Who Goes There?, 1972; Island of the Seven Hills, 1974; The Silver Leopard, 1976; A Twist in the Silk, 1980; The Man in the Shadows, 1983. Memberships: Crime Writers Association; Romantic Novelists Association, chairman, 1969-71; Society of Authors. Address: 6 Belmont Mews, Abbey Hill, Kenilworth, Warwickshire CV8 1LU, England.

LOW Rachael, b. 6 July 1923, London, England. Film Historian. Education: BSc, 1944, PhD, 1950, London School of Economics and Political Science. Appointments: Researcher, British Film Institute, London, 1945-48; Gulbenkian Research Fellow, 1968-71, Fellow Commoner, 1983, Lucy Cavendish College, Cambridge. Publications: History of the British Film 1896-1906, 1948; with Roger Manvill: History of the British Film, 1906-1914, 1949, 1914-1918, 1950, 1918-1929,

1971, 1929-1939, Vols. I and II, 1979, Vol III, 1985. Address: c/o Allen & Unwin Ltd, 40 Museum Street, London WC1, England.

LOWBURY Edward (Joseph Lister), b. 6 Dec 1913, London, England. Physician; Poet; Writer on Medical, Scientific and Literary Subjects. m. Alison Young, 12 June 1954, 3 daughters. Education: BA, 1936, BM and BCh, 1939, University College, Oxford; MA, London Hospital Medical College, 1940; DM, 1957. Appointments: Bacteriologist, Medical Research Council Burns Research Unit, Birmingham Accident Hospital, 1949-79; Founder-Honorary Director, Hospital Infection Research Laboratory, Birmingham, 1966-79. Publications: Poetry: Over 20 collections, including: Time for Sale, 1961; Daylight Astronomy, 1968; The Night Watchman, 1974; Poetry and Paradox: Poems and an Essay, 1976; Selected Poems, 1978; Selected and New Poems, 1990; Collected Poems, 1993; Mystic Bridges, 1997. Non-Fiction: Thomas Campion: Poet, Composer, Physician (with Alison Young and Timothy Salter), 1970; Drug Resistance in Antimicrobial Therapy (with G A Ayliffe), 1974; Hallmarks of Poetry (essays), 1994. Editor: Control of Hospital Infection: A Practical Handbook (with others), 1975, 3rd edition, 1992; The Poetical Works of Andrew Young (with Alison Young), 1985. Contributions to: Numerous medical, scientific, and literary publications, including reference works and journals. Honours: Newdigate Prize, 1934; Honorary Research Fellow, Birmingham University; John Keats Memorial Lecturer Award, 1973; Everett Evans Memorial Lecturer Award, 1977; DSc, Aston University, 1977; A B Wallace Memorial Lecturer and Medal, 1978; Honorary Professor of Medical Microbiology, Aston University, 1979; LL D, Birmingham University, 1980; Officer of the Order of the British Empire. Memberships: British Medical Association; Fellow, Royal College of Pathologists, Royal College of Surgeons, Royal Society of Literature; Honorary Fellow, Royal College of Physicians; Society for Applied Bacteriology; Society for General Microbiology; Others. Address: 79 Vernon Road, Birmingham B16 9SQ, England.

LOWDEN Desmond Scott, b. 27 Sept 1937, Winchester, Hants, England. m. 14 July 1962, 1 son, 1 daughter. Education: Pilgrims' School, Winchester; Marlborough College. Publications: Bandersnatch, 1969; The Boondocks, 1972; Bellman and True, 1975; Boudapesti 3, 1979; Sunspot, 1981; Cry Havoc, 1984; The Shadow Run, 1989; Chain, 1990. Honour: Silver Dagger Award, Crime Writers' Association, 1989. Membership: Crime Writers' Association. Literary Agent: Deborah Rogers. Address: c/o Deborah Rogers, Rogers, Coleridge and White Ltd, 20 Powys Mews, London W11 1JN, England.

LOWE Barry, b. 16 May 1947, Sydney, New South Wales, Australia. Playwright; Scriptwriter. Partner: Walter Figallo, 24 Dec 1972. Publications: Plays: Writers Camp, first performed, 1982; Tokyo Rose, 1989; The Death of Peter Pan, 1989; Seeing Things, 1994; Relative Merits, 1994; The Extraordinary Annual General Meeting of the Size-Queen Club, 1996. Contributions to: Short stories: Westerly; GLP; Cargo; James White Review; Included in the anthology: Flesh and the Word; Columnist: Lowe-Life, Sydney Star Observer, 1980-82. Memberships: Australian Writers Guild; Australian Society of Authors. Literary Agent: Kevin Palmer, 258 Bulwara Road, Ultimo, New South Wales 2007, Australia. Address: GPO Box 635, Sydney, New South Wales 1034, Australia.

LOWE John Evelyn, b. 23 Apr 1928, London, England. Writer. m. (1) Susan Sanderson, 1956, 2 sons, 1 daughter, (2) Yuki Nomura, 1989, 1 daughter. Education: English Literature, New College, Oxford, 1950-52. Appointments: Associate Editor, Collins Crime Club, 1953-54; Editor, Faber Furniture Series, 1954-56; Deputy Story Editor, Pinewood Studios, 1956-57; Literary Editor, Kansai Time Out Magazine, 1985-89. Publications: Thomas Chippendale, 1955; Cream Coloured Earthenware, 1958; Japanese Crafts, 1983; Into Japan, 1985; Into China, 1986; Corsica - A Traveller's Guide, 1988; A Surrealist Life - Edward James, 1991; A Short Guide to the Kyoto Museum of Archaeology, 1991; Glimpses of Kyoto Life, 1996; The Warden - A Portrait of John Sparrow, 1998; Major contribution to the Encyclopaedia Britannica and the Oxford Junior Encyclopaedia. Contributions to: American Scholar; Country Life; Listener; Connoisseur; Apollo; Others. Honours: Honorary Fellow, Royal College of Art. Memberships: Society of Antiquaries, fellow; Royal Society of Arts, fellow. Address: Paillole-Basse, 47360 Prayssas, France.

LOWE Robson, b. 7 Jan 1905, London, England. Editor; Author; Auctioneer. m. Winifred Marie Deane, 7 Mar 1928, 2 daughters. Education: Fulham Central School. Publications: Regent Catalogue of

Empire Postage Stamps, 1933; The Encyclopaedia of Empire Postage Stamps, 1935; Handstruck Postage Stamps of the Empire, 1937; The Birth of the Adhesive Postage Stamp, 1939; Masterpieces of Engraving on Postage Stamps, 1943; The Encyclopaedia of Empire Postage Stamps, 7 volumes, 1950-90; Sperati and His Work, 1956; The British Postage Stamp, 1968; Leeward Islands, 1990; The House of Stamps, Imitations, 1993. Contributions to: Many philatelic and postal journals. Address: c/o The East India Club, 16 St James' Square, London SW1, England.

LOWE Stephen, b. 1 Dec 1947, Nottingham, England. Playwright. m. (1) Tina Barclay, (2) Tany Myers, 1 son, 1 daughter. Education: BA Hons, English and Drama, 1969; Postgraduate Research, 1969-70. Appointments: Senior Tutor in Writing for Performance, Dartington College of Arts Performance, 1978-82; Resident Playwright, Riverside Studios, London, 1982-84; Senior Tutor, Birmingham University, 1987-88; Nottingham Trent University Advisory Board to Theatre Design Degree, 1987-. Publications: Touched, 1981; Cards, 1983; Moving Pictures and Other Plays, 1985; Body and Soul in Peace Plays, 2 volumes, 1985, 1990; Divine Gossip/Tibetan Inroads, 1988; Ragged Trousered Philanthropists, 1991. Contributions to: Books and journals. Honour: George Devine Award for Playwriting, 1977. Memberships: Theatre Writers Union; Writers Guild; PEN. Address: S Stroud, Judy Daish Associates, 83 Eastbourn Mews, London W2 6LQ, England.

LOWELL Susan Deborah, b. 27 Oct 1950, Chihuahua, Mexico. Writer. m. William Ross Humphreys, 21 Mar 1975, 2 daughters. Education: BA, 1972, MA, 1974, Stanford University, USA; MA, PhD, Princeton University, 1979. Appointments: University of Arizona, 1974-76, 1981; University of Texas, Dallas, 1979-80. Publications: Ganado Red: A Novella and Stories, 1988; I am Lavinia Cumming, 1993. Honours: Milkweed Editions National Fiction Prize, 1988; Mountain & Plains Booksellers Association Regional Book Award (Childrens category), 1994. Membership: Southern Arizona Society of Authors. Address: c/o Milkweed Editions, PO Box 3226, Minneapolis, MN 55403, USA.

LOWNIE Andrew James Hamilton, b. 11 Nov 1961, Kenya. Literary Agent. Education: Magdalene College, Cambridge, 1981-84; BA (Cantab); MA (Cantab); MSc, Edinburgh University, 1989. Appointments: Trustee, Iain Macleod Award, 1984; Hodder and Stoughton Publishers, 1984-85; Joined 1985, Director 1986-88, John Farquharson Literary Agents; Andrew Lownie Associates, 1988-; Denniston and Lownie, 1991-93; Director, Thistle Publishing, 1996-; Parliamentary Candidate, Monklands West, 1992. Publications: North American Spies, 1992; Edinburgh Literary Guide, 1992; John Buchan: The Presbyterian Cavalier, 1995; The Scottish Short Stories of John Buchan, editor, 1997; John Buchan's Collected Poems, editor, 1996; The Complete Short Stories of John Buchan, Volumes 1-3, editor, 1996-97. Contributions to: Times; Spectator; Telegraph; Scotland on Sunday; Introductions to John Buchan's 'Huntingtower' & 'Courts of the Morning', 1994; Introductions to John Buchan reissues Alan Sutton, 1994. Honour: English Speaking Union Scholarship to Asheville School, North Carolina, USA, 1979-80. Memberships: Royal Geographical Society, fellow; Royal Society of Arts, fellow; Society of Authors; Association of Authors' Agents. Address: 122 Bedford Court Mansions, Bedford Square, London WC1B 3AH, England.

LOWRY Lois, b. 20 Mar 1937, Honolulu, Hawaii. Writer. m. Donald Grey Lowry, 11 June 1956, div 1977, 2 sons, 2 daughters. Education: Brown University, 1954-56; BA, University of Southern Maine, 1972. Publications: Children's Books: A Summer to Die, 1977; Find a Stranger, Say Goodbye, 1978; Anastasia Krupnik, 1979; Autumn Street, 1979; Anastasia Again!, 1981; Anastasia at Your Service, 1982; Taking Care of Terrific, 1983; Anastasia Ask Your Analyst, 1984; Us and Uncle Fraud, 1984; One Hundredth Thing About Caroline, 1985; Anastasia on Her Own, 1985; Switcharound, 1985; Anastasia Has the Answers, 1986; Rabble Starkey, 1987; Anastasia's Chosen Career, 1987; All About Sam, 1988; Number the Stars, 1989; Your Move J P!, 1990; Anastasia at This Address, 1991; Attaboy Sam!. 1992; The Giver, 1993. Other: Black American Literature, 1973; Literature of the American Revolution, 1974; Values and the Family, 1977. Honours: Children's Literature Award, International Reading Association, 1978; American Library Association Notable Book Citation, 1980; Boston Globe-Horn Book Award, 1987; National Jewish Book Award, 1990; Newbery Medals, 1990, 1994. Address: 8 Lexington Avenue, Cambridge, MA 02138, USA.

LOXMITH John. See: **BRUNNER John Kilian Houston.**

LTAIF Nadine, b. 19 July 1961, Cairo, Egypt. Poet. Education: MA, French Literature, University of Montreal, 1986. Publications: Poetry: Les Métamorphoses d'Ishtar, 1987; Entre les Fleuves, 1991; Élegies du Levant, 1995; Vestige d'Un Jardin. Contributions to: Tessera; Arcade; Estuaire. Address: 2004 St Laurent 303, Montreal, Quebec H2X 2T2, Canada.

LUARD Nicholas, (James McVean), b. 26 June 1937, London, England. Writer. Education: Winchester College, 1951-54; Sorbonne, University of Paris, 1954-55; MA, Cambridge University, 1960; MA, University of Pennsylvania, 1961. Publications: Fiction: The Warm and Golden War, 1967; The Robespierre Serial, 1975; Traveling Horseman, 1975; The Orion Line, 1976; Bloodspoor, 1977; The Dirty Area, 1979; Seabird Nine, 1981; Titan, 1984. Non-Fiction: Refer to Drawer (with Dominick Elwes), 1964; The Last Wilderness: A Journey Across the Great Kalahari Desert, 1981; The Wildlife Parks of Africa, 1985. Address: 227 South Lambeth Road, London SW8, England.

LUBINGER Eva, b. 3 Feb 1930, Steyr, Austria. Writer. m. Dr Walter Myss, 7 Oct 1952, 2 sons. Appointment: Wort und Welt, Innsbruck, Austria. Publications: Paradies mit Kleinen Fehlein, 1976; Gespenster in Sir Edwards Haus, 1978; Pflucke den Wind, lyric, 1982; Verlieb Dich nicht in Mark Aurell, 1985; Zeig mir Lamorna, 1985; Flieg mit Nach Samarkand, 1987. Contributions to: Prasent, weekly newspaper. Honours: Literature Prize for lyrics, Innsbruck, 1963; Literature Prize for Drama, Innsbruck, 1969. Membership: PEN, Austria. Address: Lindenbuhelweg 16, 6020 Innsbruck, Austria.

LUCAS Celia, b. 23 Oct 1938, Bristol, England. Writer. m. Ian Skidmore, 20 Oct 1971. Education: BA, Hons, Modern History, St Hilda's College, Oxford, 1961. Publications: Prisoners of Santo Tomas, 1975, 1988, 1996; Steel Town Cats, 1987; Glyndwr Country (with Ian Skidmore), 1988; Anglesey Rambles (with Ian Skidmore), 1989; The Adventures of Marmaduke Purr Cat, 1990; The Terrible Tale of Tiggy Two, 1995. Contributions to: Numerous journals and magazines. Honours: TIR NA N-OG Award for junior fiction, 1988; Irma Chilton Award for Junior Fiction, 1995. Membership: Welsh Academy (elected 1989). Address: Aberbraint, Llanfairpwll, Isle of Anglesey, Gwynedd LL61 6BP, Wales.

LUCAS John (Randolph), b. 18 June 1929, England. Writer. m. Morar Portal, 1961, 2 sons, 2 daughters. Education: St Mary's College, Winchester; MA, Balliol College, Oxford, 1952. Appointments: Junior Research Fellow, 1953-56, Fellow and Tutor, 1960-96, Merton College, Oxford; Fellow and Assistant Tutor, Corpus Christi College, Cambridge, 1956-59; Jane Eliza Procter Visiting Fellow, Princeton University, 1957-58; Leverhulme Research Fellow, Leeds University, 1959-60; Gifford Lecturer, University of Edinburgh, 1971-73; Margaret Harris Lecturer, University of Dundee, 1981; Harry Jelema Lecturer, Calvin College, Grand Rapids, 1987; Reader in Philosophy, Oxford University, 1990-96. Publications: Principles of Politics, 1966, 2nd edition, 1985; The Concept of Probability, 1970; The Freedom of the Will, 1970; The Nature of Mind, 1972; The Development of Mind, 1973; A Treatise on Time and Space, 1973; Essays on Freedom and Grace, 1976; Democracy and Participation, 1976; On Justice, 1980; Space, Time and Causality, 1985; The Future, 1989; Space, Time and Electromagnetism, 1990; Responsibility, 1993; Ethical Economics, 1996. Contributions to: Scholarly journals. Memberships: Fellow, British Academy; British Society for the Philosophy of Science, president, 1991-93. Address: Lambrook House, East Lambrook, Somerset TA13 5HW, England.

LUCAS Stephen E, b. 5 Oct 1946, White Plains, New York, USA. Professor. m. Patricia Vore, 14 June 1969, 2 sons. Education: BA, University of California, Santa Barbara, 1968; MA, 1970, PhD, 1973, Pennsylvania State University. Appointment: Professor, University of Wisconsin at Madison. Publications: Portents of Rebellion: Rhetoric and Revolution in Philadelphia 1765-1776, 1976; The Art of Public Speaking, 1983, fifth edition, 1995; Justifying America: The Declaration of Independence as a Rhetorical Document, 1989; George Washington: The Wisdom of an American Patriot, 1997. Contributions to: Professional journals. Honour: Golden Anniversary Book Award, Speech Communication Association, 1979. Memberships: Speech Communication Association; International Society for the History of Rhetoric; Society for Eighteenth-Century Studies; Organization of American Historians. Address: Department of

Communication Arts, University of Wisconsin, Madison, WI 57306, USA.

LUCIE-SMITH John Edward McKenzie, (Peter Kershaw), b. 27 Feb 1933, Kingston, Jamaica, West Indies. Writer. Education: King's School, Canterbury; MA Hons, Modern History, Merton College, Oxford. Appointments: Education Officer, Royal Air Force, 1954-56; Advertising copywriter, 1956-66; Freelance author, journalist, and broadcaster 1966-; Consultant, curator or co-curator of a number of exhibitions in Britain and the USA and author of exhibition catalogues. Publications: Moments in Art since 1945 (entitled Late Modern in the US), 1969; A Concise History of French Painting, 1971; Symbolist Art, 1972; Eroticism in Western Art, 1972; Fantin-Latour, 1977; A Concise History of Furniture, 1979; A Cultural Calendar of the Twentieth Century, 1979; Art in the Seventies, 1980; The Story of Craft, 1981; A History of Industrial Design, 1983; A Thames and Hudson Dictionary of Art Terms, 1984; Art of the 1930s, 1985; American Art Now, 1985; Lives of the Twentieth Century Artists, 1986; Sculpture Since 1945, 1987; Art of the Eighties, 1990; Art Deco Painting, 1990; Art and Civilization, 1992; The Faber Book of Art Anecdotes, 1992; Harry Holland, 1992; Wendy Taylor, 1992; Alexander, 1992; Other publications include four collections of his own verse, two standard anthologies (the Penguin Book of Elizabethan Verse and British Poetry Since 1945), a biography of Joan of Arc, a history of piracy and an autobiography. Membership: Royal Literary Society, fellow. Address: c/o Rogers, Coleridge and White, 20 Powis Mews, London W11 1JN, England.

LUCKLESS John. See: **IRVING Clifford.**

LUDLUM Robert, (Jonathan Ryder, Michael Shepherd), b. 25 May 1927, New York, New York, USA. Author. m. Mary Ryducha, 31 Mar 1951, 2 sons, 1 daughter. Education: BA, Wesleyan University, 1951. Publications: The Scarlatti Inheritance, 1971; The Osterman Weekend, 1972; The Matlock Paper, 1973; Trevayne, 1973; The Cry of the Halidon, 1974; The Rhinemann Exchange, 1974; The Road to Gandolfo, 1975; The Gemini Contenders, 1976; The Chancellor Manuscript, 1977; The Holcroft Covenant, 1978; The Matarese Circle, 1979; The Bourne Identity, 1980; The Parsifal Mosaic, 1982; The Aquitaine Progression, 1984; The Bourne Supremacy, 1986; The Icarus Agenda, 1988; The Bourne Ultimatum, 1990; The Road to Omaha, 1992; The Scorpio Illusion, 1993; The Apocalypse Watch, 1995. Honours: Several awards and grants. Memberships: American Federation of Television and Radio Artists; Authors Guild; Authors League of America; Screen Actors Guild. Address: c/o Henry Morrison, Box 235, Bedford Hills, NY 10507, USA.

LUDWIKOWSKI Rett Ryszard, b. 6 Nov 1943, Skawina-Krakow, Poland. Professor of Law. m. Anna Ludwikowski, 19 Dec 1994, 1 son, 1 daughter. Education: LLM Law, PhD Law, Jagiellonian University. Publications: Main Currents of Polish Political Thought, 1982; The Crisis of Communism, Its Meaning, Origins and Phases, 1986; America and the World of Business, 1991; Continuity and Change in Poland, 1991: The Beginning of the Constitutional Era: A Comparative Study of the First American and European Constitutions (with William F Fox Jr), 1993; Constitution-Making in the Region of Former Soviet Dominance, 1996; Regulations of International Trade and Business, 1996. Honours: Various research grants; Residential Fellowship, Max-Planck-Institute, Hamburg, Germany, 1990.   Address: Columbus School of Law, The Catholic University of America, Washington, DC 20064, USA.

LUEBKE Frederick (Carl), b. 26 Jan 1927, Reedsburgh, Wisconsin, USA. Professor of History Emeritus. Education: BS, Concordia University, River Forest, Illinois, 1950; MA, Claremont Graduate School, 1958; PhD, University of Nebraska, 1966. Appointments: Associate Professor, 1968-72, Professor, 1972-87, Charles Mach Distinguished Professor of History, 1987-94, Professor Emeritus, 1994-, University of Nebraska; Editor, Great Plains Quarterly, 1980-84; Director, Center for Great Plains Studies, 1983-88. Publications: Immigrants and Politics, 1969; Ethnic Voters and the Election of Lincoln (editor), 1971; Bonds of Loyalty: German-Americans and World War I, 1974; The Great Plains: Environment and Culture (editor), 1979; Ethnicity on the Great Plains (editor), 1980; Vision and Refuge: Essays on the Literature of the Great Plains (co-editor), 1981; Mapping the North American Plains (co-editor), 1987; Germans in Brazil: A Comparative History of Cultural Conflict During World War I, 1987; Germans in the New World: Essays in the History of Immigration, 1990; A Harmony of the Arts: The

Nebraska State Capital (editor), 1990; Nebraska: An Illustrated History, 1995. Contributions to: Professional journals. Address: 3117 Woodsdale Boulevard, Lincoln, NE 68502, USA.

LUELLEN Valentina. See: **POLLEY Judith Anne.**

LUHRMANN Tanya Marie, b. 24 Feb 1959, Dayton, Ohio, USA. Associate Professor of Anthropology. Education: BA summa cum laude, Harvard University, 1981; MPhil, Social Anthropology, 1982, PhD, Social Anthropology, 1986, University of Cambridge. Appointments: Research Fellow, Christ's College, Cambridge, England, 1985-89; Associate Professor of Anthropology, University of California at San Diego, USA, 1989-. Publications: Persuasions of the Witch's Craft, 1989; The Good Parsi, 1996. Contributions to: Professional journals. Honours: Bowdoin Prize, 1981; National Science Foundation Graduate Fellow, 1982-85; Emanuel Miller Prize, 1983; Partingdon Prize, 1985; Stirling Prize, 1986; Fulbright Award, 1990. Memberships: American Anthropology Association; Society for Psychological Anthropology; Royal Anthropological Institute. Address: c/o Department of Anthropology, University of California at San Diego, 0101, La Jolla, CA 92093, USA.

LUKACS John Adalbert, b. 31 Jan 1924, Budapest, Hungary (US citizen, 1953). Professor of History (retired); Writer. m. (1) Helen Schofield, 29 May 1953, dec 1970, 1 son, 1 daughter, (2) Stephanie Harvey, 18 May 1974. Education: PhD, Palatine Joseph University, 1946. Appointments: Professor of History, 1974-94, Chairman, Department of History, 1947-74, Chestnut Hill College, Philadelphia; Visiting Professor, La Salle College, 1949-82; Columbia University, 1954-55; University of Toulouse, 1964-65; University of Pennsylvania, 1964, 1967, 1968, 1995-97; Johns Hopkins University, 1970-71; Fletcher School of Law and Diplomacy, 1971-72; Princeton University, 1988; University of Budapest, 1991. Publications: The Great Powers and Eastern Europe, 1953; A History of the Cold War, 1961, new edition, 1966; The Decline and Rise of Europe, 1965; Historical Consciousness, 1968, 2nd edition, 1985; The Passing of the Modern Age, 1970; The Last European War, 1939-41, 1976; 1945: Year Zero, 1978; Philadelphia: Patricians and Philistines, 1900-1950, 1981; Outgrowing Democracy: A History of the US in the 20th Century, 1984; Budapest 1900, 1988; Confessions of an Original Sinner, 1990; The Duel: Hitler vs Churchill 10 May-31 August 1940, 1991; The End of the 20th Century (and the End of the Modern Age), 1993; Destinations Past, 1994; George F Kennan and the Origins of Containment 1944-46 - The Kennan-Lukacs Correspondence, 1997; The Hitler of History, 1997. Contributions to: Professional journals. Honours: Ingersoll Prize, 1991; Cross of Merit, Republic of Hungary. Memberships: American Catholic Historical Association, president, 1977; Society of American Historians, fellow;. Address: Valley Park Road, Phoenixville, PA 19460, USA.

LUKAS J(ay) Anthony, b. 25 Apr 1933, New York, New York, USA. Journalist. m. Linda Healey, 18 Sept 1982. Education: BA, Harvard University, 1955; Postgraduate Studies, Free University of Berlin, 1955-56. Appointments: Staff, Baltimore Sun, 1958-62, New York Times, 1962-72; Nieman Fellow, Harvard University, 1968-69; Senior Editor, 1972-77, Associate Editor, 1977-78, More Journalism Review; Contributing Editor, New Times magazine, 1973-75; Visiting Lecturer, 1973, Fellow, 1973-78, Yale University; Adjunct Professor, School of Public Communication, Boston University, 1977-78, School of the Arts, Columbia University, 1995; Adjunct Lecturer, Kennedy School of Government, Harvard University, 1979-80; Editorial Board, Book-of-the-Month Club, 1989-94. Publications: The Barnyard Epithet and Other Obscenities: Notes on the Chicago Conspiracy Trial, 1970; Don't Shoot--We Are Your Children, 1971; Nightmare: The Underside of the Nixon Years, 1976; Common Ground: A Turbulent Decade in the Lives of Three American Families, 1985; Big Trouble, 1997. Contributions to: Periodicals. Honours: George Polk Memorial Award, Long Island University, 1967; Pulitzer Prizes for Local Special Reporting, 1968, and for General Non-Fiction, 1986; Page One Award, New York Newspaper Guild, 1968; Mike Berger Award, Columbia School of Journalism, 1968; Guggenheim Fellowship, 1979-80; American Book Award, 1985; National Book Critics Circle Award, 1986; Robert F Kennedy Book Award, 1986; Literary Lion, New York Public Library, 1986; Political Book of the Year Award, Washington Monthly, 1986. Memberships: Authors Guild, secretary, 1989-91, president 1995-97; Phi Beta Kappa; Signet Society; Society of American Historians, fellow. Address: 890 West End Avenue, New York, NY 10025, USA.

LUKAS Richard Conrad, b. 29 Aug 1937, Lynn, Massachusetts, USA. Historian; Professor. Education: BA, 1957, PhD, 1963, MA, 1970, Florida State University. Appointments: Research Consultant, US Air Force Historical Archives, 1957-58; Assistant Professor, 1963-66, Associate Professor, 1966-69, Professor, 1969-83, University Professor of History, 1983-89, Tennessee Technological University, Cookeville; Professor, Wright State University, Lake Campus, 1989-92; Adjunct Professor, University of South Florida, Fort Myers, 1993-. Publications: Eagles East: The Army Air Forces and the Soviet Union, 1941-45, 1970; From Metternich to the Beatles (editor), 1973; The Strange Allies: The United States and Poland 1941-45, 1978; Bitter Legacy: Polish-American Relations in the Wake of World War II, 1982; Forgotten Holocaust: The Poles under German Occupation, 1986; Out of the Inferno: Poles Remember the Holocaust, 1989; Did the Children Cry?: Hitler's War Against Jewish and Polish Children, 1994. Honours: Doctor of Humane Letters (LHD), 1987; Polonia Restituta, 1988. Address: 1344 Rock Dove Court, D-104, Punta Gorda, FL 33950, USA.

LUKE Thomas. See: **MASTERTON Graham**.

LUKER Nicholas John Lydgate, b. 26 Jan 1945, Leeds, England. University Senior Lecturer in Russian. 1 son. Education: Hertford College, Oxford, England, 1964-68; MA, French, Russian, Oxford; Lecteur d'Anglais, University of Grenoble, France, 1967; Postgraduate Scholar, Department of Slavonic Studies, 1968-70, PhD, 1971, University of Nottingham, England. Appointment: Senior Lecturer in Russian, University of Nottingham. Publications: Alexander Kuprin, 1978; Alexander Grin: The Seeker of Adventure, 1978; Alexander Grin: The Forgotten Visionary, 1980; An Anthology of Russian-Neorealism, 1982; Fifty Years on: Gorky and his Time, 1987; Alexander Grin: Selected Short Stories, 1987; From Furmanov to Sholokhov, 1988; In Defence of a Reputation, 1990; The Russian Short Story, 1900-1917, 1991; Yury Miloslavsky, Urban Romances, editor and translator, 1994; After the Watershed, 1995. Contributions to: Numerous articles in various journals in field of Russian literature. Honours: Visiting Lecturer in Russian, Victoria University of Wellington, New Zealand, 1976; Visiting Fellow, Department of Russian, University of Otago, Dunedin, New Zealand, 1991. Memberships: British Association of Slavists; Executive Committee, RLUSC for UK Universities. Address: Department of Slavonic Studies, University of Nottingham, Nottingham NG7 2RD, England.

LULUA Abdul-Wahid, b. 16 July 1931, Mowsil, Iraq. Professor of English Literature. m. Mariam Abdul-Bagi, 22 July 1962, 1 son, 1 daughter. Education: Licence-es-Lettres, English, Ecole Normale Superieure, University of Baghdad, 1952; EdM, English, Harvard University, USA, 1957; PhD, English, Western Reserve University, Cleveland, Ohio, 1962. Appointments: Lecturer, Assistant Professor, English Literature, Head, Department of European Languages, College of Education (formerly Ecole Normale Superieure), Baghdad, 1962-67; Assistant Professor, English Literature, 1967-70, Associate Professor, English Literature, Faculty of Arts, 1970-71, 1972-77, University of Kuwait; Visiting Scholar, Cambridge University, England, 1971-72; Associate Professor, English Literature, 1983, Professor, English Literature, 1983-89, Chairman, Department of English Language and Literature, 1983-84, Yarmouk University; Jordan; Professor, English Literature, United Arab Emirates University, 1989-. Publications: Critical Studies: In Search of Meaning, 1973, 2nd edition, 1983; T S Eliot, The Waste Land: The Poet and the Poem, 1980, 2nd edition, 1986; Blowing into Ashes, 1982, 2nd edition, 1989; Aspect of the Moon, 1990; Arabic Poetry and the Rise of European Love Lyrics; Various translations. Contributions to: Major Arabic magazines, Iraq and Middle East. Memberships: Modern Humanities Research Association, Cambridge; Association Internationale de Litterature Comparative. Address: c/o Riad El-Rayyes Books, 56 Knightsbridge, London SW1X 7NJ, England.

LUNARI Luigi, b. 3 Jan 1934, Milan, Italy. Writer. m. Laura Pollaroli, 8 July 1961, 1 son, 1 daughter. Education: Degree in Law, University of Milan, 1956; Diploma in Common Law, City of London College, 1958; Composition and Orchestra Conducting, Academy Chigiana, Siena, 1978. Appointments: Director, Study Office of Piccolo Teatro, 1961-82; Music and Drama Correspondent, Avanti, 1978-; Professor, History of Dramatic Art, University of Modern Languages, 1984-. Publications: L'Old Vic di Londra, 1959; Laurence Olivier, 1959; Il movimento drammatico irlandese, 1960; Il teatro irlandese: storia e antologia, 1961; Henry Irving e il teatro inglese dell'800, 1962; Maria di Nazareth, 1986. Contributions to: Il giornale nuovo, 1991. Memberships: International Society of Authors; International Society of Dramatists; PEN Club. Address: 20047 Brugherid, Via Volturno 80, Milan, Italy.

LUND Gerald Niels, b. 12 Sept 1939, Fountain Green, Utah, USA. Educator; Writer. m. Lynn Stanard, 5 June 1963, 3 sons, 4 daughters. Education: BA, Sociology, 1965, MS, Sociology, 1969, Brigham Young University; Further graduate studies, Pepperdine University. Appointment: Faculty, Brigham Young University. Publications: The Coming of the Lord, 1971; This is Your World, 1973; One in Thine Hand, 1981; The Alliance, 1983; Leverage Point, 1986; Freedom Factor, 1987; The Work and the Glory: Vol I, Pillar of Light, 1990, Vol II, Like a Fire is Burning, 1991, Vol III, Truth Will Prevail, 1992, Vol IV, Gold to Refine, 1993, Vol V, A Season of Joy, 1994. Contributions to: Monographs and magazines. Honours: Outstanding Teacher in Continuing Education, Brigham Young University, 1985; Best Novel Awards, Association of Mormon Letters, 1991, 1993. Address: 1157 East 1500 South, Bountiful, UT 84010, USA.

LUNN Janet Louise, b. 28 Dec 1928, Dallas, Texas, USA. Writer. m. Richard Lunn, 1 Mar 1950, 4 sons, 1 daughter. Education: Queen's University, Kingston, Ontario. Appointments: Writer-in-Residence, Regina Public Library, Saskatchewan, 1982-83, Kitchener Public Library, Ontario, 1987, Ottawa University, Ontario, 1993. Publications: The Country, 1967; Double Spell, 1968; Larger Than Life, 1979; The Twelve Dancing Princesses, 1979; The Root Cellar, 1981; Shadow in Hawthorn Bay, 1986; Amos's Sweater, 1988; Duck Cakes for Sale, 1989; One Hundred Shining Candles, 1990; The Story of Canada, 1992; Ghost Stories for Children (editor), 1994. Contributions to: Periodicals. Address: RR No 2, Hillier, Ontario K0K 2J0, Canada.

LUPOFF Richard Allen, b. 21 Feb 1935, New York, New York, USA. Author. m. Patricia Enid Loring, 27 Aug 1958, 2 sons, 1 daughter. Education: BA, University of Miami at Coral Gables, 1956. Appointments: Editor, Canaveral Press, 1963-70; Contributing Editor, Crawdaddy Magazine, 1968-71; Science Fiction Eye, 1988-90; Editor, Canyon Press, 1986-. Publications: Edgar Rice Burroughs: Master of Adventure, 1965; All in Color for a Dime, 1971; Sword of the Demon, 1977; Space War Blues, 1978; Sun's End, 1984; Circumpolar!, 1984; Lovecrafts Book, 1985; The Forever City, 1987; The Comic Book Killer, 1988; The Classic Car Killer, 1992; The Bessie Blue Killer, 1994; The Sepia Siren Killer, 1994; The Cover Girl Killer, 1995. Contributions to: Ramparts; Los Angeles Times; Washington Post; San Francisco Chronicle; New York Times; Magazine of Fantasy and Science Fiction. Honour: Hugo Award, 1963. Address: 3208 Claremont Avenue, Berkeley, CA 94705, USA.

LURIE Alison, b. 3 Sept 1926, Chicago, Illinois, USA. Writer. Education: Radcliffe College. Appointments: Frederic J Whiton Professor of American Literature, Cornell University; Editor, The Oxford Book of Modern Fairy Tales; Co-editor, The Garland Library of Children's Classics. Publications: Love and Friendship, 1962; The Nowhere City, 1965; Imaginary Friends, 1967; Real People, 1969; The War Between the Tates, 1974; V R Lang: Poems and Plays, 1975; Only Children, 1979; Clever Gretchen and Other Forgotten Folktales, 1980; The Heavenly Zoo, 1980; The Language of Clothes, 1981; Fabulous Beast, 1981; Foreign Affairs, 1984; The Truth About Lorin Jones, 1988; Don't Tell the Grownups: Subversive Children's Literature, 1990. Contributions to: Art and Antiques; Children's Literature; Harper's; House and Garden; Lear's; Ms; New York Times Book Review; New York Woman; Observer; Psychology Today; Times Literary Supplement; Vanity Fair; Vogue. Honours: American Academy of Arts and Letters Award in Fiction, 1984; Pulitzer Prize in Fiction, 1985; Radcliffe College Alumnae Award, 1987; Prix Femina Etranger, 1989. Address: English Department, Cornell University, Ithaca, NY 14853, USA.

LURIE Morris, b. 30 Oct 1938, Melbourne, Australia. Writer. Education: Architecture studies, Royal Melbourne Institute of Technology, 1957-60, no degree. Appointments: Writer-in-Residence, Latrobe University, 1984; Holmesglen Tafe, 1992. Publications: Rappaport, 1966; The Twenty-Seventh Annual African Hippopotamus Race, 1969; Flying Home, 1978; Outrageous Behaviour, 1984; Whole Life, 1987. Novels: Seven books for Grossmar, 1983; Madness 1991. Contributions to: Virginia Quarterly Review; The Times; Punch; Telegraph Magazine; The Age; National Times; New Yorker; Stories broadcast on BBC, and plays on ABC. Honours: State of Victoria Short Story Award, 1973; National Book Council Selection, 1980; Children's

Book Council, 1983; Bicentennial Banjo Award, 1988. Address: 2/3 Finchley Court, Hawthorn, Victoria 3122, Australia.

LUSTBADER Eric Van, b. 24 Dec 1946, New York, New York, USA. Writer. m. Victoria Lustbader. Education: BA, Columbia University, 1968. Publications: The Sunset Warrior, 1977; Shallows of Night, 1978; Dai-San, 1978; Beneath an Opal Moon, 1980; The Ninja, 1980; Sirens, 1981; Black Heart, 1982; The Miko, 1984; Jian, 1985; Shan, 1987; Zero, 1988; French Kiss, 1988; White Ninja, 1989; Angel Eyes, 1991; Black Blade, 1993; The Keishe, 1993; Batman: The Last Angel, 1994; The Floating City, 1994. Contributions to: Magazines. Address: c/o Henry Morrison Inc, Box 235, Bedford Hills, NY 10507, USA.

LUSTGARTEN Celia Sophie, b. 24 Oct 1941, New York, New York, USA. Consultant; Writer. Contributions to: Various publications. Honour: First Prize, Short Story, Alternate Realities Society and Imaginative Fiction Society, Victoria, British Columbia, 1986. Membership: Poets and Writers. Address: 317 Third Avenue, San Francisco, CA 94118, USA.

LUSTIG Arnost, b. 21 Dec 1926, Prague, Czechoslovakia. Writer; Screenwriter; Educator. m. Vera Wieislitz, 24 July 1949, 1 son, 1 daughter. Education: MA, College of Political and Social Science, Prague, 1951. Appointments: Arab-Israeli Correspondent, Radio Prague, 1948-49; Correspondent, Czechoslovak Radio, 1950-68; Screenwriter, Barrandov Film Studies, Prague, 1960-68; Writer, Kibutz Hachotrim, Israel, 1968-69; Screenwriter, Jadran Film Studio, Zagreb, 1969-70; Visiting Lecturer, English, 1971-72, Visiting Professor, English, 1972-73, Drake University; Professor, Literature and Film, American University, Washington, DC, 1973–; Head, Czechoslovak film delegation, San Sebastian Film Festival, 1968; Karlsbad Film Festival, jury member, 1965, 1996. Publications: Night and Hope, 1958; Diamonds of the Night, 1958; Street of Lost Brothers, 1959; Dita Saxova, 1962; My Acquaintance Vili Feld, 1962; A Prayer for Katarina Horovitzova, 1964; Nobody Will be Humiliated, 1964; Bitter Smells of Almonds, 1968; Darling, 1969; The Unloved (From the Diary of a Seventeen Year Old), 1986; Indecent Dreams, 1988. Films/Screenplays: Transport from Paradise, 1963; Diamonds of the Night, 1964; Dita Saxova, 1968; A Bit to Eat, 1960; The Triumph of Memory, 1989. Honour: Doctor of Hebrew Letters, Spertus College, 1986. Address: 4000 Tunlaw Road North West, Apt 825, Washington, DC 20007, USA.

LUTTWAK Edward N(icholae), b. 4 Nov 1942, Arad, Romania (US citizen, 1981). Political Scientist; Author. m. Dalya Iaari, 14 Dec 1970, 1 son, 1 daughter. Education: Carmel College, England; BSc, London School of Economics and Political Science, 1964; PhD, Johns Hopkins University, 1975. Appointments: Associate Director, Washington Center of Foreign Policy Research, District of Columbia, 1972-75; Visiting Professor of Political Science, Johns Hopkins University, 1973-78; Senior Fellow, 1976-87, Research Professor in International Security Affairs, 1978-82, Arleigh Burke Chair in Strategy, 1987-, Director, Geo-Economics, 1991-, Center for Strategic and International Studies, Washington, DC; Nimitz Lecturer, University of California, Berkeley, 1987; Tanner Lecturer, Yale University, 1989. Publications: A Dictionary of Modern War, 1971, new edition with Stuart Koehl, 1991; The Grand Strategy of the Roman Empire: From the First Century A.D. to the Third, 1976; The Economic and Military Balance Between East and West 1951-1978 (co-editor with Herbert Block), 1978; Sea Power in the Mediterranean (with R G Weinland), 1979; Strategy and Politics: Collected Essays, 1980; The Grand Strategy of the Soviet Union, 1983; The Pentagon and the Art of War: The Question of Military Reform, 1985; Strategy and History, 1985; On the Meaning of Victory: Essays on Strategy, 1986; Global Security: A Review of Strategic and Economic Issues (co-editor with Barry M Blechman), 1987; Strategy: The Logic of War and Peace, 1987; The Endangered American Dream: How to Stop the United States from Becoming a Third World Country and How to Win the Geo-Economic Struggle for Industrial Supremacy, 1993. Contributions to: Numerous books and periodicals. Address: c/o Center for Strategic and International Studies, Georgetown University, 1800 K Street North West, Washington, DC 20006, USA.

LUTYENS Mary, (Esther Wyndham), b. 31 July 1908, England. Author. Education: Queen's College, London. Publications: Forthcoming Marriages, 1933; Perchance to Dream, 1935; Rose and Thorn, 1936; Spider's Silk, 1938; Family Colouring, 1940; A Path of Gold, 1941; Together and Alone, 1942; So Near to Heaven, 1943; Julie

and the Narrow Valley, 1944; And Now There Is You, 1953; Meeting in Venice, 1956; To Be Young, 1959; Lady Lytton's Court Diary (editor), 1961; Effie in Venice, 1965; Millais and the Ruskins, 1967; Freedom from the Known by Krishnamurti (editor), 1969; The Only Revolution by Krishnamurti (editor), 1970; The Ruskins and the Grays, 1972; Cleo, 1973; Krishnamurti: The Years of Awakening, 1975; The Lyttons of India, 1979; Edwin Lutyens, 1980; Krishnamurti: The Years of Fulfilment, 1982; Krishnamurti: The Open Door, 1988; The Life and Death of Krishnamurti, 1989; Repv, 1991. Contributions to: Journals. Address: 8 Elizabeth Close, Randolph Avenue, London W9 1BN, England.

LUTYENS Mary (Esther Wyndham), b. 1908, British. Writer of Historical, Romantic, Gothic publications; Biographer. Publications: Forthcoming Marriages, 1933; Perchance to Dream, 1935; Rose and Thorn, 1936; Spider's Silk, 1938; Family Colouring, 1940; A Path of Gold, 1941; Together and Alone, 1942; So Near to Heaven, 1943; Julie and the Narrow Valley, 1944; And Now There is You, 1953; Meeting in Venice, 1956; To Be Young, 1959; editor, Lady Lytton's Court Diary, 1961; Effie in Voice, 1965; Millais and the Ruskins, 1967; editor, Freedom from the Known by Krishnamurti, 1969; editor, The Only Revolution by Krishnamurti, 1970; The Ruskins and the Grays, 1972; Cleo, 1973; Krishnamurti: The Years of Awakening, 1975; The Lyttons of India, 1979; Edwin Lutyens, 1980; Krishnamurti: The Years of Fulfilment, 1982; Krishnamurti: The Open Door, 1988; The Life and Death of Krishnamurti, 1989; Repv, 1991; Eight novels published by Mills & Boon. Contributions to: Apollo, TLS, Cornhill, Walpole Society Journal. Honours: FRSL. Literary Agent: Jane Turnbull, 13 Wendall Road, London W12 9RS. Address: 8 Elizabeth Close, Randolph Avenue, London W9 1Bn, England.

LUTZ John Thomas, b. 11 Sept 1939, Dallas, Texas, USA. Writer. m. Barbara Jean Bradley, 15 Mar 1958, 1 son, 2 daughters. Education: Meramac Community College. Publications: The Truth of the Matter, 1971; Buyer Beware, 1976; Bonegrinder, 1977; Lazarus Man, 1979; Jericho Man, 1980; The Shadow Man, 1981; Exiled with Steven Greene, 1982; The Eye with Bill Pronzini, 1984; Nightlines, 1985; The Right to Sing the Blues, 1986; Tropical Heat, 1986; Ride the Lightning, 1987; Scorcher, 1987; Kiss, 1988; Shadowtown, 1988; Time Exposure, 1989; Flame, 1990; Diamond Eyes, 1990; SWF Seeks Same, 1990; Bloodfire, 1991; Hot, 1992; Dancing with the Dead, 1992; Spark, 1993; Shadows Everywhere (short stories), 1994; Torch, 1994; Thicker Than Blood, 1994. Contributions to: Anthologies and magazines. Honours: Scroll, 1981, Edgar Award, 1983, Mystery Writers of America; Shamus Awards, 1982, 1988. Memberships: Mystery Writers of America; Private Eye Writers of America, board of directors. Address: 880 Providence Avenue, Webster Groves, MO 63119, USA.

LUX Thomas, b. 10 Dec 1946, Northampton, Massachusetts, USA. Poet; Teacher. m. Jean Kilbourne, 1983, 1 daughter. Education: BA, Emerson College, Boston, 1970; University of Iowa, 1971. Appointments: Managing Editor, Iowa Review, 1971-72, Ploughshares, 1973; Poet-in-Residence, Emerson College, 1972-75; Faculty, Sarah Lawrence College, 1975, Warren Wilson College, 1980-, Columbia University, 1980-. Publications: The Land Sighted, 1970; Memory's Handgrenade, 1972; The Glassblower's Breath, 1976; Sunday, 1979; Like a Wide Anvil From the Moon the Light, 1980; Massachusetts, 1981; Tarantulas on the lifebuoy, 1983; Half Promised Land, 1986; Sunday: Poems, 1989; The Drowned River, 1990; A Boat in the Forest, 1992; Pecked to Death by Swans, 1993; Split Horizon, 1994; The Sanity of Earth and Grass (editor with Jane Cooper and Sylvia Winner), 1994. Honours: Bread Loaf Scholarship, 1970; MacDowell Colony Fellowships, 1973, 1974, 1976, 1978, 1980, 1982; National Endowment for the Arts Grants, 1976, 1981, 1988; Guggenheim Fellowship, 1988; Kingsley Tufts Poetry Award, 1995. Address: 67 Temple Street, West Newton, MA 02164, USA.

LYALL Gavin Tudor, b. 9 May 1932, Birmingham, England. Author; Journalist. m. Katharine Whitehorn, 4 Jan 1958, 2 sons. Education: MA, Pembroke College, Cambridge, 1956; MA, 1986. Appointments: Staff, Picture Post, 1956-57; Worked on BBC TV's Tonight programme, 1958-59; Staff, Sunday Times, 1959-63. Publications: The Wrong Side of the Sky, 1961; The Most Dangerous Game, 1964; Midnight Plus One, 1965; Shooting Script, 1966; Freedom's Battle, Vol II, 1968; Venus with Pistol, 1969; Blame the Dead, 1972; Judas Country, 1975; Operation Warboard, 1976; The Secret Servant, 1980; The Conduct of Major Maxim, 1982; The Crocus List, 1985; Uncle Target, 1989; Spy's Honour, 1993; Flight from

Honour, 1996. Contributions to: Observer; Sunday Telegraph; Punch; London Illustrated News. Honours: Silver Dagger, Crime Writer's Association, 1964, 1965. Memberships: Crime Writers' Association, chairman, 1966-67; Detection Club; Society of Authors. Address: 14 Provost Road, London NW3 4ST, England.

LYKIARD Alexis (Constantine), b. 2 Jan 1940, Athens, Greece. Poet; Writer; Translator. Education: BA, 1962, MA, 1966, King's College, Cambridge. Appointments: Creative Writing Tutor, Arvon Foundation, 1974-; Writer-in-Residence, Sutton Central Library, 1976-77, Loughborough Art College, 1982-83, Tavistock, Devon Libraries, 1983-85, HMP Channings Wood, 1988-89, HMP Haslar, 1992. Publications: Lobsters, 1961; Journey of the Alchemist, 1963; The Summer Ghosts, 1964; Wholly Communion (editor), 1965; Zones, 1966; Paros Poems, 1967; A Sleeping Partner, 1967; Robe of Skin, 1969; Strange Alphabet, 1970; Best Horror Stories of J Sheridan Le Fanu (editor), 1970; Eight Lovesongs, 1972; The Stump, 1973; Greek Images, 1973; Lifelines, 1973; Instrument of Pleasure, 1974; Last Throes, 1976; Milesian Fables, 1976; A Morden Tower Reading, 1976; The Drive North, 1977; New Stories 2 (editor), 1977; Scrubbers, 1983; Cat Kin, 1985; Out of Exile, 1986; Safe Levels, 1990; Living Jazz, 1991; Beautiful is Enough, 1992; Selected Poems, 1956-96, 1997. Other: Many French translations. Address: c/o A M Heath and Co Ltd, 79 St Martin's Lane, London, EC2N 4AA, England.

LYNCH Audry Louise, b. 18 July 1933, Cambridge, Massachusetts, USA. Guidance Counsellor; Community College English Instructor. m. Gregory Lynch, 8 Sept 1956, 1 son, 2 daughters. Education: BA, Harvard University, 1955; EdM, Boston University, 1968; EdD, University of San Francisco, 1983. Publications: With Steinbeck in the Sea of Cortez, 1991; Father Joe Young: A Priest and His People, 1993. Contributions to: Yankee Magazine; West Magazine; Parade Magazine; Writer; International Herald Tribune. Memberships: California Writers Club; Writers Connection. Address: 20774 Meadow Oak Road, Saratoga, CA 95070, USA.

LYNCH Frances. See: **COMPTON D(avid) G(uy).**

LYNCH John, b. 11 Jan 1927, Boldon, England. Professor Emeritus; Historian. Education: MA, University of Edinburgh, 1952; PhD, University of London, 1955. Appointments: Lecturer in History, University of Liverpool, 1954-61; Lecturer, Reader and Professor of Latin American History, University College, London, 1961-74; Professor of Latin American History and Director of Institute of Latin American Studies, University of London, 1974-87. Publications: Spanish Colonial Administration 1782-1810: The Intendant System in the Viceroyalty of the Río de la Plata, 1958; Spain Under the Habsburgs, 2 volumes, 1964, 1967, 2nd edition, revised, 1981; The Origins of the Latin American Revolutions 1808-1826 (with R A Humphreys), 1965; The Spanish American Revolutions 1808-1826, 1973, 2nd edition, revised, 1986; Argentine Dictator: Juan Manuel de Rosas 1829-1852, 1981; The Cambridge History of Latin America (with others), Vol 3, 1985, Vol 4, 1986; Bourbon Spain 1700-1808, 1989; Caudillos in Spanish America 1800-1850, 1992; Latin American Revolutions 1808-1826: Old and New World Origins, 1994. Honours: Order of Andrés Bello, 1st Class, Venezuela, 1995; Encomienda Isabel La Católica, Spain, 1988; Doctor, Honoris Causa, University of Seville, 1990. Membership: Royal Historical Society, fellow. Address: 8 Templars Crescent, London N3 3QS, England.

LYNCH Timothy Jeremy Mahoney, b. 10 June 1952, San Francisco, California, USA. Lawyer; Classical Scholar; Author; Business Executive. Education: MS, JD, Civil Law, Taxation Law, Golden Gate University; MA, PhD, University of San Francisco, 1983; PhD, Classics, Divinity, Harvard University, 1988; JSD, Constitutional Law, Hastings Law Center, San Francisco; Postdoctoral research, Writing in Classics. Appointments: Chairman, Patristic, Biblical, Latin and Greek Literary Publications Group, Institute of Classical Studies; Chairman, Postdoctoral Research and Writing in Humanities Group, National Association of Scholars; Fellow, Harvard University Center for Hellenic Studies, 1991, 1993; Senior Research and Writing Fellow, Medieval Theological Philosophy manuscripts of St Gallen Monks, Medieval Academy of America. Publications: History of Europe, 5 volumes, 1987; Essays and Papers on US-Soviet Relations, Iran-British Relations, 1988; Legal Essays, 1990-94; Musical Papers, 1994; History of Classical Tradition, 20 volumes, 1995; Poems for children; Textbooks; Co-editor, co-author: Commentary on Classical Philology; Greek Hellenic Philosophy, Literary Translations and Commentary on Philodemus Project, 1995; 50 volumes on classical

philology, literary styles and analysis of Old Testament Exegesis, history of mediaeval and modern moral and ecumenical theological institutes. Contributions to: Journals. Honour: Member, International Platform Association; Eminent Scholar of the Year, National Association of Scholars, 1993. Memberships: American Philological Association, president, 1996-97; American Historical Association; Law Society of America; Society of Biblical Literature; American Institute of Archaeology. Address: 540 Jones Street, Suite 201, San Francisco, CA 94102-2022, USA.

LYNDS Dennis, (William Arden, Nick Carter, Michael Collins, John Crowe, Carl Dekker, Maxwell Grant, Mark Sadler), b. St Louis, Missouri, USA. Writer. m. (1) Doris Flood, div (2) Sheila McErlean, 2 daughters, (3) Gayle Hallenbeck Stone. Publications: Combat Soldier, 1962; Uptown Downtown, 1963; Why Girls Ride Sidesaddle (short stories), 1980; Freak, 1983; Minnesota Strip, 1987; Red Rosa, 1988; Castrato, 1989; Chasing Eights, 1990; The Irishman's Horse, 1991; Cassandra in Red, 1992; Crime, Punishment and Resurrection, 1992; Talking to the World, 1995; The Cadillac Cowboy, 1995. Address: 12 St Anne Drive, Santa Barbara, CA 93109, USA.

LYNN Jonathan, b. 3 Apr 1943, Bath, England. Theatre and Film Director; Actor; Writer. Education: MA, Pembroke College, Cambridge, 1964. Appointments: Artistic Director, Cambridge Theatre Company, 1976-81; Company Director, National Theatre, 1987. Publications: A Proper Man, 1976; The Complete Yes Minister, 1984; Yes Prime Minister Vol I, 1986; Yes Prime Minister Vol II, 1987; Mayday, 1993; Other: Various screenplays and television series. Address: c/o Peters, Fraser and Dunlop Ltd, The Chambers, Chelsea House, Lots Road, London SW10, England.

LYNTON Ann. See: **RAYNER Claire Berenice.**

LYON Bryce Dale, b. 22 Apr 1920, Bellevue, Ohio, USA. Professor of History. m. Mary Elizabeth Lewis, 3 June 1944, 1 son, 1 daughter. Education: AB, Baldwin-Wallace College, 1942; PhD, Cornell University, 1949. Appointments: Assistant Professor of History, University of Colorado, Boulder, 1949-51; Harvard University, 1951-56; Professor of History, University of California, Berkeley, 1959-65; Barnaby and Mary Critchfield Keeney Professor of History, 1965-, Chairman, Department of History, 1968-, Brown University. Publications: Medieval Institutions: Selected Essays, 1954; A Constitutional and Legal History of Medieval England, 1960, 2nd edition, 1980; A History of the World (with others), 1960; The High Middle Ages 1000-1300, 1964; Frankish Institutions Under Charlemagne (with M Lyon), 1968; A History of the Western World, 1969, 2nd edition, 1974; The Origins of the Middle Ages: Pirenne's Challenge to Gibbon, 1972; Studies of West European and Medieval Institutions, 1978; The Wardrobe Book of William de Norwell: 12 July 1338 to 27 May 1340 (with H S Lucas and M Lyon), 1983; The Firth of Annales History: The Letters of Lucien Febvre and Marc Bloch to Henri Pirenne 1921-1935 (with Mary Lyon), 1991. Address: Department of History, Brown University, Brown Station, Providence, RI 02912, USA.

LYON Elinor. See: **WRIGHT Elinor.**

LYONS Arthur, b. 5 Jan 1946, Los Angeles, California, USA. Writer. m. Marie Lyons. Education: BA, University of California, Santa Barbara, 1967. Publications: The Second Coming: Satanism in America, 1970; The Dead Are Discreet, 1974; All God's Children, 1975; The Killing Floor, 1976; Dead Ringer, 1977; Castles Burning, 1979; Hard Trade, 1981; At the Hands of Another, 1983; Three With a Bullet, 1985; Fast Fade, 1987; Unnatural Causes (with Thomas Noguchi), 1988; Satan Wants You, 1988; Other Poeple's Money, 1989; Physical Evidence (with Thomas Noguchi), 1990; The Blue Sense (with Marcello Truzzi), 1991; False Pretences, 1993. Address: c/o Putnam Publishing Group, 200 Madison Avenue, New York, NY 10016, USA.

LYONS Elena. See: **FAIRBURN Eleanor M.**

LYONS Garry Fairfax, b. 5 July 1956, Kingston-upon-Thames, England. Writer. m. Ruth Caroline Willis, 6 Apr 1985, 1 son, 1 daughter. Education: BA, English Literature, University of York, 1978; MA, Drama and Theatre Arts, University of Leeds, 1982. Appointments: Playwright-in-Residence, Major Road Theatre Company, 1983; Fellow in Theatre, University of Bradford, 1984-88. Major Productions: Echoes from the Valley, 1983; Mohicans, 1984; St Vitus' Boogie, 1985; Urban Jungle, 1985; The Green Violinist, 1986;

Irish Night, 1987; Divided Kingdoms, 1989; The People Museum, 1989; Dream Kitchen, 1992; Frankie and Tommy, 1992; Wicked Year, 1994. Membership: Theatre Writers' Union. Address: c/o International Creative Management, Oxford House, 76 Oxford Street, London W1N 0AX, England.

M

MA Zhuorong, b. 1 Aug 1929, Xiangtan City, Hunan, China. Research Fellow of Literature and Art. m. Chen Huixun, 15 Oct 1962, 1 son, 1 daughter. Education: Self-taught. Appointment: Chinese Hunan Comparative Literature Association Advisor, 1993. Publications: Papers on Art of Writing, 1984; A Study of Tian-Han's Dramas, 1987; Chinese-Western Religions and Literatures, 1991; A History of Religious Literatures of China, 1997; about 400 articles, poems and translations, 1948-96. Contributions to: Many magazines and journals. Honours: Hunan Literature and Art Award, 1981; Hunan Social Science Awards, 1991, 1994. Memberships: Chinese Writer's Association; Chinese Comparative Literature Association. Literary Agent: Beijing Gallant Auction Company, No 57 Bei-San-Huan Zhong-Lu, Beijing, China. Address: No 8, Mingxingli, Wuyi Road, Changsha, China.

MABBETT Ian William, b. 27 Apr 1939, London, England. University Academic. m. Jacqueline Diana June Towns, 11 Dec 1971, 2 daughters. Education: Jesus College, Oxford, 1957-63; BA (Oxon), 1960, DPhil (Oxon), 1963, MA (Oxon), 1964. Appointment: Faculty, Monash University. Publications: A Short History of India, 1968, 2nd edition, 1983; Modern China, The Mirage of Modernity, 1985; Kings and Emperors of Asia, 1985; Patterns of Kingship and Authority in Traditional Asia (editor), 1985; The Khmers (co-author), 1995. Contributions to: Hemisphere, Canberra; Asian Pacific Quarterly, Seoul; The Cambridge History of Southeast Asia. Honour: President, IXth World Sanskrit Conference, 1994. Memberships: Federation of Australian Writers; Australian Society of Authors. Address: c/o Department of History, Monash University, Clayton, Victoria 3168, Australia.

MABEY Richard Thomas, b. 20 Feb 1941, Berkhamsted, Hertfordshire, England, Writer; Broadcaster. Education: HA Hons, 1966, MA, 1971, St Catherine's College, Oxford. Appointment: Senior Editor, Penguin Books, 1966-73. Publications: The Pop Process, 1969; Food for Free, 1972; Unofficial Countryside, 1973; Street Flowers, 1976; Plants with a Purpose, 1977; The Common Ground, 1980; The Flowering of Britain, 1980; In a Green Shade, 1983; Oak and Company, 1983; Frampton Flora, 1985; Gilbert White, 1986; The Flowering of Kew, 1988; Home Country, 1990; Whistling in the Dark, 1993; Oxford Book of Nature Writing, editor, 1995; Flora Britannica, 1996. Contributions to: Times; Telegraph; Sunday Times; Observer; The Countryman; Nature; Modern Painters; The Independent. Honours: Information Book Award, Times Educational Supplement, 1977; Children's Book Award, New York Academy of Sciences, 1984; Whitbread Biography Award, 1986; Honorary DSc, University of St Andrews, 1997. Memberships: Botanical Society of British Isles, council, 1981-83; London Wildlife Trust, president, 1982-92; Plantlife, advisory council, 1990-; Open Spaces Society, advisory council, 1992-; Richard Jefferies Society, president, 1996-. Address: c/o Sheila Land Associates, 43 Doughty Street, London, England.

MAC AVOY Roberta Ann, b. 13 Dec 1949, Cleveland, Ohio, USA. Writer. Education: BA, Case Western Reserve University, 1971. Publications: Tea with the Black Dragon, Damiano, 1983; Damiano's Lute, Raphael, 1984; The Book of Kells (co-author), 1985; Twisting the Rope, 1986; The Grey Horse, 1987; The Third Eagle, 1989; Lens of the World, 1990. Address: Underhill at Nelson Farm, 1669 Nelson Road, Scotts Valley, CA 95066, USA.

MACADAMS William, b. 3 Dec 1944, Richmond, Indiana, USA. Writer. m. 2 sons. Appointment: Editor, Zygote Magazine, 1972. Publications: as Rob Morreale: Anxious to Please (novel), 1972; As William MacAdams: The Book: A Story, 1982; Ben Hecht: The Man Behind the Legend, 1990; Ben Hecht: A Biography, 1995; 701 Toughest Movie Trivia Questions of All Time, 1995. Contributions to: New York Times; Film Comment; Oui; New York Observer; Rolling Stone; Penthouse; Changes; Crawdaddy. Literary Agent: Doris Ashbrook. Address: 125 Richwood Drive, Richmond, IN 47374, USA.

MACALLAN Andrew. See: **LEASOR (Thomas) James.**

MACAULAY David (Alexander), b. 2 Dec 1946, Burton-on-Trent, England. Writer; Illustrator. m. (1) Janice Elizabeth Michel, 1970, div, 1 daughter, (2) Ruth Marris, 1978, div, (3) Charlotte Valerie. Education: Bachelor in Architecture, Rhode Island School of

Design, 1969. Publications: Cathedral: The Story of Its Construction, 1973; City: A Story of Roman Planning and Construction, 1974; Pyramid, 1975; Underground, 1976; Castle, 1977; Great Movements in Architecture, 1978; Motel of the Mysteries, 1979; Unbuilding, 1980; Electricity, 1983; Mill, 1983; BAAA, 1985; Why the Chicken Crossed the Road, 1987; The Way Things Work, 1988; Black and White, 1990; Ship, 1993; Shortcut, 1995. Honours: Caldecott Honor Books, 1973, 1977; Christopher Medal, 1991. Address: c/o Houghton Mifflin Co, 222 Berkeley Street, Boston, MA 02116, USA.

MACCARTHY Fiona, b. 23 Jan 1940, London, England. Biographer; Cultural Historian. m. David Mellor, 1966, 1 son, 1 daughter. Education: MA, English Language and Literature, Oxford University, 1961. Appointments: Reviewer, The Times, 1981-91, The Observer, 1991-. Publications: The Simple Life: C R Ashbee in the Cotswolds, 1981; The Omega Workshops: Decorative Arts of Bloomsbury, 1984; Eric Gill, 1989; William Morris: A Life for our Time, 1994; Stanley Spencer, 1996. Contributions to: Times Literary Supplement; New York Review of Books. Honours: Royal Society of Arts Bicentenary Medal, 1987; Honorary Fellowship, Royal College of Art, 1989; Honorary D Litt, University of Sheffield, 1996; Senior Fellowship, Royal College of Art, 1997; Fellow, Royal Society of Literature, 1997. Memberships: PEN Club; Royal Society of Literature. Address: The Round Building, Hathersage, Sheffield S30 1BA, England.

MACCOBY Michael, b. 5 Mar 1933, Mt Vernon, New York, USA. Consultant. m. Sandylee Weille, 19 Dec 1959, 1 son, 3 daughters. Education: BA 1954, PhD 1960, Harvard University; New College, Oxford, 1954-55; University of Chicago, 1955-56; Diploma, Mexican Institute of Psychoanalysis, 1964. Publications: Social Change and Character in Mexico and the United States, 1970; Social Character in a Mexican Village (with E Fromm), 1970, 2nd edition, 1996; The Gamesman, 1977; The Leader, 1981; Why Work, 1988, 1995; Sweden at the Edge, 1991; A Prophetic Analyst (with M Cortina), 1996. Memberships: PEN; Signet Society; Cosmos; American Psychological Association; American Anthropological Association; National Academy of Public Administration. Address: 4825 Linnean Avenue North West, Washington, DC 20008, USA.

MACCREIGH James. See: **POHL Frederik.**

MACDONALD Alastair A, b. 24 Oct 1920, Aberlour, Scotland. Poet; University Professor Emeritus. Education: MA, Aberdeen University, 1948; BLitt, Christ Church, Oxford, 1953; PhD, Manchester University, 1956. Appointments: Senior Studentship in Arts (English), Manchester, 1953-55; Professor of English, Memorial University, Newfoundland, Canada, 1955-87; Professor Emeritus, 1992. Publications: Academic: Prose and Verse in Fearful Joy, Papers from the Thomas Gray Bicentenary Conference, Ottawa, 1971, 1974; A Festschrift for Edgar Ronald Seary (co-editor, contributor), 1975; Introduction and Notes to reproduction in facsimile of Thomas Gray, An Elegy...The Eton Manuscript and First Edition 1751, 1976; Numerous essays, articles, book reviews. Poetry: Between Something and Something, 1970; Shape Enduring Mind, 1974; A Different Lens, 1981; Towards the Mystery, 1985; A Figure on the Move, 1991; Landscapes of Time: New, Uncollected and Selected Poems, 1995; Poetry in many anthologies. Other: Flavian's Fortune, (novel), 1985. Contributions to: Aberdeen University Review; Dalhousie Review; Bulletin of Humanities Association of Canada; Review of English Studies; Queen's Quarterly, Canada; Studies in Scottish Literature; The University Review, USA. Honours: Prizes and Mentions for Poetry: Honourable Mention, Stroud Festival, 1967; Canadian Author and Bookman, Prize for Best Poem in Vol 47, 1972; Prize, Best Poem in New Voices in American Poetry, 1973, Vantage Press, New York, 1973; 1st Prize for Poetry, 1976, Honourable Mention, 1978, 2nd Prize, 1982, Newfoundland Government Arts and Letters Competition; Readings of own poetry: Many public readings, including, by invitation, for Habourfront Reading Series, Toronto, Canada, 1992. Memberships: Writers' Alliance of Newfoundland and Labrador; Scottish Poetry Library Association, Edinburgh; League of Canadian Poets. Address: Department of English, Arts and Administration Building, Memorial University, St John's, Newfoundland, A1C 5S7, Canada.

MACDONALD (Margaret) Amy, b. 14 June 1951, Boston, Massachusetts, USA. Journalist. m. Thomas A Urquhart, 26 June 1976, 2 sons, 1 stepdaughter. Education: University of Pennsylvania, 1969-73; BA, Centre de Formation et Perfectionnne des Journalistes, 1982-83. Appointments: Stonecoast Writers Conference;

Teacher, Harvard University. Publications: Little Beaver and the Echo; Rachel Fister's Blister; Let's Try, Let's Make a Noise, Let's Play, Let's Do It; A Very Young Housewife. Contributions to: Parents Magazine; Earthwatch Magazine; Times; New Scientist; Guardian. Honour: Silver Stylus Award. Membership: Society of Children's Book Writers. Address: 10 Winslow Road, Falmouth, ME 04105, USA.

MACDONALD Cynthia, b. 2 Feb 1928, New York, New York, USA. Poet; Lecturer. m. E C Macdonald, 1954, div 1975, 1 son, 1 daughter. Education: BA, Bennington College, Vermont, 1950; Graduate Studies, Mannes College of Music, New York City, 1951-52; MA, Sarah Lawrence College, 1970. Appointments: Assistant Professor, 1970-74, Associate Professor and Acting Dean of Studies, 1974-75, Sarah Lawrence College; Professor, Johns Hopkins University, 1975-79; Consultant, 1977-78, Co-Director, Writing Program, 1979-, University of Houston; Guest Lecturer at various universities, colleges, seminars, etc. Publications: Amputations, 1972; Transplants, 1976; Pruning the Annuals, 1976; (W)holes, 1980; Alternate Means of Transport, 1985; Living Wills: New and Selected Poems, 1991. Contributions to: Anthologies and other publications. Honours: MacDowell Colony Grant, 1970; National Endowment for the Arts Grants, 1973, 1979; Yaddo Foundation Grants, 1974, 1976, 1979; CAPS Grant, 1976; American Academy and Institute of Arts and Letters Award, 1977; Rockefeller Foundation Fellow, 1978. Memberships: American Society of Composers, Authors, and Publishers; Associated Writing Programs. Address: c/o Alfred A Knopf Inc, 201 East 50th Street, New York, NY 10022, USA.

MACDONALD (Alexa Eleanor) Fiona, b. 25 Apr 1945, India. Writer. Publications: The Duke Who Had Too Many Giraffes; Little Bird I Have Heard. Contributions to: International Construction; Construction News; Underground Engineering. Membership: PEN. Address: 41 Donne Place, London SW3 2NH, England.

MACDONALD Malcolm. See: **ROSS-MACDONALD Malcolm John.**

MACDONOGH Giles Malachy Maximilian, b. 6 Apr 1955, London, England. Author; Journalist. Education: Balliol College, Oxford, 1975-78; BA (Hons), Modern History, Oxford University, 1978; École des Hautes Études Pratiques, France, 1980-83; MA (Oxon), 1992. Appointments: Freelance Journalist, 1983-; Editor, Made in France, 1984; Columnist, Financial Times, 1989-. Publications: A Palate in Revolution, Grimod de La Reynière and the Almanach des Gourmands, 1987; A Good German: Adam von Trott zu Solz, 1990; The Wine and Food of Austria, 1992; Brillat Savarin: The Judge and his Stomach, 1992; Syrah Grenache, Mourvèdre, 1992; Prussia, the Perversion of an Idea, 1994; Berlin, 1997. Contributions to: Reference works, books, and periodicals. Honours: Shortlisted, Andre Simon Award, 1987; Glenfiddich Special Award, 1988. Memberships: International PEN; Octagon of Wine Writers. Address: c/o Curtis Brown, 162 Regent Street, London W1, England.

MACDOUGALL Ruth Doan, b. 19 Mar 1939, Laconia, New Hampshire, USA. Writer. m. Donald K MacDougall, 9 Oct 1957. Education: Bennington College, 1957-59; BEd, Keene State College, 1961. Publications: The Lilting House, 1965; One Minus One, 1971; The Cost of Living, 1971; The Cheerleader, 1973; Wife and Mother, 1976; Aunt Pleasantine, 1978; The Flowers of the Forest, 1981; A Lovely Time Was Had By All, 1982; Snowy, 1993; Fifty Hikes in the White Mountains, 1997. Contributions to: Book Reviewer: New York Times Book Review; Newsday; Others. Honours: Winner, PEN Syndicated Fiction Project, 1983, 1984, 1985. Membership: National Writers Union. Address: 285 Range Road, Center Sandwich, NH 03227, USA.

MACDOWELL Douglas Maurice, b. 8 Mar 1931, London, England. Professor of Greek; Writer. Education: BA, 1954, MA, 1958, DLitt, 1992, Balliol College, Oxford. Appointments: Assistant Lecturer, Lecturer, Senior Lecturer, Reader in Greek and Latin, University of Manchester, England, 1958-71; Professor of Greek, University of Glasgow, Scotland, 1971-. Publications: Andokides: On the Mysteries (editor), 1962; Athenian Homicide Law, 1963; Aristophanes: Wasps (editor), 1971; The Law in Classical Athens, 1978; Spartan Law, 1986; Demosthenes: Against Meidias (editor), 1990; Aristophanes and Athens, 1995. Honours: Fellow, Royal Society of Edinburgh, 1991; Fellow, British Academy, 1993. Address: Department of Classics, University of Glasgow, Glasgow G12 8QQ, Scotland.

MACDOWELL John. See: **PARKS T(imothy) Harold.**

MACEACHERN Diane, b. 29 May 1952, Detroit, Michigan, USA. President, Vanguard Communications; Author. Education: BA, Literature, Science, Arts, 1974, MS, School of Natural Resources, 1977, University of Michigan. Publication: Save Our Planet: 750 Everyday Ways You Can Help Clean Up the Earth, 1990. Contributions to: Family Circle; Good Housekeeping; Ladies Home Journal; Self; Lady's Circle; Bottom Line; National Wildlife; Syndicated column in Washington Post Writer's Group. Honours: William J Branstrom Freshman Prize, 1970; Honorary Alumni Award, 1990. Address: 102 Tulip Avenue, Takoma Park, MD 20912, USA.

MACER-STORY Eugenia, b. 20 Jan 1945, Minneapolis, Minnesota, USA. Writer. m. Leon A Story, 1970, div 1975, 1 son. Education: BS, Speech, Northwestern University, 1965; MFA, Playwriting, Columbia University, 1968. Appointments: Fond du Lac Commonwealth Reporter, 1970; Polyarts, Boston, 1970-72; Joy of Movement, Boston, 1972-75; Magik Mirror, Salem, 1975-76; Magick Mirror Communications, Woodstock and New York City, 1977-. Publications: Congratulations: The UFO Reality, 1978; Angels of Time: Astrological Magic, 1981; Du Fu Man Chu Meets the Lonesome Cowboy: Sorcery and the UFO Experience, 1991, 2nd edition, 1992; Legacy of Daedalus, 1995; Cattle Bones and Coke Machines, (anthology), 1995; The Dark Frontier, 1997. Plays: Meister Hemmelin, 1994; Radish, 1995; Conquest of the Asteroids, 1996; Mister Shooting Star, 1997. Contributions to: Numerous publications, including Sensations magazine, 1996-97. Honour: Shubert Fellowship, 1968. Memberships: Dramatists Guild; US Psychotronics Association; Poet's House, New York City; American Society for Psychical Research. Address: Magick Mirror Communications, Box 741 - JAF Building, New York, NY 10116, USA.

MACGOWAN Christopher John, b. 6 Aug 1948, London, England. Educator. m. Catherine Levesque, 10 July 1988. Education: BA, King's College, Cambridge, 1976; MA, 1979, PhD, 1983, Princeton University, USA. Appointments: Research Assistant, The Writings of Henry D Thoreau, 1981-83; Assistant Professor, 1984-90, Associate Professor, 1990-96, Professor, 1996-, College of William and Mary, Williamsburg, Virginia; Co-editor, Editor, various works of William Carlos Williams, 1984-92. Publications: William Carlos Williams' Early Poetry: The Visual Arts Background, 1984; The Collected Poems of William Carlos Williams, Vol I, 1909-1939 (co-editor), 1986, vol II, 1939-62 (editor), 1988; William Carlos Williams' Paterson (editor), 1992. Contributions to: Reference works and journals. Honours: James Prize, King's College, Cambridge, England, 1976, 1977; Teaching Assistantship, Pennsylvania State University, 1976-77; Graduate Fellowship, Princeton University, 1977-81; Summer Grants, College of William and Mary, 1985, 1987, 1989; Summer Stipend, 1986, Fellowship 1990-91, National Endowment for the Humanities. Memberships: Modern Lanaguage Association; William Carlos Williams Society, president, 1989-91. Address: Department of English, College of William and Mary, Williamsburg, VA 23187, USA.

MACGREGOR David Roy, b. 26 Aug 1925, London, England. Author. m. Patricia Margaret Aline Purcell-Gilpin, 26 Oct 1962. Education: BA, 1948, MA, 1950, Trinity College, Cambridge University; Hammersmith School of Building, 1954-55; Associate, Royal Institute of British Architects, 1957. Publications: The Tea Clippers, 1952, revised edition, 1983; The China Bird, 1961; Fast Sailing Ships 1775-1875, 1973; Clipper Ships, 1977; Merchant Sailing Ships, 1775-1815, 1980; Merchant Sailing Ships 1815-1850, 1984; Merchant Sailing Ships 1858-1875, 1984. Contributions to: Mariner's Mirror; Journal of Nautical Archaeology. Honour: Gold Medal from Daily Express for Best Book of the Sea, 1973. Memberships: Royal Historical Society, fellow, 1957; FSA, 1975; Society of Nautical Research, council member, 1959-63, 1965-69, 1974-77, 1980-85, Hon Vice-President, 1985; Maritime Trust, 1974. Address: 99 Lonsdale Road, London SW13 9DA, England.

MACGREGOR-HASTIE Roy Alasdhair Niall, b. 28 Mar 1929, Rusholme, England. Author; University Professor. m. Maria Grazia, 25 Dec 1977, 1 son. Education: New College, Royal Military Academy, Sandhurst, 1947-48; BA, University of Manchester; MFA, University of Iowa, USA; MEd, PhD, University of Hull. Appointments: Editor, The New Nation, 1955-56, Prospice, 1967-77; Joint Editor, Miorita, 1977-. Publications: The Man from Nowhere, 1960; The Red Barbarians, 1961; Pope John XXIII, 1962; The Day of the Lion - A History of Fascism, 1964; Pope Paul VI, 1966; The Throne of Peter, 1967; Never to Be Taken Alive, 1985; Nell Gwyn, 1987; History of Western Civilisation, 1989; Getting it Right, 1990. Travel: The Compleat Migrant, 1962; Don't Send Me to Omsk, 1964; Signor Roy, 1967; Africa, 1968; Art History: Picasso, 1988. Poetry and Criticism: A Case for Poetry, 1960; Interim Statement, 1962; Eleven Elegies, 1969; Frames, 1972; The Great Transition, 1975; Poems of Our Lord and Lady, 1976; Poeme, 1980. Contributions to: Anthologies and periodicals. Honours: Victoria Poetry Prize, 1986; UNESCO Author, 1989. Memberships: PEN; Society of Authors; British Association for Romanian Studies, secretary, 1966-77, president, 1977-; International Association of Translators, president, 1978-80; Asian History Association; Scottish Record Society. Literary Agent: Kurt Singer, Anahein, California, CA 72801, USA. Address: c/o Osaka Gakuin University, Kishibe, Suita, Osaka 564, Japan.

MACHUNG Anne, b. 30 Jan 1947, Long Beach, California, USA. Sociologist. m. Ron Rothbart, 27 Sept 1986. Education: BA summa cum laude, University of Seattle, 1968; MA 1972, PhD 1983, University of Wisconsin. Publication: The Second Shift (with Arlie Hochschild), 1989. Contributions to: Journals and periodicals. Honour: Distinguished Achievement for Bay Area Women Writers', National Women's Political Caucus, 1991. Memberships: American Sociological Association; National Women's Studies Association. Address: Institute for Study of Social Change, University of California at Berkeley, Berkeley, CA 94720, USA.

MACINNES Patricia, b. 7 Apr 1954, Quantico, Virginia, USA. Writer. Education: BA, San Diego State University, 1977; MFA, Writing, University of Montana, Missoula, 1981; Stanford University, Wallace Stegner Writing Fellowship, 1984-85. Publication: The Last Night on Bikini, 1995. Contributions to: Journals. Honours: Wallace Stegner Writing Fellowship, Stanford University, 1984; Nelson Algren Award for Short Fiction, 1987; Writing Fellowship, Provincetown Fine Arts Work Center, 1988-89; Ludwig Vogelstein Grant, 1989. Literary Agent: Mary Jack Wald. Address: c/o Mary Jack Wald Associates, Suite 113, Zeckendorf Towers, 111 E 14th Street, New York, NY 10003, USA.

MACINTYRE Alasdair, b. 12 Jan 1929, Glasgow, Scotland. Philosopher; Professor; Writer. Education: BA, Queen Mary College, University of London, 1949; MA, Manchester University, 1951; MA, Oxford University, 1961. Appointments: Lecturer, Manchester University, 1951-57, Leeds University, 1957-61; Research Fellow, Nuffield College, Oxford, 1961-62; Senior Fellow, Princeton University, 1962-63; Fellow, University College, Oxford, 1963-66; Riddell Lecturer, University of Newcastle Upon Tyne, 1964; Bampton Lecturer, Columbia University, 1966; Professor of the History of Ideas, Brandeis University, 1969-72; Dean, College of Liberal Arts, 1972-73, Professor of Philosophy and Political Science, 1972-80, Boston University; Henry Luce Professor, Wellesley College, 1980-82; W Alton Jones Professor, Vanderbilt University, 1982-88; Gifford Lecturer, University of Edinburgh, 1988; Henry Luce Scholar, Yale University, 1988-89; McMahon/Hank Professor, University of Notre Dame, Indiana, 1988-94; Professor of Arts and Sciences, Duke University, 1995-. Publications: Marxism and Christianity, 1953; The Unconscious, 1957; Difficulties in Christian Belief, 1960; Short History of Ethics, 1966; The Religious Significance of Atheism, 1969; Against the Self-Images of the Age, 1971; After Virtue: A Study in Moral Theory, 1981; Is Patriotism a Virtue?, 1984; Education and Values, 1987; Whose Justice? Which Rationality?, 1988; Three Rival Versions of Moral Enquiry, 1990; First Principles, Final Ends and Contemporary Philosophy, 1990. Memberships: American Academy of Arts and Sciences; Corresponding Member, British Academy; Honorary, Phi Beta Kappa. Address: c/o Department of Philosophy, Duke University, Durham, NC 27708, USA.

MACINTYRE Stuart (Forbes), b. 21 Apr 1947, Melbourne, Victoria, Australia. Professor of History; Author. m. (1) Margaret Joan Geddes, Dec 1970, (2) Martha Adele Bruton, 26 Aug 1976, 2 daughters. Education: BA, University of Melbourne, 1968; MA, Monash University, 1969; PhD, Cambridge University, 1975. Appointments: Tutor in History, 1976, Lecturer in History, 1979, Murdoch University, Perth; Research Fellow, St John's College, Cambridge, 1977-78; Lecturer, 1980-84, Senior Lecturer, 1984-86, Reader in History, 1987-90, Ernest Scott Professor, 1990-, University of Melbourne. Publications: A Proletarian Science: Marxism in Britain 1917-1933, 1980; Little Moscows, 1980; Militant: The Life and Times of Paddy Troy, 1983; Ormond College Centenary Essays (editor), 1983; Making History (editor), 1984; Winners and Losers: The Pursuit of Social

Justice in Australian History, 1985; The Oxford History of Australia, Vol IV, 1986; The Labour Experiment, 1989; A Colonial Liberalism: The Lost World of Three Victorian Visionaries, 1990; A History for a Nation, 1995. Contributions to: Professional journals. Honours: Prizes and awards. Membership: Academy of the Social Sciences in Australia. Address: c/o Department of History, University of Melbourne, Parkville, Victoria 3052, Australia.

MACK William P, b. 6 Aug 1915, Hillsboro, Illinois, USA. Naval Officer (retired); Writer. m. Ruth McMillian, 11 Nov 1939, 1 son, 1 daughter. Education: BS, US Naval Academy; Naval War College; George Washington University. Appointments: US Naval Officer, 1935-75; Deputy Assistant Secretary of Defense, 1968-71. Publications: Non-Fiction: Naval Officers Guide, 1958; Naval Customs, Traditions and Usage, 1978; Command at Sea, 1980. Fiction: South to Java, 1988; Pursuit of the Sea Wolf, 1991; Checkfire, 1992; New Guinea, 1993; Straits of Messina, 1994. Contributions to: Various publications. Honour: Alfred Thayer Mahan for Literary Excellence, Navy League, 1982. Address: 3607 Rundelac Road, Annapolis, MD 21403, USA.

MACKAY Claire Lorraine, b. 21 Dec 1930, Toronto, Ontario, Canada. Writer. m. Jackson F Mackay, 12 Sept 1952, 3 sons. Education: BA, Political Science, University of Toronto, 1952; Postgraduate study in Social Work; University of British Columbia, 1968-69; Certificate, rehabilitation counseling, University of Manitoba, 1971. Appointment: Writer-in-Residence, Metropolitan Toronto Library, 1987. Publications: Mini-Bike Hero, 1974; Mini-Bike Racer, 1976; Mini-Bike Rescue, 1982; Exit Barney McGee, 1979; One Proud Summer, 1981; Minerva Program, 1984; Pay Cheques and Picket Lines, 1987; The Toronto Story, 1990; Touching All the Bases, 1994; Bats About Baseball, 1995; Laughs: Funny Stories, Selected by Claire Mackay, 1997. Contributions to: Newspapers and magazines. Address: 6 Frank Crescent, Toronto, Ontario M6G 3K5, Canada.

MACKAY James Alexander, (Ian Angus, William Finlay, Bruce Garden, Peter Whittington), b. 21 Nov 1936, Inverness, Scotland. Author; Journalist. m. (1) Mary Patricia Jackson, 24 Sept 1960, diss 1972, 1 son, 1 daughter, (2) Renate Finlay-Freundlich, 11 Dec 1992. Education: MA (Hons), History, 1958, DLitt, 1993, Glasgow University. Appointments: Philatelic Columnist, The New Daily, 1962-67; Collecting Wisely in Financial Times, 1967-85; Editor-in-Chief, IPC Stamp Encyclopaedia, 1968-72; Antiques Advisory Editor, Ward Lock, 1972-79; Editor, The Burns Chronicle, 1977-91, The Postal Annual, 1978-90, The Burnsian, 1986-89, Seaby Coin and Medal Bulletin, 1990-92; Consultant Editor, Antiques Today, 1992-94; Stamp and Coin Mart, 1993-, Coin News, 1994-, International Stamp and Exhibition News, 1996-. Publications: The Tapling Collection, 1964; Glass Paperweights, 1973, 3rd edition, 1988; The Dictionary of Stamps in Colour, 1973; The Dictionary of Western Sculptors in Bronze, 1977, 2nd edition, 1992; The Guinness Book of Stamps Facts and Feats, 1982, 2nd edition, 1988; Complete Works of Robert Burns, 1986; Complete Letters of Burns, 1987; Burns A-Z: The Complete Word Finder, 1990; Burns: A Biography, 1992; Vagabond of Verse: A Life of Robert W Service, 1993; William Wallace: Brave Heart, 1994; The Eye Who Never Slept: A Life of Allan Pinkerton, 1995; Michael Collins: A Life, 1996; Sounds Out of Silence: A Life of Alexander Graham Bell, 1997; 164 titles on philately, numismatics, applied and decorative arts, biography, Scottish literature, 1961-. Contributions to: Regular columns to: Stamps; Stamp Magazine; Gibbons Stamp Monthly; British Philatelic Bulletin; Stamp and Coin Mart; Coin News; Coin Monthly; Seaby Coin and Medal Bulletin; Coin Digest, Singapore; Studies in Scottish Literature, USA; Mekeel's Weekly; Stamp Collector; Scott's Monthly Journal; Canadian Stamp News; Linn's Weekly Stamp News; Occasional contributions to many others worldwide. Honours: Silver Medal Amphilex, Amsterdam, 1965; Vermeil Medals, Spellman Foundation, USA, 1982, 1987, 1990; Thomas Field Award for services to Irish Philatelic Literature, 1983; Saltire Book of the Year, 1993. Membership: The Burns Federation, executive council, 1977-95. Address: 67 Braidpark Drive, Glasgow G46 6LY, Scotland.

MACKAY Simon. See: **NICOLE Christopher Robin.**

MACKENZIE Andrew Carr, b. 30 May 1911, Oamaru, New Zealand. Journalist; Author. m. Kaarina Sisko Sihvonen, 1 Mar 1952, 1 son, 2 daughters. Education: Victoria University College, New Zealand, 1930-32. Appointment: London News Editor, Sheffield Morning Telegraph, England, 1963-76. Publications: The Unexplained, 1966; Frontiers of the Unknown, 1968; Apparitions and Ghosts, 1971;

A Gallery of Ghosts (editor), 1972; Riddle of the Future, 1974; Dracula Country, 1977; Hauntings and Apparitions, 1982; Romanian Journey, 1983; A Concise History of Romania (editor), 1985; Archaeology in Romania, 1986; The Seen and the Unseen, 1987; A Journey into the Past of Transylvania, 1990; Adventures in Time: A Study of Retrocognition, 1997. Contributions to: Journal of the Society of Psychical Research. Membership: Society for Psychical Research, Council Member, 1970-91, Vice President, 1997. Literary Agent: A M Heath, 79 St Martin's Lane, London WC2N 4AA, England. Address: 67 Woodland Drive, Hove, East Sussex BN3 6DF, England.

MACKENZIE David, b. 10 June 1927, Rochester, New York, USA. Professor of History. m. Patricia Williams, 8 Aug 1953, 3 sons. Education: AB, University of Rochester, 1951; MA and Certificate of Russian Institute, 1953; PhD, Columbia University, 1962. Appointments: US Merchant Marine Academy, 1953-58; Princeton University, 1959-61; Wells College, 1961-68; University of North Carolina, Greensboro, 1969-. Publications: The Serbs and Russian Pan-Slavism 1875-1878, 1967; The Lion of Tashkent: The Career of General M G Cherniaev, 1974; A History of Russia and the Soviet Union, 1977, 4th edition, revised, 1993; Ilija Garasanin: The Balkan Bismarck, 1985; A History of the Soviet Union, 1986, 2nd edition, revised, 1991; Ilija Garasanin Drzavnik i Diplomata, 1987; Apis: The Congenial Conspirator, 1989; Imperial Dreams/Harsh Realities: Tsarist Russian Foreign Policy, 1815-1917, 1993; From Messianism to Collapse: Soviet Foreign Policy 1917-1991, 1994; The Black Hand on Trial: Salonika, 1979, 1995; Violent Solutions: Revolutions, Nationalism, and Secret Societies in Europe to 1918, 1996; Serbs and Russians, 1996; Russia and the USSR in the Twentieth Century, 3rd edition, 1997; Solunski proces, 1997. Contributions to: Books and professional journals. Address: 1000 Fairmont Street, Greensboro, NC 27401, USA.

MACKENZIE Norman Hugh, b. 8 Mar 1915, Salisbury, Rhodesia. Educator; Writer. m. Rita Mavis Hofmann, 14 Aug 1948, 1 son, 1 daughter. Education: BA, 1934, MA, 1935, Diploma in Education, 1936, Rhodes University, South Africa; PhD, University of London, England, 1940. Appointments: Professor of English, 1966-80, Emeritus Professor, 1980-, Queen's University, Kingston, Ontario, Canada. Publications: South African Travel Literature in the 17th Century, 1955; The Outlook for English in Central Africa, 1960; Hopkins, 1968; A Reader's Guide to G M Hopkins, 1981. Editor: The Poems of Gerard Manley Hopkins (with W H Gardner), 1967, revised edition, 1970; Poems by Hopkins, 1974; The Early Poetic Manuscripts and Notebooks of Gerard Manley Hopkins in Facsimile, 1989; The Poetical Works of Gerard Manley Hopkins, 1990; The Later Poetic Manuscripts of Gerard Manley Hopkins in Facsimile, 1991; Various book chapters. Contributions to: International Review of Education; Bulletin of the Institute for Historical Research; Times Literary Supplement; Modern Language Quarterly; Queen's Quarterly; Others. Honours: Honorary DLitt, 1989; Fellow, Royal Society of Canada, 1979. Address: 416 Windward Place, Kingston, Ontario K7M 4E4, Canada.

MACKENZIE Suzanne, b. 22 Mar 1950, Vancouver, British Columbia, Canada. Professor of Geography; Writer. m. Alan Eric Nash, 29 May 1984. Education: BA, Simon Fraser University, 1976; MA, University of Toronto, 1978; DPhil, Geography, Sussex University. Appointment: Professor of Geography, Carleton University. Publications: Gender Sensitive Theory and Housing Needs of Mother Led Families (co-author), 1987; Gender and Environment in a Post-War British City, 1989; Remaking Human Geography (co-editor), 1989. Contributions to: Various publications. Memberships: Canadian Association of Geographers; International Geographic Union. Address: c/o Department of Geography, Carleton University, Ottawa, Ontario K1S 5B6, Canada.

MACKERRAS Colin Patrick, b. 26 Aug 1939, Sydney, New South Wales, Australia. Academic; Writer. m. Alyce Barbara Brazier, 29 June 1963, 2 sons, 3 daughters. Education: BA, University of Melbourne, 1961; BA, 1962, PhD, 1970, Australia National University; MLitt, Cambridge University, 1964. Appointment: Faculty, Griffith University. Publications: China Observed, 1967; The Rise of the Peking Opera 1770-1870, 1972; The Chinese Theatre in Modern Times, 1975; China: The Impact of Revolution, A Survey of Twentieth Century China, 1976; Modern China: A Chronology from 1842 to the Present, 1982; Western Images of China, 1989. Contributions to: Journals. Honour: Co-Recipient, Gold Citation, Media Peace Prize, United Nations Association of Australia, 1981. Membership: Australian

Writers' Guild. Address: c/o Division of Asian and International Studies, Griffith University, Nathan, Queensland 4111, Australia.

MACKESY Piers Gerald, b. 15 Sept 1924, Cults Aberdeenshire, Scotland. Academic; Writer. Education: BA, Christ Church, Oxford, 1950; DPhil, Oriel College, Oxford, 1953. Appointments: Harkness Fellow, Harvard University, USA, 1953-54; Fellow, 1954-87, Emeritus, 1988-, Pembroke College, Oxford, England; Visiting Fellow, Institute for Advanced Study, Princeton, New Jersey, USA, 1961-62; Visiting Professor, California Institute of Technology, 1966. Publications: The War in the Mediterranean 1803-1810, 1957; The War for America 1775-1783, 1964; Statesmen at War: The Strategy of Overthrow 1798-1799, 1974; The Coward of Minden: The Affair of Lord George Sackville, 1979; War without Victory: The Downfall of Pitt 1799-1802, 1984; British Victory in Egypt, 1801: The End of Napoleon's Conquest, 1995. Memberships: National Army Museum, council member, 1983-92; Society for Army Historical Research, council member, 1985-94; British Academy, fellow, 1988. Address: Leochel Cushnie House, Leochel Cushnie, Alford, Aberdeenshire AB33 8LJ, Scotland.

MACKIE John. See: **LEVINSON Leonard.**

MACKIE Margaret Davidson, b. 12 Nov 1914, Sydney, New South Wales, Australia. Retired Lecturer. Education: BA, Sydney, 1937; DipEd, 1940; BA, Oxford, 1940; MA, 1945. Publications: Education in the Inquiring Society, 1966; Educative Teaching, 1968; What is Right?, 1970; The Beginning Teacher, 1973; Philosophy and School Administration, 1977. Contributions to: Various education journals. Honour: OAM, 1984. Membership: Australian Society of Authors; Australian College of Education, fellow. Address: 3 Fitzgerald Avenue, Armidale, New South Wales 2350, Australia.

MACKINNON Catharine, b. 1946, USA. Professor of Law; Writer. Education: BA, Smith College, 1969; JD, 1977, PhD, 1987, Yale University. Appointments: Professor of Law, University of Michigan, 1990-; Several visiting professorships. Publications: Sexual Harrassment of Working Women, 1979; Feminism Unmodified, 1987; Toward a Feminist Theory of the State, 1989; Only Words, 1993; In Harm's Way (with Andrea Dworkin), 1997; Contributions to: Journals. Address: c/o School of Law, University of Michigan, Ann Arbor, MI 48109, USA.

MACKSEY K(enneth) J(ohn), b. 1 July 1923, Epsom, Surrey, England. Army Officer (retired); Historian. Education: Royal Military College, Sandhurst, 1943-44; British Army Staff College,1956. Appointments: Officer, Royal Tank Regiment, British Army, 1941-68, until retirement with rank of Major, 1968; Deputy Editor, History of the Second World War, History of the First World War, 1968-70. Publications: The Shadow of Vimy Ridge, To the Green Fields Beyond, 1965; Armoured Crusader: General Sir Percy Hobart, 1967; Africa Korps, Panzer Division, 1968; Crucible of Power: The Fight for Tunisia, 1969; Tank Force, Tank: A History of AFVs, 1970; Tank Warfare, Beda Fomm, 1971; The Guinness History of Land (Sea, Air) Warfare, 3 volumes, 1973-76; Battle, (in US as Anatomy of a Battle), 1974; The Partisans of Europe in the Second World War, 1975; The Guinness Guide to Feminine Achievements, 1975; Guderian: Panzer General, 1975; The Guinness Book 1952 (1953, 1954), 3 volumes, 1977-79; Kesselring, 1978; Rommel's Campaigns and Battles, 1979; The Tanks, Vol III of the History of the Royal Tank Regiment, 1979; Invasion: The German Invasion of England, July 1940, 1980; The Tank Pioneers, 1981; History of the Royal Armoured Corps 1914-1975, 1983; Commando Strike, First Clash, 1985; Technology in War, 1986; Godwin's Saga, Military Errors of World War II, 1987; Tank Versus Tank, 1988; For Want of a Nail, 1989; The Penguin Encyclopedia of Modern Warfare, 1991. Address: Whatley Mill, Beaminster, Dorset DT8 3EN, England.

MACKWORTH Cecily, b, Llantillio Pertholey, Gwent, Wales. Writer. 1 daughter. m. Marquis de Chabannes la Palice, 1956. Publications: I Came Out of France, 1942; A Mirror for French Poetry, 1942; François Villon: A Study, 1947; The Mouth of the Sword, 1949; The Destiny of Isobella Eberhardt, 1952; Spring's Green Shadow (novel), 1953; Guillaume Apollinaire and the Cubist Life, 1961; English Interludes, 1974; Ends of the World (memoirs), 1987; Lucy's Nose (novel), 1992. Contributions to: Horizon; Life and Letters Today; Poetry Quarterly; Cornhill; Twentieth Century; Cultures for all Peoples (UNESCO); Critique; Les Lettres Nouvelles. Honour: Darmstadt Award, 1965. Memberships: PEN (French); Association Internationale des Critiques Litteraires; Society of Authors of Great Britain. Literary

Agent: L Pollinger, 18 Madox Street, London, W1R 0EG. Address: 6 Rue des Countures-St-Gervais, Paris 75003, France.

MACKY Ahmad, b. 13 May 1943, Mauritius. Journalist; Editor. m. Affroze Mudhawo, 8 Aug 1988, 1 daughter. Education: LSJ, London, 1968; BA, Honours, 1990. Appointment: Editor-in-Chief, The Student's World. Publications: Six Strange Stories, 1975; Jaytoon, the Asian Woman, 1987. Contributions to: Periodicals. Memberships: International Federation of Journalists; National Union of Journalists, England. Address: Royal Road, Bel Air Rivière Séche Flacq, Mauritius.

MACLAVERTY Bernard, b. 14 Sept 1942, Belfast, Northern Ireland. Novelist. m. Madeline McGuckin, 1967, 1 son, 3 daughters. Education: BA, Hons, Queens University, Belfast, 1974. Publications: Bibliography: Secrets and Other Stories, 1977; Lamb (novel), 1980; A Time to Dance and Other Stories, 1982; Cal (novel), 1983; The Great Profundo and Other Stories, 1987; Walking the Dog and Other Stories, 1994; Grace Notes (novel), 1997. For Young Children: A Man in Search of a Pet, 1978; Andrew McAndrew, 1988, USA 1993. Radio Plays: My Dear Palestrina, 1980; Secrets, 1981; No Joke, 1983; The Break, 1988; Some Surrender, 1988; Lamb, 1992. Television Plays: My Dear Palestrina, 1980; Phonefun Limited, 1982; The Daily Woman, 1986; Sometime in August, 1989. Screenplays: Cal, 1984; Lamb, 1985. Drama Documentary: Hostages, 1992, USA 1993; Adaptation for TV: The Real Charlotte by Somerville and Ross, 1989. Honours: Northern Ireland and Scottish Arts Councils Awards; Irish Sunday Independent Award, 1983; London Evening Standard Award for Screenplay, 1984; Award from Scottish Arts Council, 1988; Joint winner, Scottish Writer of the Year, 1988; Shortlisted for The Saltire Society Scottish Book of the Year, 1994. Address: 26 Roxburgh Street, Hillhead, Glasgow G12 9AP, Scotland.

MACLEAN Arthur. See: TUBB E(dwin) C(harles).

MACLEOD Alison, b, 12 Apr 1920, Hendon, Middlesex, England. Writer. Publications: Dear Augustine, 1958; The Heretics (in US as The Heretic), 1965; The Hireling (in UK as The Trusted Servant), 1968; City of Light (in UK as No Need of the Sun), 1969; The Muscovite, 1971; The Jesuit (in US as Prisoner of the Queen), 1972; The Portingale, 1976; The Death of Uncle Joe, 1997. Address: 63 Muswell Hill Place, London N10 3RP, England.

MACLEOD Charlotte, (Alisa Craig, Matilda Hughes), b. 12 Nov 1922, Bath, England (US citizen, 1952). Writer. Publications: As Charlotte MacLeod: Mystery of the White Knight, 1964; Next Door to Danger, 1965; The Fat Lady's Ghost, 1968; Mouse's Vineyard (juvenile), 1968; Ask Me No Questions, 1971; Brass Pounder (juvenile), 1971; Astrology for Sceptics (non-fiction), 1972; King Devil, 1978; Rest You Merry, 1978; The Family Vault, 1979; The Luck Runs Out, 1979; The Withdrawing Room, 1980; We Dare Not Go a Hunting, 1980; The Palace Guard, 1981; Wrack and Rune, 1982; Cirak's Daughter (juvenile), 1982; The Bilbao Looking Glass, 1983; Something the Cat Dragged In, 1983; Maid of Honour (juvenile), 1984; The Convival Codfish, 1984; The Curse of the Giant Hogweed, 1985; The Plain Old Man, 1985; Grab Bag, 1987; The Corpse in Oozak's Pond, 1987; The Recycled Citizen, 1988; The Silver Ghost, 1988; Vane Pursuit, 1989; The Gladstone Bag, 1990. As Matilda Hughes: The Food of Love, 1965; Headlines for Caroline, 1967. As Alisa Craig: A Pint of Murder, 1980; The Grub-and-Stakers Move a Mountain, 1981; Murder Goes Mumming, 1981; The Terrible Tide, 1983; The Grub and Stakers Quilt a Bee, 1985; The Grub-and-Stakers Pinch a Poke, 1988; Trouble in the Brasses, 1989; The Grub-and-Stakers Spin and Yarn, 1990; An Owl Too Many; Something in the Water. Address: c/o Jed Mattes, 175 West 73rd Street, New York, NY 10023, USA.

MACLEOD Robert. See: KNOX William.

MACMULLEN Ramsay, b. 3 Mar 1928, New York, New York, USA. Professor (retired); Writer. m. (1) Edith Merriman Nye, 7 Aug 1954, div 1991, 2 sons, 2 daughters, (2) Margaret McNeill, 1 Aug 1992. Education: AB, 1950, AM, 1953, PhD, 1957, Harvard University. Appointments: Instructor to Assistant Professor, University of Oregon, 1956-61; Associate Professor to Professor, 1961-67, Chairman, Departments of Classics, 1965-66, Brandeis University; Fellow, Institute for Advanced Study, Princeton, New Jersey, 1964-65; Professor, 1967-93, Chairman, Department of History, 1970-72, Dunham Professor of History and Classics, 1979-93, Master, Calhoun College, 1984-90, Yale University. Publications: Soldier and Civilian in the Later Roman Empire, 1963; Enemies of the Roman Order, 1966;

Constantine, 1969; Roman Social Relations, 1974; Roman Government's Response to Crisis, 1976; Paganism in the Roman Empire, 1981; Christianizing the Roman Empire, 1984; Corruption and the Decline of Rome, 1988; Changes in the Roman Empire, 1990; Paganism and Christianity (with E N Lane), 1992; Christianity and Paganism, 1997. Contributions to: Professional journals. Honours: Fulbright Fellowship, 1960-61; Porter Prize, College Art Association, 1964; Guggenheim Fellowship, 1964; Senior Fellow, National Endowment for the Humanities, 1974-75. Memberships: Association for Documentary Editing; Association of Ancient Historians, president, 1978-81; Friends of Ancient History; Society for the Promotion of Roman Studies. Address: 25 Temple Court, New Haven, CTY 06511, USA.

MACNAB Roy Martin, b. 17 Sept 1923, Durban, South Africa. Retired Diplomat. m. Rachel Heron-Maxwell, 6 Dec 1947, 1 son, 1 daughter. Education: Hilton College, Natal, South Africa; MA, Jesus College, Oxford, England, 1955; DLitt et Phil, University of South Africa, 1981. Publications: The Man of Grass and Other Poems, 1960; The French Colonel, 1975; Gold Their Touchstone, 1987; For Honour Alone, 1988. Co-Editor: Oxford Poetry, 1947; Poets in South Africa, 1958; Journey Into Yesterday, 1962. Editor: George Seferis South African Diary, 1990; The Cherbourg Circles, 1994. Contributions to: Times Literary Supplement; Spectator; Poetry Review; History, Today. Honour: Silver Medal, Royal Society of Arts, 1958. Address: c/o Barclays Private Bank, 59 Grosvenor Street, London, W1X 9DA, England.

MACNEACAIL Aonghas, b, 7 June 1942, Uig, Isle of Skye, Scotland. Writer. m. Gerda Stevenson, 21 June 1980, 1 son. Appointments: Writing Fellowships: The Gaelic College, Isle of Skye, 1977-79, An Comunn Gaidhealachm Oban, 1979-81, Ross-Cromarty District Council, 1988-90. Publications: Poetry Quintet, 1976; Imaginary Wounds, 1980; Sireadh Bradain Sicir/Seeking Wise Salmon, 1983; An Cathadh Mor/The Great Snowbattle, 1984; An Seachnadh/The Avoiding, 1986; Rocker and Water, 1990. Contributions to: Gairm (Gaelic) Cencrastus; Words; Acuarius; Cracked Locking Glass; Chapman Lines Review; Scottish Review; Edinburgh Review; Scotsman; West Highland Free Press; Akros Poetry, Australia; Pembroke Magazine, USA; International Poetry Review, USA; Tijdschrift Voor Poezie, Belgium; Honest Ulsterman, Ireland. Honours: Grampian TV Gaelic Poetry Award; Diamond of Jubilee Award, Scottish Association for the Speaking of Verse, 1985; An Comunn Gaidhealach Literary Award, 1985. Membership: Scottish Poetry Library Association, council member, 1984-. Address: 1 Roseneath Terrace, Marchmont, Edinburgh EH9 1JS, Scotland.

MACNEIL Duncan. See: McCUTCHAN Philip Donald.

MACTHOMAIS Ruaraidh. See: THOMSON Derick S(mith).

MACVEAN Jean Elizabeth, b. Bradford, England. Poet; Writer. m. James Bernard Wright, 11 Oct 1952, 1 son, 1 daughter. Education: Sorbonne, University of Paris. Pubications: The Intermediaries (novel); Eros Reflected (poems), 1981; The Dolorous Death of King Arthur, 1992. COntributions to: Various publications. Memberships: International PEN Society, fellow; Poetry Society. Address: 21 Peel Street, London W8 7PA, England.

MACVEY John Wishart, b. 19 Jan 1923, Kelso, Scotland. Technical Information Officer (retired); Writer. Education: Diploma in Applied Chemistry, University of Strathclyde, 1951; BA, Open University, Milton Keynes, 1978. Appointments: Research Chemist, 1956-61, Plant Manager, 1961-62, Assistant Technical Information Officer, 1962-71, Technical Information Officer, Nobel's Explosives Ltd. Publications: Speaking of Space (with C P Snow, B Lovell and P Moore), 1962; Alone in the Universe?, 1963; Journey to Alpha Centauri, 1965; How We Will Reach the Stars, 1969; Whispers from Space, 1973; Interstellar Travel: Past, Present and Future, 1977; Space Weapons/Space War, 1979; Where We Will Go When the Sun Dies/, 1980; Colonizing Other Worlds, 1984; Time Travel, 1987. Address: Mellendean, 15 Adair Avenue, Saltcoats, Ayrshire KA21 5QS, Scotland.

MADDISON Tyler. See: SMITH Moe Gerard.

MADDOX Carl. See: TUBB E(dwin) C(harles).

MADELEY John, b. 14 July 1934, Salford, England. Writer; Broadcaster. m. Alison Madeley, 10 Mar 1962, 1 son, 1 daughter. Education: BA, Hons Econ, 1972. Appointments: Broadcaster, BBC and Deutsche Welle; Editor and Publisher, International Agricultural Development. Publications: Human Rights Begin with Breakfast, 1981; Diego Garcia: Contrast to the Falklands, 1982; When Aid is No Help, 1991; Trade and the Poor, 1992, 2nd edition, 1996. Contributions to: Newspapers and magazines. Membership: Society of International Development Journalists Group, secretary. Address: 19 Woodford Close, Caversham, Reading, Berks RG4 7HN, England.

MADGETT Naomi Long, b. 5 July 1923, Norfolk, Virginia, USA. Poet; Publisher; Professor of English Emeritus. m. Leonard P Andrews Sr. Education: BA, Virginia State College, 1945; MEd, English, Wayne State University; PhD, International Institute for Advanced Studies, 1980. Appointments: Research Associate, Oakland University; Lecturer in English, University of Michigan; Associate Professor to Professor of English Emeritus, Eastern Michigan University; Publisher; Editor, Lotus Press. Publications: Songs to a Phantom Nightingale, 1941; One and the Many, 1956; Star by Star, 1965; Pink Ladies in the Afternoon, 1972; Exits and Entrances, 1978; Phantom Nightingale, 1981; A Student's Guide to Creative Writing, 1990. Contributions to: Numerous anthologies and journals. Address: 16886 Inverness Avenue, Detroit, MI 48221, USA.

MADOUESSE Ti-Pique Le. See: **PARATTE Henri-Dominique.**

MADSEN Richard Paul, b. 2 Apr 1941, Alameda, California, USA. Professor of Sociology; Writer. m. Judith Rosselli, 12 Jan 1974. Education: BA, Maryknoll College, Glen Ellyn, Illinois, 1963; BD, 1967, MTh, 1968, Maryknoll Seminary, Ossining, New York; MA, 1972, PhD, 1977, Harvard University. Appointments: Ordained, Roman Catholic Priest, 1968; Maryknoll missioner, Taiwan, 1968-71; Left priesthood, 1974; Lecturer in Sociology, Harvard University, 1977-78; Assistant Professor, 1978-83, Associate Professor, 1983-85, Professor of Sociology, 1985-, University of California at San Diego, La Jolla. Publications: Chen Village: The Recent History of a Peasant Community in Mao's China (with Anita Chan and Jonathan Unger), 1984, revised edition as Chen Village Under Mao and Deng, 1992; Morality and Power in a Chinese Village, 1984; Habits of the Heart: Individualism in American Life (with Robert N Bellah, William M Sullivan, Ann Swidler and Steven M Tipton), 1985; Individualism and Commitment in American Life: A Habits of the Heart Reader (with Robert N Bellah, William M Sullivan, Ann Swidler and Steven M Tipton), 1987; Unofficial China (editor with Perry Link and Paul Pickowicz), 1989; The Good Society (with Robert N Bellah, William M Sullivan, Ann Swidler and Steven M Tipton), 1991; China and the American Dream: A Moral Inquiry, 1995. Contributions to: Journals. Honours: C Wright Mills Award, Society for the Study of Social Problems, 1985; Current Interest Book Award, Los Angeles Times, 1985; Book Award, Association of Logos Bookstores, 1986. Memberships: American Sociological Association; Association of Asian Studies, governing council for China and Inner Asia, 1989-91. Address: c/o Department of Sociology, University of California at San Diego, La Jolla, CA 92093, USA.

MAFFI Mario, b. 23 May 1947, Milan, Italy. University Professor. m. Maria Matilde Merli, 7 May 1973, 1 daughter. Education: Degree in Humanities, magna cum laude, University of Milan, 1971. Publications: La cultura underground, 1972; La giungla e il grattacielo. Gli scrittori e il "sogno americano" 1865-1920, 1982; Nel mosaico della citta. Differenze etniche e nuove culture in un quartiere di New York, 1992; Gateway to the Promised Land. Ethnic Cultures in New York's Lower East Side, 1994; New York. L'isola delle colline, 1995. Honour: Premio Libro Giovane for La cultura underground, 1975. Literary agent: Grandi & Associati, Milan. Address: istituto di Anglistica, Piazza S Alessandro 1, 20123 Milan, Italy.

MAGEE Bryan, b. 12 Apr 1930, London, England. Writer. m. Ingrid Söderlund, 1954, dec 1986, 1 daughter. Education: MA, Oxford University, 1956; Yale University, 1955-56. Appointments: Theatre Critic, The Listener, 1966-67; Regular Columnist, The Times, 1974-76. Publications: Go West Young Man, 1958; To Live in Danger, 1960; The New Radicalism, 1962; The Democratic Revolution, 1964; Towards 2000, 1965; One in Twenty, 1966; The Television Interviewer, 1966; Aspects of Wagner, 1968; Modern British Philosophy, 1971; Popper, 1973; Facing Death, 1977; Men of Ideas, 1978; The Philosophy of Schopenhauer, 1983; The Great Philosophers, 1987; On Blindness, 1995; Confessions of a Philosopher, 1997. Contributions to: Numerous

journals. Honour: Silver Medal, Royal Television Society, 1978. Memberships: Critics Circle; Society of Authors. Literary Agent: A P Watt, Ltd. Address: 12 Falkland House, Marloes Road, London W8 5LF, England.

MAGEE Wes, b. 20 July 1939, Greenock, Scotland. Poet; Writer. m. Janet Elizabeth Parkhouse, 10 Aug 1967, 1 son, 1 daughter. Education: Teaching Certificate, 1967; Advanced Certificate in Education, 1972. Publications: Poetry: Urban Gorilla, 1972; No Man's Lane, 1978; A Dark Age, 1982; Flesh of Money, 1990. Other: Oliver the Daring Birdman, 1978; The Real Spirit of Christmas, 1979; All the Day Through, 1982; Dragon's Smoke, 1985; A Shooting Star, 1985; Story Starters, 1986; A Calendar of Poems, 1986; Don't Do That, 1987; A Christmas Stocking, 1987; The Puffin Book of Christmas Poems, 1989; Morning Break, 1989; The Witch's Brew, 1989; A Big Poetry Book, 1989; Read A Poem, Write A Poem, 1989; Madtail Miniwhale, 1989; Legend of the Ragged Boy, 1992; Scribblers of Scumbagg School, 1993; The Working Children, 1994; Scumbagg School Scorpion, 1994; Sports Day at Scumbagg School, 1995; The Spookspotters of Scumbagg School, 1996; The Snowgirl and the Snowboy, 1996; The Little Dragon books (set of four), 1996; Missing!, 1996; Amanda and the Rainbow, 1997. Contributions to: Journals. Honours: New Poets Award, 1972; Poetry Book Society Recommendation, 1978; Cole Scholar (Florida, USA), 1985. Memberships: Poetry Society of Great Britain. Address: Crag View Cottage, Thorgill, Rosedale Abbey, North Yorkshire, YO18 8SG, England.

MAGNUSSON Magnus, b. 12 Oct 1929, Reykjavik, Iceland. Writer; Broadcaster. m. Mamie Baird, 1954, 1 son, 3 daughters, 1 son dec. Education: MA, Jesus College, Oxford, 1951. Publications: Introducing Archaeology, 1972; Viking Expansion Westwards, 1973; The Clacken and the Slate, 1974; Hammer of the North, 1976, 2nd edition, Viking Hammer of the North, 1980; BC, The Archaeology of the Bible Lands, 1977; Landlord or Tenant?: A View of Irish History, 1978; Iceland, 1979; Vikings!, 1980; Magnus on the Move, 1980; Treasures of Scotland, 1981; Lindisfarne: The Cradle Island, 1984; Iceland Saga, 1987. Translations (all with Hermann Palsson): Njal's Saga, 1960; The Vinland Sagas, 1965; King Herald's Saga, 1966; Laxaela Saga, 1969; (all by Halldor Laxness): The Atom Station, 1961; Paradise Reclaimed, 1962; The Fish Can Sing, 1966; World Light, 1969; Christianity under Glacier, 1973; (by Samivel) Golden Iceland, 1967. Editor: Echoes in Stone, 1983; Reader's Digest Book of Facts, 1985; Chambers Biographical Dictionary, 1990; The Nature of Scotland, 1994. Contributions to: Many books. Honours: Knight of the Order of the Falcon, 1975, Knight Commander, 1986, Iceland; Silver Jubilee Medal, 1977; Iceland Media Award, 1985; Honorary Knighthood, Great Britain, 1989; Honorary Fellow, Jesus College, Oxford, 1990; Honorary Degrees, and many other honours and awards. Memberships: Society of Antiquaries of London, fellow, 1991; Royal Scottish Geographical Society, fellow, 1991. Literary Agent: Deborah Rogers, Rogers, Coleridge & White, 20 Powis Mews, London W11 1JN, England. Address: Blairskaith House, Balmore-Torrance, Glasgow G64 4AX, Scotland.

MAGNUSSON Sigurdur A, b. 31 Mar 1928, Reykjavik, Iceland. Writer; Poet. m. (1), div, (2), div, 2 sons, 3 daughters. Education: BA, New School for Social Research, New York City, 1955. Appointments: Literary and Drama Critic, Morgunbladid, 1956-67; Editor-in-Chief, Samvinnan, 1967-74; Member, International Writing Programme, University of Iowa, 1976, 1977, International Artists' Programme, West Berlin, 1979-80, Jury, Nordic Council Prize for Literature, 1990-98. Publications: In English: Northern Sphinx: Iceland and the Icelanders from the Settlement to the Present, 1977, 2nd edition, 1984; Iceland: Country and People, 1978, 2nd edition, 1987; The Iceland Horse, 1978; The Postwar Poetry of Iceland, 1982; Icelandic Writing Today, 1982; Iceland Crucible: A Modern Artistic Renaissance, 1985; The Icelanders, 1990; The Magic of Greece, 1992. Other: Many books in Icelandic. Contributions to: Professional journals. Honours: Golden Cross of Phoenix, Greece, 1955; Cultural Council Prize for Best play, 1961, and Best Novel, 1980; European Jean Mormet Prize for Literature, 1995. Memberships: Amnesty International, Chairman, 1988-89, 1993-95; Greek-Icelandic Society, Chairman, 1985-88; Society of Icelandic Drama Critics, Chairman, 1963-71; Writers Union of Iceland, Chairman, 1971-78. Address: Baronsstig 49, 101 Reykjavik, Iceland.

MAGORIAN James, b. 24 Apr 1942, Palisade, Nebraska, USA. Writer; Poet; Author of children's stories. Education: BS, University of Nebraska, 1965; MS, Illinois State University, 1969; Graduate Studies,

Oxford University, 1972, Harvard University, 1973. Publications: Author of 56 books including: The Garden of Epicus (poetry), 1971; Distances (poetry), 1972; School Daze (children's book), 1978; Safe Passage (poetry), 1977; The Edge of the Forest (poetry), 1980; Keeper of Fire (children's book), 1984; Ground-Hog Day (children's book), 1987; The Bad Eggs (children's book), 1989; The Invention of the Afternoon Nan (children's book), 1989. Contributions to: Western Poetry Quarterly; Poetry View; Nebraska Review; San Francisco Poetry Journal; Kansas Quarterly; Louisville Review; Illinois Quarterly. Address: 1225 North 46th Street, Lincoln, NE 68503, USA.

MAGORIAN Michelle Jane, b. 6 Nov 1947, Southsea, Portsmouth, Hampshire, England. Writer; Actress. m. Peter Keith Venner, 18 Aug 1987, 2 sons. Education: Diploma, Speech and Drama, Rose Bruford College of Speech and Drama, Kent, 1969; École Internationale de Mime Marcel Marceau, Paris, France, 1969-70. Publications: Novels: Goodnight Mister Tom, 1981, US edition 1982, also book and lyrics as musical; Back Home, 1984; A Little Love Song, 1991; Cuckoo in the Nest, 1994. Poetry: Waiting for My Shorts to Dry, 1989; Orange Paw Marks, 1991. Short Story Collection: In Deep Water, 1992. Contributions to: Puffin Post. Honours: Guardian Award for Children's Fiction, UK, 1981; Commended for Carnegie Medal, UK, 1981; Children's Award, International Reading Association, USA, 1982; Notable Children's Books of 1982, Best Book of Young Adults, 1982, Young Adult Reviewers Choice, 1982, American Library Association; Western Australia Young Readers Book Award, 1983; Teachers Choice, NCTE, 1983; Best Books for Adults, American Library Association, 1984; Western Australia Young Readers Book Award, 1987. Memberships: Society of Authors; PEN; British Actors Equity. Literary Agent: Patricia White, Rogers, Coleridge and White. Address: 2 Harbour Mount, Church Road, Bembridge, Isle of Wight, PO35 5NA, England.

MAHAPATRA Jayanta, b. 22 Oct 1928, Cuttack, Orissa, India. Poet. m. Jyotsna Rani Das, 1951, 1 son. Education: MSc, Patna University, 1949. Appointments: Visiting Writer, Universities, USA, Japan, Australia, UK, Germany, Mexico, Malaysia, Indonesia, Singapore; Poet-in-Residence, Rockefeller Foundation Cultural Centre, Italy, 1986. Publications: Close the Sky, Ten by Ten, 1971; Svayamvara and Other Poems, 1971; A Rain of Rites, 1976; A Fathers Hours, 1976; Waiting, 1979; The False Start, 1980; Relationship, 1980; Life Signs, 1983; Dispossessed Nests, 1984; Selected Poems, 1987; Burden of Waves and Fruit, 1988; Temple, 1989; A Whiteness of Bone, 1992; The Best of Jayanta Mahapatra, 1995; Shadow Spacem 1997; Stories for Children and Translations. Honours: National Academy of Letters Award, New Delhi, 1981; Rockefeller Foundation Award, 1986. Address: Tinkonia, Bagicha, Cuttack 753 001, Orissa, India.

MAHARIDGE Dale (Dimitro), b. 24 Oct 1956, Cleveland, Ohio, USA. University Lecturer; Writer. Education: Cleveland State University, 1974-76; Cuyahoga Community College, 1976. Appointments: Staff, Gazette, Medina, Ohio, 1977-78; Journalist, Sacramento Bee, California, 1980-91; Assistant Professor, Columbia University, 1991-92; Lecturer, Stanford University, 1992-. Publications: Journey to Nowhere: The Saga of the New Underclass, 1985; And Their Children After Them: The Legacy of "Let Us Now Praise Famous Men", James Agee, Walker Evans, and the Rise and Fall of Cotton in the South, 1989; Yosemite: A Landscape of Life, 1990; The Last Great American Hobo, 1993. Contributions to: Periodicals. Honours: World Hunger Award, New York City, 1987; Lucius W Nieman Fellowship, Harvard University, 1988; Pulitzer Prize for General Non-Fiction, 1990; Pope Foundation Award, 1994; Freedom Forum Professors' Publishing Program Grant, 1995. Membership: Sierra Club. Address: c/o Department of Communications, Stanford University, Stanford, CA 94305, USA.

MAHESHWARI Shriram, b. 27 Nov 1931, Kanpur, India. Professor; Writer. m. Bimla, 30 May 1955, 3 sons, 2 daughters. Education: BA, 1951, MA, Economics, 1953, MA, Political Science, 1955, Agra University; MGA, Wharton School, University of Pensylvania, 1964; PhD, University of Delhi, 1965. Appointments: Professor of Political Science and Public Administration, Indian Institute of Public Administration, 1973-91; Guest faculty, Jawaharla Nehru University, New Delhi, 1979-83; Director, Centre for Political and Administrative Studies, 1991-; Visiting Professor, Department of Political Studies, University of Guelph, Ontario, Canada. Publications: Rural Development in India: A Public Policy Approach, 1986, revised edition, 1996; The Higher Civil Service in Japan, 1986; The Higher Civil Service in France, 1991; Problems and Issues in Administrative

Federalism, 1991; Administrative Reform in India, 1991; Indian Administration: An Historical Account, 1994; Major Civil Service Systems in the World, 1997; The Census Administration in India Under the Raj and After. Contributions to: Philippines Journal of Public Administration; Indian Express; Hindustan Times. Honour: Sardar Patel Prize for best work in Hindi, 1988. Memberships: Indian Public Administration Association, president, 1988-89; Indian Political Science Association. Address: 156 Golf Links, New Delhi 110003, India.

MAHFOUZ Naguib (Abdel Aziz Al-Sabilgi), b. 11 Dec 1911, Cairo, Egypt. Writer; Journalist; Civil Servant. m., 2 daughters. Education: Degree in Philosophy, University of Cairo, 1934. Appointments: Journalist, Ar-Risala; Ministry of Islamic Affairs, 1939; Department of Art; Head, State Cinema Organisation; Advisor to Minister of Culture; retired 1971. Publications: 16 collections of short stories including (in translation), The Time and the Place, 1991; 34 novels including (in translation), Midaq Alley, 1975; Mirrors, 1977; Miramar, 1978; Al-Karnak, 1979; Children of Gebelawi, (translated by Philip Stewart) 1981, new translation, 1995; The Thief and the Dogs, 1984; Wedding Song, 1984; The Beginning and the End, 1985; The Beggar, 1986; Respected Sir, 1986; The Search, 1987, Fountain and Tomb, 1988; (The Cairo Trilogy) Palace Walk, 1990, Palace of Desire, 1991, Sugar Street, 1992; The Journey of Ibn Fattouma, 1992; Adrift on the Nile, 1993; Al-Harafish, 1994; Arabian Nights and Days, 1995; Echoes of an Autobiography, 1997. Honours: Nobel Prize for Literature, 1988; Honorary Member, American Academy and Institute of Arts and Letters, 1992. Literary Agent: The American Univesity in Cairo Press. Address: 113 Sharia Kasr El Aini, Cairo, Egypt.

MAHON Derek, b. 23 Nov 1941, Belfast, Northern Ireland. Critic; Editor; Poet. Education: BA, Belfast Institute; BA, Trinity College, Dublin, 1965. Appointments: Drama Critic, Editor, Poetry Editor, New Statesman, 1981-; Poet-in-Residences. Publications: Twelve Poems, 1965; Night-Crossing, 1968; Lives, 1972; The Man Who Built His City in Snow, 1972; The Snow Party, 1975; Light Music, 1977; The Sea in Winter, 1979; Poems 1962-1978, 1979; Courtyards in Delft, 1981; The Hunt by Night, 1982; A Kensington Notebook, 1984; Antarctica, 1986. Editor: Modern Irish Poetry, 1972; The Penquin Book of Contemporary Irish Poetry, 1990. Address: c/o Rogers Coleridge & White Ltd, 20 Powis Mews, London W11 1JN, England.

MAHONEY Rosemary, b. 28 Jan 1961, Boston, Massachusetts, USA. Writer. Education: BA, Harvard College, 1983; MA, Johns Hopkins University, 1985. Publications: The Early Arrival of Dreams; A Year in China; Whoredom in Kimmage; Irish Women Coming of Age, 1993. Honours: C E Horman Prize for Fiction, Harvard College, 1982; Henfield-Transatlantics Review Award for Fiction, 1985. Contributions to: Newspapers and journals. Address: c/o Houghton Mifflin Company, 215 Park Avenue South, New York, NY 10003, USA.

MAHY Margaret, b. 21 Mar 1936, Whakatane, New Zealand. Writer; Poet. Education: BA, University of New Zealand, 1958. Appointments: Writer-in-Residence, Canterbury University, 1984, College of Advanced Education, Western Australia, 1985. Publications: Some 50 books for children, 1969-95. Honours: Several. Address: RD No 1, Lyttelton, New Zealand.

MAI Gottfried Erhard Willy, b. 11 May 1940, Finsterwalde, Germany. Theologian; Freelance Writer. m. Gunhild Flemming, 1 Sept 1962, 2 sons, 2 daughters. Education: Navigation Certificate, Nautical School, Bremen; Studied Theology and History, Universities of Bonn, Göttingen, Hamburg and Copenhagen; Dr Theol; Dr Phil. Publications: The Protestant Church and the German Emigration to North America (1815-1914), 1972; The German Federal Armed Forces 1815-1864, 1977; Die niederdeutsche Reformbewegung, 1979; Geschichte der stadt Finsterwalde, 1979; Der Überfall des Tigers, 1982; Chronicle of the 4th Minesweeper Squadron Wilhelmshaven, 1985; Buddha, 1985; Napoleon: Temptation of Power, 1986; Zwischen Polor und Wonderkreis, 1987; Lenin: The Perverted Moral, 1987. Contributions to: Books and journals. Honour: Book Prize for History of AWMM, 1983. Address: Harlinger Weg 2, D-2948 Grafschaft, Germany.

MAIBAUM Matthew, b. 14 Aug 1946, Chicago, Illinois, USA. Consulting Social Scientist; Writer. Education: AB Honours, University of California, Berkeley, 1969; MPA, University of California, Los Angeles; PhD, California School of Professional Psychology, 1975; PhD, Political Sciences, Claremont Graduate School, 1980. Publications: Sly Times (play), 1985; Wiggling in the Rain (play), 1987;

The Lilac Bush, 1990; Monographs, articles and funded studies in ethnic studies, politics, intergroup relations. Contributions to: Various journals and books. Honours: Grant Aid Award, Society for the Psychological Study of Social Issues, 1972; Best Paper, California State Psychological Association, 1975; Other awards. Memberships: Authors Guild; Dramatists Guild; Pi Gamma Mu; Sigma Xi; Society of Authors, UK. Address: 15237 Sunset Boulevard, No 24, Pacific Palisades, CA 90272, USA.

MAIDEN Jennifer, b. 7 Apr 1949, Penrith, New South Wales, Australia. Writer; Poet. m. David Toohey, 1984, 1 daughter. Education: BA, Macquarie University, New South Wales, 1974. Appointments: Tutor, University of Western Sydney, 1991. Publications: Tactics, 1974; The Occupying Forces, 1975; The Problem of Evil, 1975; Birthstones, 1978; The Border Loss, 1979; For the Left Hand, 1981; The Trust, 1988; Selected Poems of Jennifer Maiden, 1990; The Winter Baby, 1990. Novels: The Terms, 1982; Play with Knives, 1990. Short Stories: Mortal Details, 1977. Honours: Australia Council Grants or Fellowships. Address: PO Box 4, Penrith, New South Wales 2750, Australia.

MAIER Paul Luther, b. 31 May 1930, St Louis, Missouri, USA. Professor of Ancient History; Chaplain. m. Joen M Ludtke, 1967, 4 daughters. Education: MA, Harvard University, 1954; BD, Concordia Seminary, St Louis, 1955; Postgraduate Studies, Heidelberg; PhD, University of Basel, 1957. Appointments: Campus Chaplain, 1958-, Professor of Ancient History, 1961-, Western Michigan University; Lecturer. Publications: A Man Spoke, A World Listened: The Story of Walter A Maier, 1963; Pontius Pilate, 1968; First Christmas, 1971; First Easter, 1973; First Christians, 1976; The Flames of Rome, 1981; In the Fullness of Time, 1991; A Skeleton in God's Closet, 1994. Editor: The Best of Walter A Maier, 1980; Josephus: The Jewish War, 1982. Editor and Translator: Josephus: The Essential Writings, 1988; Josephus: The Essential Works, 1995. Contributions to: Many professional journals. Honours: Alumni Award for Teaching Excellence, 1974, Distinguished Faculty Scholar, 1981, Western Michigan University; Outstanding Educator in America, 1974-75; Professor of the Year, Council for the Advancement and Support of Education, 1984; Citation, Michigan Academy of Sciences, Arts and Letters, 1985; Gold Medallion Book Award, ECPA, 1989. Address: c/o Department of History, Western Michigan University, Kalamazoo, MI 49008, USA.

MAILER Norman (Kingsley), b. 31 Jan 1923, Long Beach, California, USA. Writer. m. (1) Beatrice Silverman, 1944, div 1951, 1 daughter, (2) Adele Morales, 1954, div 1962, 2 daughters, (3) Lady Jeanne Campbell, 1962, div 1963, 1 daughter, (4) Beverly Rentz Bentley, 1963, div 1980, 2 sons, 1 daughter, (5) Carol Stevens, div, 1 daughter, (6) Norris Church, 1980, 1 son. Education: BS, Harvard University. Publications: The Naked and the Dead, 1948; Barbary Shore, 1951; The Deer Park, 1955 (dramatised 1967); Advertisements for Myself, 1959; Deaths for the Ladies (poems), 1962; The Presidential Papers, 1963; An American Dream, 1964; Cannibals and Christians, 1966; Why are We in Vietnam? (novel), 1967; The Armies of the Night, 1968; Miami and the Siege of Chicago, 1968; Moonshot, 1969; A Fire on the Moon, 1970; The Prisoner of Sex, 1971; Existential Errands, 1972; St George and the Godfather, 1972; Marilyn, 1973; The Faith of Graffiti, 1974; The Fight, 1975; Some Honourable Men, 1976; Genius and Lust - A Journey Through the Writings of Henry Miller, 1976; A Transit to Narcissus, 1978; The Executioner's Song, 1979; Of Women and Their Elegance, 1980; The Essential Mailer (Selections), 1982; Pieces and Pontifications, 1982; Ancient Evenings (novel), 1983; Tough Guys Don't Dance (novel), 1983; Harlot's Ghost, 1991; How the Wimp Won the War, 1991; Oswald's Tale, 1995; Portrait of Picasso as a Young Man, 1995; The Gospel according to the Son (novel), 1997. Contributions to: Numerous journals and magazines. Honours: National Book Award for Arts and Letters, 1969; Pulitzer Prize for Non-Fiction, 1969; 14th Annual Award for Outstanding Service to the Arts, McDowell Colony, 1973. Memberships: PEN, president, 1984-86; American Academy of Arts and Letters. Literary Agent: Wylie, Aitleen, Stone, 250 West 57th St, New York, NY 10119, USA. Address: c/o Rembar, 19th West 44th Street, New York, NY 10036, USA.

MAINE David. See: **AVICE Claude (Pierre Marie).**

MAIR (Alexander) Craig, b. 3 May 1948, Glasgow, Scotland. Schoolteacher. m. Anne Olizar, 1 Aug 1970, 2 sons, 1 daughter. Education: BA, Stirling University, 1971. Publications: A Time in Turkey, 1973; A Star for Seamen, 1978; The Lighthouse Boy, 1981; Britain at War 1914-19, 1982; Mercat Cross and Tolbooth, 1988; David Angus, 1989; Stirling, The Royal Burgh, 1990; The Incorporation of Glasgow Maltmen: A History, 1990. Memberships: Scottish Society of Antiquaries, fellow; Educational Institute of Scotland; Various local history groups. Address: 21 Keir Street, Bridge of Allan, Stirling, Scotland.

MAIRS Nancy Pedrick, b. 23 July 1943, Long Beach, California, USA. Writer. m. George Anthony Mairs, 18 May 1963, 1 son, 1 daughter. Education: AB cum laude, Wheaton College, Massachusetts, 1964; MFA, 1975, PhD, 1984, University of Arizona. Publications: Instead It is Winter, 1977; In All the Rooms of the Yellow House, 1984; Plaintext, 1986; Remembering the Bone House, 1989; Carnal Acts, 1990; Ordinary Time, 1993; Voice Lessons, 1994. Contributions to: American Voice; MSS; Tri Quarterly. Honours: Western States Book Award, 1984; National Endowment for the Arts Fellowship, 1991. Memberships: Authors Guild; Poets and Writers; National Women's Studies Association. Literary Agent: Barbara S Kouts. Address: 1527 East Mabel Street, Tucson, AZ 85719, USA.

MAJA-PEARCE Adewale, b. 3 June 1953, London, England. Researcher; Consultant; Writer. Education: BA, University of Wales, University College of Swansea, 1975; MA, School of Oriental and African Studies, 1986. Appointments: Researcher, Index on Censorship, London, 1986-; Consultant, Heinemann International, Oxford, 1986-. Publications: Christopher Okigbo: Collected Poems (editor), 1986; In My Father's Country: A Nigerian Journey (non-fiction), 1987; Loyalties (stories), 1987; How Many Miles to Babylon (non-fiction), 1990; The Heinemann Book of African Poetry in English (editor), 1990; Who's Afraid of Wole Soyinka? Essays on Censorship, 1991; A Mask Dancing: Nigerian Novelists of the Eighties, 1992. Contributions to: Various periodicals. Memberships: PEN; Society of Authors. Literary Agent: David Grossman Literary Agency, London, England. Address: 33 St George's Road, Hastings, East Sussex TN34 3NH, England.

MAJOR Clarence, b. 31 Dec 1936, Atlanta, Georgia, USA. Poet; Writer; Artist; Professor. m. (1) Joyce Sparrow, 1958, div 1964, (2) Pamela Ritter. Education: BS, State University of New York at Albany, 1976; PhD, Union Graduate School, 1978. Appointments: Editor, Coercion Review, 1958-66, Writer-in-Residence, Center for Urban Education, New York, 1967-68, Teachers and Writers Collaborative-Teachers College, Columbia University, 1967-71, Aurora College, Illinois, 1974, Albany State College, Georgia, 1984, Clayton College, Denver, 1986, 1987; Associate Editor, Caw, 1967-70, Journal of Black Poetry, 1967-70; Lecturer, Brooklyn College of the City University of New York, 1968-69, 1973, 1974-75, Cazenovia Collge, New York, 1969, Wisconsin State University, 1969, Queens College of the City University of New York, 1972, 1973, 1975, Sarah Lawrence College, 1972-75, School of Continuing Education, New York University, 1975; Columnist, 1973-76, Contributing Editor, 1976-86, American Poetry Review; Assistant Professor, Howard University, 1974-76, University of Washington, 1976-77; Visiting Assistant Professor, University of Maryland at College Park, 1976, State University of New York at Buffalo, 1976; Associate Professor, 1977-81, Professor, 1981-89, University of Colorado at Boulder; Editor, 1977-78, Associate Editor, 1978-, American Book Review; Professor, 1989-, Director, Creative Writing, 1991-, University of California at Davis. Publications: Poetry: The Fires That Burn in Heaven, 1954; Love Poems of a Black Man, 1965; Human Juices, 1965; Swallow The Lake, 1970; Symptons and Madness, 1971; Private Line, 1971; The Cotton Club: New Poems, 1972; The Syncopated Cakewalk, 1974; Inside Diameter: The France Poems, 1985; Surfaces and Masks, 1988; Some Observations of a Stranger in the Latter Part of the Century, 1989; Parking Lots, 1992. Fiction: All-Night Visitors, 1969; NO, 1973; Reflex and Bone Structure, 1975; Emergency Exit, 1979; My Amputations, 1986; Such Was the Season, 1987; Painted Turtle: Woman with Guitar, 1988; Fun and Games, 1990; Dirty Bird Blues, novel, 1996. Other: Dictionary of Afro-American Slang, 1970; The Dark and Feeling: Black American Writers and Their Work, 1974; Juba to Jive: A Dictionary of African-American Slang, 1994. Editor: Writers Workshop Anthology, 1967; Man is Like a Child: An Anthology of Creative Writing by Students, 1968; The New Black Poetry, 1969; Calling the Wind: Twentieth Century African-American Short Stories, 1993; The Garden Thrives: Twentieth Century African-American Poetry, 1995. Honours: Fulbright-Hays Exchange Award, 1981-83; Western States Book Award, 1986; Pushcart Prize, 1989. Address: c/o Department of English, University of California at Davis, Davis, CA 95616, USA.

MAKARENKO Alexander Borisovich, b. 23 June 1954, Kherson, Ukraine. Physician (Psychotherapy). Education: Graduated from the Crimea Medical Institute, 1978; Doctor of Medicine, 1990. Appointments: Therapeutist, 1978-82; Physiologist, 1983-86; Head of Diagnostic Laboratory, 1987-90; Director, Research Psychotherapy Centre. Publications: Several medical books. Membership: International Psychotherapy Association, Moscow. Address: 32A Donetskaya Str, Kherson 325033, Ukraine.

MAKARSKI Henryk, b. 17 Aug 1946, Biala, Podlaska, Poland. Writer; Poet. m. Maria Anna Koziolkiewicz, 24 July 1971, 1 son, 1 daughter. Education: MA, Polish Philology, Marie-Curie-Slowdoska University of Lublin, 1969. Publications: 7 volumes of fiction, 5 volumes of poetry, various essays of literary criticism. Honours: Numerous awards. Membership: Polish Writers Association, Lublin. Address: ul Radzynska 18 m 23, 20-850 Lublin, Poland.

MAKOWIECKI Andrzej, b. 5 Aug 1938, Warsaw, Poland. Reporter; Editor; Writer. Education: State School of Music, Lodz, 1962; MA, Polish Philology, University of Lodz, 1968. Appointments: Reporter-Editor, Odgiosy, literary weekly, 1965-87; Correspondent, Polityka, weekly, 1970-72; Reporter, Zwierciadlo, weekly, 1973-75. Publications: 6 novels, 1972-87; Short stories. Contributions to: Periodicals. Honours: Various awards and prizes. Memberships: Association of Polish Authors; Association of Polish Journalists; Union of Polish Writers. Address: ul Pietrkowska 147 m 1, 90-440 Lodz, Poland.

MALINS Penelope, (Penelope Hobhouse), b. 20 Nov 1929, Castledawson, Northern Ireland. Writer; Designer. m. John Malins, 1 Nov 1965. 2 sons, 1 daughter. Education: Cambridge Hons, Economics, 1951. Publications: As Penelope Hobhouse: The Country Gardener; Colour in Your Garden; Garden Style; Flower Gardens; Guide to the Gardens of Europe; The Smaller Garden; Painted Gardens; Private Gardens of England; Borders; Flower Gardens; Plants in Garden History; Garden Style; Contributions to: The Garden; Horticulture; Vogue; Antiques; Plants and Gardens. Honour: As Penelope Hobhouse: Awarded Royal Horticultural Society Victoria Medal of Honour, 1996. Literary Agent: Felicity Bryan, Address: The Coach House, Bettiscombe, Bridport, Dorset DT6 5NT, England.

MALLET-JONES Françoise, b. 6 July 1930, Antwerp, Belgium (French citizen). Novelist. Education: Bryn Mawr College, Pennsylvania, USA, and Sorbonne, Paris, 1947-49. Appointments: Reader, Grasset Publishers, 1965-. Publications: Into the Labyrinth, 1951; The Red Room, 1955; Cordelia and Other Stories, 1956; House of Lies, 1956; Cafe Celeste, 1958; The Favourite, 1961; Signs and Wonders, 1966; The Witches: Three Tales of Sorcery, 1968; The Underground Game, 1973; Allegra, 1976; Le Rire de Laura, 1985; La Tristesse du cerf-volant, 1988; Adriana Sposa, 1989; Divine, 1991. Other: French version of Shelagh Delaney's play A Taste of Honey, 1960; A Letter to Myself, 1964; The Paper House, 1970; Juliette Greco, 1975; Marie-Paule Belle, 1987. Honours: Ordre National du Mérite, 1986. Address: c/o Flammarion et Cie, 26 rue Racine, 75278 Paris, France.

MALLINSON Jeremy John Crosby, b. 16 Mar 1937, Ilkley, Yorkshire, England. Zoological Director; Writer. m. Odette Louise Guiton, 26 Oct 1963, 1 son, 1 daughter. Appointments: Zoological Director, Jersey Wildlife Preservation Trust; Chairman, Editorial Board, International Zoo Yearbook. Publications: Okavango Adventure, 1973; Earning Your Living With Animals, 1975; Modern Classic Animal Stories (editor), 1977, US edition as Such Agreeable Friends, 1978; The Shadow of Extinction, 1978; The Facts About a Zoo, 1980; Travels in Search of Endangered Species, 1989. Contributions to: Numerous journals and magazines. Memberships: International Union for the Conservation of Nature and Natural Resources; International Union of Zoo Directors; Wildlife Preservation Trust International, Philadelphia; Wildlife Preservation Trust of Canada; Dian Fossey Gorilla Fund. Address: c/o Jersey Wildlife Preservation trust, Les Augres Manor, Trinity, Jersey, Channel Islands.

MALLON Maurus Edward, b. 10 July 1932, Greenock, Scotland. Teacher. Education: MA (Hons), University of Glasgow, 1956; BEd, Manitoba University, Canada, 1966. Publications: Basileus, 1971; The Opal, 1973; Pegaso, 1975; Way Of The Magus, 1978; Anogia, 1980; Bammer McPhie, 1984; Treasure Mountain, 1986; Postcards, 1991; Ex Novo Mundo (short stories), 1992; Compendulum, 1993; A Matter of Conscience (play), 1994. Honours: ABI Gold Record

of Excellence, 1994, 1995; ABI Lifetime Achievement Award, 1996; ABI Platinum Record for Exceptional Performance, 1997. Memberships: National Writers' Association, USA; PEN, Canada; Living Authors' Society. Literary Agents: NWA Agency. Address: Box 331, Deep River, Ontario K0J 1P0, Canada.

MALONE Joseph L(awrence), b. 2 July 1937, New York, New York, USA. Professor of Linguistics; Writer; Poet; Translator. m. 31 Jan 1964, 2 sons. Education: AB, 1963, PhD, 1967, University of California at Berkeley. Appointments: Instructor, University of California Extension, San Francisco, 1965; Instructor, 1967-68, Chairman, Department of Linguistics, 1967-, Assistant Professor, 1968-71, Associate Professor, 1971-75, Professor of Linguistics, 1975-, Barnard College and Columbia University; Consultant in Linguistics, Academic American Encyclopedia, 1977-; Editorial Board, Hellas, 1990-. Publications: The Science of Linguistics in the Art of Translation: Some Tools from Linguistics for the Analysis and Practice of Translation, 1988; Tiberian Hebrew Phonology, 1993. Contributions to: Numerous publications. Memberships: American Oriental Society; Linguistic Society of America; North American Conference on Afro-Asiatic Linguistics. Address: 169 Prospect Street, Leonia, NJ 07605, USA.

MALOUF (George Joseph) David, b. 20 Mar 1934, Brisbane, Australia. Poet; Novelist. Education: BA, University of Queensland, 1954. Appointments: Assistant Lecturer in English, University of Queensland, 1955-57; Supply Teacher, London, 1959-61; Teacher of Latin and English, Holland Park Comprehensive, 1962; Teacher, St Anselm's Grammar School, 1962-68; Senior Tutor and Lecturer in English, University of Sydney, 1968-77. Publications: Poetry: Bicycle and Other Poems, 1970; Neighbours in a Thicket: Poems, 1974; Poems, 1975-1976, 1976; Wild Lemons, 1980; First Things Last, 1981; Selected Poems, 1981; Selected Poems, 1959-1989, 1994. Fiction: Johnno (novel), 1975; An Imaginary Life (novel), 1978; Child's Play (novella), 1981; The Bread of Time to Come (novella), 1981, republished as Fly Away Peter, 1982; Eustace (short story), 1982; The Prowler (short story), 1982; Harland's Half Acre (novel), 1984; Antipodes (short stories), 1985; The Great World (novel), 1990; Remembering Babylon (novel), 1993. Play: Blood Relations, 1988. Opera Libretti: Voss, 1986; Mer de Glace; Baa Baa Black Sheep, 1993. Memoir: Twelve Edmondstone Street, 1985. Editor: We Took Their Orders and Are Dead: An Anti-War Anthology, 1971; Gesture of a Hand (anthology), 1975. Contributions to: Four Poets: David Malouf, Don Maynard, Judith Green, Rodney Hall, 1962; Australian; New York Review of Books; Poetry Australia; Southerly; Sydney Morning Herald. Honours: Grace Leven Prize for Poetry, 1974; Gold Medals, Australian Literature Society, 1975, 1982; Australian Council Fellowship, 1978; New South Wales Premier's Fiction Award, 1979; Victorian Premier's Award for Fiction, 1985; New South Wales Premier's Drama Award, 1987; Commonwealth Writer's Prize, 1991; Miles Franklin Award, 1991; Prize Femina Etranger, 1991; Inaugural International IMPAC Dublin Literary Award, 1996. Address: 53 Myrtle Street, Chippendale, New South Wales 2008, Australia.

MALZBERG Barry, (Mike Barry, Claudine Dumas, Mel Johnson, Lew W Mason, Francine de Natale, K M O'Donnell, Gerrold Watkins), b. 24 July 1939, New York, New York, USA. Writer. Education: AB, 1960, Graduate Studies, 1964-65, Syracuse University. Publications: Author or editor of over 30 books under various pseudonyns. Address: Box 61, Teaneck, NJ 07666, USA.

MAMET David (Alan), b. 30 Nov 1947, Chicago, Illinois, USA. Dramatist; Director; Writer. m. (1) Lindsay Crouse, Dec 1977, div, (2) Rebecca Pidgeon, 22 Sept 1991. Education: BA, Goddard College, Plainfield, Vermont, 1969. Appointment: Artist-in-Residence, Goddard College, 1971-73; Artistic Director, St Nicholas Theatre Co, Chicago, 1973-75; Guest Lecturer, University of Chicago, 1975, 1979, New York University, 1981; Associate Artistic Director, Goodman Theater, Chicago, 1978; Associate Professor of Film, Columbia University, 1988; Chairman of the Board, Atlantic Theater Co. Publications: Plays: The Duck Variations, 1971; Sexual Perversity in Chicago, 1973; Reunion, 1973; Squirrels, 1974; American Buffalo, 1976; A Life in the Theatre, 1976; The Water Engine, 1976; The Woods, 1977; Lone Chance, 1978; Praire du Chien, 1978; Lakeboat, 1980; Donny March, 1981; Edmond, 1982; The Disappearance of the Jews, 1983; Glengarry Glen Ross, 1984; The Shawl, 1985; Speed-the-Plow, 1987; Bobby Gould in Hell, 1989; The Old Neighborhood, 1991; Oleanna, 1992; The Cryptogram, 1994. Screenplays: The Postman Always Rings Twice, 1979; The Verdict, 1980; The Untouchables, 1986;

House of Games, 1986; Things Change (with Shel Silverstein), 1987; We're No Angels, 1987; Homicide, 1991; Hoffa, 1991; Oleanna, 1994. Novel: The Village, 1994. Poetry: The Hero Pony, 1990. Essays: Writing in Restaurants, 1986; Some Freaks, 1989; On Directing Film, 1990; The Cabin, 1992. Honours: CBS Creative Writing Fellowship, Yale University Drama School, 1976-77; Obie Awards, 1976, 1983; New York Drama Critics Circle Awards, 1976, 1987; Rockefeller Foundation Grant, 1977; Outer Critics Circle Award, 1978; Pulitzer Prize for Drama, 1987. Address: c/o Howard Rosenstone/Wender, 3 East 48th Street, 4th Floor, New York, NY 10017, USA.

MAMLEYEV Yuri, b. 11 Dec 1931, Moscow, Russia. Writer. m. Farida Mamleyev, 14 Apr 1973. Education: Forestry Institute, Moscow, 1955. Publications: The Sky Above Hell, 1980; Iznanka Gogena, 1982; Chatouny, 1986; Zivaja Smert, 1986; Golos iz Nichto, 1990; Ytopi Moyu Golovu, 1990; Vechnyi dom, 1991; Der Murder aus dem Nichts, 1992; Izbzannoe, 1993; Die Letzte Komödie, 1994. Contributions to: Periodicals. Membership: French PEN Centre. Address: 142 rue Legendre, 75017 Paris, France.

MANA Samira Al, b. 25 Dec 1935, Basra, Iraq. Librarian. m. Salah Niazi, July 1959, 2 daughters. Education: BA(Hon), University of Baghdad, 1958; Post Graduate Diploma in Librarianship, Ealing Technical College, 1976. Appointment: Assistant Editor, Alightrab Al-Adabi (Literature of the Exiled), 1985-. Publications: The Forerunners and the Newcomers, 1972; The Song, 1976; A London Sequel, 1979; Only a Half, 1979; The Umbilical Cord, 1990. Contributions to: Alightrab Al-Adabi; Many short stories in Arabic magazines; Translations in Dutch and English periodicals. Membership: PEN Club. Address: 46 Tudor Drive, Kingston-Upon-Thames, Surrey KT2 5PZ, UK.

MANCHEL Frank, b. 22 July 1935, Detroit, Michigan, USA. Writer; Editor. m. Seila Wachtel, 30 Mar 1958, 2 sons. Education: BA, Ohio State University, 1957; MA, Hunter College, 1960; EdD, Columbia University, 1966. Appointments: Editor, Journal of Popular Film and TV, 1977-, Film and History, 1996-. Publications: Terrors of the Screen, 1970; Cameras West, 1972; An Album of Great Science Fiction Films, 1976; Great Sports Movies, 1980; An Album of Modern Horror Films, 1983; Film Study: An Analytical Bibliography, 4 volumes, 1990. Contributions to: Periodicals. Memberships: American Federation of Film Societies, chairman, 1974-76; Society for Cinema Studies, treasurer, 1971-76. Address: RR 1, Box 1373, Shelburne, VT 05482, USA.

MANCHESTER William, b. 1st Apr 1922, Attleboro, Massachusetts, USA. Professor of History Emeritus; Author. m., 3 children. Education: University of Massachusetts; Dartmouth College; University of Missouri. Appointments: Served in US Marine Corps, World War II; Foreign Correspondent; Professor of History, later Professor Emeritus, Wesleyan University. Publications: Disturber of the Peace: The Life of H L Mencken, 1951; Death of a President, 1967; The Glory and the Dream: A Narrative History of America, 1968; Controversy and Other Essays in Journalism, 1976; Goodbye, Darkness, 1980; The Last Lion: Visions of Glory, 1874-1932, 1984; The Last Lion: Alone, 1932-1940, 1988; A World Lit by Fire: The Mediaeval Mind, 1992. Other: Novels and essays. Contributions to: Various publications. Honours: Several. Address: c/o Department of History, Wesleyan University, Middletown, CT 06459, USA.

MANDEL Oscar, b. 24 Aug 1926, Antwerp, Belgium (US citizen). Professor of Humanities; Writer; Dramatist; Poet. m. Adriana Schizzano, 1960. Education: BA, New York University, 1947; MA, Columbia University, 1948; PhD, Ohio State University, 1951. Appointments: Faculty, University of Nebraska, 1955-60; Fulbright Lecturer, University of Amsterdam, 1960-61; Associate Professor, 1961-65, Professor of Humanities, 1965-, California Institute of Technology, Pasadena. Publications: Fiction: Chi Po and the Sorcerer: A Chinese Tale for Children and Philosophers, 1964; Gobble-Up Stories, 1966; The Kukkurrik Fables, 1987. Verse: Simplicities, 1974; Collected Lyrics and Epigrams, 1981. Plays: Collected Plays, 2 volumes, 1970, 1972; Sigismund, Prince of Poland: A Baroque Entertainment, 1988; The Virgin and the Unicorn: Four Plays by Oscar Mandel, 1993; Two Romantic Plays, 1996. Other: A Definition of Tragedy, 1961; The Theatre of Don Juan: A Collection of Plays and Views 1630-1963 (editor), 1963; Seven Comedies by Marivaux (editor and translator), 1968; Five Comedies of Medieval France (editor and translator), 1970; Three Classic Don Juan Plays (editor and translator), 1971; Philoctetes and the Fall of Troy: Plays, Documents,

Iconography, Interpretations, including versions by Sophocles, André Gide, Oscar Mandel and Heiner Müller, 1991; Annotations to "Vanity Fair", 1981; The Book of Elaborations: Essays, 1985; August von Kotzebue: The Comedy, The Man, 1988; The Art of Alessandro Magnasco: An Essay in the Recovery of Meaning, 1994; The Cheerfulness of Dutch Art: A Rescue Operation, 1996. Contributions to: Professional journals. Memberships: College Art Association; Dramatists Guild; Modern Language Association; Société des Auteurs et Compositeurs Dramatiques. Address: c/o Division of Humanities and Social Sciences, California Institute of Technology, Pasadena, CA 91125, USA.

MANDELA Nelson, b. 1918, Transkei, South Africa. President of South Africa. m. Winnie Mandela, div 1996. Education: University of Witwatersrand. Career: Legal practice Johannesburg, 1952-; Imprisoned by South African regime, 1964, released, 1990; President of South Africa, 1994-. Publications: I Am Prepared to Die, 1965; No Easy Walk to Freedom, 1965; Nelson Mandela Speaks, 1970; The Struggle is My Life, 1978, 1986; Intensify the Struggle to Abolish Apartheid: Speeches, 1990; Long Walk to Freedom, 1994. Honours: Sakharov Prize, 1988; Nobel Peace Prize, 1993; Hon Order of Merit, 1995. Address: President's Office, Private Bag X 1000, Cape Town 8000, South Africa.

MANEA Norman, b. 19 July 1936, Suceava, Romania. Writer. m. Cella Boiangiu, 28 June 1969. Education: MS Engineering, Institute of Construction, Bucharest, 1959. Publications: In English: October, eight o'clock, 1992, On Clowns 1992-; The Black Envelope, 1995. Others: Captivi, 1970; Atrium, 1974; Anii de ucenicie ai lui August Prostul, 1979. Contributions to: New Republic; Partisan Review; Paris Review; Lettre Internationale; Vuelta; Akzente; Neue Rundschau; Sinn und Form. Honours: Guggenheim Award, 1992; MacArthur Award, 1992. Membership: American PEN. Literary Agent: Wylie, Aitken & Stone. Address: 201 West 70th Street, apt 10-I, New York, NY 10023, USA.

MANES Christopher, b. 24 May 1957, Chicago, Illinois, USA. Writer. 1 daughter. Education: BA, 1979 JD, 1992, University of California; MA, University of Wisconsin, 1981. Publications: Place of the Wild, 1994; Post Modernism and Environmental Philosophy, 1994. Contributions to: Reference works, books, journals and magazines. Memberships: California State Bar Association; Phi Beta Kappa; Writers Guild. Address: 34542 Paseo Real, Cathedral City, CA 92234, USA.

MANGUEL Alberto (Adrian), b. 13 Mar 1948, Buenos Aires, Argentina. Div, 1 son, 2 daughters. Education: Colegio Nacional de Buenos Airs, 1961-67; Universidad de Buenos Aires, 1967-68; London University, 1976. Appointments: Theatre Critic, CBLT Morning, 1984-86; Head of Contemporary Reading Group, McGill Club, 1986-89; Contributing Editor, Saturday Night, 1988, Grand Street, 1991. Publications: The Oxford Book of Canadian Ghost Stories; Black Water; Dark Arrows; The Dictionary of Imaginary Places; News from a Foreign Country Came; Other Fires; The Gates of Paradise. Contributions to: Saturday Night; Washington Post; New York Times; Village Voice; Rubicon; Whig Standard. Honours: Juan Angel Fraboschi Gold Medal; Ricardo Monner Sans Gold Medal; McKitterick Prize, 1992; Canadian Authors Association Prize, 1992; Harbourfront Prize, 1992. Memberships: Writers Union of Canada; ACTRA; PEN Canada. Address: c/o Lucinda Vardey Agency, Toronto, Ontario M5A 2T6, Canada.

MANKOWITZ Wolf, b. 7 Nov 1924, Bethnal Green, London, England. Writer; Theatrical Producer. m. Ann Margaret Seligmann, 1944, 4 sons. Education: MA, Downing College, Cambridge. Appointments: Extensive work in journalism, radio, TV, films and as Theatrical Producer; Expert in English Ceramics; Honorary Consul to Republic of Panama, Dublin, 1971; Adj Professor of Film and Theatre, University of West Mexico, 1982-89. Publications: Novels: Make Me an Offer, 1952; A Kid for Two Farthings, 1953; Laugh till You Cry, 1955; My Old Man's a Dustman, 1956; Cockatrice, 1963; The Biggest Pig in Barbados, 1965; Penguin Wolf Mankowitz, 1967; Raspberry Reich, 1978; Abracadabra!, 1980; The Devil in Texas, 1984; Gioconda, 1987; The Magic Cabinet of Professor Smucker, 1988; Exquisite Cadaver, 1989; A Night with Casanova, 1991. Short stories: The Mendelman Fire, 1958; The Blue Arabian Nights, 1972; The Day of the Women and the Night of the Men, 1975. Plays: The Bespoke Overcoat and Other Plays, 1955; Expresso Bongo, 1961; The Samson Riddle, 1972. Histories: The Portland Vase, 1953; Wedgwood, 1953; An

Encyclopedia of English Pottery and Porcelain, 1957; Dickens of London (also TV script), 1976. Biography: The Extraordinary Mr Poe, 1978; Mazeppa, 1981. Honours: Venice Film Festival Award, 1955; Hollywood Oscar, 1955; British Film Academy Awards, 1955, 1961; Critics Prize, Cork International Film Festival, 1972; Grand Prix, Cannes, 1973. Address: Bridge House, Ahakista, County Cork, Ireland.

MANN Anthony Philip, b. 7 Aug 1942, North Allerton, Yorkshire, England. Writer; Theatre Director. Education: BA, Hons, English and Drama, Manchester University, England, 1966; MA, Design and Directing, Humboldt State University, California, USA, 1969. Appointments: Trustee, New Zealand Players, 1992; Advisory Board, New Zealand Books, 1993. Publications: Eye of the Queen, 1982; Master of Paxwax, 1986; Fall of the Families, 1987; Pioneers, 1988; Wulfsyarn - A Mosaic, 1990; A Land Fit For Heroes, Vol 1, Into the Wild Wood, 1993, Vol 2, Stand Alone Stan, 1994. Contributions to: Books. Memberships: PEN, New Zealand; British Society of Dowsers; NZADIE (New Zealand Association for Drama in Education). Literary Agent: Glenys Bean, Auckland, New Zealand. Address: 22 Bruce Avenue, Brooklyn, Wellington, New Zealand.

MANN Christopher Michael Zithulele, b. 6 Apr 1948, Port Elizabeth, South Africa. Director; Writer. m. Julia Georgina Skeen, 10 Dec 1980, 1 son, 1 daughter. Education: BA, Witwatersrand University, Johannesburg, 1969; MA, Oxford University, England, 1973; MA, London University, 1974. Publications: First Poems, 1977; A New Book of South African Verse (editor with Guy Butler), 1979; New Shades, 1982; Kites, 1990; Mann Alive, video and book presentation of aural poems, 1991. Contributions to: Numerous magazines and journals. Honours: Rhodes Scholar; Newdigate Prize for Poetry, Oxford; Olive Schreiner Prize for Poetry, South African Academy of English; Hon DLitt, University of Durban-Westville. Address: Box 444, Bothas Hill, Natal, South Africa.

MANN Jessica, b. Britain. Writer. Publications: A Charitable End, 1971; Mrs Knox's Profession, 1972; The Only Security, 1973; The Sticking Place, 1974; Captive Audience, 1975; The Eighth Deadly Sin, 1976; The Sting of Death, 1978; Funeral Sites, 1981; Deadlier Than the Male, 1981; No Man's Island, 1983; Grave Goods, 1984; A Kind of Healthy Grave, 1986; Death Beyond the Nile, 1988; Faith, Hope and Homicide, 1991; Telling Only Lies, 1992; A Private Inquiry, 1996; Hanging Fire, 1997. Contributions to: Daily Telegraph; Sunday Telegraph; Various magazines and journals. Memberships: Detection Club; Society of Authors: PEN; Crime Writers Association. Literary Agent: Lavinia Trevor, 49A Goldhawk Road, London, W12 8QP, England. Address: Lambessow, St Clement, Cornwall, England.

MANNERS Alexandra. See: **RUNDLE Anne.**

MANNING Paul, b. 22 Nov 1912, Pasadena, California, USA. Author. m. Louise Margaret Windels, 22 Mar 1947, 4 sons. Education: Alumnus, Occidental College, Los Angeles. Appointments: Editor, Time-Life, New York City, 1937-38; Editor, Everyweek, 1939; Chief European Correspondent in London, Newspaper Enterprise Association and Scripps Howard Newspaper Group, 1939-42; Joined Edward R Murrow as CBS News Commentator from London, England, 1942; Only journalist to witness and broadcast both German surrender ceremonies, Reims, France, and Japanese surrender aboard USS Missouri, Tokyo Bay. Publications: Mr England, Biography of Winston Churchill, 1941; Martin Bormann, Nazi in Exile, 1986; Hirohito: The War Years, 1986; The Silent War, KGB Against the West, 1987; Years of War, 1988. Contributions to: New York Times; Reader's Digest; Saturday Evening Post; Articles to numerous journals including 8th Air Force News. Honours: Nominated for Pulitzer Prize, 1943, 1971, 1986; Special Citations, Secretary of War Robert Patterson and Secretary of Navy James Forrestal; Nominated for Congressional Medal for War Coverage, 1947. Membership: Eighth Air Force Historical Society. Address: PO Box 3129, Jersey City, NJ 07302, USA.

MANO D Keith, b. 12 Feb 1942, New York, New York, USA. Writer; Screenwriter. m. Laurie Kennedy, 18 July 1980, 2 sons. Education: BA, Columbia University, 1963; Clare College, Cambridge. Appointments: Contributing Editor, National Review, 1975-, Playboy, 1980; Book Editor, Esquire, 1979-80. Publications: Bishop's Progress, 1968; Horn, 1969; War is Heaven, 1970; The Death and Life of Harry Goth, 1971; The Proselytizer, 1972; The Bridge, 1973; Take Five, 1982; Resistance, 1984; Topless, 1991. Contributions to: Newspapers and magazines. Honours: Modern Language Association Award, 1968; Playboy Award, 1975; Literary Lion, New York Public Library, 1987.

Address: c/o National Review, 150 East 35th Street, New York, NY 10016, USA.

MANOR Jason. See: **HALL Oakley Maxwell.**

MANSEL Philip Robert Rhys, b. 19 Oct 1951. Writer. Education: Eton College, 1964-69; MA, Balliol Oxford, 1974; PhD, University College, London, 1978. Publications: Louis XVIII; The Eagle in Splendor; Sultans in Splendor; The Court of France; Le Charmeur de l'Europe: Charles Joseph de Ligne; Constantinople 1453-1924. Contributions to: History Today; Past and Present; Architectural Digest; Harpers and Queen; Spectator; International Herald Tribune; Editor, The Court Historian, Newsletter of the Society for Court Studies. Memberships: PEN; Society d' Histoire de la Restauration Assciation. Literary Agent: Curtis Brown. Address: 13 Prince of Wales Terrace, London W8 5PG, England.

MANSER Martin Hugh, b. 11 Jan 1952, Bromley, England. Reference Book Editor. m. Yusandra Tun, 1979, 1 son, 1 daughter. Education: BA, Honours, University of York, 1974; MPhil, C.N.A.A., 1977. Publications: Concise Book of Bible Quotations, 1982; A Dictionary of Everyday Idioms, 1983; Listening to God, 1984; Pocket Thesaurus of English Words, 1984; Children's Dictionary, 1984; Macmillan Student's Dictionary, 1985, 2nd edition, 1996; Penguin Wordmaster Dictionary, 1987; Guinness Book of Words, 1988; Dictionary of Eponyms, 1988; Visual Dictionary, Bloomsbury Good Word Guide, 1988; Printing and Publishing Terms, 1988; Marketing Terms, 1988; Guinness Book of Words, 1988, 2nd edition, 1991; Bible Promises: Outlines for Christian Living, 1989; Oxford Learner's Pocket Dictionary, 2nd edition, 1991; Get To the Roots: A Dictionary of Words and Phrase Origins, 1992; The Lion Book of Bible Quotations, 1992; Oxford Learner's Pocket Dictionary with Illustrations, 1992; Guide to Better English, 1994; Chambers Compact Thesaurus, 1994; Bloomsbury Key to English Usage, 1994; Collins Gem Daily Guidance, 1995; NIV Thematic Study Bible, 1996. Address: 102 Northern Road, Aylesbury, Bucks HP19 3QY, England.

MANSFIELD. See: **BROMIGE David.**

MANSFIELD-RICHARDSON Virginia, b. 26 Apr 1955, Athens, Ohio, USA. Associate Professor of Journalism. m. Brian K Richardson, 31 July 1993. Education: BA, Ohio University, 1977; MA, George Mason University, 1993; PhD, Ohio University, 1996. Publications: Articles: Statistics: An Inferential Approach, 1984; The Best of Style Plus, 1984; History of the Mass Media in the United States: An Encyclopedia, 1997. Chapter: US News Coverage of Racial Minorities: A Sourcebook, 1934 to Present, 1997. Contributions to: Washington Post; DVM, The Newsmagazine of Veterinary Medicine; City Magazine of Brussels. Honours: I D Wilson Award of 1987, for excellence in reporting veterinary issues; Sigma Delta Chi Journalism Honorary; Secretary/Treasurer, Chinese Communication Association, 1996-. Memberships: Association for Education in Journalism and Mass Communication; International Communication Association; American Association of University Professors. Address: 345 Oakley Drive, State College, PA 16803, USA.

MANSOOR Menahem, b. 4 Aug 1911, Port Said, Egypt. University Educator, Retired; Writer. m. Claire D Kramer, 29 Nov 1951, 1 son, 1 daughter. Education: University of London School of Oriental Studies, London, 1936-39; BA with Honours, 1941, MA, 1942, PhD, 1944, Trinity College, Dublin. Appointments: Chief Interpreter and Assistant Press Attache, British Embassy, Tel Aviv, 1949-54; Chairman, Department of Semitic Languages, University of Wisconsin, Madison, 1955-77; Editor, Hebrew Studies, annual of National Association of Professors of Hebrew, 1979-81. Publications: The Thanksgiving Hymns Scrolls (translation), 1961; The Dead Sea Scrolls, 1964; Political and Diplomatic History of the Arab World: 1900-1967, Chronological, 1972, Biographical, 1975, Documentary, 1978 (16 volumes); The Book of Direction to the Duties of the Heart (translated from Arabic), 1973; Jewish History and Thought: An Introduction, 1992. Other: Over 12 textbooks in Hebrew and Arabic including 2 courses for Linguaphone, London. Contributions to: Journal of Biblical Literature; Studies in the History of Religions; Biblical Research; Revue de Qumran; Hebrew Studies; Wisconsin Academy of Arts, Sciences and Letters. Honours: Fulbright Grant, 1954; Honorary Doctorate, Edgewood College, Madison, 1986; Honorary Doctorate, Hebrew Union College, Cincinnati, Ohio, 1993. Memberships: Society of Biblical Literature; Middle East Studies; Midwest President, Society of Biblical Literature, 1969-70; Midwest

President, American Oriental Society, 1970-71; Vice President, Wisconsin Academy of Arts, Sciences amd Letters, 1983. Address: 5015 Sheboygan Avenue 206, Madison, WI 53705, USA.

MANTEL Hilary (Mary), b. 6 July 1952, Derbyshire, England. Author. m. Gerald McEwen, 23 Sept 1972. Education: London School of Economics; Sheffield University; Bach Jurisprudence, 1973. Publications: Every Day is Mother's Day, 1985; Vacant Possession, 1986; Eight Months on Ghazzah Street, 1988; Fludd, 1989; A Place of Greater Safety, 1992; A Change of Climate, 1994; An Experiment in Love, 1995. Contributions to: Film column, Spectator, 1987-91; Book reviews to range of papers. Honours: Shiva Naipaul Prize, 1987; Winifred Holtby Prize, 1990; Cheltenham Festival Prize, 1990; Southern Arts Literature Prize, 1990; Sunday Express Book of the Year Award, 1992. Memberships: Royal Society of Literature, fellow; Society of Authors. Address: c/o A M Heath & Co, 79 St Martin's Lane, London WC2, England.

MANWARING Randle (Gilbert), b. 3 May 1912, London, England. Poet; Author; Retired Company Director. m. Betty Rout, 9 Aug 1941, 3 sons, 1 daughter. Education: Private Schools; MA, Keele, 1982; FSS; FPMI. Publications: Satires and Salvation (poetry), 1960; The Heart of This People, 1954; Christian Guide to Daily Work, 1963; Under the Magnolia Tree (poetry), 1965; In a Time of Unbelief (poetry), 1977; The Swifts of Maggiore (poetry), 1981; The Run of the Downs, 1984; Collected Poems, 1986; The Singing Church, 1990; Some Late Lark Singing (poetry), 1992. Contributions to: Anglo-Welsh Review; British Weekly; Poetry Review; Outposts; Envoi; This England; Country Life; The Field; South East Arts Review; John O'London's Weekly; Church of England Newspaper; The Lady; Pick; The Cricketer; Sussex Life; Limbo; Scrip; English; Oxford Magazine. Memberships: Downland Poets, chairman, 1981-83; Kent and Sussex Poetry Society; Society of Authors; Society of Sussex Authors. Address: Marbles Barn, Newick, East Sussex BN8 4LG, England.

MAPES Mary A. See: **ELLISON Virginia Howell.**

MAPLE Gordon Extra, b. 6 Aug 1932, Jersey, Channel Islands. Writer. m. Mabel Atkinson-Frayn, 29 Jan 1953, 1 son, 1 daughter. Publications: Plays: Limeade, 1963; Here's a Funny Thing, 1964; Dog, 1967; Elephant, 1968; Tortoise, 1974; Singo, 1975; Napoleon Has Feet, 1977; Pink Circle, 1984; Chateau Schloss, 1985; Popeye, 1985; Keeping in Front (memoirs), 1986; Sour Grapes (with Miles Whittier), 1986; Yet Another Falklands Film, 1987. Honours: Evening Standard Awards, 1964, 1973; Oscar nomination, 1964; SWEAT Award, 1986. Memberships: BPM, Oxford Yec; Royal Society of Literature, fellow. Literary Agent: Fraser and Dunlop Ltd (scripts). Address: The Manor, Milton, nr Banbury, Oxfordshire, England.

MAPLES Evelyn Lucille Palmer, b. 7 Feb 1919, Ponce de Leon, Missouri, USA. Editor; Author. m. William Eugene Maples, 23 Dec 1938, 2 sons, 1 daughter. Education: Southwest Missouri State University, 1936-38. Appointments: Proof Reader, Contributing Author, 1953, Copy Editor, Editor, 1963-81, Herald House. Publications: Norman Learns About the Sacraments, 1961; That Ye Love, 1971; The Many Selves of Ann-Elizabeth, 1973; Endnotes, 1989. Contributions to: Various journals; 3 Poems to Sisters in Christ, 1994. Honour: Midwestern Books Competition, 1983; Poetry Awards, 1984, 1985. Memberships: American Association of Retired Persons; Scroll Club; Missouri Writers Guild. Address: 11336 Maples Road, Niangua, MO 65713, USA.

MARAS Karl. See: **BULMER Henry Kenneth.**

MARCEAU Felicien, b. 16 Sept 1913, Cortenberg, Belgium. Author; Playwright. Publication: Plays: L'Oeuf, 1956; La Bonne Soupe, 1958; La Preuve par Quatre, 1964; Madame Princesse, 1965; La Babour, 1968; L'Homme en Question, 1973; A Nous de Jouer, 1979. Novels: Bergere Legere, 1953; Les Elans du Coeur, 1955; Creezy, 1969; Le Corps de Mon Ennemi, 1975; Appelez-moi Mademoiselle, 1984; La Carriole du Pere Juniet, 1985; Les Passions Partagees, 1987; Un Oiseau Dans Le Ciel, 1989; La Terrasse de Lucrezia, 1993; La Grande Fille, 1997. Memoirs: Les Années Courtes, 1968; Une insolente Liberte ou Les Aventures de Casanova, 1983; Les Ingenus, 1992; Le Voyage de Noce de Figaro, 1994. Honours: Prix Pellman du Théâtre, 1954; Prix Interallie, 1955; Prix Goncourt, 1969; Grand Prix Prince Pierre de Monaco, 1974; Grand Prix de Théâtre, 1975; Prix Jean Giono, 1993; Prix Jacques Audibezti, 1994. Membership:

Academie Française. Address: c/o Eds. Gallimard, 5 Rue Sebastien-Bottin, Paris 75007, France.

MARCH Jessica. See: **AFRICANO Lillian.**

MARCHANT Anyda (Sarah Aldridge). Founder and President, Naiad Press; Romantic Novelist. Publications: The Latecomer, 1974; All True Lovers, 1978; The Nesting Place, 1982; Madame Aurora, 1983; Misfortune's Friend, 1985; Magdelena, 1987; Keep To Me, Stranger, 1989; A Flight of Angels, 1992; Michaela, 1994. Address: The Naiad Press, PO Box 10543, Talahassee, FL 32302, USA.

MARCHANT Catherine. See: **COOKSON Catherine (Ann).**

MARCUS Frank, b. 30 June 1938, Breslau, Germany. Playwright; Critic; Writer. m. Jacqueline Sylvester, 1951 (d 1993), 1 son, 2 daughters. Education: St Martin's School of Art, London. Career: includes Freelance playwright: Actor, Director, Scenic Designer, Unity Theatre, Kensington; theatre critic, Sunday Telegraph, 1968-78. Publications include: The Formation Dancers, 1964; The Killing of Sister George, 1965; The Window, 1968; Mrs Mouse, Are You Within?, 1969; Notes on a Live Affair, 1972; Blank Pages, 1973; Beauty and the Beast, 1977; Blind Date, 1977; translations: Mohar, The Guardsman, 1978; Hauptmann, The Weavers, 1980; Schnitzler, La Ronde and Anatole, 1982; Television and Radio plays. Address: 79 Griffiths Road, London SW19 1ST, England.

MARCUS Jeffrey Scott, b. 4 Oct 1962, Wisconsin, USA. Novelist. Education: BA, University of Wisconsin at Madison, 1984. Publications: The Art of Cartography, 1991; The Captain's Fire. Contributins to: Newspapers and magazines. Honours: Whiting Writers Award, 1992. Address: 4735 North Woodruff Avenue, Milwaukee, WI 53211, USA.

MARCUS Joanna. See: **ANDREWS Lucilla Matthew.**

MARCUS Ruth (Barcan), b. 2 Aug 1921, New York, New York, USA. Professor of Philosophy; Writer. Div, 2 sons, 2 daughters. Education: BA, New York University, 1941; MA, 1942, PhD 1946, Yale University. Appointments: Research Associate in Anthropology, 1945-47, Reuben Post Halleck Professor of Philosophy, 1973-, Yale University; Visiting Professor, 1950-57, Professor of Philosophy, 1970-73, Northwestern University; Assistant Professor to Associate Professor, Roosevelt University, Chicago, 1957-63; Professor of Philosophy, Head, University of Illinois, Chicago, 1964-70; Fellow, Center for Advanced Study, University of Illinois, 1968-69, Center for Advanced Study in the Behavioral Sciences, Stanford, California, 1979; Visiting Fellow, Institute for Advanced Study, University of Edinburgh, 1983, Wolfson College, Oxford, 1985, 1986, Clare Hall, Cambridge, 1988; Mellon Senior Fellow, National Humanities Center, 1992-93; Visiting Distinguished Professor, University of California, Irvine, 1994. Publications: The Logical Enterprise (editor), 1975; Logic, Methodology, and Philosophy of Science, VII (editor), 1986; Modalities: Philosophical Essays, 1993. Contributions to: Scholarly books and journals. Honours: Guggenheim Fellowship, 1953-54; Medal, Collège de France, 1986; Honorary LHD, University of Illinois, 1995. Memberships: American Academy of Arts and Sciences; American Philosophical Association; President, Association for Symbolic Logic, 1981-83; President, Council on Philosophical Studies, 1985; President, Institut International de Philosophie, 1990-93; Phi Beta Kappa; Philosophy of Science Association. Address: c/o Department of Philosophy, Yale University, PO Box 208306, New Haven, CT 06525, USA.

MARCUS Steven, b. 13 Dec 1928, New York, New York, USA. Professor of English; College Dean; Writer. m. Gertrud Lenzer, 20 Jan 1966, 1 son. Education: AB, 1948, PhD, 1961, Columbia University. Appointments: Professor of English, 1966-, George Delacorte Professor of Humanities, 1976-, Chairman, Department of English and Comparative Literature, 1977-80, 1985-90, Vice-President, School of Arts and Sciences, 1993-, Dean, Columbia College, 1993-, Columbia University; Fellow, Center for Advanced Studies in the Behavioural Sciences, 1972-73; Director of Planning, 1974-76, Chairman of the Executive Committee, Board of Directors, 1976-80, National Humanities Center; Chairman, Lionel Trilling Seminars, 1976-80. Publications: Dickens: From Pickwick to Dombey, 1965; Other Victorians, 1966; Engels, Manchester and the Working Class, 1974; Representations: Essays on Literature and Society, 1976; Doing Good (with others), 1978; Freud and the Culture of Psychoanalysis, 1984.

Editor: The Life and Work of Sigmund Freud (with Lionel Trilling), 1960; The World of Modern Fiction, 2 volumes, 1968; The Continental Op, 1974. Contributions to: Professional journals and to general periodicals. Honours: Guggenheim Fellowship, 1967-68; Rockefeller Foundation Fellowship, 1980-81; National Humanities Center Fellowship, 1980-82; Fulbright Fellowship, 1982-84; Honorary DHL, Clark University, 1985. Memberships: Academy of Literary Studies, fellow; American Academy of Arts and Sciences, fellow; American Academy of Psychoanalysis; American Psychoanalytic Association, honorary; Institute for Psychoanalytic Teaching and Research, honorary. Address: c/o Department of English and Comparative Literature, Columbia University, New York, NY 10027, USA.

MARFEY Anne, b. 19 Feb 1927, Copenhagen, Denmark. Writer; Adjunct Lecturer in Danish, State University of New York at Albany. m. Dr Peter Marfey, 6 Jan 1964, dec, 1 son, 1 daughter. Education: Teachers' Certificate, Danish Teachers' College, Copenhagen, 1950; Postgraduate, Columbia University, 1961-62. Appointment: Freelance Writer, 1988-. Publications: Learning to Write, 1961; Vejen til hurtigere Laesning, 1962; Svante, 1965; Las Bedre, 1966; Amerikanere, 1967; Telefontraden, 1968; Skal Skal ikke, 1969; How Parents Can Help Their Child with Reading, 1976; Rose's Adventure, 1989; Moderne Dansk, 1989; The Duckboat, The Pump, The Pine Tree, 1994; The Chipmunk, 1994; It is the Love That Matters, 1997. Membership: Danish Writers Guild, UN Albany. Address: 9 Tudor Road, Albany, NY 12203, USA.

MARGOLIS Mac. Journalist. Education: Graduate, Trinity College, Connecticut. Appointments: Reporter in Latin America for 15 years; Special Correspondent in Rio de Janeiro, Newsweek, 1982-; Brazil Correspondent, Economist, 1993-96. Publication: The Last World: The Conquest of the Amazon Frontier, 1992. Contributions to: Various publications. Honours: Co-Winner of numerous awards. Fellowship, Alicia Patterson Foundation for Journalists, 1991. Address: c/o Newsweek, 251 West 57th Street, New York, NY 10019-1894, USA.

MARGOSHES Dave, b. 8 July 1941, New Brunswick, New Jersey, USA. Writer. m. Ilya Silbav, 29 Apr 1963. Education: BA, 1963, MFA, 1969, University of Iowa. Appointments: Writer in Residence, University of Winnipeg, 1995-96; has run numerous writers' workshops and creative writing courses. Publications: Third Impressions (short stories with Barry Dempster and Don Dickinson), 1982; Small Regrets (short stories), 1986; Walking At Brighton (poetry), 1988; Northwest Passage (poetry), 1990; Nine Lives (short stories), 1991; Saskatchewan, 1992; Long Distance Calls, 1996. Contributions to: Numerous anthologies, magazines and journals. Honours: Canadian Author and Bookman, Poem of the Year Award, 1980; Saskatchewan Writers Guild long manuscript Award, 1990; Second Prize, League of Canadian Poets' National Poetry Contest, 1991; Stephen Leacock Award for Poetry, 1996. Address: 2922 19th Avenue, Regina, Saskatchewan S4T 1X5, Canada.

MARINEAU Michele, b. 12 Aug 1955, Montreal, Quebec, Canada. Writer; Translator. Div. 1 son, 1 daughter. Education: BA, Traduction et Histoire de l'art, University of Montreal, 1988. Publications: Cassiopée ou L'été Polonais, 1988; L'été des Baleines, 1989; L'Homme du Cheshire, 1990; Pourquoi pas Istambul?, 1991; La Route de Chlifa, 1992. Honours: Prix du Gouverneur Général, 1988, 1993; Prix, Brive-Montreal, 1993; Prix, Alvine-Bélisle, 1993. Memberships: Union des Ecrivaines et Ecrivains, Quebec; Corporation Professionnelle des Traducteurs et Interprétes Agréés du Quebec; Association des Traducteurs Litteraires du Canada; Communication-Jeunesse. Literary Agent: Editions Quebec/Amérique, 425 St Jean Baptiste, Montreal, Quebec, Canada. Address: 4405 rue de Brebeuf, Montreal, Quebec H2J 3K8, Canada.

MARIZ Linda Catherine French, (Linda French), b. 27 Nov 1948, New Orleans, Louisiana, USA. Mystery Novelist. m. George Eric Mariz, 22 Aug 1970, 1 son, 1 daughter. Education: BA, History, University of Missouri, Columbia, 1970; MA, History, Western Washington University, 1973. Appointment: Creative Writing Instructor, Western Washington University, 1994. Publications: As Linda Mariz: Body English, 1992; Snake Dance, 1992. As Linda French: Talking Rain, forthcoming in 1997. Contributions to: Cash Buyer (story) in Reader, I Murdered Him Too (anthology), 1995. Memberships: Sisters in Crime; Mystery Writers of America. Literary Agent: Jane Chelius, 548 Second Street, Brooklyn, NY, USA. Address: 708 17th Street, Bellingham, WA 98225, USA.

MARK Jan(et Marjorie), b. 22 June 1943, Welwyn, Hertfordshire, England. Writer. m. Neil Mark, 1 Mar 1969, div 1989, 1 son, 1 daughter. Education: NDD, Canterbury College of Art, 1965. Appointments: Teacher, Southfields School, Gravesend, Kent, 1965-71; Arts Council Writer Fellow, Oxford Polytechnic, 1982-84. Publications: Fiction: Two Stories, 1984; Zeno was here (novel), 1987. Plays: Izzy, 1985; Interference, 1987; Captain Courage and the Rose Street Gang (with Stephen Cockett), 1987; Time and the Hour, and, Nothing to Be Afraid Of, 1990. Other: Over 20 juvenile novels, 1976-95; Over 10 juvenile story collections, 1980-93, including The Oxford Book of Children's Stories (editor), 1993; 9 picture books, 1986-95. Contributions to: Anthologies, periodicals, radio and television. Honours: Penguin/Guardian Award, 1975; Carnegie Medals, 1976, 1983; Rank Observer Prize, 1982; Angel Literary Awards, 1983, 1988. Address: 98 Howard Street, Oxford Ox4 3BG, England.

MARKERT Joy, b. 8 May 1942, Tuttlingen, Germany. Author. Publications: Asyl, 1985; Malta, 1986. Film scripts: Harlis, 1973; Der letzte Schrei, 1975; Belcanto, 1977; Das andere Lacheln (with R van Ackeren), 1978; Ich fühle was, was du nicht fühlst, 1982. Theatre: Asyl, 1984; Erichs Tag, 1985. 30 radio plays, 1976-. Contributions to: German and Austrian radio stations; Various literary publications. Honours: German Film Prize, 1972; German Film Awards, 1977, 1980; Berlin Literary Awards, 1982, 1984. Memberships: German Authors Association; Berlin Film Makers. Address: Bredowstrasse 33, D-1000 Berlin, Germany.

MARKFIELD Wallace (Arthur), b. 12 Aug 1926, New York, New York. USA. Writer. Appointment: Film Critic, New Leader, New York City, 1954-55. Publications: To an Early Grave, 1964; Teitelbaum's Window, 1970; You Could Live If They Let You, 1974; Multiple Orgasms, 1977; Radical Surgery, 1991. Address: c/o Alfred A Knopf Inc, 201 East 50th Street, New York, NY 10022, USA.

MARKHAM E(dward) A(rchibald), b. 1 Oct 1939, Montserrat, West Indies (British citizen). Editor; Poet; Writer; Dramatist; Senior Lecturer. Education: University of Wales; University of East Anglia; University of London. Appointments: Lecturer, Abraham Moss Centre, Manchester, 1976-78; Assistant Editor, Ambit Magazine, London, 1980-; Editor, Artage, 1985-87, Sheffield Thursday, 1992-; Writer-in-Residence, University of Ulster, Coleraine, 1988-91; Senior Lecturer, Sheffield Hallam University, 1991-. Publications: Poetry: Crossfire, 1972; Mad and Other Poems, 1973; Lambchops, 1976; Philpot in the City, 1976; Master Class, 1977; Love Poems, 1978; Games and Penalities, 1980; Love, Politics and Food, 1982; Family Matters, 1984; Human Rites: Selected Poems, 1970-82, 1983; Lambchops in Papua New Guinea, 1985; Living in Disguise, 1986; Towards the End of the Century, 1989; Letter from Ulster and the Hugo Poems, 1993. Plays: The Masterpiece, 1964; The Private Life of the Public Man, 1970; Dropping Outs is Violence, 1971. Short stories: Something Unusual, 1981; Ten Stories, 1994. Editor: Hinterland, 1989; The Penguin Book of Caribbean Short Stories, 1995. Honour: C Day-Lewis Fellowship, 1980-81. Address: c/o Bloodaxe Booksd Ltd, PO Box 1SN, Newcastle-upon-Tyne NE99 1SN, England.

MARKHAM Marion Margaret, b. 12 June 1929, Chicago, Illinois, USA. Writer. m. Robert Bailey Markham, 30 Dec 1955, 2 daughters. Education: BS, Northwestern University. Appointment: Contributing Editor, The Magazine Silver, 9 years. Publications: Escape from Velos, 1981; The Halloween Candy Mystery, 1982; The Christmas Present Mystery, 1984; The Thanksgiving Day Parade Mystery, 1986; The Birthday Party Mystery, 1989; The April Fool's Day Mystery, 1991; The Valentine's Day Mystery, 1992. Memberships: Society of Midland Authors; Mystery Writers of America; Authors Guild of America; Society of Children's Book Writers. Literary Agent: Alice Orr. Address: 2415 Newport Road, Northbrook, IL 60062, USA.

MARKO Katherine Dolores, b. 26 Nov 1913, Allentown, Pennsylvania, USA. Writer. m. Alex Marko, 20 Oct 1945, 2 sons, 1 daughter. Publications: The Sod Turners, 1970; God, When Will I Ever Belong?, 1979; Whales, Giants of the Sea, 1980; How the Wind Blows, 1981; God, Why Did Dad Lose His Job?, 1982; Away to Fundy Bay, 1985; Animals in Orbit, 1991; Hang Out the Flag, 1992; Pocket Babies, 1995. Contributions to: Children's Encyclopaedia Britannica; Jack and Jill; Highlights for Children; Children's Playmate; Straight; Alive; The Friend; On the Line; Childlife; Christian Science Monitor; Young Catholic Messenger; Wow. Honours: Prizes for Short Stories, 1967; Child Study Association List, 1970; Honorable Mention, Manuscript at Conference, 1973. Memberships: Childrens Reading Round Table,

Chicago; Society of Childrens Book Writers; Off Campus Writers Workshop. Address: 471 Franklin Boulevard, Elgin, IL 60120, USA.

MARKOWITZ Harry M(ax), b. 24 Aug 1927, Chicago, Illinois, USA. Economist; Professor; Writer. m. Barbara Gay. Education: PhB, 1947, MA, 1950, PhD, 1954, University of Chicago. Appointments: Research Staff, Rand Corp, Santa Monica, California, 1952-60, 1961-63; Vice-President, Institute of Management Science, 1960-62; Technical Director, Consolidated Analysis Centers Inc, Santa MOnica, California, 1963-68; Professor, University of California at Los Angeles, 1968-69; President, Arbitrage Management Co, New York City, 1969-72; Private Consultant, New York City, 1972-74; Staff, T J Watson Research Center, IBM, Yorktown Hills, New York, 1974-83; Speiser Professor of Finance, Baruch College of the City University of New York, 1982-; Director of Research, Daiwa Securities Trust Co, Jersey City, New Jersey, 1990-. Publications: Portfolio Selection: Journal of Finance, 1952; Portfolio Selection: Efficient Diversification of Investments, 1959; Simscript: A Simulation Programming Language (co-author), 1963; Studies in Process Analysis of Economic Capabilities (co-editor), 1963; Mean-Variance Analysis in Portfolio Choice, 1987. Contributions to: Professional journals and other publications. Honours: John von Neumann Theory Prize, 1989; Nobel Prize for Economics, 1990. Memberships: American Academy of Arts and Sciences; American Finance Association, president, 1982-; Econometric Society, Fellow. Address: Harry Markowitz Company, 1010 Turquoise Street, Suite 245, San Diego, CA 92109, USA.

MARKS Paula Mitchell, b. 29 Mar 1951, El Dorado, Arkansas, USA. Professor; Writer. m. Alan Ned Marks, 2 Apr 1971, 1 daughter. Education: BA, St Edwards University, Texas, 1978; MA, 1980, PhD, 1987, University of Texas. Publications: And Die in the West, 1989; Turn Your Eyes Toward Texas, 1989; Precious Dust: The American Gold Rush Era 1848-1900, 1994. Contributions to: American History Illustrated; Civil War Times; True West; Old West. Honours: T R Fehrenbach Texas History Award, 1990; Finalist, Western Writers of America, Non-Fiction Book Award, 1990; Certificate of Commendation, 1990; Kate Broocks Bates Texas History Research Award, 1991. Memberships: Authors Guild; Western Writers of America; Western History Association; Texas State Historical Association. Address: St Edwards University, 3001 South Congress, Austin, TX 78704, USA.

MARKS Richard. See: KRAUZER Steven M.

MARKS Stanley, b. London, England. Writer. Education: Coursework in Journalism, University of Melbourne. Appointments: Worked with various newspapers in Australia, UK, USA and Canada; Public Relations Manager, Australian Broadcasting Corporation, Australian Tourist Commission; Originator and Writer of the Ms cartoon series, appearing nightly in Australian and New Zealand dailies. Publications: God Gave You One Face, 1964; Fifty Years of Achievement: Three books in Children Everywhere series: Graham is an Aboriginal Boy, 1970, Rarua Lives in Papua New Guinea, 1973, Kertut Boy of Bali, 1977; Animal Olympics, 1972; St Kilda Sketchbook, 1980; Welcome to Australia, 1981; Malvern Sketchbook, 1982; Out and About in Melbourne, 1988; Montague Mouse Who Discovered Australia; Is She Fair Dinkum?; Contributions to: Newspapers and journals. Memberships: Australian Society of Authors; Australian Travel Writers; Fellowship of Australian Writers. Address: 348 Bambra Road, South Caulfield, Melbourne, Victoria 3162, Australia.

MARLATT Daphne Shirley, b. 11 July 1942, Melbourne, Victoria, Australia. Writer; Teacher. m. Gordon Alan Marlatt, 24 Aug 1963, Div. 1970, 1 son. Education: BA, English, Creative Writing, University of British Columbia, Canada, 1964; MA, Comparative Literature, Indiana University, 1968. Appointments: Writer-in-Residence, University of Manitoba, Canada, 1982, McMaster University and Hamilton Poetry Centre, 1985, University of Alberta, 1985-86, Mount Royal College, Calgary, 1987, University of Calgary, 1991; University of Western Ontario, 1993; Itinerant Instructor in English, Women's Studies, Creative Writing, at Universities of Simon Fraser, British Columbia, Victoria. Publications: Vancouver Poems, 1972; Steveston (poetry), 1974; Our Lives, 1975; Zocalo, 1977; Net Work: Selected Writing, 1980; How Hug a Stone, 1983; Touch to My Tongue, 1984; Ana Historic (novel), 1988; Ghost Works, 1993; Two Women in a Birth (with Betsy Warland), 1994. Contributions to: Origin III; Imago; Capilano Review; How(ever) I; Ellipse; Tessera Line; West Coast Line; Co-editor, Tessera Line, 1983-91. Honours: MacMillan Award; Brissenden Award; Canada Council Grants. Membership:

Writers Union of Canada. Address: c/o 24 Byerson Avenue, Toronto, Ontario M5T 2P3, Canada.

MARLIN Brigid, b. 16 Jan 1936, Washington, District of Columbia, USA. Artist; Writer. Div., 2 sons. Education: National College of Art, Dublin; Centre d'Art Sacré, Paris; Studio André L'Hôte, Paris; Beaux-Arts Académie, Montreal; Art Students League, New York; Atelier of Ernest Fuchs, Vienna. Publications: Author: From East to West, 1989; Paintings in the Mische Technique, 1990. Illustrator: King Oberon's Forest (Hilda von Stockern); Celebration of Love (Mary O'Hara); Bright Sun, Dark Sun (Nickolas Fisk); The Leap from the Chess-Board (Charles Sprague). Contributions to: Journals and magazines. Honours: Special Children's Book Award, USA, 1958; 1st Prize, America Art Appreciation Award, 1987; 1st Prize, Visions of the Future, New English Library. Memberships: PEN Club; Authors Club; Free Painters Society; Inscape Group; WIAC. Address: 15 Pixies Hill Crescent, Hemel Hempstead, Herts HP1 2BU, England.

MARLIN Henry. See: GIGGAL Kenneth.

MARLOW Joyce, b. 27 Dec 1929, Manchester, England. Writer. Appointment: Professional Actress, 1950-65. Publications: The Man with the Glove, 1964; A Time to Die, 1966; Billy Goes to War, 1967; The House on the Cliffs, 1968; The Peterloo Massacre, 1969; The Tolpuddle Martyrs, 1971; Captain Boycott and the Irish, 1973; The Life and Times of George I, 1973; The Uncrowned Queen of Ireland, 1975; Mr and Mrs Gladstone, 1977; Kings and Queens of Britain, 1977; Kessie, 1985; Sarah, 1987. Address: 109 St Albans Road, Sandridge, St Albans AL4 9LH, England.

MARLOWE Hugh. See: PATTERSON Harry.

MARLOWE Stephen, b. 7 Aug 1928, New York, New York, USA. Author. m. (1) Leigh Lang, 1950, (2) Ann Humbert, 1964, 2 daughters. Education: AB, College of William and Mary, 1949. Appointment: Writer-in-Residence, College of William and Mary, 1974-75, 1980-81. Publications: The Shining, 1962; Come Over Red Rover, 1968; The Summit, 1970; Colossus, 1972; Translation, 1976; The Valkyrie Encounter, 1978 Nineteen Fifty-Six, 1981; The Memoirs of Christopher Columbus, 1987; The Death and Life of Miguel de Cervantes, 1991. Honour: Prix Gutenberg du Livre, 1988. Address: c/o Campbell, Thompson and McLaughlin Ltd, 1 Kings Mews, London WC1N 2JA, England.

MARNY Dominique Antoinette Nicole, b. 21 Feb 1948, Neuilly, France. Novelist; Screenwriter; Journalist. m. Michel Marny, 5 Oct 1970, div, 1 daughter. Appointment: Director for J C Lattès, Mille et une femmes collection, 1993-. Publications: Crystal Palace, 1985; Les orages desirés, 1988; Les fous de lumière, 1991; Les desirs et les jours, 1993; Les courtisanes, 1994; Les belles de Cocteau, 1995. Contributions to: Madame Figaro; Vogue; Marie France. Honour: Prix Madame Europe, 1993. Membership: PEN Club. Address: 4 Avenue de New York, 75016 Paris, France.

MARON Margaret, b. Greensboro, North Carolina, USA. m. Joseph J Maron, 20 June 1959, 1 son. Education: University of North Carolina. Publications: One Coffee With, 1981; Death of a Butterfly, 1984; Bloody Kin, 1985; Death in Blue Folders, 1985; Bootlegger's Daughter, 1992; Shooting at Loons, 1994. Contributions to: Redbook; McCall's; Alfred Hitchcock. Honour: Edgar Allan Poe Award, 1993. Memberships: Mystery Writers of America; North Carolina Writers Conference. Address: c/o Vicky Bijur Literary Agency, 333 West End Avenue, Suite 5B, New York, NY 10023, USA.

MAROWITZ Charles, b. 25 Jan 1934, New York, USA. Writer. m. Jane Elizabeth Allsop, 14 Dec 1982. Appointments: Artistic Director, Malibu Stage Co, Texas Stage Co; West Coast Correspondent, Theatre Week Magazine; Senior Editor, Matzoh Ball Gazette; Theatre Critic, Los Angeles Village View. Publications: The Method as Means, 1961; The Marowitz Hamlet, 1966; The Shrew, 1972; Artaud at Rodez, 1975; Confessions of a Counterfeit Critic, 1976; The Marowitz Shakespeare, 1980; Act of Being, 1980; Sex Wars, 1983; Sherlock's Last Case, 1984; Prospero's Staff, 1986; Potboilers, 1986; Recycling Shakespeare, 1990; Burnt Bridges, 1991; Directing the Action, 1992; Cyrano de Bergerac (translation), 1995; Alarums and Excursions, 1996. Contributions to: Newspapers, journals and magazines. Honours: Order of Purple Sash, 1965; Whitbread Award, 1967; 1st Prize, Louis B Mayer Award, 1984. Memberships: Dramatists Guild; Writers Guild. Literary Agent: Gary Salt, c/o Paul Kohner

Agency, CA, USA. Address: 3058 Sequit Drive, Malibu, CA 90265, USA.

MARQUIS Max, (Edward Frank Marquis), b. Ilford, Essex, England. Author. m. (1), 1 son. (2) Yvonne Cavenne, 1953. Appointments: News Writer and Reader, RDF French Radio, 1952; Sub Editor, Columnist, Continental Daily Mail, 1952, Evening News, London, 1955; Chief British Correspondent, L'Equipe, Paris, 1970; Football Commentator, Broadcaster, Télévision Suisse-Romande, 1972. Publications: Sir Alf Ramsey: Anatomy of a Football Manager, 1970; The Caretakers, 1975; A Matter of Life, 1976; The Shadowed Heart, 1978; The Traitor Machine, 1980; Body Guard to Charles, 1989; Vengeance, 1990; The Twelfth Man, 1991; Deadly Doctors, 1992; Elimination, 1993; Undignified Death, 1994; Written in Blood, 1995. Address: c/o Rupert Crew Ltd, 1A Kings Mews, London WC1N 2JA, England.

MARR William W, b. 3 Sept 1936, China. Retired Engineer; Editor; Poet. m. Jane J Liu, 22 Sept 1962, 2 sons. Education: MS, Marquette University, 1963; PhD, University of Wisconsin, 1969. Appointments: Editing Advisor, Li Poetry Magazine, 1992; Editor, Chinese Poets, 1993. Publictions: In the Windy City, 1975; Selected Poems, 1983; White Horse, 1984; Selected Poems of Fei Ma, 1985; The Galloping Hoofs, 1986; Road, 1987; Selected Short Poems, 1991; Fly Spirit, 1992; Selected Poems, 1994; Autumn Window, 1995, 1996. Contributions to: Li Poetry Magazine; Literary Taiwan; First Line; New World Poetry; Unitas Literary Magazine; Hong Kong Literature Monthly; Renmin Wenxue; Chinese Poets. Honours: Wu Cho Liu Poetry Award, 1982; Li Poetry Translation Award, 1982; Li Poetry Award, 1984. Memberships: Li Poetry Society; First Line Poetry Society; Chinese Artists Association of North America; Past President, Chicago Poets Club; Illinois State Poetry Society; American Society of Mechanical Engineers. Address: 737 Ridgeview Street, Downers Grove, IL 60516, USA.

MARRECO Anne. See: WIGNALL Anne.

MARRIOTT-BURTON Elsie Gwedoline, b. 15 Feb 1901, Auckland, New Zealand. Journalist; Radio Broadcaster; Poet; Writer. m. Harry Marriott-Burton. Education: Commercial Art Studies, partially completed 1919-20. Appointment: Community Creative Writing Tutor, Noosa Community Queensland, 1984-. Publications: Private Diary of HRH Prince Chula, 1991; Fate Is My Journey, 1995. Contributions to: South African Newspapers, 1937-43, 1950-54; Regular contributions, Magazines, Africa, Australia a Nendw Zealand, 1937-77. Membership: FAW, Queensland Branch. Literary Agent: Ken Bullock, Buderim Queensland. Address: 269 Studio, Buderim Garden Village, Hooloolaba Road, Buderim, Queensland 4556, Australia.

MARS-JONES Adam, b. 26 Oct 1954, London, England. Education: BA, Cambridge University, 1976. Appointments: Film Critic, Reviewer, The Independent, London. Publications: Lantern Lecture and Other Stories, 1981; The Darker Proof: Stories from a Crisis (with Edmund White), 1987; Venus Envy, 1990; Monopolies of Loss, 1992; The Waters of Thirst, 1993; Blind Bitter Happiness, 1997. Editor: Mae West is Dead: Recent Lesbian and Gay Fiction. Honour: Maugham Award, 1982. Literary Agent: Peters, Fraser and Dunlop, 503-4 The Chambers, Chelsea Harbour, Lots Road, London SW10 0XF. Address: 3 Gray's Inn Square, London WC1R 5AH, England.

MARSDEN Peter Richard Valentine, b. 29 Apr 1940, Twickenham, Middlesex, England. Archaeologist. m. Frances Elizabeth Mager, 7 Apr 1979, 2 sons, 1 daughter. Education: Kilburn Polytechnic; Oxford University. Publications: Londinium, 1971; The Wreck of the Amsterdam, 1974 revised edition, 1985; Roman London, 1980; The Marsden Family of Paythorne and Nelson, 1981; The Roman Forum Site in London, 1987; The Historic Shipwrecks of South-East England, 1987. Contributions to: Geographical Magazine; Independent; Times Literary Supplement; Illustrated London News; Telegraph Colour Magazine; Various academic journals. Memberships: Society of Antiquaries, fellow; Institute of Field Archaeologists. Address: 21 Meadow Lane, Lindfield, West Sussex RH16 2RJ, Sussex.

MARSHALL Jack, b. 25 Feb 1937, New York, New York, USA. Writer; Poet. Education: Brooklyn Public Schools. Publications: The Darkest Continent, 1967; Bearings, 1970; Floats, 1972; Bits of Thirst, 1974; Bits of Thirst and Other Poems and Translations, 1976; Arriving

on the Playing Fields of Paradise, 1983; Arabian Nights, 1986. Address: 1056 Treat Avenue, San Francisco, CA 94110, USA.

MARSHALL James Vance. See: PAYNE Donald Gordon.

MARSHALL Joanne. See: RUNDLE Anne.

MARSHALL Rosalind Kay, b. Dysart, Scotland. Historian. Education: MA, Dip Ed, PhD, Edinburgh University, Scotland. Appointment: Assistant Keeper, Scottish National Portrait Gallery, 1973-. Publications: The Days of Duchess Anne, 1973; Mary of Guise, 1977; Virgins and Viragos: A History of Women in Scotland, 1983; Queen of Scots, 1986; Bonnie Prince Charlie, 1988; Henrietta Maria, 1990; Elizabeth I, 1992; Mary I, 1993. Contributions to: Various publications on social history. Honours: Hume Brown Senior Prize for PhD Thesis, 1970; Jeremiah Dalziel Prize, 1970; Scottish Arts Council New Writing Award, 1973. Memberships: Royal Society of Literature, fellow; Scottish Record Society 1993-, council member; Scots Ancestry Research Society, council member 1993-; Royal Society of Arts, fellow; Society of Antiquaries of Scotland, fellow. Address: Scottish National Portrait Gallery, Scotland.

MARSHALL Tom, b. 9 Apr 1938, Niagara Falls, Ontario, Canada. Professor of English. Education: BA, History, 1961, MA, English, 1965, Queen's University, Kingston, Ontario. Appointments: Professor of English, Queen's University, Kingston; Editor, Quarry, 1965-66, 1968-70; Poetry Editor, Canadian Forum, 1973-78. Publications: Poetry: The Beast With Three Backs, 1965; The Silences of Fire, 1969; Magic Water, 1971; The Earth-Book, 1974; The White City, 1976; The Elements: Poems 1960-1975, 1980; Playing With Fire, 1984; Dance of the Particles, 1984; Ghost Safari, 1991. Criticism: The Psychic Mariner: A Reading of the Poems of D H Lawrence, 1970; Harsh and Lovely Land: The Major Canadian Poets and the Making of a Canadian Tradition, 1979; Multiple Exposures, Promised Lands, 1992. Fiction: Fourteen Stories High, 1971; Rosemary Goal, 1978; Glass Houses, 1985; Adele at the End of the Day, 1987; Voices on the Brink, 1989; Changelings, 1991; Goddess Disclosing, 1992. Contributions to: Various journals. Memberships: Writers Union of Canada; League of Canadian Poets; PEN. Address: Department of English, Queen's University, Kingston, Ontario K7L 3N6, Canada.

MARSTEN Richard. See: LOMBINO Salvatore A.

MARTER Joan M, b. 13 Aug 1946, Pennsylvania, USA. Professor. Education: AB, Temple University, 1968; MA, 1970, PhD, 1974, University of Delaware. Appointment: Professor, Rutgers University. Publications: Vanguard American Sculpture 1913-1939, 1979; José de Rivera, 1980; Design in America, 1983; Alexander Calder, 1991; Theodore Roszak Drawings, 1992. Contributions to: Archives of American Art Journal; Sculpture Magazine; Tema Celeste; Womens Studies Quarterly. Honours: Charles F Montgomery Prize, 1984; George Wittenborn Award, 1985; Diamond Achievement Award, 1993. Memberships: International Association of Art Critics; College Art Association of America; Womens Caucus for Art. Address: Department of Art History, Voorhees Hall, Rutgers University, New Brunswick, NJ 08903, USA.

MARTI René, b. 7 Nov 1926, Frauenfeld, Switzerland. Journalist; Writer; Poet. m. Elizabeth Wahrenberger, 13 Oct 1955, 1 son, 2 daughters. Education: Commercial School, Lausanne; Cambridge Proficiency Class, Polytechnic School, London; Commercial Qualification; Diploma in French and English; Studies in Literature, Science and Philosophy, University of Konstanz. Publications: Das unauslöschliche Licht, 1954; Dom des Herzens, 1967; Die fünf unbekannten (main author), 1970; Der unsichtbare Kreis, 1975; Weg an Weg, 1979; Besuche dich in der Natur (with Lili Keller), 1983; Gedichte zum Verschenken (with Lili Keller), 1984; Stationen, 1986; Die verbrannten Schreie, 1989; Gib allem ein bisschen Zeit (with Brigitta Weiss), 1993; Lebensflamme, English translation as Vita Spark, 1995. Contributions to: Anthologies, newspapers, magazines and radio. Address: Haus am Herterberg, Haldenstrasse 5, CH-8500 Frauenfeld, Switzerland.

MARTIN (Roy) Peter, (James Melville), b. 5 Jan 1931, London, England. Author. 2 sons. Education: BA, Philosophy, 1953, MA, 1956, Birkbeck College, London University; Tübingen University, Germany, 1958-59. Appointments: Crime Fiction Reviewer, Hampstead and Highgate Express, 1983-; Occasional Reviewer, Times Literary Supplement. Publications: The Superintendent Otani mysteries, 13 in all; The Imperial Way, 1986; A Tarnished Phoenix, 1990; The Chrysanthemum Throne, 1997. Honour: Member of the Order of the British Empire, 1970. Memberships: Crime Writers Association; Mystery Writers of America; Detection Club. Address: c/o Curtis Brown, Haymarket House, London SW1Y 4SP, England.

MARTIN Alexander George, b. 8 Nov 1953, Baltimore, Maryland, USA. Writer. m. 28 July 1979, 2 sons. Education: Cambridge University, 1972-75; MA (Cantab), English; Diploma in Theatre, University College, Cardiff, 1975-76. Publications: Boris the Tomato, 1984; Snow on the Stinker, 1988; The General Interruptor, 1989; Modern Poetry, 1990; Modern Short Stories, 1991. Honour: Betty Trask Award, 1988. Membership: Society of Authors. Address: c/o David Higham Associates, 5-8 Lower John Street, London W1R 4HA, England.

MARTIN Chip. See: **MARTIN Stoddard (Hammond) Jr.**

MARTIN David (Alfred), b. 30 June 1929, London, England. Professor; Writer. m. 30 June 1962, 3 sons, 1 daughter. Education: Teacher's Diploma, Westminster College, Oxford, 1952; External Degree (BSc), 1959, PhD, 1964, University of London. Publications: Pacifism, 1966; A General Theory of Secularization, 1978; Dilemmas of Contemporary Religion, 1979; The Breaking of the Image, 1980; Divinity in a Grain of Bread, 1989; Tongues of Fire, 1990; Forbidden Revolutions, 1996; Reflections on Sociology and Theology, 1997; Does Christianity Cause War?, 1997. Contributions to: PN Review; The Times Supplement. Address: Cripplegate Cottage, 174 St John's Road, Woking, Surrey, England.

MARTIN F(rancis) X(avier), b. 2 Oct 1922, County Kerry, Ireland. Professor of Medieval History; Writer. Education: LPh, Augustinian College, Dublin, 1944; BA, 1949, MA, 1952, University College, Dublin, National University of Ireland; BD, Pontifical Gregorian University, Rome, 1951; PhD, Peterhouse College, Cambridge, 1959. Appointments: Assistant Lecturer 1959-62, Professor of Medieval History, 1962-, University College, National University of Ireland, Dublin; Chairman, Council of Trustees, National Library of Ireland, 1977-. Publications: The Problem of Giles of Viterbo 1469-1532, 1960; Medieval Studies Presented to Aubrey Gwynn (editor with J A Wyatt and J B Morrall), 1961; Friar Nugent: A Study of Francis Lavalin Nugent 1569-1635, 1962; The Irish Volunteers 1913-15 (editor), 1963; The Howth Gun-Running 1914: Recollections and Documents (editor), 1966; The Course of Irish History (editor with T W Moody), 1967, 2nd edition, 1984; Leaders and Men of the Easter Rising, Dublin 1916 (editor), 1967; The Easter Rising, Myth, Fact and Mystery, 1967; The Scholar Revolutionary: Eoin MacNeil 1867-1945 and the Making of the New Ireland (editor with F J Byrne), 1973; A New History of Ireland (editor with T W Moody and J F Byrne), Vol: III, 1974, VIII, 1982, IX, 1984, IV, 1986, II, 1987, V 1989; No Hero in the House: The Coming of the Normans to Ireland, 1977; The Conquest of Ireland by Giraldus Cambrensis (editor with A B Scott), 1978; Lambert Simnel: The Crowning of a King at Dublin, 24th May 1487, 1988; The Irish Augustinians in Rome: With Foreign Missions in 5 Continents - Europe (England and Scotland), India, Australia, North America, Africa (Nigeria and Kenya) 1656-1994 (editor with Clare O'Reilly), 1994. Address: Department of Medieval History, University College, Dublin, Dublin 4, Ireland.

MARTIN Fredric. See: **CHRISTOPHER Matthew.**

MARTIN Laurence Woodward, b. 30 July 1928, Saint Austell, England. Professor. m. Betty Parnell, 19 Aug 1951, 1 son, 1 daughter. Education: BA, History, 1948, MA, 1952, Christ's College, Cambridge; MA, International Politics, 1951, PhD with Distinction, 1955, Yale University. Publications: The Anglo-American Tradition in Foreign Affairs (with Arnold Wolfers), 1956; Peace Without Victory, 1958; The Sea in Modern Strategy, 1966; Arms and Strategy, 1973; Retreat From Empire (joint author), 1973; Strategic Thought in the Nuclear Age (editor/contributor), 1979; The Two-Edged Sword: Armed Force in the Modern World, 1982; Before the Day After, 1985; The Changing Face of Nuclear Warfare, 1987. Honours: Fellow, King's College, London, 1983-; Honorary Professor, University of Wales, 1985-; Honorary DCL, Newcastle, 1991. Memberships: International Institute of Strategic Studies; European Strategy Group. Address: Royal Institute of International Affairs, 10 St James's Square, London SW1Y 4LE, England.

MARTIN Philip (John Talbot), b. 28 Mar 1931, Melbourne, Australia. Poet; Teacher; Translator; Critic; Radio Broadcaster. Education: BA, University of Melbourne. Appointments: English tutor, University of Melbourne, 1960-62; Lecturer, Australian National University, 1963; Lecturer, Senior Lecturer, English, Monash University, 1964-88; Visiting Lecturer/Professor, University of Amsterdam, 1967, Venice, 1976, Carleton College, Northfield, Minnesota, USA, 1983. Publications: Voice Unaccompanied (poems), 1970; Shakespeare's Sonnets: Self, Love & Art (criticism), 1972; A Bone Flute (poems), 1974; Dictionary of Australian Poets (co-editor), 1980; Lars Gustafsson: Selected Poems (translation), 1982; A Flag for the Wind (poems), 1982; New and Selected Poems, 1988. Address: 25/9 Nicholson Street, Balmain 2041, Australia.

MARTIN Ralph G(uy), b. 4 Mar 1920, Chicgo, Illinois, USA. Writer. m. Marjorie Jean Pastel, 17 June 1944, 1 son, 2 daughters. Education: BJ, University of Missouri, 1941. Appointments: Managing Editor, Box Elder News Journal, Brigham, Utah, 1941; Associate Editor, The New Republic, New York City, 1945-48, Newsweek magazine, New York City, 1953-55; Executive Editor, House Beautiful, New York City, 1955-57. Publications: Boy from Nebraska, 1946; The Best is None too Good, 1948; Eleanor Roosevelt: Her Life in Pictures (with Richard Harrity), 1958; The Human Side of FDR (with Richard Harrity), 1959; Front Runner, Dark Horse (with Ed Plaut), 1960; Money, Money, Money (with Morton Stone), 1961; Man of Destiny: Charles de Gaulle (with Richard Harrity), 1962; World War II: From D-Day to VE-Day (with Richard Harrity), 1962; The Three Lives of Helen Keller (with Richard Harrity), 1962; Ballots and Bandwagons, 1964; The Bosses, 1964; President from Missouri, 1964; Skin Deep, 1964; World War II: Pearl Harbor to VJ-Day, 1965; Wizard of Wall Street, 1965; The GI War: 1941-1945, 1967; A Man for All People: Hubert H Humphrey, 1968; Jennie: The Life of Lady Randolph Churchill, 2 volumes, 1969, 1971; Lincoln Center for the Performing Arts, 1971; The Woman He Loved: The Story of the Duke and Duchess of Windsor, 1973; Cissy: The Life of Elenor Medill Patterson, 1979; A Hero of Our Time: An Intimate Study of the Kennedy Years, 1983; Charles and Diana, 1985; Golda: Golda Meir, the Romantic Years, 1988; Henry and Clare: An Intimate Portrait of the Luces, 1991; Seeds of Destruction: Joe Kennedy and His Sons, 1995. Contributions to: Books and periodicals. Memberships: Authors Guild; Century Association; Dramatists Guild; Overseas Press Club. Address: 235 Harbor Road, Westport, CT 06880, USA.

MARTIN Reginald, b. 15 May 1956, Memphis, Tennessee, USA. Editor; Director of Professional Writing Programmes; Writer. Apppointments: Feature Editor, Reporter, News, Boston, Massachusetts, 1974-77; Instructor in English, Memphis State University, 1979-80; Research Fellow, Tulsa Center for the Study of Women's Literature, 1980-81; Editor, Continental Heritage Press, 1981; Instructor in English, Tulsa Junior College; Assistant Instructor in English, University of Tulsa, 1982-83; Assistant Professor, 1983-87, Associate Professor of Composition, 1988-, Memphis State University; Visiting Lecturer, Mary Washington College, 1984; Lecturer in Literary Criticism, University of Wisconsin, Eau Claire, 1988; Director of Professional Writing Programmes, 1987-. Publications: Ntozake Shange's First Novel: In the Beginning Was the Word, 1984; Ishmael Reed and the New Black Aesthetic Critics, 1988; An Annotated Bibliography of New Black Aesthetic Criticism, 1992. Contributions to: Stories, poems, articles and reviews to various anthologies and periodicals. Honours: Winner, Mark Allen Everell Poetry Contest, 1981; Winner in Fiction, 1982, Winner in Poetry, 1983, Friends of the Library Contest; Award in Service for Education, Alpha Kappa, 1984; Award for Best Novel, Deep South Writers Competition, 1987; Award for Best Critical Article, South Atlantic Modern Language Association, 1987; Award for Best Critical Article, College English Association, 1988. Memberships: Numerous professional associations. Address: PO Box 111306, Memphis, TN 38111, USA.

MARTIN Rhona (Madeline), b. 3 June 1922, London, England. Writer; Artist. m. (1) Peter Wilfrid Alcock, 9 May 1941, div, (2) Thomas Edward Neighbour, div, 2 daughters. Appointments: Former Fashion Artist, Freelance Theatrical Designer, Cinema Manager, Secretary and Accounts Office Manager; Served on Panel of South East Arts, Regional Arts Council, 1978-84; Full-time Writer, 1979-; Part-time Tutor, Creative Writing, University of Sussex, 1986-91. Publications: Gallows Wedding, 1978; Mango Walk, 1981; The Unicorn Summer, 1984; Goodbye Sally, 1987; Writing Historical Fiction, 1988. Contributions to: London Evening News; South East Arts Review; Cosmopolitan; Prima. Honour: Georgette Heyer Historical Novel

Award, 1978. Memberships: Romantic Novelists Association; Society of Authors; Society of Women Writers and Journalists; PEN; Friends of the Arvon Foundation; Society of Limners. Literary Agent: Campbell, Thomson & McLaughlin. London, England. Address: 25 Henwood Crescent, Pembury, Kent TN2 4LJ, England.

MARTIN Robert Bernard, (Robert Bernard), b. 11 Sept 1918, La Harpe, Illinois, USA. Writer. Education: AB, University of Iowa, 1943; AM, Harvard University, 1947; BLitt, Oxford University, England, 1950. Appointments: Professor of English, Princeton University, 1950-75; Emeritus Professor, 1975; Citizens Professor of English, 1980-81, 1984-88, Emeritus Citizens Professor, 1988-, University of Hawaii. Publications: The Dust of Combat: A Life of Charles Kingsley, 1959; Enter Rumour: Four Early Victorian Scandals, 1962; The Accents of Persuasion: Charlotte Brontë's Novels, 1966; The Triumph of Wit: Victorian Comic Theory, 1974; Tennyson: The Unquiet Heart, 1980; With Friends Possessed: A Life of Edward Fitzgerald, 1985; Gerard Manley Hopkins: A Very Private Life, 1991; 3 other critical books and 4 novels. Contributions to: Numerous magazines and journals. Honours: Fellow, Acls, 1966-67; Guggenheim Fellowships, 1971-72, 1983-84; Senior Fellow, National Endowment for the Humanities, 1976-77; Fellow, Rockefeller Research Center, 1979; Duff Cooper Award, Biography, 1981; James Tait Black Award, Biography, 1981; Christian Gauss Award, 1981; DLitt, Oxford, 1987; Fellow, National Humanities Center, 1988-89. Memberships: Royal Society of Literature, fellow; Tennyson Society, honorary vice-president. Literary Agent: Curtis Brown. Address: 8 Walton Street, Oxford OX1 2HG, England.

MARTIN Ronald. See: DELIUS Anthony.

MARTIN Ruth. See: RAYNER Claire Berenice.

MARTIN Stoddard (Hammond) Jr, (Chip Martin), b. 15 Dec 1948, Bryn Mawr, Pennsylvania, USA. Writer; Editor; Lecturer. m. Edin Harper Beard, 28 Sept 1974, separated. Education: BA, History, Stanford University, 1974; PhD, University College, London, England, 1978. Appointments: Co-Founder, Editor, Starhaven Books, La Jolla, California, 1979-, Starhaven Productions, Brawley, 1983-; Guest Lecturer, California State University, 1984, University of Göttingen, 1987; Lecturer, Harvard University, 1987-. Publications: Wagner to the Wasteland: A Study of the Relationship of Wagner to English Literature, 1982; California Writers: Jack London, John Steinbeck, The Tough Guys, 1983; Art, Messianism and Crime: A Study of Antinomianism in Modern Literature and Lives, 1986; Orthodox Heresy: The Rise of Magic in Religion and its Relation to Literature, 1988. Fiction, as Chip Martin: The Jew Hater, 1979; A Revolution of the Sun, 1982-86. Contributions to: Reviews; Times Literary Supplement; Numerous articles in professional and arts journals. Literary Agent: Jane Conway-Gordon, London W11 2SE, England. Address: 601 Franklin Street, Cambridge, MA 02139, USA.

MARTIN Victoria Carolyn, b. 22 May 1945, Windsor, Berkshire, England. Writer. m. Tom Storey, 28 July 1969, 4 daughters. Education: Challow Court School, 1950-53; Silchester House School, Bucks, 1953-61; Winkfield Place, Berks, 1961-62; Byam Shaw School of Art, 1963-66. Publications: September Song, 1970; Windmill Years, 1975; Seeds of the Sun, 1980; Opposite House, 1984; Tigers of the Night, 1985; Obey the Moon, 1987. Contributions to: Woman; Woman's Own; Woman's Realm; Woman's Journal; Good Housekeeping; Woman's Weekly; Redbook; Honey, 1967-87. Literary Agent: Vanessa Holt. Address: Newells Farm House, Lower Beeding, Horsham, Sussex RH13 6LN, England.

MARTIN-JENKINS Christopher Dennis Alexander, b. 20 Jan 1945. Editor. m. Judith Oswald Hayman, 1971, 2 sons, 1 daughter. Education: BA, Modern History, MA, Fitzwilliam College, Cambridge. Appointments: Deputy Editor, 1967-70, Editor, 1981-87, Editorial Director, 1988-, The Cricketer; Sports Broadcaster, 1970-72, Cricket Correspondent, 1973-80, 1984-, BBC; Cricket Correspondent, Daily Telegraph, 1991-. Publications: Testing Time, 1974; Assault on the Ashes, 1975; MCC in India, 1977; The Jubilee Tests and the Packer Revolution, 1977; In Defence of the Ashes, 1979; Cricket Contest, 1980; The Complete Who's Who of Test Cricketers, 1980; The Wisden Book of County Cricket, 1981; Bedside Cricket, 1981; Sketches of a Season, 1981, 1989; Twenty Years On: Cricket's Years of Change, 1984; Cricket: A Way of Life, 1984; Cricketer Book of Cricket Eccentrics (editor), 1985; Seasons Past (editor), 1986; Quick Singles (joint editor), 1986; Grand Slam, 1987; Cricket Characters, 1987; Ball

by Ball, 1990; The Spirit of Cricket, 1994; World Cricketers, 1996. Address: Daily Telegraph, Canada Square, Canary Wharf, London E14 9DT, England.

MARTINET Gilles, b. 8 Aug 1916, Paris, France. Journalist; Politician; Diplomat. m. Iole Buozzi, 1938, 2 daughters. Appointments: Editor in Chief, Agence France Presse, 1944-49, Observateur, 1950-61; Director, Observateur, 1960-64; Board of Directors, Nouvel Observateur, 1964-87, Matin, 1973-81; Member, European Parliament, 1979-81; Ambassador in Italy, 1981-85; Ambassadeur de France (dignity), 1984. Publications: Le Marxisme de notre temps, 1961; La conquete des pouvoirs, 1968; Les cinq communismes, 1971; Le systeme Pompidou, 1973; L'avenir depuis vingt ans, 1975; Les sept syndicalismes, 1977; Cassandre et les tueurs, 1986; Les Italiens, 1990; Le reveil du nationalisme français, 1994. Address: 12 rue Las Cases, 75007 Paris, France.

MARTINUS Eivor Ruth, b. 30 Apr 1943, Göteborg, Sweden. Writer; Translator. m. Derek Martinus, 27 Apr 1963, 2 daughters. Education: Double Honours Degree, English and Swedish Literature, Universities of Lund and Göteberg, 1981. Publications: Five original novels in Swedish; Strindberg Translations: Thunder in the Air, 1989; The Great Highway, 1990; Chamber Plays, 1991; The Father, Lady Julie, Playing with Fire; other translations: My Life as a Dog; The Mysterious Barricades; A Matter of the Soul; Barrabas; Gertrude Markwell. Contributions to: Swedish Book Review; Swedish Books; Scandinavica. Honours: Literary Prizes from: Swedish Society of Authors; Swedish Academy; BCLA. Memberships: Society of Authors; Swedish Writers Union; Swedish Playwrights Union; Swedish English Translators Association; SVEA-BRITT. Literary Agent: Tony Peake, Peake Associates, 14 Grafton Crescent, London NW1 8SL, England. Address: 16 Grantham Road, London W4 2RS, England.

MARTONE Michael, b. 22 Aug 1955, Fort Wayne, Indiana, USA. Writer. m. Theresa Pappas, 3 Apr 1984. Education: AB, Indiana University, 1977; MA, Johns Hopkins University, 1979. Publications: Alive and Dead in Indiana, 1984; Safety Patrol, 1988; A Place of Sense, 1988; Fort Wayne is Seventh on Hitler's List, 1990; Townships, 1990; Pensees: The Thoughts of Dan Quayle, 1994; Seeing Eye, 1995. Contributions to: Antaeus; Ascent; Benzene; Shenandoah; Epoch; Iowa Review; Harper's; Northwest Review; Indiana Review; Denver Quarterly; Windless Orchard; Gargoyle; 1988. Honours: National Endowment for the Arts Literary Fellowship, 1984; PEN Syndicated Fiction Award, 1988; Ingram Merrill Foundation Award, 1988; Pushcart Prize, 1989. Memberships: National Writers Union; PEN; Associated Writing Programs. Literary Agent: Sallie Gouverneur. Address: Dept of English, University of Alabama, Tuscaloosa, AL 35406, USA.

MARTY Martin E(mil), b. 5 Feb 1928, West Point, Nebraska, USA. Professor; Writer on Religion; Editor. m. (1) Elsa Schumacher, 21 June 1952, dec, 4 sons, (2) Harriet Lindeman, 23 Aug 1982. Education: Concordia University; Washington University; AB, 1949, MDiv, 1952, Concordia Seminary; STM, Lutheran School of Theology, Chicago, 1954; PhD, University of Chicago, 1956. Appointments: Ordained Lutheran Minister; Minister, 1950-63; Senior Editor, Christian Century magazine, 1956-; Faculty, 1963-, Associate Dean, Divinity School, 1970-75, Fairfax M Cone Distinguished Service Professor, 1978-, University of Chicago; Founding President and George B Caldwell Senior Scholar-in-Residence, Park Ridge Center for the Study of Health, Faith and Ethics. Publications: A Short History of Christianity, 1959, 2nd edition, revised, 1987; The New Shape of American Religion, 1959; The Improper Opinion, 1961; The Infidel: Freethought and American Religion, 1961; Baptism, 1962; The Hidden Discipline, 1963; Second Chance for American Protestants, 1963; The Outbursts That Await Us (co-author), 1963; The Religious Press in America (co-author), 1963; Pen-Ultimates (co-author), 1963; Babylon by Choice, 1964; Church Unity and Church Mission, 1964; Varieties of Unbelief, 1964; Youth Considers "Do-It-Yourself" Religion, 1958; What Do We Believe?: The Stance of Religion in America (with Stuart E Rosenberg and Andrew Greeley), 1968; The Search for a Usable Future, 1969; The Modern Schism: Three Paths to the Secular, 1969; Righteous Empire: The Protestant Experience in America, 1970, 2nd edition, revised, as Protestantism in the United States, 1986; Protestantism, 1972; The Fire We Can Light: The Role of Religion in a Suddenly Different World, 1973; The Lutheran People, 1973; You Are Promise, 1974; What a Catholic Believes as Seen by a Non-Catholic, 1974; The Pro and Con Book of Religious America: A Bicentennial Argument, 1975; Lutheranism: A Restatement in Question and Answer Form, 1975; A Nation of Behavers, 1976; Good News in the Early Church, 1976; Religion, Awakening and Revolution, 1977; Religion in America, 1950 to the Present (with Douglas W Johnson and Jackson W Carrol), 1979; The Lord's Supper, 1980; Religious Crises in Modern America, 1980; Friendship, 1980; By Way of Response, 1981; The Public Church: Mainline, Evangelical, Catholic, 1981; Health/Medicine and the Faith Traditions: An Inquiry into Religion and Medicine (with Kenneth L Vaux), 1982; A Cry of Absence: Reflections for the Winter of the Heart, 1983, revised edition, 1993; Health and Medicine in the Lutheran Tradition: Being Well, 1983; Faith and Ferment: An Interdisciplinary Study of Christian Beliefs and Practices (with Joan D Chittister), 1983; Being Good and Doing Good, 1984; Christian Churches in the United States, 1800-1983, 1984, 2nd edition, 1987; Christianity in the New World, 1984; Pilgrims in Their Own Land: Five Hundred Years of Religion in America, 1984; The Word: People Participating in Preaching, 1984; Modern American Religion, 3 volumes, 1986, 1990, 1996; Invitation to Discipleship, 1986; Religion and Republic: The American Circumstance, 1987; The Glory and the Power: The Fundamentalist Challenge to the Modern World (with R Scott Appleby), 1992; Places Along the Way: Meditations on the Journey of Faith (with Micah Marty), 1994; A Short History of American Catholicism, 1995; Our Hopes for Years to Come (with Micah Marty), 1995. Editor: New Directions in Biblical Thought, 1960; The Place of Bonhoeffer: Problems and Responsibilities of His Thought (with Peter Berger), 1962; Religion and Social Conflict (with Robert Lee), 1964; Our Faiths, 1975; Where the Spirit Leads: American Denominations Today, 1980; Pushing the Faith: Proselytism and Civility in a Pluralistic World (with Frederick E Greenspahn), 1988; The Fundamentalism Project (with R Scott Appleby), 5 volumes, 1991-95; Civil Religion, Church and State, 1992; Missions and Ecumenical Expressions, 1992; Protestantism and Regionalism, 1992; Varieties of Protestantism, 1992; The Writing of American Religious History, 1992; Protestantism and Social Christianity, 1992; New and Intense Movements, 1992; Theological Themes in the American Protestant World, 1992; Trends in American Religion and the Protestant World, 1992; Ethnic and Non-Protestant Themes, 1993; Fundamentalism and Evangelicalism, 1993; Varieties of Religious Expression, 1993; Women and Women's Issues, 1993; Native American Religion and Black Protestantism, 1993. Contributions to: Numerous publications. Honours: Brotherhood Award, 1960; National Book Award, 1971; Christopher Award, 1985; Over 55 honorary doctorates. Memberships: American Academy of Arts and Sciences, fellow; American Academy of Religion, president, 1987; American Catholic Historical Association, president, 1981; American Philosophical Society; American Society of Church History, president, 1971. Address: 239 Scottswood, Riverside, IL 60546, USA.

MARTZ Louis Lohr, b. 27 Sept 1913, Berwick, Pennsylvania, USA. Professor; Writer. Education: AB, Lafayette College, 1935; PhD, Yale University, 1939. Appointments: Instructor, 1938-44, Assistant Professor, 1944-48, Associate Professor, 1948-54, Professor, 1954-57, Chairman of Department, 1956-62, Douglas Tracy Smith Professor, 1957-71, Sterling Professor, 1971-, Director, Beinecke Library, 1972-77, Yale University; Editorial Chairman, Yale Edition of the Works of Thomas More. Publication: The Later Career of Tobias Smollett, 1942; Pilgrim's Progress, 1949; The Poetry of Meditation, 1954; The Meditative Poem, 1963; The Paradise Within, 1964; The Poem of the Mind, 1966; The Wit of Love, 1969; Hero and Leander, 1972; Thomas More's Dialogue of Comfort, 1976; The Author in His Work, 1978; Poet of Exile (Milton), 1980; H D: Collected Poems 1912-1944, 1983; George Herbert and Henry Vaughan, 1986; H D: Selected Poems, 1988; Thomas More: The Search for the Inner Man, 1990; From Renaissance to Baroque Essays on Literature and Art, 1991; George Herbert, Selected Poems, 1994; D H Lawrence, Quetzalcoatl, 1995. Memberships: American Academy of Arts and Sciences; British Academy of Arts and Sciences. Address: 994 Yale Station, New Haven, CT 06520, USA.

MARUTA Leszek, b. 8 Nov 1930, Torun, Poland. Journalist; Writer. Div, 1 son, 1 daughter. Education: Jagellonian University, 1949-52. Appointments: Staff, later Editor, Gazeta Krakowska, 1969-71; Staff, Art Director, Scenarist, Estrada Krakowska, 1962-69; Director, WOK, Culture Centre, Tarnow, 1975-77; Staff, later Editor, Lektura magazine, 1991-93. Publications: 8 books, 1958-93. Contributions to: Numerous journals and magazines. Honours: Karuzela Literary Award, 1958; Medal of the Millennium, 1968; Polish Radio Award, 1973; Governor's Award, Tarnow, 1976; Golden Cross of Merit, 1988; Golden Badge of the City of Krakow, 1988. Memberships: Polish Journalistic Association; Polish Writers Union; Society of Authors. Address: ul Krupnicza 22/12, PL-123 Krakow, Poland.

MARVIN Blanche, b. 17 Jan 1926, New York, New York, USA. Actress; Writer; Dramatist; Critic; Publisher. m. Mark Marvin, 31 Oct 1950, 1 son, 1 daughter. Education: BA, Antioch College. Appointment: Editor and Artistic Director, Merri-Times. Publications: Over 30 plays, including 15 for children. Contributions to: Periodicals. Honours: Children's Theatre Association Award; Emmy Award. Memberships: British Association of Film and Television Artists; Equity; PMA; Royal Academy of Art; Screen Actors Guild; Theatre Writers Union; Writers Guild. Address: 21a St John's Wood High Street, London NW8 7NG, England.

MARWICK Arthur, b. 29 Feb 1936, Edinburgh, Scotland. Professor of History; Writer. Education: MA, University of Edinburgh, 1957; BLitt, Balliol College, Oxford, 1960. Appointments: Assistant Lecturer, University of Aberdeen, 1959-60; Lecturer, University of Edinburgh, 1960-69; Visiting Professor of History, State University of New York at Buffalo, 1966-67, Rhodes College, Memphis, 1991, University of Perugia, 1991; Professor of History, 1969-, Dean of Arts, 1978-84, The Open University; Visiting Scholar, Hoover Institution, and Visiting Professor, Stanford University, 1984-85; Directeur d'études invité, L'École des hautes études en sciences sociales, Paris, 1985. Publications: The Explosion of British Society 1914-1962, 1963; Clifford Allen: The Open Conspirator, 1964; The Deluge: British Society and the First World War, 1965; Britain in the Century of Total War, Peace and Social Change 1900-1967, 1968; The Nature of History, 1970, 3rd edition, 1989; War and Social Change in the Twentieth Century, 1974; The Home Front: The British and the Second World War, 1976; Women at War 1914-1918, 1977; Class: Image and Reality in Britain, France and the USA Since 1930, 1980, 2nd edition, 1990; The Thames and Hudson Illustrated Dictionary of British History (editor), 1980; British Society Since 1945, 1982, 2nd edition, 1990; Britain in Our Century: Images and Controversies, 1984; Class in the Twentieth Century (editor), 1986; Beauty in History: Society, Politics and Personal Appearance, c1500 to the Present, 1988; The Arts, Literature and Society (editor), 1990; Culture in Britain Since 1945, 1991. Contributions to: Professional journals. Address: 67 Fitzjohn's Avenue, Flat 5, Hampstead, London NW3 6PE, England.

MARX Arthur, b. 21 July 1921, New York, New York, USA. Film Writer; Television Writer; Playwright; Director; Author. Education: University of Southern California, Los Angeles, 1939-40. Publications: The Ordeal of Willie Brown, 1951; Life with Groucho, biography, 1954; Not as a Crocodile (short stories), 1958; The Impossible Years (play), 1965; Minnie's Boys (play), 1970; Son of Groucho (autobiography), 1972; Everybody Loves Somebody Sometime, Especially Himself (biography), 1974; Sugar and Spice (play), 1974; My Daughter's Rated X (play), 1975; Goldwyn, 1976; Red Skelton (biography), 1979; Groucho: A Life in Revue (play), 1986; The Nine Lives of Mickey Rooney (biography), 1986; The Ghost and Mrs Muir (play), 1987; My Life with Groucho (biography), 1988; Set to Kill (mystery novel), 1993; The Secret Life of Bob Hope (biography), 1993. Contributions to: Los Angeles Magazine; Cigar Aficionado. Honour: Laurence Olivier Award Nomination, 1987. Memberships: Authors Guild; Dramatists Guild; International Association of Crime Writers; Writers Guild of America. Address: c/o Scovil, Chichak & Galen, 381 Park Avenue South, New York, NY 10016, USA.

MASATSUGU Mitsuyuki, b. 25 Jan 1924, Taiwan. Writer. m. Kiyoko Takeda, 3 Nov 1951, 1 son, 1 daughter. Education: BS, Osaka University of Foreign Studies, Japan, 1945; Course in Industrial Management, Tokyo, 1952. Publications: How to Run a Successful Business, 1969; The Turning Point of Japanese Enterprises Overseas, 1972; The Modern Samurai Society, 1982; Zigzags to the Meiji Restoration: The Divine Puppet Dazzled the Blue-Eyed Imperialists, 1994. Contributions to: Newspapers. Address: 3-35-16 Tomioka-nishi, Kanazawa-ku, Yokohama 236, Japan.

MASCHLER Thomas Michael, b. 16 Aug 1933. Publisher. m. (1) Fay Coventry, 1970, 1 son, 2 daughters, (2) Regina Kulinicz , 1987. Appointments: Production Assistant, André Deutsch, 1955-56; Editor, MacGibbon and Kee, 1956-58; Fiction Editor, Penguin Books, 1958-60; Editorial Director, 1960-70, Chairman, 1970-, Publisher, Children's Books, 1991-, Jonathan Cape; Director, Random House, 1987-. Publications: Editor: Declarations, 1957; New English Dramatists Series, 1959-63. Address: 20 Vauxhall Bridge Road, London SW1V 2SA, England.

MASINI Eleonora Barbieri, b. 19 Nov 1928, Guatemala. Sociologist. m. Francesco Maria Masini, 31 Jan 1953, 3 sons.

Education: BA, 1948, Law Degree, 1952; Comparative Law Specialisation, 1953, Sociology Specialisation, 1969, Rome, Italy. Publications: Visions of Desirable Societies, 1983; Women - Households and Change (with Susan Stratigos), 1991; Why Future Studies?, 1992. Contributions to: Futures; Technological Forecasting and Social Change; Futurist. Memberships: World Futures Studies Federation; World Academy of Art and Sciences. Address: Via A Bertoloni 23, 00197 Rome, Italy.

MASLOW Jonathan Evan, b. 4 Aug 1948, Long Branch, New Jersey, USA. Writer. Education: BA with high honours, American Literature, Marlboro College, Vermont; MS, Columbia University Graduate School of Journalism. Publications: The Owl Papers, 1983; Bird of Life, Bird of Death: A Political Ornithology of Central America, 1986; Sacred Horses: Memoirs of a Turkmen Cowboy, 1994. Other: A Tramp in the Darien, film for BBC-WGBH-TV, 1990. Contributions to: Over 200 magazine articles to Atlantic Monthly, Saturday Review, GEO. Honours: George Varsell Award, American Academy of Arts and Letters, 1988; Guggenheim Fellowship, 1989-90. Memberships: Authors Guild; National Writers Union. Literary Agent: The Robbins Office, New York City, USA. Address: Cutter's Way, Rd 3, Woodbine, NJ 08270, USA.

MASON Bobbie Ann, b. 1 May 1940, Mayfield, Kentucky, USA. Writer. m. Roger B Rawlings, 12 Apr 1969. Education: BA, University of Kentucky, 1962; MA, State University of New York at Binghamton, 1966; PhD, University of Connecticut, 1972. Appointment: Assistant Professor of English, Mansfield State College, Pennsylvania, 1972-79. Publications: Nabokov's Garden, 1974; The Girl Sleuth: A Feminist Guide to the Bobbsey Twins, Nancy Drew and Their Sisters, 1976, 2nd edition, 1995; Shiloh and Other Stories, 1982; In Country, 1985; Spence and Lila, 1988; Love Life, 1989; Feather Crowns, 1993. Contributions to: Anthologies and magazines. Honours: Ernest Hemingway Award, 1982; National Endowment for the Arts Grant, 1983; Pennsylvania Arts Council Grants, 1983, 1989; American Academy and Institute of Arts and Letters Award, 1984; Guggenheim Fellowship, 1984; O Henry Anthology Awards, 1986, 1988; Southern Book Award, 1993. Memberships: Authors Guild; PEN. Address: c/o Amanda Urban, International Creative Management, 40 West 57th Street, New York, NY 10019, USA.

MASON Francis K(enneth), b. 4 Sept 1928, London, England. Editor; Writer; Archivist; Researcher. Education: Graduate, Royal Air Force College, Cranwell, 1951. Appointments: Editor, Flying Review International, 1963-64; Managing Director, Profile Publications Ltd, 1964-67, Alban Book Services Ltd, Watton, Norfolk; Managing Editor, Guiness Superlatives Ltd, Enfield, Middlesex, 1968-71. Publications: Author and/or Editor of some 90 books, 1961-96. Contributions to: Radio and television. Honours: International History Diploma, Aero Club of France, Paris, 1973; Founder Fellowship, Canadian Guild of Authors, 1988. Membership: Royal Historical Society, fellow. Address: Beechwood, Watton, Thetford, Norfolk IP15 6AB, England.

MASON Haydn Trevor, b. 12 Jan 1929, Saundersfoot, Pembrokeshire, Wales. Professor Emeritus of French; Writer. Education: BA, University College of Wales, 1949; AM, Middlebury College, Vermont, 1951; DPhil, Jesus College, Oxford, 1960. Appointments: Instructor, Princeton University, 1954-57; Lecturer, 1964-65, Reader, 1965-67, University of Reading; Professor of European Literature, University of East Anglia, 1967-79; Editor, Studies on Voltaire and the Eighteenth Century, 1977-95; Professor of French Literature, University of Paris III, 1979-81; Professor of French, 1981-94, Professor Emeritus, 1994-, University of Bristol; Scholar-in-Residence, University of Maryland, 1986. Publications: Pierre Bayle and Voltaire, 1963; Marivaux: Les Fausses Confidences (editor), 1964; Leibniz-Arnauld Correspondence (translator and editor), 1967; Voltaire: Zadig and Other Stories (editor), 1971; Voltaire, 1974; Voltaire: A Life, 1981; French Writers and Their Society 1715-1800, 1982; Cyrano de Bergerac: L'Autre Monde, 1984; Voltaire: Discours en vers sur l'homme (editor), 1991; Candide: Optimism Demolished, 1992; Candide (editor), 1995. Honours: Officier dans l'Ordre des Palmes Academiques, 1985; Medaille d'Argent de la Ville de Paris, 1989. Memberships: Association of University Professors of French, Chairman, 1981-82; Society for French Studies, President, 1982-84; British Society for Eighteenth-Century Studies, President, 1984-86; International Society for Eighteenth-Century Studies, President, 1991-95; Voltaire Foundation, Chairman, Board of Directors, 1989-93, Director, 1977-97. Address: c/o Department of French, University of Bristol, Bristol BS8 1TE, England.

MASON Lee W. See: MALZBERG Barry.

MASON Stanley, b. 16 Apr 1917, Blairmore, Alberta, Canada. Editor; Translator. m. Cloris Ielmini, 29 July 1944, 1 daughter. Education: MA, English Literature, Oriel College, Oxford. Appointments: Literary Editor, Graphis Magazine, 1963-83; Editor, Elements, Dow Chemical Europe House Organ, 1969-75. Publications: Modern English Structures (with Ronald Ridout), 4 volumes, 1968-72; A Necklace of Words (poetry), 1975; A Reef of Hours (poetry), 1983; Send Out the Dove (play), 1986; The Alps (verse translation of Albrecht von Haller's poem), 1987; The Everlasting Snow (poetry), 1993; Collected Poems, 1993; A German Treasury (translations), 1993. Contributions to: Adelphi; Poetry Review; Envoi; Orbis; Doors; Pennine Platform; Canadian Forum; Dalhousie Review. Address: Im Zelgli 5, 8307 Effretikon, Switzerland.

MASSIE Allan (Johnstone), b. 19 Oct 1938, Singapore. Author. m. Alison Agnes Graham Langlands, 1973, 2 sons, 1 daughter. Education: Trinity College, Glenalmond; BA, Trinity College, Cambridge. Appointments: Fiction Reviewor, The Scotsman, 1976-; Creative Writing Fellow, University of Edinburgh, 1982-84; University of Glasgow and University of Strathclyde, 1985-86; Columnist, Glasgow Herald, 1985-88, Sunday Times Scotland, 1987-, Daily Telegraph, 1991-. Publications: Novels: Change and Decay in All Around I See, 1978; The Last Peacock, 1980; The Death of Men, 1981; One Night in Winter, 1984; Augustus: The Memoirs of the Emperor, 1986; A Question of Loyalties, 1989; The Hanging Tree, 1990; Tiberius: The Memoirs of an Emperor, 1991; The Sins of the Father, 1991; These Enchanted Woods, 1993; Caesar, 1993; The Ragged Lion, 1994; King David, 1995. Other: Muriel Spark, 1979; Ill Met by Gaslight: Five Edinburgh Murders, 1980; The Caesars, 1983; Edinburgh and the Borders: In Verse (editor), 1983; A Portrait of Scottish Rugby, 1984; Eisenstadt: Aberdeen, Portrait of a City, 1984; Colette: The Woman, the Writer and the Myth, 1986; 101 Great Scots, 1987; PEN New Fiction: Thirty-Two Short Stories (editor), 1987; How Should Health Services be Financed? A Patient's View, 1988; The Novelist's View of the Market Economy, 1988; Byron's Travels, 1988; Glasgow: Portraits of a City, 1989; The Novel Today: A Critical Guide to the British Novel, 1970-1989, 1990; Edinburgh, 1994. Contributions to: Periodicals. Honours: Niven Award, 1981; Scottish Arts Council Award, 1982. Memberships: Royal Society of Literature, fellow; Scottish Arts COuncil. Address: Thirladean House, Selkirk TD7 5LU, Scotland.

MASSIE Robert K(inloch), b. 5 Jan 1929, Lexington, Kentucky, USA. Writer. m. (1) Suzanne L Tohrbach, 1954, Div 1990, 1 son, 2 daughters, (2) Deborah L Karl, 1992, 1 son. Education: BA, Yale University, 1950; BA, Oxford University, 1952. Appointments: Reporter, Collier's magazine, New York City, 1955-56; Writer, Newsweek magazine, New York City, 1956-62; Writer, USA-1 magazine, New York City, 1962; Saturday Evening Post, New York City, 1962-65; Ferris Professor of Journalism, Princeton University, 1977, 1985; Mellon Professor in the Humanities, Tulane University, 1981. Publications: Nicholas and Alexandra, 1967; Journey, 1976; Peter the Great: His Life and World, 1980; Dreadnought: Britain, Germany and the Coming of the Great War, 1991. Contributions to: Periodicals. Honours: Christopher Award, 1976; Pulitzer Prize for Biography, 1981. Memberships: Authors Guild of America, president; PEN; Society of American Historians. Address: 60 West Clinton Avenue, Irvington, NY 10533, USA.

MASSON Jeffrey Moussaieff, b. 28 Mar 1941, Chicago, Illinois, USA (as Jeffrey Lloyd Masson). Writer; Editor; Translator. Appointments: Former Professor of Sanskrit; Project Director, Sigmund Freud Archives, New York City, 1980-81; Co-Director, Freud Copyrights. Publications: The Oceanic Feeling: The Origins of Religious Sentiment in Ancient India, 1980; The Assault on Truth: Freud's Suppression of the Seduction Theory, 1984; Complete Letters of Sigmund Freud to Wilhelm Fuess, 1887-1904 (editor and translator), 1985; A Dark Science: Women, Sexuality and Psychiatry in the Nineteenth Century (editor and translator), 1987; My Father's Guru: A Journey Through Spirituality and Disillusion, 1992. Contributions to: Atlantic Monthly; International Journal of Psycho-Analysis; New York Times; New York Review of Books. Address: c/o Elaine Markson Literary Agency, 44 Greenwich Avenue, New York, NY 10011, USA.

MASTERS Hilary Thomas, b. 2 Mar 1928, Kansas City, Missouri, USA. Novelist; Short Story Writer; Essayist; Memoirist; Professor. div., 1 son, 2 daughters. Education: AB, Brown University,

1952. Appointments: Professor of English, Carnegie Mellon University; Member, Freedom to Write Committee, PEN, 1984. Publications: The Common Pasture, 1967; An American Marriage, 1969; Palace of Strangers, 1971; Last Stands: Notes from Memory, 1982; Hammertown Tales, 1985; The Harlem Valley Trio: Clemmons, 1985; Cooper, 1987; Strickland, 1990; Success, 1992; Home is the Exile, 1996. Contributions to: Sports Illustrated; North American Review; Sewanee Review; Georgia Review; New England Review; Kenyon Review. Memberships: PEN, New York Center; Authors Guild. Address: Department of English, Carnegie Mellon University, Pittsburgh, PA 15213, USA.

MASTERTON Graham (Thomas Luke), b. 16 Jan 1946, Edinburgh, Scotland. Author. m. Wiescka Walach, 11 Nov 1975, 3 sons. Publications: The Manitou, 1975; Charnel House, 1976; Rich, 1977; Railroad, 1980; Solitaire, 1983; Maiden Voyage, 1984; Tengu, 1984; Lady of Fortune, 1985; Corroboree, 1985; Family Portrait, 1986; Night Warriors, 1987; Headlines, 1987; Silver, 1987; Death Trance, 1987. Contributions to: Periodicals. Honours: Special Award, Mystery Writers of America, 1977; Silver Medal, West Coast Review of Books, 1984. Membership: Literary Guild. Literary Agent: Wiescka Masterton. Address: c/o Sphere Books, 27 Wrights Lane, London W8 5TZ, England.

MATAS Carol, b. Winnipeg, Manitoba, Canada. Writer. m. Per Brask, 2 children. Education: London, Ontario, Canada; London, England. Publications: Lisa, 1987; Jesper, 1989; The Race, 1991; Sworn Enemies, 1993; Daniel's Story, 1993; Of Two Minds (with Perry Nodelman), 1994; The Lost Locket, 1994; The Burning Time, 1994. Honours: Geoffrey Bilson Award for Historical Fiction, 1988; Canadian Library Association Notable Book Awards, 1989, 1992; New York Times Book Review Notable Book, 1990; Governor-General's Award nominee, 1993. Address: c/o Writers Union of Canada, 24 Ryerson Avenue, Toronto, Ontario M5T 2P3 Canada.

MATHERS Peter, b. 1931, Fulham, London. Novelist. Education: Sydney Technical College. Appointments: Researcher, Theatre Adviser, University of Pittsburgh, 1968. Publications: Trap, 1970; The Wort Papers, 1972; Story, A Change for the Better, 1984. Honours: Miles Franklin Award, 1967. Address: c/o Wav Publications, 499 The Parade, Magill, South Australia 5072, Australia.

MATHESON Richard (Burton), b. 20 Feb 1926, Allendale, New Jersey, USA. Writer. Education: BA, University of Missouri, 1949. Publications: Someone is Bleeding, 1953; Fury on Sunday, 1954; I Am Legend, 1954; Born of Man and Woman, 1954; Third from the Sun, 1955; The Shrinking Man, 1956; The Shores of Space, 1957; A Stir of Echoes, 1958; Ride the Nightmare, 1959; The Beardless Warriors, 1960; Shock! I, 1961; Shock! II, 1964; Shock! III, 1966; Shock Waves, 1970; Hell House, 1971; Bid Time Return, 1975; What Dreams May Come, 1978; Shock! IV, 1980; Earthbound, 1989; Collected Stories, 1989; Journal of the Gun Years, 1991; By the Gun, 1994. Address: PO Box 81, Woodland Hills, CA 91365, USA.

MATHIAS Roland Glyn, b. 4 Sept 1915, Talybont-on-Usk, Breconshire, Wales. Schoolmaster; Poet; Writer. m. Mary (Molly) Hawes, 4 Apr 1944, 1 son, 2 daughters. Education: BA, Modern History, 1936, BLitt (by thesis), 1939, MA, 1944, Jesus College, Oxford. Appointments: Schoolmaster; Editor, The Anglo-Welsh Review, 1961-76; Extra-Mural Lecturer, University College, Cardiff, 1970-77; Visiting Professor, University of Alabama at Birmingham, 1971. Publications: Poetry: Break in Harvest, 1946; The Roses of Tretower, 1952; The Flooded Valley, 1960; Absalom in the Tree, 1971; Snipe's Castle, 1979; Burning Brambles, 1983; A Field at Vallorcines, 1996. Short Stories: The Eleven Men of Egypt, 1956. Non-Fiction: Whitsun Riot, 1963; Vernon Watkins, 1974; John Cowper Powys as Poet, 1979; A Ride Through the Wood, 1985; Anglo-Welsh Literature: An Illustrated History, 1987. Contributions to: Many literary journals and periodicals. Honour: DHL, Georgetown University, Washington DC, 1985; Has volume written about him by Sam Adams, Writer of Wales series, 1995. Memberships: Welsh Arts Council; Chairman, Literature Committee, 1976-79. Address: Deffrobani, 5 Maescelyn, Brecon, Powys LD3 7NL, Wales.

MATHIEU André, (Andrew Matthew, Andrew Matthews), b. 10 Apr 1942, Beauce, Canada. Novelist. m. B Perron, 20 July 1963, 1 daughter. Education: BA, Laval University. Publications: Nathalie, 1982; La Sauvage, 1985; Aurore, 1990; Donald and Marion, 1990;

Arnold's Treasure, 1994; 20 Others. Address: CP 55, Victoriaville, Quebec, G6P 6S4, Canada.

MATHIS EDDY Darlene, b. 19 Mar 1937, Indiana, USA. Poet; Professor; Editor. m. Spencer Livingston Eddy, 23 May 1964, dec. Education: BA, Goshen College, 1959; MA, 1961, PhD, 1967, Rutgers University. Appointments: Poetry Editor, Forum, 1985-89; Poet-in-Residence, Ball State University, 1989-93; Consulting Editor, Blue Unicorn: A Tri-Quarterly of Poetry, 1995-; Founding Editor, The Hedgerow Press, Tennessee. Publications: The Worlds of King Lear, 1968; Leaf Threads Wind Rhymes, 1985; Weathering, 1991. Contributions to: Books and journals. Honours: Woodrow Wilson National Fellow, 1959-62; Rutgers University Graduate Honours Fellowship and Dissertation Award, 1964-65, 1966; Numerous Research, Creative Arts Awards; Notable Woodrow Wilson Fellow, 1991. Memberships: Associated Writing Programs; American Association of University Professors; National Council of Teachers of English; American League of PEN Women. Address: Department of English, RB 248, Ball State University, Muncie, IN 47306, USA.

MATRAY James Irving, b. 6 Dec 1948, Evergreen Park, Illinois, USA. University Professor. m. Mary Karin Heine, 14 Aug 1971, 1 son, 1 daughter. Education: BA, Lake Forest College, 1970; MA, 1973, PhD, 1977, University of Virginia. Appointments: Glenville State College, 1976-77; California State College, 1978-79; University of Texas, 1979-80; New Mexico State University, 1980-; University of Southern California, 1988-89. Publications: Truman's Plan for Victory, 1979; The Reluctant Crusade, 1941-50, 1985; Spoils of War, 1989; Historical Dictionary of the Korean War, 1991; Korea and the Cold War, 1993. Honours: Stuart L Bernath Article Award, 1980; Best Book Award, 1986; Best Reference Book Award, 1992. Memberships: American Historical Association, Pacific Coast Branch; Society for Historian of America; Foreign Relations; Organization of American Historians. Address: Box 3H Department of History, New Mexico State University, Las Cruces, NM 88003, USA.

MATSON Clive, b. 13 Mar 1941, Los Angeles, California, USA. Poet; Playwright; Teacher. Education: Undergraduate work, University of Chicago, 1958-59; MFA, Poetry, School of the Arts, Columbia University. Publications: Mainline to the Heart, 1966; Space Age, 1969; Heroin, 1972; On the Inside, 1982; Equal in Desire, 1983; Hourglass, 1987; Breath of Inspiration (essay), 1987. Contributions to: Anthologies and journals. Honour: Graduate Writing Fellowship, Columbia University, 1987-88. Memberships: Poets and Writers; Dramatists Guild; Theatre Bay Area; Bay Area Mineralogists. Literary Agent: Peter Beren, Berkeley, California, USA. Address: 472 44th Street, Oakland, CA 94609, USA.

MATSUMURA Takao, b. 7 Jan 1942, Yokohama, Japan. Professor of Economics. m. Rumiko Fukuoka, 20 May 1967, 1 son, 1 daughter. Education: BA, Economics, 1964, MA, Economics, 1966, Keio University; PhD, Social History, University of Warwick, England, 1976. Appointments: Associate Professor, 1972-81, Professor, 1982-, Department of Economics, Keio University; Visiting Fellow, Social History, Warwick University, 1987-88. Publication: The Labour Aristocracy Revisited: The Victorian Flint Glass Makers, 1850-1880, 1983. Contributions to: Journal of Historical Studies (in Japanese); Mita Economic Journal (in Japanese); Bulletin of the Society for the Study of Labour History. Honour: 7th Prize for Excellent Labour Publications, Japan Institute of Labour, 1984. Memberships: Japan Socio-Economic Society, editorial board; Japan Social Policy Society; Society for the Study of Labour History, international board. Address: 7 chome 28-2, Okusawa, Setagaya-ku, Tokyo, Japan.

MATTHEW Andrew. See: MATHIEU André.

MATTHEW Christopher Charles Forrest, b. 8 May 1939, London, England. Writer; Broadcaster. m. Wendy Mary Mallinson, 19 Oct 1979, 2 sons, 1 daughter. Education: BA (Hons), Oxford; MA (Hons), St Peter's College, Oxford. Publications: A Different World: Stories of Great Hotels, 1976; Diary of a Somebody, 1978; Loosely Engaged, 1980; The Long Haired Boy, 1980; The Crisp Report, 1981; Three Men in a Boat (annotated with Benny Green), 1982; The Junket Man, 1983; How to Survive Middle Age, 1983; Family Matters, 1987; The Simon Crisp Diaries, 1988; A Perfect Hero, 1991; The Amber Room, 1995. Radio Play: A Portrait of Richard Hillary. TV Scripts: The Good Guys, LWT, 1993. Radio Writer and Presenter: Something to Declare, 1971-82; Points of Departure, 1980-82; Invaders, 1982-83; The Travelling Show (R4), 1984-85; Fourth Column (R4), 1990-93;

Plain Tales from the Rhododendrons (R4), 1991; Cold Print (R4), 1992. Contributions to: Punch; Vogue; Daily Telegraph; Sunday Telegraph; High Life; World of Interiors; London Evening Standard; Observer. Membership: Society of Authors. Address: c/o Andrew Lownie, 122 Bedford Court Mansions, Bedford Square, London WC1B 3AH, England.

MATTHEWS Andrew. See: MATHIEU André.

MATTHEWS Patricia Anne, (P A Brisco, Patty Brisco, Laura Wylie), b. 1 July 1927, San Fernando, California, USA. Author. m. (1) Marvin Owen Brisco, 1946, div 1961, 2 sons, (2) Clayton Hartly Matthews, 1971. Education: California State University, Los Angeles. Appointments: Secretary, Administrator, California State University, 1959-77. Publications: Merry's Treasure, 1969; The Other People, 1970; The House of Candles, 1973; Mist of Evil, 1976; Love, Forever More, 1977; Raging Rapids, 1978; Love's Daring Dream, 1978; Love's Golden Destiny, 1979; Love's Many Faces (poetry), 1979; The Night Visitor, 1979; Love's Raging Tide, 1980; Love's Sweet Agony, 1980; Love's Bold Journey, 1980; Tides of Love, 1981; Embers of Dawn, 1982; Flames of Glory, 1983; Dancer of Dreams, 1984; Gambler in Love, 1985; Tame the Restless Heart, 1986; Destruction at Dawn, 1986; Twister, 1986; Enchanted, 1987; Thursday and the Lady, 1987; Mirrors, 1988; The Dreaming Tree, 1989; Sapphire, 1989; Oasis, 1989; The Death of Love, 1990; The Unquiet, 1991. With Clayton Matthews: Midnight Whispers, 1981; Empire, 1982; Midnight Lavender, 1985; The Scent of Fear, 1992; Taste of Evil, 1993; Vision of Death, 1993; The Sound of Murder, 1994. Contributions to: Short stories, poetry, articles, other writings, to magazines and anthologies. Honours: Porgie Award, West Coast Review of Books, Silver Medal, 1979, 1983, Bronze Medal, 1983; Romantic Times: Team Writing Award (with husband), 1983, Reviewers Choice Awards, Best Historical Gothics, 1986-87; Affaire de Coeur Silver Pen Readers Award, 1989. Memberships: Romantic Writers Association; Mystery Writers of America; Sisters in Crime; Novelists Ink. Address: c/o Jay Garon, 415 Central Park West, New York, NY 10025, USA.

MATTHEWS Peter John, b. 6 Jan 1945, Fareham, Hampshire, England. Editor; Writer; Television Commentator. m. Diana Randall, 1969, 2 sons. Appointments: Director, Guinness Publishing, 1981-84, 1989-96; Sports Editor, 1982-91, Editor, 1991-95, Guinness Book of Records; Athletics Commentator, ITV; Publications: Guinness Book of Athletics Facts and Feats, 1982; International Athletics Annual, 1985-; Track and Field Athletics: The Records, 1986; Guinness Encyclopaedia of Sports Records and Results, 1987-; Cricket Firsts (with Robert Brooke), 1988; Guinness International Who's Who of Sport, 1993. Co-Editor, Athletics International, 1993-. Contributions to: Athletics publications. Address: 10 Madgeways Close, Great Amwell, Ware, Hertfordshire SG12 9RU, England.

MATTHEWS William (Procter), b. 11 Nov 1942, Cincinnati, Ohio, USA. Professor of English; Writer; Poet; Translator. m. (1) Marie Murray Harris, 4 May 1963, div 1973, 2 sons, (2) Arlene Modica, 1982, (3) Patricia Smith, 1989. Education: BA, Yale University, 1965; MA, University of North Carolina at Chapel Hill, 1966. Appointments: Co-Founder and Co-Editor, Lillabulero Press and Magazine, 1966-74; Instructor, Wells College, Aurora, New York, 1968-69; Assistant Professor, Cornell University, 1969-74; Associate Professor, University of Colorado, 1974-78; Professor of English, University of Washington, Seattle, 1978-83, City College of the City University of New York, 1983-; Various visiting teaching positions. Publications: Poetry: Ruining the New Road, 1970; Sleek for the Long Flight, 1972; Sticks and Stones, 1975; Rising and Falling, 1979; Flood, 1982; A Happy Childhood, 1984; Foreseeable Futures, 1987; Selected Poems and Translations 1969-1991, 1992; Time and Money, 1995. Other: A World Rich in Anniversaries (translations of Jean Follain's prose poems with Mary Feeney), 1979; Curiosities (essays), 1989. Contributions to: Journals. Honours: National Endowment for the Arts Fellowships, 1974, 1983; Guggenheim Fellowship, 1980-81; Oscar Blumenthal Award, 1983; Ingram Merrill Foundation Fellow, 1984; Eunice Tietjens Memorial Prize, 1989; Rockefeller Foundation Study and Conference Centre Resiency, Bellagio, Italy, 1988; Hawthornden Castle International Writers Retreat, Scotland, 1990; National Book Critics' Circle Award in poetry, 1995. Memberships: Associated Writing Programs; Authors Guild; PEN; Poetry Society of America. Address: 523 West 121st Street, New York, NY 10027, USA.

MATTHIAS John Edward, b. 5 Sept 1941, Columbus, Ohio, USA. Professor; Writer; Poet. m. Diana Clare Jocelyn, 27 Dec 1967,

2 children. Education: BA, Ohio Statwe University, 1963; MA, Stanford University, 1966; Postgraduate Studies, University of London, 1967. Appointments: Visiting Fellow, 1966-77, Associate, 1977-, Clare College, Cambridge; Assistant Professor, 1966-73. Associate Professor, 1973-80, Professor, 1980-, University of Notre Dame; Visiting Professor, Skidmore College, Saratoga Springs, New York, 1975, University of Chicago, 1980. Publications: Bucyrus, 1971; Turns, 1975; Crossing, 1979; Five American Poets, 1980; Introducing David Jones, 1980; Contemporary Swedish Poetry, 1980; Bathory and Lermontov, 1980; Northern Summer: New and Selected Poems, 1984; The Battle of Kosovo, 1987; David Jones: Man and Poet: A Gathering of Ways, 1991; Reading Old Friends, 1991; Swimming at Midnight, 1995; Beltane at Aphelion, 1995. Honours: Woodrow Wilson Fellow, 1963; Fulbright Grant, 1966; Columbia University Translation Award, 1978; Swedish Institute Award, 1981; Poetry Award, Society of Midland Authors, 1984; Ingram Merrill Foundation Grants, 1984, 1990; George Bogin Memorial Award, Poetry Society of America, 1990; Lilly Endowment Fellow, 1993. Memberships: American Association of University Professors, PEN; Poetry Society of America; Poets and Writers. Address: c/o Department of English, University of Notre Dame, Notre Dame, IN 46556, USA.

MATTHIESSEN Peter, b. 22 May 1927, New York, New York, USA. Writer. m. (1) Patricia Southgate, 8 Feb 1951, div, 1 son, 1 daughter, (2) Deborah Love, 16 May 1963, dec Jan 1972, 1 son, 1 daughter, (3) Maria Eckhart, 28 Nov 1980. Education: Sorbonne, University of Paris, 1948-49; BA, Yale University, 1950. Appointment: Co-Founder and Editor, Paris Review, 1951-. Publications: Race Rock, 1954; Partisans, 1955; Wildlife in America, 1959; Raditzer, 1960; The Cloud Forest, 1961; Under the Mountain Wall, 1963; At Play in the Fields of the Lord, 1965; The Shorebirds of North America, 1967; Oomingmak: The Expedition to the Musk Ox Island in the Bering Sea, 1967; Sal Si Puedes, 1969; Blue Meridian, 1971; The Tree Where Man Was Born, 1972; Far Tortuga, 1975; The Snow Leopard, 1978; Sand Rivers, 1981; In the Spirit of Crazy Horse, 1983; Indian Country, 1984; Nine-Headed Dragon River, 1986; Men's Lives, 1986; On the River Styx and Other Stories, 1989; Killing Mister Watson, 1990; African Silences, 1991; Baikal, 1992; Shadows of Africa, 1992; East of Lo Monthang, 1995. Honours: Atlantic Prize, 1950; National Book Award, 1978; John Burroughs Medal, 1981; African Wildlife Leadership Foundation Award, 1982; Gold Medal for Distinction in Natural History, 1985. Membership: American Academy of Arts and Letters. Address: PO Box 392, Bridge Lane, Sagaponack, NY 11962, USA.

MATTINGLEY Christobel Rosemary, 26 Oct 1931, Adelaide, South Australia. Writer. m. Cecil David Mattingley, 17 Dec 1953, 2 sons, 1 daughter. Education: BA, 1st Class Hons in German, 1951; Registration Certificate and Associate of the Library Association of Australia, 1971. Publications: Numerous including: Windmill at Magpie Creek, 1971; The Great Ballagundi Damper Bake, 1975; Rummage, 1981; The Angel with a Mouth Organ, 1984; The Miracle Tree, 1985; Survival in Our Own Land: Aboriginal Experiences in South Australia since 1836, 1988; The Butcher, the Beagle and the Dog Catcher, 1990; Tucker's Mob, 1992; The Sack, 1993; No Gun for Asmir, 1993; The Race, 1995; Asmir in Vienna, 1996; Escape from Sarajevo, 1996. Contributions to: Australian Library Journal; New Zealand Libraries; Landfall; Reading Time; Classroom; Magpies; Something About the Author Autobiography Series. Honours: Advance Australia Award, 1990; Honorary Doctorate, University of South Australia, 1995; Member of the Order of Australia, 1996. Literary Agent: Hickson Associates, 128 Queen Street, Woollahra. NSW 2025, Australia. Address: 10 rosebank Terrace, Stonyfel, South Australia 5066, Australia.

MATURA Thaddee, b. 24 Oct 1922, Poland. Monk. Education: Master in Theology; Master in Biblical Studies. Publications: Celibat et Communauté, 1967; La vie religieuse au tournant, 1971; Naissance d'un charisme, 1973; Le projet évangélique de François d'Assise, 1977; Le radicalisme évangélique, 1980; Ecrits de François d'Aroise, 1981; Suivre Jésus, 1983; Ecrits de Claire d'Assise, 1985; Une absence ardente, 1988; Dieu le Père très saint, 1990. Contributions to: About 150 items to various publications. Address: 84240 Grambois, France.

MAUMELA Titus Ntsieni, b. 25 Dec 1924, Sibasa, Venda, Southern Africa. Teacher. m. Rose Maumela, 27 June 1949, 2 sons, 1 daughter. Education: BA, University of South Africa, 1961. Publications: Novels: Elelwani, 1954; Mafangambiti, 1956; Vhavenda Vho-Matshivha, 1958; Vhuhosi Vhu tou Bebelwa, 1962; Zwa Mulovha

Zwi a Fhela, 1963; Maela wa Vho-Mathavha, 1967; Musandiwa na Khotsi Vho-Liwalaga, 1968; Kanakana (youth), 1975; Ndi Vho-Muthukhuthukhu, 1977; Vho-Rammbebo, 1981; Tshiphiri Tsho Bvela Khagala, 1986; Talukanyani (youth). Dramas: Tshililo, 1957; A Hu Bebiwi Mbilu, 1975; Vhuhosi A Vhu Thetshelwi, 1975; Edzani, 1985; Tomolambilu, 1989. Short stories: Matakadzambilu, 1965; Zwiitavhathu, 1965; Maungedzo, 1972; Mihani Ya Shango, 1972; Mithetshelo, 1981; Mmbwa Ya La Inwe a i Noni, 1983; Nganea Pfufhi dza u takadza, 1989. Essay: Maanea A Pfadzaho, 1992. Folktales: Dzingaho na Dzithai dza Tshivenda, 1968; Salungano! Salungano! 1978. Language Manuals: Thikho ya Luvenda ya Fomo 1, 1970; Thikho ya Luvenda ya Fomo II, na III, 1970; Luvenda lwa Murole wa 5, 1975; Luvenda lwa Fomo I, 1975; Luvenda lwa Murole wa Fomo II, 1976; Luvenda lwa Murole wa 8, 1978; Tshivenda tsho tambaho tsha, Murole wa 5 (with Prof T W Muloiwa and B H Maumela), 1986; Gondo la Tshivenda, Murole wa 5, 1987; Gondo la Tshivenda, Murole wa 6 (with M R Madiba), 1990; Gondo la Tshivenda, Murole wa 8 (with M R Madiba and F K Maselesele), 1992; Gondo la Tshivenda, Murole wa 9 (with M R Madiba), 1992; Gondo la Tshivenda, Murole wa 10 (with M R Madiba), 1992. Address: PO Box 2, Vhufuli, Venda, Southern Africa.

MAUPIN Armistead, b. 13 May 1944, Washington District of Columbia, USA. Writer. Education: BA, University of North Carolina at Chapel Hill, 1966. Appointments: Reporter, News and Courier, Charleston, 1970-71; Associated Press, 1971-72; Columnist, Pacific Sun, San Francisco, 1974, San Francisco Chronicle, 1976-77. Publications: Tales of the City, 1978; More Tales of the City, 1980; Further Tales of the City, 1982; Babycakes, 1984; Significant Others, 1987; Sure of You, 1989; Maybe the Moon, 1992. Other: Libretto for the musical Heart's Desire, 1990. Television Programme: Armistead Maupin's Tales of the City, 1993. Contributions to: Periodicals. Honours: Best Dramatic Serial Award, Royal TV Society, 1994; George Foster Peabody Award, 1994. Address: c/o International Creative Management, 40 West 57th Street, New York, NY10019, USA.

MAVOR Elizabeth (Osborne), b. 17 Dec 1927, Glasgow, Scotland. Author. Education: St Andrews, 1940-45; St Leonard's and St Anne's College, Oxford, England, 1947-50. Publications: Summer in the Greenhouse, 1959; The Temple of Flora, 1961; The Virgin Mistress: A Biography of the Duchess of Kingston (in US as The Virgin Mistress: A Study in Survival: The Life of the Duchess of Kingston), 1964; The Redoubt, 1967; The Ladies of Llangollen: A Study in Romantic Friendship, 1971; A Green Equinox, 1973; Life with the Ladies of Llangollen, 1984; The Grand Tour of William Beckford, 1986; The White Solitaire, 1988; The American Journals of Fanny Kemble, 1990; The Grand Tours of Katherine Wilmot, France 1801-3 and Russia 1805-7, 1992; The Captain's Wife, The South American Journals of Maria Graham 1821-23, 1993. Address: Curtis Brown Ltd, 28-29 Haymarket, London SW1Y 4SP, England.

MAXWELL Glyn Meurig, b. 7 Nov 1962, Welwyn Garden City, Hertfordshire, England. Writer. Education: Worcester College, Oxford 1982-85; BA (Hons) 1st Class, English, Oxford, 1985; MA, Creative Writing, Boston University, USA, 1988. Publications: Tale of the Mayor's Son (poems), 1990; Out of the Rain (poems), 1992; Gnyss the Magnificent (verse-plays), 1993. Contributions to: Reviews to Independent; Times Literary Supplement; Vogue; Poetry Review; Verse; Poems to Times Literary Supplement; Sunday Times; Spectator; Independent; Atlantic Monthly; Partisan Review; Verse; New Yorker. Honours: Poetry Book Society Choice, 1990 and Recommendation, 1992; Shortlisted, John Llewellyn Rhys Memorial Prize, 1991; Eric Gregory Award, 1992; Somerset Maugham Travel Prize. Memberships: PEN; Poetry Society. Address: c/o Bloodaxe Books, PO Box 1SN, Newcastle-upon-Tyne NE99 1SN, England.

MAXWELL Gordon Stirling, b. 21 Mar 1938, Edinburgh, Scotland. Archaeologist. m. Kathleen Mary King, 29 July 1961, 2 daughters. Education: MA (Hons), St Andrews. Appointments: Curatorial Officer, Royal Commission for Ancient and Historical Monuments, Scotland, 1964-. Publications: The Impact of Aerial Reconnaissance on Archaeology (editor), 1983; Rome's Northwest Frontier: The Antonine Wall, 1983; The Romans in Scotland, 1989; A Battle Lost: Romans and Caledonians at Mons Graupius, 1990. Contributions to: Britannia; Proceedings of the Society of Antiquaries of Scotland; Glasgow Archaeological Journal. Memberships: Royal Society of Arts, fellow; Society of Antiquaries of London, fellow;

Society of Antiquaries of Scotland, fellow. Address: Micklegarth, 72a High Street, Aberdour, Fife KY3 0SW, Scotland.

MAXWELL Jane. See: **SMITH Jane (Marilyn) Davis**.

MAXWELL John. See: **FREEMANTLE Brian**.

MAXWELL Patricia Anne, (Jennifer Blake, Maxine Patrick, Patricia Ponder, Elizabeth Trehearne), b. 9 Mar 1942, Louisiana, USA. Author. m. Jerry R Maxwell, 1 Aug 1957, 2 sons, 2 daughters. Appointments: Writer-in-Residence, University of Northeastern Louisiana. Publications: Over 40 novels including: Love's Wild Desire, 1977; Tender Betrayal, 1979; The Storm and the Splendor, 1979; Golden Fancy, 1980; Embrace and Conquer, 1981; Royal Seduction, 1983; Surrender in Moonlight, 1984; Midnight Waltz, 1985; Fierce Eden, 1985; Royal Passion, 1986; Prisoner of Desire, 1986; Louisiana Dawn, 1987; Southern Rapture, 1987; Perfume of Paradise, 1988; Love and Smoke, 1989; Spanish Serenade, 1990; Shameless, 1994; Silver-Tongued Devil (as Jennifer Blake), 1996; Tigress (as Jennifer Blake), 1996; Garden of Scandal (as Jennifer Blake), 1997. Honour: Historical Romance Author of the Year, 1985. Address: P O Box 9218, Quitman, LA 71268, USA.

MAXWELL William, b. 16 Aug 1908, Lincoln, Illinois, USA. Author. m. Emily Gilman Noyes, 17 May 1945, 2 daughters. Education: University of Illinois, 1926-30, 1931-33; Harvard University, 1930-31. Appointments: Faculty, University of Illinois, 1931-33; Editorial Staff, New York magazine, 1936-76. Publications: Bright Center of Heaven, 1934; They Came Like Swallows, 1937; The Folded Leaf, 1945; The Heavenly Tenants, 1946; Time Will Darken It, 1948; Stories (with John Cheever, Daniel Fuchs and Jean Stafford), 1956; The Chateau, 1961; The Old Man at the Railroad Crossing, 1966; Ancestors, 1971; Over by the River, 1977. Editor: So Long, See You Tomorrow, 1979; Letters of Sylvia Townsend Warner, 1982; The Outermost Dream, 1989; Billie Dyer, 1992; All the Days and Nights, 1995; Collected Stories: All the Days and Nights, 1996; The Happiness of Getting It Down Right, Correspondance with Frank O'Connor, 1996. Contributions to: Periodicals. Honours: Honorary DLitt, University of Illinois, 1973; William Dean Howells Medal, American Academy of Arts and Letters, 1980; American Book Award, 1982; Brandeis University Creative Arts Award, 1984; Ivan Sandorf Award, National Book Critics Circle, 1994; American Academy of Arts and Letters Gold Medal for Fiction, 1995. Memberships: American Academy of Arts and Letters; National Institute of Arts and Letters, president, 1969-72. Address: 544 East 86th Street, New York NY 10028, USA.

MAY Beatrice. See: **ASTLEY Thea**.

MAY Derwent James, b. 29 Apr 1930, Eastbourne, Sussex, England. Author; Journalist. m. Yolanta Izabella Sypniewska, 1 son, 1 daughter. Education: Lincoln College, Oxford, 1949-52; MA (Oxon). Appointments: Theatre and Film Critic, Continental Daily Mail, Paris, 1952-53; Lecturer in English, University of Indonesia, 1955-58; Senior Lecturer in English, Universities of Lodz and Warsaw, 1959-63; Chief Leader Writer, Times Literary Supplement, 1963-65; Literary Editor, The Listener, 1965-86; Literary and Arts Editor, Sunday Telegraph, 1986-90; The European, 1990-91; European Arts Editor, The Times, 1992-. Publications: Novels: The Professionals, 1964; Dear Parson, 1969; The Laughter in Djakarta, 1973; A Revenger's Comedy, 1979. Non-fiction: Proust, 1983; The Times Nature Diary, 1983; Hannah Arendt, 1986; The New Times Nature Diary, 1993; Feather Reports, 1996. Contributions to: Encounter; Hudson Review. Honours: Member, Booker Prize Jury, 1978; Hawthornden Prize Committee, 1987-. Membership: Beefsteak Club; Garrick Club. Address: 201 Albany Street, London NW1 4AB, England.

MAY Gita, b. 16 Sept 1929, Brussels, Belgium. Professor of French; Writer. m. Irving May, 21 Dec 1947. Education: Hunter College, 1953; MA, 1954, PhD, 1957, Columbia University Appointments: Professor of French and Chairman, Department of French, Columbia University. Publications: Diderot Studies III (editor with O Fellows), 1961; Madame Roland and the Age of Revolution, 1970; Stendhal and the Age of Napoleon, 1977; Diderot: Essais sur la peinture, Vol XIV of his complete works (editor), 1984; Pensées détachées sur la peinture, 1995; Rebecca West, Anita Brookner, in British Writers, 1996, 1997. Contributions to: Books and professional journals. Honours: Guggenheim Fellowship, 1964; Chevalier, 1968; Officier, 1981, Ordre des Palmes Academiques; National Endowment for the Humanities Senior Fellow, 1971; Van Amringe Distinguished

Book Award, Columbia Univesity, 1971. Memberships American Society of 18th Century Studies, president, 1985-86; Modern Language Association, executive council, 1980-83. Address: c/o Department of French, Columbia University, 516 Philosophy Hall, New York, NY 10027, USA.

MAY Julian, b. 10 July 1931, Chicago, Illinois, USA. Writer. m. Thaddeus E Dikty, 1953, 2 sons, 1 daughter. Publications: The Many Colored Land, 1981; The Golden Torc, 1982; The Nonborn King, 1983; The Adversary, 1984; Intervention, 1987; Black Trillium, 1990; Jack the Bodiless, 1991; 254 other Books; Blood Trillium, 1992; Diamond Mask, 1994; Magnificat, 1996; Sky Trillium, 1997. Literary Agent: Scovil, Chichak, Galen, NY, USA. Address: Box 851 Mercer Island, WA 98040, USA.

MAY Naomi Young, b. 27 Mar 1934, Glasgow, Scotland. Novelist; Journalist; Painter. m. Nigel May, 3 Oct 1964, 2 sons, 1 daughter. Education: Slade School of Fine Art, London, England, 1953-56; Diploma, Fine Art, University of London. Publications: At Home, 1969, radio adaptation, 1987; The Adventurer, 1970; Troubles, 1976. Contributions to: Anthologies, newspapers, and magazines. Honour: History of Art Prize, Slade School of Fine Art. Membership: PEN. Address: 6 Lion Gate Gardens, Richmond, Surrey TW9 2DF, England.

MAY Robert Stephen. See: MAY Robin.

MAY Robin, (Robert Stephen May), b. 26 Dec 1929, Deal, Kent, England. Writer. 2 sons, 1 daughter. Education: Bradfield College, 1943-48; Central School of Speech and Drama, 1950-53. Publications: Operamania, 1966; Theatremania, 1967; Wit of the Theatre, 1969; Wolfe's Army, 1974; Who Was Shakespeare?, 1974; The Gold Rushes, 1977; History of the American West, 1984; History of the Theatre, 1986; A Guide to the Opera, 1987. Contributions to: Miscellaneous magazines for young people. Membership: Society of Authors. Literary Agent: Rupert Crew Ltd, Kings Mews, London WC1, England. Address: 23 Malcolm Road, London SW19 4AS, England.

MAY Stephen James, (Julian Poole), b. 10 Sept 1946, Toronto, Ontario, Canada. College Professor and Advisor; Educator; Novelist; Essayist; Historian; Critic. m. Caroline C May, 13 Oct 1972. Education: BA, 1975, MA, 1977, California State University, Los Angeles, USA; DLitt, International University, Bombay, 1992. Publications: Pilgrimage, 1987; Fire from the Skies, 1990; Footloose on the Santa Fe Trail, 1992; A Land Observed, 1993; Zane Grey: Romancing the West, 1997. Contributions to: Denver Post; Frontier Rocky Mountain News; Southwest Art; Artists of the Rockies; National Geographic. Memberships: Colorado Authors League; World Literary Academy. Literary Agent, Carl Brandt, New York City, USA. Address: 96 Hillside Terrace, Craig, CO 81625, USA.

MAYER Gerda (Kamilla), b. 9 June 1927, Carlsbad, Czechoslovakia. (British citizen). Poet. m. Adolf Mayer, 1949. Education: BA, Bedford College, London, 1963. Publications: Oddments, 1970; Gerda Mayer's Library Folder; Treble Poets 2, 1975; The Knockabourt Show, 1978; Monkey on the Analyst's Couch, 1980; The Candy Floss Tree, 1984; March Postman, 1985; A Heartache of Grass, 1988. Editor: Poet Tree Centaur: A Walthamstow Group Anthology, 1973. Address: 12 Margaret Avenue, London E4 7NP, England.

MAYER Robert, b. 24 Feb 1939, Bronx, New York, USA. Writer. m. La Donna Cocilovo, 24 Feb 1989, 1 stepdaughter. Education: BA, City College of New York, 1959; MS, Journalism, Columbia University, 1960. Appointments: Reporter, Columnist, Newsday, 1961-71; Managing Editor, Santa Fe Reporter, 1988-90. Publications: Superfolks, 1977; The Execution, 1979; Midge and Decker, 1982; Sweet Salt, 1984; The Grace of Shortstops, 1984; The Search, 1986; The Dreams of Ada, 1987; I, JFK, 1989. Contributions to: Vanity Fair; New York Magazine; Travel and Leisure; Rocky Mountain Magazine; New Mexico Magazine; Santa Fe Reporter; Newsday. Honours: National Headliner Award, 1968; Mike Berger Awards, 1969, 1971; Nominee, Edgar Allan Poe Award, 1988. Literary Agent: Philip Spitzer, New York, USA. Address: 135 Cedar Street, Santa Fe, NM 87501, USA.

MAYER Wolf, b. 23 June 1934, Stuttgart, Germany. Retired Senior Lecturer in Geology. m. Veronica Mayer, 22 Aug 1959, 2 daughters. Education: BSc, University of New Zealand, 1962; MSc,

University of Auckland, 1964; PhD, University of New England, 1972. Appointments: Senior Lecturer in Geology, retired; Visiting Scholar, University of Canberra, 1994-95; Visiting Fellow, Australian National University, Canberra, 1996-. Publications: Gemstone Identification, in Australian and New Zealand Gemstones, 1972; Gemstone Identification, in Australian Gemstones, 1974; Field Guide to Australian Rocks, Minerals and Gemstones, 1976, 3rd edition, 1992; Images in Stone: A Guide to the Building Stones of Parliament House, 1996. Contributions to: Numerous to professional journals on a variety of geological subjects. Memberships: Geological Society of Australia; History of Earth Science Society. Literary Agent: Curtis Brown, PO Box 19, Paddington, New South Wales 2021, Australia. Address: 22 Bennet Street, Spence, ACT 2615, Australia.

MAYER-KOENIG Wolfgang, b. 28 Mar 1946, Vienna, Austria. Author; University Professor. Education: Dr FA; Dr.h.c.f.litt. Appointments: Extraordinary University Professor; Founder-Director, Cultural Centre; Editor, LOG, international literary magazine. Publications: Sichtbare Pavillons, 1968; Stichmarken, 1969; Texte und Bilder, 1972; Karl Kraus als Kritiker, 1975; Sprache-Politik-Aggression, 1975; Robert Musils Moeglichkeitsstil, 1977; In den Armen unseres Waerters, 1979; Vorlaeufige Versagung, 1985; Chagrin non dechifré, 1986; Colloqui nella stanza, 1986; Schreibverantwrotung, 1986; A hatalom bonyolult angyala, 1988; Colloquios nelcuarto, 1990. Contributions to: Journals. Honours: Theodor Körner Prize for Literature; Cross for Science and Arts for Literature of the Republic of Austria; Chevalier des Arts et des Lettres de la Republique Française; Doctor of Fine Arts, State of California. Address: Hernalser Guertel 41, A-1170 Vienna, Austria.

MAYHAR Ardath, (Frank Cannon, John Killdeer, Frances Hurst), b. 20 Feb 1930, Timpson, Texas, USA. Writer; Teacher. m. Joe E Mayhar, 7 June 1958, 2 sons. Publications: How the Gods Wove in Kyrannon, 1979; Soul Singer of Tyrnos, 1981; Golden Dream: A Fuzzy Odyssey, 1982; Runes of the Lyre, 1982; Lords of the Triple Moons, 1983; Exile on Viahil, 1984; The World Ends in Hickory Hollow, 1985; The Saga of Grittel Sundotha, 1985; Medicine Walk, 1985; Carrots and Miggle, 1986; A Place of Silver Silence, 1987; Trail of the Seahawks, 1987; Feud at Sweet Water Creek, 1987; The Wall, Space and Time, 1987; Bloody Texas Trail, 1988; Texas Gunsmoke, 1988; Monkey Station, 1989; Island in the Swamp, 1993; Blood Kin, 1993; Towers of the Earth, 1994; Far Horizons, 1994; Hunters of the Plains, 1995; High Mountain Winter, 1996. Contributions to: Twilight Zone Magazine; Isaac Asimov's Science Fiction Magazine; Espionage Magazine; Mike Shayne's Mystery Magazine; Hitchcock's Mystery Magazine. Honour: Balrog Award, 1985. Memberships: Science Fiction Writers of America; Western Writers of America. Literary Agent: Jimmy Vines. Address: PO Box 180, Chireno, TX 75937, USA.

MAYNARD Christopher, b. 1949, Canada. Editor; Publisher; Writer. Appointments: Editor, Macdonald Education, 1972-74, Intercontinental Book Productions, Maidenhead, Berkshire, England, 1976-77; Director, The Strip Limited, Maynard and How Publishing, London. Publications: Planet Earth, 1974; Prehistoric World, 1974; Great Men of Science (with Edward Holmes), 1975; The Amazing World of Dinosaurs, 1976; The Real Cowboy (co-author), 1976; The Amazing World of Money, 1977; Scimitar Paperbacks (editor), 1977-78; Economy Guide to Europe (co-author), 1978; New York (with Gail Rebuck), 1978; Indians and Palefaces (with Marianne Gray), 1978; The Razzmataz Gang, 1978; Father Christmas and His Friends, 1979; The First Great Kids Catalogue, 1987. Address: 78 Carlton Mansions, Randolph Avenue, London W9, England.

MAYNARD Fredelle Bruser, b. 9 July 1922, Foam Lake, Canada. Writer; Lecturer; Television Host. div., 2 daughters. Education: BA Honours, University of Manitoba, 1942; MA, University of Toronto, 1943; PhD, Harvard University, USA, 1947. Appointments: Radcliffe Institute Scholar, USA, 1967-69; Writer-in-Residence, University of Illinois, 1974. Publications: Raisins and Almonds, 1972; Guiding Your Child to a More Creative Life, 1973; The Child Care Crisis, 1985; The Tree of Life, 1988. Contributions to: Numerous journals in USA, Canada, England, Australia, South Africa. Honours: Governor General's Medal; Fellowship, Canadian Federation of University Women; Flavelle Fellowship, Harvard University; Award for Excellence in Women's Journalism, University of Missouri; Senior Arts Award, Canada Council. Memberships: Phi Beta Kappa; Periodical Writers Association of Canada; Ontario Association of Marriage and Family Therapy; International Association for Promotion of Humanistic

Studies in Gynaecology, honorary member. Address: 25 Metcalfe Street, Toronto, Ontario M4X 1R5, Canada.

MAYNE Richard (John), b. 2 Apr 1926, London, England. Writer; Editor; Broadcaster. m. Jocelyn Mudie Ferguson, 2 daughters. Education: MA, PhD, Trinity College, Cambridge, 1947-53. Appointments: Rome Correspondent, New Statesman, 1953-54; Official of the European Community, Luxembourg and Brussels, 1956-63; Personal Assistant to Jean Monnet, Paris, 1963-66; Paris Correspondent, 1963-73, Co-Editor, 1990-94, Encounter; Visiting Professor, University of Chicago, 1970; Director, Federal Trust, London, 1971-73; Head, UK Offices of the European Commission, London, 1973-79; Film Critic, Sunday Telegraph, London, 1987-89, The European, 1990-. Publications: The Community of Europe, 1962; The Institutions of the European Community, 1968; The Recovery of Europe, 1970; The Europeans, 1972; Europe Tomorrow (editor), 1972; The New Atlantic Challenge (editor), 1975; The Memoirs of Jean Monnet (translator), 1978; Postwar: The Dawn of Today's Europe, 1983; Western Europe: A Handbook (editor), 1987; Federal Union: The Pioneers (with John Pinder), 1990; Europe: A History of its Peoples (translator), 1990; History of Europe (translator), 1993; A History of Civilizations (translator), 1994. Contributions to: Numerous in UK, USA, France and Germany. Honour: Scott-Moncrief Prize for Translation from French, 1978. Memberships: Society of Authors; Royal Institute of International Affairs; Federal Trust for Education and Research; Franco-British Council. Address: Albany Cottage, 24 Park Village East, Regent's Park, London NW1 7PZ, England.

MAYNE Seymour, b. 18 May 1944, Montreal, Quebec, Canada. Poet; Editor; Translator. Education: BA, McGill University, 1965; MA, 1966, PhD, University of British Columbia, 1972. Appointments: Managing Editor, Very Stone House, 1966-69, Editor, Ingluvin Publications, 1970-73, Mosaic Press, 1974-82. Publications: Mouth, 1970; Name, 1975; Diaporas, 1977; The Impossible Promised Land, 1981; Vanguard of Dreams, 1984; Essential Words, 1985; Children of Abel, 1986; Simple Ceremony, 1990; Killing Time, 1992; Locust of Silence, 1993; The Songs of Moses and Other Poems, 1995; Five O'Clock Shadow (co-author), 1996; Jerusalem: An Anthology, 1996. Honours: Chester Macnaghten First Prize; J I Segal Prize; York Poetry Workshop Award; American Literary Translators Association Poetry Award; Jewish Book Committee Prize. Membership: PEN. Address: Department of English, University of Ottawa, Ottawa, Ontario KIN 6N5, Canada.

MAYNE William (James Carter), b. 16 Mar 1928, Kingston upon Hull, Yorkshire, England. Writer. Appointments: Lecturer, Creative Writing, Deakin University, Geelong, Australia, 1976, 1977. Publications: About 90 stories for children and young people, 1953-. Honours: Library Association's Carnegie Medal for Best Children's Book of the Year, 1957; Guardian Award for Children's Fiction, 1993. Memberships: Fellow, Creative Writing, Rolle College, Exmouth, 1979-80. Address: c/o David Higham Associates, 5-8 Lower John Street, Golden Square, London W1R 4HA, England.

MAYOTTE Judith A (Moberly), b. 25 Jan 1937, Wichita, Kansas, USA. Author; Television Producer; Refugee Advocate; Adviser. m. Jack Parnell Mayotte, 6 Oct 1972, dec 9 Sept 1975. Education: BA, Mundelein College, Chicago; MA, PhD, Marquette University, Milwaukee, Wisconsin, 1976. Appointments: Special Adviser, US Department of State, Washington, DC; Producer, Writer, many television programmes including Portrait of America series, WTBS (Turner Broadcasting). Publication: Disposable People: The Plight of Refugees, 1992. Contributions to: Journal of International Affairs; Numerous popular journals and newspapers; Maryknoll Magazine. Honours: Emmy, 1985; Mickey Leland Award, Refugee Voices, 1994; All University Alumni Merit Award for Professional Achievement, Marquette University, 1994; Honorary Doctor of Humanities, 1994; Annual Award, Refugees International, 1994. Memberships: Women's Commission for Refugee Women and Children; International Rescue Committee; Refugees International; Senior Fellow, Policy Group; International Women's Media Foundation. Address: 1275 25th Street North West, Washington, DC 20037, USA.

MAYRÖCKER Friederike, b. 20 Dec 1924, Vienna, Austria. Writer; Poet. Publications: More than 70 books of poetry, children's books, novels, prose, radio plays, most recent being: Reise durch die Nacht, 1984; Das Herzzerreiszende der Dinge, 1985; Winterglück, 1986; Magische Blätter I, II, III, IV, 1983, 1987; Stilleben, Das Besessene Alter; Veritas, 1993; Lection, 1994; Notizen auf einem

Kamel, 1996; das zu Sehende, das zu Hörende, 1997. Contributions to: Literary journals and magazines. Honours: Roswitha-von-Gandersheim-Preis, 1982; Anton-Wildgans-Preis, 1982; Grosser Österreichischer Staatspreis, 1982; Literaturpreis des Südwestfunk, 1985; Hauptpreis für Literatur der Deutschen Industrie, 1989; Friedrich-Hölderlin Preis, 1993; Manuskripte Preis, 1994; Groszer Lit Preis der Bayerischen Akademie de Schönen Künste, 1996; Else-Lasker-Schüller-Preis, 1996; Meersburger Droste-Preis, 1997. Memberships: Österreichischer Kunstsenat Wien; Kurie für Wissenschaft und Kunst; Akademie der Künste Berlin; Internationales Künstlergremium; Grazer Autorenversammlung; Deutsche Akademie für Sprache und Dichtung Darmstadt. Address: Zentagasse 16/40, A-1050 Vienna, Austria.

MAYSON Marina. See: ROGERS Rosemary.

MAYUMI Inaba, b. 1950, Aichi Prefecture, Japan. Writer. Publications: Wakai Kage no Itami wo; Hotel Zambia; Endless Waltz; Kohaku no Machi; Dakareru; Short story collection: Koe no Shōfu (The Voice Prostitute). Honours: Prize for Young Female Authors, 1973; Sakuhin shô, 1980; Womens' Literary Award, 1992. Address: c/o Japan PEN Club, 265 Akasaka Residential Hotel, 9-1-7 Akasaka, Minato-ku, Tokyo 107, Japan.

MAZER Norma Fox, b. 15 May 1931, New York, New York, USA. m. Harry Mazer, 12 Feb 1950, 1 son, 3 daughters. Education: Antioch College; Syracuse University. Publications: I Trissy, 1971; A Figure of Speech, 1973; Saturday, The Twelfth of October, 1975; Dear Bill, Remember me, 1976; The Solid Gold Kid, 1977; Up in Seth's Room, 1979; Mrs Fish, Ape and Me and the Dump Queen, 1980; Taking Terri Mueller, 1981; When We First Met, 1982; Summer Girls, Love Boys, and Other Stories, 1982; Someone To Love, 1983; Supergirl, 1984; Downtown, 1984; A My Name is Ami, 1986; Three Sisters, 1986; B My Name is Bunny, 1987; After the Rain, 1987; Silver, 1988; Heartbeat, 1989; Babyface, 1989; C, My Name is Cal, 1990; D, My Name is Danita, 1991; Bright Days, Stupid Nights, 1992; E My Name is Emily, 1991; Out of Control, 1993. Contributions to: English Journal; Alan Review; The Writer; Signal; Writing; Redbook; Playgirl; Voice; Ingeune. Literary Agent: Elaine Markson literary Agency, 44 Greenwich Avenue, NY 10011, USA. Address: Brown Gulf Road, Jamesville, NY 13078, USA.

MAZLISH Bruce, b. 15 Sept 1923, New York, New York, USA. Professor of History; Writer. m. (1) 3 sons, 1 daughter. (2) Neva Goodwin, 22 Nov 1988. Education: BA, 1944, MA, 1947, PhD, 1955, Columbia University. Appointments: Instructor, University of Maine, 1946-48, Columbia University, 1949-50; Instructor, 1950-53, Faculty, 1955-, Professor of History, 1965-, Chairman, History Section, 1965-70, Head, Department of Humanities, 1974-79, Massachusetts Institute of Technology; Director, American School, Madrid, 1953-55. Publications: The Western Intellectual Tradition (with J Bronowski), 1960; The Riddle of History, 1966; In Search of Nixon, 1972; James and John Stuart Mill: Father and Son in the 19th Century, 1975, 2nd edition, 1988; The Revolutionary Ascetic, 1976; Kissinger: The European Mind in American Policy, 1976; The Meaning of Karl Marx, 1984; A New Science: The Breakdown of Connections and the Birth of Sociology, 1989; The Leader, the Led and the Psyche, 1990; The Fourth Discontinuity: The Co-Evolution of Humans and Machines, 1993. Editor: Psychoanalysis and History, 1963, revised edition, 1971; The Railroad and the Space Program: An Exploration in Historical Analogy, 1965; Conceptualizing Global History (with Ralph Bultjens), 1993. Contributions to: Professional journals. Honours: Clement Staff Essay Award, 1968; Toynbee Prize, 1986-87. Memberships: American Academy of Arts and Sciences, fellow; Rockefeller Family Fund, board of directors; Toynbee Prize Foundation, board of directors. Address: 11 Lowell Street, Cambridge, MA 02138, USA.

MAZZARO Jerome (Louis), b. 25 Nov 1934, Detroit, Michigan, USA. Professor of English and Comparative Literature; Author. Education: AB, Wayne University, 1954; MA, University of Iowa, 1956; PhD, Wayne State University, 1963. Appointments: Instructor, University of Detroit, 1958-61; Editor, Fresco, 1960-61, Modern Poetry Studies, 1970-79; Assistant Professor, State University of New York College at Cortland, 1962-64; Assistant Editor, North American Review, 1963-65, Noetics, 1964-65; Professor of English and Comparative Literature, State University of New York at Buffalo, 1964-96; Contributing Editor, Salmagundi, 1967-, American Poetry Review, 1972-, Italian-American, 1974-88; Poetry Editor, Helios, 1977-79. Publications: The Achievement of Robert Lowell, 1939-1959,

1960; Juvenal: Satires (translator), 1965; The Poetic Themes of Robert Lowell, 1965; Changing the Windows (verse), 1966; Modern American Poetry (editor), 1970; Transformation in the Renaissance English Lyric, 1970; Profile of Robert Lowell (editor), 1971; Profile of William Carlos Williams (editor), 1971; William Carlos Williams: The Later Poetry, 1973; Postmodern American Poetry, 1980; The Figure of Dante: An Essay on the "Vita Nuova", 1981; The Caves of Love (verse), 1985; Rubbings (verse), 1985; John Logan: The Collected Poems (editor with Al Poulin), 1989; John Logan: The Collected Fiction (editor), 1991. Contributions to: Reference works, books and journals. Honours: Guggenheim Fellowship, 1964-65; Hadley Fellowship, 1979-80. Memberships: Dante Society of America; Mark Twain Society. Address: 147 Capen Boulevard, Buffalo, NY 14226, USA.

MBURUMBA Kerina, b. 6 June 1932, Tsumeb, Namibia. Professor; Member of Parliament. m. Jane M Miller, 1957, 2 sons, 2 daughters. Education: BA, Lincoln University, Oxford, Pennsylvania, USA, 1957; Legal courses, American Extension School of Law, Chicago Correspondence School, 1953-57; Graduate courses, Graduate Faculty, New School for Social Research, New York City, 1957-59. Appointments: Diplomatic Attaché, Republic of Liberia and Ethiopia, International Court of Justice, 1960-63; Adjunct Assistant Professor, School of Education, 1968-70, Associate Professor, Afro-American Studies, 1970-71, Associate Professor, Africana Studies Department, 1972-75, Brooklyn College, City University of New York, USA; Visiting Professor, Livingston College, Rutgers University, 1970-71; Director of Communications, Namibia Foundation, Namibia, 1976-78; Member, Constituent Assembly, Namibia; Member, National Assembly of Namibia, 1990-; Consultant; Lecturer. Publications: Malcom X: The Apostle of Defiance, An African View (editor with H Newman), 1969; The Political History of Namibia 1884-1972, 1979; Namibia, The Making of a Nation. Contributions to: Ghanaian Times; New African; Africa South; Egyptian Review. Honour: PhD (honoris causa), Political Science, Padjajaran University, Bandung, Indonesia, 1962. Address: PO Box 24861, Windhoek, Namibia, South West Africa.

MCADAM Douglas John, b. 31 Aug 1951, Pasadena, California, USA. Professor of Sociology. m. Tracy Lynn Stevens, 20 Feb 1988. Education: BA, Occidental College, Los Angeles, 1963; MA, 1977, PhD, 1979, State University of New York, Stony Brook. Publications: Politics of Privacy, 1980; Political Process and the Development of Black Insurgency 1930-1970, 1982; Freedom Summer, 1988. Contributions: Numerous articles to American Journal of Sociology and American Sociological Review. Honour: Finalist, Sorokin Annual Award for Best Book in Sociology, 1989. Membership: American Sociological Association. Address: Department of Sociology, University of Arizona, Tucson, AZ 85721, USA.

MCALLISTER Casey. See: **BATTIN B W.**

MCAULEY James J(ohn), b. 8 Jan 1936, Dublin, Ireland. Professor; Poet. m. Deirdre O'Sullivan, 1982. Education: University College Dublin; University of Arkansas, Fayetteville. Appointments: Editor, Dolmen Press, Dublin, 1960-66; Professor, Eastern Washington University, Cheney, 1978-; Director, Eastern Washington University Press, 1993. Publication: Observations, 1960; A New Address, 1965; Draft Balance Sheet, 1970; Home and Away, 1974; After the Blizzard, 1975; The Exile's Recurring Nightmare, 1975; Recital, Poems, 1975-80, 1982; The Exile's Book of Hours, 1982; Coming and Going: New and Selected Poems, 1968-88, 1989. Play: The Revolution, 1966. Libretto: Praise, 1981. Honours: National Endowment for the Arts Grant, 1972; Washington Governor's Award, 1976. Address: Eastern Washington University Press, MS#14, Eastern Washington University, Cheney, WA 99004, USA.

MCBAIN Ed. See: **LOMBINO Salvatore A.**

MCCAFFREY Anne (Inez), b. 1 Apr 1926, Cambridge, Massachusetts, USA. Author. m. Wright Johnson, 14 Jan 1950, div Aug 1970, 2 sons, 1 daughter. Education: BA, Radcliffe College, 1947; University of Dublin, 1970-71. Publications: Restoree, 1967; Dragonflight, 1968; Decision at Doona, 1969; Ship Who Sang, 1969; Mark of Merlin, 1971; Dragonquest: Being the Further Adventures of the Dragonriders of Pern, 1971; Ring of Fear, 1971; To Ride Pegasus, 1973; Cooking Out of This World, 1973; A Time When, 1975; Dragonsong, 1976; Kilteran Legacy, 1975; Dragonsinger, 1977; Dinosaur Planet, 1977; Get Off the Unicorn, 1977; White Dragon, 1978; Dragondrums, 1979; Crystal Singer, 1981; The Worlds of Anne

McCaffrey, 1981; The Coelura, 1983; Moreta: Dragonlady of Peru, 1983; Dinosuar Planet Survivors, 1984; Stitch in Snow, 1984; Killashandra, 1985; The Girl Who Heard Dragons, 1985; The Year of the Lucy, 1986; Nerilka's Story, 1986; The Lady, 1987; People of Pern, 1988; Dragonsdown, 1988; Renegades of Pern, 1989; The Dragonlover's Guide to Pern (with Jody-Lynn Nye), 1989; The Rowan, 1990; Pegasus in Flight, 1990; Sassinak (with Elizabeth Moon), 1990; The Death of Sleep (with Jody-Lynn Nye), 1990; All the Weyrs of Pern, 1991; Generation Warriors, 1991; Damia, 1991; The Partnership (with Margaret Ball), 1991; Crisis at Doona (with Jody Lynn Nye), 1991; Damia, 1992; The City Who Fought (with Mercedes Lackey), 1993; Powers That Be (with Elizabeth Ann Scarborough), 1993; Chronicles of Pern: First Fall, 1993; Lyon's Pride, 1994; The Ship Who Won (with Jody-Lynn Nye), 1994; Power Lines (with Elizabeth Ann Scarborough), 1994; Dolphins of Pern, 1994; Power Play (with Elizabeth Ann Scarborough), 1995. Honours: Hugo Award, 1967; Nebula Award, 1968; E E Smith Award, 1975; Ditmar Award, 1979; Eurocon/Streso Award, 1979; Gandalf Award, 1979; Balrg Award, 1980; Golden PEN Award, 1981; Science Fiction Book Club Awards, 1986, 1989, 1991, 1992, 1993. Memberships: Authors Guild; PEN, Ireland; Science Fiction Writers of America. Address: Dragonhold Underhill, Timmore Lane, Newcastle, County Wicklow, Ireland

MCCALL Christina, b. Canada. Editor; Writer. Partner, Stephen Clarkson, 3 daughters. Education: University of Toronto. Appointments: Writer, Editor, Maclean's Saturday Night. Publications: The Man from Oxbow, 1967; Grits: A Portrait of the Liberal Party, 1982; Trudeau: L'Homme, L'Utopie, L'Historie, 1990; Trudeau and Our Times (with Stephen Clarkson), 2 volumes, 1990, 1994. Contributions to: Magazines. Honours: Southam Fellowship, University of Toronto, 1977; National Magazine Award Gold Medal, 1980; Canadian Author's Association Book of the Year, 1982; Governor-General's Literary Award for Non-Fiction, 1990; John Dafoe Prize for Distinguished Writing, 1995. Address: 59 Lowther Avenue, Toronto, Ontario M5R IC5, Canada.

MCCALL Mabel Bunny, b. 6 Feb 1923, Bronx, New York, USA. Poet. m. T Ross, 31 Oct 1947, dec 1973. Publications: Many poems, including Poems for All seasons (collection), 1991. Contributions to: Anthologies, journals and magazines. Honours: Golden Poet Awards, 1985-91, Award of Merit, 1990, World of Poetry. Memberships: American Poetry Association; International Society of Poets; World of Poetry. Address: 4112 10th Street, No 4F, Long Island City, NY 11101, USA.

MCCARRY Charles, b. 14 June 1930, Pittsfield, Massachusetts, USA. Journalist; Editor; Writer. m. Nancy Neill, 12 Sept 1953, 4 sons. Appointments: Reporter and Editor, Lisbon Evening Journal, Ohio, 1952-55; Reporter and Columnist, Youngstown Vindicator, Ohio, 1955-56; Assistant to US Secretary of Labor, Washington, DC, 1956-57; Employee, Central Intelligence Agency, 1958-67; Editor-at-Large, National Geographic magazine, 1983-90. Publications: The Miernik Dossier, 1973; The Tears of Autumn, 1975; The Secret Lovers, 1977; The Better Angels, 1979; The Last Supper, 1983; The Bride of the Wilderness, 1988; Second Sight, 1991. Non-Fiction: Citizen Nader, 1972; Double Eagle (with Ben Abruzzo, Maxie Anderson and Larry Newman), 1979; Isles of the Caribbean (co-author), 1979; The Great Southwest, 1980; Caveat, 1983; For the Record (with Donald Y Regan), 1988; Inner Circles: How America Changed the World (with Alexander M Haig Jr), 1992; Shelley's Heart, 1995. Contributions to: Periodicals. Address: c/o William Morris Agency, 1350 Avenue of the Americas, New York, NY 10019, USA.

MCCARTHY Charles Jr. See: **MCCARTHY Cormac.**

MCCARTHY Cormac, (Charles McCarthy Jr), b. 20 July 1933, Providence, Rhode Island, USA. Writer. m. Lee Holleman, 1961, div 1 child, (2) Anne deLisle, 1967, div. Publications: Novels: The Orchard Keeper, 1965; Outer Dark, 1968; Child of God, 1974; Suttree, 1979; Blood Meridian, or The Evening Redness in the West, 1985; All the Pretty Horses, 1992; The Crossing, 1994. Plays: The Gardner's Son, 1977; The Stonemason, 1994. Honours: Ingram Merrill Foundation Grant, 1960; William Faulkner Foundation Award, 1965; American Academy of Arts and Letters Travelling Fellowship, 1965-66; Rockefeller Foundation Grant, 1966; Guggenheim Fellowship, 1976; John D and Catharine T MacArthuir Foundation Fellowship, 1981; National Book Award, 1992; National Book Critics Circle Award, 1993. Address: c/o Alfred A Knopf Inc, 201 East 50th Street, New York, NY 10022, USA.

MCCARTHY Gary W, b. 23 Jan 1943, South Gate, California, USA. Western and Historical Novelist. m. Virginia Kurzwell, 14 June 1969, 1 son, 3 daughters. Education: BS, Agriculture, California State University, 1968; MS, Economics, University of Nevada, 1970. Appointments: Labour Economist, State of Nevada, Carson City, 1970-77; Economist, Copley International Corporation, La Jolla, California, 1977-79; Full-time Writer, 1979-. Publications: The Derby Man, 1976; Showdown at Snakegrass Junction, 1978; The First Sheriff, 1979; Mustang Fever, 1980; The Pony Express War, 1980; Winds of Gold, 1980; Silver Shot, 1981; Explosion at Donner Pass, 1981; The Legend of the Lone Ranger, 1981; North Chase, 1982; Rebel of Bodie, 1982; The Rail Warriors, 1983; Silver Winds, 1983; Wind River, 1984; Powder River, 1985; The Last Buffalo Hunt, 1985; Mando, 1986; The Mustangers, 1987; Transcontinental, 1987; Sodbuster, 1988. Literary Agent: Joseph Elder Agency. Address: 323 Matilija Street, No 204, Ojai, CA 93023, USA.

MCCARTHY Rosemary P, b. 21 Oct 1928, Newark, New Jersey, USA. Public Health Nurse; Retiree, NYC Health Dept; Family Historian, Genealogist, Archivist; Artist; Lecturer; Poet. Education: BSN, St John's University, 1963; MEd, Columbia University Teachers College, 1973; Catholic University of American Institute of Adult Education, 1980-81; Long Island University, Southampton Campus, Summer, 1986. Publications: Family Tree of the Connors-Walsh Family of Kiltimagh, County Mayo, Eire and USA, with Branches in Great Britain & Throughout the World, 1979; Gradma, 1986; Editor, International Family Tree Newsletter, 1979-; International Family Directory, 1983-, updated for family reunion - Kiltimagh, 1995; Life of Margaret Walsh Connors, Maternal Grandmother, forthcoming; Compiled booklets: Poetry Reading and Sing Along. Contributions to: O'Lochlainn's Journal of Irish Families; The Irish Genealogical Foundation. Memberships: Civic and historical societies. Address: 814A Jefferson Street, Alexandria, VA 22314-4255, USA.

MCCARTHY William E(dward) J(ohn), b. 30 July 1925, London, England. College Fellow; Writer. Education: Ruskin College, 1953-55; BA, Merton College, Oxford, 1957; PhD, Nuffield College, Oxford, 1959. Appointments: Research Fellow, Nuffield College, 1959-63, Staff Lecturer, Tutor, Industrial Relations, 1964-65, Fellow, Nuffield College and Centre for Management Studies, 1968-, Oxford University; Director of Research, Royal Commission on Trade and Unions and Employers Association, London, 1965-68; Senior Economic Adviser, Department of Employment, 1968-70; Special Adviser, European Economic Commission, 1974-75. Publications: The Future of the Unions, 1962; The Closed Shop in Britain, 1964; The Role of Shop Stewards in British Industrial Relations: A Survey of Existing Information and Research, 1966; Disputes Procedures in Britain (with Arthur Ivor Marsh), 1966; Employers' Associations: The Results of Two Studies (with V G Munns), 1967; The Role of Government in Industrial Relations, Shop Stewards and Workshop Relations: The Results of a Study, 1968; Industrial Relations in Britain: A Guide for Management and Unions (editor), 1969; The Reform of Collective Bargaining: A Series of Case Studies, 1971; Trade Unions, 1972, new edition, 1985; Coming to Terms with Trade Unions (with A J Collier), 1972; Management by Agreement (with N D Ellis), 1973; Wage Inflation and Wage Leadership (with J F O'Brien and V C Dowd), 1975; Making Whitley Work, 1977; Change in Trade Unions (co-author), 1981; Strikes in Post War Britain (with J W Durcun), 1985; Freedom at Work, 1985; The Future of Industrial Democracy, 1988; Employee Relations Audits, co-author, 1992; Legal Intervention in Industrial Relations, editor, 1992. Address: 4 William Orchard Close, Old Headington, Oxford, England.

MCCARTY Clifford, b. 13 June 1929, Los Angeles, California, USA. Writer; Bookseller. m. Maxine Reich, 21 July 1955, 1 son, 2 daughter. Education: BA, California State University, Los Angeles, 1952. Publications: Bogey: The Films of Humphrey Bogart, 1965; The Films of Errol Flynn (in collaboration), 1969; Published Screenplays: A Checklist, 1971; The Films of Frank Sinatra (in collaboration), 1971; Film Music 1 (editor), 1989. Contributions to: Films in Review; Film & TV Music; Notes; Pro Musica Sana; The Gissing Journal. Address: Po Box 89, Topanga, California 90290, USA.

MCCAULEY Martin, b. 18 Oct 1934, Omagh, Northern Ireland. Senior Lecturer in Politics; Writer. Education: BA, 1966, PhD, 1973, University of London. Appointments: Senior Lecturer in Soviet and East European Studies, 1968-91, Senior Lecturer in Politics, 1991-, Chairman, Department of Social Sciences, 1993-96, School of Slavonic and East European Studies, University of London.

Publications: The Russian Revolution and the Soviet State 1917-1921 (editor), 1975, 2nd edition, 1980; Khruschev and the Development of Soviet Agriculture: The Virgin Land Programme, 1953-64, 1976; Communist Power in Europe 1944-1949 (editor and contributor), 1977, 2nd edition, 1980; Marxism-Leninism in the German Democratic Republic: The Socialist Unity Party (SED), 1978; The Stalin File, 1979; The Soviet Union Since 1917, 1981; Stalin and Stalinism, 1983, 2nd edition, 1995; Origins of the Cold War, 1983, 2nd edition, 1995; The Soviet Union Since Brezhnev (editor and contributor), 1983; The German Democratic Republic Since 1945, 1984; Octobrists to Bolsheviks: Imperial Russia 1905-1917, 1984; Leadership and Succession in the Soviet Union, East Europe and China (editor and contributor), 1985; The Origins of the Modern Russian State 1855-1881 (with Peter Waldron), 1986; The Soviet Union under Gorbachev (editor), 1987; Gorbachev and Perestroika (editor), 1990; Khrushchev, 1991; The Soviet Union 1917-1991, 1991, 2nd edition, 1993; Directory of Russian MPs (editor), 1993; Longman Biographical Directory of Decision Makers in Russia and the Successor States (editor), 1994; Who's Who in Russia and the Soviet Union, 1997; Russia 1917-1941, 1997; Longman Companion to Russia since 1914, 1997. Contributions to: Professional journals. Memberships: Economic and Social Research Council; Politics and Society Group. Address: c/o School of Slavonic and East European Studies, University of London, Senate House, Malet Street, London WC1E 7HU, England.

MCCLANE Kenneth (Anderson Jr), b. 19 Feb 1951, New York, New York, USA. Professor; Poet; Writer. m. Rochelle Evette Woods, 22 Oct 1983. Education: AB, 1973, MA, 1974, MFA, 1976, Cornell University. Appointments: Instructor, Colby College, 1974-75; Luce Visiting Professor, Williams College, 1983; Associate Professor, 1983-89, Professor, 1989-93, W E B DuBois Professor, 1993-, Cornell University; Visiting Professor, Wayne State University, 1987, University of Michigan, 1989, Washington University, 1991. Publications: Take Five: Collected Poems, 1988; Walls: Essays 1985-90, 1991. Contributions to: Journals. Honours: George Harmon Coxe Award, 1973; Corson Morrison Poetry Prize, 1973. Memberships: Associated Writing Programs; Phi Beta Kappa; Poets and Writers. Address: c/o Department of English, Cornell University, Rockefeller Hall, Ithaca, NY 14853, USA.

MCCLATCHY J(oseph) D(onald Jr), b. 12 Aug 1945, Bryn Mawr, Pennsylvania, USA. Poet; Writer; Editor; Lecturer in Creative Writing. Education: AB, Georgetown University, 1967; PhD, Yale University, 1974. Appointments: Instructor, LaSalle College, Philadelphia, 1968-71; Associate Editor, Four Quarters, 1968-72; Assistant Professor, Yale University, 1974-81; Poetry Editor, 1980-91, Editor, 1991-, The Yale Review; Lecturer in Creative Writing, Princeton University, 1981-93. Publications: Anne Sexton: The Artist and Her Critics, 1978; Scenes from Another Life (poems), 1981; Stars Principal (poems), 1986; James Merrill: Recitative: Prose (editor), 1986; Kilim (poems), 1987; Poets on Painters: Essays on the Art of Painting by Twentieth-Century Poets (editor), 1988; White Paper: On Contemporary American Poetry, 1989; The Rest of the Way (poems), 1990; The Vintage Book of Contemporary American Poetry (editor), 1990; Woman in White: Selected Poems of Emily Dickinson (editor), 1991; The Vintage Book of Contemporary World Poetry, 1996; Horace: The Art of Poetry (editor and translator), 1997; Ten Commandments (poems), forthcoming. Contributions to: Anthologies and magazines. Honours: Woodrow Wilson Fellowship, 1967-68; O Henry Award, 1972; Ingram Merrill Foundation Grant, 1979; Michener Award, 1982; Gordon Barber Memorial Award, 1984, Melville Cane Award, 1991, Poetry Society of America; Witter Bynner Poetry Prize, 1985, Award in Literature, 1991; Eunice Tietjens Memorial Prize, 1985, Oscar Blumenthal Prize, 1988, Levinson Prize, 1990, Poetry Magazine; American Academy of Arts and Letters; National Endowment for the Arts Fellowship, 1986; Guggenheim Fellowship, 1988; Academy of American Poets Fellowship, 1991. Memberships: Alpha Simga Nu; International PEN; Phi Beta Kappa; Elected Chancellor, Academy of American Poets, 1996. Address: 15 Grand Street, Stonington, CT 06378, USA.

MCCLINTOCK David, b. 4 July 1913, Newcastle upon Tyne, England. Writer. m. Elizabeth Anne Dawson, 6 July 1940, 2 sons, 2 daughters. Education: BA, 1934, MA, 1940, Trinity College, Cambridge. Publications: Pocket Guide to Wild Flowers (with R S R Fitter), 1956; Supplement to Pocket Guide to Wild Flowers, 1957; Natural History of the Garden of Buckingham Palace (jointly), 1964; Companion to Flowers, 1966; Guide to the Naming of Plants, 1969, 2nd edition, 1980; Wild Flowers of Guernsey, 1975, Supplement, 1987;

Wild Flowers of the Channel Islands (with J Bichard), 1975; Joshua Gosselin of Guernsey, 1976; The Heather Garden by H van de Laar (editor and rewriter), 1978; Guernsey's Earliest Flora, 1982. Contributions to: Many books and other publications. Memberships: Botanical Society of the British Isles, president, 1971-73; Linnean Society; Ray Society, vice president, 1970-74, president, 1980-93; Royal Horticultural Society, scientific committee, 1978-95, vice chairman, 1983-93; Heather Society, president, 1990-. Address: Bracken Hill, Platt, Sevenoaks, Kent TN15 8JH, England.

MCCLURE Gillian Mary, b. 29 Oct 1948, Bradford, England. Author; Illustrator. m. 26 Sept 1971, 3 sons. Education: Horsham High School for Girls; BA, Combined Honours in French, English and History of Art, Bristol University; Teaching Diploma, Moray House. Publications: 12 children's books, 1974-94. Honours: Smarties Award, 1985; Kate Greenaway Award, 1985. Membership: CWIG Society of Authors, committee member, 1989-; PLR Advisory Committee, 1992. Literary Agent: Curtis Brown. Address: 9 Trafalgar Street, Cambridge CB4 1ET, England.

MCCLURE James (Howe), b. 9 Oct 1939, Johannesburg, South Africa. Managing Director; Writer. Appointments: Journalist, Natal, Edinburgh, Oxford, 1963-69; Deputy Editor, Oxford Times Group, 1971-74; Managing Director, Sabensa Gakula Ltd, Oxford, 1975-. Publications: The Steam Pig, 1971; The Caterpillar Cop, 1972; Four and Twenty Virgins, 1973; The Gooseberry Fool, 1974; Snake, 1975; Killers, 1976; Rogue Eagle, 1976; The Sunday Hangman, 1977; The Blood of an Englishman, 1980; Spike Island: Portrait of a British Police Division, 1980; The Artful Egg, 1984; Copworld, 1985; Imago: A Modern Comedy of Manners, 1988; The Song Dog, 1991. Honours: Gold Dagger Award, 1971, Silver Dagger Award, 1976, Crime Writers Association. Address: 14 York Road, Headington, Oxford OX3 8NW, England.

MCCLURE Michael (Thomas), b. 20 Oct 1932, Marysville, Kansas, USA. Professor; Poet; Dramatist; Writer. m. Joanna Kinnison, 1954, 1 daughter. Education: University of Wichita, 1951-53; University of Arizona, 1953-54; BA, San Francisco State College, 1955. Education: Assistant Professor, 1962-77, Associate Professor, 1977-78, Professor, 1978-, California College of Arts and Crafts, Oakland; Playwright-in-Residence, American Conservatory Theatre, San Francisco, 1975; Associate Fellow, Pierson College, Yale University, 1982. Publications: Poetry: Passage, 1956; For Artaud, 1959; Hymns to St Geryon and Other Poems, 1959; The New Book: A Book of Torture, 1961; Dark Brown, 1961; Ghost Tantras, 1964; 13 Mad Sonnets, 1964; Hail Thee Who Play, 1968, revised edition 1974; The Sermons of Jean Harlow and the Curses of Billy the Kid, 1969; Star, 1971; The Book of Joanna, 1973; Rare Angel (writ with raven's blood), 1974; September Blackberries, 1974; Jaguar Skies, 1975; Antechamber and Other Poems, 1978; The Book of Benjamin, 1982; Fragments of Perseus, 1983; Selected Poems, 1986; Rebel Lions, 1991; Simple Eyes and Other Poems, 1994. Plays: The Growl, in Four in Hand, 1964; The Blossom, or, Billy the Kid, 1967; The Beard, 1967; The Shell, 1968; The Cherub, 1970; Gargoyle Cartoons (11 plays), 1971; The Mammals, 1972; The Grabbing of the Fairy, 1973; Gorf, 1976; General Gorgeous, 1975; Goethe: Ein Fragment, 1978; The Velvet Edge, 1982; The Beard and VKTMs: Two Plays, 1985. Novels: The Mad Club, 1970; The Adept, 1971; Other: Meat Science Essays, 1963, revised edition, 1967; Freewheelin' Frank, Secretary of the Angels, as Told to Michael McClure by Frank Reynolds, 1967; Scratching the Beat Surface, 1982; Specks, 1985; Lighting the Corners: On Art, Nature, and the Visionary: Essays and Interviews, 1993. Honours: National Endowment for the Arts Grants, 1967, 1974; Guggenheim Fellowship, 1971; Magic Theatre Alfred Jarry Award, 1974; Rockefeller Foundation Fellowship, 1975; Obie Award, 1978. Address: 264 Downey Street, San Francisco, CA 94117, USA.

MCCOLLEY Diane Laurene Kelsey, b. 9 Feb 1934, Riverside, California, USA. University Professor. m. Robert M McColley, 30 Aug 1958, 1 son, 5 daughters. Education: AB, University of California; PhD, University of Illinois. Publications: Milton's Eve; A Gust for Paradise; Cambridge Companion to Milton; Medieval and Renaissance Texts and Studies. Contributions to: Milton Studies; Various Journals. Memberships: Milton Society of America; Modern Language Association; Renaissance Society of America. Address: Department of English, Rutgers, The State University of New Jersey, Camden, NJ 08102, USA.

MCCONICA James Kelsey, b. 24 Apr 1930, Luseland, Saskatchewan, Canada. Professor of History; Author. Education: BA, University of Saskatchewan, 1951; BA, 1954, MA, 1957, DPhil, 1963, Oxford University; MA, University of Toronto, 1964. Appointments: Instructor, 1956-57, Assistant Professor, 1957-62, University of Saskatchewan; Associate Professor, 1967-70, Professor of History, 1971-, Pontifical Institute of Medieval Studies, Toronto; Ordained Roman Catholic Priest, 1968; Visiting Fellow, 1969-71, 1977, Special Ford Lecturer, 1977, Research Fellow, 1978-84, Academic Dean, 1990-92, All Souls College, Oxford; Fellow, Davis Center for Historical Studies, Princeton University, 1971; Professor, University of Toronto, 1972-; President, University of St Michael's College, Toronto, 1984-90. Publications: English Humanists and Reformation Politics under Henry VIII and Edward VI, 1965; The Correspondence of Erasmus (editor), Vol III, 1976, Vol IV, 1977; Thomas More: A Short Bibliography, 1977; The History of the University of Oxford (editor), vol III, 1986; Erasmus, 1991. Contributions to: Books and professional journals. Honours: Rhodes Scholar, 1951; Guggenheim Fellowship, 1969-70; Killiam Senior Research Scholar, 1976-77; Honorary LLD, University of Saskatchewan, 1986; Honorary DLitt, University of Windsor, 1989. Memberships: American Society for Reformation Research; Canadian Society for Renaissancwe Studies; Oxfrod Historical Society; Renaissance Society of America; Royal Historical Society, fellow; Royal Society of Canada, fellow. Address: c/o Department of History, University of Toronto, Toronto, Ontario M5S 1A1, Canada.

MCCONKEY James (Rodney), b. 2 Sept 1921, Lakewood, Ohio, USA. Professor of English Literature Emeritus; Writer. m. Gladys Jean Voorhees, 6 May 1944, 3 sons. Education: BA, Cleveland College, 1943; MA, Western Reserve University, 1946; PhD, University of Iowa, 1953. Appointments: Assistant Professor to Associate Professor, Morehead State College, Kentucky, 1950-56; Director, Morehead Writer's Workshop, 1951-56, Antioch Seminar in Writing and Publishing, Yellow Springs, Ohio, 1957-60; Assistant Professor to Associate Professor, 1956-62, Professor of English, 1962-87; Goldwin Smith Professor of English Literature, 1987-92, Professor Emeritus, 1992-. Publications: The Novels of E M Forster, 1957; The Structure of Prose (editor), 1963; Night Stand, 1965; Crossroads: An Autobiographical Novel, 1968; A Journal to Sahalin (novel), 1971; The Tree House Confessions (novel), 1979; Court of Memory, 1983; To a Distant Island (novel), 1984; Chekhov and Our Age: Responses to Chekhov by American Writers and Scholars (editor), 1984; Kayo: The Authentic and Annotated Autobiographical Novel from Outer Space, 1987; Rowan's Progress, 1992; Stories from My Life with the Other Animals, 1993; The Anatomy of Memory (editor), 1996. Contributions to: Magazines. Honours: Eugene Saxton Literary Fellow, 1962-63; National Endowment for the Arts Essay Award, 1967; Ohioana Book Award, 1969; Guggenheim Fellowship, 1969-70; American Academy of Arts and Letters Award, 1979. Membership: PEN. Address: 402 Aiken Road, Trumansburg, NY 14886, USA.

MCCONVILLE Michael Anthony, b. 3 Jan 1925, Crowsborough, England. Writer. m. Beryl Anne Jerrett, 15 May 1952, 2 sons, 4 daughters. Education: Mayfield College, 1940-42; Trinity College, Dublin, 1947-50, BA (Mod); MA. Publications: Leap in the Dark, 1980; More Tales from the Mess, 1983; The Burke Foundation, 1985; A Small War in the Balkans, 1986; Ascendancy to Oblivion, 1986. Contributions to: Blackwoods, Rusi Journal, Malayan Monthly. Membership: Writers' Guild. Address: 72 Friarn Street, Bridgewater, Somerset, TA6 3ES, England.

MCCORMICK John Owen, b. 20 Sept 1918, Thief River Falls, Minnesota, USA. Professor of Comparative Literature Emeritus; Writer. m. Mairi MacInnes, 4 Feb 1954, 3 sons, 1 daughter. Education: BA, 1941, MA, 1947, University of Minnesota; PhD, Harvard University, 1951. Appointments: Senior Tutor and Teaching Assistant, Harvard University, 1946-51; Lecturer, Salzburg Seminar in American Studies, Austria, 1951-52; Professor of American Studies, Free University of Berlin, 1952-53, 1954-59; Professor of Comparative Literature, 1959-, now Emeritus, Rutgers University, New Brunswick, NJ. Publications: Catastrophe and Imagination, 1957; Versions of Censorship (with Mairi MacInnes), 1962; The Complete Aficionado, 1967; The Middle Distance: A Comparative History of American Imaginative Literature, 1919-1932, 1971; Fiction as Knowledge: The Modern Post-Romantic Novel, 1975; George Santayana: A Biography, 1987; Sallies of the Mind: Essays of Francis Fergusson, (editor, with G Gore), 1997. Contributions to: Numerous magazines and journals. Honours: Guggenheim Fellowships, 1964-65, 1980-81; Longview Award for Non-Fiction, 1960; National Endowments for the Humanities Senior

Fellow, 1983-84; American Academy and Institute of Arts and Letters Prize, 1988. Address: Hovingham Lodge, Hovingham, York YO6 4NA, England.

MCCORQUODALE Barbara Hamilton (Dame Barbara Cartland). Writer; Lecturer; Public Speaker. Publications: Over 575 books including: The Explosion of Love, 1980; A Heart is Stolen, 1980; The Power and the Prince, 1980; Free from Fear, 1980; A Song of Love, 1980; Love for Sale, 1980; Little White Doves of Love, 1980; The Perfection of Love, 1980; Lost Laughter, 1980; Punished with Love, 1980; Lucifer and the Angel, 1980; Ola and the Sea Wolf, 1980; The Pride and the Prodigal, 1980; The Goddess and the Gaiety Girl, 1980; Signpost to Love, 1980; Money, Magic and Marriage, 1980; Love in the Moon, 1980; Pride and the Poor Princess, 1980; The Waltz of Hearts, 1980; From Hell to Heaven, 1981; The Kiss of Life, 1981; Afraid, 1981; Dreams Do Come True, 1981; In the Arms of Love, 1981; For All Eternity, 1981; Pure and Untouched, 1981; Count the Stars, 1981; Kneel for Mercy, 1982; Call of the Highlands, 1982; A Miracle in Music, 1982; From Hate to Love, 1983; Lights, Laughter and a Lady, 1983; Diona and a Dalmatian, 1983; Moonlight on the Sphinx, 1984; Bride to a Brigand, 1984; Love Comes West, 1984; A Witch's Spell, 1984; White Lilac, 1984; Miracle for a Madonna, 1984; Royal Punishment, 1985; The Devilish Deception, 1985; Secrets of the Heart, 1985; A Caretaker of Love, 1985; The Devil Defeated, 1985; Love in the Ruins, 1989; The Duke's Dilemma, 1989; Beyond the Stars, 1990; Love Runs In, 1991; A Secret Passage to Love, 1992; A Train to Love, 1992; The Man of Her Dreams, 1993; Captured by Love, 1993; Love or Money, 1993; Danger to the Duke, 1993; The King without a Heart, 1993; A Battle of Love, 1993; Lovers in London, 1993. Honours: Achiever of the Year Award, National Home Furnishing Association, 1981; Bishop Wright Air Industry Award, 1984; Gold Medal for Achievement, City of Paris, 1988; Dame Commander of the Order of the British Empire, 1991. Address: Camfield Place, Hatfield, Hertfordshire, England.

MCCOURT James, b. 4 July 1941, New York, New York, USA. Author. Education: BA, Manhattan College, 1962; Graduate Studies, New York University, 1962-64, Yale University, 1964-65. Publications: Maurdew Czgowdiwz, 1975; Kaye Wayfaring, 1984; Time Remaining, 1993. Contributions to: Anthologies and magazines. Address: c/o Vincent Virga, 145 East 22nd Street, New York, NY 10003, USA.

MCCRAW Thomas, b. 11 Sept 1940, Corinth, Mississippi, USA. Professor of Business History; Writer. m. Susan Morehead, 22 Sept 1962, 1 son, 1 daughter. Appointments: Newcomen Research Fellow, Harvard University, 1973-74; Assistant Professor, 1970-74, Associate Professor, 1974-78, University of Texas; Associate Professor, 1976-78, Professor of Business, 1978-, Straus Professor of Business History, 1989-, Harvard Business School; Editor, Business History Review, 1994-. Publications: Morgan vs Lilienthal: The Feud Within in TVA, 1970; TVA and the Power Fight, 1933-39, 1971; Regulation in Perspective: Historical Essays, 1981; Prophets of Regulation, 1984; America vs Japan, 1986; The Essential Alfred Chandler, 1988; Management Past and Present, 1996; Creating Modern Capitalism, 1997. Contributions to: Professional journals. Honours: William P Lyons Masters Essay Award, 1970; Pulitzer Prize for History, 1985; Thomas Newcomen Book Award, 1985. Memberships: American Economic Association; Business History Conference; Economic History Association; Massachusetts Historical Society; Organization of American Historians. Address: c/o Harvard Business School, Soldiers Field, Boston, MA 02163, USA.

MCCREADY Jack. See: POWELL Talmage.

MCCRORIE Edward Pollitt, b. 19 Nov 1936, Central Falls, Rhode Island, USA. Professor of English. m. 27 May 1995. Education: PhD, Brown University, 1970. Publications: After a Cremation, poems, 1974; The Aeneid of Virgil, translation, 1994. Contributions to: Poems in USA journals. Address: English Department, Providence College, Providence, RI 02918, USA.

MCCRUMB Sharyn Elaine Atwood, b. 26 Feb 1948, Wilmington, North Carolina, USA. Writer. m. David McCrumb, 9 Jan 1982, 1 son, 2 daughters. Education: BA, University of North Carolina, 1970; MA, Virginia Polytechnic Institute and State University, 1987. Publications: The Hangman's Beautiful Daughter; If Ever I Return Pretty Peggy O; Bimbos of the Death Sun; Missing Susan; Highland Laddie Gone; Sick of Shadows; Lovely in Her Bones; Paying the Piper; The Windsor Knot; Zombies of the Gene Pool; MacPherson's Lament. Contributions to: Magazines. Honours: Notable Book, New York Times;

Best Appalachian Novel Award; Edgar Award; Macavity Award; Agatha Award. Memberships: Mystery Writers of America; Sisters in Crime; Appalachian Writers Association; Whimsey Foundation. Literary Agent: Dominick Abel. Address: Rowan Mountain Inc, PO Box 10111, Blacksburg, VA 24062, USA.

MCCULLAGH Sheila Kathleen, b. 3 Dec 1920, Surrey, England. Writer. Education: Bedford Froebel College, 1939-42; MA, University of Leeds, 1949. Publications: Pirate Books, 1957-64; Tales and Adventures, 1961; Dragon Books, 1963-70; One, Two, Three and Away, 1964-92; Tim Books, 1974-83; Into New Worlds, 1974; Hummingbirds, 1976-92; Whizzbang Adventures, 1980; Buccaneers, 1980-84; Where Wild Geese Fly, 1981; Puddle Lane, 1985-88; The Sea Shore, 1992. Honour: Member of the Order of the British Empire, 1987. Membership: Society of Authors. Literary Agent: A P Watt. Address: 27 Royal Crescent, Bath, Avon BA1 2CT, England.

MCCULLOUGH Colleen, b. 1 June 1937, Wellington, New South Wales, Australia. Writer. m. Ric Robinson, 1984. Education: Holy Cross College, Woollahra, Sydney University; Institute of Child Health, London University. Appointments: Neurophysiologist, Sydney, London and Yale University Medical School, New Haven, Connecticut, USA, 1967-77; Relocated to Norfolk Island, South Pacific, 1980. Publications: Tim (later filmed), 1974; The Thorn Birds (major bestseller, filmed as television series loathed by the author), 1977; An Indecent Obsession (later filmed), 1981; Cooking with Colleen McCullough and Jean Easthope, 1982; A Creed for the Third Millennium, 1985; The Ladies of Missalonghi, 1987; The First Man in Rome, 1990; The Grass Crown, 1991; Fortune's Favorites, 1993; Caesar's Women, 1996. Honour: Doctor of Letters (honoris causa), Macquarie University, Sydney, 1993. Address: Out Yenna, Norfolk Island, Oceania (via Australia).

MCCULLOUGH David (Gaub), b. 7 July 1933, Pittsburgh, Pennsylvania, USA. Historian; Author. m. Rosalee Ingram Barnes, 18 Dec 1954, 3 sons, 2 daughters. Education: BA, Yale University, 1955. Appointments: Editor, Time Inc, New York City, 1956-61, United States Information Agency, Washington, DC, 1961-64, American Heritage Publishing Co, New York City, 1964-70; Scholar-in-Residence, University of New Mexico, 1979, Wesleyan University, 1982, 1983; Host, Smithsonian World, 1984-88, The American Experience, 1988-, PBS-TV; Visiting Professor, Cornell University, 1989. Publications: The Great Bridge, 1972; The Path Between the Seas, 1977; The Johnstown Flood, 1978; Mornings on Horseback, 1981; Brave Companions, 1991; Truman, 1992. Honours: National Book Award for History, 1978; Samuel Eliot Morison Award, 1978; Cornelius Ryan Award, 1978; Francis Parkman Prizes, 1978, 1993; Los Angeles Times Prize for Biography, 1981; American Book Award for Biography, 1982; Pulitzer Prize for Biography, 1993; Harry S Truman Public Service Award, 1993; Pennsylvania Governor's Award for Excellence, 1993; St Louis Literary Award, 1993; Pennsylvania Society Gold Medal Award, 1994; Various honorary doctorates. Memberships: Jefferson Legacy Foundation; National Trust for Historic Preservation; Society of American Historians, president, 1991-; Harry S Truman Library Institute. Address: c/o Janklow & Nesbit Associates, 598 Madison Avenue, New York, NY 10022, USA.

MCCULLOUGH Ken(neth), b. 18 July 1943, Staten Island, New York, USA. Poet; Writer; Teacher. Education: BA, University of Delaware, 1966; MFA, University of Iowa, 1968. Appointments: Teacher, Montana State University, 1970-75, University of Iowa, 1983-95, Kirkwood Community College, Cedar Rapids, 1987, St Mary's University, Winona, Minnesota, 1996; Writer-in-Residence, South Carolina ETV Network, 1975-78; Participant, Artist-in-the-Schools Program, Iowa Arts Council, 1981-96. Publications: Poetry: The Easy Wreckage, 1971; Migrations, 1972; Creosote, 1976; Elegy for Old Anna, 1985; Travelling Light, 1987; Sycamore Oriole, 1991; Walking Backwards, 1997. Contributions to: Numerous publications. Honours: Academy of American Poets Award, 1966; 2nd Place, Ark River Awards, 1972; Helene Wurlitzer Foundation of New Mexico Residencies, 1973, 1994; National Endowment for the Arts Fellowship, 1974; 2nd Prize, Sri Chinmoy Poetry Awards, 1980; Writers' Voice Capricorn Book Award, 1985; 2nd Place, Pablo Neruda Award, Nimrod magazine 1990; 3rd Prize, Kudzu Poetry Contest, 1990; Ucross Foundation Residency, Wyoming, 1991; Witter Bynner Foundation for Poetry Grant, 1993; Iowa Arts Council Grants, 1994, 1996. Memberships: Associated Writing Programs; Association of American University Professors; National Association of College Academic Advisers; Renaissance Artists and Writers

Association and Renaissance International; Rocky Mountain Modern Language Association; Science Fiction Writers of America. Address: 372 Center Street, Winona, MN 55987, USA.

MCCULLY Emily Arnold, (Emily Arnold), b. 7 Jan 1939, Galesburg, Illinois, USA. Author; Illustrator. 2 sons. Education: BA, Brown University, 1961; MA, Columbia University, 1964. Publications: A Craving, 1982; Picnic, 1985; Life Drawing, 1986; Mirette on the High Wire, 1992; The Amazing Felix, 1993; Little Kit, or, the Industrious Flea Circus Girl, 1995; The Pirate Queen, 1995. Honours: O'Henry Award Collection, 1977; Caldecott Award, 1993. Memberships: PEN Society; Authors Guild. Address: c/o Harriet Wasserman, 137 East 36th Street, New York, NY 10026, USA.

MCCUNN Ruthanne Lum, b. 21 Feb 1946, San Francisco, California, USA. Writer. m. Donald H McCunn, 15 June 1965. Education: BA, 1968. Publications: Illustrated History of the Chinese in America, 1979; Thousand Pieces of Gold, 1981; Pie Biter, 1983; Sole Survivor, 1985; Chinese American Portraits, 1988; Chinese Proverbs, 1991; Wooden Fish Songs, 1995. Contributions to: Yihai and Chinese America: History and Perspectives. Honour: Before Columbus Foundation American Book Award, 1983. Memberships: Chinese Historical Society of America; Asian Women United; American Civil Liberties Union; Chinese for Affirmative Action; Amnesty International. Literary Agent: Peter Ginsberg, Curtis Brown, San Francisco, USA. Address: 1007 Castro Street, San Francisco, CA 94114, USA.

MCCUTCHEON Elsie Mary Jackson, b. 6 Apr 1937, Glasgow, Scotland. Author. m. James McCutcheon, 14 July 1962, dec, 1 daughter. Education: BA, Glasgow University, 1960; Jordanhill College of Education, 1961. Appointments: English Teacher, Glasgow, 1961-63; Publicity Officer, Norfolk Archaeological Rescue Group, 1976-78; Editor, Newsletter of Friends of the Suffolk Record Office, 1984-91. Publications: Summer of the Zeppelin; The Rat War; Smokescreen; Storm Bird; Twisted Truth. Contributions to: She; Good Housekeeping; Ideal Home; Scotland's Magazine; Scottish Field; Suffolk Fair; Eastern Daily Press. Honour: Runner-up, Guardian Award for Children's Fiction. Memberships: Bury St Edmunds Library Users Group; Writers Guild of Great Britain; Suffolk Local History Council; Suffolk Institute of Archaeology. Literary Agent: Vanessa Hamilton. Address: Wendover, Sharpers Lane, Horringer, Bury St Edmunds, Suffolk IP29 5PS, England.

MCCUTCHEON Hugh, (Hugh Davie-Martin, Griselda Wilding), b. 24 July 1909, Glasgow, Scotland. Author. Education: University of Glasgow, 1928-33; Qualified as Solicitor, 1933. Appointment: Town Clerk of Renfrew, Scotland, 1945-74. Publications: Alamein to Tunis, 1946; The Angel of Light, in US as Murder at the Angel, 1951; None Shall Sleep Tonight, 1954; Prey for the Nightingale, 1954; Cover Her Face, 1955; The Long Night Through, 1956; Comes the Blind Fury, 1957; To Dusty Death, 1960; Yet She Must Die, 1961; The Deadly One, 1962; Suddenly in Vienna, 1963; Treasure of the Sun, 1964; The Black Attendant, 1966; Killer's Moon, in US as The Moon Was Full, 1967; The Scorpion's Nest, 1968; A Hot Wind from Hell, 1969; Brand for the Burning, 1970; Something Wicked, 1970; Red Sky at Night, 1972; Instrument of Vengeance, 1975; Night Watch, 1978; The Cargo of Death, 1980. As Hugh Davie-Martin: The Girl in My Grave, 1976; The Pearl of Oyster Island, 1977; Spaniard's Leap, 1979; Death's Bright Angel, 1982. As Griselda Wilding: Promise of Delight, 1988; Beloved Wolf, 1991. Address: 19 Bentinck Drive, Troon, Ayrshire, Scotland.

MCDONALD Forrest, b. 7 Jan 1927, Orange, Texas, USA. Distinguished University Research Professor; Historian; Writer. m. (1), 3 sons, 2 daughters, (2) Ellen Shapiro, 1 Aug 1963. Education: BA, MA, 1949, PhD, 1955, University of Texas. Appointments: Executive Secretary, American History Research Centre, Madison, Wisconsin, 1953-58; Associate Professor, 1959-63, Professor of History, 1963-67, Brown University; Professor, Wayne State University, 1967-76; Professor, 1976-87, Distinguished University Research Professor, 1987-, University of Alabama, Tuscaloosa; Presidential Appointee, Board of Foreign Scholarships, Washington, DC, 1985-87; Advisor, Centre of Judicial Studies, Cumberland, Virginia, 1985-92; James Pinckney Harrison Professor, College of William and Mary, 1986-87; Jefferson Lecturer, National Endowment for the Humanities, 1987. Publications: We the People: The Economic Origins of the Constitution, 1958; Insull, 1962; E Pluribus Unum, 1965; The Presidency of George Washington, 1974; The Phaeton Ride, 1974; The Presdiency of Thomas Jefferson, 1976; Alexander Hamilton: A

Biography, 1979; Novus Ordo Seclorum, 1985; Requiem, 1988; The American Presidency: An Intellectual History, 1994. Contributions to: Professional journals. Honours: Guggenheim Fellowship, 1962-63; George Washington Medal, Freedom's Foundation, 1980; Frances Tavern Book Award, 1980; Best Book Award, American Revolution Round Table, 1986; Richard M Weaver Award, Ingersoll Foundation, 1990; First Salvatori Award, Heritage Foundation, 1992; Salvatori Book Award, Intercollegiate Studio International, 1994. Memberships: American Antiquarian Society; Philadelphia Society. Address: PO Box 155, Coker, AL 35452, USA.

MCDONALD Gregory (Christopher), b. 15 Feb 1937, Shrewsbury, Massachusetts, USA. Writer. m. Susan Aiken, 12 Jan 1963, div 1990, 2 sons. Education: BA, Harvard University, 1958. Appointment: Critic, Boston Globe, 1966-73. Publications: Fiction: Running Scared, 1964; Fletch, 1974; Confess, Fletch, 1976; Flynn, 1977; Love Among the Mashed Potatoes, 1978; Fletch's Fortune, 1978; Fletch Forever, 1978; Who Took Tony Rinaldi?, 1980; Fletch and the Widow Bradley, 1981; The Buck Passes Flynn, 1981; Fletch's Moxie, 1982; Fletch and the Man Who, 1983; Carioca Fletch, 1984; Flynn's In, 1984; Fletch Won, 1985; Safekeeping, 1985; Fletch, Too, 1986; Fletch Chronicle, 3 volumes, 1986-88; A World Too Wide, 1987; Exits and Entrances, 1988; Merely Players, 1988; The Brave, 1991; Son of Fletch, 1993; Fletch Reflected, 1994; Skylar, 1995; Skylar in Yankeeland, 1997. Non-fiction: The Education of Gregory McDonald, 1985. Editor: Last Laughs, 1986. Honours: Edgar Allan Poe Awards, Mystery Writers of America, 1975, 1977; Humanitarian of the Year Award, Tennessee Association of Federal Executives, 1989; Citizen of the Year Award, National Association of Social Workers, 1990; Roger William Straus Award, 1990; Alex Haley Award, 1992. Memberships: Authors Guild; Crime Writers Association, England; Dramatists Guild; President, Mystery Writers of America, 1985-86; Writers Guild of America. Address: c/o Arthur Greene Esquire, 101 Park Avenue, New York, NY 10178, USA.

MCDONALD Ian (A), b. 18 Apr 1933, St Augustine, Trinidad. Poet. m. Mary Angela Callender, 1948, 3 sons. Education: Queens Royal College, Trinidad; Cambridge University, 1951-55. Appointments: Director, Guyana Sugar Corporation; Director, National Art Collection; Director, Theatre Company of Guyana, Georgetown, 1981-; Chair, Demerara Publishers, 1988-. Editor: Kyk-Over-Al (West Indian Literary Journal), 1984-. Joint Editor: Heinemann Book of Caribbean Poetry, 1994. Publications: The Tramping Man (play), 1969; The Humming Bird Tree (novel), 1969; Selected Poem s, 1983; Mercy World, 1988; Essequibo (poems), 1992; Jaffo the Calypsonian (poems), 1994. Honours: Fellow, Royal Society of Literature, 1970; Guyana National Award, 1987. Address: c/o Guyana Sugar Corporation, 22 Church Street, Georgetown, Guyana.

MCDONALD J O. See: **HIBBERD Jean.**

MCDONALD Robert Francis, b. 25 Oct 1943, Vancouver, British Columbia, Canada. Writer; Broadcaster. m. Catherine Donna Napier, 28 Aug 1965. Education: BA, 1964. Publications: Pillar and Tinderbox; The Problem of Cyprus; Greece in the 1990s; Greek Privatisation. Contributions to: World Today; Economist Intelligence Unit Report on Greece and Cyprus; Viomichaniki Epitheorissis Special Survey Series. Membership: Commonwealth Journalists Association, London Management Committee. Address: 10 Chelwood Gardens, Richmond, Surrey TW9 4JQ, England.

MCDONALD Walter R(obert), b. 18 July 1934, Lubbock, Texas, USA. Horn Professor of English; Poet; Writer. m. Carol Ham, 28 Aug 1959, 2 sons, 1 daughter. Education: BA, 1956, MA, 1957, Texas Technological College; PhD, University of Iowa, 1966. Appointments: Faculties: US Air Force Academy, University of Colorado, Texas Tech University; Currently Paul W Horn Professor of English and Poet-in-Residence, Texas Tech University, Lubbock. Publications: Poetry: Caliban in Blue, 1976; One Thing Leads to Another, 1978; Anything, Anything, 1980; Working Against Time, 1981; Burning the Fence, 1981; Witching on Hardscrabble, 1985; Flying Dutchman, 1987; After the Noise of Saigon, 1988; Rafting the Brazos, 1988. Fiction: A Band of Brothers: Stories of Vietnam, 1989; Night Landings, 1989; The Digs in Escondido Canyon, 1991; All That Matters: The Texas Plains in Photographs and Poems, 1992; Where Skies Are Not Cloudy, 1993; Counting Survivors, 1995. Contributions to: Numerous journals and magazines. Honours: Poetry Awards, Texas Institute of Letters, 1976, 1985, 1987; George Elliston Poetry Prize, 1987; Juniper Prize, 1988; Western Heritage Award for Poetry, National Cowboy Hall of Fame,

1990, 1992; 1993. Memberships: Texas Association of Creative Writing Teachers; PEN; Poetry Society of America; Associated Writing Programs; Texas Institute of Letters, councillor; Past President Conference of College Teachers of English of Texas. Address: Department of English, Texas Tech University, Lubbock, TX 79409, USA.

MCDOUGALL Bonnie Suzanne, b. 12 Mar 1941, Sydney, Australia. Professor. m. H Anders Hansson, 1980, 1 son. Education: BA, 1965, MA, 1967, PhD, 1970, University of Sydney. Publications: Introduction of Western Literary Theories into China; Mao Zedong's Talks at the Yanan Conference; Popular Chinese Literature and Performing Arts; The Yellow Earth: A Film by Chen Kaige; The August Sleepwalker; Old Snow; Brocade Valley. Contributions to: Journal of the Oriental Society of Australia; Modern Chinese Literature; Renditions; Contemporary China; Stand; Grand Street; New Directions. Memberships: British Association of Chinese Studies; Universities' China Committee in London; Amnesty International. Address: Department of East Asian Studies, University of Edinburgh, 8 Buccleuch Place, Edinburgh EH8 9LW, Scotland.

MCDOUGALL Walter A(llan), b. 3 Dec 1946, Washington, District of Columbia, USA. Professor of History; Writer. m. Elizabeth Swoope, 8 Aug 1970, div 1979. Education: BA cum laude, Amherst College, 1968; MA, 1971, PhD, 1974, University of Chicago. Appointments: Assistant Professor, 1975-83, Associate Professor, 1983-87, Professor of History, 1987-, University of California, Berkeley; Vestryman, St Peter's Episcopal Church. Publications: France's Rhineland Diplomacy 1914-1924: The Last Bid for a Balance of Power in Europe, 1978; The Grenada Papers (editor with Paul Seabury), 1984; Social Sciences and Space Exploration: New Directions for University Instruction (contributor), 1984; ...The Heavens and the Earth: A Political History of the Space Age, 1985; Let the Sea Make a Noise, 1993. Contributions to: Numerous articles and reviews to periodicals. Honours: Pulitzer Prize for History, 1986; Visiting Scholar, Hoover Institution, 1986; Selected by Insight, America's Ten Best College Professors, 1987; Dexter Prize for Best Book, Society for the History of Technology, 1987. Memberships: American Church Union; Pumpkin Papers Irregulars; Delta Kappa Epsilon. Address: Department of History, University of California, Berkeley, CA 94720, USA.

MCDOWALL David Buchanan, b. 14 Apr 1945, London, England. Writer. m. 19 Apr 1975, 2 sons. Education: MA, St Johns College, Oxford. Publications: Palestine and Israel: The Uprising and Beyond; The Kurds: A Nation Denied; An Illustrated History of Britain; Britain in Close Up; The Spanish Armada; Europe and the Arabs: Discord or Symbiosis?; Lebanon: A Conflict of Minorities; A Modern History of the Kurds, 1994. Honour: The Other Award. Address: 31 Cambrian Road, Richmond, Surrey TW0 8JQ, England.

MCDOWELL Edwin (Stewart), b. 13 May 1935, Somers Point, New Jersey, USA. Journalist; Writer. m. Sathie Akimoto, 7 July 1973, 1 son, 2 daughters. Education: BS, Temple University, 1959. Appointment: Staff, New York Times. Publications: Three Cheers and a Tiger, 1966; To Keep Our Honor Clean, 1980; The Lost World, 1988. Membership: Authors Guild. Address: c/o New York Times, 229 West 43rd Street, New York, NY 10036, USA.

MCDOWELL Michael, (Nathan Aldyne, Axel Young), b. 1 June 1950, Enterprise, Alabama, USA. Author. Education: BA, Harvard University, 1972; PhD, Brandeis University, 1978. Publications: Over 20 novels, 1979-88. Address: c/o The Otte Company, 6 Golden Street, Belmont, MA 01278, USA.

MCELROY Colleen J(ohnson), b. 30 Oct 1935, St Louis, Missouri, USA. Professor; Poet; Writer. Div 1 son, 1 daughter. Education: BS, 1958, MS, 1963, Kansas State University; PhD, University of Washington, Seattle, 1973. Appointments: Editor, Dark Waters, 1973-79; Professor, University of Washington, Seattle, 1973-. Publications: Music From Home, 1976; The Halls of Montezuma, 1979; The New Voice, 1979; Winters Without Snow, 1979; Lie and Say You Love Me, 1981; Queen of the Ebony Isles, 1984; Jesus and Fat Tuesday, 1987; What Madness Brought Me Here, 1990. Contributions to: Various journals. Address: c/o Creative Writing Program, Department of English, University of Washington, Seattle, WA 98195, USA.

MCELROY Joseph (Prince), b. 21 Aug 1930, New York, New York, USA. Author. Education: BA, Williams College, 1951; MA, 1952, PhD, 1961, Columbia University. Publications: A Smuggler's Bible, 1966; Hind's Kidnap, 1969; Ancient History, 1971; Lookout Cartridge, 1974; Plus, 1977; Ship Rock, 1980; Women and Men, 1987. Address: c/o Georges Borchardt, 136 East 57th Street, New York, NY 10022, USA.

MCELROY Lee. See: KELTON Elmer Stephen.

MCEVEDY Colin (Peter), b. 6 June 1930, Stratford, England. Writer. Education: BA, 1948, BM, BCH, 1955, DM, 1970, Magdalen College, Oxford; DPM, University of London, 1963. Publications: The Penguin Atlas of Medieval History, 1961; The Penguin Atlas of Ancient History, 1967; The Atlas World History (with Sarah McEvedy), 3 volumes, 1970-73; The Penguin Atlas of Modern History, 1972; Atlas of World Population History (with Richard Jones), 1980; The Penguin Atlas of African History, 1980; The Penguin Atlas of Recent History (Europe since 1815), 1982; The Century World History FactFinder, 1984; The Penguin Atlas of North American History, 1988; The New Penguin Atlas of Medieval History, 1992. Contributions to: Bubonic Plague; Scientific American. Address: 7 Caithness Road, London W14, England.

MCEVOY Marjorie, (Gillian Bond, Marjorie Harte), b. York City, England. Novelist. m. William Noel McEvoy, 1 son, 1 daughter. Publications: Doctors in Conflict, 1962; The Grenfell Legacy, 1967; Dusky Cactus, 1969; Echoes from the Past, 1978; Calabrian Summer, 1980; Sleeping Tiger, 1982; Star of Randevi, 1984; Temple Bells, 1985; Camelot Country, 1986; The Black Pearl, 1988. Contributions to: Newspapers and magazines. Membership: Romantic Novelists Association. Address: 54 Miriam Avenue, Chesterfield, Derbyshire, England.

MCEWAN Ian Russell, b. 21 June 1948, Aldershot, Hampshire, England. Author. m. Penny Allen, 1982, 2 sons, 2 daughters. Education: BA, Honours, English Literature, University of Sussex; MA, University of East Anglia. Publications: Films: The Ploughman's Lunch, 1983; Last Day of Summer, 1984; Books: First Love, Last Rites, 1975; In Between the Sheets, 1978; The Cement Garden, 1978; The Imitation Game, 1981; The Comfort of Strangers, 1981; Or Shall We Die? (oratorio), 1982; The Innocent, 1989; Black Dogs, 1992; The Daydreamer, 1994. Address: c/o Jonathon Cape, 32 Bedford Square, London WC1B 3EL, England.

MCFARLANE James Walter, b. 12 Dec 1920, Sunderland, England. Professor of European Literature Emeritus; Writer. m. Lillie Kathleen Crouch, 1944, 2 sons, 1 daughter. Education: MA, BLitt, 1948, Oxford University. Appointments: Professor of European Literature, 1964-82, Professor Emeritus, 1982-, Founding Dean, European Studies, 1964-68, Public Orator, 1964-68, 1974-75, 1978-79, Pro-Vice Chancellor, 1968-71, Professorial Fellow, 1982-86, University of East Anglia; Editor, 1975-90, Editor-at-Large, 1991-, Scandinavica: An International Journal of Scandinavian Studies; Managing Editor, Norvik Press, 1985-. Publications: Ibsen and the Temper of Norwegian Literature, 1960; Discussions of Ibsen, 1962; Henrik Ibsen, 1970; Modernism: European Literature 1890-1930 (with Malcolm Bradbury), 1976; Ibsen and Meaning, 1989. Editor and translator: The Oxford Ibsen, 8 volumes, 1960-77; Slaves of Love and Other Norwegian Short Stories (with Janet Garton), 1982; Knut Hamsun's Letters, Vol 1 (with Harald Naess), 1990. Editor: The Cambridge Companion to Henrik Ibsen, 1994. Translator: Hamsun: Pan, 1955; Hamsun: Wayfarers, 1980; Obstfelder: A Priest's Diary, 1988. Contributions to: Professional journals. Honours: Commander's Cross, Royal Norwegian Order of St Olav, 1975; Det Norske Videnskaps-Akademie Fellow, Oslo, 1977; Festschrift published in his honour, 1985; Honorary DLitt, Loughborough, 1990; Honorary D Litt, Sunderland, 1995. Memberships: Honorary Member, Phi Beta Kappa; Foreign Member, Royal Danish Academy of Sciences and Letters; Foreign Member, Royal Norwegian Society of Sciences and Letters; Corresponding Member, Svenska Litteratursällskapet i Finland. Address: The Croft, Stody, Melton Constable, Norfolk NR24 2EE, England.

MCFEELY William S(hield), b. 25 Sept 1930, New York, New York, USA. Professor of History; Author. m. Mary Drake, 13 Sept 1952, 1 son, 2 daughters. Education: BA, Amherst College, 1952; MA, 1962, PhD, 1966, Yale University. Appointments: Assistant Professor, 1966-69, Associate Professor, 1969-70, Yale University; Professor of History, 1970-80, Rodman Professor of History, 1980-82, Andrew W

Mellon Professor in the Humanities, 1982-86, Mount Holyoke College; Visiting Professor, University College London, 1978-79; John J McCloy Professor, Amherst College, 1988-89; Richard B Russell Professor of American History, 1986-94, Abraham Baldwin Professor of the Humanities, 1994-, University of Georgia. Publications: Yankee Stepfather: General O O Howard and the Freedmen, 1968; Grant: A Biography, 1981; Ulysses S Grant: Memoirs and Selected Letters 1839-1865 (editor with Mary Drake McFeely), 1990; Frederick Douglass, 1991; Sapelo's People: A Long Walk into Freedom, 1994. Honours: Morse Fellow, 1968-69; Fellow, American Council of Learned Societies, 1974-75; Pulitzer Prize in Biography, 1982; Francis Parkman Prize, 1982; Guggenheim Fellowship, 1982-83; National Endowment for the Humanities Grant, 1986-87; Avery O Craven Award, 1992; Lincoln Prize, 1992. Memberships: American Historical Association; Authors Guild; Century Association; Organization of American Historians; PEN; Southern Historical Association. Address: 445 Franklin Street No 25, Athens, GA 30606, USA.

MCGAHERN John, b. 12 Nov 1934, Leitrim, Ireland. Author. m. Madeline Green, 1973. Education: University College, Dublin. Appointments: Research Fellow, University of Reading, 1968-71; O'Connor Professor, Colgate University, 1969, 1972, 1977, 1979, 1983, 1992; Visiting Fellow, Trinity College, 1988. Publications: The Barracks, 1963; The Dark, 1965; Nightlines, 1970; The Leavetaking, 1975; Getting Through, 1978; The Pornographer, 1979; High Ground, 1985; The Rockingham Shoot, BBC 2, 1987; Amongst Women, 1990; The Collected Stories, 1992. Address: c/o Faber & Faber, 3 Queen Square, London WC1N 3AU, England.

MCGARRITY Mark, (Bartholomew Gill), b. 22 July 1943, Holyoke, Massachusetts, USA. Author. Education: BA, Brown University, 1966; MLitt, Trinity College, Dublin, 1971. Publications: As Mark Garrity: Little Augie's Lament, 1973; A Passing Advantage, 1980; Neon Caesar, 1989, As Bartholomew Gill: McGarr and the Politician's Wife, 1977; McGarr on the Cliffs of Moher, 1978; McGarr and the P M of Belgrave Square, 1983; The Death of a Joyce Scholar, 1989; The Death of Love, 1992; Death on a Cold Wild River, 1993. Contributions to: Newspapers. Honours: Fellow, New Jersey Council of the Arts, 1981-82; First Place, New Jersey Press Association Critical Writing. Membership: PEN. Address: 159 North Shore Road, Andover, NJ 07821, USA.

MCGARRY Jean, b. 18 June 1952, Providence, Rhode Island, USA. Writer; Teacher. Education: BA, Harvard University, 1970; MA, Johns Hopkins University, 1983. Appointment: Teacher, Johns Hopkins University. Publications: Airs of Providence, 1985; The Very Rich Hours, 1987; The Courage of Girls, 1992. Contributions to: Antioch Review; Southern Review; Southwest Review; Sulfur; New Orleans Review. Honour: Short Fiction Prize, Southern Review-Louisiana State University, 1985. Membership: Associated Writing Programs. Address: 100 West University Parkway, Baltimore, MD 21210, USA.

MCGINN Bernard (John), b. 19 Aug 1937, Yonkers, New York, USA. Professor of Historical Theology and the History of Christianity. m. Patricia Ferris, 12 July 1971, 2 sons. Education: BA, St Joseph's Seminary and College, Yonkers, New York, 1959; STL, Pontifical Gregorian University, Rome, 1963; Graduate Studies, Columbia University, 1963-66; Studies, University of Munich, 1967-68; PhD, Brandeis University, 1970. Appointments: Lecturer, Regis College, Weston, Massachusetts, 1966-67; Instructor, Catholic University of America, Washington, DC, 1968-69; Instructor, 1969-70, Assistant Professor, 1970-75, Associate Professor, 1975-78, Professor of Historical Theology and the History of Christianity, 1978-, Naomi Shenstone Donnelley Professor, 1992-, Divinity School, University of Chicago. Publications: The Golden Chain: A Study in the Theological Anthropology of Isaac of Stella, 1972; The Crusades, 1973; Visions of the End: Apocalyptic Traditions in the Middle Ages, 1979; The Calabrian Abbot: Joachim of Fiore in the History of Western Thought, 1985; The Foundations of Mysticism: Origins to the Fifth Century, Vol 1 of The Presence of God: A History of Western Christian Mysticism, 1991; Apocalypticism in the Western Tradition, 1994; Antichrist: Two Thousand Years of the Human Fascination with Evil, 1994; The Growth of Mysticism: Gregory the Great through the 12th Century, 1994. Translator: Apocalyptic Spirituality, 1979; Meister Eckhart: The Essential Sermons, Commentaries, Treatises and Defense (with Edmund Colledge), 1981; Meister Eckhart: Teacher and Preacher (with Frank Tobin and Elvira Borgstadt), 1986. Editor: Three Treatises on Man: A Cistercian Anthropology, 1977; Christian Spirituality: Origins

to the Twelfth Century (with John Meyendorff and Jean Leclercq), 1985; Christian Spirituality: High Middle Ages and Reformation (with Jill Raitt and John Meyendorff), 1987; Mystical Union and Monotheistic Faith: An Ecumenical Doctrine (with Moshe Idel), 1989, 2nd edition, 1996; God and Creation: An Ecumenical Symposium (with David B Burrell), 1990; The Apocalypse in the Middle Ages (with Richard K Emmerson), 1992; Meister Eckhart and the Beguine Mystics: Hadewijch of Brabant, Mechthild of Magdeburg, and Marguerite Porete, 1994; Eriugena: East and West: Papers of the Eighth International Colloquium of the Society for the Promotion of Eriugenean Studies: Chicago and Notre Dame, 18-20 October 1991 (with Willemiem Otten), 1994. Contributions to: Articles in many books and journals. Honours: Fulbright-Hays Research Fellowship, 1967-68; AATS Research Award, 1971; Research Fellow, Institute for Advanced Studies, Hebrew University, Jerusalem, 1988-89, and Institute for Ecumenical and Cultural Research, St John's University, 1992. Memberships: American Society of Church History, President, 1995-; Eckhart Society; International Society for the Promotion of Eriugenean Studies, President; Medieval Academy of America, Fellow, 1994-. Address: 5701 South Kenwood, Chicago, IL 60637, USA.

MCGINNISS Joe, b. 9 Dec 1942, New York, New York, USA. Writer. Education: BS, Holy Cross College, 1964. Appointment: Newspaper Reporter, 1964-68. Publications: The Selling of the President, 1968; The Dream Team, 1972; Heroes, 1976; Going to Extremes, 1980; Fatal Vision, 1983; Blind Faith, 1989. Address: c/o Morton L Janklow, 598 Madison Avenue, New York, NY 10022, USA.

MCGIVERN Maureen Daly. See: DALY Maureen.

MCGOUGH Roger, b. 9 Nov 1937, Liverpool, England. Poet. m. 20 Dec 1986, 3 sons, 1 daughter. Education: St Mary's College, Crosby; BA and Graduate Certificate of Education, Hull University. Appointments: Fellow of Poetry, University of Loughborough, 1973-75; Writer-in-Residence, West Australian College of Advanced Education, Perth, 1986. Publications: The Mersey Sound (with Brian Patten and Adrian Henri), 1967; Strictly Private (editor), 1982; An Imaginary Menagerie, 1989; Blazing Fruit (selected poems 1967-87), 1990; Pillow Talk, 1990; The Lighthouse That Ran Away, 1991; You at the Back (selected poems 1967-87, vol 2), 1991; My Dad's a Fire Eater, 1992; Defying Gravity, 1992; The Elements, 1993; Lucky, 1993; Stinkers Ahoy!, 1994; The Magic Fountain, 1995; The Kite and Caitlin, 1996; Sporting Relations, 1996; Bad, Bad Cats, 1997. Honours: Honorary Professor, Thames Valley University, 1993; OBE, 1997. Address: c/o The Peters, Fraser and Dunlop Group Ltd, 5th Floor, The Chambers, Chelsea Harbour, Lots Road, London SW10 0XF, England.

MCGOVERN Ann, b. 25 May 1930, New York, New York, USA. Author. m. Martin L Scheiner, 6 June 1970, 3 sons, 1 daughter. Education: BA, University of New Mexico. Appointment: Publisher, The Privileged Traveler, 1986-90. Publications: Over 50 books including: If You Lived in Colonial Times, 1964; Too Much Noise, 1967; Stone Soup, 1968; The Secret Soldier, 1975; Sharks, 1976; Shark Lady, The Adventures of Eugenie Clark, 1978; Playing with Penguins arnd Other Adventures in Antarctica, 1994; Swimming with Sea Lions and Other Adventures in the Galapagos Islands, 1992. Contributions to: Signature; Saturday Review. Honours: Outstanding Science Books, National Science Teachers Association, 1976, 1979, 1984, 1993; Author of the Year, Scholastic Publishing Inc, 1978. Memberships: Explorers Club; PEN; Authors Guild; Society of Children's Book Writers; Society of Journalists and Authors. Literary Agent: Kirchoff Wohlberg Inc, New York, USA. Address: 30 East 62nd Street, New York, NY 10021, USA.

MCGRATH John (Peter), b. 1 June 1935, Birkenhead, Cheshire, England. Dramatist; Director. m. Elizabeth MacLennan, Mar 1962, 2 sons, 1 daughter. Education: MA, DipEd, St John's College, Oxford. Appointments: Founder-Director, 7:84 Theatre Company, 1971-88; Lecturer, Cambridge University, 1979, 1989; Founding Director, Freeway Films, 1983-. Publications: Plays: Tell Me Tell Me, 1960; Events While Guarding the Bofors Gun, 1966; Random Happenings in the Hebrides, or, The Social Democrat and the Stormy Sea, 1972; Bakke's Night of Fame, 1973; The Cheviot, the Stag, and the Black, Black Oil, 1973, revised version, 1981; The Game's a Bogey, 1975; Fish in the Sea, 1977; Little Red Hen, 1977; Yobbo Nowt, 1978; Joe's Drum, 1979; Swings and Roundabouts, 1981; Blood Red Roses, 1981; Many other non-published plays, 1958-90. Other: A Good Night Out: Popular Theatre: Audience, Class, and Form, 1981; The Bone Won't Break: On Theatre and Hope in Hard Times, 1990; Also 6 screenplays,

1967-89, and 15 television plays or series, 1961-87. Honours: Honorary Doctorate, University of Stirling, 1993; British Association of Film and Television Artists Writers Award, 1994. Address: c/o Freeway Films, 67 George Street, Edinburgh, EH2 2JG, Scotland.

MCGRATH Patrick, b. 7 Feb 1950, London, England. Author. Education: BA, University of London, 1971; Simon Fraser University, Burnaby, British Columbia. Appointment: Managing Editor, Speech Technology magazine, 1982-87. Publications: The Lewis and Clark Expedition, 1985; Blood and Water and Other Tales, 1988; The Grotesque, 1989; New York Life, or, Friends and Others, 1990; Spider, 1990; Dr Haggard's Disease, 1993. Contributions to: Periodicals. Address: 21 East Second Street, No 10, New York, NY 10003, USA.

MCGRATH Peter. Editor; Journalist. Education: Honours Graduate, Amherst College; PhD, Ethics and Society, University of Chicago, 1974.Appointments: Senior Editor, The Washingtonian magazine; Columnist, New Society, London; Writer, Senior Editor, Foreign Editor, Managing Editor, Newsweek International; Editor of New Media; Editorial Liaison to new-media initiatives by Washington Post Company, Newsweek; Executive Editor, Newsweek InterActive (production of award winning CD-ROMS, 1994-95). Contributions to: Numerous publications including: Economist; New Republic; National Observer. Honours: Newspaper Guild Page One Award for Crusading Journalism, 1982; New York State Bar Commemoration of the US Constitution, 1987; Shared Overseas Press Club Award for Foreign Coverage. Address: c/o Newsweek, 251 West 57th Street, New York, NY 10019-1894, USA.

MCGRAW Eloise Jarvis, b. 9 Dec 1915, USA. Writer. m. William Corbin McGraw, 29 Jan 1940, 1 son, 1 daughter. Education: Principia College. Publications: Sawdust in His Shoes, 1950; Moccasin Trail, 1952; Mara, Daughter of the Nile, 1953; Techniques of Fiction Writing, 1959; The Golden Goblet, 1961; Steady Stephanie, 1962; Merry Go Round in Oz, 1963; Master Cornhill, 1973; A Really Weird Summer, 1977; The Forbidden Fountain of Oz, 1980; The Money Room, 1981; Hideaway, 1983; The Seventeenth Swap, 1986; The Trouble with Jacob, 1988; The Striped Ships, 1991; Tangled Webb, 1993; The Moorchild, 1996. Contributions to: Magazines. Address: 1970 Indian Trail, Lake Oswego, OR 97034, USA.

MCGREEVY Susan Brown, b. 28 Jan 1934, Chicago, Illinois, USA. Lecturer; Writer. m. Thomas J McGreevy, 16 June 1973, 3 children. Education: Mount Holyoke College, 1951-53; BA with honours, Roosevelt University, 1969; MA, Northwestern University, 1971. Appointments: Staff Consultant, Heart of America Indian Center, Kansas City, Missouri, 1973-75; Curator of North American Ethnology, Kansas City Museum of History and Science, 1975-77; Adjunct Professor, Ottowa University, Kansas City Campus, 1976-77; Director, 1978-82, Research Associate, 1983-, Member, Board of Trustees, 1987-, Wheelwright Museum of the American Indian, Santa Fe, New Mexico; Guest Lecturer, colleges and museums, 1978-; Faculty, Northwestern University, Gallina, New Mexico, 1980-; Member, various Boards of Directors. Publications: Woven Holy People: Navajo Sandpainting Textiles (editor), 1983; Translating Tradition: Basketry Arts of the San Juan Paiutes (with Andrew Hunter Whitleford), catalogue, 1985; Guide to Microfilm Edition of the Washington N Matthews Papers (with Katherine Spencer Halpern), 1985. Contributions to: Various art journals. Honours: Grants from: National Historic Publications and Records Commission, 1980; National Endowment of the Humanities, 1981; National Endowment for the Arts, 1985. Memberships: American Anthropological Association; American Association of Museums; American Ethnological Society. Address: Route 7, Box 129-E, Santa Fe, NM 87505, USA.

MCGREGOR Iona, b. 7 Feb 1929, Aldershot, England. Writer. Education: BA Hons, University of Bristol, England, 1950. Publications: Novels: Death Wore a Diadem, 1989; Alice in Shadowtime, 1992. Historical fiction for children: An Edinburgh Reel, 1968, 4th edition, 1986; The Popinjay, 1969, 2nd edition, 1979; The Burning Hill, 1970; The Tree of Liberty, 1972; The Snake and the Olive, 1974, 2nd edition, 1978. Non-fiction: Edinburgh and Eastern Lowlands, 1979; Wallace and Bruce, 1986; Importance of Being Earnest, 1987; Huckleberry Finn, 1988. Honour: Writer's Bursary, Scottish Arts Council, 1989. Membership: Scottish PEN. Address: 9 Saxe Coburg Street, Edinburgh EH3 5BN, Scotland.

MCGRORY Edward, b. 6 Nov 1921, Stevenston, Ayrshire, Scotland. Retired Sales Consultant. m. Mary McDonald, 20 Nov 1948,

1 son, 1 daughter. Education: BA, Open University, 1985. Publications: Selected Poems, 1984; Plain and Coloured, 1985; Pied Beauty, 1986; Orchids and Daisies, 1987; Light Reflections - Mirror Images, 1988; Chosen Poems by Celebrities: Eddie McGrory's Poems, 1988; Masks and Faces, 1989; Illuminations, 1990; Letters from Flora, 1991; Candles and Lasers, 1992. Membership: Various literary societies. Address: 41 Sythrum Crescent, Glenrothes, Fife KY7 5DG, Scotland.

MCGUANE Thomas (Francis III), b. 11 Dec 1939, Wyandotte, Michigan, USA. Writer. m. (1) Portia Rebecca Crockett, 8 Sept 1962, div 1975, 1 son, (2) Margot Kidder, Aug 1976, div 1977, 1 daughter, (3) Laurie Buffett, 19 Sept 1977, 1 stepdaughter, 1 daughter. Education: University of Michigan; Olivet College; BA, Michigan State University, 1962; MFA, Yale University, 1965; Stanford University, 1966-67. Publications: The Sporting Club, 1969; The Bushwacked Piano, 1971; Ninety-Two in the Shade, 1973; Panama, 1977; An Outside Chance: Essays on Sport, 1980, new edition as An Outside Chance: Classic and New Essays on Sports, 1990; Nobody's Angel, 1982; In the Crazies: Book and Portfolio, 1984; Something to Be Desired, 1984; To Skin a Cat, 1986; Silent Seasons: Twenty-One Fishing Stories, 1988; Keep the Change, 1989; Nothing But Blue Skies, 1992. Honours: Wallace Stegner Fellowship, Stanford University, 1966-67; Richard and Hinda Rosenthal Foundation Award, American Academy of Arts and Letters, 1971; Honorary Doctorates, Montana State University, 1993, Rocky Mountain College, 1995. Address: Box 25, McLeod, MT 59052, USA.

MCGUCKIAN Medbh, b. 12 Aug 1950, Belfast, Northern Ireland. Poet; Teacher. m. John McGuckian, 1977, 3 sons, 1 daughter. Education: BA, 1972, MA, 1974, Queen's University, Belfast. Appointments: Teacher, Dominican Convent, Fortwilliam Park, Belfast, 1974; Instructor, St Patrick's College, Knock, Belfast, 1975-; Writer-in-Residence, Queen's University, Belfast, 1986-88. Publications: Poetry: Single Ladies: Sixteen Poems, 1980; Portrait of Joanna, 1980; Trio Poetry (with Damian Gorman and Douglas Marshall), 1981; The Flower Master, 1982; Venus and the Rain, 1984, revised edition, 1994; On Ballycastle Beach, 1988; Two Women, Two Shores, 1989; Marconi's Cottage, 1991; The Flower Master and Other Poems, 1993; Captain Lavender, 1994. Editor: The Big Striped Golfing Umbrella: Poems by Young People from Northern Ireland, 1985. Honours: National Poetry Competition Prize, 1979; Eric Gregory Award, 1980; Rooney Prize, 1982; Ireland Arts Council Award, 1982; Alice Hunt Bartlett Award, 1983; Cheltenham Literature Festival Poetry Competition Prize, 1989. Address: c/o Gallery Press, Oldcastle, County Meath, Ireland.

MCGUIRE Stryker. Journalist. m. Julith Jedamus, 1 son. Education: Graduated, Hamilton College, Clinton, NY, 1969. Appointments: Leader special projects team, San Antonio Light; Los Angeles Correspondent, 1978-80, Houston Bureau Chief, 1980-83, Newsweek International Senior Editor, 1983-87, Mexico City Bureau Chief and Latin America Regional Editor, 1988-89, Senior Chief of Correspondents, 1989-93, West Coast Editor, London Bureau Chief, 1996-, Newsweek. Publication: Street With No Names, 1991. Honour: Nomination, Pulitzer Prize. Address: c/o Newsweek, 251 West 57th Street, New York, NY 10019-1894, USA.

MCGURN Barrett, b. 6 Aug 1914, New York, New York, USA. Author. m. Janice Ann McLaughlin, 19 June 1962, 5 sons, 1 daughter. Education: AB, Fordham University, New York, 1935. Appointments: Reporter, New York and Paris Herald Tribune, 1935-66; Bureau Chief, Herald Tribune, Rome, Paris, Moscow, 1946-62. Publications: Decade in Europe, 1958; A Reporter Looks at the Vatican, 1960; A Reporter Looks at American Catholicism, 1966; The Supreme Court and the Press, 1997. Forthcoming: Pilgrim's Guide to Rome. Co-author: Best From Yank, 1945; Heroes For Our Times '68; 10 others. Contributions to: Reader's Digest; Catholic Digest; Commonweal; Colliers; Yank. Honours: Long Island Polk Award, 1956; Overseas Press Club Award, 1957. Memberships: Overseas Press Club of America, President, 1963-65; Foreign Press Association in Italy, President, 1961, 1962. Literary Agent: Perry Knowlton, Curtis Brown Ltd, New York, NY. Address: 5229 Duval Drive, Bethesda, MD 20816-1875, USA.

MCGWIRE Michael Kane, b. 9 Dec 1924, Madras, India. Commander, Royal Navy; Academic; Writer. m. Helen Jean Scott, 22 Nov 1952, 2 sons, 3 daughters. Education: Royal Naval College, Dartmouth, 1938-42; BSc, University of Wales, 1970. Appointments: Commander, Royal Navy, 1942-67; Professor, Dalhousie University, 1971-79; Senior Fellow, Brookings Institute, Washington, DC, 1979-90;

Visiting Professor, Global Security Programme, Cambridge University, 1990-93. Publications: Military Objectives and Soviet Foreign Policy, 1987; Perestroika and Soviet National Security, 1991. Editor: Soviet Naval Developments, 1973; Soviet Naval Policy, 1975; Soviet Naval Influence, 1977. Contribsutions to: Numerous publications. Honour: Officer of the Order of the British Empire. Address: Hayes, Durlston, Swanage, Dorset BH19 2JF, England.

MCILVANNEY William, b. 25 Nov 1936, Kilmarnock, Ayrshire, Scotland. Author; Poet. Education: MA, University of Glasgow, 1959. Publications: Fiction: Remedy is None, 1966; A Gift from Nessus, 1968; Docherty, 1975; Laidlaw, 1977; The Papers of Tony Veitch, 1983; The Big Man, 1985; Walking Wounded (short stories), 1989. Poetry: The Long Ships in Harbour, 1970; Landscapes and Figures, 1973; Weddings and After, 1984. Address: c/o John Farquharson Ltd, 162-168 Regent Street, London, W1R 5TB, England.

MCINERNEY Jay, b. 13 Jan 1955, Hartford, Connecticut, USA. Author. m. (1) Mary Reymond, 2 June 1984, (2) Helen Bransford, 27 Dec 1991. Education: BA, Williams College, 1976; Postgraduate studies, Syracuse University. Publications: Bright Lights, 1984; Ransom, 1985; Story of My Life, 1988; Brightness Falls, 1992; Savage and Son, 1995. Contributions to: Anthologies and magazines. Memberships: Authors Guild; Authors League of America; PEN; Writers Guild. Address: c/o International Creative Management, 40 West 57th Street, New York, NY 10019, USA.

MCINERNY Ralph, b. 24 Feb 1929, Minneapolis, Minnesota, USA. Professor. m, 2 sons, 4 daughters. Education: BA, St Paul Seminary, St Paul, Minnesota; MS, University of Minnesota, Minneapolis, 1953; PhL, Philosophy, 1953; PhD summa cum laude, 1954, Université Laval, Quebec, Canada. Appointments: Editor, The New Scholasticism, 1975-89; Executive Director, Homeland Foundation, 1990-92. Publications: Novels: The Priest, 1973; The Gate of Heaven, 1975; Connolly's Life, 1983; The Noonday Devil, 1985; Rigor Mortis, 1989; Four on the Floor, 1989; The Search Committee, 1990; Sisterhood, 1991; Chambre Froide, 1991; Le Demon de Midi, 1992; Desert Sinner, 1992; Basket Case, 1992; Body and Soil, 1993. Philosophical books: Art and Prudence, 1988; First Glance at Thomas Aquinas, 1989; Beothius and Aquinas, 1990; Aquinas on Human Action, 1992. Honours: Honorary Doctor of Letters, St Benedict College, 1978, University of Steubenville, 1984; Fellow, Pontifical Roman Academy of St Thomas Aquinas, 1987; Sigma National Scholastic Honour Society, 1990; Thomas Aquinas Medal, University of Dallas, 1990; St Thomas Aquinas Medallion, Thomas Aquinas College, 1991; Thomas Aquinas Medal, American Catholic Philosophical Association, 1993; Board of Governors, Thomas Aquinas College, 1993. Memberships: Authors Guild; Mystery Writers of America; Metaphysical Society of America, president, 1992-93; Fellowship of Catholic Scholars, president, 1991-93. Address: 2158 Portage Avenue, South Bend, IN 46616, USA.

MCINNIS (Harry) Don(ald), b. 18 Apr 1916, Worcester, Massachusetts, USA. Public Administrator; International Developer; Writer; Dramatist. m. Marjorie E Graber, 7 Aug 1948, 2 sons, 2 daughters. Education: AB, Clark University, 1938; Graduate studies, Clark University, 1938-39, American University, 1939-40, Johns Hopkins University, 1968-69. Publications: The Running Years, 1986; Cobwebs and Twigs, 1990; Will - Man from Stratford (play), 1992; New Work No Lines (play), 1994. Contributions to: Regularly to US personnel management journals, 1940's, 1950's. Honours: Special awards, US Government, Government of Guatemala, Republic of Korea. Memberships: Australian Writers Guild; US Dramatists Guild. Address: 22 Chauvel Circle, Chapman, ACT 2611, Australia.

MCINTIRE Dennis K(eith), b. 25 June 1944, Indianapolis, Indiana, USA. Historian (Music and Literature); Lexicographer. Education: Indiana University. Appointments: Research Editor, various general reference works, 1965-79; Editorial Associate, Nicolas Slonimsky, 1979-95; Advisor, The Oxford Dictionary of Music, 1985, 2nd edition, 1994, The New Grove Dictionary of American Music, 1986, The New Everyman Dictionary of Music, 1988, Brockhaus Riemann Musik Lexikon: Ergänzungsband, 1989, 2nd edition, 1995, Dictionnaire biographique des musiciens, 1995, The Hutchinson Encyclopedia of Music, 1995. Publications: Baker's Biographical Dictionary of Musicians (contributing editor), 7th edition, 1984, (associate editor), 8th edition, 1992; International Who's Who in Music and Musicians' Directory (consultant editor), 12th edition, 1990, (appendices editor), 13th to 15th editions, 1992-96; Baker's

Biographical Dictionary of 20th Century Classical Musicians (associate editor), 1997; International Authors and Writers Who's Who (consultant editor), 15th edition, 1997; International Who's Who in Poetry and Poets' Encyclopaedia (consultant editor), 8th edition, 1997. Contributions to: The New Grove Dictionary of American Music, 1986; Supplement to Music Since 1900, 1986; The New Grove Dictionary of Opera, 1992; Music Since 1900, 5th edition, 1994. Forthcoming: The New Grove Dictionary of Music and Musicians, revised edition. Honour: Advisor, Encyclopaedia Britannica, 1996-. Memberships: High Churchman (Conservative); Freemason; Ancient Accepted Scottish Rite; American Musicological Society; Music Library Association; Sir Thomas Beecham Society, USA. Address: 9170 Melrose Court, Indianapolis, IN 46239, USA.

MCINTYRE Arthur (Milton), b. 31 Oct 1945, New South Wales, Australia. Artist; Writer. Education: Graduated, National Art School, Sydney, 1966; Postgraduate study, Sydney University, 1971-73. Appointments: Sydney Art Critic, The Australian, 1977-78, The Age, 1981-90. Publications: Australian Contemporary Drawing, 1988; Contemporary Australian Collage and Its Origins, 1990. Contributions to: Art Monthly, UK and Australia; Art and Australia; Island; Others. Honour: VAB Grant, Australia Council, 1987. Memberships: National Gallery of Australia Association; NAVA; International Association of Art Critics. Address: 18 Malvern Avenue, Croydon, New South Wales 2132, Australia.

MCKAY Don, b. Ontario, Canada. English Teacher; Poet; Writer. Appointments: Editor, Brick Books, The Fiddlehead. Publications: Lependur, 1978; Lightning Ball Bait, 1980; Birding or Desire, 1983; Sanding Down This Rocking Chair on a Windy Night, 1987; Night Field, 1991; Apparatus, 1997. Honours: Canadian Author's Association Award for Poetry, 1983; National Magazine Award for Poetry, 1991; Governor-General's Literary Award for Poetry, 1991. Address: 434 Richmond Avenue, Victoria, British Columbia V8S 3Y4, Canada.

MCKEAN John Maule Laurie, b. 7 Nov 1943, Glasgow, Scotland. Critic; Teacher; Designer. m. Polly Eupalinos, 1 son, 1 daughter. Education: BArch (Honours), University of Strathclyde, 1968; MA, Theory of Architecture, University of Essex, 1971. Appointments: Editor, The Architects' Journal, 1971-75; UK Correspondent, Architecture, 1975-80; Architecture Correspondent, City Limits, London, 1984. Publications: Essex University: A Case Study, 1971; The First Era of Modern Architecture of the Western World, 1980; Building Materials and Architectural Quality, 1982; Style, Structure and Design, 1982; Masterpieces of Architectural Drawing, 1982; The Word Crystal, 1984; Suburban Prototype, 1986; Learning from Segal, 1987; Two Essays in Glasgow: Form, Structure and Image of the City, 1987; The Royal Festival Hall, 1990. Contributions to: Spazio e Società; Architese, Switzerland; Building Design; Architects Journal; A A Files. Honour: Elected to CICA, 1990. Memberships: Royal Society of Arts; International Building Press, UK Branch; Chartered Society of Designers; Royal Incorporation of Architects, Scotland; Design History Society; Construction History Society. Address: 34 Dukes Avenue, Muswell Hill, London N10, England.

MCKEOWN Tom S, b. 29 Sept 1937, Evanston, Illinois, USA. Independent Consultant in Writing. m. Patricia Haebig, 22 Apr 1989, 1 son, 1 daughter. Education: BA, University of Michigan, 1961; MA, University of Michigan, 1962; MFA, Vermont College, 1989. Appointments: Writer-in-Residence, Stephens College, 1968-74; Poet-in-Residence, Savannah College of Art and Design, 1982-83. Publications: The Luminous Revolver, 1973; The House of Water, 1974; Driving to New Mexico, 1974; Certain Minutes, 1978; Circle of the Eye, 1982; Three Hundred Tigers, 1994. Contributions to: The New Yorker; Atlantic; Harper's; The Nation; The New York Times; Commonweal; Chicago Tribune; Kansas City Star; The Harvard Advocate; The Yale Review. Honours: Avery Hopwood Award, 1968; Wisconsin Arts Fellowship, 1980. Address: 1220 N Gammon Road, Middleton, Wisconsin 53562, USA.

MCKINLEY Hugh, b. 18 Feb 1924, Oxford, England. Poet. m. DeboraH Waterfield, 15 Sept 1979. Appointments: Literary Editor, Athens Daily Post, 1966-77; European Editor, Poet, India, 1967-91; Editorial Panel, Bitterroot, USA, 1980-89. Publications: Poetry: Starmusic, 1976; Transformation of Faust, 1977; Poet in Transit, 1979; Exulting for the Light, 1983; Skylarking, 1994. Contributions to: Numerous publications worldwide. Honours: LittLD, International Academy of Leadership & President Marcos Medal, Philippines, 1967; DLitt, Free University of Asia, Karachi, India, 1973; Directorate,

Academia Pax Mundi, Israel, 1978. Memberships: Suffolk Poetry Society; Baha'i World Faith, life member. Address: Roseholme, Curlew Green Kelsale, Suffolk, England.

MCKINNEY Jack. See: **DALEY Brian Charles.**

MCKISSACK Frederick L(emuel), b. 12 Aug 1939, Nashville, Tennessee, USA. Children's Writer. m. Patricia McKissack, 12 Dec 1964, 3 sons. Education: BS, Tennessee Agricultural and Industrial State University, 1964. Publications: About 70 books, 1984-97. Honours: Jane Addams Children's Book Award, 1990; Boston Globe/Horn Book Award, 1993. Address: 5900 Pershing Avenue, St Louis, MO 63112, USA.

MCKISSACK Patricia (L'Ann) C(arwell), b. 9 Aug 1944, Nashville, Tennessee, USA. Children's Writer. m. Frederick L McKissack, 12 Dec 1964, 3 sons. Education: BA, Tennessee Agricultural and Industrial State University, 1964; MA, Webster University, 1975. Publications: About 90 books, 1978-97. Honours: Jane Addams Children's Book Award, 1990; Boston Globe/Horn Book Award, 1993. Address: 5900 Pershing Avenue, St Louis, MO 63112, USA.

MCKUEN Rod, b. 29 Apr 1933, Oakland, California, USA. Poet; Composer; Author; Performer; Columnist. Appointments: Many appearances, films, TV, concerts, nightclubs, and with symphony orchestras; Composer, modern classical music, film and TV scores; President, Stanyan and Discus Records, Tamarack and Stanyan Books, Rod McKuen Enterprises. Publications: Poetry: And Autumn Came, 1954; Stanyan Street and Other Sorrows, 1966; Listen to the Warm, 1967; Lonesome Cities, 1968; Twelve Years of Christmas, 1968; In Someone's Shadow, 1969; A Man Alone, 1969; With Love, 1970; Caught in the Quiet, 1970; New Ballads, 1970; Fields of Wonder, 1971; The Carols of Christmas, 1971; And to Each Season, 1972; Pastorale, 1972; Grand Tour, 1972; Come to Me in Silence, 1973; Seasons in the Sun, 1974; America, an Affirmation, 1974; Moment to Moment, 1974; Beyond the Boardwalk, 1975; The Rod McKuen Omnibus, 1975; Celebrations of the Heart, 1975; Alone, 1975; The Sea Around Me, 1977; Hand in Hand, 1977; Coming Close to the Earth, 1978; We Touch the Sky, 1979; Love's Been Good to Me, 1979; Looking for a Friend, 1980; The Power Bright and Shining, 1980; Rod McKuen's Book of Days, 1981; The Beautiful Stranger, 1981; Too Many Midnights, 1981; The Works of Rod McKuen: Vol I, Poetry 1950-1982, 1982; Watch for the Wind..., 1982; Rod McKuen-1984 Book of Days, 1983; The Sound of Solitude, 1983; Suspension Bridge, 1984; Another Beautiful Day, 2 volumes, 1984-85; Valentines, 1986. Prose: Finding My Father: One Man's Search for Identity, 1976; An Outstretched Hand, 1980. Honours: 41 Gold and Platinum Records; Grand Prix du Disque, Paris, 4 times; Grammy Award, 1969; Entertainer of the Year, 1975; Man of the Year Award, University of Detroit, 1978. Memberships: Numerous professional and civic organisations. Address: PO Box G, Beverly Hills, CA 92013, USA.

MCLANATHAN Richard, b. 12 Mar 1916, Methuen, Massachusetts, USA. Author; Art Historian. m. Jane Fuller, 3 Jan 1942. Education: AB, 1938, PhD, 1951, Harvard University. Appointments: Visiting Professor, US and European Universities; Museum Curator, Director, Trustee. Publications: Images of the Universe, 1966; The Pageant of Medieval Art and Life, 1966; The American Tradition in the Arts, 1968; The Brandywine Heritage, 1971; Art in America, 1973; The Art of Marguerite Stix, 1977; East Building, A Profile, National Gallery of Art, 1978; World Art in American Museums, 1983; Gilbert Stuart, 1986; Michelangelo, 1993. Contributions to: Numerous journals and magazines. Honours: Prix de Rome, 1948; Distinguished Service Award, United States Information Agency, 1959; Rockefeller Senior Fellowship, 1975. Literary Agent: Lucy Kroll Agency. Address: The Stone School House, Phippsburg, ME 04562, USA.

MCLAREN Colin Andrew, b. 14 Dec 1940, Middlesex, England. University Librarian. 1 son, 1 daughter. Education: BA, MPhil, Dip Arch Administration, University of London. Publications: Rattus Rex, 1978; Crows in a Winter Landscape, 1979; Mother of the Free, 1980; A Twister over the Thames, 1981; The Warriors under the Stone, 1983; Co-author, with J J Carter: Crown and Gown: An Illustrated History of the University of Aberdeen, 1994; Rare and Fair: A Visitor's History of Aberdeen University Library, 1995. Contributions to: BBC Radio 3 and 4. Honour: Society of Authors Award for Best Adaptation, 1986. Memberships: Society of Authors; Crime Writers Association. Literary Agent: A P Watt Ltd. Address: c/o The Library, University of Aberdeen, Aberdeen, Scotland.

MCLAREN John David, b. 7 Nov 1932, Melbourne, Australia. Professor; Academic. Education: BA (Hons), BEd, PhD, Melbourne University; MA, Monash University. Appointments: Associate Editor, Overland, 1968-; Editor, Australian Book Review, 1978-86; Editor, Overland, 1993-97. Publications: Our Troubled Schools, Melbourne, 1968; A Nation Apart (editor), 1983; Australian Literature: An Historical Introduction, 1989; The New Pacific Literatures: Culture and Environment in the European Pacific, 1993; Writing in Hope and Fear - Literature as Politics in Australia 1945-1972, 1997. Address: Humanities Department, Victoria University of Technology, PO Box 14428, MMC, Melbourne, Vic 3000, Australia.

MCLEISH Kenneth, b. 10 Oct 1940, Glasgow, Scotland. Author; Playwright; Translator. m. Valerie Elizabeth Heath, 30 May 1967, 2 sons. Education: BA, BMus, MA, Worcester College, Oxford, 1963. Publications: The Theatre of Aristophanes, 1980; Penguin Companion to 20th Century Arts, 1985; Listener's Guide to Classical Music, 1986; Shakespeare's People, 1986; The Good Reading Guide, 1988; Read a Book a Week, 1992; Guide to Human Thought (editor), 1993; Crucial Classics (with Valerie McLeish), 1994; Myth, 1996; Orpheus, 1997; Pocket Guide to Shakespeare's Plays (with Stephen Unwin), Guide to Greek Drama, both forthcoming. Over 50 children's books including: The Oxford First Companion to Music, 1979; Children of the Gods (Myths and Legends of Ancient Greece), 1984; Myths and Folktales of Britain and Ireland, 1986; Stories from the Bible, 1988. Translator: Aeschylus, Euripides, Ibsen, Feydeau, Labiche, Sophocles, Aristophanes. Contributions to: Periodicals. Address: c/o A P Watt, 20 John Street, London WC1N 2DR, England.

MCLELLAN David Thorburn, b. 10 Feb 1940, Hertford, England. University Teacher; Writer. m. Annie Brassart, 1 July 1967, 2 daughters. Education: MA, 1962, DPhil, 1968, St John's College, Oxford. Appointment: Faculty, Eliot College, University of Kent. Publications: The Young Hegelians and Karl Marx, 1969; Karl Marx: His Life and Thought, 1974; Engels, 1977; Marxism After Marx, 1980; Ideology, 1986; Marxism and Religion, 1987; Simone Weil: Utopian Pessimist, 1989; Unto Caesar: The Political Importance of Christianity, 1993; Political Christianity, 1997. Contributions to: Professional journals. Address: c/o Eliot College, University of Kent, Canterbury, CT2 7NS, England.

MCLEOD Wallace Edmond, b. 30 May 1931, East York, Ontario, Canada. Professor of Classics; Author. m. Elizabeth Marion Staples, 24 July 1957, 3 sons, 1 daughter. Education: BA, University of Toronto, 1949-53; AM, 1954, PhD, 1966, Harvard University, 1953-57; American School of Classical Studies, Athens, 1957-59. Appointments: Philalethes Lecturer, 1986; Prestonian Lecturer, 1986. Publications: Composite Bows from the Tomb of Tut'ankhamun, 1970; Beyond the Pillars: More Light on Freemasonry, 1973; Meeting the Challenge, 1976; Whence We Come? Freemasonry in Ontario 1784-1980, 1980; Self Bows and Other Archery Tackle from the Tomb of Tut'ankhamun, 1982; The Old Gothic Constitutions, 1985; The Grand Design: Selected Addresses and Papers, 1991. Contributions to: About 150 articles and 350 reviews. Honour: Philalethes Certificate of Literature, 1984. Memberships: Grand Abbot, Society of Blue Friars (Masonic Authors), 1991; President, Philalethes Society, 1992. Address: Victoria College, 73 Queen's Park, Toronto M5S 1K7, Canada.

MCLERRAN Alice, b. 24 June 1933, West Point, New York, USA. Writer. m. Larry Dean McLerran, 8 May 1976, 2 sons, 1 daughter. Education: BA, 1965, PhD, 1969, University of California; MS, 1973, MPH, 1974, Harvard School of Public Health. Publications: The Mountain that Loved a Bird, 1985; Secrets, 1990; Rexaboxen, 1991; I Want to go Home, 1992; Dreamsong, 1992; Hugs, 1993; Kisses, 1993; The Ghost Dance, 1995. Honour: Southwest Book Award, 1991. Memberships: Authors Guild; Society of Childrens Book Writers and Illustrators. Address: 2524 Colfax Avenue South, Minneapolis, MN 55405, USA.

MCMAHON Barrie, b. 2 June 1939, Perth, Australia. Education Public Servant. m. Jan Murphy, 7 May 1960, 2 sons. Education: Teachers Certificate; Teachers Higher Certificate; BA; MA; Graduate Diploma, Design Education and Film. Publications: (all with Robyn Quin) Exploring Images, 1984; Real Images, 1986; Stories and Stereotypes, 1987; Meet the Media, 1988; Australian Images, 1990;

Understanding Soaps, 1993. Contributions to: Australian Journal of Education; Canadian Journal of Education Communication; Education Para la Reception, Mexico; Tijdschrift voor Theaterwetenschap, Netherlands Honour: Curtin University, School of English Prize. Membership: Australian Teachers of Media. Address: PO Box 8064, Perth Business Centre, Pier Street, Perth 6849, Western Australia.

MCMANUS James, b. 22 Mar 1951, New York, USA. Poet; Writer. m. Jennifer Arra, 9 July 1992, 1 son, 1 daughter. Appointment: Professor, School of the Art Institute, Chicago, 1981-. Publications: 8 works. Contributions to: Many periodicals. Honour: Guggenheim Fellowship, 1994-95. Memberships: Associated Writing Programs; PEN. Address: c/o School of the Art Institute, 37 South Wabash, Chicago, IL 60603, USA.

MCMASTER Juliet Sylvia, b. 2 Aug 1937, Kisumu, Kenya. University Professor. m. Rowland McMaster, 10 May 1968, 1 son, 1 daughter. Education: BA, 1959, MA, 1962, St Annes College, Oxford; MA, 1963, PhD, 1965, University of Alberta. Appointments: Assistant Professor, 1965-70, Associate Professor, 1970-76, Professor, 1976-86, University Professor, 1986-, University of Alberta. Publications: Thackeray: The Major Novels, 1971; Jane Austen's Achievement, 1976; Trollope's Palliser Novels, 1978; Jane Austen on Love, 1978; The Novel from Sterne to James, 1981; Dickens the Designer, 1987; The Beautiful Cassandra, 1993; Jane Austen the Novelist, 1995. Contributions to: 19th-Century Fiction; Victorian Studies; Modern Language Quarterly; English Studies in Canada. Honours: Canada Council Post-Doctoral Fellowship, 1969-70; Guggenheim Fellowship, 1976-77; McCalla Professorship, 1982-83; University of Alberta Research Prize, 1986; Killam Research Fellowship, 1987-88; Molson Prize Winner, 1994. Memberships: Jane Austen Society of North America; Association of Canadian University Teachers of English. Address: Department of English, University of Alberta, Edmonton Alta, Canada T6G 2E5.

MCMILLAN James (Coriolanus), b. 30 Oct 1925. Journalist. m. Doreen Smith, 7 Apr 1953, 3 sons, 1 daughter. Education: MA (Economics), Glasgow University, Scotland. Publications: The Glass Lie, 1964; American Take-Over, 1967; Anatomy of Scotland, 1969; The Honours Game, 1970; Roots of Corruption, 1971; British Genius (with Peter Grosvenor), 1972; The Way We Were 1900-1950 (trilogy), 1977-80; Five Men at Nuremberg, 1984; The Dunlop Story, 1989; From Finchley to the World - Margaret Thatcher, 1990. Literary Agent: Curtis Brown, London. Address: Thurleston, Fairmile Park Road, Cobham, Surrey KT11 2PL, England.

MCMILLAN Terry, b. 18 Oct 1951, Port Huron, Michigan, USA. Writer. 1 son. Education: BS, University of California, 1979; MFA, Columbia University, 1979. Appointments: Instructor, University of Wyoming, 1987-90; Professor, University of Arizona, 1990-92. Publications: Mama, 1987; Disappearaing Acts, 1989; Breaking Ice, 1990; Waiting to Exhale, 1992; How Stella Got Her Groove Back, 1996. Contributions to: Periodicals. Honours: National Book Award; National Endowment for the Arts Fellowship; New York Foundation for the Arts Fellowship; Doubleday-Columbia University Literary Fellowship. Address: PO Box 2408, Danville, CA 94526, USA.

MCMILLEN Neil Raymond, b. 2 Jan 1939, Lake Odessa, Michigan. Professor of History; Writer. Education: BA, 1961, MA, 1963, University of Southern Mississippi; PhD, Vanderbilt University, 1969. Appointments: Assistant Professor of History, Ball State University, Muncie, 1967-69; Assistant Professor, 1969-70, Associate Professor, 1970-78, Professor of History, 1978-, University of Southern Mississippi, Hattiesburg. Publications: The Citizens' Council: Organized Resistance to the Second Reconstruction, 1971; Thomas Jefferson: Philosopher of Freedom, 1973; A Synopsis of American History (with C Sellers and H May), 1984, 7th edition 1992; Dark Journey: Black Mississippians in the Age of Jim Crow, 1989. Honour: Bancroft Prize, 1990. Address: Department of History, University of Southern Mississippi, Hattiesburg, MS 39401, USA.

MCMONIGAL Valwyn Christina, b. 6 June 1938, Sydney, New South Wales, Australia. Home Economics Teacher (retired); Writer. m. Geoffrey G McMonigal, 28 Sept 1957, 2 sons, 2 daughter. Education: School Leaving Certificate, 1954. Publications: Cookbooks: Popular Potato, 1989; Pumpkin and Other Squash, 1994; Australia Wide Cookbook (with panavisions by Ken Duncan), 1994. Contributions to: Magazines. Honours: Short Story Awards, Fellowship of Australian Writers, 1983, 1985. Memberships: Australian Society of Authors;

Patron, Girl Guide Association; Wine and Food Appreciation Society, vice-president. Address: 23 Grevillea Crs, Berkeley Vale, New South Wales 2261, Australia.

MCMURTRY Larry (Jeff), b. 3 June 1936, Wichita Falls, Texas, USA. m. Josephine Ballard, 15 July 1959, div, 1 son. Education: BA, North Texas State College; MA, Rice University; Stanford University. Appointments: Instructor and Professor of English and Creative Writing, 1961-71; Writer. Publications: Horseman Pass By (in UK as Hud), 1961; Leaving Cheyenee, 1963; The Last Picture Show, 1966, screenplay with Peter Bogdanovitch, 1971; In a Narrow Grave, 1968; Moving On, 1970; All My Firends Are Going to be Strangers, 1972; It's Always We Rambled, 1974; Terms of Endearment, 1975; Somebody's Darling, 1978; Cadillac Jack, 1982; The Desert Rose, 1983; Lonesome Dove, 1985; Texasville, 1987; Flim Flam: Essays on Hollywood, 1988; Anything For Billy, 1989; Buffalo Girls, 1990; The Evening Star, 1992; Streets of Laredo, 1993; Pretty Boy Floyd (with Diana Ossana), 1994. Honours: Jesse H Jones Award, Texas Institute of Letters, 1962; Academy of Motion Picture Arts and Sciences Award (Oscar), 1972; Pulitzer Prize for Fiction, 1986. Membership: Texas Institute of Letters. Address: c/o Simon and Schulster, 1230 Sixth Avenue, New York, NY 10020, USA.

McCALLY Terrence, b. 3 Nov 1939, St Petersburg, Florida, USA. Appointments: Stage Manager, Actors Studio, New York City, 1961; Tutor, 1961-62; Film Critic, The Seventh Art, 1963-65; Assistant Editor, Columbia College Today, 1965-66. Publications: Apple Pie, Sweet Eros Next and Other Plays, 1969; Three Plays: Cuba Si!, Bringing It All Back Home, Last Gasps, 1970; Where Has Tommy Flowers Gone?, 1972; Bad Habits: Ravenswood and Dunelawn, 1974; The Ritz and Other Plays, 1976; The Rink, 1985; And Things That Go Bump In the Night, 1990; Frankie and Jonny in the Clair de Lune, 1990; Lips Together, Teeth Apart, 1992; Until Your Heart Stops, 1993. Honours: Stanley Award, 1962; Obie Award, 1974; American Academy of Arts and Letters Citation; National Institute of Arts and Letters Citation. Address: 218 West 10th Street, New York, NY 10014, USA.

MCNAMARA Eugene Joseph, b. 18 Mar 1930, Oak Park, Illinois, uSA. Professor; Editor; Poet; Writer. m. Margaret Lindstrom, 19 July 1952, 4 sons, 1 daughter. Education: BA, MA, DePaul University; PhD, Northwestern University, 1964. Appointments: Editor, University of Windsor Review, 1965-, Mainline, 1967-72, Sesame Press, 1973-80; Professor of English, University of Windsor. Publications: Poems: For the Mean Time, 1965; Outerings, 1970; Dillinger Poems, 1970; Love Scenes, 1971; Passages, 1972; Screens, 1977; Forcing the Field, 1980; Call it a Day, 1984. Short Stories: Salt, 1977; Search for Sarah Grace, 1978; Spectral Evidence, 1985; The Moving Light, 1986. Contributions to: Queens Quarterly; Saturday Night; Chicago; Quarry; Denver Quarterly. Address: 166 Randolph Place, Windsor, Ontario N9B 2T3, Canada.

MCNEIL Florence Ann, b. 8 May 1940, Vancouver, British Columbia, Canada. Writer; Poet. m. David McNeal, 3 Jan 1973. Education: BA, 1960, MA, 1965, University of British Columbia, Vancouver. Publications: Rim of the Park, 1972; Emily, 1975; Ghost Town, 1975; A Balancing Act, 1979; The Overlanders, 1982; Miss P and Me, 1982; All Kinds of Magic, 1984; Barkerville, 1984; Catrionas Island, 1989; Breathing Each Others Air, 1994. Contributions to: Anthologies, journals, and magazines. Honours: Thea Koetner Award, 1963; MacMillan Prize, 1963; National Magazine Award for Poetry, 1980; British Columbia Book Award, 1989; Many Canada Council Grants. Memberships: British Columbia Writers Federation; Canadian Society of Children's Authors, Illustrators, and Performers; Canadian Writers Union; League of Canadian Poets. Address: 20 Georgia Wynd, Delta, British Columbia, V4M 1A5, Canada.

MCNEILL Daniel Richard, b. 1 June 1947, San Francisco, California, USA. Writer. m. Rosalind Gold, 20 Dec 1984. Education: AB, University of California at Berkeley, 1975; JD, Harvard Law School, 1982. Publication: Fuzzy Logic, 1993. Honour: Los Angeles Times Book Prize in Science and Technology, 1993. Membership: Author's Guild. Literary Agent: John Brockman. Address: 9905 Farragut, #2, Culver City, CA 90232, USA.

MCNEISH James, b. 23 Oct 1931, Auckland, New Zealand. Writer. Education: BA, University of Auckland, 1952. Appointment: Writer-in-Residence, Berlin Kunstler-program, 1983. Publications: Tavern in the Town, 1957; Fire Under the Ashes, 1965; Mackenzie, 1970; The Mackenzie Affair, 1972; Larks in a Paradise (co-author),

1974; The Glass Zoo, 1976; As for the Godwits, 1977; Art of the Pacific (with Brian Brake), 1980; Belonging: Conversations in Israel, 1980; Joy, 1982; Walking on My Feet, 1983; The Man from Nowhere: A Berlin Diary, 1985; Lovelock, 1986; Penelope's Island, 1990; The Man from Nowhere & Other Prose, 1991; My Name is Paradiso, 1995. Address: c/o James Hale, 47 Peckham Rye, London SE15 3NX, England.

MCPHEE John (Angus), b. 8 Mar 1931, Princeton, New Jersey, USA. Professor of Journalism; Author. m. (1) Pryde Brown, 16 Mar 1957, 4 daughters, (2) Yolanda Whitman, 8 Mar 1972, 2 stepsons, 2 stepdaughters. Education: AB, Princeton University, 1953; Graduate studies, Cambridge University, 1953-54. Appointments: Dramatist, Robert Montgomery Presents Television Programme, 1955-57; Associate Editor, Time magazine, New York City, 1957-64; Staff Writer, The New Yorker magazine, 1965-; Ferris Professor of Journalism, Princeton University, 1975-. Publications: A Sense of Where You Are, 1965; The Headmaster, 1966; Oranges, 1967; The Pine Barrens, 1968; A Roomful of Hovings and Other Profiles, 1969; The Crofter and the Laird, 1969; Levels of the Game, 1970; Encounters with the Archdruid, 1972; Wimbledon: A Celebration, 1972; The Deltoid Pumpkin Seed, 1973; The Curve of Binding Energy, 1974; Pieces of the Frame, 1975; The Survival of the Bark Canoe, 1975; The John McPhee Reader, 1977; Coming into the Country, 1977; Giving Good Weight, 1979; Alaska: Images of the Country (with Galen Rowell), 1981; Basin and Range, 1981; In Suspect Terrain, 1983; La Place de la Concorde Suisse, 1984; Table of Contents, 1985; Rising from the Plains, 1986; Outcroppings, 1988; The Control of Nature, 1989; Looking for a Ship, 1990; Assembling California, 1993; The Ransom of Russian Art, 1994; Irons in the Fire, 1997. Honours: American Academy and Institute of Arts and Letters Award, 1977; Woodrow Wilson Award, Princeton University, 1982; American Association of Petroleum Geologists Journalism Awards, 1982, 1986; John Wesley Powell Award, United States Geological Survey, 1988; Walter Sullivan Award, American Geophysical Union, 1993; Various honorary doctorates. Memberships: American Academy of Arts and Letters; Fellow, Geological Society of America. Address: 475 Drake's Corner Road, Princeton, NJ 08540, USA.

MCPHERSON James Alan, b. 16 Sept 1943, Savannah, Georgia, USA. Professor of English; Writer, University of Iowa. 1 daughter. Education: BA, Morris Brown College, Atlanta, 1965; LLB, Harvard University, 1968; MFA, University of Iowa, 1971. Appointments: Assistant Professor, University of California, Santa Cruz, 1969-71, Morgan State University, Baltimore, 1975-76; Associate Professor, University of Virginia, 1976-81; Visiting Scholar, Yale Law School, 1978-79; Professor of English, University of Iowa, 1981-; Lecturer, Japan, 1989-90; Staff Editor, Double Take Magazine, 1995-. Publications: Hue and Cry, 1969; Railroad, 1976; Elbow Room, 1977; Crabcakes, 1977; A World Unsuspected, 1987; The Prevailing South, 1988; Confronting Racial Differences, 1990; Lure and Loathing, 1993; Crossings, 1993. Contributions to: Periodicals. Honours: Atlantic First Award, 1968; Atlantic Grant, 1969; National Institute of Arts and Letters Award, 1970; Guggenheim Fellowship, 1972-73; John D and Catharine T MacArthur Foundation Fellowship, 1981; Excellence in Teaching Award, University of Iowa, 1991; Green Eyeshades Award, Society of Southern Journalists, 1994. Memberships: American Academy of Arts and Sciences; American Civil Liberties Union; Authors League; National Association for the Advancement of Colored People; PEN. Address: c/o Department of English, University of Iowa, Iowa City, IA 52242, USA.

MCPHERSON James Munro, b. 11 Oct 1936, Valley City, North Dakota, USA. Professor of History; Writer. m. Patricia Rasche, 28 Dec 1957, 1 daughter. Education: BA, Gustavus Adolphus College, St Peter, Minnesota, 1958; PhD, Johns Hopkins University, 1963. Appointments: Instructor, 1962-65, Assistant Professor, 1965-66, Associate Professor, 1966-72, Professor of History, 1972-82, Edwards Professor of American History, 1982-91, George Henry Davis '86 Professor of American History, 1991-, Princeton University; Commonwealth Fund Lecturer, University College, London, 1982. Publications: Struggle for Equality, 1964; The Negro's Civil War, 1965; Marching Toward Freedom: The Negro in the Civil War, 1968; Blacks in America: Bibliographical Essays, 1971; The Abolitionist Legacy: From Reconstruction to the NAACP, 1975; Ordeal by Fire: The Civil War and Reconstruction, 1981, 2nd edition, 1992; Battle Cry of Freedom: The Civil War Era, 1988; Abraham Lincoln and the Second American Revolution, 1991; Images of the Civil War, 1992; Gettysburg, 1993; What They Fought For, 1861-1865, 1994; The Atlas of the Civil

War, 1994; Drawn with the Sword: Reflections on the American Civil War, 1996; For Cause and Comrades: Why Men Fought in the Civil War, 1997. Contributions to: Professional journals. Honours: Danforth Fellow, 1958-62; Anisfield-Wolf Award, 1965; Guggenheim Fellowship, 1967-68; National Emdowment for the Humanities Fellowship, 1977-78; Pulitzer Prize in History, 1989; Several honorary doctorates. Memberships: American Historical Association; American Philosophical Society; Organization of American Historians; Phi Beta Kappa; Society of American Historians; Southern Historical Association. Address: 15 Randall Road, Princeton, NJ 08540, USA.

MCPHERSON Sandra Jean, b. 2 Aug 1943, San Jose, California, USA. Professor of English; Poet. m. (1) Henry D Carlile, 24 July 1966, div 1985, 1 daughter, (2) Walter D Pavlich, 3 Jan 1995. Education: BA, San Jose State University, 1965; Postgraduate studies, University of Washington, 1965-66. Appointments: Visiting Lecturer, University of Iowa, 1974-76, 1978-80; Holloway Lecturer, University of California, Berkeley, 1981; Teacher, Oregon Writers Workshop, Portland, 1981-85; Professor of English, University of California, Davis, 1985-. Publications: Elegies for the Hot Season, 1970; Radiation, 1973; The Year of Our Birth, 1978; Patron Happiness, 1983; Streamers, 1988; The God of Indeterminacy, 1993. Contributions to: Periodicals. Honours: Ingram Merrill Foundation Grants, 1972, 1984; National Endowment for the Arts Grants, 1974, 1980, 1985; Guggenheim Fellowship, 1976; Oregon Arts Commission Fellowship, 1984; American Academy and Institute of Art and Letters Award, 1987. Address: c/o Department of English, University of California, Davis, CA 95616, USA.

MCQUEEN Cilla, b. 22 Jan 1949, Birmingham England. Teacher; Artist; Poet. m. Ralph Hotere, 1974, 1 daughter. Education: MA, Dunedin University, Otago, 1970. Publications: Homing in, 1982; Anti Gravity, 1984; Wild Sweets, 1986; Benzina, 1988; Berlin Diary, 1990; Crikey, 1994. Play: Harlequin and Colombine, 1987. Radio Play: Spacy Calcutta's Travelling Truth Show, 1986. Honours: Robert Burns Fellowships, 1985, 1986; Goethe Institute Scholarship, 1988. Address: PO Box 69, Portobello, Dunedin, New Zealand.

MCRAE Hamish Malcolm Donald, b. 20 Oct 1943, Barnstaple, Devon, England. Journalist; Author. m. Frances Annes Cairncross, 10 Sept 1971, 2 daughters. Education: Fettes College, Edinburgh, 1957-62; Honours Degree in Economics and Political Science, Trinity College, Dublin, 1966. Appointments: Editor, Euromoney, 1972, Business and City, The Independent, 1989; Financial Editor, The Guardian, 1975; Associate Editor, The Independent, 1991. Publications: Capital City - London as a Financial Centre (with Frances Cairncross), 1973, 5th edition, 1991; The Second Great Crash (with Frances Cairncross), 1975; Japan's Role in the Emerging Global Securities Market, 1985; The World in 2020, 1994. Contributions to: Numerous magazines and journals. Honours: Financial Journalist of the Year, Wincott Foundation, 1979; Special Merit Award, Amex Bank Review Essays, 1987; Times Columnist of the Year, Periodical Publishers Association Awards, 1996. Address: 6 Canonbury Lane, London N1 2AP, England.

MCTRUSTRY Chris(tifor John), b. 29 Oct 1960, Wellington, New South Wales, Australia. Screenwriter; Novelist. m. Patricia Rose Dravine, 1 Nov 1986, 1 son, 1 daughter. Education: Bachelor of Creative Arts, 1989, Master of Creative Arts, 1990, University of Wollongong. Publications: Television: Neighbours, 1989, 1990, 1991, 1992, 1993; A Country Practice, 1991; Home and Away, 1992, 1993. Radio: Alien Evangelist, 4x30 minute comedy series, 1992. Novel: The Cat Burglar, 1995; The Card Shark, 1996; Axeman!, 1997; Frankenkid, 1997; George and the Dragon, 1997; Susie Smelly-Feet, 1997. Memberships: Australian Writers Guild; Australian National Playwrights Centre; Australian Society of Authors; Mystery Writers of America; Crime Writers Association of Australia. Address: 22 Stanleigh Crescent, West Wollongong, New South Wales 2500, Australia.

MCVEAN James. See: LUARD Nicholas.

MCWHIRTER George, b. 26 Sept 1939, Belfast, Northern Ireland. Writer; Translator; Professor. m. Angela Mairead Cold, 26 Dec 1963, 1 son, 1 daughter. Education: BA, Queen Univerity; MA, University of British Columbia. Appointments: Co-Editor-in-Chief, 1977, Advisory Editor, 1978-, Prism International Magzine; Professor, University of British Columbia, 1982-. Publications: Catalan Poems, 1971; Bodyworks, 1974; Queen of the Sea, 1976; Gods Eye, 1981;

Coming to Grips with Lucy, 1982; Fire Before Dark, 1983; Paula Lake, 1984; Cage, 1987; The Listeners, 1991; A Bad Day to be Winning, 1992; A Staircase for All Souls, 1993; Shadow Light, 1995; Musical Dogs, 1996; Fab, 1997. Contributions to: Numerous magazines and journals. Honours: McMillan Prize, 1969; Commonwealth Poetry Prize, 1972; F R Scott Prize, 1988; Ethel Wilson Fiction Prize, 1988. Memberships: League of Canadian Poets; Writers Union of Canada; PEN; Literary Translators Association of Canada. Address: 4637 West 13th Avenue, Vancouver, British Columbia V6R 2V6, Canada.

MCWHIRTER Norris Dewar, b. 12 Aug 1925, London, England. Author; Editor; Broadcaster. m. (1) Carole Eckert, 28 Dec 1957, dec 1987, 1 son, 1 daughter, (2) Tessa Mary Pocock, 26 Mar 1991. Education: BA, 1947, MA, 1948, Trinity College, Oxford. Appointments: Athletics Correspondent, Star, 1951-60, Observer, 1951-67; Editor, Athletics World, 1952-56; Founder-Editor, Guinness Book of Records, 1955. Publications: Get To Your Marks, 1951; Guinness Book of Records, 1955-86 (30 languages); Dunlop Book of Facts, 1964-73; Guinness Book of Answers, 1976-; Ross, Story of a Shared Life, 1976; Guinness Book of Essential Facts, 1979. Contributions to: Encyclopaedia Britannica; Whitakers Almanack. Honour: Commander of the Order of the British Empire, 1980. Membership: Royal Institution. Address: c/o Guinness Publishing Co, 33 London Road, Enfield, Middlesex EN2 6DJ, England.

MCWILLIAM Candia Frances Juliet, b. 1 July 1955, Edinburgh, Scotland. Writer. m. (1) Earl of Portsmouth, 10 Feb 1981, (2) F E Dinshaw, 27 Sept 1986, 2 sons, 1 daughter. Education: Sherborne School for Girls, 1968-73; BA, Girton College, Cambridge, 1976. Publications: A Case of Knives, 1988; A Little Stranger, 1989; Debatable Land, 1994. Honours: Betty Trask Prize; Scottish Arts Council Prize; Guardian Fiction Prize. Memberships: Society of Authors; PEN; Royal Society of Literature, fellow. Literary Agent: Janklow & Nesbit. Address: c/o Bloomsbury Publishing, 2 Soho Square, London W1V 5DE, England.

MCWILLIAMS Peter, b. 5 Aug 1949, Detroit, Michigan, USA. Publisher; Writer. Education: Eastern Michigan University; Maharishi International University. Publications: Come Live With Me and Be My Life, 1967; Surviving the Loss of a Love, 1971; Portraits, 1992; Life 101 and 102 series. Contributions to: Playboy. Address: c/o Prelude Press, 8159 Santa Monica Boulevard, Los Angeles, CA 90046, USA.

MEAD Matthew, b. 12 Sept 1924, Buckinghamshire, England. Poet. Appointment: Editor, Satis Magazine, Edinburgh, 1960-62. Publications: A Poem in Nine Parts, 1960; Identities, 1964; Kleinigkeiten, 1966; Identities and Other Poems, 1967; the Administration of Things, Penguin Modern Poets 16 (with Harry Guest and J Beeching), 1970; In the Eyes of the People, 1973; Minusland, 1977; The Midday Muse, 1979; A Roman in Cologne, 1986. Address: c/o Anvil Press, 69 King George Street, London SE10 8PX, England.

MEADES Jonathan Turner, b. 21 Jan 1947, Salisbury, Wiltshire, England. Journalist; Writer; Broadcaster. m. (1) Sally Browne, (2) Frances Bentley, 4 daughters. Education: Kings College, Taunton, 1960-64; Royal Academy of Dramatic Art, 1967-69. Publications: Filthy English; Peter Knows What Dick Likes; Pompey. TV: The Victorian Horse; Abroad in Britain; Further Abroad; Jerry Building; Even Further Abroad Contributions to: Times; Sunday Times; Observer; Independent. Memberships: Literary Agent: David Godwin Associates. Address: David Godwin Associates, 14 Goodwin's Court, London, WC2N 4LL, England.

MEASHAM Donald Charles, b. 19 Jan 1932, Birmingham, England. Retired Teacher, Higher Education. m. Joan Doreen Barry, 15 Dec 1954, 1 son, 1 daughter. Education: BA (Hons), Birmingham University, 1953; MPhil, Nottingham University, 1971. Appointments: Founding Editor 1983, Company Secretary, Continuing Co-editor, 1988-, Staple New Writing. Publications: Leaving, 1965; Fourteen, 1965; English Now and Then, 1965; Larger Than Life, 1967; Quattordicenni, 1967; The Personal Element, 1967; Lawrence and the Real England, 1985; Ruskin: The Last Chapter, 1989. Contributions to: Periodicals. Address: Tor Cottage, 81 Cavendish Road, Matlock, Derbyshire DE4 3HD, England.

MEDOFF Mark (Howard), b. 18 Mar 1940, Mount Carmel, Illinois, USA. Dramatist. m. Stephanie Thorne, 3 daughters. Education: BA, University of Miami, Coral Gables, 1962; MA, Stanford University, 1966. Publications: Plays: When You Comin' Back, Red Ryder?, 1973;

Children of a Lesser God, 1979; The Majestic Kid, 1981, revised edition, 1989; The Hands of Its Enemy, 1984; The Heart Outright, 986; Big Mary, 1989; Stumps, 1989; Stephanie Hero, 1990; Kringle's Window, 1991. Film scripts: Good Guys Wear Black, 1977; When You Comin' Back, Red Ryder?, 1978; Off Beat, 1985; Apology, 1986; Children of a Lesser God, 1987; Clara's Heart, 1988; City of Joy, 1992. Contributions to: Periodicals. Honours: Obie Award, 1974; Drama Desk Awards, 1974, 1980; New York Outer Critics Circle Awards, 1974, 1980; Guggenheim Fellowship, 1974-75; Antoinette Perry Award, 1980; Governor's Award for Excellence in the Arts, State of New Mexico, 1980; Distinguished Alumnus, University of Miami, 1987; California Media Access Award, 1988. Memberships: Actors Equity Association; Screen Actors Guild; Writers Guild of America. Address: Box 3585, Las Cruces, NM 88003, USA.

MEDVED Michael, b. 3 Oct 1948, Philadelphia, Pennsylvania, USA. Film Critic; Writer. m. (1) Nancy Harris Herman, 5 Aug 1972, div 1983, (2) Diane Elvenstar, 27 Jan 1985, 1 son, 2 daughters. Education: BA, Yale University, 1969; MFA, California State University at San Francisco, 1974. Appointments: Political Speech Writer, 1970-73; Creative Director, Advertising, Anrick Inc, Oakland, California, 1973-74; Co-Founder and President, Pacific Jewish Center, Venice, California, 1977-94; On-Air Film Critic, People Now, Cable News Network, 1980-83; President, Emanuel Streisand School, Venice, California, 1980-85; On-Air Film Critic and Co-Host, Sneak Previews, PBS-TV, 1985-; Chief Film Critic, New York Post, 1993-; Lecturer; Radio Talk Show Host, Seattle, Washington, 1996-. Publications: What Really Happened to the Class of '65?, 1976; The 50 Worst Films of All Time (with Harry Medved), 1978; The Shadow Presidents, 1979; The Golden Turkey Awards (with Harry Medved), 1980; Hospital, 1983; The Hollywood Hall of Shame (with Harry Medved), 1984; Son of Golden Turkey Awards (with Harry Medved), 1986; Hollywood vs America, 1992. Contributions to: Periodicals. Memberships: American Federation of Television and Radio Artists; Writers Guild of America. Address: c/o KV1, 1809 7th Avenue, Suite 200, Seattle, WA 98101, USA.

MEDVEDEV Roy (Alexandrovich), b. 14 Nov 1925, Tbilisi, Russia. Historian; Sociologist; Author. m. Galina A Gaidina, 1956, 1 son. Education: University of Leningrad; Russian Academy of Pedagogical Sciences. Appointments: Teacher of History, Ural Secondary School, 1951-53; Director, Secondary School, Leningrad Region, 1954-56; Deputy to Editor-in-Chief, Publishing House of Pedagogical Literature, Moscow, 1957-59; Head of Department, Research Institute of Vocational Education, 1960-70, Senior Scientist, 1970-71, Russian Academy of Pedagogical Sciences; People's Deputy, Supreme Soviet of the USSR, 1989-91; Member, Central Committee, Communist Party of Russia, 1990-91; Co-Chairman, Socialist Party of Labour, 1991-. Publications: A Question of Madness (with Zhores Medvedev), 1971; Let History Judge, 1972; On Socialist Democracy, 1975; Khrushchev: The Years in Power (with Zhores Medvedev), 1976; Political Essays, 1976; Problems in the Literary Biography of Mikhail Sholokhov, 1977;(editor), Samizdat Register, 2 volumes, 1977, 1980; Philip Mironov and the Russian Civil War (with S Starikov), 1978; The October Revolution, 1979; On Stalin and Stalinism, 1979; On Soviet Dissent, 1980; Nikolai Bukharin: The Last Years, 1980; Leninism and Western Socialism, 1981; An End to Silence, 1982; Khrushchev, 1983; All Stalin's Men, 1984; China and the Superpowers, 1986; Time of Change (with G Chiesa), 1990; Brezhnev: A Political Biography, 1991; Gensek s Lybianki (political biography of Andropov), 1994. Contributions to: Professional journals and general publications. Address: Abonement Post Box 258, Moscow A-475, 125475, Russia.

MEDVEDEV Zhores (Alexandrovich), b. 14 Nov 1925, Tbilisi, Russia. Biologist; Writer. m. Margarita Nikolayevna Buzina, 1951, 2 sons. Education: Timiriazev Academy of Agricultural Sciences, Moscow; Institute of Plant Physiology, Russian Academy of Sciences. Appointments: Scientist to Senior Scientist, Department of Agrochemistry and Biochemistry, Timiriazev Academy of Agricultural Sciences, Moscow, 1951-62; Head of Laboratory, Molecular Radiobiology, Institute of Medical Radiology, Obninsk, 1963-69; Senior Scientist, All-Union Scientific Research Institute of Physiology and Biochemistry of Farm Animals, Borovsk, 1970-72, National Institute for Medical Research, London, 1973-92. Publications: Protein Biosynthesis and Problems of Heredity, Development, and Ageing, 1963; Molecular-Genetic Mechanisms of Development, 1968; The Rise and Fall of T D Lysenko, 1969; The Medvedev Papers, 1970; A Question of Madness (with Roy Medvedev), 1971; Ten Years After,

1973; Khrushchev: The Years in Power (with Roy Medvedev), 1976; Soviet Science, 1978; The Nuclear Disaster in the Urals, 1979; Andropov, 1983; Gorbachev, 1986; Soviet Agriculture, 1987; The Legacy of Chernobyl, 1990. Contributions to: Many professional journals. Honour: René Schubert Prize in Gerontology, 1985. Address: 4 Osborn Gardens, London NW7 1DY, England.

MEDVEI Victor Cornelius, (C Monk), b. 6 June 1905, Budapest, Hungary. Consultant Physician. m. Sheila Mary Wiggins, 9 May 1946, dec 1989, 1 son, 2 daughters. Education: Prince Eszterhazy Gymnasium, Vienna, 1916-24; MD, University of Vienna, 1930; MRCS LRCP, St Bartholomew's Hospital, London, 1941; MRCP, 1943, FRCP, 1965. Publications: The Mental and Physical Effects of Pain, 1949; The Royal Hospital of St Bartholomew's 1923-1973 (joint editor), 1974; A History of Endocrinology, 1982, 2nd edition, 1993. Contributions to: About 80 papers for Medical Scientific Journals, 1931-92. Honours: Buckston Browne Prize, Harveian Society of London, 1948; Commander of the Order of the British Empire, 1965; Chevalier de l'ordre National du Merite, 1981; Golden MD, Diploma of the University of Vienna, 1991. Memberships: London PEN; Harveian Society, president, 1970; Osler Club of London, president, 1983; Garrick Club. Address: 38 Westmoreland Terrace, London SW1V 3HL, England.

MEEK Jay, b. 23 Aug 1937, Grand Rapids, Michigan, USA. Professor; Poet. m. Martha George, 29 Aug 1966, 1 daughter. Education: BA, University of Michigan, 1959; MA, Syracuse University, 1965. Appointments: Faculty, Wake Forest University, 1977-80, Sarah Lawrence College, 1980-82; Associate Professor, Massachusetts Institute of Technology, 1982-83; Writer-in-Residence, Memphis State University, 1984; Professor, University of North Dakota, 1985-. Publications: The Week the Dirigible Came, 1976; Drawing on the Walls, 1980; Earthly Purposes, 1984; Stations, 1989; After the Storm, 1992; Windows, 1994. Contributions to: Journals and magazines. Honours: National Endowment for the Arts Award, 1972-73; Guggenheim Fellowship, 1985-86; Bush Artist Fellowship, 1989. Address: c/o Department of English, University of North Dakota, Box 7209, University Station, Grand Forks, ND 58202, USA.

MEGGED Aharon, b. 10 Aug 1920, Wloclawek, Poland. Writer. m. Eda Zoritte, 11 May 1944, 2 sons. Appointments: Editor, MASSA, 1953-55; Literary Editor, Lamerchav Daily, 1955-68; Cultural Attaché, Israel Embassy, London, England, 1968-71; Columnist, Davar Daily, 1971-85. Publications: Hedva and I, 1953; Fortunes of a Fool, 1960; Living on the Dead, 1965; The Short Life, 1971; The Bat, 1975; Asahel, 1978; Heinz, His Son and the Evil Spirit, 1979; Journey in the Month of Av, 1980; The Flying Camel and the Golden Hump, 1982; The Turbulent Zone (essays), 1985; Foiglmann, 1987; The Writing Desk (literary essays), 1988; The Selvino Children (documentary), 1984; Anat's Day of Illumination, 1992; Longing for Olga, 1994; Iniquity, 1996. Plays: Hedva and I, 1955; Hannah Senesh, 1963; Genesis, 1965; The High Season, 1968. Contributions to: Atlantic Monthly; Encounter; Midstream; Listener; Moment; Present-Tense; Partisan Review; Ariel. Address: 26 Rupin Street, Tel Aviv 63457, Israel.

MEHROTRA Arvind Krishna, b. 16 Apr 1947, Lahore, Pakistan. Lecturer; Poet. Education: MA, University of Bombay, 1968. Appointments: Lecturer, University of Hyderbad, 1977-78. Publications: Bharatmata: A Prayer, 1966; Woodcuts on Paper, 1967; Poems, Poemes, Poemas, 1971; Nine Enclosures, 1976; Distance in Statute Miles, 1982; Middle Earth, 1984. Editor: Twenty Indian Poems, 1990; Twelve Modern Indian Poets, 1991. Honours: Homi Bhabha Fellowship, 1981. Address: Department of English Studies, University of Allahabad, Allahabad 211002, Uttar Pradesh, India.

MEHROTRA Sri Ram, b. 23 June 1931, Anantram, Etawah, UP, India. Author; Educator. m. Eva, 24 July 1957. Education: MA History, Allahabad University, 1950; PhD History, London University, 1960. Appointments: Assistant Professor, Sauger University, 1950; Lecturer, SCAS, London University, 1962; Fellow, IIAS, Shimla, 1971; Professor, Himachal Pradesh University, 1972; Visiting Professor, Wisconsin University, 1974; Visiting Fellow, St John's College, Cambridge, 1983-84; Nehru Professor, MD University, 1992. Publications: India and the Commonwealth, 1885-1929, 1965; The Emergence of the Indian National Congress, 1971; The Commonwealth and the Nation, 1978; Toward's India's Freedom and Partition, 1979; A History of the Indian National Congress, Volume One: 1885-1918, 1995. Contributions to: Journal of Commonwealth Political Studies; Journal of Development Studies; India Quarterly;

Indian Economic and Social History Review. Address: Seva, Kenfield Estate, Ambedkar Chowk, Shimla, HP 171004, India.

MEHTA Ved (Parkash), b. 21 Mar 1934, Lahore, India. Writer; Teacher. m. Linn Fenimore Cooper Cary, 1983, 2 daughters. Education: Arkansas School for the Blind; BA, Pomona College, 1956; BA, Oxford University, 1959; MA, Harvard University, 1961; MA Oxford University, 1962. Appointments: Residential Fellow, Eliot House, Harvard University, 1959-61; Staff Writer, The New Yorker magazine, 1961-94; Visiting Scholar, Case Western Reserve University, 1974; Beatty Lecturer, McGill University, 1979; Visiting Professor, Bard College, 1985, 1986, Sarah Lawrence College, 1988, New York University, 1989-90; Visiting Fellow, Balliol College, Oxford, 1988-89; Berkeley College, Yale University, 1990-93; Williams College, 1994; Vasser College, 1994-96; Senior fellow, Freedom Forum, Media Studies Center, Visiting scholar, Columbia University, 1996-97; Fellow, Center for Advanced Studies in the Behavioural Sciences, 1997-98. Publications: Face to Face, 1957; Walking the Indian Streets, 1960, revised edition, 1971; Fly and the Fly-Bottle, 1963, 2nd edition, 1983; The New Theologian, 1966; Delinquent Chacha, 1967; Portrait of India, 1970, 2nd edition, 1993; John is Easy to Please, 1971; Mahatma Gandhi and His Apostles, 1977; The New India, 1978; Photographs of Chachaji, 1980; A Family Affair: India Under Three Prime Ministers, 1982; Three Stories of the Raj, 1986. Autobiographical series: Daddyji, 1972; Mamaji, 1979; Vedi, 1982; The Ledge Between the Stream, 1984; Sound-Shadows of the New World, 1986; The Stolen Light, 1989; Up At Oxford, 1993. Contributions to: PBS-TV and BBC-TV. Honours: Guggenheim Fellowships, 1971-72, 1977-78; Ford Foundation grantee, 1971-76; Public Policy grantee, 1979-82; Association of Indians in America Award, 1978; John D and Catharine T MacArthur Foundation Fellowship, 1982-87; Distinguished Service Award, Asian/Pacific American Library Association, 1986; New York City Mayor's Liberty Medal, 1986; New York Institute for the Humanities Fellowship, 1988-92; Literary Lion Medal, New York Public Library, 1990; Literary Lion Centennial Medal, 1996; Honorary doctorates. Memberships: Council on Foreign Relations; Phi Beta Kappa. Address: 139 E 79th St, New York, NY 10021, USA.

MEIDINGER-GEISE DRIPGIE Ingeborg Lucie, b. 16 Mar 1923, Berlin, Germany. Writer; Poet; Dramatist. Education: DPhil. Publications: Over 50 works, including novels, stories, poems, essays, criticism, and radio plays. Contributions to: Various publications. Honours: Hans Sachs Drama Prize, 1976; International Mölle Literary Prize, Sweden, 1979. Memberships: Chairman, Die Kogge, 1967-88; PEN. Address: Schobertweg 1 a, D-91056 Erlangen, Germany.

MEINKE Peter, b. 29 Dec 1932, Brooklyn, New York, USA. Professor of Literature; Poet; Writer. m. Jeanne Clark, 14 Dec 1957, 2 sons, 2 daughters. Education: AB, Hamilton College, 1955; MA, University of Michigan, 1961; PhD, University of Minnesota, 1965. Appointments: Assistant Professor, Hamline University, St Paul, Minnesota, 1961-66; Professor of Literature and Director of the Writing Workshop, Eckerd College, St Petersburg, Florida, 1966-93; Fulbright Senior Lecturer, University of Warsaw, 1978-79; Visiting Distinguished Writer, University of Hawaii, 1993, University of North Carolina, Greensboro, 1996; Several Writer-in-Residencies. Publications: Lines from Neuchâtel, 1974; The Night Train and the Golden Bird, 1977; The Rat Poems, 1978; Trying to Surprise God, 1981; The Piano Tuner, 1986; Underneath the Lantern, 1987; Night Watch on the Chesapeake, 1987; Far from Home, 1988; Liquid Paper: New and Selected Poems, 1991; Scars, 1996; Campocorto, 1996. Contributions to: Periodicals. Honours: First Prize, Olivet Sonnet Competition, 1966; National Endowment for the Arts Fellowships, 1974, 1989; Gustav Davidson Memorial Award, 1976, Lucille Medwick Memorial Award, 1984, Emily Dickinson Award, 1992, Poetry Society of America; Flannery O'Connor Award, 1986; Paumanok Poetry Award, 1993; Master Artist's Fellowship, Fine Arts Work Center, Provincetown, 1995. Memberships: Academy of American Poets; National Book Critics Circle; PEN; Poetry Society of America. Address: 147 Wildwood Lane South East, St Petersburg, FL 33705, USA.

MEJIAS-LOPEZ William, b. 28 June 1959, Aguada, Puerto Rico, USA. Professor of Spanish. Education: MA, University of Puerto Rico, Aiedrat, 1983; PhD, University of California, Berkeley, 1989. Publications: Guerras de Conquista en Chile, 1990; Las Ideas de la Jerdra justa en Ercilla y La Araucana, 1992; Alnso de Escilla y prerrogativas legales, 1992; Prinicipios indigenistos de pedro de una, 1993; Ideas Reformistas en Nunez de Pineda y Basurar, 1993; Hernon Cortes y Suintoleromcia Religiosa, 1993; Testimonio jutidico de Alonso de Escilla, 1994. Honour: Ford Foundation Fellow. Memberships: Instituto de Literatura Iberuamericana; American Association of Teachers of Spanish and Portuguese. Address: Department of Espanol, Universidad de Puerto Rico, Arecibo, Puerto Rico 00613, USA.

MELCHETT Sonia. See: SINCLAIR Sonia Elizabeth.

MELCHIOR Ib (Jorgen), b. 17 Sept 1917, Copenhagen, Denmark. Author; Dramatist; Director. Education: Graduate, Stenhus College, 1936; Candidatus Philosophiae, University of Copenhagen, 1937. Appointments: Writer, Director, over 500 live and filmed TV episodes, 12 feature films, 60 documentary films, 1959-76. Publications: Order of Battle, 1972; Sleeper Agent, 1975; The Haigerloch Project, 1977; The Watchdogs of Abaddon, 1979; The Marcus Device, 1980; Hour of Vengeance, 1982; Eva, 1984; V-3, 1985; Code Name: Grand Guignol, 1987; Steps and Stairways, 1989; Quest, 1990; Hitler's Werewolves, 1991; Case by Case, 1993; Reflections on the Pool, 1997. Honours: Golden Scroll, 1976; Hamlet Award, 1982; Outstanding American-Scandinavian, 1995. Memberships: Authors Guild; Directors Guild of America; Manuscript Society; Writers Guild of America. Address: 8228 Marmont Lane, Los Angeles, CA 90069, USA.

MELDRUM James. See: BROXHOLME John Franklin.

MELEAGROU Evie, b. 28 May 1930, Nicosia, Cyprus. Author. m. Dr John Meleagrou, MD, 26 Nov 1952, 1 son, 2 daughters. Education: Diplome de la Literature Française, Athenaeum Institute, Athens; BA, University of London. Appointments: Producer, Literary Programmes, CBC, 1952-55; Editor, Cyprus Chronicles, 1960-72; Secretary, Cyprus Chronicles Cultural Centre, 1960-74; Cyprus Representative, World Writers Conference, 1965. Publications: Solomon's Family, 1957; Anonymous City, 1963; Eastern Mediterranean, 1969; Conversations with Che, 1970; Penultimate Era, 1981; Persona is the Unknown Cypriot Woman (literary essays and poetry), 1993; The Virgin Plunge in the Ocean Depths (short stories and novells), 1993; Cyprus Chronaca (historical essay), 1974-1992, 1993; Translations. Honours: Severian Literary Prize, 1945; 1st Pancyprian Prize Short Story Competition, 1952; Pancyprian Novella Competition, 1957; Cyprus National Novel Awards, 1970, 1982; Panhellenic National Novel Award, 1982. Memberships: Cyprus Chronicles Cultural Centre, general secretary; Cyprus Cultural Association of Women, General Secretary; First Cypriot Writers Association, secretary, 1961-70; Association of Greek Writers, Athens; Cyprus State Literary Awards Committee, 1969-79. Literary Agent: Dodoni Publishing House, 3 Asklipios Street, Athens, 10679, Greece. Address: 22 Messolongi Street, Nicosia, Cyprus.

MELLERS Wilfrid (Howard), b. 26 Apr 1914, Leamington, Warwickshire, England. Author; Professor of Music (retired); Composer. m. (1) Vera M Hobbs, (2) Pauline P Lewis, 3 daughters, (3) Robin S Hildyard. Education: Leamington College, 1933; BA, 1936, MA, 1938, Cambridge University; DMus, University of Birmingham, 1960. Appointments: Andrew Mellon Professor of Music, University of Pittsburgh, 1960-63; Professor of Music, University of York, 1964-81; Visiting Professor, City University, 1984-. Publications: Music and Society: England and the European Tradition, 1946; Studies in Contemporary Music, 1947; François Couperin and the French Classical Tradition, 1950, 2nd edition, revised, 1987; Music in the Making, 1952; Romanticism and the 20th Century, 1957, 2nd edition, revised, 1988; The Sonata Principle, 1957, 2nd edition, revised, 1988; Music in a New Found Land: Themes and Developments in the History of American Music, 1964, 2nd edition, revised, 1987; Harmonius Meeting: A Study of the Relationship between English Music, Poetry, and Theatre, c.1600-1900, 1965; Caliban Reborn: Renewal in Twentieth-Century Music, 1967; Twilight of the Gods: The Music of the Beatles, 1973; Bach and the Dance of God, 1980; Beethoven and the Voice of God, 1983; A Darker Shade of Pale: A Backdrop to Bob Dylan, 1984; Angels of the Night: Popular Female Singers of Our Time, 1986; The Masks of Orpheus: Seven Stages in the Story of European Music, 1987; Le Jardin Parfume: Homage to Frederico Mompou, 1989; Vaughan Williams and the Vision of Albion, 1989; The Music of Percy Grainger, 1992; Francis Poulenc, 1994. Contributions to: Reference works and journals. Honours: Honorary DPhil, City University, 1981; Officer of the Order of the British Empire, 1982. Membership: Honorary Member, Sonneck Society. Address: Oliver Sheldon House, 17 Aldwark, York, YO1 2BX, England.

MELLING John Kennedy, b. 11 Jan 1927, Westcliff-on-Sea, Essex, England. Drama Critic; Editor; Writer; Lecturer; Broadcaster; Chartered Accountant. Education: Thirsk School, 1932-38; Westcliff High School for Boys, 1938-42. Appointments: Drama Critic, The Stage, 1957-90; Editor, The Liveryman Magazine, 1970-75, Chivers Black Dagger Series of Crime Classics, 1986-91. Publications: Discovering Lost Theatres, 1969; Southend Playhouses from 1793, 1969; Discovering Theatre Ephemera, 1973; Discovering London's Guilds and Liveries, 5 editions, 1973-95; Crime Writers' Handbook of Practical Information (editor), 1989; Murder Done to Death, 1996; Scaling the High C's (with John L Brecknock), 1996. Contributions to: Newspapers and journals; Regular columnist, Crimetime. Honours: Knight Grand Cross; Order of St Michael; Crime Writers Association Award for Outstanding Services, 1989. Memberships: British Academy of Film and Television Arts; Crime Writers' Association; Fellow, Institute of Taxation; Fellow, Royal Society of Arts; Member, Fiction Awards judge, 1984-85, Committee, 1985-88, Mystery Writers of America. Address: 44 A Tranquil Vale, Blackheath, London, SE3 0BD, England.

MELLOR D(avid) H(ugh), b. 10 July 1938, England. Professor of Philosophy; Writer. Education: BA, Natural Sciences and Chemical Engineering, 1960, PhD, 1968, ScD, 1990, M in English, 1992, Pembroke College, Cambridge; MSc, Chemical Engineering, University of Minnesota, 1962. Appointments: Research Student in Philosophy, Pembroke College, 1963-68, Fellow, Pembroke College, 1965-70, University Assistant Lecturer in Philosophy, 1965-70, University Lecturer in Philosophy, 1970-83, Fellow, 1971-, and Vice-Master, 1983-87, Darwin College, University Reader in Metaphysics, 1983-85, Professor of Philosophy, 1986-, Cambridge University; Visiting Fellow in Philosophy, Australian National University, Canberra, 1975; Honorary Professor of Philosophy, University of Keele, 1989-92. Publications: The Matter of Chance, 1971; Real Time, 1981; Cambridge Studies in Philosophy, (editor), 1978-82; Matters of Metaphysics, 1991; The Facts of Causation, 1995. Contributions to: Scholarly journals. Memberships: President, Aristotelian Society, 1992-93; Fellow, British Academy; President, British Society for the Philosophy of Science, 1985-87. Address: 25 Orchard Street, Cambridge, CB1 1JS, England.

MELLOW James R(obert), b. 28 Feb 1926, Gloucester, Massachusetts, USA. Art Critic; Author. Education: BS, Northwestern University, 1950. Appointments: Staff, 1955-61, Editor-in-Chief, 1961-65, Arts Magazine; Art Critic, Art International, 1965-69, New Leader, 1969-72, New York Times, 1969-74. Publications: The Best in Arts, 1962; New York: The Art World, 1964; Charmed Circle: Gertrude Stein and Company, 1974; Nathaniel Hawthorne in His Times, 1980; Invented Lives: F Scott and Zelda Fitzgerald, 1984; Hemingway: A Life Without Consequences, 1993. Contributions to: Newspapers and journals. Honour: National Book Award, 1983. Memberships: Authors Guild; National Book Critics Circle. Address: PO Box 297, Clinton, CT 06413, USA.

MELLY (Alan) George (Heywood), b. 17 Aug 1926, Liverpool, England. Writer; Jazz Singer. Education: Private school, Buckingham. Appointments: Jazz Singer, Mick Mulligan's Band, 1949-61; Writer, Flook Strip Cartoon, 1956-71; Pop Music Critic, 1965-67; TV Critic, 1967-71, Film Critic, 1971-73, Observer Newspaper, London; Compere, George, Granada TV Show, 1974. Publications: I Flook, 1962; Owning Up, 1965; Revolt into Style, 1970; Flook by Trog, 1970; Rum, Bum and Concertina, 1977; Media Mob (with B Fantoni), 1980; Great Lovers, 1981; Tribe of One, 1981; Mellymobile, 1982; Swans Reflecting Elephants, 1982; Scouse Mouse, 1984; It's All Writ Out For You, The Life and Works of Scottie Wilson, 1986; Paris and the Surealists (with Michael Woods), 1991. Address: 33 St Lawrence Terrace, London W10 5SR, England.

MELNIKOFF Pamela Rita, b. London, England. Journalist; Author. m. Edward Harris, 29 Mar 1970. Education: North London Collegiate School. Appointments: Reporter, Feature Writer, 1960-70, Film Critic, 1970-96, The Jewish Chronicle. Publications: The Star and the Sword; Plots and Players; Prisoner in Time; The Ransomed Menorah. Librettist: Cantata Heritage, 1993. Contributions to: Jewish Quarterly; Poetry Review. Honours: Golden Pen Award; Poetry Society's Greenwood Prize. Memberships: PEN; Society of Authors; Guild of Jewish Journalists; Critics Circle. Address: 25 Furnival Street, London EC4A 1JT, England.

MELOSH Barbara, b. 19 July 1950, Salt Lake City, Utah, USA. Associate Professor of English and American Studies; Writer. m. Gary Kulik, 19 Nov 1981, 1 son. Education: AB, Middlebury College, Vermont, 1972; AM, 1975, PhD, 1979, Brown University. Appointments: Visiting Lecturer, Brown University, 1978-79; Assistant Professor, University of Wisconsin, Madison, 1979-83; Associate Curator of Medical Sciences, National Museum of American History, 1983-90; Assistant Professor, 1983-86, Associate Professor of English and American Studies, 1986-, George Mason University. Publications: The Physician's Hand: Work Culture and Conflict in American Nursing, 1983; American Nurses in Fiction (editor), 1984; Engendering Culture: Manhood and Womanhood in New Deal Public Art and Theatre, 1991; Gender and American History Since 1890 (editor), 1993. Contributions to: Books and journals. Honours: Ellen H Richards Fellow, American Association of University Women, 1976-77; Smithsonian Institution Fellow, 1980-81; George Mason-Smithsonian Fellow in New Deal Culture, 1982-83; Regents Publication Program Fellow, 1987-89. Memberships: American Historical Association; American Studies Association; Berkshire Conference on the History of Women; National Women's Studies Association; Organization of American Historians. Address: c/o Department of English, George Mason University, Fairfax, VA 22030, USA.

MELTZER David, b. 17 Feb 1937, Rochester, New York, USA. Poet; Writer; Teacher; Editor; Musician. m. Christina Meyer, 1958, 1 son, 3 daughters. Education: Los Angeles City College, 1955-56; University of California at Los Angeles, 1956-57. Appointments: Editor, Maya, 1966-71, Tree magazine and Tree Books, 1970-; Faculty, Graduate Poetics Program, 1980-, Chair, Undergraduate Writing and Literature Program, Humanities, 1988-, New College of California, San Francisco. Publications: Poetry: Poems (with Donald Schenker), 1957; Ragas, 1959; The Clown, 1960; Station, 1964; The Blackest Rose, 1964; Oyez!, 1965; The Process, 1965; In Hope I Offer a Fire Wheel, 1965; The Dark Continent, 1967; Nature Poem, 1967; Santamaya (with Jack Shoemaker), 1968; Round the Poem Box: Rustic and Domestic Home Movies for Stan and Jane Brakhage, 1969; Yesod, 1969; From Eden Book, 1969; Abulafia Song, 1969; Greenspeech, 1970; Luna, 1970; Letters and Numbers, 1970; Bronx Lil/Head of Lilian S A C, 1970; 32 Beams of Light, 1970; Knots, 1971; Bark: A Polemic, 1973; Hero/Lil, 1973; Tens: Selected Poems 1961-1971, 1973; The Eyes, the Blood, 1973; French Broom, 1973; Blue Rags, 1974; Harps, 1975; Six, 1976; Bolero, 1976; The Art, the Veil, 1981; The Name: Selected Poetry 1973-1983, 1984; Arrows: Selected Poetry 1957-1992, 1994. Novels: Orf, 1968; The Agency, 1968; The Agent, 1968; How Many Blocks in the Pile?, 1968; Lovely, 1969; Healer, 1969; Out, 1969; Glue Factory, 1969; The Martyr, 1969; Star, 1970; The Agency Trilogy, 1994; Out, 1994. Other: We All Have Something to Say to Each Other: Being an Essay Entitled "Patchen" and Four Poems, 1962; Introduction to the Outsiders, 1962; Bazascope Mother, 1964; Journal of the Birth, 1967; Isla Vista Notes: Fragmentary, Apocalyptic, Didactic Contradictions, 1970; Two-way Mirror: A Poetry Note-Book, 1977. Editor: Journal for the Protection of All Beings 1 and 3 (with Lawrence Ferlinghetti and Michael McClure), 2 volumes, 1961, 1969; The San Francisco Poets, 1971, revised as Golden Gate, 1976; Birth: An Anthology, 1973; The Secret Garden: An Anthology in the Kabbalah, 1976; Death, 1984; Reading Jazz: The White Invention of Jazz, 1993; Writing Jazz, 1997. Honours: Council of Literary Magazine Grants, 1972, 1981; National Endowment for the Arts Grants, 1974, 1975; Tombstone Award for Poetry, James Ryan Morris Memorial Foundation, 1992. Address: Box 9005, Berkeley, CA 94709, USA.

MELVILLE Anne. See: **POTTER Margaret.**

MELVILLE James. See: **MARTIN (Roy) Peter.**

MELVILLE Jennie. See: **BUTLER Gwendoline (Williams).**

MENASHE Samuel, b. 16 Sept 1925, New York, USA. Poet. Education: BA, Queen's College, Flushing, New York, 1947; Doctoral d'Universite, Sorbonne, University of Paris, 1950. Publications: The Many Named Beloved, 1961; No Jerusalem But This, 1971; Fringe of Fire, 1973; To Open, 1974; Collected Poems, 1986; Penguin Modern Poets 7, 1996. Contributions to: Periodicals. Honour: Longview Foundation Award, 1957. Membership: PEN. Address: 75 Thompson Street, Apt 15, New York, NY 10012, USA.

MENDER Mona, b. 24 May 1926, Jersey City, New Jersey, USA. Music Educator. m. Dr Irving M Mender, 25 Aug 1946, 1 son, 1 daughter. Education: BA, Mount Holyoke College; Postgraduate, Montclair College, New Jersey; The Juilliard School, New York, USA. Publications: Music Manuscript Preparation: A Concise Guide; Extraordinary Women in Support of Music. Address: PO Box 327, Basking Ridge, NJ 07920, USA.

MENDES David, (Bob Mendes), b. 15 May 1928, Antwerp, Belgium. Accountant. Education: Graduate in Accountancy, 1953. Publications: Day of Shame, 1988; The Chunnel Syndrome, 1989; The Fourth Sura, 1990; The Fraud Hunters, 1991; Vengeance, 1992; Races/Riots, 1993; Link, 1994; Merciless, 1995; Power of Fire, 1996. Translations into English and German. Honours: The Golden Halter, 1993; Dutch Award for the Best Thriller, 1993. Memberships: Flemish Writers Guild; PEN Club. Literary Agent: Dan Wright, Ann Wright Literary Agency, 136 East 56 Street, NY 10022, USA. Address: Wezelsebaan 191, B 2900 Schoten, Belgium.

MENUHIN Yehudi (Baron Stoke d'Abernon), b. 22 Apr 1916, New York, USA. (British National from 1985). m. Diana Rosamond, 1947. Education: Studied privately and with Louis Persinger, Georges Enescu and Adolph Busch. Career: Worldwide tours as violin soloist since debut at San Francisco, aged 7; Founded Menuhin School of Music at Stoke d'Abernon, Surrey, 1963; Career as Conductor from 1950s. Publications include: The Violin: Six Lessons by Yehudi Menuhin, 1971; Theme and Variationsl 1972; The Violin, 1976; Violin and Viola, (with William Primrose), 1976; Sir Edward Elgar: My Musical Grandfather, essay, 1976; Unfinished Journey, autobiography, 1977; The Music of Man, 1980; Life Class, 1986; Conversations with Menuhin, (co-author with Robin Daniels), 1979; The Complete Violinist: Thoughts, Exercises and Reflections of a Humanist Violinist, 1986. Honours include: KBE, 1965; DM, 1987; Life Peer, 1993. Address: c/o SYM Music COMpany Ltd, PO Box 6160, London SW1W 0JX, england.

MERCHANT Carolyn, b. 12 July 1936, Rochester, New York, USA. Professor; Environmental Historian. Education: AB, Vassar College, 1958; MA, History of Science, 1962, PhD, History of Science, 1967, University of Wisconsin; Doctor honoris causa, Umeå University, Sweden, 1995. Appointments: Professor of Environmental History, Philosophy, and Ethics, University of California, Berkeley; Fellowships; Consultantships; Lectureships. Publications: The Death of Nature: Women, Ecology and the Scientific Revolution, 1980, 2nd edition, 1990; Ecological Revolution: Nature, Gender, and Science in New England, 1989; Radical Ecology: The Search for a Livable World, 1992; Major Problems in Environmental History: Documents and Essays (editor), 1993; Key Concepts in Critical Theory: Ecology (editor), 1994; Earthcare: Women and the Environment, 1996. Contributions to: Scholarly journals. Honours: National Science Foundation Grants, 1976-78; National Endowment for the Humanities Grants, 1977, 1981-83; Center for Advanced Study in the Behavioural Sciences, fellow, 1978; American Council of Learned Societies Fellowship, 1978; Fulbright Senior Scholar, Umeå, Sweden, 1984; John Simon Guggenheim Fellow, 1995. Address: c/o Department of Environmental Science Policy and Management, University of California, 570 University Hall, Berkeley, CA 94720, USA.

MERCHANT William (Moelwn), b. 6 June 1913, England. Writer; Poet; Sculptor. m. Maria Eluned Hughes, 1938, 1 son, 1 daughter. Education: BA, 1st Class Honours in English, 1933, 2nd Class, 1st Division, History, 1934, MA, 1960, DLitt, 1960, University College, Cardiff. Publications: Wordsworth's Guide to the Lakes, 1952; Reynard Library Wordsworth, 1955; Shakespeare and the Artist, 1959; Creed and Drama, 1965; Comedy, 1972; Breaking the Code (poems), 1975; Essays and Studies (editor), 1977; No Dark Glass (poems), 1979; R S Thomas: A Critical Evaluation, 1979; Confrontation of Angels (poems), 1986; Jeshua (novel), 1986; Five From the Heights (novel), 1989; A Bundle of Papyrus (novel), 1989; Fragments of a Life (autobiography), 1990; Inherit the Land (short stories), 1992; Triple Heritage (novel), 1992. Contributions to: Reference works and periodicals. Honours: Honorary HLD, Wittenberg University, Ohio, 1973; Honorary Fellow, University College of Wales, 1975; Welsh Arts Council Literary Award, 1991. Membership: Fellow, Royal Society of Literature. Address: 32A Willes Road, Leamington Spa, Warwickshire, England.

MEREDITH Christopher (Laurence), b. 15 Dec 1954, Tredegar, Wales. Writer; Senior Lecturer. m. V Smythe, 1 Aug 1981, 2 sons. Education: BA (Joint Honours), Philosophy and English, University College Wales, Aberystwyth, 1976. Appointment: Senior Lecturer, University of Glamorgan. Publications: Poems: This, 1984; Snaring

Heaven, 1990. Novels: Shifts, 1988; Griffri, 1991. Contributions to: Literary magazines in Wales, England and USA. Honours: Eric Gregory Award, 1984; Welsh Arts Council Young Writer's Prize, 1985 and Fiction Prize, 1989; Griffri shortlisted for Book of the Year Award, 1992. Membership: Yr Academi Gymreig (English language Section). Address: c/o Seren Books, Wyndham Street, Bridgend, Mid Glamorgan, Wales.

MEREDITH Donald Clynton, b. 12 Apr 1938, Inglewood, California, USA. Writer. m. Jo Ann, 15 Oct 1962. Education: AA, Orange Coast College, 1959; Long Beach State College, 1959-60; San Francisco State College, 1961-62. Publications: Morning Line, 1980; Home Movies, 1982. Contributions to: Image Magazine; Texas Review; Short Story Review; Kingfisher; Folio; Slipstream; Poets and Writers; Modern Maturity Magazine; Executive Magazine. Honours: National Endowment for the Arts Grants, 1982, 1988; Pushcart Prize, 1983-84; Best Story Award, 1990. Memberships: Poets and Writers; National Writers Union. Address: 708 Gravenstein Highway North, #124, Sebastopol, CA 95472, USA.

MEREDITH William (Morris), b. 9 Jan 1919, New York, New York, USA. Poet; Professor. Education: AB, Princeton University, 1940. Appointments: Instructor in English and Woodrow Wilson Fellow in Writing, Princeton University, 1946-50; Associate Professor in English, University of Hawaii, 1950-51; Associate Professor, 1955-65, Professor in English, 1965-83, Connecticut College, New London; Instructor, Breadloaf School of English, Middlebury College, Vermont, 1958-62; Consultant in Poetry, Library of Congress, Washington, DC, 1978-80. Publications: Poetry: Love Letters from an Impossible Land, 1944; Ships and Other Figures, 1948; The Open Sea and Other Poems, 1958; The Wreck of the Thresher and Other Poems, 1964; Winter Verse, 1964; Year End Accounts, 1965; Two Pages from a Colorado Journal, 1967; Earth Walk: New and Selected Poems, 1970; Hazard, the Painter, 1975; The Cheer, 1980; Partial Accounts: New and Selected Poems, 1987. Non-Fiction: Reasons for Poetry and the Reason for Criticism, 1982; Poems Are Hard to Read, 1991. Editor: Shelley: Poems, 1962; University and College Poetry Prizes, 1964, 1966; Eighteenth-Century Minor Poets (with Mackie L Jarrell), 1968; Poets of Bulgaria (with others), 1985. Translator: Guillaume Apollinaire: Alcools: Poems, 1898-1913, 1964. Honours: Yale Series of Younger Poets Award, 1943; Harriet Monroe Memorial Prize, 1944; Rockefeller Foundation Grants, 1948, 1968; Oscar Blumenthal Prize, 1953; National Institute of Arts and Letters Grant, 1958; Loines Prize, 1966; Ford Foundation Fellowship, 1959-60; Van Wyck Brooks Award, 1971; National Endowment for the Arts Grant, 1972, Fellowship, 1984; Guggenheim Fellowship, 1975-76; International Vaptsarov Prize for Literature, Bulgaria, 1979; Los Angeles Times Prize, 1987; Pulitzer Prize in Poetry, 1988. Memberships: Academy of American Poets, chancellor; National Institute of Arts and Letters. Address: 6300 Bradley Avenue, Bethseda, MD 20817, USA.

MERRILL Christopher (Lyall), b. 24 Feb 1957, Northampton, Massachusetts, USA. Poet; Writer; Editor; Teacher. m. Lisa Ellen Gowdy, 4 June 1983, 1 daughter. Education: BA, Middlebury College, Vermont, 1979; MA, University of Washington, 1982. Appointments: Director, Santa Fe Writer's Conference, 1987-90; Founder-Director, Taos Conference on Writing and the Natural World, 1987-92, Santa Fe Literary Center, 1988-92; General Editor, Peregrine Smith Poetry Series, 1987-; Adjunct Professor, Santa Fe Community College, 1988-90; Contributing Editor, Tyuonyi, 1989-, The Paris Review, 1991-; Adjunct Faculty, Lewis and Clark College, 1993-95; Poetry Editor, Orion Magazine, 1993-; Faculty, Open Society Institute/University of Sarajevo, 1995; William H Jenks Chair in Contemporary Letters, College of the Holy Cross, 1995-. Publications: Workbook (poems), 1988; Fevers & Tides (poems), 1989; The Forgotten Language: Contemporary Poets and Nature (editor), 1991; From the Faraway Nearby: Georgia O'Keefe as Icon (with Ellen Bradbury), 1992; The Grass of Another Country: A Journey Through the World of Soccer, 1993; Watch Fire (poems), 1994; The Old Bridge: The Third Balkan War and the Age of the Refugee, 1995; What Will Suffice: Contemporary American Poets on the Art of Poetry (editor with Christopher Buckley), 1995; Only the Nails Remain: A Balkan Triptych, 1998; The Cauldron: Fifty American Poets (editor with Catherine Bowman), 1998. Contributions to: Books, journals, and periodicals. Honours: John Ciardi Fellow in Poetry, Bread Loaf Writers' Conference, 1989; Pushcart Prize in Poetry, 1990; Ingram Merrill Foundation Award in Poetry, 1991; Peter I B Lavan Younger Poets Award, Academy of American Poets, 1993. Membership: Academy of

American Poets. Address: 12 Woodstock Road, Pomfret, CT 06258, USA.

MERSSERLI Douglas John, b. 30 May 1947, Waterloo, Iowa, USA. Publisher; Poet; Writer. Education: BA, University of Wisconsin; MA, 1974, PhD, 1979, University of Maryland. Appointments: Publisher, Sun & Moon Press, 1976-; Assistant Professor, Literature, Temple University, 1979-85; Director, Contemporary Arts Education Project Inc, 1982-. Publications: Djuna Barnes: A Bibliography, 1976; Dinner on the Lawn, 1979; Some Distance, 1982; River to Rivet: A Poetic Manifesto, 1984; Language, Poetries (editor), 1987; Maxims from My Mother's Milk/Hymns to Him: A Dialogue, 1988; Silence All Round Marked: An Historical Play in Hysteria Writ, 1992; Along Without: A Film for Poetry, 1992. Contributions to: Roof; Mississippi Review; Paris Review; Boundry 2; Art Quarterly; Los Angeles Times. Membership: Modern Language Association. Address: c/o Sun & Moon Press, PO Box 481170, Los Angeles, CA 90048, USA.

MERTZ Barbara Louise Gross, (Barbara Michaels, Elizabeth Peters), b. 29 Sept 1927, Canton, Illinois, USA. Writer. div, 1 son, 1 daughter. Education: PhD, University of Chicago, 1952. Publications: Temples, Tombs & Hieroglyphs, 1964; Red Land, Black Land: The World of Ancient Egyptians, 1966; Sons of the Wolf, 1967; The Dark on the Other Side, 1970; Greygallows, 1972; The Crying Child, 1973; Wait For What Will Come, 1978; Street of the Five Moons, 1978; Summer of the Dragon, 1979; The Love Talker, 1980; The Curse of the Pharaohs, 1981; The Copenhagen Connection, 1982; Silhouette in Scarlet, 1982; Die for Love, 1984; The Mummy Case, 1985; Lion in the Valley, 1986; Trojan Gold, 1987; Deeds of the Disturber, 1988; Naked Once More, 1989; The Last Camel Died at Noon, 1991; Vanish with the Rose, 1991; Houses of Stone, 1993; The Snake, the Crocodile and the Dog, 1992; Night Train to Memphis, 1994. Contributions to: Reference works and periodicals. Honour: Doctor of Humane Letters, Hood College, 1992. Memberships: Authors Guild; Mystery Writers of America. Address: c/o Dominick Abel, 498 West End Avenue, New York, NY 10024, USA.

MERVILLON Pol-Jean. See: **NADAUS Roland.**

MERWIN W(illiam) S(tanley), b. 30 Sept 1927, New York, New York, USA. Poet; Dramatist; Writer; Translator. m. Diane Whalley, 1954. Education: AB, Princeton University, 1947. Appointments: Playwright-in-Residence, Poet's Theatre, Cambridge, Massachusetts, 1956-57; Poetry Editor, The Nation, 1962; Associate, Theatre de la Citié, Lyons, 1964-65. Publications: Poetry: A Mask for Janus, 1952; The Dancing Bears, 1954; Green with Beasts, 1956; The Drunk in the Furnace, 1960; The Moving Target, 1963; The Lice, 1967; Three Poems, 1968; Animae, 1969; The Carrier of Ladders, 1970; Signs, 1971; Writings to an Unfinished Accompaniment, 1973; The First Four Books of Poems, 1975; Three Poems, 1975; The Compass Flower, 1977; Feathers from the Hill, 1978; Finding the Islands, 1982; Opening the Hand, 1983; The Rain in the Trees, 1988; Selected Poems, 1988; Travels, 1993. Plays: Darkling Child (with Dido Milroy), 1956; Favor Island, 1957; The Gilded West, 1961; adaptations of 5 other plays. Other: A New Right Arm, n.d.; Selected Translations 1948-1968, 1968; The Miner's Pale Children, 1970; Houses and Travellers, 1977; Selected Translations 1968-1978, 1979; Unframed Originals: Recollections, 1982; Regions of Memory: Uncollected Prose 1949-1982, 1987; The Lost Upland, 1993. Editor: West Wind: Supplement of American Poetry, 1961; The Essential Wyatt, 1989. Translator: 19 books, 1959-89. Honours: Yale Series of Younger Poets Award, 1952; Bess Hokin Prize, 1962; Ford Foundation Grant, 1964; Harriet Monroe Memorial Prize, 1967; PEN Translation Prize, 1969; Rockefeller Foundation Grant, 1969; Pulitzer Prize in Poetry, 1971; Academy of American Poets Fellowship, 1973; Shelley Memorial Award, 1974; National Endowment for the Arts Grant, 1978; Bollingen Prize, 1979; Aiken Taylor Award, 1990; Maurice English Award, 1990; Dorothea Tanning Prize, 1994; Lenore Marshall Award, 1994. Memberships: Academy of American Poets; American Academy of Arts and Letters. Address: c/o Georges Borchardt Inc, 136 East 57th Street, New York, NY 10022. USA.

MESERVE Walter Joseph, b. 10 Mar 1923, Portland, Maine, USA. Distinguished Professor Emeritus; Editor; Writer. m. (1) 2 sons, 2 daughters, (2) Mollie Ann Lacey, 18 June 1981. Education: Portland Junior College, 1941-42; AB, Bates College, Lewiston, Maine, 1947; MA, Boston University, 1948; PhD, University of Washington, 1952. Appointments: Instructor to Professor, University of Kansas, 1951-68; Professor of Dramatic Literature and Theory, 1968-88, Director,

Institute for American Theatre Studies, 1983-88, Indiana University; Vice President, Feedback Services, New York City, Brooklin, Maine, 1983-; Editor-in-Chief, Feedback Theatrebooks, 1985-; Distinguished Professor, 1988-93, Distinguished Professor Emeritus, 1993-, Graduate Center, PhD Programs in Theatre and English, City University of New York; Co-Editor, American Drama and Theatre journal, 1989-93. Publications: The Complete Plays of W D Howells (editor), 1960; Outline History of American Drama, 1965, revised edition, 1994; American Satiric Comedies (co-editor), 1969; Robert E Sherwood, 1970; Modern Drama from Communist China (co-editor), 1970; Studies in Death of a Salesman (editor), 1972; Modern Literature from China (co-editor), 1974; An Emerging Entertainment: The Drama of the American People to 1828, 1977; The Revels History of Drama in English, Vol VIII: American Drama (co-author), 1977; Cry Woolf (co-author), 1982; Heralds of Promise: The Drama of the American People During the Age of Jackson 1829-1849, 1986; Who's Where in the American Theatre (co-editor), 1990, 3rd edition, 1993; A Chronological Outline of World Theatre (co-author), 1992; The Theatre Lover's Cookbook (co-editor), 1992; Musical Theatre Cookbook (co-editor), 1993. Honours: National Endowment for the Humanities Fellowships, 1974-75, 1983-84, 1988-89; Rockefeller Foundation Fellowship, 1979; Guggenheim Fellowship, 1984-85. Membership: Cosmos Club. Address: PO Box 174, Brooklin, ME 04616, USA.

MESSENT Peter Browning, b. 24 Oct 1946, Wimbledon, England. Reader in Modern American Literature. m. (1) Brenda, 10 July 1972 div, 1 son, 1 daughter, (2) Carin, 9 July 1994. Education: BA Honours, American Studies, 1969, MA, 1972, University of Manchester; PhD, University of Nottingham, 1991. Appointments: Temporary Lecturer, University of Manchester, 1972-73; Lecturer, 1973-94, Senior Lecturer in American and Canadian Studies, 1994-95, Reader in Modern American Literature, 1995-, University of Nottingham. Publications: Twentieth Century Views: Literature of the Occult (editor), 1981; New Readings of the American Novel, 1990; Ernest Hemingway, 1992; Henry James: Selected Tales (editor), 1992; Mark Twain, 1996; Criminal Proceedings (editor), 1996. Contributions to: Books, journals, and magazines. Memberships: British Association for American Studies; Mark Twain Circle. Address: c/o Department of American and Canadian Studies, University of Nottingham, Nottingham, NG7 2RD, England.

MESSER Thomas M(aria), b. 9 Feb 1920, Bratislava, Czechoslovakia (US citizen, 1944). Museum Director; Writer. m. Remedios Garcia Villa, 10 Jan 1948. Education: Institute of International Education, 1939; Thiel College, Greenville, Pennsylvania, 1939-41; BA, Boston University, 1942; Degree, Sorbonne, University of Paris, 1947; MA, Harvard University, 1951. Appointments: Director, Roswell Museum, New Mexico, 1949-52, Institute of Contemporary Art, Boston, 1957-61; Assistant Director, 1952-53, Director of Exhibitions, 1953-55, Director, 1955-56, American Federation of Arts, New York City; Adjunct Professor, Harvard University, 1960, Barnard College, 1966, 1971; Director, 1961-88, Director Emeritus, 1988-, Solomon R Guggenheim Museum, New York City; President, MacDowell Colony, 1977-78, 1993-94; Professor, Hochschule für Angewandte Kunst, Vienna, 1984, Goethe University, Frankfurt am Main, 1991-92, 1993-94, 1994-; Chief Curator, Schinn Kunsthalle, Frankfurt am Main, 1994-. Publication: Edvard Munch, 1973. Contributions to: Various museum catalogues and art journals. Honours: Chevalier, 1980, Officier, 1989, Legion d'Honneur, France. Memberships: Trustee, Fontana Foundation, Milan, 1988-; Trustee, Institute of International Education, 1991-. Address: 35 Sutton Place, New York, NY 10022, USA.

MESTAS Jean-Paul, b. 15 Nov 1925, Paris, France. Engineer; Poet; Critic; Essayist; Lecturer; Translator; Consultant. m. Christaine Schoubrenner, 23 Dec 1977, 2 sons, 1 daughter. Education: Graduated, Institute of Political Studies, Paris, 1947; LLB, 1947; BA, 1947. Publications: Soliels noirs, 1965; Part de Vivre, 1968; Resurgences, 1969; Romance Limousine, 1970; Chateau de Paille, 1971; Plaise aux souvenire, 1972; L'Aventue des choses, 1973; Le retour d'Ulysse, 1974; Traduire la Memoire, 1975; Pays Nuptial, 1977; Memoire d'Exil, 1978; Cette idee qui ne vivra pas, 1979; En ce royaume d'ombre et d'eau, 1982; Entre deux temps, 1983; En Ecoutnat vieillir les lapes, 1983; Ismene, 1984; Entre les colonns du vent, 1984; Dans la longue authomne du coeur, 1985; L'ancre et le cyclone, 1987; La terre est pleine de hailons, 1988; Entre les violons du silence, 1988; Chant pour Chris, 1989; La Lumiere arriva des mains, 1990; Roses de Sable, 1990. Contributions to: Anthologies and periodicals. Honours: Excellence in Poetry, International Poet, 1982; Premio della Cultura

Carlo Alianello, Palermo, 1991. Memberships: Associate, Emeritus Academician, International Academy of Madras; Academy of Human Sciences, Brazil; Accademia Internazionale, Naples; Life Member, International Writers and Artists, New York. Address: 65 Avenue du Parc d Proce, 44 100 Nantes, France.

MESTERHAZI Marton, b. 7 July 1941, Budapest, Hungary. Radio Drama Script Editor. m. Agnes Pécsvari, 7 July 1962, 1 son, 1 daughter. Education: MA, Hungarian, English and French, Budapest, 1964; PhD, English Literature, 1987. Publications: The World of Sean O'Casey, 1983; Sean O'Casey in Hungary, 1926-1986, 1993. Translations: The Selected Essays of Arnold J Toynbee, 1971; Ian McEwan: The Comfort of Strangers, 1984; Brian Friel: The Communication Cord, 1990. Contributions to: Nagyvilag (literary monthly). Honour: Outstanding Programmes Prizes, Hungarian Radio. Memberships: Hungarian Irish Cultural Society; Chamber of Hungarian Radio Programme Makers. Literary Agent: Artisjus, Hungarian Copywright Office. Address: Hungarian Radio, Drama H-1800, Budapest, Hungary.

METCALF John Wesley, b. 12 Nov 1938, Carlisle, England. Writer. m. Myrna Teitelbaum, 3 sons, 2 daughters. Education: BA, Bristol University, 1960. Appointments: Writer-in-Residence, University of New Brunswick, 1972-73, Loyola of Montreal, 1976, University of Ottawa, 1977, Concordia University, 1980-81, University of Bologna, 1985. Publications: The Lady Who Sold Furniture, 1970; The Teeth of My Father, 1975; Girl in Gingham, 1978; Kicking Against the Pricks, 1982; Adult Entertainment, 1986; How Stories Mean, 1993; Shooting the Stars, 1993; Freedom from Culture, 1994. Contributions to: Many Publications in Canada and USA. Honour: Canada Council Arts Awards, 1968-69, 1971, 1974, 1976, 1978, 1980, 1983, 1985. Literary Agent: Denise Bukowski, The Bukowski Agency, 125B Dupont Street, Toronto, Ontario, Canada. Address: 128 Lewis Street, Ottawa, Ontario K2P 0S7, Canada.

METZ Jerred, b. 5 May 1943, Lakewood, New Jersey, USA. Writer; Poet; Editor; Social Service Administrator. m. Sarah Barker, 14 May 1978, 1 son, 1 daughter. Education: BA, 1965, MA, 1967, University of Rhode Island; PhD, University of Minnesota, 1972. Appointment: Poetry Editor, Webster Review, 1973-. Publications: Speak Like Rain, 1975; The Temperate Voluptuary, 1976; Three Legs Up, 1977; Angels in the House, 1979; Drinking the Dipper Dry: Nine Plain-Spoken Lives, 1980; Halley's Comet: Fire in the Sky, 1985. Contributions to: Magazines and journals. Address: 56200 Jackson Street, Pittsburgh, PA 15206, USA.

METZGER Deena, b. 17 Sept 1936, Brooklyn, New York, USA. Writer; Dramatist; Teacher; Law Analyst. m. (1) H Reed Metzger, 26 Oct 1957, (2) Michael Ortiz Hill, 20 Dec 1987, 2 sons. Education: BA, Brooklyn College; MA, University of California; PhD, International College, Los Angeles. Appointments: Professor, Los Angeles Valley College, 1966-69, 1973-74, 1975-79; Faculty, California Institute of the Arts, 1970-75. Publications: In Shadows/Silence, poems, 1976; Dark Milk, 1978; The Book of Hags, 1978; The Axis Mundi, poems, 1981; What Dinah Thought, 1989; Looking for the Face of God, 1989; A Sabbath Among the Ruins, 1992; Writing for Your Life: A Guide and Companion to the Inner Worlds, 1992. Address: PO Box 186, Topanga, CA 90290, USA.

MEWSHAW Michael, b. 19 Feb 1943, Washington, District of Columbia, USA. Author; Poet. m. Linda Kirby, 17 June 1967, 2 sons. Education: MA, 1966, PhD, 1970, University of Virginia. Appointments: Instructor, 1970, Visiting Writer, 1989-91, University of Virginia; Assistant Professor of English, University of Massachusetts, 1970-71; Assistant Professor to Associate Professor of English, University of Texas, Austin, 1973-83; Visiting Artist, 1975-76, Writer-in-Residence, 1977-78, American Academy, Rome. Publications: Fiction: Man in Motion, 1970; Waking Slow, 1972; The Troll, 1974; Earthly Bread, 1976; Land Without Shadow, 1979; Year of the Gun, 1984; Blackballed, 1986; True Crime, 1991; Non-fiction: Life for Death, 1980; Short Circuit, 1983; Money to Burn: The True Story of the Benson Family Murders, 1987; Playing Away: Roman Holidays and Other Mediterranean Encounters, 1988; Ladies of the Court: Grace and Disgrace on the Women's Tennis Tour, 1993. Contributions to: Newspapers and magazines. Honours: Fulbright Fellowship, 1968-69; William Rainey Fellowship, 1970; National Endowment for the Arts Fellowship, 1974-75; Carr Collins Awards for Best Book of Non-Fiction, 1980, 1983; Guggenheim Fellowship, 1981-82; Book of the Year Award, Tennis Week, 1993. Memberships: PEN; Phi Beta Kappa;

Society of Fellows of the American Academy in Rome; Texas Institute of Letters; US Tennis Writers Association. Address: c/o William Morris Agency, 1350 Sixth Avenue, New York, NY 10019, USA.

MEYER Ben F(ranklin), b. 5 Nov 1927, Chicago, Illinois, USA. Professor of Religious Studies; Writer. m. Denise Oppliger, 27 Mar 1969. Education: BA, 1952, MA, 1953; STM, University of Santa Clara, 1958; SSL, Biblical Institute, Rome, 1961; STD, Gregorian University, Rome, 1965. Appointments: Assistant Professor of Religion, Graduate Theological Union, Berkeley, 1965-68; Associate Professor, 1969-74, Professor of Religious Studies, 1974-, McMaster University, Hamilton, Ontario. Publications: The Man for Others, 1970; The Church in Three Tenses, 1971; The Aims of Jesus, 1979; The Early Christians, 1986; Critical Realism and the New Testament, 1989; Lonergan's Hermenuetics (editor with S E McEvenue), 1989; Christus Faber: The Master Builder and the House of God, 1992; One Loaf, One Cup, 1993; Five Speeches That Changed the World, 1994; Reality and Illusion in New Testament Scholarship, 1995. Contributions to: Professional journals. Memberships: President, Canadian Society of Biblical Studies, 1988-89; Society of Biblical Literature; Studiorum Novi Testament Societas. Address: c/o Department of Religious Studies, McMaster, University, Hamilton, Ontario L8S 4K1, Canada.

MEYER E Y, b. 11 Oct 1946, Liestal, Switzerland. Novelist; Essayist; Dramatist. m. Florica Malureanu. Publications: Ein Reisender in Sachen Umsturz, 1972; In Trubschachen, 1973; Eine entfernte Aehnlichkeit, 1975; Die Ruckfahrt, 1977; Die Halfte der Erfahrung, 1980; Playdoyer, 1982; Sundaymorning, 1984; Das System des Doktor Maillard oder Die Welt der Maschinen, 1994. Contributions to: Numerous periodicals. Honours: Literature Prize of the Province of Basel, 1976; Gerhart Hauptmann Prize, 1983; Prize of the Swiss Schiller Foundation, 1984; Welti Prize for the Drama, 1985. Memberships: Swiss Writers Association; Swiss-German PEN Centre. Address: Brunnen-Gut, CH-3027 Bern, Switzerland.

MEYER June. See: **JORDAN June.**

MEYER Lynn. See: **SLAVITT David Rytman.**

MEYER Michael (Leverson), b. 11 June 1921, London, England. Writer; Dramatist; Translator. 1 daughter. Education: MA, Christ Church, Oxford. Appointments: Lecturer in English Literature, Uppsala University, 1947-50; Visiting Professor of Drama, Dartmouth College, 1978, University of Colorado, 1986, Colorado College, 1988, Hofstra University, 1989, University of California, Los Angeles, 1991. Publications: Eight Oxford Poets (editor with Sidney Keyes), 1941; Collected Poems of Sidney Keyes (editor), 1945; Sidney Keyes: The Minos of Crete (editor), 1948; The End of the Corridor (novel), 1951; The Ortolan (play), 1967; Henrik Ibsen: The Making of a Dramatist, 1967; Henrik Ibsen: The Farewell to Poetry, 1971; Henrik Ibsen: The Top of a Cold Mountain, 1971; Lunatic and Lover (play), 1981; Summer Days (editor), 1981; Ibsen on File, 1985; Strindberg: A Biography, 1985; File on Strindberg, 1986; Not Prince Hamlet (memoirs), US edition as Words Through a Windowpane, 1989; The Odd Women (play), 1993. Other: Numerous translations, including all sixteen plays by Ibsen (1960-86) and eighteen by Strindberg (1964-91). Honours: Gold Medal, Swedish Academy, 1964; Whitbread Biography Prize, 1971; Knight Commander of the Order of the Polar Star, Sweden, 1977; Royal Norwegian Order of Merit, 1995. Membership: Fellow, Royal Society of Literature. Address: 4 Montagu Square, London W1H 1RA, England.

MEYERS Jeffrey, b. 1 Apr 1939, New York, New York, USA. Writer. Education: BA, University of Michigan, 1959; MA, 1961, PhD, 1967, University of California at Berkeley. Publications: Fiction and the Colonial Experience, 1973; The Wounded Spirit: A Study of Seven Pillars of Wisdom, 1973; T E Lawrence: A Bibliography, 1975; A Reader's Guide to George Orwell, 1975; George Orwell: The Critical Heritage, 1975; Painting and the Novel, 1975; A Fever at the Core, 1976; George Orwell: An Annotated Bibliography of Criticism, 1977; Married to Genius, 1977; Homosexuality and Literature, 1890-1930, 1977; Katherine Mansfield: A Biography, 1978; The Enemy: A Biography of Wyndham Lewis, 1980; Wyndham Lewis: A Revolution, 1980; D H Lawrence and the Experience of Italy, 1982; Hemingway: The Critical Heritage, 1982; Disease and the Novel, 1860-1960, 1984; Hemingway: A Biography, 1985; D H Lawrence and Tradition, 1985; The Craft of Literary Biography, 1985; The Legacy of D H Lawrence, 1987; Manic Power: Robert Lowell and His Circle, 1987; Robert Lowell: Interviews and Memoirs, 1988; The Biographer's Art, 1989; The Spirit

of Biography, 1989; T E Lawrence: Soldier, Writer, Legend, 1989; Graham Greene: A Revaluation, 1989; D H Lawrence: A Biography, 1990; Joseph Conrad: A Biography, 1991; Edgar Allan Poe: His Life and Legacy, 1992; Scott Fitzgerald: A Biography, 1994; Edmund Wilson: A Biography, 1995; Robert Frost: A Biography, 1996; Bogart: A Life in Hollywood, 1997. Membership: Royal Society of Literature. Literary Agent: Sandy Dijkstra Agency. Address: 84 Stratford Road, Kensington, CA 94707, USA.

MEYLAKH Michael, b. 20 Dec 1944, Tashkent. Translator; Journalist; Literary Critic; Poet. m. Rita Ilukhin, 24 Dec 1989. Education: University of Leningrad, 1967; Institute of Linguistics, Academy of Sciences, 1967-70. Appointment: La Pensée Russe, Correspondent, 1988-. Publications: V Nabokov, (translations); The Language of the Troubadours; Daniel Harm's Collected Works; Alexander Vvedensky's Complete Works; Anna Akhmatova's Poems; The Lives of the Troubadours, 1994; The OBERIU Poets, 1994. Contributions to: La Pensée Russe; Financial Times; Times Literary Supplement; Continent. Honour: Political Prisoner in Russia, 1983-87. Memberships: PEN; Association Internationale d'Études Occiaties; Union of Russian Authors; Union of Russian Journalists. Address: Bolchoy 21-v, Komarovo, St Petersburg, Russia 189643.

MEYNELL Hugo Anthony, b. 23 Mar 1936, England. m. 24 Feb 1969, 1 adopted son, 3 daughters. Education: Eton College, 1949-54; Cambridge University, 1959. Appointments: Lecturer, University of Leeds, 1961-81; Visiting Professor, Emory University, 1978; Professor, Religious Studies, University of Calgary, 1981. Publications: Introduction to the Philosophy of Bernard Lonergan; The Intelligible Universe; Freud, Marx and Morals; The Art of Handel's Operas; The Nature of Aesthetic Value; Is Christianity True? Contributions to: New Scholastic; Heythrop Journal; New Blackfriars. Memberships: Canadian Society for Religious Studies; Canadian Philosophical Association; Royal Society of Canada. Address: Department of Religious Studies, University of Calgary, Calgary, Alberta T2N 1N4, Canada.

MEZEY Katalin, b. 30 May 1943, Budapest, Hungary. Poet; Writer; Journalist; Translator. m. Janos Olah, 1 Mar 1971, 2 sons, 1 daughter. Education: Philology, German Literature, Universty of Zürich, 1964; Philology, Hungarian Literature and Adult Education, Eötvös University, Budapest. Appointments: Founder-Editor, Szephalom Konyvmuhely, publishers, 1989-; Secretary, 1987-92, General Secretary, 1992-, Trade Union of Hungarian Writers. Publications: 11 books, 1970-94. Address: Pesthidegkut 2 pf 5, Budapest 1286, Hungary.

MFAUME Rogers, b. 20 June 1946, Tanga, Tanzania. Lawyer; Journalist; Editor; Writer. Education: University of Leningrad, 1988; University of Kharkov; MA, University of Tashkent. Appointment: Lecturer, Århus Centre for Kiswahili Language; Editor-in-Chief, Afro-New Magazine. Publications: Kiswahili for All, Part 1, 1990, Part 2, 1992; Juvenile Deliquency, 1994. Membership: Danish Writers' Union. Address: PO Box 2641, Arhus, DK-8200, Denmark.

MIALL Robert. See: **BURKE John Frederick.**

MICHAEL Donnelly. See: **CARROLL Paul.**

MICHAEL John. See: **CRICHTON Michael.**

MICHAEL John A, b. 5 Jan 1921, West Chester, Ohio, USA. Art Education Professor. m. Betty J Shewalter, 14 June 1958, 1 son, 1 daughter. Education: BS in Education, Ohio State University, 1942; MEd, University of Cinncinnati, 1948; DEd, Pennsylvania State University, 1959. Appointments: Teacher, Cinncinnati Public Schools, Fairview Hoffman and Hughes School, 1942-59; Art Supervisor, Finneytown Schools, 1959-61; Professor, 1961-85, Professor Emeritus, 1985-, Miami University of Ohio. Publications: Art Education in the Junior High School (editor), 1964; A Handbook for Art Instructors and Students Based Upon Concepts and Behaviours, 1970; The Lowenfeld Lectures (editor), 1982; Art and Adolescence, Teaching Art at the Secondary Level, 1983; Visual Arts Resource Handbook (editor), 1993; The National Art Education Association: Our History Celebrating 50 Years (editor/archivist), 1947-97, 1997. Contributions to: Art Teacher; Art Education; NAEA Newsletter; OAEA Journal; Ohio Artline; School Arts; Studies in Art Education: Arts and Activities; Arts at Miami; Issues in Art Education; Proceedings - Lifelong Learning; The Working Craftsman; Women's Caucus Report. Honours: Ohio Art

Educator of the Year, 1980, 1984; National Retired Art Educator of the Year, 1985; Lowenfeld Memorial Lecture Award, 1984; Marion Quin Dix Award, 1986; June King McFee Award, 1989; Miami University Achievement Award, 1991; National Art Educator of the Year, 1993; Penn State Leadership and Service Award, 1995; SRAE Marilyn Zurmuehlen Research Award, 1997. Memberships: Cincinnati McDowell Society; National Art Education Association; Ohio Art Education Association. Address: 5300 Hamilton Avenue, #203, Cincinnati, Ohio 45224-3152, USA.

MICHAEL Judith (pseudonym of husband and wife, Judith Barnard and Michael Fain). Publications: Deceptions; Possessions; Private Affairs; A Ruling Passion; Inheritance; Sleeping Beauty; Pot of Gold, 1993; A Tangled Web, 1994. Address: c/o Ann Patty, Editor-in-Chief, Crown Books, 201 East 50th Street, New York, NY 10022, USA.

MICHAELIS Bo Tao, b. 19 July 1948, Copenhagen, Denmark. Teacher; Critic; Author. m. Annette Gertrud Begtorp, 9 Oct 1976, 1 son, 1 daughter. Education: Sorbonne, University of Paris, 1969-70; University of Copenhagen. Appointments: Critic, Berlingkse Tidende, 1984-89; Reader, Gyldendal, 1985-; Chairman, Palle Rosenkrantz, 1989-; Film Critic, Teacher, Danish Filmschool, 1989-. Publications: Portrait of the Private Eye as a Petit Bourgeois; An Analysis of the Philip Marlowe Novels by Raymond Chandler; Lyst af Labyrint. Contributions to: Periodicals. Memberships: Danish Writers Union; Academy of Danish Crime Literatre; Union of Grammar School Teachers. Address: Standboulevarden 7, 4th 200 Copenhagen O, Denmark.

MICHAELS Barbara. See: **MERTZ Barbara Louise Gross.**

MICHAELS Dale. See: **RIFKIN Shepard.**

MICHAELS Kristin. See: **WILLIAMS Jeanne.**

MICHAELS Steve. See: **AVALLONE Michael (Angelo Jr).**

MICHAELS Wendy Faye, b. 25 May 1943, Melbourne, Victoria, Australia. Consultant. 3 sons. Education: BA; MA, Graduate Diploma, Educational Studies; ATCL; ASDA; MACE, PhD in progress. Publications: Played upon a Stage; When the Hurly Burly is Done; Up and Away; Inside Drama; Played upon Shakespeare's Stage; The Playwright At Work; A Deed without a Name; A Madman Shakes a Dead Geranium. Contributions to: Jeda; EQ; Nadie Journal; Australian. Membership: Australian Society of Authors. Address: 2 Marooba Road, Northbridge, New South Wales 2063, Australia.

MICHENER James Albert, b. 3 Feb 1907, New York, New York, USA. Writer. m. (1) Patti Koon, 1935, div, (2) Vange Nord, 1948, div, (3) Mari Yoriko Sabusawa, 1955. Education: Swarthmore College; Colorado State College of Education; Ohio State University; University of Pennsylvania; University of Virginia; Harvard University and St Andrews. Publications: Unit in the Social Studies, 1940; Tales of the South Pacific, 1947; The Fires of Spring, 1949; Return to Paradise, 1951; The Bridges at Toko R, 1953; Floating World, 1955; The Bridge at Andau, 1957; Selected Writings, 1957; The Hokusai Sketchbook, 1958; Japanese Prints, 1959; Report of the Country Chairman, 1961; The Source, 1965; The Quality of Life, 1970; Kent State, 1971; The Drifters, 1971; Centennial, 1974; Sports in America, 1976; Poland, 1983; Legacy, 1987; The World in My Home, 1992; Writers Handbook, 1992; My Lost Mexico, 1992; Creatures of the Kingdom, 1993; Literary Reflections, 1993; Recessional, 1994; This Noble Land: My Vision for America, 1996. Honours: Pulitzer Prize, 1947; Einstein Award, 1957; Medal of Freedom, 1977; Gold Medal Spanish Institute, 1980. Address: Texas Center for Writers, University of Texas, Austin, TX 78713, USA.

MICHIE Jonathan, b. 25 Mar 1957, London, England. Economist. m. Carolyn Downs, 5 Nov 1988, 2 sons. Education: Balliol College, Oxford University, 1976-79, 1980-85; Queen Mary College, London University, 1979-80. Publications: The Economic Legacy; Wages in the Business Cycle; Beyond the Casino Economy; The Economics of Restructuring and Intervention; Unemployment in Europe, 1994; Managing the Global Economy, 1995; Creating Industrial Capacity, 1996; Firms, Organizations and Contracts, 1997; Employment and Economic Performance, 1997; Technology, Globalisation and Economic Performance, 1997. Address: Birkbeck College, University of London, London, England.

MIDDLETON Christopher, b. 10 June 1926, Truro, Cornwall, England. University Teacher. Education: BA, 1951, DPhil, 1954, University of Oxford. Publications: Torse 3, 1962; Nonsequences, 1965; Our Flowers and Nice Bones, 1969; The Lonely Suppers of W V Balloon, 1975; Carminalenia, 1980; Serpentine, 1985; Two Horse Wagon Going By, 1986; Selected Writings, 1989; The Balcony Tree, 1992; The Pursuit of the Kingfisher Essays, 1993; Intimate Chronicles, 1996. Honours: Sir Geoffrey Faber Memorial Prize, 1963; Guggenheim Fellowship, 1974-75; Schlegel Tieck Translation Prize, 1985. Address: Germanic Languages, EPS 3 154, University of Texas at Austin, Austin, TX 78712, USA.

MIDDLETON Osman Edward, b. 25 Mar 1925, Christchurch, New Zealand. Writer; Author. m. 1949, div, 1 son, 1 daughter. Education: Auckland University College, 1946, 1948; University of Paris, 1955-56. Appointments: Robert Burns Fellow, University of Otago, 1970-71; Visiting Lecturer, University of Canterbury, 1971, also universities of Zürich, Frankfurt, Giessen, Kiel, Erlangen, Regensburg, Turin, Bologna, Pisa, Venice, Rome, 1983; Writer-in-Residence, Michael Karolyi Memorial Foundation, Vence, France, 1983. Publications: 10 Stories, 1953; The Stone and Other Stories, 1959; From the River to the Tide (juvenile), 1962; A Walk on the Beach, 1964; The Loners, 1972; Selected Stories, 1976; Confessions of an Ocelot, 1979. Contributions to: Anthologies worldwide; Numerous magazines and journals. Honours: Achievement award, 1959, Scholarship in Letters, 1965, NZ Literary Fund; Hubert Church Prose Award, 1964; Joint Winner, New Zealand Prose Fiction Award, 1976. Memberships: New Zealand Association of the Blind and Partially Blind, committee, 1970-95. Address: 20 Clifford Street, Dalmore, Dunedin, New Zealand.

MIDDLETON Roger, b. 19 May 1955, England. Economist. Education: BA, First Class Honours, Victoria University of Manchester, 1976; PhD, Cambridge University, 1981. Appointments: Lecturer in Economic History, University of Durham, 1979-87; Senior Lecturer in Economic History, University of Bristol, 1987-. Publications: Towards the Managed Economy, 1985; Government Versus the Market, 1996. Contributions to: Economic, History and Computing journals. Honours: T S Ashton Prize, Economic History Society, 1980; Choice of Outstanding Academic Book (for Government versus the Market), 1996; Royal Historical Society, fellow. Memberships: Royal Economic Society; Economic History Society; Conference of Socialist Economists; Association of History and Computing; Institute of Fiscal Studies. Address: Department of Economic and Social History, University of Bristol, Bristol BS1 1TB, England.

MIDDLETON Stanley, b. 1 Aug 1919, Bulwell, Nottingham, England. Writer. m. Margaret Shirley Charnely, 21 Dec 1951, 2 daughters. Education: BA, University of London, 1940; MEd, University of Nottingham, 1952. Publications: Harris's Requiem, 1960; Holiday, 1974; Two Brothers, 1978; In a Strange Land, 1979; Blind Understanding, 1982; Entry into Jerusalem, 1983; Recovery, 1988; Changes and Chances, 1990; Vacant Places, 1990; Valley of Decision, 1990; A Place to Stand, 1992; Married Past Redemption, 1993; Catalysts, 1994; Toward the Sea, 1995; Live and Learn, 1996; Brief Hours, 1997. Contributions to: Journals and magazines. Honours: Booker Prize, 1974; Honorary MA, University of Nottingham, 1975; M Univ, Open University. Memberships: PEN. Address: 42 Caledon Road, Sherwood, Nottingham, England.

MIDWINTER Eric, b. 11 Feb 1932, England. Educator. m. 2 sons, 1 daughter. Education: BA, Hons, History, St Catherine's College, Cambridge; MA, Education, Universities of Liverpool; DPhil, York. Appointments: Director, Liverpool Education Priority Area Project, 1968-72; Head of the Public Affairs Unit, National Consumer Council, London, 1975-80; Chair, London Regional Passengers' Committee, 1978-96; Director, Centre for Policy on Ageing, London, 1980-91; Visiting Professor of Education, Exeter University, 1993-; Chair, Community Education Development Centre, 1995-. Publications: Victorian Social Reform, 1968; Nineteenth Century Education, 1970; Old Liverpool, 1971; Social Environment and the Urban School, 1972; Priority Education, 1972; Patterns of Community Education, 1973; Education and the Community, 1975; Education for Sale, 1977; Schools in Society, 1980; W G Grace: His Life and Times, 1981; Age is Opportunity: Education and Older People, 1982; Fair Game: Myth and Reality in Sport, 1986; The Lost Seasons, 1987; The Old Order: Crime and Older People, 1990; Out of Focus: Old Age, Press and Broadcasting, 1991; Brylcreem Summer: The 1947 Summer, 1991; Illustrated History of County Cricket, 1992; Lifelines,

1994; The Development of Social Welfare in Britain, 1994; First Knock: Cricket's Opening Pairs, 1994; State Educator: The Life and Enduring Influence of W E Forster, 1995; Darling Old Oval: History of Surrey County Cricket Club, 1995. Honours: Officer of the Order of the British Empire, 1992; Honorary Doctorate, Open University. Address: Savage Club, 6 Whitehall Place, London SW14 2HD, England.

MIKHAIL Edward H(alim), b. 29 June 1926, Cairo, Egypt. Professor of English Literature; Writer. Education: BA, 1947, BEd, 1949, University of Cairo; DES, Trinity College, Dublin, 1959; PhD, University of Sheffield, 1966. Appointments: Lecturer to Assistant Professor, University of Cairo, 1949-66; Associate Professor, 1966-72, Professor of English Literature, 1972-, University of Lethbridge. Publications: The Social and Cultural Setting of the 1890's, 1969; John Galsworthy the Dramatist, 1971; Comedy and Tragedy: A Bibliography of Criticism, 1972; Sean O'Casey: A Bibliography of Criticism, 1972; A Bibliography of Modern Irish Drama 1899-1970, 1972; Dissertations on Anglo-Irish Drama, 1973; The Sting and the Twinkle: Conversations with Sean O'Casey (co-editor), 1974; J M Synge: A Bibliography of Critics, 1975; Contemporary British Drama 1950-1976: An Annotated Critical Bibliography, 1976; W B Yeats: Interviews and Recollections, 1977; J M Synge: Interviews and Recollections, 1977; English Drama 1900-1950, 1977; Oscar Wilde: An Annotated Bibliography of Criticism, 1978; A Research Guide to Modern Irish Dramatists, 1979; Oscar Wilde: Interviews and Recollections, 1979; The Art of Brendan Behan, 1979; Brendan Behan: An Annotated Bibliography of Criticism, 1980; An Annotated Bibliography of Modern Anglo-Irish Drama, 1982; Brendan Behan: Interviews and Recollections, 1982; Sean O'Casey and His Critics, 1985; The Abbey Theatre, 1987. Contributions to: Journals. Address: 6 Coachwood Point West, Lethbridge, Alberta T1J 4B3, Canada.

MIKKOLA Marja-Leena (Pirinen), b. 18 Mar 1939, Salo, Finland. Writer. Education: Candidate of Philosophy, Helsinki University, 1963. Publications: Naisia, 1962; Raskas Puuvilla, 1971; Laakarin Rouva, 1972; Anni Manninen, 1977; Maailman Virrassa, 1981; Jalkeen Kello Kymmenen, 1984. Translations of Poetry: Sylvia Plath: Sanantuojat, 1987; Dylan Thomas: Rakkaus on Viimeinen Valo, 1990; Anna Akhmatova: Runoja, 1992. Contributions to: Parnasso; Kultuurivihkot. Honours: Eino Leino Award, 1968; State Prizes for Literature, 1971, 1972, 1977, 1984. Membership: Finnish Writers Union. Literary Agent: Tammi, Helsinki. Address: Kalervonk 12 c 16, 00610 Helsinki, Finland.

MIKLOWITZ Gloria, b. 18 May 1927, New York, New York, USA. Writer. m. Julius Miklowitz, 28 Aug 1948, 2 sons. Education: Hunter College, New York City, 1944-45; BA, University of Michigan, 1948; New York University, 1948. Appointment: Instructor, Pasadena City College, 1970-80. Publications: Some 45 books for children, 1964-96. Contributions to: Newspapers, journals and magazines. Honours: Western Australia Young Book Award, 1984; Bucks Herald for Teens Publishers Award, 1990; Wyoming Soaring Eagle Award, 1993. Memberships: PEN; Society of Children's Book Writers. Address: 5255 Vista Miguel Drive, La Canada, CA 91011, USA.

MILES Betty, b. 16 May 1928, Chicago, Illinois, USA. Writer. m. Matthew B Miles, 27 Sept 1949, 1 son, 1 daughter. Education: BA, Antioch College, 1950. Publications: 14 picture books for children, 1958-95; 10 books for young adults, 1974-91. Address: 94 Sparkhill Avenue, Tappan, NY 10983, USA.

MILES Jack, b. 30 July 1942, Chicago, Illinois, USA. Journalist; Critic; Educational Administrator. m. Jacqueline Russiano, 23 Aug 1980, 1 daughter. Education: LittB, Xavier University, Cincinnati, 1964; PhB, Pontifical Gregorian University, Rome, 1966; Hebrew University, Jerusalem, 1966-67; PhD, Harvard University, 1971. Appointments: Assistant Professor, Loyola University, Chicago, 1970-74; Assistant Director, Scholars Press, Missoula, Montana, 1974-75; Postdoctoral Fellow, University of Chicago, 1975-76; Editor, Doubleday & Co, New York City, 1976-78; Executive Editor, University of California Press at Berkeley, 1978-85; Book Editor, 1985-91, Member, Editorial Board, 1991-95, Los Angeles Times; Director, Humanities Center, Claremont Graduate School, California, 1995-. Publications: Retroversion and Text Criticism, 1984; God: A Biography, 1995. Contributions to: Many periodicals. Honours: Guggenheim Fellowship, 1990-91; Research Fellow, Gould Center for Humanistic Studies, McKenna College, Claremont, California, 1991-; Pulitzer Prize in Biography, 1996. Memberships: American Academy of Religion; Amnesty International; National Books Critics Circle, president, 1990-92; PEN. Address:

Graduate Center, Claremont Graduate School, Claremont, CA 91711, USA.

MILES John. See: **BICKHAM Jack (Miles)**.

MILIONIS Christoforos, b. 4 Nov 1932, Greece. Writer. m. Tatiana Tsaliki, 28 Dec 1969, 1 daughter. Education: Diploma, Classical Greek Literature. Publications: Novels: Acrokeraunia, 1976; Dytiki Synicia, 1980; Silvestros, 1987. Short stories: The Short Stories of Trial, 1978; The Shirt of Centaur, 1982; Kalamas ke Acherontas, 1985; Chiristis Anelkystiros, 1993. Contributions to: Various publications. Honour: 1st State Award for Short Stories, 1986. Memberships: Society of Greek Writers; Union of Greek Philologists. Address: 1 Agathiou Street, Athens 11472, Greece.

MILKOMANE George Alexis Milkomanovich, (George Bankoff, George Borodin, George Braddin, Peter Conway, Alex Redwood, George Sava), b. 15 Oct 1903. Author; Consulting Surgeon. m. Jannette Hollingdale, 1939, 2 sons. 2 daughters. Publications: Autobiographical and Medical: The Healing Knife, 1937; Beauty from the Surgeon's Knife, 1938; A Surgeon's Destiny, 1939; Donkey's Serenade, 1940; Twice the Clock Round, 1941; A Ring at the Door, 1941; Surgeon's Symphony, 1944; They Come by Appointment, 1946; The Knife Heals Again, 1948; The Way of a Surgeon, 1949; Strange Cases, 1950; A Doctor's Odyssey, 1951; Patients' Progress, 1952; A Surgeon Remembers, 1953; Surgeon Under Capricorn, 1954; The Lure of Surgery, 1955; A Surgeon at Large, 1957; Surgery and Crime, 1957; All this and Surgery Too, 1958; Surgery Holds the Door, 1960; A Surgeon in Rome, 1961; A Surgeon in California, 1962; Appointments in Rome, 1963; A Surgeon in New Zealand, 1964; A Surgeon in Cyprus, 1965; A Surgeon in Australia, 1966; Sex, Surgery, People, 1967; The Gates of Heaven are Narrow, 1968; Bitter Sweet Surgery, 1969; One Russian's Story, 1970; A Stranger in Harley Street, 1970; A Surgeon and his Knife, 1978; Living with your Psoriasis (essays), 1978. Political and Historical: Rasputin Speaks, 1941; Valley of Forgotten People, 1942; The Chetniks, 1943; School for War, 1943; They Stayed in London, 1943; Russia Triumphant, 1944; A Tale of Ten Cities, 1944; War Without Guns, 1944; Caught by Revolution, 1952. Novels: Land Fit for Heroes, 1945; Link of Two Hearts, 1945; Gissy, 1946; Call it Life, 1946; Boy in Samarkand, 1950; Flight from the Palace, 1953; Pursuit in the Desert, 1955; The Emperor Story, 1959; Punishment Deferred, 1966; Man Without Label, 1967; Alias Dr Hotzman, 1968; City of Cain, 1969; The Imperfect Surgeon, 1969; Nothing Sacred, 1970; Of Guilt Possessed, 1970; A Skeleton for My Mate, 1971; The Beloved Nemesis, 1971; On the Wings of Angels, 1972; The Sins of Andrea, 1972; Tell Your Grief Softy, 1972; Cocaine for Breakfast, 1973; Return from the Valley, 1973; Sheilah of Buckleigh Manor, 1974; Every Sweet Hath Its Sour, 1974; The Way of the Healing Knife, 1976; Mary Mary Quite Contrary, 1977; Crusader's Clinic, 1977; Pretty Polly, 1977; No Man is Perfect, 1978; A Stranger in his Skull, 1979; Secret Surgeon, 1979; Crimson Eclipse, 1980; Innocence on Trial, 1981; The Price of Prejudice, 1982; The Killer Microbes, 1982; Betrayal in Style, 1983; Double Identity, 1984; A Smile Through Tears, 1985; Bill of Indictment, 1986; Rose By Any Other Name, 1987; The Roses Bloom Again, 1988; numerous novels as Geoge Broodin. Address: c/o A P Watt Ltd, 20 John Street, London WC1N 2DR, England.

MILLAR Sir Ronald (Graeme), b. 12 Nov 1919, Reading, England. Dramatist; Screenwriter; Author. Education: King's College, Cambridge. Appointments: Actor; Screenwriter, Hollywood, 1948-54. Publications: Plays: Frieda, 1946; Champagne for Delilah, 1948; Waiting for Gillian, 1954; The Bride and the Bachelor, 1956; The More the Merrier, 1960; The Bride Comes Back, 1960; The Affair (after C P Snow), 1961; The New Men (after C P Snow), 1962; The Masters (after C P Snow), 1963; Number 10, 1967; Abelard and Heloise, 1970; The Case in Question (after C P Snow), 1975; A Coat of Varnish (after C P Snow), 1982. Musicals: Robert and Elizabeth, 1964; On The Level, 1966. Autobiography: A View from the Wings, 1993. Honour: Knighted, 1980. Address: 7 Sheffield Terrace, London W8 7NG, England.

MILLARD Hamilton. See: **KIRK-GREENE Anthony**.

MILLER Arthur, b. 17 Oct 1915, New York, New York, USA. Dramatist; Writer. m. (1) Mary G Slattery, 5 Aug 1940, div 1956, 1 son, 1 daughter, (2) Marilyn Monroe, June 1956, div 1961, (3) Ingeborg Morath, Feb 1962, 1 son, 1 daughter. Education: AB, University of Michigan, 1938. Publications: Plays: Honors at Dawn, 1936; No Villain:

They Too Arise, 1937; The Man Who Had All the Luck, 1944; That They May Win, 1944; All My Sons, 1947; Death of a Salesman, 1949; The Crucible, 1953; A View from the Bridge, 1955; A Memory of Two Mondays, 1955; After the Fall, 1964; Incident at Vichy, 1964; The Price, 1968; Fame, 1970; The Reason Why, 1970; The Creation of the World and Other Business, 1972; Up From Paradise, 1974; The Archbishop's Ceiling, 1976; The American Clock, 1983; Some Kind of Love Story, 1983; Elegy for a Lady, 1983; Playing for Time, 1986; Danger Memory!, 1986; The Last Yankee, 1990; The Ride Down Mt Morgan, 1991; Broken Glass, 1994. Screenplays: The Story of G I Joe, 1945; The Witches of Salem, 1958; The Misfits, 1961; The Hook, 1975; Everybody Wins, 1990; Other: Situation Normal, 1944; Focus, 1945; Jane's Blanket, 1963; I Don't Need You Anymore, 1967; In Russia, 1969; In the Country, 1977; The Theatre Essays of Arthur Miller, 1978; Chinese Encounters, 1979; Salesman in Beijing, 1987; Timebends: A Life, 1987; The Misfits and Other Stories, 1987; Homely Girl, 1994. Honours: New York Drama Critics Circle Awards, 1947, 1949; Tony Awards, 1947, 1949, 1953; Donaldson Awards, 1947, 1949, 1953; Pulitzer Prize in Drama, 1949; Obie Award, 1958; National Institute of Arts and Letters Gold Medal, 1959; Brandeis University Creative Arts Award, 1970; George Foster Peabody Award, 1981; Emmy Awards, 1981, 1985; Literary Lion Award, New York Public Library, 1983; John F Kennedy Lifetime Achievement Award, 1984; Algur Meadows Award, Southern Methodist University, 1991. Memberships: American Academy of Arts and Letters; President, International PEN, 1965-69. Address: Tophet Road, Roxbury, CT 06783, USA.

MILLER Donald George, b. 30 Oct 1909, Braddock, Pennsylvania, USA. Clergyman. Professor. m. Eleanor Chambers, 21 July 1937, 2 sons, 1 daughter. Education: AB, Greenville College, 1930; STB, 1933; STM, 1934; MA, 1934; PhD, 1935, New York University. Appointments: Co Editor, Interpretation, 1947-62; Associate Editor, Laymans Bible Commentary, 1957-65; Editorial Board, Ex Auditu, 1985-. Publications: Fire in Thy Mouth, 1954; The Nature and Mission of the Church, 1957; The Way to Biblical Preaching, 1957; The Gospel According to Luke, 1959; The Authority of the Bible, 1972; The Scent of Eternity: On A Life of Harris Elliott Kirk of Baltimore, 1989; This Rock: A Commentary on Peter, 1993. Contributions to: Over 35 Journals. Honours: LLD, Waynesburg College, 1963; Litt D, Washington and Jefferson College, 1965. Membership: Society of Biblical Literature. Address: 401 Russell Avenue, Apt 405, Gaithersburg, MD 20877, USA.

MILLER Hugh, b. 27 Apr 1937, Wishaw, Lanarkshire, Scotland. Writer. Education: University of Glasgow; Stow College; London Polytechnic. Appointments: Editorial Assistant, Scottish ITV, Glasgow, 1958-60; Technical and Photographic Assistant to a Forensic Pathologist, University of Glasgow, 1960-62; Manager, 1963-64, Co-Owner, 1965-70, Unique Studios, London; Editor, Bulletin 1967-69, General 1968-71. Publications: A Pocketful of Miracles, 1969; Secrets of Gambling, 1970; Professional Presentations, 1971; The Open City, Levels, Drop Out, Short Circuit, Koran's Legacy, 1973; Kingpin, Double Deal, Feedback, 1974; Ambulance, 1975; The Dissector, A Soft Breeze from Hell, 1976; The Saviour, 1977; The Rejuvenators, Terminal 3, 1978; Olympic Bronze, Head of State, 1979; District Nurse, 1984; Honour a Physician, 1985; Eastenders, Teen Eastenders, 1986; Snow on the Wind, 1987; Silent Witnesses, 1988; The Paradise Club, 1989; An Echo of Justice, 1990; Home Ground, 1990; An Echo of Justice, 1991; Skin Deep 1992; Scotland Yard (co-author), 1993; Unquiet Minds, 1994; Proclaimed in Blood, 1995; Prime Target, 1996; Ballykissangel, 1997; Borrowed Time, 1997. Literary Agent: Lucas Alexander Whitley Ltd, Elsinore House, 77 Fulham Palace Road, London, W6 8JA, England. Address: The Chambers, Chelsea Harbour, London SW10 0XF, England.

MILLER Jim Wayne, b. 21 Oct 1936, Leicester, North Carolina, USA. Professor of German; Writer; Poet. m. Mary Ellen Yates, 17 Aug 1958, 2 sons, 1 daughter. Education: AB, Berea College, 1958; PhD, Vanderbilt University, 1965. Appointments: Assistant Professor, 1963-65, Associate Professor, 1965-70, Professor of German, 1970-, Western Kentucky University; Chairman, Kentucky Humanities Council, 1973-74; Various Writer-in-Residencies at colleges and universities. Publications: Poetry: The Mountains Have Come Closer, 1980; Vein of Words, 1984; Nostalgia for Seventy, 1986; Brier, His Book, 1988; The Wisdom of Folk Metaphor: The Brier Conducts a Laboratory Experiment, 1988; Round and Round with Kahlil Gibran, 1990. Other: I Have a Place (poetry anthology), (editor), 1981; Sideswipes (essays), 1988; A Jesse Stuart Reader (editor), 1988; Newfound, 1989; The Examined Life: Family, Community and Work in

American Literature, 1990; A Gathering at the Forks: Fifteen Years of the Hindman Settlement School Appalachian Writers Workshop (editor with George Ella Lyon and Gurney Norman), 1992; His First, Best Country (novel), 1993; Appalachia Inside Out (editor with Robert J Higgs and Abrose Manning), 2 volumes, 1994. Contributions to: Many books, professional journals, newspapers and magazines. Honours: Thomas Wolfe Literary Award, 1980; Appalachian Writers Association Awards, 1985, 1990; Poet Laureate of Kentucky, 1986; Zoe Kinkaid Broackman Memorial Award for Poetry, 1989; Best Book of the Year Citation, Booklist, 1989; Laurel Leaves Award, Appalachian Consortium, 1991. Memberships: American Association of Teachers of German; American Association of University Professors; Appalachian Studies Conference; Kentucky State Poetry Society; National Book Critics Circle. Address: 1512 Eastland Drive, Bowling Green, KY 42104, USA.

MILLER Jonathan (Wolfe), b. 21 July 1934, London, England. Theatre, Film, and Television Director; Writer. m. Helen Rachel Collet, 1956, 2 sons, 1 daughter. Education: MB, BCh, St John's College, Cambridge, 1959. Appointments: Theatre, film, and television director; Resident Fellow in the History of Medicine, 1970-73, Fellow, 1981-, University College, London; Associate Director, National Theatre, 1973-75; Visiting Professor in Drama, Westfield College, London, 1977-; Artistic Director, Old Vic, 1988-90; Research Fellow in Neuropsychology, University of Sussex. Publications: McLuhan, 1971; Freud: The Man, His World, His Influence (editor), 1972; The Body in Question, 1978; Subsequent Performances, 1986; The Don Giovanni Book: Myths of Seduction and Betrayal (editor), 1990. Honours: Silver Medal, Royal Television Society, 1981; Commander of the Order of the British Empire, 1983; Albert Medal, Royal Society of Arts, 1990; Honorary Doctor of Letters, University of Cambridge; Fellow of the Royal Academy; Member of American Academy of Arts and Science. Address: c/o IMG Artists, Media House, 3 Burlington Lane, London W4 2TH, England.

MILLER Karl (Fergus Connor), b. 1931, British. Appointments: Assistant Principal, HM Treasury, 1956-57; Producer, BBC Television, 1957-58; Literary Editor, The Spectator, 1958-61, The New Statesman, 1961-67; Editor, The Listener, 1967-73; Lord Northcliffe Professor of Modern English Literature, University College, London, 1974-92; Editor, 1979-89, Co-Editor, 1989-92, London Review of Books. Publications: Poetry from Cambridge 1952-54 (editor), 1955; Writing in England Today: The Last Fifteen Years (editor), 1968; A Listener Anthology August 1967 - June 1970 (editor), 1970; A Second Listener Anthology (editor), 1973; Cockburn's Millennium, 1975; Robert Burns (editor), 1981; Doubles: Studies in Literary History, 1985; Authors, 1989; Rebecca's Vest, 1993. Honour: James Tait Black Award; Scottish Arts Council Book Award. Membership: Royal Society of Literature, fellow. Address: 26 Limerston Street, London SW10, England.

MILLER Marc William, b. 29 Aug 1947, Annapolis, Maryland, USA. Writer. m. Darlene File, 24 Sept 1981, 1 son, 1 daughter. Education: BS, Sociology, University of Illinois, 1969. Appointments: Contributing Editor, Fire and Movement Magazine, 1977-84; Staff, Grenadier Magazine, 1977-79, Journal of the Traveller's Aid Society, 1979-85, Challenge Magazine, 1986-92. Publications: Traveller, 1977; Imperium, 1977; 2300 AD, 1986; Mega Traveller, 1988; Mega Traveller II, Quest for the Ancients, 1991; Spellbound, 1992. Contributions to: Journals. Honours: Several awards. Memberships: Academy of Adventure Gaming Arts and Sciences; Game Designer's Guild; Science Fiction Writers of America. Address: PO Box 193, Normal, IL 61761, USA.

MILLER Margaret J. See: **DALE Margaret Jessy**.

MILLER Merton H(oward), b. 16 May 1923, Boston, Massachusetts, USA. Professor of Banking and Finance; Writer. Education: AB, Harvard University, 1943; PhD, Johns Hopkins University, 1952. Appointments: Employee, US Treasury Department, 1944-47, Federal Reserve Board, 1947-49; Assistant Lecturer, London School of Economics and Political Science, 1952; Assistant Professor to Associate Professor, Graduate School of Industrial Administration, Carnegie Institute of Technology, Pittsburgh, 1958-61; Professor of Banking and Finance, Graduate School of Business, University of Chicago, 1961-. Publications: The Theory of Finance (with Eugene F Fama), 1972; Macroeconomics: A Neoclassical Introduction, 1974; Financial Innovation and Market Volatility, 1991. Honour: Nobel Prize for Economic Science, 1990. Memberships: American Economic

Association; President, American Finance Association, 1976; American Statistical Association; Fellow, Econometric Society. Address: c/o Graduate School of Business, University of Chicago, 1101 East 58th Street, Chicago, IL 60637, USA.

MILLER Olga Eunice, b. 27 Mar 1920, Maryborough, Queensland, Australia. Aboriginal Historian; Consultant; Artist. separated, 3 sons, 2 daughters. Education: Junior Public Examination Status, Maryborough Girls Grammar Schools, 1935. Publications: Legends of Moonie Jarl (co-author), 1964; Fraser Island Legends, 1993 new edition, 1994. TV programmes: Legends of Our Land, 1965; Across Australia, 1988. Radio programmes: This Was Our Town, 1965; Fraser Island Legends, 1983. Contributions to: Facts about Artefacts, 1965, First 200 Years, 1983, Maryborough Chronicle. Honour: Advance Australia Foundation Award, 1992. Address: 4/227 Ellena Street, Maryborough, Queensland 4650, Australia.

MILLER Seumas Roderick Macdonald, b. 11 Mar 1953, Edinburgh, Scotland, England. University Professor. Education: BA, Australia National University, 1976; MA, Oxford University, England, 1978; Diploma in Education, State College of Victoria, Australia, 1979; Higher Diploma in Journalism, Rhodes University, 1984; Doctorate in Philosophy, University of Melbourne, Australia, 1985. Publication: Re-thinking Theory, 1992. Contributions to: Numerous articles in internationally distributed professional philosophy journals and other academic journals. Address: University of Melbourne, Parkville, Vic 3052, Australia.

MILLER Sue, b. 1943, USA. Writer. Education: Radcliffe College, 1964. Publications: The Good Mother, 1986; Inventing the Abbotts and Other Stories, 1987; Family Pictures: A Novel, 1990; For Love, 1993; The Distinguished Guest, 1995. Address: c/o Alfred Knopf Inc, 201 East 50th Street, New York, NY 10022, USA.

MILLER Vassar (Morrison), b. 19 July 1924, Houston, Texas, USA. Poet. Education: BS, 1947, MA, 1952, University of Houston. Appointment: Instructor in Creative Writing, St John's School, Houston, 1975-76. Publications: Adam's Footprint, 1956; Wage War on Silence: A Book of Poems, 1960; My Bones Being Water: Poems, 1963; Onions and Roses, 1968; If I Could Sleep Deeply Enough, 1974; Small Change, Approaching Nada, 1977; Selected and New Poems, 1982; Struggling to Swim on Concrete, 1984; Despite This Flesh (editor), 1985; If I Had Wheels or Love: Collected Poems, 1991. Address: 1615 Vassar Street, Houston, TX 77006, USA.

MILLETT Kate, (Katherine Murray Millett), b. 14 Sept 1934, St Paul, Minnesota, USA. Feminist; Writer; Sculptor; Painter; Photographer. m. Fumio Yoshimura, 1965, div 1985. Education: BA, University of Minnesota, 1956; MA, St Hilda's College, Oxford, 1958; PhD, Columbia University, 1970. Appointments: Instructor in English, University of North Carolina, Greensboro, 1958; Teacher of English, Waseda University, Tokyo, 1961-63; Instructor, English and Philosophy, Barnard College, 1964-69; Instructor of Sociology, Bryn Mawr College, 1971; Distinguished Visiting Professor, State College of Sacramento, 1972-73. Publications: Sexual Politics, 1970; Prostitution Papers, 1971; Flying, 1974; Sita, 1977; The Basement, 1980; Going to Iran, 1981; The Loony-Bin Trip, 1990; The Politics of Cruelty, 1994; A.D., 1996. Contributions to: Periodicals. Memberships: Congress of Racial Equality; National Organization of Women; Phi Beta Kappa. Address: c/o Georges Borchardt Inc, 136 East 57th Street, New York, NY 10022, USA.

MILLETT Katherine Murray. See: **MILLETT Kate.**

MILLHAUSER Steven, b. 3 Aug 1943, New York, New York, USA. Novelist; Writer. m. Cathy Allis, 16 June 1986, 1 son, 1 daughter. Education: BA, Columbia College, 1965; Brown University, 1968-71. Publications: Edwin Mullhouse: The Life and Death of an American Writer, 1972; Portrait of a Romantic, 1976; In the Penny Arcade, 1986; From the Realm of Morpheus, 1986; The Barnum Museum, 1990; Little Kingdoms, 1993. Honours: Prix Medicis Etranger, 1975; Award in Literature, 1987. Address: Saratoga Springs, NY, USA.

MILLHISER Marlys (Joy), b. 27 May 1938, Charles City, Iowa, USA. Writer. m. David Millhiser, 25 June 1960, 1 son, 1 daughter. Education: BA, University of Iowa, 1960; MA, University of Colorado, 1963. Publications: Michael's Wife, 1972; Nella Waits, 1974; Willing Hostage, 1976; The Mirror, 1978; Nightmare Country, 1981; The Threshold, 1984; Murder at Moot Point, 1992; Death of the Office

Witch, 1993; Murder in a Hot Flash, 1995. Contributions to: Magazines. Honours: Top Hand Awards, 1975, 1985. Memberships: Authors Guild; Colorado Authors League; Mystery Writers of America; Sister in Crime; Western Writers of America. Address: 1843 Orchard Avenue, Boulder, CO 80304, USA.

MILLIEX Tatiana Gritsi, b. 20 Oct 1920, Athens, Greece. Writer. m. Roger Milliex, 1 June 1939, 1 son, 1 daughter. Education: Diploma, French Institute, Athens, 1938. Publications: Platia Thisiou, 1947; Sto Dromo Ton Anghelon, 1950; Kopiontes Ke Pefortismeni, 1951; Imeroloyio, 1951; Se Proto Prosopo, 1958; Allazoume?, 1958, French translation, 1985; Kai Idou Ippos Chloros, 1963; Sparagmata, 1973; H Tripoli Tou Pontou, 1977; Anadromes, 1983; Chroniko Eivos Efialti, 1986; Apo Tin Alli Oxhtictou Chronou, 1988, French translation, 1992; Onirika, 1991; To Aloni Tis Ekatis, 1993; Odiporiko Stin India, 1996. Contributions to: Variety of Greek and Cypriot magazines and journals. Honours: State Prize for short story, 1958, 1985, Novel, 1964 and 1974; Prize of Athens Academy, 1973; Prize Nikiphoros Vrettakos, 1995. Memberships: Greek Writers Society. Literary Agent: Castaniotis, odos Zalongou, 16078, Athens, Greece. Address: 20 Odos Metsovou, BP 26180 Exarchia, Athens, Greece.

MILLIGAN Terence Alan, (Spike Milligan), b. 1918, India. Playwright; Screenwriter; Humourist. Appointments: Radio and TV Personality: The Goon Show, BBC Radio; Show Called Fred, ITV; World of Beachcomber, Q5-Q10, BBC-2 Television; Curry and Chips, BBC; Oh in Colour, BBC; A Milligan for All Seasons, BBC. Publications: The Bed Sitting Room (play with J Antrobus); Oblommov (play); Son of Oblommov (play); Silly Verse for Kids, 1959; A Dustbin of Milligan, 1961; Puckoon, 1963; The Little Pot Boiler, 1963; A Book of Bits, 1965; The Bedside Milligan, 1968; Milliganimals, 1968; The Bald Twit Lion, 1970; Milligan's Ark, 1971; Adolf Hitler: My Part in His Downfall, 1971; The Goon Show Scripts, 1972; Small Dreams of a Scorpion, 1972; Rommel? Gunner Who? 1973; Badjelly the Witch, 1973; More Goon Show Scripts, 1974; Spike Milligan's Transport of Delights, 1974; Dip the Puppy, 1974; The Great McGonagal Scrapbook, 1975; The Milligan Book of Records, Games, Cartoons and Commercials (with Jack Hobbs), 1975; Monty: His Part in My Victory, 1976; Mussolini: His Part in My Downfall, 1978; A Book of Goblins, 1978; Open Heart University (verse), 1979; Indefinite Articles and Slunthorpe, 1981; The 101 Best and Only Limericks of Spike Milligan, 1982; The Goon Cartoons, 1982; Sir Nobonk and the Terrible Dragon, 1982; The Melting Pot, 1983; More Goon Cartoons, 1983; There's a Lot About, 1983; Further Transports of Delight, 1985; Floored Masterpieces and Worse Verse, 1985; Where Have All the Bullets Gone, 1985; Goodbye Soldier, 1986; The Mirror Running, 1987; Startling Verse for All the Family, 1987; The Looney, 1987; William McGonall Meets George Gershwin, 1988; It Ends with Magic..., 1990; Peacework, 1991; Condensed Animals, 1991; Dear Robert, Dear Spike, 1991; Depression and How to Survive It (with Anthony Clare), 1993; Hidden Words, 1993; The Bible - Old Testament According to Spike Milligan, 1993; Lady Chatterley's Lover According to Spike Milligan, 1994; Wuthering Heights According to Spike Milligan 1994; Spike Milligan: A Celebration, 1995; John Thomas and Lady Jane According to Spike Milligan, 1995; Black Beauty According to Spike Milligan, 1996. Honours: TV Writer of the Year Award, 1956; Golden Rose and Special Comedy Award, Montreux, 1972; Commander of the Order of the British Empire, 1992; Lifetime Achievement Award, British Comedy Awards, 1994. Address: Spike Milligan Productions, 9 Orme Court, London W2, England.

MILLINGTON Barry (John), b. 1 Nov 1951, Essex, England. Music Journalist; Writer. Education: BA, Cambridge University, 1974. Appointments: Chief Music Critic, Times; Reviews Editor, BBC Music Magazine. Publications: Wagner, 1984, 2nd edition, 1992; Selected Letters of Richard Wagner (translator and editor with S Spencer), 1987; The Wagner Compendium: A Guide to Wagner's Life and Music (editor), 1992; Wagner in Performance (editor with S Spencer), 1992; Wagner's Ring of the Nibelung: A Companion (editor, with S Spencer), 1993. Contributions to: Newspapers and magazines. Membership: Critics' Circle. Address: 50 Denman Drive South, London NW11 6RH, England.

MILLS Claudia, b. 21 Aug 1954, New York, New York, USA. Writer. m. Richard W Wahl, 19 Oct 1985, 2 sons. Education: BA, Wellesley College, 1976; MA, 1979, PhD, 1991, Princeton University. Publications: Luisa's American Dream, 1981; At the Back of the Woods, 1982; The Secret Carousel, 1983; All the Living, 1983; Boardwalk with Hotel, 1985; The One and Only Cynthia Jane Thornton,

1986; Melanie Magpie, 1987; Cally's Enterprise, 1988; Dynamite Dinah, 1990; Hannah on her Way, 1991; Dinah in Love, 1993; Phoebe's Parade, 1994; The Secret Life of Bethany Barrett, 1994. Memberships: Authors Guild; Society of Children's Book Writers. Address: 2575 Briarwood Drive, Boulder, CO 80303, USA.

MILLS Derek Henry, b. 19 Mar 1928, Bristol, England. University Fellow; Consultant. m. Florence Cameron, 26 May 1956, 1 son, 1 daughter. Education: BSc, Honours, University of London, 1949-53; MSc, University of London, 1957; PhD, University of London, 1963; FIFM; FLS. Appointments: Editor, Fisheries Management, 1974-84, John Buchan Journal, 1979-83, Walter Scott Club Bulletins, Edinburgh, 1996-; Co-Editor, Aquaculture and Fisheries Management, 1985-93, Fisheries Management and Ecology, 1994-95. Publications: Salmon and Trout: A Resource, its Ecology, Conservation and Management, 1971; Introduction to Freshwater Ecology, 1972; Scotland's King of Fish, 1980; The Salmon Rivers of Scotland, 1981, 1992; The Fishing Here Is Great!, 1985; The Ecology and Management of Atlantic Salmon, 1989; Freshwater Ecology: Principles and Applications, 1990. Contributions to: Blackwood Magazine; Field; Fly Fishers'Journal; John Buchan Journal; Salmon and Trout Magazine; Fisheries Research. Memberships: John Buchan Society; Trollope Society; Institute of Fisheries Management, Fellow; Linnean Society of London, Fellow; Walter Scott Club, Edinburgh; Atlantic Salmon Trust; Fly Fishers' Club. Address: Valerna, Aldie Crescent, Darnick, Melrose TD6 9AY, Scotland.

MILLS Ralph J(oseph) Jr, b. 16 Dec 1931, Chicago, Illinois, USA. Professor of English; Poet; Writer. m. Helen Daggett Harvey, 25 Nov 1959, 2 sons, 1 daughter. Education: BA, Lake Forest College, 1954; MA, 1956, PhD, 1963, Northwestern University; Oxford University, 1956-57. Appointments: Instructor, 1959-61, Assistant Professor, 1962-65, University of Chicago; Associate Professor, 1965-67, Professor of English, 1967-, University of Illinois at Chicago. Publications: Poetry: Door to the Sun, 1974; A Man to His Shadow, 1975; Night Road, 1978; Living with Distance, 1979; With No Answer, 1980; March Light, 1983; For a Day, 1985; Each Branch: Poems 1976-1985, 1986; A While, 1989; A Window in Air, 1993. Other: Contemporary American Poetry, 1965; On the Poet and His Craft: Selected Prose of Theodore Roethke (editor), 1965; Edith Sitwell: A Critical Essay, 1966; Kathleen Raine: A Critical Essay, 1967; Creation's Very Self: On the Personal Element in Recent American Poetry, 1969; Cry of the Human: Essays on Contemporary American Poetry, 1975. Contributions to: Books and journals. Honours: English-Speaking Union Fellowship, 1956-57; Illinois Arts Council Awards for Poetry, 1979, 1983, 1984; Society of Midland Authors Prize for Poetry, 1980; Carl Sandburg Prize for Poetry, 1984. Memberships: Phi Beta Kappa; Phi Kappa Phi. Address: 1451 North Astor Street, Chicago, IL 60610, USA.

MILLWARD Eric (Geoffrey William), b. 12 Mar 1935, Longnor, Staffordshire, England. Poet. m. Rosemary Wood, 1975. Education: Buxton College, Derbyshire, 1946-54. Publications: A Child in the Park, 1969; Dead Letters, 1978; Appropriate Noises, 1987. Honour: Arts Council Writers Award, 1978. Address: 2 Victoria Row, Knypersley, Stoke on Trent, Staffordshire ST8 7PU, England.

MILNE Christopher Robin, b. 21 Aug 1920, London, England. Author. m. Lesley Elizabeth De Selincourt, 25 July 1948, 1 daughter. Education: BA, Honours, Trinity College, Cambridge, England. Appointments: Bookseller, 1951-76; Writer, 1976-. Publications: The Enchanted Places, 1974; The Path Through the Trees, 1979; The Hollow on the Hill, 1982; The Windfall, 1985; The Open Garden, 1988. Membership: Royal Society of Arts, fellow. Address: Glebe House, Manor Way, Totnes, Devon, England.

MILOSZ Czeslaw, b. 30 June 1911, Szetejnie, Lithuania. (Naturalized US citizen, 1970). Poet; Novelist; Critic; Essayist; Translator; Professor. Education: M Juris, University of Wilno, 1934. Appointments: Programmer, Polish National Radio, Warsaw, 1934-39; Diplomatic Service, Polish Ministry of Foreign Affairs, 1945-50; Visiting Lecturer, 1960-61, Professor of Slavic Languages and Literatures, 1961-78, Professor Emeritus, 1978-, University of California at Berkeley. Publications: Poetry: Poems, 1940; Poems, 1969; Selected Poems, 1973, revised edition, 1981; Selected Poems, 1976; The Bells in Winter, 1978; The Separate Notebooks, 1984; Collected Poems, 1990; Provinces: Poems 1987-1991, 1991; Facing the River: New Poems, 1995. Novels: The Seizure of Power, 1955; The Issa Valley, 1981. Non-Fiction: The Captive Mind (essays), 1953; Native Realm: A

Search for Self-Definition (essays), 1968; The History of Polish Literature, 1969, revised edition, 1983; Emperor of the Earth: Modes of Eccentric Vision, 1977; Nobel Lecture, 1981; Visions From San Francisco Bay, 1982; The Witness of Poetry (lectures), 1983; The Land of Ulro, 1984; The Rising of The Sun, 1985; Unattainable Earth, 1986; Beginning With My Streets: Essays and Recollections, 1992. Editor and Translator: Postwar Polish Poetry: An Anthology, 1965, revised edition, 1983. Honours: Prix Littéraire Européen, Les Guildes du Livre, Geneva, 1953; Marian Kister Literary Award, 1967; Guggenheim Fellowship, 1976; Neustadt International Literary Prize, 1978; Nobel Prize for Literature, 1980; National Medal of Arts, 1990; Several honorary doctorates. Memberships: American Academy and Institute of Arts and Letters; American Academy of Arts and Sciences; American Association for the Advancement of Slavic Studies; Polish Institute of Letters and Sciences in America. Address: c/o Department of Slavic Languages and Literatures, University of California at Berkeley, CA 94720, USA.

MILWARD Alan Steele, b. 19 Jan 1935, Stoke-on-Trent, England. Professor of Economic History; Writer. m. Claudine J A Lemaitre, 1963, div 1994, 2 daughters. Education: BA, University College, London, 1956; PhD, London School of Economics and Political Science, 1960. Appointments: Lecturer, University of Edinburgh, 1960-65; Senior Lecturer, University of East Anglia, 1965-69; Associate Professor of Economics, Stanford University, 1969-71; Professor of European Studies, UMIST, 1971-83; Professor of Contemporary History, 1983-86, 1996-, European University Institute; Professor of Economic History, University of London, 1986-96; Official Historian, Cabinet Office, 1993-; Various visiting professorships. Publications: The German Economy at War, 1965; The Social and Economic Effects of the Two World Wars on Britain, 1971, 2nd edition, 1984; The New Order and the French Economy, 1972; The Fascist Economy in Norway, 1972; The Economic Development of Continental Europe 1780-1870 (with S B Paul), 1973; The Development of the Economics of Continental Europe 1870-1914 (with S B Paul), 1977; War, Economy and Society, 1977; The Reconstruction of Western Europe 1945-1951, 1984, 2nd edition, 1987; Landwirtschaft und Ernahrung im Zweiten Weltkreig (with B Martin), 1984; The European Rescue of the Nation-State, 1992; The Frontier of National Sovereignty, 1993. Contributions to: Journals and periodicals. Honour: Honorary MA, University of Manchester, 1976. Memberships: Fellow, British Academy; Economic History Association; Economic History Society; German History Society; Fellow, Royal Norwegian Academy of Letters. Address: Departimente di Storia, Istituto Universitario Europeo, Villa Schifanoia, via Boccaccio 121, Florence 50133, Italy.

MINARIK John Paul, b. 6 Nov 1947, McKeesport, Pennsylvania, USA. Engineer; Poet. Education: BS, Carnegie Mellon University, 1970; BA, University of Pennsylvania, 1978. Appointment: Editor, Academy of Prison Arts, 1973-. Publications: A Book, 1974; Patterns in the Dusk, 1977; Past the Unknown, Remembered Gate, 1980; Kicking Their Heels with Freedom, 1980; Light from Another Country, 1984. Contributions to: Periodicals. Address: 1600 Walters Mill Road, Somerset, PA 15510, USA.

MINATOYA Lydia, b. 8 Nov 1950, New York, New York, USA. Writer. 1 son. Education: BA, Lawrence University, 1972; MA, George Washington University, 1976; PhD, University of MD, 1981. Publication: Talking to High Monks in the Snow, 1992. Honours: PEN Jerard Fund Award, 1991; American Library Association Notable Book, 1992; New York Public Library Notable Book, 1992; Pacific Nova West Booksellers Award, 1993. Literary Agent: Ellen Levene Agency. Address: Harper Collins, 10 East 53rd Street, New York, NY 10022 5299, USA.

MINCHIN Devon George, b. 28 May 1919, Sydney, New South Wales, Australia. Farmer; Writer. m. Margo Slater, 2 sons, 2 daughters. Education: BA, MacQuarie University, Sydney. Publications: The Potato Man, 1944; The Money Movers, 1975; Isabel's Mine, 1989; Wartime Short Stories Collection, "The 13th Diamond". Address: Wappa Falls Farm Yandina, Queensland 4561, Australia.

MINEAR Richard H(offman), b. 31 Dec 1938, Evanston, Illinois, USA. Professor of History; Writer. m. Edith Christian, 1962, 2 sons. Education: BA, Yale University, 1960; MA, 1962, PhD, 1968, Harvard University. Appointments: Assistant Professor, Ohio State University, 1967-70; Associate Professor, 1970-75, Professor of History, 1975-,

University of Massachusetts. Publications: Japanese Tradition and Western Law, 1970; Victors' Justice, 1971; Through Japanese Eyes, 1974; Requiem for Battleship Yamato, 1985; Hiroshima: Three Witnesses, 1990; Black Eggs, 1994. Contributions to: Professional journals and general magazines. Membership: Association for Asian Studies. Address: c/o Department of History, University of Massachusetts, Amherst, MA 01003, USA.

MINER Earl (Roy), b. 21 Feb 1927, Marshfield, Wisconsin, USA. Professor; Writer. m. Virginia Lane, 15 July 1950, 1 son, 1 daughter. Education: BA, 1949, MA, 1955, PhD, University of Minnesota. Appointment: Professor, Princeton University. Publications: The Japanese Tradition in British and American Literature, 1958; Japanese Court Poetry, 1961; Dryden's Poetry, 1967; Comparative Poetics, 1992; Naming Properties, 1996. Contributions to: Professional journals. Honours: Fulbright Lectureships, 1960-61, 1966-67, 1985; American Council of Learned Societies Fellowship, 1963; Guggenheim Fellowship, 1977-78; Yamagato Banto Prize, 1988; Koizumi Yakumo Prize, 1991; Howard T Behrman Prize, 1993; Order of the Rising Sun with Gold Rays and Neck Ribbon, Government of Japan, 1994. Memberships: American Comparative Literature Association; American Society for 18th Century Studies; Association for Asian Studies; International Comparative Literature Association; Milton Society of America; Renaissance Society of America. Address: Princeton University, Princeton, NJ 08544, USA.

MINER Jane Claypool, (Jane Claypool, Veronica Ladd), b. 22 Apr 1933, McAllen, Texas, USA. Writer. m. (1) Dennis A Shelley, 1952, dec, 1 daughter, (2) Richard Yale Miner, 1962, dec. Education: BA, California State University, Long Beach, 1956. Publications: Over 60 books for teenagers. Contributions to: Numerous periodicals. Memberships: American Society of Authors and Journalists; Society of Children's Book Writers. Address: 2883 Lone Jack Road, Olivenhain, CA 92024, USA.

MINGAY G(ordon) E(dmund), b. 20 June 1923, Long Eaton, Derbyshire, England. Professor of Agrarian History Emeritus; Writer. m. Mavis Tippen, 20 Jan 1945. Education: BA, 1952, PhD, 1958, University of Nottingham. Appointments: Reader in Economic History, 1965-68, Professor of Agrarian History, 1968-85, Professor Emeritus, 1985-, University of Kent, Canterbury; Editor, Agricultural History Review, 1972-84. Publications: English Landed Society in the Eighteenth Century, 1963; The Agricultural Revolution 1750-1880 (with J D Chambers), 1966; Land, Labour, and Population in the Industrial Revolution (editor with E L Jones), 1967; Enclosure and the Small Farmer in the Age of the Industrial Revolution, 1968; Britain and America: A Study of Economic Change 1850-1939 (with Philip S Bagwell), 1970, revised edition, 1987; Fifteen Years On: The B E T Group 1956-1971, 1973; The Gentry, 1975; Arthur Young and His Times, 1975; Georgian London, 1975; Rural Life in Victorian England, 1976; The Agricultural Revolution, 1977; Mrs Hurst Dancing, 1981; The Victorian Countryside (editor), 1981; An Epic of Progress: A History of British Friesian Cattle, 1982; The Transformation of Britain 1830-1939, 1986; The Agrarian History of England and Wales, Volume VI, 1750-1850 (editor), 1989; The Rural Idyll, 1989; Editor, The Unquiet Countryside (editor), 1989; A Social History of the English Countryside, 1990; Land and Society in England 1750-1980, 1994. Contributions to: Professional journals. Honour: Fellow, Royal Historical Society. Memberships: President, British Agricultural History Society, 1987-89; Economic History Society. Address: Mill Field House, Selling Court, Selling, Faversham, Kent ME13 9RJ, England.

MINOGUE Valerie Pearson, b. 26 Apr 1931, Llanelli, South Wales. Research Professor Emeritus. m. Kenneth Robert Minogue, 15 June 1954, 1 son, 1 daughter. Education: BA, 1952, MLitt, 1956, Girton College, Cambridge. Appointments: Assistant Lecturer, University College, Cardiff, Wales, 1952-53; Contributor, Cambridge Italian Dictionary, 1956-61; Lecturer, Queen Mary College, London, England, 1962-81; Professor, 1981-88, Research Professor, 1988-96, Professor Emeritus, 1996, University of Wales, Swansea. Publications: Nathalie Sarraute: The War of the Words; Proust: Du Coté de chez Swann; Zola: L'Assommoir; Romance Studies. Contributions to: Quadrant; Literary Review; Modern Language Review; French Studies; Romance Studies; Forum for Modern Language Studies. Memberships: Association of University Professors of French; Modern Humanities Research Association; Society for French Studies; Romance Studies Institute. Address: 92 Eaton Crescent, Swansea, West Glamorgan SA1 4QP, Wales.

MINOT Susan Anderson, b. 7 Dec 1956, Boston, Massachusetts, USA. Writer. m. Davis McHenry, 30 Apr 1988, div. Education: BA, Brown University, 1978; MFA, Columbia University, 1983. Publications: Monkeys, 1986; Lost & Other Stories, 1989; Folly, 1992. Contributions to: New Yorker; Grand Street; Paris Review; Mademoiselle; Harper's; GQ; New England Monthly; Conde Nasts Traveler; Esquire; New York Times Magazine; Atlantic Monthly. Honour: Priz Femina Etranger, 1987. Literary Agent: Georges Borchardt. Address: c/o Houghton Mifflin Co, 222 Berkeley Street, Boston, MA 02116, USA.

MINTER David (Lee), b. 20 Mar 1935, Midland, Texas, USA. Professor of English; Writer. Education: BA, 1957, MA, 1959, North Texas State University; BD, 1961, PhD, 1965, Yale University. Appointments: Lecturer, University of Humburg, 1965-66, Yale University, 1966-67; Assistant Professor, 1967-69, Associate Professor 1969-74, Professor, 1974-80, 1991-, Rice University; Professor, Dean of Emory College, Vice-President for Arts and Sciences, Emory University, 1981-90. Publications: The Interpreted Design as a Structural Principle in American Prose, 1969; William Faulkner: His Life and Work, 1980; The Harper American Literature, 1986; The Norton Critical Edition of The Sound and the Fury, 1987; A Cultural History of the American Novel: Henry James to William Faulkner, 1994. Contributions to: Professional journals. Address: c/o Department of English, Rice University, PO Box 1892, Houston, TX 77251, USA.

MIRABELLI Eugene, b. 1931, USA. Author. Publications: The Burning Air, 1959; The Way In, 1968; No Resting Place, 1972; The World at Noon, 1993. Address: 29 Bennett Terrace, Delmar, NY 12054, USA.

MISTRY Rohinton, b. 1952, Bombay, India. Writer. m. Freny Elavia. Education: BSc, University of Bombay; BA, University of Toronto. Contributions to: Anthologies and periodicals. Honours: Smith/Books in Canada First Novel Award; Hart House Prizes for Fiction, 1983, 1984; Commonwealth Writer's Prizes, 1992, 1996. Address: c/o Westwood Creative Artists, 94 Harbord Street, Toronto, Ontario M5S 1G6 Canada.

MITCHELL Adrian, b. 24 Oct 1932, London, England. Writer. Education: Christ Church, Oxford. Appointments: Granada Fellow, University of Lancaster, 1968-69; Fellow, Centre for the Humanities, Wesleyan University, 1972; Resident Writer, Sherman Theatre, Cardiff, 1974-75, Unicorn Theatre for Children, 1982-83; Visiting Writer, Billericay Comprehensive School, 1978-80; Judith Wilson Fellow, Cambridge University, 1980-81. Publications: Tyger, 1971; Man Friday, 7:84, 1973; On the Beach at Cambridge, 1984; Nothingmas Day, 1984; The Pied Piper, 1986; Strawbery Drums, 1989; TV plays. Contributions to: Oxford Mail; London Magazine; Times Literary Supplement; Observer; New Yorker; Peace News Tribune; New Statesman; Sunday Times; Daily Mail; Evening Standard; Sanity. Memberships: Theatre Writers Union. Address: c/o The Peter, Fraser and Dunlop Group Ltd, 5th Floor, The Chambers, Chelsea Harbour, Lots Road, London SW10 0XF, England.

MITCHELL David John, b. 24 Jan 1924, London, England. Writer. m. 1955, 1 son. Education: Bradfield College, Berkshire; MA (Hons), Modern History, Trinity College, Oxford, 1947. Appointment: Staff Writer, Picture Post, 1947-52. Publications: Women on the Warpath, 1966; The Fighting Pankhursts, 1967; 1919 Red Mirage, 1970; Pirates, 1976; Queen Christabel, 1977; The Jesuits: A History, 1980; The Spanish Civil War, 1982; Travellers in Spain, 1990. Contributions to: Newspapers and magazines. Membership: Society of Authors. Address: 20 Mountacre Close, Sydenham Hill, London SE26 6SX, England.

MITCHELL (Sibyl) Elyne Keith, b. 30 Dec 1913, Melbourne, Victoria, Australia. Author; Grazier. m. Thomas Walter Mitchell, 4 Nov 1935, dec, 2 sons (1 dec), 2 daughters. Publications: Australia's Alps, 1942; Speak to the Earth, 1945; Soil and Civilization, 1946; Flow River, Blow Wind, 1953; Silver Brumby Series (for children), 1958-77; Kingfisher Feather (children), 1962; Winged Skis (children), 1964; Light Horse to Damascus, 1971; Light Horse, the Story of Australia's Mounted Troops, 1978; Colt from Snowy River, series, 1979-81; The Snowy Mountains, 1980; Chauvel Country, 1983; Discoverers of the Snowy Mountains, 1985; A Vision of the Snowy Mountains, 1988; Towong Hill, Fifty Years on an Upper Murray Cattle Station, 1989; Silver Brumby, Silver Dingo, 1993; Silver Brumby (film), 1993; Dancing

Brumby, 1995; Brumbies of the Night, 1996. Contributions to: Quadrant; Poetry Australia; Canberra Times; Age; Australian. Honours: Children's Book Week Award; Order of Australia Medal, 1990; Honoray Doctor of Letters, Charles Sturt University, 1993. Memberships: Australian Society of Authors. Literary Agent: Curtis Brown Ltd. Address: Towong Hill, Corryong, Victoria 3707, Australia.

MITCHELL G(eoffrey) Duncan, b. 5 June 1921, England. Professor of Sociology Emeritus. Education: BSc, University of London, 1949. Appointments: Senior Research Worker, University of Liverpool, 1950-52; Lecturer in Sociology, University of Birmingham, 1952-54; Lecturer to Senior Lecturer, 1954-67, Professor of Sociology, 1967-86, Professor Emeritus and Research Fellow, 1986-, Institute of Population Studies, University of Exeter. Publications: Neighbourhood and Community (with T Lupton, M W Hodges and C S Smith), 1954; Sociology: The Study of Social Systems, 1959, new edition, 1972; A Dictionary of Sociology (editor); A Hundred Years of Sociology, 1968; A New Dictionary of Sociology (editor), 1979; The Artificial Family (with R Snowden), 1981; Artificial Reproduction (with R and E Snowden), 1983. Contributions to: Professional journals. Honours: Member of the Order of the British Empire, 1946; Officer of the Order of the British Empire, 1964. Address: 26 West Avenue, Exeter, Devon, England.

MITCHELL Jerome, b. 7 Oct 1935, Chattanooga, Tennessee, USA. University Lecturer. Education: BA, Emory University, 1957; MA, 1959, PhD, 1965, Duke University. Appointments: Assistant Professor, University of Illinois, 1965-67; Associate Professor, 1967-72, Professor, 1972-97, University of Georgia; Fulbright Guest Professor, University of Bonn, 1972-73; Visiting Exchange Professor, University of Erlangen, 1975; Richard Merton Guest Professor, University of Regensburg, 1978-79. Publications: Thomas Hoccleve: A Study in Early 15th Century English Poetic, 1968; Hoccleve's Works: The Minor Poems, 1970; Chaucer: The Love Poet, 1973; The Walter Scott Operas, 1977; Scott, Chaucer and Medieval Romance, 1987; Old and Middle English Literature, 1994; More Scott Operas, 1996. Contributions to: Various Scholarly Journals. Memberships: South Atlantic Modern Language Association; Gesellschaft für Englische Romantik; Edinburgh Sir Walter Scott Club. Address: PO Box 1268, Athens, GA 30603, USA.

MITCHELL (Charles) Julian, b. 1 May 1935, Epping, Essex, England. Author. Education: BA 1958, Wadham College, Oxford. Appointments: Midshipman, Royal Naval Volunteer Reserve, 1953-55. Publications: Imaginary Toys, 1961; A Disturbing Influence, 1962; As Far as You Can Go, 1963; The White Father, 1964; A Heritage and Its History (play), 1965; A Family and a Fortune (play), 1966; A Circle of Friends, 1966; The Undiscovered Country, 1968; Jennie Lady Randolph Churchill: A Portrait with Letters (with Peregrine Churchill), 1974; Half-Life (play), 1977; Another Country (play), 1982, (film), 1984; Francis (play), 1983; After Aida (play), 1985; Falling Over England (play), 1994; August (adaptation of Uncle Vanya) (play), 1994, (film), 1995. Contributions to: Welsh History Review; Monmouthshire Antiquary. Literary Agent: The Peters, Fraser & Dunlop Group. Address: 47 Draycott Place, London SW3 3DB, England.

MITCHELL Juliet (Constance Wyatt), b. 4 Oct 1940, Christchurch, New Zealand. Professor; Psychoanalyst; Writer; Broadcaster. Education: BA, St Anne's College, Oxford, 1961. Appointments: Lecturer in English, University of Leeds, England, 1962-63, University of Reading, 1965-70; Luce Lecturer, Yale University, 1984-85; A D White Professor-at-Large, Cornell University, 1994-2000. Publications: Women: The Longest Revolution, 1966; Woman's Estate, 1972; Psycho-Analysis and Feminism, 1974; Rights and Wrongs of Women (co-editor), 1977; Feminine Sexuality (co-editor), 1982; Women: The Longest Revolution, 1983; What is Feminism? (co-editor), 1986; The Selected Writings of Melanie Klein (editor), 1986; Before I was I (co-editor), 1991. Literary Agent: Deborah Rogers. Address: 275 Lonsdale Road, London SW13 9QB, England.

MITCHELL Margaretta Meyer Kuhlthau, b. 27 May 1935, Brooklyn, New York, USA. Photographer. m. 23 May 1959, 3 daughters. Education: BA, Smith College, 1957; MA, University of California, 1985. Appointments: University of California Extension Program, 1976-78; City College, 1980; Civic Arts, 1980-84; Visiting Professor, Carleton College, 1988; Teacher, Academy of Art, San Francisco, 1990-94. Publications: Recollections: Gift of Place, 1969; To a Cabin, 1973; Ten Women of Photography, 1979; Dance for Life, 1985; Flowers, 1991. Contributions to: Ramparts; Vermont Life; Camera Art. Honour: Phi Beta Kappa, 1957. Membership: American

Society of Media Photographers. Address: 280 Hillcrest Road, Berkeley, CA 94705, USA.

MITCHELL Michael Robin, b. 10 Apr 1941, Rochdale, Lancashire, England. University Lecturer; Translator; Writer. m. Jane Speakman, 3 Jan 1970, 3 sons. Education: MA, 1964, BLitt, 1968, Lincoln College, Oxford. Publications: Harrap's German Grammar (co-author), 1989; Peter Hcks: Theatre for a Socialist Society, 1991; The Dedalus Book of Austrian Fantasy (editor and translator), 1992. Other: Translations of several authors. Address: 4 Mount Hope, Bridge of Allan, Stirling, Scotland.

MITCHELL Roger (Sherman), b. 8 Feb 1935, Boston, Massachusetts, USA. Poet; Teacher. 2 daughters. Education: AB, Harvard College, 1957; MA, University of Colorado, 1961; PhD, Manchester University, 1963. Appointments: Editor, Minnesota Review, 1973-81; Director, Writers Conferences, 1975-85, Creative Writing Programme, 1978-96, Indiana University. Publications: Letters from Siberia, 1971; Moving, 1976; A Clear Space on a Cold Day, 1986; Adirondack, 1988; Clear Pond, 1991; The Word for Everything, 1996; Braid, 1997. Contributions to: Periodicals. Honours: Abby M Copps Award, 1971; Midland Poetry Award, 1972; Borestone Mountain Award, 1973; PEN Award, 1977; Arvon Foundation Awards, 1985, 1987; National Endowment for the Arts Fellowship, 1986; Chester H Jones Award, 1987. Membership: Associated Writing Programs. Address: 1010 East First Street, Bloomington, IN 47401, USA.

MITCHELL William John Thomas, b. 24 Mar 1942, Anaheim, California, USA. Professor; Editor; Writer. m. Janice Misurell, 11 Aug 1968, 1 son, 1 daughter. Education: BA, Michigan State University, 1963; MA, PhD, 1968, Johns Hopkins University. Appointments: Professor of English and Art History, Chair, English Dept, 1989-92, University of Chicago; Editor, Critical Inquiry, 1979-. Publications: Blake's Composite Art, 1977; The Language of Images, 1980; The Politics of Interpretation, 1983; Against Theory, 1983; Iconology, 1986; Art and the Public Sphere, 1993; Landscape and Power, 1993; Picture Theory, 1994. Contributions to: Professional journals and general periodicals. Honours: American Philosophical Society Essay Prize, 1968; National Endowment for the Humanities Fellowships, 1978, 1986; Guggenheim Fellowship, 1983; Gaylord Donnelley Distinguished Service Professorship, 1989; College Art Association's Charles Rufus Morey Prize for distinguished book in Art History (for Picture Theory), 1996. Memberships: Academy of Literary Studies; Modern Language Association; PEN. Address: c/o Department of English and Art History, University of Chicago, 1050 East 59th Street, Chicago, IL 60637, USA.

MITCHELL W(illiam) O(rmond), b. 13 Mar 1914, Weyburn, Saskatchewan, Canada. Author; Dramatist. Education: University of Manitoba; University of Alberta, 1942. Appointments: Writer-in-Residence, University of Calgary, 1968-71, University of Windsor, Ontario, 1979-87; Director, Banff School of Fine Arts, Alberta, 1975-86. Publications: Who Has Seen the Wind?, 1947; Jake and the Kid, 1961; The Kite, 1962; The Vanishing Point, 1973; How I Spent My Summer Holidays, 1981; Since Daisy Creek, 1985; Ladybug Ladybug, 1988; According to Jake and the Kid: A Collection of New Stories, 1989; Roses Are Difficult Here, 1990. Plays: Wild Rose, 1967; Back to Beulah, 1976; The Kite, 1981; For Those in Peril on the Sea, 1982. Other: Screenplays, radio plays and television plays. Honours: Officer of the Order of Canada, 1972; Honorary DLitt, University of Ottawa, 1972; Canadian Authors Association Award, 1983. Address: c/o McClelland & Stewart Inc, 481 University Avenue, Suite 900, Toronto, Ontario M5G 2E9, Canada.

MITCHISON Naomi Margaret (Haldane), b. 1 Nov 1897, Edinburgh, Scotland. Author. m. Gilbert Richard Mitchison, 1916, 3 sons, 2 daughters. Publications: The Conquered, 1923; When the Bough Breaks, 1924; Cloud Cuckoo Land, 1925; Black Sparta, 1928; Anna Comnena, 1928; Nix-Nought-Nothing, 1928; Barbarian Stories, 1929; The Corn King and the Spring Queen, 1931; The Delicate Fire, 1932; We Have Been Warned, 1935; The Fourth Pig, 1936; Socrates (with R H S Crossman), 1937; Moral Basis of Politics, 1938; The Kingdom of Heaven, 1939; As It Was in the Beginning (with L E Gielgud), 1939; The Blood of the Martyrs, 1939; Re-Educating Scotland, 1945; The Bull Calves, 1947; Men and Herring (with D Macintosh), 1949; The Big House, 1950; Lobsters on the Agenda, 1952; Travel Light, 1952; Swan's Road, 1954; Graeme and the Dragon, 1954; Land the Ravens Found, 1955; To the Chapel Perilous, 1955; Little Boxes, 1956; Behold Your King, 1957; The Far Harbour, 1957; Other People's Worlds, 1958; Five Men and a Swan, 1958; Judy and

Lakshmi, 1959; Rib of the Green Umbrella, 1960; The Young Alexander, 1960; Karensgaard, 1961; Memoirs of a Spacewoman, 1962; The Fairy Who Couldn't Tell a Lie, 1963; When We Became Men, 1964; Return to the Fairy Hill, 1966; Friends and Enemies, 1966; African Heroes, 1968; The Family at Ditlabeng, 1969; The Africans: A History, 1970; Sun and Moon, 1970; Cleopatra's People, 1972; A Danish Teapot, 1973; A Life for Africa, 1973; Sunrise Tomorrow, 1973; Small Talk (autobiography), 1973; All Change Here (autobiography), 1975; Solution Three, 1975; Snake!, 1976; The Two Magicians, 1979; The Cleansing of the Knife and Other Poems, 1979; You May Well Ask: A Memoir 1920-40, 1979; Images of Africa, 1980; The Vegetable War, 1980; Mucking Around (autobiography) 1981; What Do You Think Yourself?, 1982; Not by Bread Alone, 1983; Among You Taking Notes, 1985; Early in Orcadia, 1987; A Girl Must Live, 1990; Sea-Green Ribbons, 1991; The Oathtakers, 1991. Honours: Commander of the Order of the British Empire, 1985; Honorary doctorates. Address: Carradale House, Carradale, Campbeltown, Scotland.

MITEHAM Hank. See: **NEWTON D(wight) B(ennett).**

MITSON Eileen Nora, b. 22 Sept 1930, Langley, Essex, England. Author. m. Arthur Samuel Mitson, 22 Sept 1951, 2 daughters, 1 dec. Education: Cambridge Technical College and School of Art, 1946-47. Appointment: Columnist, Christian Woman magazine, later Woman Alive Magazine, 1982-94. Publications: Beyond the Shadows, 1968; Amazon Adventure, 1969; The Inside Room, 1973; A Kind of Freedom, 1976; Reaching for God, 1978; Creativity (co-author), 1985. Address: 39 Oaklands, Hamilton Road, Reading, Berkshire RG1 5RN, England.

MO Timothy (Peter), b. 30 Dec 1950, Hong Kong. Writer. Education: Convent of the Precious Blood, Hong Kong; Mill Hill School, London; BA, St John's College, Oxford. Publications: The Monkey King, 1978; Sour Sweet, 1982; An Insular Possession, 1986; The Redundancy of Courage, 1991; Brownout on Breadfruit Boulevard, 1995. Contributions to: Periodicals. Honours: Gibbs Prize, 1971; Geoffrey Faber Memorial Prize, 1979; Hawthornden Prize, 1983; E M Forster Award, American Academy of Arts and Letters, 1992. Address: c/o Chatto & Windus, 20 Vauxhall Bridge Road, London SW1V 2SA, England.

MOAT John, b. 11 Sept 1936, India. Author; Poet. Education: MA, Oxford University, 1960. Publications: 6d per Annum, 1966; Heorot (novel), 1968; A Standard of Verse, 1969; Thunder of Grass, 1970; The Tugen and the Toot (novel), 1973; The Ballad of the Leat, 1974; Bartonwood, (juvenile), 1978; Fiesta and the Fox Reviews and His Prophecy, 1979; The Way to Write (with John Fairfax), 1981; Skeleton Key, 1982; Mai's Wedding (novel), 1983; Welcombe Overtunes, 1987; The Missing Moon, 1988; Firewater and the Miraculous Mandarin, 1990; Practice, 1994; Skeleton Key (complete), 1997. Address: Crenham Mill, Hartland, North Devon EX39 6HN, England.

MOCEGA-GONZALEZ Esther, b. 24 Feb 1922, Placetas, Cuba. Professor. Education: PhD, University of Havana, Cuba, 1949; PhD, University of Chicago, Illinois, USA, 1973. Appointments: Professor, Institute of Superior Education, Sancti-Spiritus, LV, Cuba, 1945-60; Sub-Director, Secondary Education, Province of Las Villas, 1959-60; Professor, Institute of Superior Education, La Vibora, Havana, Cuba, 1960-62; Professor, Universidad Central de Santa Clara, LV, Cuba, 1960-62; General Director, Secondary Education, Cuba Ministry of Education, La Habana, Cuba, 1960-62; Instructor, 1962-64, Assistant Professor, 1964-74, Associate Professor, 1974-79, Professor, 1979-90, FLD, NIU. Publications: Ideario Juvenil Martiano (co-author), 1953; La narrativa de Alejo Carpentier: su concepto del tiempo como tema fundamental, 1975; Alejo Carpentier: estudios sobre su narrativa, 1980; Hispanoamerica: El circulo perpetuo, 1988. Contributions to: Numerous articles published in refereed journals and numerous papers presented at national and international literary conferences and conventions. Memberships: Instituto Internacional de Literatura Iberoamericana; Circulo de Cultura panamericano; Instituto de Cultura Hispana, Houston, Texas; Friends of Fondren Library, Rice University, Houston, Texas. Address: 96 94 Longmont Lane, Houston, TX 77063, USA.

MODIANO Patrick Jean, b. 30 July 1945, Boulogne-Billancourt, France. Novelist. m. Dominique Zehrfuss, 1970, 2 daughters. Publications: La place de l'etoile, 1968; La ronde de nuit, 1969; Les boulevards de ceinture, 1972; Lacombe Lucien (screenplay), 1973; La polka (play), 1974; Villa triste (novel), 1975; Interrogatoire d'Emmanuel Berl, 1976; Livret de famille (novel), 1977; Rue des boutiques obscures, 1978; Une Jeunesse, 1981; Memory Lane, 1981; De si Braves Garcons (novel), 1982; Poupee blonde, 1983; Quartier perdu, 1985; Dimanches d'Aout, 1986; Une aventure de Choura, 1986; Remise de Peine, 1987; Vestiaire de l'enfance, 1989; Voyage de Noces, 1990; Fleurs de Ruine, 1991; Un Cirque Passe, 1992. Honours: Prix Roger Nimier, 1968; Prix Goncourt, 1978; Chevalier des Arts et des Lettres. Address: c/o Editions Gallimard, 5 rue Sebastien Bottin, 75007 Paris, France.

MOE Christian Hollis, b. 6 July 1929, New York City, New York, USA. Educator; Playwright. m. Carolyn Forman, 7 May 1952, 2 sons. Education: AB, College of William & Mary, 1951; MA, University of North Carolina at Chapel Hill, 1955; PhD, Cornell University, 1958. Appointments: Theater Department, Southern Illinois University, Carbondale, Chair 1958-96, Professor 1988-96. Publications: Creating Historical Drama, 1965; The Strolling Players, play, 1965; Six New Plays for Children, 1971; Three Rabbits White, play, 1975; Tom Sawyer, play adapt, 1977; Eight Plays for Youth, 1992. Contributions to: journals: Dario Fo; Bib of Theatrical Craftsmanship, 1980; House of Blue Leaves, 1996; Speech & Drama. Honours: 7 Playwriting Awards; Fulbright, 1975; American College Theatrical Festival Amoco Award, 1976; Illinois Theatre Association Award of Excellence, 1992. Memberships: Dramatists Guild; American College Theatrical Festival National Playwriting Awards Chair, 1982-86; Association of Theatrical in Higher Education Playwriting Program Chair, 1986-87; Southern Illinois Writers; McKendree Writers Conference, Vice President, 1959-62. Address: 603 South Curtis Place, Carbondale, IL 62901, USA.

MOFFAT Gwen, b. 3 July 1924, Brighton, Sussex, England. Author. m. Gordon Moffat, 1948, 1 daughter. Publications: Space Below My Feet, 1961; Two Star Red, 1964; On My Home Ground, 1968; Survival Count, 1972; Lady With a Cool Eye, 1973; Deviant Death, 1973; The Corpse Road, 1974; Hard Option, 1975; Miss Pink at the Edge of the World, 1975; Over the Sea to Death, 1976; A Short Time to Live, 1976; Persons Unknown, 1978; Hard Road West, 1981; The Buckskin Girl, 1982; Die Like a Dog, 1982; Last Chance Country, 1983; Grizzly Tail, 1984; Snare, 1987; The Stone Hawk, 1989; The Storm Seekers, 1989; Rage, 1990; The Raptor Zone, 1990; Pit Bull, 1991; Veronica's Sisters, 1992; The Outside Edge, 1993; Cue the Battered Wife, 1994. Contributions to: Newspapers and magazines. Memberships: Crime Writers Association; Mystery Writers of America; Society of Authors. Address: c/o Laurence Pollinger Ltd, 18 Maddox Street, Mayfair, London W1R 0EU, England.

MOFFEIT Tony A, b. 14 Mar 1942, Claremont, Oklahoma, USA. Librarian; Poet. Education: BSc, Psychology, Oklahoma State University, 1964; MLS, University of Oklahoma, 1965. Appointments: Assistant Director, Library, 1980-, Poet-in-Residence, 1986-95, University of Southern Colorado; Director, Pueblo Poetry Project, 1980-. Publications: La Nortenita, 1983; Outlaw Blues, 1983; Shooting Chant, 1984; Coyote Blues, 1985; Hank Williams Blues, 1985; The Spider Who Walked Underground, 1985; Black Cat Bone, 1986; Dancing With the Ghosts of the Dead, 1986; Pueblo Blues, 1986; Boogie Alley, 1989; Luminous Animal, 1989; Poetry is Dangerous, the Poet is an Outlaw, 1995. Contributions to: Journals and magazines. Honours: Jack Kerouac Award, 1986; National Endowment for the Arts Fellowship, 1992. Membership: American Library Association. Address: 1501 East 7th, Piebloe, CO 81001, USA.

MOFFETT Judith, b. 30 Aug 1942, Louisville, Kentucky, USA. Poet; Writer; Teacher. m. Edward B Irving, 1983. Education: BA, Hanover College, Indiana, 1964; MA, Colorado State University, 1966; University of Wisconsin at Madison, 1966-67; MA, 1970, PhD, 1971, University of Pennsylvania. Appointments: Fulbright Lecturer, University of Lund, Sweden, 1967-68; Assistant Professor, Behrend College, Penn State University, 1971-75; Visiting Lecturer, University of Iowa, 1977-78; Visiting Lecturer, 1978-79, Assistant Professor, 1979-86, Adjunct Assistant Professor, 1986-88, Adjunct Associate Professor, 1988-, University of Pennsylvania. Publications: Poetry: Keeping Time, 1976; Whinny Moor Crossing, 1984. Fiction: Pennterra, 1987; The Ragged World, 1991; Time, Like an Ever-Rolling Stream, 1992; Two That Came True, 1992; Other: James Merrill: An Introduction to the Poetry, 1984; Homestead Year: Back to the Land in the Suburbs, 1995. Honours: Fulbright Grants, 1967, 1973; American Philosophical Society Grant, 1973; Eunice Tiejens Memorial Prize, 1973; Borestone Mountain Poetry Prize, 1976; Levinson Prize, 1976;

Ingram Merrill Foundation Grants, 1977, 1980; Columbia University Translation Prize, 1978; Bread Loaf Writers Conference Tennessee Williams Fellowship, 1978; Swedish Academy Translation Prize, 1982; National Endowment for the Humanities Translation Fellowship, 1983; National Endowment for the Arts Fellowship, 1984; Swedish Academy Translation Grant, 1993. Address: 951 East Laird Avenue, Salt Lake City, UT 84105, USA.

MOHAMED N P, b. 1 July 1929, Calicut, India. Author. m. 27 Nov 1954, 4 sons, 3 daughters. Education: Intermediate, Madras University. Appointments: Assistant Editor, Kerala Kaumundi, 1987. Publications: Thopplyum Thattavum 1952; Maram, 1959; Hiranya Kashipu, 1976; Abudabi-Dubai, 1978; Ennapadem, 1981; Avar Nalupaer, 1987. Contributions to: Journals and peridocials. Honours: Madras Government Award, Short Stories, 1959; Kerala Sahitya Academy Awards, 1969, 1981. Memberships: Kerala Sahitya Academy, executive committee; Central Academy of Letters, advisory member in Malayasian. Address; Suthalam, Calicut-Pin 6730007, Kerala, India.

MOHLER James A(ylward), b. 22 July 1923, Toledo, Ohio, USA. Roman Catholic Priest; Professor of Religious Studies Emeritus; Writer. Education: LittB, Xavier University, 1946; PhL, 1949, STL, 1956, Bellarmine School of Theology; MSIR Loyola University, 1960; PhD, University of Ottawa, 1964; STD, University of St Paul, 1965. Appointments: Entered Society of Jesuits, 1942; Ordained Roman Catholic Priest, 1955; Instructor, 1960-65, Assistant Professor, 1965-69, Associate Professor, 1969-74, Professor of Religious Studies, 1974-94, Professor Emeritus, 1994-, John Carroll University, Cleveland; Visiting Scholar, Union Theological Seminary, New York City, 1966; Various research fellowships in colleges and universities in the US and overseas. Publications: Man Needs God: An Interpretation of Biblical faith, 1966; The Beginning of Eternal Life: The Dynamic Faith of Thomas Aquinas, Origins and Interpretation, 1968; Dimensions of Faith, Yesterday and Today, 1969; The Origin and Evolution of the Priesthood, 1970; The Heresy of Monasticism: The Christian Monks, Types and Anti-Types, 1971; The School of Jesus: An Overview of Christian Education, Yesterday and Today, 1973; Cosmos, Man, God, Messiah: An Introduction to Religion, 1973; Dimensions of Love, East and West, 1975; Sexual Sublimation and the Sacred, 1978; The Sacrament of Suffering, 1979; Dimensions of Prayer, 1981; Love, Marriage and the Family, Yesterday and Today, 1982; Paradise: Gardens of the Gods, 1984; Health, Healing and Holiness: Medicine and Religion, 1986; Late Have I Loved You: Augustine on Human and Divine Relations, 1991; A Speechless Child is the Word of God: Augustine on the Trinity, Christ, Mary, Church and Sacraments, Prayer, Hope and the Two Cities, 1992. Contributions to: Religious journals. Memberships: American Academy of Religion; American Association of University Professors; Association for Asian Studies; Catholic Theological Society of America; College Theology Society. Address: John Carroll University, University Heights, Cleveland, OH 44118, USA.

MOHR Steffen, b. 24 July 1942, Leipzig, Germany. Author. 3 sons, 4 daughters. Education: Diplomas in Theatre, University of Leipzig and Institute of Literature, Leipzig. Publications: 8 books, 1975-89; Screenplays; Television films; Radio plays. Memberships: Free Society of Literature; Union of Crime Writers. Address: Liechtensteinstrasse 35, Leipzig, Germany.

MOHRT Michel, b. 28 Apr 1914, Morlaix, France. Writer; Editor. m. Françoise Jarrier, 1955, 1 son. Education: Law School, Rennes. Appointments: Lawyer, Marseilles Bar until 1942; Professor, Yale University, 1947-52; Editor, Head of English Translations, Les Editions Gallimard, 1952-. Publications: Novels: Le repit: Mon royaume pour un cheval, 1949; La prison martitime, 1961; La campagne d'Italie, 1965; L'ours des Adirondacks, 1969; Deux Americaines a Paris, 1974; Les moyens du bord, 1975; La guerre civile, 1986; Le Telesieje, 1989. Essays: Montherlant, homme libre, 1943; Le nouveau Roman American, 1956; L'air du large,1969; Vers l'Ouest, 1988; Benjamin ou Lettes sur l'Inconstance, 1989. Plays: Une jeu d'enfer, 1970; La maison du père, 1979; Vers l'Ouest, 1988; On Liquide et on s'en Va, 1992. Honours: Officier, Legion d'honneur, Croix de guerre; Grand Prix du roman de l'Académie Française, 1962; Grand Prix de la Critique Litteraire, 1970; Grand prix du Litteraure de l'Académie Française, 1983. Memberships: Académie Française, 1985; Garrick Club. Address: Editions Gallimard, 5 rue Sebastien-Bottin, Paris 75007, France.

MOJTABAI Ann Grace, b. 8 Jun 1937, New York, New York, USA. Author; Educator. m. Fathollah Motabai, 27 April 1960, div 1966, 1 son, 1 daughter. Education: BA, Philosophy, Antioch College, 1958; MA, Philosophy, 1968, MS in Library Science, 1970, Columbia University. Appointments: Lecturer in Philosophy, Hunter College, 1966-68; Briggs-Copeland Lecturer on English, Harvard University, 1978-83; Writer in Residence, University of Tulsa, 1983-. Publications: Mundome, 1974; The 400 Eels of Sigmund Freud, 1976; A Stopping Place, 1979; Autumn, 1982; Blessed Assurance, 1986; Ordinary Time, 1989; Called Out, 1994. Contributions to: New York Times Book Review; New Republic; Philosophy Today; Philosophical Journal. Honours: Radcliffe Institute Fellow, 1976-78; Guggenheim Fellowship, 1981-82; Richard and Hinda Rosenthal Award, American Academy and Institute of Arts and Letters, 1983; Lillian Smith Award, Southern Regional Council, 1986; Academy Award in Literature, American Academy of Arts and Letters, 1993. Memberships: Mark Twain Society; PEN; Texas Institute of Letters; Phi Beta Kappa. Literary Agent: Georges Borchardt. Address: 2102 South Hughes, Amarillo, TX 79109, USA.

MOKYR Joel, b. 26 July 1946, Leyden, the Netherlands. Professor of Economics and History. m. Margalit B Mokyr PhD, 29 Sept 1969, 2 daughters. Education: BA, Hebrew University, 1968; PhD, Yale University, 1974. Publications: Industrialization in the Low Countries, 1976; Why Ireland Starved, 1983; The Lever of Riches, 1990; The British Industrial Revolution, 1993. Memberships: Fellow, American Academy of Arts and Sciences, 1996. Address: Department of Economics, Northwestern University, Evanston, IL 60208, USA.

MOLBJERG Lis Guri Nostahl, b. 26 July 1920, Copenhagen, Denmark. Danish Government Official. m. Hans Molbjerg, 1944, 1 daughter. Education: Bachelor degree of Public Administration, 1974. Publications: Member of the Party (Euro-Communist Party - experiences from politics), 1995; Two Minutes Silence, poetry, 1995. Contributions to: Poetry in: Wild Wheat; Politiken newspaper. Membership: Society of Danish Authors, 1995-. Address: Krogerrupgade 59 3, 2200 Copenhagen N, Denmark.

MOLDON Peter Leonard, b. 31 Mar 1937, London, England. Writer; Freelance Designer. Education: Hampton Grammar School, 1948-55; Regent Street Polytechnic, 1958-59. Publications: Your Book of Ballet (illustrated and designed by author), 1974, revised edition 1980; Nureyev (designed by author), 1976; The Joy of Knowledge Encyclopaedia (ballet articles), 1976. Contributions to: Dancing Times. Honours: Children's Book of the Year, National Book League, 1974. Address: 11 Oxlip Road, Witham, Essex CM8 2XY, England.

MOLE John Douglas, b. 12 Oct 1941, Taunton, Somerset, England. Teacher; Writer. m. Mary Norman, 22 Aug 1968, 2 sons. Education: MA, Magdalene College, Cambridge, 1964. Publications: In and Out of the Apple, 1984; Homing, 1987; Boo to a Goose (for children), 1987; Passing Judgements: Poetry in the Eighties (critical essays), 1989; The Mad Parrot's Countdown, 1990; The Conjuror's Rabbit, 1992; Depending on the Light, 1993; Selected Poems, 1995; Hot Air (for children), 1996. Contributions to: Periodicals. Honours: Eric Gregory Award, 1970; Signal Award, for the year's outstanding contribution to children's poetry, 1988; Cholmondeley Award, 1994. Membership: Society of Authors. Address: 11 Hill Street, St Albans, Hertfordshire AL3 4QS, England.

MOLLENKOTT Virginia Ramey, b. 1932, USA. Professor of English. Appointments: Faculty Member, Shelton College, 1955-63, Nyack College, 1963-67; Assistant Editor, Seventeenth Century News, 1964-73; Professor of English, William Paterson College of New Jersey, 1967-97. Publications: Adamant and Stone Chips: A Christian Humanist Approach to Knowledge, 1967; In Search of Balance, 1969; Adam Among the Television Trees: An Anthology of Verse by Contemporary Christian Poets (editor), 1971; Women, Men and the Bible, 1977, revised edition, 1988; Is the Homosexual My Neighbour (with Letha Scanzoni), 1978, updated and expanded edition, 1994; Speech, Silence, Action, 1980; Views From the Intersection (with Catherine Barry), 1983; The Divine Feminine: Biblical Imagery of God as Female, 1983; Godding: Human Responsibility and the Bible, 1987; Women of Faith in Dialogue (editor), 1987; Sensuous Spirituality: Out from Fundamentalism, 1992. Memberships: Modern Language Association; Milton Society of America; Evangelical and Ecumenical Women's Caucus. Address: 11 Yearling Trail, Hewitt, NJ 07421, USA.

MOLLOY Michael (John), b. 22 Dec 1940, England. Jounalist; Editor. m. Sandra June Foley, 1964, 3 daughters. Appointments: Staff, 1962-70, Assistant Editor, 1970-75, Deputy Editor, 1975, Editor, 1975-85, Daily Mirror; Director, 1976-, Editor-in-Chief, 1985-, Mirror Group Newspapers; Editor, Sunday Mirror, 1986. Publications: The Black Dwarf, 1985; The Kid from Riga, 1986; The Harlot of Jericho, 1988; The Century. Address: 62 Culmington Road, London W13, England.

MOMADAY Navarre Scott, b. 27 Feb 1934, Lawton, Oklahoma, USA. Writer; Painter; Professor. m. Regina Heitzer, 21 July 1978, 4 daughters. Education: BA, University of New Mexico, 1958; MA, 1960, PhD, 1963, Stanford University. Appointments: Visiting Professor, Columbia University, Princeton University, 1979; Writer-in-Residence, Southeastern University, 1985, Aspen Writers Conference, 1986. Publications: House Made of Dawn, 1968; The Way to Rainy Mountain, 1969; The Names, 1976; The Gourd Dancer, 1976; The Ancient Child, 1989; In the Presence of the Sun, 1992; Enchanted Circle, 1993; The Native Americans (with Linda Hozan), 1993. Honours: Pulitzer Prize in Fiction, 1969; Premio Mondello, Italy, 1979; Honorary Degrees, various universities. Membership: PEN. Address: c/o Julian Bach Literary Agency, New York, USA.

MOMI Balbir Singh, b. 20 Nov 1935, Amagarh, India. Retired Teacher and Education Officer; Writer; Translator. m. Baldev Kaur, 28 Oct 1954, 4 daughters. Education: Honours in Punjabi, 1953, MA, 1970, in Punjabi, Honours in Persian, 1974, PhD registration, 1977, Panjab University, Chandigarh. Appointments: School Teacher, 1954-71; Education Officer, 1976-93; Lecturer and Research Assistant, GND University, Amritsar, 1974-76; Literary Editor, Perdesi Canafi Ajit Punjab, Toronto, Ontario, Canada, 1982-97. Publications: Short stories, novels, plays and translations. Contributions to: Many publications. Honours: Vrious literary awards. Memberships: International Cultural Forum, India and Canada, Senior International Vice-President, 1993-; International Perdesi Punjab, Sahit Sabha, Toronto, and Ajit Sahit Sa, 1982-97. Address: 17 Donaldson Drive, Brampton, Ontario L6Y 3H1, Canada.

MOMMSEN Katharina Zimmer, b. 18 Sep 1925, Berlin, Germany. Professor of Literature. m. Momme H Mommsen, 23 Dec 1948. Education: Abitur, 1943, DrPhilHabil, 1962, University of Berlin; DPhil, University of Tübingen, 1956. Appointments: Researcher, German Academy of Sciences, Berlin, 1949-61; Docent, Professor, Free University of Berlin, 1962-70; Professor, German Literature, Carleton University, Ottawa, 1970-74, Stanford University, 1974-93. Publications: Goethe und 1001 Nacht, 1960; Goethe und Diez, 1961; Goethe und der Islam, 1964; Natur und Fabelreich in Faust II, 1968; Schillers Anthologie, 1973; Kleists Kampf mit Goethe, 1974; Gesellschraftkritik bei Fontane und Thomas Mann, 1974; Herders Journal Meiner Reise, 1976; Hofsmannsthal und Fontane, 1978; Who is Goethe?, 1983; Goethe - Warum?, 1984; Goethes Marchen, 1984; Goethe und die arabische Welt, 1988. Contributions to: Numerous journals and magazines. Honours: Guggenheim Fellowship, 1976; Alexander von Humboldt Forschungspreis, 1980; Bundesverdienskreuz 1 Klasse, 1985; Endowed Chair as Albert Guerard Professor of Literature, Stanford University. Memberships: Various professional organisations. Address: 980 Palo Alto Avenue, Palo Alto, CA 94301, USA.

MONACO James Frederick, b. 15 Nov 1942, New York, USA. Writer; Publisher. m. Susan R Schenker, 24 Oct 1976, 2 sons, 1 daughter. Education: BA, Muhlenberg College, 1963; MA, Columbia University, 1964. Publications: How to Read a Film, 1977, 3rd edition, 1995; American Film Now, 1979, 2nd edition, 1984; The New Wave, 1976; Media Culture, 1977; Celebrity, 1977; Connoisseurs Guide to the Movies, 1985; The International Encyclopedia of Film, 1991; The Movie Guide, 1992; Cinemania: Interactive Movie Guide, 1992. Contributions to: Numerous publications. Memberships: Authors Guild; Writers Guild. Literary Agent: Virginia Barber. Address: UNET Inc, 31 East 12th Street, New York, NY 10003, USA.

MONCURE Jane Belk, b. 16 Dec 1926, Orlando, Florida, USA. Teacher; Author: Consultant. m. James Ashby Moncure, 14 June 1952, 1 son. Education: BS, Virginia Commonwealth University, 1952; MA, Columbia University, 1954. Appointments: Instructor, Early Childhood Education, University of Richmond, Virginia, 1972-73; Burlington Day School, Burlington, North Carolina, 1974-78. Publications: First Steps to Reading - Sound Box Books/The Child's World (24 books), 1970's; Magic Castle Books/ The Child's World (27 books), 1980's; First Steps to Math (10 books), 1980's; Word Bird (27 books), 1980's and 1990's; Discovery World (15 books), 1990's. Honours: Outstanding Service to Young Children, 1979; C S Lewis Gold Medal Award, Best Children's Book of the Year, 1984. Address: Cove Cottage, Seven Lakes Box 3336, West End, NC 27376, USA.

MONETTE Madeleine, b. 3 Oct 1951, Montreal, Quebec, Canada. Author. m. William R Leggio, 27 Dec 1979. Education: MA, Literature, University of Quebec. Publications: Le Double Suspect, 1980; Petites Violences, 1982; Fuites et Poursuites, 1982; Plages, 1986; L'Aventure, la Mesaventure, 1987; Amandes et melon, 1991; Nouvelles de Montreal, 1992; La Femme furieuse, 1997. Contributions to: Periodicals. Honours: Robert-Cliche Award, 1980; Grants, Canadian Council of Arts, the Conseil des Arts et des Lettres du Quebec, Fonds Gabrielle-Roy. Memberships: Quebec Writers Union; PEN. Address; 2 Charlton Street, 11K, New York, NY 10014, USA.

MONEY David Charles, b. 5 Oct 1918, Oxford, England. Schoolmaster. m. Madge Matthews, 30 Nov 1945, 1 son. Education: Honours Degree, Chemistry, 1940, Honours Degree, Geography, 1947, St John's College, Oxford University. Publications: Human Geography, 1954; Climate, Soils and Vegetation, 1965; The Earth's Surface, 1970; Patterns of Settlement, 1972; Environmental Systems (series), 1978-82; Foundations of Geography, 1987; Climate and Environmental Systems, 1988; China - The Land and the People, 1984, revised edition, 1989; China Today, 1987; Australia Today, 1988; Environmental Issues - The Global Consequences, 1994; China in Change, 1996. Honour: Geographical Association, honorary member. Memberships: Farmer's Club; Royal Geographical Society, fellow. Address: 52 Park Avenue, Bedford MK40 2NE, England.

MONEY Keith, b. 1934, Auckland, New Zealand. Author; Artist; Photographer. Publications: Salute the Horse, 1960; The Horseman in Our Midst, 1963; The Equestrian World, 1963; The Art of the Royal Ballet, 1964; The Art of Margot Fonteyn, 1965; The Royal Ballet Today, 1968; Fonteyn: The Making of a Legend, 1973; John Curry, 1978; Anna Pavlova: Her Life & Art, 1982; The Bedside Book of Old Fashioned Roses, 1985; Some Other Sea: The Life of Rupert Brooke, 1988-89; Margot, assoluta, 1993; Fonteyn and Nureyev: The Great Years, 1994. Other: Screenplays. Contributions to: Anthologies, journals, and magazines. Address: Carbrooke Hall Farm, Thetford, Norfolk, England.

MONGRAIN Serg, b. 15 Jan 1948, Trois Rivieres, Quebec, Canada. Writer; Photographer. Educations: Mathematical Université du Quebec a Trois Rivieres, 1972. Publications: L'Oeil du l'idée, 1988, 1991; Le calcul des heures, 1993. As Photographer: Lis: écris, 1981; L'image titre, 1981; Agrestes, 1988; Many exhibition catalogues in art. Contributions to: Periodicals. Membership: Union des écrivains du Quebec. Address: 994 rue Sainte Cecile, Trois Rivieres, Quebec G9A 1L3, Canada.

MONK C. See: MEDVE Victor Cornelius.

MONOD Jean, b. 19 Oct 1941, Paris, France. Writer; Ethnologist; Filmmaker; Editor. m. (1) Marie Laure Chaude, 1962, (2) Kagumi Onodera, 1989, 3 sons, 2 daughters. Education: University of Paris, 1974. Appointments: Lecturer, 1970-; Editor-in-Chief, Aiou, 1987-. Publications: Several books. Contributions to: Journals and periodicals. Honours: Prix Georges Sadoul; Prix Louis Marinde l'Académie des Sciences; d'Ortre-Mer. Address: L'Espinassounel, 48330 Saint Etienne Valle Française, France.

MONSARRAT Ann Whitelaw, b. 8 Apr 1937, Walsall, England. Journalist; Writer. m. Nicholas Monsarrat, 22 Dec 1961. Appointments: Journalist, West Kent Mercury, 1954-58, Daily Mail, London, 1958-61, Tatler, 1993-, UNESCO Courier, 1994; Assistant Editor, Stationery Trade Review, 1961. Publications: And the Bride Wore ... The Story of the White Wedding, 1973; An Uneasy Victorian: Thackeray the Man, 1980. Address: San Lawrenz, Gozo, Malta.

MONTAG Tom b. 31 Aug 1947, Fort Dodge, Iowa, USA. Poet; Editor; Publisher. Education: BA, Dominican College of Racine, 1972. Appointments: Formerly Researcher, Centre for Venture Management; Editor, Publisher, Monday Morning Press, Milwaukee, 1971-; Editor, Publisher, Margins Books, 1974-. Publications: Wooden Nickel, 1972; Twelve Poems, 1972; Measurers, 1972; To Leave This Place, 1972; Making Hay, 1973; The Urban Ecosystem: A Holistic Approcah (editor with F Stearns), 1974; Making Hay and Other Poems, 1975; Ninety

Notes Toward Partial Images and Lover Prints, 1976; Concerns: Essays and Reviews: 1977; Letters Home, 1978: The Essential Ben Zen, 1992. Address: c/o Sparrow Press, 193 Waldron Street, West Lafayette, IN 47906, USA.

MONTAGU OF BEAULIEU Edward John Barrington Douglas-Scott-Montagu, 3rd Baron, b. 20 Oct 1926, London, England. Museum Administrator; Author. m. (1) Elizabeth Belinda, 1959, div 1974, 1 son, 1 daughter, (2) Fiona Herbert, 1974, 1 son. Education: St Peter's Court, Broadstairs; Ridley College, St Catharines, Ontario; Eton College; New College, Oxford. Appointments: Founder, Montagu Motor Car Museum, 1952, world's first Motor Cycle Museum, 1956, National Motor Museum, Beaulieu, 1972; Founder-Editor, Veteran and Vintage magazine, 1956-79; Chairman, Historic Buildings and Monuments Commission, 1983-92. Publications: The Motoring Montagus, 1959; Lost Causes of Motoring, 1960; Jaguar: A Biography, 1961, revised edition, 1986; The Gordon Bennett Races, 1963; Rolls of Rolls-Royce, 1966; The Gilt and the Gingerbread, 1967; Lost Causes of Motoring: Europe, 2 volumes, 1969, 1971; More Equal Than Others, 1970; History of the Steam Car, 1971; The Horseless Carriage, 1975; Early Days on the Road, 1976; Behind the Wheel, 1977; Royalty on the Road, 1980; Home James, 1982; The British Motorist, 1987; English Heritage, 1987; The Daimler Century, 1995. Memberships: Federation of British Historic Vehicle Clubs, president, 1989-; Federation Internationale des Voitures Anciennces, president, 1980-83; Historic Houses Association, president, 1973-78; Museums Association, president, 1982-84; Union of European Historic Houses, president, 1978-81. Address: Palace House, Beaulieu, Brockenhurst, Hants SO42 7ZN, England.

MONTAGUE John (Patrick), b. 28 Feb 1929, New York, New York, USA. Poet; Writer; Lecturer. Education: BA, 1949, MA, 1953, University College, Dublin; Postgraduate Studies, Yale University, 1953-54; MFA, University of Iowa, 1955. Appointment: Lecturer in Poetry, University College, Cork. Publications: Forms of Exile, 1958; The Old People, 1960; Poisoned Lands and Other Poems, 1961; The Dolmen Miscellany of Irish Writing (editor), 1962; Death of a Chieftain and Other Stories, 1964; All Legendary Obstacles, 1966; Patriotic Suite, 1966; A Tribute to Austin Clarke on His Seventieth Birthday, 9th May 1966 (editor with Liam Miller), 1966; Home Again, 1967; A Chosen Light, 1967; Hymn to the New Omagh Road, 1968; The Bread God: A Lecture, with illustrations in Verse, 1968; A New Siege, 1969; The Planter and the Gael (with J Hewitt), 1970; Tides, 1970; Small Secrets, 1972; The Rough Field (play), 1972; The Cave of Night, 1974; O'Riada's Farewell,1974; The Faber Book of Irish Verse (editor), 1974; A Slow Dance, 1975; The Great Cloak, 1978; Selected Poems, 1982; The Dead Kingdom, 1984; Mount Eagle, 1989. Address: Department of English, University College, Cork, Ireland.

MONTE Bryan Robert, b. 3 Nov 1957, Cleveland, Ohio, USA. Writer. Editor. Education: BA, English Literature, University of California, Berkeley, 1983; MA, Graduate Writing Programme, Brown University, 1986. Appointments: California Poet-in-the-Schools, 1983-84; Editor, No Apologies, 1983-; University Fellow, Brown University, 1984-86; Assistant Bibliographer, John Carter Brown Library, 1986; Writing Specialist, Massachusetts Public Schools, 1986-87. Publcations: Poetry: The Mirror of the Medusa, 1987; Neurotika, 1988. Contributions to: James White Review; Bay Windows; Advocate. Honours: Youth and Creative Arts Award, Saints Herald, 1976-78; Joan Lee Yang Memorial Poetry Prize, University of California, 1982; many other honours and awards. Literary Agent: Jayne Walker. Address: 1835 Ednamary Way, No E, Mountain View, CA 94040, USA.

MONTELEONE Thomas Francis, b. 14 Apr 1946, Baltimore, Maryland, USA. Writer. m. Elizabeth, 2 sons, 1 daughter. Education: BS, Psychology, 1964, MA, English Literature, 1973, University of Maryland. Publications: The Time Swept City, 1977; The Secret Sea, 1979; Night Things, 1980; Dark Stars and Other Illuminations, 1981; Guardian, 1981; Night Train, 1984; Lyrica, 1987; The Magnificent Gallery, 1987; Crooked House, 1988; Fantasma, 1989; Borderlands, 1990; Borderlands 2, 1991; Borderlands 3, 1992; The Blood of the Lamb, 1992; Borderlands 4, 1993. Contributions to: Anthologies and magazines. Honours: Nebula Awards, best short story, 1976, 1977; Gabriel Award, best television drama, 1984; Bronze Award, International Film and TV Festival, New York, best television drama, 1984; Bram Stoker Award for Superior Achievement - novel, 1993. Memberships: Science Fiction Writers of America; Horror Writers of America. Address: c/o Howard Morhaim, 175 Fifth Avenue, New York, NY 10010, USA.

MONTGOMERY Marion H Jr, b. 16 Apr 1925, Thomaston, Georgia, USA. Professor of English; Writer; Poet. m. Dorothy Carlisle, 20 Jan 1952, 1 son, 4 daughters. Education: AB, 1950, MA, 1953, University of Georgia; Creative Writing Workshop, University of Iowa, 1956-58. Appointments: Assistant Director, University of Georgia Press, 1950-52; Business Manager, Georgia Review, 1951-53; Instructor, Darlington School for Boys, 1953-54; Instructor, 1954-60, Assistant Professor, 1960-67, Associate Professor, 1967-70, Professor of English, 1970-, University of Georgia; Writer-in-Residence, Converse College, 1969. Publications: Fiction: The Wandering of Desire, 1962; Darrell, 1964; Ye Olde Bluebird, 1967; Fugitive, 1974. Poetry: Dry Lightening, 1960; Stones from the Rubble, 1965; The Gull and Other Georgia Scenes, 1969. Non-Fiction: Ezra Pound: A Critical Essay, 1970; T S Eliot: An Essay on the American Magus, 1970; The Reflective Journey Toward Order: Essays on Dante, Wordsworth, Eliot and Others, 1973; Eliot's Reflective Journey to the Garden, 1978; The Prophetic Poet and the Spirit of the Age, Vol 1: Why Flannery O'Connor Stayed Home, 1980, Vol II: Why Poe Drank Liquor, 1983, Vol III: Why Hawthorne Was Melancholy, 1984; Possum, and Other Receipts for the Recovery of "Southern" Being, 1987; The Trouble with You Innerleckchuls, 1988; The Men I Have Chosen for Fathers: Literary and Philosophical Passages, 1990; Liberal Arts and Community: The Feeding of the Larger Body, 1990; Virtue and Modern Shadows of Turning: Preliminary Agitations, 1990; Romantic Confusions of the Good: Beauty as Truth, Truth Beauty, 1997; Practical Liberal Arts and the Decline of Higher Education, 1997. Contributions to: Anthologies and magazines. Honours: Eugene Saxton Memorial Award, 1960; Georgia Writers Association Award for Fiction; Earhart Foundation Fellowship, 1973-74. Address: Box 115, Crawford, GA 30630, USA.

MONTI Nicolas, b. 8 Jan 1956, Milan, Italy. Architect; Writer. Education: Liceo Gonzaga, Milan, 1974; Paris VI University, 1976; Polytechnic School of Architecture, Milan, 1984. Publications: Mediterranean Houses; Cunha Moraes, Viagens en Angola; Italian Modern: A Design Heritage; Africa Then; Emilio Sommariva; Luca Comerio, Fotografo e Cineasta; Design Ethno, 1994; Il Gioco della Seduzione, 1996. Contributions to: Various publications. Honour: Study Tour of Japan essay contest. Memberships: Ordine degli Architetti; Collegio degli Ingegneri; Società degli Architetti; Studio Professionnale Associati. Literary Agent: Melanie Jackson Agency, 250 West 57th Street, New York, New York, USA. Address: Via Borghetto 5, 20122 Milan, Italy.

MONTPETIT Charles, b. 3 Jan 1958, Montreal, Quebec, Canada. Novelist; Scriptwriter; Cartoonist. Education: BA, Communications, Concordia University, 1979. Publications: Moi ou la planète, 1973; Une Conquête de plus, 1981; Temps perdu, 1984; Temps mort, 1989; La Première Fois, 1991; Copie carbone, 1993; The First Time, 1995; The First Time, Australian version, 1996. Contributions to: Numerous Magazines and Journals. Honours: Actuelle-Jeunesse Prize, 1973; Four Radio-Canada Scriptwriting Competitions, 1978, 1979, 1991, 1995; Governor General Award, 1989; White Raven, 1992; Signet d'or, 1993. Memberships: Communication jeunesse; Canadian Society of Children's Authors, Illustrators and Performers; Canadian Children's Book Centre; SF Canada; Union des écrivaines et écrivains du Québec. Address: 4282C Fullum Street, Montreal, Quebec H2H 2J5, Canada.

MOONEY Bel, b. 8 Oct 1946, Liverpool, England. Writer; Broadcaster. m. Jonathan Dimbleby, 23 Feb 1968, 1 son, 1 daughter. Education: BA, 1st Class Honours, English Language and Literature, University College, London, 1969; Fellow, 1994. Appointments: Columnist, Daily Mirror, 1979-80, Sunday Times, 1982-83, The Listener, 1984-86; Television interview series, television films and radio programmes; Governor, Bristol Polytechnic, 1989-91. Publications: Novels: The Windsurf Boy, 1983; The Anderson Question, 1985; The Fourth of July, 1988; Lost Footsteps, 1993; Intimate Letters, 1997. Children's Books: Liza's Yellow Boat, 1980; I Don't Want To!, 1985; The Stove Haunting, 1986; I Can't Find It!, 1988; It's Not fair!, 1989; A Flower of Jet, 1990; But You Promised!, 1990; Why Not?, 1990; I Know!, 1991; The Voices of Silence, 1994; I'm Scared!, 1994; I Wish!, 1995; The Mouse with Many Rooms, 1995; Why Me?, 1996; I'm Bored!, 1997; Joining the Rainbow, 1997; The Green Man, 1997. Other: The Year of the Child, 1979; Differences of Opinion, 1984; Father Kissmass and Mother Claws (with Gerald

Scarfe), 1985; Bel Mooney's Somerset, 1989; From this Day Forward, 1989; Perspectives for Living, 1992. Address: c/o David Higham Associates, 5 Lower John Street, London W1R 3PE, England.

MOONMAN Eric, b. 29 Apr 1929, Liverpool, England. Visiting Professor in Systems Science. m. Jane Moonman, 10 Sept 1962, div 1991, 2 sons, 1 daughter. Education: Christ Church, Southport; Diploma in Social Sciences, University of Liverpool, 1955; University of Manchester. Appointments: Senior Lecturer in Industrial Relations, South Western Essex Technical College, 1962-64; Senior Research Fellow in Management Sciences, University of Manchester, 1964-66; Member of Parliament, Labour Party, Billericay, 1966-70, Basildon, 1974-79; Director, Centre for Contemporary Studies, 1979-90; Consultant, International Red Cross, 1991-94; Chairman, Essex Radio, 1991-; Visiting Professor of Systems Science, City University, 1992-; Chairman, Academic Response to Anti-Semitism and Racism, 1994-. Publications: The Manager and the Organization, 1961; Employee Security, 1962; European Science and Technology, 1968; Communication in an Expanding Organization, 1970; Reluctant Partnership, 1970; Alternative Government, 1984; The Violent Society (editor), 1987. Contributions to: Newspapers and periodicals. Honour: Order of the British Empire. Memberships: Institute of Management, Fellow; Royal Society of Arts, Fellow. Address: 1 Beacon Hill, London N7 9LY, England.

MOORCOCK Michael (John), (Edward P Bradbury, Desmond Read), b. 18 Dec 1939, Mitcham, Surrey, England. Writer. Appointments: Editor, Tarzan Adventures, 1956-58, Sexton Blake Library, 1959-61, New Worlds, London, 1964-79. Publications: The Stealer of Souls and Other Stories (with James Cawthorn), 1961; Caribbean Crisis, 1962; The Fireclown, 1965, as The Winds of Limbo, 1969; The Sundered World, 1965, as The Blood Red Game, 1970; Stormbringer, 1965; Michael Kane series: Warriors of Mars, 1965, as The City of the Beast, 1970; The Distant Suns (with Philip James), 1975; The Quest for Tanelorn, 1975; The Adventures of Una Persson and Catherine Cornelius in the Twentieth Century, 1976; The End of All Songs, 1976; Moorcock's Book of Martyrs, 1976; The Lives and Times of Jerry Cornelius, 1976; Legends from the End of Time, 1976; The Sailor on the Seas of Fate, 1976; The Transformation of Miss Mavis Ming, 1977, as Messiah at the End of Time, 1978; The Weird of the White Wolf, 1977; The Bane of the Black Sword, 1977; Sojan (for children), 1977; Condition of Muzak, 1977; Glorianna, 1978; Dying for Tomorrow, 1978; The Golden Barge, 1979; My Experiences in the Third World War, 1980; The Russian Intelligence, 1980; The Great Rock'n'Roll Swindle, 1980; Byzantium Endures, 1981; The Entropy Tanga, 1981; The Warhound and the World's Pain, 1981; The Brothel in Rosenstrasse, 1982; The Dancers at the End of Time (omnibus), 1983; The Retreat from Liberty, 1983; The Language of Carthage, 1984; The Opium General and Other Stories, 1984; The Chronicles of Castle Brass, 1985; Letters from Hollywood, 1986; The City in the Autumn Stars, 1986; The Dragon in the Sword, 1986; Death is No Obstacle, 1992. Editor: The Best of New Worlds, 1965; England Invaded, 1977; New Worlds: An Anthology, 1983. Address: c/o Anthony Sheil Associates, 43 Doughty Street, London WC1N 2LF, England.

MOORE Brian, b. 25 Aug 1921, Belfast, Northern Ireland. Author. m. Jean Denney, Oct 1967, 1 son. Education: Saint Malachy's College, Belfast. Publications: The Lonely Passion of Judith Hearne, 1955; The Feast of Lupercal, 1957; The Luck of Ginger Coffey, 1960; An Answer from Limbo, 1962; The Emperor of Ice-Cream, 1965; I am Mary Dunne, 1968; Fergus, 1970; The Revolution Script, 1971; Catholics, 1972; The Great Victorian Collection, 1975; The Doctor's Wife, 1976; The Mangan Inheritance, 1979; The Temptation of Eileen Hughes, 1981; Cold Heaven, 1983; Black Robe, 1985; The Color of Blood, 1987; Lies of Silence, 1990; No Other Life, 1993. Honours: Que, Literary Prize, 1958; Guggenheim Fellowship, 1959; American Academy of Arts and Letters Award, 1961; Fiction Award, Governor General of Canada, 1961; Canada Council Senior Fellowships, 1962, 1976; W H Smith Award, 1973; Scottish Arts Council International Fellowship, 1983; Heinemann Award, Royal Society of Literature, 1986; Sunday Express Book of the Year Award, 1987; Hon D.Litt, Queen's University of Belfast, 1989; Hon D.Litt, National University of Ireland, University College, Dublin, 1991. Address: 33958 Pacific Coast Highway, Malibu, CA 90265, USA.

MOORE Charles Hilary, b. 31 Oct 1956. Journalist; Editor; Writer. m. Caroline Mary Baxter, 1981, 1 son, 1 daughter. Education: BA, Trinity College, Cambridge. Appointments: Joined Editorial Staff,

1979, Leader Writer, 1981-83, Deputy Editor, 1990-92, The Daily Telegraph; Assistant Editor, Political Columnist, 1983-84, Editor, 1984-90, Fortnightly Columnist, 1990-95, The Spectator; Weekly Columnist, The Daily Express, 1987-90; Editor, The Sunday Telegraph, 1992-95; Editor, The Daily Telegraph, 1995-. Address: 16 Thornhill Square, London N1 1BQ, England.

MOORE Christopher Hugh, b. 9 June 1950, Stoke-on-Trent, England. Historian; Writer. m. Louise Brophy, 7 May 1977. Education: BA, Honours, University of British Columbia, 1971; MA, University of Ottawa, 1977. Publications: Louisbourg Portraits, 1982; The Loyalists, 1984; The Illustrated History of Canada (co-author), 1987; Many Radio Documentaries, School Texts, Educational Software Programmes, Historical Guidebooks on Canadian History. Contributions to: Numerous scholarly journals and magazines. Honours: Governor General's Literary Award, 1982; Canadian Historical Association Award of Merit, 1984; Secretary of State's Prize for Excellence in Canadian Studies, 1985. Memberships: Writers Union of Canada; Canadian Historical Association; Ontario Historical Society; Heritage Canada Foundation. Address: 620 Runnymede Road, Toronto, Ontario M6S 3A2, Canada.

MOORE Eric. See: **BRUTON Eric.**

MOORE John Evelyn (Captain), b. 1 Nov 1921, Sant'Ilario, Italy. Editor; Author; Retired Naval Officer. m. (1) Joan Pardoe, 1945, 1 son, 2 daughters, (2) Barbara Kerry. Appointments: Editor, Jane's Fighting Ships, 1972-87, Jane's Naval Review, 1982-87. Publications: Jane's Major Warships, 1973; The Soviet Navy Today, 1975; Submarine Development, 1976; Soviet War Machine (jointly), 1976; Encyclopaedia of World's Warships (jointly), 1978; World War 3 (jointly), 1978; Seapower and Politics, 1979; Warships of the Royal Navy, 1979; Warships of the Soviet Navy, 1981; Submarine Warfare: Today and Tomorrow (jointly), 1986. Membership: Royal Geographical Society, fellow. Address: Elmhurst, Rickney, Hailsham, Sussex BN27 1SF, England.

MOORE Patrick Alfred Caldwell, b. 4 Mar 1923, Pinner, Middlesex, England. Astronomer; Author. Appointments: BBC TV Series, The Sky at Night, 1957-; Radio Braodcasts; Editor, Year Book of Astronomy, 1962-; Director, Armagh Planetarium, 1965-68; Composer, Perseus and Andromeda (opera), 1975; Theseus, 1982. Publications: Guide to the Moon, 1976; Atlas of the Universe, 1980; History of Astronomy, 1983; Guinness Book of Astronomy, revised edition, 1983; The Story of the Earth (with Peter Cattermole), 1985; Halley's Comet (with Heather Couper), 1985; Patrick Moore's Armmchair Astronomy, 1985; Stargazing, 1985; Exploring the Night Sky with Binoculars, 1986; The A-Z of Astronomy, 1986; Astronomy for the Under Tens, 1987; Stargazing, 1988; Men of the Stars, 1988; The Planet Neptune, 1989; Mission to the Planets, 1990; A Passion for Astronomy, 1991; The Earth for Under Tens, 1992; Fireside Astronomy, 1992. Honours: Goodacre Medal, British Astronomical Association, 1968; Officer of the Order of the British Empire, Jackson Gwilt Gold Medal, Royal Astronomical Society, 1977; Klumpke Medal, Astronomical Society of the Pacific, 1979; Commander of the Order of the British Empire, 1988; Minor Planet No 2602 named "Moore" in his honour. Membership: British Astronomical Association. Address: Farthings, 39 West Street, Selsey, West Sussex, England.

MOORE Peter Dale, b. 20 June 1942, Nantyglo, Wales. University Lecturer. m. Eunice P Jervis, 18 Dec 1966, 2 daughters. Education: BSc, 1963, PhD, 1966, University of Wales. Publications: Peatlands; Biography; Pollen Analysis; Atlas of Living World; Encylopedia of Animal Ecology; Mitchell Beazeley Guide to Wild Flowers; European Mires; Methods in Plant Ecology. Contributions to: New Scientist; Nature; Plants Today; Journal of Ecology. Memberships: British Ecological Society; Cambridge Philosophic Society; Botanical Society of British Isles. Address: Division of Life Sciences, Kings College, Campden Hill Road, London W8 7AH, England.

MOORE Ruth Nulton, b. 19 June 1923, Easton, Pennsylvania, USA. Writer. m. Carl Leland Moore, 15 June 1946, 2 sons. Education: BA, Bucknell University; MA, Columbia University. Publications: Frisky the Playful Pony, 1966; Hiding the Bell, 1968; Peace Treatry, 1977; Ghost Bird Myster, 1977; Mystery of the Lost Treasure, 1978; Tomas and the Talking Birds, 1979; Wilderness Journey, 1979; Mystery at Indian Rocks, 1981; The Sorrel Horse, 1982; Danger in the Pines, 1983; In Search of Liberty, 1983; Mystery of the Missing Stallions,

1984; Mystery of the Secret Code, 1985; The Christmas Surprise, 1989; Mystery at the Spanish Castle, 1990; Distant Thunder, 1991; Mystery at Captain's Cove, 1992. Contributions to: Jack and Jill; Children's Activities. Honours: C S Lewis Honor Book Medal, 1983; Religion in Media Silver Angel Award, 1984. Membership: Children's Authors and Illustrators of Philadelphia. Literary Agent: McIntosh and Otis, Address: 3033 Center Street, Bethlehem, PA 18017, USA.

MOORE Sally, b. 12 Feb 1936, Buffalo, New York, USA. Writer; Photographer. m. Richard E Moore, 10 Dec 1960, 1 son, 2 daughters. Education: Mount Holyoke College; Sarah Williston Scholar. Publication:Country Roads of Pennsylvania, 1993. Contributions to: Travel Articles: US Air Magazine, Delta Sky Magazine, Snow Country, New York Times. Memberships: Society of American Travel Writers; American Association of Journalists and Authors. Address: 1226 Blossom Terrace, Boiling Springs, PA 17007, USA.

MOORE Susanna, b. 9 Dec 1948, Bryn Mawr, Pennsylvania, USA. Writer. m., 1 daughter. Publications: My Old Sweetheart, 1982; The Whiteness of Bones, 1990; Sleeping Beauties, 1994; In the Cut, 1995. Honours: PEN/Ernest Hemingway Citation; Sue Kaufman Prize, American Academy of Arts and Letters, 1983. Address: c/o International Creative Management, 40 West 57th Street, New York, NY 10019, USA.

MOOREHEAD Caroline, b. 28 Oct 1944, London, England. Journalist; Writer. Education: BA, University of London, 1965. Appointments: Reporter, Time Magazine, Rome, 1968-69; Feature Writer, Telegraph Magazine, London, 1969-70, The Times, London, 1973-88; Features Writer, Times Educational Supplement, 1970-73; Human Rights Columnist, The Independent, 1988-. Publications: Myths and Legends of Britain (editor and translator), 1968; Fortune's Hostages, 1980; Sidney Bernstein: A Biography, 1983; Freya Stark: A Biography, 1985; Troublesome People, 1986; Betrayal: Children in Today's World, 1989; Bertrand Rundei: A Biography, 1992. Address: 36 Fitzroy Road, London NW1, England.

MOORHOUSE Frank, b. 21 Dec 1938, Nowra, Queensland, Australia. Writer. Education: University of Queensland; WEA. Appointments: President, Australian Society of Authors, 1979-82; Chairman, Copyright Council of Australia, 1985. Publications: Futility and Other Animals, 1969; The Americans, Baby, 1972; The Electrical Experience, 1974; Conference-Ville, 1976; Tales of Mystery and Romance, 1977; Days of Wine and Rage, 1980; Room Service, 1986; Forty-Seventeen, 1988; Lateshows, 1990. Contributions to: Bulletin. Honours: Henry Lawson Short Story Prize, 1970; National Award for Fiction, 1975; Awgie Award, 1976; Gold Medal for Literature, Australian Literary, 1989. Memberships: Australian Royal Automobile Club, Sydney; Crouchos Club, London; Member, Order of Australia. Address: c/o Rosemary Cresswell, Private Bag 5, PO Balmain, New South Wales 2041, Australia.

MOORHOUSE Geoffrey, b. 29 Nov 1931, Bolton, Lancashire, England. Author. m. Marilyn Isobel Edwards, 2 sons, 1 daughter. previous marriage. Publications: The Other England, 1963; Against All Reason, 1969; Calcutta, 1971; The Missionaries, 1973; The Fearful Void, 1974; The Diplomats, 1977; The Boat and the Town, 1979; The Best Loved Game, 1979; Lord's 1983; Indian Britannica, 1983; To the Frontier, 1984; Apples in the Snow, 1990; Hell's Foundation: A Town, it's Myth and Gallipolis, 1992. Contributions to: Guardian; Times; Observer; London Magazine; Books and Bookmen. Honours: Cricket Society Literary Award, 1979; Thomas Cook Literary Award, 1984. Memberships: Royal Geographical Society, fellow; Royal Society of Literature, fellow. Literary Agent: A P Watt Ltd, London. Address: Park House, Gayle, Near Hawes, North Yorks DL8 3RT, England.

MORA Sonia Marta, b. 1 July 1953, San José, Costa Rica. University Researcher; Writer. m. Heian Mora Corrales, 13 July 1974, 3 daughters. Education: DEA, 1988, PhD, 1990, Université Paul Valéry, France, 1988; MA, Universidad de Costa Rica, San José, 1989. Publications: La palabra al margen; La enseñanza del Español en aristo (co-author), 1986; Las poetas del buen amor, 1991; Indomitas voces: las poetas de Costa Rica (anthology) (co-author), 1994; De la sujccion colonial a la patria criolla; El Perigvillo Sarniento y los origenes de la novela hispanoamericana, 1995; Cultura y desarrollo (essay), 1996. Contributions to: Journal of Philosophy, 1997; Journals in Canada, France, and America. Honours: Fulbright Visiting Scholarship, 1987; International Visitor's Programme, US Government, 1996. Memberships: Instituto Internacional de Literatura, 1988;

International Institute of Sociocriticism, France, 1990; National Committee, UNESCO, 1994. Address: PO Box 511-2350 San José, Costa Rica.

MORAES Dominic, b. 19 july 1938, Bombay, India. Writer; Poet. Education: Jesus College, Oxford. Appointments: Managing Editor, Asia Magazine, 1972-; Consultant, United Nations Fund for Population Activities, 1973-. Publications: A Beginning, 1957; Gone Away, 1960; My Son's Father (autobiography), 1968; The Tempest Within, 1972; The People Time Forgot, 1972; A Matter of People, 1974; Voices for Life (essays), 1975; Mrs Gandhi, 1980; Bombay, 1980; Ragasthan: Splendour in the Wilderness, 1988. Other: Poetry and travel books. Honour: Hawthornden Prize, 1957. Address 521 Fifth Avenue, New York, NY 10017, USA.

MORAN John Charles, b. 4 Oct 1942, Nashville, Tennessee, USA. Librarian; Editor; Foundation Director; Researcher. Education: BA, 1967, MLS, 1968, George Peabody College for Teachers. Appointments: Director, F Marion Crawford Memorial Society, 1975-; Editor, The Romantist, 1977-; The Worthis Library, 1980-. Publications: In Memoriam: Gabriel Garcia Moren 1875-1975, 1975; Seeking Refuge in Torre San Nicola, 1980; An F Marion Crawford Companion, 1981; Anne Crawford von Rabe: A Shadow on a Wave (editor), 1981, 2nd edition, 1997; Bibliography of Marketing of Fruits and Vegetables in Honduras 1975-1985 (author, compiler), 1985. Contributions to: Professional journals and to general magazines; Current Research, History of Honduras in the Nineteenth Century. Honours: A Special Guest, Il Magnifico Crawford - Conference on Francis Marion Crawford, Sant' Agnelio Di Sorrento. Address: c/o F Marion Crawford Society, Sarascinesca House, 3610 Meadowbrook Avenue, Nashville, TN 37205, USA.

MORAY WILLIAMS Ursula, b. 19 Apr 1911, Petersfield, Hampshire, England. Writer of Children's Books. m. Conrad Southey John, 28 Sept 1935, 4 sons. Education: Winchester Art College. Publications: Approximately 70 titles, 1931-, including: Jean-Pierre; Adventures of the Little Wooden Horse; Gobbolino the Witch's Cat; Further Adventures of Gobbolino and the Little Wooden Horse; Nine Lives of Island Mackenzie; The Noble Hawks; Bogwoppit; Jeffy the Burglar's Cat; Good Little Christmas Tree; Cruise of the Happy-Go-Gay; Bellabelinda and the No-Good Angel; The Moonball. Contributions to: Magazines. Membership: West of England Writers Guild. Literary Agent: Curtis Brown, London, England. Address: Court Farm House, Beckford, near Tewkesbury, Gloucestershire, England.

MOREAU Ron. Journalist. Education: Graduate, University of California, Berkeley. Appointments: Member, International Voluntary Services, went to Vietnam, 1969; Stringer, Washington Post; Correspondent, Saigon Bureau, 1972, transferred to Hong Kong, 1974, Buenos Aires Bureau Chief, 1976-78, Head of Mideast Bureau, Cairo, 1978, Correspondent, Paris Bureau, 1983, Miami Bureau Chief, 1983-87, Bangkok Bureau Chief, 1987-, Newsweek. Address: c/o Newsweek, 251 West 57th Street, New York, NY 10019-1894, USA.

MORENCY Pierre, b. Lauzon, Quebec, Canada. Writer. Education: BA, College de Levis, 1963; Licence es Lettres, Université Laval, Quebec, 1966. Appointment: Freelance Writer, Radio Canada, 1967-91. Publications: Les Passeuses, 1976; Effets Personnels, 1986; Quand nous serons, 1988; L'Oeil Americain, 1989; A Season for Birds (selected poems), 1990; The Eye is an Eagle, 1992; Glimmer on the Mountain, 1992; Lumière des Oiseaux, 1992; Les Paroles qui Marchent dans la Nuit, 1994; La Vie Entière, 1996. Honours: Prix Alain Grandbois, 1987; Prix Quebec-Paris, 1988; Prix Ludger Duvernay, 1991; Prix France Quebec, 1992; Chevalier, Ordere des Arts et des Lettres de France. Memberships: PEN Club; Union des Ecrivains Quebecois. Address: 155 Wilfrid-Avenue Laurier, Quebec G1R 2K8, Canada.

MORENO Armando, 19 Dec 1932, Porto, Portugal. University Professor; Physician; Writer; Poet; Dramatist. m. Maria Guinot Moreno, 3 Oct 1987. Education: Licentiate in Medicine, 1960; MD, 1972; Aggregation in Medicine, 1984; Licentiate in Literature, 1986. Appointments: 1st Congresso Luso-Brasilerio de Literaturea, Porto, 1984; Oration Sapientia, Universidad Tecnica de Lisboa, Lisbon; 1st Congresso Internacional de Lingua Portuguesa, Lisbon, 1989; Ciclo de Conferencias O Corpo Morfologica, Porto, 1990. Publications: Historias Quase Clinicas (short stories), 3 volumes, 1982, 1984, 1988; A Chamada (short stories), 1982; As Carreiras (romance), 1982; O Bojador (romance) 1982; Biologia do Conto (literary study), 1987; Cais do Sodre (short stories), 1988; O Animal Que deupla Mente, 1993; Contos Oeirenses (short stories), 1994; A Governaçao pela Competencia, 1995. Other: Medical books, poetry and plays. TV Series: Historias quase Clinicas, 1988; Médicos Escritores (author and introducer); Viver com Saude, 1993, 1994, 1995; Historia da Medicine Portuguesa; Arte e Medicina no Mundo; Médicos Artistas Portugueses. Contributions to: Noticias Medicas; Geofarma; Espaco Medico; Intercidades; O Diario; Journal de Letras; Letras e Letras. Honours: Theatre Play Award, Fialho de Almeida, 1982; Literary Award, Abel Salazar, 1986; Great Award to Romance, Cidade de Amadora, 1990. Memberships: Associacao Portuguesa de Escritories; Sociedade Portugeusa de Escritores Medocos; Sociedade de Ciencias Medicas de Lisboa; Sociedade Portuguesa de Anatomia; President, Sociedade de Escritores e Artistas Médicos; President, Associaçao dos Avicultores de Portugal; Vice President, International Union of Medical Writers; President, Uniao de Médicos Escritores e Artistas Lusofonos. Address: Rua Almirante Matos Moreira 7, 2775 Carcavelos, Portugal.

MORETON John. See: **COHEN Morton Norton.**

MORGAN Claire. See: **HIGHSMITH (Mary) Patricia.**

MORGAN David Henry, b. 28 Sept 1928, Invercargill, New Zealand. Consultant; Trainer; Technical Writer. m. Patricia Margaret Taylor, 30 Dec 1961, 2 sons, 1 daughter. Education: MA, University of New Zealand, 1961. Publications: Thinking and Writing, 1966; Effective Business Letters, 1970; Working with Words, 1989; Resource Packages and Distance Education Packages on Writing and Communication. Contributions to: Professional journals. Memberships: Council for Programs in Technical and Scientific Communication. Address: PO Box 687, Civic Square ACT 2608, Australia.

MORGAN Edwin (George), b. 27 Apr 1920, Glasgow, Scotland. Titular Professor of English Emeritus; Poet; Writer. Education: MA, University of Glasgow, 1947. Appointments: Assistant Lecturer, 1947-50, Lecturer, 1960-65, Senior Lecturer, 1965-71, Reader, 1971-75, Titular Professor of English, 1975-80, Professor Emeritus, 1980-, University of Glasgow; Visiting Professor, University of Strathclyde, 1987-90; Honorary Professor, University College, Wales, 1991-95. Publications: Poetry: The Vision of Cathkin Braes, 1952; The Cape of Good Hope, 1955; Starryveldt, 1965; Scotch Mist, 1965; Sealwear, 1966; Emergent Poems, 1967; The Second Life, 1968; Gnomes, 1968; Proverbfolder, 1969; Penguin Modern Poets 15 (with Alan Bold and Edward Brathwaite), 1969; The Horseman's Word: A Sequence of Concrete Poems, 1970; Twelve Songs, 1970; The Dolphin's Song, 1971; Glasgow Sonnets, 1972; Instamatic Poems, 1972; The Whittrick: A Poem in Eight Dialogues, 1973; From Glasgow to Saturn, 1973; The New Divan, 1977; Colour Poems, 1978; Star Gate: Science Fiction Poems, 1979; Poems of Thirty Years, 1982; Grafts/Takes, 1983; Sonnets from Scotland, 1984; Selected Poems, 1985; From the Video Box, 1986; Newspoems, 1987; Themes on a Variation, 1988; Tales from Limerick Zoo, 1988; Collected Poems, 1990; Hold Hands Among the Atoms, 1991; Sweeping Out the Dark, 1994. Other: Essays, 1974; East European Poets, 1976; Hugh MacDiarmid, 1976; Twentieth Century Scottish Classics, 1987; Nothing Not Giving Messages (interviews), 1990; Crossing the Border: Essays in Scottish Literature, 1990; Language, Poetry and Language Poetry, 1990; Evening Will Come They Will Sew the Blue Sail, 1991. Editor: Collins Albatross Book of Longer Poems: English and American Poetry from the Fourteenth Century to the Present Day, 1963; Scottish Poetry 1-6 (co-editor), 1966-72; New English Dramatists 14, 1970; Scottish Satirical Verse, 1980; James Thomson: The City of Dreadful Night, 1993. Translator: Beowulf, 1952; Poems fron Eugenio Montale, 1959; Sovpoems, 1961; Vladimir Mayakovsky: Wi the Haill Voice, 1972; Fifty Renascence Love Poems, 1975; Rites of Passage, 1976; Platen: Selected Poems, 1978; Master Peter Pathelin, 1983; Edmond Rostand: Cyrano de Bergerac: A New Verse Translation, 1992; Collected Translations, 1996. Honours: Cholmondeley Award for Poets, 1968; Scottish Arts Council Book Awards, 1968, 1973, 1975, 1977, 1978, 1983, 1984, 1991, 1992; Hungarian PEN Memorial Medal, 1972; Soros Translation Award, 1985. Address: 19 Whittingehame Court, Glasgow G12 0BG, Scotland.

MORGAN (George) Frederick, b. 25 Apr 1922, New York, New York, USA. Poet; Writer; Editor. m. (1) Constance Canfield, 1942, div 1957, 6 children, (2) Rose Fillmore, 1957, div 1969, (3) Paula Deitz, 1969. Appointments: Co-Founder, 1947, Editor, 1947-, The Hudson Review; Chair, Advisory Council, Department of Romance Languages and Literatures, Princeton University, 1973-90. Publications: Poetry:

A Book of Change, 1972; Poems of the Two Worlds, 1977; Death Mother and Other Poems, 1979; The River, 1980; Northbrook, 1982; Eleven Poems, 1983; Poems, New and Selected, 1987. Other: The Tarot of Cornelius Agrippa, 1978; The Fountain and Other Fables, 1985. Editor: The Hudson Review Anthology, 1961; The Modern Image: Outstanding Stories from "The Hudson Review", 1965. Honour: Chevalier de l'Ordre des Arts et des Lettres, France, 1984. Address: c/o The Hudson Review, 684 Park Avenue, New York, NY 10021, USA.

MORGAN Memo. See: **AVALLONE Michael (Angelo Jr).**

MORGAN Michaela, b. 7 Apr 1951, Manchester, England. Writer; Teacher. m. Colin Holden, 1 son. Education: BA, University of Warwick, 1973; PGCE, University of Leicester, 1975. Appointment: Writer-in-Residence, HM Prisons, Ashwell and Stocken, Leicester, 1992. Publications: The Monster is Coming; The Edward Stories; Dinostory; The Helpful Betty Stories;. Harraps Junior and Longmans Project. Contributions to: Poetry anthologies for children. Honours: Children's Book of the Year; Children's Choice, International Reading Association and United Kingdom Reading Association Award. Memberships: Society of Authors; NAWE. Literary Agent: Rosemary Sandberg, Bowerdean Street, London SW6, England. Address: 9 Main Street, Bisbrooke, Oakham, Rutland, Leics LE15 9EP, England.

MORGAN Mihangel. See: **MORGAN-FINCH Mihangel Ioan.**

MORGAN (Colin) Pete(r), b. 7 June 1939, Leigh, Lancashire, England. Poet. Education: Normanton School, Buxton, 1950-57. Appointments: Creative Writing for Northern Arts, Loughborough University, 1975-77. Publications: A Big Hat or What, 1968; Loss of Two Anchors, 1970; Poems for Shortie, 1973; The Grey Mare Being the Better Steed, 1973; I See You on My Arm, 1975; Ring Song, 1977; The Poets Deaths, 1977; Alpha Beta, 1979; The Spring Collection, 1979; One Greek Alphabet, 1980; Reporting Back, 1983; A Winter Visitor, 1984; The Pete Morgan Poetry Pack, 1984. Plays: Still the Same Old Harry, 1972; All the Voices Going Away, 1979. Television Documentaries. Honours: Arts Council of Great Britain Award, 1973. Address: c/o Fordon Fraser Publications, Eastcotts Road, Bedford MK4Z 0JX, England.

MORGAN Robert, b. 3 Oct 1944, Hendersonville, North Carolina, USA. Professor of English; Poet; Writer. m. Nancy K Bullock, 1965, 1 son, 2 daughters. Education: Emory College, Oxford, 1961-62; North Carolina State University, Raleigh, 1962-63; BA, University of North Carolina at Chapel Hill, 1965; MFA, University of North Carolina at Greensboro, 1968. Apointments: Instructor, Salem College, Winston-Salem, North Carolina, 1968-69; Lecturer, 1971, Assistant Professor, 1973-78, Associate Professor, 1978-84, Professor, 1984-92, Kappa Alpha Professor of English, 1992-, Cornell University. Publications: Poetry: Zirconia Poems, 1969; The Voice in the Crosshairs, 1971; Red Owl, 1972; Land Diving, 1976; Trunk & Thicket, 1978; Groundwork, 1979; Bronze Age, 1981; At the Edge of the Orchard Country, 1987; Sigodlin, 1990; Green River: New and Selected Poems, 1991. Fiction: The Blue Valleys: A Collection of Stories, 1989; The Mountains Won't Remember Us and Other Stories, 1992; The Hinterlands: A Mountain Tale in Three Parts, 1994; The Truest Pleasure, 1995. Non-Fiction: Good Measure: Essays, Interviews and Notes on Poetry, 1993. Honours: National Endowment for the Arts Fellowships, 1968, 1974, 1981, 1987; Southern Poetry Review Prize, 1975; Eunice Tietjins Award, 1979; Jacaranda Review Fiction Prize, 1988; Guggenheim Fellowship, 1988-89; Amon Liner Prize, 1989; James G Hanes Poetry Prize, 1991; North Carolina Award in Literature, 1991. Address: c/o Department of English, Goldwin Smith Hall, Cornell University, Ithaca, NY 14853, USA.

MORGAN Robin (Evonne), b. 29 Jan 1941, Lake Worth, Florida, USA. Journalist; Editor; Writer; Poet. 1 child. Education: Columbia University. Appointments: Editor, Grove Press, 1967-70; Visiting Chair and Guest Professor, New College, Sarasota, Florida, 1973; Editor and Columnist, 1974-87, Editor-in-Chief, 1989-93, Ms Magazine; Distinguished Visiting Scholar and Lecturer, Rutgers University, 1987. Publications: Sisterhood is Powerful: An Anthology of Writings from the Women's Liberation Movement (editor), 1970; Going Too Far: The Personal Chronicle of a Feminist, 1978; The Anatomy of Freedom: Feminism, Physics and Global Politics, 1982, 2nd edition, 1994; Sisterhood is Global: The International Women's Movement Anthology (editor), 1984; The Demon Lover: On the Sexuality of Terrorism, 1989; The Word of a Woman: Feminist Dispatches 1968-91, 1992, 2nd edition, 1994. Fiction: Dry Your Smile: A Novel, 1987; The Mer-Child: A New Legend, 1991. Poetry: Monster, 1972; Lady of the Beasts, 1976; Death Benefits, 1981; Depth Perception: New Poems and a Masque, 1982; Upstairs in the Garden: Selected and New Poems, 1968-88, 1990. Plays: In Another Country, 1960; The Duel, 1979. Contributions to: Magazines and periodicals. Honours: National Endowment for the Arts Grant, 1979-80; Yaddo Grant, 1980; Ford Foundation Grants, 1982, 1983, 1984; Feminist of the Year Award, Fund for a Feminist Majority, 1990. Memberships: Feminist Writers' Guild; Media Women; North American Feminist Coalition; Sisterhood is Global Institute, co-founder. Address: 230 Park Avenue, New York, NY 10169, USA.

MORGAN-FINCH Mihangel Ioan, (Mihangel Morgan), b. 7 Dec 1959, Aberdare, Wales, England. University Lecturer. Education: BA, University of Wales, 1990; PhD, University of Wales, 1995. Publications: Diflaniad Fy Fi, 1988; Beth Yw Rhif Ffôn Duw, 1991; HenLwybr A Storiau Eraill, 1992; Saith Pechod Marwol, 1993; Dirgel Ddyn, 1993; Te Gyda'r Frenhines, 1994; Tair Ochr Geiniog, 1996. Contributions to: Barn; Barddas; Taliesin; Tu Chwith; Poetry Wales. Honours: Prose Medal, Eisteddfod, 1993; BBC Wales Arts Awards, Runner Up, 1993; Welsh Arts Council, Book of the Year Short List, 1993-94. Memberships: Gorsedd Beirdd; Ynys Prydain. Address: Porth Ceri, Talybont, Aberystwyth, Dyfed, Wales.

MORIARTY J. See: **KELLY Tim.**

MORITZ A(lbert) F(rank), b. 15 Apr 1947, Niles, Ohio, USA. Writer; Poet; Editor; Publisher. m. Theresa Carrothers, 1 son. Education: BA, 1969, MA, 1972, PhD, 1975, Marquette University. Publications: Signs and Certainties, 1979; Music and Exile, 1980; Black Orchid, 1981; The Pocket Canada (with Theresa Moritz), 1982; Canada Illustrated: The Art of Nineteenth-Century Engraving, 1982; Between the Root and the Flower, 1982; The Visitation, 1983; America the Picturesque: The Art of Nineteenth-Century Engraving, 1983; Stephen Leacock: A Biography, 1985; The Oxford Illustrated Literary Guide to Canada, 1987; Song of Fear, 1992. Contributions to: Periodicals. Honour: American Academy of Arts and Letters Fellow, 1991. Address: 31 Portland Street, Toronto, Ontario M5V 2V9, Canada.

MORLAND Dick. See: **HILL Reginald (Charles).**

MORLEY Don, b. 28 Jan 1937, Derbyshire, England. Photographer; Journalist. m. Josephine Mary Munro, 17 Sept 1961, 2 sons. Education: National Certificates, Electrical Engineering, Photography. Appointments: Former Picture Editor, The Guardian; Former Chief Photographer, Sports World Magazine, British Olympic Association; Chief Photographer, Moto Course; Founder Member/Director All Sport Photographic Ltd, 1975. Publications: Action Photography, 1975; Motorcycling, 1977; Everyone's Book of Photography, 1977; Everyone's Book of Motorcycling, 1981; The Story of the Motorcycle, 1983; Motorbikes, 1983; Classic British Trial Bikes, 1984; Classic British Moto Cross Machines, 1985; The Classic British Two Stroke Trials Bikes, 1987; The Spanish Trials Bikes, 1987; Trials: A Rider's Guide, 1990; BSA (History in Colour), 1990; Triumph (History in Colour), 1990; Norton (History in Colour), 1990; BMW (History in Colour), 1993. Contributions to: Magazines and journals worldwide. Honours: 17 national and international photography awards. Memberships: Professional Sports Photographers Association, founder, chairman, and honorary life member; Guild of Motoring Writers; Sports Writers Association of Great Britain. Address: 132 Carlton Road, Reigate, Surrey RH2 0JF, England.

MORLEY Patricia Marlow, b. 25 May 1929, Toronto, Ontario, Canada. Writer; Educator. m. Lawrence W Morley, div, 3 sons, 1 daughter. Education: BA Hon, English Language and Literature, University of Toronto, 1951; MA, English, Carleton University, 1967; PhD, English Literature, University of Ottawa, 1970. Appointments: Assistant Professor, 1972-75, Associate Professor, 1975-80, Fellow, 1979-89, Professor of English and Canadian Studies, 1980-89, Lifetime Honorary Fellow, 1989-, Simone de Beauvoir Institute, Concordia University. Publications: The Mystery of Unity: Theme and Technique in the Novels of Patrick White, 1972; The Immoral Moralists: Hugh MacLennan and Leonard Cohen, 1972; Robertson Davies: Profiles in Canadian Drama, 1977; The Comedians: Hugh Hood and Rudy Wiebe, 1977; Morley Callaghan, 1978; Kurelek: A Biography, 1986; Margaret Laurence, The Long Journey Home, 1991; As Though Life Mattered: Leo Kennedy's Story, 1994. Contributions to:

Professional and mainstream journals. Honours: Award for Non-fiction, 1987; Ottawa-Carleton Literary Award, 1988; D S Litt (Doctor of Sacred Letters), Thorneloe College, Laurentian University, 1992. Membership: Writer's Union of Canada. Address: Box 137, Manotick, Ontario K4M 1A2, Canada.

MORLEY Sheridan Robert, b. 5 Dec 1941, Ascot, Berkshire, England. Journalist; Biographer; Broadcaster. m. Margaret Gudejko, 18 July 1965, div. 1990, 1 son, 2 daughters. Education: MA (Hons), Merton College, Oxford, 1964. Appointments: Arts Editor, Punch, 1974-88; Drama Critic, International Herald Tribune, 1975-; Drama Critic, Spectator, 1992-; Film Critic, Sunday Express, 1992-94. Publications: A Talent to Amuse (1st biography of Noel Coward), 1969; The Other Side of the Moon (1st biography of David Niven), 1979; Odd Man Out (1st biography of James Mason), 1984; Gladys Cooper; Gertrude Lawrence; Oscar Wilde; Tales From the Hollywood Raj; Elizabeth Taylor; Marlene Dietrich; Katherine Hepburn; Review Copies; Our Theatres in the 80's; Spread a Little Happiness, 1986; Shooting Stars: Our Theatres in the Eighties, 1990; Methuen Book of Theatrical Short Stories, 1992; Robert My Father, 1993; Audrey Hepburn, 1993; Methuen Book of Movie Stories, 1994; Dirk Bogarde, 1996; Gene Kelly, 1996. Contributions to: Times; Punch; Herald Tribune; Spectator; Sunday Times; Playbill, USA; Variety, USA; Australian. Honour: BP Arts Journalist of the Year, 1990. Memberships: Critics Circle; Garrick Club. Literary Agent: Curtis Brown, 28 Haymarket London, SW1 45P. Address: 5 Admiral Square, Chelsea Harbour, London SW10 0UU, England.

MORPURGO Jack Eric, b. 26 Apr 1918, London, England. Author; Literary Agent; University Professor. m. Catherine Noel Kippe Cammaerts, 16 July 1947, dec 1993, 3 sons, 1 daughter. Education: Christ's Hospital, England; University of New Brunswick, Canada; BA, College of William and Mary, USA, 1938; Durham University, England, 1939; Institute of Historical Research, 1946. Appointments: Editor, Penguin Books, 1945-69, Penguin Parade, 1949-50; General Editor, Penguin History of England and Penguin History of the World, 1949-69; Assistant Director, Nuffield Foundation, 1951-54; Director General, National Book League, 1954-69; Professor of American and Canadian Studies, University of Geneva, Switzerland, 1968-70; Professor of American Literature, University of Leeds, England, 1969-83. Publications: American Excursion, 1949; Leigh Hunt: Autobiography (editor), 1949; Charles Lamb and Elia, 1949; The Christ's Hospital Book (with Edmund Blunden), 1952; History of the United States (co-author), 2 volumes, 1955; The Road to Athens, 1963; Barnes Wallis: A Biography, 1972; Their Majesties: Royall Colledge, 1976; Allen Lane: King Penguin, 1979; Christ's Hospital (with G A T Allan), 1986; Master of None: An Autobiography, 1990; Christ's Hospital: An Introductory History, 1990; Charles Lamb and Elia, 1993; Editions of Trelawny, Keats, Cobbett, Fenimore Cooper, Lewis Carroll, Marlowe and others. Contributions to: Times Literary Supplement; Daily Telegraph; Yorkshire Post; Quadrant, Australia; Mayfair, Canada. Honours: 5 honorary doctorates, USA institutions; Special Literary Award, Yorkshire Post, 1980. Memberships: Army and Navy Club; Pilgrims. Literary Agent: Sexton Agency and Press Ltd. Address: Managing Director, P & M Youngman Carter Ltd, 12 Laurence Mews, Askew Road, London W12 9AT, England.

MORRELL David, b. 24 Apr 1943, Kitchener, Ontario, Canada. Author. m. Donna Maziarz, 10 Oct 1965, 1 son, dec, 1 daughter. Education: BA, University of Waterloo, 1966; MA, 1967, PhD, 1970, Penn State University. Appointments: Assistant Professor, 1970-74, Associate Professor, 1974-77, Professor of American Literature, 1977-86, University of Iowa. Publications: Fiction: First Blood, 1972; Testament, 1975; Last Reveille, 1977; The Totem, 1979; Blood Oath, 1982; The Hundred-Year Christmas, 1983; The Brotherhood of the Rose, 1984; Rambo: First Blood, Part II, 1985; The Fraternity of the Stone, 1985; The League of Night and Fog, 1987; Rambo III, 1988; The Fifth Profession, 1990; The Covenant of the Flame, 1991; Assumed Identity, 1993; Desperate Measures, 1994; Extreme Denial, 1996. Non-fiction: John Barth: An Introduction, 1976; Fireflies, 1988. Contributions to: Journals and magazines. Honours: Distinguished Recognition Award, Friends of American Writers, 1972; Best Novella Awards, Horror Writers of America, 1989, 1991. Memberships: Horror Writers of America; Writers Guild of America. Address: c/o Henry Morrison, PO Box 235, Beford Hills, NY 10507, USA.

MORRIS Desmond John, b. 24 Jan 1928, Purton, Wiltshire, England. Zoologist. m. Ramona Baulch, 30 July 1952, 1 son. Education: BSc, Birmingham University, 1951; DPhil, Oxford

University, 1954. Publications: The Biology of Art, 1962; The Naked Ape, 1967; The Human Zoo, 1969; Manwatching, 1977; Catwatching, 1986; Dogwatching, 1986; The Animal Contract, 1990; Animal-Watching, 1990; Babywatching, 1991; Christmas Watching, 1992; The World of Animals, 1993; The Human Animal, 1994; The World Guide to Gestures, 1994. Contributions to: Many journals and magazines. Membership: Scientific Fellow, Zoological Society of London. Address: c/o Jonathan Cape, Random Century House, 20 Vauxhall Bridge Road, London SW1V 2SA, England.

MORRIS Jan, (James Morris), b. 2 Oct 1926. Writer. Appointments: Editorial Staff: The Times, 1951-56; The Guardian, 1957-62. Publications: (as James Morris) Coast to Coast, 1956; Sultan in Oman, 1957; The Market of Seleukia, 1957; Coronation Everest, 1958; South African Winter, 1958; The Hashemite Kings, 1959; Venice, 1960; The Upstairs Donkey (for children), 1962; The Road to Huddersfield, 1963; Cities, 1963; The Presence of Spain, 1964; Oxford, 1968; Pax Britannica, 1968; The Great Port, 1970; Places, 1972; Heaven's Command, 1973; Farewell the Trumpets, 1978. (As Jan Morris), Conundrum, 1974; Travels, 1976; The Oxford Book of Oxford, 1978; Spain, 1979; Destinations; The Venetian Empire, My Favourite Stories of Wales, 1980; The Small Oxford Book of Wales, Wales the First Place; A Venetian Bestiary; Spectacle of Empire, 1982; Stones of Empire, 1983; Journeys, 1984; The Matter of Wales, 1984; Among the Cities, 1985; Last Letters from Hav, 1985; Stones of Empire: The Buildings of the Raj, 1986; Manhattan '45, 1987; Hong Kong, 1988; Pleasures of a Tangled Life (autobiography), 1989; Ireland, Your Only Place, 1990; City to City, 1990; Sydney, 1992; A Machynlleth Triad, 1993; Fisher's Face, 1995. Honours: Commonwealth Fellowship, USA, 1954; George Polk Memorial Award for Journalism, USA, 1961; Heinemann Award for Literature; Honorary Fellow, University College of Wales, Aberystwyth; Honorary DLitt, University of Wales; Honorary D Litt, University of Glamorgan. Membership: Yr Academi Gymreig. Address: Trefan Morys, Llanystumdwy, Cricieth, Gwynedd, LL52 0LP, Wales.

MORRIS Janet Ellen, (Casey Prescott, Daniel Stryker), b. 25 May 1946, Boston, Massachusetts, USA. Writer. m. 31 Oct 1970. Publications: Silistra Quartet, 1976-78, 1983-84; Dream Dance Trilogy, 1980-83; I the Sun, 1984; Heroes in Hell, 10 volumes, 1984-88; Beyond Sanctuary, 3 volumes, 1985-86; Warlord, 1986; The Little Helliad, 1986; Outpassage, 1987; Kill Ratio, 1987; City at the Edge of Time, 1988; Tempus Vabound, 1989; Target (with David Drake), 1989; Warrior's Edge, 1990; Threshold, 1991; Trust Territory, 1992; American Warrior, 1992; The Stalk, 1994. Contributions to: Various publications. Honour: Hellva Award for Best Novel, 1985. Memberships: Science Fiction Writers of America; Mystery Writers of America; BMI (Broadcast Music Inc); New York Academy of Science; National Intelligence Study Center; Association of Old Crows. Literary Agent: Perry Knowlton. Address: c/o Curtis Brown Ltd, 10 Astor Place, New York, NY 10003, USA.

MORRIS Julian. See: **WEST Morris.**

MORRIS Mary, b. 14 May 1947, Chicago, Illinois, USA. Writer. m. Larry O'Connor, 20 Aug 1989, 1 daughter. Education: BA, Tufts College, 1969; MA, 1973, MPhil, 1977, Columbia University. Appointments: Teacher, Princeton University, 1980-87, 1991-94; New York University, 1988-94; Sarah Lawrence College, 1994. Publications: Nothing to Declare: Memoirs of a Woman Travelling Alone, 1989; Wall to Wall: From Beijing to Berlin by Rail, 1992; A Mother's Love, 1993; Maiden Voyages, 1993; House Arrest, 1996; The Lifeguard, 1997. Contributions to: Periodicals. Honours: Rome Prize; Guggenheim Fellowship. Memberships: American PEN; Authors Guild; Friends of the American Academy in Rome. Address: Ellen Levine Literary Agency, 15 E 26th St, New York, NY 10010, USA.

MORRIS Mervyn, b. 1937, Kingston, Jamaica. Lecturer; Poet. Education: University of West Indies, Kingston; St Edmund Hall, Oxford. Appointments: Senior Lecturer, University of West Indies, 1970; Reader, West Indian Literature. Publications: The Pond, 1973; On Holy Week, 1976; Shadowboxing, 1979. Editor: Seven Jamaican Poets, 1971; Jamaica Women: An Anthology of Poems, 1980; Focus, 1983; An Anthology of Contemporary Jamaican Writing; The Faber Book of Contemporary Caribbean Short Stories, 1990. Honour: Institute of Jamaica Musgrave Medal, 1976. Address: Department of English, University of West Indies, Mona, Kingston 7, Jamaica.

MORRIS Sara. See: **BURKE John Frederick.**

MORRIS Vera. See: **KELLY Tim.**

MORRISON (Philip) Blake, b. 8 Oct 1950, Burnley, Lancashire, England. Literary Editor; Poet; Writer. m. Katherine Ann Drake, 1976, 2 sons, 1 daughter. Education: BA, University of Nottingham, 1972; PhD, University College, London, 1978. Appointments: Literary Editor, The Observer, 1987-89, The Independent on Sunday, 1990-. Publications: The Movement: English Poetry and Fiction of the 1950's, 1980; Seamus Heaney, 1982; The Penguin Book of Contemporary British Poetry (co-editor), 1982; Dark Glasses, 1984-89; The Ballad of the Yorkshire Ripper and Other Poems, 1987; The Yellow House, 1987; And When Did You Last See Your Father?, 1994. Honours: Somerset Maughan Award, 1984; Dylan Thomas Prize, 1985; J R Ackerley Prize, 1994. Membership: Royal Society of Literature, fellow. Address: c/o The Independent on Sunday, 40 City Road, London EC1Y 2DB, England.

MORRISON Anthony (Tony) James, b. 5 July 1936, England. Television Producer; Writer. Appointments: Partner, South American Pictures; Director, Nonesuch Expeditions Ltd. Publications: Steps to a Fortune (co-author), 1967; Animal Migration, 1973; Land Above the Clouds, 1974; The Andes, 1976; Pathways to the Gods, 1978; Lizzie: A Victorian Lady's Amazon Adventure (co-editor), 1985; The Mystery of the Nasca Lines, 1987; Margaret Mee, In Search of Flowers of the Amazon (editor), 1988; QOSQO, Navel of The World, 1995. Membership: Margaret Mee Amazon Trust. Address: 48 Station Road, Woodbridge, Suffolk IP12 4AT, England.

MORRISON Bill, b. 22 Jan 1940, Ballymoney, Northern Ireland. Playwright; Theatre Director. Div, 1 son, 1 daughter. Education: LLB (Honours), Queen's University, Belfast, 1962. Appointments: Resident Playwright, Victoria Theatre, Stoke-on-Trent, England, 1968-71, Everyman Theatre, Liverpool, 1976-79; Associate Director, 1981-83, Artistic Director, 1983-85, Liverpool Playhouse. Publications: Stage plays: Flying Blind, 1979; Scrap, 1982; Be Bop a Lula, 1988; A Love Song for Ulster, 1993; Patrick's day, 1972; Cavern of Dreams, (with Carol Ann Duffy), 1984; Drive On, 1996; Radio and stage plays: Sam Slade Is Missing, 1971; The Love of Lady Margaret, 1972; Ellen Cassidy, 1975; The Emperor of Ice Cream, 1977; Blues in a Flat, 1989; The Little Sister, 1990. Radio plays: The Great Gun-Running Episode, 1973; Simpson and Son, 1977; Maguire, 1978; The Spring of Memory, 1981; Affair, 1991; Three Steps to Heaven, 1992; Waiting for Lefty, 1994; Murder at the Cameo, 1996. TV plays: McKinley and Sarah, 1974; Joggers, 1979; Potatohead Blues, 1980; Shergar, 1986; A Safe House, 1990; Force of Duty, 1992; C'mon Everybody, 1996. Honour: Best Programme, Pye Radio Awards, 1981. Address: c/o Alan Brodie Presentation, 211 Piccadilly, London W1V 9LD England.

MORRISON Dorothy Jean Allison, b. 17 Feb 1933, Glasgow, Scotland. Author; Lecturer. m. James F T Morrison, 12 Apr 1955, 1 son, 1 daughter. Education: MA (Honours), Glasgow University. Appointments: Principal Teacher of History, Montrose Academy, 1968-73; Lecturer in History, Dundee College of Education, 1973-83; Advisor to Scottish History series, History at Hand series, Scotland's War series, Scottish TV. Publications: Old Age, 1972; Young People, 1973; Health and Hospitals, 1973; The Civilian War (with M Cuthbert), 1975; Travelling in China, 1977; The Romans in Britain, 1978, 2nd edition, 1980; Billy Leaves Home, 1979; Story of Scotland (with J Halliday), I, 1979, 1980, II, 1982; The Great War, 1914-18, 1981; Historical Sources for Schools, I Agriculture, 1982; History Around You, 1983; People of Scotland, I, 1983, II, 1985; Ancient Greeks (with John Morrison), 1984; Handbook on Money Management, 1985; Modern China, 1987; The Rise of Modern China, 1988; Montrose Old Church - A History, 1991; Scotland's War, 1992; A Sense of History - Castles, 1994; Ancient Scotland, 1996; The Wars of Independence, 1996. Address: Craigview House, Usan, Montrose, Angus DD10 9SD, Scotland.

MORRISON Sally, b. 29 June 1946, Sydney, New South Wales, Australia. Writer. 1 son. Education: BSc (Hons), Australian National University, 1970. Publications: Who's Taking You to the Dance? (novel), 1979; I Am a Boat (short stories), 1989; Mad Meg (novel), 1994. Contributions to: Bulletin; Australian Literary Supplement; Overland; Quadrant; Island; Sydney Morning Herald; Age Monthly Review. Honours: Project Assistance Grants, Victorian Ministry of the Arts, 1988, 1993, 1994; Writer's Grants, Australia Council Literary Board, 1990, 1991, 1992; Winner, National Book Council Banjo Award for Fiction, for Mad Meg, 1995. Memberships: Fellowship of Australian Writers; Australian Society of Authors; Victorian Writers Centre.

Address: c/o Margaret Connolly and Associates, PO Box 495, Wahroonga, New South Wales 2021, Australia.

MORRISON Toni, b. 18 Feb 1931, Lorain, Ohio, USA. Professor; Author. m. Harold Morrison, 1958, div 1964, 2 sons. Education: BA, Howard University, 1953; MA, Cornell University, 1955. Appointments: Instructor, Texas Southern University, Houston, 1955-57, Howard University, 1957-64; Senior Editor, Random House Inc, New York City, 1965-85; Associate Professor, State Unversity of New York at Purchase, 1971-72; Visiting Lecturer, Yale University, 1976-77, Bard College, 1986-88; Albert Schweitzer Chair in Humanities, State University of New York at Alabany, 1984-89; Robert F Goheen Professor in the Council of Humanities, Princeton University 1989-; Clark Lecturer, Trinity College, Cambridge, 1990; Massey Lecturer, Harvard University, 1990. Publications: Fiction: The Bluest Eye, 1969; Sula, 1973; Song of Solomon, 1977; Tar Baby, 1981; Beloved, 1987; Jazz, 1992; Play. Dreaming Emmett, 1986. Other; The Black Book (editor), 1974; Playing in the Dark: Whiteness and the Literary Imagination (lectures), 1992; Race-ing Justice, En-Gendering Power: Essays on Anita Hill, Clarence Thomas, and the Construction of Social Reality (editor), 1992; Nobel Prize Speech, 1994. Honours: Ohioana Book Award, 1975; American Academy and Institute of Arts and Letters Award, 1977; Pulitzer Prize in Fiction, 1988; Nobel Prize for Literature, 1993; National Book Foundation Medal, 1995. Memberships: American Academy of Arts and Letters; American Academy of Arts and Sciences; Authors Guild; Authors League of America; National Council on the Arts. Address: c/o Department of Creative Writing, Princeton University, Princeton, NJ 08544, USA.

MORRISON Wilbur Howard, b. 21 June 1915, Plattsburgh, New York, USA. Freelance Writer. Education: Plattsburgh State Normal School, 1922-30; Plattsburgh High School, 1930-34. Publications: Hellbirds, the Story of the B-29s in Combat, 1960; The Incredible 305th: The Can Do Bombers of World War II, 1962; Wings Over the Seven Seas: US Naval Aviation's Fight For Survival, 1974; Point of No Return: The Story of the Twentieth Air Force, 1979; Fortress Without a Roof: The Allied Bombing of the Third Reich, 1982; Above and Beyond, 1941-45, 1983; Baja Adventure Guide, 1990; The Elephant and the Tiger: The Full Story of the Vietnam War, 1990; Donald W Douglas: A Heart With Wings, 1991; Twentieth Century American Wars, 1993; The Adventure Guide to the Adirondacks and Catskills, 1995. Honour: Papers, Manuscripts, Memorabilia, housed in American Heritage Center, University of Wyoming. Membership: Dramatists Guild. Address: 2036 East Alvarado Street, Fallbrook, CA 92028, USA.

MORRISS Frank, b. 28 Mar 1923, Pasadena, California, USA. Writer; Teacher. m. Mary Rita Moynihan, 11 Feb 1950, 1 son, 3 daughters. Education: BS, Regis College, Denver, 1943; JD, Georgetown University School of Law, Washington, DC, 1948; Doctor of Letters, Register College of Journalism, Denver 1953. Appointments: News Editor, Denver Catholic Register, 1960, National Register, 1963; Associate Editor, Vermont Catholic Tribune, 1961; Founding Editor, Twin Circle, 1967; Contributing Editor, Wanderer, St Paul, Minnesota, 1968-. Publications: The Divine Epic, 1973; The Catholic as Citizen, 1976; A Neglected Glory, 1976; Abortion (co-author), 1979; The Forgotten Revelation: A Christmas Celebration (editor and contributor), 1985; A Little Life of Our Lord, 1993. Membership: Fellowship of Catholic Scholars (USA). Address: 3505 Owens Street, Wheat Ridge, CO 80033, USA.

MORT Graham Robert, b. 11 Aug 1955, Middleton, England. Poet. m. Maggie Mort, 12 Feb 1979, 3 sons. Education: BA, Liverpool University, 1977; St Martin's College, Lancaster, 1980. Appointment: Creative Writing Course Leader, Open College of the Arts, 1989-. Publications: A Country on Fire; Into the Ashes; A Halifax Cider Jar; Sky Burial; Snow from the North; Starting to Write; The Experience of Poetry, Storylines. Contributions to: Numerous literary magazines and journals. Honours: 1st Prizes, Cheltenham Poetry Competition, 1979, 1982; Duncan Lawrie Prizes, Arvon Poetry Competition, 1982, 1992, 1994; Major Eric Gregory Award, 1985; Authors Foundation Award, 1994. Memberships: Society of Authors; National Association of Writers in Education. Address: The Beeches, Riverside, Clapham, Lancaster LA2 8DT, England.

MORTIMER John Clifford (Geoffrey Lincoln), b. 21 Apr 1923, London, England. Barrister; Playwright; Novelist. m. (1) Penelope Ruth Fletcher, 1 son, 1 daughter, (2) Penelope Gallop, 2 daughters. Education: Brasenose College, Oxford. Appointments: Called to the Bar, 1948; QC, 1966; Master of the Bench, Inner Temple, 1975.

Publications: Charade, 1947; Rumming Park, 1948; Answer Yes or No, 1950; Like Men Betrayed, 1953; Three Winters, 1956; Will Shakespeare, 1977; Rumpole of the Bailey, 1978; The Trials of Rumpole, 1979; Rumpole's Return, 1981; Clinging to the Wreckage (autobiography), 1982; In Character, 1983; Rumpole and the Golden Thread, 1983; Rumpole's Last Case, 1986; Paradise Postponed, 1986; Character Parts (interviews), 1986; Summer's Lease, 1988; Rumpole and the Age of Miracles, 1988; Titmuss Regained, 1989; Rumpole à la Carte, 1990; Rumpole on Trial, 1992; Dunster, 1992; Rumpole and the Angel of Death, 1996; Felix in the Underworld, 1997; Murderers and Other Friends (autobiography), forthcoming. Plays: The Dock Brief and Other Plays, 1959; The Wrong Side of the Park, 1960; Two Stars for Comfort, 1962; The Judge, 1967; Come As You Are, 1970; The Bells of Hell; Villians, 1992. Film scripts: John and Mary, 1970; Edwin, 1984. TV series: Rumpole of the Bailey, 6 series; Brideshead Revisited, 1981; Unity Mitford, 1981; The Ebony Tower, 1984; Paradise Postponed, 1986; Summer Lease, 1989; Titmuss Regained, 1991; Under the Hammer, 1993. Contributions to: Various periodicals. Honours: Italia Prize, Short Play, 1958; British Academy Writers Award, 1979; Writer of the Year, BAFTA, 1980; Book of the Year, Yorkshire Post, 1982; Susquehanna University, 1985; Commander of the Order of the British Empire, 1986; Hon LLD: Exeter, 1986, St Andrew, 1987; Hon DLitt, Nottingham. Memberships: Howard League for Penal Reform, president, 1991-; Royal Court Theatre, chairman, 1990-; Royal Society of Literature, president, 1989-. Address: c/o The Peter Fraser and Dunlop Group Ltd, 5th Floor, The Chambers, Chelsea Harbour, Lofts Road, London SW10, England.

MORTIMER Penelope (Ruth), (Penelope Dimont, Ann Temple), b. 19 Sept 1918, Rhyl, Flint, Wales. Author. Education: University College, London. Appointment: Film Critic, The Observer, London, 1967-70. Publications: Johanna, 1947; A Villa in Summer, 1954; The Bright Prison, 1956; With Love and Lizards (with John Mortimer), 1957; Daddy's Gone A-Hunting, US edition as Cave of Ice, 1958; Saturday Lunch with the Brownings, 1960; The Pumpkin Eater, 1962; My Friend Says It's Bullet-Proof, 1967; The Home, 1971; Long Distance, 1974; About Time: An Aspect of Autobiography, 1979; The Handyman, 1983; Queen Elizabeth: A Life of the Queen Mother, 1986; Portrait of a Marriage (screenplay), 1990; About Time Too (autobiography), 1993. Honour: Whitbread Prize, 1979; Literary Agent: Anthony Sheil, 43 Doughty Street, London WC1N 2LF, England. Address: 19 St Gabriel's Road, London NW2 4DS, England.

MORTIMER-DUNN Gloria Dawn Cecilia, b. 22 July 1928, Sydney, New South Wales, Australia. Designer; Teacher. m. Bernard Mortimer-Dunn, 24 Dec 1954. Education: Honours Diploma in Art (Design and Craft), East Sydney Technical College. Publications: Pattern Design, 1960; Fashion Making, 1964; Fashion Design, 1972, UK Edition as ABC of Fashion; Pattern Design for Children, 1995. Address: 15 Roberts Street, Rose Bay, New South Wales 2029, Australia.

MORTON Frederic, b. 5 Oct 1924, Vienna, Austria. Author. m. Marcia Colman, 28 Mar 1957, 1 daughter. Education: BS, College of the City of New York, 1947; MA, New School for Social Research, New York City. Publications: The Rothschilds, 1962; A Nervous Splendour, 1978; The Forever Street, 1987; Thunder at Twilight, 1991. Contributions to: Newspapers and journals. Memberships: Authors Guild; PEN Club. Address: c/o Lantz Office Ltd, 888 Seventh Avenue, New York, NY 10019, USA.

MORTON G L. See: FRYER Jonathan.

MORTON Harry Edwin Clive, (Pindar Pete), b. 24 Mar 1931, Gordonvale, Queensland, Australia. Sugar Cane Grower. m. Desma Baird, 18 Jan 1958, 1 son, 2 daughters. Education: Cairns High School. Publications: The Cane Cutters (with G Burrows), 1986; Smoko the Farm Dog, 1989; By Strong Arms, 1995. Contributions to: Australian, UK and Canadian magazines; Australian, Italian and US anthologies; Short stories and features, Australian Cane Grower, 1960-. Honours: Fellowship of Australian Writers Regional History, 1986; Vaccari Historical Trust, 1987. Address: PO Box 166, Gordonvale, North Queensland 4865, Australia.

MORTON Henry (Harry) Albert, b. 20 July 1925, Gladstone, Manitoba, Canada. Writer. Associate Professor of History (retired). Education: BA, BEd, University of Manitoba; MA, University of Cambridge, England; PhD, University of Otago, New Zealand. Publications: And Now New Zealand, 1969; The Wind Commands,

1975; Which Way New Zealand, 1975; Why Not Together?, 1978; The Whale's Wake, 1982; The Farthest Corner, 1988. Honour: Sir James Wattie Award, Book of the Year, 1976. Memberships: Blenheim Club; PEN New Zealand; Royal New Zealand Airforce Association. Address: 55B Brooklyn Drive, Blenheim, Marlborough, New Zealand.

MOSBY Aline, b. 27 July 1922, Missoula, Montana, USA. Journalist. Education: BA, University of Montana School of Journalism, 1943; Postgraduate studies, Columbia University, 1965. Appointments: Journalist, Time magazine, 1943; Journalist, Foreign Correspondent, United Press International, 1943-85; Freelance Writer, Paris, France, 1985-; Lecturer, Guest Instructor, University of Montana. Publication: The View from Number 13 People's Street. Address: 1 Rue Maître Albert, Paris 75005, France.

MOSCA Julius. See: **HEDMAN Dag Sven Gustav.**

MOSES Elbert Raymond Jr, b. 31 Mar 1908, New Concord, Ohio, USA. Professor Emeritus. m. (1) Mary M Sterrett, 21 Sept 1933, dec 1984, 1 son, (2) Caroline M Chambers, 19 June 1985. Education: AB, University of Pittsburgh; MSc, PhD, University of Michigan. Publications: A Guide to Effective Speaking, 1956, 1957; Phonetics: History and Interpretation, 1964; Three Attributes of God, 1983; Adventure in Reasoning, 1988; Beating the Odds, 1992; The Range, Great Poems of Our Time, 1993; Where Is Virtue, 1993; Reflections Within, 1993. Contributions to: American Speech and Hearing Magazine; Journal of American Speech; Speech Monographs; Veterans Voices. Honours: Paul Harris Fellow, Rotary, 1971; Certificate, Humanitarian Services, Nicaraguan Government, 1974; Phi Delta Kappa Service Key, 1978; Certificate, Services to Education, 1981; Life Patron, 1985, Grand Ambassador, 1985, American Biographical Institute; World Literary Academy, life fellow, 1987. Membership: International Society of Poets, 1993. Address: 2001 Rocky Dells Drive, Prescott, AZ 86303, USA.

MOSKOWITZ Faye Stollman, b. 31 July 1930, Detroit, Michigan, USA. English Professor; Writer, m. Jack Moskowitz, 29 Aug 1948, 2 sons, 2 daughters. Education: BA, George Washington University, 1970; MA, 1979; PhD (abd), 1974. Publications: A Leak in the Heart; Whoever Finds This; I Love You; And the Bridge is Love; Her Face in the Mirror: Jewish Women Write about Mothers and Daughters (editor), 1994. Contributions to: New York Times; Washington Post; Chronicle of Higher Education; Womans Day; Feminist Studies; Calyx; Christian Science Monitor; Wigwag Magazine. Honours: Michael Karolyi Foundation: Breadloaf Scholar; EdPress Merit Award; Pen Syndicated Fiction Award. Membership: Jenny McKean Moore Fund for Writers. Literary Agent: Russell & Volkenning. Address: 3306 Highland Place, North West, Washington, DC 20008, USA.

MOSLEY Jonathan Philip, b. 8 June 1947, Grimsby, England. University Professor. m. Shu Ching Huang, 11 Aug 1988. Education: BA, University of Leeds, 1968; MA, 1970, PhD, 1976, University of East Anglia. Publications: Ingmar Bergman: The Cinema as Mistress; Bruges-La-Morte; Tea Masters, Tea Houses; Georges Rodenbach: Critical Essays; October Long Sunday. Contributions to: Journals. Memberships: British and International Comparative Literature Associations; Society for Cinema Studies. Address: Pennsylvania State University, Worthington Scranton Campus, 120 Ridge View Drive, Dunmore, PA 18512, USA.

MOSLEY Nicholas (Lord Ravensdale), b. 25 June 1923, London, England. Author. Education: Balliol College, Oxford, 1946-47. Publications: Spaces of the Dark, 1951; The Rainbearers, 1955; Corruption, 1957; African Switchback, 1958; The Life of Raymond Raynes, 1961; Meeting Place, 1962; Accident, 1965; Experience and Religion: A Lay Essay in Theology, 1965; Assassins, 1966; Impossible Object, 1968, screenplay, 1975; Natalie, Natalia, 1971; The Assassination of Trotsky, 1972, screenplay, 1973; Julian Grenfell: His Life and the Times of His Death 1888-1915, 1976; Catastrophe Practice, 1979; Imago Bird, 1980; Serpent, 1981; Rules of the Game: Sir Oswald and Lady Cynthia Mosley 1896-1933, 1982; Beyond the Pale: Sir Oswald Mosley and Family 1933-1980, 1983; Judith, 1986; Hopeful Monsters, 1990; Efforts at Truth, 1994; Children of Darkness and Light, 1996. Honour: Whitbread Prize. Address: 2 Gloucester Crescent, London NW1 7DS, England.

MOSLEY Walter, b. 1952, Los Angeles, California, USA. m. Joy Kellman. Education: Goddard College; Johnson State University; City College, New York. Publications: Devil in a Blue Dress, 1990; A Red Death, 1991; White Butterfly, 1992; Black Betty, 1994; R L's Dream, 1995; The Little Yellow Dog; The Bad Boy Bobby Brown. Address: c/o Paramount Publishing, Pocket Books, 1230 Avenue of the Americas, New York, NY 10020, USA.

MOSS Norman Bernard, b. 30 Sept 1928, London, England. Journalist. m. Hilary Sesta, 21 July 1963, 2 sons. Education: Hamilton College, New York City, 1946-47. Appointments: Staff Journalist with newspapers, news agencies and radio networks. Publications: Men Who Play God - The Story of the Hydrogen Bomb, 1968; A British-American Dictionary, 1972, 5th edition, revised, 1994; The Pleasures of Deception, 1976; The Politics of Uranium, 1982; Klaus Fuchs: The Man Who Stole the Atom Bomb, 1987; Monograph: The Politics of Global Warming, 1992. Honour: Magazine Writer of the Year, Periodical Publishers Association, 1982. Memberships: International Institute of Strategic Studies; Society of Authors. Literary Agent: Michael Shaw, Curtis Brown Group. Address: 21 Rylett Crescent, London W12 9RP, England.

MOTION Andrew Peter, b. 26 Oct 1952, London, England. Writer. m. Jan Dalley, 9 June 1985, 2 sons, 1 daughter. Education: BA (1st Class Honours), MLitt, University College, Oxford, 1970-76. Appointments: Editor, Poetry Review, 1980-82; Editorial Director, Chatto and Windus, 1982-89; Professor of Creative Writing, University of East Anglia, 1995-. Publications: Dangerous Play, Selected Poems, 1979-84; The Lamberts (biography), 1986; Natural Causes (poems), 1987; The Pale Companion (novel), 1989; Love in a Life (poems), 1991; Famous for the Creatures (novel), 1991; Philip Larkin: A Writer's Life, 1993; The Price of Everything (poems), 1994; Salt Water, (poems), 1997. Contributions to: Times Literary Supplement; The Observer; LRB. Honours: ARVON/Observer Prize; John Llewelyn Rhys Prize; Dylan Thomas Prize; Somerset Maugham Award; Whitbread Prize for Biography; Honorary DLitt, University of Hull. Memberships: Royal Society of Literature, Fellow; Chair, Literature Panel, Arts Council. Literary Agent: Pat Kavanagh, The Peters, Frazer and Dunlop Group Ltd. Address: c/o Faber and Faber, 3 Queen Square, London WC1 3AU, England.

MOTT Michael, (Charles Alston), b. 8 Dec 1930, London, England. Professor of English Emeritus; Writer; Poet. m. (1) Margaret Ann Watt, 6 May 1961, dec 1990, 2 daughters, (2) Emma Lou Pwers, 16 Nov 1992. Education: Diploma, Central School of Arts and Crafts, London; Intermediate Law Degree, Law Society, London; BA, History of Art, Courtauld and Warburg Institutes, London. Appointments: Editor, Air Freight, 1954-59, Thames and Hudson publishers, 1961-64; Assistant Editor, Adam International Review, 1956-66, The Geographical Magazine, 1964-66; Poetry Editor, The Kenyon Review, 1966-70; Visiting Professor and Writer-in-Residence, Kenyon College, 1966-70, State University of New York at Buffalo, 1968, Concordia University, Montreal, Quebec, 1970, 1974, Emory University, 1970-77, College of William and Mary, 1978-79, 1985-86; Professor of English, 1980-92, Professor Emeritus, 1992-, Bowling Green State University. Publications: Fiction: The Notebooks of Susan Berry, 1962; Master Entrick, 1964; Helmet and Wasps, 1964; The Blind Cross, 1968. Poetry: Absence of Unicorns, Presence of Lions, 1977; Counting the Grasses, 1980; Corday, 1986; Piero di Cosimo: The World of Infinite Possibility, 1990; Taino, 1992. Non-fiction: The Seven Mountains of Thomas Merton, 1984. Contributions to: Journals and newspapers. Honours: Governor's Award in Fine Arts, State of Georgia, 1974; Guggenheim Fellowship, 1979-80; Christopher Award, 1984; Ohioana Book Award, 1985; Olscamp Research Award, 1985; Nancy Dasher Book Award, 1985; Phi Beta Kappa, Alpha Chapter, 1994. Memberships: Amnesty International; British Lichen Society; Royal Geographical Society. Address: 122 The Colony, Williamsburg, VA 23185, USA.

MOTTRAM Eric, b. 1920, England. Professor; Poet. Education: Cambridge University. Appointments: Professor, Kings College, University of London, 1983; Other University Appointments in USA, India, Europe. Publications: Inside the Whale, 1970; The He Expression, 1973; Local Movement, 1973; Two Elegies, 1974; Against Tyranny, 1975; 1922 Earth Raids and Other Poems, 1973-75, 1976; Homage to Braque, 1976; Spring Ford, 1977; Tunis, 1977; Elegy 15: Neruda, 1978; Precipe of Fishes, 1979; 1980 Mediate; Elegies, 1981; A Book of Herne, 1975-81; Interrogation Rooms: Poems, 1980-81; Address, 1983; Three Letters, 1984; The Legal Poems, 1984; Selected Poems, 1989; Peace Projects and Brief Novels, 1989; Studies and Editions of American Literature. Address: Department of English,

King's College, University of London, The Strand, London WC2R 2LS, England.

MOULD Daphne Desiree Charlotte Pochin, b. 15 Nov 1920, Salisbury, England. Author. Education: BSc 1st Class Honours, Geology, 1943, PhD, Geology, 1946, University of Edinburgh. Publications: The Celtic Saints, 1956; The Irish Saints (critical biographies), 1963; The Aran Islands, 1972; Ireland from the Air, 1972; Irish Monasteries, 1976; Captain Roberts of the Sirius, 1988; Discovering Cork, 1991. Contributions to: Numerous publications; Broadcaster on Radio Telefis Eireann. Honours: LLD, National University of Ireland, 1993. Membership: Aircraft Owners and Pilots Association. Address: Aherla House, Aherla, County Cork, Ireland.

MOUNT William Robert Ferdinand, b. 2 July 1939, London, England. Novelist; Journalist; Editor. m. Julia Lucas, 20 July 1968, 2 sons, 1 daughter. Education: BA, Christ Church, Oxford, 1961. Appointments: Political Correspondent, 1977-82, Literary Editor, 1984-85, Spectator; Head of Prime Minister's Policy Unit, 1982-84; Columnist, Daily Telegraph, 1985-90; Editor, Times Literary Supplement, 1991-. Publications: Very Like a Whale, 1967; The Theatre of Politics, 1972; The Man Who Rode Ampersand, 1975; The Clique, 1978; The Subversive Family, 1982; The Selkirk Strip, 1987; Of Love and Asthma, 1991; The British Constitution Now, 1992; Umbrella, 1994; The Liquidator, 1995. Contributions to: Spectator; Encounter; National Interest; Politique Internationale. Honour: Hawthornden Prize, 1992. Address: 17 Ripplevale Grove, London N1, England.

MOUNTFIELD David. See: GRANT Neil.

MOURE Erin, b. 17 Apr 1955, Calgary, Alberta, Canada. Poet. Education: University of Calgary, 1972-73; University of British Columbia, 1974-75. Publications: Domestic Fuel, 1985; Wanted Alive, 1985; Furious, 1988; WSW (West South West), 1989; Sheepish Beauty, 1992; Civilian Love, 1992; The Green Word, 1994; Search Procedures, 1996. Contributions to: Various publications. Honours: Governor-General's Award; Pat Lowther Memorial Award; National Magazine Award. Memberships: League of Canadian Poets; Writers Union of Canada. Address: c/o Writers Union of Canada, 24 Ryerson Avenue, Toronto, Ontario M5T 2P3, Canada,

MOWAT David, b. 16 Mar 1943, Cairo, Egypt. (British citizen). Playwright. Education: BA, New College, Oxford, 1964. Publications: Jens, 1965; Pearl, 1966; Anna Luse, 1968; Dracula, 1969; Purity, 1969; The Normal Woman, and Tyypi, 1970; Adrift, 1970; The Others, 1970; Most Recent Least Recent, 1970; Inuit, 1970; The Diabolist, 1971; John, 1971; Amalfi (after Webster), 1972; Phoenix-and-Turtle, 1972; Morituri, 1972; My Relationship with Jayne, 1973; Come, 1973; Main Sequence, 1974; The Collected Works, 1974; The Memory Man, 1974; The Love Maker, 1974; X to C, 1975; Kim, 1977; Winter, 1978; The Guise, 1979; Hiroshima Nights, 1981; The Midnight Sun, 1983; Carmen, 1984; The Almas, 1989; Jane, or The End of the World, 1992. Radio Plays. Honour: Arts Council Bursaries. Address: 7 Mount Street, Oxford OX2 6DH, England.

MOXHAM Gwenyth Constance, b. 3 Sept 1943, Adelaide, South Australia, Australia. Teacher. m. Kenneth Ewing Moxham, 14 May 1966, 1 son, 1 daughter. Education: Associate in Arts and Education, 1965, BA, 1966, University of Adelaide; Diploma of Teaching, Adelaide Teachers College, 1966; TO; MACE. Publication: They Built South Australia: Engineers, Technicians, Manufacturers, Contractors and their Work (with D A Cumming), 1986. Contribution to: Australian Dictionary of Biography, Volume 4, 1940-1980, Sir Claude Gibb, 1996. Memberships: Australian Reading Association; Australian College of Education. Address: 6 Barr Smith Drive, Urrbrae, South Australia 5064, Australia.

MOYERS Bill, b. 5 June 1934, Hugo, Oklahoma, USA. Journalist; Broadcaster. m. Judith Davidson, 18 Dec 1954, 2 sons, 1 daughter. Education: BJ, University of Texas, 1956; Graduate Studies, University of Edinburgh, 1956-57; MTh, Southwestern Baptist Theological Seminary, 1959. Appointments: Personal Assistant, Senator Lyndon B Johnson, 1960; Associate Director, 1961-62, Deputy Director, 1963, Peace Corps; Special Assistant, 1963-67, Press Secretary, 1965-67, President Lyndon B Johnson; Publisher, Newsday, Garden City, New York, 1967-70; Editor-in-Chief, Bill Moyers Journal, Public-TV, 1971-76, 1978-81; Chief Correspsondent, CBS Reports, CBS-TV, 1976-78; Senior News Analyst, CBS News,

CBS-TV, 1981-86; Founder and Executive Director, Public Affairs TV Inc, 1987-; Various special series, PBS-TV. Publications: Listening to America, 1971; Report from Philadelphia, 1987; The Secret Government, 1988; Joseph Campbell and the Power of the Myth, 1988; A World of Ideas, 1989, 2nd edition, 1990; Healing and the Mind, 1993; Genesis, 1996. Honours: George Foster Peabody Awards, 1976, 1980, 1985, 1986, 1988, 1989, 1990; The Charles Frankel Prize on the Humanities, 1996; Silver Baton Awards, Gold Baton Award, 1991, DuPont-Columbia University; George Polk Awards, 1981, 1986; Regents Medal of Excellence, Board of Regents, State of New York; Religious Liberty Award, American Jewish Committee, 1995; Communicator of the Decade Award, Religious Communications Congress, 1990; TV Hall of Fame, 1995; Career Achievement Award, International Documentary Association; Nelson Mandela Award for Health and Human Rights, 1996; Numerous Emmy Awards. Membership: American Academy of Arts and Sciences, Fellow; Society of American Historians; American Philosophical Society, Fellow. Address: c/o Public Affairs TV Inc, 356 West 58th Street, New York, NY 10019, USA.

MOYES Gertrude Patricia, b. 19 Jan 1923, Bray, Ireland. Author. m. (1) John Moyes, 29 Mar 1952, (2) John Haszard, 13 Oct 1962. Publications: Henry Tibbett mystery series, 1959-89; Several other books, 1989-95. Contributions to: Magazines. Honour: Edgar Special Scroll, Mystery Writers of America. Memberships: Authors Guild; Crime Writers Association; Detection Club; Mystery Writers of America. Address: Po Box 1, Virgin Gorda, British Virgin Islands.

MOYNIHAN Daniel Patrick, b. 16 Mar 1927, Tulsa, Oklahoma, USA. United States Senator; Writer. m. Elizabeth Therese Brennan, 29 May 1955, 2 sons, 1 daughter. Education: City College of New York, 1943; BA, Tufts University, 1948; MA, 1949, PhD, 1961, Fletcher School of Law and Diplomacy. Appointments: Special Assistant, 1961-62, Executive Assistant, 1962-63, to the US Secretary of Labor; Assistant Secretary of Labor, 1963-65; Fellow, Center for Advanced Studies, Wesleyan University, 1965-66; Professor of Education and Urban Politics, 1966-73, Senior Member, 1966-77, Professor of Government, 1973-77, Kennedy School of Government, Harvard University; Assistant for Urban Affairs, 1969-70, Counsellor, 1969-70, Consultant, 1971-73, to the President of the US; US Ambassador to India, 1973-75; US Permanent Representative to the United Nations, 1975-76; US Senator (Democrat) from the State of New York, 1977-. Publications: Beyond the Melting Pot (with Nathan Glazer), 1963; The Defenses of Freedom: The Public Papers of Arthur J Goldberg (editor), 1966; Equal Educational Opportunity (co-author), 1969; On Understanding Poverty: Perspectives for the Social Sciences (editor), 1969; The Politics of a Guaranteed Income, 1973; Coping: On the Practice of Government, 1974; Ethnicity: Theory and Experience (editor with Nathan Glazer), 1975; A Dangerous Place (with S Weaver), 1978; Counting Our Blessings: Reflections on the Future of America, 1980; Loyalties, 1984; Family and Nation, 1986; Came the Revolution: Argument in the Reagan Era, 1988; On the Law of Nations, 1990; Pandaemonium: Ethnicity in International Politics, 1993. Contributions to: Professional journals. Honours: Meritorious Service Award, US Department of Labor, 1965; Centennial Medal, Syracuse University, 1969; International League for Human Rights Award, 1975; John LaFarge Award for Interracial Justice, 1980; Medallion, State University of New York at Albany, 1984; Henry Medal, Smithsonian Institution, 1985; SEAL Medallion, Central Intelligence Agency, 1986; Laetare Medal, Notre Dame University, 1992; Thomas Jefferson Award, 1993; Numerous honorary doctorates. Address: c/o United State Senate, Washington DC 20510, USA.

MOYNIHAN John Dominic, b. 31 July 1932, London, England. Journalist; Author. 1 son, 2 daughters. Education: Chelsea School of Art. Appointments: Bromley Mercury, 1953-54; Evening Standard, 1954-63; Daily Express, 1963-64; The Sun, 1964-65; Assistant Literary Editor, Sports Correspondent, Sunday Telegraph, 1965-89; Freelance, The Sunday Telegraph, The Sunday Times, The Independent on Sunday, The Daily Express, 1989-. Publications: The Soccer Syndrome, 1966, 2nd edition, 1987; Not All a Ball (autobiography), 1970; Park Football, 1970; Football Fever, 1974; Soccer, 1974; The Chelsea Story, 1982; The West Ham Story, 1984; Soccer Focus, 1989; Kevin Keegan: Black and White, 1993. Contributions to: Newspapers and magazines. Memberships: Society of Authors; Sports Writers Association; Football Writers Association; Lawn Tennis Writers Association; Chelsea Arts Club; Scribes. Address: 102 Ifield Road, London SW10, England.

MPHAHLELE Ezekiel (Es'kia Mphahlele), b. 17 Dec 1919, Pretoria, South Africa. Author; Professor of African Literature. Education: MA, University of South Africa, Pretoria, 1956. Appointments: Teacher of English and Afrikaans, Orlando High School, Johannesburg, 1942-52; Fiction Editor, Drum magazine, Johannesburg, 1955-57; Lecturer in English Literature, University of Ibadan, Nigeria, 1957-61; Director of African Programmes, International Association for Cultural Freedom, Paris, 1961-63; Director, Chem-chemi Creative Centre, Nairobi, Kenya, 1963-65; Lecturer, University College, Nairobi, 1965-66, University of Denver, 1966-74, University of Pennsylvania, 1974-77; Professor of African Literature, University of the Witwatersrand, Johannesburg, 1979-. Publications: Man Must Live and Other Stories, 1947; Down Second Avenue (autobiography), 1959; The Living Dead and Other Stories, 1961; The African Image (essays), 1962, 2nd edition, 1974; Modern African Stories (editor with E Komey), 1964; African Writing Today (editor), 1967; In Corner B and Other Stories, 1967; The Wanderers (novel), 1971; Voices in the Whirlwind and Other Essays, 1972; Chirundu (novel), 1979; The Unbroken Song, 1981; Bury Me at the Marketplace, 1984; Father Come Home, 1984; Afrika My Music: An Autobiography 1957-1983, 1986. Address: African Studies Institute, University of the Witwatersrand, Johannesburg 2001, South Africa.

MUAMBA Muepu, b. 23 Nov 1946, Tshilundu, Belgian Congo. Journalist; Writer. Education: Institut St Ferdinand, Jernappes, Belgium. Appointments: Literary Director, Editions Les Presses Africaines, Kinshasa, Zaire; Literary Critic, Salongo and Elima. Publications: Ventre Creux, short stories; Suppliqué; Anthologie d'une jeune littérature (selected by Oliver Dubuis); Afrika in eigener Sache (with Jochen Klicker and Klaus Paysan), essays on Africa, 1980; Poems in various anthologies; Devoir d'ingérence, nouvelles et poèmes, 1988; Ma Terre d'O, poems, in press. Contributions to: Salongo; Elima; Culture et Authenticité, Kinshasa; Beto, Dusseldorf; Estuaires, Luxembourg; Etoiles d'afrique, Paris. Memberships: Maison Africaine de la Poesie Internationale Dakar-Senegal; Societé Française des Gens de Lettres, Paris; Union Internationale des Journalistes et de la Presse de la Langue Française, Paris; Royal African Society, London. Address: c/o Dr.Phil M Kohlert-Neméth, Schaumainkai 99, 6000 Frankfurt am Main 70, Germany.

MUEHL Lois Baker, b. 29 Apr 1920, Oak Park, Illinois, USA. Freelance Writer; Retired Teacher. m. Siegmar Muehl, 15 Apr 1944, 2 sons, 2 daughters. Education: BA, English, Oberlin College, 1941; MA, English, Education, University of Iowa, 1965. Appointments: Associate Professor of Rhetoric, 1966-85; Teacher of Creative Writing in Conferences and Adult Education among others; Taught Reading, Speech and Writing in English in Thailand, 1980, 1982, Korea, 1985, China, 1987-88. Publications: My Name is ..., 1959; Worst Room in the School, 1961; The Hidden Year of Devlin Bates, 1967; Winter Holiday Brainteasers, 1979; A Reading Approach to Rhetoric, 1983; Trading Cultures in the Classroom (with Siegmar Muehl), 1993; Talkable Tales, 1993. Other: Poems and quips in Meadowbrook Press books and in Reader's Digest (prose only). Contributions to: Light verse and poetry in Capper's; Country Woman; Saturday Evening Post; Wall Street Journal; 100 Works, among others; Academic articles in Library Chronicle, Journal of Reading, Journal of Negro Education, and Language and Speech among others. Honours: Phi Beta Kappa, 1941; Old Gold Creative Fellowship, 1970; Community Service Commendation, Merced, California, 1984. Memberships: President, University Women's Writers Group; Treasurer, National League of American Pen Women; Iowa Poetry Association. Address: 430 Crestview Avenue, Iowa City, IA 52245-5222, USA.

MUGGESON Margaret Elizabeth, (Margaret Dickinson, Everatt Jackson), b. 30 Apr 1942, Gainsborough, Lincolnshire, England. Writer; Partner in Retail Store. m. Dennis Muggeson, 19 Sept 1964, 2 daughters. Education: Lincoln College of Technology, 1960-61. Publications: Pride of the Courtneys, 1968; Brackenbeck, 1969; Portrait of Jonathan, 1970; The Road to Hell (as Everatt Jackson), 1975; Abbeyford Trilogy, 1981; Lifeboat!, 1983; Beloved Enemy (as Margaret Dickinson), 1984; Plough the Furrow, 1994. Membership: Romantic Novelists Association. Literary Agent: Darley Anderson, Darley Anderson Books, Estelle House, 11 Eustace Road, London SW6 1JB, England. Address: 17 Seacroft Drive, Skegness, Lincolnshire PE 25 3AP, England.

MÜHRINGER Doris Agathe Annemarie, b. 18 Sept 1920, Graz, Austria. Writer; Poet. Publications: Gedichte I, 1957; Das Marchen von den Sandmannlein (children's picture book), 1961; Gedichte II, 1969;

Staub offnet das Auge: Gedichte III, 1976; Tag, mein Jahr (with H Valencak), 1983; Vogel, die ohne Schlaf sind: Gedichte IV, 1984; Tanzen unter d Netz, short prose, 1985; Das hatten die Ratten vom Schatten: Ein Lachbuch, 1989, 2nd edition, 1992; Reisen wir (Ausgewählte Gedichte aus vier Jahrzehnten), 1995. Contributions to: Numerous literary magazines in 9 countries. Honours: Georg Trakl Prize, 1954; Award of Achievement, Vienna, 1961; Lyrics Prize of Steiermark, 1973; Austrian State Scholarship, 1976; Award of Achievement, Board of Austrian Literar-Mechana, 1984; Großer Literaturpreis des Landes Steiermark, 1985. Memberships: PEN; Association of Austrian Writers; Poium; Kogge. Address: Goldeggasse 1, A-1040 Vienna, Austria.

MUIR Richard, b. 18 June 1943, Yorkshire, England. Author; Photographer. Education: 1st class honours, Geography, 1967, PhD, 1970, Aberdeen University, Scotland. Appointment: Editor, National Trust Regional Histories and Countryside Commission National Park Series. Publications: Over 25 books, including: Modern Political Geography, 1975; Hedgerows: Their History and Wildlife (with N Muir), 1987; Old Yorkshire, 1987; The Countryside Encyclopaedia, 1988; Fields (with Nina Muir), 1989; Portraits of the Past, 1989; Barleycorn (fiction), 1989; The Dales of Yorkshire, 1991; The Villages of England, 1992; The Coastlines of Britain, 1993; Political Geography: A New Introduction, 1997; The Yorkshire Countryside: A Landscape History, 1997. Contributions to: Geographical Magazine; Sunday Times Magazine; Observer Magazine; Various academic articles. Honour: Yorkshire Arts Literary Prize, 1982-83. Address: Waterfall Close, Station Road, Birstwith, Harrogate, Yorkshire, England.

MUKHERJEE Bharati, b. 27 July 1940, Calcutta, India (Canadian citizen, 1972). Associate Professor; Author. m. Clarke Blaise, 19 Sept 1963, 2 sons. Education: BA, University of Calcutta, 1959; MA, University of Baroda; MA, PhD, University of Iowa. Appointment: Associate Professor, McGill University, Montreal, Canada, 1966-. Publications: Tiger's Daughter, 1972; Wife, 1975; Kautilya's Concept of Diplomacy, 1976; Days and Nights in Calcutta (with Clark Blaise), 1977; The Middleman, 1989. Honour: National Book Critics Circle Award, 1988. Address: Department of English, McGill University, Montreal, Quebec, Canada.

MULDOON Paul, b. 20 June 1951, Armagh, Ireland. Radio Producer; Poet. Education: BA, Queen's University, Belfast. Appointments: Radio Producer, BBC Northern Ireland; Lecturer, Princeton University, USA; Various teaching posts, USA, 1987-; Professor, Princeton University, 1995. Publications: Knowing My Place, 1971; Poetry Introduction 2, 1972; New Weather, 1973, new edition, 1994; Spirit of Dawn, 1975; Mules, 1977; Names and Addresses, 1978; Why Brownlee Left, 1980; Immram, 1980; Quoof, 1983; Faber Poetry Cassette with Ted Hughes, 1983; The Wishbone, 1984; Selected Poems of Paul Muldoon, 1986; Faber Book of Contemporary Irish Poetry (editor), 1986; Meeting the British, 1987; Madoc: A Mystery, 1990; Shining Brow (opera libretto), 1993; The Annals of Chile, 1994; The Last Thesaurus, 1995; New Selected Poems, 1996; The Noctuary of Narcissus Batt, 1997. Address: Faber and Faber, 3 Queen Square, London WC1N 3AU, England.

MULFORD Wendy, b. 1941, England. Lecturer; Poet. m. John James. Education: BA, MA, Cambridge University; M Phil, University of London. Appointment: Senior Lecturer, Thames Polytechnic, London, 1968-82. Publications: Bravo to Girls and Heroes, 1977; No Fee: A Line or Two for Free, 1979; Reactions to Sunsets, 1980; The Light Sleepers: Poems, 1980; Some Poems, 1968-78, 1982; River Whose Eyes, 1982; The ABC of Writing and Other Poems, 1985; Late Spring Next Year, 1979-85; This Narrow Place: Sylvia Townsend Warner, Valentine Ackland: Life, Letters and Politics, 1930-51, 1988; The Virago Book of Love Poetry (editor), 1990; Lusus Naturae, 1990. Address: c/o Curtis Brown Ltd, Haymarket House, 28-29 Haymarket, London SW1Y 4SP, England.

MULISCH Harry, b. 29 July 1927, Haarlem, Netherlands. Novelist; Poet; Dramatist. Education: Haarlem Lyceum. Publications: 22 books of fiction, 1952-92, poetry collections and plays. Honour: Knight, Order of Orange Nassau, 1977. Address: Van Miereveldstraat 1, 1071 DW Amsterdam, Netherlands.

MULLIN Chris(topher John), b. 12 Dec 1947, Chelmsford, England. Member of Parliament. m. Nguyen Thi Ngoc, 14 Apr 1987, 1 daughter. Publications: Error of Judgement; The Truth About the Birmingham Bombings; A Very British Coup; The Last Man Out of

Saigon; The Year of the Fire Monkey. Honours: For the TV version of A Very British Coup: BAFTA Awards; US Emmy, Best Drama. Literary Agent: Pat Kavanagh, Peters, Frazer and Dunlop. Address: The House of Commons, London SW1, England.

MULVIHILL Maureen Esther, b 2 Oct 1944, Detroit, Michigan, USA. Writer; Scholar; Teacher. m. Daniel R Harris, 18 June 1983. Education: BPhil, Monteith College, 1966; MA, Wayne State University, 1968; PhD, University of Wisconsin at Madison, 1983; Postdoctoral Studies, Yale Centre for British Art, 1986, Columbia University Rare Book School, 1986. Appointments: Corporate Communications Director, Gruntal & Co Inc, New York City, 1983-85; Communications Consultant, New York City, 1985-; Visiting Scholar and Lecturer, various colleges and universities. Publications: British Women Writers, 1989; Essays in Restoration, 1989; British Women Writers, 1989; Scriblerian, 1989; Encyclopedia of Continental Women Writers, 1991; Curtain Calls, 1991; Poems by Ephelia, 1992; Studies in 18th-Century Culture, 1992. Honours: National Endowment for the Humanities Fellowship; Awards and scholarships. Memberships: American Society for 18th-Century Studies; Bibliographical Society of America; Institute for Research in History; Modern Language Associaton; Princeton Research Forum; Society for Textual Scholarship. Address: 45 Plaza Street West, Park Slope, Brooklyn, NY 11217, USA.

MUNONYE John (Okechukwu), b. 22 Apr 1929, Akokwa, Nigeria. Novelist. m. Regina Nwokeji, 1957, 1 son, 1 daughter. Education: Cert Ed, University of London, 1953. Appointments: Chief Inspector of Education, East Central State, 1973-76, Imo State, 1976-77. Publications: The Only Son, 1966; Obi, 1969; Oil Man of Obange, 1971; A Wreath for Maidens, 1973; A Dancer of Fortune, 1974; Bridge to a Wedding, 1978. Short Stories: Silent Child, 1973; Pack Pack Pack, 1977; Man of Wealth, 1981; On a Sunday Morning, 1982; Rogues, 1985. Honours: Member, Order of the Niger, 1980. Address: PO Box 436 Orlu, Imo State, Nigeria.

MUNRO Alice, b. 10 July 1931, Wingham, Ontario, Canada. Novelist; Story Writer. Education: University of Western Ontario, 1949-51. Appointments: Artist in Residence, University of Western Ontario, 1974-75, University of British Columbia, Vancouver, 1980. Publications: Novel: Lives of Girls and Women, 1971. Stories: Dance of the Happy Shades, 1973; Something I've Been Meaning to Tell You: 13 Stories, 1974; Personal Fictions, 1977; Who Do You Think You Are?, 1979; The Moons of Jupiter, 1982; The Progress of Love, 1986; Friends of My Youth, 1990. Play: How I Met My Husband, 1974. Honours: Governor-General's Award; Canada-Australia Literary Prize, 1978; D Litt, University of Western Ontario, 1976; WH Smith Literary Award, 1996. Address: c/o Writers Union of Canada, 24 Ryerson Street, Toronto, Ontario M5T 2PW, Canada.

MUNRO David Mackenzie, b. 28 May 1950. Freelance Geographical Reference Editor. m. Wendy Jane Nimmo, 22 Nov 1985. Education: BSc, 1973, PhD, 1983, University of Edinburgh. Appointment: Editor, Chambers World Gazetteer, 1984-. Publications: Chambers World Gazetteer (editor), 1988; Ecology and Environment in Belize (editor), 1989; A World Record of Major Conflict Areas (with Alan J Day), 1990; The Hutchinson Guide to the World (associate editor), 1990; Contributor: Longman's Encyclopedia; Hutchinson's Encyclopedia; Oxford Encyclopaedic English Dictionary. Contributions to: Geographical Magazine. Address: Department of Geography, University of Edinburgh, Drummond Street, Edinburgh EH8 9XP, Scotland.

MUNRO John Murchison, b. 29 Aug 1932, Wallasey, Cheshire, England. University Administrator. m. Hertha Ingrid Bertha Lipp, 12 Aug 1956, 2 sons, 2 daughters. Education: BA, English Literature, University of Durham, 1955; PhD, English Literature, Washington University, St Louis, 1960. Appointments: Part-time Instructor of English, Washington University, St Louis, 1956-60; Instructor, University of North Carolina, 1960-63; Assistant Professor, University of Toronto, Canada, 1963-65; Professor, American University of Beirut, Lebanon, 1965-87; Director, Outreach Services, Professor of Mass Communications, 1987-, Associate Dean for External Affiars, 1990-, American University, Cairo, Egypt. Publications: English Poetry in Transition, 1968; Arthur Symons, 1969; The Decadent Poets of the 1890's, 1970; Selected Poems of Theo Marzials, 1974; James Elroy Flecker, 1976; A Mutual Concern: The Story of the American University of Beirut, 1977; Cyprus: Between Venus and Mars (with Z Khuri), 1984; Selected Letters of Arthur Symons (with Karl Beckson),

1988; Theatre of the Absurd: Lebanon, 1982-88, 1989; Middle East Times (senior editor). Contributions to: Scholarly journals and general periodicals. Honour: Fulbright Research Award, University of California, Los Angeles, 1987. Address: American University in Cairo, 113 Kasr el Aini Street, Cairo, Egypt.

MUNRO Rona, b. 7 Sept 1959, Aberdeen, Scotland. Playwright. Education: MA, Edinburgh University, 1980. Appointment: Literary Associate, Hampstead Theatre, Lodndon, 1996-. Publications: Fugue, 1983; Piper's Cave, 1985; Saturday at the Commodore, 1989; Bold Girls, 1990; Your Turn to Clear the Stair, 1992; The Maiden Stone, 1995; Plays for Stage, Radio and Film. Honour: Evening Standard Award, 1991. Address: Casarotto Ramsay Ltd, National House, 60-66 Wardour Street, London W1V 3HP, England.

MUNRO Ronald Eadie. See: **GLEN Duncan Munro.**

MUNSCH Robert N(orman), b. 11 Jun 1945, Pittsburgh, Pennsylvania, USA. Writer. m. Ann D Metta, 20 Jan 1973, 1 son, 2 daughters. Education: BA, History, Fordham University, 1969; MA, Anthropology, Boston University, 1971; MEd, Child Studies, Tufts University, 1973. Appointments: Lecturer, 1975-80, Assistant Professor, 1980-84, University of Guelph; Full-time writer, 1984-. Publications: 29 books, including: The Paper Bag Princess, 1980; Love You Forever, 1986; Stephanie's Ponytail, 1996. Honour: Canadian Bookseller's Association Author of the Year, 1991. Memberships: Writer's Union of Canada; Canadian Association of Children's Authors, Illustrators and Performers; Canadian Author's Association. Address: c/o Writers Union of Canada, 24 Ryerson Avenue, Toronto, Ontario M5T 2P3, Canada.

MURA David (Alan), b. 17 June 1952, Great Lakes, Illinois, USA. Poet; Writer; Teacher. m. Susan Sencer, 18 June 1983, 1 daughter. Education: BA, Grinnell College, 1974; Graduate Studies, University of Minnesota, 1974-79; MFA, Vermont College, 1991. Appointments: Instructor, 1979-85, Associate Director of the Literature Program, 1982-84, Writers and Artists-in-the-Schools, St Paul, Minnesota; Faculty, The Loft, 1984-, St Paul, Minnesota; Instructor, St Olaf College, 1990-91; Visiting Professor, University of Oregon, 1991; Various poetry readings. Publications: A Male Grief: Notes on Pornography and Addiction, 1987; After We Lost Our Way (poems), 1989; Turning Japanese, 1991; The Colors of Desire (poems), 1995. Contributions to: Anthologies and magazines. Honours: Fanny Fay Wood Memorial Prize, American Academy of Poets, 1977; US/Japan Creative Artist Fellow, 1984; National Endowment for the Arts Fellowship, 1985; Discovery/Nation Award, 1987; National Poetry Series Contest, 1988; Pushcast Prize, 1990; Minnesota State Arts Board Grant and Fellowship, 1991; New York Times Notable Book of the Year, 1991; Loft McKnight Award of Distinction, 1992. Memberships: Asian-American Renaissance Conference; Center for Arts Criticism, president, 1991-92; Jerome Foundation; Phi Beta Kappa. Address: 1920 East River Terrace, Minneapolis, MN 55414-3672, USA.

MURATA Kiyoaki, b. 19 Nov 1922, Ono, Hyogo, Japan. Educator; Author. m. (1) Minako Iesaka, 1960, div 1981, 2 sons, 1 daughter, (2) Kayoko Matsukura, 1987. Education: MA, University of Chicago, USA. Appointments: Editorial Writer, 1957-66, Managing Editor, 1971-76, Executive Editor, 1976-77, Managing Director, 1976-83, Editor-in-Chief, 1977-83, The Japan Times; Director, Japan Graphic Inc, 1977-82; Professor, International Communications, Yachiyo International University, 1988. Publications: Japan's New Buddhism - An Objective Account of Soka Gakkai, 1969; Japan - The State of the Nation, 1979; Kokuren Nikki-Suppon Wan no Kaiso (UN Diary - Recollections of Turtle Bay), 1985; An Enemy Among Friends, 1991. Honours: Honorary LLD, Carleton College; Vaughn Prize, Japan Newspaper Editors and Publishers Association. Address: 19-12 Hiroo 2 chome, Shibuya-ku, Tokyo 150, Japan.

MURDOCH Dame (Jean) Iris, b. 15 July 1919, Dublin, Ireland. Writer; Philsopher. m. John O Bayley. Education: Somerville College, Oxford. Publications: Sartre: Romantic Rationalist, 1953; Under the Net, 1954; The Flight from the Enchanter, 1955; The Sandcastle, 1957; The Bell, 1958; A Severed Head, 1961, play, 1963; An Unofficial Rose, 1962; The Unicorn, 1963; The Italian Girl, 1964, play, 1967; The Red and the Green, 1964; The Time of the Angels, 1966; The Nice and the Good, 1968; Bruno's Dream, 1969; A Fairly Honourable Defeat, 1970; The Sovereignty of Good, 1970; The Servants and the Snow (play), 1970; An Accidental Man, 1971; The Three Arrows (play), 1972; The

Black Prince, 1973; The Sacred and Profane Love Machine, 1974; A Word Child, 1975; Henry and Cato, 1976; The Sea, the Sea, 1978; The Fire and the Sun, 1978; Nuns and Soldiers, 1980; Art and Eros (play), 1980; The Philosopher's Pupil, 1983; The Good Apprentice, 1985; Acastos, Platonic Dialogues, 1986; The Book of the Brotherhood, 1987; The Message to the Planet, 1989; Metaphysics as a Guide to Morals, 1992. Honours: Honorary DLitt, Universities of Sheffield, Belfast, East Anglia (Norwich), Caen, London; Fellow, 1948-63, Honorary Fellow, 1963, St Anne's College, Oxford; James Tait Black Prize for Fiction, 1974; Whitbread Literary Award for Fiction, 1974; Booker Prize for Fiction, 1978; Gifford Lecture, University of Edinburgh, 1982; Dame Commander of the Order of the British Empire, 1987. Memberships: Various professional organisations. Address: c/o Ed Victor Ltd, 162 Wardour Street, London W1V 4AT, England.

MURNANE Gerald, b. 1939, Melbourne, Victoria, Australia. Novelist. m. 3 sons. Education: BA, University of Melbourne, 1969. Appointments: Lecturer, Victoria College, Melbourne; Senior Lecturer, Deakin University, Melbourne. Publications: Tamarisk Row, 1974; A Lifetime on Clouds, 1976; The Plains, 1982; Landscape with Landscape, 1985; Inland, 1988; Velvet Waters (stories), 1990; Emerald Blue (stories), 1995. Address: 2 Falcon Street, Macleod, VA 3085, Australia.

MURPHEY Rhoads, b. 13 Aug 1919, Philadelphia, Pennsylvania, USA. Professor of History and Asian Studies. m. Eleanor Albertson, 12 Jan 1952, 2 sons, 2 daughters. Education: AB, 1941, AM, 1942, History, AM, China, 1948, PhD, Eastern History and Geography, 1950, Harvard University. Publications: Shanghai: Key to Modern China, 1953; A New China Policy, 1965; Approaches to Modern Chinese History, 1967; Introduction to Geography, 1969, 4th edition 1978; Scope of Geography, 1969, 4th edition, 1987; Treaty Ports, 1975; Mozartian Historian, 1976; Outsiders, 1977; Fading of the Maoist Vision: The Chinese, 1986; The Human Adventure, 1990; 50 Years of China to Me, 1994; A History of Asia, 1995; Civilizations of the World, 1995; East Asia: A New History, 1997. Contributions to: Various professional journals. Honour: Best Book of Year, 1978. Membership: Association of Asian Studies, president, 1986-. Address: Department of History, University of Michigan, Ann Arbor, MI 48109, USA.

MURPHY C L. See: **MURPHY Lawrence Agustus.**

MURPHY Clive, b. 28 Nov 1935, Liverpool, England. Writer. Education: BA, LLB, Trinity College, Dublin, 1958; Incorporated Law Society of Ireland, 1958. Publications: Freedom for Mr Mildew and Nigel Someone; Summer Overtures; Oral history: The Good Deeds of a Good Woman; Born to Sing; Four Acres and a Donkey; Love, Dears!; A Funny Old Quist; Oiky; At the Dog in Dulwich; A Stranger in Gloucester; Dodo, 1993; Endsleigh, 1994. Contributions to: Over 21; PEN Broadsheet; Cara; Books and Bookmen; Panurge. Honour: Adam International Review 1st Novel Award. Memberships: PEN; Society of Authors; Royal Society of Literature, associate. Address: 132 Brick Lane, London E1 6RU, England.

MURPHY Jim, b. 25 Sep 1947, Newark, New Jersey, USA. Writer; Children's Book Editor. m. Elaine Kelso, 12 Dec 1970. Education: BA, Rutgers University; Radcliffe College. Publications: Weird and Wacky Inventions, 1978; Rat's Christmas Party, 1979; Harold Thinks Big, 1980; Death Run, 1982; Two Hundred Years of Bicycles, 1983; The Indy 500, 1983; Trackers, 1984; Baseball's All-Time Stars, 1984; Guess Again: More Weird and Wacky Inventions, 1985; The Long Road to Gettysburg, 1992. Contributions to: Cricket. Honour: Golden Kite Award Society of Children's Book Writers and Illustrators, 1993. Address: 138 Wildwood Avenue, Upper Montclair, NJ 07043, USA.

MURPHY Lawrence Agustus, (Steven C Lawrence, C L Murphy), b. 17 May 1924, Brockton, Massachusetts, USA. Educator; Author. Education: BS, Massachusetts Maritime Academy, 1944; BS, Journalism, 1950, MA, English and American Literature, 1951, Boston University. Appointments: English Teacher/Department Chairman, South Junior High School, Brockton, Massachussets, 1951-87; Instructor in Creative Writing, Stonehill College, North Easton, Massachussets, 1967. Publications: The Naked Range, 1956: Saddle Justice, 1957; Brand of a Texan, 1958; The Iron Marshal, 1960; Night of the Gunmen, 1960; Gun Fury, 1961; With Blood in their Eyes, 1961; Slattery, 1961; Bullet Welcome for Slattery, 1961; Walk a Narrow Trail,

1962; A Noose for Slattery, 1962; Longhorns North, 1962; Slattery's Gun Says No, 1962; A Texan Comes Riding, 1966; Buffalo Grass (with C L Murphy), 1966; That Man From Texas, 1972; Edge of the Land, 1974; Six-Gun Junction, 1974; North to Montana, 1975; Slattery Stands Alone, 1976; Trial for Tennihan, 1976; A Northern Saga, 1976; Day of the Commancheros, 1977; Gun Blast, 1977. Memberships: Navy League of the United States; US Naval Institute; Battle of Nomandy Foundation; US Navy Memorial Foundation; Christian Coalition; American Air Museum in Britain; Massachussetts Maritime Academy Alumni Association; Boston University Alumni Association; Liberty Ship - John W Brown Memorial; Merchant Marine Veterans of World War II. Address: MA, USA.

MURPHY Walter Francis, b. 21 Nov 1929, Charleston, South Carolina, USA. Professor of Jurisprudence Emeritus; Writer. m. Mary Therese Dolan, 28 June 1952, 2 daughters. Education: AB, University of Notre Dame, 1950; AM, George Washington University, 1954; PhD, University of Chicago, 1957. Appointments: Research Fellow, Brookings Institution, Washington, DC, 1957-58; Assistant Professor, 1958-61, Associate Professor, 1961-65, Professor of Politics, 1965-95, McCormick Professor of Jurisprudence, 1968-95, Professor Emeritus, 1995-, Princeton University. Publications: Courts, Judges and Politics (editor with C Herman Pritchett), 1961, 4th edition, 1986; Congress and the Court, 1962; American Democracy (co-author), 4th edition, 1963, to 10th edition, 1983; Elements of Judicial Strategy, 1964; Wiretapping on Trial, 1965; Modern American Democracy (with M N Danielson), 1969; The Study of Public Law (with Joseph Tanehaus), 1972; Public Evaluations of Constitutional Courts (co-author), 1974; Comparative Constitutional Law (co-author), 1977; The Vicar of Christ, 1979; Basic Cases in Constitutional Law (editor with W D Lockard), 1980, 3rd edition, 1991; The Roman Enigma (fiction), 1981; American Constitutional Interpretation (with J Fleming and S A Barber), 2nd edition, 1995. Contributions to: Professional journals. Honours: Distinguished Service Cross; Purple Heart; Birkhead Award, 1958; Merriam-Cobb-Hughes Award, 1963; Guggenheim Fellowship, 1973-74; National Endowment for the Humanities Fellowship, 1978-79; Chicago Foundation for Literature Award, 1980; Lifetime Achievement Award, Law and Courts Section, American Political Science Association, 1995. Memberships: American Academy of Arts and Sciences, fellow; American Political Science Association. Address: 1533 Eagle Ridge Drive North East, Albuquerque, NM 87122, USA.

MURRAY Albert, b. 12 May 1916, Nokomis, Alabama, USA. Writer. m. 31 May 1941, 1 daughter. Education: BS, Tuskegee University, 1939; MA, New York University, 1948. Publications: The Omni-Americans, 1970; South to a Very Old Place, 1971; The Hero and the Blues, 1973; Train Whistle Guitar, novel, 1974; Stomping the Blues, 1976; Good Morning Blues, 1985; The Spyglass Tree, novel, 1991; The Seven League Boots, novel; The Blue Devils of Nada, 1996. Honours: Honorary DLitt, Colgate University, 1975; Lillian Smith Award for Fiction, 1977; ASCAP-Deems Taylor Award, 1977; Lincoln Center Alumni Emeirto Award, 1991; Honorary D Humane Letters, Spring Hill College, 1996; Honorary DLitt, Hamerton College, 1997. Memberships: American PEN; Authors Guild. Literary Agents: Wylie, Aitken and Stone. Address: 45 West 132nd Street, New York, NY 10037, USA.

MURRAY Frances. See: **BOOTH Rosemary Sutherland.**

MURRAY Les(lie Allan), b. 17 Oct 1938, Nabiac, New South Wales, Australia. Poet; Writer; Translator. Education: BA, University of Sydney, 1969. Apointments: Co-Editor, Poetry Australia, 1973-80; Poetry Reader, Angus and Robertson Publishers, 1976-91; Literary Editor, Quadrant, 1990-. Publications: Poetry: The Ilex Tree (with Geoffrey Lehmann), 1965; The Weatherboard Cathedral, 1969; Poems Against Economics, 1972; Lunch and Counter Lunch, 1974; Selected Poems: The Vernacular Republic, 1976, 2nd edition, 1982; Ethnic Radio, 1978; The Boys Who Stole the Funeral, 1980; Equanimities, 1982; The People's Otherworld, 1983; Persistence in Folly, 1984; The Australian Year (with Peter Solness), 1986; The Daylight Moon, 1986; Dog Fox Field, 1990; Collected Poems, 1991; The Rabbiter's Bounty, 1992; Translations from the Natural World, 1991. Prose: The Peasant Mandarin, 1978; Blocks and Tackles, 1991; The Paperbark Tree: Selected Prose, 1992. Editor: The New Oxford Book of Australian Verse, 1986; Collins Dove Anthology of Australian Religious Verse, 1986; Fivefathers: Five Australian Poets of the Pre-Academic Era, 1994. Contributions to: Many publications. Honours: Grace Leven Prizes, 1965, 1980, 1990; Cook Bicentennial Prize, 1970; National Book Awards, 1974, 1984, 1985, 1991, 1993; C J Dennis Memorial Prize, 1976; Gold Medal, Australian Literary Society, 1984; New South

Wales Premier's Prize, 1984; Canada-Australia Award, 1985; Australian Broadcasting Corporation Bicentennial Prize, 1988; National Poetry Award, 1988; Order of Australia, 1989; New South Wales Premier's Prize, 1993; Victorian Premier's Prize, 1993; Petrarca Preis, Germany, 1995; T S Eliot Prize, UK, 1997; Honorary doctorates. Membership: Poetry Society of Great Britain, honorary vice-president. Address: c/o Margaret Connolly and Associates, 16 Winton Street, Warrawee, New South Wales 2074, Australia.

MURRAY Rona, b. 10 Feb 1924, London, England. Lecturer; Poet. m. Walter Dexter, 1972. Education: MA, University of British Columbia, Vancouver, 1965; PhD, University of Kent, Canterbury, 1972. Appointment: Lecturer, University of Victoria, 1977-82. Publications: Poetry: The Enchanted Adder, 1965; The Power of the Dog and Other Poems, 1968; Ootischenie, 1974; Selected Poems, 1974; An Autumn Journal, 1980; Journey, 1981; Adam and Eve in Middle Age, 1984. Other: One, Two, Three, Alary, play, 1970; The Art of Earth: An Anthology (co-editor), 1979; Creatures, play, 1980; The Indigo Dress and Other Stories, 1986; Journey Back to Peshawar, memoirs/travel, 1992. Honours: Canada Council Grants; Pat Lowther Award, 1982. Address: 3825 Duke Road, RR4, Victoria, British Columbia V9B 5T8, Canada.

MURRELL John, b. 15 Oct 1945, USA (Canadian citizen). Playwright. Education: BA, University of Calgary. Appointment: Head, Theatre Section, Canada Council, 1988. Publications: Metamorphosis, 1970; Haydn's Head, 1973; Power in the Blood, 1975; Arena, 1975; Teaser, 1975; A Great Noise, A Great Light, 1976; Memoir, 1977; Uncle Vanya (after Chekhov), 1978; Mandragola (after Machiavelli), 1978; Bajazet (after Racine), 1979; The Seagull (after Chekhov), 1980; Farther West, 1982; New World, 1985; October, 1988; Democracy, 1991. Address: c/o Talonbooks, 201-1019 East Cordova, Vancouver, British Columbia V6A 1MB, Canada.

MURTI Kotikalapudi Venkata Suryanarayana, b. 31 May 1929, Parlakemidi, India. Retired Professor of English; Teacher; Research Guide; Researcher; Creative Writer; Journalist; Linguist. Education: MA, English Language and Literature, 1963, PhD, English, 1972, Andhra University; Certificate in Linguistics, Central Institute of English and Foreign Languages, Hyderabad, 1969. Publications: Books of poetry in English: Allegory of Eternity, 1975; Triple Light, 1975; Sparks of the Absolute, 1976; Spectrum, 1976; Symphony of Discords, 1977; Araku, 1982; Comic and Absolute, 1995; Convex-Image and Concave-Mirror, 1995. Other works: Waves of Illumination, 1978; Poetry in Telugu: Iham lo Param, 1979; Lillahela, 1981; Sword and Sickle: A Study of Mulk Raj Anand's Novels, 1983; Kohinoor in the Crown: Critical Studies in Indian English Literature, 1987; Old Myth and New Myth: Letters from MRA to KVS, 1991; Pranavam tho Pranayam, 1994. Address: 43-21-9A Venkatarazu Nagar, Visakhapatnam 530 016, (AP), India.

MUSGRAVE Susan, b. 12 Mar 1951, Santa Cruz, California, USA. Poet; Writer; Teacher. m. Stephen Douglas Reid, 1986, 2 daughters. Education: Oak Bay High School. Appointments: Instructor and Writer-in-Residence, University of Waterloo, Ontario, 1983-85; Instructor, Kootenay School of Writing, British Columbia, 1986, Camosun College, Victoria, British Columbia, 1988-90; Writer-in-Residence, University of New Brunswick, Fredericton, 1985, Vancouver Public Library, 1986, Sidney Public Library, British Columbia, 1989, University of Western Ontario, 1992-93, University of Toronto, 1995; Writer-in-Electronic-Residence, York University, 1991-94. Publications: Poetry: Songs of the Sea-Witch, 1970; Skuld, 1971; Birthstone, 1972; Entrance of the Celebrants, 1972; Equinox, 1973; Kung, 1973; Grave-Dirt and Selected Strawberries, 1973; Against, 1974; Two Poems, 1975; The Impstone, 1976; Kiskatinaw Songs (with Séan Virgo), 1977; Selected Strawberries and Other Poems, 1977; For Charlie Beaulieu..., 1977; Two Poems for the Blue Moon, 1977; Becky Swan's Book, 1978; A Man to Marry, A Man to Bury, 1979; Conversation During the Omelette aux Fines Herbes, 1979; When My Boots Drive Off in a Cadillac, 1980; Taboo Man, 1981; Tarts and Muggers: Poems New and Selected, 1982; The Plane Put Down in Sacramento, 1982; I do not know if things that happen can be said to come to pass or only happen, 1982; Cocktails at the Mausoleum, 1985; Desireless: Tom York (1947-1988), 1988; Musgrave Landing, 1988; The Embalmer's Art: Poems New and Selected, 1991; In the Small Hours of the Rain, 1991; Forcing the Narcissus, 1994. Fiction: The Charcoal Burners, 1980; Hag Head, 1980; The Dancing Chicken, 1987. Other: Great Musgrave, 1989; Cleacut Words: Writer for Clayquot (editor), 1993; Because You Loved

Being a Stranger: 55 Poets Celebrate Patrick Lane (editor), 1994; Musgrave Landing: Musings on the Writing Life, 1994. Honours: Canada Council Grants, 1969, 1972, 1976, 1979, 1983, 1985, 1989, 1991; National Magazine Award, Silver, 1981; Nichol Poetry Chapbook Award, 1991; British Columbia Cultural Fund Grants, 1991, Reader's Choice Award, Prairie Schooner, 1993. Address: 10301 West Saanich Road, Po Box 2421, Sidney, British Columbia V8L 3Y3, Canada.

MUSGROVE Frank, b. 16 Dec 1922, Nottingham, England. Professor of Education Emeritus; Writer. m. Dorothy Ellen Nicholls, 1 daughter. Education: BA, Magdalen College, Oxford, 1947; PhD, University of Nottingham, 1958. Appointments: Lecturer, University of Leicester, 1957-62; Senior Lecturer, University of Leeds, 1963-65; Professor of Research in Education, University of Bradford, 1965-70; Sarah Fielden Professor of Education, 1970-82, Professor Emeritus, 1982-, University of Manchester; Co-Editor, Research in Education, 1971-76; Honorary Professor, University of Hull, 1985-88; Various guest lectureships. Publications: The Migratory Elite, 1963; Youth and the Social Order, 1964; The Family, Education and Society, 1966; Society and the Teacher's Role (with P H Taylor), 1969; Patterns of Power and Authority in English Education, 1971; Ectasy and Holiness, 1974, new edition, 1994; Margins of the Mind, 1977; School and the Social Order, 1979; Education and Anthropology, 1982; The North of England: A History from Roman Times to the Present, 1990. Contributions to: Professional journals. Honour: Doctor of Letters, Open University, 1982. Memberships: Royal Anthropological Institute; Fellow, Royal Society of Arts. Address: Dib Scar, the Cedar Grove, Beverley, East Yorkshire, HU17 7EP, England.

MUSICA Barbara, b. 25 Dec 1943, Los Angeles, California, USA. Writer; Professor. m. Mauro E Mujica, 26 Dec 1966, 1 son, 2 daughters. Education: BA, University of California, 1964; MA, Middlebury Graduate Program in Paris, 1965; PhD, New York University, 1974. Appointments: Book Review Editor, Americas Magazine; Senior Associate Editor, The Washington Review. Publications: Iberian Pastoral Characters, 1986; Characters, 1986; The Deaths of Don Bernardo (fiction), 1990; Texto y Vida: Introduction a la Literatura Espanola, criticism, 1990; Et in Arcadia Ego, 1990; Antologia de la Literatura Espanola, Vol I & II, 1991; Looking at the Comedia, 1993; Far From My Mother's Home, fiction, 1996. Contributions to: Los Angeles Times; Literary Review; Antetam Review; What is Secret; Two Worlds Walking; Where Angels Glide at Dawn; New Southern Literary Messenger. Honours: Poets and Writers, 1984; Pushcart Nominee, 1986; New York Times 50 Best Op Eds of the Decade, 1990; E L Doctorow International Fiction Award, 1992. Literary Agent: Chadd-Stevens. Address: Department of Spanish and Portuguese, Georgetown University, ICC 405, Washington DC 20057-0989, USA.

MUSKE Carol Anne (Carol Muske Dukes), b. 17 Dec 1946, St Paul, Minnesota, USA. Professor; Writer; Poet. m. David Dukes, 31 Jan 1983, 1 stepson, 1 daughter. Education: BA, Creighton University, 1967; MA, State University of California, San Francisco. Appointments: Professor, University of Southern California at Los Angeles; Founder, Art W/O Walls. Publications: Dear Digby, 1989; Red Trouseau (poems), 1993; Saving St Germ (novel), 1993. Contributions to: Periodicals. Honours: Castanola Award, 1979; Guggenheim Fellowship, 1981; National Endowment for the Arts Fellowship, 1984; Ingram Merrill Foundation Award, 1988. Memberships: Authors Guild; PEN; Poetry Society of America. Address: c/o Department of English, University of Southern California, University Park, Los Angeles, CA 90089, USA.

MUSSEY Viginia T H. See: **ELLISON Virginia Howell**.

MUSSON Cecile Norma. See: **SMITH Cecile Norma Musson**.

MYERS Jack Elliot, b. 29 Nov 1941, Lynn, Massachusetts, USA. Professor of English. m. Thea Temple, 25 Sept 1993, 3 sons, 1 daughter. Education: BA, University of Massachusetts, 1970; MFA, University of Iowa, 1972. Appointments: Professor, Southern Methodist University; Poetry Editor, Cimarron Review, 1989; Distinguished Writer-in-Residence, Wichita State University, 1992, University of Idaho, 1993. Publications: Black Sun Abraxas, 1970; Will It Burn?, 1974; The Family War, 1977; I'm Amazed That You're Still Singing, 1981; A Trout in the Milk, 1982; New American Poets of the '80's, 1984; The Longman Dictionary & Handbook of Poetry, 1985; As Long As You're Happy, 1986; New American Poets of the '90's, 1991; A Profile of 20th Century American Poetry, 1992; Blindsided, 1993; Leaning House Poets, volume 1, 1996. Contributions: Journals and magazines. Honours: Texas Institute of Letters Poetry Awards, 1978, 1993; Elliston Book Award, 1978; National Endowment for the Arts Fellowships, 1982, 1986. Memberships: Associated Writing Programs, vice-president, 1991-94; PEN; Texas Association of Creative Writing Teachers. Address: Department of English, Southern Methodist University, Dallas, TX 75275, USA.

MYRE André, b. 14 Aug 1939, Montreal, Canada. Titular Professor. Education: PhD, Hebrew Union College. Publication: Un Souffle Subversif, 1987. Memberships: SBL; SNTS. Address: Theology University of Montreal, CP 6128, PO Box Centre Ville, Montreal, Quebec H3C 3J7, Canada.

N

NABOKOV Dmitri, b. 10 May 1934, Berlin, Germany. Operatic Bass; Writer; Translator. Education: AB cum laude, Harvard University; Longy School of Music, 1955-57. Appointments: Has sung leading bass operatic roles and performed in concert in many theatres in many countries of North and South America and Europe. Publications: Translations, including numerous works of Vladimir Nabokov, 1957-; Translator, editor and commentator: The Man from the USSR and Other Plays (Vladimir Nabokov), 1984; The Enchanter (Vladimir Nabokov), 1986; The Selected Letters of Vladimir Nabokov, 1940-1977, 1989. Contributions to: Articles and essays to various collections and periodicals. Honours: Cum Laude Society; Winner, International Opera Contests, Reggio Emilia, 1960, Parma, 1966; Participant, award-winning recording of Madrigals by Gesualdo, 1963. Memberships: Offshore Powerboat Racing Association; American Powerboat Racing Association; American Alpine Club; Ferrari Club, Switzerland; Chevalier du Tastevin. Literary Agent:, Smith and Skolnik, New York, USA. Address: Chemin de la Caudraz, CH-1820 Montreux, Switzerland.

NADAUS Roland, (Pol-Jean Mervillon), b. 28 Nov 1945, Paris, France. Professor. m. Simone Moris, 9 Sept 1967, 1 daughter. Education: Professor, 1966; President, Jury du Prix International Emile Snyder de St Quentin-en-Yvelins. Publications: Maison de Paroles, 1969; Journal - Vrac, 1981; Je ne Tutoie que Dieu et ma femme (poems), 1992; Dictionnaire initiatique de l'orant, 1993; L'homme que tuèrent les mouches, 1996. Contributions to: Several journals. Honour: Prix Gustave Gasser, 1993. Membership: Pen Club of France. Address: 20 route de Troux, 78280 Guyancourt, France.

NADICH Judah, b. 13 May 1912, Baltimore, Maryland, USA. Rabbi; Writer. m. Martha Hadassah, The City of Ribaloe, 26 Jan 1947, 3 daughters. Education: AB, College of New York, 1932; Jewish Theological Seminary of America, 1932-36; MA, Columbia University, 1936; Rabbi, Master of Arts, Doctor of Hebrew Literature, 1953. Publications: Eisenhower and the Jews, 1953; Menachem Ribalow: The Flowering of Modern Hebrew Literature (translator), 1957; Louis Ginzberg: Al Halakhah Ve-Aggadah (editor), 1960; Jewish Legends of the Second Commonwealth, 1983; Legends of the Rabbis, 1994. Contributions to: Reference works, books, and journals. Honour: OBE, 1944; Croix de Guerre, 1945; Doctor of Divinity, honoris causa, 1966. Memberships: Jewish Book Council of America, president, 1970-72; Rabbinical Assembly, president, 1972-74. Address: Park Avenue Synagogue, 50 East 87th Street, New York, NY 10028, USA.

NADOLNY Sten, b. 29 July 1942, Zehdenick/Havel, Germany. Author. Education: Abitur, 1961; Dr phil, Modern History, 1977. Publications: Netzkarte, 1981; Die Entdeckung der Langsamkeit, 1983; Selim oder die Gabe der Rede, 1990; Das Erzählen und die guten Absichten, 1990; Ein Gott der Frechheit, 1994. Honours: Ingeborg Bachmann Prize, 1980; Hans Fallada Prize, 1985; Vallombrosa Prize, Florence, 1986; Ernst Hoferichter Prize, 1995. Memberships: PEN; Bayerische Akademie der Schönen Künste. Literary Agent: Agence Hoffman, Bechsteinstrasse 2, D-80804 Munich, Germany. Address: Kollatzstrasse 19, D-14059 Berlin, Germany.

NAGARAJA RAO C K, (Haida, Haritas, Rajanna), b. 12 June 1915, Chellakere, India. Author; Journalist. m. Rajamani Nagarajo Rao, 18 May 1934, 2 sons, 6 daughters. Education: Intermediate Engineering Exam, Mysore University, 1933; Hindi Preaveshika Exam, 1937. Publications: Wild Jasmine, 1937; Mushrooms, 1942; Shoodramuni, 1943; Dayadadavanala, 1944; Sangama, 1944; Place and Date of Mahakavi Lakshmeesha, 1969; Pattamahadevi Shantaladevi, 1978; Sankole Basava, 1979; Sampanna Samaja, 1979; Savilladavaru, 1982; Kuranganayani, 1983; Ekalavya, 1988; Veeranganga Vishnuvardhana, 1992. Contributions to: Various publications. Honours: Award for Research and Criticism, 1969-70, Best Creative Literature of the Year, 1978, Karnataka State Sahitya Akademi; Moorthidevi Sahitya Puraskar of Bharatiya Jnanpith, 1983. Memberships: Kannada Sahitya Parishat; Karnataka Lekhakar Sangha; PEN All India Centre; Mythic Society; Authors Guild of India. Address: 7/61/2 Mandaara, 1 Main Road, Padmanabhanagar, Bangalore 560 070, India.

NAGATSUKA Ryuji, b. 20 Apr 1924, Nagoya, Japan. Professor. m. 20 July 1949. Education: Graduated, Section of French Literature, University of Tokyo, 1948. Appointments: Professor, Nihon University, 1968-. Publications: Napoleon tel qu'il était, 1969; J'étais un kamikaze, 1972; George Sand, sa vie et ses oeuvres, 1977; Napoleon, 2 volumes, 1986; Talleyrand, 1990. Contributions to: Yomiuri Shimbun. Honours: Prix Pierre Mille, 1972; Prix Senghor, 1973. Membership: Association Internationale des Critiques Littéraires, Paris. Address: 7-6-37 Oizumigakuen-cho, Nerima-ku, Tokyo, Japan.

NAGEL Paul C(hester), b. 14 Aug 1926, Independence, Missouri, USA. Historian; Writer. m. Joan Peterson, 19 Mar 1948, 3 sons. Education: BA, 1948, MA, 1949, PhD, 1952, University of Minnesota. Appointments: Historian, Strategic Air Command, US Air Force, Omaha, 1951-53; Assistant Professor, Augustana College, Sioux Falls, South Dakota, 1953-54; Assistant Professor to Associate Professor, Eastern Kentucky University, Richmond, 1954-61; Visiting Professor, Amherst College, 1957-58, Vanderbilt University, 1959, University of Minnesota, 1964; Faculty, 1961-65, Professor of History, 1965-69, Dean, College of Arts and Sciences, 1965-69, University of Kentucky; Special Assistant to the President for Academic Affairs, 1969-71, Professor of History, 1969-78, Vice-President for Academic Affairs, 1971-74, University of Missouri; Professor of History and Head, Department of History, University of Georgia, 1978-80; Director, Virginia Heritage Society, Richmond, 1981-85; Distinguished Lee Scholar, Lee Memorial Foundation, 1986-90; Visiting Scholar, Duke University, 1991-92, University of Minnesota, 1992-, Carleton College, 1993-. Publications: One Nation Indivisible: The Union in American Thought 1776-1861, 1964, 2nd edition, 1980; This Sacred Trust: American Nationality 1798-1898, 1971, 2nd edition, 1980; Missouri: A History, 1977, 2nd edition, 1988; Descent from Glory: Four Generations of the John Adams Family, 1983; Extraordinary Lives: The Art and Craft of American Biography (co-author), 1986; The Adams Women: Abigail and Louisa Adams, Their Sisters and Daughters, 1987; George Caleb Bingham (co-author), 1989; The Lees of Virginia: Seven Generations of an American Family, 1990; Massachusetts and the New Nation (co-author), 1992; John Quincy Adams: A Public Life, A Private Life, 1997. Contributions to: Professional journals and general publications. Honours: Best Book Award, 1977; Book of the Month Club Main Selection, 1983; Laureate of Virginia, 1988. Memberships: Massachusetts Historical Society; Pilgrim Society; Society of American Historians; Southern Historical Association, president, 1984-85. Address: 1314 Marquette Avenue, Apt 2206, Minneapolis, MN 55403, USA.

NAGEL Thomas, b. 4 July 1937, Belgrade, Yugoslavia (US citizen, 1944). Professor of Philosophy and Law; Writer. m. (1) Doris Blum, 18 June 1958, div 1973, (2) Anne Hollander, 26 June 1979. Education: BA, Cornell University, 1958; BPhil, Corpus Christi College, Oxford, 1960; PhD, Harvard University, 1963. Appointments: Assistant Professor of Philosophy, University of California at Berkeley, 1963-66; Assistant Professor, 1966-69, Associate Professor, 1969-72, Professor, 1972-80, Princeton University; Tanner Lecturer, Stanford University, 1977; Tanner Lecturer, Oxford University, 1979; Professor of Philosophy, 1980-, Chairman, Department of Philosophy, 1981-86, Professor of Philosophy and Law, 1986-, New York University; Howison Lecturer, University of California at Berkeley, 1987; Thalheimer Lecturer, Johns Hopkins University, 1989; John Locke Lecturer, Oxford University, 1990; Hempel Lecturer, Princeton University, 1995; Whitehead Lecturer, Harvard University, 1995; Immanuel Kant Lecturer, Stanford University, 1995. Publications: The Possibility of Altruism, 1970; Mortal Questions, 1979; The View from Nowhere, 1986; What Does It All Mean?, 1987; Equality and Partiality, 1991; Other Minds: Critical Essays, 1969-94, 1995; The Last Word, 1996. Contributions to: Scholarly journals. Honours: Guggenheim Fellowship, 1966-67; National Endowment for the Humanities Fellowships, 1978-79, 1984-85; Honorary Fellow, Corpus Christi College, Oxford, 1992-. Memberships: American Academy of Arts and Sciences, Fellow; British Academy, Fellow. Address: c/o School of Law, New York University, 40 Washington Square South, New York, NY 10012, USA.

NAGORSKI Andrew. Journalist. m. Christina Nagorski, 4 children. Education: BA, magna cum laude, Phi Beta Kappa, Amherst College, 1969; University of Cracow. Appointments: Teacher in Social Studies, Wayland High School, Massachusetts; Associate Editor, 1973, Assistant Managing Editor of the Atlantic, Pacific and Latin America Editions, 1977, Hong Kong-based Asia Regional Editor, 1978, Hong Kong Bureau Chief, 1979, Newsweek International magazine;

Leader of Bureaus in Bonn, Rome, Hong Kong and Moscow, Newsweek; Senior Associate, Carnegie Endowment for International Peace, Washington, DC, 1988; Warsaw Bureau Chief, 1990, assigned to Moscow, 1991, Moscow Bureau Chief, 1995, Berlin Bureau Chief, 1996-, Newsweek; TV and radio appearances. Publications: Reluctant Farewell: An American Reporter's Candid Look Inside the Soviet Union, 1982; The Birth of Freedom, 1993. Address: c/o Newsweek, 251 West 57th Street, New York, NY 10019-1894, USA. Honours: 3 Awards/Citations for Reporting, Overseas Press Club;

NAGY Paul, b. 23 Aug 1934, Hungary. Writer. Div. Education: Bachelor's degree, Hungary, 1953; Diploma, French Language and Literature, Sorbonne, Paris, 1962. Appointments: Co-Founder, Atelier Hongrois, 1962; Co-Founder, p'ART video-review, 1987. Publications: Books: Les faineants de Hampstead, 1969; Sadisfaction IS, 1977; Journal in-time, 1984; Points de Repères "Postmodernes": Lyotard, Habermas, Derrida, 1993; Journal in-time II, 1994; Projections-performances, 1978-; Visual multimedia works, 1980-. Contributions to: Change; Change International; Rampike; Lotta poetica. Membership: Union des Ecrivains Français. Address: 141 Avenue Jean Jaures, 92120 Montrouge, France.

NAHAL Chaman, b. 2 Aug 1927, Sialkot, India. Writer. Appointments: Member, Department of English, Delhi University, 1963-; Columnist, Talking About Books, The Indian Express newspaper, 1966-73; Associate Professor of English, Long Island University, New York, USA, 1968-70. Publications: The Weird Dances (short stories), 1965; A Conversation with J Kristnamurti, 1965; D H Lawrence: An Eastern View, 1970; Drugs and the Other Self (editor), 1971; The Narrative Pattern in Ernest Hemingway's Fiction, 1971; The New Literatures in English, 1985; The Bhagavad-Gita: A New Rendering, 1987. Novels: My True Faces, 1973; Azadi, 1975; Into Another Dawn, 1977; The English Queens, 1979; The Crown and the Loincloth, 1982; Sunrise in Fiji, 1988; The Salt of Life, 1990. Address: 2/1 Kalkaji Extension, New Delhi 110019, India.

NAIFEH Steven (Woodward), b. 19 June 1952, Tehran, Iran. Art Lecturer; Public Relations Consultant. Education: AB, Princeton University; MA, JD, Harvard University. Publications: Culture Making: Money, Success, and the New York Art World, 1976; Moving Up in Style, 1980; Gene Davis, 1981; From Primitive to Modern: One Hundred Years of Nizenzu Art, c. 1982 ; The Arts Book, c. 1982; What Every Client Needs to Know About Using a Lawyer, 1982; Pillars of Wisdom: New Buildings for the World of Islam, c. 1983; Why Can't Men Open Up?, 1984; The Best Lawyers in America: Directory of Experts, 1990; Jackson Pollock: An American Saga (with Gregory White Smith), 1990; The Best Doctors in America, 1992; Final Justice, 1993. Honours: Pulitzer Prize in Biography, 1991. Address: 129 First Avenue South West, Aiken, SC 29801, USA.

NAIMAN Anatoly G, b. 23 Apr 1936, Leningrad, Russia. Poet; Writer. m. Galina Narinskaia, 1969, 1 son, 1 daughter. Education: Degree in Organic Chemistry, Leningrad Technological Institute, 1958; Postgraduate Diploma in Screenwriting, Moscow, 1964. Appointments: Visiting Professor in Russian and Poetry, Bryn Mawr College, USA, 1991; Visiting Fellow, All Souls College, Oxford, 1991-92. Publications: Remembering Anna Akhmatova, 1989; The Poems of Anatoly Naiman, 1989; The Statue of a Commander and Other Stories, 1992; Translations into Russian of various books. Contributions to: New Worlds; October; The Star; Literaturnaia Gazeta; Russkaia Mysl; L'Espresso; Times Literary Supplement. Honour: Lativian Union of Writers Translators Prize. Memberships: Leningrad Four (group of Poets), 1960-66; Writers Committee, Leningrad, 1965-70, Moscow, 1970-; PEN Club, France, 1989-. Literary Agent: Andrew Nurnberg Associates, London. Address: Dmitrovskoye Schosse 29 fl 56, Moscow, Russia.

NAIPAUL Vidiadhar Surajprasad, b. 17 Aug 1932, Trinidad. Writer. m. Patricia Hale, 1955. Education: BA, Honours, English, University College, Oxford, 1954. Publications: The Mystic Masseur, 1957; The Suffrage of Elvira, 1958; Miguel Street, 1959; A House for Mr Biswas, 1961; The Middle Passage, 1962; Mr Stone and the Knights Companion, 1963; An Area of Darkness, 1965; The Mimic Men, 1967; A Flag on the Island, 1967; The Loss of Eldorado, 1969; In a Free State, 1971; India: A Wounded Civilization, 1977; A Bend in the River, 1979; The Return of Eva Perion, 1980; Among the Believers, 1981; Finding the Centre, 1984; The Enigma of Arrival, 1987; A Turn in the South, 1989. Contributions to: Various journals and magazines. Honours: Rhys Memorial Prize, 1958; W H Smith Literary Award,

1968; Booker Prize, 1971; Bennet Award, 1980; Jerusalem Prize, 1983; DLitt, Cambridge University, 1983; Ingersoll Prize, 1986. Memberships: Royal Society of Literature, fellow; Society of Authors. Literary Agent: Gillon Aitken. Address: c/o Aitken & Stone, 29 Fernshaw Road, London SW10 0TG, England.

NAKAYAMA Kiyoshi, b. 30 Mar 1935, Japan. Professor of English, 1 son, 1 daughter. Education: BA, French, Tenri University, Nara, 1955; MA, English Literature, Kansai University, Osaka, 1962. Publications: Selected Essays of John Steinbeck, 1981; Tanoshi Mokuyobi, 1984; Uncollected Stories of John Steinbeck, 1986; John Steinbeck's Writings: The California Years, 1989; John Steinbeck: Asian Perspectives, 1992; Steinbeck in Japan: A Bibliography, 1992; Of Mice and Men: A Play in Three Acts (co-editor), 1993. Contributions to: Kansai University English Literature Society Bulletin; San Jose Studies; Essays on Collecting John Steinbeck's Books; Steinbeck Quarterly; Monterey Life. Honour: Richard W and Dorothy Burkhardt Award, 1992. Memberships: John Steinbeck Society of Japan, executive director; International John Steinbeck Society, executive board; Japan-American Literature Society, executive board, 1994-. Address: 594 Takabatake Honyakushi-cho, Nara-shi, Nara 630, Japan.

NAKAYAMA Shigeru, b. 22 June 1928, Japan. Professor. m. Motoko Watanabe, 8 July 1962, 1 son, 1 daughter. Education: BA, Tokyo University, 1951; PhD, Harvard University, 1959. Publications: History of Japanese Astronomy, 1969; Chinese Science, 1973; Science and Society in Modern Japan, 1974; Characteristics of Scientific Development in Japan, 1977; Academic and Scientific Traditions, 1984; Science, Technology and Society in Postwar Japan, 1991. Memberships: International Council for Science Policy Studies; Académie Internationale d'Histoire des Sciences; President, International Society of the History of East Asian Science, Technology and Medicine. Address: 3-7-11 Chuo, Nakano, Tokyo, Japan.

NANDA Bal Ram, b 11 Oct 1917, Rawalpindi, India. Historian; Writer. m. Janak Khosla, 24 May 1946, 2 sons. Education: MA, History, 1st class, University of Punjab, Lahore, 1939. Appointment: Director, Nehru Memorial Museum and Library, New Delhi, 1965-79. Publications: Mahatma Gandhi, A Biography, 1958; The Nehrus, Motilal and Jawaharlal, 1962; Gandhi, A Pictorial Biography, 1972; Gokhale, The Indian Moderates and the British Raj, 1977; Jawaharlal Nehru, A Pictorial Biography, 1980; Gandhi and His Critics, 1986; Gandhi, Pan-Islamism, Imperialisn and Nationalism in India, 1989; In Gandhi's Footsteps: Life and Times of Jamnalal Bajaj, 1990; Jawaharal Nehrw: Rebel and Statesman, 1996. Editor: Socialism in India, 1972; Indian Foreign Policy: The Nehru Years, 1975; Science and Technology in India, 1977; Essays in Modern Indian History, 1980; Mahatma Gandhi: 125 Years, 1995. Contributions to: Numerous newspapers, magazines and journals. Honours: Rockefeller Fellowship, 1964; National Fellowship, Indian Council of Social Science Research, New Delhi, 1979; Dadabhai Naoroji Memorial Prize, 1981; Padma Bhushan, 1988. Memberships: Institute for Defence Studies and Analyses, New Delhi; Authors Guild of India; Indian International Centre. Address: S-174 Panchshila Park, New Delhi 110017, India.

NANNEN Henri, b. 25 Dec 1913, Emden. Journalist; Publisher; Editor; Founder of Museum Kunsthalle in Emden. m. (1) Martha Kimm, 1947, (2) Eske Nagel, 1990, 1 son. Education: Studied Art History in Munich. Publications: Kleines Musikbrevier, 1943; Glanz von Innen, 1949; Ludolf Backhyusen, Monographie, 1985. Contributions to: Publisher, Editor, Hannoversche Neueste Nachrichten, 1947; Abendpost, Hannover; Editor & Publisher, Stern, Hamburg, 1948-83. Honours: ZDF (German Television) Order of Merit, 1971; Order of Merit of German Republic, 1989; Order of Merit of Lower Saxony, 1992; Mentor-Award, 1993; Maecenas-Award, 1995. Address: Kunsthalle in Emden, Hinter dem Rahmen 13, 26721 Emden, Germany.

NANSE. See: KUO Nancy.

NAPIER William (Bill) McDonald, b. 29 June 1940, Perth, Scotland. Astronomer. m. Nancy Miller Baillie, 7 July 1965, 1 son, 1 daughter. Education: BSc, 1963; PhD, 1966. Publications: The Cosmic Serpent, 1982; The Cosmic Winter, 1990; The Origin of Comets, 1990. Contributions to: New Scientist; Astronomy Today. Honour: Joint recipient, Arthur Beer Memorial Prize, 1986-87. Membership: Royal Astronomical Society, fellow. Address: Royal Observatory, Blackford Hill, Edinburgh EH9 3HJ, Scotland.

NARAIN Vineet, b. 18 Apr 1956, Khurja, UP, India. Journalism. m. Dr Meeta Narain, 4 Aug 1982, 2 sons. Education: PhD, Agra University, Agra, India, 1983. Publication: My Hawala Kurushetra, in printing. Contributions to: Indian leading newspapers and magazines. Address: C 6/28 Safdarjung Dev Area, New Delhi 110016, India.

NARANG Gopi Chand, b. 1 Jan 1931, Dukki, Baluchistan, India. Professor. m. Manorama Narang, 9 Dec 1973, 2 sons. Education: Honours, 1st in 1st Class, Urdu, 1948, Honours, 1st in 1st Class, Persian 1958, Punjab University; MA, 1st in 1st Class, Urdu, 1954, PhD, 1958, Diploma in Linguistics, 1st Division, 1961, University of Delhi; Postdoctoral courses in Acoustic Phonetics and Transformational Grammar, Indiana University, USA, 1964. Appointment: Professor of Urdu Language and Literature, Delhi University; Acting Vice Chancellor, Jamia Millia University, 1981-82; Visiting Professor, Indian Studies, University of Wisconsin, Madison, 1963-63, 1968-70. Publications: Karkhandari Dialect of Delhi Urdu, 1961; Puranon Ki Kahaniyan, 1976; Anthology of Modern Urdu Poetry, 1981; Urdu Afsana, Riwayat aur Masail, 1982; Safar Ashna, 1982; Usloobiyat-e-Mir, 1985; Saniha-e-Karbala bataur Sheri Istiara, 1987; Amir Khusrau ka Hindavi Kalaam, 1988; Adabi Tanqeed aur Usloobiyat, 1989; Rajinder Singh Bedi (anthology), 1990; Urdu Language and Literature: Critical Perspectives, 1991; Sakhtiyat, Pas-Sakhtiyat, Mashriqi Sheriyat, 1993; Balwant Singh, anthology, 1995; Hindustan ke Urdu Musannifin aur Shoara, 1996. Address: D-252 Sarvodaya Enclave, New Delhi 110017, India.

NARAYAMA Fujio, b. 13 June 1948, Iwate, Japan. Author; Poet. Education: Graduate in Drama, Arts Department, Toho Gakuen Junior College, 1970. Publications: Manhattan Ballad, 1977; Sanctuary of Evil, 1979; Lay Traps in the Winter, 1981; The Scarred Bullet, 1989; Neverending Night, 1992. Honours: 21st Iwate Arts Festival Award, for The Woman Carrying Straw, 1967; 23rd Iwate Arts Festival Incentive Award, for The Summer Opposition, 1969; 46th All Yomimono New Writer's Award, for New York Samurai, 1975. Memberships: Japan Writers Association; Mystery Writers of Japan; Sino-Japanese Cultural Exchange Society; Mystery Writers of America. Literary Agent: Woodbell Co Ltd. Address: 2-1-11 Veruzone 2-B, Nukui, Nerima-ku, Tokyo, Japan.

NARAYAN Rasipuram Krishnaswamy, b. 10 Oct 1906, Madras, India. Novelist. Education: Maharajas College, Mysore, 1930. Appointment: Owner, Indian Thought Publications, Mysore. Publications: Swami and Friends: A Novel of Malgudi, 1935; The Bachelor of Arts, 1937; The Dark Room, 1939; The English Teacher, 1945; The Financial Expert, 1952; The Guide, 1958; The Man Eater of Malgudi, 1962; The Vendor of Sweets, 1967; The Painter of Signs, 1976; Talkative Man, 1986; The World of Nagaraj. Stories: Malgudi Days, 1943; Cyclone and Other Stories, 1944; An Astrologer's Day and Other Stories, 1947; Lawley Road, 1956; A Horse and Two Goats, 1970; Essays, Travel Writing and Memoirs. Honours: English Speaking Union Award, 1975; D Litt, University of Delhi; Fellow, Royal Society of Literature, 1980. Address: 15 Vivekananda Road, Yadavagiri, Mysore 2, India.

NARDON Anita Lucia, b. 2 Apr 1931, Belgium. Multi-Lingual Secretary; Art Critic. div., 3 sons. Appointments: Staff, Peau de Serpent, 1962-78, Le Drapeau Rouge, 1980-91, IDEART, 1989, Saison, 1989. Publications: Poetry: 18 Booklets; La Chanson d'Isis; Tale: Contes pour Yannick; Art Books: more than 14 artist's monographies; 50 Artistes de Belgique, Vol IV, V, VI. Contributions: Various monthly art magazines. Honours: Médaille d'argent Arthur Rimbaud; Prix Ville de Toulon, France; Prix Silarus Francia; Médaille de Bronze, Poésiades de Paris. Memberships: PEN; Association International des Critiques d'Art. Address: Rue Jourdan 57, 1060 Brussels, Belgium.

NARULA Surinder Singh, b. 8 Nov 1917, Amritsar, India. Writer; Poet; Teacher. m. Pritama, 10 Apr 1950, 3 daughters. Education: MA, English, 1942. Appointments: Former Principal and Head, Post Graduate Department of English and American Literatures, Government College, Ludhiana. Publications: 13 novels, 6 collections of short stories, 8 books of literary criticism, 3 collections of poetry and 12 books on socio-cultural subjects. Contributions to: Numerous professional journals. Honours: Rattingon Gold Medalist, 1938; J S Hailey Prizeman, 1938; Panjab Government Shiromani Sahityakar; Panjab Arts Council Award; Sahitya Shri Award, Bhartiya Bhasha Sangam; Rotary International Award; Panjabi Sahitya Akademi Silver Jubilee Robe of Honour; Vishav Panjabi Sammelan Gold Medal; many other honours and awards. Memberships: Various professional organisations. Address: 684 Gurdevnagar, Civil Lines, Ludhiana 141001, India.

NASH Gary Baring, b. 27 July 1933, Philadelphia, Pennsylvania, USA. Professor of History; Writer. m. (1) Mary Workum, 20 Dec 1955, div, 1 son, 3 daughters, (2) Cynthia Shelton, 24 Oct 1981. Education: BA, 1955, PhD, 1964, Princeton University. Appointments: Assistant to the Dean, Graduate School, 1959-61, Instructor, 1964-65, Assistant Professor, 1965-66, Princeton University: Assistant Professor, 1966-68, Associate Professor, 1969-72, Professor of History, 1972-, Dean, Undergraduate Curriculum Development, 1984-91, University of California at Los Angeles; Associate Director, 1988-94, Director, 1994-, National Center for History in the Schools; Co-Chairman, National History Studies Project, 1992-95. Publications: Quakers and Politics: Pennsylvania, 1681-1726, 1968, revised edition, 1993; Class and Society in Early America, 1970; The Great Fear: Race in the Mind of America (editor with Richard Weiss), 1970; Red, White, and Black; The Peoples of Early America, 1974, 3rd edition, 1991; The Urban Crucible: Social Change, Political Consciousness, and the Origins of the American Revolution, 1979; Struggle and Survival in Colonial America (editor with David Sweet), 1980; The Private Side of American History (co-editor), 2 volumes, 1983, 1987; The American People: Creating a Nation and a Society (with J R Jeffrey), 2 volumes, 1985, 1989, 3rd edition, 1993, 4th edition, 1997; Retracing the Past, 2 volumes, 1985, 1989, 1993, 1997; Race, Class and Politics: Essays on American Colonial and Revolutionary Society, 1986; Forging Freedom: The Formation of Philadelphia's Black Comunity, 1720-1840, 1988; Race and Revolution, 1990; Freedom by Degrees: Emancipation and Its Aftermath in Pennsylvania (with Jean R Soderlund), 1991; American Odyssey: The United States in the 20th Century, 1991, revised edition, 1993; History on Trial: Culture Wars and the Teaching of the Past, co-author Charlotte Crabtree and Ross Dunn, 1997. Contributions to: Professional journals. Honours: Guggenheim Fellowship, 1969-70; American Antiquarian Society; American Historical Association; Institute of Early American History and Culture; Organization of American Historians, president, 1994-95; Society of American Historians. Address: 16174 Alcima Avenue, Pacific Palisades, CA 90272, USA.

NASH Gerald David, b. 16 July 1928, Berlin, Germany (US citizen, 1944). Historian; Distinguished Porfessor. m. Marie L Norris, 19 Aug 1967, 1 daughter. Education: BA, New York University, 1950; MA, Columbia Universty, 1952; PhD, University of California at Berkeley, 1957. Appointments: Instructor, 1957-58, Visiting Assistant Professor, 1959-60, Stanford University; Assistant Professor, Northern Illinois University, DeKalb, 1958-59; Postdoctoral Fellow, Harvard University, 1960-61; Faculty, 1961-68, Professor of History, 1968-85, Chairman, Department of History, 1974-80, Presidential Professor, 1985-90, Distinguished Professor, 1990-, University of New Mexico: Visting Associate Professor, New York University, 1965-66; Editor, The Historian, 1974-84; George Bancroft Professor of American History, University of Gottingen, 1990-91. Publications: State Government and Economic Development, 1964; Issues in American Economic History (editor), 1964, 3rd edition, 1984; F D Roosevelt (editor), 1967; US Oil Policy, 1968; Perspectives on Administration, 1969; The Great Transition, 1971; The American West in the 20th Century, 1973; The Great Depression and World War II, 1979; Urban West (editor), 1979; The American West Transformed: The Impact of World War II, 1985; Social Security in the US: The First Half Century (editor with Noel Pugach and Richard Tomasson), 1988; Perspectives on the 20th Century West (editor with Richard Etulain), 1989; World War II and the West: Reshaping the Economy, 1990; Creating the West: Historical Interpretations (editor), 1991; A P Gianinni and the Bank of America, 1992; The Crucial Era, 1992; Research Opportunities in 20th Century Western History (editor with Richard Etulain), 1996. Contributions to: Professional journals. Honours: Newberry Library Fellow, 1959; Huntington Library Grant, 1979; National Endowment for the Humanities Senior Fellow, 1981; Project 87 Fellow, 1982-83; Phi Beta Kappa. Memberships: Agricultural History Society; American Historical Association; Business History Society; Organisation of American Historians; Western History Association. Address: c/o Department of History, University of New Mexico, Albuquerque, NM 87131, USA.

NASH Padder. See: **SEWART Alan.**

NASSAR Eugene Paul, b. 20 June 1935, Utica, New York, USA. Professor of English. m. Karen Nocian, 30 Dec 1969, 1 son, 2 daughters. Education: BA, Kenyon College, 1957; MA, Worcester College, Oxford, 1960; PhD, Cornell University, 1962. Appointments: Instructor in English, Hamilton College, 1962-64; Assistant Professor of English, 1964-66, Associate Professor, 1966-71, Professor, 1971-, Utica College, Syracuse University; Director, Ethnic Heritage Studies Center. Publications: Wallace Stevens: An Anatomy of Figuration, 1965, 2nd edition, 1968; The Rape of Cinderella: Essays in Literary Continuity, 1970; Selections from a Prose Poem: East Utica, 1971; The Cantos of Ezra Pound: The Lyric Mode, 1975; Wind of the Land: Two Prose Poems, 1979; Essays: Critical and Metacritical, 1983; Illustrations to Dante's Inferno, 1994; Editor of several books. Contributions to: Various publications. Address: 704 Lansing Street, Utica, NY 13501, USA.

NASSAUER Rudolf, b. 8 Nov 1924, Frankfurt am Main, Germany. Writer; Poet. Education: University of Reading, 1943-45. Publications: Poems, 1947; The Holigan, 1959; The Cuckoo, 1962; The Examination, 1973; The Unveiling, 1975; The Agents of Love, 1976; Midlife Feasts, 1977; Reparations, 1981; Kramer's Goats, 1986. Address: 51 St James' Gardens, London W11, England.

NATALE Francine de. See: MALZBERG Barry.

NATHAN David, b. 9 Dec 1926, Manchester, England. Journalist. m. Norma Ellis, 31 Mar 1957, 2 sons. Appointments: Copy Boy, Copy Taker, News Chronicle, Manchester, 1942-44, 1947; Reporter, St Helen's Reporter, 1947-49; Reporter, Feature Writer, Theatre Critic, London Editor, Nottingham Guardian, 1949-52; Daily Mail, 1952-54; Associated Press, 1954-55; Reporter, Feature Writer, Theatre Critic, Daily Herald/Sun, 1955-69; Theatre Critic, 1970-, Deputy Editor, 1978-91, Jewish Chronicle. Publications: Hancock (with Freddie Hancock), 1969; A Good Human Story (television play), 1978; The Freeloader (novel), 1970; The Laughtermakers, 1971; The Story So Far (novel), 1986. Radio Plays: The Belman of London, 1982; The Bohemians, 1983; Glenda Jackson, a critical profile, 1984; John Hurt, An Actor's Progress, 1986. Contributions to: Prospect Applause; Times Saturday Review; Daily Telegraph; Sunday Telegraph; Independent; Harper's and Queens; TV Times; Observer Colour Magazine. Honour: Highly Commended, Writer's Award, Royal Television Society, 1978. Membership: Critics Circle, president, 1986-88. Literary Agent: Giles Gordon, Curtis Brown Ltd. Address: 16 Augustus Close, Brentford Dock, Brentford, Middlesex, England.

NATHAN Edward Leonard, b. 8 Nov 1924, Los Angeles, California, USA. Teacher; Poet. m. Carol G Nash, 27 June 1949, 1 son, 2 daughters. Publications: Western Reaches, 1958; Glad and Sorry Seasons, 1963; The Day the Perfect Speakers Left, 1969; Returning Your Call, 1975; Dear Blood, 1980; Holding Patterns, 1982; Carrying On: New & Selected Poems, 1985; Diary of a Left-Handed Bird Watcher, 1996. Translations: First Person, Second Person by Agyeya, 1971; The Transport of Love, 1976; Grace and Mercy in Her Wild Hair, 1982; Songs of Something Else, 1982; Happy as a Dog's Tail, 1986; With the Skin (translation with C Milosz of poetry of Aleksander Wat), 1989; Talking to My Body (translation with C Milosz of Anna Swir), 1996. Contributions to: Salmagundi; New Yorker; New Republic; Kenyon Review. Honours: National Institute of Arts and Letters Award, 1971; Guggenheim Fellowship, 1976-77. Address: 40 Beverly Road, Kensington, CA 94707, USA.

NATHAN Robert S(tuart), b. 13 Aug 1948, Johnstown, Pennsylvania, USA. Writer. Education: BA, Amherst College, 1970. Appointment: Producer, Law and Order series, NBC-TV. Publications: Amusement Park, 1977; Rising Higher, 1981; The Religion, 1982; The Legend, 1986; The White Tiger, 1988; In the Deep Woods, 1989; Other: In the Deep Woods (television film), 1992. Contributions to: Periodicals and National Public Radio. Address: c/o William Morris Agency, 1350 Avenue of the Americas, New York, NY 10019, USA.

NATUSCH Sheila Ellen, b. 14 Feb 1926, Invercargill, New Zealand. Writer; Illustrator. m. Gilbert G Natusch, 28 Nov 1950. Education: MA, Otago University, 1948. Publications: Animals of New Zealand, 1967; Brother Wohlers, 1969, 2nd edition, 1992; New Zealand Mosses, 1970; Wild Fare for Wilderness Foragers, 1970; Native Plants, revised edition, 1976; Hell and High Water, 2nd edition, 1992; The Cruise of the Acheron, 1978; On the Edge of the Bush, 1978; Wellington, 1981; A Bunch of Wild Orchids, 3rd edition, 1983; A Pocketful of Pebbles, 1983; Southward Ho, 1985; William Swainson of

Fern Grove, 1987; Roy Traill of Stewart Island, 1991; An Island Called Home, 1992; The Natural World of the Traills, 1995. Contributions to: New Zealand Dictionary of Biography; The Past Today; The German Connection. Honours: Hubert Church Award for Brother Wohlers, PEN New Zealand, 1969. Address: 46 Owhiro Bay Parade, Wellington 6002, New Zealand.

NAUMOFF Lawrence Jay, b. 23 Jul 1946, Charlotte, North Carolina, USA. Author. Div, 1 son. Education: BA, University of North Carolina, Chapel Hill, 1969. Publications: The Night of the Weeping Women, 1988; Rootie Kazootie, 1990; Taller Women, 1992; Silk Hope, NC, 1994. Contributions to: Various literary magazines, short stories. Honours: Thomas Wolfe Memorial Award, 1969; National Endowment for the Arts Grant, 1970; Whiting Foundation Writers Award, 1990. Membership: PEN. Literary Agents: Barbara Lowenstein (USA); Adam Stein (UK). Address: PO Box 901, Carrboro, NC 27510, USA.

NAVASKY Victor S, b. 5 July 1932, New York, New York, USA. Editor; Writer. m. Anne Dandy Strongin, 27 Mar 1966, 1 son, 2 daughters. Education: AB, Swarthmore College, 1954; JD, Yale Law School, 1959. Publications: Kennedy Justice, 1971; Naming Names, 1980. Contributions to: Many magazines and journals. Honour: American Book Award, 1981. Memberships: American PEN; Authors Guild; Committee to Protect Journalists. Address: 33 West 67th Street, New York, NY 10023, USA.

NAVON Robert, b. 18 May 1954, New York, New York, USA. Editor; Philosopher. Education: BA, Lehman College, City University of New York, 1975; MS, State University of New York, Geneseo, 1978; MA studies, New School for Social Research, New York City, 1982-86; PhD candidate, University of New Mexico, 1991-. Publications: Patterns of the Universe, 1977; Autumn Songs: Poems, 1983; The Pythagorean Writings, 1986; Healing of Man and Woman, 1989; Harmony of the Spheres, 1991; Cosmic Patterns, Vol I, 1993; Great Works of Philosophy, 7 volumes (editor). Honours: New York State Regents Scholar, 1971; Phi Beta Kappa, 1975; Intern, Platform Association, 1980. Memberships: Society of Ancient Greek Philosophy; American Philosophical Association. Address: PO Box 81702, Albuquerque, NM 87198, USA.

NAYAK Harogadde Manappa, b. 5 Feb 1931, Hosamane, India. Teacher. m. Yashodharamma, 11 May 1955, 1 son, 1 daughter. Education: BA, Honours, University of Mysore, 1955; MA, Calcutta University, 1959; PhD, Indiana University, Indiana, USA, 1964. Appointments: Editor, Prabuddha Karnataka, 1967-84; Adviser, Grantha Loka, 1976-. Publications: Over 60 books. Contributions to: Various publications. Honours: Calcutta University Gold Medal, 1959; Mysore University Jubilee Award, 1978; Karnataka State Award, 1982; Karnataka Sahitya Akademy Award, 1985. Memberships: Indian National Academy of Letters; National Book Trust, India; Indian PEN; Kannada Sahitya Parisht; Karnataka Janapada Parisht. Address: Godhuli, Jayalakshmi Puram, Mysore 570-021, Karnataka, India.

NAYLOR Gloria, b. 25 Jan 1950, New York, New York, USA. Author; President of Film Production Company. Education: BA, Brooklyn College of the City University of New York, 1981; MA, Yale University, 1983. Appointments: Writer-in-Residence, Cummington Community of the Arts, 1983; Visiting Professor, George Washington University, 1983-84, Princeton University, 1986-87, Boston University, 1987; United States Information Agency Cultural Exchange Lecturer, India, 1985; Visiting Writer, New York University, 1986; Fannie Hurst Visiting Professor, Brandeis University, 1988; Senior Fellow, Society for the Humanities, Cornell University, 1988; President, One Way Productions films, New York City, 1990-. Publications: The Women of Brewster Place: A Novel in Seven Stories, 1982; Lindin Hills, 1985; Mama Day, 1988; Bailey's Cafe, 1992; Children of the Night: The Best Short Stories by Black Writers, 1967 to the Present (editor), 1995. Contributions to: Magazines. Honours: National Book Award for Best First Novel, 1983; Distinguished Writer Award, Mid-Atlantic Writers Association, 1983; National Endowment for the Arts Fellowship, 1985; Candace Award, National Coalition of 100 Black Women, 1986; Guggenheiim Fellowship, 1988; Lillian Smith Award, 1989. Address: c/o One Way Productions, 638 2nd Street, Brooklyn, NY 11215, USA.

NAYLOR Phyllis, b. 4 Jan 1933, Anderson, Indiana, USA. Writer. Education: Diploma, Joliet Junior College, 1953; BA, American University, 1963. Publications: Over 90 books for adults or children, 1965-96. Honour: Newbery Medal, American Library Association, 1992. Address: 9910 Holmhurst Road, Bethesda, MD 20817, USA.

NEAL Ernest Gordon, b. 20 May 1911, Boxmoor, Hertfordshire, England. Retired School Teacher; Biologist. m. Helen Elizabeth Thomson, 30 Apr 1937, 3 sons. Education: BSc, MSc, PhD, London University and Extension, 1931-35. Publications: Exploring Nature with a Camera, 1946; The Badger, 1948; Woodland Ecology, 1953; Topsy and Turvy: My Two Otters, 1961; Uganda Quest, 1971; Biology for Today (with K R C Neal), 1974; Badgers, 1977; Badgers in Closeup, 1984; Natural History of Badgers, 1986; On Safari in East Africa: A Background Guise, 1991; The Badger Man: Memoirs of a Biologist, 1994; Badgers, co-author Chris Cheesman, 1996. Contributions to: Country Life; The Field; Illustrated London News; Times; Wildlife Magazine; Sunday Times; Countryman; Countryside Magazine; Mammal Review. Honours: Fellow, Institute of Biology, 1965; Stamford Raffles Award, Zoological Society of London, 1965; Member of the Order of the British Empire, 1976. Memberships: Society of Authors; Mammal Society; British Ecological Society; Somerset Wildlife Trust. Address: 42 Park Avenue, Bedford MK40 2NF, England.

NEEDLE Jan, b. 8 Feb 1943, Holybourne, England. Writer. Education: Drama Degree, Victoria University of Manchester, 1971. Publications: Albeson and the Germans, 1977; My Mate Shofiq, 1978; A Fine Boy for Killing, 1979; The Size Spies, 1979; Rottenteeth, 1980; The Bee Rustlers, 1980; A Sense of Shame, 1980; Wild Wood, 1981; Losers Weepers, 1981; Another Fine Mess, 1981; Brecht (with Peter Thomson), 1981; Piggy in the Middle, 1982; Going Out, 1983; A Game of Soldiers, TV serial, 1983, book, 1985; A Pitiful Place, 1984; Great Days at Grange Hill, 1984; Tucker's Luck, 1984; Behind the Bike Sheds, 1985; Tucker in Control, 1985, TV Series, 1985; Wagstaffe, The Wind-Up Boy, 1987; Soft Soap, TV play, 1987, TV series, 1988; Truckers, TV series, 1987; Uncle in the Attic, 1987; Skeleton at School, 1987; In the Doghouse, 1988; The Sleeping Party, 1988; Mad Scramble, 1989; As Seen on TV, 1989; The Thief, TV series, 1989; The Thief, novel, 1990; The bully, novel, 1992; The Bill, TV series, 1992. Literary Agents: Rochelle Stevens and Co, London, England; David Higham Associates, 5-8 Lower John Street, London W1R 4HA, England. Address: c/o Rochell Stevens and Co, 2 Terretts Place, Upper Street, London N1 1QZ, England.

NEELY Mark Edward Jr, b. 10 Nov 1944, Amarillo, Texas, USA. Writer; Editor; Professor. m. Sylvia Eakes, 15 June 1966. Education: BA, 1966, PhD, 1973, Yale University. Appointments: Director, Louis A Warren Lincoln Library and Museum, Fort Wayne, Indiana; Visiting Instructor, Iowa State University, 1971-72; Editor, Lincoln Lore, 1973-; Professor, St Louis University. Publications: The Abraham Lincoln Encyclopedia, 1981; The Lincoln Image: Abraham Lincoln and the Popular Print (with Harold Holzer and Gabor S Boritt), 1984; The Insanity File: The Case of Mary Todd Lincoln (with R Gerald McMurty), 1986; The Confederate Image: Prints of the Large Cause, 1987; The Lincoln Family Album: Photographs from the Personal Collection of a Historic American Family, 1990; The Fate of Liberty: Abraham Lincoln and Civil Libertires, 1991; The Last Best Hope on Earth: Abraham Lincoln and the Promise of America, 1993; Mine Eyes Have Seen the Glory: The Civil War in American Art (with Harold Holzer), 1993. Honour: Pulitzer Prize for History, 1992. Memberships: Abraham Lincoln Association; Indiana Association of Historians, president, 1987-88; Society of Indiana Archivists, president, 1980-81. Address: c/o Department of History, St Louis University, 221 North Grand Avenue, St Louis, MO 63103, USA.

NEESER Andreas, b. 25 Jan 1964, Schlossrued, Switzerland. Teacher. Education: Studies in German Language and Literature, English Literature, Literary Criticism, University of Zürich; Degree, 1990; Teacher's Diploma, 1994. Publications: Schattensprünge (novel), 1995; Treibholz (poems), 1997. Honours: Grants, Cantons of Aargau, 1991, 1992. Memberships: Swiss Writers' Union, Zurich; PEN Switzerland. Literary Agent: Pendo-Verlag, Wolfbachstr 9, CH-8032 Zürich, Switzerland. Address: Neugutstrasse 4, CH-5000 Aarau, Switzerland.

NEHAMAS Alexander, b. 22 Mar 1946, Athens, Greece (Spanish citizen). Professor in the Humanities, Philosophy, and Compartive Literature; Author. m. Susan Glimcher, 22 June 1983, 1 son. Education: BA, Swarthmore College, 1967; PhD, Princeton University, 1971. Appointments: Assistant Professor, 1971-76, Associate Professor, 1976-81, Professor of Philosophy, 1981-86, University of Pittsburgh; Visiting Fellow, 1978-79, Professor of Philosophy, 1988, 1990-, Edmund N Carpenter II Class of 1943 Professor in the Humanities, 1989-, Professor of Comparative Literature, 1990-, Princeton University; Mills Professor of Philosophy,

University of California, Berkeley, 1983; Visiting Scholar, 1983-84, Professor of Philosophy, 1986-90, University of Pennsylvania; Sather Professor of Classical Literature, University of California, Berkeley, 1993. Publications: Nietzsche: Life as Literature, 1985; Plato's "Symposium" (translator and editor with Paul Woodruff), 1989; Gregory Vlastos: Socrates: Ironist and Moral Philosopher (translator and editor with Paul Kalligas), 1993; Aristotle's "Rhetoric": Philosophical Essays (co-editor with D J Furley), 1994; Plato's "Phaedrus" (translator and editor with Paul Woodruff), 1995; Virtues of Authenticity: Essays on Plato and Socrates, 1997. Contributions to: Books and professional journals. Honours: National Endowment for the Humanities Fellowship, 1978-79; Guggenheim Fellowship, 1983-84; Romanell-Phi Beta Kappa Professor in Philosophy, 1990-91; Phi Beta Kappa Visiting Scholar, 1995. Memberships: American Academy of Arts and Sciences; American Society for Aesthetics; Modern Greek Studies Association; North American Nietzsche Society. Address: 692 Pretty Brook Road, Princeton, NJ 08540, USA.

NEIL Andrew, b. 21 May 1949, Paisley, Scotland. Newspaper Editor; Broadcaster. Education: MA, University of Glasgow. Appointments: Reporter and Correspondent, Economist, 1973-82; London Editor, 1982-83, Editor, 1983-94, Sunday Times; Executive Editor and Chief Correspondent, Fox News Network, 1994; Contributing Editor, Vanity Fair, New York, 1995; Regular appearances on current affairs programmes in London and New York; Editor-in-Chief, Scotsman, Edinburgh, The European, London, 1997. Publications: The Cable Revolution, 1982; Britain's Free Press: Does It Have One?, 1988; Full Disclosure (autobiography), 1996. Address: Glenburn Enterprises Ltd, PO Box 584, London SW7 3QY, England.

NELSON Marguerite. See: FLOREN Lee.

NELSON Richard, b. 17 Oct 1950, Chicago, Illinois, USA. Dramatist; Screenwriter. Education: BA, Hamilton College, 1972. Appointments: Literary Manager, BAM Theatre Co, Brooklyn, 1979-81; Associate Director, Goodman Theatre, Chicago, 1980-83; Dramaturg, Guthrie Theatre, Minneapolis, 1981-82. Publications: The Vienna Notes (in Word Plays I), 1980; Il Campiello (adaptation), 1981; An American Comedy and Other Plays, 1984; Between East and West (in New Plays USA 3), 1986; Principia Scriptoriae, 1986; Strictly Dishonorable and Other Lost American Plays (editor), 1986; Rip Van Winkle, 1986; Jungle Coup (in Plays from Playwrights Horizons), 1987; Accidental Death of an Anarchist (adaptation), 1987. Address: 32 South Street, Rhinebeck, NY 12572, USA.

NELSON-HUMPHRIES Tessa, (Luisa-Teresa Nelson-Humphries), b.Yorkshire, England. Professor; Writer; Poet. m. (1) Kenneth Nelson Brown, 1 June 1957, dec 1962, (2) Cecil H Unthank, 26 Sept 1963, dec 1979. Education: BA, MA, University of North Carolina, 1965; PhD, University of Liverpool, 1974. Appointments: Director of English, Windsor College, Buenos Aires; Professor of English, Cumberland College, Williamsburg, Kentucky, 1964-90; Part-Time Faculty, New Mexico State University, Las Cruces, 1990-92. Contributions to: Various publications. Honours: Several prizes and honorable mentions. Memberships: American Association of University Women; Society of Children's Book Writers, USA; Society of Women Writers and Journalists, England. Address: 3228 Jupiter Road, 4 Hills, Las Cruces, NM 88012-7742, USA.

NEUBERGER Julia Babette Sarah, b. 27 Feb 1950, London, England. Rabbi; Author; Broadcaster. m. Anthony John Neuberger, 17 Sept 1973, 1 son, 1 daughter. Education: Newnham College, Cambridge, 1969-73; BA, Assyriology, Hebrew, Cambridge, MA, 1975; Rabbinic Ordination, Leo Baeck College, 1977. Publications: Judaism, for children, 1986; Caring for Dying People of Different Faiths, 1987; Days of Decision, 4 vols (editor), 1987; Whatever's Happening to Women? 1991; A Necessary End (editor with John White), 1991; Ethics and Healthcare: Research Ethics Committees in the UK, 1992; The Things that Matter, an anthology of Women's Spiritual Poetry (editor), 1993; On Being Jewish, 1995. Contributions to: Jewish Chronicle; Times; Irish Times; Irish Sunday Tribune; Vogue; Cosmopolitan; Sunday Times; Telegraph; Sunday Express; Mail on Sunday; Evening Standard. Membership: Royal Society of Arts, fellow. Literary Agent: Carol Smith. Address: 28 Regent's Park Road, London NW1 7TR, England.

NEUGEBOREN Jay (Michael), b. 30 May 1938, New York, New York, USA. Writer. Education: BA, Columbia University, 1959; MA, Indiana University, 1963. Appointments: Visiting Writer, Stanford

University, 1966-67; Writer-in-Residence, University of Massachusetts, 1971-. Publications: Big Man, 1966; Corky's Brother, 1969; Sam's Legacy, 1974; The Stolen Jew, 1981; Before My Life Began, 1985. Contributions to: Magazines. Honours: Transatlantic Review Novella Award, 1967; National Endowment for the Arts Fellowships, 1967; Guggenheim Fellowship, 1978; Present Tense Award for Best Novel, 1981; PEN Syndicated Fiction Prizes, 1982-88; Wallant Memorial Prize for Best Novel, 1985. Memberships: Authors Guild; PEN. Address: 35 Harrison Avenue, Northampton, MA 01060, USA.

NEUMEYER Peter F(lorian), b. 4 Aug 1929, Munich, Germany. Professor; Writer. m. Helen Wight Snell, 28 Dec 1952, 3 sons. Education: BA, 1951, MA, 1955, PhD, 1963, University of California at Berkeley. Appointments: Assistant Professor, Harvard University, 1963-69; Associate Professor, State University of New York at Stony Brook, 1969-75; Professor and Chairman, Department of English, West Virginia University, 1975-78; Professor, San Diego State University, 1978-. Publications: Kafka's The Castle, 1969; Donald and the ..., 1969; Donald Has a Difficulty, 1970; The Faithful Fish, 1971; Elements of Fiction (co-editor), 1974; Homage to John Clare, 1980; Image and Makers (co-editor), 1984; The Phantom of the Opera (adaptation), 1988; The Annotated Charlotte's Web, 1994. Contributions to: Journals. Address: 45 Marguerita Road, Kensington, CA 94707, USA.

NEUSTADT Richard E(lliott), b. 26 June 1919, Philadelphia, Pennsylvania, USA. Professor Emeritus; Writer. m. (1) Bertha Frances Cummings, 21 Dec 1945, dec 1984, 1 son, 1 daughter, (2) Shirley Williams, 19 Dec 1987. Education: AB, University of California at Berkeley, 1939; MA, 1941, PhD, 1951, Harvard University. Appointments: Economist, US Office of Price Administration, 1942, US Bureau of the Budget,1946-50, White House, Washington, DC, 1950-54; Professor of Public Administration, Cornell University, 1953-54; Professor of Government, Columbia University, 1954-64; Visiting Professor, Princeton University, 1957, University of California at Berkeley, 1986, Cornell University, 1992, University of Essex, 1994-95; Visiting Lecturer, 1961-62, Associate Member, 1965-67, 1990-92, Nuffield College, Oxford; Consultant to President John F Kennedy, 1961-63, President Lyndon B Johnson, 1964-66; Professor of Government, 1965-78, Lucius N Littauer Professor of Public Administration, 1978-87, Douglas Dillon Professor, 1987-89, Professor Emeritus, 1989-, Harvard University; Fellow, Center for Advanced Study in the Behavioral Sciences, 1978-79. Publications: Presidential Power, 1960, revised edition, 1990; Allied Politics, 1970; The Swine Flu Affair (with Harvey V Fineberg), 1978, republished as the Epidemic That Never Was, 1982; Thinking in Time (with Ernest R May), 1986. Contributions to: Professional journals. Memberships: American Academy of Arts and Sciences, fellow; American Philosophical Society; American Political Science Association; Council on Foreign Relations; Institute for Strategic Studies; National Academy of Public Administration. Address: 79 JFK Street, Cambridge, MA 02138, USA.

NEUSTATTER Angela Lindsay, b. 24 Sept 1943, Buckinghamshire, England. Journalist. Author. 2 sons. Education: Regent Street Polytechnic, London; Diploma in Journalism. Publications: Twiggy - Health and Beauty, 1985; Mixed Feelings, 1986; Hyenas in Petticoats: A Look at 20 Years of Feminism, 1989. Contributions to: Guardian; Times; Observer; Sunday Telegraph; Daily Telegraph. Honours: Feminist Top Twenty List, 1986; Institute for the Study of Drug Dependency Award, 1994. Literary Agent: Jane Bradish-Ellames, Curtis Brown. Address: 32 Highbury Place, London N5, England.

NEVES Augusto. See: **CARDOSO PIRES Joao.**

NEVEU Angéline, b. 2 Sept 1946, France. Writer; Poet. Publications: Synthese, 1976; Lyrisme Télévisé, 1982; Rêve, 1982; Désir, 1985; Le Vent Se Fieau Vent, 1994. Contributions to: International and national journals. Honour: Bourse du Centre National des Lettres, Paris, 1986. Membership: Union Nationale des Ecrivains du Québec. Address: 809 Bloomfield, Apt 701, Outremont, Québec H2V 3S5, Canada.

NEVILLE Robert Cummings, b. 1 May 1939, St Louis, Missouri, USA. Professor of Philosophy and Religion; Author. m. Elizabeth E Neville, 1963, 3 daughters. Education: BA, 1960, MA, 1962, PhD, 1963, Yale University. Appointments: Instructor, 1963-65, Yale University; Assistant Professor, 1965-68, Associate professor, 1968-71, Fordham University; Associate Professor, 1971-74, Professor

of Philosophy, 1974-77, State University of New York College at Purchase; Adjunct Professor of Religious Studies and Research Professor, 1977-78, Professor of Philosophy and Professor of Religious Studies, 1978-87, State University of New York at Stony Brook; Professor, Departments of Religion and Philosophy, and School of Theology, 1987-, Dean, School of Theology, 1988-, Boston University. Publications: God the Creator: On the Transendence and Prescence of God, 1968, new edition, 1992; The Cosmology of Freedom, 1974, new edition, 1995; Soldier, Sage, Saint, 1978; Creativity and God: A Challenge to Process Theology, 1980, new edition, 1995; Reconstruction of Thinking, 1981; The Tao and the Daimon: Segments of a Religious Enquiry, 1982; The Puritan Smile, 1987; Recovery of the Measure, 1989; Behind the Masks of God, 1991; A Theology Primer, 1991; The Highroad Around Modernism, 1992; Eternity's and Time's Flow, 1993; Normative Cultures, 1995; The Truth of Broken Symbols, 1996. Editor: Operating on the Mind: The Psychosurgery Conflict (with Willard Gaylin and Joel Meister), 1975. Associate Editor, Encyclopedia of Bioethics, 1978; New Essays in Metaphysics, 1987; The Recovery of Philosophy in America, (with Thomas Rasulis), 1997. Contributions to: Books, professional journals, and periodicals. Memberships: American Academy of Religion, President, 1992; American Philosophical Association; American Theological Society; Boston Theological Society; Institute of Society, Ethics, and the Life Sciences; Society for Studies of Process Philosophies; Society of Philosophers in America; International Society for Chinese Philosophy, President, 1993; Metaphysical Society of America, President, 1989. Address: 5 Cliff Road, Milton, MA 02186, USA.

NEVINS Francis M(ichael) (Jr), b. 6 Jan 1943, Bayonne, New Jersey, USA. Professor of Law; Writer. m. (1) Muriel Walter, 6 June 1966, div 1978, (2) Patricia Brooks, 24 Feb 1982. Education: AB, St Peter's College, 1964; JD, New York University, 1967. Appointments: Admitted to the New Jersey Bar, 1967; Assistant Professor, 1971-75, Associate Professor, 1975-78, Professor, 1978-, St Louis University School of Law. Publications: Novels: Publish and Perish, 1975; Corrupt and Ensnare, 1978; The 120 - Hour Clock, 1986; The Ninety Million Dollar Mouse, 1987; Into the Same River Twice, 1996. Non-fiction: Detectionary (with 4 co-authors), 1971; Royal Bloodline: Elley Queen, Author and Detective, 1974; Missouri Probate: Intestacy, Wills and Basic Administration, 1983; The Films of Hopalong Cassidy, 1988; Cornell Woolrich: First You Dream , Then You Die, 1988; Bar-20: The Life of Clarence E Mulford, Creator of Hopalong Cassidy, 1993; The Films of the Cisco Kid, 1997. Fiction edited or co-edited: Nightwebs, 1971; The Good Old Stuff, 1983; Exeunt Murderers, 1983; Buffet for Unwelcome Guests, 1983; More Good Old Stuff, 1985; Carnival of Crime, 1985; Hitchcock in Prime Time, 1985; The Best of Ellery Queen, 1985; Leopold's Way, 1985; The Adventures of Henry Turnbuckle, 1987; Better Mousetraps, 1988; Mr President- Private Eye, 1988; Death on Television, 1989; Little Boxes of Bewilderment, 1989; The Night My Friend, 1991. Non-fiction edited or co-edited: The Mystery Writer's Art, 1970; Mutiplying Villainies, 1973. Honours: Edgar Awards, Mystery Writers of America, 1975, 1988. Address: 7045 Cornell, University City, MO 63130, USA.

NEVZGLIADOVA Elena Vsevolodovna, (Elena Ushakova), b. 2 June 1939, Leningrad, Russia; Poet; Literary Critic. m. Aleksandr Semyonovich Kushner, 1 son. Education: Graduate, 1962, PhD, 1974, Philological Faculty, Leningrad University. Publication: Nochnoe Solntse (A Night Sun), 1991. Contributions to: Neva; Znamya; Syntaxis; Raduga; Zvezda; Novii Mir; Almanakh Petropol. Membership: Writers' Union. Address: Kaluzhskii per 9 apt 48, St Petersburg 193015, Russia.

NEW Anthony Sherwood Brooks, b. 14 Aug 1924, London, England. Architect. m. Elizabeth Pegge, 11 Apr 1970, 1 son, 1 daughter. Education: Northern Polytechnic School of Architecture, 1941-43, 1947-51. Publications: Observer's Book of Postage Stamps, 1967; Observer's Book of Cathedrals, 1972; A Guide to the Cathedrals of Britain, 1980; Property Service Agency Historic Buildings Register, Volume II (London), 1983; A Guide to the Abbeys of England and Wales, 1985; New Observer's Book of Stamp Collecting, 1986; A Guide to the Abbeys of Scotland, 1988. Memberships: Society of Antiquaries, fellow; Royal Institute of British Architects, fellow; Institution of Structural Engineers. Address: 26 Somerset Road, New Barnet, Herts EN5 1RN, England.

NEWBY Eric, b. 6 Dec 1919, England. m. Wanda Skof, 1946, 1 son, 1 daughter. Education: St Paul's School. Appointments: Travel

Editor, The Observer, London; General Editor, Time Off Books, 1963-73; Traveller and freelance writer. Publications: The Last Grain Race, 1956; A Short Walk in the Hindu Kush, 1958; Something Wholesale, 1962; Time Off Guide to Southern Italy, 1966; Slowly Down the Ganges, 1966; My Favourite Stories of Travel, 1967; Grain Race, 1968; Wonders of Britain, 1968; Wonders of Ireland, 1969; Love and War in the Apennines, 1971; Ganga, 1973; World Atlas of Exploration, 1975; Great Ascents, 1977; The Big Red Train Ride, 1978; A Traveller's Life, 1982; On the Shores of the Mediterranean, 1984; A Book of Travellers' Tales, 1986; Round Ireland in Low Gear, 1987; What the Traveller Saw, 1989; A Small Place in Italy, 1994; A Merry Dance Around the World, 1995. Honours: MC, 1945; Commander of the Order of the British Empire, 1994. Address: Pine View House, 4 Pine View Close, Chilworth, Surrey GU4 8RS, England.

NEWBY (Percy) Howard, b. 25 June 1918, Crowborough, Sussex, England. Author. m. 12 July 1945, 2 daughters. Education: St Paul's College, Cheltenham. Publications: A Journey to the Interior, 1945; The Picnic at Sakkara, 1955; Something to Answer For, 1968; Kith, 1977; Feelings Have Changed, 1981; Leaning in the Wind, 1986; Coming in with the Tide, 1991; Something About Women, 1995; 12 other novels; 3 historical studies; 2 works of literary criticism; 2 children's books. Honours: Atlantic Award, 1946; Somerset Maugham Prize, 1948; Yorkshire Post Fiction Award, 1968; Booker Prize, 1969; Commander of the Order of the British Empire, 1972. Membership: Society of Authors. Literary Agent: David Higham Associates. Address: Garsington House, Garsington, Oxford OX44 9AB, England.

NEWCOMER James William, b. 14 Mar 1912, Gibsonburg, Ohio, USA. College Professor; Vice Chancellor Emeritus. m. 17 Aug 1946, 1 son, 2 daughters. Education: PhB, Kenyon College; MA, University of Michigan; PhD, University of Iowa. Publications: Criticism: Maria Edgeworth the Novelist, 1967; Maria Edgeworth, 1973; Lady Morgan the Novelist, 1990. Poetry: The Merton Barn Poems, 1979; The Resonance of Grace, 1984. Other: The Grand Duchy of Luxembourg (history), 1984; The Nationhood of Luxembourg (essays), 1996; Luxembourg (essays), 1995. Contributions to: College English; Nineteenth Century Fiction; Criticism; Books at Iowa; Arlington Quarterly; Descant; Sands. Honours: Phi Beta Kappa; Commander in Order of Merit and Honorary Member, L'Institut Grand-Ducal, Duchy of Luxembourg. Address: 1100 Elizabeth Boulevard, Fort Worth, TX 76110, USA.

NEWLANDS Willy, (William Newlands of Lauriston), b. 5 Nov 1934, Perth, Scotland. Travel Writer. m. (1) 1 son, 2 daughters, (2) Dorothy Straton Walker, 1985. Appointments: Scripwriter, Presenter, TV travel series, Grampian/STV, 1993-94. Contributions to: Daily Telegraph; Observer; Mail on Sunday; Guardian; Times; Daily Express; Field. Honours: Churchill Fellow, 1968; Travel Writer of the Year, 1983-84, 1987-88. Address: Lauriston Castle, by Montrose, Angus DD10 0DJ, Scotland.

NEWMAN Andrea, b. 7 Feb 1938, Dover, England. Writer. Div. Education: BA, Honours, English, 1960, MA, 1972, London University. Publications: A Share of the World, 1964; Mirage, 1965; The Cage, 1966; Three Into Two Won't Go, 1967; Alexa, 1968; A Bouquet of Barbed Wire, 1969; Another Bouquet, 1977; An Evil Streak, 1977; Mackenzie, 1980; A Sense of Guilt, 1988; Triangles, 1990; A Gift of Poison, 1991. Contributions to: Woman; Woman's Own; Woman's Realm; Marie-Claire; GQ; Living; TV Scripts for Bouquet of Barbed Wire; Another Bouquet; Mackenzie; A Sense of Guilt. Memberships: PEN; Writers' Guild. Address: c/o A P Watt, 20 John Street, London WC1N 2DR, England.

NEWMAN Arnold Clifford, b. 10 Apr 1941, New York, New York, USA. Naturalist; Author. m. Arlene Ruth Newman (Ash), 7 Dec 1963, 1 son, 1 daughter. Education: BBA, 1962; PhD, 1996. Publications: The Tropical Rainforest: The Lungs of the Planet, 1987; Tropical Deforestation: Global Consequences and Alternatives, (co-author with Dr Brent Blackwelder) 1989; Tropical Rainforest - A World Survey of Our Most Valuable and Endangered Habitat with a Blueprint for it's Survival, 1990. Honours: Decorated by USSR Academy of Sciences for Service to Earth's Species, Congressional Acclimation for Conservation, 1987; Humanitarian Award from Southern California Motion Picture Council, 1994; National Humanity Award, Honoring America's Best Role Models, 1995. Address: 3931 Camino de la Cumbre, Sherman Oaks, CA 91423, USA.

NEWMAN Aubrey N(orris), b. 14 Dec 1927, London, England. Professor of History; Writer. Education: MA, University of Glasgow, 1949; BA, 1953, MA, DPhil, 1957, Wadham College, Oxford. Appointments: Research Fellow, Bedford College, University of London, 1954-55; Professor of History, University of Leicester. Publications: The Parliamentary Diary of Sir Edward Knatchbull, 1722-1730, 1963; The Stanhopes of Chevening: A Family Biography, 1969; A Bibliography of English History, 1485-1760; The United Synagogue, 1870-1970, 1977; The Jewish East End, 1840-1939, 1981; The Board of Deputin, 1760-1985: A Brief Survey, 1987; The World Turned Insde Out: New Views on George II, 1988. Memberships: Jewish Historical Society of England, president, 1977-79. Address: c/o Department of History, University of Leicester, Leicester LE1 7RH, England.

NEWMAN G F, b. 22 May 1945, England. Writer. Publications: Sir, You Bastard, 1970; You Nice Bastard, 1972; You Flash Bastard, 1974; The Govnor, 1977; The Nation's Health, 1982; Law and Order, 1977, 1983; The List, 1984; The Men with Guns, 1985; Set a Thief, 1986; The Testing Ground, 1987; Operation Bad Apple (play); An Honourable Trade (play). Address: Wessington Court, Woolhope, Hereford HR1 4QN, England.

NEWMAN John Kevin, b. 17 Aug 1928, Bradford, Yorkshire, England. Classics Educator. m. Frances M Stickney, 8 Sept 1970, 1 son, 2 daughters. Education: BA, Lit Humaniores, 1950, BA, Russian, 1952, MA, 1953, Oxford University; PhD, Bristol University, 1967. Appointments: Classics Master, St Francis Xavier College, Liverpool, 1952-54; Downside School, Somerset, 1955-69; Faculty, 1969-, Professor of Classics, 1980-, University of Illinois, Urbana, USA; Editor, Illinois Classical Studies, 1982-87. Publications: Augustus and the New Poetry, 1967; The Concept of Vates in Augustan Poetry, 1967; Latin Compositions, 1976; Golden Violence, 1976; Dislocated: An American Carnival, 1977; Pindar's Art, 1984; The Classical Epic Tradition, 1986; Roman Catullus, 1990; Lelio Guidiccioni, Latin Poems, 1992; Augustan Propertius, 1997. Honours: Silver Medals, Vatican, Rome, 1960, 1962, 1965. Membership: Senior Common Room, Corpus Christi College Oxford, 1985-86. Address: 703 West Delaware Avenue, Urbana, IL 61801, USA.

NEWMAN Leslea, b. 5 Nov 1955, Brooklyn, New York, USA. Writer; Teacher of Women's Writing Workshops. Education: BS, Education, University of Vermont, USA, 1977; Certificate in Poetics, Naropa Institute, 1980. Appointment: Massachusetts Artists Fellowship in Poetry, 1989. Publications: Good Enough to Eat, 1986; Love Me Like You Mean It, 1987; A Letter to Harvey Milk, 1988; Heather Has Two Mommies, 1989; Bubbe Meisehs by Shayneh Maidelehs, 1989; Secrets, 1990; In Every Laugh a Tear, 1992; Writing from the Heart, 1992; Every Woman's Dream, 1994; Fat Chance, 1994; Too Far Away to Touch, 1995; A Loving Testimony: Remembering Loved Ones Lost to AIDS, 1995; The Feminine Mystique, 1995; Remember That, 1996; My Lover is a Woman: Contemporary Lesbian Love Poems, 1996; Out of the Closet and Nothing to Wear, 1997. Contributions to: Magazines. Honour: 2nd Place Finalist, Raymond Carver Short Story Competition, 1987; National Endowment for the Arts, poetry fellowship, 1997. Memberships: Authors Guild; Authors League of America; Poets and Writers. Address: PO Box 815, Northampton, MA 01061, USA.

NEWMAN Margaret. See: **POTTER Margaret.**

NEWMAN Peter Charles, b. 19 May 1929, Vienna, Austria. Journalist; Writer. Education: MA, Economics, University of Toronto; McGill University. Appointments: Assistant Editor, The Financial Post, 1951-55; Ottawa Editor, 1955-64, Editor-in-Chief, 1971-82, Maclean's Magazine; Ottawa Editor, 1964-69, Editor-in-Chief, 1969-71, Toronto Daily Star; Director, Maclean Hunter Ltd, 1972-83; Host, weekly interview programme, Global TV Network, 1981-87. Publications: Flame of Power, 1959; The Distemper of Our Times, 1968; The Canadian Establishment, 1975; The Establishment Man, 1982; Company of Adventurers, 1985; Caesars of the Wilderness, 1987; Empire of the Bay, 1989. Honours: Quill Award, Journalist of the Year, 1977; Knight Commander, Order of St Lazarus, 1983; National Business Writing Achievement Award, 1986; Bob Edwards Award, 1989. Address: 2594 Panorama Drive, Deep Cove, North Vancouver, British Columbia, V7G 1V5, Canada.

NEWTON David Edward, b. 18 June 1933, Grand Rapids, Michigan, USA. University Educator; Science Writer. Education: AS, Grand Rapids Junior College, 1953; BS with high distinction,

Chemistry, 1955, MA, Education, 1961, University of Michigan; DEd, Science Education, Harvard University, 1971; Various short courses, Cornell University, Oregon State University, Atlanta University, Hampshire College. Publications: Chemistry Problems, 1962, 3rd edition, 1984; Understanding Venereal Disease, 1973, 2nd edition, 1978; Math in Everyday Life, 1975, 2nd edition, 1991; Scott Foresman Biology (with Irwin Slesnick, A LaVon Blazar, Alan McCormack and Fred Rasmussen), 1980, 2nd edition, 1985; Science and Social Issues, 1983, 3rd edition, 1992; Biology Updated, 1984, 2nd edition, 1987; Chemistry Updated, 1985, 2nd edition, 1989; An Introduction to Molecular Biology, 1986; Science Ethics, 1987; Particle Accelerators, 1989; Taking a Stand Against Environmental Pollution, 1990; Land Use, 1991; James Watson and Francis Crick: A Search for DNA and Beyond, 1992; Contributions to: Books and journals. Honours: Sloane Scholarship, University of Michigan, 1958; Star '60 Award, National Science Teachers Association; William Payne Scholar, Horace Rackham Graduate School, University of Michigan, 1961-62; Shell Merit Fellow, 1964; Outstanding Young Science Educator of the Year, AETS, 1968. Memberships: Phi Beta Kappa; Phi Kappa Phi; Phi Lambda Upsilon; Delta Pi Alpha; National Science Teachers Association; Association for the Education of Teachers in Science; American Association for the Advancement of Science; National Association of Science Writers; Children's Science Book Review Committee. Address: Instructional Horizons Inc, 297 Addison Street, San Francisco, CA 94131, USA.

NEWTON Suzanne, b. 8 Oct 1936, Bunnlevel, North Carolina, USA. Children's Writer. Education: AB, Duke Unversity, 1957. Appointments: Consultant in Creative Writing, North Carolina Public Schools, 1972; Writer-in-Residence, Meredith College, Raleigh, North Carolina. Publications: Some 10 books, 1971-95. Address: 841-A Barringer Drive, Raleigh, NC 27606, USA.

NEY James W(alter Edward Colby), b. 28 July 1932, Nakaru, Kenya. Professor of English; Writer. m. Joan Marie Allen, 12 June 1954, 2 sons, 1 daughter. Education: AB, 1955, AM, 1957, Wheaton College; EdD, University of Michigan, 1963. Appointments: Visiting Professor, University of Montreal, 1962, George Peabody College for Teachers, Nashville, Tennessee, 1965, University of Hawaii, 1967, Western New Mexico University, 1971; Faculty, University of Ryukyus, Okinawa, 1962-64; Assistant Professor, Michigan State University at Hunt Valley, 1964-69; Professor of English, Arizona State University, Tempe, 1969-. Publications: Readings on American Society, 1969; Exploring in English, 1972; Discovery in English, 1972; American English for Japanese Students, 1973; Linguistics, Language, Teaching and Composition in the Grades, 1975; Semantic Structures for the Syntax of the Modal Auxiliaries and Complements in English, 1982; Transformational Grammar: Essays for the Left Hand, 1988; American College Life in English Communication, 1991; American English in a Situational Context, 1991; GMAT Study Guide and Time Saver, 1993; English Proficiency through American Culture, 1994. Contributions to: Books and professional journals. Memberships: American Linguistic Association; Canadian Linguistic Association; National Council of Teachers of English. Address: 13375 North 96th Place, Scottsdale, AZ 85260, USA.

NEYREY Jerome H(enry), b. 5 Jan 1940, New Orleans, Louisiana, USA. Professor. Education: BA, 1963; MA, 1964; MDiv, 1970; MTh, 1972; PhD, 1977; STL, 1987. Appointments: Weston School of Theology, 1977-92; University of Notre Dame, Indiana, 1992-. Publications: The Passion According to Luke, 1983; Christ is Community, 1983; An Ideology of Revolt, 1988; Calling Jesus Names, 1988; The Resurrection Stories, 1988; Paul, In Other Words, 1990; The Social World of Luke - Acts, 1991. Contributions to: Catholic Biblical Quarterly; Journal of Biblical Literature; Biblica; Novum Testamentum; New Testament Studies. Honours: Bannan Fellowship, Santa Clara University, 1984-85; Young Scholars Grant, 1984; ATS Grant, 1989; Visiting Professor, Pontifical Biblical Institute, Rome, 1989; Lilly Foundation, 1989; Plowshares, 1990. Memberships: Catholic Biblical Association; Society of Biblical Literature, New England Region President 1990; Context Group, executive secretary. Address: Department of Theology, University of Notre Dame, Notre Dame, IN 46556, USA.

NEZZLE. See: SAUNDERS Nezzle Methelda.

NGUGI J(ames) T, (Ngugi wa Thiong'o), b. 5 Jan 1938, Kamiriithu, Kenya. Literary and Political Journalist; Author. Education: University College, Kampala; Leeds University, Yorkshire.

Appointment: Former Editor, Penpoint magazine, Kampala, Uganda. Publications: As J T Ngugi or Ngugi wa Thiong'o: The Black Hermit (play), 1962; This Time Tomorrow (play), 1964; Weep not, Child, 1964; The River Between, 1965; A Grain of Wheat, 1967; Homecoming: Essays on African and Caribbean Literature, Culture and Politics, 1972; Secret Lives, 1974; Petals of Blood, 1977; The Trial of Dedan Kimathi (with M G Mugo), 1977; Writers in Politics, 1980; Devil on the Cross, 1981; Detained: A Writer's Prison Diary, 1981; Education for a National Culture, 1981; I Will Marry When I Want (play), 1982; Barrel of a Pen: Resistance to Repression in Neo-Colonial Kenya, 1983. Contributions to: Sunday Nation, Nairobi. Address: c/o William Heinemann Ltd, 10 Upper Grosvenor Street, London W1X 9PA, England.

NGUGI WA THIONG'O. See: NGUGI J(ames) T.

NI CHUILLEANAIN Eilean, b. 28 Nov 1942. Lecturer; Writer; Poet. m. Macdara Woods, 27 June 1978, 1 son. Education: BA, 1962, MA, 1964, University College, Cork; BLitt, Lady Margaret Hall, Oxford, 1969. Appointments: Lecturer in Mediaeval and Renaissance English, Trinity College, Dublin, 1966-; Professor of American History and Institutions, Oxford University, 1969-78. Publications: Acts and Monuments, 1972; Site of Ambush, 1975; Cork, 1977; The Second Voyage, 1977; The Rose-Geranium, 1981; Irish Women: Image and Achievement (editor), 1985; The Magdalene Sermon, 1989; The Brazen Serpent, 1994. Contributions to: Cyphers Literary Magazine; Journal of Ecclesiastical History; Poems in many magazines. Honours: Irish Times Poetry Prize, 1966; Patrick Kavanagh Pize, 1972. Address: 2 Quarry Hollow, Headington, Oxford OX3 8JR, England.

NICHOLLS Christine Stephanie, b. 23 Jan 1943, Bury, Lancashire, England. Writer. m. Anthony James Nicholls, 12 Mar 1966, 1 son, 2 daughters. Education: BA, 1964, MA, 1968, Lady Margaret Hall, Oxford; DPhil, St Antony's College, Oxford, 1968. Appointments: Henry Charles Chapman Research Fellow, Institute of Commonwealth Studies, London University, 1968-69; Freelance Writer, BBC, 1970-74; Research Assistant, 1975-76; Joint Editor, 1961-89, Editor, 1989-95, Dictionary of National Biography Supplements, including: Missing Persons, 1990; Hutchinson Encyclopaedia of Biography, editor, 1996-; Sutton Pocket Biographies, editor, 1996-; Dictionary of National Biography, supplements, 1961-90; The Swahili Coast, 1971; Cataract (with P Awdry), 1985; Power: A Political History of the 20th Century, 1990; Hutchinson Encyclopaedia of Biography, 1996; Missing Persons (editor), 1990. Address: 27 Davenant Road, Oxford OX2 8BU, England.

NICHOLS (Joanna) Ruth, b. 4 Mar 1948, Toronto, Ontario, Canada. Theologian; Author. m. W N Houston, 21 Sept 1974. Education: BA, University of British Columbia; MA, Religious Studies, 1972, PhD, Theology, 1977, McMaster University. Publications: Ceremony of Innocence, 1969; A Walk Out of the World, 1969; The Marrow of the World, 1972; Song of the Pearl, 1976; The Left-handed Spirit, 1978; The Burning of the Rose, 1989; What Dangers Deep: A Story of Philip Sidney, 1992. Honours: Shankar International Literay Contest Awards, 1963, 1965; Woodrow Wilson Fellowship, 1968; Fellow, 1971-72, Research Fellow, 1978, Canada Council; Gold Medal, Canadian Association of Children's Librarians, 1972. Address: 276 Laird Drive, Toronto, Ontario M6Y 3XY, Canada.

NICHOLS Grace, b. 18 Feb 1950, Guyana. Writer; Poet; Journalist; Teacher. Education: University of Guyana, Georgetown. Publications: I is a Long Memories Woman, 1983; The Fat Black Woman's Poems, 1984; Come on Into My Tropical Garden, 1988; Black Poetry (editor), 1988; Lazy Thoughts of a Lazy Woman, 1989; Whole of a Morning Sky (novel), 1989; Other: Children's stories. Honour: British Arts Council Bursary, 1988. Address: c/o Curtis Brown Ltd, Haymarket House, 28-29 Haymarket, London SW1Y 4SP, England.

NICHOLS John (Treadwell), b. 23 July 1940, Berkeley, California, USA. Writer; Photographer. 1 son, 1 daughter. Education: BA, Hamilton College, New York, 1962. Publications: The Sterile Cuckoo, 1965; The Wizard of Loneliness, 1966; The Milagro Beanfield War, 1974; The Magic Journey, 1978; A Ghost in the Music, 1979; If Mountains Die, 1979; The Nirvana Blues, 1981; The Last Beautiful Days of Autumn, 1982; On the Mesa, 1986; American Blood, 1987; A Fragile Beauty, 1987; The Sky's the Limit, 1990; An Elegy for September, 1992; Keep It Simple, 1993; Conjugal Bliss, 1994; The Holiness of Water, 1995. Address: Box 1165, Taos, NM 87571, USA.

NICHOLS Pamela Amber McCurdy, b. 25 June 1956, Columbus, Ohio, USA. Nurse. m. Jerry Lee Nichols, 26 June 1974, 1 son, 1 daughter. Education: Nursing degree, WVNCC, Wheeling, West Virginia, 1994. Literary Appointment: Teacher of Poetry, Monroe County School, 1980. Publications: After the Battle, 1979; Touch the Sun, 1982; Lampslight, 1986; Oh Beloved, My Beloved (Part 1), 1987; For My Persecuted Brethren, 1988; Wedding Song, 1989. Contributions to: International Marriage Encounter Magazine; Northern Lights Literary Magazine WVNCC. Honours: Awards of Merit, 1986, 1987, 1988. Membership: National Society of Published Poets; ABI. Address: 46430 Buckio Road, Woodsfield, OH 43793, USA.

NICHOLS Peter Richard, b. 31 July 1927, Bristol, England. Playwright. m. Thelma Reed, 1960, 1 son, 3 daughters (1 dec). Appointments: Actor, 1950-55; Teacher, Primary and Secondary Schools, 1958-60; Arts Council Drama Panel, 1973-75; Playwright in Residence, Guthrie Theater, Minneapolis, Minnesota, USA, 1976. Publications: TV plays: Walk on the Grass, 1959; Promenade, 1960; Ben Spray, 1961; The Reception, 1961; The Big Boys, 1961; Continuity Man, 1963; Ben Again, 1963; The Heart of the Country, 1963; The Hooded Terror, 1963; When the Wind Blows, 1964, later adapted for radio; The Brick Umbrella, 1968; Daddy Kiss It Better, 1968; The Gorge, 1968; Hearts and Flowers, 1971; The Common, 1973. Films: Catch Us If You Can, 1965; Georgy Girl, 1967; Joe Egg, 1971; The National Health, 1973; Privates on Parade, 1983. Stage plays: A Day in the Death of Joe Egg, 1967; The National Health, 1969; Forget-me-not Lane, 1971; Chez Nous, 1973; The Freeway, 1974; Privates on Parade, 1977; Born in the Gardens, 1979, televised, 1986; Passion Play, 1980, Poppy, musical, 1982; A Piece of My Mind, 1986; Blue Murder, 1995. Autobiography: Feeling You're Behind, 1984. Honours: Standard Best Play Awards, 1967, 1969, 1983; Evening Standard Best Comedy, Society of West End Theatre Best Comedy, Ivor Novello Best Musical Awards, 1977; Society of West End Theatre Best Musical, 1982; Tony Award, 1985. Membership: Royal Society of Literature, fellow. Literary Agent: Rochelle Stevens, 2 Terrett's Place, London N1 8PS, England. Address: 22 Belsize Park Gardens, London NW3 4LH, England.

NICHOLS Roger (David Edward), b. 6 April 1939, England. m. Sarah Edwards, 1964, 2 sons, 1 daughter. Education: Harrow School; MA, Worcester College, Oxford. Appointments: Master at St Michael's College, Tenbury, 1966-73; Lecturer, Open University, 1974-80, University of Birmingham, 1974-80; Freelance writer and broadcaster, 1980-. Publications: Debussy, 1973; Through Greek Eyes (with Kenneth McLeish), 1974; Messiaen, 1975; Through Roman Eyes, 1976; Ravel, 1977; Greek Everyday Life (with Sarah Nichols), 1978; Ravel Remembered, 1987; Debussy: Letters (editor and translator), 1987; Claude Debussy: Pelléas et Mélisande (with Richard Langham Smith), 1989; Debussy Remembered, 1992. Address: The School House, The Square, Kington, Herefordshire HR5 3BA, England.

NICHOLSON Christina. See: NICOLE Christopher Robin.

NICHOLSON Geoffrey Joseph, b. 4 Mar 1953, Sheffield, England. Writer. Education: MA, English, Gonville and Caius College, Cambridge, 1975; MA, Drama, University of Essex, Colchester, 1978. Publications: Street Sleeper, 1987; The Knot Garden, 1989; What We Did On Our Holidays, 1990; Hunters and Gatherers, 1991; Big Noises, 1991; The Food Chain, 1992; Day Trips to the Desert, 1992; The Errol Flynn Novel, 1993; Still Life with Volkswagens, 1994; Everything and More, 1994; Footsucker, 1995; Bleeding London, 1997. Contributions to: Ambit magazine; Grand Street; Tiger Dreams; Night; Twenty Under 35; A Book of Two Halves. Honour: Shortlisted, Yorkshire 1st Work Award, 1987. Literary Agent: A P Watt, London, England. Address: 23 Sutherland Avenue, London W9 2HE, England.

NICHOLSON Margaret Beda. See: YORKE Margaret.

NICHOLSON Robin. See: NICOLE Christopher Robin.

NICK Dagmar, b. 30 May 1926, Breslau, Germany. Writer; Poet. Education: Psychology and Graphology studies, Munich, 1947-50. Publications: Poetry: Martyrer, 1947; Das Buch Holofernes, 1955; In den Ellipsen des Mondes, 1959; Zeugnis und Zeichen, 1969; Fluchtlinien, 1978; Gezählte Tage, 1986; Im Stillstand der Stunden, 1991; Gewendete Masken, 1996. Prose: Einladung nach Israel, 1963; Rhodos, 1967; Israel gestern und heute, 1968; Sizilien, 1976; Götterinseln der Ägäis, 1981; Medea, ein Monolog, 1988; Lilith, eine Metamorphose, 1992. Contributions to: Zeit; Frankfurter Allgemeine Zeitung; Akzente; Merian; Westermanns Monatshefte; Horen; Chicago Review; International Poetry Review; Chariton Review. Honours: Liliencron Prize, Hamburg, 1948; Eichendorff Prize, 1966; Honorary Award, Gryphius Prize, 1970; Roswitha Medal, 1977; Kulturpreis Schlesien des Landes Niedersachsen, 1986; Gryphius Prize, 1993. Memberships: PEN Club; Association of German Writers. Address: Kuglmüllerstrasse 22, D 80638 Munich, Germany.

NICOL Dominik, b. 25 Sept 1930, North Oltenia, Rumania. Writer; Photographer. Education: Baccalaureat Diploma, Rm Valcea Lyceum, 1949; Diploma in Technology and Chemistry of Antibiotics, Bucharest, 1954. Publications: Self encounter, 1979; Vacuum (colocviu de abis), 1979; Ten Oneiric sketches, 1980; Rendez-Vous sau Intalnire cu mine insumi, 1987; Vacuum-Void (bilingual edition), play, 1988; Pe portativul vietii - journal literar - 1992. Contributions to: Magazines. Address: PO Box 411, Times Square Sta, New York, NY 10108, USA.

NICOL Donald MacGillivray, b. 4 Feb 1923, England. Historian; Professor Emeritus. m. Joan Mary Campbell, 1950, 3 sons. Education: MA, PhD, Pembroke College, Cambridge. Appointments: Scholar, British School of Archaeology, Athens, 1949-50; Lecturer in Classics, University College, Dublin, 1952-64; Visiting Fellow, Dumbarton Oaks, Washington DC, 1964-65; Visiting Professor of Byzantine History, Indiana University, 1965-66; Senior Lecturer and Reader in Byzantine History, University of Edinburgh, 1969-70; Koraes Professor of Modern Greek and Byzantine History, Language and Literature, 1970-88, Assistant Principal, 1977-80, Vice Principal, 1980-81, Professor Emeritus, 1988-, King's College, University of London; Editor, Byzantine and Modern Greek Studies, 1973-83; Birbeck Lecturer, Cambridge University, 1976-77; Director, Gennadius Library, Athens, 1989-92. Publications: The Despotate of Epiros, 1957; Meteora: The Rock Monasteries of Thessaly, 1963, revised edition, 1975; The Byzantine Family of Kantakouzenos (Cantacuzenus) ca 1100-1460: A Genealogical and Prosopographical Study, 1968; Byzantium: Its Ecclesiastical History and Relations with the Western World, 1972; Last Centuries of Byzantium 1261-1453, 1972, 2nd edition, 1993; Church and Society in the Last Centuries of Byzantium, 1979; The End of the Byzantine Empire, 1979; The Despotate of Epiros 1267-1479: A Contribution to the History of Greece in the Middle Ages, 1984; Studies in Late Byzantine History and Prosopography, 1986; Byzantium and Venice: A Study in Diplomatic and Cultural Relations, 1988; Joannes Gennadios - The Man: A Biographical Sketch, 1990; A Biographical Dictionary of the Byzantine Empire, 1991; The Immortal Emperor: The Life and Legend of Constantine Palaiologos, last Emperor of the Romans, 1992; The Byzantine Lady: Ten Portraits 1250-1500, 1994. Contributions to: Professional journals. Membership: British Academy, fellow. Address: 16 Courtyards, Little Shelford, Cambridge CB2 5ER, England.

NICOLE Christopher (Robin), (Daniel Adams, Leslie Arlen, Robin Cade, Peter Grange, Nicholas Grant, Caroline Gray, Mark Logan, Simon Mackay, Christina Nicholson, Robin Nicholson, Alan Savage, Alison York, Andrew York), b. 7 Dec 1930, Georgetown, Guyana. Novelist. m. Diana Bachmann, 8 May 1982, 4 sons, 3 daughters. Education: Harrison College, Barbados; Queen's College, Guyana; Fellow, Canadian Bankers Association. Publications: As Christopher Nicole: Ratoon, 1962; Caribee Series, 1974-78; Byron, 1979; The Haggard Series, 1980-82; The China Series, 1984-86; The Japan Series, 1984-86; Black Majesty, 2 volumes, 1984-85; The Old Glory series, 1986-88; Ship with No Name, 1987; The High Country, 1988; The Regiment, 1988; The Pearl of the Orient, 1988. As Andrew York: The Eliminator Series, 1966-75; The Operation Series, 1969-71; Where the Cavern Ends, 1971; Dark Passage, 1976; The Tallant Series, 1977-78; The Combination, 1984. As Peter Grange: King Creole, 1966; The Devil's Emissary, 1968. As Robin Cade: The Fear Dealers, 1974. As Mark Logan: The Tricolour Series, 1976-78. As Christina Nicholson: The Power and the Passion, 1977; The Savage Sands, 1978; The Queen of Paris, 1983. As Alison York: The Fire and the Rape, 1979; The Scented Sword, 1980. As Robin Nicholson: The Friday Spy, 1981. As Leslie Arlen: The Borodin Series, 1980-85. As Daniel Adams: The Brazilian Series, 1982-83. As Simon Mackay: The Anderson Series, 1984-85. As Caroline Gray: First Class, 1984; Hotel de Luxe, 1985; White Rani, 1986; Victoria's Walk, 1986; The Third Life, 1988; Shadow of Death, 1989; Blue Water, Black Depths, 1990; The Daughter, 1992; Golden Girl, 1992; Spares, 1993; Spawn of the Devil, 1993. As Christopher Nicole: The Happy Valley, 1989; The Triumph, 1989; The Command, 1989; Dragon'd Blood, 1989; Dark Sun, 1990; Sword of Fortune, 1990; Sword of Empire, 1990; Days of Wine &

Roses, 1991; The Titans, 1992; Resumption, 1992; The Last Battle, 1993. As Alan Savage: Ottoman, 1990; Mughal, 1991; The Eight Banners, 1992; Queen of Night, 1993; The Last Bannerman, 1993. As Nicholas Grant: Khan, 1993. Also several books written jointly with wife, Diana Bachmann. Contributions to: Numerous journals and magazines. Memberships: Society of Authors; Literary Guild of America; Mark Twain Society. Literary Agent: David Higham Associates Ltd, 5-8 Lower John Street, Golden Square, London W1R 4HA, England. Address: Curtis Brown & John Farquharson Ltd, 162-168 Regent Street, London W1R 5TB, England.

NICOLSON Nigel, b. 19 Jan 1917, London, England. Author. m. Philippa Janet, 1953, div 1970, 1 son, 2 daughters. Education: Eton College, 1930-35; Balliol College, Oxford, 1936-39. Publications: The Grenadier Guards, 1939-45, 1949; People and Parliament, 1958; Lord of the Isles, 1960; Great Houses of Britain, 1965, revised edition, 1978; Harold Nicolson: Diaries and Letters (editor), 3 volumes, 1966-68; Great Houses, 1968; Alex (F M Alexander of Tunis), 1973; Portrait of a Marriage, 1973; The Himalayas, 1975; Letters of Virginia Woolf (editor), 6 volumes, 1975-80; Mary Curzon, 1977; Napoleon, 1812, 1985; The World of Jane Austen, 1991; Vita and Harold: The Letters of Vita Sackville-West and Harold Nicolson, 1910-1962 (editor), 1992. Honours: Member of the Order of the British Empire, 1945; Whitbread Award. Memberships: Royal Society of Literature, fellow; Society of Arts, fellow. Address: Sissinghurst Castle, Kent, England.

NIEDZIELSKI Henryk Zygmunt, b. 30 Mar 1931, Troyes, France. Educator. m. 26 July 1977, 3 sons, 1 daughter. Education: BA, 1959, MA, 1963, PhD, 1964, Romance Philology, University of Connecticut, USA. Appointments: Editor-in-Chief, Language & Literature in Hawaii, 1967-72; Correspondent, France Amerique, 1969-72; Editorial Board, Conradiana, 1971-76, Science et Francophonie, 1985-91; Associate Editor, The Phonetician, 1994-. Publications: Le Roman de Helcanus, 1966; The Silent Language of France, 1975; Studies on the Seven Sages of Rome, 1978; Jean Misrahi Memorial Volume, 1978; The Silent Language of Poland, 1989. Contributions to: Professional journals. Honours: Distinguished Fellow, University of Auckland, New Zealand, Foundation, 1989; Silver Cross of Merit, Polish People's Republic, 1989. Memberships: Medieval Academy of America; International Arthurian Society; American Association of Teachers of French, 1981-83; Hawaii Association of Translators, founding president, 1982; International Association of Teachers of English as a Foreign Language; Chopin Society of Hawaii, founding director, 1990. Address: 2425 West Orange Avenue, Anaheim, CA 92804, USA.

NIEMANN Linda Grant, b. 22 Sep 1946, Pasadena, California, USA. Railroad Brakeman. Education: BA, University of California, Santa Cruz, 1968; PhD, University of California, Berkeley, 1975. Publication: Boomer: Railroad Memoirs, 1990. Honour: Non-Fiction Award, Bay Area Book Reviewers Association, 1991. Memberships: PEN West; National Writers Union. Address: PO Box 7409, Santa Cruz, CA 95061, USA.

NIEMINEN Kai Tapani, b. 11 May 1950, Helsinki, Finland. Poet; Translator. m. 1991, 1 daughter. Education: Philosophy and Musicology, 1970-72; Private studies in Japanese, 1971. Publications: 14 books of poetry, 1971-97; Several translations from Japanese poetry and drama. Contributions to: Various publications. Honour: National Literary Awards, Ministry of Culture, 1986, 1990. Memberships: Authors Society; Finnish PEN, president, 1991-94. Address: Baggbole 99A, 07740 Gammelby, Finland.

NIGG Joseph Eugene, b. 27 Oct 1938, Davenport, Iowa, USA. Editor; Writer. m. (1) Gayle Madsen, 20 Aug 1960, div 1979, 2 sons, (2) Esther Muzzillo, 27 Oct 1989. Education: BA, Kent State University, 1960; MFA, Writers Workshop, University of Iowa, 1963; PhD, University of Denver, 1975. Appointments: Assistant Editor, Essays in Literature, 1974-75; Associate Editor, Liniger's Real Estate, 1979-85; Fiction Editor, Wayland Press, 1985-92. Publications: The Book of Gryphons, 1982; The Strength of Lions and the Flight of Eagles, 1982; A Guide to the Imaginary Birds of the World, 1984; Winegold, 1985; The Great Balloon Festival, 1989; Wonder Beasts, 1995. Contributions to: Various journals and magazines. Honours: Non-fiction Book of the Year Awards, Colorado Authors League, 1983, 1985, 1989; Mary Chase Author of the Year, Rocky Mountain Writers Guild, 1984. Memberships: Colorado Authors League; Rocky Mountain Writers Guild. Address: 1114 Clayton Street, Denver, CO 80206, USA.

NIKOSI Lewis, b. 5 Dec 1936, Natal, South Africa. Writer; Dramatist. Education: M C Sultan Technical College, 1954-55; Harvard University, 1961-62; Diploma in Literature, University of London, 1974; University of Sussex, 1977. Appointments: Staff, Ilange Lae Natal (Zulu newspaper), Durban, 1955-56, Drum magazine and Golden City Post, Johannesburg, 1956-60, South African Information Bulletin, Paris, 1962-68; Radio Producer, BBC Transcription Centre, London, 1962-64; Literary Editor, New African magazine, London, 1965-68. Publications: The Rhythm of Violence, 1964; Home and Exile (essays), 1965; The Transplanted Heart: Essays on South Africa, 1975; Tasks and Masks: Themes and Styles of African Literature, 1981; Mating Birds (novel), 1986. Address: Flat 4, Burgess Park Mansions, Fortune Green Road, London NW6, England.

NILE Dorothea. See: AVALLONE Michael (Angelo Jr).

NIMS John Frederick, b. 20 Nov 1913, Chicago, Illinois, USA. Professor; Editor of Poetry. m. Bonnie Larkin, 1 son, 1 daughter. Education: AB, 1937, MA, 1939, University of Notre Dame; PhD, University of Chicago, 1945. Appointments: Professor, numerous Universities including: University of Notre Dame, University of Florence, University of Madrid, University of Illinois, Harvard University, Williams College; Editor, Poetry Chicago, 1978-84. Publications: The Iron Pastoral, 1947; A Fountain in Kentucky, 1950; The Poems of St John of the Cross (translator), 1958, 3rd edition, 1979; Knowledge of the Evening, 1960; Of Flesh and Bone, 1967; Sappho to Valery: Poems in Translation, 1971, 3rd edition, 1992; Western Wind: An Introduction to Poetry, 1974, 3rd edition, 1992; The Harper Anthology of Poetry, 1981; The Kiss: A Jambalaya (poems), 1982; Selected Poems, 1982; A Local Habitation: Essays on Poetry, 1985; The Six-Cornered Snowflake, 1991; Zany in Denim, 1991. Contributions to: Numerous magazines, journals and reviews. Honours: National Institute of Arts and Letters Award, 1967; Creative Arts Poetry Award, Brandeis University, 1972; Fellowship, Academy of American Poets, 1982; Guggenheim Fellowship, 1986-87; Aiken-Taylor Award, 1991; Melville Cane Award, 1992; Hardison Poetry Prize, 1993. Address: 3920 Lake Shore Drive, Chicago, IL 60613, USA.

NIOSI Jorge Eduardo, b. 8 Dec 1945, Buenos Aires, Argentina. University Professor. m. Graciela Ducatenzeiler, 25 Nov 1971, 2 daughters. Education: Licence, Sociology, National University of Buenos Aires, 1967; Advanced Degree, Economics, IEDES, Paris, 1970; Doctorate, Sociology, Ecole Pratique, Paris, 1973. Publications: Les entrepeneurs dans la politique argentine, 1976; The Economy of Canada, 1978; Canadian Capitalism, 1981; Firmes Multinationales et autonomie nationale, 1983; Canadian Multinationals, 1985; La montee de l'ingenierie canadienne, 1990; Technology and National Competitiveness, 1991; New Technology Policy and Social Innovation in the Firm (editor), 1994. Contributions to: Journals and magazines. Honours: John Porter Award, Canadian Sociology and Anthropology Association, 1983; Fellow, Statistics Canada, 1989-92; Fellow, Fulbright Programme. Memberships: International Sociological Association; Canadian Sociology and Anthropology Association; International Management of Technology Association; Royal Society of Canada. Address: CREDIT, UQAM, Box 8888, Station Centre Ville, Montreal, Quebec H3C 3P8, Canada.

NISBET Jim, b. 20 Jan 1947. Writer. Publications: Poems for a Lady, 1978; Gnachos for Bishop Berkeley, 1980; The Gourmet (novel), 1980; Morpho (with Alaistair Johnston), 1982; The Visitor, 1984; Lethal Injection (novel), 1987; Death Puppet (novel), 1989; Laminating the Conic Frustum, 1991; Small Apt, 1992; Ulysses' Dog, 1993; Sous le Signe de la Razoir, 1994. Address: c/o William Morris Agency, 1350 Avenue of the Americas, New York, NY 10019, USA.

NISH Ian Hill, b. 3 June 1926, Edinburgh, Scotland. Professor (retired). m. Rona Margaret Speirs, 29 Dec 1965, 2 daughters. Education: University of Edinburgh, 1943-51; University of London, 1951-56. Appointments: University of Sydney, New South Wales, Australia, 1957-62; London School of Economics and Political Science, England, 1962-91. Publications: Anglo-Japanese Alliance, 1966; The Story of Japan, 1968; Alliance in Decline, 1972; Japanese Foreign Policy, 1978; Anglo-Japanese Alienation 1919-52, 1982; Origins of the Russo-Japanese War, 1986; Contemporary European Writing on Japan, 1988; Japan's Struggle with Internationalism, 1931-33, 1993. Honours: Commander of the Order of the British Empire, 1990; Order of the Rising Sun, Japan, 1991. Memberships: European Association of Japanese Studies, president, 1985-88; British Association of

Japanese Studies, president, 1986. Address: Oakdene, 33 Charlwood Drive, Oxshott, Surrey KT22 0HB, England.

NIVEN Alastair Neil Robertson, b. 25 Feb 1944, Edinburgh, Scotland. Director of Literature of the Arts Council of England; Writer. m. Helen Margaret Trow, 22 Aug 1970, 1 son, 1 daughter. Education: BA, 1966, MA, 1968, University of Cambridge; MA, University of Ghana, 1968; PhD, University of Leeds, 1972. Appointments: Lecturer, English, University of Ghana, 1968-69, University of Leeds, England, 1969-70; Lecturer, English Studies, University of Stirling, Scotland, 1970-78; Visiting Professor, Aarhus University, Denmark, 1975-76; Honorary Lecturer, University of London, 1979-84; Editor, Journal of Commonwealth Literature, 1979-92; Chapman Fellow, Institute of Commonwealth Studies, 1984-85; Visiting Fellow, Australian Studies Centre, London, 1985; Director of Literature, Arts Council of Great Britain, 1987-94, Arts Council of England, 1994-. Publications: D H Lawrence: The Novels, 1978; The Yoke of Pity: The Fictional Writings of Mulk Raj Anand, 1978; The Commonwealth of Universities (with Hugh W Springer), 1987; Truth into Fiction or Raja Rao's The Serpent and the Rope, 1988. Editor: The Commonwealth Writer Overseas, 1976; Under Another Sky, 1987. Study guides on William Golding, R K Narayan, Elechi Amadi. Contributions to: Times; Ariel; Literary Criterion; Commonwealth Essais et Etudes. Honours: Commonwealth Scholar, 1966-68; Laurence Olivier Awards Panel, 1989-91; Judge, Booker Prize, 1994. Memberships: Greater London Arts Association Literature Advisory Panel, chairman, 1980-84; Association for Commonwealth Literature and Language Studies, secretary, 1986-89; UK Council for Overseas Student Affairs, executive committee chairman, 1987-92; Commonwealth Trust. Address: Eden House, 28 Weathercock Lane, Woburn Sands, Buckinghamshire MK17 8NY, England.

NIVEN Larry (Laurence Van Cott), b. 30 Apr 1938, Los Angeles, California, USA. m. Marilyn Joyce Wisowaty, 6 Sept 1969. Education: California Institute of Technology, 1956-58; BA, Mathematics, Washburn University, Kansas, 1962. Publications: Neutron Star, 1966; Ringworld, 1970; Inconstant Moon, 1971; The Hole Man, 1974; Protector, 1974; The Borderland of Sol, 1975; Dream Park (with Steven Barnes), 1981; Football (with Jerry Pournelle), 1985; Playgrounds, 1991; The Gripping Hand (with Jerry Pournelle), 1993. Contributions to: Books and magazines. Honours: Honorary Doctor of Letters, Washburn University, 1984; Science Fiction Achievement Awards, 1966, 1970, 1971, 1974, 1975; Nebula Best Novel, 1970; Australian Best International Science Fiction, 1972, 1974; Inkpot Award, San Diego Comic Convention, 1979. Literary Agent: Eleanor Wood. Address: c/o Spectrum Literary Agency, 111 8th Vanalden Avenue, Tarzana, CA 91356, USA.

NJEMOGA-KOLAR Ana, b. 5 July 1951, Padina, Yugoslavia. Writer. m. Samo Kolar, 5 Apr 1980. Education: Faculty of Philosophy, Novi Sad University; Qualified Secondary School Teacher of Slovak Language and Literature. Appointments: Junior Journalist, Radio Novi Sad, 1976-81; Senior Journalist, Editor, TV Novi Sad, 1981-82; Co-Founder, Editorial Board Member, IGROPIS magazine (on children's theatre), 1990. Contributions to: Magazines, radio and television. Honours: 2nd Prize, Yugoslav Competition for Best Children's Play, Radio Sarajevo, 1988; 2nd and 3rd Prizes, Competition for Best Children's Radio Story, Radio Novi Sad, 1988-89; 2nd Prize, Competition for Best Children's Story, Pioneers magazine, 1990; 1st Prizes, Republic Competition for Best Children's Story, 1990, 1991; 1st Prize, Competition for Best Theatre Play for Adults, New Life literary magazine, 1991. Membership: Vojvodina Journalists Association. Address: PO Box 11, 07 801 Secovce, Slovakia.

NOAKES Vivien, b. 16 Feb 1937, Twickenham, England. Writer. m. Michael Noakes, 9 July 1960, 2 sons, 1 daughter. Education: MA, English, Senior Scholar, Somerville College, Oxford University. Publications: Edward Lear: The Life of a Wanderer, 1968, 3rd edition, 1985; Edward Lear 1812-1888, The Catalogue of the Royal Academy Exhibition, 1985; The Selected Letters of Edward Lear, 1988; The Painter Edward Lear, 1991. Contributions to: Times; Times Literary Supplement; Daily Telegraph; New Scientist; Punch; Harvard Magazine; Tennyson Research Bulletin. Literary Agent: Watson, Little Limited. Address: 146 Hamilton Terrace, London NW8 9UX, England.

NOBLE Jayne. See: **DOWNES Mary Raby.**

NOBUKO Takagi, b. 1946, Yamaguchi Prefecture, Japan. Writer. Education: Tokyo Women's University. Publications: Sono

Hosoki Michi (published in Bungakkai magazine); Tsuta Moe; Suimyaku; Novels: Hikari idaku tomoyo; Hakô kirameku hate; Black noddy ga sumu ki; Toki wo aoku somete; Aika wa nagareru; Southern Squall; Kore we zange de wa naku; Ayagumo no mine. Honours: Akutagawa Literary Prize, 1984; Shimase Award for Love Fiction; Women's Literary Award. Address: c/o Japan PEN Club, 265 Akasaka Residential Hotel, 9-1-7 Akasaka, Minato-ku, Tokyo 107, Japan.

NOEL. See: **ADAMS Douglas.**

NOEL Arthur. See: **RAVEN Simon.**

NOEL Lise, b. 19 Apr 1944, Montreal, Quebec, Canada. Writer; Former Professor; Columnist. Education: BA, 1965, Licence in Letters, 1970, MA, History, 1975, PhD, History, 1982, University of Montreal; University of Aix-en-Provence, France. Publication:Intolerance: The Parameters of Oppression, 1994. Contributions to: Critère; Liberté; Possibles; Service Social; Le Devoir. Honours: Hachette-Larousse, 1967; Governor General's Award, Non Fiction, 1989; The Myers Centre Award for the Study of Human Rights in North America, 1994. Address: 2608 Chemin Cote Sainte Catherine, Montreal, Quebec H3T 1B4, Canada.

NOL-HUME Ivor, b. 1927, London, England. Archaeologist; Writer. Education: St Lawrence College, Kent, 1942-44. Appointments: Archaeologist, Guildhall Museum Corp, London, 1949-57; Chief Archaeologist, 1957-64, Director, Department of Archaeology, 1964-72, Resident Archaeologist, 1972-87, Colonial Williamsburg; Research Associate, Smithsonian Institution, Washington, DC, 1959-; Guest Curator, Steuben Glass Co, 1990; Director, Roanoke Project, 1991-93; Chairman, Jamestown Rediscovery Advisory Board, 1994-95. Publications: Archaeology in Britain, 1953; Tortoises, Terrapins and Turtles (with Audrey Noël-Hume), 1954; Treasure in the Thames, 1956; Great Moments in Archaeology, 1957; Here Lies Virginia, 1963, new edition, 1994; 1775: Another Part of the Field, 1966; Historical Archaeology, 1969; Artifacts of Early America, 1970; All the Best Rubbish, 1974; Early English Delftware, 1977; Martin's Hundred, 1982; The Virginia Adventure, 1994; Shipwreck: History from the Bermuda Reeds, 1995. Films: Doorway to the Past, 1968; The Williamsburg File, 1976; Search for a Century, 1981. Contributions to: Professional journals. Honours: Award for Historical Archaeology, University of South Carolina, 1975; Achievement Award, National Society of the Daughters of the Founders and Patriots of America, 1989, National Society of the Daughters of the American Colonists, 1990; Officer of the Order of the British Empire, 1992. Memberships: American Antiquarian Society; Society of Antiquaries, London, fellow; Society of Historical Archaeology; Society for Post-Medieval Archaeology; Virginia Archaeological Society. Address: 2 West Circle, Williamsburg, VA 23185, USA.

NOF Shimon Y, b. 22 Mar 1946, Haifa, Israel. Professor of Industrial Engineering. m. Nava C Vardinon, 1972, 2 daughters. Education: BSc, 1969, MSc, 1972, Industrial Engineering and Management, Technicon, Haifa, Israel; PhD, Industrial and Operations Engineering, University of Michigan, Ann-Arbor, USA, 1976. Appointments: Deputy Editor, Computor and Knowledge Engineering, 1984-; Special Issue Editor, Material Flow, 1984-85; Consulting Editor, Encyclopedia of Robotics, 1984-88; Editorial Board, Handbook of Industrial Engineering, 1989-92, International Journal of Production Planning and Control, 1991-, International Journal of Industrial Engineering, 1993-, Computing and Emerging Methodologies/IIE Transactions, 1993-. Publications: Handbook of Industrial Robotics, 1985; Robotics and Material Flow, 1986; International Encyclopedia of Robotics and Automation, 1988; Advanced Information Technology for Industrial Material Flow Systems, 1989; Concise Encyclopedia of Robotics and Automation (co-editor), 1990. Contributions to: Journals and Proceedings. Honours: Fulbright Grant, 1972; Silent Hoist Doctoral Award, 1975; American Association of Publishers Awards of Excellence, 1975, 1988. Memberships: Institute of Industrial Engineers, fellow; Association of Computing Machinary; Institute of Management Science; Japan Industrial Management Association; Society of Manufacturing Engineers; International Federation of Production Research. Address: 1287 Grissom Hall, Purdue University, West Lafayette, IN 47907, USA,

NOLAN Patrick, b. 2 Jan 1933, Bronx, New York, USA. Teacher. 3 sons. Education: MA, University of Detroit; PhD, English Literature, Bryn Mawr College. Appointments: Instructor, University of Detroit; Professor, Villanova University. Publications: Films: Hourglass

Moment, 1969; Jericho Mile, 1978. Plays: Chameleons, 1981; Midnight Rainbows, 1991. Honours: Emmy Award, 1979; Citation, Teaching Excellence, Philadelphia Magazine, 1980. Membership: Writes Guild of America, West; Dramatists Guild. Literary Agent: Matthew Rosenberger, 8623 Germantown Avenue, Chestnut Hill, PA 19118, USA. Address: English Department, Villanova University, Villanova, PA 19085, USA.

NOLAN William F(rancis), (Frank Anmar, Mike Cahill, F E Edwards, Michael Phillips), b. 6 Mar 1928, Kansas City, Missouri, USA. Writer; Poet. Education: Kansas City Art Institute, 1946-47; San Diego State College, 1947-48; Los Angeles City College, 1953. Publications: Numerous books, including: Barney Oldfield, 1961; Phil Hall: Yankee Champion, 1962; Impact 20 (stories), 1963; John Huston: King Rebel, 1965; Sinners and Superman, 1965; Death is for Losers, 1968; Dashiell Hammett: A Casebook, 1969; Alien Horizons (stories), 1974; Hemingway: Last Days of the Lion, 1974; Wonderworlds (stories), 1977; Hammett: A Life on the Edge, 1983; Things Beyond Midnight (stories), 1984; Dark Encounters (poems), 1986; Logan: A Trilogy, 1986; How to Write Horror Fiction, 1990; Six in Darkness (stories), 1993; Night Shapes (stories), 1993. Address: c/o Loni Perkins Associates Literary Agency, 301 West 53rd Street, New York, NY 10019, USA.

NONHEBEL Clare, b. 7 Nov 1953, London, England. m. Robin Nonhebel, 30 Aug 1975. Education: BA (Honours), French Studies, University of Warwick. Appointments: Freelance Feature Writer, 1980-84. Publications: Cold Showers, 1985; The Partisan, 1986; Incentives, 1988; Child's Play, 1991. Contributions to: Newspapers, journals, and magazines. Honour: Joint Winner, Betty Trask Award, 1984. Address: c/o Curtis Brown, Haymarket House, 28/29 Haymarket, London SW1Y 4SP, England.

NOON Ed. See: **AVALLONE Michael Angelo.**

NOONE Edwina. See: **AVALLONE Michael (Angelo Jr).**

NORDBRANDT Henrik, b. 21 Mar 1945, Copenhagen, Denmark. Writer. Education: Turkish and Arabic Studies. Publications: Digte, 1966; Miniaturer, 1967; Syvsoverne, 1969; Omgivelser, 1972; Opbrud ogankomstr, 1974; Ode til blaeksprutten, 1976; Guds hus, 1977; Selected Poems, 1978; Amenia, 1982; Violinbyggernes by, 1985; Glas, 1986; Istid, 1987. Contributions to: Various journals and magazines. Honours: 12 Literary Awards. Address: Gyldendal, Klareboderne 3, Copenhagen 1001 K, Denmark.

NORLING Bernard, b. 23 Feb 1924, Hunters, Washington, USA. Retired University Professor. m. Mary Pupo, 30 Jan 1948. Education: BA, Gonzaga University, 1948; MA, 1949, PhD, 1955, Notre Dame University. Appointments: Instructor, 1952-55, Assistant Professor, 1955-61, Associate Professor, 1961-71, Professor, 1971-86, History Department, University of Notre Dame. Publications: Towards a Better Understanding of History, 1960; Timeless Problems in History, 1970; Understanding History Through the American Experience, 1976; Return to Freedom, 1983; Behind Japanese Lines, 1986; The Nazi Impact on a German Village, 1993; Lapham's Raiders, 1996. Contributions to: Magazines and journals. Honour: Best Teacher of Freshman, University of Notre Dame, 1968. Memberships: Indiana Association of Historians; Michiana Historians, president, 1972. Address: 504 East Pokagon, South Bend, IN 46617, USA.

NORMAN Barry Leslie, b. 21 Aug 1933, London, England. Writer; Broadcaster. m. Diana Narracott, 1957, 2 daughters. Appointments: Entertainments Editor, Daily Mail, London, 1969-71; Weekly Columnist, The Guardian, 1971-80; Writer and Presenter, BBC 1 Film, 1973-81, 1983-88, The Hollywood Greats, 1977-79, 1984, The British Greats 1980, Omnibus, 1982, Film Greats, 1985, Talking Pictures, 1988; Radio 4 Today, 1974-76, Going Places, 1977-81, Breakaway, 1979-80. Publications: Novels: The Matter of Mandrake, 1967; The Hounds of Sparta, 1968; End Product, 1975; A Series of Defeats, 1977; To Nick a Good Body, 1978; Have a Nice Day, 1981; Sticky Wicket, 1984. Non-fiction: Tales of the Redundance Kid, 1975; The Hollywood Greats, 1979; The Movie Greats, 1981; Talking Pictures, 1987; 100 Best Films of the Century, 1992; Thriller, The Birddog Tape, 1992; The Mickey Mouse Affair, 1995. Honours: British Association of Film and Television Artists Richard Dimbleby Award, 1981; Honorary DLitt, University of East Anglia, 1991, University of Hertfordshire, 1996; Magazine Columnist of the Year, 1991. Address:

c/o Curtis Brown Ltd, Haymarket House, 28-29 Haymarket, London SW1Y 4SP, England.

NORMAN Geraldine (Lucia), (Geraldine Keen, Florence Place), b. 13 May 1940, Wales. Journalist. m. Frank Norman, July 1971. Education: MA (Honours), Mathematics, St Anne's College, Oxford, 1961; University of California at Los Angeles, USA, 1961-62. Publications: The Sale of Works of Art (as Geraldine Keen), 1971; 19th Century Painters and Paintings: A Dictionary, 1977; The Fake's Progress (co-author), 1977; The Tom Keating Catalogue (editor), 1977; Mrs Harper's Niece (as Florence Place), 1982; Biedermeier Painting, 1987; Top Collectors of the World (co-author), 1993. Contributions to: The Independent on Sunday, Sunday Times and others. Honour: News Reporter of the Year, 1976. Literary Agent: Gillon Aitken. Address: 5 Seaford Court, 220 Great Portland Street, London W1, England.

NORMAN Hilary, b. London, England. Writer. Education: Queen's College, London. Appointments: Director, Henry Norman textile manufacturing and retail firm, London, 1971-79; Production Assistant, Capital Radio, London, 1980-82, British Broadcasting Corporation, 1982-85; Writer, 1985-. Publications: Novels: In Love and Friendship, 1986; Château Ella, 1988; Shattered Stars, 1991; Fascination, 1992; Spellbound, 1993; Laura, 1994; Susanna, 1996; The Pact, 1997; As Alexandra Henry: If I Should Die, 1995. Contributions to: Woman's Own. Literary Agents: John Hawkins Associates, 71 West 23rd Street, New York, NY 10010, USA; A M Heath Co. Address: c/o A M Heath Co Ltd, 79 St Martins Lane, London WC2N 4AA, England.

NORMAN John, b. 20 July 1912, Syracuse, New York, USA. Professor Emeritus; Writer; Poet. m. Mary Lynott, 28 Dec 1948, 4 daughters. Education: BA, 1935, MA, 1938, Syracuse University; PhD, Clark University, 1942. Publications: Edward Gibbon Wakefield: A Political Reappraisal, 1963; Labor and Politics in Libya and Arab Africa, 1965. Contributions to: Anthologies, reference books, and journals. Honour: World Poetry Prize, 1991. Address: 94 Cooper Road, John's Pond, Ridgefield, CT 06877, USA.

NORMAN Marsha, b. 21 Sept 1947, Louisville, Kentucky, USA. Dramatist; Writer. m. (1) Michael Norman, div 1974, (2) Dann C Byck Jr, Nov 1978, div, (3) Timothy Dykman, 1 son, 1 daughter. Education: BA, Agnes Scott College, 1969; MAT, University of Louisville, 1971. Appointments: Teacher, Kentucky Arts Commission, 1972-76; Book Reviewer and Editor, Louisville Times, 1974-79. Publications: Plays: Getting Out, 1977; Third and Oak: The Laudromat (and) The Pool Hall, 1978; 'Night, Mother, 1982; Four Plays by Marsha Norman, 1988. Novel: The Fortune Teller, 1987. Musical: The Secret Garden, 1991. Honours: National Endowment for the Arts Grant, 1978-79; John Gassner New Playwrights Medallion, Outer Critics Circle, 1979; George Oppenheimer-Newsday Award, 1979; Rockefeller Foundation Playwright-in-Residence Grant, 1979-80; Susan Smith Blackburn Prize, 1982; Pulitzer Prize in Drama, 1983; Tony Award for Best Book of a Musical, 1991. Address: c/o The Tantleff Offce, 375 Greenwich Street, No 700, New York, NY 10013, USA.

NORRIE Philip Anthony, b. 5 Feb 1953, Sydney, New South Wales, Australia. Medical Practitioner. m. Belinda Jill Vivian, 6 June 1974, 2 sons. Education: MB BS, University of New South Wales, 1977; Certificate, Family Planning Association, 1980; MSc, University of Sydney, 1993; MSocSc honours degree in progress, Charles Sturt University. Appointments: Wine Writer for various publications; Editorial Board, Alcohol in Moderation, 1992. Publications: Vineyards of Sydney, Cradle of Australian Wine Industry, 1990; Lindeman - Australia's Classic Winemaker, 1993; Penfold - Time Honoured, 1994; Australia's Wine Doctors, 1994; Wine and Health, 1995; Leo Buring - Australia's Wine Authority, 1996. Contributions to: Australasian Journal of Psychopharmacology; Australian Doctor; Australian Medical Observer; Journal of Medical Biography; Australian; Alcohol in Moderation; Hunter Valley Wine Society Journal. Memberships: Australian Medical Association; Australian National Trust; Royal Australian Historical Society; Australian Society of the History of Medicine; New South Wales Society Medical History Society; Australian Medical Friends of Wine Society, founder-president; FIBA; Wine Press Club of New South Wales. Address: 22 Ralston Road, Palm Beach, New South Wales 2108, Australia.

NORRIS Ken, b. 3 Apr 1951, Bronx, New York, USA. Associate Professor; Poet. m. Susan Hamlett, 1987. Education: PhD, McGill University, Montreal, 1980. Appointment: Associate Professor,

Canadian Literature, University of Maine. Publications: Report on the Second Half of the Twentieth Century, 1977; The Perfect Accident, 1978; The Book of Fall, 1979; Autokinesis, 1980; Sonnets and Other Dead Forms, 1980; To Sleep, To Love, 1982; Eight Odes, 1982; Whirlwinds, 1983; The Better Part of Heaven: Pacific Writings, 1984; One Night, 1985; In the Spirit of the Times, 1986; Islands, 1986; In the House of No, 1991; Editions of Canadian poetry. Honours: Canada Council Arts Grant, 1982. Address: Department of English, University of Maine, 304 Neville Hall, Orno, ME 04469, USA.

NORRIS Leslie, b. 21 May 1921, Merthyr Tydfil, Wales. Professor; Poet; Writer. m. Catherine Mary Morgan, 1948. Education: MPhil, University of Southampton, 1958. Appointments: Principal Lecturer, West Sussex Institute of Education, 1956-74; Professor, Brigham Young University, Provo, Utah, 1981-. Publications: Tongue of Beauty, 1941; Poems, 1944; The Loud Winter, 1960; Finding Gold, 1964; Ransoms, 1970; Mountains, Polecats, Pheasants and Other Hegies, 1973; Selected Poems, 1986; Collected Poems, 1996. Contributions to: Various publications. Honours: British Arts Council Award, 1964; Alice Hunt Bartlett prize, 1969; Chomondeley Poetry Prize, 1979; Katherine Mansfield Award, 1981. Memberships: Royal Society of Literature, fellow; Welsh Academy, fellow. Address: 849 South Carterville Road, Orem, UT 84058, USA.

NORSE Harold George, b. 6 July 1916, New York, New York, USA. Professor; Writer; Poet. Education: BA, Brooklyn College, 1938; MA, New York University, 1951. Appointments: Instructor, Cooper Union College, New York, 1949-52, Lion School of English, Rome, Italy, 1956-57, United States Information Service School, Naples, Italy, 1958-59; Instructor in Creative Writing, San Jose State University, California, 1973-75; Professor in Creative Writing, New College of California, 1994-95. Publications: The Roman Sonnets of Giuseppe Gioacchino Belli (translator), 1960, 2nd edition, 1974; Karma Circuit (poems), 1967; Hotel Nirvana (poems\, 1974; Carnivorous Saint (poems), 1977; Mysteries of Magritte (poems), 1984; Love Poems, 1986; Memoirs of a Bastard Angel (autobiography), 1989; Seismic Events (poems), 1993. Contributions to: Journals and magazines. Honours: National Endowment for the Arts Fellowship, 1974; R H de Young Museum Grant, 1974; Lifetime Achievement Award in Poetry, National Poetry Association, 1991. Membership: PEN. Address: 157 Albion Street, San Francisco, CA 94110, USA.

NORTH Andrew. See: NORTON André.

NORTH Elizabeth (Stewart), b. 20 Aug 1932, Hampshire, England. Author; Teacher of Creative Writing. Education: BA, University of Leeds, 1973. Appointment: Writer-in-Residence, Bretton Hall College of Higher Education, 1984-85. Publications: Make Thee an Ark (radio play), 1969; Wife Swopping (radio play), 1969; The Least and Vilest Things (novel), 1971; Pelican Rising (novel), 1975; Enough Blue Sky (novel), 1977; Everything in the Garden (novel), 1978; Florence Avenue (novel), 1970; Dames (novel), 1981; Ancient Enemies (novel), 1982; The Real Tess (radio feature), 1984; Jude the Obscure (adaptation for radio), 1985. Address: 8 Huby Park, Huby, Leeds, England.

NORTHCUTT Wayne, b. 5 July 1944, New Orleans, Louisiana, USA. Professor of History; Writer. Education: BA, History, 1966, MA, History, 1968, California State University, Long Beach; PhD, European History, University of California, Irvine, 1974. Publications: The French Socialist and Communist Party Under the Fifth Republic: From Opposition to Power, 1985; Mitterrand: A Political Biography, 1992; Historical Dictionary of the French 4th and 5th Republics 1946-1991, 1992; The Regions of France: A Reference Guide to History and Culture, 1996. Contributions to: Contemporary French Civilization; West European Politics; French Historical Studies. Honours: Camargo Fellowship, 1986; National Endowment for the Humanities Grant, 1993. Address: Department of History, Niagara University, NY 14109, USA.

NORTON André, (Andrew North), b. 17 Feb 1912, Cleveland, Ohio, USA. Author. Education: Western Reserve University, 1930-32. Appointment: Children's Librarian, Cleveland Public Library. Publications: Over 150 books, 1934-97. Address: High Hallack, 4911 Celtkiller Highway, Monterey, TN 38574, USA.

NORTON Augustus Richard, b. 2 Sept 1946, New York, USA. Professor; Army Officer (Colonel). m. Deanna J Lampros, 27 Dec 1969, 1 son. Education: BA, magna cum laude 1974, MA, Political Science 1974, University of Miami; PhD, Political Science, University of Chicago, 1984. Publications: Studies in Nuclear Terrorism, 1979; International Terrorism, 1980; NATO, 1985; Touring Nam: The Vietnam War Reader, 1985; Amal and the Shia: Struggle for the Soul of Lebanon, 1987; The International Relations of the Palestine Liberation Organization, 1989; UN Peacekeepers: Soldiers with a Difference, 1990; Political Tides in the Arab World, 1992. Contributions to: Survival & Foreign Policy; Current History; New Outlook; New Leader; Middle East Journal. Address: Department of Social Science, United States Military Academy, West Point, NY 10996, USA.

NORWICH John Julius, b. 15 Sept 1929, London, England. Writer; Broadcaster. m. (1) Anne Clifford, 5 Aug 1952, 1 son, 1 daughter, (2) Mollie Philipps, 14 June 1989. Education: University of Strasbourg, 1947; New College, Oxford, 1949-52. Publications: Mount Athos, 1966; Sahara, 1968; The Normans in the South, 1967; The Kingdom in the Sun, 1970; A History of Venice, 1977; Christmas Crackers 1970-79, 1980; Glyndebourne, 1985; The Architecture of Southern England, 1985; A Taste for Travel, 1985; Byzantium: The Early Centuries, 1988; More Christmas Crackers 1980-89, 1990; Venice: A Traveller's Companion (editor), 1990; The Oxford Illustrated Encyclopaedia of the Arts, editor, 1990; Byzantium, the Apogee, 1991; Byzantine Decline and Fate, 1995. Contributions to: Numerous magazines and journals. Honours: Commander, Royal Victorian Order; Commendatore, Ordine al Merito della Repubblica Italiana. Memberships: Royal Society of Literature, fellow; Royal Geographical Society, fellow; Beefsteak. Literary Agent: Felicity Bryan, 2A North Parade, Oxford, England. Address: 24 Blomfield Road, London W9 1AD, England.

NOSKOWICZ-BIERON Helena, b. 5 July 1931, Sobolow, Poland. Journalist. m. Wladystaw Bieron, 27 Dec 1956, 2 sons. Education: BA, Journalism, Jangiellonian University, Krakow, 1964; MA, Journalism, University of Warsaw, 1964. Appointments: Reporter, Polish Radio, 1953-63; Columnist, Echo Krakowa, daily, 1964-81, Gazeta Krakowska and Dziennik Polski, 1989-; Editor, Underground Press, 1981-89. Publications: Ciagle czekaja z obiadem, 1978; Kto Ukradl Zloty Fon, 1991. Contributions to: Periodicals. Honours: Book of the Year, 1978; Association of Polish Journalists prizes and awards. Membership: Association of Polish Journalists. Address: ul Batorego 19/16, 31-135 Krakow, Poland.

NOTLEY Alice, b. 8 Nov 1945, Bisbee, Arizona, USA. Poet. m. Douglas Oliver, 10 Feb 1988, 2 sons. Education: BA Barnard College, 1967; MFA, The Writers' Workshop, University of Iowa, 1970. Publications: Alice Ordered Me to Be Made, 1976; When I Was Alive, 1980; How Spring Comes, 1981; Waltzing Matilda, 1981; Margaret and Dusty, 1985; At Night the States, 1988; Beginning with a Stain; Homer's Art, 1991; The Scarlet Cabinet (with Douglas Oliver), 1992. Contributions to: Scarlet. Honours: National Endowment for the Arts Award, 1979; Poetry Center Book Award, 1982; General Electric Foundation Award, 1984; NYFA Fellowship, 1991. Address: 61 rue Lepic, 75018, France.

NOVAK Maximillian Erwin, b. 26 Mar 1930, New York, New York, USA. University Professor. m. Estelle Gershgoren, 21 Aug 1966, 2 sons, 1 daughter. Education: PhD, University of California, 1958; DPhil, St John's University, Oxford, 1961. Appointments: Assistant Professor, University of Michigan, 1958-62; Assistant Professor to Professor, University of California, Los Angeles, 1962-. Publications: Economics and the Fiction of Daniel Defoe, 1962; Defoe and the Nature of Man, 1963; Congreve, 1970; Realism Myth and History in the Fiction of Daniel Defoe, 1983; Eighteenth Century English Literature, 1983. Editor: The Wild Man Within, 1970; English Literature in the Age of Disguise, 1977; California Dryden, Vols X and X111, 1971, 1984. Contributions to: Professional journals. Address: Deparment of English, University of California, Los Angeles, CA 90095, USA.

NOVAK Michael (John), b. 9 Sept 1933, Johnstown, Pennsylvania, USA. Professor; Author; Editor. m. Karen Ruth Laub, 29 June 1963, 1 son, 2 daughters. Education: AB, Stonehill College, North Easton, Massachusetts, 1956; BT, Gregorian University, Rome, 1958; MA, Harvard University, 1966. Appointments: Assistant Professor, Stanford University, 1965-68; Associate Editor, Commonweal magazine, 1966-69; Associate Professor of Philosophy and Religious Studies, State University of New York at Old Westbury, 1968-71; Provost, Disciplines College, State University of New York at Old Westbury, 1969-71; Associate Director for Humanities, Rockefeller Foundation, New York City, 1973-75; Writer-in-Residence, Washington Star, 1976; Syndicated Columnist, 1976-80, 1984-89; Resident Scholar in Religion and Public Policy, 1978-, George Frederick Jewett Chair in Public Policy Research, 1983-, Director, Social and Political Studies, 1987-, American Enterprise Institute, Washington, DC; Head (with rank of Ambassador), US Delegation, United Nations Human Rights Commission, Geneva, 1981, 1982, Conference on Security and Cooperation in Europe, 1986; Founder-Publisher, 1982-96, Editor-in-Chief, 1993-96, Crisis; Faculty, University of Notre Dame, 1986-87; Columnist, Forbes magazine, 1989-94; Various lectureships. Publications: The Tiber was Silver (novel), 1961; A New Generation, 1964; The Experience of Marriage, 1964; The Open Church, 1964; Belief and Unbelief, 1965, 3rd edition, 1994; A Time to Build, 1967; Vietnam: Crisis of Conscience (with Brown and Herschel), 1967; American Philosophy and the Future, 1968; A Theology for Radical Politics, 1969; Naked I Leave (novel), 1970; The Experience of Nothingness, 1970; Story in Politics, 1970; All the Catholic People, 1971; Ascent of the Mountain, Flight of the Dove, 1971; Politics: Realism and Imagination, 1971; A Book of Elements, 1972; The Rise of the Unmeltable Ethnics, 1972; Choosing Our King, 1974; The Joy of Sports, 1976, revised edition, 1994; The Guns of Littimer, 1978; The American Vision, 1978; Rethinking Human Rights I, 1981, II, 1982; The Spirit of Democratic Capitalism, 1982; Confession of a Catholic, 1983; Moral Clarity in the Nuclear Age, 1983; Freedom with Justice, 1984; Human Rights and the New Realism, 1986; Will It Liberate?: Questions About Liberation Theology, 1986; Character and Crime, 1986; The New Consensus on Family and Welfare, 1987; Taking Glasnost Seriously: Toward an Open Soviet Union, 1988; Free Persons and the Common Good, 1989; This Hemisphere of Liberty, 1990; The Spirit of Democratic Capitalism, 1991; Choosing Presidents, 1992; The Catholic Ethic and the Spirit of Capitalism, 1993; To Empower People: From State to Civil Society, 1996; Business as a Calling, 1996. Contributions to: Numerous publications. Honours: Freedom Award, Coalition for a Democratic Majority, 1979; George Washington Honor Medal, Freedom Foundation, 1984; Award of Excellence, Religion in Media, 1985; Ellis Island Medal of Honor, 1986; Anthony Fisher Prize, 1992; Templeton Prize for Progress in Religion, 1994; International Award, Institution for World Capitalism, Jacksonville University, Florida, 1994; Many honorary doctorates. Memberships: American Academy of Religion; Catholic Theological Society; Council on Foreign Relations; Institute for Religion and Democracy, director, 1981-; National Center of Urban and Ethnic Affairs, director, 1982-86; Society of Christian Ethics; Society of Religion in Higher Education. Address: c/o American Enterprise Institute, 1150 17th Street North West, Washington, DC 20036, USA.

NOVAK Robert. See: **LEVINSON Leonard.**

NOWRA Louis, b. 1950, Melbourne, Victoria, Australia. Playwright. Education: La Trobe University, Victoria. Appointment: Co-Artistic Director, Lighthouse Company, Sydney, 1983. Publications: Albert Names Edward, 1975; Inner Voices, 1977; Visions, 1978; Inside the Island, 1980; The Precious Woman, 1980; The Song Room, 1981; Royal Show, 1982; The Golden Age, 1985; Whitsunday Opera Libretto, 1988; Byzantine Flowers, 1989; Summer of the Aliens, 1989; Cosi, 1992; Radiance, 1993; Crow, 1994. Novels: The Misery of Beauty, 1976; Palu, 1987; Red Nights, 1997. Other: Radio, television and screenplays. Honours: Australian Literature Board Fellowships. Address: Hilary Linstead & Associates, Level 18, Plaza 11, 500 Oxford Street, Bondi Junction, New South Wales 2022, Australia.

NOYE Laurence Richard (Larry), F1)b. 28 July 1928, Melbourne, Australia. Journalist; Retired. Appointments: Staff Journalist, Footscray Mail, 1946-52; Bendigo Advertiser, 1952-55; Geelong Advertiser, 1955-56; Australian United Press, 1958-59; Larnceston Examiner, 1959-60; Hobart Mercury, 1960-64; Western Suburbs Advertiser, 1964-80; Temporary Journalist, ABC, AAP, Depts Transport, Primary Industry, 1981-93. Publications: Articles, Political Insight, The Strategy, newspaper monthly, 1992-96. Memberships: Fellowship of Australian Writers. Address: 92 Simmons Drive, Altona, Vic, Australia.

NOYES Stanley Tinning, b. 7 Apr 1924, San Francisco, California, USA. Teacher; Writer. m. Nancy Black, 12 Mar 1949, 2 sons, 1 daughter. Education: BA, English, 1950, MA, English, 1951, University of California, Berkeley. Appointment: Literary Arts Coordinator, New Mexico Arts Division, 1972-86. Publications: No Flowers for a Clown (novel), 1961; Shadowbox (novel), 1970; Faces and Spirits (poems), 1974; Beyond the Mountains (poems), 1979; The Commander of Dead Leaves (poems), 1984; Los Comanches: The Horse People, 1751-1845, 1993. Contributions to: San Francisco

Review; New Mexico Quarterly; Sumac; Cold Mountain Review; San Marcos Review; Puerto del Sol; Greenfield Review; High Plains Literary Review; Floating Island. Honour: MacDowell Fellow, 1967. Membership: PEN American Center. Literary Agent: Maria Theresa Caen, 2901 Scott Street, San Francisco, CA 94123, USA. Address: 634 East Garcia, Santa Fe, NM 87501, USA.

NOZICK Robert, b. 16 Nov 1938, New York, USA. Professor of Philosophy; Writer. m. Gjertrud Schnackenberg, 5 Oct 1987, 1 son, 1 daughter. Education: AB, Columbia College, 1959; PhD, Princeton University, 1963. Appointments: Assistant Professor, Princeton University, 1964-65; Assistant Professor, 1965-67, Professor, 1969-, Arthur Kingsley Professor of Philosophy, 1985-, Harvard University; Associate Professor, Rockefeller University, 1967-69. Publications: Anarchy, State & Utopia, 1974; Philosophical Explanations, 1981; The Examined Life, 1989; The Nature of Rationality, 1993; Socratic Puzzles, 1997. Honours: National Book Award, 1975; Ralph Waldo Emerson Award, 1982. Memberships: PEN; American Academy of Arts and Sciences; American Philosophical Association; British Academy. Address: Emerson Hall, Harvard University, Cambridge, MA 02138, USA.

NUDELSTEJER Sergio, b. 24 Feb 1924, Warsaw, Poland. Journalist; Writer. m. Tosia Malamud. Education: National University of Mexico. Publications: Theodor Herzl: Prophet of Our Times, 1961; The Rebellion of Silence, 1971; Albert Einstein: A Man in His Time, 1980; Franz Kafka: Conscience of an Era, 1983; Rosario Castellanos: The Voice, the Word, the Memory (anthology), 1984; Borges: Getting Near to His Literary Work, 1987; Elias Canetti: The Language of Passion, 1990; Spies of God: Authors at the End of the Century, 1992; Stefan Zweig: The Conscience of Man, 1992; Everlasting Voices: Latinamerican Writers, 1996; Jerusalem: 3000 Years of History, 1997. Contributions to: Periodicals. Address: Heraclito 331, Apt 601, Poanco 11560, Mexico.

NUGENT Neill, b. 22 Mar 1947, Newcastle-upon-Tyne, England. Professor. m. Maureen Nugent, 12 Sept 1969, 2 daughters. Education: BA, Politics, Social Administration, University of Newcastle, 1969; MA, Government, University of Kent, 1970; London School of Economics, 1970-71. Publications: The British Right (with R King); Respectable Rebels (with R King); The Left in France (with D Lowe); The Government and Politics of the European Union, 1994; The European Business Environment (with R O'Donnell), 1994; The European Union: Annual Review of Activities, 1992, 1993, 1994, 1995. Contributions to: Professional journals and edited books. Memberships: Political Studies Association; University Association for Contemporary European Studies; European Community Studies Association, USA. Address: Department of Politics and Philosophy, Manchester Metropolitan University, Geoffrey Manton Building, Rosamond Street West, Manchester M15 6LA, England.

NULAND Sherwin, b. 8 Dec 1930, New York, New York, USA. Surgeon; Professor; Author. m. Sarah Peterson, 29 May 1977, 2 sons, 2 daughters. Education: BA, New York University, 1951; MD, Yale University, 1955. Appointments: Surgeon, Yale-New Haven Hospital, Connecticut, 1962-91; Clinical Professor of Surgery, Yale School of Medicine, 1962-. Publications: The Origins of Anesthesia, 1983; Doctors: The Biography of Medicine, 1988; Medicine: The Art of Healing, 1991; The Face of Mercy, 1993; How We Die: Reflections on Life's Final Chapter, 1994. Honour: National Book Award for Non-Fiction, 1994. Memberships: American College of Surgeons, fellow; Associates of the Yale Medical School Library, chairman, 1982-94; New England Surgeons Society; Yale-China Association, chairman, 1988-93. Address: 29 Hartford Turnpike, Hamden, CT 06517, USA.

NUNIS Doyce Blackman Jr, b. 30 May 1924, Cedartown, Georgia, USA. Professor of History Emeritus; Writer; Editor. Education: BA, University of California at Los Angeles, 1947; MS, 1950, MEd, 1952, PhD, 1958, University of Southern California at Los Angeles. Appointments: Lecturer, 1951-56, Associate Professor, 1965-68, Professor of History, 1968-89, Professor Emeritus, 1989-, University of Southern California at Los Angeles; Instructor, El Camino College, 1956-59; Assistant Professor, University of California at Los Angeles, 1959-65; Editor, Southern California Quarterly, 1962-. Publications: Andrew Sublette: Rocky Mountain Prince, 1960; Josiah Belden: 1841 California Overland Pioneer, 1962; The Golden Frontier: The Recollections of Herman Francis Rinehart, 1851-69 (editor), 1962; The California Diary of Faxon Dean Atherton, 1836-39 (editor), 1964;

Letters of a Young Miner (editor), 1964; The Journal of James H Bull (editor), 1965; The Trials of Isaac Graham, 1967; The Medical Journey of Pierre Garnier in California, 1851, 1967; Past is Prologue: Centennial Profile of Pacific Mutual Life Insurance Company, 1968; Hudson's Bay Company's First Fur Brigade to the Sacramento Valley: Alexander McLeod's 1829 Hunt, 1968; Sketches of a Journey on Two Oceans by Abbe Henri - J A Alric, 1850-1867 (editor), 1971; San Francisco 1856 Vigilance Committee: Three Views (editor), 1971; The Drawings of Ignatio Tirsh, S J (editor), 1972; Los Angeles and Its Environs in the Twentieth Century: A Bibliography of a Metropolis, 1973; A History of American Political Thought, 2 volumes, 1975; The Mexican War in Baja, California, 1977; Henry F Hoyt's A Frontier Doctor (editor), 1979; Los Angeles From the Days of the Old Pueblo (editor), 1981; The Letters of Jacob Baegert, 1749-1761: Jesuit Missionary in Baja, California (editor), 1982; Transit of Venus: The First Planned Scientific Expedition in Baja, California, 1982; Men, Medicine and Water: The Building of the Los Angeles Acqueduct, 1908-1913, 1982; Frontier Fighter by George W Coe (editor), 1984; Southern California Historical Anthology (editor), 1984; The Life of Tom Horn (editor), 1987; A Guide to the History of California (co-editor), 1988; Great Doctors of Medicine, 1990; The Bidwell- Bartleson Party, 1991; The Life of Tom Horn Revisited, 1992; Southern California's Spanish Heritage, 1992; Southern California Local History: A Gathering of W W Robinson's Writings (editor), 1993; From Mexican Days to the Gold Rush, 1993; Tales of Mexican California (editor), 1994; Women in the Life of Southern California, 1995. Contributions to: Professional journals. Honours: Henry E Huntington Library Grant, 1960; Guggenheim Fellowship, 1963-64; American Philosophical Society Grant, 1969; Papal Medal, 1984; Franciscan History Award, 1990; Distinguished Emeritus Award, Univeristy of Southern California at Los Angeles, 1993; Knight Commander of St Gregory, 1993; Phi Order of Isabel the Catholic (Spain), 1995; Alpha Theta; Pi Sigma Alpha. Memberships: American Antiquarian Society; American Historical Association; California Historical Society, vice-president, 1989-93; Historical Society of Southern California; Organization of American Historians; Western Historical Association. Address: 4426 Cromwell Avenue, Los Angeles, CA 90027-1250, USA.

NUNN Frederick McKinley, b. 29 Oct 1937, Portland, Oregon, USA. Professor of History; Writer. m. (1) Tey Diana Rebolledo, 10 Sept 1960, div 1973, 1 daughter, (2) Susan Karant Boles, 8 Feb 1974, 1 daughter. Education: BA, University of Oregon, 1959; MA, 1963, PhD, 1963, University of New Mexico. Appointments: Assistant Professor, 1965-67, Associate Professor, 1967-72, Professor of History, 1972-, Portland State University, Oregon. Publications: Chilean Politics, 1920-31: The Honorable Mission of the Armed Forces, 1970; The Miltary in Chilean History: Essays on Civil-Miltary Relations, 1810-1973, 1976; Yesterday's Soldiers: European Military Professionalism in South America, 1890-1940, 1983; The Time of the Generals: Latin American Professional Militarism in World Perspective, 1992. Contributions to: Professional journals. Address: c/o Department of History, Portland State University, PO Box 751, Portland, OR 92707, USA.

NUSSBAUM Martha (Craven), b. 6 May 1947, New York, New York, USA. Philosopher; Classicist; Professor; Writer. m. Alan Jeffrey Nussbaum, Aug 1968, div 1987, 1 daughter. Education: BA, New York University, 1969; MA, 1971, PhD, 1973, Harvard University. Appointments: Assistant Professor of Philosophy and Classics, 1975-80, Associate Professor, 1980-83, Harvard University; Visiting Professor, Wellesley College, 1983-84; Associate Professor of Philosophy and Classics, 1984-85, Professor of Philosophy, Classics, and Comparative Literature, 1985-87, David Benedict Professor of Philosophy, Classics, and Comparative Literature, 1987-89, Professor, 1989-95, Brown University; Visiting Fellow, All Souls College, Oxford, 1986-87; Gifford Lecturer, University of Edinburgh, 1993; Visiting Professor of Law, 1994, Professor of Law and Ethics, 1995-, University of Chicago. Publications: Aristotle's De Motu Animalium, 1978; Language and Logic (editor), 1983; The Fragility of Goodness, 1986; Love's Knowledge, 1990; Essays on Aristotle's De Anima (editor with A Rorty), 1992; The Quality of Life (editor with A Sen), 1993; Passions and Perceptions (editor with J Brunschwig), 1993; The Therapy of Desire, 1994; Women, Culture, and Development (editor), 1995. Honours: Guggenheim Fellowship, 1983; Creative Arts Award, Brandeis University, 1990; Spielvogel-Diamondstein Award, 1991. Memberships: Fellow, American Academy of Arts and Sciences; American Philological Association; American Philosophical Association; American Philosophical Society; PEN. Address: c/o Law

School, University of Chicago, 1111 East 60th Street, Chicago, IL 60637, USA.

NUTTALL Jeffrey, b. 8 July 1933, Clitheroe, Lancashire, England. Artist. Div., 5 sons, 1 daughter. Education: Intermediate Examination, Arts and Crafts, Hereford School of Art, 1951; NDD, Painting (Special Level), Bath Academy of Art, Corsham, 1953; ATD, Institute of Education, London University, 1954. Appointments: Sergeant Instructor, Royal Army Education Corps, 1954-56; Art Master, Secondary Modern Schools, Leominster, 1956-59, East Finchley, London, 1956-63, Barnet, 1963-67; English Master, Greenacre Secondary Modern, Great Yarmouth, 1967-68; Lecturer, Foundation Course, Bradford College of Art, 1968-70; Senior Lecturer, Fine Art, Leeds Polytechnic, 1970-81; Head, Fine Art Department, Liverpool Polytechnic, 1981-84; Part-time teaching, 1984-; Occasional broadcasts, London Weekend TV, Granada TV, Yorkshire TV, BBC Radio; Exhibited paintings in numerous exhibitions. Publications: Verse: Objects, 1973; Sun Barbs, 1974; Grape Notes/Apple Music, 1979; Scenes and Dubs, 1987; Mad with Music, 1987. Fiction: The Gold Hole, 1968; Snipe's Spinster, 1973; The Patriarchs, 1975; Anatomy of My Father's Corpse, 1976; What Happened to Jackson, 1977; Muscle, 1980; Teeth, 1994. Non-fiction: King Twist, A Portrait of Frank Randle, 1978; Performance Art, Vol I: Memoirs, 1979, Vol II: Scripts, 1979; The Pleasures of Necessity, 1989; The Bald Soprano, 1989. Graphics: Come Back Sweet Prince, 1965; Oscar Christ and the Immaculate Conception, 1970; The Fox's Lair, 1972. Contributions to: Newspapers and journals. Honours: No 3 Winner, Teeth, Novel in a Day Competition, Groucho Club, 1994. Address: 71 White Hart Lane, Barnes, London SW13 0PP, England.

NUWER Henry (Hank) Joseph, b. 19 Aug 1946, Buffalo, New York, USA. Author. m. (1) Alice Cerniglia, 28 Dec 1968, div 1980, 1 son, (2) Jenine Howard, 9 Apr 1982, 1 son. Education: BS, State University College of New York, Buffalo, 1968; MA, New Mexico Highlands University, 1971; PhD equivalency, Ball State University, 1988. Appointments: Assistant Professor of English, Clemson University, 1982-83; Associate Professor of Journalism, Ball State University, 1985-89; Senior Writer, Rodale Press Book Division, Emmaus, Pennsylvania, 1990-91; Historian, Cedar Crest College, 1991-93; Editor, Arts Indiana Magazine, 1993-95; Visiting Associate, Professional Journalism, University of Richmond, 1995-. Publications: Non-fiction: Come Out, Come Out Wherever You Are (with Carole Shaw), 1982; Strategies of the Great Football Coaches, 1987; Strategies of the Great Baseball Managers, 1988; Rendezvous with Contemporary Authors, 1988; Recruiting in Sports, 1989; Steroids, 1990; Broken Pledges: The Deadly Rite of Hazing, 1990; Sports Scandals, 1994; How To Write Like an Expert, 1995. Fiction: The Bounty Hunter series (with William Boyles), 4 volumes, 1980-82. Editor: Rendezcous at the Ezra Pound Centennial Conference, 1982. Address: Arts Indiana, 47 South Pennsylvania, Suite 701, Indianapolis, IN 46204, USA.

NYE Joseph, b. 19 Jan 1937, South Orange, New Jersey, USA. Professor; Writer. m. Molly Harding, 3 sons. Education: AB, summa cum laude, Princeton University, 1958; BA, Oxford University, 1960; PhD, Harvard University, 1964. Appointments: Instructor, 1964-66, Assistant Professor, 1966-69, Associate Professor, 1969-71, Professor, 1971-, Director, Center for International Affairs, 1989-93, Dean, John F Kennedy School of Government, 1995-, Harvard University; Deputy to Under-Secretary of State for Security Assistance, Science and Technology, 1977-79; Assistant Secretary of Defense for International Security Affairs, 1994-95. Publications: Pan-Africanism and East African Integration, 1965; Peace in Parts: Integration and Conflict in Regional Organization, 1971; Conflict Management by International Organizations, 1972; Power and Independence, 1977; Living with Nuclear Weapons, 1983; The Making of America's Soviet Policy, 1985; Hawks, Doves and Owls (co-author), 1985; Nuclear Ethics, 1986; Bound to Lead: The Changing Nature of American Power, 1990; Global Competition After the Cold War: A Reassessment of Trilateralism (with Kurt Bidenkopf and Motoo Shiina), 1991; After the Storm: Lessons from the Gulf War (editor with Roger L Smith), 1992; Understanding International Conflicts: An Introduction to Theory and History, 1993. Contributions to: Professional journals, magazines and newspapers. Honours: Distinguished Honor Award, US Department of State; Several US Government Distinguished Service Medals. Memberships: American Academy of Arts and Sciences, fellow; Academy of Diplomacy, fellow; Aspen Institute, senior fellow; Executive Committee, Trilateral Commission. Address: c/o John F

Kennedy School of Government, Harvard University, 79 John F Kennedy Street, Cambridge MA 02138, USA.

NYE Robert, b. 15 Mar 1939, London, England. Poet; Novelist; Literary Critic. Appointments: Poetry Editor, The Scotsman, 1967-; Poetry Critic, The Times, London, 1971-. Publications: Juvenilia, 1 (poems), 1961, 2 (poems), 1963; Taliesin (juvenile), 1966; March Has Horse's Ears (juvenile), 1966; Doubtfire (novel), 1967; Beowulf, 1968; Tales I Told My Mother, 1969; Sawney Bean (with Bill Watson), 1969; Sisters, 1969; Darker Ends (poems), 1969; Wishing Gold, 1970; Fugue (screenplay), 1971; Poor Pumpkin, 1971; A Choice of Sir Walter Raleigh's Verse, 1972; The Mathematical Princess and Other Stories, 1972; Cricket, 1972; A Choice of Swinburne's Verse; The Faber Book of Sonnets, 1976; Penthesilia, 1976; Falstaff (novel), 1976; The English Sermon 1750-1850, 1976; Divisions on a Ground (poems), 1976; Out of the World and Back Again (juvenile), 1977; Merlin (novel), 1978; The Bird of the Golden Land, 1980; Faust (novel), 1980; Harry Pay the Pirate (juvenile), 1981; The Voyage of the Destiny (novel), 1982; The Facts of Life and Other Fictions, 1983; Three Tales (for children), 1983; PEN New Poetry 1 (editor), 1986; William Barnes, selected poems (editor), 1988; The Memoirs of Lord Byron (novel), 1989; A Collection of Poems 1955-1988, 1989; The Life and Death of My Lord Gilles de Rais (novel), 1990; First Awakenings: The Early Poems of Laura Riding (editor with Elizabeth Friedmann and Alan J Clark), 1992; Mrs Shakespeare (novel), 1993; A Selection of the Poems of Laura Riding (editor), 1994; 14 Poems, 1994; Spine Chilling Tales (juvenile), 1995; Henry James and Other Poems, 1995; Collected Poems, 1995. Honours: Gregory Award for Poetry, 1963; Guardian Fiction Prize, 1976; Hawthornden Prize, 1977; Travel Scholarship, Society of Authors, 1991. Membership: Royal Society of Literature, fellow, 1976. Address: c/o Sheil Land Associates Ltd, 43 Doughty Street, London WC1N 2LF, England.

NYE Simon Beresford, b. 29 July 1958, Burgess Hill, Sussex, England. Writer. Education: BA, French, German, Bedford College, London University, 1980; Diploma, Technical Translation, Polytechnic of Central London, 1985. Publications: Men Behaving Badly, 1994-97, as situation comedy, 5 series, Thames TV, 1992, BBC, 1994; Wideboy, 1991, as comedy drama series Frank Stubbs Promotes, Carlton TV, Series I, 1993, Series 2, 1994; Situation comedy: Is It Legal?, 2 series on ITV, 1995, 1996; Translator: The Vienna Opera, 1985; Braque, 1986; Matisse: Graphic Works, 1987. Contributions to: Sunday Times; Guardian; Others. Honour: Winner, Best ITV Sitcom, for Men Behaving Badly, ITV Comedy Awards, 1993; Winner, Best Sitcom for "Is It Legal?", 1995; Winner, Best Comedy Series, Men Bahaving Badly, Writers Guild of Great Britain, 1995, and Royal Television Society, 1996; Nominated, International Emmy Award, Best Comedy, for Men Bahaving Badly, 1996. Literary Agent: Rod Hall, A P Watt Ltd, London, England. Address: 55 South Hill Park, London NW3 2SS, England.

NYLUND Anna Kristina, b. 1 Dec 1911, Petalax, Finland. Elementary School Teacher. m. Gunnar Nylund, 25 Aug 1947, 2 daughters. Education: Elementary School Teacher's Examination, 1933. Publications: Sanna, 1978; Sommarens Fotspar, 1981; Dold Visdom Och Gömd Skatt, Petalax Historia I, 1982; Blommis Maj, Petalax Historia II, 1983; Ur Bykiston, 1981. Contributions to: Landhöjning, 1977; Havtorn, 1980; Strandspar, 1989; Ordskott, 1993. Membership: Svenska Österbottens Litteraturförening; Finlands Svenska Författareförening RF. Address: Strandgatan 7B, Fin 65100 Vasa, Finland.

NYLUND Gunnar Isak Georg, b. 2 June 1916, Nykarleby Ytterjeppo, Finland. Elementary School Teacher. m. Anna Nordman Holm, 25 Aug 1947, 2 daughters. Education: Elementary School Teacher's Examination, 1944. Publications: Alla de Dagar, 1978; Såsom Blommor På Röd Jord, 1981; Solvarv, 1982; Oändlighetens Eftermiddag, 1984; Vår by Vid Älven - Ytterjeppo, 1985; Gnistor av Liv, 1987; Sällsamma Samtal, 1994. Contributions to: Anthologies: Landhöjning, 1977; Havtorn, 1980; Strandspår, 1989; Ordskott, 1993. Membership: Svenska Österbottens Litteraturförening; Finlands Svenska Författareförening RF. Address: Strandgatan 7B, Fin 65100 Vasa, Finland.

O

O'BALANCE Edgar, b. 1918. Writer; Journalist. Publications: The Arab-Israeli War, 1956; The Sinai Campaign, 1956; The Story of the French Foreign Legion, 1961; The Red Army of China, 1962; The Indo-China War 1945-1954, 1964; The Red Army of Russia, 1964; The Greek Civil War 1948-1960, 1966; The Algerian Insurrection 1954-1962, 1967; The Third Arab-Israeli War 1967, 1972; The Kurdish Revolt 1961-1970, 1973; Arab Guerilla Power, 1974; The Electronic War in the Middle East 1968-1970, 1974; The Wars in Vietnam 1954-1972, 1975; The Secret War in the Sudan 1955-1972, 1977; No Victor, No Vanquished, 1978; The Language of Violence, 1979; Terror in Ireland, 1979; The Tracks of the Bear, 1982; The Gulf War, 1988; The Cyanide War, 1989; Terrorism in the 1980s, 1989; Wars in Afghanistan: 1839-1990, 1991; The Second Gulf War; The Civil War in Yugoslavia; Civil War in Bosnia: 1992-1994; The Kurdish Struggle: 1920-94, 1995; Islamic Fundamentalist Terrorism, 1996; Wars in the Caucasus: 1990-95, 1996; The Palestinian Intifada, forthcoming. Membership: Former Chairman, Military Commentators Circle. Address: Wakebridge Cottage, Wakebridge, Matlock, Derbyshire, England.

O'BRIAN Geoffrey, b. 4 May 1948, New York, New York, USA. Writer; Poet; Translator. m. Kaalii Francis, 18 March 1977. Education: Yale University; BA, State University of New York at Stony Brook; Nichibei Kaiwa Gaku-in, Tokyo. Appointments: Co-Editor, Pony Tail, 1968-70, Montemora, 1975-76; Editor, Frogpond, 1981; Executive Editor, Library of America. Publications: Selected Poetry of Vincente Huidobro, 1981; Hard Boiled America: The Lurid Years of Paperbacks, 1981; Dream Time: Chapters from the Sixties, 1988; The Book of Maps, 1989. Contributions to: Anthologies and periodicals. Address: c/o W W Norton Co, 500 Fifth Avenue, New York, NY 10110, USA.

O'BRIEN (William) Tim(othy), b. 1 Oct 1946, Austin, Minnesota, USA. Writer. m. Anne O'Brien. Education: BA, Macalester College, 1968; Graduate Studies, Harvard University. Publications: If I Die in a Combat Zone, Box Me Up and Ship Me Home, 1973; Northern Lights, 1975; Going After Cacciato, 1978; The Nuclear Age, 1981; The Things They Carried: A Work of Fiction, 1990; In the Lake of Woods, 1994. Contributions to: Magazines. Honours: O Henry Memorial Awards, 1976, 1978; National Book Award, 1979; Vietnam Veterans of America Award, 1987; Heartland Prize, Chicago Tribune, 1990; Phi Beta Kappa. Address: c/o International Creative Managment, 40 West 57th Street, New York, NY 10019, USA,

O'BRIEN Conor Cruise (Donat O'Donnell), b. 3 Nov 1917, Dublin, Ireland. Writer; Editor. m. (1) Christine Foster, 1939, div 1962, 1 son, 1 daughter, (2) Màire MacEntee, 1962, 1 adopted son, 1 adopted daughter. Education: BA, 1940, PhD, 1953, Trinity College, Dublin. Appointments: Member, Irish diplomatic service, 1944-61; Vice-Chancellor, University of Ghana, 1962-65; Albert Schweitzer Professor of Humanities, New York University, 1965-69; Member, Labour Party, Dublin North-east, Dail, 1969-77, Senate, Republic of Ireland, 1977-79; Visiting Fellow, Nuffield College, Oxford, 1973-75; Minister for Posts and Telegraphs, 1973-77; Pro-Chancellor, University of Dublin, 1973-; Fellow, St Catherine's College, Oxford, 1978-81; Editor-in-Chief, The Observer, 1979-81; Visiting Professor and Montgomery Fellow, Dartmouth College, New Hampshire, USA, 1993-94. Publications: Maria Cross, 1952; Parnell and His Party, 1957; The Shaping of Modern Ireland (editor), 1959; To Katanga and Back, 1962; Conflicting Concepts of the UN, 1964; Writers and Politics, 1965; The United Nations: Sacred Drama, 1967; Murderous Angels (play), 1968; Power and Consciousness, 1969; Conor Cruise O'Brien Introduces Ireland, 1969; Albert Camus, 1969; The Suspecting Glance (with Màire Cruise O'Brien), 1970; A Concise History of Ireland, 1971; States of Ireland, 1972; King Herod Advises (play), 1973; Neighbours: The Ewart-Biggs Memorial Lectures 1978-79, 1980; The Siege: The Saga of Israel and Zionism, 1986; Passion and Cunning, 1988; God Land: Reflections on Religion and Nationalism, 1988; The Great Melody: A Thematic Biography and Commented Anthology of Edmund Burke, 1992; Ancestral Voices, 1994. Honours: Valiant for Truth Media Award, 1979; Honorary doctorates. Memberships: Royal Irish Academy; Royal Society of Literature. Address: Whitewater, Howth Summit, Dublin, Ireland.

O'BRIEN Edna, b. 15 Dec 1936, Tuamgraney, County Clare, Ireland. Author. m. 1954, div 1964, 2 sons. Education: Pharmaceutical College of Ireland. Publications: The Country Girls, 1960, film, 1983; The Lonely Girl, 1962; Girls in Their Married Bliss, 1963; August is a Wicked Month, 1964; Casualties of Peace, 1966; The Love Object, 1968; A Pagan Place, 1970, play, 1971; Night, 1972; A Scandalous Woman (short stories), 1974; Mother Ireland, 1976; Johnny I Hardly Knew You (novel), 1977; Arabian Days, 1977; Mrs Reinhardt and Other Stories, 1978; The Wicked Lady (screenplay), 1981; Virginia (play), 1981; Returning: A Collection of New Tales, 1982; A Christmas Treat, 1982; Home Sweet Home (play), 1984; Stories of Joan of Arc (film), 1984; A Fanatic Heart, Selected Stories, 1985; Flesh and Blood (play), 1987; Madame Bovary (play), 1987; Vanishing Ireland, 1987; The High Road, 1989; Lantern Slides (short stories), 1990; Time and Tide, 1992. Honours: Yorkshire Post Novel Award, 1971; Kingsley Amis Award. Address: c/o Douglas Rae Management, 28 Charing Cross Road, London WC2 0DB, England.

O'BRIEN Stephen. See: **LEVINE Stuart (George).**

O'BRIEN CORDOBA Esteban. See: **LEVINE Stuart.**

O'CASEY Brenda. See. **HAYCRAFT Anna (Margaret).**

O'CONNELL Richard (James), b. 25 Oct 1928, New York, New York, USA. Poet; Educator. Education: BS, Temple University, 1956; MA, Johns Hopkins University, 1957. Publications: Brazilian Happenings, 1966; Terrane, 1967; Epigrams From Martial, 1976; Hudson's Fourth Voyage, 1978; Irish Monastic Poems, 1984; Temple Poems, 1985; Hanging Tough, 1986; Battle Poems, 1987; Selected Epigrams, 1990; New Epigrams from Martial, 1991; The Caliban Poems, 1992; RetroWorlds, 1993; Simulations, 1993; Voyages, 1995. Contributions to: New Yorker; Paris Review; Atlantic Monthly; National Review; Quarterly Review of Literature; Littack; Acumen; Texas Quarterly. Honours: Fulbright Lecturer, University of Brazil, 1960, University of Navarre, Pamplona, Spain, 1962-63; Contemporary Poetry Prize, 1972; Yaddo Foundation Writing Residencies, 1974, 1975. Memberships: American PEN Club; Modern Language Association. Address: 1150 Hillsboro Mile, #815, Hillsboro Beach, FL 33062, USA.

O'CONNOR Patrick, b. 8 Sept 1949, London, England. Writer; Editor. Appointments: Deputy Editor, Harpers and Queen, 1981-86; Contributing Editor, F M R, 1986; Editor-in-Chief, Publications, Metropolitan Opera Guild, 1987-89; Consulting Editor, The New Grove Dictionary of Opera, 1989-91. Publications: Josephine Baker (with B Hammond), 1988; Toulouse-Lautrec: The Nightlife of Paris, 1991; The Amazing Blonde Woman, 1991. Contributions to: Times Literary Supplement; Literary Review; Daily Telegraph; Gramophone; Opera; House and Garden; Music and Letters; Independent. Memberships: National Union of Journalists; PEN. Literary Agent: Deborah Rodgers. Address: c/o Rodgers, Coleridge and White, 20 Powis Mews, London W11 1JN, England.

O'CONNOR Robert Patrick. See: **PATRICK Robert.**

O'DONNELL Donat. See: **O'BRIEN Conor Cruise.**

O'DONNELL K M. See: **MALZBERG Barry.**

O'DONNELL M R. See: **ROSS-MACDONALD Malcolm John.**

O'DONNELL Michael, b. 20 Oct 1928. Author; Broadcaster. m. Catherine Dorrington Ward, 1953, 1 son, 2 daughters. Education: MBBChir, St Thomas' Hospital Medical School, London, England. Appointments: Editor, Cambridge Writing, 1948, World Medicine, 1966-82; Scriptwriter, BBC Radio, 1949-52; General Medical Practitioner, 1954-64. Publications: O Lucky Man, 1972; Inside Cambridge Anthology, 1952; The Europe We Want, 1971; My Medical School, 1978; The Devil's Prison, 1982; Doctor! Doctor! An Insider's Guide to the Games Doctors Play, 1986; The Long Walk Home, 1988; Dr Michael O'Donnell's Executive Health Guide, 1988. Other: Television plays and documentaries; Radio scripts. Contributions to: Punch; New Scientist; Vogue; Times; Sunday Times; Daily Telegraph; Daily Mail; Listener. Literary Agent: A P Watt. Address: Handon Cottage, Markwick Lane, Loxhill, Godalming, Surrey GU8 4BD, England.

O'DONNELL Peter, (Madeleine Brent), b. 11 Apr 1920, London, England. Author. Education: Catford Central School, London. Appointments: Writer of Strip Cartoons, Garth, 1953-66, Tug Transom, 1964-66, Romeo Brown, 1956-62, Modesty Blaise, 1963-. Publications: Modesty Blaise, 1965; Sabre-Tooth, 1966; I, Lucifer, 1967; A Taste for Death, 1969; The Impossible Virgin, 1971; Pieces of Modesty (short stories), 1972; The Silver Mistress, 1973; Murder Most Logical (play), 1974; Last Day in Limbo, 1976; Dragon's Claw, 1978; The Xanadu Talisman, 1981; The Night of Morningstar, 1982; Dead Man's Handle, 1985; Cobra Trap, 1996. As Madeleine Brent: Tregaron's Daughter, 1971; Moonraker's Bride, 1973; Kirkby's Changeling, 1975; Merlin's Keep, 1977; The Capricorn Stone, 1979; The Long Masquerade, 1981; A Heritage of Shadows, 1983; Stormswift, 1984; Golden Urchin, 1986. Address: 49 Sussex Square, Brighton BN2 1GE, England.

O'DONOVAN Joan Mary, b. 31 Dec 1914, Mansfield, England. Retired. Appointment: Former General Advisor for Education, Oxfordshire, retired 1977. Publications: Dangerous Worlds, 1958; The Visited, 1959; Shadows on the Wall, 1960; The Middle Tree, 1961; The Niceties of Life, 1964; She, Alas, 1965; Little Brown Jesus, 1970; Argument with an East Wind, 1986. Contributions to: Times Educational Supplement; Guardian; Punch; Vogue; Harper's and Queen. Memberships: Society of Authors; International PEN. Address: 14 Rue du Four, 24600 Ribérac, France.

O'DRISCOLL Dennis, b. 1 Jan 1954, Thurles, County Tipperary, Ireland. Editor: Poet. m. Julie O'Callaghan, 1985. Education: University College Dublin, 1972-75. Appointments: Literary Organiser, Dublin Arts Festival, 1977-79; Editor, Poetry Ireland Review, 1986-87. Publications: Kist, 1982; Hidden Extras, 1987. Co Editor, The First Ten Years: Dublin Arts Festival Poetry, 1979. Honour: Irish Arts Council Bursary. Address: Ketu, Breffni Gate, Church Road, Dalkey, County Dublin, Ireland.

O'FAOLAIN Julia, b. 6 June 1932, London, England. Writer. m. Lauro Rene Martines, 14 Dec 1957, 1 son. Education: BA, 1952, MA, 1953, University College, Dublin; University of Rome, 1952-53; Sorbonne, Paris, 1953-55. Publications: We Might See Sights! and Other Stories, 1968; Godded and Codded, 1970; Not in God's Image: Women in History from the Greeks to the Victorians (editor with Lauro Rene Martines), 1973; Man in the Cellar, 1974; Women in the Wall, 1975; No Country for Young Men, 1980; Daughters of Passion, 1982; The Obedient Wife, 1982; The Irish Signorina, 1984; The Judas Cloth, 1992. Contributions to: Newspapers and magazines. Membership: Society of Authors. Address: c/o Deborah Rogers Ltd, 20 Powis Mews, London W11 1JN, England.

O'FARRELL Patrick James, b. 17 Sept 1933, Greymouth, New Zealand. Professor of History. m. Deirdre Genevieve MacShane, 29 Dec 1956, 3 sons, 2 daughters. Education: MA, University of New Zealand, 1956; PhD, Australian National University, 1961. Appointments: Professor, School of History, University of New South Wales, Australia. Publications: The Catholic Church in Australia: A Short History, 1968; Documents in Australian Catholic History, 2 volumes, 1969; Harry Holland: Militant Socialist, 1969; Ireland's English Question, 1971; England and Ireland since 1800, 1975; Letters from Irish Australia, 1984; The Catholic Church and Community: An Australian History, 1985; The Irish in Australia, 1986; Vanished Kingdoms: Irish in Australia and New Zealand, 1990; Through Irish Eyes: Australian and New Zealand Images of the Irish, 1788-1948, 1994. Contributions to: Historical, literary and religious journals. Honour: New South Wales Premier's Literary Award, 1987. Memberships: Australian Society of Authors; Australian Academy of the Humanities, fellow. Address: School of History, University of New South Wales, Sydney 2052, New South Wales, Australia.

O'FLAHERTY Patrick Augustine, b. 6 Oct 1939, Long Beach, Newfoundland, Canada. Professor; Writer. 3 sons. Education: BA (Hons); MA; PhD. Publications: The Rock Observed, 1979; Part of the Main: An Illustrated History of Newfoundland and Labrador (with Peter Neary), 1983; Summer of the Greater Yellowlegs, 1987; Priest of God, 1989; A Small Place in the Sun, 1989; By Great Waters (with Peter Neary); Come Near at Your Peril: A Visitor's Guide to the Island of Newfoundland, 1992, revised edition, 1994; Benny's Island, 1994. Contributions to: Weekend Magazine; Saturday Night; Canadian Forum; Queen's Quarterly; Globe and Mail; Ottawa Citizen; others. Membership: Writers Union of Canada. Address: Box 2676, St Johns, Newfoundland A1C 6K1, Canada.

O'GRADY Desmond James Bernard, b. 27 Aug 1935, Limerick, Ireland. Poet; Writer; Translator. 1 son, 2 daughters. Education: MA, 1964, PhD, 1982, Harvard University. Appointments: Secondary School Teacher, University Professor, 1955-82. Publications: Chords and Orchestrations, 1956; Reilly, 1961; Professor Kelleher and the Charles River, 1964; Separazioni, 1965; The Dark Edge of Europe, 1967; The Dying Gaul, 1968; Off Licence (translator), 1968; Hellas, 1971; Separations, 1973; Stations, 1976; Sing Me Creation, 1977; The Gododdin (translator), 1977; A Limerick Rake (translator), 1978; The Headgear of the Tribe, 1979; His Skaldcrane's Nest, 1979; Grecian Glances (translator), 1981; Alexandria Notebook, 1989; The Seven Arab Odes (translator), 1990; Tipperary, 1991; Ten Modern Arab Poets (translator), 1992; My Fields This Springtime, 1993; Alternative Manners (translator), 1993; Trawling Tradition: Collected Translations, 1954-1994, 1994; Il Galata Morente, 1996; The Road Taken: Poems, 1956-96, 1996. Prose Memoirs: Ezra Pound, Patrick Kavanagh, Samuel Beckett, Olga Rudge, Anna Akhmatova. Essays: On poetry, poets, translating poetry. Contributions to: Anthologies and magazines. Memberships: Ireland's Aosdána of Literature and the Arts. Address: Ardback, Kinsdale, County Cork, Ireland.

O'GRADY Tom, b. 26 Aug 1943. Teacher; Poet; Vintner. Education: BA, University of Baltimore, 1966; MA, Johns Hopkins University, 1967; Advanced Studies of English and American Literature, University of Delaware, 1972-74. Appointments: Lecturer in English, Johns Hopkins University, 1966-67; Catonsville College, 1969-71, University of Delaware, 1972-74, Hampden-Sydney College, 1974-76; Adjunct Professor of English, Poet-in-Residence, Hampden-Sydney College, 1976-. Publications: Establishing a Vineyard (sonnet sequence), 1977; Photographs, 1980; The Farmville Elegies, 1981; In the Room of the Just Born (poems), 1989; The Hampden-Sydney Poetry Anthology (editor), 1990; Carvings of the Moon, A Cycle of Poems, 1991; Shaking the Tree: A Book of Works and Days, 1993; Sun, Moon and Stars (Poems), 1996; The Gardens of November (Full-length Play), 1996; Tubes: 3 One-Act Plays, 1997. Contributions to: Newsletters; Dryad; Enoch; Scene; Pyx; Nimrod; New Laurel Review. Address: PO Box 126, Hampden-Sydney, VA 23943, USA.

O'HEHIR Diana, b. 23 May 1922, USA. Writer; Professor of English. Div, 2 sons. Education: MA, Aesthetics of Literature, 1957; PhD, Humanities, 1970, Johns Hopkins University. Publications: Novels: I Wish This War Were Over, 1984; The Bride Who Ran Away, 1988. Poetry: Summoned, 1976; The Power to Change Geography, 1979; Home Free, 1988. Honours: Devins Award for Poetry, 1974; Helen Bullis Poetry Award, 1977; Di Castagnola Award in Poetry, 1981; Guggenheim Fellowship, 1984; National Endowment for the Humanities Fellowship in Fiction, 1984. Memberships: Poetry Society of America; Modern Language Association; Authors Guild; Poets and Writers. Literary Agent: Ellen Levine. Address: English Department, Mills College, Oakland, CA 94613, USA.

O'LEARY Liam, b. 25 Sept 1910, Youghal, County Cork, Eire. Film Historian. Education: University College, Dublin. Appointments: Editorial Staff, Ireland Today, 1936-37. Publications: Invitation to the Film, 1945; The Silent Cinema, 1965; Rex Ingram, Master of the Silent Cinema, 1980; International Dictionary of Films and Filmmakers, 1985; Cinema Ireland: A History. Contributions to: Ireland Today, Film Critic; Irish Times; Films and Filming; Kosmorama; The Leader; Irish Press; Envoy; The Bell. Honours: Medal for services in film section, Brussels International Film Fair, 1958; Medal for contribution to Irish Film Industry, National Film Studios of Ireland. Address: The Garden Flat, 2 Otranto Place, Sandycove, County Dublin, Ireland.

O'LEARY Rosemary, b. 26 Jan 1955, Kansas City, Missouri, USA. Professor; Author; Writer. m. Larry Schroeder, 8 July 1989, 1 daughter. Education: BA, English Literature, 1978, MPA, Public Administration, 1982, JD, Law, 1981, University of Kansas; PhD, Public Administration, Maxwell School of Citizenship & Public Affairs, Syracuse University, New York, 1988. Publications: Emergency Planning: Local Government and the Community Right to Know Act, 1993; Environmental Change: Federal Courts and the EPA, 1993, 1995; Public Administration and Law, 2nd edition, 1996. Contributions to: Handbook of Public Administration; ICMA Municipal Yearbook; Environmental Law and Policy in the European Union and the United States; Globalization and Decentralization; Public Administration Review; Publius; The Handbook of Public Law and Public Administration. Honours: State of Kansas Board of Regents Merit Scholarship, 1973; Justice Donnan Stephenson American Judicature

Society Award for Leadership, 1980, 1981; American Bar Association Award for Excellence, 1981; Syracuse University Graduate Student Scholar, 1985-87; James C Webb Award, 1990; Professor of the Year Award, 1990-91; Lilly Foundation Award, 1992; William E Mosher and Frederick C Mosher Award, 1992; Daniel Patrick Moynihan Award, 1993; Undergraduate Core Teaching Award, 1996; Distinguished Service Award, 1996; Excellence in Teaching Award, 1996. Address: School of Public and Environmental Affairs, Indiana University, Bloomington, IN 47505, USA.

O'MALLEY Mary, b. 19 Mar 1941, Bushey, Hertfordshire, England. Playwright. Appointments: Resident Writer, Royal Court Theatre, 1977. Publications: Superscum, 1972; A 'Nevolent Society, 1974; Oh If Ever a Man Suffered, 1975; Once a Catholic, 1977; Look out, Here Comes Trouble, 1978; Talk of the Devil, 1986. Honour: Evening Standard Award, 1978. Address: Knockeven, Cliffs of Moher, County Clare, Ireland.

O'NEILL Michael Stephen Charles, b. 2 Sept 1953, Aldershot, England. Reader in English. m. Rosemary Ann McKendrick, 1977, 1 son, 1 daughter. Education: Exeter College, Oxford, 1972-75; BA (Hons), Class I, English, 1975; MA (Oxon), 1981; DPhil (Oxon), 1981. Appointments: Co-Founder, Editor, Poetry Durham, 1982-94; Former Reader in English, now Professor, 1995-, University of Durham. Publications: The Human Mind's Imaginings: Conflict and Achievement in Shelley's Poetry, 1989; Percy Bysshe Shelley: A Literary Life, 1989; The Stripped Bed (poems), 1990; Auden, MacNeice, Spender: The Thirties Poetry (with Gareth Reeves), 1992; Shelley Special Issue, Durham University Journal, 1993; Shelley (critical reader, editor), 1993; The 'Defence of Poetry' Fair Copies, 1994; Keats: Bicentenary Reader, editor, 1997; Fair Copies of Shelley's Manuscripts, co-editor with Donald H Reiman, 1997; Romanticism and the Self-Conscious Poem, forthcoming. Honours: Eric Gregory Award, 1983; Cholmondeley Award, 1990. Address: Department of English, University of Durham, Durham DH1 3JT, England.

O'NEILL Patrick Geoffrey, b. 9 Aug 1924, London, England. Professor of Japanese Emeritus; Writer. m. Diana Howard, 1951, 1 daughter. Education: BA, 1949, PhD, 1957, School of Oriental and African Studies, University of London. Appointments: Lecturer in Japanese, 1949-68, Professor of Japanese, 1968-86, Professor Emeritus, 1986-, School of Oriental and African Studies, University of London. Publications: A Guide to No, 1954; Early No Drama, 1958; Introduction to Written Japanese (with S Yanada), 1963; A Programmed Course on Respect Language in Modern Japanese, 1966; Japanese Kana Workbook, 1967; A Programmed Introduction to Literary-style Japanese, 1968; Japanese Names, 1972; Essential Kanji: 2000 Japanese Characters, 1973; Tradition and Modern Japan (editor), 1982; A Dictionary of Japanese Buddhist Terms (editor with H Inagaki), 1984; A Reader of Handwritten Japanese, 1984; T Kawatake: Japan on Stage (translator), 1990; Annotated plate supplement in H Plutschow: Matsuri - The Festivals of Japan, 1996. Address: 44 Vine Road, East Molesey, Surrey KT8 9LF, England.

O'NEILL Paul, b. 26 Oct 1928, St John's, Newfoundland, Canada. Author. Education: National Academy of Theatre Arts, New York. Publications: Spindrift and Morning Light, 1968; The City in Your Pocket, 1974; The Oldest City, 1975; Seaport Legacy, 1976; Legends of a Lost Tribe, 1976; Breakers, 1982; The Seat Imperial, 1983; A Sound of Seagulls, 1984; Upon This Rock, 1984. Other: Radio and Stage plays; TV and film scripts. Contributions to: Many periodicals. Honours: Literary Heritage Award, Newfoundland Historical Society; Robert Weaver Award, National Radio Producers Association of Canada, 1986; Honorary Doctor of Laws, Memorial University of Newfoundland, 1988; Order of Canada, 1990; Newfoundland and Labrador Arts Hall of Honour, 1991; Canada Commemorative Medal, 1992. Memberships: Canadian Authors Association; Canadian Radio Producers Association; Newfoundland and Labrador Arts Council, chairman, 1988-89; Newfoundland Writers Guild; Writers Union of Canada. Address: 115 Rennies Mill Road, St John's, Newfoundland, A1B 2P2, Canada.

O'ROURKE Andrew Patrick, b. 26 Oct 1933, Plainfield, New Jersey, USA. County Executive; Writer. Separated, 1986, 1 son, 2 daughters. Education: BA, Fordham College, 1954; JD, Fordham Law School, 1962; LLM, New York University Graduate Law School, 1965. Publications: Red Banner Mutiny, 1986; Hawkwood, 1989. Contributions to: Bar journals and digests; The Proceedings of the Naval Institute; Journal of Ancient and Medieval Studies. Honours:

Honorary DHL, Mercy College, 1984; Honorary LLD, Manhattanville College, 1986; Honorary JD, Pace University, 1988. Address: 148 Martine Avenue, White Plains, NY 10601, USA.

O'SULLIVAN Vincent (Gerard), b. 28 Sept 1937, Auckland, New Zealand. Editor; Poet. Education: MA, University of Auckland, 1959; B Litt, Lincoln College, Oxford, 1962. Appointments: Visiting Fellow, Yale University, New Haven; Writer-in-Residence, University of Virginia. Publications: Our Burning Time, 1965; Revenants, 1969; Bearings, 1973; From the Indian Funeral, 1976; Brother Jonathan, Brother Kafka, 1980; The Rose Ballroom and Other Poems, 1982; The Butcher Papers, 1982; The Pilate Tapes, 1986. Plays: Shuriken, 1985; Jones and Jones, 1989. Fiction: Miracle: A Romance, 1976; The Boy, the Bridge, the River, 1978; Dandy Edison for Lunch and Other Stories, 1981. Non-Fiction: New Zealand Poetry in the Sixties, 1973; Katherine Mansfield's New Zealand, 1974; Editions of New Zealand Literature. Honour: New Zealand Book Award, 1981. Address: c/o John McIndoe Ltd, 51 Crawford Street, PO Box 694, Dunedin, New Zealand.

O'TOOLE James (Joseph), b. 15 Apr 1945, San Francisco, California, USA. Business Educator; Writer. m. Marilyn Louise Burrill, 17 June 1967, 2 children. Education: BA, University of Southern California at Los Angeles, 1966; DPhil, Oxford University, 1970. Appointments: Director, Twenty Year Forecast Project, Center for Futures Research, 1973-81; University Professor of Management, 1980-; Host, Why in the World Television Programmes, 1981, 1983; Executive Director, The Leadership Institute, 1991; Senior Fellow, Aspen Institute, Colorado, 1994. Publications: Work, Learning and the American Future, 1977; Tenure (with others), 1979; Making America Work, 1981; Working: Changes and Choices (editor), 1981; Vanguard Management: Redesigning the Corporate Future, 1985; The Executive's Compass: Business and the Good Society, 1993. Address: 19912 Pacific Coast Highway, Malibu, CA 90265, USA.

OAKES John Bertram, b. 23 Apr 1913, Elkins Park, Pennsylvania, USA. Journalist. m. Margery C Hartman, 1945, 1 son, 3 daughters. Education: Princeton University; Queen's College, Oxford; AM; ILD. Appointments: Reporter, Trenton Times, 1936-37; Political Reporter, Washington Post, 1937-41; Editor, Review of The Week, Sunday New York Times, 1946-49; Editorial Board, 1949-61, Editorial Page Editor, 1961-76, Senior Editor, 1977-78, Contributing Columnist, 1977-90, New York Times. Publication: The Edge of Freedom, 1961. Contributions to : Essays Today, 1955; Foundations of Freedom, 1958; Tomorrow's American, 1977; On The Vineyard, 1980; The March to War, 1991; Cast a Cold Eye, 1991. Address: 1120 Fifth Avenue, New York, NY 10128, USA.

OAKES Philip, b. 31 Jan 1928, Burslem, Staffordshire, England. Author; Poet. Appointments: Scriptwriter, Granada TV and BBC, London, 1958-62; Film Critic, The Sunday Telegraph, London, 1963-65; Assistant Editor, Sunday Times Magazine, 1965-67; Arts Columnist, Sunday Times, London, 1969-80. Publications: Unlucky Jonah: Twenty Poems, 1954; The Punch and Judy Man (with Tony Hancock), screenplay, 1962; Exactly What We Want (novel), 1962; In the Affirmative (poems), 1968; The God Botherers, US edition as Miracles: Genuine Cases Contact Box 340 (novel), 1969; Married/Singular (poems), 1973; Experiment at Proto (novel), 1973; Tony Hancock: A Biography, 1975; The Entertainers (editor), 1975; A Cast of Thousands (novel), 1976; The Film Addict's Archive, 1977; From Middle England (memoirs), 1980; Dwellers All in Time and Space (memoirs), 1982; Selected Poems, 1982; At the Jazz Band Ball: A Memory of the 1950's, 1983; Shopping for Women (novel), 1994. Address: Fairfax Cottage, North Owersby, Lincolnshire LN8 3PX, England.

OAKLEY Ann (Rosamund), b. 17 Jan 1944, London, England. Professor of Sociology and Social Policy; Writer. 1 son, 2 daughters. Education: MA, Somerville College, Oxford, 1965; PhD, Bedford College, London, 1974. Appointments: Research Officer, Social Research Unit, Bedford College, London, 1974-79; Wellcome Research Fellow, Radcliffe Infirmary, National Perinatal Epidemiology Unit, Oxford, 1980-83; Deputy Director, Thomas Coram Research Unit, 1985-90, Director, Social Science Research Unit, 1990-, Professor of Sociology and Social Policy, 1991-, University of London. Publications: Sex, Gender and Society, 1972; The Sociology of Housework, 1974; Housewife, 1974, US edition as Women's Work: A History of the Housewife, 1975; The Rights and Wrongs of Women (editor with Juliet Mitchell), 1976; Becoming a Mother, 1980; Women Confined, 1980, Subject Women, 1981; Miscarriage (with A McPherson and H

Roberts), 1984; Taking It Like a Woman, 1984; Telling the Truth about Jerusalem, 1986; What Is Feminism (editor with Juliet Mitchell), 1986; The Men's Room, 1988; Only Angels Forget, 1990; Matilda's Mistake, 1990; Helpers in Childbirth: Midwifery Today (with S Houd), 1990; The Secret Lives of Eleanor Jenkinson, 1992; Social Support and Motherhood: The Natural History of a Research Project, 1992; Essays on Women, Medicine and Health, 1992; Scenes Originating in the Garden of Eden, 1993; Young People, Health and Family Life (with J Brennen, K Dodd and P Storey), 1994; The Politics of the Welfare State (editor with S Williams), 1994. Contributions to: Professional journals. Address: c/o Tessa Sayle Ltd, 11 Jubilee Place, London SW3, England.

OAKLEY Graham, b. 27 Aug 1929, Shrewsbury, England. Children's Writer. Education: Warrington Art School, 1950. Appointments: Scenic artist, theatres and Royal Opera House, London; Designer, BBC-TV, 1962-77. Publications: Church Mice series, 1972-87; Graham Oakley's Magical Changes, 1980; Once Upon a Time: A Prince's Fantastic Journey, 1990. Address: c/o Macmillan Children's Books, 4 Little Essex Street, London WC2R 3LF, England.

OANDASAN William Cortes, b. 17 Jan 1947, Santa Rosa, California, USA. Poet; Educator. m. 28 Oct 1973, 2 daughters. Education: BA, 1974; MA, 1981; MFA, 1984; Instructor Credential, 1989. Appointments: Editor, A Publications, 1976-; Senior Editor, American Indian Culture and Research Journal, University of California, Los Angeles, 1981-86; Instructor, English Department, University of Orleans, Louisiana State University, 1988-90. Publications: Moving Inland, 1983; Round Valley Songs, 1984; Summer Night, 1989; The Way to Rainy Mountain: Internal and External Structures, in Approaches to Teaching World Literature, 1988; Poetry in Harper's Anthology of 20th Century Native American Poetry, 1988. Contributions to: Colorado Review; Southern California Anthology; California Courier; American Indian Culture and Research Journal. Honours: Publishing Grant, National Endowment for the Arts, 1977; American Book Award, 1985; Summer Scholar Award for Writers, 1989; Research Council Grant, 1989. Memberships: Associated Writing Programs; A Writers Circle; Modern Language Association; Society for the Study of Multi-Ethnic Literatures; Association for the Study of American Indian Literatures; National Association on Ethnic Studies; Philological Society of the Pacific Coast. Address: 3832 West Avenue 43, No 13, Los Angeles, CA 90041, USA.

OATES Joyce Carol, b. 16 June 1938, Millersport, New York, USA. Author; Dramatist; Poet; Professor; Publisher. m. Raymond Joseph Smith, 23 Jan 1961. Education: BA, Syracuse University, 1960; MA, University of Wisconsin at Madison, 1961. Appointments: Instructor, 1961-65, Assistant Professor, 1965-67, University of Detroit; Faculty, Department of English, University of Windsor, Ontario, Canada, 1967-78; Co-Publisher (with Raymond Joseph Smith), Ontario Review, 1974-; Writer-in-Residence, 1978-81, Professor, 1987-, Princeton University. Publications: Fiction: With Shuddering Fall, 1964; A Garden of Earthly Delights, 1967; Expensive People, 1968; Them, 1969; Wonderland, 1971; Do With Me What You Will, 1973; The Assassins: A Book of Hours, 1975; Childwold, 1976; Son of the Morning, 1978; Unholy Loves, 1979; Cybele, 1979; Angel of Light, 1981; Bellefleur, 1980; A Bloodsmoor Romance, 1982; Mysteries of Winterthurn, 1984; Solstice, 1985; Marya: A Life, 1986; You Must Remember This, 1987; Lives of the Twins, 1987; Soul-Mate, 1989; American Appetites, 1989; Because It Is Bitter, and Because It Is My Heart, 1990; Snake Eyes, 1992; Black Water, 1992; Foxfire, 1993; What I Lived For, 1994; Zombie, 1995; You Can't Catch Me, 1995; First Love: A Gothic Tale, 1996. Stories: By the North Gate, 1963; Upon the Sweeping Flood and Other Stories, 1966; The Wheel of Love, 1970; Cupid and Psyche, 1970; Marriages and Infidelities, 1972; A Posthumous Sketch, 1973; The Girl, 1974; Plagiarized Material, 1974; The Goddess and Other Women, 1974; Where Are You Going, Where Have You Been?: Stories of Young America, 1974; The Hungry Ghosts: Seven Allusive Comedies, 1974; The Seduction and Other Stories, 1975; The Poisoned Kiss and Other Stories from the Portuguese, 1975; The Triumph of the Spider Monkey, 1976; Crossing the Border, 1976; Night-Side, 1977; The Step-Father, 1978; All the Good People I've Left Behind, 1979; Queen of the Night, 1979; The Lamb of Abyssalia, 1979; A Middle-Class Education, 1980; A Sentimental Education, 1980; Last Day, 1984; Wild Saturday and Other Stories, 1984; Wild Nights, 1985; Raven's Wing, 1986; The Assignation, 1988; Heat and Other Stories, 1991; Where Is Here?, 1992; Haunted Tales of the Grotesque, 1994. Plays: Three Plays:

Ontological Proof of My Existence, Miracle Play, The Triumph of the Spider Monkey, 1980; Twelve Plays, 1991; The Perfectionist and Other Plays, 1995. Poetry: Women in Love and Other Poems, 1968; Anonymous Sins and Other Poems, 1969; Love and Its Derangements, 1970; Wooded Forms, 1972; Angel Fire, 1973; Dreaming America and Other Poems, 1973; The Fabulous Beasts, 1975; Seasons of Peril, 1977; Women Whose Lives Are Food, Men Whose Lives Are Money, 1978; Celestial Timepiece, 1980; Nightless Nights: Nine Poems, 1981; Invisible Women: New and Selected Poems 1970-1982, 1982; Luxury of Sin, 1984; The Time Traveller: Poems 1983-1989, 1989. Other: The Edge of Impossibility: Tragic Forms in Literature, 1972; The Hostile Sun: The Poetry of D H Lawrence, 1973; New Heaven, New Earth: The Visionary Experience in Literature, 1974; The Stone Orchard, 1980; Contraries: Essays, 1981; The Profane Art: Essays and Reviews, 1983; Funland, 1983; On Boxing, 1987, expanded edition, 1994; (Woman) Writer: Occasions and Opportunities, 1988. Editor: Scenes from American Life: Contemporary Short Fiction, 1973; The Best American Short Stories 1979 (with Shannon Ravenel), 1979; Night Walks: A Bedside Companion, 1982; First Person Singular: Writers on Their Craft, 1983; Story: Fictions Past and Present (with Boyd Litzinger), 1985; Reading the Fights (with Daniel Halpern), 1988. Honours: National Endowment for the Arts Grants, 1966, 1968; Guggenheim Fellowship, 1967; O Henry Awards, 1967, 1973, and Special Awards for Continuing Achievement, 1970, 1986; Rosenthal Award, 1968; National Book Award, 1970; Rea Award, 1990; Heideman Award, 1990; Bobst Lifetime Achievement Award, 1990; Walt Whitman Award, 1995. Membership: American Academy of Arts and Letters. Address: 185 Nassau Street, Princeton, NJ 08540, USA.

OATES Stephen B(aery), b. 5 Jan 1936, Pampa, Texas, USA. Professor; Writer. m. (1), 1 son, 1 daughter, (2) Marie Philips. Education: BA, 1958, MA, 1960, PhD, 1969, University of Texas at Austin. Appointments: Instructor, 1964-67, Assistant Professor, 1967-68, Arlington State College; Assistant Professor, 1968-70, Associate Professor, 1970-71, Professor of History, 1971-80, Adjunct Professor of English, 1980-85, Paul Murray Kendall Professor of Biography, 1985-, University of Massachusetts at Amherst; Various guest lectureships. Publications: Confederate Cavalry West of the River, 1961; John Salmon Ford: Rip Ford's Texas (editor), 1963; The Republic of Texas (general editor), 1968; Visions of Glory, Texas on the Southwestern Frontier, 1970; To Purge This Land with Blood: A Biography of John Brown, 1970, 2nd edition, revised, 1984; Portrait of America (editor): Vol I, From the European Discovery to the End of Reconstruction, Vol II, From Reconstruction to the Present, 1973, 6th edition, 1994; The Fires of Jubilee: Nat Turner's Fierce Rebellion, 1975; With Malice Toward None: The Life of Abraham Lincoln, 1977; Our Fiery Trial: Abraham Lincoln, John Brown, and the Civil War Era, 1979; Let the Trumpet Sound: The Life of Martin Luther King, Jr, 1982; Abraham Lincoln: The Man Behind the Myths, 1984; Biography as High Adventure: Life-Writers Speak on Their Art (edior), 1986; William Faulkner: The Man and the Artist, a Biography, 1987; A Woman of Valor: Clara Barton and the Civil War, 1994; The Approaching Fury: Voices of the Storm, 1820-1861, 1997. Contributions to: Professional journals. Honours: Texas State Historical Association Fellow, 1968; Texas Institute of Letters Fellow, 1969; Guggenheim Fellowship, 1972; Christopher Awards, 1977, 1982; Barondess/Lincoln Award, New York Civil War Round Table, 1978; National Endowment for the Humanities Fellow, 1978; Robert F Kennedy Memorial Book Award, 1983; Institute for Advanced Studies in the Humanities Fellow, 1984; Kidger Award, New England History Teachers Association, 1992; Nevins-Freeman Award, Chicago Civil War Round Table, 1993; Phi Beta Kappa. Memberships: American Antiquarian Society; Society of American Historians; Texas Institute of Letters. Address: 10 Bridle Path, Amherst, MA 01002, USA.

OBARSKI Marek, b. 2 July 1947, Poznan, Poland. Writer; Poet; Critic; Editor; Translator. m. Aleksandra Zaworska, 27 Mar 1982, 2 sons, 2 daughters. Appointments: Director, Flowering Grass Theatre, 1974-79, Literary Department, Nurt magazine, 1985-90; Critic, Art for Child magazine, 1989-90; Editor, 1991-93, Translator, 1993-, Rebis Publishing House; Editor, Europe, 1992-94. Publications: 10 volumes, 1969-97. Contributions to: Journals and magazines. Honours: Medal of Young Artists, 1984; Stanislaw Pietak Award, 1985. Memberships: Ecologic Association of Creators; Union de Gens de Lettres Polonaises. Address: os Wl Lokietka 13 F m 58, 61-616 Poznan, Poland.

OBERG Leon Erik, b. 5 Jan 1944, Goulborn, New South Wales, Australia. Newspaper Editor. m. Tricia Noakes, 14 Oct 1967, 2 sons, 2 daughters. Publications: Locomotives of Australia, 1975, 3rd edition, 1996; Diesel Locomotives of Australia, 1980; Trains, 1984; Motive Power, 1995; Australian Rail at Work, 1995. Contributions to: Magazines.Memberships: Australian Media Arts; Australian Entertainment Alliance. Address: 102 Taralga Road, Bradfordville, New South Wales, Australia.

OBSTFELD Raymond, (Pike Bishop, Jason Frost, Don Pendleton, Carl Stevens), b. 22 Jan 1952, Williamsport, Pennsylvania, USA. Assistant Professor of English; Wrier; Poet; Dramatist; Screenwriter. Education: BA, Johnston College, University of Redlands, 1972; MA, University of California at Davis, 1976. Appointments: Lecturer to Assistant Professor of English, Orange Coast College, 1976-. Publications: Fiction: The Golden Fleece, 1979; Dead-End Option, 1980; Dead Heat, 1981; Dead Bolt, 1982; The Remington Factor, 1985; Masked Dog, 1986; Redtooth, 1987; Brainchild, 1987; The Whippin Boy, 1988. As Pike Bishop: Diamondback, 1983; Judgement at Poisoned Well, 1983. As Jason Frost: Warlord series, 1983-85; Invasion USA, 1985; As Don Pendleton: Bloodsport, 1982; Flesh Wounds, 1983; Savannah Swingsaw, 1985; The Fire Eaters, 1986. As Carl Stevens: The Centaur Conspiracy, 1983; Ride of the Razorback, 1984. Poetry: The Cat With Half a Face, 1978. Contributions to: Anthologies and other publications. Membership: Mystery Writers of America. Address: 190 Greenmoor, Ivine, CA 92714, USA.

ODA Makoto, b. 2 June 1932, Osaka, Japan. Novelist; Writer. m. Hyon Sune, Dec 1982, 1 daughter. Education: University of Tokyo, Japan, 1957; Harvard University, 1958-59. Publications: Nihon no Chishikizin (essay), 1964; Hiroshima (novel), 1981; Far From Vietnam (novel), 1992; Thought on the Earthquake and War (critical essay), 1996. Honour: Lotus Prize, Afro-Asian Writers Association, 1987. Address: 1-41-501 Ohama-cho, Nishinomiya, Japan.

ODAGA Asenath (Bole), b. 5 July 1937, Rarieda, Kenya. Author. Education: Kikuyu Teacher Training College, 1955-56; BA, 1974, Diploma in Education, 1974, MA, 1981, University of Nairobi. Appointments: Tutor, Church Missionary Society Teacher Training College, Ngiya, 1957-58; Teacher, Butere Girls School, 1959-60; Headmistress, Nyakach Girls School 1961-63; Assistant Secretary, Kenya Dairy Board, Nairobi, 1965-67; Secretary, Kenya Library Services, Nairobi, 1968; Advertising Assistant, East African Standard Newspaper and Kerr Downey and Selby Safaris, both Nairobi, 1969-70; Assistant Director, Curriculum Development Programme, Christian Churches Educational Association, Nairobi, 1974-75; Research Fellow, Institute of African Studies, University of Nairobi, 1976-81. Publications: God, Myself and Others (editor with David Kirui and David Crippen), 1976; Kip Goes to the City (children's fiction), 1977; Poko Nyar Mugumba (Poko Mugumba's Daughter, children's folktale), 1978; Thu Tinda: Stories from Kenya (folktales), 1980; The Two Friends (folktales), 1981; Miaha (in Luo: The Bride, play), 1981; Simbi Nyaima (The Sunken Village, play), 1982; Oral Literature: A School Certificate Course (school text book), 1982; Ange ok Tel (Regret Never Comes First, children's fiction), 1982; Kenyan Folk Tales, 1982; Sigendini gi Timbe Luo Moko (Stories and Some Customs of the Luo), 1982; A Reed on the Roof, Block Ten, With Other Stories (fiction), 1982; Mouth and Pen: Literature for Children and Young People in Kenya, 1983; My Home (reader), 1983; The Shade Changes (fiction), 1984; Yesterday's Today: The Story of Oral Literature, 1984; The Storm (fiction), 1986; Nyamgondho the Son of Ombare and Other Luo Stories, 1986; Between the Years (fiction), 1987; A Bridge in Time (fiction), 1987; Munde and his Friends (children's fiction), 1987; Munde Goes to the Market (children's fiction), 1987; The Rag Ball (children's fiction), 1987; The Silver Cup (children's fiction), 1988; The Storm (adolescent's fiction), 1988; Rianan (fiction), 1990; A Night on a Tree (fiction), 1991; Luo Sayings, 1992. Address: PO Box, 1743 Kisumu, Kenya, Africa.

ODELL Peter Randon, b. 1 July 1930, Coalville, England. Professor of International Energy Studies Emeritus; Writer. m. Jean Mary McKintosh, 1957, 2 sons, 2 daughters. Education: BA, 1951, PhD, 1954, University of Birmingham; AM, Fletcher School of Law and Diplomacy, Cambridge, Massachusetts, 1958. Appointments: Economist, Shell International Petroleum Co, 1958-61; Lecturer, 1961-65, Senior Lecturer, 1965-68, Visiting Professor, 1983-, London School of Economics and Political Science; Professor of Economic Geography, 1968-81, Director, Centre for International Energy Studies,

1981-90, Professor Emeritus, 1991-, Erasmus University, Rotterdam; Stamp Memorial Lecturer, London University, 1975; Faculty, College of Europe, Bruges, 1983-90; Scholar-in-Residence, Rockefeller Centre, Bellagio, Italy, 1984; European Editor, Energy Journal, 1988-90; Killam Visiting Scholar, University of Calgary, 1989. Publications: An Economic Geography of Oil, 1963; Oil: The New Commanding Height, 1966; Natural Gas in Western Europe: A Case Study in the Economic Geography of Energy Resources, 1969; Oil and World Power: A Geographical Interpretation, 1970, 8th edition, 1986; Economies and Societies in Latin America (with D A Preston), 1973, 2nd edition, 1978; Energy: Needs and Resources, 1974, 2nd edition, 1977; The North Sea Oil Province (with K E Rosing), 1975; The West European Energy Economy: The Case for Self-Sufficiency, 1976; The Optimal Development of the North Sea Oilfields (with K E Rosing), 1976; The Pressures of Oil: A Strategy for Economic Revival (with L Vallenilla), 1978; British Offshore Oil Policy: A Radical Alternative, 1980; The Future of Oil, 1980-2080 (with K E Rosing), 1980, 2nd edition, 1983; Energie: Geen Probleem? (with J A van Rayn), 1981; The International Oil Industry: An Interdisciplinary Perspective (editor with J Rees), 1986; Global and Regional Energy Supplies: Recent Fictions and Fallacies Revisited, 1991. Honours: Canadian Council Fellow, 1978; International Association for Energy Econs Prize, 1991; Royal Scottish Geographical Society Centenary Medal, 1993. Address: 7 Constitution Hill, Ipswich IPI 3RG, England.

ODELL Robin Ian, b. 19 Dec 1935, Totton, Hampshire, England. Editor. m. Joan Bartholomew, 19 Sept 1959. Publications: Jack the Ripper in Fact and Fiction, 1965; Exhumation of a Murder, 1975; Jack the Ripper: Summing-up and Verdict (with Colin Wilson), 1977; The Murderers' Who's Who (with J H H Gaute), 1979; Lady Killers, 1980; Murder Whatdunit, 1982; Murder Whereabouts, 1986; Dad Help Me Please (with Christopher Berry-Dee), 1990; A Question of Evidence, 1992; Lady Killer, 1992; The Long Drop, 1993. Contributions to: Crimes and Punishment; The Criminologist. Honours: FCC Watts Memorial Prize, 1957; International Humanist and Ethical Union, 1960; Edgar Award, Mystery Writers of America, 1980. Memberships: Paternosters; Our Society; Crime Writers Association. Literary Agent: Curtis Brown. Address: 11 Red House Drive, Sonning Common, Reading RG4 9NT, England.

ODGERS Darrel Allan, b. 7 Mar 1957, Smithton, Tasmania, Australia. Secretary; Manager; Writer. m. Sally P Farrell, 26 May 1979, 1 son, 1 daughter. Education: School Board Certificate. Publication: Timedetector 1995; Dad's New Path, 1995; Maria's Diary, 1996; Theft in Time, forthcoming; Timedetectors II, forthcoming; CD and the Giant Cat, forthcoming, all co-written with Sally Odgers. Membership: Australian Society of Authors. Address: PO Box 41, Latrobe, Tasmania 7307, Australia.

ODGERS Sally Farrell, (Tegan James), b. 26 Nov 1957, Latrobe, Tasmania, Australia. Freelance Writer and Lecturer. m. Darrel Allan Odgers, 26 May 1979, 1 son, 1 daughter. Publications: Dreadful David, 1984; Five Easy Lessons, 1989; Kayak, 1991; Shadowdancers, 1994; Timedetector (with D Odgers), 1995. Contributions to: Lucky; Organic Growing; Australian Women's Weekly; Good House Keeping; Australian Author; Writer's News. Honour: Journalism Award, Circular Head Festival, 1993. Memberships: Australian Society of Authors; Society of Women Writers. Address: PO Box 41, Latrobe, Tasmania 7307, Australia.

OE Kenzaburo, b. 31 Jan 1935, Ehime, Shikoku, Japan. Author. m. Yukari Kenzaburo, 2 children. Education: Degree in French Literature, University of Tokyo, 1959. Publications: Fiction: Shiiku, 1958, English translation as the Catch, 1966; Memushiri kouchi, 1958, English translation as Nip the Buds, Shoot the Kids, 1995; The Perverts, 1963; Adventures in Daily Life, 1964; Kojinteki na taiken, 1964, English translation as A Personal Matter, 1968; Man'en gannen no futoburu, 1967, English translation as The Silent Cry, 1974; Pinchi ranna chosho, 1976, English translation as The Pinch Runner Memorandum, 1995; Teach Us to Outgrow Our Madness (also includes Aghwee the Sky Monster, the Day He Himself Shall Wipe My Tears Away, and Prize Stock), 1977; The Crazy Iris and Other Stories of the Atomic Aftermath, 1984. Non-Fiction: Hiroshima Notes, 1963; Japan, the Ambiguous, and Myself: The Nobel Prize Speech and Other Lectures, 1995. Other: Many fiction and non-fiction books in Japanese. Honours: Akutagawa Prize, Japanese Society for the Promotion of Literature, 1958; Shinchosha Literary Prize, 1964; Tanizaki Prize, 1967; Europelia Arts Festival Literary Prize, 1989; Nobel Prize for

Literature, 1994. Address: 585 Seijo-machi, Setagaya-Ku, Tokyo, Japan.

OFFEN Yehuda, b. 4 Apr 1922, Altona, Germany. Writer; Poet. m. Tova Arbisser, 28 Mar 1946, 1 daughter. Education: BA, London University, 1975; MA, Comparative Literature, Hebrew University, Jerusalem, 1978. Publications: L'Lo L'An, 1961; Har Vakhol, 1963; Lo Agadat Khoref, 1969; Nofim P'nima, 1979; B'Magal Sagur (short stories), 1979; N'Vilat Vered, 1983; Shirim Bir'hov Ayaif, 1984; P'Gishot Me'ever Lazman, 1986; Massekhet Av, 1986; Stoning on the Cross Road (short stories), 1988; Who Once Begot a Star, 1990; Silly Soil, 1992; Back to Germany, 1994. Contributions to: Various publications. Honours: ACUM Prizes for Literature, 1961, 1979, 1984; Talpir Prize for Literature, 1979; Efrat Prize for Poetry, 1989. Memberships: Hebrew Writers Association, Israel; International Academy of Poets, USA; PEN Centre, Israel; ACUM (Société des Auteurs, Compositeurs et Editeurs en Israel); National Federation of Israeli Journalists; International Federation of Journalists, Brussels. Address: 8 Gazit Street, Tel-Aviv 69417, Israel.

OFFERMANN Bill, b. 15 Sept 1935, Düren, Germany. Art Brut-Author. m. 6 Sept 1966, 2 sons, 1 daughter. Education: Wire-Weaver, Chief. Publications: Tötliche Liebe, autobiografie, 1993; Fund-orte 3:Im Falle eines Falles, 1996; Soiree brut, 1994. Contributions to: Literaturzeitschrift orte: 84, 91, 93, 95, 99. Memberships: SSV; Schweiz Schriftstellerverband. Literary Agent: Werner Bucher, Wolfhalden. Address: Rest Fernsichet, 9427 Zelg-Wolfhalden, Switzerland.

OGBURN Charlton, b. 15 Mar 1911, Atlanta, Georgia, USA. Writer. m. (1) Mary C Aldis, 6 June 1945, div 1951, 1 son, (2) Vera Weidman, 24 Feb 1951, 2 daughters. Education: SB, cum laude, Harvard University, 1932; Graduate, National War College, 1952. Publications: The White Falcon, 1955; The Bridge, 1957; Big Caesar, 1958; The Marauders, 1959; US Army, 1960; The Gold of The River Sea, 1965; The Winter Beach, 1966; The Forging of Our Continent, 1968; The Continent in Our Hands, 1971; Winespring Mountain, 1973; The Southern Appalachians: A Wilderness Quest, 1975; The Adventure of Birds, 1976; Railroads: The Great American Adventure (National Geographical Society), 1977; The Mysterious William Shakespeare: The Myth and the Reality, 1984, second edition, 1992. Contributions to: Magazines and Journals. Address: 403 Hancock Street, Beaufort, SC 29902, USA.

OGILVY George. See: **AYERST David**.

OJALA Ossi Arne Atos, b. 22 Mar 1933, Savonlinna, Finland. Author; Playwright. Education: BA, University of Helsinki. Publications: 7 novels, 1966-85; Over 30 plays broadcast. Contributions to: Several publications. Honours: Otava Prize, 1964; 1st prize, Novel Competition, 1966; Best Finnish Novel for Young People, 1967. Memberships: Several literary organizations. Address: Keskustie 39, 19600 Hartola, Finland.

OKARA Gabriel (Imomotimi Gbaingbain), b. 21 Apr 1921, Bumodi, Ijaw District, Rivers State, Western Nigeria. Publishing Director; Poet. Education: Government College Umuahia. Appointments: Director, Rivers State Publishing House, Port Harcourt, 1972-. Publications: The Voice (novel), 1964; Poetry from Africa, 1968; The Fisherman's Invocation, 1978. Honour: Commonwealth Poetry Prize, 1979. Address: PO Box 219, Port Harcourt, Nigeria.

OKON Zbigniew Waldemar, b. 21 July 1945, Chelm, Poland. Teacher; Writer; Poet. m. Halina Pioro Maciejewska, 6 Oct 1969, 2 sons, 1 daughter. Education: Marie Curie-Sklodowska University, Lublin. Publications: Outlooks and Reflections, 1968; The Soldiers of the Chalk Hills, 1970; Impatience of the Tree, 1979; Intimidation By Twilight, 1986; Calling Up the Darkness, 1987; In a Halfway, 1996; Grandpa Tudrey's Cavalry, 1997. Contributions to: Poetry in various journals and magazines. Honours: 1st Prize Winner, Poetry Competitions, 1964, 1966, 1968, 1974; Czechowicz Literary Prize, 1987. Memberships: Stowarzyszenie Ziemi Chelmskiej; Pryzmaty; Union of Polish Literary Men. Address: Ul Kolejowa 86/19, 22-100 Chelm, Poland.

OKRI Ben, b. 1959, Minna, Nigeria. Novelist; Poet; Short Story Writer. Education: Urohobo College, Warri, Nigeria; University of Essex, Colchester. Appointments: Broadcaster, Network Africa, BBC World Service, 1984-85; Poetry Editor, West Africa, 1981-87; Fellow Commoner in Creative Arts, Trinity College, Cambridge; Writer and Reviewer, New Statesman, Observer, Guardian, The Times, London, New York Times and many International newspapers, journals and magazines. Publications: Flowers and Shadows, 1980; The Landscapes Within, 1982; The Famished Road, 1991; Songs of Enchantment, 1993. Short Stories: Incidents at the Shrine, 1986; Stars of the Curfew, 1988. Poetry: An African Elegy. Honours: Booker Prize Winner, 1991; Paris Review for Fiction; Premio Letterario Internazionale Chianti Ruffino-Antico Fattore, 1993; Premio Grinzane Cavour Prize, 1994. Address: c/o Jonathan Cape Ltd, 20 Vauxhall Bridge Road, London SW1V 2SA, England.

OLDKNOW Antony, b. 15 Aug 1939, Peterborough, England. Poet; Literary Translator; Professor. Education: BA, University of Leeds, 1961; Postgraduate Diploma, Phoenetics, University of Edinburgh, 1962; PhD, University of North Dakota, USA, 1983. Appointments: Editor, Publisher, Scopcraeft Press Inc, 1966-; Travelling Writer, The Great Plains Book Bus, 1979-81; Writer-in-Residence, Wisconsin Arts Board, 1980-83; Poetry Staff, Cottonwood, 1984-87; Professor of Literature, Eastern New Mexico University, 1987-; Associate Editor, Blackwater Quarterly, 1993. Publications: Lost Allegory, 1967; Tomcats and Tigertails, 1968; The Road of the Lord, 1969; Anthem for Rusty Saw and Blue Sky, 1975; Consolations for Beggars, 1978; Miniature Clouds, 1982; Ten Small Songs, 1985; Clara d'Ellébeuse (translated novel), 1992; The Villages and Other Poems (translated book), 1993. Contributions to : Numerous Journals, Magazines and Reviews; Poems in American Poetry Review, 1992 and Men of Our Time, 1993. Address: Department of Languages and Literature, Eastern New Mexico University, Portales, NM 88130, USA.

OLDS Sharon, b. 19 Nov 1942, San Francisco, California, USA. Poet; Associate Professor. Education: BA, Stanford University, 1964; PhD, Columbia University, 1972. Appointments: Lecturer-in-Residence on Poetry, Theodor Herzl Institute, New York, 1976-80; Adjunct Professor, 1983-90, Director, 1988-91, Associate Professor, 1990-, Graduate Program in Creative Writing, New York University; Fanny Hurst Chair in Literature, Brandeis University, 1986-87. Publications: Satan Says, 1980; The Dead and the Living, 1984; The Gold Cell, 1987; The Matter of This World: New and Selected Poems, 1987; The Sign of Saturn, 1991; The Father, 1992; The Wellspring, 1996. Honours: Creative Arts Public Service Award, 1978; Madeline Sadin Award, 1978; Guggenheim Fellowship, 1981-82; National Endowment for the Arts Fellowship, 1982-83; Lamont Prize, 1984; National Book Critics Circle Award, 1985; T S Eliot Prize Shortlist, 1993; Lila Wallace-Reader's Digest Fellowship, 1993-96. Address: Alfred A Knopf Inc, 201 East 50th Street, New York, NY 10025, USA.

OLDSEY Bernard, b. 18 Feb 1923, Wilkes-Barre, Pennsylvania, USA. Professor, Editor; Writer. m. Ann Marie Re, 21 Sep 1946, 1 son, 1 daughter. Education: BA, 1948, MA, 1949, PhD, 1955, Pennsylvania State University. Appointments: Instructor to Associate Professor, English, Pennsylvania State University, 1951-69; Senior Fulbright Professor, American Literature, Universidad de Zaragoza, Spain, 1964-65; Professor, English, West Chester University of Pennsylvania, 1969-90; Editor, College Literature, 1974-90; University Professor, University of Innsbruck, Austria, 1985. Publications: From Fact to Judgement, 1957; The Art of William Golding, 1967; The Spanish Season (novel), 1970; Hemingway's Hidden Craft, 1979; Ernest Hemingway: Papers of a Writer, 1981; British Novelists, 1930-1960, 1983; Critical Essays on George Orwell, 1985; The Snows of Yesteryear, novel. Address: 520 William Ebbs Lane, West Chester, PA 19380, USA.

OLIVER (Symmes) Chad(wick), b. 1928, USA. Author. Publications: Shadows in the Sun, 1954; Mists of Dawn (juvenile fiction), 1952; Another Kind (short stories), 1955; The Winds of Time, 1957; Unearthly Neighbors, 1960; Ecology and Cultural Continuity as Contributing Factors in the Social Organization of the Plains Indians, 1962; The Wolf is My Brother (western novel), 1967; The Shores of Another Sea, 1971; The Edge of Forever (short stories), 1971; Giants in the Dust, 1976; Cultural Anthropology: The Discovery of Humanity, 1980; Broken Eagle, 1989. Honour: Western Heritage Award for Best Novel, 1989. Address: 301 Eanes Road, Austin, TX 78746, USA.

OLIVER Douglas Dunlop, b. 14 Sept 1937, Southampton, England. Poet; Novelist; Prosodist. m. (1) Janet Hughes, July 1962, (2) Alice Notley, Feb 1988, 2 stepsons, 2 daughters. Education: BA, Literature, 1975, MA, Applied Linguistics, 1982, University of Essex.

Appointments: Journalist, newspapers in England, Agence France-Presse, Paris, 1959-72; University Lecturer, Literature, English, various, 1975-; Editorial Board, Franco-British Studies; Co-Editor, Scarlet magazine. Publications: Oppo Hectic, 1969; The Harmless Building, 1973; In the Cave of Succession, 1974; The Diagram Poems, 1979; The Infant and the Pearl, 1985; Kind, 1987; Poetry and Narrative in Performance, 1989; Three Variations on the Theme of Harm, 1990; Penniless Politics, 1991; The Scarlet Cabinet (with Alice Notley), 1992. Contributions to: Anthologies including: A Various Art, 1987; The New British Poetry 1968-1988, 1988; Numerous poems, articles, fiction, to magazines and journals. Honours: Eastern Arts Grant, 1977; South-East Arts Grant, 1987; Fund for Poetry Grants, 1990, 1991. Literary Agent: John Parker, MBA Associates, 45 Fitzroy Street, London W1P 5HR, England. Address: c/o British Institute in Paris, 11 Rue de Constantine, 75007 Paris, France.

OLIVER Mary, b. 10 Sept 1935, Cleveland, Ohio, USA. Poet; Educator. Education: Ohio State University; Vassar College. Appointments: Mather Visting Professor, Case Western Reserve University, 1980, 1982; Poet-in-Residence, Bucknell University, 1986; Elliston Visiting Professor, University of Cinncinnati, 1986; Margaret Banister Writer-in-Residence, Sweet Briar College, 1991-95; William Blackburn Visiting Professor of Creative Writing, Duke University, 1995. Publications: No Voyage, and Other Poems, 1963, augmented edition, 1965; The River Styx, Ohio, and Other Poems, 1972; The Night Traveler, 1978; Twelve Moons, 1978; Sleeping in the Forest, 1979; American Primitive, 1983; Dream Work, 1986; Provincetown, 1987; House of Light, 1990; New and Selected Poems, 1992; A Poetry Handbook, 1994; White Pine: Poems and Prose Poems, 1994; Blue Pastures, 1995. Contributions to: Periodicals in the US and England. Honours: Poetry Society of America 1st Prize, 1962; Devil's Advocate Award, 1968; Shelley Memorial Award, 1972; National Endowment for the Arts Fellowship, 1972-73; Alice Fay di Castagnola Award, 1973; Guggenheim Fellowship, 1980-81; American Academy and Institute of Arts and Letters Award, 1983; Pulitzer Prize in Poetry, 1984; Christopher Award, 1991; L L Winship Award, 1991; National Book Award for Poetry, 1993. Memberships: PEN; Poetry Society of America. Address: c/o Molly Malone Cook Literary Agency, Box 338, Provincetown, MA 02657, USA.

OLIVER Paul H(ereford), b. 25 May 1927, Nottingham, England. Author; Lecturer in Architecture and Popular Music. m. Valerie Grace Coxon, 19 Aug 1950. Education: Drawing Exam Distinction, 1945; Painting Exam, National Diploma in Design, 1947; Art Teachers' Diploma, 1948, Diploma in Humanities, History of Art, Distinction, 1955, University of London, England. Appointments: Editor, Architectural Association Journal, 1961-63; Reviewer, Arts Review, 1965-70; Member, Cambridge University Press Popular Music Editorial Board, 1980-. Publications: Bessie Smith, 1959; Blues Fell This Morning, 1960, revised edition, 1990; Conversation with the Blues, 1965, revised edition, 1997; Screening the Blues, 1968; The Story of the Blues, 1969, revised edition, 1997; Shelter and Society (editor), 1970; Savannah Syncopators: African Retentions in the Blues, 1970; Shelter in Africa, 1971; Shelter in Greece, co-editor Orestis Doumanis, 1994; Shelter, Sign and Symbol, 1975; Dunroamin: The Suburban Semi and Its Enemies (with Ian Davis and Ian Bentley), 1981; Early Blues Songbook, 1994; Songsters and Saints: Vocal Traditions on Race Records, 1984; Blues Off the Record: Thirty Years of Blues Commentary, 1984; Dwellings: The House Across the World, 1987; Black Music in Britain (editor), 1990; Blackwell's Guide to Blues Records (editor), 1990; Architecture - An Invitation (with Richard Hayward), 1990; The New Blackwell Guide to Recorded Blues, co-editor John Cowley, 1996; The Encyclopedia of Vernacular Architecture of the World, editor, 1997. Contributions to: Journals and magazines. Honours: Prix d'Etrangers, Paris, 1962; Prix du Disque, Paris, 1962; Honorary Fellow, AmCAS University of Exeter, 1986; Honorary Fellow, Oxford Polytechnic, 1988; Sony Radio Award Best Special Music Programme, 1988; Katherine Briggs Folklore Award, 1990; Honorary Doctor of Arts, Oxford Brookes University, 1995. Memberships: Fellow, Royal Anthropological Institute; Architectural Association; International Association for the Study of Popular Music; International Association for the Study of Traditional Environments;Vernacular Architecture Group UK. Address: Wootton-by-Woodstock, Oxon, England.

OLIVER Reginald Rene St John, b. 7 July 1952, London, England. Actor; Dramatist. Education: BA Hons, University College, Oxford, 1975. Appointments: Literary Consultant to Drama Panel, Arts Council of Great Britain, 1983-86; Director of Publications, Seeds Ltd,

1986-. Publications: Zuleika, 1975; Interruption to the Dance, 1977; You Might as Well Live, 1978; The Shewstone, 1981; Passing Over, 1982; Absolution, 1984; Back Payments, 1985; Rochester, 1986; A Portrait of Two Artists, 1986; Imaginary Lines, 1987. Contributions to: Numerous magazines and journals. Honours: Time Out Award Best Fringe Play; International Theatre Award, 1985. Memberships: Dramatist's Club; British Actors Equity; Theatre Writers Union. Literary Agent: Margaret Ramsay Ltd. Address: The Bothy, Wormington Grange, Broadway, Worcs, England.

OLIVER Roland Anthony, b. 30 Mar 1923, Srinagar, Kashmir. Professor of the History of Africa; Author. m. (1) Caroline Florence, 1947, dec 1983, 1 daughter, (2) Suzanne Doyle, 1990. Education: MA, PhD, King's College, Cambridge. Appointments: Foreign Office, 1942-45; R J Smith Research Studentship, King's College, Cambridge, 1946-48; Lecturer, School of Oriental and African Studies, 1948-58; Reader in African History, 1958-63, Professor of the History of Africa, 1963-86, University of London; Editor (with J D Fage), Journal of African History, 1960-73; Francqui Professor, University of Brussels, 1961; Visiting Professor, Northwestern University, 1962, Harvard University, 1967. Publications: The Missionary Factor in East Africa, 1952; Sir Harry Johnston and the Scramble for Africa, 1957; The Dawn of African History (editor), 1961; A Short History of Africa (with J D Fage), 1962; A History of East Africa (editor with Gervase Mathew), 1963; Africa since 1800 (with A E Atmore), 1967; The Middle Age of African History (editor), 1967; Papers in African Prehistory (with J D Fage), 1970; Africa in the Iron Age (with B M Fagen), 1975; The Cambridge History of Africa (general editor with J D Fage), 8 volumes, 1975-86; The African Middle Ages, 1400-1800 (with A E Atmore), 1981; The African Experience, 1991; In the Realms of the Gold: Pioneering in African History, 1997. Contributions to: Scholarly journals. Honours: Haile Selassie Prize Trust Award, 1966; Distinguished Africanist Award, American African Studies Association, 1989; Honorary Fellow, School of Oriental and African Studies, 1992. Memberships: Académie Royale des Sciences d'Outremer, Brussels, corresponding member; African Studies Association, president, 1967-68; British Academy, fellow; British Institute in Eastern Africa, president, 1981-93; International Congress of Africanists; Royal African Society, vice-president, 1965-. Address: Frilsham Woodhouse, Thatcham, Berkshire RG18 9XB, England.

OLLARD Richard (Laurence), b. 9 Nov 1923, Bainton, Yorkshire, England. Historian; Writer. Education: MA, New College, Oxford, 1952. Appointments: Lecturer, 1948-52, Senior Lecturer in History and English, 1952-59, Royal Naval College, Greenwich; Senior Editor, William Collins and Sons, London, 1960-83. Publications: Historical Essays 1600-1750 (editor with H E Bell), 1963; The Escape of Charles II, 1967; Man of War: Sir Robert Holmes and the Restoration Navy, 1969; Pepys, 1974, new illustrated edition, 1991; War Without an Enemy: A History of the English Civil Wars, 1976; The Image of the King: Charles I and Charles II, 1979; An English Education: A Perspective of Eton, 1982; For Veronica Wedgwood These: Studies on 17th Century History (editor with Pamela Tudor Craig), 1986; Clarendon and His Friends, 1987; Fisher and Cunningham: A Study in the Personalities of the Churchill Era, 1991; Cromwell's Earl: A Life of Edward Montagu, 1st Earl of Sandwich, 1994; Dorset: A Pimlico County History Guide, 1995; The Sayings of Samuel Pepys, 1996. Memberships: Royal Society of Literature, fellow; Society of Antiquaries, fellow. Address: c/o Curtis Brown Ltd, Haymarket House, 28-29 Haymarket, London SW1Y 4SP, England.

OLMSTEAD Andrea Louise, b. 5 Sep 1948, Dayton, Ohio, USA. Musicologist. m. Larry Thomas Bell, 2 Jan 1982. Education: BM, Hartt College of Music, 1972; MA, New York University, 1974. Appointments: Faculty, The Juilliard School, 1972-80; Boston Conservatory, 1981-. Publications: Roger Sessions and His Music, 1985; Conversations With Roger Sessions, 1987; The New Grove 20th Century American Masters, 1987; The Correspondence of Roger Sessions, 1992. Contributions to: Journal of the Arnold Schoenberg Institute; American Music; Musical Quarterly; Tempo; Musical America; Perspectives of New Music; Music Library Association Notes. Honours: National Endowment for the Humanities Grants; Outstanding Academic Book Choice, 1986. Memberships: Sonneck Society; Pi Kappa Lambda. Address: 73 Hemenway Street, Apt 501, Boston, MA 02115, USA.

OLSEN Lance, b. 14 Oct 1956, USA. Writer; Poet; Critic; Teacher. m. Andrea Hirsch, 3 Jan 1981. Education: BA Hons, University of Wisconsin, 1978; MFA, University of Iowa, 1980; MA,

1982, PhD, 1985, University of Virginia. Appointment: Professor of Creative Writing and Contemporary Fiction, University of Idaho, 1996; Idaho Writer-in-Residence, 1996. Publications: Ellipse of Uncertainty, 1987; Circus of the Mind in Motion, 1990; Live From Earth, 1991; William Gibson, 1992; My Dates With Franz, 1993; Natural Selections (poems with Jeff Worley), 1993; Scherzi, I Believe, 1994; Tonguing The Zeitgeist, 1994; Lolita, 1995; Burnt, 1996; Time Famine, 1996. Contributions to: Magazines and journals. Address: Bear Creek Cabin, 1490 Ailor Road, Deary, ID 83823, USA.

OLSEN Theodore Victor, (Joshua Stark, Christopher Storm, Cass Willoughby), b. 25 Apr 1932, Rhinelander, Wisconsin, USA. Writer. m. Beverly Butler, 25 Sept 1976. Education: BSc English, University of Wisconsin, 1955. Publications: Haven of the Hunted, 1956; The Rhinelander Story, 1957; The Man from Nowhere, 1959; McGivern, 1960; High Lawless, 1960; Gunswift, 1960; Ramrod Rider, 1960; Brand of the Star, 1961; Brothers of the Sword, 1962; Savage Sierra, 1962; The Young Duke, 1963; Break the Young Land, 1964; The Sex Rebels, 1964; A Man Called Brazos, 1964; Canyon of the Gun, 1965; Campus Motel, 1965; The Stalking Moon, 1965; The Hard Men, 1966; Autumn Passion, 1966; Bitter Grass, 1967; The Lockhart Breed, 1967; Blizzard Pass, 1968; Arrow in the Sun, 1969; Keno, 1970; A Man Named Yuma, 1971; Eye of the Wolf, 1971; There Was a Season, 1973; Mission to the West, 1973; Run to the Mountain, 1974; Track the Man Down, 1975; Day of the Buzzard, 1976; Westward They Rode, 1976; Bonner's Stallion, 1977; Rattlesnake, 1979; Roots of the North, 1979; Allegories for One Man's Moods, 1979; Our First Hundred Years, 1981; Blood of the Breed, 1982; Birth of a City, 1983; Red is the River, 1983; Lazlo's Strike, 1983; Lonesome Gun, 1985; Blood Rage, 1987; A Killer is Waiting, 1988; Under the Gun, 1989; The Burning Sky, 1991; The Golden Chance, 1992. Contributions to: 20 short stories in Ranch Romances, 1956-57. Honour: Award of Merit, State Historical Society of Wisconsin, 1983; Western Writers of America Spur Award for Best Western Paperback Novel, 1992. Membership: Western Writers of America. Literary Agent: Jon Tuska, Golden West Literary Agency, 2327 S E Salmon St, Portland, OR 97214. Address: PO Box 856, Rhinelander, WI 54501, USA.

OLSON Toby, (Merle Theodore Olson), b. 17 Aug 1937, Berwyn, Illinois, USA. Poet; Author. m. (1) Ann Yeomans, 1963, div 1965, (2) Miriam Meltzer, 1966. Education: BA, Occidental College, Los Angeles, 1964; MA, Long Island University, New York, 1966. Appointments: Associate Director, Aspen Writers Workshop, Colorado, 1964-67; Assistant Professor, Long Island University, 1966-74; Faculty, New School for Social Research, New York City, 1967-75; Poet-in-Residence, State University of New York at Cortland, 1972, Friends Seminary, New York, 1974-75; Professor of English, Temple University, Philadelphia, 1984. Publications: Poetry: The Brand, 1969; Worms into Nails, 1969; The Hawk-Foot Poems, 1969; Maps, 1969; Pig's Book, 1970; Cold House, 1970; Poems, 1970; Tools, 1971; Shooting Pigeons, 1971; Vectors, 1972; Fishing, 1973; The Wrestlers and Other Poems, 1974; City, 1974; A Kind of Psychology, 1974; Changing Appearances: Poems 1965-1970, 1975; A Moral Proposition, 1975; Priorities, 1975; Seeds, 1975; Standard-4, 1975; Home, 1976; Three and One, 1976; Doctor Miriam: Five Poems by Her Admiring Husband, 1977; Aesthetics, 1978; The Florence Poems, 1978; Birdsongs: Eleven New Poems, 1980; Two Standards, 1982; Still/Quite, 1982; Unfinished Building, 1993. Fiction: The Life of Jesus, 1976; Seaview, 1982; The Woman Who Escaped from Shame, 1986; Utah, 1987; Dorit in Lesbos, 1990; At Sea, 1993. Editor: Margins 1976, 1976; Writing Talks: Views on Teaching Writing from Across the Professions (with Muffy E A Siegal), 1983. Honours: Creative Artists Public Service Grant, 1975; PEN Faulkner Award for Fction, 1983; Pennsylvania Council on the Arts Fellowship, 1983; Guggenheim Fellowship, 1985; Yaddo Colony Fellowship, 1985; National Endowment for the Arts Fellowship, 1985; Rockefeller Foundation Fellowship, 1987. Address: 329 South Juniper Street, Philadelphia, PA 19107, USA.

OLSON Walter Karl, b. 20 Aug 1954, Detroit, Michigan, USA. Writer; Editor. Education: BA, Yale University, 1975. Publications: New Directions in Liability Law (editor), 1988; The Litigation Explosion, 1991. Literary Agent: Writers' Representatives Inc, 25 West 19th Street, New York, NY10011-4202, USA. Address: Manhattan Institute, 52 Vanderbilt Avenue, New York, NY 10017, USA.

OLUDHE-MACGOYE Marjorie Phyllis, b. 21 Oct 1928, Southampton, England. Writer; Poet; Bookseller. m. D G W Oludhe-Macgoye, 4 June 1960, dec 1990, 3 sons, 1 daughter.

Education: BA, English, 1948, MA, 1953, London University. Publications: Growing Up at Lina School (juvenile), 1971, 2nd edition, 1988; Murder in Majengo (novel), 1972; Song of Nyarloka and Other Poems, 1977; Coming to Birth (novel), 1986; The Story of Kenya (history), 1986; The Present Moment (novel), 1987; Street Life (novella), 1988; Victoria and Murder in Majengo, 1993; Homing In (novel), 1994; Moral Issues in Kenya, 1996; Chire (novel), 1997. Contributions to: London Magazine; Literary Review; Ghala; Zuka; Alfajiri; Most anthologies of East African poetry; Heinemann Book of African Poetry in English. Honours: BBC Arts in Africa Poetry Award (3), 1982; Sinclair Prize for Fiction, 1986. Address: PO Box 70344, Nairobi, Kenya.

OMAN Julia Trevelyan, b. 11 July 1930, Kensington, England. Designer. m. Sir Roy Strong, 10 Sept 1971. Education: Royal College of Art, London. Appointments: Designer, BBC Television, 1955-57; Art Director, The Charge of the Light Brigade, 1967; Laughter in the Dark, 1968; Designer, Brief Lives, 1967, 40 Years On, 1968, Enigma Variations, 1968; Production Designer, Julius Caesar, 1969, The Merchant of Venice, 1970, Eugene Onegin, 1971, The Straw Dogs, 1971, Othello, 1971, Samuel Pepys, 1971, Getting On, 1971, Un Ballo in Maschera, 1973, La Boheme, 1974, The Importance of Being Ernest, 1976, Die Fledermaus, 1977, Hayfever, 1980, Otello, 1983, The Consul, 1985, Mr and Mrs Nobody, 1986, A Man for All Seasons, 1987, The Best of Friends, 1988. Publications: Street Children; Elizabeth R; Mary Queen of Scots; The English Year. Contributions to: Architectural Review; Vogue; Honours: Commander of the Order of the British Empire, 1986; Honorary DLitt, University of Bristol, 1986. Membership: Chartered Society of Designers, fellow. Literary Agent: Felicity Bryan. Address: Oman Productions Limited, The Laskett, Much Birch, Hereford HR2 8HZ, England.

OMOLEYE Mike, b. 26 Jan 1940, Oyo Ekiti, Ondo State, Nigeria. Journalist; Publisher. m. M A Omoleye, 1970, 4 sons, 3 daughters. Education: Diploma in Journalism. Appointments: Freelance Journalist, 1960-63; Reporter, Morning Post and Sunday Post, 1964-69; Special Roving Features Writer, 1969-71, News Editor, 1972-73, Assistant Editor, 1974-76, Daily Sketch and Sunday Sketch; Managing Director, Omoleye Publishing Company Ltd, 1976-; Publisher, Sunday Glory, 1986-. Publications: You Can Control Your Destiny, 1974; Fascinating Folktales, 1976; Great Tales of the Yorubas, 1977; Mystery World Under the Sea, 1979; Awo As I Know Him, 1982; The Book of Life, 1982; Self Spiritual Healing, 1982; Issues at Stake, 1983; Make the Psalms Perform Wonders for You, 1990; Awo Speaks of Revolution, 1991. Contributions to: Newspapers. Address: GPO 1265, Ibadan, Oyo State, Nigeria.

OMURA Jimmie Matsumoto, b. 27 Nov 1912, Winslow, Washington, USA. Journalist; Editor; Publisher. m. Haruko Motoishi, 8 Mar 1951, 2 sons. Education: Broadway High School, Seattle. Appointments: Editor, New Japanese American News, Los Angeles, 1933-34, New World Daily News, San Francisco, 1935-36; Publisher, Current Life Magazine, San Francisco, 1940-42; Editor and Public Relations, The Rocky Shimpo, Denver, 1944, 1947. Contributions to: Numerous periodicals. Honour: Lifetime Achievement Award, Asian American Journalists Association, 1989. Address: 1455 South Irving Street, Denver, CO 80219, USA.

ONDAATJE (Philip) Michael, b. 12 Sept 1943, Colombo, Ceylon. Poet; Novelist; Dramatist; Teacher; Film Director. Education: St Thomas' College, Colombo; Dulwich College, London; Bishop's University, Lennoxville, Quebec, 1962-64; BA, University of Toronto, 1965; MA, Queen's University, Kingston, Ontario, 1967. Appointments: Teacher, University of Western Ontario, 1969-71; Glendon College, York University, Toronto, 1971-; Visting Professor, University of Hawaii, 1979; Brown University, Providence, Rhode Island, 1990; Film Director. Publications: The Dainty Monsters, 1967; The Man With Seven Toes, 1969; Left Handed Poems, 1970; Rat Jelly, 1973; Elimination Dance, 1978, revised edition, 1980; There's a Trick with a Knife I'm Learning to Do: Poems, 1963-1978, 1979; Claude Glass, 1979; Tin Roof, 1982; Secular Love, 1984; All Along the Mazinaw: Two Poems, 1986; The Cinnamon Peeler: Selected Poems, 1989. Novels: The Collected Works of Billy the Kid, 1970; Coming Through Slaughter, 1976; In the Skin of a Lion, 1987; The English Patient, 1992. Criticism: Leonard Cohen, 1970. Non-Fiction: Running in the Family, 1982; Editor: The Broken Ark, verse, 1971, revised edition as A Book of Beasts, 1979; Personal Fictions: Stories by Monroe, Wiebe, Thomas, and Blaise, 1977; The Long Poem Anthology, 1979; Brushes With Greatness: An Anthology of Chance Encounters with Greatness (with Russell Banks and David Young), 1989; The Brick Anthology (with Linda Spalding), 1989; From Ink Lake: An Anthology of Canadian Short Stories, 1990; The Faber Book of Contemporary Canadian Short Stories, 1990. Honours: Ralph Gustafson Award, 1965; Epstein Award, 1966; E J Pratt Medal, 1966; Canadian Governor-General's Awards for Literature, 1971, 1980, 1992; W H Smith/Books in Canada First Novel Award, 1977; Canada-Australia Prize, 1980; City of Toronto Arts Award, 1987; Trillium Book Awards, 1987, 1992; Ritz-Hemingway Prize Nomination, 1987; Booker McConnell Prize, British Book Council, 1992; Canadian Authors Association Author of the Year Award, 1993; Commonwealth Prize (regional), international nomination, 1993; Chianti Ruffino-Antonio Fattore International Literary Prize, 1994; Nelly Sachs Award, 1995; Premio Grinzane Cavour, 1996. Address: c/o Ellen Levine Literary Agency, 15 East 26th Street, Suite 1801, New York, NY 10010, USA.

ONG Walter Jackson,b. 30 Nov 1912, Kansas City, MO, USA. Priest; Society of Jesus; University Professor. Education: BA, Rockhurst College, 1933; PhL, 1940, MA, 1941, STL, 1948, St Louis University; PhD, Harvard University, 1955; Various Honorary Doctorates. Appointments include: Professor, 1959-, Professor of Humanities in Psychiatry, 1970-, University Professor of Humanities, 1981-, Emeritus Professor, 1984-, St Louis University; Visiting Professor at various universities; Lincoln Lecturer, 1974, Zaire, Cameroun, Nigeria, Senegal; Wolfson College Lecturer, Oxford University, 1985; Lecturer, Finland, Austria, 1968; Israel, Egypt, 1969; USIA Lecturer, Sweden, Tunisia, Morocco, 1975; Korea, Japan, 1980. Publications include: Rhetoric, Romance and Technology, 1971; Interfaces of the Word, 1977; Fighting for Life: Contest, Sexuality and Consciousness, 1981; Orality and Literacy, 1982; Hopkins, The Self and God, 1986; Faith and Contexts, 3 Volumes, 1995. Contributions to: Over 300 articles across the USA, Europe and other continents. Address: St Louis University, St Louis, MO 63103, USA.

ONWY. See: EVANS Donald.

ONYEAMA Charles Dillibe Ejiofor, b. 6 Jan 1951, Enugu, Nigeria. Publisher; Author; Journalist. m. Ethel Ekwueme, 15 Dec 1984, 4 sons. Education: Premier School of Journalism, Fleet Street, London, England. Appointments: Board of Directors, Star Printing and Publishing Company Ltd, 1992-94; Managing Director, Delta Publications (Nigeria) Ltd. Publications: Nigger at Eton, 1972; John Bull's Nigger, 1974; Sex is a Nigger's Game, 1975; The Book of Black Man's Humour, 1975; I'm the Greatest, 1975; Juju, 1976; Secret Society, 1977; Revenge of the Medicine Man, 1978; The Return, 1978; Night Demon, 1979; Female Target, 1980; The Rules of the Game, 1980; The Story of an African God, 1982; Modern Messiah, 1983; Godfathers of Voodoo, 1985; African Legend, 1985; Correct English, 1986; Notes of a So-Called Afro-Saxon, 1988. Contributions to: Books and Bookmen; Spectator; Times; Daily Express; Sunday Express; Drum; West Africa; Roots; Guardian; Evening News. Memberships: President, Delta Book Club; Councillor, 5-man Caretaker Committee, Udi Local Government Council, Enugu State, 1994-. Literary Agent: Elspeth Cochrane Agency, London, England. Address: 8B Byron Onyeama Close, New Haven, PO Box 1171, Enugu, Enugu State, Nigeria.

OPATRNY Josef, b. 19 Nov 1945, Skryje, Czechoslovakia. Historian; Teacher; Writer. m. Olga Titerová-Opatrná, 20 Feb 1970, 1 son, 2 daughters. Education: MA, 1968, PhD, 1969, Professor in History (Professor Doctor), 1995, Charles University, Prague. Publications: Válka Severu proti Jihu (American Civil War), 1986; Objevitelé, dobyvatelé, osadníci (Discoverers, Conquerors, Colonists), 1992; US Expansionism and Cuban Annexationism in the 1850s, 1993; Amerika presidenta Granta (President Grant's America), 1994; Historical Pre-Conditions of the Origin of the Cuban Nation, 1994; Cuba - Algunes Problemas de su Historia (editor), 1995. Contributions to: Revista de Indias; Cuban Studies; Ibero-Americana Pragensia; Estudios Migratorios Latinoamericanos. Honour: Czechoslovakian Literary Fund Award, 1987. Memberships: Executive Committee, 1990-93, Vice President, 1996-, European Latinoamericanists Association; New York Academy of Sciences. Address: Bulharská 12, 101 00 Prague 10, Czech Republic.

OPIE Iona, b. 13 Oct 1923, Colchester, England. Writer. Publications: A Dictionary of Superstitions (with Moira Tatem), 1989; The People in the Playground, 1993; With Peter Opie: The Oxford Dictionary of Nursery Rhymes, 1951; The Oxford Nursery Rhyme Book, 1955; The Lore and Language of Schoolchildren, 1959; Puffin

Book of Nursery Rhymes, 1963; A Family Book of Nursery Rhymes, 1964; Children's Games in Street and Playground, 1969; The Oxford Book of Children's Verse, 1973; Three Centuries of Nursery Rhymes and Poetry for Children, 1973; The Classic Fairy Tales, 1974; A Nursery Companion, 1980; The Oxford Book of Narrative Verse, 1983; The Singing Game, 1985; Babies: an unsentimental anthology, 1990. Honours: Honorary MA (Oxon), 1962; Honorary MA, Open University, 1987; Honorary DLitt, Southampton, 1987; Honorary DLitt, Nottingham, 1991. Address: Westerfield House, West Liss, Hampshire GU33 6JQ, England.

OPITZ May, (May Ayim), b. 3 May 1960, Hamburg, Germany. Poet; Educator; Speech Therapist. Education: Adult Education, MA, 1986; Speech Therapist Diploma, 1990. Appointments: Vaterland-Mutterprache, Berlin, 1991; CELAFI, Toronto, 1992; Black Bookfair, London, 1993; Zesde Internationale MEP-festival, Utrecht, Netherlands, Panafst Ghana, 1994. Publications: Showing our Colors, 1992; Entfernte Verbindungen, 1993; Daughters of Africa, 1992; Schwarze Frauen der Welt, 1994. Contributions to: Books and journals. Memberships: Co-founder, Literatue frauen, 1989; Deutscher Schriftstellerverband; Co-founder, Initiative of Black Germans, 1986. Literary Agent: Orlanda Frauenverlag, Grobgörschenstr 40, 10827 Berlin, Germany. Address: Hohenstaufenstrasse 63, 10781 Berlin, Germany.

ORFALEA Gregory Michael, b. 9 Aug 1949, Los Angeles, California, USA. Writer; Editor. m. Eileen Rogers, 4 Aug 1984, 3 sons. Education: AB with honours, English, Georgetown University; MFA, Creative Writing, University of Alaska. Appointments: Reporter, Northern Virginia Sun, 1971-72; Professor, Santa Barbara City College, California,1974-76; Editor, Political Focus, 1979-81, Small Business Administration, 1985-91, Resolution Trust Corporation, 1991-95; Federal Deposit Insurance Corporation, 1995-96; Comptroller of the Currency, 1996-97; Freddie Mac, 1997-. Publications: Before the Flames, 1988; The Capital of Solitude, 1988; Grape Leaves, 1988; Imagining America: Stories of the Promised Land, 1991; Messengers of the Lost Battalion, 1997. Contributions to: Washington Post; Triquarterly; Cleveland Plain-Dealer; Christian Science Monitor. Honours: California Arts Council Award, 1976; American Middle East Peace Research Award, 1983; District of Columbia Commission on the Arts and Humanities Award, 1991, 1993. Membership: American PEN. Address: 6001 34th Place North West, Washington, DC 20015, USA.

ORGEL Doris, (Doris Adelberg), b. 15 Feb 1929, Vienna, Austria. Writer. m. Shelley Orgel, 25 June 1949, 2 sons, 1 daughter. Education: BA, Barnard College, 1960. Appointments: Senior Staff Writer,Editor, The Publications and Media Group of The Bank Sheer College of Education, 1961-. Publications: Sarah's Room, 1963; The Devil in Vienna, 1978; My War with Mrs Galloway, 1985; Whiskers Once and Always, 1986; Midnight Soup and a Witch's Hat, 1987; Starring Becky Suslow, 1989; Nobodies and Somebodies, 1991; Next Time I Will, 1993; The Mouse Who Wanted To Marry, 1993; Ariadne, Awake, 1994; Some 30 others - retellings, translations, light verse and original stories for children; Novels for young adults: Risking Love, 1985; Crack in the Heart, 1989. Contributions to: Cricket magazine. Address: c/o Writers House, 21 West 26th Street, New York, NY 10010, USA.

ORIOL Jacques, (Jacques F G Vandievoet), b. 1 Oct 1923, Brussels, Belgium. Geography Teacher (retired); Poet; Essayist; Critic. 1 son. Education: Agregation, secondary school teaching, 1951. Publications: Quarantaine, 1983; Dédicaces, 1984; Midi, déjè Minuit, 1985; Nous ferons se lever une clarté très haute, 1985; L'Un, Le Multiple et le Tout, 1985; Voyage, 1986; Co-author with Années Quatre-Vingts group: L'an prochain a Valparaiso, 1986; Etat critique, 1987; Bruxelles a venir, 1987; Poète aujourd'hui, comment dire?, 1989; Douze chants pour renouer les liens d'amour en floréal, 1989; Demi-deuil, 1990; Contre la réforme de l'orthographe (collective work), 1990; Un un mot comme en cent (ana), 1992; Dilecta, 1993. Contributions to: Reviews to various literary journals. Honours: 1st Prize, Classical Poetry, Rosati, Arras, 1985; Cup, Nord Pas-de-Calais Regional Council, 1986; François Villon Prize, National Association of French Writers, 1986; Silver Medal, High School of French Contemporary Culture, 1987; 1st Prize, Classical Poetry, École de la Loire, Blois, 1989. Memberships: Belgian Section, PEN Club; Association of Belgian Authors; Union of Walloon Writers and Artists; Sociedad de Escritores de Chile; Années Quatre-Vingts Group; Association pour la au suavegarde et l'expansion de la langue française. Address: 210 avenue Moliere, boite 10, B-1060 Brussels, Belgium.

ORLEDGE Robert Francis Nicholas, b. 5 Jan 1948, Bath, Somerset, England. Professor of Music. Education: Associate, Royal College of Organists, 1964; Clare College, Cambridge; BA (Hons), Music, 1968, MA, 1972, PhD, 1973, Cambridge University. Appointment: Professor of Music, University of Liverpool. Publications: Gabriel Fauré, 1979, revised edition, 1983; Debussy and the Theatre, 1982; Charles Koechlin (1867-1950): His Life and Works, 1989, revised edition, 1995; Satie the Composer, 1990; Satie Remembered, 1995. Contributions to: Music and Letters; Musical Quarterly; Musical Times; Music Review; Current Musicology; Journal of the Royal Musical Association. Memberships: Royal Musical Association; Centre de Documentation Claude Debussy; Association des Amis de Charles Koechlin; Fondation Erik Satie. Address: Windermere House, Windermere Terrace, Liverpool L8 3SB, England.

ORLOVA Alexandra (Anatolrevna), b. 22 Feb 1911, Ekaterinoslav, Russia (US citizen, 1984). Musicologist. m. (1) Georgi Orlov, 1935, dec 1940, 2 sons, (2) Mikhail Glukh, 23 Apr 1963, dec 1973. Education: Leningrad Institute of Art History, 1928-30; Extra-mural studies, Leningrad University, 1930-33. Appointments: Freelance Writer, 1950-. Publications: Glinka: Literary Legacy, Vol I, 1952, Vol II, 1953; Glinka in the Memory of Contemporaries, 1955; Rimsky-Korsakov, Chronicle of His Life and Works (in Russian), 4 volumes, 1969-71; Glinka in Petersburg, 1971; Musorgsky in Petersburg, 1974; Mikhail Glinka: Essay on His Life and Works, 1977; Musorgsky: Days and Works, 1983; Glinka's Life in Music, 1988; Tchaikovsky: A self-portrait, 1990; Musorgsky Remembered, 1991. Contributions to: Numerous contributions to collections, newspapers and magazines, USSR, USA, France, Germany. Address: 97 Van Wagenen Avenue, Apt 1D, Jersey City, NJ 07306, USA.

ORLOWSKI Wladyslaw, b. 27 June 1922, Warsaw, Poland. Writer. m. Halina Radzikowska, 4 Nov 1954, 2 sons. Education: MA, University of Lodz, 1947; PhD, Institute of Art, Polish Academy of Sciences, Warsaw, 1970. Publications: From the Book to the Screen, 1961; The Justice in Kyoto (play), 1961; Other's Love, Other's Suffering, 1976; Call From the Empty Space, 1982; The Splinters, 1987; Sunrise of the Passed Day, 1988. Contributions to: Numerous journals and magazines. Honours: Literary Prizes, Minister of Defence, 1965, City of Lodz, 1987. Membership: Society of Polish Writers. Address: ul Brzezna 18 m 5, 90-303 Lodz, Poland.

ORMEROD Roger, b. 17 Apr 1920, Wolverhampton, Staffordshire, England. Author. Publications: Time to Kill, 1974; The Silence of the Night, 1974; Full Fury, 1975; A Spoonful of Luger, 1975; Sealed with a Loving Kill, 1976; The Colour of Fear, 1976; A Glimpse of Death, 1976; Too Late for the Funeral, 1977; The Murder Come to Mind, 1977; A Dip into Murder, 1978; The Weight of Evidence, 1978; The Bright Face of Danger, 1979; The Amnesia Trap, 1979; Cart Before the Hearse, 1979; More Dead than Alive, 1980; Double Take, 1980; One Breathless Hour, 1981; Face Value, 1983; Seeing Red, 1984; The Hanging Doll Murder, 1984; Dead Ringer, 1985; Still Life with Pistol, 1986; A Death to Remember, 1986; An Alibi Too Soon, 1987; The Second Jeopardy, 1987; An Open Window, 1988; By Death Possessed, 1988; Guilt on the Lily, 1989; Death of an Innocent, 1989; No Sign of Life, 1990; Hung in the Blance, 1990; Farewell Gesture, 1990. Address: c/o Constable, 10 Orange Street, London WC2H 7EG, England.

ORMONDE Paul Fraser, b. 7 Feb 1931, Sydney, New South Wales, Australia. Journalist; Public Relations Consultant. m. Marie Therese Kilmartin, 27 Aug 1955, 2 sons, 2 daughters. Education: St Patricks' College, Strathfield, Sydney. Appointments: Editorial Board, Catholic Worker, Melbourne, 1959-76; Feature writer/leader writer, Melbourne Herald, 1970-81; Vice Chairman, Victorian Writers Centre, 1993-. Publications: The Movement, 1972; A Foolish Passionate Man, 1981; Catholics in Revolution, 1988. Contributions to: Meanjin; Overland; Eureka Street; Sydney Morning Herald; The Age, Sunday Age (Melbourne); Catholic Worker (Melbourne). Memberships: Fellowship of Australian Writers; Victorian Writers Centre, Vice Chair, 1993-; National Book Council Committee. Address: 23/2A Robe Street, St Kilda, Victoria, 3182 Australia.

ORMSBY Frank, b. 30 Oct 1947, Enniskillen County, Fermanagh, Northern Ireland. Schoolmaster. Education: BA, English, 1970, MA, 1971, Queen's University, Belfast, Northern Ireland.

Appointment: Editor, The Honest Ulsterman, 1969-89. Publications: A Store of Candles, 1977; Poets from the North of Ireland (editor), 1979, new edition, 1990; A Northern Spring, 1986; Northern Windows: An Anthology of Ulster Autobiography (editor), 1987; The Long Embrace: Twentieth Century Irish Love Poems (editor), 1987; Thine in Storm and Calm: An Amanda McKittrick Ros Reader (editor), 1988; The Collected Poems of John Hewitt (editor), 1991; A Rage for Order: Poetry of the Northern Ireland Troubles (editor), 1992; The Ghost Train, 1995. Address: 36 Strathmore Park North, Belfast BT15 5HR, Northern Ireland.

ORNSTEIN Robert E, b. 17 Feb 1942, New York, New York, USA. Assisstant Professor of Medical Psychology; President, Langley Porter Institute. Education: BA, Queens College, City of New York; PhD, Stanford University. Publications: On the Experience of Time, 1968; On the Psychology of Meditation, 1971; Psychology of Consciousness, 1974; The Healing Brain (co-author), 1987; New World, New Mind: Moving Towards Conscious Evolution (co-author), 1989; The Roots of the Self, 1993. Contributions to: Psychonomic Science; Psychophysiology; Psychology Today. Honours: Creative Talent Award, American Institute for Research, 1968; UNESCO Award, Best Contribution to Psychology, 1972; Media Award, American Psychological Foundation, 1973. Memberships: International Society for the Study of Time; Institute for the Study of Human Consciousness; Biofeedback Society. Address: Langley Porter Institute, 401 Parnassus, San Francisco, CA 94143, USA.

ORR Gregory (Simpson), b. 3 Feb 1947, Albany, New York, USA. Professor of English; Poet; Writer. m. Trisha Winer, 1973, 2 daughters. Education: BA, Antioch College, 1969; MFA, Columbia University, 1972. Appointments: Assistant Professor, 1975-80, Associate Professor, 1980-88, Professor of English, 1988-, University of Virginia; Poetry Consultant, Virginia Quarterly Review, 1976-; Visting Writer, University of Hawaii at Manoa, 1982. Publications: Poetry: Burning the Empty Nests, 1973; Gathering the Bones Together, 1975; Salt Wings, 1980; The Red House, 1980; We Must Make A Kingdom of It, 1986; New and Selected Poems, 1988; City of Salt, 1995; Non-Fiction: Stanley Kunitz: An Introduction to the Poetry, 1985; Richer Entanglements: Essays and Notes on Poetry and Poems, 1993. Honours: Academy of American Poets Prize, 1970; YM-YWHA Discovery Award, 1970; Bread Loaf Writers Conference Transatlantic Review Award, 1976; Guggenheim Fellowship, 1977; National Endowment for the Arts Fellowships, 1978, 1989; Fulbright Grant, 1983. Address: c/o Department of English, University of Virginia, Charlottesville, VA 22903, USA.

ORR Wendy Ann, b. 19 Nov 1953, Edmonston, New Brunswick, Canada. Author (Children's and Young Adult). m. Thomas Orr, 11 Jan 1975, 1 son, 1 daughter. Education: Diploma of Occupational Therapy, 1975; BSc, 1982. Publications: Amanda's Dinosaur, 1988; The Tin Can Puppy, 1990; Bad Martha, 1991; Leaving It To You, 1992; Aa-Choo!, 1992; Micki Moon & Daniel Day, 1993; Ark in the Park, 1994; Mind-Blowing (Aus)/A Light in Space (Canada), 1994; The Great Yackandandah Billy Cart Race, 1994; Yasou Nikki, 1995; The Bully Biscuit Gang, 1995; Jessica Joan, 1995; Dirtbikes, 1995; Grandfather Martin, 1995; Peeling the Onion, 1996; Alroy's Very Nearly Clean Bedroom, 1996. Honours: Australian Children's Book Council Book of the Year, Younger Readers: Shortlist 1993, Winner 1995. Memberships: Australian Society of Authors; Australian Children's Book Council (Victoria). Literary Agent: Debbie Golvan, Golvan Arts Management, PO Box 766, Kew 3101, Australia. Address: RMB 1257, Cobram, Victoria 3644, Australia.

ORSZÁG-LAND Thomas, b. 12 Jan 1938, Budapest, Hungary. Writer. Publications: Berlin Proposal, 1990; Free Women, 1991. Translations: Bluebeard's Castle, 1988; Splendid Stags, 1992; 33 Poems by Radnoti, 1992; Poems by Mezei, 1995. Contributions to: Nature; Contemporary Review; Spectator; New York Times; Observer; Guardian; Financial Times; Times Higher Education Supplement. Memberships: Fellow, International PEN; Foreign Press Association; Royal Institute of International Affairs; Society of Authors. Address: PO Box 1213, London N6 5HZ, England.

ORTEGA Julio, b. 29 Sept 1942, Peru. Professor; Writer. m. Claudia J Elliott, 21 Mar 1986. Education: Doctorate in Literature, Catholic University, Lima, Peru. Appointments: Professor, University of Texas at Austin, 1978-86, Brandeis University, 1987-. Publications: La Contemplation y la fiesta, 1969; Mediodia, 1970; Figuracion de la persona, 1971; Relato de la Utopia, 1973; Ceremonias, 1974; Rituales,

1976; The Land in the Day, 1978; Latin America in its Literature, 1980; Poetics of Change, 1984; Adios Ayachucho, 1986; La Lima del 900, 1986; Teoria poetica de Vallejo, 1986; Antolgia de la poesia hispanoamericana, 1987. Contributions to: Journals and magazines. Honours: Guggenhei Fellowship, 1974; Prizes. Memberships: Archives de la Litterature Latinoamericaine, Paris; Latin American Studies Association; Peruvian Association of Culture, president. Address: c/o Department of Romance and Comparative Literature, Brandeis University, Waltham, MA 02254, USA.

ORTIZ Simon J(oseph), b. 27 May 1941, Albuquerque, New Mexico, USA. Poet; Writer. m. Marlene Foster, Dec 1981, div Sept 1984, 3 children. Education: Fort Lewis College, 1961-62; University of New Mexico, 1966-68; University of Iowa, 1968-69. Appointments: Instructor, San Diego State University, 1974; Institute of American Arts, Santa Fe, New Mexico, 1974; Navajo Community College, Tsaile, Arizona, 1975-77; College of Marin, Kentfield, California, 1976-79; University of New Mexico, Albuquerque, 1979-81; Sinte Gleska College, Mission, South Dakota, 1985-86; Lewis and Clark College, Portland, Oregon, 1990; Consulting Editor, Navajo Comunity College Press, Tsaile, 1982-83; Pueblo of Acoma Press, Acoma, New Mexico, 1982-84; Arts Coordinator, Metropolitan Arts Commission, Portland, Oregon, 1990. Publications: Naked in the Wind (poetry), 1971; Going for the Rain (poetry), 1976; A Good Journey, poetry, 1977; Howbah Indians (short stories), 1978; Song, Poetry, Language (essays), 1978; Fight Back: For the Sake of the People, For the Sake of the Land (poetry and prose), 1980; From Sand Creek: Rising in This Heart Which is Our America (poetry), 1981; A Poem is a Journey, 1981; The Importance of Childhood, 1982; Fightin': New and Collected Stories, 1983; Woven Stone: A 3-in-1 Volume of Poetry and Prose, 1991; After and Before the Lightning (poems), 1994. Editor: Califa: The California Poetry (co-editor), 1978; A Ceremony of Brotherhood (co-editor), 1980; Earth Power Coming, anthology of Native American short fiction, 1983. Contributions to: Various anthologies and textbooks. Honours: National Endowment for the Arts Discovery Award, 1969; Fellowship, 1981; Honored Poet, White House Salute to Poetry and American Poets, 1980; New Mexico Humanities Council Humanitarian Award for Literary Achievement, 1989. Address: 3535 North 1st Avenue, #R-10, Tucson, AZ 85719, USA.

OSBORN Betty Olive, b. 15 July 1934, Melbourne, Victoria, Australia. Writer; Historian. m. Bruce Jamieson Osborn, 23 Apr 1962, 1 son, 3 daughters. Education: BA, University of Melbourne, 1959. Appointments: Journalist, Argus, 1952-57; Book Editor, Melbourne University Press, 1958-62. Publications: History of Holy Trinity Bacchus Marsh, 1971; The Bacchus Story, 1973; Pieces of Glass (play), 1977; Maryborough, A Social History 1854-1904 (with Trenear DuBourg), 1985; Maryborough: Against the Odds 1905-1961, 1995. Contributions to: Argus Weekend Magazine; Age Literary Supplement; Wimmera-Mallee Country Bulletin. Honour: Montague Grover Prize, 1955. Memberships: Fellowship of Australian Writers (Victoria) Inc; Graduate Union, Melbourne University; Committee Member, Midlands Historical Society; Life Member, Bacchus Marsh and District Historical Society. Address: 18 Douglass Street, Maryborough, Victoria 3465, Australia.

OSBORNE Charles Thomas, b. 24 Nov 1927, Brisbane, Australia. Author; Critic; Musicologist. Education: Brisbane High School, 1941-44; Griffith University, 1944. Appointments: Assistant Editor, The London Magazine, 1958-66; Literature Director, Arts Council of Great Britain, 1966-86; Chief Theatre Critic, London Daily Telegraph, 1987-92. Publications: The Complete Operas of Verdi, 1969; W H Auden: The Life of a Poet, 1980; Letter to W H Auden and Other Poems, 1984; Giving It Away, 1986; The Bel Canto Operas, 1994; Volumes on Mozart, Wagner, Puccini and Strauss. Contributions to: Times Literary Supplement; Encounter; Spectator; Encyclopedia dell Speltacolo; Annual Register, Harvard Advocate. Honour: Gold Medal, 1993. Memberships: PEN; Royal Society of Literature; Critics' Circle. Literary Agent: Aitken & Stone, 29 Fernshaw Road, London SW10 0TG, England. Address: 125 St George's Road, London SE1 6HY, England. 192.

OSBORNE Maggie, (Margaret Osborne), b. 10 June 1941, Hollywood, California, USA. Writer. m. George M Osborne II, 27 Apr 1972, 1 son. Publications: Alexa, 1980; Salem's Daughter, 1981; Portrait in Passion, 1981; Yankee Princess, 1982; Rage to Love, 1983; Flight of Fancy, 1984; Castles and Fairy Tales, 1986; Winter Magic, 1986; The Heart Club, 1987; Where There's Smoke, 1987; Chase the Heart, 1987; Heart's Desire, 1988; Dear Santa, 1989; Partners (with

Carolyn Bransford), 1989; Jigsaw, 1990; American Pie, 1990; Lady Reluctant, 1991; Emeral Rain, 1991; Happy New Year Darling, 1992; Murder By the Book, 1992; The Pirate and His Lady, 1992; Cache Poor, 1993; A Wish and a Kiss, 1993; The Accidental Princess, 1994; The Drop in Bride, 1994; The Wives of Bowie Stone, 1994. Address: Box E, Dillon, CO 80435, USA.

OSBORNE Mary Pope, b. 20 May 1949, Fort Sill, Oklahoma, USA. Writer. m. Will Osborne, 16 May 1976. Education: BA, University of North Carolina. Publications: Run, Run, As Fast As You Can, 1982; Love Always, Blue, 1983; Best Wishes, Joe Brady, 1984; Mo to the Rescue, 1985; Last One Home, 1986; Beauty and the Beast, 1987; Christopher Columbus, Admiral of the Ocean Sea, 1987; Pandora's Box, 1987; Jason and the Argonauts, 1988; The Deadly Power of Medusa (with Will Osborne), 1988; Favorite Greek Myths, 1989; A Visit to Sleep's House, 1989; Mo and His Friends, 1989; American Tall Tales, 1990; Moonhorse, 1991; Spider Kane Series, 1992; Magic Treehouse Series, 1993; Mermaid Tales, 1993; Molly and the Prince, 1994; Haunted Waters, 1994; Favourite Norse Myths, 1996; One World, Many Religions, 1996; Rockinghorse Christmas, 1997. Address: Brandt & Brandt Agancy, 1501 Broadway, No 2310, New York, NY 10036, USA.

OSBOURNE Ivor Livingstone, b. 6 Nov 1951, Porus, Jamaica. Author; Publisher. Partner, Charline Mertens, 2 daughters. Publications: Novels: The Mercenary, 1976; The Mango Season, 1979, 2nd edition, 1987; Prodigal, 1987; The Rasta Cookbook, Optima, 1990; The Exotic Cookbook of Optima, 1990. Contributions to: Various journals and magazines. Literary Agent: Peter Bryant Writers, 3 Kidderpire Gardens, Hampstead, London, England. Address: 27c Chippenham Road, Maida Vale, London W9 2AH, England.

OSERS Ewald, b. 13 May 1917, Prague, Czechoslovakia. Translator; Author. m. Mary Harman, 3 June 1942, 1 son, 1 daughter. Education: Prague University; BA (Hons), University of London. Appointments: Chairman, Translators Association, 1971, 1980-81; Translators Guild, 1975-79; Vice-Chairman, Institute of Linguists, 1975-80; Vice-President, International Federation of Translators, 1977-81, 1984-87; Editorial Director, Babel, 1979-87; Member, International Book Committee, 1981-87. Publications: Poetry: Wish You Were Here, 1976; Arrive Where We Started, 1995; Volume of own poetry translated into Czech, 1986; Translator, over 110 books including 34 volumes of poetry; English translation of Jaroslav Seifert, Czech Nobel Prize Winner. Contributions to: Magazines. Address: 33 Reades Lane, Sonning Common, Reading, Berkshire RG4 9LL, England.

OSOFISAN Femi, (Babafemi Adeyemi), b. 16 June 1946, Erunwon, Nigeria. Playwright; Author. Education; BA, 1969, PhD, 1974, University of Ibadan. Appointments: Professor, University of Ibadan; Visiting Professor, American Universities. Publications: You Have Lost Your Fine Face, 1969; Red is the Freedom Road, 1974; A Restless Run of Locusts, 1975; The Chattering and the Song, 1974; Once upon Four Robbers, 1978; Farewell to a Cannibal Rage, 1978; Birthdays Are Not for Dying, 1981; The Oriki of a Grasshopper, 1981; No More the Wasted Breed, 1982; Midnight Hotel, 1982; Aringindin and the Nightwatchman, 1989; Another Raft, 1989; Yungba Yungba and the Dance Contest. TV Plays. Novels: Kolera Kolej, 1975; Cordelia, 1990. Verse: Minted Coins, 1986. Honours: Fulbright Fellowships, 1986. Address: Department of Theatre Arts, University of Ibadan, Ibadan, Nigeria.

OSTRIKER Alicia Suskin, b. 11 Nov 1937, New York, New York, USA. Professor of English; Poet; Writer. m. 2 Dec 1958, 1 son, 2 daughters. Education: BA, Brandeis University, 1959; MA, 1960, PhD, 1964, University of Wisconsin. Appointment: Assistant Professor to Professor of English, Rutgers University , 1965-. Publications: Poetry: Songs, 1969; Once More Out of Darkness and Other Poems, 1974; A Dream of Springtime: Poems, 1970-77, 1978; The Mother-Child Papers, 1980; A Woman Under the Surface, 1983; The Imaginary Lover, 1986; Green Age, 1989; The Nakedness of the Fathers, 1994; The Crack in Everything, 1996. Criticism: Vision and Verse in William Blake, 1965; Writing Like a Woman, 1982; Stealing the Language, 1986; Feminist Revision and the Bible, 1993. Contributions to: Professional journals and general publications. Honours: National Endowment for the Arts Fellowship, 1977; Guggenheim Fellowship, 1984-85; William Carlos Williams Prize, Poetry Society of America, 1986; Strousse Poetry Prize, Prairie Schooner, 1987; Anna Rosenberg Poetry Award, 1994; Nominee,

National Book Award, 1996. Memberships: Modern Languages Association; PEN; Poetry Society of America, board of governors, 1988-91. Address: 33 Philip Drive, Princeton, NJ 08540, USA.

OSTROM Hans Ansgar, b. 29 Jan 1954, USA. Writer; Poet; Teacher. m. Jacqueline Bacon, 18 July 1983, 1 son. Education: BA, 1975, PhD, English, 1982, University of California, Davis. Appointments: Contributing Reviewer, Choice, 1987-; Columnist, Morning News Tribune, Tacoma, Washington, 1990-. Publications: The Living Language, 1984; Lives and Moments, 1991; Three to Get Ready, 1991; The Coast Starlight, 1992; Water's Night (with Wendy Bishop), 1992; Colors of a Different Horse, 1993; Langston Hughes: The Short Fiction, 1993. Contributions to: Reviews, poems, stories to: Ploughshares; San Francisco Chronicle; Poetry Northwest; Webster Review; San Francisco Review of Books. Honours: Harvest Prize in Poetry, 1978; Redbook Prize in Fiction, 1985. Memberships: National Book Critics Circle; Modern Language Association; Mystery Writers of America. Address: English Department, University of Puget Sound, Tacoma, WA 98416, USA.

OTTEN Charlotte F(lennema), b. 1 Mar 1926, Chicago, Illinois, USA. Professor of English. m. Robert T Otten, 21 Dec 1948, 2 sons. Education: AB, 1949; MA, 1969; PhD, 1971. Publications: Environ: D With Eternity, 1985; A Lycanthropy Reader, 1986; The Voice of the Narrator in Children's Literature, 1989; English Women's Voices, 1991; The Virago Book of Birth Poetry, 1993; Bantam Book of Birth Poetry, 1995; January Rides the Wind, 1997; Classic Werewolf Stories, 1997. Contributions to: Amherst Review; Anglican Theological Review; Commonweal; South Florida Poetry Review; Christian Century; Snowy Egret; South Coast Poetry Review; Manhattan Poetry Review; Descant; Kentucky Poetry Review; MacGuffin; Interim; Southern Humanities Review; Whiskey Island Magazine; Shakespeare Quarterly; Shakespeare Newsletter; Milton Studies; Notes and Queries; English Literary Renaissance; Huntington Library Quarterly; English Studies; Chaucer Review; Signal; Concerning Poetry. Address: English Department, Calvin College, Grand Rapids, MI 49546, USA.

OUELLETTE (Marie Léonne) Francine, b. 11 Mar 1947, Montreal, Quebec, Canada. Writer. 1 daughter. Education: Fine Arts Diploma in Sculpture, 1968; Pilot Licence, 1973. Publications: Au Nom du Père et du Fils, 1984; Le Sorcier, 1985; Sire Gaby du Lac, 1989; Les Ailes Du Destin, 1992; Le Grand Blanc, 1993. Honours: France-Québec, Jean Hamelin, 1986; Prix, Du Grand Public, 1993. Memberships: Union des écrivains Québécois UNEQ. Literary Agent: Michel Ouellette. Address: CP 30, 1044 ch Presquîle, Lac Des Iles, Québec J0W 1J0, Canada.

OUSMANE Sembene, b. 1 Jan 1923, Ziguinchor, Casamance Region, Senegal. Writer; Filmmaker. Education: Studied Film Production under Marc Donski, USSR. Appointments: Plumber; Bricklayer; Apprentice Mechanic; Founder, Editor, 1st Wolof Language Monthly, Kaddu. Publications: Novels: Le docker noir, 1956; O Pays mon beau peuple, 1957; Les bouts de bois de Dieu, 1960; Voltaïque, 1962; L'harmattan, 1964; Vehi-Ciosane suivi du mandat, 1966; Xala, 1974; Fat ndiay Diop, 1976; Dernier de l'empire, 1979. Honours: 1st Prize for Novelists, World Festival of Negro Arts, Dakar, 1966; Grand Prix pour les lettres, President of Republic of Senegal, 1993; Numerous international awards. Memberships: Association des Ecrivain du Sénégal; Societé des Gens de Lettres, France; Société Africaine de Culture; Corresponding Member, German Academy of Letters; President, International PEN Club, Senegal Section. Address: PO Box 8087, Yoff, Dakar, Senegal.

OVERY Paul (Vivian), b. 14 Feb 1940, Dorchester, England. Art Critic; Writer. Education: BA, 1962, MA, 1966, King's College, Cambridge. Appointments: Art Critic, The Listener, London, 1966-68, The Financial Times, London, 1968-70; Literary Editor, New Society, London, 1970-71; Chief Art Critic, The Times, London, 1973-78; Freelance critic and writer, 1978-. Publications: Edouard Manet, 1967; De Stijl, 1969; Kandinsky: The Language of the Eye, 1969; Paul Neagu: A Generative Context, 1981; The Rietveld Schroder House (co-author), 1988; De Stijl, 1991; The Complete Rietveld Furniture (with Peter Vöge), 1993; A Recognition of Restrictions (essay), 1994; Designing for the Modern World, De Stijl: The Red Blue Chair and the Schröder House (essay), in Investigating Modern Art, 1996. Contributions to: Books and journals. Memberships: National Union of Journalists; Society of Authors. Address: 92 South Hill Park, London NW3 2SN, England.

OVESEN Ellis, b. 18 July 1923, New Effington, South Dakota, USA. Writer; Artist; Composer. m. Thor Lowe Smith, 27 Aug 1949, 2 sons. Education: MA, cum laude, University of Wisconsin, 1948; California Teachers Credential, San Jose State University, 1962; Extra classes in poetry writing. Appointments: Teacher of English, University of Wisconsin, 1946-48, San Jose State University, 1962-63; Teaching Poetry, 1963-90. Publications: Gloried Grass, 1970; Haloed Paths, 1973; To Those Who Love, 1974; The Last Hour: Lives Touch, 1975; A Time for Singing, 1977; A Book of Praises, 1977; Beloved I, 1980, II, 1990; The Green Madonna, 1984; The Flowers of God, 1985; The Keeper of the Word, 1985; The Wing Brush, 1986; The Year of the Snake, 1989; The Year of the Horse, 1990. Contributions to: Poet India; Los Altos Town Crier; Paisley Moon; Fresh Hot Bread; Samvedana; Plowman. Honours: National Honour Society, 1941; Los Altos Hills Poet, 1976-90; Honorary Doctorate, World Academy of Arts and Culture, 1986; Dame of Merit, Knights of Malta, 1988; Golden Poet Awards, 1988, 1989, 1991; World Poet Award, 1989; Research Fellow, 1992. Memberships: National Writers Club; California Writers Club; Poetry Society of America; California State Poetry Society. Address: Box 482, Los Altos, CA 94023, USA.

OVNI. See: **TORRES Luiz Rebouças.**

OVSTEDAL Barbara Kathleen, (Rosalind Laker), b. England. Writer. m. Inge Ovstedal, 1945, 1 son, 1 daughter. Education: West Sussex College of Art. Publications: As Rosalind Laker: The Warwyck Trilogy, 1979-80; This Shining Land, 1985; The Silver Touch, 1987; To Dance With Kings, 1988; The Golden Tulip, 1991; The Venetian Mask, 1992; The Sugar Pavilion, 1993; The Fortuny Gown, 1995; The Fragile Hour, 1996. Contributions to: Good Housekeeping; Country Life; Woman; Woman's Own; Woman's Weekly. Memberships: Society of Authors; Romantic Novelists Association. Address: c/o Laurence Pollinger Ltd, 18 Maddox Street, London W1R 0EU, England.

OWEN Charles, b. 14 Nov 1915, England. Author; Management Consultant; Royal Navy Officer (retired). m. Felicity, 14 Feb 1950, 1 son, 1 daughter. Education: Royal Navy Colleges, Dartmouth and Greenwich, England. Publications: Independent Traveller, 1966; Britons Abroad, 1968; The Opaque Society, 1970; No More Heroes, 1975; The Grand Days of Travel, 1979; Just Across the Channel, 1983; Plain Yarns from the Fleet, 1997. Contributions to: Various magazines and journals. Honour: Distinguished Service Cross, 1943. Memberships: Society of Authors; Writers Guild of Great Britain; PEN. Address: Flat 31, 15 Portman Square, London W1H 9HD, England.

OWEN Douglas David Roy, b. 17 Nov 1922, Norton, Suffolk, England. University Professor (retired). m. Berit Mariann Person, 31 July 1954, 2 sons. Education: University College, Nottingham, 1942-43; BA, 1948, MA, 1953, PhD, 1955, Cambridge; Sorbonne and Collège de France, Paris, 1950-51. Appointment: Founder, General Editor, Forum for Modern Language Studies, 1965-. Publications: The Evolution of the Grail Legend, 1968; The Vision of Hell, 1970; The Song of Roland (translation), 1972, new expanded edition, 1990; The Legend of Roland: A Pageant of the Middle Ages, 1973; Noble Lovers, 1975; Chrétien de Troyes: Arthurian Romances (translation), 1987; Guillaume le Clerc: Fergus of Galloway (translation), 1989; A Chat Round the Old Course (by DDRO), 1990; Eleanor of Aquitaine: Queen and Legend, 1993; The Romance of Reynard the Fox, 1994. Editor with R C Johnston: Fabliaux, 1957; Two Old French Gauvain Romances, 1972. Contributions to: Books and journals. Memberships: International Arthurian Society; Société Rencesvals; International Courtly Literature Society. Address: 7 West Acres, St Andrews, Fife KY16 9UD, Scotland.

OWEN Eileen, b. 27 Feb 1949, Concord, New Hampshire, USA. Editor; Writer. m. John D Owen, 19 June 1971. Education: BA, Spanish, University of New Hampshire, 1971; BA, English, 1979, MA, Creative Writing, 1981, University of Washington. Publication: Facing the Weather Side, 1985. Contributions to: Poetry Northwest; Dark Horse; Tar River Review of Poetry; Passages North; Sojourner; Welter; Seattle Review; Mississippi Mud; Hollow Springs Review; Signpost; Back Door Travel; Arts and Artists. Honour: Artist-in-Residence, Ucross Foundation, Wyoming, 1984. Address: 18508 90th Avenue West, Edmonds, WA 98020, USA.

OWENS Rochelle, b. 2 Apr 1936, Brooklyn, New York, USA. Poet; Dramatist; Critic; Professor; Translator. m. (1) David Owens, 30 Mar 1956, diss 1959, (2) George Economou, 17 June 1962. Education: Theatre Arts, Herbert Berghof Studio, New York City; New School for

Social Research, New York City; University of Montreal, Alliance Française, Paris, New York City. Appointments: Visiting Lecturer, University of California at San Diego, 1982; Writer-in-Residence, Brown University, Providence, Rhode Island, 1989; Currently, Adjunct Professor in Creative Writing, University of Oklahoma, Norman. Publications: Poetry: Not Be Essence That Cannot Be, 1961; Four Young Lady Poets (with others), 1962; Salt and Core, 1968; I Am the Babe of Joseph Stalin's Daughter: Poems 1961-1971, 1972; Poems From Joe's Garage, 1973; The Joe 82 Creation Poems, 1974; The Joe Chronicles, Part 2, 1979; Shemuel, 1979; French Light, 1984; Constructs, 1985; W C Fields in French Light, 1986; How Much Paint Does the Painting Need, 1988; Black Chalk, 1992; Rubbed Stones and Other Poems, 1994; New and Selected Earlier Poems, 1961-1990, forthcoming. Plays: Futz and What Came After, 1968; The Karl Marx Play and Others, 1974; Emma Instigated Me, 1976; The Widow and the Colonel, 1977; Mountain Rites, 1978; Chucky's Hunch, 1982. Editor: Spontaneous Combustion: Eight New American Plays, 1972; Tramnslator: Liliane Atlan: The Passerby, 1993. Contributions to: Poems in many anthologies and periodicals; Critical articles and essays in various journals. Honours: Rockefeller Grants, 1965, 1976; Obie Awards, 1965, 1967, 1982; Yale School of Drama Fellowship, 1968; American Broadcasting Corporation Fellowship, 1968; Guggenheim Fellowship, 1971; National Endowment for the Arts Award, 1976; Villager Award, 1982; Franco-Anglais Festival de Poesie, Paris, 1991; Rockefeller Foundation Resident Scholar, Bellagio, Italy, 1993. Memberships: American Society of Composers, Authors, and Publishers; Authors League; Dramatists Guild; New York Theatre Strategy; Women's Theatre Council. Address: 1401 Magnolia, Norman, OK 73072, USA.

OXLEY William, b. 29 Apr 1939, Manchester, England. Poet; Philosopher; Translator; Actor; Traveller; Freelance Writer. Education: Manchester College of Commerce, 1953-55. Publications: The Dark Structures, 1967; New Workings, 1969; Passages from Time: Poems from a Life, 1971; The Icon Poems, 1972; Sixteen Days in Autumn (travel), 1972; Opera Vetera, 1973; Mirrors of the Sea, 1973; Eve Free, 1974; Mundane Shell, 1975; Superficies, 1976; The Exile, 1979; The Notebook of Hephaestus and Other Poems, 1981; Poems of a Black Orpheus, 1981; The Synopthegms of a Prophet, 1981; The Idea and Its Imminence, 1982; Of Human Consciousness, 1982; The Cauldron of Inspiration, 1983; A Map of Time, 1984; The Triviad and Other Satires, 1984; The Inner Tapestry, 1985; Vitalism and Celebration, 1987; The Mansands Trilogy, 1988; Mad Tom on Tower Hill, 1988; The Patient Reconstruction of Paradise, 1991; Forest Sequence, 1991; In the Drift of Words, 1992; The Playboy, 1992; Cardboard Troy, 1993; The Hallsands Tragedy, 1993; Collected Longer Poems, 1994; Completing the Picture (editor), 1995; The Green Crayon Man, 1997. Contributions to: Anthologies and periodicals. Address: 6 The Mount, Furzeham, Brixham, South Devon TQ5 8QY, England.

OZ Amos, b. 4 May 1939, Jerusalem, Israel. Author. m. Nily Zuckerman, 5 Apr 1960, 1 son, 2 daughters. Education: BA cum laude, Hebrew Literature, Philosophy, Hebrew University, Jerusalem, 1965. Appointments: Teacher, Literature, Philosophy, Hulda High School and Givat Brenner Regional High School, 1963-86; Visiting Fellow, St Cross College, Oxford, England, 1969-70; Writer-in-Residence, Hebrew University, Jerusalem, 1975, 1990; Visiting Professor, University of California, Berkeley, USA, 1980; Writer-in-Residence, Professor of Literature, The Colorado College, Colorado Springs, 1984-85; Writer in Residence, Visiting Professor of Literature, Boston University, Massachusetts, 1987; Full Professor of Hebrew Literature, Ben Gurion University, Beer Sheva, Israel, 1987-. Publications: Over 15 books, 1962-96. Address: c/o Deborah Owen Ltd, 78 Narrow Street, London E14, England.

OZICK Cynthia, b. 17 Apr 1928, New York, New York, USA. Author. m. Bernard Hallote, 7 Sept 1952, 1 daughter. Education: BA, cum laude, English, New York University, 1949; MA, Ohio State University, 1950.Publications: Trust, 1966; The Pagan Rabbi and Other Stories, 1971; Bloodshed and Three Novellas, 1976; Levitation: Five Fictions, 1982; Art and Ardor: Essays, 1983; The Cannibal Galaxy, 1983; The Messiah of Stockholm, 1987; Metaphor and Memory: Essays, 1989; The Shawl, 1989; The Pagan Rabbi & Other Stories, 1991. Contributions to: Poetry, criticism, reviews, translations, essays and fiction in numerous periodicals and anthologies. Honours: Guggenheim Fellowship, 1982; Mildred and Harold Strauss Living Award, American Academy of Arts and Letters, 1983; Honorary doctorates. Memberships: PEN; Authors League; American Academy of Arts and Sciences; American Academy and Institute of Arts and

Letters; Phi Beta Kappa. Address: c/o Raines & Raines, 71 Park Avenue, New York, NY 10016, USA.

P

PAANANEN Eloise (Katherine), b. 12 Apr 1923, Seattle, Washington, USA. Author. m. (1) P R Engle, 1 son, 1 daughter, (2) Lauri A Pannanen, 26 Oct 1973. Education: BA, George Washington University, 1947. Publications: Some 30 books on military history, culture, travel, etc. Contributions to: Newspapers and magazines. Honours: Several awards. Memberships: American Society of Journalists and Authors; Society of Women Geographers. Address: 6348 Crosswoods Drive, Falls Church, VA 22044, USA.

PACK Robert, b. 29 May 1929, New York, New York, USA. Professor; Poet; Writer. m. (1) Isabelle Miller, 1950, (2) Patricia Powell, 1961, 2 sons, 1 daughter. Education: BA, Dartmouth College, 1951; MA, Columbia University, 1953. Appointments: Teacher, Barnard College, 1957-64; Abernathy Professor, Middlebury College, Vermont, 1970-; Director, Bread Loaf Writers Conferences, 1973-. Publications: Poetry: The Irony of Joy, 1955; A Stranger's Privilege, 1959; Guarded by Women, 1963; Selected Poems, 1964; Home from the Cemetery, 1969; Nothing But Light, 1972; Keeping Watch, 1976; Waking to My Name: New and Selected Poems, 1980; Faces in a Single Tree: A Cycle of Monologues, 1984; Clayfield Rejoices, Clayfield Laments: A Sequence of Poems, 1987; Before It Vanishes: A Packet for Professor Pagels, 1989; Fathering the Map: New and Selected Later Poems, 1993. Other: Wallace Stevens: An Approach to His Poetry and Thought, 1958; Affirming Limits: Essays on Morality, Choice and Poetic Form, 1985; The Long View: Essays on the Discipline of Hope and Poetic Craft, 1991. Editor: The New Poets of England and America (with Donald Hall and Louis Simpson), 1957, 2nd edition, 1962; Poems of Doubt and Belief: An Anthology of Modern Religious Poetry (with Tom Driver), 1964; Literature for Composition on the Theme of Innocence and Experience (with Marcus Klein), 1966; Short Stories: Classic, Modern, Contemporary (with Marcus Klein), 1967; Keats: Selected Letters, 1974; The Bread Loaf Anthology of Contemporary American Poetry (with Sydney Lea and Jay Parini), 1985; The Bread Loaf Anthology of Contemporary American Short Stories (with Jay Parini), 2 volumes, 1987, 1989; Poems for a Small Planet: An Anthology of Nature Poetry (with Jay Parini), 1993. Honours: Fulbright Fellowship, 1956; American Academy of Arts and Letters Grant, 1957; Borestone Mountain Poetry Awardf, 1964; National Endowment for the Arts Grant, 1968. Address: c/o Middlebury College, Middlebury, VT 05742, USA.

PACNER Karel, b. 29 Mar 1936, Janovice-n-Uhl, Czechoslovakia. Science Journalist. m. 1971-73. Education: Dipl Ing (Master's degree), Economics, Economics University, Prague, 1959. Appointments: Mlada fronta (now Mlada fronta Dnes) daily newspaper, 1959-. Publications: In Czech: On both sides of Space, 1968; ... and the giant leap for mankind (Apollo 11), 1971, 1972; We are Searching Extra-Terrestrial Civilisation, 1976; Columbuses of Space, 1976; Soyuz is Calling Apollo, 1976; The Constructor-in-Chief, 1977; Nine Space Days, 1978; Message of Space Worlds, 1978; The Trip on Mars; Towns in Space, 1986; The Humanized of Galaxy, 1987; Discovered Secrets of UFO, 1991; The Secret Race on the Moon, 1996. Contributions to: Several Czech magazines especially Letectvi a kosmonautika. Honours: Literary awards for several books from publishing houses. Memberships: Community of Writers in Czech Republic; Czechoslovak Society of Arts and Sciences in USA, Czechoslovak Branch. Address: K Vidouli 216, 15500 Prague 5, Czech Republic.

PADEL Ruth, b. 8 May 1946, London, England. Poet; Writer. m. Myles Burnyeat, 15 Aug 1984, 1 daughter. Education: BA, 1969, MA, 1975, PhD, 1976, Oxford University. Publications: Poetry: Alibi, 1985; Summer Snow, 1990; Angel, 1993; Fusewire, 1996. Other: In and Out of the Mind: Greek Images of the Tragic Self, 1992; Whom Gods Destroy: Elements of Greek and Tragic Madness, 1995. Contributions to: Anthologies, journals, newspapers and periodicals including: International Journal of Psycho-analysis, 1996; Essays on Paul Durcan, Irish Poet, 1996; Arion, 1996. Honours: Prizes, National Poetry Competition, 1985, 1992, 1994, First Prize, 1996; Royal Literary Fund Grant, 1991; Wingate Fellowship, 1992; Poetry Book Society Recommendation, 1993; Bursary from Arts Council, Great Britain for Writers Bursary for Fusewire. Memberships: Hellenic Society; PEN; Royal Zoological Society; Society of Authors. Address: 38 Lisburne Road, London NW3 2NR, England.

PADFIELD Peter Lawrence Notton, b. 3 Apr 1932, Calcutta, India. Author. m. Dorothy Jean Yarwood, 23 Apr 1960, 1 son, 2 daughters. Publications: The Titanic and the Californian, 1965; An Agony of Collisions, 1966; Aim Straight: A Biography of Admiral Sir Percy Scott, 1966; Broke and the Shannon: A Biography of Admiral Sir Philip Broke, 1968; The Battleship Era, 1972; Guns at Sea: A History of Naval Gunnery, 1973; The Great Naval Race: Anglo-German Naval Rivalry 1900-1914, 1974; Nelson's War, 1978; Tide of Empires: Decisive Naval Campaigns in the Rise of the West, Volume I 1481-1654, 1979, Volume II 1654-1763, 1982; Rule Britannia: The Victorian and Edwardian Navy, 1981; Beneath the Houseflag of the P & O, 1982; Dönitz, The Last Führer, 1984; Armada, 1988; Himmler, Reichsführer - SS, 1990; Hess: Flight for the Führer, 1991, revised, updated edition, 1993; War beneath the Sea: Submarine Conflict 1939-1945, 1995. Novels: The Lion's Claw, 1978; The Unquiet Gods, 1980; Gold Chains of Empire, 1982; Salt and Steel, 1986. Address: Westmoreland Cottage, Woodbridge, Suffolk, England.

PADGETT Tim. Journalist. m. Yolaluis Perez-Padgett. Education: BA, Wabash College, Indiana; Studied in London, 1983, and in Venezuela, 1985-86; MA, Medill Graduate School of Journalism, Northwestern University, 1985. Appointments: Reporter and Copy Editor, Topics Newspapers, Indianapolis, Indiana, 1980; Intern, Newsday, 1982, 1983; News Reporter, Chicago Sun-Times, 3 years; Chicago Correspondent, 1988-90, Mexico City Bureau Chief, 1990-, Newsweek. Honour: Co-Winner, First Place Award for Newswriting, Illinois UPI, 1986; Co-Winner, Bartolome Mitre Award for Distinguished Journalism, Inter-American Press Association, 1994. Address: c/o Newsweek, 251 West 57th Street, New York, NY 10019-1894, USA.

PADHY Pravat Kumar, b. 27 Dec 1954, India. Geologist; Poet. m. Namita Padhy, 6 Mar 1983, 2 daughters. Education: MSc, 1979; MTech, Mineral Exploration, 1980; PhD, Applied Geology, 1992. Appointment: Geologist, ONGC, Baroda, Gujarat. Publication: Silence of the Seas, 1992. Contributions to: Anthologies and periodicals. Honour: Certificate of Honour, Writer's Life Line, Canada, 1986. Address: 166 HIG Complex, Sailashri Vihar, Bhubaneshwar 751016, Orissa, India.

PADOVANO Anthony Thomas, b. 18 Sept 1934, Harrison, New Jersey, USA. Professor of American Literature; Writer. m. Theresa P Lackamp, 1 Sept 1974, 3 sons, 1 daughter. Education: BA magna cum laude, Seton Hall University, 1956; STB magna cum laude, 1958, STL magna cum laude, 1960, STD magna cum laude, 1962, Pontifical Gregorian University, Rome; PhL, St Thomas Pontifical International University, Rome, 1962; MA, New York University, 1971; PhD, Fordham University, 1980. Appointments: Professor of Systematic Theology, Darlington School of Theology, Mahuah, New Jersey, 1962-74; Professor of American Literature, Ramapo College of New Jersey, 1971-; Various visiting professorships. Publications: The Cross of Christ, The Measure of the World, 1962; The Estranged God, 1966; Who Is Christ?, 1967; Belief in Human Life, 1969; American Culture and the Quest for Christ, 1970; Dawn Without Darkness, 1971; Free to Be Faithful, 1972; Eden and Easter, 1974; A Case for Worship, 1975; Presence and Structure, 1975; America: Its People, Its Promise, 1975; The Human Journey: Thomas Merton, Symbol of a Century, 1982; Trilogy, 1982; Contemplation and Compassion, 1984; Winter Rain: A Play in One Act and Six Scenes, 1985; His Name is John: A Play in Four Acts, 1986; Christmas to Calvary, 1987; Love and Destiny, 1987; Summer Lightening: A Play in Four Acts and Four Seasons, 1988; Conscience and Conflict, 1989; Reform and Renewal: Essays on Authority, Ministry and Social Justice, 1990; A Celebration of Life, 1990; The Church Today: Belonging and Believing, 1990; Scripture in the Street, 1992; A Retreat with Thomas Merton: Biography as Spiritual Journey, 1995. Contributions to: Books and periodicals. Honours: Awards and citations. Memberships: Catholic Theological Society of America; International Federation of Married Priests; International Thomas Merton Society; Priests for Equality; Honorary Member, Sigma Tau Delta Literature Honour Society; Theta Alpha Kappa, National Honour Society for Religious Studies and Theology. Address: c/o School of American and International Studies, Ramapo College of New Jersey, Mahwah, NJ 07430, USA.

PAGE Eleanor. See: **COERR Eleanor (Beatrice).**

PAGE Emma. See: **TIRBUTT Honoris.**

PAGE Geoff(rey Donald), b. 7 July 1940, Grafton, New South Wales, Australia. Teacher; Writer. m. Carolyn Mau, 4 Jan 1972, 1 son. Education: BA (Hons); DipEd. Appointments: Writer-in-Residence, Australian Defence Force Academy, Curtin University, Wollongong University and Edith Cowan University. Publications: The Question, in Two Poets, 1971; Smalltown Memorials, 1975; Collecting the Weather, 1978; Cassandra Paddocks, 1980; Clairvoyant in Autumn, 1983; Shadows from Wire: Poems and Photographs of Australians in the Great War (editor), 1983; Benton's Conviction (novel), 1985; Century of Clouds: Selected Poems of Guillaume Apollinaire (translator with Wendy Coutts), 1985; Collected Lives, 1986; Smiling in English, Smoking in French, 1987; Footwork, 1988; Winter Vision (novel), 1989; Invisible Histories (stories and poems), 1990; Selected Poems, 1991; Gravel Corners, 1992; On the Move (editor), 1992; Human Interest, 1994. Honours: Literature Board Grants, Australia Council, 1974, 1983, 1987, 1989, 1992. Memberships: Australian Society of Authors; Australian Teachers Union. Address: 8 Morehead Street, Curtin, Australian Capital Territory 2605, Australia.

PAGE Katherine Hall, b. 9 July 1947, New Jersey, USA. Writer. m. Alan Hein, 5 Dec 1975, 1 son. Education: AB, Wellesley College, 1969; EdM, Tufts University, 1974; EdD, Harvard University, 1985. Publications: Faith Fairchild mystery series: The Body in the Belfry, 1990; The Body in the Bouillon, 1991; The Body in the Kelp, 1991; The Body in the Vestibule, 1992; The Body in the Cast, 1993, 1994; The Body in the Basement, 1994, 1995; The Body in the Bog, 1996, 1997; Christie & Company, (juvenile), 1996, 1997; Christie & Company Down East, (juvenile), 1997. Honours: Agatha for Best First Domestic Mystery, 1991. Memberships: Mystery Readers International; Mystery Writers of America; Authors Guild; Sisters in Crime; American Crime Writers League; Society of Children's Bookwriters and Illustrators; International Association of Crime Writers. Literary Agent: Faith Hamlin, Greenburger Associates Inc, New York, NY, USA. Address: c/o Faith Hamlin, Sanford J Greenburger Associates Inc, 55 Fifth Avenue, New York, NY 10003, USA.

PAGE Louise, b. 7 Mar 1955, London, England. Playwright. Education: BA, University of Birmingham, 1976. Appointment: Resident Playwright, Royal Court Theatre, 1982-83. Publications: Want Ad, 1977; Glasshouse, 1977; Tissue, 1978; Lucy, 1979; Hearing, 1979; Flaws, 1980; House Wives, 1981; Salonika, 1982; Real Estate, 1984; Golden Girls, 1984; Beauty and the Beast, 1985; Diplomatic Wives, 1989; Adam Wasxa Gardener, 1991; Like to Live, 1992; Hawks and Doves, 1992; Radio and TV plays. Honour: George Devine Award, 1982. Address: 6J Oxford & Cambridge Mansions, Old Marylebone Road, London NW1 5EC, England.

PAGE Norman, b. 8 May 1930, Kettering, Northamptonshire, England. Professor of Modern English Literature; Author. m. Jean Hampton, 29 Mar 1958, 3 sons, 1 daughter. Education: BA, 1951, MA, 1955, Emmanuel College, Cambridge; PhD, University of Leeds, 1968. Appointments: Principal Lecturer in English, Ripon College of Education, Yorkshire, 1960-69; Assistant Professor, 1969-70, Associate Professor, 1970-75, Professor of English, 1975-85, University of Alberta; Professor of Modern English Literature, University of Nottingham, 1985-. Publications: The Language of Jane Austen, 1972; Speech in the English Novel, 1973, 2nd edition, 1988; Thomas Hardy, 1977; A E Housman: A Critical Biography, 1983; A Kipling Companion, 1984; E M Forster, 1988; Tennyson: An Illustrated Life, 1992. Contributions to: Professional journals. Honours: Guggenheim Fellowship, 1979; University of Alberta Research Prize, 1983. Membership: Royal Society of Canada, fellow; Thomas Hardy Society; Newstead Abbey Byron Society; Tennyson Society. Address: 23 Braunston Road, Oakham, Rutland LE15 6LD, England.

PAGE P(atricia) K(athleen), b. 23 Nov 1916, Swanage, Dorset, England. Writer; Poet; Painter. m. W Arthur Irwin, 16 Dec 1950, 1 stepson, 2 stepdaughters. Education: Studied art with Frank Schaeffer, Brazil, Charles Seliger, New York; Art Students League, New York; Pratt Graphics, New York. Appointments: Scriptwriter, National Film Board, Canada, 1946-50; Conducted writing workshops, Toronto, 1974-77; Teacher, University of Victoria, British Columbia, 1977-78. Publications: As Ten as Twenty, 1940; The Sun and the Moon (novel), 1944; The Metal and the Flower, 1954; Cry Ararati: Poems New and Selected, 1967; The Sun and the Moon and Other Fictions, 1973; Poems Selected and New, 1974; To Say the Least (editor), 1979; Evening Dance of the Grey Flies, 1981; The Glass Air (poems, essays, and drawings), 1985; Brazilian Journal (prose), 1988; I-Sphinx: A Poem for Two Voices, 1988; A Flask of Sea Water (fairy story), 1989;

The Glass Air: Poems Selected and New, 1991; The Travelling Musicians (children's book), 1991; Unless the Eye Catch Fire (short story), 1994; The Goat That Flew (fairy story), 1994; Hologram: A Book of Glosas, 1994; A Children's Hymn for the United Nations, 1995. Contributions to: Journals and magazines. Honours include: Governor-General's Award for Poetry, 1954; Officer of the Order of Canada, 1977; national Magazines Gold Award for Poetry, 1986; Banff Centre School of Fine Arts National Award, 1989; National Magazines Silver Award for Poetry, 1990; Subject of National Film Board film Still Waters, 1991; Readers' Choice Award, Prairie Schooner, 1994; Subject of 2-part sound feature The White Glass, CBC, 1996; Subject of special issue of Malahat Review, 1997; Honorary doctorates. Address: 3260 Exeter Road, Victoria, British Columbia, V8R 6A6, Canada.

PAGE Robin, b. 3 May 1943, Cambridgeshire, England. Writer. Publications: Down with the Poor, 1971; The Benefits Racket, 1972; Down Among the Dossers, 1973; The Decline of an English Village, 1974; The Hunter and the Hunted, 1977; Weather Forecasting: The Country Way, 1977; Cures and Remedies: The Country, 1978; Weeds: The Country Way, 1979; Animal Cures: The Country Way, 1979; The Journal of a Country Parish, 1980; Journeys into Britain, 1982; The Country Way of Love, 1983; The Wildlife of the Royal Estates, 1984; Count One to Ten, 1986; The Fox's Tale, 1986; The Duchy of Cornwall, 1987; The Fox and the Orchid, 1987. Address: Bird's Farm, Barton, Cambridgeshire, England.

PAGLIA Camille (Anna), b. 2 Apr 1947, Endicott, New York, USA. Professor of Humanities; Writer. Education: BA, State University of New York at Binghamton, 1968; MPhil, 1971, PhD, 1974, Yale University. Appointments: Faculty, Bennington College, Vermont, 1972-80; Visiting Lecturer, Wesleyan University, 1980; Visiting Lecturer, Yale University, 1980-84; Assistant Professor, 1984087, Associate Professor, 1987-91, Professor of Humanities, 1991-, College of the Performing Arts, later the University of Arts; Several visiting lectureships. Publications: Sexual Personae: Art and Decadence from Nefertiti to Emily Dickinson, 1990; Sex, Art, and American Culture: Essays, 1992; Vamps and Tramps: New Essays, 1994. Contributions to: Journals and periodicals and Internet communications. Address: c/o Department of Humanities, University of the Arts, 320 South Broad Street, Philadelphia, PA 19102, USA.

PAINE Lauran Bosworth, b. 25 Feb 1916, Duluth, Minnesota, USA. Author. m. Mona Margarette Lewellyn, 26 June 1982, 1 son, 4 daughters. Education: Pacific Military Academy, 1930-32; St Alban's Episcopal School, 1932-34. Publications: Over 700 westerns, 1950-92, 79 mysteries, 1958-75, 119 romances, and non-fiction books. Address: 9413 North Highway 3, Fort Jones, CA 96032, USA.

PAJOR JohnJoseph, b. 5 Feb 1948, South Bend, Indiana, USA. Poet. m. Cass Peters-Pajor, 18 Nov 1989, 3 sons, 1 daughter. Education: Technical College. Appointments include: Readings; Poetry Concerts; Drama radio; Cable TV broadcasts, 1965-96. Publications: Dies Faustus, revised edition, 1976; In Transit, 1978; A Collection of 3, 1979; Auditions, 1979; Traveler, 1979; Works: On Tour; African Violets, 1989; Challenger, 1990; Sacred Fire, 1990; Chiaroscuro, 1991; Wilderness - land of the raining moon, 1991. Poetry Collections, 1976-94. Contributions to: University publications. Honour: Literary Honoraruim, National Poetry Awards, 1978. Address: 848 51st Street, Port Townsend, WA 98368, USA.

PALEY Grace, b. 11 Dec 1922, New York, New York, USA. Author; Poet; College Instructor (retired). m. (1) Jess Paley, 20 June 1942, div, 1 son, 1 daughter, (2) Robert Nichols, 1972. Education: Hunter College, New York City, 1938-39; New York University. Appointments: Teacher, Columbia University, Syracuse University, Sarah Lawrence College, City College of the City University of New York. Publications: Fiction: The Little Disturbances of Man: Stories of Women and Men at Love, 1968; Enormous Changes at the Last Minute, 1974; Later the Same Day, 1985; The Collected Stories, 1994. Poetry: Long Walks and Intimate Talks (includes stories), 1991; New and Collected Poems, 1992. Other: Leaning Forward, 1985; Three Hundred Sixty-Five Reasons Not to Have Another War: 1989 Peace Calender (with Vera B Williams), 1988. Contributions to: Books, anthologies and magazines. Honours: Guggenheim Fellowship, 1961; National Institute of Arts and Letters Award, 1970; Edith Wharton Citation of Merit as the first State Author of New York, New York State Writers Institute, 1986; National Endowment for the Arts Senior Fellowship, 1987; Vermont Governor's Award for Excellence in the

Arts, 1993. Membership: American Academy of Arts and Letters. Address: Box 620, Thetford Hill, VT 05074, USA.

PALIN Michael Edward, b. 5 May 1943, Sheffield, Yorkshire, England. Freelance Writer and Actor. m. Helen M Gibbins, 1966, 2 sons, 1 daughter. Education: BA, Brasenose College, Oxford, 1965. Appointments: Actor, Writer: Monty Python's Flying Circus, BBC TV, 1969-74; Ripping Yarns, BBC TV 1976-80; Writer, East of Ipswich, BBC TV, 1986; Films: Actor and Joint Author: And Now for Something Completely Different, 1970; Monty Python and the Holy Grail, 1974; Monty Python's Life of Brian, 1978; Time Bandits, 1980; Monty Python's The Meaning of Life, 1982; Actor, Writer, Co-Producer, The Missionary, 1982; Around the World in 80 Days, BBC, 1989; Actor: Jabberwocky, 1976; A Private Function, 1984; Brazil, 1985; A Fish Called Wanda, 1988; Contributor, Great Railway Journeys of the World, BBC TV, 1980; Actor, Co-Writer, American Friends (film), 1991; Actor, GBH (TV Channel 4), 1991. Publications: Monty Python's Big Red Book, 1970; Monty Python's Brand New Book, 1973; Dr Fegg's Encyclopaedia of All World Knowledge, 1984; Limericks, 1985; For Children: Small Harry and the Toothache Pills, 1981; The Mirrorstone, 1986; The Cyril Stories, 1986; Around the World in 80 Days, 1989; Pole to Pole, 1992. Honour: Writers Guild, Best Screenplay Award, 1991. Address: 68a Delancey Street, London NW1 7RY, England.

PALMER Alan Warwick, b. 28 Sept 1926, Ilford, Essex, England. Schoolmaster (retired); Writer. m. Veronica Mary Cordell, 1 Sept 1951. Education: MA, 1950, MLitt, 1954, Oriel College, Oxford. Publications: Alexander I, Tsar of War and Peace, 1974; The Chancelleries of Europe, 1982; Crowned Cousins: The Anglo-German Royal Connection, 1986; The East End, 1989; Bernadotte: Napoleon's Marshal, Sweden's King, 1990; The Penguin Dictionary of Twentieth Century History, 4th edition, 1990; The Decline and Fall of the Ottoman Empire, 1992; Twilight of the Hapsburgs, 1994; Dictionary of the British Empire and Commonwealth, 1996. Contributions to: Journals. Memberships: International PEN; Royal Society of Literature, fellow. Address: 4 Farm End, Woodstock, Oxford OX20 1XN, England.

PALMER Diana. See: KYLE Susan (Eloise Spaeth).

PALMER Frank Robert, b. 9 Apr 1922, Westerleigh, Gloucestershire, England. Linguist; Professor (retired). m. Jean Elisabeth Moore, 1948, 3 sons, 2 daughters. Education: MA, New College, Oxford, 1948; Graduate Studies, Merton College, Oxford, 1948-49. Appointments: Lecturer in Linguistics, School of Oriental and African Studies, University of London, 1950-52, 1953-60; Professor of Linguistics, University College of North Wales, Bangor, 1960-65; Professor and Head, Department of Linguistic Science, 1965-87, Dean, Faculty of Letters and Social Sciences, 1969-72, University of Reading. Publications: The Morphology of the Tigre Noun, 1962; A Linguistic Study of the English Verb, 1965; Selected Papers of J R Firth, 1951-1958 (editor), 1968; Prosodic Analysis (editor), 1970; Grammar, 1971, 2nd edition, 1984; The English Verb, 1974, 2nd edition, 1987; Semantics, 1976, 2nd edition, 1981; Modality and the English Modals, 1979, 2nd edition, 1990; Mood and Modality, 1986; Grammatical Roles and Relations, 1994. Contributions to: Professional journals. Memberships: Academia Europaea; British Academy, fellow; Linguistic Society of America; Philological Society. Address: Whitethorns, Roundabout Lane, Winnersh, Wokingham, Berkshire, RG41 5AD, England.

PALMER John, b. 13 May 1943, Sydney, Nova Scotia, Canada. Playwright; Director. Education: BA, English, Carleton University, Ottawa, Canada, 1965. Appointments: Dramaturge, Associate, Factory Theatre Lab, Toronto, 1970-73; Co-Founder, Co-Artistic Director, Toronto Free Theatre, 1972-76; Resident Playwright, Canadian Repertory Theatre, Toronto, 1983-87; Course Director, Final Year Playwrighting, York University, Toronto, 1991-93; Resident Playwright, National Theatre School of Canada, 1993-94. Publications: 2 Plays: The End, and A Day at the Beach, 1991; Before the Guns, Memories for my Brother, Part I, Dangerous Traditions: Four Passe-Muraille Plays, 1992; Henrik Ibsen On the Necessity of Producing Norwegian Drama, 1992-93; Selected Plays. Contributions to: Various publications. Address: 32 Monteith Street, Toronto, Ontario M4Y 1K7, Canada.

PALMER Peter John, b. 20 Sept 1932, Melbourne, Victoria, Australia. Teacher. m. Elizabeth Fischer, 22 Dec 1955, 1 son, 1 daughter. Education: BA, 1953, BEd, 1966, University of Melbourne. Publications: The Past and Us, 1957; The Twentieth Century, 1964;

Earth and Man, 1980; Man on the Land, 1981; Man and Machines, 1983; Macmillan Australian Atlas (executive editor), 1983, 4th edition, 1993; Challenge, 1985; Geography 10 (author, illustrator), 1992. Editor, contributor, illustrator: Confrontation, 1971; Interaction, 1974; Expansion, 1975; Survival, 1976; Three Worlds, 1978. Address: 34 Ardgower Court, Lower Templestowe, Victoria 3107, Australia.

PALMER Tony, b. 29 Aug 1941, London, England. Film Director; Author. Publications: Born Under A Bad Sign; Trials of Oz; Electric Revolution; Biography of Liberace; All You Need Is Love; Charles II; Julian Bream, A Life on the Road; Menuhin, A Family Portrait. Contributions to: Observer; Sunday Times; New York Times; Spectator; Punch; Daily Mail; Life Magazine. Honours: Italia Prize, twice; Gold Medal, New York Film and TV Festival, 6 times; Fellini Prize; Critics Prize, São Paulo; Special Jury Prize, San Francisco. Membership: Garrick Club. Address: Nanjizal, St Levan, Cornwall, England.

PALOMINO JIMENEZ Angel, b. 2 Aug 1929, Toledo, Spain. Novelist; Journalist; Television Writer. Education: Linguistics, Science and Chemistry studies, Central University, Madrid; Technician in Management. Publications: Numerous works of poetry, short stories, essays and novels including: El Cesar de Papel, 1957; Zamora y Gomora, 1968; Torremolinos Gran Hotel, 1971; Memorias de un Intelectual Antifranquista, 1972; Un Jaguar y una Rubia, 1972; Madrid Costa Fleming, 1973; Todo Incluido, 1975; Divorcio para une Virgen Rota, 1977; La Luna Se Llama Perez, 1978; Plan Marshall para 50 Minutos, 1978; Las Otras Violaciones, 1979; Adiós a los Vaqueros, 1984; Este muerto no soy yo, 1989; Caudillo, 1992; De carne y sexo, 1993. Contributions to: Estafeta Literaria; ABC; Semana. Honours: International Prize, Press Club, 1966; Miguel de Cervantes National Literary Prize, 1971; Finalist, Planeta Prize, 1977. Memberships: Royal Academy of Fine Arts and Historical Sciences; National Academy of Gastronomy; Spanish Association of Book Writers; International Federation of Tourism Writers; International Association of Literary Critics. Literary Agent: Editorial Planeta, Barcelona, Spain. Address: Conde de Penalver 17, 28006 Madrid, Spain.

PALSSON Einar, b. 10 Nov 1925, Reykjavik, Iceland. Headmaster. m. Birgitte Laxal, 24 Dec 1948, 2 sons, 1 daughter. Education: Cand phil, University of Iceland, 1946; Certificate of Merit, Royal Academy of Dramatic Art, London, 1948; BA, Danish and English Literature, Univrersity of Iceland, 1957. Appointments: Chairman, Reykjavik City Theatre (Leikfélag Reykjaviku), 1950-53; Play Producer, Reykjavik City Theatre, National Theatre and Icelandic State Radio, 1952-63. Publications: Spekin og Sparifotin (essays), 1963; The Roots of Icelandic Culture, 10 volumes, 1969-91. Contributions to: Various publications. Membership: Nordic Society, director, 1966-69. Address: Solvallagata 28, 101 Reykjavik, Iceland.

PAMA Cornelis, b. 5 Nov 1916, Rotterdam, Netherlands. Editor; Author. m. Heather Myfanwy Woltman, 1 Mar 1977, 1 son, 2 daughters. Education: Dutch Publishing Diploma. Appointments: Manager, Bailliere, Tindall & Cox Ltd, London, 1948-55; General Manager, W & G Foyle, Cape Town, South Africa, 1955-67; Honorary Editor: Arma, 1955-, Familia, 1965-; Director, A A Balkema Publishers, Cape Town, 1967-72; Editor, Tafelberg Publishers, Cape Town, 1972-80; Editor-in-Chief, Nederlandse Post, Cape Town, 1980-. Publications: Lions and Virgins, 1964; Genealogies of Old South African Families, 3 volumes, 2nd edition, 1966; The South African Library 1810-1968, 1968; The Heraldry of South African Families, 1970; Vintage Cape Town, 1973; Bowler's Cape Town, 1975; Regency Cape Town, 1978; Handboek der Heraldiek, 5th edition, 1987; 21 other books on genealogy and heraldry. Contributions to: Historical, genealogical and heraldic journals. Honours: Extraordinary Gold Medal, South African Academy of Arts and Sciences, 1966; J Bracken Lee Award, Salt Lake City; Gold Medal Pro Merito Genealogicae, Deutsche Zentralstelle für Familiengeschichte, Germany, 1976; Distinguished Fellow, American College of Heraldry; Distinguished Fellow, New Zealand Heraldry Society. Memberships: PEN South African Centre; South African Academy of Arts and Sciences; Afrikaanse Skrywerskring. Address: PO Box 4839, Cape Town 8000, South Africa.

PAMPEL Martha Maria, b. 4 Apr 1913, Muhlheim, Ruhr, Germany. Author. m. Adolf Pampel, 1 June 1936, 1 daughter. Education: Business Training - Wholesale trade with exam (balance-sheet-safety); Correspondence Course, English; Organist's Examination; International Famous Writers School. Publications: Die

Tur Steht offen, 1965, 1976; Heilige mitkleinen Fehlern, 1977; Land der dunklen Walder, 1977; Wer in der Liebe bleibt, 1978; Ein Streiter vor dem Herrn, 1979; Das Freuen lernen, 1979, recorded on tape, 1983; 7 small volumes, series, Die Feierabendstende; Various little books: Die Kleinen Freuden des Alltags, 1986; Nur mit dem Herzen sieht man gut, 1990; Da sich das herz zum Herzen findet, 1992; Calendars, children's devotions book. Contribution: Der Redliche Ostpreuße. Honours: Diploma of Merit, Universityie delle Arti, Italy, 1982; Albert Einstein Academy Bronze Medal, peace proposition, Universal Intelligence Data Bank of America, 1986; Honorary Doctorate, International University Foundation, USA, 1986. Membership: Freie-r Deutscher Autorenverband. Address: Lortzingstrasse 9, Bad Sachsa, D-37441, Germany.

PANICHAS George Andrew, b. 21 May 1930, Springfield, Massachusetts, USA. Educator; Literary Critic; Scholar. Education: BA, American International College, 1951; MA, Trinity College, Hartford, Connecticut, 1952; PhD, Nottingham University, UK, 1962. Appointments: Instructor, Assistant/Associate Professor, Professor of English, University of Maryland, 1962-. Editor, Modern Age, quarterly review; Advisory editor, Continuity, history journal. Publications: Adventure in Consciousness: The Meaning of D H Lawrence's Religious Quest, 1964; Renaissance and Modern Essays (co-editor) 1966; Epicurus, 1967; The Reverent Discipline: Essays in Literary Criticism and Culture, 1974; The Burden of Vision: Dostoevsky's Spiritual Art, 1977; The Courage of Judgement: Essays in Literary Criticism, Culture and Society, 1983; Editor of numerous books. Contributions to: Books and journals. Honours: Royal Society of Arts, UK, fellow, 1971-; Grant, Earhart Foundation, 1982. Memberships: Awards committee, Richard M Weaver Fellowship, 1983-; Jury panel, Ingersoll Prizes, 1986-; Academic Board, National Humanities Institute, 1985-. Address: Department of English, University of Maryland, College Park, MD 20742, USA.

PANIKER Ayyappa, b. 12 Sept 1930, Kavalam, India. Professor. m. Sreeparvathy Paniker, 6 Dec 1961, 2 daughters. Education: BA Honours, Travancore, 1951; MA, Kerala, 1959; CTE, Hyderabad, 1966; AM, PhD, Indiana University, USA, 1971. Appointments: Founder Editor, Kerala Kavita, 1965; General Editor, Kerala Writers in English; Editor, World Classics Retold in Malayalam, Indian Journal of English Studies; Chief Editor, Medieval Indian Literature. Publications: Ayyappa Panikerude Kritikal 1, 1974, 1981; Ayyappa Panikerude Lekhanangal, 1982; Ezhukavitalum Patanagalam, 1984; Ayyappa Panikerude Kritikal II, 1984; Cuban Poems (translation), 1984; Granth Sahib (translation), 1986; Mayakovski's Poems, 1987; Dialogues, 1988; Vallathol: A Centenary Perspective; Ayyappa Panikerude Kritikal III 1981-89, 1989; Pattu Kavitakal Patanagalum, 1989; Thakazhi Sivasankara Pillai, 1989; Gotrayanam, 1989; Indian Literature in English, A Perspective of Malayalain Literature, 1990; Spotlight on Comparative Indian Literature, 1992; Avatarikakal, 1993. Address: 111 Gandhinagar, Trivandrum 695014, India.

PANIKER Salvador, b. 1 Mar 1927, Barcelona, Spain. Publisher; Writer. Education: Lic Philos; Doctor of Industrial Engineering. Publications: Conversaciones en Cataluna, 1966; Los Signos y las Cosas, 1968; Conversaciones en Madrid, 1969; La Dificultad de Ser Español, 1979; Aproximacion al Origen, 1982; Primer Testamento, 1985; Ensayos retroprogresivos, 1987; Segunda Memoria, 1988; Lectura de los Griegos, 1992. Contributions to: La Vanguardia; El País; Revista de Occidente. Honour: International Press Prize, 1969. Address: Numancia 117-121, Barcelona 08029, Spain.

PAOLUCCI Anne (Attura), b. c.1930, Rome, Italy. Poet; Writer; Dramatist; Editor; Professor. m. Henry Paolucci. Education: BA, Barnard College; MA, PHD, Columbia University, 1963. Appointments: Assistant Professor of English and Comparative Literature, City College of the City University of New York, 1959-69; Research Professor, 1969-; Professor of English, 1975-; Chairperson of the English Department, 1982-91, Director of the Doctor of Arts Degree Program in English, 1982-, St John's University, Jamaica, New York; Visiting Lecturer at various universities in the US and abroad; Founder-Editor Director, Council on National Literatures, 1974-. Publications: Poetry: Poems Written for Sbek's Mummies, Marie Menken, and Other Important Persons, Places and Things, 1977; Riding the Mast Where it Swings, 1980; Tropic of the Gods, 1980; Gorbachev in Concert (and Other Poems), 1991; Age Hasn't Withered My Charms and Other Poems, 1994. Fiction: Eight Short Stories, 1977; Sepia Tones: Seven Short Stories, 1986; Grandma, Pray For Me (with Nishan Paolucci), 1990. Non-Fiction: Hegel on Tragedy, 1962; A

Short History of American Drama, 1966; Eugene O'Neill, Arthur Miller, Edward Albee, 1967; From Tension to Tonic: The Plays of Edward Albee, 1972; Pirandello's Theater: The Recovery of the Modern Stage for Dramatic Art, 1974; Dante and the "Quest for Eloquence" in India's Vernacular Languages (with Henry Paolucci), 1984. Editor: Canada, 1977; Dante's Influence on American Writers, 1977; India: Review of National Literatures (with Ronald Warwick), 1979; Contemporary Literary Theory: An Overview, 1987; Columbus: Modern Views of Columbus and His Time: Essays, Poems, Reprints (with Henry Paolucci), 1990. Plays: The Short Season, 1970; Minions of the Race, 1972; Incidents at the Great Wall, 1976; In the Green Room with Machiavelli, 1980; Cipango!: A One-Act Play in Three Scenes About Christopher Columbus, 1985; The Actor in Search of His Mask, 1987. Contributions to: Stories, articles, reviews, and poems in various journals. Honours; Fulbright Scholarship, 1951-52; Woodbridge Honorary Fellow, Columbia University, 1961-62; Yaddo Colony Residency, 1965; American Council of Learned Societies Grant, 1978; Cavaliere, 1986, Commendatore, 1992, Order of Merit, Italy; Alpha Psi Omega. Memberships: American Comparative Literature Association; American Institute of Italian Studies, advisory board, 1977-; American Society of Italian Legions of Merit, board of directors 1990; Byron Society of America and England, founder-member, advisory board, 1973-; Dante Society of America, council member, 1974-76, vice president, 1976-77; International Comparative Literature Association; International Shakespeare Association; Modern Language Association, executive committee, 1975-77; National Graduate Fellows Program, fellowship board, 1985-86; National Society of Literature and the Arts; PEN American Center; Pirandello Society of America, vice-president, 1968-79, president, 1979-; Shakespeare Association of America; World Centre for Shakespeare Studies, board of directors, 1972-. Address: c/o Department of English, St John's University, Jamaica, NY 11439, USA.

PAPAGEORGIOU Kostas G, b. 4 July 1945, Athens, Greece. Author; Producer, Greek Radio. Education: Law Diploma, 1968; Literature, Philology, University of Athens, 1969-72. Appointments: Editor, Grammata ke Technes, 1982-; Member, Commission for Literary Awards, Ministry of Culture, 1982-84, Commission for Authors' Pensions, 1991-. Publications: Piimata, 1966; Sillogi, 1970; Epi pigin Kathise, 1972; Ichnographia (poetry), 1975; To Giotopato (prose), 1977; To Ikogeniako dendro (poetry), 1978; To skotomeno ema, 1982; Kato ston ipno (poetry), 1986; I genia tou 70, 1989; Rammemo Stoma (poetry), 1990. Contributions to: Anti; Diavazo; Lexi; Dendro; Tram; Tomes; Chronico. Membership: Eteria sigrafeon (Greek Authors Union). Literary Agent: Kedros Publishing House, Athens, Greece. Address: Kerasountos 8, 11528 Athens, Greece.

PAPAKOU-LAGOU Avgi, b. 1923, Phthiotida, Greece. Writer. Education: Pedagogical Academy, Lamia. Publications: Fairy Tales: The Fairy Child and Other Fairy tales, 1962, 3rd edition, 1979; In the Chestnut Grove, 1979, 3rd edition, 1994; What and Where, the Brave Mouse, 1988, 3rd edition, 1994; The Forest and its Animals and Other Fairy Tales, 1991; The Animals' Warning, 1983, 3rd edition, 1994; The Little Robot of Understanding, 1995. Novels: The Father's Secret, 1980; The Forest and its World, 1986; Don't Cry My Little One, 1988, 2nd edition, 1990; Theodora, the Princess from Trebizond, 1994; The Personalities and Works of Greek Children's Literature (biographies), 1987. Short stories: The Festival Stories, 1980, 2nd edition, 1989; The Grandfather's Fairy Tale, 1980, 2nd edition, 1989; The Flower of Love, 1980, 2nd edition, 1989; Alexis' Photographs, 1995. Plays: A Different Kind of Summer (for children), 1976, 3rd edition, 1991; The Joyful Return (for children), 1968; A Game with Father (for children), 1991; Shall We Play Theater? (for children), 1996. Other: The Poems of Katerina, 1994; Folkloric Approaches, 1996. Honours include: Penelope Delta Award, Children's Book Circle of Greece; Evgenia Kleidara Prize, Aeolian Letters. Memberships: Children's Book Circle of Greece; Society of Greek Authors; Union of Authors and Illustrators of Greek Children's Books; Greek Folklore Society; Group of Authors and Writers of Phthiotida. Address: 121 Pandossias Street, N Ionia, GR-14232 Athens, Greece.

PAPALEO Joseph, b. 13 Jan 1926, New York, New York, USA. Professor of Literature and Writing; Fiction Writer. m. 4 sons. Education: BA, Sarah Lawrence College, 1949; Diploma di Profitto, University of Florence, Italy, 1951; MA, Columbia University, 1952. Appointments: Teacher, Fieldston Prep School, 1952-60; Professor, Literature and Writing, Sarah Lawrence College, 1960-68, 1969-92; Guest Professor, Laboratorio de Cibernetica, Naples, Italy, 1968-69. Publications: All the Comforts (novel), 1968; Out of Place (novel),

1971; Picasso at Ninety One, 1988; The Bronx Book of the Dea, short stories; My Life Story (Sicilian Zen Version), short stories in 3 anthologies: Delphinium Blossoms, From the Margin, Imagining America, 1991, 1992. Contributions to: Journals and magazines. Honours: Guggenheim Fellowship, 1974; Ramapo College Poetry Prize, 1986. Memberships: Authors Guild; Italian American Writers Association; American Association of University Professors. Address: 60 Puritan Avenue, Yonkers, NY 10710, USA.

PAPAS William, b. 1927, South Africa. Author. Education: South Africa; Beckham, England. Appointments: Formerly Cartoonist, The Guardian, The Sunday Times Newspapers, Punch Magazine; Book Illustrator, Painter, Print Maker. Publications: The Press, 1964; The Story of Mr Nero, 1965; The Church, 1965; Parliament, 1966; Freddy the Fell-Engine, 1966; The Law, 1967; Tasso, 1967; No Mules, 1967; Taresh, the Tea Planter, 1968; A Letter from India, 1968; A Letter from Israel, 1968; Theodore, or, The Mouse Who Wanted to Fly, 1969; Elias the Fisherman, 1970; The Monk and the Goat, 1971; The Long-Haired Donkey, 1972; The Most Beautiful Child, 1973; The Zoo, 1974; People of Old Jerusalem, 1980; Papas' America, 1986; Papas' Portland, 1994. Membership: Savage Club, London. Address: 422 North West 8th Avenue, Portland, OR 97209, USA.

PAPASTRATU Danae, b. 20 Mar 1936, Patras, Greece. Author; Journalist. Education: Diploma, Law, Athens University, 1959; Greek-American Institute, 1965; Université de Paris-Sorbonne, 1969. Appointments: Protevoussa Journal; News of Municipalitis; Collector Magazine; Nautical Greece. Publications: Travels with the Polar Book, 1978; A vol d'oiseau, 1979; We Will See in Philippi, 1981; Without Periphrasis (poems), 1981; An Essay about Poetry, 1983; Diadromes sto Horo and Hrono (travel book), 1989; Anichnetsis (essays), 1992; A Little Odyssey - Translation. Contributions to: Many publications. Memberships: Society of Greek Writers. Address: Bouboulinas 1a, Hilioupolis 16345, Athens, Greece.

PAPAZOGLOU Orania, b. 13 July 1951, Bethel, Connecticut, USA. Writer. m. William L DeAndrea, 1 Jan 1984, 2 sons. Education: AB, Vassar College, 1973; AM, University of Connecticut, 1975; Doctoral Study, Michigan State University, 1975-80. Publications: Sweet, Savage Death (novel), 1984; Wicked Loving Murder (novel), 1985; Death's Savage Passion (novel), 1986; Sancify (novel), 1986; Rich, Radiant Slaughter, 1988. Contributions to: Magazines. Address: c/o Meredith Bernstein, 470 West End Avenue, New York, NY 10024, USA.

PAPINEAU David Calder, b. 30 Sept 1947, Como, Italy. Philosopher. m. Rose Wild, 6 July 1986, 1 son, 1 daughter. Education: BSc (Hons), University of Natal, 1967; BA (Hons), 1970, PhD, Cambridge University. Appointments: Professor, King's College, London, 1990-; Editor, British Journal for the Philosophy of Science, 1993-. Publications: For Science in the Social Sciences, 1978; Theory and Meaning, 1979; Reality and Representation, 1987; Philosophical Naturalism, 1993. Membership: British Society for the Philosophy of Science, president, 1993-95. Address: Department of Philosophy, King's College, London WC2R 2LS, England.

PARATTE Henri-Dominique, (Ti-Pique le Madouesse), b. 19 Mar 1950, Berne, Switzerland. Professor; Writer; Translator; Journalist. m. Genevieve Houet, 1974, 2 sons, 1 daughter; Partner, Martine L Jacquet, 1981. Education: Licence ès lettres, 1969; Maîtrise, Strasbourg, 1970; Doctorat IIIe cycle, Lille, 1974; Certified Translator, ATINS, 1992; Certified Literary Translator, Canada Council, 1986. Appointments: Jury, Prix Suisse-Canada, 1980-85; Editor, Swiss-French Studies, 1980-86; Literary Editor, Les Editions du Grand-Pré, 1984-97; Editorial board of various journals; Juries, Canada Council; Chair, Canadian Status of the Artist Federal Commission, 1986-92; President, Société de la Presse Acadienne, 1996-97; Board Member, cultural organizations. Publications: Virgie Tantra Non Arpadar, 1972; La Mer Ecartelée, 1979; Jura-Acadie, 1980; Dis Moi la Nuit, 1982; Cheval des iles, 1984; Alexandre Voisard, 1985; Anne: la maison aux pignons verts, 1987; Acadians, 1991, reprinted, 1997; Confluences, 1996. Contributions to: Eloizes; Ecritare; Ven'd'Est; Rivière; Feux Chalins; Poéme-USA; Littéréalite; Envols; Mensuil 25; Etudes Irlandaises; Cahiers Ramz; Various anthologies. Honours: Literary Awards, Canton de Berne, Switzerland, 1972, 1979; Honorable Mention, John Glassco Award, 1985. Memberships: Writers' Federation of Nova Scotia, executive member, 1979-82; Association des Ecrivains Acadiens, executive, 1980-85, president, 1985-87; Conseil Culturel Acadien de la Nouvelle-Ecosse, president, 1993-95;

Association des Artistes Acadiens de la Nouvelle-Ecosse, 1992-96. Address: 23 Highland Avenue, Wolfville, Nova Scotia B0P 1X0, Canada.

PARES Marion, (Judith Campbell, Anthony Grant), b. 7 Nov 1914, West Farleigh, Kent, England. Writer. m. Humphrey Pares, 5 June 1937, 4 daughters. Publications: Family Pony, 1962; The Queen Rides, 1965; Horses in the Sun, 1966; Police Horse, 1967; World of Horses, 1969; World of Ponies, 1970; Anne: Portrait of a Princess, 1970; Family on Horseback (with N Toyne), 1971; Princess Anne and Her Horses, 1971; Elizabeth and Philip, 1972; The Campions, 1973; Royalty on Horseback, 1974; The World of Horses, 1975; Anne and Mark, 1976; Queen Elizabeth II, 1979; The Mutant, 1980; Charles: A Prince of His Time, 1980; The Royal Partners, 1982; Royal Horses, 1983; Ponies, People and Palaces (autobiography). Address: c/o A M Heath Ltd, 79 St Martin's Lane, London WC2N 4AA, England.

PARINI Jay (Lee), b. 2 Apr 1948, Pittston, Pennsylvania, USA. Poet; Novelist; Literary Critic; Professor. m. Devon Stacey Jersild, 21 June 1981. Education: AB, Lafayette College; B Phil, PhD, University of St Andrew. Appointments: Editor, North Star poetry series; Member, Vermont Council on the Humanities and Social Sciences, 1975-; Vermont Council of the Arts, 1980-82; Editorial Committee, Juniper Prize for Poetry, University of Massachussetts Press, 1984-. Publications: Poetry: Singing in Time, 1972; Anthracite Country, 1982; Town Life, 1988. Novels: The Love Run, 1980; The Patch Boys, 1988; The Last Station, 1990. Other: Theodore Roeyuke: An American Romantic, 1979; A Vermont Christmas, 1988; The Columbia History of American Poetry (editor), 1993; Biography of John Steinbeck, 1995; editor of several poetry anthologies. Address: Rt 1, Box 195, Middlebury, VT 05753, USA.

PARIS Bernard Jay,b. 19 Aug 1931, Baltimore, Maryland, USA. University Professor. m. Shirley Helen Freedman, 1 Apr 1949, 1 son. Education: AB, 1952, PhD, 1959, Johns Hopkins University. Appointments: Instructor, Lehigh University, 1956-60; Assistant Professor, 1960-64, Associate Professor, 1964-67, Professor, 1967-81, Michigan State University; Professor, English, University of Florida, 1981-; Professor, English, University of Florida, 1981-96; Director, Institute for Psychological Study of the Arts, 1985-92, International Karen Horney Society, 1991-. Publications: Experiments in Life, George Eliot's Quest for Values, 1965; A Psychological Approach to Fiction: Studies in Thackeray, Stendhal, George Eliot, Dosteovsky and Conrad; Psychoanalysis Search for Self-Understanding, 1974; Character and Conflict in Jane Austen's Novels, 1978; Editor: Third Force Psychology and the Study of Literature, 1986; Shakespeare's Personality (co-editor), 1989; Bargains with Fate: Psychological Crises and Conflicts in Shakespeare and His Plays, 1991; Character as a Subversive Force in Shakespeare: The History and the Roman Plays, 1991; Karen Horney: A Psychoanalyst's Search for Self-Understanding, 1994. Contributions to: Numerous essays in scholarly and literary journals; Editorial Board, The American Journal of Psychoanalysis. Honours: Phi Beta Kappa, 1952; National Endowment of the Humanities Fellow, 1969; Guggenheim Fellowship, 1974.Memberships: Modern Language Association of America; Honorary Member, Association for the Advancement of Psychoanalysis; Scientific Associate, American Academy of Psychoanalysis. Address: 1430 North West 94th Street, Gainesville, FL 32606, USA.

PARIS I Mark, b. 28 Feb 1950, Baltimore, Maryland, USA. Translator. Life Partner: John L Gibbons. Education: Baltimore Polytechnic Institute, 1963-67; BA, Johns Hopkins University, 1971; MA, 1973, MPhil, 1974, Columbia University. Appointments: Instructor in French, Barnard College, New York City, 1975-80; Freelance Translator, 1976-. Publications: Translator of 20 books, 1977-96 includingParadise on Earth: The Gardens of Western Europe, Gabrielle van Zuylen, 1995; Weather: Drama of the Heavens, René Chaboud, 1996. Honours: Maryland Senatorial Scholar, 1967-71; Woodrow Wilson Fellow, 1971; National Defense Education Act Fellow, 1971-74; President's Fellow, Columbia University, 1975-76; F J E Woodbridge Distinguished Fellow, Columbia University, 1975-76. Memberships: Phi Beta Kappa.

PARISI Joseph Anthony, b. 18 Nov 1944, Duluth, Minnesota, USA. Editor; Writer; Consultant. Education: BA Honours, College of St Thomas, 1966; MA, 1967, PhD Honours, University of Chicago, 1973. Appointments: Associate Editor, 1976-83, Acting Editor, 1983-85, Editor, 1985-, Poetry Magazine; Writer and Producer, Poets in Person series, National Public Radio, 1991. Publications: The Poetry Anthology 1912-77 (editor), 1978; Marianne Moore: The Art of a Modernist, 1989; Voices & Visions Reader's Guide, 1987; Poets in Person Reader's Guide, 1992. Contributions to: Yale Review; Georgia Review; Shenandoah; Modern Philology; TriQuarterly; Booklist; Poetry; Mandarin Oriental; Chicago Tribune Book World; Chicago Sun-Times Book Week; Sewanee Review. Honours: Fellowship, University of Chicago, 1966-69; Alvin M Bentley Scholarship; Delta Epsilon Sigma. Memberships: Society of Midland Authors; Modern Language Association. Address: c/o Poetry, 60 West Walton Street, Chicago, IL 60610, USA.

PARK (Rosina) Ruth (Lucia), b. Australia. Author; Playwright. Publications: The Uninvited Guest (play), 1948; The Harp in the South, 1948; Poor Man's Orange, US edition, as 12 and a Half Plymouth Street), 1949; The Witch's Thorn, 1951; A Power of Roses, 1953; Pink Flannel, 1955; The Drums Go Bang (autobiographical with D'Arcy Niland), 1956; One-a-Pecker, Two-a-Pecker (US edition, The Frost and the Fire), 1961; The Good Looking Women, 1961; The Ship's Cat, 1961 (US edition, Serpent's Delight, 1962); Uncle Matt's Mountain, 1962; The Road to Christmas, 1962; The Road Under the Sea, 1962; The Muddle-Headed Wombat series, 11 volumes, 1962-76; The Hole in the Hill (US edition, The Secret of the Maori Cave), 1964; Shaky Island, 1962; Airlift for Grandee, 1964; Ring for the Sorcerer, 1967; The Sixpenny Island (US edition, Ten-Cent Island), 1968; Nuki and the Sea Serpent, 1969; The Companion Guide to Sydney, 1973; Callie's Castle, 1974; The Gigantic Balloon, 1975; Swords and Crowns and Rings, 1977; Come Danger, Come Darkness, 1978; Playing Beatie Bow, 1980; When the Wind Changed, 1980; The Big Brass Key, 1983; The Syndey We Love, 1983; Missus, 1985; My Sister Sif, 1986; The Tasmania We Love, 1987; Callie's Family: James, 1991; A Fence Around the Cuckoo, 1992; Fishing in the Styx, 1993; Home Before Dark, 1995. Address: c/o Curtis Brown Pty Ltd, PO Box 19, Paddington, New South Wales 2021, Australia.

PARKER Franklin, b. 2 June 1921, New York, New York, USA. Professor of Education Emeritus; Writer. m. Betty Parker, 12 June 1950. Education: BA, Berea College, 1949; MS, University of Illinois, 1950; EdD, Peabody College of Vanderbilt University, 1956. Appointments: Librarian, Ferrum College, Virginia, 1950-52, Belmont College, Nashville, 1952-54, George Peabody College for Teachers, Vanderbilt University, 1955-56; Associate Professor of Education, State University of New York at New Paltz, 1956-57, University of Texas at Austin, 1957-64; Professor of Education, University of Oklahoma, 1964-68; Benedum Professor of Education, 1968-86, Professor Emeritus, 1986-, West Virginia University, Morgantown; Distinguished Visiting Professor, Northern Arizona University, 1986-89, Western Carolina University, 1989-94. Publications: African Development and Education in Southern Rhodesia, 1960, 2nd edition, 1974; Africa South of the Sahara, 1966; George Peabody: A Biography, 1971, revised edition, 1995; The Battle of the Books: Kanawha Country, 1975; What Can We Learn from the Schools of China?, 1977; British Schools and Ours, 1979; Co-Author: John Dewey: Master Educator, 2nd edition, revised, 1961; Government Policy and International Education, 1965; Church and State in Education, 1966; Strategies for Curriculum Change: Cases from 13 Nations, 1968; Dimensions of Physical Education, 1969; International Education: Understandings and Misunderstandings, 1969; Understanding the American Public High School, 1969; Education in Southern Africa, 1970; Curriculum for Man in an International World, 1971; Administrative Dimensions of Health and Physical Education Programs, Including Athletics, 1971; Education and the Many Faces of the Disadvantaged, 1972; The Saber-Tooth Curriculum, 1972; Accelerated Development in Southern Africa, 1974; Myth and Reality: A Reader in Education, 1975; Six Questions: Controversy and Conflict in Education, 1975; Crucial Issues in Education, 6th edition, revised, 1977; Censorship and Education, 1981; Academic Profiles in Higher Education, 1993. Editor: American Dissertations on Foreign Education: A Bibliography with Abstracts, 20 volumes, 1971-90; Education in Puerto Rico and of Puerto Ricans in the USA (with Betty June Parker), 2 volumes, 1978, 1984; Women's Education: A World View: Annotated Bibliography of Doctoral Dissertations, 2 volumes, 1979, 1981; US Higher Education: A Guide to Information Sources, 1980; Education in the People's Republic of China, Past and Present: Annotated Bibliography, 1986; Education in England and Wales: An Annotated Bibliography. Contributions to: Reference works, books and professional journals, several articles in Tennessee Encyclopaedia, Tennessee Historical Society, forthcoming. Honours: Fulbright Senior Research Fellow, 1961-62; Distinguished Alumnus Award, Peabody

College of Vanderbilt University, 1970, Berea College, 1989. Memberships: African Studies Association; American Academy of Political and Social Sciences; American Educational Research Association; Comparative and International Education Society; History Education Society. Address: PO Box 100, Pleasant Hill, TN 38578, USA.

PARKER Gordon, b. 28 Feb 1940, Newcastle, England. Author; Playwright. Education: Newcastle Polytechnic, 1965-68. Appointment: Book Reviewer, BBC Radio and ITV. Publications: The Darkness of the Morning, 1975; Lightning in May, 1976; The Pool, 1978; Action of the Tiger, 1981. Radio plays: The Seance, 1978; God Protect the Lonely Widow, 1982. Address: 14 Thornhill Close, Seaton Delaval, Northumberland, England.

PARKER Jean. See: **SHARAT CHANDRA Gubbi Shankara Chetty.**

PARKER Robert B(rown), b. 17 Sept 1932, Springfield, Massachusetts, USA. Author. m. Joan Hall, 26 Aug 1956, 2 sons. Education: BA, Colby College, 1954; MA, 1957, PhD, 1971, Boston University. Appointments: Lecturer, Boston University, 1962-64; Faculty, Lowell State College, 1964-66, Bridgwater State College, 1966-68; Assistant Professor 1968-73, Associate Professor 1973-76, Professor of English 1976-79, Northeastern University. Publications: Fiction: The Godwulf Manuscript, 1973; God Save the Child, 1974; Mortal Stakes, 1975; Promised Land, 1976; The Judas Goat, 1978; Wilderness, 1979; Looking for Rachel Wallace, 1980; Early Autumn, 1981; A Savage Place, 1981; Surrogate, 1982; Ceremony, 1982; The Widening Gyre, 1983; Love and Glory, 1983; Valediction, 1984; A Catskill Eagle, 1985; Taming a Sea Horse, 1986; Pale Kings and Princes, 1987; Crimson Joy, 1988; Playmates, 1989; Poodle Springs (completion of unfinished novel by R Chandler), 1989; Stardust, 1990; Perchance to Dream, 1991; Pastime, 1991; Double Deuce, 1992; All Our Yesterdays, 1994; Walking Shadow, 1994. Other: The Personal Response to Literature, 1971; Order and Diversity, 1973; Three Weeks in Spring, with Joan Parker, 1978. Address: c/o Helen Brann Agency, 94 Curtis Road, Bridgewater, CT 06752, USA.

PARKES Joyce Evelyne, (J E Dubois), b. 30 June 1930, Serang, West Java, Indonesia. Writer; Archivist. 1 son, 2 daughters. Education: Archivist's course, Java, 1948-49. Publications: The Land of Sand and Stone, 1977; Silver and Gold, 1977; Changes, 1977. Contributions to: Numerous including: Midland Review; Pen International, UK; Fremantle Arts Review; Poetry Australia; Sydney Morning Herald. Memberships: Fellowship of Australian Writers; PEN; W B Yeats Society; KSP Foundation of Western Australia. Address: 16 John Street, Darlington, Western Australia 6070, Australia.

PARKES Roger Graham, b. 15 Oct 1933, Chingford, Essex, England. Novelist; Scriptwriter. m. Tessa Isabella McLean, 5 Feb 1964, 1 son, 1 daughter. Education: National Diploma of Agriculture. Appointments: Staff Writer, Farming Express and Scottish Daily Express, 1959-63; Editor, Farming Express, 1963; Staff Script Editor, Drama, BBC-TV, London 1964-70. Publications: Death Mask, 1970; Line of Fire, 1971; The Guardians, 1973; The Dark Number, 1973; The Fourth Monkey, 1978; Alice Ray Morton's Cookham, 1981; Them and Us, 1985; Riot, 1986; Y-E-S, 1986; An Abuse of Justice, 1988; Troublemakers, 1990; Gamelord, 1991; The Wages of Sin, 1992. Contributions to: Daily Express; Sunday Express. Honour: Grand Prix de Littérature, Paris, 1974. Memberships: Writers Guild of Great Britain; Magistrates Association. Literary Agents: Watson Little Ltd, London England; The Sharland Organisation, London, England. Address: Cartlands Cottage, Kings Lane, Cookham Dean, Berkshire SL6 9AY, England.

PARKINSON Michael, b. 28 Mar 1935, Yorkshire, England. TV Presenter; Writer. m. Mary Heneghan, 3 sons. Appointments: Staff, The Guardian, Daily Express, Sunday Times, Punch, Listener; Joined Granada TV as interviewer/reporter, 1965; Executive Producer and Presenter, London Weekend TV, 1968; Presenter, Cinema, 1969-70, Tea Break, Where in the World, 1971; Hosted own chat show "Parkinson", BBC, 1972-82, "Parkinson One to One", Yorkshire TV, 1987-; Presenter, Give Us a Clue, 1984-, All Star Secrets, 1985, Desert Island Discs, 1986-88, Parky, 1989, LBC Radio, 1990; Help Squad, 1991, Daily Telegraph, 1991-. Publications: Football Daft, 1968; Cricket Mad, 1969; Sporting Fever, 1974; George Best: An Intimate Biography, 1975; A-Z of Soccer (joint author), 1975; Bats in the Pavilion, 1977; The Woofits, 1980; Parkinson's Lore, 1981; The

Best of Parkinson, 1982; Sporting Lives, 1992; Sporting Profiles, 1995. Address: c/o Michael Parkinson Enterprises Ltd, IMG, Axis Centre, Burlington Lane, London W4 2TH, England.

PARKS Suzan-Lori, b. 1964, USA. Dramatist; Instructor in Playwrighting. Education: Mt Holybrooke College; Drama Studios, London, England. Publications: Plays: Imperceptible Mutabilities in the Third Kingdom, 1989; Betting on the Dust Commander, 1990; Death of the Last Black Man in the Whole World, 1990; Devotees of the Garden of Love, 1992. Other: Video, film, and radio items. Honours: Obie Award, 1990; Whiting Writer's Award, 1992; Numerous grants and fellowships. Address: c/o Giles Whiting Foundation, 30 Rockefeller Plaza, New York, NY 10112, USA.

PARKS T(imothy) Harold (John MacDowell), b. 19 Dec 1954, Manchester, England. Educator; Translator; Author. Education: BA, Cambridge University, 1977; MA, Harvard University, 1979. Publications: Tongues of Flame, 1985; Loving Roger, 1986; Home Thoughts, 1987; Family Planning, 1989; Cara Massimina (as John MacDowell), 1990; Goodness, 1991; Italian Neighbours, 1992; Shear, 1993. Short stories: Keeping Distance, 1988; The Room, 1992. Translations; La Cosa (short stories), 1985; Notturno indiano (novel), 1988; L'uomo che guarda (novel), 1989; Viaggio a Romas, 1989; Il filo dell'orrizonto (novel), 1989; La donna di Porto Pim, I volatili del Beato Angelico (short story collections), 1991; C'un punto della terra, 1991; I beati anni del castigo (novel), 1991; Le nozze di Cadmo e Armonia, 1993; La strada di San Giovanni (stories), 1993. Contributions to: Numerous articles, reviews and talks for BBC Radio 3. Honours: Somerset Maugham, 1986; Betty Trash 1st Prize, 1986; Llewellyn Rhys, 1986; John Floria Prize for Best Translation from Italian. Membership: Authors Society. Literary Agent: Curtis Brown. Address: Via delle Primule 6, Montorio, 37033 Verona, Italy.

PARLAKIAN Nishan, b. 11 July 1925, New York, New York, USA. Professor of Drama; Playwright. m. Florence B Mechtel, 1 son, 1 daughter. Education: BA, Syracuse University, 1948; MA, 1950, MA, 1952, PhD, 1967, Columbia University. Appointments: Editorial Board, Ararat, 1970-, MELUS, 1977-80; Editor, Pirandello Society Newsletter, Armenian Church Magazine; Associate Editor, Pirandello Society Annual. Publications: Original plays: The Last Mohigian, 1959; Plagiarized, 1962; What Does Greta Garbo Mean to You?, 1973; Grandma, Pray for Me, 1988. Translated plays: For the Sake of Honor, 1976; Evil Spirit, 1980; The Bride, 1987; Be Nice, I'm Dead, 1990. Contributions to: Armenian Literature Between East and West; Review of National Literature, 1984. Honours: Prizewinner, Stanley Awards, 1961; International Arts Award for Playwriting, Columbus Countdown, 1992. Memberships: Modern Language Association; President, Pirandello Society of America, 1995. Literary Agent: Ann Elmo. Address: 415 W 115th Street, New York City, NY 10025, USA.

PARMELEE David Freeland, b. 20 June 1924, Oshkosh, Wisconsin, USA. Research Curator; Former Professor. m. Jean Marie Peterson, 4 Dec 1943, 1 daughter. Education: BA, Lawrence University, Appleton, Wisconsin, 1950; MSc, University of Michigan, Ann Arbor, 1952; PhD, University of Oklahoma, Norman, 1957. Appointments: Professor, University of Minnesota, 1970-92; Research Curator of Ornithology, University of Nevada, Las Vegas, 1992-. Publications: The Birds of West-Central Ellesmere Island and Adjacent Areas, 1960; The Birds of Southeastern Victoria Island and Adjacent Small Islands, 1967; Bird Island in Antarctic Waters, 1980; Antarctic Birds, 1992. Contributions to: Arctic; Antarctic Journal US; Auk; Beaver; Bird-Banding; Condor; Ibis; Living Bird; Loon; Wilson Bulletin. Honours: Antarctic Place Name 'Parmelee Massif' at 70°58' S, 62°10'W, Geographic Names Division, Defense Mapping Agency, Topographic Center, Washington, DC, 1977; Native Son Award, Michigan Rotary International, 1982. Memberships: Organization of Biological Field Stations; British Ornithological Society; Cooper's Ornithological Society; Wilson Ornithological Society; Fellow, Explorers Club; British Ornithologists' Club. Address: Marjorie Barrick Museum of Natural History, 4505 Maryland Parkway, Box 454012, Las Vegas, NV 89154, USA.

PARMET Herbert Samuel, b. 28 Sept 1929, New York, New York, USA. Professor of History Emeritus; Writer. m. Joan Kronish, 12 Sept 1948, 1 daughter. Education: BS, State University of New York at Oswego, 1951; MA, Queens College, New York City, 1957; Postgraduate Studies, Columbia University, 1958-62. Appointments: Professor of History 1968-83, Distinguished Professor of History 1983-95, Professor Emeritus 1995-, Graduate School, City University

of New York; Consultant, ABC-TV, New York City, 1983, KERA-TV, Dallas, 1986-91, WGBH-TV, Boston, 1988-91. Publications: Aaron Burr: Portrait of an Ambitious Man, 1967; Never Again: A President Runs for a Third Term, 1968; Eisenhower and the American Crusades, 1972; The Democrats: The Years after FDR, 1976; Jack: The Struggles of John F Kennedy, 1980; JFK: The Presidency of John F Kennedy, 1983; Richard Nixon and His America, 1990; George Bush: The Life of a Lone Star Yankee, 1997. Contributions to: Professional journals. Honour: National Endowment for the Humanities Grant, 1987. Memberships: American Historical Association; Authors Guild; Authors League; Organization of American Historians; Society of American Historians, Fellow. Address: 36 Marsten Lane, Hillsdale, NY 12529, USA.

PARQUE Richard (Anthony), b. 8 Oct 1935, Los Angeles, California, USA. Writer; Poet; Teacher. m. Vo Thi Lan, 1 May 1975, 3 sons. Education: BA, 1958, MA, 1961, California State University, Los Angeles; California State Teaching Credential, 1961; Postgraduate studies, University of Redlands. Publications: Sweet Vietnam, 1984; Hellbound, 1986; Firefight, 1987; Flight of the Phantom, 1988; A Distant Thunder, 1989. Contributions to: Journals, magazines and newspapers. Honours: Bay Area Poets Award, 1989; Vietnam novels have been placed in the Colorado State University Vietnam War Collection. Memberships: Authors Guild; Academy of American Poets. Address: PO Box 327, Verdugo City, CA 91046, USA.

PARRINDER (John) Patrick, b. 11 Oct 1944, Wadebridge, Cornwall, England. Literary Critic. 2 daughters. Education: Christ's College, 1962-65, Darwin College, 1965-67, Cambridge; MA, PhD, Cambridge University. Appointments: Fellow, King's College, Cambridge, 1967-74; Lecturer in English, 1974-80, Reader, 1980-86, Professor, 1986-, University of Reading. Publications: H G Wells, 1970; Authors and Authority, 1977, 2nd enlarged edition, 1991; Science Fiction: Its Criticism and Teaching, 1980; James Joyce, 1984; The Failure of Theory, 1987; Shadows of the Future, 1995. Editor: H G Wells: The Critical Heritage, 1972; Science Fiction: A Critical Guide, 1979; Shadows of the Future, 1995. Contributions to: London Review of Books; Many academic journals. Honour: President's Award, World Science Fiction, 1987. Memberships: Vice-President, H G Wells Society; Science Fiction Foundation. Address: Department of English, University of Reading, PO Box 218, Reading, Berkshire RG6 6AA, England.

PARTLETT Launa, (Launa Gillis), b. 19 May 1918, Miles, Queensland, Australia. Retired Editress; Writer; Poet. m. Charles Henry Partlett, 19 June 1943, dec, 1 son, 1 daughter. Education: Art Classes; Writing courses. Appointments: Social Editress, St George Call Newspaper, starting 1960; Freelance articles, The Leader Newspaper. Publications: Guluguba Pioneers - Stories from Queensland Rural Community, 1986; John Jones and Family: Rocky River Gold (co-author), 1987. Contributions to: Anthologies, magazines, and newspapers. Honour: Newshound Certificate, Leader Newspaper, 1984; Gold Medal, 1995, Certificate, ABI, USA; Certificate, IBC. Memberships: Miles Historical Society; Former Member: Art Society of New South Wales; Bankstown Art Society; Australian Stockmans Hall of Fame; Canterbury and District Historical Society; Life Member, British Bible Society; Honorary Ranger, National Parks and Wildlife Service; Dorcas Society. Address: 3/11 Parry Avenue, Narwee, New South Wales 2209, Australia.

PARTNOY Alicia, b. 7 Feb 1955, Bahia Blanca, Argentina. Literature Professor; Translator; Human Rights Lecturer. m. Antonio Leiva, 2 daughters. Education: Certificate of Translation, English/Spanish, American University, USA, 1986; MA, Latin American Literature, Catholic University of America, Washington, DC, 1991. Appointments: Acquisitions Editor, Cleis Press, San Francisco, 1989-; Lecturer on Latin American Literature, Maryland Institute - College of Arts, Baltimore, 1992. Publications: The Little School: Tales of Disappearance and Survival in Argentina, 1986; You Can't Drown the Fire: Latin American Women Writing in Exile (editor), 1988; Revenge of the Apple - Venganza de la Manzana, 1992. Membership: Amnesty International. Address: PO Box 21425, Washington, DC 20009, USA.

PARTRIDGE Derek, b. 24 Oct 1945, London, England. Professor of Computer Science. m. 27 Aug 1971, 2 daughters. Education: BSc, Chemistry, University College, London, 1968; PhD, Computer Science, Imperial College, London, 1972. Appointments: Professor, University of Exeter, England; Editor, Computational Science, book series, Ablex Publishing Corporation, Norwood, New Jersey, USA. Publications:

Artificial Intelligence: Applications in the Future of Software Engineering, 1965; A New Guide to Artificial Intelligence, 1991; Engineering Artificial Intelligence Software, 1992. Contributions to: More than 100 articles to professional magazines and journals. Memberships: American Association for Artificial Intelligence; Society for Artificial Intelligence and Simulation of Behaviour. Address: Department of Computer Science, University of Exeter, Exeter EX4 4PT, England.

PARTRIDGE Frances Catherine, b. 15 Mar 1900, London, England. Writer. m. Ralph Partridge, 2 Mar 1933, 1 son. Education BA (Hons), English, Moral Sciences, Newnham College, Cambridge, 1921. Appointment: Editor, The Greville Memoirs (with Ralph Partridge), 1928-38; Translator, 20 books from French and Spanish. Publications: A Pacifist's War, 1978; Memories, 1981; Julia, 1983; Everything to Lose, 1985; Friends in Focus, 1987; The Pasque Flower, 1990; Hanging On, 1990; Other People, 1993; Good Company, 1994. Contributions to: Many book reviews and obituaries to various publications. Memberships: Royal Society of Literature, fellow; International PEN. Address: 15 West Halkin Street, London SW1X 8JL, England.

PASCALIS Stratis, b. 4 Mar 1958, Athens, Greece. Poet; Translator. m. Sophie Phocas, 28 Feb 1982, 2 daughters. Education: Graduated, Political Sciences, University of Athens, 1983. Publications: Poetry: Anactoria, 1977; Excavation, 1984; Hermaphrodite's Night, 1989; Sour Cherry Trees in the Darkness, 1991; Translations: 49 Scholia on the poems of Odysseus Elytis, by Jeffrey Carson, 1983; Phaedra, by Racine, 1990; The Horla and Other Stories of Madness and Terror, by Guy de Maupassant, 1992. Contributions to: Magazines and newspapers. Honour: Maris P Ralli Prize for 1st Book of a Young Poet, 1977. Membership: Society of Greek Writers. Address: Diamandidou 36, Palio Psychiko, Athens 15452, Greece.

PASCHE Jean-Robert, b. 15 Aug 1950, Lausanne, Switzerland. Writer; Analyst of Dreams; Researcher. m. 26 Apr 1977, 2 d. Education: Higher educ, Switzerland. Publications: Les rêves ou la Connaissance Intérieure, 1987; Etre selon ses Rêves, 1992. Contributions to: Articles to newspapers and magazines, France, Belgium, Switzerland. Memberships: Société Suisse des Ecrivains; Société Genevoise des Ecrivains; Pro Litteris, Switzerland. Literary Agent: Editions Buchet/Chastel, 18 rue de Condé, 75006 Paris, France. Address: Centre International d'études et de recherche sur les Rêves, case postale 473, 1211 Geneva, Switzerland.

PASCHEN Elise Maria, b. 4 Jan 1959, Chicago, Illinois, USA. Arts Administrator; Poet. Education: BA with honours, Harvard University, 1982; MPhil, 1984, DPhil, 1988, Oxford University, England. Appointment: Executive Director, Poetry Society of America. Publications: Houses: Coasts, 1985; Infidelities, 1996; Houses: Coasts. Contributions to: Poetry Magazine; Poetry Review, England; Oxford Magazine; Poetry Ireland Review; Oxford Poetry; Harvard Advocate; New Yorker; Mation; New Republic; Poetry. Honours: Lloyd McKim Garrison Medal for Poetry, Harvard University, 1982; Joan Grey Untermyer Poetry Prize, Harvard/Radcliffe, 1982; Richard Selig Prize for Poetry, Magdalen College, Oxford, 1984; Nicholas Roerich Poetry Prize, 1996; Lloyd McKim Garrison Medal. Membership: National Arts Club. Address: Poetry Society of America, 15 Gramercy Park, New York, NY 10003, USA.

PASKANDI Géza, b. 18 May 1933, Szatmarhegy-Viile Satumare, Romania. Writer. m. Anna-Maria Sebök, 24 Apr 1970, 1 daughter. Education: University Bolyai-Kolozsvar-Cluj, 1953-57. Appointments: Journalist, Szatmarnemeti, Bucharest, Kolozsvar, 1949-54; Editor, Editions Kriterion, Kolozsvar, 1970-73; Review Kortars, Budapest, Hungary. Publications: Tales, Radio Plays, Screenplays, 1970-90; Drama, 1970, 1975, 1987; Poetry, 1972, 1979, 1989; Essays, 1984; Novels, 1988, 1989. Contributions to: Magazines and journals. Honours: Award, Romanian Writers Assocation, 1970; Jozsef Attila Award, Hungary, 1977; Award for Hungarian Art, 1991; Kossuth Award, Hungary, 1992. Memberships: PEN Club; Hungarian Writers Association; Moricz Zsigmond Literary Society; Hungarian Academy of Arts. Address: Nagyszalonta utca 50, 1112 Budapest, Hungary.

PASSMORE Jacki, b. 2 July 1947, Queensland, Australia. Food Writer; Cookbook Author. 1 daughter. Career: Food Writer; Queensland Newpapers, Sunday Mail, Courier Mail, 1993. Publications: Asia: The Beautiful Cookbook, 1987; The Encyclopedia of

Asian Food and Cooking, 1990; The Complete Spanish Cookbook, 1992; Festival Foods of Thailand, 1992; The Noodle Shop Cookbook, 1994; 15 others. Memberships: Queensland Wine Writers Club; International Association of Culinary Professionals, USA. Literary Agent: Judith Weber, Sobel Weber Associates Inc, 146 East 19th Street, New York, NY 10003, USA. Address: 50 Turin Street, West End, Brisbane, Queensland 4101, Australia.

PATCHETT Ann, b. 2 Dec 1963, Los Angeles, California, USA. Writer. Education: BA, Sarah Lawrence College, 1984; MFA, University of Iowa, 1987. Appointments: Writer-in-Residence, Allegheny College, 1989-90; Visiting Assistant Professor, Murray State University, 1992. Publications: The Patron Saint of Liars, 1992; Taft, 1994. Contributions to: Anthologies and periodicals. Honours: James A Michener/Copernicus Award, University of Iowa, 1989; Yaddo Fellow, 1990; Millay Fellow, 1990; Resident Fellow, Fine Arts Work Center, Provincetown, Massachusetts, 1990-91; Notable Book, American Library Association, 1992. Address: c/o Carol Fass Ivy Publishing, 201 East 50th Street, New York, NY 10022, USA.

PATEL Gieve, b. 18 Aug 1940, Bombay, India. Poet; Dramatist; Painter. m. Toni Diniz, 1969, 1 daughter. Education: St Xaviers College, Bombay; Grant Medical College, Bombay. Publications: Poems, 1966; How Do You Withstand, Body, 1976; Mirrored, Mirroring, 1990. Plays, Princes, 1971; Savaska, 1982; Mister Behram, 1987. Honours: Woodrow Wilson Fellowship, 1984. Address: 5E Malabar Apartments, Nepean Road, Bombay 400 036, India.

PATERAKIS Yolanda, b. 27 Oct 1934, Greece. Writer. m. Andreas Paterakis, 14 Sept 1963, 1 son, 1 daughter. Education: Greek Literary Certificate, 1954; University of Cambridge, England, 1958. Publications: Some 25 books, 1976-96 including: Once in Macedonia, Novel, 1994; The Moonman, Tale, 1995. Contributions to: Many publications in NEA ESTIA. Memberships: Children's Book Circle of Greece; National Society of Greek Authors, General Secretary, 1979-. Address: 17 Kritonis Street, 11634 Athens, Greece.

PATERSON Aileen (Francis), b. 30 Nov 1934, Burntisland, Fife, Scotland. Author; Illustrator of Children's Books. m. Hamish Paterson, 5 Apr 1963, 2 sons, 4 daughters. Education: DA, Edinburgh, 1955; Moray House Teaching Qualification, 1961. Publications: Maisie Comes to Morningside, 1984; Maisie Goes to School, 1988; Maisie in the Rainforest, 1992; Maisie and the Puffer, 1992; Maisie Goes to Hollywood, 1994. Contributions to: Scotsman; Scotland on Sunday; Scotland's Languages Magazine; Insider. Membership: Society of Authors in Scotland. Literary Agent: Gina Pollinger. Address: 8 Carlyle Place, Edinburgh EH7 5SR, Scotland.

PATERSON Alistair Ian, b. 28 Feb 1929, Nelson, New Zealand. Poet; Writer; Educational Consultant. m. Dec 1984, 2 sons, 3 daughters. Education: BA, University of New Zealand, 1961; Diploma in Education, University of Auckland, 1972. Appointments: Royal New Zealand Navy, 1954-74; Dean of General Studies, New Zealand Police, 1974-78; Tertiary Inspector, New Zealand Department of Education, 1979-89; Educational Consultant, 1990-. Publications: Caves in the Hills, 1965; Birds Flying, 1973; Cities and Strangers, 1976; The Toledo Room: A Poem for Voices, 1978; 15 Contemporary New Zealand Poets (editor), 1980; Qu'appelle, 1982; The New Poetry, 1982; Incantations for Warriors, 1982; Oedipus Rex, 1986; Short Stories from New Zealand (editor), 1988; How to be a Millionaire by Next Wednesday (novel), 1994. Contributions to: Various publications. Honours: Fulbright Fellowship, 1977; John Cowie Reid Award, University of Auckland, 1982; Katherine Mansfield Award for Fiction, 1993; New Zealand Creative Writing Grant, 1995. Memberships: PEN; Wellington Poetry Society. Address: PO Box 9612, Newmarket, Auckland, New Zealand.

PATERSON Katherine (Womeldorf), b. 31 Oct 1932, Qing Jiang, China. Public School Teacher; Writer. m. John Barstow Paterson, 2 sons, 2 adopted daughters. Education: AB, King College; MA, Presbyterian School of Christian Education; MRS, Kobe University School of Japanese Language, Union Theological Seminary. Publications: Sign of the Chrysanthemum, 1973; The Great Gilly Hopkins, 1978; Jacob Have I Loved, 1980; Consider the Lilies: Plants of the Bible, 1986; Park's Quest, 1988; The Spying Heart, 1989; Tale of the Mandarin Ducks, 1990; The King's Equal, 1992; Flip-Flop Girl, 1994; Angel and the Donkey, 1996. Honours: American Library Association Awards, 1974, 1976, 1977, 1978; Newbery Medals, 1978, 1981; National Book Award, 1979; Christopher Award, 1979; Parents

Choice Award, 1983; Laura Ingalls Wilder Award, 1986; Regina Medal Award, Catholic Library Association, 1988; Boston Globe/Horn Book Award, 1991. Address: c/o Dutton Children's Books, 375 Hudson Street, New York, NY 10014, USA.

PATILIS Yannis, b. 21 Feb 1947, Athens, Greece. Teacher of Literature; Poet. m. Elsa Liaropoulou, 2 sons. Education: Degree, Law School, 1971, Department of Byzantine and Neo-Hellenic Studies, 1977, University of Athens. Appointments: Co-Founder and Co-Editor, Nesus, poetry and music journal, 1983-85; Editor and Publisher, Planodion, literature and the politics of culture journal, 1986-. Publications: 8 volumes of poetry, 1970-93, including collected poems, 1993; Camel of Darkness, Selected Poems of Yannis Patilis, 1970-1990, 1997. Contributions to: Various publications. Membership: Society of Greek Writers. Address: 23 G Mistriotou Street, 112 55 Athens, Greece.

PATON WALSH Jill, b. 29 Apr 1937, London, England. Children's Author. Education: Diploma in Education, 1959, MA, St Anne's College, Oxford. Publications: Over 30 books, 1966-93. Address: 72 Water Lane, Histon, Cambridge CB4 4LR, England.

PATRICK Maxine. See: **MAXWELL Patricia Anne.**

PATRICK Susan. See: **CLARK Patricia Denise.**

PATRICK William. See: **HAINING Peter Alexander.**

PATTEN Brian, b. 7 Feb 1946, Liverpool, England. Poet; Writer. Appointment: Regents Lecturer, University of California at San Diego. Publications: Poetry: The Mersey Sound: Penguin Modern Poets 10, 1967; Little Johnny's Confession, 1967; The Home Coming, 1969; Notes to the Hurrying Man: Poems, Winter '66-Summer '68, 1969; The Irrelevant Song, 1970; At Four O'Clock in the Morning, 1971; Walking Out: The Early Poems of Brian Patten, 1971; The Eminent Professors and the Nature of Poetry as Enacted Out by Members of the Poetry Seminar One Rainy Evening, 1972; The Unreliable Nightingale, 1973; Vanishing Trick, 1976; Grave Gossip, 1979; Love Poems, 1981; New Volume, 1983; Storm Damage, 1988; Grinning Jack: Selected Poems, 1990; Armada, 1996. Editor: Clare's Countryside: A Book of John Clare, 1981. Children's Books: Prose: The Jumping Mouse, 1972; Mr Moon's Last Case, 1975; Emma's Doll, 1976; Jimmy Tag-along, 1988; Grizzelda Frizzle, 1992; Impossible Parents, 1994. Poetry: Gargling With Jelly, 1985; Thawing Frozen Frogs, 1990; The Puffin Book of 20th Century Children's Verse, 1991; The Magic Bicycle, 1993; The Utter Nutters, 1994. Contributions to: Journals and newspapers. Honour: Special Award, Mystery Writers of America (for Mr Moon's Last Case), 1977. Membership: Chelsea Arts Club. Address: c/o Puffin Penguin Books, 27 Wrights Lane, London W8 5TZ, England.

PATTERSON Henry (Harry), (Martin Fallon, James Graham, Jack Higgins, Hugh Marlowe), b. 27 July 1929, Newcastle upon Tyne, England. Author. m. (1) Amy Margaret Hewitt, 1958, div. 1984, 1 son, 3 daughters, (2) Denise Lesley Anne Palmer, 1985. Education: Certificate in Education, Carnegie College, 1958; BSc, London School of Economics and Political Science, 1962. Appointments: NCO, The Blues, 1947-50, 1950-58. Publications: As Jack Higgins: Prayer for the Dying, 1973, filmed, 1985; The Eagle Has Landed, 1975, filmed, 1976; Storm Warning, 1976; Day of Judgement, 1978; Solo, 1980; Luciano's Luck, 1981; Touch the Devil, 1982; Exocet, 1983; Confessional, 1985, filmed, 1985; Night of the Fox, 1986, filmed, 1990; Season in Hell, 1989; Coldharbour, 1990; The Eagle Has Flown, 1991. As Harry Patterson: The Valhalla Exchange, 1978; To Catch a King, 1979, filmed, 1983; Dillinger, 1983. Many others under pseudonyms, including: The Violent Enemy, filmed, 1969; The Wrath of God, filmed, 1972; Some books translated into 42 languages. Address: c/o Ed Victor, 162 Wardour Street, London W1V 3AT, England.

PATTERSON (Horace) Orlando (Lloyd), b. 5 June 1940, Jamaica, West Indies. Professor of Sociology; Writer. Education: BSc, University of West Indies, 1962; PhD, London School of Economics and Political Science, 1965. Appointments: Professor of Sociology 1971-, John Cowles Professor of Sociology 1993, Harvard University; Associate Editor, American Sociological Review, 1989-92. Publications: Fiction: The Children of Sisyphus, 1964; An Absence of Ruins, 1967; Die the Long Day, 1972. Non-Fiction: The Sociology of Slavery: Jamaica 1655-1838, 1967; Ethnic Chauvinism: The Reactionary Impulse, 1977; Slavery and Social Death: A Comparative Study, 1982; Freedom, 2 volumes, 1991, 1995. Contributions to: Books

and professional journals. Honours: Best Novel in English Award, Dakar Festival of Negro Arts, 1965; Walter Channing Cabot Faculty Prize, Harvard University, 1983; Co-Winner, Ralph Bunche Award, American Political Science Association, 1983; Distinguished Contribution to Scholarship Award, American Sociological Association, 1983; National Book Award for Non-Fiction, 1991; University of California at Los Angeles Medal, 1992. Memberships: American Academy of Arts and Sciences, Fellow; American Sociological Association. Address: c/o Department of Sociology, Harvard University, Cambridge, MA 02138, USA.

PATTERSON James, b. 22 Mar 1947, Newburgh, New York, USA. Author. Education: BA, Manhattan College, 1969; MA, Vanderbilt University, 1970. Publications: The Thomas Berryman Number, 1976; The Season of the Machete, 1977; The Jericho Commandment, 1979; Virgin, 1980; Black Market, 1986; The Midnight Club, 1989; The Day America Told the Truth, 1991; Along Came the Spider, 1993; The Second American Revolution, 1994; Kiss the Girls, 1995; Miracle on the 17th Green, 1996; Jack & Jill, 1996. Address: c/o Warner Books, 1271 Avenue of the Americas, New York, NY 10020, USA.

PATTERSON Michael Wyndham (formerly Michael Wyndham Richards), b. 7 Sept 1939, London, England. University Professor. m. (1) Ellinor von Einsiedel, (2) Diana (Dixi) Patterson, (3) Jane Prentice, 3 sons, 5 daughters. Education: BA, Mediaeval and Modern Languages, 1962, DPhil, 1968, Oxford. Publications: German Theatre Today, 1976; The Revolution in German Theatre 1900-1933, 1981; Peter Stein, 1981; Georg Büchner: Collected Works (editor), 1987; The First German Theatre, 1990; German Theatre: A Bibliography, 1996. Address: Department of Visual and Performing Arts, De Montfort University, Leicester LE1 9BH, England.

PATTERSON Richard North, b. 22 Feb 1947, Berkeley, California, USA. Novelist. m. Laurie Anderson Patterson, 13 Apr 1993, 4 sons, 2 daughters. Education: BA, History, Ohio Wesleyan Universty, Delaware, Ohio, 1968; JD, Case Western Reserve Law School, Cleveland, Ohio. Publications: The Lasko Tangent, 1979; The Outside Man, 1981; Escape the Night, 1983; Private Screening, 1985; Degree of Guilt, 1993; Eyes of a Child, 1995; The Final Judgement, 1995; Silent Witness, 1997. Contributions to: Magazines, journals and newspapers. Honours: Edgar Allen Poe Award, The Lasko Tangent, 1979; French Grand Prix de Litterateur Policiere, 1995; President's Award to Distinguished Alumni, Case Western Reserve University, 1997. Membership: Board of Directors, PEN; Board of Trustees, Ohio Wesleyan University; Dean's National Advisory Committee, Case Western Reserve School of Law; Regional Committee for the Selection of White House Fellows, 1997. Literary Agent: Frederick Hill; Frederick Hill Associates, San Francisco, California.

PATTISON Robert, b. 28 Oct 1945, Orange, New Jersey, USA. Teacher. Education: AB, Yale University; MA, University of Sussex, 1968; PhD, Columbia University, 1974. Appointments: Adjunct Lecturer, Richmond College, City University of New York, 1974; Adjunct Instructor, Queensborough Community College, City University of New York, 1974-75; Instructor, English, St Vincent's College, St John's University, New York, 1975-77; Professor of English, Southampton College, Long Island University, New York, 1978-. Publications: The Child Figure in English Literature, 1978; Tennyson and Tradition, 1980; On Literacy, 1982; The Triumph of Vulgarity, 1987; The Great Dissent: John Henry Newman and the Liberal Heresey, 1991. Contributions to: Nation; ADE Bulletin; University of Toronto Quarterly; Mosaic; New York Times; Dickens Studies Newsletter; Various edited volumes. Honours: Long Island University Trustees Awards for Scholarship, 1979, 1985; Rockefeller Foundation Fellowship, 1980-81; Guggenheim Fellowship, 1988-87. Address: PO Box 2106, Southampton, NY 11969, USA.

PATTRICK William. See: **HAINING Peter.**

PATZERT Rudolph, b. 15 Oct 1911, New York, New York, USA. Master Marinek. m. Theresa Levis, 2 sons. Education: De Smouitime Institute, 1940-41. Publication: Running the Palestine Blockade. Address: 1756 Belle Meade Road, Encinitas, CA 92024, USA.

PAUL Barbara Jeanne, b. 5 June 1931, Maysville, Kentucky, USA. Writer. Div. 1 son. Education: AB, Bowling Green State University, 1955; MA, University of Redlands, 1957; PhD, University of Pittsburgh, 1969. Appointment: Mellon Fellow, University of Pittsburgh, 1967-69. Publications: An Exercise for Madmen, 1978; The

Fourth Wall, 1979; Pillars of Salt, 1979; Bibblings, 1979; First Gravedigger, 1980; Under the Canopy, 1980; Your Eyelids Are Growing Heavy, 1981; Liars and Tyrants and People Who Turn Blue, 1982; A Cadenza for Caruso, 1984; The Renewable Virgin, 1984; Prima Donna at Large, 1985; Kill Fee, 1985; But He Was Already Dead When I Got There, 1986; A Chorus of Detectives, 1987; The Three-Minute Universe, 1988; He Huffed and He Puffed, 1989; Good King Sauerkraut, 1989; In-Laws and Out Laws, 1990; You Have the Right to Remain Silent, 1992; The Apostrophe Thief, 1993. Contributions to: Magazines and journals. Memberships: American Crime Writers League; Science Fiction and Fantasy Writers of America; Sisters in Crime; Mystery Writers of America. Address: c/o Scott Meredith Literary Agency, 845 Third Avenue, New York, NY 10022, USA.

PAUL Jeremy, b. 29 July 1939, Bexhill, Sussex, England. Writer. m. Patricia Garwood, 26 Nov 1960, 4 daughters. Education: King's, Canterbury and St Edmund Hall, Oxford. Publications: Numerous TV plays, series and adaptations, 1960-, including: Upstairs, Downstairs, 1971-75; Country Matters, 1972; The Duchess of Duke Street, 1976; Danger, UXB, 1977; A Walk in the Forest, 1980; The Flipside of Dominick Hide (with Alan Gibson), 1980; Sorrell and Son, 1983; The Adventures, Return and Memoirs of Sherlock Holmes, 1984-94; Lovejoy, 1991-94. Theatre: David Going Out, 1971; Manoeuvres, 1971; Visitors (with Carey Harrison), 1980; The Secret of Sherlock Holmes, 1988; The Watcher, 1989. Film: Countess Dracula, 1970. Membership: Writers Guild of Great Britain. Address: c/o William Morris Agency, 31-32 Soho Square, London W1V 5DG, England.

PAULIN Tom, (Thomas Neilson Paulin), b. 25 Jan 1949, Leeds, Yorkshire, England. Poet; Critic; Lecturer in English Literature. m. Munjiet Kaut Khosa, 1973, 2 sons. Education: BA, University of Hull; BLitt, Lincoln College, Oxford. Appointments: Lecturer, 1972-89, Reader in Poetry, 1989-94, University of Nottingham; G M Young Lecturer in English Literature, University of Oxford, 1994-; Fellow, Hertford College, Oxford, 1994-. Publications: Poetry: Theoretical Locations, 1975; A State of Justice, 1977; Personal Column, 1978; The Strange Museum, 1980; The Book of Juniper, 1981; Liberty Tree, 1983; The Argument at Great Tew, 1985; Fivemiletown, 1987; Selected Poems 1972-90, 1993; Walking a Line. 1994. Other: Thomas Hardy: The Poetry of Perception, 1975; Ireland and the English Crisis, 1984; The Faber Book of Political Verse (editor), 1986; Hard Lines 3 (co-editor), 1987; Minotaur: Poetry and the Nation State, 1992. Honours: Eric Gregory Award, 1978; Somerset Maugham Award, 1978; Faber Memorial Prize, 1982; Fulbright Scholarship, 1983-84. Address: c/o Faber & Faber, 3 Queen Square, London WC1N 3AU, England.

PAULSON Ronald (Howard), b. 27 May 1930, Bottineau, North Dakota, USA. Professor of Humanities; Writer. m. Barbara Lee Appleton, 25 May 1957, div 1982, 1 son, 1 daughter. Education: BA, 1952, PhD, 1958, Yale University. Appointments: Instructor 1958-59, Assistant Professor, 1959-62, Associate Professor, 1962-63, University of Illinois; Professor of English, 1967-75, Chairman, Department of English, 1968-75, Andrew W Mellon Professor of Humanities, 1973-75, Mayer Professor of Humanities, 1984-, Chairman, Department of Humanities, 1985-91, Johns Hopkins University; Professor of English, Yale University, 1975-84. Publications: Theme and Structure in Swift's Tale of a Tub, 1960; Fielding: The Critical Heritage (editor with Thomas Lockwood), 1962; Fielding: 20 Century Views (editor), 1962; Hogarth's Graphic Works, 1965, 3rd edition, revised, 1989; The Fictions of Satire, 1967; Satire and the Novel, 1967; Satire: Modern Essays in Criticism, 1971; Hogart: His Life, Art and Times, 1971; Rowlandson: A New Interpretation, 1972; Emblem and Expression: Meaning in Eighteenth Century English Art, 1975; The Art of Hogarth, 1975; Popular and Polite Art in the Age of Hogarth and Fielding, 1979; Literary Landscape: Turner and Constable, 1982; Book and Painting: Shakespeare, Milton and the Bible, 1983; Representations of Revolution, 1983; Breaking and Remaking, 1989; Figure and Abstraction in Contemporary Painting, 1990; Hogarth: Vol I, The Modern Moral Subject, 1991, Vol II, High Art and Low, 1992, Vol III, Art and Politics, 1993; The Beautiful, Novel and Strange: Aesthetics and Heterodoxy, 1996. Contributions to: Professional journals. Honours: Guggenheim Fellowships, 1965-66, 1986-87; National Endowment for the Humanities Fellow, 1977-78. Memberships: American Academy of Arts and Sciences, Fellow; American Society of 18th Century Studies, President, 1986-87. Address: 2722 St Paul Street, Baltimore, MD 21218, USA.

PAUWELS Rony (Claude Van De Berge), b. 30 Apr 1945, Assenede, Belgium. Docent of Declamation; Writer; Poet. m. Drongen Pauwells, 30 Jan 1973. Education: Koninklijk Conservatorium, Gent. Appointments: Docent Declamation, Academy of Arts, Ecklo; Universities of Brussels, Gent, Louvain-La-Neuve; University of Bonn, Germany, 1989. Publications: De koude wind du over het zand waeut, 1977; Het bewegen van her hoge gras op de top van de hevvel, 1981; Hiiumaa, 1987; Attu, 1988; Aztlan, 1990. Poetry: De zang van de maskers, 1988; De Mens in der ster, 1991; Het Silhouet, 1993. Contributions to: Journals and magazines. Honours: Several literary prizes. Membership: VVF (Flemish Writers). Address: Oude Molenstraat 2, 9960 Assenede, Belgium.

PAVEY Don, (Jack Adair), b. 25 July 1922, London, England. Senior Lecturer of Art and Design (retired); Writer. Education: ARCA, Royal College of Art, 1946; University of London, 1956-59. Appointments: Senior Lecturer of Art and Design, Kingston Polytechnic; Editor, Athene, Journal of the Society for Education Through Art, 1972-80. Publications: Methuen Handbook of Colour and Colour Dictionary (editor), 1963, 3rd edition, 1978; Art-Based Games, 1979; Genius, 1980; Colour, 1981; The Artist's Colourmen's Story, 1985; Virtual Genius, 1986. Contributions to: Journals. Honour: Freedom of the City of London, Guild of Painter Stainers, 1987. Memberships: Colour Group, Great Britain; Design Research Society; Junior Arts and Science Centres, Founder-Chairman, 1970-80; National Art Education Archives, Bretton Hall, Wakefield, Founder-Trustee, 1985-86; Royal Society of Arts, Life Fellow; Society for Education Through Art, Council Member, 1972-83. Address: 30 Wayside, Sheen, London SW14 7LN, England.

PAVLOVICH. See: AKSENOV Vasilii.

PAXTON Lois. See: LOW Lois Dorothea.

PAYNE Donald Gordon, (Ian Cameron, Donald Gordon, James Vance Marshall), b. 3 Jan 1924, London, England. Author. m. Barbara Back, 20 Aug 1947, 4 sons, 1 daughter. Education: MA, History, Oxford. Publications: Walkabout, 1959; A River Ran Out of Eden, 1963; The Island at the Top of the World, 1970; To the Farthest Ends of the Earth, History of the Royal Geographical Society, 1980; Mountains of the Gods, 1984; Lost Paradise: The Exploration of the Pacific, 1987; Many other books. Contributions to: Reader's Digest; National Geographic. Literary Agent: John Johnson. Address: Pippacre, Westcott Heath, Dorking RH4 3JZ, Surrey, England.

PAYNE Laurence, b. 5 June 1919, London, England. Author; Actor. Education: London Schools. Appointments: Numerous stage, film, television and radio roles; Drama Teacher, Royal College of Music, London, St Catherine's School, Guildford, Surrey. Publications: The Nose of My Face, 1962; Too Small for His Shoes, 1962; Deep and Crisp and Even, 1964; Birds in the Belfry, 1966; Spy for Sale, 1969; Even My Foot's Asleep, 1971; Take the Money and Run, 1982; Malice in Camera, 1983; Vienna Blood, 1984; Dead for a Ducat, 1985; Late Knight, 1987. Address: c/o Hodder and Stoughton, 47 Bedford Square, London WC1B 3DP, England.

PAYNE Peggy, b. 8 Jan 1949, Wilmington, North Carolina, USA. Writer. m. Dr Bob Dick, 8 Dec 1983. Education: AB, English, Duke University. Publications: Revelation, 1988; The Healing Power of Doing Good (co-author), 1992. Contributions to: Cosmopolitan; Ms; Family Circle; Travel & Leisure; New York Times; Washington Post; McCall's. Honours: Annual Fiction Award, Crucible, 1978; National Endowment for the Humanities Fellowship, 1979; Indo-American Fellowship, 1991-92. Memberships: American Society of Journalists and Authors; Authors Guild. Address: 512 St Mary's Street, Raleigh, NC 27605, USA.

PAZ Octavio, b. 31 Mar 1914, Mexico City, Mexico. Poet; Philosopher; Essayist; Critic; Director; Revista Vuelta. m. Marie José Tramini, 1 daughter. Education: National University of Mexico. Appointments: Secretary, Mexican Embassy, Paris, 1946; New Delhi, 1952; Chargé d'Affaires ad interim, Japan, 1952; Posted Minister Secretariat for External Affairs, Mexico, 1953-58; Extraordinary and Plenipotentiary Minister to Mexican Embassy, Paris, 1959-62; Ambassador to India, 1962-68; Simon Bolivar Professor of Latin American Studies, Cambridge, 1970; Visiting Professor of Spanish American Literature, University of Texas, Austin, and University of Pittsburgh, 1969-70; Charles Eliot Norton Professor of Poetry, Harvard University, 1971-72; Editor, Plural Mexico City, 1971-75. Publications:

Poetry: Hombre, 1937; Libertad bajo Palabra, 1949; Aguila o Sol?, 1951; Semillas para un Himno, 1956; Piedra de Sol, 1957; La Estacion Violenta, 1958; Discos Visuales, 1968; Ladera Este, 1969; La Centena, 1969; Topoemas, 1971; Renga, 1971; New Poetry of Mexico (anthology), 1972; Pasado en Claro, 1975; Vuelta, 1976; Poemas 1935-1975, 1979; Arbol adentro, 1987. In English: Early Poems (1935-57), 1963; Configurations, 1971; A Draft of Shadows and Other Poems, 1979; Airborn/Hijos del Aire, 1981; Selected Poems, 1984; Collected Poems (1957-87), 1987. Prose: El Laberinto de la soledad, 1950; El Arco y la Lira, 1956; Las Peras del Olmo, 1957; Postdata, 1970; El Mono Gramatico, 1971. Honours: Guggenheim Fellowship, 1944; International Poetry Grand Prix, 1963; National Prize for Literature, Mexico, 1977; Golden Eagle, Nice, 1978; Ollin Yoliztli, Mexico, 1980; Cervantes, Spain, 1982; Neustadt International Prize for Literature, USA, 1982; T S Eliot Prize, Ingersoll Foundation, USA, 1987; Nobel Prize for Literature, 1990. Address: c/o Revista Vuelta, Presidente Canonza 210, Coyascan, Mexico 4000 DF, Mexico.

PEARCE Ann Philippa, b. Great Shelford, Cambridgeshire, England. Freelance Writer of Childrens Books. m. Martin James Christie, 9 May 1963, 1 daughter. Education: MA, Cambridge University. Appointments: Script Writer, Producer, School Broadcasting, Radio, 1945-58; Children's Editor, André Deutsch Ltd, 1960-67. Publications: Minnow on the Say, 1954; Tom's Midnight Garden 1958; Mrs Cockle's Cat, 1961; A Dog So Small, 1962; The Children of the House (with Sir Brian Fairfax-Lucy), 1968, reissued as The Children of Charlecote, 1989; The Squirrel Wife, 1971; What the Neighbours Did and Other Stories, 1972; The Shadow Cage and Other Stories of the Supernatural, 1977; The Battle of Bubble and Squeak, 1978; The Elm Street Lot, 1979; The Way to Sattin Shore, 1983; Lion at School and Other Stories, 1985; Who's Afraid? and Other Strange Stories, 1986; Emily's Own Elephant, 1987; The Toothball, 1987; Freddy, 1988; Old Belle's Summer Holiday, 1989; Here Comes Tod, 1992; Editor, Dread and Delight: A Century of Children's Ghost Stories, 1995. Contributions to: Times Literary Supplement; Guardian. Honours: Carnegie Medal, 1959; New York Herald Tribune Spring Festival Prize, 1962; Whitbread Prize, 1979; Honorary Doctor of Letters, (DLitt), Hull University, 1995. Membership: Society of Authors; Fellow, Royal Society of Literature, 1994. Address: c/o Laura Cecil, 17 Alwyne Villas, London N1 2HG, England.

PEARCE Brian Leonard, (Joseph Redman), b. 8 May 1915, Weymouth, Dorset, England. Translator. m. (1) Lilla Fox, 1940, 1 son, 2 daughters, (2) Fanny Greenspan, 1954, (3) Margaret Mills, 1966. Education: University College, London, 1934-37; BA Honours (Upper IInd), History, London, 1937. Appointments: Honorary Visiting Fellow: Aberdeen University; Glasgow University; School of Slavonic and East European Studies, University of London, 1992. Publications: How Haig Saved Lenin, 1987; The Staroselsky Problem, 1994. Translations: The New Economics (E Preobrazhensky), 1965; Islam and Capitalism (M Rodinson), 1974; The Communist Movement, Part 1 (F Claudin), 1975; How the Revolution Armed (L D Trotsky), 1979-81; The Thinking Reed (Boris Kagarlitsky), 1988; Bread and Circuses (Paul Veyne), 1990; The Staroselsky Problem, 1994; Others. Contributions to: Sbornik and its successor Revolutionary Russia. Honours: Scott-Moncrieff Prizes, 1975, 1979, 1990. Membership: Translators Association. Address: 42 Victoria Road, New Barnet, Herts EN4 9PF, England.

PEARCE Brian Louis, b. 4 June 1933, West London, England. Poet; Novelist; Lecturer; Former College Librarian. m. Margaret Wood, 2 Aug 1969, 1 daughter. Education: University College, London. Appointments: Examiner in English Literature, Library Association, 1964-70; Member, Writers in Schools Scheme, Greater London Arts; Occasional Lecturer, National Portrait Gallery, London, 1990-. Publications: Fiction: Victoria Hammersmith (novel), 1988; London Clay (stories), 1991; The Bust of Minerva, 1992; A Man in his Room, 1992; Battersea Pete, 1994; The Servant of his Country, 1994; Tufnell Triptych, 1997. Poetry: Selected Poems 1951-73, 1978; The Vision of Piers Librarian, 1981; Office Hours, 1983; Browne Study, 1984; Dutch Comfort (poetry, prose, translations), 1985; Gwen John Talking, 1985, 2nd edition, 1996; Jack o'Lent, 1991; Leaving the Corner: Selected Poems 1973-1985, 1992; City Whiskers in The Playing of Easter Music (with Caws and Caseley, 1996; The Proper Fuss, 1996. Criticism and Non-fiction: Palgrave: Selected Poems (editor), 1985; Thomas Twining of Twickenham, 1988; The Fashioned Reed: The Poets of Twickenham from 1500, 1992; Thames Listener: Poems 1949-89, 1993; Varieties of Fervour: Portraits of Victorian and Edwardian poets, 1996. Plays: The Eagle and the Swan, 1966; Shrine Rites, 1990; Dame Ethel Walker: An Essay in Reassessment, 1997; The Palgraves and John

Murray: Letters (editor), 1997. Contributions to: Various publications. Honours: 5th-6th Place, 1-Act Verse Play Competition, Poetry Society, 1964; 1st Prize, Christian Poetry Competition, 1989. Memberships: Browning, Hopkins, Masefield and Palgrave Societies; PEN; RSL; Library Association, fellow; Royal Society of Arts, fellow. Address: 72 Heathfield South, Twickenham, Middlesex TW2 7SS, England.

PEARCE Mary Emily, b. 7 Dec 1932, London, England. Writer. Publications: Apple Tree Lean Down, 1973; Jack Mercybright, 1974; The Sorrowing Wind, 1975; Cast a Long Shadow, 1977; The Land Endures, 1978; Seedtime and Harvest, 1980; Polsinney Harbour, 1983; The Two Farms, 1985; The Old House at Railes, 1993. Memberships: Society of Authors. Address: Owls End, Shuthonger, Tewkesbury, Gloucestershire, England.

PEARSALL Derek Albert, b. 28 Aug 1931, Birmingham, England. Professor of English. m. Rosemary Elvidge, 30 Aug 1952, 2 sons, 3 daughters. Education: BA, 1951, MA, 1952, University of Birmingham. Appointments: Assistant Lecturer, Lecturer, King's College, University of London, 1959-65; Lecturer, Senior Lecturer, Reader, 1965-76, Professor, 1976-87, University of York; Visiting Professor, 1985-, Gurney Professor of English, 1987-, Harvard University, Cambridge, Massachusetts, USA. Publications: John Lydgate, 1970; Landscapes and Seasons of the Medieval World (with Elizabeth Salter), 1973; Old English and Middle English Poetry, 1977; Langland's Piers Plowman: An Edition of the C-Text, 1978; The Canterbury Tales: A Critical Study, 1985; The Life of Geoffrey Chaucer: A Critical Biography, 1992. Memberships: Council Member, Early English Text Society; Medieval Academy of America, Fellow; New Chaucer Society, President, 1988-90; American Academy of Arts and Sciences, Fellow. Address: Harvard University, Department of English, 11 Prescott Street, Cambridge, MA 02138, USA.

PEARSALL Ronald, b. 20 Oct 1927, Birmingham, England. Author. Education: Birmingham College of Art, 1952-54. Publications: Is That My Hook in Your Ear?, 1966; Worm in the Bud, 1969; The Table-Rappers, 1972; The Possessed, 1972; The Exorcism, 1972; Diary of Vicar Veitch, 1972; A Day at the Big Top, 1973; The Wizard and Elidog, 1973; Victorian Sheet Music Covers, 1973; Victorian Popular Music, 1973; Edwardian Life and Leisure, 1973; Collecting Mechanical Antiques, 1973; Collecting Scientific Instruments, 1974; Inside the Antique Trade (with Graham Webb), 1974; Edwardian Popular Music, 1975; Night's Black Angels, 1975; Collapse of Stout Party, 1975; Popular Music of the 1920s, 1976; Public Purity Private Shame, 1976; The Alchemists, 1976; The Belvedere, 1976; Conan Doyle, 1977; Antique Hunter's Handbook, 1978; Tides of War, 1978; Thomas en Olihond, 1979; The Iron Sleep, 1979; Making and Managing an Antique Shop, 1979, revised edition, 1986; Tell Me Pretty Maiden, 1981; Practical Painting, 1983, 4 volumes, 1990; Joy of Antiques, 1988; The Murder in Euston Square, 1989; Antique Furniture for Pleasure and Profit, 1990; Lifesaving, 1991; Painting Abstract Pictures, 1991; Encyclopedia of Everyday Antiques, 1992; Antique Furniture Almanac, 1992. Address: Sherwell, St Teath, Bodmin, Cornwall PL30 3JB, England.

PEARSE Lesley Margaret, b. 24 Feb 1945, Rochester, Kent, England. Novelist. 3 daughters. Education: Northbrook School Lee, London. Publications: Georgia, 1992; Tara, 1993; Clarity, 1994. Contributions to: Periodicals. Membership: Romantic Writers Association; RNA, West Country Writers Association. Literary Agent: Darley Anderson, Estelle House, 11 Eustace Road, Fulham SW6 1JB, London. Address: 16 Withleigh Road, Knowle, Bristol BS4 2LQ, England.

PEARSON Ridley, b. 13 Mar 1953, Glen Cove, New York, USA. Author. Education: Kansas University, 1972; Brown University, 1974. Publications: Never Look Back, 1985; Blood of the Albatross, 1986; The Seizing of Yankee Green Mall, 1987; Undercurrents, 1988; Probable Cause, 1990; Hard Fall, 1992; The Angel Maker, 1993; No Witnesses, 1994; Chain of Evidence, 1995. Honour: Fulbright Fellow, 1990-91. Memberships: Writers Guild of America; Mystery Writers of America; Authors Guild; International Crime Writers Association. Literary Agent: Al Zuckerman. Address: PO Box 670, Hailey, ID 83333, USA.

PEARSON William Harrison (Bill), b. 18 Jan 1922, Greymouth, New Zealand. Writer; Retired University Teacher. Education: Greymouth Technical High School, 1934-38; MA, Canterbury University College, Christchurch, 1948; PhD, King's College, University of London, England, 1952. Publications: Coal Flat, 1963, 5th edition, 1985; Henry Lawson Among Maoris, 1968; Fretful Sleepers and Other Essays, 1974; Rifled Sanctuaries, 1984; Six Stories, 1991. Honours: Co-Recipient, Landfall Readers Award, 1960; New Zealand Book Award for Non-Fiction, 1975. Address: 49 Lawrence Street, Herne Bay, Auckland, New Zealand.

PECK John (Frederick), b. 13 Jan 1941, Pittsburgh, Pennsylvania, USA. Poet. m. Ellen Margaret McKee, 1963, div, 1 daughter. Education: AB, Allegheny College, Meadville, Pennsylvania, 1962; PhD, Stanford University, 1973. Appointments: Instructor, 1968-70, Visiting Lecturer, 1972-75, Princeton University; Assistant Professor, 1977-79, Professor of English, 1980-82, Mount Holyoke College, South Hadley, Massachusetts. Publications: Poetry: Shagbark, 1972; The Broken Blockhouse Wall, 1978; Argura, 1993. Other: The Poems and Translations of Hi-Lo, 1991. Honours: American Academy of Arts and Letters Award, 1975, and Rome Fellowship, 1978; Guggenheim Fellowship, 1981. Address: c/o Englisches Seminar, Plattenstrasse 47, 8032 Zürich, Switzerland.

PECK M(organ) Scott, b. 22 May 1936, New York, New York, USA. Psychiatrist; Writer. m. Lily Ho, 27 Dec 1959, 1 son, 2 daughters. Education: Middlebury College, 1954-56; AB, Harvard University, 1958; MD, Case Western Reserve University, 1963. Appointments: US Army, 1963-72; Psychiatric practice, New Preston, Connecticut, 1972-84; Medical Director, New Milford Hospital Mental Health Clinic, 1973-81; Co-Founder and Board Member, Foundation for Community Encouragement, Ridgefield, Connecticut, 1984-93. Publications: The Road Less Traveled: A New Psychology of Love, Traditional Values and Spiritual Growth, 1978; People of the Lie: The Hope for Healing Human Evil, 1983; What Return Can I Make?: The Dimensions of the Christian Experience (with Marilyn von Waldener and Patricia Kay), 1985; The Different Drum: Community Making and Peace, 1985; A Bed by the Window: A Novel of Mystery and Redemption, 1990; The Friendly Snowflake: A Fable of Faith, Love and Family, 1992; Further Along the Road Less Traveled: The Unending Journey toward Spiritual Growth, 1993; A World Waiting to Be Born: Civility Rediscovered, 1993; Meditations from the Road: Daily Reflections from the Road Less Traveled and the Different Dru, 1993. Address: Bliss Road, New Preston, CT 06777, USA.

PECK Richard (Wayne), b. 5 Apr 1934, Decatur, Illinois, USA. Writer. Education: BA, DePauw University, 1956; MA, Southern Illinois University, 1959. Publications: Don't Look and It Won't Hurt, 1972; The Ghost Belonged to Me, 1975; Are You in the House Alone?, 1976; Secrets of the Shopping Mall, 1979; Amanda/Miranda, 1980; New York Time, 1981; Close Enough To Touch, 1981; This Family of Women, 1983; Remembering the Good Times, 1985; Blossom Culp and the Sleep of Death, 1986; Princess Ashley, 1987; Those Summer Girls I Never Met, 1988; Unfinished Portrait of Jessica, 1991. Contributions to: New York Times; School Library Journal. Honours: Edgar Allan Poe Award, American Society of Mystery Writers, 1977; American Library Association Margaret Edwards Young Adult Author Award, 1990. Memberships: Authors Guild; Authors League. Literary Agent: Sheldon Fogelman, New York. Address: 155 E 72nd St, New York, NY 10021, USA.

PECK Robert Newton, b. 17 Feb 1928, Vermont, USA. Author. Education: AB, Rollins College, 1953; Cornell University. Appointment: Director, Rollins College Writers Conference, 1978-. Publications: A Day No Pigs Would Die, 1972; Millie's Boy, 1973; Path of Hunters: Animal Struggle in a Meadow, 1973; Soup, 1974; Soup for Me, 1975; Wild Cat, 1975; Bee Tree and Other Stuff (verse), 1975; Fawn, 1975; I Am the King of Kazoo, 1976; Rabbits and Redcoats, 1976; Hamilton, 1976; Hang for Treason, 1976; King of Kazoo (music and lyrics), play, 1976; Last Sunday, 1977; Trig, 1977; Patooie, 1977; The King's Iron, 1977; Soup for President, 1978; Eagle Fur, 1978; Trig Sees Red, 1978; Basket Case, 1979; Hub, 1979; Mr Little, 1979; Clunie, 1979; Soup's Drum, 1980; Secrets of Successful Fiction, 1980; Trig Goes Ape, 1980; Soup of Wheels, 1981; Justice Lion, 1981; Trig or Treat, 1982; Banjo, 1982; Soup in the Saddle, 1983; Soup's Goat, 1984; Spanish Hoof, 1985; Soup on Ice, 1985; Jo Silver, 1985; Soup on Fire, 1987; My Vermont, 1987; Hallaporosa, 1988; Arly, 1989; Soup's Hoop, 1990; Higbee's Halloween, 1990; Little Soup's Hayride, 1991; Little Soup's Birthday, 1991; Arly II, 1991; Soup in Love, 1994; Soup Ahoy, 1994; A Part of the Sky, 1994; Soup 1776, 1995. Honour: Mark Twain Award, Missouri, 1981. Address: 500 Sweetwater Club Circle, Longwood, FL 32779, USA.

PECKHAM Morse, b. 17 Aug 1914, Yonkers, New York, USA. Distinguished Professor Emeritus of English and Comparative Literature. Education: BA, University of Rochester, 1935; MA, 1938, PhD, 1947, Princeton University. Appointments: Instructor, 1946-47, Assistant Professor 1948-49, Rutgers University; Assistant Professor, 1949-52, Associate Professor, 1952-61, Director, Institute for Humanistic Education for Business Executives, 1953-54, University Press, 1953-55, Professor, 1961-67, University of Pennsylvania, Philadelphia; Distinguished Professor of English and Comparative Literature, 1967-80, Distinguished Professor Emeritus, 1980-, University of South Carolina, Columbia. Publications: On the Origin of Species: A Variorum Text, by Charles Darwin (editor), 1959; Humanistic Education for Business Executives: An Essay in General Education, 1960; Word, Meaning, Poem: An Anthology of Poetry (editor with Seymour Chapman), 1961; Beyond the Tragic Vision: The Quest for Identity in the Nineteenth Century, 1962; Man's Rage for Chaos: Biology, Behaviour and the Arts, 1965; Romanticism: The Culture of the Nineteenth Century (editor), 1965; Paracelsus, by Robert Browning (editor), 1969; Art and Pornography: An Experiment in Explanation, 1969; The Triumph of Romanticism; Speculation on Some Heroes of a Culture Crisis, 1970; Pippa Passes, by Robert Browning (editor), 1971; Luria, by Robert Browning (editor), 1973; Romanticism and Behaviour: Collected Essays II, 1976; Sordello, by Robert Browning (editor), 1977; Explanation and Power: The Control of Human Behavior, 1979; Romanticism and Ideology, 1985; The Birth of Romanticism, 1986. Address: 6478 Bridgewood Road, Columbia, SC 29206, USA.

PEDEN William Creighton, b. 25 July 1935, Concord, North California, USA. Professor of Philosophy. m. (2) Harriet McKnight Peden, 6 Oct 1978, 1 stepson, 2 daughters. Education: BA, Davidson College, 1957; MA, University of Chicago, 1960; BD, 1962; PhD, St Andrews University, Scotland, 1965. Appointments: Founding Editor, Journal of Social Philosophy, 1970-83; Founding Co-Editor, American Journal of Theology & Philosophy, 1980-91; General and Co-Editor, Social Philosophy Today, Book Series, 1985-95; General Co-Editor, American Liberal Religious Thought Book Series, 1993-. Publications: Wieman's Empirical Process Philosophy, 1977; Whitehead's View of Reality, 1981; The Chicago School: Voices of Liberal Religious Thought, 1987; The Philosopher of Free Religion: Francis Ellingwood Abbot 1836-1903, 1992; Civil War Pulpit to World's Parliament of Religion: The Thought of William James Potter 1829-1893, 1996; Editor, 21 books. Contributions to: Over 100 articles to scholarly journals. Address: 295 Bonnie Drive, Highlands, NC 28741, USA.

PEDERSEN Ellen Miriam Kamp, b. 16 Feb 1948,Copenhagen, Denmark. Writer; Translator. Education: MA, English and Phonetics, 1972-76; Danish Degree. Literary Appointment: Summer Course on Science Fiction, Danish Adult Education Centre, 1989. Publications: Slaver of New York, 1989; Black Robe (Danish translation), 1992; Denny Alice, 1993; Numerous translations and articles; Book and taped interviews for Radio. Contributions to: Mind & Behavior; Studies in the Humanities; Danish Newspapers, Journals and Magazines. Honour: Danish Award for theory and criticism, 1980. Memberships: Danish Translators Association; Danish Writers Guild. Address: Jerichausgade 49.2, 1777 Copenhagen V, Denmark

PEDERSEN Liselotte, b. 31 May 1957, Bellinger, Denmark. Aurthor; Poet; Painter; Teacher. Education: Cand PhK in Danish Literature and Language; Studies in Arts and Philosophy. Publication: In the Flight, 1986. Contributions to: Anthologies, magazines and journals. Honour: Travel Legacy, 1988. Membership: Dansk Forfatterforening.

PEET Bill, (William Bartlett Peet), b. 29 Jan 1915, Grandview, Indiana, USA. Children's Writer. Education: John Herron Art Institute, Indianapolis, 1933-36. Appointments: Formerly Artist and Screenwriter for Walt Disney Productions. Publications: Hubert's Hair-Raising Adventure, 1959; Huge Harold, 1961; Smokey, 1962; The Pinkish Purplish Bluish Egg, 1963; Ella, 1964; Randy's Dandy Lions, 1964; Kermit the Hermit, 1965; Chester the Worldly Pig, 1965; Capyboppy, 1966; Farewell to Shady Glade, 1966; Jennifer and Josephine, 1967; Buford the Little Big-Horn, 1967; Fly Homer Fly, 1969; The Whingdingdilly, 1970; The Wump World, 1970; How Droofus the Dragon Lost His Head, 1971; The Caboose Who Got Loose, 1971; Countdown to Christmas, 1972; The Ant and the Elephant, 1972; The Spooky Tail of Preewit Peacock, 1973; Merle the High Flying Squirrel, 1974; The Gnats of Knotty Pine, 1975; Big Bad Bruce, 1976; Eli, 1978; Cowardly Clyde, 1979; Encore for Eleanor, 1981; The Luckiest One of

All, 1982; No Such Things, 1983; Pamela Camel, 1984; The Kweeks of Kookatumdee, 1985; Zella Zack and Zodiak, 1986; Jethro and Joel Were a Troll, 1987; Bill Peet - An Autobiography, 1989; Cock-A-Doodle Dudley, 1990. Address: Houghton Mifflin Co, 1 Beacon Street, Boston, MA 02107, USA.

PEIRCE Neal R, b. 5 Jan 1932, USA. Writer; Editor. Education: AB, Princeton University, 1954; Graduate Studies, Harvard University, 1957-58. Appointments: Political Editor, Congressional Quarterly, 1960-69; Co-Founder, Contributing Editor, The National Journal, Washington, DC, 1969-; Fellow, Woodrow Wilson Center for Scholars, 1971-74; Syndicated Columnist, Washington Post Writers Group. Publications: The People's President, 1968, 2nd edition, 1981; The Megastates of America, 1972; The Pacific States of America, 1972; The Great Plains States of America, 1973; The Deep South States of America, 1974; The Border South States, 1975; The New England States, 1976; The Mid-Atlantic States of America, 1977; The Great Lakes States of America, 1980; The Book of America, 1983; Corrective Capitalism, 1987; Enterprising Communities, 1989; Citisates, 1993; Breakthroughs: Recreativity the American City, 1994. Address: 610 G Street South West, Washington, DC 20024, USA.

PELIKAN Jaroslav Jan, b. 17 Dec 1923, Akron, Ohio, USA. Professor of History; Writer. m. Sylvia Burica, 9 June 1946, 2 sons, 1 daughter. Education: Graduated, Concordia Junior College, Ft Wayne, Indiana, 1942; BD, Concordia Theological Seminary, St Louis, 1946; PhD, University of Chicago, 1946. Appointments: Faculty, Valparaiso University, 1946-49, Concordia Seminary, St Louis, 1949-53, University of Chicago, 1953-62; Titus Street Professor of Ecclesiastical History, 1967-72, Sterling Professor of History, 1972-, Dean, Graduate School, 1973-78, Director, Division of Humanities, 1974-75, Chairman, Medieval Studies, 1974-75, 1978-80, William Clyde DeVane Lecturer, 1984-86, Yale University; Various guest lectureships. Publications: From Luther to Kierkegaard, 1950; Fools for Christ, 1955; The Riddle of Roman Catholicism, 1959; Luther the Expositor, 1959; The Shape of Death, 1961; The Light of the World, 1962; Obedient Rebels, 1964; The Finality of Jesus Christ in an Age of Universal History, 1965; The Christian Intellectual, 1966; Spirit Versus Structure, 1968; Development of Doctrine, 1969; Historical Theology, 1971; The Christian Tradition, 5 volumes, 1971-89; Scholarship and Its Survival, 1983; The Vindication of Tradition, 1984; Jesus Through the Centuries, 1985; The Mystery of Continuity, 1986; Bach Among the Theologians, 1986; The Excellent Empire, 1987; The Melody of Theology, 1988; Confessor Between East and West, 1990; Imago Dei, 1990; Eternal Feminines, 1990; The Idea of the University: A Reexamination, 1992; Christianity and Classical Culture, 1993; Faust the Theologian, 1995; The Reformation of the Bible/The Bible of the Reformation, 1996; Mary Through the Centuries, 1996; Editor: Makers of Modern Theology, 5 volumes, 1966-68; The Preaching of Chrysostom, 1967; Interpreters of Luther, 1968; Twentieth-Century Theology in the Making, 3 volumes, 1969-70; The Preaching of Augustine, 1973; The World Treasury of Modern Religious Thought, 1991; Sacred Writings, 7 volumes, 1992. Contributions to: Numerous books and professional journals. Honours: Abingdon Award, 1959; John Gilmary Shea Prize, American Catholic Historical Association, 1971; National Award, Slovak World Congress, 1973; Religious Book Award, Catholic Press Association, 1974; Christian Unity Award, Atonement Friars, 1975; Senior Fellow, Carnegie Foundation for the Advancement of Teaching, 1982-83; Festschrifts published in his honour, 1984, 1996; Haskins Medal, Medieval Academy of America, 1985; Award for Excellence, American Academy of Religion, 1989; Umanita Award, Newberry Library, 1990; Joseph A Sittler Award, 1993; Various honorary doctorates and other honours. Memberships: American Academy of Arts and Sciences, President, 1994-97; American Historical Association; American Philosophical Society; American Society of Church History, President, 1965; International Congress of Luther Research, President, 1971; Medieval Academy of America, Fellow; Phi Beta Kappa. Address: 156 Chestnut Lane, Hamden, CT 06518, USA.

PELUFFO Luisa, b. 20 Aug 1941, Buenos Aires, Argentina. Writer. m. Pablo Masilorens, 24 Apr 1971, 2 sons. Education: Drawing Teacher's degree, National Fine Arts School, 1959; Stage Direction, National Drama School, 1975. Appointments: Staff: Panorama Magazine, Buenos Aires, 1969-70; Channel 7 TV, Buenos Aires, 1970-71; La Nacion newspaper, 1971-76; Leader, Literary Workshops, San Carlos de Bariloche Municipal Art School, 1985-97; Director, Seminars of Writing, Buenos Aires, 1993-97. Publications: Materia Viva (poems), 1976; Conspiraciones (short stories), 1st edition, 1982, 2nd edition, 1989; Materia de Revelaciones (poems) 1983; Todo Eso

Oyes (novel), 1989; La Otra Orilla (poems), 1991; La Doble Vida, (novel), 1993; Work included in the following anthologies: 38 Cuento Breves Argentino Siglo XXI, 1978; Sur del Mundo, Narradores de la Patagonia, 1992. Contributions to: La Nación; La Prensa; Rio Negro; Puro Cuento; Ronda Aerolineas Argentinas. Honours: Special Mention in the Culture Bureau National Poetry Contest, 1976; 1st Prize, Victoria Ocampo Literary Contest, 1980; Emecé Prize, 1988-89; Regional Prize, 30th Anniversary of the National Arts Foundation, 1991; Finalist with Special Jury recognition, Latin American Pegaso Prize for Literature, 1993. Address: Palacios 465 (8400) Bariloche, Provincia de Rio Negro, Argentina.

PEMBERTON Margaret, b. 10 Apr 1943, Bradford, England. Writer. m. 1 son, 4 daughters. Publications: Harlot, 1981; Lion of Languedoc, 1981; The Flower Garden, 1982; Silver Shadows, Golden Dreams, 1985; Never Leave Me, 1986; Multitude of Sins, 1988; White Christmas in Saigon, 1990; An Embarrassment of Riches, 1992; Zadruga, 1993; Moonflower Madness, 1993; Tapestry of Fear, 1994; The Londoners, 1995; Magnolia Square, 1996; Yorkshire Rose, 1996; The Londoners, 1995; Magnolia Square, 1996; Coronation Summer, 1997. Memberships: Crime Writers Association; Romantic Novelists Association; PEN; Society of Authors. Literary Agent: Carol Smith, England.

PENA MUNOZ Margarita, b. 21 Aug 1937, Mexico. Writer; Scholar. m. B Lima, 6 Nov 1971, 1 son. Education: BD, Hispanic Literature, 1963, MD, Hispanic Literature, 1965, University of Mexico; PhD, El Colegio de Mexico, 1968. Appointments: Researcher, Literary Researching Centre, 1969-75, Professor, 1975-87, University of Mexico. Publications: Living Again, 1980; Flores de varia poesia, 1980; America's Discovery and Conquest, An Anthology of Chronicles, 1982; To Pass Over in Silence, 1983; Mofarandel, 1986. Contributions to: Journals, periodicals and magazines. Memberships: International Hispanists Association; PEN; International Institute of Latin-American Literature; Latin-American Linguistics Association, University of Mexico. Address: Cerrada del Convento 45, Casa 2, Tlalpan, Mexico DF 14420, Mexico.

PENDLETON Don. See: **OBSTFELD Raymond.**

PENN John. See: **TROTMAN Jack.**

PENNANT-REA Rupert Lascelles, b. 23 Jan 1948, Southern Rhodesia. Economist. m. Helen Jay, 2 sons, 1 daughter, 2 stepdaughters. Education: BA, Economics, Trinity College, Dublin, 1970; MA, University of Manchester, 1972. Appointments: Economics Correspondent, 1977, Economics Editor, 1981, Editor, 1986-93, The Economist; Deputy Governor, Bank of England, London, 1993-. Publications: Gold Foil, 1978; Who Runs the Economy? (co-author), 1979; The Pocket Economist, 1983; The Economist Economics, 1986. Honour: Wincott Prize for Financial Journalism, 1984. Memberships: Reform Club; MCC; Harare. Literary Agent: Curtis Brown Ltd, London. Address: Bank of England, Threadneedle Street, London EC2R 8AH, England.

PEPPE Rodney Darrell, b. 24 June 1934, Eastbourne, East Sussex, England. Author; Artist. m. Tatjana Tekkel, 16 July 1960, 2 sons. Education: Eastbourne School of Art, 1951-53, 1955-57; London County Council Central School of Art, 1957-59; NDD, Illustration (special subject) and Central School Diploma. Publications: The Alphabet Book, 1968; The House That Jack Built, 1970; Odd One Out, 1974; Henry series, 1975-84; The Mice Who Lived in a Shoe, 1981; The Kettleship Pirates, 1983; The Mice and the Clockwork Bus, 1986; Huxley Pig series, 1989; The Mice and the Travel Machine, 1993. Contributions to: Periodicals. Membership: Society of Authors. Address: Barnwood House, Whiteway, Stroud, Gloucestershire GL6 7ER, England.

PEPPERCORN Lisa Margot, b. 2 Oct 1913, Franfurt am Main, Germany. (Brazilian citizen). Musicologist. m. Lothar Bauer, 9 Apr 1938. Education: Abitur; Degree, History of Music, Royal Conservatory, Brussels. Appointments: Worked in London until 1938; Music Correspondent, New York Times, Rio de Janeiro, 1939-46, Musical America, 1940-47; Market Researcher, RCA Victor, Camden, New Jersey, and 25 other companies, 1946-52; Research work, Villa-Lobos, Zürich, Switzerland, 1961-. Publications: A Villa Lobos Opera, 1940; Musical Education in Brazil, 1940; Violin Concerto by Villa Lobos, 1941; New Villa Lobos Works, 1942; Villa-Lobos in Paris, 1985; Villa-Lobos: Collected Studies, 1992; Letters, 1994; The World of Villa-Lobos in Pictures and Documents, 1996. Contributions to: Numerous articles. Honours include: Outstanding Academic Book, Choice Magazine, 1992. Address: Schulhaus Strasse 53, 8002 Zurich, Switzerland.

PERERA Victor Haim, b. 12 Apr 1934, Guatemala. Writer. m. Padma Hejmadi, 8 Aug 1960, div 1974. Education: BA, Brooklyn College, 1956; MA, University of Michigan, 1958. Appointments: Editorial Staff, The New Yorker, 1963-66; Reporter, The New York Times Magazine, 1971-75; Contributing Editor, Present Tense, 1974-89; Editorial Board, Tikkun, 1990-. Publications: The Conversion, 1970; The Loch-Ness Monster Watchers, 1974; The Last Lords of Palenque (with Robert D Bruce), 1982; Rites: A Guatemalan Boyhood, 1986; Testimony: Death of a Guatemalan Village, by Victor Montejo (translator), 1987; Unfinished Conquest: The Guatemalan Tragedy, 1993; The Cross and the Pear Tree: A Sephardic Journey, 1995. Contributions to: New Yorker; Atlantic Monthly; Nation; New York Review; Partisan Review. Honours: Avery Hopwood Major Award in the Essay, 1962; National Endowment of the Arts Writing Award, 1980; PEN Fiction (Short Story) Award, 1984; Present Tense/Joel Cavior Award in Biography, 1987; Lila Wallace, Reader's Digest Writing Award, 1992-94. Membership: PEN American Centre. Address: c/o Watkins-Loomis Agency, 133 East 35th Street, New York, NY 10016, USA.

PERI ROSSI Chistina, b. 12 Nov 1941, Montevideo, Uruguay. Writer. Education: Professor of Comparative Literature, 1963. Appointments: Professor of Literature, Montevideo, 1963-72; Professor of Comparative Literature and Latin American Literature, Universidad Autonoma de Barcelona, Spain, 1983. Publications: La Nave de los locos, novel; Solitano de amor, novel; Babel barbara, poetry; El museo de los esfuerzos inutiles, short stories; La rebelion de los ninos, short stories; Europa despues de la Uwia, poetry; Una pasion prohibida, short stories; La tarde del dinosaurio, short stories. Contributions to: Marcha, Uruguay; In Spain: Quimera; El Viejo Topo; El Pais; La Vanguardia; Efe. Honours: ARCA Prize, Uruguay, 1968; 1st Prize, MARCHA, Uruguay, 1969; Inventarios Provisionales de Poesia, 1974; Civdad de Palma, 1975; Benito Perez Galdos Prize, 1979; Cibtat de Barcelona Award, 1991; Award for Babel barbara in English, Quarterly Review of Literature Poetry Series, Princeton, New Jersey, 1992. Membership: Asociacion Colegial de Escritores de Espana. Literary Agent: International Editors, Barcelona, Spain. Address: Travessera de les Corts No 171 4o 1a, 08028 Barcelona, Spain.

PERKINS George Burton, b. 16 Aug 1930, Lowell, Massachusetts, USA. University Professor. m. Barbara Miller, 9 May 1964, 3 daughters. Education: AB, Tufts College, 1953; MA, Duke University, 1954; PhD, Cornell University, 1960. Appointments: Teaching Assisstant, Cornell University, 1957-60; Assisstant Professor, Farleigh Dickinson University, 1963-66; Lecturer, American Literature, Edinburgh University, 1966-67; Professor, Eastern Michigan University, 1967-; General Editor, Journal of Narrative Technique, 1970-92. Publications: Writing Clear Prose, 1964; The Theory of the American Novel, 1970; Realistic American Short Fiction, 1972; American Poetic Theory, 1972; The American Tradition in Literature (with Bradley, Beatty, Long and Perkins), 4th to 9th editions, 1974-99; The Practical Imagination (with Frye, Baker), 1985; Contemporary American Literature (with B Perkins), 1991; Kaleidoscope (with B Perkins), 1993; Women's Work (with Perkins and Warhol), 1994; The Harper Handbook to Literature (with Frye, Baker, Perkins), 1997. Contributions to: Professional journals. Honours: Duke University Fellow 1953-54; Cornell University Fellow, 1954-55; Phi Kappa Phi, 1956; Distinguished Faculty Award, Eastern Michigan University, 1978; Fellow, Institute for Advanced Studies in the Humanities, Edinburgh University, 1981; Senior Fulbright Scholar, University of Newcastle, Australia, 1989. Memberships: Various professional organisations. Address: 1316 King George Boulevard, Ann Arbor, MI 48108, USA.

PERKINS Michael, b. 3 Nov 1942, Lansing, Michigan, USA. Writer. m. Renie (Shoemaker) McCune, 20 June 1960, 1 son, 2 daughters. Education: Ohio University, Athens, 1963; New School for Social Research, 1962; City College New York, 1966. Appointments: Editor, Tompkins Square Press, 1966-68, Croton Press Ltd, 1969-72, Ulster Arts Magazine, 1978-79; Programme Director, Woodstock Guild, 1985-95; Senior Editor, Masquerade Books, New York City, 1992-. Publications: Evil Companions, 1968; Down Here, 1969; The Secret Record, 1977; The Persistence of Desire, 1977; The Good Parts, 1994; Gift of Choice, 1994; Dark Matter, Novel, 1996; Coming Up, Editor of Anthology, 1996. Contributions to: Notre Dame Review,

1996; Para*Doxa, 1996; Periodicals. Memberships: Authors Guild; National Book Critics Circle. Literary Agent. Claudia Menza. Address: 750 Ohayo Mt Road, Glenford, NY 12433, USA.

PERRETT Bryan, b. 9 July 1934, Liverpool, England. Author; Military Historian. m. Anne Catherine Trench, 13 Aug 1966. Education: Liverpool College. Appointment: Defence Correspondent to Liverpool Echo, during Falklands War and Gulf War. Publications: The Czar's British Squadron (with A Lord), 1981; A History of Blitzkrieg, 1983; Knights of the Black Cross - Hitler's Panzerwaffe and its Leaders, 1986; Desert Warfare, 1988; Encyclopaedia of the Second World War (with Ian Hogg), 1989; Canopy of War, 1990; Liverpool: A City at War, 1990; Last Stand - Famous Battles Against the Odds, 1991; The Battle Book - Crucial Conflicts in History from 1469 BC to the Present, 1992; At All Costs - Stories of Impossible Victories, 1993; Seize and Hold - Master Strokes of the Battlefield, 1994; Iron Fist - Crucial Armoured Engagements, 1995; Against All Odds! More Dramatic Last Stand Actions, 1995; Impossible Victories - Ten Unlikely Battlefield Successes, 1996. Contributions to: War Monthly; Military History; World War Investigator; War in Peace (partwork); The Elite (partwork). Memberships: Rotary Club of Ormskirk; Royal United Services Institute. Literary Agent: Watson Little Ltd, London, England; McIntosh and Otis, New York, USA. Address: 7 Maple Avenue, Burscough, Nr Ormskirk, Lancashire L40 5SL, England.

PERRIAM Wendy Angela, b. 23 Feb 1940, London, England. Author. m. (1) 22 Aug 1964, 1 daughter, (2) John Alan Perriam, 29 July 1974. Education: St Anne's College, Oxford, 1958-61; BA (Hons), History, 1961, MA, 1972, Oxford; London School of Economics, 1963-64. Publications: Novels: Absinthe for Elevenses, 1980; Cuckoo, 1981; Born of Woman, 1983; The Stillness The Dancing, 1985; Sin City, 1987; Devils, for a Change, 1989; Fifty-Minute Hour, 1990; Bird Inside, 1992; Michael, Michael, 1993; Breaking and Entering, 1994; Coupling, 1996. Contributions to: Anthologies, newspapers and magazines including: She; Cosmopolitan; Penthouse; Sunday Times; Evening Standard; Daily Mail; Poems and short stories in Arts Council Anthology and South East Arts Anthologies; Seven Deadly Sins, 1992. Memberships: PEN; Society of Authors; British Actors Equity Association. Address: c/o Curtis Brown, 4th Floor, Haymarket House, 28/29 Haymarket, London SW1Y 4SP, England.

PERRIE Walter, b. 5 June 1949, Lanarkshire, Scotland. Poet; Author; Critic. Education: MA Honours, Mental Philosophy, University of Edinburgh, 1975; MPhil, English Studies, University of Stirling, 1989. Appointments: Editor, Chapman, 1970-73; Scottish-Canadian Exchange Fellow, University of British Columbia, Canada, 1984-85; Managing Editor, Margin: International Arts Quarterly, 1985-90; Stirling Writing Fellow, University of Stirling, 1991. Publications: Metaphysics and Poetry (with Hugh MacDiarmid), 1974; Poem on a Winter Night, 1976; A Lamentation for the Children, 1977; By Moon and Sun, 1980; Out of Conflict, 1982; Concerning the Dragon, 1984; Roads that Move: A Journey Through Eastern Europe, 1991; Thirteen Lucky Poems, 1991; From Milady's Wood and Other Poems, 1997. Contributions to: Journals and periodicals. Honours: Scottish Arts Council Bursaries, 1976, 1983, 1994, and Book Awards, 1976, 1983; Eric Gregory Award, 1978; Merrill Ingram Foundation Award, 1987. Memberships: PEN, Scotland; Society of Authors. Address: 10 Croft Place, Dunning, Perthshire PH2 0SB, Scotland.

PERRY George Cox, b. 7 Jan 1935, London, England. Writer. m. 1 July 1976, 1 son. Education: BA, 1957, MA, 1961, Trinity College, Cambridge. Appointment: Film Critic, Illustrated London News, 1982-. Publications: The Films of Alfred Hitchcock, 1965; A Competitive Cinema (co-author), 1966; Penguin Book of Comics, 1967; The Great British Picture Show, 1974; Rule Britannia - The Victorian World, 1974; Hitchcock, 1975; Movies From the Mansion, 1976; Forever Ealing, 1981; Diana- A Celebration, 1982; Life of Python, 1984; Rupert: A Bear's Life, 1985; Bluebell, 1986; The Complete Phantom of the Opera, 1987. Contributions to: Times; Sunday Times; Radio Times; Los Angeles Times. Literary Agent: Deborah Rogers Ltd, London, England. Address: 7 Roehampton Lane, London SW15 5LS, England.

PERRY Ritchie, (John Allen), b. 7 Jan 1942, King's Lynn, Norfolk, England. Teacher; Author. Education: BA, St John's College, Oxford, 1964. Publications: The Fall Guy, 1972; Nowhere Man, US edition as A Hard Man to Kill, 1973; Ticket to Ride, 1973; Holiday with a Vengeance, 1974; Your Money and Your Wife, 1975; One Good Death Deserves Another, 1976; Dead End, 1977; Brazil: The Land and Its People, 1977; Copacabana Stud (as John Allen), 1977; Dutch

Courage, 1978; Bishop's Pawn, 1979; Up Tight (as John Allen), 1979; Grand Slam, 1980; Fool's Mate, 1981; Foul Up, 1982; MacAllister, 1984; Kolwezi, 1985; Presumed Dead, 1988; Comeback, 1991. Children's books: George H Ghastly, 1982; George H Ghastly to the Rescue, 1982; George H Ghastly and the Little Horror, 1985; Fenella Fang, 1986; Fenella Fang and the Great Escape, 1987; Fenella Fang and the Wicked Witch, 1989; The Creepy Tale, 1989; Fenalla Fang and the Time Machine, 1991; The Runton Werewolf, 1994. Literary Agent: Peters, Fraser and Dunlop. Address: The Linhay, Water Lane, West Runton, Norfolk NR27 9QP, England.

PERUTZ Kathrin, b. 1 July 1939, New York, New York, USA. Author; Executive. Education: BA, Barnard College, 1960; MA, New York University, 1966. Appointments: Executive Director, Contact Program Inc. Publications: The Garden, 1962; A House on the Sound, 1964; The Ghosts, 1966; Mother is a Country: A Popular Fantasy, 1968; Beyond the Looking Glass: America's Beauty Culture, 1970; Marriage is Hell: The Marriage Fallacy, 1972; Reigning Passions, 1978; Writing for Love and Money, 1991. Also as Johanna Kingsley: Scents, 1985; Faces, 1987. Memberships: PEN; Authors Guild. Literary Agent: Elaine Markson. Address: 16 Avalon Road, Great Neck, NY 10021, USA.

PERVIN Alice. See: **LIST Annelise.**

PESETSKY Bette, b. 16 Nov 1932, Milwaukee, Wisconsin, USA. Writer. m. Irwin Pesetsky, 25 Feb 1956, 1 son. Education: BA, Washington University, 1954; MFA, University of Iowa, 1959. Publications: Stories Up to a Point, 1982; Author from a Savage People, 1983; Midnight Sweets, 1988; Digs, 1988; Confessions of a Bad Girl, 1989; Late Night Muse, 1991; Cast a Spell, 1993. Contributions to: New Yorker; Vanity Fair; Ms; Vogue; Paris Review; Ontario Review; Stand. Honours: Creative Writing Fellowship, National Endowment for the Arts, 1979-80; Creative Writing Public Service Award, New York Council for the Arts, 1980-81. Membership: PEN. Literary Agent: Goodman Associates, USA. Address: Hilltop Park, Dobbs Ferry, NY 10522, USA.

PETE Pindar. See: **MORTON Harry Edwin Clive**

PETECKI Bohdan Antoni, b. 5 July 1931, Krakow, Poland. Writer. m. Janina Rogowska, 19 July 1966, 1 daughter. Education: MA, Oriental Studies, Jagiellonian University, Kracow. Journalist, Polish Radio Station, Katowice, 1958-68; Sub-Editor, TV Broadcasting Station, Katowice, 1968-72; 1st Sub-Editor, Polish Radio Broadcasting Station, 1972-75; Sub-Editor, Panorama magazine, 1978-. Publications: 11 books, 1975-83. Contributions to: Various journals and magazines. Honours: Diploma of Honour, National Publishers Iskry, Warsaw, 1977; Novel of the Year, Magzine Fantastyka, 1984. Membership: Polish Writer's Association, Katowice. Address: ul Baltycka 51A, 40-778 Katowice, Poland.

PETERFREUND Stuart Samuel, b. 30 June 1945, Brooklyn, New York, USA. Professor of English; Poet. m. 12 Sept 1981. Education: AB, Cornell University, 1966; MFA, University of California, Irvine, 1968; PhD, University of Washington, 1974. Appointments: University of Arkansas, 1975-78; Assistant Professor, 1978-82, Associate Professor 1982-91, Full Professor, 1991-, Chair, 1991-, Northeastern University. Publications: The Hanged Knife and Other Poems, 1970; Harder Than Rain (poems), 1977; Interstatements (poems), 1986; Literature and Science: Theory and Practice, 1990. Contributions to: Journals. Address: Department of English 406 HO, Northeastern University, 360 Huntington Avenue, Boston, MA 02115, USA.

PETERKIEWICZ Jerzy, b. 29 Sept 1916, Fabianki, Poland. Novelist; Poet. Education: University of Warsaw; MA, University of St Andrews, Scotland, 1944; PhD, King's College, London, England, 1947. Publications: Prowincja, 1936; Wiersze i poematy, 1938; Pogrzeb Europy, 1946; The Knotted Cord, 1953; Loot and Loyalty, 1955; Polish Prose and Verse, 1956; Antologia liryki angielskiej, 1958; Future to Let, 1958; Isolation, 1959; Five Centuries of Polish Poetry (with Burns Singer), 1960, enlarged edition, 1970; The Quick and the Dead, 1961; That Angel Burning at My Left Side, 1963; Poematy Londynskie, 1965; Inner Circle, 1966; Green Flows the Bile, 1969; The Other Side of Silence (The Poet at the Limits of Language), 1970; The Third Adam, 1975; Easter Vigil and Other Poems, by Karol Wojtyla (Pope John Paul II) (editor, translator), 1979; Kula magiczna, Poems 1934-52, 1980; Collected Poems, by Karol Wojtyla (Pope John Paul

II) (editor, translator), 1982; Poezje wybrane, Selected Poems, 1986; Literatura polska w perspektywie europejskiej (essays translated from English), 1986; Modlitwy intelektu (poems), 1988; Messianic Prophecy, 1991; In the Scales of Fate (autobiography), 1993; The Place Within: The Poetry of Pope John Paul II (editor and translator) 1994. Essays; Poems; Radio plays, BBC 3. Contributions to: Numerous periodicals. Literary Agent: John Johnson Ltd, 45-47 Clerkenwell Green, London EC1R 0HT, England. Address: 7 Lyndhurst Terrace, London NW3 5QA, England.

PETERS Catherine Lisette, b. 30 Sept 1930, London, England. Lecturer; Writer. m. (1) John Glyn Barton, 14 Jan 1952, 3 sons, (2) Anthony Storr, 9 Oct 1970. Education: BA 1st Class Honours, 1980, MA, 1984, Oxford University. Appointments: Editor, Jonathan Cape, 1960-74; Lecturer in English, Somerville College, Oxford, 1981-92. Publications: Thackeray's Universe, 1987; The King of Inventors: A Life of Wilkie Collins, 1991. Contributions to: Books and journals. Memberships: Wilkie Collins Society; Society of Authors; Fellow, Royal Society of Literature; International PEN. Literary Agent: Michael Sissons, Peters, Fraser and Dunlop. Address: 45 Chalfont Road, Oxford OX2 6TJ, England.

PETERS Elizabeth. See: **MERTZ Barbara Louise Gross.**

PETERS Ellis. See: **PARGETER Edith.**

PETERS Lance, b. 8 May 1934, Auckland, New Zealand. Author; Screenwriter. m. Laura Chiang, 25 Feb 1981, 2 sons. 2 daughters. Appointments: London Representative, Seymour Theatre Centre, 1973-74; Feature Writer, TV Times London Correspondent, 1974-76. Publications: Carry On Emmannuelle, 1978; The Dirty Half Mile, 1981; Cut-Throat Alley, 1982; Enemy Territory, 1988; God's Executioner, 1988; The Civilian War Zone, 1989; The Red Collar Gang, 1989; The Dirty Half Mile (Again), 1989; Gross Misconduct, 1993; Savior in the Grave, 1994; Extensive TV writing: comedy, documentary and drama; 5 feature film screenplays; Assault with a Deadly Weapon, stage play. Contributions to: Numerous popular magazines. Memberships: Honorary Life Member, Australian Writers Guild, president, 1970-72; Australian Society of Authors; Writers Guild of Great Britain; British Academy of Film and Television Arts. Literary Agents: Gelfman and Schneider, 250 W 5th Street, New York, NY 10107, USA; Catherine Hanen, Attorney, 2049 Century Park East, Suite 3100, Century City, CA 90067, USA (personal manager). Address: 291 Fitzwilliam Road, Vaucluse, Sydney, New South Wales 2030, Australia.

PETERS Margot McCullough, b. 13 May 1933, USA. Writer; Professor. 1 son, 1 daughter. Education: BA, 1961, MA, 1965, PhD, 1969, University of Wisconsin-Madison. Appointments: Kathe Tappe Vernon Professor of Biography, Dartmouth College, 1978; Professor Emerita, University of Wisconsin; Reviewer, New York Times Book Review. Publications: Charlotte Brontë, Style in the Novel, 1973; Unquiet Soul: A Biography of Charlotte Brontë, 1975; Bernard Shaw and the Actresses, 1980; Mrs Pat: The Life of Mrs Patrick Campbell, 1984; The House of Barrymore, 1990; Wild Justice, (as Margret Pierce), 1995; Co editor, Unpublished Shaw, 1996; May Sarton, A Biography, 1997. Contributions to: Biography; Language and Style; Annual of Bernard Shaw Studies; Southwest Review: British Studies Monitor; Harvard magazine; Brontë Society Transactions. Honours: Best Prose Award, Friends of American Writers, 1975; Banta Awards, 1980, 1984; George Freedley Memorial Awards for Best Drama Book, 1980, 1984; English Speaking Union Ambassador Award, 1990; American Council of Learned Societies Fellow; Guggenheim Fellow; Wisconsin Institute for the Humanities Fellow; Rockefeller Fellow. Memberships: Bernard Shaw Society; Brontë Society; Tennessee Williams Society; Authors Guild. Literary Agent: Janklow and Nesbit, New York. Address: 511 College Street, Lake Mills, WI 53551, USA.

PETERS Mark. See: **TAYLOR Peter Mark.**

PETERS Maureen, (Victoria Black, Catherine Darby, Belinda Grey, Levannah Lloyd, Judith Rothman, Sharon Whitby), b. 3 Mar 1935, Caernarvon, North Wales. Writer. Education: BA and Diploma in Education, University College of North Wales, 1956. Publications: Over 40 books, fiction and non-fiction, 1980-90. Address: 45-47 Clerkenwell Green, London EC1R 0HT, England.

PETERS Richard. See: **HAINING Peter.**

PETERS Richard Stanley, b. 31 Oct 1919, Missouri, India. Emeritus Professor. m. Margaret Lee Duncan, 16 July 1943, 1 son, 2 daughters. Education: Queen's College, Oxford; Birkbeck College, London; BA (Oxon); BA, London; PhD, London, 1949. Appointments: Part-time Lecturer, 1946-49, Full-time Lecturer, 1949-58, Reader in Philosophy, 1958-62, Birkbeck College, University of London; Visiting Professor, Harvard University, USA, 1961; Professor, Philosophy of Education, 1962, Emeritus Professor, 1982-, Institute of Education, London; Part-time Lectureships, Bedford College, London, and London School of Economics, 1966; Visiting Fellow, Australian National University, Canberra, 1969. Publications: Ethics and Education, 1945; Hobbes, 1956; Social Principles of the Democratic State (co-author), 1958; Authority, Responsibility and Education, 1960; Logic of Education (co-author), 1970; Reason and Compassion, 1973; Psychology and Ethical Development, 1974; Essays on Educators, 1981; Moral Education and Moral Development, 1981. Editor: International Library of the Philosophy of Education. Address: Flat 3, 16 Shepherd's Hill, Highgate, London N6 5AQ, England.

PETERS Robert Louis, b. 20 Oct 1924, Eagle River, Wisconsin, USA. Professor of English; Poet; Writer. Div, 3 sons, 1 daughter. Education: BA, 1948, MA, 1949, PhD, 1952, University of Wisconsin at Madison. Appointments: Instructor, University of Idaho, 1952-53, Boston University, 1953-55; Assistant Professor, Ohio Wesleyan University, 1955-58; Associate Professor, Wayne State University, 1958-63; Professor of English, University of California at Riverside, 1963-68, and Irvine, 1968-. Publications: The Drowned Man to the Fish, 1978; Picnic in the Snow: Ludwig of Bavaria, 1982; What Dillinger Meant to Me, 1983; Hawker, 1984; Kane, 1985; Ludwig of Bavaria: Poems and a Play, 1986; The Blood Countess: Poems and a Play, 1987; Haydon, 1988; Brueghel's Pigs, 1989; Poems: Selected and New, 1992; Goodnight Paul: Poems, 1992; Snapshots for a Serial Killer: A Fiction and Play, 1992; Zapped: 3 Novellas, 1993; Nell: A Woman from Eagle River, 1994; Lili Marlene: A Memoir of World War II, 1995. Other: Victorians in Literature and Art, 1961; The Crowns of Apollo: Swinburne's Principles of Literature and Art, 1965; The Letters of John Addington Symonds (co-editor), 3 volumes, 1967-69; Gabriel: A Poem by John Addington Symonds, 1974; The Collected Poems of Amnesia Glassclock: John Steinbeck , (editor), 1977; Letter to a Tutor: The Tennyson Family Letters to Henry Graham Dakyns (editor), 1988. Contributions to: Professional journals. Honours: Guggenheim Fellowship, 1966-67; Yaddo, MacDowell Colony, and Ossabaw Island Project Fellowships, 1973-74; National Endowment for the Arts Grant, 1974. Membership: American Society for Aesthetics; PEN; Writer's Guild. Address: 9431 Krepp Drive, Huntington Beach, CA 92646, USA.

PETERSEN Peter James, b. 23 Oct 1941, Santa Rosa, California, USA. Writer; Teacher. m. Marian Braun, 6 July 1964, 2 daughters. Education: AB, Stanford University; MA, San Francisco State University; PhD, University of New Mexico. Appointments: English Instructor, Shasta College. Publications: Would You Settle for Improbable, 1981; Nobody Else Can Walk It for You, 1982; The Boll Weevil Express, 1983; Here's to the Sophomores, 1984; Corky & the Brothers Cool, 1985; Going for the Big One, 1986; Good-bye to Good O'Charlie, 1987; The Freshman Detective Blues, 1987; I Hate Camping, 1991; Liars, 1992; The Sub, 1993; I Want Answers and a Parachute, 1993; Some Days, Other Days, 1994. Honour: National Endowment for the Humanities Fellowship, 1976-77. Membership: Society of Children's Book Writers. Literary Agent: Ruth Cohen, PO Box 7626, Menlo Park, CA 94025, USA. Address: 1243 Pueblo Court, Redding, CA 96001, USA.

PETERSON Donald Macandrew, b. 23 June 1956. Lecturer in Cognitive Science. Education: MA, Philosophy and Psychology, Edinburgh University, 1978; PhD, Philosophy, University College London, 1985, MSc, Dic, in Foundations of Advanced Information Technology, Imperial College, London, 1986. Publication: Wittgenstein's Early Philosophy - Three Sides of the Mirror, 1990. Contributions to: Professional journals and magazines. Membership: Society of Artificial Intelligence and the Simulation of Behaviour. Address: Department of Computer Science, University of Birmingham, Birmingham B15 2TT, England.

PETERSON Robert, b. 2 June 1924, Denver, Colorado, USA. 1 daughter. Education: BA, University of California, Berkeley, 1947; MA, San Francisco State College, 1956. Appointment: Writer-in-Residence, Reed College, Protland, Oregon, 1969-71. Publications: Home for the Night, 1962; The Binnacle, 1967; Wondering Where You Are, 1969; Lone Rider, 1976; Under Sealed Orders, 1976; Leaving Taos, 1981;

The Only Piano Player in La Paz, 1985; Waiting for Garbo: 44 Ghazals, 1987; All The Time in the World, 1996. Honours: Grant in Poetry, National Endowment for the Arts, 1967; Amy Lowell Travelling Fellowship, 1972-73; National Poetry Series, Leaving Taos, 1981. Memberships: Authors Guild; PEN. Address: PO Box 417, Fairfax, CA 94978, USA.

PETERZEN (Anna Karin) Elisabet, b. 15 Apr 1938, Stockholm, Sweden. Author, 1 daughter. Education: London School of Foreign Trade, 1960; Stockholm University, 1980-83. Appointment: Women's Committee, Swedish Union of Authorss, 1985-88. Publications: Marmor och Ebenholts, 1964; Njutning, 1967; Trygghet, 1968; Aktenskaps Brott, 1969; Den konstgjorda mannen, 1973; En mans liv (Mustafa Said), 1974; Roman, 1976; Ljusnatten, 1981; Lura Livet, 1981; Sista Sticket, 1983; Mamsell Caroline, 1986; Djursager, 1987; Nubiens Hjarta, 1989. Honours: 1st Prize, Best 2nd World Novel, 1976; 1st Prize, Best Book Club Novel, 1986. Membership: Swedish Union of Authors, 1970-. Address: Osmo, Sweden.

PETOCZ Andras, b. 27 Aug 1959, Budapest, Hungary. Editor; Writer; Poet. 2 daughters. Education: Graduated, Lorand Eötvös University, Budapest, 1986. Appointments: Chief Editor, Jelenlet, literary periodical, 1981-83; Editor and Publisher, Medium Art, underground literary periodical during the Communist regime, 1983-89; Editor, Magyar Muhley, literary periodical, 1989-91. Publications: Poems, essays, and children's poems. Contributions to: Periodicals. Honour: Several literary prizes. Memberships: Art Association of the Hungarian Republic; Hungarian Writers Association. Address: Studio of Medium Art, Donati u 6, H-1015 Budapest, Hungary.

PETROSKI Catherine, b. 7 Sept 1939, St Louis, Missouri, USA. Writer. m. Henry Petroski, 15 July 1966, 1 s, 1 d. Education: BA, MacMurray College, 1961; MA, University of Illinois, 1962. Appointments: National Endowment for the Arts Writing Fellowship, 1978-79, 1983-84; Publications: Gravity and Other Stories, 1981; Beautiful My Mane in the Wind, 1983; The Summer That Lasted Forever, 1984; Chalk Ginger Blue: The Honeymoon Diary of Susan Hawthorn, 1997. Contributions to: Short fiction in Virginia Quarterly Review, Mississippi Review, Southern Humanities Review, North American Review, Prairie Schooner and others; reviews of fiction and non-fiction to Chicago Tribune and others. Honours: Berlin Prize, 1960; Texas Institute of Letters Prize, 1976; PEN Syndicated Fiction Prizes, 1983-85, 1988. O Henry Award, 1989; AAUW North Carolina Literary and Historical Association Book Prize; 1984 Honorary DLitt conferred by MacMurray College. Memberships: The Author's Guild; National Book Critics Circle. Address: 2528 Wrightwood Avenue, Durham, NC 27705, USA.

PETROSKI Henry, b. 6 Feb 1942, New York, USA. Engineer; Teacher; Writer. m. Catherine Ann Groom, 15 July 1966, 1 son, 1 daughter. Education: BME, Manhattan College, 1963; MS, 1964, PhD, 1968, University of Illinois. Appointment: Faculty, School of Engineering, Duke University. Publications: To Engineer is Human, 1985; Beyond Engineering, 1986; The Pencil, 1990; The Evolution of Useful Things, 1992; Design Paradigms, 1994; Engineers of Dreams, 1995; Invention by Design, 1996. Memberships: American Society of Civil Engineers; American Society of Mechanical Engineers; National Academy of Engineering. Address: School of Engineering, Duke University, Durham, NC 27708-0287, USA.

PETROVITS Loty, b. 12 Aug 1937, Athens, Greece. Author. m. Andreas Andrutsopoulos, 23 July 1966, 1 son, 1 daughter. Education: University of Michigan; Istituto Italiano di Cultura in Atene, 1960. Appointments: Editorial Correspondent, Phaedrus, 1980-88; Associate Editor, Bookbird, 1982-; Co-Editor, Diadromes, 1986-. Publications: O Mikros Adelfos, 1976, Japanese translation, 1988; Tris Fores Ki Enan Kero, 1977; Gia Tin Alli Patrida, 1978; Sto Tsimentenio Dasos, 1981; Zetete Mikros, 1982; Istories pou kanenas den xerei, 1984; Spiti Gia Pente, 1987, Japanese translation, 1990; Istories me tous dodeca mines, 4 volumes, 1988; Lathos Kyrie Noyger!, 1989; 13 more books for children and 4 for adults; Translations from English into Greek include: Blowfish Live in the Sea, by Paula Fox, 1979; The Camelthorn Papers, by Ann Thwaite, 1987. Contributions to: Phaedrus; Bookbird; Diadromes; Efthini; Diavazo; Kypriaki Martyria; Helidonia; Gia Hara. Address: 129 Aristotelous Street, GR 11251 Athens, Greece.

PETTIFER James Milward, b. 6 Apr 1949, Hereford, England. Writer; Teacher. m. 7 June 1974, 1 son, 1 daughter. Education: Hertford College, Oxford, MA, 1971. Appointments: Co-Editor, "Albania

Life" magazine; Member, Royal Institute of International Affairs, London; Senior Associate Member, St Antony's College, Oxford; Currently Visiting Professor, Institute of Balkan Studies, Aristotle University of Thessalonika, Greece. Publications: Blue Guide/Guide Bleu to Albania, 1991; The Greeks - Land and People Since the War, 1993; Blue Guide to Bulgaria, 1996; Albania: From Anarchy to a Balkan Identity (with M Vickers). Contributions to: Regular Writer for The Times (London), Wall Street Journal; The Economist, others. Memberships: Institute of Balkan Studies, Greece; Institute of Balkan History, Sofia, Bulgaria. Literary Agent: Curtis Brown Ltd, 28-29 Haymarket, London SW1Y 4SP, England.

PETTIFER Julian, b. 21 July 1935, Malmesbury, England. Freelance Writer; Broadcaster. Education: St John's College, Cambridge, 1955-58. Appointments: TV Reporter, Writer, Presenter: Southern TV, 1958-62; Tonight, 1962-64, 24 Hours, 1964-69, Panorama, 1969-75, BBC; Presenter, Cuba - 25 Years of Revolution, series, 1984, Host, Busman's Holiday, 1985-86, ITV; Numerous TV documentaries including: Vietnam War Without End, 1970; The World About Us, 1976; The Spirit of 76, 1976; Diamonds in the Sky, 1979; Nature Watch, 5 series, 1981-90; Automania, 1984; The Living Isles, 1986; Africawatch, 1989; Missionaries, 1990; BBC Assignment, 1993-94; BBC Correspondent, 1994-95. Publications: Diamonds in the Sky: A Social History of Air Travel (co-author), 1979; Nature Watch, 1981; Automania, 1984; The Nature Watchers, 1985; Missionaries, 1990; Nature Watch, 1994. Honour: Reporter of the Year Award, Guild of Television Directors and Producers, 1968. Memberships: Royal Society for Nature Conservation, vice-president, 1992-; Royal Botanic Gardens, Kew, trustee, 1993-; Royal Society for the Protection of Birds, president, 1994. Address: c/o Curtis Brown, 28/29 Haymarket, London SW1Y 4SP, England.

PEYREFITTE (Pierre) Roger, b. 17 Aug 1907, Castres (Tarn), France. Author. Education: BA, Ecole des Sciences Politiques, Paris. Publications: Les amitiés particulières, 1944-45; Mademoiselle de Murville, 1946; Le prince des neiges, 1947; L'oracle, 1948; Les amours singulières, 1949; La Mort d'une mère, 1950; Les ambassades, 1951; Du Vesuve a l'Etna, 1952; Les clés de St Pierre, 1955; Jeunes Proies, 1956; Chevaliers de Malte, 1957; L'exile de Capri, 1959; Le Spectateur nocturne, 1960; Les fils de la lumière, 1961; La nature du prince, 1963; Les Juifs, 1965; Notre Amour, 1967; Les Americains, 1968; Des Francais, 1970; La Coloquinte, 1971; Manouche, 1972; La muse garçonnière, 1973; Tableaux de chasse ou la vie extraordinaire de Fernand Legros, 1976; Propos secrets, 1977; La Jeunesses d'Alexandre, 1977; L'enfant de coeur, 1978; Roy, 1979; Les conquêtes d'Alexandre, 1979; Propos Secrets II, 1980; Alexandre Le Grand, 1981; L'illustre ecrivain, 1982; La soutane rouge, 1983; Henry de Montherlent- Roger Peyrefitte correspondence, 1983; Voltaire, sa Jeunesse et son Temps, 1985; L'Innominato, nouveaux propos secrets, 1989; Reflexion sur De Gaulle, 1992. Honour: Prix Theophaste Renaudot. Address: 9 Avenue du Marechal Manoury, 75016, Paris, France.

PEYTON Kathleen Wendy, (Kathleen Herald, K M Peyton), b. 2 Aug 1929, Birmingham, England. Writer. m. Michael Peyton, 1950, 2 daughters. Education: ATD, Manchester School of Art. Publications: As Kathleen Herald: Sabre, the Horse from the Sea, 1947; The Mandrake, 1949; Crab the Roan, 1953. As K M Peyton: North to Adventure, 1959; Stormcock Meets Trouble, 1961; The Hard Way Home, 1962; Windfall, 1963; Brownsea Silver, 1964; The Maplin Bird, 1964, USA, 1965; The Plan for Birdsmarsh, 1965; Thunder in the Sky, 1966; Flambards Trilogy, 1969-71; The Beethoven Medal, 1971; The Pattern of Roses, 1972; Pennington's Heir, 1973; The Team, 1975; The Right-Hand Man, 1977; Prove Yourself a Hero, 1977; A Midsummer Night's Death, 1978; Marion's Angels, 1979; Flambards Divided, 1981; Dear Fred, 1981; Going Home, 1983; The Last Ditch, 1984; Froggett's Revenge, 1985; The Sound of Distant Cheering, 1986; Downhill All the Way, 1988; Darkling, 1989; Skylark, 1989; No Roses Round the Door, 1990; Poor Badger, 1991; Late to Smile, 1992; The Boy Who Wasn't There, 1992; The Wild Boy and Queen Moon, 1993; Snowfall, 1994. Honours: New York Herald Tribune Award, 1965; Carnegie Medal, 1969; Guardian Award, 1970. Address: Rookery Cottage, North Fambridge, Chelmsford, Essex CM3 6LP, England.

PEYTON Richard. See: **HAINING Peter Alexander**.

PFANNER (Anne) Louise, b. 6 Mar 1955, Sydney, New South Wales, Australia. Illustrator; Writer. m. (1) Glenn Woodley, 24 Dec 1976, (2) Tim Maddox, 12 Jan 1987, 4 sons. Education: Diploma,

Graphic Design, 1977; BA, Visual Communication, 1986; MA, Children's Literature and Literacy, 1997. Appointment: Regular exhibits of illustrations. Publications: Louise Builds a Boat, 1986; Louise Builds a House, 1987; The Little Red Hen, 1997; The Country Mouse, 1997; Illustrator: Your Book of Magic Secrets (R Deutch), 1991; I'm a Little Teapot, 1995; First Book of Gardening, 1995; Mean Charlotte the Good Idea, 1996; Sing Book, infants section, 1996; Contributing Illustrator: Under the Clock, 1996. Contributions to: Illustrations in various publications. Memberships: Society of Book Illustrators, Sydney; Australian Society of Authors; Australian Society of Authors. Literary Agent: Barbara Mobbs, PO 126, Edgecliffe, New South Wales 2027, Australia. Address: 4 Catalpa Avenue, Avalon, New South Wales 2107, Australia

PFEFFER Susan Beth, b. 17 Feb 1948, New York, New York, USA. Children's Writer. Education: BA, New York University, 1969. Publications: Some 40 books, 1970-96. Address: 14 South Railroad Avenue, Middletown, NJ 10940, USA.

PHILANDERSON Flavian Titus, (Johnny Goad, Flavian P Stimulus, John Stimulus), b. 3 Mar 1933, Penang, British Malaya. High School Teacher; Freelance Journalist; Writer. m. Martha Bernadette Pillai, 29 Dec 1956, 2 sons, 2 daughters. Education: Overseas School Certificate A, University of Cambridge, 1951; Teacher Training, Ministry of Education, British Administration, Malaya; Fiction Writing, Premier School of Journalism, Fleet Street, London. Publications: A Course in Primary English (co-author), set texts for ESL students, 1969; Sun Never Sets; Zigzags; Optics of Being; Window in the Sky, novel, 1982; Diary of a Sydney Girl, 1992; All Flesh Is Grass, 1995. Contributions to: Various publications. Memberships: Australian Society of Authors; Royal Australian Historical Society; History Teachers Association; Fellowship of Australian Writers; Independent Teachers Association; National Geographical Association. Address: 32 Hillcrest Avenue, Winston Hills, Sydney, New South Wales 2153, Australia.

PHILLIPS Caryl, b. 13 Mar 1958, St Kitts, West Indies. British Citizen. Playwright; Novelist. Education: BA, Oxford University, 1979. Appointments: Visiting Writer, 1990, Professor English, Amherst College, Massachusetts, 1994. Publications: Strange Fruit, 1980; Where There is Darkness, 1982; The Shelter, 1983; The Wasted Years, 1984; The Final Passage, 1985; A State of Independence, 1986; Higher Ground, 1989; Cambridge, 1991; Crossing the River, 1993. Non-Fiction: The European Tribe, 1987. Other: Playing Away (screenplay), 1987; Radio and television plays. Honours: Martin Luther King Memorial Prize, 1987; Guggenheim Fellow, 1992; James Tait Black Memorial Prize, 1993; Lannan Foundation Fiction Award, 1994; AM (Hon), Amherst College, Massachusetts, 1995. Address: c/o Curtis Brown Ltd, Haymarket House, 28-29 Haymarket, London SW1Y 4SP, England.

PHILLIPS Edward O, b. 26 Nov 1931, Montreal, Quebec, Canada. Teacher; Writer. Education: BA, McGill University, 1953; LL.L. University of Montreal, 1956; AMT, Harvard University, 1957; MA, Boston University, 1962. Publications: Sunday's Child, 1981; Where There's a Will, 1984; Buried on Sunday, 1986; Hope Springs Eternal, 1988; Sunday Best, 1990; The Landlady's Niece, 1992; The Mice Will Play, Novel, 1996. Contributions to: Short stories to various Canadian journals. Honour: Arthur Ellis Award, 1986. Memberships: Canadian Writers Union; PEN. Literary Agent: Livingstone Cooke, Inc. Address: 425 Wood Avenue, Westmount, Quebec H3Y 3J3, Canada.

PHILLIPS Jayne Anne, b. 19 July 1952, Buckhannon, West Virginia, USA. Writer. m. Mark Brian Stockman, 26 May 1985, 1 son, 2 stepsons. Education: BA, West Virginia University, 1974; MFA, University of Iowa, 1978. Appointments: Adjunct Associate Professor of English, Boston University, 1982-; Fanny Howe Chair of Letters, Brandeis University, 1986-87. Publications: Sweethearts, 1976; Counting, 1978; Black Tickets, 1979; How Mickey Made It, 1981; Machine Dreams, 1984; Fast Lanes, 1984; Shelter, 1994. Honours: Pushcart Prizes, 1977, 1979, 1983; Fels Award in Fiction, Coordinating Council of Literary Magazines, 1978; National Endowment for the Arts Fellowships, 1978, 1985; St Lawrence Award for Fiction, 1979; Sue Kaufman Award for Fiction, American Academy and Institute of Arts and Letters, 1980; O Henry Award, 1980; Bunting Institute Fellowship, Radcliffe College, 1981; Notable Book Citation, American Library Association, 1984; Best Book Citation, New York Times, 1984. Memberships: Authors Guild; Authors League of America; PEN.

Address: c/o International Creative Management, 40 West 57th Street, New York, NY 10019, USA.

PHILLIPS Michael. See: **NOLAN William.**

PHILLIPS Robert Schaeffer, b. 2 Feb 1938, Milford, Delaware, USA. Professor of English; Writer; Poet. m. Judith Anne Bloomingdale, 16 June 1963, 1 son. Education: BA, 1960, MA, 1962, Syracuse University. Publications: The Pregnant Man (poems), 1978; Running on Empty (poems), 1981; Public Landing Revisited (fiction), 1982; Personal Accounts: New & Selected Poems, 1986; Breakdown Lane (poems), 1994; Others: The Land of Lost Content, 1970; Aspects of Alice, 1971. Contributions to: New Yorker; Hudson Review; Paris Review; Encounter; Poetry; Partisan Review; Boulevard; New York Times Book Review. Honour: American Academy of Arts Letters Award, 1987. Memberships: American PEN; Author's Guild; Poets' House; Poetry Society of America; The Players. Literary Agent: Wieser & Wieser, 118 E 25th Street, New York, NY 10010, USA. Address: 1908 Banks Street, Houston, TX 77098, USA.

PHILLIPS Shelley, b. 18 Mar 1934, Melbourne, Victoria, Australia. Psychological Consultant; Writer. 2 daughters. Education: BA (Hons), English, History, University of Melbourne; BA, Psychology, University of Western Australia; PhD, Sydney University, 1972; Visiting Scientist, Programme Associate, Tavistock Clinic, London, 1975-76, 1978-79, 1982-83. Publications: Young Australian: The Attitudes of Our Children, 1979; Relations With Children: The Psychology of Human Development in a Changing World, 1986; Beyond the Myths: Mother-Daughter Relations in Psychology, History, Literature and Everyday Life, 1991. Contributions to: Books and professional journals. Honours: Prox Accesit Arts Convocation Prize, University of Western Australia, 1959; Honorary academic appointments: University of Birmingham, England, 1975, Georgia State University, USA, 1975, University of Alberta, Canada, 1976, London University Institute of Education, 1979, Institute of Early Childhood Studies, Melbourne, 1982; University College, London, 1983; Research grants. Memberships: Australian Society of Authors; Society of Women Writers; Jane Austen Society; National Trust; Australian Psychological Society; College of Educational and Developmental Psychologists. Address: Sydney, New South Wales, Australia.

PHILLIPSON (Charles) Michael, b. 16 June 1940, Gatley, Cheshire, England. Freelance Painter; Writer. m. Julia Hauxwell, 1 Sept 1971, 1 son, 2 daughters. Education: BA, 1961, MA, 1964, Nottingham University. Publications: Making Fuller Use of Survey Data, 1968; Sociological Aspects of Crime and Delinquency, 1971; New Directions in Sociological Theory (co-author), 1972; Understanding Crime and Delinquency, 1974; Problems of Reflexivity and Dialectics in Sociological Inquiry (co-author), 1975; Painting, Language and Modernity, 1985; In Modernity's Wake, 1989. Contributions to: Numerous including: Reviews to sociology journals; Articles and reviews to Artscribe International, 1986-88; To Ceramise, Catalogue Essay in Ceramic Contemporaries 2, 1996. Address: Derlwyn, Glandwr, Hebron, Whitland, Pembrokeshire SA34 0YD, Wales.

PHILP Peter, b. 10 Nov 1920, Cardiff, Wales. Writer. m. 25 Sept 1940, 2 sons. Publications: Beyond Tomorrow, 1947; The Castle of Deception, 1952; Love and Lunacy, 1955; Antiques Today, 1960; Antique Furniture for the Smaller Home, 1962; Furniture of the World, 1974. Contributions to: Times; Antique Dealer and Collectors Guide; Antique Collecting; Antique Furniture Expert (with Gillian Walkling), 1991. Honours: Arts Council Award, 1951; C H Foyle Award, 1951. Membership: Society of Authors. Address: 77 Kimberley Road, Cardiff CF2 5DP, Wales.

PHIPPS Christine, b. 5 Dec 1945, Bristol, England. University Lecturer; Counsellor. Div. Education: BA 1st Class Honours, Hull University, 1968; MLitt, St Hugh's College, Oxford University, 1971; Advanced Diploma in Linguistics, Lancaster University, 1986; Advanced Diploma in Counselling, Wigan College of Technology, 1989. Publication: Buckingham: Public and Private Man (George Villiers 1628-1687), 1985. Contributions to: Notes and Queries Journal. Address: 21 Hurstway, Fulwood, Preston, Lancashire PR2 9TT, England.

PHIPSON Joan. See: **FITZHARDINGE Joan Margaret.**

PICANO Felice, b. 22 Feb 1944, New York, New York, USA. Author. Education: BA cum laude, Queens College, City University of New York, 1960. Publications: Smart as the Devil, 1975; Eyes, 1976; Deformity Lover and Other Poems, 1977; The Lure, 1979; Late in the Season, 1980; An Asian Minor, 1981; Slashed to Ribbons in Defense of Love and Other Stories, 1982; House of Cards, 1984; Ambidextrous, 1985; Men Who Loved Me, 1989; To the Seventh Power, 1989; The New Joy of Gay Sex, 1992; Dryland's End, 1995; Like People in History, 1995. Contributions to: Men on Men; Violet Quill Reader; Numerous magazines and journals. Honours: Finalist, Ernest Hemingway Award; PEN Syndicated Short Fiction Award; Chapbook Award, Poetry Society of America. Memberships: PEN Club; Writers Guild of America; Authors Guild; Publishing Triangle. Literary Agent: Malaga Baldi. Address: 95 Horatio Street 423, New York, NY 10014, USA.

PICARD Barbara Leonie, b. 4 Dec 1917, Richmond, Surrey, England. Author. Publications: Ransom for a Knight, 1956; Lost John, 1962; One is One, 1965; The Young Pretenders, 1966; Twice Seven Tales, 1968; Three Ancient Kings, 1972; Tales of Ancient Persia, reprinted, 1993; The Iliad, 1991; The Odyssey, 1991; French Legends, Tales and Fairy Stories, 1992; German Hero-sagas and Folk-tales, 1993; Tales of the Norse Gods, 1994; Selected Fairy Tales, 1994; The Deceivers, 1996. Address: Oxford University Press, Walton Street, Oxford, England.

PICARD Robert George, b. 15 July 1951, Pasadena, California, USA. Professor; Author. m. Elizabeth Carpelan, 15 Sept 1979, 2 daughters, 1 son. Education: BA, Loma Linda University, 1974; MA, California State University, Fullerton, 1980; PhD, University of Missouri, 1983. Appointments: Editor, Journal of Media Economics, 1988-97; Associate Editor, Political Communication and Persuasion, 1989-91. Publications: The Press and the Decline of Democracy, 1985; Press Concentration and Monopoly, 1988; The Ravens of Odin: The Press in the Nordic Nations, 1988; In the Camera's Eye: News Coverage of Terrorist Events, 1991; Media Portrayals of Terrorism: Functions and Meaning of News Coverage, 1993; The Cable Networks Handbook, 1993; Joint Operating Agreements: The Newspaper Preservation Act and its Application, 1993; The Newspaper Publishing Industry, 1997. Address: 2806 Gertrude Street, Riverside, CA 92506, USA.

PICK Frederick Michael, 21 June 1949, Leicestershire, England. Antique Dealer; Designer/Director; Author; Lecturer. Education: MA, History and Law, Gonville and Caius College, Cambridge. Publications: The English Room, 1985; The National Trust Pocket Guide to Furniture, 1985; The English Country Room, 1988. Contributions to: Periodicals. Honour: 1969 Exhibitioner in History, Gonville and Caius, Cambridge. Memberships: Society of Authors; Twentieth Century Society; Royal Society for Asian Affairs; British Antique Dealer Association; Lansdowne Club. Address: 114 Mount Street, London W1Y 5RA, England.

PICKARD Tom, b. 7 Jan 1946, Newcastle upon Tyne, England. Writer; Director. m. Joanna Voit, 22 July 1978, 2 sons, 1 daughter. Publications: Guttersnipe: City Lights (novella), 1971; Hero Dust (poems), 1979; Jarrow March (oral history), 1982; Custom and Exile (poems), 1985; We Make Ships (oral history), 1989. Contributions to: Television documentaries and series. Honour: Arts Council Writer-in-Residence, Warwick University, 1979-80. Membership: ACTT, General Council. Address: c/o Judy Daish Associates, 2 St Charles Place, London W10 6EG, England.

PICKERING Sir Edward (Davies), b. 4 May 1912, England. Journalist; Publishing Executive. m. (1) Margaret Soutter, 1936, div 1947, 1 daughter, (2) Rosemary Whitton, 1955, 2 sons, 1 daughter. Education: Middlesborough High School. Appointments: Chief Sub-Editor, 1939, Managing Editor, 1947-49, Daily Mail; Managing Editor, 1951-57, Editor, 1957-62, Daily Express; Director, Beaverbrook Newspapers, 1956-64, Scottish Daily Record and Sunday Mail Ltd, 1966-69, Times Newspapers Holdings Ltd, 1981-, William Collins Sons & Co Ltd, 1981-89, Harper Collins Publishers Ltd, 1989-; Editorial Director, Daily Mirror Newspapers Ltd, 1964-68; Director 1966-75, Chairman, Newspaper Division, 1968-70, and Magazines, 1970-74, International Publishing Corporation; Chairman, Mirror Group Newspapers, 1975-77, Times Supplements Ltd, 1989-; Executive Vice-Chairman, Times Newspapers Ltd, 1982-. Honours: Knighted, 1977; Honorary Freeman, Stationers' and Newspaper Makers' Company, 1985; Astor Award for Distinguished Service to the

Commonwealth Press, 1986; Honorary DLitt, City University of London, 1986. Memberships: Commonwealth Press Union, Chairman of the Council, 1977-86; Fédèration Internationale de la Presse Periodique, Treasurer, 1971-75; Press Council, Vice Chairman, 1976-82. Address: Chatley House, Norton St Philip, Somerset, England.

PICKERING Howard Charles, b. 14 April 1943, Brisbane, Australia. Teacher. m. Lorraine Pickering (Purdy), 13 Dec 1965, 1 son, 1 daughter. Education: Advanced Trade. Publications: Senior Graphics, 1988; Junior Graphics, 1989; Introducing Graphics, 1990. Memberships: Industrial Technology and Design Teachers Association of Queensland; President, Secretary, Treasurer, Editor, Institute of Technology Education New South Wales; Queensland Society for Information Technology. Address: 11 Kiriwina Street, Fig Tree Pocket, Queensland 4069, Australia.

PICKERING Paul Granville, b. 9 May 1952, Rotherham, England. Novelist; Playwright. m. Alison Beckett, 11 Dec 1983, 1 daughter. Education: Royal Masonic Schools; BA (Hon) Psychology, Leicester University. Publications: Wild About Harry, 1985; Perfect English, 1986; The Blue Gate of Babylon, 1989; Charlie Peace, 1991. Anthologies: Winters Tales (contributed short story), 1989; Play: After Hamlet, New Grove Theatre, London, 1994. Contributions to: Times; Sunday Times; Indepedent. Membership: Society of Authors. Address: 20 Brackebury Gardens, London W6 0BP, England.

PIECHOCKI Stanislaw Ryszard, b. 8 Feb 1955, Olsztyn, Poland. Lawyer. m. Elzbieta Piechocki, 27 Oct 1979, 1 daughter. Education: MSc, Department of Law, University of Torun, 1978. Publications: Na krancu drogi (On the End of Way), story, 1975; Przedostatni przystanek (The Last But One Stop), novel, 1980; Tekturowe czolgi (The Cardboard Tanks), novel, 1983; Przysposobienie dziecka (Adoption of Child), science material, 1983; Przyladek burz (Cape of Storm), novel, 1989; Czysciec zwany Kortau (Purgatory called Kortau), report, 1993; Dzieje olsztynskich ulic (History of Streets in Olsztyn), tales, 1st Edition, 1994, 2nd Edition, 1995. Contributions to: Various publications. Honours: Ignacy Krasicki Memorial Medal for Best First Novel, 1980; Award, Minister of Culture and Art, 1984. Memberships: Polish Writers Association; Polish Lawyers Association; Society of the Friends of Warmia and Masuriás Literature. Address: ul Iwaszkiewicza 16 m 28, 10-089 Olsztyn, Poland.

PIELMEIER John, b. 3 Feb 1949, Altoona, Pennsylvania, USA. Dramatist; Actor. m. Irene O'Brian, 9 Oct 1982. Education: BA, Catholic University of America; MFA, Pennsylvania State University. Publications: Agnes of God, 1983; Haunted Lives (A Witches Brew, A Ghost Story, A Gothic Tale), 1984. Honours: Christopher Award, 1984; Humanitas Award, 1984. Memberships: Writers Guild of America; Dramatists Guild; American Federation of Television and Radio Artists; Actors Equity Association. Address: c/o Artists Agency, 230 West 55th Street, New York, NY 10019, USA.

PIERARD Richard V(ictor), b. 29 May 1934, Chicago, Illinois, USA. Professor of History; Writer. m. Charlene Burdett, 15 June 1957, 1 son, 1 daughter. Education: BA 1958, MA 1959, California State University, Los Angeles; University of Hamburg, 1962-63; PhD, University of Iowa, 1964. Appointments: Instructor, University of Iowa, 1964; Assistant Professor 1964-67, Associate Professor 1967-72, Professor of History 1972-, Indiana State University, Terre Haute; Research Fellow, University of Aberdeen, 1978; Fulbright Professor, University of Frankfurt, 1984-85, University of Halle 1989-90. Publications: Protest and Politics: Christianity and Contemporary Affairs (with Robert G Clouse and Robert D Linder), 1968; The Unequal Yoke: Evangelical Christianity and Political Conservatism, 1970; The Cross and the Flag (editor with Robert G Clouse and Robert D Linder), 1972; Politics: A Case for Christian Action (with Robert D Linder), 1973; The Twilight of the Saints: Christianity and Civil Religion in Modern America (with Robert D Linder), 1977; Streams of Civilization, Vol II (with Robert G Clouse), 1980; Bibliography on the Religious Right in America, 1986; Civil Religion and the Presidency (with Robert D Linder), 1988; Two Kingdoms: The Church and Culture Through the Ages (with Robert G Clouse and E M Yamauchi), 1993; The Revolution of the Candles (with Joerg Swoboda), 1996. Contributions to: Many books, reference works, and professional journals. Honour: Research and Creativity Award, Indiana State University, 1994. Memberships: American Historical Society; American Society of Church History; American Society of Missiology; Baptist World Alliance, Baptist Heritage Study Committee, 1990-2000; Evangelical Theological Society, President, 1985; Greater Terre Haute Church Federation, President, 1987-88; International Association of Mission Studies. Address: c/o Department of History, Indiana State University, Terre Haute, IN 47809, USA.

PIERCE Meredith Ann, b. 5 July 1958, Seattle, Washington, USA. Writer. Education: AA, Liberal Arts, 1976, BA, English, 1978, MA, English, 1980, University of Florida. Publications: The Darkangel, 1982; A Gathering of Gargoyles, 1984; The Woman Who Loved Reindeer, 1985; Birth of the Firebringer, 1985; Where the Wild Geese Go, 1988; Rampion, 1989; The Pearl of the Soul of the World, 1990. Contributions to: Magazines. Honours: Several citations and awards for children's and young adult's literature. Memberships: Author's Guild; Phi Beta Kappa; Science Fiction Writers of America. Address: 703 North West 19th Street, Gainesville, FL 32603, USA.

PIERCY Marge, b. 31 Mar 1936, Detroit, Michigan, USA. Poet; Writer. m. (3) Ira Wood, 2 June 1982. Education: AB, University of Michigan, 1957; MA, Northwestern University, 1958. Appointments: Poet-in-Residence, University of Kansas, 1971; Distinguished Visiting Lecturer, Thomas Jefferson College and Grand Valley State College, Allendale, Michigan, 1975-76, 1978, 1980; Staff, Fine Arts Work Center, Provincetown, Massachusetts, 1976-77; Writer-in-Residence, College of the Holy Cross, Worcester, Massachusetts, 1976; Butler Professor of Letters, State University of New York at Buffalo, 1977; Fiction Writer-in-Residence, Ohio State University, 1985; Elliston Poetry Fellow, University of Cincinnati, 1986; Poetry Editor, Tikkun Magazine, 1988-; DeRoy Distinguished Visiting Professor, University of Michigan, 1992; Guest, University of North Dakota Writers Conference, 1995, Florida Suncoast Writers Conference, 1996. Publications: Poetry: Breaking Camp, 1968; Hard Loving, 1969; To Be of Use, 1973; Living in the Open, 1976; The Twelve-Spoke Wheel Flashing, 1978; The Moon is Always Female, 1980; Circles on the Water: Selected Poems of Marge Piercy, 1982; Stone, Paper, Knife, 1983; My Mother's Body, 1985; Available Light, 1988; Mars and Her Children, 1992; The Eight Chambers of the Heart: Selected Poems, 1995; What Are Big Girls Made Of?, 1997. Fiction: Going Down Fast, 1969; Dance the Eagle to Sleep, 1970; Small Changes, 1973; Woman on the Edge of Time, 1976; The High Cost of Living, 1978; Vida, 1980; Braided Lives, 1982; Fly Away Home, 1984; Gone to Soldiers, 1987; Summer People, 1989; He, She and It, 1991; The Longings of Women, 1994; City of Darkness, City of Light, 1996; Parti-Colored Blocks for a Quilt: Poems on Poetry, 1982; Early Ripening: American Women Poets Now, 1988. Contributions to: Anthologies and periodicals. Honours: Borestone Mountain Poetry Awards, 1968, 1974; National Endowment for the Arts Award, 1978; Carolyn Kizer Poetry Prizes, 1986, 1990; Sheaffer Eaton-PEN New England Award, 1989; Brit ha-Darot Award, Shalom Center, 1992; Arthur C Clarke Award, 1992. Memberships: Authors Guild; Authors League; National Organization for Women; National Writers Union; New England Poetry Club; Poetry Society of America. Address: Box 1473, Wellfeet, MA 02667, USA.

PIERRE José, b. 24 Nov 1927, Bénesse-Maremne, France. Writer. m. Nicole Pierre, 5 Sept 1953. Education: Docteur ès-Lettres, Sorbonne, Paris, 1979. Appointment: Director of Research, Centre National de la Recherche Scientifique. Publications: Qu'est-ce que Thérèse? -C'est les marronniers en fleurs (novel), 1974; Gauguin aux Marquises (novel), 1982; L'Univers Surréaliste (history of art), 1983; André Breton et la peinture, 1987; L'Univers Symboliste (history of art and literature), 1991. Plays: Magdeleine LeClerc, le dernier amour du Marquis de Sade, 1993. Contributions to: La Quinzaine Littéraire, 1969-76. Memberships: Société des Gens de Lettres; Association Internationale des Critiques d'Art, Section France. Address: 2 rue Cournot, 75015 Paris, France.

PIETRASS Richard Georg, b. 11 June 1946, Lichtenstein, Sachsen. Poet; Translator; Psychologist. m. Erika Schulze, dec 22 Dec 1993, 26 Aug 1982, 2 sons, 1 daughter. Education: Practical training in a hospital, 1965-66; Military Service, Diploma in Psychology, Humboldt University, Berlin, 1975. Publications: Poesiealbum 82, 1974; Notausgang, 1980; Freiheitsmuseum, 1982; Spielball, 1987; Was mir zum Glück fehlt (selected poems), 1989; Weltkind (selected poems), 1990; Letzte Gestalt, 1994; Randlage, 1996. Honours: Ehrengabe der Schillerstiftung Weimar, 1992; Literaturpreis des Kulturkreises der Deutschen Wirtschaft, 1994. Memberships: Verband Deutscher Schriftsteller; Deutsches PEN - Zentrum. Address: Schleusinger Str 13, D-12687 Berlin, Germany.

PIGUET-CUENDET Suzanne, (Suzanne Deriex), b. 16 Apr 1926, Yverdon, Switzerland. Writer. m. Jean-François Piguet, 7 May 1949, 3 sons. Education: Bacc Latin/Greek, 1944; Lic Math Sc; Semi-lic theol, University Lausanne, Switzerland. Publications: Corinne (novel), 1961; San Domenico (novel), 1964; L'enfant et la mort (novel), 1968; L'homme n'est jamais seul (novel), 1983; Les sept vies de Louise Croisier née Moraz (novel), 1986; Un arbre de vie (novel), 1995. Honours: Prize of Jubilé du Lyceum Club de Suisse, 1963; Prix Veillon, 1968; Prix Pro Helvetia, 1983; Prix Alpes-Jura and Prix des Murailles, 1988; Prix du Livre vaudois, 1990. Memberships: PEN Club; ADELF; SSE; SGDLF; Lyceum; FU; AECEF. Address: Rte de Lausanne 11, 1096 Cully, Switzerland.

PIKE Charles R. See: **HARKNETT Terry.**

PIKE Charles R. See: **BULMER Henry Kenneth.**

PIKE (Dag) Roderick Douglas, b. 26 Jan 1933, Surrey, England. Writer; Consultant. m. Catherine B C Bennett, 24 Aug 1978, 1 son, 2 daughters. Education: Master's Certificate of Competency, Sutton Grammar School. Appointments: International Editor, Work Boat World, 1984; Power Editor, Boat International, 1993; Editor, World of Power, 1993; International Editor, RIB International, 1995. Publications: Electronics Afloat, 1986; Practical Motor Cruising, 1988; Fast Boats and Rough Seas, 1989; Fast Boat Navigation, 1990; Electronic Afloat, 1991; Boat Electrical Systems, 1992; Motor Sailers, 1993; RORC Manual of Safety and Survival, 1993; RORC Manual of the Weather, 1993; Inflatables, 1994; The Sextant Simplified, 1995. Contributions to: Boat International; RIB International; Small Ships; Motor Boats Monthly; Motorboat & Yachting; Sunday Times; Yachting (US); Motor Boating & Sailing (US); Skipper (Spain); Motorboote (Holland); Boote (Germany); Asian Marine (Singapore). Honours: Fellow, Royal Institute of Navigation; Fellow, Royal Geographical Society. Membership: Yachting Journalists Association. Address: 8 Lower Street, Stroud, Gloucester GL5 2HT, England.

PILCHER Rosamunde, (Jane Fraser), b. 22 Sept 1924, Lelant, Cornwall, England. Writer. m. Graham Pilcher, 4 children. Publications: April, 1957; On My Own, 1965; Sleeping Tiger, 1967; Another View, 1969; The End of the Summer, 1971; Snow in April, 1972; The Empty House, 1973; The Day of the Storm, 1975; Under Gemini, 1977; Wild Mountain Thyme, 1978; The Carousel, 1981; Voices in Summer, 1984; The Blue Bedroom and Other Stories, 1985; The Shell Seekers, 1988; September, 1989; Flowers in the Rain, 1991; Coming Home, 1996. Contributions to: Woman and Home; Good Housekeeping. Honour: RNA Award, Coming Home, 1996. Address: Penrowan, L:ongforgan, Perthshire DD2 5ET, Scotland.

PILGRIM Anne. See: **ALLAN Mabel Esther.**

PILKINGTON Roger Windle, b. 17 Jan 1915, St Helens, England. Author. m. (1) Miriam Jaboor, 27 July 1937, (2) Ingrid Geijer, 11 Oct 1972. Education: Magdalene College, Cambridge, 1933-37; MA (Cantab); PhD. Publications: 20 volumes in Small Boat series, including: Small Boat Down the Years, 1988; Small Boat in the Midi, 1989; Scientific philosophy and Christianity, notably: World Without End, 1960; Heavens Alive, 1962; Children's books including: The Ormering Tide, 1974; I Sailed on the Mayflower, 1990; One Foot in France, 1992; View from the Shore, 1995. Contributions to: Sunday Telegraph; Guardian. Honours: Chevalier, Compagnons du Minervois. Membership: Master, Glass Sellers Company, 1968. Address: Les Cactus, Moutouliers 34 310, France.

PILLING Christopher (Robert), b. 20 Apr 1936, Birmingham, England. Writer; Poet; Teacher. m. Sylvia Hill, 6 Aug 1960, 1 son, 2 daughters. Education: BA Hons, University of Leeds, 1957; Diplôme d'Etudes Françaises, Université de Poitiers, 1955; Certificate of Education, Loughborough College, 1959. Appointments: Assistant d'Anglais, Ecole Normale d'Instituteurs, Moulins, Allier, France, 1957-58; Teacher, French, Physical Education, Wirral Grammar School, Cheshire, England, 1959-61; King Edward's Grammar School for Boys, Camp Hill, Birmingham, 1961-62; Teacher, French, Housemaster, Ackworth School, Yorkshire, 1962-73; Reviewer, Times Literary Supplement, 1973-74; Head, Modern Languages, Housemaster, Knottingley High School, West Yorkshire, 1973-78; Tutor, English Literature and Art and Poetry, Newcastle University Department of Adult Education, 1978-80; Head, French, Teacher, German, Latin, Keswick School, Cumbria, 1980-88. Publications: Snakes and Girls, 1970; In All the Spaces on All the Lines, 1971;

Foreign Bodies, 1992; Cross Your Legs and Wish, 1994; These Jaundiced Loves (translation of Les Amours Jaunes, by Tristan Corbière), 1995. Various broadsheets. Contributions to: Books: Oxford Book of Christmas Poems; The Oxford Book of Verse in English Translation; PEN Anthologies; Peterloo Anthologies; Four Poetry and Audience Poets, 1971; 21 Years of Poetry & Audience, 1975; Adam's Dream, 1981; Between Cornets, 1984; Speak to the Hills, 1985; Voices of Cumbria, 1987; New Christian Poetry, 1990; Northern Poetry 2, The New Lake Poets, 1991; Poetry Book Society Anthology, 1992; The Forward Book of Poetry, 1994; Glitter When You Jump, 1996; Robinson (Figures Mythiques), 1996. Journals and newspapers: New Welsh Review; Observer; Times Literary Supplement; London Magazine; New Statesman; Critical Quarterly; Encounter; Ambit; Arts Council New Poetry Anthologies; Spectator; Lettres d'Europe; Independent; Poetry Review; Pennine Platform; Lancaster Literature Festival Anthologies; A Mandeville 15; Stand Magazine; Critical Survey; Blade; Modern Poetry in Translation 8 and 9 (translations); Le Quatrièm Tristan et l'Aile de Marcelle (essay); Tristan Cornière en 1995 (essay); Max and the Onion (essay), 1995. Address: 25 High Hill, Keswick, Cumbria CA12 5NY, England.

PILON Jean-Guy, b. 12 Nov 1930, St Polycarpe, Québec, Canada. Writer; Poet; Radio Producer and Broadcaster. Education: Law Graduate, University of Montreal, 1954. Appointments: Founder, 1959, Director, 1959-79, Review, Liberte; Head, Cultural Broadcast Service, 1970-85, Producer, Radio Canada. Publications: Poetry: La Fiancee du Matin, 1953; Les Cloitres de l'Ete, 1955; L'Homme et le Jour, 1957; La Mouette et le Large, 1960; Recours au Pays, 1961; Pour Saluer une Ville, 1963; Comme eau retenue, 1969, revised edition, 1985; Saisons pour la Continuelle, 1969; Silences pour une Souveraine, 1972. Contributions to: Various publications. Honours: Québec Poetry Prize, Prix David, 1956; Louise Labe Prize, 1969; France-Canada Prize, 1969; Van Lerberghe Prize, Paris, 1969; Governor-General of Canada Prize, 1970; Athanase David Prize, 1984; Officer, Order of Canada, 1987; Officier de l'Ordre national du Québec, 1988; Memberships: President, International Québec Writers Union; Royal Society of Canada; Officer de l'Ordre des Arts et des lettres (France), 1993. Address: 5724 Cote Saint-Antoine, Montréal, Québec H4A 1R9, Canada.

PINCHER (Henry) Chapman, b. 29 Mar 1914, Ambala, India. Freelance Writer; Novelist; Business Consultant. m. (1) 1 daughter, 1 son, (2) Constance Wolstenholme, 1965. Education: BSc Honours, Botany, Zoology, 1935. Appointments: Staff, Liverpool Institute, 1936-40; Royal Armoured Corps, 1940; Defence, Science and Medical Editor, Daily Express, 1946-73; Assistant Editor, Daily Express, Chief Defence Correspondent, Beaverbrook Newspapers, 1972-79. Publications: Breeding of Farm Animals, 1946; A Study of Fishes, 1947; Into the Atomic Age, 1947; Spotlight on Animals, 1950; Evolution, 1950; It's Fun Finding Out (with Bernard Wicksteed), 1950; Sleep and How to Get More of It, 1954; Sex in Our Time, 1973; Inside Story, 1978; Their Trade is Treachery, 1981; Too Secret Too Long, 1984; The Secret Offensive, 1985; Traitors - the Labyrinth of Treason, 1987; A Web of Deception, 1987; The Truth about Dirty Tricks, 1991; One Dog and Her Man, 1991; Pastoral Symphony, 1993; A Box of Chocolates, 1993; Life's a Bitch!, 1996. Novels: Not with a Bang, 1965; The Giantkiller, 1967; The Penthouse Comspirators, 1970; The Skeleton at the Villa Wolkonsky, 1975; The Eye of the Tornado, 1976; The Four Horses, 1978; Dirty Tricks, 1980; The Private World of St John Terrapin, 1982; Contamination, 1989. Honours: Granada Award, Journalist of the Year, 1964; Reporter of the Decade, 1966; Honorary DLitt, Newcastle-upon-Tyne, 1979. Address: The Church House, 16 Church Street, Kintbury, Near Hungerford, Berkshire RG15 0TR, England.

PINGET Robert, b. 19 July 1919, Geneva, Switzerland. Writer; Dramatist. Education: University of Geneva. Appointments: Former Barrister, later Painter; Teacher, French in England; literary career, 1951-. Publications: Fantoine et Agapa, 1951; Mahu et la Materiau, 1952; Le renard et la Loussoule, 1955; Graal Filibuste, 1956; Baga, 1958; Le Fiston, 1959; Lettre morte (play), 1959; La manivelle (play), 1960; Clope au dossier, 1961; Architruc (play), 1961; L'hypothese (play), 1961; L'inquisitore, 1962; Quelqu'un, 1965; Autour de Mortin (dialogue), 1965; Le libera, 1968; La passacaille, 1969; Fable, 1971 Identite, Abel et Bela (play), 1971; Paralchimie, 1973; Cette voix, 1975; L'Apocryphe, 1980; Monsieur Songe, 1982; Le harnais, 1984. Honours: Prix des Critiques, 1963; Prix Femina, 1965. Address: c/o Editions de Minuit, 7 rue Bernard-Palissey, 75006, Paris, France.

PINNER David John, b. 6 Oct 1940. Writer. m. Catherine, 23 Oct 1965, 1 son, 1 daughter. Education: Royal Academy of Dramatic Art, 1959-60. Publications: Stage plays: Dickon, 1965; Fanghorn, 1966; The Drums of Snow, 1969; The Potsdam Quartet, 1973; An Evening with the GLC, 1974; The Last Englishman, 1975; Lucifer's Fair, 1979; Screwball, 1985; The Teddy Bears' Picnic, 1988. TV plays: Juliet and Romeo, 1975; 2 Crown Courts, 1978; The Potsdam Quartet, 1980; The Sea Horse. Novels: Ritual, 1967; With My Body, 1968; Corgi, 1969; There'll Always Be an England, 1984. Address: Barnes, London, England.

PINNEY Lucy Catherine, b. 25 July 1952, London, England. Author; Journalist. m. Charles Pinney, 14 June 1975, 2 sons, 1 daughter. Education: BA Honours, English, Education, York University, 1973. Publications: The Pink Stallion, 1988; Tender Moth, 1994; Short story in The Best of the Fiction Magazine Anthology, 1986. Contributions to: Sunday Times; Observer; Daily Mail; Telegraph; Company; Cosmopolitan; Country Living; Country Homes and Interiors; She magazine. Honour: Runner-up, Betty Trask Prize, 1987. Membership: West Country Authors Association. Literary Agent: A P Watt Ltd. Address: Egremont Farm, Payhembury, Honiton, Devon EX14 0JA, England.

PINNOCK Winsome, b. 1961, London. Playwright. Education: BA, Goldsmiths College, London, 1982; MA, Birkbeck Coll, London. Appointments: Playwright-in-Residence, Tricycle Theatre, Kilburn, 1990, Royal Court Theatre, London, 1991, Clean Break Theatre Company, 1994. Publications: The Wind of Change, 1987; Leave Taking, 1988; Picture Palace, 1988; A Rock in Water, 1989; A Hero's Welcome, 1989; Talking in Tongues, 1991. TV Plays: Episodes in South of the Border and Chalkface Series. Screenplay: Bitter Harvest. Honours: Thames TV Award, 1991; George Devine Awd, 1991. Address: c/o Lemon, Unna and Durbridge, 24 Pottery Lane, Holland Park, London W11 4LZ, England.

PINSDORF Marion Katheryn, b. 22 June 1932, Teaneck, New Jersey, USA. Corporate Officer; Journalist; Senior Fellow in Communications. Div. Education: BA cum laude, Drew University, 1954; MA, 1967, PhD, 1976, New York University. Appointments: Vice President, 1971-77, Senior Consultant, 1988-90, Co-ordinator, Hill and Knowlton Inc; Vice President for Corporate Communications, Textron Inc, 1977-80, Ina Corporation, 1980-82; Adjunct Assistant Professor in Brazilian Studies, Brown University, 1979-; Member, Board of Directors, AMFAC Inc, 1982-88; Senior Fellow in Communications, Graduate School of Business, Fordham University, 1988-. Publications: Communicating When Your Company is Under Seige: Surviving Public Crises, 1987, new edition, 1997; German-Speaking Entrepreneurs: Builders of Business in Brazil, South, 1990. Contributions to: Academic journals and general publications. Memberships: Americas Society; Arthur Page Society; Authors Guild; Northeast Brazilianists. Address: 114 Leonia Avenue, Leonia, NJ 07605, USA.

PINSON William Meredith Jr, b. 3 Aug 1934, Fort Worth, Texas, USA. Educator; Executive; Minister. m. Bobbie Ruth Judd, 1 June 1955, 2 daughters. Education: BA, University of North Texas, 1955; MDiv, 1959, ThD, 1963, Southwestern Baptist Theological Seminary. Publications: Twenty Centuries of Great Preaching, 1970; Five Worlds of Youth, 1974; Applying the Gospel, 1975; Families with Purpose, 1978; Youth Affirm the Biblical Vicar and the Family, 1981; Word Topical Bible, 1981; Biblical View of the Family, 1981; Ready to Minister, 1984. Contributions to: Journal of Church and State; Southwestern Journal of Theology; Baptist Standard; Report From the Capitol. Honour: Distinguished Alumni Award, University of North Texas, 1980. Address: 333 North Washington, Dallas, TX 75246, USA.

PINTER Harold, b. 10 Oct 1930, London, England. Actor; Playwright; Author; Poet. m. Lady Antonia Fraser. Publications: Plays: The Room, 1957; The Birthday Party, 1957; The Dumb Waiter, 1957; The Hothouse, 1958; A Slight Ache, 1958; A Night Out, 1959; The Caretaker, 1959; Night School, 1960; The Dwarfs, 1960; The Collection, 1961; The Lover, 1962; Tea Party, 1964; The Homecoming, 1964; The Basement, 1966; Landscape, 1967; Silence, 1968; Old Times, 1970; Monologue, 1972; No Man's Land, 1974; Betrayal, 1978; Family Voices, 1980; A Kind of Alaska, 1982; Victoria Station, 1982; One for the Road, 1984; Mountain Language, 1988; The New World Order, 1991; Party Time, 1991; Moonlight, 1993. Screenplays: The Caretaker, 1962; The Servant, 1963; The Pumpkin Eater, 1963; The Quiller Memorandum, 1965; Accident, 1966; The Birthday Party, 1967;

The Go-Between, 1969; The Homecoming, 1969; Langrishe Go Down, 1970; A la Recherche de Temps Perdu, 1972; The Last Tycoon, 1974; The French Lieutenant's Woman, 1980; Betrayal, 1981; Victory, 1982; The Turtle Diary, 1984; The Hamdmaid's Tale, 1987; The Heat of the Day, 1988; Reunion, 1989; The Trial, 1989; The Comfort of Strangers, 1989. Honours: Evening Standard Drama Award, 1960; Best British Screenplay, Screenwriters Guild, 1963; Italia Prize, 1963; Best Screen Writing of Year, New York Film Critics, 1964; British Film Academy Award, 1964; Whitbread Award, 1967; Writers Guild Prize, Best Screenplay Award, 1971; Donatello Prize and Ennio Flaiano Award, Italy, 1982. Memberships: Fellow, Royal Society of Literature; Honorary Member, American Academy and Institute of Arts and Letters. Address: c/o Judy Daish Associates Ltd, 83 Eastbourne Mews, London W2 6LQ, England.

PIONTEK Heinz, b. 15 Nov 1925, Kreuzburg, Silesia, Germany. Writer; Poet. m. Gisela Dallman, 1951. Education: Theologisch-Philosophische Hochschule, Dillengen. Publications: Poetry: Die Furt, 1952; Die Rauchfahne, 1953; Miteiner Kranichfeder, 1962; Klartext, 1966; Früh im September, 1982; Helldunkel, 1987. Novels: Die mittleren Jahre, 1967; Dichterleben, 1976; Juttas Neffe, 1979. Anthology: Leid und Zeit Ewigkeit, 1987. Non-Fiction: Windrichtungen, 1963; Liebeserklarungen, 1969. Honours: Tukan Prize, 1971; Georg Büchner Prize, 1976; Werner Egk Prize, 1981. Address: Duffer Strasse 97, 8000 Munich 50, Germany.

PIRIE David Tarbat, b. 4 Dec 1946, Dundee, Scotland. Writer. m. Judith Harris, 21 June 1983, 1 son, 1 daughter. Education: University of York; University of London. Appointments: Tutor; Film Critic, Editor, Time Out Magazine, 1980-84. Publications: Heritage of Horror, 1974; Mystery Story, 1980; Anatomy of the Movies, 1981. Films: Rainy Day Women, 1984; Wild Things, 1988; Black Easter, 1993; Wildest Dreams, 1995; Element of Doubt, 1996; The Woman in White, 1997. TV: Never Come Back, BBC serial, 1989; Ashenden, BBC serial, 1990; Natural Lies, TV serial, 1991. Contributions to: Various journals. Honours: Drama Prize, New York Festival, 1985; Best Network Series Prize, Chicago Film Festival, 1990; Best TV Feature: Black Easter, Chicago Film Television Festival, 1996; Best TV Feature Film, Chicago Film Festival, 1996. Membership: Screenwriters Studio, Dartington Hall, 1990. Literary Agent: Stephen Durbridge. Address: c/o Lemon Unna and Durbridge, 24 Pottery Lane, London W11, England.

PIRSIG Robert Maynard, b. 6 Sept 1928, Minneapolis, Minnesota, USA. Author. m. (1) Nancy Ann James, 10 May 1954, div Aug 1978, 2 sons, (2) Wendy Kimball, 28 Dec 1978, 1 daughter. Education: BA, 1950, MA, 1958, University of Minnesota. Publications: Zen and the Art of Motorcycle Maintenance, 1974; Lila, 1991. Honours: Guggeneheim Fellowship, 1974; AAAL Award, 1979. Address: c/o Bantam Books, 1540 Broadway, New York, NY 10036, USA.

PISKOR Stanislaw, b. 13 Aug 1944, Poland. Writer. m. 29 Sept 1969, 1 son, 1 daughter. Education: Degree in History of Art, Adam Mickiewicz University, Poznan, 1969; Doctor, Philology, Silesian University, Katowice, 1985. Appointment: Editor-in-Chief, Studio magazine, 1981-93. Publications: Confessions, 1975; Dispute Over Poetry, 1977; The Moveable Country, 1980; The Polish Identity, 1988; On the Bridge of Europe, 1992; Transfiguracja, 1993. Plays: The Glass Pane, 1976; The Overflow, 1979; The Slaughter House, 1980. Contributions to: Magazines. Honours: Award of publisher Epoka, Warsaw, 1988; Award of Literary Foundation, Warsaw, 1988; Literary Award of Solidarity, Katowice, 1993. Memberships: Association of Polish Writers, Department Katowice, president; Association of Art Historians in Poland. Address: Ul Jaworznicka 38, 32-520 Jaworzno, Poland.

PISTORIUS Vladimir, b. 10 Jan 1951, Ostrava, Czechoslovakia. Editor. m. Jitka Pistoriusova, 17 Apr 1976, 1 son. Education: Graduated, Faculty of Mathematics and Physics, Charles University, Prague, 1974. Appointments: Directed KE-78, one of Czech samizdat book editions, 1978-89; Editor-in-Chief, Mlada fronta Publishers, 1990-. Publications: A prece, 1978; Jak se chyta slunce, 1981; Filkovi na kalhoty, 1984; Starnouci literatura, 1991. Contributions to: Kriticky sbornik; Literani noviny; Lidove noviny. Membership: Czech Writer's Society. Address: Skalecka 17, 170 00 Prague 7, Czechoslovakia.

PITCHER Harvey John, b. 26 Aug 1936, London, England. Writer. Education: BA, 1st Class Honours, Russian, Oxford University. Publications: Understanding the Russians, 1964; The Chekhov Play:

A New Interpretation, 1973; When Miss Emmie was in Russia, 1974; Chekhov's Leading Lady, 1979; Chekhov: The Early Stories, 1883-1888 (with Patrick Miles), 1982; The Smiths of Moscow, 1984; Lily: An Anglo-Russian Romance, 1987; In Russian translation: Muir and Merrieless: The Scottish Partnership that became a Household Name in Russia, 1994; Witnesses of the Russian Revolution, 1994. Contributions to: Times Literary Supplement. Address: 37 Bernard Road, Cromer, Norfolk NR27 9AW, England.

PITT Barrie William Edward, b. 7 July 1918, Galway, Ireland. Historian. m. (1) Phyllis Kate Edwards, 1 son, dec, (2) Sonia Deidre Hoskins, 1953, div 1971, (3) Frances Mary Moore, 1983. Appointments: Historical Consultant to the BBC series, The Great War, 1963. Publications: The Edge of Battle, 1958; Zeebrugge, St George's Day, 1918, 1958; Coronel and Falkland, 1960; The Last Act, 1962; Purnell's History of the Second World War (editor), 1964; Ballantine's Illustrated History of World Warr II (editor-in-chief), 1967; Purnell's History of the First World War (editor), 1969; Ballantine's Illustrated History of the Violent Century (editor-in-chief), 1971; British History Illustrated (editor), 1974-78; The Battle of the Atlantic, 1977; The Crucible of War: Western Desert, 1941, 1980; The Crucible of War: Year of Alamein, 1942, 1982; Special Squadron, 1983. Contributions to: Encyclopaedia Britannica; Sunday Times. Address: 10 Wellington Road, Taunton, Somerset TA1 4EG, England.

PITT David C(harles), b. 15 Aug 1938, Wellington, New Zealand. Sociologist; Writer. m. Carol Haigh, 13 Feb 1959, 3 sons, 4 daughters. Education: BA, University of New Zealand, 1961; BLitt, 1963, DPhil, 1965, MLitt, 1980, Oxford University. Appointments: Assistant Professor of Anthropology and Sociology, University of Victoria, British Columbia, 1966-67; Professor of Sociology and Head, Department of Sociology, University of Waikato, Hamilton, New Zealand, 1968-71; Professor of Sociology, Head, Department of Sociology, Chairman, European Studies Committee, University of Auckland, 1971-79; Charge de Recherches and Member of the Executive Council, Institut International de Recherches pour la Paix, Geneva, 1982-; Consultant to various world organizations. Publications: Tradition and Economic Progress in Samoa: A Case Study in the Role of Traditional Social Institutions in Economic Development, 1970; Historical Documents in Anthropology and Sociology, 1972; Emerging Pluralism (with C Macpherson), 1975; Social Dynamics of Development, 1976; Development from Below: Anthropologists and Development Situations (editor), 1976; Social Class in New Zealand (editor), 1977; Child Labour: A Threat to Health and Development (editor), 1981; Children and War (editor), 1983; Culture and Conservation, 1984; The Nature of United Nations Bureaucracies (editor), 1984; Rethinking Population, Environment and Development, 1986; Nuclear Free Zones (editor), 1987; New Ideas in Environmental Education (editor), 1988; Deforestation: Social Dynamics in Watersheds and Mountain Ecosystems (editor), 1988; The Future of the Environment (editor), 1988; The Anthropology of War and Peace (editor), 1989; Mountain Worlds in Danger (with Sten Nilsson), 1991. Contributions to: Professional journals. Memberships: International Sociological Association; International Union of Anthropological and Ethnological Sciences; Royal Anthropological Institute. Address: c/o Institut International de Recherches pour la Paix, 34 Boulevard du Pont d'Arve, Geneva 1205, Switzerland.

PITT David George, b. 12 Dec 1921, Musgravetown, Newfoundland, Canada. Author; University Professor (retired). m. Marion Woolfrey, 5 June 1946, 1 son, 1 daughter. Education: BA (Hons) English, Mt Allison University, 1946; MA, 1948, PhD, 1960, University of Toronto. Appointment: Professor of English Literature, Memorial University of Newfoundland, 1949-83. Publications: Elements of Literacy, 1964; Windows of Agates, 1966; Critcal Views on Canadian Writers: E J Pratt, 1969; Toward the First Spike: The Evolution of a Poet, 1982; Goodly Heritage, 1984; E J Pratt: The Truant Years, 1984; E J Pratt: The Master Years, 1987; Tales From the Outer Fringe, 1990. Honours: Medal for Biography, University of British Columbia, 1984; Artist of the Year, Newfoundland Arts Council, 1988; Honorary LLD, Mt Allison University, 1989. Memberships: Association of Canadian University Teachers of English; Humanities Association of Canada. Address: 7 Chestnut Place, St John's, Newfoundland A1B 2T1, Canada.

PITT-KETHLEY Fiona, b. 21 Nov 1954, Edgware, Middlesex, England. Writer; Poet. Education: BA Hons, Fine Art, Chelsea School of Art, 1976. Publications: The Perfect Man, 1984; The Tower of Glass, 1985; Gesta, 1986; Sky Ray Lolly, 1986; Private Parts, 1987; Journeys

to the Underworld, 1988; The Misfortunes of Nigel, 1991; The Literary Companion to Sex, 1992; The Pan Principle, 1994; The Literary Companion to Low Life, 1995; Double Act, 1996. Contributions to: Numerous magazines and newspapers including Times and Telegraph. Honours: Calouste Gulbenkian Award, 1995. Memberships: Chelsea Arts Club; Film Artistes Association. Address: 7 Ebenezer Road, Hastings, East Sussex TN34 3BS, England.

PITTOCK Murray George Hornby, b. 5 Jan 1962, Nantwich, England. Academic. m. Anne Grace Thornton Martin, 15 Apr 1989, 2 daughters. Education: MA, 1st Class, English Language and Literature, Glasgow University, 1983; Snell Exhibitioner, Balliol College, Oxford, 1983-86; DPhil, Oxford, 1986; British Academy Postdoctoral Research Fellow, University of Aberdeen, 1988-89. Appointments: Junior Research Fellow, Linacre College, Oxford, 1988-; Lecturer, University of Edinburgh, 1989-94; Reader in English Literature, University of Edinburgh, 1994-96; Chair in Literature, University of Strathclyde, 1996-. Publications: The Invention of Scotland, 1991; Clio's Clavers, 1992; Spectrum of Decadence, 1993; Poetry and Jacobite Politics, 1994; The Myth of the Jacobite Clans, 1995; Poetry and Jacobite Politics in Eighteenth Century Britain and Ireland, 1996. Contributions to: Over 100 articles to journals including: Victorian Poetry; Scottish Literary Journal; Irish University Review; Nineteenth-Century Fiction; British Journal for Eighteenth-Century Studies; Editor, Scottish Literay Journal; Press, radio and TV appearances, UK, USA. Honours: Society of Arts, Scotland, 1995. Winner, 1 of 10 1st Prizes, National Children's Writing Contest, 1973; Buchanan Prize, 1979; Bradley Medal, 1983; English-Speaking Union Scholar, 1984; BP Humanities Research Prize, Royal Society of Edinburgh, 1992; FSA Scot, 1995.Memberships: Council, Association for Scottish Literary Studies; Royal Historical Society, Fellow. Address: Department of English Studies, University of Strathclyde, Glasgow G1 1XH, Scotland.

PLACE Florence. See: NORMAN Geraldine.

PLAIN Belva, b. 9 Oct 1919, New York, New York, USA. Writer. m. Irving Plain, 14 June 1941, dec 1982, 3 children. Education: Barnard College. Publications: Evergreen, 1978; Random Winds, 1980; Eden Burning, 1982; Crescent City, 1984; The Golden Cup, 1987; Tapestry, 1988; Blessings, 1989; Harvest, 1990; Treasures, 1992; Whispers, 1993; Daybreak, 1994; The Carousel, 1995. Address: c/o Delacourte Press, 1540 Broadway, New York, NY 10036, USA.

PLANO Jack Charles, b. 25 Nov 1921, Merrill, Wisconsin, USA. Professor of Political Science Emeritus; Writer. m. Ellen L Ruehlow, 25 June 1954, 2 sons, 1 daughter. Education: AA, Merrill Commercial College, 1940; AB, Ripon College, 1949; MA, 1950, PhD, 1954, University of Wisconsin. Appointments: Assistant Professor, 1952-57, Associate Professor, 1957-63, Professor of Political Science, 1963-87, Chairman, Department of Political Science, 1979-84, Professor Emeritus, 1987-, Western Michigan University, Kalamazoo; Assistant State Director, Michigan Citizenship Clearing House, 1957-60; Co-Director, Associated Educators, Troy, Alabama, 1961-69; Visiting Fellow, Institute for the Study of International Organizations, University of Sussex, 1971-72; Managing Editor, Personality Press, 1990-. Publications: The Content of the Introductory International Politics Course: Basic Framework and Concepts, 1958; The American Political Dictionary (with Milton Greenberg), 1962, 10th edition 1997; The United Nations and the Indian-Pakistan Dispute, 1966; Forging World Order: The Politics of International Organization (with Roy Olton), 1967, 2nd edition, 1971; The International Relations Dictionary (with Roy Olton), 1969, 5th edition (with Lawrence Irving), 1996; Political Science Dictionary (with Milton Greenberg, Roy Olton, and Robert E Riggs), 1973; Dictionary of Political Analysis (with Robert E Riggs), 1973, 2nd edition (with Robert E Riggs and H S Robin), 1982; United Nations Capital Development Fund: Poor and Rich Worlds in Collision (with Marjon Vashti Kamara), 1974; Experiments in Undergraduate Teaching (co-author), 1976; The Latin American Political Dictionary (with Ernest E Rossi), 1980, 2nd edition 1993; The Public Administration Dictionary (with Ralph C Chandler), 1982, 2nd edition, 1988; The Soviet and East European Political Dictionary (with Barbara McCrea and George Klein), 1984; The United Nations: International Organization and World Politics (with Robert E Riggs), 1988, 2nd edition, 1993; Memoirs: Vol I, Fishhooks, Apples and Outhouses: Memories of the 1920's, 1930's and 1940's, 1991, Vol II, Life in the Educational Trenches: Memories of College and University Days (1946-1952), 1991, Vol III, Pulling the Weeds and Watering the Flowers (1952-1993), 1993. Honours: Several grants and awards. Memberships: Academy of Political Science; American Academy of

Political and Social Science; American Association for the United Nations; International Studies Association. Address: 705 Weaver Circle, Kalamazoo, MI 49006, USA.

PLANTE David (Robert), b. 4 Mar 1940, Providence, Rhode Island, USA. Writer. Education: University of Louvain, Belgium, 1959-60; BA, Boston College, 1961. Appointments: Writer-in-Residence, University of Tulsa, 1979-82; Visiting Fellow, University of Cambridge, 1984-85; L'Université de Québec à Montreal, 1990; Gorky Institute of Literature, Moscow, Russia, 1991. Publications: Fiction: The Ghost of Henry James, 1970; Slides, 1971; Relatives, 1974; The Darkness of the Body, 1974; Figures in Bright Air, 1976; The Family, 1978; The Country, 1981; The Woods, 1982; The Foreigner, 1984; The Catholic, 1986; The Native, 1988; The Accident, 1991; Annunciation, 1994; Non-Fiction: Difficult Women: A Memoir of Three, 1983. Contributions to: Anthologies and magazines. Honours: Henfield Fellow, University of East Anglia, 1975; British Arts Council Grant, 1977; Guggenheim Fellowship, 1983; American Academy and Institute of Arts and Letters Award, 1983. Address: 38 Montagu Square, London W1, England.

PLANTEY Alain b. 19 July 1924, Mulhouse, France; Author; Councellor of State; Diplomat; Chairman of The International Court of Arbitration, International Chamber of Commerce. m. Christiane Wioland, 4 daughters. Education: University of Bordeaux; LLD, University of Paris, 1949; Diploma, National School of Public Administration, Paris, 1949. Appointments: Diplomat; Councillor of State; Honorary Chairman, International Court of Arbitration, International Chamber of Commerce. Publications: Traite Pratique de La Fonction Publique, 1953, 3rd edition, 1971; Prospective de L'Etat Paris, 1974; La Fonction Publique Internationale Paris, 1977; La Negociation Internationale, 1980, 1994; International Civil Service, 1981; La Funcion Publica Internacional y Europea, 1982; De la Politique les Etats, 1987, 2nd edition, 1992; Tratado de Derecho Diplomatico, 1991; La Fonction Publique, Traite Général, 1992. Contributions to: Various journals and magazines: including: Le Monde. Honours: Award, Academy of Moral and Political Sciences, 1979; Award, Académie Française, 1982; Commander, Légion d'Honneur, Palmes Academiques. Memberships: French Academie des Sciences Morales et Politiques; Various professional organizations. Address: 6 Avenue Sully Prudhomme, Paris 75007, France.

PLANTINGA Alvin, b. 15 Nov 1932, Ann Arbor, Michigan, USA. Professor of Philosophy; Writer. m. Kathleen Ann DeBoer, 16 June 1955, 2 sons, 2 daughters. Education: AB, Calvin College, Grand Rapids, 1954; MA, University of Michigan, 1955; PhD, Yale University, 1958. Appointments: Instructor, Yale University, 1957-58; Associate Professor, Wayne State University, 1958-63; Professor, Calvin College, 1963-82; Fellow, Center for Advanced Study in the Behavioral Sciences, 1968-69; Visiting Fellow, Balliol College, Oxford, 1975-76; John A O'Brien Professor of Philosophy, 1982-, Director, Center for Philosophy of Religion, 1983-, University of Notre Dame, Indiana; Gifford Lecturer, University of Edinburgh, 1987. Publications: God and Other Minds, 1967; The Nature of Necessity, 1974; God, Freedom, and Evil, 1974; Does God Have a Nature?, 1980; Faith and Rationality, 1983; Warrant: The Current Debate, 1993; Warrant and Proper Function, 1993. Honours: Guggenheim Fellowship, 1971-72; National Endowment for the Humanities Fellowships, 1975-76, 1987, 1995-96; Honorary doctorates. Memberships: American Philosophical Association; President, Society of Christian Philosophers, 1983-86. Address: c/o Department of Philosophy, University of Notre Dame, Notre Dame, IN 46556, USA.

PLATE Andrea, (Andrea Darvi), b. 29 July 1952, Los Angeles, California, USA. Teacher; Writer. m. Thomas Plate, 22 Sept 1979, 1 daughter. Education: MA, Journalism, University of Southern California, Los Angeles; BA, English, University of California, Berkeley. Appointments: Assistant Professor, Communications Department, Fordham University, 1988-90; Senior Lecturer, Journalism, University of Southern California, 1990-92, Santa Monica College, 1993-; English Teacher, Oakwood School, 1994-. Publication: Secret Police, 1981. Contributions to: Periodicals. Address: 812 16th Street, #2, Santa Monica, CA 90403, USA.

PLATER Alan Frederick, b. 15 Apr 1935, Jarrow on Tyne, County Durham, England. Writer; Dramatist. m. (1) Shirley Johnson, 1958, div 1985, 2 sons, 1 daughter, (2) Shirley Rubinstein, 1986, 3 sons. Education: King's College, Durham, 1953-57; University of

Newcastle. Contributions to: Stage, screen, radio, television, anthologies and periodicals. Honours: Various stage, radio and television drama awards. Memberships: Royal Society of Literature, fellow; Royal Society of Arts, fellow; Writer's Guild of Great Britain, president, 1991-95. Address: c/o 200 Fulham Road, London SW10 9PN, England.

PLATT Charles, b. 1944. Author; Poet; Freelance Writer. Publications: The Garbage World, 1967; The City Dwellers, 1970; Highway Sandwiches (poetry), 1970; The Gas (poetry), 1970; Planet of the Voles, 1971; New Worlds 6 (editor with Michael Moorcock), 1973 (in USA as New Worlds 5, 1974); New Worlds 7 (editor with Hilary Bailey), 1974 (in US as New Worlds 6, 1975); Sweet Evil, 1977; Dream Makers: The Uncommon People Who Write Science Fiction, 1980. Address: c/o Gollancz, 14 Henrietta Street, London WC2E 8QJ, England.

PLAYER Corrie Lynne (Oborn), b. 14 Oct 1942, Ogden, Utah, USA. Journalist; Writer; Teacher. m. Gary Farnsworth Player, 5 sons, 3 daughters. Education: AA, Weber College; BA, 1964, MA, 1965, Stanford University. Publication: Anchorage Altogether, 1972, revised edition, 1977. Contributions to: Magazines and newspapers. Honours: Non-Fiction Book Awards, Oklahoma Writers Federation, 1986, 1988. Memberships: Oklahoma Writers Federation; League of Utah Writers; National Writers Club; National Foster Parents Association. Address: 429 400th South, Cedar City, UT 84720, USA.

PLAYER Trezevant. See: **YEATMAN Ted P.**

PLEIJEL Agneta, b. 26 Feb 1940, Stockholm, Sweden. Author. m. Maciej Zaremba, 27 Nov 1982, 1 daughter. Education: MA, 1970. Publications: Kollontay (play), 1979; Angels, Dwarfs (poetry), 1981; The Hill on the Black Side of the Moon (film), 1983; Eyes of a Dream (poetry), 1984; He Who Observeth the Wind (novel), 1987; Dog Star (novel), 1989. Contributions to: Several, mostly in Sweden/Scandinavia. Memberships: President, Swedish PEN Club. Address: Tantogatan 45, 117 42 Stockholm, Sweden.

PLIMPTON George (Ames), b. 18 Mar 1927, New York, New York, USA. Writer; Editor. m. (1) Freddy Medora Espy, 1968, div 1988, 1 son, 2 daughter, (2) Sarah Whitehead Dudley, 1991, 2 daughters. Education: AB, Harvard University, 1948; MA, Cambridge University, 1952. Appointments: Editor-in-Chief, Paris Review, 1953-, Paris Review Editions, 1965-72, 1987-; Instructor, Barnard College, 1956-58; Associate Editor, Horizon magazine, 1959-61, Harper's magazine, 1972-81; Director, American Literary Anthology programme, 1967-71; Host, various television specials. Publications: Rabbit's Umbrella, 1956; Out of My League, 1961; Paper Lion, 1966; The Bogey Man, 1968; Mad Ducks and Bears, 1973; One for the Record, 1974; Shadow-Box, 1976; One More July, 1976; Sports! (with Neil Leifer), 1978; A Sports Bestiary (with Arnold Roth), 1987; The X-Factor, 1990; The Best of Plimpton, 1990. Editor: Writers at Work, 9 volumes, 1957-92; American Journey: The Times of Robert Kennedy (with Jean Stein), 1970; Pierre's Book, 1971; The Fancy, 1973; Edie: An American Biography (with Jean Stein), 1982; D V (with Christopher Hemphill), 1984; The Paris Review Anthology, 1989; The Writer's Chapbook, 1989; Women Writers at Work, 1989; Poets at Work, 1989; The Norton Book of Sports, 1992; Chronicles of Courage (with Jean Kennedy Smith), 1992. Contributions to: Numerous publications. Honours: Distinguished Achievement Award, University of Southern California, 1967; Blue Pencil Award, Columbia Spectator, 1981; Mark Twain Award, International Platform Association, 1982; Chancellor's Award, Long Island University, 1986; L'Ordre des Arts et des Lettres, France, 1994. Memberships: American Pyrotechnics Association; Explorers Club; Linnean Society; Mayflower Descendants Society; PEN; National Football League Alumni Association; Pyrotechnics Guild International. Address: c/o Paris Review Inc, 541 East 72nd Street, New York, NY 10021, USA.

PLINGE Walter. See: **THURGOOD Nevil.**

PLOWDEN Alison, b. 18 Dec 1931, Simla, India. Writer. Publications: Over 16 books, 1971-96. Contributions to: Radio and television. Honours: Writers Guild of Great Britain Award; Best British Educational TV Script, 1972. Address: c/o John Johnson, Clerkenwell House, 45-47 Clerkenwell Green, London EC1R 0HT, England.

PLUCKROSE Henry Arthur, (Richard Cobbett), b. 23 Oct 1931, London, England. Teacher; Children's Writer. Education: St Mark and St John College, London, 1952-54; Institute of Education, London, 1958-60; FCP, College of Preceptors, 1976. Appointments: Teacher, Elementary School, Inner London, 1954-68; Head, Education, Prior Weston School, London, 1968-; Editor, Let's Go Series. Publications: Over 50 books, 1965-90. Address: 3 Butts Lane, Danbury, Essex, England.

PLUMB Sir John (Harold), b. 20 Aug 1911, Leicester, England. Professor of Modern English History Emeritus; Writer. Education: University College, Leicester; Christ's College, Cambridge; BA, University of London, 1933; PhD, University of Cambridge, 1936. Appointments: Ehrman Research Fellow, King's College, Cambridge, 1939-46; Fellow, 1946-, Steward, 1948-50, Tutor, 1950-59, Vice-Master, 1964-68, Master, 1978-82, Christ's College, Cambridge; University Lecturer in History, 1946-62; Reader in Modern English History, 1962-65, Professor of Modern English History, 1966-74, Professor Emeritus, 1974-, University of Cambridge; Various visiting professorships; Editor, History of Human Society, 1959-, Pelican Social History of Britain, 1982-; Historical Advisor, Penguin Books, 1960-92. Publications: English in the Eighteenth Century, 1950; West African Explorers (with C Howard), 1952; Chatham, 1953; Studies in Social History (editor), 1955; Sir Robert Walpole, 2 volumes, 1956, 1960; The First Four Georges, 1956; The Renaissance, 1961; Men and Places, 1962; Crisis in the Humanities, 1964; The Growth of Political Stability in England, 1675-1725, 1967; Death of the Past, 1969; In the Light of History, 1972; The Commercialisation of Leisure, 1974; Royal Heritage, 1977; New Light on the Tyrant, George III, 1978; Georgian Delights, 1980; Royal Heritage: The Reign of Elizabeth II, 1980; The Birth of a Consumer Society (with Neil McKendrick and John Brewer), 1982; Collected Essays: Vol I, The Making of a Historian, 1988, Vol II: The American Experience, 1989. Contributions to: Books and journals. Honours: Festschrift published in his honour, 1974; Knighted, 1982; Honorary doctorates. Memberships: British Academy, fellow; Royal Historical Society, fellow; Royal Society of Literature, fellow. Address: c/o Christ's College, Cambridge CB2 3BU, England.

PLUMME Don E. See: **KATZ Bobbi.**

PLUNKETT James, b. 21 May 1920, Dublin, Ireland. Novelist. Education: Dublin College of Music. Appointments: Senior Producer, Radio Telefis Eireann, 1974-85. Publications: Strumpet City, 1969; The Gems She Wore: A Book of Irish Places, 1972; Farewell Companions, 1977; The Circus Animals, 1990. Short Stories: The Trusting and the Maimed, Other Irish Stories, 1959; Collected Short Stories, 1977. Plays: Homecoming 1954; Big Jim, 1954; The Risen People, 1958; Radio Plays; TV Plays and Programmes. Other: Boy on the Back Wall and Other Essays, 1987. Honours: Jacob's Award (Television Feature), 1963, 1969; Yorkshire Poet Award, 1969; President, Irish Academy of Letters, 1980-82; Sunday Independent, Irish Life Award, Literature, 1990; Irish Butler Award, Literature, Irish-American Cultural Institute, 1993. Memberships: President, Irish Academy of Letters, 1980-81; Society of Irish Playwrights; Aosdana. Literary Agent: Peter Fraser and Dunlop Group, 503-4 the Chambers, Chelsea Harbour, Lots Road, London SW10 0XF. Address: 29 Parnell Road, Bray, County Wicklow, Ireland.

POAGUE Leland Allen, b. 15 Dec 1948, San Francisco, California, USA. Professor of English; Writer. m. Susan Aileen Jensen, 24 Aug 1969, 2 daughters. Education: BA, San Jose State College, 1970; PhD, University of Oregon, 1973. Appointments: Instructor, 1973-74, Assistant Professor, 1974-78, State University of New York at Geneseo; Visiting Assistant Professor, University of Rochester, 1977; Assistant Professor, 1978-81, Associate Professor, 1981-86, Professor of English, 1986-, Iowa State University. Publications: The Cinema of Frank Capra: An Approach to Film Comedy, 1975; The Cinema of Earnest Lubitsch: The Hollywood Films, 1978; Billy Wilder and Leo McCarey, 1980; Howard Hawks, 1982; Film Criticism: A Counter Theory (with William Cadbury), 1982; A Hitchcock Reader (editor with Marshall Deutelbaum), 1986; Another Frank Capra, 1994; Conversations with Susan Sontag (editor), 1995. Contributions to: Various journals. Address: c/o Department of English, Iowa State University, Ames, IA 50011, USA.

POCOCK Tom, (Thomas Allcot Guy Pocock), b. 18 Aug 1925, London, England. Author; Journalist. m. Penelope Casson, 26 Apr 1969, 2 daughters. Publications: Nelson and His World, 1968; Chelsea Reach, 1970; Fighting General, 1973; Remember Nelson, 1977; The Young Nelson in the Americas, 1980; 1945: The Dawn Came Up Like Thunder, 1983; East and West of Suez, 1986; Horatio Nelson, 1987;

Alan Moorehead, 1990; The Essential Venice, 1990; Sailor King, 1991; Rider Haggard and the Lost Empire, 1993; Norfolk, 1995; Edited, Travels of a London Schoolboy, 1996; Travels of a London Schoolboy, (editor),1996; A Thirst for Glory, 1996. Contributions to: Numerous newspapers and magazines. Literary Agent: Andrew Lownie. Address: 22 Lawrence Street, London SW3 5NF, England.

PODHORETZ Norman, b. 16 Jan 1930, Brooklyn, New York, USA. Editor; Writer. m. Midge Rosenthal Decter, 21 Oct 1956, 1 son, 3 daughters. Education: AB, Columbia University, 1950; BHL, Jewish Theological Seminary, 1950; BA, 1952, MA, 1957, Cambridge University. Appointments: Associate Editor, 1956-58, Editor-in-Chief, 1960-95, Editor-at-Large, 1995-, Commentary Magazine; Member, University Seminar on American Civilization, Columbia University, 1958; Editor-in-Chief, Looking Glass Library, 1959-60; Chairman, New Directions Advisory Committee, United States Information Agency, 1981-87; Senior Fellow, Hudson Institute, 1995-. Publications: Doings and Undoings: The Fifties and After in American Writing, 1964; The Commentary Reader (editor), 1966; Making It, 1968; Breaking Ranks, 1979; The Present Danger, 1980; Why We Were in Vietnam, 1982; The Bloody Crossroads, 1986. Contributions to: Periodicals. Honours: Fulbright Fellowship, 1950-51; Kellet Fellow, Cambridge University, 1952; Honorary LHD, Hamilton College, 1969, Yeshiva University, 1991, Boston University, 1995, Adelphi University, 1996; Honorary LLD, Jewish Theological Seminary, 1980. Membership: Council on Foreign Relations. Address: c/o Commentary Magazine, American Jewish Committee, 165 East 56th Street, New York, NY 10022, USA.

POGREBIN Letty Cottin, b. 9 June 1939, New York, New York, USA. Writer; Editor. m. Bertrand Pogrebin, 1963, 1 son, 2 daughters. Education: BA, Brandeis University, 1959. Appointments: Columnist for various periodicals, 1970-; Editor, MS magazine, 1971- . Publications: How to Make it in a Man's World, 1970; Getting Yours, 1975; Growing Up Free, 1980; Stories for Free Children (editor), 1982; Family Politics, 1983; Among Friends, 1986; Free to be...A Family (editor), 1987. Contributions to: Anthologies and periodicals. Honours: Emmy Award, 1974; Matrix Award, 1981. Memberships: Author's Guild; National Women's Political Caucus; Jewish Fund for Justice; Women's Action Alliance. Address: c/o Ms Magazine, 1 Times Square, New York, NY 10036, USA.

POHL Frederik (James MacCreigh), b. 26 Nov 1919, New York, New York, USA. Writer; Editor. Education: Public Schools. Appointments: Book Editor and Associate Circulation Manager, Popular Science Co, New York City, 1946-49; Literary Agent, New York City, 1949-53; Editor, Galaxy Publishing Co, New York City, 1960-69; Executive Editor, Ace Books, New York City, 1971-72; Science Fiction Editor, Bantam Books, New York City, 1973-79. Publications: Author or editor of over 45 books, 1953-95. Memberships: Author's Guild; Science Fiction Writers of America, President, 1974-76; World Science Fiction, President, 1980-82. Address: c/o World, 855 South Harvard Drive, Palatine, IL 60067, USA.

POIDEVIN Leslie Oswyn Sheridan, b. 28 Jan 1914, Cremorne, New South Wales, Australia. Medical Doctor (Gynaecologist and Obstetrician). m. Rosemarie Slaney Poole, 18 Sept 1946, 2 daughters. Education: Sydney Grammar School; Faculty of Medicine, Sydney University, 1932-37; MBBS, 1938; MRCOG, 1951, FRCOG (London), 1961; MD, 1961, MS, 1965, University of Adelaide. Appointments: Head of Department of Obstetrics, University of Adelaide, 1952-58. Publications: Caesarean Section Scars, 1965; Samurais and Circumcision, 1985; Goodbye Doctor, 1986; Doctor Goes Farming, 1987; The Lucky Doctor, 1988; Doctor in Heaven, 1989; Come In Doctor, 1990; And The Winner Is..., 1992. Contributions to: The Lancet, British Medical Journal, Journal of Obstetrics and Gynaecology of British Empire, Medical Journal of Australia, 1951-83. Address: 9 St Albans Drive, Burnside, South Australia 5066, Australia.

POIRIER Louis, (Julien Grace), b. 27 July 1910, St Florent le Vieil, Maine et Loire, France. Education: Ecole des Science, Politiques, 1933; Ecole Normale Superieure, 1934. Appointments: Professor, Numerous Public Schools in France; Assistant to Faculty, Caen University, 1935-47; Professor, Lycee Claude Bernard, Paris, 1947-70; Guest Professor, University of Wisconsin, USA, 1970; Writer, 1939-. Publications: Au château d'Angol, 1939; Un Beau Ténébreux, 1945; Liberto Grande, 1946; Le Rivage du Syrtes, 1951; Un Balcon un Forêt, 1958; Lettrines, 1967; La Presqu'ile, 1974; Les Eaux Etroites, 1976; En Lisant, en Ecrivant, 1981; La Forme d'une Ville, 1985;

Cannets du Grand Chemin, 1992. Honour: Prix Goncourt, 1951. Address: 61 Rue de Grenelle, 75007 Paris, France.

POIRIER Richard, b. 9 Sept 1925, Gloucester, Massachusetts, USA. Literary Critic. Education: University of Paris, 1946; BA, Amherst College, 1949; MA, Yale University, 1950; Fulbright Scholar, Cambridge University, England, 1952; PhD, Harvard University, 1960. Appointments: Williams College, 1950-52; Harvard University, 1955-62; Rutgers University, 1962-; Editor, Partisan Review, 1963-71, Raritan Quarterly, 1980-; Vice-President, Founder, Library of America, 1980-. Publications: Comic Sense of Henry James, 1960; In Defense of Reading (co-editor), 1962; A World Elsewhere, 1966; The Performing Self, 1971; Norman Mailer, 1976; Robert Frost: The Work of Knowing, 1977; The Renewal of Literature, 1987; Poetry and Pragmatism, 1992. Contributions to: Daedalus; New Republic; Partisan Review; New York Review; London Review of Books; Times Literary Supplement. Honours: Phi Beta Kappa, 1949; Fulbright Fellow, 1952; Bollingen Fellow, 1963; Guggenheim Fellowship, 1967; National Endowment for the Humanities Fellow, 1972; HHD, Amherst College, 1978; Award, American Academy of Arts and Letters, 1980; Literary Lion of New York, 1992. Memberships: Poets, Playwrights, Editors, Essayists and Novelists; American Academy of Arts and Sciences; Century Club. Address: 104 West 70th Street, 9B, New York, NY 10023, USA.

POL Lotte Constance van de, b. 11 May 1949, Enschede, Netherlands. Historian. m. Egmond Elbers, 15 Mar 1985, 2 daughters. Education: MA, History and English 1977, University of Amsterdam, 1996; phD, History, Erasmus University, Rotterdam. Appointments: Teacher of History, Hervormd Lyceum, Amsterdam, 1977-78; Rijks Pedagogische Academie (Teacher Training College), Amersfoort, 1977-81; Research Fellow, Department of History, Erasmus University, Rotterdam, 1982-88. Publications: Daar was laatst een meisje loos Nederlandse vrouwen als matrozen en soldaten: Een historisch onderzoek (co-author), 1981; F L Kersteman, De Bredasche Heldinne (co-author), 1988; The Tradition of Female Transvestism in Early Europe (co-author), 1989; Vrouwen in mannenkleren. De geschiedenis van een tegendraadse traditie: Europa 1500-1800 (co-author), 1989; Frauen in Männerkleidern: Weibliche Transvestiten und ihre Geschichte (co-author), 1990; Kvinnor i manskläder: En avvikande tradition, Europa 1500-1800 (co-author), 1995. Het Amsterdams Hoerdom: Prostitutie in de 17e, 1996. 1650-1750, 1995. Contributions to: Books and professional journals. Address: Jan van Scorelstraat 127, 3583 CM Utrecht, The Netherlands.

POLAND Dorothy Elizabeth Hayward, (Alison Farely, Jane Hammond), b. 3 May 1937, Barry, Wales. Author. Publications: As Alison Farely: The Shadows of Evil, 1963; Plunder Island, 1964; High Treason, 1966; Throne of Wrath, 1967; Crown of Splendour, 1968; The Lion and the Wolf, 1969; Last Roar of the Lion, 1969; Leopard From Anjou, 1970; King Wolf, 1974; Kingdom under Tyranny, 1974; Last Howl of the Wolf, 1975; The Cardinal's Nieces, 1976; The Tempestuous Countess, 1976; Archduchess Arrogance, 1980; Scheming Spanish Queen, 1981; Spain for Mariana, 1982; As Jane Hammond: The Hell Raisers of Wycombe, 1970; Fire and the Sword, 1971; The Golden Courtesan, 1975; Shadow of the Headsman, 1975; The Doomtower, 1975; Witch of the White House, 1976; Gunpowder Treason, 1976; The Red Queen, 1976; The Queen's Assassin, 1977; The Silver Madonna, 1977; Conspirator's Moonlight, 1977; Woman of Vengeance, 1977; The Admiral's Lady, 1978; The Secret of Petherick, 1982; The Massingham Topaz, 1983; Beware the King's Enchantress, 1983; Moon in Aries, 1984; Eagle's Talon, 1984; Death in the New Forest, 1984. Address: Horizons, 99 Dock View Road, Barry, Glamorgan, Wales.

POLE J(ack) R(ichon), b. 14 Mar 1922, England. Historian; Writer. m. Marilyn Louise Mitchell, 31 May 1952, div 1988, 1 son, 2 daughters. Education: BA, Oxford University, 1949; PhD, Princeton University, 1953; MA, Cantab, 1963. Appointments: Instructor, Princeton University, 1952-53; Assistant Lecturer to Lecturer in American History, University College, London, 1953-63; Reader in American History and Government, Cambridge University, Fellow of Churchill College, 1963-79, Vice Master, 1975-78; Fellow, Center for Advanced Study in the Behavioral Sciences, USA, 1969-70; Guest Scholar, Woodrow Wilson International Centre, Washington, DC, 1978-79; Rhodes Professor of American History and Institutions, Oxford University, 1979-89; Fellow, St Catherine's College, Oxford, 1979-; Senior Research Fellow, College of William and Mary, Virginia, 1991; Leverhulme Trust Emeritus Fellow, 1991-93. Publications:

Abraham Lincoln and the Working Classes of Britain, 1959; Abraham Lincoln, 1964; Political Representation in England and the Origins of the American Republic, 1966; The Advance of Democracy (editor), 1967; The Seventeenth Century: The Origins of Legislative Power, 1969; The Revolution in America: Documents of the Internal Development of America in the Revolutionary Era, (editor) 1971; The Meanings of American History (co-editor), 1971; Foundations of American Independence, 1763-1815, 1972; American Historical Documents (general editor), 1975; The Decision for American Independence, 1975; The Idea of Union, 1977; The Pursuit of Equality in American History, 1978, 2nd edition, revised, 1993; Paths to the American Past, 1979; The Gift of Government: Political Responsibility from the English Restoration to American Independence, 1983; Colonial British America: Essays in the New History of the Early Modern Era, (co-editor), 1983; The American Constitution: For and Against: The Federalist and Anti-Federalist Papers (editor), 1987; The Blackwell Encyclopedia of the American Revolution (Co-editor), 1991. Contributions to: Reference works and professional journals. Memberships: British Academy, Fellow; Royal Historical Society, Fellow. Address: 20 Divinity Road, Oxford OX4 1LJ, England.

POLIAKOFF Stephen, b. 1952, London, England. Dramatist; Director. m. Sandy Welch, 1983, 1 son, 1 daughter. Education: Westminster School; Cambridge University. Publications: Plays: Clever Soldiers, 1974; The Carnation Gang, 1974; Hitting Town, 1975; City Sugar, 1976; Strawberry Fields, 1978; Shout Across the River, 1978; The Summer Party, 1980; Favourite Nights, 1981; Breaking the Silence, 1984; Coming into Land, 1987; Playing with Trains, 1989; Sienna Red, 1992. Other: Films and television plays. Honours: Several awards and prizes. Address: 33 Donia Devonia Road, London N1 8JQ, England.

POLING-KEMPES Lesley Ann, b. 9 Mar 1954, Batavia, New York, USA. Writer. m. James Kempes, 31 May 1976, 1 son, 1 daughter. Education: BA cum laude, University of New Mexico, 1976. Publications: Harvey Girls: Women Who Opened The West, 1989; Canyon of Remembering, Novel, 1996; Valley of Shining Stone: The Story of Abiguiu, 1997. Contributions to: Puerta del Sol; Writer's Forum 16; Best of the West 3; Higher Elevations; Articles to New Mexico Magazine. Honour: Zia Award for Excellence, New Mexico Press Women, 1991. Literary Agent: Lois de la Haba. Address: PO Box 36, Abiquiu, NM 87510, USA.

POLLAND Madelaine Angela, (Frances Adrian), b. 31 May 1918, Kinsale, County Cork, Ireland. Novelist; Short Story Writer; Children's Fiction Writer. Appointment: Assistant Librarian, Hertfordshire, 1939-42, 1945-46. Publications: Children of the Red King, 1961; Beorn the Proud, 1962; The White Twilight, 1962; Chuiraquimba and the Black Robes, 1962; City of the Golden House, 1963; The Queen's Blessing, 1963; Flame over Tara, 1964; Thicker Than Water, 1964; Mission to Cathay, 1965; Queen Without Crown, 1965; Deirdre, 1967; The Little Spot of Bother (US edition as Minutes of a Murder), 1967; To Tell My People, 1968; Stranger in the Hills, 1968; Random Army (US edition as Shattered Summer), 1969; To Kill a King, 1970; Alhambra, 1970; A Family Affair, 1971; Package to Spain, 1971; Daughter to Poseidon (US edition as Daughter of the Sea, 1972; Prince of the Double Axe, 1976; Double Shadow (as Francis Adrian), 1977; Sabrina, 1979; All Their Kingdoms, 1981; The Heart Speaks Many Ways, 1982; No Price Too High, 1984; As It Was in the Beginning, 1987; Rich Man's Flowers, 1990; The Pomegranate House, 1992. Literary Agent: A P Watt Limited, 20 John Street, London, WC1N 2DR. Address: Edificio Hercules 634, Avenida Gamonal, Arroyo de La Miel, Malaga, Spain.

POLLARD Jane (Jane Jackson, Dana James), b. 22 Nov 1944, Goole, Yorkshire, England. Author. m. (3) Michael Pollard, 2 June 1992, 2 sons, 1 daughter. Publications: Historical Romances: Harlyn Tremayne, 1984; The Consul's Daughter, 1986; Contemporary Romance: Doctor in The Andes, 1984; Desert Flower, 1986; Doctor in New Guinea, 1986; Rough Waters, 1986; The Marati Legacy, 1986; The Eagle and the Sun, 1986; Heart of Glass, 1987; Tarik's Mountain, 1988; Snowfire, 1988; Pool of Dreaming, 1988; Dark Moon Rising, 1989; Love's Ransom, 1989; A Tempting Shore, 1992; Bay of Rainbows, 1993; Mystery: Deadly Feast, 1997; Historical Romance: A Place of Birds, 1997. Contributions to: Falmouth Packet; West Briton; Western Morning News; Woman's Way; Radio Cornwall; BFBS Gibraltar, GIB TV. Memberships: Executive, Royal Cornwall Polytechnic Society; Romantic Novelists Association; Society of Authors. Literary Agent: Dorothy Lumley, Dorian Literary Agency,

Upper Thornehill, 27 Church Street, St Marychurch, Torquay, Devon, TQ1 4QY. Address: 32 Cogos Park, Comfort Road, Mylor, Falmouth, Cornwall TR11 5SF, England.

POLLARD John (Richard Thornhill), b. 1914, United Kingdom. Retired Senior Lecturer in Classics. Publications: Journey to the Styx, 1955; Adventure Begins in Kenya, 1957; Africa for Adventure, 1961; African Zoo Man, 1963; Wolves and Werewolves, 1964, 2nd edition, 1991; Helen of Troy, 1965; Seers, Shrines and Sirens, 1965; The Long Safari, 1967; Virgil: The Aeneid Appreciation (with C Day-Lewis), 1969; Birds in Greek Life and Myth, 1977; Divination and Oracles: Greece, Civilization of the Ancient Mediterranean, 1986; No County to Compare, 1994. Address: The Yard, Red Wharf Bay, Anglesey, LL75 8RX, Wales.

POLLEY Judith Anne, (Valentina Luellen, Helen Kent, Judith Stewart), b. 15 Sep 1938, London, England. Author. m. Roy Edward Polley, 28 Mar 1959, 1 son. Education: High School, Belgravia and Maida Vale, London. Publications: About 50 Modern and Historical Romance novels, including: To Touch the Stars, 1980; Beloved Enemy, 1980; Don't Run From Love, 1981; Moonshadow, 1981; Prince of Deception, 1981; Beloved Adversary, 1981; Shadow of the Eagle, 1982; Silver Salamander, 1982; The Wind of Change, 1982; The Measure of Love, 1983; The Peaceful Homecoming, 1983; The Valley of Tears, 1984; Moonflower, 1984; Elusive Flame of Love, 1984; Mistress of Tanglewood, 1984; Black Ravenswood, 1985; The Lord of Darkness, 1985; Devil of Talland, 1985; Passionate Pirate, 1986; Where the Heart Leads, 1986; Love the Avenger, 1986; The Devil's Touch, 1987; My Lady Melisande, 1987; Dark Star, 1988; Love and Pride (Book 1), 1988; The Web of Love (Book 2), 1989; Winter Embers, Summer Fire, 1991; To Please a Lady, 1992; One Love, 1993; Hostage of Love, 1994; many foreign editions and translations. Contributions to: Woman's Weekly Library; Woman's Realm; Woman's Weekly Fiction series; Museum of Peace and Solidarity, Samarkand, Uzbekistan. Membership: Founding Member, English Romantic Novelists Association. Address: Calcada, 8150 Sao Braz de Alportel, Algarve, Portugal.

POLLITT Katha, b. 14 Oct 1949, New York, New York, USA. Writer; Poet; Editor. Div, 1 child. Education: BA, Harvard University, 1972; MFA, Columbia University, 1975. Appointments: Literary Editor, 1982-84, Contributing Editor, 1986-92, Associate Editor, 1992-, The Nation; Junior Fellow, Council of Humanities, Princeton University, 1984; Lecturer, New School for Social Research, New York City, 1986-90, Poetry Center, 92nd Street YMHA and WYHA, New York City, 1986-95. Publications: Antarctic Traveller, 1982; Reasonable Creatures: Essays on Women and Feminism, 1994. Contributions to: Journals and periodicals. Honours: National Book Critics Circle Award, 1983; I B Lavan Younger Poet's Award, Academy of American Poets, 1984; National Endowment for the Arts Grant, 1984; Guggenheim Fellowship, 1987; Whiting Fellowship, 1993. Address: 317 West 93rd Street, New York, NY 10025, USA.

POLLOCK John (Charles), b. 9 Oct 1923, London, England. Clergyman; Writer. m. Anne Barrett-Lennard, 4 May 1949. Education: Charterhouse, Godalming; BA, 1946, MA, 1948, Trinity College, Cambridge; Ridley Hall, Cambridge. Appointments: War Service, Coldstream Guards 1943-45, (Captain, Staff Supreme Commander, South East Asia); Assistant Master of History and Divinity, Wellington College, Berkshire, 1947-49; Ordained Anglican Deacon, 1951, Priest, 1952; Curate, St Paul's Church, Portman Square, London, 1951-53; Rector, Horsington, Somerset, 1953-58. Publications: Candidate for Truth, 1950; A Cambridge Movement, 1953; The Cambridge Seven, 1955, new edition, 1996; Way to Glory: The Life of Havelock of Lucknow, 1957, revised edition, 1996; Shadows Fall Apart, 1958; The Good Seed, 1959; Earth's Remotest End, 1960; Hudson Taylor and Maria, 1962, new edition, 1996; Moody Without Sankey, 1963, new edition, 1995; The Keswick Story, 1964; The Christians from Siberia, 1964; Billy Graham, 1966, revised edition, 1969; The Apostle: A Life of Paul, 1969, revised edition, 1985; Victims of the Long March, 1970; A Foreign Devil in China: The Life of Nelson Bell, 1971, new edition, 1988; George Whitefield and the Great Awakening, 1972; Wilberforce, 1977, new edition, 1988; Billy Graham: Evangelist to the World, 1979; The Siberian Seven, 1979; Amazing Grace: John Newton's Story, 1981; The Master: A Life of Jesus, 1984, new editions, 1992, 1996; Billy Graham: Highlights of the Story, 1984; Shaftesbury: The Poor Man's Earl, 1985, new edition, 1990; A Fistful of Heroes: Great Reformers and Evangelists, 1988; John Wesley, 1989; On Fire for God: Great Missionary Pioneers, 1990; Fear No Foe: A Brother's

Story, 1992; Gordon: The Man Behind the Legend, 1993. Contributions to: Reference works and religious periodicals. Membership: English Speaking Union Club. Address: Rose Ash House, South Molton, Devonshire EX36 4RB, England.

POLOMÉ Edgar (Ghislain) C(harles), b. 31 July 1920, Brussels, Belgium (US citizen, 1966). Professor of Liberal Arts (retired); Author. m. (1) Julia Joséphine Schwindt, 22 June 1944, dec 29 May 1975, 1 son, 1 daughter, (2) Barbara Baker Harris, 11 July 1980, div Jan 1991, (3) Sharon Looper Rankin, 8 Feb 1991. Education: BA, 1940, PhD, 1949, Free University of Brussels; MA, Catholic University of Louvain, 1943. Appointments: Professor of Germanic Languages, Athénée Adolphe Max, Brussels, 1942-56; Professor of Dutch, Belgian Broadcasting Corp, Brussels, 1954-56; Professor of Linguistics, University of the Belgian Congo, 1956-61; Visiting Associate Professor, 1961-62, Professor of Germanic, Oriental and African Languages and Literatures, 1961-90, Director, Center for Asian Studies, 1962-72, Christie and Stanley Adams Jr Centennial Professor of Liberal Arts, 1984-90, University of Texas at Austin; Co-editor, 1973-, Managing Editor, 1987-, Journal of Indo-European Studies; Co-Editor, Mankind Quarterly, 1980-. Publications: Swahili Language Handbook, 1967; Language Surveys in the Developing Nations (editor with Sirarpi Ohannessian and Charles Ferguson), 1974; Linguistics and Literary Studies in Honor of Archibald A Hill (editor with M A Jazayery and Werner Winter), 1976; Language in Tanzania (editor with C P Hill), 1980; Man and the Ultimate: A Symposium (editor), 1980; The Indo-Europeans in the Fourth and Third Millennia (editor), 1982; Language, Society and Paleoculture, 1982; Essays on Germanic Religion, 1989; Guide to Language Change (editor), 1990; Reconstructing Languages and Cultures (editor), 1992. Contributions to: Scholarly books and professional journals. Honour: Fulbright-Hays Scholar, University of Kiel, 1968. Memberships: American Anthropological Association; American Institute of Indian Studies; American Oriental Society; Indogermanische Gesellschaft; Linguistics Society of America; Modern Language Association; Societas Linguistica Europea; Société de Linguistique de Paris. Address: 2701 Rock Terrace Drive, Austin, TX 78704, USA.

POLONSKY Antony (Barry), b. 23 Sept 1940, Johannesburg, South Africa. Lecturer in International History; Writer. Education: BA, University of the Witwatersrand, 1960; MA, DPhil, Oxford University, 1967. Appointments: Lecturer in East European History, University of Glasgow, 1968-70; Lecturer in International History, London Schools of Economics and Political Science, 1970-, London University, 1981-. Publications: Politics in Independent Poland, 1972; The Little Dictator, 1975; The Great Powers and the Polish Question, 1976; The Beginnings of Communist Rule in Poland (with B Druckier), 1978; The History of Poland since 1863 (co-author), 1981; My Brother's Keeper?: Recent Polish Debates on the Holocaust, 1990; Jews in Eastern Poland and the USSR (editor with Norman Davies), 1991; From Shtetl to Socialism: Studies from Polin, 1994. Contributions to: Professional journals. Address: 27 Dartmouth Park Road, London NW5, England.

POLUNIN Nicholas (Vladimir), b. 26 June 1909, Hammonds Farm, Checkendon, Oxfordshire, England. Environmentalist; Writer; Editor; Foundation President. m. Helen Eugenie Campbell, 3 Jan 1948, 2 sons, 1 daughter. Education: BA, First Class Honours, 1932, MA, 1935, DPhil, 1935, DSc, 1942, Christ Church, Oxford; MS, Yale University, 1934. Appointments: Fellow, Harvard University, 1950-54; Guest Professor, University of Geneva, 1959-61, 1975-76; Professor of Botany and Ecology, University of Ife, Ibadan, Nigeria, 1962-66; Founder-Editor, Biological Conservation, 1967-74, Environmental Conservation, 1974-95; President, Foundation for Environmental Conservation, 1975-; World Council for the Biosphere, 1984-; Originator of first Biosphere Day, 21 Sept 1991, subsequently held yearly on the same date worldwide. Publications: Author of more than 600 scientific papers, editorials, reviews and books; Editor of more than 30 further books; World Who Is Who and Does What in Environment and Conservation (editor), 1996. Honours: Many awards and prizes, including Commander of the order of the British Empire, 1976; International Environment Prize. Address: Foundation for Environmental Conservation, Floors 7 & 8, Chemin Taverney, 1218 Grand-Saconnex, Geneva, Switzerland.

PONDER Patricia. See: MAXWELL Patricia Anne.

POOLE Josephine. See: HELYAR Jane Penelope Josephine.

POOLE Julian. See: MAY Stephen James.

POPE Dudley Bernard Egerton, b. 29 Dec 1925, Kent, England. Author. m. Kathleen Patricia Hall, 17 Mar 1954, 1 daughter. Education: Ashford Grammer School. Publications: The Ramage Series (18 volumes), the York series (5 volumes), The Battle of the River Plate, 1956; 73 North, 1958; England Expects, 1959; At 12 Mr Byng Was Shot, 1962; The Black Ship, 1963; Ramage Series includes: Ramage's Trial, 1984; Ramage's Challenge, 1985; Ramage and the Dido, 1989. Address: c/o Campbell Thomson and McLaughlin, 31 Newington Green, London N16 9PU, England.

POPE Pamela Mary Alison, b. 26 Apr 1931, Lowestoft, Suffolk, England. Novelist. m. Ronald Pope, 3 Apr 1954, 2 daughters. Education: Newland High School, Hull. Publications: The Magnolia Seige, 1982; The Candleberry Tree, 1982; Eden's Law, 1983; The Wind in the East, 1989; The Rich Pass By, 1990; Neither Angels Nor Demons, 1992; A Collar of Jewels, 1994. Contributions to: Good Housekeeping; Woman; Woman's Realm; Vanity Fair; True; Loving; Hampshire Magazine; Hampshire Life; London Evening News. Memberships: Romantic Novelists Association; Society of Women Writers and Journalists. Address: 1 Rhiners Close, Sway, Lymington, Hampshire, SO41 6BZ.

POPESCU Christine (Christine Pullein-Thompson), b. 30 Oct 1930, London, England. Author. m. Julian Popescu, 6 Oct 1954, 2 sons, 2 daughters. Appointment: Speaker, Eastern Arts, 1984. Publications: 95 books for children including Phantom Horse series, 1956; Pony Patrol series 1970's; Black Pony Inn series; Father Unknown, 1980; A Home for Jessie series, 1986; Stay at Home Ben, Careless Ben, 1987; The Road Through the Hills, 1988; Across the Frontier, 1990; The Long Search, 1991; I Want That Pony, 1993; Collection: Horse and Pony Stories. Contributions to: Riding magazines. Memberships: PEN; Society of Authors; Eastern Arts; The Book Trust; Chairman Mellis Parish Council. Literary Agent: Jennifer Luithlen Agency. Address: The Old Parsonage, Mellis, Eye, Suffolk, IP23 8EE, England.

PORAD Francine Joy, b. 3 Sept 1929, Seattle, Washington, USA. Poet; Painter. m. Bernard L Porad, 12 June 1949, 3 sons, 3 daughters. Education: BFA, University of Washington, 1976. Appointment: Editor, Brussels Sprout, Haiku Journal, 1988-95, Red Moon Anthologies, 1996-; Co-editor, Sunlight Through Rain Anthology, 1996. Publications: Pen and Inklings, 1986; Connections, 1986; After Autumn Rain, 1987; Blues on the Run, 1988-95; Free of Clouds, 1989; Without Haste, 1990; Round Renga Round, 1990; A Mural of Leaves, 1991; Hundreds of Wishes, 1991; Joy is My Middle Name, 1993; The Patchwork Quilt, 1993; Waterways (edited by Leroy Gorman, 1995; All Eyes, 1995; Ladles and Jellyspoons, 1996; Extended Wings, 1996. Contributions to: Leading Haiku journals in the USA, Canada, Croatia, Australia, Japan, England and Romania, Croatia and Australia, (total of 60 poetry publications). Honours: Cicada Chapbook Award, 1990; San Francisco International Haiku Honorable Mention, 1991; International Tanka Awards (3) 1991; International Tanka Awards, 1992, 1993; 1st Prize, Poetry Society of Japan International Tanka Competition, 1993; Haiku Society of America Merit Book Award, 1994; Winner, Haiku Oregon PEN Women Award, 1995. Memberships: Haiku Society of America, president, 1993-95; Association of International Renku; National League of American Pen Women. Address: 6944-SE 33rd, Mercer Island, WA 98040, USA.

PORÉE-KURRER Philippe Lucien-Marie, b. 30 Apr 1954, Fécamp, France. Writer. m. Marylis DuFour, 14 Feb 1976, 4 sons, 2 daughters. Publications: Les Portes du Paradis, 1986; Le Retour de l'Orchidée, 1990; La Promise du Lac, 1992; La Quête de Nathan Barker, 1994; Shalóm, 1996. Contributions to: Jerusalem Post; DeVoir. Honour: Prix du Public, Québec, 1993. Membership: UNEQ. Address: 17 Avenue Garry, Blenheim, Ontario N0P 1A0, Canada.

PORTAL Ellis. See: POWE Bruce Allen.

PORTER Bern(ard Harden), b. 14 Feb 1911, Porter Settlement, Maine, USA. Writer. Education: BS, Colby College, 1932; ScM, Brown University, 1933. Publications: Author, 86 books including: Dieresis, 1976; The Wastemaker, 1980; I've Left, 1982; The Book of Do's, 1984; Here Comes Everybody's Don't Book, 1984; Sweet End, 1984; Last Acts, 1985; Dear Me, 1985; Gee-Whizzels, 1986; H L Mencken: A Bibliography, 1987; First Publications of F Scott Fitgerald, 1987; Sounds That Arouse, 1992. Contributions to: Various magazines, 1932-89. Honours: Carnegie Authors Award, 1976; PEN Award, 1976; National Endowment for the Arts Award, 1981. Memberships: Fellow,

Society of Programmed Instruction, 1970-; Maine Writers and Publishers Alliance, 1980-. Address: 50 Salmond Street, Belfast, ME 04915, USA.

PORTER Bernard (John), b. 5 June 1941, Essex, England. Professor of Modern History; Writer. m. Deidre O'Hara, 29 July 1972, 1 son, 2 daughters. Education: BA, 1963, MA, PhD, 1967, Corpus Christi College, Cambridge. Appointments: Fellow, Corpus Christi College, Cambridge, 1966-68; Lecturer, 1968-78, Senior Lecturer, 1978-87, Reader, 1987-92, University of Hull; Professor of Modern History, University of Newcastle, 1992-. Publications: Critics of Empire: British Radical Attitudes to Colonialism in Frica 1896-1914, 1968; The Lion's Share: A Short History of British Imperialism 1850-1970, 1976, 2nd edition, revised 1984; The Refugee Question in Mid-Victorian Politics, 1979; Britain, Europe and the World 1850-1982: Delusions of Grandeur, 1983, 2nd edition, 1987; The Origins of the Vigilant State: The London Metropolitan Police Special Branch Before the First World War, 1987; Plots and Paranoia: A History of Political Espionage in Britain 1790-1988, 1989; Britannia's Burden: The Political Development of Britain 1857-1990, 1994. Contributions to: Professional journals. Address: c/o Department of History, University of Newcastle, Newcastle upon Tyne, NE 7RU, England.

PORTER Brian (Ernest), b. 5 Feb 1928, Seasalter, Kent, England. Lecturer; Writer. Education: BSc, 1954, PhD, 1962, London School of Economics and Political Science. Appointments: Lecturer in Political Science, University of Khartoum, 1963-65; Lecturer, 1965-71, Senior Lecturer in International Politics, 1971-85, University College, Aberystwyth; Acting Vice-Counsel, Muscat, 1967; Honorary Lecturer in International Relations, University of Kent, Canterbury, 1984-. Publications: Britain and the Rise of Communist China, 1967; The Aberystwyth Papers: International Politics 1919-1969 (editor), 1972; The Reason of States (joint author), 1982; Home Fires and Foreign Fields: British Social and Military Experience in the First World War (joint author), 1985; The Condition of States (joint author), 1991; Martin Wright's International Theory (co-editor), 1991. Address: Rutherford College, University of Kent, Canterbury, Kent, England.

PORTER Burton F(rederick), b. 22 June 1936, New York, New York, USA. Professor of Philosophy; Academic Dean; Writer. m. (1) Susan Jane Porter, 10 May 1966, div 1974, 1 daughter, (2) Barbara Taylor Metcalf, 31 Dec 1980, 1 son, 1 stepdaughter. Education: BA, University of Maryland, 1959; Postgraduate Studies, Oxford University, 1962; PhD, St Andrews University, Scotland, 1969. Appointments: Assistant Professor, University of Maryland Overseas Division, London, 1966-69; Associate Professor, King's College, Wilkes-Barre, Pennsylvania, 1969-71; Professor of Philosophy, Russell Sage College, Troy, New York, 1971-87, rexel University, 1987-91; Dean of Arts and Sciences, Western New England College, Springfield, Massachusetts, 1991-. Publications: Deity and Morality, 1968; Philosophy: A Literary and Conceptual Approach, 1974, 3rd edition, 1995; Personal Philosophy: Perspectives on Living, 1976; The Good Life: Alternatives in Ethics, 1980, 3rd edition, 1994; Reasons for Living: A Basic Ethics, 1988; Religion and Reason, 1993. Contributions to: Professional journals. Honour: Outstanding Educator of America, 1973. Memberships: American Philosophical Association; Modern Language Association. Address: c/o Office of the Dean of Arts and Sciences, Western New England College, Springfield, MA 01119, USA.

PORTER Catherine Marjorie, b. 27 June 1947, Oxford, England. Writer; Translator. 1 son, 1 daughter. Education: BA, Hons, Russian, Czech, School of Slavonic Studies, University of London, 1970. Publications: Fathers and Daughters, 1976; Alexandra Kollontai: A Biography, 1980; Blood and Laughter: Images of the 1905 Revolution, 1983; Moscow in World War 2, 1987; Women in Revolutionary Russia, 1987; Larissa Reisner: A Biography, 1988. Translations: Love of Worker Bees, 1977; A Great Love, 1981; Ship of Widows, 1985; Sofia Tolstoya's Diary, 1985; Arise and Walk, 1990; The Best of Ogonoyok, 1990; Little Vera, 1990. Contributions to: Independent; Guardian; New Statesman and Society; Independent on Sunday. Honours: Various translation awards. Membership: Society of Authors. Address: c/o Curtis Brown Ltd, Haymarket House, 28-29 Haymarket, London SW1Y 4SP, England.

PORTER Joshua Roy, b. 1921, England. Theologian; Writer. Appointments: Fellow, Chaplain and Tutor, Oriel College, Oxford and University Lecturer in Theology, Oxford University, 1949-62; Canon and Prebendary of Wightring, Chichester Cathedral and Theological Lecturer, 1965-88; Dean, Faculty of the Arts 1968-71, Department

Head and Professor of Theology 1972-86, University of Exeter. Publications: Eight Oxford Poets (with J Heath-Stubbs and S Keyes), 1941; Poetry from Oxford in War-Time (with W Bell) 1944; World in the Heart, 1944; Promise and Fulfilment (with F F Bruce), 1963; Moses and Monarchy, 1963; The Extended Family in the Old Testament, 1967; A Source Book of the Bible for Teachers (with R C Walton), 1970; Proclamation and Presence (editor with J I Durham), 1970; The Non-Juring Bishops, 1973; The Journey to the Other World (with H R E Davidson), 1975; The Book of Leviticus, 1976; Animals in Folklore (editor with W D M Russell), 1978; The Monarchy, the Crown and the Church, 1978; Tradition and Interpretation (with G W Anderson), 1979; A Basic Introduction to the Old Testament (with R C Walton), 1980; Folklore Studies in the Twentieth Century (co-editor), 1980; Divination and Oracles (with M Loewe and C Blacker), 1981; The Folklore of Ghosts (with H R E Davidson), 1981; Israel's Prophetic Tradition (co-author), 1982; Tracts for Our Times (co-author), 1983; The Hero in Tradition and Folklore (with C Blacker), 1984; Arabia and the Gulf: From Traditional Society to Modern States (with I Netton), 1986; Schöpfung und Befreiung, co-author, 1989; Synodical Government in the Church of England, 1990; Christianity and Conservatism, co-author, 1990; Oil of Gladness, 1993; Boundaries and Thresholds (with H R E Davidson), 1993; World Mythology, 1993; The Illustrated Guide to the Bible, 1995. Memberships: Wiccamical Canon and Prebendary of Exceit, Chichester Cathedral, 1988-; Society for Old Testament Study, President, 1983; Society of Biblical Literature; Folklore Society, President, 1976-79; Prayer Book Society, Vice-Chairman, 1987-96. Address: 36 Theberton Street, Barnsbury, London N1 OQX, England.

PORTER Michael E, b. 23 May 1947, Ann Arbor, Michigan, USA. Advisor of Business Administration; Writer. m. Deborah Zylberberg, 26 Oct 1985, 2 daughters. Education: BSE, Princeton University, 1969; MBA,1971, PhD, 1973, Harvard University. Appointments: Assistant Professor, 1973-77, Associate Professor, 1977-82, Professor of Business Administration 1982-90, C Roland Christensen Professor of Business Administration, 1990-, Harvard University; Consultant to various businesses and governments. Publications: Interbrand Choice, Strategy, and Bilateral Market Power, 1976; Studies in Canadian Industrial Organization (with A M Spence, R E Caves and J M Scott), 1977; Competitive Strategy: Techniques for Analyzing Industries and Competitors, 1980; Competition in the Open Economy (with A M Spence and R E Caves), 1980; Cases in Competitive Strategy, 1982; Competitive Advantage: Creating and Sustaining Superior Performance, 1985; Business Policy: Text and Cases (with C R Christensen, K R Andrews, R L Hammermesch, and J L Bower), 6th edition, 1986; Competition in Global Industries (editor), 1986; The Competitive Advantage of Nations, 1990; Upgrading New Zealand's Competitive Advantage (with Graham T Crocombe and Michael J Enright), 1991; Strategy: Seeking and Securing Competitive Advantage (editor with Cynthia A Montgomery), 1991; Advantage Sweden (with Orjan Solbell and Ivo Zander), 1991; International Wettbewerbsvorteile: Ein Strategisches Konzept für die Schweiz (with Silvio Borner, Rolf Weder, and Michael J Enright), 1991; Capital Choices: Changing the Way America Invests in Industry (editor), 1992. Contributions to: Professional journals and general publications. Honours: McKinsey Foundation Awards, 1979, 1987; Graham and Dodd Award, Financial Analysts Federation, 1980; International Academy of Management Fellow, 1985; George F Terry Award, 1985, Fellow 1988, Academy of Management; Distinguished Professional Award, Society of Competitor Intelligence Professionals, 1989; Charles Coolidge Parlin Award, American Marketing Association, 1991; Honorary doctorates. Memberships: American Economic Association; American Marketing Association; Phi Beta Kappa; Royal Academy of Engineering Sciences; Sigma Xi; Tau Beta Pi. Address: c/o School of Business, Harvard University, Aldrich 200, Boston, MA 02163, USA.

PORTER Peter Neville Frederick, b. 16 Feb 1929, Brisbane, Queensland, Australia. Writer; Poet. m. Jannice Henry, 1961, dec 1974, 2 daughters. Publications: Once Bitten, Twice Bitten, 1961; Penguin Modern Poets 2, 1962; Poems, Ancient and Modern, 1967; A Porter Folio, 1969; The Last of England, 1970; Preaching to the Converted, 1972; After Martial (translator), 1972; Jonah (with Arthur Boyd), 1973; The Lady and the Unicorn, 1975; Living in a Calm Country, 1975; New Poetry I (joint editor), 1975; The Cost of Seriousness, 1978; English Subtitles, 1981; Collected Poems, 1983; Fast Forward, 1984; Narcissus (with Arthur Boyd), 1985; Possible Worlds, 1989; The Chain of Babel, 1992. Honour: Duff Cooper Prize, 1983. Address: 42 Cleveland Square, London W2, England.

PORTIS Charles McColl, b. 28 Dec 1933, El Dorado, Arkansas, USA. Writer. Education: BA, University of Arkansas, 1958. Publications: Novels: Norwood, 1966; True Grit, 1968; The Dog of the South, 1979; Masters of Atlantis, 1985; Gringos, 1991. Address: 7417 Kingwood, Little Rock, AR 72207, USA.

PORTOCALA Radu, b. 27 Mar 1951, Bucharest, Romania. Writer; Journalist. m. Delphine Beaugonin, 21 Dec 1987, 2 daughters. Education: Master of International Relations, Paris, 1986; BA, Romanian, Paris, 1986. Publications: Autopsie Du Coup D'Etat Roumain, 1990; Câlâtorie in Cusca Hidrelor, 1994; La Chute Dans L'Enthousiasme, 1995; Several volumes of poetry in Romanian. Contributions to: Le Point; Est & Ouest; Cuvintul, Bucharest; Voice of America; Radio France Internationale. Address: 7 Rue Du Docteur Roux, 75015 Paris, France.

PORTWAY Christopher (John), b. 30 Oct 1923, Halstead, Essex, England. Travel Journalist; Author; Novelist; Travel Correspondent. m. Jaroslava Krupickova, 4 Apr 1957, 1 son, 1 daughter. Publications: Journey to Dana, 1955; The Pregnant Unicorn, 1969; All Exits Barred, 1971; Corner Seat, 1972; Lost Vengeance, 1973; Double Circuit, 1974; The Tirana Assignment, 1974; The Anarchy Pedlars, 1976; The Great Railway Adventure, 1983; Journey Along the Spine of the Andes, 1984; The Great Travelling Adventure, 1985; Czechmate, 1987; Indian Odyssey, 1993; A Kenyan Adventure, 1993; Pedal for Your Life, 1996. Contributions to: Daily Telegraph; Country Life; Lady; Railway Magazine; In-Flight Magazines; Glasgow Herald; Scotsman; Liverpool Daily Post. Various holiday and travel magazines including: Morning and Leisure Magazine. Honours: TD; FRGS; Winston Churchill Fellow, 1993. Address: 22 Tower Road, Brighton BN2 2GF, England.

POSNER Gerald, b. 20 May 1954, San Francisco, California, USA. Attorney; Writer. m. Trisha D Levene, Apr 1984. Education: BA, University of California, 1972-75; JD, Hastings College of Law, 1975-78. Publications: Mengele: The Complete Story, 1986; Warlords of Crime, 1988; Bio-Assassins, 1989; Hitler's Children, 1991; Case Closed, 1993. Contributions to: New York Times; New Yorker; Chicago Tribune; US News & World Report. Honour: Pulitzer Finalist, 1993. Memberships: National Writers Union; Authors Guild; PEN. Literary Agent: Andrew Wylie. Address: 250 West 57th Street, Suite 2114, New York, NY 10019, USA.

POSTER Mark, b. 6 July 1941, New York, New York, USA. Professor of History; Writer. Education: BS, University of Pennsylvania, 1962; MA, 1965, PhD, 1968, New York University. Appointments: Assistant Professor, 1969-74, Associate Professor, 1974-78, Professor of History, 1978-, University of California at Irvine; Member, Editorial Board, The 18th Century: A Journal of Interpretation. Publications: The Utopian Thought of Restif de la Bretonne, Harmonian Man: Selected Writings of Charles Fourier (editor), 1971; Existential Marxism in Postwar France, 1976; Critical Theory of the Family, 1978; Satre's Marxism, 1979; Foucalt, Marxism and History, 1984; Baudrillard: Selected Writings (editor), 1988; Critical Theory and Poststructuralism, 1989; The Mode of Information, 1990; Postsuburban California: The Social Transformation of Orange County Since 1945 (editor with Rob King and Spencer Olin), 1991. Address: History Department, University of California at Irvine, Irvine, CA 92717, USA.

POSTMA Johannes (Menne), b. 14 Jan 1935, Friesland, Netherlands. University Professor. Education: BA, Graceland College, 1962; MA, University of Kansas, 1964; PhD, Michigan State University, 1970. Appointments: Instructor, Western Michigan University, 1964-68; Assistant Professor to full Professor, Mankato State University, 1969-; Visiting Professor, Leiden Rijksunversiteit, 1986-87. Publication: The Dutch in the Atlantic Slave Trade, 1600-1815, 1990. Memberships: American Historical Association; Social Science History Association; Royal Institute of Linguistics and Anthropology. Address: 50 Woodview Drive, Mankato, MN 56001, USA.

POTOK Chaim, b. 17 Feb 1929, New York, New York, USA. Writer. m. Adena Sara Mosevitsky, 8 June 1958, 1 son, 2 daughters. Education: BA, Yeshiva University, 1950; MHL, Rabbinic Ordination, Jewish Theological Seminary, 1954; PhD, University of Pennsylvania, 1965. Appointments: Visiting Professor, University of Pennsylvania, 1983-92, 1995; Visiting Professor, John Hopkins University, 1994, 1996. Publications: The Chosen, 1967; The Promise, 1969; My Name is Asher Lev, 1972; In the Beginning, 1975; Wanderings, 1978; The Book of Lights, 1981; Davita's Harp, 1985; The Gift of Asher Lev, 1990;

I am the Clay, 1992; The Tree of Here, 1993; The Sky of Now, 1995; The Gates of November, 1996. Contributions to: New York Times Sunday Book Review; Esquire; Commentary; Triquarterly; Philadelphia Enquirer Book Review; Forward; Moment. Honours: Wallant Prize, 1967; Athenaeum Award, 1970; National Jewish Book Award, 1991; National Foundation for Jewish Culture Award, 1997. Memberships: PEN; Drama Guild; Writers Guild. Literary Agent: Owen Laster, William Morris Agency. Address: 20 Berwick Road, Merion, PA 19066, USA.

POTTER Beverly Ann, b. 3 Mar 1944, Summit, New Jersey, USA. Psychologist; Publisher; Business Executive. Education: BA, 1966, MS, 1968, San Francisco State University; PhD, Stanford University, 1974. Publications: Chlorella: The Amazing Alchemist; Turning Around: Keys to Motivation and Productivity, 1980; Beating Job Burnout: How to Transform Work Pressure into Productivity, 1980, 2nd Edition, 1993; The Way of the Ronin: Riding the Waves of Change at Work, 1985; Preventing Job Burnout: A Work Book, 1987, 2nd Edition, 1995; Drug Testing at Work: A Guide for Employers and Employees, 1990; Brain Boosters: Foods & Drinks That Make You Smarter, 1993; Finding a Path With a Heart, 1994; From Conflict to Co-operation: How to Mediate a Dispute, 1996; The Worry Wart's Companion: Twenty One Ways to Soothe Yourself and Worry Smart, 1997. Contributions to: Journals and magazines. Memberships: North California Booksellers Association; Bay Area Organisation Development Network. Address: PO Box 1035, Berkeley, CA 94701, USA.

POTTER Jeremy (Ronald), b. 25 Apr 1922, London, England. Writer; Publisher. m. 11 Feb 1950, 1 son, 1 daughter. Education: MA, Queen's College, Oxford. Publications: Good King Richard?, 1983; Pretenders, 1986; Independent Television in Britain, volume 3: Politics and Control 1968-80, 1989 and volume 4: Companies and Programmes 1968-80, 1990; Tennis and Oxford, 1994. Novels: Hazard Chase, 1964; Death in Office, 1965; Foul Play, 1967; The Dance of Death, 1968; A Trail of Blood, 1970; Going West, 1972; Disgrace and Favour, 1975; Death in the Forest, 1977; The Primrose Hill Murder, 1992; The Mystery of the Campden Wonder, 1995. Address: The Old Pottery, Larkins Lane, Headington, Oxford OX3 9DW, England.

POTTER Margaret, (Anne Betteridge, Anne Melville, Margaret Newman), b. 21 Jun 1926, Harrow, Middlesex, England. Author. m. Jeremy Potter, 11 Feb 1950, 1 son, 1 daughter. Education: Major Scholar, Modern History, St Hugh's College, Oxford; MA, Oxon; Book Production course, London School of Printing. Publications: As Margaret Newman: The Boys Who Disappeared; Trouble on Sunday; The Motorway Mob; Tilly and the Princess; Unto the Fourth Generation. As Anne Betteridge: A Portuguese Affair; A Little Bit of Luck; Shooting Star; Love in a Rainy Country; The Girl Outside; Journey From a Foreign Land; A Time of Their Lives, short stories; The Temp; A Place for Everyone; The Tiger and the Goat. As Anne Melville: The Lorimer Line; The House of Hardie; Grace Hardie; The Hardie Inheritance; The Dangerfield Diaries; The Tantivy Trust; A Clean Break; The Russian Tiara; Standing Alone; The Longest Silence; Role Play; Snapshots, short stories. Contributions to: Fiction Reviews; Travel articles; Short stories in magazines. Memberships: Writers in Oxford Society of Authors. Address: c/o Peters, Fraser and Dunlop, 5th Floor, The Chambers, Chelsea Harbour, Lots Road, London SW10 0XF, England.

POULIN Gabrielle, b. 21 June 1929, St Prosper, Quebec, Canada. Writer; Poet. Education: MA, University of Montreal; DLitt, University of Sherbroke. Appointment: Writer-in-Residence, Ottawa Public Library, 1988. Publications: Les Miroirs d'un poète: Image et reflets de Paul Eluard, 1969; Cogne la caboche, 1979, English translation as All the Way Home, 1984; L'Age de l'interrogation, 1937-52, 1980; Les Mensonges d'Isabelle (novel), 1983; La Couronne d'oubli (novel), 1990; Petites Fugues pour une saison seche (poems), 1991; Le Livre de déraison (novel), 1994; Mon père aussi était horloger (poetry), 1996. Contributions to: Periodicals. Honours: Swiss Embassy Prize, 1967; Il Arts Council of Canada Grants, 1968-83, 1985; Champlain Literary Prize, 1979; Carleton Literary Prize, Ottawa, 1983; Alliance Française Literary Prize, 1984; Salon du Livre de Toronto Literary Prize, 1994. Memberships: Société des écrivains canadiens de l'Outaouias; Union Quebecois Writers. Address: 1997 Avenue Quincy, Ottawa, Ontario K1J 6B4, Canada.

POULSEN Morten. See: VIZKI Morti.

POUPLIER Erik, b. 16 June 1926, Svendborg, Denmark. Writer. m. Annalise Hansen, 28 Sept 1947, 1 daughter. Education: Trained as journalist. Publications: In Danish: Lend Me Your Wife, 1957; My Castle in Ardèche, 1968; The Gentle Revolt, 1970; The Discreet Servant of the Death, 1972; The Adhesive Pursuer, 1973; Murder, Mafia and Pastis'er, 1974; My Castle in Provence, 1979; The Old Man in Provence, 1980; The Clumsy Kidnappers, 1981; The World of Annesisse, 1982; The Galic Cock, 1984; My Own Provence, 1984; The Cuisine of Provence, 1985; Panic in Provence, 1986; All Year Round in Provence, 1987; Machiavelli, 1987; The Anaconda-Coup in Provence, 1988; Long Live the Grandparents, 1988; Barbaroux and the Flood, 1989; Always Around the Next Corner (memoirs), 1990; Pearls of Provence, 1991; Barbaroux and the Nuns, 1992; Merry-Go-Round, 1993; The 4 Seasons of Provence, 1995; The Hangman, 1996. Contributions to: Jyllands Posten, Denmark. Memberships: Danish Author's Society; Société d'Ecrivains de Nice et de Cannes; Danish Press Association. Address: Les Charmettes, Chemin de Plateau, 83550 Vidauban, France.

POURNELLE Jerry Eugene, (Wade Curtis), b. 7 Aug 1933, Shreveport, Louisiana, USA. Writer; Lecturer; Consultant. Education: University of Iowa, 1953-54; BS, 1955, MS, 1957, PhD, Psychology, 1960, PhD, Political Science, 1964, University of Washington. Publications: Red Heroin (as Wade Curtis), 1969; The Strategy of Technology: Winning the Decisive War (with Stefan Possony), 1970; Red Dragon (as Wade Curtis), 1971; A Spaceship for the King, 1973; Escape From the Planet of the Apes (novelization of screenplay), 1973; The Mote in God's Eye (with Larry Niven), 1974; 20/20 Vision (editor), 1974; Birth of Fire, 1976; Inferno (with Larry Niven), 1976; West of Honor, 1976; High Justice (short stories), 1977; The Mercenary, 1977; Lucifer's Hammer (with Larry Niven), 1977; Exiles to Glory, 1978; Black Holes (editor), 1979; A Step Further Out (non-fiction), 1980; Janisseries, 1980; Oath of Fealty (with Larry Niven), 1981; Clan and Crown (with Roland Green), 1982; There Will Be War (co-editor), 1983; Mutual Assured Survival (with Dean Ing), 1984; Men of War (co-editor), 1984; Blood and Iron (co-editor), 1984; Day of the Tyrant (co-editor), 1985; Footfall (with Larry Niven), 1985; Warriors (co-editor), 1986; Imperial Stars: The Stars at War, Republic and Empire (co-editor), 2 volumes, 1986-87; Guns of Darkness (co-editor), 1987; Storms of Victory (with Roland Green), 1987; Legacy of Hereot (with Larry Niven), 1987; Prince of Mercenaries, 1989; The Gripping Hand (with Larry Niven), 1993. Contributions to: Magazines. Memberships: Fellow, Operations Research Society of America; Fellow, American Association for the Advancement of Science; Science Fiction Writers of America, president, 1974. Address: 121901 1/2 Ventura Boulevard, Box 372, Studio City, CA 91604, USA.

POWE Bruce Allen, (Ellis Portal), b. 9 June 1925, Edmonton, Alberta, Canada. Business Executive; Writer. Education: BA, 1949, MA, 1951, University of Alberta. Appointments: Special Assistant, Minister of Mines and Technical Surveys, 1951-57; Editorial Assistant, Imperial Oil Ltd, 1957-60; Executive Director, Ontario Liberal Association, 1960-63; Vice President, Public Relations, Baker Advertising Ltd, 1964-66; Vice President of Public Affairs, Canadian Life and Health Insurance Association, Toronto, 1966-90. Publications: Expresso '67, 1966; Killing Ground: The Canadian Civil War (as E Portal), 1968, under own name, 1972; The Last Days of the American Empire, 1974; The Aberhart Summer, 1983; The Ice Eaters, 1987. Address: 158 Ridley Boulevard, Toronto, Ontario M5M 3M1, Canada.

POWE Bruce William, b. 23 Mar 1955, Ottawa, Ontario, Canada. Author; Teacher. m. Robin Leslie Mackenzie, 7 Sept 1991, sep Dec 1996, 1 son, 1 daughter. Education: BA, Special Honours, York University, Toronto; MA, University of Toronto. Appointment: Academic Advisor, York University, Toronto, 1994-. Publications: A Climate Charged, 1984; The Solitary Outlaw, 1987, reprint 1996; Noise of Time, text for Glenn Gould Profile, 1989; A Tremendous Canada of Light, 1993, reprint 1997; Outage: A Journey into Electric City, 1995. Contributions to: Globe and Mail; Toronto Star; Grail; Antigonish Review; Bennington Review; Exile; Modern Drama. Honours: York University Book Award, 1977; Special MA Scholarship to University of Toronto, 1979; Explorations Grant, Canada Council, 1980; Maclean-Hunter Fellowship, 1989; Ontario Arts Council Awards, 1990, 1991, 1992, 1994; 1996. Address: 625 Myrtle Road West, Ashburn, Ontario L0B 1A0, Canada.

POWELL Anthony (Dymoke), b. 21 Dec 1905, London, England. Writer. m. Lady Violet Pakenham, 1934, 2 sons. Education: Eton; Balliol College, Oxford. Appointments: With Duckworth

Publishers, 1926-35; Literary Editor, Punch, 1953-59; Trustee, National Portrait Gallery, 1962-76. Publications: A Dance to the Music of Time (sequence of 12 novels), from A Question of Upbringing, 1959, to Hearing Secret Harmonies, 1975; The Soldier's Art, 1966; The Military Philosophers, 1968; The Garden God and the Rest I'll Whistle: The Text of Two Plays, Books Do Furnish a Room, 1971; Temporary Kings, 1973; Infants of the Spring, 1976; Messengers of Day, 1978; Faces in My Time, 1980; The Strangers All Are Gone, 1982; O, How the Wheel Becomes It!, 1983; To Keep the Ball Rolling (abridged memoirs), 1983; The Fisher King, 1986; Miscellaneous Verdicts (criticism), 1990; Under Review (criticism), 1992; Journals 1982-1986, 1996; Journals 1987-1989, 1996; Journals 1990-1992, 1997. Honours: Commander of the Order of the British Empire, 1956; Companion of Honour, 1988; Orders of White Lion (Czechoslovakia), Leopold II (Belgium), Oaken Crown and Croix de Guerre (Luxembourg); James Tait Black Prize; Hon DLitt: Sussex, Leicester, Kent, Oxford, Bristol, University of Wales, Bath; Honorary Fellow, Balliol College, Oxford, 1974; W H Smith Award, 1974; The Hudson Review Bennett Award, 1984; Ingersoll Foundation; Hon DLitt, Wales, 1992. Address: The Chantry, Near Frome, Somerset BA11 3LJ, England.

POWELL Bill. Journalist. Education: Degree in History, Northwestern University, 1979. Appointments: Correspondent for Pittsburgh, Houston and Boston, Staff Editor, BusinessWeek, 1979-85; General Editor, 1985-87, New York-based Senior Writer in Business Section, 1987-89, Asia Economics Editor, 1989-94, Tokyo Bureau Chief, 1991-94, Berlin Bureau Chief, 1994-, Moscow Bureau Chief, 1996-, Newsweek. Contributions to: Journals. Honours: Gerald Loeb Award for media story, Civil War at CBS, 1986; Winner, Morton Frank Award for Best Business/Economic Reporting from Abroad, Overseas Press Club, 1992; Co-winner with Marcus Mabry, Morton Frank Award for Best Business Reporting, Overseas Press Club, 1996. Address: c/o Newsweek, 251 West 57th Street, New York, NY 10019-1894, USA.

POWELL (John) Enoch, b. 16 June 1912, Birmingham, England. Politician; Writer. Education: BA, MA, Trinity College, Cambridge, 1937. Appointments: Conservative Member of Parliament for Wolverhampton South-West, 1950-74; Ulster Unionist Member of Parliament (UK) for South Down, Northern Ireland, 1976-87. Publications: The Rendel Harris Papyri, 1936; First Poems, 1937; A Lexicon to Herodotus, 1938; The History of Herodotus, 1939; Casting Off and Other Poems, 1939; Herodotus, Book VIII, 1939; Llyfr Blegywryd, 1942; Thucydidis Historia, 1942; Herodotus (translation), 1949; One Nation (with others), 1950; Dancer's End and the Wedding Gift, poetry, 1951; The Social Services: Needs and Means, 1952; Change Is Our Ally (with others), 1954; Biography of a Nation (with A Maude), 1955; Saving in a Free Society, 1960; Great Parliamentary Occasions, 1960; A Nation Not Afraid, 1965; A New Look at Medicine and Politics, 1966; The House of Lords in the Middle Ages (with K Wallis), 1968; Freedom and Reality, 1969; Income Tax at 4/3 in the Pound, 1970; The Common Market: The Case Against, 1971; Still To Decide, 1972; No Easy Answers, 1973; Wrestling With the Angel, 1977; Joseph Chamberlain, 1977; A Nation or No Nation, 1978; Collected Poems, 1990; Enoch Powell on 1992, 1992; Evolution of the Gospel, 1994. Honour: Member of the Order of the British Empire, 1943. Address: 33 South Eaton Place, London SW1W 9EN, England.

POWELL Geoffrey Stewart, (Tom Angus), b. 25 Dec 1914, Scarborough, Yorkshire, England. Soldier; Writer. m. Felicity Wadsworth, 15 July 1944, 1 son, 1 daughter. Education: Scarborough College, 1923-31; Army Staff College, 1945-46; United States Command and General Staff College, 1950-51; Joint Services Staff College, 1953-54; BA, Open University, 1981. Publications: The Green Howards, 1966; The Kandyan Wars, 1973; Men at Arnhem, 1978, (1st edited under the pseudonym Tom Angus); Suez: The Double War (with Roy Fullick), 1979; The Book of Campden, 1982; The Devil's Birthday: The Bridges to Arnhem, 1984; Plumer: The Soldier's General, 1990; The Green Howards: 300 Years of Service, 1992; Buller: A Scapegoat: A Life of General Sir Redvers Buller, VC, 1994. Contributions to: Journals and magazines. Honour: Fellow, Royal Historical Society, 1989. Literary Agent: A M Heath and Company. Address: c/o Army and Navy Club, Pall Mall, London SW1, England.

POWELL Joseph Michael, b. 27 Dec 1938, Bootle, England. University Professor. m. Suzanne Margaret Geehman, 28 Dec 1967, 1 son, 1 daughter. Education: BA Hons, 1960, MA, 1962, Liverpool University; PhD, 1969, DLitt, 1993, Monash University, Victoria, Australia. Publications: Public Lands of Australia Felix, 1970; Environmental Management in Australia, 1976; Mirrors of the New World, 1977; Historical Geography of Modern Australia, 1988; Watering the Garden State, 1989; Plains of Promise, Rivers of Destiny, 1991; 'MDB' The Emergence of Bioregionalism in the Murray-Darling Basin, 1993. Honour: Fellow, Academy of Social Science of Australia, 1985. Address: Department of Geography and Environmental Science, Monash University, Clayton, Victoria 3168, Australia.

POWELL Neil, b. 11 Feb 1948, London, England. Writer; Editor. Education: BA, 2:1 English and American Literature, 1966-69, MPhil, English Literature, 1969-71, University of Warwick. Publications: At the Edge (poems), 1977; Carpenters of Light (criticism), 1979; A Season of Calm Weather (poems), 1982; Selected Poems of Fulke Greville (editor), 1990; True Colours: New and Selected Poems, 1991; Unreal City (novel), 1992; The Stones on Thorpeness Beach (poems), 1994; Roy Fuller: Writer and Society (critical biography), 1995; Gay Love Poetry (editor), 1997; The Language of Jazz, 1997; Selected Poems, forthcoming. Contributions to: Critical Quarterly; Encounter; Gay Times; Guardian; Listener; London Magazine; New Statesman; PN Review; Poetry Review; Times Literary Supplement. Honours: Gregory Award, Society of Authors, 1969; Authors' Foundation Award, 1992. Memberships: Poetry Society; Society of Authors. Address: c/o Carcanet Press Ltd, 4th Floor, Conavon Court, 12-16 Blackfriars Street, Manchester M3 5BD, England.

POWELL Padgett, b. 25 Apr 1952, Gainesville, Florida, USA. Professor of Creative Writing. m. Sidney Wade, 22 May 1984, 2 daughters. Education: BA, College of Charleston 1975; MA, University of Houston, 1982. Appointment: Professor of Creative Writing, University of Florida, Gainesville, 1984-. Publications: Edisto (novel), 1984; A Woman Named Drown (novel), 1987; Typical (stories), 1991; Edisto Revisited (novel), 1996; Aliens of Affection (stories), forthcoming. Contributions to: Periodicals; Harper's Magazine. Honours: Best Book Citation, Time Magazine, 1984; Whiting Foundation Writers' Award, 1986; American Academy and Institute of Arts and Letters Rome Fellowship in Literature 1987. Memberships: PEN; Authors Guild; Writers Guild of America, East. Literary Agent: Cynthia Cannell, Janklow & Nesbit, 598 Madison Avenue, NY 10022, USA. Address: Department of English, University of Florida, Gainesville, FL 32611, USA.

POWELL Talmage, b. 4 Oct 1920, Hendersonville, North Carolina, USA. Writer. Education: University of North Carolina. Publications: Co author: Cabins & Castles, 1981; Wild Game, 1994; Western Ghosts, 1990; New England Ghosts, 1990; Murder for Halloween, 1994; Encyclopedia Mysteriosa, 1994; Six-Gun Ladies, Stories of Women on the American Western Frontier, 1996. Contributions to: Anthologies, films, and television. Address: 33 Caledonia Road, Kenilworth, Asheville, NC 28803, USA.

POWELL Violet Georgiana, b. 13 Mar 1912, London, England. Writer. Education: Private girls' school, Bushey. Publications: Five out of Six, 1960; A Substantial Ghost, 1967; The Irish Cousins, 1970; A Compton-Burnett Compendium, 1973; Within the Family Circle, 1976; Margaret, Countess of Jersey, 1978; Flora Annie Steel, Novelist of India, 1981; The Constant Novelist, 1983; The Album of Anthony Powell's Dance to the Music of Time (editor), 1987; The Life of a Provincial Lady: A Study of E M Delafield and Her Works, 1988; A Jane Austen Compendium, 1993. Address: The Chantry, Nr Frome, Somerset BA11 3LJ, England.

POWELL-SMITH Vincent, (Francis Elphinstone, Jucticiar, Santa Maria), b. 28 Apr 1939, Kent, England. Arbitrator; Advocate. m. Martha Marilyn Du Barry, 4 Apr 1989, 1 daughter. Education: LLB; LLM; MCL; PhD; DLitt. Appointments: Editorial Consultant, Butterworth & Co, 1984; Editor, Construction Law Reports, 52 volumes, 1959, Asia-Pacific Law Reports, 1992; Consultant, Malayan Law Journal. Publications: Law of Boundaries and Fences, 1966, 2nd edition, 1972; Building Contract Claims, 2nd edition, 1988; Malaysian Standard Form of Building Contract, 1990; Building Contract Dictionary, 2nd edition, 1990; Building Regulations Explained and Illustrated, 10th edition, 1995. Contributions to: Contract Journal; Times; Field, Building, Architect's Journal; Malaysian Law Journal; Construction Law Journal; International Journal of Construction Law; Islamic Studies. Address: #B1 Menara Impian, 68000 Ampang, Selangor, Malaysia.

POWER Edward, b. near Waterford, Ireland. Writer; Freelance Journalist; Personalised Children's Book-Seller. Contributions to: Books, anthologies and periodicals. Memberships: National Union of

Journalists; Royal British Legion. Address: Laurel Cottage, Dowlin, Piltown, Carrick-on-Suir, Ireland.

POWERS M L. See: **TUBB E(dwin) C(harles).**

POWNALL David, b. 19 May 1938, Liverpool, England. Author; Dramatist. m. 1) Glenys Elsie Jones, 1961, div, 3 sons, (2) Mary Ellen Ray, 1981, (3) Alex Sutton, 3 sons, 1993. Education: BA, University of Keele, 1960. Appointments: Resident Writer, Century Theatre, 1970-72; Resident Playwright, Duke's Playhouse, Lancaster, 1972-75; Founder-Resident Writer, Paines Plough Theatre, London, 1975-80. Publications: Fiction: The Raining Tree War, 1974; African Horse, 1975; The Dream of Chief Crazy Horse, 1975; God Perkins, 1977; Light on a Honeycomb, 1978; Beloved Latitudes, 1981; The White Cutter, 1989; The Gardener, 1990; Stagg and His Mother, 1991; The Sphinx and the Sybarites, 1994. Plays: Over 40 stage plays, 1969-96; Radio and television plays. Honours: Edinburgh Festival Fringe Awards, 1976, 1977; Giles Cooper Awards, 1981, 1985; John Whiting Award, Arts Council of Great Britain, 1982; Sony Gold and Silver Awards for Original Radio Drama, 1994, 1995. Membership: Royal Society of Literature, Fellow. Address: c/o John Johnson Ltd, 45-47 Clerkenwell Green, London EC1R 0HT, England.

POYER Joe (Joseph John Poyer), b. 30 Nov 1939, Battle Creek, Michigan, USA. Writer; Editor; Publisher. m. Bonnie Prichard, Oct 1987. Education: BA, Michigan State University, 1961. Appointments: North Cape Publications: Publisher/Editor, Safe and Secure Living; International Military Review; International Naval Review. Publications: Fiction: North Cape, 1968; Balkan Assignment, 1971; Chinese Agenda, 1972; Shooting of the Green, 1973; The Contract, 1978; Tunnel War, 1979; Vengeance 10, 1980; Devoted Friends, 1982; Time of War, 2 volumes, 1983, 1985. Non-Fiction: The 45-70 Springfield, 1991; US Winchester Trench and Riot Guns, 1993; Pocket Guide 45-70 Springfield, 1994; The Migarand, 1936 to 1957, 1995; The SKS Carbine, 1997. Contributions to: Journals. Address: PO Box 1027, Tustin, CA 92681, USA.

POYNDER Edward. See: **GRIGG John.**

PRABHASHANKAR T G (Premi), b. 7 May 1942, Tumkur, India. Professor of Hindi. m. Anu Prabha, 16 Mar 1969, 1 son, 1 daughter. Education: MA Hindi, Mysore University, 1965; PhD, Karnatak University, Dharwar, 1977. Appointments: Professor of Hindi, Bangalore University; Editor, Basava Marg, half yearly Hindi Magazine, Bangalore. Publications: Kavyabala (poetry in Hindi), 1975; Kannada Aur Hindi Sahitya Ka Tulanatmak Adyayan, 1977; Adhunik Hindi Kavita Par Gandhivad Ka Prabhav, 1981; Basava Darshan (essay, translation), 1983; Shresta Jeevania (biographies), 1984; Talash (poetry in Hindi), 1988; Kanasugala Kannadi, poetry in Kannada. Contributions to: Hindi Poems and articles to leading Hindi magazines: Kadambini; Aaj Kal; Samakaleen Bharatia Sahitya; Bhasha. Honours: Karnatak State Monetary Award for translation of Basava Darshan, 1983; Souhardh Samman Cash Award, Uttar Pradesh Government, 1990. Memberships: Vice-President, Poets International, Bangalore; Convenor, Authors Guild of India, Bangalore Chapter. Address: Prabhu Priya 391, VI Main 111 Block 111 Stage, Basavaeswar Nagar, Bangalore 5600079, India.

PRALL Stuart Edward, b. 2 June 1929, Saginaw, Michigan, USA. Professor of History; Author. m. Naomi Shafer, 20 Jan 1958, 1 son, 1 daughter. Education: BA, Michigan State University, 1951; MA, University of Rhode Island, 1953; University of Manchester, England, 1953-54; PhD, Columbia University, 1960. Appointments: Queens College and Graduate School, University Center, City University of New York, 1955-58, 1960-; Newark State College, New Jersey, 1958-60; Executive Officer, PhD Program in History, Graduate School, City University of New York, 1988-94. Publications: The Agitation for Law Reform during the Puritan Revolution, 1640-1660, 1966; The Puritan Revolution: A Documentary History, 1968; The Bloodless Revolution: England, 1688, 1972; A History of England, 1984; Church and State in Tudor and Stuart England, 1993. Contributions to: The Development of Equity in Tudor England; American Journal of Legal History. Honours: Fulbright Scholar, University of Manchester, 1953-54; Fellow, Royal Historical Society, 1978. Memberships: American Historical Association; North American Conference on British Studies. Address: 1479 Court Place, Hewiett, NY 11557, USA.

PRANTERA Amanda, b. 23 Apr 1942, England. Author. Publications: Strange Loop, 1984; The Cabalist, 1985; Conversations

with Lord Byron on Perversion, 163 Years After His Lordship's Death, 1987; The Side of the Moon, 1991; Pronto-Zoe, 1992; The Young Italians, 1993. Address: Jane Conway Gordon, 1 Old Compton Street, London, W1V 5PH, England.

PRASAD Madhusudan, b. 3 Jan 1950, Allahabad, India. Reader in English; Writer. m. Kiran Srivastava, 29 May 1971, 4 daughters. Education: BA, 1967, MA, English, 1969, DPhil, 1974, University of Allahabad. Publications: D H Lawrence: A Study of His Novels, 1980; Anita Desai: The Novelist, 1981; In the Dark (stories), 1982; Indian-English Novelists: An Anthology of Critical Essays (editor), 1982; Contemporary Indian-English Stories (editor), 1983, 3rd edition, 1988; Perspectives on Kamala Markanddaya (editor), 1984; The Poetry of Jayanta Mahapatra: A Critical Study (editor), 1986; Living Indian-English Poets: An Anthology of Critical Essays (editor), 1989. Contributions to: Numerous research papers published in journals, magazines and books; Poems, Pacific Quarterly Ploana (New Zealand), Rimu (New Zealand). Address: 134-112 Kothaparcha off G T Road, Allahabad 211 003, India.

PRATCHETT Terry, b. 28 Apr 1948, Beaconsfield, England. Author. m. Lyn Pratchett, 1 daughter. Publications: Adult Fiction: The Dark Side of the Sun, 1976; Strata, 1981; The Colour of Magic, 1983; The Light Fantastic, 1986; Equal Rites, 1987; Mort, 1987; Sourcery, 1989; Wyrd Sisters, 1988; Pyramids, 1989; Eric (illustrated by Josh Kirby), 1989; Guards! Guards!, 1989; Moving Pictures, 1990; Reaper Man, 1991; Witches Abroad, 1991; Small Gods, 1992; Lords and Ladies, 1993; Men at Arms, 1993; Soul Music, 1994; Interesting Times, 1994; The Discworld Companion (with Stephen Briggs), 1994; Maskerade, 1995; Discworld Mapp (with Stephen Briggs), 1995; Feet of Clay, 1996; Hogfather, 1996; The Pratchett Portfolio (illustrated by Paul Kidby), 1996. Juvenile Fiction: The Carpet People, 1971, revised edition, 1992; Truckers, 1989; Diggers, 1990; Wings, 1990; Only You Can Save Mankind, 1992; Johnny and the Dead, 1993. Other: The Unadulterated Cat (illustrated by Gray Joliffe), 1989; Good Omens: The Nice and Accurate Predictions of Agnes Nutter, Witch (with Neil Gaiman), 1990. Honours: British Science Fiction Awards, 1989, 1990. Address: c/o Colin Smythe Ltd, PO Box 6, Gerrards Cross, Buckinghamshire SL9 8XA, England.

PRATHER Richard S(cott), (David Knight, Douglas Ring), b. 9 Sept 1921, Santa Ana, California, USA. Writer. Education: Riverside Junior College, California, 1940-41. Publications: Over 50 books, 1950-88. Address: c/o Tor Books, 175, Fifth Avenue, New York, NY 10010, USA.

PRATT John Clark, b. 19 Aug 1932, St Albans, Vermont, USA. Writer; Educator. m. (2) Doreen Goodman, 28 June 1968, 1 son, 5 daughters. Education: BA, University of California, 1954; MA, Columbia University, 1960; PhD, Princeton University, 1965. Appointments: Instructor, English, 1960-65, Assistant Professor, 1965-69, Associate Professor, 1969-73, Professor, 1973-75, United States Air Force Academy; Professor, Colorado State University, 1975-; President, Pratt Publishing Company, 1989-. Publications: The Meaning of Modern Poetry, 1962; John Steinbeck, 1970; One Flew Over the Cuckoo's Nest (editor), 1973, revised edition, 1996; Middlemarch Notebooks (co-editor), 1978; Vietnam Voices, 1984, revised edition 1998; The Laotian Fragments, 1985; Reading the Wind: The Literature of the Vietnam War (co-author), 1986; Writing from Scratch: The Essay, 1987; The Quiet American (editor), 1996. Contributions to: Vietnam War Literature; Vietnam-Perkasie; Fourteen Landing Zones; Unaccustomed Mercy. Honours: Fulbright Lecturer, University of Lisbon, Portugal, 1974-75; Fulbright Lecturer, Leningrad State University, USSR, 1980; Honours Professor, Colorado State University, 1989; Award for Excellence in the Arts. The Vietnam Veterans of America, 1995. Address: Department of English, Colorado State University, Ft Collins, CO 80523, USA.

PRAWER Siegbert Salomon, b. 15 Feb 1925, Cologne, Germany. Professor of German (retired); Author; Editor; Artist. Appointments: Professor of German, Westfield College, London University, 1964-69; Taylor Professor of German, Oxford University, 1969-85; Co-Editor, Oxford German Studies, 1971-75; Anglica Germanica, 1973-79; Dean of Degress, Queen's College, Oxford, 1974-92. Publications: German Lyric Poetry, 1952; Mörike und seine leser, 1960; Heine's Buch der Lieder: A Critical Study, 1960; Heine: The Tragic Satirist, 1962; The Penguin Book of Lieder (editor), 1964; Essays in German Language, Culture and Society (co-editor), 1969; The Romantic Period in Germany (editor), 1970; Seventeen Modern

German Poets (editor), 1971; Comparative Literary Studies, 1973; Karl Marx and World Literature, 1976; Caligan's Children: The Film as Tale of Terror, 1980; Heine's Jewish Comedy, 1983; Frankenstein's Island: England and the English in the Writings of Heinrich Heine, 1986; Israel at Vanity Fair: Jews and Judaism in the Writings of W M Thackeray, 1992. Contributions to: Professional journals. Honours: 2 Goethe Medals; Gundolf Prize, German Academy of Language and Literature; Honorary doctorates, University of Birmingham and University of Cologne. Memberships: British Academy, fellow; London University Institute of Germanic Studies, fellow, honorary director, 1965-68; British Comparative Literature Association, fellow, president, 1984-86; German Academy of Language and Literature, corresponding fellow; Queen's College, Oxford, honorary fellow; Jesus College, Cambridge, honorary fellow; British Comparative Literature Association, fellow, president 1990-92. Address: c/o Queen's s College, Oxford, England.

PREBBLE John (Edward Curtis), b. 23 June 1915, Edmonton, Middlesex, England. Author. Publications: Where the Sea Breaks, 1944; The Edge of Darkness (US edition as, The Edge of the Night), 1948; Age Without Pity, 1950; The Mather Story, 1954; The Brute Streets, 1954; The High Girders (US edition as Disaster at Dundee), 1956; My Great-Aunt Appearing Day, 1958, reissued with additions as Spanish Stirrup, 1973; Mongaso (with John A Jordan) (US edition as Elephants and Ivory), 1959; The Buffalo Soldiers, 1959; Culloden, 1961; The Highland Clearances, 1963; Glencoe, 1966; The Darien Disaster, 1968; The Lion in the North, 1971; Mutiny, 1975; John Prebble's Scotland, 1984; The King's Jaunt: George IV in Edinburgh, 1988; Landscapes and Memories, 1993. Honours: McVitie Award, Scottish Writer of the Year, 1993; Honorary DLitt, Glasgow, 1997. Memberships: Royal Society of Literature, fellow; Royal Society of Arts, fellow; Society of Authors; International PEN; Writer's Guild. Literary Agent: Curtis Brown. Address: 905 Nelson House, Dolphin Square, London SW1V 3PA, England.

PRELUTSKY Jack, b. 8 Sept 1940, Brooklyn, New York, USA. Writer; Poet. m. Carolynn Prelutsky, 1979. Education: Hunter College, New York City. Publications: Over 40 books for young readers, 1967-96. Honours: Many citations and awards. Address: c/o Greenwillow Books, 1350 Avenue of the Americas, New York, NY 10019, USA.

PRENTIS Malcolm David, b. 27 June 1948, Auchenflower, Queensland, Australia. Academic. m. Marion Anne Bird, 7 Jan 1978, 2 sons, 1 daughter. Education: University of Queensland, 1966; University of Sydney, 1967-69; BA Hons 1970; Macquarie University, 1970-74, 1977; MA Hons, 1973; PhD, 1980; University of New England, 1980-81; Diploma Tertiary Education, 1982. Publications: Fellowship, 1977; St Davids Kirk, 1977; Continuity and Change, 1982; The Scots in Australia, 1983; A Study in Black and White, 2nd edition, 1988; The Scottish in Australia, 1987; Warringah History (editor and contributor), 1989; Scots to the Fore, 1993; The Forest Kirk, 1993; An All Round Man, forthcoming; The Ties that Bind, (editor and contributor), forthcoming. Contributions to: numerous. Address: 15 Dakara Drive, French's Forest, NSW 2086, Australia.

PRESCOTT Casey. See: **MORRIS Janet Ellen.**

PRESCOTT J(ohn) R(obert) V(ictor), b. 1931, Newcastle upon Tyne, England. Professor Emeritus. Education: BSc, 1952, Diploma in Education, 1955, MA, 1957, University of Durham; PhD, Birbeck College, London, 1961. Appointments: Lecturer, University College, Ibadan, 1956-61; Lecturer to Reader, 1961-85, Professor of Geography, 1985-, University of Melbourne. Publications: The Geography of Frontiers and Boundaries, 1965, revised edition as Frontiers and Boundaries, 1978; The Geography of State Policies, 1968; The Evolution of Nigeria's International and Regional Boundaries 1861-1971, 1971; Political Geography, 1972; The Political Geography of the Oceans, 1975; The Map of Mainland Asia by Treaty, 1975; Our Fragmented World: An Introduction to Political Geography (with W G East), 1975; The Frontiers of Asia and Southwest Asia (with H J Collier and D F Prescott), 1976; The Last of Lands: Antartica (with J Lovering), 1979; Austrlai's Continental Shelf (with other), 1979; Maritime Jurisdiction in Southeast Asia, 1981; Australia's Maritime Boundaries, 1985; The Maritime Political Boundaries of the World, 1985; Political Frontiers and Boundaries, 1987; Aboriginal Frontiers and Boundaries in Australia (with S Davis), 1992; A Geographical Description of the Spratly Islands and an Account of Hydrographic Surveys Amongst Those Islands (with David Hancox), 1995. Address:

Department of Geography, University of Melbourne, Parkville, Victoria 3052, Australia.

PRESS John Bryant, b. 11 Jan 1920, Norwich, England. Retired Officer of the British Council. m. Janet Crompton, 20 Dec 1947, 1 son, 1 daughter. Education: Corpus Christi College, Cambridge, England. Publications: The Fire and the Fountain, 1955; The Chequer'd Shade, 1958; A Map of Modern English Verse, 1969; The Lengthening Shadows, 1971; John Betjeman, 1974; Poets of World War II, 1984; A Girl with Beehive Hair, 1986. Contributions to: Encounter; Southern Review; Art International. Honours: Royal Society of Literature Heinemann Award, 1959; 1st Prize, Cheltenham Poetry Festival, 1959. Membership: Royal Society of Literature, fellow. Address: 5 South Parade, Frome, Somerset BA11 1EJ, England.

PRESS Lloyd Douglas Jr, (Skip Press), b. 26 July 1950, Commerce, Texas, USA. Writer. m. Debra Ann Hartsog, 30 July 1989, 1 son, 1 daughter. Education: Honours Programme, East Texas State University, Commerce. Publications: A Woman's Guide to Firearms, 1986; Cliffhanger,1992; The Devil's Forest Fire, 1993; Knucklehead, 1993; A Rave of Snakes, 1993; The Importance of Mark Twain, 1993. Contributions to: Boy's Life; Disney Adventures; Reader's Digest; Writer's Digest; many others. Honour: Siver Medal, New York International Film Festival, 1987. Memberships: Dramatist's Guild; Poets and Writers; Independent Writers of Southern California, vice-president, 1990-91; Poets, Essayists and Novelists. Address: 2132 Palos Verdes Drive West 6, Palos Verdes Estates, CA 90274, USA.

PRESTON Ivy Alice Kinross, b. 11 Nov 1913. Writer. m. Percival Edward James Preston, 14 Oct 1937, 2 sons, 2 daughters. Publications: The Silver Stream (autobiography), 1958; Hospital on the Hill, 1967; Voyage of Destiny, 1974; The House Above the Bay, 1976; Fair Accuser, 1985; Stranger From the Sea, 1987; 40 romance novels, reprinted in 9 languages and 130 editions. Contributions to: Many publications. Memberships: South Canterbury Writers Guild; New Zealand Women Writers Society; South Island Writers Association. Romance Writers of America; Romantic Novelists Association, London. Literary Agent: Robert Hale Ltd, London England. Address: 95 Church Street, Timaru, Southe Canterbury, New Zealand.

PRESTON Peter John, b. 23 May 1938. Editorial Director, Guardian Media Group. m. Jean Mary Burrell, 1962, 2 sons, 2 daughters. Education: MA English Literature, St John's College, Oxford. Appointments: Editorial Trainee, Liverpool Daily Post, 1960-63; The Guardian: Political Reporter, 1963-64; Education Correspondent, 1965-66, Diary Editor, 1966-68, Features Editor, 1968-72; Production Editor, 1972-75; Editor, 1975-95, The Guardian; Editor-in-Chief, The Guardian & The Observer, 1995-96; Executive Chairman and World Chairman, International Press Institute. Honours: Hon DLitt, Loughborough, 1982; DU, Essex, 1994. Address: The Guardian and Observer, 119 Farringdon Road, London EC1R 3ER, England.

PRESTON Richard McCann, b. 5 Aug 1954, Cambridge, Massachusetts, USA. Writer. m. 11 May 1985. Education: BA summa cum laude, Pomona College, 1977; PhD, English and American Literature, Princeton University, 1983. Appointments: Lecturer in English, Princeton University, 1983; Visiting Fellow, Princeton University Council of the Humanities, 1994-95. Publications: First Light, 1987; American Steel, 1991; The Hot Zone, 1994. Contributions to: Newspapers and magazines. Honours: American Institute of Physics Science Writing Award, 1988; Asteroid 3686 named 'Preston', 1989; AAAS, Westinghouse Award, 1992; MIT McDermott Award, 1993. Membership: Authors Guild. Address: c/o Lynn Nesbit, Janklow & Nesbit Associates, 598 Madison Avenue, New York, NY 10022, USA.

PRESTON-MAFHAM Rodney Arthur, b. 14 June 1942, Harrow, England. Author; Photographer. m. Jean Brown, 31 July 1969, 1 son, 2 daughters. Education: University College, London, 1960-63; BSc, Zoology, Wye College, University of London, 1963-68; MSc, PhD. Publications: Spiders of the World, 1984; Spiders: An Illustrated Guide, 1991; Cacti: The Illustrated Dictionary, 1991; The Encyclopedia of Land Invertebrate Behaviour, 1993; The Natural History of Insects, 1996; The Natural History of Spiders, 1996. Address: Amberstone, 1 Kirland Road, Bodmin, Cornwall, PL30 5JQ, England.

PREUSS Paul F, b. 7 Mar 1942, Albany, Georgia, USA. Writer. m. (1) Marsha May Pettit, 1963, 1 daughter, (2) Karen Reiser, 1973,

(3) Debra Turner, 1993. Education: BA cum laude, Yale University, 1966. Publications: The Gates of Heaven, 1980; Re-entry, 1981; Broken Symmetries, 1983; Human Error, 1985; Venus Prime series (with Arthur C Clarke), 1987-91; Starfire, 1988; The Ultimate Dinosaur, 1992; Core, 1993; Secret Passages, 1997. Contributions to: Books and newspapers; The New York Review of Science Fiction. Memberships: Northern California Science Writers Association; Science Fiction and Fantasy Writers of America; Bay Area Book Reviewers' Association. Literary Agent: Jean V Naggar, New York; The New York Review of Science Fiction. Address: 304 Donahue Street, Sausalito, CA 94965, USA.

PRICE A(lice) Lindsay, b. 21 Oct 1927, Augusta, Georgia, USA. Writer; Artist; Publisher. Education: BA, Oklahoma State University, 1949; MA, University of Tulsa, 1970. Appointment: Scholar-in-Residence, Voices and Visions, 1990, 1992. Publications: Faces of the Waterworld, 1976; Our Dismembered Shadow, 1982; Swans of the World in Nature, History, Myth and Art, 1994. Contributions to: Enwright House; Rhino; Commonweal; Gryphon; Phoenix; Nimrod; Greenfield Review; Suncatcher. Honours: Fist Award, Nimrod, 1970; Pegasus Award, 1981; Arts and Humanities Literary Award, 1992. Membership: Poets And Writers. Address: 3113 South, Florence Avenue, Tulsa, OK 74015, USA.

PRICE (Alan) Anthony, b. 16 Aug 1928, Hertfordshire, England. Author; Journalist; Editor. m. (Yvonne) Ann Stone, 1953, 2 sons, 1 daughter. Education: Exhibitioner, MA, Merton College, Oxford, 1952. Appointment: Editor, The Oxford Times, 1972-88. Publications: The Labryinth Makers, 1970; The Alamut Ambush, 1971; Colonel Butler's Wolf, 1972; October Men, 1973; Other Paths to Glory, 1974; Our Man in Camelot, 1975; War Game, 1976; The '44 Vintage, 1978; Tomorrow's Ghost, 1979; The Hour of the Donkey, 1980; Soldier No More, 1981; The Old Vengeful, 1982; Gunner Kelly, 1983; Sion Crossing, 1984; Here Be Monsters, 1985; For the Good of the State, 1986; A New Kind of War, 1987; A Prospect of Vengeance, 1988; The Memory Trap, 1989; The Eyes of the Fleet, 1990. Honours: Silver Dagger, 1970, Gold Dagger, 1974, Crime Writers Association; Swedish Academy of Detection Prize, 1978. Literary Agent: A P Watt. Address: Wayside Cottage, Horton cum Studley, Oxford OX33 1AW, England.

PRICE Glanville, b. 16 June 1928, Rhaeadr, Wales. University Professor. m. Christine Winifred Thurston, 18 Aug 1954, 3 sons, 1 daughter. Education: University of Wales, Bangor, 1946-50; University of Paris, 1950-53; BA, Wales, 1949; MA, Wales, 1952; Docteur de l'Université de Paris, 1956. Appointments: Professor of French, University of Stirling, 1967-72, University of Wales, Aberystwyth, 1972-92; Research Professor, 1992-95; Professor Emeritus, 1995-, University of Wales; Joint Editor, The Year's Work in Modern Language Studies, 1972-92. Publications: The Present Position of Minority Languages in Western Europe, 1969; The French Language, Present and Past, 1971; William, Count of Orange: Four Old French Epics (editor), 1975; Romance Linguistics and the Romance Languages (with Kathryn F Bach), 1977; The Languages of Britain, 1984; Ireland and the Celtic Connection, 1987; An Introduction to French Pronunciation, 1991; A Comprehensive French Grammar, 1992; After The Celtic Connection (editor), 1992; Hommages offerts à Maria Manoliu, (editor with Coman Lupu), 1994. Contributions to: Journals. Memberships: Modern Humanities Research Association, chairman, 1979-90; Philological Society; Society for French Studies. Address: Department of European Languages, University of Wales, Aberystwyth, Ceredigion SY23 3DY, Wales.

PRICE Jennifer. See: HOOVER Helen Mary.

PRICE Reynolds, b. 1 Feb 1933, Macon, North Carolina, USA. Professor; Author; Poet; Dramatist. Education: AB, Duke University, 1955; BLitt, Merton College, Oxford, 1958. Appointments: Faculty, 1958-61, Assistant Professor, 1961-68, Associate Professor, 1968-72, Professor, 1972-77, James B Duke Professor, 1977-, Duke University; Writer-in-Residence, University of North Carolina at Chapel Hill, 1965, University of Kansas, 1967, 1969, 1980, University of North Carolina at Greensboro, 1971; Glasgow Professor, Washington and Lee University, 1971; Faculty, Salzburg Seminar, 1977. Publications: A Long and Happy Life, 1962; The Names and Faces of Heroes, 1963; A Generous Man, 1966; Love and Work, 1968; Permanent Errors, 1970; Things Themselves, 1972; The Surface of Earth, 1975; Early Dark, 1977; A Palpable God, 1978; The Source of Light, 1981; Vital Provisions, 1982; Private Contentment, 1984; Kate Vaiden, 1986; The Laws of Ice, 1986; A Common Room, 1987; Good Hearts, 1988; Clear

Pictures, 1989; The Tongues of Angels, 1990; The Use of Fire, 1990; New Music, 1990; The Foreseeable Future, 1991; Conversations with Reynolds Price, 1991; Blue Calhoun, 1993; Full Moon, 1993; The Collected Stories, 1993; A Whole New Life, 1994; The Promise of Rest, 1995; Three Gospels, 1996. Honours: William Faulkner Foundation Award for Notable First Novel, 1962; Sir Walter Raleigh Awards, 1962, 1976, 1981, 1984, 1986; Guggenheim Fellowship, 1964-65; National Endowment for the Arts Fellow, 1967-68; National Institute of Arts and Letters Award, 1971; Bellamann Foundation Award, 1972; North Carolina Award, 1977; National Book Critics Circle Award, 1986; Elmer H Bobst Award, 1988; R Hunt Parker Award, North Carolina Literary and Historical Society, 1991. Memberships: American Academy of Arts and Letters; Phi Beta Kappa; Phi Delta Theta. Address: PO Box 99014, Durham, NC 27708, USA.

PRICE Roger (David), b. 7 Jan 1944, Port Talbot, Wales. Professor of Modern History; Writer. Education: BA, University of Wales, University College of Swansea, 1965. Appointments: Lecturer, 1968-82, Senior Lecturer, 1982-83, Reader in Social History, 1984-91, Professor, European History, 1991-94, University of East Anglia; Lecturer, then Professsor of European History, University of East Anglia, 1968-94; Professor of Modern History, University of Wales, Aberystwyth, 1994-. Publications: The French Second Republic: A Social History, 1972; The Economic Modernization of France, 1975; Revolution and Reaction: 1848 and The Second French Republic (editor and contributor), 1975; 1848 in France, 1975; An Ecomomic History of Modern France, 1981; The Modernization of Rural France: Communications Networks and Agricultural Market Structures in 19th Century France, 1983; A Social History of 19th Century France, 1987; The Revolutions of 1848, 1989; A Concise History of France, 1993; Documents on the French Revolution of 1848, 1996; Napoleon III and the French Second Empire, 1997. Contributions to: Numerous Magazines and Journals. Honours: DLitt, University of East Anglia, 1985. Membership: Fellow, Royal Historical Society, 1983. Address: Department of History and Welsh History, University of Wales, Aberystwyth, Dyfed SY23 3DY, Wales.

PRICE Stanley, b. 12 Aug 1931, London, England. Writer. m. Judy Fenton, 5 July 1957, 1 son. Education: MA, University of Cambridge, England. Publications: Novels: Crusading for Kronk, 1960; A World of Difference, 1961; Just for the Record, 1962; The Biggest Picture, 1964. Stage plays: Horizontal Hold, 1967; The Starving Rich, 1972; The Two of Me, 1975; Moving, 1980; Why Me?, 1985. Screenplays: Arabesque, 1968; Gold, 1974; Shout at the Devil, 1975. TV plays: All Things Being Equal, 1970; Exit Laughing, 1971; Minder, 1980; The Kindness of Mrs Radcliffe, 1981; Moving, 1985; Star Quality, series, 1986; Close Relations, 1986-87; The Bretts, 1990. Contributions to: Observer; Sunday Telegraph; New York Times; Los Angeles Times; Punch; Plays and Players; New Statesman; Independent; Town. Memberships: Writer's Guild; Dramatists Club. Address: Douglas Rae, 28 Charing Cross Road, London WC2, England.

PRICE Susan, b. 8 July 1955, Brades Row, England. Children's Fiction Writer. Education: Tividale, England. Publications: Devil's Piper, 1973; Twopence a Tub, 1975; Sticks and Stones, 1976; Home from Home, 1977; Christopher Uptake, 1981; The Carpenter (stories), 1981; In a Nutshell, 1983; From Where I Stand, 1984; Ghosts at Large, 1984; Odin's Monster, 1986; The Ghost Drum, 1987; The Bone Dog, 1989; Forbidden Doors, 1990. Honours: The Other Award, 1975; Carnegie Medal, 1987. Membership: Society of Authors. Literary Agent: A M Heath & Co Ltd, 79 St Martins Lane, London. Address: c/o Faber & Faber Ltd, 3 Queen Square, London WC 1N 3AU, England.

PRICE Victor, b. 10 Apr 1930, Newcastle, County Down, Northern Ireland. Education: BA Hons, Modern Languages (French and German), Queen's University, Belfast, 1947-51. Appointments: With the BBC, 1956-90, ending as Head of German Language Service. Publications: Novels: The Death of Achilles, 1963; The Other Kingdom, 1964; Caliban's Wooing, 1966; The Plays of Georg Büchner, 1971; Two Parts Water (poems), 1980. Contributions to: Financial Times; Scotsman; BBC World Service; Deutschland Funk; Channel Four. Address: 22 Oxford Gardens, London W4 3BW, England.

PRIEST Christopher (McKenzie), b. 1943, United Kingdom. Freelance Writer. Publications: Indoctrinaire, 1970; Fugue for a Darkening Island, US edition as Darkening Island, 1972; Inverted World, 1974; Your Book of Film-Making, 1974; Real-Time World, 1974; The Space Machine, 1976; A Dream of Wessex, US edition as The

Perfect Lover, 1977; Anticipations (editor), 1978; An Infinite Summer, 1979; Stars of Albion (co-editor), 1979; The Affirmation, 1981; The Glamour, 1984; The Quiet Woman, 1990; The Prestige, 1995. Honours: James Tait Black Memorial Prize for Fiction, 1995. Memberships: Management Committee, Society of Authors, 1985-88. Literary Agent: Antony Harwood, Aitken Stone and Wylie. Address: c/o Aitken Stone & Wylie Ltd, 29 Fernshaw Road, London, SW10 0TG, England.

PRIESTLEY Brian, 10 July 1946, Manchester, England. Writer; Musician. Education: BA (Hon) French; Diploma of Education, Leeds University. Publications: Mingus, A Critical Biography, 1982; Jazz Piano, 6 volumes, 1983-90; Charlie Parker, 1984; John Coltrane, 1987; Jazz: The Essential Companion (with Ian Carr and Digby Fairweather), 1987; Jazz on Record, A History, 1988; Jazz - The Rough Guide (with Ian Carr and Digby Fairweather), 1995. Contributions to: Reviews and articles; The Gramophone; New Grove Encyclopedia of Jazz; The Cambridge Companion to the Piano; The International Directory of Black Composers. Literary Agent: Barbara Levy. Address: 120A Farningham Road, Caterham, Surrey CR3 6LJ, England.

PRINCE Alison (Mary), b. 26 Mar 1931, Kent, England. Writer. m. Goronwy Siriol Parry, 26 Dec 1957, 2 sons, 1 daughter. Education: Beckenham Grammar School; Slade School Diploma, London University; Art Teacher's Diploma, Goldsmith's College. Appointment: Fellow in Creative Writing, Jordanhill College, Glasgow, 1988-90. Publications: The Doubting Kind (young adults), 1974; How's Business (children's book), 1985; The Ghost Within (supernatural stories), 1987; The Blue Moon Day (children's book), 1989; The Necessary Goat (essays on creativity), 1992; Kenneth Grahame: An Innocent in the Wild Wood (biography), 1994; The Witching Tree (novel), 1996; The Sherwood Hero (children's book), 1996. Contributions to: New Statesman; Scotsman; Herald; Scottish Child; various educational journals. Honour: Runner-up for Smarties Prize, 1986; Guardian Fiction Award, 1996. Memberships: Scottish PEN; Society of Authors. Address: Burnfoot, Whiting Bay, Isle of Arran KA27 8QL, Scotland.

PRINCE F(rank) T(empleton), b. 13 Sept 1912, Kimberley, Cape Province, South Africa. Professor of English (retired); Poet. m. Pauline Elizabeth Bush, 10 Mar 1943, 2 daughters. Education: BA, Balliol College, Oxford, 1934. Appointments: Visiting Fellow, Princeton University, USA, 1935-36, All Souls College, Oxford, 1968-69; Lecturer, 1945-55, Reader, 1955-56, Professor of English, 1957-74, University of Southampton; Clark Lecturer, Cambridge University, 1972-73; Professor of English, University of the West Indies, Mona, Kingston, Jamaica, 1975-78; Fannie Hurst Visiting Professor, Brandeis University, Waltham, Massachusetts, 1978-80; Visiting Professor, Washington University, St Louis, 1980-81; Sana'a University, North Yemen, 1981-83; Writer-in-Residence, Hollins College, Virginia, 1984. Publications: Poetry: Poems, 1938; Soldiers Bathing and Other Poems, 1954; The Stolen Heart, 1957; The Doors of Stone: Poems, 1938-1962, 1963; Memoirs of Oxford, 1970; Penguin Modern Poets 20 (with John Heath-Stubbs and Stephen Spender), 1971; Drypoints of the Hasidim, 1975; Afterword on Rupert Brooke, 1976; Collected Poems, 1979; The Yuan Chen Variations, 1981; Later On, 1983; Fragment Poetry, 1986; Walks in Rome, 1987; Collected Poems, 1935-92, 1993. Other: The Italian Element in Milton's Verse, 1954. Editor: John Milton: Samson Agonistes, 1957; William Shakespeare: The Poems, 1960; John Milton: Paradise Lost, Books I and II, 1962; John Milton: Comus and Other Poems, 1968. Contributions to: Keats Country (poem), PN Review 106, 1995. Honours: DLitt, University of Southampton, 1981, University of York, 1982; American Academy and Institute of Arts and Letters Award, 1982. Address: 32 Brookvale Road, Southampton, Hampshire S017 1QR, England.

PRINGLE-JONES Jennifer Suzanne, b. 26 May 1946, Tasmania, Australia. Journalist. m. 21 July 1967, 1 son, 2 daughters. Education: Dux of School, St Michael's Collegiate School, 1962. Appointments: Staff, Mercury Newspaper, 1962-67; Journalist, ABC Radio/TV 1967-71, TAS/TV 1978-86, Commonwealth Scientific and Industrial Research Organisation, 1986-. Publications: Discovering Tasmania, 1981; Explore Tasmania, 1983, 2nd edition, 1989; Tasmania is a Garden, 1985; Tasmania the Beautiful Island, 1989. Contributions to: Various publications. Honours: Numerous scripting awards; National Tourism Award; TV News Reporters Award. Membership: Australian Journalists Association; Australian Day Council; Queen Elizabeth II Silver Jubilee Trust for Young Australians; Advisory Board, St John's Hospital. Address: 29 Amanda Crescent, Sandy Bay, Tasmania 7005, Australia.

PRIOR Allan, b. 13 Jan 1922, Newcastle upon Tyne, England. Author. Education: Newcastle upon Tyne; Blackpool. Publications: A Flame in the Air, 1951; The Joy Ride, 1952; The One-Eyed Monster, 1958; One Away, 1961; The Interrogators, 1965; The Operators, 1966; The Loving Cup, 1968; The Contract, 1970; Paradiso, 1972; Affair, 1976; Never Been Kissed in the Same Place Twice, 1978; Theatre, 1981; A Cast of Stars, 1983; The Big March, 1983; Her Majesty's Hit Man, 1986; Führer - the Novel, 1991; The Old Man and Me, 1994; The Old Man and Me Again, 1996. Address: Summerhill, 24 Waverley Road, St Albans, Herts, England.

PRITCHARD Margaret (Marged) Jones, b. 29 Aug 1919, Tregaron, Dyfed, Wales, England. Modern Languages Teacher; Lecturer for Welsh Learners. m. Robert Gwilym Pritchard, 5 Apr 1949, 1 son. Education: Honours Degree in French, 1940; First Class Teaching Diploma, Bangor, 1941. Appointment: Literary Adjudicator, Welsh Arts Council, 1991; Adjudicator for the main Novel Competition, National Eisteddfod, 1996. Publications: Cregyn Ar y Traeth, 1974; Gwylanod yn y Mynydd, 1975; Clymau and Disgwyl, 1976; Mid Mudan Mo'r Môr, 1976; Enfys y Bore, 1980; Nhw Oedd Yno, 1986; Adar Brith; Unwaith Eto (Short Stories), 1994. Contributions to: Taliesin; Traethodydd; Barn; y Genhinen; y Faner. Honour: Welsh Arts Council Prize, 1975. Membership: Welsh Academy, Adjudicator of Prose, 1993. Literary Agent: Gomer Press, Dyfed. Address: Glaslyn, Minffordd, Penrhyndeudraeth, Gwynedd LL48 6HL, Wales.

PRITCHARD R(obert) John, b. 30 Nov 1945, Los Angeles, California, USA. Freelance Writer and Broadcaster. m. (1) Sonia Magbanna Zaide, 15 Aug 1969, div 1984, 1 son, 1 daughter, (2) Lady Elayne Antonia Lodge, 20 Dec 1989. Education: AB, University of California, 1967; MA, 1968, PhD, 1980, London School of Economics, England; LLB, University of Kent at Canterbury, England. Appointments: Managing Editor, Millennium: Journal of International Studies, 1974-78; Consultant Editor/Compiler, Tokyo War Trial Project, London School of Economics, 1981-87; Director/Company Secretary, Integrated Dictionary Systems Ltd, 1988-90; Lecturer in History, University of Kent, 1990-93; Fellow in War Studies, Kings College, London, 1990-93; Simon Senior Research Fellow in History, University of Manchester, 1993-94; Director, Historical Enterprises, 1993-; Chairman of the Board, Robert M Kempner Collegium, 1996-. Publications: Reichstag Fire and Ashes of Democracy, 1972; Tokyo War Crimes Trial Complete Transcripts, Proceedings of International Military Tribunal for Far East (with S M Zaide), 22 volumes, 1981; Tokyo War Crimes Trial, Index and Guide (with S M Zaide), 5 volumes, 1981-87; General History of the Philippines (co-author), vol 1, American Half Century 1898-1946, 1984; The Tokyo War Crimes Trial: An International Symposium (co-author), 1984, 1986; Far Eastern Influences on British Strategy Towards the Great Powers 1937-39, 1987; Overview of the Historical Importance of the Tokyo War Trial, 1987; Total War: Causes and Causes of the Second World War (co-author), 1989, 1995; Japan and the Second World War (with Lady Toshiko Marks), 1989; The Japanese Army's Secret of Secrets (co-author), 1989; From Pearl Harbour to Hiroshima (co-author), 1993; La Déportation: La Système Concentrationnaire Nazi (co-author), 1995; Wada umi no Koe wo Kiku: senso sekinin to Ningen no Tsumi; to no Ma (Harken to the Cries at Our Birth: The Intervals Separating War Responsibility and Crimes of Humanity,(co-author), 1996; Handbook of the Literature and Research of World War Two (co-author), 1997; International Criminal Law (co-author), 1997. Contributions to: International Criminal Law (3 volumes), 1996; Encyclopedia of Terrorism (3 volumes, 1996); Handbook of the Literature and Research of World War Two (2 volumes), 1996. Literary Agent: Sheila Watson, Watson, Little Ltd, 12 Egbert Street, London, NW1 8LJ. Address: 11 Charlotte Square, Margate, Kent, CT9 1LR, England.

PRITCHARD William H(arrison), b. 12 Nov 1932, Binghamton, New York, USA. Professor of English; Writer. m. 24 Aug 1957, 3 sons. Education: BA, Amherst College, 1953; MA, PhD, Harvard University, 1960. Appointments: Faculty 1958-, later Henry Clay Folger Professor of English, Amherst College. Publications: Wyndham Lewis, 1968; Seeing Through Everything: English Writers, 1918-1940, 1977; Lives of the Modern Poets, 1980, 2nd edition, 1997; Frost: A Literary Life Reconsidered, 1984, 2nd edition, 1994; Randall Jarrell: A Literary Life, 1990; Playing It By Ear: Literary Essays and Reviews, 1994; English Papers: A Teaching Life, 1995; Lives of the Modern Poets, 2nd edition, 1996; English Papers: A Teaching Life, 1996. Contributions to: Various publications. Honours: American Council of Learned Societies Fellowship; Guggenheim Fellowship; National Endowment for the

Humanities Fellowship. Membership: Association of Literary Scholars and Critics. Address: 62 Orchard Street, Amherst, MA 01002, USA.

PRITZKER Andreas E M, b. 4 Dec 1945, Baden, Switzerland. Physicist. m. Marthi Ehrlich, 4 Dec 1970. Education: PhD, Physics, Swiss Federal Institute of Technology, Zürich. Publications: Filberts Verhaengnis, 1990; Das Ende der Taeuschung, 1993. Membership: Swiss Writers Association. Address: Rebmoosweg 55, CH-5200 Brugg, Switzerland.

PROCASSION Michael, b. 1946, USA. Playwright. Publications: The Shadow Box, 1977; Black Angel, 1984; The Lady and the Clarinet, 1985; Ice; Breaking Up; The Bonfire of the Vanities. Honours: Pulitzer Prize in Drama, 1978; Tony Award, 1978. Address: c/o Dramatists Play Service, 440 Park Avenue South, New York, NY 10016, USA.

PROSSER Harold Lee, b. 31 Dec 1944, Springfield, Missouri, USA. Author; Composer; Interfaith Minister. m. (1), div 1988, 2 daughters, (2) Debra Cunningham Phipps, 6 Dec, 1994. Education: AA, Santa Monica College, 1968; BS, 1974, MSED, 1982, Southwest Missouri State University; Ordained Interfaith Minister, New Mexico Theological Seminary, 1994. Publications: Dandelion Seeds: 18 Stories, 1974; Goodbye Lon Chaney Jr, Goodbye, 1977; Desert Woman Visions: 100 Poems, 1987; Jack Bimbo's Touring Circus Poems, 1988; Charles Beaumont (biography), 1994; Numerous musical compositions for publication. Contributions to: Honours: Manuscripts permanently housed and stored at the following universities under title: The H L Prosser Collection: 1. Golden Library, Eastern New Mexico University at Portales, New Mexico; 2. Archival Heritage Centre, University of Wyoming at Laramie, Wyoming; 3. Donnelly Library, New Mexico Highlands University at Las Vegas, New Mexico. Memberships: American Society of Composers, Authors, and Publishers; Vedanta Society. Address: 1313 South Jefferson Avenue, Springfield, MO 65807, USA.

PROULX E(dna) Annie, b. 22 Aug 1935, Norwich, Connecticut, USA. Writer. m. James Hamilton Lang, 22 June 1969, div 1990, 3 sons. Education: BA, University of Vermont, 1969; MA, Sir George Williams University, Montreal, 1973. Publications: Heart Songs and Other Stories, 1988; Postcards, 1992; The Shipping News, 1993; Accordion Crimes, 1996. Contributions to: Periodicals. Honours: Guggenheim Fellowship, 1992; PEN/Faulkner Award, 1993; National Book Award for Fiction, 1993; Chicago Tribune Heartland Award, 1993; Irish Times International Fiction Award, 1993; Pulitzer Prize in Fiction, 1994. Memberships: Phi Alpha Theta; Phi Beta Kappa; PEN American Centre. Address: c/o Simon and Schuster Inc, 1230 Avenue of the Americas, New York, NY 10020, USA.

PRUITT William O(badiah) Jr, b. 1 Sept 1922, Easton, Pennsylvania, USA. University Professor; Senior Scholar. m. Erna Nauert, 5 Feb 1951, 1 son, 1 daughter. Education: BSc, University of Maryland, 1947; MA, University of Michigan, 1948; PhD, University of Michigan, 1952. Publications: Wild Harmony; Boreal Ecology; Author of 65 Scientific Papers; Author of 40 Popular Articles. Honours: Fellow, Arctic Institute of North America; Fellow, Explorers Club; Seton Medal, Manitoba Naturalists Society; Northern Science Award and Centenary Medal, Government of Canada; Stefansson Award, University of Manitoba; DSc (Hon) University of Alaska, 1993. Memberships: American Society of Mammalogists, Arctic Institute; Sigma Xi. Address: Department of Zoology, University of Manitoba, Winnipeg, Manitoba R3T 2N2, Canada.

PRUTER Robert, b. 1 July 1944, Philadelphia, Pennsylvania, USA. Editor. m. 22 July 1972, 1 daughter. Education: BA, 1967, MA, 1976, Roosevelt University. Publications: Chicago Soul, 1991; Blackwell Guide to Soul Recordings (editor and contributor), 1993; Doowop: The Chicago Scene, 1996. Contributions to: Chicago History; Living Blues; Goldmine; Juke Blues; Record Collectors' Monthly. Address: 576 Stratford Avenue, Elmhurst, IL 60126, USA.

PRUTKOV Kozma. See: **SNODGRASS W D.**

PRVULOVICH Zika Rad, (Dr Peters), b. 4 Dec 1920, Vlahovo, Serbia, Yugoslavia. Retired University Senior Lecturer. m. Janet Mary Atkins, 11 Aug 1959, 1 son, 1 daughter. Education: BA (Mod), Trinity College, Dublin, 1951; BA (Oxon), 1952; DPhil (Oxon), 1956; MA (Oxon), 1957. Publications: Njegoseva Teorija Saznauja i Sistem, 1981; Prince-Bishop Hjegosh's Religious Philosophy, 1984; Serbia between the Swastika and the Red Star, 1986; Tajna Boga i Tajna

Sveta, 1991; The Ray of the Microcosm, translation of Prince-Bishop Njegosh's poem Luca Mikrokozma (bilingual edition with critical commentary and introduction in English), 1992. Contributions to: Many contributions to various literary, political, religious and philosophical journals and magazines. Honour: Wray Prize in Philosophy, Dublin University, 1951. Memberships: Honorary Librarian, Dublin University Philosophical Society; PEN, English Section; Honorary Member, Serbian Writers Club; Society of Serbian Writers and Artist, England; Philosophy of Education Society of Great Britain; Oriel Society; University of Birningham Common Room. Address: 26 Wheeler's Lane, King's Heath, Birmingham B13 0SA, England.

PRYCE-JONES David, b. 15 Feb 1936, Vienna, Austria. m. 29 July 1959, 1 son, 2 daughters. Education: BA, MA, Magdalen College, Oxford, 1956-59. Appointments: Literary Editor: Time & Tide, 1961; Spectator, 1964. Publications: Owls & Satyrs, 1961; The Sands of Summer, 1963; Next Generation, 1964; Quondam, 1965; The Stranger's View, 1967; The Hungarian Revolution, 1969; Running Away, 1969; The Face of Defeat, 1971; The England Commune, 1973; Unity Mitford, 1976; Vienna, 1978; Shirley's Guild, 1981; Paris in the Third Reich, 1983; Cyril Connolly, 1984; The Afternoon Sun, 1986; The Closed Circle, 1989; Inheritance, 1992; You Can't Be Too Careful, 1993; The War That Never Was, 1995. Contributions to: Numerous journals and magazines. Honour: Wingate Prize, 1986; Sunlight Literary Prize, 1989. Memberships: Royal Society of Literature. Literary Agent: The Peters Fraser and Dunlop Group Ltd. Address: Lower Pentwyn, Gwenddwr, Powys LD2 3LQ, Wales.

PRYNNE J(eremy) H(alvard), b. 24 June 1936, England. Education: Graduate, Jesus College, Cambridge, 1960. Appointments: Frank Knox Fellow, Harvard University, 1960-61; Fellow, University Lecturer, and Librarian, Cambridge University, 1962-. Publications: Kitchen Poems, 1968; Day Light Songs, 1968; The White Stones, 1969; Brass, 1971; Into the Day, 1972; Wound Response, 1974; High Pink on Chrome, 1975; News of Warring Clans, 1977; Down where changed, 1979; Poems, 1982; The Oval Window, 1983; Bands Around the Throat, 1987; Word Order, 1989; Not-You, 1993; Her Weasles Wild Returning, 1994. Address: Gonville & Caius College, Cambridge CB2 1TA, England.

PRYOR Adel. See: **WASSERFALL Adel.**

PRYOR Bonnie Helen, b. 22 Dec 1942, Los Angeles, California, USA. Author. m. Robert E Pryor, 2 sons, 4 daughters. Publications: Grandpa Bear, 1985; Rats, Spiders and Love, 1986; Amanda and April, 1986; Grandpa Bear's Christmas, 1986; Mr Z and the Time Clock, 1986; Vinegar Pancakes and Vanishing Cream, 1987; House on Maple Street, 1987; Mr Munday and Rustlers, 1988; Seth of Lion People, 1989; Plumtree War, 1989; Porcupine Mouse, 1989; Perfect Percy, 1989; Mr Munday and Space Creatures, 1989; Merry Christmas Amanda and April, 1990; 24 Hour Lipstick Mystery, 1990; Greenbrook Farm, 1991; Jumping Jenny, 1992; Beaver Boys, 1992; Lottie's Dream, 1992; Poison Ivy and Eyebrow Wigs, 1993; Horses in the Garage, 1993; Birthday Blizzard, 1993; Marvelous Marvin and the Werewolf Mystery, 1994; Marvelous Marvin and the Pioneer Ghost, 1995; Dream Jar, 1996. Contributions to: Magazines, Childrens Literature. Honours: Children's Choice, 1986; Outstanding Book List, National Society of Science Teachers and National Society of Social Studies, 1987; Irma Simonton Black Award, Bank Street College, 1989; National Society of Science Teachers Award for Seth of Lion People, 1990; Ohioana Alice Louise Wood Award for Contributions to Children Literature. Membership: Society of Children's Book Writers. Address: 19600 Baker Road, Gambier, OH 43022, USA.

PRZYBYSZ Janusz Anastzy, b. 31 May 1926, Poznan, Poland. Journalist; Writer. m. Danuta Maria Magolewska, 10 Sept 1951, 1 daughter. Education: University of Poznan, 1950. Publications: Several books and short story collections, 1962-90. Contributions to: Periodicals. Honours: Reymont Literary Prize, 1987; City of Poznan Prize, 1988. Memberships: Association of Authors and Composers; Polish Journalists Association. Address: ul Galileusza 6A m.6, 60-159 Poznan, Poland.

PRZYMANOWSKI Janusz, b. 20 Jan 1922, Warsaw, Poland. Author; Journalist. m. Aleksandra Nowinska, 2 June 1984, 1 daughter. Education: University of Warsaw, 1964. Publications: Over 15 books and 200 songs. Contributions to: Various publications and television. Honours: Literary Prizes, Ministry of National Defence, 1959, 1961, 1966, 1967, 1987, Ministry of Culture and Art, 1967, and the Prime

Minister, 1977. Membership: Union of Polish Authors. Address: ul Deuga, 30/34m 00-238 Warsaw, Poland.

PRZYPKOWSKI Andrzej Jozef, b. 9 July 1930, Poland. Writer. m. Halina Sienska, 17 Mar 1980, 1 daughter. Education: University of Warsaw, 1952. Publications: Gdzies we Francji, 1966; Gdy Wrocisz do Montpellier, 1969; Na ma jutra w Saint-Nazaire, 1971; Taniec marihuany, 1977; Palm City, 1978; Victoria, 1980; 18 novels, 1 travel book, including latest novel Miraz, 1987. Contributions to: Nike; Argumenty. Honour: Order of Polonia Restituta, 1980. Memberships: Union of Polish Writers; National Council of Culture. Literary Agent: Authors Agency Ltd, Warsaw. Address: Graniczna 62, 05-540 Zalesie Gorne, Poland.

PUGH Dan(iel Lovelock), b. 11 Mar 1924, England. Engineer's Buyer (retired); Poet. m. Doris Irene Wheatcroft, 22 Sep 1951, 1 son, 4 daughters. Education: Evening and Correspondence Courses in Trades Unionism and Local Government, 1944-46; Old Testament, New Testament, Art of Teaching, Preaching, Child Psychology, 1951-55; Work Study, 1974. Contributions to: Poetry and creative articles to various publications, mainly UK, also South Africa, New Zealand, USA. Honours: Poem in top 5% Rhyme Revival Competition, 1981, published in 1982 Anthology; Haiku in Top 100 (of 5200), BHA-JA: Contest, 1991; Sonnet recommended, Age Concern Competition, 1991; Winner, Hrafnhon Magazine International Literary Competition, 1991; Mirrors, Tanka Award Poet, (USA), 1992. Memberships: Christian Writers Forum; Fellowship of Christian Writers. Literary Agent: Gerald England, New Hope International (overseas placements). Address: 8 Wyvern Terrace, Melton Mowbray, Leicestershire, LE13 1AD, England.

PUGLISI Angela Aurora, b. 28 Jan 1949, Messina, Italy. Professorial University Lecturer; Writer. Education: BA, Dunbarton College, 1972; MFA, Painting, 1974, MA, Art History, MA, Language and Literature, 1977, PhD, Comparative Literature, 1983. Appointments: Education Consultant, US Government, 1983-86; Faculty, Georgetown University, Washington, DC, 1986-; Education Specialist, US Government 1993-. Publications: Towards Excellence in Education Through Liberal Arts, 1984; Homage, 1985; Nature's Canvas, 1985; Sonnet, 1985; Primavera, 1986; Sand Dunes, 1986; Sun's Journey, 1986; Jet d'Eau, 1986; Ocean Waves, 1986; Prelude, 1987; Woodland Revisited, 1988; Ethics in Journalism, 1989; Ethics in Higher Education, 1995; Homage II, in Voce Italiana, 1996. Other: Artistic publications, 1989-90. Honour: Certificate for Outstanding Service to Education and Education Reform. Memberships: Catholic Academy of Sciences; Corcoran College of Art Association; Italian Cultural Center, Casa Italiana, founding member; SEE; Lady of the Holy Sepulchre of Jerusalem. Address: 2843 Cedar Lane, Vienna, VA 22180, USA.

PUJUN Zhang. See: **LUO Bin Ji.**

PULLEIN-THOMPSON Christine. See: **POPESCU Christine.**

PULSFORD Petronella, b. 4 Feb 1946, Leeds, Yorkshire, England. Actress; Writer; Director. Education: BA, Hons, English, St Hilda's College, Oxford. Publication: Lee's Ghost (novel), 1990. Honour: Constable Trophy for Fiction, 1989. Memberships: Society of Authors; Equity. Address: 8 Thomas Street West, Savile Park, Halifax, West Yorks HX1 3HF, England.

PUNNOOSE Kunnuparambil P, b. 26 Mar 1942, Kottayam, India. Editor. m. Santhamma, 9 Jan 1967, 1 son, 2 daughters. Education: College Graduate, 1962. Appointments: Managing Editor, Concept Publishing Company, 1974-75, Asian Literary Market Review, 1975-; Director, Darsan Books Ltd, 1983-; General Convener, Kottayam International Book Fair, 1984-. Publications: Directory of American University Presses, 1979; American Book Trade in India, 1981; Bookdealers in India and the Orient, 1992; Studying in India, 1994. Contributions to: Over 100 articles on the art and craft of writing and the business of book and magazine publishing. Honours: Kottayam International Book Fair Awards, 1989, 1994. Memberships: Authors Guild of India; Kerala Book Society; Afro-Asian Book Council, New Delhi. Literary Agent: Jaffe Publishing Management Service. Address: Kunnuparambil Buildings, Kurichy, Kottayam 686549, India.

PURCELL Sally (Anne Jane), b. 1 Dec 1944, England. Poet. Education: MA, Lady Margaret Hall, Oxford, 1970. Publications: The Devil's Dancing Hour, 1968; The Holly Queen, 1972; Provençal

Poems, 1969; Dark of Day, 1977; By the Clear Fountain, 1980; Guenever and the Looking Glass, 1984; Lake & Labyrinth, 1985; Four Poems, 1985; Heraldic Symbols (co-author), 1986; Through Lent with Blessed Ramon Lull, 1994. Other: The Happy Unicorns, 1971; George Peele, 1972; Monarchs and the Muse, 1972; The Poems of Charles of Orleans, 1973; The Early Italian Poets, 1981. Translations: Dante, De Vulgari Eloquentia, 1979; Gaspara Stampa, 1985; Nikos Gatsos, Amorgós, 1986. Contributions to: Acumen; Swansea Review; Outposts; William Oxley's anthology Completing the Picture, 1995. Honour: Arts Council Award, 1971. Address: c/o Anvil Press Poetry, 69 King George Street, London SE10 8PX, England.

PURDUE Arthur William, b. 29 Jan 1941, North Shields, England. University Lecturer. m. 29 Aug 1979, 1 daughter. Education: BA Hons, History, King's College, London, 1962; Diploma of Education, King's College, Durham University, 1963; Master of Letters, University of Newcastle-upon-Tyne, 1974. Publications: The Civilization of the Crowd (with J M Golby), 1984; The Making of the Modern Christmas (with J M Golby), 1986; The Monarchy and the British People (with J M Golby), 1988. Contributions to: Salisbury Review; Times Higher Education Supplement; New Society; Country Life; Northern History; International Review of Social History. Memberships: Trollope Society; Fellow, Royal Historical Society. Address: The Old Rectory, Allendale, Hexham, Northumberland NE47 9DA, England.

PURDY Al(fred Wellington), b. 30 Dec 1918, Wooler, Ontario, Canada. Poet; Author; Editor. m. Eurithe Mary Jane Parkhurst, 1941, 1 son. Education: Albert College, Belleville, Ontario; Trenton Collegiate Institute. Appointments: Visiting Associate Professor, Simon Fraser University, 1970; Writer-in-Residence, Loyola College, 1973-74, University of Western Ontario, 1977-78, University of Toronto, 1987-88. Publications: Poetry: The Enchanted Echo, 1944; Pressed on Sand, 1956; The Crafte so Longer to Lerne, 1959; Poems for All the Annettes, 1962; The Blur in Between, 1963; The Cariboo Horses, 1965; North of a Summer, 1967; Wild Grape Wine, 1968; Love in a Burning Building, 1970; Hiroshima Poems, 1972; Selected Poems, 1972; On the Bearpath Sea, 1973; In Search of Owen Roblin, 1974; Sex and Death, 1973; The Poems of Al Purdy, 1976; Sun Dance at Dusk, 1976; At Marsport Drugstore, 1977; No Other Country, 1977; A Handful of Earth, 1977; Being Alive: Poems, 1958-78, 1978; No Second Spring, 1978; Moths in the Iron Curtain, 1979; The Stone Bird, 1981; Bursting into Song: An Al Purdy Omnibus, 1982; Birdwatching at the Equator, 1983; Piling Blood, 1984; Collected Poems, 1986; The Woman on the Shore, 1990; Naked with Summer in Your Mouth, 1994. Other: A Splinter in the Heart (novel), 1990; Margaret Laurence--Al Purdy: A Friendship in Letters, 1993; Starting from Ameliasburgh: Collected Prose, 1995. Honours: Governor-General's Awards, 1966, 1987; Order of Canada, 1982; Order of Ontario, 1987. Address: RR No 1, Ameliasburgh, Ontario K0K 1A0, Canada.

PURDY Carol Ann, b. 5 Jan 1943, Long Beach, California, USA. Writer; Psychotherapist in Private Practice. m. John Purdy, 8 June 1963, 1 son, 2 daughters. Education: BA, California State University, Long Beach, 1964; MSW, California State University, Sacramento, 1990. Publications: Iva Dunnit and the Big Wind, 1985; Least of All, 1987; The Kid Power Program, Groups for High Risk Children, 1989; Mrs Merriwether's Musical Cat, 1994; Nesuya's Basket, 1997. Memberships: Society of Children's Book Writers; National Association of Social Workers. Literary Agent: Faith Hamlin, Stanford J Greenburger Literary Agency. Address: Kid Power, 645 Antelope Blvd #22, Red Bluff, CA 96080, USA.

PURDY James (Amos), b. 17 July 1923, Ohio, USA. Author; Poet; Dramatist. Education: University of Chicago; University of Puebla, Mexico. Publications: Novels: 63: Dream Palace, 1956; Malcolm, 1959; The Nephew, 1961; Cabot Wright Begins, 1964; Eustace Chisholm and the Works, 1967; Jeremy's Version, 1970; I Am Elijah Thrush, 1972; The House of the Solitary Maggot, 1974; Color of Darkness, 1974; Malcolm, 1974; In a Shallow Grave, 1976; Narrow Rooms, 1978; Mourners Below, 1981; On Glory's Course, 1984; In the Hollow of His Hand, 1986; Candles of Your Eyes, 1986; Garments the Living Wear, 1989; Out with the Stars, 1992. Story Collections: Don't Call Me by My Right Name and Other Stories, 1956; 63: Dream Palace: A Novella and Nine Stories, 1957; Children Is All, 1962; An Oyster Is a Wealthy Beast, 1967; Mr Evening: A Story and Nine Poems, 1968; On the Rebound: A Story and Nine Poems, 1970; A Day After the Fair: A Collection of Plays and Stories, 1977; The Candles of Your Eyes and Thirteen Other Stories, 1987; 63: Dream Palace:

Selected Stories, 1957-1987, 1991. Poetry: The Running Sun, 1971; Sunshine Is an Only Child, 1973; Lessons and Complaints, 1978; Sleep Tight, 1979; The Brooklyn Branding Parlors, 1985; Collected Poems, 1990 Plays: Cracks, 1963; Wedding Finger, 1974; Two Plays, 1979; Scrap of Paper, 1981; The Berrypicker, 1981; Proud Flesh, 1981. Honours: National Institute of Arts and Letters Grant, 1958; Guggenheim Fellowships, 1958, 1962; Ford Foundation Grant, 1961; Morton Dauwen Zabel Fiction Award, American Academy of Arts and Letters, 1993. Address: 236 Henry Street, Brooklyn, NY 11201, USA.

PURNELL Kathryn Isabell, b. Vancouver, British Columbia, Canada. Writer; Poet; Editor; Tutor. m. William Ernst Purnell, 2 daughters. Education: Melbourne University, Australia. Career: Editor, Society of Women Writers, Australia, 1980-91; Writer in Community, City of Melbourne, East Melbourne Library, Victoria, 1993. Publications: Larpent - The History of a Ship and a District, 1989. Poetry: Pandora, 1979; Safari, 1979; Trillium, 1981; Otway Country, 1984; Fairy Trees, 1990; A Harpsicord of Water, 1994. Essays on poetry: Magic Perhaps; The Perpetual Evaluation. Editor, poetry anthologies: Spin of Pink Health, 1980; Spin of Gold Wattle, 1982. Editor, prose anthologies, 1984-89: Journeys; Arrivals; Remember. Series Editor, Gold Wattle Poets Nos 1-32, 1983-92; The Beautiful Hill, 1993. Contributions to: Magazines. Honours: Prose Award, 1967; Poetry Awards, 1972, 1973, 1975, 1976, 1979. Memberships: Society of Women Writers, Australia; International PEN; Victorian Writers Centre. Address: East Melbourne, Victoria, Australia.

PURSER Philip John, b. 28 Aug 1925, Letchworth, England. Journalist; Author. m. Ann Elizabeth Goodman, 18 May 1957, 1 son, 2 daughters. Education: MA, St Andrews University, 1950. Appointments: Staff, Daily Mail, 1951-57; Television Critic, Sunday Telegraph, 1961-87. Publications: Peregrination 22, 1962; Four Days to the Fireworks, 1964; The Twentymen, 1967; Night of Glass, 1968; The Holy Father's Navy, 1971; The Last Great Tram Race, 1974; Where is He Now?, 1978; A Small Explosion, 1979; The One and Only Phyllis Dixey, 1978; Halliwell's Television Companion (with Leslie Halliwell), 1982, 2nd edition, 1986; Shooting the Hero, 1990; Poeted: The Final Quest of Edward James, 1991; Done Viewing, 1992. Contributions to: Numerous magazines and journals. Memberships: Writers Guild of Great Britain; British Academy of Film and Television Arts; Academy Club. Literary Agent: David Highams Associates. Address: 10 The Green, Blakesley, Towcester, Northamptonshire NN12 8RD, England.

PURVES Libby (Elizabeth Mary), 2 Feb 1950, London, England. Journalist/Broadcaster. m. Paul Heiney, 2 Feb 1980, 1 son, 1 daughter. Education: BA 1st class honours, Oxford, 1971. Appointments: Presenter/Writer, BBC, 1975-; Editor, Tatler, 1983. Publications: Adventures Under Sail (editor), 1962; Britain at Play, 1982; The Sailing Weekend Book, 1984; How Not to Be a Perfect Mother, 1987; One Summer's Grace, 1989; How Not to Raise a Perfect Child, 1991; Casting Off, 1995; A Long Walk in Wintertime, 1996; Home Leave, 1997. Contributions to: Columnist in: Times, Sunday Express; magazines in Britain and Australia. Honour: Best Book of the Sea, 1984. Literary Agent: A P Watt, 20 John Street, London WC1, England. Address: Vale Farm, Middleton, Saxmundham, Suffolk 1P17 3LT, England.

PUZO Mario, b. 15 Oct 1920, New York, New York, USA. Author; Screenwriter. m. Erika Lina Broske, 1946, 3 sons, 2 daughters. Education: New School for Social Research, New York City; Columbia University. Publications: The Dark Arena, 1955, revised edition, 1985; The Fortunate Pilgrim, 1964; The Godfather, 1969; Fools Die, 1978; The Sicilian, 1984; The Fourth K, 1991; The Last Don, 1996. Screenplays: The Godfather (with Francis Ford Coppola), 1972; The Godfather, Part II (with Francis Ford Coppola), 1974; Earthquake (with George Fox), 1974; Superman (with Robert Benton, David Newman and Leslie Newman), 1978; Superman II (with David Newman and Leslie Newman), 1981; The Godfather, Part III (with Francis Ford Coppola), 1990; Christopher Columbus: The Discovery (with Cary Bates and John Briley), 1992. Other: The Godfather Papers and Other Confessions, 1972; Inside Las Vegas, 1977. Contributions to: Many magazines. Honours: Academy Awards, 1972, 1974; Golden Globe Awards, 1973, 1990. Address: c/o Random House Inc, 201 East 50th Street, New York, NY 10022, USA.

PYBUS Rodney, b. 5 June 1938, Newcastle upon Tyne, Northumberland, England. Lecturer; Poet. m. Ella Johnson, 1961, 2 sons. Education: MA, Gonville and Caius College, Cambridge, 1965.

Appointments: Lecturer, Macquarie University, Sydney, 1976-79; Literature Officer, Northern Arts, Cumbria, 1979-81. Publications: In Memoriam Milena, 1973; Bridging Loans and Other Poems, 1976; At the Stone Junction, 1978; The Loveless Letters, 1981; Wall, 1981; Talitha Cumi, 1983; Cicadas in Their Summers, 1965-85, 1988; Flying Blues, 1994. Co-Editor: Adams Dream, 1981. Honours: Arts Council Fellowships. Address: 21 Plough Lane, Sudbury, Suffolk CO10 6AU, England.

PYENSON Lewis Robert, b. 26 Sept 1947, Pt Pleasant Beach, New Jersey, USA. University Professor; Administrator. m. Susan Ruth Sheets, 19 Aug 1973, 2 sons, 1 daughter. Education: BA Honors Physics, Swarthmore College, 1969; MSc Physics, University of Wyoming, 1970; PhD, History of Science, Johns Hopkins University, 1974. Appointments: Lecturer to Professor, Université de Montréal, Canada, 1973-86; Professor of History, University of Montreal, 1986-95; Professor of History and Mathematics and Dean of the Graduate School, University of Southwestern Louisiana, 1995-. Publications: Neohumanism and the Persistance of Pure Mathematics in Wilhelmian Germany, 1983; The Young Einstein, 1985; Cultural Imperialism and Exact Sciences, 1985; Empire of Reason, 1989; Civilizing Mission, 1993. Contributions to: History of Science; Annals of Science; THES; ISIS; Historical Studies in the Physical and Biological Sciences. Honours: Sigma Xi, 1985; Royal Society, Canada, fellow. 1994. Memberships: History of Science Society; X Club. Address: Graduate School, University of Southwestern Louisiana, Lafayette, LA 70504, USA.

PYNCHON Thomas (Ruggles Jr), b. 8 May 1937, Glen Cove, Long Island, New York, USA. Author. Education: BA, Cornell University, 1958. Publications: V, 1963; The Crying of Lot 49, 1965; Gravity's Rainbow, 1973; Mortality and Mercy in Vienna, 1976; Low-lands, 1978; Slow Learner (short stories), 1984; In the Rocket's Red Glare, 1986; Vineland, 1990. Contributions to: Periodicals. Honours: Rosenthal Foundation Award, National Institute of Arts and Letters, 1967; Howells Medal, American Academy of Arts and Letters, 1975; John D and Catharine T MacArthur Foundation Fellowship, 1988. Address: c/o Melanie Jackson Agency, 250 West 57th Street, Suite 1119, New York, NY 10107, USA.

Q

QAZI Moin, b. 4 Apr 1956, Nagpur, India. Bank Executive; Author; Poet. m. Nahid Qazi, 30 Dec 1984, 2 sons. Education: LLB, 1983; MA, 1989; PhD, 1993. Publication: A Wakeful Heart (poems), 1990; The Real Face, 1991; The Elegant Costumes of the Deccan; The Mission of Muhammad. Contributions to: About 1000 articles and 150 poems to Indian and foreign publications; Northern Perspectives (Australia), BBC London. Honours: Politics Essay Gold Medal, 1977; DLitt, World Congress of Poets, 1991; International Eminent Poet Award, 1991; Nominated International Poet of the Year, International Poetry Association (Washington), 1995; Awarded Michael Madhusudan Poetry Award, 1996; Nominated as expert for Evaluation of doctoral theses in English Literature at Nagpur University. Address: Gandhi Chourk Sadar, Nagpur 440001, India.

QUANDT William B(auer), b. 23 Nov 1941, Los Angeles, California, USA. Professor of Government and Foreign Affairs; Writer. m. (1) Anna Spitzer, 21 June 1964, div 1980, (2) Helena Cobban, 21 Apr 1984, 1 daughter. Education: BA, Stanford University, 1963; PhD, Massachusetts Institute of Technology, 1968. Appointments: Researcher, Rand Corporation, Santa Monica, California, 1967-72; Staff Member, 1972-74, Senior Staff Member, 1977-79, National Security Council, Washington, DC; Associate Professor, University of Pennsylvania, 1974-76; Senior Fellow, Brookings Institution, Washington, DC, 1979-94; Senior Associate, Cambridge Energy Research Associates, Massachusetts, 1983-90; Professor of Government and Foreign Affairs, University of Virginia, 1994-. Publications: Revolution and Political Leadership: Algeria 1954-68, 1969; The Politics of Palestinian Nationalism, 1973; Decade of Decisions, 1977; Saudi Arabia in the 1980's, 1981; Camp David: Peacemaking and Politics, 1986; The Middle East: Ten Years After Camp David, 1988; The United States and Egypt, 1990; Peace Process: American Diplomacy and the Arab-Israeli Conflict Since 1967, 1994; The Algerian Crisis, with Andrew Preire, 1996. Contributions to: Professional journals. Honours: Phi Beta Kappa, 1963; NDEA Fellow, 1963; Social Science Research Council Fellow, 1966; Council on Foreign Relations Fellow, 1972. Memberships: Council on Foreign Relations; Middle East Institute; Middle East Studies Association, president, 1987-88. Address: c/o Department of Government and Foreign Affairs, University of Virginia, Cabell Hall 255, Charlottesville, VA 22901, USA.

QUARTUS Appleton. See: **CREGAN David.**

QUEEN Ellery. See: **POWELL Talmage.**

QUICK Barbara, b. 28 May 1954, Los Angeles, California, USA. Writer. m. John Quick, 1 Aug 1988. Education: BA, Hons, Literature, University of California, Santa Cruz. Publication: Northern Edge (novel) 1990, revised edition, 1995; Forthcoming Publications: The Stolen Child (novel), 1997. Contributions to: New York Times Book Review. Honours: 2nd place, Ina Coolbrith Poetry Prize, 1977; Citation, B Dalton Bookseller, 1990. Literary Agent: Elizabeth Wales, Levant & Wales. Address: c/o Elizabeth Wales, 108 Hayes Street, Seattle, WA 98109, USA.

QUILLER Andrew. See: **BULMER Henry Kenneth.**

QUIN Robyn, b. 10 June 1954, Perth, Western Australia, Australia. Academic. m. Rod Quin. Education: Teachers Certificate; BA; MA; Graduate Diploma, Film and TV. Publications: (All with Barrie McMahon) Exploring Images, 1984; Real Images, 1986; Stories and Stereotypes, 1987; Meet the Media, 1989; Australian Images, 1990; Understanding Soaps, 1993. Contributions to: Australian Journal of Education; Canadian Journal of Educational Communication; Education Para la Reception, Mexico; Tijdschrift voor Theaterwetensschap, Germany. Honour: Cuitin University School of English Prize. Membership: Australian Teachers of Media, Western Australia. Address: PO Box 8064, Perth Business Centre, Pier Street, Perth 6849, Western Australia.

QUINE Willard Van Orman, b. 25 June 1908, Akron, Ohio, USA. Professor of Philosophy; Writer. m. (1) Naomi Ann Clayton, 19 Sept 1930, 2 daughters, (2) Marjorie Boynton, 2 Sept 1948, 1 son, 1 daughter. Education: AB in Mathematics summa cum laude, Oberlin College, 1930; AM, 1931, PhD, 1932, in Philosophy, Harvard University; MA, Oxford University, 1953. Appointments: Instructor, Tutor, 1936-41, Associate Professor, 1941-48, Professor of Philosophy, 1948-, Chairman, Department of Philosophy, 1952-53, Edgar Pierce Professor of Philosophy, 1955-78, Harvard University; Visiting Professor, University of São Paulo, 1942, Rockefeller University, 1968, Collège de France, 1969; George Eastman Visiting Professor, Oxford University, 1953-54, University of Tokyo, 1959; Member, Institute for Advanced Study, Princeton University, 1956-57; Fellow, Center for Advanced Study in the Behavioral Sciences, 1958-59, Center for Advanced Studies, Wesleyan University, 1965; Gavin David Young Lecturer in Philosophy, University of Adelaide, 1959; Paul Carus Lecturer, American Philosophical Association, 1971; Hagerstrom Lecturer, University of Uppsala, 1973; Sir Henry Savile Fellow, Merton College, Oxford, 1973-74; Ferrater Mora Lecturer, Gerona, Spain, 1990. Publications: A System of Logistics, 1934; Mathematical Logic, 1940; Elementary Logic, 1941; O Sentido da Nova Logica, 1944; Methods of Logic, 1950; From a Logical Point of View, 1953; Word and Object, 1960; Set Theory and Its Logic, 1963; The Ways of Paradox, 1966; Selected Logic Papers, 1966; Ontological Relativity, 1969; Philosophy of Logic, 1970; The Web of Belief (with J S Ullian), 1970; The Roots of Reference, 1974; Theories and Things, 1981; The Time of My Life, 1985; Quiddities, 1987; La Scienza e i Dati di Senso, 1987; Pursuit of Truth, 1989; The Logic of Sequences, 1990; From Stimulus to Science, 1995. Contributions to: Scholarly books and journals. Honours: Nicholas Murray Butler Gold Medal, Columbia University, 1970; Rockefeller, Bellagio, Italy, 1975; František Polacky Gold Medal, Czech Republic, 1991; Silver Medal, Charles University, Prague, 1993; Rolf Schock Prize in Philosophy, Sweden, 1993; Kyoto Prize, 1996; Many honorary doctorates. Memberships: Academie Internationale de la Philosophie de Science; American Academy of Arts and Sciences; American Philosophical Association; Association of Symbolic Logic, President, 1953-56; British Academy, Fellow; Institut de France, corresponding member; Institut Internationale de Philosophie; National Academy of Sciences; Phi Beta Kappa. Address: c/o Department of Philosophy, Emerson Hall, Harvard University, Cambridge, MA 02138, USA.

QUINNEY Richard, b. 16 May 1934, Elkhorn, Wisconsin, USA. University Professor. Education: BS, Caroll College, 1956; MA, Nortwestern University, 1957; PhD, University of Wisconsin, 1962. Appointments: Instructor, Department of Sociology and Anthropology, St Lawrence University, 1960-62; Assistant Professor, Department of Sociology, University of Kentucky, 1962-65; Associate Professor, 1965-70, Professor 1970-73, Department of Sociology, New York University; Research and writing leaves, Department of Sociology, University of North Carolina at Chapel Hill, Sabbatical, New York University, 1971-74; Visiting Professor, 1975-78, Adjunct Professor, 1980-83, Department of Sociology, Brown University; Distinguished Visiting Professor, 1978-79, Adjunct Professor, 1980-83, Department of Sociology, Boston College; Professor, Department of Sociology, Northen Illinois University, 1983-. Publications: Criminology: Analysis and Critique of Crime in America, 1975; Class, State and Crime: On the Theory and Practice of Criminal Justice, 1977; Capitalist Society: Readings for a Critical Sociology (editor), 1979; Providence: The Reconstruction of Social and Moral Order, 1980; Marxism and Law (co-editor with Piers Beirne), 1982; Social Existence: Metaphysics, Marxism and the Social Sciences, 1982; Criminology as Peacemaking (co-editor with Harold E Pepinsky), 1991; Journey to a Far Place: Autobiographical Reflections, 1991. Contributions to: Professional journals. Honours: Edwin Sutherland Award, for contributions to criminological theory, American Society of Criminology, 1984; Fulbright Award, Lectureship at University College, Galway, Ireland, 1986; President's Award, Western Society of Criminology, 1992. Address: Department of Sociology, Northern Illinois University, Dekalb, IL 60115, USA.

QUINTAVALLE Uberto Paolo, b. 1 Nov 1926, Milan, Italy. Writer. m. Josephine Hawke, 1970, 5 sons. Education: D Litt, University of Milan, 1949; Playwriting, Yale Drama School, 1950. Publications: La festa, 1953; Segnati a dito, 1956; Capitale Mancata, 1959; Tutti compromessi, 1961; Rito Romano, rito ambrosiano, 1964; Carolinda, 1974; Il Dio riciclato, 1989; La Corriere della sera; Il Gionale; Le Diecimila Canzoni di Putai, 1992; Fastoso Degrado, 1993; Il Memoriale di Pinocchio, 1993; Filottete, 1994; Milano Perduta, 1994; Incerca di Upamanyu, 1995; Le Erinni, 1996. Contributions to: Il Corriere Della Sera; Il Ciornale. Membership: PEN Club, Secretary General of the Italian Division; Vice President, PEN Club, Italy. Address: Via Mangili 2, 20121 Milan, Italy.

QUIRK Sir Randolph (Lord), b. 12 July 1920, Isle of Man, England. Academic. Education: BA, 1947, MA, 1949, PhD, 1951, DLitt, 1961, University College, London; Yale University, USA. Publications: The Use of English, 1968; Elicitation Experiments in English, 1970; Grammar of Contemporary English, 1972; University Grammar of English, 1974; The Linguist and the English Language, 1974; Style and Communication in the English Language, 1982; Comprehensive Grammar of the English Language, 1985; Words at Work, 1987; A Student's Grammar of the English Language, 1990; English in Use, 1990; An Introduction to Standard English, 1993; Grammatical and Lexical Variance in English, 1995. Honours: Commander of the Order of the British Empire, 1976; Knighted, 1985; Life Peerage, 1994; Honorary Doctorates: Paris and over 20 other Universities. Membership: British Academy, past president. Address: University College London, Gowen Street, London WC1E 6BT, England.

QURESHI Bashir, b. 25 Sept 1935. Doctor; Writer. Education: FRCGP; DCH; AFOM(RCP); FRSH; MICGP; FRIPHH; MFFP(RCOG). Appointments: Editor, Faculty News, Royal College of General Practitioners, 1981-86; Editor, London Medicine, 1986-88; Editor, Writer, Journal of the GP Writer Association, 1992; Editor, Faculty Newsletter, Faculty of Community Health, 1988-92. Publications: Transcultural Medicine - Dealing wiwth Patients from Different Cultures, 1989. Contributions to: Rehabilitation of the Elderly, 1989; Health Care for Asians, 1990; Screening and Surveillance in General Practice, 1992; RCGP Members References Books, 1983, 1985; The British Medical Annual, 1984, 1986; British Medical Journal; Sunday Times; Journal of the Royal Society of Medicine; Pulse; GP and Doctor; Journal of the Royal Society of Health. Memberships: Society of Authors; PEN; Council Member, Royal College of General Practitioners; Deputy Chairman, 1996-97, Chairman, 1997-98, Royal Society of Health. Address: 32 Legrace Avenue, Houslow West, Middlesex TW4 7RS, England.

R

RABAN Jonathan, b. 14 June 1942, Fakenham, Norfolk, England. Writer. Education: BA, University of Hull, 1963. Publications: The Technique of Modern Fiction: Essays in Practical Criticism, 1968; Mark Twain: Huckleberry Finn, 1969; Technique of Modern Fiction, 1969; The Society of the Poem, 1971; Soft City, 1974; Robert Lowell's Poems: A Selection (editor), 1974; Arabia: A Journey Through the Labyrinth, 1979; Old Glory: An American Voyage, 1981; Foreign Land (novel), 1985; Coasting, 1986; For Love and Money: A Writing Life, 1987; God, Man and Mrs Thatcher, 1989; Hunting Mr Heartbreak, 1991; The Oxford Book of the Sea (editor), 1992; Bad Land: An American Romance, 1996. Other: Plays for radio and television. Contributions to: Periodicals and journals including: Harper's; Esquire; New Republic; New York Review of Books; Outside; Granta; New York Times Book Review; Vogue. Honours: Heinemann Award, Royal Society of Literature, 1982; Thomas Cook Award, 1982; Thomas Cook Award II, 1992; National Book Critics Circle Award, 1997. Memberships: Fellow, Royal Society of Literature; Society of Authors. Address: c/o Aitken Stone and Wylie, 29 Fernshaw Road, London SW10 0TG, England.

RABE Berniece, b. 11 Jan 1928, Parma, Missouri, USA. Author. m. 30 July 1946, 3 sons, 1 daughter. Education: BSEd, National College; Graduate work in Psychology and Administration, Northern Illinois and Roosevelt Universities; Master's degree, Columbia College, Chicago. Appointments: Writing Instructor, Columbia College, Chicago; Consultant, Missouri Council of the Arts. Publications: Rass, 1973; Naomi, 1975; The Girl Who Had No Name, 1977; The Orphans, 1978; Who's Afraid, 1980; Margaret's Moves, 1987; A Smooth Move, 1987; Rehearsal for the Bigtime, 1988; Where's Chimpy, 1988; Tall Enough to Own the World, 1988; Magic Comes In It's Time, 1993; The Legend of the First Candy Cares, 1994. Picture books: The Balancing Girl, 1982; Can They See Me; Two Peas in a Pod. 2 film scripts. Contributions to: Short stories and articles. Honours: Honor Book, 1975, Golden Kite Award, 1977, National Society of Children's Book Writers; Midland Author's Award, 1978; Notable Book of the Year, American Library Association, 1982; National Children's Choice Award, 1987. Memberships: Board of Directors, Society of Midland Authors; Board of Directors, Off Campus Writers; Board of Directors, Fox Valley Writers. Address: Denton, TX 76205, USA.

RABIE Mohamed, b. 5 June 1940, Yazour, Palestine. Professor; Author. m. Maha El-Halabie, 23 June 1969, 1 son, 2 daughters. Education: BSc, Agricultural Economics, 1962; MA, Rural Sociology, 1965; MA, Economics, 1968; PhD, Economics, 1970; Studies in Jordan, Egypt, Germany and USA. Appointments: Assistant Professor, Texas Southern University, Houston, 1968; Associate Professor, Kuwait University, 1973; Adjunct Professor, Georgetown University, Johns Hopkins American University, 1982, 1984, 1986. Publications: 16 books including: Economics and Society (Arabic), 1973; The Politics of Foreign Aid (English), 1987; The Other Side of Arab Defeat (Arabic), 1987; The Making of US Foreign Policy (Arabic), 1990; The New World Order (English), 1992; Conflict Resolution and Ethnicity (English), 1994; US-PLO Dialogue (English and Arabic), 1995. Contributions to: Several articles to journals in the USA, Germany, Austria and Arab countries. Honours: Kuwait's Council and Higher Art and Literature; Von Humboldt; Stiftung, Germany. Memberships: Arab Thought Forum; Contemporary Authors; Palestinian Writers and Journalists Association. Address: 7416 Helmsdale Road, Bethesda, MD 20817, USA.

RACHLIN Nahid, b. 6 June 1944, Abadan, Iran. Writer; Instructor. m. Howard Rachlin, 1 daughter. Education: BA, Psychology, Lindenwood College, St Charles, Missouri, USA; 24 credits in Creative Writing, Columbia University. Appointments: New York University, School of Continuing Education, 1978-90; Marymount Manhattan College, 1986-87; Hofstra University, 1988-90; Yale University, 1989-90; Hunter College, 1990; Barnard College, 1991-. Publications: Foreigner, 1978; John Murray, 1978; Married to a Stranger, 1983; Veils, 1992. Contributions to: Redbook; Shenandoah; Crosscurrents; Fiction; Prism International; Ararat; Confrontation; Minnesota Review; Four Quarters; Columbia Magazine; New Laurel Review; Blueline; New Letters; Mississippi Mud; City Lights Journal; Pleiades; North Atlantic Review; Chanteh. Honours: Doubleday-Columbia Fellowship; Stegner Fellowship, Stanford University; National Endowment for the Arts

Grant; Bennet Certificate Award; PEN Syndicated Fiction Project. Membership: PEN. Address: 501 East 87th Street, Apt PHC, New York, NY 10128, USA.

RADLEY Sheila. See: ROBINSON Sheila Mary.

RADTKE Günter, b. 23 Apr 1920, Berlin, Germany. Author. Education: Trainee Journalist. Publications: Davon Kommst du Nicht Los, 1971; Die Dunne Haut der Luftballons, 1975; Der Krug auf Dem Weg Zum Wasser, 1977; Gluck aus Mangel an Beweisen, 1978; Suchen Wer Wir Sind, 1980; Gedanken zum Selbermachen, 1987; Wolkenlandschaften, 1988; Nicht so ernst wie es ist, 1990; Notizen zur greifbaren Nähe, 1993. Contributions to: Numerous literary magazines, newspapers and broadcasting stations. Honours: German Short Story Prize, 1971; George Mackensen Prize, 1973; First Roman Literature Prize, 1975; Literature Prize, Markische Culture Conference, 1979; Prize, European Writers Corporation DIE KOGGE, 1993. Memberships: Die Kogge; Association of German Writers; NGL Hamburg and Berlin; PEN. Literary Agent: Deutsche Verlags-Anstalt. Address: Postfach 86, Keitum/Sylt, Germany.

RAE Hugh Crauford, (James Albany, Robert Crawford, R B Houston, Stuart Stern, Jessica Stirling), b. 22 Nov 1935, Glasgow, Scotland. Novelist. m. Elizabeth Dunn, 3 Sept 1960, 1 daughter. Publications: Skinner, 1965; Night Pillow, 1966; A Few Small Bones, 1968; The Saturday Epic, 1970; Harkfast, 1976; Sullivan, 1978; Haunting at Waverley Falls, 1980; Privileged Strangers, 1982. As Jessica Stirling: The Spoiled Earth, 1974; The Hiring Fair, 1976; The Dark Pasture, 1978; The Deep Well at Noon, 1980; The Blue Evening Gone, 1982; The Gates at Midnight, 1983; Treasures on Earth, 1985; Creature Comforts, 1986; Hearts of Gold, 1987; The Good Provider, 1988; The Asking Price, 1989; The Wise Child, 1990; The Welcome Light, 1991; Lantern for the Dark, 1992; Shadows on the Shore, 1993; The Penny Wedding, 1994; The Marrying Kind, 1995; The Workhouse Girl, 1996; The Island Wife, 1997. As James Albany: Warrior Caste, Mailed Fist, Deacon's Dagger, 1982; Close Combat, Matching Fire, 1983; Last Bastion, Borneo Story, 1984. Membership: Scottish Association of Writers. Address: Drumore Farm Cottage, Balfron Station, Stirlingshire, Scotland.

RAE John Malcolm, b. 20 Mar 1931, London, England. Education: MA, Sidney Sussex College, Cambridge University, 1955; PhD, King's College, London University. Publications: The Custard Boys, 1960; Conscience and Politics, 1970; The Golden Crucifix, 1974; The Treasure of Westminster Abbey, 1975; Christmas is Coming, 1976; Return to the Winter Place, 1979; The Third Twin: A Ghost Story, 1980; The Public School Revolution, 1981; Letters from School, 1987; Too Little, Too Late?, 1989; Delusions of Grandeur, 1993; Letters to Parents, forthcoming. Contributions to: Encounter; Times Literary Supplement; Times Educational Supplement; Times; Sunday Telegraph. Honour: United Nations Award for Film Script, Reach for Glory, 1962. Literary Agent: The Peters Fraser Dunlop Group Ltd. Address: 26 Cedar Lodge, Lythe Hill Park, Haslemere, Surrey GU27 3TD, England.

RAELIN Joseph A(lan), b. 10 Apr 1948, Cambridge, Massachusetts, USA. Professor of Management. m. Abby P Dolin, 4 Aug 1974, 2 sons. Education: Diploma, University of Paris, Sorbonne, 1969; BA, 1970, EdM, 1971, Tufts University; PhD, State University of New York, Buffalo, 1977. Appointments: Professor, Wallace E Carroll School of Management, Boston College, Massachusetts, 1976-. Publications: Building a Career: The Effect of Initial Job Experiences and Related Attitudes on Later Employment, 1980; The Salaried Professional: How to Make the Most of Your Career, 1984; The Clash of Cultures: Managers Managing Professionals, 1986, paperback, 1991; Co-editor: Management Learning. Contributions: 70 articles in professional journals, proceedings and magazines. Honour: Best Paper in Management Education Award, Academy of Management, 1994. Membership: Academy of Management (US). Address: Wallace E Carroll School of Management, Boston College, Chestnut Hill, MA 02167, USA.

RAFFEL Burton (Nathan), b. 27 Apr 1928, New York, New York, USA. Distinguished Professor of Humanities and Professor of English; Lawyer; Writer; Poet; Editor; Translator. m. Elizabeth Clare Wilson, 16 Apr 1974, 3 sons, 3 daughters. Education: BA, Brooklyn College, 1948; MA, Ohio State University, 1949; JD, Yale University, 1958. Appointments: Lecturer, Brooklyn College, 1950-51; Editor, Foundation News, 1960-63; Instructor, 1964-65, Assistant Professor,

1965-66, State University of New York at Stony Brook; Associate Professor, State University of New York at Buffalo, 1966-68; Visiting Professor, Haifa University, 1968-69, York University, Toronto, 1972-75, Emory University, 1974; Professor of English and Classics, University of Texas at Austin, 1969-71; Senior Tutor (Dean), Ontario College of Art, Toronto, 1971-72; Professor of English, 1975-87, Lecturer in Law, 1986-87, University of Denver; Editor-in-Chief, Denver Quarterly, 1976-77; Contributing Editor, Humanities Education, 1983-87; Director, Adirondack Mountain Foundation, 1987-89; Advisory Editor, The Literary Review, 1987-; Distinguished Professor of Humanities and Professor of English, University of Southwestern Louisiana, 1989-. Publications: Non-fiction: The Development of Modern Indonesian Poetry, 1967; The Forked Tongue: A Study of the Translation Process, 1971; Introduction to Poetry, 1971; Why Re-Create?, 1973; Robert Lowell, 1981; T S Eliot, 1982; American Victorians: Explorations in Emotional History, 1984; How to Read a Poem, 1984; Ezra Pound: The Prime Minister of Poetry, 1985; Politicians, Poets and Con Men, 1986; The Art of Translating Poetry, 1988; Artists All: Creativity, the University, and the World, 1991; From Stress to Stress: An Autobiography of English Prosody, 1992; The Art of Translating Prose, 1994. Fiction: After Such Ignorance, 1986; Founder's Fury (with Elizabeth Raffel), 1988; Founder's Fortune (with Elizabeth Raffel), 1989. Poetry: Mia Poems, 1968; Four Humours, 1979; Changing the Angle of the Sun-Dial, 1984; Grice, 1985; Evenly Distributed Rubble, 1985; Man as a Social Animal, 1986. Other: Numerous translations. Contributions to: Professional journals. Honours: Frances Steloff Prize for Fiction, 1978; American-French Foundation Translation Prize, 1991; Several grants. Memberships: National Faculty; Phi Kappa Phi. Address: 203 South Mannering Avenue, Lafayette, LA 70508, USA.

RAIJADA Rajendrasinh, b. 1 July 1943, Sondarda, India. Educator. m. Gulabkumari Raijada, 21 Feb 1969, 2 sons, 1 daughter. Education: BEd, Gujarati, 1973, MA, Gujarati, 1975, Saurashtra University, Rajkot; PhD, Mysticism in Modern Gujarati Poetry, Sardar Patel University, Vallabhvidyanagar, 1979. Appointments: Central Committee Member, Gujarati Sahitya Parishad, Amdavad, 1975-77; Language Expert, Gujarat State Text Book Board, Gandhinagar, 1975-82; Resource Person, National Education Policy, 1986; Adviser, Gujarat Sahitya Academy, Gandhinagar, 1991; Central Committee Member, Gujarat State Text Book Board, Gandhinagar, 1997-2000. Publications: Radha Madhav (translation from Hindi), 1970; Farva avyo chhun (poetry), 1976; Gulmahor ni niche (short stories), 1977; Rahasyavad (essays), 1980; Hun, Kali chhokari ane Suraj (poetry), 1982; Darsdhan ane Itishas (collection of articles), 1983; Sant Parampara Vimarsh (criticism), 1989; Tantra Sadhana, Maha Panth Ane Anya Lekho (collection of articles), 1993. Address: Sondarda, via Kevadra 362227, Gujarat, India.

RAILSBACK Brian Evan, b. 24 Sep 1959, Glendale, California, USA. Assistant Professor of English. m. Sandra Lea Railsback, 6 Aug 1983, 2 sons, 1 daughter. Education: AA, 1981; BA, Journalism, 1982; MA, English, 1985; PhD, English, 1990. Appointments: John Cady Fellow, Ohio University, 1989; Assistant Professor, English, Western Carolina University, North Carolina, 1990-. Contributions to: Scholarly articles to: San Jose Studies; Steinbeck Quarterly; Short story to Tamaqua; Reviews to various Magazines and journals. Memberships: American Writing Programs; Modern Language Association; International Steinbeck Society. Address: PO Box 1001, Cullowhee, NC 28723, USA.

RAINE Craig Anthony, b. 3 Dec 1944, Shildon, England. Writer. m. Ann Pasternak Slater, 27 Apr 1972, 3 sons, 1 daughter. Education: Honours Degree, English Language and Literature, Oxford, 1966; BPhil, English Studies, Oxford, 1968. Appointments: Reviews Editor, The New Review, 1977-79; Editor, Quarto, 1979-80; Poetry Editor, New Statesman, 1981; Faber, 1981-91. Publications: The Onion Memory, 1978; A Martian Sends a Postcard Home, 1979; Rich, 1984; The Electrification of The Soviet Union, 1987; 1953, 1990; Haydn and the Valve Trumpet, 1990; History: The Home Movie, 1994; Clay: Whereabouts Unknown, 1996. Contributions to: Observer; Sunday Times; Independent on Sunday; New Statesman; Listener; Encounter; London Review of Books; Times Literary Supplement; Literary Review; Grand Street; New Yorker; Financial Times. Honours: Southern Arts Literature Award, 1980; Cholmondeley Award, 1983; Fellow, New College, Oxford, 1991-. Memberships: PEN; Royal Society of Literature. Literary Agent: David Godwin. Address: New College, Oxford, England.

RAINE Kathleen (Jessie), b. 14 June 1908, London, England. Poet; Critic; Editor; Translator. m. (1) Hugh Skyes Davies, div, (2) Charles Madge, div, 1 son, 1 daughter. Education: MA, Girton College, Cambridge, 1929. Appointment: Founder, Temenos Academy, 1990. Publications: Poetry: Stone and Flower: Poems, 1935-1943, 1943; Living in Time, 1946; The Pythoness and Other Poems, 1948; Selected Poems, 1952, revised edition, 1989; The Year One, 1953; Collected Poems of Kathleen Raine, 1956; The Hollow Hill and Other Poems, 1960-64, 1965; Ninfa Revisited, 1968; Six Dreams and Other Poems, 1968; A Question of Poetry, 1969; The Lost Country, 1971; Three Poems Written in Ireland, 1973; On a Deserted Shore, 1973; The Oracle in the Heart and Other Poems, 1975-1978, 1980; Collected Poems, 1935-1980, 1981; The Presence: Poems, 1984-87, 1988; Living with Mystery: Poems, 1987-1991, 1992; Non-Fiction: Poetry in Relation to Traditional Wisdom, 1958; Blake and England, 1960; Defending Ancient Springs, 1967; The Written Word, 1967; Blake and Tradition, 2 volumes, 1968; William Blake, 1970; Faces of Day and Night (autobiography), 1972; Yeats, the Tarot, and the Golden Dawn, 1972, revised edition, 1976; Farewell Happy Fields: Memories of Childhood, 1973; Death-in-Life and Life-in-Death: Cuchulain Comforted and News for the Delphic Oracle, 1974; A Place, a State, 1974; David Jones, Solitary Perfectionist, 1974, enlarged edition, 1975; The Land Unknown (autobiography), 1975; The Lion's Mouth: Concluding Chapters of Autobiography, 1977; From Blake to a Vision, 1978; David Jones and the Actually Loved and Known, 1978; Blake and the New Age, 1979; Cecil Collins, Painter of Paradise, 1979; What is Man?, 1980; The Human Face of God: William Blake and the Book of Job, 1982; The Inner Journey of the Poet and Other Papers, 1982; Yeats the Initiate: Essays on Certain Themes in the Writings of W B Yeats, 1984; Poetry and the Frontiers of Consciousness, 1985; The English Language and the Indian Spirit: Correspondence between Kathleen Raine and K D Sethna, 1986; India Seen Afar, 1991; Golgonooza, City of Imagination: Last Studies in William Blake, 1991. Editor: Aspects de la litterature anglaise (with Max-Pol Fouchet), 1947; The Letters of Samuel Taylor Coleridge, 1952; Selected Poems and Prose of Coleridge, 1957; Coleridge: Letters, 1969; Selected Writings of Thomas Taylor the Platonist (with George Mills Harper), 1969; A Choice of Blake's Verse, 1974; Shelley, 1974. Contributions to: Books and journals. Honours: Harriet Monroe Memorial Prize, 1952; Arts Council Award, 1953; Oscar Blumenthal Prize, 1961; Cholmondeley Award, 1970; W H Smith & Son Literary Award, 1972; Foreign Book Prize, France, 1979; Queen's Gold Medal for Poetry, 1993. Address: 47 Paultons Square, London SW3, England.

RAJA P, b. 7 Oct 1952, Pondicherry, India. Writer. Lecturer in English. m. Periyanayaki, 6 May 1976, 2 sons, 1 daughter. Education: BA, English, 1973; MA, English Language and Literature, 1975; PhD, Indian Writing in English, 1992. Appointments: Literary Editor, Pondicherry Today; Editorial Associate, Indian Book Chronicle. Publications: From Zero to Infinity (poems), 1987; Folktales of Pondicherry, 1987; A Concise History of Pondicherry, 1987; Tales of Mulla Nasruddin, 1989; The Blood and Other Stories, 1991; M P Pandit: A Peep Into His Past, 1993; Many Worlds of Manoj Das, 1993; The Best Woman in My Life and Other Stories, 1994; Sudden Tales the Folks Told, 1995. Translations from Tamil: The Stupid Guru and his Foolish Disciples, 1981, The Sun and the Stars, 1982; The works of Tamil poet Bharathidasan co-translator). Contributions to: Numerous journals. Honours: Literary Award, Pondicherry University, 1987; International Eminent Poet Award, Madras, 1988; Michael Madhusudan Academy Award, Calcutta, 1991. Address: 74 Poincare Street, Olandai-Keerapalayam, Pondicherry 605004, India.

RAJANNA. See: NAGARAJA RAO C K.

RAJIC Negovan, b. 24 June 1923, Belgrade, Yugoslavia (Canadian citizen). Writer. m. Mirjana Knezevic, 28 Mar 1970, 1 son, 1 daughter. Education: University of Belgrade, 1945-46; Diplome d'etudes techniques superieures, 1962, Diploma in Electrical Engineering, 1968, Conservatoire des Arts et Metiers, Paris. Appointments: Fought with Resistance during World War II, escaped Yugoslavia 1946, arrived Paris, 1947, resumed studies in Engineering; Research Engineer, Physical Laboratory, Ecole Polytechnique de Paris, 1956-63; Researcher in Electronics, France, 1963-69; Came to Canada, 1969, becoming Professor of Mathematics, Cegep Trois Rivieres to 1987. Publications: Les Hommes-taupes (novel), 1978, translated by David Lodbell as The Mole Men, 1980; Propos d'un vieux radoteur (short story collection), 1982, translated by David Lobdell as The Master of Strappado, 1984; Sept Roses pour une boulangere: Recit, 1987, translated by David Lobdell as Seven Roses for a Baker,

1988; Service penitentiaire national (short story collection), 1988, translated by David Lobdell as Shady Business, 1989; Numerous articles and short stories. Contribution to: De la philosphie comme passion de la liberte, 1984. Honours: Prix Esso du Cercle du Livre de France, 1978; Prix Air Canada for best short story, 1980; Prix Slobodan Yovanovitch Association des ecrivains et artistes serbes en exile, 1984; Prix litteraire de Trois-Rivieres, 1988. Memberships: PEN International; Association of Writers of Quebec; Honorary Member, Association of Serbian Writers, Belgrade. Address: 300 Dunant, Trois-Rivieres, Quebec G8Y 2W9, Canada.

RAJU Chethput, b. 28 Jan 1916, Vellore, North Arcot District, Tamil Nadu, India. Retired Commercial Executive and Manager; Poet. m. Eashwari Raju, 14 Nov 1947, 2 sons. Education: BA English (Special), 1957. Publications: This Modern Age and Other Poems, 1954; No Exit, 1970. Contributions to: Poetry Review, London; Poetry Nippon, Japan; National Library of Poetry, USA; Purpose, USA; Others. Honours: Prizewinner, All India Poetry Contests, 1991, 1992. Memberships: PEN India; Associate, Chartered Insurance Institute; LCC, London. Adddress: 3 Ganga Vihar, 318 Bhalchandra Road, Matunga, CR, Bombay 400 019, India.

RAKUSA Ilma, b. 2 Jan 1946, Rimavska Sobota, Slovakia. Writer; Translator; Literary Critic. 1 son. Education: Slavic Languages and Literatures, University of Zurich, Switzerland; PhD, 1971. Publications: Die Insel, 1982; Miramar, 1986; Steppe, 1990; Jim, 1993; Farbband und Randfigur, 1994; Einsamkeiten, 1996; Ein Lesebuch, 1996; Ein Strich durch alles, 1997. Translations of Marguerite Duras, Marina Tsvetaeva, Danilo Kiš and others. Honour: Petrarca Award for Translation, 1991. Membership: Deutsche Akademie für Sprache und Dichtung, Darmstadt. Address: Richard Kissling-Weg 3, CH-8044 Zurich, Switzerland.

RAMA RAO Vadapalli Vijaya Bhaskara, b. 1 Jan 1938, Srikakulam District, A P, India. Educator. m. Ramani Rama Rao, 15 Apr 1959, 1 son, 3 daughters. Education: BA, Economics, 1957; BA, English, 1958; MA, English, 1961; Diploma in Teaching English, 1966; Diploma in French, 1979; PhD, 1980. Publications: In English: Poosapati Ananda Gajapati Raju (biography), 1985; Tapaswi (novel), 1989; Graham Greene's Comic Vision (criticism), 1990; Into That Heaven of Freedom (novel), 1991; Warm Days Will Never Cease. Translation: Trapped (novel, from English to Telugu), 1991; 6 novels in Telugu: Sparasarekhalu, 1977; Neetikireetalu, 1977; Maguvalu - Manasulu, 1980; Gaalipadagalu - Deepakalikalu, 1981; Tapaswi, 1985; The Joy of the Divine, 1994; The Drunken Boat, 1994; Malapalli (English translation), 1994; Unnava, Sahitya Akademi (monograph), 1994. Contributions to: 15 literary reviews in English and about 125 short fiction in Telugu to magazines and journals; About 400 English and about 20 Telugu feature and newspaper articles. Address: 19-5-13 Kanukurti Street, Vizianagaram 535 002, India.

RAMA RAU Santha, (Rama Rau Wattles), b. 24 Jan 1923, Madras, India. Freelance Writer. m. (1) Faubion Bowers, 24 Oct 1951, div 1966, 1 son, (2) Gurdon W Wattles, 1970. Education: BA, Honours, Wellesley College, USA, 1945. Publications: Home to India, 1945; East of Home, 1950; This India, 1953; Remember the House, 1955; View to the South-East, 1957; My Russian Journey, 1959; A Passage to India (dramatisation of E M Forster's novel), 1962; Gifts of Passage, 1962; The Cooking of India, 1970; The Adventuress, 1970; A Princess Remembers, 1976; An Inheritance, 1977. Contributions to: Numerous journals and magazines. Honours: Honorary Degrees: Bates College, 1960, Roosevelt University, 1962, Brandeis University, 1962, Russell Sage College, 1965; Awards: Mlle Mag Merit Award, 1965; Association of Indians in America, 1977. Address: c/o William Morris Agency, 1350 6th Avenue, New York, NY 10019, USA.

RAMAMURTI Krishnamurthy Sitaraman, (Madhuram Ramamurti), b. 4 Nov 1930, Madras, India. Professor of English; Dean. m. Rajesnari Ramamurti, 4 July 1958, 2 daughters. Education: BSc, Physics, 1950, MA, English Language and Literature, 1954, University of Madras; MA, English Literature, Muslim University, Aligarh, 1963; Diploma, Teaching of English, Central Institute of English, Hyderabad; PhD, Madurai University, 1975. Appointments: Lecturer, English, St Aloysius College, Mangalore, 1954-65; Professor, Head, Department of English, Sri Palaniasndowar Arts College, Palmi, 1965-76; Lecturer, 1976-78, Reader, 1978-84, Professor, 1984-91, Dean, College Development Council, 1991-, Bharathidasan University, Tiruchirapalli. Publications: Thomas Kyd: The Spanish Tragedy (editor), 1978; Vazhithunai (novel), 1980; Perspectives on Modern

English Prose, 1985; Rise of the Indian Novel, 1986; Variety in Short Stories, 1988. Contributions to: About 12 short novels and short stories in Tamil to leading journals; about 12 feature articles to leading newspapers including: The Hindu; Indian Express; about 70 research papers to standard literary journals; about 20 book reviews and review articles. Honour: Prize for novel, 1980. Memberships: Indian Association of English Teachers; Comparative Literature Association of India; Executive Committee, Indian Association of Canadian Studies. Address: Bharatidasan University, Tiruchirapalli 620024, India.

RAMDIN Ronald Andrew, b. 20 June 1942, Marabella, Trinidad. Historian; Writer; Lecturer. m. Irma de Freitas, 20 Dec 1969, 1 son. Education: Diploma in Speech and Drama, New Era Academy of Drama and Music, 1963; Diploma in Industrial Relations and Trade Union Studies, University of Middlesex, 1977; BSc, Economics, London School of Ecnomics and Political Science, 1982; DLitt, University of London, 1995. Publications: From Chattel Slave to Wage Earner, 1982; Introductory Text: The Black Triangle, 1984; The Making of the Black Working Class in Britain, 1987; Paul Robeson: The Man and His Mission, 1987; World in View: West Indies, 1990; Arising From Bondage: A History of East Indians in the Caribbean 1838-1991; The Other Middle Passage, 1995. Contributions to: Anglo-British Review; City Limits; Dragon's Teeth; Race Today; Caribbean Times; West Indian Digest; History Workshop Journal. Honours: Scarlet Ibis Medal, Gold Award, Trinidad and Tobago High Commission, London, 1990; Hansib, Caribbean Times, Community Award, Britain, 1990. Memberships: Society of Authors; Royal Historical Society. Literary Agent: Faith Evans Associates. Address: The British Library, Humanities and Social Science Section, Great Russell Street, London WC1B 3DG, England.

RAMIREZ-DE-ARELLANO Diana, b. 3 June 1919, New York, New York, USA. Professor Emeritus; Poet; Writer. Education: BA, University of Puerto Rico, 1941; MA TC, University of Columbia, 1946; Licentiate Degree and Title, University of Madrid, 1959; Doctorate Degree and Title, 1952 and 1961. Appointments: Poetry Chair, City College, City University of New York, 1970-; President and Director of Publications, Ateneo de Puerto Rico en New York; Professor, Graduate Center, CUNY, 1972. Publications: Los Ramirez de Arellano de Lope de Vega, 1954; Caminos de la Creación Poética en Pedro Salinas (literary criticism), 1957; Angeles de Ceniza (poetry) 1958; Privilegio (poetry), 1959; Poesía Contemporánea en Lengua Española, 1961; Tree at Vespers (bilingual poetry, editor), 1987; Un Vuelo Casi Humano (poetry); Albatros Sobre el Alma (poetry); Adelfazar (Elegía), 1995. Contributions to: Numerous journals in Puerto Rico and Spain. Honours: First Prize in Literature, 1958, Prize for Literary Criticism, 1961, Institute of Literature, Puerto Rico; Order of Merit, Republic of Ecuador, 1971; International Prize for Poetry, Ministry of Education and Arts, Bolivia, 1964; Professor Emeritus, City University of New York, 1984; Diploma La Gloire, Academia Leonardo de Vinci, Rome; Laurel Clara Lair, Association of Writers; Premio Al Margen for Literature. Memberships: Hispanic Society of America; American Association of Spanish and Portuguese (Professor Emeritus); President, Atenio Puertorriqueño de Nueva York; President, Josefina Romo Arregui Memorial Foundation; PEN Club International; Royal Academy of Doctors of Madrid. Literary Agent: Edificio Acapulco, 25 Avenue Marina Española, Playa de Poniente, Benidorm, Alicante, Spain. Address: 23 Harbor Circle, Centerport, NY 11721, USA.

RAMKE Bin, b. 19 Feb 1947, Pt Neches, Texas, USA. Teacher; Editor; Poet. m. 31 May 1967, 1 son. Education: BA, Louisiana State University, 1970; MA, University of New Orleans, 1971; PhD, Ohio University, 1975. Appointments: Professor of English, Columbus College, Georgia, 1976-85, University of Denver, 1985-; Editor, Contemporary Poetry Series, University of Georgia Press, 1984-; Poetry Editor, 1985-, Editor, 1994-, The Denver Quarterly. Publications: The Difference Beteewn Night And Day, 1978; White Monkeys, 1981; The Language Student, 1987; The Erotic Light of Gardens, 1989; Massacre of the Innocents, 1995. Contributions to: Poetry; New Yorker; Paris Review; Essays and reviews in Georgia Law Review; Denver Quarterly. Honours: Yale Younger Poets Award, 1977; Texas Institute of Arts and Letters Award, poetry, 1978; Iowa Poetry Award, 1995. Memberships: PEN, American Centre; Associated Writing Programs; National Book Critics' Circle. Address: Department of English, University of Denver, Denver, CO 80208, USA.

RAMNEFALK (Sylvia) Marie Louise, b. 21 Mar 1941, Stockholm, Sweden. Poet; Writer. Education: FK, 1964, FL, 1968, FD,

1974, Stockholm University. Appointments: Script Supervisor, TV-Theatre, 1967-68; University Teacher, Stockholm University, 1960s; Umea University, 1970s; School for Librarians, Boras, 1970s, 1980s; Karlstad University, 1986-87; Literary critic, several papers and magazines. Publications: 7 poetry books; Opera librettos. Contributions to: Numerous newspapers and magazines. Honours: Recipient of several Scholarships. Memberships: Forfattarforlaget, executive board, 1977-82; president, 1982-84; Sveriges Forfattarforbund, executive board, 1979-83; Forfattarnas Fotokopieringsfond, president, 1985-87; Swedish PEN. Address: Vastra Valhallavagen 25A, S-182 Djursholm, Sweden.

RAMPERSAD Arnold, b. 13 Nov 1941, Trinidad, West Indies. University Professor. m. 1985, 1 child. Education: BA, MA, Bowling Green State University; MA, PhD, Harvard University. Publications: Melville's Israel Potter: A Pilgrimage and Progress, 1969; The Art and Imagination of W E B Dubois, 1976; Life of Langston Hughes, Vol I 1902-1941: I Too Sing America, 1986, Vol II 1941-1967: I Dream a World, 1988; Slavery and the Literary Imagination (co-editor), 1989; Days of Grace: A Memoir (with Arthur Ashe), 1993. Honours: Ansfield Wolf Book Award in Race Relations, Cleveland Foundation, 1987; Clarence L Hotte Prize, Phelps Stoke Fund, 1988; Pulitzer Prize Finalist, 1989; American Book Award, 1990. Address: Department of English, Princeton University, Princeton, NJ 08544, USA.

RAMPLING Anne. See: **RICE Anne.**

RAMSAY Jay. See: **RAMSAY-BROWN John Andrew.**

RAMSAY-BROWN John Andrew, (Jay Ramsay), b. 20 Apr 1958, Guildford, Surrey, England. Poet; Writer; Translator; Administrator; Editor; Teacher. Education: Charterhouse School; BA Honours, English Language and Literature, Pembroke College, Oxford, 1980; Foundation Year diploma in Psychosynthesis, London Institute, 1987. Appointments: Co-founder and Administrator, Angels of Fire, 1983-88; Project Director, Chrysalis - The Poet In You, 1990. Publications: Psychic Poetry: a Manifesto, 1985; Angels of Fire (co-editor), 1986; Raw Spiritual: Selected Poems, 1986; Trwyn Meditations, 1987; The White Poem, 1988; Transformation: The Poetry of Spiritual Consciousness (editor), 1988; The Great Return, books 1 to 5, 2 volumes, 1988; Transmissions, 1989; Strange Days, 1990; Journey to Eden (with Jenny Davis), 1991; For Now (with Geoffrey Godbert), 1991; The Rain, the Rain, 1992; St Patrick's Breastplate, 1992; Tao Te Ching: a New Translation, 1993; I Ching, 1995; Kuan Yin, 1995; Chuang Tzu (with Martin Palmer), 1996; Alchemy: The Art of Transformation, 1996; Earth Ascending - An Anthology of New and Living Poetry (editor), 1996. Contributions to: Poetry Review; Literary Review; City Limits; Acumen; Resurgence; Jungle, Paris; Apart, Germany; Island, Athens; Forum. Memberships: Poetry Society; Psychosynthesis Education and Trust, London; College of Psychic Studies, London. Address: c/o Susan Mears, The Old Church, Monkton Deverill, nr Warminster, Wiltshire BA12 7EX, England.

RAND Peter, b. 23 Feb 1942, San Francisco, California, USA. Writer. m. Bliss Inui, 19 Dec 1976, 1 son. Education: MA, Johns Hopkins University, 1975. Appointments: Fiction Editor, Antaeus, 1970-72; Editor, Washington Monthly, 1973-74; Teaching Fellow, Johns Hopkins University, 1975; Lecturer-in-English, Columbia University, 1976-91. Publications: Firestorm, 1969; The Time of the Emergency, 1977; The Private Rich, 1984; Gold From Heaven, 1988; Deng Xiaoping: Chronicle of an Empire, by Ruth Ming (editor and translator with Nancy Liu and Lawrence R Sullivan), 1994; China Hands: The Adventures and Ordeals of the American Journalists and Joined Forces with the Great Chinese Revolution, 1995. Contributions to: Periodicals. Honour: CAPS, 1977. Memberships: PEN; Authors Guild; Poets and Writers; East Asian Institute, Columbia University; Research Associate, Fairbank Center, Harvard University. Literary Agent: Wendy Weil. Address: 24 Winslow Road, Belmont, MA 02178, USA.

RANDALL Clay. See: **ADAMS Clifton.**

RANDALL Rona, b. Birkenhead, Cheshire, England. Writer. m. 1 son. Publications: 57 published novels, including: Dragonmede, 1974; The Watchman's Stone, 1976; The Eagle at the Gate, 1978; The Mating Dance, 1979; The Ladies of Hanover Square, 1981; Curtain Call, 1982; The Drayton Trilogy: The Drayton Legacy, 1985; The Potter's Niece, 1987; The Rival Potters, 1990. Non-fiction: Jordan and the Holy Land, 1968; The Model Wife, 19th Century Style, 1989;

Writing Popular Fiction, 1992. Honours: Romantic Novelists Association Award, 1969; US Literary Guild Exclusive Selection, 1975. Memberships: Society of Authors; International PEN; Society of Women Writers and Journalists; Society of Sussex Authors. Address: Conifers, Pembury Road, Tunbridge Wells, Kent TN2 4ND, England.

RANSLEY Peter, b. 12 Oct 1931, Leeds, England. Writer; Dramatist. m. Cynthia Harris, 14 Dec 1974, 1 son, 1 daughter. Education: Queen Mary College, London, 1950-52. Publications: The Price, 1988; Bright Hair About the Bone, 1989. Theatre: Ellen and Disabled, 1972; Runaway, 1974. Other: Numerous television plays and series, including Bread or Blood, 1982; The Price, 1985; Underbelly, 1991; Seaforth, 1994. Film: The Hawk, 1992. Honours: Gold Medal, 1st Commonwealth TV Film Festival, 1980; Royal Television Society Writer's Award, 1981. Address: The Chambers, Chelsea Harbour, Lots Road, London SW10, England.

RANSOM Bill, b. 6 June 1945, Puyallup, Washington, USA. Writer; Poet. 1 daughter. Education: BA, University of Washington, 1970. Appointments: NDEA Title IV Fellow, American Minority Literature, University of Nevada, Reno, 1971-72; Poetry in the Schools, Master Poet, National Endowment for the Arts, 1974-77. Publications: Novels: The Jesus Incident, 1979; The Lazarus Effect, 1983; The Ascension Factor, 1988; Jaguar, 1990; Viravax, 1993; Burn, 1995. Poetry: Finding True North, 1974; The Single Man Looks at Winter, 1983; Last Call, 1984; Waving Arms at the Blind, 1975; Last Rites, 1979; Semaphore, 1993. Other: Learning the Ropes (poetry, essays and short fiction), 1995. Contributions: The Woman Who Played Imaginary Piano for her Potato, Puerto del Sol, 1996; Numerous journals and magazines. Honours: National Endowment for the Arts Discovery Award, 1977. Memberships: Poetry Society of America; Poets, Essayists and Novelists; International Association of Machinists and Aerospace Workers; Science Fiction, Fantasy Writers of America; Poets and Writers Inc. Literary Agent: Ralph Vicinanza, New York. Address: PO Box 284, Grayland, WA 98547, USA.

RANZ HORMAZABAL Mario de los Candelas, b. 23 Aug 1950. Writer. m. Agustin Garcia Alonso, 2 sons, 1 daughter. Education: Colegio de Religiosas de Duenas, Palencia. Appointments: Writer, La Valderia and Andrade. Publications: Poetry: Al principio del camino, 1962; Andurina 1; Spighe dorate (in Italian); Como la luz de la aurora, 1982; Efluvios liricos; Petalos de mis rosas, 1983; La Campina 2, 1983; La esencia del mar, 1983; Mis poemas, 1983; De verso en verso de flor en flor, 1984; Armor incompleto, 1984; Il turbamento dell' Amore (in Italian), 1984; Armor incompleto, 4th and 5th editions, 1985; Caprichosas protuberancias poeticas, 1986; Alondra-10, 1986; Sonetos, 1994. Other: Pequenas biografias de grandes personajes, 1982; Desde mi butaca. Critica de cine, 1982; Conoce usted a...., 1983; Les presento a..., 1983. Contributions to: Periodicals. Honour: Premio de poesia, Concurso El Paisaje de Dibujo del Centro Cultural Aga (Vizcaya), 1974. Memberships: Club El Paisaje; Centro Cultural Literario y Artistico AGA; Academia O jornal de Felgueiras; Founder member, secretary, Association Cultural La Marcilla (Leon). Address: Entre los Rios, 10 24760 Castrocalbon, Léon, Spain.

RAO Raja, b. 5 Nov 1908, Hassan, Mysore, India. Author. Education: BA, University of Madras, 1929; Sorbonne, University of Paris, 1930-33. Appointment: Professor, University of Texas at Austin, 1965. Publications: Kanthapura, 1938; The Cow of the Barricades and Other Stories, 1947; The Serpent and the Rope, 1960; The Cat and Shakespeare: A Tale of India, 1965; Comrade Krilov, 1976; The Policeman and the Rose, 1978; The Chess Master and His Moves, 1978; Alien Poems and Other Stories, 1983; On the Ganga Ghat, 1989. Honour: Neustadt International Prize, 1988. Address: c/o University of Texas at Austin, Austin, TX 78712, USA.

RAPHAEL Adam Eliot Geoffrey, b. 22 Apr 1938, London, England. Journalist. m. Caroline Rayner Ellis, 15 May 1970, 1 son, 1 daughter. Education: BA Honours, History, Oxford University. Appointments: London, 1965-68, Foreign Correspondent in USA, 1969-73, Guardian; Political Correspondent, 1976-82, Political Editor, 1982-87, Observer; Presenter, BBC Newsnight, 1987-88; Executive Editor, Observer, 1988-93; Writer on Home Affiars, Economist, 1994-. Publications: My Learned Friends,non-fiction, 1989; Grotesque Libels, 1991; Ultimate Risk, non-fiction, 1994. Honours: Journalist of the Year, Granada Awards, 1973; Journalist of the Year, IPC Awards, 1973. Address: 50 Addison Avenue, London W11 4QP, England.

RAPHAEL Frederic Michael, b. 14 Aug 1931, Chicago, Illinois, USA. Writer. m. 17 Jan 1955, 2 sons, 1 daughter. Education: St John's College, Cambridge, England. Publications: Obbligato, 1956; The Earlsdon Way, 1958; The Limits of Love, 1960; The Trouble With England, 1962; The Graduate Wife, 1962; Lindmann, 1963; Darling, 1965; Orchestra and Beginners, 1967; Two for the Road (film script with preface), 1968; Like Men Betrayed, 1970; Who Were You With Last Night?, 1971; April, June and November, 1972; Richard's Things, 1973; California Time, 1975; The Glittering Prizes, 1976; Somerset Maugham (biography), 1977; Sleeps Six (short stories), 1979; Cracks in the Ice: Views and Reviews, 1979; Oxbridge Blues (short stories), 1980; Byron (biography), 1982; Heaven and Earth, 1985; Think of England I, 1990; A Double Life, 1993; Of Gods and Men (Greek mythology revisited), 1993; The Latin Lover (short stories), 1994; Old Scores, 1995. Translations (with Kenneth McLeish): The Poems of Catullus, 1978; The Plays of Aeschylus, 2 volumes, 1991. Contributions to: Sunday Times (London); Times Literary Supplement; Prospect. Honours: Lippincott Prize, 1961; Writers' Guild, 1965, 1966; USA Academy Award, 1966; British Academy Award, 1966; Royal TV Society Award, 1976; ACE (US Cable TV) Awards, 1985, 1991. Membership: Fellow, Royal Society of Literature. Address: c/o Deborah Rogers, Rogers, Coleridge and White, 20 Powis Mews, London W11 1JN, England.

RASKY Harry, b. 9 May 1928, Toronto, Ontario, Canada. Writer; Director; Producer; Commentator. m. Ruth Arlene Werkhoven, 21 Mar 1965, 1 son, 1 daughter. Education: BA, 1949, LLD, 1982, University of Toronto. Publications: Nobody Swings on Sunday, 1980; Tennessee Williams - A Portrait in Laughter and Lamentation; Teresa Stratas: Prophecy, 1995; 40 feature-length documentaries including: Tennessee Williams' South, 1972; Homage to Chagall - The Colours of Love, 1975; The War Against the Indians, 1992. Contributions to: Nation; Saturday Night; Financial Post; Directors Guild of America News. Honours: Canadian Radio Award, 1951; Nominations, Writers Guild of America Award, 1972, 1978, 1980; 10 Awards, Writers Guild of Canada; Hollywood Interational Angel Gold Prize; Munich International Film Festival Prize. Memberships: Writers Guild of Canada; Writers Guild of America; Writers Union of Canada; Directors Guild of America; Academy of Motion Pictures Arts and Sciences, Hollywood; Academy of TV Arts and Sciences, New York; Academy of Canadian Cinema, Toronto. Literary Agent: Lucinda Vardy Agency. Address: CBC, Box 500, Terminal A, Toronto, Ontario, Canada.

RATHER Dan, b. 31 Oct 1931, Wharton, Texas, USA. Broadcast Journalist. m. Jean Goebel, 1 son, 1 daughter. Education: BA in Journalism, Sam Houston State College, Huntsville, Texas, 1953; University of Houston; South Texas School of Law. Appointments: Staff, United Press International, Houston Chronicle, KTRH Radio, Houston, KHOU-TV, Houston; White House Correspondent, 1964-65, 1966-74, Chief, London Bureau, 1965-66, CBS-TV; Anchorman-Correspondent, CBS Reports, 1974-75; Co-Editor, 60 Minutes, CBS-TV, 1975-81; Anchorman, Dan Rather Reporting, CBS Radio, 1977-; Anchorman, many CBS News special programmes. Publications: The Palace Guard (with Gary Gates), 1974; The Camera Never Blinks (with Mickey Herskowitz), 1977; Memoirs: I Remember (with Peter Wyden), 1991; The Camera Never Blinks Twice: The Further Adventures of a Television Journalist, 1994. Honours: Many Emmy Awards; Dan Rather Communications Building named in his honour, Sam Houston State University, Huntsville, Texas. Address: c/o CBS News, 524 West 57th Street, New York, NY 10019, USA.

RATNER Rochelle, b. 2 Dec 1948, Atlantic City, New Jersey, USA. Poet; Novelist; Critic. Appointments: Poetry Columnist, Soho Weekly News, 1976-82; Executive Editor, American Book Review, 1978-; Small Press Columnist, Library Journal, 1985. Publications: A Birthday of Waters, 1971; False Trees, 1973; Pirate's Song, 1976; The Tightrope Walker, 1977; Quarry, 1978; Combing the Waves, 1979; Sea Air in a Grave Ground Hog Turns Toward, 1980; Hide and Seek, 1980; Practicing to Be a Woman: New and Selected Poems, 1982; Trying to Understand What it Means to be a Feminist, 1984; Bobby's Girl, 1986. Contributions to: New York Times; Hanging Loose; Shenandoah; Antaeus; Salmagundi. Memberships: PEN; National Book Critics Circle; Poetry Society of America. Address: 314 East 78th Street, New York, NY 10021, USA.

RAVEN Simon, (Arthur Noel), b. 28 Dec 1927, London, England. Author; Dramatist. m. Susan Mandeville Kilner, 1951, div, 1 son. Education: Honours Degree in Classics, King's College, Cambridge, 1952. Publications: Alms for Oblivion, 10 volumes,

1964-76; Shadows on the Grass, memoirs, 1982; The First Born of Egypt, 7 volumes, 1984-92; Bird of Ill Omen, 1989; Is There Anybody There? Said the Traveller, Memories of a Private Nuisance, 1991. Other: Various television scripts: including Edward and Mrs Simpson, The Palliseus. Contributions to: Periodicals. Membership: Royal Society of Literature, Fellow, 1993-. Address: 4th Floor, Haymarket House, 28/29 Haymarket, London SW1Y 4SP, England.

RAVIV Dan, b. 27 Sept 1954, New York, USA. News Correspondent. m. Dori Phaff, 27 June 1982, 1 son, 1 daughter. Education: BA, cum laude, Harvard University, 1976. Publications: Behind the Uprising: Israelis, Jordanians, Palestinians, 1988; The Imperfect Spies, 1989; Every Spy a Prince: Complete History of Israel's Intelligence Community, 1990; Friends in Deed: Inside the US-Israel Alliance, 1994. Honour: Overseas Press Club of America Award, 1987. Literary Agent: Russell Galen of Scovil-Chichak-Galen, New York. Address: CBS News, 4770 Biscayne Boulevard, Miami, FL 33137, USA.

RAVVIN Norman, b. 26 Aug 1963, Calgary, Alberta, Canada. Novelist; University Instructor. Education: BA (Hons), 1986, MA, English, 1988, University of British Columbia; PhD, University of Toronto, 1994. Publication: Café des Westens (novel), 1991. Contributions to: Various publications. Honours: Alberta Culture and Multiculturalism New Fiction Award, 1990; PhD Fellowship, Social Sciences and Humanities Research Council of Canada. Memberships: Writers Guild of Alberta; Association of Canadian College and University Teachers of English; Modern Language Society of America. Address: c/o Red Deer College Press, 56 Avenue and 32nd Street, Box 5005, Red Deer, Alberta, T4N 5H5, Canada.

RAWLS John (Bordley), b. 21 Feb 1921, Baltimore, Maryland, USA. Professor of Philosophy; Writer. m. Margaret Warfield Fox, 28 June 1949, 2 sons, 2 daughters. Education: AB, 1943, PhD, 1950, Princeton University; Cornell University, 1947-48. Appointments: Instructor in Philosophy, Princeton University, 1950-52; Assistant Professor to Associate Professor of Philosophy, Cornell University, 1953-59; Visiting Professor, 1959-60, Professor of Philosophy, 1962-, Harvard University; Professor of Philosophy, Massachusetts Institute of Technology, 1960-62. Publications: A Theory of Justice, 1971; Justice as Fairness, 1991; Two Concepts of Rules, 1991; Political Liberalism, 1993. Contributions to: Books and philosophical journals. Honours: Fulbright Fellow, Oxford University, 1952-53; Phi Beta Kappa Ralph Waldo Emerson Award, 1972. Memberships: American Academy of Arts and Sciences; President, American Association of Political and Legal Philosophy, 1970-72; American Philosophical Association; American Philosophical Society. Address: c/o Department of Philosophy, Harvard University, Cambridge, MA 02138, USA.

RAWLS Philip. See: LEVINSON Leonard.

RAWORTH Thomas Moore, b. 19 July 1938, London, England. Poet; Writer. m. Valarie Murphy, 4 sons, 1 daughter. Education: MA, University of Essex, 1970. Appointments: Poet-in-Residence, University of Essex, 1969, Northeastern University, Chicago, 1973-74; King's College, Cambridge, 1977-78; Lecturer, Bowling Green State University, Ohio, 1972-73; Visiting Lecturer, University of Texas, 1974-75, University of Cape Town, 1991, University of San Diego, 1996. Publications: The Relation Ship, 1967; The Big Green Day, 1968; A Serial Biography, 1969; Lion, Lion, 1970; Moving, 1971; Act, 1973; Ace, 1974; Common Sense, 1976; Logbook, 1977; Sky Tails, 1978; Nicht Wahr, Rosie?, 1979; Writing, 1982; Levre de Poche, 1983; Heavy Light, 1984; Tottering State: Selected Poems, 1963-83, 1984, UK edition, 1987; Lazy Left Hand, 1986; Visible Shivers, 1987; All Fours, 1991; Catacoustics, 1991; Eternal Sections, 1991; Survival, 1991; Clean and Well Lit: Selected Poems 1987-1995; 1996. Contributions to: Periodicals. Honours: Alice Hunt Bartlett Prize, 1969; Cholmondeley Award, 1971; International Committee on Poetry Award, New York, 1988. Membership: PEN. Address: 3 St Philip's Road, Cambridge CB1 3AQ, England.

RAWSON Claude Julien, b. 8 Feb 1935, Shanghai, China. Professor of English; Writer. m. Judith Ann Hammond, 14 July 1959, 3 sons, 2 daughters. Education: Magdalen College, Oxford, England, 1952-57; BA, 1955; MA, BLitt, 1959. Appointments: George M Bodman Professor of English, Yale University; Editor, Modern Language Review, and Yearbook of English Studies, 1974-88; General Editor, Unwin Critical Library, 1975-; Executive Editor, Cambridge History of Literary Criticism, 1983-; General Editor, Blackwell Critical

Biographies, 1986-; Chairman and General Editor, Yale Editions of the Private Papers of James Boswell, 1990-. Publications: Henry Fielding, 1968; Focus Swift, 1971; Henry Fielding and the Augustan Ideal under Stress, 1972, 2nd edition, 1991; Gulliver and the Gentle Reader, 1973, 2nd edition, 1991; Fielding: A Critical Anthology, 1973; The Character of Swift's Satire, 1983; English Satire and the Satiric Tradition, 1984; Order from Confusion Sprung: Studies in 18th Century Literature, 1985, 2nd edition, 1994; Thomas Parnell's Collected Poems (editor with F P Lock), 1989; Satire and Sentiment 1660-1800, 1994; Jonathan Swift: A Collection of Critical Essays (editor), 1995. Memberships: British Society for 18th Century Studies, president, 1974-75; American Society for 18th Century Studies, Clifford Lecturer, 1992; Modern Humanities Research Association, Committee member, 1974-88. Literary Agent: The Peters, Fraser and Dunlop Group Ltd. Address: 50 Malthouse Lane, Kenilworth, Warwickshire CV8 1AD, England.

RAY David Eugene, b. 20 May 1932, Sapulpa, Oklahoma, USA. Professor of English Emeritus; Writer; Poet. m. Suzanne Judy Morrish, 21 Feb 1970, 1 son, 3 daughters. Education: BA, 1952, MA, 1957, University of Chicago. Appointments: Instructor, Wright Junior College, 1957-58, Northern Illinois University, 1958-60; Assistant Professor, Reed College, Portland, Oregon, 1964-66; Lecturer, Writer's Workshop, University of Iowa, 1969-70; Visiting Associate Professor, Bowling Green State University, 1970-71; Professor of English, 1971-95, Professor Emeritus, 1995-, University of Missouri, Kansas City; Senior Academy Professor, University of Arizona, 1996-; Visiting Professor, Syracuse University, 1978-79, University of Rajasthan, India, 1981-82; Exchange Professor, University of Otago, New Zealand, 1987; Visiting Fellow, University of Western Australia, 1991. Publications: X-Rays, 1965; Dragging the Main and Other Poems, 1968; A Hill in Oklahoma, 1972; Gathering Firewood: New Poems and Selected, 1974; Enough of Flying: Poems Inspired by the Ghazals of Ghalib, 1977; The Tramp's Cup, 1978; The Farm in Calabria and Other Poems, 1979; The Touched Life, 1982; Not Far From the River, 1983; On Wednesday I Cleaned Out My Wallet, 1985; Elysium in the Halls of Hell, 1986; Sam's Book, 1987; The Maharani's New Wall, 1989; Wool Highways, 1993; Kangaroo Paws, 1994. Short Stories: The Mulberries of Mingo, 1978. Contributions to: Journals and newspapers. Honours: William Carlos Williams Awards, Poetry Society of America, 1979, 1993; PEN Syndicated Fiction Awards, 1982-86; Bernice Jennings Award for Traditional Poetry, Amelia Magazine, 1987; Emily Dickinson Award, Poetry Society of America, 1988; Maurice English Poetry Award, 1988; National Poetry Award, Passaic Community College, 1989; 1st Prize, Stanley Hanks Memorial Contest, St Louis Poetry Centre, 1990; New England Poetry Club Daniel Varoujan Award, 1996; New Millenium Poetry Award, 1997. Memberships: Academy of American Poets; PEN; Phi Kappa Phi; Poetry Society of America. Address: 2033 East 10th Street, Tucson, AZ 85719, USA.

RAY Robert Henry, b. 29 Apr 1940, San Saba, Texas, USA. Professor of English. m. Lynette Elizabeth Dittmar, 1 Sept 1962, 2 daughters. Education: BA, 1963, PhD, 1967, University of Texas at Austin. Appointments: Assistant Professor of English, 1967-75, Associate Professor of English, 1975-85, Professor of English, 1985-, Baylor University. Publications: The Herbert Allusion Book, 1986; Approaches to Teaching Shakespeare's King Lear, 1986; A John Donne Companion, 1990; A George Herbert Companion, 1995. Contributions to: Various publications. Honour: Phi Beta Kappa, 1962. Memberships: Modern Language Association of America; John Donne Society. Address: Department of English, PO Box 97406, Baylor University, Waco, TX 76798, USA.

RAY Robert J, b. 15 May 1935, Amarillo, Texas, USA. Teacher; Writer. m. (1) Ann Allen, div, (2) Margot M Waale, July 1983. Education: BA, 1957, MA, 1959, PhD, 1962, University of Texas, Austin. Appointments: Instructor, 1963-65, Assistant Professor, 1965-68, Associate Professor, 1968-75, Professor, 1976, Beloit College, Beloit, Wisconsin; Writing Teacher, Valley College, 1984-88, University of California, Irvine, 1985-88; Adjunct Professor, Chapman College, 1988-. Publications: The Art of Reading: A Handbook on Writing (with Ann Ray), 1968; The Heart of the Game (novel), 1975; Cage of Mirrors (novel), 1980; Small Business: An Entrepreneur's Plan (with L A Eckert and J D Ryan), 1985; Bloody Murdock (novel), 1987; Murdock for Hire (novel), 1987; The Hitman Cometh (novel), 1988; Dial M for Murder (novel), 1988; Murdock in Xanadu (novel), 1989. Membership: Mystery Writers of America. Address: c/o Ben Kamsler, H N Swanson Inc, 8523 Sunset Boulevard, Los Angeles, CA 90069, USA.

RAYMOND Derek. See: **COOK Robert William Arthur.**

RAYMOND Diana Joan, b. 25 Apr 1916, London, England. Novelist. m. Ernest Raymond, 20 Aug 1940, 1 son. Publications: Over 25 books, 1958-96. Honour: Books Society Choice, 1954. Membership: Society of Authors. Address: 22 The Pryors, East Heath Road, London NW3 1BS, England.

RAYMOND Mary. See: **KEEGAN Mary Constance.**

RAYMOND Patrick Ernest, b. 25 Sep 1924, Cuckfield, Sussex, England. Royal Air Force Officer (retired); Writer. m. Lola Pilpel, 27 May 1950, 1 son. Education: Art School, Cape Town, South Africa. Appointments: Royal Air Force, rising to Group Captain, 1942-77. Publications: A City of Scarlet and Gold, 1963; The Lordly Ones, 1965; The Sea Garden, 1970; The Last Soldier, 1974; A Matter of Assassination, 1977; The White War, 1978; The Grand Admiral, 1980; Daniel and Esther, 1989. Literary Agent: A P Watt Limited. Address: 24 Chilton Road, Chesham, Buckinghamshire HP5 2AU, England.

RAYNER Claire Berenice, (Sheila Brandon, Ann Lynton, Ruth Martin), b. 22 Jan 1931, London, England. Writer; Broadcaster. m. Desmond Rayner, 23 June 1957, 2 sons, 1 daughter. Education: State Registered Nurse, Gold Medal, Royal Northern Hospital, London, 1954; Midwifery, Guy's Hospital. Publications: Over 90 books, ranging from medical to fiction, 1965-96. Contributions to: Professional journals, newspapers, radio, and television. Honours: Freeman, City of London, 1981; Medical Journalists Association Award, 1987; Honorary Fellow, University of North London, 1988; Best Specialist Consumer Columnist Award, 1988; Order of the British Empire, 1996. Memberships: Royal Society of Arts, Fellow; Royal Society of Medicine, Fellow; Society of Authors. Address: Holly Wood House, Rosborough Avenue, Harrow-on-the-Hill, Middlesex HA1 3BU, England.

RAYNER Mary Yoma, b. 30 Dec 1933, Mandalay, Burma. Author. m. (1) Eric Rayner, 6 Aug 1960, 2 sons, 1 daughter, (2) Adrian Hawksley, 9 Mar 1985. Education: Honours Degree, English, University of St Andrews, Scotland. Publications: Witch-Finder, 1975; Mr and Mrs Pig's Evening Out, 1976; Garth Pig and the Icecream Lady, 1977; The Rain Cloud, 1980; Mrs Pig's Bulk Buy, 1981; Crocodarling, 1985; Mrs Pig Gets Cross, 1986; Reilly, 1987; Oh Paul!, 1988; Rug, 1989; Marathon and Steve (USA), 1989; Bathtime for Garth Pig, 1989; Open Wide, 1990; The Echoing Green, 1992; Garth Pig Steals the Show, 1993; One by One, Ten Pink Piglets, 1994. Memberships: Society of Authors; Member of Advisory Committee, Public Lending Right, 1989-93. Literary Agent: Laura Cecil. Address: c/o Pan Macmillan Ltd, Cavaye Place, London SW10 9PG, England.

RAYSON Hannie, b. 31 Mar 1957, Brighton, Melbourne, Australia. Playwright. Education: BA, University of Melbourne, 1977; Dip Art in Dramatic Arts, Victoria College of Arts, 1980. Appointments: Writer-in-Residence, various institutions; Literature Board, Australia Council, 1992-95. Publications: Please Return to Sender, 1980; Mary, 1981; Leave it Till Monday, 1984; Room to Move, 1985; Hotel Sorrento, 1990; SLOTH (television play), 1992; Falling From Grace, 1994. Honours: Australian Writers Guild Awards, 1986, 1991; New South Wales Premier's Literary Award; Sidney Myer Performing Arts Award, 1996. Address: Hilary Linstead & Associates, Level 18, Plaza 2, 500 Oxford Street, Bondi Junction, New South Wales 2022, Australia.

RAZ Joseph, b. 21 Mar 1939, Haifa, Palestine. Professor of the Philosophy of Law; Writer. Education: Magister Juris, Hebrew University, Jerusalem, 1963; DPhil, Oxford University, 1967. Appointments: Lecturer, Hebrew University, Jerusalem, 1967-70; Research Fellow, 1970-72, Nuffield College, Oxford; Tutorial Fellow, 1972-85, Professor of the Philosophy of Law, 1985-, Balliol College, Oxford. Publications: The Concept of a Legal System, 1970, 2nd edition, 1980; Practical Reason and Norms, 1975, 2nd edition, 1990; The Authority of Law, 1979; The Morality of Freedom, 1986; Ethics in the Public Domain, 1994. Contributions to: Professional journals and other publications. Honours: W J M Mackenzie Book Prize, Political Studies Association, UK, 1987; Elaine and David Spitz Book Prize, Conference for the Study of Political Thought, New York, 1987; Honorary Doctorate, Katolieke University, Brussels, 1993. Memberships: American Academy of Arts and Sciences, honorary foreign member; British Academy, Fellow. Address: c/o Balliol College, Oxford OX1 3BJ, England.

READ Miss. See: **SAINT Dora Jessie**.

READ Anthony, b. 21 Apr 1935, Staffordshire, England. Writer. m. Rosemary E Kirby, 29 Mar 1958, 2 daughters. Education: Central School of Speech and Drama, London, 1952-54. Publications: The Theatre, 1964; Operation Lucy (with David Fisher), 1980; Colonel Z (with David Fisher), 1984; The Deadly Embrace (with David Fisher), 1988; Kristallnacht (with David Fisher), 1989; Conspirator (with Ray Bearse), 1991; The Fall of Berlin (with David Fisher), 1992; Berlin: The Biography of a City (with David Fisher), 1994. Over 100 television films, plays and serials. Honours: Pye Colour TV Award, 1983; Wingate Literary Prize, 1989. Membership: Writers Guild of Great Britain. Literary Agent: Books: Murray Pollinger. TV & Film: Stephen Durbridge, Lemon, Unna & Durbridge Ltd. Address: 7 Cedar Chase, Taplow, Buckinghamshire, England.

READ Desmond. See: **MOORCOCK Michael (John)**.

READ Piers Paul, b. 7 Mar 1941, Beaconsfield, England. Writer. m. Emily Albertine Boothby, 29 July 1967, 2 sons, 2 daughters. Education: MA, St John's College, Cambridge, England. Publications: Game in Heaven (with Tussy Marx), 1966; The Junkers, 1968; Monk Dawson, 1969; The Upstart, 1973; A Married Man, 1979; The Free Frenchman, 1986; The Professor's Daughter, 1975; Polonaise, 1976; The Villa Golitsyn, 1981; A Season in the West, 1988; On the Third Day, 1990. Non-Fiction: Alive, 1974; The Train Robbers, 1978; Quo Vadis?: The Subversion of the Catholic Church, 1991; Ablaze, 1993; A Patriot in Berlin, 1995 (published as The Patriot, USA, 1996). Contributions to: Spectator; Tablet. Honours: Sir Geoffrey Faber Memorial Prize, 1968; Hawthornden Prize, 1969; Somerset Maugham Award, 1969; Thomas More Award, 1976; James Tait Black Memorial Prize, 1988. Memberships: Society of Authors; Royal Society of Literature, fellow. Literary Agent: Aitken and Stone. Address: 50 Portland Road, London W11 4LG, England.

READE Hamish. See: **GRAY Simon (James Holliday)**.

READING Peter, b. 27 July 1946, Liverpool, England. Poet. m. Diana Gilbert, 5 Oct 1968, 1 daughter. Education: BA, Liverpool College of Art, 1967. Appointments: Teacher, large comprehensive school in Liverpool; Lecturer, Department of Art History, Liverpool College of Art, 1968-70; Fellowship, Sunderland Polytechnic, 1981-83. Publications: Water and Waste, 1970; For the Municipality's Elderly, 1974; The Prison Cell and Barrel Mystery, 1976; Nothing for Anyone, 1977; Fiction, 1979; Tom O'Bedlam's Beauties, 1981; Diplopic, 1983; 5 x 5 x 5 x 5 x 5, 1983; C, 1984; Ukulele Music, 1985; Stet, 1986; Essential Reading, 1986; Final Demands, 1988; Perduta Gente, 1989; Shitheads, 1989; Evagatory, 1992; 3 in 1, 1992; Last Poems, 1993. Honours: Cholmondeley Award for Poetry, 1978; First Dylan Thomas Award, 1983; Whitbread Award, Poetry Category, 1986; Lannan Foundation, USA, Literary Fellowship Award, 1990. Membership: Royal Society of Literature, fellow. Address: 1 Ragleth View, Little Stretton, Shropshire, England.

READSHAW Grahame George Cochrane, b. 23 Feb 1933, Toowoomba, Queensland, Australia. Medical Practitioner. m. Laurel Gray, 27 Oct 1956, 2 sons, 2 daughters. Education: MB, BS, 1955; Diploma of Ophthalmology, 1964; Fellow, Royal Australian College of Ophthalmology, 1978. Publications: Looking Up, Looking Back at Old Brisbane (with R Wood), 1987; Keep It Simple System for Watercolour Painting, 1992. Contributions to: Medical Journal of Australia; Australian Journal of Ophthalmology; Australian Artist Magazine. Honour: Grumbacher Gold Medallion for Painting, 1983. Memberships: Royal Queensland Art Society; Watercolour Society of Queensland; Australian Medical Association; Royal Australian College of Ophthalmologists; Aviation Medical Society of Australia and New Zealand. Address: 44 Victoria Avenue, Chelmer, Queensland 4068, Australia.

REAKES Janet Elizabeth, b. 26 Jan 1952, Bristol, England. Genealogist. Education: Diploma of Family History Studies; Accredited Genealogist (GSU). Publications: How To Trace Your Convict Ancestors, 1986; A to Z of Genealogy: A Handbook, 1987, 3rd edition, 1993; How to Trace Your Family Tree and Not Get Stuck on a Branch, 1987; How to Trace Your English Ancestors, 1987; How to Trace Your Irish Ancestors, reprinted, 1993; How to Write the Family Story, 1993. Contributions to: Columnist, Sunday Mail, Queensland, Australia; Former Columnist, Sunday Sun; Telegraph; Mirror; New Idea; Womens Weekly; Herald; Sun. Membership: Australian Authors.

Address: PO Box 937, Hervey Bay, Queensland, Australia.

REANEY James Crear, b. 1 Sept 1926, South Easthope, Ontario, Canada. Professor; Poet; Dramatist. m. 29 Dec 1951, 2 sons, 1 daughter. Education: BA, 1948, MA, 1949, University of Toronto. Appointments: Faculty, University of Manitoba, Winnipeg, 1948-60; Professor, Middlesex College, University of Western Ontario, 1960-. Publications: Poetry: The Red Heart, 1949; A Suit of Nettles, 1958; Twelve Letters to a Small Town, 1962; The Dance of Death at London, 1963; Poems, 1972; Selected Shorter and Longer Poems, 1975-76; Performance Poems, 1990. Plays: Night Blooming Cereus, 1959; The Killdeer, 1960; One Masque, 1960; The Sun and the Moon, 1965; Listen to the Wind, 1966; The Canada Tree, 1967; Genesis, 1968; Masque, 1972; The Donnellys: A Trilogy, 1973-75; Baldoon, 1976; King Whistle, 1979; Antler River, 1980; Gyroscope, 1981; I, the Parade, 1982; The Canadian Brothers, 1983; Alice Through the Looking Glass (adaptation of Lewis Carroll's book), 1994. Opera Libretto: The Shivaree (music by John Beckwith), 1982; The Box Social and Other Stories, 1996. Contributions to: Books, journals and periodicals. Honours: Governor-General's Awards, 1949, 1958, 1963; University of Alberta Award for Letters, 1974; Order of Canada, 1975. Memberships: Association of Canadian University Teachers, president, 1959-60; Playwright's Union of Canada; League of Canadian Poets. Literary Agent: John Miller, Cultural Support Services, 14 Earl Street, 1st Floor, Toronto, Ontario M4Y 1M3, Canada. Address: Department of English, University of Western Ontario, London, Ontario N6A 3K7, Canada.

RECHEIS Kathe, b. 11 Mar 1928, Engelhartszell, Austria. Freelance Writer of Children's and Young People's Literature. Publications: Geh heim und vergiss Alles, 1964; Fallensteller am Bibersee, 1972; London 13 Juli, 1974; Der weite Weg des Nataiyu, 1978; Wo die Wolfe glücklich sind, 1980; Der Weisse Wolf, 1982; Weisst du dass die Baume reden, 1983; Lena - Unser Dorf und der Krieg, 1987; Tomasita, 1989; Wolfsaga, 1994. Honours: Austrian State Prizes for Children's and Young People's Literature, 1961, 1963, 1964, 1967, 1971, 1972, 1975, 1976, 1979, 1980, 1984, 1987, 1992, 1995; Österreichischer Würdigungspreis für Kinder-und Jugendliteratur for Complete Works, 1986; IBBY Certificate of Honour, 1978, 1982, 1987, 1994. Memberships: Austrian Writers Association; PEN Club. Address: Rembrandtstrasse 1/28, A 1020 Vienna, Austria.

REDDY T Vasudeva, b. 21 Dec 1943, Mittapalem, India. Lecturer in English. m. 5 Nov 1970, 2 sons, 1 daughter. Education: BSc, 1963; MA English, 1966; PhD English, 1985; PGDTE, 1983. Appointment: Lecturer in English, 1966-. Publications: When Grief Rains (poems), 1982; The Vultures (novel), 1983; The Broken Rhythms (poems), 1987; Jane Austen, 1987; Jane Austen: Matrix of Matrimony, 1987; The Fleeting Bubbles (poems), 1989. Contributions to: Poems, critical articles and reviews to various journals and magazines. Honours: Award of International Eminent Poet, 1987; Honorary DLitt, World Academy of Arts and Culture, California, 1988; State Award for Best Teacher, University College Teachers, Andhra Pradesh, India, 1991. Memberships: International Poets Academy, Madras; World Poetry Society, California; American Biographical Institute, USA; Government College Teachers Association, Andhra Pradesh, India. Address: Narasingapuram Post, Via Chandragiri, Pin 517 102, AP, India.

REDGROVE Peter William, b. 2 Jan 1932, Kingston-on-Thames, Surrey, England. Analytical Psychologist; Poet; Writer. m. (1) 1 daughter, (2) Penelope Shuttle, 2 sons, 1 daughter. Education: Queen's College, Cambridge. Appointments: Visiting Poet, University of Buffalo, 1961-62; Gregory Fellow in Poetry, University of Leeds, 1962-65; O'Connor Professor of Literature, Colgate University, 1974-75; Writer-at-Large, North Cornwall Arts, 1988. Publications: Poetry: The Collector, 1960; The Nature of Cold Weather, 1961; At the White Monument, 1963; The Force, 1966; Penguin Modern Poets 11, 1968; Work in Progress, 1969; Dr Faust's Sea-Spiral Spirit, 1972; Three Pieces for Voices, 1972; The Hermaphrodite Album (with Penelope Shuttle), 1973; Sons of My Skin: Selected Poems, 1975; From Every Chink of the Art, 1977; Ten Poems, 1977; The Weddings at Nether Powers, 1979; The Apple Broadcast, 1981; The Working of Water, 1984; The Man Named East, 1985; The Mudlark Poems and Grand Buveur, 1986; In the Hall of the Saurians, 1987; The Moon Disposes: Poems 1954-1987, 1987; The First Earthquake, 1989; Dressed as for a Tarot Pack, 1990; Under the Reservoir, 1992; The Laborators, 1993; The Cyclopean Mistress, 1993; My Father's Trapdoors, 1994; Abyssophone, 1995; Assembling a Ghost, 1996; The

Best of Redgrove, 1996; Orchard End, 1997; What the Black Mirror Saw, 1997. Novels: In the Country of the Ski, 1973; The Terrors of Dr Treviles (with Penelope Shuttle), 1974; The Glass Cottage, 1976; The Sleep of the Great Hypnotist, 1979; The God of Glass, 1979; The Beekeepers, 1980; The Facilitators, 1982; Tales from Grimm, 1989. Other: Plays for stage, radio and television; Non-fiction: The Wise Wound (with Penelope Shuttle), 1978, 2nd edition, 1986; The Black Goddess and the Sixth Sense, 1987; Alchemy for Women (with Penelope Shuttle), 1995; Honours: George Rylands' Verse-Speaking Prize, 1954; Poetry Book Society Choices, 1961, 1966, 1979, 1981; 5 Arts Council Awards, 1969-82; Guardian Fiction Prize, 1973; Prudence Farmer Poetry Award, 1977; Cholmondeley Award, 1985; Queen's Gold Medal for Poetry, 1996. Membership: Royal Society of Literature, Fellow. Address: c/o David Higham Associates, 5-8 Lower John Street, Golden Square, London W1R 4HA, England.

REDMAN Joseph. See: **PEARCE Brian Leonard.**

REDWOOD Alex. See: **MILKOMANE George Alexis Milkomanovich.**

REED Eliot. See: **AMBLER Eric.**

REED Ishmael (Scott), b. 22 Feb 1938, Chattanooga, Tennessee, USA. Writer; Poet; Publisher; Editor; Teacher. m. (1) Priscilla Rose, 1960, div 1970, 1 daughter, (2) Carla Blank-Reed, 1970, 1 daughter. Education: University of Buffalo, 1956-60. Appointments: Lecturer, University of California at Berkeley, 1967-, University of Washington, 1969-70, State University of New York at Buffalo, 1975, 1979, University of Arkansas, 1982, Columbia University, 1983, Harvard University, 1987, University of California at Santa Barbara, 1988; Chairman and President, Yardbird Publishing Company, 1971-; Director, Reed Cannon and Johnson Communications, 1973-; Visiting Professor, 1979, Associate Fellow, 1983-, Calhoun House, Yale University; Visiting Professor, Dartmouth College, 1980; Co-Founder (with Al Young) and Editor, Quilt Magazine, 1981-; Associate Fellow, Harvard University Signet Society, 1987-. Publications: Fiction: The Free-Lance Pallbearers, 1967; Yellow Black Radio Broke-Down, 1969; Mumbo-Jumbo, 1972; The Last Days of Louisiana Red, 1974; Flight to Canada, 1976; The Terrible Twos, 1982; Reckless Eyeballing, 1986; The Terrible Threes, 1989; Japanese by Spring, 1993. Poetry: Catechism of a Neoamerican Hoodoo Church, 1970; Conjure: Selected Poems 1963-1970, 1972; Chattanooga, 1973; A Secretary to the Spirits, 1978; New and Collected Poems, 1988. Other: The Rise, Fall and ...? of Adam Clayton Powell (with others), 1967; Shrovetide in Old New Orleans, 1978; God Made Alaska for the Indians, 1982; Cab Calloway Stands in for the Moon, 1986; Ishmael Reed: An Interview, 1990; Airin' Dirty Laundry, 1993. Editor: 19 Necromancers from Now, 1970; Yardbird Reader, 5 volumes, 1971-77; Yardbird Lives! (with Al Young), 1978; Calafia: The California Poetry, 1979; Quilt 2-3 (with Al Young), 2 volumes, 1981-82; Writin' is Fightin': Thirty-Seven Years of Boxing on Paper, 1988; The Before Columbus Foundation Fiction Anthology: Selections from the American Books Awards, 1980-1990 (with Kathryn Trueblood and Shawn Wong), 1992. Honours: National Endowment for the Arts Grant, 1974; Rosenthal Foundation Award, 1975; Guggenheim Fellowship, 1975; American Academy of Arts and Letters Award, 1975; Michaux Award, 1978. Membership: Before Columbus Foundation, president, 1976-. Address: c/o Ellis J Freedman, 415 Madison Avenue, New York, NY 10017, USA.

REED Jeremy, b. 1951, Jersey, Channel Islands. Poet; Writer. Education: BA, University of Essex, Colchester. Publications: Target, 1972; Saints and Psychotics: Poems 1973-74, 1974; Vicissitudes, 1974; Diseased Near Deceased, 1975; Emerald Cat, 1975; Ruby Onocentaur, 1975; Blue Talaria, 1976; Count Bluebeard, 1976; Jacks In His Corset, 1978; Walk on Through, 1980; Bleecker Street, 1980; No Refuge Here, 1981; A Long Shot to Heaven, 1982; A Man Afraid, 1982; By the Fisheries, 1984; Elegy for Senta, 1985; Skies, 1985; Border Pass, 1986; Selected Poems, 1987; Engaging Form, 1988; The Escaped Image, 1988; Nineties, 1990; Dicing for Pearls, 1990. Novels: The Lipstick Boys, 1984; Blue Rock, 1987; Madness: The Price of Poetry, 1990. Honours: Somerset Maugham Award, 1985. Address: c/o Jonathan Cape Ltd, 20 Vauxhall Bridge Road, London SW1V 2SA, England

REED John (Reginald), b. 30 May 1909, Aldershot, Hampshire, England. Retired Schoolmaster; Music Critic. m. Edith Marion Hampton, 30 Oct 1936, 2 sons, 2 daughters. Education: County High

School, Aldershot, 1920-27; Diploma of Education, 1930, BA Hons, English Language and Literature, 1935, London University. Appointment: Music Critic, The Guardian, 1974-81. Publications: Schubert: The Final Years, 1972; Schubert (Great Composers Series), 1978; The Schubert Song Companion, 1985; Schubert (Master Musicians Series), 1986. Contributions to: Newspapers and journals. Honours: Duckles Award for best reference book on a musical topic published in 1985, Music Library Association of America, 1987; Honorary Member, International Franz Schubert Institute of Vienna, 1989. Membership: Schubert Institute UK, chairman, 1991-94. Address: 130 Fog Lane, Didsbury, Manchester M20 0SW, England.

REED Michael Arthur, b. 25 Apr 1930, Aylesbury, Buckinghamshire, England. University Professor. m. Gwynneth Vaughan, 1 Oct 1955, 1 son. Education: BA, 1954, MA, 1958, University of Birmingham; LLB, University of London, 1966; PhD, University of Leicester, 1973. Appointment: Professor, Loughborough University. Publications: The Buckinghamshire Landscape, 1979; The Georgian Triumph, 1983; The Age of Exuberance, 1986; The Landscape of Britain, 1990; A History of Buckinghamshire, 1993. Contributions to: Journals. Memberships: Fellow, Royal Historical Society, 1985; Fellow, Society of Antiquaries of London, 1985. Address: Department of Information and Library Studies, Loughborough University, Loughborough, Leicestershire, England.

REEDER Carolyn, b. 16 Nov 1937, Washington, District of Columbia, USA. Writer; Teacher. m. Jack Reeder, 15 Aug 1959, 1 son, 1 daughter. Education: BA, 1959, MEd, 1971, The American University. Publications: Historical fiction for children: Shades of Grey, 1989; Grandpa's Mountain, 1991; Moonshiner's Son, 1993. Adult fiction, co-authored with Jack Reeder: Shenandoah Heritage, 1978; Shenandoah Vestiges, 1980; Shenandoah Secrets, 1991. Honours: Scott O'Dell Award for Historical Fiction, 1989; Child Study Association Award, 1989; American Library Association Notable Book, 1989; Honour Book for the Jane Addam's Children's Book Award, 1989; Notable Trade Book in the Language Arts, 1989; Jefferson Cup Award, 1990; International Reading Association Young Adult Choice for 1991; Joan G Sugarman Children's Book Award, 1992-93; Hedda Seisler Mason Honor Award, 1995. Membership: Children's Book Guild of Washington DC, former treasurer. Address: 7314 University Avenue, Glen Echo, MD 20812, USA.

REEDER Hubert, b. 17 Mar 1948, Plainfield, New Jersey, USA. Poet; Writer. Education: BS, 1989. Publications: Gates Found I, 1977; Gates Found II, 1982. Honours: Awards of Merit, World of Poetry, 1984, 1985, 1987, 1988; Editor's Choice Award, National Library of Poetry, 1989; Poet of Merit Award, American Poetry Society. Memberships: American Poetry Society; World of Poetry. Address: PO Box 128, East Orange, NJ 07019, USA.

REEMAN Douglas Edward, (Alexander Kent), b. 15 Oct 1924, Thames Ditton, Surrey, England. Author. m. Kimberley June Jordan, 5 Oct 1985. Publications: A Prayer for the Ship, 1958; High Water, 1959; Send a Gunboat, 1960; Dive in the Sun, 1961; The Hostile Shore, 1962; The Last Raider, 1963; With Blood and Iron, 1964; HMS Saracen, 1965; Path of the Storm, 1966; The Deep Silence, 1967; The Pride and the Anguish, 1968; To Risks Unknown, 1969; The Greatest Enemy, 1970; Against the Sea, 1971; Rendezvous - South Atlantic, 1972; Go In and Sink!, 1973; The Destroyers, 1974; Winged Escort, 1975; Surface with Daring, 1976; Strike from the Sea, 1978; A Ship Must Die, 1979; Torpedo Run, 1981; Badge of Glory, 1982; The First to Land, 1984; D-Day: A Personal Reminiscence, 1984; The Volunteers, 1985; The Iron Pirate, 1986; In Danger's Hour, 1988; The White Guns, 1989; Killing Ground, 1990; The Horizon, 1993; Sunset, 1994; The Douglas Reeman Omnibus, 1994; A Dawn Like Thunder, 1996. As Alexander Kent: To Glory We Steer, 1968; Form Line of Battle, 1969; Enemy in Sight!, 1970; The Flag Captain, 1971; Sloop of War, 1972; Command a King's Ship, 1974; Signal - Close Action! 1974; Richard Bolitho - Midshipman, 1975; Passage to Mutiny, 1976; In Gallant Company, 1977; Midshipman Bolitho and the 'Avenger', 1978; Captain Richard Bolitho, RN, 1978; The Inshore Squadron, 1978; Stand Into Danger, 1980; A Tradition of Victory, 1981; Success to the Brave, 1983; Colours Aloft!, 1986; Honour This Day, 1987; With All Despatch, 1988; The Only Victor, 1990; The Bolitho Omnibus, 1991; Beyond the Reef, 1992; The Darkening Sea, 1993; For My Country's Freedom, 1995; Cross of St. George, 1996. Contributions to: Various journals and magazines. Address: Peters, Fraser & Dunlop, The Chambers, Chelsea Harbour, London SW10 0XF, England.

REES Barbara Elizabeth, b. 9 Jan 1934, Worcester, England. Writer. m. Larry Herman, 1 Sept 1967, div 1978, 1 daughter. Education: BA Honours, English Language and Literature, University of Oxford; MA. Appointment: Arts Council of Great Britain Creative Writer-in-Residence, North London Polytechnic, 1976-78. Publications: Try Another Country (3 short novels), 1969; Diminishing Circles, 1970; Prophet of the Wind, 1973; George and Anna, 1976; The Victorian Lady, 1977; Harriet Dark, 1978. Contributions to: Good Housekeeping; Melbourne Herald; Annabella; Det Nye; Woman's Own. Honour: Arts Council Award, 1974. Address: 102 Savernake Road, London NW3 2JR, England.

REES Brian, b. 20 Aug 1929, Strathfield, Sydney, Australia. Parliamentary Researcher; Writer. m. (1) Julia Birley, 17 Dec 1959, dec, (2) Juliet Akehurst, 3 Jan 1987, 2 sons, 3 daughters. Education: First Class Historical Tripos, Parts I and II, Trinity College, Cambridge. Appointments: Assistant Master, Eton College, 1952-65; Headmaster, Merchant Taylor's School, 1965-73, Charterhouse, 1973-81, Rugby School, 1981-84. Publications: A Musical Peacemaker (biography of Sir Edward German), 1987; History and Idealism (editor), 1990. Forthcoming Publications: Stowe: History of a Public School; Biography of Camille Saint-Saens. Address: 52 Spring Lane, Flore, Northamptonshire NN7 4LS, England.

REES David Benjamin, b. 1 Aug 1937, Llanddewi Brefi, Dyfed, Wales. Minister of Religion. m. Meinwen Rees, 31 July 1963, 2 sons. Education: BA, BD, MSc, University of Wales, University of Liverpool and University of Salford. Appointments: Editor, Angor, 1979-; Peacelinks, 1986-96, Reconciliation Quarterly, 1990-. Publications: Wales: the Cultural Heritage, 1981; Preparation for Crisis: Adult Education 1945-80, 1982; Hanes Phwyf Llanddewi Brefi, 1984; Liverpool Welsh and Their Religion, 1984; Owen Thomas: A Welsh Preacher in Liverpool, 1991; Liverpool and Politics: 1800-1911, 1996. Contributions to: Planet; New Wales Review; Y Faner; Traethodydd; Inheritance; Treasury. Honour: University of Wales Ellis Griffith Prize, 1979. Memberships: George Borrow Society; Tolkein Society; Dorothy L Sayers Society; William Cobbett Society. Address: 32 Garth Drive, Liverpool L18 6HW, England.

REES-MOGG Lord William, b. 14 July 1928, Bristol, England. Journalist; Editor; Writer. m. Gillian Shakespeare Morris, 1962, 2 sons, 3 daughters. Education: Balliol College, Oxford. Appointments: Staff, 1952-55, Chief Leader Writer, 1955-60, Assistant Editor, 1957-60, The Financial Times; City Editor, 1960-61, Political and Economic Editor, 1961-63, Deputy Editor, 1964-67, The Sunday Times; Editor, The Times, 1967-81; Director, The Times Ltd, 1968-81; Vice-Chairman, BBC Board of Governors, 1981-86; Chairman, Arts Council, 1982-89, Broadcasting Standards Council, 1988-. Publications: The Reigning Error: The Crisis of World Inflation, 1974; An Humbler Heaven, 1977; How to Buy Rare Books, 1985; Blood in the Streets, 1988; The Great Reckoning, 1991; Picnics on Vesuvius, 1992; The Sovereign Individual: How to Survive and Thrive During the Collapse of the Welfare State (with James Dale Davidson), 1997. Contributions to: Periodicals. Memberships: Oxford Union, President, 1951; Pontifical Council for Culture, 1983-87; Trollope Society, President. Address: 17 Pall Mall, London SW1, England.

REEVE F(ranklin) D(olier), b. 18 Sept 1928, Philadelphia, Pennsylvania, USA. Professor of Letters; Writer; Poet. Education: PhD, Columbia University, 1958. Appointments: Professor of Letters, Wesleyan University, 1970-; Visiting Lecturer, Yale University, 1972-86; Editor, Poetry Review, 1982-84; Visiting Professor, Columbia University, 1988. Publications: Anthology of Russian Plays (translator), 2 volumes, 1961, 1963; The Russian Novel, 1966; In the Silent Stones, 1968; The Red Machines, 1968; Just Over the Border, 1969; The Brother, 1971; The Blue Cat, 1972; White Colors, 1973; Nightway, 1987; An Arrow in the Wall, 1987; The White Monk, 1989; The Garden, 1990; Concrete Music, 1992; The Trouble with Reason, 1993; A Few Rounds of Old Maid and Other Stories, 1995. Contributions to: Many journals and periodicals. Honours: American Academy of Arts and Letters Award, 1970; PEN-Syndicated Fiction Awards, 1985, 1986; Golden Rose, New England Poetry Society, 1994. Memberships: PEN, American Centre; Poetry Society of America, Vice-President, 1982-84; Poets House; Vermont Centre for the Book. Address: Box 206, Wilmington, VT 05363, USA.

REGAN Dian Curtis, b. 17 May 1950, Colorado Springs, Colorado, USA. Children's Book Author. m. John Regan, 25 Aug 1979. Education: BS Honours, Education, University of Colorado, Boulder,

1980. Appointments: Speaker, numerous writers' conferences, USA. Publications: I've Got Your Number, 1986; The Perfect Age, 1987; Game of Survival, 1989; The Kissing Contest, 1990; Jilly's Ghost, 1990; Liver Cookies, 1991; The Class With the Summer Birthdays, 1991; The Curse of the Trouble Dolls, 1992; My Zombie Valentine, 1993; Princess, 1993; Cripple Creek Ghost Mine, 1993; Thirteen Days of Halloween, 1993. Contributions to: Magazines and children's publications. Honours: Children's Choice Award, 1987; Pick of The List, American Library Association, 1989; Oklahoma Cherubim Awards, 1990, 1991, 1992. Memberships: Authors Guild; Society of Children's Book Writers; Oklahoma Writers Federation. Address: c/o Curtis Brown Ltd, 10 Astor Place, 3rd Floor, New York, NY 10003, USA.

REGISTER Cheri, (Cheryl Lynn Register), b. 30 Apr 1945, Albert Lea, Minnesota, USA. Writer; Freelance Teacher. m. 1966-85, 2 daughters. Education: BA Honours, 1967, MA Honours, 1968, PhD Honours, 1973, University of Chicago. Appointments: Co-founder, organizer and workshop leader, Emma Willard Task Force on Education, Minnesota, 1970-73; Co-ordinator of Women's Center, University of Idaho, Moscow, 1973-74; Assistant Professor of Women's Studies and Scandinavian Languages and Literatures, University of Minnesota - Twin Cities, Minneapolis, 1974-80; Writer and Freelance Teacher, 1980-. Publications: As Cheri Register: Sexism in Education (co-author), 1971; Kvinnokamp och litteratur i USA och Sverige (Women's Liberation and Literature in the United States and Sweden), 1977; A Telling Presence: Westminster Presbyterian Church 1857-1982 (editor), 1982; Mothers, Saviours, Peacemakers: Swedish Women Writers in the Twentieth Century, 1983; Living With Chronic Illness: Days of Patience and Passion, 1987; Are Those Kids Yours?: American Families With Children Adopted from Other Countries, 1990. Contributions to: Various edited volumes and to magazines. Honour: Jerome Foundation Travel and Study Grant, 1991; Minnesota Historical Society Research Grant, 1996. Address: 4226 Washburn Avenue South, Minneapolis, MN 55410, USA.

REICHI Ali. See: **KATZ Bobbi.**

REID Alastair, b. 22 Mar 1926, Whithorn, Wigtonshire, Scotland. Writer; Translator; Poet. Education: MA, University of St Andrews, Scotland, 1949. Appointments: Visiting Lecturer at Universities in the UK and USA; Staff Writer, Correspondent, New Yorker, 1959-. Publications: To Lighten my House, 1953; Oddments, Inklings, Omens Moments, 1959; Passwords: Places, Poems, Preoccupations, 1963; Mother Goose in Spanish, 1967; Corgi Modern Poets in Focus 3, 1971; Weathering: Poems and Translations, 1978; Whereabouts: Notes on Being a Foreigner, 1987; An Alastair Reid Reader, 1995; Stories for Children and Translations from Spanish of Pablo Neruda, Jorge Luis Borges and other writers. Honour: Scottish Arts Council Award, 1979. Address: c/o New Yorker, 20 West 43rd Street, NY 10036, USA.

REID Christina, b. 12 Mar 1942, Belfast, Northern Ireland. Playwright. Education: Queens University, Belfast, 1982-83. Appointments: Writer-in-Residence, Lyric Theatre, Belfast, 1983-84, Young Vic Theatre, London, 1988-89. Publications: Did You Hear the One About the Irishman?, 1980; Tea in a China Cup, 1983; Joyriders, 1986; The Last of a Dyin' Race, 1986; The Belle of The Belfast City, 1986; My Name? Shall I Tell You My Name?, 1987; Les Miserables (after Hugo), 1992; Clowns, 1996: Plays produced in England, Ireland, Europe (in translation) and USA. Honours: Ulster TV Drama Award, 1980; Giles Cooper Award, 1986; George Devine Award, 1986. Address: c/o Alan Brodie Representation, 211 Piccadilly, London W1V 9LD, England.

REID Loren, b. 26 Aug 1905, Gilman City, Missouri, USA. Professor Emeritus of Communication. m. Augusta Towner, 28 Aug 1930, 3 sons, 1 daughter. Education: BA, Grinnell College, 1927; MA, 1930, PhD, 1932, University of Iowa. Appointments: University of Missouri, 1935-39, 1939-75; Syracuse University, 1939-44; Emeritus Professor, 1975-. Publications: Teaching Speech, 4 editions, 1960-71; Speaking Well, 4 editions, 1962-82; Hurry Home Wednesday, 1978; Finally It's Friday, 1981; Professor on the Loose, 1992; Reflections, 1995. Contributions to: School and Society; History Today; Kansas City Star; Quarterly Journal of Speech; Parliamentary History. Honours: Distinguished Research/Service Awards, Grinnell College, University of Missouri. Memberships: Missouri Writers Guild; Missouri Library Association; Central States Speech Association; National Communication Association. Address: 200 East Brandon Road, Columbia, MO 65203, USA.

REID Lady Michaela Ann, b. 14 Dec 1933, Tean Staffordshire, England. Author. m. Alexander James Reid, 15 Oct 1955, 1 son, 3 daughters. Education: Law Tripos, Part 1, Girton College, Cambridge University. Publications: Ask Sir James: Sir James Reid, Personal Physician to Queen Victoria and Physician-in-Ordinary to Three Monarchs, 1987, 4th edition, 1996. Address: Lanton Tower, Jedburgh, Roxburghshire, Scotland.

REID Philip. See: **INGRAMS Richard Reid.**

REIF Stefan Clive, b. 21 Jan 1944, Edinburgh, Scotland. Academic. m. Shulamit Stekel, 19 Sept 1967, 1 son, 1 daughter. Education: BA Hons, 1964, PhD, 1969, University of London; MA, University of Cambridge, England, 1976. Appointments: Editor, Cambridge University Library's Genizah Series, 1978-. Publications: Shabbethai Sofer and his Prayer-book, 1979; Interpreting the Hebrew Bible, 1981; Published Material from the Cambridge Genizah Collections, 1988; Genizah Research after Ninety Years, 1992; Judaism and Hebrew Prayer, 1993; Hebrew Manuscipts at Cambridge University Library, 1996. Contributions to: Over 190 articles in Hebrew and Jewish studies. Address: Taylor-Schechter Genizah Research Unit, Cambridge University Library, West Road, Cambridge CB3 9DR, England.

REIN Evgeny Borisovich, b. 29 Dec 1935, St Petersburg, Russia. Poet; Writer. m. Nadejda Rein, 21 Jan 1989, 1 son. Education: Graduated, Mechanical Engineer, Leningrad Technological Institute, 1959. Publications: Poetry: The Names of Bridges, 1984; Shore Line, 1989; The Darkness of Mirrors, 1989; Irretrievable Day, 1991; Counter-Clockwise, 1992. Contributions to: Russian, European and US magazines. Honours: Smena Magazine Award, 1970; Tallinn Magazine Award, 1982. Memberships: Russia Writers Union; Russian PEN Centre. Address: ulitza Kuusinena 7, Apt 164, 123308 Moscow, Russia.

REINER Annie, b. 11 May 1949, New York, New York, USA. Writer; Psychotherapist. Education: BA, University of California at Los Angeles, 1973; MSW, University of Southern California, 1975. Publications: A Visit to the Art Galaxy, 1991; The Naked I, 1994; Dancing in the Park, 1995; This Nervous Breakdown is Driving Me Crazy, 1996; The Long Journey of the Little Seed, 1996; Infancy and the Essential Nature of Work, 1996. Contributions to: Journals. Honours: Various awards. Literary Agent: Charlotte Gusay Literary Agency. Address: 10553 Almayo Avenue, Los Angeles, CA 90064, USA.

REITER David Philip, b. 30 Jan 1947, Cleveland, Ohio, USA. Publisher; Writer. m. Cherie Lorraine Reiter, 26 Apr 1992. Education: BA, Independent Study, University of Oregon; MA, American Literature, University of Alberta, Canada; PhD, Creative Writing, University of Denver, 1982. Appointments: Lecturer, Cariboo University College, Canada, 1975-84, University of British Columbia, 1984, British Columbia Institute of Technology, 1984, University of Canberra, Australia, 1986-90. Publications: The Snow in Us, 1989; Changing House, 1991; The Cave After Saltwater Tide, 1992. Contributions to: Australian, Canadian, US and UK journals. Honours: Queensland Premier's Poetry Award, 1989; Imago-QUT Short Story Competition, 1990. Literary Agent: Debbie Golvan, Melbourne, Victoria, Australia. Address: 15 Gavan Street, Ashgrove, Queensland 4060, Australia.

REKAI Kati, b. 20 Oct 1921, Budapest, Hungary. Journalist; Broadcaster. m. John Rekai, 15 Aug 1941, 2 daughters. Education: High School, Budapest. Publications: 22 travel books for children. Contributions to: Magazines and radio. Honours: Award for Canadian Unity, 1979; Knighthood of St Ladislaus, 1980; Prix Saint-Exupery-Valeur Jeunesse, 1988; Rakoczi Foundation Award, 1991; Cross of the Order of Merit, Republic of Hungary, for Contribution to the Development of Canadian-Hunagrian Cultural Relations, 1993; Order of Canada, 1993. Memberships: Canadian Scene; Ethnic Journalists and Writers Club; Writers Union of Canada; The Arts and Letters Club; Toronto Historical Board. Address: 623-21 Dale Avenue, Toronto, Ontario M4W 1K3, Canada.

REMEC Miha, b. 10 Aug 1928, Pluj, Yugoslavia. Journalist; Writer; Dramatist; Poet. m. Mira Iskra, 1 July 1970, 3 sons. Appointment: Editorial Staff, Daily Newspaper, Delo, 1953-. Publications: Novels: Solstice, 1969; Recognition, 1980; Iksion, 1981; Mana, 1985; The Big Carriage, 1986; Two Short Novels: The Hunter and The Unchaste Daughter, 1987. Dramas: The Dead Kurent, 1959;

The Happy Dragons, 1963; Workshop of Clouds, 1966; The Plastionic Plague, 1982; Other: Stories; Poems. Contributions to: Articles in numerous professional magazines and journals. Honours: Literary Awards for Drama, 1950, 1976; SFera Awards, 1981, 1987. Memberships: Slovene Writers Association; World Science Fiction Organization; SFera Science Fiction Club. Literary Agent: Ziga Leskovsek, Ljubljana, Slovenia. Address: Pod lipami 58, Ljubljana 61000, Slovenia.

REMNICK David, b. 1959, USA. Journalist; Writer. m. 2 sons. Education: Princeton University. Publication: Lenin's Tomb: The Last Days of the Soviet Empire, 1993. Contributions to: Newspapers and periodicals. Honours: Pulitzer Prize for General Non-Fiction, 1994; Helen Bernstein Award, New York Public Library, 1994. Address: c/o Random House Inc, 201 East 50th Street, New York, NY 10022, USA.

REMY Pierre-Jean. See: **ANGREMY Jean-Pierre.**

RENAS Y. See: **ELBERG Yehuda.**

RENAUD (Ernest) Hamilton Jacques, b. 10 Nov 1943, Montreal, Quebec, Canada. Author; Poet; Translator; Speaker. 2 sons, 1 daughter. Appointments: Critic and Researcher, Radio Canada, 1965-67; Reporter, Metro-Express, Montreal, 1966; Critic, Le Devoir, Montreal, 1975-78; Teacher, Creative Writing Workshop, University of Quebec, 1980-89; Spokesman, Equality Party, 1989; Researcher, Senator Jacques Hebert, 1990. Publications: 20 books, including: Electrodes (poems), 1962; Le Casse (stories), 1964; Clandestines (novel), 1980; L'espace du Diable (stories), 1989; Les Cycles du Scorpion (poems), 1989; La Constellation du Bouc Emissaire (non-fiction), 1993. Contributions to: Various publications. Address: 205 Ivy Crescent 3, Ottawa, Ontario K1M 1X9, Canada.

RENDELL Ruth, (Barbara Vine), b. 17 Feb 1930, London, England. Writer. m. (1) David Rendell, div, (2) 1977, 1 son. Education: Loughton High School, Essex, England. Publications: From Doon with Death, 1964; To Fear a Painted Devil, 1965; Vanity Dies Hard, 1966; A New Lease of Life, 1967; Wolf to the Slaughter, 1967 (televised 1987); The Secret House of Death, 1968; The Best Man to Die, 1969; A Guilty Thing Surprised, 1970; One Across Two Down, 1971; No More Dying Then, 1971; Murder Being Once Done, 1972; Some Lie and Some Die, 1973; The Face of Trespass, 1974 (televised, An Affair in Mind, 1988); Shake Hands for Ever, 1975; The Fallen Curtain (short stories), 1976; A Sleeping Life, 1978; Make Death Love Me, 1979; Means of Evil (short stories), 1979; The Lake of Darkness, 1980 (televised, Dead Lucky, 1988); Put on by Cunning, 1981; Master of the Moor, 1982; The Fever Tree (short stories), 1982; The Speaker of Mandarin, 1983; The Killing Doll, 1984; The Tree of Hands, 1984 (film 1989); An Unkindness of Ravens, 1985; The New Girl Friend (short stories), 1985; Live Flesh, 1986; A Dark-Adapted Eye (as Barbara Vine), 1987; Heartstones, 1987; Talking to Strange Men, 1987; A Fatal Inversion (as Barbara Vine), 1987 (televised 1992); A Warning to the Curious - The Ghost Stories of M R James (editor), 1987; Collected Short Stories, 1987; The House of Stairs (as Barbara Vine), 1988; The Veiled One, 1988 (televised 1989); The Bridesmaid, 1989; Ruth Rendell's Suffolk, 1989; Undermining the Central Line (with Colin Ward), 1989; Going Wrong, 1990; Gallowglass (as Barbara Vine), 1990 (televised 1993); The Copper Peacock, 1991; King Solomon's Carpet, 1991; Kissing the Gunner's Daughter, 1992. Honours: Arts Council National Book Award for Genre Fiction, 1981; Cartier Diamond Dagger Award, Crime Writers Association, 1991. Address: Nussteads, Polstead, Suffolk CO6 5DN, England.

RENÉE, (Renée Gertrude Taylor), b. 19 July 1929, Napier, New Zealand. Playwright. Education: BA, University of Auckland, 1979. Appointments: Member of women's writers collective groups, 1979-84; Director and actress with the Napier Repertory Players; Robert Burns Fellowship, University of Otago, 1989; Writers Fellowship, University of Waikato and Creative NZ, 1995. Publications: Secrets: Two One-Woman Plays, 1982; Breaking Out, 1982; Setting the Table, 1982; What Did You Do in the War, Mummy?, 1982; Asking For It, 1983; Dancing, 1984; Wednesday to Come, 1984; Groundwork, 1985; Pass It On, 1986; Born to Clean, 1987; Jeannie Once, 1990; Touch of the Sun, 1991; Missionary Position, 1991; The Glass Box, 1992; Tiggy Tiggy Touchwood, 1992; Willy Nilly (novel), 1990; Daisy and Lily, 1993; Does This Make Sense To You?, 1995. Other: Television plays and short stories. Honours: Queen Elizabeth II Arts Council Grant and Award; Project Grant, 1991; QEII Arts Council Scholarship in Letters, 1993; Others. Literary Agent: (Plays) Playmarket, PO Box 9767,

Wellington, New Zealand. Address: 3/45 Whites Line West, Woburn, Lower Hutt, New Zealand.

RENIER Elizabeth. See: **BAKER Betty (Lou).**

RENO Dawn Elaine, b. 15 Apr 1953, Waltham, Massachusetts, USA. Writer. m. Robert G Reno, 25 Feb 1978, 1 daughter, 3 stepsons, 1 stepdaughter. Education: AA cum laude, Liberal Arts, Bunker Hill Community College, Boston, 1976; BA summa cum laude, Liberal Studies, Johnson State College, Vermont, 1990; MFA, Vermont College, 1996. Appointments: Reporter, New England County Antiques, 1979-86; Assistant Editor, Vermont Woman, 1988-91; Columnist, Daytona Beach News Journal, 1992-93. Publications: Jenny Moves, 1984; Jenny's First Friend, 1984; Collecting Black Americana, 1986; American Indian Collectibles, 1989; American Country Collectibles, 1991; All That Glitters, 1992; Collecting Advertising, 1993; Native American Collectibles, 1994; The Silver Dolphin, 1994; Collecting Romance Novels, 1995; Contemporary Native American Artists, 1996; Encyclopaedia of Black Collectibles, 1996. Contributions to: Journals. Honours: Semi-finalist, Writer's Digest Non-Fiction Contest, 1986; Fiction Award, Johnson State College, 1990; Virginia Centre for the Creative Arts Fellowship, 1990; Vermont Studio Colony Fellowship, 1993. Memberships: League of Vermont Writers; National Writers Union; Society of Children's Book Writers; Romance Writers of America; Novelists Inc. Address: 3280 Shingler Terrace, Deltona, FL 32738, USA.

REPLANSKY Naomi, b. 23 May 1918, Bronx, New York. USA. Poet. Education: BA, University of California, Los Angeles, 1956. Appointments: Poet-in-Residence, Pitzer College, Claremont, California, 1981. Publications: Ring Song, 1952; Twenty-One Poems, Old and New, 1988; The Dangerous World, New and Selected Poems, 1994. Contributions to: Ploughshares; Missouri Review; Nation; Feminist Studies. Honour: Nominated for National Book Award, 1952. Memberships: PEN American Center; Poetry Society of America. Address: 711 Amsterdam Avenue, No 8E, New York, NY 10025, USA.

RESCHER Nicholas, b. 15 July 1928, Hagen, Westphalia, Germany (US citizen, 1944). Professor of Philosophy; Writer. m. (1) Frances Short, 5 Sept 1951, 1 daughter, (2) Dorothy Henle, 10 Feb 1968, 2 sons, 1 daughter. Education: BS, Queens College, New York City, 1949; PhD Princeton University, 1951. Appointments: Instructor in Philosophy, Princeton University, 1951-52; Associate Professor of Philosophy, Lehigh University, Bethlehem, Pennsylvania, 1957-61; University Professor of Philosophy, 1961-, Vice Chairman, Center for the Philosophy of Science, 1985-, University of Pittsburgh; Secretary General, International Union of the History and Philosophy of Science, United Nations Educational, Scientific, and Cultural Organization, 1969-75; Honorary Member, Corpus Christi College, Oxford, 1977-; Founder-Editor, American Philosophical Quarterly, History of Philosophy Quarterly, and Public Affairs Quarterly. Publications: The Coherence Theory of Truth, 1973; Scientific Progress, 1978; The Limits of Science, 1985; A System of Pragmatic Idealism, 3 volumes, 1992-93; Predicting the Future, 1997. Contributions to: Various scholarly journals. Honours: Honorary doctorates, Loyola University, Chicago, 1970, University of Córdoba, Argentina, 1992, Lehigh University, 1993, University of Konstanz, Germany, 1995; Alexander von Humboldt Prize, Germany, 1983. Memberships: Académie Internationale de Philosophie des Sciences; American Philosophical Association; G W Leibnitz Society of America; Institut International de Philosphie; Royal Asiatic Society. Address: c/o Department of Philosophy, University of Pittsburgh, 1012 Cathedral, Pittsburgh, PA 15260, USA.

RESTAK Richard Martin, b. 4 Feb 1942, Wilmington, Delaware, USA. Physician; Author. m. Carolyn Serbent, 18 Oct 1968, 3 daughters. Education: MD, Georgetown Medical School, 1966; Trained in Neurology and Psychiatry. Appointments: Consultant, Encyclopedia of Bioethics, 1978; Special Contributing Editor, Science Digest, 1981-85; Editorial Board, Integrative Psychiatry: An International Journal for the Synthesis of Medicine and Psychiatry, 1986. Publications: Premeditated Man: Bioethics and the Control of Future Human Life, 1975; The Brain: The Last Frontier: Explorations of the Human Mind and Our Future, 1979; The Self Seekers, 1982; The Brain, 1984; The Infant Mind, 1986; The Mind, 1988; The Brain Has a Mind of Its Own, 1991; Receptors, 1994; Modular Brain, 1994. Contributions to: Anthologies, journals, and periodicals. Honours: Summer Fellowship, National Endowment for the Humanities, 1976; Claude Bernard Science Journalism Award, National Society for

Medical Research, 1976; Distinguished Alumni Award, Gettysburg College, 1985. Memberships: American Academy of Neurology; American Academy of Psychiatry and the Law; American Psychiatric Association; Behavioral Neurology Society; New York Academy of Sciences; International Neuropsychological Society; National Book Critics Circle; International Brotherhood of Magicians; Philosophical Society of Washington; International Platform Association. Literary Agent: Sterling Lord, One Madison Avenue, New York, USA. Address: 1800 R Street North West, Suite C-3, Washington, DC 20009, USA.

REUTHER David Louis, b. 2 Nov 1946, Detroit, Michigan, USA. Children's Book Publisher; Writer. m. Margaret Alexander Miller, 21 July 1973, 1 son, 1 daughter. Education: BA, Honours, University of Michigan, Ann Arbor, 1968. Publications: The Hidden Game of Baseball (co-author), 1984; Total Baseball, 1989, revised edition, 1991; The Whole Baseball Catalog, 1990. Co-Editor: The Armchair Quarterback, 1982; The Armchair Aviator, 1983; The Armchair Mountaineer, 1984; The Armchair Book of Baseball, 1985; The Armchair Angler, 1986; The Armchair Traveler, 1989. Children's Books: Fun to Go, 1982; Save-the-Animals Activity Book, 1982. Contributions to: The Horn Book, 1984. Memberships: American Booksellers Asociation-CBC Joint Committee, 1990-93; American Library Association; Authors Guild; Children's Book Council, Board of Directors, 1985-88, 1991-94, Chairman, 1993; Society of Children's Book Writers. Address: 271 Central Park West, New York, NY 10024, USA.

REYES Carlos, b. 2 June 1935, Marshfield, Missouri, USA. Poet; Teacher. m. (1) Barbara Ann Hollingsworth, 13 Sept 1958, div 1973, 1 son, 3 daughters, (2) Karen Ann Stoner, 21 May 1979, div 1992, (3) Elizabeth Atly, 27 Dec 1993. Education: BA, University of Oregon, 1961; MA, ABD, University of Arizona, 1965. Appointments: Governor's Advisory Committee on the Arts, Oregon, 1973; Poet to the City of Portland, 1978; Poet-in-Residence, in various public schools in Oregon and Washington; Editor, Hubbub, 1982-90. Publications: The Shingle Weaver's Journal, 1980; The Prisoner, 1973; At Doolin Quay, 1982; Nightmarks, 1990; A Suitcase Full of Crows, 1995. Contributions to: Various journals and magazines. Honours: Oregon Arts Commission Individual Artist Fellowship, 1982; Yaddo Fellowship, 1984. Memberships: Board, Portland Poetry Festival Inc, 1974-84; PEN Northwest, co-chair, 1992-93. Address: 3222 North East Schuyler, Portland, OR 97212, USA.

REYNOLDS Arlene V, b. 26 Feb 1947, Pittsfield, Massachusetts, USA. Actress; Author. m. (1) 27 Aug 1964, div 18 Oct 1993, 1 son, 1 daughter, (2) R W King, 2 Mar 1997. Education: AA, Cypress College, California, 1979. Appointments: Member, Company A Productions, performing historical recreations of nineteenth century people, specializing in Elizabeth Custer, wife of General Custer, and other nineteenth century women; First person shows: Personal Reminiscences of the Civil War; Garrison Life on the Plains; Westward the Women; Along the Oregon Trail; Tales Not for the Timid; Lizzie Borden Breaks Her Silence; General Sheridan in Washington Territory; Custer's Last Fight and the Indian's Greatest Victory; East of Gettysburg; Then You'll Remember Me. Publication: The Civil War Memories of Elizabeth Bacon Custer, 1994. Honour: John M Carroll Literary Award, 1994. Address: PO Box 2762, Everett, WA 98203-0762, USA.

REYNOLDS Graham (Arthur), b. 10 Jan 1914, Highgate, London, England. Writer; Art Historian. Education: BA Honours, Queens College, Cambridge University. Publications: Nicholas Hilliard and Isaac Oliver, 1947, 1971; English Portrait Miniatures, 1952, revised edition, 1988; Painters of the Victorian Scene, 1953; Catalogue of the Constable Collection, Victoria and Albert Museum, 1960, revised edition, 1973; Constable, The Natural Painter, 1965; Victorian Painting, 1966, revised edition, 1987; Turner, 1969; Concise History of Watercolour Painting, 1972; Catalogue of Portrait Miniatures, Wallace Collection, 1980; The Later Paintings and Drawings of John Constable, 2 volumes, 1984; English Watercolours, 1988; The Earlier Paintings of John Constable, 2 volumes, 1996; Catalogue of Portrait Miniatures, Metropolitan Museum of Art, New York, 1996. Contributions to: Times Literary Supplement; Burlington Magazine; Apollo; New Departures. Honours: Mitchell Prize, 1984; Officer of the Order of the British Empire, 1984; British Academy, fellow, 1993; Honorary Keeper of Minatures, Fitzwilliam Museum, Cambridge, 1994. Literary Agent: A M Heath & Company Limited. Address: The Old Manse, Bradfield St George, Bury St Edmunds, Suffolk IP30 0AZ, England.

REYNOLDS Keith (Kev) Ronald, b. 7 Dec 1943, Ingatestone, Essex, England. Author; Photojournalist; Lecturer. m. Linda Sylvia Dodsworth, 23 Sept 1967, 2 daughters. Publications: Walks and Climbs in the Pyrenees, 1978, 1983, 1993; Mountains of the Pyrenees, 1982; The Weald Way and Vanguard Way, 1987; Walks in the Engadine, 1988; The Valais, 1988; Walking in Kent, 1988; Classic Walks in the Pyrenees, 1989; Classic Walks in Southern England, 1989; The Jura, 1989; South Downs Way, 1989; Eye on the Hurricane, 1989; The Mountains of Europe, 1990; Visitors Guide to Kent, 1990; The Cotswold Way, 1990; Alpine Pass Route, 1990; Classic Walks in the Alps, 1991; Chamonix to Zermatt, 1991; The Bernese Alps, 1992; Walking in Ticino, 1992; Central Switzerland, 1993; Annapurna, A Trekkers' Guide, 1993; Walking in Kent Volume II, 1994; Everest, A Trekkers' Guide, 1995. Contributions to: The Great Outdoors; Climber and Hill Walker; Environment Now; Trail Walker; Country Walking; High. Membership: Outdoor Writers' Guild. Address: Freshfields, Crockham Hill, Edenbridge, Kent TN8 6RT, England.

REYNOLDS Kimberley Kay Griffith, b. 8 Jan 1955, Columbus, Ohio, USA. Lecturer in English. m. Peter Lloyd Reynolds, 9 Oct 1976, 1 son, 1 daughter. Education: BA summa cum laude, C W Post College, Long Island, New York, 1975; BA, 1984, MA, 1985, PhD, 1988, University of Sussex. Publications: Girls Only? Gender and Popular Children's Fiction, 1880-1910; An Illustrated Dictionary of Art Terms. Contributions to: Books and journals. Address: 10 Dorset Road, Lewes, East Sussex BN7 1TH, England.

REYNOLDS Vernon, b. 14 Dec 1935, Berlin, Germany. University Teacher. m. Frances Glover, 5 Nov 1960, 1 son, 1 daughter. Education: BA, PhD, London University; MA, Oxford University. Publications: Budongo: A Forest and its Chimpanzees, 1965; The Apes, 1967; The Biology of Human Action, 1976, 2nd edition, 1980; The Biology of Religion (with R Tanner), 1983; Primate Behaviour: Information, Social Knowledge and the Evolution of Culture (with D Quiatt), 1993. Memberships: Fellow, Royal Anthropological Institute; Chairman, Biosocial Society; Primate Society of Great Britain; Society for the Study of Human Biology. Address: Institute of Biological Anthropology, Oxford University, 58 Banbury Road, Oxford OX2 6QS, England.

RHODES Anthony (Richard Edward), b. 24 Sep 1916, Plymouth, Devon, England. Writer. m. Rosaleen Forbes, 9 Apr 1956. Education: Royal Military Academy, Woolwich; MA, Trinity College, University of Cambridge, England; Licence et Lettres, University of Geneva, Switzerland. Publications: Sword of Bone, 1942; The Uniform, 1949; A Sabine Journey, 1952; A Ball in Venice, 1953; The General's Summer House, 1954; The Dalmation Coast, 1955; Where the Turk Trod, 1956; The Poet as Superman: A Life of Gabriele D'Annunzio, 1959; Rise and Fall of Louis Renault, 1966; The Prophet's Carpet, 1969; Princes of the Grape, 1970; Art Treasures of Eastern Europe, 1971; The Vatican in the Age of the Dictator, 1922-45, 1973; Propaganda in the Second World War, 1976; The Vatican in the Age of the Liberal Democracies, 1983; The Vatican in the Age of the Cold War, 1992; 15 book-length translations from French, Italian and German. Contributions to: Encounter; Sunday Telegraph. Honour: Cavaliere Commendatore del'Ordine di San Gregorio Magno (Papal Title). Memberships: Society of Authors; PEN; Bucks Club; Beefsteak Club. Literary Agent: Anthony Sheil. Address: 46 Fitzjames Avenue, London W14, England.

RHODES Philip, b. 2 May 1922, Sheffield, England. Medical Practitioner; Professor, Postgraduate Medical Education (retired). m. Elizabeth Worley, 26 Oct 1946, 3 sons, 2 daughters. Education: Clare College, Cambridge University, England, 1940-43; St Thomas' Hospital, London, England, 1943-46, MA (Cantab) 1946; MB Chir (Cantab) 1946; FRCS (Eng) 1953; FRCOG 1964; FRACMA 1976; FFOM 1990; FRSA 1990. Publications: Fluid Balance in Obstetrics, 1960; Introduction to Gynaecology and Obstetrics, 1967; Woman: A Biological Study, 1969; Reproductive Physiology, 1969; The Value of Medicine, 1976; Dr John Leake's Hospital, 1978; Letters to a Young Doctor, 1983; Outline History of Medicine, 1985; The Oxford Companion to Medicine (associate editor), 1986; Wakerley, A Village in Northamptonshire, 1994; A Short Story of Clinical Midwifery, 1995; Gynaecology for Everywoman, 1996. Contributions to: Lancet; British Medical Journal; British Journal of Obstetrics and Gynaecology; Practitioner. Honours: Annual Prize, Brontë Society, 1972. Memberships: Medical Committee, Society of Authors; British Medical Association. Address: 1 Wakerley Court, Wakerley, Oakham, Leicester LE15 8PA, England.

RHODES Richard (Lee), b. 4 July 1937, Kansas City, Kansas, USA. Writer. Education: BA cum laude, Yale University, 1959. Publications: Non-fiction: The Inland Ground, 1970; The Ozarks, 1974; Looking for America, 1979; The Making of the Atomic Bomb, 1988; A Hole in the World, 1990; Making Love, 1992; Dark Sun, 1995; How to Write, 1995. Fiction: The Ungodly, 1973; Holy Secrets, 1978; The Last Safari, 1980; Sons of Earth, 1981. Contributions to: Numerous journals and magazines. Honours: National Book Award in Non-fiction, 1987; National Book Critics Circle Award in Non-fiction, 1987; Pulitzer Prize in Non-fiction, 1988. Membership: Authors Guild. Address: c/o Janklow and Nesbit Associates, 598 Madison Avenue, New York, NY 10022, USA.

RHONE Trevor Dave, b. 24 Mar 1940, Kingston, Jamaica, West Indies. Playwright; Director; Screenwriter. m. Camella King, 5 Mar 1974, 2 sons, 1 daughter. Education: Diploma, Speech and Drama, Rose Bruford College of Speech and Drama, 1963. Appointment: Resident playwright, Barn Theatre, Kingston, 1968-75. Publications: Old Time Story, 1981; Two Can Play, 1984. Honours: Silver Musgrave Medal, Institute of Jamaica, 1972; Commander of the Order of Distinction, National Honour, Jamaica, 1980; Gold Musgrave Medal, 1988; Academy Award, Film Canada, 1989. Literary Agents: Yvonne Brewster, 32 Buckley Road, London, NW6 7LU, England; I C M, New York, USA. Address: 1 Haining Mews, Kingston 5, Jamaica, West Indies.

RICARD Charles, b. 9 Jan 1922, Gap, France. Author; Poet. m. J Balmens, 28 July 1951. Education: Professeur de Lettres. Publications: Novels: Le puits, 1967; La derniere des revolutions, 1968; A propos d'un piano casse, 1977; Le Pot-a-Chien, 1979; Alerte rouge aux cités soleils, 1985; Le mercredi des Cendres, 1986; Le Chemin des Oiseaux, 1991; Rédé, 1992; Les Mysteres du Villaret, 1993. Poetry: Si j'avais su, 1960; Je Voudrais, 1963; Les ombres du chemin, 1964. Contributions to: Various magazines and journals. Honours: Gold Medal, International Competition of Clubs of Cote d'Azur; Gold Medal, International Competition, Lutece, 1976; Prix Diamant, 1985; Prix du Vimeu, 1986. Memberships: Academy of the French Provinces; Associate, Society of French Poets; Associate, Gens de Lettres de France. Address: 20 rue du Super-Gap, 05000 Gap, France.

RICCHIUTI Paul B(urton), b. 4 July 1925, Redford Township, Michigan, USA. Writer. Education: Andrews University, 1949-52; Loma Linda University, 1953. Appointments: Layout and Design Artist, Pacific Press Publishing Association, 1955-. Publications: For Children: I Found a Feather, 1967; Whose House is It?, 1967; Up in the Air, 1967; When You Open Your Bible, 1967; Jeff, 1973; Amy, 1975; Five Little Girls, 1975; Let's Play Make Believe, 1975; My Very Best Friend, 1975; Elijah Jeremiah Phillip's Great Journey, 1975; Yankee Dan, 1976; General Lee, 1978; Mandy, 1978; Mike, 1978; Jimmy and the Great Balloon, 1978; Charlie Horse, 1992; Mrs White's Secret Sock, 1992. Other: Ellen (adult biography of Ellen G White), 1977; End of the World Man and Other Stories, 1989; Rocky and Me, 1989; New Dog in Town, 1991. Contributions to: Anthologies, newspapers, and magazines. Address: 5702 East Powerline, Nampa, ID 83687, USA.

RICE Anne, (Anne Rampling, A N Roquelaure), b. 4 Oct 1941, New Orleans, Louisiana, USA. Writer. m. Stan Rice, 14 Oct 1961, 1 son, 1 daughter, dec. Education: Texas Women's University, 1959-60; BA, 1964, MA, 1971, San Francisco State College; Graduate Studies, University of California, Berkeley, 1969-70. Publications: Interview with the Vampire, 1976; The Feast of All Saints, 1980; Cry to Heaven, 1982; The Claiming of Sleeping Beauty, 1983; Beauty's Punishment, 1984; Beauty's Release: The Continued Erotic Adventures of Sleeping Beauty, 1985; Exit to Eden, 1985; The Vampire Lestat, 1985; Belinda, 1986; The Queen of the Damned, 1988; The Mummy: Or Ramses the Damned, 1989; The Witching Hour, 1990; Tale of the Body Thief, 1992; Lasher, 1993; Taltos, 1994; Memnoch the Devil, 1995; Servant of the Bones, 1996. Membership: Authors Guild. Address: c/o Alfred A Knopf Inc, 201 East 50th Street, New York, NY 10022,USA.

RICH Adrienne (Cecile), b. 16 May 1929, Baltimore, Maryland, USA. Professor of English and Feminist Studies; Poet; Writer. m. Alfred H Conrad, 1953, dec 1970, 3 sons. Education: AB, Radcliffe College, 1951. Appointments: Visiting Poet, Swarthmore College, 1966-68; Adjunct Professor, Columbia University, 1967-69, Lecturer, 1968-70, Instructor, 1970-71, Assistant Professor, 1971-72, Professor, 1974-75, City College of New York; Fannie Hurst Visiting Professor, Brandeis University, 1972-73; Professor of English, Douglass College,

New Brunswick, New Jersey, 1976-78; A D White Professor-at-Large, Cornell University, 1981-85; Clark Lecturer and Distinguished Visiting Professor, Scripps College, Claremont, California, 1983; Visiting Professor, San Jose State UIniversity, California, 1985-86; Burgess Lecturer, Pacific Oaks College, Pasadena, California, 1986; Professor of English and Feminist Studies, Stanford University, 1986-. Publications: Poetry: A Change of World, 1951; (Poems), 1952; The Diamond Cutters and Other Poems, 1955; Snapshots of a Daughter-in-Law: Poems 1954-1962, 1963; Necessities of Life: Poems 1962-1965, 1966; Selected Poems, 1967; Leaflets: Poems 1965-1968, 1969; The Will to Change: Poems 1968-1970, 1971; Diving into the Wreck: Poems 1971-1972, 1973; Poems Selected and New, 1975; Twenty-One Love Poems, 1976; The Dream of a Common Language: Poems 1974-1977, 1978; A Wild Patience Has Taken Me This Far: Poems 1978-1981, 1981; Sources, 1983; The Fact of a Doorframe: Poems Selected and New 1950-1984, 1984; Your Native Land, Your Life, 1986; Time's Power: Poems 1985-1988, 1989; An Atlas of the Difficult World: Poems 1988-1991, 1991; Collected Early Poems 1950-1970, 1993; Dark Fields of the Republic, 1995. Other: Of Woman Born: Motherhood as Experience and Institution, 1976; Women and Honor: Some Notes on Lying, 1977; On Lies, Secrets and Silence: Selected Prose 1966-1978, 1979; Compulsory Heterosexuality and Lesbian Existence, 1980; Blood, Bread and Poetry: Selected Prose 1979-1985, 1986; What Is Found There: Notebooks on Poetry and Politics, 1993. Honours: Yale Series of Younger Poets Award, 1951; Guggenheim Fellowships, 1952, 1961; American Academy of Arts and Letters Award, 1961; Bess Hokin Prize, 1963; Eunice Tietjens Memorial Prize, 1968; National Endowment for the Arts Grant, 1970; Shelley Memorial Award, 1971; Ingram Merrill Foundation Grant, 1973; National Book Award, 1974; Fund for Human Dignity Award, 1981; Ruth Lilly Prize, 1986; Brandeis University Creative Arts Award, 1987; Elmer Holmes Bobst Award, 1989; Commonwealth Award in Literature, 1991; Frost Silver Medal, Poetry Society of America, 1992; Los Angeles Times Book Award, 1992; Lenore Marshall/Nation Award, 1992; William Whitehead Award, 1992; Lambda Book Award, 1992; Harriet Monroe Prize, 1994; John D and Catharine T MacArthur Foundation Fellowship, 1994; Tanning Prize, 1996; Honorary doctorates. Address: c/o W W Norton & Company, 500 Fifth Avenue, New York, NY 10110, USA.

RICH Elaine Sommers, b. 8 Feb 1926, Indiana, USA. Writer. m. Dr Ronald L Rich, 14 June 1953, 3 sons, 1 daughter. Education: BA, Goshen College, 1947; MA, Michigan State University, 1950. Publications: Breaking Bread Together, 1958; Hannah Elizabeth, 1964; Tomorrow, Tomorrow, Tomorrow, 1966; Am I This Countryside, 1981; Mennonite Women 1683-1983, 1983; Spiritual Elegance, 1987; Prayers for Everyday, 1989; Walking Together in Faith, 1993. Contributions to: Fortnightly column, Thinking With, in Mennonite Weekly Review, 1973-. Address: 112 South Spring Street, Bluffton, OH 45817, USA.

RICH Frank Hart, b. 2 June 1949, Washington, USA. Critic. m. (1) Gail Winston, 1976, 2 sons, (2) Alexandra Rachelle Witchel, 1991. Education: BA, Harvard University, 1971. Appointments: Co-Editor, Richmond Mercury, Virginia, 1972-73; Senior Editor and Film Critic, New York Times Magazine, 1973-75; Film Critic, New York Post, 1975-77; Film and Television Critic, Time Magazine, 1977-80; Chief Drama Critic, 1980-93, Op-Ed Columnist, 1994-, New York Times; Columnist, New York Times Sunday Magazine, 1993. Publication: The Theatre Art of Boris Aronson (with others), 1987. Contributions to: Newspapers and periodicals. Address: c/o The New York Times, 229 West 43rd Street, New York, NY 10036, USA.

RICHARD Mark, b. 1955, Lousiana, USA. Writer. Education: BA, Washington and Lee University. Publications: The Ice at the Bottom of the World: Stories, 1989; Fishboy: A Ghost's Story, 1993. Contributions to: Anthologies and periodicals. Honours: Whiting Writer's Award, 1990; Ernest Hemingway Foundation Award, 1990. Address: c/o Doubleday & Co Inc, 1540 Broadway, New York, NY 10036, USA.

RICHARDS Alun, b. 27 Oct 1929, Pontypridd, Wales. Author. m. Helen Howden, 8 July 1956, 3 sons, 1 daughter. Education: Diploma, Social Science and Education, University of Wales. Appointment: Editor, Penguin Book of Welsh Short Stories and Penguin Book of Sea Stories, Vols 1-11. Publications: The Elephant You Gave Me, 1963; The Home Patch, 1966; A Woman of Experience, 1969; Home to An Empty House, 1974; Ennal's Point, 1979; Dai Country, 1979; The Former Miss Merthyr Tydfil and Other Stories, 1980; Barque Whisper,

1982; Days of Absence (autobiography), 1987. Contributions to: Guardian; Planet; Western Mail. Honours: Arts Council Prize for Collected Short Stories, 1974; Royal National Lifeboat Institution Public Relations Award, 1983; Japan Foundation Fellowship, 1984. Membership: Writers Guild of Great Britain. Literary Agent: Harvey Unna and Stephen Durbridge Limited. Address: 326 Mumbles Road, Swansea SA3 5AA, Wales.

RICHARDS David Adams, b. 17 Oct 1950, Newcastle, New Brunswick, Canada. Education: St Thomas University, New Brunswick, Canada. Publications: The Coming of Winter, 1974; Blood Ties, 1976; Dancers at Night, 1978; Lives of Short Duration, 1981; Road to the Stilt House, 1985; Nights Below Station Street, 1988; Evening Snow Will Bring Such Peace, 1990; For Those Who Hunt the Wounded Down, 1993. Honours: Norman Epstein Prize; Governor General's Award, 1988; Maclean's Award; Canada Authors Association Literary Award, 1991; Canada-Australian Literary Award, 1992. Address: c/o The Canada Council, 350 Albert Street, PO Box 1047, Ottawa, Ontario K1P 5V8, Canada.

RICHARDS Denis George, b. 10 Sept 1910, London, England. Writer. m. Barbara Smethurst, 6 Jan 1940, 4 daughters. Education: Trinity Hall, Cambridge, 1928-31; Ist Class Hons BA, 1931; MA, 1935. Publications: An Illustrated History of Modern Europe, 1938; An Illustrated History of Modern Britain, 1951; Royal Air Force, 1939-45 (with H St G Saunders), 3 volumes, 1953, 1954; Offspring of the Vic: A History of Morley College, 1958; Britain Under the Tudors and Stuarts, 1958; The Battle of Britain: The Jubilee History (with Richard Hough), 1989; The Few and the Many, 1990; The Hardest Victory: RAF Bomber Command in the Second World War, 1994. Contributions to: Books and Bookmen; Daily Telegraph Supplement; Financial Times. Honours: C P Robertson Memorial Trophy, 1956; Officer of the Order of the British Empire, 1990. Memberships: PEN, Honorary Treasurer; Arts Club; Society of Authors; Garrick Club; RAF Club. Address: 16, Broadlands Road, London N6 4AN, England.

RICHARDS Hubert John, b. 25 Dec 1921, Weilderstadt, Germany. Lecturer; Writer. m. 22 Dec 1975, 1 son, 1 daughter. Education: STL (Licence in Theology), Gregorian University, Rome; LSS (Licence in Scripture), Biblical Institute, Rome. Publications: The First Christmas: What Really Happened?, 1973; The Miracles of Jesus: What Really Happened?, 1975; The First Easter: What Really Happened?, 1977; Death and After: What Will Really Happen?, 1979; What Happens When You Pray?, 1980; Pilgrim to the Holy Land, 1985; Focus on the Bible, 1990; The Gospel According to St Paul, 1990; God's Diary, 1991; Pilgrim to Rome, 1993. Contributions to: Regular articles and reviews in various publications. Membership: Chairman, Norfolk Theological Society. Address: 59 Park Lane, Norwich, Norfolk NR2 3EF, England.

RICHARDS Sir James, (Jim Cladpole), b. 13 Aug 1907, London, England. Editor; Journalist; Writer; Historian. Education: Diploma, Architectural Association, School of Architecture, London, 1929; Associate, Royal Institute of British Architects, 1930. Appointments: Editor, Architectural Review, 1937-71, European Heritage, 1974-75; Architectural Correspondent, The Times, 1947-71. Publications: High Street, 1938; Introduction to Modern Architecture, 1940; The Castles on the Ground, 1946; The Functional Tradition, 1958; The Anti-Rationalists (editor), 1973; Who's Who in Architecture (editor), 1977; Eight Hundred Years of Finnish Architecture, 1978; Memoirs of An Unjust Fella, 1980; Goa, 1981; National Trust Book of English Architecture, 1981; National Trust Book of Bridges. Contributions to: Architectural Review; Architects Journal; Times; Times Literary Supplement; Listener; New Statesman; Country Life. Honours: Commander of the Order of the British Empire, 1959; Bicentenary Medal, Royal Society of Arts, 1971; Knighted, 1972; Honorary Fellow, American Institute of Architects, 1984; Commander, Order of the White Rose of Finland, 1985. Literary Agent: Curtis Brown Ltd. Address: 29 Fawcett Road, London SW10, England.

RICHARDS Ronald Charles William, (Allen Saddler), b. 15 Apr 1923, London, England. Writer; Dramatist; Critic. Publications: Novels: The Great Brain Robbery, 1965; Gilt Edge, 1966; Talking Turkey, 1968; Betty, 1974. Other: Children's books, radio and television dramas. Contributions to: Newspapers, magazines, and journals. Memberships: South West Arts; Writers Guild. Address: 5 St John's Hall, Station Road, Totnes, Devon TQ9 5HW, England.

RICHARDS Sean. See: **HAINING Peter.**

RICHARDSON Joanna, b. London, England. Biographer. Education: The Downs School, Seaford, Sussex; MA, St Anne's College, Oxford. Publications: Fanny Brown, 1952; Théophile Gautier: His Life and times, 1958; The Pre-Eminent Victorian: A Study of Tennyson, 1962; The Everlasting Spell: A Study of Keats and His Friends, 1963; Essays by Divers Hands (editor), 1963; Introduction to Victor Hugo: Choses Vues, 1964; Edward Lear, 1965; George IV: A Portrait, 1966; Creevey and Greville, 1967; Princess Mathilde, 1969; Verlaine, 1971; Enid Starkie, 1973; Verlaine (translator, poems), 1974; Baudelaire (translator, poems), 1975; Victor Hugo, 1976; Zola, 1978; Keats and His Circle: An Album of Portraits, 1980; Paris Under Siege, 1982; Colette, 1983; The Brownings, 1986; Judith Gautier, 1987; Portrait of a Bonaparte, 1987; Baudelaire, 1994. Honours: Chevalier de l'Ordre des Arts et des Lettres, 1987; Prix Goncourt de la biographie, 1989. Membership: Royal Society of Literature, fellow. Address: c/o Curtis Brown Ltd, Haymarket House, 28-29 Haymarket, London SW1Y 4SP, England.

RICHARDSON Ruth, b. 19 Dec 1951, London, England. Historian. Education: BA Honours, English Literature, 1977; MA, History, 1978; DPhil, History, 1985. Appointments: Research Officer, Institute of Historical Research, University of London, 1985-; Wellcome Research Fellow, Department of Anatomy, University College, London. Publications: Death, Dissection and the Destitute, 1988; The Builder Illustrations Index, 1843-83 (with Robert Thorne), 1994. Contributions to: Books and journals. Honours: Leverhulme Research Fellowship, 1992-93; Monkton Copeman Medal, Society of Apothecaries, London, 1993. Memberships: Folklore Society; Museum of Soho, trustee; Royal Historical Society, fellow; Society of Authors. Address: c/o Institute of Historical Research, University of London, London WC1E 7HU, England.

RICHÉ Pierre, b. 4 Oct 1921, Paris, France. Professor Emeritus; Writer. m. Suzanne Grenier, 20 Dec 1953. Education: Agregé, History, 1948; Docteur es lettres, 1962. Appointment: Professor, later Professor Emeritus, University of Paris X. Publications: Education et Culture dans l'Occident Barbare, 1962; Ecoles et Enseignement dans le Haut Moyen Age, 1970; La Vie Quotidienne dans l'Empire Carolingien, 1973; Dhuoda Manuel pour Mon Fils (editor and translator, 1975; Les Carolingiens une Famille Qui fit l'Europe, 1983; Gerbert d'Aurillac Pape de l'an Mil, 1987; Petite Vie de Saint Bernard, 1989; Japanese L'Europe Barbare de 476 a 774, 1989. Contributions to: Professional journals. Honours: Officier des Palmes Académiques; Prix Gobert, 1963; Prix de Courcel, 1969, 1988; Prix George Goyau, 1974. Memberships: Centre International de Recherche et de Documentation sur le monarchisme Celtique, honorary president; Comité des Travaux Historiques et Scientifiques, Section d'Histoire Medievale et de Philologie; Société d'Histoire de France; Société Nationale des Antiquaries de France. Address: 99 Rue Bobillot, Paris 75013, France.

RICHESON Cena Golder, b. 11 Apr 1941, Oregon, USA. Author; Poet. m. Jerry Dale Richeson, 3 June 1961, 2 sons. Education: AA, Diablo Valley College, 1962; BA, California State University, 1972. Appointments: Instructor, Shasta College, California, 1974-76, Liberty Union High School, Brentwood, California, 1984-85; Columnist, Anderson Press Weekly Newspaper, California, 1976-78; Frontier Correspondent, National Tombstone Epitaph, Tucson, 1986-; Book Reviewer, Publishers Weekly, 1994-95. Contributions to: Anthologies and periodicals. Honours: Several awards. Memberships: California Writers Club, president, 1991-92; Society of Children's Book Writers; Zane Grey's West Society. Address: PO Box 268, Knightsen, CA 94548, USA.

RICHIE Donald (Steiner), b. 17 Apr 1924, Lima, Ohio, USA. Critic; Writer. m. Mary Evans, Nov 1961, div 1965. Education: Antioch College, 1942; US Maritime Academy, 1943; BS, Columbia University, 1953. Appointments: Film Critic, Pacific Stars and Stripes, Tokyo, 1947-49; Arts Critic, Saturday Review of Literature, New York City, 1950-51; Film Critic, 1953-69, Literary Critic, 1972-, Japan Times, Tokyo; Lecturer in American Literature, Waseda University, Tokyo, 1954-59; Arts Critic, The Nation, New York City, 1959-61; Newsweek Magazine, New York City, 1973-76; Time Magazine, 1997; Curator of Film, Museum of Modern Art, New York City, 1968-73; Toyoda Chair, University of Michigan, 1993; Lecturer, Film, Telemark University, 1996-97. Publications: Where Are the Victors? (novel), 1956, new edition, 1986; The Japanese Film: Art and Industry (with Joseph L Anderson), 1959, expanded edition, 1982; The Japanese Movie: An Illustrated History, 1965, revised edition, 1982; The Films of Akira Kurosawa, 1965, revised edition, 1995; Companions of the Holiday

(novel), 1968, new edition, 1977; George Stevens: An American Romantic, 1970; The Inland Sea, 1971, new edition, 1993; Japanese Cinema, 1971; Three Modern Kyogen, 1972; Ozu: The Man and His Films, 1974; Ji: Signs and Symbols of Japan (with Mana Maeda), 1975; The Japanese Tatoo, 1980; Zen Inklings: Some Stories, Fables, Parables, Sermons and Prints with Notes and Commentaries, 1982; A Taste of Japan: Food Fact and Fable, What the People Eat, Customs and Etiquette, 1985; Viewing Film, 1986; Introducing Tokyo, 1987; A Lateral View, 1987, new edition, 1992; Different People: Pictures of Some Japanese, 1987; Tokyo Nights, 1988, new edition, 1994; Japanese Cinema: An Introduction, 1990; The Honorable Visitors, 1994; Partial Views, 1995; The Temples of Kyoto, 1995. Honours: Citations from the government of Japan, 1963, 1970; Citation, US National Society of Film Critics, 1970; Kawakita Memorial Foundation Award, 1983; Citations, Government of Japan, 1983; Presidential Citation, New York University, 1989; Novikoff Award, San Francisco Film Festival, 1990; Tokyo Metropolitan Government Cultural Award, 1993; John D Rockefeller III Award, 1994; Japan foundation Prize, 1995. Address: Ueno 2, 12.18 (801), Taito-ku, Tokyo 110, Japan.

RICHLER Mordecai, b. 27 Jan 1931, Montreal, Quebec, Canada. Writer; Dramatist. m. Florence Wood, 1960, 3 sons, 2 daughters. Education: Sir George Williams University. Appointments: Writer-in-Residence, Sir George Williams University, 1968-69; Visiting Professor, Carleton University, 1972-74. Publications: Novels: The Acrobats, 1954; Son of a Smaller Hero, 1955; A Choice of Enemies, 1957; The Apprenticeship of Duddy Kravitz, 1959; The Incomparable Atuk, 1963; Cocksure, 1968; St Urbain's Horseman, 1971; Images of Spain, 1978; Joshua Then and Now, 1980; Solomon Grusky Was Here, 1989; Broadsides, 1991; Jacob Two-Two's First Spy Case, 1995. Stories: The Street, 1972. Other: Essays, film scripts, television plays, and children's books. Honours: Canada Council Junior Arts Fellowships, 1959, 1960, Senior Arts Fellowship, 1967; Guggenheim Fellowship, 1967; Governor-General's Award for Fiction, 1969; Golden Bear, Berlin Film Festival, 1974. Address: 1321 Sherbrooke Street West, Apt 80C, Montreal, Quebec H3G 1J4, Canada.

RICHTER Anne, b. 25 June 1939, Brussels, Belgium. Writer; Teacher of French. Widow, 1 daughter. Education: Licence of Philosophy and Letters, Free University of Brussels, 1963. Publications: Short stories: La Fourmi a Fait le Coup, 1954, English translation, 1956; Les Locataires, 1967; La Grande Pitié de la Famille Zintram, 1986. Essays: Georges Simenon et l'Homme Désintégré, 1964; Milosz, 1965; Le Fantastique Féminin, Un Art Sauvage, 1984; Simenon Malgré Lui, 1993. Anthologies: L'Allemagne Fantastique, 1973; Les Contes Fantastiques de Guy de Maupassant, 1974; Le Fantastique Féminin, 1977; Histoires de Doubles et de Miroirs, 1981; Roger Bodart: La Route du Sel, 1993. Contributions to: Journals. Honours: Prizes, Belgian Academy of French Literature and Language. Memberships: PEN International; Association of Belgian Authors; International Association of Literary Critics. Address: 93 Boulevard Louis Schmidt, bte 13, 1040 Brussels, Belgium.

RICHTER Harvena, b. 13 Mar 1919, Reading, Pennsylvania, USA. University Lecturer (retired); Writer; Poet. Education: BA, University of New Mexico, 1938; MA, 1955, PhD, 1966, New York University. Appointments: Lecturer, New York University, 1955-66, University of New Mexico, 1969-89. Publications: The Human Shore, 1959; Virginia Woolf: The Inward Voyage, 1970; Writing to Survive: The Private Notebooks of Conrad Richter, 1988; The Yaddo Elegies and Other Poems, 1995; Green Girls: poems early and late, 1996. Contributions to: Magazines and newspapers. Honours: Grants and fellowships. Memberships: Authors Guild; Kappa Kappa Gamma. Address: 1932 Candelaria Road North West, Albuquerque, NM 87107, USA.

RICHTER Milan, b. 25 July 1948, Bratislava, Czechoslovakia. Writer; Poet; Translator; Diplomat. m. Adreinna Matejovova, 1 Oct 1980, 1 son, 2 daughters. Education: German and English Linguistics and Literature, Comenius University, Bratislava, 1967-72; PhD, 1985. Appointments: Part-Time Editor, Dotyky Literary Magazine, 1988-89; Revue Svetovej Literatury, 1991; Fulbright Research Scholar, University of California at Los Angeles, 1990; Head, Slovak Embassy, Oslo, 1993. Publications: Poetry books in Slovak and German; Translations into Slovak of various writers. Contributions to: Anthologies, magazines, and journals. Address: Sidlisko 714, CS 900 42 Dunajska Luzna, Slovakia.

RICKS Christopher (Bruce), b. 18 Sept 1933, London, England. Professor of English; Writer; Editor. m. (1) Kirsten Jensen, 1956, div 1975, 2 sons, 2 daughters, (2) Judith Aronson, 1977, 1 son, 2 daughters. Education: BA, 1956, BLitt, 1958, MA, 1960, Balliol College, Oxford. Appointments: Lecturer, Oxford University, 1958-68; Visiting Professor, Stanford University, 1965, University of California at Berkeley, 1965, Smith College, 1967, Harvard University, 1971, Wesleyan University, 1974, Brandeis University, 1977, 1981, 1984; Professor of English, University of Bristol, 1968-75, University of Cambridge, 1975-86, Boston University, 1986-. Publications: Milton's Grand Style, 1963; Tennyson, 1972, revised edition, 1987; Keats and Embarrassment, 1974; The Force of Poetry, 1984; Eliot and Prejudice, 1988; Beckett's Dying Words, 1993; Essays in Appreciation, 1996. Editor: Poems and Critics: An Anthology of Poetry and Criticism from Shakespeare to Hardy, 1966; A E Housman: A Collection of Critical Essays, 1968; Alfred Tennyson: Poems, 1842, 1968; John Milton: Paradise Lost and Paradise Regained, 1968; The Poems of Tennyson, 1969, revised edition, 1987; The Brownings: Letters and Poetry, 1970; English Poetry and Prose, 1540-1674, 1970; English Drama to 1710, 1971; Selected Criticism of Matthew Arnold, 1972; The State of the Language (with Leonard Michaels), 1980, new edition, 1990; The New Oxford Book of Victorian Verse, 1987; Inventions of the March Hare: Poems 1909-1917 by T S Eliot, 1996. Contributions to: Professional journals, Memberships: American Academy of Arts and Sciences, fellow; British Academy, fellow; Tennyson Society, vice-president. Address: 39 Martin Street, Cambridge, MA 02138, USA.

RIDGWAY Judith Anne, b. 10 Nov 1939, Stalybridge, England. Writer. Education: BA Class II, Division 1, Keele University, 1962. Publications: Home Cooking for Money, 1983; Making the Most of Rice, 1983; Making the Most of Pasta, 1983; Making the Most of Potatoes, 1983; Making the Most of Bread, 1983; Making the Most of Eggs, 1983; Making the Most of Cheese, 1983; The Little Lemon Book, 1983; Barbecues, 1983; Cooking Round the World, 1983; Cooking with German Food, 1983; The Little Bean Book, 1983; Frying Tonight, 1984; Running Your Own Wine Bar, 1984; Sprouting Beans and Seeds, 1984; Man in the Kitchen, 1984; The Little Rice Book, 1984; Successful Media Relations, 1984; Running Your Own Catering Company, 1984; Festive Occasions, 1986; The Vegetable Year, 1985; Nuts and Cereals, 1985; Cooking Without Gluten, 1986; Vegetarian Wok Cookery, 1986; Wining and Dining at Home, 1985; Cheese and Cheese Cookery, 1986; 101 Ways With Chicken Pieces, 1987; The Wine Lovers Record Book, 1988; Pocket Book of Oils, Vinegars and Seasoning, 1989; The Little Red Wine Book, 1989; The Vitamin and Mineral Diet Cookbook, 1990; Catering for a Wedding, 1991; Vegetarian Delights, 1992; Quick After Work Pasta Cookbook, 1993; Best Wine Buys in the High Street, 1991, 5th edition, 1995; Food for Sport, 1994; Quick After Work Vegetarian Cookbook, 1994; The Noodle Cookbook, 1994; The Catering Management Handbook, 1994; Best Wine Buys in the High Street, 1996; Practical Media Relations, 1996. Memberships: Society of Authors; Guild of Food Writers; Circle of Wine Writers. Literary Agent: Lisa Eveleigh. Address: 46 Gloucester Square, London W2 2TQ, England.

RIDLER Anne (Barbara), b. 30 July 1912, Rugby, Warwickshire, England. Author; Poet. m. Vivian Ridler, 1938, 2 sons, 2 daughters. Education: Diploma in Journalism, King's College, University of London, 1932. Publications: Poetry: Selected Poems, 1961; Some Time After, 1972; Ten Oxford Poets (with others), 1978; New and Selected Poems, 1988; Collected Poems, 1994. Plays: The Jesse Tree (libretto), 1972; The King of The Golden River (libretto), 1975; The Lambton Worm (libretto), 1978. Other: A Measure of English Poetry (criticism), 1991. Translations: Così fan Tutte, 1986; Gluck's Orpheus, 1988; Don Giovanni, 1990; Figaro, 1991; Coronation of Poppea, 1992; Operas of Monteverdi (contributor), 1992; Tancredi, 1993. Biography: A Victorian Family Postbag, 1988. Editor: A Little Book of Modern Verse, 1941; Best Ghost Stories, 1945; Supplement to Faber Book of Modern Verse, 1951; The Image of the City and Other Essays by Charles Williams, 1958; Shakespeare Criticism, 1963; Poems of James Thomson, 1963; Thomas Traherne, 1966; Best Stories of Church and Clergy (with Christopher Bradby), 1966; Selected Poems of George Darley, 1979; Poems of William Austin, 1983. Address: 14 Stanley Road, Oxford OX4 1QZ, England.

RIDLEY Jasper Godwin, b. 25 May 1920, West Hoathly, Sussex, England. Author. m. Vera Pollakova, 1 Oct 1949, 2 sons, 1 daughter. Education: Sorbonne, University of Paris, 1937; Magdalen College, Oxford University, 1938-39; Certificate of Honour, Council of Legal Education, 1945. Publications: Nicholas Ridley, 1957; Thomas

Cranmer, 1962; John Knox, 1968; Lord Palmerston, 1970; Mary Tudor, 1973; Garibaldi, 1974; The Roundheads, 1976; Napolean III and Eugenie, 1979; The History of England, 1981; The Statesman and the Fanatic, 1982; Henry VIII, 1984; Elizabeth I, 1987; The Tudor Age, 1988; The Love Letters of Henry VIII, 1988; Maximillian and Juárez, 1992; Tito, 1994; History of the Carpenters' Company, 1995. Contributions to: The Prime Ministers, 1975; Garibaldi Generale Della Liberta, 1984; Childhood in Sussex, 1988; Sussex Women, 1995; English Heritage Journal, 1989. Honour: James Tait Black Memorial Prize, 1970. Memberships: English PEN; Fellow, Royal Society of Literature; Life President, Tunbridge Wells Writers Circle; Sussex Authors; Court of Assistants, Worshipful Company of Carpenters, master, 1988, 1990. Literary Agent: Curtis Brown (London and New York). Address: 6 Oakdale Road, Tunbridge Wells, Kent TN4 8DS, England.

RIDPATH Ian (William), b. 1 May 1947, Ilford, Essex, England. Writer; Broadcaster. Publications: Over 30 books, including: Worlds Beyond, 1975; Encyclopedia of Astronomy and Space (editor), 1976; Messages From the Stars, 1978; Stars and Planets, 1978; Young Astronomer's Handbook, 1981; Hamlyn Encyclopedia of Space, 1981; Life Off Earth, 1983; Collins Guide to Stars and Planets, 1984; Gem Guide to the Night Sky, 1985; Secrets of the Sky, 1985; A Comet Called Halley, 1985; Longman Illustrated Dictionary of Astronomy and Astronautics, 1987; Monthly Sky Guide, 1987; Star Tales, 1989; Norton's Star Atlas (editor), 1989; Book of the Universe, 1991; Atlas of Stars and Planets, 1992. Address: 48 Otho Court, Brentford Dock, Brentford, Middlesex TW8 8PY, England.

RIES Hans, b. 22 Dec 1941, Gilching, Germany. Research Scientist. m. Gitta Maikl, 24 May 1968, 1 son. Appointments: Wilhelm Busch Museum, Hannover, 1980-; Vice-President, International Youth Library, Munich, 1992-. Publications: Wilhelm Buschals Zeichner nach der Natur, 1982; Zwischen Hausse und Baisse, Börse und Geld in der Karikatur, 1987; Illustration und Illustratoren 1871-1914, 1992. Other: Allgemeines Künstlerlexikon, 1985-. Contributions to: Börsenblatt für den Deutschen Buchhandel, Aus dem Antiquariat. Address: Römerstrasse 93, D 82205 Gilching, Germany.

RIFBJERG Klaus Thorvald, b. 15 Dec 1931, Copenhagen, Denmark. Author. m. Inge Merete Gerner, 28 May 1955, 1 son, 2 daughters. Education: Princeton University, 1950-51; University of Copenhagen, 1951-56. Appointments: Library Critic, Information, 1955-57, Politiken, 1959-; Editor, Vindrosen, 1959-64; Literary Director, Gyldendal Publishers, 1985-92. Publications: Anna (Jeg) Anna, 1970; Marts, 1970, 1970; Leif den Lykkelige JR, 1971; Til Spanien, 1971; Lena Jorgensen, Klintevej 4, 2650, Hvidovre, 1971; Brevet til Gerda, 1972; RR, 1972; Spinatfuglene, 1973; Dilettanterne, 1973; Du skal ikke vaere ked af det Amalia, 1974; En Hugorm i solen, 1974; Vejen ad Hvilken, 1975; Tak for turen, 1975; Kiks, 1976; Tango, 1978; Dobbeltgoenger, 1978; Drengene, 1978; Joker, 1979; Voksdugshjertet, 1979; Det sorte hul, 1980. Short stories: Og Andre Historier, 1964; Rejsende, 1969; Den Syende Jomfru, 1972; Sommer, 1974. Non-fiction: I medgang Og Modgang, 1970. Plays: Gris Pa Gaflen, 1962; Hva' Skal Vi Lave, 1963; Udviklinger, 1965; Hvad en Mand Har brug For, 1966; Voks, 1968; Ar, 1970; Narrene, 1971; Svaret Blaeser i Vinden, 1971; Det Korte af det lange, 1976; Twist, 1976; Et bortvendt ansigt, 1977; Deres majestaet!, 1977. Poems: Livsfrisen, 1979. Honours: Danish Dramatists, 1966; Danish Academy Award, 1966; Golden Laurels, 1967; Grand Prize, Danish Academy of Arts and Letters, 1968; Soren Gyldendal Award, 1969; Nordic Council Award, 1971; Grant of Honour, Danish Writers Guild, 1973; PH Prize, 1979; Holberg Medal, 1984; H C Andersen Prize, 1987; Doctor honoris causa, Luna University, 1992. Membership: Danish Academy of Arts and Letters. Address: Kristianiagade 22, DK 2100, Copenhagen, Denmark.

RIGHTMIRE G Philip, b. 15 Sept 1942, Boston, Massachusetts, USA. Professor of Anthropology. m. Berit Johansson, 20 Aug 1966, 1 son, 1 daughter. Education: BA, Harvard University, 1964; MS, 1966, PhD, 1969, University of Wisconsin. Appointments: Assistant Professor, Associate Professor, Professor, State University of New York, Binghamton. Publication: The Evolution of Homo Erectus, 1990. Contributions to: Reference works and professional journals. Memberships: American Association for the Advancement of Science; Sigma Xi. Address: 4004 Fuller Hollow Road, Vestal, NY 13850, USA.

RILEY James Andrew, b. 25 July 1939, Sullivan County, Tennessee, USA. Author; Feature Writer. m. Dorothy Elizabeth Taylor,

14 Oct 1960, 2 sons. Education: BS, 1961, MA, 1966, East Tennessee State University; EdS, Nova University, 1982. Publications: The All-Time All-Stars of Black Baseball, 1983; Dandy, Day, and the Devil, 1987; The Hundred Years of Chet Hoff, 1991; Biographical Encyclopedia of the Negro Baseball Leagues, 1994; Buck Leonard: The Black Lou Gehrig, 1995; Nice Guys Finish First: the Autobiography of Monte Irvin, 1996. Contributions to: Reference books and journals; Athlon Baseball, 1995; African-American Sports Greats: A Biographical Dictionary, 1995; Negro Leagues Baseball Yearbook, 1993, 1994. Honours: Society for American Baseball Research Awards, 1990, 1994. Membership: Society for American Baseball Research. Address: PO Box 560968, Rockledge, FL 32956-0968, USA.

RILEY Samuel Gayle III, b. 8 Oct 1939, Raleigh, North Carolina, USA. University Professor. m. Mary Elaine Weisner, 14 May 1966, div 1986, 1 son, 1 daughter. Education: AB, Davidson College, 1961; MBA, 1962, PhD, Mass Communication Research, 1970, University of North Carolina, Chapel Hill. Appointments: Assistant Professor, Journalism, Temple University, 1970-74; Associate Professor, Journalism, Georgia Southern University, 1971-81; Professor, Communication Studies, Virginia Polytechnic Institute and State University, 1981-. Publications: Magazines of the American South, 1986; Index to Southern Periodicals, 1986; American Magazine Journalists (Dictionary of Literary Biography), 4 volumes, 1988, 1989, 1990, 1994; Index to City and Regional Magazines of the United States, 1989; Regional Interest Magazines of the United States, 1991; GR8 PL8S, 1991; Corporate Magazines of the United States, 1992; Consumer Magazines of the British Isles, 1993; The Best of the Rest, 1993; Biographical Dictionary of American Newspaper Columnists, 1995. Contributions to: Reference books, professional journals, newspapers, and magazines. Memberships: Association for Education in Journalism and Mass Communications; Research Society of American Periodicals; American Journalism Historians Association. Address: 1865 Mountainside Drive, Blacksburg, VA 24060, USA.

RINALDI Nicholas Michael, b. 2 Apr 1934, Brooklyn, New York, USA. Professor; Writer; Poet. m. Jacqueline Tellier, 29 Aug 1959, 3 sons, 1 daughter. Education: AB, Shrub Oak College, 1957; MA, 1960, PhD, 1963, Fordham University. Appointments: Instructor to Assistant Professor, St John's University, 1960-65; Lecturer, City University of New York, 1966; Associate Professor, Columbia University, 1966; Assistant Professor to Professor, Fairfield University, 1966-; Professor, University of Connecticut, 1972. Publications: The Resurrection of the Snails, 1977; We Have Lost Our Fathers, 1982; The Luftwaffe in Chaos, 1985; Bridge Fall Down, 1985. Contributions to: The Virginia Quarterly Review; Periodicals. Honours: Joseph P Slomovich Memorial Award for Poetry, 1979; All Nations Poetry Awards, 1981, 1983; New York Poetry Forum Award, 1983, Eve of St Agnes Poetry Award, 1984; Charles Angoff Literary Award, 1984. Memberships: Associated Writing Programs; Poetry Society of America. Address: 190 Brookview Avenue, Fairfield, CT 06432, USA.

RING Douglas. See: PRATHER Richard Scott.

RINGELL Susanne Gun Emilia, b. 28 Feb 1955, Helsinki, Finland. Author. m. Anders Larsson, 6 June 1992. Education: Theater Academy of Helsinki, 1977-81; Actress Diploma. Publications: Det Förlovade Barnet, 1993; Vestalen, The Vestal Virgin, 1994; Gall eller Våra Osynliga Väntrum, 1994; Vara Sten, 1996. Plays: Edelweiss, 1989; Pantlånekontoret, 1992. Radio Plays: Vendettan, 1990; Vestalen, 1994. Contributions to: Fågel Fenix; Blå; Transit. Honour: Granberg Sumeliuska Priset, 1994; Prix Italia, 1995. Membership: Finlands Svenska Författareförening RF. Literary Agent: Söderström & Co Förlags AB. Address: Snellmansgatan 16 B 24, 00170 Helsinki, Finland.

RINHART Marion Hutchinson, b. 20 Feb 1916, Bradley Beach, New Jersey, USA. Author; Historian. m. Lloyd, 3 Mar 1935, dec 1996, 1 son. Education: Research and study, Washington, DC. Appointments: Seminar, University of Georgia, 1977; Lecturing Professor, Ohio State University, 1985, 1986. Publications: American Daguerrian Art, 1967; American Miniature Case Art, 1969; America's Affluent Age, 1971; Summertime, 1978; The American Daguerrotype, 1981; America's Centennial Celebration, 1976; Victorian Florida, 1986. Contributions to: Art in America; Antiques Journal; Modern Photography; Camera; American West; History of Photography an International Quarterly; American History; Iowa Heritage. Honour: Fiest

Daguerrian Society Award, 1990. Address: 242B Jefferson Court, Lakewood, NJ 08701, USA.

RIO-SUKAN Isabel del, b. 8 Sep 1954, Madrid, Spain. Writer; Poet; United Nations Translator; Literary Translator. m. H B Sukan, 31 July 1981, 2 daughters. Education: Lic Cc Inf, Madrid Central University, 1972-77; Incorporated Linguist, Institute of Linguists, London, 1985. Appointments: Editor, Arts and Literary Programmes, Spanish Section, BBC World Service, 1978-82; Currently full-time Translator, International Maritime Organisation, United Nations agency, London, England. Publications: BBC Get By In Spanish, 1992; Ciudad del interior, 1993; La duda, 1995. Translations: The Secret Garden, by F H Burnett, 1990; Poetry by Sylvia Plath and T L Beddoes. Contributions to: Articles on translation matters in professional journals. Honours: Finalist, Nuevos Narradores Competition, 1994; Finalist, Premio Icaro, 1995. Memberships: Society of Authors; Translators Association; Institute of Linguists; Institute of Translation and Interpreting; AITC, Geneva. Literary Agent: Tusquets Editores, Iradier 24, Barcelona 08017, Spain; The Caroline Davidson Literary Agency, 5 QWueen Anne's Gardens, London W4 1TU, England. Address: PO Box 10314, London W14 0FT, England.

RIOS Juan, b. 28 Sep 1914, Barranco, Lima, Peru. Poet; Dramatist; Journalist; Critic. m. Rosa Saco, 16 Sep 1946, 1 daughter. Publications: Cancion de Siempre, 1941; Malstrom, 1941; La Pintura Contempranea en el Peru, 1946; Teatro (1), 1961; Ayar Manko, 1963; Primera Antologia Poetica, 1981. Honours: National Prizes, Playwriting, 1946, 1950, 1952, 1954, 1960; National Poetry Prizes, 1948, 1953. Memberships: Writers' Fellowship, UNESCO, Europe and Egypt, 1960-61; Academia Peruana de la lengua Correspondiente a la Espanola. Address: Bajada de Banos 109, Barranco, Lima 04, Peru.

RIPLEY Alexandra (Braid), b. 8 Jan 1934, Charleston, South Carolina, USA. Author. m. (1) Leonard Ripley, 1958, div 1963, (2) John Graham, 1981, 2 daughters. Education: AB, Vassar College, 1955. Publications: Who's That Lady in the President's Bed?, 1972; Charleston, 1981; On Leaving Charleston, 1984; The Time Returns, 1985; New Orleans Legacy, 1987; Scarlett: The Sequel to Margaret Mitchell's Gone With the Wind, 1991; From the Fields of Gold, 1994; A Love Devine, 1996. Address: c/o Janklow-Nesbit Associates, 598 Madison Avenue, New York, NY 10022, USA.

RIPLEY Michael David, (Mike Ripley), b. 29 Sep 1952, Huddersfield, England. Critic; Writer. m. Alyson Jane White, 8 July 1978, 2 daughters. Education: BA Honours, Economic History, University of East Anglia. Appointments: Crime Fiction Critic, The Sunday Telegraph, 1989-91; Crime Critic, The Daily Telegraph, 1991-. Publications: Just Another Angel, 1988; Angel Touch, 1989; Angel Hunt, 1990; Angels in Arms, 1991. Short stories: The Body of the Beer, 1989; Smeltdown, 1990; Gold Sword, 1990. Contributions to: The 'Britcrit' Column in Mystery Scene, 1991. Honours: Scholarship to public school; Runner-up, Punch Magazine Awards for Funniest Crime Novel, 1988; Last Laugh Awards, Crime Writers Association, 1989, 1991; Angel Literary Award for Fiction, 1990. Memberships: Crime Writers Association; Sisters in Crime, USA; Dorothy L Sayers Society. Address: c/o David Higham Associates, 5-8 Lower John Street, London W1R 4HA, England.

RIPPON Angela, b. 12 Oct 1944, Plymouth, Devon, England. Television and Radio Presenter; Writer. m. Christopher Dare, 1967. Education: Grammar School, Plymouth, England. Appointments: Editor, Presenter, Producer, Westward Television, 1969-73; News Reporter, National News, 1973-76; Newsreader, Nine O'Clock News, 1976-81; Arts and Entertainment Officer, WNEV-TV, Channel 7, Boston, USA, 1984-85; Hostess, The Health Show, BBC Radio 5, 1989-90; Anchorwoman, Angela Rippon Morning Report, 1990-92, Angela Rippon's Drive Time Show, 1992-. Publications: Riding, 1980; In the Country, 1980; Mark Phillips: The Man and His Horses, 1982; Angela Rippon's West Country, 1982; Victoria Plum, 1983; Badminton: A Celebration, 1987; Many recordings. Honours: Radio and Television Industries Awards for Newsreader of the Year, 1976, 1977, 1978; Television Personality of the Year, 1977; Sony Award, 1990. Memberships: International Club for Women in Television, vice-president, 1979-; English National Ballet Association, chairman; American College, London, board member. Address: c/o International Management Group, Media House, 3 Burlington Lane, Chiswick, London W4 2TH, England.

RITCHIE David. See: CALDER Nigel.

RITCHIE Elisavietta Artamonoff, b. 29 June 1932, Kansas City, Missouri, USA. Writer; Poet; Translator; Teacher; Editor; Photographer. m. (1) Lyell Hale Ritchie, 2 sons, 1 daughter, (2) Clyde Henri Farnsworth, 22 June 1991. Education: Degré Supérieur, Mention Très Bien, Sorbonne, Paris, 1951; Cornell University, 1951-53; BA, University of California, Berkeley, 1954; MA, French Literature, minor Russian Studies, American University, 1976; Advanced Russian courses, Georgetown University. Appointments: US Information Agency Visiting Poet, Brazil, 1972; Far East 1977; Yugoslavia, Bulgaria, 1979; Founder, Director, The Wineberry Press, 1983-; President, Washington Writers Publishing House, 1986-89; Leader, Creative Writing Workshops. Publications: Timbot, 1970; Tightening the Circle Over Eel Country, 1974; A Sheath of Dreams and Other Games, 1976; Moving to Larger Quarters, 1977; Raking the Snow, 1982; The Problem With Eden, 1985; Flying Time: Stories and Half-Stories, 1992; A Wound-Up Cat and Other Bedtime Stories, 1993; Wild Garlic: The Journal of Maria X, 1995; Elegy for the Other Woman, 1996; The Arc of the Storm, 1996. Contributions to: Canadian Women Studies; When I'm An Old Woman I Shall Wear Purple; Confrontations; Anthologies and periodicals. Honours: New Writer's Award for Best 1st Book of Poetry, Great Lakes Colleges Association, 1975-76; Graduate Teaching Fellowship, American University; Fellow, Virginia Center for the Creative Arts; 4 times PEN Syndicated Fiction Winner; 4 Individual Artist Grants, Washington, DC, Commission for the Arts; Two Annual Awards, Poetry Society of America. Memberships: Writer's Center; Washington Independent Writers; PEN; Amnesty International; Poetry Society of America; Poets and Writers; Environmental organisations. Address: 3207 Macomb Street North West, Washington, DC 20008, USA.

RITTER Erika, b. 1948, Saskatchewan, Canada. Playwright. Education: BA, McGill University, Montreal, 1968; MA, University of Toronto, 1970. Appointments: Dramatist in Residence, Stratford Festival, Ontario, 1985. Publications: A Visitor from Charleston, 1975; The Splits, 1978; Winter, 1671, 1979; The Automatic Pilot, 1980; The Passing Scene, 1982; Urban Scrawl, 1984; Murder at McQueen, 1986; Ritter in Residence, 1987; Essays and Sketches. Honour: ACTRA Award, 1982. Address: c/o Shain Jaffe, Great North Artists, 350 Dupont Street, Toronto, Ontario M5R 1V9, Canada.

RITTERBAND Olly, b. 28 Dec 1923, Miercurea-Niraj, Romania. Artist; Author. m. Daniel Ritterband, 25 Dec 1949, 2 daughters. Education: Royal Danish Academy of Fine Arts, Copenhagen; École Nationale Superieure des Beaux-Arts, Paris; Accademia del Mosaico, Ravenna, Italy. Appointment: Teacher, Royal Danish Academy of Fine Arts, Copenhagen. Publications: I Will Not Die, 1982; The Will to Survive, 1990. Contributions to: Publications on the Holocaust. Memberships: Danish Authors Association; Friends of Mosaic Art, president; Gentofte Society of Culture; Society of Jewish History. Address: Niels Andersensvej 65, Hellerup, DK-2900, Denmark.

RITVO Harriet, b. 19 Sept 1946, Cambridge, Massachusetts, USA. Historian. Education: AB, 1968, PhD, 1975, Harvard University. Appointment: Professor of History and Writing, Arthur J Conner Professor of History, Massachusetts Institute of Technology. Publications: The Animal Estate: The English and Other Creatures in the Victorian Age; The Macropolitics of 19th-Century Literature (co-editor with Jonathan Arac). Contributions to: Numerous essays and reviews on 18th and 19th-Century cultural history, and on the relationship between humans and other animals. Honour: Whiting Writers' Award, 1990. Memberships: PEN American Center; American Historical Association; History of Science Society; Society for the History of Natural History. Address: E51-285 Massachusetts Institute of Technology, Cambridge, MA 02139, USA.

RIVA Maria Elizabeth, b. 13 Dec 1924, Berlin, Germany (US citizen). Author; Former Actress. m. William Riva, 4 July 1947, 4 sons. Publication: Marlene Dietrich by Her Daughter, 1992. Contributions to: Various. Honours: Various acting awards, 1946-55. Address: 133 RR2, Wassaic, NY 12592, USA.

RIVARD Ken J, b. 30 June 1947, Montreal, Quebec, Canada. Special Education Teacher; Poet; Writer. m. Micheline Rivard, 19 Sept 1972, 2 daughters. Education: BEd, University of Montreal, 1970; MEd, McGill University, 1974. Publications: Poetry: Kiss Me Down to Size, 1983; Losing His Thirst, 1985; Frankie's Desires, 1987. Fiction: Working Stiffs, 1990; If She Could Take All These Men, 1995. Contributions to: Anthologies and periodicals. Memberships: Writers

Guild of Alberta; League of Canadian Poets. Address: 120 Whiteview Place North East, Calgary, Alberta T1Y 1R6, Canada.

RIVKIN J F, b. 1951, USA. Publications: Silverglass, 1986; Web of Wind, 1987; Witch of Rhostshyl, 1989; Mistress of Ambiguities, 1991; The Dreamstone, 1991. Membership: Science Fiction and Fantasy Writers of America. Address: 1430 Massachusetts Avenue, Suite 306, Cambridge, MA 02138, USA.

RIVOYRE Christine Berthe Claude Denis de, b. 29 Nov 1921. Journalist; Author. Education: University of Syracuse, USA. Appointments: Journalist, Le Monde, 1950-55; Literary Director, Marie-Claire, 1955-65; Member, Haut Comité de la Langue Française, Conseil Superieur des Lettres, Prix Medicis Jury. Publications: L'alouette au miroir, 1956; La mandarine, 1957; La tete en fleurs, 1960; La glace a l'ananas, 1962; Les sultans, 1964; Le petit matin, 1968; Le seigneur des chevaux (with A Kalda), 1969; Fleur d'agonie, 1970; Boy, 1973; Le voyage a l'envers, 1977; Belle alliance, 1982; Reine-Mere, 1985. Honours: Chevalier, Legion d'honneur; Chevalier, des Arts et des Lettres Prix Paul Morand, 1984. Address: Dichats Ha, Onesse Laharie, 40110, Morceux, France.

RIZKALLA John Ramsay, b. 2 Nov 1935, Manchester, England. Writer. Education: Baccalaureat Francais, 1st and 2nd part, 1952-53; BA Hons, Manchester University, 1958. Publication: The Jericho Garden, 1988. Contributions to: Books, magazines and radio. Membership: Society of Authors. Address: c/o Murray Polinger, 222 Old Brompton Road, London SW5 0BZ, England.

ROBB Graham Macdonald, b. 2 June 1958, Manchester, England. Writer. m. Margaret Robb, 2 May 1986. Education: BA 1st Class Honours, 1981; PGCE, Goldsmiths College, London, 1982; PhD, Vanderbilt University, Nashville, Tennessee, USA, 1986. Publications: Le Corsaire - Satan en Silhouette, 1985; Baudelaire Lecteur de Balzac, 1988; Scenes de La Vie de Boheme (editor), 1988; Baudelaire, (translation), 1989; La Poésie de Baudelaire et La Poésie Française, 1993; Balzac, 1994; Unlocking Mallarmé, 1996. Contributions to: Times Literary Supplement; Revue d'Histoire Litteraire de La France; French Studies. Honours: Postdoctoral Research Fellow; British Academy Fellowship, 1987-90. Memberships: Society of Authors; Societe d'Histoire Litteraire de La France. Address: 139 Hollow Way, Oxford OX4 2NE, England.

ROBB James Harding, b. 28 Apr 1920, Gisborne, New Zealand. Sociologist; Professor Emeritus, Victoria University of Wellington. m. Margaret Ruth Storkey, 6 Feb 1946, 2 sons, 2 daughters. Education: MA, New Zealand, 1947; BSc (Econ), London, 1948; PhD, London, 1951. Publications: Working Class Anti-Semite, 1954; The Life and Death of Official Social Research in New Zealand, 1936-1940, 1987. Contributions to: Numerous articles in professional journals. Address: 9 Allen Terrace, Tawa, Wellington, New Zealand.

ROBBE-GRILLET Alain, b. 18 Aug 1922, Brest, France. Writer; Filmmaker; Agronomist. m. Catherine Rstakian, 1957. Education: Institute Agronomique. Publications: Novels: Les Gommes, 1953; Le Voyeur, 1955; La Jalousie, 1957; Dans le Labyrinthe, 1959; La Maison de Rendez-vous, 1965; Projet pour une Revolution a New York, 1970; Topologie d'une Cite Fantome, 1976; La Belle Captive, 1977; Un Regicide, 1978; Souvenirs du Triangle d'Or, 1978; Djinn, 1981; Le Miroir qui Revient, 1984; Angélique ou l'Enchantment, 1987; Les Derniers Jours de Corinthe, 1994. Short stories: Instantanes, 1962. Essay: Pour un Nouveau Roman, 1964. Films: L'Annee Derniere a Marienbad, 1961. Films Directed: L'Immortelle, 1963; Trans-Europ-Express, 1967; L'Homme qui Ment, 1968; L'Eden et Apres, 1970; Glissements Progressifs du Plaisir, 1974; Le Jeu Avec le Feu, 1975; La Belle Captive, 1983; Un Bruit qui rend fou, 1995. Honours: Chevalier, Legion d'Honneur; Officier, Ordre National du Merite; Prix Louis Delluc, 1963. Memberships: Various professional organisations. Address: 18 Boulevard Maillot, 92200 Neuilly-sur-Seine, France.

ROBBINS Harold, b. 21 May 1916, New York, New York, USA. Author. m. (1) Lillian Machnivitz, div, (2) Grace Palermo, div, 2 daughters, (3) Jan Stapp. Education: New York Public Schools. Publications: Never Love a Stranger, 1948; The Dream Merchants, 1949; A Stone for Danny Fisher, 1951; Never Leave Me, 1953; 79 Park Avenue, 1955; Stiletto, 1958; The Carpetbaggers, 1961; Where Love Has Gone, 1962; The Adventurers, 1966; The Inheritors, 1969; The Betsy, 1971; The Pirate, 1974; The Lonely Lady, 1976; Dreams Die

First, 1977; Memories of Another Day, 1979; Goodbye Janette, 1981; Spellbinder, 1982; Descent for Xanadu, 1984; The Storyteller, 1985; The Piranhas, 1991; The Raiders, 1994; The Stallion, 1996. Address: c/o McIntosh & Otis, 310 Madison Avenue, New York, NY 10017, USA.

ROBBINS Kenneth Randall, b. 7 Jan 1944, Douglasville, Georgia, USA. Associate Professor; Writer; Dramatist. m. Dorothy Dodge, 14 May 1988, 1 son, 1 daughter. Education: AA, Young Harris College, 1964; BSEd, Georgia Southern University, 1966; MFA, University of Georgia, 1969; PhD, Southern Illinois University at Carbondale, 1982. Appointments: Assistant Professor, Jacksonville University, Florida, 1974-79; Associate Professor, Newberry College, South Carolina, 1977-85, University of South Dakota, 1985-; Presenter, Black Hills Writers Conference, 1986-90; Editor, Wayne S Knutson Dakota Playwriting Series. Publications: The Dallas File (play), 1982; Buttermilk Bottoms (novel), 1987. Contributions to: Journals and radio. Honours: Toni Morrison Prize for Fiction, 1986; Associated Writing Programs Novel Award, 1986; Festival of Southern Theatre Awards, 1987, 1990. Memberships: American College Theatre Festival; Association of Theatre in Higher Education; Dramatists Guild; The Loft, Minneapolis; Playwright's Centre, Minneapolis; Society for Humanities and Technology; Southeastern Theatre Conference. Address: 118 Willow, Vermillion, SD 57069, USA.

ROBBINS Tom, (Thomas Eugene Robbins), b. 1936, Blowing Rock, North Carolina, USA. m. (1), (2) Terrie Robbins, div, 1 son. Education: Washington and Lee University, 1954-56; Degree in Social Science, Richmond Professional Institute, Virginia, 1959; University of Washington, 1963. Publications: Guy Anderson, 1965; Another Roadside Attraction, 1971; Even Cowgirls Get the Blues, 1976; Still Life with Woodpecker, 1980; Jitterbug Perfume, 1984; Skinny Legs and All, 1990; Half Asleep in Frog Pajamas, 1994. Address: PO Box 338, La Conner, WA 98257, USA.

ROBERSON John Royster, b. 7 Mar 1930, Roanoke, Virginia, USA. Editor; Writer. m. Charlene Grace Hale, 17 Sept 1966, 1 son, 1 daughter. Education: BA, 1950, MA, 1953, University of Virginia; Certificates of French Studies, 1st and 2nd Degrees, University of Grenoble, France, 1952; Diploma in Mandarin Chinese, US Army Language School, Monterey, California, 1956. Appointments: From Assistant to Senior Editor, Holiday, 1959-70; Copywriter, N W Ayer Advertising, 1971-76; From Associate to Senior Staff Editor, Reader's Digest Condensed Books, 1976-95. Publications: China from Manchu to Mao 1699-1976, 1980; Japan from Shogun to Sony 1543-1984, 1985; Transforming Russia 1692-1991, 1992. Contributions to: Atlantic; Holiday; Reader's Digest; Studies in Bibliography; Virginia Magazine of History and Biography. Honours: Raven Society, University of Virginia, 1950; Rotary International Fellowship, University of Grenoble, 1951-52. Memberships: International House of Japan; US China People's Friendship Society; Director of Publications, Science Education Center, Fairfield County, Connecticut. Address: 16 Hassake Road, Old Greenwich, CT 06870, USA.

ROBERT Adrian. See: JOHNSTON Norma.

ROBERTS Andrew, b. 13 Jan 1963, London, England. Author. Education: MA 1st Class Honours, Modern History, Gonville and Caius College, Cambridge, 1985. Publications: The Holy Fox: A Biography of Lord Halifax; Eminent Churchillians, 1994; The Aachen Memorandum, 1995. Contributions to: Spectator; Literary Review; Columnist, Sunday Times. Memberships: Beefsteak Club; University Pitt Club, Cambridge; Brooks. Literary Agent: Georgina Capel, Simpson Fox. Address: 2 Tite Street, London SW3 4HY, England.

ROBERTS Brian, b. 19 Mar 1930, London, England. Writer. Education: Teacher's Certificate, St Mary's College, Twickenham, 1955; Diploma in Sociology, University of London, 1958. Appointments: Teacher of English and History, 1955-65. Publications: Ladies in the Veld, 1965; Cecil Rhodes and the Princess, 1969; Churchills in Africa, 1970; The Diamond Magnates, 1972; The Zulu Kings, 1974; Kimberley: Turbulent City, 1976; The Mad Bad Line: The Family of Lord Alfred Douglas, 1981; Randolph: A Study of Churchill's Son, 1984; Cecil Rhodes: Flawed Colossus, 1987; Those Bloody Women: Three Heroines of the Boer War, 1991. Address: North Knoll Cottage, 15 Bridge Street, Frome BA11 1BB, England.

ROBERTS Eirlys Rhiwen Cadwaladr, b. 3 Jan 1911, United Kingdom. Journalist. m. John Cullen, 1941. Education: BA Honours, Classics, Girton College, Cambridge. Appointments: Editor, Which?

magazine, 1958-73; Head of Research and Editorial Division, Consumers' Association. Publication: Consumers, 1966. Contributions to: Various journals and magazines. Honours: Office of the Order of the British Empire, 1971; Commander of the Order od the British Empire, 1977. Membership: Royal Society of Arts. Address: 8 Lloyd Square, London, WC1X 9BA, England.

ROBERTS Irene, (Roberta Carr, Elizabeth Harle, I M Roberts, Ivor Roberts, Iris Rowland, Irene Shaw), b. 27 Sept 1925, London, England. Writer. Education: London schools. Appointments: Woman's Page Editor, South Hams Review, 1977-79; Tutor, Creative Writing, Kingsbridge Community College, 1978-. Publications: Shadows on the Moon, 1968; Thunder Heights, 1969; Surgeon in Tibet, 1970; Birds Without Bars, 1970; The Shrine of Fire, 1970; Sister at Sea, 1971; Gull Haven, 1971; Moon Over the Temple, 1972; The Golden Pagoda, 1972; Desert Nurse, 1976; Nurse in Nepal, 1976; Stars Above Raffael, 1977; Hawks Burton, 1979; Syphony of Bells, 1980; Nurse Moonlight, 1980; Weave Me a Moonbeam, 1982; Jasmine for a Nurse, 1982; Sister on Leave, 1982; Nurse in the Wilderness, 1983; Moonpearl, 1986; Sea Jade, 1987; Kingdom of the Sun, 1987; Song of the Nile, 1987. Juvenile: Holiday's for Hanbury, 1964; Laughing is for Fun, 1964. As Ivor Roberts: Jump into Hell, 1960; Trial by Water, 1961; Green Hell, 1961; as Iris Rowland: Blue Feathers, 1967; Moon Over Moncrieff, 1969; Star Drift, 1970; Rainbow River, 1970; The Wild Summer, 1970; Orange Blossom for Tara, 1971; Blossoms in the Snow, 1971; Sister Julia, 1972; Golden Bubbles, 1976; Hunter's Dawn, 1977; Golden Triangle, 1978; Forgotten Dreams, 1978; Temptation, 1983; Theresa, 1985. As Roberta Carr: Sea Maiden, 1965; Fire Dragon, 1967; Golden Interlude, 1970. As Elizabeth Harle: Golden Rain, 1964; Gay Rowan, 1965; Sandy, 1967; Spray of Red Roses, 1971; The Silver Summer, 1971; The Burning Flame, 1979; Come to Me Darling, 1983. As Irene Shaw: Moonstone Manor, 1968, US edition as Murder Mansion 1976; The Olive Branch, 1968; As I M Roberts: The Throne of the Pharoahs, 1974; Hatsheput, Queeen of the Nile, 1976; Hour of the Tiger, 1985; Jezebel Street, 1994; Limehouse Lady, 1995; More Laughter Than Tears, 1996; London's Pride in Progress, 1997. Membership: Founder Member, romantic Novelists Association. Address: Alpha House, Higher Town, Marlborough, Kingsbridge, South Devon TQ7 3RL, England.

ROBERTS John Morris, b. 14 Apr 1928, Bath, England. Academic; Writer. m. Judith Cecilia Mary Armitage, 1964, 1 son, 2 daughters. Education: BA, 1949, MA, 1952, DPhil, 1953, Oxford University. Appointments: Member, Institute of Advanced Study, Princeton, New Jersey, 1960-61; Council, European University Institute, 1980-88; USA/UK Education Commission (Fulbright), 1981-87; Visiting Professor, University of South Carolina, 1961; Secretary, Harmsworth Trust, 1962-68; Senior Proctor, Oxford University, 1967-68; Vice-Chancellor and Professor, Southampton University, 1979-85; Honorary Fellow, 1981-84, 1994-, Warden, 1985-94, Merton College, Oxford; Governor, BBC, 1988-93. Publications: French Revolution Documents i, 1966; Europe 1880-1945, 1967, new edition, 1990; The Mythology of the Secret Societies, 1972; The Paris Commune from the Right, 1973; Revolution and Improvement: The Western World 1775-1847, 1976; History of the World, 1976, revised edition, 1993; The French Revolution, 1978; The Triumph of the West, 1985; Shorter Illustrated History of the World, 1994. Contributions to: Professional journals. Honours: Honorary DLitt, Southampton University, 1987; Cavalier, Order of Merit, Italian Republic, 1989; Commander of the Order of the British Empire, 1996. Memberships: National Portrait Gallery, trustee, 1984-; Royal Literary Fund; Society of Authors; Royal Historical Society. Address: c/o Merton College, Oxford OX1 4JD, England.

ROBERTS Keith John Kingston, (Alistair Bevan), b. 10 Sept 1935, Kettering, Northamptonshire, England. Author; Freelance Graphic Designer and Advertising Copywriter. Education: National Diploma in Design, Northampton School of Art, 1956; Leicester College of Art, 1956-57. Appointments: Assistant Editor, Science Fantasy, 1965-66; Assistant Editor, 1965-66, Managing Editor, 1966, Science Fiction Impulse. Publications: The Furies, 1966; Pavane, 1968; The Inner Wheel, 1970; Anita, 1970; The Boat of Fate, 1971; Machines and Men, 1973; The Chalk Giants, 1974; The Grain Kings, 1975; Ladies from Hell, 1979; Molly Zero, 1980; Kiteworld, 1985; Kaeti and Company, 1986; The Lordly Ones, 1986. Address: 23 New Street, Henley-on-Thames, Oxford RG9 2BP, England.

ROBERTS Kevin E(rnest) A(lbert), b. 8 Mar 1940, Adelaide, Australia. Poet; Author; Dramatist. Education: BA, University of

Adelaide, 1962; MA, Simon Fraser University, 1968. Appointment: Instructor, Malaspina University College. Publications: Cariboo Fishing Notes (poetry), 1973; Five Poems, 1974; West Country (poetry), 1975; Deepline (poetry), 1978; S'Ney'mos (poetry), 1980; Heritage (poetry), 1981; Stonefish (poetry), 1982; Flash Harry and The Daughters of Divine Light (fiction), 1982; Black Apples (play), 1983; Nanoose Bay Suite (poetry), 1984; Picking the Morning Colour (fiction), 1985; Tears in a Glass Eye (novel), 1989; Red Centre Journal (art and poetry show), 1985. Address: Box 55, Lantzville, British Columbia, Canada V0R 2H0.

ROBERTS Michèle, b. 29 May 1949, Bushey, Hertfordshire, England. Poet; Writer; Dramatist. Education: BA, Oxford University, 1970; Library Associate, University of London, 1970. Publications: Fiction: A Piece of the Night, 1978; Tales I Tell My Mother, 1978; The Wild Girl, 1984; The Book of Mrs Noah, 1986; More Tales I Tell My Mother, 1989; The Seven Deadly Sins, 1989; The Seven Cardinal Virtues, 1990; In the Red Kitchen, 1990; God, 1992; Daughters of the House, 1993. Poetry: The Mirror of the Mother, 1986; Psyche and the Hurricane, 1991. Play: The Journey Woman, 1988. Screenplay: The Heavenly Twins, 1992. Contributions to: Anthologies and other publications. Honour: W H Smith Literary Award, 1993. Address: c/o W H Smith Literary Award, Strand House, 7 Holbein Place, London SW1W 8NR, England.

ROBERTS Nora, b. 10 Oct 1950, Washington, District of Columbia, USA. Writer. m. (1) Ronald Aufdem-Brinker, 17 Aug 1968, div 1985, 2 sons, (2) Bruce Wilder, 6 July 1985. Education: Graduated, High School, 1968. Publications: Irish Thoroughbred, 1981; This Magic Moment, 1983; The MacGregors, 1985; Hot Ice, 1987; Sacred Sins, 1987; Brazen Virtue, 1988; The O'Harleys, 1988; Sweet Revenge, 1989; Public Secrets, 1990; The Calhoun Women, 1991; Genuine Lies, 1991; Carnal Innocence, 1992; Honest Illusions, 1992; Divine Evil, 1992; Private Scandals, 1993; Hidden Riches, 1994; True Betrayals, 1995; Montana Sky, 1996. As J D Robb: glory in death, 1995; Naked in Death, 1995; Immortal in Death, 1996. Honours: Romance Writers of America, Golden Medallions, 1982, 1983, 1984, 1986; Hall of Fame, 1986, and Rita Award, 1990; Waldenbooks Awards, 1986, 1987, 1989, 1990, 1991; B Dalton Awards, 1990, 1991; RITA Awards, 1993, 1994, 1995. Memberships: Romance Writers of America; Mystery Writers of America; Novelists Inc; Crime Writers; Sisters-in-Crime. Address: c/o Writers House, 21 West 26th Street, New York, NY 10010, USA.

ROBERTS Willo Davis, b. 29 May 1928, Grand Rapids, Michigan, USA. Freelance Writer. m. David Roberts, 20 May 1949, 2 sons, 2 daughters. Appointment: Literary council Member, Pacific Northwest Writers Conference. Publications: 88 books including: Murder at Grand Bay, 1955; The Girl Who Wasn't There, 1957; Nurse Kay's Conquest, 1966; The Tarot Spell, 1970; King's Pawn, 1971; White Jade, 1975-; 8 volumes in The Black Pearl Series, 1978-80; The Search for Willie, 1980; A Long Time To Hate, 1982; Keating's Landing, 1984; The Annalise Experiment, 1985; To Share a Dream, 1986; Madawaska, 1988. Books for children and young adults: The View from the Cherry Tree, 1975; Don't Hurt Laurie, 1977; The Girl with the Silver Eyes, 1980; The Pet Sitting Peril, 1983; Eddie and the Fairy God Puppy, 1984; Baby Sitting is a Dangerous Job, 1985; The Magic Book, 1986; Sugar Isn't Everything, 1987; Megan's Island, 1988; Nightmare, 1989; Scared Stiff, 1991; Dark Secrets, 1991; Twisted summer, 1996. Honours: Mark Twain Award, 1980; Pacific Northwest Writers Achievement Award, 1986; Edgar Allan Poe Award, 1988, 1995; Florida Sunshine State Award, 1994. Memberships: Mystery Writers of America; Society of Children's Book Writers; Seattle Freelancers; Pacific Northwest Writers Conference. Address: 12020 West Engebretson Road, Granite Falls, WA 98252, USA.

ROBERTSON Barbara, b. 20 July 1931, Toronto, Ontario, Canada. Writer. Education: BA, University of Toronto, 1953; MA, Queen's University of Kingston, 1957. Publications: The Wind Has Wings (editor, with M A Downie), 1968, enlarged edition as The New Wind Has Wings, 1984; Wilfrid Laurier: The Great Conciliator, 1971, new edition, 1991; The Well-Filled Cupboard (with M A Downie), 1987; Doctor Dwarf and Other Poems for Children (editor, with M A Downie), 1990; Ottawa at War: The Grant Dexter Memoranda 1939-1945, (co-editor F W Gibson), 1994. Contributions to: Periodicals. Address: 52 Florence Street, Kingston, Ontario K7M 1Y6, Canada.

ROBERTSON Charles, b. 22 Oct 1940, Glasgow, Scotland. Parish Minister; Chaplain to Her Majesty the Queen in Scotland, (Clergyman). m. 30 July 1965, 1 son, 2 daughters. Education: MA,

Edinburgh University, 1964. Publications: Editor, contributor: Common Order; Saint Margaret Queen of Scotland and her Chapel; Singing the Faith; Worshipping Together; Hymns for a Day; Songs of God's People. Contributions to: Record of Church Service Society; Scottish Journal of Theology (reviewer). Memberships: Chairman, Joint Liturgical Group; Secretary, Panel on Worship. Address: Manse of Canongate, Edinburgh EH8 8BR, Scotland.

ROBERTSON Denise, b. 9 June 1933, Sunderland, England. Writer; Broadcaster. m. (1) Alexander Robertson, 19 Mar 1960, (2) John Tomlin, 3 Nov 1973, 5 sons. Publications: Year of Winter, 1986; Land of Lost Content, 1987; Blue Remembered Hills, 1987; Second Wife, 1988; None to Make You Cry, 1989; Remember the Moment, 1990. Contributions to: Numerous. Honour: Constable Fiction Trophy, 1985. Address: 9 Springfield Crescent, Seaham, County Durham, England.

ROBERTSON James (Irvin Jr), b. 18 July 1930, Danville, Virginia, USA. Professor of History. m. Elizabeth Green, 1 June 1952, 2 sons, 1 daughters. Education: BA, Randolph-Macon College, 1954; MA, 1955, PhD, 1959, Emory University; LittD, Randolph-Macon College, 1980. Appointments: Associate Professor of History, University of Montana, 1965-67; Professor, Head, History Department, 1967-75, C P Miles Professor of History, 1976-, Virginia Polytechnic Institute and State University; C P Miles Professor of History, 1976-92; Alumni Distinguished Professor in History, 1992-. Publications: The Stonewall Brigade, 1963; The Civil War Letters of General Robert McAllister, 1965; Recollections of a Maryland Confederate Soldier, 1975; Four Years in the Stonewall Brigade, 1978; The 4th Virginia Infantry, 1980; Civil War Sites in Virginia: A Tour-Guide, 1982; The 18th Virginia Infantry, 1983; Tenting Tonight: The Soldiers' View, 1984; General A P Hill, 1987; Soldiers Blue and Gray, 1988; Civil War! American Becomes One Nation, 1992; Jackson and Lee: Legends in Gray (with Mort Kunstler), 1995. Contributions to: More than 150 articles in historical journals and history magazines; Regular appearances in Civil War programmes on television and radio. Honours: Freeman-Nevins Award, 1981; Bruce Catton Award, 1983; William E Wine Award for Teaching Excellence, 1983; A P Andrews Memorial Award, 1985; James Robertson Award of Achievement, 1985; Jefferson Davis Medal, United Daughters of the Confederacy. Memberships: Virginia Historical Society; Organization of American Historians; Southern Historical Association; Confederate Memorial Society. Address: Department of History, Virginia Polytechnic Institute and State University, Blacksburg, VA 24061, USA.

ROBERTSON Thomas. See: GILES Frank.

ROBINETTE Joseph Allen, b. 8 Feb 1939, Rockwood, Tennessee, USA. College Professor; Playwright. m. Helen M Seitz, 27 Aug 1965, 4 sons, 1 daughter. Education: BA, Carson-Newman College, 1960; MA, 1966, PhD. 1972, Southern Illinois University. Publications: The Fabulous Fable Factory, 1975; Once Upon a Shoe (play), 1979; Legend of the Sun Child (musical), 1982; Charlotte's Web (dramatization), 1983; Charlotte's Web (musical with Charles Strouse), 1989; Anne of Green Gables (dramatization), 1989; The Lion, the Witch and the Wardrobe (dramatization), 1989; The Trial of Goldilocks (operetta), 1990; Dorothy Meets Alice (musical), 1991; Stuart Little (dramatization), 1992; The Trumpet of the Swan (dramatization), 1993; The Adventures of Beatrix Potter and Her Friends (musical), 1994; The Littlest Angel (musical), 1994; The Jungle Book (dramatization), 1995. Contributions to: Children's Theatre News; Opera For Youth News. Honour: Charlotte Chorpenning Cup, National Children's Playwriting Award, 1976. Memberships: American Society of Composers, Authors and Publishers; American Association for Theatre in Education; Opera for Youth. Address: Department of Theatre and Dance, Rowan College, Glassboro, NJ 08028, USA.

ROBINS Patricia. See: CLARK Patricia Denise.

ROBINSON David Bradford, b. 14 Apr 1937, Richmond, Virgina, USA. Poet; Author. Education: HS, 1955; BS, 1959; MS, Hons, 1961; AA, 1970; BA, 1973; DD, 1977; DSc, 1978; PhD, 1979; MA, 1995; JD, 1995. Publications: Characteristics of Cesium, 1978; Lyric Treasure One, 1978; Collected Poems, 1987; Praise the Wilderness, Nineteen Original New Poems to Survival, 1990. Contributions to: From the Barren Sky; The School Musician, 1980; For the Aesthete, 1981; A Blast for Wagner, 1981;Highflying Eagle; Simcoe Review, 1982; The Fairy Flower; Seeds of Light, 1986. Honours: Golden Poet Award, 1987; Pegasus Time Capsule Award, 1991; Albert Einstein

Medal, 1994; World Lifetime Achievement Award, 1996. Membership: International Society of Poets. Address: PO Box 1414, Miami Shores, FL 33153-1414, USA.

ROBINSON David Julien, b. 6 Aug 1930. Film Critic. Education: BA Hons, King's College, Cambridge. Appointments: Associate Editor, Sight and Sound, Editor, Monthly Film Bulletin, 1956-58; Programme Director, NFT, 1959; Film Critic, Financial Times, 1959-74, The Times, 1974-93; Editor, Contrast, 1962-63. Publications: Hollywood in the Twenties, 1969; Buster Keaton, 1969; The Great Funnies, 1972; World Cinema, 1973, 2nd edition, 1980 (US edition as The History of World Cinema, 1974, 1980); Chaplin: The Mirror of Opinion, 1983; Chaplin: His Life and Art, 1985; Music of the Shadows, 1990; Masterpieces of Animation, 1991; Richard Attenborough, 1992; Georges Méliès, 1993; Lantern Images: Iconography of the Magic Lantern, 1993. Contributions to: Times; Guardian; Australian; Sight and Sound. Honours: Roger Machin Prize, 1985; Commise Prize, 1987-88; Diego Fabbri Prize, 1989; Fellini Prize, 1991. Address: 96-100 New Cavendish Street, London W1M 7FA, England.

ROBINSON Ian, b, 1 July 1934, Manchester, England. Writer; Poet. m. Adelheid Armbrüster, 21 Dec 1959, 1 son, 1 daughter. Education: MA, Oriel College, Oxford, 1955-58. Appointments: Editor, Oasis Magazine, 1969-; Publisher, Oasis Books, 1970-; Deputy Chairman, Poetry Society of Great Britain, 1977-78. Publications: Poetry: Accidents, 1974: Three, 1978; Short Stories, 1979; Maida Vale Elegies, 1983; Journal, 1987. Fiction: Obsequies, 1979; Fugitive Aromas, 1979; Blown Footage, 1980; Dissolving Views, 1986. Graphic Book: The Glacier in the Cupboard, 1995. Contributions to: Prism International, Vancouver; Canadian Fiction Magazine; London Magazine; Prospice; Blue Cage; Poesie Europe, Germany; Osiris, USA; 200 others. Memberships: Association of Little Presses: Society of Fulham Artists. Address: 12 Stevenage Road, London SW6 6ES, England.

ROBINSON Jancis Mary, b. 22 Apr 1950, Carlisle, Cumbria, England. Writer; Broadcaster. m. Nicholas Laurence Lander, 1981, 1 son, 2 daughters. Education: MA, St Anne's College, Oxford, 1971. Appointments: Editor, Wine and Spirit, 1976-80, Which Wine Guide, 1980-82; Founder-Editor, Drinker's Digest, later Which Wine? Monthly, 1977-82; Freelance Radio and Television Broadcaster, 1983-; Wine Correspondent, Sunday Times, 1987-88, Evening Standard, 1987-88; Contributor, 1989-, Financial Times. Publications: The Wine Book, 1979, revised edition, 1983; The Great Wine Book, 1981; Masterglass, 1983, revised edition, 1987; How to Choose and Enjoy Wine, 1984; Vines, Grapes and Wines, 1986; Food and Wine Adventures, 1987; The Demon Drink, 1988; Vintage Timecharts, 1989; The Oxford Companion of Wine (editor), 1994; Jancis Robinson's Wine Course, 1995; Jancis Robinson's Guide to White Grapes, 1996; Confessions of a Wine Lover, 1997. Contributions to: Periodicals. Honours: Glenfiddich Trophy, 1983, 1996; Master of Wine, 1984; Andre Simon Memorial Prizes, Wine Guild Awards, Clicquot Book of the Year, 1986, 1996; Honorary Doctorate, Open University, 1997. Address: c/o A P Watt, 20 John Street, London WC1N 2DR, England.

ROBINSON Jeffrey, b. 19 Oct 1945, New York, New York, USA. Author. m. Aline Benayoun, 27 Mar 1985, 1 son, 1 daughter. Education: BS, Temple University, Philadelphia, Pennsylvania. Publications: Bette Davis, Her Stage and Film Career, 1983; Teamwork, 1984; The Risk Takers, 1985; Pietrov and Other Games (fiction), 1985; Minus Millionaires, 1986; The Ginger Jar (fiction), 1986; Yamani: The Inside Story, 1988; Rainier and Grace, 1989; The Risk Takers: Five Years On, 1990; The End of the American Century, 1992; The Laundrymen, 1994; Bardot: Two Lives, 1994; The Margin of the Bulls (fiction), 1995. Contributions to: More than 700 articles and short stories published in major magazines and journals worldwide. Honours: Overseas Press Club, 1984; Benedictine After Dinner Speaker of the Year, 1990. Membership: PEN. Address: c/o Mildred Marmur Associates Ltd., 2005 Palmer Avenue, Larchmont, NY 10538, USA.

ROBINSON Kim Stanley, b. 23 Mar 1952, Waukegan, Illinois, USA. Author. Education: BA, 1974, PhD, 1982, University of California at San Diego; MA, Boston University, 1975. Appointments: Visiting Lecturer, University of California at San Diego, 1982, 1985, University of California at Davis, 1982-84, 1985. Publications: The Novels of Philip K Dick, 1984; The Wild Shore, 1984; Icehenge, 1985; The Memory of Whiteness, 1985; The Planet on the Table, 1986; The Gold Coast, 1989; Green Mars, Red Mars, 1994. Contributions to:

Periodicals. Address: 17811 Romelle Avenue, Santa Ana, CA 92705, USA.

ROBINSON Robert Henry, b. 17 Dec 1927, Liverpool, England. Writer; Broadcaster. m. Josephine Mary Richard, 1958. 1 son, 2 daughters. Education: MA, Exeter College, Oxford. Publications: Landscape With Dead Dons, 1956; Inside Robert Robinson, 1965; The Conspiracy, 1968; The Dog Chairman, 1982; Everyman Book of Light Verse (editor), 1984; Bad Dreams, 1989; Prescriptions of a Pox Doctor's Clerk, 1991; Skip All That: Memoirs, 1996. Contributions to: Newspapers, radio and television. Address: 16 Cheyne Row, London SW3, England.

ROBINSON Roland (Edward), b. 1912, British. Poet; Writer. Appointments: Member, Kirsova Ballet, 1944-47; Ballet Critic, 1956-66, Book Reviewer, Sydney Morning Herald; Editor, Poetry Magazine, Sydney; President, Poetry Society of Australia. Publications: Beyond the Grass-Tree Spears (verse), 1944; Language of the Sand, 1948; Legend and Dreaming: Legends of the Dream-Time of the Australian Aborigines, 1952; Tumult of the Swans, 1953; The Feathered Serpent: The Mythological Genesis and Recreative Ritual of the Aboriginal Tribes of the Northern Territory of Australia, 1956; Black-Feller, White-Feller, 1958; Deep Well, 1962; The Man Who Sold His Dreaming, 1965; Grendel, 1967; The Australian Aborigine in Colour, Wandjina: Children of the Dreamtime: Aboriginal Myths and Legends, 1968; Selected Poems, 1971; The Drift of Things 1914-1952, 1973; The Shift of Sands 1952-62, 1976; A Letter to Joan, 1978; Selected Poems, 1984; Selected Poems, 1989; The Nearest the White Man Gets, 1989. Address: 10 Old Main Street, Belmont North, New South Wales 2280, Australia.

ROBINSON Sheila Mary, (Sheila Radley, Hester Rowan), b. 18 Nov 1928, Cogenhoe, Northamptonshire, England. Writer. Education: BA, University of London. Publications: Death and the Maiden, 1978; The Chief Inspector's Daughter, 1981; A Talent for Destruction, 1982; Blood on the Happy Highway, 1983; Fate Worse Than Death, 1985. Address: c/o Curtis Brown Ltd., Haymarket House, 28-29 Haymarket, London SW1Y 4SP, England.

ROBINSON Spider, b. 24 Nov 1948, New York, New York, USA. Writer. Education: BA, State University of New York at Stony Brook, 1972. Publications: Telempath, 1976; Callahan's Crossing Saloon, 1977; Stardance (with Jeanne Robinson), 1979; Antinomy, 1980; Time Travelers Strictly Cash, 1981; Mindkiller, 1982; Melancholy Elephants, 1984; Night of Power, 1985; Callahan's Secret, 1986; Time Pressure, 1987; Callahan and Company, 1987; Lady Slings the Booze, 1993; Off the Wall at Callahan's, 1994. Address: c/o Ace Books, 200 Madison Avenue, New York, NY 10016, USA.

ROBLES Harold Edgar, b. 8 Oct 1948, Paramaribo, Surinam. President, Founder, Albert Schweitzer Institute for the Humanities. m. Ruth D'Agostino, 2 sons, 1 daughter. Education: BA, MBA, University of Rotterdam. Appointments: Secretary-General, International Albert Schweitzer Association, 1975-81; Founder, President, Albert Schweitzer Center, The Netherlands, 1973-81; Founder, President, Albert Schweitzer Institute for the Humanities, Wallingford. Publications: Bosch & Keuning (for adults), 1975; J H Kok (for children), 1978; Reverence for Life: The Words of Albert Schweitzer (for adults), 1993;An Adventurer of Humanity (for children), 1994; Eerbied voor het Leven (for adults), 1994. Contributions to: Journals in USA and Holland. Honours: Medal, City of Krakow, Poland, 1978; Swedish Albert Schweitzer Award, 1980; Pro Merito Order (Gold), Austria, 1986; United Way Gold Award, 1987; Ehrenzeichen für Wissenschaft und Kunst, Austria, 1988; Knight Commander, Order of Saint Andrew, England, 1988; Cordon Bleu du Saint-Esprit, Landau, Germany, 1990; Tiffany Apple of New York, 1993; Special Citation, State of Connecticut, 1994; Commendation, US House of Representatives, 1995; DHL, Albertus Magnus College, 1996. Memberships: The War and Peace Foundation; Genesis, Georgian Foundation for Health Services, Tbilisi, Georgia; Foundation of Friends for the Center of Cerebral Palsy and Child Development, Belgrade. Address: c/o Albert Schweitzer Institute for the Humanities, PO Box 550, Wallingford, CT 06492, USA.

ROCHARD Henri. See: CHARLIER Roger Henri.

ROCHE Billy, (William Michael Roche), b. 11 Jan 1949, Wexford, Ireland. Playwright; Author. Education: Christian Brothers Secondary School, 1966. Appointments: Singer, the Roach Band,

1975-80; Playwright-in-Residence, Bush Theatre, London, 1988. Publications: Plays: A Handful of Stars, 1987; Amphibians, 1987; Poor Beast in the Rain, 1989; Belry, 1991; The Cavalcaders, 1993. Novel: Tumbling Down, 1986; Film Script: Trojan Eddie, 1997. Honours: London Theatre Fringe Award, 1992; Time Out Award, 1992. Address: c/o Leah Schmidt, The Agency, 24 Pottery Lane, Holland Park, London W11 4LZ, England.

ROCHE George Charles III, b. 16 May 1935, Denver, Colorado, USA. College President. m. June Bernard, 2 sons, 2 daughters. Education: BS, Regis College, CO, 1956; MA, 1961, PhD, 1965, University of Colorado. Appointment: President, Hillsdale College, Michigan. Publications: The Bewildered Society, 1972; Going Home, 1986; A World Without Heroes: A Modern Tragedy, 1987; A Reason for Living, 1989; One by One, 1990. Contributions to: Newspapers and magazines. Honour: Freedom Leadership Award, Freedoms Foundation, 1972. Memberships: Mont Pelerin Society; Philadelphia Society; American Association of Presidents of Independent Colleges and Universities. Address: Hillsdale College, Hillsdale, MI 49242, USA.

ROCHE Sylviane, b. 10 June 1949, Paris, France. Teacher of French Literature. m. Christophe Calame, 1 Feb 1985, 1 son, 1 daughter. Education: MA, Lausanne University, Switzerland. Appointments: Director and Editor, Ecriture literary review. Publications: Les Passantes, 1987; Le Salon Pompadour, 1990; Septembre, 1992; Maroussia va á l'école, 1993. Contributions to: Numerous. Honours: Prix du Jubilé UBS, 1989; Prix de la commission francophone du canton de Berne. Membership: Société Suisse des écrivains. Address: 53 avenue de Rumine, 1005 Lausanne, Switzerland.

ROCHE William Michael. See: **ROCHE Billy.**

ROCKWELL John (Sargent), b. 16 Sept 1940, Washington, District of Columbia, USA. Music Critic. Education: BA, Harvard University, 1962; Graduate Studies, University of Munich, 1962-63; MA, 1964, PhD, 1972, University of California at Berkeley. Appointments: West Coast Correspondent, Opera News, 1968-72; Music and Dance Critic, Oakland Tribune, California, 1969; Assistant Music and Dance Critic, Los Angeles Times, 1970-72; Music Critic, New York Times, 1974; Lecturer in Cultural History, Princeton University, 1977-79; Lecturer in Music, Brooklyn College of the City University of New York, 1980; Adviser, The New Grove Dictionary of American Music, 1986. Publications: Robert Wilson: A Theater of Images (with Robert Stearns), 1980; All American Music: Composition in the Late Twentieth Century, 1983; Sinatra: An American Classic, 1984. Contributions to: Books and periodicals. Honours: German Academic Exchange Fellowship, 1962-63; Woodrow Wilson Fellowship, 1963-64; National Book Critics Circle Award Nomination, 1983. Memberships: Music Critics Association, treasurer, 1977-81; Phi Beta Kappa. Address: c/o New York Times, 229 West 43rd Street, New York, NY 10036, USA.

RODDY Lee, b. 22 Aug 1921, Marion County, Illinois, USA. Writer. m. Cicely Price, 17 Oct 1947, 1 son, 1 daughter. Education: AA, Los Angeles City College, 1945. Publications: The Life and Times of Grizzly Adams, 1977; The Lincoln Conspiracy, 1977; Jesus, 1979; Ghost Dog of Stoney Ridge, 1985; Dooger, Grasshopper Hound, 1985; The City Bear's Adventures, 1985; The Hair Pulling Bear Dog, 1985; Secret of the Shark Pit, 1988; Secret of the Sunken Sub, 1989; The Overland Escape, 1989; The Desperate Search, 1989; Danger on Thunder Mountain, 1990; Secret of the Howland Cave, 1990; The Flaming Trap, 1990; Mystery of the Phantom Gold, 1991; The Gold Train Bandits, 1992. Other: Several books made into films and television programmes. Honours: Various awards and book club selections. Memberships: Authors Guild of America; Authors League; National Society of Children's Book Writers. Address: PO Box 700, Penn Valley, CA 95946, USA.

RODEFER Stephen, (Jean Calais), b. 20 Nov 1940, Bellaire, Ohio, USA. Writer; Lecturer. 3 sons. Education: BA, Amherst College, 1963; MA, State University of New York, Buffalo, 1967; MA, San Francisco State University, 1981. Appointments: Teaching Fellow, 1963-66, Instructor, 1966-67, State University of New York, Buffalo; Assistant Professor, Co-Director of Writing Programme, University of New Mexico, 1967-71; Editor, Duende Press, Placitas, New Mexico, 1972-75; Language Arts Specialist, Berkeley Unified School District, California, 1976-81; Lecturer, San Francisco State University, California, 1981-85, University of California at Berkeley, 1990-;

Curator, Archive for New Poetry, 1985-87, Lecturer in Poetry, 1985-89, University of California, San Diego. Publications: The Knife, 1965; Villon (as Jean Calais), 1976; One or Two Love Poems From the White World, 1976; The Bell Clerk's Tears Keep Flowing, 1978; Plane Debris, 1981; Four Lectures, 1982; Oriflamme Day (with Benjamin Friedlander), 1984; Safety (translations of Sappho and the Greek Anthology), 1985; Emergency Measures, 1987. Contributions to: Sulfur; Conjunctions; Temblor; Oblek; Writing; This; Sur. Honours: Faculty Fellowship for Poetry, Research Foundation, State University of New York, Buffalo, 1967; Co-winner, Annual Book Award for Four Lectures, American Poetry Centre, San Francisco, 1983; Public Arts Council Grant, 1987; Fund for Poetry Award, New York, 1988. Memberships: American Literary Translators Association; American Association of University Professors; Poets Theatre. Address: 6434 Raymond Street, Oakland, CA 94611, USA.

RODGERS Carolyn Marie, b. 14 Dec 1942, Chicago, Illinois, USA. Professor; Writer; Poet; Editor. Education: BA, Roosevelt University, 1981; MA, University of Chicago, 1983. Appointments: Professor of Afro-American Literature, 1969, Lecturer in English and Co-Ordinator of Poetry Workshop, 1970, Columbia College; Poet-in-Residence, University of Washington, 1970, Indiana University, 1974, Roosevelt University, 1983; Founder-Editor, Eden Press, 1991, Rare Form newsletter, 1994-. Publications: Paper Soul, 1968; Songs of a Blackbird, 1970; How I Got Ovah, 1976; The Heart as Evergreen, 1978; Translation, 1980; A Little Lower Than the Angels, 1984; Morning Glory, 1989; The Religious Poetry of Carolyn M Rodgers, 1993; Daughters of Africa, 1993; We're Only Human, 1994; A Train Called Judah, 1996; Chosen to Believe, 1996. Contributions to: Journals and magazines. Honours: National Endowment for the Arts Award, 1970; Conrad Kent Rivers Award, 1970; Society of Midland Authors Award, 1970; Carnegie Writer's Grant, 1980; Television Gospel Tribute, 1982; PEN Grant, 1987. Memberships: Gwendolyn Brooks Writing Workshop; Organization of Black American Culture. Address: PO Box 804271, Chicago, IL 60680, USA.

RODGERS Daniel Tracy, b. 29 Sept 1942, Darby, Pennsylvania, USA. Professor of History. m. Irene Wylie Rodgers, Dec 1971, 2 sons. Education: AB-BSc, Engineering, Brown University, 1965; PhD, History, Yale University, 1973. Appointment: Professor of History, Princeton University. Publications: The Work Ethic in Industrial America 1850-1920, 1978; Contested Truths: Keywords in American Politics since Independence, 1987. Contributions to: Professional journals. Reviews in American History; Journal of American History. Honour: Frederick Jackson Turner Award, Organization of American Historians, 1978. Address: Department of History, Princeton University, Princeton, NJ 08544, USA.

RODRIGUES Santan Rosario, b. 23 Sept 1948, Goa. Public Relations Expert; Poet; Editor. m. Patricia Rodrigues, 23 Sept 1983. Education: MA, English Literature, University of Bombay. Appointments: Founder-Editor, Kavi India Poetry Quarterly, 1976-83; Poetry Editor, Imprint, 1977-78, Gomanta Times, 1989-90. Publications: I Exist, 1976; 3 Poets, 1978; The Householder Yogi, 1982. Contributions to: Anthologies and periodicals. Memberships: Asiatic Society; Association of Business Communicators of India; Bombay English Association; PEN India. Address: 7 Gautam Apts, 45-624 Kastur Park, Shimpoli Road, Borivali, Bombay 400092, India.

RODRIGUEZ Judith, b. 13 Feb 1936, Perth, Western Australia. Poet; Dramatist; Librettist; Editor; Lecturer. m. (1) Fabio Rodriguez, 1964, div 1981, 4 children, (2) Thomas Shapcott, 1982. Education: BA, University of Queensland, Brisbane, 1957; MA, Girton College, Cambridge, 1962; Certificate of Education, University of London, 1968. Appointments: Lecturer in External Studies, University of Queensland, Brisbane, 1959-60; Lecturer in English, Philippa Fawcett College of Education, London, 1962-63; University of the West Indies, Kingston, Jamaica, 1963-65; Teacher of English as a Foreign Language, St Giles School of English, London, 1965-66; Lecturer in English, St Mary's College of Education, Twickenham, 1966-68; Lecturer, 1969-75, Senior Lecturer in English, 1977-85, La Trobe University, Bundoora, Australia; Writer-in-Residence, Rollins College, Florida, 1986; Lecturer in English, Macarthur Institute of Higher Education, Milperra, Sydney, 1987-88, Royal Melbourne Institute of Technology, 1988-89, Victoria College, 1989-92; Poetry Series Editor, Penguin Books Australia; Senior Lecturer, Deakin University, 1993-. Publications: Poetry: Four Poets, 1962; Nu-Plastik Fanfare Red, 1973 and Other Poems, 1973; Water Life, 1976; Shadow on Glass, 1978; Arapede, 1979; Mudcrab at Gambaro's, 1980; Witch Heart, 1982; Floridian Poems, 1986; The

House by Water: Selected and New Poems, 1988; The Cold, 1992. Play: Poor Johanna (with Robyn Archer), 1994. Opera Libretto: Lindy, 1994. Editor: Mrs Noah and the Minoan Queen, 1982; Poems Selected from the Australian's 20th Anniversary Competition (with Andrew Taylor), 1985; Modern Swedish Poetry (with Thomas Shapcott), 1985; Collected Poems of Jennifer Rankin, 1990. Contributions to: Numerous publications. Honours: Arts Council of Australia Fellowships, 1974, 1978, 1983; Government of South Australia Biennial Prize for Literature, 1978; International PEN Peter Stuyvesant Prize for Poetry, 1981; Order of Australia, 1994; Christopher Brennan Award, Fellowship of Australian Writers, 1994. Memberships: Association for the Study of Australian Literature; Australian Society of Authors; International PEN; South Pacific Association for Commonwealth Language and Literature Studies; Melbourne PEN Centre; Victorian Writer's Centre. Literary Agent: Australian Literary Management, 2A Armstrong Street, Middle Park, Victoria 3206. Address: PO Box 231, Mont Albert, Victoria 3127, Australia.

RODRIGUEZ Lazara Ana, b. 17 Apr 1938, Bejucal, Havana, Cuba. Doctor in Medicine. Education: University of Havana School of Medicine, 1958-61; Medical Degree, CETEC University, Dominican Republic, 1983; Medical Degree, USA, 1986. Publications: Diary of a Survivor: Nineteen Years in a Cuban Women's Prison, 1995; Unpublished poems and short stories. Literary Agent: Jane Dystel Literary Management, New York, New York, USA. Address: 47 Alhambra Circle, Apt 4, Coral Gables, Florida 33134, USA.

RODWAY Anne. See: BRENNAN Patricia Winifred.

ROEBUCK Derek, b. 22 Jan 1935, Stalybridge, England. Professor of Comparative Law; Writer. m. Susanna Leonie Hoe, 18 Aug 1981, 2 sons, 1 daughter. Education: MA (Oxon), 1960; MCom, Victoria University of Wellington, 1965. Publications: Author of 34 books on law and legal history, translated into ten languages, including: Credit and Security in Asia, 10 volumes (with D E Allan and M E Hiscock), 1973-80; Whores of War: Mercenaries Today (with Wilfred Burchett), 1976; The Background of the Common Law, 2nd edition, 1990; Hong Kong Digest of Contract, 1995; Hong Kong Digest of Criminal Law, 3 volumes, 1995-96; Hong Kong Digest of Criminal Procedure, 3 volumes, 1996-97. Contributions to: Over 30 articles on law and language. Membership: Selden Society. Address: 20A Plantation Road, Oxford OX2 6JD, England.

ROECKER William Alan, b. 17 Jan 1942, Madison, Wisconsin, USA. Writer; Poet. m. Debbie Sue Huntsman, 31 Dec 1985. Education: BS, 1966, MFA, 1967, University of Oregon. Appointments: Assistant Editor, Northwest Review, 1967; Instructor, Associate Professor, English, University of Arizona, 1968-74; Editor, Windsport Magazine, 1981-82; Saltwater Editor, Today's Fishermen, 1985, Fishing and Hunting News, 1993; Associate Editor, South Coast Sportfishing, 1987; Senior Editor, South Coast Sportfishing, 1988; Senior Managing Editor, California Angler Magazine, 1992. Publications: Willamette (poems), 1970; Stories that Count, 1971; You Know Me (poems), 1972; Closer to the Country (poems), 1976; Standup Fishing: Saltwater Methods, Tackle & Techniques, 1990. Contributions to: Numerous journals and magazines. Honours: Haycox Award, 1966; Neubergr Award, 1967; Runner Up, Yale Younger Poets, 1971; National Endowment for the Arts Award, 1973; Gray Prize, Hang Gliding Journalism, 1984. Memberships: Outdoor Writers Association of America; Outdoor Writers Association of California. Address: PO Box 586071, Oceanside, CA 92058, USA.

ROGERS Floyd. See: SPENCE William (John Duncan).

ROGERS Ingrid, b. 3 May 1951, Rinteln, Germany. Pastor; Teacher; Writer. m. H Kendall Rogers, 9 June 1972, 1 son, 1 daughter. Education: DUEL, Sorbonne Nouvelle, Paris, France, 1971; Oxford University, England, 1972-73; Staatsexamen, 1974, PhD, 1976, Philipps University, Marburg; Doctor of Ministry Degree, Bethany Theological Seminary, 1988. Publications: Tennessee Williams: A Moralist's Answer to the Perils of Life, 1976; Peace Be Unto You, 1983; Swords into Plowshares, 1983; In Search of Refuge, 1984; Glimpses of Clima, 1989. Honours: Christopher Book Award, 1985; Angel Award of Excellence, 1985; Evangelische Studienwerk Villigst Fellowships, 1971-74, 1974-76. Address: Manchester College, Box 64, North Manchester, IN 46962, USA.

ROGERS Jane Rosalind, b. 21 July 1952, London, England. Writer. 1 son, 1 daughter. Education: BA Honours, English Literature,

New Hall, Cambridge, 1974; Postgraduate Certificate in Education, Leicester University, 1976. Appointments: Writer-in-Residence, Northern College, Barnsley, South Yorkshire, 1985-86; Sheffield Polytechnic, 1987-88; Judith E Wilson Fellow, Cambridge, 1991. Publications: Separate Tracks, 1983; Her Living Image, 1984; The Ice is Singing, 1987; Mr Wroe's Virgins, 1991; Promised Lands, 1995. Screenplay: Dawn and the Candidate, 1989. Other: Mr Wroe's Virgins (BBC serial), 1993. Contributions to: Magazines. Honours: North West Arts Writers Bursary, 1985; Somerset Maugham Award, 1985; Samuel Beckett Award, 1990; Writers' Guild Award, Best Fiction Book, for Promised Lands, 1996. Memberships: Royal Society of Literature, Fellow; Society of Authors. Address: c/o Pat Kavanagh, The Peters, Fraser & Dunlop Group Ltd, 503/4 The Chambers, Chelsea Harbour, London SW10 0XF, England.

ROGERS Linda (Hall), b. 10 Oct 1944, Port Alice, British Columbia, Canada. Poet; Writer; Lecturer. m., 3 sons. Education: MA, English Literature, University of British Columbia. Appointments: Lecturer, University of British Columbia, University of Victoria, Camosun College, Malaspina College. Publications: Some Breath, 1978; Queens of the Next Hot Star, 1981; I Like to Make a Mess, 1985; I Think I Am Ugly, 1985; Witness, 1985; Setting the Hook, 1986; Singing Rib, 1987; Worm Sandwich, 1989; Brown Bag Blues, 1991; Letters from the Doll Hospital, 1992; Hard Candy, 1994; The Half Life of Radium, 1994; Frank Zapper and the Disappearing Teacher, 1994; Molly Brown is Not a Clown, 1996; Love in the Rainforest (selected poetry), 1996. Contributions to: Journals, magazines, and newspapers. Honours: Aya Poetry Prize, 1983; Canada Council Arts Awards, 1987, 1990; British Columbia Writers Poetry Prize, 1989; Cultural Services Award, 1990; Governor-General's Centennial Medal for Poetry and Performance, 1993; Stephen Leacock Award for Poetry, 1994; Dorothy Livesay Award for Poetry, 1995; Peoples Poetry Award, 1996. Memberships: Federation of British Columbia Writers, president; League of Canadian Poets; Society of Canadian Composers; Writers Union of Canada. Address: 1235 Styles Street, Victoria, British Columbia V9A 3Z6, Canada.

ROGERS Michael Alan, b. 29 Nov 1950, Santa Monica, California, USA. Novelist; Journalist. Education: BA, Creative Writing, Stanford University, 1972. Appointments: Associate Editor, Rolling Stone, 1972-76; Editor-at-Large, Outside, 1976-78; Visiting Lecturer in Fiction, University of California, 1981-82; Senior Writer, Newsweek, 1983-94; Contributing Editor, Newsweek, 1994-; Vice President, Post-Newsweek New Media, 1994-. Publications: Mindfogger, 1973; Do Not Worry about the Bear, 1978; Biohazard, 1979; Silicon Valley, 1983; Forbidden Sequence, 1989. Contributions to: Magazines. Honours: Distinguished Science Writing Award, American Association for the Advancement of Science, 1974; Computer Press Association, 1987; Software Publishers Association, 1991. Membership: Authors Guild. Address: c/o Newsweek, 388 Market Street, Suite 1650, San Francisco, CA 94111, USA.

ROGERS Pat, b. 17 Mar 1938, Beverley, Yorkshire, England. Professor; Writer. Education: BA, 1961, MA, 1965, PhD, 1968, Fitzwilliam College, Cambridge. Appointments: Fellow, Sidney Sussex College, Cambridge, 1964-69; Lecturer, King's College, University of London, 1969-73; Professor of English, University College of North Wales, Bangor, 1973-76, University of Bristol, 1977-86; DeBartolo Professor, Liberal Arts, University of South Florida, Tampa, 1986-. Publications: Daniel Defoe: A Tour Through Great Britain, 1971; Grub Street: Studies on a Sub-culture, 1980, revised edition as Hacks and Dunces, 1980; Daniel Defoe: The Critical Heritage (editor), 1972; The Augustan Vision: An Introduction to Pope, 1976; The Eighteenth Century (editor), 1978; Henry Fielding: A Biography, 1979; Swift: Complete Poems, Literature and Popular Culture in the Eighteenth Century (editor), 1983; Eighteenth-Century Encounters, 1985; The Oxford Illustrated History of English Literature (editor), 1987; The Economy of Arts in the 18th Century, 1989; An Outline of English Literature, 1992; Essays on Pope, 1993; Johnson and Boswell in Scotland, 1993. Address: Department of English, University of South Florida, Tampa, FL 33620, USA.

ROGERS Robert Frederick, b. 26 May 1930, San Diego, California, USA. Writer; Consultant. 3 sons. Education: BS, West Point; PhD, Georgetown. Publication: Destiny's Landfall: A History of Guam, 1995. Honour: Guam Magalahe Award, 1996. Address: PO Box 5364, UOG Station, Mangilao, Guam 96923, USA.

ROGERS Rosemary, (Marina Mayson), b. 7 Dec 1932, Sri Lanka. Writer. m. (1) Summa Navaratnam, 16 Jan 1953 div, 2 sons, 2 daughters, (2) Leroy Rogers, 1957, div 1964, (3) Christopher M Kadison, 1984. Education: BA, English, 1952. Publications: Sweet Savage Love, 1974; Wildest Heart, 1974; Dark Fires, 1975; Wicked Loving Lies, 1976; The Crowd Pleasers, 1978; The Insiders, 1979; Lost Love, Last Love, 1980; Love Play, 1981; Surrender to Love, 1982; The Wanton, 1984; Bound by Desire, 1988. Contributions to: Star Magazine; Good Housekeeping. Memberships: Writers Guild of America; Authors Guild. Address: 300 East 56th Street, Apt 27J, New York, NY 10022, USA.

ROGERS Samuel Shepard, (Sam Shepard), b. 5 Nov 1943, Fort Sheridan, Illinois, USA. Actor; Playwright. m. (1) O-Lan Johnson, 9 Nov 1969, div, 1 son, (2) domestic partner, Jessica Lange, 1 son, 1 daughter. Education: Mount Antonio Junior College. Publications: Five Plays, 1967; La Turista, 1968; Operation Sidewinder, 1970; The Unseen Hand and Other Plays, 1971; Mad Dog Blues and Other Plays, 1971; Hawk Moon, 1973; The Tooth of Crime, 1974; Geography of a Horse Dreamer, 1974; Action, 1975; The Unseen Hand, 1975; Angel City and Other Plays, 1976; Rolling Thunder Logbook, 1977; Buried Child and Other Plays, 1979; Four One-Act Plays, 1980; True West, 1981; Seven Plays, 1981; Motel Chronicles, 1982; Fool for Love and Other Plays, 1984; A Lie of the Mind, 1985; Curse of the Starving Class, 1990; States of Shock, 1992; Simpatico, 1994. Honours: Obie Awards, 1966, 1967, 1968, 1973, 1975, 1977, 1979, 1984; National Institute and American Academy of Arts and Letters Award, 1974; Pulitzer Prize in Drama, 1979; New York Drama Critics Circle Award, 1986. Membership: American Academy of Arts and Letters. Address: c/o Loris Berman, Little Theatre Building, 240 West 44th Street, New York, NY 10036, USA.

ROGGEMAN Willem Maurits, b. 9 July 1935, Brussels, Belgium. Journalist. m. 8 Jan 1975, 1 son, 1 daughter. Education: Economic Sciences, University of Ghent. Publications: Poetry: Rhapsody in Blue, 1958; Baudelaire Verliefd, 1964; Memoires, 1985; Een Leegte die Verdwijnt, 1985; Al Wie Omkÿkt is Gezien, 1988; De Uitvinding van de Tederheid, 1994. Novels: De Centauren, 1963; De Verbeelding, 1966; De belegering van een Luchtkasteel, 1990. Essays: Cesare Pavese, 1961; Beroepsgeheim, 1975. Contributions to: De Vlaamse Gids; Nieuw Vlaams Tijdschrift; Avenue; De Gids. Honours: Dirk Martensprize, 1963; Louis Paul Boon Prize, 1974; Prize, City of Brussels, 1975. Memberships: Vereniging van Vlaamse Letterkundigen; Flemish PEN Centre. Address: Luchtlaan 4, 1700 Dilbeek, Belgium.

ROHEN Edward, (Bruton Connors), b. 10 Feb 1931, Dowlais, South Wales. Poet; Writer. m. Elizabeth Jarrett, 4 Apr 1961, 1 daughter. Education: ATD, Cardiff College of Art, 1952. Appointments: Art Teacher, Ladysmith High, British Columbia, Canada, 1956-57; Head of Art, St Bonaventures, London, 1958-73, Ilford County High for Boys, Essex, 1973-82. Publications: Nightpriest, 1965; Bruised Concourse, 1973; Old Drunk Eyes Haiku, 1974; Scorpio Broadside 15, 1975; Poems/Poemas, 1976; A 109 Haiku and One Seppuku for Maria, 1987; Sonnets for Maria Marriage, 1988; Sonnets: Second Sequence for Maria, 1989. Contributions to: Anthologies and magazines. Memberships: Academician, Centro Cultural Literario e Artistico de o Jornal de Felgeiras, Portugal; Korean War Veterans Writers and Arts Society; Welsh Academy. Address: 57 Kinfauns Road, Goodmayes, Ilford, Essex IG3 9QH, England.

ROHRBACH Peter Thomas, (James Cody), b. 27 Feb 1926, New York, New York, USA. Writer. m. Sheila Sheehan, 21 Sept 1970, 1 daughter. Education: BA, MA, Catholic University of America. Publications: 17 books, including: Conversation with Christ, 1981; Stagecoach East, 1983; American Issue, 1985; The Largest Event: World War II, 1993; National Issue, 1994. Contributions to: Encyclopedias and periodicals. Memberships: Authors Guild of America; Poets, Playwrights, Editors, Essayists and Novelists; Washington Independent Writers. Address: 9609 Barkston Court, Potomac, MD 20850, USA.

ROKKAN Elizabeth Gwenllian Clough, b. 26 May 1925, Lampeter, Wales. University Lecturer; Translator. m. Stein Rokkan, 14 Oct 1950, 1 son, 1 daughter. Education: BA, 1945, MA, 1957, University of Wales. Appointment: Associate Professor, Department of English, University of Bergen, Norway, 1986-90. Publications: Translations: Cora Sandel: Alberta & Jacob, 1962; Alberta & Freedom, 1963; Alberta Alone, 1965; Tarjei Vesaas: The Ice Palace, 1966; The Great Cycle, 1968; The House in the Dark, 1976; The Silken Thread, 1982; View from the Window (short stories), 1986; Johan Borgen: The Scapegoat, 1993; Jostein Gaarder: The Christmas Mystery, 1996. Contributions to various publications. Honour: St Olavs Medal, Norway, 1995. Membership: Translators' Association/Society of Authors. Address: 7 Maynard Court, Fairwater Road, Llandaff, Cardiff CF5 2LS, Wales.

ROLAND Alex, b. 7 Apr 1944, Providence, Rhode Island, USA. Historian. m. 31 June 1979, 3 sons. Education: BS, US Naval Academy, 1966; MA, University of Hawaii, 1970; PhD, Duke University, 1974. Publications: Underwater Warfare in the Age of Sail, 1978; Model Research: The National Advisory Committee for Aeronautics, 1985; Men in Arms: A History of Warfare and its Interrelationships with Western Society, 1991. Memberships: Society of Military History; Society for the History of Technology; History of Science Society. Address: Department of History, Duke University, Durham, NC 27708, USA.

ROLLS Eric Charles, b. 25 Apr 1923, Grenfell, New South Wales, Australia. Author; Farmer. m. (1) Joan Stephenson, 27 Feb 1954, dec 1985, 2 sons, 1 daughters, (2) Elaine van Kempen, 1988. Publications: Sheaf Tosser, 1967; They All Ran Wild, 1969; Running Wild, 1973; The River, 1974; The Green Mosaic, 1977; Miss Strawberry Verses, 1978; A Million Wild Acres, 1981; Celebration of the Senses, 1984; Doorways: A Year of the Cumberdeen Diaries, 1989; Selected Poetry, 1990; Sojourners, 1993; Flowers and the Wide Sea, 1992; From Forest to Sea, 1993; Citizens, 1996. Contributions to: Bulletin; Overland; National Times; Age; Sydney Morning Herald; Independent Monthly; Sydney Morning Herald; Sun Herald; various others. Honours: David Myer Trust Award for Poetry, 1968; Captain Cook Bicentennial Award for Non-Fiction, 1970; John Franklin Award for Children's Books, 1974; Braille Book of the Year, 1975; The Age Book of the Year, 1981; Talking Book of the Year, 1982; Fellow, Australian Academy of the Humanities, 1985, 1986; Australian Creative Fellow, 1991; Order of Australia, 1991, 1992; Honorary Doctorate University of Canbenna, 1995. Memberships: Australian Society of Authors; National Book Council. Address: PO Box 2038, North Haven, New South Wales 2443, Australia.

ROLOFF Michael, b. 19 Dec 1937, Berlin, Germany (US citizen, 1952). Playwright. Education: BA, Haverford College, USA, 1958; MA, Stanford University, 1960. Appointments: Editor, Farrar, Straus and Giroux, 1966-70; Staff, Lantz-Donadio Literary Agency, 1970-72; Senior Editor, Continuum Books, 1972-75; Publicity Manager, Urizen Books, 1975-81. Publications: Screenplays: Feelings, 1982; Darlings and Monsters, 1983; Graduation Party, 1984. Plays: Wolves of Wyoming, 1985; Palombe Blue, 1985; Schizzohawk, 1986. Poetry: Headshots, 1984; It Won't Grow Back, 1985. Fiction: Darlings and Monsters Quartet, 4 titles, 1986-; Numerous translations from German. Address: Box 6754, Malibu, CA 90264, USA.

ROMAINE-DAVIS Ada, b. 7 June 1929, Cumberland, Maryland, USA. Nurse Educator; Medical Historian. m. John F Davis, 1 Aug 1953, 2 sons, 1 daughter. Education: Diploma, Kings County Hospital School of Nursing, Brooklyn, New York; BS, MS, PhD, University of Maryland, Baltimore and College Park; MD, College Park; Post-doctoral Studies, History of Science and Technology/Medicine, University of Maryland; Certified Adult Nurse Practitioner, American Nurses Certification Center. Appointment: Associate Professor, Johns Hopkins University School of Nursing, Baltimore. Publications: John Gibbon and His Heart-Lung Machine, 1992; Home Health Care: An Annotated Bibliography, 1992; Home Health Care: Brief Bibliography, 1994; Encyclopedia of Home Care for the Elderly (editor), 1995. Contributions to: American Journal of Nursing; Health Care Trends & Transitions; Nurse Practitioner; Journal of the Academy of Nurse Practitioners. Honour: Honorable Mention, American Medical Writers Association, 1993. Memberships: American Historical Association; Society for the History of Medicine; National Organization of Nurse Practitioner Faculties; American Academy of Nurse Practitioners; Sigma Theta Tau. Address: 6400 Wilmett Road, Bethesda, MD 20817, USA.

ROMBOTIS Anastasios, (Tasos Korfis), b. 12 Oct 1929, Corfu, Greece. Vice-Admiral (retired); Writer; Poet. m. Helen Moniakis, 5 Feb 1959, 1 son, 1 daughter. Education: Various professional schools and academies, Greece and in USA; NATO Defence College, Rome, 1971-72. Appointments: Director, Prosperos book publishers, 1973 ; Director, Anacyclisis literary magazine, 1985-90. Publications: Poetry:

Diary 1, 1963; Diary 2, 1964; Diary 3, 1968; Diarios, 1971; Handiwork, 1977; Poems, 1983; Pafsilipa, 1987; 153 Graffiti, 1992. Prose: Journey without Polar Star, 1953; A Desert House, 1973; Knowledge of the Father, 1984. Essays: The Poet Romos Filyras, 1974; The Poet Nikos Kavadias, 1978; Glances at the Poets 1920-1940, 1978; Deposits in Short Terms, 1982; The Poet Napoleon Lapathiotis, 1985; Glances at the Literature 1920-1940, 1991. Translations: Lustra (Ezra Pound), 1977; Poems (William Carlos Williams), 1979; Poems (Ezra Pound), 1981. Other: Coexistences, 1982; The Writer Stratis Doukas 1895-1936 (biography), 1988. Contributions to: Diagenios, 1958-80; Numerous poems, prose pieces and essays to Greek magazines. Honours: Several awards. Membership: Society of Writers. Address: Alkiviadou 9, 10439 Athens, Greece.

ROMER Stephen Charles Mark, b. 20 Aug 1957, Bishops Stortford, Hertfordshire, England. University Lecturer; Poet. m. Bridget Stevens, 17 July 1982, 1 son. Education: Radley College, 1970-74; English Tripos, Double First, Trinity Hall, Cambridge, 1975-78; Harvard University, 1978-79; British Institute, Paris, 1980-81; PhD, Cantab, 1985. Publications: The Growing Dark, 1981; Firebird 3, 1985; Idols, 1986; Plato's Ladder, 1992. Contributions to: Anthologies, journals, and periodicals. Honour: Gregory Award for Poetry, 1985. Address: 6 rue de Verneuil, 75007 Paris, France.

ROMERIL John, b. 26 Oct 1945, Melbourne, Victoria, Australia. Playwright. Education: BA, Monash University, Clayton, 1970. Appointments: Writer-In-Residence, various Australian groups and National University, Singapore, 1974-87. Publications: A Nameless Concern, 1968; The Litchen Table, 1968; The Man from Chicago, 1969; In a Place Like Somewhere Else, 1969; Chicago Chicago, 1970; Marvellous Melbourne, 1970; Dr Karl's Kure, 1970; Whatever Happened to Realism, 1971; Rearguard Action, 1971; Hackett Gets Ahead, 1972; Bastardy, 1972; Waltzing Matilda, 1974; The Floating World, 1974; The Golden Holden Show, 1975; The Accidental Poke, 1977; Mickey's Moomba, 1979; Centenary Dance, 1984; The Kelly Dance, 1984; Definitely Not the Last, 1985; Koori Radio, 1987; Top End, and History of Australia (co-author), 1989; Lost Weekend, 1989; Black Cargo, 1991; The Reading Boy, 1991; Working Out, 1991; Television plays. Honours: Victorian Government Drama Fellowship, 1988. Address: Almost Managing, PO Box 1034, Carlton, Victoria 3053, Australia.

ROMERO Julia Graciela, b. 17 Feb 1961, La Plata, Buenos Aires, Argentina. Translator; Writer. Div 1992, 1 son. Education: Professor of Letters, Estoy Hacienda el Doctorado en Manuel Puig; Lugar de Trabajo: Facultad de Humanidades y Ciencias de la Educacion Universidad Nacional de la Plata. Publications: A Notaciones en Collage; De Mologo al Estallido de la Voz; La Imaginacion Melodramatica Sentimento y Vida Nacional; Las Traiciones de Manuel Puig; Puig la Seduccion y la Historia. Membership: Instituto International de Litertura Iberoamericana. Address: 54 #990, PA, CP 1900, La Plata, Buenos Aires, Argentina.

ROMEU Jorge Luis (Beltran de Quiros), b. 10 Dec 1945, Havana, Cuba. Educator; Writer. m. Zoila Barreiro, 25 July 1970, 3 sons. Education: Diplomas: Language, 1964, Literature, 1966, Teaching, 1970, Alliance Française de La Havane; Licendiado en Matematicas, University of Havana, 1973; MS, 1981, MPh, 1987, PhD, 1990, Syracuse University, USA. Appointments: Editor, Club Las Palmas Newsletter; Monthly Column, Syracuse Post Standard; Radio Commentator, WAER-FM, Syracuse University Public Radio Station; Associate Professor of Statistics, State University of New York, Cortland. Publications: Los Unos, Los Otros y El Seibo, 1971; La Otra Cara de la Moneda, 1984; Thinking of Cuba (collected op-ed pieces). Contributions to: Professional journals and general periodicals. Address: PO Box 6134, Syracuse, NY 13217, USA.

ROMTVEDT David William, b. 7 June 1950, Portland, Oregon, USA. Writer. m. Margo Brown, 30 May 1987. Education: BA, Reed College, 1972. Appointment: State Literature Consultant, Wyoming, 1987. Publications: Free and Compulsory for All, 1984; Moon, 1984; Letters from Mexico, 1987; Black Beauty and Kiev the Ukraine, 1987; Crossing The River, Poets of the Western US, 1987; How Many Horses, 1988; A Flower Whose Name I Do Not Know, 1992; Crossing Wyoming, 1992. Contributions to: Paris Review; Canadian Forum; American Poetry Review; Poets and Writers Magazine. Honours: National Endowment for the Arts Residency Award, 1979, and Fellowship, 1987; Pushcart Prize, 1991; National Poetry Series Award, 1991. Address: 457 North Main, Buffalo, WY 82834, USA.

ROMVARY Susan, b. 20 Aug 1925, Miskolc, Hungary. Bookkeeper; Controller. m. John Romvary, 22 Nov 1947, 1 son. Education: Pazmany Peter University, Budapest, 1947-49; Thomas More Institute, Montreal, 1973; Concordia University, 1975. Publication: Zsuzsa not Zsazsa: Balance with a Smile, 1992. Contributions to: Anthologies and journals. Honours: 1st Prizes, Canadian Authors Association, 1987, 1988; 1st Prize, Hungarian Literary Association, 1988. Memberships: Canadian Authors Association; Hungarian Authors Association. Address: 4000 De Maisonneuve West, Westmount, Quebec H3Z 1J9, Canada.

RONAY Egon, b. Pozsony, Hungary. Journalist. m. (1), 2 daughters, (2) Barbara Greenslade, 1967, 1 son. Education: LLD, University of Budapest; Academy of Commerce, Budapest. Appointments: General Manager, The Marquee Restaurant, London, 1952-55; Columnist on food, wine, eating-out and tourism, Daily Telegraph, Sunday Telegraph, 1954-60; Columnist, Evening News, 1968-74; Food Columnist, Sunday Times, 1986-91. Publications: Egon Ronay's Guide to Hotels and Restaurants (annual), 1956-87; Egon Ronay's Just a Bite (annual), 1979-85; Egon Ronay's Pub Guide (annual), 1980-85; Egon Ronay's Guide to 500 Good Restaurants in Europe's Main Cities (annual), 1983-85; The Unforgettable Dishes of My Life, 1989; Many other tourist guides. Honours: Médaille de la Ville de Paris from Jacques Chirac, 1983; Chevalier de l'Ordre du Mérite Agricole, 1987. Memberships: Académie des Gastronomes, France; British Academy of Gastronomes, founder-president, 1983; International Academy of Gastronomy, founder-vice-president, 1987. Address: 37 Walton Street, London SW3 2HT, England.

RONDINI Adele, b. 30 Jan 1921, Italy. Headmaster (retired); Writer. m. 1 Dec 1951, 2 sons. Education: Degree in Arts; Postgraduate Qualifications in Arts and French. Appointments: Various positions, 1965-. Publications: Fosombron Sparita, 1969; Fosombron Spareta, 1970; Le Journal de Jean Pierre; Rimpianto a Due Voci, 1972; La tombola Di Papa (editor), 1983. Contributions to: Various magazines and journals. Honours: Picchio d'Argento delle Monde for Poetry, Rome, 1971; Accademia Tiberina, Roma Caripodoglio for Poetry, 1968; 1st Prize for Poetry, G Pascoli, 1979. Memberships: President, Fondaz Artistica Monassi, 1981-; Le Rondini Cultural Club, 1987-; Vice-president, Le Migliori Mondo, Rome; Public Relations, CIAS, Rome. Address: Via Mondragone u/12, 00179 Rome, Italy.

ROOKE Daphne Marie, b. 6 Mar 1914, Boksburg, South Africa. Writer. m. 1 June 1937, 1 daughter. Publications: A Grove of Fever Trees, 1950, reprint, 1989; Mittee, 1951, reprint, 1987; Ratoons, 1953, reprint, 1990; Wizards Country, 1957; Beti, 1959; A Lover for Estelle, 1961; The Greyling, 1962; Diamond Jo, 1965; Boy on the Mountain, 1969; Margaretha de la Porte, 1976. Contributions to: Journals. Honours: 1st Prize, APB Novel Competition, 1946; Doctor of Literature, honoris causa, University of Natal, 1997. Address: 54 Regatta Court, Oyster Row, Cambridge CB5 8NS, England.

ROOKE Leon, b. 11 Sept 1934, Roanoke Rapids, North Carolina, USA. Author. Appointments: Writer-in-Residence, University of North Carolina, 1965-66, University of Victoria, 1972-73, University of Southwest Minnesota, 1974-75, University of Toronto, 1984-85, University of Western Ontario, 1990-91; Visiting Professor, University of Victoria, 1980-81. Publications: Novels: Last One Home Sleeps in the Yellow Bed, 1968; Vault, 1974; The Broad Back of the Angel, 1977; The Love Parlour, 1977; Fat Woman, 1980; The Magician in Love, 1980; Death Suite, 1982; The Birth Control King of the Upper Volta, 1983; Shakespeare's Dog, 1983; Sing Me No Love Songs I'll Say You No Prayers, 1984; A Bolt of White Cloth, 1984; How I Saved the Province, 1990; The Happiness of Others, 1991; A Good Baby, 1991; Who Do You Love?, 1992. Stage Plays: A Good Baby, 1991; The Coming, 1991; 4 others. Contributions to: About 300 short stories in leading North American journals. Honours: Canada and Australia Literary Prize, 1981; Best Paperback Novel of the Year, 1981; Governor-General's Award, 1984; North Carolina Award for Literature, 1990. Memberships: PEN; Writers' Union of Canada. Address: 209 Main Street, Eden Mills, Ontario N0B 1P0, Canada.

ROOM Adrian Richard West, b. 27 Sept 1933, Melksham, England. Writer. Education: Honours Degree, Russian, 1957, Diploma, Education, 1958, University of Oxford. Publications: Place-Names of the World, 1974; Great Britain: A Background Studies English-Russian Dictionary (Russian Language), 1978; Room's Dictionary of Confusibles, 1979; Place-Name Changes since 1900, 1980; Naming Names, 1981; Room's Dictionary of Distinguishables, 1981; Dictionary of Trade Name Origins, 1982; Room's Classical Dictionary, 1983; Dictionary of Cryptic Crossword Clues, 1983; A Concise Dictionary of Modern Place-Names in Great Britain and Ireland, 1983; Guide to British Place-Names, 1985; Dictionary of Changes in Meaning, 1986; Dictionary of Coin Names, 1988; Guinness Book of Numbers, 1989; Dictionary of Dedications, 1990; A Name for Your Baby, 1992; The Street Names of England, 1992; Brewer's Dictionary of Names, 1992; Corporate Eponymy, 1992; Place-Name Changes 1900-91, 1993; The Naming of Animals, 1993; Hutchinson Pocket Dictionary of First Names, 1994; Hutchinson Pocket Dictionary of Confusible Words, 1994; African Place-Names, 1994; Cassell Dictionary of Proper Names, 1994; A Dictionary of Irish Place-Names, 1994; Cassell Dictionary of First Names, 1995; Hutchinson Pocket Dictionary of Place Names, 1995; Brewer's Dictionary of Phrase and Fable, revised edition, 1995; Literally Entitled, 1996; An Alphabetical Guide to the Language of Name Studies, 1996; Placenames of Russia and the Former Soviet Union, 1996. Memberships: Royal Geographical Society; Society of Authors; English Place-Name Society; American Name Society; Translators Association; Britain-Russia Centre. Address: 12 High Street, St Martin's, Stamford, Lincolnshire PE9 2LF, England.

ROONEY Lucy, b. 13 July 1926, Liverpool, England. Former Lecturer; Religious Sister of Notre Dame de Namur. Education: Teaching Certificate, Universities of Manchester and Liverpool; City and Guilds Advanced Handloom Weaver, 1965. Publications: Co-author: Mary, Queen of Peace, 1984; Medjugorje Unfolds, 1986; Medjugorje Journal, 1987; Lord Jesus Teach Me To Pray, 1988; Medjugorje Retreat, 1989; Our Lady Comes to Scottsdale, 1992; Return to God: The Scottsdale Message, 1993; Medjugorje Unfolds in Peace and in War, 1994; Finding Jesus in the World: Prayer with leilhard de Chardin, 1996. Contributions to: Religious Journals. Address: 52 Warriner Gardens, London SW11 4DU, England.

ROOSE-EVANS James Humphrey, b. 11 Nov 1927, England. Writer; Dramatist; Director. Education: BA, 1952, MA, 1957, Oxford University; Ordained non-stipendiary priest, Anglican Church, 1981. Appointments: Founder, Hampstead Theatre, 1959; Founder-Artistic Director, Bleddfa Trust, Centre for Caring and the Arts in the Welsh Marches; Distinguished Visiting Fellow, Ohio State University; Gian-Carlo Menotti Artist-in-Residence, Charleston College, South Carolina. Publications: Darling Ma: The Letters of Joyce Grenfell (editor), 1988; The Time of My Life: War Memoirs of Joyce Grenfell (editor), 1989; Inner Journey, Outer Journey, most recent edition, 1989; A Pride of Players, 1993; Passages of the Soul, 1994; Adaptations for the stage: 84 Charing Cross Road, 1983; Cider With Rosie, 1994; One Foot on the Stage: Biography of Richard Wilson, 1996; Eminently a Victorian (play), 1997; Directing a Play; Experimental Theatre; Various adult and 7 children's books. Creative Works: Many theatre productions in the West End, Broadway and Europe including: Private Lives; Cider With Rosie; Under Milk Wood; The Best of Friends; An Ideal Husband. Contributions to: Newspapers, magazines, radio, and television. Honours: Directing awards. Memberships: Dramatists Club; Garrick Club. Address: c/o Conway Van Gelder, 18-21 Jermyn Street, London SW1Y 6HP, England.

ROOT William Pitt, b. 28 Dec 1941, Austin, Texas, USA. Professor; Poet. m. Pamela Uschuk, 6 Nov 1988, 1 daughter. Education: BA, University of Washington, 1964; MFA, University of North Carolina at Greensboro, 1966. Appointments: Stegman Fellow, Stanford University, 1967-68; Assistant Professor, Michigan State University, 1967-68; Visiting Writer-in-Residence, Amherst College, 1971, University of Southwest Louisiana, 1976, Wichita State University, 1976, University of Montana, 1978, 1980, 1982-85, Pacific Lutheran University, 1990; Professor, Hunter College of the City University of New York, 1986-. Publications: The Storm and Other Poems, 1969; Striking the Dark Air for Music, 1973; A Journey South, 1977; Reasons for Going It on Foot, 1981; In the World's Common Grasses, 1981; Invisible Guests, 1984; Faultdancing, 1986; Trace Elements from a Recurring Kingdom, 1994; Selected Odes of Pablo Neruda, 1997. Contributions to: Magazines and periodicals. Honours: Academy of American Poetry Prize, 1967; Rockefeller Foundation Grant, 1969-70; Guggenheim Fellowship, 1970-71; National Endowment for the Arts Grant, 1973-74; Pushcart Awards, 1977, 1980, 1985; US-UK Exchange Artist, 1978-79; Stanley Kunitz Poetry Award, 1981; Guy Owen Poetry Award, 1984. Address: c/o Department of English, Hunter College of the City University of New York, 695 Park Avenue, New York, NY 10021, USA.

ROPER David, b. 30 Nov 1954, Hessle, Yorkshire, England. Critic. Education: MA, AKC, King's College, London. Appointments: Editor, Square One, 1978, Gambit, 1978-85, Platform, 1981-82, Plays and Players, 1983-84; Drama Editor, Event, 1981-82; Theatre Critic, Daily Express, 1982-87; Arts Correspondent, BBC, 1987-90; Channel 4 TV, 1990-93; Director, Heavy Entertainment Ltd, 1993-. Publications: The Pineapple Dance Book, 1983; Bart! (biography of Lionel Bart), 1994. Contributions to: Tatler; Event; Time Out; Sunday Telegraph; Daily Express; Sunday Express; Daily Mail; Harper's and Queen. Address: PO Box 5055, London W12 0ZX, England.

ROQUELAURE A N. See: **RICE Anne.**

RORTY Richard (McKay), b. 4 Oct 1931, New York, New York, USA. Philosopher; Professor; Writer. m. (1) Amelie Sarah Oksenberg, 15 June 1954, div 1972, 1 son, (2) Mary R Varney, 4 Nov 1972, 1 son, 1 daughter. Education: BA, 1949, MA, 1952, University of Chicago; PhD, Yale University, 1956. Appointments: Instructor, Yale University, 1955-57; Instructor, 1958-60, Assistant Professor, 1960-61, Wellesley College; Faculty, 1961-70, Professor of Philosophy, 1970-81, Stuart Professor of Philosophy, 1981-82, University Professor of Humanities, 1982-, University of Virginia. Publications: Philosophy and the Mirror of Nature, 1979; Consequences of Pragmatism, 1982; Contingency, Irony, and Solidarity, 1989; Objectivity, Relativism, and Truth, 1991; Essays on Heidegger and Others, 1991; Essays on Aristotle's De Anima (editor with Martha Nussbaum), 1992. Honours: Guggenheim Fellowship, 1973-74; MacArthur Foundation Fellow, 1981-86. Memberships: American Academy of Arts and Sciences; American Philosophical Association. Address: c/o University of Virginia, 412 Cabell Hall, Charlottesville, VA 22903, USA.

ROSCA Ninotchka, b. Philippines. Writer. Education: AB, Comparative Literature, University of the Philippines; Graduate Studies in Khmer Civilization. Publications: Novels: State of War, 1988; Twice Blessed, 1992. Short Stories: Bitter Country, 1972; Monsoon Collection, 1982. Honour: New York Foundation for the Arts Fiction Fellowships, 1986, 1991. Memberships: Board of Directors, PEN International; PEN American Center. Address: c/o Sterling Lord Literistic, 1 Madison Avenue, NY 10010, USA.

ROSE Andrew Wyness, b. 11 Feb 1944, Headingley, Leeds, England. Barrister. Education: Trinity College, Cambridge, 1963-67; MA; LLM; Called to Bar, Grays Inn, London, 1968. Appointments: Barrister, 1968-88. Publications: Stinie: Murder on the Common, 1985; Scandal at the Savoy, 1991. Honour: Shortlisted, Golden Dagger Award for Non-fiction, Crime Writers Association. Membership: Elected Member, The Crimes Club, 1996. Address: Brock House, 26 The Street, Sutton Waldron, Blandford Forum, Dorset DT11 8N2, England.

ROSE Daniel Asa, b. 20 Nov 1949, New York, New York, USA. Writer. m. (1) Laura Love, 30 Nov 1974, div, 2 sons, (2) Shelley Roth, 5 Sept 1993. Education: AB, English, Honours, Brown University, 1971. Appointments: Travel Columnist, Esquire; Travel Editor, Dimension. Publications: Flipping for it, 1987; Small Family with Rooster, 1988; Various Screenplays, poems, stories, reviews and literary essays. Contributions to: Newspapers and magazines. Honours: O Henry Prize, 1980; PEN Literary Awards, 1987, 1988. Address: 138 Bay State Road, Renoboth, MA 02769, USA.

ROSE Joel Steven, b. 1 Mar 1948, Los Angeles, California, USA. Writer. m. Catherine Texier, 2 daughters. Education: BA, Hobart College, 1970; MFA, Columbia University. Publications: Kill the Poor (novel), 1988; Between C and D (co-editor), 1988; Love is Strange (co-editor), 1993. Contributions to: Newspapers and magazines. Honours: National Endowment for the Arts Award, 1986; New York State Council on the Arts Award, 1986-87. Memberships: Coordinating Council of Literary Magazines; Poets and Writers; Writers Guild of America. Address: 255 East 7th Street, New York, NY 10009, USA.

ROSE Kenneth Vivian, b. 15 Nov 1924, Bradford, Yorkshire, England. Writer. Education: Repton School; Scholar, MA, New College, Oxford, 1948. Appointments: Assistant Master, Eton College, 1948; Editorial Staff, Daily Telegraph, 1952-60; Founder, Writer, Albany Column, Sunday Telegraph, 1961-. Publications: Superior Person: A Portrait of Curzon and his Circle in Late Victorian England, 1969; The Later Cecils, 1975; William Harvey: A Monograph, 1978; King George V, 1983; Kings, Queens and Courtiers: Intimate Portraits of the Royal House of Windsor, 1985; Harold Nicolson,1992. Contributions to: Dictionary of National Biography. Honours: Fellow,

Royal Society of Literature, 1976; Wolfson Award for History, 1983; Whitbread Award for Biography, 1983; Yorkshire Post Biography of the Year Award, 1984. Address: 38 Brunswick Gardens, London W8 4 AL, England.

ROSE Mark Allen, b. 4 Aug 1939, New York, New York, USA. Professor of English; Writer. Div, 1 son. Education: AB, Princeton University, 1961; BLitt, Merton College, 1963; PhD, Harvard University, 1967. Appointments: Instructor to Associate Professor of English, Yale University, 1967-74; Professor of English, University of Illinois, 1974-77, University of California at Santa Barbara, 1977-; Director, University of California Humanities Research Institute, 1989-94. Publications: Heroic Love, 1968; Golding's Tale, 1972; Shakespearean Design, 1972; Spenser's Art, 1975; Alien Encounters, 1981; Authors and Owners, 1993. Editor: Twentieth Century Views of Science Fiction, 1976; Twentieth Century Interpretations of Antony and Cleopatra, 1977; Bridges to Science Fiction (with others), 1980; Shakespeare's Early Tragedies, 1994. Honours: Woodrow Wilson Fellow, 1961; Henry Fellow, 1961-62; Dexter Fellow, 1966; Morse Fellow, 1970-71; National Endowment for the Humanities Fellowships, 1979-80, 1990-91. Memberships: Modern Language Association; Phi Beta Kappa; Renaissance Society of America; Shakespeare Society of America. Address: 1135 Oriole Road, Montecito, CA 93108, USA.

ROSE Mitchell, b. 22 Nov 1951, Pennsylvania, USA. Literary Agent; Editor. Education: BA, Bard College, 1974; MFA, Goddard College, 1980. Appointments: Freelance Writer, 1975-80; Editor and Managing Editor for trade magazines, 1980-83; Editor, New American Library, 1983-86; Literary Agent and Editor, 1986-. Publications: The Victorian Fairy Tale Book, 1988; The Wizard of Oz: The Official Pictorial History, 1989; Gone With the Wind: The Definitive Illustrated History, 1989; The Film Encyclopaedia, 1990; Dr Deming, 1990; At Dawn We Slept, 1991; Harper Dictionary of American Government and Politics, 1992; Lawrence of Arabia, 1992; Judy Garland, 1992; Healing Through Nutrition, 1993; Kennedy as President, 1993. Contributions to: Boston Phoenix. Membership: Authors Guild. Address: Mitchell S Rose Literary Agency, 688 Avenue of the Americas, New York, NY 10010, USA.

ROSE Richard, b. 9 Apr 1933, St Louis, Missouri, USA. Professor of Public Policy. m. Rosemary J Kenny, 14 Apr 1956, 2 sons, 1 daughter. Education: BA distinction, Johns Hopkins University, USA; DPhil, Oxford University, England, 1960. Appointments: Editor, Journal of Public Policy, 1985-. Publications: Politics in England, 1964, 5th edition, 1989; Governing Without Consensus: An Irish Perspective, 1971; Electoral Behaviour, 1974; International Almanac of Electoral History (with T T Mackie), 1972, 3rd edition, 1991; Problem of Party Government, 1974; Managing Presidential Objectives, 1976; Can Government Go Bankrupt? (with B G Peters), 1978; Do Parties Make a Difference?, 1980; Presidents and Prime Ministers (co-editor), 1980; Understanding the United Kingdom, 1982; Understanding Big Government, 1984; Nationwide Competition for Votes, 1984; Public Employment in Western Nations, 1985; Voters Begin to Choose (with D McAllister), 1986; Ministers and Ministries, 1987; Taxation by Political Inertia, 1987; The Post-Modern President, 1988; Ordinary People in Public Policy, 1989; The Loyalty of Voters, with d McAllister, 1990; Lesson Drawing in Public Policy, 1993; Inheritance in Public Policy, 1994; What is Europe?, 1995. Contributions to: Times; Telegraph; New Society; Economist; Various TV Stations. Honours: Guggenheim Fellowship, 1974; Fellow, Woodrow Wilson International Centre, Washington, DC, USA, 1974; Japan Foundation Fellow, 1984; Fellow, British Academy, 1992; Honorary Foreign Member, Finnish Academy of Arts and Sciences; American Academy of Arts and Sciences. Address: CSPP, University of Strathclyde, Glasgow G1 1XH, Scotland.

ROSEN Michael Wayne (Landgrave of Hesse), b. 7 May 1946, Harrow, England. Writer; Performer. m. 30 Nov 1987, 3 sons, 2 stepdaughters. Education: Middlesex Hospital Medical School, 1964-65; Wadham College, Oxford, 1965-69; National Film School, 1973-76. Appointments: Writer-in-Residence, Vauxhall Manor Comprehensive School, 1976-77, London Borough of Brent, 1983-84, John Scurr Primary School, 1984-87, 1988-90, Western Australia College of Advanced Education, 1987. Publications: Mind Your Own Business, 1974; Quick Let's Get Out Of Here, 1983; Don't Put the Mustard in the Custard, 1984; The Kingfisher Book of Poetry, 1984; The Hypnotiser, 1988; We're Going on a Bear Hunt, 1989. Contributions to: New Statesman; Guardian; Times Educational Supplement; Jewish Socialist. Honours: Signal Poetry Award, 1982;

The Other Award, 1984; Smarties Award, 1989. Membership: Equity. Address: c/o The Peters Fraser and Dunlop Group Limited, 5th Floor, The Chambers, Chelsea Harbour, Lots Road, London SW10 0XF, England.

ROSEN Norma, b. 11 Aug 1925, New York, New York, USA. Writer; Teacher. m. Robert S Rosen, 1960, 1 son, 1 daughter. Education: BA, Mt Holyoke College, 1946; MA, Columbia University, 1953. Appointments: Teacher, Creative Writing, New School for Social Research, New York City, 1965-69, University of Pennsylvania, 1969, Harvard University, 1971, Yale University, 1984, New York University, 1987-. Publications: Joy to Levine!, 1962; Green, 1967; Touching Evil, 1969; At the Center, 1982; John and Anzia: An American Romance, 1989; Accidents of Influence: Writing as a Woman and a Jew in America (essays), 1992. Contributions to: Anthologies and other publications. Honours: Saxton, 1960; CAPS, 1976; Bunting, 1971-73. Memberships: PEN; Authors Guild; Phi Beta Kappa. Literary Agent: Gloria Loomis. Address: 133 East 35th Street, New York, NY 10016, USA.

ROSENBERG Bruce Alan, b. 27 July 1934, New York, New York, USA. Teacher; Writer. m. Ann Harleman, 20 June 1981, 3 sons. Education: BA, Hofstra University, 1955; MA, Pennsylvania State University, 1960; PhD, Ohio State University, 1965. Publications: The Art of the American Folk Preacher, 1970; Custer and the Epic of Defeat, 1975; The Code of the West, 1982; The Spy Story, 1987; Can These Bones Live?, 1988; Ian Fleming, 1989; The Neutral Ground, 1995. Contributions to: Over 60 professional journals. Honours: James Russell Lowell Prize, 1970; Chicago Folklore Prizes, 1970, 1975. Membership: Folklore Fellows International. Address: 55 Summit Avenue, Providence, RI 02906, USA.

ROSENBERG Greta. See: **GUT-RUSSENBERGER Margrit.**

ROSENBERG Liz, b. 3 Feb 1957, Glen Cove, New York, USA. Associate Professor of English. m. (1) John Gardner, 14 Feb 1982, (2) David Bosnick, 8 Dec 1985, 1 son. Education: BA, Bennington College; MA, Johns Hopkins University. Appointment: Associate Professor of English, State University of New York at Binghamton. Publications: Poetry: The Fire Music, 1986; Children of Pardin, 1993. Children's Books: Adelaide and the Night Train, 1989; Window, Mirror Man, 1990; The Scrap Doll, 1991; Monster Mama, 1993. Contributions to: New York Times; New Yorker; Nation; Southern Review; Poetry. Honours: Atlantic 1st Award, 1976; Pennsylvania Council of the Arts Award, 1982; National Kelloggs Fellowship, 1982-85; Agnes Starrett Poetry Prize, 1985. Memberships: Association of Writers and Poets; Poets and Writers. Address: c/o English Department, State University of New York, Binghamton, NY 13902, USA.

ROSENBERG Nancy Taylor, b. 9 July 1946, Dallas, Texas, USA. Writer. m. (1) Calvin S Kyrme, div, 2 sons, 1 daughter, (2) Jerry Rosenberg, 2 daughters. Education: Gulf Park College; University of California at Los Angeles. Publications: Mitigating Circumstances, 1993; Interest of Justice, 1993; The Eyewitness, 1994; First Offense, 1994; California Angel, 1995. Address: c/o Dytton Publicity, 375 Hudson Street, New York, NY 10014, USA.

ROSENBERG Peter Michael, b. 11 July 1958, London, England. Writer. Education: BSc, University of Sussex, 1979. Publications: The Usurper (co-author), 1988; Kissing Through a Pane of Glass, 1993; Touched By a God or Something, 1994; Because It Makes My Heart Beat Faster, 1995; Daniel's Dream, 1996. Contributions to: Journals and magazines. Honour: 2nd Prize, Betty Trask Award, 1992. Literary Agent: 48 Walham Grove, London SW6 1QR, England. Address: 430 St Ann's Road, London N15 3JJ, England.

ROSENBLATT Joe, (Joseph Rosenblatt), b. 26 Dec 1933, Toronto, Ontario, Canada. Editor; Poet; Writer. m. Faye Smith, 1970, 1 son. Education: Central Technical School, Toronto; George Brown College, Toronto. Appointments: Editor, Jewish Dialog magazine, 1969-; Writer-in-Residence, University of Western Ontario, London, 1979-80, University of Victoria, British Columbia, 1980-81, Saskatoon Public Library, Saskatchewan, 1985-86; Visiting Lecturer, University of Rome, 1987, University of Bologna, 1987. Publications: Poetry: Voyage of the Mood, 1963; The LSD Leacock, 1966; Winter of the Luna Moth, 1968; The Bumblebee Dithyramb, 1972; Blind Photographer: Poems and Sketches, 1973; Dream Craters, 1974; Virgins and Vampires, 1975; Top Soil, 1976; Loosely Tied Hands: An Experiment in Punk, 1978; Snake Oil, 1978; The Sleeping Lady, 1979;

Brides of the Stream, 1983; Poetry Hotel: Selected Poems 1963-1985, 1985; Gridi nel Buio, 1990; Beds & Consenting Dreamers, 1994; A Tentacled Mother, 1995; The Rosenblatt Reader, 1995; The Voluptuous Gardener, 1996; Madre Tentacolare, 1995. Fiction: Tommy Fry and the Ant Colony, 1979. Other: Doctor Anaconda's Solar Fun Club: A Book of Drawings, 1977; Escape from the Glue Factory: A Memoir of Paranormal Toronto Childhood in the Late Forties, 1985; The Kissing Goldfish of Siam: A Memoir of Adolescence in the Fifties, 1989; Joe Rosenblatt Reader, 1995; A Tentacled Mother, 1995; Madre Tentacolare, 1995. Honours: Canada Council Grants, 1966, 1968, 1980, 1982; Ontario Arts Council Award, 1970; Governor-General's Award, 1976; BC Book Award, 1986. Address: c/o Olichan Books, Box 10, Lantzville, British Columbia, Canada V0R 2H0.

ROSENBLUM Martin Jack, b. 19 Aug 1946, Appleton, Wisconsin, USA. Poet; Writer. m. Maureen Rice, 6 Sept 1970, 2 daughters. Education: BS, 1969, MA, 1971, PhD, 1980, University of Wisconsin. Appointments: Guest Lecturer, University of East Anglia, Norwich, England, 1975; Poet-in-Residence, Wisconsin Review, University of Wisconsin at Oshkosh, 1987. Publications: Home, 1971; On, 1972; The Werewolf Sequence, 1974; Brite Shade, 1984; Conjuction, 1987; The Holy Ranger: Harley-Davidson Poems, 1989. Non-Fiction: Harley-Davidson Inc, 1903-1993: An Historical Overview, 1994; Down on the Spirit Farm (CD of music and poetry), 1994. Honour: Wisconsin Award, Best Poet of 1995. Address: 2521 East Stratford Court, Shorewood, WI 53211, USA.

ROSENFELD Albert Hyman, b. 31 May 1920, Philadelphia, USA. Science Writer. m. 24 Aug 1948, 1 son, 1 daughter. Education: BA, History and Social Science, New Mexico State University. Appointments: Associate Editor, 1956-58, Senior Science Editor, 1958-60, Life; Managing Editor, Family Health, 1969-71; Senior Science Editor, Saturday Review, 1973-80; Contributing Editor, Geo, 1979-81, Science Digest, 1980-82. Publications: The Quintessence of Irving Langmui, 1962; The Second Genesis: The Coming Control of Life, 1969; Prolongevity, 1976; Mind and Supermind (editor), 1977; Science, Invention and Social Change (editor), 1978; Responsible Parenthood (with G W Kliman), 1980; Prolongevity II, 1985. Contributions to: Magazines. Honours: Aviation Space Writers Award, 1964; Westinghouse Writing Award AAAS, 1966; Lasker Award, 1967; Claude Bernard Science Journalism Award, 1974; National Magazine Award, 1975; James P Grady Medal, American Chemical Society, 1981; Honorary DLitt, New Mexico State University. Memberships: Council for the Advancement of Science Writing; National Association of Science Writers; Authors Guild. Address: 25 Davenport Avenue, New Rochelle, NY 10805, USA.

ROSENGARTEN Theodore, b. 17 Dec 1944, Brooklyn, New York, USA. Writer. m. 1974, 1 son. Education: AB, Amherst College, 1966; PhD, Harvard University, 1975. Publication: All God's Dangers: The Life of Nate Shaw, 1974. Honour: National Book Award, 1975. Address: PO Box 8, McClellanville, SC 29458, USA.

ROSENSTAND Peder Tuxen, b. 2 Nov 1935, Copenhagen, Denmark. Poet; Artist; Painter; Professor. m. Anni Rosenstand, 1960, 3 sons, 1 daughter. Education: Royal Danish Academy of Art, Copenhagen; University of Copenhagen, Denmark. Publications: Osteklokken, 1974; Blik, 1988. Other: Dramatic Works for Danish, Swedish and Norway TV; Painting Exhibitions Held in Germany, England, New York, USA, Sweden, Denmark, Italy, 1962-94. Contributions to: Essays, Articles to Pinqvinen. Membership: Authors Society, Copenhagen. Address: Gl Mollerup, 4673 Rodvig Stevns, Tlf 53707030, Denmark.

ROSENTHAL Barbara Ann, b. 17 Aug 1948, Bronx, New York, USA. Writer; Artist. 2 daughters. Education: BFA, Carnegie-Mellon University, 1970; MFA, Queens College, City University of New York, 1975. Career: Editor-in-Chief, Patterns, 1967-70; Adjunct Lecturer in English, College of Staten Island of the City University of New York, 1990-. Publications: Clues to Myself, 1982; Sensations, 1984; Old Address Book, 1985; Homo Futurus, 1986; In The West of Ireland, 1992; Soul and Psyche: The Zygotes of Art, 1996; In the Round; Children's Shoes, 1993. Contributions to: Anthologies and journals. Contributions to: Numerous professional journals and lit-art magazines including: Feelings, 1990-91; Poetry Motel, 1993; Spit, 1990, 1993; Parting Gifts, 1993; Cradle and All, 1990; MacGuffin Reader; Bohemian Chronicle, 1993. Honours: Various awards and residencies. Address: 727 Avenue of the Americas, New York, NY 10010, USA.

ROSENTHAL Jack Morris, b. 8 Sept 1931, Manchester, England. Dramatist; Writer. m. Maureen Lipman, 18 Feb 1973, 1 son, 1 daughter. Education: BA, Sheffield University. Publications: Over 300 television scripts, 1963-97; 5 stage plays; Film screenplays include: Lucky Star, 1980; Yentl (with Barbara Streisand), 1983; The Chain, 1985; The Wedding Gift, 1994. Television: Eskimo Day, 1996. Honours: British Academy of Film and Television Artists Arts Award, 1976; Royal Television Society Writer's Award, 1976, and Hall of Fame, 1993; Honorary MA, University of Salford, 1994; Commander of the Order of the British Empire, 1994; Hon DLitt, University of Manchester, 1995; DLitt, University of Manchester, 1995; Associate Professor in Theatre, University of Sheffield, 1997. Address: c/o Casartto Co Ltd, 60-66 Wardour Street, London W1, England.

ROSS Alan, b. 6 May 1922, Calcutta, India. Author; Publisher; Journalist. m. Jennifer Fry, 1949, div 1985, 1 son. Education: St John's College, Oxford. Appointments: Royal Navy, 1942-45; Staff, The Observer, 1950-71, toured Australia as Correspondent, 1964-65, West Indies 1960-68; Editor, London Magazine, 1961-; Managing Director, London Magazine Editions (Publishers), 1965-. Publications: The Derelict Day, 1947; Time Was Away, 1948; The Forties, 1950; The Gulf of Pleasure, 1951; The Bandit on the Billiard Table, 1954; Something of the Sea, 1954; Australia 55, 1956, 2nd edition 1983; Abroad (editor), 1957; Cape Summer and the Australians in England, 1957, 2nd edition 1986; To Whom It May Concern, 1958; The Onion Man, 1959; Through the Caribbean, 1960; The Cricketer's Companion (editor), 1960; Danger on Glass Island, 1960; African Negatives, 1962; Australia, 63, 1963; West Indies at Lord's, 1963, 2nd edition 1986; North from Sicily, 1965; Poems 1942-1967, 1968; Tropical Ice, 1972; The Taj Express, 1973; London Magazine Stories 1-11 (editor), 1964-80; Living in London (editor), 1974; Open Sea, 1975; Selected Poems of Lawrence Durrell (editor), 1977; Death Valley and Other Poems, 1980; The Turf (editor), 1982; Colours of War, 1983; Ranji, 1983; Living Out of London (editor), 1984; Blindfold Games, 1986; The Emissary, 1986; Coastwise Lights, 1988; After Pusan, 1996. Honours: Atlantic Award for Literature, Rockefeller Foundation, 1946; Commander of the Order of the British Empire, 1982. Membership: Royal Society of Literature, fellow. Address: 4 Elm Park Lane, London SW3, England.

ROSS Angus. See: **GIGGAL Kenneth**.

ROSS Catherine. See: **BEATY Betty Joan Campbell Smith**.

ROSS Gary Earl, b. 12 Aug 1951, Buffalo, New York, USA. Writing Educator. m. 23 Dec 1970, div 1994, 2 sons, 1 daughter. Education: BA, 1973, MA, 1975, State University of New York at Buffalo. Appointments: Associate Professor for EOC in Writing, 1995; Writing Educator, State University of New York Educational Opportunity Center at Buffalo, 1977-. Publications: Guiding the Adult Learner (editor), 1979; Developmental Perspectives (editor), 1981; Practical Considerations for Computer-Assisted Writing Instruction for Disadvantaged Learners, 1990; Teaching Creative Writing, 1990. Contributions to: Professional journals and general periodicals; Buffalo News; ELF; Artvoice. Honours: Hearts on Fire Award, American Poetry Association, 1983; Writer-in-Residences, Just Buffalo Literary Organization, 1987, 1992; LIFT Program Fiction Fellowship, 1989. Memberships: International Society for the Exploration of Teaching Alternatives; Just Buffalo Literary Organization; Niagara-Erie Writers, board chair, 1987-89; United University Professions. Address: c/o State University of New York Educational Opportunity Center at Buffalo, 465 Washington Street, Buffalo, NY 14203, USA.

ROSS Helaine. See: **DANIELS Dorothy**.

ROSS James. See: **WELCH Colin**.

ROSS John Munder, b. 20 June 1945, New York, New York, USA. Psychoanalyst; Writer. m. 1 son. Education: BA magna cum laude, Harvard University, 1967; MA, 1973, PhD, 1974, Clinical Psychology, New York University; Certificate in Psychoanalysis, New York University Medical Centre, 1984. Publications: Father and Child, 1982; Tales of Love, Sex and Danger, 1986; The Oedipus Papers, 1988; The Male Paradox, 1992; What Men Want, 1993. Contributions to: Professional journals and general periodicals. Address: 243 West End Avenue, Suite 101, New York, NY 10023, USA.

ROSS Jonathon. See: **ROSSITER John**.

ROSS Leonard Q. See: **ROSTEN Leo C.**

ROSS Malcolm. See: **ROSS-MACDONALD Malcolm John.**

ROSS Michael Elsohn, b. 30 June 1952, Utica, New York, USA. Writer; Naturalist. m. 20 July 1977, 1 son. Education: BS, Conservation of Natural Resources, University of California at Berkeley, 1974;Multi-Subject Teaching Credential, California State University at Fresno, 1981. Publications: Cycles, Cycles, Cycles, 1979; What Makes Everything Go?, 1979; Easy Day Hikes in Yosemite, 1985; Faces in all Kinds of Places, 1986; Yosemite Fun Book, 1987; Become a Bird and Fly, 1992; The World of Small, 1993; Sand Box Scientist, 1995; Happy Camper Handbook, 1995; Rolypolyology, 1996; Wormology, 1996. Honours: Awards of Excellence and Honorable Mentions, US National Park Service. Membership: Society of Children's Books Writers and Illustrators. Literary Agent: Andrea Brown. Address: PO Box 295, El Portal, CA 95318, USA.

ROSS-MACDONALD J(ohn), (Malcolm Macdonald, Malcolm Ross, M R O'Donnell, Malcolm Ross), b. 29 Feb 1932, Chipping, Sodbury, Gloucestershire, England. Freelance Writer; Editor; Designer. m. Ingrid Giehr, 2 daughters. Education: Falmouth School of Art, 1950-54; Diploma, University College, London, 1958. Appointments: Lektor, Folk University, Sweden, 1959-61; Executive Editor, Aldus Books, 1962-65; Visiting Lecturer, Hornsey College of Art, 1965-69. Publications: The Big Waves, 1962; Macdonald Illustrated Encyclopaedia, 10 volumes (executive editor), 1962-65; Spare Part Surgery (co-author), 1968; Machines in Medicine, 1969; The Human Heart, 1970; World Wildlife Guide, 1971; Beyond the Horizon, 1971; Every Living Thing, 1973; World from Rough Stones, 1974; Origin of Johnny, 1975; Life in the Future, 1976; The Rich Are With You Always, 1976; Sons of Fortune, 1978; Abigail, 1979; Goldeneye, 1981; The Dukes, 1982; Tessa'd'Arblay, 1983; In Love & War, 1984; Mistress of Pallas, 1986; Silver Highways, 1987; The Sky with Diamonds, 1988; A Notorious Woman, 1988; His Father's Son, 1989; An Innocent Woman, 1989; Hell Hath No Fury, 1990; A Woman Alone, 1990; The Captain's Wives, 1991; A Woman Scorned, 1991; A Woman Possessed, 1992; All Desires Known, 1993; To the End of Her Days, 1993; Dancing on Snowflakes, 1994; For I Have Sinned, 1994; Kernow & Daughter, 1994; Crissy's Family, 1995. Contributions to: Sunday Times; New Scientist; Science Journal; Month; Jefferson Encyclopaedia. Memberships: Authors Guild; Society of Authors. Address: c/o David Higham Ltd, 5-8 Lower John Street, London W1R 4HA, England.

ROSSI Bruno. See: **LEVINSON Leonard.**

ROSSI Maria Francesca (Francesca Duranti), b. 2 Jan 1935, Genoa, Italy. Writer. m. (1) Enrico Magnani, 1956, (2) Massimo Duranti, 1970, 1 son, 1 daughter. Education: Studied jurisprudence, University of Pisa. Publications: La bambina, 1976; Piazza, Mia Bella Piazza, 1978; The House on Moonlake, 1984; Happy Ending, 1987; Effetti Personalia, 1988; Ultima Stesura, 1991. Contributions to: Il Secoloxx; Il Giornale; Il Messaggero. Honours: Martina Franca Citta di Milano, Bagutta, 1984; Basilicata Hemingway Campiello, 1988; Prix Lectrices d'Elle, Castiglioncello, 1991. Address: Villa Rossi, Gattaiola, Lucca, Italy.

ROSSITER John. See: **CROZIER Brian Rossiter.**

ROSSITER John, (Jonathan Ross), b. 2 Mar 1916, Devonshire, England. Writer. Education: Preparatory and military schools, Wooolwich and Bulford, 1924-32. Appointments: Detective Chief Superintendent, Wiltshire Constabulary, 1939-69; Flight Lieutenant, RAF/VR, 1943-46; Columnist, Wiltshire Courior, Swindon, 1963-64. Publications include: As Jonathon Ross: The Blood Running Cold, 1968; Diminished by Death, 1968; Dead at First Hand, 1969; The Deadest Thing You Ever Saw, 1969; Death's Head, 1982; Dead Eye, 1983; Dropped Dead, 1984; Fate Accomplished, 1987; Sudden Departures, 1988; A Time for Dying, 1989; Daphne Dead and Done For, 1990; Murder be Hanged, 1992; The Body of a Woman, 1994; Murder! Murder! Burning Bright, 1996; Here Lies Nancy Frail; The Burning of Billy Toober; I Know What Its Like to Die; A Rattling of Old Bones; Dark Blue and Dangerous; Burial Deferred. As John Rossiter: The Victims, 1971; A Rope for General Dietz, 1972; The Manipulators, 1973; The Villains, 1974; The Golden Virgin, 1975; The Man Who Came Back, 1978; Dark Flight, 1981. Contributions to: Police Review. Membership: Crime Writers Association. Literary Agent: Murray Pollinger, 222 Old Brompton Road, London SW5 0BZ, England.

Address: 3 Leighton Home Farm Court, Wellhead Lane, Westbury, Wilts BA13 3PT, England.

ROSSNER Judith (Perelman), b. 1 Mar 1935, New York, New York, USA. Writer. m. (1) Robert Rossner, 13 June 1954, div, (2) Mort Persky, 9 Jan 1979, div, 1 son, 1 daughter. Education: City College, New York City, 1952-55. Publications: To the Precipice, 1966; Nine Months in the Life of an Old Maid, 1969; Any Minute I Can Split, 1972; Looking for Mr Goodbar, 1975; Attachments, 1977; Emmeline, 1980; August, 1983; His Little Women, 1990; Olivia or the Weight of the Past, 1994. Contributions to: Magazines and journals. Memberships: Authors Guild; PEN. Address: c/o Julian Bach Literary Agency, 747 Third Avenue, New York, NY 10017, USA.

ROSTON Murray, b. 10 Dec 1928, London, England. Professor of English; Writer. Education: MA, Queen's College, Cambridge, 1952; MA, 1954, PhD, 1961, Queen Mary College, London. Appointment: Professor of English, Bar-Ilan University, Ramat Gan, Israel, 1956-. Publications: Prophet and Poet: The Bible and the Growth of Romanticism, 1965; Biblical Drama in England from the Middle Ages to the Present Day, 1968; The Soul of Wit: A Study of John Donne, 1974; Milton and the Baroque, 1980; Sixteenth-Century English Literature, 1982; Renaissance Perspectives in Literature and the Visual Arts, 1987; Changing Perspectives in Literature and the Visual Arts, 1650-1820, 1990; Victorian Contexts in Literature and the Visual Arts, 1995. Contributions to: Professional journals. Address: 51 Katznelson Street, Kiryat Ono, Israel.

ROTBLAT Joseph, b. 4 Nov 1908, Warsaw, Poland. Professor Emeritus; Writer. Education: MA, University of Warsaw; PhD, University of Liverpool. Appointments: Professor, 1950-76, Professor Emeritus, 1976-, Medical College of St Batholomew's Hospital, University of London; Editor, Physics in Medicine and Biology, 1960-73; President, Pugwash Conferences on Science and World Affairs, 1988-. Publications: Radioactivity and Radioactive Substances (with Sir James Chadwick), 1961; Science and World Affairs, 1962; The Uses and Effects of Nuclear Energy (co-author), 1964; Aspects of Medical Physics (editor), 1966; Pugwash: The First Ten Years, 1967; Scientists in the Quest for Peace: A History of the Pugwash Conferences, 1972; Nuclear Reactors: To Breed or Not to Breed, 1977; Nuclear Energy and Nuclear Weapon Proliferation, 1979; Nuclear Radiation in Warfare, 1981; Scientists, The Arms Race and Disarmament, 1982; The Arms Race at a Time of Decision, 1984; Nuclear Strategy and World Security, 1985; World Peace and the Developing Countries, 1986; Strategic Defence and the Future of the Arms Race, 1987; Co-existence, Co-operation and Common Security, 1988; Verification of Arms Reductions, 1989; Global Problems and Common Security, 1989; Nuclear Proliferation: Technical and Economic Aspects, 1990; Global Security Through Co-Operation, 1990; Towards a Secure World in the 21st Century, 1991; Striving for Peace, Security and Development in the World, 1992; A Nuclear-Weapon-Free World: Desirable? Feasible?, 1993. Honours: Commander of the Order of the British Empire, 1965; Albert Einstein Peace Prize, 1992; FRS, 1995; Nobel Peace Prize, 1995. Address: 8 Asmara Road, London NW2 3ST, England.

ROTH Andrew, b. 23 Apr 1919, New York, New York, USA. Political Correspondent. m. Mathilda Anna Friederich, 1949, div 1984, 1 son, 1 daughter. Education: BSS, City College of New York, 1939; MA, Columbia University, 1940; Harvard University. Appointments: Reader, City College, 1939; Research Associate, Institute of Pacific Relations, 1940; Editorial Writer, The Nation, 1945-46; Foreign Correspondent, Toronto Star Weekly, 1946-50; London Correspondent, France Observateur, Sekai, Singapore Standard, 1950-60; Director, Parliamentary Profiles, 1955-; Political Correspondent, Manchester Evening News, 1972-84; Political Correspondent, New Statesman, 1984-. Publications: Japan Strikes South, 1941; French Interests and Policies in the Far East, 1942; Dilemma in Japan, 1945; The Business Background of MPs, 1959, 7th edition, 1980; The MPs Chart, 1967, 6th edition, 1987; Enoch Powell: Tory Tribune, 1970; Can Parliament Decide..., 1971; Heath and the Heathmen, 1972; Lord on the Board, 1972; Sir Harold Wilson: Yorkshire Walter Mitty, 1977; Parliamentary Profiles, Vols I-IV, 1984-85, 2nd edition, 1988-90; New MPs of '92, 1992; Mr Nice Guy and His Chums, 1993. Address: 34 Somali Road, London NW2 3RL, England.

ROTHE-VALLBONA Rima Gretel, b. 15 Mar 1931, San José, Costa Rica. Writer; College Professor. m. Dr Carlos Vallbona, 26 Dec 1956, 1 son, 1 daughter. Education: BA, BS Colegio Superior de

Senoritas, San José, Costa Rica, 1948; Diploma, Professor of French in a Foreign Country, University of Paris, Sorbonne, 1953; Diploma in Spanish Philology, University of Salamanca, Spain, 1954; MA, University of Costa Rica, 1962; DML, Doctor in Modern Languages, Middlebury College, USA, 1981. Appointments: Visiting Professor, Rice University, 1980-83, University of St Thomas Summer Program in Argentina, 1972; Rice University Summer Program in Spain, 1974; Cullen Foundation Professor of Spanish, 1989-; Emeritus Professor, 1995-. Publications: Noche en vela (novel), 1968; Polvo del camino (short stories), 1971; Yolanda Oreamuno (literary essay), 1972; La Salamandra Rosada (short stories), 1979; La Obra en prosa de Eunice Odio (literary essay), 1981; Mujeres y agonias (short stories), 1982; Las sombres que perseguimos (novel), 1983; Baraja de soledades (short stories), 1983; Cosecha de pecadores (short stories), 1988; El arcangel del perdon (short stories), 1990; Mundo, demonio y mujer (novel), 1991; Los infiernos de la mujer y algo mas (short stories), 1992; Vida y sucesos de la Monja Alferez (critical edition), 1992; Flowering Inferno: Tales of Sinking Hearts (short stories), 1993. Honours: Ancora Award, 1983-84; Medal of Civil Service, 1989. Memberships: Board of Directors, Houston Public Library, 1984-86; Pannelist in Cultural Arts Council of Houston, 1984-86, Board of Directors, 1990. Address: 3706 Lake Street, Houston, TX 77098, USA.

ROTHENBERG Jerome (Dennis), b. 11 Dec 1931, New York, New York, USA. Professor of Visual Arts and Literature; Poet; Writer. m. Diane Brodatz, 25 Dec 1952, 1 son. Education: BA, City College, New York City, 1952; MA, University of Michigan, 1953. Appointments: Professor of English and Comparative Literature, State University of New York at Binghamton, 1986-88; Professor of Visual Arts and Literature, University of California at San Diego, 1988-. Publications: New Young German Poets, 1959; White Sun, Black Sun, 1960; Technicians of the Sacred, 1968; Poems for the Game of Silence: Selected Poems, 1971; Shaking the Pumpkin, 1972, 2nd edition, 1986; America: A Prophecy, 1973; Poland/1931, 1974; Revolution of the Word, 1974; A Big Jewish Book, 1977; A Seneca Journal, 1978; Numbers and Letters, 1980; Vienna Blood, 1980; Pre-Faces, 1981; That Dada Strain, 1983; Symposium of the Whole, 1983; 15 Flower World Variations, 1984; A Merz Sonata, 1985; New Selected Poems, 1970-85, 1986; Exiled in the Word, 1989; Khurbn and Other Poems, 1989; Further Sightings and Conversations, 1989; The Lorca Variations, 1994; Gematria, 1994; Poems for the Millenium, Vol I, 1995; Pictures of the Crucifixion, 1996; Seedings and Other Poems, 1996; The Book: Spiritual Instrument, 1996. Contributions to: Various publications. Honours: National Endowment for the Arts Fellowship, 1975; Guggenheim Fellowship, 1976; American Book Award, 1982; Translation Award, PEN Center, USA West, 1994; Josephine Miles Literary Awards, PEN Oakland, 1994, 1996. Memberships: New Wilderness Foundation; PEN Internationa. Address: c/o Department of Visual Arts, University of California at San Diego, La Jolla, CA 92093, USA.

ROTHMAN Judith. See: **PETERS Maureen.**

ROTHSTEIN Sir John Knewstub Maurice, b. 11 July 1901, England. Art Gallery Director (retired); Writer. Education: MA, Oxford University, 1927; PhD, University College, London, 1931. Appointments: Director, various art galleries, including The Tate, 1938-64. Publications: An Introduction to Painting, 1934; Augustus John, 1944; Modern English Painters, 3 volumes, 1952-74, revised edition, 1984; Turner, 1960; Sickert, 1961; Paul Nash, 1961; Summer's Lease, 1965; Brave Day, Hideous Night, 1966; Francis Bacon, 3 volumes, 1967; Time's Thievish Progress, 1970; Edward Burra, 1972; Stanley Spencer, the Man, 1979; John Nash, 1983; Stanley Spencer, 1989. Honours: Commander of the Order of the British Empire, 1948; Knighted, 1952; Knight Commander, Order of the Aztec Eagle, Mexico, 1953; Honorary Fellow, Worcester College, Oxford, 1953; Fellow, University College, London, 1976; Knight Commander, Order of St Gregory the Great, 1977. Address: Beauforest House, Newington, Dorchester-on-Thames, Oxford OX9 8AG, England.

ROTIMI (Emmanuel Gladstone) Ola(wale), b. 13 Apr 1938, Sapele, Nigeria. Playwright. Education: BFA, Boston University, 1963; MFA, Yale University, 1966. Appointment: Head, Department of Creative Arts, University of Port Harcourt, 1982-. Publications: Our Husband Has Gone Mad Again, 1966; The Gods Are Not To Blame, 1968; Kurunmi: An Historical Tragedy, 1969; Holding Talks, 1970; Ovonramwen Nogbaisi, 1971; Imitation into Madness, 1973; Grip Am, 1973; Akassi Youmi, 1977; If: A Tragedy of the Ruled, 1979; Hopes of the Living - Dead, 1985. Honours: Oxford University Press Prize, 1970.

Address: Department of Creative Arts, University of Port Harcourt, PMB 5323, Port Harcourt, Rivers State, Nigeria.

ROUDINESCO Elisabeth, b. 10 Sept 1944, Paris, France. Historian; Writer. Education: State Doctor of Letters Degree, History and Human Science, University of Paris; École des Hautes Études en Sciences, Paris. Publications: Histoire de la Psychanalyse en France, 1885-1995, 2 volumes, 1982, 1986; Madness and Revolution, 1991; Jacques lacan Esquisse d'une vie Historie d'une Systéme de Pensée, 1993. Contributions to: Various publications. Memberships: Comité de la Maison des Ecrivains, Paris; Société International d'histoire de la Psychiatrie et de la Psychanalyse, Paris. Address: 89 avenue Denfert-Rochereau, 75014 Paris, France.

ROUNDTREE Owen. See: **KRAUZER Steven M**.

ROUSSEAU George (Sebastian), b. 23 Feb 1941, New York, New York, USA. Professor of English Literature; Writer. Education: BA, Amherst College, 1962; MA, 1964, PhD, 1966, Princeton University. Appointments: Osgood Fellow in English Literature, 1965-66, Woodrow Wilson Dissertation Fellow, 1966, Princeton University; Book Reviewer, The New York Times, 1967-; Instructor, Harvard University, 1966-68; Assistant Professor, 1968-69, Associate Professor, 1969-76, Professor of English, 1976-94, University of California at Los Angeles; Fulbright Resident Professor, West Germany, 1970; Honorary Fellow, Wolfson College, Cambridge, 1974-75; Overseas Fellow, Cambridge University, 1979; Visiting Fellow Commoner, Trinity College, Cambridge, 1982; Senior Fulbright Resident Scholar, Sir Thomas Browne Institute, Netherlands, 1983; Visiting Exchange Professor, King's College, Cambridge, 1984; Senior Fellow, National Endowment for the Humanities, 1986-87; Visiting Fellow and Waynflete Lecturer, Magdalen College, Oxford, 1993-94; Regius Professor of English Literature, King's College, University of Aberdeen, 1994-. Publications: This Long Disease My Life: Alexander Pope and the Sciences (editor with Marjorie Hope Nicolson), 1968; John Hill's Hypochondriasis, 1969; English Poetic Satire: Wyatt to Byron (with N Rudenstine), 1969; The Augustan Milieu: Essays Presented to Louis A Landa (editor with Eric Rothstein), 1970; Tobias Smollett: Bicentennial Essays Presented to Lewis M Knapp (co-editor), 1971; Organic Form: The Life of an Idea (editor), 1972; Goldsmith: The Critical Heritage, 1974; The Renaissance Man in the 18th Century, 1978; The Ferment of Knowledge: Studies in the Historiography of Eighteenth Century Science (editor with Roy Porter), 1980; The Letters and Private Papers of Sir John Hill, 1981; Tobias Smollett: Essays of Two Decades, 1982; Literature and Science (editor), 1985; Science and the Imagination: The Berkeley Conference (editor), 1985; Sexual Underworlds of the Enlightenment (editor with Roy Porter), 1987; The Enduring Legacy: Alexander Pope Tercentenary Essays (editor with P Rogers), 1988; Exoticism in the Enlightenment (with Roy Porter), 1990; Perilous Enlightenment: Pre- and Post-Modern Discources: Sexual, Historical, 1991; Enlightenment Crossings: Pre- and Post-Modern Discources: Anthropological, 1991; Enlightenment Borders: Pre- and Post-Modern Discources: Medical, Scientific, 1991; Hysteria Before Freud (co-author), 1993. Contributions to: Professional journals and general publications. Honour: Clifford Prize, 1987. Memberships: Many professional organizations. Address: c/o Department of English, Taylor Building, King's College, University of Aberdeen, Aberdeen AB24 3UB, Scotland.

ROUX Jean-Louis, b. 18 May 1923, Montreal, Quebec, Canada. Dramatic Artist; Director; Playwright; Founder and Director of Cultural Organisations. m. Monique, 25 Oct 1950, 1 son. Education: BA cum laude, Convent of Hochelaga, Mont Jésus Marie, Collège sainte-Marie, 1942; Certificat d'études in chemistry, physics and biology, Université de Montréal, 1943; Medical studies, 1943-46. Appointments: Amateur theatricals at the Collège Sainte-Marie, 1933-42; Compagnons de Saint-Laurent, 1939-42; Compagnie Ludmilla Pitoeff, 1942-46; Theatre, in Paris, and tours in France, Belgium, Switzerland and Tunisia, 1946-51; Co-Founder, Le Théatre du Nouveau Monde, Secretary General 1953-63, Artistic Director 1966-82; Toured many productions as actor, director and manager in France, Belgium, Switzerland, Luxembourg, Czechoslovakia, USSR, New York, Canada, 1955-82; Director General, National Theatre School of Canada, 1982; Full-time acting, directing and writing plays, 1987. Publications: Rose Latulippe (romantic comedy), 1951; Bois-Brulés, 1967; On n'a pas tué Joe Hill, 1967; Nuit des rois, 1968; Chien Limier, 1978; Camille et Caroline, 1982; Coeurs de soeurs, 1982; Rita veut s'éduquer, 1988. Honours: Kiwanis Certificate, 1962; Centennial confederation medal, 1967; Molson Prize, 1977; World Theatre Award, 1985; Chevalier de l'Ordre national du Québec, 1988. Memberships: Union des artistes; Société des Auteurs et Compositeurs dramatiques et Compositeurs; Alliance of Canadian Cinema, Television and Radio Artists; Canadian Actors' Equity Association; Royal Society of Canada. Address: 4145 Blueridge Crescent, Apt 2, Montreal, Quebec H3H 1S7, Canada.

ROVNER Arkady, b. 28 Jan 1940, Odessa, Russia. Writer; Publisher; Teacher. m. Victoria Andreyeva, 5 Aug 1969, 1 son. Education: MA, Philosophy, 1965, Moscow University; Graduate Programme, Department of German and English, 1965-67, Moscow Pedagogical Institute; Graduate Programme, Department of Foreign Studies, American University, Washington, DC, 1974-75; Doctoral Studies, Department of Religion, Columbia University, 1976-87. Appointments: Publisher, Gnosis Press, 1978-; Instructor, Faculty Member, New York University, 1981-85; Instructor, New School for Social Research, New York, 1981-. Publications: Gostii iz oblastii, 1975; Kalalatsy, 1980; Khod korolyom, 1989; Etagy Gadesa, 1992; Tretya Kultura, book of essays, 1996. Contributions to: Various publications. Honours: Cammington Community of the Arts, USA, 1983; Mme Karolyi Foundation, Vance, France, 1984. Membership: American PEN Center; Union of Russian Writers. Address: PO Box 42, Prince Street Station, New York, NY 10012, USA.

ROWAN Deidre. See: **WILLIAMS Jeanne.**

ROWAN Hester. See: **ROBINSON Sheila Mary.**

ROWBOTHAM David Harold, b. 27 Aug 1924, Toowoomba, Queensland, Australia. Author; Poet; Journalist. m. Ethel Jessie Matthews, 14 Jan 1952, 2 daughters. Education: BA, University of Queensland, 1965; MA (QUAL), 1969. Appointments: Australian Delegate, World Congress of Poets, 1981; Cultural Visitor, USA, Library of Congress, 1988; Commonwealth Literary Fund Lecturer in Australian Literature, 1956, 1961, 1964; National Book Reviewing Panel, Australian Broadcasting Commission, 1954-63; Literary Editor, Brisbane Courier-Mail, 1980-87. Publications: Ploughman and Poet (poems), 1954; Town and City (stories), 1956; Inland (poems), 1958; The Man in the Jungle (novel), 1964; All the Room (poems), 1964; Bungalow and Hurricane (poems), 1967; The Makers of the Ark (poems), 1970; The Pen of Feathers (poems), 1971; Mighty Like a Harp (poems), 1974; Selected Poems, 1975; Maydays (poems), 1980; New and Selected Poems, 1945-93, 1994; The Ebony Gates: New & Wayside Poems, 1996. Contributions to: Numerous magazines and journals. Honours: Pacific Star, World War II, 1945; Emeritus Fellow of Australian Literature, Australia Council, 1989; Second Prize for Poetry, NSW Captain Cook Bi-Centenary Celebrations Literary Competition, 1970; Grace Leven Prize, 1964; Ford Memorial Medal for Poetry, University of Queensland, 1948; Order of Australia, Queen's Birthday Honours, 1991. Memberships include: Foundation Councillor, Australian Society of Authors, 1964-; Australian Journalists Association; International Federation of Journalists; President, State Branch, Fellowship of Australian Writers, 1982. Address: 28 Percival Terrace, Holland Park, Brisbane, Queensland 4121, Australia.

ROWE Brian. See: **CRESSWELL Helen.**

ROWETT Helen Graham Quiller, b. 30 Dec 1915, London, England. Retired Lecturer. Education: Girton College, Cambridge, 1935-39; BA, Natural Science, 1938; Part II, Zoology, 1939; MA, 1942. Publications: Guides to Dissection Parts 1-5, 1950-53; The Rat as a Small Mammal, 1960, 3rd edition, 1974; Guide to Dissection, 1962, revised edition, 1970; Histology and Embryology, 1962; Basic Anatomy and Physiology, 1959, 3rd edition, revised, 1988; Two Moorsway Guide, 1976, 5th edition, revised, 1996; Roundabout Family Rambling, 1995. Honour: Grisedale Research Scholarship, Manchester, 1939-40. Memberships: Society of Authors; West Country Writers; Institute of Biology; Royal Society of Arts, fellow. Address: 3 Manor Park, Dousland, Yelverton, Devon PL20 6LX, England.

ROWINSKI Alexander, b. 9 Mar 1931, Poland. Author. m. Hanna Gis, 13 Sep 1975, 1 son, 1 daughter. Education: BA, Philosophical and Social Sciences, Warsaw University, 1953. Appointments: Staff, Dziennik Zachodni, 1954-57, Prawo i Zycie, 1959-70, Kultura, 1972-78; Editor in Chief, Przeglad Tygodniowy, 1982-83. Publications: Wstapcie do klasztoru, 1966, 2nd edition, 1970; Anioly Warszawy, 1970, 3rd edition, 1974; Swiat sie konczy, 1972; Rozkoszny Pantoffelland, 1974; Wlepszym towarzystwie, 1975; Tamci zolnierze, 1979, 2nd edition, 1988; Spadek po synach slonca, 1987. Contributions to: Numerous magazines and journals. Honours: Julian Brun Award, 1960; Polish

Journalists Association Award, 1966; Award, Zycie Literackie, 1969; Ksawery Pruszynski Award, 1975. Membership: Polish Authors Association. Address: ul Jazgarzewska 10, 00-730 Warsaw, Poland.

ROWLAND Iris. See: **ROBERTS Irene.**

ROWLAND J(ohn) R(ussell), b. 10 Feb 1925, Armidale, New South Wales, Australia. Diplomat; Poet. Education: BA, University of Sydney, 1945. Appointments: Australian Ambassador to France, 1978-82; Visiting Fellow, Australian National University, 1982-83. Publications: The Feast of Ancestors, 1965; Snow, 1971; Time and Places: Poems of Locality, 1975; The Clock Inside, 1979; Sixty, 1989; Granite Country, 1994. Translator: The Sculptor of Candles, 1985. Honour: Officer, Order of Australia, 1981. Address: 15 Grey Street, Deakin, Australian Capital Territory 2600, Australia.

ROWLAND Peter Kenneth, b. 26 July 1938, London, England. Writer. Education: Graduate, University of Bristol, 1960. Publications: The Last Liberal Governments: The Promised Land 1905-1910, 1968; The Last Liberal Governments: Unfinished Business 1911-1914, 1971; Lloyd George, 1975; Macaulay's History of English in the 18th Century (editor), 1980; Macaulay's History of England from 1485 to 1685 (editor), 1985; Autobiography of Charles Dickens (editor), 1988; The Disappearance of Edwin Drood, 1991; Thomas Day 1748-1789: Virtue Almost Personified, 1996; The Life and Times of Thomas Day 1748-1789, 1996. Address: 18 Corbett Road, Wanstead, London E11 2LD, England.

ROWLAND Robin F, b. 17 June 1950, Tanga, Tanzania. Writer. Education: Lawrence Park Collegiate, Toronto, Canada; BA, Anthropology, York University, Toronto, 1973; Bachelor of Journalism, Carleton University, Ottawa, 1975. Appointments: Reporter, Sudbury Star, Ontario, Canada, 1975-76; Editor, CBC National Radio News, Toronto, 1977-80; Writer, Editor, CBC Teletext, Toronto, 1982-85; Freelance Writer, CTV National News, Toronto, 1988-. Publications: King of the Mob, Rocco Perri and the Women Who Ran His Rackets, 1987; Undercover: Cases of the RCMP's Most Secret Operative (with James Dubro), 1991. Radio Plays: A Truthful Witness, 1985; King of the Bootleggers, 1986; Hot Coffee, 1988. Membership: Science Fiction and Fantasy Writers of America. Address: Eridani Productions, Suite 1005, 268 Poplar Plains Road, Toronto, Ontario M4V 2P2, Canada.

ROWLAND-ENTWISTLE (Arthur) Theodore (Henry), b. 30 July 1925, Clayton-le-Moors, Lancashire, England. Writer. Education: BA (Hons), Open University. Publications: Famous Composers (with J Cooke), 1974; Animal Worlds (with J Cooke), 1975; Famous Explorers (with J Cooke), 1975; Facts and Records Book of Animals, 1975; Famous Kings and Emperors (with J Cooke), 1977; The World You Never See: Insect Life, 1976; Our Earth, 1977; The Restless Earth, 1977; Exploring Animal Homes, 1978; Seashore Life (as T E Henry), 1983; Fishes (as James Hall-Clarke), 1983; Fact Book of British History (with J Cooke), 1984; Heraldry, 1984; Houses, 1985; World of Speed, 1985; Confucius, 1986; Stamps, 1986; Nebuchadnezzar, 1986; Rivers and Lakes, 1986; Focus on Rubber, 1986; Great British Architects, 1986; Great British Inventors, 1986; Great British Kings and Queens, 1986; Great British Reformers, 1986; Focus on Coal, 1987; The Royal Marines, 1987; The Secret Service, 1987; The Special Air Service, 1987; Jungles and Rainforests, 1987; Three-Dimensional Atlas of the World, 1988; Flags, 1988; Guns, 1988; Focus on Silk, 1989; Weather and Climate, 1991; Funfax History of Britain, 1993; Question and Answer Quiz Book (with A Kramer), 1995; World Events and Dates, 1995. Contributions to: Various encyclopaedias and periodicals. Memberships: Royal Geographical Society, fellow; Zoological Society, fellow. Address: West Dene, Stonestile Lane, Hastings, Sussex TN35 4PE, England.

ROWSE A(lfred) L(eslie), b. 4 Dec 1903, St Austell, Cornwall, England. Historian; Poet; Professor Emeritus. Education: MA, Christ Church, Oxford, 1929. Appointments: Fellow, All Souls College, Oxford, 1925-74; Research Associate, Huntington Library, San Marino, California, USA, 1962-69. Publications: Poetry: Poems of a Decade, 1941; Poems Chiefly Cornish, 1944; Poems Partly American, 1959; The Road to Oxford, 1978; A Life: Collected Poems, 1981; Transatlantic: Later Poems, 1989. Other: Tudor Cornwall: Portrait of a Society, 1941; A Cornish Childhood, 1942; The England of Elizabeth, 1950; The Churchills: The Story of a Family, 1956-58; William Shakespeare: A Biography, 1963; Christopher Marlowe: A Biography, 1964; Shakespeare's Southampton, 1965; The Cornish in America, 1969; The Elizabethan Renaissance, 1971-72; Shakespeare the Man,

1973; Oxford in the History of the Nation, 1975; Matthew Arnold, Poet and Prophet, 1976; Homosexuals in History, 1977; The Byrons and Trevanions, 1978; A Man of the Thirties, 1979; Memories of Men and Women, 1980; Shakespeare's Globe: His Intellectual and Moral Outlook, 1981; Eminent Elizabethans, 1983; Shakespeare's Self-Portrait, 1984; Froude the Historian, 1987; The Poet Auden, 1987; Discovering Shakespeare, 1989; The Sayings of Shakespeare, 1993; Fowl Caroline Portraits, 1993; All Souls in My Time, 1993; Historians I Have Known, 1995. Honours: Benson Medal, Royal Society of Literature, 1982; Honorary doctorates. Memberships: British Academy, fellow; English Association, president, 1952; Royal Society of Literature, fellow; Shakespeare Club, Stratford-upon-Avon, president, 1970-. Address: Trenarren House, St Austell, Cornwall PL26 6BH, England.

ROYCE Kenneth. See: **GANDLEY Kenneth Royce.**

RUAS Charles Edward, b. 14 Nov 1938, Tientsin, China. Author. m. Agneta Danielsson, 10 June 1967, div 1976, 1 son. Education: BA, 1960, MA, 1963, PhD, 1970, Princeton University; Sorbonne, University of Paris, 1964. Publications: Conversations With American Writers, 1986; Entering the Dream: Lewis Carroll, 1994. Other: Several translations. Contributions to: Newspapers and magazines. Honours: Fulbright Lecturer, 1992; Fellowships and awards. Memberships: PEN International; Writers Room. Address: c/o Curtis Brown Ltd, 10 Astor Place, 3rd Floor, New York, NY 10003, USA.

RUBENS Bernice Ruth, b. 26 July 1923, Cardiff, Wales. Author. m. Rudi Nassauer, 1947, 2 daughters. Education: BA, University of Wales, 1944. Appointments: Author, Director, documentary films on Third World subjects. Publications: Novels: Set on Edge, 1960; Madame Sontsatzka, 1962; Mate in Three, 1964; The Elected Member, 1968; Sunday Best, 1970; Go Tell the Lemming, 1972; I Sent a Letter to My Love, 1974; Ponsonby Post, 1976; A Five-year Sentence, 1978; Spring Sonata, 1979; Birds of Passage, 1980; Brothers, 1982; Mr Wakefield's Crusade, 1985; Our Father, 1987; Kingdom Come: A Solitary Grief, 1991; Mother Russia, 1992; Autobiopsy, 1993; Yesterday in the Back Lane, 1995. Honours: Booker Prize, 1970; American Blue Ribbon (documentary film), 1972; Hon DLitt, University of Wales. Membership: Fellow, University College, Cardiff. Address: Flat 3, 111 Canfield Gardens, London NW6 3DY, England.

RUBIN Larry Jerome, b. 14 Feb 1930, Bayonne, New Jersey, USA. Professor of English; Writer; Poet. Education: BA, 1951, MA, 1952, PhD, 1956, Emory University. Appointments: Instructor, 1956-58, Assistant Professor, 1958-65, Associate Professor, 1965-73, Professor of English, 1973-, Georgia Institute of Technology, Atlanta; Smith-Mundt Fellow, University of Krakow, 1961-62; Fulbright Lecturer, University of Bergen, 1966-67; Visiting Professor, Free University of West Berlin, 1969-70, University of Innsbruck, 1971-72. Publications: Poetry: The World's Old Way, 1963; Lanced in Light, 1967; All My Mirrors Lie, 1975. Contributions to: Many professional journals, anthologies, and periodicals. Honours: Poetry Society of America Awards, 1961, 1973; Sidney Lanier Award, Oglethorpe University, 1964; Georgia Poet of the Year Awards, 1967, 1975; Kansas City Star Award, 1969; Georgia Writers Association Award, 1973; Georgia Authors Series Award, 1975; All Nations Poetry Award, Triton College, 1980. Memberships: Poetry Society of America; Georgia Poetry Society. Address: Box 15014, Druid Hills Branch, Atlanta, GA 30333, USA.

RUBIN Rivka Leah Jacobs, b. 22 Feb 1952, Philadelphia, Pennsylvania, USA. Writer. m. Gerald E Rubin, 25 Nov 1981, 1 son. Education: BA, History, 1981, MA, Sociology, 1982, Marshall University. Publications: Experimentum Crucis, 1981; The Boy From the Moon, 1985; The Milk of Paradise, 1985; Morning on Venus, 1985. Memberships: Science Fiction Writers of America; West Virginia Sociological Association. Address: 1285 26th Street, Huntington, WV 25705, USA.

RUBINSTEIN Gillian Margaret, b. 29 Aug 1942, Berkhamsted, England. Author. m. Philip Rubinstein, 1973, 1 son, 2 daughters. Education: BA, MA, Modern Languages, Oxford University, 1961-64; Postgraduate Certificate of Education, University of London, 1972. Publications: Space Demons, 1986; Beyond the Labyrinth, 1988; Answers to Brut, 1988; Melanie and the Night Animal, 1988; Skymaze, 1989; Flashback, 1990; At Ardilla, 1991; Dog In, Cat Out, 1991;

Squawk and Screech, 1991; Galax-Arena, 1992; Keep Me Company, 1992; Mr Plunkett's Pool, 1992; The Giant's Tooth, 1993; Foxspell, 1994. Honours: Honour Books, Australian Children's Book Council, 1987, 1989; Senior Fellowships, Australia Council, 1988, 1989-92; National Children's Book Awards, 1988, 1990; New South Wales Premier's Award, 1988; Book of the Year, CBA, 1989. Membership: Australian Society of Authors. Address: c/o Australian Literary Management, 2a Armstrong Street, Middle Park, Victoria 3206, Australia.

RUBINSTEIN Hilary Harold, b. 24 Apr 1926, London, England. Literary Agent; Writer. m. Helge Kitzinger, 6 Aug 1955, 3 sons, 1 daughter. Education: Cheltenham College; MA, Merton College, Oxford. Appointments: Director, Victor Gollancz Ltd, 1953-63; Deputy Editor, The Observer Magazine, 1964-65; Managing Director, A P Watt Ltd, 1965-92, Hilary Rubinstein Books, 1992-. Publications: The Complete Insomniac, 1974; Hotels and Inns (editor), 1984; The Good Hotel Guide (founder-editor), 1978-. Contributions to: Newspapers and magazines. Memberships: Arts Council, literature panel, 1973-79; literature national committee, 1975-77; Open College of the Arts, trustee, 1987-; Society of Authors. Address: 32 Labbroke Grove, London W11 3BQ, England.

RUDKIN James David, b. 29 June 1936, London, England. Dramatist. m. Alexandra Margaret Thompson, 3 May 1967, 2 sons, 2 daughters. Education: MA, St Catherine's College, Oxford, 1957-61. Appointment: Judith E Wilson Fellow, University of Cambridge, 1984. Publications: Afore Night Come (stage play), 1964; Schoenberg's Moses und Aron (translation for Royal Opera), 1965; Ashes (stage play), 1974; Cries From Casement as His Bones are Brought to Dublin (radio play), 1974; Penda's Fen (TV film), 1975; Hippolytus (translation from Euripides), 1980; The Sons of Light (stage play), 1981; The Triumph of Death (stage play), 1981; Peer Gynt (translation from Ibsen), 1983; The Saxon Shore (stage play), 1986; Rosmersholm (translation from Ibsen), 1990; When We Dead Waken (translation from Ibsen), 1990. Opera libretti: The Grace of Todd, Gordon Crosse, 1969; Inquest of Love, Jonathan Harvey, 1993. Contributions to: Drama; Tempo; Encounter. Honours: Evening Standard Most Promising Dramatist Award, 1962; John Whiting Drama Award, 1974; Obie Award, New York, 1977; New York Film Festival Gold Medal for Screenplay, 1987; Sony Silver Radio Drama Award, 1994. Memberships: Hellenic Society; PEN. Address: c/o Casarotto Ramsay Ltd, National House, 60-66 Wardour Street, London W1V 3HP, England.

RUDMAN Mark, b. 11 Dec 1948, New York, New York, USA. Poet; Critic; Editor; Translator; Adjunct Professor. m. Madeleine Bates, 1 son. Education: BA, New School for Social Research, 1971; MFA, Columbia University, 1974. Appointments: Poetry and Criticism Editor, 1975-, Editor-in-Chief, 1984-, Pequod Journal; Writer-in-Residence, University of Hawaii, 1978, State University of New York at Buffalo, 1979, and Wabash College, 1979; Adjunct Lecturer, Queens College, 1980-81; Lecturer, Parsons School of Design, 1983; Poet-in-Residence and Associate Professor, York College, 1984-88; Assistant Director and Adjunct Professor, Graduate Creative Writing Program, New York University, 1986-; Adjunct Professor of Creative Writing, Columbia University, 1988-91; Poet-in-Residence, State University of New York, Purchase, 1991; Adjunct Professor, Columbia University, 1992-. Publications: In The Neighboring Cell (poems), 1982; The Mystery in the Garden (poetry chapbook), 1985; By Contraries and Other Poems: 1970-1984, Selected and New, 1986; The Ruin Revived (poetry chapbook), 1986; The Nowhere Steps (poems), 1990; Literature and the Visual Arts, 1990; Diverse Voices: Essays on Poetry, 1993; Rider, 1994; Realm of Unknowing: Meditations on Art, Suicide, Uncertainty, and Other Transformations, 1995; The Millennium Hotel (poems), 1996. Contributions to: Poems and essays in many anthologies and other publications. Honours: Academy of American Poets Award, 1971; Yaddo Residencies, 1977, 1983; Ingram Merrill Foundation Fellowship, 1983-84; New York Foundation of the Arts Fellowship, 1988; National Book Critics Circle Award in Poetry, 1994; National Endowment for the Arts Fellowship, 1995; Guggenheim Fellowship, 1996-97. Memberships: PEN; Board of Governors, Poetry Society of America, 1984-88. Address: 817 West End Avenue, New York, NY 10025, USA.

RUDOLF Anthony, b. 6 Sept 1942, London, England. Writer; Translator. Div, 1 son, 1 daughter. Education: BA, Trinity College, Cambridge, 1964; Diploma, British Institute, Paris, 1964. Appointments: Co-Founder and Editor, Menard Press, London, 1969;

Advisory Editor, Modern Poetry in Translation, 1973-; Adam Lecturer, Kemp College, London, 1990; Member of Jury, Neustady International Prize, Oklahoma, 1986. Publications: The Same River Twice, 1976; After the Dream: Poems 1964-79, 1980; Primo Levi's War Against Oblivion, 1990; Mandorla, 1997. Other: Translations of poetry. Contributions to: Periodicals. Address: 8 The Oaks, Woodside Avenue, London N12 8AR, England.

RUDOLPH Lee (Norman), b. 28 Mar 1948, Cleveland, Ohio, USA. Mathematician; Poet; Writer. Education: BA, Princeton University, 1969; PhD, Massachusetts Institute of Technology, 1974. Publications: Curses and Songs and Poems, 1974; The Country Changes, 1978. Contributions to: Professional journals, anthologies, and periodicals. Honours: Several awards. Memberships: Alice James Poetry Cooperative; National Writers Union. Address: PO Box 251, Adamsville, RI 02801, USA.

RUDOMIN Esther. See: **HAUTZIG Esther.**

RUELL Patrick. See: **HILL Reginald (Charles).**

RUELLAND Jacques G, b. 14 Aug 1948, Spa, Belgium. Professor; Writer. m. Krystyna Brylska-Ruelland, 17 Nov 1977, 1 daughter. Education: BA, Philosophy, 1975; MA, Philosophy, 1983; MA, History, 1985; PhD, History of Science, 1994. Appointment: Professor of History and Philosophy of Science. Publications: Pierre du Calvet 1735-1786, 1986; Orwell et 1984: Trois approches, 1988; Valentin Jautard 1736-1787, 1989; De l'épistémologie à la politique, 1991; Histoire de la guerre sainte, 1993; La Moisson littéraire, 1993; Civilisation occidentale: histoire et héritages, 1995; Philosopher à Montréal, 1995; Tolérance, 1996; Lueur dans les ténèbres, 1996. Contributions to: Various publications. Honours: Honorary Member, Société de Philosophie de Montréal; Prix Percy-W-Roy, 1987, 1988; Prix du Ministre, 1995. Memberships: Fondation Aérovision, Quebec, honorary member; Musée des arts graphiques, Montreal, president, 1986-95; Société des arts et des lettres, Brossard, president, 1993-; Société des écrivains canadiens, chairman, 1993-. Address: 360 rue de Venise, Brossard, Quebec J4W 1W7, Canada.

RUIZ Bernardo, b. 6 Oct 1953, Mexico City, Mexico. Author; Poet. m. Virginia Abrin Batule, 18 Nov 1978, 2 sons. Education: BA, Spanish and Latin American Literature, Universidad Nacional Autonoma de Mexico. Appointments: Editor, Universidad Autonoma Metropolitana, 1979, Ministry of Labour, 1985-88; Director, INBA, Centro Nacional de Informacion y Promocion de la Literatura, 1992. Publications: Fiction: Viene la Muerte, 1976; La otra orilla, 1980; Olvidar tu nombre, 1982; Vals sins fin, 1982, revised edition, 1986; Los caminos del hotel, 1991. Poetry: El Tuyo, el mismo, 1986; Juego de Cartas, 1992. Contributions to: Various publications. Memberships: Asociacion de Criticos de Mexico; Asociacion de Escritores de Mexico; Sociedad General de Escritores de Mexico. Address: Arizona 94-6, Col Napoles, CP 03810, Mexico DF.

RUKEYSER Louis (Richard), b. 30 Jan 1933, New York, New York, USA. Economic Writer and Broadcaster. m. Alexandra Gill, 3 Mar 1962, 3 daughters. Education: AB, Princeton University, 1954. Appointments: Reporter, Baltimore Sun Newspapers, 1954-65; Chief Political Correspondent, Baltimore Evening Sun, 1957-59; Chief, London Bureau, 1959-63, Chief Asian Correspondent, 1963-65, Baltimore Sun; Senior Correspondent and Commentator, 1965-73, Paris Correspondent, 1965-66, Chief, London Bureau, 1966-68, Economic Editor and Commentator, 1968-73, ABC News; Host, Wall $treet Week With Louis Rukeyser, PBS-TV, 1970-; Syndicated Economic Columnist, McNaught Syndicate, 1976-86, Tribune Media Services, 1986-93; Editor-in-Chief, Louis Rukeyser's Wall Street, 1992-, Louis Rukeysers's Mutual Funds, 1994-. Publications: How to Make Money in Wall Street, 1974, 2nd edition, 1976; What's Ahead for the Economy: The Challenge and the Chance, 1983, 2nd edition, 1985; Louis Rukeyser's Business Almanac, 1988, 2nd edition, 1991. Honours: Overseas Press Club Award, 1963, and Citation, 1964; G M Loeb Award, University of Connecticut, 1972; George Washington Honor Medals, Freedoms Foundation, 1972, 1978; Janus Award, 1975; Literary Guild Selections, 1974, 1976, 1984; New York Financial Writers Association Award, 1980; Free Enterprise Man of the Year, Texas A & M University, 1987; Women's Economic Round Table Award, 1990; Several honorary doctorates. Address: 586 Round Hill Road, Greenwich, CT 06831, USA.

RULE Jane, b. 28 Mar 1931, Plainfield, New Jersey, USA. Writer; Teacher. Education: Mills College, Oakland, California. Appointments: Teacher of English, Concord Academy, Massachusetts, 1954-56; Assistant Director, International House, 1958-59; Intermittent Lecturer in English, 1959-70; Visiting Lecturer in Creative Writing, University of British Columbia, Vancouver, 1972-73. Publications: The Desert of the Heart, 1964; This Is Not You, 1970; Against the Season, 1971; Lesbian Images, 1975; Themes for Diverse Instruments, 1975; The Young in One Another's Arms, 1977; Contract With the World, 1980; Outlander, 1981; Inland Passage, A Hot-Eyed Moderate, 1985; Memory Board, 1987; After the Fire, 1989. Honours: Canadian Author's Association Best Novel of the Year, 1978, Best Story of the Year, 1978; US Gay Academic Union Literature Award, 1978; Canadian Institute for the Blind, 1991; Fund for Human Dignity Award of Merit, 1983; Honorary Doctor of Letters, University of British Columbia, 1994. Memberships: Writers' Union of Canada; PEN. Literary Agent: Anne Borchardt, Georges Borchardt Inc, 136 East 57th Street, New York, NY 10022, USA. Address: The Fork, Rte 1, S19 C 17, Galiano, British Columbia V0N 1P0, Canada.

RUMBAUT Helen Elizabeth, b. 8 Oct 1949, Deland, Florida, USA. Writer; Public Information Specialist. m. Carlos Alberto Rumbaut, 5 July 1970, 1 daughter. Education: BA, French, University of Kansas, 1971. Publications: Dove Dream (young adult novel), 1994. Contributions to: Quick Picks brochure; Lone Star Quarterly; Crossing Press, Women and Food. Memberships: Authors' Guild; PEN West; Society of Children's Book Writers & Illustrators; Austin Writers' League.

RUMENS Carol Ann, b. 10 Dec 1944, Forest Hill, London, England. Writer; Poet. m. David Rumens, 30 July 1965, div, 2 daughters. Education: University of London, 1964-65. Appointments: Writing Fellow, University of Kent, 1983-85; Northern Arts Writing Fellow, 1988-90; Writer-in-Residence, Queen's University, Belfast, 1991-. Publications: A Strange Girl in Bright Colours, 1973; Unplayed Music, 1981; Star Whisper, 1983; Direct Dialling, 1985; Selected Poems, 1987; Plato Park, 1988; The Greening of the Snow Beach, 1988; From Berlin to Heaven, 1990. Contributions to: Periodicals. Honours: Alice Hunt Bartlett Prize (jointly), 1981; Prudence Farmer Award, 1983; Cholmondeley Award, 1984. Memberships: International PEN; Royal Society of Literature, fellow; Society of Authors. Address: 100A Tunis Road, London W12 7EY, England.

RUNDLE Anne, (Marianne Lamont, Alexandra Manners, Joanne Marshall, Jeanne Sanders), b. United Kingdom. Writer. Publications: The Moon Marriage, 1967; Swordlight, 1968; Cuckoo at Candlemass (as J Marshall), 1968; Cat on a Broomstick (as J Marshall), The Dreaming Tower (as J Marshall), Dragonscale, 1969; Rakehell, Tamlane, Dark Changeling (as M Lamont), Green Glass Moon (as M Lamont), Flower of Silence (as J Marshall), 1970; Babylon Was Dust (as J Marshall), Bitter Bride Bed (as M Lamont), 1971; Lost Lotus, Amberwood, 1972; Wildboar Wood (as J Marshall), The Trelised Walk, Sea-Song, The Stone Maiden (as A Manners), 1973; Candles in the Wood (as A Manners), Heron Brook, Spindrift (as J Sanders), Follow a Shadow (as J Marshall), Valley of Tall Chimneys (as J Marshall), 1974; The Singing Swans (as A Manners), 1975; Judith Lammeter, 1976; Sable Hunter (as A Manners), Nine Moons Wasted (as M Lamont), 1977; Grey Ghyll, The Peacock Bed (as J Marshall), Wildford's Daughter (as A Manners), 1978 (in UK as The White Moths, 1979); Horns of the Moon (as M Lamont), 1979; Echoing Yesterday (as A Manners), 1981; Trilogy, Karran Kinrade (as A Manners), 1982; A Serpent's Tooth (as M Lamont), 1983; Trilogy, The Red Bird (as A Manners), Trilogy, The Gaming House (as A Manners), 1984; Moonbranches, 1986. Address: Cloy Cottage, Knowe Road, Brodick, Isle of Arran, Scotland.

RUNHAM. See: **ACKROYD Peter.**

RUSAN Otila Valeria. See: **BLANDIANA Ana.**

RUSCH Barbara Lynn, b. 7 July 1949, Toronto, Ontario, Canada. Ephemerist. m. Donald Zaldin, 24 May 1991, 1 son, 1 daughter, 2 stepsons, 2 stepdaughters. Education: BA, French Literature, 1971, MA, French Literature, 1976, University of Toronto. Publications: Canadian Printed Ephemera: An Historical Survey, 1988; Patterns of Alienation in 19th Century Manuscript Ephemera (editor), Ephemera Canada, 1991-; Collecting Victorian Ephemera, 1991; Blue Boxes Devour Paper Past, 1993; The Art of Persuasion: Images of Victorian Advertising Ephemera, 1994; Factory View Trade Cards:

Image of a New Social Order, 1996. Honours: True Davidson Memorial Award for Excellence, Bootmakers of Toronto, 1986; Warren Carlton Memorial Award, Bootmakers of Toronto, 1988, 1989; Maurice Rickards Award, Ephemera Society of America, 1989; Samuel Pepys Award, Ephemera Society, UK, 1992. Memberships: Ephemera Society of Canada, Founder & Pres, 1987-; Ephemera Society of America, Director 1993-96; The Bootmakers of Toronto, Director 1987-91; 1997. Address: 36 Macauley Drive, Thornill, Ontario L3T 5S5, Canada.

RUSH Norman, b. 24 Oct 1933, San Francisco, California, USA. Writer. m. Elsa Rush, 10 July 1955, 1 son, 1 daughter. Education: BA, Swarthmore College, 1956. Appointments: Instructor in English and History and Co-Director of College A, Rockland Community College, Suffern, New York, 1973-78; Co-Director, US Peace Corps, Botswana, 1978-83. Publications: Whites (stories), 1986; Mating (novel), 1991. Contributions to: Anthologies and periodicals. Membership: PEN American Center. Address: 10 High Tor Road, New City, NY 10956, USA.

RUSHDIE (Ahmed) Salman, b. 19 June 1947, Bombay, India. Writer. m. (1) Clarissa Luard, 1976, div 1987, 1 son, (2) Marianne Wiggins, 1988. Education: MA, King's College, Cambridge. Appointments: Actor, Fringe Theatre, London, 1968-69; Advertising Copywriter, 1969-73; Part-time Copywriter, 1976-80. Publications: Grimus, 1975; Midnight's Children, 1981; Shame, 1983; The Jaguar Smile: A Nicaraguan Journey, 1987; The Satanic Verses, 1988; Haroun and the Sea of Stories, 1990; Imaginary Homelands: Essays and Criticism 1981-1991 (essays), 1991; The Wizard of Oz, 1992; The Moor's Last Sigh; East West (stories), 1995. Television films: The Painter and the Pest, 1985; The Riddle of Midnight, 1988. Contributions to: New York Times; Guardian; Granta; New Yorker. Honours: Booker McConnell Prize for Fiction, 1981; Arts Council Literature Bursary, 1981; English Speaking Union Literary Award, 1981; James Tait Black Memorial Book Prize, 1981; Prix du Meilleur Livre Etranger, 1984; Nominated for Whitbread Prize, 1988; Booker Prize, 1993. Memberships: PEN; Production Board, British Film Institute; Advisory Board, Institute of Contemporary Arts; Fellow, Royal Society of Literature. Address: c/o Aitken and Stone Ltd, 29 Fernshaw Road, London SW10 0TG, England.

RUSSELL Irwin Peter, b. 16 Sept 1921, Bristol, England. Poet. m. (1) 1951, (2) 1974, 2 sons, 2 daughters. Education: Malvern College; Queen Mary College, London. Appointments: Poet-in-Residence, University of Victoria, British Columbia, 1972-74; Purdue University, Lafayette, Indiana, 1976-77; Teaching Fellow, Imperial Academy of Philosophy, Tehran, Iran, 1977-79. Publications: An Examination of Ezra Pound, 1950, 1975; Elegies of Quintilius, 1954, 3rd edition, 1996; Venice Poems, 1965, 2nd edition, 1995; All for the Wolves, Selected Poems 1947-74, 1984; Theories and Other Lyrics, 1990; Over 100 books and pamphlets including Dante and Islam, 1992. Contributions to: Magazines and journals. Honours: Premio internazionale Le Muse, City of Florence, 1990; Premio Internazionale Dante Alighieri, 1993. Address: 52026 Pian di Sco, Arezzo, Italy.

RUSSELL James. See: **HARKNETT Terry**.

RUSSELL John, b. 22 Jan 1919, Fleet, England. Art Critic; Writer. Education: BA, Magdalen College, Oxford, 1940. Appointments: Honorary Attaché, Tate Gallery, 1940-41; Staff, Ministry of Information, 1941-43, Naval Intelligence Division, Admiralty, London, 1943-46; Contributor, 1945-49, Art Critic, 1949-74, The Sunday Times; Art Critic, 1974-82, Chief Art Critic, 1982-, The New York Times. Publications: Shakespeare's Country, 1942; British Portrait Painters, 1945; Switzerland, 1950; Logan Pearsall Smith, 1950; Erich Kleiber, 1956; Paris, 1960, 2nd edition, 1983; Seurat, Private View (with Bryan Robertson and Lord Snowdon), 1965; Max Ernst, 1967; Henry Moore, 1968; Ben Nicholson, 1969; Pop Art Redefined (with Suzi Gablik), 1969; The World of Matisse, 1970; Francis Bacon, 1971; Édouard Vuillard, 1971; The Meanings of Modern Art, 1981, new and enlarged edition, 1990; Reading Russell, 1989; London, 1994. Contributions to: Various publications; Chief Art Critic, New York Times, 1982-91. Honour: Member, American Academy of Arts and Letters, 1996. Address: 166 East 61st Street, New York, NY 10021, USA.

RUSSELL Martin James, b. 25 Sept 1934, Bromley, Kent, England. Writer. Publications: No Through Road, 1965; The Client, 1975; Mr T, 1977; Death Fuse, 1980; Backlash, 1981; The Search for

Sara, 1983; A Domestic Affair, 1984; The Darker Side of Death, 1985; Prime Target, 1985; Dead Heat, 1986; The Second Time is Easy, 1987; House Arrest, 1988; Dummy Run, 1989; Mystery Lady, 1992; Leisure Pursuit, 1993. Memberships: Crime Writers' Association; Detection Club. Address: 15 Breckonmead, Wanstead Road, Bromley, Kent BR1 3BW, England.

RUSSELL Nicholas, b. 9 Oct 1938, Teddington, Middlesex, England. University Professor; Journalism Teacher. m. Sharon Elizabeth Plows, 20 June 1964, 2 sons. Education: BA English Honours, McGill University, 1966; MA English Honours, University of London, 1966; PhD Journalism, University of Wales, 1994. Publications: Monographs, Trials and Tribulations, 1986; The Quarrymen of History, 1987; Morals and the Media, 1994. Contributions to: Many Magazines and Journals. Memberships: Commonwealth Association of Journalists; Commonwealth Association of Journalism Educators; Association for Education in Journalism. Address: School of Journalism, University of Regina, Regina, Saskatchewan S4S OA2, Canada.

RUSSELL Ray, b. 4 Sept 1924, Chicago, Illinois, USA. Author; Editor. m. Ada Beth Stevens, 5 Sept 1950, 1 son, 1 daughter. Education: Chicago Conservatory; Goodman Theatre School of Drama (division of Art Institute, Chicago). Publications: Sardonicus, 1961; The Case Against Satan, 1962; The Little Lexicon of Love, 1966; Unholy Trinity, 1967; The Colony, 1969; Sagittarius, 1971; Prince of Darkness,1971; Incubus, 1976; Holy Horatio, 1976; Princess Pamela, 1979; The Book of Hell, 1980; The Devil's Mirror, 1980; The Bishop's Daughter, 1981; Haunted Castles, 1985; The Night Sound (poetry), 1987; Dirty Money, 1988; Absolute Power, 1992. Contributions to: Anthologies, textbooks, journals, and films. Honours: Sri Chinmoy Poetry Award, 1977; World Fantasy Lifetime Achievement Award, 1991; Bram Stoker Award, 1993. Address: c/o H N Swanson Inc, 8523 Sunset Boulevard, Los Angeles, CA 90069, USA.

RUSSELL Sherman Apt, b. 23 July 1954, California, USA. Teacher; Writer. m. Peter Russell, 24 Jan 1981, 1 son, 1 daughter. Education: BS, Conservation and Natural Resources, University of California at Berkeley; MFA, English and Creative Writing, University of Montana. Publications: Built to Last (co-author), 1986; Frederick Douglass, 1987; Songs of the Fluteplayer, 1991; The Humpbacked Fluteplayer, 1993; Kill the Cowboy: A Battle of Mythology in the West, 1993; When the Land was Young: Reflections on American Archaeology, 1996. Contributions to: Newspapers and magazines. Literary Agent: Sharon Friedman. Address: 1113 West Street, Silver Sity, NM 88061, USA.

RUSSELL Willy, (William Martin Russell), b. 23 Aug 1947, Liverpool, England. Author. m. Ann Seagroatt, 1969, 1 son, 2 daughters. Education: Certificate of Education, St Katherine's College of Education, Liverpool. Appointments: Teacher, 1973-74; Fellow, Creative Writing, Manchester Polytechnic, 1977-78. Publications: Theatre: Blind Scouse, 1971-72; When the Reds (adaptation), 1972; John, Paul, George, Ringo and Bert (musical), 1974; Breezeblock Park, 1975; One for the Road, 1976; Stags and Hens, 1978; Educating Rita, 1979; Blood Brothers (musical), 1983; Our Day Out (musical), 1983; Shirley Valentine, 1986. Television Plays: King of the Castle, 1972; Death of a Young Young Man, 1972; Break In (for schools), 1974; Our Day Out, 1976; Lies (for schools), 1977; Daughter of Albion, 1978; Boy With Transistor Radio (for schools), 1979; One Summer (series), 1980. Radio Play: I Read the News Today (for schools), 1979. Screenplays: Band on the Run, 1979; Educating Rita, 1981. Honours: Honorary MA, Open University; Honorary Director, Liverpool Playhouse. Address: c/o Margaret Ramsay Ltd, 14A Goodwin's Court, St Martin's Lane, London WC2, England.

RUSSO Albert, b. 26 Feb 1943, Kamina, Zaire. Writer; Poet. 1 son, 1 daughter. Education: Abschluss Diplom, Heidelberg; BSc, General Business Administration, New York University, USA. Appointments: Member, Jury of the Prix de l'Europe, 1982-; Jury Member, Neustadt International Prize for Literature, 1996. Publications: Incandescences, 1970; Eclats de malachite, 1971; La Pointe du diable, 1973; Mosaïque New Yorkaise, 1975; Albert Russo Anthology, 1987; Mixed Blood (novel), 1990; Le Cap des illusions (novel), 1991; Futureyes/Dans la nuit bleu fauve (poetry in English and in French), 1992; Kaleidoscope (poetry collection), 1993; Éclipse sur le Lac Tanganyika (novel), 1994; Venetian Thresholds, stories and poems, 1995; Painting the Tower of Babel, poetry collection, 1996; Zapinette Vidio, novel, 1996. Contributions to: Professional journals and BBC World Service. Honours: Willie Lee Martin Short Story Award, USA, 1987; Marguerette Cummins Award for Poetry, USA. Memberships: PEN; Authors Guild of America; Writers and Poets; Association of French Speaking Writers. Address: BP 640, 75826 Paris Cedex 17, France.

RUTSALA Vern, b. 5 Feb 1934, McCall, Idaho, USA. Writer; Teacher. m. Joan Colby, 6 May 1957, 2 sons, 1 daughter. Education: BA, Reed College, 1956; MFA, University of Iowa, 1960. Publications: The Window, 1964; Small Songs, 1969; The Harmful State, 1971; Laments, 1975; The Journey Begins, 1976; Paragraphs, 1978; The New Life, 1978; Walking Home from the Icehouse, 1981; Backtracking, 1985; The Mystery of Lost Shoes, 1985; Ruined Cities, 1987; Selected Poems, 1991; Little-Known Sports, 1994. Contributions to: New Yorker; Esquire; Poetry; Hudson Review; Harper's; Atlantic; American Poetry Review; Paris Review. Honours: National Endowment for the Arts Fellowships, 1974, 1979; Northwest Poetry Prize, 1976; Guggenheim Fellowship,1982; Carolyn Kizer Poetry Prize, 1988; Master, Fellowship, Oregon Arts Commission, 1990; Hazel Hall Award, 1992; Juniper Prize, 1993; Duncan Lawrie Prize, Arvon Foundation, 1994. Memberships: PEN; Poetry Society of America; AWP. Address: 2404 North East 24th Avenue, Portland, OR 97212, USA.

RUTTER Michael Llewellyn, b. 15 Aug 1933, Brummanna, Lebanon. Professor of Child Psychiatry; Writer. m. Marjorie Heys, 27 Dec 1958, 1 son, 2 daughters. Education: MB ChB, 1950-55, MD, 1963, University of Birmingham; DPM, University of London, 1961. Appointments: Professor of Child Psychiatry, University of London; Director, MRC Child Psychiatry Unit, and of the Social, Genetic and Developmental Psychiatry Research Centre. Publications: Depression in Young People: Development and Clinical Perspectives (co-editor), 1986; Language Development and Disorders (co-editor), 1987; Treatment of Autistic Children (co-editor), 1987; Parenting Breakdown: The Making and Breaking of Intergenerational Links (co-author), 1988; Assessment and Diagnosis in Child Psychopathology, 1988; Straight and Devious Pathways From Childhood to Adulthood, 1990; Biological Risk Factors for Psychosocial Disorders, 1991; Developing Minds: Challenge and Continuity Across the Lifespan, 1993; Stress, Risk and Resilience in Children and Adolescents, Processes, Mechanisms and Interventions, co-editor, 1994; Psychosocial Disorders in Young People: Time Trends and Their Causes, co-editor, 1995; Child and Adolescent Psychiatry: Modern Approaches (co-editor), 3rd edition, 1994; Development Through Life: A Handbook for Clinicians (co-editor), 1994; Psychosocial Disorders in Young People: Time Trends and their Causes (co-editor), 1995; Behavioural Genetics (co-author), 3rd edition, 1997. Contributions to: Numerous professional journals. Honours: Knight Baronet, 1992; Several honorary doctorates; American Psychological Association Distinguished Scientific Contribution Award, 1995; Castilla del Pino Prize for Achievement in Psychiatry, Cordoba, Spain, 1995; Honorary Doctorate of Psychology, University of Syvaskylä, Finland, 1996; Royal Society of Medicine, honorary fellow, 1996; Royal College of Paediatrics and Child Health, honorary founding fellow, 1996; Society for Research in Child Development, president elect, 1997. Memberships: American academy of Arts and Sciences, honorary foreign member; Royal College of Psychiatrists, fellow; Royal College of Physicians, fellow. Address: MRC Child Psychiatry Unit, Institute of Psychiatry, De Crespigny Park, Denmark Hill, London SE5 8AF, England.

RUYS Andrew John, b. 17 July 1964, Adelaide, South Australia. Research Scientist. m. Juanita Feros, 14 May 1988, 1 son. Education: BEng Hons I, 1987, DPhil, 1992, University of New South Wales, Australia. Appointment: Fellowship in Bioceramics, Australian Research Council, 1994. Publications: Founding Editor, International Ceramic Monographs, 1994; Contributing Editor, Phase Diagrams for Ceramists, handbook series, 1994. Contributions to: Over 80 published papers in journals and conference proceedings to Australia, UK, USA, Germany and Singapore. Honours: Alcan Research Award, 1988; Young Achiever Finalist, 1990. Memberships: Australasian, American and Japanese Ceramic Societies; Pacific Rim 1996 Conference, Editor. Address: 6 Hereford Place, West Pymble, Sydney 2073, Australia.

RUYSLINCK Ward. See: DE BELSER Raymond.

RUZICKA Penelope Susan, (Penny Kane), b. 23 Jan 1945, Kenya. Consultant; Writer. m. Ladislav Ruzicka, 21 Mar 1984. Education: MSc, Economics, University of Wales, 1986. Publications: Choice Not Chance, 1978; The Which? Guide to Birth Control, 1983;

Asking Demographic Questions, 1985; China's One Child Family (editor), 1985; Tradition, Development and the Individual, 1986; The Second Billion: Population and Family Planning in China, 1987; Famine in China, 1959-61, 1988; Differential Mortality, 1989; Women's Health: From Womb to Tomb, 1991; Victorian Families in Fact and Fiction, 1994. Contributions to: Various publications. Membership: International Union for the Scientific Study of Population. Address: The Old School, Majors Creek near Braidwood, New South Wales 2622, Australia.

RYAN Francis Patrick, b. 23 July 1944, Limerick, Ireland. Doctor; Writer. m. Barbara, 1968, 1 son, 1 daughter. Education: MB, ChB (Hons), Sheffield, 1970; MRCP (London), 1973; FRCP, 1985; FRSH, 1993. Appointments: Ex Sectional Editor, Royal Society Medicine; Ex-Editorial Director, Swift Publishers. Publications: Tuberculosis: The Greatest Story Never Told. Co-Author: The Eskimo Diet; Tiger, Tiger; Goodbye Baby Blue; Sweet Summer; The Walnut Diet & Fitness Plan; Virus X. Contributions to: Various newspapers and journals in UK, USA; Scientific articles for medical and scientific journals. Membership: Society of Authors; Royal College of Physicians; Royal Society for Health; Lansdowne Club. Literary Agent: Bill Hamilton, AM Heath.

RYAN John Gerald Christopher, b. 4 Mar 1921, Edinburgh, Scotland. Artist; Writer. m. Priscilla Ann Blomfield, 3 Jan 1950, 1 son, 2 daughters. Education: Ampleforth College, York, 1930-40; Regent Street Polytechnic Art School, 1946-47. Appointment: Cartoonist, Catholic Herald, 1965-. Publications: 14 children's picture books, Captain Pugwash, 1956-86; Tiger Pig; 12 Noah's Ark Stories; 2 Dodo books; Mabel and the Tower of Babel, 1990; Adventures of Sir Cumference, 1990; Jonah, a Whale of a Tale, 1994; Soldier Sam and Trooper Ted, 1994. Contributions to: Magazines. Membership: Society of Authors. Literary Agent: Jane Gregory. Address: Gungarden Lodge, Rye, East Sussex TN31 7HH, England.

RYBICKA Zofia, b. 28 Nov 1920, Klony, Poland. Writer; Critic; Translator. m. Waldemar Jerzy Rybicki, 2 Jan 1955, div 1958. Education: Secondary School for Kindergarten Teachers, 1934-37; ITT Lyceum, 1945-46; Secondary School Certificate, 1946, Gdansk-Wrzeszcz; Graduated, Diplomatic Consular Faculty, Academy of Political Science, Warsaw, 1950; Diploma, Organ, High Music School, Gdansk-Wrzeszcz, 1952; MPh, Polish Philology and Literature Faculty, Warsaw University, 1953. Appointments: Polish Army, 1944-45; Proof Reader, Press House, Gdansk, 1947-50; Grammar School Teacher, Lyceum for Kindergarten Teachers, Gdansk-Wreszcz, 1952-55; Editor, Ministry of National Defence Publishing House, Warsaw, 1955-75; Head, German and Scandinavian Department, Polish Publishing House, PIW, Warsaw, 1975-81. Publications: Translations of numerous works into Polish. Contributions to: Various publications. Honours: Silver Cross of Merit, 1975; Knight's Cross, Polonia Restituta, 1979; Several military orders. Memberships: Polish Writers Union; ZAIKS; Stowarzyszenie Tlumacy Polskich; Polish Association of Editors. Address: ul Dzika 19/23 m 88, 00-172 Warsaw, Poland.

RYCE-MENUHIN Joel, b. 11 June 1933, USA. Analytical Psychologist; Former International Concert Pianist. m. Yaltah Menuhin, 11 June 1960. Education: BMus, 1953; BSc Honours, 1976; MPhil, 1982. Publications: The Self in Early Childhood, 1988; Jungian Sandplay: The Wonderful Therapy, 1992; Jung and the Monotheisms, 1993. Contributions to: Clinical Papers in Journal of Analytical Psychology; Harvest; Chiron; Free Association Journal; British Journal of Projective Psychology; Guild of Pastoral Psychology. Memberships: IAAP, PEN; Founding Director, British and Irish Sandplay Society. Address: 85 Canfield Gardens, London NW6 3EA, England.

RYDELL Forbes. See: FORBES Stanton.

RYDER Jonathan. See: LUDLUM Robert.

RYDER Susan Margaret, (Baroness Ryder of Warsaw, Sue Ryder), b. 3 July 1923, Leeds, England. Social Worker; Writer. m. Lord Cheshire of Woodhall, 5 Apr 1959, dec, 1 son, 1 daughter. Appointments: Co-Founder, Ryder Cheshire Foundation; Founder, Sue Ryder Foundation. Publications: And the Morrow is Theirs (autobiography); Child of My Love (autobiography), 1986. Honours: Member of the Order of the British Empire, 1957; Member, 1965, Commander's Cross, 1992, Order of Polonia Restituta; Companion of the Order of St Michael and St George, 1976; Created Baroness Ryder of Warsaw in Poland and of Cavendish in Suffolk, England, 1978; Several honorary doctorates. Memberships: Special Operations Executive Club; World War Memorial Fund for Disaster Relief, trustee. Address: Sue Ryder Home, Cavendish, Sudbury, Suffolk CO10 8AY, England.

RYLANT Cynthia, b. 6 June 1954, Hopewell, Virginia, USA. Writer. m., div, 1 son. Education: BA, Morris Harvey College; MA, Marshall University; MLS, Kent State University. Appointments: Children's Librarian; Lecturer in English. Honours: English Speaking Union Book-Across-the-Sea Ambassador of Honour Award, 1984; Child Study Association of America Best Book, 1985; National Council for Social Studies Best Book, 1985; Boston Globe Book Award, 1991; Newbery Award, 1993. Address: c/o Dell Publishing, 1540 Broadway, New York, NY 10036, USA.

RYZMAN Leonard, b. Melbourne, Victoria, Australia. Professional Speaker; Author. Education: BEc, BA, DipEd, Monash University; Graduate Diploma in Human Relations Education, Melbourne University. Publications: Leonardo Da Vinci 1452-1519: The Concise Biography, 1983; Murder on the Management Express, 1985; Make Your Own Rainbow, 1990; All You Need Is Life, 1994. Play: All Things Must Pass But Here Comes the Sun. Contributions to: Numerous magazines. Membership: National Speakers Association of Australia. Address: c/o Curtis Brown (Australia), PO Box 19, Paddington, New South Wales, Australia.

S

S Elizabeth Von. See: **FREEMAN Gillian.**

SABAT-RIVERS Georgina, b. 20 June, Santiago, Cuba. Professor of Latin American Literature. m. (1) 3 sons, 1 daughter, (2) Elias L Rivers, 1969. Education: Universidad de Oriente, Santiago, Cuba; Université de Paris, Sorbonne, France; Masters, 1967, PhD, 1969, Johns Hopkins University, Baltimore. Appointments: Western Maryland College, 1973-78; State University of New York at Stony Brook, 1978-93. Publications: Author of several books. Honours: Numerous. Memberships: Modern Language Association; Editorial Board, 1987-90, Revista Iberoamericana; CLAR, Editorial Board. Address: Department of Hispanic Languages and Literature, State University of New York at Stony Brook, Stony Brook, NY, USA.

SACHS Marilyn (Stickle), b. 18 Dec 1927, New York, New York, USA. Writer. m. Morris Sachs, 26 Jan 1947, 1 son, 1 daughter. Education: BA, Hunter College, New York City, 1949; MLS, Columbia University, 1953. Publications: Over 35 books, 1964-96. Honours: Many citations, prizes and awards. Address: 733 31st Avenue, San Francisco, CA 94121, USA.

SACHS Murray, b. 10 Apr 1924, Toronto, Ontario, Canada. Literary Scholar; Teacher. m. Miriam Blank, 14 Sept 1961, 1 son, 1 daughter. Eduction: BA Modern Languges, University of Toronto, 1946; MA, French, 1947, DPhil, French, 1953, Columbia University, New York, USA. Career includes: Assistant Professor of Romanic Languages, Williams College, 1954-60; Professor of French and Comparative Literature, Brandeis University, 1960-. Publications: The Career of Alphonse Daudet, 1965; The French Short Story in the 19th Century, 1969; Anatole France: The Short Stories, 1974; Ghosts in the Family, 1995; Another Day, 1997. Contributions to: Books and professional journals; Kaleidoscope. Memberships: American Comparative Literature Association; Association of Literary Scholars and Critics. Address: c/o Department of Romance and Comparative Literature, Shiffman Humanities Center, Brandeis University, Waltham, MA 02254, USA.

SACKS Oliver (Wolf), b. 9 July 1933, London, England. Neurologist; Writer. Education: BA, 1954, MA, 1958, BM, 1958, BCh, 1958, Queen's College, Oxford; University of California at Los Angeles, 1962-65. Appointments: Intern, Middlesex Hospital, London, 1958-60, Mt Zion Hospital, San Francisco, 1961-62; Resident in Neurology, University of California at Los Angeles, 1962-65; Fellow in Neurochemistry and Neuropathology, 1965-66, Instructor, 1966-75, Assistant Professor, 1975-78, Associate Professor, 1978-85, Clinical Professor of Neurology, 1985, Albert Einstein College of Medicine, Yeshiva University, New York City; Staff Neurologist, Beth Abraham Hospital, New York City, 1966-. Publications: Migraine, 1970, revised edition, 1985; Awakenings, 1973, new edition, 1990; A Leg to Stand On, 1984; The Man Who Mistook His Wife for a Hat and Other Clinical Tales, 1985; Seeing Voices: A Journey into the World of the Deaf, 1989, revised edition, 1991; An Anthropologist on Mars: Seven Paradoxical Tales, 1995; The Island of the Colour-blind, 1996. Contribdutions to: Newspapers and journals. Honours: Hawthornden Prize, 1974; Oskar Pfister Award, American Psychiatric Association, 1988; Guggenheim Fellowship, 1989; Harold D Vursell Memorial Award, American Academy and Institute of Arts and Letters, 1989; Odd Fellows Book Award, 1990; Scriptor Award, University of Southern California, 1991; Professional Support Award, National Headache Foundation, 1991; Presidential Citation, American Academy of Neurology, 1991; Honorary doctorates. Address: 2 Horatio Street #3G, New York, NY 10014, USA.

SADDLEMYER (Eleanor) Ann, b. 28 Nov 1932, Prince Albert, Saskatchewan, Canada. Critic; Theatre Historian; Educator. Education: BA, 1953, Honours, English Diploma, 1955, University of Saskatchewan; MA, Queen's University, 1956; PhD, Bedford College, University of London, England, 1961. Appointments: Faculty, University of Victoria, British Columbia, 1960-71; Faculty, Victoria College, 1971-, Director, Graduate Centre for the Study of Drama, 1972-77, 1985-88, Master, Massey College, 1988-95, Professor and Master Emeritus, 1995, University of Toronto; Berg Chair, New York University, 1975. Publications: The World of W B Yeats, 1965; In Defence of Lady Gregory, Playwright, 1966; J M Synge Plays, Books I and II, 1968; Synge and Modern Comedy, 1968; Letters to Molly: J M Synge to Marie O'Neill, 1971; Lady Gregory Plays, 4 volumes, 1971; Theatre Business, 1982; The Collected Letters of J M Synge, 2 volumes, 1983-84; Lady Gregory Fifty Years After, 1987; Early Stages: Essays on the Theatre in Ontario 1800-1914, 1990; Synge's Playboy of the Western World and other Plays, 1995; Later Stages: Essays on the Theatre in Ontario, World War I to the 1950's, 1997. Contributions to: Professional journals. Honours: Honorary LLD, Queen's, 1977; British Academy Rosemary Crawshay Award, 1986; FRSC, 1976; Fellow, Royal Society of Arts, 1987; DLitt, Victoria, 1989; DLitt, McGill, 1989, Windsor, 1990, Saskatchewan, 1991; Alumni Award of Excellence, University of Toronto, 1991; WEoman of Distinction, 1994; Officer of the Order of Canada, 1995. Memberships: Former President, International Association for Study of Anglo-Dutch Literature; Association for Canadian Theatre Research, Founding President; Board, Canadian Theatre Museums Association. Address: 10876 Madrona Drive, Sidney, British Columbia V8L 5N9, Canada.

SADDLER Allen. See: **RICHARDS Ronald Charles William.**

SADGROVE Sidney Henry, (Lee Torrance), b. 1920, British. Artist; Teacher; Writer. Publications: You've Got To Do Something, 1967; A Touch of the Rabbits, The Suitability Factor, 1968; Stanislaus and the Princess, 1969; A Few Crumbs, 1971; Stanislaus and the Frog, Paradis Enow, 1972; Stanislaus and the Witch, 1973; The Link, 1975; The Bag, Half Sick of Shadows, Bleep, All in the Mind, 1977; Icary Dicary Doc, Angel, 1978; Filling, 1979; First Night, Only on Friday, 1980; Hoodunnit, 1984; Pawn en Prise, 1985; Just for Comfort, 1986; Tiger, 1987; State of Play, 1988; Warren, 1989; Dear Mrs Comfett, 1990. Membership: Writers Guild of Great Britain. Address: Pimp Barn, Withyham, Hartfield, Sussex, TN7 4BB, England.

SADIE Stanley (John), b. 30 Oct 1930, Wembley, Middlesex, England. Musicologist; Lexicographer; Writer. m. (1) Adèle Bloom, 10 Dec 1953, dec 1978, 2 sons, 1 daughter, (2) Julie Anne McCormack, 18 July 1978, 1 son, 1 daughter. Education: BA, 1953, Mus B, 1953, MA, 1957, PhD, 1958, Cambridge University. Appointments: Faculty, Trinity College of Music, London, 1957-65; Music Critic, The Times of London, 1964-81; Editor, The Musical Times, 1967-87. Publications: Handel, 1962; The Pan Book of Opera (with Arthur Jacobs), 1964, 3rd edition, 1984; Mozart, 1966; Beethoven, 1967, 2nd edition, 1974; Handel, 1968; Handel Concertos, 1972; The New Grove Dictionary of Music and Musicians (editor), 20 volumes, 1980, revised edition, 24 volumes, 1999; The New Grove Dictionary of Musical Instruments (editor), 1984; The Cambridge Music Guide (with Alison Latham), 1985; The New Grove Dictionary of American Music (editor with H Wiley Hitchcock), 4 volumes, 1986; Mozart Symphonies, 1986; The Grove Concise Dictionary of Music (editor), 1988; Handel Tercentenary Collection (editor with A Hicks), 1988; History of Opera (editor), 1989; Performance Practice (editor with Howard M Brown), 2 volumes, 1989; Man and Music (general editor), 8 volumes, 1989-93; Music Printing and Publishing (co-editor), 1990; The New Grove Dictionary of Opera (editor), 4 volumes, 1992; Wolfgang Amadè Mozart: Essays on His Life and Music (editor), 1995. Contributions to: Professional journals and general publications. Honours: Commander of the Order of the British Empire, 1982; Honorary LittD, 1982. Memberships: Critics Circle; International Musicological Society, president, 1992-97; Royal College of Music, fellow; Royal Academy of Music, honorary; Royal Musical Association, president, 1989-94. Address: 12 Lyndhurst Road, London NW3 5NL, England.

SADLER Mark. See: **LYNDS Dennis.**

SAEE John Islamudin, b. 12 Sept 1959, Panjsher, Afghanistan (Australian citizen). Lecturer in Management of Consumer Science. Education: Certificate, German Language and Literature, Hamburg University, Germany; BA, Social Sciences, Flinders University, South Australia, 1980; MCom, University of New South Wales, 1983; PhD, International Management, University of Technology, New South Wales, in progress. Publications: AMP Management Requirements Definition Study (co-author), 1986; Sales Unit Management System User's Reference Manual, 1986; User's Acceptance Testing Specifications, 1986-87. Contributions to: Various books and journals. Memberships: Australian Institute of Management; Professional Member, Australian and New Zealand Academy of Management; International Communication Association. Address: Thorpe, Melbourne, Victoria, Australia.

SAFIRE William, b. 17 Dec 1929, New York, New York, USA. Columnist; Writer. m. Helene Belmar Julius, 16 Dec 1962, 1 son, 1 daughter. Education: Syracuse University, 1947-49. Appointments: Reporter, New York Herald-Tribune Syndicate, 1949-51; Correspondent, Europe and the Middle East, WNBC-WNBT, 1951; Radio-TV Producer, WMBC, New York City, 1954-55; Vice-President, Tex McCrary Inc, 1955-60; President, Safire Public Relations, 1960-68; Special Assistant to President Richard M Nixon, 1969-73; Columnist, The New York Times, 1973-. Publications: The Relations Explosion, 1963; Plunging into Politics, 1964; Safire's Political Dictionary, 1968, 3rd edition, 1978, new edition as Safire's New Political Dictionary, 1993; Before the Fall, 1975; Full Disclosure, 1977; Safire's Washington, 1980; On Language, 1980; What's the Good Word?, 1982; Good Advice on Writing (with Leonard Safire), 1982, new edition, 1992; I Stand Corrected, 1984; Take My Word for It, 1986; You Could Look It Up, 1988; Language Maven Strikes Again, 1990; Leadership (with Leonard Safire), 1990; Fumblerules, 1990; The First Dissident, 1992; Lend Me Your Ears, 1992; Quoth the Maven, 1993; Safir's New Political Dictionary, 4th edition, 1993; In Love with Norma Loquendi, 1994; Sleeper Spy, 1995. Contributions to: Newspapers and magazines. Honour: Pulitzer Prize for Distinguished Commentary, 1978. Membership: Pulitzer, board, 1995-. Address: c/o The New York Times, 1627 Eye Street North West, Washington, DC 20006, USA.

SAGAN Françoise, b. 21 June 1935, Carjac, France. Novelist; Playwright. Education: Sorbonne, Paris. Publications: Bonjour Tristesse, 1954; A Certain Smile, 1956; Those Without Shadows, 1957; Aimez-vous Brahms, 1959; Wonderful Clouds, 1961; La Chamade, 1965; The Heart-Keeper, 1968; A Few Hours of Sunlight, 1969; Scars on the Soul, 1972; Lost Profile, 1974; Silken Eyes, 1976; The Unmade Bed, 1977; Le Chien Couchant, 1980; Incidental Music, 1981; The Painted Lady, 1981; The Still Storm, 1983; Engagements of the Heart, 1985; La Maison de Raquel Vega, 1985; Painting in Blood, 1987; The Leash, 1989; Les Faux-fuyants, 1991. Plays: Castle in Sweden, 1960; Les Violons parfois, 1962; Landru (screenplay for Claude Chabrol), 1963; Bonheur, impair et passe, 1964; The Dizzy Horse, 1966; Un piano dans l'herbe, 1970; Le Sang doré des Borgia (screenplay), 1977; Il fait beau jour et nuit, 1978; Opposite Extremes, 1987. Other: Mirror of Venus, 1965; Réponses 1954-74, autobiographical conversations, 1974; Brigitte Bardot, 1975; Sand et Musset: Lettres d'amour, 1985; Dear Sarah Bernhardt, 1987; La Sentinelle de Paris, 1988; The Eiffel Tower, 1989. Address: c/o Edition Juilliard, 20 rue des Grands Augustins, 75006 Paris, France.

SAGGS Henry William Frederick, b. 2 Dec 1920, Weeley, Essex, England. Professor of Semitic Languages. m. Joan Butterworth, 21 Sep 1946, 4 daughters. Education: King's College, London, 1939-42, 1946-48; School of Oriental and African Studies, London, 1949-52; BD, 1942, MTh, 1948; MA, 1950; PhD, 1953. Appointments: Lecturer, then Reader in Akkadian, School of Oriental and African Studies, London, 1953-66; Professor of Semitic Languages, University College Cardiff, University of Wales, 1966-83. Publications: The Greatness That Was Babylon, 1962, revised edition, 1987; Everyday Life in Babylon and Assyria, 1965, 2nd edition, 1987; The Encounter With the Divine in Mesopotamia and Israel, 1978; The Might That Was Assyria, 1984, 2nd edition, 1990; Civilization Before Greece and Rome, 1989; Babylonians, 1995. Contributions to: Iraq; Sumer; Journal of Cuneiform Studies; Journal of Theological Studies; Archiv für Oreintforschung; Revue d'Assyriologie; Journal of Semitic Studies; Bibliotheca Orientalis. Memberships: Society of Authors; Society of Antiquaries; British School of Archaeology in Iraq, Council Member; Savage Club; Royal Asiatic Society. Address: Eastwood, Bull Lane, Long Melford, Suffolk CO10 9EA, England.

SAHAY Akhoweri Chittaranjan, b. 2 Jan 1925, Muzaffarpur, India. Associate Professor of English (retired); Editor; Poet; Writer. m. Akhowi Priyamvada Sahay, 17 June 1945, 3 sons, 1 daughter. Education: BA, Honours, Distinction, 1945, MA, English, 1947, Patna University; MDEH, National University of Electro Homeopathy, Kanpur, 1964; PhD, English, Stanton University, New York, 1985. Appointments: Lecturer and Head, Department of English, Rajendra College, Chapra, 1948-68; Lecturer, L S College, Muzaffarpur, 1968-74; Associate Professor of English, Bihar University, Muzaffarpur, 1974-85; Chief Editor, Kavita India quarterly, 1987-. Publications: Poetry: Van Yoothi, 1939; Van Shepali, 1941; Van Geet, 1943; Ajab Desh, 1945; Roots and Branches, 1979; Emerald Foliage, 1981; Pink Blossoms, 1983; Golden Pollens, 1985; Vernal Equinox, 1987; Summer Clouds, 1989. Short stories for children: Dick Aur Ostrich, 1946; Motilal Tota, 1948; Rani Sahiba, 1964. Prose: The Rubaiyat and Other Essays, 1980; My Interest in Occultism, 1982. Contributions to: Numerous anthologies and journals. Honours: Many prizes, medals and certificates of merit. Memberships: International Writers and Artists Association, USA; PEN All-India Centre; Poetry Society, India and UK; Theosophical Society, Madras; United Writers Association, Madras; World Poetry Society; Writers Club, Madras. Address: Kavita India House, South-East Chaturbhujasthn, Muzaffarpur 842001, Bihar, India.

SAHGAL Nayantara (Pandit), b. 10 May 1927, Allahabad, Uttar Pradesh, India. Writer. m. (1), 2 Jan 1949, div, 1 son, 2 daughters, (2), 17 Sept 1979. Education: BA, History, Wellesley College, Massachusetts, 1947. Appointments: Advisory Panel for English, Sahitya Akademi, 1972-75; Writer-in-Residence, Southern Methodist University, Dallas, 1973, 1977; Research Scholar, Radcliffe (now Bunting) Institute, Cambridge, Massachusetts, 1976; Member, Indian delegation to the United Nations, 1978; Fellow, Woodrow Wilson International Center for Scholars, Washington, DC, 1981-82, National Humanities Center, North Carolina, 1983-84; Jury, Commonwealth Writers Prize, 1990, 1991. Publications: Fiction: A Time to Be Happy, 1958; This Time of Morning, 1965; Storm in Chandigarh, 1969; The Day in Shadow, 1972; A Situation in New Delhi, 1977; Rich Like Us, 1985; Plans for Departure, 1986; Mistaken Identity, 1988. Non-Fiction: Prison and Chocolate Cake, 1954, new revised edition, 1998; From Fear Set Free, 1962; The Freedom Movement in India, 1970; Indira Gandhi: Her Road to Power, 1982; Relationship: Extracts from a Correspondence (with E N Mangat Rai), 1994; Point of View, 1997. Contributions to: Newspapers and magazines. Honours: Book Society Recommendation, 1959; Sinclair Prize for Fiction, 1985; Sahitya Akademi Award, 1986; Commonwealth Writers Prize, Eurasia, 1987; Honorary Doctor of Letters, University of Leeds, 1997. Memberships: American Academy of Arts and Sciences, 1990. Address: 181 B Rajpur Road, Dehra Dun 248009, Uttar Pradesh, India.

SAID Edward, b. 1 Nov 1935, Jerusalem, Palestine. Professor; Writer. m. Mariam Cortas, 14 Dec 1970, 2 children. Education: AB, Princeton University, 1957; AM, 1960, PhD, 1964, Harvard University. Appointments: Instructor, 1963-65, Assistant Professor, 1965-67, Associate Professor, 1967-70, Professor, 1970-77, Parr Professor of English and Comparative Literature, 1977-89, Old Dominion Foundation Professor of Humanities, 1989-, University Professor, 1992-, Columbia University; Visiting Professor, Harvard University, 1974, Johns Hopkins University, 1979, Yale University, 1985; Fellow, Center for Advanced Study in the Behavioural Sciences, Palo Alto, California, 1975-76; Christian Gauss Lecturer in Criticism, Princeton University, 1977; Carpenter Professor, University of Chicago, 1983; T S Eliot Lecturer, University of Kent, Canterbury, 1985; Northrop Frye Chair, University of Toronto, 1986; Messenger Lecturer, Cornell University, 1986; Wilson Lecturer, Wellesley College, 1991; Amnesty Lecturer, Oxford University, 1992; Lord Northcliffe Lecturer, University College, London, 1993; Reith Lecturer, BBC, London, 1993. Publications: Joseph Conrad and the Fiction of Autobiography, 1966; Beginnings: Intention and Method, 1975; Orientalism, 1978; The Question of Palestine, 1979; Literature and Society, 1979; Covering Islam, 1981; The World, the Text and the Critic, 1983; After the Last Sky, 1986; Blaming the Victims, 1988; Muscial Elaborations, 1991; Culture and Imperialism, 1993; Representations of the Intellectual, 1994; The Politics of Dispossession, 1994; Ghazzah-Arihah: Salam Amriki, 1994. Contributions to: Professional journals and other publications. Honours: Guggenheim Fellowship, 1972-73; Soicial Science Research Fellow, 1975; Lionel Trilling Awards, Columbia University, 1976, 1994; Rene Wellek Award, American Comparative Literature Association, 1985. Memberships: American Academy of Arts and Sciences; American Comparative Literature Association; Association of Arab-American University Graduates; Council on Foreign Relations; Modern Language Association; PEN, executive board, 1989-. Address: c/o Department of English, Columbia University, New York, NY 10027, USA.

SAIL Lawrence Richard, b. 29 Oct 1942, London, England. Poet; Writer. m. (1) Teresa Luke, 1966, div 1981, 1 son, 1 daughter, (2) Helen Bird, 1994. Education: BA, Honours, Modern Languages, St John's College, Oxford, 1964. Appointments: Teacher of Modern Languages, Lenana School, Nairobi, 1966-71, Millfield School, 1973-74, Blundell's School, Devon, 1975-81, Exeter School, 1982-91; Editor, South West Review, 1981-85; Chairman, Arvon Foundation, 1990-94; Programme Director, Cheltenham Festival of Literature, 1991; Jury Member, European (Aristeion) Literature Prize, 1994-96. Publications: Opposite Views, 1974; The Drowned River, 1978; The

Kingdom of Atlas, 1980; South West Review: A Celebration (editor), 1985; Devotions, 1987; Aquamarine, 1988; First and Always (editor), 1988; Out of Land: New and Selected Poems, 1992; Building into Air, 1995. Contributions to: Anthologies, magazines and newspapers. Honours: Hawthornden Fellowship, 1992; Arts Council Writer's Bursary, 1993. Memberships: Authors' Society; St John's College, Oxford, senior common room management committee; Poetry Society. Address: Richmond Villa, 7 Wonford Road, Exeter, Devon EX2 4LF, England.

SAINSBURY Maurice Joseph, b. 18 Nov 1927, Sydney, New South Wales, Australia. Consultant Psychiatrist. m. Erna June Hoadley, 22 Aug 1953, 1 son, 2 daughters. Education: MB, BS, University of Sydney, 1952; DPM, Royal College of Physicians and Surgeons, 1960; MHP, University of New South Wales, 1980. Appointments: Consultant Psychiatrist, Australian Army, 1976-86, Chelmsford Royal Commission, 1988-90. Publication: Key to Psychiatry, 1973, 4th edition (with L G Lambeth), 1988. Contributions to: Professional journals. Honours: Reserve Force Decoration, 1985; Member of the Order of Australia, 1987. Memberships: After Care Association of New South Wales, past president; Guardianship Board, New South Wales; Mental Health Review Tribunal, New South Wales; Royal Australian and New Zealand College of Psychiatrists, fellow; Royal College of Psychiatrists, fellow. Address: 3 Bimbil Place, Killara, New South Wales 2071, Australia.

SAINT Dora Jessie (Miss Read), b. 17 Apr 1913, Surrey, England. Novelist; Short Story and Children's Fiction Writer. Education: Homerton College, 1931-33. Publications: Village School, 1955; Village Diary, 1957; Storm in the Village, 1958; Hobby Horse Cottage, 1958; Thrush Green, 1959; Fresh From the Country, 1960; Winter in Thrush Green, 1961; Miss Clare Remembers, 1962; The Market Square, 1966; The Howards of Caxley, 1967; Country Cooking, 1969; News from Thrush Green, 1970; Tyler's Row, 1972; Christmas Mouse, 1973; Battles at Thrush Green, 1975; No Holly for Miss Quinn, 1976; Village Affairs, 1977; Return to Thrush Green, 1978; The White Robin, 1979; Village Centenary, 1980; Gossip From Thrush Green, 1981; A Fortunate Grandchild, 1982; Affairs at Thrush Green, 1983; Summer at Fairacre, 1984; At Home in Thrush Green, 1985; Time Remembered, 1986; The School at Thrush Green, 1987; The World at Thrush Green, 1988; Mrs Pringle, 1989; Friends at Thrush Green, 1990; Changes at Fairacre, 1991; Celebrations at Thrush Green, 1992; Farewell to Fairacre, 1993; Tales From a Village School, 1994. Membership: Society of Authors. Address: Strouds, Shefford Woodlands, Newbury, Berkshire RG16 7AJ, England.

SAINT-AMAND Pierre, b. 22 Feb 1957, Port-au-Prince, Haiti. Professor of French Studies and Comparative Literature. Education: BA, 1978; MA, Romance Languages, 1980; PhD, Romance Languages, 1981. Appointments: Assistant Professor, Yale University, 1981-82; Stanford University, 1982-86; Associate Professor, 1986-90, Professor, 1990 Brown University: Francis Wayland Professor, 1997-. Publications: Diderot: Le Labyrinthe de la Relation, 1984; Séduire ou la Passion des Lumieres, 1986; Les Lois de L'Hostilite, 1992; The Libertine's Progress, 1994; The Laws of Hostility, 1996; Editor: Diderot, 1984; Le Roman au dix-huitième siècle, 1987; Autonomy in the Age of Enlightenment, 1993. Honour: Guggenheim Foundation, 1989. Memberships: Modern Language Association; American Society for Eighteenth Century Studies. Address: French Studies, Box 1961, Brown University, Providence, RI 02912, USA.

SAINT-DENIS Janou, b. 6 May 1930, Montreal, Quebec, Canada. Actress; Poet. m. 30 Oct 1952, dec, 25 Apr 1956, 1 son, 1 daughter. Education: Diploma-es Lettres et Sciences, Couvent d'Hochelaga, Montreal, 1946; Diploma, Conservatoire Lassalle (theatre), 1950; Diploma, Université du Théatre des Nations, Paris, France, 1962. Appointments: Established Poetry Readings in Montreal, 1959, Paris, 1961-71; Started Poetry Shows, 1975, named "Place aux Poetes"; Founder, Les Productions du Soudain (Poetry Company). Publications: Mots a dire, Mauxa dire, 1972; Claude Gauvreau, le Cygne, 1977; Place aux Poetes, 1977; Les Carnets de l'Audace, 1981; La Roue du Feu Secret, 1985; Hold-Up Mental, 1988; Memoire Innee, 1990. Contributions to: Various publications. Honours: Membre d'Honneur de l'U.N.E.Q. Memberships: Union des Ecrivaines et Ecrivans du Quebec; Société des Ecrivains Canadiens, Montreal Section; Société Littéraire de Laval; Union des Artistes; Société canadienne des auteurs, compositeurs et éditeurs de musique. Address: 4445 Rue St Dominique, Montreal, Quebec H2W 2B4, Canada.

SAKAMOTO Yoshikazu, b. 16 Sept 1927, USA. Professor; Writer m. Kikuko Ono, 2 June 1956, 2 daughters. Education: University of Tokyo, 1948-51; Graduate Studies, University of Chicago, 1955-56. Appointments: Research Fellow, 1951-54, Associate Professor, 1954-64, Professor of International Politics, 1964-88, Professor Emeritus, 1988-, University of Tokyo; Professor of Peace and World Order Studies, Meiji Gakuin University, Tokyo, 1988-. Publications: Elements of World Instability: (co-editor), 1981; Democratizing Japan: The Allied Occupation of Japan (co-editor), 1987; Strategic Doctrines and Their Alternatives (editor), 1987; Asia: Militarization and Regional Conflict (editor), 1988; The Emperor System as a Japan Problem (editor), 1989; Global Transformation: Challenge to the State System (editor), 1994. Other: Various books in Japanese. Contributions to: Books and professional journals. Honours: Rockefeller Foundation fellow, 1956-57; Eisenhower fellow, 1964; Special Fellow, United Nations Institute for Training and Research, 1972-74; Mainichi Press National Book Award, 1976. Memberships: American Political Science Association; Asian Peace Research Association, secretary general, 1983-90; International Peace Research Association, secretary general, 1979-83; Japanese Political Science Association. Address: 8-29-19 Shakujii-machi, Nerima-ku, Tokyo 177, Japan.

SAKYA Manju Ratna, b. 1 June 1946, Kathmandu, Nepal. Journalist. m. Subha Luxmi Sakya, 1966, 1 son, 1 daughter. Education: MCom, Trubhuvan University, Nepal, 1967. Publications: An Approach to Nepalese Currency; many articles, books on media published. Contributions to: Chief Editor, Arpan Weekly. Honours: Coronation Medal; Gorkha Dashin Bahu Second Class; Third SAARC Medal; Order of the White Rose, Finland; King Birendra's 51st Birthday Medal. Memberships: Asian Mass Communicatio, Research and Information Centre, Singapore; Press Foundation of Asia, Manila; International Organisation of Journalists, Prague; Society of Professional Journalists, USA; International Press Institute, Austria; World Invest News, Arizona, USA. Address: PO Box 285, Maitighar, Kathmandu, Nepal.

SALAHI Emran, b. 22 Feb 1947, Tehran, Iran. Chief Librarian. m. Hayedeh Vahabzadeh, 21 Jan 1975, 1 son, 1 daughter. Education: Diploma, English, Farsi Translation, 1972. Publications: Iranian Contemporary Satirists (with B Assadipour); Crying Under Water; A Train Among Fog; A Station By the Road; Stone Comes Through the Window (in Turkish); Seventieth; The Dreams of the Blue Man; You May Not Believe. Contributions to: Donyaye-Sokhan (in Iran). Membership: Association of Iranian Poets and Writers. Address: No 16 Hosseini Alley 21, Bahman Street, Azadi, Tehran 13417, Iran.

SALE (John) Kirkpatrick, b. 27 June 1937, Ithaca, New York, USA. Editor; Writer. m. Faith Apfelbaum Sale, 21 June 1962, 2 daughters. Education: BA, Cornell University, 1958. Appointments: Editor, The New Leader, 1959-61, New York Times Magazine, 1965-68, The Nation, 1981-82; Contributing Editor, The Nation, 1986-. Publications: SDS, 1973; Power Shift, 1975; Human Scale, 1980; Dwellers in the Land: The Bioregional Vision, 1985; The Conquest of Paradise: Christopher Columbus and the Columbian Legacy, 1990; The Green Revolution: The American Environmental Movement 1962-1992, 1993; Rebels Against the Future: The Luddites and Their War on the Industrial Revolution, 1995. Memberships: Learning Alliance; PEN American Centre, board member, 1976-; E F Schumacher Society, secretary, 1980-86, co-director, 1986-. Address: 113 West 11th Street, New York, NY 10011, USA.

SALINGER J(erome) D(avid), b. 1 Jan 1919, New York, New York, USA. Author. m. Claire Douglas, 1953, div 1967, 1 son, 1 daughter. Education: Valley Forge Military Academy; Columbia University. Publications: The Catcher in the Rye, 1951; Nine Stories, 1953; Franny and Zooey, 1961; Raise High the Roof-Beam, Carpenters and Seymour: An Introduction, 1963. Contributions to: Magazines. Address: c/o Harold Ober Associates, 425 Madison Avenue, New York, NY 10017, USA.

SALISBURY Frank B(oyer), b. 3 Aug 1926, Provo, Utah, USA. Professor of Plant Physiology; Writer. m. (1) Lois Marilyn Olson, 1 Sept 1949, 5 sons, 2 daughters, (2) Mary Thorpe Robinson, 28 June 1991. Education: BS, 1951, MA, 1952, University of Utah; PhD, California Institute of Technology. Appointments: Assistant Professor of Botany, Pomona College, Claremont, California, 1954-55; Assistant Professor, 1955-61, Professor of Plant Physiology, 1961-66, Colorado State University, Fort Collins; National Science Foundation Postdoctoral Fellow, University of Tübingen, University of Innsbruck,

1962-63; Professor of Plant Physiology, 1966-, Head, Department of Plant Science, 1966-70, Distinguished Professor of Agriculture, 1987-, Utah State University, Logan; Technical Representative in Plant Physiology, US Atomic Energy Commission, Germantown, Maryland, 1973-74; Visiting Professor, University of Innsbruck, 1983; Lady Davis Fellow, Hebrew University of Jerusalem, 1983; Member, Life Sciences Advisory Committee, 1986-88, Aerospace Medicine Advisory Committee, 1988-93, Director, Controlled Ecological Life Support System Discipline Working Group, 1989-, National Aeronautics and Space Administration; Editor, Americas and the Pacific Rim, Journal of Plant Physiology, 1989-. Publications: The Flowring Process, 1963; Vascular Plants: Form and Function (with R V Parke), 1964, 2nd edition, 1970; Truth by Reason and by Revelation, 1965; Plant Physiology (with C Ross), 1969, 4th edition, 1992; The Biology of Flowering, 1971; Botany: An Ecological Approach (with W Jensen), 1972, 2nd edition, 1984; The Utah UFO Display: A Biologist's Report, 1974; The Creation, 1976; Biology (with others), 1977; Units, Symbols and Terminology for Plant Physiology (editor and contributor), 1996. Contributions to: Professional journals and general publications. Honours: Merit Award, Botanical Society of America; Founder's Award, American Society for Gravitational and Space Biology, 1994. Memberships: American Academy of Arts and Sciences, fellow; American Institute of Biological Sciences, governing board, 1976-79; American Society for Gravitational and Space Biology; American Society of Plant Physiologists, editorial board, 1967-92; Botanical Society of America; Phi Kappa Phi; Sigma Xi; Utah Academy of Science, Arts and Letters. Address: 2020 North 1250 East, North Logan, UT 84322, USA.

SALISBURY John. See: **CAUTE David.**

SALISBURY Robert H(olt), b. 29 Apr 1930, Elmhurst, Illinois, USA. Professor of Political Science; Writer. Education: AB, Washington and Lee University, 1951; MA, 1952, PhD, 1955, University of Illinois. Appointments: Faculty, Washington University, 1955-97; Chairman, Department of Political Science, 1966-73, 1986-92; Sovers Professor of American Government, 1982-97, Professor Emeritus, 1997-. Publications: Functions and Policies of American Government (co-author), 1958, 3rd edition, 1967; American Government: Readings and Problems (with Eliot, Chambers and Prewitt), 1959, 2nd edition, 1965; Democracy in the Mid-Twentieth Century (editor with Chambers), 1960; State Politics and the Public Schools (with Masters and Eliot), 1964; Interest Group Politics in America, 1970; Governing America: Public Choice and Political Action, 1973; Citizen Participation in the Public Schools, 1980; Interest and Institutions: Substance and Structure in American Politics, 1992; The Hollow Core (with Heinz, Laumann and Nelson), 1993. Contributions to: Professional journals. Honours: Guggenheim Fellowship, 1990; Rockefeller Visiting Scholar, Bellagio, Italy, 1990. Address: 709 S Skinker, St Louis, MO 63105, USA.

SALOM Philip, b. 8 Aug 1950, Bunbury, Western Australia, Australia. Lecturer; Poet. Education: BA, Curtin University, Perth, 1976; Dip Ed, 1981. Appointments: Tutor and Lecturer, Curtin University, 1982-93; Writer-in-Residence, Singapore National University, 1989, B R Whiting Library/Studio, Rome, 1992; Lecturer, Murdoch University, 1994-. Publications: The Silent Piano, 1980; The Projectionist: Sequence, 1983; Sky Poems, 1987; Barbecue of the Primitives, 1989; Playback, 1991; Tremors, 1992; Feeding the Ghost, 1993; Drama/Play, Always Then and Now, 1993. Honours: Commonwealth Poetry Prizes, 1981, 1987; Western Australian Premier's Prize (fiction) 1992; Australia/New Zealand Literary Exchange Award, 1992; Australia Council Fellowships. Address: 795 Mills Road, Glen Forest, Western Australia, 6071 Australia.

SALTER Charles A, b. 12 Oct 1947, Fort Worth, Texas, USA. US Army Officer; Research Psychologist; Writer. m. 13 May 1972, 1 son, 2 daughters. Education: BS magna cum laude, Tulane University, 1969; MA, 1970, PhD, 1973, University of Pennsylvania; MS, 1987, SD, 1989, Harvard University School of Public Health. Appointments: US Army Officer; Editor, Alternative Careers for Academics Bulletin, 1978; Syndicated Columnist, Suburban Features, 1983-85. Publications: Psychology for Living, 1977; The Professional Chef's Guide to Kitchen Management (editor), 1985; Knight's Foodservice Dictionary (editor), 1987; Foodservice Standards in Resorts, 1987; On the Frontlines, 1988; Getting it Off, Keeping it Off, 1988; Literacy and the Library, 1991; Looking Good, Eating Right, 1991; The Vegetarian Teen, 1991; Food Risks and Controversies, 1993; The Nutrition-Fitness Link, 1993. Membership: American Society of

Journalists and Authors. Address: MCMR-PLC, Fort Detrick, MD 21702, USA.

SALTER James, b. 10 June 1925, New York New York, USA. Writer. m. Ann Altemus, 5 June 1951, div 1976, 2 sons, 3 daughters. Publications: The Hunters, 1957; The Arm of Flesh, 1960-; A Sport and a Pastime, 1967; Light Years, 1976; Sold Faces, 1980; Dusk and Other Stories, 1989. Contributions to: Paris Review; Antaeus; Grand Street; Vogue; Esquire. Honours: Grant, American Academy of Arts and Letters, 1982; PEN-Faulkner Award, 1989. Membership: PEN USA. Address: Box 765, Bridgehampton, NY 11932, USA.

SALTER Mary Jo, b. 15 Aug 1954, Grand Rapids, Michigan, USA. Lecturer; Poet; Editor. m. Brad Leithauser, 1980, 2 daughters. Education: BA cum laude, Harvard University, 1976; MA, Cambridge University, 1978. Appointments: Instructor, Harvard University, 1978-79; Staff Editor, Atlantic Monthly, 1978-80; Poet-in-Residence, Robert Frost Place, 1981; Lecturer in English, 1984-, Emily Dickinson Lecturer in Humanities, 1995-, Mount Holyoke College, South Hadley, Massachusetts; Poetry Editor, The New Republic, 1992-95. Publications: Henry Purcell in Japan, 1985; Unfinished Painting, 1989; The Moon Comes Home, 1989; Sunday Skaters: Poems, 1994. Contributions to: Periodicals. Honours: Discovery Prize, The Nation, 1983; National Endowment for the Arts Fellow, 1983-84; Lamont Prize in Poetry, 1988; Guggenheim Fellowship, 1993; National Book Critics Circle Award Nomination, 1994. Membership: International PEN. Address: c/o Alfred A Knopf Inc, 201 East 50th Street, New York, NY 10022, USA.

SALTMAN Judith, b. 11 May 1947, Vancouver, British Columbia, Canada. Associate Professor of Children's Literature and Librarianship; Writer. m. Bill Barringer, 1 daughter. Education: MA, Simmons College, 1982. Appointments: Children's Librarian, Toronto Public Library, 1970-72, West Vancouver Memorial LIbrary, 1973-79, Vancouver Public Library, 1980-83; Assistant Professor, 1983-88, Associate Professor of Children's Literature and Librarianship, 1988-, University of British Columbia. Publications: The Riverside Anthology of Children's Literature (editor), 6th edition, 1985; Goldie and the Sea, 1987; Modern Canadian Children's Books, 1987; The New Republic of Childhood, 1990. Contributions to: Various publications. Address: School of Library, Archival and Information Studies, University of British Columbia, 831-1956 Main Mall, Vancouver, British Columbia V6T 1Z1, Canada.

SALTZMAN Arthur Michael, b. 10 Aug 1953, Chicago, Illinois, USA. Professor; Writer. m. Marla Jane Marantz, 26 July 1980, 1 daughter. Education: AB, 1971, AM, 1976, PhD, 1979, University of Illinois. Appointments: Teaching Fellow, University of Illinois, 1975-80; Assistant Professor, 1981-86, Associate Professor, 1986-92, Professor, 1992-, Missouri Southern State College. Publications: The Fiction of William Gass: The Consolation of Language, 1986; Understanding Raymond Carver, 1988; Designs of Darkness in Contemporary American Fiction, 1990; The Novel in the Balance, 1993; This Mad "Instead": Governing Metaphors in Contemporary American Fiction, 1997. Contributions to: Professional Journals and general periodicals. Honours: Several awards. Memberships: Modern Language Association; PEN; Phi Beta Kappa. Address: 2301 West 29th Street, Joplin, MO 64804, USA.

SAMBROOK Arthur (James), b. 5 Sept 1931, Nuneaton, Warwickshire, England. Professor of English; Writer. m. Patience Ann Crawford, 25 Mar 1961, 4 sons. Education: BA, 1955, MA, 1959, Worcester College, Oxford; PhD, University of Nottingham, 1957. Appointments: Lecturer, St David's College, Lampeter, Wales, 1957-64; Lecturer, 1964-71, Senior Lecturer, 1971-75, Reader, 1975-81, Professor of English, 1981-92, Emeritus Professor, 1992-, University of Southampton. Publications: A Poet Hidden: The Life of R W Dixon, 1962; The Scribleriad, etc (editor), 1967; William Cobbett, 1973; James Thomson: The Seasons (editor), 1981; English Pastoral Poetry, 1983; The Eighteenth Century: The Intellectual and Cultural Context of English Literature 1700-1789, 1986, 2nd edition, 1993; Liberty, the Castle of Indolence and Other Poems, 1986; James Thomson 1700-1748: A Life: Biographical, Critical, 1992; William Cowper: The Task and Other Poems (editor), 1994; With the Rank and Pay of a Sapper, 1997. Contributions to: Reference books, professional journals and general periodicals. Address: c/o Department of English, University of Southampton, Highfield, Southampton, Hampshire SO9 5NH, England

SAMPSON Anthony Terrell Seward, b. 3 Aug 1926, Durham, England. Writer. m. 31 May 1965, 1 son, 1 daughter. Education: Christ Church, Oxford University, 1947-50. Appointments: Editor, Drum Magazine, South Africa, 1951-55; Staff, Observer, 1955-66; Editorial Advisor, Brandt Commission, 1978-80; Columnist, Newsweek International, 1977-. Publications: Drum, 1956; Anatomy of Britain, 1962; New Europeans, 1968; The Sovereign State of ITT, 1973; The Seven Sisters, 1975; The Arms Bazaar, 1977; The Money Lenders, 1981; Black and Gold, 1987; The Midas Touch, 1989; The Essential Anatomy of Britain: New Patterns of Power in the Nineties, 1992; Company Man: The Rise and Fall of Corporation Life, 1995. Contributions to: Numerous journals. Honour: Prix International de la Presse, Nice, 1976. Memberships: Society of Authors, chairman, 1992-94. Address: 27 Ladbroke Grove, London W11, England.

SAMPSON Geoffrey (Richard), b. 27 July 1944, Broxbourne, Hertfordshire, England. University Lecturer; Writer. Education: MA, St John's College, Cambridge; Yale University; Oxford University. Appointments: Fellow, Queen's College, Oxford, 1969-72; Lecturer, London School of Economics, 1972-74; Lecturer, 1974-76, Reader, 1976-84, University of Lancaster; Professor of Linguistics, University of Leeds, 1985-90; Director, Centre for Advanced Software Applications, University of Sussex, 1991-. Publications: The Form of Language, 1975; Liberty and Language, 1979; Making Sense, School of Linguistics, 1980; An End to Allegiance, 1984; Writing Systems, 1985; The Computational Analysis of English (with Garside and Leech), 1987; English for the Computer, 1995. Membership: MBCS. Address: School of Cognitive and Computing Sciences, University of Sussex, Falmer, Brighton BN1 9QH, England.

SAMPSON Ronald Victor, b. 12 Nov 1918, St Helen's, Lancashire, England. Writer. m. 9 Jan 1943, 2 daughters. Education: Keble College, Oxford, 1936-39, 1946-47, 1948-51; Nuffield College, Oxford; MA, 1947, DPhil, 1951. Publications: Progress in the Age of Reason, 1957; Equality and Power, 1965; Tolstoy: The Discovery of Peace, 1973. Contributions to: Books, professional journals and periodicals. Membership: English PEN. Address: Beechcroft, Hinton Charterhouse, Bath, Avon, England.

SAMS Eric, b. 3 May 1926, London, England. Civil Servant (retired); Writer. m. Enid Tidmarsh, 30 June 1952, 2 sons. Education: BA, 1st Class Honours, Corpus Christi College, Cambridge, 1950; PhD, 1972. Appointments: Civil Servant, 1950-78; Visiting Professor, McMaster University, Hamilton, Ontario, Canada, 1976-77. Publications: The Songs of Hugo Wolf, 1961, 3rd edition, 1993; The Songs of Robert Schumann, 1969, 3rd edition, 1993; Brahms Songs, 1971; Shakespeare's Edmund Ironside, 1985; The Real Shakespeare, 1995; Shakespeare's Edward III, 1996. Contributions to: Reference works and journals. Honour: Leverhulme Grant, 1984. Membership: Guildhall School of Music and Drama, honorary member, 1983-. Address: 32 Arundel Avenue, Sanderstead, Surrey CR2 8BB, England.

SAMUELS Warren Joseph, b. 14 Sept 1933, New York, New York, USA. Professor of Economics; Writer. Education: BBA, University of Miami at Coral Gables, 1954; MS, 1955, PhD, 1957, University of Wisconsin. Appointments: Assistant Professor, University of Missouri, 1957-58, Georgia State College, Atlanta, 1958-59; Assistant Professor, 1959-62, Associate Professor of Economics, 1962-68, University of Miami at Coral Gables; Professor of Economics, Michigan State University, 1968-; Editor, Journal of Economic Issues, 1971-81. Publications: The Classical Theory of Economic Policy, 1966; A Critique of Administrative Regulation of Public Utilities (editor with H M Trebing), 1972; Pareto on Policy, 1974; The Economy as a System of Power (editor), 2 volumes, 1979; Taxing and Spending Policy (co-editor), 1980; The Methodology of Economic Thought (editor), 1980; Research in the History of Economic Thought and Methodology (editor), 1983. Contributions to: Professional journals. Memberships: Association for Social Economics, president, 1988; Economics Society of Michigan, president, 1972-73; History of Economics Society, president, 1981-82. Address: 4397 Cherrywood Drive, Okemos, MI 48864, USA.

SAMUELSON Robert J. Journalist. m. Judith Herr, 2 sons, 1 daughter. Education: BA, Government, Harvard University, 1967. Appointments: Reporter, Washington Post's Business Desk, 1969-73; Freelance Reporter, Sunday Times (London), Los Angeles Times, New Republic and Columbia Journalism Review, 1973-76; Economics Correspondent, 1976-81, Columnist - Economic Focus, Contributing Editor, 1981-84, National Journal; Contributing Editor and Columnist,

Newsweek, 1984-; Bi-weekly column, Washington Post, Los Angeles Times, Boston Globe and other papers (columns sold in syndication by Washington Post Writers Group). Publication: The Good Life and Its Discontents: The American Dream and the Age of Entitlement 1945-1995, book, 1996. Honours: National Magazine Award, 1981; Gerald Loeb Award, 1983; Gerald Loeb Awards for Best Commentary, 1986, 1993; National Headliner Award for Consistently Outstanding Column on One Subject, 1987, 1992, 1993, 1995; John Hancock Award for Best Business and Financial Columnist, 1993; Clarion Award for Best MagazineEditorial/Opinion Column, Women in Communications, 1994. Address: c/o Newsweek, 1750 Pennsylvania Avenue NW, Washington DC 20006, USA.

SANBORN Margaret, b. 7 Dec 1915, Alameda, California, USA. Writer. Education: San Francisco Conservatory of Music, 1924-28; College of Marin, California, 1932-34; California School of Fine Arts, 1934-36. Publications: Robert E Lee: A Portrait, 1807-1861, 1966, revised edition, 1995; Robert E Lee: The Complete Man 1861-1870, 1967, revised edition, 1995; The American: River of El Dorado, 1974; The Grand tetons, 1978; Yosemite: Its Discovery, Its Wonders and Its People, 1981; Mark Twain: The Bachelor Years, 1990. Address: 527 Northern Avenue, Mill Valley, CA 94941, USA.

SANCHEZ Sonia, b. 9 Sept 1934, Birmingham, Alabama, USA. Professor of English; Poet; Dramatist; Writer. m. Etheridge Knight, div, 2 sons, 1 daughter. Education: BA, Hunter College, 1955; New York University, 1959-60; PhD, Wilberforce University, 1972. Appointments: Instructor, San Francisco State College, 1967-69; Lecturer, University of Pittsburgh, 1969-70, Rutgers University, 1970-71, Manhattan Community College, 1971-73, City University of New York, 1972; Associate Professor, Amherst College, 1972-73, University of Pennsylvania, 1976-77; Associate Professor, 1977-79, Professor of English, 1979- Temple University. Publications: Poetry: Homecomeing, 1969; WE a BaddDDD People, 1970; Liberation Poem, 1970; It's a New Day: Poems for Young Brothas and Sistuhs, 1971; Ima Talken bout the Nation of Islam, 1971; Love Poems, 1973; A Blues Book for Blue Black Magical Women, 1974; I've Been a Woman: New and Selected Poems, 1978, revised edition, 1985; Homegirls and Handgrenades, 1984; Under a Soprano Sky, 1987; Wounded in the House of a Friend, 1995. Plays: The Bronx is Next, 1968; Sister Son/ji, 1969; Dirty Hearts '72, 1973; Uh, Uh: But How Do it Free Us?, 1974. Stories: A Sound Investment, 1980. Other: Crisis in Culture, 1983. Editor: Three Hundred Sixty Degrees of Blackness Comin' at You, 1972; We Be Word Sorcerers: 25 Stories by Black Americans, 1973. Honours: PEN Award, 1969; American Academy of Arts and Letters Award, 1970; National Endowment for the Arts Award, 1978; Smith College Tribute to Black Women Award, 1982; Lucretia Mott Award, 1984; Before Columbus Foundation Award, 1985; PEN Fellow, 1993. Address: c/o Department of English, Temple University, Philadelphia, PA 19041, USA.

SANDEN Einar, b. 8 Sept 1932, Tallinn, Estonia. Writer; Historian. m. Dr Elizabeth Gorell, 6 Sept 1994. Education: MA, 1983, PhD, 1984, USA. Appointments: Managing Director, Owner, Boreas Publishing House, 1975; Councillor, Estonian Government in Exile, 1975-90. Publications: KGB Calling Eve, 1978; The Painter From Naissaar, 1985; Ur Eldinum Til Islands, 1988; An Estonian Saga, 1995. Contributions to: Editor of various Estonian periodicals. Honours: Distinguished Freedom Writer, UPLI, Manila, the Philippines, 1968; Cultural Award, Fraternity Sakala, Toronto, 1984. Memberships: PEN Centre for Writers in Exile, 1954-80; Royal Society of Literature, London, 1960; Association of Estonian Writers Abroad, 1970; English PEN, 1976; Estonian National Council, 1959; Association for the Advancement of Baltic Studies, USA, 1980; Estonian Academic Association of War History, Tallinn, 1988. Address: Boreas House, 63 Ninian Road, Cardiff CF2 5EL, Wales.

SANDERS (James) Ed(ward), b. 17 Aug 1939, Kansas City, Missouri, USA. Poet; Writer; Singer; Lecturer. m. Miriam Kittell, 5 Oct 1961, 1 child. Education: BA, New York University, 1964. Appointments: Editor-Publisher, Fuck You/A Magazine of the Arts, 1962-65; Founder-Lead Singer, The Fugs, satiric folk-rock-theatre group, 1964-69; Owner, Peace Eye Bookstore, New York City, 1964-70; Visiting Professor of Language and Literature, Bard College, Annadale-on-Hudson, New York, 1979, 1983; Lectures, readings, performances throughout the US and Europe. Publications: Poetry: Poem from Jail, 1963; A Valorium Edition of the Entire Extant Works of Thales!, 1964; King Lord/Queen Freak, 1964; The Toe Queen Poems, 1964; The Fugs' Song Book (with Ken Weaver and Betsy

Klein), 1965; Peace Eye, 1965; Egyptian Hieroglyphics, 1973; 20,000 A.D., 1976; The Cutting Prow, 1981; Hymn to Maple Syrup and Other Poems, 1985; Poems for Robin, 1987; Thirsting for Peace in a Raging Century: Selected Poems 1961-1985, 1987; Hymn to the Rebel Cafe: Poems 1987-1991, 1993; Chekov: A Biography in Verse, 1995. Editor: Poems for Marilyn, 1962. Compiler and Contributor: Bugger: An Anthology of Buttockry, 1964; Despair: poems to come down by, 1964; Fiction: Shards of God: A Novel of the Yippies, 1970; Tales of Beatnik Glory (short stories), 2 volumes, 1975, 1990; Fame and Love in New York, 1980. Non-Fiction: The Family: The Story of Charles Manson's Dune Buggy Attack Battalion, 1971; Vote! (with Abbie Hoffman and Jerry Rubin), 1972; Investigative Poetry, 1976; The Z-D Generation, 1981. Other: Musicals: Recordings with The Fugs; Solo recordings. Honours: Frank O'Hara Prize, Modern Poetry Association, 1967; National Endowment for the Arts Awards, 1966, 1970, Fellowship, 1987-88; Guggenheim Fellowship, 1983-84; American Book Award, 1988. Memberships: New York Foundation for the Arts; PEN. Address: PO Box 729, Woodstock, NY 12498, USA.

SANDERS Jeanne. See: **RUNDLE Anne**.

SANDERSON John Michael, b. 23 Jan 1939, Glasgow, Scotland. University Reader. Education: MA, 1963, PhD, 1966, Queens' College, Cambridge, 1957-63. Appointments: Reader, University of East Anglia; General Editor, Cambridge University Press Economic History Society Studies in Economic and Social History Series, 1992-; Council, Economic History Society, 1994. Publications: The Universities and British Industry, 1850-1970, 1972; The Universities in the 19th Century, 1975; Education, Economic Change and Society in England, 1780-1870, 1983, 2nd edition, 1992, Japanese edition, 1993; From Irving to Olivier, A Social History of the Acting Profession in England, 1880-1983, 1984; Educational Opportunity and Social Change in England, 1900-1980s, 1987; The Missing Stratum, Technical School Education in England, 1900-1990s, 1994. Contributions to: Economic History Review; Journal of Contemporary History; Contemporary Record; Business History; Northern History; Past and Present. Membership: Economic History Society. Address: School of Economic and Social Studies, University of East Anglia, Norwich, Norfolk, England.

SANDERSON Stewart F(orson), b. 23 Nov 1924, Blantyre, Malawi. Folklorist; Writer. Education: MA, University of Edinburgh. Appointments: Secretary-Archivist, 1952-58, Senior Research Fellow, Editor, Scottish Studies, 1957-60, University of Edinburgh; Lecturer in Folk Life Studies and Director, Folk Life Survey, 1960-64, Director, Institute of Dialect and Folk Life Studies, 1964-83, Chairman, School of English, 1980-, University of Leeds. Publications: Hemingway, 1961, 2nd edition, 1970; The City of Edinburgh (with others), 1963; Studies in Folk Life (with others), 1969; The Secret Common-Wealth and A Short Treatise of Charms and Spells (editor), 1976; To Illustrate the Monuments (with others), 1976; The Linguistic Atlas of England (editor with H Orton and J Widdowson), 1978; Ernest Hemingway: For Whom the Bell Tolls, 1980. Contributions to: Journals. Memberships: British Institute of Recorded Sound; Folklore Society, president, 1971-73; Society of Folk Life Studies. Address: c/o School of English, University of Leeds, Leeds LS2 9JT, England.

SANDFORD Jeremy. Playwright; Author; Journalist; Musician; Performer. m. (1) Nell Dunn, 1956, 3 sons, (2) Philippa Finnis, 1987. Education: Eton; Oxford. Appointments: Director, Hatfield Court New Age Conference Centre; Editor, Romano Drom (Gypsy Newspaper), 1970-73. Publications: Synthetic Fun, 1967; Cathy Come Home, 1967; Whelks and Chromium, 1968; Edna the Inebriate Woman, 1971; Down and Out in Britain, 1971; In Search of the Magic Mushroom, 1972; Gypsies, 1973; Tomorrow's People, 1974; Prostitutes, 1975; Smiling David, 1975; Figures and Landscapes: The Art of Lettice Sandford, 1991; Hey Days in Hay, 1992; Songs from the Roadside, 100 Years of Gypsy Music in the West Midlands, 1995. Contributor to: Guardian; Sunday Times; Observer. Honours: Italia Prize, 1967; Writers Guild, Best Television Play, 1967, 1971; BECTU (then ACTT) Best Television Plays, 1967. Memberships: Writers Guild; BECTU, Hereford Traveller Support Group. Address: Hatfield Court, Near Leominster HR6 0SD, England.

SANDOZ (George) Ellis (Jr), b. 10 Feb 1931, New Orleans, Louisiana, USA. Professor of Political Science; Writer. m. Therese Alverne Hubley, 31 May 1957, 2 sons, 2 daughters. Education: BA, 1951, MA, 1953, Louisiana State University; University of North Carolina, 1950; Georgetown University, 1952-53; University of Heidelberg, 1956-58; PhD, University of Munich, 1965. Appointments: Instructor to Professor, Louisiana Polytechnic Institute, 1959-68; Professor and Head, Department of Political Science, East Texas State University, 1968-78; Professor of Political Science, 1978-, Director, Eric Voegelin Institute for American Renaissance Studies, 1987-, Louisiana State University. Publications: Political Apocalypse: A Study of Dostoevsky's Grand Inquisitor, 1971; Conceived in Liberty: American Individual Rights Today, 1978; A Tide of Discontent: The 1980 Elections and Their Meaning, editor, 1981; The Voegelianian Revolution: A Biographical Introduction, 1981; Eric Voegelin's Thought: A Critical Appraisal (editor), 1982; Election '84: Landslade Without a Mandate? (editor with Cecil V Crabb Jr), 1985; A Government of Laws: Political Theory, Religion and the American Founding, 1990; Political Sermons of the American Founding Era, 1730-1805 (editor), 1991, index, 1996; Eric Voegelin's Significance for the Modern Mind (editor), 1991; The Roots of Liberty: Magna Carta, Ancient Constitution, and the Anglo-American Tradition of Rule of Law (editor), 1993; The Political and Constitutional Writings of Sir John Fortescue (editor), 1997. Contributions to: The Collected Works of Eric Voegelin (principal editor, 1986-), scholarly books and professional journals. Honours: Germanistic Society of America Fellow, 1964-65; Fulbright Scholar, 1964-65; Henry E Huntington Library Fellow, 1986-87; Fulbright 40th Anniversary Distinguished American Scholar, Italy, 1987; Distinguished Research Master and University Gold Medal, Louisiana State University, 1993; Medal and Rector's Certificate, 1994, Honorary PhD, 1995, Palacky University, Olomouc, Czech Republic. Memberships: American Historical Association; American Political Science Association; Federalist Society; Organization of American Historians; Philadelphia Society; Southern Political Science Association; Southwestern Political and Social Science Associations; Eric Voegelin Society, founder-secretary 1985-. Address: c/o Eric Voegelin Institute for American Renaissance Studies, Louisiana State University, 240 Stubbs Hall, Baton Rouge, LA 70803, USA.

SANDS Martin. See: **BURKE John Frederick**.

SANDY Stephen, b. 2 Aug 1934, Minneapolis, Minnesota, USA. Professor; Writer; Poet. m. Virginia Scoville, 1 son, 1 daughter. Education: BA, Yale University, 1955; MA, 1959, PhD, 1963, Harvard University. Appointments: Lecturer in American Literature, University of Tokyo, 1967-68; Visiting Professor, Brown University, 1968-69; Harvard University, 1986-88; Faculty, Bennington College, Vermont, 1969-; Director, Poetry Workshop, Chautauqua Institution, New York, 1975, 1977; McGee Visiting Distinguished Professor of Writing, Davidson College, North Carolina, 1994. Publications: Stresses in the Peaceable Kingdom, 1967; Roofs, 1971; Riding to Greylock, 1983; To a Mantis, 1987; Man in the Open Air, 1988; The Epoch, 1990; Thanksgiving Over the Water, 1992; A Cloak for Hercules (translation of Seneca's Hercules Oetaeus), 1995; Vale of Academe: A Prose Poem for Bernard Malamud, 1996; Works and Days New and Selected Poems, 1998. Contributions to: Journals and magazines. Honours: Yaddo Residencies, 1976, 1993; MacDowell Colony Fellowships, 1983, 1993; National Endowment for the Arts Poet-in-Residence, Poetry Center, Philadelphia, 1985; Ingram Merrill Foundation Fellowship, 1985; Vermont College on the Arts Fellowship, 1988; National Endowment for the Arts Fellowship, 1988. Address: Box 524, North Bennington, VT 05257, USA.

SANDYS Elspeth Somerville, b. 18 Mar 1940, Timaru, New Zealand. Writer. 1 son, 1 daughter. Education: MA, Auckland, New Zealand; LTCL (Music); FTCL (Speech, Drama). Publications: Catch a Falling Star, 1978; The Broken Tree, 1981; Love and War, 1982; Finding Out, 1991; Best Friends'(short stories), 1993; River Lines, 1995. Other: Radio plays. Contribution to: Magazines. Honours: Frank Sargeson Fellow, Auckland, 1992; Burns Fellow, Otago University, 1995. Memberships: Writers Guild; Society of Authors. Address: Box 60028, Titirangi, Auckland 7, New Zealand.

SANER Reg(inald Anthony), b. 30 Dec 1931, Jacksonville, Illinois, USA. Poet; Writer; Professor. m. Anne Costigan, 16 Aug 1958, 2 sons. Education: BA, St Norbert College, Wisconsin, 1950; MA, 1954, PhD, 1962, University of Illinois at Urbana; Università per Stranieri, Perugia, 1960-61; Università di Firenze, Florence, 1960-61. Appointments: Assistant Instructor, 1956-60, Instructor in English, 1961-62, University of Illinois at Urbana; Assistant Professor, 1962-67, Associate Professor, 1967-72, Professor of English, 1972-, University of Colorado at Boulder. Publications: Poetry: Climbing into the Roots, 1976; So This is the Map, 1981; Essay on Air, 1984; Red Letters, 1989. Non-Fiction: The Four-Cornered Falcon: Essays on the Interior

West and the Natural Scene, 1993. Contributions to: Poems and essays in numerous anthologies and other publications. Honours: Fulbright Scholar to Florence, Italy, 1960-61; Borestone Mountain Poetry Awards, 1971, 1973; Walt Whitman Award, 1975; National Endowment for the Arts Creative Writing Fellowship, 1976; Pushcart Prize II, 1977-78; Colorado Governor's Award for Excellence in the Arts, 1983; Quarterly Review of Literature Award, 1989; Rockefeller Foundation Resident Scholar, Bellagio, Italy, 1990; Hazel Barnes Award, University of Colorado, 1993. Memberships; Dante Society; PEN; Renaissance Society; Shakespeare Association. Address: 1925 Vassar, Boulder, CO 80303, USA.

SANTA MARIA. See: **POWELL-SMITH Vincent.**

SANTINI Rosemarie, b. New York, New York, USA. Writer. Education: Hunter College, New York City. Appointments: Senior Editor, True Story Magazine; Lecturer, New School of Social Research. Publications: The Secret Fire, 1978; A Swell Style of Murder, 1986; The Disenchanted Diva, 1988; Blood Sisters, 1990; Private Lies, 1991. Contributions to: New Mystery Magazine; Many anthologies and magazines. Honours: New Mystery Mag Award, 1997. Memberships: Authors Guild; Dramatists Guild; International Association of Crime Writers; Mystery Writers of America; National Academy of Television Arts and Sciences; Novelists Inc; PEN; Poetry Society of America; Poets and Writers; Sisters in Crime; Society of American Journalists and Authors. Address: c/o Pratt University, 295 Lafayette Street, New York, NY 10012, USA.

SANTOS Helen. See: **GRIFFITHS Helen.**

SAPERSTEIN David, b. Brooklyn, New York, USA. Author; Screenwriter; Film Director. m. Ellen-Mae Bernard, 1 son, 1 daughter. Education: City College, New York City. Appointments: Assistant Professor of Film, Graduate Film and Television School, New York University, 1992-93; Manhattan Marymount College, 1996-97. Publications: Cocoon, 1985; Fatal Reunion, 1987; Metamorphosis: The Cocoon Story Continues, 1988; Red Devil, 1989; Five-a-Rama, 1995; Dark Again, 1997. Other: 23 screenplays; Librettist and Lyricist, 3 shows, 70 published songs. Honour: Writers Guild of America Best Story for the Screen Nomination, 1985; Cocoon, New York Times Best Seller, 1985; Cocoon, Winner of 2 AcademyAwards, 1985; Fatal Reunion, Selection, Sweden Book of the Month Club, 1988. Memberships: Directors Guild of America; Writers Guild of America; National Honour Society BMI. Address: c/o Ebbets Field Productions, PO Box 42, Wykagyl Station, New Rochelle, NY 10804, USA.

SAPP (Eva) Jo (Barnhill), b. 4 Feb 1944, San Antonio, Texas, USA. Writer; Editor. m. David Paul Sapp, 1 son, 1 daughter. Education: BA Honours, English and Creative Writing, 1976, MA, 1982, PhD coursework completed, 1985, University of Missouri. Appointments: Editorial Assistant, 1978-80, Senior Fiction Advisor, 1980-81, Associate Editor, Special Projects, 1981-92, and Fiction, 1986-88, Missouri Review; Editorial Consultant, Cultural Plan of Action, 1987-. Publications: Missouri Review Online (co-editor), 1986-88; The Best of the Missouri Review: Fiction 1978-90 (co-editor), 1991. Contributions to: Anthologies and magazines. Honours: McKinney Prize, 1984; Editor's Book Awards Nominee, 1988; Missouri Arts Council Grant, 1988; Elmer Holmes Bobst Award Nominee, 1992. Memberships: Associated Writing Programs; Columbia Commission on the Arts, secretary, 1986-87, vice-chair, 1987-88, chair, 1988-; Poets and Writers. Address: c/o Columbia Commission on the Arts, Columbia, MO 65211, USA.

SARAC Roger. See: **CARAS Roger (Andrew).**

SARAH Robyn (Belkin), b. New York, New York, USA. Writer; Teacher. Publications: The Touchstone (poems), 1992; A Nice Gazebo (stories), 1992. Address: c/o Véhicule Press, POB 125 Station du Parc, Montreal H2W 2M9, Canada.

SARANTI Galatia, b. 8 Nov 1920, Greece. Writer. m. Stavros Patsouris, 26 Dec 1948, 2 sons. Education: Law Faculty, University of Athens, 1947. Publications: Novels: Lilacs, 1949; The Book of Johannes and Maria, 1952; Return, 1953; Our Old House, 1959; The Limits, 1966; Cracks, 1979; The Waters of Euripoe, 1989. Short stories: Bright Colours, 1962; Remember Vilna, 1972. Contributions to: Nea Hestia; Helliniki Ahmiozptia; Epoches; Diabazo. Honours: Kostas Ouranis Prize, 1953; State Prizes, 1957, 1974; Academy of Athens Literature Prize, 1979. Memberships: National Society of Greek

Writers; PEN Club. Address: Kallidromidy 87-89, 10683 Athens, Greece.

SARGENT Lyman Tower, b. 9 Feb 1940, Rehoboth, Massachusetts, USA. Professor of Political Science; Writer. m. (1) Patricia McGinnis, 27 Dec 1961, div, 1 son, (2) Mary T Weiler, 14 Aug 1985, div. Education: BA, International Relations, Macalester College, 1961; MA, American Studies, 1962, PhD, Political Science, 1965, University of Minnesota. Appointments: Faculty, University of Wyoming, 1964-65; Professor of Political Science, University of Missouri-St Louis, 1965-; Visiting Professor, University of Exeter, 1978-79, 1983-84, London School of Economics and Political Science, 1984-85; Stout Research Centre for the Study of New Zealand Society, History and Culture, Victoria University of Wellington, 1995-96; Editor, Utopian Studies, 1988-; Stout Research Centre, Victoria University of Wellington, New Zealand, 1995-96. Publications: Contemporary Political Ideologies: A Comparative Analysis, 1969, 10th edition, 1993, 1996; Techniques of Political Analysis: An Introduction, 1970; New Left Thought: An Introduction, 1972; British and American Utopian Literature 1516-1975: An Annotated Bibliography (editor), 1979, revised edition, 1988; IVR NORTHAM IV Consent: Concept, Capacity, Conditions, Constraints (editor), 1979; Contemporary Political Ideologies: A Reader (editor), 1990; Extremism in America: A Reader, editor, 1995; Political Thought in the United States: A Documentary History, editor, 1997; New Zealand Utopian Literature: An Annotated Bibliography, 1997; New Zealand International Communities: A Research Guide; Extremism in America: A Reader, 1995. Contributions to: Professional journals. Address: c/o Department of Political Science, University of Missouri-St Louis, 8001 Natural Bridge Road, St Louis, MO 63121, USA.

SARGESSON Jenny. See: **DAWSON Jennifer.**

SARKAR Anil Kumar, b. 1 Aug 1912, India. Professor Emeritus. m. Aruna Sarkar, 1 Nov 1941 dec, 1 son, 3 daughters. Education: MA 1st Class, 1935, PhD, 1946, D.Litt, 1960, Patna University. Appointments: Professor, Rajendra College, 1940-44; Senior Lecturer, University of Ceylon, Colombo and Perdeniya, 1944-64; Visiting Professor, University of New Mexico, Albuquerque, USA, 1964-65; Full Professor of Philosophy and West-East Philosophy, 1965-82, California State University, Hayward, USA; Research Director, Professor of Asian Studies, 1968-80, Professor Emeritus, 1980-, California Institute of Integral Studies, San Francisco, 1980-. Publications: An Outline of Whitehead's Philosophy, 1940; Changing Phases of Buddhist Thought, 1968, 4th edition, 1996; Whitehead's Four Principles From West-East Perspectives, 1974, 2nd edition, enlarged, 1994; Dynamic Facets of Indian Thought, vol 1, 1980, Vols 2-4, 1987-88; Experience in Change and Prospect Pathways from War to Peace, 1989; Sri Aurobindo's Vision of the Super Mind - Its Indian and Non-Indian Interpreters, 1989; Buddhism and Whitehead's Process: Philosophy, 1990; Zero: Its Role and Prospects in Indian Thought and its Impact on Post-Einsteinian Astrophysics, 1992; The Mysteries of Vajrayana Buddhism: From Atisha to Dalai Lama, 1993; Triadic Avenues of India's Cultural Prospects: Philosophy, Physics and Politics, 1995; Shaping of Euro-Indian Philosophy, 1995; Yoga, Mathematics and Computer Sciences in Change Confronting Twenty-First Century. Contributions to: Indian, American and other journals. Address: B/B/12/15-7 Kalyani, Df Nadia, West Bengal, India.

SARNA Jonathan D(aniel), b. 10 Jan 1955, Philadelphia, Pennsylvania, USA. Professor of Jewish American History; Writer. m. Ruth Langer, 8 June 1986, 1 son, 1 daughter. Education: BHL Honours, Hebrew College, Boston, 1974; BA summa cum laude, Highest Honours, Judaic Studies and History, 1975, MA, Judaic Studies, 1975, Brandeis University; MA, 1976, MPhil, History, 1978, PhD, History, 1979, Yale University. Appointment: Joseph H and Belle R Braun Professor of American Jewish History, Brandeis University. Publications: Jews in New Haven (editor), 1978; Mordecai Manuel Noah: Jacksonian Politician and American Jewish Communal Leader, 1979; Jacksonian Jew: The Two Worlds of Mordecai Noah, 1981; Jews and the Founding of the Republic (co-editor), 1985; The American Jewish Experience: A Reader (editor), 1986; American Synagogue History: A Bibliography and State-of-the-Field Survey (with Alexandra S Korros), 1988; JPS: The Americanization of Jewish Culture: A History of the Jewish Publication Society 1888-1988, 1989; The Jews of Cincinnati (with Nancy H Klein), 1989; Ethnic Diversity and Civic Identity: Patterns of Conflict and Cohesion in Cincinnati Since 1820, 1992; Yuhude Artsot ha-Berit, 1992; Jesus of Boston, with Ellen Smith, 1995. Contributions to: Books, professional journals and general periodicals. Address: c/o Brandeis University, Waltham, MA 02254, USA.

SARNA Nahum Mattathias, b. 27 Mar 1923, London, England. Professor of Biblical Studies Emeritus; Writer. m. Helen Horowitz, 13 Mar 1947, 2 sons. Education: BA, 1944, MA, 1946, University of London; PhD, Dropsie College, Philadelphia, 1955. Appointments: University College, London, 1946-49; Gratz College, Philadelphia, 1951-57; Jewish Theological Seminary, New York City, 1957-65; Visiting Professor, Columbia University, 1964-65, 1992, Yale University, 1992-94; Faculty, 1965-67, Dora Golding Professor of Biblical Studies, 1967-85, Professor Emeritus, 1985-, Brandeis University; Distinguished Professor, Florida Atlantic University, 1995-. Publications: Understanding Genesis, 1966; Exploring Exodus, 1985; Commentary on Genesis, 1989; Commentary on Exodus, 1991; Songs of the Heart: An Introduction to the Book of Psalms, 1993. Contributions to: Professional journals. Honours: Jewish Book Council Award, 1967; American Council of Learned Societies Senior Fellow, 1971-72; Fellow, Institute for Advanced Studies, Hebrew University, 1982-83; Honorary doctorates. Memberships: American Academy for Jewish Research, Fellow; American Oriental Society; Association for Jewish Studies; Dead Sea Scrolls Foundation, board of advisors; Israel Exploration Society; Palestine Exploration Society; World Union of Jewish Studies. Address: 7886 Chula Vista Crescent, Boca Raton, FL 33433, USA.

SAROYAN Aram, b. 25 Sept 1943, New York, New York, USA. Writer. m. Gailyn McClanahan, 9 Oct 1968, 1 son, 2 daughters. Education: University of Chicago; New York University; Columbia University. Publications: Aram Saroyan, 1968; Pages, 1969; Words and Photographs, 1970; The Street: An Autobiographical Novel, 1974; Genesis Angels: The Saga of Lew Welch and the Beat Generation, 1979; Last Rites: The Death of William Saroyan, 1982; William Saroyan, 1983; Trio: Portrait of an Intimate Friendship, 1985; The Romantic, 1988; Friends in the World: The Education of a Writer, 1992; Rancho Mirage: An American Tragedy of Manners, Madness and Murder, 1993; Forthcoming Publications: Day and Night: Bolimas Poems, 1972-81, (1998). Contributions to: New York Times Book Reivew; Los Angeles Times Book Review; Nation Village Voice; Mother Jones; Paris Review. Honours: Poetry Awards, National Endowment for the Arts, 1967, 1968. Memberships: President, PEN Center USA West, 1992-93. Address: 1107 15th Street, Santa Monica, CA 90403, USA.

SATTERTHWAIT Walter, b. 23 Mar 1946, Philadelphia, Pennsylvania, USA. Writer. 1 daughter. Education: Reed College, 1969-72. Publications: Cocain Blues, 1980; The Aegean Affair, 1981; Wall of Glass, 1987; Miss Lizzie, 1989; At Ease With the Dead, 1990; Wilde West, 1991; A Flower In the Desert, 1992; The Hanged Man, 1993 (UK edition as The Death Card, 1994). Contributions to: Alfred Hitchcock's Mystery Magazine; Santa Fe Reporter. Memberships: Mystery Writers of America; Private Eye Writers of America. Address: PO Box 5452, Clearwater, FL 34618, USA.

SAUNDERS Ann Loreille, (Ann Cox-Johnson), b. 23 May 1930, London, England. Historian. m. Bruce Kemp Saunders, 4 June 1960, 1 son, 1 daughter. Education: Plumptre Scholar, Queen's College, London, 1946-48; BA Hons, University College, London, 1951; PhD, Leicester University, 1965. Appointments: Archivist, Marylebone Public Library, London, 1956-63; Honorary Editor, Costume Society, 1967-; London Topographical Society, 1975-. Publications: London, City and Westminster, 1975; Art and Architecture of London, 1984, John Bacon, R A, 1740-1799; St Martin-in-the-Fields, 1989; The Royal Exchange, 1991. Contributions to: Magazines. Honours: Prize for Best Specialist Guide Book of the Year, British Tourist Board, 1984; Fellow, University College, London, 1992. Memberships: Fellow, Society of Antiquaries; Costume Society; London Topographical Society. Address: 3 Meadway Gate, London NW11 7LA, England.

SAUNDERS James (Arthur), b. 8 Jan 1925, London, England. Playwright. m. Audrey Cross, 1951, 1 son, 2 daughters. Education: University College, Southampton, 1946-49. Publications: Plays: Moonshine, 1958; Alas, Poor Fred and The Ark, 1959; Committal, Barnstable and Return to a City, 1960; A Slight Accident, 1961; Double Double, 1962; Next Time I'll Sing To You, The Pedagogue and Who Was Hilary Maconochie?, 1963; A Scent of Flowers and Neighbours, 1964; Triangle and Opus, 1965; A Man's Best Friend and The Borage Pigeon Affair, 1969; After Liverpool, 1970; Games and Savoury

Meringue, 1971; Hans Kohlhaas, 1972; Bye Bye Blues, 1973; The Island, 1975; Bodies, 1977; Birdsong, 1979; Fall, 1981; Emperor Waltz, 1983; Scandella, 1985; Making It Better, 1992; Retreat, 1995. Television: Watch Me I'm a Bird, 1964; Bloomers (series), 1979; TV adaptations of works by D H Lawrence, Henry James, H E Bates and R F Delderfield. Screenplays: Sailor's Return; The Captain's Doll. Honours: Arts Council of Great Britain Drama Bursary, 1960; Evening Standard Drama Award,1963; Writer's Guild TV Adaptation Award, 1966; Arts Council Major Bursary, 1984; BBC Radio Play Award, 1986; Molière Award, Paris, 1990. Address: c/o Casarotto Ramsay Ltd, 60-66 Wardour Street, London W1V 3HP, England.

SAUNDERS Nezzle Methelda, (Nezzle), b. 26 May 1940, Smithville, Jamaica, West Indies. Writer. m. 27 July 1960, 3 sons, 4 daughters. Education: Diploma, Office Practice, South Nottingham College of Further Education, 1976; City and Guilds Certificate, Community Care, 1989. Appointments: Schools and Community Centres Radio Programmes, 1986-94; Channel 4 TV Programme, 1988; Lecturer, Afro-Caribbean Family and Friends, 1990-93. Publications: Divine Inspiration, 1986; Insight, 1987; Children's and Student's Anthology, 1988. Contributions to: Periodicals. Honour: Bursary Award, Nottinghamshire County Council Leisure Services. Membership: Arts Development Group, president, 1987-. Address: 48 Finsbury Avenue, Sneinton Dale, Nottingham NG2 4LL, England.

SAUVAIN Philip (Arthur), b. 28 Mar 1933, Burton on Trent, Staffordshire, England. Writer. m. June Maureen Spencley, 27 July 1963, 1 son, 1 daughter. Education: MA, Cambridge University, 1956; Postgraduate Certificate in Education, University of London, 1957. Appointments: Senior Lecturer in Geography, James Graham College, Leeds, 1963-68; Head, Environmental Studies Department, Charlotte Mason College of Education, Ambleside, 1968-74. Publications: Looking Around Town and Country, 1975; A First Look at Winds, 5 volumes, 1975-78 Inagining the Past: First Series, 6 volumes, 1976, second series, 6 volumes, 1979; The British Isles, 1980; The Story of Britain Series, 4 volumes, 1980; Britain's Living Heritage, 1982; The History of Britain, 4 volumes, 1982; Theatre, 1983; Macmillan Junior Geography, 4 volumes, 1983; Hulton New Geographies, 5 volumes, 1983; History Map Books, 2 volumes, 1983, 1985; Hulton New Histories, 5 volumes, 1984-85; France and the French, 1985; European and World History, 1815-1919, 1985; Modern World History, 1919 Onwards, 1985; How History Began, 1985; Castles and Crusaders, 1986; What to Look For, 4 volumes, 1986; British Economic and Social History, 2 volumes, 1987; Exploring Energy, 4 volumes, 1987; GCSE History Companion Series, 3 volumes, 1988; How We Build, 3 volumes, 1989; The World of Work, 3 volumes, 1989; Skills for Geography, 1989; Skills for Standard Grade History, 1990; Exploring the Past: Old World, 1991; The Way it Works, 3 volumes, 1991; Changing World, 1992; Breakthrough: Communications, 1992; History Detectives, 3 volumes, 1992-93; Great Battles and Sieges, 4 volumes, 1992-93; Expanding World, 1993; The Era of the Second World War, 1993; Robert Scott in the Antarctic, 1993; Target Geography, 14 volumes, 1994-95; The Tudors and Stuarts, 1995; Britain Since 1930, 4 volumes, 1995; Geography Detective, 4 volumes, 1995-96; Famous Lives, 2 volumes, 1996; Key Themes of the Twentieth Century, 1996; Key Themes of the Twentieth Century: Teacher's Guide, 1996. Address: 70 Finborough Road, Stowmarket, Suffolk IP14 1PU, England.

SAVA George. See: **MILKOMANE George Alexis Milkomanovich**.

SAVAGE Alan. See: **NICOLE Christopher Robin**.

SAVAGE Thomas, (Tom Savage), b. 14 July 1948, New York, New York, USA. Poet; Critic; Editor. Education: BA, English, Brooklyn College of the City University of New York, 1969; MLS, Columbia University School of Library Science, 1980. Appointments: Teaching Assistant, Naropa Institute School of Poetics, 1975; Editor, Roof Magazine, 1976-78, Gandhabba Magazine, 1981-93; Teacher, Words, Music, Words for Poets and Composers, St Mark's Poetry Project, 1983-85. Publications: Personalities, 1978; Filling Spaces, 1980; Slow Waltz on a Glass Harmonica, 1980; Housing Preservation and Development, 1988; Processed Words, 1990; Out of the World, 1991; Political Conditions and Physical States, 1993; Precipice, 1994. Contributions to: Magazines and journals. Honours: PEN Grant, 1978; Coordinating Council of Literary Magazine Grant, 1981-82. Membership: Coordinating Council of Literary Magazines. Address: 622 East 11th Street, No 14, New York, NY 10009, USA.

SAVOY Douglas Eugene (Gene), b. 11 May 1927, Bellingham, Washington, USA. Bishop; Writer; Educator; Explorer. m. Sylvia Ontaneda, 7 July 1971, 2 sons, 1 daughter. Publications: Antisuyo: The Search for the Lost Cities of the High Amazon, 1970; The Child Christ, 1973; The Decoded New Testament, 1974; On the Trail of the Feathered Serpent, 1974; The Prophecies of Jamil, 7 volumes, 1976-83; The Secret Sayings of Jamil: The Image and the World, 7 volumes, 1976-87; The Essaei Document: Secrets of an Eternal Race, 1978; The Lost Gospel of Jesus: Hidden Teachings of Christ, 1978. Other: 39 texts, 400 audio tapes: Lectures on Religious Systems and Theology, 3 documentary videos. Contributions to: Various publications. Honours: Over 40 Flag Awards, Andean Explorers Foundation, 1958-94; Silver Hummingbird Award, Ministry Industry and Tourism of Peru, 1987; Explorer of the Century Trophy, Andean Explorers Foundation, 1988; Decorated Officer, Order of the Grand Cross, Republic of Peru, 1989; Medal of Merit Andres Reyes, 1989; Award, City of Ica, Peru, 1995. Memberships: Authors Guild; Explorers Club, New York City; Geographical Society, Lima, Peru; Andean Explorers Foundation and Ocean Sailing Club. Address: 2025 LaFond Drive, Reno, NV 89509, USA.

SAWYER Robert J(ames), b. 29 Apr 1960, Ottawa, Ontario, Canada. Writer. m. Carolyn Joan Clink, 11 Dec 1984. Education: BAA, Ryerson Polytechnical Institute, 1982. Publications: Golden Fleece, 1990; Far-Seer, 1992; Fossil Hunter, 1993; Foreigner, 1994; End of an Era, 1994; The Terminal Experiment, 1995. Honours: Aurora Award, Canadian Science Fiction and Fantasy Association, 1992; Homer Awards, 1992, 1993; Writer's Reserve Grant, Ontario Arts Council, 1993. Memberships: Crime Writers of Canada; Mystery Writers of America; Science Fiction and Fantasy Writers of America; Writers Union of Canada. Address: 7601 Bathurst Street, No 617, Thornhill, Ontario L4J 4H5, Canada.

SAWYER Roger Martyn, b. 15 Dec 1931, Stroud, England. Author. m. Diana Margaret Harte, 30 Aug 1952, 2 sons. Education: BA Hons, Diploma in Education, Wycliffe College, University of Wales, 1952-58; PhD, History, Southampton University, 1979. Publications: Casement: The Flawed Hero, 1984; Slavery in the Twentieth Century, 1986; Children Enslaved, 1988; The Island from Within (editor), 1990; 'We are but Women': Women in Ireland's History, 1993. Contributions to: Immigrants and Minorities; South. Honour: Airey Neave Award, 1985. Memberships: Anti-Slavery International (council member); Society of Authors. Address: Ducie House, Darts Lane, Bembridge, Isle of Wight PO35 5YH, England.

SAY Allen, b. 28 Aug 1937, USA. Children's Author and Illustrator. m. Deirdre Myles, 18 Apr 1974, 1 child. Publications: Author and Illustrator: Dr Smith's Safari, 1972; Once Under the Cherry Blossom Tree: An Old Japanese Tale, 1974; The Feast of Lanterns, 1976; The Bicycle Man, 1982; A River Dream, 1988; The Lost Lake, 1989; Tree of Cranes, 1991; Grandfather's Journey, 1993; The Stranger in the Mirror, 1995. Author: The Innkeeper's Apprentice, 1989; El Chino, 1990. Illustrator: 7 books, 1971-88. Honours: Christopher Award, 1985; Boston Globe-Horn Book Awards, 1988, 1994; Caldecott Honor Book, 1989; Caldecott Medal, 1994. Address: c/o Houghton Mifflin Children's Books, 222 Berkeley Street, Boston, MA 02116, USA.

SAYER Ian Keith Terence, b. 30 Oct 1945, Norwich, Norfolk, England. Company Director; Author. 2 sons, 3 daughters. Publications: Nazi Gold: The Story of the World's Greatest Robbery, 1984; America's Secret Army: The Untold Story of the Counter Intelligence Corps, 1989; Hitler's Last General: The Case Against Wilhelm Mohnke, 1989. Contributions to: Freight News Express (Columnist), 1984-89; The Sunday Times; The Sunday Times Magazine. Address: c/o FRX International, FRX House, 760-762 Bath Road, Cranford, Middlesex TW5 9TY, England.

SAYLOR Steven (Warren), b. 23 Mar 1956, Port Lavaca, Texas, USA. Writer. Registered domestic partner, Richard K Solomon, 15 Mar 1991. Education: BA, University of Texas at Austin, 1978. Publications: Roman Blood, 1991; Arms of Nemesis, 1992; Catilina's Riddle, 1993; The Venus Throw, 1995; A Murder on the Appian Way, 1996; House of the Vestals, 1997. Contributions to: Books and periodicals. Honours: Robert L Fish Memorial Award, Mystery Writers of America, 1993; Lambda Literary Award, 1994. Membership: Mystery Writers of America. Address: 1711 Addison Street, Berkeley, CA 94703, USA.

SCAGLIONE Aldo D(omenico), b. 10 Jan 1925, Turin, Italy. Professor of Literature; Writer. m. (1) Jeanne M Daman, 28 June 1952, dec 1986, (2) Marie M Burns, Aug 1992. Education: DLitt, University of Turin, 1948. Appointments: Faculty, University of California at Berkeley, 1952-68; W R Kenan Professor, University of North Carolina at Chapel Hill, 1969-87; Professor, 1987-91, Erich Maria Remarque Professor of Literature, 1991-, New York University. Publications: Nature and Love in the Late Middle Ages, 1963; Ars Grammatica, 1970; The Classical Theory of Composition, 1972; The Theory of German Word Order, 1981; The Liberal Arts and the Jesuit College System, 1986; Knights at Court, 1991. Contributions to: Professional journals. Honours: Knight of the Order of Merit, Republic of Italy; Fulbright Scholar, 1951; Guggenheim Fellowship, 1958; Newberry Fellow, 1964; Fellow, University of Wisconsin Institute for the Humanities, 1981. Memberships: American Association for Italian Studies, honorary president, 1989; Boccaccio Association of America, president, 1980-83; Medieval Academy of America. Address: 3 Reading Avenue, Frenchtown, NJ 08825, USA.

SCALAPINO Robert A(nthony), b. 19 Oct 1919, Leavenworth, Kansas, USA. Professor of Government Emeritus; Writer. m. Ida Mae Jessen, 23 Aug 1941, 3 daughters. Education: BA, Santa Barbara College, 1940; MA, 1943, PhD, 1948, Harvard University. Appointments: Lecturer, Santa Barbara College, 1940-41; Instructor, Harvard University, 1948-49; Assistant Professor, 1949-51, Associate Professor, 1951-56, Robson Research Professor of Government and Director, Institute of East Asian Studies, 1978-90, Professor Emeritus, 1990-, University of California at Berkeley; Editor, Asian Survey, 1962-96. Publications: Democracy and the Party Movement in Pre-War Japan, 1953, 2nd edition, 1967; The Chinese Anarchist Movement (with George T Yu), 1961; North Korea Today (editor), 1963; The Japanese Communist Movement, 1920-1966, 1967; The Communist Revolution in Asia (editor), 1969, 2nd edition, 1977; Communism in Korea (with Chong-Sik Lee), 1972; Elites in the People's Republic of China (editor), 1972; Asia and the Road Ahead, 1975; The Foreign Policy of Modern Japan (editor), 1977; The United States and Korea: Looking Ahead, 1979; North Korea Today: Strategic and Domestic Issues (editor with Jun-Yop Kim), 1983; The Early Japanese Labor Movement, 1984; The Politics of Development: Perspectives on Twentieth Century Asia, 1989; The Last Leninists: The Uncertain Future of Asia's Communist States, 1992. Contributions to: Many scholarly books and journals. Honours: Carnegie Foundation Grant, 1951-53; Social Science Research Council, Fellow, 1952-53; Ford Foundation Grant, 1955; Rockefeller Foundation Grants, 1956-59, 1961; Guggenheim Fellowship, 1965-66; Woodrow Wilson Award, American Political Science Association, 1973; Order of the Sacred Treasure, Japan, 1988; Presidential Order, Republic of Korea, 1990; Berkeley Fellow, 1990; Honorary doctorates. Memberships: American Academy of Arts and Sciences; American Political Science Association; Association for Asian Studies; Council on Foreign Relations; Foreign Policy Association; Western Political Science Association; Member of Board, Asia Foundation, Atlantic Council, Pacific Forum, CSIS. Address: 2850 Buena Vista Way, Berkeley, CA 94708, USA.

SCAMMELL William, b. 2 Jan 1939, Hythe, Hampshire, England. Poet; Critic. m. Jacqueline Webb, 15 Aug 1964, 2 sons. Education: BA, University of Bristol, 1967. Appointments: Lecturer in English, University of Newcastle, 1975-91; Chairman, Northern Arts Literature Panel, 1982-85. Publications: Yes and No, 1979; A Second Life, 1982; Time Past, 1982; Jouissance, 1985; Eldorado, 1987; Keith Douglas: A Study, 1988; Bleeding Heart Yard, 1992; The Game: Tennis Poems, 1992; Five Easy Pieces, 1993; Barnacle Bill, 1994. Editor: Between Comets: for Norman Nicholson at 70, 1984; This Green Earth: Nature Poetry 1400-1980, 1992; The New Lake Poets, 1992; The Poetry Book Society Anthology 3, 1992; Winter Pollen: Occasional Prose of Ted Hughes, 1994. Honours: British Arts Council Award, 1985; Northern Arts Writers Awards, 1988, 1991, 1994. Address: Centre for Continuing Education, The University, Newcastle upon Tyne NE1 7RU, England.

SCANNELL Vernon, b. 23 Jan 1922, Spilsby, Lincolnshire, England. Author; Poet. m. 4 Oct 1954, 3 sons, 2 daughters. Appointments: Visiting Poet, Shrewsbury School, 1973-75; Writer-in-Residence, Berinsfield, Oxfordshire, 1975-76; Poet-in-Residence, King's School, Canterbury, 1979. Publications: Fiction: The Fight, 1952; The Wound and the Scar, 1953; The Face of the Enemy, 1960; The Big Time, 1967; Ring of Truth, 1983. Poetry: New and Collected Poems, 1980; Winterlude, 1983; Funeral Games,

1987; Soldiering On, 1989; A Time for Fires, 1991; Collected Poems 1950-1993, 1994. Non-Fiction: The Tiger and the Rose, 1971; Argument of Kings, 1987; Drums of Morning, Growing Up in the 30's, 1992; The Black and White Days, poems, 1996. Contributions to: Periodicals; Sunday Telegraph; London Magazine; Observer; Poets Review. Honours: Heinemann Award for Literature, 1960; Cholmondeley Poetry Prize, 1974. Membership: Royal Society of Literature, Hon Fellow. Address: 51 North Street, Otley, West Yorkshire LS21 1AH, England.

SCARBOROUGH William Kauffman, b. 17 Jan 1933, Baltimore, Maryland, USA. University Professor; Historian. m. Patricia Estelle Carruthers, 16 Jan 1954, 1 son, 1 daughter. Education: AB, 1954, PhD, 1962, University of North Carolina; MA, Cornell University, 1957. Publications: The Overseer: Plantation Management in the Old South, 1966; The Diary of Edmund Ruffin, 3 volumes, 1972-89. Contributions to: Books and professional journals. Honours: Phi Beta Kappa, 1953; Mississippi Historical Society president, 1979-80; Jules and Frances Landry Award for The Diary of Edmund Ruffin, Vols I-III, Louisiana State University Press, 1989. Honour: Charles W Moorman Distinguished Alumni Professor in the Humanities, 1996-98. Memberships: Organization of American Historians; Southern Historical Association; Agricultural History Society; Mississippi Historical Society; St George Tucker Society; Southern Carolina Historical Society. Address: Department of History, University of Southern Mississippi, Southern Station, Box 5047, Hattiesburg, MS 39406, USA.

SCARF Margaret, (Maggie Scarf), b. 13 May 1932, Philadelphia,Pennsylvania, USA. Writer. m. Herbert Eli Scarf, 28 June 1953, 3 daughters. Education: BA, South Connecticut State University, 1989. Appointments: Contributing Editor, The New Republic, 1975-; Fellow, Center for Advanced Study, Stanford, California, 1977-78, 1985-86; Writer-in-Residence, Jonathan Edwards College, Yale University, 1992-. Publications: Body, Mind, Behavior, 1976; Unfinished Business, 1980; Intimate Partners, 1987; Member Advisory Board, Paynter Fellowship in Journalism, Yale University, 1994-; Intimate Worlds: Life Inside the Family, 1995. Contributions to: Magazines and journals. Honours: Ford Foundation Fellow, 1973-74; Nieman Fellow, Harvard University, 1975-76; Alicia Patterson Fellow, 1978-79; Smith Richardson Foundation Grants, 1991, 1992, 1993, 1994. Memberships: Connecticut Society of Psychoanalytic Psychologists; PEN. Address: c/o Jonathan Edwards College, Yale University, 68 High Street, New Haven, CT 06517, USA.

SCARFE Allan (John), b. 30 Mar 1931, Caulfield, Victoria, Australia. Writer. m. Wendy Scarfe, 6 Jan 1955, 4 children. Education: BA; DipEd; TPTC. Appointments: Teacher, Warrnambool Secondary College, retired; Writer. Publications: With Wendy Scarfe: A Mouth of Petals, 1967; Tiger on a Rein, 1969; People of India, 1972; The Black Australians, 1974; Victims or Bludgers?: Case Studies in Poverty in Australia, 1974; J P: His Biography, 1975; Victims or Bludgers?: A Poverty Inquiry for Schools, 1978; Arms Kindi, 1978, abridged and enlarged edition, 1996; Labor's Titan: The Story of Percy Brookfield 1878-1921, 1983; All That Grief: Migrant Recollections of Greek Resistance to Facism 1941-49, 1994. Contributions to: Several publications. Honours: With Wendy Scarfe: Australia Literature Boards Grants, 1980, 1988. Address: 8 Bostock Street, Warrnambool, Victoria 3280, Australia.

SCARFE Norman, b. 1 May 1923, Felixstowe, England. Education: MA Hons, History, Oxford, 1949. Appointments: Chairman, Centre of East Anglia Studies, University of East Anglia; Founder, Honorary General Editor, Suffolk Records Society, 1958-92. Publications: Suffolk, 1960, 2nd edition, 1988; Essex, 1968, 2nd edition, 1982; Cambridgeshire, 1983; The Suffolk Landscape, 1972, 2nd edition, 1987; Suffolk in the Middle Ages, 1986; A Frenchman's Year in Suffolk (1784), 1988; Innocent Espionage: The La Rochefoucauld Brothers' Tour of England in 1785, 1995. Contributions to: Proceedings, Suffolk Institute of Archaeology; Aldeburgh Festival Annual Programme Book; Country Life; The Book Collector;Dictionary of National Biography. Honours: Hon Litt D, University of East Anglia, 1989; Member of the Order of the British Empire, 1994. Memberships: International PEN; Founder Chairman, Suffolk Book League, 1982; Fellow, Society of Antiquaries. Literary Agent: John Welch, Milton House, Milton, Cambridge, CB4 6AD, England. Address: The Garden Cottage, 3 Burkitt Road, Woodbridge, Suffolk IP12 4JJ, England.

SCARFE Wendy (Elizabeth), b. 21 Nov 1933, Adelaide, South Australia. Writer; Poet. m. Allan Scarfe, 6 Jan 1955, 4 children. Education: BA; BLitt; ATTC. Appointments: Teacher, Warrnambool Secondary College, retired; Writer; Poet. Publications: Novels: The Lotus Throne, 1976; Neither Here Nor There, 1978; Laura My Alter Ego, 1988; The Day They Shot Edward, 1991; The Sculptor, novel in progress. Poetry: Shadow and Flowers, 1964, enlarged edition, 1984; With Allan Scarfe: A Mouthful of Petals, 1967; Tiger on a Rein, 1969; People of India, 1972; The Black Australians, 1974; Victims or Bludgers?: Case Studies in Poverty in Australia, 1974; J P: His Biography, 1975; Victims or Bludgers?: A Poverty Inquiry for Schools, 1978; Arms Kindi, 1978, abridged and enlarged edition, 1996; Labor's Titan: The Story of Percy Brookfield, 1878-1921, 1983; All That Grief: Migrant Recollections of Greek Resistance to Fascism, 1941-1949, 1994; The Sculptor, in progress; No Taste for Carnage, biography with Allan Scarfe, in progress; Remembering Jayaprakash, biography with Allan Scarfe, in progress. Contributions to: Overland; Australian Short Stories; Age. Honours: With Allan Scarfe, Australia Literature Board Grants, 1980, 1988. Membership: Fellowship of Australian Writers. Address: 8 Bostock Street, Warrnambool, Victoria 3280, Australia.

SCHALLER George B(eals),b. 26 May 1933, Berlin, Germany. m. Kay Morgan, 26 Aug 1957, 2 sons. Education: BS Zoology, BA, Anthropology, University of Alaska; MS, PhD, University of Wisconsin. Appointments: Professor; Researcher. Publications: The Year of the Gorilla, 1964; The Serengati Tiger, 1972; Stones of Silence: Journeys in the Himalayas, 1980; The Last Panda, 1993. Contributions to: Zoological journals and popular periodicals. Honour: National Book Award, 1973. Address: The Wildlife Conservation Society, Bronx Park, NY 10460, USA.

SCHAU Jens Michael, b. 25 May 1948, Ronne, Bornholm, Denmark. Psychologist; Writer; Dramatist; Screenwriter. Education: BA, History, 1974, PhD, Psychology, 1978, University of Copenhagen. Publications: I Familiens Skod, 1982; Byen og Oen, 1983; Himlen begynder ved Jorden, 1984; Far, Mor og Børn, 1988; En lille Prins, 1994. Television films: Boksning; Naeste Sommer Maske, 1988. Radio Play: Sonner, 1984. Contributions to: Magazines and journals. Honours: Statens Kunstfond, 1983, 1984, 1985. Address: c/o Tiderne Skifter and Gyldendal Publishers, Klareboderne 3, 1115 Copenhagen K, Denmark.

SCHEIBER Harry N(oel), b. 1935, New York, New York, USA. Professor of Law; Writer. Education: BA, Columbia University, 1955; MA, 1957, PhD, 1961, Cornell University. Appointments: Fellow, Centre for Advanced Study in the Behavioural Sciences, 1966, 1971; Professor of Law, later Stefan Reisenfeld Professor of Law and History, University of California at Berkeley; Academic Chair for History and Civics, National Assessment of Educational Progress, 1986-88. Publications: The Wilson Administration and Civil Liberties, 1960; United States Economic History, 1964; America: Purpose and Power (co-author), 1965; The Condition of American Federalism, 1966; The Frontier in American Development (co-editor), 1969; The Old Northwest, 1969; The Ohio Canal Era 1820-1861, 1969, 2nd edition, 1987; Black Labor in American History, 1972; Agriculture in the Development of the Far West, 1975; American Economic History (co-author), 1976; American Law and the Consitutional Order, 1978, 2nd edition, 1990; Perspectives on Fedralism (editor), 1987; Power Divided (co-editor), 1989; The Federalism of the Judicial Mind (editor), 1993; Legal Culture and the Legal Profession (co-author), 1995. Contributions to: Professional journals. Honours: Guggenheim Fellowships, 1967, 1989; Distinguished Fulbright Lecturer, Australia, 1984; National Endowment for the Humanities Fellow, 1984; University of California Humanities Research Institute Fellow, 1989. Address: c/o School of Law, University of California at Berkeley, Berkeley, CA 94708, USA.

SCHELL Orville Hickok, b. 20 May 1940, New York, New York, USA. Writer. 3 sons. Education: BA magna cum laude, Harvard College; MA, PhD (ABD), University of California at Berkeley; Currently Dean, Graduate School of Journalism, University of California, Berkeley. Publications: 6 books, including Mandate of Heaven, 1994. Contributions to: Magazines. Honours: Alice Patterson Fellowship, 1981; MacDowell Colony Fwellowships, 1984, 1987; Guggenheim Fellowship, 1989-90; Freedom Forum Media Studies Center, Columbia University, senior fellow, 1996. Memberships: Authors Guild; PEN; Council on Foreign Relations. Address: c/o International Creative Management, 40 West 57th Street, New York, NY 10019, USA.

SCHELLENBERG James Arthur, b. 7 June 1932, Vinland, Kansas, USA. Social Scientist. m. 28 Dec 1974, 3 sons, 1 daughter. Education: AB, Baker University, 1954; MA, 1955, PhD, 1959, University of Kansas. Publications: An Introduction to Social Psychology, 1970, revised edition, 1974; Masters of Social Psychology, 1978; The Science of Conflict, 1982; Conflict Between Communities, 1987; Primitive Games, 1990; An Invitation to Social Psychology, 1993; Exploring Social Behaviour, 1993. Address: 124 Madison Boulevard, Terre Haute, IN 47803, USA.

SCHEPISI Frederic Alan, b. 26 Dec 1939, Melbourne, Victoria, Australia. Film Writer; Producer; Director. m. (1) Joan Mary Ford, (2) Rhonda Elizabeth Finlayson, 1973, 3 sons, 4 daughters, (3) Mary Rubin, 1984. Appointments: TV Production Manager, Patron Advisory Service, Melbourne, 1961-64; Victorian Manager, Cinesound Productions, Melbourne, 1964-66; Managing Director, 1964-66; Governing Chairman, 1979-, The Film House, Melbourne. Publications: Films: The Devil's Playground, 1975; The Chant of Jimmie Blacksmith, 1978; Barbarosa, 1981; Iceman, 1983; Plenty, 1984-85; Roxanne, 1986; Evil Angels, 1987; Russia House, 1989; Mr Baseball, 1991; Six Degrees of Separahon, 1993; IQ, 1994. Honours: Australian Film Awards, Best Film, 1975; Australian Film Awards, Best Film, Best Achievement in Direction, Best Screenplay adapted from another source and the AFI Members Prize Special Award, 1989. Address: 159 Eastern Road, South Melbourne, Victoria, Australia 3205.

SCHEVILL James (Erwin), b. 10 June 1920, Berkeley, California, USA. Writer; Poet; Dramatist; Professor. m. (1) Helen Shaner, 1942, div. 1966, 2 daughters, (2) Margot Blum, 1966. Education: BS, Harvard University, 1942; MA, Brown University. Appointments: Assistant Professor of Humanities, California College of Arts and Crafts, Oakland, 1951-59; Associate Professor of English, San Francisco State University, 1959-68; Professor of English, 1968-88, Professor Emeritus, 1988-, Brown University. Publications: Tensions (poems), 1947; The American Fantasies, poems, 1951; Sherwood Anderson: His Life and Work, 1951; High Sinners, Low Angels (musical play), 1953; The Right to Greet (poems), 1956; The Roaring Market and the Silent Tomb (biography of Bern Porter), 1956; The Bloody Tenet (verse play), 1957; Selected Poems, 1945-62, 1962; Voices of Mass and Capital A (play), 1962; The Stalingrad Elegies (poems), 1964; The Black President, and Other Plays, 1965; Violence and Glory: Poems 1962-67, 1969; Lovecraft's Follies (play), 1971; Breakout! In Search of New Theatrical Environments, 1972; The Buddhist Car and Other Characters (poems), 1973; The Arena of Ants (novel), 1977; The Mayan Poems, 1978; The American Fantasies: Collected Poems 1945-1982, 1983; Oppenheimer's Chair (play), 1985; Collected Short Plays, 1986; Ambiguous Dancers of Fame: Collected Poems 1945-1986, 1987; Where to Go, What to Do, When You Are Bern Porter: A Personal Biography, 1992; 5 Plays 5, 1993; Winter Channels (poems), 1994; The Complete American Fanatasies (poems), 1996. Honours: Ford Foundation Grant, 1960-61; William Carlos Williams Award, 1965; Guggenheim Fellowship, 1981; Centennial Review Poetry Prize, 1985; Honorary DHL, Rhode Island College, 1986; Pawtucket Arts Council Award for Poetry and Theatre, 1987; American Academy and Institute of Arts and Letters Award, 1991. Literary Agent: Helen Merrill. Address: 1309 Oxford Street, Berkeley, CA 94709, USA.

SCHEVING Hans, b. 27 June 1958, Copenhagen, Denmark. Architect. Education: Architect, Royal Academy of Fine Arts, School of Architecture, Copenhagen, 1984. Publications: Rome: A Guide to Rome, 1988; London: A Guide to London, 1993. Contributions to: Danish Architects Journal, Arkitekten; Danish Weekly Journal, Weekend Avisen. Memberships: Danish Architects Association. Address: Rojenvaengets Hoveovej 29, DK 2100, Copenhagen, Denmark.

SCHIFF James Andrew, b. 6 Dec 1958, Cincinnati, Ohio, USA. Teacher; Writer. m. 24 June 1989, 2 sons. Education: AB, Duke University, 1981; MA, 1985, PhD, 1990, New York University. Appointment: Visiting Instructor, University of Cincinnati, 1989-. Publications: Updike's Version: Rewriting The Scarlet Letter, 1992; Understanding Reynolds Price, 1996; John Updike Revisited, 1998; Critical Essays on Reynolds Price, 1998. Contributions to: Southern Review; American Literature; South Atlantic Review; Studies in American Fiction; Critique. Memberships: Modern Language Association; SAMLA. Address: 2345 East Hill Avenue, Cincinnati, OH 45308, USA.

SCHLAFLY Phyllis (Stewart), b. 15 Aug 1924, St Louis, Missouri, USA. Lawyer; Columnist; Author. m. Fred Schlafly, 20 Oct 1949, 4 sons, 2 daughters. Education: BA, Washington University, St Louis, 1944; MA, Harvard University, 1945. Appointments: Conservative Political Activist; Editor, The Phyllis Schlafly Report, 1967-; Syndicated Columnist, Copley News Service, 1976-. Publications: A Choice, Not an Echo, 1964; The Gravediggers, 1964; Strike from Space, 1965; Safe, Not Sorry, 1967; The Betrayers, 1968; Mindszenty the Man, 1972; Kissinger on the Couch, 1975; Ambush at Vladivostok, 1976; The Power of the Positive Woman, 1977; Child Abuse in the Classroom (editor), 1984; Equal Pay for Unequal Work, 1984; Pornography's Victims, 1987; Who Will Rock the Cradle?, 1989; First Reader, 1994. Contributions to: Journals, magazines, radio and television. Honours: 10 Honours Awards, Freedom Foundation. Memberships: American Bar Association; Commission on the Bicentennial of the US Constitution, 1985-91; Daughters of the American Revolution; Illinois Bar Association; Phi Beta Kappa; Pi Sigma Alpha. Address: 68 Danforth Road, Alton, IL 62002, USA.

SCHLESINGER Arthur M(eier) Jr, b. 15 Oct 1917, Columbus, Ohio, USA. Historian; Professor; Author. m. (1) Marian Cannon, 1940, div 1970, 2 sons, 2 daughters, (2) Alexandra Emmet, 1971, 1 son. Education: AB, Harvard University, 1938; Postgraduate Studies, Cambridge University, 1938-39. Appointments: Associate Professor, 1946-54, Professor of History, 1954-61, Harvard University; Special Assistant to President John F Kennedy, 1961-64; Visiting Fellow, Institute for Advanced Study, Princeton, New Jersey, 1966; Schweitzer Professor of Humanities, City University of New York, 1966-95; Chairman, Franklin Delano Roosevelt Four Freedoms Foundation, 1983-. Publications: Orestes A Brownson: A Pilgrim's Progress, 1939; The Age of Jackson, 1945; The Vital Center, 1949; The General and the President (with R H Revere), 1951; The Age of Roosevelt, Vol I, The Crisis of the Old Order 1919-1933, 1957, Vol II, The Coming of the New Deal, 1958, Vol III, The Politics of Upheaval, 1960; Kennedy or Nixon: Does It Make Any Difference?, 1960; The Politics of Hope, 1963; The National Experience (with John Blum), 1963; A Thousand Days: John F Kennedy in the White House, 1965; The Bitter Heritage: Vietnam and American Democracy 1941-66, 1967; The Crisis of Confidence, 1969; The Imperial Presidency, 1973; Robert Kennedy and His Times, 1978; The Cycles of American History, 1986; The Disuniting of America, 1991. Editor: The Harvard Guide to American History, 1954; Guide to Politics, 1954; Paths to American Thought, 1963; The Promise of American Life, 1967; The Best and Last of Edwin O'Connor, 1970; The History of American Presidential Elections (with F L Israel), 1971, new edition, 1986; The Coming to Power, 1972; The Dynamics of World Power: A Documentary History of United States Foreign Policy 1945-1972, 1973; History of US Political Parties, 1973; The American Statesman, 1982; The Almanac of American History, 1983; Running for President, 1994. Contributions to: Professional journals. Honours: Francis Parkman Prize, Society of American Historians, 1957; Bancroft Prize, Columbia University, 1958; Pulitzer Prize in Biography, 1966; National Book Awards, 1966, 1979; National Institute and American Academy of Arts and Letters Gold Medal in History and Biography, 1967; Ohio Governor's Award for History, 1973; Fregene Prize for Literature, Italy, 1983; Grants, fellowships and honorary doctorates. Memberships: American Academy and Institute of Arts and Letters, president, 1981-84, chancellor, 1984-87; American Civil Liberties Union; American historical Association; American Philosophical Society; Americans for Democratic Action, chairman, 1952-54; Colonial Society of Massachusetts; Council on Foreign Relations; Franklin and Eleanor Roosevelt Institute, co-chairman, 1983-; Organization of American Historians; Phi Beta Kappa. Address: 455 East 51st Street, New York, NY 10022, USA.

SCHMIDMAN Jo Ann, b. 18 Apr 1948, Omaha, Nebraska, USA. Theatre Director; Playwright. Education: BFA, Boston University, 1970. Appointments: Producing Artistic Director, Omaha Magic Theatre, 1968-; Team Member, Artist-in-Schools, Nebraska Arts Council, 1994. Publications: Plays: This Sleep Among Women, 1974; Running Gag, 1980; Astro Bride, 1985; Velveeta Meltdown, 1985; Right Brain (editor with M Terry and S Kimberlain), 1992. Other: Various unpublished but produced plays, 1978-93. Address: 2309 Hanscom Boulevard, Omaha, NE 68105, USA.

SCHMIDT-NIELSEN Knut, b. 24 Sept 1915, Trondheim, Norway (US citizen, 1950). Scientist; Writer. Education: PhD, University of Copenhagen, 1946. Appointments: Faculty, Department of Zoology, Duke University; Editor, scientific journals. Publications: Desert

Animals, 1964; How Animals Work, 1972; Animal Physiology, 1975, 5th edition, 1997; Scaling: Why is Animal Size So Important?, 1984. Contributions to: Many professional journals. Honours: Honorary MD, University of Lund, 1983; Honorary PhD, University of Trondheim, 1993. Memberships: Acadèmie des Sciences, Paris; National Academy of Sciences, USA; Royal Society, London. Address: c/o Department of Zoology, Duke University, Durham, NC 27708-0325, USA.

SCMITZ Dennis (Mathew), b. 11 Aug 1937, Dubuque, Iowa, USA. Professor of English; Poet. m. Loretta D'Agostino, 1960, 2 sons, 3 daughters. Education: BA, Loras College, Dubuque, Iowa, 1959; MA, University of Chicago, 1961. Appointments: Instructor, Illinois Institute of Technology, Chicago, 1961-62, University of Wisconsin at Milwaukee, 1962-66; Assistant Professor, 1966-69, Poet-in-Residence, 1966-, Associate Professor, 1969-74, Professor of English, 1974-, California State University at Sacramento. Publications: We Weep for Our Strangeness, 1969; Double Exposures, 1971; Goodwill, Inc, 1976; String, 1980; Singing, 1985; Eden, 1989; About Night: Selected and New Poems, 1993. Honours: New York Poetry Center Discovery Award, 1968; National Endowment for the Arts Fellowships, 1976, 1985, 1992; Guggenheim Fellowship, 1978; di Castagnola Award, 1986; Shelley Memorial Award, 1988. Address: c/o Department of English, California State University at Sacramento, 6000 Jay Street, Sacramento, CA 95819, USA.

SCHMOOKLER Andrew Bard, b. 19 Apr 1946, Long Branch, New Jersey, USA. Writer; Speaker; Consultant. m. 28 Sept 1986, 2 sons, 1 daughter. Education: BA summa cum laude, Harvard College, 1967; PhD, Thelogical Union and University of California, 1977. Publications: The Parable of the Tribes, The Problem of Power in Social Evolution, 1984, 2nd edition, 1995; Out of Weakness: Healing the Wounds that Drive us to War, 1988; Sowing and Reapings: The Cycling of Good and Evil in the Human System, 1989; The Illusion of Choice: How the Market Economy Shapes Our Destiny, 1992; Fools Gold: The Fate of Values in a World of Goods, 1993. Honour: Erik H Erikson Prize, International Society for Political Psychology, 1984. Literary Agent: Jane DystaL, Jane Dystel Literary MAnagement, One Union Square West, New York, NY 19993, USA. Address: 86 Sunset Ridge Road, Broadway, VA 22815, USA.

SCHNAPPER Dominique Aron, b. 9 Nov 1934, Paris, France. Director of Studies. m. Antoine Schnapper, 28 Nov 1958, 1 son, 2 daughter. Education: IEP, 1957; Doctorate, Sorbonne, 1967; Doctorat d'Etat, 1979. Appointments: Director of Studies, École des Hautes Études en Sciences Sociales, Paris. Publications: L'Italie Rouge et Noire, 1971; Juifs et Israelites, 1980; L'épreuve du Chomage, 1981; La France de L'Intégration, 1991; L'Europe des Immigrés, 1992; La Communauté des Citoyens, 1994. Memberships: President, Société Française de Sociologie; Société Française de Sciences Politiques; Society of Friends of Raymond Aron. Address: 75 Bd St Michel, 75005 Paris, France.

SCHNEEBAUM Tobias, b. 25 Mar 1922, New York, New York, USA. Writer; Lecturer. Education: BA, City College of New York, 1942; MA, Cultural Anthropology, Goddard College, 1977. Publications: Keep the River on Your Right, 1969; Wild Man, 1979; Life with the Asmat, 1981; Asmat Images, 1985; Where the Spirits Dwell, 1988; Embodied Spirits, 1990. Contributions to: Various publications. Honours: Fulbright Fellowship, 1955; Ingram Merrill Foundation Grants, 1982, 1989; Ludwig Vogelstein Foundation Grant, 1985. Memberships: Explorers Club; PEN. Address: 463 West Street, No 410A, New York, NY 10014, USA.

SCHOEMPERLEN Diane Mavis, b. 9 July 1954, Thunder Bay, Ontario, Canada. Writer; Teacher. 1 son. Education: BA, English, Lakehead University, Ontario, 1976. Appointments: Teacher, Kingston School of Writing, Queens University, Ontario, 1986-93, St Lawrence College, Kingston, 1987-, University of Toronto Summer Writers' Workshop, 1992; Editor, Coming Attractions, Oberton Press, 1994-. Publications: Double Exposures, 1984; Frogs and Other Stories, 1986; Hockey Night in Canada, 1987; The Man of My Dreams, 1990; Hockey Night in Canada and Other Stories, 1991; In the Language of Love, 1994. Contributions to: Anthologies. Honours: WGA Award for Short Fiction, 1987; Silver National Magazine Award, 1989; The Man of my Dreams shortlisted for Governor-General's Award and Trillium Award. Membership: Writer's Union of Canada. Address: 32 Dunlop Street, Kingston, Ontario, K7L 1L2, Canada.

SCHOENEWOLF Gerald Frederick, b. 23 Sept 1941, Fredericksburg, Texas, USA. Psychoanalyst; Writer. m. (1) Carol Slater, 1964-69. 1 daughter, (2) Theresa Lamb, 1979-84. Education: BA, Goddard College, Plainfield, Vermont; MA, California State University, Dominguez Hills; PhD, Union Institute, Cincinnati, Ohio. Publications: 101 Common Therapeutic Blinders (with R Robertiello), 1987; 101 Therapeutic Successes, 1989; Sexual Animosity between Men and Women, 1989; Turning Points in Analytic Therapy: The Classic Cases, 1990; Turning Points in Analytic Therapy: From Winnicott to Kernberg, 1990; The Art of Hating, 1991; Jennifer and Her Selves, 1991; Counterresistance, 1993; Erotic Games: Bringing Intimacy Back into Relationships, 1995; The Couple Who fell in Hate and Other Tales of Eccleotic Psychotherapy, 1996. Contributions to: Numerous papers and short stories to various publications. Memberships: American Psychological Association; National Association for the Advancement of Psychoanalysis. Address: R.R.I, Box 304F, Bushkill, PA 18324, USA.

SCHOFIELD Caroline (Carey), b. 29 Dec 1953, Surrey, England. Writer. m. Laurence King, 14 June 1985. Education: BA Cantab, 1976. Publications: Mesrine, 1980; Jagger, 1984; Russia at War, 1987; Inside the Soviet Army, 1991; The Russian Elite: Inside Spetsnaz and the Airborne Forces, 1993. Contributions to: Various publications. Memberships: International Institute of Strategic Studies; Royal United Services Institute. Address: 6 St Martins Road, London SW9, England.

SCHOFIELD Michael, b. 24 June 1919, Leeds, England. Sociologist; Writer. Education: MA, Cambridge University, 1940. Publications: The Sexual Behaviour of Young People, 1965; The Sociological Aspects of Homosexuality, 1965; Society and the Young School Leaver, 1967; Drugs and Civil Liberties, 1968; Social Research, 1969; Behind the Drug Scene (co-author), 1970; The Strange Case of Pot, 1971; The Rights of Children (co-author), 1972; The Sexual Behaviour of Young Adults, 1973; Promiscuity, 1976; The Sexual Containment Act, 1978. Address: 28 Lyndhurst Gardens, London NW3 5NW, England.

SCHOFIELD Paul. See: TUBB E(dwin) C(harles).

SCHOFIELD William Greenough, b. 13 June 1909, Providence, Rhode Island, USA. Author. m. 21 Nov 1934, 2 sons, 1 daughter. Appointments: Feature Writer, Providence Journal, 1936-40; Chief Editorial Writer, Columnist, Foreign Correspondent, Boston Traveler, 1940-67; Manager, Editorial Services, Raytheon Co., 1967-70; Director, Public Information Consultant, Public Affairs, Publications Editor, Boston University, 1970-79. Publications: Ashes in the Wilderness, 1942; The Cat in the Convoy, 1946; Payoff in Black, 1947; The Deer Cry, 1948; Seek for a Hero, 1956; Sidewalk Statesman, 1959; Destroyers: 60 Years, 1962; Treason Trail, 1964; Eastward the Convoys, 1966; Freedom by the Bay, 1974; Frogmen: First Battles, 1987. Contributions to: Reader's Digest; Catholic Digest; Redbook; Skipper; Information; Boston Sunday Herald. Honour: Achievement Award, US Department of Interior, 1976. Address: 16 Hunnewell Circle, Newton, MA 02158, USA.

SCHOLEY Arthur (Edward), b. 17 June 1932, Sheffield, England. Children's Writer; Playwright. Publications: The Song of Caedmon (with Donald Swann), 1971; Christmas Plays and Ideas for Worship, 1973; The Discontented Dervishes, 1977; Sallinka and the Golden Bird, 1978; Twelve Tales for a Christmas Night, 1978; Wacky and His Fuddlejig (with Donald Swann), 1978; Singalive (with Donald Swann) 1978; Herod and The Rooster(with Ronald Chamberlain) 1979; The Dickens Christmas Carol Show, 1979; Baboushka (with Donald Swann) 1979; Candletree (with Donald Swann) 1981; Five Plays for Christmas, 1981; Four Plays About People, 1983; Martin the Cobbler, 1983; The Hosanna Kids, 1985; Make a Model Christmas Crib, 1988; Who'll Be Brother Donkey?, 1990; Brendan Ahoy!, (with Donald Swann), 1994. Address: 1 Cranbourne Road, London N10 2BT, England.

SCHOONOVER Jason Brooke Rivers Morgan, b. 14 Sept 1946, Melfort, Saskatchewan, Canada. Author; Anthropologist. Education: BA, English, Simon Fraser University, Burnaby, British Columbia, Canada. Appointments: Announcer, CKOM Radio, Saskatoon, 1970-71; Announcer, Music Director, Promotion Manager, Producer, CFQC Radio, Saskatoon, 1972-77; CBC Broadcaster, 1972-77; President, Schoononer Properties, 1975-. Publications: The Bangkok Collection, 1988; Thai Gold, 1989. Honours: B'nai B'rith

Media Human Rights Award, on behalf of CFQC Radio, 1976. Hobbies: Travel; Outdoors; Reading. Address: 720 University Drive, Saskatoon, Saskatchewan S7N 0J4, Canada.

SCHOULTZ Solveig von, b. 5 Aug 1907, Borga, Finland. Author. m. Erik Bergman, 7 July 1961. Education: Teacher's Qualification; PhD, honouris causa, 1986. Publications: Poetry: Eko av ett rop, 1946; Natet, 1956; Sank ditt ljus, 1963; De fyra flojtspelarna, 1975; Bortom traden hors havet, 1980; En enda minut, 1981; Vattenhjulet, 1986; Alla trãd vantar faglar, 1988; Ett sått att räkna tiden, 1989; Samtal med en fjäril, 1994; Molnskuggan; Short Novels: Ingenting ovanligt, 1948; Narmare nagon, 1951; Den blomstertid, 1958; Aven dina kameler, 1965; Rymdbruden, 1970; Somliga mornar, 1976; Kolteckning, ofullbordad, 1983; Ingen dag forgaves, 1984; Nåsta dag, 1991; Långs vattenbrynet, 1992; Samtal med en fjäril, 1994. Other: Plays for TV and Radio. Address: Berggatan 22C, Helsinki 10, Finland.

SCHRAG Peter, b. 24 July 1931, Karlsruhe, Germany. Journalist; Editor. Education: BA, Amherst College, 1953; Graduate Studies, Amherst College and University of Massachusetts, 1957-59. Appointments: Reporter, El Paso Herald Post, Texas, 1953-55; Assistant Secretary, Amherst College, 1956-66; Associate Education Editor, 1966-68, Executive Editor, 1968-73, Saturday Review, New York City; Editor, Change, New York City, 1969-70; Lecturer, University of Massachusetts, 1970-72, University of California at Berkeley, 1990-; Editor, Editorial Page, Sacramento Bee, California, 1978-; Contributing Editor, The American Prospect. Publications: Voices in the Classroom, 1965; Village School Downtown, 1967; Out of Place in America, 1970; The Decline of the WASP, UK edition The Vanishing American, 1972; The End of the American Future, 1973; Test of Loyalty, 1974; The Myths of the Hyperative Child (with Diane Divorky), 1975; Mind Control, 1978. Contributions to: Newspapers and magazines. Honour: Guggenheim Fellow, 1971-72. Membership: National Conference of Editorial Writers. Literary Agent: Ellen Levine, Ellen Levine Literary Agency, 15 East 26th Street, Suite 1801, New York, NY 10010, USA. Address: c/o Sacramento Bee, 21st and Q Streets, Sacramento, CA 95816, USA.

SCHRAMM David, b. 25 Oct 1945, St Louis, Missouri, USA. Vice President for Research; Professor in the Physical Sciences; Writer; Editor. m. Judith Jane Gibson, 20 June 1986, 2 sons. Education: SB, Physics, Massachusetts Institute of Technology, 1967; PhD, Physics, California Institute of Technology, 1971. Appointments: Faculty, later Louis Block Professor in the Physical Sciences, University of Chicago; Associate Editor, American Journal of Physics, 1978-81; Editor, Theoretical Astrophysics Series, University of Chicago Press, 1981-; Astrophysics Editor, Physics Reports, 1981-I; Correspondent, Comments on Nuclear and Particle Astrophysics, 1984-; Receiving Editor, New Astronomy, 1995-. Publications: From Quarks to the Cosmos: Tools of Discovery (co-author), 1989; The Shadows of Creation: Dark Matter and the Structure of the Universe, 1991; The Big Bang and Other Explosions in Nuclear and Particle Astrophysics, 1996. Contributions to: Professional journals. Honours: 1st Annual Robert J Trumpler Award, Astronomical Society of the Pacifc, 1974; Helen B Warner Prize, American Astronomical Society, 1978; 1st Prize, Gravity Research Foundation, 1980; Richtmyer Memorial Award Lecturer, American Association of Physics Teachers, 1984; Alexander von Humboldt Award, 1988; Einstein Medal, Eotvos University, Budapest, 1989; Aspen Center for Physics Chair, Colorado, 1992-95; Lilienfeld Award, American Physical Society, 1993; University of Chicago Graduate Teaching Award, 1994. Memberships: American Academy of Arts and Sciences, fellow; American Association for the Advancement of Science, fellow; American Astronomical Society; American Physical Society, fellow; Hungarian Academy of Science; International Astronomical Union; Meteorotical Society, fellow; National Academy of Sciences. Address: c/o University of Chicago, 5640 South Ellis Avenue, AAC 140, Chicago, IL 60637, USA.

SCHRAMM Werner, b. 28 Apr 1926, Germany. Author; Painter. Education: Teacher Training Institute; Langemarck Studies (wounded during World War II). Publications: Stefan Zweig, 1961; Das antike Drama 'Die Bacchantinnen' in der Neugestaltung durch H Wolfgang Philipp, 1980; Hugo Wolfgang Philipps Tragikomödie 'Der Clown Gottes', 1983; Moderner deutscher Roman, 1983; Stefan Zweig: Bildnis eines genialen Charakters, 1984. Honours: Cultural Doctorate in Literature, 1991; Research Advisor of the Year, 1991; Professional of The Year, 1991; Grand Ambassador of Achievement, 1991; Silver Shield of Valor, 1992; Doctor of Arts, Albert Einstein International Academy Foundation, 1993; Man of the Year, 1993; Pictorial

Testimonial of Achievement and Distinction, 1993; Gold Record of Achievement, 1994; Order of International Ambassadors, 1995. Memberships: American Biographical Institute Research Association's Board of Governors, 1989; Fellowship of the International Biographical Association, 1989; American Biographical Institute Research Board of Governors, 1989; IBC Advisory Council, 1990; International Order of Merit, 1990; Lifetime Achievement Academy, 1991; ABI Research Board of Advisors, 1991; Men's Inner Circle of Achievement, 1993. Address: Eckenerweg 8, D 25524 Itzehoe, Germany.

SCHREINER Samuel Agnew, Jr., b. 6 June 1921, Mt Lebanon, Pennsylvania, USA. Author. m. Doris Moon, 22 Sept 1945, 2 daughters. Education: AB, Summa cum laude, Princeton University, 1942. Publications: Thine is the Glory, 1975; The Condensed World of the Reader's Digest, 1977; Pleasant Places, 1977; Angelica, 1978; The Possessors and the Possessed, 1980; The Van Alens, 1981; A Place Called Princeton, 1984; The Trials of Mrs Lincoln, 1987; Cycles, 1990; Mayday! Mayday!, 1990; Code of Conduct (with Everett Alvarez), 1992; Henry Clay Frick: The Gospel of Greed, 1995. Contributions to: Reader's Digest; Woman's Day; McCalls; Redbook; Parade. Address: 111 Old Kings Highway South, Darien, Ct 06820, USA.

SCHRIEBERG David. Journalist. Education: Graduate, Georgetown University. Appointments: Staff Writer, San Jose Mercury News, 1984-90; Mexico City Bureau Chief, Sacramento Bee/McClatchy News Service; Buenos Aires Bureau Chief, Newsweek, 1994-. Contributions to: Atlantic Monthly; New Republic; Washington Magazine. Honours: Co-Winner, Pulitzer Prize for General News Reporting, 1990; George Polk Award for Regional Reporting, 1990; Inter-American Press Association Prize for Best Coverage of Latin America in a US Daily, 1993; Knight Journalism Fellow, Stanford University, 1993-94. Address: c/o Newsweek, 251 West 57th Street, New York, NY 10019-1894, USA.

SCHUCHMAN Joan. See: **FEINBERG Joan Miriam**.

SCHULBERG Budd, b. 27 Mar 1914, New York, New York, USA. Author. m. (1) Virginia Ray, 23 July 1936, div 1942, 1 daughter, (2) Victoria Anderson, 17 Feb 1943, div 1964, 2 sons, (3) Geraldine Brooks, 12 July 1964, dec 1977, (4) Betsy Anne Langman, 9 July 1979, 1 son, 1 daughter. Education: AB cum laude, Dartmouth College, 1936. Appointments: Founder-President, Schulberg Productions; Founder-Director, Watts Writers Workshop, Los Angeles, 1965-; Founder-Chairman, Frederick Douglass Creative Arts Center, New York City, 1971-. Publications: What Makes Sammy Run?, 1941; The Harder They Fall, 1947; The Disenchanted, 1950; Some Faces in the Crowd, 1953; Waterfront, 1955; Sanctuary V, 1969; The Four Seasons of Success, 1972; Loser and Still Champion: Muhammad Ali, 1972; Swan Watch, 1975; Everything That Moves, 1980; Moving Pictures: Memories of a Hollywood Prince, 1981; Love, Action, Laughter and Other Sad Tales, 1990; Sparring with Hemingway and Other Stories of the Fight Game, 1995. Editor: From the Ashes: Voices of Watts, 1967. Screenplays: Little Orphan Annie (with Samuel Ornitz), 1938; Winter Carnival (with F Scott Fitzgerald), 1939; Weekend for Three, 1941; City Without Men (with Martin Berkeley), 1943; Government Girl, 1943; On the Waterfront, 1954; A Face in the Crowd, 1957; Wind Across the Everglades, 1958. Contributions to: Magazines. Honours: Academy Award, 1954; New York Critics Circle Award, 1954; Screen Writers Guild Award, 1954; Venice Film Festival Award, 1954; Christopher Award, 1955; German Film Critics Award, 1957; B'hai Human Rights Award, 1968; Prix Literaire, Deauvile Festival, 1989; Westhampton Writers Lifetime Achievement Award, 1989; World Boxing Association Living Legend Award, 1990; Southampton Cultural Center 1st Annual Literature Award, 1992. Memberships: American Civil Liberties Union; American Society of Composers, Authors and Publishers; Authors Guild; Dramatists Guild; PEN; Phi Beta Kappa; Writers Guild East. Address: c/o Miriam Altschuler Literary Agency, RR1, Box 5, Old Post Road, Red Hook, NY 12571, USA.

SCHULLER Gunther (Alexander), b. 22 Nov 1925, New York, New York, USA. Composer; Conductor; Music Educator; Publisher. m. Marjorie Black, 8 June 1948, dec 1992, 2 sons. Education: St Thomas Choir School, New York City, 1938-44. Appointments: Teacher, Manhattan School of Music, New York City, 1950-63; Teacher, 1963-84, Artistic Co-Director, 1969-74, Director, 1974-84, Berkshire Music Center, Tanglewood, Massachusetts; Faculty, Yale School of Music, 1964-67; President, New England Conservatory of Music, Boston, 1967-77; Music Publisher, 1975-; Artistic Director, Festival at Sandpoint, 1985-. Publications: Horn Technique, 1962, 2nd edition,

1992; Early Jazz: Its Roots and Musical Development, 3 volumes, 1968-; Musings, 1985; The Swing Era, 1988. Contributions to: Various publications. Honours: Guggenheim Fellowship, 1962-63; ASCAP-Deems Taylor Award, 1970; Rodgers and Hammerstein Award, 1971; William Schuman Award, Columbia University, 1989; John D and Catharine T MacArthur Foundation Fellowship, 1991; Pulitzer Prize in Music, 1994; Honorary doctorates. Memberships: American Academy of Arts and Sciences; American Academy of Arts and Letters. Address: 167 Dudley Road, Newton Centre, MA 02159, USA.

SCHULTZ John (Ludwig), b. 28 July 1932, Columbia, Missouri, USA. Writer; Teacher. m. (1) Anne Gillian Bray, 10 Dec 1962, div Nov 1975, (2) Betty E Schiflett, 9 May 1992, 1 son, 1 daughter. Appointments: Chair Fiction Writing Department, 1967-, Head, Master in Teaching Writing, 1983-, Head, Master in Fine Arts in Creative Writing, 1990-, Columbia College, Chicago. Publications: The Tongues of Men, 1969; No One Was Killed, 1969; Motion Will be Denied, 1972; Writing from Start to Finish, 1982, new edition, 1990; The Chicago Conspiracy Trial, 1993. Contributions to: Journals. Memberships: Associated Writing Programs; Modern Language Association. Address: 3636 North Janssen, Chicago, IL 60613, USA.

SCHULZ Max (Frederick), b. 15 Sept 1923, Cleveland, Ohio, USA. Professor of English; Writer. Education: University of Chicago, 1947-48; AB, 1949, MA, 1950, University of Pittsburgh; Postgraduate Studies, University of Minnesota, 1950-51; PhD, Wayne State University, 1959. Appointments: Professor of English, 1963-94, Chairman, Department of English, 1968-80, Curator, Fisher Gallery, 1993-, University of Southern California at Los Angeles; Associate Editor, Critique Magazine, 1971-85. Publications: The Poetic Voices of Coleridge, 1963, revised edition, 1965; Essays in American and English Literature Presented to Bruce Robert McElderry Jr (editor), 1967; Radical Sophistication: Studies in Contemporary Jewish-American Novelists,, 1969; Bruce Jay Friedman, 1973; Black Humor Fiction of the Sixties: A Pluralistic Definition of Man and His World, 1973; Paradise Preserved: Recreations of Eden in 18th and 19th Century England, 1985; The Muses of John Barth: Tradition and Metafiction from Lost in the Funhouse to the Tidewater Tales, 1990; Exhibition Catalogue: Edgar Ewing, the Classical connection, 1993; The Mythic Present of Chagoya, Valdez and Gronk, 1995. Contributions to: Professional journals. Address: c/o Fisher Gallery, University of Southern California at Los Angeles, Los Angeles, CA 90089, USA.

SCHUNCK Christian, b. 28 Mar 1972, Cologne, Germany. Journalist; Student. Education: Abitur, Collegium Josephinum; Bonn Gymnasium, 1991; MBA, Clark University, Worcester, Massachusetts. Appointment: Junior Supervisor, Enzyklopädie der Martimen Philatelie, 1993-94. Publications: Wirtschaft und Umwelt in Trier als Europäischer Grenzregion (co-author), 1994; Enzyklopädie der Maritimen Philatelie, Ergänzungslieferung (co-author), 1993; Contributor to Diemels Welt Lexikon und Reisehandbuch, 1995. Contributions to: Topical Time; Heer; Medienspiegel; Michel-Rundschau. Honours: Navicula-Verdienstspange Silver, 1994; BDPh-Ehrennadel Bronze, 1994. Memberships: AIJP; ACUNS; PWS; APS Writers Unit No 30; VNJ. Address: Im Litzelholz 60, 54293 Trier, Germany.

SCHUNCKE Michael, b. 8 May 1929, Dresden, Germany. Special Teacher; Author; Consultant. m. Dorothea Czibulinski-Dressler, 22 Dec 1956, 2 daughters. Education: Theory of Music, 1945-49; Advertising, Academy of Mannheim, 1953-54; Seminars in writing, advertising, marketing. Appointment: Vice Chairman, Poetical Ludwig-Finckh-Freundeskreis Gaienhofen, 1989-93. Publications: Wanderer Zwischen, 1975; Sprecht die Sprache der Adressaten, 1982; Schlüsselworte erfolgreicher Anzeigen, 1986; Praktische Werbehilfe, 1987; Atmosphäre eines Jugend in Baden-Baden, 1995. Honours: Goldene Hans Buchholz Medaille, 1974; Awards in Community. Memberships: Gesellschaft für Deutsche Sprache; Poetical Ludwig-Finckh-Freundeskreis Gaienhofen; Robert Schumann Gesellschaft; Mendelssohn Gesellschaft. Address: Lichtental, Heschmattweg 11, D 76534 Baden Baden, Germany.

SCHWANDT Stephen (William), b. 5 Apr 1947, Chippewa Falls, Wisconsin, USA. Educator. m. Karen Sambo, 13 June 1970, 2 sons. Education: BA, Valparaiso University, 1969; BS, St Cloud State University, 1972; MA, University of Minnesota - Twin Cities, 1972. Appointments: Teacher of Composition and American Literature, Irondale High School, New Brighton, Minnesota, 1974-; Instructor,

Concordia College, St Paul, Minnesota, 1975-80, Normandale Community College, 1983-. Publications: The Last Goodie, 1985; A Risky Game, 1986; Holding Steady, 1988; Guilt Trip, 1990; Funnybone, 1992. Contributions to: Various newspapers. Memberships: National Education Association; Authors Guild; Book Critics Circle; National Council for Teachers of English; The Loft. Address: Marilyn Marlow, Curtis Brown Ltd, 10 Astor Place, New York, NY 10003, USA.

SCHWARTZ Eli, b. 2 Apr 1921, New York, New York, USA. Professor of Economics (retired). m. Renee S Kartiganer, 29 Aug 1948, 1 son, 1 daughter. Education: BS, University of Denver, 1943; Army, USA, 1943-46; MA, University of Connecticut, 1948; PhD, Brown University, 1952. Appointments: Instructor, University of Rhode Island, 1947-48; Assistant Instructor, Brown University, 1948-51; Chief Regional Economist, Office of Price Stabilization, Boston, 1951-53; Lecturer, Michigan State University, 1953-54; Assistant Professor, 1954-58, Associate Professor, 1958-62, Professor of Economics, 1962-78, Chairman, Department of Economics, 1978-84, Charles Macfarlane Professor of Economics, 1978-91, Lehigh University. Publications: Corporate Finance, 1962; Trouble in Eden: A Comparison of the British and Swedish Economies, 1980; Managing Municipal Finance (editor), 1980, 4th edition, 1996; Restructuring the Thrift Industry, 1989; Theory and Application of the Interest Rate, 1993. Contributions to: Professional journals. Honours: Senior Teaching Grant, Lehigh University, 1972; Earhart Foundation Grant, 1978. Memberships: American Economics Association; American Finance Association; National Association of Forensic Economists. Address: Rauch Business Centre. 621 Taylor Street, Lehigh University, Bethlehem, PA 18015, USA.

SCHWARTZ Elliott (Shelling), b. 19 Jan 1936, Brooklyn, New York, USA. Composer; Professor of Music; Writer. m. Dorothy Rose Feldman, 26 July 1960, 1 son, 1 daughter. Education: AB, 1957, MA, 1958, EdD, 1962, Columbia University. Appointments: Instructor, University of Massachusetts, 1960-64; Assistant Professor, 1964-70, Associate Professor, 1970-75, Professor of Music, 1975-, Bowdoin College; Distinguished Visiting Professor, Ohio State University, 1985-86; Visiting Professor of Music, Ohio State University, 1988-92; Visiting Fellow, Robinson College, Cambridge, England, 1993-94, 1997-98. Publications: The Symphonies of Ralph Vaughan Williams, 1964; Contemporary Composers on Contemporary Music (editor with Barney Childs), 1967; Electronic Music: A Listener's Guide, 1973, 2nd edition, revised, 1976; Music: Ways of Listening, 1982; Music Since 1945: Issues, Materials and Literature (with Daniel Godfrey), 1993. Contributions to: Professional journals. Honours: Guaudeamus Prize, Netherlands, 1970; Maine State Award in the Arts and Humanities, 1970; National Endowment for the Arts Grants, 1978-83; Rockefeller Foundation Residencies, Bellagio, Italy, 1980, 1989. Memberships: American Society of University Composers; College Music Society, president. Address: 10 Highview Road, PO Box 451, South Freeport, ME 04078, USA.

SCHWARTZ John (Burnham), b. 8 May 1965, New York, New York, USA. Writer. Education: BA, East Asian Studies, Harvard University, 1987. Publication: Bicycle Days, 1989. Contributions to: Periodicals. Honour: Lyndhurst Prize, 1991. Memberships: Authors Guild; Poet's Theatre, Cambridge, Massachusetts. Address: c/o International Creative Management, 40 West 57th Street, New York, NY 10019, USA.

SCHWARTZ Lynne Sharon, b. 19 Mar 1939, Brooklyn, New York, USA. Author; Poet. m. Harry Schwartz, 22 Dec 1957, 2 daughters. Education: BA, Barnard College, 1959; MA, Bryn Mawr College, 1961; New York University, 1967-72. Publications: Rough Strife, 1980; Balancing Acts, 1981; Disturbances in the Field, 1983; Acquainted with the Night (stories), 1984; We Are Talking About Homes (stories), 1985; The Melting Pot and Other Subversive Stories, 1987; Leaving Brooklyn, 1989; A Lynne Sharon Schwartz Reader: Selected Prose and Poetry, 1992; The Fatigue Artist, 1995; Ruined by Reading: A life in Books, 1996. Contributions to: Periodicals. Honours: National Endowment for the Arts Fellowship, 1984; Guggenheim Fellowship, 1985; New York State Foundation for the Arts Fellowship, 1986. Memberships: Authors Guild; National Book Critics Circle; National Writers Union; PEN American Centre.

SCHWARTZ Ros, b. 24 Oct 1952, London, England. Translator. Partner, Andrew Cowen, 1 son, 1 daughter. Education: Licence-ès-Lettres, Universite de Paris VIII, 1978. Publications:

Translations: I Didn't Say Goodbye (Claudine Vegh), 1984; The Blue Bicycle (Régine Deforges), 1985; Black Docker (Ousmane Sembéne), 1987; Desperate Spring (Fettouma Touati), 1987; The Net (Ilie Nastase), 1987; Cuisine Extraordinaire, 1988; Return to Beirut (Andrée Chedid), 1989; Women in Evidence (Sébastien Japrisot), 1990; Dining with Proust (Anne Borel), 1992; The Dragon Book (Ciruelo), 1992. Memberships: Translators Association, chairwoman, 1991-92; Society of Authors; Institute of Translation and Interpreting; Women in Publishing. Address: 34 Uplands Road, London N8 9NL, England.

SCHWARTZ Sheila, b. 15 Mar 1936, New York, USA. Professor; Writer. Div, 1 son, 1 daughter, 1 dec. Education: BA, Adelphi University; MA, Teachers College, Columbia University; EdD, New York University. Appointment: Professor, State University of New York College at New Paltz. Publications: How People Lived in Ancient Greece and Rome, 1967; How People Lived in Mexico, 1969; Teaching the Humanities, 1970; Earth in Transit, 1977; Like Mother, Like Me, 1978; Growing Up Guilty, 1978; Teaching Adolescent Literature, 1979; The Solid Gold Circle, 1980; One Day You'll Go, 1981; Jealousy, 1982; The Hollywood Writer's Wars, 1982; Bigger is Better, 1987; Sorority, 1987; The Most Popular Girl, 1987; The Children of Izieu, documentary film, Writer/Producer, 1992. Contributions to: Writing in America, 1989. Honours: Fulbright Fellowship; Teaching awards; Fellows Award, Adolescent Literature Association, 1979; UUP/New York State Medal for Excellence, 1991; New York State English Council 1979 Award for Excellence in Letters; New York State English Council Award for Excellence in Teaching, 1980; Fellows Award, New York State English Council. Membership: International PEN, Newsletter Committee, Women's Committee Address: c/o State University of New York College at New Paltz, New Paltz, NY 12561, USA.

SCHWARZ Daniel Roger, b. 12 May 1941, Rockville Centre, New York, USA. Professor of English; Writer. 2 sons. Education: BA, Union College, 1963; MA, 1965, PhD, 1968, Brown University. Appointments: Professor of English, Cornell University, 1968-; Distinguished Visiting Cooper Professor, University of Arkansas at Little Rock, 1988; Citizen's Chair in Literature, University of Hawaii, 1992-93; Visiting Eminent Scholar, University of Alabama, Huntsville, 1996. Publications: Disraeli's Fiction, 1979; Conrad: Almayer's Folly to Under Western Eyes, 1980; Conrad: The Later Fiction, 1982; The Humanistic Heritage: Critical Theories of the English Novel from James to Hillis Miller, 1986; Reading Joyce's Ulysses, 1987, revised 1991; The Transformation of the English Novel 1890-1930: Studies in Hardy, Conrad, Joyce, Lawrence, Forster and Woolf, 1989, revised new edition and paperback, 1995; The Case for a Humanistic Poetics, 1991; Narrative and Representation in the Poetry of Wallace Stevens, 1993; Reconfiguring Modernism: Explorations in the Relationship Between Modern Art and Literature, 1997. Contributions to: Professional journals. Honours: American Philosophical Society Grant, 1981; 9 National Endowment for the Humanities Summer Seminars for College and High School Teachers Grants, 1984-93; USIA Lecturer and Academic Specialist Lecturer, Australia, 1993. Membership: International Association of University Professors of English. Address: c/o Department of English, 304 Rockefeller Hall, Cornell University, Ithaca, NY 14853, USA.

SCHWERIN Doris Belle, b. 24 June 1922, Peabody, Massachusetts, USA. Author; Composer. m. Jules V Schwerin, 2 Mar 1946, 1 son. Education: Boston University; New England Conservatory of Music; Diploma, Julliard School of Music, 1943; Student of George Antheil and Stefan Wolpe. Publications: Diary of a Pigeon Watcher, 1976; Leanna (novel in 6 movements), 1978; The Tomorrow Book (children's book), 1984; Rainbow Walkers, UK edition as The Missing Years; The Tree That Cried (children's book), 1988; Cat and I (memoir), 1990. Contributions to: MS Magazine. Honour: Charles Sergal National Play Award, University of Chicago, 1971. Memberships: PEN; Assocation of American Composers, Authors and Publishers; Authors Guild; Authors League. Literary Agent: Patricia Collins, 157 East 72nd Street, New York, NY 10021, USA. Address: 317 West 83rd Street, New York, NY 10024, USA.

SCHWERNER Armand, b. 11 May 1927, Antwerp, Belgium. Professor of English and Speech; Poet; Writer; Musician. m. Doloris Holmes, 13 Jan 1961, div 1978, 1 child. Education: Cornell University, 1945-47; University of Geneva, 1947-48; BS, 1950, MA, 1964, Columbia University. Appointments: Instructor, Long Island University, New York City, 1963-64; Instructor, 1964-66, Assistant Professor, 1966-69, Associate professor, 1969-73, Professor of English and Speech, 1973-, College of Staten Island of the City University of New

York. Publications: Poetry: The Lightfall, 1963; The Tablets I-VIII, 1968; (if personal), 1968; Seaweed, 1968; The Tablets I-XV, 1971; Bacchae Sonnets, 1974; The Tablets XVI, XVII, XVIII, 1975; The Triumph of the Will, 1976; This Practice: Tablet XIX and Other Poems, 1976; Bacchae Sonnets 1-7, 1977; The Work, the Joy and the Triumph of the Will, 1977; Sounds of the River Naranjana and The Tablets I-XXIV, 1983; The Tablets I-XXVI, 1989. Other: Stendhal's "The Red and the Black": Notes and Criticism, 1963; The Domesday Dictionary (with Donald M Kaplan), 1963; A Farewell to Arms: A Critical Commentary, 1963; Billy Budd and Typee: Critical Commentary, 1964; The Sound and the Fury: A Critical Commentary (with Jerome Neibrief), 1964; John Steinbeck's "Of Mice and Men", 1965; John Steinbeck's "The Red Pony" and "The Pearl", 1965; Andre Gide's "The Immoralist", "Strait is the Gate", and Other Works: A Critical Commentary, 1966; Dos Passos's "U.S.A." and Other Works, 1966; Albert Camus' "The Stranger": A Critical Commentary, 1970; Redspell: Eleven American Indian Adaptations (translator), 1975. Contributions to Anthologies, professional journals and general periodicals. Honours: Numerous grants and fellowships including: Faculty Research Fellowships, State University of New York, 1970, 1972, City University of New York, 1971; National Endowment for the Arts Creative Writing Fellowships, 1973, 1979, 1987; Creative Incentive Fellowship, PSC/CUNY, 1986, 1992; Greater NY Arts Development Fund Grant for Poetry (SICA), 1987; Fund for Poetry: Grant for Contribution to Contemporary American Poetry, 1991. Memberships: Modern Language Association; National Book Critics Circle; National Council of Teachers of English; PEN America Centre; Poets House, New York City. Address: 20 Bay Street Landing, Apt B-3C, Staten Island, NY 10301, USA.

SCIARRILLO Carmen Francisca Maria Vivern, b. 8 Jul 1919. Author; Piano Teacher. Publications: La Educacion Musical En La Escuela Primaria, 1964; Cuentos Musicales Escenificados, 1965; Marcha Para Mi Escuela, La Escarapela, 1967; Cinco Canciones Para Jardin de Infantes, 1969; Canciones Para Mi Escuela, 1970; Cancionero Didactico Escolar, 1970; Comedias Musicales Escolares, 1972; La Educacion Musical En La Escuela Primaria, 1979. Honours: Ten Confs. by LRA Radio Nacional; Narrator and Coordinator, Firsts Musical Educational Congress at The Medical University, 1970. Literary Agent: Rogelio Sciarrillo. Address: Ignacio Fermin Rodriguez 2427, Capital Federal CP 1406, Buenos Aires, Argentina.

SCOFIELD Jonathan. See: **LEVINSON Leonard.**

SCOFIELD Sandra (Jean), b. 5 Aug 1943, Wichita Falls, Texas, USA. Writer. m. (1) Allen Scofield, dec, 1 daughter, (2) Bill Ferguson, 10 July 1975. Education: BA, University of Texas, 1964; MA, 1978, PhD, 1979, University of Oregon. Appointments: Teacher, Elementary and High School, Texas, Illinois, California and Oregon; Assistant Professor of Education, 1979-80, Adjunct Professor of English, 1991-, Southern Oregon State College; Writer. Publications: Gringa, 1989; Beyond Deserving, 1991; Walking Dunes, 1992; More Than Allies, 1993; Opal on Dry Ground, 1994; A Chance to See Egypt, 1996. Contributions to: Periodicals. Honours: 2nd Place, Katherine Anne Porter Fiction Prize, 1985; New American Writing Award, 1989; American Academy and Institute of Arts and Letters 1st Fiction Award Nomination, 1989; Creative Writing Fellowship, National Endowment for the Arts, 1989; National Book Award Nomination, 1991; American Book Award, 1992; Oregon Book Award Nomination, 1994; Texas Institute of Letters Fiction Award, 1997. Memberships: PEN; Authors Guild; Oregon Institute of Literary Arts; Austin Writers League. Hobbies: Reading; Visiting Museums and Galleries. Literary Agent: Emma Sweeney, 280 Riverside Drive, New York, NY 10025, USA. Address: PO Box 3329, Ashland, OR 97520, USA.

SCOTT Arthur Finley, b. 30 Nov 1907, Kronstad, Orange Free State, South Africa. University Teacher (retired); Author. m. (1) Margaret Ida Scott, June 1935, dec, (2) Margaret Clare Scott, Jan 1954, dec, 2 daughters. Education: BA, 1930, MA, 1934, Cambridge University; Graduate Studies, Oxford University, 1930. Appointments: Senior Lecturer in English, Borough Road College of Education, London, 1952-73; Faculty, London University, 1968-73; Director, Scott and Finley Ltd. Publications: Over 130 books, 1938-83. Honour: Life Fellow, International Biographical Association. Memberships: Kettering Three Arts Society; National Book League; Royal Society of Literature; Society of Authors. Address: 59 Syon Park Gardens, Isleworth, Middlesex TW7 5NE, England.

SCOTT Donald Fletcher, b. 29 Nov 1930, Norfolk, England. Medical Consultant (retired). m. (1) Adrienne Mary Moffett, 2 Sept 1967, dec 1992, (2) Dr Mary Paterson, 5 Jan 1994, 1 son, 1 daughter. Education: MB, ChB, Edinburgh University, Scotland, 1951-57; DPM, London University, 1965. Publications: About Epilepsy, 1969; Fire and Fire Raisers, 1974; Understanding EEG, 1975; Coping With Suicide, 1989; Beating Job Burnout, 1989; The History of Epileptic Therapy, 1992. Contributions to: Over 100 articles mainly to medical/psychological journals. Honour: Fellow, Royal College of Physicians, 1979. Memberships: Electro-Encephalogram Society; Association of British Neurologists; Association of British Clinical Neurophysiology; British Society of Clinical Neurophysiology; Association of British Neurologists. Address: 25 Park Gate, Blackheath, London SE3 9XF, England.

SCOTT Gail, b. 20 Jan 1945, Ottawa, Ontario, Canada. Writer. 1 daughter. Education: BA, Queen's University, Kingston, Ontario, 1966; University of Grenoble. Appointments: Journalist, Montreal Gazette, The Globe and Mail, 1970-79; Writing Instructor, 1981-90; Writer-in-Residence, Concordia University, Montreal, 1991-92, University of Alberta, Edmonton, 1994-95. Publications: Spare Parts, 1982; Heroine, 1987; La Theorie, un Dimanche, 1988; Spaces Like Stairs, 1989; Serious Hysterics (anthology), 1992; Resurgences (anthology), 1992; Main Brides, 1994. Contributions to: Journals and other publications. Honours: Shortlisted, Quebec Society for the Promotion of English Language Literature, 1987, 1994. Memberships: L'Union des Ecrivains Quebecois; Writer's Union of Canada. Address: c/o Coach House Press, 401 Heron Street, Toronto, Ontario M5S 2G5, Canada.

SCOTT John A, b. 23 Apr 1948, Littlehampton, Sussex, England. University Lecturer; Poet; Writer. Education: BA, DipEd, Monash University, Victoria, Australia. Appointments: Lecturer, Swinburne Institute, 1975-80, Canberra College of Advanced Education, 1980-89, University of Wollongong, New South Wales, 1989-. Publications: The Barbarous Sideshow, 1976; From the Flooded City, 1981; Smoking, 1983; The Quarrel with Ourselves, 1984; Confession, 1984; St Clair, 1986, revised edition, 1990; Blair, 1988; Singles: Shorter Works 1981-1986, 1989; Translation, 1990; What I Have Written, 1993. Contributions to: Various publication. Honours: Poetry Society of Australia Award, 1970; Mattara Poetry Prize, 1984; Wesley Michel Wright Awards, 1985, 1988; Victorian Premier's Prize for Poetry, 1986; ANA Award, fellowship of Australian Writers, 1990. Address: c/o McPhee Gribble Publishers, 56 Claremont Street, South Yarra, Victoria 3141, Australia.

SCOTT John Peter, b. 8 Apr 1949, London, England. Professor of Sociology; Writer. m. Jill Wheatley, 4 Sept 1971, 1 son, 1 daughter. Education: Kingston College of Technology, 1968-71; BSc, Sociology, London University, 1971; London School of Economics and Political Science, 1971-72; PhD, University of Strathclyde, 1976. Appointments: Lecturer, University of Strathclyde, 1972-76; Lecturer, 1976-87, Reader, 1987-91, Professor of Sociology, 1991-94, University of Leicester; Editor, Network Newsletter, British Sociological Association, 1985-89, Social Studies Review, later Sociology Review, 1986-; Professor of Sociology, University of Essex, 1994-. Publications: Corporations, Classes and Capitalism, 1979, 2nd edition, 1985; The Upper Classes, 1982; The Anatomy of Scottish Capital (with M Hughes), 1982; Directors of Industry, (with C Griff), 1984; Networks of Corporate Power (co-editor), 1985; Capitalist Property and Financial Power, 1986; A Matter of Record, 1990; The Sociology of Elites (editor), 3 volumes, 1990; Who Rules Britain, 1991; Social Network Analysis, 1992; Power (editor), 3 volumes, 1994; Poverty and Wealth, 1994; Sociological Theory, 1995; Stratification and Power, 1996; Corporate Business and Capitalist Classes, 1997; Class, editor, 4 volumes, 1997. Contributions to: Professional journals and general periodicals. Honour: Sociological Theory listed an an Outstanding Sociology Book of the Year, Choice. Membership: British Sociological Association, secretary, 1991-92, chairperson, 1992-93, treasurer, 1997-. Address: c/o Department of Sociology, University of Essex, Colchester CO4 3SQ, England.

SCOTT Jonathan Henry, b. 22 Jan 1958, Auckland, New Zealand. Historian; Writer; Poet. Education: BA, 1980, BA Honours, 1981, Victoria University of Wellington; PhD, Cambridge University, 1986. Appointment: Faculty, Downing College, Cambridge. Publications: Algernon Sidney and the English Republic, 1623-1677, 1988; Algernon Sidney and the Restoration Crisis 1677-1683, 1991. Contributions to: Books, professional journals and literary publications

including: Albion, 25, 4, 1993; Britain and the Netherland XI: The Exchange of Ideas, Simon Groenveld and Michael Wintle (editors), 1994; The Certainty of Doubt: Essays in Honour of Peter Munza, M Fairburn and W H Oliver (editors), 1996; The Stuart Court and Europe, Malcolm Smuts (editor), 1996. Literary Agent: Charles Taylor, Peters Fraser and Dunlop. Address: c/o Downing College, Cambridge CB2 1DQ, England.

SCOTT Nathan A(lexander) Jr, b. 24 Apr 1925, Cleveland, Ohio, USA. Professor of English Emeritus; Minister; Writer. m. Charlotte Hanley, 21 Dec 1946, 2 children. Education: AB, University of Michigan, 1944; BD, Union Theological Seminary, 1946; PhD, Columbia University, 1949. Appointments: Dean of the Chapel, Virginia Union University, 1946-47; Instructor, 1948-51, Assistant Professor, 1951-53, Associate Professor of Humanities, 1953-55, Howard University; Assistant Professor, 1955-58, Associate Professor, 1958-64, Professor of Theology and Literature, 1964-72, Professor of English, 1967-76, Shailer Mathews Professor of Theology and Literature, 1972-76, University of Chicago; Ordained Priest, Episcopal Church, 1960; Co-editor, Journal of Religion, 1963-77; Canon Theologian, Cathedral of St James, Chicago, 1967-76; Commonwealth Professor of Religious Studies, 1976-81, Professor of English, 1976-90, William R Kenan Professor of Religious Studies, 1981-90, Professor Emeritus, 1990-, University of Virginia. Publications: Rehearsals of Discomposure: Alienation and Reconciliation in Modern Literature, 1952; The Tragic Vision and the Christian Faith, 1957; Modern Literature and the Religious Frontier, 1958; Albert Camus, 1962; Reinhold Niebuhr, 1963; The New Orpheus: Essays Toward a Christian Poetic, 1964; The Climate of Faith in Modern Literature (editor), 1964; Samuel Beckett, 1965; Four Ways of Modern Poetry (editor), 1965; Man in the Modern Theatre (editor), 1965; The Broken Center: Studies in the Theological Horizon of Modern Literature, 1966; Ernest Hemingway, 1966; The Modern Vision of Death (editor), 1967; Adversity and Grace: Studies in Recent American Literature (editor), 1968; Craters of the Spirit: Studies in the Modern Novel (editor), 1968; Negative Capability: Studies in the New Literature and the Religious Situation (editor), 1969; The Unquiet Vision: Mirrors of Man is Existentialism, 1969; Nathanael West, 1971; The Wild Prayer of Longing: Poetry and the Sacred, 1971; Three American Moralists: Mailer, Bellow, Trilling, 1973; The Legacy of Reinhold Niebuhr (editor), 1975; The Poetry of Civic Virtue: Eliot, Malraux, Auden, 1976; Mirrors of Man in Existentialism, 1978; The Poetics of Belief: Studies in Coleridge, Arnold, Pater, Santayana, Stevens and Heidegger, 1985; Visions of Presence in Modern American Poetry, 1993; Reading George Steiner (with Ronald Sharp), 1994. Contributions to: Professional journals and other publications. Honours: Many honorary doctorates. Memberships: American Academy of Arts and Sciences, fellow; American Academy of Religion, president, 1986; Modern Language Association; Society for Values in Higher Education; Society of Arts, Religion and Contemporary Culture. Address: 1419 Hilltop Road, Charlottesville, VA 22903, USA.

SCOTT Paul Henderson, b. 7 Nov 1920, Edinburgh, Scotland. Essayist; Historian; Critic; Former Diplomat. Education: MA, MLitt, Edinburgh University. Publications: 1707: The Union of Scotland and England, 1979; Walter Scott and Scotland, 1981; John Galt, 1985; Towards Independence: Essays on Scotland, 1991; Andrew Fletcher and the Treaty of Union, 1992; Scotland: A Concise Cultural History (editor), 1993; Defoe in Edinburgh, 1994. Contributions to: Newspapers and journals. Honour: Andrew Fletcher Prize, 1993. Memberships: International PEN, president, Scottish Centre; Saltire Society; Advisory Council for the Arts in Scotland; Association for Scottish Literary Studies. Address: 33 Drumsheugh Gardens, Edinburgh EH3 7RN, Scotland.

SCOTT Rosie, b. 22 Mar 1948, New Zealand. Writer. m. 28 Nov 1987, 2 daughters. Education: MA, Honours, English, 1968; Graduate Diploma, Drama, 1984. Publications: Fiction: Glory Days, 1988; Queen of Love (stories), 1989; Nights With Grace, 1990; Feral City, 1992; Lives on Fire, 1993; Movie Dreams, 1995. Poetry: Flesh and Blood, 1984. Contributions to: Various publications in New Zealand, Australia, France, Germany, UK, USA. Honours: Sunday Times Award for play; Novels shortlisted for New Zealand National Book Awards, Australian National Book Awards, Banyon Patterson, Christina Stead National Book Awards, Biennial National Book Awards, Adelaide; Sunday Times-Bruce Mason Award, 1986; Australian Writers Fellowship, 1992; ASIT. Memberships: Australian Society of Authors, Committee Member, 1994-; Greenpeace; PEN New Zealand. Address: 21 Darghan Street, Glebe, New South Wales 2037, Australia.

SCOTT Roy Vernon, b. 26 Dec 1927, Wrights, Illinois, USA. Professor of History; Writer. Education: BS, Iowa State College, 1952; MA, 1953, PhD, 1957, University of Illinois. Appointments: Assistant Professor, University of Southwestern Louisiana, 1957-58, University of Missouri, 1959-60; Assistant Professor, 1960-62, Associate Professor, 1962-64, Professor of American History, 1964-, Distinguished Professor, 1979-, Mississippi State University. Publications: The Agrarian Movement in Illinois 1880-1896, 1962; The Reluctant Farmer: The Rise of Agricultural Extension to 1914, 1970; The Public Career of Cully A Cobb: A Study in Agricultural Leadership (with J G Shoalmire), 1973; Southern Agriculture Since the Civil War (with George L Robinson Jr), 1979; Railroad Development Programs in the Twentieth Century, 1985; The Great Northern Railway: A History (with others), 1988; Eugene Beverly Ferris and Agricultural Science in the Lower South, 1991; Wal-Mart: A History of Sam Walton's Retail Phenomenon (with Sandra S Vance), 1994. Contributions to: Professional journals. Memberships: American Historical Association; Organization of American Historians; Southern Historical Association; Economic History Association; Agricultural History Society, President, 1978-79; Mississippi Historical Society, Presidnet, 1989-90. Address: c/o Department of History, Mississippi State University, Mississippi State, MS 39762, USA.

SCOTT Sally Elisabeth, b. 30 May 1948, London, England. Writer; Illustrator. Education: BA, Hons, Philosophy and English Literature, York University, 1970. Publications: The Elf King's Bride, 1981; The Magic Horse, 1985; The Three Wonderful Beggars, 1987. Illustrator: Tales and Legends of India. Membership: Society of Authors. Address: c/o David Higham Associates Ltd, 5-8 Lower John Street, Golden Square, London W1R 4HA, England.

SCOTT Tom, b. 6 June 1918, Glasgow, Scotland. Poet; Children's Writer. Education: MA, PhD, University of Edinburgh. Appointment: Former Editor, Scottish Literature Series, Pergamon Press, Oxford. Publications: Seeven Poems o Maister Francis Vilton, 1953; An Ode til New Jerusalem, 1956; The Ship and Ither Poems, 1963; A Possible Solution to the Scottish Question, 1963; Dunbar: A Critical Exposition of the Poems, 1966; The Oxford Book of Scottish Verse (with J McQueen), 1966; Late Medieval Scots Poetry: A Selection from the Makars and their Heirs Down to 1610, 1967; At the Shrine o the Unkent Sodger: A Poem for Recitation, 1968; Tales of Robert the Bruce, 1969; The Penguin Book of Scottish Verse, 1970; Brand the Builder, 1975; The Tree, 1977; Tales of Sir William Wallace, 1981; The Dirty Business, 1986; Collected Shorter Poems, 1993. Address: Duddingston Park, Edinburgh 15, Scotland.

SCOTT William Neville, (Bill Scott), b. 4 Oct 1923, Bundaberg, Queensland, Australia. Author. Publications: Focus on Judith Wright, 1967; Some People (short stories), 1968; Brother and Brother (verse), 1972; The Continual Singing: An Anthology of World Poetry, 1973; Portrait of Brisbane, 1976; The Complete Book of Australian Folklore, 1976; Bushranger Ballads, 1976; My Uncle and Other People (short stories), 1977; Boori (children's fiction), 1978; Tough In yhe Old Days (autobiography), 1979; Ned Kelly After a Century of Acrimony (with John Meredith), 1980; The Second Penguin Australian Songbook, 1980; Darkness Under the Hills (children's fiction), 1980; Reading 360 series (The Blooming Queensland Side, On the Shores of Botany Bay, The Golden West, Bound for South Australia, Upon Van Diemen's Land, The Victorian Bunyip), 6 volumes, 1981; Australian Bushrangers, 1983; Penguin Book of Australian Humorous Verse, 1984; Shadows Among the Leaves (children's fiction), 1984; The Long and the Short and the Tall (folklore), 1985; Following the Gold (children's poems), 1989; Many Kinds of Magic (short stories), 1990; Hey Rain (cassette, songs and poems), 1992; The Currency Lad (fiction) 1994; Songbird in Your Pocket (cassette, songs and poems) 1994; Pelicans and Chihuahuas (folklore), 1995; The Banshee, the Bollocky and the Boiler (short stories), 1995. Address: 157 Pratten Street, Warwick, Queensland 4370, Australia.

SCOTT TANNER Amoret, b. 27 Mar 1930, Vancouver, British Columbia, Canada. Social Historian. m. Ralph Tanner, 24 Aug 1985. Publications: Hedgerow Harvest, 1979; Parrots, 1982; With Christopher Scott: Collecting Bygones, 1964; Tobacco and the Collector, 1966; Dummy Board Figures, 1966; Discovering Smoking Antiques, 1970, 2nd edition, 1981; Discovering Stately Homes, 1973, 3rd edition, 1989; Staffordshire Figures (Shire Album), 1986, 2nd edition, 1993. Contributions to: Saturday Book; Country Life; Antique Collector; Antiquarian Book Monthly. Honour: Medal of the Order of Australia, 1992. Membership: Founder Member, Member of Council,

Ephemera Society. Address: The Footprint, Padworth Common, Reading RG7 4QG, England.

SCOTT-STOKES Natascha (Norton), b. 11 Apr 1962, Munich, Germany. Travel Writer. m. Benoit Le Blanc, 27 Feb 1992. Education: BA Hons Humanities, Middlesex Polytechnic; MA Latin American Studies, University of London. Appointments: Associate Editor, Writer's Newsletter, 1989-90. Publications: An Amazon and a Donkey, 1991. Co-Author: Germany, the Rough Guide, 1989; The Cadogan Guide to Central America, 1992; The Amber Trail, 1993. Contributions to: Lima Times; Writers Newsletter. Memberships: Writers Guild of Great Britain; PEN English Centre; Fellow, Royal Geographical Society. Address: 55 Leconfield Road, London N5 2RZ, England.

SCOVELL E(dith) J(oy), b. 1907, Sheffield, Yorkshire, England. Poet. m. Charles Elton, 1937. Education: BA, Somerville College, Oxford, 1930. Publications: Shadows of Chrysanthemums and Other Poems, 1944; The Midsummer Meadow and Other Poems, 1946; The River Steamer and Other Poems, 1956; The Space Between, 1982; Ten Poems, 1984; Listening to Collared Doves, 1986; Collected Poems, 1988; Selected Poems, 1991. Honour: Cholmondeley Award, 1989. Address: 51 Diamond Court, Oxford OX2 TAA, England.

SCRUTON Roger, b. 27 Feb 1944, Burlingthorpe, England. Philosopher; Author; Journalist; Editor; Publisher. Education: BA, 1965, PhD, 1979, Jesus College, Cambridge. Appointments: Professor of Philosophy, Birbeck College, London, Boston Univeristy, USA; Editor, The Salisbury Review; Founder, Publisher and Director, Claridge Press; Radio and television broadcasts. Publications: Art and Imagination, 1974; The Aesthetics of Architecture, 1979; The Meaning of Conservatism, 1980; The Politics of Culture and Other Essays, 1981; Fortnight's Anger (novel), 1981; A Short History of Modern Philosophy, 1982, 2nd edition, 1995; A Dictionary of Political Thought, 1982, 2nd edition, 1996; The Aesthetic Understanding, 1983; Kant, 1983; Untimely Tracts, 1985; Thinkers of the New Left, 1986; Sexual Desire, 1986; Spinoza, 1987; A Land Held Hostage: Lebanon and the West, 1987; The Philosopher on Dover Beach and Other Essays, 1989; Francesca (novel), 1991; A Dove Descending and Other Stories, 1991; Xanthippic Dialogues, 1993; Modern Philosophy, 1994; The Classical Vernacular: Architectural Principles in an Age of Nihilism, 1995; Animal Rights and Wrongs, 1996; The Intelligent Person's Guide to Philosophy, 1996; The Aesthetics of Music, 1997. Contributions to: Newspapers and journals. Address: Sunday Hill Farm, Brinkworth, Wilts SN15 5AS, England.

SCULLY Vincent (Joseph Jr), b. 21 Aug 1920, New Haven, Connecticut, USA. Professor of Art History Emeritus; Writer. m. Catherine Lynn, 30 Dec 1980, 4 children. Education: BA, 1940, PhD, 1949, Yale University. Appointments: Instructor, Assistant Professor, Associate Professor, 1947-61, Col John Trumbull Professor of Art History, 1961-83, Sterling Professor of History of Art, 1983-91, Sterling Professor Emeritus, 1991-; Host, New World Visions: American Art and the Metropolitan Museum 1650-1914, PBS-TV, 1983; Visiting Professor, University of Miami at Coral Gables, 1992-97; Mellon Visiting Professor of History, California Institute of Technology, 1995. Publications: The Architectural Heritage of Newport, Rhode Island (with Antoinette Forrester Downing), 1952, 2nd edition, revised, 1967; The Shingle Style: Architectural Theory and Design from Richardson to the Origins of Wright, 1955, revised edition as The Shingle Style and the Stick Style: Architectural Theory and Design from Downing to the Origins of Wright, 1971; Frank Lloyd Wright, 1960; Modern Archiecture: The Architecture of Democracy, 1961, revised edition, 1974; Louis I Kahn, 1962; The Earth, the Temple and the Gods: Greek Sacred Architecture, 1962, 3rd edition, revised, 1980; American Architecture and Urbanism, 1969, revised edition, 1988; Pueblo Architecture of the Southwest, 1971; The Shingle Style Today: or, The Historian's Revenge, 1974; Pueblo: Mountain, Village, Dance, 1975, 2nd edition, 1989; Robert Stern (with David Dunster), 1981; Wesleyan: Photographs, 1982; Michael Graves, Buildings and Projects, 1966-1981, 1982; The Villas of Palladio, 1986; The Architecture of the American Summer: The Flowering of the Shingle Style, 1987; New World Visions of Household Gods and Sacred Places: American Art and the Metropolitan Museum 1650-1914, 1988; The Architecture of Robert Venturi (with others), 1989; The Great Dinosaur Mural at Yale: The Age of Reptiles (with others), 1990; Architecture: The Natural and the Manmade, 1991; French Royal Gardens: The Design of André Le Notre (with Jeannie Baubion-Maclere), 1992; Robert A M Stern, Buildings and Projects 1987-1992, 1992; Mother's House: The Evolution of Vanna Venturi's House in Chestnut Hill (with Robert

Venturi), 1992. Honours: National Endowment for the Humanities Senior Fellowship, 1972-73; American Institute of Architects Medal, 1976; Thomas Jefferson Medal, University of Virginia, 1982; Topaz Award, Association of Collegiate Schools of Architecture/American Institute of Architects, 1986; Literary Lion, New York Public Library, 1992; Governor's Arts Awards Medal, State of Connecticut, 1993; American Academy in Rome Award, 1994; Thomas Jefferson Lecturer, Kennedy Center, Washington, DC; National Endowment for the Humanities, 1995; Honorary doctorates. Memberships: American Institute of Architects, honorary member; National Trust for Historic Preservation, trustee; Royal Institute of British Architects, honorary fellow. Address: 252 Lawrence Street, New Haven, CT 06511, USA.

SCUPHAM John Peter, b. 24 Feb 1933, Liverpool, England Writer; Poet. m. Carola Nance Braunholtz, 6 Aug 1957, 3 sons, 1 daughter. Education: Honours Degree, English, Emmanuel College, Cambridge, 1957. Appointments: Founder-Publisher, The Mandeville Press. Publications: The Snowing Globe, 1972; Prehistories, 1975; The Hinterland, 1977; Summer Places, 1980; Winter Quarters, 1983; Out Late, 1986; The Air Show, 1989; Watching the Perseids, 1990; Selected Poems, 1990; The Ark, 1994. Contributions to: Anthologies and magazines. Membership: Royal Society of Literature, fellow. Address: Old Hall, Norwich Road, South Burlingham, Norfolk NR13 4EY, England.

SEAGER Ralph William, b. 3 Nov 1911, Geneva, New York, USA. University Teacher (retired); Poet; Writer. m. Ruth M Lovejoy, 1932, 3 sons. Education: University of California at Berkeley, 1949-51; University of New Hampshire Writers Conference, 1954; Harvard University, 1956. Appointments: Assistant Professor of English, 1960-77, Professor Emeritus, 1977-, Keuka College; Judge, Arizona Poetry Society, 1992-94. Publications: Songs from a Willow Whistle, 1956; Beyond the Green Gate, 1958; Christmas Chimes in Rhymes, 1962; Cup, Flagon and Fountain, 1965; A Choice of Dreams, 1970; Wheatfields and Vineyards, 1975; The Manger Mouse and Other Christmas Poems, 1977; Hiding in Plain Sight, 1982; The Love Tree, 1985; The First Quartet (with 3 other poets), 1988; My Folks and the One-Room Schoolhouse (anthology), 1993. Prose: The Sound of an Echo, 1963; Little Yates and the United States, 1976; The First Baptist Church: One Hundred Fifty Years (co-author), 1980. Contributions to: Periodicals. Honour: Honorary DLitt, 1970. Membership: World Parnassian Guild International, Honorary Director, 1995. Address: 311 Keuka Street, Penn Yan, NY 14527, USA.

SEAGRAVE Sterling, b. 15 Apr 1937, Columbus, Ohio, USA. Writer. m. (1) Wendy Law-Yone, 1967, (2) Peggy Sawyer, 1982, 1 son, 1 daughter. Education: University of Miami, 1956; University of Mexico, 1957; University of Venezuela, 1958. Publications: Yellow Rain, 1981; Soldiers of Fortune, 1981; The Soong Dynasty, 1985; The Marcos Dynasty, 1988; Dragon Lady, 1992. Contributions to: Atlantic: Far Eastern Economic Review; Esquire; Time; Smithsonian. Membership: Authors Guild. Address: c/o William Morris Agency, 31 Soho Sq, London W1V 5DG, England.

SEAL Basil. See: **BARNES Julian Patrick.**

SEALEY Leonard George William, b. 7 May 1923, London, England. Educational Author, Consultant. m. (1) Joan Hearn, Mar 1944, dec, (2) Nancy Verre, August 1972, 5 sons. Education: Teachers Certificate, Peterborough College, England; DipED, MEd, University of Leicester. Publications: The Creative Use of Mathematics, 1961; Communication and Learning (co-author), 1962; Exploring Language, 1968; Basic Skills in Learning, 1970; Introducing Mathematics, 1970; The Lively Readers, 1973; Our World Encyclopedia (editor), 1974; Open Education, 1977; Children's Writing, 1979. Memberships: Fellow, Royal Society of Arts; Phi Delta Kappa. Address: 136 Sandwich Road, Plymouth, MA 02360, USA.

SEALTS Merton M(iller) Jr, b. 8 Dec 1915, Lima, Ohio, USA. Professor of English Emeritus; Writer. Education: BA, College of Wooster, 1937; PhD, Yale University, 1942. Appointments: Instructor, University of Missouri, 1941-42, Wellesley College, 1946-48; Assistant Professor, 1948-51, Associate Professor, 1951-58, Professor of English, 1958-65, Lawrence College/University; Professor of English, 1965-75, Henry A Pochmann Professor of English, 1975-82, Professor Emeritus, 1982-, University of Wisconsin at Madison. Publications: Melville as Lecturer, 1957; Herman Melville: Billy Budd, Sailer (editor with Harrison Hayford), 1962; The Journals and Miscellaneous Notebooks of Ralph Waldo Emerson (editor), Vol V, 1965, Vol X, 1973;

Melville's Reading, 1966, revised edition, 1988; Emerson's Nature: Origin, Growth, Meaning (editor with Alfred R Ferguson), 1969, 2nd edition, enlarged, 1979; The Early Lives of Melville: Nineteenth-Century Biographical Sketches and Their Authors, 1974; Pursuing Melville, 1940-1980: Chapters and Essays, 1982; Emerson on the Scholar, 1992; Beyond the Classroom: Essays on American Authors, 1996. Contributions to: Scholarly books and journals. Honours: Ford Foundation Fellow, 1953-54; Guggenheim Fellowship, 1962-63; National Endowment for the Humanities Senior Fellow, 1975; Jay B Hubbell Award, Modern Language Association, 1992; Distinguished Alumni Award, College of Wooster, 1994; Distinguished Achievement Award, Ralph Waldo Emerson Society, 1995. Memberships: Ralph Waldo Emerson Society; Melville Society, President, 1953; Thoreau Society; American Literature Association; Modern Language Association of America; Phi Beta Kappa. Address: 6209 Mineral Point Road, Apt 1106/08, Madison, WI 53705-4556, USA.

SEARLE John R(ogers), b. 31 July 1932, Denver, Colorado, USA. Professor of Philosophy; Writer. m. Dagmar Carboch, 24 Dec 1958, 2 sons. Education: University of Wisconsin, 1949-52; BA, 1st Class Honours, 1955, MA, 1959, DPhil, 1959, Oxford University. Appointments: Lecturer in Philosophy, Christ Church, Oxford, 1956-59; Professor of Philosophy, later Mills Professor of the Philosophy of Mind and Language, University of California at Berkeley, 1959-; Visiting Professor at various US and European universities; Lecturer throughout the world. Publications: Speech Acts: An Essay in the Philosophy of Language, 1969; The Campus War, 1971; Expression and Meaning: Studies in the Theory of Speech Acts, 1979; Intentionality: An Essay in the Philosophy of Mind, 1983; Minds, Brains and Science, 1984; The Foundations of Illocutionary Logic (with D Vanderveken), 1985; The Rediscovery of the Mind, 1992; The Construction of Social Reality, 1995. Contributions to: Scholarly journals. Honours: Rhodes Scholar, 1952-55; Guggenheim Fellowship, 1975-76; Fulbright Awards, 1983, 1985; Honorary Doctor of Humane Letters, Adelphi University, 1993, University of Wisconsin, 1994. Memberships: American Academy of Arts and Sciences; American Council of Learned Societies, board of directors, 1979-87; American Philosophical Association; Council for Philosophical Studies; National Humanities Center, board of trustees, 1976-90. Address: c/o Department of Philosophy, University of California at Berkeley, Berkeley, CA 94720, USA.

SEARLE Ronald, (William Fordham), b. 3 Mar 1920, Cambridge, England. Writer. Education: Cambridge School of Art, 1939. Publications: Forty Drawings, 1946; Le Nouveau Ballet Anglais, 1947; Hurrah for St Trinian's, 1948; The Female Approach, 1949; Back to the Slaughterhouse, 1951; Souls in Torment, 1953; Rake's Progress, 1955; Merry England, 1956; Which Way Did He Go?, 1961; Searle in the Sixties, 1965; From Frozen North to Filthy Lucre, 1964; Pardong M'sieur, 1965; Searle' Cats, 1969; Hommage à Toulouse Lautrec, 1969; Secret Sketchbook, 1970; The Addict, 1971; More Cats, 1975; Drawings From Gilbert and Sullivan, 1975; The Zoodiac, 1977; Ronald Searle, 1978; The King of Beasts, 1980; The Big Fat Cat Book, 1982; Winespeak, 1983; Ronald Searle in Perspective, 1984; Ronald Searle's Golden Oldies, 1985; To the Kwai - and Back, 1986; Something in the Cellar, 1986. Ah Yes I Remember it Well: Paris 1961-1975, 1987; The Non-Sexist Dictionary, 1988; Slightly Foxed - but still desirable, 1989; The Curse of St Trinian's, 1993; Marquis de Sade meets Goody Two Shoes, 1994. Address: c/o Tessa Sayle, 11 Jubilee Place, London SW3 3TE, England.

SEAWIND Jay. See: **WYNN John Charles.**

SEDGWICK Eve Kosofsky, b. 2 May 1950, Dayton, Ohio, USA. Professor of English; Writer. Education: BA, Cornell University, 1971; MPhil, 1974, PhD, 1975, Postdoctoral Studies, 1976-78, Yale University. Appointments: Instructor, Yale University, 1975-76; Assistant Professor of English and Creative Writing, Hamilton College, Clinton, New York, 1978-81; Assistant Professor, Boston University, 1981-83; Faculty Fellow, Mary Ingraham Bunting Institute, Cambridge, Massachusetts, 1983-84; Associate Professor of English and Women's Studies, Amherst College, 1984-88; Professor of English, 1988-92, Newman Ivey White Professor of English, 1992-, Duke University; Research Fellow, National Humanities Center, 1991-92. Publications: The Coherence of Gothic Conventions, 1980; Between Men: English Literature and Male Homosocial Desire, 1985; Epistemology of the Closet, 1990; Tendencies, 1993; Performativity and Performance (editor with Andrew Parker), 1994; Fat Art, Thin Art, 1994.

Contributions to: Anthologies, professional journals and literary publications. Honours: Mellon Fellow, 1976-78; Kirkland Endowment Grants, 1980, 1981; Co-Winner, Crompton-Noll Award in Gay and Lesbian Studies, Modern Language Association, 1984; Guggenheim Fellowship, 1987-88. Memberships: Dickens Society, board of trustees, 1991-94; English Institute, board of trustees, 1992-97; Modern Language Association. Address: c/o Department of English, Duke University, Durham, NC 27708, USA.

SEDGWICK Fred, b. 20 Jan 1945, Dublin, Ireland. Lecturer in Education; Poet. Education: St Luke's College, Exeter; MA, University of East Anglia at Norwich, 1984. Appointments include: Head of Downing Primary School, Suffolk; Education Lecturer. Publications: Really in the Dark, 1980; From Another Part of the Island, 1981; A Garland for William Cowper, 1984; The Living Daylights, 1986; Falernian, 1987; This Way, That Way: A Collection of Poems for Schools (editor), 1989; Lighting Up Time: On Children's Writing, 1990.Address: 1 Mornington Avenue, Ipswich, Suffolk IP1 4LA, England.

SEDLEY Kate. See: **CLARKE Brenda (Margaret Lilian).**

SEE Carolyn, (Monica Highland), b. 13 Jan 1934, Pasadena, California, USA. Writer. m. (1) Richard See, 18 Feb 1954, (2) Tom Sturak, 30 Apr 1960, 2 daughters. Education: PhD, University of California at Los Angeles, 1953. Appointment: Professor of English, University of California at Los Angeles. Publications: The Rest is Done with Mirrors, 1970; Blue Money, 1974; Mothers, Daughters, 1977; Rhine Maidens, 1980; Golden Days, 1985; When Knaves Meet, 1988; The Mirrored Hall in the Hollywood Dance Hall, 1991; Dreaming: Hard Luck and Good Times in America, 1995. As Monica Highland: Lotus Land, 1983; 1-10 Shanghai Road, 1985; Greetings From Southern California, 1987; Precious Cargo, 1990; Two Schools of Thought (with John Espey), 1991. Contributions to: Newspapers and Magazines. Honours: Samuel Goldwyn Award, 1963; Sidney Hillman Award, 1969; National Endowment for the Arts Grant, 1974; Bread and Roses Award, National Womens Political Caucus, 1988; Vesta Award, 1989; Guggenheim Fellowship in Fiction, 1989; Lila Wallace Grant, 1993. Memberships: PEN Centre USA West, president, 1993-94. Address: PO Box 107, Topanga, CA 90290, USA.

SEED Cecile Eugenie, (Jenny Seed), b. 18 May 1930, Cape Town, South Africa. Author. m. Edward (Ted) Robert Seed, 31 Oct 1953, 3 sons, 1 daughter. Publications: The Great Thirst, 1985; The Great Elephant, 1986; Place Among the Stones, 1987; Hurry, Hurry, Sibusiso, 1988; The Broken Spear, 1989; The Prince of the Bay, 1989; The Big Pumpkin, 1990; Old Grandfather Mantis, 1992; The Hungry People, 1993; A Time to Scatter Stones, 1993; Lucky Boy, 1995; The Strange Large Egg, 1996. Honour: MER Award, 1987. Address: 10 Pioneer Crescent, Northdene, Kwazulu-Natal 4093, South Africa.

SEGAL Erich, b. 16 June 1937. Adjunct Professor of Classics; Honorary Research Fellow. m. Karen James, 1975, 1 son, dec, 2 daughters. Education: AB, 1958, AM, 1959, PhD, 1965, Harvard University. Appointments: Teaching Fellow, Harvard, 1959-64; Lecturer in Classics, Yale, 1964; Assistant Professor 1965-68, Associate Professor 1968-73, Visiting Professor in Classics, University of Munich, 1973; Princeton University, 1974-75; Tel Aviv, 1976-77; Visiting Professor in Contemporary Literature, Dartmouth College, 1976-78, 1979-80, Member, Common Room, 1984-, Wolfson College, Oxford. Publications: Roman Laughter: The Comedy of Plautus, 1968, revised edition, 1987; Euripides: A Collection of Critical Essays (editor), 1968; Plautus: Three Comedies (editor and translator), 1969, revised edition 1985; Oxford Readings in Greek Tragedy (editor), 1983; Caesar Augustus: seven aspects (editor, with Fergus Millar, 1984; Plato's Dialogues (editor), 1985; Oxford Readings in Aristophanes, 1994; Plautus: Four Comedies (editor and translator), 1996. Novels: Love Story, 1970; Fairy Tale (for children), 1973; Oliver's Story, 1977; Man, Woman and Child, 1980; The Class, 1973; Doctors, 1988; Acts of Faith, 1992; Prizes, 1995; Only Love, 1997. Honours: Boylston Prize, 1957; Bowdoin Prize, 1959; Golden Globe Award, 1970; Premio San Valentin de Terni, 1989. Address: Wolfson College, Oxford, OX2 6UD, England.

SEGAL Lore (Groszmann), b. 8 Mar 1928, Vienna, Austria. Writer. m. David I. Segal, 3 Nov 1960, dec, 1 son, 1 daughter. Education: BA, English, Bedford College, University of London, England, 1948. Appointments: Professor, Writing Division, School of Arts, Columbia University, Princeton University, Sarah Lawrence

College, Bennington College; Professor of English, University of Illinois; Ohio State University. Publications: Novels: Other People's Houses, 1964; Lucinella, 1976; Her First American, 1985. Children's books: Tell Me a Mitzi, 1977; The Story of Mrs Brubeck and How She Looked for Trouble and Where She Found Him, 1981; The Story of Mrs Lovewright and Purrless Her Cat, 1985. Translations: Gallows Songs (with W D Snodgrass), 1968; The Juniper Tree and Other Tales from Grimm, 1973; The Book of Adam to Moses; The Story of King Soul and King David. Contributions to: Periodicals. Honours: Guggenheim Fellowship, 1965-66; National Endowment for the Arts Grant, 1982; National Endowment for the Humanities Grant, 1983; Academy of Arts and Letters Award, 1986; grantee, Ohio Arts Council, 1996. Address: 280 Riverside Drive, New York, NY 10025, USA.

SEGHERS Greta Irene Pieter, b. 11 Feb 1942, Beveren-Waas, Belgium. Writer; History Teacher. m. Ludo de Cock, 12 July 1966, 1 son, 1 daughter. Education: Secondary Teacher Training, Dutch, History. Appointments: Member, Editorial staff, Dietsche Warande en Belfort, 1984; Member, Literary Commission, East Flanders, 1991. Publications: Het blauwe meisje (stories), 1980; Wat ge leest en schrijft, dat zijt ge zelf (essay), 1985; Het eigenzinnige leven van Angèle Manteau (biography), 1992. Novels: Afkeer van Faulkner, 1977; Omtrent de man die wederkwam, 1978; Ontregeling en Misverstand, 1983; De zijpaden van het paradijs, 1988; Hoe moordend is mijn school, 1990. Stories: Een Dunne Wand, 1994. Contributions to: Various publications. Honours: Best Debut Prize, 1977; Yang Prize, 1977; Prize, 1983, Honorable Mention, 1985, Province of East Flanders. Membership: Dietsche Warande en Belfort. Address: Tuinlaan 14, 9120, Vrasene, Belgium.

SEIDMAN Hugh, b. 1 Aug 1940, New York, New York, USA. Writer; Poet; Teacher. m. Jayne Holsinger, 2 June 1990. Education: BS, Mathematics, Polytechnic Institute of Brooklyn, 1961; MS, Physics, University of Minnesota, 1964; MFA, Poetry, Columbia University, 1969. Appointments: Faculty, New School for Social Research, New York City, 1976-; Assistant Professor, Washington College, 1979; Visiting Lecturer, University of Wisconsin, 1981, Columbia University, 1985, Poet-in-Residence, College of William and Mary, 1982; Visiting Poet, Writers Voice, New York City, 1988. Publications: Collecting Evidence, 1970; Blood Lord, 1974; Throne/Falcon/Eye, 1982; People Live, They Have Lives, 1992; Selected Poems 1965-1995, 1995. Contributions to: Many publications. Honours: Yale Series of Younger Poets Prize, 1969; National Endowment for the Arts Grant, 1970, and Fellowships, 1972, 1985; Yaddo Fellowships, 1972, 1976, 1986; MacDowell Colony Fellowships, 1974, 1975, 1989; Writers Digest Poetry Prize, 1982; New York Foundation for the Arts Poetry Fellowship, 1990. Memberships: American PEN; Authors Guild; Authors League; Poetry Society of America. Address: 463 West Street, No H-822, New York, NY 10014, USA.

SEIFMAN Eli, b. 4 Aug 1936, Brooklyn, New York, USA. Professor of Social Sciences; Writer. Education: BA, 1957, MS, 1959, Queens College, City University of New York; PhD, New York University, 1965. Appointments: Instructor, 1964-65, Assistant Professor, 1965-67, Associate Professor, 1967-70, Professor, later Distinguished Professor of Social Sciences, 1970-, State University of New York at Stony Brook. Publications: History of the New York State Colonization Society, 1966; Social Studies: Structure, Models and Strategies, 1969; Teacher's Handbook, 1971; Towards a New World Outlook, 1976; Education and Socialization Modernization, 1987. Contributions to: Professional journals. Honour: Phi Lamda Theta Book Award, 1973. Memberships: American Historical Association; Kappa Delta Pi; National Council for Social Studies; Phi Alpha Theta; Phi Beta Kappa; Royal Society for Asian Affairs. Address: c/o Department of Social Sciences, State University of New York at Stony Brook, Stony Brook, NY 11794, USA.

SELBOURNE David, b. 4 June 1937, London, England. Writer; Playwright. Publications: The Play of William Cooper and Edmund Dew-Nevett, 1968; The Two-Backed Beast, 1969; Dorabella, 1970; Samson and Alison Mary Fagan, 1971; The Damned, 1971; Class Play, 1973; Brook's Dream: The Politics of Theatre, 1974; What's Acting? and Think of a Story Quickly!, 1977; An Eye to India, 1977; An Eye to China, 1978; Through the Indian Looking Glass, 1982; The Making of a Midsummer Night's Dream, 1983; Against Socialist Illusion: A Radical Argument, 1985; In Theory and In Practice: Essays on the Politics of Jayaprakash Narayan, 1986; Left Behind: Journeys into British Politics, 1987; A Doctor's Life: The Diaries of Hugh

Selbourne MD 1960-63, 1989; Death of the Dark Hero: Eastern Europe 1987-90, 1990; The Spirit of the Age, 1993; Not an Englishman: Conversations With Lord Goodman, 1993; The Principle of Duty, 1994. Honour: Member, Academy of Savignano, Italy, 1994. Address: c/o Christopher Sinclair-Stevenson, 3 South Terrace, London SW7, England.

SELBY Stephen, b. 5 June 1952, Darley Dale, Derbyshire, England. Playwright. m. Ann Spence, 6 Mar 1982, 1 daughter. Education: Social Science and Philosophy. Appointments: Writer, Director, Producer, Noc On Theatre, 1987-, Hurdles of Time Theatre, 1991-; Dramaturgo, La Edel de Oro Theatre Company. Publications: Better Looking Corpse; Contentious Work; Archie Pearson the One Legged Shoemaker; Eviction; Cuts: Nottingham by the Sea; Hurdles of Time; Erewash Giants, 1993; The Concrete Silver Band, 1995; Tontos Sabios y Ladrones Honestos, 1996. Memberships: Theatre Writers Union; Camasiiey Theatre Directors Association. Address: 53 Percival Road, Sherwood, Nottingham NG5 2FA, England.

SELLMAN Roger Raymond, b. 24 Sept 1915, London, England. Schoolmaster; Lecturer; Devon County Inspector of Schools (retired). m. Minnie Coutts, 10 Aug 1938. Education: MA, Dip Ed, Oxford University; PhD, Exeter University. Publications: Methuen's Outline Series: Castles and Fortresses, 1954; The Crusades, 1955; Roman Britain, 1956; English Churches, 1956; The Vikings, 1957; Elizabethan Seamen, 1957; Prehistoric Britain, 1958; Civil War and Commonwealth, 1958; The Anglo Saxons, 1959; Ancient Egypt, 1960; Norman England, 1960; Medieval English Warfare, 1960; The First World War, 1961; The Second World War, 1964; Garibaldi and the Unification of Italy, 1973; Bismarck and the Unification of Germany, 1973; The Prairies, 1974. Historical Atlases and Textbooks: Outline Atlas of Eastern History, 1954; Outline Atlas of World History, 1970; Modern World History, 1972; Students Atlas of Modern History, 1973; Modern British Economic and Social History, 1973; Historical Atlas for First Examinations, 1973; Modern European History, 1974. Local History: Illustrations of Dorset History, 1960; Illustrations of Devon History, 1962; Devon Village Schools in the Nineteenth Century, 1968; Aspects of Devon History, 1985. Contributions to: Victorian Countryside, 1981; Devon Historian ; Devon and Cornwall Notes and Queries. Address: Pound Down Corner, Whitestone, Exeter EX4 2HP, England.

SELTZER Joanne, b. 21 Nov 1929, Detroit, Michigan, USA. Writer; Poet. m. Stanley Seltzer, 10 Feb 1951, 1 son, 3 daughters. Education: BA, University of Michigan, 1951; MA, College of St Rose, 1978. Publications: Adirondack Lake Poems, 1985; Suburban Landscape, 1988; Inside Invisible Walls, 1989. Contributions to: Journals and magazines. Honours: All Nations Poetry Contest Award, 1978; World Order of Narrative and Formalist Poets Competitions Prizes, 1986, 1988, 1990, 1992, 1993, 1994; Tucumari Literary Review Poetry Contest Award, 1989. Memberships: American Literary Translators Association; Associated Writing Programs; Hudson Valley Writers Guild; Poetry Society of America; Poets & Writers. Address: 2481 McGovern Drive, Schenectady, NY 12309, USA.

SEMMLER Clement William, b. 23 Dec 1914, Eastern Well, South Australia. Broadcaster; Writer. m. (1) div, 1 son, 1 daughter, (2) Catherine Helena Wilson, 20 Dec 1974, 1 daughter. Education: MA, University of Adelaide, 1938. Appointment: Fellow, College of Fine Arts, University of New South Wales. Publications: For the Uncanny Man (essays), 1963; Barcroft Boake, 1965; Literary Australia (editor), 1965; The Banjo of the Bush, 1966; Kenneth Slessor, 1966; Twentieth Century Australian Literary Criticism (editor), 1967; The Art of Brian James, 1972; Douglas Stewart, 1974; The ABC-Aunt Sally and the Sacred Cow, 1981; A Frank Hardy Swag (editor), 1982; The War Diaries of Kenneth Slessor, 1985; The War Dispatches of Kenneth Slessor, 1987; Pictures on the Margin (memoirs), 1991. Contributions to: Periodicals and journals. Honours: DLitt, University of New England, Armidale, 1968; Officer of the Order of the British Empire, 1972; AM, 1988. Address: The Croft, St Clair Street, Bowral, New South Wales 2576, Australia.

SEN Amartya Kuman, b. 3 Nov 1933, Santiniketan, India. Professor of Economics and Philosophy; Writer. m. (1) Nabaneeta Dev, 1960, div 1974, (2) Eva Colorni, 1977, dec 1985, (3) Emma Rothschild, 1991, 4 children. Education: BA, Presidency College, Calcutta, 1953; BA, 1955, MA, PhD, 1959, Trinity College, Cambridge. Appointments: Professor of Economics, Jadavpur University, Calcutta, 1956-58; Fellow, Trinity College, Cambridge, 1957-63, All Souls

College, Oxford, 1980-88; Professor of Economics, Delhi University, 1963-71, London School of Economics and Political Science, 1971-77; Professor of Economics, 1977-80, Drummond Professor of Political Economy, 1980-88, Oxford University; Andrew D White Professor at Large, Cornell University, 1978-85; Lamont University Professor and Professor of Economics and Philosophy, Harvard University, 1988-. Publications: Choice of Techniques, 1960; Collective Choice and Welfare, 1970; Guidelines for Project Evaluation (with P Dasgupta and Stephen Marglin), 1972; On Economic Inequality, 1973; Employment, Technology and Development, 1975; Poverty and Famines: An Essay on Entitlement and Deprivation, 1981; Choice, Welfare and Measurement, 1982; Resources, Values and Development, 1984; Commodities and Capabilities, 1985; On Ethics and Economics, 1987; The Standard of Living (with others), 1987; Hunger and Public Action (with Jean Dreze), 1989; Jibanayatra o arthaniti, 1990; The Political Economy of Hunger (editor with Jean Dreze), 3 volumes, 1990-91; Money and Value: On the Ethics and Economics of Finance/Denaro e valore: Etica ed economia della finanza, 1991; Inequality Reexamined, 1992; The Quality of Life (editor with Martha Nussbaum), 1993; Economic Development and Social Opportunity (with Jean Dreze), 1995. Contributions to: Professional journals. Honours: Mahalanobis Prize, 1976; Honorary Doctor of Literature, University of Saskatchewan, 1979. Memberships: American Academy of Arts and Sciences;American Economic Association, president, 1994-; British Academy, fellow; Development Studies Association; Econometric Society, fellow; Indian Economic Association; International Economic Association, president, 1986-88, honorary president, 1988-; Royal Economic Society. Address: c/o Department of Economics, Littauer Building, Harvard University, Cambridge, MA 02138, USA.

SENGUPTA Preety, b. 17 May 1944, Ahmedabad, India. Writer; Poet. m. Chandan Sengupta, 21 June 1975. Education: MA in English Literature. Publications: Some 18 works. Contributions to: Various publications. Honours: Several literary awards. Memberships: PEN India; Poetry Society of America. Address: 15 Stewart Place, White Plains, NY 10603, USA.

SEPAMLA (Sydney) Sipho, b. 1932, Johannesburg, South Africa. Editor; Writer; Poet. Education: Studied as teacher. Appointments: Editor, New Classic and S'ketsh magazines. Publications: Hurry Up To It, 1975; The Blues Is You In Me, 1976; The Soweto I Love, 1977; The Root Is One, 1979; Children of the Earth, 1983; Selected Poems, 1984. Novels: A Ride on the Whirlwind, 1981; Third Generation, 1986. Address: c/o Skotaville Publishers, PO Box 32483, Braamfontein 2017, South Africa.

SEQUIERA Isaac J F, b. 5 Jan 1930, Hyderabad, India. University Professor. Education: BA, 1955; MA, 1958; PhD, 1970, Utah. Publications: The Theme of Initiation in Modern American Fiction, 1975; A Manifesto for Humour, 1985; Popular Culture: East and West, 1991; Studies in American Literature, 1991; Viewpoints USA, 1992; Essays in American Studies, 1992; The Closing of the American frontier, 1994; American Studies Today, 1995. Contributions to: 70 papers in research journals in USA, Korea and India. Honours: Seaton Scholar, 1947; Fulbright Smith-Mundt Award, 1966; American Council of Learned Societies Fellow, 1979; UGC Council Lecturer, 1983, Professor Emeritus, 1991. Memberships: Modern Language Association, USA; Indian Association of American Studies; American Studies Association, USA; Poetry Society, president, 1975-80; Dramatic Circle, Hyderabad, president, 1980-. Address: American Studies Research Centre, ASRC, Hyderabad 500007, AP, India.

SEROTE Mongane Wally, b. 8 May 1944, Johannesburg, South Africa. Cultural Attaché; Poet. Education: MFA, Columbia University, New York, 1979. Appointment: Cultural Attaché, Department of Arts and Culture, African National Congress, South Africa. Publications: Yakhal'imkomo, 1972; Tsetlo, 1974; No Baby Must Weep, 1975; Behold Mama, Flowers, 1978; The Night Keeps Winking, 1982; Selected Poems, 1982; A Tough Tale, 1987. Novel: To Every Birth Its Blood, 1981. Honour: Fulbright Scholarship. Address: 28 Penton Road, PO Box 38, London N1 9PR, England.

SERVADIO Gaia Cecilia, b. 13 Sept 1938, Padua, Italy. Writer; Journalist. 2 sons, 1 daughter. Education: St Martin's School of Art, London; National Diploma in Graphic Art. Appointments: Lecturer, Associazione Italiana, 1970, Manchester Museum, 1982; Italian Foreign Minister, Australia, 1992, India, 1995; Consultant Editor, Editore, Italy, 1987; Director of Debates and Literary Talks, Accademia Italiana, 1988-94. Publications: Melinda, 1968; Don Juan/Salome,

1969; Il Metodo, 1970; Mafioso, 1972; A Siberian Encounter, 1973; Luchino Visconti: A Biography, 1985; A Profile of a Mafia Boss: Insider Outsider, 1986; To a Different World: La donna nel Rinascimento, 1986; Il Lamento di Arianna, 1987; Una infanzia diversa, 1988; The Story of R, 1990; Edward Lear's Italian Castles, editor, 1990; La Vallata, 1991; Incontri (essays), 1993; The Real Traviata, 1994; La mia umbria (editor), 1994. Contributions to Il Corriere della Sera; The Observer. Honour: Cavaliere Ufficiale della Republica Italiana, 1980. Memberships: Foreign Press Association, vice-president, 1974-79; Society of Authors. Address: 31 Bloomfield Terrace, London SW1 8PQ, England.

SERVICE Alastair Stanley Douglas, b. 8 May 1933, London, England. Writer. m. (1) Louisa Anne Hemming, 28 Feb 1959, div 1983, 1 son, 1 daughter, (2) Zandria Madeleine Pauncefort, 21 Feb 1992. Education: Modern History, Queen's College, Oxford, 1953-55. Appointments: Banker, Publisher, 1958-75; Organiser, Law Reform Campaigns on Family Planning, Divorce, Abortion, Adoption, 1964-75. Publications: A Birth Control Plan for Britain, 1972; Edwardian Architecture and its Origins, 1975; London 1900, 1978; Architects of London: 1066 to Today, 1979; The Megaliths of Europe: A Guide, 1979; Lost Worlds, 1980; Anglo-Saxon and Norman Buildings: A Guide, 1981; Edwardian Interiors, 1981; Victorian/Edwardian Hampstead, 1990; Standing Stones of Europe: The Great Neolithic Monuments, 1993. Contributions to: Journals and newspapers. Honour: Commander of the Order of the British Empire, 1995. Memberships: Family Planning Association, national chairman, 1975-80; Health Education Authority, vice-chairman, 1978-89; Society of Architectural Historians of Great Britain; Victorian Society; Wessex NHS Region, regional chairman, 1993-94; Wiltshire and Bath Health Commission, chairman, 1992-96; Wiltshire Health Authority, Chairman, 1996-. Address: Swan House, Avebury, Near Marlborough, Wilts SN8 1RA, England.

SERVIEN Louis-Marc, Comte de Boisdauphin, Lord of Quendon, b. 8 Jan 1934, Yverdon, Switzerland. Writer; Editor; Journalist. Education: Licence in Law, Economics and Commercial Sciences, University of Lausanne; Dr Acc, Rome, Italy. Publications: Les Fonds de Placement Collectif en Suisse, 1958; Le Régime Fiscal des Fonds de Placement en Suisse, 1959; Les Sociétés d'Investissement ou Fonds de Placement: Nouvelle Formule d'Epargne, 1962; Le Fisc et l'Investment Trust, ou Quelques Réflexions à Propos du XVIIe Congres de l'IFA, Athens, 1962; Mutual Funds, Why Not? A Survey of International Investment Funds, 1968; Quelques Réflexions à Propos du Nouveau Statut Juridique des Fonds de Placement Suisses, 1969; Fondos de Inversion, Una Nueva Formula de Ahorro, 1970; Fondi di Investimento in Svizzera, 1972; Gibraltar: Tax on the Rock..., 1986. Contributions to: Society magazines, at home and Europe. Honours: Concordia Order, Sao Paulo, Brazil; Gold Medal, Arts, Science et Lettres, Paris. Memberships: Union Internationale des Journalistes et de la Presse de Langue Française, Paris; Syndicat des Journalistes et Ecrivains, Paris; Association Indépendante des Journalistes Suisses, Lausanne; Club Diplomatique de Genève. Address: Quendon Hall, 23 Chemin du Levant, CH-1005, Lausanne, Switzerland.

SETH Vikram, b. 20 June 1952, Calcutta, India. Poet; Novelist. Education: BA, 1975, MA, 1978, Corpus Christi College, Oxford; MA, 1979, PhD, Economics, Stanford University, USA. Appointment:Senior Editor, Stanford University Press, 1985-86. Publications: Mappings (poetry), 1982; From Heaven Lake: Travels Through Sianking and Tibet (non-fiction), 1983; The Humble Administrator's Garden (poetry), 1985; All You Who Sleep Tonight (poetry translation), 1985; The Golden Gate (verse novel), 1986; A Suitable Boy, 1994. Honours: Guggenheim Fellowships; Thomas Cook Travel Book Award, 1983; Commonwealth Poetry Prize, 1986; W H Smith Literary Award, 1994. Address: c/o Anthony Sheil Associates, 42 Doughty Street, London WC1N 2LF, England.

SETTANNI Harry Eugene, b. 8 Mar 1945, Chicago, Illinois, USA. Professor. Education: BS English, St Joseph's University, Philadelphia, 1967; MA, Philosophy, Villanova University, Pennsylvania, 1972; PhD, Philosophy, Saint John's University, Jamaica, New York, 1976. Publications: Holism, A Philosophy for Today, Anticipating The Twenty-First Century, 1990; What is Man? 1991; What is Morality? 1992; Five Philosophers: How Their Lives Influenced Their Thought, 1992; Controversial Questions in Philosophy, 1996; Scientific Knowledge, 1992; What is Freedom of Choice? 1992; The Probabilist Theism of John Stuart Mill, 1991; The

Philosophic Foundation of Paranormal Phenomena, 1992; Logic Workbook, 1993; Five Primers in the Social Sciences, 1996; Essays in Psychology and Epistemology, 1996; Knowledge and Reality, 1996; Miscellaneous Essays, 1996. Address: 122 Copley Road, Upper Darby, PA 19082, USA.

SETTLE Mary Lee, b. 29 July 1918, Charleston, West Virginia, USA. Writer; Editor. m. (1) Rodney Weathersbee, 1939, div 1946, (2) Douglas Newton, 1946, div 1956, (3) William Littleton Tazewell, 2 Sept 1978, 1 son. Education: Sweet Briar College, 1936-38. Appointments: Assistant Editor, Harper's Bazaar, New York City, 1945; English Correspondent, Flair Magazine, 1950-51; Editor, American Heritage, New York City, 1961-; Associate Professor, Bard College, 1965-76; Visiting Lecturer, Iowa Writer's Workshop, 1976, University of Virginia, 1978; Founder, PEN-Faulkner Award, 1980. Publications: Fiction: The Love Eaters, 1954; The Kiss of Kin, 1955; O Beulah Land, 1956; Know Nothing, 1960; Fight Night on a Sweet Saturday, 1964; The Clam Shell, 1971; Prisons, 1973; Blood Tie, 1977; The Scapegoat, 1980; The Killing Ground, 1982; Celebration, 1986; Charley Bland, 1989. Play: Juana La Loca, 1965. Non-Fiction: All the Brave Promises: Memories of Woman 2nd Class 2146391 (autobiography), 1966; Turkish Reflections (autobiography), 1991. Contributions to: Anthologies and magazines. Honours: Guggenheim Fellowships, 1958, 1960; Ingram Merrill Foundation Award, 1975; National Book Award, 1978; Janet Heidinger Kafka Prize, 1983; American Academy of Arts and Letters Award, 1994. Address: 544 Pembroke Avenue, Norfolk, VA 23507, USA.

SEWART Alan, (Padder Nash), b. 26 Aug 1928, Bolton Lancashire, England. Writer. m. Dorothy Teresa Humphreys, 13 Oct 1962, 2 sons, 1 daughter. Education: LLB, University of London. Publications: Tough Tontine, 1978; A Ribbon for My Repute, 1978; The Salome Syndrome, 1979; The Women of Morning, 1980; In That Rich Earth. 1981; Smoker's Cough, 1982; Death Game - Five Players, 1982; If I Should Die, 1983; Dead Man Drifting, 1984; The Educating of Quinton Quinn, 1984. Non-fiction: Murder in Lancashire, 1988; Leisure Guides, Lancashire (with Dorothy Sewart), 1989. As Alan Sewart Well: Mr Crumblestone's Eden, 1980; Where Lionel Lies, 1984; Candice is Dead, 1984; As Padder Nash: Grass, 1983; Coup de Grass, 1983; Wayward Seeds of Grass, 1983; Grass and Supergrass, 1984. Contributions to: Police Review. Membership: Crime Writers Association. Address: 7 Knott Lane, Easingwold, York YO6 3LX, England.

SEWELL Elizabeth, b. 9 Mar 1919, Coonoor, India. Writer; Lecturer. Education: BA, 1942, MA, 1945, PhD, 1949, Cambridge University. Publications: The Orphic Voice; The Field of Nonsense; Paul Valéry: The Mind in the Mirror; An Idea; The Structure of Poetry; The Dividing of Time; The Singular Hope; Now Bless Thyself; The Unlooked-For, novel, 1995. Contributions to: USA, Canada, England, France, Austria, Netherlands. Honours: Honorary Doctorates; National Award; Zoe Kincaid Brockman Award. Memberships: PEN; Lewis Carroll Society of North America; North Carolina Writers Network. Address: 854 West Bessemer Avenue, Greensboro, NC 27408, USA.

SEWELL Stephen, b. 1953, Sydney, New South Wales, Australia. Playwright. Education: BS, University of Sydney, 1975. Appointment: Chairman, Australian National Playwrights Centre. Publications: The Father We Loved on a Beach by the Sea, 1976; Traitors, 1979; Welcome the Wright World, 1983; The Blind Giant is Dancing, 1983; Burn Victim (with others), 1983; Dreams in an Empty City, 1986; Hate, 1988; Miranda, 1989; Sisters, 1991; King Golgrutha, 1991; In the City of Grand-Daughters, 1993; Dust, 1993. Honour: New South Wales Premier's Award, 1985. Address: Hilary Linstead and Associates Pty Ltd, Level 18, Plaza II, 500 Oxford Street, Bondi Junction, New South Wales 2022, Australia.

SEXTON Rosemary, b. 20 Dec 1946, Haileybury, Ontario, Canada. Writer. m. J Edgar, 9 May 1979, 1 son, 2 stepsons, 1 daughter, 1 stepdaughter. Education: Havergal College; BA, Laurentian University, 1968; Interim High School Assistant Certificate, Type B, College of Education, 1969; Specialist Guidance Certificate, 1973; BA, Honours, University of Toronto, 1972; MA, York University, 1976; LLB, Osgoode Hall Law School, 1976. Appointments: Teacher of English and Latin, New Liskeard SS, 1968-69, and West Hill SS, 1969-72; Articled with law firm, Holden Murdoch Finlay Robinson, 1976-77; Called to the Bar of Ontario, 1977; Tax Editor, CCH (Canada) Ltd, 1977-78; Society Columnist, The Globe and Mail, 1988-93. Publications: The Glitter Girls, 1993; Confessions of a Society

Columnist, 1995. Memberships: Served on various Boards, 1982-87: Family Day Care Services of Metro Toronto; Toronto Symphony Women's Committee; Toronto Pops Orchestra; Canadian Psychiatric Awareness Committee; Arthritis Society, Rosedale Branch; Wellesley Hospital Auxilliary; Society for Educational Visits and Exchanges in Canada; St George-St David PC Riding Association; Laurentian University. Address: 211 Queen's Quay West, Suite 1107, Toronto, Ontario M5J 2M6, Canada.

SEYERSTED Per, b. 18 May 1921, Oslo, Norway. Professor of American Literature (retired); Writer. Education: MA, Harvard University, 1959; PhD, University of Oslo, 1969. Appointments: Professor of American Literature, University of Oslo, 1973-91; Associate Editor, Studies in American Fiction, 1985-95. Publications: Gilgamesj, 1967, 4th edition, 1996; Kate Chopin: A Critical Biography, 1969, 4th edition, 1994; The Complete Works of Kate Chopin (editor), 1969, 3rd edition, 1993; A Kate Chopin Miscellany (editor), 1979; Leslie Marmon Silko, 1980; Scando-Americana: Papers on Scandinavian Emigration to the United States (editor), 1980; Dakky Kiaer (editor), 1982; From Norwegian Romantic to American Realist: Studies in the Life and Writings of Hjalmar Hjorth Boyesen, 1984; The Arctic: Canada and the Nordic Countries (editor), 1991. Contributions to: Journals. Honours: American Council of Learned Societies Fellow, 1964-66; Norwegian Research Council for Science and Letters Fellow, 1966-69. Memberships: Modern Language Association of America; Nordic Association for American Studies, president, 1973-79; Nordic Association for Canadian Studies, vice-president, 1984-93; Norsk faglitterarer forfatterforening; Norwegian Academy for Science and Letters. Address: c/o Department of British and American Studies, University of Oslo, PB 1003 Blindern, 0315 Oslo, Norway.

SEYMOUR Alan, b. 6 June 1927, Perth, Western Australia, Australia. Playwright. Education: Perth Modern School. Appointments: Former Actor, Theatre Critic and Journalist. Publications: Swamp Creatures, 1958; The One Day of the Year, 1960; The Gaiety of Nations, 1965; A Break in the Music, 1966; The Pope and the Pill, 1968; Oh Grave, Thy Victory, 1973; Structures, 1973; The Wind from the Plain, 1974; The Float, 1980 (plays produced in Australia, Adelaide, London, Glasgow, Europe and Japan). Radio and Television plays. Novels: The One Day of the Year, 1967; The Coming Self-Destruction of the United States, 1969. Honour: Australia Council for the Arts Grant. Address: 74 Upland Road, London SE22 0DB, England.

SEYMOUR Arabella Charlotte Henrietta, b. 8 Dec 1948, London, England. Author. 1 daughter. Education: West Ham College of Technology. Publications: A Passion in the Blood, 1985; Dangerous Deceptions, 1986; The Sins of Rebeccah Russell, 1988; The End of the Family, 1990; No Sad Songs (as Sarah Lyon, 1990; Princess of Darkness, 1991; A Woman of Pleasure, 1994; Sins of the Mother, 1996. Contributions to: Woman's Day, Australia. Membership: Society of Authors. Literary Agent: Sheil Land Associates Ltd. Address: Sondes House, Patrixbourne, Canterbury, Kent CT4 5DD, England.

SEYMOUR-SMITH Martin, b. 24 April 1928, England. Writer. m. Janet de Glanville, 1952; 2 daughters. Education: MA, St Edmund Hall, Oxford. Appointments: Schoolmaster, 1954-60; Freelance writer, 1960-; General Editor, Gollancz Classics, 1967-69; Visiting Professor, University of Wisconsin at Parkside, 1971-72. Publications: Robert Graves, 1956; Tea With Miss Stockport, 24 Poems, 1963; Bluff Your Way in Literature, 1966; A New Canon of English Poetry (co-editor), 1967; Fallen Women, A Sceptical Enquiry into the Treatment of Prostitutes, Their Clients and Their Pimps in Literature, 1969; Poets Through Their Letters, 1969; Reminiscences of Norma, Poems 1963-70, 1971; Guide to Modern World Literature, 1973; Sex and Society, 1973; Who's Who in 20th Century Literature, 1976; Fifty European Novels, 1979; Novels and Novelists, 1980; The New Astrologer, 1981; Robert Graves: His Life and Work, 1982, revised, 1995; Rudyard Kipling, 1989; Everyman Dictionary of Fictional Characters, 1990; Hardy, 1994; Wilderness (poems), 1994; editions of Marvell, Shakespeare (Sonnets, 1963); Ben Jonson, Longer Elizabethan Poems, 1970; Whitman, Hardy and Conrad (The Secret Agent, 1984). Address: 36 Holliers Hill, Bexhill on Sea, East Sussex TN40 2DD, England.

SHAABAN Bouthaina, b. 1 Apr 1953, Syria. Associate Professor; Writer. m. Khalil Jawad, 2 Sept 1981, 2 daughters. Education: BA, English Literature, Damascus University, 1975; MA, 1978; PhD, 1982, English Literature, Warwick University.

Appointments: Lecturer, Constantine University, Algeria, 1982-84; Lecturer, 1985-90, Associate Professor, 1991-, Damascus University; Fulbright Professor, Duke University, 1990-91. Publications: Both Right and Left-Handed Arab Women Talk About Their Lives, 1988; Poetry and Politics: Shelley and the Chartist Movement, 1993. Contributions to: Various publications. Honour: Rockefeller Foundation Appointment, Rice University, Houston, Texas 1992-93. Memberships: FIT, Arab Writers Union; International PEN; Keats-Shelley Society. Address: c/o Arab Writers Union, PO Box 3230, Damascus, Syria.

SHADBOLT Maurice (Francis Richard), b. 4 June 1932, Auckland, New Zealand. Novelist. m. Bridget Armstrong, 1978. Education: University of Auckland. Appointments: Journalist, New Zealand, 1952-54; Documentry Screenwriter, Director, New Zealand Film Unit, 1954-57; Full Time Writer, 1957-. Publications: Among the Cinders, 1965; This Summer's Dolphin, 1969; An Ear of the Dragon, 1971; Danger Zone, 1975; The Lovelock Version, 1980; Season of the Jew, 1986; Monday's Warrior, 1990. Story Collections: The New Zealander: A Sequence of Stories, 1959; Summer Fires and Winter Country, 1963; The Presence of Music: Three Novellas; Figures in Light: Selected Stories. Play: Once on Chunk Bair, 1982. Guides and Histories of New Zealand. Honours: James Wattie Awards, 1973, 1991; New Zealand Book Award, 1981; Officer of the Order of the British Empire, 1989. Address: Box 60028 Titirangi, Auckland 7, New Zealand.

SHAFER Neil, b. 24 Apr 1933, Chicago, Illinois, USA. m. Edith Oelsher, 7 June 1964, 2 sons, 1 daughter. Education: BA, Education, Arizona State College, 1955; MMus, Catholic University of America, 1959. Publications: United States Territorial Coinage for the Philippine Islands, 1961; A Guide Book of Philippine Paper Money, 1964; A Guide Book of Modern US Currency, 8 editions, 1965-79;Guide Book of Philippine Paper Money, 1964; Philippine Emergency and Guerilla Currency of World War II, 1974; Standard Catalog of World Paper Money (co-editor), 1981-97; Standard Catalog of Depression Scrip of the US (co-author), 1985. The Wonderful World of Paper Money, 1992; College Currency (editor), 1993; Contributions to: Associate Editor, Whitman Numismatic Journal, 1964-68; Editor-in-Chief, New England Journal of Numismatics, 1985-87; Monthly column on paper money, Bank Note Reporter, 1987-, Numismatic News, 1996-. Honours: Various Awards, Numismatic Literary Guild, 1986, 1988, 1996; Medal of Merit, American Numismatic Association, 1988; Various Awards, Society of Paper Money Collectors. Memberships: Numismatic Literary Guild, 1968-; American Numismatic Association; International Bank Note Society; Society of Paper Money Collectors. Address: PO Box 17138, Milwaukee, WI 53217, USA.

SHAFFER Anthony (Joshua), b. 15 May 1926, Liverpool, England. Playwright; Writer. m. Diane Cilento, 1985. Education: Graduated Trinity College, Cambridge, 1950. Appointments: Former Barrister and Journalist. Publications: The Savage Parade, 1963, revised edition, 1987; Sleuth, 1970; Murderer, 1970; The Wicker Man, 1974; Masada, 1974; Widow's Weeds, 1977; Death on the Nile, 1978; Absolution, 1979; Evil Under the Sun, 1982; Appointment with Death, 1988; Sommersby, 1994. Novels: How Doth the Little Crocodile (with Peter Shaffer), 1952; Withered Murder (with Peter Shaffer), 1955; The Wicker Man, 1978; Absolution, 1979. Honours: Tony Award, 1971; 6 Edgar Allan Poe Awards, Mystery Writers of America; Grande Prix Filmes Fantastique Paris. Address: c/o Peters, Fraser and Dunlop Group, 503-504 The Chambers, Chelsea Harbour, Lots Road, London SW10 0XF, England.

SHAFFER Harry George, b. 28 Aug 1919, Vienna, Austria. Professor Emeritus of Economics. m. Betty Shaffer, 7 June 1987, 3 sons, 1 daughter. Education: BS, 1947, MA, 1948, PhD, 1958, New York University. Publications: The Soviet Economy, 1963; The Soviet System, 1965, revised edition, 1984; The Communist World, 1967; The Soviet Treatment of Jews, 1974; Soviet Agriculture, 1977; Women in the Two Germanies, 1981. Contributions to: Over 75 articles in professional, semi-professional and other periodicals in such countries as America, England, France, Germany, and Italy. Honours: Beta Gamma Sigma; Hill Teacher, Best Professor. Address: Department of Economics, University of Kansas, Lawrence, KS 66045, USA.

SHAFFER Peter Levin, b. 15 May 1926, Liverpool, England. Playwright. Education: BA, Trinity College, Cambridge, 1947-50. Appointments: Literary critic, Truth, 1956-57; Music Critic, Time and Tide, 1961-62. Publications: Plays: Five Finger Exercise, 1958; The Private Ear and the Public Eye, 1962; The Royal Hunt of the Sun,

1964; Black Comedy, 1965; White Lies, 1967; Shrivings, 1970; Equus, 1973; Amadeus, 1979; The Collected Plays of Peter Shaffer, 1982; Yonadab, 1985; Lettice and Lovage, 1987; Whom Do I Have the Honour of Addressing?, 1990; The Gift of the Gorgon, 1992. Honours: Standard Drama Awards, 1958, 1979; New York Drama Critics Circle Awards, 1960, 1975; Antoinette Perry Awards, 1975, 1981; Academy Award (Oscar), 1984; Commander of the Order of the British Empire, 1987; Hambourg Shakespeare Prize, 1987; William Inge Award for Distinguished Contribution to American Theatre, 1992. Address: London Management, 2-4 Noel Street, London W1V 3RB, England.

SHAH Tahir, b. 16 Nov 1966, London, England. Writer. Education: BA, International Relations, US International University. Publications: Various monographs; Books: Beyond the Devil's Teeth, 1995; Middle East Bedside Book, 1991; Journey Through Namibia, 1994; Spectrum Guide to Jordan, 1994; The Islamic Legacy of Timbuktu, monography. Contributions to: Newspapers and magazines. Memberships: Association of Cryto-Zoology, Arizona; Institute for Cultural Research, London; Institute for the Study of Human Knowledge, San Francisco; Wig and Pen Club, London. Address: PO Box 2227, London NW2 3BP, England.

SHAHED Husne Ara, 11 Oct 1943, Noakhali, Bangladesh. Teacher. m. A F Shahed Ali, 16 Oct 1966, 2 sons, 1 daughter. Education: MA, Philosophy, Dhaka University, 1965. Publications include: Tran Shibirer Din Ratri (Life in the Relief Camp), 1997; Pathaker Mon (The Pulse of the Readers), 1997; Rebecca, 1997. Contributions to: Dainik Bangla; Dainik Sangbad; Sev national dailies, weekly and monthly periodicals. Memberships: National Institute for Development of Bengali Language & Literature; Asiatic Society of Bangladesh; PEN. Address: Shere Bangla Girls College, 20 Hatkhola Road, Wari, Dhaka 1203, Bangladesh.

SHAHEEN Jack G(eorge), b. 21 Sept 1935, Pittsburgh, Pennsylvania, USA. Professor of Mass Communication; Writer. m. Bernice Marie, 22 Jan 1966, 1 son, 1 daughter. Education: BFA, Carnegie Institute of Technology, 1957; MA, Penn State University, 1964; PhD, University of Missouri, 1967. Appointments: Professor of Mass Communication, Southern Illinois University at Edwardsville, 1969-; Arts Critic, WSIE Radio, 1970-85; Consultant, CBC News, 1993. Publications: Nuclear War Films, 1978; The TV Arab, 1984. Contributions to: Newspapers and magazines. Honours: Fulbright Scholar, 1974, 1981; Scholar-Diplomat, US Department of State, 1978; Outstanding Book of the Year Citation, Choice Magazine, 1984. Address: 1 Dahlgren Lane, Hilton Head Island, SC 29928-3939, USA.

SHAHEEN Mohammad Yousef, b. 17 Feb 1938, Halhul, Jordan. Professor of English Literature. Education: PhD, Cambridge University, England. Appointment: Professor of English, University of Jordan. Publications: George Meredith, A Reappraisal of the Novels, 1981; The Impact of Eliot on Sayyah, 1992; Tayyeb Salih's Season of Migration to the North, 1993; Myth and Literature, 1996; Selected Letters of George Meredith, 1997. Contributions to: Review of English Studies; Modern Language Review; Twentieth Century; Modern Fiction. Address: PO Box 13073, University of Jordan, Amman, Jordan.

SHAHRYAR Faridoon (Khusro), b. 1 June 1975, Aligarh. Student. Education: Final Year, English Hons, AMU. Appointment: Literary Secretary, Aligarh Muslim University, 1996. Contributions to: Poetry Nottingham International; WIRE; Surrey; New Hope International Writing, Cheshire; IOTA, Derbyshire; Weyfarers, Surrey; Prophetic Voices, California, USA; Several Indian journals and magazines. Memberships: Expansion Unlimited, Nottingham; Poetry Society; New Delhi; Literary Quest; Ranchi, India. Address: AB-83, Medical Colony, Aligarh Muslim University, Aligarh-2, India.

SHANE John. See: **DURST Paul.**

SHANGE Ntozake (born Paulette Williams), b. 18 Oct 1948, Trenton, New Jersey, USA. Poet; Dramatist; Writer; Associate Professor of Drama. 1 daughter. Education: BA, Barnard College, 1970; MA, University of Southern California at Los Angeles, 1973. Appointments: Faculty, Sonoma State College, Rohnert Park, California, 1973-75, Mills College, Oakland, California, 1975, City College of the City University of New York, 1975, Douglass College, New Brunswick, New Jersey, 1978; Artist-in-Residence, Equinox Theater, Houston, 1981-; Associate Professor of Drama, University of Houston, 1983-. Publications: Poetry: Melissa and Smith, 1976; Natural Disasters and Other Festive Occasions, 1977; Happy Edges,

1978; Some Men, 1981; A Daughter's Geography, 1983; From Okra to Greens, 1984; Ridin' the Moon in Texas: Word Paintings, 1988; The Love Space Demands: A Continuing Saga, 1992. Plays: For Colored Girls Who Have Considered Suicide When the Rainbow is Enuf, 1976; Photograph: Lovers-in-Motion, 1981; Spell #7, 1981; Boogie Woogie Landscapes, 1981. Fiction: Sassafrass: A Novella, 1977; Sassafrass, Cypress and Indigo, 1982; Betsey Brown, 1985; Liliane: Resurrection of the Daughter, 1995. Non-Fiction: See No Evil: Prefaces, Essays and Accounts 1976-1983, 1984. Honours: New York Drama Critics Circle Award, 1977; Obie Awards, 1977, 1980; Columbia University Medal of Excellence, 1981; Guggenheim Fellowship, 1981. Address: c/o St Martin's Press, 175 Fifth Avenue, New York, NY 10010, USA.

SHAPCOTT Thomas W(illiam), b. 21 Mar 1935, Ipswich, Queensland, Australia. Poet; Writer; Administrator. m. (1) Margaret Hodge, 1960, (2) Judith Rodriguez, 1982, 1 son, 3 daughters. Education: BA, University of Queensland, 1968. Appointments: Director, Australia Council Literature Board, 1983-90; Executive Director, National Book Council, 1992-97; Professor of Creative Writing, Adelaide University, 1997. Publications: Poetry: Sonnets, 1960-63, 1963; A Taste of Salt Water, 1967; Inwards to the Sun, 1969; Fingers at Air, 1969; Begin with Walking, 1973; Shabbytown Calendar, 1975; 7th Avenue Poems, 1976; Selected Poems, 1978; Make the Old Man Sing, 1980; Welcome!, 1983; Travel Dice, 1987; Selected Poems, 1956-1988, 1989; In the Beginning, 1990; The City of Home, 1995. Novels: The Birthday Gift, 1982; White Stag of Exile, 1984; Hotel Bellevue, 1986; The Search for Galina, 1989; Mona's Gift, 1993. Plays: The 7 Deadly Sins, 1970. Editor: New Impulses in Australian Poetry (with R Hall), 1967; Australian Poetry Now, 1970; Contemporary American and Australian Poetry, 1975; Poetry as a Creative Learning Process, 1978. Contributions to: Newspapers and journals. Honours: Grace Leven Prize, 1961; Sir Thomas White Memorial Prize, 1967; Sidney Myer Charity Trust Awards, 1967, 1969; Churchill Fellowship, 1972; Canada-Australia Literary Prize, 1978; Officer of the Order of Australia, 1989; Honorary DLitt, Macquarie University, 1989; Gold Wreath, Struga International Poetry Festival, 1989; Christopher Brennan Award for Poetry, 1994. Memberships: Australia Book Review, Chairman; Australian Society of Authors; International PEN. Address: PO Box 231, Mont Albert, Victoria 3127, Australia.

SHAPIRO David (Joel), b. 2 Jan 1947, Newark, New Jersey, USA. Poet; Art Critic; Teacher. m. Lindsey Stamm, 1970, 1 child. Education: BA, 1968, PhD, 1973, Columbia University; BA, 1970, MA, 1974, Clare College, Cambridge. Appointments: Violinist in various orchestras, 1963-; Instructor and Assistant Professor of English, Columbia University, 1972-80; Visiting Professor, Brooklyn College of the City University of New York, 1979, Princeton University, 1982-83; Visting Faculty, Cooper Union, New York City, 1980-; Currently: Full Professor, Art History, William Paterson College, Wayne, New Jersey. Publications: Poetry: January: A Book of Poems, 1965; Poems from Deal, 1969; A Man Holding an Acoustic Panel, 1971; The Page-Turner, 1973; Lateness, 1977; To an Idea, 1984; House, Blown Apart, 1988; After a Lost Original, 1990. Other: John Ashbery: An Introduction to the Poetry, 1979; Jim Dine: Painting What One Is, 1981; Jasper Johns: Drawings 1954-1984, 1984; Mondrian Flowers, 1990; Alfred Leslie: The Killing Cycle (with Judith Stein), 1991. Honours: Bread Loaf Writers Conference Robert Frost Fellowship, 1965; Ingram Merrill Foundation Fellowship, 1967; Book-of-the-Month Club Fellowship, 1968; Kellett Fellow, Clare College, Cambridge, 1968-70; Creative Artists Public Service Grant, 1974; Morton Dauwen Zabel Award, 1977; National Endowment for the Arts Grants, 1979; National Endowment for the Humanities Fellowships, 1980; Graham Foundation Grant, for research in Architecture and Poetry; Foundation for Contemporary Performance Arts, grant, 1996; Milton Asery Professor Bard Graduate School of the Arts, 1996. Address: 3001 Henry Hudson Parkway, Riverdale, NY 10463, USA.

SHAPIRO Harvey, b. 27 Jan 1924, Chicago, Illinois, USA. Editor; Poet. m Edna Kaufman, 23 July 1953, 2 sons. Education: BA, Yale University, 1947; MA, Columbia University, 1948. Appointments: Staff, Commentary, 1955-57, The New Yorker, 1955-57, New York Times Magazine, 1957-64; Assistant Editor, 1964-75, Editor, 1975-83, New York Times Book Review; Deputy Editor, New York Times Magazine, 1983-. Publications: The Eye, 1953; The Book, 1955; Mountain Fire Thornbush, 1961; Battle Report, 1966; This World, 1971; Lauds, 1975; Lauds and Nightsounds, 1978; The Light Holds, 1984; National Cold Storage Company: New and Selected Poems, 1988; A Day's Portion, 1994; Selected Poems, 1997. Contributions to: Periodicals. Honour:

Rockefeller Grant for Poetry, 1967. Address: c/o The New York Times Magazine, 229 West 43rd Street, New York, NY 10036, USA.

SHAPIRO Karl (Jay), b. 10 Nov 1913, Baltimore, Maryland, USA. Professor of English (retired); Poet; Writer. m. Sophie Wilkins, 25 Apr 1985. Education: Johns Hopkins University, 1937-39. Appointments: Consultant in Poetry, Library of Congress, Washington, DC, 1946-47; Associate Professor, Johns Hopkins University, 1947-50; Editor, Poetry, 1950-56, Prairie Schooner, 1956-66; Professor of English,University of Nebraska, 1956-66, University of Illinois, Circle Campus, Chicago, 1966-68, University of California at Davis, 1968-85. Publications: Poetry: Poems, 1935; New and Selected Poems, 1940-46, 1946; Trial of a Poet, 1947; Poems, 1940-53, 1953; Poems of a Jew, 1958; Selected Poems, 1968; White-Haired Lover, 1968; Adult Bookstore, 1976; Collected Poems, 1940-78, 1978; New and Selected Poems, 1940-86, 1987. Novel: Edsel, 1971. Non-Fiction: Beyond Criticism, 1953; In Defense of Ignorance, 1960; Prose Keys to Modern Poetry (with James E Miller Jr and Bernice Slote), 1962; The Bourgeois Poet, 1964; A Prosody Handbook (with Robert Beum), 1964; To Abolish Children, 1968; The Poetry Wreck, 1975; The Younger Son (autobiography), 1988; Reports of My Death (autobiography), 1990; The Old Horsefly, 1993. Honours: Jeanette S Davis Prize, 1942; Levinson Prize, 1943; Contemporary Poetry Prize, 1943; Pulitzer Prize in Poetry, 1945; Shelley Memorial Prize, 1945; Guggenheim Fellowships, 1945-46, 1953-54; Bollingen Prize for Poetry, 1969; Robert Kirsch Award, Los Angeles Times, 1989; Charity Randall Citation, 1990. Memberships: American Academy of Arts and Letters; American Academy of Arts and Sciences. PEN. Address: 211 West 106th Street, No 11C, New York, NY 10025, USA.

SHAPIRO Laura. Journalist. m. John Stratton Hawley, 1 daughter. Education: BA, Radcliffe College. Appointments: Writer and Columnist, The Real Paper, Cambridge, Massachusetts, 1969-76; Dance Critic, Boston Globe, 1975-77; Journalist, Seattle Weekly, 1978-84; Associate Editor, 1984, General Editor, 1987, Senior Writer, 1992-, Newsweek. Publication: Perfection Salad: Women and Cooking at the Turn of the Century, 1986. Honours: Exceptional Media Merit Award, National Women's Political Caucus, 1992; National Headliner Award for Consistently Outstanding Feature Writing, Press Club of Atlantic City, 1992; James Beard Journalism Award for Excellence, 1994. Address: c/o Newsweek, 251 West 57th Street, New York, NY 10019-1894, USA.

SHARAT CHANDRA Gubbi Shankara Chetty, (Jean Parker), b. 5 Mar 1938, Nanjangud, India. Professor of English; Poet; Writer. m. Jane Sharat Chandra, 8 Jan 1966, 1 son, 2 daughters. Education: BA, 1956, BL, 1968 University of Mysore; MS, State University of New York, 1964; LLM, University of Toronto, 1966; MFA, University of Iowa, 1968. Appointments: Editor, Kamadhenu, 1970-75, South Asian Review, 1989-; Assistant Professor, Washington State University, 1972-80; Fulbright Professor, Malaysia, 1978, Bangladesh, 1989; Assistant Professor, 1983-87, Associate Professor, 1987-92, Professor of English, 1992-, University of Missouri, Kansas City. Publications: April in Nanjangud, 1971; Once or Twice, 1974; The Ghost of Meaning, 1978; Heirloom, 1982; Family of Mirrors, 1993; Immigration of Loss, 1993. Contributions to: Newspapers, magazines and journals. Honours: Florida State Poetry Award, 1980; National Endowment for the Arts Fellowship, 1981. Memberships: Associated Writing Programs; Modern Language Association; South Asian Language Association. Address: 9916 Juniper, Overland Park, KS 66207, USA.

SHARMA Vera, b. 10 Feb 1926, Bombay, India. Writer; Poet; Dramatist. m. 10 Mar 1949, 1 daughter. Publications: Stories, poems and plays; Aaher, short stories in Marathi translation, 1996. Contributions to: Various publications. Honours: Several prizes. Memberships: Asiatic Society of Bombay; PEN Bombay. Address: Bhairavi, 106 6th Road, Tilaknagar, Goregaon W, Bombay 400 062, India.

SHARP Ronald A(lan), b. 19 Oct 1945, Cleveland, Ohio, USA. Perofessor of English; Writer. m. Inese Brutans, 22 June 1968, 2 sons. Education: Syracuse University, 1963-64; BA, Kalamazoo College, 1967; Instituto Internacional, Madrid, 1965-66; MA, University of Michigan, 1968; University of Edinburgh, 1971; PhD, University of Virginia, 1974. Appointments: Instructor, Western Michigan University, 1968-70; Instructor, 1970-72, Assistant Professor, 1974-78, Associate Professor, 1978-85, Professor of English, 1985-90, John Crowe Ransom Professor of English, 1990-, Kenyon College; Visiting Professor, Concordia University, 1978; Co-Editor, The Kenyon Review,

1978-82. Publications: Keats, Scepticism and the Religion of Beauty, 1979; Friendship and Literature: Spirit and Form, 1986; The Norton Book of Friendship (with Eudora Welty), 1991; Reading George Steiner (with Nathan A Scott Jr), 1994. Contributions to: Books and journals. Honours: Ford Foundation Grant, 1971; English Speaking Union fellowship, 1973; Mellon Grant, 1980; National Endowment for the Humanities Fellowships, 1981-82, 1984, 1985, 1986-87, 1994, 1996; National Humanities Center Fellowship, 1986-87; Various grants. Memberships: Keats-Shelley Association; Modern Language Association; Wordsworth-Coleridge Association. Address: c/o Department of English, Kenyon College, Gambier, OH 43022, USA.

SHARPE Tom, (Thomas Ridley Sharpe), b. 30 Mar 1928, London, England. Author. m. Nancy Anne Looper, 6 Aug 1969. 3 d. Education: Lancing College, 1942-46; Pembroke College, Cambridge, 1948-52. Publications: Riotous Assembly, 1971; Indecent Exposure, 1973; Porterhouse Blue, 1974; Blott on the Landscape, 1975; Wilt, 1976; The Great Pursuit, 1977; The Throwback, 1978; The Wilt Alternative, 1979; Ancestral Vices, 1980; Vintage Stuff, 1982; Wilt on High, 1984. Contributions to: Numerous magazines and journals. Honours: Laureat Le Grand Prix de L'Humour Noir, Paris, 1986; Le Legion de l'Humour, Aphia, Paris, 1986. Membership: Society of Authors. Address: 38 Tunwells Lane, Great Shelford, Cambridge CB2 5LT, England.

SHATTUCK Roger (Whitney), b. 20 Aug 1923, New York, New York, USA.Writer; Translator; Poet; Editor; Professor. m. Nora Ewing White, 20 Aug 1949, 4 children. Education: BA, Yale University, 1947. Appointments: Reporter, Chicago Daily News, Paris Office, 1948-49; Assistant Trade Editor, Harcourt, Brace & Co, New York City, 1949-50; Society of Fellows, 1950-53, Instructor in French, 1953-56, Harvard University; Assistant Professor, 1956-59, Associate Professor of Romance Languages, 1959-62, Professor of French and English, 1962-71, Chairman of the Department of French and Italian, 1968-71, University of Texas at Austin; Commonwealth Professor of French, University of Virginia, 1974-88; University Professor and Professor of Modern Foreign Languages, Boston University, 1988-; Lecturer at many universities, colleges, art museums and other venues. Publications: Non-Fiction: The Banquet Years: The Origins of the Avant-Garde in France, 1885 to World War One, 1958, revised edition, 1968; Proust's Binoculars: A Study of Memory, Time, and Recognition in A La Recherche du Temps Perdu, 1963; Marcel Proust, 1974; The Forbidden Experiment: The Story of the Wild Boy of Aveyron, 1980; The Innocent Eye on Literature and the Arts, 1984; Forbidden Knowledge: From Prometheus to Pornography, 1996. Poetry: Half Tame, 1964; Editor and Translator: René Daumal: Mount Analogue: A Novel of Symbolically Authentic Non-Euclidean Adventures in Mountain Climbing, 1960; The Selected Writings of Guillaume Apollinaire, 1963, revised edition, 1971; Paul Valéry: Occasions (with Frederick Brown), 1970. Editor: The Craft and Context of Translation (with William Arrowsmith), 1961; Selected Writings of Alfred Jarry: Ubu Cuckolded, Exploits and Opinions of Dr Faustroll, Pataphysician, and Other Writings (with Simon Watson Taylor), 1966. Translator: René Daumal: A Fundamental Experiment, 1987. Contributions to: Essays, short stories, and poems in various publications. Honours: Guggenheim Fellowship, 1958-59; Fulbright Research Fellow, 1958-59; American Council of Learned Societies Research Fellow, 1969-70; National Book Award, 1975; American Academy and Institute of Arts and Letters Award, 1987; Doctorat honoris causa, University of Orléans, France, 1990. Memberships: National Translation Center, advisory board, 1964-69, chairman, 1966-69; National Humanities Faculty, 1972-73; Publications of the Modern Language Association, editorial board, 1977-78; American Academy of Arts and Sciences, 1990-; Association of Literary Scholars and Critics, president, 1995-96. Address: c/o University Professors Program, Boston University, 745 Commonwealth Avenue, Boston, MA 02215, USA.

SHAVELSON Melville, b. 1 April 1917, New York, New York, USA. Writer; Director. m. Lucille T Myers, 2 Nov 1938, 1 son, 1 daughter. Education: AB, Cornell University, 1937. Publications: Screenplays: The Princess and the Pirate, 1944; Wonder Man, 1944; Room for One More, 1951; I'll See You in My Dreams, 1952. Writer, Director: The Seven Little Foys, 1954; Beau James, 1956; Houseboat, 1957; The Five Pennies, 1958; It Started in Naples, 1959; On the Double, 1960; Yours, Mine and Ours, 1968; The War Between Men and Women, 1972; The Legend of Valentino, 1975; Deceptions, 1985. Writer, Director, Producer: The Pigeon That Took Rome, 1962; A New Kind of Love, 1963; Cast a Giant Shadow, 1966; Mixed Company, 1974; The Great Houdinis, 1976; Ike, 1979. Broadway Musical: Jimmy,

1969. Books: How to Make a Jewish Movie, 1970; Lualda, 1975; The Great Houdinis, 1976; The Eleventh Commandment, 1977; Ike, 1979; Don't Shoot It's Only Me, 1990. Honours: Screenwriters Guild Award, 1959; Christopher Award, 1959; Award of Merit, United Jewish Appeal, 1966. Address: 11947 Sunshine Terrace, Studio City, CA 91604, USA.

SHAW Brian. See: **TUBB E(dwin) C(harles).**

SHAW Bynum (Gillette), b. 10 July 1923, Alamance County, North Carolina, USA. Professor of Journalism. m. (1) Louise N Brantley, dec, 30 Aug 1948, (2) Emily P Crandall, dec, 19 June 1982, (3) Charlotte E Reeder, 26 Nov 1986, 2 daughters. Education: BA, Wake Forest College, 1951. Publications: The Sound of Small Hammers, 1962; The Nazi Hunter, 1968; Divided We Stand, The Baptists in American Life, 1974; Days of Power, Nights of Fear, 1980; W W Holden: A Political Biography (with Edgar E Folk), 1982; The History of Wake Forest College, Vol IV, 1988; Oh, Promised Land!, 1992. Contributions to: Esquire; New Republic; Moneysworth; New York Times; The Baltimore Sun. Honour: Sir Walter Raleigh Award in Fiction, 1969. Membership: North Carolina Writers Conference, chairman, 1972. Address: 2700 Speas Road, Winston-Salem, NC 27106, USA.

SHAW Irene. See: **ROBERTS Irene.**

SHAWCROSS William (Hartley Hume), b. 28 May 1946, England. Writer. m (1) Marina Warner, 1971, div, 1 son, 1 daughter, (2) Michal Levin, 1981, div, (3) Hon Olga Polizzi, 1993. Education: Exeter College, Oxford. Appointments: Writer for Washington Post, Sunday Times, Spectator, New Statesman; Chairman, Article 19, International Centre on Censorship. Publications: Dubcek, 1970; Crime and Compromise, 1974; Sideshow: Kissinger, Nixon and the Destruction of Cambodia, 1979; The Quality of Mercy: Cambodia, Holocaust and Modern Memory, 1984; The Shah's Last Ride, 1989; Kowtow: A Plea on Behalf of Hong Kong, 1989; Murdoch, 1992; Cambodia's New Deal, 1994. Address: Friston Place, East Dean, East Sussex, BN20 OAH, England.

SHEARER Jill, b. 14 Apr 1936, Melbourne, Victoria, Australia. Playwright. Publications: The Trouble with Gillian, 1974; The Foreman, 1976; The Boat, 1977; The Kite, 1977; Nocturne, 1977; Catherine, 1978; Stephen, 1980; Release Lavinia Stannard, 1980; A Woman Like That, 1986; Shimada, 1987; Comrade, 1987; The Family, 1994. Honours: Australia Council Grant, 1987; Arts Queensland Fellowship, 1993. Address: c/o Playlab Press, PO Box 185, Ashgrove, Brisbane 4060, Queensland, Australia.

SHEEHAN Neil, b. 27 Oct 1936, Holyoke, Massachusetts, USA. Writer. m. Susan Margulies, 30 Mar 1965, 2 daughters. Education: AB cum laude, Harvard University, 1958. Appointments: Vietnam Bureau, United Press International, Saigon, 1962-64; Reporter, New York Times, 1964-72. Publications: The Arnheiter Affair, 1972; A Bright Shining Lie: John Paul Vann and America in Vietnam, 1988; After the War Was Over: Hanoi and Saigon, 1992. Contributions to: Newspapers and journals. Honours: 1st Annual Drew Pearson Award, 1971; Honorary LittD, Columbia College, Chicago, 1972; Sidney Hillman Foundation Awards, 1972, 1988; Columbia Journalism Awards, 1972, 1989; Guggenheim Fellowship, 1973-74; Adlai Stevenson Fellow, 1973-75; Lehrman Institute Fellow, 1975-76; Rockefeller Foundation Fellow, 1976-77; Woodrow Wilson International Center for Scholars Fellow, 1979-80; National Book Award, 1988; Pulitzer Prize for General Non-Fiction, 1989; Robert F Kennedy Book Award, 1989; Ambassador Award, English Speaking Union, 1989; John F Kennedy Award, 1989; Honorary LHD, American INternational College, 1990, University of Lowell, 1991; Literary Lion, New York Public Library, 1992. Memberships: Society of American Historians; American Academy of Achievement. Address: 4505 Klingle Street North West, Washington, DC 20016, USA.

SHEEHY Gail, b. 27 Nov 1937, Mamaroneck, New York, USA. Journalist; Editor; Writer. m. (1) Albert Sheehy, 20 Aug 1960, div, 1 daughter, (2) Clay Felker, 1985, 1 adopted daughter. Education: BA, University of Vermont; Columbia University. Contributions to: Periodicals. Honours: Front Page Awards, Newswoman's Club of America, 1964, 1973; National Magazine Award, 1972; Anisfield-Wolf Book Award, 1986. Memberships: Authors Guild; Authors League of America; Common Cause; National Organization for Women; Newswoman's Club of New York; PEN American Center. Address: c/o

William Morrow Publishing, 1350 Avenue of the Americas, New York, NY 10019, USA.

SHELBOURNE Cecily. See: **EBEL Suzanne.**

SHELBY Graham, b. 1940, England. Writer. Publications: The Knights of Dark Renown, 1969; The Kings of Vain Intent, 1970; The Villains of the Piece, 1972; The Devil is Loose, 1973; The Wolf at the Door, 1975; The Cannaways, 1978; The Cannaway Concern, 1980; The Edge of the Blade, 1986; Demand the World, 1990. Address: c/o A P Watt Ltd, 20 John Street, London WC1N 2DR, England.

SHELDON John. See: **BLOCH Robert.**

SHELDON Lee. See: **LEE Wayne C.**

SHELDON Roy. See: **TUBB E(dwin) C(harles).**

SHELDON Sidney, b. 11 Feb 1917, Chicago, Illinois, USA. Author; Screenwriter; Playwright. m. (1) Jorja Curtright, 1951, dec 1985, (2) Alexandra Kostoff, 1989. Education: Northwestern University. Appointments: Television Show Creator, Producer and Writer, 1963-; Creator, Writer, Producer, I Dream of Jeannie (TV show); Creator, Hart to Hart (TV show). Publications: The Merry Widow (operetta) (adaptor with Ben Roberts), 1943; Jackpot, 1944; Deam with Music, 1944; Alice in Arms, 1945; The Bachelor and the Bobby-Soxer (screenplay), 1947; Easter Parade (screenplay) (with Albert Hackett and Frances Goodrich), 1948; Annie Get Your Gun (screenplay), 1950; Rich, Young and Pretty (screenplay), 1951; Dream Wife, 1953; Anything Goes (screenplay), 1956; Never Too Young, 1956; The Buster Keaton Story (screenplay), 1957; Redhead, 1959; Roman Candle, 1960; Billy Rose's Jumbo (screenplay), 1962. Novels: The Naked Face, 1970; The Other Side of Midnight, 1974; Bloodline, 1977; Rage of Angels, 1980; The Master of the Game, 1982; If Tomorrow Comes, 1985; Windmills of the Gods, 1986; The Sands of Time, 1988; Memories of Midnight, 1990; The Doomsday Conspiracy, 1991; The Stars Shine Down, 1992; Nothing Lasts Forever, 1994; Morning, Noon and Night, 1995. Honours: Academy Award, 1947; Screen Award, Writers Guild of America, 1948, 1950, 1959. Address: c/o Press Relations, William Morrow & Co, 1350 Avenue of the Americas, New York, NY 10019, USA.

SHELTON Mark Logan, b. 19 May 1958, Chicago, Illinois, USA. Writer. m. Eve Shelnutt, 29 May 1982. Education: AB, Western Michigan University, 1980; MFA, University of Pittsburgh, 1982. Publications: Working in a Very Small Place, 1989; The Next Great Thing: The Sun, the Stirling Engine and the Drive to Change the World, 1994. Contributions to: Newspapers and journals. Honours: Best Sports Stories, Sport News; 12 Sigma Delta Chi Awards. Membership: Judge, Ohioana Library Association Book Awards, 1990-. Address: 25 Andover Street, Worcester, MA 01606, USA.

SHEPARD Sam. See: **ROGERS Samuel Shepard.**

SHEPHERD Michael. See: **LUDLUM Robert.**

SHEPHERD Robert James, b. 14 Feb 1949, Solihull, Warwickshire, England. Author; Journalist; TV Producer; Director. Education: BA, MA, 1968-72, University of Kent. Appointments: Leader and Features Writer, Investors Chronicle, 1983; Editorial Team, Producer, A Week in Politics, 1983-88; Parliamentary Lobby Correspondent, 1984-87; Producer, documentaries. Publications: Public Opinion and European Integration, 1975; A Class Divided, 1988; Ireland's Fate, 1990; The Power Brokers, 1991; Iain Macleod, 1994. Contributions to: Political Quarterly; New Statesman; Investors Chronicle; Marxism Today; Guardian; The Times; The Irish Independent; The Sunday Press; Ireland of the Welcomes. Honours: Prix Stendhal (television), 1993; Reuter Fellowship, Oxford University, 1995. Memberships: Society of Authors; International PEN; National Union of Journalists; BECTU. Address: c/o Curtis Brown Ltd, Haymarket House, 28-29 Haymarket, London SW1Y 4SP, England.

SHEPPARD Right Reverend David (Stuart), b. 6 Mar 1929, Reigate, Surrey, England. Bishop. m. Grace Isaac, 19 June 1957, 1 d. Education: MA, Trinity Hall, Cambridge. Publications: Parson's Pitch, 1964; Built as a City, 1974; Bias to the Poor, 1983; Better Together (with Archbishop Derek Worlock), 1988; With Christ in the Wilderness (with Archbishop Derek Worlock), 1990; With Hope in Our Hearts (with Archbishop Derek Worlock), 1994. Contributions to: Various publications. Honours: Honorary LLD, Liverpool University, 1981; Honorary DTech, Liverpool Polytechnic, 1987; Hon DD, Cambridge University; Freeman of the City of Liverpool. Memberships: Chairman, Church of England Board for Social Resposibilty, 1991-96. Address: Bishop's Lodge, Woolton Park, Liverpool L25 6DT, England.

SHER Antony, b. 14 June 1949, South Africa. Actor; Writer; Artist. Education: Webber-Douglas Academy of Dramatic Art, London, 1969-71. Appointments: Repertory seasons at Nottingham, Edinburgh and Liverpool; Actor, National Theatre, London, in plays by Brecht and Chekov; Associate Artist, Royal Shakespeare Company, 1982-; Appearances in films and on television. Publications: Year of the King, 1985; Middlepost (novel), 1988; Characters (paintings and drawings), 1989; Changing Step (TV film script), 1989; The Indoor Boy (novel), 1991; Cheap Lives (novel), 1995. Honours: Best Actor Award, Drama Magazine, 1984; Olivier Award, London Evening Standard, 1985. Address: c/o Hope and Lyne, 108 Leonard Street, London EC2A 4RH, England.

SHER Steven Jay, b. 28 Sept 1949, USA. Writer; Poet. m. Nancy Green, 11 Mar 1978, 1 son, 1 daughter. Education: BA, City College of the City University of New York, 1970; MA, University of Iowa, 1972; MFA, Brooklyn College of the City University of New York, 1978. Appointments: Director, Creative Writing, Spalding University, 1979-81, Oregon State University, 1981-86, University of North Carolina at Wilmington, 1986-89; Visiting Writer, Western Oregon State College, 1991-95, Willamette University, 1993. Publications: Nickelodeon, 1978; Persnickety, 1979; Caught in the Revolving Door, 1980; Trolley Lives, 1985; The Man With a Thousand Eyes and Other Stories, 1989; Traveler's Advisory, 1994; Co-Editor: Northwest Variety: Personal Essays by 14 Regional Authors, 1987. Contributions to: Anthologies and periodicals. Honours: All Nations Poetry Contest, 1977; Weymouth Centre Residency, 1988; North Carolina Writers Network Writers and Readers Series Competition, 1989; Oregon Book Awards Finalist in Poetry, 1994. Memberships: Academy of American Poets; Associated Writing Programs; Poetry Society of America; Poets and Writers; Willamette Literary Guild, President. Address: 3930 North West Witham Hill Drive, No 133, Corvallis, OR 97330, USA.

SHERATON Mimi, b. 10 Feb 1926, Brooklyn, New York, USA. Food Critic; Writer. m. (1) William Sheraton, 10 Aug 1945, div 1954, (2) Richard Falcone, 30 July 1955, 1 son. Education: BS, New York University, 1947. Appointments: Managing Editor, Supplemental Division, House Beautiful, New York City, 1954-56; Food Critic, New York Magazine, 1967-75, New York Times, 1975-83, Time Magazine, 1984; Publisher, Mimi Sheraton's Taste Newsletter, 1987-90; Food Editor, Condé Nast Traveler, 1987-91; Contributing Editor, Harper's Bazaar, 1993-95, New Woman, 1994-. Publications: The Seducer's Cookbook, 1962; City Portraits, 1963; The German Cookbook, 1965; Visions of Sugar Plums, 1968; From My Mother's Kitchen, 1979, new edition, 1991; Mimi Sheraton's New York Times Guide to New Restaurants, 1983; Is Salami and Eggs Better Than Sex? (with Alan King), 1985; Mimi Sheraton's Favorite New York Restaurants, 1986, new edition, 1989; The Whole World Loves Chicken Soup, 1995. Contributions to: Magazines. Honours: Penney Missouri Award, University of Missouri at Columbia, 1974; Front Page Award, Newswomen's Club of New York, 1977. Address: c/o William Morris Agency, 1350 Avenue of the Americas, New York, NY 10019, USA.

SHERMAN Eileen Bluestone, b. 15 May 1951, Atlantic City, New Jersey, USA. Author; Playwright; Lyricist. m. Neal Jonathan Sherman, 10 June 1973, 1 son, 1 daughter. Education: BA, Finch College, New York, 1973; MA, State University of New York at Albany, 1976. Publications: The Odd Potato, 1984; Monday in Odessa, 1986; Independence Avenue, 1990. Others: Musical plays; The Magic Door (television series), 1987-90. Honours: Outstanding Social Studies Trade Book Award, 1986; National Jewish Book Award for Children's Literature, 1986; Emmy Awards, 1988, 1989; Teacher's Choice Award, 1991. Memberships: Authors Guild; Dramatists Guild; National League of American PEN Women; Society of Children's Book Writers. Address: 5049 Wornall Road, Kansas City, MO, USA.

SHERMAN William David, b. 24 Dec 1940, Philadelphia, Pennsylvania, USA. Poet; Writer. m. Barbara Beaumont, 22 July 1970, div 1978. Education: AB, Temple University, 1962; MA, 1964, PhD, 1968, State University of New York at Buffalo; Dickinson School of Law, 1974-75. Appointments: Teacher, Instructor, and Lecturer in USA and England; Editor; Publisher; Poetry readings. Publications: The Landscape of Contemporary Cinema (with Leon Lewis), 1967; The

Cinema of Orson Welles, 1967; The Springbok (poems), 1973; The Hard Sidewalk (poems), 1974; The Horses of Gwyddno Garanhir (poems), 1976; Mermaids, I, 1977, revised edition, 1985, and II, 1985 (poems); Heart Attack and Spanish Songs in Mandaine Land (poems), 1981; Duchamp's Door (poems), 1983; She Wants to Go to Pago-Pago, 1986; The Tahitian Journals, 1990; A Tale for Tusitala, 1993. Contributions to: Anthologies; Numerous poems, articles and reviews in periodicals. Address: 4805 B Street, Philadelphia, PA 19120, USA.

SHERRIN Ned (Edward George Sherrin), b. 18 Feb 1931, Low Ham, Somerset, England. Director; Producer; Writer. Education: MA, Oxford University; Barrister-at-Law. Publications: Cindy-Ella (with Caryl Brahms), 1962; Rappel (with Caryl Brahms), 1964; Benbow Was His Name (with Caryl Brahms), 1967; Ooh La (with Caryl Brahms), 1973; After You Mr Feydeau (with Caryl Brahms), 1975; A Small Thing Like an Earthquake, 1983; Song by Song (with Caryl Brahms), 1984; Cutting Edge, 1984; 1956 and All That (with Neil Shand), 1984; The Metropolitan Mikado (with Alistair Beaton), 1985; Too Dirty for the Windmill (with Caryl Brahms), 1986; Loose Neds, 1990; Theatrical Anecdotes, 1991; Ned Sherrin in His Anecdotage, 1993; The Oxford Dictionary of Humorous Quotations, 1995; Sherrin's Year, diary, 1996; Scratch an Actor, novel, 1996. Address: c/o Scott Ferris Associates, 15 Gledhow Gardens, London SW5 0AY, England.

SHERRY (Michael) Norman, b. 6 July 1935, Tirana, Albania. Writer; Professor of Literature. Education: BA, English Literature, University of Durham, England; PhD, University of Singapore, 1963. Appointments: Lecturer in English Literature, University of Singapore, 1961-66; Lecturer, Senior Lecturer, University of Liverpool, England, 1966-70; Professor of English, University of Lancaster, 1970-82; Fellow, Humanities Research Center, North Carolina, USA, 1982; Mitchell Distinguished Professor of Literature, Trinity University, San Antonio, Texas, 1983-. Publications: Conrad's Eastern World, 1966; Jane Austen, 1966; Charlotte and Emily Brontë, 1969; Conrad's Western World, 1971; Conrad and His World, 1972; Conrad: The Critical Heritage, 1973; Conrad in Conference, 1976; The Life of Graham Greene, Vol 1 1904-39, 1989, Vol 2 1939-55, 1994. Editor: An Outpost of Progress and Heart of Darkness, 1973; Lord Jim, 1974; Nostromo, 1974; The Secret Agent, 1974; The Nigger of the Narcissus, Typhoon, Falk and Other Stories, 1975; Joseph Conrad: A commemoration, 1976. Contributions to: Academic American Encyclopedia; Guardian; Daily Telegraph; Oxford Magazine; Modern Language Review; Review of English Studies; Notes and Queries; BBC; Times Literary Supplement; Observer. Honours: Fellow, Royal Society of Literature, 1986; Edgar Allan Poe Award, 1989; Guggenheim Fellowship, 1989-90. Memberships: Savile. Address: Trinity University, 715 Stadium Drive, San Antonio, TX 78212, USA.

SHERWIN Byron L(ee), b. 18 Feb 1946, New York, New York, USA. Professor; Author. m. Judith Rita Schwartz, 24 Dec 1972, 1 son. Education: BS, Columbia University; BHL, 1966, MHL, 1968, Rabbi, 1970, Jewish Theological Seminary; MA, New York University, 1969; PhD, University of Chicago, 1978. Appointments: Assistant Professor, 1970-74, Associate Professor, 1974-78, Professor of Jewish Philosophy and Mysticism, 1978-, Vice-President for Academic Affairs, 1984-, Spertus College of Judaica, Chicago; Visiting Professor, Mundelein College, 1974-82; Director, Holocaust Studies Project, National Endowment for the Humanities, 1976-78. Publications: Judaism: The Way of Sanctification (with Samuel H Dresner), 1978; Abraham Joshua Heschel, 1979; Encountering the Holocaust: An Interdisciplinary Survey (editor with Susan G Ament), 1979; Garden of the Generations, 1981; Jerzy Kosinski: Literary Alarmclock, 1982; Mystical Theology and Social Dissent: The Life and Works of Judah Loew of Prague, 1982; The Golem Legend: Origins and Implications, 1985; Contexts and Content: Higher Jewish Education in the United States, 1987; Thank God: Prayers of Jesus and Christians Together, 1989; In Partnership with God: Contemporary Jewish Law and Ethics, 1990; No Religion Is an Island (with Harold Kasimov), 1991; Towards a Jewish Theology, 1992; How to Be a Jew: Ethical Teaching of Judaism (with Seymour J Cohen), 1992; The Spiritual Heritage of Polish Jews, 1995; Sparks Amongst the Ashes: The Spiritual Legacy of Polish Jewry, 1997. Contributions to: Professional journals. Honours: Man of Reconciliation Award, Polish Council of Christians and Jews, 1992; Presidential Medal, Officer of the Order of Merit, Republic of Poland, 1995; Doctor of Hebrew Letters, honoris causa, Jewish Theological Seminary of America, 1996. Memberships: American Academy of Religion; American Association of University Professors; Rabbinical Assembly of America; American Philosophical

Association; Society for Business Ethics. Address: 6702 North Sheridan Road, Chicago, IL 60626, USA.

SHIELDS Carol Ann, b. 2 June 1935, Oak Park, Illinois, USA (Canadian citizen, 1974). Professor; Author; Poet. m. Donald Hugh Shields, 20 July 1957, 1 son, 4 daughters. Education: BA, Hanover College, 1957; MA, University of Ottawa, 1975. Appointments: Editorial Assistant, Canadian Slavonic Papers, Ottawa, 1972-74; Lecturer, University of Ottawa, 1976-77, University of British Columbia, 1978-90; Professor, University of Manitoba, 1980-; The Canada Council, 1994-. Publications: Fiction: Small Ceremonies, 1976; The Box Garden, 1977; Happenstance, 1980; A Fairly Conventional Woman, 1982; Various Miracles (short stories), 1985; Swann: A Mystery, 1987; The Orange Fish (short stories), 1989; A Celibate Season (with Blanche Howard), 1991; The Republic of Love, 1992; The Stone Diaries, 1993. Poetry: Others, 1972; Intersect, 1974; Coming to Canada, 1992. Plays: Women Waiting, 1983; Departures and Arrivals, 1984; Thirteen Hands, 1993; Fashion Power Guilt (with Catherine Shields), 1995. Honours: Canada Council Grants, 1973, 1976, 1978, 1986; Canadian Authors Association Fiction Prize, 1976; Canadian Broadcasting Corporation Prizes, 1983, 1984; National Magazine Award, 1985; Arthur Ellis Award, 1987; Governor-General's Award, 1993; National Book Critics Circle Award, 1994, 1995; Pulitzer Prize in Fiction, 1995; Honorary Doctorates, Universities of Ottawa, Winnipeg, Hanover College, British Columbia, 1995; Lire Magazine Book of the Year, France, 1995. Memberships: Jane Austen Society; PEN; Writers Guild of Manitoba; Writers Union of Canada; Canada Council. Address: 701-237 Wellington Crescent, Winnipeg, Manitoba R3M 0A1, Canada.

SHIPLER David K(arr), b. 3 Dec 1942, Orange, New Jersey, USA. Journalist; Correspondent; Writer. m. Deborah S Isaacs, 17 Sept 1966, 2 sons, 1 daughter. Education: AB, Dartmouth College, 1964. Appointments: News Clerk, 1966-67, News Summary Writer, 1967-68, Reporter, 1968-73, Foreign Correspondent, Saigon, 1973-75, and Moscow, 1975-, Bureau Chief, Moscow, 1977-79, and Jerusalem, 1979-84, Correspondent, Washington, DC, 1985-87, Chief Diplomatic Correspondent, 1987-88, The New York Times; Guest Scholar, Brookings Institution, 1984-85; Senior Associate, Carnegie Endowment for International Peace, 1988-90; Adjunct Professor, School of International Service, American University, Washington, DC, 1990; Ferris Professor of Journalism and Public Affairs, 1990-91, Woodrow Wilson Visiting Fellow, 1990-, Princeton University. Publications: Russia: Broken Idols, Solemn Dreams, 1983; Arab and Jew: Wounded Spirits in a Promised Land, 1986. Contributions to: Newspapers and journals. Honours: Distinguished Reporting Award, Society of Silurians, 1971; Distinguished Public Affairs Reporting Award, American Political Science Association, 1971; Co-Winner, George Polk Award, 1982; Pulitzer Prize for General Non-Fiction, 1987; Alfred DuPont-Columbia University Award for Broadcast Journalism, 1990. Membership: Human Rights Watch, Middle East. Address: 4005 Thornapple Street, Chevy Chase, MD 20815, USA.

SHOR Ira Neil, b. 2 June 1945, New York, New York, USA. Professor of English; Writer. Education: BA, 1966, MA, 1968, University of Michigan; PhD, University of Wisconsin, 1971. Appointment: Professor of English, City University of New York. Publications: A Pedagogy for Liberation, 1986; Freire for the Classroom, 1987; Critical Teaching and Everyday Life, 1987; Culture Wars: School and Society in the Conservative Restoration, 1969-91, 1992; Empowering Education, 1992; When Students Have Power: Negotiating Authority in a Critical Pedagogy, 1996. Contributions to: Professional journals. Honours: Fellowships, 1966, 1982, 1983; Chancellor's Scholar, City University of New York, 1985. Address: c/o English Doctoral Program, City University of New York, 33 West 42nd Street, New York, NY 10036, USA.

SHORT Brian Michael, b. 27 Feb 1944, Canterbury, Kent, England. University Senior Lecturer. m. (1) 2 sons, (2) Valerie, 17 Dec 1979, 1 son. Education: North Western Polytechnic, 1963-73. Publications: The South East From AD100; The English Rural Community. Contributions to: Professional journals. Honours: Fellow, Royal Society of Arts; Fellow, Royal Geographical Society. Memberships: Agricultural History Society; Sussex Archeaological Society. Address: CCS, University of Sussex, Falmer, Brighton BN1 9QW, England.

SHREEVE James Marion, b. 26 Feb 1951, Ohio, USA. Writer. m. Christine Kuethe, 8 June 1985, 1 daughter, 1 stepson, 1 stepdaughter. Education: BA, Brown University, 1973; MFA, University

of Iowa, 1979. Publications: The Sex Token, 1976; Nature: The Other Earthlings, 1987; Lucy's Child (co-author), 1989. Contributions to: Discover; MD; Science, Science Illustrated. Address: 10549 St Paul Street, Kensington, MD 20895, USA.

SHRIMSLEY Bernard, b. 13 Jan 1931, London, England. Newspaper Editor. m. Norma Jessie Alexandra Porter, 1952, 1 daughter. Education: England. Appointments: Assistant Editor, Daily Mirror, London, 1964-68; Editor, Liverpool Daily Post, 1968-69, The News of the World, London, 1975-80; Deputy Editor, 1969-72, Editor, 1972-75, The Sun, London; Editor-designate/Editor, The Mail on Sunday, London, 1980-82; Associate Editor, Daily Express, London, 1983-96; Judge, British Press Awards, 1989-96. Publications: The Candidates, 1968; Lion Rampant, 1984. Contributions to: Newspapers and journals. Memberships: British Press Council, Vice-Chairman, 1989-90; Society of Authors. Address: c/o Daily Express, Ludgate House, 245 Blackfriars Road, London SE1 9UX, England.

SHUBIN Seymour, b. 14 Sept 1921, Philadelphia, Pennsylvania, USA. Author. m. Gloria Amet, 27 Aug 1957, 1 son, 1 daughter. Education: BS, Temple University. Appointments: Managing Editor, Official Detective Stories Magazine, Psychiatric Reporter. Publications: Anyone's My Name, 1953; Manta, 1958; Wellville, USA, 1961; The Captain, 1982; Holy Secrets, 1984; Voices, 1985; Never Quite Dead, 1989; Remember Me Always, 1994. Contributions to: Saturday Evening Post; Reader's Digest; Redbook; Family Circle; Story; Ellery Queen's Mystery Magazine; Emergency Medicine; Official Detective Stories Magazine; Perspective in Biology and Medicine. Honours: Edgar Allan Poe, Special Award; Special Citation for Fiction, Athenaeum of Philadelphia; Certificate of Honor, Temple University. Memberships: American Society of Authors and Journalists; Authors Guild; Mystery Writers of America; PEN, American Center. Address: 122 Harrogate Road, Wynnewood, PA 19096, USA.

SHUKMAN Harold, b. 23 Mar 1931, London, England. Lecturer in Modern Russian History; Writer. m. (1) Ann King Farlow, 1956, div 1970, 2 sons, 1 daughter, (2) Barbara King Farlow. Education: BA Hons, University of Nottingham, 1956; MA, 1961, DPhil, 1961, Oxford University. Appointments: Fellow, 1961-, Lecturer in Modern Russian History, 1969-, St Antony's College, Oxford. Publications: Lenin and the Russian Revolution, 1977; Blackwells Encyclopedia of the Russian Revolution (editor), 1988; Andrei Gromyko: Memories (editor and translator), 1989; Stalin: Triumph and Tragedy (editor and translator), 1991; Lenin: His Life and Legacy (editor and translator), 1994; Trotsky: Eternal Revolutionary (editor and translator), 1996; Rasputin, 1997; Seven Leaders: From Lenin to Gorbachev (editor and translator), 1998. Contributions to: Professional journals and general periodicals. Memberships: Authors Society; Royal Historical Society, Fellow; Translators Association. Address: St Antony's College, Oxford OX2 6JF, England.

SHUMSKY Zena. See: **COLLIER Zena**.

SHUPE Anson (David Jr), b. 21 Jan 1948, Buffalo, New York, USA. Sociology Professor. m. Janet Ann Klickua, 27 June 1970, 1 son, 1 daughter. Education: BA, College of Wooster, Ohio, 1970; MA, 1972, PhD, 1975, Indiana University. Publications: Moonies in America, 1979; The New Vigilantes, 1980; Strange Gods, 1981; The Family Secret, 1983; The Mormon Corporate Empire, 1985; The Darker Side of Virtue, 1991; In the Name of All That's Holy: A Theory of Clergy Malfeasance, 1995. Co-Editor: The Politics of Religion and Social Change; Secularization and Fundamentalism Reconsidered; The Violent Couple, 1994. Contributions to: Newspapers and magazines. Memberships: American Sociological Association; Association for the Sociology of Religion; Society for the Scientific Study of Religion; Religious Research Association. Address: Sociology and Anthropology Department, Indiana University-Purdue University, Fort Wayne, IN 46805, USA.

SHUSTERMAN Richard M(ark), b. 3 Dec 1949, Philadelphia, Pennsylvania, USA. Professor of Philosophy; Writer. m. Rivka Nahmani, 16 Aug 1970, div 1986, 2 sons, 1 daughter. Education: BA magna cum laude, 1971, MA magna cum laude, 1973, Hebrew University of Jerusalem; DPhil, St John's College, Oxford, 1979. Appointments: Lecturer, Bezalael Academy of Art, 1980-81; Visiting Lecturer, Hebrew University of Jerusalem, 1980-82; Lecturer, 1980-82, Senior Lecturer in English and Philosophy, 1983-87, Ben-Gurion University of the Negev, Beersheba, Israel; Visiting Fellow, St John's College, Oxford, 1984-85; Visiting Associate Professor, 1985-87,

Associate Professor of Philosophy, 1987-91, Full Professor, 1992, Temple University, Philadelphia; Director of Studies, École des Hautes Études en Sciences Sociales, 1990; Visiting Professor, 1990, Director of Studies, 1995-, College International de Philosophie, 1990. Publications: The Object of Literary Criticism, 1984; Sources for the Study of Philosophy in High School, Vol V: Aesthetics, 1989; The Interpretive Turn: Philosophy, Science, Culture (editor with D Hiley and J Bohman), 1991; Pragmatist Aesthetics: Living Beauty, Rethinking Art, 1992; L'Art á L'Etat Vif, 1992; Kunst Leben, 1994; Sons l'interprétation, 1994; Practicing Philosophy: Pragmatism and the Philosophical Life. Contributions to: Books and journals. Honours: American Council of Learned Societies Grant, 1988; National Endowment for the Humanities Grant, 1988, Fellowship, 1990; Fulbright. Memberships: American Philosophical Association; American Society for Aesthetics. Address: 339 West 19th Street, New York, NY 10011, USA.

SHUTTLE Penelope Diane, b. 12 May 1947, Staines, Middlesex, England. Writer. m. Peter Redgrove, 16 Sept 1980, 1 daughter. Publications: Novels: An Excusable Vengeance, 1967; All the Usual Hours of Sleeping, 1969; Wailing Monkey Embracing a Tree, 1974; The Terrors of Dr Treviles (with Peter Redgrove), 1974; The Glass Cottage, 1976; Rainsplitter in the Zodiac Garden, 1976; The Mirror of the Giant, 1979. Poetry: The Hermaphrodite Album (with Peter Redgrove), 1973; The Orchard Upstairs, 1980; The Child-Stealer, 1983; The Lion From Rio, 1986; Adventures With My Horse, 1988; Taxing the Rain, 1992. Psychology and sociology: The Wise Wound: Menstruation and Everywoman (with Peter Redgrove) 1978, 4th edition, revised, 1990; Alchemy For Women (with Peter Redgrove), 1995; Building a City for Jamie, poems, 1996. Numerous pamphlet collections, broadsheets, radio dramas, recordings, readings and television features. Contributions to: Various publications. Honours: Arts Council Awards, 1969, 1972, 1985; Greenwood Poetry Prize, 1972; E C Gregory Award, 1974. Address: c/o David Higham Associates Ltd, 5-8 Lower John Street, London W1R 4HA, England.

SIATOPOULOS Dimitrios, b. 1 Apr 1917, Athens, Greece. Attorney-at-Law; Journalist; Writer. m. 27 Dec 1947, 1 son, 1 daughter. Education: Law degree, 1944, Science of Political Economics degree, University of Athens. Publications: Over 35 books, including historical and biographical volumes, 1954-95. Contributions to: Newspapers and magazines. Honours: National Prize for Young Writers, 1954; 1st Prize, Academy of Athens, 1971; 1st National Prize for Literature, 1978. Memberships: International Association for Literature Critics, president, Greek Section; Various Greek literary organisations. Address: 20 Omirou Street, 106 72 Athens, Greece.

SIDDONS Anne Rivers, b. 9 Jan 1936, Atlanta, Georgia, USA. Writer. m. Heyward L Siddons, 11 June 1966, 4 sons. Education: BAA, Auburn University, 1958. Publications: John Chancellor Makes Me Cry, 1975; Heartbreak Hotel, 1976; The House Next Door, 1978; Homeplace, 1986; Peachtree Road, 1988; King's Oak, 1990; Outer Banks, 1991; Colony, 1992; Hill Towns, 1993; Downtown, 1994; Fault Lines, 1995; Up Island, 1997. Contributions to: Magazines. Honours: Georgia Author of the Year Award, 1988; Honorary Doctor of Letters, 1992; Honorary Doctor of Letters, 1997. Memberships: Authors Guild; International Womans Forum; Woodward Academy, Dalethorpe University. Address: 3767 Vermont Road North East, Atlanta, GA 30319, USA.

SIEPMANN Mary Aline, (Mary Wesley), b. 24 June 1912. Writer. m. (1) 2nd Baron Swinfen, 1937, div 1945, 2 sons, (2) Eric Siepmann, 1952 dec 1970, 1 son. Education: London School of Economics and Political Science. Publications: Speaking Terms (for children), 1968; The Sixth Seal (for children), 1968; Haphazard House (for children), 1983; Jumping the Queue, 1983; The Camomile Lawn, 1984; Harnessing Peacocks, 1985; The Vacillations of Poppy Carew, 1986; Not That Sort of Girl, 1987; Second Fiddle, 1988; A Sensible Life, 1990; A Dubious Legacy, 1992; An Imaginative Experience, 1994. Honours: Honorary Degrees, Open University, University of Exeter; Fellow, London School of Economics and Political Science; Commander of the Order of the British Empire, 1995. Membership: PEN. Address: c/o Transworld Publishers Ltd, London W5 5SA, England.

SIGAL Clancy, b. 6 Sept 1926, Chicago, Illinois, USA. Writer. Education: BA, University of California at Los Angeles, 1950. Publications: Weekend in Diplock, 1960; Going Away; A Report, A

Memoir, 1963; Zone of the Interior, 1976. Address: c/o Jonathon Cape, 30 Bedford Square, London WC1B 3EL, England.

SIGGINS Maggie, b. Toronto, Ontario, Canada. Appointments: Former Magazine Writer; Political Columnist; Television Producer; Journalism Professor; Writer. Publications: Basset: A Biography, 1979; Brian and the Boys: A Story of Gang Rape, 1984; A Canadian Tragedy: JoAnn and Colin Thatcher, 1985; Revenge of the Land, 1991. Honours: Southam Fellowship, 1974-75; Max Bell Chair in Journalism, 1983-84; Arthur Ellis Award, Crime Writers of Canada, 1986; Governor-General's Award for Non-Fiction, 1992. Address: 2831 Retallack Street, Regina, Saskatchewan S4S 1S8, Canada.

SILKIN Jon, b. 2 Dec 1930, London, England. Poet; Critic; Editor; Professor of English and American Literature. m. Lorna Tracy, div, 3 sons, 1 dec, 1 daughter. Education: BA Honours, English, University of Leeds, 1962. Appointments: Tutor, Writers Workshop, University of Iowa, 1968, 1969, 1991, Creative Writing, College of Idaho, 1978; Visiting Lecturer, University of Sydney, 1974; Visiting Poet, University of Notre Dame, 1985, University of North Alabama, 1987; Distinguished Writer-in-Residence, American University, 1989; Literary Fellow, Dumfries and Galloway Arts Association, 1990; Professor of English and American Literature, University of Tsukuba, 1991-. Publications: The Peaceable Kingdom, 1954, 2nd edition, 1975; The Two Freedoms, 1958; The Reordering of the Stones, 1961; Nature with Man, 1965; Poems New and Selected, 1966; Amana Grass, 1971; Out of Battle: Criticism of Poets of World War I, 1972, 2nd edition, 1987; Poetry of the Committed Individual (anthology), 1973; The Principal of Water, 1974; The Little Time-Keeper, 1976; The Penguin Book of First World War Poetry (editor), 1979; The Psalms with Their Spoils, 1980; Selected Poems, 1980, enlarged edition, 1988; Gurney (verse play), 1985; The War Poems of Wilfred Owen (editor), 1985, 2nd edition, 1994; The Ship's Pasture, 1986; The Penguin Book of First World War Prose (editor with Jon Glover), 1989; The Lens-Breakers, 1992; Selected Poems, 1994; The Life of Metrical and Free Verse in Twentieth Century Poetry, 1996. Contributions to: Various publications. Honours: Gregory Fellowship in Poetry, University of Leeds, 1958; Geoffrey Faber in Poetry, University of Leeds, 1958; Geoffrey Faber Memorial Prize, 1966. Membership: Royal Society of Literature, fellow. Address: 13 Queens Terrace, Newcastle upon Tyne NE2 2PJ, England.

SILKO Leslie Marmon, b. 1948, Albuquerque, New Mexico, USA. Professor of English; Writer; Poet. 2 sons. Education: BA in English, University of New Mexico, 1969. Appointments: Teacher, University of New Mexico; Professor of English, University of Arizona at Tucson, 1978-. Publications: Fiction: Cremony, 1977; Almanac of the Dead, 1991; Yellow Woman, 1993. Poetry: Laguna Woman, 1974; Storyteller, 1981. Other: The Delicacy and Strength of Lace: Letters Between Leslie Marmon Silko and James A Wright, 1986; Sacred Water: Narratives and Pictures, 1993. Honours: National Endowment for the Arts Grant, 1974; Chicago Review Award, 1974; Pushcart Prize, 1977; John D and Catharine T MacArthur Foundation Fellowship, 1983. Address: c/o Department of English, University of Arizona at Tucson, Tucson, AZ 85721, USA.

SILLIMAN Ron(ald Glenn), b. 8 May 1946, Pasco, Washington, USA. Editor; Poet. m. (1) Rochelle Nameroff, 1965, div 1972, (2) Krishna Evans, 1986, 2 sons. Education: Merritt College, 1965, 1969-72; San Francisco State College, 1966-69; University of California at Berkeley, 1969-71. Appointments: Editor, Tottel's, 1970-81; Director of Research and Education, Committee for Prisoner Humanity and Justice, San Rafael, California, 1972-76; Project Manager, Tenderloin Ethnographic Research Project, San Francisco, 1977-78; Director of Outreach, Central City Hospitality House, San Francisco, 1979-81; Lecturer, San Francisco University, 1981; Visiting Lecturer, University of California at San Diego, La Jolla, 1982; Writer-in-Residence, New College of California, San Francisco, 1982; Director of Public Relations and Development, 1982-86, Poet-in-Residence, 1983-90, California Institute of Integral Studies, San Francisco; Executive Editor, Socialist Review, 1986-89; Managing Editor, Computer Land, 1989-. Publications: Poetry: Moon in the Seventh House, 1968; Three Syntactic Fictions for Dennis Schmitz, 1969; Crow, 1971; Mohawk, 1973; Nox, 1974; Sitting Up, Standing Up, Taking Steps, 1978; Ketjak, 1978; Tjanting, 1981; Bart, 1982; ABC, 1983; Paradise, 1985; The Age of Huts, 1986; Lit, 1987; What, 1988; Manifest, 1990. Other: A Symposium on Clark Coolidge (editor), 1978; In the American Tree (editor), 1986; The New Sentence, 1987. Honours: Hart Crane and Alice Crane Williams Award, 1968; Joan Lee

Yang Awards, 1970, 1971; National Endowment for the Arts Fellowship, 1979; California Arts Council Grants, 1979, 1980; Poetry Center Book Award, 1985. Address: 1819 Curtis, Berkeley, CA 94702, USA.

SILLITOE Alan, b. 4 Mar 1928, Nottingham, England. Writer; Poet; Dramatist. m. Ruth Esther Fainlight, 19 Nov 1959, 1 son, 1 daughter (adopted). Education: Principally self-taught. Appointments: Writer, 1948-. Publications: Without Beer or Bread (poems), 1957; Saturday Night and Sunday Morning (novel), 1958, revised edition, 1968; The General (novel), 1960; The Rats and Other Poems, 1960; Key to the Door (novel), 1961; Road to Volgograd (travel), 1964; A Falling Out of Love and Other Poems, 1964; The Death of William Posters (novel), 1965; A Tree on Fire (novel), 1967; A Start in Life (novel), 1967; Shaman and Other Poems, 1968; Love in the Environs of Voronezh and Other Poems, 1968; Travel in Nihilon (novel), 1971; Raw Material (memoir), 1972; The Flame of Life(novel), 1974; Storm and Other Poems, 1974; Barbarians and Other Poems, 1974; Mountains and Caverns: Selected Essays, 1975; The Widower's Son (novel), 1976; The Storyteller (novel), 1979; The Lost Flying Boat (novel), 1983; Down from the Hill (novel), 1984; Sun Before Dearture (poems), 1984; Life Goes On (novel), 1985; Tides and Stone Walls (poems), 1986; Out of the Whirlpool (novel), 1987; The Open Door (novel), 1989; Lost Loves (novel), 1990; Leonard's War, 1991; Snowstop, 1993. Other: Short stories and plays. Honours: Author's Club Prize, 1958; Hawthornden Prize, 1960; Honorary Fellow, Manchester Polytechnic, 1977. Memberships: Royal Geographical Society, fellow; Savage Club; Society of Authors; Writers Action Group. Address: c/o Savage Club, 1 Whitehall Place, London SW1A 2HD, England.

SILLS Leslie Elka, b. 26 Jan 1948, Brooklyn, New York, USA. Artist; Author; Lecturer. m. Robert J Oresick, 9 July 1978, 1 son. Education: BA, Psycholgy, Boston University, 1969; MA, School of the Museum of Fine Arts, Boston, 1973. Publications: Inspirations: Pilgrims and Pioneers: New England Women in the Arts, 1987; Inspirations: Stories About Women Artists, 1989; Visions: Stories About Women Artists, 1994. Contributions to: Pilgrims and Pioneers: New England Women in the Arts, 1987; Magazines. Honours: 1 of 10 Best Books for Children Citation, Parenting Magazine, 1989; Pick of the Lists, American Bookseller, 1989, 1993; Recommended List, New York Public Library, 1989, 1993; Editor's Choice, Best Books, 1989, 1993; Notable Book Awards, American Library Association, 1989, 1994; Best Book Citation, School Library Journal, 1993. Memberships: National Women's Caucus for Art; New England Authors and Illustrators of Children's Books. Address: 38 St Paul Street, Brookline, MA 02146, USA.

SILLS-DOCHERTY Jonathon John, (John Docherty), b. 7 Jan 1941, Bowden, Cheshire, England. Humorous Writer; Lyricist; Poet. Education: Fielden Park College, West Didsbury, Manchester, 1977; Poetry Workshop, 1981, Extramural Department, 1986-87, University of Manchester. Appointments: Editor, Guardian Society, 1974; Reporter, Dun & Bradstreet, 1975; Proof Reader, sub-editor, biography compiler, Odd Fellow Magazine. Publications: A Walk Around the City & Other Groans, 1969, revised edition, 1973; Words on Paper, 1977; From Bottoms to Tops & Back Again, 1977, limited edition, 1987; Ballads of Ecstasy & Perspicacity, 1987; Ballads of North West John (plus cassette tape), 1987; tribute ballads to Nigel Mansell and Eddie 'The Eagle' Edwards, and other lyrics. Contributions to: Newspapers and magazines. Honours: North West Arts Poetry Award, 1978; Double prizewinner, Tribute for St George's Day, Granada TV, 1978. Memberships: Turner Society; Court School of Dancing; Independent Order of Odd Fellows; Friend, North West Arts, Manchester City Art Gallery; Authors North; Subscriber, Manchester Academy of Fine Arts. Address: 5 Farm Avenue, Stretford, Manchester M32 9TW, England.

SILMAN Roberta, b. 29 Dec 1934, Brooklyn, New York, USA. Writer. m. Robert Silman, 14 June 1956. Education: BA, English Literature, Cornell University, 1956; MFA, Writing, Sarah Lawrence College, 1975. Publications: Somebody Else's Child, 1976; Blood Relations, 1977; Boundaries, 1979; The Dream Dredger, 1986; Beginning the World Again, 1990. Contributions to: Numerous magazines in USA and UK. Honours: Child Study Association Award, Best Children's Book, 1976; Janet Kafka Prizes, 1978, 1980; Guggenheim Fellowship, 1979; National Endowment for the Arts, Fellowship, 1983; PEN Syndicated Fiction Project Awards, 1983, 1984. Memberships: PEN; Authors Guild; Poets and Writers; Phi Beta Kappa. Address: 18 Larchmont Street, Ardsley, NY 10502, USA.

SILVER Richard. See: **BULMER Henry Kenneth.**

SILVERSTEIN Shel(by), b. 1932, Chicago, Illinois, USA. Cartoonist; Writer; Dramatist; Poet; Composer. Div, 1 daughter. Appointments: Cartoonist, Pacific Stars and Stripes; Writer and Cartoonist, Playboy, 1956-. Publications: Self-Illustrated: Now Here's My Plan: A Book of Futilities, 1960; Uncle Shelby's ABZ Book: A Primer for Tender Young Minds, 1961; Playboy's Teevee Jeebies, 1963; Uncle Shelby's Story of Lafcadio, The Lion Who Shot Back, 1963; The Giving Tree, 1964; Uncle Shelby's Giraffe and a Half (verse), 1964; Uncle Shelby's Zoo: Don't Bump the Glump! (verse), 1964; Who Wants a Cheap Rhinoceros!, 1964; More Playboy's Teevee Jeebies: Do-It-Yourself Dialog for the Late Late Show, 1965; Where the Sidewalk Ends: The Poems and Drawings of Shel Silverstein, 1974; The Missing Piece, 1976; Different Dances, 1979; A Light in the Attic, 1981; The Missing Piece Meets the Big O, 1981; Falling Up, 1996. Plays: The Lady or the Tiger, 1981; Gorilla, 1983; Wild Life, 1983; Remember Crazy Zelda, 1984; The Crate, 1985; The Happy Hour, 1985; One Tennis Shoe, 1985; Little Feet, 1986; Wash and Dry, 1986; The Devil and Billy Markham, 1989. Screenplay: Things Change (with David Mamet), 1988. Contributions to: The Best American Short Plays 1992-1993: The Theatre Annual Since 1937, 1993; Other: Composer and lyricist of many songs. Honours: New York Times Outstanding Book Award, 1974; School Library Journal Best Books Award, 1981; International Reading Association's Children's Choice Award, 1982; Buckeye Awards, 1983, 1985; William Allen White Award, 1984. Address: c/o Grapefruit Productions, 106 Montague Street, Brooklyn, NY 11201, USA.

SILVIS Randall Glenn, b. 15 July 1950, Rimersburg, Pennsylvania, USA. Novelist; Playwright. m. Rita Lynne McCanna, 25 Sept 1982, 2 sons. Education: BS, Clarion University, 1973; MEd, Indiana University, 1976. Appointments: James Thurber Writer-in-Residence, Thurber House, Columbus, Ohio, 1989; Visiting Writer, Mercyhurst College, Pennsylvania, 1989-90, Ohio State University, 1991, 1992. Publications: The Luckiest Man in the World; Excelsior; An Occasional Hell; Under the Rainbow; Dead Man Falling; Screenplays: An Occasional Hell; Believe the Children. Contributions to: Magazines. Honours: National Endowment for the Arts Fellowship; Drue Heinz Literature Prize; National Playwright Showcase Award; Fulbright Senior Scholar Research Grant. Literary Agent: Novels: Peter Rubie, L Perkins Associates, 5800 Arlington Avenue, Sute 18J, Riverdale, NY 10471, USA; Stage Plays and Movie scripts: Jonathan Westover, The Gage Group Inc, 9255 Sunset Boulevaard, Suite 515, Los Angeles, CA 90069, USA. Address: PO Box 297, St Petersburg, PA 16054, USA.

SIMIC Charles, b. 9 May 1938, Belgrade, Yugoslavia (US citizen, 1971). Associate Professor of English; Poet; Writer. m. Helen Dubin, 1964, 1 son, 1 daughter. Education: University of Chicago, 1956-59; BA, New York University, 1967. Appointments: Faculty, California State College, Hayward, 1970-73; Associate Professor of English, University of New Hampshire, 1973-. Publications: Poetry: What the Grass Says, 1967; Somewhere Among Us a Stone is Taking Notes, 1969; Dismantling the Silence, 1971; White, 1972, revised edition, 1980; Return to a Place Lit by a Glass of Milk, 1974; Biography and a Lament, 1976; Charon's Cosmology, 1977; Brooms: Selected Poems, 1978; School for Dark Thoughts, 1978; Classic Ballroom Dances, 1980; Shaving at Night, 1982; Austerities, 1982; Weather Forecast for Utopia and Vicinity: Poems: 1967-1982, 1983; The Chicken Without a Head, 1983; Selected Poems 1963-1983, 1985, revised edition, 1990; Unending Blues, 1986; The World Doesn't End: Prose Poems, 1989; In the Room We Share, 1990; The Book of Gods and Devils, 1990; Hotel Insomnia, 1992; A Wedding in Hell, 1994. Other: The Uncertain Certainty: Interviews, Essays and Notes on Poetry, 1985; Wonderful Words, Silent Truth, 1990; Dimestore Alchemy, 1992; Unemployed Fortune Teller, 1994. Editor: Another Republic: 17 European and South American Writers (with Mark Strand), 1976; The Essential Campion, 1988. Translator: 12 books, 1970-92. Honours: PEN Awards, 1970, 1980; Guggenheim Fellowship, 1972; National Endowment for the Arts Fellowships, 1974, 1979; Edgar Allan Poe Award, 1975; American Academy of Arts and Letters Award, 1976; Harriet Monroe Poetry Award, 1980; Fulbright Fellowship, 1982; Ingram Merrill Foundation Fellowship, 1983; John D and Catharine T MacArthur Foundation Fellowship, 1984; Pulitzer Prize in Poetry, 1990. Address: c/o Department of English, University of New Hampshire, Durham, NH 03824, USA.

SIMIONESCU Mircea Horia, b. 23 Jan 1928, Targoviste, Romania. Writer. m. Teodora Dinca, 26 Feb 1953, 2 daughters. Education: BA, Literature, Bucharest University, 1964. Publications: The Well Tempered Ingenious Man, 4 volumes, 1969, 1970, 1980, 1983; After 1900, About Noon, 1974; Ganymede's Kidnapping, 1975; Endless Dangers, 1982; Advice for the Dauphin, 1979; Ulysse and the Shadow, 1982; The Banquet, 1982; The Cutaway, 1984; Sale By Auction, 1985; Three Looking Glasses, 1987; The Siege of the Common Place, 1988; The Angel with the Apron, 1992. Contributions to: Magazines, journals, radio, and television. Honours: Writers Union of Romania Prize, 1974. Memberships: Writers Union of Romania; Journalists Union of Romania. Address: 3 Belgrad Str, Bucharest, CD 71248, Romania.

SIMKIN Tom, b. 11 Nov 1933, Auburn, New York, USA. Geologist; Writer. m. Sharon Russell, 3 July 1965, 1 son, 1 daughter. Education: BS, Swarthmore College, 1955; MSE, 1960, PhD, 1965, Princeton University. Appointment: Staff, Smithsonian Institution, Washington, DC. Publications: Volcanoes of the World, 1981, 2nd edition, 1994; Krakatau 1883: The Volcanic Eruption and Its Effects, 1983; Volcano Letter, 1987; Global Volcanism 1975-85, 1989; Paricutin: The Volcano Born in a Mexican Cornfield, 1993. Contributions to: Scientific journals. Honour: Choice Outstanding Academic Book Award, 1984. Memberships: American Geophysical Union; Charles Darwin Foundation for the Galapagos Isles; Geological Society of Washington, president, 1990; International Association of Volcanology. Address: c/o Smithsonian Institution, Museum of Natural History, Washington, DC 20560, USA.

SIMMERMAN Jim, b. 5 Mar 1952, Denver, Colorado, USA. Associate Professor of English; Poet. Education: 1973, MA, English, 1976, University of Missouri; MFA, Creative Writing, University of Iowa, 1980. Appointments: Instructor, 1977-78, Assistant Professor, 1983-86, Associate Professor of English and Director of Creative Writing, Northern Arizona University; Editorial Board, Pushcart Prize Series, 1985-. Publications: Home, 1983; Bad Weather, 1987; Once Out of Nature, 1989; Moon Go Away, I Don't Love You Anymore, 1994; Yoyo, 1994; Dog Music: Poetry About Dogs, co-editor, 1996. Contributions to: Anthologies and journals. Honours: Arizona Commission on the Arts Fellowships for Poetry, 1983, 1987; National Endowment for the Arts Fellowship, 1984; Pushcart Writers Choice Selection, 1984, and Prize, 1985; Fine Arts Work Center Poetry Fellowship, 1984-85; Best of the Small Presses Book Fair Selection, 1990; Fellowship, Hawthornden Castle International Retreat for Writers, Scotland, 1996. Memberships: Associated Writing Programs, board of directors, 1992-95, secretary, 1994-95; Rocky Mountain Modern Language Association. Address: 3601 Mountain Drive, Flagstaff, AZ 86001, USA.

SIMMONS Michael, b. 17 Oct 1935, Watford, England. Journalist. m. Angela Thomson, 20 Apr 1963, 2 sons. Eduaction: BA Honours, University of Manchester, 1960. Appointments: Political Correspondent, Glasgow Herald, 1964-67; East Europe Correspondent, Financial Times, 1968-72; Third World Editor, 1978-81, East Europe Editor, 1983-89, Diplomatic Correspondent, 1989-92, Community Affairs, 1993-95, Deputy Editor, Society, 1994-, The Guardian. Publications: Voices From the South (co-editor), 1983; Berlin: Dispossessed City, 1988; The Unloved Country: Portrait of East Germany, 1989; Reluctant President: A Political Life of Vaclav Havel, 1991; Behind the Hill: Poverty in Rural England, forthcoming. Contributions to: Newspapers and journals. Memberships: Society of Authors; Trinity Cricket Club. Address: c/o The Guardian, London EC1 3ER, England.

SIMMS Suzanne. See: GUNTRUM Suzanne Simmons.

SIMON Barney, b. 13 Apr 1933, Johannesburg, South Africa. Playwright. Education: Studied in Johannesburg. Appointments: Co-Founder and Director, The Market Theatre, Johannesburg, 1978. Publications: Phiri, 1972; Hey Listen, 1973; People, and People Too, 1973; Joburg Sis, 1974; Storytime, 1975; Medea (after Grillparzer), 1978; Cincinatti, 1979; Call me Woman, 1980; Cold Stone Jug, 1980; Marico Moonshine and Manpower, 1981; Woza Albert, 1981; Black Dogonj Mayama, 1984; Born in the RSA, 1985; Outers, 1985; Written by Hand, 1987; Score Me with Ages, 1989; Eden and Other Places, 1989; Inyanga- About Women in Africa, 1989; Singing the Times, 1992 (all plays created in collaboration with participants); Television plays. Honours: Edinburgh Festival Fringe Awards, 1982, 1987; Los Angeles

Critics Award, 1982; Rockefeller Grants. Address: c/o The Market Theatre, PO Box 8656, Johannesburg 2000, South Africa.

SIMON Claude, b. 10 Oct 1913, Madagascar. Writer. Education: College Stanislas, Paris. Publications: Le tricheur, 1945; La corde raide, 1947; Gulliver, 1952; Le sacre de printemps, 1954; Le vent, 1957; L'herbe, 1958; La route des Flandres, 1960; Le palace, 1962; Histoire, 1967; La bataille de Pharsale, 1969; Orion aveugle, 1970; Les corps conducteurs, 1971; Tryptyque, 1973; Lecon de choses, 1975; Les Georgiques, 1981; Le chevelure de Bérénice, 1984; Discours de Stockholm, 1986; L'invitation, 1987; L'acacia, 1989; The Georgies, 1989. Honours: Prix de l'Express, 1960; Prix Medicis, 1967; Doctor (honoris causa), University of Bologna, 1989; Grand Croix Ordre National du Mérite, 1990. Address: Editions de Minuit, 7 rue Bernard-Palissey, 75006 Paris, France.

SIMON Herbert A(lexander), b. 15 June 1916, Milwaukee, Wisconsin, USA. Economist; Professor of Computer Science and Psychology; Author. m. Dorothea Isobel Pye, 25 Dec 1937, 1 son, 2 daughters. Education: BA, 1936, PhD, 1943, University of Chicago. Appointments: Assistant Professor, 1942-47, Professor of Political Science, 1947-49, Illinois Institute of Technology, Chicago: Professor of Administration, 1949-62, Professor of Administration and Psychology, 1962-65, Richard King Mellon University Professor of Computer Science and Psychology, Carnegie Institute of Technology, later Carnegie-Mellon University; Various visiting lectureships. Publications: Administrative Behaviour, 1947, 4th edition, 1977; Public Administration (with Donald W Smithburg and Victor A Thompson), 1950, with new introduction, 1991; Fundamental Research in Administration (with others), 1953; Models of Man, 1958; Organizations (with James G March and H Guetzkow), 1958, 2nd edition, 1993; Planning Production, Inventories, and Work Force (with C C Holt, F Modigliani, and J Muth), 1960; The New Science of Management Decision, 1960, revised edition, 1977; The Shape of Automation, 1965; The Sciences of the Artificial, 1969, 3rd edition, 1996; Human Problem Solving (with Allen Newell), 1972; Representation and Meaning: Experiments with Information Processing (editor with L Siklossy), 1972; Models of Discovery, and Other Topics in the Methods of Science, 1978; Models of Thought, Vol 1, 1979, Vol 2, 1989; Models of Rationality, Vol 1, 1982, Vol 2, 1982, Vol 3, 1997; Reason in Human Affairs, 1983; Protocol Analysis: Verbal Reports as Data (with K Anders Ericsson), 1984, revised edition, 1993; Scientific Discovery: Computational Explorations of the Creative Processes (with Pat Langley, Gary L Bradshaw, and Jan M Zytow), 1987; Models of My Life (autobiography), 1991; Economics, Bounded Rationality, and the Cognitive Revolution (with Ricardo Viale, Massimo Egidi and Robin Marris), 1992. Contributions to: Books, professional journals and many other publications. Honours: Distinguished Scientific Contributions Award, 1969, and Gold Medal Award in Psychology, 1988, American Psychological Association; Nobel Prize in Economic Science, 1978; James Madison Award, American Political Science Association, 1984; National Medal of Science, 1986; John Von Neumann Theory Prize, Operations Research Society of America and Institute of Management Science, 1988; Research Excellence Award, International Joint Conference on Artificial Intelligence, 1995; Dwight Waldo Award, American Society for Public Administration, 1995; Many honorary doctorates; Phi Beta Kappa; Sigma Xi. Memberships: American Academy of Arts and Sciences, fellow; American Association for the Advancement of Science, fellow; American Association of University Professors; American Economic Association, distinguished fellow; American Psychological Association; American Philosophical Society; American Political Science Association; William James Fellow; American Sociological Association, fellow; Econometric Society, fellow; Institute of Management Sciences, vice-president, 1954; National Academy of Sciences, council member, 1978-81, 1983-86; Foreign Member, Chinese Academy of Sciences; Operations Research Society of America; Psychonomic Society. Address: 128 N Craig Street, Apt 504, Pittsburgh, PA 15213, USA.

SIMON Neil, b. 4 July 1927, New York, New York, USA. Dramatist; Screenwriter. m. (1) Joan Balm, 30 Sept 1953, dec, (2) Marsha Mason, 1973, div, (3) Diane Lander, 1987. Education: New York University, 1946. Publications: Plays: Come Blow Your Horn, 1961; Barefoot in the Park, 1963; The Odd Couple, 1965; The Star-Spangled Girl, 1966; Plaza Suite, 1968; The Last of the Red Hot Lovers, 1969; The Gingerbread Lady, 1970; The Prisoner of Second Avenue, 1971; The Sunshine Boys, 1972; The Good Doctor, 1973; God's Favorite, 1974; California Suite, 1976; Chapter Two, 1977; I Ought to Be in Pictures, 1980; Fools, 1981; The Brighton Beach

Memoirs, 1983; Biloxi Blues, 1985; Broadway Bound, 1986; Rumors, 1988; Lost in Yonkers, 1991; Jake's Woman, 1992; Laughter on the 23rd Floor, 1993; London Suite, 1995. Screenplays: After the Fox, 1966; The Out-of-Towners, 1970; The Heartbreak Kid, 1973; Murder by Death, 1976; The Goodbye Girl, 1977; The Cheap Detective, 1978; Seems Like Old Times, 1980; Max Dugan Returns, 1983; The Lonely Guy, 1984; The Sluggers Wife, 1984; The Marrying Man, 1991; Also many adaptions of his plays for films. Lyrics for Musicals: Little Me, 1962, revised version, 1982; Sweet Charity, 1966; Promises, Promises, 1968; They're Playing Our Song, 1979; The Goodbye Girl, 1993. Other: Rewrites: A Memoir, 1996. Honours: Tony Awards, 1965, 1985, 1991; Evening Standard Drama Award, 1967; Sam S Shubert Award, 1968; Writers Guild Screen Awards, 1968, 1970, 1975, and Laurel Award, 1979; Pulitzer Prize in Drama, 1991. Memberships: Dramatists Guild; Writers Guild of America. Address: c/o A DaSilva, 502 Park Avenue, New York, NY 10022, USA.

SIMON Robert. See: **MUSTO Barry**.

SIMON Sheldon (Weiss), b. 31 Jan 1937, St Paul, Minnesota, USA. Professor of International Politics; Writers. m. Charlann Scheid, 23 Apr 1962, 1 son. Education: BA, 1958, PhD, 1964, University of Minnesota; MA, Princeton University, 1960. Appointents: Visiting Professor, University of British Columbia, 1972-73, 1979-80, Carleton University, 1976, American Graduate School of International Management, 1991-92; Monetary Institute of International Studies, 1991, 1996; Professor of International Politics, Arizona State University, Tempe. Publications: The Broken Triangle: Peking, Djakarta and the PKI, 1969; War and Politics in Cambodia, 1974; Asian Neutralism and US Policy, 1975; The Military and Security and in the Third World, 1976; Asian Security in the Post-Cold War Era, 1993; Southern Asian Security in the New Millenium, 1996. Contributions to: Professional journals. Address: c/o Department of Political Science, Arizona State University, Tempe, AZ 85287-2001, USA.

SIMON Werner, b. 5 June 1914, Bremen, Germany. Psychiatrist. m. Elizabeth Strawn, 24 Apr 1939. Education: Medical School, University of Frankfurt, Germany, 1932-36; MD Degree, University of Bern, Switzerland, 1937. Appointments: Chief of Psychiatry, Veterans Administration Medical Center, Minneapolis, 1948-71; Consultant, Hennepin County Medical Center, Minneapolis, 1971-; Emeritus Professor of Psychiatry, University of Minnesota Medical School. Publications: Differential Treatment and Prognosis in Schizophrenia, 1959; Suicide Among Physicians, 1989. Contributions to: Books and professional journals. Memberships: Minnesota Psychiatric Society, president 1967-69; American Psychiatric Association, Life Fellow; American College of Physicians, Fellow; International Association for Suicide Prevention; Minnesota Society of Neurological Sciences. Address: 8915 River Ridge Road, Minneapolis, MN 55425, USA.

SIMPSON Alan, b. 27 Nov 1929, England. Scriptwriter; Author. m. Kathleen Phillips, 1958, dec 1978. Appointments: Scriptwriter, author with Ray Galton, 1951-; Various television programmes, 1954-. Publications: Hancock, 1961; Steptoe and Son, 1963; The Reunion and Other Plays, 1966; Hancock Scripts, 1974; The Best Of Hancock, 1986; Film scripts and theatre works. Honours: Scriptwriter of the Year, Guild of TV Producers and Directors, 1959; Best Comedy TV Series Awards, Screenwriters Guild, 1962-65; John Logie Baird Award, 1964; Best Comedy Series Award, Dutch TV, 1966; Best Comedy Screenplay Award, Scriptwriters Guild, 1972; Portugal Golden Globe Best TV Series Award, for Camilo and Filho (Steptoe and Son), 1995. Address: c/o Tessa Le Bars Management, 54 Birchwood Road, Petts Wood, Kent BR5 1NZ, England.

SIMPSON Dorothy (née Preece), b. 20 June 1933, Blaenavon, Monmouthshire, Wales. Author. Education: BA, 1954, Teaching Diploma, 1955, University of Bristol. Appointments: Teacher of English and French, Dartford Grammar School for Girls, Kent, 1955-59, Erith Grammer School, Kent, 1959-61; Teacher of English, Senacre School, Maidstone, Kent, 1961-62. Publications: Harbinger of Fear, 1977; The Night She Died, 1981; Six Feet Under, 1982; Puppet for a Corpse, 1983; Close Her Eyes, 1984; Last Seen Alive, 1985; Dead on Arrival, 1986; Element of Doubt, 1987; Suspicious Death, 1988; Dead by Morning, 1989; Doomed to Die, 1991; Wake the Dead, 1992; No Laughing Matter, 1993. Honour: Silver Dagger Award, 1985. Address: c/o Curtis Brown Ltd, 4th Floor, Haymarket House, 28/29 Haymarket, London SW1Y 4SP, England.

SIMPSON Elizabeth Robson, b. 16 Oct 1910, Sydney, New South Wales, Australia. Zoologist; Painter; Writer. m. Alfred Moxon Simpson, 3 Aug 1938, 1 son. Education: BSc, 1931, 1st Class Honours, 1933, MSc, 1935. University of Adelaide, South Australia. Publications: The Hahndorf Walkers and the Beaumont Connection, 1983; The Clelands of Beaumont, 1986; Beaumont House, the Land and its People, 1993. Contributions: 10 papers on larval trematodes, in Transactions of Royal Society of South Australia. Honours: John Bagot Scholarship and Medal, University of Adelaide, 1929; Fellow, Royal South Australian Society of Arts; Award, Genealogical Society of South Australia, 1987. Memberships: Queen Adelaide Club; Lyceum Club of South Australia Inc; Tatlers; Fellow, Royal Society of South Australia, 1938-46. Address: Beaumont Press, 2nd Floor, 135 Waymouth Street, Adelaide, South Australia 5000, Australia.

SIMPSON Jerry Howard, Jr, b. 11 Dec 1925, Providence, Rhode Island, USA. President, Bike Tour, France. m. Jane Coral Augustine Simpson, 4 Sept 1973, 1 son, 1 daughter. Education: BA History/Languages, Moravian College for Men, University of North Carolina. Publications: Torn Land, 1970; Cycling France, 1992; Notes on the French Revolution, 1994; Paris in Winter, 1995; Pensées Impolies (in French), 1996. Contributions to: Reader's Digest; American History Illustrated; Bicycling; Wall Street Journal; Bike World. Honour: 1st Place, Virginia Press Association, 1969-70. Membership: Comenian Literary Society. Literary Agent: E E Richey 303-1399 Barclay Street, Vancouver, British Columbia V6E 1H6, Canada.

SIMPSON John Cody Fidler, b. 9 Aug 1944, Cleveleys, England. Television Journalist. m. Diane Jean Petteys, 14 Aug 1965, separated, 2 daughters. Education: MA, Magdalene College, Cambridge, 1963-66. Appointments: Editor, Granta, 1965; Trainee, sub-editor, producer, reporter, BBC Radio News, 1966-72; BBC correspondent, Dublin, 1972, Brussels, 1975, Johannesburg, 1977; Political editor, 1980; Diplomatic editor, BBC TV and Radio, 1988-; Contributing editor, The Spectator, 1990-. Publications: The Best of Granta, 1967; Moscow Requiem (novel), 1981; A Fine and Private Place (novel), 1983; The Disappeared, 1985; Behind Iranian Lines, 1988; Despatches from the Barricades, 1990; From the House of War: Baghdad and the Gulf, 1991; The Darkness Crumbles: The Death of Communism, 1992; In the Forests of the Night: Encounters with Terrorists, Drug-Runners and the Oppressors in Peru, 1993. Contributions to: Listener, Harper's; Granta; Spectator. Honour: Commander of the Order of the British Empire, 1991. Membership: Athenaeum; Chelsea Arts Club. Address: c/o BBC Television News, Television Centre, Wood Lane, London W12, England.

SIMPSON Louis Aston Marantz, b. 27 Mar 1923, Jamaica, West Indies. Professor of English (retired); Writer; Poet. m. (1) Jeanne Rogers, 1949, div 1954, 1 son, (2) Dorothy Roochvarg, 1955, div 1979, 1 son, 1 daughter, (3) Miriam Bachner Butensky, 23 June 1985. Education: BSc, 1944, MA, 1950, PhD, 1959, Columbia University. Appointments: Associate Editor, Bobbs-Merrill Publishing Co, 1950-55; Instructor to Assistant Professor of English, Columbia University, 1955-59; Professor of English, University of California at Berkeley, 1959-67, State University of New York at Stony Brook, 1967-93. Publication: Poetry: The Arrivistes: Poems 1940-1949, 1949; Good News of Death and Other Poems, 1955; A Dream of Governors, 1959; At the End of the Open Road, 1963; Selected Poems, 1965; Adventures of the Letter I, 1971; Searching for the Ox, 1976; Caviare at the Funeral, 1980; The Best Hour of the Night, 1983; People Live Here: Selected Poems, 1949-1983, 1985; Collected Poems, 1988; In the Room We Share, 1990; There You Are, 1995. Other: The New Poets of England and America (editor), 1957; James Hogg: A Critical Study, 1962; An Introduction to Poetry (editor), 1967; Three on a Tower: The Lives and Works of Ezra Pound, T S Eliot and William Carlos Williams, 1975; A Revolution in Taste, 1978; A Company of Poets, 1981; The Character of the Poet, 1986; Selected Prose, 1989. Contributions to: Various publications. Honours: Hudson Review Fellowship, 1957; Prix de Rome Fellowship, 1957; Guggenheim Fellowships, 1962, 1970; Pulitzer Prize for Poetry, 1964; Jewish Book Council Award, 1981; Elmer Holmes Bobst Award, 1987. Address: 186 Old Field Road, Setauket, NY 11733, USA.

SIMPSON Matt(hew William), b. 13 May 1936, Lancashire, England. Lecturer; Writer. m. Monika Ingrid Weydert, 13 Dec 1962, 1 son, 1 daughter. Education: Cambridge University, 1955-58; Liverpool University, 1958-59. Appointments: Literature Panel, Merseyside Arts Association, 1970-75; Chairman, Executors of the Widows Project,

1980-; Poet-in-Residence, Tasmanian Poetry Festival, 1994. Publications: Making Arrangements, 1982; An Elegy for the Galosherman, 1990; The Pig's Thermal Underwear, 1992; To Tasmania with Mrs Meredith, 1994; Catching Up with History, 1995; On the Right Side of the Earth, 1995. Contributions to: Anthologies, journals and magazines. Membership: Poetry Society of Great Britain. Address: 29 Boundary Drive, Liverpool L25 0QB, England.

SIMPSON N(orman) F(rederick), b. 29 Jan 1919, London, England. Author. Education: BA, University of London, 1954. Appointments: Teacher and Extramural Lecturer, Westminster College, London, 1946-62; Literary Manager, Royal Court Theatre, London, 1976-78. Publications: The Hole, 1958; One Way Pendulum, 1960; The Form, 1961; The Hole and Other Plays and Sketches, 1964; The Cresta Run, 1966; Some Tall Tinkles: Television Plays, 1968; Was He Anyone, 1973; Harry Bleachbaker (novel), 1974, US edition as Man Overboard, 1976; Inner Voices, 1983. Address: c/o Mrs Holder, Hillview, Lower Inkpen, Berkshire RG15 0DX, England.

SIMPSON Ronald Albert, b. 1 Feb 1929, Melbourne, Victoria, Australia. m. Pamela Bowles, 27 Aug 1955, 1 son, 1 daughter. Education: Trained Primary Teachers' Certificate, 1951; Associate Diploma in Fine Art, Royal Melbourne Institute of Technology, 1966. Appointments: Teacher, Junior and Secondary Schools, Australia and England, 1951-68; Lecturer, Senior Lecturer, The Chisholm Institute of Technology, Melbourne, Victoria, 1968-87. Publications: The Walk Along the Beach, 1960; This Real Pompeii, 1964; After the Assassination, 1968; Diver, 1972; Poems from Murrumbeena, 1976; The Forbidden City, 1979; Poems From the Age (editor), 1979; Selected Poems, 1981; Words for a Journey, 1986; Dancing Table, 1992. Honours: Australia Council for Travel, 1977, Category A Fellowship to write poetry, 1987; FAW Christopher Brennan Award, 1992. Membership: Australian Society of Authors. Address: 29 Omama Road, Murrumbeena, Melbourne, Victoria 3163, Australia.

SIMS George Frederick Robert, b. 3 Aug 1923, Hammersmith, London, England. Rare Book Dealer; Author. m. Beryl Simcock, 2 sons, 1 daughter. Education: Lower School of John Lyon, Harrow, 1934-40. Publications: The Terrible Door, 1964; Sleep No More, 1966; The Last Best Friend, 1967; The Sand Dollar, 1969; Deadhand, 1971; Hunters Point, 1973; The End of the Web, 1976; Rex Mundi, 1978; Who Is Cato? 1981; The Keys of Death, 1982; Coat of Arms, 1984; The Rare Book Game, 1988; Last of the Rare Book Game, 1990; The Despain Papers, 1992. Contributions to: Black Mask; Saturday Book; London Magazine; American Book Collector; Book Collector; Antiquarian Book Monthly Review. Memberships: Crime Writers Association; Detection Club. Address: Peacocks, Hurst, Reading, Berkshire RG10 0DR, England.

SINCLAIR Andrew Annandale, b. 21 Jan 1935, Oxford, England. Writer; Historian. m. Sonia Melchett, 25 July 1984, 2 sons. Education: Major Scholar, BA, PhD, Trinity College, Cambridge, 1955-59; Harkness Fellow, Harvard University, 1955-59; American Council of Learned Societies Fellow, Stanford University, 1964-65. Appointments: Founding Fellow, Churchill College, 1961-63; Lecturer, University College, London, 1966-68; Publisher, Lorrimer Publishing, 1968-89. Publications: The Breaking of Bumbo, 1959; My Friend Judas, 1959; Prohibition: The Era of Excess, 1961; Gog, 1967; Magog, 1972; Jack: A Biography of Jack London, 1977; The Other Victoria, 1981; King Ludd, 1988; War Like A Wasp, 1989; The War Decade: An Anthology of the 1940's, 1989; The Need to Give, 1990; The Far Corners of the Earth, 1991; The Naked Savage, 1991; The Strength of the Hills, 1991; The Sword and the Grail, 1992; Francis Bacon: His Life and Violent Times, 1993; In Love and Anger, 1994. Contributions to: Sunday Times; Times; New York Times; Atlantic Monthly. Honours: Somerset Maugham Prize, 1967; Venice Film Festival Award, 1971. Memberships: Fellow, Society of American Historians, 1970; Fellow, Royal Literary Society, 1968. Address: 16 Tite Street, London SW3 4HZ, England.

SINCLAIR Iain Macgregor, b. 11 June 1943, Cardiff, Wales. Poet; Writer. m. Anna Hadman, 4 Mar 1967, 1 son, 2 daughters. Education: Trinity College, Dublin; Courtauld Institute, London. Publications: Poetry: Back Garden Poems, 1970; Muscat's Wurm, 1972; The Birth Rug, 1973; Lud Heat, 1975; Brown Clouds, 1977; Suicide Bridge, 1979; Fluxions, 1983; Fresh Eggs and Scalp Metal, 1983; Autistic Poses, 1985; Significant Wreckage, 1988; Selected Poems, 1970-87, 1989; Jack Elam's Other Eye, 1992. Fiction: White Chappell, Scarlet Tracings, 1987; Downriver, 1991; Radon Daughters,

1994; Essays: Lights Out for the Territory, 1997. Address: 28 Albion Drive, London E8 4ET, England.

SINCLAIR Olga Ellen, (Ellen Clare, Olga Daniels), b. 23 Jan 1923, Norfolk, England. Writer. m. Stanley George Sinclair, 1 Apr 1945, 3 sons. Publications: Gypsies, 1967; Hearts By the Tower, 1968; Bitter Sweet Summer, 1970; Dancing in Britain, 1970; Children's Games, 1972; Toys, 1974; My Dear Fugitive, 1976; Never Fall in Love, 1977; Master of Melthorpe, 1979; Gypsy Girl, 1981; Ripening Vine, 1981; (as Olga Daniels), Lord of Leet Castle, 1984; (as Olga Daniels), The Gretna Bride, 1985; When Wherries Sailed By, 1987; The Bride From Faraway, 1987; The Untamed Bride, 1988; Gretna Green; A Romantic History, 1989; (as Olga Daniels), The Arrogant Cavalier, 1991. Memberships: Society of Authors; Romantic Novelists Association; Society of Women and Journalists; President, Norwich Writer's Circle. Address: Dove House Farm, Potter Heigham, Norfolk NR29 5LJ, England.

SINCLAIR Sonia Elizabeth, (Sonia Graham, Sonia Melchett), b. 6 Sept 1928, Nainital, India. Writer. m. (1) Julian Mond, Lord Melchett, dec June 1973, 1 son, 2 daughters, (2) Andrew Sinclair, 1984. Education: Royal School, Bath; Queen's Secretarial College, Windsor, England. Appointments: Writer, Member of Board of Directors, English Stage Company. Publications: (as Sonia Graham) Tell Me Honestly (nonfiction), 1964; (as Sonia Melchett) Someone is Missing (nonfiction), 1987; (as Sonia Melchett) Passionate Quests - Five Contemporary Women Travellers, 1989. Contributions to: Periodicals. Honour: Prizewinner, Short Story Competition, Raconteur Magazine. Address: 16 Tite Street, London SW3 4HZ, England.

SINDEN Donald, b. 9 Oct 1923, Plymouth, Devon, England. Actor; Writer. m. Diana Mahony, 1948, 2 sons. Appointments: Professional Actor, 1942-; Films for the Rank Organisation, 1952-60; Associate Artist, Royal Shakespeare Company, 1967-. Publications: A Touch of the Memoirs, 1982; Laughter in the Second Act, 1985; Everyman Book of Theatrical Anecdotes (editor), 1987; The English Country Church, 1988; The Last Word (editor), 1994. Honour: Commander of the Order of the British Empire, 1979. Memberships: Council of British Actors Equity, 1966-77, Trustee, 1988-; Chairman, Theatre Museum Advisory Board, 1971-80; Drama Panel, 1973-77, Advisory Board, 1982-86, Arts Council; Federation of Playgoers' Societies, president, 1968-93; President, Royal Theatrical Fund, 1983-; Fellow, Royal Society of Arts, 1966-. Address: 60 Temple Fortune Lane, London NW11 7UE, England.

SINGER Adam. See: KARP David.

SINGER June Flaum, b. 17 Jan 1932, Jersey City, New Jersey, USA. Writer. m. Joseph Singer, 7 Sep 1950, 1 son, 3 daughters. Education: Ohio State University, Columbus, 1948-50. Publications: The Bluffer's Guide to Interior Decorating, 1972; The Bluffer's Guide to Antiques, (American editor), 1972; The Debutantes, 1981; Star Dreams, 1982; The Movie Set, 1984; The Markoff Women, 1986; The President's Women, 1988; Sex in the Afternoon, 1990; Till the End of Time, 1991; Brilliant Divorces, 1992. Memberships: Southern California Society of Women Writers; PEN West; Authors Guild. Address: 780 Stone Canyon Road, Bel-Air, CA 90077, USA.

SINGER Marilyn, b. 3 Oct 1948, New York, New York, USA. Children's Writer. m. Steven Aronson, 31 July 1971. Education: BA, Queens College of the City University of New York, 1969; MA, New York University, 1979. Publications: 49 books; The Morgans Dream, 1995; A Wasp is not a Bee, 1995. Contributions to: Periodicals. Honours: Several awards for children's books. Memberships: Authors Guild; PEN American Centre; Society of Children's Book Writers and Illustrators. Address: 42 Berkeley Place, Brooklyn, NY 11217, USA.

SINGER Peter (Albert David), b. 6 July 1946, Melbourne, Australia. Professor of Philosophy; Writer. m. Renata Diamond, 16 Dec 1968, 3 daughters. Education: BA with Honours, 1967, MA, 1969, University of Melbourne; BPhil, University College, Oxford, 1971. Appointments: Lecturer in Philosophy, University College, Oxford, 1971-73; Visiting Assistant Professor of Philosophy, New York University, 1973-74; Senior Lecturer in Philosophy, La Trobe University, Bundoora, Victoria, Australia, 1974-76; Professor of Philosophy, Monash University, Clayton, Victoria, 1977-; Director, 1983-91, Deputy Director, 1992-, Centre for Human Bioethics, Clayton, Australia; Co-Editor, Bioethics, 1986-. Publications: Democracy and Disobedience, 1973; Animal Rights and Human Obligations (editor with

Thomas Regan), 1975, 2nd edition, 1989; Animal Liberation: A New Ethics for Our Treatment of Animals, 1975, 2nd edition, 1990; Practical Ethics, 1979, 2nd edition, 1993; Marx, 1980; The Expanding Circle: Ethics and Sociobiology, 1981; Test-Tube Babies (editor with William Walters), 1982; Hegel, 1983; The Reproduction Revolution: New Ways of Making Babies (with Deane Wells), 1984, 2nd edition as Making Babies: The New Science and Ethics of Conception, 1985; In Defence of Animals (editor), 1985; Should the Baby Live? The Problem of Handicapped Infants (with Helga Kuhse), 1985; Applied Ethics (editor), 1986; Animal Liberation: A Graphic Guide (with Lori Gruen), 1987; Animal Factories (with Jim Mason), 1990; Embryo Experimentation (editor), 1990; Companion to Ethics (editor), 1991; How Are We to Live?, 1993; The Great Ape Project: Equality Beyond Humanity (editor with Paola Cavalieri), 1993; Rethinking Life and Death, 1994; Ethics (editor), 1994; The Greens, 1996. Contributions to: Philosophy journals. Address: c/o Centre for Human Bioethics, Monash University, Wellington Road, Clayton, Victoria, Vic 3168, Australia.

SINGER Sarah Beth, b. 4 July 1915, Brooklyn, New York, USA. Poet; Writer. m. Leon E Singer, 23 Nov 1938, 1 son, 1 daughter. Education: BA, New York University, 1934; Graduate Studies, New School for Social Research, New York City, 1960-64. Appointments: Teacher, poetry seminars and workshops, 1968-74, 1981-83; Consulting Editor, Poet Lore, 1976-81. Publications: After the Beginning, 1975; Of Love and Shoes, 1987; The Gathering, 1992; Filtered Images (anthology), 1992. Contributions to: Anthologies, newspapers and journals. Honours: Stephen Vincent Benét Narrative Poetry Awards, 1968, 1971; 5 Poetry Society of America Awards, 1972-76; National League of American Penwomen Awards, 1976-92; Washington Poets Association Award, 1989; Haiku Award, Brussels Sprouts, 1992. Memberships: National League of American Penwomen; Poetry Society of America, vice-president, 1974-78. Address: 2360 43rd Avenue East, Seattle, WA 98112, USA.

SINGH Amritjit, b. 20 Oct 1945, Rawalpindi, India. Teacher; Translator; Editor. m. Prem Singh, 24 Mar 1968, 1 son, 1 daughter. Education: BA, Panjab University, 1963; MA, Kurukshetra University, 1965; PhD, New York University, 1973. Appointments: Professor of English, University of Delhi, 1965-68, City University of New York, 1970-71, 1973-74, New York University, 1972-73, Hofstra University, 1984-86, Rhode Island College, 1986-. Publications: The Novels of the Harlem Renaissance, 1976; India: An Anthology of Contemporary Writing, 1983; The Magic Circle of Henry James, 1989; The Harlem Renaissance: Revaluations, 1989; Memory, Narrative and Identity, 1994; Conversations with Ralph Ellison, 1995; Conversations with Ishmael Reed, 1995; Memory and Cultural Politics, 1996. Contributions to: Numerous essays and reviews in American Literature, Indian Literature and African American Studies. Honours: Fulbright Fellowship, 1968-69; National Endowment for the Humanities Fellowship, 1991-92. Memberships: President, Melus, 1994-97; Modern Language Association. Address: Department of English, Rhode Island College, Providence, RI 02908, USA.

SINGH Charu Steel, b. 15 May 1955, Uttar Pradesh, India. Teacher. m. Maya, 6 June 1987, 1 son. Education: BA, 1974; MA, 1976; PhD, 1978. Appointments: MBS College, Gangapur, 1977-79; Lecturer, 1979-91, Reader, 1991-, Kashi Vidyapith University. Publications: The Chariot of Fire; Auguries of Evocation; Contemporary Literary Theory; Literary Theory: Possibilities and Limits; Four Collections of poems; Confederate Gestures: Search for Method in Indian Literature Studies, editor, 1993; Self-Reflexive Materiality; Concentric Imagination; Theory and Interpretation of Literature, editor, 1996. Contributions to: Literary Criterion; Journal of Literary Criticism; Modern Language Review; Years Work in English Studies. Honours: British Council Fellowship, 1982-83; Prestigious University Grants; University grants Commission Research Scientist 'B', 1986-91; Fellowship, Indian Institute of Advanced Study, Shimla, 1993; Fellowship, Indioan Institute of Advanced Study, Shimla, 1996-97. Memberships: American Studies Research Centre; Indian PEN. Address: 36-20/A-36, Brahmanand Nagar, Ext 1, Durga Kund, Varanasi 221005, India.

SINGH Ram Krishna, b. 31 Dec 1950, Varanasi, India. Teacher; Writer; Poet; Editor. m. Durga Bulli, 1 Mar 1978, 1 son, 1 daughter. Education: BA, University of Gorakhpur, 1970; MA, Banras Hindu University, 1972; PhD in English, Kashi Vindyapith, 1981. Appointments: Journalist, Press Trust of India, 1973-74; Lecturer, Royal Bhutam Polytechnic, 1974-76; Faculty, Indian School of Mines, Dhanbad, 1976-; Guest Editor, Language Forum, New Delhi, 1986;

Board of Advisors, Canopy, 1986-; Co-Editor, Creative Forum, 1987-; General Editor, Creative Forum New Poets' Series, 1992-; Editorial Associate, Indian Book Chronicle, 1992-; Associate Editor, Young Poets, 1994-; Indian Journal of Applied Linguistics, 1994-; Indian Editor, The Hearts of the Handmaidens, 1995-. Publications: Savitri: A Spiritual Epic, 1984; My Silence, 1985; Using Contemporary English Idioms, 1985-86; Sound and Silence (editor), 1986; Indian English Writing, 1981-1985 (editor), 1987; Using English in Science and Technology, 1988; Memories Unmemoried, 1988; Practising English in Science and Technology, 1990; Flight of Phoenix, 1990; Music Must Sound, 1990; Recent Indian English Poets: Expressions and Beliefs (editor), 1992; I Do Not Question, 1994; Krishna Scrivinas: The Poet of Inner Aspiration, 1994; My Silence and Other Selected Poems, 1995; General English Practice, 1995; Writing Your Thesis and Research Papers, 1996. Contributions to: Indian Journal of English Studies; Literary Endeavour; Language Forum; Journal of Indian Writing in English; Commonwealth Quarterly; Poet; Indian Literature; Prophetic Voices; Forum; Creative Inspiration; International Poetry; Canopy; World Poetry; Creative Forum; Poetry; Young Poets; Micropress Yates (Australia); Twilight Ending (USA); Amber (Canada); Indian Literary Panorama. Honours: Honorary DLitt, World Academy of Arts and Culture, 1984; Eminent Poet and Fellowship, International Poets Academy, Madras, 1987; Certificates of Excellence, International Writers and Artists Association, 1987, 1988; Michael Madhusudan Award, Michael Madhusudan Academy, Calcutta, 1994. Memberships: International Poets Academy, Madras; International Writers and Artists Association; PEN, Bombay; World Poetry Society; International Association of Teachers of English as a Foreign Language, UK. Address: c/o Indian School of Mines, Dhanbad 826004, India.

SIONIL JOSE Francisco, b. 3 Dec 1924, Rosales, Pangasinan, Philippines. Novelist. m. Tersita G Jovellanos. Appointments: Publisher, Editor, Solidarity Magazine, 1966-; Manager, Solidaridad Galleries, Manila, 1967-. Publications: The Pretenders, 1962; Tree, 1978; My Brother, My Executioner, 1979; Mass, 1982; Po-on, 1985; Ermita, 1988; Spiderman, 1991. Story Collections: The Pretenders and Other Stories, 1962; The God Stealer and Other Stories, 1968; Waywaya and Other Short Stories for the Philippines, 1980; Two Filipino Women, 1982; Platinum and Other Stories, 1983; Olvidon and Other Stories, 1988. Honours: National Press Club Awards; British Council Grant, 1967; Rockefeller Foundation Bellagio Award, 1979; Ramon Magsaysay Memorial Award for Literature, 1980; International House of Japan Fellowship, 1983. Address: Solidaidad Publishing House, 531 Padre Faura, Ermita PO Box 3959, Manila, Philippines.

SIPHERD Ray, b. 27 Aug 1935, Uniontown, Pennsylvania, USA. Writer. m. Anne Marie Foran, 4 Oct 1986. Education: BA, Yale University, 1957. Publications; The White Kite, 1972; Ernie and Bert's Telephone Call, 1978; The Count's Poem, 1979; Down on the Farm with Grover, 1980; Sherlock Hemlock and the Outer Space Creatures, 1981; Big Bird's Animal Alphabet, 1987; When is My Birthday, 1988; The Courtship of Peggy McCoy, 1990; The Christmas Store, 1993; Dance of the Scarecrows, 1996. Honours: Emmy Awards, 1969, 1974, 1985. Memberships: American Society of Composers, Authors and Publishers; Writers Guild of America. Address: PO Box 366, Newtown, CT 06470, USA.

SIROF Harriet Toby, b. 18 Oct 1930, New York, New York, USA. Writer; Teacher. m. 18 June 1949, 1 son, 1 daughter. Education: BA, New School for Social Research, New York City, 1962. Publications: A New-Fashioned Love Story, 1977; The IF Machine, 1978; The Junior Encyclopedia of Israel, 1980; Save the Dam!, 1981; That Certain Smile, 1981; The Real World, 1985; Anything You Can Do, 1986; Because She's My Friend, 1993; The Road Back: Living With a Physical Disability, 1993; Bring Back Yesterday, 1996. Contributions to: Colorado Review; Descent; Inlet; Maine Review; North American Review; New Orleans Review; Sam Houston Review; San Jose Studies; Woman; Voices of Brooklyn. Honour: Junior Literary Guild Selection, 1985. Memberships: Authors Guild; Society of Children's Book Writers. Address: 792 East 21 Street, Brooklyn, NY 11210, USA.

SISKEL Gene, (Eugene Karl Siskel), b. 26 Jan 1946, Chicago, Illinois, USA. Film Critic. m. Marlene Iglitzen, 1980, 2 daughters. Education: BA, Yale University, 1967; Postgraduate Studies, Department of Defence Information School, 1968. Appointments: Fellow, Coro Foundation, 1968; Film Critic, Chicago Tribune, 1969-; WBBM-TV, Chicago, 1974-, CBS This Morning, 1990-; Co-Host,

Sneak Previews, WTTW-TV, Chicago, 1977-82, At the Movies, syndicated television programme, 1982-86; Siskel and Ebert, syndicated television programme, 1986-; Host, Nightwatch, WTTW-TV, Chicago, 1979-80. Publication: The Future of the Movies (with Roger Ebert), 1991. Contributions to: Newspapers and magazines. Honour: Honorary PhD of Letters, Illinois College, 1989. Membership: Arts Club, Chicago. Address: c/o Chicago Tribune, Box 25340, Chicago, IL 60625, USA.

SISLER Harry Hall, b. 13 Mar 1917, Ironton, Ohio, USA. Chemist; Educator; Dean Emeritus. m. (1) Helen E Shaver, 29 Jun 1940, 2 sons, 2 daughters, (2) Hannelore L Wass, 13 Apr 1978. Education: BSc, Honours, Ohio State University, 1936; MSc, Chemistry, 1937; PhD, 1939, University of Illinois. Appointments: Board of Publication, Journal of Chemical Education, 1956-58; Editor, Reinhold Publication Corporation, 1958-78; Consulting Editor, Dowden, Hutchinson and Ross, 1971-78; Assistant to the Editor, Death Studies, 1978-. Publications: Chemistry in Non-Aqueous Solvents, 1961; Electronic Structure, Properties and the Periodic Law, 1963; The Chloramination Reaction, 1977; Chemistry: A Systematic Approach, 1980; Nitrogen Compounds, Encyclopedia of Inorganic Chemistry, Vol 7, 1993. Poems: Starlight, 1976; Of Outer and Inner Space, 1980; Earth, Air, Fire and Water, 1989; Autumn Harvest, 1996; Numerous others. Contributions to: Over 200 articles in major scientific and scholarly journals, including Chemistry of Inorganic Nitrogen Compounds, 1994. Address: 6014 North West 54th Way, Gainesville, FL 32653-3265, USA.

SISSON C(harles) H(ubert), b. 22 Apr 1914, Bristol, England. Poet; Writer; Translator; Editor; Retired Civil Servant. m. Nora Gilbertson, 19 Aug 1937, 2 daughters. Education: BA, 1st Class Honours, University of Bristol, 1934; Postgraduate studies, University of Berlin and Freiburg, 1934-35, Sorbonne, University of Paris, 1935-36. Appointments: Assistant Principal, 1936-42, Principal, 1945-53, Assistant Secretary, 1953-62, Undersecretary, 1962-68, Assistant Undersecretary of State, 1968-71, Director of Occupational Safety and Health, 1971-73, Ministry of Labour. Publications: Poetry: Poems, 1959; Twenty-One Poems, 1960; The London Zoo, 1961; Numbers, 1965; The Discarnation: Or, How the Flesh Became Word and Dwelt Among Us, 1967; Metamorphoses, 1968; Roman Poems, 1968; In the Trojan Ditch: Collected Poems and Selected Translations, 1974; The Corridor, 1975; Anchises, 1976; Exactions, 1980; Selected Poems, 1981; Night Thoughts and Other Poems, 1983; Collected Poems, 1943-1983, 1984; God Bless Karl Marx!, 1987; Antidotes, 1991; Nine Sonnets, 1991; The Pattern, 1993; What and Who, 1994: Novels: An Asiatic Romance, 1953; Christopher Homm, 1965: Non-Fiction: The Spirit of British Administration and Some European Comparisons, 1959, 2nd edition, 1966; Art and Action (essays), 1965; Essays, 1967; English Poetry 1900-1950: An Assessment, 1971; The Case of Walter Baghot, 1972; David Hume, 1976; The English Sermon: An Anthology, Vol 2, 1976; The Avoidance of Literature: Collected Essays, 1978; Anglican Essays, 1983; The Poet and the Translator, 1985; On the Look-Out: A Partial Autobiography, 1989; In Two Minds: Guesses at Other Writers, 1990; English Perspectives: Essays on Liberty and Government, 1992; Is There a Church of England?, 1993. Translator: Versions and Perversions of Heine, 1955; The Poetry of Catullus, 1966; The Poetic Art: A Translation of Horace's "Ars Poetica", 1975; Lucretius: De Rerum Natura: The Poem on Nature, 1976; Jean de La Fontaine: Some Tales, 1979; Dante Alighieri: The Divine Comedy, 1981; The Song of Roland, 1983; Joachim du Bellay: The Regrets, 1984; Virgil: The Aeneid, 1986; Jean Racine: Britannicus, Phaedra, Athaliah, 1987. Editor: David Wright: South African Album, 1976; Jonathan Swift: Collected Poems, 1977; Thomas Hardy: Jude the Obscure, 1979; Philip Mairet: Autobiographical and Other Papers, 1981; Christina Rossetti: Selected Poems, 1984; Jeremy Taylor: Selected Writings, 1990. Contributions to: Agenda; London Magazine; London Review of Books; New Criterion; New York Times Review of Books; Poetry Nation Review; Spectator; Times Literary Supplement. Honours: Senior Simon Research Fellow, University of Manchester; Fellow, Royal Society of London, 1975; Honorary DLitt, University of Bristol, 1980; Companion of Honour, 1993. Address: Moorfield Cottage, The Hill, Langport, Somerset TA10 9PU, England.

SISSON Rosemary Anne, b. 13 Oct 1923, London, England. Writer. Education: BA, Honours, University College, London; MLit, Newnham College, Cambridge. Appointments: Junior Lecturer, University of Wisconsin, 1949-50; Lecturer, University College, London, 1950-53, University of Birmingham, 1953-54; Drama Critic,

Stratford-upon-Avon Herald, 1954-57. Publications: The Exciseman, 1972; The Killer of Horseman's Flats, 1973; The Stratford Story, 1975; Escape From the Dark, 1976; The Queen and the Welshman, 1979; The Manions of America, 1981; Bury Love Deep, 1985; Rosemary for Remembrance, 1985; Beneath the Visting Moon, 1986; The Bretts, 1987; The Young Indiana Jones Chronicles, 1993-. Contributions to: Newspapers and journals. Honour: Laurel Award, Writers Guild of Great Britain. Memberships: Academy Club; Honorary Secretary, Dramatists Club; Writers Guild of Great Britain, President; Council Member, BAFTA. Address: 167 New King's Road, Parson's Green, London SW6, England.

SIZER John, b. 14 Sept 1938, Grimsby, England. Chief Executive. m. 1965, 3 sons. Education: BA, Nottingham University, 1964; DLitt, Loughborough University of Technology, 1989. Publications: An Insight into Management Accounting, 3rd edition, 1989; A Casebook of British Management Accounting, 2 volumes, 1984-85; Institutional Responses to Financial Reductions in University Sector DES, 1987. Contributions to: Professional journals. Honour: Commander of the Order of the British Empire, 1989. Memberships: Chartered Institute of Management Accountants, fellow; Royal Society of Arts, fellow; Vice President, Society for Research into Higher Education, 1995. Address: c/o Scottish Higher Education Funding Council, Donaldson House, 97 Haymarket Terrace, Edinburgh EH12 5HD, Scotland.

SKALDASPILLIR Sigfriour. See: BROXON Mildred Downey.

SKELTON Geoffrey David, b. 11 May 1916, Springs, South Africa. Writer; Translator. m. Gertrude Klebac, 4 Sept 1947, 2 sons. Education: Plymouth College, City of London School, 1927-34. Appointments: BBC, England, 1956-67. Publications: Wagner at Bayreuth, 1965, 2nd edition, 1976; Wieland Wagner, 1971; Paul Hindemith, 1975; Richard and Cosima Wagner, 1982; Wagner in Thought and Practice (essays), 1991; Cosima Wagner's Dairies: An Abridgement, 1994; Selected Letters of Paul Hindemith, 1995. Translations from German: The Marat-Sade, play by Peter Weiss (with Adrian Mitchell), 1964; Cosima Wagner's Diaries, 1978, 1980; Works by Max Frisch, Freidrich Heer, Günter Herburger, Robert Lucas; Training Ground, novel by Siegfried Lenz, 1991. Honours: American PEN Prize for Translation (with Adrian Mitchell), 1967; Schlegel-Tieck Translation Prizes, 1973, 1992; Yorkshire Post Music Award, 1975. Memberships: Radiowriters Association, executive committee 1969-72; Translators Association, executive committee 1972-74, 1979-81, chairman, 1974. Address: 49 Downside, Shoreham, West Sussex BN43 6HF, England.

SKOCPOL Theda, b. 4 May 1947, Detroit, Michigan, USA. Sociologist; Political Scientist; Writer. m. 1 son. Appointment: Faculty, Harvard University, 1986-. Contributions to: Books and professional journals. Honours: J David Greenstone Award and Woodrow Wilson Foundation Award, American Political Association, 1993; Allan Sharlin Memorial Award, Social Science History Association, 1993; Political Sociology Book Award, American Sociological Association, 1993; Ralph Waldo Emerson Prize, Phi Beta Kappa, 1995; C Wright Mills Award, 1979; Co-winner, American Sociologists Association Award for Distinguished Contribution to Scholarship, 1980. Address: c/o Department of Government, Harvard University, Cambridge, MA 02138, USA.

SKRZYNECKI Peter, b. 6 Apr 1945, Imhert, Germany (Australian citizen). Lecturer; Poet. m. Kate Magrath, 1 son, 2 daughters. Education: University of Sydney. Appointments: Lecturer, University of Western Sydney, 1987. Publications: Poetry: There, Behind the Lids, 1970; Headwaters, 1972; Immigrant Chronicle, 1975; The Aviary: Poems, 1975-77, 1978; The Polish Immigrant, 1982; Night Swim, 1989. Other: Joseph's Coat: An Anthology of Multicultural Writing, 1985; Short Story, The Wild Dogs, 1987; The Beloved Mountain (novel), 1988. Honour: Captain Cook Bicentenary Award, 1970. Address: 6 Sybil Street, Eastwood, New South Wales 2122, Australia.

SKUNCKE Marie-Christine, b. 20 Jan 1951, Paris, France. Associate Professor (Docent) in Comparative Literature; Writer. Education: French Baccalauréat, 1968; Fil Mag, University of Lund, Sweden, 1970; BA, 1973, PhD, 1980, Cambridge University. Appointment: Associate Professor (Docent) in Comparative Literature, Uppsala University, Sweden. Publications: Sweden and European Drama 1772-1796, 1981; Gustaf III: Det Offentliga Barnet (Gustaf III:

A Royal Childhood), 1993. Contributions to: Scholarly and popular articles on Swedish eighteenth century literature and history; Scholarly articles on nineteenth century women writers in Sweden and Poland. Honours: Shortlisted, Swedish August Prize, 1993; Prizes, Swedish Academy, 1994, Royal Swedish Academy of Letters, 1994, Swedish Literary Society of Finland, 1996. Memberships: President, Swedish Society for Eighteenth-Century Studies, 1990-94; Executive Committee, International Society for Eighteenth-Century Studies, 1995-99. Address: Tegnérgatan 27C, S-752 26 Uppsala, Sweden.

SKVORECKY Josef (Vacláv), b. 27 Sept 1924, Nachod, Czechoslovakia (Canadian citizen). Professor of English (retired); Author. Education: PhD, Charles University, Prague, 1951. Appointments: Professor of English, University of Toronto, 1975-90. Publications: The Views in the February Night, 1948; The Cowards, 1958; Murder for Luck, 1962; The Menorah, 1964; The Life of High Society, 1965; The Bass Saxophone, 1967; A Babylonian Story, 1967; The End of the Nylon Age, 1967; Miss Silver's Past, 1969; The Bitter World: Selected Stories, 1946-67, 1969; The Tank Battalion, 1969; The Miracle Game, 1972; Sins for Father Knox, 1973; The Swell Season, 1975; The Engineer of Human Souls, 1977; Dvorák Society, 1985; A Bride From Texas, 1992. Other: God in Your House (play), 1980; Screenplays, television plays, essays and translations. Honour: Honorary Citizen, City of Prague, 1990. Address: 487 Sackville Street, Toronto, Ontario MM4X 1T6, Canada.

SLATER Ian David, b. 1 Dec 1941, Queensland, Australia. Author; Lecturer. m. Marian Ella Wray Johnston, 18 Dec 1968, 1 son, 1 daughter. Education: BA, 1972, MA, 1972, PhD, 1977, University of British Columbia. Appointments: Editor, Pacific Affairs; Lecturer, University of British Columbia; Visiting Lecturer, University of Ljubljana, 1984; Writer-in-Residence, Simon Fraser University, 1986, Sechelt Festival of the Arts, 1988. Publications: 16 books, radio plays. Honours: Royal Institute Scholarship; Mark Eastman United Nations Award. Membership: Authors Guild of America. Address: 4074 West 17th Avenue, Vancouver, British Columbia V6S 1A6, Canada.

SLATTA Richard Wayne, b. 22 Oct 1947, North Dakota, USA. Professor of History; Writer. m. Maxine P Atkinson, 25 June 1982, 1 son. Education: BA cum laude, Pacific Lutheran University, 1969; MA, Portland State University, 1974; PhD, History, University of Texas at Austin, 1980. Appointments: Professor of History, North Carolina State University; Staff Writer, Cowboys and Indiana magazine, 1994-; Staff Writer, Persimmon Hill, 1996-. Publications: Gauchos and the Vanishing Frontier, 1992; Cowboys of the Americas, 1994; The Cowboy Encyclopedia, 1994, paperback edition, 1996; Comparing Cowboys and Frontiers, 1997. Contributions to: Cowboys and Indians; History Microcomputer Review; Professional journals. Honours: Hubert Herring Book Prize, 1984; Western Heritage Award for Non-Fiction, National Cowboy Hall of Fame, 1991; Best Reference Work, American Library Association and Library Journal,1994. Memberships: American Historical Association; Conference on Latin American History; Western History Association. Address: c/o Department of History, Box 8108, North Carolina State University, Raleigh, NC 27695-8108, USA.

SLAVITT David R(ytman), (David Benjamin, Henry Lazarus, Lynn Meyer, Henry Sutton), b. 23 Mar 1935, White Plains, New York, USA. Novelist; Poet; Translator; Lecturer. m. (1) Lynn Nita Meyer, 27 Aug 1956, div 1977, 2 sons, 1 daughter, (2) Janet Lee Abraham, 16 Apr 1978. Education: BA, magna cum laude, Yale University, 1956; MA, Columbia University, 1957. Appointments: Instructor in English, Georgia Institute of Technology, Atlanta, 1957-58; Staff, Newsweek magazine, 1958-63; Assistant Professor, University of Maryland, College Park, 1977; Associate Professor of English, Temple University, Philadelphia, 1978-80; Lecturer in English, Columbia University, 1985-86; Lecturer, Rutgers University, 1987-; Lecturer in English and Classics, University of Pennsylvania, 1991-; Visiting Professorships; Many university and college poetry readings. Publications: Novels: Rochelle, or Virtue Rewarded, 1966; Feel Free, 1968; Anagrams, 1970; ABCD, 1972; The Outer Mongolian, 1973; The Killing of the King, 1974; King of Hearts, 1976; Jo Stern, 1978; Cold Comfort, 1980; Ringer, 1982; Alice at 80, 1984; The Agent, 1986; The Hussar, 1987; Salazar Blinks, 1988; Lives of the Saints, 1989; Turkish Delights, 1993; The Cliff, 1994. As Henry Sutton: The Exhibitionist, 1967; The Voyeur, 1969; Vector, 1970; The Liberated, 1973; The Sacrifice: A Novel of the Occult, 1978; The Proposal, 1980. As Lynn Meyer: Paperback Thriller, 1975; As Henry Lazarus: That Golden Woman, 1976. As David Benjamin: The Idol, 1979. Non-fiction: Understanding Social Life: An Introduction to Social Psychology (with

Paul F Secord and Carl W Backman), 1976; Physicians Observed, 1987; Virgil, 1991. Other: Editor: Adrien Stoutenburg: Land of Superior Mirages: New and Selected Poems, 1986; Short Stories Are Not Real Life: Short Fiction, 1991. Translator: The Eclogues of Virgil, 1971; The Eclogues and the Georgics of Virgil, 1972; The Tristia of Ovid, 1985; Ovid's Poetry of Exile, 1990; Seneca: The Tragedies, 1992; The Fables of Avianus, 1993; The Metamorphoses of Ovid, 1994. Contributions to: Various other books as well as periodicals. Honours: Pennsylvania Council on the Arts Award, 1985; National Endowment for the Arts Fellowship, 1988; American Academy and Institute of Arts and Letters Award, 1989; Rockefeller Foundation Artist's Residence, 1989. Address: 523 South 41st Street, Philadelphia, PA 19104, USA.

SLIDE Anthony Clifford, b. 7 Nov 1944, Birmingham, England. Film Historian; Archivist; Writer. Appointments: Editor, Filmmakers, 1982-; Book Reviewer, Classic Images, 1989-. Publications include: Early American Cinema, 1970; Early Women Directors, 1977; The Vaudevillians, 1981; The American Film Industry: A Historical Dictionary, 1986; The Big V: A History of the Vitagraph Company, 1987; Silent Portrait, 1990; Nitrate Won't Wait: A History of Film Preservation in the United States, 1992; Before Video: A History of the Non-Theatrical Film, 1992; Gay and Lesbian Characters and Themes in Mystery Novels, 1993; The Encyclopedia of Vaudeville, 1994. Contributions to: Periodicals. Honours: Outstanding Reference of the Year Citation, American Library Association, 1987, 1994; Honorary DLitt, Bowling Green University, 1990. Address: 4118 Rhodes Avenue, Studio City, CA 91604, USA.

SLOAN Allan. Journalist. m. Nancy Sloan, 3 children. Education: BA, Brooklyn College, 1966; MS, Graduate School of Journalism, Columbia University, 1967. Appointments: Writer, syndicated business column, including Washington Post; Boston Globe; Dallas Morning News; Los Angeles Times; Denver Post; Business Reporter, Detroit Free Press, 1972-78; Staff Writer, Associate Editor, 1979-81, Senior Editor, 1984-88, Forbes magazine; Staff Writer, Money magazine, 1982-84; Wall Street Editor, Newsweek, 1995-. Honours: Four-time Winner, Gerald Loeb Award; John Hancock Award for Excellence in Business and Financial Journalism. Address: c/o Newsweek, 251 West 57th Street, New York, NY 10019-1894, USA.

SLOAN Carolyn, b. 15 Apr 1937, London, England. Freelance Journalist; Children's Author. m. David Hollis, 15 May 1961, 2 sons. Education: Harrogate College; Tutorial Schools, Newcastle, Guildford. Publications: Carter is a Painter's Cat, 1971; The Penguin and the Vacuum Cleaner, 1974; Shakespeare, Theatre Cat, 1982; Skewer's Garden, 1983; Helen Keller, 1984; An Elephant for Muthu, 1986; The Sea Child, 1987; Don't Go Near the Water, 1988; Gracie, 1994; Incredible Journey, 1996. Contributions to: Newspapers and journals. Membership: Society of Authors. Address: 7 Dapdune Road, Guildford, Surrey GU1 4NY, England.

SLOMAN Anne, b. 24 Apr 1944, London, England. Journalist. m. Martyn Sloman, 22 Apr 1972, 2 sons. Education: BA, Honours, Politics, Philosophy and Economics, St Hilda's College, Oxford University, 1963-66. Appointments: Radio Producer 1967-72, TV Producer, 1972-73, Senior Producer, Radio, Current Affairs, Executive Producer, General Election and US Presidential Results Coverage, 1973-81, Assistant Editor, Today Programme, 1981-82, Editor, Special Current Affairs, 1983-, BBC; Editor, Special Current Affairs, 1983-94; Deputy Head of Weekly Programmes (TV & Radio) BBC, News & Current Affairs, 1994-. Publications: Co-author: British Political Facts 1900-79, 1980; No Minister, 1982; But Chancellor, 1983; With Respect Ambassador, 1985; The Thatcher Phenomenon, 1986. Honours: Award, Outstanding Programme Contribution, Broadcasting Guild of Journalists; Broadcasting Press Guild Radio Award, Outstanding Programme, 1985; Outstanding Contribution, 1988. Address: 29 Church Crescent, London N10, England.

SLOTKIN Richard Sidney, b. 8 Nov 1942, Brooklyn, New York, USA. Professor of English; Writer. m. Iris F Shupack, 23 June 1963, 1 son. Education: BA, Brooklyn College of the City University of New York, 1963; PhD, Brown University, 1967. Appointments: Faculty, 1966-76, Professor of English, 1976-, Chairman, Department of American Studies, 1976-, Olin Professor, 1982-, Wesleyan University. Publications: Regeneration Through Violence: The Mythology of the American Frontier, 1600-1860, 1973; So Dreadful a Judgement: Puritan Responses to King Philip's War, 1675-1677 (with J K Folsom), 1978; The Crater: A Novel of the Civil War, 1980; The Fatal Environment: The Myth of the Frontier in the Age of Industrialization,

1800-1890, 1985; The Return of Henry Starr, 1988; Gunfighter Nation: The Myth of the Frontier in Twentieth Century America, 1992. Contributions to: Professional journals. Honours: Albert J Beveridge Award, American Historical Association, 1973; National Endowment for the Humanities Fellowship, 1973-74; Rockefeller Foundation Fellowship, 1976-77; Little Big Horn Association Award, 1986. Memberships: American Association of University Professors; American Film Institute; American Historical Association; American Studies Association; Authors Guild; Modern Language Association; Organization of American Historians; PEN; Society of American Historians, fellow; Western History Association. Address: c/o Department of English, Wesleyan University, Middletown, CT 06459, USA.

SMALL Ernest. See: **LENT Blair**.

SMALL Michael Ronald, b. 3 Jan 1943, Croydon, Surrey, England. Teacher; Short Story Writer; Poet; Textbook Writer. Education: BA, London University; BEd, La Trobe University, Australia; MA, University of Windsor, Canada. Publications: Her Natural Life and Other Stories, 1988; Film: A Resource Book for Studying Film as Text (with Brian Keyte), 1994; A History of the ootscray Football Club: Unleashed, (with John Lack, Chris McConville, Damien Wright), 1996. Contributions to: Numerous journals and magazines. Membership: Victorian Fellowship of Australian Writers. Address: 71 Strabane Avenue, Box Hill North, Victoria 3129, Australia.

SMALLEY Stephen Stewart, b. 11 May 1931, London, England. Clerk in Holy Orders. m. Susan Jane Paterson, 13 July 1974, dec 3 Nov 1995. Education: BA, 1955, MA, 1958, PhD, 1979, Jesus College, Cambridge; BD, 1957, Eden Theological Seminary, USA; Deacon, 1958, Priest, 1959, Ridley Hall, Cambridge. Appointments: Assistant Curate, St Paul's, Portman Square, London, 1958-60; Chaplain, Peterhouse, Cambridge, 1960-63, Acting Dean, 1962-63, Lecturer and Senior Lecturer, University of Ibadan, Nigeria, 1963-69; Lecturer and Senior Lecturer, University of Manchester, 1970-77; Warden of St Anselm Hall, 1972-77; Canon Residentiary and Precentor, 1977-86, Vice-Provost 1986, Coventry Cathedral; Dean, Chester Cathedral, 1987-. Publications: The Spirit's Power, 1972; Christ and Spirit in the New Testament (editor), 1973; John: Evangelist and Interpreter, 1978; 1, 2, 3 John, 1984; Thunder and Love: John's Revelation and John's Community, 1994. Contributions to: Learned journals. Honours: Foundation and Lady Kay Scholar, Jesus College, Cambridge, 1948, 1955; Select Preacher, University of Cambridge, 1963-64; Manson Memorial Lecturer, University of Manchester, 1986. Memberships: Archbishops' Doctrine Commission of the Church of England, 1981-86; Studiorum Novi Testamenti Societas; Chester City Club. Address: The Deanery, 7 Abbey Street, Chester CH1 2JF, England.

SMARANDACHE Florentin, b. 10 Dec 1954, Balcesti, Vilcea, Romania. Mathematician; Writer. Education: MA, Mathematics and Computer Science, University of Craiova. Publications: Nonpoems, 1990; Circles of Light, Dark Snow, 1992; Philosophia Paradoxae, 1995; FUGIT, 1995. Other: Books in Romanian and French. Contributions to: Anthologies and other publications. Memberships: Romanian Mathmatical Association; US Mathematical Association. Address: 2456 S Rose Park Drive, Tucson, AZ 85710, USA.

SMEDS Dave, b. 23 Feb 1955, Reedley, California, USA. Author. m. Connie Willeford, 26 June 1982, 1 son, 1 daughter. Education: BA, English, Psychology, Sonoma State University. Publications: The Sorcery Within, 1985; The Schemes of Dragons, 1989. Contributions to: Anthologies and magazines. Memberships: Authors Guild; Science Fiction Writers of America. Address: 164 Jack London Drive, Santa Rosa, CA 95409, USA.

SMEED John William, b. 21 Feb 1926, London, England. Emeritus Professor in German. m. Gay Jones, 24 Mar 1952. Education: BA, MA, PhD, University of Wales. Publications: Jean Paul's Dreams, 1966; Faust in Literature, 1975; The Theophrastan Character, 1985; German Song and its Poetry, 1987; Don Juan: Variations on a Theme, 1990; Famous Poets, Neglected Composers, Songs to Lyrics by Goethe, Heine, Mörike and others, 1992. Contributions to: Literary Periodicals in England, Germany and USA. Honours: University of Wales Fellowship, 1953; Leverhulme Research Fellowship, 1983. Address: 53 Claypath, Durham DH1 1QS, England.

SMELSER Neil Joseph, b. 22 July 1930, Kahoka, Missouri, USA. Professor of Sociology Emeritus; Writer. m. (1) Helen Thelma Margolis, 10 June 1954, div 1965, 1 son, 1 daughter, (2) Sharin Fateley, 20 Dec 1967, 1 son, 1 daughter. Education: BA, 1952, PhD, 1958, Harvard University; BA, 1954, MA, 1959, Magdalen College, Oxford; Graduate, San Francisco Psychoanalytic Institute, 1971. Appointments: Advisory Editor, American Journal of Sociology, 1960-82; Editor, American Sociological Review, 1962-65, 1989-90; Faculty, 1958-62, Professor of Sociology, 1962-72, University Professor of Sociology, 1972-94, Professor Emeritus, 1994-, University of California at Berkeley; Durector, Center for Advanced Study in the Behavioral Sciences, Stanford, 1994-. Publications: Economy and Society (with T Parsons), 1956; Social Change in the Industrial Revolution, 1959; Theory of Collective Behavior, 1962; The Sociology of Economic Life, 1963, 2nd edition, 1975; Essays in Sociological Explanation, 1968; Sociological Theory: A Contemporary View, 1971; Comparative Methods in the Social Sciences, 1976; The Changing Academic Market (with Robin Content), 1980; Sociology, 1981, 5th edition, 1995; Social Paralysis and Social Change, 1991; Effective Committee Service, 1993. Editor: Personality and Social Systems (with W T Smelser), 1963, 2nd edition, 1971; Social Structure and Mobility in Economic Development (with S M Lipset), 1966; Sociology: A Survey Report (with James Davis), 1969; Karl Marx on Society and Social Change, 1973; Public Higher Education in California (with Gabriel Almond), 1974; Themes of Work and Love in Adulthood (with Erik Erikson), 1980; The Micro-Macro Link (with others), 1987; Handbook of Sociology, 1988; Social Change and Modernity (with Hans Haferkamp), 1992; Theory of Culture (with Richard Munch), 1992; The Handbook of Economic Sociology (with Richard Swedberg), 1994; Problematics of Sociology, 1997. Honours: Rhodes Scholar, 1952-54; Junior Fellow, Society of Fellows, Harvard University, 1955-58; Russell Sage Foundation Fellow, 1989-90. Memberships: American Academy of Arts and Sciences, honorary member; American Philosophical Society, honorary member; National Academy of Sciences, honorary member; American Sociological Association, president, 1996-97; International Sociological Association, vice-president, 1990-94; Pacific Sociological Association. Address: 400 El Escarpado, Stanford, CA 94305, USA.

SMIRNOV Igor Pavlovich, b. 19 May 1941, Leningrad, Russia. Professor of Russian Literature. m. Johanna Renate Luise Elisabeth Döring-Smirnov, 16 July 1979. Education: MA, Leningrad State University, 1963; Dr Phil Sci, Institute of Russian Literature, Leningrad, 1967. Appointments: Editorial Board, Elementa, Journal of Slavic Studies and Comparative Cultural Semiotics, Los Angeles, 1992; New Literary Review, Moscow, 1992; Professor of Russian Literature, University of Konstanz. Publications: Meaning in Art and the Evolution of Poetic Systems, 1977; The Emergence of the Inter-text, 1985; Towards a Theory of Literature, 1987; Being and Creating, 1990; On Old Russian Culture, Russian National Specificity and the Logic of History, 1991; Psychohistory of Russian Literature from Romanticism Till Now, 1995; Der Welt der Slaven, 1995. Contributions to: Russian Literature; Wiener Slawistischer Almanach; Mesto pechati. Address: Guerickestrasse 35, 80 805 Munich, Germany.

SMITH A(nthony) C(harles) H(ockley), b. 31 Oct 1935, Kew, England. Writer. Education: MA, Cambridge University. Appointments: Literary Associate, Royal Shakespeare Co, 1964-74; Senior Research Associate, University of Birmingham, 1965-69; Director, Cheltenham Festival of Literature, 1978-79; Chairman, Playwrights Company, 1979-83; Visiting Professor, Emory University, Atlanta, Georgia, 1986, University of Texas, 1990-91, 1994. Publications: The Crowd, 1965; Zero Summer, 1971; Orghast at Persepolis, 1972; Paper Voices, 1975; Treatment, 1976; The Jericho Gun, 1977; Edward and Mrs Simpson, 1978; Extra Cover, 1981; The Dark Crystal, 1982; Wagner, 1983; Sebastian the Navigator, 1985; Lady Jane, 1985; Labyrinth, 1986. Contributions to: Newspapers, magazines, and television. Honours: Arts Council Writing Awards, 1970-71, 1974-75, 1980; University of Bristol Drama Fellowship, 1976-79. Membership: Writers' Guild of Great Britain. Address: 21 West Shrubbery, Bristol BS6 6TA, England.

SMITH Barbara Herrnstein, b. 6 Aug 1932, New York, New York, USA. Professor of Comparative Literature and English; Writer. m (1) R J Herrnstein, 28 May 1951, div 1961, (2) T H Smith, 21 Feb 1964, div 1974, 2 daughters. Education: BA, 1954, MA, 1955, PhD, English and American Literature, 1965, Brandeis University. Appointments: Faculty, Bennington College, Vermont, 1961-73, University of Pennsylvania, 1973-87; Professor of Comparative Literature and English, Duke University, 1987-; Northrop Frye Chair, University of Toronto, 1990. Publications: Poetic Closure: A Study of How Poems End, 1968; On the Margins of Discourse: The Relation of

Literature to Language, 1978; Contingencies of Value: Alternative Perspectives for Critical Theory, 1988; The Politics of Liberal Education (co-editor), 1991. Contributions to: Professional journals. Address: c/o Department of English, Duke University, Durham, NC 27706, USA.

SMITH Bernard William, b. 3 Oct 1916, Sydney, New South Wales, Australia. Art Historian and Critic. m. (1) Kate Beatrice Hartley Challis, 16 May 1941, 1 son, 1 daughter, (2) Margaret Patricia Thompson, 30 July 1995. Education: BA, Sydney University, 1952; Warburg Institute, London, England, 1948-50; PhD, Australian National University, 1956. Appointment: Category A Literary Fellowship, Australia Council, 1990-91. Publications: Place, Taste and Tradition, 1945; European Vision and the South Pacific, 1960; Australian Painting, 1962; The Architectural Character of Glebe, Sydney (with K Smith), 1973; Documents on Art and Taste in Australia, 1975; The Boy Adeodatus, 1984; The Art of Captain Cook's Voyages (with R Joppien), 3 volumes, 1985-87; The Death of the Artist as Hero, 1988; The Critic as Advocate, 1989; Imagining the Pacific, 1992; Noel Counitian, 1993; Poems, 1996. Contributions to: Journal of the Wartburg and Courtauld Institutes, Modern Painters (London); Meanjin, Scripsi, Australian Society. Honours: Co-Recipient, Ernest Scott Prize for History, Melbourne, 1962; Henry Lawson Prize for Poetry, 1964; Honorary LittD, University of Melbourne, 1976; Australian National Book Council Prize, Nettie Palmer Prize for Non-Fiction and Talking Book Award, 1984. Memberships: Australian Society of Authors; Australian Academy of the Humanities, president, 1977-80; Australian Humanities Research Council, secretary, 1962-65; Fellow, Society of Antiquaries; UNESCO Committee for Letters, Australia, 1963-69. Address: 168 Nicholson Street, Fitzroy, Victoria 3065, Australia.

SMITH Bradley F, b. 5 Oct 1931, Seattle, Washington, USA. Writer; Teacher. m. 31 Dec 1983, 2 daughters. Education: BA, 1957, MA, 1960, University of California at Berkeley. Publications: Adolf Hitler: His Family, Childhood, and Youth, 1967; Himmler Geheimreden, 1974; Reaching Judgement at Nuremberg, 1977; Operation Sunrise (with Elena Agarossi), 1979; The American Road to Nuremberg, 1981; The Road to Nuremberg, 1981; The Shadow Warriors, 1983; The War's Long Shadow, 1986; The Ultra-Magic Deals and the Special Relationship, 1940-46, 1992; Sharing Secrets with Stalin, Anglo-American Intelligence Cooperation with the USSR 1941-1945, 1996. Contributions to: Newspapers and journals. Honours: Observer Book of the Year, 1977; Shortlisted for Los Angeles Times Book of the Year, 1981; Phi Beta Kappa. Membership: Authors Guild. Address: 104 Regents Park Road, London NW1 8UG, England.

SMITH Bryan. See: KNOTT William Cecil.

SMITH Cecile Norma Musson, (Cecile Norma Musson), b. 13 Aug 1914, Bermuda. Educator; Journalist; Welfare Activist. m. James A C Smith, dec, 23 Nov 1955. Education: Cambridge University, 1935; Graduate, Ontario Business College; Certificates, Queens University, University of Maryland, Bermuda College. Appointments: Founder, President, Bermuda Writers Club, 1957; Honorary Representative, Centro Studies S Leonardo da Vinci, 1963-80. Publications: Thoughts in Verse, 1937; Acclaimed, 1942; BWC History, 1942; Island Life, 1951; When I Began, 1994. Contributions to: World Fair Anthology of Verse; South and West USA; Bermuda Review; Poetic Voices of America. Honour: CSSI Great Prize, Rome. Memberships: LFABIRA; Deputy Governor, United Poets Laureate. Address: Cavendish Apt 2, Block 7, Hibiscus, Devonshire DV03, Bermuda.

SMITH C(larice) Holly, b. 12 July 1931, Sydney, New South Wales, Australia. Editor; Writer; Creative Writing Tutor. Education: Teachers Certificate, New South Wales Department of Education, 1954; International Correspondence School courses, Short Story, Radio Playwriting, TV Scriptwriting, Public Relations, 1960-96, Diploma, 1996; Certificate, Advertising Copywriting, 1988; Diploma, Journalism, 1989. Appointments: Own business, Proofreading and Editing Services, 1988-; Planned, wrote, conducted 2 series of radio interviews, Meet the Authors (14 interviews), 1990, 1993; Tutor, The Writing School, 1991-. Publication: The Metric Primer, 1973. Contributions to: Newspapers and journals. Honours: Best Newsletter Award for Editing, New South Wales Fellowship of Australian Writers, 1993. Memberships: Actors Equity; Fellowship of Australian Writers. Address: 6 Park Avenue, Avalon Beach, New South Wales 2107, Australia.

SMITH Dave, b. 19 Dec 1942, Portsmouth, Virginia, USA. Professor; Poet. m. Deloras M Weaver, 31 Mar 1966, 1 son, 2 daughters. Education: BA, English, University of Virginia, 1965; MA, English, Southern Illinois University, 1969; PhD, English, Ohio University, 1976. Appointments: Teacher, Poquoson High School, Poquoson, Virginia, 1965-67; Teaching Assistant, Southern Illinois University, 1967-69, Ohio University, 1971-72, 1975-76; Instructor, Western Michigan University, 1973-74; Assistant Professor, Cottey College, Missouri, 1974-75; Assistant Professor/Director, Creative Writing, University of Utah, 1975-77; Associate Professor/Director, Creative Writing, University of Utah, 1977-79; Visiting Professor, State University of New York, Binghamton, 1979-80; Associate Professor/Director, Creative Writing, University of Florida, 1980-81; Professor, Virginia Commonwealth University, 1981-90, Louisiana State University, 1990-. Publications: Onliness, 1981; In the House of the Judge, 1983; Southern Delights, 1983; Gray Soldiers, 1984; The Morrow Anthology of Younger American Poets, 1985; The Roundhouse Voices: Selected and New Poems, 1985; Local Assays: On Contemporary American Poetry, 1985; Cuba Night, 1990; The Essential Poem, 1991; Night Pleasures: New and Selected Poems, 1992; Fate's Kite: Poems 1991-95, 1996; Floating on Solitude: Three Books of Poetry, 1996. Contributions to: American Scholar; Kenyon Review; Georgia Review; Paris Review; Partisan Review; New Yorker; Nation; Poetry. Honours: National Endowment for the Arts Fellowship, 1976, 1981; Academy of Arts and Letters Award, 1979; Reader's Poetry Prize, Prairie Schooner, 1980, 1995; Guggenheim Fellowship, 1981; Lyndhurst Fellowship, 1987-89. Memberships: Poetry Society of America; Associated Writing Programs; Fellowship of Southern Authors. Address: Editor, The Southern Review, 43 Allen Hall, Louisiana State University, Baton Rouge, LA 70803, USA.

SMITH David Lawrence, b. 3 Dec 1963, London, England. Lecturer in History. Education: Eastbourne College, 1972-81; Selwyn College, Cambridge, BA 1st Class Hons, 1985, MA, 1989, PhD, 1990. Appointment: Fellow, Selwyn College, Cambridge, 1988-. Publications: Oliver Cromwell, 1991; Louis XIV, 1992; Constitutional Royalism and the Search for Settlement, 1994; The Theatrical City, 1995. Contributions to: Historical Journal; Historical Research; Journal of British Studies; Transactions of the Royal Historical Society. Honour: Alexander Prize, Royal Historical Society, 1991. Membership: Fellow, Royal Historical Society, 1992. Address: Selwyn College, Cambridge CB3 9DQ, England.

SMITH Delia. Cookery Writer and Broadcaster. m. Michael Wynn Jones. Appointments: Several BBC TV Series; Cookery Writer, Evening Standard, later the Standard, 1972-85; Columnist, Radio Times. Publications: How to Cheat at Cooking, 1971; Country Fare, 1973; Recipes from Country Inns and Restaurants, 1973; Family Fare, book 1, 1973, book 2, 1974; Evening Standard Cook Book, 1974; Country Recipes from "Look East", 1975; More Country Recipes from "Look East", 1976; Frugal Food, 1976; Book of Cakes, 1977; Recipes from "Look East", 1977; Food for Our Times, 1978; Cookery Course, part 1, 1978, part 2, 1979, part 3, 1981; The Complete Cookery Course, 1982; A Feast for Lent, 1983; A Feast for Advent, 1983; One is Fun, 1985; Food Aid Cookery Book (editor), 1986; A Journey into God, 1988; Delia Smith's Christmas, 1990; Delia Smith's Summer Collection, 1993. Contributions to: Consultant Food Editor, Sainsbury's The Magazine. Honours: Andre Simon Memorial Fund Special Award, 1994; Officer of the Order of the British Empire, 1995. Address: c/o Deborah Owen Ltd, 78 Narrow Street, London E14 8BP, England.

SMITH Sir Dudley, b. 14 Nov 1926, Cambridge, England. Former Journalist; Member of Parliament. m. (1), div, 1 son, 2 daughters, (2) Catherine Amos, 1976. Appointments: Journalist and Senior Executive, various provincial and national newspapers, 1943-66; Assistant News Editor, Sunday Express, 1953-59; Divisional Director, Beecham Group, 1966-70; Member of Parliament; Deputy Lieutenant, Warwickshire; Secretary-General, European Democratic Group, Council of Europe, 1985-; President, Western European Assembly, 1993-. Publications: They Also Served, 1945; Harold Wilson: A Critical Biography, 1964. Honours: Knighted, 1983; Honorary DL, 1989. Address: Church Farm, Weston under Wetherley, Near Leamington Spa, Warwickshire, England.

SMITH Emma, b. 21 Aug 1923, Newquay, Cornwall, England. Writer. m. Richard Llewellyn Stewart-Jones, 31 Jan 1951, dec 1957, 1 son, 1 daughter. Publications: Maiden's Trip, 1948; The Far Cry, 1949; Emily, 1959; Out of Hand, 1963; Emily's Voyage, 1966; No Way of Telling, 1972; The Opportunity of a Lifetime, 1978. Contributions to:

Various magazines. Honours: Atlantic Award, short stories, 1948; John Llewellyn Rhys Memorial Prize, 1948; James Tait Black Memorial Prize, 1949. Address: c/o Curtis Brown Ltd, Haymarket House, 28-29 Haymarket, London SW1Y 4SP, England.

SMITH Genevieve Douglas, b. 14 Aug 1923, McKees Rocks, Pennsylvania, USA. Educator: Education Administrator; Writer. m. William Reeves Smith, 6 Jan 1946, 1 daughter. Education: BBA, Westminster College, Pennsylvania, 1945; MS, 1971, EdD, 1973, University of Tennessee. Publications: Techniques and Activities for Teaching Business Skills: Featuring the Mini-Company, 1977; Genevieve Smith's Deluxe Handbook for the Executive Secretary, 1979; I'd Rather Be the Boss!, 1992. Contributions to: Journals and magazines. Honours: Pi Lambda Theta; Phi Delta Kappa. Memberships: American Education Research Association; International Women's Writing Guild; Knoxville Writers' Guild; National Business Education Association; Society of Children's Book Writers; Tennessee Writers' Alliance. Address: 1205 Snowdon Drive, Knoxville, TN 37912, USA.

SMITH Gregory Blake, b. 24 July 1951, Torrington, Connecticut, USA. Professor; Writer. m. Martha L Smith, 13 Apr 1987, 1 son. Education: AB, Bowdoin College, 1975, MA, Boston University, 1981; MFA, University of Iowa, 1983. Appointment: Professor, Carleton College. Publications: The Devil in the Dooryard, 1986; The Divine Comedy of John Venner, 1992; Nietzsche, Heidegger and the Transition to Postmodernity, 1995. Honours: Stegner Fellowship, Stanford University, 1985; National Endowment for the Arts Fellowship, 1988. Address: c/o Department of English, Carleton College, Northfield, MN 55057, USA.

SMITH Hedrick (Lawrence), b. 9 July 1933, Kilmacolm, Scotland. Journalist; Writer; Television Commentator; Lecturer. m. (1) Ann Bickford, 29 June 1957, div Dec 1985, 1 son, 3 daughters, (2) Susan Zox, 7 Mar 1987. Education: Graduated, Choate School, 1951; BA, Williams College, 1955; Postgraduate Studies, Balliol College, Oxford, 1955-56. Appointments: Staff, United Press International, 1959-62; Diplomatic News Correspondent, 1962-64, 1966-71, Middle East Correspondent, 1964-66, Chief, Moscow Bureau, 1971-74, Washington Bureau, 1976-79, Deputy National Editor, 1975-76, Washington Correspondent, 1980-85, New York Times; Panelist, Washington Week in Review, PBS-TV, 1969-; Visiting Journalist, American Enterprise Institute, 1985-87; Fellow, Foreign Policy Institute, School of Advanced International Studies, Johns Hopkins University, 1989-; Various PBS-TV documentaries; Many lectures. Publications: The Russians, 1975; The Power Game: How Washington Works, 1988; The New Russians, 1990; Rethinking America, 1995. With others: The Pentagon Papers, 1972; Reagan the Man, the President, 1981; Beyond Reagan: The Politics of Upheaval, 1986; Seven Days That Shook the World, 1991. Honours: Nieman Fellow, Harvard University, 1969-70; Pulitzer Prize for International Reporting, 1974; Overseas Press Club Award, 1976, and Citation, 1991; George Polk Award, 1990; Gold Baton Award, DuPont-Columbia University, 1990; George Foster Peabody Award, 1991; Hillman Award, 1996. Memberships: Gridiron Club; Phi Beta Kappa. Address: c/o Foreign Policy Institute, School of Advanced International Studies, Johns Hopkins University, Baltimore, MD 21218, USA.

SMITH Iain Crichton, b. 1 Jan 1928, Isle of Lewis, Scotland. Poet; Writer. m. Donalda Gillies Smith, 16 July 1977, 2 stepsons. Education: MA, Honours, English, Aberdeen University, 1949. Publications: Poetry: Thistles and Roses, 1961; The Law and the Grace, 1969; From Bourgeois Land, 1969; Love Poems and Elegies, 1972; Selected Poems, 1982; A Life, 1985; The Village and Other Poems, 1989; Collected Poems, 1992. Fiction: Consider the Lilies, 1968; The Last Summer, 1969; The Black and the Red (short stories), 1973; On the Island (short stories), 1974; The Hermit and Other Stories, 1977. Contributions to: Journals and magazines. Honours: PEN Poetry Award, 1970; Poetry Society Recommendations, 1972, 1975, 1989, 1992, and Choice, 1984; Commonwealth Poetry Prize, 1986; Saltire Award, 1992. Memberships: Royal Literature Society, fellow; Scottish Arts Council, main body, 1985-88, literature committee, 1985-91. Address: Tigh Na Fuaran, Taynuilt, Argyll, Scotland.

SMITH Jane (Marilyn) Davis, (Jane Maxwell), b. 18 May 1949, LaPorte, Indiana, USA. Writer. m. Donald Lee Smith, 15 Apr 1967, 2 sons, 2 daughters. Education: Certified Dental Assistant, Elkhart University of Medical Dental Technique, 1964; Graduate, Institute of Children's Literature, 1981; National Writers' Club Magazine Course,

1981; Fiction and non-fiction courses, Writers' Digest School, 1984-85, Rocky Mountain Writers' Institute, 1985-86. Appointments: Typist, University of Notre Dame Graduate School, 1971; Professional Children's Book Writer, 1979. Publication: Syndee The Chipmunk (children's book). Contributions to: New York Daily News; Central Coast Parent (California); Parentguide Magazine (New York). Honour: Third Place (Honorable Mention), Byline Magazine Prose Essay Contest, 1985. Memberships: National Writers Association; International Platform Association. Address: 139 Timber Lane, South Bend, IN 46615, USA.

SMITH Julie, b. 25 Nov 1944, Annapolis, Maryland, USA. Writer. Education: BA, University of Mississippi, 1965. Publications: Death Turns a Trick, 1982; Huckleberry Fiend, 1987; New Orleans Mourning, 1990; Axeman's Jazz, 1991; Jazz Funeral, 1993; New Orleans Beat, 1994; House of Blues, 1995. Contributions to: Periodicals. Honour: Edgar Allan Poe Award, Mystery Writers of America, 1991. Address: c/o Mystery Writers of America, 174 East 47th Street, New York, NY 10017, USA.

SMITH Lee, b. 1 Nov 1944, Grundy, Virginia, USA. University Teacher; Writer. m. (1) James E Seay, June 1967, div, 2 children, (2) Hal Crowther, June 1985. Education: BA, Hollins College, Virginia, 1967. Appointments: Staff, Tuscaloosa News, Alabama, 1968-69; Teacher, Harpeth Hall School, Nashville, Tennessee, 1971-73; Carolina Friends School, Durham, 1974-77; Lecturer in Creative Writing, University of North Carolina at Chapel Hill, 1977-81; Faculty, Department of English, North Carolina State University, Raleigh, 1981-; Fellow, Center for Documentary Studies, Duke University, 1991-93. Publications: The Last Day the Dogbushes Bloomed, 1968; Something in the Wind, 1971; Fancy Strut, 1973; Black Mountain Breakdown, 1980; Cakewalk (short stories), 1980; Oral History, 1983; Family Linen, 1985; Fair and Tender Ladies, 1988; Me and My Baby View the Eclipse (short stories), 1990; The Devil's Dream, 1992; Saving Grace, 1994. Honours: Book-of-the Month Club Fellowship, 1967; O Henry Awards, 1979, 1981, 1984; John Dos Passos Award, 1984; Sir Walter Raleigh Award, 1984; North Carolina Award for Literature, 1985; Lyndhurst Prize, 1990-92; Robert Penn Warren Prize, 1991. Memberships: North Carolina Writers Network; PEN. Address: c/o Department of English, North Carolina University, Raleigh, NC 27695, USA.

SMITH Lew. See: **FLOREN Lee.**

SMITH Moe Sherrard (Tyler Maddison), b. 22 June 1939, Leeds, England. Author; Journalist; Adjudicator; Literary Agent. m. Thomas Maddison Smith, 14 Mar 1962. Appointments: Staff, Scribe magazine, 1975-78, Driving Mirror Magazine, 1975-84, Pocklington Post, 1988-90; Principal, Writing Tutorial, 1975-. Publications: Write a Successful Novel; The Essential Guide to Novel Writing; Cold Blast of Winter; Rubbings; Wholly Love; Yorkshire Air Museum Guide Book. Contributions to: Various publications. Memberships: Various writers groups. Address: c/o Sherrard Smith Associates, Garthend House, Illington, York YO4 2TX, England.

SMITH Patrick D(avis), b. 8 Oct 1927, Mendenhall, Mississippi, USA. Writer; Lecturer. m. Iris Doty, 1 Aug 1948, 1 son, 1 daughter. Education: BA, 1947, MA, 1959, University of Mississippi. Appointments: Director, Public Relations, Hinds Community College, 1959-62; Director, Public Information, University of Mississippi, 1962-66; Director, College Relations, Brevard Community College, 1966-88. Publications: A Land Remembered; Allapattah; Angel City; Forever Island; The River Is Home; The Beginning. Contributions to: More than 1000. Honours: Tebeay Prize; Outstanding Author Award; Outstanding Florida Author Award; Best Writer Award; Toastmasters International Communication Achievement Award; Environmental Writers Award; Medal of Honor; Order of the South Award, Southern Academy of Arts, Letters and Sciences, 1995; Florida Ambassador of the Arts Award, Florida Department of State, 1996. Memberships: Space Coast Writers Guild; Authors Guild; Poets and Writers. Address: 1370 Island Drive, Merritt Island, FL 32952, USA.

SMITH Peter Charles Horstead, b. 15 Oct 1940, North Elmham, Norfolk, England. Author. Appointment: Editor, Photo Precision Ltd, printers and publishers, 1972-75. Publicatons: Destroyer Leader, 1968; Task Force 57, 1969, 2nd edition, 1994; Pedestal, 1970, 3rd edition, 1994; Stuka at War, 1970, 2nd edition, 1980; Hard Lying, 1971; British Battle Cruisers, 1972; War in the Aegean (with Edwin Walker), 1974; Heritage of the Sea, 1974; Battle of the Malta Striking Forces (with

Edwin Walker), 1974; Destroyer Action (editor and contributor), 1974; R A F Squadron Badges, 1974; The Story of the Torpedo Bomber, 1974; The Haunted Sea (editor), 1974; Per Mare Per Terram: A History of the Royal Marines, 1974; Arctic Victory, 1975, 2nd edition, 1994; The Battle of Midway, 1976; Fighting Flotilla, 1976; Undesirable Properties (editor and contributor), 1977; The Great Ships Pass. 1977; Hit First, Hit Hard, 1979; The Phantom Coach (editor and contributor), 1979; Action Imminent, 1980; Haunted Shores (editor and contributor), 1980; Impact: The Dive Bomber Pilots Speak, 1981; Cruisers in Action (with J R Dominy), 1981; Dive Bomber, 1982; Rendezvous Skerki Bank (fiction), 1982; Hold the Narrow Sea, 1984; Uninvited Guests, 1984; H M S Wild Swan, 1985; Into the Assault, 1985; Vengeance, 1986; Jungle Dive Bombers at War, 1987; Victoria's Victories, 1987; Dive Bombers in Action, 1988; The Royal Marines: A Pictorial History (with Derek Oakley), 1988; Battleship Royal Sovereign, 1988; Stuka Squadron, 1990; Close Air Support, 1990; T-6: The Harvard, Texan and Wirraway, 1995; Eagle's War, 1996; Ship Strike, 1996. Contributions to: Various publications. Honour: Royal Marines Historical Society Award, 1987-88. Memberships: Society of Authors, London; Royal Marines Historical Society, Eastney; American Aviation Historical Society. Address: Foxden, 12 Brooklands Road, Riseley, Bedford MK44 1EE, England.

SMITH Ralph Bernard, b. 9 May 1939, Bingley, England. Professor; Writer. Education: BA, 1959, PhD, 1963, University of Leeds. Appointments: Lecturer, later Reader in the History of South East Asia, 1962-88, Professor of the International History of Asia, 1988-, School of Oriental and African Studies, University of London. Publications: Vietnam and the West, 1968; Land and Politics in the England of Henry VIII, 1970; An International History of the Vietnam War, 3 volumes, 1983, 1985, 1991. Contributions to: Professional journals and general periodicals. Address: c/o School of Oriental and African Studies, University of London, Russell Square, London WC1, England.

SMITH Sandra Lee, b. 28 June 1945, San Francisco, California, USA. Writer; Teacher. m. Edward Leroy Smith Jr, 4 Mar 1967. Education: BA, 1967; Masters Degree, Bilingual/Multicultural Education, 1980. Publications: Loves Miracles (fiction), 1988; Coping with Decision Making, 1989; Dream Song (fiction), 1990; Value of Self Control, 1990; Drug Abuse Prevention, 1995; Discovering Personal Resources; Setting Goals; Discovering Own Space. Contributions to: Poetry and Articles. Honour: Silver Pen Award, 1990. Address: 5433 South Mill Avenue, Tempe, Arizona, USA.

SMITH Terry Lamson, b. 10 Nov 1937, Sydney, New South Wales, Australia. Journalist; Author. m. Sybilla Smith, 24 Feb 1970, 2 sons. Education: Shore School, Sydney. Publications: The Complete Book of Australian Golf, 1975, 3rd edition, 1988; Australian Golf: The First 100 Years, 1982; Aussie Golf Trivia, 1985; Path to Victory: Wallaby Rugby Power in the 80s, 1987; More Aussie Golf Trivia, 1988; The Champions: Australia's Sporting Greats, 1990; The Bedside Book of Cricket Centuries, 1991; I Love Youse All: The Jeff French Story, 1993. Contributions to: Newspapers and periodicals. Membership: Elanora Country Club. Address: 6 Shannon Avenue, Killarney Heights, Sydney, New South Wales 2087, Australia.

SMITH Vivian (Brian), b. 3 June 1933, Hobart, Tasmania, Australia. Lecturer; Poet; Editor. m. Sybille Gottwald, 15 Feb 1960, 1 son, 2 daughters. Education: MA, 1955, PhD, 1970, University of Sydney. Appointments: Lecturer, University of Tasmania, 1955-66; Literary Editor, Quadrant magazine, Sydney, 1975-90; Reader, University of Sydney, 1982-. Publications: The Other Meaning, 1956; An Island South, 1967; The Poetry of Robert Lowell, 1975; Familar Places, 1978; Tide Country, 1982; Tasmania and Australian Poetry, 1984; Selected Poems, 1985; New Selected Poems, 1995. Contributions to: Newspapers and magazines. Honours: Grace Leven Prize; New South Wales Premiers Prize, 1983. Membership: Australian Society of Authors. Address: 19 McLeod Street, Mosman, New South Wales 2088, Australia.

SMITH Wilbur Addison, b. 9 Jan 1933, Zambia (British citizen). Author. m. Danielle Smith, 2 sons, 1 daughter. Education: BComm, Rhodes University, 1953. Appointments: Former business executive; Professional writer, 1961-; Publications: When the Lion Feeds, 1964; The Dark of the Sun, 1965; The Sound of Thunder, 1966; Shout at the Devil, 1968; Gold Mine, 1970; The Diamond Hunters, 1971; The Sunbird, 1972; Eagle in the Sky, 1974; The Eye of the Tiger, 1975; Cry Wolf, 1976; A Sparrow Falls, 1977; Hungry as the Sea, 1978; Wild

Justice, 1979; A Falcon Flies, 1980; Men of Men, 1981; The Angels Weep, 1982; The Leopard Hunts in Darkness, 1984; The Burning Shore, 1985; Power of the Sword, 1986; Rage, 1987; The Courtneys, 1987; The Courtneys in Africa, 1988; A Time to Die, 1989; Golden Fox, 1990; Elephant Song, 1991; River God, 1993; The Seventh Scroll, 1995; Birds of Prey, 1997. Contributions to: Numerous journals and magazines. Address: c/o Charles Pick, Flat 3, 3 Bryanston Place, London, W1H 7FN, England.

SMITH William Jay, b. 22 Apr 1918, Winnfield, Louisiana, USA. Professor of English Emeritus; Poet; Writer. m. (1) Barbara Howes, 1947, div 1965, 2 sons, (2) Sonja Haussmann, 1966, 1 stepson. Education: BA, 1939, MA, 1941, Washington University, St Louis; Institut de Touraine, Tours, France, 1938; Columbia University, 1946-47; Wadham College, Oxford, 1947-48; University of Florence, 1948-50. Appointments: Instructor, 1946-47, Visiting Professor, 1973-75, Columbia University; Instructor, 1951, Poet-in-Residence and Lecturer, 1959-64, 1966-67, Williams College; Writer-in-Residence, 1965-66, Professor of English, 1967-68, 1970-80, Professor Emeritus, 1980-, Hollins College, Virginia; Consultant in Poetry, 1968-70, Honorary Consultant, 1970-76, Library of Congress, Washington, DC; Lecturer, Salzburg Seminar in American Studies, 1974; Fulbright Lecturer, Moscow State University, 1981; Poet-in-Residence, Cathedral of St John the Divine, New York City, 1985-88. Publications: Poetry: Poems, 1947; Celebrations at Dark, 1950; Snow, 1953; The Stork, 1954; Typewriter Birds, 1954; The Bead Curtain: Calligrams, 1957; The Old Man on the Isthmus, 1957; Poems 1947-1957, 1957; Prince Souvanna Phouma: An Exchange Between Richard Wilbur and William Jay Smith, 1963; Morels, 1964; The Tin Can and Other Poems, 1966; New and Selected Poems, 1970; A Rose for Katherine Anne Porter, 1970; At Delphi: For Allen Tate on His Seventy-Fifth Birthday, 19 November 1974, 1974; Venice in the Fog, 1975; Verses on the Times (with Richard Wilbur), 1978; Journey to the Dead Sea, 1979; The Tall Poets, 1979; Mr Smith, 1980; The Traveler's Tree: New and Selected Poems, 1980; Oxford Doggerel, 1983; Collected Translations: Italian, French, Spanish, Portuguese, 1985; The Tin Can, 1988; Journey to the Interior, 1988; Plain Talk: Epigrams, Epitaphs, Satires, Nonsense, Occasional, Concrete and Quotidian Poems, 1988; Collected Poems 1939-1989, 1990; Also 16 books of poetry for children, 1955-90. Stories: Ho for a Hat!, 1989. Other: The Spectra Hoax, 1961; The Skies of Venice, 1961; Children and Poetry: A Selective Bibliography (with Virginia Haviland), 1969, revised edition, 1979; Louise Bogan: A Woman's Words, 1972; The Streaks of the Tulip: Selected Criticism, 1972; Green, 1980; Army Brat: A Memoir, 1980. Editor: Herrick, 1962; The Golden Journey: Poems for Young People (with Louise Bogan), 1965, revised edition, 1990; Poems from France, 1967; Poems from Italy, 1972; A Green Place: Modern Poems, 1982. Contributions to: Journals and magazines. Honours: Rhodes Scholar, 1947-48; Ford Foundation Fellowship, 1964; Henry Bellamann Major Award, 1970; National Endowment for the Arts Grant, 1972; National Endowment for the Humanities Grants, 1975, 1989; Gold Medal of Labor, Hungary, 1978; Ingram Merrill Foundation Grant, 1982. Membership: American Academy of Arts and Letters, vice-president for literature, 1986-89. Address: 63 Luther Shaw Road, Cummington, MA 01026, USA.

SMITH Z Z. See: WESTHEIMER David.

SMITHYMAN (William) Kendrick, b. 9 Oct 1922. Poet; Writer. m. (1) Mary Stanley Smithyman, dec 1980, 3 sons, (2) Margaret Ann Edgcumbe, 1981. Education: Seddon Memorial Technical College, Auckland; Auckland Teachers College, Auckland University College. Appointment: Visiting Fellow, Commonwealth Literature, University of Leeds, England, 1969. Publications: Seven Sonnets, 1946; The Blind Mountain, 1951; The Gay Trapeze, 1955; The Night Shift: Poems on Aspects of Love (co-author), 1957; Inheritance, 1962; Flying to Palmerston, 1968; Earthquake Weather, 1974; The Seal in the Dolphin Pool, 1974; Dwarf with a Billiard Cue, 1978; Stories about Wooden Keyboards, 1985; Are You Going to the Pictures?, 1987; Selected Poems, 1989; Auto/Biographies, 1992. Editor: Novels by William Satchell, 1971, 1985; Short stories by Greville Texidor, 1987. Contributions to: Academic journals; Anthologies. Honour: DLitt, University of Auckland, 1986. Address: 66 Alton Avenue, Northcote, Auckland, New Zealand.

SMITTEN Richard, b. 22 Apr 1940, Bronx, New York, USA. Writer. 1 daughter. Education: BA, University of Western Ontario. Publications: Twice Killed, 1987; The Man Who Made it Snow (with Max Mermelstein and Robin Moore), 1990; Godmother, 1990; Bank of

Death, 1993; Legal Tender, 1994. Address: 3675 Skyline Drive, Jensen Beach, FL 34957, USA.

SMUCKER Barbara (Claassen), b. 1 Sept 1915, Newton, Kansas, USA. Writer; Librarian. m. 21 Jan 1939, 2 sons, 1 daughter. Education: BS, Kansas State University, 1936. Publications: Henry's Red Sea, 1955; Cherokee Run, 1957; Wigwam in the City, 1966; Runaway to Freedom, 1979; Days of Terror, 1979; Amish Adventure, 1983; Incredible Jumbo, 1990; Garth and the Mermaid, 1992. Contributions to: Various publications. Address: 20 Pinebrook Drive, Bluffton, OH 45817, USA.

SMYTH Dacre, b. 5 May 1923, London, England. Former Naval Officer. m. Jennifer Haggard, 11 Jan 1952, 1 son, 4 daughters. Education: RAN College, 1940. Publications: The Bridges of the Yarra, 1979; The Lighthouses of Victoria, 1980; Historic Ships of Australia, 1982; Old Riverboats of the Murray, 1982; Views of Victoria, 1984; The Bridges of Kananook Creek, 1986; Waterfalls of Victoria, 1988; Gallipoli Pilgrimage, 1990; Immigrant Ships to Australia, 1992; Pictures in My Life, 1994. Honour: Runner-up, Griffin Press Literary Award, 1990. Memberships: Fellowship of Australian Writers; Victoria Artists Society; Australian Guild of Realist Artists. Address: 22 Douglas Street, Toorak, Victoria 3142, Australia.

SMYTHE Colin Peter, b. 2 Mar 1942, Maidenhead, Berkshire, England. Editor; Publisher; Literary Agent. Education: Bradfield College, Berkshire, 1955-59; BA, 1963, MA, 1966, Trinity College, Dublin. Appointment: General Editor, Irish Literary Studies series. Publications: The Coole Edition of Lady Gregory's Writings (general editor), 1970-; A Guide to Coole Park: Home of Lady Gregory, 1973, 3rd edition, 1995; Lady Gregory: Our Irish Theatre (editor), 1973; Lady Gregory: Poets and Dreamers (editor), 1974; Lady Gregory: Seventy Years 1852-1922 (editor), 1974; The Collected Works of G W Russell - AE (general editor with Henry Summerfield), 1978-; Robert Gregory 1881-1918 (editor), 1981; Lady Gregory Fifty Years After (editor with Ann Saddlemyer), 1986; Oxford Companion to Irish Literature (associate editor), 1996. Honours: Various orders and medals including: Knight, Order of Our Lady of the Conception of Vila Viçosa, Portugal. Memberships: Athenaeum Club; American Conference for Irish Studies; British Association for Irish Studies; Canadian Association for Irish Studies; International Association for the Study of Irish Literature; Mark Twain Society, honorary member; Royal Society of Arts, fellow. Address: PO Box 6, Gerrards Cross, Bucks SL9 8XA, England.

SNEYD Lola. Poet; Short Story Writer; Journalist. Publications: The Asphalt Octopus, 1983; The Concrete Giraffe, 1984; Ringette is Fun, 1985; Nature's Big Top, 1987; Classy Cats, 1991. Memberships: Canadian Authors' Association; Canadian Society of Children's Authors, Illustrators & Performers; League of Canadian Poets. Honours: Canadian Children's Book Centre Our Choice; Lynn Harrington Award, Canadian Authors' Association, 1983. Address: 7 Wheeler Avenue, Toronto, Ontario M4L 3V3, Canada.

SNODGRASS W(illiam) D(e Witt), (S S Gardons, Will McConnell, Kozma Prutkov), b. 5 Jan 1926, Wilkinsburg, Pennsylvania, USA. Poet; Writer; Dramatist; Professor. m. (1) Lila Jean Hank, 6 June 1946, div Dec 1953, 1 daughter, (2) Janice Marie Ferguson Wilson, 19 Mar 1954, div Aug 1966, 1 son, (3) Camille Rykowski, 13 Sept 1967, div 1978, (4) Kathleen Ann Brown, 20 June 1985. Education: Geneva College, 1943-44, 1946-47; BA, 1949, MA, 1951, MFA, 1953, University of Iowa. Appointments: Instructor in English, Cornell University, 1955-57; Instructor, University of Rochester, New York, 1957-58; Assistant Professor of English, Wayne State University, Detroit, 1959-67; Professor of English and Speech, Syracuse University, New York, 1968-77; Visiting Professor, Old Dominion University, Norfolk, Virginia, 1978-79; Distinguished Professor, 1979-80, Distinguished Professor of Creative Writing and Contemporary Poetry, 1980-94, University of Delaware, Newark; Various lectures and poetry readings. Publications: Poetry: Heart's Needle, 1959; After Experience, 1967; As S S Gardons, Remains: A Sequence of Poems, 1970, revised edition, 1985; The Fuehrer Bunker, 1977; If Birds Build With Your Hair, 1979; D D Byrde Calling Jennie Wrenne, 1984; A Colored Poem, 1986; The House the Poet Built, 1986; A Locked House, 1986; The Kinder Capers, 1986; Selected Poems, 1957-87, 1987; W D's Midnight Carnival (with DeLoss McGraw), 1988; The Death of Cock Robin (with DeLoss McGraw), 1989; Each in His Season, 1994; The Fuehrer Bunker: The Complete Cycle, 1995. Essay: In Radical Pursuit, 1975. Play: The Fuehrer

Bunker, 1978. Other: Translations of songs. Contributions to: Essays, reviews, poems to many periodicals. Honours: Ingram Merrill Foundation Award, 1958; Longview Foundation Literary Award, 1959; National Institute of Arts and Letters Grant, 1960; Pulitzer Prize in Poetry, 1960; Yaddo Resident Awards, 1960, 1961, 1965; Guinness Poetry Award, 1961; Ford Foundation Grant, 1963-64; National Endowment for the Arts Grant, 1966-67; Guggenheim Fellowship, 1972-73; Government of Romania Centennial Medal, 1977; Honorary Doctorate of Letters, Allegheny College, 1991. Memberships: National Institute of Arts and Letters; Poetry Society of America; International PEN. Address: RD 1, Box 51, Erieville, NY 13061, USA.

SNOWMAN Daniel, b. 4 Nov 1938, London, England. BBC Producer. m. Janet Linda Levison, 1 son, 1 daughter. Education: BA (Double First Class) History, Cambridge, 1961; MA, Government, Cornell University, New York, USA. 1963. Appointments: Lecturer in History and American Studies, University of Sussex, 1963-67; BBC Producer 1967-; currently Chief Producer, BBC Radio Features and Arts, until 1995; Visiting Professor of History, California State University, 1972-73. Publications: America Since 1920, 1968; Eleanor Roosevelt, 1970; Kissing Cousins (British and American Culture), 1977; If I Had Been.... Ten Historical Fantasies, 1979; The Amadeus Quartet, 1981; The World of Placido Domingo, 1985; Beyond the Tunnel of History, 1990; Pole Positions: The Polar Regions and the Future of the Planet, 1993; Plácido Domingo's Tales From the Opera, 1994. Contributions to: Books, newspapers and journals. Membership: Regular singer with London Philharmonic Choir 1967-, former Chairman. Address: 46 Molyneux Street, London W1H 5HW, England.

SNYDER Francis Gregory, b. 26 June 1942, Madison, Wisconsin, USA. Professor of Law; Writer. m. Sian Miles, 20 Aug 1967, 1 son. Education: BA, Yale University, 1964; Fulbright Scholar, Institut d'Études Politiques de Paris, 1964-65; JD, Harvard Law School, 1968; Certificat de Droit et Economie des Pays d'Afrique, 1969; Doctorat de Spécialité, University of Paris I, 1973. Appointments: US Attorney, Massachusetts, 1968; Professor of Law, European University Institute, San Domenico di Fiesole, Italy. Publications: One-Party Government in Mali, 1965; Law and Population in Senegal, 1977; Capitalism and Legal Change, 1981; Law of the Common Agricultural Policy, 1985; International Law of Development (co-editor), 1987; Labor, Law and Crime (co-editor), 1987; The Political Economy (co-editor), 1987; Policing and Prosecution in Britain 1750-1850 (co-editor), 1989; New Directions in European Community Law, 1990; European Community Law, 2 volumes, 1993. Contributions to: Professional journals. Honours: Research Associate, International Development Research Center, 1978; Officier dans l'Ordre des Palmes Academiques, 1988. Membership: Law and Society Association. Address: c/o Department of Law, European University Institute, Badia Fiesolana I-50016, San Domenico di Fiesole, Italy.

SNYDER Gary (Sherman), b. 8 May 1930, San Francisco, California, USA. Poet; Writer; Teacher. m., 2 sons, 2 stepdaughters. Education: BA, Reed College, Portland, Oregon, 1951; Graduate Studies in Linguistics, Indiana University, 1951; Graduate School, Department of East Asian Languages, University of California, Berkeley, 1953-56; Studied Zen Buddhism and East Asian culture in Japan. Appointment: Faculty, University of California, Davis, 1986-. Publications: Poetry: Riprap and Cold Mountain Poems, 1959; Myths and Texts, 1960; A Range of Poems, 1966; Three Worlds, Three Realms, Six Roads, 1966; The Back Country, 1968; The Blue Sky, 1969; Regarding Wave, 1970; Manzanita, 1971; Plute Creek, 1972; The Fudo Trilogy: Spell Against Demons, Smokey the Bear Sutra, The California Water Plan, 1973; Turtle Island, 1974; All in the Family, 1975; Songs for Gaia, 1979; Axe Handles, 1983; Left Out in the Rain: New Poems, 1947-1986, 1986; The Practice of the Wild, 1990; No Nature: New and Selected Poems, 1992; Mountains and Rivers Without End, 1996. Prose: Earth House Hold: Technical Notes and Queries to Fellow Dharma Revolutionaries, 1969; The Old Ways: Six Essays, 1977; He Who Hunted Birds in His Father's Village: The Dimensions of a Haida Myth, 1979; The Real Work: Interviews and Talks, 1964-1979, 1980; Passage Through India, 1984; A Place in Space, 1995. Contributions to: Anthologies. Honours: Scholarship, First Zen Institute of America, 1956; American Academy of Arts and Letters Award, 1966; Bollingen Foundation Grant, 1966-67; Frank O'Hara Prize, 1967; Levinson Prize, 1968; Guggenheim Fellowship, 1968-69; Pulitzer Prize in Poetry, 1975; Finalist, National Book Award, 1992. Memberships: American Academy of Arts and Letters; American Academy of Arts and Sciences. Address: 18442 Macnab Cypress Road, Nevada City, CA 95959, USA.

SNYDER Zilpha Keatley, b. 11 May 1927, Lemoore, California, USA. Writer. m. 18 June 1950, 2 sons, 1 daughter. Education: BA, Whittier College, 1948. Publications: Season of Ponies, 1964; The Velvet Room, 1965; Black and Blue Magic, 1966; The Egypt Game, 1967; The Changeling, 1970; The Headless Cupid, 1971; The Witches of Worm, 1972; The Princess and the Giants, 1973; The Truth About Stone Hollow, 1974; The Famous Stanley Kidnapping Case, 1979; Blair's Nightmare, 1984; The Changing Maze, 1985; And Condors Danced, 1987; Squeak Saves the Day and Other Tooley Tales, 1988; Janie's Private Eyes, 1989; Libby on Wednesday, 1990; Song of the Gargoyle, 1991; Fool's Gold, 1993; Cat Running, 1994; The Trespasser, 1995; Castle Court Kids, 1995; The Diamond War; The Box and the Bone; Ghost Invasion; Secret Weapons. Honour: Beatty Award for Cat Running, 1995. Address: 52 Miller Avenue, Mill Valley, CA 94941, USA.

SOCOLOFSKY Homer Edward, b. 20 May 1922, Tampa, Kansas, USA. Emeritus Professor of History. m. Helen Margot Wright, 23 Nov 1946, 4 sons, 2 daughters. Education: BS, 1944, MS, 1947, Kansas State University; PhD, University of Missouri, 1954. Appointments: Professor of History, later Professor Emeritus, Kansas State University; History Editor, Kansas Quarterly, 1969-92; Book Review Editor, Journal of the West, 1978-92. Publications: Arthur Capper, Publisher, Politician, Philanthropist, 1962; Historical Atlas of Kansas (with Huber Self), 1972, 2nd edition, 1989; Landlord William Scully, 1979; The Presidency of Benjamin Harrison (with Allan Spetter), 1987; Governors of Kansas, 1990; Kansas History: An Annotated Bibliography (with Virgil Dean), 1992. Contributions to: Over 40 articles in journals and anthologies. Address: Department of History, Kansas State University, Manhattan, KS 66506, USA.

SODERHIELM Ulf Stefan, b. 21 July 1934, Goldingen, Letland. Agronomist. m. Kelly Else Marjatta Viherva, 24 Oct 1965, 1 son, 2 daughters. Education: Agronomist, Helsingfors University Faculty of Agro-Forestry. Publications: Sval Fristad, 1956; Hog Sjo Och Marviol, 1962; Angslycka, 1971; Motljus, 1994. Address: 07930 Perna, Finland.

SOFOLA Zulu, b. 22 June 1935, Issele-Uku, Nigeria. Playwright. Education: PhD, University of Ibadan, 1977. Appointment: Head, Department of the Performing Arts, University of Ilorin, Kwara State, Nigeria, 1989-. Publications: The Disturbed Peace of Christmas, 1969; Wedlock of the Gods, 1971; The Operators, 1973; King Emene, 1975; Old Wines are Tasty, 1975; The Sweet Trap, 1975; The Wizard of Law, 1976; The Deer and the Hunter's Pearl, 1976; Memories in the Moonlight, 1977; Song of a Maiden, 1977; Queen Umu-Ako of Oligbo, 1989; Eclipse and the Fantasia, 1990; Lost Dreams, 1991; The Showers, 1991. Honour: Fulbright Fellowship, 1988. Address: Department of the Performing Arts, University of Ilorin, Ilorin, Kwara State, Nigeria.

SOHAIL Khalid, b. 9 July 1952, Pakistan. Psychiatrist; Writer; Poet. Education: MBBS, Pakistan, 1974; FRCP(C), Canada, 1982. Publications: Discovering New Highways in Life (psychotherapy), 1991; From One Culture to Another (essays), 1992; Literary Encounters (interviews), 1992; Pages of my Heart (poems), 1993; A Broken Man (stories), 1993; Collections of poems, stories, essays and translations of world literature. Contributions to: Anthologies and journals. Honours: Honourary Cultural Doctorate in Literature, World University, USA, 1993; Rahul Award, Calcutta, India, 1994. Memberships: Writers Union of Canada; Fellow, Royal College of Physicians and Surgeons, Canada. Address: PH6 100 White Oaks Court, Whitby, Ontario L1P 1B7, Canada.

SOHOLM Ejgil, b. 19 Apr 1936, Nykobing Mors, Denmark. Librarian; Author; Translator; Freelance Journalist. m. Kirsten Kynne Frandsen, 28 Apr 1961, 2 sons, 1 daughter. Education: MA, Universty of Århus, 1963. Appointments: Lecturer in Danish Literature, University of Århus, 1968-73; Senior Librarian, State and University Library, Århus, 1968-; Editor, DF-Revy, 1978-82. Publications: Roman om en forbrydelse, 1976; Fra frihedskamp til lighedstrom, 1979; Storm P for Ping, 1986; Ordkvartet Århus, 1990; Angli giorde det, 1992. Other: Translations of children's books. Contributions to: Periodicals. Membership: Danish Writers Union. Address: PO Box 1302, DK-8210 Århus V, Denmark.

SOKOL Lech Andrzej, b. 21 Feb 1942, Koprzywnica, Poland. Historian of Literature and Theatre; Diplomat. m. Anna Lisowska, 26 Dec 1965, 1 son, 1 daughter. Education: Polish Philology, 1959-64, MA, 1964, University of Warsaw; PhD, 1972, Habilitation, 1990,

Institute of Art, Polish Academy of Sciences and Humanities. Appointments: Editor, State Publishing House PIW, 1963-69; Research Worker, Institute of Art, Polish Academy of Sciences and Humanities, Department of Theatre, 1969-91; Lecturer in Modern Drama and Theatre Aesthetics, State Academy of Drama, Warsaw, 1972-91; Polish Ambassador to Norway, 1991-96, and Iceland, 1992-96. Publications: Books in Polish: The Grotesque in the Drama of S I Witkiewicz, 1973; August Strindberg, 1981; Witkiewicz and Strindberg: A Comparative Study, 1990, also published in book form as Witkacy and Strindberg: Distant and Close, 1995. Other: Editor of 5 volumes of Strindberg's plays and short stories with introductions, 2 volumes of short stories by XIXth century Polish Writers with introductions and commentaries, and 2 volumes of plays by Polish playwrights Rózewicz and Witkiewicz; Author of about 160 essays and articles in Polish, English, French, Norwegian and Swedish published in Poland, Germany, Norway, Sweden Switzerland and UK; Author of poetry in Polish translated into Norwegian; Translator of American, French and Swedish poetry into Polish. Contributions to: Various publications, including: Pamietnik Teatralny; Pamietnik Literacki; Dialog; Teatr; Theatre Research International (UK); Ergo (Norway). Membership: International Theatre Institute. Address: Sapiezynska 5 m 18, 00-215 Warsaw, Poland.

SOLOW Robert M(erton), b. 23 Aug 1924, Brooklyn, New York, USA. Professor of Economics Emeritus; Writer. m. Barbara Lewis, 19 Aug 1945, 2 sons, 1 daughter. Education: BA, 1947, MA, 1949, PhD, 1951, Harvard University. Appointments: Faculty, 1949-58, Professor of Economics, 1958-95, Professor Emeritus, 1995-, Massachusetts Institute of Technology; Senior Economist, 1961-62, Consultant, 1962-68, US Council of Economic Advisors; Marshall Lecturer and Fellow Commoner, Peterhouse, Cambridge University, 1963-64; Eastman Visiting Professor, Oxford University, 1968-69; Senior Fellow, Society of Fellows, Harvard University, 1975-89; Deming Professor, New York University, 1996-97. Publications: Linear Programming and Economic Analysis, (with R Dortman and P Samuelson), 1958; Capital Theory and the Rate of Return, 1963; The Sources of Unemployment in the United States, 1964; Growth Theory, 1970; Price Expectations and the Behaviour of the Prive Level, 1970; Made in America (with M Dertouzos and R Lester), 1989; The Labor Market as a Social Institution, 1990; A Critical Essay on Modern Macroeconomic Theory (with F Hahn), 1995. Contributions to: Professional journals. Honours: David A Wells Prize, Harvard University, 1951; Seidman Award in Political Economy, 1983; Nobel Prize for Economic Science, 1987; Numerous honorary doctorates. Memberships: American Academy of Arts and Sciences; American Economics Society, vice-president, 1968, president, 1979; American Philosophical Society; Brtish Academy, corresponding fellow; Econometric Society, president, 1964; National Academy of Science, council member, 1977-80, 1995. Address: 528 Lewis Wharf, Boston, MA 02110, USA.

SOLZHENITSYN Aleksandr Isayevich, b. 11 Dec 1918, Kislovodsk, Russia. Writer; Poet. m. (1) Natalya Reshetovskaya, 27 Apr 1940, div (2) 1956, div 1972, (3) Natalya Svetlova, Apr 1973, 3 sons, 1 stepson. Education: Correspondence course in Philology, Moscow Institute of History, Philosophy, and Literature, 1939-41; Degree in Mathematics and Physics, University of Rostock, 1941. Appointments: Writer as a youth; Secondary School Teacher; Commander, Soviet Army during World War II; Held in prisons and labour camp, 1945-53; Exiled as a teacher, Kok-Terek, Kazakhstan, 1953-56; Teacher, Mathematics and Physics, Riazan; Exiled from Soviet Union, 1974-94. Publications: One Day in the Life of Ivan Denisovich (novella), 1962; For the Good of the Cause (novella), 1963; We Never Make Mistakes (novel), 1963; The First Circle (novel), 1968; Cancer Ward (novel), 2 volumes, 1968-69; The Love Girl and the Innocent (play), 1969; Candle in the Wind (play), 1969; The Rights of the Writer, 1969; The Red Wheel (novel cycle), 1971-, including August 1914, October 1916, March 1917, April 1917; Stories and Prose Poems by Aleksandr Solzhenitsyn, 1971; Six Etudes by Aleksandr Solzhenitsyn, 1971; Nobel Lecture by Aleksandr Solzhenitsyn, 1972; A Lenten Letter to Pimen, Patriarch of All Russia, 1972; The Gulag Archipelago, 1918-1956: An Experiment in Literary Investigation, 3 volumes, 1974, 1976, 1979; Peace and Violence, 1974; Prussian Nights: Epic Poems Written at the Forced Labor Camp, 1950, 1974; Letter to the Soviet Leaders, 1974; Solzhenitsyn: A Pictorial Autobiography, 1974; The Oak and the Calf (memoir), 1975; Lenin in Zürich, 1975; American Speeches, 1975; From Under the Rubble (with others), 1975; Warning to the West, 1976; A World Split Apart, 1979; The Mortal Danger, 1981; Victory Celebrations: A Comedy in Four Acts and Prisoners: A Tragedy (plays), 1983;

Rebuilding Russia: Towards Some Formulations, 1991; The Russian Question Toward the End of the Century, 1995; November 1969, forthcoming. Honours: Prix du Meilleur Livre Etranger, France, 1969; Nobel Prize for Literature, 1970; Freedoms Foundation Award, Stanford University, 1976; Many honorary degrees. Membership: American Academy of Arts and Sciences. Address: PO Box 121, Cavendish, VT 05142, USA.

SOMERS Suzanne. See: **DANIELS Dorothy.**

SOMERSET FRY Peter George Robin Plantagenet, b. 3 Jan 1931, Kent, England. Author; Journalist. m. (2) Daphne Diana Elizabeth Caroline Yorke, 1958, dec 1961, (3) Hon Mrs Leri Butler, 1961, div 1973, (4) Pamela Fiona Ileene Whitcombe, 1974. Education: Lancing College; St Thomas's Hospital Medical School, London; St Catherine's College, Oxford. Appointments: Editorial staffs, Atomics & Nuclear Energy, 1957-58, Tatler & Bystander, 1958; Information Officer, Ministry of Public Buildings and Works, 1967-70; Head of Information, COSIRA, 1970-74; Editor of Books, HM Stationery Office, 1975-80; General editor, Macmillan History in Pictures series, 1977-80. Publications: Mysteries of History, 1957; The Cankered Rose, 1959; Rulers of Britain, 1967, 3rd edition, 1973; They Made History, 1971, 2nd edition, 1973; The World of Antiques, 1970, 4th edition, 1972; Antique Furniture, 1971; Children's History of the World, 1972, 11th edition, 1987; Zebra Book of Famous Men, 1972: Zebra Book of Famous Women, 1972; Collecting Inexpensive Antiques, 1973, 5th edition, 1980; British Medieval Castles, 1974; Great Caesar, 1974; 1000 Great Lives, 1975, 9th edition, 1987; 2000 Years of British Life, 1976; Chequers: The Country Home of Britain's Prime Minsters, official history, 1977; 3,000 Questions and Answers, 1977, 12th edition, 1984; Boudicca, 1978; The David and Charles Book of Castles, 1980; Beautiful Britain, 1981; Great Cathedrals, 1982; The History of Scotland (with Fiona Somerset Fry), 1982, 3rd edition, 1992; Rebellion Against Rome, 1982; Roman Britain: History & Sites, 1984; Junior Illustrated Dictionary, 1987; A History of Ireland (with Fiona Somerset Fry), 1988, 2nd edition, 1991; Castles of the British Isles, 1990; The Tower of London, 1990; Kings and Queens of England and Scotland, 1990, 4th edition, 1993; Handbook of Antique Furniture, 1992; Dorling Kindersley History of the World, 1994. Memberships: Congress of Independent Archaeologists, founder-member, 1985-; Wolfson College, Cambridge, senior member, 1980-. Address: Wood Cottage, Wattisfield, Bury St Edmunds, Suffolk IP22 1NE, England.

SOMLYÓ György, b. 28 Nov 1920, Balatonboglar, Hungary. Writer; Poet. Div, 1 son. Education: University of Budapest, 1945-46; Sorbonne, University of Paris, 1947-48. Appointments: Director, Literary Section, Radio Budapest, 1954-55, Arion Magazine, 1966-87. Publications: Over 17 books, including novels, poetry and essays in Hungarian, 1977-96. Contributions to: Various publications. Address: Irinyi 3. u 39, Budapest H-1111, Hungary.

SONENBERG Maya, b. 24 Feb 1960, New York, New York, USA. Writer; Professor. Education: BA, Wesleyan University, 1982; MA, Brown University, 1984. Appointments: English Department Instructor, Sonoma State University, 1986; Lecturer, Chabot College, 1989-90; Assistant Professor, Oregon State University, 1990-93, University of Washington, 1993-. Publication: Cartographies, 1989. Contributions to: The Writer; Grand Street; Chelsea; The Cream City Review; Columbia; Gargoyle. Honours: McDowell Colony Fellow, 1987; Drue Heinz Literature Prize, 1989; Centre for the Humanities Faculty Fellow, Oregon State University, 1992-93. Memberships: Associated Writing Programs; Modern Language Association. Literary Agent: Claire Needell, The Wendy Weil Literary Agency, 232 Madison Avenue, Suite 1300, New York, NY 10016, USA. Address: English Department, Box 354330, University of Washington, Seattle, WA 98195, USA.

SONTAG Susan, b. 16 Jan 1933, New York, New York, USA. Novelist; Essayist. m. Philip Rieff, 1950, div 1958, 1 son. Education: BA, University of Chicago, 1951; MA, English, 1954, MA, Philosophy, 1955, Harvard University. Publications: The Benefactor (novel), 1963; Against Interpretation (essays), 1966; Death Kit (novel), 1967; Trip to Hanoi (essays), 1968; Styles of Radical Will (essays), 1969; On Photography (essays), 1977; Illness as Metaphor (essays), 1978; I, etcetera (stories), 1978; Under the Sign of Saturn (essays), 1980; A Sontag Reader, 1982; AIDS and Its Metaphors (essays), 1989; The Way We Live Now (story), 1991; The Volcano Lover: A Romance, 1992; Alice in Bed: A Play, 1993. Contributions to: Various publications. Honours: Rockefeller Foundation Fellowships, 1965,

1974; Guggenheim Fellowships, 1966, 1975; National Book Critics Circle Award, 1978; Officier de l'Ordre des Arts et des Lettres, France, 1984; John D and Catherine T MacArthur Foundation Fellowship, 1990-95; Malaparte Prize, Italy, 1992; Honorary Doctorates, Columbia University, 1993, Harvard University, 1993; Montblanc Cultural Achievement Award, 1994. Memberships: American Academy of Arts and Letters; PEN American Center, president, 1987-89. Address: c/o Wylie, Aitken & Stone, 250 West 57th Street, Suite 2114, New York, NY 10107, USA.

SOR-REIME Geir, b. 11 June 1953, Stavanger, Norway. Archaeologist; Philatelic Writer. m. Anne Kari Skar, 25 June 1976. Education: Magister Artium, Nordic Archaeology, University of Bergen, 1982. Publication: Avaldsnes, Norges Eldste Kongesete, 1989. Contributions to: Gibbons Stamp Monthly; Mekeel's Weekly Stamp News (USA); Phil forum. Address: Salvagergata 9, N-4006 Stavanger, Norway.

SORENSEN Knud, b. 10 Mar 1928, Hjorring, Denmark. Writer. m. Anne Marie Dybro Jorgensen, 4 July 1950, 2 sons. Education: Graduate, Royal Veterinary and Agricultural University, Copenhagen, 1952. Publications: Over 30 books, in Danish, 1965-96. Contributions to: Various publications. Honours: Several literary awards. Memberships: Autorenkreiss Plesse; The Danish Writers' Union. Address: Skelholmvehj 2, DK-7900 Nykobing Mors, Denmark.

SORENSEN Preben, b. 17 Feb 1939, Tved, Denmark. Editor; Chief of Information. m. Inge Lunding, 11 Mar 1961, 1 son, 1 daughter. Appointments: Journalist, 1967; Editor, 1971-. Publications: Fagpressen: Fretidens Medie, 1980; Arbejdsmarkedsordbog, 1987; De Udelukkede, 1989; Nordisk Arbejdsmarkedsordbog, 1990; Under Herrer og Mestre, 1992; Pas Yo Pressen, 1995. Contributor to: Editor, Nyt fra Arbejdermüseet and Radio-TV NYT. Memberships: Danish Writers' Union; Danish Union of Journalists; Danish Listeners and Viewers Organisation, chairman. Address: Ny Ostergade 34, 2 tv, 1101 Copenhagen K, Denmark.

SORENSEN Villy, b. 13 Jan 1929, Frederiksberg, Denmark. Writer. Education: Philosophical and Philological Studies, Copenhagen, Freiburg im Breisgau. Publications: 27 books in Danish; Titles translated into English: Strange Stories, 1956; Seneca, 1984; Tutelary Tales, 1988; Downfall of the Gods, 1989; Another Metamorphosis and other Fictions, 1990; Four Biblical Tales, 1991; Harmless Tales, 1991. Honours: Danish Academy Prize; Henrik Steffens Prize; Swedish Academy Nordic Prize. Membership: Danish Academy. Address: Bredebovej 31, 2800 Lyngby, Denmark.

SORESTAD Glen Allan, b. 21 May 1937, Vancouver, British Columbia, Canada. Writer; Poet; Publisher. m. Sonia Diane Talpash, 17 Sept 1960, 3 sons, 1 daughter. Education: BEd, 1963, MEd, 1976, University of Saskatchewan. Appointments: Elementary School Teacher, 1957-69; Senior English Teacher, 1969-81; President, Thistledown Press, 1975-. Publications: Some 10 poetry publications; Hold the Rain in Your Hands: Poems Selected and New, 1985; Icons of Flesh, 1996; Birchbark Meditations, 1996. Contributions to: Numerous newspapers, journals, and periodicals. Honours: Canada Council Writing Grant; SWG Founder's Award; Hilroy Fellowship; Saskatchewan Arts Board Writing Grant. Memberships: Association of Canadian Publishers; Literary Press Group; Saskatchewan Writers Guild; Writers Union of Canada; League of Canadian Poets; International PEN. Address: 668 East Place, Saskatoon, Saskatchewan S7J 2Z5, Canada.

SORRENTINO Gilbert, b. 27 Apr 1929, Brooklyn, New York, USA. Novelist; Poet; Professor. m. (1) Elsene Wiessner, div, (2) Vivian V Ortiz, 3 children. Education: Brooklyn College, 1950-51, 1955-57. Appointments: Editor, Publisher, Neon Magazine, New York City, 1956-60; Editor, Grove Press, New York City, 1965-70; Teacher, Columbia University, 1965, Aspen Writers Workshop, 1967, Sarah Lawrence College, 1971-72, New School for Social Research, New York City, 1976-79; Edwin S Quain Professor of Literature, University of Scranton, 1979; Professor of English, Stanford University, 1982-. Publications: Novels: The Sky Changes, 1966; Steelwork, 1970; Imaginative Qualities of Actual Things, 1971; Splendide-Hotel, 1973; Mulligan Stew, 1979; Aberration of Starlight, 1980; Crystal Vision, 1981; Blue Pastoral, 1983; Odd Number, 1985; Rose Theatre, 1987; Misterioso, 1989; Under the Shadow, 1991; Red the Fiend, 1995. Poetry: The Darkness Surrounds Us, 1960; Black and White, 1964; The Perfect Fiction, 1968; Corrosive Sublimate, 1971; A Dozen

Oranges, 1976; White Sail, 1977; The Orangery, 1977; Selected Poems, 1958-1980, 1981. Essays: Something Said, 1984. Play: Flawless Play Restored: The Masque of Fungo, 1974. Translator: Sulpiciae Elegidia/Elegiacs of Sulpicia: Gilbert Sorrentino Versions, 1977. Contributions to: Various anthologies and periodicals. Honours: Guggenheim Fellowships, 1973-74, 1987-88; Samuel S Fels Award, 1974; Creative Artists Public Service Grant, 1974-75; Ariadne Foundation Grant, 1975; National Endowment for the Arts Grants, 1975-76, 1978-79, 1983-84; John Dos Passos Prize, 1981; Mildred and Harold Strauss Livings, 1982 (declined); American Academy and Institute of Arts and Letters Award, 1985; Lannan Literary Award for Fiction, 1992. Membership: PEN American Center. Address: Department of English, Stanford University, Stanford, CA 94305, USA.

SOSKIN V H. See: **ELLISON Virginia Howell.**

SOSUKE Shibasaki. See: **CIVASAQUI Jose**.

SOTO Gary, b. 12 Apr 1952, Fresno, California, USA. Writer; Poet. m. Carolyn Sadako Oda, 24 May 1975, 1 daughter. Education: BA, California State University at Fresno, 1974; MFA, University of California at Irving, 1976. Appointments: Assistant Professor, 1979-85, Associate Professor of English and Ethnic Studies, 1985-92, Part-time Senior Lecturer in English, 1992-93, University of California at Berkeley; Elliston Professor of Poetry, University of Cincinnati, 1988; Martin Luther King/Cesar Chavez/Rosa Park Visiting Professor of English, Wayne State University, 1990. Publications: Poetry: The Elements of San Joaquin, 1977; The Tale of Sunlight, 1978; Where Sparrows Work Hard, 1981; Black Hair, 1985; Who Will Know Us?, 1990; A Fire in My Hands, 1990; Home Course in Religion, 1992; Neighborhood Odes, 1992; Canto Familiar/Familiar Song, 1994; New and Selected Poems, 1995. Other: Living Up the Street: Narrative Recollections, 1985; Small Faces, 1986; Lesser Evils: Ten Quartets, 1988; California Childhood: Recollections and Stories of the Golden State (editor), 1988; A Summer Life, 1990; Baseball in April and Other Stories, 1990; Taking Sides, 1991; Pacific Crossing, 1992; The Skirt, 1992; Pieces of the Heart: New Chicano Fiction (editor), 1993; Local News, 1993; The Pool Party, 1993; Crazy Weekend, 1994; Jesse, 1994; Boys at Work, 1995; Chato's Kitchen, 1995; Everyday Seductions (editor), 1995; Summer on Wheels, 1995; The Old Man and His Door, 1996; Snapshots of the Wedding, 1996; Buried Onions, 1997. Contributions to: Magazines. Honours: Academy of American Poets Prize, 1975; Discovery/The Nation Prize, 1975; United States Award, International Poetry Forum, 1976; Bess Hokin Prize for Poetry, 1978; Guggenheim Fellowship, 1979-80; National Endowment for the Arts Fellowships, 1981, 1991; Levinson Award, Poetry Magazine, 1984; American Book Award, Before Columbus Foundation, 1985; California Arts Council Fellowship, 1989; Carnegie Medal, 1993. Address: 43 The Crescent, Berkeley, CA 94708, USA.

SOULE Gardner (Bosworth), b. 16 Dec 1913, Paris, Texas, USA. Author. m. (1) Janie Lee McDowell, 20 Sept 1940, dec, (2) Mary Muir Dowhing, 23 Apr 1994. Education: BA, Rice University, 1933; BSc, 1935, MSc, 1936, Columbia University. Appointments: Associated Press, 1936-41; US Naval Reserve, 1942-45; Managing Editor, Better Homes & Gardens, 1945-50. Publications: Tomorrow's World of Science, 1963; The Maybe Monsters, 1963; The Mystery Monsters, 1965; Trail of the Abominable Snowman, 1965; The Ocean Adventure, 1966; UFO's and IFO's, 1967; Wide Ocean, 1970; Men Who Dared the Sea, 1976; The Long Trail, How Cowboys and Longhorns Opened the West, 1976; Mystery Monsters of the Deep, 1981; Mystery Creatures of the Jungle, 1982; Antarctica, 1985; Christopher Columbus, 1989. Contributions to: Popular Science Monthly; United Features; London Express Syndicate; Boy's Life; Illustrated London News. Honour: Navy League Commendation, 1956. Memberships: Sigma Delta Chi; Columbia University Club. Address: 517 West 113th Street, Apt 53, New York, NY 10025, USA.

SOULE Maris Anne, b. 19 June 1939, Oakland, California, USA. Writer; Teacher. m. William L Soule, 11 May 1968, 1 son, 1 daughter. Education: BA, University of California, Davis, 1961; Secondary Teaching Credential, University of California, Berkeley. Publications: First Impressions, 1983; No Room for Love, 1984; Lost and Found, 1985; Sounds Like Love, 1986; A Winning Combination, 1987; The Best of Everything, 1988; The Law of Nature, 1988; Storybook Hero, 1989; Jared's Lady, 1991; No Promises Made, 1994; Stop the Wedding!, 1994. Memberships: Romance Writers of America; Novelists Inc. Address: RRI, Box 173B, Fulton, MI 49052, USA.

SOURELIS Grigoriadou, b. 18 June 1930, Kavala, Northern Greece. Author. m. 1968, 2 sons, 2 daughters. Education: The Damascus School of Journalism; The Greek School of Social Workers. Publications: The Sparrow in the Red Vest, 1982; Game with No Rules, 1982; Before the Final Whistle, 1982; It Matters to Me, 1990; The Great Farewell, 1990. Others: The Emperor's Ring; Katerina for a Place in Heaven; The Crazy Boat Without a Rudder; The Moon, the Stamp and Me; Dancing in the Forest; The Wind Plays the Flute; Alexis and the Wooden Horse; The 12 Moons. Contributions to: Diadromes Magazine (co-founder and co-editor); The Metropolis of Piraeus. Honours: European Honours List, University of Padua, 1973; Ourani Award, 1978; International Board of Books for Young People, Honours List, 1978; Greek Society of Christian Letters Award, 1989; Special Award, The Smyrnians Union, 1990; Hans Christian Andersen International Award, Greek Nominee, 1992. Memberships: The Womans Literary Club; The Greek Society of Christian Letters; The National Association of Greek Authors; The Smyrnian Union. Address: 37 Aharnon Str, 145 61 Kifissia, Athens, Greece.

SOUSTER (Holmes) Raymond, (John Holmes), b. 15 Jan 1921, Toronto, Ontario, Canada. Bank Clerk (retired); Writer; Poet. m. Rosalia L Geralde, 24 June 1947. Education: University of Toronto Schools, 1932-37; Humberside Collegiate Institute, 1938-39. Appointment: Canadian Imperial Bank of Commerce, retired, 1964. Publications: 100 Poems of 19th Century Canada (editor with D Lochhead), 1974; Sights and Sounds (editor with R Wollatt), 1974; These Loved, These Hated Lands (editor with R Wollatt), 1974; The Poetry of W W Campbell (editor), 1978; The Best-Known Poems of Archibald Lampman (editor), 1979; Collected Poems of Raymond Souster, 7 volumes, 1980-92; Powassan's Drum: Selected Poems of Duncan Campbell Scott (editor with D Lochhead), 1983; Queen City: Toronto in Poems and Pictures (with Bill Brooks), 1984; Windflower: The Selected Poems of Bliss Carmen (editor with D Lochhead), 1986; Riding the Long Black Horse, 1993; Old Bank Notes, 1993; No Sad Songs Wanted Here, 1995; Close to Home, 1997. Contributions to: Magazines. Honours: Governor-General's Award for Poetry in English, 1964; President's Medal, University of Western Ontario, 1967; Centennial Medal, 1967; City of Toronto Book Award, 1979; Silver Jubilee Medal, 1977; Officer of the Order of Canada, 1995. Membership: League of Canadian Poets: Founding Member and First Chairman, 1968-72, Life Member, 1996. Address: 39 Baby Point Road, Toronto, Ontario M6S 2G2, Canada.

SOUTHALL Ivan Francis, b. 8 June 1921, Melbourne, Victoria, Australia. Writer. m. (1) Joy Blackburn, 8 Sept 1945 div, 1 son, 3 daughters, (2) Susan Westerlund Stanton, 11 Nov 1976. Appointments: Whitall Poetry and Literature Lecturer, Library of Congress, Washington, DC, USA, 1973; May Hill Arbuthnot Honour Lecturer, University of Washington, USA, 1974; Writer-in-Residence, Macquarie University, Sydney, 1979. Publications: They Shall Not Pass Unseen, 1956; Softly Tread the Brave, 1960; Hills End, 1962; Ash Road, 1965; To the Wild Sky, 1967; Let the Balloon Go, 1968; Josh, 1971; Head in the Clouds, 1972; Matt and Jo, 1973; What About Tomorrow?, 1977; City Out of Sight, 1984; Christmas in the Tree, 1985; Rachel, 1986; Blackbird, 1988; The Mysterious World of Marcus Leadbeater, 1990; Ziggurat, 1996. Honours: Australian Children's Book of the Year, 1966, 1968, 1971, 1976; Australian Picture Book of the Year, with Ted Greenwood, 1969; Children's Welfare and Culture Encouragement Award, Japan, 1969; Carnegie Medal, 1971; Silver Griffel, Netherlands, 1972; Australia Writers Award, 1974; IBBY Honour Book, 1974, 1979; Order of Australia, 1981; National Children's Book Award, Australia, 1986; Australia Council Emeritus Award, 1993; Others. Memberships: Australian Society of Authors; Fellowship of Australian Writers. Address: PO Box 25, Healesville, Victoria 3777, Australia.

SOUTHAM B(rian) C(harles), b. 15 Sept 1931, London, England. Publisher. Education: BA, 1956, MA, 1960, BLitt, 1965, Lincoln College, Oxford. Appointments: Lecturer in English Literature, University of London, 1961-63; Currently Publisher, The Athlone Press, London. Publications: Volume the Second (editor), 1963; Jane Austen's Literary Manuscripts, 1964; Selected Poems of Lord Tennyson (editor), 1964; Jane Austen: The Critical Heritage (editor), 2 volumes, 1966, 1987; Critical Essays on Jane Austen (editor), 1968; Minor Works of Jane Austen (editor with R W Chapman), 1969; A Student's Guide to the Selected Works of T S Eliot, 1969, 6th edition, 1994; Tennyson, 1971; Jane Austen Sanditon (editor), 1975; Jane Austen: Northanger Abbey and Persuasion (editor), 1976; Jane Austen: Sense and Sensibility, Pride and Prejudice, and Mansfield

Park (editor), casebooks, 3 volumes, 1976; Jane Austen: Sir Charles Grandison, editor, 1980; T S Eliot (editor), 1981. Membership: Chairman, Jane Austen Society. Address: 3 West Heath Drive, London NW11 7QG, England.

SOWANDE Bode, b. 2 May 1948, Kaduna, Nigeria. Playwright. Education: Universities of Ife, Dakar and Sheffield; MA, 1974; PhD, 1977. Appointment: Senior Lecturer, Department of Theatre Arts, University of Ibadan, 1977-90. Publications: The Night Before, 1972; Lamps in the Night, 1973; Bar Beach Prelude, 1976; A Sanctus for Women, 1976; Afamoko - the Workhorse, 1978; Farewell to Babylon, 1978; Kalakuta Cross Currents, 1979; The Master and the Frauds, 1979; Barabas and the Master Jesus, 1980; Flamingo, 1982; Circus of Freedom Square, 1985; Tornadoes Full of Dreams, 1989; Arede Owo (after L'Avare by Molière), 1990; Mammy-Water's Wedding, 1991; Ajantala-Pinocchio, 1992; Novels: Our Man the President, 1981; Without a Home, 1982; The Missing Bridesmaid, 1988; Stage Adaptation of Amos Tutuola's novel, My Life In the Bush of Ghosts in Africa '95 Festival, London, 1995; Radio and Television plays. Honours: Association of Nigerian Authors Drama Awards; Chevalier de l'Ordre des Arts et des Lettres, France, 1991; Patron of the Arts Award, Pan African Writers Association, 1993. Address: c/o Odu Themes Meridian, 33 Oyo Road, Orita, PO Box 14369, Post Office UI, Ibadan, Nigeria.

SOYINKA Wole (Akinwande Oluwole), b. 13 July 1934, Isara, Nigeria. Poet; Dramatist; Writer; Professor. Education: University of Ibadan; BA, Leeds University, 1959. Appointments: Research Fellow in Drama, 1960-61, Chairman, Department of Theatre Arts, 1969-72, University of Ibadan; Lecturer in English, 1962-63, Professor in Dramatic Literature, 1972, Professor of Comparative Literature, 1976-85, University of Ife; Senior Lecturer in English, University of Lagos, 1965-67; Political prisoner, 1967-69; Fellow, Churchill College, Cambridge, 1973-74; Goldwin Smith Professor of Africana Studies and Theatre, Cornell University, 1988-92; Exiled by the Nigerian military government, 1995. Publications: Poetry: Idanre and Other Poems, 1967; Poems from Prison, 1969, augmented edition as A Shuttle in the Crypt, 1972; Ogun Abibiman, 1976; Mandela's Earth and Other Poems, 1989. Plays: The Invention, 1955; A Dance of the Forests, 1960; Longi's Harvest, 1966; The Trials of Brother Jero, 1967; The Strong Breed, 1967; Madmen and Specialists, 1970; Before the Blackout, 1971; Camwood on the Leaves, 1973; Collected Plays, 2 volumes, 1973, 1974; Death and the King's Horseman, 1975; Opera Wonyosi, 1981; A Play of Giants, 1984; Six Plays, 1984; Requiem for a Futurologist, 1985; From Zia with Love, 1992; A Scourge of Hyacinths, 1992; The Beatification of Area Boy, 1995. Novels: The Interpreters, 1965; Season of Anomy, 1973. Other: The Man Died: Prison Notes of Wole Soyinka, 1972; Myth, Literature and the African World, 1976; Ake: The Years of Childhood (autobiography), 1981; Art, Dialogue and Outrage, 1988; Isara: A Voyage Around "Essay", 1989; The Open Score: A Personal Narrative of the Nigerian Crisis, 1996. Editor: Plays from the Third World: An Anthology, 1971; Poems of Black Africa, 1975. Honours: Rockefeller Foundation Grant, 1960; John Whiting Drama Prize, 1966; Jock Campbell Award, 1968; Nobel Prize for Literature, 1986. Memberships: International Theatre Institute; Union of Writers of the African Peoples; National Liberation Council of Nigeria. Address: c/o Random House Inc, 201 East 50th Street, 22nd Floor, New York, NY 10022, USA.

SPACKS Patricia Meyer, b. 17 Nov 1929, San Francisco, California, USA. Professor of English. 1 daughter. Education: BA, Rollins College, 1949; MA, Yale University, 1950; PhD, University of California at Berkeley, 1955. Appointments: Instructor in English, Indiana University, 1954-56; Instructor in Humanities, University of Florida, 1958-59; Instructor, 1959-61, Assistant Professor, 1961-63, Associate Professor, 1965-68, Professor of English, 1968-79, Wellesley College; Professor of English, 1979-89, Chairman, Department of English, 1985-88, Yale University; Edgar F Shannon Professor of English, 1989-, Chairman, Department of English, 1991-, University of Virginia. Publications: The Varied God, 1959; The Insistence of Horror, 1962; 18th Century Poetry (editor), 1964; John Gay, 1965; Poetry of Vision, 1967; Late Augustan Prose (editor), 1971; An Argument of Images, 1971; Late Augustan Poetry (editor), 1973; The Female Imagination, 1975; Imagining a Self, 1976; Contemporary Women Novelists, 1977; The Adolescent Idea, 1981; Gossip, 1985; Desire and Truth, 1990; Boredom: The Literary History of a State of Mind, 1995. Honour: American Academy of Arts and Sciences, 1994. Membership: Modern Language Association, president, 1994. Address: Department of English, 219 Bryn Hall, University of Virginia,

Charlottesville, VA 22903, USA.

SPARK David Brian, b. 5 Oct 1930, Darlington, England. Journalist. m. 20 Sept 1958, 1 son, 1 daughter. Education: MA Modern Languages, Trinity Hall, Cambridge, 1948-51. Appointments: Assistant Editor, The Northern Echo, 1965-66; Leadwriter, Westminster Press, 1967-86; Editor, National Press Agency, 1972-82; Assistant London Editor, Westminster Press, 1982-86; Editor, Commonwealth Journalists Association Newsletter, 1986-. Publications: Practical Newspaper Reporting, 1966, new edition, 1993; How to Ask about Developing Countries, 1992; A Journalist's Guide to Sources, 1996. Contributions to: Financial Times; The Independent. Memberships: Commonwealth Journalists Association; Association of British Science Writers. Address: 47 Seagry Road, Wanstead, London E11 2NH, England.

SPARK Dame Muriel (Sarah), b. 1 Feb 1918, Edinburgh, Scotland. Author; Poet. m. S O Spark, 1937, diss, 1 son. Education: James Gillespies's School for Girls, Edinburgh; Heriot Watt College, Edinburgh. Appointments: Political Intelligence Department, British Foreign Office, 1944-45; General Secretary, Poetry Society, 1947-49; Founder, Forum literary magazine, and Editor, Poetry Review, 1949. Publications: Fiction: The Comforters, 1957; Robinson, 1958; Memento Mori, 1959; The Ballad of Peckham Rye, 1960; The Bachelors, 1960; Voices at Play, 1961; The Prime of Miss Jean Brodie, 1961; Territorial Rights, 1979; Loitering with Intent, 1981; Bang-Bang You're Dead and Other Stories, 1982; The Only Problem, 1984; The Stories of Muriel Spark, 1985; A Far Cry from Kensington, 1988; Symposium, 1990; The French Window and the Small Telephone, 1993; Omnibus 1, 1993; Omnibus II, 1994. Poetry: The Fanfarlo and Other Verse, 1952; Collected Poems I, 1967; Going Up to Sotheby's and Other Poems, 1982. Play: Doctors of Philosophy, 1962. Non-Fiction: Child of Light: A Reassessment of Mary Wollstonecraft Shelley, 1951, revised edition as Mary Shelley, 1987; Emily Brontë: Her Life and Work, 1953; John Masefield, 1953; Curriculum Vitae (autobiography), 1992; The Essence of the Brontës, 1993. Editor: Tribute to Wordsworth, 1950; A Selection of Poems of Emily Brontë, 1952; My Best Mary: The Letters of Mary Shelley, 1953; The Letters of the Brontës: A Selection, 1954; Letters of John Henry Newman, 1957. Contributions to: Various periodicals. Honours: Prix Italia, 1962; Yorkshire Post Book of the Year Award, 1965; James Tait Black Memorial Prize, 1966; Officer of the Order of the British Empire, 1967; 1st Prize, FNAC La Meilleur Recueil des Nouvelles Etrangères, 1987; Scottish Book of the Year Award, 1987; Officier de l'Ordre des Arts et des Lettres, France, 1988; Ingersoll Foundation T S Eliot Award for Creative Writing, 1992; Dame Commander of the Order of the British Empire, 1993. Address: c/o David Higham Associates Ltd, 5-8 Lower John Street, Golden Square, London, W1R 4HA, England.

SPARSHOTT Francis (Edward), b. 19 May 1926, Chatham, Kent, England. Philosopher; Writer; Poet; Professor. m. Kathleen Elizabeth Vaughn, 7 Feb 1953, 1 daughter. Education: BA, MA, Corpus Christi College, Oxford, 1950. Apointments: Lecturer, 1950-55, Assistant Professor, 1955-62, Associate Professor, 1962-64, Professor, 1964-91, of Philosophy, University of Toronto. Publications: An Enquiry into Goodness and Related Concepts, 1958; The Structure of Aesthetics, 1963; The Concept of Criticism: An Essay, 1967; Looking for Philosophy, 1972; The Theory of the Arts, 1982; Off the Ground: First Steps in the Philosophy of the Art of Dance, 1988; Taking Life Seriously: A Study of the Argument of the Nicomachean Ethic, 1994; A Measured Place: Towards a Philosophical Understanding of the Art of Dance, 1995. Poetry: A Divided Voice, 1965; A Cardboard Garage, 1969; The Rainy Hills: Verses After a Japanese Fashion, 1979; The Naming of the Beasts, 1979; New Fingers for Old Dikes, 1980; The Cave of Trophonius and Other Poems, 1983; The Hanging Gardens of Etobicoke, 1983; Storms and Screens, 1986; Sculling to Byzantium, 1989; Views from the Zucchini Gazebo, 1994. Contributions to: Various books and periodicals. Honours: American Council of Learned Societies Fellowship, 1961-62; Canada Council Fellowship, 1970-71; Killam Research Fellowship, 1977-78; 1st Prize for Poetry, CBC Radio Literary Competition, 1981; Centennial Medal, Royal Society of Canada, 1982; Connaught Senior Fellowship in the Humanities, 1984-85. Memberships: American Philosophical Association; American Society for Aesthetics, president, 1981-82; Aristotelian Society; Canadian Classical Association; Canadian Philosophical Association, president, 1975-76; League of Canadian Poets, president, 1977-78; PEN International, Canadian Centre; Royal Society of Canada, fellow, 1977. Address: 50 Crescentwood Road, Scarborough, Ontario M1N 1E4, Canada.

SPENCE Alan, b. 5 Dec 1947, Glasgow, Scotland. Dramatist; Writer; Poet. Education: University of Glasgow, 1966-69, 1973-74. Appointments: Writer-in-Residence, University of Glasgow, 1975-77, Traverse Theatre, Edinburgh, 1982, University of Edinburgh, 1989-92, 1990; University of Aberdeen, 1996-. Publications: Plays: Sailmaker, 1982; Space Invaders, 1983; Changed Days, 1991. Fiction: Its Colours They Are Fine (short stories), 1977; The Magic Flute (novel), 1990; Stone Garden (stories), 1995. Poetry: Plop (15 Haiku), 1970; Glasgow Zen, 1981. Honours: Scottish Arts Council Book Awards, 1977, 1990, 1996; People's Prize, 1996; TMA Martini Prize, 1996. Address: 21 Waverley Park, Edinburgh EH8 8ER, Scotland.

SPENCE Bill. See: **SPENCE William (John Duncan).**

SPENCE Jonathan (Dermott), b. 11 Aug 1936, Surrey, England. Professor of History; Writer. m. (1) Helen Alexander, 15 Sept 1962, div 1993, 2 sons, (2) Chin Annping, 12 Aug 1993. Education: BA, Cambridge University, 1959; PhD, Yale University, 1965. Appointments: Assistant Professor, 1966-71, Professor of History, 1971-, Yale University; Wiles Lecturer, Queen's University, Belfast, 1985; Gauss Lecturer, Princeton University, 1987; Visiting Professor, Beijing University, 1987; Honorary Professor, Nanjing University, 1993. Publications: Ts'Ao Yin and the K'Ang-Hsi Emperor, 1966; To Change China, 1969; Emperor of China, 1974; The Death of Woman Wang, 1978; The Gate of Heavenly Peace, 1981; The Memory Palace of Matteo Ricci, 1984; The Question of Hu, 1988; The Search for Modern China, 1990; Chinese Roundabout, 1992; God's Chinese Son, 1996. Contributions to: Professional journals and periodicals. Honours: Yale Fellow in East Asian Studies, 1962-65, 1968-70; John Adison Porter Prize, 1965; Christopher Award, 1975; Devane Teaching Medal, 1978; Guggenheim Fellowship, 1979-80; Los Angeles Times Book Award, 1982; Vurseli Prize, American Academy and Institute of Arts and Letters, 1983; Comisso Prize, Italy, 1987; John D and Catherine T MacArthur Foundation Fellowship, 1988-93; Gelber Prize, Canada, 1990; Honorary doctorates. Memberships: American Academy of Arts and Sciences; American Philosophical Society; Association of Asian Studies. Address: 691 Forest Road, New Haven, CT 06515, USA.

SPENCE William (John Duncan), (Jessica Blair, Jim Bowden, Kirk Ford, Floyd Rogers, Bill Spence), b. 20 Apr 1923, Middlesborough England. Author. m. Joan Mary Rhoda Ludley, 8 Sept 1944, 1 son, 3 daughters. Education: St Mary's Teachers Training College, 1940-42. Publications: Numerous books, including: Romantic Rydale (with Joan Spence), 1977, new edition, 1987; Harpooned, 1981; The Medieval Monasteries of Yorkshire (with Joan Spence), 1981; Stories from Yorkshire Monasteries (with Joan Spence), 1992; As Jessica Blair: The Red Shawl, 1993; A Distant Harbour, 1993; Storm Bay, 1994; The Restless Spirit, 1996; 36 Westerns; 3 war novels, others. Membership: Society of Authors. Address: Post Office, Ampleforth College, York YO6 4EZ, England.

SPENCER Elizabeth, b. 19 July 1921, Carrollton, Mississippi, USA. Writer. m. John Arthur Rusher, 29 Sept 1956. Education: AB, cum laude, Belhaven College, 1942; MA, Vanderbilt University, 1943. Appointments: Writer-in-Residence, Adjunct Professor, 1977-86, Concordia University, Montreal; Visiting Professor, University of North Carolina at Chapel Hill, 1986-92. Publications: Fire in the Morning, 1948; This Crooked Way, 1952; The Voice at the Back Door, 1956; The Light in the Piazza, 1960; No Place for an Angel, 1967; Ship Island and Other Stories, 1968; The Snare, 1972; The Stories of Elizabeth Spencer, 1981; The Salt Line, 1984; Jack of Diamonds, 1988; For Lease or Sale (drama), 1989; The Night Travellers, 1991. Contributions to: Journals, including New Yorker; Atlantic; Southern Review; Kenyon Review. Address: 402 Longleaf Drive, Chapel Hill, NC 27514, USA.

SPENCER LaVyrle, b. 17 Aug 1943, Browerville, Minnesota, USA. Writer. m. Daniel F Spencer, 10 Feb 1962, 2 daughters. Education: High School, Staples, Minnesota. Publications: The Fulfillment, 1979; The Endearment, 1982; Hummingbird, 1983; Twice Loved, 1984; Sweet Memories, 1984; A Heart Speaks, 1986; Tears, 1986; Years, 1986; The Gamble, 1987; Separate Bed, 1987; Vows, 1988; Morning Glory, 1988; Bitter Sweet, 1990; Forgiving, 1991; November of the Heart, 1992; Bygones, 1993; Family Blessings, 1994; That Camden Summer, 1996. Honours: Historical Romance of the Year Awards, Romance Writers of America, 1983, 1984, 1985. Address: 6701 79th Avenue, Brooklyn Park, MN 55445, USA.

SPIEGELMAN Art, b. 15 Feb 1948, Stockholm, Sweden. Cartoonist; Editor; Writer. m. Françoise Mouly, 12 July 1977, 2 children. Education: Harpur College, Binghamton, New York. Appointments: Creative Consultant, Artist, Designer, Editor, and Writer, Topps Chewing Gum Inc, Brooklyn, New York, 1966-88; Editor, Douglas Comix, 1972; Instructor, San Francisco Academy of Art, 1974-75, New York School of the Visual Arts, 1979-87; Contributing Editor, Arcade, The Comics Revue, 1975-76; Founder-Editor, Raw, 1980-; Artist and Contributing Editor, The New Yorker, 1992-. Publications: Author and Illustrator: The Complete Mr Infinity, 1970; The Viper Vicar of Vice, Villainy, and Vickedness, 1972; Ace Hole, Midge Detective, 1974; The Language of Comics, 1974; Breakdowns: From Maus to Now: An Anthology of Strips, 1977; Work and Turn, 1979; Every Day Has Its Dog, 1979; Two-Fisted Painters Action Adventure, 1980; Maus: A Survivor's Tale, 1986; Read Yourself Raw (with F Mouly), 1987; Maus, Part Two, 1992; The Wild Party, 1994. Honours: Playboy Editorial Award for Best Comic Strip, 1982; Joel M Cavior Award for Jewish Writing, 1986; Stripschappening Award for Best Foreign Comics Album, 1987; Pulitzer Prize Special Citation, 1992; Alpha Art Awrd, Angouleme, France, 1993. Address: c/o Raw Books and Graphics, 27 Greene Street, New York, NY 10013, USA.

SPILLANE Mickey, (Frank Morrison Spillane), b. 9 Mar 1918, New York, New York, USA. Author. m. (1) Mary Ann Pearce, 1945, div, 2 sons, 2 daughters, (2) Sherri Malinou, 1964, div, (3) Jane Rodgers Johnson, 1983. Education: Kansas State College. Publications: I, the Jury, 1947; Vengeance is Mine!, 1950; My Gun is Quick, 1950; The Big Kill, 1951; One Lonely Night, 1951; The Long Wait, 1951; Kiss Me, Deadly, 1952; Tough Guys, 1960; The Deep, 1961; The Girl Hunters, 1962; Day of the Guns, 1964; The Snake, 1964; Bloody Sunrise, 1965; The Death Dealers, 1965; The Twisted Thing, 1966; The By-Pass Control, 1967; The Delta Factor, 1967; Body Lovers, 1967; Killer Mine, 1968; Me, Hood!, 1969; Survival: Zero, 1970; Tough Guys, 1970; The Erection Set, 1972; The Last Cop Out, 1973; The Flier, 1973; Tomorrow I Die, 1984; The Killing Man, 1989; Back Alley, 1996. Editor: Murder is My Business, 1994. TV Series: Mike Hammer, 1984-87. Children's Books: The Day the Sea Rolled Back, 1979; The Ship That Never Was, 1982. Address: c/o E P Dutton, 375 Hudson Street, New York, NY 10014, USA.

SPOONER John D. Investment Advisor; Novelist. m. 3 children. Appointments: Director, The Atlantic Monthly and David Godine Publishers; Member, Massachusetts Cultural Council; Senior Vice President, Smith Barney Inc. Publications: Confessions of a Stockbroker; Smart People; Sex and Money; Playboy; Manhattan Inc; The Atlantic, 1995; Esquire; The Boston Globe; A Book for Boston; Contributing Editor, Worth; Business Editor, Boston Magazine. Address: Smith Barney Inc, Exchange Place, 53 State Street, Boston, MA 02109, USA.

SPRIGEL Oliver. See: **AVICE Claude (Pierre Marie).**

SPRIGGE Timothy Lauro Squire, b. 14 Jan 1932, London, England. Professor of Philosophy; Writer. m. Giglia Gordon, 4 Apr 1959, 1 son, 2 daughters. Education: BA, 1955, MA, PhD, 1961, Cantab. Appointment: Professor of Philosophy, University of Edinburgh. Publications: The Correspondence of Jeremy Benthan (editor), 1968; Facts, Words and Beliefs, 1970; Santayana: An Examination of His Philosophy, 1974; The Vindication of Absolute Idealism, 1983; Theories of Existence, 1984; The Rational Foundation of Ethics, 1987; James and Bradley: American Truth and British Reality, 1993. Contributions to: Professional journals and periodicals. Honour: Fellow, Royal Society of Edinburgh. Memberships: Mind Association; Scots Philosophical Club. Address: c/o David Hume Tower, University of Edinburgh, George Square, Edinburgh EH8 9JX, Scotland.

SPRING Michael, b. 14 Oct 1941, New York, New York, USA. Editor; Writer. Div, 2 sons. Education: BA, Haverford College, Pennsylvania, 1964; MA, English Literature, Columbia University, 1970. Appointments: Vice President and Editorial Director, Fodor's Travel Publications; Contributing Editor, Condé Nast's Traveler magazine; Travel Expert, CNN-TV Travel Show, 1992-. Publications: The American Way of Working (editor), 1980; Barron's Book Notes series (editor), 50 volumes, 1984; A Student's Guide to Julius Caesar, 1984; The Great Weekend Escape Book, 3rd edition, 1987, 4th edition, 1990; Great European Itineraries, 1987, 3rd edition, 1994. Contributions to: Magazines, periodicals and journals. Honour: Distinguished Achievement Award in Educational Journalism,

Educational Press Association of America, 1987. Address: c/o Random House Inc, 201 East 50th Street, New York, NY 10022, USA.

SPRINGER Nancy, b. 5 July 1948, New Jersey, USA. Novelist. m. Joel H Springer, 13 Sept 1969, 1 son, 1 daughter. Education: BA, English Literature, Gettysburg College, 1970. Appointments: Personal Development Plan Instructor, University of Pittsburgh, 1983-85; Leisure Learning Instructor, York College, Pennsylvania, 1986-91; Education Instructor, Franklin and Marshall College, 1988-. Publications: The Sable Moon, 1981; The Black Beast, 1982; The Golden Swan, 1983; Wings of Flame, 1985; Chains of Gold, 1986; A Horse to Love (juvenile), 1987; Madbond, 1987; Chance and Other Gestures of the Hand of Fate, 1987; The Hex Witch of Seldom, 1988; Not on a White Horse (juvenile), 1988; Apocalypse, 1989; They're All Named Wildfire (juvenile), 1989; Red Wizard (juvenile), 1990; Colt (juvenile), 1991; The Friendship Song (juvenile), 1992; The Great Pony Hassle (juvenile), 1993; Stardark Songs (poetry), 1993; Larque on the Wing, 1994; The Boy on a Black Horse (juvenile), 1994; Metal Angel, 1994; Music of Their Hooves (poetry, juvenile), 1994. Contributions to: Magazines and journals. Honours: Distinguished Alumna, Gettysburg College, 1987; Nominee, Hugo Award, 1987; Nominee, World Fantasy Award, 1987; International Reading Association Children's Choice, 1988; Joan Fassler Memorial Book Award, 1992; International Reading Association Young Adult's Choice, 1993. Memberships: Society of Children's Book Writers; Central Pennsylvania Writers' Organization; Children's Literature Council of Pennsylvania; Pennwriters, president, 1992-93; Novelists Inc; Society of Children's Book Writers. Jean V Naggar. Address: c/o Virginia Kidd Agency, Box 278, 538 East Harford Street, Milford, PA 18337, USA.

SPRINKLE Patricia Houck, b. 13 Nov 1943, Bluefield, West Virginia, USA. Writer. m. Robert William Sprinkle, 12 Sept 1970, 2 sons. Education: AB, Vassar College, 1965. Publications: Fiction: Murder at Markham, 1988; Murder in the Charleston Manner, 1990; Murder on Peachtree Street, 1991; Somebody's Dead in Snellville, 1992; Death of a Dunwoody Matron, 1993; A Mystery Bred in Buckhead, 1994; Deadly Secrets on the St Johns, 1995; When Did We Lose Harriet?, 1997. Non-fiction: Hunger: Understanding the Crisis Through Games, 1980; In God's Image: Meditations for the New Mother, 1988; Housewarmings: For Those Who Make a House a Home, 1992; Women Who Do Too Much: Stress and the Myth of the Superwoman, 1992; Children Who Do Too Little, 1993; A Gift From God, 1994; Women Home Alone: Learning to Thrive, 1996; Sign of the Times, short story, 1995. Contributions to: Magazines. Memberships: Mystery Writers of America; Penwoman; Publicity Chairperson, Sisters in Crime. Address: 15086 South West 113th Street, Miami, FL 33196, USA.

SPURLING John (Antony), b. 17 July 1936, Kisumu, Kenya. Dramatist; Novelist; Art Critic. m. Hilary Forrest, 4 Apr 1961, 2 sons, 1 daughter. Education: BA, St John's College, Oxford, 1960. Publications: Plays: MacRune's Guevara (as Realised by Edward Hotel), 1969; In the Heart of the British Museum, 1971; Shades of Heathcliff and Death of Captain Doughty, 1975; The British Empire, Part One, 1982. Novels: The Ragged End, 1989; After Zenda, 1995. Other: Beckett: A Study of His Plays (with John Fletcher), 1972, 3rd edition, revised, as Beckett, the Playwright, 1985; Graham Greene, 1983. Contributions to: Books, newspapers, periodicals, theatre (14 plays produced, 1969-94), radio (8 plays, 1976-93), and television (4 plays, 1970-73). Honour: Henfield Writing Fellowship, University of East Anglia, 1973. Address: c/o MLR Ltd, 200 Fulham Road, London SW10 9PN, England.

SRIVASTAVA Ramesh Kumar, b. 2 Jan 1940, Banpur, India. m. Usha Rani Srivastava, 27 June 1959, 2 sons. Education: BA, 1957; MA, 1961; PhD, 1972. Appointments: Editor, The Summit, 1970-72; Associate Editor, 1976-88, Editor, 1988-93, The Punjab Journal of English Studies. Publications: Love and Animality: Stories, 1984; Cooperative Colony: Stories, 1985; Neema (novel), 1986; Six Indian Novelists in English, 1987; Games They Play and Other Stories, 1989; Critical Studies in English and American Literature, 1993; Under the Lamp: Stories, 1993. Contributions to: Newspapers and journals. Honours: Fulbright Fellowship, 1969; Senior Fulbright Grant, 1984. Memberships: Authors Guild of India; Indian PEN; Modern Language Association. Address: B 16 Guru Nanak Dev University, Amritsar 143005, India.

ST AUBYN Giles R (The Hon), b. 11 Mar 1925, London, England. Writer. Education: Wellington College; MA, Trinity College,

Oxford University. Publications: Lord Macaulay, 1952; A Victorian Eminence, 1957; The Art of Argument, 1957; The Royal George, 1963; A World to Win, 1968; Infamous Victorians, 1971; Edward VII, Prince and King, 1979; The Year of Three Kings 1483, 1983; Queen Victoria: A Portrait, 1991. Honour: LVO. Memberships: Fellow, Royal Society of Literature; Society of Authors. Address: Saumarez Park Manor, Apt 2, Route de Saumarez, Câtel, Guernsey GY5 7TH, Channel Islands.

ST CLAIR Elizabeth. See: COHEN Susan.

ST CLAIR William, b. 7 Dec 1937, London, England. Author. 2 daughters. Education: St John's College, Oxford, 1956-60. Appointments: Formerly, 1985, Huntington Library, San Marino, California, 1985; Fellow, All Souls College, Oxford, 1992-96; Visiting Fellow Commoner, Trinity College, Cambridge, 1997. Publications: Lord Elgin and the Marbles, 1967, revised edition, 1983; That Greece Might Still Be Free, 1972; Trelawny, 1978; Policy Evaluation: A Guide for Managers, 1988; The Godwins and the Shelleys: The Biography of a Family, 1989; Executive Agencies: A Guide to Setting Targets and Judging Performance, 1992. Honours: Heinemann Prize, Royal Society of Literature, 1973; Time-Life Prize, 1990; MacMillan Silver Pen, 1990. Memberships: British Academy, fellow; Byron Society, international president; Royal Society of Literature, fellow. Address: 52 Eaton Place, London SW1, England.

ST DAWN Grace Galasso, b. 24 Apr 1921, Paterson, New Jersey, USA. Poet; Speaker. 1 son. Education: Hon PhD, National Academy of Management, China; Litt World Academy of Arts and Culture. Publications: God Gave Me His Peace - Love God Truat God. Honours: Various awards, medals, 4 honorary doctorates. Memberships: American Biographical Research Institute, life fellow; International Biographical Centre, life fellow; International Platform Association, life fellow; World Poetry, life fellow; Knights of Malta, life fellow. Address: 340 Elliot Place, Paramus, NJ 07652, USA.

ST JOHN David. See: HUNT Everette Howard.

ST JOHN Lucia. See: DIORIO Mary Ann Lucia.

ST JOHN Nicole. See: JOHNSTON Norma.

STACEY Tom, (Thomas Charles Gerard Stacey), b. 11 Jan 1930, Bletchingly, England. Author. m. Caroline Clay, 5 Jan 1952, 1 son, 4 daughters. Education: Eton College, Oxford. Appointments: Writer and Foreign Correspondent, Daily Express, London, 1954, 1956-60; Correspondent, Montreal Star, 1955-56; Chief Roving Correspondent, Sunday Times, London, 1960-65; Columnist, Evening Standard, London, 1965-67; Managing Director, Correspondents World Wide, London, 1967-71; Tom Stacey Ltd, later Stacey International, London, 1969-. Publications: Fiction: The Brothers M, 1960; The Living and The Dying, 1976; The Pandemonium, 1980; The Twelfth Night of Ramadan, 1983; The Worm in the Rose, 1985; Deadline, 1988; Decline, 1991; Film Screenplay: Deadline, 1988; Radio Play: Affair in Riyadh. Non-fiction: The Hostile Sun: A Malayan Journey, 1953; Summons to Ruwenzori, 1965; Immigration and Enoch Powell, 1970. Other: Today's World: A Map Notebook for World Affairs (editor), 1968; Correspondents World Wide (with Caroline Hayman), 1968; Chambers' Encyclopedia Yearbook (editor-in-chief), 1969-72; Here Come the Tories, 1970; Peoples of the World (editorial director), 20 volumes, 1971-73. Contributions to: Books, newspapers, and periodicals. Honours: John Llewllyn Rhys Memorial Prize, 1954; Granada Award, 1961. Memberships: Royal Geographical Society, fellow; Royal Society of Literature, fellow. Address: 128 Kensington Church Street, London W8, England.

STACK George Joseph, b. New York, New York, USA. Professor of Philosophy Emeritus; Writer. m. Claire Avena, dec, 1 son, 1 daughter. Education: BA, Pace University, 1960; MA, 1962, PhD, 1964, Penn State University. Appointments: Instructor, Penn State University, 1962-63; Instructor, 1963-64, Assistant Professor, 1964-67, Long Island University; Assistant Professor, 1967-68, Associate Professor, 1968-70, Professor of Philosophy, 1970-95, Professor Emeritus, 1995-, State University of New York at Brockport. Publications: Berkeley's Analysis of Perception, 1970, 2nd edition, 1992; On Kierkegaard: Philosophical Fragments, 1976; Kierkegaard's Existential Ethics, 1977, 2nd edition, 1992; Sartre's Philosophy of Social Existence, 1978; Lange and Nietzsche, 1983. Contributions to: Books and professional journals. Memberships: American Philosophical Association; North American Nietzsche Society; Society for the Advancement of American Philosophy. Address: PO Box 92, Grapevine, TX 76099, USA.

STADTLER Beatrice, b. 26 June 1921, Cleveland, Ohio, USA. Educator; Writer. m. Oscar Stadtler, 31 Jan 1945, 1 son, 2 daughters. Education: Diploma, Sunday School Teacher, 1957; Bachelor, Judaic Studies, 1971; MSc, Religious Education, 1983; Master of Jewish Studies, 1989. Appointments: Columnist, Cleveland Jewish News for Youth, 1962, Boston Jewish Advocate, 1975. Publications: The Holocaust: A History of Courage and Resistance, 1975; Significant Lives, 1976; Rescue From the Sky, 1978; The Story of Dona Gracia Mendes, 1969; The Adventures of Gluckel of Hameln, 1967; Once Upon a Jewish Holiday, 1965. Contributions to: Books and periodicals; Shofar Magazine; Young Judean; Israel Philatelist; Kadima. Honour: The Holocaust was winner of the Jewish Book Council Award for Best Jewish Juvenile in America, 1975; Award for book, A History of Israel Through Her Postage Stamps, Third National Canadian Philatelic Literature Exhibition. Membership: Society of Israel Philatelists, co-editor, Israel Philatelist; Jewish Educator's Assembly. Address: 24355 Tunbridge Lane, Beachwood, OH 44122, USA.

STAINES David, b. 8 Aug 1946, Toronto, Ontario, Canada. Educator; Writer. Education: BA, University of Toronto, 1967; AM, 1968, PhD, 1973, Harvard University. Appointments: Assistant Professor of English, Harvard University, 1973-78; Honorary Research Fellow, University College, London, 1977-78; Associate Professor, 1978-85, Professor of English, 1985-, University of Ottawa; Five College Professor of Canadian Studies, Smith College, 1982-84. Publications: Editor: The Canadian Imagination: Dimensions of a Literary Culture, 1977; Stephen Leacock: A Reappraisal, 1986; The Forty-Ninth and Other Parallels: Contemporary Canadian Perspectives, 1986. Author: Tennyson's Camelot: The Idylls of the King and Its Medieval Sources, 1982. Translator: The Complete Romances of Chretien de Troyes, 1990; Beyond the Provinces: Literary Canada at Century's End, 1995. Contributions to: Profesional journals. Address: Department of English, University of Ottawa, Ottawa, Ontario K1N 6N5, Canada.

STAINES Trevor. See: **BRUNNER John Kilian Houston.**

STALLWORTHY Jon (Howie), b. 18 Jan 1935, London, England. Professor of English Literature; Poet; Writer. m. Gillian Waldock, 25 June 1960, 3 children. Education: BA, 1958, BLitt, 1961, Magdalen College, Oxford. Appointments: Editor, 1959-71, Deputy Academic Publisher, 1974-77, Oxford University Press; Visiting Fellow, All Souls College, Oxford, 1971-72; Editor, Clarendon Press, Oxford, 1972-77; John Wendell Anderson Professor of English Literature, Cornell Unversity, Ithaca, New York, 1977-86; Reader in English Literature, 1986-92; Professor of English, 1992-, Oxford Unversity. Publications: Poetry: The Earthly Paradise, 1958; The Astronomy of Love, 1961; Out of Bounds, 1963; The Almond Tree, 1967; A Day in the City, 1967; Root and Branch, 1969; Positives, 1969; A Dinner of Herbs, 1970; Hand in Hand, 1974; The Apple Barrel: Selected Poems, 1955-63, 1974; A Familiar Tree, 1978; The Anzac Sonata: Selected Poems, 1986; The Guest from the Future, 1995. Other: Between the Lines: Yeats's Poetry in the Making, 1963; Vision and Revision in Yeats's Last Poems, 1969; The Penguin Book of Love Poetry (editor), 1973; Wilfred Owen: A Biography, 1974; Poets of the First World War, 1974; Boris Pasternak: Selected Poems (translator with France), 1982; The Complete Poems and Fragments of Wilfred Owen (editor), 1983; The Oxford Book of War Poetry (editor), 1984; The Poems of Wilfred Owen (editor), 1985; First Lines: Poems Written in Youth from Herbert to Heaney (editor), 1987; Henry Reed: Collected Poems (editor), 1991; Louis MacNeice, 1995. Contributions to: Professional journals. Memberships: British Academy, fellow; Royal Society of Literature, fellow. Address: Wolfson College, Oxford OX 2 6UD, England.

STAMM Gret. See: **GUT-RUSSENBERGER Margrit.**

STAMPER Alex. See: **KENT Arthur (William Charles).**

STANBROUGH Harvey Ernest, b. 19 Nov 1952, Alamogordo, New Mexico, USA. US Marine (retired); College Instructor; Poet; Editor. m. Mona Griffith, 23 June 1984, 3 sons, 2 daughters. Education: BA, English, 1996. Publication: Melancholy and Madness, 1993; Partners in Rhyme, 1996; On Love and War and Other Fantasies, 1997. Contributions to: Anthologies and other publications. Honours:

Contest awards; Phi Theta Kappa. Address: 810 South Michigan, Roswell, NM 88201, USA.

STANFIELD Anne. See: **COFFMAN Virginia (Edith).**

STANGL (Mary) Jean, b. 14 May 1928, Irondale, Missouri, USA. Education: BA, University of LaVerne, 1975; MA, California State University at Northridge, 1977. Publications: Over 20 books, 1975-96. Honours: Several. Memberships: Beatrix Potter Society; National Association for the Education of Young Children; Society of Children's Book Writers and Illustrators. Address: 1658 Calle La Cumbre, Camarillo, CA 93010, USA.

STANLEY Autumn Joy, b. 21 Dec 1933, Vinton County, Ohio, USA. Writer. m. (1) F Blair Simmons, 6 June 1955, div 1971, 1 son, 3 daughters, (2) John Morgan Daniel, 1 Jan 1973, div 1984. Education: AB, high distinction, Transylvania College, 1955; MA, English and American Literature, Stanford University, 1967. Appointments: Instructor, Pacific Lutheran University, Tacoma, 1957-58, Canada College, Redwood City, California, 1969-70; Editor, Stanford University Press, California, 1969-74; Development Editor, Wadsworth Publishers, Belmont, California, 1974-80; Affiliated Scholar, Center for Research on Women and Gender, Stanford University, California, 1984-88. Publications: Asparagus: The Sparrowgrass Cookbook, 1977; 'Mainder the Buttercup, 1977; The Enchanted Quill, 1978; Mothers and Daughters of Invention, 1993; Contributions to: Anthologies, magazines and journals. Honour: Distinguished Service Award, Transylvania University, 1995. Memberships: Institute for Historical Study; National Women's Studies Association. Address: 241 Bonita Los Trancos Woods, Portola Valley, CA 94028-8103, USA.

STANLEY Bennett. See: **HOUGH Stanley Bennett.**

STANLEY Julian Cecil, Jr, b. 9 July 1918, Macon, Georgia, USA. Professor of Psychology; Writer. m. (1) Rose Roberta Sanders, 18 Aug 1946, dec 1978, 1 daughter, (2) Barbara S Kerr, 1 Jan 1980. Education: BS, Physical Science, Georgia Southern University, 1937; EdM, 1946, EdD, Experimental and Educational Psychology, 1950, Harvard University; Postdoctoral Fellow, University of Chicago, 1955-56; Fulbright Act Research Scholar, University of Louvain, Belgium, 1958-59, University of New Zealand, 1974. Appointments: Professor of Education and Psychology, 1967-71, Professor of Psychology, 1971-, Johns Hopkins University; Founder and Director, Study of Mathematically Precocious Youth (SMPY), Johns Hopkins University, 1971-; Visiting Lecturer at Universities in Australia, 1980, 1992; Visiting Distinguished Professor, University of North Texas, 1990. Publications: Author, Co-Author or Editor of 13 books and about 500 professional articles, technical notes, chapters, reviews, and technical letters to editors. Honours: Life Member, Johns Hopkins University Chapter Recognition Award, 1979, Phi Delta Kappa; Fellow, American Statistical Association; American Association for the Advancement of Science; American Psychological Association; American Psychological Society Distinguished Teacher, White House Commission on Presidential Scholars, 1987, 1992; James McKeen Cattell Fellow Award in Applied Psychology, 1994; Phi Beta Kappa; Sigma Xi; Honorary Doctorates, University of North Texas, 1990, State University of West Georgia, 1997. Memberships: American Educational Research Association; National Academy of Education; National Association for Gifted Children. Address: Johns Hopkins University, Baltimore, MD 21218, USA.

STANLEY Patricia. Professor of German. Education: PhD, 1975. Publications: The Realm of Possibilities, 1988; Wolfgang Hildesheimer and His Critics, 1993. Contributions to: South Atlantic Review; Monatshefte; German Studies Review; Germanic Review; Denver Quarterly; Literary Review; Colloquium Germanica; Seminar. Honour: Fulbright Fellow. Address: Department of Modern Languages and Linguistics, Florida State University, Tallahassee, FL 32306-1020, USA.

STANTON Vance. See: **AVALLONE Michael (Angelo Jr).**

STARK Joshua. See: **OLSEN Theodore Victor.**

STARK ADAM Pegie, b. 4 July 1949, South Bend, Indiana, USA.Designer; Artist; Teacher. m. Dr G Stuart Adam, 23 Feb 1994. Education: BFA, 1975, MA, School of Journalism, 1981, PhD in Mass Communications, Indiana University, 1984. Publications: Co-Author and Designer: Eyes on the News, 1990; Color, Contrast and

Dimension in News Design, 1995. Designer: Contemporary Newspaper Design, 2nd edition, 1992; Designer: Newspaper Evolutions, 1997. Contributions to: IFRA journal, Germany; Society of Newspaper Design journal. Honours: Society of Newspaper Design, 17 awards, 1987-88; 1st Place, Florida Design Competition, 1991. Memberships: Society of Newspaper Design; Association for the Education of Journalism and Mass Communication. Address: 4D Castlebrook Lane, Nepean, Ontario K2G 5E3, Canada.

STARNES John Kennett, b. 5 Feb 1918, Montreal, Quebec, Canada. Retired Diplomat. m. Helen Gordon Robinson, 10 May 1941, 2 sons. Education: Institute Sillig, Switzerland, 1935-36; University of Munich, Germany, 1936; BA, Bishop's University, 1939. Appointments: Counsellor, Canadian Embassy, Bonn, 1953-56; Head of Defence Liaison, Ottawa, 1958-62; Ambassador, Federal Republic of Germany, 1962-66, United Arab Republic and The Sudan, 1966-67; Assistant Undersecretary of State for External Affairs, 1967-70; Director General, Royal Canadian Mounted Police Security Service, 1970-73; Member Council, International Institute for Strategic Studies, 1977-85. Publications: Deep Sleepers, 1981; Scarab, 1982; Orion's Belt, 1983; The Cornish Hug, 1985; Latonya (novel), 1994. Contributions to: Numerous Newspapers, journals and periodicals. Honours: Centennial Medal; Honorary Doctor of Civil Law, Bishop's University, 1975; Commemorative Medal for 125th Anniversary of the Confederation of Canada, 1992. Memberships: International Institute of Strategic Studies; Canadian Institute of International Affairs; Canadian Writers Foundation. Address: 100 Rideau Terrace, Apt 9, Ottawa, Ontario K1M 0Z2, Canada.

STAROBINSKI Jean, b. 17 Nov 1920, Geneva, Switzerland. Writer. m. Jacqueline Sirman, 15 Aug 1954, 3 sons. Education: PhD, Geneva, 1958; MD, Lausanne, 1960. Publications: Jean Jacques Rousseau: La Transparence et L'Obstacle, 1957; La Relation Critique, 1970; 1789: Les Emblemes de La Raison: Montaigne en Mouvement, 1983; Le Remede dans Le Mal, 1989; Largesse, 1994. Contributions to: Newspapers and journals. Honours: Chevalier Legion D'Honneur, 1980; Prix Européen de L'Essai, 1983; Balzan Prize, 1984; Prix de Monaco, 1988; Goethe Prize, 1994. Memberships: President, Rencontres International; Institut de France, Paris. Address: Universite de Geneva, CH-1211 Geneva 4, Switzerland.

STARR Paul (Elliot), b. 12 May 1949, New York, New York, USA. Professor of Sociology; Writer; Editor. m. Sandra Luire Stein, 12 Apr 1981. Education: BA, Columbia University, 1970; PhD, Harvard University, 1978. Appointments: Junior Fellow, Harvard Society of Fellows, 1975-78; Assistant Professor, Harvard University, 1978-82; Associate Professor, 1982-85, Professor of Sociology, 1985-; Princeton University; Founder-Co-Editor, The American Prospect; Founder, Electronic Policy Network, 1995. Publications: The Discarded Army: Veterans After Vietnam, 1974; The Social Transformation of American Medicine, 1983; The Logic of Health-Care Reform, 1992. Contributions to: Professional journals. Honours: Guggenheim Fellowship, 1981-82; C Wright Mills Award, 1983; Pulitzer Prize in General Non-Fiction, 1984; Bancroft Prize, 1984. Address: c/o Department of Sociology, Princeton University, Princeton, NJ 08544, USA.

STARR Renata. See: CORTEN Irina H Shapiro.

STARRATT Thomas, b. 6 Oct 1952, Holyoke, Massachusetts, USA. Teacher; Writer. m. Patricia, 7 Apr 1994, 3 sons, 2 daughters. Education: BSc, Plymouth State Teachers College, Plymouth, New Hampshire, 1975; MEd, University of New Hampshire, 1980; Numerous graduate courses from various schools. Appointments: Teacher, Oyster River Middle School, 1976-77, Rochester Junior High School, 1977-81; Reading Improvement Specialist, Mannheim Middle School, 1981-91; Teacher/Assistant Principal, A T Mahan High School, Iceland, 1991-95; Spangdahlem Middle School, 1995-.Publications: Poetry: Nightwatch, 1994; Amsterdam, 1994; Summer on the Lava Plain, 1994; Eye to Your Storm, 1995; Passages, 1995; Excess, 1995; Sumer Days, 1995; Amsterdam Revisited, 1995; Washed Up, 1996. Contributions to: Professional journals. Honour: Excellence in Reading Award, 1990. Membership: ASCD; International Reading Association. Address: PSC 09, Box 1383, APO AE, D-09123 Germany.

STAVE Bruce M(artin), b. 17 May 1937, New York, New York, USA. Historian. m. Sondra T Astor, 16 June 1961, 1 son. Education: AB, Columbia College, 1959; MA, Columbia University, 1961; PhD, University of Pittsburgh, 1966. Appointments: Professor, 1975-;

Director, Center for Oral History, 1981-, Chairman, Department of History, 1985-94, University of Connecticut. Publications: The New Deal and the Last Hurrah, 1970; The Discontented Society (co-editor), 1972; Socialism and the Cities (contributing editor), 1975; The Making of Urban History, 1977; Modern Industrial Cities, 1981; Talking About Connecticut, 1985, 2nd edition, 1990; Mills and Meadows: A Pictorial History of Northeast Connecticut (co-author), 1991; From the Old Country: An Oral History of European Migration to America (co-author), 1994. Contributions to: Journal of Urban History; Americana Magazine; International Journal of Oral History. Honours: Fulbright Professorships, India, 1968-69, Australia, New Zealand, Philippines, 1977, China, 1984; National Endowment for the Humanities Fellowship, 1974; Homer Bubbidge Award for From Your Old Country, Association for the Study of Connecticut History, 1995. Memberships: American Historical Association; Organization of American Historians; Immigration History Society; New England Historical Association, president, 1994-95; New England Association of Oral History. Address: 200 Broad Way, Coventry, CT 06238, USA.

STEAD C(hristian) K(arlson), b. 17 Oct 1932, Auckland, New Zealand. Poet; Writer; Critic; Editor; Professor. m. Kathleen Elizabeth Roberts, 8 Jan 1955, 1 son, 3 daughters. Education: BA, 1954, MA, 1955, University of New Zealand; PhD, University of Bristol, 1961; DLitt, University of Auckland, 1982. Appointments: Lecturer in English, University of New England, Australia, 1956-57; Lecturer, 1960-61, Senior Lecturer, 1962-64, Associate Professor, 1964-67, Professor of English, 1967-86, Professor Emeritus, 1986-, University of Auckland; Chairman, New Zealand Literary Fund Advisory Committee, 1972-75, New Zealand Authors' Fund Committee, 1989-91. Publications: Poetry: Whether the Will is Free, 1964; Crossing the Bar, 1972; Quesada: Poems 1972-74, 1975; Walking Westward, 1979; Geographies, 1982; Poems of a Decade, 1983; Paris, 1984; Between, 1988; Voices, 1990. Fiction: Smith's Dream, 1971; Five for the Symbol, 1981; All Visitors Ashore, 1984; The Death of the Body, 1986; Sister Hollywood, 1989; The End of the Century at the End of the World, 1992; The Singing Whakapapa, 1994. Criticism: The New Poetic: Yeats to Eliot, 1964, revised edition, 1987; In the Glass Case: Essays on New Zealand Literature, 1981; Pound, Yeats, Eliot and the Modernist Movement, 1986; Answering to the Language: Essays on Modern Writers, 1989. Editor: World's Classics: New Zealand Short Stories, 1966, 3rd edition, 1975; Measure for Measure: A Casebook, 1971, revised edition, 1973; Letters and Journals of Katherine Mansfield, 1977; Collected Stories of Maurice Duggan, 1981; The New Gramophone Room: Poetry and Fiction (with Elizabeth Smither and Kendrick Smithyman), 1985; The Faber Book of Contemporary South Pacific Stories, 1994. Contributions to: Poetry, fiction and criticism to various anthologies and periodicals. Honours: Katherine Mansfield Prize, 1960; Nuffield Travelling Fellowship, 1965; Katherine Mansfield Menton Fellowship, 1972; Jessie Mackay Award for Poetry, 1972; New Zealand Book Award for Poetry, 1975; Honorary Research Fellow, University College, London, 1977; New Zealand Book Awards for Fiction, 1985, 1995; Commander of the Order of the British Empire, 1984; Queen Elizabeth II Arts Council Scholarship in Letters, 1988-89; Queen's Medal for services to New Zealand literature, 1990; Fellow, Royal Society of Literature, 1995; Senior Visiting Fellow, St John's College, Oxford, 1996-97. Membership: New Zealand PEN, Chairman, Auckland branch, 1986-89, National Vice President, 1988-90. Address: 37 Tohunga Crescent, Auckland 1, New Zealand.

STEANE J(ohn) B(arry), b. 12 April 1928, Coventry, England. Music Journalist; Writer. Education: English, Cambridge University. Appointments: Teacher of English, Merchant Taylors' School, Northwood, 1952-88; Reviewer: Gramophone, 1973-, Musical Times (with Alec Sanders), 1988-, Opera Now, 1989-. Publications: Marlowe: A Critical Study, 1964; Dekker: The Shoemaker's Holiday (editor), 1965; Tennyson, 1966; Jonson: The Alchemist (editor), 1967; Marlowe: The Complete Plays, 1969; Nashe: The Unfortunate Traveller and Other Works, 1972; The Grand Tradition: Seventy Years of Singing on Record, 1973, revised 1993; Voices: Singers and Critics, 1992; Singers of the Century, 1996. Co-author: Opera on Record, 3 volumes, 1979-85; Song on Record, 2 volumes, 1986-88; Choral Music on Record, 1991; Elisabeth Schwarzkopf: A Career on Record, 1995. Contributions to: New Grove Dictionary of Music, 1980; New Grove Dictionary of Opera, 1992. Address: 32 Woodland Avenue, Coventry, England.

STEARNS Peter, b. 3 Mar 1936, London, England. m. Carol Stearns, 26 Mar 1978, 1 son, 3 daughters. Education: AB, 1957, AM, 1959, PhD, 1963, Harvard University. Appointment: Dean, College of

Humanities and Social Science, Carnegie Mellon University. Publications: European Society in Upheaval, 1967; The Impact of the Industrial Revolution, 1972; Old Age in European Society, 1977; The Other Side of Western Civilization, 1984; Be a Man: Males in Modern Society, 1990; American Cool, 1994. Contributions to: Professional journals. Honours: Phi Beta Kappa; Social Science Research Council Fellowship; American Philosophical Society Grant; Guggenheim Fellowship; Koren Prize; Newcomen Special Award; Elliott Dunlap Smith Teaching Award. Memberships: American Historical Association; International Society for Research. Address: Carnegie Mellon University, Pittsburgh, PA 15213, USA.

STEBEL Sidney Leo, (Leo Bergson, Steve Toron), b. 28 June 1923, Iowa, USA. Writer. m. Jan Mary Dingler, 10 Sept 1954, 1 daughter. Education: BA, English Literature, University of Southern California, Los Angeles, 1949. Appointment: Adjunct Professor, Masters of Professional Writing, University of Southern California, Los Angeles, 1991. Publications: The Widowmaster, 1967; The Collaborator, 1968; Main Street, 1971; The Vorovich Affar, 1975; The Shoe Leather Treatment, 1983; Spring Thaw, 1989; The Boss's Wife, 1992; Double Your Creative Power, 1996. Contributions to: Anthologies, newspapers and magazines. Honour: 2nd Place, Fiction Award, Spring Thaw, PEN Center West, 1989. Memberships: Australian Writers Guild; Authors Guild; Former International Secretary, PEN Centre, USA West; Writers Guild of America; Author's League. Literary Agent: Don Congdon, Don Congdon Associates Inc, 156 Fifth Avenue #625, New York, NY 10010, USA. Address: 1963 Mandeville Canyon Road, Los Angeles, CA 90049, USA.

STEEL Danielle (Fernande), b. 14 Aug 1947, New York, New York, USA. Writer. Education: Parsons School of Design, New York City, 1963-67. Appointments: Vice-President for Public Relations and New Business, Supergirls Ltd, New York City, 1968-71; Copywriter, Grey Advertising, San Francisco, 1973-74. Publications: Going Home, 1973; Passion's Promise, 1977; Now and Forever, 1978; The Promise, 1978; Season of Passion, 1979; Summer's End, 1979; To Love Again, 1980; The Ring, 1980; Loving, 1980; Love, 1981; Remembrance, 1981; Palomino, 1981; Once in a Lifetime, 1982; Crossings, 1982; A Perfect Stranger, 1982; Thurston House, 1983; Changes, 1983; Full Circle, 1984; Having a Baby, 1984; Family Album, 1985; Secrets, 1985; Wanderlust, 1986; Fine Things, 1987; Kaleidoscope, 1987; Zoya, 1988; Star, 1988; Daddy, 1989; Message from Nam, 1990; Heartbeart, 1991; No Greater Love, 1991; Jewels, 1992; Mixed Blessings, 1992; Vanished, 1993; Accident, 1994; The Gift, 1994; Wings, 1994; Lightning, 1995; Five Days in Paris, 1996; Malice, 1996. Contributions to: Periodicals. Address: PO Box 1637, New York, NY 10156, USA.

STEEL Ronald Lewis, b. 25 Mar 1931, Morris, Illinois, USA. Professor of International Relations; Writer. Education: BA magna cum laude, Northwestern University, 1953; MA, Harvard University, 1955. Appointments: Vice Consul, US Foreign Service, 1957-58; Editor, Scholastic Magazine, 1959-62; Senior Associate, Carnegie Endowment for International Peace, 1962-83; Visiting Fellow, Yale University, 1971-73; Visiting Professor, University of Texas, 1977, 1979, 1980, 1985, Wellesley College, 1978, Rutgers University, 1980, University of California at Los Angeles, 1981, Dartmouth College, 1983, Princeton University, 1984; Fellow, Woodrow Wilson International Center for Scholars, 1984-85, Wissenschaftskolleg zu Berlin, Federal Republic of Germany, 1988; Professor of International Relations, University of Southern California at Los Angeles, 1986-; Shapiro Professor of International Relations, George Washington University, 1995-96. Publications: The End of Alliance: America and the Future of Europe, 1964; Tropical Africa Today (with G Kimble), 1966; Pax Americana, 1967; Imperialists and Other Heroes, 1971; Walter Lippman and the American Century, 1980; Temptations of a Superpower, 1995. Contributions to: Professional journals and general publications. Honours: Sidney Hillman Prize, 1968; Guggenheim Fellowship, 1973-74; Los Angeles Times Book Award, 1980; Washington Monthly Book Award, 1980; National Book Critics Circle Award, 1981; Bancroft Prize, Columbia University, 1981; American Book Award, 1981. Memberships: American Historical Association; Council on Foreign Relations; Society of American Historians. Address: c/o School of International Relations, University of Southern California, Los Angeles, CA 90089, USA.

STEELE Shelby, b. 1946, Chicago, Illinois, USA. Professor of English; Writer. Education: Coe College, 1968; M in Sociology, Southern Illinois University, 1971; PhD in English, University of Utah, 1974. Appointment: Professor of English, San Jose State University.

Publication: The Content of Our Character: A New Vision of Race in America, 1991. Contributions to: Journals. Honour: National Book Critics Circle Award, 1991. Address: c/o Department of English, San Jose State University, Washington Square, San Jose, CA 95192, USA.

STEFFLER John Earl, b. 13 Nov 1947, Toronto, Ontario, Canada. Professor of English Literature; Poet; Writer. m. Shawn O'Hagan, 30 May 1970, 1 son, 1 daughter. Education: BA, University of Toronto, 1971; MA, University of Guelph, 1974. Publications: An Explanation of Yellow, 1980; The Grey Islands, 1985; The Wreckage of Play, 1988; The Afterlife of George Cartwright, 1991. Contributions to: Journals and periodicals. Honours: Books in Canada First Novel Award, 1992; Newfoundland Arts Council Artist of the Year Award, 1992; Thomas Raddall Atlantic Fiction Award, 1992; Joseph S Stauffer Prize, 1993. Memberships: League of Canadian Poets; PEN; Writers Alliance of Newfoundland and Labrador. Address: c/o Department of English, Memorial University of Newfoundland, Corner Brook, Newfoundland A2H 6PN, Canada.

STEIN Clarissa Ingeborg, (Sara Cristiens), b. 3 Sept 1948, Munich, Germany. Editor; Poet. m. Herbert Stein, 26 May 1981, 1 daughter. Education: Diplom Finanzwirt- (FH), Beamtenfachhochschule, Herrsching, Bavaria, 1975. Appointments: Editor, Papyrus Publishing, 1991-. Publications: New Melodies Neue Melodien, 1992; Notes from My Land (poems), 1993; Billy Tea and Sand Ballet (poems), 1996. Contributions to magazines and journals in Australia and overseas. Memberships: Deakin Literary Society, Deakin University; General Member, Victorian Committee National Book Council. Address: 16 Grand View Crescent, Upper Ferntree Gully, Victoria 3156, Australia.

STEIN Peter Gonville, b. 29 May 1926, Liverpool, England. Professor of Law; Writer. m. (1), div, 3 daughters, (2) Anne M Howard, 16 Aug 1978. Education: BA, 1949, LLB, 1950, Gonville and Caius College, Cambridge; Admitted as Solicitor, 1951; University of Pavia, 1951-52. Appointments: Professor of Jurisprudence, University of Aberdeen, 1956-68; Regius Professor of Civil Law, University of Cambridge, 1968-93. Publications: Regulae Iuris: From Juristic Rules to Legal Maxims, 1966; Legal Values in Western Society (with J Shand), 1974; Legal Evolution: The Story of an Idea, 1980; Legal Institutions: The Development of Dispute Settlement, 1984; The Character and Influence of the Roman Civil Law, 1988; The Teaching of Roman Law in England Around 1200 (with F de Zulueta), 1990; Römisches Recht und Europa: Die Geschichte einer Rechtskultur, 1996. Contributions to: Professional journals. Honours: Honorary Dr Iuris, University of Göttingen, 1980; Honorary Dott Giur, University of Ferrara, 1991; Honorary QC, 1993. Memberships: British Academy, fellow; Belgian National Academy; Italian National Academy, foreign fellow; Selden Society, vice-president, 1984-87; Society of Public Teachers of Law, president, 1980-81. Address: c/o Queen's College, Cambridge, CB3 9ET, England.

STEINBACH Meredith Lynn, b. 18 Mar 1949, Ames, Iowa, USA. Novelist; Associate Professor. m. Charles Ossian Hartman, 5 May 1979, div 1991, 1 son. Education: BGS, 1973, MFA, 1976, University of Iowa. Literary Appointments: Teaching Fellow, University of Iowa, 1975-76; Writer in Residence, Antioch College, 1976-77; Lecturer, Fiction, Northwestern University, 1977-79; Visiting Assistant Professor, University of Washington, 1979-82; Bunting Fellow, Radcliffe-Harvard, 1982-83; Assistant Professor to Associate Professor, Brown University, 1983-. Publications: Novels: Zara, 1982, 1996; Here Lies the Water, 1990; The Birth of the World as We Know It, 1996. Short stories: Reliable Light, 1990. Contributions to: Tri-Quarterly Magazine; Antaeus; Massachusetts Review; Antioch Review; South West Review; Black Warrior Review. Honours: Pushcart Prize, Best of the Small Presses, 1977; National Endowment for the Arts Fellowship, 1978; Bunting Fellow, Bunting Summer Fellow, Mary Ingraham Bunting Institute, Radcliffe College, Harvard, 1982-83; Rhode Island Artists Fellowship, 1986-87; O Henry Award, 1990. Memberships: PEN; Associated Writing Programs; Amnesty International. Literary Agent: Kathleen Anderson, Scovil, Chichak and Galen Literary Agency Inc. Address: c/o 381 Park Avenue, New York, NY 10016, USA.

STEINER-ISENMANN Robert, b. 19 May 1955, Basel, Switzerland. Writer. 1 daughter. Education: Theology, University of Zürich. Publications: Gaetano Donizetti: Sein Leben und seine Opern, 1982; Espoirs-hopfnungen (revue), 1988, new edition, 1993; Windspiel der Leidenschaft (poems), 1994. Contributions to: Anthologies, magazines and journals. Memberships: Association Suisse des

Écrivains: Association Valaisanne des Écrivains; PEN Club. Address: Café de la Rosablanche, 1996 Basse-Nendaz/VS, Switzerland.

STEINHARDT Nancy R Shatzman, b. 14 July 1954, St Louis, Missouri, USA. Art Historian. m. Paul Joseph Steinhardt, 1 July 1979, 3 sons, 1 daughter. Education: AB, Washington University, St Louis, 1974; AM, 1975, PhD, 1981, Harvard University. Appointment: Faculty, University of Pennsylvania. Publications: Chinese Traditional Architecture, 1984; Chinese Imperial City Planning, 1990; Liao Architecture, 1997. Contributions to: Professional journals and general periodicals. Memberships: Association for Asian Studies; College Art Society; Society of Architectural Historians. Address: c/o Department of Asian and Middle Eastern Studies, University of Pennsylvania, Philadelphia, PA 19104, USA.

STENDAL Grant Vincent, b. 8 Dec 1955, Rochdale, England. Writer. Education: BA, Flinders University of South Australia, 1982; BA (Honours), University of Tasmania, 1985; PhD candidate, University of Adelaide, 1994-. Publications: At Work: Australian Experiences, 1984; Job Representatives Handbook, revised edition, 1989. Contributions to: Journals, newspapers and periodicals. Honour: International Travel Grant, Australian Industrial Relations Society, 1994. Membership: Australian Industrial Relations Society. Address: Department of Politics, University of Adelaide, Adelaide, South Australia 5005, Australia.

STEPHAN John Jason,b. 8 Mar 1941, Chicago, Illinois, USA. Professor; Historian. m. 22 June 1963. Education: BA, 1963, MA, 1964, Harvard University; PhD, University of London, England, 1969. Appointments: Far Eastern Editor, Harvard Review, 1962; Visiting Fellow, St Antony's College, Oxford, 1977; Professor of History, University of Hawaii, 1980-; Visiting Professor of History, Stanford University, 1986; Research Fellow, Kennan Institute of Advanced Russian Studies, 1987; Editor, Encyclopedia of Siberia, 1988-. Publications: Sakhalin: A History, 1971; The Kuril Islands: Russo-Japanese Frontier in the Pacific, 1974; The Russian Fascists, 1978; Hawaii Under the Rising Sun, 1984; Soviet-American Horizons in the Pacific (with V.P. Chichkanov), 1986; The Russian Far East: A History, 1994. Contributions to: Washington Post; Modern Asian Studies; American Historical Review; Pacific Affairs; Pacific Community; Journal for Asian Studies; New York Times; Siberica; Pacifica; Australian Slavic and East European Studies. Honours: Fulbright Fellowship, 1967-68; Japan Culture Translation Prize, 1973; Japan Foundation Fellowship, 1977; Sanwa Distinguished Scholar, Fletcher School of Law and Diplomacy, Tufts University, 1989; Distinguished Invited Speaker, Canadian Historical Association, 1990. Memberships: Authors Guild; PEN; International House of Japan, Life Member; American Association for the Advancement of Slavic Studies, Life Member; American Historical Association; Canadian Historical Association. Address: Department of History, University of Hawaii, 2530 Dole Street, Honolulu, HI 96822, USA.

STEPHEN Ian, b. 29 Apr 1955, Stornoway, Isle of Lewis, Scotland. Writer; Artist. m. Barbara Ziehm, 9 Nov 1984, 2 sons. Education: BEd (with distinction) and Hons in English, Aberdeen University, 1980. Appointments: Inaugural Robert Louis Stevenson/ Christian Salvesen Fellow, Grez Sur Loing, France, 1995. Publications: Malin, Hebrides, Minches, 1983; Varying States of Grace, 1989; Siud an T-Eilean (editor), 1993; Providence II, 1994; Broad Bay, 1997. Numerous exhibitions poetry/texts with visual arts. Contributions to: Poems; Fiction; Reviews - The Scotsman; The Edinburgh Review; periodicals in Australia, Belgium, Canada. Honours: Scottish Arts Council Bursaries, 1981, 1995. Membership: PEN, Scotland. Literary Agent: Alec Finlay, Morning Star Publications, Edinburgh. Address: Last House, 1 Benside, Isle of Lewis HS2 0DZ, Scotland.

STEPHENS Michael Gregory, b. 4 Mar 1946, USA. University Lecturer; Writer. 1 daughter. Education: BA, MA, 1976, City College of the City University of New York; MFA, Yale University, 1979. Appointments: Lecturer, Columbia University, 1977-91, Princeton University, 1979-85, New York University, 1989-91; Assistant Professor, Fordham University, 1979-85. Publications: After Asia (poems), 1993; The Brooklyn Book of the Dead (novel), 1994; Green Dreams: Essays Under the Influence of the Irish, 1994. Contributions to: Newspapers, journals, and magazines. Honour: Associated Writing Programs Award in Creative Non-Fiction, 1993. Membership: PEN. Address: c/o Spuyten Duyvil Press, Box 1852, New York, NY 10025, USA.

STEPHENS Reed. See: **DONALDSON Stephen Reeder.**

STEPHENSON Hugh, b. 18 July 1938, England. Writer; Journalist; Teacher. m. (1) Auriol Stevens, 1962, 2 sons, 1 daughter, (2) Diana Eden, 1990. Education: MA, New College, Oxford; University of California, Berkeley, USA. Appointments: HM Diplomatic Service, 1964-69; Staff, The Times, 1968; Editor, The Times Business News, 1972-81, New Statesman, 1982-86; Professor of Journalism, City University, 1986-. Publications: The Coming Clash, 1972; Mrs Thatcher's First Year, 1980; Claret and Chips, 1982. Address: c/o Department of Journalism, City University, Northampton Square, London EC1, England.

STERLING Maria Sandra. See: **FLOREN Lee.**

STERN Gerald, b. 22 Feb 1925, Pittsburgh, Pennsylvania, USA. Poet; Teacher. m. Patricia Miller, 1952, 1 son, 1 daughter. Education: BA, University of Pittsburgh, 1947; MA, Columbia University, 1949. Appointments: Instructor, Temple University, Philadelphia, 1957-63; Professor, Indiana University of Pennsylvania, 1963-67, Somerset County College, New Jersey, 1968-82; Visiting Poet, Sarah Lawrence College, 1977; Visiting Professor, University of Pittsburgh, 1978, Columbia University, 1980, Bucknell University, 1988, New York Universty, 1989; Faculty, Writer's Workshop, University of Iowa, 1982-94; Distinguished Chair, University of Alabama, 1984; Fanny Hurst Professor, Washington University, St Louis, 1985; Bain Swiggert Chair, Princeton University, 1989; Poet-in-Residence, Bucknell University, 1994. Publications: The Naming of Beasts and Other Poems, 1973; Rejoicings, 1973; Lucky Life, 1977; The Red Coal, 1981; Paradise Poems, 1984; Lovesick, 1987; Leaving Another Kingdom: Selected Poems, 1990; Two Long Poems, 1990; Bread Without Sugar, 1992; Odd Mercy, 1995. Honours: National Endowment for the Arts Grants, 1976, 1981, 1987; Lamont Poetry Selection Award, 1977; Governor's Award, Pennsylvania, 1980; Guggenheim Fellowship, 1980; Bess Hokin Award, 1980; Bernard F Connor Award, 1981; Melville Cane Award, 1982; Jerome J Shestack Prize, 1984; Academy of Poets Fellowship, 1993; Ruth Lilly Poetry Prize, 1996. Address: c/o Department of English, University of Iowa, Iowa City, IA 52242, USA.

STERN Richard G(ustave), b. 25 Feb 1928, New York, New York, USA. Writer; Professor. m. (1) Gay Clark, (2) Alane Rollings, 3 sons, 1 daughter. Education: BA, University of North Carolina; MA, Harvard University; PhD, University of Iowa. Publications: Noble Rot Stories, 1949-89; Golk, 1960; Europe or Up and Down with Baggish and Schreiber, 1961; In Any Case, 1962; Stich, 1965; Other Man's Daughters, 1973; A Father's Words, 1986; The Position of the Buoy, 1986; Shares and Other Fictions, 1992; One Person and Another, 1993; Sistermoney, 1995. Contributions to: Journals and magazines. Honours: Longwood Award, 1954; American Academy of Arts and Letters Award, 1968; Friends of Literature Award, 1968; Sandburg Award, 1979; Award of Merit for the Novel, 1985. Address: 1050 East 59th Street, Chicago, IL 60637, USA.

STERN Richard Martin,b. 17 Mar 1915, Fresno, California, USA. Writer. m. Dorothy Helen Atherton, 20 Dec 1937, 1 daughter (adopted). Education: Harvard College, 1933-36. Appointment: Editorial Board, The Writer, 1976-. Publications: Bright Road to Fear, 1958; Search for Tabatha Carr, 1960; These Unlucky Deeds, 1960; High Hazard, 1962; Cry Havoc, 1963; Right Hand Opposite, 1963; I Hide, We Seek, 1964; The Kessler Legacy, 1967; Brood of Eagles, 1969; Merry Go Round, 1969; Manuscript for Murder, 1970; Murder in the Walls, 1971; Stanfield Harvest, 1972; Death in the Snow, 1973; The Tower, 1973; Power, 1974; The Will, 1976; Snowbound Six, 1977; Flood,1979; The Big Bridge, 1982; Wildfire, 1985; Tsunami, 1988; Tangled Murders, 1989; You Don't Need an Enemy, 1989; Missing Man, 1990; Interloper, 1990. Contributions to: Magazines. Honour: Edgar Award, Mystery Writers of America, 1958. Memberships: Past President, Mystery Writers of America; Crime Writers Association, UK; Authors Guild, USA. Address: Route 9, Box 55, Santa Fe, NM 87505, USA.

STERN Steve, b. 21 Dec 1947, Memphis, Tennessee, USA. Associate Professor of English; Writer. Education: BA, Rhodes College, 1970; MFA, University of Arkansas, 1977. Appointments: Visiting Lecturer, University of Wisconsin, 1987; Associate Professor of English, Skidmore College, Saratoga Springs, New York, 1994-. Publications: Isaac and the Undertaker's Daughter, 1983; The Moon and Ruben Shein, 1984; Lazar Malkin Enters Heaven, 1986; Mickey and the Golem, 1986; Hershel and the Beast, 1987; Harry Kaplan's

Adventures Underground, 1991; Plague of Dreamers, 1994. Contributions to: Magazines and journals. Honours: O Henry Prize, 1981; Pushcart Writers Choice Award, 1984; Edward Lewis Wallant Award, 1988. Address: c/o Department of English, Skidmore College, Saratoga Springs, NY 12866, USA.

STERN Stuart. See: RAE Hugh Crauford.

STERNBERG Robert J(effrey), b. 8 Dec 1949, Newark, New Jersey, USA. Psychology Educator; Writer. m. Alejandra Campos, 11 Aug 1991, 1 son, 1 daughter. Education: BA summa cum laude, Yale University, 1972; PhD, Stanford University, 1975. Appointments: Faculty, Department of Psychology, Yale University; Associate Editor, Intelligence, 1977-82, Child Development, 1981-84; Editor, Psychological Bulletin, 1991-96. Publications: Beyond IQ: A Triarchic Theory of Human Intelligence, 1985; Intelligence Applied: Understanding Your Intellectual Skills, 1986; Practical Intelligence: The Nature and Origins of Competance in the Everyday World (editor with Richard K Wagner), 1986; The Triangle of Love, 1987; The Triarchic Mind, 1988; The Nature of Creativity (editor), 1988; Metaphors of Mind: Conceptions of the Nature of Intelligence, 1990; Successful Intelligence, 1996. Contributions to: Professional journals. Honours: Distinguished Scholar Award, National Association for Gifted Children, 1985; Outstanding Book Award, American Educational Research Association, 1987; Sylvia Scribner Award, American Educational Research Association; Award for Excellence, Mensa Education and Research Foundation, 1989. Memberships: American Association for the Advancement of Science, fellow; American Educational Research Association; American Psychological Association, fellow; Society for Research in Child Development; American Academy of Arts and Sciences, fellow. Address: c/o Department of Psychology, Yale University, Box 208205, New Haven, CT 06520, USA.

STERNLICHT Sanford, b. 20 Sept 1931, New York, New York, USA. Professor of English; Literary Critic; Poet. m. Dorothy Hilkert, 7 June 1956, dec 1977, 2 sons. Education: BS, State University of New York at Oswego, 1953; MA, Colgate University, 1955; PhD, Syracuse University, 1962. Appointments: Instructor, 1959-60, Assistant Professor, 1960-62, Associate Professor, 1962, Professor of English, 1962-72, Professor of Theatre, 1972-86, State University of New York College at Oswego; Leverhulme Foundation Visiting Fellow, University of York, England, 1965-66; Professor of English, Syracuse University, 1986-. Publications: Poetry: Gull's Way, 1961; Love in Pompeii, 1967. Non-Fiction: Uriah Philips Levy: The Blue Star Commodore, 1961; The Black Devil of the Bayous: The Life and Times of the United States Steam-Sloop Hartford (with E M Jameson), 1970; John Webster's Imagery and the Webster Canon, 1974; John Masefield, 1977; McKinley's Bulldog: The Battleship Oregon, 1977; C S Forester, 1981; USF Constellation: Yankee Racehorse (with E M Jameson), 1981; Padraic Colum, 1985; John Galsworthy, 1987; R F Delderfield, 1988; Stevie Smith, 1990; Stephen Spender, 1992; Siegfried Sassoon, 1993; All Things Herriot: James Herriot and His Peaceable Kingdom, 1995; Jean Rhys, 1996. Editor: Selected Stories of Padraic Colum, 1985; Selected Plays of Padraic Colum, 1989; In Search of Stevie Smith, 1991; New Plays from the Abbey Theatre 1993-1995, 1996. Contributions to: Books, professional journals and general periodicals. Honours: Prizes, fellowships and grants. Memberships: Modern Language Association; PEN; Poetry Society of America, fellow; Shakespeare Association of America. Address: 128 Dorset Road, Syracuse, NY 13210, USA.

STERNMAN William, b. 26 Apr 1935. Writer. Education: Degree in Advertising, Charles Morris Price School of Advertising and Journalism, Philadelphia. Publications: Stories in: Weber Studies; Writers Journal; The Panhandler; The Mark; The Advocate; Pinehurst Journal; Dream International Quarterly; Monocacy Valley Review; PBW; Riding Out; Contemporary Writing (Australia); Foolscap (England); The Chronicle (South Africa); Brainwave (Pakistan); Menzed (New Zealand); Asztal Lap (Hungary); Regular column, Playback in Audience, A Film Journal (on staff, 1976-); Articles and reviews in Films in Review; Boston Herald; Houston Chronicle; Philadelphia Inquirer; St Petersburg Times; The Drummer. Honour: Fellowship Grant in Literature, Pennsylvania Council on the Arts, 1993.

STEVENS Carl. See: OBSTFELD Raymond.

STEVENS Graeme Roy, b. 17 July 1932, Lower Hutt, New Zealand. Palaeontologist. m. Diane Louise Morton Ollivier, 20 Oct 1962, 2 sons, 1 daughter. Education: BSc, 1954, MSc 1st Class, 1956,

University of New Zealand; PhD, University of Cambridge, England, 1960; Fellowship, Royal Society of New Zealand, 1976. Appointments: UNESCO Sub Commission for the Natural Sciences, 1976; Advisory Committee on Adult Education, 1979; Book Resources Panel, National Library of New Zealand, 1981. Publications: Rugged Landscape, 1974; Geology of the Tararuas, 1975; Geology of New Zealand, 1978; New Zealand Adrift, 1980; Lands in Collision, 1985; Prehistoric New Zealand, 1988; The Great New Zealand Fossil Book, 1990; On Shaky Ground, 1991; Life and Landscapes, 1991. Contributions to: 154 scientific papers to professional journals. Honours: Hamilton Prize, Royal Society of New Zealand, 1959; Wattie Book of the Year Awards for Non-Fiction, 1974, 1980; Doctor of Science, Victoria University of Wellington, 1989; Queen's Service Order, 1994. Memberships: Royal Society of New Zealand, Home Secretary; Geological Society of New Zealand, Publisher. Address: 19A Wairere Road, Belmont, Lower Hutt, New Zealand.

STEVENS John. See: TUBB E(dwin) C(harles).

STEVENS Lynsey. See: HOWARD Lynette Desley.

STEVENS Peter, b. 17 Nov 1927, Manchester, England. Canadian Citizen. Professor; Poet. Education: BA, Nottingham University; MA, McMaster University, 1963; PhD, University of Saskatchewan, 1968. Appointment: Professor, University of Windsor, 1973. Publications: Plain Geometry, 1968; Nothing But Spoons, 1969; A Few Myths, 1971; Breadcrusts and Glass, 1972; Family Feelings and Other Poems, 1974; Momentary Stay, 1974; The Bogman Pavese Tactics, 1977; An All That Jazz, 1980; Coming Back, 1981; Revenge of the Mistresses, 1981; Out of the Willow Trees, 1986; Editor of Literary Volumes. Honours: Canada Council Award, 1969. Address: Department of English, University of Windsor, Windsor, Ontario N9B 3P4, Canada.

STEVENS William Christopher. See: ALLEN Stephen Valentine.

STEVENSON David, b. 30 Apr 1942, Largs, Ayrshire, Scotland. Professor of History; Writer. m. Wendy McLeod, 2 sons. Education: BA, University of Dublin, 1966; PhD, University of Glasgow, 1970; DLitt, University of Glasgow, 1989. Appointments: Faculty, University of Aberdeen, University of St Andrews; Editor, Northern Scotland, 1980-90. Publications: The Scottish Revolution, 1973; Revolution and Counter-Revolution in Scotland, 1977; Alastair MacColla and the Highland Problem, 1980; Scottish Covenanters and Irish Confederates, 1981; The Origins of Freemasonry, 1988; The First Freemasons, 1988; King or Covenant: Voices from Civil War, 1996; Scotland's Last Royal Wedding, 1997; Union, Revolution and Religion in 17th Century Scotland, 1997. Contributions to: Historical journals. Membership: Royal Society of Edinburgh, Fellow. Address: St John's House, University of St Andrews, St Andrews KY16 9QW, Scotland.

STEVENSON John, (Mark Denning), b. 8 May 1926, London, England. Writer; Teacher. m. Alison Stevenson, 1951, div. Appointments: Fiction Editor, 1981-82, Book Review Columnist, 1982-90, Mystery News; Instructor, Writer's Digest Schools, 1989-. Publications: Some 30 books, including Die Fast, Die Happy, 1976; Beyond the Prize, 1978; Merchant of Menace, 1980; Writing Commercial Fiction, 1983; Ranson, 1989. Contributions to: Journals and magazines. Honours: 4th Prize, Crime Writers International Congress, Stockholm, 1981; Life Membership, Mystery Writers of America, 1993. Address: 2005 Ivar Avenue, No 3, Los Angles, CA 90068, USA.

STEWARD Hal David, b. 2 Dec 1918. Author; Journalist. Education: LLB, La Salle Extension University, Chicago, 1948; BS, Boston University, 1961; PhD, Columbia Pacific University, San Rafael, California, 1979. Appointments: Correspondent, Newsletter on Newsletters, Rhinebeck, New York, 1985-; Former Executive Editor, Daily Chronicle, Centralia, Washington, 1975-79; Retired US Army Lieutenant Colonel, Combat Veteran of World War II and Korean War. Publications: The Successful Writer's Guide, 1970; Money Making Secrets of the Millionaires, 1972; Winning in Newsletters, 1989; 2 novels; 2 military histories. Contributions to: More than 500 articles to national magazines. Honour: Copley Journalism Award, 1963. Memberships: Authors Guild; Society of Professional Journalists; National Press Club; San Diego Press Club; Investigative Reporters and Editors. Address: 5240 Fiore Terrace, #J-306, San Diego, CA 92122, USA.

STEWART Bruce Robert, b. 4 Sept 1925, Auckland, New Zealand. Writer; Dramatist. m. Ellen Noonan, 16 Oct 1950, 3 sons, 3 daughters. Education: BA, University of Auckland. Publications: A Disorderly Girl, 1980; The Turning Tide, 1980; The Hot and Copper Sky, 1982. Other: Various plays for stage, radio and television, including Me and My Shadow, 1988; The Dog That Went to War, 1989; Speak Low, 1993. Contributions to: Newspapers, magazines and journals. Honours: Edgar Allan Poe Award, Mystery Writers of America, 1963; Charles Henry Foyle Award, UK, 1968. Memberships: British Film Institute; Writers Guild of Australia; Writers Guild of Great Britain, co-chairman, 1979-81. Address: c/o Harvey Unna, 24 Pottery Lane, Holland Park, London W11, England.

STEWART David. See: **HIGHAM Robin.**

STEWART Harold Frederick, b. 14 Dec 1916, Sydney, Australia. Poet; Writer; Translator. Education: University of Sydney. Appointments: Broadcaster, Australian Broadcasting Commission; Lecturer, Victorian Council of Adult Education. Publications: Poetry: The Darkening Ecliptic (with James McAuley), 1944; Phoenix Wings: Poems 1940-46, 1948; Orpheus and Other Poems, 1956; The Exiled Immortal: A Song Cycle, 1980; By the Old Walls of Kyoto: A Year's Cycle of Landscape Poems with Prose Commentaries, 1981; Collected Poems (with Ern Malley), 1993. Translator: A Net of Fireflies: Japanese Haiku and Haiku Paintings, 1960; A Chime of Windbells: A Year of Japanese Haiku, 1969; Tannisho: Passages Deploring Deviations of Faith (with Bando Shojun), 1980; The Amida Sutra Mandala (with Inagaki Hisao), 1995. Honours: Sydney Morning Herald Prize for Poetry, 1951; Australia Council Grant, 1978; Senior Emeritus Writers Fellow, Australia Council, 1982; Christopher Brennan Prize for Poetry, 1988. Address: 501 Keifuku Dai-ni Manshon, Yamabana-icho Dacho 7-1, Shugakuin, Sakyo-ku, Kyoto 606, Japan.

STEWART Judith. See: **POLLEY Judith Anne.**

STEWART Leslie, b. 23 May 1949, Benghazi, Libya. Scriptwriter; Director; Author; Lyricist. 2 sons. Education: St Edward's College, Malta. Publications: Novel: Two of Us, 1989. Plays: Three Minute Heroes, 1985; Good Neighbours, 1987; Wide Games, 1987. TV Films and Plays: Three Minute Heroes, 1982; Wide Games, 1984; The Amazing Miss Stella Estelle, 1984; Good Neighbours, 1984; Space Station: Milton Keynes, 1985; The Little Match Girl, 1986; Janna, Where Are You?, 1987; Boogie Outlaws (TV serial), 1987; Two of Us, 1988; Q.P.R. Askey Is Dead, 1989; That Green Stuff, 1990. Radio: The Key To My Father's House, 1992; Canada Park, 1994. Stage: Shoot-Up At Elbow Creek (musical), 1976; The Little Match Girl (musical), 1977; The Soldier, 1983; The Little Match Girl, 1983; Shoot-Up at Elbow Creek, 1985; A Game Of Soldiers, 1987; The Little Match Girl (director), 1995. TV Films: Space Station: Milton Keynes (with Colin Rogers), 1985; That Green Stuff, 1990; A Foot In The Door, 1992. Other: Lola, Terry, She's Not There (with Colin Rogers), TV shorts, 1985; Filigree (TV documentary), 1993. Honours: Emmy Nomination, 1987; Ivor Novello Award, 1988; Richard Imison Memorial Award Shortlist, 1992. Memberships: Writer's Guild of Great Britain; British Academy of Film and Television Arts; Associate Member, Performing Rights Society. Literary Agent: Jane Annakin, William Morris Agency (UK) Ltd. Address: York Villa, Station Road, Haddenham, Cambridgeshire CB6 3XD, England.

STEWART Lady Mary Florence Elinor, b. 17 Sept 1916, Sunderland, England. Writer. m. Frederick Henry Stewart, 24 Sept 1945. Education: BA, 1938, DipEd, 1939, MA, 1941, Durham University. Publications: Madam, Will You Talk?, 1954; Thunder on the Right, 1957; My Brother Michael, 1959; The Moonspinners, 1962; The Crystal Cave, 1970; A Walk in Wolf Wood, 1970; The Little Broomstick, 1971; Touch Not the Cat, 1976; Thornyhold, 1988; Frost on the Window and Other Poems, 1990; Stormy Petrel, 1991; The Prince and the Pilgrim, 1995. Contributions to: Many articles to various magazines. Honours: Frederick Niven Prize; Scottish Arts Council Award; Honorary Fellow, Newnham College, Cambridge. Memberships: PEN; New Club. Address: 79 Morningside Park, Edinburgh EH10 5EZ, Scotland.

STIBBE Mark W G, b. 16 Sept 1960, London, England. Clerk in Holy Orders. m. Alison Heather Stibbe, 30 July 1983, 2 sons, 1 daughter. Education: BA/MA, Cambridge University, 1982; PhD, Nottingham University, 1989. Publications: John as Storyteller, 1992; The Gospel of John as Literature, 1993; John: A New Biblical Commentary, 1993; A Kingdom of Priests, 1994; John's Gospel, 1994;

Explaining Baptism in the Holy Spirit, 1995; Chapter in The Impact of Toronto, 1995; O Brave New Church, 1996; Times of Refreshing, 1996; Know Your Spiritual Gifts, 1997. Contributions to: Numerous articles to Renewal; Anglicans for Renewal; Various New Testament journals; Journal of Pentecostal Theology; Soul Survivor. Honours: MA; Dip.Th; PhD. Address: St Andrew's Vicarage, 39 Quickley Lane, Chorley Wood, Herts WD3 5AE, England.

STICKLAND Caroline Amanda, b. 10 Oct 1955, Rinteln, Germany. Writer. m. William Stickland, 3 Aug 1974, 1 d. Education: BA Hons, English and American Literature, University of East Anglia, 1977. Publications: The Standing Hills, 1986; A House of Clay, 1988; The Darkness of Corn, 1990; An Ancient Hope, 1993; The Darkening Leaf, 1995. Honours: Betty Trask Award, 1985. Memberships: Society of Authors; Mrs Gaskell Society; Thomas Hardy Society. Literary Agent: Vivien Green, Richard Scott Simon Ltd, 43 Doughtly Street, London WC1N 2LF, England. Address: 81 Crock Lane, Bothenhampton, Bridport, Dorset DT6 4DQ, England.

STILES Martha Bennett, b. 30 Mar 1933, Manila, Philippines. Writer. m. Martin Stiles, 18 Sept 1954, 1 son. Education: BS, University of Michigan, 1954. Publications include: The Strange House at Nowburyport, 1963; Darkness Over the Land, 1966; The Star in the Forest, 1977; Sarah the Dragon Lady, 1986; Kate of Still Waters, 1990. Contributions to: Journals and periodicals. Honours include: Society of Children's Book Writers Grant, 1988; Al Smith Fellowship, Kentucky Arts Council, 1992. Memberships include: Authors Guild; King Library Associates; Paris Arts Club. Literary Agent: Russell and Volkening. Address: 861 Hume-Bedford Road, Paris, KY 40361, USA.

STILLINGER Jack (Clifford), b. 16 Feb 1931, Chicago, Illinois, USA. Professor of English; Writer. m. (1) Shirley Louise Van Wormer, 30 Aug 1952, 2 sons, 2 daughters, (2) Nina Zippin Baym, 21 May 1971. Education: BA, University of Texas, 1953; MA, Northwestern University, 1954; PhD, Harvard University, 1958. Appointments: Assistant Professor, 1958-61, Associate Professor, 1961-64, Professor of English, 1964-, University of Illinois; Editor, Journal of English and Germanic Philiology, 1961-72; Member, Center for Advanced Study, University of Illinois, 1970-. Publications: The Early Draft of John Stuart Mill's Autobiography (editor), 1961; Anthony Munday's Zelauto (editor), 1963; William Wordsworth: Selected Poems and Prefaces (editor), 1965; The Letters of Charles Armitage Brown (editor), 1966; Twentieth Century Interpretations of Keats' Odes (editor), 1968; John Stuart Mill: Autobiography and Other Writings (editor), 1969; The Texts of Keats' Poems, 1974; The Poems of John Keats, 1978; Mill's Autobiography and Literary Essays (editor), 1981; John Keats: Complete Poems (editor), 1982; The Norton Anthology of English Literature (editor), 1986, 6td edition, 1993; John Keats: Poetry Manuscripts at Harvard, 1990; Multiple Authorship and the Myth of Solitary Genius, 1991; Coleridge and Textual Instability: The Multiple Versions of the Major Poems, 1994. Contributions to: Professional journals. Honours: National Woodrow Wilson Fellow, 1953-54; Guggenheim Fellowship, 1964-65; Distinguished Scholar Award, Keats-Shelley Association of America, 1986; Phi Beta Kappa. Memberships: American Academy of Arts and Sciences, fellow; Byron Society; Keats-Shelley Association of America; Modern Language Association. Address: 806 West Indiana Avenue, Urbana, IL 61801, USA.

STIMULUS Flavian P. See: **PHILANDERSON Flavian Titus.**

STIMULUS John. See: **PHILANDERSON Flavian Titus.**

STIRLING Jessica. See: **RAE Hugh Craufdord.**

STIVENS Dal(las George), b. Blayney, 1911, Australia. Author. Literary Appointments: Australian Department of Information, 1944-50; Press Officer, Australia House, London, England, 1949-50; Foundation President, 1963-64, Vice-President, 1964-66, President, 1967-73, Australian Society of Authors; Chairman, Literary Committee, Captain Cook Bicentenary Celebrations, 1969-70; Member, New South Wales Advisory Committee, ABC, 1971-73. Publications: The Tramp and Other Stories, 1936; The Courtship of Uncle Henry: Short Stories, 1946; The Gambling Ghost and Other Stories, 1946; Jimmy Brockett: Portrait of a Notable Australian, 1951; Ironbark Bill, 1955; The Wide Arch, 1958; Coast to Coast: Australian Stories, 1957-58 (editor), 1959; A Guide to Book Contracts (with B Jefferis), 1967; Three Persons Make A Tiger, 1968; A Horse of Air, 1970; The Incredible Egg: A Billion Year Journey, 1974; The Unicorn and Other Tales, 1976; The Bushranger, 1979; The Demon Bowler and Other Cricket Stories,

1979. Address: 5 Middle Harbour Road, Lindfield 2070, New South Wales, Australia.

STOKER Alan, (Alan Evans), b. 2 Oct 1930, Sunderland, England. Writer. m. Irene Evans, 30 Apr 1960, 2 sons. Education: Grammar School. Publications: End of the Running, 1966; Mantrap, 1967; Bannon, 1968; Vicious Circle, 1970; The Big Deal, 1971; Thunder at Dawn, 1978; Ship of Force, 1979; Dauntless, 1980; Seek Out and Destroy, 1982; Deed of Glory, 1984; Audacity, 1985; Eagle at Taranto, 1987; Night Action, 1989; Orphans of the Storm, 1990; Sink or Capture, 1993; Sword at Sunrise, 1994. Other: Short stories; Children's books. Contributions to: Newspapers and magazines. Membership Society of Authors. Address: 9 Dale Road, Walton on Thames, Surrey KT12 2PY, England.

STOKER Richard, b. 8 Nov 1938, Castleford, Yorkshire, England. Composer; Author. m. (2) Dr Gillian Patricia Watson, 10 July 1986. Education: Huddersfield School of Music, 1953-58; Royal Academy of Music, with Lennox Berkeley, 1958-62; Composition with Nadia Boulanger, Paris, 1962-63; Also private study. Appointments: Professor of Composition, 1963-87, Tutor, 1970-80, Royal Academy of Music; Composition Teacher, St Paul's School, Hammersmith, London, 1973-76; Composition Teacher, Magdalene College, Cambridge, 1983-96. Publications: Portrait of a Town, 1970; Words Without Music (Outposts), 1975; Open Window-Open Door (autobiography), 1985; Tanglewood (novel), 1994; Diva (novel), 1997; Collected Short Stories, 1997. Contributions to: Records and Recording; Books and Bookmen; Guardian; Performance; The Magistrate; Editor, The Composer, 1969-80. Honours: BBC Music Award, 1952; Eric Coates Award, 1962; Mendelssohn Scholarship, 1962; Dove Prize, 1962; Associate, 1965, Fellow, 1971, Royal Academy of Music; Editor's Award, American National Library, 1995, 1997. Memberships: Executive Committee, Composers' Guild; Association of Professional Composers; Royal Society; PRS; MCPS; Royal Academy of Music; Magistrates' Association; Founder Member, Atlantic Council of the UK; European Atlantic Group. Address: c/o Ricordi, 210 New Kings Road, London SW6 4NZ, England.

STOLOFF Carolyn, b. 14 Jan 1927, New York, New York, USA. Poet; Painter; Teacher. Education: Dalton School; University of Illinois, 1944-46; BS, Painting, Columbia University School of General Studies, 1949; Art Studies with Xavier Gonzales, Eric Isenburger and Hans Hofmann; Poetry studies with Stanley Kunitz. Appointments: Teacher, Manhattanville College, 1957-74, Chairman, Art History and Studio Art, 1960-65, Baird House, 1973, Stephen's College, 1975, Hamilton College, 1985, University of Rochester, 1985; Poets in Public Service, 1989-90; School Volunteer Program, 1995-96. Publications: Stepping Out, 1971; In the Red Meadow, 1973; Dying to Survive, 1973; Lighter-Than-Night Verse, 1977; Swiftly Now, 1982; A Spool of Blue: New and Selected Poems, 1983; You Came to Meet Someone Else, 1993. Contributions to: Anthologies and journals. Honours: MacDowell Colony Residence Grants, 1961, 1962, 1970, 1976; Theodore Roethke Award, Poetry Northwest, 1967; National Council on the Arts Award, 1968; Helene Wurlitzer Foundation Grants, 1972-74; Silver Anniversary Medal, Audubon Artists, 1967; Michael M Engel Sr Memorial Award, 1982; Robert Philipps Award, 1990; Bader-Rowney Award for Oil Painting, 1994; Art Student's League Award for Oil Painting, 1995. Membership: Poetry Society of America. Address: Address: 24 West 8th Street, New York, NY 10011, USA.

STONE Gerald Charles, b. 22 Aug 1932, Surbiton, Surrey, England. University Lecturer; Writer; Editor. m. Vera Fedorovna Konnova, 10 Apr 1974, 2 sons, 2 daughters. Education: BA, 1964, PhD, 1969, School of Slavonic and East European Studies, London University. Appointment: Editor, Oxford Slavonic Papers, 1982-. Publications: The Smallest Slavonic Nation: The Serbs of Lusatia, 1972; The Russian Language Since the Revolution (with Bernard Comrie), 1978; An Introduction to Polish, 1980, 2nd edition, 1992; The Formation of the Slavonic Literary Languages (editor with Dean Worth), 1985; Serbska poezija: Kěrluše (editor), 1995; A Dictionarie of the Vulgar Russe Tongue: Attributed to Mark Ridley (editor), 1996; Serbska poezija: Kjarliže, (editor), 1996; The Russian Language in the Twentieth Century (with Bernard Comrie and Maria Polinsky), 1996; Kerluse (editor), 1995. Contributions to: Professional journals. Memberships: British Academy, fellow; Philosophical Society, council member, 1981-86; Society for Slovene Studies; Maćica Serbska. Address: 6 Lathbury Road, Oxford OX2 7AU, England.

STONE Joan Elizabeth, b. 22 Oct 1930, Port Angeles, Washington, USA. Assistant Professor of English; Poet; Writer. m. James A Black, 30 July 1990, 4 sons, 1 daughter. Education: BA, 1970, MA, 1974, PhD, 1976, University of Washington. Appointments: Visting Professor of Poetry, University of Montana, 1974; Director, Creative Writing Workshop, University of Washington, 1975; Assistant Professor of English, Colorado College, 1977-. Publications: The Swimmer and Other Poems, 1975; Alba, 1976; A Letter to Myself to Water, 1981; Our Lady of the Harbor, 1986. Contributions to: Journals and magazines. Honours: Academy of American Poets Awards, 1969, 1970, 1972; Borestone Mountain Awards, 1973, 1974. Address: 312 East Yampa Street, Colorado Springs, CO 80903, USA.

STONE Lawrence, b. 4 Dec 1919, Epsom, Surrey, England (US citizen, 1970). Professor of History (retired); Writer. m. Jeanne Caecilia Fawtier, 24 July 1943, 1 son, 1 daughter. Education: Sorbonne, University of Paris, 1938; BA, MA, Christ Church, Oxford, 1946. Appointments: Lecturer, University College, 1947-50, Fellow, Wadham College, 1950-63, Oxford; Member, Institute for Advanced Study, Princeton, New Jersey, 1960-61; Dodge Professor of History, 1963-90, Director, Shelby Cullom Davis Center for Historical Studies, 1968-90, Princeton Univeristy. Publications: Sculpture in Britain: The Middle Ages, 1955; An Elizabethan: Sir Horatio Palavicino, 1956; The Crisis of the Aristocracy, 1558-1641, 1965; The Causes of the English Revolution 1529-1642, 1972, revised edition, 1986; Family and Fortune Studies in Aristocratic Finance in the Sixteenth and Seventeenth Centuries, 1973; Family, Sex and Marriage in England 1500-1800, 1977; The Past and Present Revisited, 1987; Road to Divorce: England 1530-1987, 1990; Uncertain Unions: Marriage in England 1660-1753, 1992; Broken Lives: Marital Separation and Divorce in England 1660-1857, 1993. Contributions to: Professional journals. Memberships: American Academy of Arts and Sciences, fellow; American Philosophical Society; British Academy, corresponding member. Address: 266 Moore Street, Princeton, NJ 08540, USA.

STONE Peter Bennet, b. 6 July 1933, Oldham, Lancashire, England. Environmental Journalist. m. Jennifer Jane Wedderspoon, 29 July 1964, 2 daughters. Education: BA (Hons), MA, Balliol College, Oxford (Open Scholar, Science), 1951-55. Appointments: Producer, BBCTV, 1958-64; Senior Information Advisor, UN Conference on Environment, 1972; Editor-in-Chief, UN Development Forum, 1972-84; Director of Information, Brundtland Commisssion, 1984. Publications: Japan Surges Ahead, 1967; The Great Ocean Business, 1971; Did We Save the Earth at Stockholm, 1972; State of the World's Mountains: Global Report, 1992. Contributions to: Ceres, FAO; Economist; Many newspapers. Memberships: Scientific and sporting societies; Fellow, Royal Geographical Society; FGS; Alpine Club. Address: 6 Eyot Green, Chiswick Mall, London W4 2PT, England.

STOPPARD Miriam, b. 12 May 1937, Newcastle upon Tyne, England. Physician; Writer; Broadcaster. m. Tom Stoppard, 1972, div 1992, 2 sons, 2 stepsons. Education: Royal Free Hospital School of Medicine, University of London; MB, BS, 1962, University of Durham; MD, King's College Medical School, University of Newcastle upon Tyne, 1966. Appointmments: Senior House Officer in Medicine, Royal Victoria Infirmary, King's College Hospital, Newcastle upon Tyne, 1962-63; Research Fellow, Department of Chemical Pathology, 1963-65, Registrar in Dermatology, 1965-66, Senior Registrar in Dermatology, 1966-68, University of Bristol; Television series, Where There's Life, 1981-, Baby and Co, 1984-, Woman to Woman, 1985, Miriam Stoppard's Health and Beauty Show, 1988-. Publications: Miriam Stoppard's Book of Baby Care, 1977; Miriam Stoppard's Book of Health Care, 1979; The Face and Body Book, 1980; Everywoman's Lifeguide, 1982; Your Baby, 1982; Fifty Plus Lifeguide, 1982; Your Growing Child, 1983; Baby Care Book, 1983; Pregnancy and Birth Book, 1984; Baby and Child Medical Handbook, 1986; Everygirl's Lifeguide, 1987; Feeding Your Family, 1987; Miriam Stoppard's Health and Beauty Book, 1988; Every Woman's Medical Handbook, 1988; Lose 7lbs in 7 Days, 1990; Test Your Child, 1991; The Magic of Sex, 1991; Conception, Pregnancy and Birth, 1993; The Menopause, 1994; The Breast Book, 1996. Contributions to: Medical journals. Memberships: British Association of Rheumatology and Rehabilitation; Heberden Society; Royal Society of Medicine. Address: Iver Grove, Iver, Buckinghamshire, England.

STOPPARD Tom, (Thomas Straussler), b. 3 July 1937, Zin, Czechoslovakia (British citizen). Dramatist. m. (1) Jose Ingle, 1965, div 1972, 2 sons, (2) Miriam Moore-Robinson, 1972, div 1992, 2 sons. Publications: Novel: Lord Malaquist and the Moon, 1965. Plays: A

Walk on the Water, 1963; Rosencrantz and Guildenstern Are Dead, 1966; The Real Inspector Hound, 1968; Jumpers, 1972; Travesties, 1974; Dirty Linen, 1976; Every Good Boy Deserves Favour, 1977; Night and Day, 1978; The Real Thing, 1982; Arcadia, 1993; Indian Ink, 1995. Also film, radio and television scripts. Honours: John Whiting Award, Arts Council, 1967; Evening Standard Awards, 1967, 1972, 1978, 1982, 1993; New York Drama Critics Award, 1968; Italia Prize, 1968; Tony Awards, 1968, 1976, 1984; Shakespeare Prize, 1979. Address: c/o The Peters, Fraser and Dunlop Group Ltd, The Chambers, Chelsea Harbour, Lots Road, London SW10 0XF, England.

STOREY David (Malcolm), b. 13 July 1933, England. FreelanceNovelist; Playwright; Screen Writer. Education: Slade School of Fine Art, London. Publications: This Sporting Life, 1960; Flight into Camden, 1961; The Restoration of Arnold Middleton, 1967; In Celebration, 1969; The Contractor, 1970; Home, 1970; The Changing Room, 1971; Pasmore, 1972; The Farm, 1973; Cromwell, 1973; A Temporary Life, 1973; Life Class, 1974; Mother's Day, 1976; Saville, 1976; Early Days, Sisters, Life Class, 1980; A Prodigal Child, 1982; Present Times, 1984; Storey's Lives, Poems 1951-91, 1992. Honour: Booker Prize, 1976. Address: c/o Jonathan Cape, Random Century House, 20 Vauxhall Bridge Road, London SW1V 2SA, England.

STORM Christopher. See: OLSEN Theodore Victor.

STORR (Charles) Anthony, b. 18 May 1920, Bentley, England. Psychiatrist; Author. m. (1) Catherine Cole, 6 Feb 1942, 3 daughters, (2) Catherine Barton, 9 Oct 1970. Education: Winchester College; MB BChir, Cantab, 1944, MA Cantab, 1946, Christ's College, Cambridge. Publications: The Integrity of the Personality, 1960; Sexual Deviation, 1964; Human Aggression, 1968; Human Destructiveness, 1972; The Dynamics of Creation, 1972; Jung, 1973; The Art of Psychotherapy, 1979; The Essential Jung,1983; Solitude: A Return to the Self, 1988; Churchill's Black Dog and Other Phenomena of the Human Mind (US edition as Churchill's Black Dog, Kafka's Mice and Other Phenomena of the Human Mind), 1989; Freud, 1989; Music and the Mind, 1992; Feet of Clay, 1996. Contributions to: Newspapers. Honours: Fellow, Royal Society of Literature, 1990; Honorary Fellow, Royal College of Psychiatrists, 1993. Memberships: Fellow, Green College, Oxford, 1979, Emeritus, 1984. Address: 45 Chalfont Road, Oxford OX2 6TJ, England.

STORR Catherine (Lady Balogh), b. 21 July 1913, London, England. Psychiatrist (retired); Author Education: Newnham College, Cambridge, 1932-41; West London Hospital, 1941-44. Appointment: Assistant Editor, Penguin Books, London, 1966-70. Publications: Clever Polly Series, 4 volumes, 1952-80; Stories for Jano, 1952; Marianne Dreams, 1958; Marianne and Mark, 1959; Robin, 1962; Flax Into Gold (libretto), 1964; Lucy, 1964; The Catchpole Story, 1965; Rufus, 1969; Puss and the Cat, 1969; Thursday, 1971; Kate and the Island, 1972; Black God, White God, 1972; Children's Literature (editor), 1973; The Chinese Egg, 1975; The Painter and the Fish, 1975; Unnatural Fathers, 1976; The Story of the Terrible Scar, 1976; Tales from the Psychiatrist's Couch (short stories), 1977; Winter's End, 1978; Vicky, 1981; The Bugbear, 1981; February Yowler, 1982; The Castle Boy, 1983; Two's Company, 1984; Cold Marble (short stories), 1985; Daljit and The Unqualified Wizard, 1989; The Spy Before Yesterday, 1990; We Didn't Think of Ostriches, 1990; Babybug, 1992; Finn's Animal, 1992; The Mirror Image Ghost, 1994; Stephen and the Family Nose, 1995; Watcher at the Window, 1995. Honour: Prize, Friends of the Earth, 1985. Membership: Royal Society of Medicine. Address: Flat 5, 12 Frognal Gardens, London NW3, England.

STOTT Mike, b. 2 Jan 1944, Rochdale, Lancashire, England. Playwright. Education: Manchester University. Appointments: Resident Writer, Hampstead Theatre Club, 1975. Publications: Mata Hari, 1965; Erogenous Zone, 1969; Funny Peculiar, 1973; Lenz (after Büchner), 1974; Plays for People Who Don't Move Much, 1974; Midnight, 1974; Other People, 1974; Lorenzaccio (after De Musset), 1976; Followed by Oysters, 1976; Soldiers Talking Cleanly, 1978; The Boston Strangler, 1978; Grandad, 1978; Strangers, 1979; Ducking Out, 1982; Dead Men, 1982; Penine Pleasures, 1984; The Fling, 1984; The Fancy Man, 1988; Radio and television plays. Address: c/o Michael Imison Playwrights, 28 Almeida Street, London N1 1TD, England.

STOW (Julian) Randolph, b. 28 Nov 1935, Geraldton, Western Australia. Education: Universities of Western Australia and Sydney, 1956. Appointments: Lecturer, English University of Leeds, Yorkshire, 1962, 1968-69, University of Western Australia, 1963-64; Harkness

Fellow, USA, 1964-66; Resident in England, 1966-. Publications: A Haunted Land, 1956; The Bystander, 1957; To the Islands, 1958; Tourmaline, 1963; The Merry Go Round in the Sea, 1965; Midnite (for children), 1967; Visitants, 1979; The Girl Green as Elderflower, 1980; The Suburbs of Hell, 1984. Librettos to Music by Peter Maxwell Davies: Eight Songs for a Mad King, 1969; Miss Donnithorne's Maggot, 1974. Verse Collections: Act One, 1957; Outrider: Poems, 1956-62, 1962; A Counterfeit Silence: Selected Poems, 1969; Randolph Stow (omnibus volume, edited by A J Hassall), 1990. Honours: Miles Franklin Award, 1958; Britannica-Australia Award, 1966; Grace Leven Prize, 1969; Arts Council of Great Britain Bursary, 1969; Commonwealth Literary Fund Grant, 1974; Patrick White Award, 1979. Address: Richard Scott Simon Ltd, 43 Doughty Street, London WC1N 2LF, England.

STRAND Mark, b. 11 Apr 1934, Summerside, Prince Edward Island, Canada. Poet; Writer; Professor. m. (1) Antonia Ratensky, 14 Sep 1961, div June 1973, 1 daughter, (2) Julia Rumsey Garretson, 15 Mar 1976, 1 son. Education: AB, Antioch College, 1957; BFA, Yale University, 1959; MA, University of Iowa, 1962. Appointments: Instructor, University of Iowa, 1962-65; Fulbright Lecturer, University of Brazil, 1965; Assistant Professor, Mount Holyoke College, 1966; Visiting Professor, University of Washington, 1967, University of Virginia, 1977, California State University at Fresno, 1977, University of California at Irvine, 1978 and Wesleyan University, 1979-80; Adjunct Professor, Columbia University, 1968-70; Visiting Lecturer, Yale University, 1969-70 and Harvard University, 1980-81; Associate Professor, Brooklyn College, 1971; Bain Swiggett Lecturer, Princeton University, 1972; Fanny Hurst Professor of Poetry, Brandeis University, 1973; Professor, 1981-86 and Distinguished Professor, 1986-94, University of Utah; Poet Laureate of the USA, 1990-91; Elliot Coleman Professor of Poetry, Johns Hopkins University, 1994-. Publications: Poetry: Sleeping With One Eye Open, 1964; Reasons for Moving, 1968; Darker, 1970; The Sargentville Notebook, 1973; The Story of Our Lives, 1973; The Late Hour, 1978; Selected Poems, 1980; The Continuous Life, 1990; Dark Harbor, 1993. Fiction: Mr and Mrs Baby (short stories), 1985. Prose: The Monument, 1978; The Art of the Real, 1983; William Bailey, 1987; Hopper, 1994. Anthologies: The Contemporary American Poets, 1969; New Poetry of Mexico (with Octavio Paz), 1970; Another Republic (with Charles Simic), 1976; The Best American Poetry 1991 (with David Lehman), 1992. Translations: Halty Ferguson: 18 Poems from the Quechua, 1971; Rafael Alberti: The Owl's Insomnia (poems), 1973; Carlos Drummond de Andrade: Souvenir of the Ancient World (poems), 1976; Travelling in the Family: The Selected Poems of Carlos Drummond de Andrade, 1986. Children's Books: The Planet of Lost Things, 1982; The Night Book, 1985; Rembrandt Takes a Walk, 1986. Contributions to: Poems, book reviews, art reviews, essays on poetry and painting and interviews in numerous periodicals. Honours: Fulbright Scholarship to Italy, 1960-61; Ingram Merill Fellowship, 1966; National Endowment for the Arts Fellowships, 1967-68, 1977-78; Rockefeller Fellowship, 1968-69; Edgar Allan Poe Prize, 1974; Guggenheim Fellowship, 1974-75; National Institute of Arts and Letters Award, 1975; Academy of American Poets Fellowship, 1979; Writer-in-Residence, American Academy, Rome, 1982; John D and Catherine T MacArthur Fellowship, 1987-92; Utah Governor's Award in the Arts, 1992; Bobbitt National Prize for Poetry, 1992; Bollingen Prize for Poetry, 1993. Memberships: American Academy and Institute of Arts and Letters, 1980-; National Academy of Arts and Sciences, 1995-. Address: The Writing Seminars, Johns Hopkins University, 3400 North Charles Street, Baltimore, MD 21218, USA.

STRANDBERG Keith (William), b. 21 Aug 1957, Toledo, Ohio, USA. Screenwriter; Author. m. Carol Anne Hartman, 25 Sept 1982, 2 sons. Education: BA, Chinese Language and Literature, 1979; BA, Physical Education, 1979; MA, Film and Screenwriting, 1997. Publications: Stir Fry Cooking, 1985; Action Film Making Master Class, 1993. Films: No Retreat, No Surrender, 1986; Raging Thunder, 1987; Blood Brothers, 1989; The King of the Kickboxers, 1990; American Shaolin, 1991; American Dragons, 1997; Superfights, 1996; Bloodmoon, 1997. Contributions to: Many publications. Honours: International Martial Arts Hall of Fame, 1993; World Martial Arts Hall of Fame, 1994. Memberships: National Martial Arts Advisory Board; National Writers Club. Address: 3634 Peregrine Circle, PA 17554, USA.

STRANGER Joyce. See: WILSON Joyce Muriel.

STRASSER Steven. Journalist. m. Joyce Barnathan, 2 sons, 1 daughter. Education: BA, Political Science, University of Nebraska; MA, Graduate School of Journalism, Columbia University. Appointments: Reporter, Miami Herald, 1973-77; Associate Editor, Foreign Affairs Department, Deputy Foreign Editor, 1981-83, Senior Writer in National Affairs, Moscow Correpsondent, 1985-88, Hong Kong Bureau Chief and Asia Regional Editor, 1992-, Asia Editor, 1996-, Newsweek; Senior Writer, 1981, Senior Editor, 1988, Managing Editor, 1990, Newsweek International. Honours: Shared Citation, Overseas Press Club Awards, 1981; Co-Winner, Overseas Press Club Awards, 1982, 1989; National Headliner Award for Outstanding Coverage of a Major News Event. Address: c/o Newsweek, 251 West 57th Street, New York, NY 10019-1894, USA.

STRATTON Thomas. See: **DE WEESE Thomas Eugene "Gene".**

STRAUB Peter Francis, b. 2 Mar 1943, Milwaukee, Wisconsin, USA. Novelist. m. 27 Aug 1966. Education: BA, University of Wisconsin, 1965; MA, Columbia University, 1966. Publications: Open Air (poetry), 1972; Marriage, 1973; Julia, 1975; If You Could See Me New, 1977; Ghost Story, 1979; Shadowland, 1980; Floating Dragon, 1983; The Talisman (with Stephen King), 1984; Koko, 1988; Mystery, 1989; Houses Without Doors, 1990; The Throat, 1993; The Hellfire Club, 1996. Contributions to: Times Literary Supplement; New Statesman; Washington Post. Honours: British Fantasy Award, 1983; Auguest Derleth Award , 1983; World Fantasy Award Best Novel Awards, 1988, 1993; Bram Stoker Award, Best Novel, 1993. Memberships: Mystery Writers of America; Horror Writers of America; PEN. Literary Agent: David Gernert. Address: 53 West 85th Street, New York, NY 10024, USA.

STRAUS Dennis David, (Ascher/Straus), b. New York, USA. Writer. Education: MA, Columbia University. Publications: Letter to an Unknown Woman; The Other Planet; The Menaced Assassin; Red Moon/Red Lake. Contributions to: Chicago Review; Paris Review; Epoch; Top Stories; Chelsea; Exile; Calyx; Zone; Confrontation; Central Park; New American Writing; Asylum Annual; Red Moon/Red Lake; Top Top Stories (anthology); 15 Years in Exile (anthology); Likely Stories (anthology); The Living Underground (anthology). Honours: Panache Experimental Fiction Prize; Pushcart Prize; Caps Fellowship. Address: PO Box 176, Rockaway Park, NY 11694, USA.

STRAUS/ASCHER. See: **ASCHER Sheila.**

STRAUSS Jennifer, b. 30 Jan 1933, Heywood, Western Australia. Lecturer; Poet. m. Wermer Strauss, 1958, 3 sons. Education: BA, University of Melbourne, 1954; University of Glasgow, 1957-58; PhD, Monash University, 1992. Appointments include: Senior Lecturer, 1971-, Associate Professor, 1992-, Monash University, Melbourne. Publications: Children and other Strangers, 1975; Winter Driving, 1981; Middle English Verse: An Anthology (co-editor), 1985; Labour Ward, 1988; Boundary Conditions: The Poetry of Gwen Harwood, 1992; The Oxford Book of Australian Love Poems (editor), 1993; Judith Wright, 1995. Memberships: Victorian Ministry for the Arts, 1983-85; Premiers Literary Awards Committee. Address: 2-12 Tollingtom Avenue, East Malvern, Western Australia 3145, Australia.

STRAUSS Susan, b. 21 Dec 1954, New York, New York, USA. Author; Storyteller. m. Ted Wise, 22 June 1991, 1 daughter. Education: BA, English, 1977, MA, English Education, 1980, University of Virginia. Publications: Coyote Stories for Children: Tales from Native America, 1991; Wolf Stories: Myth and True Tales from Around the World, 1994; The Passionate Fact: Storytelling in Natural History and Cultural Interpretation, 1996. Contributions to: Children's Writers and Illustrators Market, 1994. Address: PO Box 1141, Bend, OR 97709, USA.

STRAUSSLER Thomas. See: **STOPPARD Tom.**

STRAWSON Galen John, b. 5 Feb 1952, Oxford, England. Philosopher. m. Jose Said, 20 July 1974, diss, 1994, 1 son, 2 daughters. Education: BA, Philosophy, 1973, MA, 1977, Cambridge; BPhil, 1977, DPhil, 1983, Oxford. Appointments: Assistant Editor, 1978-87, Consultant, 1987-, Times Literary Supplement, London. Publications: Freedom and Belief, 1986; The Secret Connection, 1989; Mental Reality, 1994. Contributions to: Times Literary Supplement; Sunday Times; Observer; London Review of Books; Independent on Sunday; Mind; American Philosophical Quarterly; Inquiry; Analysis, Philosophical Studies. Honours: R A Nicholson Prize for Islamic

Studies, Cambridge, 1971; T H Green Prize for Moral Philosophy, Oxford, 1983; Fellow, Jesus College, Oxford. Membership: Mind Association. Address: Jesus College, Oxford OX1 3DW, England.

STRAWSON Sir Peter (Frederick), b. 23 Nov 1919, London, England. Professor of Metaphysical Philosophy (retired); Author. m. Grace Hall Martin, 1945, 2 sons, 2 daughters. Education: Christ's College, Finchley; St John's College, Oxford. Appointments: Assistant Lecturer in Philosophy, University College of North Wales, 1946; John Locke Scholar, Oxford University, 1946; Lecturer in Philosophy, 1947, Fellow and Praelector, 1948, Fellow, 1948-68, Honorary Fellow, 1979-, University College, Oxford; Visiting Professor, Duke University, 1955-56; Fellow of the Humanities Council and Visiting Associate Professor, 1960-61, Visiting Professor, 1972, Princeton University; Reader, 1966-68, Waynflete Professor of Metaphysical Philosophy, 1968-87, Oxford University; Fellow, 1968-87, Honorary Fellow, 1989, Magdelen College, Oxford; Woodbridge Lecturer, Columbia University, 1983; Immanuel Kant Lecturer, University of Munich, 1985; Visiting Professor, Collège de France, 1985. Publications: Introduction to Logical Theory, 1952; Individuals, 1959; The Bounds of Sense, 1966; Philosophical Logic (editor), 1966; Studies in the Philosophy of Thought and Action (editor), 1968; Logico-Linguistic Papers, 1971; Freedom and Resentment, 1974; Subject and Predicate in Logic and Grammar, 1974; Scepticism and Naturalism: Some Varieties, 1985; Analyse and Métaphysique, 1985, English translation as Analysis and Metaphysics, 1992. Contributions to: Scholarly journals. Honour: Knighted 1977. Memberships: Academia Europaea; American Academy of Arts and Sciences, honorary member; British Academy, fellow. Address: 25 Farndon Road, Oxford OX2 6RT, England.

STREET Pamela, b. 3 Mar 1921, Wilton, Wiltshire, England. Writer. Div, 1 daughter. Education: Salisbury and South Wiltshire College of Further Education, 1967-69. Publications: My Father, A G Street, 1969, 2nd edition, 1984; Portrait of Wiltshire, 1971, new edition, 1980; Arthur Bryant: Portrait of a Historian, 1979; Light of Evening, 1981; The Stepsisters, 1982; Morning Glory, 1982; Portrait of Rose, 1986; The Illustrated Portrait of Wiltshire, 1984, paperback edition, 1994; Personal Relations, 1987; The Mill-Race Quartet, 1988; The Timeless Moment, 1988; The Beneficiaries, 1989; Doubtful Company, 1990; Guilty Parties, 1991; Late Harvest, 1991; The Colonel's Son, 1992; Hindsight, 1993; Keeping it Dark, 1994; King's Folly, 1995; The General's Wife, 1996. Contributions to: Newspapers and magazines. Address: 47 South Street, Flt 5, London W1Y 5PD, England.

STREETEN Paul Patrick, b. 18 July 1917, Vienna, Austria. University Professor. m. Ann H Higgins, 9 June 1951, 1 stepson, 2 daughters. Education: MA, Aberdeen University, 1944; BA (Oxon), 1947; MA (Oxon), 1952; DLitt, 1976. Publications: Economic Integration, 1961, 2nd edition, 1964; Frontiers of Development Studies, 1972; Development Perspectives, 1981; First Things First, 1981; What Price Food?, 1987; Mobilizing Human Potential, 1989; Thinking About Development, 1995. Contributions to: Magazines and journals. Honours: Honorary Fellow, Institute of Development Studies, 1980; Honorary Fellow, Balliol College, 1986; Development Prize, Justus Liebig University, 1987; Honorary LLD, Aberdeen University, 1980; Honorary DLitt, University of Malta, 1992. Address: Box 92, Spencertown, NY 12165, USA.

STRESHINSKY Shirley, b. 7 Oct 1934, Alton, Illinois, USA. Writer. m. Ted Streshinsky, 16 June 1966, 1 son, 1 daughter. Education: BA, University of Illinois. Publications: And I Alone Survived, 1978; Hers the Kingdom, 1981; A Time Between, 1984; Gift of the Golden Mountain, 1988; The Shores of Paradise (novel), 1991; Audubon: Life and Art in The American Wilderness, 1993. Contributions to: Journals and magazines. Honours: Best Human Interest Article, Society Magazine Writers Association, 1968; Educational Press Award, 1968. Membership: Authors Guild. Address: PO Box 674, Berkeley, CA 94701, USA.

STROM Robert Duane, b. 21 Jan 1935, Chicago, Illinois, USA. Professor of Psychology; Writer. m. Shirley Kaye Mills, Apr 1962, 2 sons. Education: BS, Macalester College, 1958; MA, University of Minnesota, 1959; PhD, University of Michigan, 1962. Appointment: Professor of Psychology, Arizona State University, Tempe. Publications: Teaching in the Slum School, 1965; Psychology for the Classroom, 1969; Teachers and the Learning Process, 1971; Education for Affective Achievement (with E P Torrance), 1973; Values and Human Development, 1973; Learning Processes, 1976; Parent and Child Development, 1978; Growing Through Play: Parents and

Children, 1981; Educational Psychology, 1982; Human Development and Learning, 1989; Becoming a Better Grandparent, 1991; Grandparent Education, 1991; Achieving Grandparent Potential, 1992. Contributions to: Over 250 articles to professional journals. Honours: NATO Scholar, University of Ankara, Turkey, 1967; Fulbright Scholar, University of the Philippines, 1974, Canberra, Australia, 1975; Fulbright Scholar, University of Stockholm, Sweden, 1985; Research Fellow, Japan Society for the Promotion of Science, 1995; Research Fellow, Japan Ministry of Education, Science and Culture, 1995. Membership: American Psychological Association. Address: Arizona State University, Tempe, AZ 85287, USA.

STRONG Eithne, b. 23 Feb 1923, West Limerick, Ireland. Poet; Writer. m. Rupert Strong, 12 Nov 1943, 2 sons, 7 daughters. Education: BA, Trinity College, Dublin. Publications: Short stories: Patterns, 1981; Circt Oibre, 1980; Fuil agus Fallat, 1983; Songs of Living, 1965; Sarah in Passing, 1974; Flesh the Greatest Sin, 1989; My Darling Nei nbour, 1985. Fiction: Degrees of Kindred, 1979; Poetry: Aoife Faoi Ghlas, 1990; An Sagart Pinc, 1990; Let Live, 1990; Spatial Nosing, 1993; Fiction: The Love Riddle, 1993. Contributions to: Anthologies, journals and magazines. Memberships: Conradh Na Gaeilge; Irish PEN; Irish Writers Union; Poetry Ireland; Aosdána. Address: 17 Eaton Square, Monkstown, Dublin, Ireland.

STRONG Jonathan, b. 13 Aug 1944, Evanston, Illinois, USA. Writer; University Teacher. Education: Harvard University, 1969. Appointment: Faculty, Tufts University. Publications: Tike, 1969; Ourselves, 1971; Elsewhere, 1985; Secret Words, 1992; Companion Pieces, 1993; An Untold Tale, 1993; Offspring, novel, 1995; The Old World, novel, 1997. Contributions to: American Literature; Journals and magazines. Honours: O Henry Story Awards, 1967, 1970; Rosenthal Award, 1970; National Endowment for the Arts Award, 1986. Memberships: New England Gilbert and Sullivan Society; Sir Arthur Sullivan Society. Address: c/o Department of English, Tufts University, Medford, MA 02155, USA.

STRONG Pat. See: **HOUGH Richard Alexander.**

STRONG Sir Roy (Colin), b. 23 Aug 1935, London, England. Art Historian; Writer; Lecturer. m. Julia Trevelyan Oman. Education: Queen Mary College, London; Warburg Institute, London. Appointments: Assistant Keeper, 1959, Director, Keeper and Secretary, 1967-73, National Portrait Gallery, London; Ferens Professor of Fine Art, University of Hull, 1972; Walls Lecturer, J Pierpoint Morgan Library, New York, 1974; Director, Victoria and Albert Museum, London, 1974-87; Director, Oman Publications Ltd. Publications: Portraits of Queen Elizabeth I, 1963; Holbein and Henry the VIII, 1967; The English Icon: Elizabethan and Jacobean Portraiture, 1969; Tudor and Jacobean Portraits, 1969; Van Dyck: Charles I on Horseback, 1972; Splendour at Court: Renaissance Spectacle and the Theatre of Power, 1973; Nicholas Hilliard, 1975; The Renaissance Garden in England, 1979; Britannia Triumphans: Inigo Jones, Rubens and Whitehall Palace, 1980; Henry, Prince of Wales and England's Lost Renaissance, 1986; Creating Small Gardens, 1986; Gloriana: Portraits of Queen Elizabeth I, 1987; A Small Garden Designer's Handbook, 1987; Cecil Beaton: The Royal Portraits, 1988; Creating Small Formal Gardens, 1989; Lost Treasures of Britain, 1990; A Celebration of Gardens (editor), 1991; The Garden Trellis, 1991; Small Period Gardens, 1992; Royal Gardens, 1992; A Country Life, 1994; Successful Small Gardens, 1994; William Larkin: Vanitù giacobite, Italy, 1994; The Tudor and Stuart Monarchy, 2 volumes, 1994-95; The English Vision: Country Life 1897-1997; The Story of Britain, 1996; The Tudor and Stuart Monarchy, 3 volumes 1995-97. Co-Author: Leicester's Triumph, 1964; Elizabeth R, 1971; Mary Queen of Scots, 1972; Inigo Jones: The Theatre of the Stuart Court, 1973; An Early Victorian Album: The Hill-Adamson Collection, 1974; The English Miniature, 1981; The English Year, 1982; Artists at the Tudor Court, 1983. Honours: Fellow, Queen Mary College, 1976; Knighted, 1982; Senior Fellow, Royal College of Artists, 1983; Honorary doctorates. Memberships: Arts Council of Great Britain, Chairman, Arts Panel, 1983-87; British Council, Fine Arts Advisory Committee, 1974-87; Royal College of Artists, Council, 1979-87; Westminster Abbey Architectural Panel, 1975-89. Address: The Laskett, Much Birch, Herefords HR2 8HZ, England.

STROUHAL Eugen, b. 24 Jan 1931, Prague, Czechoslovakia. Anthropologist; Archaeologist; Medical Historian. m. Martina Piplova, 5 Aug 1965, 1 son, 1 daughter. Education: Dr Med, 1956; Dr Phil, 1959; CSc (PhD), 1968; Dr Hab, 1990, University of Warsaw; DSc,

1991; Assistant Professor, 1992; Full Professor, 1995. Appointments: Institute of Egyptology, 1961-68; Department of Antiquity, National Museum of Prague, 1969-92; First Medical Faculty, Charles University, Prague, 1990-. Publications: Egyptian Mummies in Czechoslovak Collections (with L Vyhnánek), 1979; Die Anthrop Untersuchung d C-Gruppen und Pan-Gräber-Skelette (with J Jungwirth), 1984; Begegnungen mit Alaska, 1990; Life in Ancient Egypt (Life of the Ancient Egyptians), 1992; Secondary Cemetery in the Mastaba of Ptahshepses at Abusir (with L Bareš), 1993. Honours: Hrdlička Medal, 1981; Michalowski Medal, 1987. Memberships: Member of 10 Czech and 15 international or foreign scientific societies. Address: Na Truhlarce 24, 18000 Prague-Liben, Czechoslovakia.

STRYKER Daniel. See: **MORRIS Janet Ellen.**

STUART Dabney, b. 4 Nov 1937, Richmond, Viginia, USA. Professor of English; Editor; Poet; Writer. m. (3) Sandra Westcott, 1983, 2 sons, 1 daughter. Education: AB, Davidson College, North Carolina, 1960; AM, Harvard Universty, 1962. Appointments: Instructor, College of William and Mary, Williamsburg, Virginia, 1961-65; Instructor, 1965-66, Assistant Professor, 1966-69, Associate Professor, 1969-74, Professor, 1974-91, S Blount Mason Professor of English, 1991-, Washington and Lee University, Lexington, Virginia; Poetry Editor, 1966-76, Editor-in-Chief, 1988-95, Shenandoah; Visiting Professor, Middlebury College, 1968-69; McGuffey Chair of Creative Writing, Ohio University, 1972; Visiting Poet, University of Virginia, 1981, 1982-83; Poetry Editor, New Virginia Review, 1983. Publications: Poetry: The Diving Bell, 1966; A Particular Place, 1969; Corgi Modern Poets in Focus 3, 1971; The Other Hand, 1974; Friends of Yours, Friends of Mine, 1974; Round and Round: A Triptych, 1977; Rockbridge Poems, 1981; Common Ground, 1982; Don't Look Back, 1987; Narcissus Dreaming, 1990; Light Years: New and Selected Poems, 1994; Second Sight: Poems for Paintings by Carol Cloar, 1996. Fiction: Sweet Lucy Wine: Stories, 1992. Non-Fiction: Nabokov: The Dimensions of Parody, 1978. Honours: Dylan Thomas Prize, Poetry Society of America, 1965; Borestone Mountain Awards, 1969, 1974, 1977; National Endowment for the Arts Grant, 1969, and Fellowships, 1974, 1982; Virginia Governor's Award, 1979; Guggenheim Fellowship, 1987-88; Individual Artists Fellowship, Virginia Commission for the Arts, 1996. Address: c/o Department of English, Washington and Lee University, Lexington, VA 24450, USA.

STUART Sidney, See: **AVALLONE Michael (Angelo Jr).**

STUBBS Jean, b. 23 Oct 1926, Denton, Lancashire, England. Author. m.(1) Peter Stubbs, 1 May 1948, 1 son, 1 daughter, (2) Roy Oliver, 5 Aug,1980. Education: Manchester School of Art, 1944-47; Diploma, Loreburn Secretarial College, Manchester, 1947. Appointments: Copywriter, Henry Melland, 1964-66; Reviewer, Books and Bookmen, 1965-76; Writer-in-Residence for Avon, 1984. Publications: The Rose Grower, 1962; The Travellers, 1963; Hanrahan's Colony, 1964; The Straw Crown, 1966; My Grand Enemy, 1967; The Passing Star, 1970; The Case of Kitty Ogilvie, 1970; An Unknown Welshman, 1972; Dear Laura, 1973; The Painted Face, 1974; The Golden Crucible, 1976; Kit's Hill,1979; The Ironmaster, 1981; The Vivian Inheritance, 1982; The Northern Correspondent, 1984; 100 Years Around the Lizard, 1985; Great Houses of Cornwall,1987; A Lasting Spring, 1987; Like We Used To Be, 1989; Summer Secrets, 1990; Kelly Park, 1992; Charades, 1994. Contributions to: Anthologies and magazines. Honours: Tom Gallon Trust Award for short story writing, 1964; Daughter of Mark Twain, 1973. Memberships: PEN; Society of Women Writers and Journalists; Detection Club; Lancashire Writers Association; West Country Writers. Literary Agent: Jennifer Kavanagh, 44 Langham Street, London W1N 5RG, England. Address: Trewin, Nancegollan, Helston, Cornwall TR13 0AJ, England.

STUCCHI PRINETTI Emanuela, b. 22 Oct 1954, Milan, Italy. Writer. 2 sons. Education: Graphic design; Music; Languages. Publications: Pasta Sauces, 1992; Salads, 1993; Italian Vegetarian Cooking, 1994. Literary Agent: Susan Lesher, Lesherland Lesher, New York, USA. Address: Loc Badia A Coultibuono, 53013 Gaiole, Chianti, Italy.

STUEWE Paul William,b. 5 Oct 1943, Rochester, New York, USA. Editor; Writer. m. Denna Groetzinger, 30 Aug 1976, 1 son, 2 daughters. Education: BA, Columbia University, 1965; MA, University of Toronto, 1993. Appointments: Contributing Editor, Quill & Quire, 1979-90; Editor, Books in Canada, 1990-. Publications: Don't Deal Five

Deuces; The Storms Below; Hugh Garner's Life and Works; Clearing the Ground. Contributions to: Various publications. Honour: Shortlisted, City of Toronto Book Award. Membership: Canadian Society of Magazine Editors. Address: 149 Essex Street, Toronto, Ontario M6G 1T6, Canada.

STYLES (Frank) Showell, (Glyn Carr), b. 14 Mar 1908, Four Oaks, Warwickshire, England. Author. m. Kathleen Jane Humphreys, 1954, 1 son, 2 daughters. Appointments: Royal Navy, 1939-46 (retired as Commander); Professional author, 1946-76; Led 2 private Arctic expeditions, 1952-53; Himalayan expedition, 1954. Publications: A Tent on Top, 1971; Vincey Joe at Quiberon, 1971; Admiral of England, 1973; A Sword for Mr Fitton, 1975; Mr Fitton's Commission, 1977; The Baltic Convoy, 1979; A Kiss for Captain Hardy, 1979; Centurion Comes Home, 1980; The Quarterdeck Ladder, 1982; Seven-Gun Broadside, 1982; The Malta Frigate, 1983; Mutiny in the Caribbean, 1984; The Lee Shore, 1985; Gun-Brig Captain, 1987; HMS Cracker, 1988; Nelson's Midshipman, 1990; A Ship for Mr Fitton, 1991; The Independent Cruise, 1992; Mr Fitton's Prize, 1993; Mr Fitton and the Black Legion, 1994; Mr Fitton in Command, 1995; The 12-Gun Cutter, 1996. Other: First on the Summits, 1970; First up Everest, 1970; The Forbidden Frontiers: A Survey of India from 1765-1949, 1970; Welsh Walks and Legends, 1972; Snowdon Range, 1973; The Mountains of North Wales, 1973; Glyder Range, 1974; Backpacking: A Comprehensive Guide, 1976; Backpacking in the Alps and Pyrenees, 1976; Backpacking in Wales, 1977; Welsh Walks and Legends: South Wales, 1977. As Glyn Carr: Death on Milestone Buttress, 1951; Murder on the Matterhorn, 1951; The Youth Hostel Murders, 1952; The Corpse in the Crevasse, 1952; A Corpse at Camp Two, 1955; Murder of an Owl, 1956; The Ice-Axe Murders, 1958; Swing Away, Climber, 1959; Holiday With Murder, 1961; Death Finds a Foothold, 1962; Lewker in Norway, 1963; Death of a Weirdy, 1965; Lewkwer in Tirol, 1967; Fat Man's Agony, 1969. Honour: Fellow, Royal Geographic Society, 1954. Address: Trwyn Cae Iago, Borth y Gest, Porthmadog, Gwynedd LL49 9TW, Wales.

STYLIANOPOULOS Orestis, (Orestis Helianos), b. 11 May 1950, Athens, Greece. Writer. m. Claudine Bandelier, 13 Jan 1979. Education: Faculty of Medicine, University of Athens, 1968-72; Faculty of Psychology, University of Geneva, 1974-76. Publications: Orthogenesis (novel), 1987; The Genuine Story of H S (novel), 1989; The Children of Alexander the Great (travelogue), 1989; Aspects of the Past and Present of Greeks, 1991; Condamnation for Life (short stories), 1991; The Secret of Immortality (tales), 1995. Contributions to: Rizospastis; Kathimerini; Diavazo; I Lexi; Tote; Le Regard Cretois; Nea Ecologia. Memberships: Society of Swiss Writers; The Friends of Nikos Kazantzaki Society, president, 1996. Address: Archarnon 95, 104 40 Athens, Greece.

STYRON William (Clark) Jr, b. 11 June 1925, Newport News, Virginia, USA. Writer. m. Rose Burgunder, 4 May 1953, 1 son, 3 daughters. Education: LLD, Davidson College, 1942-43; AB, LLD, Duke University, 1943-47. Publications: Lie Down in Darkness, 1951; The Long March, 1953; Set This House on Fire, 1960; The Confessions of Nat Turner, 1967; Sophie's Choice, 1979; This Quiet Dust, 1982; Darkness Visible, 1990; A Tidewater Morning, 1993. Contributions to: Articles, essays and reviews to numerous journals. Honours: Pulitzer Prize for Fiction, 1968; Howells Medal, 1970; American Book Award, 1980; Prix Mondial Cino del Duca, 1985; Commandeur Ordre des Arts et des lettres, 1985; Edward MacDowell Medal, 1988; Decorated Commandeur Legion d'Honneur, France, 1988; Elmer Holmes Bobst Award for fiction, 1989; National Medal of Arts, 1993; National Arts Club Gold Medal, 1995; Common Wealth Award, 1995. Memberships: Honorary Member, Academie Goncourt, France; American Academy of Arts and Letters; American Academy of Arts and Sciences. Address: 12 Rucum Road, Roxbury, CT 06783, USA.

SUBRAMAN Belinda, (Mary Bumgarner), b. USA. Poet; Editor. Education: BA, Regents College, New York, 1987; MA, California State University, 1990. Appointment: Poetry Editor, Gypsy Magazine and Vergin Press, 1983-. Publications: Nurnberg Poems, 1983; Heather and Mace, 1985; Eye of the Beast, 1986; Fighting Woman, 1986; Body Parts, 1987; He Dreams His Playmate, 1987; Skin Divers (with Lyn Lifshin), 1988; Halloween, 1989; The Jesuit Poems, 1989; Elephants and Angels, 1991; The Innocents, 1991; Finding Reality in Myth, 1996. Contributions to: Anthologies, magazines and journals. Address: PO Box 370322, El Paso, TX 79937, USA.

SUDAMA Bhikkhoo. See: **GOKANI Pushkar Haridas.**

SUGIMOTO Yoshio, b. 7 Dec 1939, Nishinomiya, Japan. Professor of Sociology; Writer. m. Machiko Satow, 19 June 1966, 1 son, 2 daughters. Education: Graduate, Political Science, Kyoto University, 1964; PhD, University of Pittsburgh, 1973. Appointments: Lecturer, 1973-75, Senior Lecturer, 1975-82, Reader, 1982-88, Professor of Sociology, 1988-, La Trobe University, Bundoora, Melbourne. Publications: Popular Disturbance in Postwar Japan, 1981; Images of Japanese Society, 1986; Democracy in Contemporary Japan, 1986; The Japanese Trajectory, 1988; Constructs for Understanding Japan, 1989; The MFP Debate, 1990; Japanese Encounters with Postmodernity, 1995; An Introduction to Japanese Society, 1997. Contributions to: Professional journals. Honour: Japan Intercultural Publications Award, 1987. Membership: Australian Academy of the Humanities, Fellow. Address: c/o School of Sociology, Politics and Anthropology, La Trobe University, Bundoora, Melbourne, Victoria 3083, Australia.

SUHRAWARDY (Rizvi) Nilofar, b. 25 Feb 1963, Allahbad, India. Writer; Journalist. Education: BA, University of Delhi, 1984; MA, JNU, 1986; MPhil, JNU, 1989; MA, School of Journalism and Mass Communication, UW-Madison, USA, 1992. Appointments: Editor, Eagle Heights Newsletter, Madison, Wisconsin, USA, 1991-92; Assistant Editor (Jr), The Times of India, 1994-95; Assistant Editor, The Pioneer, 1995-96, The Statesman, 1996-. Contributions to: Wisconsin State Journal; Austin-American Statesman; The Badger Herald, USA; Arab News, Saudi Arabia; Impact International, England. Indian publications include: The Pioneer; Mainstream; The Times of India; The Pioneer; The Statesman; Hindustan Times; The Sunday Mail; The Indian Post; Free Press Journal; The Evening News; Mid-Day; National Herald; Women's Era. Membership: Association for Education in Journalism and Mass Communication, USA. Address: 375-B, Pocket II, Mayur Vihar I, Delhi-91, India.

SUKNASKI Andrew, b. 30 July 1942, Wood Mountain, Saskatchewan, Canada. Editor; Poet. Education: University of British Columbia, Vancouver, 1967-68. Appointment: Editor, Three Legged Coyote, Wood Mountain, 1982-. Publications: This Shadow of Eden, 1970; Circles, 1970; Rose Wayn in the East, 1972; Old Mill, 1972; The Zen Pilgrimage, 1972; Four Parts Sand: Concrete Poems, 1972; Wood Mountain Poems, 1973; Suicide Notes, Booke One, 1973; These Fragments I've Gathered for Ezra, 1973; Leaving, 1974; Blind Man's House, 1975; Leaving Wood Mountain, 1975; Octomi, 1976; Almighty Voice, 1977; Moses Beauchamp, 1978; The Ghosts Call You Poor, 1978; Two for Father, 1978; In the Name of Narid: New Poems, 1981; Montage for an Interstellar Cry, 1982; The Land They Gave Away: Selected and New Poems, 1982; Silk Trail, 1985. Honour: Canada Council Grants. Address: c/o Thistledown Press, 668 East Place, Saskatoon, Saskatchewan S7J 2Z5, Canada.

SULERI GOODYEAR Sara, b. 12 June 1953, Karachi, Pakistan. Editor; Professor of English. m. Austin Goodyear, 6 July 1993, 1 stepson, 2 stepdaughters. Education: BA Hons, Kinnaird College, 1974; PhD, Indiana University, 1983. Appointments: Editor, The Yale Journal of Criticism, 1987-97. Publications: Meatless Days, 1989; The Rhetoric of English India, 1993. Memberships: Editorial Board: Yale Review, 1991-, Transition, 1992-. Address: HCR 64, Box 474, Reach Road, Brooklyn, ME 04616, USA.

SULLIVAN Thomas William, b. 20 Nov 1940, Highland Park, Michigan, USA. Author; Teacher. 1 son, 1 daughter. Education: BA, 1964. Publications: Diapason, 1978; The Phases of Harry Moon, 1988; Born Burning, 1989; The Martyring, 1997. Contributions to: Magazines. Honours: Cash Awards, Hemingway Days Festival Literary Contest, 1985; DADA Literary Contest, 1985, 1987. Memberships: Science Fiction Writers of America; MENSA; Literary Guild; Society of the Black Bull; Arcadia Mixture. Literary Agent: Jim Hornfischer, The Literary Group, 1300 Guadalupe Street, Suite 208, Austin, TX 78701, USA. Address: 17376 Catalpa, Lathrup Village, MI 48076, USA.

SULLOWAY Frank Jones, b. 2 Feb 1947, Concord, New Hampshire, USA. Psychologist and Historian of Science; Psychologist; Writer. 1 son. Education: AB summa cum laude, 1969, AM, History of Science, 1971, PhD, History of Science, 1978, Harvard University. Appointments: Junior Fellow, Harvard University Society of Fellows, 1974-77; Member, Institute for Advanced Study, Princeton, New Jersey, 1977-78; Research Fellow, Miller Institute for Basic Research in Science, University of California at Berkeley, 1978-80; Research

Fellow, 1980-81, Visiting Scholar, 1989-, Massachusetts Institute of Technology; Postdoctoral Fellow, 1981-82, Visiting Scholar, 1984-89, Harvard University; Research Fellow, University College, London, England, 1982-84; Vernon Professor of Biography, Dartmouth College, 1986. Publications: Freud, Biologist of the Mind, 1979; Darwin and His Finches, 1982; Freud and Biology: The Hidden Legacy, 1982; Darwin's Conversion, 1982; Darwin and the Galapagos, 1984; Darwin's Early Intellectual Development, 1985; Reassessing Freud's Case Histories, 1991; Born to Rebel: Birth Order, Family Dynamics and Revolutionary Genius, 1996. Contributions to: Professional journals. Honours: Pfizer Award, History of Science Society, 1980; National Endowment for the Humanities Fellowship, 1980-81; National Science Foundation Fellowship, 1981-82; Guggenheim Fellowship, 1982-83; John D and Catherine T MacArthur Foundation Fellowship, 1984-89; Golden Plate Award, American Academy of Achievement, 1997; James Randi Award, Skeptics Society, 1997. Memberships: American Association for the Advancement of Science, Fellow; American Psychological Society; History of Science Society; Human Behavior and Evolution Society. Address: Massachusetts Institute of Technology, Programme in Science, Technology and Society, Building E51-093, Cambridge, MA 02139, USA.

SUMMERS Anthony (Bruce), b. 21 Dec 1942, Bournemouth, England. Author; Journalist. m. (4) 27 Jun 1992, 3 sons. Education: BA, Modern Languages, New College Oxford, 1964. Appointments: Researcher, World In Action Programme, Granada TV, 1963; Newsreader, Writer, Swiss Broadcasting Corporation 1964-65; Scriptwriter, BBC-TV News, 1965; BBC-TV Current Affairs Programmes, 1965-73, rising to Senior Film Producer. Publications: The File On the Tsar (with Tom Mangold), 1976; Conspiracy (Who Killed President Kennedy?), 1980; Goddess: The Secret Lives of Marilyn Monroe, 1985; Honeytrap: The Secret Worlds of Stephen Ward (with Stephen Dorril), 1987; Official and Confidential, The Secret Life of J Edgar Hoover, 1993. Contributions to: Sunday Times; Observer; Independent. Honour: Golden Dagger, Crime Writers Association, for best Non-Fiction, 1980; Memberships: PEN; Authors Guild; NVJ; BECTV. Address: One Madison Avenue, New York City, NY 10010, USA.

SUNDERLAND Eric, b. 18 Mar 1930, Ammanford, Dyfed, Wales. Former Vice Chancellor, University College, Bangor. m. 19 Oct 1957, 2 daughters. Education: BA Class 1, Geography with Anthropology, University of Wales; MA Anthropology (by thesis), University of Wales; PhD Anthropology (by thesis), University College, London. Publications: Elements of Human and Social Geography: Some Anthropological Perspectives, 1973; Genetic Variation in Britain (co-editor), 1973; The Operation of Intelligence: Biological Pre-Conditions for the Operation of Intelligence (co-editor), 1980; Genetic and Population Studies in Wales (co-editor), 1986. Contributions to: Journals and periodicals. Address: Bryn, Ffriddoedd Road, Bangor, Gwynedd LL57 2EH, Wales.

SUTHERLAND Margaret, b. 16 Sept 1941, Auckland, New Zealand. Writer. m. 2 sons, 1 daughter. Education: Registered Nurse. Publications: The Fledgling, 1974; Hello, I'm Karen (children's book), 1974; The Love Contract, 1976; Getting Through, 1977, US edition as Dark Places, Deep Regions, 1980; The Fringe of Heaven, 1984; The City Far From Home, 1992. Contributions to: Journals and magazines. Honours: Literary Fellow, Auckland University, 1981; Scholarships in Letters, New Zealand, 1981, 1984; Australia Council Writers Fellowships, 1992, 1995. Memberships: Australian Society of Authors; Federation of Australian Writers. Address: 10 Council Street, Speers Point, New South Wales 2284, Australia.

SUTHERLAND SMITH Beverley Margaret, b. 1 July 1935, Australia. Writer. Div, 2 sons, 2 daughters. Appointments: A Taste For All Seasons, 1975, revised edition, 1991; A Taste of Class, 1980; A Taste in Time, 1981; Gourmet Gifts, 1985; Chocolates and Petit Fours, 1987; Delicious Desserts, 1989; Oriental Cookbook, 1990; Simple Cuisine, 1992; Vegetables, 1994. Contributions to: Gourmet Magazine; Epicurean Magazine; The Age; Golden Wings; German Geographical Magazine; Herald and Weekly Times. Memberships: International Association of Culinary Professionals; Ladies Wine and Food Society of Melbourne; Chaine des Rotisseurs; Wine Press Club; Amities Gastronomiques Internationales. Address: 29 Regent Street, Mount Waverley, Melbourne, Victoria 3149, Australia.

SÜTO András, b. 17 June 1927, Pusztakamaras, Transylvania, Romania. Journalist; Editor; Writer; Dramatist. m. Eva Szabo, 1949, 2

children. Appointments: Contributor, later Editor-in-Chief, Falvak Népe, 1949-54; Deputy Chief Editor, Igaz Szo literary monthly, 1955-57; Chief Editor, Uj Elet, pictorial, 1957-89. Publications: Some 20 volumes, including novels, short stories, essays and plays, 1953-96. Honours: State Prizes, Romania, 1953, 1954; Herder Prize, Vienna, 1979; Kossuth Prize, Hungary, 1992. Address: Marosvásárhely, Str Marasti Nr 36, 4300 Tirgu Mures, Romania.

SUTTON Henry. See: SLAVITT David Rytman.

SUTTON Keith Ashley, b. 27 Jan 1944, Moorabbin, Victoria, Australia. Editor; Writer. div., 1 son. Education: BA, Australian National University, Canberra, 1972; Associate Diploma in Professional Writing, Canberra College of Advanced Education, 1974. Appointments: Editor, Publications, Department of Foreign Affairs, Canberra, 1977-85; Editor to Australian Auditor-General, Canberra, 1985-88. Publications: How to Stuff Up a Small Business (with Gavin Byrne and Neville O'Neill), 1990; Blueprint for the Casino Industry: Federal Hotels and Wrest Point, 1992; Australia's Coins and Notes, 1993. Memberships: Australian Society of Authors; Canberra Society of Editors; National Press Club. Address: 29 Lucy Street, Ashfield, New South Wales 2131, Australia.

SUTTON Shaun Alfred Graham, b. 14 Oct 1919, England. Stage and Television Director; Producer; Writer. m. Barbara Leslie, 1948, 1 son, 3 daughters. Education: Embassy School of Acting, London; Royal Navy, 1940-46. Appointments: Director, Buxton Repertory Theatre, Latymer Upper School, London, Embassy Theatre, 1947-51, On Monday Next, Comedy Theatre, 1949; Entered BBC TV service, 1952; Head, BBC Drama Serials Department, 1966-68, BBC TV Drama Group, 1969-81; Producer, 1981-92; Script Consultant Director, Primetime Television. Publications: Queen's Champion (children's novel), 1961; The Largest Theatre in the World, 1982. Other: A Christmas Carol (stage adaptation), 1949. Honour: Officer of the Order of the British Empire, 1979. Memberships: British Academy of Film and Television Arts; Royal Television Society, Fellow. Address: 15 Corringham Court, Corringham Road, London NW11 7BY, England.

SVENNINGSEN Poul Flöe, b. 23 May 1919, Vejle, Denmark. Journalist; Artist. m. Karen Bröchner, 17 Mar 1956, 3 sons, 1 daughter. Publications: Little Stranger, 1951; Little Nuisance, 1952; Anglers Angle, 1953; Snooze, 1954; Little Angel, 1961; Jagt og Tone, 1975; Sejlads mellem Öerne, 1977; Mille: A Very Special Dog, 1979; Kåre Lord Fjeldmose (novel), 1979. Contributions to: Numerous translations, exhibitions of drawings and paintings and contributions to anthologies; Commentator and columnist, Berlingske Tidende, Copenhagen. Memberships: Danish Journalists' Association; Society of Danish Authors. Address: Dämringsvej 15, DK 2900 Hellerup, Denmark.

SVOBODA Terese, b. 5 Sept 1950, Ogallala, Nebraska, USA. Poet; Writer; Videomaker. m. Stephen M Bull, 18 July 1981, 3 sons. Education: University of Nebraska, 1968; Montreal Museum of Fine Arts, 1968; Manhattanville, 1968-70; Oxford University, 1969; University of Colorado, 1970; Stanford University, 1971; BFA, University of British Columbia, 1973; MFA, Columbia University, 1978. Appointments: Rare Manuscript Curator, McGill University, 1969; Co-Producer, PBS-TV series Voices and Visions, 1980-82; Distinguished Visiting Professor, University of Hawaii, 1992; Professor, Sarah Lawrence College, 1993. Publications: Poetry: All Aberration, 1985; Laughing Africa, 1990; Mere Mortal, 1995; Fiction: Cannibal, 1995. Contributions to: Poems, fiction, essays, and translations to periodicals. Honours: Writer's Choice Column Award, New York Times Book Review, 1985; Iowa Prize, 1990; Bobst Prize, 1995. Memberships: PEN; Poets and Writers; Poet's House, founding member and advisory board member, 1986-91. Address: 56 Ludlow Street, New York, NY 10002, USA.

SWAMY M R Kumara, b. 23 Jan 1938, Mysore, India. Financial Management Researcher; Editor. m. Shaila, 25 Aug 1966, 1 son, 1 daughter. Education: BA, Hons, Economics, India; MA, Economics, India, 1958; PhD, Economics, USA, 1965. Appointments: Advising Oil Economist, Qatar Government, Arabia, 1967-69; Senior Research Officer, Commerce Research Bureau, India, 1969-77; Professor and Head, Institute of Management and Technology and Anambra State University of Technology, Nigeria, 1977-87; Managing Editor/Director, Journal of Financial Management and Analysis, Om Sai Ram Centre for Financial Management Research, India, 1987-. Publications: Founder, Editor, Nigerian Journal of Financial Management, 1982-87; Journal of Financial Management and Analysis (Third World's first and world's second Financial Management Journal), 1987-; Blueprint on Cooperative Development in Nigeria's Fourth Five Year Plan (based on Professor Swamy's Measure of Welfare Gap); Report of the Committee of Experts on Low Cost Housing Through Cooperative Societies (Anambra State Government of Nigeria Policy Document, 1981. Contrbutions to: 165 scholarly papers in professional journals. Honours: Distinguished Economist Guest Lecturer, with Italian Academy of Sciences, University of Rome, 1965-66; Financial Management Association; Lisle Fellowship; Indian E C Association. Address: Managing Editor/Director, Journal of Financial Management and Analysis, Om Sai Ram Centre for Financial Management Research, 15 Prakash Cooperative Housing Society, Relief Road, Santacruz (West), Mumbai 400054, India.

SWAN Gladys, b. 15 Oct 1934, New York, New York, USA. Writer; Associate Professor. m. 9 Sept 1955, 2 daughters. Education: BA, Western New Mexico University, 1954; MA, Claremont Graduate School. Appointments: Distinguished Visiting Writer-in-Residence, University of Texas, El Paso, 1984-85; Visiting Professor, Ohio University, 1986-87; Associate Professor, University of Missouri, 1987-. Publications: On the Edge of the Desert (short stories), 1979; Carnival for the Gods (novel), 1986; Of Memory and Desire (short stories), 1989; Do You Believe in Cabeza de Vaca?, 1991; Ghost Dance: A Play of Voices, 1992. Contributions to: Magazines. Honours: Fulbright Fellowship, Writer-in-Residence, Yugoslavia, 1988; Honorary Doctorate of Humane Letters, Western North Mexico University, 1992. Memberships: Authors Guild; Associated Writing Programs; PEN American Center. Address: 2601 Lynwood Drive, Columbia, MO 65203, USA.

SWAN Robert Arthur, b. 2 Oct 1917, Broken Hill, Australia. Retired Civil Servant. m. Marie Kathleen McClelland, 14 Oct 1949, dec 1984, 1 daughter. Education: BA, University Of Melbourne, 1950. Publications: Argonauts Returned And Other Poems, 1946; Australia In The Antarctic: Interest, Activity And Endeavour, 1961; To Botany Bay: If Policy Warrants The Measure, 1973; 12 Collections of Poems, 1982- 1994. Contributions: Royal Historical Society Of Victoria; Royal Australian Historical Society; Australia Defence 2000; Australia And World Affairs; Australian Dictionary Of Biography; British National Biography. Membership: Fellow, Royal Geographical Society, London; United Services Institute, Sydney; Commando Association, Australia; Z Special Unit Association, Australia. Address: 64 Beach Drive, Woonona, NSW 2517, Australia.

SWAN Susan, b. 9 June 1945, Ontario, Canada. Novelist. m. Barry Haywood, 25 Mar 1969, 1 daughter. Education: BA, McGill University. Appointment: Professor, York University. Publications: The Biggest Modern Woman of the World; The Wives of Bath; The Last of the Golden Girls; Unfit for Paradise. Honour: Best First Novelist Finalist, 1983. Literary Agent: Anne McDermid and Associates, 78 Albany Avenue, Toronto, Ontario M5R 3C3, Canada. Address: 151 Robert Street, Toronto, Ontario M5S 2K6, Canada.

SWANN Lois, b. 17 Nov 1944, New York, New York, USA. Author; Reader, Calliope's Chamber; Teacher. m. (1) T G Swann, 15 Aug 1964, 1 son, 1 daughter, div 1979, (2) Kenneth E Arndt, 3 Sept 1988. Education: BA, Marquette University, 1966. Publications: The Mists of Manittoo, 1976; Torn Covenants, 1981; John Milton: The True Wayfaring Christian, 1986. Contributions to: Magazines. Honours: Ohioana Library Association Award for First Novelists, 1976; Papers archived in Twentieth Century Collection, Boston University. Memberships: Authors Guild; Poets and Writers. Address: 22 Sagamore Road, Bronxville, NY 10708, USA.

SWANSON Judith Ann, b. 4 Nov 1957, Los Angeles, California, USA. Assistant Professor of Political Philosophy; Writer. m. David R Mayhew, 20 Nov 1987. Education: BA, Colorado College, 1979; MSc with distinction, London School of Economics and Political Science, 1980; PhD, University of Chicago, 1987. Appointments: Lecturer, Yale University, 1985-86; Assistant Professor, University of Georgia, 1986-88; Assistant Professor of Political Philosophy, Boston University, 1988-. Publication: The Public and the Private in Aristotle's Political Philosophy, 1992. Contributions to: Professional journals. Honours: Earhart Foundation Fellowship, 1980-84; Josephine de Karnan Fellowship, 1983-84; National Endowment for the Humanities Fellowship, 1990-91. Memberships: American Philosophical Association; American Political Science Association; Claremont Institute Society for the Study of Political Philosophy and Statesmanship; Conference for the Study of Political Thought;

International Association for Greek Philosophy; Society for Greek Political Thought. Address: c/o Department of Political Science, Boston University, 232 Bay State Road, Boston, MA 02215, USA.

SWANTON Ernest William, b. 11 Feb 1907, London, England. Author. m. Ann Marion Carbutt, 11 Feb 1958. Appointments: Staff, Evening Standard, 1927-39, Daily Telegraph, 1946-75; Editorial Director, 1965-89, President, 1990-, The Cricketer. Publications: The History of Cricket, 1938-1962 (with H S Altham), 1962; Barclays World of Cricket, 1966, 3rd edition, 1986; As I Said at the Time, 1983; The Essential E W Swanton, 1990. Contributions to: Newspapers and periodicals. Honours: Officer of the Order of the British Empire, 1965; Commander of the Order of the British Empire, 1994. Address: Delt House, Sandwich, Kent CT13 9HB, England.

SWARD Robert (Stuart), b. 23 June 1933, Chicago, Illinois, USA. Poet; Writer; University Lecturer. 2 sons, 3 daughters. Education: BA, University of Illinois, 1956; MA, University of Iowa, 1958; Postgraduate Studies, Middlebury College, Vermont, 1959-60, University of Bristol, 1960-61. Appointments: Poet-in-Residence, Cornell University, 1962-64, University of Victoria, British Columbia, 1969-73, University of California at Santa Cruz, 1987-; Writer-in-Residence, Foothill Writers Conference, summers 1988-; Writer, Writing Programme, Language Arts Department, Cabrillo College, 1989-. Publications: Uncle Dog and Other Poems, 1962; Kissing the Dancer and Other Poems, 1964; Half a Life's History: New and Selected Poems 1957-83, 1983; The Three Roberts (with Robert Zend and Robert Priest), 1985; Four Incarnations: New and Selected Poems 1957-91, 1991; Family (with David Swanger, Tilly Shaw and Charles Atkinson), 1994; Earthquake Collage, 1995; A Much-Married Man (novel), 1996. Contributions to: Anthologies, newspapers and magazines; Contributing Editor, Blue Penny Quarterly and other Internet literary publications. Honours: Fulbright Fellowship, 1960-61; Guggenheim Fellowship, 1965-66; D H Lawrence Fellowship, 1966; Djerassi Foundation Residency, 1990; Way Cool Site Award, editing eSCENE 1996, Internet literary magazine. Memberships: League of Canadian Poets; Modern Poetry Association; National Writers Union, USA; Writers Union of Canada. Address: PO Box 7062, Santa Cruz, CA 95061-7062, USA.

SWARTZ Jon David, b. 28 Dec 1934, Houston, Texas, USA. Educator; Psychologist; Writer. m. Carol Joseph Hampton, 20 Oct 1966, 2 sons, 1 daughter. Education: BA, 1956, MA, 1961, PhD, 1969, Postgraduate Fellow, 1973-74, University of Texas at Austin. Appointments: Assistant Professor, University of Texas at Austin, 1969-72; Editorial Associate, Current Anthropology, 1971-77; Book Review Editor, Journal of Biological Psychology, 1972-80; Associate Editor, American Corrective Therapy Journal, 1971-81, Exceptional Children, 1982-84; Associate Professor and Chairman of Psychology, University of Texas, Permian Basin, 1974-79; Professor of Education and Psychology, Associate Dean, Libraries and Learning Resources, Southwestern University, Georgetown, Texas, 1978-90; Coordinator and Administrative Head, Killeen Office, 1990-91, Chief of Psychological Services, Temple Office, 1991-, Central Counties Center for MHMR Services, Texas. Publications: Administrative Issues in Institutions for the Mentally Retarded, 1972; Multihandicapped Mentally Retarded, 1973. Co-Author: Inkblot Perception and Personality, 1961; Mental Retardation: Approaches to Institutional Change, 1969; Personality Development in Two Cultures, 1975; Holtzman Inkblot Technique: An Annotated Bibliography, 1956-1982, 1983, Supplement, 1988; Handbook of Old-Time Radio: A Comprehensive Guide to Golden Age Radio Listening and Collecting, 1993. Co-Editor: Profoundly Mentally Retarded, 1976; Research with the Profoundly Retarded, 1978. Contributions to: Professional journals and general magazines; Handbook of Texas, 1996. Honours: US Office of Education Fellow, 1964-66; Franklin Gilliam Prize, University of Texas, 1965; Spencer Fellow, National Academy of Education, 1972-74; Faculty Fellowship Award, Southwestern University, 1981. Memberships: American Academy on Mental Retardation; American Association for the Advancement of Science, Fellow; American Psychological Society, Fellow; Western Research Conference on Mental Retardation; Society for Personality Assessment; Southwestern Psychological Association. Address: 1704 Vine Street, Georgetown, TX 78626-7228, USA.

SWEARER Donald Keeney, b. 2 Aug 1934, Wichita, Kansas, USA. Professor of Religion. m. 17 June 1964, 1 son, 1 daughter. Education: AB cum laude, 1956, MA, 1965, PhD, 1967, Princeton University. Publications: Buddhism in Transition, 1970; Secrets of the

Lotus, 1971; Wat Haripunjaya: The Royal Temple of the Buddha's Relic, 1976; Dialogue, the Key to Understanding Other Religions, 1977; Buddhism, 1977; Buddhism and Society in Southeast Asia, 1981; For the Sake of the World: The Spirit of Buddhist and Christian Monasticism, 1989; Me-and-Mine, Selected Essays of Bhikkhu Buddhadasa, 1989; Ethics, Wealth and Salvation, 1989. Contributions to: Journal of the American Academy of Religion; Journal of Ecumenical Studies; Journal of Religious Ethics; Philosophy East and West; Journal of the Siam Society; Religious Studies Review. Honours: Phi Beta Kappa, 1956; Kent Fellow, 1964-65; Asian Religions Fellowship, Society for Religion in Higher Education, 1967-68; Senior Fellowship, National Endowment for the Humanities, 1972-73; Humanities Fellowship, Rockefeller Foundation, 1985-86; Senior Research Fellowship, Fulbright (CIES), 1989-90; Charles and Harriet Cox McDowell Professor of Religion, 1992-; Fulbright-Hays Fellowship, 1994; Guggenheim Fellowship, 1994. Memberships: American Academy of Religion; Association for Asian Studies; American Society for the Study of Religion; Society for Buddhist-Christian Studies. Address: 109 Columbia Avenue, Swarthmore, PA 19081, USA.

SWEDE George, b. 20 Nov 1940, Riga, Latvia. Professor; Poet; Writer. m. Anita Krumins, 23 July 1974, 2 sons. Education: BA, University of British Columbia, 1964; MA, Dalhousie University, 1965; PhD, Greenwich University, 1996. Appointments: Instructor, Vancouver City College, 1966-67; Instructor, 1968-73, Professor of Psychology, 1973-, Ryerson Polytechnic University; Director, Poetry and Things, 1969-71, Developmental Psychology, Open College, 1973-75; Poetry Editor, Poetry Toronto, 1980-81, Writers' Magazine, 1988-90; Reviews and Poetry Editor, Writers' Quarterly, 1982-88. Publications: Poetry including: Tell-Tale Feathers, 1978; Wingbeats, 1979; A Snowman, Headless, 1979; This Morning's Mockingbird, 1980; Eye to Eye with a Frog, 1981; All of Her Shadows, 1982; Tick Bird, 1983; Flaking Paint, 1983; Bifids, 1984; Time is Flies, 1984; The Space Between (co-author), 1986; I Eat a Rose Petal, 1987; Multiple Personality, 1987; Where Even the Factories Have Lawns (co-author), 1988; Leaping Lizzard, 1988; Holes in My Cage, 1989; I Want to Lasso Time, 1991; Leaving My Loneliness, 1992; Five O'Clock Shadows, co-author, 1996. Non-fiction: The Modern English Haiku, 1981; Creativity: A New Psychology, 1993; Psychology of Art; An Experimental Approach, editor, 1994; Fiction: Moonlit Gold Dust, 1979; Quilby: The Porcupine Who Lost His Quills (co-author), 1980; Missing Heirloom, 1980; Seaside Burglaries, 1981; Downhill Theft, 1982; Undertow, 1982; Dudley and the Birdman, 1985; Dudley and the Christmas Thief, 1986. Contributions to: Magazines worldwide. Honours: Book Award, Haiku Society of America, 1980; High/Coo Press Chapbook Competition Winner, 1982; 3 Museum of Haiku Literature Awards; 5 Canadian Children's Book Centre Our Choice Awards; 1st Prize, Haiku in English, Mainichi Daily News, 1993. Memberships: PEN; Canadian Society of Children's Authors, Illustrators and Performers; League of Canadian Poets; Haiku Canada, Co-founder, 1977; Haiku Society of America; Writers Union of Canada. Address: Box 279, Station P, Toronto, Ontario M5S 2S8, Canada.

SWEENEY Matthew, b. 6 Oct 1952, County Donegal, Ireland. Poet. m. Rosemary Barber, 1979. Education: University College, Dublin, 1970-78; BA, Polytechnic of North London, 1978. Appointments: Writer-in-Residence, Farnham College, Surrey, 1984-85; Writing Fellowship, University of East Anglia, 1986; Publicist and Events Assistant, Poetry Society, 1988-90; Poet in Residence, Hereford and Worcester, 1991; Writer in Residence, South Bank Centre, 1994-95. Publications: Without Shores, 1978; A Dream of Maps, 1981; A Round House, 1983; The Lame Waltzer, 1985; The Chinese Dressing Gown (for children), 1987; Blue Shoes, 1989; The Flying Spring Onion (for children0, 1992; Cacti, 1992; The Snow Vulture (for children), 1992; Fatso in the Red Suit (for children), 1995; Emergency Kit: Poems for Strange Times (co-edited with Jo Shapcott), 1996; Writing Poetry (co-written with John Hartley Williams), 1997; The Bridal Suite, 1997; Penguin Modern Poets 12, 1997. Honours: Prudence Farmer Prize, 1984; Cholmondeley Award, 1987; Arts Council Literature Award, 1992. Address: 11 Dombey Street, London WC1N 3PB, England.

SWETZ Frank Joseph, b. 7 July 1937, New York, New York, USA. Professor of Mathematics; Writer. Education: BA, Marist College, 1962; MA, Fordham University, 1963; DEd, Columbia University, 1972. Appointments: Instructor, Columbia University Teachers College, 1967-69; Professor of Mathematics, Penn State University, 1969-. Publications: Mathematics Education in China, 1974; Was Pythagoras Chinese?, 1977; Socialist Mathematics Education, 1979; Capitalism and Arithmetic, 1987; Mathematical Modelling in School Curriculum, 1991; The History of Mathematics: A Collection of Readings, 1992; The Sea Island Mathematical Manual, 1992; From Five Fingers to Infinity, 1994. Contributions to: Professional journals. Honours: Edpress Awards, 1971, 1984; Fulbright Research Fellowship, 1985; Outstanding Research Awards, Penn State University, 1986, 1989; Fulbright Lectureship, Malaysia, 1995. Memberships: International Study Group on the History of Pedagogy of Mathematics; National Council of Teachers of Mathematics; Pennsylvania Council of Teachers of Mathematics. Address: 616 Sandra Avenue, Harrisburg, PA 17109, USA.

SWIFT Graham Colin, b. 4 May 1949, London, England. Author. Education: Queens' College, Cambridge, 1967-70; MA, York University, 1973. Publications: The Sweet Shop Owner, 1980; Shuttlecock, 1981; Learning to Swim and Other Stories, 1982; Waterland, 1983; The Magic Wheel (editor with David Profumo), 1986; Out of This World, 1988; Ever After, 1992; Last Orders, 1996. Honours: Nominated for Booker Prize, 1983; Geoffrey Faber Memorial Prize, 1983; Guardian Fiction Award, 1983; Royal Society of Literature Winifred Holtby Award, 1983; Premio Grinzane Cavour, Italy, 1987; Prix du Meilleur Livre Étranger, France, 1994; Booker Prize for Fiction, 1996. Address: 20 John Street, London WC1N 2DR, England.

SWIFT Robert. See: **KELLY Tim.**

SWINBURNE Richard Granville, b. 26 Dec 1934, Smethwick, Staffordshire, England. Professor of Philosophy; Author. m. Monica Holmstrom, 1960, separated 1985, 2 daughters. Education: BA, 1957, BPhil, 1959, Dip Theol, 1960, MA, 1961, Oxford University. Appointments: Fereday Fellow, St John's College, Oxford, 1958-61; Leverhulme Research Fellow in the History and Philosophy of Science, University of Leeds, 1961-63; Lecturer to Senior Lecturer in Philosophy, University of Hull, 1963-72; Visiting Associate Professor of Philosophy, University of Maryland, 1969-70; Professor of Philosophy, University of Keele, 1972-84; Distinguished Visiting Scholar, University of Adelaide, 1982; Nolloth Professor of the Philosophy of the Christian Religion, Oxford University, 1985-; Visiting Professor of Philosophy, Syracuse University, 1987; Visiting Lecturer, Indian Council for Philosophical Research, 1992. Publications: Space and Time, 1968, 2nd edition, 1981; The Concept of Miracle, 1971; An Introduction to Confirmation Theory, 1973; The Coherence of Theism, 1977, revised edition, 1993; The Existence of God, 1979, revised edition, 1991; Faith and Reason, 1981; Personal Identity (with S Shoemaker), 1984; The Evolution of the Soul, 1986, revised edition, 1997; Responsibility and Atonement, 1989; Revelation, 1992; The Christian God, 1994; Is There a God?, 1996. Contributions to: Scholarly journals. Honour: Fellow, British Academy, 1992. Address: c/o Oriel College, Oxford OX1 4EW, England.

SWINDELLS Robert Edward, b. 20 Mar 1939, Bradford, England. Writer. Education: Teacher's Certificate, Huddersfield Polytechnic, 1972. Publications: Some 20 books, 1973-95. Honours: Children's Book Award, 1980; Children's Rights Workshop Other Award, 1984; Carnegie Medal, 1994. Address: c/o The Library Association, 7 Ridgmount Street, London WC1E 7AE, England.

SYLVESTER (Anthony) David (Bernard), b. 21 Sept 1924, England. m. Pamela Briddon, 3 daughters. Appointments: Visiting Lecturer, Slade School of Fine Arts, 1953-57, Royal College of Arts, 1960-70, Swarthmore College, Penn, 1967-68; Chairman of Art Panel, Arts Council of Great Britain, 1980-82; Organizer of modern art exhibitions at the Tate, Hayward and Serpentine Galleries, London (Henry Moore, Magritte, Miro and Giacometti), Palais des Beaux Arts at Brussels and the Musée National d'Art Moderne, Paris; film and television presentations of Giacometti, Matisse and Magritte. Publications: Henry Moore, 1968; Magritte, 1969; Interviews with Francis Bacon, 1975, enlarged edition, 1980; Looking at Giacometti, 1994. Honours: Commander of the Order of the British Empire, 1983; Fellow, Royal Academy, 1986; Golden Lion of Venice for film criticism, 1993. Address: c/o The Tate Gallery (Exhibitions), London, England.

SZABÓ István, b. 18 Feb 1938, Budapest, Hungary. Film Director; Scenario Writer. m. Vera Gyurey. Education: Budapest Academy of Theatre and Film Arts. Appointments: Member, various Hungarian film studios; Tutor, College of Theatre and Film Arts, Budapest. Publications: Many works, including plays, films, documentaries and television productions. Honours: Various theatre and film awards, including Academy Award (AMPAS) for best foreign language film, 1981; UK Critics' Prize, 1982; British Academy of Film and Television Artists Award, 1986; Silver Bear of Berlin Award, 1992; European Script Writer of the Year Award, 1992. Memberships: Academy of Motion Picture Arts and Sciences; Akademie der Künste, Berlin. Address: ISL Films, Róua-uta 174, 1149 Budapest, Hungary.

SZABO Magda, b. 5 Oct 1917, Hungary. Writer; Dramatist; Poet. m. Tibor Szobotka, 1948. Education: Teacher's Certificate, 1940; PhD, Classical Philology. Appointments: Teacher, secondary schools, 1940-44, 1950-59. Publications: Novels, plays, radio dramas, poems, essays and film scripts, many translated into English and other languages. Honours: Jozsef Attila Prizes, 1959, 1972; Kossuth Prize, 1978; Getz Corporation Prize, USA, 1992. Memberships: Academy of Sciences of Europe; Hungarian Szechenyi Academy of Arts. Address: Julia-utca 3, H-1026 Budapest, Hungary.

SZÁNTÓ András, b. 1 Jan 1964, Budapest, Hungary. Sociologist; Media Researcher; Arts Writer. Education: BA, Budapest University of Economics, 1988; MA, 1990, MPhil, 1990; PhD, Columbia University, 1996. Appointment: Associate Director, National Arts Journalism Programme, Columbia University, New York. Publications: Kitörö Eberséggel (with T Dessewffy), 1989; The Crucial Facts (with J Horvát), 1993; From Silence to Polyphony, 1995. Contributions to: Actes de la Recherche en Sciences Sociales; Theory and Society; Imago; Uj Müvészet; Boston Globe. Address: 135 Perry Street, #9, New York, NY 10014, USA.

SZASZ Imre, b. 19 Mar 1927, Budapest, Hungary. Writer; Translator. m. Elizabeth Windsor, 23 Sept 1965, 2 daughters. Education: Degree in English and Hungarian Literature, Budapest University, 1950. Appointments: Publishing House Editor, 1949-68; Literary Editor, Cultural Weekly, Budapest, 1968-90; General Secretary, Hungarian PEN Centre, 1989-94. Publications: Come at Nine, 1969; Dry Martini, 1973; One Went Hunting, 1985; Menesi Street, 1986; This is the Way the World Ends, 1986; Self-portrait with Background, 1986; I'll Go When You Dismiss Me, 1991. Contributions to: Magazines and journals. Honours: Jozef Attila Awards, 1954, 1989; Book of the Year, 1989. Memberships: Hungarian Writers Union; Hungarian PEN Centre; Hungarian Journalists Union. Address: Szeher ut 82, Budapest 1021, Hungary.

SZIRTES George Gabor Nicholas, b. 29 Nov 1948, Budapest, Hungary. Poet. m. Clarissa Upchurch, 11 July 1970, 1 son, 1 daughter. Education: BA (1st class Honours), Fine Art, Leeds College of Art, England. Publications: The Slant Door, 1979; November and May, 1981; The Kissing Place, 1982; Short Wave, 1984; The Photographer in Winter, 1986; Selected Poems, 1987; Metro, 1988; Bridge Passages, 1991; Blind Field, 1994. Translations from Hungarian: Imre Madach's Tragedy of Man, 1987; Dezsö Kosztolányi's Anna Édes, 1992; Ottó Orbán's The Blood of the Walsungs, 1993; Zsuzsa Rakovszky's New Life, 1994. Contributions to: Numerous journals and magazines. Honours: Faber Memorial Prize, 1980; Arts Council Bursary, 1984; British Council Fellowship, 1985; Cholmondeley Award, 1987; Dery Prize for Translation, 1991; Decorated, Hungarian Republic, 1991; Shortlisted, Whitbread Poetry Prize, 1992. Memberships: Fellow, Royal Society of Literature; PEN. Address: 20 Old Park Road, Hitchin, Hertfordshire SG5 2JR, England.

SZYMBORSKA Wisława, b. 2 July 1923, Bnin, Poland. Poet; Critic; Translator. Education: Jagellonian University, Kraków, 1945-48. Appointment: Editorial Styaff, Zycie Literackie magazine, 1953-81. Publications: Dlatego zyjemy (That's Why We Are Alive), 1952, 2nd edition, 1985; Pytania zadawane sobie (Questioning Oneself), 1954; Wolanie do Yeti (Calling Out to Yeti), 1957; Sól (Salt), 1962; Wiersze wybrane (Selected Verses), 1964; Poezje wybrane (Selected Poems), 1967; Sto pociech (No End of Fun), 1967; Poezje (Poems), 1970; Wszelki wypadek (Could Have), 1972; Wybór wierszy (Selected Verses), 1973; Tarsjusz i inne wiersze (Tarsius and Other Verses), 1976; Wielka liczba (A Large Number), 1977; Poezje wybrane II (Selected Poems II), 1983; Ludzie na moscie (The People on the Bridge), 1986; Wieczór autorski: Wiersze (Authors' Evening: Verses), 1992; Koniec i poczatek (The End and the Beginning), 1993. Poetry in English: Sounds, Feelings, Thoughts: Seventy Poems, 1981; People on a Bridge, 1990; View with a Grain of Sand, 1995. Contributions to: Poetry and criticism in various publications. Honours: City of Kraków Prize for Literature, 1954; Polish Ministry of Culture Prize, 1963; Goethe Prize, 1991; Herder Prize, 1995; Honorary doctorate, Adam Mickiewicz University, Poznań, 1995; Nobel Prize for Literature, 1996;

Polish PEN Club Prize, 1996. Address: Ul Krolewska 82/89, 30-079 Kraków, Poland.

T

TABORI George, b. 24 May 1914, Budapest, Hungary (British citizen). Playwright. Education: Zrinyl Gymnasium, Hungary. Publications: Flight into Egypt, 1952; The Emperor's Clothes, 1953; Miss Julie (version of Strindberg), 1958; Brouhaha, 1958; Brecht on Brecht, 1962; The Resistible Rise of Arturo Ui (after Brecht), 1963; Andora (after Max Frisch), 1963; The Niggerlovers, 1967; The Cannibals, 1968; Mother Courage (after Brecht), 1970; Clowns, 1972; Talk Show, 1976; Changes, 1976; Mein Kampf: A Farce, 1989; Weisman and Copperface, 1991. Novels: Beneath the Stone the Scorpion, 1945; Companions of the Left Hand, 1948; Original Sin, 1947; The Caravan Passes, 1951; The Journey: A Confession, 1958; The Good One, 1960. Screenplays. Address: c/o Suhrkamp Verlag, Lindenstrasse 29-35, Postfach 4229, 6000 Frankfurt am Main, Germany.

TABORSKI Boleslaw, b. 7 May 1927, Torun, Poland. Writer; Translator; Broadcaster. m. Halina Junghertz, 20 June 1959, 1 daughter. Education: BA, Bristol University. Appointments: Producer, Polish Section, 1959-89, Editor, Arts in Action, 1985-93, BBC World Service; Visiting Professor, Graduate Center, City University of New York, New York City, 1982. Publications: Poetry: Times of Passing, 1957 Grains of Night, 1958; Crossing the Border, 1962; Lesson Continuing, 1967; Voice of Silence, 1969; Selected Poems, 1973; Web of Words, 1977; For the Witnesses, 1978; Observer of Shadows, 1979; Love, 1980; A Stranger's Present, 1983; Art, 1985; The Stillness of Grass, 1986; Life and Death, 1988; Politics, 1990; Shakespeare, 1990; Goodnight Nonsense, 1991. Criticism: New Elizabethan Theatre, 1967; Polish Plays in English Translations, 1968; Byron and the Theatre, 1972; The Inner Plays of Karol Wojtyla, 1989. Co-Author: Crowell's Handbook of Contemporary Drama, 1971; Polish Plays in Translation, 1983; Numerous translations into English and Polish. Contributions to: Gambit; Stand; Theatre Research; Theatre Quarterly; Miesiecznik Literacki, Tulanr Drama Review; Polish Review; Dialog; Kultura; Wiez; Teatr. Honours: Polish Writers Association Abroad Award, 1954; Jurzykowski Foundation Award, New York, 1968; Merit for Polish Culture Badge and Diploma, Warsaw, 1970; Koscielski Foundation Award, Geneva, 1977; SI Witkiewicz ITI Award, Warsaw, 1988; ZAIKS Translation Award, Warsaw, 1990. Memberships: Honorary Committee Leon Shiller Foundation, 1987-; Association of Authors, ZAIKS, 1985-; Council Gallery in the Provinces Foundation, Lublin, 1990-; Association of Polish Writers, Warsaw, 1991-; Council, Pro Europa Foundation, Warsaw, 1994-; World Association of Polish Home Army (AK), Ex-Servicemen, Warsaw, 1992-. Address: 66 Esmond Road, Bedford Park, London W4 1JF, England.

TADEUSZ Rozewicz, b. 9 Oct 1921, Radomsko, Poland. Poet; Playwright. m. Wiestawa Koztowska, 1949. Education: University of Kraków. Publications: Face of Anxiety; Conversation with the Prince; The Green Rose; The Card Index; The Witnesses; White Marriage; The Trap. Contributions to: Various Journals. Honours: State Prizes, 1955, 56; Literary Prize, City of Kraków, 1959; Prize of Minister of Culture and Art, 1962; State Prize, 1st Class, 1966; Prizes, Minister of Foreign Affairs, 1974, 1987; Austrian National Prize, European Literature, 1982; German Literary Award, 1994. Membership: Bavarian Academy of Fine Arts. Address: Authors Agency, ul Hispoteozna 2, Warsaw, Poland.

TADEUSZ T. See: **WITTLIN Thaddeus.**

TAGLIABUE John, b. 1 July 1923, Cantu, Italy. College Teacher (retired); Poet; Writer. m. Grace Ten Eyck, 11 Aug 1946, 2 daughters. Education: BA, 1944, MA, 1945, Advanced Graduate Work, 1947-48, Columbia University. Appointments: Teacher, American University, Beirut, Lebanon, 1945, State College of Washington, 1946-47, Alfred University, New York, 1948-50, University of Pisa, Italy, 1950-52, Bates College, Maine, 1953, University of Tokyo, 1958-60; Fulbright Lecturer, University of Indonesia, 1993. Publications: Poems, 1959; A Japanese Journal, 1966; The Buddha Uproar, 1970; The Doorless Door, 1970; The Great Day, 1984; New and Selected Poems 1942-97, 1997. Contributions to: Journals, magazines, and periodicals. Memberships: Academy of American Poets; Maine Writers and Publishers Alliance; PEN; Poetry Society of America. Address: 12 Abbott Street, Lewiston, ME 04240, USA.

TAIT Arch, b. 6 June 1943, Glasgow, Scotland. Translator; University Lecturer. Education: MA, 1966, PhD, 1971, Trinity Hall, Cambridge. Appointments: Lecturer, University of East Anglia, 1970; Lecturer, University of Birmingham, 1983; Editor, Glas: New Russian Writing, 1991. Publications: Lunacharsky, The Poet Commissar, 1984; Translated: The Russian Style, 1991; Is Comrade Bulgakov Dead?, 1993; Baize-Covered table with Decanter, 1995. Memberships: Translators Association; Society of Authors; British Association for Slavonic and East European Studies. Address: Department of Russian Literature, University of Birmingham, Birmingham B15 2TT, England.

TALBOT Michael (Owen), b. 4 Jan 1943, Luton, Bedfordshire, England. Professor of Music; Writer. m. Shirley Mashiane, 26 Sept 1970, 1 son, 1 daughter. Education: ARCM, Royal College of Music, London, 1960-61; BA, 1964, BMus, 1965, PhD, 1969, Clare College, Cambridge. Appointments: Lecturer, 1968-79, Senior Lecturer, 1979-83, Reader, 1983-86, James and Constance Alsop Professor of Music, 1986-, University of Liverpool. Publications: Vivaldi, 1978, 4th edition, revised, 1993; Albinoni: Leben und Werk, 1980; Antonio Vivaldi: A Guide to Research, 1988; Tomaso Albinoni: The Venetian Composer and His World, 1990; Benedetto Vinaccesi: A Musician in Brescia and Venice in the Age of Corelli, 1994; The Sacred Vocal Music of Antonio Vivaldi, 1995. Contributions to: Professional journals. Honours: Cavaliere del Ordine el Merite della Repubblica Italiana, 1980; Oldman Prize, 1990. Memberships: British Academy, fellow; Royal Musical Association; Vivaldi Society, historical adviser. Address: 36 Montclair Drive, Liverpool L18 0HA, England.

TALBOT Norman Clare, b. 14 Sept 1936, Gislingham, Suffolk, England. Poet; Writer; Editor; Literary Consultant; Professor. m. 17 Aug 1960, 1 son, 2 daughters. Education: BA, Durham University, Hatfield College, 1959; PhD, Leeds University, 1962. Appointments: Lecturer, 1968, Associate Professor, 1968, Professor, 1973-, in English, Newcastle University College, University of New South Wales, Australia; Visiting Professor, Yale University, 1967-68, University of East Anglia, 1975-76, University of Århus, 1976, University of Oregon, 1983, University of Leicester, 1984, Linacre College, Oxford, 1987-88, University of Exeter, 1992. Publications: Poetry: Poems for a Female University, 1968; Son of a Female University, 1972; The Fishing Boy, 1975; Find the Lady, 1978; Where Two Rivers Meet, 1981; The Kelly Haiku, 1985; Four Zoas of Australia, 1992. Criticism: The Major Poems of John Keats, 1967. Editor: A Glossary of Poetic Terms, 1980, revised edition, 1982; Another Site to Be Mined: The New South Wales Anthology, 1986; Spelling English in Australia (with Nicholas Talbot), 1989; Weaving the Heterocosm: An Anthology of British Narrative Poetry, 1989; Roland Robinson: The Nearest the White Man Gets, 1989; T H Naisby: The Pink Tongue, 1990. Contributions to: Numerous periodicals. Honours: E C Gregory Memorial Award for Poetry, 1965; American Council of Learned Societies Fellowship, 1967-68. Memberships: William Morris Society; Former President, Australian Studies Association. Address: Department of English, Newcastle University College, University of New South Wales, New South Wales 2308, Australia.

TALLENT Elizabeth (Ann), b. 8 Aug 1954, Washington, District of Columbia, USA. Writer; Professor of English. m. Barry Smoots, 28 Sept 1975, 1 son. Education: BA, Illinois State University at Normal, 1975. Appointment: Professor of English, University of California at Davis. Publications: Married Men and Magic Tricks, 1982; In Constant Flight, 1983; Museum Pieces, 1985; Time With Children, 1987; Honey, 1993. Contributions to: Magazines. Honours: Bay Area Book Reviewers Association Fiction Award; National Endowment for the Arts Fellowship, 1992. Membership: Poets and Writers. Address: c/o Department of English, University of California at Davis, Davis, CA 95616, USA.

TALMAGE Anne. See: **POWELL Talmage**.

TAN Amy, b. 19 Feb 1952, Oakland, California, USA. Writer. m. Lou DeMattei, 6 Apr 1974. Education: BA, 1973, MA, 1974, San Jose State College; Postgraduate studies, University of California at Berkeley, 1974-76. Publications: The Joy Luck Club (novel), 1989; The Kitchen God's Wife (novel), 1992; The Moon Lady (children's book), 1992; The Chinese Siamese Cat (children's book), 1994; The Hundred Secret Senses (novel), 1995. Contributions to: Various periodicals. Honours: Commonwealth Club Gold Award for Fiction, San Francisco, 1989; Booklist Editor's Choice, 1991; Marian McFadden Memorial Lecturer, Indianapolis, 1996. Address: c/o G P Putnam's Sons, 200 Madison Avenue, New York, NY 10016, USA.

TANG Victor, b. 12 Apr 1942, China. Business Executive, IBM. m. Wendy Chu, 3 June 1968, 1 son, 2 daughters. Education: BSEE, 1963, MS, Mathematical Physics, 1965, Purdue University; Advanced Research and Studies, Pennsylvania State University, 1967-69; MBA, Columbia University, 1983. Publications: The Silverlake Project, 1992;Competitive Marketing, Part I and II (with Philip Kotler), 1993. Contributions to: Books and professional journals. Memberships: Eta Kappa Nu, Electrical Engineering Honour Society; Pi Mu Epsilon, Mathematics Honour Society; Beta Gamma Sigma, Business Honour Society; Sigma Pi Sigma, Physics Honour Society. Address: 55 Deerfield Lane South, Pleasantville, NY 10570, USA.

TANNER Jacqueline, b. 23 June 1943, Geneva, Switzerland. Laboratory Assistant. m. François Clement, 18 Sept 1986. Appointment: Laboratory Assistant. Publications: Aurore Petrifiee, 1979; Melanie la Nuit, 1980; La Maryssee, 1984; Moraine Infiniment, 1989. Contributions to: Nota Bene; Levant; Le Passe-Muraille. Honours: Schiller Prize, 1980; Michel Dentan Prize, 1984. Memberships: Societe suisse des Ecrivains; Association vaudoise des ecrivains; International Parliament of Writers; PEN Club International; Societe Bernoise des Ecrivains. Address: Avenue du Leman 39, 1005-CH Lausanne, Switzerland.

TANNER Paul Antony, (Tony Tanner), b. 18 Mar 1935, Richmond, Surrey, England. Professor of English and American Literature; Writer. m. Nadia Fusini, 1979. Education: MA, PhD, Jesus College, Cambridge. Appointments: Fellow, King's College, Cambridge, 1960-, Center for Advanced Studies in the Behavioral Sciences, Stanford, California, 1974-75; American Council of Learned Societies Fellow, University of California at Berkeley 1962-63; University Lecturer, Cambridge, 1966-80; Reader in American Literature, 1980-89, Professor of English and American Literature, 1989-, University of Cambridge. Publications: The Reign of Wonder, 1965; Mansfield Park, 1966; Henry James: Modern Judgements, 1968; City of Words 1950-1970, 1971; Adultery in the Novel: Contact and Transgression, 1979; Thomas Pynchon, 1982; Henry James, 1985; Jane Austen, 1986; Scenes of Nature, Signs of Men, 1987; Venice Desired, 1992; Henry James and the Art of Non-Fiction, 1995. Address: c/o King's College, Cambridge CB2 1ST, England.

TANSKA Natalie, (Jala Danková), b. 30 Dec 1929, Prague, Czechoslovakia. Writer. m. Jan Válek, 20 Oct 1960. Education: Academy of Performing Arts, Prague, 1954. Appointments: Theatre Critic, 1956-63; Script Writer, Film Studios, Koliba, 1965-68. Publications: Several books in Czech. Contributions to: Periodicals. Honours: Several awards. Membership: PEN. Address: Vikova 7, Prague 140 00, Czech Republic.

TAPPLY William G(eorge), b. 16 July 1940, Waltham, Massachusetts, USA. Writer. m. Cynthia Ehrgott, 7 Mar 1970, 1 son, 2 daughters. Education: BA, Amherst College, 1962; MAT, Harvard University, 1963; Tufts University, 1965-67. Appointments: High School History Teacher, Lexington, Massachusetts, 1963-65; Director of Economic Education, Tufts University, 1967-68; Housemaster and Teacher, Lexington High School, 1969-90; Editorial Associate, Writer's Digest School, 1992-. Publications: Fiction: Death at Charity's Point, 1984; The Dutch Blue Error, 1985; Follow the Sharks, 1985; The Marine Corpse, 1986; Dead Meat, 1987; The Vulgar Boatman, 1987; A Void in Hearts, 1988; Dead Winter, 1989; Client Privilege, 1989; The Spotted Cats, 1991; Tight Lines, 1992; The Snake Eater, 1993; The Seventh Enemy, 1995. Non-Fiction: Those Hours Spent Outdoors, 1988; Opening Day and Other Neuroses, 1990; Home Water Near and Far, 1992; Sportsman's Legacy, 1993; The Elements of Mystery Fiction, 1995. Contributions to: Magazines. Honour: Scribner Crime Novel Award, 1984. Memberships: Authors Guild; Mystery Writers of America; Private Eye Writers of America. Address: 47 Ann Lee Road, Harvard, MA 01451, USA.

TARN Nathaniel, b. 30 June 1928, Paris, France. Professor Emeritus; Poet; Writer. m. (1), div, 2 children, (2) Janet Rodney, 1981. Education: BA, 1948, MA, 1952, Cambridge University; MA, 1952, PhD, 1957, University of Chicago. Appointments: Visiting Professor, State University of New York at Buffalo, 1969-70, Princeton University 1969-70, University of Pennsylvania, 1976, Jilin University, China, 1982; Professor of Comparative Literature, 1970-85, Professor Emeritus, 1985-, Rutgers University. Publications: Poetry: Old Savage/Young City, 1964; Penguin Modern Poets 7 (with Richard Murphy and Jon Silkin), 1966; Where Babylon Ends, 1968; The Beautiful Contradictions, 1969; October: A Sequence of Ten Poems

Followed by Requiem Pro Duabus Filiis Israel, 1969; The Silence, 1970; A Nowhere for Vallejo: Choices, October, 1971; Lyrics for the Bride of God, 1975; Narrative of This Fall, 1975; The House of Leaves, 1976; From Alaska: The Ground of Our Great Admiration of Nature, 1977; The Microsm, 1977; Birdscapes, with Seaside, 1978; The Forest (with Janet Rodney), 1979; The Land Songs, 1981; Weekends in Mexico, 1982; The Desert Mothers, 1984; At the Western Gates, 1985; Palenque: Selected Poems 1972-1984, 1986; Seeing America First, 1989; The Mothers of Matagalpa, 1989; Flying the Body, 1993. Non-fiction: Views from the Weaving Mountain: Selected Essays in Poetics & Anthropology, 1991. Honours: Guinnes Prize, 1963; Wenner Gren Fellowships, 1978, 1980; Commonwealth of Pennsylvania Fellowship, 1984; Rockefeller Foundation Fellowship, 1988. Address: PO Box 8187, Santa Fe, NM 87504, USA.

TARNAS Richard Theodore, b. 21 Feb 1950, Geneva, Switzerland. Writer; Lecturer; Educator. m. Heather Malcolm, 28 May 1982, 1 son, 1 daughter. Education: AB, Harvard University, 1972; PhD, Saybrook Institute, 1976. Publication: The Passion of the Western Mind, 1991. Literary Agent: Frederick Hill Associates. Address: California Institute of Integral Studies, 9 Peter Yorke Way, San Francisco, CA 94109, USA.

TARRANT John. See: **EGLETON Clive Frederick William.**

TART Indrek, (Julius Ürt), b. 2 May 1946, Tallinn, Estonia. Physicist; Poet; Literary Critic. m. Aili Arelaid Tart, 7 Feb 1980, 1 son, 1 daughter. Education: Tallinn 4th Secondary School; Tartu University. Appointments: Institute of Cybernetics, 1969-80; Institute of Chemical Physics and Biophysics, Estonian Academy of Sciences, 1980-92; Tallinn Pedagogical University, 1992-; Director of Information, Estonian National Commission for UNESCO, 1992-93. Publications: Haljendav Ruumala, 1981; Väike Luuletaja ja Teised, 1993; Various translations. Contributions to: Anthologies and other publications. Honour: Honorary Fellow, Writing, University of Iowa. Membership: Estonian Writers Union. Address: Kurni 17-1, Tallinn, EE0016, Estonia.

TARUSKIN Richard, b. 2 Apr 1945, New York, New York, USA. Professor; Musicologist; Critic; Author. Education: PhD, Columbia University, 1975. Appointments: Assistant Professor, 1975-81, Associate Professor of Music, 1981-87, Columbia University; Visiting Professor, University of Pennsylvania, 1985; Associate Professor, 1986-89, Professor, 1989-, University of California at Berkeley; Hanes-Willis Visiting Professor, University of North Carolina at Chapel Hill, 1987. Publications: Opera and Drama in Russia, 1981, new edition, 1994; Busnoi: The Latin-Texted Works (editor with commentary), 2 volumes, 1990; Musorgsky: Eight Essays and an Epilogue, 1993; Stravinsky and the Russian Traditions: A Biography of the Works Through Mavra, 2 volumes, 1995; Text and Act: Essays on Music and Performance, 1995. Contributions to: The New Grove Dictionary of Opera, 1992; Many articles and reviews in professional journals and general periodicals. Honours: Fulbright-Hays Traveling Fellowship, 1971-72; Guggenheim Fellowship, 1987; Dent Medal, England, 1987; ASCAP-Deems Taylor Award, 1989. Membership: American Musicological Society. Address: c/o Department of Music, University of California at Berkeley, Berkeley, CA 94720, USA.

TATE James (Vincent), b. 8 Dec 1943, Kansas City, Missouri, USA. Poet; Professor. Education: University of Missouri, 1963-64; BA, Kansas State University, 1965; MFA, University of Iowa, 1967. Appointments: Instructor in Creative Writing, University of Iowa, 1966-67; Visiting Lecturer, University of California, Berkeley, 1967-68; Poetry Editor, Dickinson Review, 1967-76; Trustee and Associate Editor, Pym-Randall Press, 1968-80; Assistant Professor of English, Columbia University, 1969-71; Associate Professor, then Professor of English, 1971-, University of Massachusetts, Amherst; Poet-in-Residence, Emerson College, 1970-71; Associate Editor, Barn Dream Press. Publications: Poetry: Cages, 1966; The Destination, 1967; The Lost Pilot, 1967; Notes of Woe: Poems, 1968; Camping in the Valley, 1968; The Torches, 1968, revised edition, 1971; Row with Your Hair, 1969; Is There Anything?, 1969; Shepherds of the Mist, 1969; Amnesia People, 1970; Are You Ready Mary Baker Eddy? (with Bill Knot), 1970; Deaf Girl Playing, 1970; The Oblivion Ha-Ha, 1970; Wrong Songs, 1970; Hints to Pilgrims, 1971, 2nd edition, 1982; Absences, 1972; Apology for Eating Geoffrey Movius' Hyacinth, 1972; Hottentot Ossuary, 1974; Viper Jazz, 1976; Riven Doggeries, 1979; Land of Little Sticks, 1981; Constant Defender, 1983; Reckoner, 1986; Distance from Loved Ones, 1990; Selected Poems, 1991; Worshipful Company of Fletchers, 1993. Novel: Lucky Darryl, 1977. Contributions to: Numerous books and periodicals. Honours: Yale Younger Poets Award, 1966; Poet of the Year, Phi Beta Kappa, 1972; National Institute of Arts and Letters Award, 1974; Massachusetts Arts and Humanities Fellow, 1975; Guggenheim Fellowship, 1976; National Endowment for the Arts Fellowship, 1980; Pulitzer Prize in Poetry, 1992; National Book Award for Poetry, 1994. Membership: Bollingen Prize Committee, 1974-75. Address: Department of English, University of Massachusetts, Amherst, MA 01003, USA.

TATEMATSU Wahei, b. 15 Dec 1947, Utsunomiya, Tochigi, Japan. Author. 1 son, 1 daughter. Education: Graduate in Economics, Waseda University, 1971. Publications: Distant Thunder, 1980; Market of Delight, 1981; Sexual Apolcalypse, 1985; Poison, 1997; Valley of Grace, 1997. Honours: Waseda University New Writer Award, for Bicycle, 1970; Second Noma Arts New Writer Award, for Distant Thunder, 1980; Afro-Asian Writers Association 1985 Lotus Award for Young Writers, 1986; Eighth Tsubota Joji Literary Award, for Washing Eggs, 1993. Memberships: Japan Writers Association; Japan Pen Club. Literary Agent: Woodbell Co Ltd. Address: 3-23-10 Ebisu, Shibuya-ku, Tokyo, Japan.

TAUCHID Mohamad, b. 16 Jan 1934, Kediri, Java, Indonesia. Geologist; Geochemist; Writer; Independent Consultant. m. Gisèle Emard, 26 Sept 1964, 3 daughters. Education: Candidate, Geology, Bandung Institute of Technology, Indonesia, 1955-59; BSc Honours, Geology, St Francis Xavier University, Antigonish, 1959-61; MSc, Geochemistry, Ottawa University, Ontario, 1961-65; Completed PhD programme, Economic Geology, Geochemistry, Carleton University, Ottawa, Ontario, 1965-68. Appointments: Project Manager of UNDP funded International Atomic Energy Agency project in Colombia, 1978-80; Senior Officer, Vienna based International Atomic Energy Agency, 1980-94, retired; Independent Consultant, 1994-. Contributions to: Uranium Deposits in Asia and the Pacific: Geology and Exploration, 1988; Global geochemical database, UNESCO Earth Sciences, 1995; International Atomic Energy Agency atlas, 1995; Many contributions to publications as editor and/or contributor. Honour: Distinguished Service Award, International Atomic Energy Agency, 1985. Memberships: Fellow, Society of Economic Geology; Fellow, Geological Association of Canada; Association of Exploration Geochemist; Canadian Institute of Mining, Metallurgy and Petroleum; Propsectors and Developers Association of Canada. Hobbies: Cycling; Badminton; Skiing; Travel. Address: 44 Thare Crescent, Nepean, Ontario K2J 2P4, Canada.

TAVIRA Luis de, b. 1 Sept 1948, Mexico. Dramatist; Poet; Theatre Director. 3 sons. Education: Licentiate, Literature and Dramatic Arts, Univeridad Nacional Autónoma de México, 1972; Master of Philosophy, Instituto Libre de Filosofía, Mexico, 1976. Appointments: Director, Centro Universitario de Teatro, Universidad Nacional Autónoma de México, 1978-82, Centro de Experimentación Teatral, INBA, Mexico, 1985-90, Caso del Teatro, AC, Mexico, 1990-. Publications: 7 plays, 1982-91; 3 poetry books, 1972, 1978, 1992. Contributions to: Journals. Honours: Best play and best director awards. Address: Offico 59, Prados de Coyoacan, Mexico DF 04810, Mexico.

TAYLOR Andrew (John Robert), b. 14 Oct 1951, Stevenage, England. Writer. m. Caroline Jane Silverwood, 8 Sept 1979, 1 son, 1 daughter. Education: BA, 1973, MA, 1976, Emmanuel College, Cambridge; MA, University of London, 1979. Publications: Waiting for the End of the World, 1984; Our Father's Lies, 1985; Freelance Death, 1987; The Second Midnight, 1987; Blacklist, 1988; Toyshop, 1990; Double Exposure, 1990; Blood Relation, 1993; Odd Man Out, 1993; The Invader, 1994; An Air That Kills, 1994; The Mortal Sickness, 1995; The Four Last Things, 1997; The Lover of the Grave, 1997. Honour: John Creasey Award, 1982. Memberships: Crime Writers Association, Committee Member, 1996-; Society of Authors; Detection Club. Address: c/o Richard Scott Simon Ltd, 43 Doughty Street, London WC1N 2LF, England.

TAYLOR Andrew MacDonald, b. 19 Mar 1940, Warnambool, Victoria, Australia. Professor; Poet; Writer. m. Beate Josephi, 1981, 1 son, 1 daughter. Education: BA, 1961, MA, 1970, University of Melbourne. Appointments: Lockie Fellow, University of Melbourne, 1965-68; Lecturer, 1971-74, Senior Lecturer, 1974-91, Associate Professor, 1992, University of Adelaide; Professor, Edith Cowan University, 1992-. Publications: Reading Australian Poetry, 1987; Selected Poems, 1960-85, 1988; Folds in the Map, 1991; Sandstone, 1995. Contributions to: Newspapers, journals, and magazines.

Honours: Several prizes and awards; Member of the Order of Australia. Memberships: Association for the Study of Australian Literature; Australian Society of Authors; PEN. Address: c/o Department of English, Edith Cowan University, Mount Lawley, Western Australia 6050, Australia.

TAYLOR Beverly White, b. 30 Mar 1947, Grenada, Mississippi, USA. Professor of English; Writer. Education: BAE, University of Mississippi, 1969; MA, 1970, PhD, 1977, Duke University. Appointments: Assistant Professor, 1977-84, Associate Professor 1984-92, Professor of English, 1992-, University of North Carolina at Chapel Hill. Publications: The Return of King Arthur, 1983; Arthurian Legend and Literature, 1984; Francis Thompson, 1987; The Cast of Consciousness, 1987; Gender and Discourse in Victorian Literature and Art, 1992. Contributions to: Periodicals and Encyclopaedias on 19th century and Arthurian literature. Memberships: Victorians Institute, president, 1989-90; Tennyson Society; Browning Institute; Modern Language Association; International Arthurian Society. Address: Department of English, University of North Carolina, Chapel Hill, NC 27599, USA.

TAYLOR H Baldwin. See: WAUGH Hillary Baldwin.

TAYLOR John Laverck, b. 25 May 1937, Yorkshire, England. Educator; Writer. m. Jennifer Margaret Green, 21 Sept 1981, 1 son, 2 daughters. Education: DipArch, University of Leeds, 1960; MSc, Urban Design, Columbia University, 1963; PhD, University of Sheffield, 1969. Appointments: College Principal; Bramley Professor; Various visiting professorships. Publications: Planning for Urban Growth, 1972; Simulation in the Classroom, 1974; Learning and the Simulation Game, 1978; Guide on Simulation and Gaming for Environmental Education, 1984; Feedback on Instructional Simulation Systems, 1992. Contributions to: Professional journals. Honours: Fulbright Fellow, 1962-64; Salzburg Fellow, 1965-66; Nuffield School Science Fellow, 1968-74; Officer of the Order of the British Empire, 1990. Memberships: Several professional organisations. Address: Tapton Hall Barn, Balmoak Lane, Chesterfield, Derbyshire, S41 OTH, England.

TAYLOR John Russell, b. 1935, England. Critic; Writer. Appointments: Professor of the Cinema Division, University of Southern California at Los Angles, 1972-78; Art Critic, The Times, 1978-. Publications: Anger and After: A Guide to the New British Drama, 1962; Anatomy of a Television Play, 1962; Cinema Eye, Cinema Ear: Some Key Film Makers of the 1960s, 1964; Penguin Dictionary of the Theatre, 1966; The Art Nouveau Book in Britian, 1966; Art in London: A Guide, 1966; The Rise and Fall of the Well-Made Play, 1967; Look Back in Anger: A Casebook, 1968; The Art Dealers, 1969; Harold Pinter, 1969; The Hollywood Musical, 1971; The Second Wave: British Dramatists for the Seventies, 1971; David Storey, 1974; Fifty Superstars, 1974; Peter Shaffer, 1975; Directors and Directions: Cinema for the Seventies, 1978; Hitch: The Life and Times of Alfred Hitchcock, 1978; Impressionism, 1981; Strangers in Paradise: The Hollywood Emigres 1933-50, 1982; Ingrid Bergman, 1983; Alec Guiness: A Celebration, 1984; Vivien Leigh, 1984; Hollywood 1940s, 1985; Portraits of the British Cinema, 1985; Orson Welles, 1986; Edward Wolfe, 1986; Great Movie Moments, 1987; Impressionist Dreams, 1990; Bernard Meninsky, 1990; Liz Taylor, 1991; Ricardo Cinalli, 1992; Heart on Her Sleeve, 1993; Monet: Artist in Context, 1995. Address: c/o The Times (reviews), Pennington Street, London E1 9XN, England.

TAYLOR John Vernon, b. 11 Sept 1914, Cambridge, England. Retired Bishop; Writer. m. Peggy Wright, 5 Oct 1940, Oxford, 1 son, 2 daughters. Education: MA, Trinity College, Cambridge University; MA, St Catherine's College, Oxford University; D Ed, London University Institute of Education. Publications: Christianity and Politics in Africa, 1955; The Growth of the Church in Buganda, 1958; The Primal Vision, 1963; The Go Between Goti, 1972; Enough is Enough, 1975; Weep Not For Me, 1986; A Matter of Life and Death, 1986; A Christmas Sequence and Other Poems, 1989; Kingdom Come, 1989; The Christlike God, 1992. Honours: Honorary Doctor of Divinity, 1962; Collins Religious Book Prize, 1974; Honorary Fellow, New College and Magdalen College, Oxford, 1986, Trinity College, Cambridge, 1987; Honorary Doctor of Literature, 1991. Address: 65 Aston Street, Oxford OX4 1EW, England.

TAYLOR John W(illiam) R(ansom), b. 8 June 1922, Ely, England. Editor; Writer. m. Doris Alice Haddrick, 1946, 1 son, 1 daughter. Appointments: Correspondent, Contributing Editor, Editor, various journals; Editor-in-Chief, Janes All the World's Aircraft, 1959-89 Editor Emeritus and Section Compiler, 1989-... Publications: Spitfire, 1946; Civil Aircraft Markings, 1950-78; Military Aircraft Recognition, 1953-79; Science in the Atomic Age, 1956; Pictorial History of the Royal Air Force, 1968-70, 1980; Civil Aircraft of the World, 1970-79; The History of Aviation, 1973, new edition, 1978; Helicopters of the World, 1976-79; Aircraft, Strategy and Operations of the Soviet Air Force, 1986; CFS: Birthplace of Air Power, 1987; Soviet Wings, 1991; Fairey Aviation, 1997. Honours: Officer of the Order of the British Empire; Honorary Doctorate; Order of Merit, WAEO, 1981; Freeman of the City of London, 1987; Lauren D Lyman Award, 1990. Memberships: Royal Aeronautical Society, fellow; Royal Historical Society, fellow. Address: 36 Alexandra Drive, Surbiton, Surrey KT5 9AF, England.

TAYLOR Judy, (Julia Marie Hough), b. 12 Aug 1932, Minton, Swansea, Wales. Writer. m. Richard Hough, 1980. Appointments: Bodley Head Publishers, 1951-; Director, Bodley Head Ltd, 1967-84, Chatto, Bodley Head and Jonathan Cape Ltd, 1973-80, Chatto, Bodley Head & Jonathan Cape Australia Pty Ltd, 1977-80; Consultant to Penguin, Beatrix Potter, 1981-87. Publications: Sophie and Jack, 1982; My First Year: A Beatrix Potter Baby Book, 1982; Sophie and Jack in the Snow, 1984; Dudley and the Monster, 1986; Dudley Goes Flying, 1986; Dudley in a Jam, 1986; Dudley and the Strawberry Shake, 1986; That Naughty Rabbit Beatrix Potter and Peter Rabbit, 1987; Beatrix Potter 1866-1943, 1989; Beatrix Potter's Letters: A Selection, 1989; So I Shall Tell You a Story, 1993. Contributions to: Numerous professional journals. Honour: Member of the Order of the British Empire, 1971. Memberships: Publishers Association Council; Book Development Association; UNICEF International Art Committee; UK UNICEF Greetings Card Committee; Beatrix Potter Society; Royal Society of Authors, fellow. Address: 31 Meadowbank, Primrose Hill Road, London NW3 1AY, England.

TAYLOR Laurie Aylma, b. 3 Sept 1939, Tappan, New York, USA. Writer. m. Allen Sparer, 17 July 1971, 2 daughters. Education: BA, Ohio Wesleyan University, 1960. Publications: Footnote to Murder; Only Half a Hoax; Deadly Objectives; Shed Light on Death; The Blossom of Erda; Changing the Past; Love of Money; Poetic Justice; A Murder Waiting to Happen; Cats Paw. Contributions to: Anthologies. Honours: Minnesota Voices Project; Lois Phillips Hudson Prize. Memberships: Poets and Writers; Mystery Writers of America; Science Fiction and Fantasy Writers of America. Literary Agent: Frances Collin. Address: 4000 York Avenue South, Minneapolis, MN 55410, USA.

TAYLOR Peter Mark, (Mark Peters), b. 5 Dec 1936, Huddersfield,England. Author. m. Rosemary Hughes Grey, 21 July 1958, 1 son. Education: Huddersfield College. Appointments: Managing Director, Arrow Books, 1966-70; Managing Director, Hutchinson, Australia, 1970-74, Methuen, Australia, 1974-76. Publications: More than 20 books, including: An End to Silence: The Building of the Overland Telegraph Line, 1980; Australia: The First Twelve Years, 1982; Pastoral Properties of Australia, 1984; An Australian Country Life, 1986; Station Life in Australia, 1988; An Atlas of Australian History, 1990. Contributions to: Sydney Morning Herald; The Australian; This Australia. Membership: Union Club, Sydney. Address: 36 Sundance Way, Runaway Bay, Queensland 4216, Australia.

TAYLOR Renée (Gertrude). See: RENÉE.

TAYLOR Theodore Langhans, b. 23 June 1921, Statesville, North Carolina, USA. Writer. m. (1) Gwen Goodwin, 25 Oct 1946, 2 sons, 1 daughter, (2) Flora Gray, 18 Apr 1982. Publications: The Magnificent Mitscher, 1954; Fire on the Beaches, 1957; The Cay, 1968; The Children's War, 1971; The Maldonado Miracle, 1973; Teetoncey, 1974; Jule, 1979; The Trouble with Tuck, 1981; Battle of the Midway Island, 1982; HMS Hood vs Bismarck, 1983; Battle in the English Channel, 1984; Sweet Friday Island, 1984; The Cats of Shambala, 1985; Walking Up a Rainbow, 1986; The Stalker, 1987; The Hostage, 1988; Sniper, Monocolo, 1989; Tuck Triumphant, 1990; The Weirdo, 1991; Maria, 1992; To Kill a Leopard, 1993; Timothy of the Clay, 1993; The Bomb, 1996; Rogue Wave, 1996. Contributions to: Saturday Evening Post; McCall's; Ladies Home Journal; Saturday Review of Literature; Argosy. Honours: Lewis Carroll Shelf Award; Jane Addams Peace and Freedom Foundation Award; Western Writers of America Award; George G Stone Center Award; Edgar Allan Poe Award; International Association of School Librarians Award; Best

Books, American Library Association, 1993, 1995; Scott O'Dell Historical Novel. Literary Agent: Gloria Loomis, Watkins-Loomis, New York City, USA. Address: 1856 Catalina Street, Laguna Beach, CA 92651, USA.

TCHRSINA Ludmila Andreevna, b. 2 Jan 1946, Ukraine. Engineer; Chemist Technologist. m. Khraplivy Anatoly Petrovich, 6 July 1968, 2 daughters. Education: Odessa Technological Institute, 1968; Candidate Degree, 1974; Associate Professor, 1979; Doctors Degree, 1990; Professor, 1991. Publications: On Nature of Thermodynamic Agent of Vat Dye Leuco Compounds to the Viscose Fibre, 1974; The Process of Cotton Yarn Dying with Vat Dyes, 1988; Chemical Composition and Dying Properties of Vat Dyes, 1989; Resource Savings of Dying Yarn in Packs, 1993; Resource Savings in the Branch of Primary Processing of Bast Fibres, 1995. Address: Zala Egerseg Street 5, Floor 29, Kherson 325005, Ukraine.

TEALE Ruth. See: FRAPPELL Ruth Meredith.

TEBBEL John, b. 16 Nov 1912, Boynce City, USA. Writer; Retired Professor. m. 29 Apr 1939, 1 daughter. Education: BA, 1935, Central Michigan University; MS, Columbia University. Publications: The Life and Good Times of William Randolph Hearst, 1952; George Horace Lorimer and the Saturday Evening Post, 1952; History of Book Publishing in the United States, Vol I, 1972, Vol IV, 1981; The Media in America, 1974; The Press and the Presidency, 1985; Between Covers, 1987; The Magazine in America, 1991; Turning the World Upside Down, 1993; Over 40 others. Contributions to: Over 500 articles in national magazines and professional journals. Honours: Graduate, School of Journalism, Columbia University, 50th Anniversary Awards, 1963; Alumni Award, 1975; Publishing Hall of Fame, 1985. Memberships: Society of Professional Journalists; Authors Guild. Literary Agent: William B Goodman. Address: 4033 The Forest at Duke, 2701 Pickett Road, Durham, NC 27705, USA.

TELFER Barbara Jane, b. 13 Aug 1945, Wellington, New Zealand. Author. m. Maxwell Bryant Telfer, 14 Mar 1970, 2 daughters. Education: New Zealand School Dental Nurse Certificate, 1965. Publications: The Great New Zealand Puzzle Book, 1987; The Great International Puzzle Book, 1988; The Great Crafty Ideas Book, 1988; A Book of Australian Puzzles, 1988; The Great Number Puzzle Book, 1990; Summertime Puzzles, 1992; Astro Puzzles, 1992; World of Puzzles, 1992; Mystery Word Puzzles, 1993; The Windsor Street Mystery, 1993; The Great Christmas Activity Book, 1993; The Great Junior Puzzle Book, 1994; The Second Great Number Puzzle Book, 1994; The Zoo Mystery, 1994; The Greenhouse Mystery, 1994; Barbara Telfer's Paper Fun, 1995. Contributions to: Magazines. Address: 9 Regent Street, Rotorua, New Zealand.

TELFER Tracie. See: CHAPLIN Jenny.

TEMKO Allan Bernard, b. 4 Feb 1926, New York, New York, USA. Professor (retired); Architecture Critic; Writer. m. Elizabeth Ostroff, 1 July 1950, 1 son, 1 daughter. Education: AB, Columbia University, 1947; Postgraduate Studies, Sorbonne, University of Paris, 1948-49, 1951-52, University of California at Berkeley, 1949-51. Appointments: Lecturer, Sorbonne, University of Paris, 1953-54, École des Arts et Metiers, Paris, 1954-55; Assistant Professor of Journalism, 1956-62, Lecturer in City Planning and Social Sciences, 1966-70, Lecturer, Graduate School of Journalism, 1991, University of California at Berkeley; West Coast Editor, Architectural Forum, 1959-62; Architecture Critic, 1961-93, Art Editor, 1979-82, San Francisco Chronicle; Professor of Art, California State University at Hayward, 1971-80; Lecturer in Art, Stanford University, 1981, 1982. Publications: Notre Dame of Paris, 1955; Eero Saarinen, 1962; No Way to Build a Ballpark and Other Irreverent Essays on Architecture, 1993. Contributions to: Newspapers and magazines. Honours: Guggenheim Fellowship, 1956-57; Gold Medal, 1956, Silver Medal, 1994, Commonwealth Club of California; Rockefeller Foundation Grant, 1962-63; Manufacturers Hanover/Art World 1st Prize in Architectural Criticism, 1986, and Critics' Award, 1987; National Endowment for the Arts Fellowship, 1988; Professional Achievement Award, Society of Professional Journalists, 1988; Pulitzer Prize for Criticism, 1990. Address: 1015 Fresno Avenue, Berkeley, CA 94707, USA.

TEMPLE Ann. See: MORTIMER Penelope (Ruth).

TEMPLE Dan. See: NEWTON D(wight) B(ennett).

TEMPLE Nigel Hal Longdale, b. 21 Jan 1926, Lowestoft, Suffolk, England. Painter; Architectural and Garden Historian; Photographer; Lecturer. m. Judith Tattersill, 1 son, 1 daughter. Education: National Diploma in Design, 1951; Art Teacher's Diploma, Sheffield, 1953; MLitt, Architecture, University of Bristol, 1978; PhD, University of Keele, 1985. Publications: Farnham Inheritance, 1956, 2nd edition, 1965; Farnham Buildings and People, 1963, 2nd edition, 1973; Looking at Things, 1968; Seen and Not Heard, 1970; John Nash and the Village Picturesque, 1979; Blaise Hamlet, 1986; George Repton's Pavilion Notebook: A Catalogue Raisonné, 1993. Contributions to: Country Life; Journal of Garden History; Architectural Review; Garden History; Georgian Group Journal. Honours: Fellow, National Society for Art Education, 1964; Companion, Guild of St George. Memberships: Royal West of England Academy; Council Member, Garden History Society. Address: 4 Wendover Gardens, Christchurch Road, Cheltenham, Gloucestershire GL50 2PA, England.

TEMPLE Norman Joseph, b. 28 Apr 1947, London, England. University Professor. m. Frances Farquhar, 3 Aug 1971, div, 1 son. Education: PhD Biochemistry, Wolverhampton University, 1980. Publications: Western Diseases: Their Dietary Prevention and Reversibility (with D Burkitt), 1994; Diet for the New Century (with H Diehl and A Ludington), 1996. Contributions to: 36 papers in peer-reviewed journals. Address: Athabasca University, Athabasca, Alberta T9S 1A1, Canada.

TEMPLE Paul. See: **DURBRIDGE Francis Henry**.

TEMPLE (Robert) Philip, b. 20 Mar 1939, Yorkshire, England. Author. m. Daphne Evelyn Keen, 12 June 1965, div., 1 son, 1 daughter. Appointments: Editor, New Zealand Alpine Journal, 1968-70, 1973; Associate Editor, Landfall, 1972-75; Katherine Mansfield Memorial Fellowship, Menton, France, 1979; Robert Burns Fellowship, University of Otago, Dunedin, New Zealand, 1980; Berliner Kunstlerprogramm Fellowship, West Berlin, 1987. Publications: The World at Their Feet, 1969; Ways to the Wilderness, 1977; Beak of the Moon, 1981; Sam, 1984; New Zealand Explorers, 1985; Kakapo, 1988; Making Your Vote Count, 1992; Dark of the Moon, 1993; Temple's Guide to the New Zealand Parliament, 1994; Kotuku, 1994; The Book of the Kea, 1996. Honours: Arts Council Non-Fiction Bursary, 1994; AIM Honour Award, 1995 New Zealand Library Research Fellowship, 1996. Memberships: PEN, New Zealand Centre, 1970-; PEN Representative, New Zealand Authors Advisory Committee, 1986-88, 1993-; New Zealand Alpine Club, 1960-86. Literary Agent: John Johnson Ltd, London, England. Address: 147a Tomahawk Road, Dunedin, New Zealand.

TEMPLE Wayne C(alhoun), b. 5 Feb 1924, Richwood, Ohio, USA. Historian; Archivist; Author. m. Sunderline (Wilson) Mohn, 9 Apr 1979, 2 stepsons. Education: AB cum laude, Senior Class Honours and Honours in History, 1949, AM, 1951, PhD, 1956, University of Illinois, Champaign-Urbana. Appointments: Editor-in-Chief, 1958-73, Editorial Board, 1973-, Lincoln Herald; Board of Advertisers, The Lincoln Forum. Publications: Indian Villages of the Illinois Country, 1958-; Campaigning with Grant, 1961; Stephen A Douglas: Freemason, 1982; The Building of Lincoln's Home and its Saga, 1984; Lincoln's Connections with the Illinois and Michigan Canal, 1986; Illinois' Fifth Capitol (with Sunderine Temple), 1988; Abraham Lincoln: From Skeptic to Prophet, 1995. Contributions to: Numerous journals including many to the Lincoln Herald. Honours: Gold Honor Key, Sigma Tau Delta; Lincoln Diploma of Honor; Lincoln Medallion from the National Sesquicentennial Commission; Sigma Tau Delta (English honorary). Membership: Abraham Lincoln Association. Address: 1121 South 4th Street Court, Springfield, Illinois 62703, USA.

TEMPLETON Fiona, b. 23 Dec 1951, Scotland. Theatre Director; Poet; Writer. Education: MA, University of Edinburgh, 1973; MA, New York University, 1985; Publications: Elements of Performance Art, 1976; London, 1984; You The City, 1990; Delirium of Interpretations, 1997; Cells of Release, 1997; Hi Cowboy, 1997. Contributions to: Anthologies and journals. Honours: Grants, fellowships and awards. Memberships: New Dramatists; Poets and Writers. Address: 100 St Mark's Place, No 7, New York, NY 10009, USA.

TENNANT Emma Christina, (Catherine Aydy), b. 20 Oct 1937, London, England. Author. 1 son, 2 daughters. Publications: The Colour of Rain, 1963; The Crack, 1973; The Last of the Country House Murders, 1975; Hotel De Dream, 1976; The Bad Sister, 1978; Wild Nights, 1979; Woman Beware Woman, 1983; Black Marina, 1984; The

Adventures of Robina, 1986; The House of Hospitalities, 1987; A Wedding of Cousins, 1988; The Bad Sister, 1989; Sisters and Strangers, 1990; Faustine, 1991; The ABC of Writing, 1992; Tess, 1993; Pemberley, 1993; An Unequal Marriage, 1994; Elinor-Marianne, 1996. Contributions to: London Review of Books; London Quarterly. Honour: Honorary degree in Literature, Aberdeen University Membership: Fellow, Royal Society of Literature. Address: c/o Curtis Brown and Associates, Haymarket House, 28/29 Haymarket, London SW1Y 4SP, England.

TERKEL Studs, (Louis Terkel), b. 16 May 1912, New York, New York, USA. Author; Broadcaster. m. Ida Goldberg, 2 July 1939, 1 son. Education: PhB, 1932, JD, 1934, University of Chicago. Appointments: Actor in stage productions; Host, Studs Terkel Almanac radio interview programme, Chicago, 1952-. Publications: Giants of Jazz, 1957, revised edition, 1975; Division Street: America, 1967, 2nd edition, 1993; Hard Times: An Oral History of the Great Depression, 1970; Working: People Talk About What They Do All Day and How They Feel About What They Do, 1974; Talking to Myself: A Memoir of My Times, 1977; American Dreams: Lost and Found, 1980; "The Good War": An Oral History of World War II, 1984; Envelopes of Oral Sound: The Art of Oral Recording (with others), 1985, 2nd edition, 1990; The Neon Wilderness (with Nelson Algren), 1986; Chicago, 1986; The Great Divide: Second Thoughts on the American Dream, 1988; RACE: How Blacks and Whites Think and Feel About the American Obesession, 1992; Coming of Age, 1995. Contributions to: Newspapers and magazines. Honours: Ohio State University Award, 1959; UNESCO Prix Italia Award, 1962; University of Chicago Alumni Association Communicator of the Year Award, 1969; George Foster Peabody Award, 1980; Society of Midland Authors Awards, 1982, 1983; Eugene V Debs Award, 1983; Pulitzer Prize in Non-Fiction, 1985; Hugh M Hefner First Amendment Award for Lifetime Achievement, 1990. Address: 850 West Castlewood Terrace, Chicago, IL 60640, USA.

TERLECKI Tymon Tadeusz Julian, b. 10 Aug 1905, Przemysl, Poland. Writer; Professor Emeritus. m. (1) Antonia Kopczynskam 1946, dec 1983, (2) Nina Taylor, 1987. Education: PhD, King John Casimir University, 1932. Appointments: Senior Lecturer, 1952-68, Professor of Polish Literature, 1968-81, Polish University Abroad; Visiting Professor, 1964-65, Professor of Polish Literature and Theatre, 1965-72, Senior Visiting Professor, 1972-77, University of Chicago. Publications: Rodowód poetycki Ryszarda Berwinskiego, 1937; Krytyka Personalistyczna, 1957; Egzystencjalizm chrzescijanski, 1958; Pani Helena, 1962; Stanislaw Wyspianski, 1983; Rzeczy teatralne, 1984; Szukanie Rownowagi, 1985; Londyn-Paryz, 1987. Contributions to: Kultura, Paris; Wiadomósci; Many Polish periodicals. Honours: Theatrical Book of the Year, 1985; Stanislaw Vincenz Prize, 1985; Radziszewski Prize, Catholic University of Lublin, 1990; Honorary Doctorate, University of Wroclaw, 1990. Memberships: Polish History-Literary Society of Paris, 1950; Co-Founder, Union of Polish Writers Abroad, Chairman, 1955-59, 1965-66; Co-Founder, Association of Polish Writers; Polish Society of Arts and Sciences Abroad, 1952-; Polish Institute of Arts and Sciences of America. Address: 325 Woodstock Road, Oxford OX2 7NX, England.

TERLECKI Wladyslaw Lech, b. 18 May 1933, Czestochowa, Poland. Writer. m. Lucyna Basaj, 1955, 1 son, 1 daughter. Education: University of Wroclaw. Appointments: Staff: Wspolczesnosc, 1958-65; Drama Section, Polish Radio, 1965-70. Publications: Cobble Stones, 1956; Fire, 1962; The Conspiracy, 1966; High Season, 1966; The Wormwood Star, 1968; Two Heads of a Bird, 1970; Pilgrims, 1972; Return from Tzarskoe Selo, 1973; Black Romance, 1974; Rest After the Race, 1975; Tea with the Man Who is Not Here, 1976; The Forest Grows, 1977; Cien Karla, Cien Olbrzyma, 1983; Lament, 1983; Pismak, 1984; Zwierzeta Zostaly Oplacone, 1987; Kill the Tzar, 1992; Numerous film scripts and theatre plays. Honours: Koscielski Prize, Switzerland, 1973; ODRA Award, 1978; Literatura Award, 1981; Drama Award, Teatr Polski, 1987. Memberships: PEN; Polish Film-Makers Union; Association of Polish Writers. Address: ul Mazurska 1, 05-806 Komorow, Poland.

TERRILL Ross, b. 24 Aug 1938, Melbourne, Victoria. Australia (US citizen, 1979). Writer. Education: Wesley College, 1956; BA, University of Melbourne, 1962; PhD, Harvard University, 1970. Appointments: Teaching Fellow, 1968-70, Lecturer, 1970-74, Research Associate, East Asian Studies, 1970-, Harvard University; Contributing Editor, Atlantic Monthly, 1970-84; Research Fellow, Asia Society, 1978-79. Publications: 800,000,000: The Real China, 1972; R H

Tawney and His Times, 1973; Flowers on the Iron Tree: Five Cities of China, 1975; The Future of China After Mao, 1978; Mao, 1980, 2nd edition, 1993; The White Boned Demon, 1984, 2nd edition, 1992; The Australians, 1987; China in Our Time, 1992. Contributions to: Newspapers and magazines. Honours: Frank Knox Memorial Fellowship, 1965; Sumner Prize, 1970; George Polk Memorial Award, 1972; National Magazine Award, 1972. Address: 200 Saint Botolph Street, Boston, MA 02115, USA.

TERRY William. See: **HARKNETT Terry.**

TESH Ruby Nifong, b. 5 Oct 1917, Winston-Salem, North Carolina, USA. Organ and Piano Teacher; Choir Director; Poet. m. Luther E Tesh, 27 Sept 1936, 2 sons. Education: Winston-Salem Public Schools. Publications: Fleeting Inspiration, 1988; Random Thoughts, 1992. Contributions to: Anthologies and periodicals. Honour: Honorary Charter Membership for Outstanding Achievement in Poetry, International Society of Poets. Address: 2409 Friedberg Church Road, Winston-Salem, NC 27127, USA.

TETSURO Miura, b. 1931, Aomori Prefecture, Japan. Writer.Education: Degree in French Literature, Waseda University, Tokyo, 1957. Appointments: Editor, Public Relations Company, Tokyo, 1960; Professional Writer, 1961-. Publications: Jûgo-sai no shuu-i; Shinobugawa (novel); Kenjû to jûgo no tanpen (collection of short stories); Shônen Sanka: Byakuya wo yuku; Jinenjo; Tanpen-shû Mosaic; Minomushi (novel). Honours: Second Shinchô Dôjin Zasshi Prize; Akutagawa Literary Prize; Nome Literary Prize, 1976; Grand Prize for Japanese Literature, 1983; Osaragi Jirô Award, 1985; Kawabata Yasunari Literary Awards, 1990, 1992; Itoh Sei Literary Award, 1991. Memberships: Japan Academy of Art; Board Member, Japan Writers Association. Address: c/o Japan Writers' Association, Bungei Shunjyu Building, 9th Floor, 3-23 Kioi-cho, Chiyoda-ku, Tokyo 102, Japan.

THALER M N. See: **KERNER Fred.**

THAMEZ Lorraine D, b. 26 Nov 1950, Pueblo, Colorado, USA. Writer; Poet. 2 sons, 1 daughter. Education: AA, Literature, 1997. Publications: Prairie Woman; Dangerous Games; Together Forever; One Heart - One Hand (poetry). Contributions to: Purgatoire Magazine (poetry editor); Permeable Press (editor). Memberships: PEN; Poets and Writers; Western Writers' Guild. Literary Agent: American Literary Agency. Address: 121 Chanlon Road, New Providence, NJ 07974, USA.

THAYER Geraldine. See: **DANIELS Dorothy.**

THELLE Notto Reidar, b. 19 Mar 1941, Hong Kong. Professor of Theology; Writer. m. Mona Irene Ramstad, 19 June 1965, 2 sons, 3 daughters. Education: Candidate of Theology, 1966, Degree in Practical Theology, 1966, DTheol, 1982, University of Oslo. Appointments: Missionary, Scandinavian East Asia Mission, Kyoto, Japan, 1969-85; Editor, Japanese Religions, 1974-85, Norsk Tidskrift for Misjon, 1988-96; Associate Director, National Christian Council Center for the Study of Japanese Religions, Kyoto, 1974-85; Professor of Theology, University of Oslo, 1986-. Publications: Buddhism and Christianity in Japan: From Conflict to Dialogue, 1854-1899, 1987; Hvem kan stoppe vinden?, 1991; Mennesket og mysteriet, 1992, revised edition, 1997; Ditt ansikt söker jeg, 1993. Contributions to: Religious and cultural journals. Address: Skinstadveien, 3370 Vikersund, Norway.

THELWELL Norman, b. 3 May 1923, Berkenhead, Cheshire, England. Artist; Writer; Cartoonist. m. 11 Apr 1949, 1 son, 1 daughter. Education: NDA, ADT, Liverpool College of Art, 1947-50. Appointment: Art Teacher, Wolverhampton College of Art, 1950-57. Publications: Angels on Horseback, 1957; Thelwell Country, 1959; A Place of Your Own, 1960; Thelwell in Orbit, 1961; A Leg at Each Corner, 1962; The Penguin Thelwell, 1963; Top Dog, 1964; Thelwell's Riding Academy, 1965; Drawing Ponies, 1966; Up the Garden Path, 1967; The Compleat Tangler, 1967; The Thelwell Book of Leisure, 1968; This Desirable Plot, 1970; The Effluent Society, 1971; Penelope, 1972; Three Sheets in the Wind, 1973; Belt Up, 1975; Thelwell Goes West, 1976; Thelwell's Brat Race, 1978; A Plank Bridge by a Pool, 1979; Thelwell's Gymkhana, 1980; Pony Calvalcade, 1981; A Mill Stone Round My Neck, 1982; Some Damn Fool's Signed the Rubens Again, 1983; Magnificat, 1984; Thelwell's Sporting Prints, 1985; Wrestling with a Pencil, 1986; Play It As It Lies, 1987; Penelope Rides Again, 1988;

The Cat's Pyjamas, 1992. Contributions to: Punch, 1952-77; Cartoonist for News Chronicle, 1956-60, Sunday Dispatch, 1960-62, Sunday Express, 1962-72; Numerous other journals and magazines. Literary Agent: Momentum Licensing Ltd, London, England. Address: Herons Mead, Timsbury, Romsey, Hampshire SO51 0NE, England.

THEROUX Paul Edward, b. 10 Apr 1941, Medford, Massachusetts, USA. Writer. m. (1) Anne Castle, 4 Dec 1967, div 1993, 2 sons, (2) Sheila Donnelly, 18 Nov 1995. Education: BA, University of Massachusetts. Appointments: Lecturer, University of Urbino, Italy, 1963, Soche Hill College, Malawi, 1963-65; Faculty, Department of English, Makerere University, Uganda, 1965-68, University of Singapore, 1968-71; Visiting Lecturer, University of Virginia, 1972-73. Publications: Fiction: Waldo, 1967; Fong and the Indians, 1968; Girls at Play, 1969; Murder in Mount Holly, 1969; Jungle Lovers, 1971; Sinning with Annie, 1972; Saint Jack, 1973; The Black House, 1974; The Family Arsenal, 1976; The Consul's File, 1977; Picture Palace, 1978; A Christmas Card, 1978; London Snow, 1980; World's End, 1980; The Mosquito Coast, 1981; The London Embassy, 1982; Half Moon Street, 1984; O-Zone, 1986; My Secret History, 1988; Chicago Loop, 1990; Millroy the Magician, 1993; My Other Life, 1996. Non-Fiction: V S Naipaul, 1973; The Great Patagonian Express, 1979; The Kingdom by the Sea, 1983; Sailing Through China, 1983; Sunrise with Sea Monsters, 1985; The White Man's Burden, 1987; Riding the Iron Rooster, 1988; The Happy Isles of Oceania, 1992; The Pillars of Hercules, 1995. Honours: Editorial Awards, Playboy magazine, 1972, 1976, 1977, 1979; Whitbread Award, 1978; James Tait Black Award, 1982; Yorkshire Post Best Novel Award, 1982; Thomas Cook Travel Prize, 1989; Honorary doctorates. Memberships: Royal Geographical Society; Royal Society of Literature, fellow. Address: c/o Hamish Hamilton Ltd, 27 Wrights Lane, London W8 5TZ, England.

THEVOZ Jacqueline, b. 29 Apr 1926, Estavayer-le-Lac, Switzerland. m. Jacques Congnard, 12 Nov 1960, 2 daughters. Education: Catholic Institute, Lausanne; University of Lausanne; Lausanne Conservatory. Appointments: Founder, Centre de Choregraphic Musicale; Founder, Movement for the Return to the Former Catholic Liturgy; Swiss Delegate, Académie Internationale de Lutèce, Paris. Publications: Aloys Fornerod, mon maître, 1973; Jean Dawint, l'extraordinaire chatelain de Cernex; Le Chateau de Paradis, 1979; Les Termites, 1982; Passage d'une comète, 1993. Contributions to: La Suisse; Le Republicain; Espaces; La Tribune de Lausanne; Le Semeur; Memento-Enfants; La Femme d'Aujourd 'hui. Honours: Prix Folloppe de la Faculté des Lettres de Lausanne, 1949; Prix de l'Academie des Treize, 1983; Knight of the Internationale des Arts; Dr Ad Honorem; Vice President, Société Fribourgeoise des Ecrivains. Address: Hermone, Verossier Haut, F 74500 Larringes-sur-Evian.

THEYTAZ Jean-Marc, b. 6 Nov 1955, Sion, Switzerland. Journalist. m. Claudia Glassey, 24 Oct 1980, 1 son, 1 daughter. Education: Licency of Letters, University of Fribourg, 1982. Publications: Litanies de L'arrière Saison, 1981; Fernand Martignoni, 1983; La Voix des Ages, 1987; Pierre de Planchouet, 1991; Blanches Etendues, 1994. Contributions to: Magazines and journals. Honours: Poetry Prize, 1989; Renaissance Française, 1994. Memberships: AVE; Swiss Writers Society. Literary Agent: Roger Salamin, Monographic, 3960 Sierre. Address: Rue de l'Etrier 6, 1950 Sion, Switzerland.

THIELE Colin Milton, b. 16 Nov 1920, Eudunda, South Australia, Australia. Author. m. Rhonda Gladys Gill, 17 Mar 1945, 2 daughters. Education: BA, DipEd, DipT, University of Adelaide. Publications: 90 books including: The Sun on the Stubble; Storm Boy; Blue Fin; The Fire in the Stone; Seashores and Shadows. Contributions to: Newspapers and journals. Honours: Companion, Order of Australia; Grace Levin Poetry Prize; Austrian State Prize; Australian Children's Book of the Year Award; Netherlands Silver Pencil Award. Memberships: Australian Society of Authors; Australian College of Education. Address: Endeavour Lane, King Scrub, via Dayboro, Queensland 4521, Australia.

THIRY August, b. 24 Apr 1948, Grazen, Belgium. Professor. m. Simonne Rutten, 28 July 1972, 2 daughters. Education: MA, Germanic Languages, 1972; Slavonic Languages, Russian, 1975. Appointments: Editor, Cultural Magazine, 1976-82; Reviewer, Russian Literature, 1990-. Publications: Het Paustovski Syndroom; Onder Assistenten; Russische Literatuur in de zoste Eeuw; Montagne Russe; Byzantijns Blauw, 1996; Grand Trunk Road in Pakistan, 1996. Contributions to: Periodicals. Honours: De Brakke Hond Story Award; Guido Gezelle

Novel Award. Literary Agent: Lionel Deflo. Address: Dorenstraat 196, 3020 Herent, Belgium.

THISTLETHWAITE Frank, b. 24 July 1915, Emeritus Professor. m. Jane Hosford, 1940, 2 sons, 1 dec, 3 daughters. Education: Exhibitioner and Scholar, St John's College, Cambridge; BA 1st class honours, History, English Literature, 1938; Commonwealth Fund Fellow, University of Minnesota, 1938-40; MA (Cantab), 1941. Appointments include: Editor, The Cambridge Review, 1937; British Press Service, New York, USA, 1940-41; Various university teaching positions; Founding Chancellor, 1961-80, Emeritus Professor, 1980-, University of East Anglia, Norwich, England; Visiting Scholar, various American universities. Publications: The Great Experiment: An Introduction to the History of the American People, 1955; The Anglo-American Connection in the Early Nineteenth Century, 1958; Dorset Pilgrims, 1989; A Lancashire Family Inheritance, 1996. Contributions to: Books and history journals; Migration from Europe Overseas, in A Century of European Migrations 1830-1930. Honours: Honorary LHD, Colorado, 1972; Honorary Fellow, RIBA, St John's College, Cambridge, 1974; Commander of the Order of the British Empire, 1979; Honorary DCL, East Anglia, 1980; Honorary Professor of History, University of Mauritius, 1981; Honorary ScD, University of Minnesota, 1994. Memberships: Founding Chairman, British Association of American Studies; Fellow, Royal Historical Society. Address: 15 Park Parade, Cambridge CB5 8AL, England.

THOM James Alexander, b. 28 May 1933, Gosport, Indiana, USA. Novelist. m. Dark Rain, 20 May 1990. Education: AB, Butler University, Indianapolis, 1961. Appointments: Reporter and Columnist, The Indianapolis Star, 1961-67; Lecturer in Journalism, Indiana University, 1978-80. Publications: Spectator Sport, 1978; Long Knife, 1979; Follow the River, 1982; From Sea to Shining Sea, 1984; Staying Out of Hell, 1985; Panther in the Sky, 1989; The Children of First Man, 1994; The Spirit of the Place, 1995. Contributions to: Magazines. Honour: Honorary DHL, Butler University, 1995. Memberships: Authors Guild; Western Writers of America. Literary Agent: Mitch Douglas, International Creative Management, New York. Address: 10061 West Stogsdill Road, Bloomington, IN 47404, USA.

THOMANECK Jürgen (Karl Albert), b. 12 June 1941, Stettin, Germany. Professor in German; Writer. m. Guinevere Ronald, 3 Aug 1964, 2 daughters. Education: University of Tübingen, 1962; Dr phil, University of Kiel, 1966; MEd, University of Aberdeen. Appointments: Lecturer, 1969-88, Senior Lecturer in German, 1988-92, Professor, 1992-, University of Aberdeen. Publications: Deutsches Abiturienten Lexikon, 1974; Fremdsprachenunterricht und Soziolinguistik, 1981; Police and Public Order in Europe, 1985; The German Democratic Republic, 1989; Plenzdorf's Die Neuen Leiden des Jungen W, 1991. Contributions to: Learned journals. Membership: Royal Society for the Arts, fellow. Address: 17 Elm Place, Aberdeen AB25 3SN, Scotland.

THOMAS David Arthur, b. 6 Feb 1925, Wanstead, England. Retired Marketing Executive. m. Joyce Irene Petty, 3 Apr 1948, 1 daughter. Education: Northampton Polytechnic, 1948-53. Publications: With Ensigns Flying, 1958; Submarine Victory, 1961; Battle of the Java Sea, 1968; Crete 1941: The Battle at Sea, US edition as Nazi Victory, 1972; Japan's War at Sea, 1978; Royal Admirals, 1982; Compton Mackenzie: A Bibliography, 1986; Companion to the Royal Navy, 1988; Illustrated Armada Handbook, 1988; The Atlantic Star, 1990; Christopher Columbus, Master of the Atlantic, 1991; Churchill: The Member for Woodford, 1995. Membership: Fellow, Royal Society of Arts. Address: Cedar Lodge, Church Lane, Sheering, Bishop's Stortford, Hertfordshire, England.

THOMAS Donald Michael, b. 27 Jan 1935, Redruth, Cornwall, England. Poet; Novelist. 2 sons, 1 daughter. Education: BA 1st Class Honours, English, MA, New College, Oxford. Appointments: Schoolteacher, 1959-63; Lecturer, Hereford College of Education, 1964-78. Publications: Poetry: Penguin Modern Poets 11, 1968; Two Voices, 1968; Logan Stone, 1971; Love and Other Deaths, 1975; The Honeymoon Voyage, 1978; Dreaming in Bronze, 1981; Selected Poems, 1983; Puberty Tree, 1992. Novels: The Flute Player, 1979; Birthstone, 1980; The White Hotel, 1981; Ararat, 1983; Swallow, 1984; Sphinx, 1986; Summit, 1987; Pictures at an Exhibition, 1993; Eating Pavlova, 1994. Translations: Requiem, and Poem Without a Hero (Akhmatova), 1976; Way of All the Earth (Akhmatova), 1979; Bronze Horseman (Pushkin), 1982. Fiction: Lying Together, 1990; Flying into Love, 1992. Address: The Coach House, Rashleigh Vale, Tregolis Road, Truro TR1 1TJ, England.

THOMAS Elizabeth Marshall, b. 13 Sept 1931, Boston, Massachusetts, USA. Writer. m. 14 Jan 1956, 1 son, 1 daughter. Education: AB, Radcliffe College, 1954; MA, George Washington University, 1980. Publications: The Hill People, 1953; The Harmless People, 1959; Warrior Herdsmen, 1966; Reindeer Moon, 1987; The Animal Wife, 1990; The Old Way, 1990; The Hidden Life of Dogs, 1993; The Tribe of Tiger: Cats and Their Culture, 1994; Certain Poor Shepherds, 1996. Contributions to: Journals. Honours: Brandeis University Creative Arts Award, 1968; PEN Hemingway Citation, 1988; Radcliffe College Alumni Recognition Award, 1989; Honorary DLitt, Franklin Pierce College, 1992. Memberships: PEN; Society of Women Geographers. Address: 80 East Mountain Road, Peterborough, NH 03458, USA.

THOMAS Evan. Journalist. m. Oscie Thomas, 2 daughters. Appointments: Correspondent, Writer, Editor, Time magazine, 9 years; Washington Bureau Chief, 1986-, Assistant Managing Editor, 1991-, Newsweek; Numerous television appearances. Publications: The Wise Men: Six Friends and the World They Made (co-author), 1986; The Man to See (biography of Edward Bennett Williams), 1991; The Very Best of Men: Four Who Dared: The Early Years of the C.I.A., 1995. Honours: 1st Place, National Headliner Award, 1989. Address: c/o Newsweek, 251 West 57th Street, New York, NY 10019-1894, USA.

THOMAS Franklin Richard, b. 1 Aug 1940, Indiana, USA. Professor. m. Sharon Kay Myers, 2 June 1962, 1 son, 1 daughter. Education: AB, MA, Purdue University; PhD, Indiana University, 1970. Appointments: Purdue University, 1969-70; Professor, Michigan State University, 1971-; Research Associate, Indiana University, 1978-79. Publications: Poetry: Fat Grass, 1970; Frog Praises Night, 1980; Alive With You This Day, 1980; The Landlocked Heart: Poems from Indiana, 1980; Heart Climbing Stairs, 1986; Corolla, Stamen and Style, 1986; The Whole Mystery of the Bregn, 1989; Miracles, 1996. Non-Fiction: The Literary Admirers of Alfred Stieglitz, 1983; Americans in Denmark, 1989. Fiction: Prism: The Journal of John Fish, 1992. Contributions to: Numerous journals and magazines. Honours: MacDowell Colony Fellowship; Fulbright Teaching Awards to Denmark, 1974-75, 1985-86; Michigan Council for the Arts Award for Poetry, 1990. Address: Department of American Thought and Language, Michigan State University, East Lansing, MI 48824, USA.

THOMAS Lee. See: **FLOREN Lee**.

THOMAS Rich. Journalist. Education: Graduate in English and Economics, University of Michigan; University of Frankfurt, Germany. Appointments: Economic and General News Reporter, United Press International, 1957; Financial Editor, New York Post; Associate Editor, Business Department, Chief Economic Correspondent in Washington, DC, 1970-, Newsweek; Various television appearances. Contributions to: Reader's Digest; International Economy; Atlantic Monthly; Cato Institute. Honours: Won or shared in over 12 awards, including Two Gerald Loeb Awards. Address: c/o Newsweek, 251 West 57th Street, New York, NY 10019-1894, USA.

THOMAS Rosie, (Janey King), b. 22 Oct 1947, Denbigh, Wales. Novelist. m. Caradoc King, 1975, 1 son, 1 daughter. Education: BA, St Hilda's College, Oxford, 1976. Publications: Love's Choice, 1982; Celebration, 1982; Follies, 1983; Sunrise, 1984; The White Dove, 1985; Strangers, 1986; Bad Girls, Good Women, 1988; A Woman of Our Times, 1990; All My Sins Remembered, 1991; Other People's Marriages, 1993; A Simple Life, 1996. Honour: Romantic Novel of the Year Award, Romantic Novelists Association, 1985. Hobbies: Skiing; Gardening; Cooking; Socialising. Literary Agent: Caradoc King. Address: c/o AP Watt Ltd, 20 John Street, London WC1, England.

THOMAS Victoria. See: **DE WEESE Thomas Eugene (Gene)**.

THOMEY Tedd, b. 19 July 1920, Butte, Montana, USA. Journalist; Author. m. Patricia Natalie Bennett, 11 Dec 1943, 1 daughter. Education: BA, University of California, 1943. Appointments: Publicity Director, San Diego State College, 1941-42; Reporter, San Diego Union-Tribune, 1942; Reporter, Assistant Editorial Promotion Manager, San Francisco Chronical, 1942-43, 1945-48; News Editor, Columnist, Long Beach Press Telegram, 1950-; Creative Writing Instructor, Long Beach City College; Guest Lecturer, University of Southern California; Consultant, 20th Century Fox Studios. Publications: And Dream of Evil, 1954; Jet Pilot, 1955; Killer in White, 1956; Jet Ace, 1958; I Want Out, 1959; Flight to Takla-Ma, 1961; The Loves of Errol Flynn, 1961; The Sadist, 1961; Doris Day (biography),

1962; All the Way, 1964; The Glorious Decade, 1971; The Prodigy Pilot, 1987; The Big Love (co-author), 1986; Hollywood Uncensored, 1965; Hollywood Confidential, 1967; The Comedians, 1970. Play: The Big Love (co-author), 1991; Immortal Images, 1996. Contributions to: Many magazines. Honours: 1st Place, Distinguished Newspaper Feature Writing, Theta Sigma Phi Journalism Society, 1952; Award, Best Front Page, California Newspaper Publishers. Literary Agent: Scott Meredith, New York, USA. Address: 7228 Rosebay Street, Long Beach, CA 90808, USA.

THOMPSON Diana Pullein. See: **FARR Diana**.

THOMPSON Ernest Victor, b. 14 July 1931, London, England. Author. m. Celia Carole Burton, 11 Sept 1972, 2 sons. Publications: Chase the Wind, 1977; Harvest of the Sun, 1978; The Music Makers, 1979; Ben Restallick, 1980; The Dream Traders, 1981; Singing Spears, 1982; The Restless Sea, 1983; Cry Once Alone, 1984; Polrudden, 1985; The Stricken Land, 1986; Becky, 1988; God's Highlander, 1988; Lottie Trago, 1989; Cassie, 1990; Wychwood, 1991; Blue Dress Girl, 1992; Mistress of Polrudden, 1993; The Tolpuddle Woman, 1994; Various books on Cornish and West Country subjects. Contributions to: Approximately 200 short stories to magazines. Honour: Best Historical Novel, 1976. Memberships: Society of Authors; Vice-President, West Country Writers Club; Patron, Cornwall Drama Association; Vice-Patron, Mevagissey Male Choir; Royal Society of Literature. Address: Parc Franton, Pentewan, St Austell, Cornwall, England.

THOMPSON Jean Louise, b. 1 Jan 1950, Chicago, Illinois, USA. Writer. Education: BA, University of Illinois, 1971; MFA, Bowling Green State University, 1973. Appointments: Graduate Assistant, Bowling Green State University, 1971-73; Professor, University of Illinois, 1973-; Warren Wilson College, 1988; Distinguished Visiting Writer, Wichita State University, 1991; San Francisco State University, 1992. Publications: The Woman Driver; Little Face and Other Stories; My Wisdom; The Gasoline Wars. Contributions to: Journals and magazines. Honours: Reader, Associated Writing Programs Novel Contest; Guggenheim Fellow; McGinnis Memorial Award; National Endowment for the Arts Fellowship; Canarad Fellow; Pushcart Prizes. Literary Agent: Harriet Wasserman. Address: 203 Smith Road, Urbana, IL 61801, USA.

THOMPSON Judith, b. 20 Sept 1954, Montreal, Quebec, Canada. Playwright. Education: BA, Kingston University, Ontario, 1976; National Theatre School at Montreal, 1976-79. Publications: The Crackwalker, 1980; White Biting Dog, 1984; Pink, 1986; Tornado, 1987; I am Yours, 1987; The Other Side of the Dark, 1989; Lion in the Streets, 1990; Hedda Gabler (after Ibsen), 1991; Radio and television plays. Honours: Governor-General's Awards. Address: c/o Great North Artists, 350 Dupont Street, Toronto, Ontario M5R 1V9, Canada.

THOMPSON Lloyd A(rthur), b. 24 June 1932, Barbados. Professor of Classics and Ancient History; Writer. m. Alma Rosalind Platten, 1 Sept 1956, 2 sons. Education: BA, 1956, MA, 1960, St John's College, Cambridge. Appointments: Assistant Lecturer, 1956-59, Lecturer, 1959-64, Senior Lecturer, 1964-65, Associate Professor, 1965-66, Professor of Classics and Ancient History, 1966-95, University of Ibadan, Nigeria; Visiting Fellow, St John's College, Cambridge, 1964; Editor, Museum Africum, 1972-84. Publications: Studies in Cicero (with J Ferguson, A R Hands, and W A Laidlaw), 1962; Africa in Classical Antiquity (editor with J Ferguson), 1969; Romans and Blacks, 1989; Culture and Civilization (editor), 1991; Democracy, Democratisation and Africa (editor), 1994. Honour: American Book Award, 1990. Membership: American Philological Association. Address: 31 Acrefield Drive, Cambridge CB4 1JW, England.

THOMPSON Tom, (Eduarde Batarde), b. 21 Oct 1953, Parkes, New South Wales, Australia. Publisher; Writer. m. Elizabeth Butel, 20 Nov 1984, 1 daughter. Education: BA, Macquarie University. Appointments: Publisher, Australian Bicentennial Authority, 1984-; Publisher, Literature, Angus & Robertson. Publications: Island Hotel Dreams, 1977; Neon Line, 1978; From Here, 1978; The View from Tinsel Town, 1985; Growing Up in the Sixties, 1986. Contributions to: Sydney Morning Herald; Australian; Australian Book Review; Age; National Times. Membership: Australian Society of Authors. Address: PO Box 157, Kings Cross, New South Wales 2011, Australia.

THOMSON Derick S(mith), (Ruaraidh MacThòmais), b. 5 Aug 1921, Stornoway, Isle of Lewis, Scotland. Professor of Celtic (retired); Poet; Writer. m. Carol Galbraith, 1952, 5 sons, 1 daughter. Education: MA, University of Aberdeen, 1947; BA, Emmanuel College, Cambridge, 1948. Appointments: Assistant in Celtic, University of Edinburgh, 1948-49; Lecturer in Welsh, 1949-56, Professor of Celtic, 1963-91, University of Glasgow; Editor, Gairm Gaelic Literary Quarterly, 1952-; Reader in Celtic, University of Aberdeen, 1956-63. Publications: An Dealbh Briste, 1951; Eadar Samhradh is Foghar, 1967; An Rathad Cian, 1970; The Far Road and Other Poems, 1971; An Introduction to Gaelic Poetry, 1974, new edition, 1990; Saorsa agus an Iolaire, 1977; Creachadh na Clarsaich, 1982; The Companion to Gaelic Scotland, 1983, new edition, 1994; European Poetry in Gaelic Translation, 1990; Smeur an Dochais, 1992; Gaelic Poetry in the Eighteenth Century, 1993; Meall Garbh/The Rugged Mountain, 1995. Contributions to: Books, journals and magazines. Honours: Publication Awards, Scottish Arts Council, 1971, 1992; Ossian Prize, FVS Foundation, Hamburg, 1974; Saltire Scottish Book of the Year Award, 1983; Honorary DLitt, University of Wales, 1987, University of Aberdeen, 1994. Memberships: British Academy, fellow; Glasgow Arts Club; Scottish Gaelic Texts Society, president. Address: 15 Struan Road, Cathcart, Glasgow G44 3AT, Scotland.

THOMSON Edward. See: **TUBB E(dwin) C(harles)**.

THOMSON Elizabeth (Mary), (Liz Thomson), b. 12 Sept 1957, London, England. Writer; Editor. Education: BA Honours, Music, University of Liverpool, 1979. Appointments: Staff Writer, Publishing News; Editor, Books; Numerous radio appearances, BBC and IBA. Publications: Conclusions on the Wall: New Essays on Bob Dylan, 1980; Folk Songs and Dances of England/Folk Songs and Dances of Scotland (arranger), 1982; With David Gutman: The Lennon Companion, 1987; The Dylan Companion, 1990; The Bowie Companion, 1993. Contributions to: Newspapers and journals; Chic; Mojo. Memberships: Society of Authors; National Union of Journalists; International Association for the Study of Popular Music; Charter 88; Labour Party. Address: 24 Grosvenor Park Road, Walthamstow, London E17 9PG, England.

THOMSON June Valerie, b. 24 June 1930, Sandgate, Kent, England. Writer. Div, 2 sons. Education: BA (Hons), English, Bedford College, University of London. Publications: Not One of Us, 1972; A Question of Identity, 1978; Deadly Relations, 1979; Shadow of a Doubt, 1981; To Make a Killing, 1982; A Dying Fall, 1985; No Flowers by Request, 1987; Rosemary for Remembrance, 1988; The Spoils of Time, 1989; Past Reckoning, 1990; The Secret Files of Sherlock Holmes, 1990; Foul Play, 1991; The Secret Chronicles of Sherlock Holmes, 1992; The Secret Journals of Sherlock Holmes, 1993; Holmes and Watson - A Study in Friednship, 1994. Contributions to: Several short stories to various magazines. Honour: Prix du Roman d'Aventures, France, 1983. Memberships: Crime Writers Association; Detection Club. Literary Agent: Michael Shaw, Curtis Brown and Associates, Haymarket House, 28/29 Haymarket, London SW1Y 4SP, England. Address: 177 Verulam Road, St Albans, Hertfordshire AL3 4DW, England.

THORBURN James Alexander, b. 24 Aug 1923, Martins Ferry, Ohio, USA. Professor of English and Linguistics Emeritus; Writer; Poet; Translator. m. (1) Lois McElroy, 3 July 1954, 1 son, 1 daughter, (2) June Yingling, 18 Apr 1981. Education: BA, 1949, MA, 1951, Ohio State University; PhD, Linguistics, Louisiana State University, 1977. Appointments: Instructor in English, Louisiana State University, 1961-70, Professor of English and Linguistics, 1970-89, Professor Emeritus, 1989-, Southeastern Louisiana University. Contributions to: Many anthologies, journals, and periodicals. Honours: Several. Memberships: Numerous professional organizations. Address: Southeastern Louisiana University, Hammond, LA 70402, USA.

THORNE Nicola. See: **ELLERBECK Rosemary Anne L'Estrange**.

THORNHILL Richard. See: **POLLARD John**.

THORNTON Margaret Rose. Professor of Law and Legal Studies. Education: BA Hons, Sydney; LLB, New South Wales; LLM, Yale University. Publications: The Liberal Promise: Anti-Discrimination in Australia, 1990; Public and Private: Feminist Legal Debates, 1995; Dissonape and Distrust: Women in the Legal Profession, 1996. Contributions to: International Journal of the Sociology of Law; Journal of Law and Society; Australian Feminist Law Journal. Address: School of Law and Legal Studies, La Trobe University, Bundoora, Victoria 3083, Australia.

THORPE David Richard, b. 12 Mar 1943. Schoolmaster; Political Biographer. Education: BA (Hons), 1965, MA, 1969, Selwyn College, Cambridge. Appointment: Appointed Official Biographer of Lord Home of the Hirsel, 1990. Publications: The Uncrowned Prime Ministers: A Study of Sir Austen Chamberlain, Lord Curzon and Lord Butler, 1980; Selwyn Lloyd, 1989; Alec Douglas-Home, 1996. Contributions to: The Blackwell Biographical Dictionary of British Political Life in the 20th Century, 1990. Memberships: Johnson Club; United Oxford and Cambridge University Club. Literary Agent: Graham C Greene, CBE (Ed Victor). Address: Brooke Hall, Charterhouse, Godalming, Surrey GU7 2DS, England.

THORPE Dobbin. See: **DISCH Thomas M.**

THORSTENSEN Alana. See: **DI SCIASCIO Eve Francesca.**

THRING Meredith Wooldridge, b. 17 Dec 1915, Melbourne, Victoria, Australia. Professor of Engineering. m. 14 Dec 1940, 2 sons, 1 daughter. Education: BA 1st Class Honours, Physics, Trinity College, Cambridge, 1937; ScD, Cambridge, 1964. Publications: Man, Machines and Tomorrow, 1973; Machines: Master or Slaves of Man?, 1973; How to Invent, 1977; The Engineer's Conscience, 1980, reprinted, 1992; Robots and Telechirs, 1983. Contributions to: More than 150 scientific and technical articles to journals. Memberships: Fellow, Royal Academy of Engineering; Fellow, Institution of Electrical Engineers; Fellow, Institution of Mechanical Engineers; Fellow, Institute of Physics; Fellow, Institution of Chemical Engineers; Senior Fellow, Institute of Energy, president, 1962-63. Address: Bell Farm, Brundish, Suffolk IP13 8BL, England.

THUBRON Colin Gerald Dryden, b. 14 June 1939, London, England. Writer. Publications: Mirror to Damascus, 1967; The Hills of Adonis: A Quest in Lebanon, 1968; Jerusalem, 1969; Journey Into Cyprus, 1975; The God in the Mountain (novel), 1977; Emperor (novel), 1978; The Venetians, 1980; The Ancient Mariners, 1981; The Royal Opera House Covent Garden, 1982; Among the Russians, 1983; A Cruel Madness, 1984; Behind the Wall: A Journey Through China, 1987; Falling, 1989; Turning Back the Sun, 1991; The Lost Heart of Asia, 1994. Contributions to: Times; Times Literary Supplement; Independent; Sunday Times; Sunday Telegraph; New York Times; Granta. Honours: Fellow, Royal Society of Literature, 1969; Silver Pen Award, 1985; Thomas Cook Award, 1988; Hawthornden Prize, 1989. Memberships: PEN. Literary Agent: Gillow Aitken and Stone. Address: Garden Cottage, 27 St Ann's Villas, London W11 4RT, England.

THURGOOD Nevil, (Walter Plinge), b. 29 Dec 1919, Stansted Mountfitcher, Essex. Self Employed Actor; Director; Writer. m. Eva Mary Hopper, 23 Aug 1941, 4 sons. Education: Technical College Certificate, 1936. Publications: The Furtive Fortunes of Fickle Fate and Sir Jaspers Revenge, 1984; Good Evening Ladies & Gentlemen, 1988; Sleeping Beauty, unpublished; Thurgood, A family history, private publication. Memberships: Life Member, Actors Equity; Australian Writers Guild; British Music Hall Society. Address: The Croft, 329 Mount Macedon Road, Mount Macedon, Victoria 3441, Australia.

TIBBER Robert. See: **FRIEDMAN Rosemary.**

TIBBER Rosemary. See: **FRIEDMAN Rosemary.**

TICKLE Phyllis A(lexander), b. 12 Mar 1934, Johnson City, Tennessee, USA. Writer. m. Dr Samuel M Tickle, 17 June 1955, 3 sons, 4 daughters. Education: BA, East Tennessee State University; MA, Furman University. Appointments: Poet-in-Residence, Memphis Brooks Museum, 1977-85; Director, St Lukes Press, 1975-89; Director, Trade Publishing Group, The Wimmer Companies, 1989; Director Emeritus, 1992-; Religion Editor, Publishers Weekly, 1992-. Publications: The Story of Two Johns, 1976; American Genesis, 1976; On Beyong Koch, 1981; The City Essays, 1983; Selections, 1984; What the Heart Already Knows, 1985; Final Sanity, 1987; Ordinary Time, 1988; The Tickle Papers, 1989; Re-discovering the Sacred: Spirituality in America, 1995; My Father's Prayer: A Remembrance, 1995. Contributions to: Episcopalian; Tennessee Churchman; Dixie Flyer; Feminist Digest; 365 Meditations for Women, 1989; Disciplines, 1989. Honours: Individual Artists Fellowship in Literature, 1983; Book of Excellence Award, Body, Mind and Spirit Magazine, for My Father's

Prayer. Memberships: Vice President, President, Tennessee Literary Arts Association; Chair, Publishers Association of the South; Academy of Christian Editors, 1995-; Religion Newswriters Association, 1995-. Address: 3522 Lucy Road South, Lucy Community, Millington, TN 38053, USA.

TIEDE Tom (Robert), b. 24 Feb 1937, Huron, South Dakota, USA. Journalist; Author. 1 son, 1 daughter. Education: BA, Washington State University, 1959. Appointments: Instructor, Lecturer in Field, 1965-; Currently, Senior Editor, National Correspondent, Newspaper Enterprise Association, the Scripps-Howard Syndicate; Publisher, "The News", Georgia. Publications: Your Men at War, 1966; Coward, 1968; Calley: Soldier or Killer?, 1970; Welcome to Washington, Mr Witherspoon, 1982; The Great Whale Rescue, 1986; American Tapestry, 1990; The Man Who Discovered Pluto, 1991; Fosser, 1994. Honours: Ernie Pyle Memorial Award for War Reporting; National Headlines Award for Feature Writing; Freedom's Foundation Award; George Washington Medal. Address: Mill Run Bourne, Box 1919, Richmond Hill, GA 31324, USA.

TIGAR Chad. See: **LEVI Peter.**

TIGHE Carl, b. 26 Apr 1950, Birmingham, England. Writer. Education: BA Hons, English, 1973, MA, 1974, University College, Swansea; PDESL, Leeds University, 1979. Appointments: Script Reader, BBC Wales Radio and TV, 1985-87. Publications: Little Jack Horner, 1985; Baku!, 1986; Gdansk: National Identity in the Polish-German Borderlands, 1990; Rejoice! And Other Stories, 1992; For BBC Radio: Polish Poet, 1995; Day Out, 1994; April Fool, 1996. Contributions to: Anthologies and journals. Honours: Welsh Arts Council Literary Bursary, 1983; All London Drama Prize, 1987; British Council Travel Bursary, 1990; Shortlisted for Irish Times First Fiction Prize, 1993. Memberships: PEN; Writers Guild; Welsh Union of Writers; Welsh Academy. Literary Agent: Mic Cheetham, 138 Buckingham Palace Road, London SW1W 9SA, England. Address: 36 Oak Road, Withington, Manchester M20 9DA, England.

TILL Christa Maria, b. 23 Jan 1946, Vienna, Austria. Language Teacher. m. Dr Hans Heinrich Schiesser, 27 Sept 1974. Education: Dr Phil, Studies, German and French, University of Vienna. Publications: David, David Supermann, 1986; E Wie Emma, 1989; Wiener Altwaren Vendetta, 1995. Contributions to: Poems in Rund um den Kreis, 1996. Honour: KOELA, 1978. Memberships: Swiss Writers Association; I G Autoren, Vienna, Austria. Address: Fehrenstr 12, CH-8032, Zürich, Switzerland.

TILLMAN Barrett, b. 24 Dec 1948, Pendleton, Oregon, USA. Writer. Education: Oregon State University, 1967-68; BS, Journalism, University of Oregon, 1971. Appointments: Founder-Publisher, Champlin Museums Press, 1982-87; Managing Editor, The Hook Magazine, 1986-89. Publications: The Dauntless Dive Bomber of World War II, 1976; Avenger at War, 1979; Corsair: The F4U in World War II and Korea, 1979; Hellcat: The F6F in World War II, 1979; On Yankee Station, 1987; Warriors, 1990; Pushing the Envelope: The Career of Fighter Ace and Test Pilot Marion Carl, 1994. Contributions to: Journals and magazines. Honours: US Air Force Historical Foundation Writing Award, 1981; Captain Emile Louis Bonnot Award for Lifetime Achievement in Naval Writing, Naval Order of the United States, 1994; Admiral Arthur W Radford Award for Naval History and Literature, 1994. Memberships: Association of Naval Aviation; Conference of Historic Aviation Writers, founder; Tailhook Association; US Naval Institute, life member. Address: Box 567, Athena, OR 97813, USA.

TINDALL Gillian Elizabeth, b. 4 May 1938, London, England. Novelist; Biographer; Historian. m. Richard G Landown, 1 son. Education: BA 1st Class, MA, University of Oxford. Publications: Novels: No Name in the Street, 1959; The Water and the Sound, 1961; The Edge of the Paper, 1963; The Youngest, 1967; Someone Else, 1969; Fly Away Home, 1971; The Traveller and His Child, 1975; The Intruder, 1979; Looking Forward, 1983; To the City, 1987; Give Them All My Love, 1989; Spirit Weddings, 1992; Celestine, 1996. Short stories: Dances of Death, 1973; The China Egg and Other Stories, 1981. Biography: The Born Exile on George Gissing, 1974; Journey of a Lifetime and Other Stories, 1990. Non-fiction: A Handbook on Witchcraft, 1965; The Fields Beneath, 1977; City of Gold: The Biography of Bombay, 1981, 2nd edition, 1992; Rosamund Lehmann, an Appreciation, 1985; Countries of the Mind, the Meaning of Place to Writers, 1991; Celestine: Voices from a French Village, 1995, 1996.

Contributions to: Newspapers and journals. Honours: Somerset Maugham Award, 1972; Enid McLead Prize, 1995. Memberships: Fellow, Royal Society of Literature; PEN; Fellow, Royal Society of Arts. Address: c/o Curtis Brown Ltd, 28/29 Haymarket, London SW1Y 4SP, England.

TINNISWOOD Peter, b. 21 Dec 1936, Liverpool, England. Writer. Publications: A Touch of Daniel, 1969; Mog, 1970; I Didn't Know You Cared, 1973; Except You're A Bird, 1974; Tale from a Long Room, 1981-82; The Brigadier Down Under, 1983; The Brigadier in Season, 1984; Call it a Canary, 1985; The Village Fete; The Brigadier and Uncle Mort; Radio and Television Plays. Honours: Best First Novel of the Year, 1969; Book of the Month Choice, 1969; Winfred Holiby Award, 1974; Sony Award for Radio, 1987; Giles Cooper Award, 1987; Writers Guild Comedy Award, 1991. Membership: Royal Society of Literature. Address: c/o Jonathan Clowes Agency, Ironbride Bridge House, Bridge Approach, London NW1 8BD, England.

TIPTON David John, b. 28 Apr 1934, Birmingham, England. Author. m. twice, div., 2 sons, 3 daughters. Education: Saltley College, Birmingham, 1957-59; Essex University, 1976-77. Appointments: Editor, Rivelin Press, 1974-84, Redbeck Press, 1984-. Publications: Poetry: Peru, The New Poetry (translations), 1970; Millstone Grit, 1972; Nomads and Settlers, 1980; Wars of the Roses, 1984; Green and Purple, 1993; The South American Poems, 1994. Biography, fiction: Atahualpa, 1976; Freak Summer, 1984. Contributions to: Ambit; London Magazine; Stand; Poetry Review; Poetry, Chicago; Evergreen Review; Twentieth Century; Tribune; Outposts. Address: 24 Aireville Road, Frizinghall, Bradford BD9 4HH, Yorkshire, England.

TIRBUTT Honoria, (Emma Page). Author. Publications: In Loving Memory, 1970; Family and Friends, 1972; A Fortnight by the Sea, 1973, US edition as Add a Pinch of Cyanide; Element of Chance, 1975; Missing Woman, 1980; Every Second Thursday, 1981; Last Walk Home, 1982; Cold Light of Day, 1983; Scent of Death, 1985; Final Moments, 1987; A Violent End, 1988; Deadlock, 1991; Mortal Remains, 1992; In the Event of My Death, 1994; Murder Comes Calling, 1995; Hard Evidence, 1996. Address: c/o The Crime Club, Harper Collins Publishers, 77-85 Fulham Palace Road, London W6 8JB, England.

TIRION Wil, b. 19 Feb 1943, Breda, Netherlands. Uranographer; Graphic Artist. m. Cokkie van Blitterswijk, 23 Dec 1975, 1 son, 1 daughter. Education: High School, 1959; Famous Artists Schools, 1968; Self-taught, Uranography. Publications: Sky Atlas 2000.0, 1981; Bright Star Atlas 2000.0, 1989; Cambridge Star Atlas 2000.0, 1991. Co-author: Collins Guide to Stars and Planets, 1984, 2nd edition, 1993; Uranometria 2000.0, Vol I, 1987, Vol II, 1988; Monthly Sky Guide, 1987; Binocular Astronomy, 1992; The Southern Sky Guide, 1993. Contributions to: Books and journals. Honour: Dr J van der Bilt Prize, Netherlands, 1987. Memberships: NVWS (Dutch Organisation of Amateur Astronomers); British Astronomical Association. Address: Wisselspoor 221, 2908 AD Capelle A/D IJsell, Netherlands.

TLALI Miriam (Masoli), b. 1933, Sophiatown, Johannesburg, South Africa. Novelist. Education: University of the Witwatersrand, Johannesburg. Publications: Miriam at the Metropolitan, 1975; Amandla, 1980. Stories: Mihloti, 1984; Footprints in the Quag, Stories and Dialogues from Soweto, 1989. Address: c/o Pandora Press, 77-85 Fulham Palace Road, London W6 8JB, England.

TOBIN Meryl Elaine, (Meryl Brown Tobin), b. 26 Aug 1940, Melbourne, Australia. Writer. m. Hartley Tobin, 6 Jan 1962, 2 sons, 1 daughter. Education: BA, 1961, Dip Ed, 1962, Melbourne. Publications: Author of 11 books including: Puzzles Galore, 1978, 1993; Exploring Outback Australia, 1988; Puzzleways: Grammar and Spelling, 1990; Puzzle Round Australia, 1992; More Puzzles Galore!, 1980, 1994; CarLoads of Fun, 1983; Animal Puzzle Parade, 1991; Puzzling Cats, 1994; Pets to Puzzle, 1995; Puzzles Ahoy!, 1995; Play with Words, 1996. Contributions to: 45 short stories; Hundreds of articles and puzzles; poetry, cartoons and comic strips. Honours: Seven awards. Memberships: Australian Society of Authors; Fellowship of Australian Writers; Society of Women Writers, Australia (Victoria Branch). Address: Ningan, Bass Highway, The Gurdies, Victoria 3984, Australia.

TOCH Henry, b. 15 Aug 1923. Tax Consultant. m. Margaret Schwarz, 3 Apr 1958. Education: Bachelor of Commerce, 2nd Class Honours (Upper Division), London School of Economics and Political Science, University of London, 1950. Appointment: Formerly Monthly Columnist, Law for Business. Publications: How to Pay Less Income Tax, 1958, 4 editions, re-issued, 1986; Tax Savings for Businessmen, 1960, 3 editions; Income Tax, handbook, 1966, 14 editions; Economics for Professional Studies, 1974, 3 editions; How to Survive Inflation, 1977; How to Pass Examinations in Taxation, 1979; Cases in Income Tax, 1981; Essentials of British Constitution and Government, 1983; Taxation Made Simple, 1985, 2 editions. Contributions to: Cooperative News; Journal of Business Law. Membership: Financial Intermediaries Manager and Brokers Regulatory Association. Address: Candida, 49 Hawkshead Lane, North Mymms, Hatfield, Herts AL9 7TD, England.

TOFFLER Alvin (Eugene), b. 4 Oct 1928, New York, New York, USA. Author. m. Adelaide Elizabeth (Heidi) Farrell Toffler, 29 Apr 1950, 1 daughter. Education: BA, New York University. Appointments: Associate Editor, Fortune Magazine, 1959-61; Visiting Scholar, Russell Sage Foundation, 1969-70. Publications: (mostly in collaboration with Heidi Toffler): The Culture Consumers, 1964; The Schoolhouse in the City, 1968; Future Shock, 1970; The Futurists (editor), 1972; Learning for Tomorrow (editor), 1973; The Eco-Spasm Report, 1975; The Third Wave, 1980; Previews and Premises, 1983; The Adaptive Corporation, 1984; Power Shift, 1990; War and Anti-War, 1993; Creating a New Civilization, 1994-95. Contributions to: Newspapers, journals and magazines. Honours: Medal, President of Italy; Author of the Year, American Society of Journalists and Authors; Prix de Meilleur Livre Etranger; Officer de l'Ordre des Arts et Sciences; Honorary doctorates. Memberships: Ameriacn Association for the Advancement of Science, fellow; American Society of Journalists and Authors; International Institute for Strategic Studies; World Future Studies Federation. Address: c/o Curtis Brown Ltd, 10 Astor Place, New York, NY 10003, USA.

TOFFLER Heidi, b. 1 Aug 1929, New York, New York, USA. Author. m. Alvin Toffler, 29 Apr 1950, 1 daughter. Education: BA, Long Island University. Publications: (with Alvin Toffler) The Culture Consumers, 1964; Future Shock, 1970; The Futurists (editor), 1972; Learning for Tomorrow (editor), 1973; The Third Wave, 1980; Previews and Premises, 1983; The Adaptive Corporation, 1984; Powershift, 1990; War and Anti-War, 1993; Creating a New Civilization. Contributions to: Newspapers, journals and periodicals. Honours: Medal, President of Italy; Honorary doctorates. Address: c/o Curtis Brown Ltd, 10 Astor Place, New York, NY 10003, USA.

TOMALIN Claire, b. 20 June 1933, London, England. Author. m. (1) Nicholas Tomalin, dec 1973, (2) Michael Frayn, 5 children. Education: MA, Newnham College, Cambridge, 1954. Appointment: Literary Editor, The Sunday Times, London, 1980-85. Publications: The Life and Death of Mary Wollstonecroft, 1974; Shelley and His World, 1980; Parents and Children, 1981; Katherine Mansfield: A Secret Life, 1987; The Invisible Woman: The Story of Nelly Teman and Charles Dickens, 1990; Mrs Jordan's Profession: The Story of a Great Actress and Future King, 1991; The Winter Wife, 1991. Honours: Whitbread First Book Prize, 1974; James Tait Black Memorial Prize, 1990; Hawthornden Prize, 1991. Address: 57 Gloucester Crescent, London NW1 7EG, England.

TOMASZEWSKA Marta, b. 10 Apr 1933, Warsaw, Poland. Author. Education: MA, University of Warsaw, 1956. Publications: Over 40 novels, 1974-96. Contributions to: Various publications. Honours: Polish Prime Minister's Award, 1981; Cross of the Order of Polonia Restituta, 1987; XII Premio Europeo di Litteratura Giuvanile-Lista d'Oneren Arrativa, 1988; Ibby Awards Certificate of Honour, 1988. Memberships: Association of Polish Writers; Polish Writers Union; ZAIKS. Address: Natolinska 3 m 64, Warsaw 00-562, Poland.

TOMLINSON (Alfred Charles, b. 8 Jan 1927, Stoke-on-Trent,Staffordshire, England. Professor of English Emeritus; Poet; Writer. m. 23 Oct 1948, 2 daughters. Education: BA, Queens' College, Cambridge; MA, London. Appointments: Lecturer, 1956-68, Reader, 1968-82, Professor of English, 1982-92, Professor Emeritus, 1992-, University of Bristol; Visiting Professor, University of New Mexico, 1962-63; O'Connor Professor, Colgate University, New York, 1967-68, 1989-90; Visiting Fellow of Humanities, Princeton University, 1981; Lamont Professor, Union College, New York, 1987. Publications: Poetry: Relations and Contraries, 1951; The Necklace, 1955; Seeing is Believing, 1958; A Peopled Landscape, 1963; American Scenes, 1966; The Poem as Initiation, 1968; The Way of a World, 1969; Written on Water, 1972; The Way In, 1974; The Shaft, 1978; Selected Poems, 1951-74, 1978; The Flood, 1981; Notes from New York, 1984;

Collected Poems, 1985, enlarged edition, 1987; Annunciations, 1989; The Door in the Wall, 1992; Jubilation, 1995; Selected Poems 1955-97, 1997. Other: In Black and White, 1976; The Oxford Book of Verse in English Translation (editor), 1980; Some Americans: A Literary Memoir, 1981; Poetry and Metamorphosis, 1983; Eros Englished: Erotic Poems from the Greek and Latin (editor), 1991. Contributions to: Books, professional journals, and other publications. Honours: Bess Hokin Prize, 1956; Oscar Blumenthal Prize, 1960; Inez Boulton Prize, 1964; Frank O'Hara Prize, 1968; Cheltenham Poetry Prize, 1976; Cholmondeley Poetry Award, 1979; Wilbur Award for Poetic Achievement, 1982; Premio Europeo di Cittadella, Italy, 1991; Bennett Award for Poetry, 1992; Honorary doctorates. Memberships: Academic and literary organisations. Address: Brook Cottage, Ozleworth Bottom, Wotton-under-Edge, Glos GL12 7QB, England.

TOMLINSON Catherine Twaddle Dimond, b. 1 Mar 1917, Ipswich, Queensland, Australia. Home Economics Teacher; Author. m. (1) D J Linton, Jan 1944 (killed in action, 1945), (2) H F B Tomlinson, Dec 1950, 1 son, 1 daughter. Education: 3-year Trained Teacher, Queensland Education Department, 1934-36; Diploma, Domestic Science, Department of Public Instruction of Queensland, Technical Branch, 1942; BA, University of Queensland, St Lucia, Brisbane, 1987. Publications: Recipes with a Difference, 1962; Competitive Cookery, 1972; Successful Cookery, 1983. Contributions to: Journal of Home Economics Association, Australia; Queensland Home Economics Association magazine; A Centenary History of Home Economics Education in Queensland 1881-1991; History of South Brisbane College of Technical and Further Education, 1988; Home Economics Education 1881-1981; Honours: Listed in Who's Who of Australian Writers, 1991, 2nd edition, 1995; Australian Dictionary of Biography, 1993; International Authors and Writers Who's Who, 14th edition. Memberships: Australian Society of Authors; Alumni Association of the University of Queensland Inc; Standing Committee, Women's College, University of Queensland; Life Member, Ipswich (Queensland) Girls' Grammar School Old Girls' Association. Address: 12 Wiseman Street, Kenmore, Queensland 4069, Australia.

TOMLINSON Gerald (Arthur), b. 24 Jan 1933, Elmira, New York, USA. Writer; Editor; Publisher. m. (Mary) Alexis Usakowski, 19 Aug 1966, 2 sons. Education: BA, Marietta College, Ohio, 1955; Columbia Law School, New York City, 1959-60. Appointments: Associate Editor, Business and Professional Books, Prentice Hall, 1960-63, School Department, Harcourt Brace Jovanovich, 1963-66; Senior Editor, English Department, Holt, Rinehart and Winston, 1966-69; Executive Editor, K-12 English, Silver Burdett and Ginn, 1969-82; Publisher, Home Run Press, 1985-. Publications: On a Field of Black (novel), 1980; School Administrator's Complete Letter Book, 1984; Baseball Research Handbook, 1987; Speaker's Treasury of Sports Anecdotes, Stories and Humor, 1990; Encyclopedia of Religious Quotations, 1991; The New Jersey Book of Lists (co-author), 1992; Murdered in Jersey, 1994. Contributions to: Magazines and journals. Honours: Best Detective Stories of the Year, E.P. Dutton, 1976; Mystery Writers of America Annual Anthologies, 5 appearances, 1977-87. Memberships: Authors Guild; Mystery Writers of America; Society for American Baseball Research. Address: 19 Harbor Drive, Lake Hopatcong, NJ 07849, USA.

TOMLINSON Mary Teresa, b. 15 Aug 1935, England. Journalist; Public Relations/Lecturer; Specialist in European Community Affairs and Tourism. m. Noel Tomlinson, 15 Aug 1959, 1 son, 1 daughter. Education: English, Accountancy and Economics Diploma; School of Economics, 1952-54; School of Drama and Music; School of Art, 1955-56. Appointment: Partner, Ays Press and Public Relations. Publications: Around the World in Cookery and Cakes, 1980; Wool on the Back (with Peter Taylor), 1987. Contributions to: Newspapers and journals. Honours: Nominee, Woman of Europe Award, 1990; Member, Club of Rhodes, UK, 1991-; MCIJ. Memberships: Society of Women Writers and Journalists; Institute of Journalists; Officer; Chartered Institute of Journalists. Address: Mayfield Cottage, 51 Ebrington, nr Campden, Glos GL55 6NQ, England.

TOOMEY Jeanne Elizabeth, b. 22 Aug 1921, USA. Writer. 1 son, 1 daughter. Education: BA, Southampton College of Long Island University, 1976. Publications: How to Use Your Dreams to Solve Your Problems, 1970; Murder in the Hamptons, 1994. Contributions to: True Detective; Inside Detective; Family Circle; Family Weekly; AP Newsfeatures, New Jersey. Honours: Woman of the Year, lower courts, New York; Women's Press Club, 1960; Nevada State Press Association Award, 1960-61.

TOONA GOTTSCHALK Elin-Kai, b. 12 July 1937, Tallinn, Estonia. Freelance Writer. m. Donald Frederick Gottschalk, 9 Oct 1967, 1 son. Publications: Puuingel, 1965; Lotukata, 1968; Sipelgas Sinise Kausi All, 1973; In Search of Coffee Mountains, 1977; Lady Cavaliers, 1977; Pictures, and DP Camp Child: Poetry in Visions, 1988; Kalevikula Vimne Tutar (novel), 1988; Kolm Valget Tuvi (novel), 1992. Contributions to: Estonia; Regular column for The Coastal Illustrated, St Simons Island, Georgia, 1974-75; Coastal Quarterly, Georgia; Indian River Life, Florida; Lady's Circle, New York; Talent Magazine, International Platform Association; St Petersburg Times; New Writers Magazette, Florida; Storyteller Magazine; Eesti Haal, London; Vaba Eesti Sona, New York; Tulimuld, Sweden; Mana, Canada/USA; Triinu; Aim; Reminisce; Estonia. Scripts for Radio Liberty, Voice of America. Honours: 1st Prize for Young Estonian Writers in England, 1952; Certificate of Merit, Storyteller Magazine, London, 1962; 1st Prize for Short Story Competition 13, Writer's Review, London, 1966; The H Visnapuu Literary Award for Estonians, World Association of Estonians, 1966; Ennu Literary Prize, USA, 1968; Certificate of Commendation, Golden Windmill Radio Drama Contest, Radio Nederland Wereldomroep, 1971; 1st Prize, National Examiner Contest, 1983; 1st Prize for Non-Fiction and 2nd Prize for Photo Journalism, Floriad State Awards, National League of American Pen Women, 1985; Honourable Mention, Short Story Contest, National League of American Women, 1988; Lauri Literary Prize, 1993. Memberships: International PEN, Estonian Branch; All Estonian Literary Associations Worldwide; Fellow, International Biographical Association; National League of American Pen Women; International Platform Association. Address: 27554 US 19N, #37 Clearwater, FL 33761, USA.

TOPOLSKI Daniel, b. 4 June 1945, London, England. Writer; Broadcaster. Partner, Susan Gilbert, 2 daughters. Education: BA Geography, Diploma Social Anthropology, MA Geography, New College, Oxford, 1964-68. Publications: Muzungu: One Man's Africa, 1976; Travels with my Father: South America, 1983; Boat Race: The Oxford Revival, 1985; True Blue: The Oxford Mutiny, 1988; Henley: The Regatta, 1989. Contributions to: Telegraph; Times; 'You' Magazine; Hello; Radio Times; Tatler; Vogue; Life; Madamoiselle; Daily Mail; Observer; Evening Standard; BBC; Broadcaster TV and Radio, Sport and Travel. Honours: Sports Book of the Year, 1990; Radio Travel Program of the Year, 1994. Memberships: Churchill Fellow; Fellow, Royal Geographical Society; Henley Steward; Leander Club; London RC. Literary Agent: Lucas Alexander Whitley, Elsinor House, 77 Fulham Palace Road, London W6 HJA. Address: 69 Randolph Avenue, London W9 1DW, England.

TOPSOE Vilhelm, b. 20 July 1944, Copenhagen, Denmark. Lawyer. m. Elisabeth, 12 Dec 1981, 2 daughters. Education: Cand jur, 1968. Publications: Dømt, 1973; SR II, 1975; To Familier, 1980; De Sorte Fugle, 1984; Orn Harriet, 1987; Svampejagten, 1995. Contributions to: Berlingske Tidende; Weekend-Avisen. Address: Rosenvængets Sidealle 3, DK 2100 Copenhagen 0, Denmark.

TORANSKA Teresa, b. 1 Jan 1946, Wolkowysk, Poland. Journalist. m. Leszek Sankowski, 17 Jan 1989. Education: MA Law, 1969, Journalism, 1972, Warsaw University, Poland; Visiting Scholar, Harvard University, USA, 1989. Publications: Europa Za 100 Dolarow (Europe for a $100), 1975; Widziane Z Dolu (View from the Bottom), 1979; Oni (Them), 1986; My (We), 1994. Television apperances: Changing the Guard, Channel 4, UK, 1990; Now You Channel 2, Poland, 1996. Contributions to: Kultura; Polityka; Granta. Memberships: Association of Polish Authors; International Federation of Journalists. Literary Agent: Leszek Sankowski. Address: Zywnego 12/102, 02-701 Warsaw, Poland.

TOREKULOVICH. See: AITMAYOV Chingiz.

TORON Steve. See: STEBEL Sidney Leo.

TORRANCE Lee. See: SADGROVE Sidney Henry.

TORRANCE Thomas F(orsythe), b. 30 Aug 1913, Chengdu, China. Minister of Religion; Professor of Theology. m. Margaret Edith Spear, 2 Oct 1946, 2 sons, 1 daughter. Education: MA, 1934; BRD 1937; DrTheol, 1946; DLitt, 1971. Appointments: Founder-Editor, Journal of Theology, 1948-88; Moderator, General Assembly, Church of Scotland, 1976-77. Publications: The Doctrine of Grace, 1949; Calvin's Doctrine of Man, 1949; Kingdom and Church, 1956; Conflict and Agreement in the Church, 2 volumes, 1959-60; Theology in

Reconstruction, 1965; Theological Science, 1969; God and Rationality, 1971; Theology in Reconciliation, 1975; Space, Time and Resurrection, 1976; Space, Time and Incarnation, 1979; The Ground and Grammar of Theology, 1980; Christian Theology and Scientific Culture, 1980; Divine and Contingent Order, 1981; Reality and Scientific Theology, 1984; The Humanity of John Calvin, 1987; The Trinitarian Faith, 1988; The Christian Frame of Mind, Reason, Order and Openness in Theology and Natural Science, 1989; Karl Barth, Biblical and Evangelical Theological Theologian, 1990; Senso del divino e scienza mnoderna, 1992; Theological Dialogue between Orthodox and Reformed Churches (editor), 1993; Royal Priesthood, 1993; Divine Meaning: Studies in Patristic Hermeneutics, 1994; Trinitarian Perspectives: Toward Doctrinal Agreement, 1994; The Christian Doctrine of God, One Being Three Persons, 1996; Scottish Theology, From John Knox to John McLeod Campbell, 1996. Contributions to: Numerous. Honours: Honorary doctorates; Honorary DD, Edinburgh, 1996. Memberships: British Academy; International Academy of Religious Sciences, president, 1972-81; International Academy of the Philosophy of Sciences; Center of Theological Inquiry, Princeton, New Jersey; Royal Society of Edinburgh. Address: 37 Braid Farm Road, Edinburgh EH10 6LE, Scotland.

TORRES Ana Teresa, b. 6 July 1945, Caracas, Venezuela. Writer. m. Gaston Carvallo, 10 Jan 1975, 1 son, 1 daughter. Education: Psychology degree, 1968; Clinical psychology diploma, 1973; Psychoanalyst diploma, 1982. Publications: Novels: El Exilio del Tiempo, 1990; Dona Ines contra el Olvido, 1992; Vagas Desapariciones, 1995; Malena de cinco mundos, 1997. Other: El Amor como sintoma (essay), 1993; Elegir la Neurosis (essay), 1992. Contributions to: Imagen; Venezuela Literary Journal; Inti. Honours: Municipal, 1992; Narrativa, 1992; Picon-Salas, 1992. Literary Agent: Dr Ray Gude Mertin, Frankfurt, Germany. Address: POBA International 1-20034, PO Box 02-5255, Miami, FL 33102, USA.

TORRES Luiz Rebouças, (Ovni, Rebouças, Tórres), b. 13 Dec 1948, Ibicuipeba, Ceara, Brazil. Language Teacher; Interpreter; Translator; Writer. Education: Scholarship, Bates College, Lewiston, Maine, USA, 1970-72; Graduate, Letters Course in English and Portuguese, Federal University of Rio Grande do Norte (UFRN), Natal, Brazil, 1994; Law School, Federal University of Pernambuco; Currently studying Journalism, UFRN. Appointments: Teacher of English, Portuguese, and Spanish; Interpreter, Brazil, and Africa, 1977; Translator of English/Portuguese; Writer; Artist; Painter; Poet; Ufologist; Lecturer; Polyglot; 'Zine Writer; Politician; Various appearances on Brazilian radio and television. Publications: Ovni, Un ET Diferente, De Betaflex Para A Terra (Ovni, a Different ET, From Betaflex to the Earth), 1992; Ufology, 1993; Informe Ovni (magazine). Contributions to: Poems in Hora Do Povo (newspaper), 1980, Journal De Natal (newspaper), 1996; Un Dia, A Poesia (A Day, The Poetry), by Ayres Marques (book and video), 1996; Articles in Brazilian and international press. Honour: Distinguished Finalist, 3rd Place, Ufologist Short Story Contest, Argentina, 1996. Hobbies: Reading; Writing. Address: Caixa Postal 2655, Natal, RN 59022-970, Brazil.

TORRES Tereska. See: LEVIN Torres.

TOURNOER Michel Edouard, b. 19 Dec 1924, Paris, France. Author. Publications: Friday or The Other Island, 1969; The Erl King (The Ogre), 1972; Gemini, 1981; The Four Wise Men, 1982; The Fetishist, 1984; Gilles et Jeanne, 1987; The Golden Droplet, 1987. Honours: Grand Prix du Roman, Académie Française, 1967; Prix Goncourt. Memberships: Académie Goncourt, France; Akademie der Künste, Berlin, Germany. Address: 78460 Choisel, Chevreuse, France.

TOWNSEND John Rowe, b. 10 May 1922, Leeds, Yorkshire, England. Author and Critic. m. Vera Lancaster, 3 July 1948, dec 9 May 1973, 1 son, 2 daughters. Education: BA, 1949, MA, 1954, Emmanuel College, Cambridge. Appointments: Sub-Editor, 1949-54, Art Editor, 1954-55, Manchester Guardian; Editor, 1955-59, Children's Book Editor (part-time), 1968-78, Columnist, 1968-81, Manchester Guardian Weekly; Permanent Visiting Faculty Member, Center for Children's Literature, Simmons College, 1978-84; Several visiting lectureships. Publications: Written for Children: An Outline of English-Language Children's Literature, 1965, 4th edition, revised, 1992; A Sense of Story: Essays on Contemporary Writers for Children, 1971; A Sounding of Storytellers: New and Revised Essays on Contemporary Children's Writers, 1979. Other: 10 children's books, 1961-86; 17 young adult's books, 1963-92. Contributions to: Books and periodicals.

Honours: Silver Pen Award (English PEN), 1969; Christopher Award (USA), 1982; Edgar Allan Poe Award, 1982. Memberships: British Society of Authors; Children's Writers Group, chairman, 1975-76, 1990-91. Address: 72 Water Lane, Histon, Cambridge CB4 4LR, England.

TOWNSEND Peter Wooldridge, b. 22 Nov 1914, Rangoon, Burma. Author. m. Marie Luce Jamagne, 21 Dec 1959, 1 son, 2 daughter. Education: Haileybury; Royal Air Force College, 1933-35; Royal Air Force Staff College, 1942-43. Publications: Earth my Friend, 1960; Duel of Eagles, 1970; The Last Emperor, 1975; Time and Chance, 1978; The Smallest Pawns in the Game, 1979-80; The Girl in the White Ship, 1982; The Postman of Nagasaki, 1984; Duel in the Dark, 1986; Nostalgia Britannica, 1994. Contributions to: Daily Telegraph; Daily Mail; Daily Express; Sunday Express; Evening Standard; Paris Match; Journal du Dimanche; Le Figaro; Le Figaro Litteraire; Madame Figaro; Le Temps Retrouve. Membership: European Academy of Science, Arts and Letters. Address: La Mare aux Oiseaux, 78610 St Leger en Yvelines, France.

TOWNSEND Sue, b. 4 Feb 1946, Leicester, England. Author. Publications: The Secret Diary of Adrian Mole Aged Thirteen and Three-Quarters, 1982; The Growing Pain of Adrian Mole, 1984; The Diaries of Adrian Mole, combined volume issued in USA, 1986; Bazaar and Rummage, Groping for Words, Womberang: Three Plays, 1984; True Confessions of Adrian Albert Mole; Mr Bevan's Dream, 1989; Ten Tiny Fingers, Nine Tiny Toes (play), 1989; Adrian Mole from Minor to Major, 1991; The Queen and I, 1992; Adrian Mole: The Wilderness Years, 1993. Contributions to: London Times; New Statesman; Observer; Sainsburys Magazine, 1993. Memberships: Writers Guild; PEN; Fellow, Royal Society of Literature. Literary Agent: Giles Gordon, Curtis Brown Ltd. Address: 6 Ann Street, Edinburgh EH4 1PJ, Scotland.

TOWNSEND Tom, (Thomas L Townsend), b. 1 Jan 1944, Waukegan, Illinios, USA. Novelist. m. Janet L Simpson, 17 Apr 1965. Education: Arkansas Military Academy. Publications: Texas Treasure Coast, 1978; Where the Pirates Are, 1985; Trader Wooly, 1987; Trader Wooly and the Terrorists, 1988; Queen of the Wind, 1989; Battle of Galveston, 1990; Trader Wooly and the Ghost in the Colonel's Jeep, 1991; The Holligans, 1991; Bubba's Truck, 1992; The Ghost Flyers, 1993; A Fair Wind to Glory, 1994. Honours: Friend of American Writers Award, 1986; Texas Blue Bonnet Master List, 1986; Silver Award, Best Children's Video, Houston International Film Festival, 1986. Address: PO Box 905, Kemah, TX 77565, USA.

TOYNBEE Polly (Mary Louisa), b. 27 Dec 1946, Isle of Wight, England. Journalist; Writer. m. Peter Jenkins, 1970, 1 son, 2 daughters, 1 stepdaughter. Education: St Anne's College, Oxford. Literary appointments: Reporter, The Observer, 1968-71; Editor, Washington Monthly, USA, 1972-73; Feature Writer, Observer, 1974-76; Columnist, The Guardian, 1977-88; Social Affairs Editor, BBC, 1988-. Publications: Leftovers, 1966; A Working Life, 1970; Hospital, 1977; The Way We Live Now, 1981; Lost Children, 1985. Honours: Catherine Pakenham Award for Journalism, 1975; British Press Awards, 1977, 1982. Address: BBC TV, TV Centre, Wood Lane, London W12, England.

TRACEY Hugh. See: EVANS Stuart.

TRACHTENBERG Paul, b. 25 Oct 1948, Los Angeles, California, USA. Poet. Education: AA, Fullerton Junior College, 1966; California State Polytechnic University, Pomona, 1968. Publications: Short Changes for Loretta, 1982; Making Waves, 1986; Ben's Exit, 1993. Address: 9431 Krepp Drive, Huntington Beach, CA 92646, USA.

TRANTER Nigel Godwin, (Nye Tregold), b. 23 Nov 1909, Glasgow, Scotland. Author. m. May Jean Campbell Grieve, 11 July 1933, 1 son, dec, 1 daughter. Publications: Numerous historical, romantic, Western, adventure, children's and non-fiction books; Lord in Waiting, 1994; Highness in Hiding, 1995; Honours Even, 1995; A Rage of Regents, 1996. Honours: Officer of the Order of the British Empire, 1983; Scot of the Year Award, 1991; Honorary doctorate. Memberships: PEN Scottish Centre, president, 1962-66; Scottish Teachers of History Association, Honorary President, 1990; Honorary Society of Authors, president, 1966-72; Honorary President, Saltire Society; Honorary Memberm Scottish Library Association. Address: Quarry House, Aberlady, East Lothian, EH32 OQB, Scotland.

TRAPIDO Barbara (Louise), b. 5 Nov 1941, Cape Town, South Africa. Writer. m. Stanley Trapido, 29 Apr 1963, 1 son, 1 daughter. Education: BA Hons, English; Postgraduate Certificate, London. Publications: Brother of the More Famous Jack, 1982; Noah's Ark, 1985; Temples of Delight, 1990; Juggling, 1994. Contributions to: Spectator; Sunday Telegraph; Sunday Times. Honours: Whitbread Award, 1982; Shortlisted for Sunday Express Book of the Year Award, 1990. Literary Agent: Alexandra Pringle, Toby Eady Associates. Address: 3rd Floor, 9 Orme Court, London W2 4RL, England.

TRASK Jonathan. See: **LEVINSON Leonard**.

TRAVIS Jack, b. 2 Mar 1952, Newellton, Louisiana, USA. Architect; Writer. m. Chandra Llewellyn-Travis, 28 Sept 1996. Education: BArch, Arizona State University, 1977; MArch, University of Illinois, 1978. Appointments: Architect, own firm, 1985-; Adjunct Professor, Fashion Institute of Technology, Parsons School of Design; Founder, Studio for Afri-Culturalism in Architecture and Design; Lecturer; Panelist, Judge, Juror and Organizer of several competitions and events; Exhibitor. Publications: African American Architects: In Current Practice (monograph), 1992; I, An Architect Too! (monograph), in progress. Contributions to: Various journals; Many feature articles in various magazines. Honours: Numerous recognitions of merit. Memberships: National Organization of Minority Architects; New York Coalition of Black Architects; South American Institute of Architects, NCARB; Studio Museum of Harlem; National AIA Task Force on Diversity. Address: 103 East 125 Street, Harlem, NY 10035-1641, USA.

TRAVIS Millicent Elizabeth. See: **LANE M Travis**.

TREANOR Oliver, b. 1 May 1949, Warrenpoint, Northern Ireland. Catholic Priest. Education: Queen's University, Belfast; BA (Hons); PGCE; Dip Phil; Pont Università Gregoriana, Rome; STB, 1977, STL, 1979, STD, 1984. Publication: Mother of the Redeemer, Mother of the Redeemed, 1988; Seven Bells to Bethlehem: The O Antiphons of Advent, 1995. Contributions to: Observatore Romano, Vatican City; Priests and People, Durham, England; Theology Digest, USA; Religious Life Review, Dublin.Address: St Malachy's College, Belfast BT15 2AE, Northern Ireland.

TREASE (Robert) Geoffrey, b. 11 Aug 1909, Nottingham, England. Author. m. Marian Granger Boyer, 11 Aug 1933, 1 daughter. Education: Open Scholar in Classics, Queen's College, Oxford, 1928-29. Publications: 107 books including: Bows Against the Barons, 1934; Cue for Treason, 1940; Tales Out of School, 1948; No Boats on Bannermere, 1949; A Whiff of Burnt Boats: An Early Autobiography, 1971; Laughter at the Door: A Continued Autobiography, 1974; Tomorrow is a Stranger, 1987; The Arpino Assignment, 1988; A Flight of Angels, 1988; Shadow Under the Sea, 1990; Calabrian Quest, 1990; Aunt Augusta's Elephant, 1991; Song for a Tattered Flag, 1992; Fire on the Wind, 1993; Bring Out the Banners, 1994; No Horn at Midnight, 1995; Cruise on the Sea, 1996. Contributions to: Daily Telegraph; Times Literary Supplement; Times Educational Supplement; The Author. Honours: New Play Prize, Welwyn Theatre Festival, 1938; New York Herald Tribune Award, 1966; Fellow, Royal Society of Literature, 1979. Memberships: Society of Authors, chairman, 1972-73, council member, 1973-; PEN. Address: c/o Murray Pollinger, 222 Old Brompton Road, London SW5 0BZ, England.

TREBORLANG Robert, b. 19 Dec 1943, Jerusalem, Israel. Writer; Poet. m. Moi Moi Cumines, 6 May 1971. Education: BA, Language, University of Sydney, 1968. Publications: How to Survive in Australia, 1985; How to be Normal in Australia, 1987; How to Make it Big in Australia, 1989; She Vomits Like a Lady, 1991; Staying Sane in Australia, 1991; Men, Women and Other Necessities, 1992; A Hop Through Australia's History, 1993; How to Mate in Australia, 1993; The Little Book of Aussie Wisdom, 1994; The Little Book of Aussie Insults, 1994. Contributions to: 24 Hours; Australian; Australian Jewish Times. Honour: Literature Grant, Australia, 1976. Memberships: Australian Journalist Association, Section of Media; Entertainment and Arts Alliance. Address: PO Box 997, Potts Point, New South Wales 2011, Australia.

TREGLOWN Jeremy Dickinson, b. 24 May 1946, Anglesey, North Wales. Professor of English; Biographer; Editor; Critic. m. (1) Rona Bower, 1970, div,1982, 1 son, 2 daughters, (2) Holly Urquhart Eley, 1984. Education: BLitt, MA (Oxon); PhD, London. Appointments: Lecturer in English, Lincoln College, Oxford, 1974-77; University College, London, 1977-80; Assistant Editor, 1980-82, Editor, 1982-90, Times Literary Supplement; Chairman of Judges, Booker Prize, 1991; Ferris Professor of Journalism, Princeton University, USA, 1992; Professor of English, University of Warwick, England, 1993-. Publications: Letters of John Wilmot, Earl of Rochester (editor), 1980; Spirit of Wit: Reassessments of Rochester (editor), 1982; Introduction, R L Stevenson, In the South Seas, 1986; Selection, and Introduction, The Lantern Bearers: Essays by Robert Louis Stevenson, 1987; Introductions to reprints of complete novels of Henry Green, 1991-; Roald Dahl: A Biography, 1994. Contributions to: Numerous magazines and journals. Membership: Council, Royal Society of Literature. Literary Agent: Rogers, Coleridge and White. Address: Gardens Cottage, Ditchley Park, Enstone, Nr Chipping Norton, Oxon OX7 4EP, England.

TREGOLD Nye. See: **TRANTER Nigel Godwin**.

TREHEARNE Elizabeth. See: **MAXWELL Patricia Anne**.

TRELFORD Donald Gilchrist, b. 9 Nov 1937, Coventry, England. Journalist; Broadcaster. m. (1) Janice Ingram, 1963, 2 sons, 1 daughter, (2) Katherine Louise Mark, 1963, 1 daughter. Education: MA, Selwyn College, Cambridge. Appointments: Pilot Officer, RAF, 1956-58; Staff, newspapers in Coventry and Sheffield, 1961-63; Editor, Times of Malawi and Correspondent in Africa, The Times, Observer, BBC, 1963-66; Deputy News Editor, 1966, Assistant Managing Editor, 1968, Deputy Editor, 1969-75, Director, Editor, 1976-93, Observer; Professor of Journalism Studies, Sheffield University, 1993-. Publications: Siege; County; Champions; Sunday Best; Snookered, 1985; Child or Change (with Gary Kasparov), 1988; Len Hutton Remembered, 1992. Contributions to: The Queen Observed, 1986; Saturday's Boys, 1990. Honours: Editor, Newspaper of the Year, Granada TV Press Awards, 1982; Commended, International Editor of the Year, 1984; Honorary DLitt, Sheffield University, 1990. Memberships: British Executive Committee, International Press Institute, 1976-; Fellow, Royal Society of Arts, 1988-. Address: c/o Michael Sissons, Peters, Fraser and Dunlop Group, 503/4 Chelsea Harbour, London SW10 0XF, England.

TREMBLAY Gail Elizabeth, b. 15 Dec 1945, Buffalo, New York, USA. Poet; Artist; College Teacher. Education: BA, Drama, University of New Hampshire, 1967; MFA, Creative Writing, University of Oregon, 1969. Appointment: Faculty, Evergreen State College, Olympia, Washington. Publications: Night Gives Woman the Word, 1979; Talking to the Grandfathers, 1980; Indian Singing in 20th Century America, 1990. Contributions to: Wooster Review; Denver Quarterly; Calyx; Northwest Review; Maize; Studies: American Indian Literature, Volume 7, No 4, 1995. Honour: Alfred E Richards Poetry Prize, 1967. Memberships: Board Member, Woman's Caucus for Art; Vice-President of the Board, Indian Youth of America; Native American Writers Circle of the Americas; Board Member, National Committee United States of American/International Association of Art, UNESCO. Address: Seminar 3127, The Evergreen State College, Olympia, WA 98505, USA.

TREMLETT George William, b. 5 Sept 1939, England. Author; Journalist; Bookseller. m. Jane Mitchell, 1971, 3 sons. Publications: 17 biographies of rock musicians, 1974-77; Living Cities, 1979; Caitlin (with Mrs Caitlin Thomas), 1986; Clubmen, 1987; Homeless, Story of St Mungo's, 1989; Little Legs (with Roy Smith), 1989; Rock Gold, 1990; Dylan Thomas: In the Mercy of His Means, 1991; Gadaffi: The Desert Mystic, 1993; David Bowie, 1994. Honour: Officer of the Order of the British Empire. Membership: Advisory Panel, BBC Community Programme Unit, 1985-. Literary Agents: A M Heath & Co Ltd, London, England; Tony Secunda, San Francisco, USA. Address: Corran House, Laugharne, Carmarthen, Dyfed SA33 4SJ, Wales.

TRENHAILE John Stevens, b. 29 Apr 1949, Hertford, England. Writer. Education: BA, 1971, MA, 1975, Magdalen College, Oxford. Publications: Kyril, 1981; A View from the Square, 1983; Nocturne for the General, 1985; The Mahjong Spies, 1986; The Gates of Exquisite View, 1987; The Scroll of Benevolence, 1988; Kyrsalis, 1989; Acts of Betrayal, 1990; Blood Rules, 1991; The Tiger of Desire, 1992; A Means to Evil, 1993. Address: c/o Blake Friedman, Literary Agents, 37-41 Gower Street, London WC1E 6HH, England.

TRENTON Gail. See: **GRANT Neil**.

TRESILLIAN Richard. See: **ELLIS Royston**.

TREVELYAN (Walter) Raleigh, b. 6 July 1923, Port Blair, Andaman Islands. Author; Publisher; Editorial Director. Appointment: Publisher, 1948-88. Publications: The Fortress, 1956; A Hermit Disclosed, 1960; Italian Short Stories: Penguin Parallel Texts (editor), 1965; The Big Tomato, 1966; Princes Under the Volcano, 1972; The Shadow of Vesuvius, 1976; A Pre-Raphaelite Circle, 1978; Rome '44, 1982; Shades of the Alhambra, 1984; The Golden Oriole, 1987; La Storia dei Whitaker, 1989; Grand Dukes and Diamonds, 1991; A Clear Premonition, 1995; The Companion Guide to Sicily, 1996. Contributions to: Newspapers and journals. Honours: John Florio Prize for translation from Italian, The Outlaws by Luigi Meneghello; 1967. Memberships: Committee Member, Fellow, Vice Chairman, PEN; Fellow, Royal Society of Literature; Brooks's; Lansdowne Club; Groucho Club; Chairman, Anglo-Italian Society for Protection of Animals. Literary Agent: A M Heath, 79 St Martin's Lane, London WC2N 4AA, England. Addresses: 18 Hertford Street, London W1Y 7DB, England; St Cadix, St Veep, Lostwithiel, Cornwall PL22 0PB, England.

TREVOR (Lucy) Meriol, b. 15 Apr 1919, London, England. Author. Education: BA, St Hugh's College, Oxford, 1942. Publications: Newman: The Pillar of the Cloud, Newman: Light in Winter, 2 volumes, 1962; Pope John, 1967; The Arnolds, 1973; The City and the World, 1970; The Golden Palaces, 1985; James II: The Shadow of a Crown, 1988; 16 historical novels, 1956-; 2 biographical books; 12 books for older children, 1949-66. Contributions to: Reviewer for Times Literary Supplement, 1960s, 1970s. Honours: James Tait Black Memorial Prize, 1962; Elected Fellow, Royal Society of Literature, 1967. Address: 41 Fitzroy House, Pulteney Street, Bath BA2 4DW, England.

TREVOR William. See: **COX William Trevor.**

TRICKETT (Mabel) Rachel, b. 20 Dec 1923, Lathom, Lancashire, England. Author. Education: MA, Lady Margaret Hall, Oxford, 1947. Appointment: Principal, St Hughe's College, Oxford, 1973-91. Publications: The Return Home, 1952; The Course of Love, 1954; Point of Honour, 1958; A Changing Place, 1962; The Elders, 1966; The Visit to Timon, 1970. Plays: Antigone, 1954; Silas Marner, 1960. Non-Fiction: The Honest Muse: A Study in Augustan Verse, 1967; Browning's Lyricism, 1971; Tennyson's Craft, 1981. Honours: Rhys Memorial Prize, 1953; Honorary Fellow, Lady Margaret Hall, 1978. Address: Flat 4, 18 Norham Gardens, Oxford OX2 6QB, England.

TRIER MORCH Dea, b. 9 Dec 1941, Copenhagen, Denmark. Writer; Graphic Artist. m. Troels Trier, 1 son, 2 daughters. Education: Graduated, Royal Academy of Fine Arts, Copenhagen, 1964; Postgraduate Studies, Academies of Fine Arts, Warsaw, Kraków, Belgrade, Leningrad, Prague, 1964-67. Publications: 15 books in Danish, 1968-95, including Winter's Child, translated into 22 languages. Other: Various graphic works exhibited worldwide. Honours: Danish Author of the Year Award, 1977; Danish Government Stipends for Life, 1985, and for Works, 1994. Memberships: Danish Writers Association, chairman, 1990-91; PEN Club, Denmark; Union of Danish Graphic Artists; The Artists Association, Denmark. Address: Jens Juels Gade 7, 2100 Copenhagen, Denmark.

TRIGGER Bruce Graham, b. 18 June 1937, Cambridge, Ontario, Canada. Professor of Anthropology. m. Barbara Marian Welch, 7 Dec 1968, 2 daughters. Education: BA, University of Toronto, 1959; PhD, Yale University, 1964. Appointments: Assistant Professor, Northwestern University, 1963-64; Assistant Professor, 1964-67, Associate Professor, 1967-69, Professor, 1969-, McGill University. Publications: History and Settlement in Lower Nubia, 1965; Late Nubian Settlement at Arminna West, 1967; Beyond History, 1968; The Huron: Farmers of the North, 1969, revised edition, 1990; Cartier's Hochelaga and the Dawson Site, 1972; Nubia Under the Pharaohs, 1976; The Children of Aataentsic, 1976, revised edition, 1987; Time and Traditions, 1978; Handbook of North American Indians, Vol 15, Northeast 1978; Gordon Childe, 1980; Natives and Newcomers, 1985; The History of Archaeological Thought, 1989; Early Civilizations: Ancient Egypt in Context, 1992. Contributions to: Antiquity; American Antiquity; World Archaeology; Man. Editor, Native and Northern Series, McGill-Queen's University Press. Honours: Canadian Silver Jubilee Medal, 1977; Cornplanter Medal, 1979; Innis-Gerin Medal, Royal Society of Canada, 1985; DSc, University of New Brunswick, 1987; John Porter Prize, 1988; DLitt, University of Waterloo, 1990; Prix du Québec, 1991; Honorary Member, Prehistoric Society, England, 1991; Honorary Fellow, Society of Antiquaries of Scotland, 1993; LLD,

University of Western Ontario, 1995. Memberships: Various professional organizations. Address: Department of Anthropology, McGill University, 855 Sherbrooke Street West, Montreal, Quebec H3A 2T7, Canada.

TRILLIN Calvin (Marshall), b. 5 Dec 1935, Kansas City, Missouri, USA. Journalist; Critic; Author. m. Alice Stewart, 13 Aug 1965, 2 daughters. Education: BA, Yale University, 1957. Appointments: Reporter, later Writer, Time magazine, 1960-63; Staff Writer, The New Yorker magazine, 1963-; Columnist, The Nation magazine, 1978-85; King Features Syndicate, 1986-. Publications: An Education in Georgia: Charlayne Hunter, Hamilton Holmes, and the Integration of the University of Georgia, 1964; Barnett Frummer is an Unbloomed Flower and Other Adventures of Barnett Frummer, Rosalie Mondle, Roland Magruder, and Their Friends, 1969; US Journal, 1971; American Fried: Adventures of a Happy Eater, 1974; Runestruck, 1977; Alice, Let's Eat: Further Adventures of a Happy Eater, 1978; Floater, 1980; Uncivil Liberties, 1982; Third Helpings, 1983; Killings, 1984; With All Disrespect: More Uncivil Liberties, 1985; If You Can't Say Something Nice, 1987; Travels with Alice, 1989; Enough's Enough (and Other Rules of Life), 1990; American Stories, 1991; Remembering Denny, 1993; Deadline Poet, 1994; Too Soon to Tell, 1995. Contributions to: Magazines. Honours: Deadline Poet, 1994; Too Soon to Tell, 1995. Contributions to: Magazines. Honours: National Book Award Nomination, 1980; Books-Across-the-Sea Ambassador of Honor Citation, English-Speaking Union, 1985. Address: c/o The New Yorker, 25 West 43rd Street, New York, NY 10036, USA.

TRIPP Miles Barton, (John Michael Brett, Michael Brett), b. 5 May 1923, Ganwick Corner, England. Writer. Publications: Kilo Forty, 1963; The Eighth Passenger, 1969; A Man Without Friends, 1970; High Heels, 1987; The Frightened Wife, 1987; The Cords of Vanity, 1989; Video Vengeance, 1990; The Dimensions of Deceit, 1993. Memberships: Society of Authors; Crime Writers Association, chairman, 1968-69; Detection Club. Address: The Peters Fraser and Dunlop Group Ltd, 5th Floor, The Chambers, Chelsea Harbour, Lots Road, London SW10 0XF, England.

TRISTRAM Uvedale Francis Barrington, b. 20 Mar 1915. Journalist. m. Elizabeth Frances Eden-Pearson, 8 Sept 1939, 1 daughter. Appointments: Morning Post; Assistant Editor, Aeropilot; Managing Editor, Hulton Publications, 1960-61; Editorial Manager, Longacre Press, 1961-62; Director of Information and Broadcasting, Basutoland, 1962-67; Director of Information, UK Freedom from Hunger Campaign, 1967-73; Founder, Editor, World Hunger. Publications: Adventure in Oil, 1958; John Fisher; Basutoland, 1961. Contributions to: Sunday Telegraph; Time and Tide; Tablet; Universe; Catholic Herald; Commercial Times. Honours: Rics Awards, Best Property Column in Weekly Paper, 1988, 1991; ISVA Provincial Property of the Year, 1990. Memberships: Guild of Catholic Writers, Master of the Keys, 1987-91; Deputy Master 1991-93; Institute of Journalists. Address: 19 Mallards' Reach, Weybridge, Surrey KT13 9HQ, England.

TROLLOPE Joanna, (Caroline Harvey), b. 9 Dec 1943, England. Writer. m. (1) David Roger William Potter, 1966, 2 daughters, (2) Ian Bayley Curteis, 1985, 2 stepsons. Education: MA, St Hugh's College, Oxford, 1972. Appointments: Information and Research Department, Foreign Office, 1965-67; Teaching posts, Farnham Girl's Grammar School, Adult education, English for Foreigners and Daneshill School, 1967-79. Publications: Eliza Stanhope, 1978; Parson Harding's Daughter, 1979; Mistaken Virtues (US edition of Parson Harding's Daughter),1979; Leaves from the Valley, 1980; The City of Gems, 1981; The Steps of the Sun, 1983; Britannia's Daughters: A Study of Women in the British Empire, 1983; The Taverners' Place, 1986; The Choir, 1988; A Village Affair, 1989; A Passionate Man, 1990; The Rector's Wife, 1991; The Men and the Girls, 1992; A Spanish Lover, 1992; The Best of Friends, 1992; The Country Habit: An Anthology, 1993; Next of Kin, 1996. As Caroline Harvey: Legacy of Love, 1992; A Second Legacy, 1993; The Brass Dolphin, 1997. Contributions to: Newspapers and magazines. Honours: Romantic Historical Novel of the Year, 1980; Officer of the Order of the British Empire, 1996. Address: c/o Peters, Fraser and Dunlop, Fifth Floor, The Chambers, Chelsea Harbour SW10 0XF, England.

TRONSKI Bronislaw, b. 24 Sept 1921, Wilno, Poland. Journalist; Writer. m. Janina Zajacowna, 3 July 1980, 1 son, 1 daughter. Education: Academy of Political Sciences, 1946-48; MA, Law, Jagiellonian University, Kraków, 1949. Appointments: Staff,

Socjalistyczna Agencja Prasowa, 1946-48, Agencja Robotnicza, 1948-64, Polska Agencja Prasowa, 1964; Foreign Correspondent, Far East, 1959-60, Balkan Countries, 1972-76, Algieria and Tunisia, 1980-82; Special Correspondent, European countries. Publications: Tedy przeszta Smierc, 1957; Na Dachu Swiata, 1961; Stonce Nad Stara Planina, 1979; W Cieniu Nadziei, 1980; Trucja Bez Tajemnic, 1981; Algierskie Osobliwosci, 1984; Test Pan Wolny, 1987; Tanczacy prezydent, 1988; Mozaika sródziemnomorska, 1988; Smak ziemi obiecanej, 1990; Stambul, 1992; I w Ostrej swiecisz Bramie, sladami mlodego Adama Mickiewicza, 1993; Translations of dramas. Contributions to: Numerous journals and magazines. Honours: Award, President of Polish Parliament; Awards, Parliament Reporters Club, 1965, 1966; Award, Polonia Club, Polish Journalists Association, 1985; Award, Weekly Kultura, 1988; Award, Counsel Fund of Literature, 1988; Award, International Publishers Club, 1990. Memberships: Polish Writers Association; Polish Journalists Association; Authors and Composers Association; Vice-President, Union of Warsaw Insurgents, 1991-. Address: Rakowiecka Street 33, App 30, 02-519 Warsaw, Poland.

TROTMAN Jack, (John Penn), b. Canada. Writer. Appointments: Officer, British Army Intelligence Corps, 1940-46; Foreign Office, 1946-48; Joint Intelligence Bureau, Ottawa, Canada, 1949-65; Canadian Department of National Defence, 1965-73; NATO International Staff, Paris, France, 1973-77; President, National Trust for Jersey, Channel Islands, 1984-87, 1990-92. Publications: Notice of Death, US edition as An Ad for Murder, 1982; Deceitful Death, US edition as Stag-Dinner Death, 1983; A Will to Kill, 1983; Mortal Term, 1984; A Deadly Sickness, 1985; Unto the Grave, 1986, Barren Revenge, 1986; Accident Prone, 1987; Outrageous Exposures, 1988; A Feast of Death, 1989; A Killing to Hide, 1990; A Knife Ill-Used, 1991; Death's Long Shadow, 1991; A Legacy of Death, 1992; A Haven of Danger, 1993; Widow's End, 1993; The Guilty Party, 1994; So Many Steps to Death, 1995; Bridal Shroud, 1996. Address: c/o Murray Pollinger, 222 Old Brompton Road, London SW5 0BZ, England.

TROW George W S, b. 28 Sept 1943, Greenwich, Connecticut, USA. Writer; Dramatist. Education: AB, Harvard University, 1965. Appointments: Staff Writer, The New Yorker, 1966-. Publications: Bullies (stories), 1980; Within the Context of No Context (essays), 1981; The City in the Mist (novel), 1984. Other: Several plays. Contributions to: Anthologies and periodicals. Honours: Jean Stein Awards, American Academy and Institute of Arts and Letters, 1981, 1984, 1986; Guggenheim Fellowship, 1994-95. Address: c/o The New Yorker, 20 West 43rd Street, New York, NY 10036, USA.

TRUCK Robert-Paul (Count), b. 3 May 1917, Calais, France. Poet; Critic; Historian. m. Jeanne Brogniart, 24 July 1942, 1 daughter. Education: Baccalaureat, 1935; French Naval School, 1938. Publications: Poetry: Heures Folles, 1938; Au Bord de la Nuit, 1948; Intersignes, 1953; Vertiges, 1989; Bois des Iles, 1992; Marche des Rois, 1993; Cicatrices, 1995. Non-Fiction: Médecins de la Honte (with Betty Truck), 1975; Memngele, l'ange de la mort (with Betty Truck), 1976. Contributions to: Anthologies and other publications. Honours: Various medals, diplomas and certificates. Memberships: Academia Leonardo da Vinci; Institut Académique de Paris; International Academy of Poets; Société des Poètes Français; World Literary Academy. Address: Varouna, 49 Rue de Lhomel, 62600 Berck-Plage, France.

TRUMAN Jill, b. 12 June 1934, Enfield, Middlesex, England. Teacher; Writer; Dramatist. m. Tony Truman, 31 Mar 1956, dec 1975, 1 son, 3 daughters. Education: BA, English Literature, 1955; Postgraduate Certificate in Drama, 1979. Publication: Letter to My Husband, 1988. Other: Radio plays: Letter to My Husband, 1986; Gone Out-Back Soon, 1988; Travels in West Africa, 1990; Flit, 1992; For Lizzie, 1994. Theatre: The Web, 1991. Musical: Kings of the Night, 1993. Contributions to: Magazines. Membership: Writers Guild of Great Britain. Literary Agent: Peters, Fraser and Dunlop. Address: 2 Ellesmere Road, Bow, London E3 5QX, England.

TRZEBINSKI Errol Georgia, b. 24 June 1936. Biographer. m. Zbigniew Wacław Trzebinski, 2 sons, 1 daughter. Education: School Certificate, Wimborne Convent School, 1953. Appointments: Consultant for BBC, including From an Immgrant's Notebook and 6-part series Hemingway; Consultant, World Without Walls (documentary on Beryl Markham), USA; Consultant, Out of Africa (feature film). Publications: Silence Will Speak: The Life of Denys Finch Hatton and His Relationship With Karen Blixen, 1977; The

Kenya Pioneers, 1985; The Lives of Beryl Markham, 1993. Contributions to: Periodicals and journals. Membership: Society of Authors, London. Literary Agent: Vivienne Schuster, Curtis Brown Ltd, London. Address: PO Box 84045, Mombasa, Kenya.

TSALOUMAS Dimitris, b. 13 Oct 1921, Leros, Greece. Teacher; Poet. m. Isle Wulff, 1958, 2 sons, 2 daughters. Appointments: Teacher, Victorian Schools, 1958-82; Writer-in-Residence, Oxford University, 1989, Melbourne University, Queensland University, La Trobe University. Publications: Resurrection, 1967; Triptych for a Second Coming, 1974; Observations for a Hypochondriac, 1974; The House with the Eucalyptus, 1975; The Sick Barber and Other Characters, 1979; The Book of Epigrams, 1981; The Observatory: Selected Poems, 1983; Falcon Drinking: The English Poems, 1988; Portrait of a Dog, 1991; The Barge, 1993. Editor, Translator of Poetry. Honours: Australia Council Grant and Fellowship; National Book Council Award, 1983; Wesley M Wright Prize for Poetry, 1994; Patrick White Award, 1994. Address: 72 Glenhuntly Road, Elwood, VA 3184, Australia.

TSCHABOLD Matthias, b. 16 Apr 1956, Lausanne, Switzerland. Poet. m. Anne-Marie Haddad, 8 May 1986. Education: Licence en Théologie, University of Lausanne, 1980; Licence es Lettres, 1993, Pedagogical Diploma, 1997, University of Zürich. Publications: Poetry: La Dépossession, 1981; Le Transfuge, 1992. Contributions to: Journal de Geneva, 1984; Repères. Membership: Société Suisse des écrivains. Address: Zweiackerstrasse, 8053 Zürich, Switzerland.

TSCHUMI Jean-Raymond, b. 21 Oct 1953, Berne, Switzerland. Teacher of Spanish and German. m. Hélène Veyre, 19 May 1994, 3 daughters. Education: Licence ès Lettres, University of Lausanne, 1979. Publications: Poetry: Résurgences, 1990; L'Été Disloqué, 1994; Un An A Vif, 1996. Contributions to: La Poésie Suisse Romande, anthology; Nouveau Quotidien, 1995-96. Honour: Prix Claude Sernet, France, 1991. Memberships: Swiss Writers' Association; Association Vaudoise des Écrivains. Address: Chemin du Village 1, CH-1012 Lausanne, Switzerland.

TSURUMI Shunsuke. Writer. Publications: Tayu Saizo Pen: A History of Slapstick Comedy, 1980; An Intellectual History of Wartime Japan, 1986; Amaho Dzome Dan: The Biography of a Stripper, 1989; Shirwateki Jikan: Mythological Time, 1994; Conversation in 10 volumes, 1996. Honours: Takaao Choei Prize; Osalagi Jiro Prize; Asalui Prize; Mystery Story Writers Prize. Address: 230-99 Nagafanicho Iwakura, Sakyo-ku, Kyoto, Japan.

TUBB E(dwin) C(harles), (Chuck Adams, Jud Cary, J F Clarkson, James S Farrow, James R Fenner, Charles S Graham, Charles Grey, Volsted Gridban, Alan Guthrie, George Holt, Gill Hunt, E F Jackson, Gregory Kern, King Lang, Mike Lantry, P Lawrence, Chet Lawson, Arthur MacLean, Carl Maddox, M L Powers, Paul Schofield, Brian Shaw, Roy Sheldon, John Stevens, Edward Thomson, Douglas West, Eric Wilding), b. 15 Oct 1919, London, England. Writer. Publications: Over 100 under various pseudonyms; Science fiction/fantasy: Saturn Patrol, 1951; Argentis, 1952; Planetoid Disposals Ltd, 1953; The Living World, 1954; Alien Dust, 1955; The Space-Born, 1956; Touch of Evil, 1959; Moon Base, 1964; Ten From Tomorrow (short stories), 1966; Death is a Dream, 1967; COD Mars, 1968; STAR Flight, 1969; The Jester at Scar, 1970; Lallia, 1971; Century of the Manikin, 1972; Mayenne, 1973; Veruchia, 1973; Zenya, 1974; Atilus the Slave, 1975; Jack of Swords, 1976; Haven of Darkness, 1977; Incident on Ath, 1978; Stellar Assignment, 1979; The Luck Machine, 1980. Suspense and Western novels: The Fighting Fury, 1955; Scourge of the South, 1956; Wagon Trail, 1957; Target Death, 1961; Too Tough to Handle, 1962; Airborne Commando, 1963; The Quillian Sector, 1978; Web of Sand, 1979; Iduna's Universe, 1979; The Terra Data, 1980; World of Promise, 1980; Nectar of Heaven, 1981; The Terridae, 1981; The Coming Event, 1982; Earth is Heaven, 1982; Melome, 1983; Stardeath, 1983; Angado, 1984; Symbol of Terra, 1984; The Temple of Truth, 1985; Pandora's Box, 1996. Contributions to: 230 stories to magazines and journals. Literary Agent: Carnell Literary Agency. Address: 67 Houston Road, London SE23 2RL, England.

TUCKER Eva Marie, b. 18 Apr 1929, Berlin, Germany. Writer. m. 11 Mar 1950 (widowed 1987), 3 daughters. Education: BA Honours, German, English, University of London. Appointments: C Day Lewis Writing Fellow, Vauxhall Manor School, London, 1978-79; Hawthornden Writing Fellowship, 1991. Publications: Contact (novel), 1966; Drowning (novel), 1969; Radetzkymarch by Joseph Roth (translation), 1974. Contributions to: BBC Radio 3 and 4; Encounter; London Magazine; Woman's Journal; Vogue; Harpers; Spectator; Listener; PEN International. Memberships: English PEN; Turner Society; Society of Authors. Literary Agent: Paul Marsh. Address: 63B Belsize Park Gardens, London NW3 4JN, England.

TUCKER Helen, b. 1 Nov 1926, Raleigh, North Carolina, USA. Writer. Education: BA, Wake Forest University, 1946; Graduate Studies, Columbia University, 1957-58. Appointments: Reporter, Times-News, Burlington, 1946-47, Times-News, Twin Falls, 1948-49, Statesman, Boise, 1950-51, Raleigh Times, 1955-57; Continuity Writer, Radio KDYL, Salt Lake City, Utah, 1952-53; Continuity Supervisor, Radio WPTF, Raleigh, 1953-55; Editorial Assistant, Columbia University Press, 1959-60; Director of Publicity and Publications, North Carolina Museum of Art, Raleigh, 1967-70. Publications: The Sound of Summer Voices, 1969; The Guilt of August Fielding, 1972; No Need of Glory, 1973; The Virgin of Lontano, 1974; A Strange and Ill-Starred Marriage, 1978; A Reason for Rivalry, 1979; A Mistress to the Regent: An Infamous Attachment, 1980; The Halverton Scandal, 1980; A Wedding Day Deception, 1981; The Double Dealers, 1982; Season of Dishonor, 1982; Ardent Vows, 1983; Bound by Honor, 1984; The Lady's Fancy, 1991; Bold Impostor, 1991. Contributions to: Lady's Circle; Ellery Queen Mystery Magazine; Alfred Hitchcock M ystery Magazine; Ladies Home Journal; The Crecent Review; Montevallo Review. Honours: Woman to receive the Distinguished Alumni Award, Wake Forest University, 1971; Franklin County Artist of the Year Award, 1992. Literary Agent: McIntosh and Otis, 310 Madison Avenue, New York, NY 10017, USA. Address: 2930 Hostetler Street, Raleigh, NC 27609, USA.

TUCKER Martin, b. 8 Feb 1928, Philadelphia, Pennsylvania, USA. Professor of English; Writer; Poet. Education: BA, 1949, PhD, 1963, New York University; MA, University of Arizona, 1954. Appointments: Faculty, Long Island University, 1956-; Editor, Confrontation magazine, 1970-. Publications: Modern British Literature (editor), Vols I-IV, 1967-76; Africa in Modern Literature, 1967; The Critical Temper (editor), Vols I-V, 1970-89; Joseph Conrad, 1976; Homes of Locks and Mysteries (poems), 1982; Literary Exile in the United States, 1991; Sam Shepard, 1992; Attention Spans (poetry), 1997; Modern American Literature (editor), 1997. Contributions to: Professional journals and general periodicals. Honours: National Endowment for the Arts/Coordinating Council and Literary Magazine Awards for Editorial Distinction, 1976, 1984; English-Speaking Union Award, 1982; Phi Beta Kappa. Memberships: African Literature Association; African Studies Association; Authors Guild; Modern Language Association; National Book Critics Circle; PEN, executive board, 1973-96; Poetry Society of America. Address: 90-A Dosoris Lane, Glen Cove, NY 11542, USA.

TUCKMAN Bruce W(ayne), b. 24 Nov 1938, New York, New York, USA. Psychologist; Professor; Writer. Education: BS, Psychology, Rensselaer Polytechnic Institute, 1960; MA, Psychology, 1962, PhD, Psychology, 1963, Princeton University. Appointments: Research Associate, Princeton University, 1963; Adjunct Professor, University College, University of Maryland, 1963-65; Research Psychologist, Naval Medical Research Institute, Bethesda, Maryland, 1963-65; Associate Professor of Education, 1965-70, Professor of Education, 1970-78, Director of Research, Graduate School of Education, 1975-78, Rutgers University; Dean, School of Education, Baruch College of the City University of New York, 1978-82; Senior Research Fellow, Center for Advanced Study in Education, City University of New York, 1982-83; Dean, 1983-85, Professor, 1985-, College of Education, Florida State University; Consulting Editor, 1987-93, Executive Editor, 1993-, Journal of Experimental Education. Publications: Conducting Educational Research, 1972, 4th edition, 1994; Testing for Teachers, 1975, 2nd edition, 1988; Evaluating Instructional Programs, 1979, 2nd edition, 1985; Analyzing and Designing Educational Research, 1985; Effective College Management, 1987; Road to Boston (novel), 1988; Educational Psychology, 1992. Contributions to: Journals. Honours: National Institute of Mental Health Fellowship, 1961-63; New Jersey Association of English Teachers Author's Award, 1969; Phi Delta Kappa Research Award, 1973; Outstanding Teaching Award, 1993; Florida State University Teaching Award, 1993. Memberships: Fellow, American Psychological Association; American Educational Research Association; Gulf Winds Track Club. Address: Department of Educational Research, Florida State University, Tallahassee, FL 32306-3030, USA.

TUDOR Andrew Frank, b. 19 Nov 1942, Edinburgh, Scotland. University Lecturer. Education: BA, Sociology, 1965. Publications: Theories of Film, 1973; Image and Influence, 1974; Beyond Empiricism, 1982; Monsters and Mad Scientists, 1989. Contributions to: Film Critic for New Society, 1975-82. Address: Department of Sociology, University of York, Heslington, York YO1 5DD, England.

TUDOR-CRAIG Pamela Wynn (Pamela, Lady Wedgwood), b. 26 June 1928, London, England. Art Historian; Writer. m. (1) Algernon James Riccarton Tudor-Craig, 27 July 1956, dec 1969, 1 daughter, (2) Sir John Wedgwood, 1 May 1982, dec 1989. Education: 1st Class Honours degree, 1949, PhD, 1952, Courtauld Institute, University of London. Appointments: Teacher, several US colleges; Presenter, The Secret Life of Paintings television series, 1986; Arts page, Church Times, 1988-. Publications: Richard III, 1973; The Secret Life of Paintings (co-author), 1986; Bells Guide to Westminster Abbey (co-author), 1986; Exeter Cathedral, 1991; Anglo-Saxon Wall Paintings, 1991. Contributions to: Books and professional journals. Honour: Honorary Doctor of Humanities, William Jewell College, 1983. Memberships: Cathedrals Advisory Commission, 1975-90; English-Speaking Union, Cultural Affairs Committee; Society of Antiquaries, Fellow, 1958-, Council Member, 1989-92. Address: 9 St Anne's Crescent, Lewes, East Sussex BN7 1SB, England.

TUFTY Barbara Jean, b. 28 Dec 1923, Iowa City, Iowa, USA. Conservation Writer and Editor. m. Harold G Tufty, 29 Dec 1948, 2 sons, 1 daughter. Education: BA, Botany, Duke University; Postgraduate classes, New School for Social Research, New York City, 1946; Sorbonne, University of Paris, 1948; University of Colorado, 1949, 1950, 1951. Appointments: Science Writer, Science Service, 1948-72, National Academy of Sciences, 1970-72; Editor, National Science Foundation, 1972-84; Conservation Writer and Editor, Audubon Naturalist Society, 1986-. Publications: 1001 Questions Answered About Natural Land Disasters, 1969; 1001 Questions Answered About Storms, 1970; Cells, Units of Life, 1973; Wildflowers of the Washington-Baltimore Area (co-author), 1995. Contributions to: Reference books, journals, and magazines. Honours: Chi Delta Phi, 1945; Honorary Life Member (1st Woman), Bombay Natural History Society, 1960; Thomas Stokes Honourable Mention Writing Award, 1972; Catherine O'Brien Honourable Mention Writing Award, 1972; Writing Fellowships at Ossabaw Island Institute, Library of Congress. Memberships: Washington Independent Writers; National Association of Science Writers; Nature Conservancy; Washington Environmental Writers Association; Environmental Writers Association; Environmental Defence Fund; Earthwatch. Address: 3812 Livingston Street North West, Washington, DC 20015, USA.

TUGENDHAT Julia. See: DOBSON Julia Lissant.

TULLY (William) Mark, b. 24 Aug 1935, Calcutta, India. Journalist. m. Margaret Tully, 13 Aug 1960, 2 sons, 2 daughters. Education: Trinity Hall, Cambridge, 1956-59. Publications: Amritsar; Mrs Gandhi's Last Battle; Raj to Rajiv; No Full Stops in India; The Heart of India, 1995. Honours: Officer of the Order of the British Empire; Dimbleby Award, British Academy of Film and Television Arts; Broadcasting Press Guild; Padmashri. Literary Agent: Gill Coleridge. Address: 1 Nizamuddin East, New Delhi 110013, India.

TUOHY John Francis (Frank), b. 2 May 1925, Uckfield, Sussex, England. Writer. Education: MA Honours, King's College, Cambridge, 1946. Publications: The Animal Game, 1957; The Warm Nights of January, 1960; The Ice Saints, 1964; Portugal, 1970; W B Yeats, 1976; Collected Stories, 1984. Contributions to: Numerous magazines and journals. Honours: Katherine Mansfield Prize, 1960; James Tait Black Memorial Prize, 1964; Geoffrey Faber Memorial Prize, 1964; William Heinemann Award, 1978. Memberships: PEN; Society of Authors. Literary Agent: The Peters Fraser and Dunlop Group Ltd, London, England. Address: Shatwell Cottage, Yarlington, Nr Wincanton, Somerset BA9 8DL, England.

TUQAN Fadwa, b. 1 Mar 1917, Nablus, Palestine. Publications: My Brother Ibrahim, 1946; Alone with Days, 1952; Give Us Love, 1960; Before the Closed Door, 1967; Night and Knights, 1969; Alone at the Top of the World, 1973; I Found It, 1975; An Arduous Mountain Journey (autobiography), 1985; Adonis and the Other Thing, 1989; Difficult Journey, 1993. Contributions to: Innumerable contributions through the Arab World. Literary Agent: Dar Al-Adab, Beirut, Lebanon; Dar Al-Shorouq, Amman, Jordan. Address: PO Box 31, Nablus, Palestine, Via Israel.

TURBILL Janice Betina, b. 13 Mar 1944, Sydney, New South Wales, Australia. University Lecturer. Education: BA, Macquarie University, 1979; MED, Sydney University, 1985; PhD, Wollongong University, 1994. Publications: No Better Way To Teach Writing, 1982; Now We Want To Write, 1983; Towards a Reading Writing Classroom (with Andrea Butler), 1984; Coping with Chaos (with B Cambourne), 1987; Responsive Evaluation (with B Cambourne), 1994. Contributions to: Books and journals. Memberships: Society of Authors of Australia; Fellow, Australian College of Education. Address: Faculty of Education, University of Wollongong, New South Wales, Australia 2522.

TURK Frances Mary, b. 14 Apr 1915, Huntingdon, England. Novelist. Publications: Paddy O'Shea, 1937; The Precious Hours, 1938; Paradise Street, 1939; Lovable Clown, 1941; Angel Hill, 1942; The Five Grey Geese, 1944; Salutation, 1949; The Small House at Ickley, 1951; The Gentle Flowers, 1952; The Dark Wood, 1954; The Glory and the Dream, 1955; Dinny Lightfoot, 1956; No Through Road, 1957; The White Swan, 1958; The Secret Places, 1961; The Guarded Heart, 1964; Legacy of Love, 1967; Fair Recompense, 1969; Goddess of Threads, 1975; A Visit to Marchmont, 1977; Candle Corner, 1986. Contributions to: Many periodicals. Memberships; Romantic Novelists Association; Many other professional organisations. Address: Hillrise, Brampton Road, Buckden, Huntingdon PE18 9UH, England.

TURNBULL Gael Lundin, b. 7 Apr 1928, Edinburgh, Scotland. Poet; Former Medical Practitioner. m. (1) Jonnie May Draper, 1952, 3 daughters, (2) Pamela Jill Iles, 1983. Education: BA, Cambridge University, 1948; MD, University of Pennsylvania, 1951. Publications: A Trampoline, 1968; Scantlings, 1970; A Gathering of Poems, 1950-80, 1983; A Year and a Day, 1985; A Winter Journey, 1987; While Breath Persist, 1992; For Whose Delight, 1995. Contributions to: Numerous journals and magazines. Honour: Alice Hunt Bartlett Award, 1969. Address: 12 Strathearn Place, Edinburgh EH9 2AL, Scotland.

TURNER Alberta Tucker, b. 22 Oct 1919, New York, New York, USA. Professor Emerita; Poet; Writer. m. William Arthur Turner, 9 Apr 1943, 1 son, 1 daughter. Education: BA, Hunter College, New York City, 1940; MA, Wellesley College, Massachusetts, 1941; PhD, Ohio State University, 1946. Appointments: Lecturer to Professor, 1964-90, Director, Poetry Center, 1964-90, Professor Emerita, 1990-, Cleveland State University; Associate Editor, Field, Contemporary Poetry and Poetics, 1970-. Publications: Poetry: Need, 1971; Learning to Count, 1974; Lid and Spoon, 1977; A Belfry of Knees, 1983; Beginning with And: New and Selected Poems, 1994. Other: 50 Contemporary Poets: The Creative Process (editor), 1977; Poets Teaching, editor, 1981; To Make a Poem, 1982; 45 Contemporary Poems: The Creative Process (editor), 1985; Responses to Poetry, 1990. Contributions to: Journals and magazines. Honours: MacDowell Colony Fellowship, 1985; Cleveland Arts Prize, 1985; Ohio, Poetry Award, 1986; Ohio Governor's Award for Arts in Education, 1988. Memberships: Milton Society of America; PEN American Center. Address: 482 Caskey Court, Oberlin, OH 44074, USA.

TURNER Billie Lee II, b. 22 Dec 1945, Texas City, Texas, USA. Professor of Geography; Writer. m. Linda Lee Van Zandt, 1 son, 1 daughter. Education: BA, Geography, 1968, MA, Geography, 1969, University of Texas; PhD, Geography, University of Wisconsin, Madison, 1974. Publications: Pre-Hispanic Maya Agriculture (co-editor), 1978; Once Beneath the Forest, 1983; Pulltrouser Swamp, 1985; Comparative Farming Systems (co-editor), 1987; The Earth as Transformed by Human Action (co-editor), 1990; Population Growth and Agricultural Change in Africa, 1993; Changes in Land Use and Land Cover: A Global Perspective (co-editor), 1994; Regions at Risk: Comparisons of Threatened Environments (co-editor), 1995. Contributions to: Over 100 on science, economy and botany in various publications. Honours: Guggenheim Fellowship, 1981; Fellow, CASBS, 1994; Honours, Association of American Geography, 1995; National Academy of Sciences, 1995; Higgins Chair of Environment and Society; Centenary Medal, Royal Scottish Geographical Society, 1996. Address: 19 Farnun Street, Worcester, MA 01602, USA.

TURNER Brian (Lindsay), b. 4 Mar 1944, Dunedin, New Zealand. Editor; Poet. Education: Otago Boys High School, 1957-61. Appointments: Managing Editor, John McIndoe Ltd, Dunedin, 1975-86. Publications: Poetry: Ladders of Rain, 1978; Ancestors, 1981; Listening to the River, 1983; Bones, 1985; All That Blue Can Be, 1989; Beyond, 1992. Other: New Zealand High Country: Four Seasons, 1983; The Guide to Trout Fishing in Otago, 1994. Honours: Robert Burns Fellowship, 1984; New Zealand Book Award for Poetry, 1993; Scholarship in Letters, 1994. Membership: New Zealand Society of Authors. Address: 2 Upper Junction Road, Sawyers Bay, Dunedin, New Zealand.

TURNER Frederick, b. 19 Nov 1943, East Haddon, Northamptonshire, England. Professor of Humanities; Writer. m. Mei Lin Chang, 25 June 1966, 2 sons. Education: BA, 1965, MA, 1967, BLitt, 1967, English Language and Literature, Oxford University. Appointments: Assistant Professor of English, University of California, Santa Barbara, USA, 1967-72; Associate Professor of English, Kenyon College, 1972-85; Editor, Kenyon Review, 1978-83; Visiting Professor of English, University of Exeter, England, 1984-85; Founders Professor of Arts and Humanities, University of Texas at Dallas, Richardson, USA, 1985-. Publications: Shakespeare and the Nature of Time, 1971; Between Two Lives, 1972; The Return, 1979; The New World, 1985; The Garden, 1985; Natural Classicism, 1986; Genesis: An Epic Poem, 1988; Rebirth of Value, 1991; Tempest, Flute and Oz, 1991; April Wind, 1991; Beauty, 1991; Foamy Sky: The Major Poems of Miklos Radnoti (translator with Zsuzanna Ozsvath), 1992; The Culture of Hope, 1995. Contributions to: Journals and periodicals. Honours: Ohioana Prize for Editorial Excellence, 1980; Djerassi Foundation Grant and Residency, 1981; Levinson Poetry Prize, 1983; Missouri Review Essay Prize, 1986; PEN Golden Pen Award, 1992. Memberships: PEN; Modern Language Association. Address: 2668 Aster Drive, Richardson, TX 75082, USA.

TURNER George (Reginald), b. 8 Oct 1916, Melbourne, Australia. Appointments: Employment Officer, Commonwealth Employment Service, Melbourne, 1945-49, Wangaratta, VA, 1949-50; Textile Technician, Bruck Mill, Wangaratta, 1951-64; Senior Employement Officer, Volkswagen Ltd, 1964-67. Publications: Young Man of Talent, 1959; A Stranger and Afraid, 1961; A Waste of Shame, 1965; The Lame Dog Man, 1967; Beloved Son, Transit of Cassidy, 1978; Vaneglory, 1982; Yesterdays Men, 1983; The Sea and Summer, 1987; A Pursuit of Miracles, 1990; The Destiny Makes, 1993. Honours: Miles Franklin Award, 1962; Arthur C Clarke Award, 1987. Membership: Australian Society of Authors. Literary Agent: Cherry Weiner, 28 Kipling Way, NJ, USA. Address: 4/296 Inkerman Street, East St Kilda, VA 3183, Australia.

TURNER George William, b. 26 Oct 1921, Dannevirke, New Zealand. University Teacher (retired). m. Beryl Horrobin, 18 Apr 1949, 2 sons. Education: BA, 1944, MA, 1948, New Zealand; Diploma, New Zealand Library School, 1948; Diploma in English Linguistic Studies, University College, London, England, 1964. Appointments: Tutor and Lecturer, University of Canterbury, New Zealand, 1955-64; Reader, University of Adelaide, 1965-86. Publications: The English Language in Australia and New Zealand, 1966, 2nd edition, 1972; Good Australian English (editor), 1972; Stylistics, 1973; Australian Pocket Oxford Dictionary, 2nd edition (editor), 1984; Australian Concise Oxford Dictionary (editor), 1986; The Australian Oxford Paperback Dictionary (co-editor with Beryl Turner), 1989. Contributions to: Books and journals. Honours: Fellow, Australian Academy of the Humanities, 1974; Festschrift: Lexicographical and linguistic studies, (edited by T L and Jill Burton, D S Brewer), 1988. Address: 3 Marola Avenue, Rostrevor, South Australia 5073, Australia.

TURNER Len. See: **FLOREN Lee.**

TURNER L A (Leslie-Anne), b. 6 May 1969, Quebec, Canada. Journalist; Writer. Education: Ontario, Canada; Undertaking MA in Arts Criticism/Media. Appointments: Freelance journalist and writer, 1987-89; Report writer, 1989-91; Freelance journalist, feature writer, film critic, 1991-94; Journalist and editor, 1994; Freelance journalist, feature writer and interviewer, reviewer, scriptwriter, 1994-. Publications: When Technology Fails, 1993. Contributions to: Telegraph; Various consumer and professional journals on film and aviation, UK and international. Address: Knight's Cottage, Knight's Place Farm, Nr Cobham, Rochester, Kent ME2 3UB, England.

TURNER Mary. See: **LAMBOT Isobel Mary.**

TURNER Philip William, (Stephen Chance), b. 3 Dec 1925, Rossland, British Columbia, Canada. Writer; Dramatist. m. Margaret Diana Samson, 23 Sept 1950, 2 sons, 1 daughter. Education: BA/MA, English Lanaguage and Literature, Oxford University, 1946. Publications: The Grange at High Force, 1965; The Bible Story, 1968; Septimus & the Danedyke Mystery, 1973; The Candlemass Treasure,

1988. Plays: Christ in the Concrete City, 1956; How Many Miles to Bethlehem?, 1987. Honour: Carnegie Medal, 1965. Literary Agent: Watson Little, London, England. Address: St Francis, 181 West Malvern Road, Malvern, Worcs, England.

TURNILL Reginald, b. 12 May 1915, Dover, England. Writer; Broadcaster. m. 10 Sept 1938, 2 sons. Education: Fleet Street Reporter. Appointments: Reporter, Industrial Correspondent, Press Association, London, 1930-56; Industrial Correspondent, 1956-58; Aerospace and Defence Correspondent, 1958-75, BBC. Publications: The Language of Space, 1970; Observer's Book of Manned Spaceflight, 1972, 3rd edition, 1978; Observer's Unmanned Spaceflight, 1974; Observer's Spaceflight Directory, 1978; Space Age, 1980; Jane's Spaceflight Directory, 1984, 4th edition, 1988; Space Technology International, 1989, 4th edition, 1992; World Aerospace Development, 1993; Celebrating Concorde, 1994. Contributions to: Zodiac; Executive Travel; Aerospace; Aviation Week; Space Technology. Memberships: British Interplanetary Society; Royal Aeronautical Society. Address: Somerville Lodge, Hillside, Sandgate, Kent CT20 3DB, England.

TURQUE Bill, b. 1954, New York, New York, USA. Journalist. Education: BA, English, University of Michigan, 1977. Appointments: Reporter, Kansas City Star, Dallas Times Herald; General Editor, National Affairs Section, 1989, Senior Writer, National Affairs Section, 1992, White House Correspondent, 1994-, Newsweek. Honours: National Magazine Award Nomination, 1993; Co-recipient, several awards with Newsweek. Address: c/o Newsweek, 251 West 57th Street, New York, NY 10019-1894, USA.

TUSIANI Joseph, b. 14 Jan 1924, Foggia, Italy (US citizen, 1956). Professor (retired); Writer; Poet. Education: Dottore in Lettere summa cum laude, University of Naples, 1947. Appointments: Chairman, Italian Department, College Mount St Vincent, 1948-71; Lecturer in Italian, Hunter College, New York City, 1950-62; Visiting Associate Professor, New York University, 1956-64, City University of New York, 1971-83; NDEA Visiting Professor of Italian, Connecticut State College, 1962; Professor, Herbert H Lehman College, New York City, 1971-83. Publications: Dante in Licenza, 1952; Two Critical Essays on Emily Dickinson, 1952; Melos Cordis, Poems in Latin, 1955; Odi Sacre: Poems, 1958; The Complete Poems of Michelangelo, 1960; Lust and Liberty: The Poems of Machiavelli, 1963; Tasso's Jerusalem Delivered (verse translation), 1970; Italian Poets of the Renaissance, 1971; The Age of Dante, 1973; Tasso's Creation of the World, 1982; Rosa Rosarum (poems in Latin), 1984; In Exilio Rerum (poems in Latin), 1985; La Parola Difficile, 3 volumes, 1988, 1991, 1992; Carmina Latina, 1994; Leopardi's Canti, translation, 1994; Le Poesie Inglesi di G A Borgese, 1995. Contributions to: Books and journals. Honours: Greenwood Prize for Poetry, 1956; Cavaliere ufficiale, Italy, 1973; Leone di San Marco Award, 1982; Joseph Tusiani Scholarship Fund founded in his honour, Lehman College, 1983; Congressional Medal of Merit, 1984; Progresso Medal of Liberty, 1986; Outstanding Teacher Award, American Association of Teachers of Italian; Renoir Literary Award, 1988; An International Homage, 1994; Festschrift published in his honour, 1995; Enrico Fermi Award, 1995. Memberships: Catholic Poetry Society of America; Poetry Society of America. Address: 308 East 72nd Street, New York, NY 10021, USA.

TUTTLE Lisa, b. 16 Sept 1952, Houston, Texas, USA. Writer. Education; BA, Syracuse University, 1973. Publications include: Windhaven, 1981; Familiar Spirit, 1983; Catwitch, 1983; Children's Literary Houses, 1984; Encyclopedia of Feminism, 1986; A Spaceship Built of Stone and Other Stories, 1987; Heroines: Women Inspired by Women, 1988; Lost Futures, 1992; Memories of the Body, 1992; Panther in Argyll, 1996; The Pillow Friend, 1996. Contributions to: Magazines. Honour: John W Campbell Award, 1974. Literary Agent: Abner Stein. Address: 10 Roland Gardens, London SW7, England.

TUTTLE William McCullough, b. 7 Oct 1937, Detroit, Michigan, USA. Professor of History. m. (1) Linda Lee Stumpp, 12 Dec 1959, div, 2 sons, 1 daughter, (2) Kathryn Nemeth, 6 May 1995. Education: BA, Denison University, 1959; MA, 1964, PhD, 1967, University of Wisconsin. Appointments: Assistant Professor, 1967-70, Associate Professor, 1970-75, Professor of History, 1975-, University of Kansas; Senior Fellow in Southern and Negro History, Johns Hopkins University, 1969-70; Research Fellow, Harvard University, 1972-73; Associate Fellow, Stanford Humanities Center, 1983-84; Research Associate, University of California, Berkeley, 1986-88. Publications: Race Riot: Chicago in the Red Summer of 1919, 1970; W E B DuBois,

1973; Plain Folk (co-author), 1982; Daddy's Gone to War: The Second World War in the Lives of America's Children, 1993. Contributions to: Journal of American History; American Studies; Labor History; Technology and Culture. Honours: National Endowment for the Humanities, Younger Humanist Fellowship, 1972-73; Award of Merit, American Association for State and Local History, 1972; Guggenheim Fellowship, 1975-76; Evans Grant, 1975-76; Beveridge Grant, 1982; Fellowship for Independent Study and Research, 1983-84; National Endowment for the Humanities, Projects Research Grant, 1986-89; Hall Humanities Research Fellow, 1990. Memberships: Society of American Historians; American Historical Association; Organization of American Historians. Address: 21 Winona Avenue, Lawrence, KS 66046, USA.

TUTUOLA Amos, b. June 1920, Abeokuta, Western Nigeria. Novelist. Education: Anglican Central School, Abeokuta. Appointment: Visiting Research Fellow, University of Ife, 1979. Publications: The Palm Wine Drinkard, His Dead Palm Wine Tapester in the Dead's Town, 1952; My Life in the Bush of Ghosts, 1954; Simbi and the Styr of the Dark Jungle, 1955; Ajaiyi and His Inherited Poverty, 1967; The Witch Herbalist of the Remote Town, 1981; The Wild Hunter in the Bush of the Ghosts, 1982; Pauper, Brawler and Slanderer, 1987; T Yoruba Folktales, 1986; The Village Witchdoctor and Other Stories, 1990. Co-Editor: Winds of Change: Modern Stories from Black Africa, 1977. Address: PO Box 2251, Ibadan, Nigeria.

TWINING William Lawrence, b. 22 Sept 1934, Kampala, Uganda. Professor of Law; Writer. m. Penelope Elizabeth Wall Morris, 31 Aug 1957, 1 son, 1 daughter. Education: BA, 1955, MA, 1960, DCL, 1990, Brasenose College, Oxford; JD, University of Chicago, 1958. Appointments: Professor of Law, University College, London; Editor, Law in Context Series, 1965-, Jurists Series, 1979-. Publications: Karl Llewellyn and the Realist Movement, 1973, 2nd edition, 1985; Law, Publishing and Legal Information, 1981; Theories of Evidence, 1985; Learning Lawyers' Skills, 1989; Rethinking Evidence, 1990; Analysis of Evidence, 1991; How to Do Things With Rules, 1991; Evidence and Proof, 1992; Blackstone's Tower, 1994; Law in Context: Enlarging a Discipline, 1997. Contributions to: Professional journals. Honours: Honorary LLD, University of Victoria, 1980, University of Edinburgh, 1994. Memberships: Commonwealth Legal Education Association; Society of Public Teachers of Law; UK Association for Legal and Social Philosophy. Address: c/o Faculty of Law, University College, 4 Endsleigh Gardens, London WC1H 0EG, England.

TWUM Michael Kyei, b. 30 Apr 1954, Writer; Poet. m. Maureen Twum, 22 Aug 1986, 1 son. Education: Modern School of Commerce, Ghana, 1974; University of Bonn, West Germany, 1981. Appointments: Lifetime Deputy Governor, ABIRA, USA, 1987. Publications: Golden Poems from Africa, 1982; Beyond Expectations, 1983; Great Adventures of an African, 1983. Contributions to: Several Magazines and Newspapers. Honours: Silver Medal, 1985, Gold Medal, 1987, ABI, USA; Certificates, IBC, England. Memberships: National Association of Writers; World Institute of Achievement; IBC; PEN International. Literary Agent: Vantage Press, New York, USA. Address: 78 Acacia Road, Mitcham, Surrey CR4 1ST, England.

TYLER Anne, b. 25 Oct 1941, Minneapolis, Minnesota, USA. Writer. m. Taghi M Modaressi, 3 May 1963, 2 children. Education: BA, Duke University, 1961; Postgraduate Studies, Columbia University, 1962. Publications: If Morning Ever Comes, 1964; The Tin Can Tree, 1965; A Slipping Down Life, 1970; The Clock Winder, 1972; Celestial Navigation, 1974; Searching for Caleb, 1976; Earthly Possessions, 1977; Morgan's Passing, 1980; Dinner at the Homesick Restaurant, 1982; The Best American Short Stories, 1983 (editor with Shannon Ravenel), 1983; The Accidental Tourist, 1985; Breathing Lessons, 1988; Saint Maybe, 1991; Tumble Tower (juvenile), 1993; Ladder of Years, 1995. Honours: National Book Critics Circle Award for Fiction, 1985; Pulitzer Prize for Fiction, 1989. Memberships: American Academy of Arts and Letters; American Academy of Arts and Sciences. Literary Agent: Timothy Seldes, Russell & Volkening Inc. Address: 222 Tunbridge Road, Baltimore, MD 21212, USA.

TYLER W T. See: **HAMRICK Samuel J, Jr.**

TYSON Remer Hoyt, b. 2 July 1934, Statesboro, Georgia, USA. Journalist. m. Virginia Curtin Knight, 18 Feb 1984, 1 son, 1 daughter. Education: Georgia Teacher College, 1952-54; University of Georgia, 1954-56; Art degree, Harvard University, Nieman Fellow, 1967-68; Harvard Business School, 1981. Publication: They Love a Man in the

Country, 1988. Memberships: Foreign Correspondents Association of Southern Africa; East Africa Foreign Correspondents Association. Address: 3 Woking Drive, Northwood, Mt Pleasant, Harare, Zimbabwe.

U

UGGLA Andrzej Nils, b. 30 Mar 1940, Warsaw, Poland. Researcher. m. Margaretha Backman, 20 Dec 1969, 1 son, 1 daughter. Education: MA, Gdansk University, 1966; DPhil, University of Uppsala, 1977. Publications: Strindberg och den polska teatern, 1890-1970, 1977; Polen i svensk press under andra världskriget, 1986; Den svenska polenbilden och Polsk prosa i Sverige 1939-1960, 1986; Från Politik till litteratur, 1989; Sverige och polska skalder, 1990; Polacy w Szwecji w latach II wojny swiatowej, 1996. Memberships: Union of Polish Writers Abroad; Stowarzyszenie Pisarzy Polskich; Sveriges Författarförbund. Address: Hovtångsv 10, 756 48 Uppsala, Sweden.

UHNAK Dorothy, b. 1933, Bronx, New York, USA. Writer. Education: City College, New York City; BS, John Jay College of Criminal Justice of the City University of New York, 1968. Appointments: Detective, New York City Transit Police Department, 1953-67. Publications: Policewoman, 1964; The Bait, 1968; The Witness, 1969; The Ledger, 1970; Law and Order, 1973; The Investigation, 1977; False Witness, 1981; Victims, 1985; The Ryer Avenue Story, 1993. Contributions to: Newspapers and magazines. Honours: Edgar, Mystery Writers of America, 1969; Legrande Prix de la Litterateur Policiere, 1971. Memberships: PEN; Writers Guild of America. Address: c/o Simon and Schuster Inc, 1230 Sixth Avenue, NY 10020, USA.

ULAM Adam B(runo), b. 8 Apr 1922, Lwow, Poland (US citizen, 1949). Professor of History and Political Science Emeritus; Writer. 2 sons. Education: AB, Brown University, 1943; PhD, Harvard University, 1947. Appointments: Faculty, 1947-59, Professor of Government, 1959-92, Gurney Professor of History and Political Science, 1979-92, Professor Emeritus, 1992-, Research Associate, 1948-, Director, 1973-76, 1980-92, Russian Research Center, Harvard University. Publications: The Bolsheviks and Lenin, 1965; Stalin: The Man and His Era, 1972, 2nd edition, 1987; Expansion and Coexistence, 1973; Dangerous Relations: The Soviet Union in World Politics, 1970-82, 1983; The Kirov Affair, 1988; The Communists: The Story of Power and Lost Illusions, 1948-91, 1992. Contributions to: Professional journals. Honours: Guggenheim Fellowships, 1956, 1969; Rockefeller Foundation Fellowships, 1957, 1960; Honorary LLD, Brown University, 1983. Memberships: American Academy of Arts and Sciences; American Philosophical Society. Address: c/o Russian Research Center, Harvard University, Cambridge, MA 02138, USA.

ULRICH Laurel Thatcher, b. 11 July 1938, Sugar City, Idaho, USA. Professor of History. m. Gael Dennis Ulrich, 22 Sept 1958, 3 sons, 2 daughters. Education: BA, University of Utah, 1960; MA, Simmons College, 1971; PhD, University of New Hampshire, 1980. Appointments: Assistant Professor, 1980-88, Associate Professor, 1988-92, Professor of History, 1992-, University of New Hampshire; Phillips Professor of Early American History and Professor of Women's Studies, Harvard University 1995-. Publications: A Midwife's Tale: The Life of Martha Ballard, 1990; Good Wives, 1991. Contributions to: Journals and magazines. Honours: John S Dunning Prize, 1990; Pulitzer Prize for History, 1991; Bancroft Prize, 1991; Gary Lindberg Award, 1991; New England Historical Association Award, 1991; Guggenheim Fellowship, 1991-92; Charles Frankel Award, 1993. Membership: American Historical Association. Address: Department of History, Robinson Hall, Harvard University, Cambridge, MA 02138, USA.

UNDERHILL Charles. See: **HILL Reginald (Charles)**.

UNDERWOOD Michael. See: **EVELYN John Michael**.

UNGER Barbara, b. 2 Oct 1932, New York, New York, USA. Professor of English and Creative Writing; Poet. m. (1), 2 daughters, (2) Theodore Kiichiro Sakano, 31 July 1987. Education: BA, 1954, MA, 1957, City College of New York. Appointment: Professor of English and Creative Writing, Rockland Cmmunity College, State University of New York, 1969-. Publications: Basement: Poems 1959-63, 1975; The Man Who Burned Money, 1980; Inside the Wind, 1986; Learning to Foxtrot, 1989; Blue Depression Glass, 1991. Contributions to: Journals and magazines. Honours: Breadloaf Scholar, 1978; National Poetry Competition Award, 1982; Ragdale Foundation Fellowships, 1985, 1986; Goodman Award in Poetry, 1989; Anna Davidson Rosenberg

Award for Poems on the Jewish Experience, 1990; Djerassi Foundation Literature Residency, 1991; JH G Roberts Writing Award in Poetry, 1991. Membership: Poetry Society of America. Address: 101 Parkside Drive, Suffern, NY 10901, USA.

UNGER J(ames) Marshall, b. 28 May 1947, Cleveland, Ohio, USA. Professor of Japanese; Writer. m. Mutsuyo Okumura Unger, 18 Oct 1976. Education: AB, 1969, AM 1971, University of Chicago; MA, 1972, PhD, 1975, Yale University. Appointments: Senior Lecturer in Japanese, University of Canterbury, Christchurch, New Zealand, 1975-76; Assistant Professor, 1977-82, Associate Professor, 1982-87, Professor of Japanese, 1987-92, University of Hawaii at Manoa; Visiting Scholar, University of Tokyo, 1985; Visiting Porfessor, University of Tsukuba, 1989, National Museum of Ethnology, Osaka, 1991; Professor of Japanese, University of Maryland at College Park, 1992-96, Ohio State University, 1996-. Publications: Studies in Early Japanese Morphophonemics, 1977, 2nd edition, 1993; The Fifth Generation Fallacy: Why Japan is Betting Its Future on Artificial Intelligence, 1987; Literacy and Script Reform in Occupation Japan: Reading Between the Lines, 1996. Editor: Language, Writing Systems, and Literacy (with Sakiyama Osamu and Umesao Tadao), 1992; A Framework for Introductory Japanese Language Curricula in American High Schools and Colleges (with Fred C Lorish, Mari Noda, and Yasuko Wada), 1993. Contributions to: Numerous books and journals. Honours; Various grants and fellowships. Memberships: American Oriental Society; Association for Asian Studies; Association of Teachers of Japanese; International House of Japan; Linguistic Society of America. Address: 204 Cunz Hall, 1841 Millikin Road, OH 43210, USA.

UPDIKE John (Hoyer), b. 18 Mar 1932, Shillington, Pennsylvania, USA. Writer; Poet; Critic. m. (1) Mary Entwistle Pennington, 26 June 1953, div 1977, 2 sons, 2 daughters, (2) Martha Ruggles Bernhard, 30 Sept 1977, 3 stepchildren. Education: AB, Harvard University, 1954; Ruskin School of Drawing and Fine Art, Oxford, 1954-55. Publications: Novels: The Poorhouse Affair, 1959; Rabbit, Run, 1960; The Centaur, 1963; Of the Farm, 1965; Couples, 1968; Rabbit Redux, 1971; A Month of Sundays, 1975; Marry Me: A Romance, 1976; The Coup, 1978; Rabbit is Rich, 1981; The Witches of Eastwick, 1984; Roger's Version, 1986; S, 1988; Rabbit at Rest, 1990; Memories of the Ford Administration, 1992; Brazil, 1994; Short stories: Pigeon Feathers and Other Stories, 1962; Museums and Women and Other Stories, 1972; Too Far to Go: The Maples Stories, 1979; Problems and Other Stories, 1979; Your Lover Just Called: Stories of Joan and Richard Maple, 1980; The Chaste Planet, 1980; People One Knows: Interviews with Insufficiently Famous Americans, 1980; Invasion of the Book Envelopes, 1981; Bech is Back, 1982; The Beloved, 1982; Confessions of a Wild Bore, 1984; More Stately Mansions: A Story, 1987; Trust Me: Short Stories, 1987; The Afterlife and Other Stories, 1994; Poetry: Telephone Poles and Other Poems, 1963; Midpoint and Other Poems, 1969; Seventy Poems, 1972; Six Poems, 1973; Tossing and Turning, 1977; Sixteen Sonnets, 1979; Five Poems, 1980; Spring Trio, 1982; Jester's Dozen, 1984; Facing Nature: Poems, 1985; Collected Poems 1953-1993, 1993. Essays and criticism among others: Picked-Up Pieces, 1975; Hub Fans Bid Kid Adieu, 1977; Talk from the Fifties, 1979; Ego and Art in Walt Whitman, 1980; Hawthorne's Creed, 1981; Hugging the Shore: Essays and Criticism, 1983; Emersonianism, 1984; Just Looking: Essays on Art, 1989; Self-Consciousness: Memoirs, 1989; Odd Jobs, 1991. Play: Buchanan Dying, 1974. Contributions to: Many periodicals. Honours: Guggenheim Fellowship, 1959; National Book Award for Fiction, 1966; Prix Medicis Etranger, 1966; O Henry Awards for Fiction, 1966, 1991; MacDowell Medal for Literature, 1981; Pulitzer Prizes in Fiction, 1982, 1991; National Book Critics Circle Awards for Fiction, 1982, 1991, and for Criticism, 1984; PEN/Malamud Memorial Prize, 1988; National Medal of Arts, 1989. Memberships: American Academy of Arts and Letters; American Academy of Arts and Sciences. Address: c/o Alfred A Knopf Inc, 201 East 50th Street, New York, NY 10022, USA.

URE Jean Ann, b. 1 Jan 1943, Caterham, Surrey, England. Writer. m. Leonard Gregory, 12 Aug 1967. Eduction: Webber Douglas Academy of Dramatic Art, 1965-66. Publications: Plague 99, 1989; Skinner Melon and Me, 1996; Captain Cranko and the Crybaby, 1993; The Children Next Door, 1994. Honour: Lanc Book Award, 1989. Membership: Society of Authors. Address: 88 Southbridge Road, Croydon CR0 1AF, England.

URIS Leon (Marcus), b. 3 Aug 1924, Baltimore, Maryland, USA. Author. m. 1) Betty Katherine Beck, 5 Jan 1945, div 1968, 2 sons, 1

daughter, (2) Margery Edwards, 1968, dec 1969, (3) Jill Peabody, 15 Feb 1970, 1 daughter. Education: Baltimore City College. Publications: Battle Cry, 1953; The Angry Hills, 1955; Exodus, 1957; Exodus Revisited, 1959; Mile 18, 1960; Armageddon, 1964; Topaz, 1967; The Third Temple, 1967; QB VII, 1970; Ireland: A Terrible Beauty, 1975; Trinity, 1976; Jerusalem, Song of Songs (with Jill Uris), 1981; The Haj, 1984; Mitla Pass, 1988; Redemption, 1995. Screenplays: Battle Cry, 1954; Gunfight at the OK Corral, 1957. Adaptation: Ari (musical play), 1971. Honours: National Institute of Arts and Letters Grant, 1959; Daroff Memorial Award, 1959; John F Kennedy Medal, Irish-American Society of New York, 1977; Gold Medal, Eire Society of Boston, 1978; Jobotinsky Medal, State of Israel, 1980; Hall Fellow (with Jill Uris), Concord Academy, 1980; Scopus Award, Hebrew University of Jerusalem, 1981; Honorary Doctorates. Address: c/o Doubleday & Co Inc, 666 Fifth Avenue, New York, NY 10103, USA.

URQUHART Jane, b. 21 June 1949, Geraldton, Ontario, Canada. Writer. m. (1) Paul Brian Keele, 6 Jan 1969, (2) Tony Urquhart, 5 May 1976, 1 daughter. Education: BA, English, 1971, BA, History, 1975, University of Guelph. Appointments: Writer-in-Residence, University of Ottawa, 1990, Memorial University, St John's, Newfoundland, 1992; Writer-in-Residence, University of Toronto, 1997-. Publications: False Shuffles, 1982; The Little Flowers of Madame Montespan, 1984; The Whirlpool, 1986; Storm Glass, 1987; Changing Heaven, 1990; Away (novel), 1993. Contributions to: Brick Magazine; Globe and Mail Book Pages; Quill and Quire; Malahat Review. Honours: Short listed for Seal First Novel Award, Le Prix de Meilleur Livre Etranger, France, 1992; Trillium Award, Canada, 1993; Marian Engel Award for Outstanding Prose Writing by a Canadian Woman, 1994. Memberships: Writer's Union of Canada; PEN International; Board Member, PEN Canada. Address: c/o Writers Union of Canada, 24 Ryerson Avenue, Toronto, Ontario M5T 2P3, Canada.

URSELL Geoffrey Barry, b. 14 Mar 1943, Moose Jaw, Saskatchewan, Canada. Writer; Editor. m. Barbara Davies, 8 July 1967. Education: BA, University of Manitoba, 1965; MA, 1966, PhD, University of London, 1973. Appointments: Writer-in-Residence, Saskatoon Public Library, 1984-85, Winnipeg Public Library, 1989-90; Editor, Grain, 1990. Publications: Way Out West; The Look Out Tower; Perdue; Trap Lines; Saskatoon Pie; The Running of the Deer. Contributions to: This Magazine; Saturday Night; Canadian Forum; Quarry; Border Crossings; Canadian Fiction Magazine; NeWest Review; Western People. Honours: Clifford E Lee National Playwriting Award; Special Commendation in Commonwealth Poetry Prize; Books in Canada First Novel Award. Memberships: PEN; Writers Union of Canada; Playwright's Union of Canada; Saskatchewan Writers Guild; Sk Playwrights Centre. Address: c/o Coteau Books, 401-2206 Dewdney Avenue, Regina, Saskatchewan S4R 1H3, Canada.

ÜRT Julius. See: **TART Indrek.**

USHAKOVA Elena. See: **NEVZGLIADOVA Elena Vsevolodovna.**

USHERWOOD Elizabeth (Ada), b. 10 July 1923, London, England. Writer. m. Stephen Usherwood, 24 Oct 1970. Publications: Visit Some London Catholic Churches (with Stephen Usherwood), 1982; The Counter-Armada, 1596: The Journal of the "Mary Rose" (with Stephen Usherwood), 1983; We Die for the Old Religion (with Stephen Usherwood), 1987; Women First, 1989; A Saint in the Family (with Stephen Usherwood), 1992. Address: 24 St Mary's Grove, London N1 2NT, England.

USTINOV Sir Peter, b. 16 April 1921, London, England. Author; Actor; Playwright; Director. m. (3rd) Helene du Lau d'Allemans, 1972. Education: Westminster School. Appointments: Author, Actor Playwright and Director, 1940-; Goodwill Ambassador, UNICEF, 1969-. Publications: House of Regrets, 1942; Blow Your Own Trumpet, 1943; Beyond, 1943; The Bambury Nose, 1944; Plays About People, 1950; The Love of Four Colonels, 1951; The Moment of Truth, 1951; Romanoff and Juliet, 1956; And a Dash of Pity: Short Stories, 1959; The Loser (novel), 1961; Photo Finish, 1962; Five Plays, 1965; The Frontiers of the Sea, 1966; The Unknown Soldier and his Wife: Two Acts of War Separated by a Truce for Refreshment, 1967; Halfway up the Tree, 1967; The Wit of Peter Ustinov, 1969; Kumnagel (novel), 1971; R Love J, 1973; Dear Me (memoirs), 1977; My Russia (memoirs/travel), 1983; Ustinov in Russia, 1987; The Disinformer (novella), 1989; The Old Man and Mr Smith, 1990; Ustinov at Large,

1991; Still at Large, 1993. Honours: Commander of the Order of the British Empire, 1975; Knighted, 1990. Address: 11 Rue de Silly, 92100 Boulogne, France.

V

VACHSS Andrew Henry, b. 19 Oct 1942, New York, New York, USA. Attorney at Law; Consultant; Writer. Education: BA, Case Western Reserve University, 1965; JD magna cum laude, New England School of Law, 1975. Appointments: Attorney, private practice, New York City, 1976-; Adjunct Professor, College of New Resources, New York City, 1980-81; Numerous consultancy appointments. Publications: The Life-Style Violent Juvenile: The Secure Treatment Approach, 1979; Strega, 1987, 1988, 1996; Blue Belle, 1988, 1990, 1995; Hard Candy, 1989, 1990, 1995; The Child Abuse-Delinquency Connection: A Lawyer's View, 1989; Blossom, 1990, new edition, 1996; Sacrifice, 1991; Ivy, 1991; Shella, 1993, new edition, 1994; The Ultimate Evil, 1995; Footsteps of the Hawk, 1995, 1996; False Allegations, 1996. Contributions to: Anthologies and magazines. Honours: Grand Prix de Litterature Policiere, 1988; Falcon Award, 1988; Deutschen Krimi Preis, 1989. Memberships: American Professional Society on the Abuse of Children; American Society of Criminology; National Association of Counsel for Children; PEN American Centre; Board of Counselors: CIVITAS Childlaw Center, Loyola School of Law, Chicago, CIVITAS ChildTrauma Programs, Bayalor College of Medicine, Houston. Address: 299 Broadway, Suite 1803, NEw York, NY 10007, USA.

VAGGE Ornello, (Lionello Grifo), b. 10 Aug 1934, Rome, Italy. Poet; Writer; Translator. Education: Doctor of Political and Social Sciences, Brussels, 1958. Publications: Poems and short stories, 1980-95. Contributions to: Journals and magazines. Honours: Several poetry prizes. Memberships: Many literary organizations. Address: c/o Blue Jay Press, Apdo Correos 32, E-30380 La Manga del Mar Menor, Spain.

VALENCAK Hannelore, b. 23 Jan 1929, Donawitz, Austria. Writer. m. (2) Viktor Mayer, 28 Apr 1962, 1 son. Education: PhD, Physics, University of Graz, Styria, Austria. Publications: Novels: Die Hohlen Noahs, 1961; Ein Fremder Garten, 1964; Zuflucht hinter der Zeit, 1967; Vorhof der Wirklichkeit, 1972; Das magische Tagebuch, 1981; various short stories, poetry and books for young people. Contributions to: Neue Deutsche Hefte; Literatur und Kritik; Dimension, USA; Others. Honours: National Advancement Award, 1957; Peter Rosegger Prize, Styrian Regional Government, 1966; Austrian Children's Book Prize, 1977; Amade Prize, Monaco, 1978. Memberships: Austrian PEN Club; Austrian Writers Union; Styrian Writers Union; Podium. Address: Schwarzspanierstrasse 15/2/8, A-1090 Vienna, Austria.

VALENTINE Alec. See: **ISAACS Alan**.

VALENTINE Jean, b. 27 Apr 1934, Chicago, Illinois, USA. Poet; Teacher. m. James Chace, 1957, div 1968, 2 daughters. Education: BA, Radcliffe College, 1956. Appointments: Teacher, Swarthmore College, 1968-70, Barnard College, 1968, 1970, Yale University, 1970, 1973-74, Hunter College of the City University of New York, 1970-75, Sarah L:awrence College, Columbia University, 1974-. Publications: Poetry: Dream Barker and Other Poems, 1965; Pilgrims, 1969; Ordinary Things, 1974; Turn, 1977; The Messenger, 1979; Home, Deep, Blue: New and Selected Poems, 1988; Night Lake, 1992; The River at Wolf, 1992. Honours: Yale Series of Younger Poets Award, 1965; National Endowment for the Arts Grant, 1972; Guggenheim Fellowship, 1976. Address: c/o Department of Writing, Columbia University, New York, NY 10027, USA.

VALERIO Anthony, b. 13 May 1940, USA. Author. 1 son, 2 daughters. Education: BA, Columbia College, 1962. Appointments: Book Editor, Major Publishing Houses, 1966-72; Instructor of Writing, 1986-88. Publications: Bart: A Life of A Bartlett Giamatti; Valentino and the Great Italians; The Mediterranean Runs Through Brooklyn. Contributions to: Paris Review; Philadelphia Magazine; Patterson Review; Anthologies; Dream Streets; Columbus Review. Membership: PEN. Address: 106 Charles Street, 14 New York, NY 10014, USA.

VALERY Anne. See: **FIRTH Anne Catherine**.

VALGARDSON William Dempsey, b. 7 May 1939, Winnipeg, Manitoba, Canada. Writer; Professor. Div. 1 son, 1 daughter. Education: BA, United College, 1961; BEd, University of Manitoba,

1966; MFA, University of Iowa, 1969. Appointments: Associate Professor, 1970-74, Professor, University of Victoria, 1974-; Fiction Editor, Canadian Author, 1996-. Publications: Bloodflowers; God is Not a Fish Inspector; Gentle Sinners, What Can't Be Changed, Should'nt be Mourned; The Girl with the Botticelli Face; Red Dust; The Carpenter of Dreams; In the Gutting Shed; Thor, 1994; Sarah and the People opf Sand River, 1996. Contributions to: Magazines. Honours: Presidents Medal; First Prize CBC Annual Literary Competition; First Novel Award; CAA Silver Medal; Ethel Wilson Literary Prize, 1992; Mr Christie Prize, 1995. Membership: Writers Union of Canada. Lite rary Agent: Donna-wong Juliana, PO Box 2050, MPO, Vancouver, BC V6B 3R6,Canada. Address: 1908 Waterloo Road, Victoria, British Columbia V8P 1J3, Canada.

VALLBONA (Rothe) de Rima Gretchen, b. 15 Mar 1931, San José, Costa Rica. Professor; Author. m. Carlos Vallbona, 26 Dec 1956, 1 son, 3 daughters. Education: BA, BS, Colegio Superior de Senoritas, San José, 1948; MA, University of Costa Rica, 1962; DML, Middlebury College, 1981. Appointments: Professor, Hispanic Literature, Liceo J.J. Vargas Calvo, Costa Rica, 1955-56, University of St Thomas, Houston, 1964-; Member, Editorial Board: Letras Femeninas, 1975-, Alba de America, 1981-, Foro Literario, 1979-89; Co-Director, Foro, 1984-89;Contributing Editor, The America's Review, 1989-. Publications: Noche en vela, 1968; Polvo del camino, 1971; Yolanda Oreamuno, 1972; La Salamandra Rosada, 1979; La obra en prosa de Eunice Odio, 1981; Mujeres y agonias, 1982; Las sombras que perseguimos, 1983; Cosecha de pecadores, 1988; El aréngel del perdòn, 1990; Mundo demonio y mujer, 1991; Los infiernos de la mujer y algo mas, 1992; Vida i sucesos de la Morja Alférez, 1992; Flowering Inferno - Tales of Sinking Hearts, 1993. Contributions to: Professional journals and general magazines. Honours: Aquileo J Echeverria Costa Rican Novel Prize, 1968; Agripina Montes del Valle Novel Prize, Colombia, 1978; Ancora Literary Award, Costa Rica, 1984; El Lazo de Dama de la Orden del Mérito Civil, Spain, 1988; Cullen Foundation Professor of Spanish, 1989; Emeritus Professor, University of St Thomas, 1995. Memberships: Comunidad de Escritores Latinoamericanos de Costa Rica; Associacion de Literatura Femenina Hispanica; National Writers Association; Instituto Literario y Cultural Hispanico. Address: University of St Thomas, 3800 Montrose Boulevard, Houston, TX 77006, USA.

VALTINOS Thanassis, b. 16 Dec 1932, Arcadia, Greece. Author; Screenwriter. 1 daughter. Education: Cinematography studies, Athens, 1950-53. Publications: Various books and screenplays, 1972-92. Contributions to: Periodicals. Honours: Screenwriter's Prize, Cannes Film Festival, 1984; Greek State Prize for Literature, 1989. Memberships: European Academy of Science and Arts; Greek Society of Playwrights; Greek Society of Writers; International Theatre Institute. Literary Agent: Jane Assimakopoulos, 2nd kil, Pedini-Ambelia, Ioannina 45500, Greece. Address: Astydamantos 66-68, Athens 11634, Greece.

VAN COTT Laurence. See: **NIVEN Larry**.

VAN DE BERGE Claude. See: **PAUWELS Rony**.

VAN DE LAAR Waltherus Antonius Bernardinus, (Victor Vroomkoning), b. 6 Oct 1938, Boxtel, Netherlands. Teacher; Poet. m. Inge Gorris, 22 Jan 1968, 1 son, 1 daughter. Education: Master's degree, Dutch Linguistics and Literature, 1978. Appointments: Contact publishing house, Amsterdam, 1966-67; Teacher, Interstudie teachers' training college, Arnhem, 1977-83; Co-Writer, Kritisch Literatur Lexicon reference book for literature, 1981-. Publications: De einders tegemoet, 1983; De laatste dingen, 1983; Circuit des souvenirs, 1984; Klein museum, 1987; Groesbeek Tijdrit, 1989; Echo van een echo, 1990; Oud zeer, 1993. Contributions to: Magazines and periodicals. Honour: Pablo Neruda Prize, 1983. Membership: Lira. Address: Aldenhof 70-17, 6537 DZ Nijmegen, Netherlands.

VAN DER VAT Dan, b. 28 Oct 1939, Alkmaar, Netherlands. Author; Journalist. m. Christine Mary Ellis, 1962, 2 daughters. Education: BA, honours, Classics, University of Durham, England, 1960. Appointments: The Journal, Newcastle Upon Tyne, 1960; Daily Mail, 1963; The Sunday Times, 1965; The Times, 1967, including ten years as foreign correspondent; The Guardian, 1982-88; Chief Foreign Leader-Writer; Full-time author, 1989-. Publications: The Grand Scuttle, 1982; The Last Corsair, 1983; Gentlemen of War, 1984; The Ship That Changed the World, 1985; The Atlantic Campaign, 1939-45, 1988; The Pacific Campaign, 1941-45, 1991; Freedom was Never Like

This: A Winter's Journey in East Germany, 1991; Stealth at Sea - History of the Submarine, 1994; The Riddle of the Titanic (with Robin Gardiner), 1995. Contributions to: Newspapers, magazines, radio and TV. Honours: Best First Work Award, Yorkshire Post, 1982; Best Book of the Sea Award, King George's Fund for Sailors, 1983. Memberships: Society of Authors; Campaign for Freedom of Information. Literary Agent: Michael Shaw, Curtis Brown. Address: 28/29 Haymarket, London SW1Y 4SP, England.

VAN DER WEE Herman (Frans Anna), Baron, b. 10 July 1928, Lier, Belgium. Professor of Social and Economic History; Writer. m. Monique Verbreyt, 27 Feb 1954, 1 son, 1 daughter. Education: BA, Philosophy, 1949, LLD, 1950, Licentiaat, Political and Social Sciences (MA Status), 1951, Doctor in Historical Sciences 1963, University of Leuven; Graduate Studies, Sorbonne, University of Paris, London School of Economics and Political Science. Publications: Prix et salaires: Manuel Méthodologie, 1956; La Banque Nationale de Belgique et la politique monétaire entre le deux guerres, 1975; Prosperity and Upheaval: The World Economy, 1945-1980, 1986; Histoire economique mondiale, 1945-1990, 1990; The Low Countries in Early Modern Age, 1993; History of European Banking, 1994; The Paramount Challenge, 1822-1997, 1997. Contributions to: Books and professional journals. Honours: De Stassart Prize, Royal Academy of Belgium, 1968; Fulbright-Hayes Awards, 1975, 1981; Quinquennial Solvay Prize, National Foundation of Scientific Research, Belgium, 1981; Amsterdam Prize, Royal Academy of the Netherlands, 1992; Honorary doctorates, University of Brussels, 1994, University of Leicester, 1995; Knighted (Baron), 1994; Golden Medal for Special Merits, Flemish Parliament, 1996. Memberships: American Academy of Sciences, honorary foreign member; British Academy, corresponding fellow; Leuven Institute for Central and East European Studies, president, advisory council, 1990-94; International Economic History Association, president, 1986-90, honorary president, 1990-; Royal Academy of Belgium, full member; Royal Academic of Sciences of the Netherlands, foreign member. Address: De Hettinghe, B-9170 St Pauwels, Belgium.

VAN DUYN Mona (Jane), b. 9 May 1921, Waterloo, Iowa, USA. Poet; Writer; Critic; Editor; Reviewer; Lecturer. m. Jarvis A Thurston, 31 Aug 1943. Education: BA, Iowa State Teachers College, 1942; MA, State University of Iowa, 1943. Appointments: Reviewer, Poetry magazine, 1944-70; Instructor in English, State University of Iowa, 1945, University of Louisville, 1946-50; Founder-Editor (with Jarvis A Thurston), Perspective: A Quarterly of Literature, 1947-67; Lecturer in English, 1950-67, Adjunct Porfessor, 1983, Visiting Hurst Professor, 1987, Washington University, St Louis; Poetry Advisor, College English, 1955-57; Lecturer, Salzburg Seminar in American Studies, 1973; Poet-in-Residence, Breadloaf Writing Conferences, 1974, 1976; Poet Laureate of the USA, 1992-93; Numerous poetry readings. Publications: Valentines to the Wide World: Poems, 1959; A Time of Bees, 1964; To See, To Take, 1970; Bedtime Stories, 1972; Merciful Disguises: Poems Published and Unpublished, 1973; Letters From a Father and Other Poems, 1982; Near Changes: Poems, 1990; Lives and Deaths of the Poets and Non-Poets, 1991; If It Be Not I: Collected Poems, 1992; Firefall, 1993. Contributions to: Many anthologies; Poems, criticism, reviews, and short stories in various periodicals. Honour: Eunice Tietjens Memorial Prize, 1956; National Endowment for the Arts Grants, 1966-67, 1985; Harriet Monroe Memorial Prize, 1968; Hart Crane Memorial Award, 1968; 1st prize, Borestone Mountain Awards, 1968; Bollingen Prize, 1970; National Book Award for Poetry, 1971; Guggenheim Fellowship, 1972-73; Loines Prize, National Institute of Arts and Letters, 1976; Fellow, Academy of American Poets, 1981; Sandburg Prize, Cornell College, 1982; Shelley Memorial Award, Poetry Society of America, 1987; Ruth Lilly Prize, 1989; Pulitzer Prize in Poetry, 1991. Memberships: Academy of American Poets, chancellor, 1985; National Institute of Arts and Letters. Address: 7505 Teasdale Avenue, St Louis, MO 63130, USA.

VAN HEERDEN Etienne Roché, b. 3 Dec 1954, Johannesburg, South Africa. University Professor. m. Karin Reuter, 8 Dec 1979, 2 daughters. Education: BA (Law); BA Hons (cum laude); MA (cum laude); LLB; PhD; Attorney of Supreme Court of South Africa. Publications: My Kubaan, 1983; Toorberg, 1986; Liegfabriek, 1988; Lasspirs en Camparis, 1991; Die Stoetmeester, 1993; Obiter Dictum; Oin re Awol; Die Loaste Kreef. Contributions to: More than 120 contributions internationally. Honours: Perskor Prize, 1980; Eugene Marais Prize, 1983; Hertzog Prize, 1986; CNA Prize (twice), 1986, 1988; Hofaeyr Prize, 1986; ATKV Prizes, 1986, 1988; Rapport Prize, 1993; Honourable Mention Noina Award. Literary Agent: Carole Blake,

Blake Friedman, London, England. Address: Department of Afrikaans, Rhodes University, Box 94, Grahamstown, 6140, USA.

VAN OVER Raymond, b. 29 June 1934, Inwood, Long Island, New York, USA. Writer. Appointments: Editor, Garrett/Helix Press, 1962-65. International Journal of Parapsychology, 1965-68; Film and Story Editor, 20th Century Fox and Columbia Pictures, 1968-72; Instructor, Hofstra University, 1973-76, New York University, 1973-76. Publications: Explorer of the Mind, 1967; I Ching, 1971; A Treasury of Chinese Literature, 1972; Psychology and Extrasensory Perception, 1972; Unfinished Man, 1972; The Chinese Mystics, 1973; Taoist Tales, 1973; Total Meditation, 1973; The Psychology of Freedom, 1974; Eastern Mysticism, 2 volumes, 1977; Sun Songs, 1980; Smearing the Ghost's Face With Ink, 1983; Monsters You Never Heard Of, 1983; Khomeini: A Biography, 1985; The Twelfth Child, 1990; Whisper, 1991; In a Father's Rage, 1991. Other: Screenplays and documentaries. Contributions to: Journals and magazines. Memberships: American Society for Psychical Research; Author's Guild. Address: 2905 Rittenhouse Street North West, Washington, DC 20015, USA.

VAN TOORN Penelope, b. 19 Dec 1952, Sydney, New South Wales, Australia. University Lecturer (literary critic). Education: BA Hons, 1980, MA Hons, 1984, University of Sydney; PhD, University of British Columbia, 1991. Publications: Rudy Wiebe and the Historicity of the Word, 1995; Speaking Positions: Aboriginality, Gender and Ethnicity in Australian Cultural Studies (co-editor), 1995; Neil Bissoondath, Canadian Writers and Their Works, Vol 11, 1997. Contributions to: Southern Review; Meanjin; Southerly; SPAN Journal of Commonwealth Literature; Literature and Theology; Canadian Literature; New Literatures Review. Address: Department of English, University of Sydney, New South Wales 2006, Australia.

VANCE William L(ynn), b. 19 Apr 1934, Dupree, South Dakota, USA. Professor of English; Writer. Education: AB, Oberlin College, 1956; MA, English Language and Literature, 1957, PhD, English Language and Literature, 1962, University of Michigan. Appointments: Assistant Professor, 1962-67, Associate Professor, 1967-73, Professor of English, 1973-, Boston University. Publications: American Literature (co-editor), 2 volumes, 1970; America's Rome, Vol I, Classical Rome, 1989, Vol II, Catholic and Contemporary Rome, 1989; The Faber Book of America (co-editor), 1992; Immaginari a confronto (co-editor), 1993. Honours: Association of American Publishing Prize, 1989; Ralph Waldo Emerson Prize, Phi Beta Kappa, 1990; Guggenheim Fellowship, 1990-91; Honorary LLD, University of South Dakota, 1992. Membership: Modern Language Association. Address: 255 Beacon Street, Boston, MA 02116, USA.

VANDERHAAR Gerard A(nthony), b. 15 Aug 1931, Louisville, Kentucky, USA. Professor. m. Janice Marie Searles, 22 Dec 1969. Education: BA 1954, Providence College; STD 1965, University of St Thomas, Rome. Appointments: Faculty, St John's University, New York, 1964-65, Providence College, 1965-68, Wesleyan University, 1968-69, Christian Brothers University, 1971-. Publications: A New Vision and a New Will for Memphis, 1974; Christians and Nonviolence in the Nuclear Age, 1982; Enemies and How to Love Them, 1985; Way of Peace: A Guide to Nonviolence (co-editor), 1987; The Philippines: Agony and Hope (co-author), 1989; Active Nonviolence: A Way of Personal Peace, 1990; Why Good People Do Bad Things, 1994. Booklets: Nonviolence, Theory and Practice, 1980; Nonviolence in Christian Tradition, 1983. Contributions to: Reference books and journals. Honours: Outstanding Educators of America, 1971; Distinguished Service Award, United Nations Association, 1981; Catholic Press Association Book Award for Spirituality, 1991; Tennessee Higher Education Commission Award for Community Service, 1994. Memberships: American Academy of Religion; American Association of University Professors; Pax Christi; National Conference of Christians and Jews; Fellowship of Reconcilliation; War Registers League. Address: 3554 Boxdale, Apt 3, Memphis, TN 38118, USA.

VANDERKAM James Claire, b. 15 Feb 1946, Cadillac, Michigan, USA. Professor. m. Mary Vander Molen, 24 Aug 1967, 2 sons, 1 daughter. Education: AB, Calvin College, 1968; BD, Calvin Theological Seminary, 1971; PhD, Harvard University, 1976. Publications: Textual and Historical Studies in the Book of Jubilees, 1977; Enoch and the Growth of Apocalyptic Tradition, 1984; The Book of Jubilees, 2 volumes, 1989; The Dead Sea Scrolls Today, 1994; Enoch: A Man for All Generations, 1995. Honours: Distinguished Research and Literary Publication Award, College of Humanities and

Social Sciences, North Carolina State University, 1991; Biblical Archaeology Society Publication Award for Best Popular Book on Archaeology, 1995. Address: Department of Theology, University of Notre Dame, Notre Dame, IN 46556, USA.

VANDIEVOET Jacques F G. See: **ORIOL Jacques**.

VANDIVER Frank Everson, b. 9 Dec 1925, Austin, Texas, USA. Professor of History. m. Renée Aubry, 21 Mar 1980, 1 son, 2 daughters. Education: BA, University of Texas, 1949; PhD, Tulane University, 1951; MA, Oxford University, 1963; Dr of Humanities, Hon, Austin College, 1977; DHL, Lincoln College, 1991; BA Hon, Lincoln College, 1995. Appointments: Harmsworth Professor of American History, Oxford University, 1963-64; Visiting Professor of Military History, US Military Academy, New York, 1973-74. Publications: Mighty Stonewall, 1957; Fields of Glory (with W H Nelson), 1960; Their Tattered Flags: The Epic of the Confederary, 1970; Black Jack: The Life and Times of John J Pershing, 1977; Blood Brothers: A Short History of the Civil War, 1992; Shadows of Vietnam: Lyndon Johnsons Wars, 1997. Honour: Carr P Collins Award, 1957; Guggenheim and Rockefeller Fellowships. Membership: President, Southern Historical Society, 1972-73. Address: PO Box 10600, College Station, TX 77842-0600, USA.

VANE Brett. See: **KENT Arthur (William Charles)**.

VANICEK Zdeněk, (Alois Bocek), b. 24 June 1947, Chlumec, Czechoslovakia. Diplomat; Professor; Poet; Writer. Div, 1 son, 1 daughter. Education: BA, College of Economics, Prague, 1972; MA, LLD, Charles University, Prague, 1979; PhD, Diplomatic Academy, Prague, 1981. Appointments: Czechoslovak Diplomatic Service, 1972-91; Professor of International Relations and Law, 1993-. Publications: The Theory and the Practice of British Neo-Conservatism, 1988; Amidst the Ruins of Memories, 1990; To the Ends of the Earth, 1992; On the Edge of Rain, 1994; Under the Range of Mountains of Five Fingers, 1996; Seven Thousand Years Chiselled in Limestone, A collection of travel sketches from Malta, Prague 1996. Contributions to: Newspapers and magazines. Honours: Several awards, medals, and honorary memberships. Membership: Poetry Society, England; Royal Society for Literature, MRSL, UK, 1996. Address: Vladislova 8, 110 00 Prague 1, Czech Republic.

VANSITTART Peter, b. 27 Aug 1920, Bedford, England. Author. Education: Worcester College, Oxford. Publications: I Am the World, 1942; Enemies, 1947; The Overseer, 1949; Broken Canes, 1950; A Verdict of Treason, 1952; A Little Madness, 1953; The Game and the Ground, 1956; Orders of Chivalry, 1958; The Tournament, 1959; A Sort of Forgetting, 1960; Carolina, 1961; Sources of Unrest, 1962; The Friends of God, 1963; The Siege, The Lost Lands, 1964; The Dark Tower, 1965; The Shadow Land, 1967; The Story Teller, 1968; Green Knights Black Angels, 1969; Landlord, 1970; Vladivostok: Figures in Laughter, 1972; Worlds and Underworlds, 1974; Quintet, 1976; Flakes of History, 1978; The Death of Robin Hood, 1980; Voices from the Great War, 1981; Three Six Seven, 1982; Voices 1870-1914, John Masefield's Letters from the Front, 1984; The Ancient Mariner and the Old Sailor, 1985; Happy and Glorious, 1987; Parsifal, 1988; Voices of the Revolution, 1989; The Wall, 1990; A Choice of Murder, 1992; London, 1992; A Safe Conduct, 1995. Contributions to: Guardian; Times; London Magazine. Honour: Honorary Fellowship, Worcester College, Oxford, 1996. Membership: Royal Society of Literature, fellow. Literary Agent: Anthony Shiel. Address: 9 Upper Park Road, Hampstead, London NW3, England.

VARMING Ole, b. 24 Mar 1929, Frederiksberg, Denmark. Psychologist. m. Ellen Michaelsen, 1 July 1961, 1 son, 1 daughter. Education: Graduate, Applied Psychology, University of Copenhagen, 1960; PhD, Royal Danish School of Education, 1984; Doctor's Thesis, University of Lund, Sweden, 1988. Publications: Educationally Subnormal Children, 1979; Psychological-Pedagogical (co-author); Dictionary, 11th edition, 1997; Discipline in School - From Without or Within?, 1978; Self-Esteem and Self-Esteem Development, 1995. Membership: Danish Writers' Union. Literary Agent: Gyldendal, Copenhagen, Denmark. Address: GL Torv 11, 4880 Nysted, Denmark.

VARVERIS Yannis, b. 25 Nov 1955. Writer. m. 6 Oct 1982, 1 son. Education: University of Athens; Sorbonne III, Paris. Publications: In Imagination and Reason; The Leak; Invalids of War; Death Extends; Bottoms Piano; Mr Fog (poetry), 1993; The Girl from Samos (translation), 1993. Contributions to: Many publications. Memberships:

Society of Writers; Greek Union of Theatrical Critics; Grece ITI. Address: 51 Omirou Street, 10672 Athens, Greece.

VASSANJI Moyez, b. 30 May 1950, Nairobi, Kenya. Writer. m. Nurzehan Aziz, 14 July 1979, 1 child. Education: BS, Massachusetts Institute of Technology, 1974; PhD, University of Pennsylvania, 1978. Appointments: Lecturer and Researcher, University of Toronto; Writer-in-Residence, University of Iowa, 1989. Publications: A Meeting of Streams: South Asian Canadian Literature (essays, editor), 1985; The Gunny Sack, 1989; No New Land, 1991; Uhuru Street, 1992; The Book of Secrets, 1994. Honours: Commonwealth Regional Prize for Best First Novel, 1990; Griller Prize, 1994; F G Bressani Literary Prize, 1994; Harbourfront Literary Award, 1994. Address: 39 Woburn Avenue, Toronto, Ontario M5M 1K5, Canada.

VEGE Nageswara Rao, b. 18 Jan 1932, Peda, India. Physician; Surgeon; Poet; Writer. Education: BA, Andhra University; MD, University of Parma. Publications: Poetry: Pace e Vita, 1963; Life and Love, 1965; Santi Priya, 1966; The Light of Asoka, 1970; Peace and Love, 1981; Templi Trascurati, 1983; The Best of Vege, 1992. Other: 100 Opinions of Great Men on Life, 1992. Contributions to: Newspapers and magazines. Honours: Giuseppe Ungaretti Award, 1982; Grand Prix Mediterranee, 1982; Schiller Award, 1985; Greenwood Poetry Forum Award, 1985; La Ballata Award, 1991; Viareggio Award, 1992. Memberships: International PEN; Italian Writers Association; Scrittori della Svizzera Italiana; Swiss Writers Association; World Doctors Writers Association. Address: Via Monte Ceneri 20, 6516 Gerra Paino TI, Switzerland.

VELARDO Joseph Thomas, b. 27 Jan 1923, Newark, New Jersey, USA. Biomedical Scientist; Professor; Writer. m. Forresta M M Monica Power, 12 Aug 1948, dec 1976. Education: AB, University of Northern Colorado, 1948; Miami University, Oxford, Ohio, 1949; PhD, Harvard Univerity, 1952. Appointments: Editor, Contributor, Twenty Niner, B-29 Newspaper; Weekly Column, News and Notes, New Jersey Italian-American and Jersey Press Newspapers, 1940-43; Writer, Columnist, Air Force, Greeley Daily Tribune, 1943; Columnist, Mirror Newspaper, 1946-48. Publications: 2 Radio Plays, 1946-48; Endocrinology of Reproduction, 1958; Essentials of Human Reproduction, 1958; Enzymes in the Female Genital System, 1963; The Ovary (co-author), 1963; Biology of Reproduction, Basic and Clinical Studies (co-author and co-editor), 1973; Human Reproduction, 1973. Contributions to: Co-Editor, Continuing Medical Education (CME); Endocrinology; Journal of Endocrinology; American Journal of Physiology; Anatomical Record; Journal of Clinical Endocrinology and Metabolism; Science and Nature; Journal of Histochemistry and Cytochemistry; Ecology; Science (AAAS), USA (reviewer). Honours: US Presidential Unit Citation, 2 Bronze Stars, World War II; Rubin Award, American Society for the Study of Sterility, Harvard and Yale Universities, 1954; Lederle Medical Faculty Award, Harvard and Yale Universities, 1955-58; Honorary Citizen, São Paulo, Brazil, 1973. Address: c/o Wilson House, 607 East Wilson Avenue, Old Grove East, Lombard, IL 60148-4062, USA.

VENDLER Helen Hennessy, b. 30 Apr 1933, Boston, Massachusetts, USA. Professor; Poetry Critic. 1 son. Education: AB, Emmanuel College, 1954; PhD, Harvard University, 1960. Appointments: Instructor, Cornell University, 1960-63; Lecturer, Swarthmore College and Haverford College, Pennsylvania, 1963-64; Associate Professor, 1966-68, Professor, 1968-85, Boston University; Fulbright Lecturer, University of Bordeaux, 1968-69; Poetry Critic, The New Yorker, 1978-; Overseas Fellow, Churchill College, Cambridge, 1980; Senior Fellow, Harvard Society of Fellows, 1981-93, Visiting Professor, 1981-85, Kenan Professor, 1985-, Associate Academic Dean, 1987-92, Porter University Professor, 1990-, Harvard University; Charles Stewart Parnell Fellow, 1996, Honorary Fellow, 1996-, Magdalene College, Cambridge. Publications: Yeat's Vision and the Later Plays, 1963; On Extended Wings: Wallace Stevens' Longer Poems, 1969; The Poetry of George Herbert, 1975; Part of Nature, Part of Us: Modern American Poets, 1980; The Odes of John Keats, 1983; Wallace Stevens: Words Chosen Out of Desire, 1984; The Harvard Book of Contemporary American Poetry (editor), 1985; Voices and Visions: The Poet in America, 1987; The Music of What Happens, 1988; Soul Says, 1995; The Given and the Made, 1995; The Breaking of Style, 1995; Poems, Poets, Poetry, 1995. Contributions to: Professional journals. Honours: Lowell Prize, 1969; Guggenheim Fellowship, 1971-72; American Council of Learned Societies Fellow, 1971-72; National Institute of Arts and Letters Award, 1975; Radcliffe College Graduate Society Medal, 1978; National Book Critics Award,

1980; National Endowment for the Humanities Fellowships, 1980, 1985, 1994; Keats-Shelley Association Award, 1994; Truman Capote Award, 1996; Many honorary doctorates; Phi Beta Kappa. Memberships: American Academy of Arts and Letters; American Academy of Arts and Sciences, vice-president, 1992-95; American Philosophical Society; English Institute; Modern Language Association, president, 1980. Address: 54 Trowbridge Street, No 2, Cambridge, MA 02138, USA.

VENN George Andrew Fyfe, b. 10 Dec 1943, Tacoma, Washington, USA. Professor; Writer; Editor; Poet; Critic. m. Elizabeth Cheney, 1 son, 1 daughter. Education: BA, College of Idaho, 1967; MFA, Creative Writing, University of Montana, 1970; also attended Central University, Quito, Ecuador; University of Salamanca, Spain; City Literary Institute, London. Appointments: Writer-on-Tour, Western States Arts Foundation, 1977; Foreign Expert, Changsha Railway University, Hunan, China, 1981-82; General Editor, Oregon Literature Series, 1989-94; Writer-in-Residence, Eastern Oregon State College. Publications: Sunday Afternoon: Grande Ronde, 1975; Off the Main Road, 1978; Marking the Magic Circle, 1988; Oregon Literature Series, 1992-94; many poems, essays, stories. Contributions to: Oregon Humanities; Writer's Northwest Handbook; North West Review; Northwest Reprint Series; Poetry Northwest; Willow Springs; Clearwater Journal; Oregon East; Portland Review. Honours: Pushcart Prize, 1980; Oregon Book Award, 1988; Stewart Holbrook Award, 1994. Memberships: Executive Board, Oregon Council of Teachers of English; Editorial Board, Northwest Folklore. Address: Department of English, Eastern Oregon State College, La Grande, OR 97850, USA.

VENTURI Robert, b. 25 June 1925, Philadelphia, Pennsylvania, USA. Architect; Writer. m. Denise Scott Brown, 23 July 1967, 1 son. Education: AB summa cum laude, 1947, MFA, 1950, Princeton University. Appointments: Designer, 1950-58; Assistant to Associate Professor of Architecture, University of Pennsylvania, 1957-65; Partner, Venturi, Cope and Lippincott, Philadelphia, 1958-61, Venturi and Short, Philadelphia, 1961-64, Venturi and Rauch, Philadelphia, 1964-80, Venturi, Rauch and Scott Brown, Philadelphia, 1980-89, Venturi, Scott Brown and Associates Inc, Philadelphia, 1989-; Charlotte Shepherd Davenport Professor of Architecture, Yale University, 1966-70. Publications: Complexity and Contradiction in Architecture, 1966, 2nd edition, 1977; Learning from Las Vegas (with Denise Scott Brown and Steven Izenour), 1972, 2nd edition, 1977; A View from the Campidoglio: Selected Essays, 1953-84 (with Denise Scott Brown), 1984; Iconography and Electronics Upon a Generic Architecture. Contributions to: Numerous publications. Honours: Rome Prize Fellow, American Academy in Rome, 1954-56; Commendatore of the Order of Merit, Republic of Italy, 1986; Pritzker Architecture Prize, 1991; National Medal of Arts, Manufacturers and Commerce, 1993; Phi Beta Kappa; Several honorary doctorates. Memberships: American Academy of Arts and Sciences; Royal Institute of British Architects, honorary member. Address: c/o Venturi, Scott Brown and Associates Inc, 4236 Main Street, Philadelphia, PA 19127, USA.

VERCOUTTER Jean, b. 2 Jan 1911, Lambersart, France. Egyptologist. m. Odette Gaiddon, 26 Jan 1943, 1 son, 1 daughter. Education: Docteur es Lettres, Sorbonne, Paris, 1953. Publications: Les Objets égyptiens du mobilier funéraire carthaginois, 1945; L'Egypte ancienne, 1946; Essai sur les relations entre Egytiens et Préhellènes, 1954; L' Egypte et le Monde égéen préhellénique; Etude critique des sources égyptiennes, 1956; Textes biographiques du Serapéum de Memphis, 1962; A la recherche de l'Egypte oubliée, 1986; L'Egypte et la chambre noire, 1992; L'Egypte et la Vallée du Nil I: Des origines à la fin de l'Ancien Empire, 1992. Contributions to: Periodicals. Honour: Prix Bordin et Prix Saintour, 1946. Membership: L'Institut. Address: 25 rue de Trévise, 75009 Paris, France.

VERDUIN John Richard Jr, b. 6 July 1931, Muskegon, Michigan, USA. University Professor. m. Janet M Falk, 26 Jan 1963, 1 son, 1 daughter. Education: BS, Science, University of Albuquerque, 1954; MA, Education Administration, 1959, PhD, Curriculum, 1962, Michigan State University. Publications: Cooperative Curriculum Improvement, 1967; Conceptual Models in Teacher Education, 1967; Adults Teaching Adults, 1977; The Adult Educator, 1979; Curriculum Building for Adult Learning, 1980; The Lifelong Learning Experience, 1986; Adults and Their Leisure, 1984; Handbook for Differential Education for the Gifted, 1986; Differentielle Erziehung Besonders Begabter, 1989; Distance Education: The Foundation of Effective Practice, 1991; Uzaktan Egitim: Etkin Uygulama Esaslari, 1994;

Helping Students Develop Investigative, Problem Solving and Thinking Skills in a Cooperative Setting, 1996. Contributions to: Lifelong Learning; Leisure Quarterly; Gifted Education Press Newsletter; Dialogue on Aging; Science Education; NAPCAE Exchange; Illinios Career Education Journal. Memberships: American Association for Supervision and Curriculum Development; IACEA; Phi Delta Kappa. Address: 107 North Lake Lane, Carbondale, IL 62901, USA.

VERMA Daya Nand, b. 12 Dec 1930, Multan City. Author; Palmist. m. 28 Jan 1951, 1 daughter. Publications: Yaun Vyavhar Anusheelan; Zindabad Murdabad; Kam Bhav Ki Nayee Vyakhya; Palmistry Ke Goorh Rahsya; Mansik Saphalta; Hum Sab Aur Voh; Dhyn Toga; Palmistry Ke Anubhoot Praypg. Contributions to: Gyanodya; Hamara Mun; Prakashit Man; All The Sec rets of Palmistry, 1992; Palmistry: How to Master It, 1994. Honours: Literary Award; Honoured Vishva Yoga Conference. Memberships: Authors Guild of India; Film Writers Association; Bhartiya Lekhak Sangathan; PEN; AKhil Bhartiya Hindi Prakahak Sangh; Creater Kailash Residents Association; All Indian Hindi Publishers Association; Afro Asian Book Council. Address: W21 Greater Kailash 1, New Delhi 110048, India.

VERMEIREN Koen, b. 18 Dec 1953, Antwerp, Belgium. Education: Study Germanic Philogy, 1978; Doctor of Literature & Philosophy, 1984. Appointments: Teacher, Writers Academy of Antwerp. Publications: Hermans and Wittgenstein; De Vrolijke Eenzaamheid; Schaduwen; Dood Spoor; De Droomexpres; De Kus Van Selena; Herr Ludwig; De Gek op De Heuvel. Contributions to: Numerous publications. Honours: ANV Visser Neerlandia Award; August Beernaert Award. Address: Visbeekbaan 32, 2275 Wechelderzande, Belgium.

VERMES Geza, b. 22 June 1924, Mako, Hungary. Professor Emeritus; Emeritus Fellow. m. Pamela Curle, 12 May 1958, dec. Education: Universities of Budapest and Louvain, 1945-52; DTheol; MA; DLitt; Honorary DD; Honorary DLitt. Appointments: Editor, Journal of Jewish Studies, 1971; Director, Forum for Qumran Research, Oxford Centre for Hebrew Studies, 1991-; Professor of Jewish Studies and Emeritus Fellow, Wolfson College, Oxford. Publications: Scripture and Tradition in Judaism, 1961,2nd edition, 1973; The Dead Sea Scrolls in English, 1962, 3rd edition, 1987, 1995; Jesus the Jew, 1973, 3rd edition, 1994; Postbiblical Jewish Studies, 1975; Jesus and the World of Judaism, 1982; The Religion of Jesus the Jew, 1993; The Dead Sea Scrolls: Qumran in Perspective, 1994. Editor: The History of the Jewish People in the Age of Jesus Christ by E Schuerer, 3 volumes, 1973-87. Contributions to: Journal of Jewish Studies; Journal of Semitic Studies; Jewish Chronicle; Times; Times Literary Supplement; New York Review of Books. Honour: Fellow, British Academy. Memberships: British Association for Jewish Studies; European Association for Jewish Studies. Literary Agent: Peters, Fraser, Dunlop. Address: West Wood Cottage, Foxcombe Lane, Boars Hill, Oxford OX1 5DH, England.

VERNON Annette Robyn. See: **CORKHILL Annette Robyn**.

VESTER Frederic, b. 23 Nov 1925, Saarbrücken, Germany. Biochemist. m. Anne Pillong, 2 Feb 1950, 1 son, 2 daughters. Education: University of Mainz, 1945; Licence es sciences, Sorbonne, University of Paris, 1950; PhD, University of Hamburg, 1953. Publications: Krebs Fehlgesteuertes Leben, 1977; Denken, Lernen, Vergessen, 1978; Phaenomen Stress, 1978; Unsere Welt ein Vernetztes System, 1983; Neuland des Denkens, 1984; Januskopf Landwirtschaft, 1986; Wasser Leben, 1987; Ausfahrt Zukunft, 1991; Crashtest Hobilität, 1995. Contributions to: Professional journals. Honours: Adolf Grimme Prize, 1974; German Environmental Protection Medal, 1975; Deutsche Umweltmedaille, 1992. Memberships: Various professional organizations; Club of Rome. Address: c/o Studiengruppe für Biologie, und Umwelt GmbH, Nussbaumstrasse 14, 80336, Munich, Germany.

VICARION Palmiro (Count). See: **LOGUE Christopher**.

VICKERS Hugo (Ralph), b. 12 Nov 1951, London, England. Writer. m. Elizabeth Anne Blyth, 23 Sept 1995. Education: University of Strasbourg, 1970-71; Appointments: Broadcaster, Radio and Television, 1973-; Director, Burkes Peerage, 1974-79. Publications: We Want the Queen, 1977; Gladys, Duchess of Marlborough, 1979; Debretts Book of the Royal Wedding, 1981; Cocktails and Laughter (editor), 1983; Cecil Beaton: The Authorised Biography, 1985; Vivien Leigh, 1988; Loving Garbo, 1994; Royal Orders, 1994; The Private

World of the Duke and Duchess of Windsor, 1995; The Kiss, 1996. Contributions to: The Times; Books and periodicals. Honour: Stern Prize for Non-Fiction, PEN, 1996. Memberships: Commemorate Collectors Society; Historic Houses Association; Royal Society of Literature. Address: 62 Lexham Gardens, London W8 5JA, England.

VICKY. See: **BHARGAVA Vishal**.

VIDAL Gore, (Edgar Box), b. 3 Oct 1925, West Point, New York, USA. Writer. Education: Graduate, Phillips Exeter Academy, 1943. Publications: Novels: Williwaw, 1946; In a Yellow Wood, 1947; The City and the Pillar, 1948; The Season of Comfort, 1949; A Search for the King, 1950; Dark Green, Bright Red, 1950; The Judgment of Paris, 1952; Messiah, 1954; Julian, 1964; Washington, DC, 1967; Myra Breckinridge, 1968; Two Sisters, 1970; Burr, 1973; Myron, 1974; Kalki, 1978; Creation, 1981; Duluth, 1983; Lincoln, 1984; Empire, 1987. Stories: A Thirsty Evil, 1956. Play: Visit to a Small Planet, 1957. Television and Broadway productions: The Best Man, 1960; Romulus, 1966; Weekend, 1968; An Evening with Richard Nixon, 1972; Gore Vidal's Lincoln, 1988. Essays: Rocking the Boat, 1962; Reflections upon a Sinking Ship, 1969; Homage to Daniel Shays, 1973; Matters of Fact and of Fiction, 1977; The Second American Revolution, 1982; Armageddon?, 1987; United States: Essays 1952-1992, 1993. Memoir: Palimpsest, 1995. Films: The Catered Affair, 1956; The Left-Handed Gun, 1958; The Best Man, 1964. Teleplays: The Death of Billy the Kid, 1958; Dress Gray, 1986. Honour: National Book Award, 1993. Address: c/o Random House, 201 East 50th Street, New York, NY 10022, USA.

VIDOR Miklos Janos, (Nicholas John), b. 22 May 1923, Budapest, Hungary. Writer. m. 22 Aug 1972. Education: Doctor of German and Hungarian Literature and Aesthetics, 1947. Publications: Over 3 books, 1947-95.Contributions to: Various publications. Honours: Jozsef Attila Prize, 1955; Officer's Cross, Hungarian Republic, 1993; Stephanus Prize, 1995. Memberships: Hungarian Art Foundation; Hungarian PEN Club, vice-president, 1994; Union of Hungarian Writers. Address: 17 Pushkin u, H-1088 Budapest, Hungary.

VIERBECK Peter (Robert Edwin), b. 5 Aug 1916, New York, New York, USA. Historian; Poet; Professor. m. (1) Aanya de Markov, June 1945, div May 1970, 1 son, 1 daughter, (2) Betty Martin Falkenberg, 30 Aug 1972. Education: BS, 1937, MA, 1939, PhD, 1942, Harvard University; Graduate Study as a Henry Fellow, Christ Church, Oxford, 1937-38. Appointments: Instructor, Tutor, Harvard University, 1946-47; Assistant Professor of History, 1947-48, Visiting Lecturer in Russian History, 1948-49, Smith College, Northampton, Massachusetts; Associate Professor, 1948-55, Professor of Modern European and Russian History, 1955-65, Mount Holyoke Alumnae Foundation Chair of Interpretive Studies, 1965-79, and William R Kenan Chair of History, 1979-, Mount Holyoke College; Whittal Lecturer in Poetry, Library of Congress, Washington, DC, 1954, 1963; Fulbright Professor in American Poetry and Civilization, University of Florida, 1955; Elliston Chair and Poetry Lecturer, University of Cincinnati, 1956; Visiting Lecturer, University of California at Berkeley, 1957, 1964, and City College of the City University of New York, 1964; Visiting Research Scholar in Russian for the Twentieth Century Fund, 1962-63; Director, Poetry Workshop, New York Writers Conferences, 1965-67. Publications: History: Metapolitics: From the Romanitics to Hitler, 1941, revised editions as Metapolitics: The Roots of the Nazi Mind, 1961, 2nd revised edition, 1965, updated edition, 1982; Conservatism Revisited: The Revolt Against Revolt, 1815-1949, 1949, 2nd edition as Conservatism Revisited and the New Conservatism: What Went Wrong?, 1962, 3rd edition, 1972; Shame and Glory of the Intellectuals: Babbitt, Jr Versus the Rediscovery of Values, 1953; The Unadjusted Man: A New Hero for Americans: Reflections on the Distinction Between Conserving and Conforming, 1956; Conservatism: From John Adams to Churchill, 1956, revised edition, 1962; Inner Liberty: The Stubborn Grit in the Machine, 1957; Conservatism from Burke and John Adams till 1982: A History and an Anthology, 1982. Poetry: Terror and Decorum: Poems 1940-1948, 1948; Strike Through thr Mask: Lyrical Poems, 1950; The First Morning: New Poems, 1952; Dream and Responsibility: The Tension Between Poetry and Society, 19853; The Persimmon Tree, 1956; The Tree Witch: A Poem and a Play (First of All a Poem), 1961; New and Selected Poems, 1932-1967, 1967; Archer in the Marrow: The Applewood Cycles of 1967-1987, 1987; Tide and Continuities: Last and First Poems, 1995-1938, 1995. Play: Opcomp: A Modern Medieval Miracle Play, 1993. Contributions to: Monographs, essays, reviews and poems to

numerous periodicals. Honours: Pulitzer Prize in Poetry, 1949; Guggenheim Fellowship, 1959-60; Rockefeller Foundation Research Grant, 1958; National Endowment for the Humanities Senior Research Fellowship, 1969; Poetry Award, Massachusetts Artists Foundation, 1978; Sadin Prize, New York Quarterly, 1980; Golden Rose Award, 1981, Varoujan Poetry Prize, 1983, New England Poetry Club; Ingram Merrill Foundation Fellowship in Poetry, 1985. Memberships: American Committee for Cultural Freedom, executive committee; American Historical Association; Committee for Basic Education, charter member; Oxford Society; PEN; Phi Beta Kappa; Poetry Society of America. Address: 12 Silver Street, South Hadley, MA 01075, USA.

VIERROS Tuure Johannes, b. 20 Dec 1927, Kankaanpaa, Finland. Teacher; Writer. m. Enni Luodetlahti, 22 June 1954, 4 sons, 1 daughter. Education: University of Helsinki, 1952. Publications: Over 40 books, including some 20 textbooks, 1959-97. Contributions to: Journals and magazines. Honours: Several literary prizes. Memberships: Authors in Helsinki; Finnish Society of Authors; PEN. Address: Untuvaisentie 7 G 94, 00820 Helsinki, Finland.

VILLA GILBERT Mariana Soledad Magdalena, b. 21 Feb 1937, Croydon, England. Writer. Publications: Mrs Galbraith's Air, 1963; My Love All Dressed in White, 1964; Mrs Cantello, 1968; A Jingle Jangle Song, 1968; The Others, 1970; Manuela: A Modern Myth, 1973; The Sun in Horus, 1986. Address: 28 St Martins Road, Canterbury, Kent CT1 1QW, England.

VINCENT John James, b. 29 Dec 1929, Sunderland, England. Methodist Minister. m. Grace Johnston Stafford, 4 Dec 1958, 2 sons, 1 daughter. Education: BD, Richmond College, London University, 1954; STM, Drew University, 1955; DeTheol, Basel University, 1960; Ordained, Methodist Church, 1956. Appointments: Director, Urban Theology Unit, 1969-; Editor, New City Journal, 1971-; Adjunct Professor, New York Theological Seminary, 1979-87; Honorary Lecturer, Sheffield University, 1990-. Publications: Christ and Methodism, 1964; Here I Stand, 1967; Secular Christ, 1968; The Race Race, 1970; The Jesus Thing, 1973; Stirrings, Essays Christian and Radical, 1975; Alternative Church, 1976; Disciple and Lord, 1976; Starting all over Again, 1981; Into the City, 1982; OK Let's Be Methodists, 1984; Radical Jesus, 1986; Mark at Work, 1986; Britain in the 90's, 1989; Liberation Theology fron the Inner City, 1992; A Petition of Distress from the Cities, 1993; A British Liberation Theology, annual volumes, 1995-. Memberships: Studiorum Novi Testamenti Societas; Alliance of Radical Methodists; Methodist Church of Great Britain, 1989-90. Address: 178 Abbeyfield Road, Sheffield S4 7AY, England.

VINCENT Richard Charles, b. 1 Mar 1949, Allentown, Pennsylvania, USA. University Professor; Author; Editor. m. Christine M LaCaruba, 29 Jan 1972, 2 daughters. Education: BA, Mansfield University, 1972; MA, Temple University, 1977; PhD, University of Massachusetts, Amherst, 1983. Appointments: Temple University, 1974; University of Massachusetts, 1977; Slippery Rock State College, 1979; Western Illinois University, 1981; Southern Illinois University - Carbondale, 1983; University of Hawaii-Manoa, 1986-. Publications: Financial Characteristics of Selected B Film Productions of Albert J Cohen, 1951-1957, 1980; Global Glasnost: Toward a New International Information/Communication Order?, 1992; Towards Equity in Global Communication: MacBride Update, 1996; USA Glasnost: Missing Political Themes in US Media Discourse, 1997. Contributions to: Journalism Quarterly; Journalism Monographs; Political Communication; Journal of the University Film Association; Assorted book chapters. Honour: Fulbright, fellow, 1994-95. Memberships: International Association of Mass Communications Researchers; American Educators in Journalism and Mass Communication; International Communication Association; Asian Mass Communication Research and Information Association; Pacific Telecommunications Council. Address: Department of Communication, University of Hawaii-Manoa, Honolulu, Hawaii 96822, USA.

VINE Barbara. See: **RENDELL Ruth**.

VINGE Vernor Steffen, b. 2 Oct 1944, Waukesha, Wisconsin, USA. Writer; Teacher. Education: PhD, Mathematics, University of California, San Diego. Publications: True Names; Marooned in RealTime; Peace War; Threats and Other Promises; Witling; Tatja Grimm's World. Address: Department of Mathematical Sciences, San Diego State University, San Diego, CA 92182, USA.

VIRTUE Noel, b. 3 Jan 1947, Wellington, New Zealand. Author. Education: New Zealand secondary schools. Publications: The Redemption of Elsdon Bird, 1987; Then Upon the Evil Season, 1988; Among the Animals: A Zookeeper's Story, 1988; In the Country of Salvation, 1990; Always the Islands of Memory, 1991; The Eye of the Everlasting Angel, 1993; Sandspit Crossing, 1994. Address: c/o Hutchinson, 20 Vauxhall Bridge Road, London SW1V, England.

VISTICA Gregory. m. Joan Amero Vistica, 2 daughters. Education: BA, International Affairs, Graduate Studies in International Relations, San Francisco State University. Appointments: Reporter, San Diego Union-Tribune; National Security Correspondent, Newsweek, 1995-; Consultant, ABC News' investigative show, PrimeTime Live; Appearances on Nightline and other television news programs; Guest appearances on numerous radio talk shows both in USA and abroad. Publication: Fall From Glory: The Men Who Sank the US Navy, 1996. Honours: Two-times Winner, George Polk Award; Twice nominated for the Pulitzer Prize. Address: c/o Newsweek, 251 West 57th Street, New York, NY 10019-1894, USA.

VISWANATHAN Subrahmanyam, b. 23 Oct 1933, Sholavandan, Tamil Nadu, India. Professor. m. Nirmala Nilakantan, 26 June 1960, 1 daughter. Education: BA, 1953, MA, 1958, University of Madras; PhD, Sri Venkateswara University, 1977. Appointments: Lecturer, Sri Venkateswara University, 1959-77; Reader, 1977-82, Professor, 1982-, University of Hyderabad. Publications: The Shakespeare Play as Poem, 1980; Critical Essays, 1982; Shakespeare in India, 1987; On Shakespeare's Dramaturgy, 1992. Contributions to: Professional journals. Honours: Indian UGC National Lecturer in English Literature, 1986-87; Emeritus Fellow, UGC, 1995-. Address: A14 Staff Quarters, University of Hyderabad, Hyderabad 500134, India.

VITIELLO Justin, b. 14 Feb 1941, New York, USA. Professor of Italian. Education: BA, Brown University 1963; PhD, University of Michigan, 1970. Appointments: Assistant Professor of Comparative Literature, University of Michigan, 1970-73; Assistant, Associate then Full Professor of Italian, Temple University, 1974-. Publications: Il carro del pesce di Vanzetti, 1989; Vanzetti's Fish Cart, 1991; Sicily Within, 1992; Confessions of a Joe Rock, 1992; Subway Home, 1994. Contributions to: Professional journals. Address: Clivo Delle Mura Vaticane, 23-00136 Rome, Italy.

VIVIAN Daisy. See: **KENYON Bruce Guy.**

VIZINCZEY Stephen, b. 12 May 1933, Kaloz, Hungary. Writer. m. Sept 1963, 3 daughters. Education: University of Budapest, 1949-50; Academy of Theatre Arts, Budapest, 1951-56. Appointments: Editor, Exchange Magazine, 1960-61; Producer, Canadian Broadcasting Corporation, 1962-65. Publications: In Praise of Older Women, 1965; The Rules of Chaos, 1969; An Innocent Millionaire, 1983; Truth and Lies in Literature, 1986; The Man with the Magic Touch, 1994. Contributions to: Currently; Observer; ABC. Membership: PEN. Address: 70 Coleherne Court, Old Brompton Road, London SW5 0EF, England.

VIZKI Morti (Morten Poulsen), b. 18 Jan 1963, Copenhagen, Denmark. Author. Education: Japanese, University of Copenhagen. Publications: Himmelstormere, 1986; Begge Ben, 1990; Det Sidste Rum, 1993; Vingens Kniv, 1993; Sol, 1997. Honours: Klaus Rifbderg Award, 1986; Nordic Radio Prize, 1989; Laureate of State, 1990; Marguerite Viby Award, 1994. Address: Sankt Jorgens Alle 7, 1669 Copenhagen V, DK, Denmark.

VLAD Alexandru, b. 31 July 1950, Romania. Author. m. Maria Vlad, 4 Mar 1985, 2 sons. Education: BA, Cluj Napoca University. Appointment: Assistant Editor, Vatra, 1990-. Publications: The Giffins Wing, 1981; The Way to the South Pole, 1985; In The Cold of the Summer, 1985; Atena, Atena, 1994; Reinventing Politics, 1994. Contributions to: Steaua; Vatra; Amfiteatru; Astra; Trubuna; New Glass; 22; Romania Literara. Memberships: Union of Writers; N Steinhardt Memorial Foundation. Address: Str Lugoslaviei Nr 72 Bl, B4 Ap23 3400 Cluj Napoc, Romania.

VOGASSARIS Angleo-Eftihios (Felix), b. 6 May 1935, Piraeus, Greece. Teacher; Writer; Playwright. Div. Education: Degree in Philosophy and Greek Literature, University of Athens; Diploma, German Academy, Munich; Diplomas in English and French. Appointments: Editor; High School Teacher; Educational Advisor.

Publications: Over 40 works, including novels, plays, poems, and essays, 1968-92. Contributions to: Newspapers and magazines. Memberships: Association of Greek Writers; Piraeus Literary and Arts Society, president. Address: 1-3 Aristotelous Street, GR 18535 Piraeus, Greece.

VOGEL Paula Anne, b. 18 Nov 1951, Washington, District of Columbia, USA. Dramatist; Teacher. Education: BA, Catholic University of America, Washington, DC. Appointments: Consultant on Playwrighting and Theatre Arts; Faculty, Brown University. Honours: National endowment for the Arts, 1980, 1991; AT&T Award, 1992; Obie Award, 1992; Fund for New American Plays, 1994; Guggenheim Fellow, 1995; Pew Charitable Trust Senior Artist Residency, 1995-97; Lucille Lortel Award, 1997. Address: c/o Department of English, Brown University, Providence, RI 02912, USA.

VOIGT Ellen Bryant, b. 9 May 1943, Danville, Virginia, USA. Poet; Teacher. m. Francis G W Voigt, 5 Sept 1965, 1 son, 1 daughter. Education: BA, Converse College, Spartanburg, South Carolina, 1964; MFA, University of Iowa, Iowa City, 1966. Appointments: Faculty Member, Iowa Wesleyan College, 1966-69, Goddard College, 1969-79, Massachusetts Institute of Technology, 1979-82, Warren Wilson College, 1981-; Participant, Indiana, Tucson, Napa Valley, Catskills and Breadloaf Writers Conferences. Publications: Claiming Kin, 1976; The Forces of Plenty, 1983; The Lotus Flowers, 1987; Two Trees, 1992; Kyrie, 1996. Contributions to: New Yorker; Atlantic; American Poetry Review; Antioch Review; Partisan Review; Pequod; Ploughshares; Georgia Review; Ohio Review; Poetry; New Republic. Honours: National Endowment for the Arts Fellowship, 1975; Guggenheim Fellowship, 1978; Pushcart Prize, 1983, 1987; Honorable Mention, The Poets' Prize, 1987; Emily Clark Balch Award, 1987; Honorary Doctor of Literature, Converse College, 1989; Haines Award for Poetry, Fellowship of Southern Writers, 1993; Finalist, National Book Critics Circle Award, 1996. Address: Box 16, Marshfield, VT 05658, USA.

VOLLMAN William T, b. 28 July 1959, Santa Monica, California, USA. Author. Education: Deep Springs College, 1977-79; BA summa cum laude, Cornell University, 1981; Graduate Studies, Unversity of California at Berkeley, 1982-83. Publications: You Bright and Risen Angels: A Cartoon, 1987; The Rainbow Stories, 1989; Seven Dreams: A Book of North American Landscapes, 7 volumes, 1990-; Whores for Gloria, or, Everything Was Beautiful Until the Girls Got Anxious, 1991; Thirteen Stories and Thirteen Epitaphs, 1991; An Afghanistan Picture Show, or, How I Saved the World, 1992; Butterfly Stories, 1993. Honours: Ella Lyman Cabot Trust Fellowship, 1982; Regent's Fellow, University of California at Berkeley, 1982-83; Ludwig Vogelstein Award, 1987; Whiting Writers' Award, 1988; Shiva Naipaul Memorial Prize, 1989. Address: c/o Viking-Penguin, 375 Hudson Street, New York, NY 10014, USA.

VON SCHROEDER Urs Rudolf, b. 4 May 1943, Uzwil, Switzerland. Editor-in-Chief; Writer. m. Patricia Lardi, 4 June 1991. Education: Certificate of Commerce, Switzerland, 1962; Linguistic studies in UK, France and USA. Publications: Kein Grund zur Panik (short stories), 1983; Gestern Hongkong - morgen New York (non-fiction), 1984; Walter Matysiak (monograph), 1986; SR 308 - Startbereit (non-fiction), 1989; Kitso Ketsudan (non-fiction), 1991. Contributions to: Signature, Japan; Others. Memberships: Swiss Writers' Association; PEN Centre, Switzerland. Address: Im Stemmerli 9, CH-8200 Schaffhausen, Switzerland.

VON STRASSER Karl. See: **CAIDIN Martin.**

VONARBURG Elisabeth, b. 1947, France. Teacher; Editor; Writer. Education: PhD, Creative Writing. Appointments: Teacher of Literature, colleges and universities, Quebec; Literary Editor, Solaris, 1979-90. Publications: The Silent City, 1986; Comment écrire des histoires, 1986; Histoires de la Princess et du Dragon, 1991; Ailleurs et au Fapon, 1992. Honours: Grand Prix de la Science-Fiction Française, Prix Rosny Ainé, and Prix Boréal, 1982; Casper Awards for Best Science Fiction Short Story in French, 1987, 1990, 1991; Best Science Fiction Book Awards, 1991, 1992. Address: 266 Beleau, Chicoutini, Quebec G7H 2Y8, Canada.

VONNEGUT Kurt Jr, b. 11 Nov 1922, Indianapolis, Indiana, USA. Author. m. (1) Jane Marie Cox, 1 Sept 1945, div 1979, 1 son, 2 daughters, 3 adopted nephews, (2) Judith Krementz, 1979, 1 daughter. Education: Cornell University, 1940-42; University of Chicago,

1945-47, MA in Anthropology, 1971. Appointments: Lecturer, Writers Workshop, University of Iowa, 1965-67; Lecturer in English, Harvard University, 1970; Distinguished Professor, City College of the City University of the New York, 1973-74. Publications: Novels: Player Piano, 1951; Sirens of Titan, 1959; Mother Night, 1961; Cat's Cradle, 1963; God Bless You, Mr Rosewater, 1964; Slaughterhouse-Five, 1969; Breakfast of Champions, 1973; Slapstick, or Lonesome No More, 1976; Jailbird, 1979; Deadeye Dick, 1982; Galapagos, 1985; Bluebeard, 1987; Hocus Pocus, 1990; Timequake, 1997. Short stories: Welcome to the Monkey House, 1968. Play: Happy Birthday, Wanda Jane, 1970. Television script: Between Time and Timbuktu, or Prometheus-5, 1972. Non-fiction: Wampeters, Foma and Granfallons, 1974; Palm Sunday, 1981; Fates Worse Than Death, 1991. Contributions to: Journals and magazines. Honours: Guggenheim Fellowship, 1967-68; National Institute of Arts and Letters Award, 1970. Membership: American Academy of Arts and Letters. Address: c/o Donald C Farber, 150 East 58th Street, 39th Floor, New York, NY 10135, USA.

VOYLE Mary. See: **MANNING Rosemary**.

VROOMKONING Victor. See: **VAN DE LAAR Waltherus Antonius Bernardinus**.

VUONG Lynette Dyer, b. 20 June 1938, Owosso, Michigan, USA. Author; Lecturer. m. Ti Quang Vuong, 9Jan 1962, 2 sons, 2 daughters. Education: University of Wisconsin, Milwaukee, 1958-61; Graduated, Registered Nurse, Milwaukee County Hospital School of Nursing, 1959. Publications: The Brocaded Slipper and Other Vietnamese Tales, 1982; A Friend for Carlita, 1989; The Golden Carp and Other Tales from Vietnam, 1993; Sky Legends of Vietnam, 1993. Contributions to: Various publications. Honours: Romance Writers of America Golden Heart Award, 1st Place in Mainstream Division, unpublished manuscript; Catholic Library Association's Ann Martin Book Award, 1991. Memberships: Associated Authors of Children's Literature, Houston; Romance Writers of America; Society of Children's Book Writers; Golden Key National Honor Society, Classical Association of Houston. Address: 1521 Morning Dove Drive, Humble, TX 77396, USA.

W

WADDELL Evelyn Margaret, (Lyn Cook), b. 4 May 1918, Weston, Ontario, Canada. Children's Librarian; Writer. m. Robb John Waddell, 19 Sept 1949, 1 son, 1 daughter. Education: BA, English Language and Literature, Bachelor in Library Science, University of Toronto. Publications: All as Lyn Cook: The Bells on Finland Street, 1950, 2nd edition, 1991; The Little Magic Fiddler, 1951; Rebel on the Trail, 1953; Jady and the General, 1955; Pegeen and the Pilgrim, 1957; The Road to Kip's Cove, 1961; Samantha's Secret Room, 1963, 2nd edition, 1991; The Brownie Handbook for Canada, 1965; The Secret of Willow Castle, 1966, 1984; The Magical Miss Mittens, 1970; Toys from the Sky, 1972; Jolly Jean-Pierre, 1973; If I Were All These, 1974; A Treasure for Tony, 1980; The Magic Pony, 1981; Sea Dreams, 1981; The Hiding Place, 1990, 1994; A Canadian ABC (poems), 1990; Where Do Snowflakes Go?, 1994. Honours: Honorary Member, Academy of Canadian Writers; Vicky Metcalf Award, 1978. Membership: Canadian Society of Children's Authors, Illustrators and Performers. Address: 72 Cedarbrae Blvd, Scarborough, Ontario M1J 2K5, Canada.

WADDINGTON FEATHER John Joseph, b. 10 July 1933, Keighley, Yorkshire, England. Anglican Priest; Publisher. m. Sheila Mary Booker, 23 July 1960, 3 daughters. Education: BA, Leeds University. Appointment: Co- Editor, Orbis, 1971-80. Publications: Yorkshire Dialect, 1969; Garlic Lane, 1970; Easy Street, 1971; One Man's Road, 1979; Quills Adventures in the Great Beyond, 1980; Tall Tales from Yukon, 1983; Khartoum Trilogy, 1985; Quill's Adventures in Wasteland, 1986; Quill's Adventures in Grozzieland, 1988; Six Christian Monologues, 1990; Shropshire, 1994. Contributions to: Various Journals and Magazines. Honours: Brontë Society Prize, 1963; Cyril Hodges Poetry Award, 1976. Memberships: Yorkshire Dialect Society; Bronte Society; Royal Society of Arts. Address: Fair View, Old Coppice, Lyth Bank, Shrewsbury, Shropshire SY3 0BW, England.

WADE David, b. 2 Dec 1929, Edinburgh, Scotland. Writer. Education: Queen's College, Cambridge, 1952. Appointments: Radio Critic, The Listener, 1965-67; The Times, 1967-89. Publications: Trying to Connect You; The Cooker; The Guthrie Process; The Gold Spinners; Three Blows in Anger; The Ogden File; The Carpet Maker of Samarkand; The Nightingale; Summer of 39; The Facts of Life; A Rather Nasty Crack; On Detachment; The Tree of Strife; Power of Attorney; Alexander. Membership: Society of Authors. Literary Agent: MBA Ltd, 45 Fitzroy Street, London W1P 5HR, England. Address: Willow Cottage, Stockland Green Road, Southborough, Kent TN3 0TL, England.

WAELTI-WALTERS Jennifer (Rose), b. 13 Mar 1942, Wolverhampton, England. Professor of French and Women's Studies; Writer. Education: BA, Hons, 1964, PhD, 1968, University of London; Licence-ès-Lettres, University of Lille, France, 1965. Appointment: Professor of French and Women's Studies, University of Victoria, British Columbia. Publications: Alchimie et Litterature, 1975; J M G Le Clézio, 1977; Michel Butor: A View of His World and a Panorama of His Work, 1977; Fairytales and the Female Imagination, 1982; Jeanne Hyvrard (with M Verthuy), 1989; Feminist Novelists of the Belle Epoque, 1991; Michel Butor, 1992; Feminisms of the Belle Epoque (with S Hause), 1994; Jeanne Hyvrard, Theorist of the Modern World, 1996; Dead Girl in a Lace Dress by J Hyvrard, translated with J-P Mentha. Contributions to: Professional journals and general magazines. Honour: Association des Professeurs de Français des Universités et Colleges Canadiens Prize for the Best Book of Literary Criticism in French, 1989. Memberships: Association des Professeurs de Français des Universités et Colleges Canadiens; Canadian Research Institute for the Advancement of Women; Canadian Women's Studies Association. Address: c/o Department of Women's Studies, University of Victoria, Victoria, British Columbia V8W 3P4, Canada.

WAGNER-MARTIN Linda, b. 1936, USA. Professor of English and Comparative Literature; Writer; Editor. Appointments: Faculty, Wayne State University, Bowling Green State University, Ohio, Michigan State University; Hanes Professor of English and Comparative Literature, University of North Carolina at Chapel Hill; Editor, The Centennial Review. Publications: The Poems of William Carlos Williams, 1964; The Prose of William Carlos Williams, 1970; Phyllis McGinley, 1971; William Faulkner: Four Decades of Criticism (editor), 1973; T S Eliot (editor), 1974; Ernest Hemingway: Five Decades of Criticism (editor), 1974; Hemingway and Faulkner: Inventors/Masters, 1975; Introducing Poems (with C David Mead), 1976; Ernest Hemingway: A Reference Guide, 1978; Dos Passos: Artist as American, 1979; American Modern, 1980; Songs for Isadora, 1981; Ellen Glasgow: Beyond Convention, 1982; Sylvia Plath: Critical Essays, 1984; Ernest Hemingway: Six Decades of Criticism (editor), 1987; Sylvia Plath: A Biography, 1987; Sylvia Plath: The Critical Heritage (editor), 1988; Anne Sexton: Critical Essays (editor), 1989; The Modern American Novel, 1914-45, 1989; The Heath Anthology of American Literature (co-editor), 1989, 2nd edition, 1994; Denise Levertov: Critical Essays (editor), 1990; Telling Women's Lives: The New Biography, 1994; The Oxford Companion to Women's Writing in the United States (co-editor), 1995; Favored Strangers: Gertrude Stein and Her Family, 1995; New Essays on Go Down Moses, 1995. Contributions to: Professional journals. Address: c/o Department of English, University of North Carolina at Chapel Hill, Chapel Hill, NC 27514, USA.

WAGONER David (Russell), b. 5 June 1926, Massillon, Ohio, USA. Professor of English; Poet; Author. m. (1) Patricia Parrott, 1961, div 1982, (2) Robin Heather Seyfried, 1982. Education: BA, Penn State University, 1947; MA, Indiana University, 1949. Appointments: Instructor, DePauw University, 1949-50, Penn State University, 1950-53; Assistant Professor, 1954-57, Associate Professor, 1958-66, Professor of English, 1966-, University of Washington, Seattle; Editor, Poetry Northwest, 1966-; Elliston Professor of Poetry, University of Cincinnati, 1968. Publications: Poetry: Dry Sun, Dry Wind, 1953; A Place to Stand, 1958; Poems, 1959; The Nesting Ground, 1963; Staying Alive, 1966; New and Selected Poems, 1969; Working Against Time, 1970; Riverbed, 1972; Sleeping in the Woods, 1974; A Guide to Dungeness Spit, 1975; Travelling Light, 1976; Collected Poems, 1956-1976, 1976; Who Shall be the Sun?: Poems Based on the Love, Legends, and Myths of Northwest Coast and Plateau Indians, 1978; In Broken Country, 1979; Landfall, 1981; First Light, 1983; Through the Forest: New and Selected Poems, 1977-1987, 1987. Fiction: The Man in the Middle, 1954; Money, Money, Money, 1955; Rock, 1958; The Escape Artist, 1965; Baby, Come on Inside, 1968; Where Is My Wandering Boy Tonight?, 1970; The Road to Many a Wonder, 1974; Tracker, 1975; Whole Hog, 1976; The Hanging Garden, 1980. Editor: Straw for the Fire: From the Notebooks of Theodore Roethke 1943-1963, 1972. Honours: Guggenheim Fellowship, 1956; Ford Foundation Fellowship, 1964; American Academy of Arts and Letters Grant, 1967; National Endowment for the Arts Grant, 1969; Morton Dauwen Zabel Prize, 1967; Oscar Blumenthal Prize, 1974; Fels Prize, 1975; Eunice Tietjens Memorial Prize, 1977; English-Speaking Union Prize, 1980; Sherwood Anderson Prize, 1980. Membership: Academy of American Poets, chancellor, 1978. Address: 5416-154th Pl SW, Edmonds, WA 98026, USA.

WAHLBECK Jan-Christer, b. 10 July 1948, Vasa, Finland. Psychologist; Family Therapist; Consultant. m. Liisa Ryyppö, 1 Dec 1978, 1 son, 2 daughters. Education: MA, 1976; Advanced Family Therapist, 1988; Organizational Consultant, 1988. Publications: Steg På Hållplatsen (poetry), 1977; Bussen Stannar Bakom Hörnet (poetry), 1979; Mognadens Opera (poetry), 1981; Näckrosor Och Bränt Vatten (novel), 1983; Katastrof Efter Katastrof (poetry), 1984; Pojken Och Korpen, illustrated fairy tale, 1988; Bilen Och Lidelserna (poetry), 1991; Huset Och Luftens Musik (poetry), 1993. Honour: Villa Biaudet Fellowship, 1985-88. Memberships: The Finlandssvede Union of Writers. Address: Brunnsgatan 12, Fin-06100 Borgå, Finland.

WAINWRIGHT Geoffrey, b. 16 July 1939, Yorkshire, England. Professor of Systematic Theology; Methodist Minister. m. Margaret Wiles, 20 Apr 1965, 1 son, 2 daughters. Education: BA, 1960, MA, 1964, BD, 1972, DD, 1987, Cambridge University; DrThéol University of Geneva, 1969. Appointments: Editor, Studia Liturgica, 1974-87; Professor of Systematic Theology, The Divinity School, Duke University, Durham, North Carolina. Publications: Christian Initiation, 1969; Eucharist and Eschatology, 1971, 2nd edition, 1981; The Study of Liturgy (co-editor), 1978, 2nd edition, 1992; Doxology, 1980; The Ecumenical Moment, 1983; The Study of Spirituality (co-editor), 1986; On Wesley and Calvin, 1987; Keeping the Faith: Essays to Mark the Centenary of Lux Mundi (editor), 1989; The Dictionary of the Ecumenical Movement (co-editor), 1991; Methodists in Dialogue, 1995; Worship With One Accord, 1997; For Our Salvation, 1997. Contributions to: Reference books and theological journals. Honours:

Numerous named lectureships worldwide. Memberships: American Theological Society, secretary, 1988-95, president, 1996-97; International Dialogue Between the World Methodist Council and the Roman Catholic Church, chairman; Societas Liturgica, president, 1983-85; World Council of Churches Faith and Order Commission, 1976-91. Address: The Divinity School, Duke University, Durham, NC 27708, USA.

WAINWRIGHT Jeffrey, b. 19 Feb 1944, Stoke on Trent, England. Poet; Dramatist; Translator; Lecturer. m. Judith Blatt, 22 July 1967, 1 son, 1 daughter. Education: BA, 1965, MA, 1967, University of Leeds. Appointments: Assistant Lecturer, Lecturer, University of Wales, 1967-72; Visiting Instructor, Long Island University, 1970-71; Senior Lecturer, Manchester Polytechnic, 1972-; Northern Theatre Critic, The Independent, 1988-. Publications: Poetry: The Important Men, 1970; Heart's Desire, 1978; Selected Poems, 1985. Plays: For the stage, film and television. Other: Translations of various plays into English. Contributions to: Anthologies; BBC Radio; Many periodicals. Honour: Judith E Wilson Visiting Fellow, Cambridge University, 1985. Memberships: National Association of Teachers in Further and Higher Education; Writers Guild of Great Britain. Address: 11 Hesketh Avenue, Didsbury, Manchester M20 8QN, England.

WAITE Peter Busby, b. 12 July 1922, Toronto, Ontario, Canada. Professor of History. m. Masha Maria Gropuzzo, 22 Aug 1958. Education: BA (Hons), 1948, MA, 1950, University of British Columbia; PhD, University of Toronto, 1954. Publications: The Life and Times of Confederation, 1864-1867, 1962; Canada 1874-1896, 1971; John A Macdonald, His Life and World, 1975; The Man from Halifax: Sir John Thompson, Prime Minister, 1985; Lord of Point Grey: Larry MacKenzie of UBC, 1987; Between Three Oceans: Challenges of a Continental Destiny, 1840-1900, Chapter IV, Illustrated History of Canada, 1988; The Loner: The Personal Life and Ideas of R B Bennett 1870-1947, 1992; The Lives of Dalhousie University: Volume I, Lord Dalhousie's College, 1818-1925, 1994. Contributions to: Some 55 articles to numerous magazines and journals. Honours: Fellow, Royal Society of Canada, 1972; Runner-up, Governor-General's Gold Medal Prize, 1985; Lieutenant-Governor's Medal, British Columbia, 1987; LL.D Dalhousie University, 1991; D.Litt, University of New Brunswick, 1991, Memorial University of Newfoundland, 1991, Carleton University, 1993; Officer of the Order of Canada, 1993. Memberships: Canadian Historical Association, president, 1968-69; Humanities Research Council, chairman, 1968-70; Aid to Publications Committee, Social Science Federation, chairman, 1987-89. Address: 960 Ritchie Drive, Halifax, Nova Scotia B3H 3P5, Canada.

WAKEFIELD Dan, b. 21 May 1932, Indianapolis, Indiana, USA. Author; Screenwriter. Education: BA, Columbia University, 1955. Appointments: News Editor, Princeton Packet, New Jersey, 1955; Staff Writer, The Nation magazine, 1956-59; Staff, Bread Loaf Writers Conference, 1964, 1966, 1968, 1970, 1986; Visiting Lecturer, University of Massachusetts at Boston, 1965-66, University of Illinois, 1968; Contributing Editor, The Atlantic Monthly, 1969-80; Writer-in-Residence, Emerson College, 1989-92; Contributing Writer, GQ magazine, 1992-; Distinguished Visiting Writer, Florida International University, 1995-. Publications: Island of the City: The World of Spanish Harlem, 1959; Revolt in the South, 1961; Ananthology, 1963; Between the Lines, 1966; Supernation at Peace and War, 1968; Going All the Way, 1970; Starting Over, 1973; All Her Children, 1976; Home Free, 1977; Under the Apple Tree, 1982; Selling Out, 1985; Returning: A Spiritual Journey, 1988; The Story of Your Life: Writing a Spiritual Autobiography, 1990; New York in the Fifties, 1992; Expect a Miracle, 1995; Creating from the Spirit, 1996. Editor: The Addict: An Anthology, 1963. Television: James at 15, 1977-78; The Seduction of Miss Leona, 1980; Heartbeat, 1988. Honours: Bernard DeVoto Fellow, Bread Loaf Writers Conference, 1957; Rockefeller Foundation Grant, 1968; Short Story Prize, National Council of the Arts, 1968. Memberships: Authors Guild of America. Address: c/o Janklow & Nesbit, 598 Madison Avenue, New York, NY 10022, USA.

WAKEMAN (Frederic) Evans (Jr), b. 12 Dec 1937, Kansas City, Kansas, USA. Professor of Asian Studies; Writer. Div, 2 sons, 1 daughter. Education: BA, Harvard College, 1959; Postgraduate Studies, Institut d'Etudes Politiques, University of Paris, 1959-60; MA, 1962, PhD, 1965, University of California at Berkeley. Appointments: Assistant Professor, 1965-67, Associate Professor, 1968-70, Professor of History, 1970-89, Director, Center of Chinese Studies, 1972-79, Haas Professor of Asian Studies, 1989-, Director, Institute of East Asian Studies, 1990-, University of California at Berkeley; Humanities Research Professor and Visiting Scholar, Corpus Christi College, Cambridge, 1976-77, Beijing University, 1980-81, 1985. Publications: Strangers at the Gate: Social Disorder in South China, 1839-1861, 1966; Nothing Concealed: Essays in Honor of Liu Yu-Yun, 1970; History and Will, 1973; The Fall of Imperial China (co-editor), 1976; Ming and Qing Historical Studies in the People's Republic of China, 1981; The Great Enterprise: The Manchu Reconstruction of Imperial Order in Seventeenth Century China, 2 volumes, 1985; Shanghai Sojourners (co-editor), 1992; Policing Shanghai, 1995. Contributions to: Professional journals. Honours: American Council of Learned Societies, fellow, 1967-68; Guggenheim Fellowship, 1973-74; Levenson Prize, 1986. Memberships: American Academy of Arts and Sciences; American Historical Association; Association for Asian Studies; Council on Foreign Relations. Address: c/o Institute of East Asian Studies, University of California at Berkeley, Berkeley, CA 94720, USA.

WAKEMAN John, b. 29 Sept 1928, London, England. Editor; Writer. m. Hilary Paulett, 15 Mar 1957, 4 sons, 1 daughter. Education: Associate, British Library Association, 1950; BA, 1989, MA, 1990, University of East Anglia. Publications: World Authors, 1950-75, 1975; World Authors, 1970-75, 1980; A Room for Doubt, 1985; The Rialto, 1985; World Film Directors, 1987; The Beach Hut, 1987. Contributions to: Newspapers and magazines. Honours: Library Journal Best Reference Book Selection, 1988, and Outstanding Academic Book Selection, 1989, Eastern Arts Travel Bursary, 1991; Hawthornden Fellowship, 1992. Address: The Rectory, Toormore, Schull, County Cork, Ireland.

WALCOTT Derek (Alton), b. 23 Jan 1930, Castries, St Lucia, West Indies. Poet; Dramatist; Visiting Professor. m. (1) Fay Moyston, 1954, div 1959, 1 son, (2) Margaret Ruth Maillard, 1962, div, 2 daughters, (3) Norline Metivier, 1982. Education: St Mary's College, Castries, 1941-47; BA, University College of the West Indies, Mona, Jamaica, 1953. Appointments: Teacher, St Mary's College, Castries, 1947-50, 1954, Grenada Boy's Secondary School, St George's, 1953-54, Jamaica College, Kingston, 1955; Feature Writer, Public Opinion, Kingston, 1956-57; Founder-Director, Little Carib Theatre Workshop, later Trinidad Theatre Workshop, 1959-76; Feature Writer, 1960-62, Drama Critic, 1963-68, Trinidad Guardian, Port-of-Spain; Visiting Professor, Columbia Universitry, 1981, Harvard University, 1982, 1987; Assistant Professor of Creative Writing, 1981, Visiting Professor, 1985-, Brown University. Publications: Poetry: 25 Poems, 1948; Epitaph for the Young: XII Cantos, 1949; Poems, 1951; In a Green Night: Poems 1948-1960, 1962; Selected Poems, 1964; The Castaway and Other Poems, 1965; The Gulf and Other Poems, 1969; Another Life, 1973; Sea Grapes, 1976; The Star-Apple Kingdom, 1979; Selected Poems, 1981; The Fortunate Traveller, 1981; The Caribbean Poetry of Derek Walcott and the Art of Romare Bearden, 1983; Midsummer, 1984; Collected Poems 1948-1984, 1986; The Arkansas Testament, 1987; Omeros, 1989; Collected Poems, 1990; Poems 1965-1980, 1992; Derek Walcott: Selected Poems, 1993. Plays: Cry for a Leader, 1950; Senza Alcun Sospetto or Paolo and Francesca, 1950; Henri Christophe: A Chronicle, 1950; Robin and Andrea or Bim, 1950; Three Assassins, 1951; The Price of Mercy, 1951; Harry Dernier, 1952; The Sea at Dauphin, 1954; Crossroads, 1954; The Charlatan, 1954, 4th version, 1977; The Wine of the Country, 1956; The Golden Lions, 1956; Ione: A Play with Music, 1957; Ti-Jear and His Brothers, 1957; Drums and Colours, 1958; Malcochon, or, The Six in the Rain, 1959; Jourmard, or, A Comedy till the Last Minute, 1959; Batai, 1965; Dream on Monkey Mountain, 1967; Franklin: A Tale of the Islands, 1969, 2nd version, 1973; In a Fine Castle, 1970; The Joker of Seville, 1974; O Babylon!, 1976; Remembrance, 1977; The Snow Queen, 1977; Pantomime, 1978; Marie Laveau, 1979; The Isle is Full of Noises, 1982; Beef, No Chicken, 1982; The Odyssey: A Stage Version, 1993. Non-Fiction: The Antilles: Fragments of Epic Memory: The Nobel Lecture, 1993. Honours: Rockefeller Foundation Grants, 1957, 1966, and Fellowship, 1958; Arts Advisory Council of Jamaica Prize, 1960; Guinness Award, 1961; Ingram Merrill Foundation Grant, 1962; Borestone Mountain Awards, 1964, 1977; Heinemann Awards, Royal Society of Literature, 1966, 1983; Cholmondeley Award, 1969; Eugene O'Neill Foundation Fellowship, 1969; Gold Hummingbird Medal, Trinidad, 1969; Obie Award, 1971; Officer of the Order of the British Empire, 1972; Guggenheim Fellowship, 1977; Welsh Arts Council International Writers Prize, 1980; John D and Catharine T MacArthur Foundation Fellowship, 1981; Los Angeles Times Book Prize, 1986; Queen's Gold Medal for Poetry, 1988; Nobel Prize for Literature, 1992. Memberships: American Academy of Arts and

Letters, honorary member; Royal Society of Literature, fellow. Address: 165 Duke of Edinburgh Avenue, Diego Martin, Trinidad and Tobago.

WALDENFELS Hans, b. 20 Oct 1931, Essen, Ruhr, Germany. University Professor. Education: Lic Phil, 1956; Lic Theol, 1964; Dr Theol, 1968; Dr Theol Habil, 1976; Ordained Roman Catholic Priest, 1963. Publications: Faszination des Buddhismus, 1982; Kontextuelle Fundamentaltheologie, 1988; An der Grenze des Denkbaren, 1988; Lexikon der Religionen, 1989; Begegnung der Religionen, 1990; Phänomen Christentum, 1994; Gott, 1995; Einführung in die Theologie der Offenbarung, 1996. Honour: Dr Theol hc, Warsaw. Memberships: Internationales Institut für Missionswissenschaftliche Forschungen; International Association for Mission Studies; Deutsche Vereinigung für Religionsgeschichte; Deutsche Gesellschaft für Missioswissenschaft; Rotary Club. Address: Grenzweg 2, D 4000 Dusseldorf 31, Germany.

WALDROP Rosmarie, b. 24 Aug 1935, Kitzingen/Main, Germany. Writer; Poet; Translator; Editor. m. 21 Jan 1959. Education: Undergraduate studies, Universities of Würzburg, Freiburg and Aix-Marseille; MA, 1960, PhD, 1966, University of Michigan, USA. Appointments: Editor, Publisher, Burning Deck Press, USA, 1963-; Wesleyan University, 1964-70; Southern Methodist University, 1977; Brown University, 1977-78, 1983, 1990-91; Tufts University, 1978-81. Publications: Edmond Jabes: The Book of Questions (translator), 7 volumes bound as 4, 1976-84; The Road is Everywhere or Stop This Body, 1978; Streets Enough to Welcome Snow (poems), 1986; The Reproduction of Profiles (poems), 1987; The Hanky of Pippin's Daughter (novel); A Form/of Taking/It All (novella), 1990; Lawn of Excluded Middle (poems), 1993. Contributions to: Conjunctions; Sulfur; Oblek; Denver Quarterly; Temblor. Honours: Major Hopwood Award in Poetry, 1963; Howard Fellowship, 1974-75; Columbia Translation Center Award, 1978; National Endowment for the Arts Award, 1988; Award from the Fund for Poetry, 1990; Deutscher Akademischer Austauschdienst Fellowship, 1993; Harold Morton Landon Translation Award, 1994. Membership: PEN. Address: 71 Elmgrove Avenue, Providence, RI 02906, USA.

WALKER Alexander, b. 22 Mar 1930, Portadown, Northern Ireland. Journalist; Film Critic. Education: BA, Queen's University, Belfast; College d'Europe, Belgium; University of Michigan. Appointments: Lecturer, University of Michigan, 1952-54; Features Editor, Birmingham Gazette, 1954-56; Critic, Evening Standard, 1960-; Columnist, Vogue Magazine, 1974-86; Broadcaster, Co-Producer, television programmes. Publications: The Celluloid Sacrifice: Aspects of Sex in the Movies, 1966; Stardom: The Hollywood Phenomenon, 1970; Stanley Kubrick Directs, 1971; Hollywood, England: British Film Industry in the 60s, 1974; Rudolph Valentino, 1976; Double Jakes, 1978; Superstars, 1978; The Shattered Silents, 1978; Garbo, 1980; Peter Sellers: Authorised Biography, 1981; Joan Crawford, 1983; Dietrich, 1984; No Bells on Sunday: The Journals of Rocket Roberts, 1984; National Heroes: British Cinema in the 70's and 80's, 1985; Bette Davis, 1986; Vivien: The Life of Vivien Leigh, 1987; It's Only a Movie, Ingrid, 1988; Elizabeth: The Life of Elizabeth Taylor, 1990; Zinnemann, 1991; Fatal Charm: The Life of Rex Harrison, 1992; Audrey: Her Real Story, 1994. Contributions to: Magazines. Honours: Critic of the Year Awards, 1970, 1974; Chevalier de l'Ordre des Arts et des Letters, France, 1981. Memberships: British Film Institute; British Screen Advisory Council. Address: 1 Marlborough, 38-40 Maida Vale, London W9 1RW, England.

WALKER Alice (Malsenior), b. 9 Feb 1944, Eatonton, Georgia, USA. Author; Poet. m. Melvyn R Leventhal, 17 Mar 1967, div 1976, 1 daughter. Education: BA, Sarah Lawrence College, 1966. Appointments: Writer-in-Residence and Teacher of Black Studies, Jackson State College, 1968-69, Tougaloo College, 1970-71; Lecturer in Literature, Wellesley College, 1972-73, University of Massachusetts at Boston, 1972-73; Distinguished Writer, Afro-American Studies Department, University of California at Berkeley, 1982; Fannie Hurst Professor of Literature, Brandeis University, 1982; Co-Founder and Publisher, Wild Trees Press, Navarro, California, 1984-88. Publications: Once, 1968; The Third Life of Grange Copeland, 1970; Five Poems, 1972; Revolutionary Petunias and Other Poems, 1973; In Love and Trouble, 1973; Langston Hughes: American Poet, 1973; Meridian, 1976; Goodnight, Willie Lee, I'll See You in the Morning, 1979; You Can't Keep a Good Woman Down, 1981; The Color Purple, 1982; In Search of Our Mother's Gardens, 1983; Horses Make a Landscape Look More Beautiful, 1984; To Hell With Dying, 1988; Living by the Word: Selected Writings, 1973-1987, 1988; The Temple

of My Familiar, 1989; Her Blue Body Everything We Know: Earthling Poems, 1965-1990, 1991; Finding the Green Stone, 1991; Possessing the Secret of Joy, 1992; Warrior Marks (with Pratibha Parmar), 1993; Double Stitch: Black Women Write About Mothers and Daughters (with others), 1993; Everyday Use, 1994. Editor: I Love Myself When I'm Laughing... And Then Again When I'm Looking Mean and Impressive, 1979. Honours: Bread Loaf Writer's Conference Scholar, 1966; Ingram Merrill Foundation Fellowship, 1967; McDowell Colony Fellowships, 1967, 1977-78; National Endowment for the Arts Grants, 1969, 1977; Richard and Hinda Rosenthal Pound Award, American Academy and Institute of Arts and Letters, 1974; Guggenheim Fellowship, 1977-78; Pulitzer Prize for Fiction, 1983; American Book Award, 1983; O Henry Award, 1986; Nora Astorga Leadership Award, 1989; Freedom to Write Award, PEN Center, West, 1990; Honorary doctorates. Address: c/o Wendy Weil Agency Inc, 232 Madison Avenue, Suite 1300, New York, NY 10016, USA.

WALKER Andrew Norman, b. 19 May 1926, Looe, Cornwall, England. Retired BBC Journalist. m. Avril Anne Elizabeth Dooley, 20 June 1956, 2 sons, 2 daughters. Publications: The Modern Commonwealth, 1975; The Commonwealth: A New Look, 1978; A Skyful of Freedom, 1992. Contributions to: Janes Defence Weekly; Commonwealth Magazine. Membership: Commonwealth Journalists Association. Address: 9 Chartwell Court, Brighton, East Sussex BN1 2EW, England.

WALKER David Maxwell, b. 9 Apr 1920, Glasgow, Scotland. Professor of Law Emeritus; Writer. m. Margaret Knox, 1 Sept 1954. Education: MA, 1946, LLB, 1948, LLD, 1985, University of Glasgow; PhD, 1952, LLD, 1960, University of Edinburgh; LLB, 1957, LLD, 1968, University of London. Appointments: Advocate, Scottish Bar, 1948; Professor of Jurisprudence, University of Glasgow, 1954-58; Barrister, Middle Temple, 1957; Director, Scottish University Law Institute, 1974-80; Regius Professor of Law, 1958-90, Professor Emeritus and Senior Research Fellow, 1990-, University of Glasgow. Publications: Law of Damages in Scotland, 1955; The Scottish Legal System, 1959, 6th edition, 1992; Law of Delect in Scotland, 1966, 2nd edition, 1981; Scottish Courts and Tribunals, 1969, 5th edition, 1985; Principles of Scottish Private Law, 2 volumes, 1970, 4th edition, 4 volumes, 1988-89; Law of Prescription and Limitation in Scotland, 1973,1996; Law of Civil Remedies in Scotland, 1974; Law of Contracts in Scotland, 1979, 3rd edition, 1995; The Oxford Companion of Law, 1980; Stair's Institutions (editor), 6th edition, 1981; Stair Tercentenary Studies (editor), 1981; The Scottish Jurists, 1985; The Legal History of Scotland, 4 volumes, 1988, 1990, 1995. Contributions to: Books and legal journals. Honours: Honorary LLD, University of Edinburgh, 1974; Commander of the Order of the British Empire, 1986; Festschrift published in his honour, 1990. Memberships: British Academy, fellow; Faculty of Advocates; Royal Society of Edinburgh, fellow; Scottish History Society; Society of Antiquarians of Scotland; Society of the Middle Temple; Stair Society. Address: 1 Beaumont Gate, Glasgow G12 9EE, Scotland.

WALKER Geoffrey De Quincey, b. 24 Oct 1940, Waratah, New South Wales, Australia. Professor of Law. m. Patricia Mary Kehoe, 7 Dec 1990. Education: LLB, 1962; LLM, 1963; SJD, 1966. Appointment: Professor of Law, University of Queensland, 1985-. Publications: Australian Monopoly Law, 1967; Initiative and Referendum: The People's Law, 1987; The Rule of Law: Foundation of Constitutional Democracy, 1988. Contributions to: Over 60 Articles. Honour: Gowen Fellow, University of Pennsylvania, 1966. Address: T C Beirne School of Law, University of Queensland, Qld 4072, Australia.

WALKER George F(rederick), b. 23 Aug 1947, Toronto, Ontario, Canada. Playwright. Education: Graduated Riverdale Collegiate, Toronto, 1965. Appointment: Resident Playwright, New York Shakespeare Festival, 1981. Publications: The Prince of Naples, 1971; Ambush at Tether's End, 1971; Sacktown Rag, 1972; Baghdad Saloon, 1973; Beyond Mozambique, 1974; Ramona and the White Slaves, 1976; Gossip, 1977; Zastrozzi: The Master of Discipline, 1977; Filthy Rich, 1979; Rumours of our Death (musical), 1980; Theatre of the Film Noir, 1981; Science and Madness, 1982; The Art of War: An Adventure, 1983; Criminals in Love, 1984; Better Living, 1986; Beautiful City, 1987; Nothing Sacred, after Turgenev, 1988; Love and Anger, 1990; Radio and television plays. Honour: Canada Council Grants. Address: c/o Great North Artists, 350 Dupont Street, Toronto, Ontario M5V 1V9, Canada.

WALKER Harry. See: **WAUGH Hillary Baldwin.**

WALKER Lou Ann, b. 9 Dec 1952, Hartford City, Indiana, USA. Writer. m. Speed Vogel, 8 Sept 1986, 1 daughter. Education: Attended Ball State University, 1971-73; Degree in French Language and Literature, University of Besancon, 1975; BA, Harvard University, 1976. Appointments: Reporter, Indianapolis News, 1976; Assistant to Executive Editor, New York (magazine), New York, 1976-77; Assistant Editor, Esquire Magazine, 1977-79; Assistant to Executive Editor, Cosmopolitan, New York City, 1979-80; Associate Editor, Diversion (magazine), New York City, 1980-81; Editor, Direct (magazine), New York City, 1981-82; Sign Language Interpretor for New York Society for the Deaf; Consultant to Broadway's Theater Development Fund and sign language advisor on many Broadway shows, 1984-; Contributing Editor, New York Woman, 1990-92; Publications: Amy: The Story of a Deaf Child, 1985; A Loss for Words: The Story of Deafness in a Family (autobiography), 1986; Hand, Heart and Mind, 1994; Roy Lichtenstein: The Artist at Work, 1994. Contributions to: New York Times Book Review; Chicago Sun-Times (Book Reviews); Esquire; New York Times Magazine; New York Woman; Life. Honours: Rockefeller Foundation Humanities Fellowship, 1982-83; Christopher Award, 1987; National Endowment for the Arts Creative Writing Grant, 1988. Membership: Authors Guild. Address: c/o Darhansoff & Verrill, 179 Franklin Street, 4th Floor, New York, NY 10013, USA.

WALKER Ted, (Edward Joseph Walker), b. 28 Nov 1934, Lancing, England. Professor of Creative Writing Emeritus; Author; Poet. m. (1) Lorna Ruth Benfell, 11 Aug 1956, dec 1987, 2 sons, 2 daughters, (2) Audrey Joan Hicks, 8 July 1988. Education: BA, Hons, Modern and Mediaeval Languages, St John's College, Cambridge, 1956, MA, 1977. Appointments: Assistant Master, North Paddington School, London, 1956-58; Head, French Department, Southall Technical Grammar School, 1958-63; Modern Languages Department, Bognor Regis School, 1963-65; Professor of Creative Writing, 1971-92, Professor Emeritus, 1992-, New England College. Publications: Fox in a Barn Door, 1965; The Solitaries, 1967; The Night Bathers, 1970; Gloves to the Hangman, 1973; Burning the Ivy, 1978; The Lion's Calvacade, 1980; The High Path, 1982; You've Never Heard Me Sing, 1985; Hands at a Live Fire, 1987; In Spain, 1987; The Last of England, 1992; Grandad's Seagulls, 1993. Screenplays: The Wind in the Willows, 1995; The Willows in Winter, 1996 Contributions to: Newspapers, journals and magazines. Honours: Eric Gregory Award, 1964; Cholmondeley Award, 1966; Alice Hunt Bartlett Award, 1967; Major Award, Arts Council of Great Britain, 1969; Campion Prize, 1974; Honorary DLitt, University of Southampton, 1995. Memberships: Cholmondeley Award for Poetry, chairman of the judges, 1973-91; Royal Society of Literature, fellow. Literary Agent: Sheil Land Associates Ltd, 43 Doughty Street, London WC1N 2LF, England. Address: Argyll House, The Square, Eastergate, Chichester, West Sussex PO20 6UP, England.

WALKER Wilbert Lee, b. 22 July 1925, Durham, North Carolina, USA. Retired Public Administrator. m. Grace Clayborne, 15 June 1951, 1 son. Education: BA, Morgan State University, 1950; MSW, SocialWork, Howard University, Washington, DC, 1954. Publications: We Are Men, 1972; The Pride of Our Hearts, 1978; Stalemate at Panmunjon, 1980; Servants of All, 1982; The Deputy's Dilemma, 1987. Honours: Trinity Presbyterian Church Literary Award, 1978; Alpha Phi Alpha Literary Award, 1979. Memberships: Mid Atlantic Writers Association; Committee of Small Magazines, Editors and Publishers; National Association of Social Workers, life member; Delta Lambda Chapter, Alpha Phi Alpha Fraternity, Past President. Address: PO Box 18625, Baltimore, MD 21216, USA.

WALL Ethan. See: HOLMES Bryan John.

WALL Geoffrey. See: CHADWICK Geoffrey.

WALL Mervyn, b. 23 Aug 1908, Dublin, Ireland. Retired Chief Executive, Irish Arts Council. m. Fanny Freehan, 25 Apr 1950, 1 son, 3 daughters. Education: BA, National University of Ireland, 1928. Appointments: Civil Servant, 1934-48; Programme Officer, Radio Eireann, 1948-57; Chief Executive, Irish Arts Council, 1957-75; Book Reviewer, Radio Critic, Radio Broadcaster. Publications: The Unfortunate Fursey, 1946; The Return of Fursey, 1948; No Trophies Raise, 1956; Forty Foot Gentlemen Only, 1962; A Flutter of Wings, 1974; The Garden of Echoes, 1988; Plays. Contributions to: Journals. Honour: Best European Novel of Year, 1952. Memberships: Irish Academy of Letters; Irish Writers Union. Literary Agent: Jonathan Williams. Address: 2 The Mews, Sandycove Avenue West, Sandycove, County Dublin, Ireland.

WALLACE Betty Frances, b. 28 June 1926, Gastonia, North Carolina, USA. Retired Teacher/Educator; Librarian; Writer; Poet. m. William Andrew Wallace Jr, 4 Sept 1948, 1 son, 2 daughters. Education: BFA Degree, Painting, University of Georgia, 1948; Postgraduate Study, Georgia State University, 1967-69, 1972-73; Tift College, 1976; Elementary Certification, Art Certification, Georgia State University, 1976; Teacher of Gifted Certification, West Georgia College, 1981. Publications: Through a Time Sieve, 1984; With Wings Afire, 1990. Poetry: The Bayeaux Tapestry, 1980; House of the Muses, 1980; The Lo Moth, 1983; Retreat without Maximilian, 1983; Ballade for the Lady, 1984; Posture of Sleep, 1988. Contributions to: Anthologies and periodicals. Honours: New York Poetry Forum, Villanelle, 1983; Daniel Whitehead Hicky National Awards, 1983, 1988; Author of Year in Poetry, 1985; Free Verse, Nevada State Poetry Society, 1987; Teacher of Year, 1987; Blue Ribbon Award, Southern Poetry Association, 1989. Memberships: Georgia State Poetry Society, Charter Member; Southern Poetry Association; American Association of University Women; National Geographics Association. Address: 30 Woodlawn Avenue, Hampton, GA 30228, USA.

WALLACE Ian Robert, b. 31 Mar 1950, Ontario, Canada. Author; Illustrator. Education: Ontario College of Art, 1969-74. Publications: Julie News, 1974; The Sandwich (co-author), 1975; The Christmas Tree House, 1976; Chin Chiang and the Dragon's Dance, 1984; The Sparrow's Song, 1986; Morgan the Magnificent, 1987; Architect of the Moon, 1988; Mr Kneebone's New Digs, 1991. Contributions to: New Advocate; Quill & Quire. Honours: Runner Up, City of Toronto Book Awards, 1976; IODE Book Award, 1985; Canadian Library Association's Amelia Francis Howard-Gibbon Award, 1985; Ibby Honour Book, 1986; American Library Association Notable Book, 1986; White Raven Book, Bologna Children's Book Fair, 1987; Mr Christie's Award, 1990; Elizabeth Mrazik-Cleaver Award, 1990; Hans Christian Anderson Award Nominee (Illustration), 1992. Membership: Writers Union. Address: 184 Major Street, Toronto, Ontario M5S 2L3, Canada.

WALLACE Ronald William, b. 18 Feb 1945, Cedar Rapids, Iowa, USA. Poet; Professor of English. m. Margaret Elizabeth McCreight, 3 Aug 1968, 2 daughters. Education: BA, College of Wooster, 1967; MA, 1968, PhD, 1971, University of Michigan. Appointments: Director of Creative Writing, University of Wisconsin, Madison, 1975-; Series Editor, Brittingham Prize in Poetry, 1985-; Director, Wisconsin Institute for Creative Writing, 1986-. Publications: Henry James and the Comic Form, 1975; Installing the Bees, 1977; Cucumbers, 1977; The Last Laugh, 1979; The Facts of Life, 1979; Plums, Stones, Kisses and Hooks, 1981; Tunes for Bears to Dance to, 1983; God Be With the Clown, 1984; The Owl in the Kitchen, 1985; People and Dog in the Sun, 1987; Vital Signs, 1989; The Makings of Happiness, 1991; Time's Fancy, 1994. Contributions to: New Yorker; Atlantic; Nation; Poetry; Southern Review; Poetry Northwest. Honours: Hopwood Award for Poetry, 1970; Council for Wisconsin Writers Awards, 1978, 1979, 1984, 1985, 1986, 1988; Helen Bullis Prize in Poetry, 1985; Robert E Gard Award for Excellence in Poetry, 1990; Posner Poetry Prize, 1992; Gerald A Bartell Award in the Arts, 1994. Memberships: Poets and Writers; Associated Writing Programs. Address: Department of English, University of Wisconsin, Madison, WI 53706, USA.

WALLACE-CRABBE Chris(topher Keith), b. 6 May 1934, Richmond, Victoria, Australia. Professor of English; Poet. m. Sophie Feil, 1 son, 1 daughter. Education: BA, 1956, MA, 1964, University of Melbourne. Appointments: Reader in English, 1976-88, Professor of English, 1988-, University of Melbourne. Publications: Poetry: No Glass Houses, 1956; The Music of Division, 1959; Eight Metropolitan Poems, 1962; In Light and Darkness, 1964; The Rebel General, 1967; Where the Wind Came, 1971; Selected Poems 1955-72, 1973; Act in the Noon, 1974; The Shapes of Gallipoli, 1975; The Foundations of Joy, 1976; The Emotions are not Skilled Workers, 1979; The Amorous Cannibal and Other Poems, 1985; I'm Deadly Serious, 1988. Novel: Splinters, 1981. Other: Melbourne or the Bush: Essays on Australian Literature and Societty, 1973. Editor, volumes of Australian poetry. Honour: Dublin Prize, 1986. Address; c/o Department of English, University of Melbourne, Melbourne, Victoria 3052, Australia.

WALLER Jane Ashton, b. 19 May 1944, Bucks, England. Writer; Ceramist. m. Michael Vaughan Rees, 11 June 1982. Education: Oxford Art College, 1962-63; Sir John Cass Colleg, 1966-69; MA, Royal College of Art, 1982; BA, Hornsey Art College, 1985. Publications: A Stitch in Time, 1972; Some Things for the Children,

1974; Some Dinosaur Poems for Children, 1975; A Man's Book, 1977; The Thirties Family Knitting Book, 1981; Below the Green Pond, 1982; The Man's Knitting Book, 1984; Women in Wartime (with Michael Vaughan-Rees), 1987; Women in Uniform (with Michael Vaughan-Rees), 1989; Handbuilt Ceramics, 1990; Blitz: the Civilian War (with Michael Vaughan-Rees), 1990 Saving the Dinosaurs, 1994; The Sludgegulpers, 1996. Contributions to: Ceramic Review. Honour: Herbert Read Literary Award, 1981. Address: 22 Roupell Street, Waterloo, London SE1 8SP, England.

WALLER Robert James, b. 1 Aug 1939, USA. Writer. m. Georgia Ann Wiedemeier, 1 son. Education: University of Iowa, 1957-58; University of Northern Iowa, 1958; PhD, Indiana University, 1968. Appointments: Professor of Management, 1968-91, Dean, School of Business, 1979-85, University of Northern Iowa. Publications: Just Beyond the Firelight: Stories and Essays, 1988; One Good Road is Enough: Essays, 1990; The Bridges of Madison County, 1992; Slow Waltz in Cedar Bend, 1993; Old Songs in a New Cafe: Selected Essays, 1994; Border Music, 1995. Honour: Literary Lion Award, New York Public Library, 1993. Address: c/o Aaron Priest Literary Agency, 708 Third Avenue, 23rd Floor, New York, NY 10017, USA.

WALLEY Byron. See: CARD Orson Scott.

WALLINGTON Vivienne Elizabeth, (Elizabeth Duke), b. 8 Feb 1937, Adelaide, South Australia. Former Librarian; Writer. m. John Wallington, 18 Apr 1959, 1 son, 1 daughter. Education: Matriculated, Girton G.S., Adelaide, 1954; Library Registration, Prelim + 6 Subjects, 1954-59. Publications: Somewhere, 1982; Butterfingers, 1986; Names are Fun, 1990; Outback Legacy, 1993; Shattered Wedding, 1994; To Catch a Playboy, 1995; Heartless Stranger, 1996; Takeover Engagement, 1997. Contributions to: Newspapers. Honour: Finalist, Heart of Romance Award, USA, 1996. Memberships: Society of Women Writers; Romance Writers of America; Romance Writers of Australia; Romantic Novelists Association. Address: 38 Fuller Street, Mitcham, Victoria 3132, Australia.

WALLS Ian Gascoigne, b. 28 Apr 1922, Glasgow, Scotland. Horticulturist. m. Eleanor McIntosh McCaig, 11 Aug 1947, 2 daughters. Education: West of Scotland Agricultural College, 1949. Appointments: Gardening Writer, Glasgow Herald. Publications: Gardening Month by Month, 1962; Creating Your Garden, 1967; Tomato Growing Today, 1972; The Complete Book of the Greenhouse, 1973, 5th edition, 1993; A-Z of Garden Pests and Problems, 1979; Modern Greenhouse Methods, 1984; Profit from Growing Vegetables, Fruits and Flowers, 1988; Simple Tomato Growing, 1988; Simple Vegetable Growing, 1988; Growing Tomatoes, 1989; Making Your Garden Pay: Low Cost Gardening, 1992. Memberships: Glasgow Wheelers CC; Milngavie Horticultural Society. Address: 17 Douglaston Avenue, Milngavie, Glasgow G62 6AP, Scotland.

WALSER Martin, b. 24 Mar 1927, Wasserburg, Germany. Writer. Education: Theological Philosophical College, Regensburg; PhD, University of Tübingen. Publications: Ehen in Philippsburg, 1957; Halbzeit, 1960; Das Einhorn, 1966; Der Sturz, 1973; Jenseits de Liebe, 1976; Ein Fliehendespferd, 1978; Das Schwanenhaus, 1980; Brief on Lord Liszt, 1982; Messmers Gedanken, 1985; Die Vej Teidigung Derkindheit, 1991; Ohne einander, 1993. Honours: Grip 47 Prize, 1955; Hermann Hesse Prize, 1957; Gerhardt Hauptmann Prize, 1962; Schiller Prize, 1965; Georg Büchner Prize, 1981; Order pour le Merite für Wissensdaften und Künste, 1993; Officer de l'ordre des Arts et des Lettres, 1994. Memberships: German Academy for Language and Literature; Association of German Writers; PEN; Academy of Arts, Berlin. Address: 777 Uberlingen Nussdorf, Zum Hecht 36, Germany.

WALSH Sheila, (Sophie Leyton), b. 10 Oct 1928, Birmingham, England. Writer. Education: Southport College of Art, 1945-48. Publications: The Golden Songbird, 1975; The Sergeant Major,s Daughter, 1977; A Fine Silk Purse, 1978; The Incomparable Miss Brady, 1980; The Rose Domino, 1981; A Highly Respectable Marriage, 1983; The Runaway Bride, 1984; Cousins of a Kind, 1985; The Incorrigible Rake, 1985; An Insubstantial Pageant, 1986; Bath Intrigue, 1986; Lady Aurelia's Bequest, 1987; Minerva's Marquis, 1988; The Nabob, 1989-90; A Woman of Little Importance, 1991; Until Tomorrow, 1993; Remember Me, 1994; A Perfect Bride, 1994. Honour: Best Romantic Novel of Year, 1983. Memberships: Romantic Novelists Association; Soroptimist International of Southport. Address: 35 Coudray Road, Southport, Merseyside PR9 9NL, England.

WALSHE Aubrey Peter, b. 12 Jan 1934, Johannesburg, South Africa. Professor of Political Science. m. Catherine Ann Pettifer, 26 Jan 1957, 1 son, 3 daughters. Education: BA Hons, Wadham College, Oxford, 1956; DPhil, St Antony's College, Oxford, 1968. Appointments: Lecturer, University of Lesotho, 1959-62; Professor of Political Science, University of Notre Dame, Indiana, 1967-. Publications: The Rise of African Nationalism in South Africa, 1971; Black Nationalism in South Africa, 1974; Church Versus State in South Africa, 1983; Prophetic Christianity and the Liberation Movement in South Africa, 1996. Contributions to: Cambridge History of Africa, 1986, professional journals and newspapers. Address: c/o Department of Government, University of Notre Dame, Notre Dame, IN 46556, USA.

WALTER Richard, b. 11 July 1944, New York, New York, USA. Writer; Educator. m. Patricia Sandgrund, 18 June 1967, 1 son, 1 daughter. Education: BA History 1965, Harpur College, State University of New York; MS Communications 1966, Newhouse School of Public Communications, Syracuse University; Postgraduate Study, Department of Cinema, University of Southern California, 1967-70. Appointments: Professor and Screenwriting Chairman, Department of Film and Television, University of California, Los Angeles, 1977-. Publications: Barry and the Persuasions, 1976; Screenwriting: The Art, Craft and Business of Film and Television Writing, 1988; The Whole Picture, 1995. Screenplays: Group Marriage; Return of Zorro; Dynamite Lady; Mrs Charlie; Split; Young Love; Marked Man; Jackie Whitefish. Contributions to: Asian Wall Street Journal; Los Angeles Times; Los Angeles Herald Examiner. Memberships: Writers Guild of America; PEN Centre West; University Film and Video Association. Address: Department of Film and Television, University of California, Los Angeles, CA 90095, USA.

WALTERS Huw, b. 25 Dec 1951, Glanaman, Dyfed, Wales. Librarian; Bibliographer. Education: BLib, 1978; PhD, 1985. Appointments: Leverhulme Research Assistant, Department of Bibliographical Studies, College of Librarianship Wales, Aberystwyth, 1979; Assistant Librarian, Bibliographical Services Division, Department of Printed Books, National Library of Wales, Aberystwyth, 1981. Publications: Erwau'r Glo, 1976; Brinli: Cyfreithiwr, Bardd, Archdderwydd, 1981; Ysgol Glanaman, y Ganrif Gyntaf, 1984; Canu'r Pwll a'r Pulpud, 1987; John Morris-Jones, 1864-1929: Llyfryddiaeth Anodiadol, 1987; The Welsh Periodical Press, 1987; The Amman Valley Long Ago, 1987; Evan David Jones, 1903-1987: Llyfryddiaeth, 1987; A Bibliography of Welsh Periodicals, 1735-1850, 1993; Yr Adolygydd a'r Beirniad: eu Cynnwys a'u Cyfranwyr, 1996. Contributions to: The Oxford Companion to the Literature of Wales; The Dictionary of Welsh Biography; The New Dictionary of National Biography; Annual Bibliography of the History of the Printed Book and Libraries; Bibliographies of the published works of the following scholars published in various Festschrift: Gomer Morgan Roberts, Thomas John Morgan, Bedwyr Lewis Jones, Dafydd James Bowen, Robert (Bobi) Maynard Jones, Meredydd Evans, Robert Geraint Gruffydd, Brynley Francis Roberts. Honours: National Eisteddfod of Wales Prizes, 1974, 1979; University of Wales, Sir Ellis (Jones) Ellis-Griffith Memorial Prize, 1988; University of Wales, W L Davies Award, 1988; Welsh Arts Council Literary Prize, 1988; Honorary Member, Gorsedd of Bards, 1990; Honorary President Amman Valley History Society, 1990. Address: Bryn-teg, 10 Dinas Terrace, Aberystwyth, Dyfed SY23 1BT, Wales.

WALVIN James, b. 2 Jan 1942, Manchester, England. Historian; Professor. m. Jennifer, 2 sons. Education: BA, Keele University, 1964; MA, McMaster University, 1970. Publications: Black-White, The Negro and English Society, 1973; The People's Game, Social History of Football, 1975; Slavery and the Slave Trade, 1983; England, Slaves and Freedom, 1986; Victorian Values, 1987; Black Ivory, A History of British Slavery, 1993. Honour: Martin Luther King Memorial Prize, 1974. Membership: Royal Historical Society. Address: Department of History, University of York, Heslington, York YO1 5DD, England.

WALWICZ Ania, b. 19 May 1951, Swidnica, Poland (Australian citizen). Artist; Poet. Education: Dip Ed, University of Melbourne, 1984; Diploma and Graduate Diploma, Victorian College of the Arts. Appointment: Writer-in-Residence, Deakin and Murdoch Universities, 1987-88. Publications: Writing, 1982; Boat, 1989. Plays: Girlboytalk, 1986; Dissecting Mice, 1989; Elegant, 1990; Red Roses, 1992. Contributions to: 71 anthologies. Honours: Australian Council Literature Board grants; Fellowship, 1990; New Writing Prize, Victorian Premier's Literary Awards, 1990. Address: 9 Cremorne Street, Fitzroy, Victoria 3065, Australia.

WALWORTH Arthur Clarence Jr, b. 9 July 1903, Newton, Massachusetts, USA. Historian. Education: Phillips Andover Academy, 1921; BA, Yale College, 1925. Publications: Black Ships Off Japan, 1946; Cape Breton: Isle of Romance, 1948; Woodrow Wilson: Vol 1, American Prophet, Vol 2, World Prophet, 1958; America's Moment: 1918, 1977; Wilson and His Peacemakers: American Diplomacy at the Paris Peace Conference, 1986; Guide to the Diary, Reminiscences, and Memoirs of Colonel Edward M House in Manuscripts and Archives, 1994. Contributions to: Book reviews; travel articles; Considerations on Woodrow Wilson and Edward M House in Presidential Studies Quarterly, Winter 1994. Honour: Pulitzer Prize in Biography, 1958. Address: 28 Howe Street, Wellesley, MA 02181, USA.

WALZER Michael (Laban), b. 3 Mar 1935, New York, New York, USA. Professor of Social Science; Writer. m. Judith Borodovko, 17 June 1956, 2 daughters. Education: BA, Brandeis University, 1956; PhD, Harvard University, 1961. Appointments: Assistant Professor of Politics, Princeton University, 1962-66; Associate Professor, 1966-68, Professor of Government, 1968-80, Harvard University; Professor of Social Science, Institute for Advanced Study, Princeton, New Jersey, 1980-; Editor, Dissent, 1976-. Publications: The Revolution of the Saints: A Study in the Origins of Radical Politics, 1965; The Political Imagination in Literature (editor with Philip Green), 1968; Obligations: Essays on Disobedience, War and Citizenship, 1970; Political Action: A Practical Guide to Movement Politics, 1971; Regicide and Revolution: Speeches at the Trial of Louis XVI (editor; Marian Rothstein, translator), 1974; Just and Unjust Wars: A Moral Argument with Historical Illustrations, 1977; Radical Principles: Reflections of an Unreconstructed Democrat, 1980; Spheres of Justice: A Defense of Pluralism and Equality, 1983; Exodus and Revolution, 1985; Interpretation and Social Criticism, 1987; The Company of Critics: Social Criticism and Political Commitment in the Twentieth Century, 1989; What it Means to be an American, 1992; Thick and Thin: Moral Argument at Home and Abroad, 1994; Pluralism, Justice and Equality (with David Miller), 1995. Contributions to: Professional journals and general publications. Honours: Fulbright Fellow, Cambridge University, 1956-57; Harbison Award, 1971. Memberships: Conference on the Study of Political Thought; Society of Ethical and Legal Philosophy. Address: 103 Linwood Circle, Princeton, NJ 08520, USA.

WAMBAUGH Joseph (Aloysius Jr), b. 22 Jan 1937, Pittsburgh, Pennsylvania, USA. Writer. m. Dee Allsup, 26 Nov 1955, 1 son, 1 daughter. Education: BA, 1960, MA, 1968, California State University, Los Angeles. Publications: The New Centurions, 1971; The Blue Knight, 1972; The Onion Field, 1973; The Choirboys, 1975; The Black Marble, 1978; The Glitter Dome, 1981; The Delta Star, 1983; Lines and Shadows, 1984; The Secrets of Harry Bright, 1985; Echoes in the Darkness, 1987; The Blooding, 1989; The Golden Orange, 1990; Fugitive Nights, 1992; Finnegan's Week, 1993; Floaters, 1996. Honours: Edgar Allan Poe Award, 1974; Rodolfo Walsh Prize, International Association of Crime Writers, 1989. Address: c/o William Morrow & Co, 105 Madison Avenue, New York, NY 10016, USA.

WANDOR Michelene Dinah, b. 20 Apr 1940, London. Writer. m. Edward Victor, 1963, div, 2 sons. Education: BA, Newnham College; MA, University of Essex; LTCL, DipTCL, Trinity College of Music. Appointment: Poetry Editor, Time Out, 1971-82. Publications: Carry on Understudies, 1981; Five Plays, 1984; Routledge, 1986; Look Back in Gender, 1987; Guests in the Body, 1987; Gardens of Eden, 1990; Five Plays, 1984. Contributions to: Listener; Sunday Times. Honour: International Emmy, 1987. Membership: Writers Guild. Address: 71 Belsize Lane, London NW3 5AU, England.

WANG Zhecheng, (Qi Fang), b. 22 Mar 1936, Hangzhou, China. Writer; Editor. m. Wen Xiaoyu, 24 Jan 1962, 1 daughter. Education: Graduated, Chinese Language and Literature Department, Beijing University, 1958. Appointments: Editor, Prairie, 1958; Professional Novelist, Inner Mongolia Writers Association, 1982; Professor-Novelist, Zhejiang Writer's Association, 1986; Vice-Chairman, 1992; Chief-Editor and President of Jiangnan, 1992. Publications: Play: People in the Greater Xingen Mountains, 1963. Novelettes: Soil (joint work with wife), 1981; Farewell, Puncture Vine, 1982; Sonato of the Heart, 1982; Worries of the Small Sun, 1982. Contributions to: China Youth; Shanghai Literature; Harvest; The Current; Writers; Guang Ming Daily; Wen Hui Daily. Honours: 1st National Excellent Novelette Award Winner, 1981; 2nd National Excellent Novelette Award Winner, 1983; 10 other prizes. Memberships: Chinese Writers Association; Vice Chairman, Zhejiang Writers Association; Committee Member,

Zhejiang Literature and Art Union; Council Member, Chinese Current Literature Research Association. Address: 105 Nanshan Road, Hangzhou Zhejiang 310002, China.

WARD John Hood, b. 16 Dec 1915, Newcastle upon Tyne, England. Civil Service Senior Principal (retired); Writer; Poet. m. Gladys Hilda Thorogood, 27 July 1940, 1 son, 2 daughters. Education: Royal Grammar School, Newcastle, 1925-33. Appointment: Senior Principal, Department of Health and Social Security, retired, 1978. Publications: A Late Harvest, 1982; The Dark Sea, 1983; A Kind of Likeness, 1985; The Wrong Side of Glory, 1986; A Song at Twilight, 1989; Grandfather Best and the Protestant Work Ethic, 1991; Tales of Love and Hate, 1993; The Brilliance of Light, 1994; Winter Song, 1995; Selected Poems, 1968-95, 1996. Contributions to: Anthologies and periodicals. Honours: Imperial Service Order, 1977; Poetry Prize, City of Westminster Arts Council, 1977; Open Poetry Prize, Wharfedale Music Festival, 1978; Lancaster Festival Prizes, 1982, 1987, 1988, 1989, 1994, 1995; 1st Prize, Bury Open Poetry Competition, 1987; 1st Prizes, High Peak Open Competition, 1988, 1989; 1st Prize, May and Alfred Wilkins Memorial Prize, 1995. Memberships: Manchester Poets; Society of Civil Service Authors. Address: 42 Seal Road, Bramhall, Stockport, Cheshire SK7 2JS, England.

WARD Philip, b. 10 Feb 1938, Harrow, England. Chartered Librarian; Professional Writer. m. 4 Apr 1964, 2 daughters. Education: University for Foreigners, Perugia; Coimbra University. Appointments: Honorary Editor, The Private Library, 1958-64; Coordinator, Library Services, Tripoli, Libya, 1963-71; Director, National Library Services, 1973-74. Publications: The Oxford Companion to Spanish Literature, 1978; A Dictionary of Common Fallacies, 1978-80; Lost Songs, 1981; A Lifetime's Reading, 1983; Japanese Capitals, 1985; Travels in Oman, 1987; Sofia: Portrait of a City, 1989; Wright Magic, 1990; Bulgaria, 1990. Honours: Fellow, Royal Geographical Society; Royal Society of Arts; Guinness Poetry Award, 1959; 1st Prize, International Travel Writers Competition, 1990. Membership: Private Libraries Association. Address: c/o Oxford University Press, Walton Street, Oxford OX2 6DP, England.

WARD Ronald Bentley, b. 6 Oct 1928, Sydney, New South Wales, Australia. University Lecturer. m. Brenda Madden, 7 Jan 1955, 1 son, 1 daughter. Education: Trades Certificate, 1948; Diploma, Sydney Technical College, 1955; BEng, University of New South Wales, 1961; MBA, Macquarie University, 1975; PhD, 1994. Appointment: Lecturer, School of Mechanical Engineering, University of Technology, Sydney. Publications: The Engineering of Management, 1987; The Engineering of Communication, 1988, revised edition, 1989; A Plant for Appropriate Technology, 1991; Contributions to: Various conference proceedings and symposia, Australia and overseas. Memberships: Institution of Engineers, Australia; Australian Institute of Management. Address: 13 Landscape Avenue, Forestville, New South Wales 2087, Australia.

WARDLE (John) Irving, b. 20 July 1929, Bolton, England. Drama Critic. m. (1) Joan Notkin, 1958, div, (2) Fay Crowder, 1963, div, 2 sons, (3) Elizabeth Grist, 1975, 1 son, 1 daughter. Education: BA, Wadham College, Oxford, 1949; ARCM, Royal College of Music, London, 1955. Appointments: Sub Editor, Times Educational Supplement, 1956; Deputy Theatre Critic, The Observer, 1960; Drama Critic, The Times, 1963-89; Editor, Gambit, 1973-75; Theatre Critic, The Independent on Sunday, 1989. Publications: The Houseboy, 1974; The Theatres of George Devine, 1978; Theatre Criticism, 1992. Address: 51 Richmond Road, New Barnet, Herts, England.

WARE Armytage. See: **BARNETT Paul le Page.**

WARE Wallace. See: **KARP David.**

WARNER Francis, (Robert Le Plastrier), b. 21 Oct 1937, Bishopthorpe, Yorkshire, England. Poet; Dramatist; Academic. m. (1) Mary Hall, 1958, div 1972, 2 daughters, (2) Penelope Anne Davis, 1983, 1 son, 1 daughter. Education: BA, MA; Christ's Hospital; St Catharine's College, Cambridge. Appointments: Lord White Fellow and Tutor, 1965-, University Lecturer, 1965-, Vice Master, 1987-89, St Peter's College, Oxford; Pro Proctor, Oxford University, 1989-90, 1996-97. Publications: Poetry: Perennia, 1962; Early Poems, 1964; Experimental Sonnets, 1965; Madrigals, 1967; The Poetry of Francis Warner, 1970; Lucca Quartet, 1975; Morning Vespers, 1980; Spring Harvest, 1981; Epithalamium, 1983; Collected Poems 1960-1964, 1985; Nightingales, 1997. Plays: Maquettes, 1972; Meeting Ends,

1974; Killing Time, 1976; A Conception of Love, 1978; Light Shadows, 1980; Moving Reflections, 1983; Living Creation, 1985; The Athens of Pericles, 1988; Byzantium, 1990; Virgil and Caesar, 1993; Agora, 1994; King Francis I, 1995; Goethe's Weimar, 1997. Contributions to: Anthologies and journals. Honours: Messing International Award, 1972; Benemerenti Silver Medal, Knights of St George, Constantinian Order, Italy, 1990. Address: St Peter's College, Oxford OX1 2DL, England.

WARNER Marina, b. 9 Nov 1946, England. m. (1) Hon William Hartley Hume Shawcross, 1972, div 1980, (2) John Piers Dewe Mathews, 1981. Education: MA, Lady Margaret Hall, Oxford. Appointments: Reviewer, various London and New York publications; Tinbergen Professor, Erasmus University, Rotterdam, 1991; Reith Lecturer, 1994; Visiting Professor, Queen Mary and Westfield College, London, 1994-; University of Ulster, 1994-95; University of York, 1996-. Publications: The Dragon Empress, 1972; Alone of All Her Sex: The Myth and Cult of the Virgin Mary, 1976; Queen Victoria's Sketchbook, 1980; Joan of Arc: The Image of Female Heroism, 1981; Monuments and Maidens: The Allegory of the Female Form, 1985; Into the Dangerous World: Childhood and its Costs, 1991; Managing Monsters: Six Myths of Our Time, 1994; From the Beast to the Blonde: On Fairy Tales and Their Tellers, 1995. Fiction: In a Dark Wood, 1977; The Skating Party, 1983; The Lost Father, 1988; Indigo, 1992; The Mermaids in the Basement (short stories), 1993; Opera libretto for John Woolrich, 1996. Honour: Fawcett Prize, 1986. Address: c/o Rogers, Coleridge and White, 20 Powis Mews, London W11 1JN, England.

WARNER Val, b. 15 Jan 1946, Middlesex, England. Writer; Poet. Education: BA, Somerville College, Oxford, 1968. Appointments: Writer-in-Residence, University College, Swansea, 1977-78, University of Dundee, 1979-81. Publications: These Yellow Photos, 1971; Under the Penthouse, 1973; The Centenary Corbiere (translator), 1975; The Collected Poems and Prose of Charlotte Mew (editor), 1981, 1983; Before Lunch, 1986. Contributions to: Many journals and periodicals. Honour: 3rd Prize, Lincolnshire Literature Festival Poetry Competition, 1995. Membership: PEN. Address: c/o Carcanet Press Ltd, 402-406 Corn Exchange, Manchester M4 3BY, England.

WARNOCK Baroness (Helen Mary Warnock), b. 14 April 1924, England. m. Sir Geoffrey Warnock, 1949, dec 1995. Education: MA, BPhil, Lady Margaret Hall, Oxford. Appointments: Fellow, Tutor in Philosophy, St Hugh's College, Oxford, 1949-66; Headmistress, Oxford High School, 1960-72; Senior Research Fellow, St Hugh's College, Oxford, 1976-84; Mistress of Girton College, Cambridge, 1985-92. Publications: Ethics Since 1900, 1960; The Philosophy of Jean Paul Sartre, 1963; Existentialist Ethics, 1966; Imagination, 1975; Schools of Thought, 1977; Education: A Way Forward, 1979; Memory, 1987; A Common Policy for Education, 1988; The Universities: Knowing Our Minds, 1990; The Uses of Philosophy, 1992; Imagination and Understanding, 1993; Imagination and Time, 1994; Women Philosophers, 1996. Honours: Dame Commander of the Order of the British Empire, 1984. Address: 3 Church Street, Great Bedwyn. Nr Marlborough, Wiltshire SN8 3PE, England.

WARREN Rosanna, b. 27 July 1953, Fairfield, Connecticut, USA. Associate Professor of English; Poet; Writer. m. Stephen Scully, 1981, 2 daughters, 1 stepson. Education: BA summa cum laude, Yale University, 1976; MA, Johns Hopkins University, 1980. Appointments: Assistant Professor, Vanderbilt University, 1981-82; Visiting Assistant Professor, 1982-88, Assistant Professor, 1989-95, Associate Professor of English, 1995-, Boston University; Poetry Consultant and Contributing Editor, Partisan Review, 1985-; Poet-in-Residence, Robert Frost Farm, 1990. Publications: The Joey Story, 1963; Snow Day, 1981; Each Leaf Shines Separate, 1984; The Art of Translation: Voices from the Field (editor), 1989; Stained Glass, 1993; Eugenio Montale's Cuttlefish Bones (editor), 1993; Euripides' Suppliant Women (translator with Stephen Scully), 1995. Contributions to: Many journals and magazines. Honours: National Discovery Award in Poetry, 92nd Street YMHA-YWCA, New York City, 1980; Yaddo Fellow, 1980; Ingram Merrill Foundation Grants, 1983, 1993; Guggenheim Fellowship, 1985-86; American Council of Learned Societies Grant, 1989-90; Lavan Younger Poets Prize, 1992, and Lamont Poetry Prize, 1993, Academy of American Poets; Lila Wallace Writers' Fund Award, 1994; Witter Bynner Prize in Poetry, American Academy of Arts and Letters, 1994; May Sarton Award, New England Poetry Club, 1995. Membership: Modern Language Association; American Literary Translators Association; Association of Literary Scholars and Critics;

PEN. Address: c/o University Professors Program, Boston University, 745 Commonwealth Avenue, Boston, MA 02215, USA.

WARSH Lewis, b. 9 Nov 1944, New York, New York, USA. Poet; Writer; Publisher; Teacher. m. Bernadette Mayer, Nov 1975, 1 son, 2 daughters. Education: BA, 1966, MA, 1975, City College of the City University of New York. Appointments: Co-Founder and Co-Editor, Angel Hair magazine and Angel Hair Books, New York City, 1966-77; Co-Editor, Boston Eagle, Massachusetts, 1973-75; Teacher, St Marks in the Bowery Poetry Project, 1973-75; Co-Founder and Publisher, United Artists magazine and United Artists Books, New York, 1977-; Lecturer, Kerouac School of Disembodied Poetics, Boulder, Colorado, 1978, New England College, 1979-80, Queens College, 1984-86, Farleigh Dickinson University, 1987-; Adjunct Associate Professor, Long Island University, 1987-. Publications: Poetry: The Suicide Rates, 1967; Highjacking: Poems, 1968; Moving Through Air, 1968; Chicago (with Tom Clark), 1969; Dreaming as One: Poems, 1971; Long Distance, 1971; Immediate Surrounding, 1974; Today, 1974; Blue Heaven, 1978; Hives, 1979; Methods of Birth Control, 1982; The Corset, 1986; Information from the Surface of Venus, 1987; A Free Man, 1991; Avenue of Escape, 1995. Other: Part of My History (autobiography), 1972; The Maharajah's Son (autobiography), 1977; Agnes and Sally (fiction), 1984. Honours: Poet's Foundation Award, 1972; Creative Artists Public Service Award in Fiction, 1977; National Endowment for the Arts Grant in Poetry, 1979; Coordinating Council of Literary Magazines Editor's Fellowship, 1981. Address: 701 President Street, No 1, Brooklyn, NY 11215, USA.

WARTOFSKY (William) Victor, b. 15 June 1931, New York, USA. Writer. m. Tamar Chachik, 1957, 1 son, 2 daughters. Education: George Washington University, 1950-52; BA, American University, 1963. Publications: Mr Double and Other Stories; Meeting the Pieman; Year of the Yahoo; The Passage; Prescription for Justice; Terminal Justice. Screenplays: Death be my Destiny; The Hellbox; Feathers. Contributions to: USIA America; Fifty Plus; Macabre; Quartet; True. Address: 8507 Wild Olive Drive, Potomac, MD 20854, USA.

WASSERFALL Adel, (Adel Pryor), b. 2 Dec 1918, Haugesund, Norway. Writer; Housewife. m. Education: Cape Technical College, South Africa. Appointments: English Teacher in Copenhagen; Involved with Sudan Interior Mission in South Africa for many years; Associated with Cape Town Children's Service Mission for 9 years. Publications: Novels: Tangled Paths, 1959; Clouded Glass, 1961; Hidden Fire, 1962; Out of the Night, 1963; Hearts in Conflict, 1965; Forgotten Yesterday, 1966; Valley of Desire, 1967; Sound of the Sea, 1968; Free of a Dream, 1969; A Norwegian Romance, 1976; All Is Not Gold, 1979; Flame of Jealousy. Honours: English Composition Prize, 1934; Sir William Thorne Award, 1937; Short Story Contest Award, 1946. Address: 8 Iona Street, Milnerton 7441, Cape, South Africa.

WATERMAN Andrew (John), b. 28 May 1940, London, England. Senior Lecturer in English; Poet. Div, 1 son. Education: BA, 1st Class Hons, English, University of Leicester, 1966; Worcester College, Oxford, 1966-68. Appointments: Lecturer, 1968-78, Senior Lecturer in English, 1978-, University of Ulster, Coleraine, Northern Ireland. Publications: Living Room, 1974; From the Other Country, 1977; Over the Wall, 1980; Out for the Elements, 1981; The Poetry of Chess (editor), 1981; Selected Poems, 1986; In the Planetarium, 1990; The End of the Pier Show, 1995. Contributions to: Anthologies, journals and periodicals. Honours: Poetry Book Society Choice, 1974 and Recommendation, 1981; Cholmondeley Award for Poetry, 1977; Arvon Poetry Competition Prize, 1981. Address: 15 Hazelbank Road, Coleraine, County Derry BT51 3DX, Northern Ireland.

WATERS John Frederick, b. 27 Oct 1930, Somerville, Massachusetts, USA. Writer. Education: BS, University of Massachusetts. Publications: Marine Animal Collectors, 1969; The Crab From Yesterday, 1970; The Sea Farmers, 1970; What Does An Oceanographer Do, 1970; Saltmarshes and Shifting Dunes, 1970; Turtles, 1971; Neighborhood Puddle, 1971; Some Mammals Live in the Sea, 1972; Green Turtle: Mysteries, 1972; The Royal Potwasher, 1972; Seal Harbour, 1973; Hungry Sharks, 1973; Giant Sea Creatures, 1973; The Mysterious Eel, 1973; Camels: Ships of the Desert, 1974; Carnivorous Plants, 1974; Exploring New England Shores, 1974; The Continental Shelves, 1975; Creatures of Darkness, 1975; Victory Chimes, 1976; Maritime Careers, 1977; Fishing, 1978; Summer of the Seals, 1978; The Hatchlings, 1979; Crime Labs, 1979; A Jellyfish is Not a Fish, 1979; Flood, 1991; Watching Whales, 1991; The Raindrop Journey, 1991; Deep Sea Vents, 1994; Night Raiders Along the Cape,

1996; Sharks, 1996. Contributions to: Cape Cod Compass. Honours: Junior Literary Book Choice (twice); Outstanding Science books for Children Awards (7 times). Memberships: Southeastern Massachusetts Creative Writers Club; Organizer, Cape Cod Writers; 12 O'Clock Scholars; Society of Children's Book Writers; Authors Guild Inc. Address: Box 735, Chatham, MA 02633, USA.

WATERTON Betty Marie, b. 31 Aug 1923, Oshawa, Ontario, Canada. Children's Writer. m. Claude Waterton, 7 Apr 1942, 1 son, 2 daughters. Publications: A Salmon for Simon, 1978; Pettranetta, 1980; Mustard, 1983; The White Moose, 1984; Quincy Rumpel, 1984; Orff, 27 Dragons (and a Snarkel !), 1984; The Dog Who Stopped the War, (adaptation and translation), 1985; Starring Quincy Rumpel, 1986; Quincy Rumpel, PI, 1988; Morris Rumpel and the Wings of Icarus, 1989; Plain Noodles, 1989; Quincy Rumpel and the Sasquatch of Phantom Cove, 1990; Quincy Rumpel and the Woolly Chaps, 1992; Quincy Rumpel and the Mystifying Experience, 1994; Quincy Rumpel and the All-day Breakfast, 1996. Honour: Co-winner, Canada Council Award for Children's Literature, 1978. Memberships: Canadian Society of Children's Authors, Illustrators and Performers; Federation of British Columbia Writers. Address: 10135 Tsaykum Road, RR1, Sidney, British Columbia V8L 3R9, Canada.

WATKINS Floyd C, b. 19 Apr 1920, Cherokee County, Georgia, USA. Professor Emeritus; Writer; Farmer. m. Anna E Braziel, 14 June 1942, 1 son, 2 daughters. Education: BS, Georgia Southern University, 1946; AM, Emory University, 1947; PhD, Vanderbilt University, 1952. Appointments: Instructor, 1949-61, Professor, 1961-80, Candler Professor of American Literature, 1980-88, Professor Emeritus, 1988-, Emory University; Visiting Professor, Southeastern University, Oklahoma, 1961, 1970, Texas A & M University, 1980. Publications: The Literature of the South (co-editor), 1952; Thomas Wolfe's Characters, 1957; Old Times in the Faulkner Country (co-author), 1961; The Flesh and the Word, 1971; In Time and Place, 1977; Then and Now: The Personal Past in the Poetry of Robert Penn Warren, 1982; Some Poems and Some Talk About Poetry (co-author), 1985; Talking About William Faulkner, co-author, 1996. Address: 519 Druand Drive North East, Atlanta, GA 30307, USA.

WATKINS Gerrold. See: **MALZBERG Barry**.

WATKINS Karen Christna, (Catrin Collier, Katherine John), b. 30 May 1948, Pontypridd, Wales. Writer. m. Trevor John Watkins, 28 Dec 1968, 2 sons, 1 daughter. Education: Teaching Certificate, 1969, Swansea College. Publications: Without Trace, 1990; Hearts of Gold, 1992; One Blue Moon, 1993; Six Foot Under; A Silver Lining, 1994; Murder of a Dead Man, 1994; All That Glitters, 1995; Such Sweet Sorrow, 1996; By Any Other Name, 1995. Memberships: PEN; Society of Authors; Crime Writers Association. Address: c/o A M Heath and Co, 79 St Martin's Lane, London WC2N 4AA. England.

WATKINS Nicholas, b. 17 Sept 1946, Bath, England. Art Historian. m. Nadia Daskalaff, 16 July 1970, 2 daughters. Education: BA, Hons, History of European Art, 1966, MPhil, 1979, Courtauld Institute of Art. Publications: Matisse, 1984; Bonnard, 1994. Contributions to: Burlington Magazine; Apollo; TLS; Art Monthly.

WATMOUGH David, b. 17 Aug 1926, London, England. Author. Education: Theology Major, King's College, University of London, 1945-49. Appointments: War Service, Royal Naval Volunteer Reserve, 1944-45. Publications: Ashes for Easter (stories), 1972; Love and the Waiting Game(stories), 1975; From a Cornish Landscape (stories), 1975; No More into the Garden (novel), 1978; Fury (stories), 1984; The Connecticut Countess (stories), 1984; The Unlikely Pioneer (opera), 1985; Vibrations in Time, (stories), 1986; The Year of Fears (novel), 1987; Thy Mother's Glass (novel), 1992; The Time of the Kingfishers (novel), 1994; Hunting with Diana (stories), 1996. Contributions to: Encounter; Spectator; New York Times Book Review; Saturday Night, Canada; Canadian Literature; Dalhousie Review; Connoisseur, New York; Malahat Review; Vancouver Step. Honours: Senior Literary Arts Awards, Canada Council, 1976, 1986; Winner, Best Novel of Year Award, Giovanni's Room, Philadelphia, 1979. Memberships: Writers Union of Canada; Federation of British Columbia Writers. Literary Agent: Robert Drake, Drake Literary Agency, 314 South Iseminger Street, Philadelphia, PA 19107-5904, USA. Address: 3358 West First Avenue, Vancouver, British Columbia V6R 1G4, Canada.

WATSON John Richard, b. 15 June 1934, Ipswich, England. Professor. m. Pauline Elizabeth Roberts, 21 July 1962, 1 son, 2 daughters. Education: BA, MA, Magdalen College, Oxford; PhD, University of Glasgow, 1966. Publications: Everymans Book of Victorian Verse, 1982; Wordworth's Vital Soul, 1982; The Poetry of Gerard Manley Hopkins, 1986; Wordsworth, 1983; Companion to Hymns and Psalms, 1988; English Poetry of the Romantic Period 1789-1830, 1985, 2nd edition, 1992; A Handbook to English Romanticism, 1992. Contributions to: Critical Quarterly; Essays in Criticism; Collections of Essays. Membership: Modern Humanities Research Association, Chairman; Charles Wesley Society, Vice-President; International Association of University Professor of English, President. Address: Stoneyhurst, 27 Western Hill, Durham DH1 4RL, England.

WATSON Lynn, b. 5 June 1948, Woodland, California, USA. Teacher; Writer; Poet. Education: University of California, Berkeley, 1966-68; BA English, Sonoma State University, 1975; MFA Fiction Writing 1977, University of Iowa, Writers Workshop, 1977. Appointments: Freelance Writer for various print media and publications; Teacher, University of Iowa, College of the Desert, Sonoma State University, Santa Rosa Junior College; Artist/Facilitator, State Prison, California, 1981. Publications: Alimony or Death of the Clock (novel), 1981; Amateur Blues (poetry), 1990; Catching the Devil (poetry), 1995. Contributions to: Journals and periodicals. Honours: First Place, Poetry, National Poetry Association, San Francisco, 1990; Honorable Mention, World of Poetry Contest, Sacramento, 1991. Membership: California Poets in the Schools. Address: PO Box 1253, Occidental, CA 95465, USA.

WATSON Richard Allan, b. 23 Feb 1931, New Market, Iowa, USA. Professor of Philosophy; Writer. m. Patty Jo Andersen, 30 July 1955, 1 daughter. Education: BA, 1953, MA, 1957, PhD, Philosophy, 1961, University of Iowa; MS, Geology, University of Minnesota, 1959. Appointments: Instructor, University of Michigan, 1961-64; Assistant Professor, 1964-67, Associate Professor, 1967-74, Professor of Philosophy, 1974-, Washington University, St Louis; President, Cave Research Foundation, Mammoth Cave, Kentucky, 1965-67; Trustee, National Parks and Conservation Association, Washington, DC, 1969-81; Editor, Classics in Speleology, 1968-73, Speleologia, 1974-79, Cave Books, 1980-, Journal of the History of Philosophy, 1983, Journal of the History of Philosophy Monograph Series, 1985-95. Publications: The Downfall of Cartesianism, 1966; Man and Nature (with Patty Joe Watson), 1969; The Longest Cave (with Roger W Brucker), 1976; Under Plowman's Floor (novel), 1978; The Runner (novel), 1981; The Philosopher's Diet, 1985; The Breakdown of Cartesian Metaphysics, 1987; The Philosopher's Joke, 1990; Writing Philosophy, 1992; Niagara (novel), 1993; Caving, 1994; The Philosopher's Demise, 1995; Representational Ideas, 1995; Good Teaching, 1997. Contributions to: Professional journals. Honours: American Council of Learned Societies Fellow, 1967-68; Center for Advanced Study in the Behavioral Sciences Fellowships, 1967-68, 1981-82, 1991-92; National Endowment for the Humanities Grant, 1975; Center for International Studies Fellow, Princeton, New Jersey, 1975-76; Camargo Foundation Fellow, 1995. Memberships: American Academy of Arts and Sciences; American Philosophical Association; Cave Research Foundation; National Speleological Society, honorary life member; Authors League of America. Address: c/o Department of Philosophy, Washington University, St Louis, MO 63130, USA.

WATSON Will. See: **FLOREN Lee**.

WATT-EVANS Lawrence, b. 26 July 1954, Arlington, Massachusetts, USA. Freelance Writer. m. Julie F McKenna, 30 Aug 1977, 1 daughter, 1 son. Education: Princeton University, 1972-74, 1975-77. Publications: The Lure of the Basilisk, 1980; The Seven Altars of Dûsarra, 1981; The Cyborg and the Sorcerers, 1982; The Sword of Bheleu, 1983; The Book of Silence, 1984; The Chromosomal Code, 1984; The Misenchanted Sword, 1985; Shining Steel, 1986; With a Single Spell, 1987; The Wizard and the War Machine, 1987; Denner's Wreck, 1988; Nightside City, 1989; The Unwilling Warlord, 1989; The Nightmare People, 1990; The Blood of a Dragon, 1991; The Rebirth of Wonder, 1992; Crosstime Traffic, 1992; Taking Flight, 1993; The Spell of the Black Dagger, 1993; Split Heirs (with Esther Friesner), 1993; Out of This World, 1994; In the Empire of Shadow, 1995; The Reign of the Brown Magician, 1996. Contributions to: Journals and magazines. Honours: Isaac Asimov's Science Fiction Readers Poll Award, 1987; Science Fiction Achievement Award (Hugo) for Best Short Story of 1987, 1988. Memberships: Science Fiction Writers of America; Horror Writers Association. Address: c/o Russell Galen,

Scott Meredith Literary Agency, 845 Third Avenue, New York, NY 10022, USA.

WATTLES Rama Rau. See: RAMA RAU Santha.

WATTS Nigel John, b. 24 June 1957, Winchester, England. Writer. m. Sahera Chohan, 10 Aug 1991. Publications: The Life Game, 1989; Billy Bayswater, 1990; We All Live in a House Called Innocence, 1992; Twenty Twenty, 1995. Honour: Betty Trask Award, 1989. Address: 260 Ashburnham Road, Ham Richmond, Surrey, England.

WATTS Victor Ernest, b. 18 Apr 1938, Bristol, England. University Teacher. m. Mary Curtis, 4 Apr 1964, 1 son, 2 daughter. Education: Merton College, Oxford, 1957-61; University College, London, 1961-62; MA, Oxford, 1964; FSA. Appointments: Lecturer, 1962-74, Senior Lecturer, 1974-, Durham University; Master of Grey College, Durham University, 1989-. Publications: Boethius The Consolation of Philosophy, 1969; The Cambridge Dictionary of English Place Names. Contributions to: Medium Aevum; Nomina; Journal of the English Placename Society. Memberships: English Place Name Society; Architectural and Archaeological Society of Durham and Northumberland. Address: The Masters House, High Close, Hollingside Lane, Durham DH1 3TN, England.

WAUGH Auberon, b. 17 Nov 1939, England. Writer. m. Lady Teresa Onslow, 1961, div 1971, 2 sons, 2 daughters. Education: Christ Church, Oxford. Appointments: Columnist, Private Eye, 1970-86, The Spectator, 1976-; Chief Book Reviewer, Daily Mail, 1981-86; Editor, Literary Review, 1986; Book Reviewer, Sunday Telegraph, 1990-; Way of the World Columnist, Daily Telegraph, 1990-; Editor, Literary Review, 1986. Publications: The Foxglove Saga, 1960; The Path of Dalliance, 1963; Who Are the Violets Now?, 1966; Consider the Lillies, 1968; A Bed of Flowers, 1971; Four Crowded Years: The Diaries of Auberon Waugh, 1972-76, A Turbulent Decade 1976-85, 1985; Waugh on Wine, 1986; Will This Do? (autobiography), 1991; Way of the World (collected journalism), 1995. Honour: Granada TV What the Papaers Say Columnist of the Year, 1978, 1988. Address: Combe Florey House, Combe Florey, Taunton, Somerset.

WAUGH Hillary Baldwin (Elissa Grandower, H Baldwin Taylor, Harry Walker), b. 22 June 1920, New Haven, Connecticut, USA. Author. m. (1) Diana Taylor, 16 June 1951, div 1980, 1 son, 2 daughters, (2) Shannon O Cork, 11 June 1983, div 1995. Education: BA, Yale University, 1942. Publications: Last Seen Wearing..., 1952; The Missing Man, 1964; Rivergate House, 1980; The Glenna Powers Case, 1981; The Doria Rafe Case, 1981; The Billy Cantrell Case, 1982; The Nerissa Claire Case, 1983; The Veronica Dean Case, 1984; The Priscilla Copperwaite Case, 1985. Honours: Grand Master, Swedish Academy of Detection, 1981; Grand Master, Mystery Writers of America, 1989. Memberships: Mystery Writers of America; Crime Writers Association, England. Address: 9 Marshall Avenue, Guilford, CT 06437, USA.

WAYMAN Thomas (Ethan), (Tom Wayman), b. 13 Aug 1945, Hawkesbury, Ontario, Canada. Poet; Professor. Education: BA, University of British Columbia, 1966; MFA, University of California at Irvine, 1968. Appointments: Instructor, Colorado State University, Fort Collins, 1968-69; Writer-in-Residence, University of Windsor, Ontario, 1975-76; Assistant Professor of English, Wayne State University, Detroit, 1976-77; Writer-in-Residence, University of Alberta, Edmonton, 1978-79; Instructor, David Thompson University Centre, Nelson, British Columbia, 1980-82; Writer-in-Residence, Simon Fraser University, Burnaby, British Columbia, 1983; Instructor, Kootenay School of Writing, Vancouver, 1984-87; Kwantlen College, Surrey, British Columbia, 1988-89; Professor, Okanagan College, Kelowna, British Columbia, 1990-91, 1992-; Instructor, Kootenay School of the Arts, 1991-92. Publications: Mindscapes (with others), 1971; Waiting for Wayman, 1973; For and Against the Moon: Blues, Yells and Chuckles, 1974; Beaton Abbott's Got the Contract: An Anthology of Working Poems (editor), 1974; Money and Rain: Tom Wayman Live!, 1975; Routines, 1976; Transport, 1976; A Government Job at Last: An Anthology of Working Poems, Mainly Canadian (editor), 1976; Kitchener-Chicago/Saskatoon, 1977; Free Time: Industrial Poems, 1977; A Planet Mostly Sea, 1979; Living on the Ground: Tom Wayman Country, 1980; Introducing Tom Wayman: Selected Poems 1973-1980, 1980; Going for Coffee: Poetry on the Job (editor), 1981; The Nobel Prize Acceptance Speech, 1981; Counting the Hours: City Poems, 1983; Inside Job: Essays on the New Work Writing, 1983; The Face of Jack Munro, 1986; In a Small House on the Outskirts of Heaven, 1989;

East of Main: An Anthology of Poetry from East Vancouver (co-editor with Calvin Wharton), 1989; Paperwork: Contemporary Poems from the Job, 1991; A Country Not Considered: Canada, Culture, Work, 1993; Did I Miss Anything? Selected Poems, 1973-1993, 1993; The Astonishing Weight of the Dead, 1995. Honours: Several prizes and awards. Address: PO Box 163, Winlaw, British Columbia VOG 2JO, Canada.

WEARNE Alan Richard, b. 23 July 1948, Melbourne, Australia. Poet; Verse Novelist. Education: BA, Latrobe University, 1973; DipEd SCV Rusden, 1977. Appointments: Poetry Editor, Meanjin, 1984-87; Writer in Residence, University of Newcastle, New South Wales, 1989. Publications: Public Relations, 1972; New Devil, New Parish, 1976; The Nightmarkets, 1986; Out Here, 1987. Contributions to: Scripsi; Meanjin; Book Reviews in the Age. Honours: National Book Council Award, 1987; Gold Medal, Association for the Study of Australian Literature, 1987. Address: 83 Edgevale Road, Kew Melbourne Victoria 3101, Australia.

WEBB Bernice Larson, b. Ludell, Kansas, USA. Retired Professor; Consultant; Poet; Writer. m. Robert MacHardy Webb, 14 July 1961, 1 son, 1 daughter. Education: AB, 1956, MA, 1957, PhD, 1961, University of Kansas; University of Aberdeen, Scotland, 1959-60. Appointments: Assistant Instructor, University of Kansas, 1958-59, 1960-61; Assistant Professor, 1961-67, Associate Professor, 1967-80, Professor, 1980-87, Consultant, 1987-, University of Southwestern Louisiana; Editor, Cajun Chatter, 1964-66, The Magnolia, 1967-71, Louisiana Poets, 1970-89; Book Reviewer, Journal of American Culture, 1980-87, Journal of Popular Culture, 1980-87. Publications: The Basketball Man, 1973 (translated into Japanese), revised edition, 1994; Beware of Ostriches, 1978; Poetry on the Stage, 1979; Lady Doctor on a Homestead, 1987; Two Peach Baskets, 1991; Spider Webb, 1993; Born to Be a Loser (with Johnnie Allen), 1993; Mating Dance, 1996. Contributions to: Various publications. Honours: Many poetry awards and prizes. Memberships: Deep South Writers Conference, board member; Louisiana State Poetry Society, president; Phi Beta Kappa, president; South Central College English Association, president, 1986-87. Address: 159 Whittington Drive, Lafayette, LA 70503, USA.

WEBB Phyllis, b. 8 Apr 1927, Victoria, British Columbia, Canada. Professor; Poet; Retired. Education: BA, University of British Columbia at Vancouver, 1949; McGill University, Montreal. Appointment: Adjunct Professor, University of Victoria, British Columbia. Publications: Trio, 1954; Even Your Right Eye, 1956; The Sea is Also a Garden, 1962; Naked Poems, 1965; Selected Poems 1954-65, 1966; Wilson's Bowl, 1980; Sunday Water: Thirteen Anti Ghazals, 1982; The Vision Tree: Selected Poems, 1982; Water and Light: Ghazals and Anti Ghazals, 1984; Hanging Fire, 1990; Nothing but Brush Strokes, selected prose, 1995; Talking, essays, 1982. Honours: Canada Council Awards; Governor General's Award, 1982; Officer of the Order of Canada, 1992. Address: 128 Menhinick Drive, Salt Spring Island, British Columbia V8K 1W7, Canada.

WEBER Eugen (Joseph), b. 24 Apr 1925, Bucharest, Romania. Professor of Modern European History; Writer. m. Jacqueline Brument-Roth, 12 June 1950. Education: Institut d'études politiques, Paris, 1948-49, 1951-52; MA, 1954, MLitt, 1956, Emmanuel College, Cambridge. Appointments: Assistant Professor, University of Iowa, 1955-56; Assistant Professor, 1956-59, Associate Professor, 1959-63, Professor, 1963-, Dean, College of Letters and Sciences, 1977-82, Joan Palevsky Professor of Modern European History, 1984-, University of California at Los Angeles; Visiting Professor, Collège de France, Paris, 1983; Director d'études, École des hautes études, Paris, 1984-85; Christian Gauss Lecturer, Princeton University, 1990. Publications: Nationalist Revival in France, 1959; Paths to the Present, 1960; Satan Franc-Maçon, 1964; Varieties of Fascism, 1964; The European Right (with H Rogger), 1965; A Modern History of Europe, 1971; Europe Since 1715, 1972; Peasants into Frenchmen, 1976; La Fin des Terroirs, 1983; France Fin-de-siècle, 1986; My France, 1990; Movements, Currents, Trends, 1991; The Hollow Years, 1994; La France des années trente, 1995; The Western Tradition, 1995. Contributions to: Professional journals. Honours: Fulbright Fellowships, 1952, 1982-83; American Philosophical Society Research Fellow, 1959; American Council of Learned Societies Research Fellow, 1962; Guggenheim Fellowship, 1963-64; National Endowment for the Humanities Senior Fellowships, 1973-74, 1982-83; Commonwealth Prizes of California, 1977, 1987; Prix de la Société des gens de lettres, France, 1984; Prix litteraire Etats-Unis/France, 1995; Prix Maurice

Beaumont, 1995. Memberships: American Academy of Arts and Sciences; American Historical Association; Association française de science politique; Phi Beta Kappa; Société d'histoire moderne; Society of French Historical Studies. Address: c/o Department of History, University of California at Los Angeles, Los Angeles, CA 90095, USA.

WEBER George Richard, b. 7 Feb 1929, The Dalles, Oregon, USA. Certified Public Accountant. m. Nadine Hanson, 12 Oct 1957, 3 daughters. Education: BS, Oregon State University, 1950; MBA, University of Oregon, 1962. Publications: Small Business Long-Term Finance, 1962; A History of the Coroner and Medical Examiner Offices, 1963; CPA Litigation Service References, 1991. Contributions to: Cost and Management; Hyacinths & Biscuits. Honours: Bronze Star Medal with V, US Army, 1953; Selected by AICPA as one of One Hundred Future Leaders of Accounting Profession in the USA, 1963; Knightly Association of St George the Martyr, 1986. Memberships: American Institute of CPA's; Oregon Society of CPA's; Portland Committee on Foreign Relations. Address: 2603 North East 32nd Avenue, Portland, OR 97212, USA.

WEBSTER Ernest, b. 24 Oct 1923, Harbrough, England. Retired Director; Writer. m. 8 Oct 1942, 2 daughters. Education: London Matric, History and Economics. Publications: The Friulan Plot; Madonna of the Black Market; Cossack Hide Out; Red Alert; The Venetian Spy Glass; The Verratoli Inheritance; Million Dollar Stand in; The Watches. Address: 17 Chippendale Rise, Otley, West Yorkshire LS21 2BL, England.

WEBSTER Jan, b. 10 Aug 1924, Blantyre, Scotland. Writer. m. 10 Aug 1946, 1 son, 1 daughter. Education: Hamilton Academy. Publications: Trilogy: Colliers Row, 1977; Saturday City, 1978; Beggarman's Country, 1979; Due South, 1981; Muckle Annie, 1985; One Little Room, 1987; Rags of Time, 1987; A Different Woman, 1989; Abercrombie's Aunt and Other Stories, 1990; I Only Can Dance with You, 1990; Bluebell Blue, 1991; Lowland Reels, 1992; Tallies War, 1993; Makalienski's Bones, 1995; Pinkmount Drive, 1996. Address: c/o Robert Hale, 45-47 Clerkenwell Green, London EC1R 0HJ, England.

WEBSTER Jesse. See: **CASSILL R(onald) V(erlin)**.

WEBSTER John (Jack) Barron, b. 8 July 1931, Maud, Aberdeenshire, Scotland. Journalist. m. Eden Keith, 17 Feb 1956, 3 sons. Education: Maud School; Peterhead Academy; Robert Gordon's College, Aberdeen. Publications: The Dons, 1978; A Grain of Truth, 1981; Gordon Strachan, 1984; Another Grain of Truth, 1988; Alistair MacLean: A Life, 1991; Famous Ships of the Clyde, 1993. Television: The Webster Trilogy, 1993. The Flying Scots, 1994; The Express Years, 1994; In the Driving Seat, 1996; The Herald Years, 1996. TV Film: John Brown: The Man Who Drew a Legend, 1994. Honours: Bank of Scotland Awards: Columnist of the Year, 1996; UK Speaker of the Year, 1996. Address: 58 Netherhill Avenue, Glasgow G44 3XG, Scotland.

WEBSTER Noah. See: **KNOX William**.

WEBSTER Norman William, b. 21 Aug 1920, Barrow in Furness, Cumbira, England. Retired Physicist. m. Phyllis Joan Layley, 17 Feb 1945, 2 daughters. Education: BSc, University of London. Publications: Joseph Locke, Railway Revolutionary, 1970; Britain's First Trunk Line: The Grand Junction Railway, 1972; Horace Reactor, 1972; The Great North Road, 1974; Blanche of Lancaster, 1990. Contributions to: Cumbria; The Book Collector. Memberships: Jane Austen Society; European Movement. Address: 15 Hillcrest Drive, Slackhead, Milnthorpe, Cumbria LA7 7BB, England.

WECKESSER Elden Christian, b. 31 Mar 1910, Marshallville, Ohio, USA. Emeritus Professor of Surgery. m. Kathryn Tuttle Weckesser, 17 Mar 1937, 4 daughters. Education: Duke University, 1928-29; Adelbert College Western Reserve University, 1930-33; BA, Case Western Reserve Medical School, 1932-36, MD 1936. Publications: Treatment of Hand Injuries, 1974; The Department of Surgery, Case Western Reserve University, 1843-1986, 1986; His Name Was Mudd, 1991; Co-author, Flynn's Hand Surgery, 1966, 1975, 1982, 1991; Medicine in Cleveland and Cuyahoga Co, 1810-1976, 1977. Contributions to: Numerous articles to medical journals. Honour: Distinguished Alumnus Case Western Reserve University, 1981. Address: 129 Manor Brook Drive, Chagrin Falls, OH 44022, USA.

WECKMANN Luis, b. 7 Apr 1923, Durango, Mexico. Retired Diplomat; Professor of History Emeritus. Education: MA, History, 1944; PhD, History, 1949, Lic Law, 1950, National University of Mexico; Dr, International Public Law, Paris, 1951. Appointments: Mexican diplomatic service, 1952-89; Assistant Secretary-General, United Nations, New York City, 1974-75; Professor of History Emeritus, University of the Americas, 1990. Publications: Las Bulas Alejandrinas de 1493, 1949, reprinted as Constantino el Grande y Cristobal Colon, 1993; El Pensamiento Político Medieval, 1950, 2nd edition, 1993; Panorma de la Cultura Medieval, 1962; La Herencia Medieval de Mexico, 2 volumes, 1982, 2nd edition, 1994; Carlota de Belgica: Archivos, 1989; La herencia medieval del Brasil, 1994. Address: Villa del Cardo, Cardo 4, San Miguel de Allende, Gto 37700, Mexico.

WEDDE Ian, b. 17 Oct 1946, Blenheim, New Zealand. Poet; Novelist; Critic. m. Rosemary Beauchamp, 1967, 3 sons. Education: MA, Auckland University, 1968. Appointment: Writer-in-Residence, Victoria University, Wellington, 1984. Publications: Homage to Matisse, 1971; Made Over, 1974; Pathway to the Sea, 1974; Earthly: Sonnets for Carlos, 1975; Don't Listen, 1977; Spells for Coming Out, 1977; Castaly and Other Poems, 1980; Tales of Gotham City, 1984; Georgicon, 1984; Driving into the Storm: Selected Poems, 1987; Tendering, 1988. Novels: Dick Seddon's Great Dive, 1976; Symmes Hole, 1986. Plays, Eyeball, Eyeball, 1983; Double or Quit: The Life and Times of Percy Topliss, 1984. Editor of Volumes of Poetry. Honour: New Zealand Book Award.

WEDGWOOD BENN Anthony Neil. See: **BENN Tony**.

WEHRFRITZ George. Journalist. m. Diana Lou Grant. Education: Degree in Economics, University of California, Davis; Participant, Yale-China International Asian Studies Program, University of Hong Kong, 1983-84. Apointments: Political Correspondent, International Community Radio Taipei, 11 months; Taiwan Correspondent, United Press International, 1992-93; Freelance Writer for various publications including Newsweek, Business Week, Christian Science Monitor, and Far Eastern Review, until 1993; Beijing Bureau Chief, Newsweek, 1994. Publication: Southwest China Off the Beaten Track, 2nd edition, 1996. Address: 251 West 57th Street, New York, NY 10019-1894, USA.

WEHRLI Peter, b. 30 July 1939, Switzerland, Writer; Television Producer. Education: University of Zürich; University of Paris. Publications: Ankunfte, 1970; Catalogue of the 134 Most Important Observations during a Long Railway Journey, 1974; Zelluloid Paradies, 1978; Tingeltangel, 1982; Alles von Allem, 1985; La Farandula, 1986; This Book is Free of Charge; 18th Xurumbambo, 1992. Contributions to: Magazines and Journals. Honours: Award of the Government of Zürich; Distinguished Service Citation. Memberships: PEN; Swiss Writers Association; Gruppe Olten; International Federation of Journalists; International Association of Art Critics. Address: Weinbergstrasse 100, 8006 Zürich, Switzerland.

WEIGEL George, b. 17 Apr 1951, Baltimore, Maryland, USA. Roman Catholic Theologian. m. Joan Balcombe, 21 June 1975, 1 son, 2 daughters. Education: BA Philosophy 1973, St Mary's Seminary and University, Baltimore, 1973; MA, Theology, University of St Michael's College, Toronto, 1975. Appointments: Fellow, Woodrow Wilson International Centre for Scholars, 1984-85; Editorial Boards, First Things, The Washington Quarterly, and Orbis. Publications: Tranquillitas Ordinis: The Present Failure and Future Promise of American Catholic Thought on War and Peace, 1987; Catholicism and the Renewal of American Democracy, 1989; American Interests, American Purpose: Moral Reasoning and US Foreign Policy, 1989; Freedom and Its Discontents, 1991; Just War and the Gulf War (co-author), 1991; The Final Revolution: The Resistance Church and the Collapse of Communism, 1992; Idealism Without Illusions: US Foreign Policy in the 1990's, 1994; Soul of the World: Notes on the Future of Public Catholicism, 1995. Contributions to: Numerous publications. Memberships: Catholic Theological Society of America; Council on Foreign Relations. Literary Agent: Loretta Barret, Loretta Barrett Books Inc, 101 Fifth Avenue, New York, NY 10003, USA. Address: Ethics and Public Policy Centre, 1015 15th Street North West, Suite 900, Washington, DC 20005, USA.

WEIN Elizabeth Eve (Gatland), b. 2 Oct 1964, New York, New York, USA. Writer; Folklorist. m. Tim Gatland, 1 Jan 1996. Education: BA, Yale University, 1986; MA, 1989, PhD, 1994, University of Pennsylvania. Publications: The Winter Prince, 1993; Fire, in Writers of the Future, Vol 9 (short stories), 1993; New Years Eve, in Not the Only One, 1995; The Bellcaster's Apprentice, in The Horns of Elfland, 1997. Honours: Jacob K Javits Fellow, 1988-92; Carolyn Field Award, Runner Up, 1994. Memberships: Authors Guild; Society of Children's Book Writers and Illustrators; Science Fiction and Fantasy Writers of America. Literary Agent: Shawna McCarthy. Address: 41A Oak Tree Road, Marlow, Bucks SL7 3ED, England.

WEINBERG Gerhard L(udwig), b. 1 Jan 1928, Hannover, Germany. Professor of History; Writer. m. Janet I White, 29 Apr 1989, 1 son. Education: BA, New York State College for Teachers, 1948; MA, 1949, PhD, 1951, University of Chicago. Appointment: Professor of History, University of North Carolina at Chapel Hill. Publications: Germany and the Soviet Union, 1939-41, 1954; Hitlers Zweites Buch, 1961; The Foreign Policy of Hitler's Germany, 1933-36, 1970; The Foreign Policy of Hitler's Germany, 1937-39, 1980; A World in the Balance: Behind the Scenes of World War II, 1981; A World at Arms: A Global History of World War II, 1994; Germany, Hitler and World War II, 1995. Contributions to: Professional journals. Honours: AHA Beer Prizes, 1971, 1994; GSA Halverson Prize, 1981; Honorary Doctor of Humane Letters, 1989. Memberships: American Historical Association; Conference Group for Central European History; German Studies Association; World War II Studies Association. Address: c/o Department of History, University of North Carolina at Chapel Hill, Chapel Hill, NC 27599-3195, USA.

WEINBERG Steven, b. 3 May 1933, New York, New York, USA. Professor of Science; Author. m. Louise Goldwasser, 6 July 1954, 1 daughter. Education: BA, Cornell University, 1954; Postgraduate Studies, Copenhagen Institute of Theoretical Physics, 1954-55; PhD, Princeton University, 1957. Appointments: Research Associate and Instructor, Columbia University, 1957-59; Research Physicist, Lawrence Radiation Laboratory, Berkeley, 1959-60; Faculty, 1960-64, Professor of Physics, 1964-69, University of California at Berkeley; Visiting Professor, 1967-69, Professor of Physics, 1979-83, Massachusetts Institute of Technology; Higgins Professor of Physics, Harvard University, 1973-83; Senior Scientist, Smithsonian Astrophysics Laboratory, 1973-83; Josey Professor of Science, University of Texas at Austin, 1982-; Senior Consultant, Smithsonian Astrophysics Observatory, 1983-; Various visiting professorships and lectureships. Publications: Gravitation and Cosmology: Principles and Application of the General Theory of Relativity, 1972; The First Three Minutes: A Modern View of the Origin of the Universe, 1977; The Discovery of Subatomic Particles, 1982; Elementary Particles and the Laws of Physics (with R Feynman), 1987; Dreams of a Final Theory, 1992; The Quantum Theory of Fields, Vol I, Foundations, 1995, Vol II, Modern Applications, 1996. Contributions to: Books, periodicals and professional journals. Honours: J Robert Oppenheimer Memorial Prize, 1973; Dannie Heineman Prize in Mathematical Physics, 1977; American Institute of Physics-US Steel Foundation Science Writing Award, 1977; Nobel Prize in Physics, 1979; Elliott Cresson Medal, Franklin Institute, 1979; Madison Medal, Princeton University, 1991; National Medal of Science, National Science Foundation, 1991. Memberships: American Academy of Arts and Sciences; American Mediaeval Academy; American Philosophical Society; American Physical Society; Council on Foreign Relations; History of Science Society; International Astronomical Union; National Academy of Science; Phi Beta Kappa; Philosophical Society of Texas, president, 1994; Royal Society; Texas Institute of Letters. Address: c/o Department of Science, University of Texas at Austin, Austin, TX 78712, USA.

WEINFIELD Henry (Michael), b. 3 Jan 1949, Montreal, Quebec, Canada. Associate Professor in Liberal Studies; Poet; Writer. Education: BA, City College of New York, 1970; MA, State University of New York, Binghamton, 1973; PhD, City University of New York, 1985. Appointments: Lecturer, State University of New York, Binghamton, 1973-74; Adjunct Lecturer, Lehman College, 1974-77; Baruch College, 1979-81; City College of New York, 1982-83; Adjunct Lecturer, 1983-84, Special Lecturer, 1984-91, New Jersey Institute of Technology; Assistant Professor, 1991-96, Associate Professor, 1996-, in Liberal Studies, University of Notre Dame. Publications: Poetry: The Carnival Cantata, 1971; In the Sweetness of New Time, 1980; Sonnets Elegiac and Satirical, 1982. Other: The Poet Without a Name: Gray's Elegy and the Problem of History, 1991; The Collected Poems of Stéphane Mallarmé, translated with commentary, 1995. Contributions to: Articles, poems, translations in many publications. Honours: Coordinating Council of Literary Magazines Award, 1975; National Endowment for the Humanities Fellowship, 1989. Memberships:

Coordinating Council of Literary Magazines, 1972-76; Modern Language Association, 1985-94; Poetry Society of America, 1988-92. Address: Program of Liberal Studies, University of Notre Dame, Notre Dame, IN 46556, USA.

WEINREICH Beatrice, (Beatrice Sliverman-Weinreich), b. 14 May 1928, New York, New York, USA. Folklorist. m. Uriel Weinreich, 26 June 1949, dec 1967, 1 son, 1 daughter. Education: BA, Brooklyn College, 1949; Graduate Studies, Folklore and Ethnography, University of Zürich, 1950; MA, Anthropology, Columbia University, 1956. Publications: Yidisher Folklor (co-editor), 1954; Yiddish Language and Folklore: A Selective Bibliography (co-editor), 1959; Yiddish Folktales, 1988; The Language and Culture Atlas of Ashkenzic Jewry, Vol II, Research Tools (co-editor), 1993. Contributions to: Books and journals. Memberships: American Folklore Society; International Society for Folk Narrative Research; New York Folklore Society. Address: 555 West 57 Street, New York, NY 10019, USA.

WEINSTEIN Michael Alan, b. 24 Aug 1942, Brooklyn, New York, USA. Political Philosopher. m. Deena Schneiweiss, 31 May 1964. Education: BA summa cum laude 1964, New York University; MA, 1965, PhD 1967, Western Reserve University. Appointments: Assistant Professor, Western Reserve University, 1967, Virginia Polytechnic Institute, 1967-68, Purdue University, 1972-; Distinguished Professor of Political Science, University of Wyoming, 1979. Publications: The Polarity of Mexican Thought: Instrumentalism and Finalism, 1976; The Tragic Sense of Political Life, 1977; Meaning and Appreciation: Time and Modern Political Life, 1978; The Structure of Human Life: A Vitalist Ontology, 1979; The Wilderness and the City: American Classical Philosophy as a Moral Quest, 1982; Unity and Variety in the Philosophy of Samuel Alexander, 1984; Finite Perfection: Reflections on Virtue, 1985; Culture Critique: Fernand Dumont and the New Quebec Sociology, 1985; Data Trash, 1994; Culture/Flesh: Explorations of Postcivilized Modernity, 1995. Contributions to: Magazines and journals. Honours: Best Paper Prize, Midwest Political Science Association, 1969; Guggengeim Fellowship, 1974-75; Rockefeller Foundation Humanities Fellowship, 1976. Address: Department of Political Science, Purdue University, West Lafayette, IN 47907, USA.

WEINTRAUB Stanley, b. 17 Apr 1929, Philadelphia, Pennsylvania, USA. Professor of Arts and Humanities; Writer; Editor. m. Rodelle Horwitz, 6 June 1954, 2 sons, 1 daughter. Education: BS, West Chester State College, Pennsylvania, 1949; MA, Temple University, 1951; PhD, Penn State University, 1956. Appointments: Instructor, 1953-59, Assistant Professor, 1959-62, Associate Professor, 1962-65, Professor of English, 1965-70, Research Professor, 1970-86, Evan Pugh Professor of Arts and Humanities, 1986-, Penn State University; Director, Institute for Arts and Humanistic Studies, 1970-90; Visiting Professor, University of California at Los Angeles, 1963, University of Hawaii, 1973, University of Malaya, 1977, National University of Singapore, 1982. Publications: Private Shaw and Public Shaw: A Dual Portrait of Lawrence of Arabia and George Bernard Shaw, 1963; The War in the Wards: Korea's Forgotten Battle, 1964; The Art of William Golding (with B S Oldsey), 1965; Reggie: A Portrait of Reginald Turner, 1965; Beardsley: A Biography, 1967; The Last Great Cause: The Intellectuals and the Spanish Civil War, 1968; Evolution of a Revolt: Early Postwar Writings of T E Lawrence (with R Weintraub), 1968; Journey to Heartbreak: The Crucible Years of Bernard Shaw 1914-1918, 1971; Whistler: A Biography, 1974; Lawrence of Arabia: The Literary Impulse (with R Weintraub), 1975; Aubrey Beardsley: Imp of the Perverse, 1976; Four Rossettis: A Victorian Biography, 1977; The London Yankees: Portraits of American Writers and Artists in England 1894-1914, 1979; The Unexpected Shaw: Biographical Approaches to G B Shaw and His Work, 1982; A Stillness Heard Round the World: The End of the Great War, 1985; Victoria: An Intimate Biography, 1987; Long Day's Journey into War: December 7, 1941, 1991; Bernard Shaw: A Guide to Research, 1992; Disraeli: A Biography, 1993; The Last Great Victory: The End of World War II, July/August 1945, 1995; Shaw's People, Victoria to Churchill, 1996; Albert, Uncrowned King, 1997. Editor: Unfinished novel by George Bernard Shaw, 1958; C P Snow: A Spectrum, 1963; The Yellow Book: Quintessence of the Nineties, 1964; The Savoy: Nineties Experiment, 1966; The Court Theatre, 1966; Biography and Truth, 1967; The Literary Criticism of Oscar Wilde, 1968; Shaw: An Autobiography, 1969-70; Bernard Shaw's Nondramatic Literary Criticism, 1972; Directions in Literary Criticism (with Philip Young), 1973; Saint Joan Fifty Years After: 1923/24-1973/74, 1973; The Portable Bernard Shaw, 1977; The

Portable Oscar Wilde (with Richard Aldington), 1981; Modern British Dramatists 1900-1945, 2 volumes, 1982; The Playwright and the Pirate: Bernard Shaw and Frank Harris: A Correspondence, 1982; British Dramatists Since World War II, 2 volumes, 1982; Bernard Shaw: The Diaries, 1885-1897, 1986; Bernard Shaw on the London Art Scene 1885-1950, 1989. Contributions to: Professional journals. Honours: Guggenheim Fellowship, 1968-69; Distinguished Humanist Award, Pennsylvania Humanities Council, 1985. Memberships: Authors Guild; PEN. Address: c/o Penn State University, 202 Ihlseng Building, University Park, PA 16802, USA.

WEISSBORT Daniel, b. 1 May 1935, London, England. Professor; Poet; Translator; Editor. Education: BA, Queen's College, Cambridge, 1956. Appointments: Co-Founder (with Ted Hughes), Modern Poetry in Translation, 1965-83; Professor, University of Iowa, 1980-. Publications: The Leaseholder, 1971; In an Emergency, 1972; Soundings, 1977; Leaseholder: New and Collected Poems, 1965-85, 1986; Inscription, 1990; Lake, 1993. Other: Editor and translator of Russian literature. Honour: Arts Council Literature Award, 1984. Address: c/o Department of English, University of Iowa, Iowa City, IA 52242, USA.

WELCH Ann Courtenay, b. 20 May 1917, London, England. Aviation Writer. m. (1) 2 daughters, (2) P P Lorne Elphinstone Welch, 24 June 1953, 1 daughter. Appointments: Editor, Bulletin, Fédération Aéronautique Internationale, 1979-89, Royal Aero Club Gazette, 1984-. Publications: The Woolacombe Bird, 1964; Story of Gliding, 1965; New Soaring Pilot, 1970; Pilot's Weather, 1973; Gliding, 1976; Hang Glider Pilot, 1977; Book of Air Sports, 1978; Accidents Happen, 1978; Soaring Hang Gliders, 1981; Complete Microlight Guide, 1983; Happy to Fly (autobiography), 1984; Complete Soaring Guide, 1986. Contributions to: Flight International, UK; Aeroplane, UK; Royal Aero Club Gazette; Pilot; Flight Safety Bulletin. Honours: Officer, Order of the British Empire; Silver Medal, Royal Aero Club; 4 Medals, Fédération Aéronautique Internationale. Memberships: Fellow, Royal Aeronautical Society; Royal Meteorological Society; Royal Institute of Navigation. Address: 14 Upper Old Park Lane, Farnham, Surrey GU9 0AS, England.

WELCH James, b. 1940, Browning, Montana, USA. Writer; Poet. m. Lois M Welch. Education: Northern Montana College; BA, University of Montana. Publications: Fiction: Winter in the Blood, 1974; The Death of Jim Loney, 1979; Fool's Crow, 1986; The Indian Lawyer, 1990. Poetry: Riding the Earthboy 40, 1971, revised edition, 1975. Non-Fiction: Killing Custer: The Battle of the Little Bighorn and the Fate of the Plains Indians (with Paul Stekler), 1994. Editor: Richard Hugo: The Real West Marginal Way: A Poet's Autobiography (with Ripley S Hugg and Lois M Welch), 1986. Contributions to: Periodicals. Honours: National Endowment for the Arts Grant, 1969; Los Angeles Times Book Prize, 1987; Pacific Northwest Booksellers Association Book Award, 1987. Address: 2321 Wylie Street, Missoula, MT 59802, USA.

WELCH Liliane, b. 20 Oct 1937, Luxembourg. Professor of French Literature; Poet; Writer. m. Cyril Welch, 1 daughter. Education: BA, 1960, MA, 1961, University of Montana; PhD, Penn State University, 1964. Appointments: Assistant Professor, East Carolina University, 1965-66, Antioch College, Ohio, 1966-67; Assistant Professor, 1967-71, Associate Professor, 1971-72, Professor of French Literature, 1972-, Mount Allison University. Publications: Emergence: Baudelaire, Mallarmé, Rimbaud, 1973; Winter Songs, 1973; Syntax of Ferment, 1979; Assailing Beats, 1979; October Winds, 1980; Brush and Trunks, 1981; From the Songs of the Artisans, 1983; Manstoma, 1985; Rest Unbound, 1985; Word-House of a Grandchild, 1987; Seismographs: Selected Essays and Reviews, 1988; Fire to the Looms Below, 1990; Life in Another Language, 1992; Von Menschen und Orten, 1992; Dream Museum, 1995; Fidelities, 1997. Contributions to: Professional and literary journals. Honours: Alfred Bailey Prize, 1986; Bressani Prize, 1992. Memberships: Association of Italian-Canadian Poets; Federation of New Brunswick Writers; League of Canadian Poets; Letzebuerger Schriftsteller Verband; Writers Union of Canada. Address: Box 246, Sackville, New Brunswick E0A 3C0, Canada.

WELDON Fay, b. 22 Sept 1931, Alvechurch, Worcestershire, England. Writer. m. (1) Ron Weldon, 12 June 1961, 4 daughters, (2) Nick Fox, 1994. Education: MA, St Andrews University, 1952. Publications: Fat Woman's Joke, 1968; Down Among the Women, 1971; Female Friends, 1975; Remember Me, 1976; Praxis, 1978; Puffball, 1980; The President's Child, 1982; Letters to Alice, 1984; Life

and Loves of a She Devil, 1984; Rebecca West, 1985; The Sharpnel Academy, 1986; The Hearts and Lives of Men, 1987; Leader of the Band, 1988; Wolf of the Mechanical Dog, 1989; The Cloning of Joanna May, 1989; Pary Puddle, 1989; Moon Over Minneapolis or Why She Couldn't Stay, 1991; Life Force, 1992; Growing Rich, 1992; Affliction, 1994. Contributions to: Numerous Journals and Magazines. Memberships: Royal Society of Authors; Writers Guild of Great Britain. Address: c/o Giles Gordon, 6 Ann Street, Edinburgh E4 1PS, Scotland.

WELLINGTON Fred. See: **PURDY A F.**

WELLS Martin John, b. 24 Aug 1928, London, England. Zoologist; Educator. m. Joyce Finlay, 8 Sept 1953, 2 sons. Education: BA, 1952; MA, 1956; ScD, 1966. Publications: Brain and Behaviour in Cephalopods, 1962; You, Me and the Animal World, 1964; Lower Animals, 1968; Octopus: Physiology and Behaviour of an Advanced Invertebrate, 1978. Contributions to: Several Journals. Honours: Silver Medal, Zoological Society, 1968; Fellow, Churchill College, Cambridge. Memberships: Philosophical Society; Marine Biology Association. Address: The Bury Home End, Fulbourn, Cambridge, England.

WELLS Peter, b. 12 Jan 1919, London, England. Writer; Poet. m. (1) Elisabeth Vander Meulen, dec 1967, (2) Gillian Anne Hayes-Newington, 1988, 1 daughter. Education: Privately; Universities of London and Manchester; Dip Soc, London, 1970; Cert in Psychiatric Social Work, Manchester, 1973. Publication: Co-Editor, Poetry Folios 1942-46, 1951. Contributions to: Anthologies, newspapers and magazines. Memberships: PEN; Society of Authors; Free Painters and Sculptors. Address: Model Farm, Linstead Magna, Halesworth, Suffolk, England.

WELLS Peter Frederick, (John Flint), b. 28 Feb 1918. Retired Professor; Writer. m. (1) Jeanne Chiles, 17 Feb 1945, 3 sons, (2) Rita Vincent, 26 Apr 1994. Education: MA (Wales), 1948; DipEd (Wales), 1949; DPhil, University of Waikato, New Zealand, 1971. Appointments: Head, Language Studies Department, University of Waikato, 1961-73; Director, Institute of Modern Languages, James Cook University of North Queensland, 1974-84. Publications: Let's Learn French, 1963; Les Quatre Saisons, 1966; Let's Learn Japanese, 1968; Nihongo no Kakikata, 1971; A Description of Kalaw Kawaw Ya, 1976. Other: Anthology of Poems by Ishikawa Takuboku, 1972; Phonetics and Orthography of French, 1975. Contributions to: Journal of Modern Languages and Literature; Bulletin de L'Association G Budé; New Zealand Journal of French Studies; Education; LINQ; English Language and Literature Association. Honour: Order of the Sacred Treasure, Japan. Membership: Founder, President, New Zealand-Japan Society, Hamilton. Address: 249 Bankwood Road, Chartwell, Hamilton, New Zealand.

WELLS Robert, b. 17 Aug 1947, England. Teacher; Translator; Poet. Education: King's College, Cambridge, 1965-68. Appointment: Teacher, Leicester University, 1979-82. Publications: Shae Mariners, 1970; The Winter's Task, 1977; Selected Poems, 1986; Translations of the Georgics by Virgil and the Idyll by Theocritus. Address: c/o Carcanet Press, 208-212 Corn Exchange Buildings, Manchester M4 3BQ, England.

WELLS Roger, b. 30 Jan 1947, London, England. University Lecturer, div, 1 daaughter. Education: BA, 1969, Dphil, 1978, University of York. Appointments: Lecturer, University of Wales, 1972-73, University of Exeter, 1973-75, University of York, 1975-76, Senior Lecturer, University of Brighton, 1976-95; Reader in History, Christ Church College, Canterbury, 1995-. Publications: Death and Distress in Yorkshire, 1793-1801, 1977; Riot and Political Disaffection in Nottinghamshire in the Age of Revolutions 1776-1803, 1983; Wretched Faces: Famine in Wartimes England, 1793-1801, 1988; Class, Conflict and Protest in the English Countryside, 1700-1880, 1990; Victorian Village, 1992. Contributions to: Social History; Rural History; Southern History; Northern History; Policing and Society; Journal of Peasant Studies; Journal of Historical Geography; Local Historian; English Historical Review; Agricultural History Review; London Journal; Labour History Bulletin; Journal of Social Policy. Membership: Royal Historical Society. Address: Christ Church College, Canterbury, Kent CT1 1QU, England.

WELLS Rosemary, b. 29 Jan 1943, New York, New York, USA. Author and Illustrator of Young Reader's Books. 2 daughters. Education: Museum School, Boston. Publications: Over 40 books,

1969-95. Honours: Many awards. Address: 738 Sleepy Hollow Road, Briarcliff Manor, NY 10510, USA.

WELLS Tobias. See: **FORBES Stanton.**

WELLS William K. See: **GARSIDE Jack Clifford.**

WELTON Anthony. See: **JOY David.**

WELTY Eudora, b. 13 Apr 1909, Jackson, Mississippi, USA. Author. Education: Mississippi State College for Women; BA, University of Wisconsin, 1929; Postgraduate Studies, Columbia School of Advertising, 1930-31. Publications: A Curtain of Green, 1941; The Robber Bridegroom, 1942; The Wide Net, 1943; Delta Wedding, 1946; Music From Spain, 1948; Short Stories, 1949; The Golden Apples, 1949; The Ponder Heart, 1954; The Bride of the Innisfallen, 1955; Place in Fiction, 1957; The Shoe Bird, 1964; Thirteen Stories, 1965; A Sweet Devouring, 1969; Losing Battles, 1970; One Time, One Place, 1971; The Optimist's Daughter, 1972; The Eye of the Story, 1978; The Collected Stories of Eudora Welty, 1980; One Writer's Beginnings, 1985; Eudora Welty Photographs, 1989; The Norton Book of Friendship (editor with Ronald A Sharp), 1991; A Writer's Eye: Collected Book Reviews, 1994; Monuments to Interruption: Collected Book Reviews, 1994. Contributions to: The New Yorker. Honours: Guggenheim Fellowship, 1942; O Henry Awards, 1942, 1943, 1968; National Institute of Arts and Letters Grant, 1944, and Gold Medal, 1972; William Dean Howells Medal, American Academy of Arts and Letters, 1955; Christopher Book Award, 1972; Pulitzer Prize in Fiction, 1973; Presidential Medal of Freedom, 1980; National Medal for Literature, 1980; Notable Book Award, American Library Association, 1980; American Book Awards, 1981, 1984; Commonwealth Medal, Modern Language Association, 1984; National Medal of Arts, 1987; Chevalier de l'Ordre des Arts et Lettres, France, 1987. Membership: American Academy of Arts and Letters. Address: 1119 Pinehurst Street, Jackson, MS 39202, USA.

WENDT Albert, b. 27 Oct 1939, Apia, Western Samoa. Professor of English; Writer; Poet; Dramatist. 1 son, 2 daughters. Education: MA in History, Victoria University, Wellington, 1964. Appointments: Professor of Pacific Literature, University of the South Pacific, Suva, Fiji, 1982-87; Professor of English, University of Auckland, 1988-. Publications: Sons for the Return Home, 1973; Pouliuli, 1977; Leaves of the Banyan Tree, 1979; Ola, 1990; Black Rainbow, 1992. Short stories: Flying-Fox in a Freedom Tree, 1974; The Birth and Death of the Miracle Man, 1986. Plays: Comes the Revolution, 1972; The Contract, 1972. Verse: Inside us the Dead: Poems 1961-74; Shaman of Visions, 1984. Honours: Landfall Prize, 1963; Wattie Award, 1980. Address: Department of English, University of Auckland, Private Bag, Auckland, New Zealand.

WENTWORTH Wendy. See: **CHAPLIN Jenny.**

WERTH Lloyd E. See: **DOAN Eleanor Lloyd.**

WESCOTT Roger Williams, b. 28 April 1925, Philadelphia, Pennsylvania, USA. Anthropologist; Writer; Poet. m. 12 Apr 1964. Education: BA, English and History, 1945, MA, Oriental Studies, 1947, PhD, Linguistic Science, 1948, Princeton University; MLitt, Social Anthropology, Oxford University, 1953. Appointments: Director, University Playreaders, Ibadan, Nigeria, 1955-56; Assistant Professor of English, Massachusetts Institute of Technology, USA, 1956-57; Associate Professor of English, Michigan State University, 1957-62; Evaluator, National Endowment for the Humanities, 1975-; Associate Editor, Thoughts for All Seasons, USA, 1988-. Publications: The Divine Animal, 1969; Visions: Selected Poems, 1975; Sound and Sense, 1980; Language Families, 1986; Getting it Together, 1990. Co-Author: The Creative Process, 1974; Poems for Children, 1975; Literary and Linguistic Studies, 1978; Anthropological Poetics, 1990. Honours: Rhodes Scholar, Oxford University, 1948-50; First Holder, Endowed Chair of Excellence in Humanities, University of Tennessee, 1988-89. Memberships: International Society for the Comparative Study of Civilsations, president, 1992-; Linguistic Association of Canada and the US, president, 1976-77. Address: 16-A Heritage Crest, Southbury, CT 06488, USA.

WESKER Arnold, b. 24 May 1932, England. Writer; Dramatist. m. Dusty Bicker, 1958, 2 sons, 2 daughters. Education: Upton House School, Hackney. Appointments: Director, Centre 42: Centre for the Arts, London, 1961-70; Chairman, British Section, 1978-85, President,

Playwrights' Permanent Committee, 1980-85, International Theatre Institute. Publications: Chicken Soup with Barley, 1959; Roots, 1959; I'm Talking About Jerusalem, 1960; The Kitchen, 1960; Chips With Everything, 1962; Their Very Own Golden City, 1966; The Four Seasons, 1966; The Friends, 1970; Fears of Fragmentation, 1970; Six Sundays in January, 1971; The Old Ones, 1972; Love Letters on Blue Paper, 1974; Say Goodbye, You May Never See Them Again, 1974; The Journalists, 1975; The Plays of Arnold Wesker, 2 Volumes, 1976-77; Words as Definition of Experience, 1977; Journey into Journalism, 1977; The Merchant, 1977; Said the Old Man to the Young Man, stories, The Journalists, a Triptych, 1979; Collected Plays and Stories, 5 Volumes, 1980; Caritas, 1981; Annie Wobbler, 1983; Distinctions (essays) 1985; Four Portraits, 1987; Lady Othello and Other Plays, 1987; The Wedding Feast, Shylock, The Mistress, One More Ride on the Merry Go Round, When God Wanted a Son and Bluey: six volumes of collected plays, 1990; As Much as I Dare (utobiography) 1994; Wild Spring, collected plays, volume 7. Honours: Royal Society of Literature, fellow, 1985; Honorary LittD, University of East Anglia; Honorary Fellow, Queen Mary University, London; Honorary LittD, Denison University, Ohio. Address: 37 Ashley Road, London N19 3AG, England.

WESLEY James. See: **RIGONI Orlando Joseph.**

WESLEY Mary. See: **SIEPMANN Mary Aline.**

WESLEY-SMITH Peter, b. 10 June 1945, Adelaide, South Australia. Professor of Law. Education: LLB, University of Adelaide, 1969; BA Hons in History, University of Adelaide, 1970; PhD, University of Hong Kong, 1976. Publications: The Ombley-Tombley, 1969; Hocus Pocus, 1975; Unequal Treaty 1898-1997, 1980; The Ombley-Gombley, 1969; Constitutional and Administrative Law in Hong Kong, 2nd edition, 1993; The Sources of Hong Kong Law, 1994; An Introduction to the Hong Kong Legal System, 2nd edition, 1993; Foul Fowl, 1995; The Hunting of the Snark: Second Expedition, 1996. Address: Faculty of Law, University of Hong Kong, Hong Kong.

WEST Anthony C(athcart Muir), b. 1 July 1910, County Down, Northern Ireland. Novelist. m. Olive Mary Burr, 1940, 11 children. Publications: River's End and Other Stories, 1958; The Native Moment, 1959; Rebel to Judgement, 1962; The Ferret Fancier, 1963; As Towns with Fire, 1968; All the King's Horses and Other Stories, 1981. Honours: Atlantic Award, 1946. Address: c/o Poolbeg Press, Knocksdean House, Forrest Great, Swords, County Dublin, Ireland.

WEST Ben, b. 30 Nov 1963, London, England. Writer. m. Bryony Imogen Menzies Clack, 14 Oct 1989, 1 son, 1 daughter. Publication: London for Free. Contributions to: Guardian; Daily Telegraph; Independent; Sunday Times; Sunday Telegraph; Daily Mail; Daily Express; Evening Standard. Address: 37 Vanbrugh Park, London, SE3 7AA, England.

WEST Cornel (Ronald), b. 2 June 1953, Tulsa, Oklahoma, USA. Professor of Afro-American Studies and the Philosophy of Religion; Writer. m. (1), div, 1 son, (2) div, (3) Elleni West. Education: AB, Harvard University, 1973; MA, 1975, PhD, 1980, Princeton University. Appointments: Assistant Professor of the Philosophy of Religion, Union Theological Seminary, New York City, 1977-83, 1988; Associate, Yale University Divinity School, 1984-87, University of Paris, 1987; Professor of Religion and Director of African American Studies, Princeton University, 1989-94; Professor of Afro-American Studies and the Philosophy of Religion, Harvard University, 1994-. Publications: Theology in the Americas: Detroit II Conference Papers (editor with Caridad Guidote and Margaret Coakley), 1982; Prophesy Deliverance!: An Afro-American Revolutionary Christianity, 1982; Post-Analytic Philosophy (with John Rajchman), 1985; Prophetic Fragments, 1988; The American Evasion of Philosophy: A Genealogy of Pragmatism, 1989; Breaking Bread: Insurgent Black Intellectual Life (with Bell Hooks), 1991; The Ethical Dimensions of Marxist Thought, 1991; Out There: Marginalization and Contemporary Cultures (co-editor), 1991; Race Matters, 1993; Keeping Faith: Philosophy and Race in America, 1993; Beyond Eurocentrism and Multiculturalism, 1993. Contributions to: Newspapers and magazines. Address: c/o Harvard University, Cambridge, MA 02138, USA.

WEST Douglas. See: **TUBB E(dwin) C(harles).**

WITT Harold Vernon, b. 6 Feb 1923, Santa Ana, California, USA. Freelance Writer; Editor. m. Beth Hewitt, 8 Sept 1948, 1 son, 2

daughters. Education: BA, 1943, BLS, 1953, University of California, Berkeley; MA, University of Michigan, 1947. Appointments: Co-Editor, California State Poetry Quarterly, 1976; Blue Unicorn, 1977-; Consulting Editor, Poet Lore, 1976-91. Publications: The Death of Venus, 1958; Beasts in Clothes, 1961; Now Swim, 1974; Suprised by Others at Fort Cronkhite, 1975; Winesburg by the Sea, 1979; The Snow Prince, 1982; Flashbacks and Reruns, 1985; The Light at Newport, 1992; American Literature, 1994. Contributions to: Journals and periodicals. Honours: Hopwood Award, 1947; Phelan Award, 1960; 1st Prize, San Francisco Poetry Centre poetic drama competition, 1963; Emily Dickinson Award, Poetry Society of America, 1972; Various Awards, World Order of Narrative Poets. Address: 39 Claremont Avenue, Orinda, CA 94563, USA.

WEST Morris (Langlo), (Morris East, Julian Morris), b. 26 Apr 1916, Melbourne, Victoria, Australia. Author. m. Joyce Lawford, 1953, 3 sons, 1 daughter. Education: University of Melbourne. Publications: Gallows on the Sand, 1955; Kundu, 1956; Children of the Sun, 1957; The Crooked Road (English Title, The Big Story), 1957; The Concubine, 1958; Backlash (English Title, The Second Victory), 1958; The Devil's Advocate, 1959 (filmed 1977); The Naked Country, 1960; Daughter of Silence (novel and play), 1961; The Shoes of the Fisherman, 1963; The Ambassador, 1965; The Tower of Babel, 1968; The Heretic, a Play in Three Acts, 1970; Scandal in the Assembly (with Robert Francis), 1970; Summer of the Red Wolf, 1971; The Salamander, 1973; Harlequin, 1974; The Navigator, 1976; Proteus, 1979; The Clowns of God, 1981; The World is Made of Glass, 1983 (play 1984); Cassidy, 1986; Masterclass, 1988; Lazarus, 1990; The Lovers, 1993; Vanishing Point, 1996; A View from the Ridge, 1996. Honours: National Brotherhood Award, National Council of Christians and Jews, 1960; James Tait Black Memorial Prize, 1960; Royal Society of Literature, Heinemann Award, 1960; Hon DLitt, Santa Clara University, 1969, Mercy College, New York, 1982, University of Western Sydney, 1993, Australian National University, 1995; Order of Australia, 1985. Memberships: Fellow, Royal Society of Literature; World Academy of Arts and Science. Address: PO Box 102, Avalon, New South Wales 2107, Australia.

WEST Nigel, b. 8 Nov 1951, London, England. Historian. m. 15 June 1979, 1 son, 1 daughter. Education: University of Grenoble; University of Lille; London University. Appointments: BBC TV, 1977-82. Publications: A Matter of Trust M15 1945-72, 1982; Unreliable Witness, 1984; Carbo M15, 1981, M16, 1983, 1985; GCHQ, 1986; Molehunt, 1986; The Friends, 1987; Games of Intelligence, 1990; Seven Spies who Changed the World, 1991; Secret War, 1992; The Illegals, 1993; Faber Book of Espionage, 1993; Faber Book of Treachery, 1995. Contributions to: Times; Intelligence Quarterly. Honour: The Experts Expert, Observer, 1989. Address: Westintel Research Ltd, PO Box 2, Goring on Thames, Berks RG8 9SB, England.

WEST Sally. See: HASTREITER Marge Thielman.

WESTHEIMER David, (Z Z Smith), b. 11 Apr 1917, Houston, Texas, USA. Writer. m. Doris Rothstein Kahn, 9 Oct 1945, 2 sons. Education: BA, Rice Institute, Houston, 1937. Publications: Summer on the Water, 1948; The Magic Fallacy, 1950; Watching Out for Dulie, 1960; This Time Next Year, 1963; Von Ryan's Express, 1964; My Sweet Charlie, 1965; Song of the Young Sentry, 1968; Lighter Than a Feather, 1971; Over the Edge, 1972; Going Public, 1973; The Aulia Gold, 1974; The Olmec Head, 1974; Von Ryan's Return, 1980; Rider on the Wind, 1984; Sitting it Out, 1992. Memberships: Authors Guild; PEN; California Writers Club; Retired Officers Association; Writers Guild of America West. Address: 11722 Darlington Avenue, No 2, Los Angeles, CA 90049, USA.

WESTON Corinne Comstock, b. 8 Dec 1919, Maine, USA. Professor of History. m. Arthur Weston, 17 Oct 1947. Education: BA History, University of Maine, 1941; PhD, History, Columbia University, 1951. Appointment: Membership, Fulbright-Hays National Screening Committee, 1974-78. Publications: Cardinal Documents in British History, 1951; British Constitutional History Since 1832, 1957; English Constitutional Theory and the House of Lords 1556-1832, 1965; Subjects and Sovereigns: The Grand Controversy Over Legal Sovereignty in Stuart England, 1981; The House of Lords and Ideological Politics, 1995. Honours: Phi Beta Kappa, 1941; Royal Historical Society, 1973-97; American Historical Association; American Philosophical Society, John Frederick Lewis Award, and Speaker, 1995; City University of New York Research Awards, 1979-88;

National Endowment for the Humanities Research Travel Grant, 1986; University of Paris, 1986 Annales, Special Recognition for Original Research. Address: 200 Central Park South, New York, NY 10019-1415, USA.

WESTON Helen Gray. See: DANIELS Dorothy.

WESTRICK Elsie Margaret Beyer, b. 12 Nov 1910, Fort William, Ontario, Canada. Poet; Writer. m. Roswell G Westrick, 6 Oct 1945, 5 daughters, 2 stepsons, 1 stepdaughter. Education: Diploma, Institute of Childrens Literature, 1976; Diploma, Writing for Young People, 1985; Diploma, Writing Self Fiction, 1989, Writers Digest School. Publications: Poetry: On This Holy Night, 1949; Tender Foliage of Summer, 1972; The Photograph, 1975; Beauty on a Beach, 1983; Memories of Childhood, 1983; The Breath of Fall, 1986; Call of the Blue Jay, 1987; The Breath of Fall, 1986; My Last Love, 1989; The Old Lighthouse, 1990; My Special Place, 1993; All We Hold Dear, 1996. Honours: Golden Poet Awards, World of Poetry, 1985, 1986; Award for Poetic Achievement, 1988; Silver Poet Award, World of Poetry, 1990. Address: 3751 Wheeler Road, Snover, MI 48472, USA.

WEVILL David (Anthony), b. 15 Mar 1935, Yokohama, Japan. Lecturer; Poet. m. Assia Gutman, 1960. Education: BA, Caius College, Cambridge, 1957. Appointment: Lecturer, University of Texas, Austin. Publications: Penguin Modern Poets, 1963; Birth of a Spark, 1964; A Christ of the Ice Floes, 1966; Firebreak, 1971; Where the Arrow Falls, 1973; Other Names for the Heart: New and Selected Poems, 1964-84, 1985; Figures of Eight, 1987; Translator of Hungarian Poetry. Honour: Arts Council Prize and Bursaries. Address: Department of English, University of Texas at Austin, TX 78712, USA.

WEYL Brigitte Ruth, b. Munich, Germany. Publisher. Education: MD, 1951, Freiburg; Medical State Examination, 1950; Medical Examination for Foreigners, Basel. Appointments: Medical Work, 1951-56; Editor, Die Presse, Vienna, 1957-68; Publisher, Sudkurier, Konstanz, 1959-89; Sudverlag und Universitatsverlag Konstanz, 1959-; Founder, Publisher, UVK Fachverlag für Wissenschaft und Studium GmbH, 1993. Contributions to: Die Presse; Sudkurier; Publizistik. Honours: Honorary President, Deutsch Französische Vereinigung Konstanz, 1979-; Officer de l'Order National du Merite, 1983; Bundesverdienstkreuz 1K1, 1984; Ehrensenatorin Universitat Konstanz, 1991; Honorary President, Gesellschaft der Freunde und Forderer der Universität Konstanz, 1995-. Memberships: International Press Institut; Gesellschaft der Freunde und Forderer der Universitat Konstanz; Stifervereinigung für die Deutsche Wissenschaft, Landeskuratorium Baden Württemberg; Vereinigung Deutsch Franzosischer Gesellschaften in Deutschland und Frankreich, Kuratorium. Address: PO Box 1020 51, D-78420 Konstanz, Germany.

WHALEN Philip (Glenn), b. 20 Oct 1923, Portland, Oregon, USA. Poet; Novelist; Zen Buddhist Priest. Education: BA, Reed College, Portland, Oregon, 1951. Appointments: Writer, 1951-; Ordained Zen Buddhist Priest, 1973; Head Monk, Dharma Sangha, Santa Fe, New Mexico, 1984-87; Abbot, Hartford Street Zen Center, San Francisco, 1987-. Publications: Poetry: Three Satires, 1951; Self-Portrait from Another Direction, 1959; Memoirs of an Interglacial Age, 1960; Like I Say, 1960; Hymnus ad Patrem, 1963; Three Mornings, 1964; Monday in the Evening, 1964; Goddess, 1964; Every Day, 1965; Highgrade: Doodles, Poems, 1966; T/o, 1967; The Invention of the Letter: A Beastly Morality Being an Illuminated Moral History for the Edification of Younger Readers, 1967; Intransit: The Philip Whalen Issue, 1967; On Bear's Head, 1969; Severance Pay, 1970; Scenes of Life at the Capital, 1971; The Kindness of Strangers: Poems, 1969-74, 1976; Prolegomena to a Study of the Universe, 1976; Decompressions: Selected Poems, 1978; Enough Said: Poems 1974-1979, 1981; Heavy Breathing: Poems 1967-1980, 1983. Novels: You Didn't Even Try, 1967; Imaginary Speeches for a Brazen Head, 1971. Other: Off the Wall: Interviews with Philip Whalen, 1978; The Diamond Noodle, 1980. Contributions to: Anthologies and many periodicals. Honours: Poets Foundation Award, 1962; V K Ratcliff Award, 1964; American Academy of Arts and Letters Grants-in-Aid, 1965, 1991; Committee on Poetry Grants, 1968, 1970, 1971; Morton Dauwen Zabel Award for Poetry, 1986; Fund for Poetry Awards, 1987, 1991, Address: c/o Hartford Street Zen Center, 57 Hartford Street, San Francisco, CA 94114, USA.

WHALEN Terry Anthony, b. 1 Feb 1944, Halifax, Nova Scotia, Canada. Professor of English; Editor. m. Maryann Antonia Walters, 30 Feb 1966, 2 sons, 2 daughters. Education: BA, Honours, Saint Mary's

University, 1965; MA, Honours, University of Melbourne, 1968; International Graduate Seminar Certificate, Oxford University, 1970; PhD, University of Ottawa, 1980. Appointments: Tutor, University of Sydney, 1966, University of Melbourne, 1967; Lecturer, 1968-70, Assistant Professor, 1970-76, 1978-80, Associate Professor, 1981-85, Professor of English, 1985-, St Mary's University; Teaching Fellow, University of Ottawa, 1976-77; Editor, Atlantic Provinces Book Review, 1980-90. Publications: Philip Larkin and English Poetry, 1986, reprinted 1990; Bliss Carman and His Works, 1983; The Atlantic Anthology: Criticism (editor), 1985; Charles G D Roberts and His Works, 1989; Poutledge Encyclopaedia of Post-Colonial Literature in English (contributor), 1994. Contributions to: Books, journals and periodicals. Honours: British Commonwealth Scholarship, 1966-68; Election to Council Member Status, Writers' Federation of Nova Scotia; Grants: Canada Council; Social Sciences and Humanities Research Council of Canada; Canadian Federation for the Humanities. Memberships: Writers Federation of Nova Scotia; Association of Canadian University Teachers of English; Northeast Modern Language Association; Modern Language Association. Address: 26 Oceanview Drive, Purcells Cove, Halifax, Nova Scotia B3P 2H3, Canada.

WHAM David Buffington, b. 25 May 1937, Evanston, USA. Political Writer. m. 3 Mar 1968, 1 son, 1 daughter. Education: BA, Harvard. Appointments: Co-author, Offical Report on Poor People's March for Jobs and Income, 1968; Speech Writer, Congressman James R Mann, 1970-76; Speech Writer, Adlai E Stevenson III, Democratic Candidate for Governor, Illinois, 1986. Publication: There is a Green Hill, 1967. Contributions to: December Magazine; Story Quarterly; Woodwind; The Fair Brandy, a Novella, 1966; Maelstrom; Means; Pilgrimage; etc. Honours: 1st Prize, Maelstrom Magazine, 1968. Literary Agent: Gerald McCauley, New York City. Address: 860 Hinman Avenue #724, Evanston, IL 60202, USA.

WHEATCROFT John Stewart, b. 24 July 1925, Philadelphia, Pennsylvania, USA. College Professor; Writer; Poet. m. (1) Joan Mitchell Osborne, 10 Nov 1952, div. 1974, 2 sons, 1 daughter, (2) Katherine Whaley Warner, 14 Nov 1992. Education: BA, Bucknell University, 1949; MS, 1950, PhD, 1960, Rutgers University. Appointment: Director, Stadler Center for Poetry, Bucknell University, Lewisbug, Pennsylvania. Publications: Poetry: Death of a Clown, 1963; Prodigal Son, 1967; A Voice from the Hump, 1977; Ordering Demons, 1981; The Stare on the Donkey's Face, 1990. Novels: Edie Tells, 1975; Catherine, Her Book, 1983; The Beholder's Eye, 1987; Killer Swan, 1992. Other: Slow Exposures (stories), 1986; Our Other Voices (editor), interviews with poets, 1991; Mother of All Loves, 1994; Trio with Four Players, 1995. Contributions to: Newspapers and magazines. Honours: Alcoa Playwriting Award, 1966; National Educational Television Award, 1967; Fellowships: Yaddo, 1972, 1985; MacDowell Colony, 1973; Virginia Center for the Creative Arts, 1976, 1978, 1980, 1982. Memberships: Poetry Society of America; PEN. Address: Stadler Center for Poetry, Bucknell University, Lewisburg, PA 17837, USA.

WHEELWRIGHT Julie Diana, b. 2 June 1960, Farnborough, Kent, England. Writer; Broadcaster. Education: BA, University of British Columbia; MA, University of Sussex. Appointments: Reporter, Vancouver Sun, 1980; President, Canadian University Press, 1981; Consultant, Open University, 1991. Publications: Amazons and Military Maids, 1989, 2nd edition, 1994; The Fatal Lover, 1992. Contributions to: Newspapers and journals. Honours: Canada Council Non Fiction Writers Grants, 1990-91, 1994-95. Memberships: Writers Guild; Institute of Historical Research; Honorary Research fellow, Royal Holloway, University of London. Address: 5 Cleaver Street, London SE11 4DP, England.

WHELAN Peter, b. 3 Oct 1931, Newcastle-under-Lyme, England. Playwright. Education: Graduated, Keele University, Staffordshire, 1955. Appointments: Advertising Copywriter and Director, 1959-90. Publications: Lakota (co-author), 1970; Double Edge (co-author), 1975; Captain Swing, 1978; The Accrington Pals, 1981; Clay, 1982; A Cold Wind Blowing Up (co-author), 1983; Worlds Apart, 1986; The Bright and Bold Design, 1991; The School of Night, 1992. Honours: Two Writers Guild Best Play Nominations. Address: c/o Lemon, Unna, and Durbridge, 24 Pottery Lane, Holland Park, London W11 4LZ, England.

WHETTON Peter, b. 30 Nov 1939, Manchester, England. Natural Therapist; Teacher. m. Maureen, 28 Dec 1965, 1 son. Publications: Can You Cope, 1978; Getting a Job, 1979; In ihe Job, 1979; Enhanced

Eduk Brain Gym, 1985; Accelerated Learning, 1992; Partners in Responsible Behaviour, 1993; Lifetime Learning for Pre Schoolers, 1990. Contributions to: Times Educational Supplement; SIT Journal; Special Education. Membership: Australian Society of Authors. Address: PO Box 343, Clarendon, 5157 Australia.

WHISTLER (Alan Charles) Laurence, b. 21 Jan 1912, Eltham, Kent. Writer; Glass Engraver; Poet. m. Jill Furse, 1939, dec 1944. Education: BA, Balliol College, Oxford, 1934. Publications: Children of Hertha and Other Poems, 1929; Armed October and Other Poems, 1932; Four Walls, 1934; The Emperor Heart, 1936; The Burning Glass, 1941; Who Live in Unity, 1944; The World's Room: The Collected Poems of Laurence Whistler, 1949; The View from This Window, 1956; Audible Silence, 1961; Fingal's Cave, 1963; To Celebrate Her Living, 1967; For Example: Ten Sonnets in Sequence to a New Pattern, 1969; A Bridge on the Usk, 1976; Enter, 1987. Other: Sir John Vanbrugh: Architect and Dramatist, 1664-1726, 1938; Rex Whistler, 1905-1944: His Life and His Drawings, 1948; The Initals in the Heart, 1964; The Image on the Glass, 1975; The Laughter and the Urn: The Life of Rex Whistler, 1985. Honours: Officer of the Order of the British Empire, 1955; Commander of the Order of the British Empire, 1973; Honorary Fellow, Balliol College, Oxford, 1973. Address: c/o The College Secretary, Balliol College, Oxford, England.

WHITBY Sharon. See: PETERS Maureen.

WHITE Edmund (Valentine III), b. 13 Jan 1940, Cincinnati, Ohio, USA. Writer. Education: BA, University of Michigan, 1962. Appointments: Writer, Time-Life Books, New York City, 1962-70; Senior Editor, Saturday Review, New York City, 1972-73; Assistant Professor of Writing Seminars, Johns Hopkins University, 1977-79; Adjunct Professor, Columbia University School of the Arts, 1981-83; Executive Director, New York Institute for the Humanities, 1982-83; Professor, Brown University, 1990-92. Publications: Fiction: Forgetting Elena, 1973; Nocturnes for the King of Naples, 1978; A Boy's Own Story, 1982; Aphrodisiac (with others), stories, 1984; Caracole, 1985; The Darker Proof: Stories from a Crisis (with Adam Mars-Jones), 1987; The Beautiful Room is Empty, 1988; Skinned Alive, stories, 1995; The Farewell Symphony, 1997. Non-Fiction: The Joy of Gay Sex: An Intimate Guide for Gay Men to the Pleasures of a Gay Lifestyle (with Charles Silverstein), 1977; States of Desire: Travels in Gay America, 1980; The Faber Book of Gay Short Fiction (editor), 1991; Genet: A Biography, 1993; The Selected Writings of Jean Genet (editor), 1993; The Burning Library, essays, 1994; Our Paris, 1995. Contributions to: Many periodicals. Honours: Ingram Merrill Foundation Grants, 1973, 1978; Guggenheim Fellowship, 1983; American Academy and Institute of Arts and Letters Award, 1983; Chevalier de l'ordre des arts et lettres, France, 1993; American Academy of Arts and Letters. Address: c/o Maxine Groffsky Literary Agency, 2 Fifth Avenue, New York, NY 10011, USA.

WHITE Gillian Mary, b. 13 Jan 1936, Essex, England. Retired University Professor. m. Colin A Fraser, 1 Apr 1978. Education: LLB, 1957; PhD, 1960, Barrister, Grays Inn, 1960. Appointment: Professor of Law, University of Manchester. Publications: The Use of Experts by International Tribunals, 1965; Principles of International Economic Law, 1988; International Economic Law and Developing States, 1992; International Law in Transition, 1992; Good Faith, 1994. Memberships: British Institute of International and Comparative Law; International Law Association; American Society of International Law; Royal Society of Arts. Address: c/o Faculty of Law, University of Manchester, Manchester M13 9PL.

WHITE Jon (Ewbank) Manchip, b. 22 June 1924, Cardiff, Glamorganshire, Wales. Writer; Poet; Professor of English. m. Valerie Leighton, 2 children. Education: St Catherine's College, Cambridge, 1942-43, 1946-50; Open Exhibitioner in English Literature; MA with Honours in English, Prehistoric Archaeology, and Oriental Languages (Egyptology), and University Diploma in Anthropology. Appointments: Story Editor, BBC-TV, London, 1950-51; Senior Executive Officer, British Foreign Service, 1952-56; Independent Author, 1956-67, including a period as screenwriter for Samuel Bronston Productions, Paris and Madrid, 1960-64; Professor of English, University of Texas, El Paso, 1967-77; Lindsay Young Professor of English, University of Tennessee, Knoxville, 1977-94. Publications: Novels: Mask of Dust, 1953; Build Us a Dam, 1955; The Girl from Indiana, 1956; No Home But Heaven, 1957; The Mercenaries, 1958; Hour of the Rat, 1962; The Rose in the Brandy Glass, 1965; Nightclimber, 1968; The Game of Troy, 1971; The Garden Game, 1973; Send for Mr Robinson, 1974;

The Moscow Papers, 1979; Death by Dreaming, 1981; The Last Grand Master, 1985; Whistling Past the Churchyard, 1992. Poetry: Dragon and Other Poems, 1943; Salamander and Other Poems, 1945; The Rout of San Romano, 1952; The Mountain Lion, 1971. Other: Ancient Egypt, 1952; Anthropology, 1954; Marshal of France: The Life and Times of Maurice, Comte de Saxe, 1962; Everyday Life in Ancient Egypt, 1964; Diego Velázquez, Painter and Courtier, 1969; The Land God Made in Anger: Reflections on a Journey Through South West Africa, 1969; Cortés and the Downfall of the Aztec Empire, 1971; A World Elsewhere: One Man's Fascination with the American Southwest, 1975; Everyday Life of the North American Indians, 1979; What to do When the Russians Come: A Survivors' Handbook (with Robert Conquest), 1984; The Journeying Boy: Scenes from a Welsh Childhood, 1991. Memberships: Texas Institute of Letters, 1970; Honorary, Phi Beta Kappa, 1992; Welsh Academy, 1995. Literary Agent: Wallace Agency, 177 East 70th Street, New York, NY 10021, USA. Address: 6817 Northshore Drive, Knoxville, TN 37919, USA.

WHITE Kenneth, b. 28 Apr 1936, Glasgow, Scotland. Professor of 20th Century Poetics; Poet; Writer. m. Marie Claude Charfut. Education: MA, University of Glasgow, 1959; University of Munich; University of Paris. Appointments: Lecturer in English, Institut Charles V, Paris, 1969-83; Professor of 20th Century Poets, Sorbonne, University of Paris, 1983-. Publications: Poetry: Wild Coal, 1963; En Toute Candeur, 1964; The Cold Wind of Dawn, 1966; The Most Difficult Area, 1968; A Walk Along the Shore, 1977; Mahamudra, 1979; Le Grand Rivage, 1980; Terre de diament, 1983; Atlantica: Mouvements et meditations, 1986; L'esprit nomade, 1987; The Bird Bath: Collected Longer Poems, 1989; Handbook for the Diamond Country: Collected Shorter Poems 1960-1990, 1990. Fiction: Letters from Gourgounel, 1966; Les Limbes Incandescents, 1978; Le Visage du vent d'Est, 1980; La Route Bleue, 1983; Travels in the Drifting Dawn, 1989; Pilgrim of the Viod, 1994. Other: Essays. Contributions to: Various publications. Honour: Grand Prix de Rayonnement, French Academy, 1985. Address: Gwenved, Chemin du Goaquer, 22560 Trebeurden, France.

WHITE Robert Rankin, b. 8 Feb 1942, Houston, Texas, USA. Historian; Writer. Education: BA, Geology, University of Texas, Austin, 1964; MS, Hydrology, University of Arizona, 1971; PhD, American Studies, University of New Mexico, 1993. Publications: The Lithographs and Etchings of E Martin Hennings, 1978; The Taos Society of Artists, 1983; Bert Geer Phillips and the Taos Art Colony (co-author), 1994. Contributions to: Journals and periodicals. Memberships: New Mexico Book League, president, 1994, executive director, 1996-; First Friday; Historical Society of New Mexico, president, 1991-93. Address: 1409 Las Lomas Road North East, Albuquerque, NM 87106, USA.

WHITE W(illiam) Robin(son), b. 12 July 1928, Kodaikanal, South India. Author. m. Marian Biesterfeld, 3 Feb 1948, 2 sons, 1 daughter. Education: BA, Yale University, 1950; Bread Loaf Fellow, Middlebury College, 1956; Stegner Creative Writing Fellow, Stanford University, 1956-57; MA, California State Polytechnic University. Appointments: Editor-in-Chief, Per-Se International Quarterly, Stanford University Press, 1965-69; Instructor, Photojournalism, 1973, Director, Creative Writing Seminar, 1984, Mendocino Art Center; Lecturer, Writing Programme, Scripps College, 1984; Fiction Editor, West-word literary magazine, 1985-90; Instructor, Writer's Programme, University of California, Los Angeles, 1985-; Research Reader, The Huntington Library, 1985-86; Lecturer, Writing Programme and CompuWrite, California State Polytechnic University, 1985-93. Publications: House of Many Rooms, 1958; Elephant Hill, 1959; Men and Angels, 1961; Foreign Soil, 1962; All In Favor Say No, 1964; His Own Kind, 1967; Be Not Afraid, 1972; The Special Child, 1978; The Troll of Crazy Mule Camp, 1979; Moses the Man, 1981; The Winning Writer, 1997. Contributions to: Journals and magazines. Honours: Harper Prize, 1959; O Henry Prize, 1960; Coordinating Council of Literary Magazines Award, 1968; Distinguished Achievement Award, Educational Press, 1974; Spring Harvest Poetry Awards, 1992, 1994, 1995. Memberships: Authors Guild; California State Poetry Society. Literary Agent: Curtis Brown. Address: 1940 Fletcher Avenue, South Pasadena, CA 91300, USA.

WHITEHORN Katharine (Elizabeth), b. 2 Mar 1928, London, England. Writer. Education: BA, Newham College, London, 1950; Graduate Studies, Cornell University, Ithaca, New York, 1954-55. Appointments: Staff, Picture Post, London, 1956-57, Womans Own, London, 1958, Spectator, 1959-61; Fashion Editor, 1960-63,

Columnist, 1963-, The Observer; Board Member, British Airports Authority, 1972-77; Rector, St Andrews University, 1982-85; Board Member, Nationwide Building Society, 1983-91. Publications: Cooking in a Bedsitter, 1960; Roundabout, 1961; Only on Sundays, 1966; Whitehorn's Social Survival, 1968; Observations, 1970; How to Survive in Hospital, 1972; How to Survive Children, 1975; How to Survive in the Kitchen, 1979; How to Survive Your Money Problems, 1983; View from a Column, 1991. Contributions to: Newspapers and magazines. Address: 119 Farringdon Road, London EC1R 3ER, England.

WHITEHOUSE David Bryn, b. 15 Oct 1941, Worksop, England. Writer; Editor. Education: BA, 1963, MA, 1964, PhD, 1967, Cambridge University. Appointments: Correspondent, Archeologia Medievale; Editor, Journal of Glass Studies, 1988-; Advisory Editor, American Early Medieval Studies, 1991-; Advisory Board, Encyclopedia of Islamic Archaeology, 1991. Publications: Author: Glass of the Roman Empire, 1988; Glass: A Pocket Dictionary, 1993; English Cameo Glass, 1994. Co-Author: Archaeological Atlas of the World, 1975; Aspects of Medieval Lazio, 1982; Mohammed, Charlemagne and the Origins of Europe, 1983; Glass of the Caesars, 1987; The Portland Vase, 1990; Treasures from the Corning Museum of Glass, 1992. Contributions to: Books, journals, and other publications. Memberships: Accademia Fiorentina delle Arti del Disegno; International Association for the History of Glass, president, 1991-94; Keats-Shelley Memorial Association, Rome, president, 1982-83; Pontificia Accademia Romana di Archeologia; Royal Geographical Society; Society of Antiquaries of London; Unione Internazione degli istituti di Archeologia, Storia e Storia dell'Arte in Roma, president, 1980-81. Address: c/o Corning Museum of Glass, One Museum Way, Corning, NY 14830-2252, USA.

WHITFIELD Stephen Jack, b. 3 Dec 1942, Houston, Texas, USA. University Teacher; Writer. m. Lee Cone Hall, 15 Dec 1984. Education: BA, Tulane University, 1964; MA, Yale University, 1966; PhD, Brandeis University, 1972. Appointments: Faculty, Brandeis University; Book Review Editor, American Jewish History, 1979-86; Contributing Editor, Moment Magazine, 1980-87. Publications: Scott Nearing: Apostle of American Radicalism, 1974; Into the Dark: Hannah Arendt and Totalitarianism, 1980; A Critical American: The Politics of Dwight Macdonald, 1984; Voices of Jacob, Hands of Esau: Jews in American Life and Thought, 1984; American Space, Jewish Time, 1988; A Death in the Delta: The Story of Emmett Till, 1988; The Culture of the Cold War, 1991. Contributions to: Journals. Honours: Kayden Prize, 1981; Rockefeller Foundation Fellow, Bellagio, Italy, 1991. Memberships: American Humor Studies Association; American Jewish Historical Society; American Studies Association. Address: c/o Department of American Studies, Brandeis University, Waltham, MA 02254, USA.

WHITMAN Ruth (Bashein), b. 28 May 1922, New York, New York, USA. Poet; Editor; Translator; Teacher. m. (1) Cedric Whitman, 13 Oct 1941, div 1958, 2 daughters, (2) Firman Houghton, 23 July 1959, div. 1964, 1 son, (3) Morton Sacks, 6 Oct 1966. Education: BA, Radcliffe College, 1944; MA, Harvard University, 1947. Appointments: Editorial Assistant, 1941-42, Educational Editor, 1944-45, Houghton Mifflin Co, Boston; Freelance Editor, Harvard University Press, 1945-60; Poetry Editor, Audience magazine, 1958-63; Director, Poetry Workshop, Cambridge Center for Adult Education, 1964-68, and Poetry in the Schools Program, Massachusetts on the Arts, 1970-73; Scholar-in-Residence, Radcliffe Institute, 1968-70; Instructor in Poetry, Radcliffe College, 1970-, and Harvard University Writing Program, 1979-84; Writer-in-Residence and Visiting Lecturer at various colleges and universities; many poetry readings. Publications: Blood and Milk Poems, 1963; Alain Bosquet: Selected Poems (translator with others), 1963; Isaac Bashevis Singer: The Seance (translator with others), 1968; The Marriage Wig, and Other Poems, 1968; The Selected Poems of Jacob Glatstein (editor and translator), 1972; The Passion of Lizzie Borden: New and Selected Poems, 1973; Poemaking: Poets in Classrooms, editor, 1975; Tamsen Donner: A Woman's Journey, 1975; Permanent Address: New Poems, 1973-1980, 1980; Becoming a Poet: Source, Process, and Practice, 1982; The Testing of Hanna Senesh, 1986; The Fiddle Rose: Selected Poems of Abraham Sutzkever (translator), 1989; Laughing Gas: Poems New and Selected, 1963-1990, 1991; Hatsheput, Speak to Me, 1992. Contributions to: Anthologies and periodicals. Honours: MacDowell Colony Fellowships, 1962, 1964, 1972-74, 1979, 1982; Kovner Award, Jewish Book Council of America, 1969; Guiness International Poetry Award, 1973; National Endowment for the Arts Grant, 1974-75; John Masefield Award, 1976; Senior Fulbright Fellowship, 1984-85; Urbanarts Award, 1987; Phi Beta

Kappa. Memberships: Authors Guild; Authors League of America; New England Poetry Club; PEN; Poetry Society of America. Address: 40 Tuckerman Avenue, Middletown, RI 02840, USA.

WHITTEN Leslie H(unter) Jr, b. 21 Feb 1928, Jacksonville, Florida, USA. Writer; Journalist. m. Phyllis Webber, 11 Nov 1951, 3 sons, 1 daughter. Education: BA, English and Journalism, Lehigh University. Publications: Progeny of the Adder, 1965; Moon of the Wolf, 1967; Pinion, The Golden Eagle, 1968; The Abyss, 1970; F Lee Bailey, 1971; The Alchemist, 1973; Conflict of Interest, 1976; Washington Cycle (poems), 1979; Sometimes a Hero, 1979; A Killing Pace, 1983; A Day Without Sunshine, 1985; The Lost Disciple, 1989; The Fangs of Morning, 1994. Contributions to: Newspapers and literary magazines. Honours: Doctor, Humane Letters, Lehigh University, 1989; Journalistic Awards, Edgerton Award, American Civil Liberties Union. Memberships: Washington Independent Writers; Investigative Reporters and Editors; Authors Guild. Address: 114 Eastmoor Drive, Sliver Spring, MD 20901, USA.

WHITTEN Norman E(arl) Jr, b. 23 May 1937, Orange, New Jersey, USA. Professor of Anthropology and Latin America. m. Dorothea S Whitten, 4 Aug 1962. Education: BA, Colgate University, 1959; MA, 1961, PhD, 1964, University of North Carolina, Chapel Hill. Appointments: Associate Professor, 1970-73, Professor of Anthropology, 1973- University of Illinois; Editor, Boletin de Antropologia Ecuatoriana, 1973-76, Anthropology Newsletter, Latin American Anthropology Group, 1973-76; American Ethnologist, 1979-84. Publications: Class Kinship and Power in an Ecuadorian Town, 1965; Afro-American Anthropology (editor), 1970; Sacha Runa: Ethnicity and Adaptation of Ecuadorian Jungle Quichua, 1976; Cultural Transformations and Ethnicity in Modern Ecuador (editor), 1981; Amazonia Ecuatoria, La Otro Cara del Progreso, 1981; BlackFrontiersmen: Afro-Hispanic Culture of Ecuador and Colombia, 1985; Sicuanga Runa: The Other Side of Development in Amazonian Ecuador, 1985; Art, Knowledge and Health (with Dorothea S Whitten), 1985; From Myth to Creation: Art from Amazonian Ecuador (with Dorothea S Whitten), 1988; Pioneros Negros: La Cultura Afro-Latinoamericana del Ecuador y de Colombia, 1992; Imagery and Creativity: Ethnoaesthetics and Art Worlds in the Americas (with Dorothea S Whitten), 1993; Transformaciones Culturales y Etnicidad en la Sierra Ecuatoriana, 1993. Contributions to: Professional journals. Honours: Author's Award in Anthropology, New Jersey Teachers Association, 1966; Society of Sigma Xi. Memberships: American Anthropological Association, 1975-78, Representative to American Association for the Advancement of Science, executive board, 1990-95; American Ethnological Association, executive board 1980-84; Latin American Studies Association, executive board 1983-87; Society of Cultural Anthropology; Royal Anthropological Institute. Address: 507 Harding Drive, Urbana, IL 61801, USA.

WHITTINGTON Peter. See: MACKAY James Alexander.

WIATER Stanley, b. 21 May 1953, Northampton, Massacusetts, USA. Author; Editor. m. Iris D Arroyo, 21 Sept 1985, 1 daughter. Education: Bachelor's Degree, Magna Cum Laude, University of Massachusetts, Amherst, 1975. Publications: Night Visions 7 (editor), 1989; Dark Dreamers: Conversations with the Masters of Horror, 1990; The Official Teenage Mutant Ninja Turtles Treasury, 1991; Dark Visions: Conversations with the Masters of the Horror Film, 1992; After the Darkness (editor), 1993; Comic Book Rebels: Conversations with the Creators of the New Comics (with Stephen R Bissette), 1993. Contributions to: Fangoria; Fear; New Blood; Horrorstruck; Twilight Zone Magazine; Cemetery Dance. Honour: Bram Stoker Award for Superior Achievement in Non-fiction, 1991. Memberships: Horror Writers Association, 1984; National Writers Union, 1990. Literary Agent: Tal Literary Agency, PO Box 1837, Leesburg, VA 20177, USA.

WICK Carter. See: WILCOX Colin.

WICKERT Erwin, b. 7 Jan 1915, Bralitz, Germany. Author; Retired Ambassador. m. Ingelborg Weides, 2 Oct 1939, 2 sons, 1 daughter. Education: Friedrich Wilhelm University, Berlin, 1934-35; BA, Dickinson College, 1936; PhD, University of Heidelberg, 1939. Publications: Der Auftrag des Himmels, 1961; Der Purpur, 1966; Mut und Ubermut, 1981; China von innen gesehen, 1982; Der verlassene Tempel, 1985; Der Kaiser und der Grosshistoriker, 1987; Zappas oder die Wiedeckehr des Herrn,1995. Contributions to: Frankfurter Allgemeine Zeitung; Die Welt. Honours: Radio Play Award, 1952; Grosses Bundesverdienstkreuz, 1979; State Prize of Literature.

Memberships: PEN, 1963-95; Academy of Science and Literature. Address; Rheinhöhenweg 22, Oberwinter, D 53424 Remagen, Germany.

WICKHAM Glynne, (William Gladstone), b. 15 May 1922, Capetown, South Africa. Writer; Broadcaster. Education: BA, 1946, MA, 1947, PhD, 1951, New College, Oxford. Appointments: Professor of Drama, Bristol University, 1960-82; Chairman, Radio West, 1979-84; National Commission to NESCO, 1984-86. Publications: The Relationship Between Universities and Radio, Film and Television, 1956; Drama in the World of Science, 1962; Early English Stages 3 vols in 4, 1959-81; The Medieval Theatre, 1974; English Moral Interludes, 1975, 2nd edition, 1985; The Theatre in Europe, 1979; A History of the Theatre, 1985, 2nd edition, 1992. Memberships: Polish Academy of Arts and Science; Hon Fellow, Britsol University, 1996-. Address: 6 College Road, Bristol 8, Avon, England.

WIDDOWSON John David Allison, b. 22 June 1935, Sheffield, England. University Lecturer. m. Carolyn Lois Crawford, 1 Sept 1960, 2 sons, 1 daughter. Education: BA, 1959, MA, 1963, Oxford University; MA, Leeds University, 1966; PhD, Newfoundland University, 1972. Appointments: Editor, Lore and Language, 1969; Member, Editorial Advisory Board, Rural History, 1990. Publications: Learning About Linguistics, 1974; The Linguistic Atlas of England, 1978; Language, Culture and Tradition, 1981; Dictionary of Newfoundland English, 1982; Studies in Linguistic Geography, 1985; Word Maps, 1987; Studies in Newfoundland Folklore, 1991; Survey of English Dialects: The Dictionary and Grammar, 1994; Folktales of Newfoundland, 1996; An Atlas of English Dialects, 1996. Contributions to: Numerous Articles and Reviews, 1962-. Honours: Certificate of Merit; Regional History Award; Folklore Fellows International. Memberships: Devonshire Association; Folklore Society, President, 1987-90, Vice President, 1990-; Societas Linguisticla Europaeia; American Folklore Society; Oral History Society; Canadian Oral History Society; Folklore Studies Association of Canada; Yorkshire Dialect Society. Address: The Centre for English Cultural, Tradition and Language, The University, Sheffield S10 2TN, England.

WIEMANN Marion Russell Jr, b. 7 Sept 1929, Chesterton, Indiana, USA. Biologist; Microscopist. 1 daughter. Education: BS, Indiana University, 1959; Cultural Doctorate, Biological Sciences, World University Roundtable, 1991; ScD, London Institute for Applied Research, 1994; ScD, World Academy, Germany, 1995; Professor of Science, Australian Institute for Coordinated Research, Australia, 1995. Publications: Tooth Decay: It's Cause and Prevention Through Controlled Soil Composition, 1985; Soil Fertility and Permanent Agriculture (in 3 parts), 1983; The Mechanism of Tooth Decay, 1985. Contributions to: Periodicals and journals. Honours: Award of Merit, 1973, Distinguished Technical Communicator Award, 1974, Society for Technical Communication. Membership: Fellow, World Literary Academy. Address: 418 South 9th Street, PO Box 1016, Chesterton, IN 46304, USA.

WIENER Joel Howard, b. 23 Aug 1937, New York, USA. Professor of History. m. Suzanne Wolff, 4 Sept 1961, 1 son, 2 daughters. Education: BA, New York University, 1959; Research Fellow, University of Glasgow, 1961-63; PhD, Cornell University, 1965; Associate Editor, New Dictionary of National Biogeaphy. Publications: The War of the Unstamped, 1969; A Descriptive Finding List of Unstamped Periodicals 1830-36, 1970; Great Britain: Foreign Policy and the Span of Empire (editor), 1972; Great Britain: The Lion at Home (editor), 1974; Radicalism and Freethought in 19th Century Britain, 1983; Innovators and Preachers: The Role of the Editor in Victorian England (editor), 1985; Papers for the Millions: The New Journalism in Britain c. 1850's-1914 (editor), 1988; William Lovett, 1989. Contributions to: Labor History; Journal of Social History; New Society; Victorian Periodicals Review; Albion; Journal of Modern History; Choice; English Literature In Transition; Victorian Studies; Listener; American Journalism; Nineteenth-Century Prose. Honour: Fellow, Royal Historical Society, 1974. Memberships: Research Society for Victorian Periodicals, president; American Historical Association; City University of New York, Academy for the Humanities and Sciences; American Journalism Historians Association; Conference on British Studies. Address: 267 Glen Court, Teaneck, NJ 07666, USA.

WIENERS John (Joseph), b. 6 Jan 1934, Milton, Massachusetts, USA. Poet; Dramatist; Writer. Education: BA, Boston College, 1954; Black Mountain College, North Carolina, 1955-56; State University of New York, Buffalo, 1965-69. Publications: The Hotel

Wentley Poems, 1958, revised edition, 1965; Still-Life (play), 1961; Asphodel in Hell's Despite, 1963; Ace Pentacles, 1964; Chinoiserie, 1965; Hart Crane, Harry Crosby, I See You Going Over the Edge, 1966; Anklesox and Five Shoelaces (play), 1966; King Solomon's Magnetic Quiz, 1967; Pressed Water, 1967; Selected Poems, 1968; Unhired, 1968; A Letter to Charles Olson, 1968; Asylum Poems, 1969; Untitled Essay on Frank O'Hara, 1969; A Memory of Black Mountain College, 1969; Nerves, 1970; Youth, 1970; Selected Poems, 1972; Woman, 1972; The Lanterns Along the Wall, 1972; Playboy, 1972; We Were There!, 1972; Holes, 1974; Behind the State Capitol, or, Cincinnati Pike, 1985; A Superficial Estimation, 1986; Conjugal Contraries and Quart, 1986; Cultural Affairs in Boston: Poetry and Prose, 1956-1985, 1988. Contributions to: Numerous periodicals. Honours: Poet's Foundation Award, 1961; New Hope Foundation Award, 1963; National Endowment for the Arts Grants, 1966, 1968, 1984; Academy Award, 1968; Guggenheim Fellowship, 1985. Address: 44 Joy Street, Apt 10, Boston, MA 02114, USA.

WIESEL Elie(zer), b. 30 Sept 1928, Sighet, Romania (US citizen). Professor; Author; Journalist. Appointments: Distinguished Professor of Judaic Studies, City College, City University of New York, 1972-76; Andrew W Mellon Professor in the Humanities, Professor of Religion, Professor of Philosophy, Boston University, Massachusetts, 1976-; Henry Luce Visiting Scholar in the Humanities and Social Thought, Whitney Humanities Centre, Yale University, 1982-83; Distinguished Visiting Professor of Literature and Philosophy, Florida International University, 1982; Journalist for Israeli, French and US Newspapers. Publications: Night (memoir), 1960; Dawn (novel), 1966; The Jews of Silence (personal testimony), 1966; Legends of Our Time (essays and stories), 1968; A Beggar in Jerusalem (novel), 1970; One Generation After (essays and stories), 1970; Souls on Fire: Portraits and Legends of the Hasidic Masters, 1972; The Oath (novel), 1973; Zalmen or the Madness of God (play), 1974; Messengers of God: Portraits and Legends of Biblical Heroes, 1976; Four Hasidic Masters, 1978; A Jew Today (essays, stories, dialogues), 1978; The Trial of God (play), 1979; The Testament (novel), 1980; Images from the Bible, 1980; Five Biblical Portraits, 1981; Somewhere a Master (Hasidic tales), 1982; Paroles d'etranger (essays, stories, dialogues), 1982; The Golem, retelling of Legend, 1983; The Fifth Son (novel), 1985; Signes d'Exode (essays, stories, dialogues), 1985; Against Silence: The Voice and Vision of Elie Wiesel (collected writings), 1985; Job ou Dieu dans la Tempete (dialogue and commentary with Josy Eisenberg), 1986; The Nobel Address, 1987; Twilight (novel), 1988; The Six Days of Destruction (with Albert Friedlander), 1988; Silences et memoire d'hommes (essays), 1989; L'Oublie (novel), 1989; From the Kingdom of Memory (reminiscences), 1990; Evil and Exile (dialogues with Philippe-Michael de Saint-Cheron), 1990; Sages and Dreamers, Portraits and Legends from the Bible, the Talmud and the Hasidic Tradition, 1991; Celebration Talmudique, Portraits of Talmudic Masters, 1991; The Forgotten, 1992; A Passover Hagaddah, 1993; All Rivers Run to the Sea, Memoirs, 1995; Memoir in Two Voices (with François Mitterand), 1996; Et la mer n'est pas remplie, memoirs, 1996. Honours: Congressional Gold Medal, 1984; Nobel Peace Prize, 1986; Presidential Medal of Freedom, 1992; Numerous others. Memberships: Various literary societies, including PEN. Address: 745 Commonwealth Avenue, Boston, MA 02215, USA.

WIESENFARTH Joseph John, b. 20 Aug 1933, Brooklyn, New York, USA. Professor of English. m. Louise Halpin, 21 Aug 1971, 1 son. Education: BA, Catholic University of America, 1956; MA, University of Detroit, 1959; PhD, Catholic University of America, 1962. Appointments: Assistant Professor, La Salle College, Philadelphia, 1962-64; Assistant Professor, 1964-67, Associate Professor, 1967-70, Manhattan College, New York; Associate Professor, 1970-76, Professor, 1976-, University of Wisconsin, Madison; Associate Editor, Renascence, 1972-76, 1992-; Associate Dean, Graduate School, 1995-96. Publications: Henry James and the Dramatic Analogy, 1963; The Errand of Form: An Essay of Jane Austen's Art, 1967; George Eliot's Mythmaking, 1977; George Eliot: A Writer's Notebook 1854-1879, 1981; Gothic Manners and the Classic English Novel, 1988. Contributions to: Numerous articles on British and American Fiction. Honours: Phi Beta Kappa, 1956; Fellow, National Endowment for the Humanities, 1967-68; Institute for Research in Humanities Fellow, 1975; Fulbright Fellow, 1981-82; Christian Gauss Prize Award Committee, 1986-88, 1989-90. Memberships: Modern Language Association; Jane Austen Society of North America; Henry James Society, Katherine Anne Porter Society. Address: Department of English, University of Wisconsin, 600 North Park Street, Madison, WI 53706, USA.

WIESENTHAL Simon, b. 31 Dec 1908, Poland. Writer. m. Cyla, 1 daughter. Education: Architectural Studies, Prague, Lvov. Appointment: Editor, Ausweg, 1960-. Publications: KZ Mauthausen, 1946; Head Mufti, 1947; Agent of the Axis, 1947; The Murderes Among Us, 1967; Sunflower, 1969; Sails of Hope, 1973; The Case of Krystyna Jaworska, 1975; Every Day Remembrance Day, 1986; Justice, Not Vengeance, 1989. Honours: Dutch Medal for Freedom; Jean Moulin Medaille; Kaj Munk medal; Commander Oranje Nassau, Queen Juliana of the Netherlands; Justice Brandeis Awards; Knight, Legion of Honour, France; Numerous others. Membership: Austrian PEN. Address: Salztorgasse 6, 1010 Vienna, Austria.

WIGG T I G. See: **McCUTCHAN Philip Donald.**

WIGNALL Anne, (Alice Acland, Anner Marreco), b. 12 June 1912, London, England. Writer. m. (1) Francis Egerton Grosvenor, Fifth Baron of Ebury, July 1933, div, 2 sons, (2) Barton Wignall, 12 Nov 1947, dec, 1 daughter, (3) Anthony Marreco, 1961, div. Education: Private. Publications: As Alice Acland: Biography: Caroline Norton, 1948; Novels: Templeford Park, 1954; A Stormy Spring, 1955; A Second Choice, 1956; A Person of Discretion, 1958; The Corsican Ladies, 1974; The Secret Wife, 1975; The Ruling Passion, 1976. As Anne Marreco: Biography: The Rebel Countess, 1967; Novels: The Charmer and The Charmed, 1963; The Boat Boy, 1964. Address: c/o Curtis Brown Ltd, Haymarket House, 28-29 Haymarket, London SW1Y 4SP, England.

WIKAN Unni, b. 18 Nov 1944, Ibesfad, Norway. Professor. m. Fredrik Barth, 30 Jan 1973, 1 son. Education: BA, Bergen University, 1968; PhD, Oslo University, 1980. Publications: Life Among the Poor in Cairo, 1980; Behind the Veil in Arabia: Women in Oman, 1982; Managing Turbulent Hearts: A Balinese Formula for Living, 1990; Tomorrow, God Willing: Self-Made Destinies in Cairo, 1996. Contributions to: American Anthropologist; American Ethnologist; Man; Ethos; Current Anthropology; Cultural Anthropology; Social Science and Medicine; Culture, Medicine and Psychiatry. Memberships: Norwegian Association of Professional Authors; American Anthropological Association; Society for Psychological Anthropology; European Association for Social Anthropologists. Address: Ethnographic Museum, Frederiksgate 2, Ol64, Oslo, Norway.

WIKHOLM-OSTLING Gungerd Helene, b. 14 Oct 1954, Karis, Finland. Writer; Journalist; Poet. m. Tom Seth Ostling, 14 Sept 1990, 2 daughters. Education: Svenska Social-Och Kommunalhogskolan, Helsingor, 1974-77. Appointment: Cultural Journalist, Finnish Broadcasting Company, 1977-. Publications: Torplandet (poetry), 1982; Aria (poetry), 1987; Anhalter, Svarta Och Roda (poetry), 1990; Ur Vattnets Arkiv (poetry), 1993; Stora Dagen, Lilla Natten (poetry), 1995. Contributions to: Columnes for Hufvudstadsbladet. Honours: Svenska Litteratursallskapet, 1988; Langmanska Fonden, 1993. Membership: Finlands Svenska Forfattareforening. Literary Agent: The Editor, Soderstroms-forlag. Address: Kilavägen 29 A3, Karis, Finland.

WILBUR Richard (Purdy), b. 1 Mar 1921, New York, New York, USA. Poet; Writer; Translator; Editor; Professor. m. Mary Charlotte Hayes Ward, 20 June 1942, 3 sons, 1 daughter. Education: AB, Amherst College, 1942; AM, Harvard University, 1947. Appointments: Assistant Professor of English, Harvard University, 1950-54; Associate Professor of English, Wellesley College, 1955-57; Professor of English, Wesleyan University, 1957-77; Writer-in-Residence, Smith College, 1977-86; Poet Laureate of the USA, 1987-88; Visiting Lecturer at various colleges and universities. Publications: Poetry: The Beautiful Changes and Other Poems, 1947; Ceremony and Other Poems, 1950; Things of This World, 1956; Poems, 1943-1956, 1957; Advice to a Prophet and Other Poems, 1961; The Poems of Richard Wilbur, 1963; Walking to Sleep: New Poems and Translations, 1969; Digging to China, 1970; Seed Leaves: Homage to R F, 1974; The Mind-Reader: New Poems, 1976; Seven Poems, 1981; New and Collected Poems, 1988. For Children: Loudmouse, 1963; Opposites, 1973; More Opposites, 1991; A Game of Catch, 1994; Runaway Opposites, 1995. Non-Fiction: Anniversary Lectures (with Robert Hillyer and Cleanth Brooks), 1959; Emily Dickinson: Three Views (with Louise Bogan and Archibald MacLeish), 1960; Responses: Prose Pieces, 1953-1976, 1976. Editor: Modern American and Modern British Poetry (with Louis Untermeyer and Karl Shapiro), 1955; A Bestiary, 1955; Poe: Complete Poems, 1959; Shakespeare: Poems (with Alfred Harbage), 1966, revised edition, 1974; Poe: The Narrative of Arthur Gordon Pym, 1974; Witter Bynner: Selected Poems, 1978. Translator: Molière: The Misanthrope, 1955; Molière: Tartuffe, 1963; Molière: The School for

Wives, 1971; Molière: The Learned Ladies, 1978; Racine: Andromache, 1982; Racine: Phaedra, 1986; Molière: The School for Husbands, 1992; Molière: Amphitryon, 1995. Honours; Harriet Monroe Memorial Prizes, 1948, 1978; Oscar Blumenthal Prize, 1950; Guggenheim Fellowships, 1952-53, 1963-64; Prix de Rome Fellowship, American Academy of Arts and Letters, 1954; Edna St Vincent Millay Memorial Award, 1957; Pulitzer Prizes in Poetry, 1957, 1989; National Book Award for Poetry, 1957; Ford Foundation Fellowship, 1960; Bollingen Prizes, 1963, 1971; Brandeis University Creative Arts Award, 1971; Shelley Memorial Award, 1973; Drama Desk Award, 1983; Chevalier, Ordre des Palmes Academiques, 1983; Los Angeles Times Books Prize, 1988; Gold Medal for Poetry, American Academy and Institute of Arts and Letters, 1991; Edward Mac Dowell Medal, 1991; National Medal of Arts, 1994. Memberships: Academy of American Poets, chancellor; American Academy of Arts and Letters, president, 1974-76, chancellor, 1976-78, 1980-81; American Academy of Arts and Sciences; American Society of Composers, Authors and Publishers; Authors League of America; Dramatists Guild; Modern Language Association, honorary fellow. Address: 87 Dodwells Road, Cummington, MA 01206, USA.

WILBY Basil Leslie, (Gareth Knight), b. 1930, Colchester, Essex, England. Appointments: University Sales Manager, 1970-76; Longman Group Publishing Manager, 1976-91; Freelance Publishing Consultant, 1991-93. Publications: A Practical Guide to Qabalistic Symbolism, 1965; The New Dimensions Red Book, 1968; The Practice of Ritual Magic, 1969; Occult Exercises & Practices, 1969; Meeting the Occult, 1973; Experience of the Inner Worlds, 1975; The Occult: An Introduction, 1975; The Secret Tradition in Arthurian Legend, 1983; The Rose Cross and the Goddess, 1985; The Treasure House of Images, 1986; The Magic World of the Tarot, 1991; Magic and the Western Mind, 1991; Evoking the Goddess, 1993; Dion Fortune's Magical Battle of Britain, 1993. Address: 8 Acorn Avenue, Braintree, Essex, England.

WILCOX James, b. 4 Apr 1949, Hammond, Louisiana, USA. Author. Education: BA, Yale University. Publications: Modern Baptists, 1983; North Gladiola, 1985; Miss Undine's Living Room, 1987; Sort of Rich, 1989; Guest of a Sinner, 1993. Contributions to: Periodicals. Memberships: Authors Guild; PEN. Address: c/o International Creative Management, 40 West 57th Street, New York, NY 10019, USA.

WILD Peter, b. 25 Apr 1940, Northampton, Massachusetts, USA. Professor of English; Poet; Writer. m. (1) Sylvia Ortiz, 1966, (2) Rosemary Harrold, 1981. Education: BA, 1962, MA, 1967, University of Arizona; MFA, University of California at Irvine, 1969. Appointments: Assistant Professor, Sul Ross State University, Alpine, Texas, 1969-71; Assistant Porfessor, 1971-73, Associate Professor, 1973-79, Professor of English. 1979-, University of Arizona; Contributing Editor, High Country News, 1974-; Consulting Editor, Diversions, 1983-. Publications: Poetry: The Good Fox, 1967; Sonnets, 1967; The Afternoon in Dismay, 1968; Mica Mountain Poems, 1968; Joining Up and Other Poems, 1968; Mad Night with Sunflowers, 1968; Love Poems, 1969; Three Nights in the Chiricahuas, 1969; Poems, 1969; Fat Man Poems, 1970; Term and Renewals, 1970; Grace, 1971; Dilemma, 1971; Wild's Magical Book of Cranial Effusions, 1971; Peligros, 1972; New and Selected Poems, 1973; Cochise, 1973; The Cloning, 1974; Tumacacori, 1974; Health, 1974; Chihuahua, 1976; The Island Hunter, 1976; Pioneers, 1976; The Cavalryman, 1976; House Fires, 1977; Gold Mines, 1978; Barn Fires, 1978; Zuni Butte, 1978; The Lost Tribe, 1979; Jeanne d'Arc: A Collection of New Poems, 1980; Rainbow, 1980; Wilderness, 1980; Heretics, 1981; Bitteroots, 1982; The Peaceable Kingdom, 1983; Getting Ready for a Date, 1984; The Light on Little Mormon Lake, 1984; The Brides of Christ, 1991; Easy Victory, 1994. Other: Pioneer Conservationists of Western America, 2 volumes, 1979, 1983; Enos Mills, 1979; Clarence King, 1981; James Welch, 1983; Barry Lopez, 1984; John Haines, 1985; John Nicholas, 1986; The Saguaro Forest, 1986; John C Van Dyke: The Desert, 1988; Alvar Núñez Cabeza de Vaca, 1991; Ann Zwinger, 1993. Editor: New Poetry of the American West (with Frank Graziano), 1982. Honours: Writer's Digest Prize, 1964; Hart Crane and Alice Crane Williams Memorial Fund Grant, 1969; Ark River Review Prize, 1972; Ohio State University President's Prize, 1982. Address: 1547 East Lester, Tucson, AZ 85719, USA.

WILDER Cherry. See: **GRIMM Barbara Lockett.**

WILDING Eric. See: **TUBB E(dwin) C(harles).**

WILDING Griselda. See: **McCUTCHEON Hugh.**

WILDING Michael, b. 5 Jan 1942, Worcester, England. Professor. Education: BA, 1963, MA, 1968, University of Oxford. Appointments: Lecturer, 1963-66, Senior Lecturer, 1969-72, Reader, 1972-92, Professor, 1993-, University of Sydney; Lecturer, University of Birmingham, 1967-68; Visiting Professor, University of California, 1987. Publications: Aspects of the Dying Process, 1972; Living Together, 1974; Short Story Embassy, 1975; West Midland Underground, 1975; Scenic Drive, 1976; The Phallic Forest, 1978; Pacific Highway, 1982; Reading the Signs, 1984; The Paraguyan Experiment, 1985; The Man of Slow Feeling, 1985; Under Saturn, 1988; Great Climate, 1990; Social Visions, 1993; The Radical Tradition, Lawson, Furphy, Stead, 1993; This is for You, 1994; Book of the Reading, 1994; The Oxford Book of Australian Short Stories, 1994. Honours: Senior Fellowship, Literature Board, Australia Council, 1978; Elected Fellow, Australian Academy of the Humanities, 1988. Address: Department of English, University of Sydney, Sydney, New South Wales 2006, Australia.

WILENTZ Robert Sean, b. 20 Feb 1951, New York, USA. Historian. m. Mary Christine Stansell, 30 Jan 1980, 1 son, 1 daughter. Education: BA, Columbia College, 1972; BA, University of Oxford, 1974; PhD, Yale University, 1980. Publications: Chants Democratic, 1984; Rites of Power, 1985; The Key of Liberty, 1993; The Kingdom of Matthias, 1994. Contributions to: New Republic; Dissent. Honours: Beveridge Award, 1984; Turner Award, 1985. Membership: Society of American Historians. Address: 7 Edgehill Street, Princeton, NJ 08540, USA.

WILFORD John Noble, b. 4 Oct 1933, Murray, Kentucky, USA. Journalist; Writer. m. Nancy Watts Paschall, 25 Dec 1966, 1 daughter. Education: BS, Journalism, University of Tennessee, 1955; MA, Political Science, Syracuse University, 1956; International Reporting Fellow, Columbia University, 1961-62. Appointments: Science Reporter, 1965-73, 1979-, Assistant National Editor, 1973-75, Director of Science News, 1975-79, Science Correspondent, 1979-, New York Times, New York City; Mc Graw Distinguished Lecturer in Writing, Princeton University, 1985; Professor of Science Journalism, University of Tennessee, 1989-90. Publications: We Reach the Moon, 1969; The Mapmakers, 1981; The Riddle of the Dinosaur, 1985; Mars Beckons, 1990; The Mysterious History of Columbus, 1991. Contributions to: Nature; Wilson Quarterly; New York Times Magazine; Science Digest; Popular Science. Honours: Westinghouse-American Association for the Advancement of Science Writing Award, 1983; Pulitzer Prize for National Reporting, 1984, shared 1987. Memberships: Century Club, New York City; National Association of Science Writers; American Geographical Society, council member, 1994-. Address: New York Times, 229 West 43rd Street, New York, NY 10036, USA.

WILFRED Leopold. See: **PETERS Lenrie.**

WILKERSON Cynthia. See: **LEVINSON Leonard.**

WILKINSON Doris, b. Lexington, Kentucky, USA. Professor of Sociology; Writer. Education: BA, University of Kentucky, 1958; MA, 1960, PhD, 1968, Case Western Reserve University; MPH, Johns Hopkins University, 1985; Postdoctoral Studies, Harvard University, 1991. Appointments: Assistant Professor, 1968-70, Professor of Sociology, 1985-, University of Kentucky; Associate Professor to Professor, Macalester College, 1970-77; Executive Associate, American Sociological Association, Washington, DC, 1977-80; Professor of Medical Sociology, Howard University, 1980-84; Visiting Professor, University of Virginia, 1984-85; Visiting Scholar, 1989-90, Visiting Professor, 1992, 1993, 1994, Harvard University; Rapoport Visiting Professor of Social Theory, Smith College, 1995. Publications: Workbook for Introductory Sociology, 1968. Editor: Black Revolt: Strategies of Protest, 1969. Co-Editor: The Black Male in America, 1977; Alternative Health Maintenance and Healing Systems, 1987; Race, Gender and the Life Cycle, 1991. Contributions to: Professional journals. Honours: Woodrow Wilson Foundation Fellowship, 1959-61; I Peter Gellman Award, Eastern Sociological Society, 1987; Dubois-Johnson-Frazier Award, American Sociological Association, 1988; American Council of Learned Societies Fellowship, 1989-90; Ford Foundation Fellowship, 1989-90; National Endowment for the Humanities Fellowship, 1991; Distinguished Scholar Award, Association of Black Sociologists, 1993; Great Teacher Award, 1992. Memberships: Alpha Kappa Delta; American Sociological Association;

Eastern Sociological Society, president, 1992-93; Phi Beta Kappa; Society for the Study of Social Problems, president, 1987-88; Southern Sociological Society. Address: c/o Department of Sociology, University of Kentucky, Lexington, KY 40506, USA.

WILKINSON Richard Herbert, b. 26 Apr 1951, Skipton, Yorkshire, England. Egyptologist. m. Anna Wagner, 27 July 1975, 2 sons. Education: PhD, University of Minnesota. Appointment: Faculty, University of Arizona. Publications: Reading Egyptian Art, 1992; Symbol and Magic in Egyptian Art, 1994. Contributions to: Professional journals and general periodicals. Honours: Numerous. Membership: International Association of Egyptologists. Address: c/o University of Arizona, Harvil 347, Box 10, Tucson, AZ 85721, USA.

WILL Clifford Martin, b. 13 Nov 1946, Hamilton, Ontario, Canada. Physicist. m. Leslie Carol Saxe, 26 June 1970, 2 daughters. Education: BSc, Applied Mathematics, Theoretical Physics, McMaster University, 1968; PhD, Physics, California Institute of Technology, 1971. Appointment: Faculty, Washington University, St Louis. Publications: Theory and Experiment in Gravitational Physics, 1981, 2nd edition, 1993; Was Einstein Right?, 1986, 2nd edition, 1993. Contributions to: Periodicals. Honours: Fellowship, Alfred P Sloan Foundation, 1975-79; Science Writing Award, American Institute of Physics, 1987. Memberships: Fellow, American Institute of Physics; American Astronomical Society; International Society on General Relativity and Gravitation. Address: Department of Physics, Campus Box 1105, Washington University, St Louis, MO 63130, USA.

WILL Frederic, b. 4 Dec 1928, New Haven, Connecticut, USA. Professor of Comparative Literature; Poet. Education: AB, Indiana University, 1949; PhD, Yale University, 1954. Appointments: Instructor in Classics, Dartmouth College, 1953-55; Assistant Professor of Classics, Pennsylvania State University, 1954-59, University of Texas, 1960-64; Associate Professor of English and Comparative Literature, 1964-66, Professor of Comparative Literature, University of Massachusetts at Amherst, 1971-; Visiting Lecturer in poetry and criticism at many colleges and universities; Many poetry readings. Publications: Intelligible Beauty in Aesthetic Thought: From Winckelmann to Victor Cousin, 1958; Mosaic and Other Poems, 1959; A Wedge of Words (poems), 1962; Kostes Palamas: The Twelve Words of the Gypsy (translator), 1964; Hereditas: Seven Essays on the Modern Experience of the Classical (editor), 1964; Metaphrasis: An Anthology from the University of Iowa Translation Workshop, 1964-65 (editor), 1965; Flumen Historicum: Victor Cousin's Aesthetic and Its Sources, 1965; Literature Inside Out: Ten Speculative Essays, 1966; Planets, poems 1966; Kostes Palamas: The King's Flute, translator, 1967; From a Year in Greece, 1967; Archilochos, 1969; Herondas, 1972; Brandy in the Snow (poems), 1972; Theodor Adorno: The Jargon of Authenticity (translator with Knut Tarnowski), 1973; The Knife in the Stone, 1973; The Fact of Literature, 1973; Guatemala, 1973; Botulism (poems), 1975; The Generic Demands of Greek Literature, 1976; Belphagor, 1977; Epics of America (poems), 1977; Our Thousand Year Old Bodies: Selected Poems, 1956-1976, 1980; Shamans in Turtlenecks: Selected Essays, 1984; The Sliced Dog, 1984; Entering the Open Hole, 1989; Recoveries, 1993. Contributions to: Many poems and articles in various periodicals. Honours: Fulbright Grants, 1950-51, 1955, 1956-57, 1975-76, 1980-81; American Council of Learned Societies Grant, 1958; Voertman Poetry Awards, Texas Institute of Letters, 1962, 1964; Bollingen Foundation Grant; National Endowment for the Arts Grant. Address: Department of Comparative Literature, University of Massachusetts at Amherst, Amherst, MA 01003, USA.

WILL George Frederick, b. 4 May 1941, Champaign, Illinios, USA. Author; Syndicated Columnist. 3 sons, 1 daughter. Education: BA with honours, Religion, Trinity College, Hartford, Connecticut, 1962; Magdalen College, Oxford, England; BA (Oxon), Politics, Philosophy, Economics, 1964; PhD, Politics, Princeton University, New Jersey, 1967. Appointments: Editor, The National Review, Washington, DC, 1973-76; Syndicated Columnist, The Washington Post, 1974-; Contributing Editor, Newsweek Magazine, 1976-; Occasional Op-Ed Page Contributor, The London Daily Telegraph, 1987-. Publications: The Pursuit of Happiness and Other Sobering Thoughts, 1978; The Pursuit of Virtue and Other Tory Notions, 1982; Statecraft as Soulcraft: What Government Does, 1983; The Morning After: American Successes and Excesses, 1986; The New Season: A Spectator's Guide to the 1988 Election, 1987; Men at Work: The Craft of Baseball, 1990; Suddenly: The American Idea Abroad and at Home, 1990; Restoration: Congress, Term Limits and the Recovery of Deliberative

Democracy, 1992; The Leveling Wind, 1994. Honours: Pulitzer Prize for Commentary, 1977; LLD, University of San Diego, 1977; DLitt, Dickinson College, Carlisle, Pennsylvania, 1978; DLitt, Georgetown University, Washington, DC, 1978; University of Illinois, 1988, Doctor of Humane Letters, Duke University, 1991, College of William and Mary, 1994; Cronkite Award, Arizona State University, 1991; Madison Medal Award, Princeton University, 1992; William Allen White Award, University of Kansas, William Allen White School of Journalism, 1993. Memberships: Emil Verban Society; Trustee, Little League Foundation, 1992; Advisory Board, Institute of United States Studies University of London, 1993. Address: c/o Writers Group, The Washington Post, 1150 Fifteenth Street North West, Washington, DC 20071, USA.

WILLETT Frank, b. 18 Aug 1925, Bolton, England. Archaeologist; Art Historian. m. M Constance Hewitt, 24 July 1950, 1 son, 3 daughters. Education: BA, 1947, MA, 1951, Oxford University. Appointments: Editorial Secretary, Manchester Literary and Philosophical Society, 1950-58; Editorial Board, West African Journal of Archaeology, 1970-, Journal of African Studies, 1973-; Curator, Royal Society of Edinburgh, 1992-97. Publications: Ife in the History of West African Sculpture, 1967; African Art, 1971, revised edition, 1993; The Arts of the African People, 1974; Treasures of Ancient Nigeria, 1980. Contributions to: Professional journals, books and other publications. Honours: Commander of the Order of the British Empire, 1985; Leadership Award of the Arts Council of African Studies Association. Memberships: Manchester Literary and Philosophical Society; Royal Anthropological Institute; Royal Society of Edinburgh, fellow. Address: c/o The Hunterian Museum, University of Glasgow, Glasgow G12 8QQ, Scotland.

WILLIAM John. See: **CROSSLEY-HOLLAND Kevin.**

WILLIAMS Alberta Norine (Sonia Davis), b. 22 Apr 1908, Olds, Alberta, Canada. Writer; Songwriter; Author; Poet; Rancher. m. Billy D Williams, 4 Sept 1928, 1 son, 1 daughter. Education: Business College, Fayetteville, Arkansas, 1921; GED, Two Spanish Courses, Creative Writing, Local History, Pueblo Community College, 1960; 2 Corres Courses, Writer's Digest and Will Heideman. Appointments: National Library of Poetry; Famous Poet Society; Mile High Poetry; Drurys Publishing Co; Ivill Books; World of Poetry; Poetry Society of Colorado. Publications: Pearls of a Lady, 1976; Potpourri of a Poet, 1992; Prairie Bird (life story) 1994. Compiler, Rye Home Church History, 1975. Other: Songs, limericks, plays, short stories, haikus, book reports, articles. Contributions to: Buzzard Roost Ranch, 1994; Territorial Daughters Book II; Fence Post. Honour: Inducted, International World Writers Hall of Fame, 1997. Memberships: President, Verses of the Valley; Secretary, Territorial Daughters; DAR; Rye Home United Methodist Church; Huerfano County Cowbelles; Chair, Rye Women's Club, various posts; Green Horn Valley Art Society. Address: Lascar Route, Box 75, Rye, CO 81069, USA.

WILLIAMS Bert Nolan, b. 19 Aug 1930, Toronto, Ontario, Canada. Writer; Teacher. m. Angela Babando, 6 Dec 1952, 1 son. Education: Self-taught. Publications: Food for the Eagle, 1970; Master of Ravenspur, 1970; The Rocky Mountain Monster, 1972; Sword of Egypt, 1977; Brumaire (play), 1982; Poetry, Popular Songs (music and lyrics), Short Stories, Magazine Articles. Contributions to: Journals and magazines. Address: 10 Muirhead Road, Apt 504, North York, Ontario M2J 4P9, Canada.

WILLIAMS C(harles) K(enneth), b. 4 Nov 1936, Newark, New Jersey, USA. Poet; Professor. m. Catherine Justine Mauger, Apr 1975, 1 son, 1 daughter. Education: BA, University of Pennsylvania, 1959. Appointments: Visiting Professor, Franklin and Marshall College, Lancaster, Pennsylvania, 1977, University of California at Irvine, 1978, Boston University, 1979-80; Professor of English, George Mason University, 1982; Visiting Professor, Brooklyn College, 1982-83; Lecturer, Columbia University, 1982-85; Holloway Lecturer, University of California at Berkeley, 1986; Professor, Princeton University, 1996-. Publications: A Day for Anne Frank, 1968; Lies, 1969; I Am the Bitter Name, 1972; The Sensuous President, 1972; With Ignorance, 1977; The Women of Trachis (co-translator), 1978; The Lark, the Thrush, the Starling, 1983; Tar, 1983; Flesh and Blood, 1987; Poems 1963-1983, 1988; The Bacchae of Euripides (translator), 1990; A Dream of Mind, 1992; Selected Poems, 1994. Contributions to: Akzent; Atlantic; Carleton Miscellany; Crazyhorse; Grand Street; Iowa Review; Madison Review; New England Review; New Yorker; Seneca Review; Transpacific Review; TriQuarterly. Honours: Guggenheim Fellowship; National Book Critics Circle Award, 1983; National Endowment for the

Arts Fellowship, 1985; Pushcart Press Prizes, 1982, 1983, 1987; Morton Dawen Zabel Prize, 1988; Lila Wallace Writers Award, 1993. Membership: PEN. Address: 82 Rue d'Hauteville, 75010 Paris, France.

WILLIAMS David, b. 8 June 1926, Bridgend, Mid Glamorgan, Wales. Novelist. m. Brenda Yvonne Holmes, 18 Aug 1952, 1 son, 1 daughter. Education: Cathedral School, Hereford, 1938-43; St John's College, Oxford, 1943-44, 1947-48. Publications: Unholy Writ; Murder for Treasure; Wedding Treasure; Murder in Advent; Holy Treasure; Treasure by Degrees; Copper, Gold and Treasure; Treasure Preserved; Advertise for Treasure; Prescription for Murder; Divided Treasure; Treasure By Post; Planning on Murder; Banking on Murder; Last Seen Breathing; Death of a Prodigal; Dead in the Market, 1996. Contributions to: Numerous Short Stories. Honour: Elected Member, Welsh Academy, 1995. Memberships: Society of Authors; Crime Writers Association; Mystery Writers of America; Carlton Club; Wentworth G C; Detection Club. Address: Blandings, Pinewood Road, Virginia Water, Surrey GU25 4PA, England.

WILLIAMS David Larry, b. 22 June 1945, Souris, Manitoba, Canada. Professor of English; Writer. m. Darlene Olinyk, 22 July 1967, 2 sons. Education: Pastor's Diploma, Briercrest Bible Institute, Saskatchewan, 1965; BA, Honours, University of Saskatchewan, 1968; MA, Amherst College, 1970; PhD, University of Massachusetts, 1973. Appointments: Lecturer, 1972-73, Assistant Professor, 1973-77, Associate Professor, 1977-83, Professor, 1983-, English, University of Manitoba, Winnipeg; Editorial Board, Canadian Review of American Studies, 1976-86; Guest Professor, Indian Association for Canadian Studies, MS University of Baroda, 1992. Publications: The Burning Wood (novel), 1975; Faulkner's Women: The Myth and the Muse (criticism), 1977; The River Horsemen (novel), 1981; Eye of the Father (novel), 1985; Chapter in Trace: Prairie Writers on Writing, 1986; To Run with Longboat: Twelve Stories of Indian Athletes in Canada (with Brenda Zeman), 1988; Confessional Fictions: A Portrait of the Artist in the Canadian Novel, 1991. Contributions to: Books and professional journals. Honours: Woodrow Wilson Fellow, 1968-69; Canada Council Fellow, 1969-72; Canada Council Arts Grant 'B', 1977-78, 1981-82; Touring Writer in Scandinavia for External Affairs, Canada, 1981; RH Institute Award for Research in Humanities, 1987; Olive Beatrice Stanton Award for Excellence in Teaching, 1992. Memberships: Writers' Union of Canada; National Council of Prairie Region, 1978-79, 1984-85; PEN International. Address: Department of English, St Paul's College, University of Manitoba, Winnipeg R3T 2M6, Canada.

WILLIAMS Heathcote, b. 15 Nov 1941, Helsby, Cheshire, England. Playwright. Appointments: Associate Editor, Transatlantic Review, New York and London. Publications: The Local Stigmatic, 1967; AC/DC, 1970; Remember the Truth Dentist, 1974; The Speakers, 1974; Very Tasty - a Pantomime, 1975; An Invitation to the Official Lynching of Abdul Malik, 1975; Anatomy of a Space Rat, 1976; Hancock's Last Half-Hour, 1977; Playpen, 1977; The Immortalist, 1977; At It, 1982; Whales, 1986. Verse: Whale Nation, 1988; Falling for a Dolphin, 1988; Sacred Elephant, 1989; Autogeddon, 1991. Other: The Speakers, 1964; Manifestoes, Manifestern, 1975; Severe Joy, 1979; Elephants, 1983. Honours: Evening Standard Award, 1970. Address: Judy Daish Associates, 83 Eastbourne Mews, London W2 6LQ, England.

WILLIAMS Herbert Lloyd, b. 8 Sept 1932, Aberystwyth, Wales. Writer. m. Dorothy Maud Edwards, 13 Nov 1954, 4 sons, 1 daughter. Publications: The Trophy, 1967; A Lethal Kind of Love, 1968; Come Out Wherever You Are, 1976; Stage Coaches in Wales, 1977; The Welsh Quiz Book, 1978; Railways in Wales, 1981; The Pembrokeshire Coast National Park, 1987; Stories of King Arthur, 1990; Ghost Country, 1991; Davies the Ocean, 1991; The Stars in Their Courses, 1992. TV Drama and Documentaries: Taff Acre, HTV, 1981; A Solitary Mister, BBC2, 1983; Alone in a Crowd, BBC2, 1984; Calvert in Camera, HTV, 1990. Radio Dramas: Doing the Bard, BBC Radio Wales, 1986; Bodyline, BBC Radio 4, 1991. TV Drama and Documentaries: The Great Powys, HTV, 1994; Arouse All Wales, HTV, 1996. Contributions to: New Welsh Review; Anglo-Welsh Review; Planet; Transatlantic Review; Poetry Wales; Cambrensis; Tribune; Acumen, Western Mail. Honours: Welsh Arts Council Short Story Prize, 1972, and Bursary, 1988; Aberystwyth Open Poetry Competition, 1990; Hawthornden Poetry Fellowship, 1992; Rhys Davies Short Story Award, 1995. Memberships: Writers Guild of Great Britain; Welsh Academy; Welsh Union of Writers. Address: 20 Amesbury Road, Penylan, Cardiff CF2 5DW, Wales.

WILLIAMS Hugo (Mordaunt), b. 20 Feb 1942, Windsor, Berkshire, England. Writer; Critic; Poet. m. Hermine Demoriane, 12 Oct 1966, 1 daughter. Education: Eton College, 1955-60. Appointments: Assistant Editor, London Magazines, 1961-69; Television Critic, New Statesman, 1982-87; Theatre Critic, Sunday Correspondent, 1989-90; Film Critic, Harpers & Queen, 1993-. Publications: Symptoms of Loss, 1965; All the Time in the World, 1966; Sugar Daddy, 1970; Some Sweet Day, 1975; Love Life, 1979; No Particular Place to Go, 1981; Writing Home, 1985; Self-Portrait with a Slide, 1990. Contributions to: Newspapers and periodicals. Honours: Eric Gregory Award, 1965; Cholmondeley Award, 1970; Geoffrey Faber Memorial Prize, 1979. Membership: Royal Society of Literature. Address: 31 Raleigh Street, London N1 8NW, England.

WILLIAMS J(eanne) R, (Megan Castell, Jeanne Creasey, Jeanne Crecy, Jeanne Foster, Kristin Michaels, Deidre Rowan), b. 10 Apr 1930, Elkhart, Kansas, USA. Author. Education: University of Oklahoma, 1952-53. Publications: To Buy a Dream, 1958; Promise of Tomorrow, 1959; Coyote Winter, 1965; Beasts with Music, 1967; Oil Patch Partners, 1968; New Medicine, 1971; Trails of Tears, 1972; Freedom Trail, 1973; Winter Wheat, 1975; A Lady Bought with Rifles, 1977; A Woman Clothed in Sun, 1978; Bridge of Thunder, 1978; Daughter of the Sword, 1979; The Queen of a Lonely Country (as Megan Castell), 1980; The Valiant Women, 1981; Harvest of Fury, 1982; The Heaven Sword, 1983; A Mating of Hawks, 1984; The Care Dreamers, 1985; So Many Kingdoms, 1986; Texas Pride, 1987; Lady of No Man's Land, 1988; No Roof but Heaven, 1990; Home Mountain, 1990; The Island Harp, 1991; The Longest Road, 1993; Daughter of the Storm, 1994; The Unplowed Sky, 1994; Home Station, 1995. As J R Williams: Mission in Mexico, 1960; The Horsetalker, 1961; The Confederate Fiddle, 1962; River Guns, 1962; Oh Susanna, 1963; Tame the Wild Stallion, 1967. As Jeanne Crecy: Hands of Terror, UK edition as Lady Gift, 1972; The Lightning Tree, 1972; My Face Beneath Stone, 1975; The Winter-Keeper, 1975; The Night Hunters, 1975. As Deirdre Rowan: Dragon's Mount, 1973; Silver Wood, 1974; Shadow of the Volcano, 1975; Time of the Burning Mask, 1976; Ravensgate, 1976. As Kristin Michaels: To Begin with Love, 1976; Enchanted Journey, 1977; Song of the Heart, 1977; Make Believe Love, 1978. As Jeanne Foster: Deborah Leigh, 1981; Eden Richards, 1982; Woman of Three Worlds, 1984; The Island Harp, 1991. Contributions to: Journals. Honours: Texas Institute of Letters Best Children's Book, 1958; Four Western Writers of America Spur Awards; Best Novel of the West, 1981, 1990; Lew Strauss Golden Saddleman Award for Lifetime Achievement, 1988. Memberships: Author's Guild; Western Writers of America, president, 1974-75. Literary Agent: Phyllis Westling, Harold Obers Associates. Address: Box 335, Portal, AZ 85632, USA.

WILLIAMS John Hoyt, b. 26 Oct 1940, Darien, Connecticut, USA. Professor of History. m. 27 Jan 1963, 1 son, 1 daughter. Education: BA, 1963, MA, History 1965, University of Connecticut; PhD, Latin American History 1969, University of Florida. Appointments: Assistant Professor of History 1969-73, Associate Professor of History, 1973-78, Professor of History, 1978-, Indiana State University. Publications: Rise and Fall of the Paraguayan Republic 1800-1870, 1979; A Great and Shining Road, 1988; Sam Houston: A Biography of the Father of Texas, 1993. Contributions to: Atlantic Monthly; Christian Century; Americas; National Defense; Current History; Hispanic American Historical Review. Address: History Department, Indiana State University, Terre Haute, IN 47809, USA.

WILLIAMS Malcolm David, b. 9 Apr 1939, South Wales. Author. Widower, 1 daughter. Education: Birmingham University Institute of Education, 1951-61. Publications: Yesterday's Secret, 1980; Poor Little Rich Girl, 1981; Debt of Friendship, 1981; Another Time, Another Place, 1982; Mr Brother's Keeper, 1982; The Stuart Affair, 1983; The Cordillera Conspiracy, 1983; The Girl from Derry's Bluff, 1983; A Corner of Eden, 1984; Sorrow's End, 1984; A Stranger on Trust, 1987; Shadows From the Past, 1989. Contributions to: Several Hundred Short Stories and serials to various magazines, newspapers; Poetry published in UK and USA; Contributor of articles in UK. Honours: 1st Prize, Short Story Competition, 1961, 1969. Memberships: Society of Authors; West Country Writers Association; Fellow, World Literary Academy. Address: 40 Longlands Road, Bishops Cleeve, Cheltenham, Glos GL52 4JP, England.

WILLIAMS Miller, b. 8 Apr 1930, Hoxie, Arkansas, USA. University Press Director; Writer; Poet. m. Lucille Day, 29 Dec 1951, 1 son, 2 daughters. Education: BS, Arkansas State College, 1950; MS,

University of Arkansas, 1952. Appointments: Founder-Editor, 1968-70, Advisory Editor, 1975-, New Orleans Review; Contributing Editor, Translation Review, 1976-80. Publications: A Circle of Stone, 1964; Southern Writing in the Sixties (with J W Corrington), 2 volumes, 1966; So Long at the Fair, 1968; Chile: An Anthology of New Writing, 1968; The Achievement of John Ciardi, 1968; The Only World There Is, 1968; The Poetry of John Crowe Ransom, 1971; Contemporary Poetry in America, 1972; Halfway from Hoxie: New and Selected Poems, 1973; How Does a Poem Mean? (with John Ciardi), 1974; Railroad (with James Alan McPherson), 1976; Why God Permits Evil, 1977; A Roman Collection, 1980; Distraction, 1981; Ozark, Ozark: A Hillside Reader, 1981; The Boys on Their Bony Mules, 1983; Living on the Surface: New and Selected Poems, 1989; Adjusting to the Light, 1992; Points of Departure, 1995. Contributions to: Various publications. Honours: Henry Bellaman Poetry Award, 1957; Bread Loaf Fellowship in Poetry, 1961; Fulbright Lecturer, 1970; Prix de Rome, American Academy of Arts and Letters, 1976; Honorary Doctor of Humanities, Lander College, 1983; National Poets Prize, 1992; John William Corrington Award for Excellence in Literature, Centenary College, Louisiana, 1994; American Academy of Arts and Letters Award, 1995; Honorary Doctor of Humane Letters, Hendrix College, 1995; Inaugural Poet, Presidential Inauguration, 1997. Address: c/o University of Arkansas Press, Fayetteville, AR 72701, USA.

WILLIAMS Nigel, b. 20 Jan 1948, Cheadle, Cheshire, England. Novelist; Playwright. Education: Oriel College, Oxford. Publications: Novels: My Life Closed Twice, 1977; Jack be Nimble, 1980; Charlie, 1984; Star Turn, 1985; Witchcraft, 1987; Breaking Up, 1988; Black Magic, 1988; The Wimbledon Poisoner, 1990; They Came from SW19, 1992. Plays: Double Talk, 1976; Snowwhite Washes Whiter, 1977; Class Enemy, 1978; Easy Street, 1979; Sugar and Spice, 1980; Line 'em, 1980; Trial Run, 1980; WCPC, 1982; The Adventures of Jasper Ridley, 1982; My Brother's Keeper, 1985; Deathwatch (after Genet), 1985; Country Dancing, 1986; As It Was, 1987; Nativity, 1989. Television plays. Honour: Somerset Maugham Award for fiction, 1978. Address: c/o Faber and Faber, 3 Queen Square, London WC1N 3AU, England.

WILLIAMS Philip F C, b. 5 Apr 1956, Little Rock, Arkansas, USA. University Professor. m. Yenna Wu, 23 Nov 1990, 1 son. Education: BA, University of Arkansas, 1978; MA, 1981, PhD, 1985, University of California at Los Angeles. Appointments: Assisting Professor of Foreign Languages, 1986-93, Associate Professor of Languages and Literature, 1993-, Arizona State University; Postdoctoral Fellow, Harvard University, 1990-91; Assistant Professor, University of Vermont, 1991-92. Publication: Village Echoes: The Fiction of Wu Zuxiang, 1993. Contributions to: Scholarly journals. Honour: Humanities Research Award, Arizona State University, 1989. Memberships: Southwest Conference of Asian Studies, President, 1996; Phi Beta Kappa, Arizona Beta Chapter Vice President, 1996; American Association for Chinese Comparative Literature, Executive Committee Member, 1995-. Address: Department Languages and Literatures, Box 870202, Arizona State University, Tempe, AZ 85287-0202, USA.

WILLIAMS Tony, b. 11 Jan 1946, Swansea, Wales. Academic. m. Kathleen Ensor, 1 June 1980. Education: Teachers Certificate, Swansea College of Education, 1967; First Class Honours, Biblical Studies, 1970; PhD, Theology, Manchester University, 1974; MA, Film Studies, Warwick University, 1979. Publications: Italian Western: Opera of Violence (co-author), 1975; Jack London: The Movies, 1992; Vietnam War Films (co-editor), 1994; Hearths of Darkness: The Family in the American Horror Film, 1996; Radical Allegories: The Films of Larry Cohen, 1997; The Making of the Warner Brothers Sea Wolf (co-editor), 1997. Contributions to: Cinema Journal; Wide Angle; Movie: Cineaction; Film History; Vietnam Generation; Jump Cut; Science Fiction Studies; Jack London Journal. Honour: Jack London Man of the Year, 1988. Memberships: Society for Cinema Studies; Aizen. Address: English Department, Southern Illinois University, Carbondale, IL 62701, USA.

WILLIAMSON Joel R, b. 27 Oct 1929, Anderson County, South Carolina, USA. Professor; Writer. m. Betty Anne Woodson, 18 Nov 1986, 1 son, 2 daughters. Education: AB 1949, MA 1951, University of South Carolina; PhD, University of California, Berkeley, 1964. Appointment: Instructor, 1950-64, Assistant Professor, 1964-66, Associate Professor, 1966-69, Professor, 1969-85, Linberger Professor in Humanities, 1985-, Department of History, University of North Carolina, Chapel Hill. Publications: After Slavery: The Negro in

SC During Reconstruction, 1965; Origins of Segregation, 1968; New People: Miscegenation and Mulattoes in the US, 1980; The Crucible of Race, 1984; A Rage for Order, 1986; William Faulkner and Southern History, 1993; Forthcoming publications: Elvis Presley: A Study in Southern and American Culture; Emeline: A Study in Elite Miscegenation; The Souls of White Folk: The Evolution of Southern White Culture in the 20th Century. Contributions to: various publications. Honours: Parkman, Emerson, Owsley, Kennedy, Mayflower Awards; Mayflower Cup, 1994; Pulitzer Prize finalist in History, 1994. Memberships: Society of American Historians; Southern Historical Association; Organizations of American Historians; Numerous fellowships. Address: 211 Hillsborough St, Chapel Hill, NC 27514, USA.

WILLIAMSON Jack, (John Stewart Williamson), b. 29 Apr 1908, Bisbee, Arizona, USA. Writer. m. Blanche Slaten Harp, 15 Aug 1947, dec 1985, 2 stepchildren. Education: BA, MA, 1957, Eastern New Mexico University; PhD, University of Colorado, 1964. Appointment: Professor of English, Eastern New Mexico University, Portales, 1960-77. Publications Science Fiction: The Legion of Space, 1947; Darker Than You Think, 1948; The Humanoids, 1949; The Green Girl, 1950; The Cometeers, 1950; One Against the Legion, 1950; Seetee Shock, 1950; Seetee Ship, 1950; Dragon's Island, 1951; The Legion of Time, 1952; Dome Around America, 1955; The Trial of Terra, 1962; Golden Blood, 1964; The Reign of Wizadry, 1965; Bright New Universe, 1967; Trapped in Space, 1968; The Pandora Effect, 1969; People Machines, 1971; The Moon Children, 1972; H G Wells: Critic of Progress, 1973; Teaching Science Fiction, 1975; The Early Williamson, 1975; The Power of Blackness, 1976; The Best of Jack Williamson, 1978; Brother to Demons, Brother to Gods, 1979; Teaching Science Fiction: Education for Tomorrow, 1980; The Alien Intelligence, 1980; The Humanoid Touch, 1980; Manseed, 1982; The Queen of a Legion, 1983; Wonder's Child: My Life in Science Fiction, 1984; Lifeburst, 1984; Firechild, 1986; Mazeway, 1990; Beachhead, 1992; Demon Moon, 1994. Co-author with Frederik Pohl: Undersea Quest, 1954; Undersea Fleet, 1955; Undersea City, 1956; The Reefs of Space, 1964; Starchild, 1965; Rogue Star, 1969; The Farthest Star, 1975; Wall Around a Star, 1983; Land's End, 1988. With James Gunn: Star Bridge, 1955. With Miles J Breuer: The Birth of a New Republic, 1981. Honours: Pilgrim Award, Science Fiction Research Association, 1968; Grand Master Nebula Award, 1976; Hugo Award, 1985. Memberships: Science Fiction Writers of America, president 1978-80; Science Fiction Research Association; World Science Fiction Planetary Society. Address: PO Box 761, Portales, NM 88130, USA.

WILLIAMSON Robert Clifford, b. 25 Apr 1916, Los Angeles, California, USA. Professor of Sociology; Writer. m. Virginia M Lorenzini, 11 Apr 1953, 2 sons. Education: BA, Psychology, 1938, MA, Psychology, 1940, University of California, Los Angeles; PhD, Sociology, University of Southern California, 1951. Publications: Social Psychology (with S S Sargent), 1958, 3rd edition, 1982; El Estudiante Colombiano y sus Aetitudes, 1962; Marriage and Family Relations, 1966, 2nd edition, 1972; Sex Roles in Contemporary Culture, 1970; Bilingualism and Minority Languages, 1991; Early Retirement: Promises and Pitfalls (with A Rinehart and T Blank), 1992; Latin American Societies in Transition, 1997. Contributions to: American Journal of Sociology; Social Forces; Journal of Marriage and the Family; Revista Mexicana de Sociologia; Western Political Quarterly; Sociology and Social Research. Address: Department of Sociology, Lehigh University, 681 Taylor Street, Bethlehem, PA 18015, USA.

WILLIAMSON Robin, b. 24 Nov 1943, Edinburgh, Scotland. Writer; Musician; Storyteller. m. Bina Jasbinder Kaur Williamson, 2 Aug 1989, 1 son, 1 daughter. Publications: Home Thoughts from Abroad, 1972; Five Denials on Merlin's Grave, 1979; Selected Writings, 1980-83, 1984; The Craneskin Bag, 1989. Other: Music books, spoken word cassettes and recordings. Address: BCM 4797, London WC1N 3XX, England.

WILLIS Meredith Sue, b. 31 May 1946, Clarksburg, West Virginia, USA. Writer; Teacher. m. Andrew B Weinberger, 9 May 1982, 1 son. Education: BA, Barnard College, 1969; MFA, Columbia University, 1972. Publications: A Space Apart, 1979; Higher Ground, 1981; Personal Fiction Writing, 1984; Only Great Changes, 1985; Quilt Pieces, 1990; Blazing Pencils, 1991; Deep Revision, 1993; In the Mountains of America, 1994. Honours: National Endowment for the Arts, Fellowship, 1978; New Jersey Literary Fellowship, 1989, 1995. Memberships: PEN; Authors Guild; National Writers Union. Address: 311 Prospect Street, South Orange, NJ 07079, USA.

WILLOUGHBY Cass. See: **OLSEN Theodore Victor.**

WILLOUGHBY Lee Davis. See: **AVALLONE Michael (Angelo Jr).**

WILMER Clive, b. 10 Feb 1945, Harrogate, Yorkshire, England. Freelance Teacher; Lecturer; Writer; Broadcaster. m. Diane Redmond, 12 Sept 1971, div 1986, 1 son, 1 daughter. Education: BA 1st Class Hons, English, 1967, MA, 1970, King's College, Cambridge. Appointments: Exhibition Committee, Pound's Artists, Tate Gallery, London and Kettle's Yard, Cambridge, 1984-85; Visiting Professor, Creative Writing, University of California, Santa Barbara, 1986; Editor, Numbers, 1986-90; Presenter of BBC Radio 3 Series, Poet of the Month, 1989-92; Mikimoto Memorial Ruskin Lecturer, University of Lancaster, 1996. Publications: Poems: The Dwelling Place, 1977; Devotions, 1982; Of Earthly Paradise, 1992. Translator with G Gömöri: Miklós Radnóti, Forced March, 1979; György Petri, Night Song of the Personal Shadow, 1991. Editor: Thom Gunn: The Occasions of Poetry, 1982; John Ruskin: Unto This Last and Other Writings, 1985; Dante Gabriel Rossetti: Selected Poems and Translations, 1991; William Morris: News From Nowhere and Other Writings, 1993; Poets Talking: The 'Poet of the Month', Interviews from BBC Radio 3, 1994; Selected Poems, 1995; My Manifold City, translated with George Gömöri, 1996. Contributions to: PN Review; Times Literary Supplement; The Times; Southern Review; Agenda; Others. Honours: Writer's Grant, Arts Council of Great Britain, 1979; Author's Foundation Grant, 1993. Membership: Companion of the Guild of St George, 1995. Address: 57 Norwich Street, Cambridge CB2 1ND, England.

WILOCH Thomas, b. 3 Feb 1953, Detroit, Michigan, USA. Writer; Editor. m. Denise Gottis, 10 Oct 1981. Education: BA, Wayne State University, 1978. Appointments: Associated with Gale Research Inc, 1977-; Freelance Writing and Editing; Columnist, Retrofuturism, 1991-93; Book Reviewer, Anti-Matter Magazine, 1992-94; Columnist, Photo Static, 1993-94. Publications: Stigmata Junction, 1985; Paper Mask, 1988; The Mannikin Cypher, 1989; Tales of Lord Shantih, 1990; Decoded Factories of the Heart, 1991, new edition, 1994; Night Rain, 1991; Narcotic Signature, 1992; Lyrical Brandy, 1993; Mr Templeton's Toyshop, 1995; Neon Trance, 1997. Contributions to: More than 200 magazines. Honours: Nomination, Pushcart Prize, 1988, 1990; Nomination, Rhysling Award, 1992, 1996. Address: 43672 Emrick Drive, Canton, MI 48187, USA.

WILSON A(ndrew) N, b. 27 Oct 1950, England. Author. m. (1) Katherine Duncan-Jones, 2 daughters, (2) Ruth Alexander Guilding, 1991. Education: MA, New College, Oxford. Appointments: Lecturer, St Hugh's College and New College, Oxford, 1976-81; Literary Editor, The Spectator, 1981-83. Publications: The Sweets of Pimlico (novel), 1977; Unguarded Hours (novel), 1978; Kindly Light (novel), 1979; The Laird of Abbotsford, 1980; The Healing Art (novel), 1980; Who Was Oswald Fish (novel), 1981; Wise Virgin (novel), 1982; A Life of John Milton, 1983; Scandal (novel), 1983; Hilaire Belloc, 1984; Gentlemen in England (novel), 1985; Love Unknown (novel), 1986; co-author, The Church in Crisis, 1986; Stray (novel), 1987; Landscape in France, 1987; Incline Our Hearts (novel), 1987; Penfriends from Porlock, Essays and Reviews, 1977-86, 1988; Tolstoy: A Biography, 1988; Eminent Victorians, 1989; C S Lewis: A Biography, 1990; A Bottle in the Smoke (novel), 1990; Against Religion, 1991; Daughters of Albion (novel), 1991; Jesus, 1992; A Vicar of Sorrows (novel), 1993; The Faber Book of Church and Clergy, 1992; The Rise and Fall of the House of Windsor, 1993; The Faber Book of London (editor), 1993; Hearing Voices (novel), 1995. Honours: Royal Society of Literature, fellow, 1981; Whitbread Biography Award, 1988. Address: 91 Albert Street, London NW1 7LX, England.

WILSON August, b. 27 Apr 1945, Pittsburgh, Pennsylvania, USA. Dramatist. 1 daughter. Appointment: Founder, Black Horizons Theatre Co, Pittsburgh, 1968. Publications: The Homecoming, 1979; The Coldest Day of the Year, 1979; Fullerton Street, 1980; Black Bart and the Sacred Hills, 1981; Jitney, 1982; Ma Rainey's Black Bottom, 1984; Fences, 1985; Joe Turner's Come and Gone, 1986; The Piano Lesson, 1987; Two Trains Running, 1990; Seven Guitars, 1995. Honours: New York Drama Critics Circle Awards, 1985, 1986, 1988, 1990, 1996; Whiting Writer's Award, 1986; American Theatre Critics Outstanding Play Awards, 1986, 1990, 1992; Drama Desk Awards, 1986, 1990; Pulitzer Prizes for Drama, 1987, 1990; Tony Award, 1987; Outer Critics' Circle Award, 1987; Literary Lion Award, New York Public Library, 1988. Membership: American Academy of Arts and

Letters. Address: 1285 Avenue of the Americas, New York, NY 10019, USA.

WILSON Barbara. See: **HARRIS Laurence Mark.**

WILSON Budge Marjorie, b. 2 May 1927, Halifax, Nova Scotia, Canada. Writer. m. Alan Wilson, 31 July 1953, 2 daughters. Education: BA, 1949, Diploma in Education, 1952, Dalhousie University. Publications: The Best-Worst Christmas Present Ever, 1984; A House Far from Home, 1986; Mr John Bertrand Nijinsky and Charlie, 1986; Mystery Lights at Blue Harbour, 1987; Breakdown, 1988; Going Bananas, 1989; Thirteen Never Changes, 1989; Madame Belzile and Ramsay Hitherton-Hobbs, 1990; Lorinda's Diary, 1991; The Leaving, 1990; Oliver's Wars, 1992; The Courtship (adult short fiction), 1994; Cassandra's Driftwood, 1994; Cordelia Clark and Other Stories, 1994; Many adult and children's short stories. Contributions to: University of Windsor Review, The Dress, 1993; Pottersfield Portfolio, Elliot's Daughter, 1994; The Dandelion Garden, 1995; Harold and Harold, 1995; Mothers and Other Strangers, 1996. Honours: CBC Literary Competition, 1981; Atlantic Writing Competition, 1986; City of Dartmouth Book Award, 1991; Young Adult Book Award, Canadian Library Association, 1991; Marianna Dempster Award, Canadian Authors Association, 1992; Ann Connor Brimer Award, 1993. Memberships: Board Member, Writers Federation of Nova Scotia; Canadian Authors Association; Writers Union of Canada; Secretary, Atlantic Representative, Canadian Society of Children's Authors, Illustrators and Performers; Councillor-East (Canada), International Board on Books for Young Children. Address: North West Cove, RR1, Hubbards, Nova Scotia B0J 1T0, Canada.

WILSON Christopher Richard Maclean, b. 6 Jan 1934, Minehead, Somerset, England. Educator. m. Alma Louis Oliver, 5 Sept 1964, 2 sons. Education: BA, 1957, MA, 1961, St Catharine's College, Cambridge; Clifton Theological School, Bristol, 1960; Episcopal Theological School, Cambridge, Massachusetts, USA; MA 1971, PhD 1977, University of Toronto. Appointment: Director, Board and Management Services, Ontario Hospital Association, 1978-92. Publications: Hospital-wide Quality Assurance, 1987; Governing with Distinction, 1988; New on Board, 1991; Strategies in Health Care Quality, 1992. Monographs: Quality Assurance-Getting Started, 1985; Annotated Bibliography on Hospital Governance, 1989; Risk Management for Canadian Health Care Facilities, 1990. Contributions to: Professional journals. Honours: Writer of the Year, Canadian Association for Quality in Health Care, 1990; Honorary Fellow, University of Manchester 1992-94. Address: 10 St Mary Street, Toronto, Ontario M4Y 1P9, Canada.

WILSON Colin Henry, b. 26 July 1931, Leicester, England. Author. m. (1) Dorothy Betty Troop, 1 son, (2) Joy Stewart, 2 sons, 1 daughter. Appointments: Visiting Professor, Hollins College, Virginia, 1966-67, University of Washington, Seattle, 1967, Dowling College, Majorca, 1969, Rutgers University, New Jersey, 1974. Publications: The Outsider, 1956; Religion and the Rebel, 1957; The Age of Defeat, 1959; Ritual in the Dark, 1960; The Strength to Dream, 1962; Origins of the Sexual Impulse, 1963; Necessary Doubt, 1964; Eagle and the Earwig, 1965; The Glass Cage, 1966; Sex and the Intelligent Teenager, 1966; Voyage to a Beginning, 1969; Hermann Hesse, 1973; Strange Powers, 1973; The Space Vampires, 1976; Mysteries, 1978; Starseekers, 1980; Access to Inner Worlds, 1982; Psychic Detectives, 1983; The Essential Colin Wilson, 1984; Rudolf Steiner: The Man and His Work, 1985; An Encyclopedia of Scandal (with Donald Seaman), 1986; Spider World: The Tower, 1987; Aleister Crowley - The Man and the Myth, 1987; An Encyclopedia of Unsolved Mysteries (with Damon Wilson), 1987; Marx Refuted, 1987; Written in Blood (with Donald Seaman), 1989; The Misfits - A Study of Sexual Outsiders, 1988; Beyond the Occult, 1988; The Serial Killers, 1990; Spiderworld: The Magician, 1991; The Strange Life of P D Ouspensky, 1993. Contributions to: The Times; Literary Review; The Gramophone; Evening Standard Daily Mail. Membership: Society of Authors. Address: Tetherdown, Trewallock Lane, Gorran Haven, Cornwall, England.

WILSON Dave. See: **FLOREN Lee.**

WILSON Des, b. 1941, New Zealand. Writer. Appointments: Journalist, Broadcaster, 1957-67; Director, Shelter National Campaign for the Homeless, 1967-71; Columnist, The Guardian, 1968-70, The Observer, 1971-75; Head of Public Affairs, Royal Shakespeare Company, London, 1974-76; Editor, Social Work Today, 1976-79;

Deputy Editor, Illustrated London News, 1979-81; Chairman, Campaign for Lead Free Air, 1981-85; Friends of the Earth, 1982-86; Freedom of Information, 1984-91; President, Liberal Party, 1986-87; General Election Campaign Director, Liberal Democrats, 1991-92. Publications: I Know It Was the Place's Fault, 1970; Des Wilson's Minority Report, 1973; So You Want to be Prime Minister, 1979; The Lead Scandal, 1982; Pressure: The A to Z of Campaigning in Britain, 1984; The Enviornmental Crisis, 1984; The Secrets File, 1984; Costa del Sol, 1990; Campaign: 1992; Campaigning, The A to Z of Public Advocacy, 1994. Address: 48 Stapleton Hall Road, Stroud Green, London N4 3QG, England.

WILSON Edward Osborne, b. 10 June 1929, Birmingham, Alabama, USA. Biologist; Professor; Writer. m. Irene Kelley, 30 Oct 1955, 1 daughter. Education: BS, 1949, MS, 1950, University of Alabama; PhD, Harvard University, 1955. Appointments: Junior Fellow, Society of Fellows, 1953-56, Faculty, 1956-76, Curator, Entomology, 1971-, Baird Professor of Science, 1976-94, Pellegrino University Professor, 1994-, Harvard University; Board of Directors, World Wildlife Fund, 1983-94, Organization of Tropical Studies, 1984-91, New York Botanical Gardens, 1991-95, American Museum of Natural History, 1992-, American Academy of Liberal Education, 1993-, Nature Conservancy, 1994-, Conservation International, 1997-. Publications: The Insect Societies, 1971; Sociobiology: The New Synthesis, 1975; On Human Nature, 1978; Promethean Fire (with C J Lumsden), 1983; Biophilia, 1984; The Ants (with Bert Holldobler), 1990; Success and Dominance in Ecosystems, 1990; The Diversity of Life, 1991; Journey to the Ants (with Bert Holldobler), 1994; Naturalist, 1994; Others. Contributions to: Professional journals. Honours: National Medal of Science, 1976; Pulitzer Prizes in Non-Fiction, 1979, 1991; Tyler Ecology Prize, 1984; Weaver Award for Scholarly Letters, Ingersoll Foundation, 1989; Crafoord Prize, Royal Swedish Academy of Sciences, 1990; Prix d'Institut de la Vie, Paris, 1990; International Prize for Biology, Government of Japan, 1993; Audubon Medal, Audubon Society, 1995; Phi Beta Kappa Prize for Science, 1995; Los Angeles Times Book Prize for Science, 1995; Schubert Prize, Germany, 1996; Many honorary doctorates; Others. Memberships: American Academy of Arts and Sciences, fellow; American Genetics Association; American Humanist Society; American Philosophical Society; British Ecological Society, honorary life member; Entomological Society of America, honorary life member; National Academy of Science; Royal Society of London; Finnish Academy of Science and Letters; Russian Academy of Natural Sciences. Address: 9 Foster Road, Lexington, MA 02173, USA.

WILSON Edwin James (Peter), b. 27 Oct 1942, Lismore, New South Wales, Australia. Community Relations, Royal Botanic Gardens, Sydney. m. Cheryl Lillian Turnham, 1 Sept 1975, 2 sons, 1 daughter. Education: BSc, University of New South Wales. Publications: Banyan, 1982; Liberty, Egality, Fraternity, 1984; The Dragon Tree, 1985; Discovering the Domain, 1986; Wild Tamarind, 1987; Falling Up Into Verse, 1989; Songs of the Forest, 1990; The Rose Garden, 1991; The Wishing Tree, 1992; The Botanic Verses, 1993; Contributions to: Poetry Australia; Australian Folklore, Vol 9, 1994, Vol10, 1995, Vol 11, 1996. Membership: New South Wales Poets Union. Address: PO Box 32, Lane Cove, New South Wales 2066, Australia.

WILSON Gina, b. 1 Apr 1943, Abergele, North Wales. Children's Writer; Poet. Education: MA, University of Edinburgh, 1965; Mount Holyoke College, 1965-66. Appointments: Assistant Editor, Scottish National Dictionary, 1967-73, Dictionary of the Older Scottish Tongue, 1972-73. Publications: Cora Ravenwing, 1980; A Friendship of Equals, 1981; The Whisper, 1982; All Ends Up, 1984; Family Feeling, 1986; Just Us, 1988; Polly Pipes Up, 1989; I Hope You Know, 1989; Jim Jam Pyjamas, 1990; Wompus Galumpus, 1990; Riding the Great White, 1992; Prowlpuss, 1994. Address: c/o David Higham Ltd, 5-8 Lower John Street, Golden Square, London W1R 4HA, England.

WILSON Jacqueline, b. 17 Dec 1945, Bath, Somerset, England. Writer. m. William Millar Wilson, 28 Aug 1965, 1 daughter. Publications: Nobody's Perfect, 1982; Waiting for the Sky to Fall, 1983; The Other Side, 1984; Amber, 1986; The Power of the Shade, 1987; This Girl, 1988; Stevie Day Series, 1987; Is There Anybody There?, 1990; The Story of Tracy Beaker, 1991; The Suitcase Kid, 1992; Deep Blue, 1993; The Bed and Breakfast Star, 1994; Cliffhanger, 1995; The Dinosaur's Packed Lunch, 1995; Double Act, 1995; Bad Girls, 1996. Honours: Oak Tree Award, 1992; Winner, Smarties Award, 1995. Address: 1B Beaufort Road, Kingston on Thames, Surrey KT1 2TH, England.

WILSON Joyce Muriel, (Joyce Stranger), b. 26 May 1921, London, England. Writer; Dog Trainer. m. Dr Kenneth Bruce Wilson, 28 Feb 1944, 2 sons, 1 daughter. Education: BSc, University College, London, 1942. Publications: Over 65 books; Thursday's Child, 1994; A Cry on the Wind, 1995. Contributions to: Various publications; Smart Dogs; Dog Training Weekly. Memberships: Humane Education Society; People and Dogs Society, President; Canine Concern, President; UK Register of Canine Behaviourists; Association of Pet Dog Trainers; Chartered Institute of Journalists; Society of Authors. Literary Agent: Brian Stone, Aiken & Stone Ltd. Address: 29 Fernshaw Road, London SW10 0TG, England.

WILSON Keith, b. 26 Dec 1927, Clovis, New Mexico, USA. Poet; Writer. m. Heloise Brigham, 15 Feb 1958, 1 son, 4 daughters. Education: BS, US Naval Academy, 1950; MA, University of New Mexico, 1956. Publications: Homestead, 1969; Thantog: Songs of a Jaguar Priest, 1977; While Dancing Feet Shatter the Earth, 1977; The Streets of San Miguel, 1979; Retables, 1981; Stone Roses: Poems from Transylvania, 1983; Meeting at Jal (with Theodore Ensliu), 1985; Lion's Gate: Selected Poems 1963-1986, 1988; The Wind of Pentecost, 1991; Graves Registry, 1992; The Way of the Dove, 1994. Contributions to: Journals. Honours: National Endowment for the Arts Fellowship; Fulbright-Hays Fellowship; D H Lawrence Creative Writing Fellowship. Address: 1500 South Locust Street, No C-21, Las Cruces, NM 88001, USA.

WILSON Leslie Erica, b. 10 Aug 1952, Nottingham, England. Novelist. m. David Wilson, 20 July 1974, 2 daughters. Education: BA, Durham University; PGCE, Oxford. Publications: Morning is Not Permitted, 1990; Malefice, 1992; US Publications, 1993; The Mountain of Immoderate Desires, 1994. Contributions to: Orbis; Writing Women; Guardian; Iron; Good Housekeeping Sunday Times; Independent on Sunday; London Rewiew of Books; Literary Review. Memberships: Poetry Society; Society of Authors; PEN; Royal Society of Literature.

WILSON Lorraine Margaret, b. 18 May 1939, Echuca, Victoria, Australia. Educational Consultant. Education: Trained Infant Teacher's Certificate; Certificate A, Education Department of Victoria. Appointment: Public Lending Right Committee. Publications: City Kids, series, 1978-86; Write Me A Sign, 1979; Country Kids, series, 1982-87; You Can't Make a Book in a Day (with B Scarffe, 1988); My Mum Has False Teeth and Other Stories, 1990; An Integrated Approach to Learning (with D Malmgren, S Ramage, L Schulz), 1990; Write Me a Poem, 1994; Footy Kids, series, 1995; I Have Two Dads, 1995; I Speak Two Languages, 1995; James and Jessie Series, 1995. Contributions to: Curriculum and Research Bulletin; Australian Journal of Reading; Primary Education; Reading Teacher; Teaching K-8. Honour: ALEA Medal, 1996. Memberships: Australian Society of Authors; Australian Literacy Educators Association; Convenor of Special Interest Group, "Teachers Applying Whole Language"; International Reading Association; Australian Education Network. Address: 81 Amess Street, North Carlton, Victoria 3054, Australia.

WILSON Peter John, b. 24 Apr 1944, Sydney, New South Wales, Australia. Mathematics Tutor. m. Sau Ching Au, 27 Apr 1988. Education: BSc, 1964, MA, 1989, University of Sydney. Publications: Australia's Insect Life, 1970; Modelling the SR 71A, 1976; The Living Bush: A Naturalist's Guide, 1977; Australia's Butterflies, 1977; Darkness, No Darkness, 1978; The Convair F106 Delta Dart, 1978; World of Insects, 1979; Depth of Field, 1980; Extreme Close-up Photography, 1981; Insect Photography, 1985; Butterflies of the Rainforest, 1986; Going It Alone, 1989. Address: 49 Despointes St, Marrickville, New South Wales 2204, Australia.

WINCH Donald Norman, b. 15 Apr 1935, London, England. University Professor. m. 5 Aug 1983. Education: BSc, London School of Economics, 1956; PhD, Princeton University, 1960. Publications: Classical Political Economy and Colonies, 1965; Economics and Policy, 1969, 1972; Economic Advisory Council, 1976; Adam Smith's Politics, 1978; That Noble Science of Politics, 1983; Malthus, 1987; Riches and Poverty, 1996. Contributions to: Many Learned Journals. Honours: Fellow, British Academy, 1986; Royal Historical Society, 1987. Memberships: Royal Economic Society; Economic Journal; Royal Economic Society. Address: University of Sussex, Falmer, Brighton, Sussex BN1 9QN, England.

WINCH Gordon Clappison, b. 6 Feb 1930, Kyogle, New South Wales, Australia. Author; Consultant. m. Diana Elizabeth May Vernon, 20 Dec 1956, 1 son, 2 daughters. Education: BA (Syd), 1956; MA

(Syd), 1967; MEd (Syd), 1964; PhD (Wisc), 1971. Publications: Teaching Reading: A Language Experience (editor with Valerie Hoogstad), 1985; Give Them Wings: The Experience of Children's Literature (editor with Maurice Saxby), 1987, 2nd edition, 1991; Samantha Seagull's Sandals, 1985; Enoch the Emu, 1986; Primary Grammar Handbook (with Gregory Blaxell), 1994. Contributions to: English in Australia; Journal of Australian Association for Teaching of English; Journals of Australian Reading Association; Primary English Teachers' Association. Honour: Head, Department of English, Kuring-gai, University of Technology, Sydney, New South Wales. Memberships: Primary English Teachers' Association, New South Wales, Foundation President; Australian Literary Educators' Association; Children's Book Council of Australia; Australian Society of Authors. Address: 186 Beecroft Road, Cheltenham, New South Wales 2119, Australia.

WINCH Peter Guy, b. 14 Jan 1926, London, England. Professor of Philosophy. m. Jan 1947, 2 sons. Education: MA; BPhil, 1951, St Edmund Hall, Oxford. Publications: The Idea of a Social Science, 1951; Ethics and Action, 1972; Trying to Make Sense, 1987; Simone Weil: The Just Balance, 1989. Editor: Studies in the Philosophy of Wittgenstein, 1969; Wittgenstein: Attention to Particulars, 1990; The Political Responsibility of Intellectuals, 1990. Contributions to: Numerous Journals, magazines and periodicals. Honours: Senior Research Fellow, Leverhulme Trust, 1976-77; Fellow, King's College, London, 1985-; Corresponding Member, Institut für die Wissenschaften vom Menschen, Vienna, 1986-; Honorary Fellow, University College of Swansea, 1990-. Memberships: Aristotelian Society, president, 1980-81; American Philosophical Association; Association of University Teachers; American Association of University Professors. Address: 310 West Hill Street 3W, Champaign, IL 61820, USA.

WINCHESTER Jack. See: **FREEMANTLE Brian**.

WINDSOR Patricia, (Colin Daniel), b. 21 Sept 1938, New York, USA. Writer; Lecturer; Teacher. 1 son, 1 daughter. Appointments: Faculty, Institute of Children's Literature, University of Maryland Writers Institute; Editor-in-Chief, The Easterner, Washington, DC; Co-Director, Wordspring Literary Consultants; Director, Summertree Studios, Savannah. Publications: The Summer Before, 1973; Something's Waiting for You, Baker D, 1974; Home is Where Your Feet Are Standing, 1975; Mad Martin, 1976; Killing Time, 1980; The Sandman's Eyes, 1985; The Hero, 1988; Just Like the Movies, 1990; The Christmas Killer, 1991. Contributions to: Anthologies and magazines. Honours: American Library Association Best Book Award, 1973; Outstanding Book for Young Adults Citation, New York Times, 1976; Edgar Allan Poe Award, Mystery Writers of America, 1986. Memberships: Authors Guild; Childrens Book Guild; International Writing Guild; Mystery Writers of America; Poetry Society of Georgia; Savannah Storytellers. Address: c/o Writers House, 21 West 26th Street, New York, NY 10010, USA.

WINEGARTEN Renee, b. 23 June 1922, London, England. Literary Critic; Author. m. Asher Winegarten, dec 1946. Education: MA, 1943, PhD, 1950, Girton College, Cambridge. Publications: French Lyric Poetry in the Age of Malherbe, 1954; Writers and Revolution, 1974; The Double Life of George Sand, 1978; Madame de Staël, 1985; Simone de Beauvoir: A Critical View, 1988. Contributions to: Journals. Memberships: Friends of George Sand; Society of Authors; Authors Guild. Address: 12 Heather Walk, Edgware, Middlesex HA8 9TS, England.

WINGATE John Allan, b. 15 Mar 1920, Cornwall, England. Author. 1 son, 1 daughter. Publications: Submariner Sinclair Series, 1959-64; Sinclair Action Series, 1968, 1969, 1971; HMS Belfast, In Trust for the Nation, 1972; In the Blood, 1973; Below the Horizon, 1974; The Sea Above Them, 1975; Oil Strike, 1976; Black Tide, 1976; Avalanche, 1977; Red Mutiny, 1977; Target Risk, 1978; Seawaymen, 1979; Frigate, 1980; Carrier, 1981; Submarine, 1982; William the Conqueror, 1984; Go Deep, 1985; The Windship Race, 1987; The Fighting Tenth, 1990; The Man Called Mark, 1996. Honour: Mentioned in Dispatches, 1942; Distinguished Service Cross, 1943. Membership: Nautical Institute. Address: c/o Lloyd Bank Plc, Waterloo Place, Pall Mall, London SW1Y 5NJ.

WINSTON Sarah, (Sarah E Lorenz), b. 15 Dec 1912, New York, New York, USA. Writer. m. Keith Winston, 11 June 1932, 2 sons. Education: New York University, 1929, 1930; Philosophy and Appreciation of Art course, The Barnes Foundation, 1966, 1967; Art

Seminars (research), 1967-89. Publications: And Always Tomorrow, 1963; Everything Happens for the Best, 1969; Our Son, Ken, 1969; Not Yet Spring (poems), 1976; V-Mail: Letters of the World War II Combat Medic, 1985; Summer Conference, 1990; Of Apples and Oranges, 1993. Contributions to: Journals. Honours: 1st Prize Awards, 1972, 1974, National League of American Pen Women. Membership: National League of American Pen Women. Address: 1801 Morris Road, No C110, Blue Bell, PA 19422, USA.

WINTER Michael John, b. 5 Aug 1964, Sydney, New South Wales, Australia. Writer; Actor; Executive Story Consultant. Education: Picton High School; New South Wales Police Academy. Publications: Effortless Way (rock musical), 1986; Radio Nemesis, 1990; Blue Heelers (television series), 1992-95; Water Rats, 1995. Memberships: Australian Writers Guild; Australian Film Institute; Actors Equity; MEAA. Address: 22 Castlereagh Street, Tahmoor, New South Wales 2573, Australia.

WINTERSON Jeanette, b. 27 Aug 1959, Manchester, England. Writer. Education: MA, St Catherine's College, Oxford, 1981. Publications: Oranges Are Not the Only Fruit, 1985; The Passion, 1987; Sexing the Cherry, 1989; Written on the Body, 1992; Art and Lies; Art Objects, 1994, essays, 1995. Screenplay: Great Moments in Aviation, 1993. Honours: Whitbread Award for Best First Novel, 1985; John Llewellyn Rhys Memorial Book Prize, 1987; E M Forster Award, American Academy of Arts and Letters, 1989. Address: c/o Bloomsbury, 2 Soho Square, London W1V 5DE, England.

WISEMAN Christopher Stephen, b. 31 May 1936, Hull, England. University Teacher. Education: MA, Cambridge University; PhD, University of Strathclyde. Publications: Waiting for the Barbarians, 1971; The Barbarian File, 1975; Beyond the Labyrinth: A Study of Edwin Muir's Poetry, 1978; The Upper Hand, 1981; An Ocean of Whispers, 1982; Postcards Home, 1988; Missing Persons, 1989; Remembering Mr Fox, 1995. Contributions to: Journals and periodicals. Honours: Alberta Achievement Award for Excellence, 1988; Writers Guild of Alberta Award for Poetry, 1988; Alberta Culture Poetry Prize, 1988. Address: Department of English, University of Calgary, Calgary, Alberta T2N 1N4, Canada.

WISEMAN David, (Jane Julian), b. 13 Jan 1916, Manchester, England. Writer. m. Cicely Hilda Mary Richards, 2 Sept 1939, 2 sons, 2 daughters. Education: BA, 1937, Teaching Diploma, 1938, Manchester University. Appointment: Editor, Adult Education, 1947-50. Publications: Jeremy Visick, 1981; The Fate of Jeremy Visick, 1982; Thimbles, 1982; Blodwen and the Guardians, 1983; Adams Common, 1984; Pudding and Pie, 1986; Jumping Jack, 1988; Badge of Honour, 1989; The Devil's Cauldron, 1989; Mum's Winning Streak, 1990; Moonglow, 1990; Goliath Takes the Bait, 1993. As Jane Julian: Ellen Bray, 1985; As Wind to Fire, 1989; The Sunlit Days, 1990. Membership: Society of Authors. Address: 24 Ravenswood Drive, Auckley, Doncaster DN9 3PB, England.

WITTICH John Charles Bird, (Charles Bird), b. 18 Feb 1929, London, England. Retired Librarian. m. June Rose Taylor, 10 July 1954, 1 son, 1 daughter. Education: BA, 1951. Publications: Off Beat Walks In London, 1969, revised, 1995; Curiosities of London, 1973, revised, 1996; London Villages, 1992; Curiosities of Surrey, 1994; Exploring Cathedrals, 1996. Contributions to: Periodicals, journals and magazines. Address: 88 Woodlawn Street, Whitstable, Kent CT5 1HH, England.

WOESSNER Warren (Dexter), b. 31 May 1944, Brunswick, New Jersey, USA. Attorney; Editor; Poet; Writer. m. Iris Freeman, 6 Jan 1990. Education: BA, Cornell University, 1966; PhD, 1971, JD, 1981, University of Wisconsin. Appointments: Founder, Editor, and Publisher, 1968-81, Senior Editor, 1981-, Abraxas Magazine; Board of Directors, 1988-92, President, 1989-92, Coffee House Press; Contributing Editor, Pharmaceutical News. Publications: The Forest and the Trees, 1968; Landing, 1974; No Hiding Place, 1979; Storm Lines, 1987; Clear to Chukchi, 1996. Contributions to: Anthologies, magazines, periodicals and journals. Honours: National Endowment for the Arts Fellowship, 1974; Wisconsin Arts Board Fellowship, 1975, 1976; Loft-McKnight Fellowship, 1985; Minnesota Voices, Literary Competition for Poetry, 1986. Address: 34 West Minnehaha Parkway, Minneapolis, MN 55419, USA.

WOHLLEBEN Rudolf, b. 4 June 1936, Bad Kreuznach, Germany. Antenna Telecommunications Engineer; Writer. m. Walburg

B Groehler, 27 Aug 1967, 2 sons. Education: BSEE, Techn, Hochschule, Karlsruhe, 1957; MSEE, Techn, Hochschule, Munich, 1960; Dr Ing, RWTH, Aachen, 1969; Lecturer Antennas, Microwaves, radar, 1980 ; University of Kaiserslautern, Germany. Appointment: Commissary, Division for Electronics, Max-Planck-Institut fuer Radioastronomie, Bonn, Germany, 1971-. Publications: Antennas for Elliptical Polarisation and It's Measuring Techniques, 1968; Farfield Array Antenna Pattern Simulation on an Analog Computer, 1970; Farfield Array Antenna Pattern Simulation on The hybrid analog computer, 1973; Interferometrie in Radioastronomie u Radar, 1973; Corps Alemannia Karlsruhe in 250 Semestern (editor), 1988; Interferometry in Radioastronomy and Radar Techniques, Dondrecht, NL, 1991; Fruehe Spaetlese, Poems, 1953-1997, 1997. Contributions to: 67 scientific papers in telecommunications periodicals in Germany, USA, England; 126 book reviews in German, Swiss periodicals. Membership: US-Planetary Society, Germany. Literary Agent: Robert Wohlleben, Holstentwiete 1, D 22763 Hamburg, Germany. Address: Max-Planck-Institut fuer Radioastronomie, PB 2024, D53010 Bonn, German.

WOLFE Christopher, b. 11 Mar 1949, Boston, Massachusetts, USA. Professor of Political Science; Writer. m. Anne McGowan, 17 June 1972, 5 sons, 5 daughters. Education: BA, University of Notre Dame, 1971; PhD, Boston College, 1978. Appointments: Instructor, Assumption College, Worcester, Massachusetts, 1975-78; Assistant Professor, 1978-84, Associate Professor, 1984-92, Professor of Political Science, 1992-, Marquette University; Founder, American Public Philosophy Institute, 1990. Publications: The Rise of Modern Judicial Review: From Constitutional Interpretation to Judge-Made Law, 1986, revised edition, 1994; Faith and Liberal Democracy, 1987; Judicial Activism: Bulwark of Freedom or Precarious Security?, 1991; Liberalism at the Crossroads (editor with John Hittinger), 1994; How to Interpret the Constitution, 1996. Contributions to: Professional journals and general periodicals. Honours: Woodrow Wilson Fellowship, 1971; Institute for Educational Affairs Grants, 1982, 1983; Bradley Foundation Grant, 1986; National Endowment for the Humanities Fellowship, 1994. Memberships: American Political Science Association; Federalist Society; Fellowship of Catholic Scholars; Phi Beta Kappa. Address: c/o Department of Political Science, Marquette University, Box 1881, Milwaukee, WI 53201-1881, USA.

WOLFE Gary Kent, b. 24 Mar 1946, Sedalia, Missouri, USA. Educator; Critic. Education: BA, University of Kansas, 1968; MA, 1969, PhD, 1971, University of Chicago. Appointments: Editorial Board, Science-Fiction Studies, 1984-, Journal of the Fantastic in the Arts, 1988-. Publications: The Known and the Unknown: The Iconography of Science Fiction, 1979; David Lindsay, 1982; Critical Terms for Science Fiction and Fantasy, 1986. Co-author: Elements of Research, 1979. Editor: Science Fiction Dialogues, 1982. Contributions to: Books, reference works, and journals. Honours: Eaton Award for Science Fiction Criticism, 1981; Pilgrim Award, Science Fiction Research Association, 1987; James Friend Memorial Award for Literary Criticism, Friends of Literature, 1992. Memberships: Committee Director, International Association for the Fantastic in the Arts, 1985-; Board of Directors, Friends of the Chicago Public Library, 1990-93. Address: 1450 East 55th Place, Apt 420 South, Chicago, IL 60637, USA.

WOLFE Peter, b. 25 Aug 1933, New York, New York, USA. Professor; Writer. m. Marie Paley, 22 Dec 1962, div 1969, 2 sons. Education: BA, City College of New York, 1955; MA, LeHigh Universty, 1957; PhD, University of Wisconsin, 1965. Publications: Dashiell Hammett, 1980; Laden Choirs: Patrick White, 1983; Something More Than Night: Raymond Chandler, 1985; John le Carré, 1987; Yukio Mishima, 1989; Alarms and Epitaphs: Eric Ambler, 1993; In the Zone: Rod Serling's Twilight Vision, 1996; A Vision of His Own: William Gaddis, 1997. Contributions to: Weekend Australian; Sydney Morning Herald; New Zealand Listener; Calcutta Statesman; New York Times Book Review; Chicago Tribune. Hnours: Fulbright Award to India, 1987, Poland, 1991; University of Missouri, President's Award for Creativity and Research, 1995. Address: 4466 West Pine, Apt 18B, St Louis, MO 63108, USA.

WOLFERS Michael, b. 28 Sept 1938, London, England. Writer; Translator. Education: Wadham College, Oxford University, 1959-62; South Bank Polytechnic, 1990-91. Appointments: Journalist, The Times, London, 1965-72; Visiting Senior Lecturer, African Politics and Government, University of Juba, 1979-82. Publications: Black Man's Burden Revisited, 1974; Politics in the Organisation of African Unity,

1976; Luandino Vierira, The Real Life of Domingos Xavier, 1978; Poems for Angola, 1979; Samir Amin, Delinking: Towards a Polycentric World, 1990; Hamlet and Cybernetics, 1991. Contributions to: Numerous Publications. Memberships: Royal Institute of International Affairs; Gyosei Institute of Management. Address: 66 Roupell Street, London SE1 8SS, England.

WOLFF Edward (Nathan), b. 10 Apr 1946, Long Branch, New Jersey, USA. Professor of Economics; Writer. m. Jane Zandra Forman, 27 Nov 1977, 1 son, 1 daughter. Education: AB, Harvard College, 1968; MPhil, 1972, PhD, 1974, Yale University. Appointments: Assistant Professor, 1974-79, Associate Professor, 1979-84, Professor of Economics, 1984-, New York University; Managing Editor, Review of Income and Wealth, 1987-; Associate Editor, Structural Change and Economic Dynamics, 1989-, Journal of Population Economics, 1990-. Publications: Growth, Accumulation and Unproductive Activity: An Analysis of the Post-War US Economy, 1987; International Comparisons of the Distribution of Household Wealth (editor), 1987; Productivity and American Leadership: The Long View (co-author), 1989; The Information Economy: The Implications of Unbalanced Growth (co-author), 1989; Internation Perspectives on Profitability and Accumulation (co-editor), 1992; Competitivenss, Convergence and International Specialization (co-author), 1993; Top Heavy: A Study of the Increasing Inequality of Wealth in America, 1995; The Night in Question, 1996; Vintage Book of American Stories, editor, 1995. Contributions to: Books and professional journals. Memberships: American Economic Association; Conference on Research in Income and Wealth; International Association for Research in Income and Wealth, council member, 1987-94; International Institute of Public Finance; International Input-Output Association, council member. Address: c/o Department of Economics, New York University, New York, NY 10012, USA.

WOLFF Tobias, (Jonathan Ansell), b. 19 June 1945, Birmingham, Alabama, USA. Writer. m. Catherine Dolores Spohn, 1975, 2 sons, 1 daughter. Education: BA, 1972, MA, 1975, Oxford University; MA, Stanford University, 1978. Publications: In the Garden of the North American Martyrs (short stories), 1981; Matters of Life and Death: New American Stories (editor), 1982; The Barracks Thief, 1984; Back in the World, 1985; A Doctor's Visit: The Short Stories of Anton Checkhov (editor), 1987; This Boy's Life, a memoir, 1989; In Pharaoh's Army, Memories of the Lost War, 1994; Best American Short Stories (editor), 1994; Picador Book of Contemporary American Stories (editor). Contributions to: TriQuarterly; Missouri Review; Ploughshares; Atlantic Monthly; Esquire; Vanity Fair; Antaeus. Honours: Wallace Stegner Fellowship, 1975-76; National Endowment for the Arts Fellowships, 1978, 1985; Mary Roberts Rinehart Grant, 1979; Arizona Council on the Arts and Humanities Fellowship, 1980; O Henry Short Story Prizes, 1980, 1981, 1985; Guggengeim Fellowship, 1982; St Lawrence Award for Fiction, 1982; PEN/Faulkner Award for Fiction, 1985; Rea Award for the Short Story, 1989; Whiting Foundation Award, 1989; Los Angeles Times Book Prize, 1989; Lila Wallace Foundation Award, 1994; Lyndhurst Foundation Award, 1994. Memberships: Authors Guild; PEN. Address: 214 Scott Avenue, Syracuse, NY 13224, USA.

WOLKSTEIN Diane, b. 11 Nov 1942, New York, New York, USA. Writer; Storyteller. m. Benjamin Zucker, 7 Sept 1969, 1 daughter. Education: BA, Smith College, 1964; MA, Bank Street College of Education, 1967. Appointments: Hostess, Stories from Many Lands with Diane Wolkstein, WNYC-Radio, New York City, 1967-; Instructor, Bank Street College, 1970-; Teacher, New York University, 1983-; Teacher, Sarah Lawrence College, 1984, New School for Social Research, New York City, 1989; Leader, many storytelling workshops. Publications: 8,000 Stones, 1972; The Cool Ride in the Sky: A Black-American Folk Tale, 1973; The Visit, 1974; Squirrel's Song: A Hopi-Indian Story, 1975; Lazy Stories, 1976; The Red Lion: A Persian Sufi Tale, 1977; The Magic Orange Tree and Other Haitian Folk Tales, 1978; White Wave: A Tao Tale, 1979; The Banza: A Haitian Folk Tale, 1980; Inanna, Queen of Heaven and Earth: Her Stories and Hymns from Summer (with Samuel Noah Kramer), 1983; The Magic Wings, A Chinese Tale, 1983; The Legend of Sleepy Hollow, 1987; The First Love Stories, 1991; Oom Razoom, 1991; Little Mouse's Painting, 1992; Step by Step, 1994; Esther's Story, 1996; Bouki Danus the Kokioko, 1997; White Wave, 1996; The Magic Orange Tree, 1997. Contributions to: Periodicals and recordings. Honours: Several citations and awards. Address: 10 Patchin Place, New York, NY 10011, USA.

WOMACK Peter, b. 27 Jan 1952, Surrey, England. Lecturer. Education: BA, Oxford University, 1973; PhD, Edinburgh University, 1984. Appointment: Lectureship, 1988-96 Senior Lectureship, 1996-, University of East Anglia. Publications: Ben Jonson, 1986; Improvement and Romance, 1989; English Drama: A Cultural History (with Simon Shepherd), 1996. Contributions to: Textual Practice, 1987; New Theatre Quarterly, 1989; Culture and History, 1350-1600; David Aers, 1992. Address: School of English and American Studies, University of East Anglia, Norwich NR4 7TJ, England.

WOOD Charles (Gerald), b. 6 Aug 1932, St Peter Port, Guernsey, Channel Islands. Playwright. Education: Birmingham College of Art, 1948-50. Publications: Prisoner and Escort, 1961; Cockade, 1963; Tie Up the Ballcock, 1964; Don't Make Me Laugh, 1965; Meals on Wheels, 1965; Fill Up the Stage with Happy Hours, 1966; Dingo, 1967; Labour, 1968; H, Being Monologues at Front of Burning Cities, 1979; Collier's Wood, 1970; Welfare, 1971; Veterans; or, Hair in the Gates of the Hellespont, 1972; The Can Opener, 1974; Jingo, 1975; The Script, 1976; Has "Washington" Legs?, 1978; The Garden, 1982; Red Star, 1984; Across for the Garden of Allah, 1986; Tumbledown, 1988; The Plantagenets (after Shakespeare), 1988; Man, Beast and Virtue (after Pirandello), 1989. Screenplays: The Knack, 1965; Help (co-author), 1965; How I Won the War, 1967; The Charge of the Light Brigade (co-author), 1968; The Long Day's Dying, 1968; The Bed-Sitting Room (co-author), 1968; Fellini Satyricon, 1969; Cuba, 1980; Vile Scripts, 1981. Television scripts. Honours Prix Italia, RAI, 1988; British Acedemy for Film and Television Arts Award, 1988. Address: Long Barn, Sibford Gopwer, Near Banbury, Oxfordshire OX15 5RT, England.

WOOD David Bernard, b. 21 Feb 1944, Sutton, England. Writer; Actor; Theatre Producer; Director; Composer. m. Jacqueline Stanbury, 21 Jan 1975, 2 daughters. Education: BA, Worcester College, Oxford. Publications: Musical Plays for Children: The Owl and the Pussycat Went to Sea, 1970; The Plotters of Cabbage Patch Corner, 1973; Hijack Over Hygenia, 1974; The Papertown Paperchase, 1976; Larry the Lamb in Toytown, 1976; Books: The Gingerbread Man, 1977; Old Father Time, 1977; Mother Goose's Golden Christmas, 1978; Cinderella, 1980; Dick Whittington and Wondercat, 1982; Meg and Mog Show, 1985; Dinosaurs and all that Rubbish, 1986; The Gingerbread Man, 1985; The Discorats, 1985; The See Saw Tree, 1987; Sidney the Monster, 1988; Happy Birthday Mouse, 1991; Save the Human, 1991; The BFG, 1992; Baby Bears Buggle Ride, 1993; The BFG Plays for Children, 1993; The Witches, 1994. Honour: Nottinghamshire Childrens Book of Year Award, 1989. Memberships: Society of Authors; British Actors Equity Association; Green Room Club. Address: c/o Margaret Ramsey Ltd, 14A Goodwins Court, St Martins Lane, London WC2, England.

WOOD Edgar Allardyce, (Kerry Wood), b. 2 June 1907, New York, New York, USA (Canadian citizen, 1973). Author; Journalist. Appointments: Correspondent and Columnist, newspapers including: Edmonton Bulletin, Edmonton Journal, Calgary Herald and Calgary Albertan, 1926-73. Publications: Robbing the Roost: The Marquis of Roostburg Rules Governing the Ancient and Dishonourable Sport, 1938; I'm a Gaggle Man Myself, 1940; Three Mile Bend, 1945; Birds and Animals in the Rockies, 1946; A Nature Guide for Farmers, 1947; The Magpie Menace, 1949; Cowboy Yarns for Young Folk, 1951; The Sanctuary, 1952; A Letter from Alberta, 1954; A Letter from Calgary, 1954; Wild Winter (autobiography), 1954; The Map-Maker: The Story of David Thompson, 1955; Willowdale, 1956; The Great Chief Maskepetoon Warrior of the Crees, 1957; The Queen's Cowboy: Colonel Macleod of the Mounties, 1960; Great Horned MacOwl, 1961; The Boy and the Buffalo, 1963; Mickey the Beaver and Other Stories, 1964; A Lifetime of Service: George Moon, 1966; A Corner of Canada: A Personalized History of the Red Deer River Country, 1966; A Time for Fun, 1967; The Medicine Man, 1968; Samson's Long Ride, 1968; The Creek, 1970; The Icelandic-Canadian Poet Stephan G Stephansson: A Tribute, 1974; Red Deer, A Love Story, 1975; Bessie, the Coo, 1975; A Legacy of Laughter, 1986. Honours: Governor-General's Medals, Juvenile Literature, 1955, 1957; 1st Vicky Metcalf Award, 1963; Alberta Historical Society Award, 1965; Honorary Doctorate, University of Alberta, 1969; Honorary Life Member, Alberta Federation of Naturalists, 1970; Alberta Achievement Award, 1975; Loran L Goulden Memorial Award, 1987; Order of the Bighorn, Edmonton, Alberta, 1987; Distinguished Service Award, Interpretration, Red Deer, Alberta,1988; Member of the Order of Canada, 1990; Confederation Commemoration Medal, 1992. Memberships: Life Member, Red Deer River Naaturalists; Life Member, Alberta

Federation of Naturalists. Address: Site 3, RR2, Red Deer, Alberta T4N 5E2, Canada.

WOOD John Cunningham, b. 12 July 1952, Perth, Western Australia. Economist. m. Caoline D'Cruz, 5 June 1976, 1 son, 2 daughters. Education: B Econ, University of Western Australia, 1973; PhD, Oxford University, 1978. Appointment: Professor, University of Notre Dame, Western Australia Publications: British Economists and the Empire, 1860-1914, 1983; Editor of 21 books on great economists, 1983. Honours: Shell Scholarship, University of Oxford, 1975-78; Nuffield College, Studentship, 1977-78; Duke of Edinburgh's Third Commonwealth Study Conference, 1986. Memberships: CEDA; Economic Society of Western Australia; Royal Institute of Public Administration; Helm Wood Publishers Pty Limited. Address: c/o University of Notre Dame, 19 Mouat Street, Fremantle, Western Australia 6060, Australia.

WOOD Ronald Francis James, b. 30 Nov 1921. Ophthalmologist; Medical Practitioner. m. Mary Lynette Young, 21 Feb 1948, 3 sons, 2 daughters. Education: Bachelor of Medicine and Bachelor of Surgery, 1944; Fellow, Royal Australian College of Ophthalmologists, 1969; Fellow, Royal Australasian College of Surgeons, 1977; Foundation Fellow, Royal College of Ophthalmologists, 1987. Publications: Australia's Quest for Colonial Health, 1983; Looking Up and Looking Back at Old Brisbane, 1987; (with others) Earnest Sandford Jackson, 1987; Pioneer Medicine in Australia, 1988; Some Milestones of Australian Medicine, 1994. Contributions to: Journal of the Royal Historical Society of Queensland; Australian Journal of Ophthalmology; Australian and New Zealand Journal of Ophthalmology. Memberships: Royal Historical Society of Queensland; Queensland Club. Address: 120 Queenscroft Street, Chelmer 4068, Brisbane, Australia.

WOOD Susan, b. 31 May 1946, Commerce, Texas, USA. Poet. m. Cliff L Wood, 2 June 1967, div 1982, 1 son, 1 daughter. Education: BA, East Texas State University, 1968; MA, University of Texas at Arlington, 1970; Graduate Studies, Rice University, 1973-75. Publications: Bazaar, 1981; Campo Santo, 1990. Contributions to: Newspapers and periodicals. Address: c/o Maxine Groffsky Literary Agency, 2 Fifth Avenue, New York, NY 10011, USA.

WOOD Victoria, b. 19 May 1953, Prestwich, Lancashire, England. Writer; Comedienne. m. Geoffrey Durham, 1980, 1 son, 1 daughter. Education: BA, Drama, Theatre Arts, University of Birmingham. Publications: Victoria Wood Song Book, 1984; Lucky Bag, 1985; Up to You Porky, 1986; Barmy, 1987; Mens Sana in Thingummy Doodah, 1990; Pat and Margaret, screenplay, 1994; Chunky, 1996. Honours: British Academy of Film and Television Arts Awards, Broadcasting Press Awards; Variety Club BBC Personality of the Year, 1987; Hon DLitt, Lancaster, 1989; DLitt, Sunderland, 1994; BPG Award for Best Screenplay, 1994; Honorary DLitt, Bolton 1995; Honorary DLitt, Birmingham, 1996. Address: c/o Richard Stone, 25 Whitehall, London SW1, England.

WOODCOCK Joan, b. 6 Feb 1908, Bournemouth, England. Poet; Artist; Genealogist. m. Alexander Neville Woodcock, 18 Sept 1937, 2 sons, 1 daughter. Publications: The Wandering Years, 1990; Borrowing From Time, 1992; Stabbed Awake, 1994. Contributions to: Anthologies; journals. Honours: Awards - Envoi, Rhyme International (Orbis); World Order of Narrative and Formalist Poets, New York, 1991; Writers Forum, Scotland; Others. Memberships: Poetry Society; British Haiku Society; Associate member, Peterloo Poets; Founder Member, Calne Writers' Circle; Verse Writers Guild of Ohio, USA; National Federation of State Poetry Societies Inc, USA; Scottish Genealogy Society; Birmingham and Midland Society for Genealogy and Heraldry; Wiltshire and other Family History Societies. Address: 6 Hudson Road, Malmesbury, Wiltshire SN16 0BS, England.

WOODCOCK John Charles, b. 7 Aug 1926, Longparish, Hampshire, England. Cricket Writer. Education: Trinity College, Oxford; MA, Oxon. Appointments: Staff, Manchester Guardian, 1952-54; Cricket Correspondent, The Times, 1954-; Editor, Wisden Cricketer's Almanack, 1980-86. Publications: The Ashes, 1956; Barclays World of Cricket, 1980. Contributions to: Country Life; The Cricketer. Honour: Sportswriter of the Year, British Press Awards, 1987. Address: The Curacy, Longparish, Nr Andover, Hants SP11 6PB, England.

WOODCOTT Keith. See: BRUNNER John Kilian Houston.

WOODEN Rodney John, b. 16 July 1945, London, England. Playwright. Publications: Woyzeck (adaptation of Büchner's play), 1990; Your Home in the West, 1991; Smoke, 1993; Moby Dick, 1993. Honours: 1st Prize, Mobil International Playwriting Competition, 1990; John Whiting Award, 1991; Mobil Writer-in-Residence Bursary, 1991-92. Membership: PEN International. Address: c/o Micheline Steinberg Playwrights, 110 Forgnal, London NW3 6XU, England.

WOODFORD Peggy, b. 19 Sept 1937, Assam, India. Writer. m. Walter Aylen, 1 Apr 1967, 3 daughters. Education: MA, St Anne's College, Oxford. Publications: Please Don't Go, 1972; Mozart: His Life and Times, 1977; Schubert: His Life and Times, 1978; Rise of the Raj, 1978; See You Tomorrow, 1979; The Girl With a Voice, 1981; Love Me, Love Rome, 1984; Misfits, 1984; Monster in Our Midst, 1987; Out of the Sun, 1990; Blood and Mortar, 1994; Cupid's Tears, 1995; On the Night, 1997; Jane's Story, forthcoming. Memberships: Society of Authors; Royal Society of Literature. Address: c/o David Higham Associates, 5-8 Lower John Street, London W1R 4HA, England.

WOODHEAD Peter Anthony, b. 11 Nov 1944, Shipley, Yorkshire, England. m. Sylvia Ann, 24 Aug 1970, 1 son, 1 daughter. Education: BA, University College, London, 1966; MA, University of Sheffield, 1969; M Phil, University of Leicester, 1985. Publications: Keyguide to Information Sources in Archaeology, 1985; Keyguide to Information Sources in Museum Studies (co-author), 1989, 2nd edition, 1994. Contributions to: Various articles on library topics in librarianship periodicals. Honour: Outstanding Reference Book, Choice, 1990. Membership: Library Association. Address: 81 Uppingham Road, Houghton on the Hill, Leicestershire LE7 9HL, England.

WOODRING Carl, b. 29 Aug 1919, Terrell, Texas, USA. Educator. m. Mary Frances Ellis, 24 Dec 1942. Education: BA, 1940, MA, 1942, Rice University; AM, 1947, PhD, 1949, Harvard University. Publications: Victorian Samplers, 1952; Virginia Woolf, 1966; Wordsworth, 1965, revised, 1968; Politics in English Romantic Poetry, 1970; Nature into Art, 1989; Table Talk of Samuel Taylor Coleridge, 1990; Columbia History of British Poetry (editor), 1993; Columbia Anthology of British Poetry (co-editor), 1995. Contributions to: Western Review; Virginia Quarterly Review; Keats-Shelley Journal; Comparative Drama. Honours: Guggenheim Fellowship, 1955; American Council of Learned Societies, fellow, 1965; Phi Beta Kappa Gauss Prize, 1971; PKB Visiting Scholar, 1974-75; Senior Mellon Fellow, 1987-88. Memberships: American Academy of Arts and Sciences; International Association of University Professors of English (IAUPE); Grolier Club. Address: 2838 Montebello Road, #20, Austin, TX 78746, USA.

WOODS Jeannie Marlin, b. 6 Oct 1947, Shreveport, Louisiana, USA. College Professor; Stage Director; Author. m. Daniel Carl Woods, 7 Sept 1973. Education: BA, Theatre, University of Idaho, 1970; MA, Hunter College, 1987; MPh, 1988, PhD, Theatre, 1989, City University of New York. Appointments: Lecturer, Baruch College and City College of New York, 1987, 1988; Assistant/Associate Professor of Theatre, Winthrop University, 1989-. Publications: Theatre to Change Men's Souls - The Artistry of Adrian Hall, 1993; Maureen Stapleton: A Bio-Bibliography, 1992. Contributions to: Theatre Topics; Theatre Journal; Southern Theatre; Soviet and East European Performance. Honours: Dissertation Year Fellowship, City University of New York, 1988-89; Named Outstanding Junior Professor, Winthrop University, 1995. Address: Department of Theatre and Dance, Winthrop University, Rock Hill, SC 29733, USA.

WOODS P F. See: **BAYLEY Barrington John.**

WOODS Stockton. See: **FORREST Richard.**

WOODWARD Bob, (Robert Upshur Woodward), b. 26 Mar 1943, Geneva, Illinois, USA. Journalist; Writer. m. Elsa Walsh, 25 Nov 1989, 1 child. Education: BA, Yale University, 1965. Appointments: Reporter, Montgomery County Sentinel, Maryland, 1970-71; Reporter, 1971-78, Metropolitan Editor, 1979-81, Assistant Managing Editor, 1981-, Washington Post. Publications: All the President's Men (with Carl Bernstein), 1973; The Final Days (with Carl Bernstein), 1976; The Brethren (with Carl Armstrong), 1979; Wired, 1984; Veil: The Secret Wars of the CIA, 1987; The Commanders, 1991; The Man Who Would Be President (with David S Broder), 1991; The Agenda: Inside the Clinton White House, 1994; The Choice, 1996. Honour: Pulitzer Prize Citation, 1972. Address: c/o Washington Post, 1150 15th Street North West, Washington, DC 20071, USA.

WOODWARD C(omer) Vann, b. 13 Nov 1908, Vanndale, Arkansas, USA. Professor of History Emeritus; Author. m. Glenn Boyd MacLeod, 21 Dec 1937, dec 1982, 1 son, dec. Education: AB, Emory University, 1930; MA, Columbia University, 1932; PhD, University of North Carolina, 1937. Appointments: Instructor in English, Georgia School of Technology, 1930-31, 1932-33; Assistant Professor of History, University of Florida, 1937-39; Scripps College, Claremont, California, 1940-43; Visiting Professor of History, 1939, James W Richard Lecturer in History, 1954, University of Virginia; Professor of History, Johns Hopkins University, 1946-61; Commonwealth Lecturer, University of London, 1954; Harold Vyvyan Harmsworth Professor of American History, Oxford University, 1954-55; Sterling Professor of History, 1961-77, Professor Emeritus, 1977-, Yale University; Jefferson Lecturer in Humanities, 1978. Publications: Tom Watson: Agrarian Rebel, 1938, 3rd edition, 1990; The Battle for Leyte Gulf, 1947; Reunion and Reaction: The Compromise of 1877 and the End of Reconstruction, 1951, 2nd edition, revised, 1991; Origins of the New South 1877-1913, 1951, revised edition, 1971; The Strange Career of Jim Crowe, 1955, 3rd edition, revised, 1974; The Burden of Southern History, 1960, 3rd edition, revised, 1993; The National Experience (with others), 1963; The Comparative Approach to American History (editor), 1968; American Counterpoint: Slavery and Racism in the North-South Dialogue, 1971; Responses of the Presidents to Charges of Misconduct, 1974; Oxford History of the United States (general editor), 11 volumes, 1982-; Thinking Back: The Perils of Writing History, 1986; The Future of the Past, 1988; The Old World's New World, 1991. Contributions to: Books and professional journals. Honours: Bancroft Prize, 1952; National Institute of Arts and Letters Award, 1954; American Council of Learned Societies, 1962; Brandeis University Creative Arts Award, 1982; Pulitzer Prize in History, 1982; American Historical Society Life Work Award, 1986; American Academy of Arts and Letters Gold Medal for History, 1990; Honorary doctorates. Memberships: American Academy of Arts and Letters; American Academy of Arts and Sciences, vice-president, 1988-89; American Historical Association, president, 1969; American Philosophical Society; British Academy; Organization of American Historians, president, 1968-69; Royal Historical Society; Southern Historical Association, president, 1952. Address: 83 Rogers Road, Hamden, CT 06517, USA.

WOODWARD Kenneth L. Journalist. Education: Graduated with Honours,Notre Dame University, 1957; University of Michigan Law School; MA, English, University of Iowa; European Literature, University of Strasbourg, France. Appointments: Instructor in English, University of Maryland Overseas Division, 1959-60; Stringer, Time magazine, 1959-60; Chief Feature Writer, Sun Special, Omaha, 1962-64; Associate Editor in Charge, 1964, General Editor, 1969, Senior Writer, 1974, Newsweek. Contributions to: Major contributor to The Bible in America. Honours: Outstanding Citizenship Award, Omaha Urban League, 1964; National Magazine Award, American Society of Magazine Editors; 7 Wilbur Awards, Religious Public Relations Council; William E Leidt Award, National Council of the Episcopal Church, 1965, 1981; National Media Award, American Psychological Foundation, 1976; Co-recipient, National Magazine Award, 1978; Clarion Award, Women in Communications, 1979; Schachern Memorial Award, Religion Newswriters' Association, 1992. Address: c/o Newsweek, 251 West 57th Street, New York, NY 10019-1894, USA.

WOODWORTH Steven E(dward), b. 28 Jan 1961, Akron, Ohio, USA. Assistant Professor of History; Writer. m. Leah Dawn Bunke, 13 Aug 1983, 5 sons. Education: BA, Southern Illinois University at Carbondale, 1982; University of Hamburg, 1982-83; PhD, Rice University, 1987. Appointments: Adjunct Instructor, Houston Community College, 1984-87; Instructor in History, Bartlesville Wesleyan College, Oklahoma, 1987-89; Assistant Professor of History, Toccoa Falls College, Georgia, 1989-97; Assistant Professor of History, Texas Christian University, 1997-. Publications: Jefferson Davis and His Generals: The Failure of Confederate Command in the West, 1990; The Essentials of United States History, 1841 to 1877; Westward Expansion and the Civil War, 1990; The Essentials of United States History, 1500 to 1789: From Colony to Republic, 1990; The Advanced Placement Examination in United States History, 1990; Davis and Lee at War, 1995; Leadership and Command in the American Civil War (editor), Vol I, 1995; The American Civil War: A Handbook of Literature and Research (editor), 1996. Contributions to: Books and professional journals. Honour: Fletcher Pratt Award, 1991, 1996. Memberships: Grady Mcwhiney Research Foundation, fellow; American Historical Association; Organization of American Historians;

Southern Historical Association; Organization of Military Historians; Society of Civil War Historians. Address: c/o Department of History, Texas Christian University, TCU Box 297260, Fort Worth, TX 76129, USA.

WORSLEY Dale, b. 3 Nov 1948, Louisiana, USA. Writer; Dramatist. m. Elizabeth Fox, 14 July 1991. Appointment: Writing Programme, Columbia University, New York City, 1992. Publications: The Focus Changes of August Previco, 1980; The Art of Science Writing, 1989. Plays: Cold Harbor, 1983; The Last Living Newspaper, 1993. Honours: Fellowship in Fiction, 1986, Fellowship in Playwriting, 1989, National Endowment for the Arts. Membership: Dramatists Guild. Address: 150 Lafayette Ave 1, Brooklyn, NY 11238, USA.

WORSTHORNE Sir Peregrine Gerard, b. 22 Dec 1923, Chelsea, London, England. Journalist. m. (1) 1950, dec, 1 daughter, (2) Lucinda Lambton, 1992. Education: Peterhouse, Cambridge; BA, Magdalen College, Oxford. Appointments: Editorial Staff, Glasgow Herald, 1946-48; Washington Correspondent, 1948-50, Leader Writer, The Times, 1952-55; Daily Telegraph, 1955-61; Assistant Editor, 1961-86, Editor, 1986-89, Editor, Comment Section, 1989-91, Columnist, 1991-, Sunday Telegraph. Publications: The Socialist Myth, 1972; Peregrinations, 1980; By the Right, 1987; Tricks of Memory, 1993. Contributions to: Newspapers and journals. Honours: Granada Columnist of Year, 1980; Knighted, 1991. Memberships: Garrick Club; Beefsteak Club; Pratts Club. Address: The Old Rectory, Hedgerley, Buckinghamshire SL2 3VY, England.

WORTH Anthony. See: **WEST William Alexander**.

WORTHINGTON Edgar Barton, b. 13 Jan 1905, London, England. Ecologist. m. (1) Stella Johnson, 23 Aug 1930, (2) Harriett Stockton, 21 June 1980, 3 daughters. Education: MA, PhD, Rugby, Gonville and Caius, Cambridge. Appointments: Fishery Survey of Lake Victoria, 1927, of Lakes Albert and Kioga, 1928; Leader of Cambridge Expedition to African Lakes and Balfour Student, 1930-31; Scientist to Lord Hailey's African Survey, 1933-37; Director of Freshwater Biological Association, 1937-46; Scientific Adviser to Middle East Supply Council, 1939-45; Secretary of Colonial Research Committee and Development Adviser, Uganda, 1946, to East Africa High Commission, 1947-50; Secretary-General to Scientific Council for Africa, 1951-56; Deputy-Director General, Nature Conservancy, 1956-62; Director of International Biological Programme, 1962-72. Publications: Inland Waters of Africa (with Stella Worthington), 1933; Science in Africa, 1937; Life in Lakes and Rivers (with T T Macan), 1951; Science in the Development of Africa, 1958; The Ecological Century - A Personal Appraisal, 1983; The Ecological Century Review, 1998. Honours: Commander of the Order of the British Empire, 1962; Tot Ridder, Order of the Golden Ark, Netherlands, 1976; Honorary Member, International Union for Conservation of Nature Medal of UNESCO, 1994. Memberships: Linnaean Society of London; Royal African Society.

WORTIS Avi, (Avi), b. 23 Dec 1937, New York, New York, USA. Children's Author. m. (1) Joan Gabriner, div, 2 sons, (2) Coppelia Kahn. Education: BA, 1959, MA, 1962, University of Wisconsin at Madison; MS in Library Science, Columbia University, 1964. Appointments: Librarian, New York Public Library, 1962-70, Trenton State College, New Jersey, 1970-86; Conducted over 800 workshops and seminars with children, parents and educators. Publications: Things That Sometimes Happen, 1970; Snail Tale, 1972; No More Magic, 1975; Captain Grey, 1977 Emily Upham's Revenge, 1978; Night Journeys, 1979; History of Helpless Harry, 1980; Who Stole the Wizard of Oz?, 1981; Sometimes I Think I Hear My Name, 1982; Shadrach's Crossing, 1983; Devil's Race, 1984; SOR Losers, 1984; The Fighting Ground, 1984; Bright Shadow, 1985; Wolf Rider, 1986; Romeo and Juliet--(Together (and Alive!)--At Last, 1987; Something Upstairs, 1988; The Man Who Was Poe, 1989; True Confessions of Charlotte Doyle, 1990; Windcatcher, 1991; Nothing But the Truth, 1991; Blue Heron, 1992; 'Who Was That Masked Man, Anyway?, 1992; Punch With Judy, 1993; City of Light, City of Dark, 1993; The Bird, the Frog, and the Light, 1994; The Barn, 1994; Tom, Babette & Simon, 1995; Poppy, 1995; Finding Providence, 1996; Beyond the Western Sea, 1996. Contributions to: Periodicals. Honours: American Library Association Notable Book Awards, 1984, 1991, 1992, 1993, 1995, 1996; One of the Best Books of the Year Awards, Library of Congress, 1989, 1990; Newbery Honor Book Awards, 1991, 1992; Many others. Membership: Authors Guild. Address: 2205a Grove Street, Boulder, CO 30203, USA.

WOUK Herman, b. 27 May 1915, New York, New York, USA. Writer. m. Betty Sarah Brown, 9 Dec 1945, 3 sons, 1 dec.Education: AB, Columbia University, 1934. Appointments: Visiting Professor of English, Yeshiva University, 1952-57; Scholar-in-Residence, Aspen Institute of Humanistic Studies, Colorado, 1973-74. Publications: Fiction: Aurora Dawn, 1947; The City Boy, 1948; Slattery's Hurricane, 1949; The Caine Muntiny, 1951; Marjorie Morningstar, 1955; Lomokome Papers, 1956; Youngblood Hawke, 1962; Don't Stop the Carnival, 1965; The Winds of War, 1971; War and Remembrance, 1978; Inside, Outside, 1985; The Hope, 1993; The Glory, 1994. Plays: The Traitor, 1949; The Caine Mutiny Court-Martial, 1953; Nature's Way, 1957. Television Screenplays: The Winds of War, 1983; War and Remembrance, 1986. Non-Fiction: This is My God, 1959. Honours: Pulitzer Prize in Fiction, 1952; Columbia University Medal for Excellence, 1952; Alexander Hamilton Medal, 1980; University of California at Berkeley Medal, 1984; Washington Book Award, 1986; Golden Plate Award, American Academy of Achievement, 1986; US Naval Memorial Foundation Lone Sailor Award, 1987. Memberships: Authors League; PEN; Writers Guild of America. Address: c/o B S W Literary Agency, 3255 North Street North West, Washington, DC 20007, USA.

WRIGHT A(mos) J(asper III), b. 3 Mar 1952, Gadsden, Alabama, USA. Medical Librarian. m. Margaret Dianne Vargo, 14 June 1980, 1 son, 1 daughter. Education: BA, Auburn University, 1973; MLS 1983, University of Alabama. Publications: Frozen Fruit (poetry), 1978; Right New I Feel Like Robert Johnson (poetry), 1981; Criminal Activity in the Deep South, 1800-1930, 1989. Contributions to: Anaesthesiology; Anaesthesia and Analgesia; Poem; Aura; Old West. Memberships: Medical Library Association; Anaesthesia History Association. Address: 119 Pintail Drive, Pelham, AL 35124, USA.

WRIGHT Anthony David, b. 9 June 1947, Oxford, England. Historian. Education: City of London School, 1958-65; BA, Merton College, 1968; MA, British School at Rome, 1973; D Phil, Brasenose College, 1973. Appointments: General Editor, A History of the Papacy. Publications: The Counter Reformation, 1982; Catholicism and Spanish Society, 1991. Contributions to: Professional journals. Honours: Accademia di San Carlo, 1978; Fellowship, Royal Historical Society, 1980; Visiting Fellowship, Edinburgh University, 1983. Memberships: Athenaeum, Ecclesiastical History Society. Address: School of History, University of Leeds, Leeds LS2 9JT, England.

WRIGHT C(arolyn) D, b. 6 Jan 1949, Mountain Home, Arkansas, USA. Poet; Professor. m. Forrest Gander, 23 Sept 1983, 1 son. Education: BA Memphis State University, 1971; MFA, University of Arkansas, 1976. Publications: Terrorism, 1979; Translations of the Gospel Back Into Tongues, 1981; Further Adventures with God, 1986; String Light, 1991; Just Whistle, 1993; The Lost Roads Project: A Walk-in Book of Arkansas, 1994; The Reader's Map of Arkansas, 1994. Contributions to: Journals. Honours: National Endowment for the Arts Fellowships, 1981, 1987; Witter Bynner Prize for Poetry, 1986; Guggenheim Fellowship, 1987; Mary Ingraham Bunting Fellowship, 1987; General Electric Award for Younger Writers, 1988; Whiting Writers Award, 1989; Rhode Island Governors Award for Arts, 1990; Lila Wallace - Reader's Digest Writers Award, 1992. Address: 351 Nayatt Road, Barrington, RI 02806, USA.

WRIGHT Charles Penzel Jr, b. 25 Aug 1935, Pickwick Dam, Tennessee, USA. Writer; Teacher. m. Holly McIntire, 6 Apr 1969, 1 son. Education: BA, Davidson College, 1957; MFA, University of Iowa, 1963; Postgraduate, University of Rome, Italy, 1963-64. Appointments: University of California, Irvine, 1966-83; University of Virginia, 1983-. Publications: Grave of the Right Hand, 1970; Hard Freight, 1973; Bloodlines, 1975; China Trace, 1977; Southern Cross, 1981; Country Music (selected early poems), 1982; Other Side of the River, 1984; Zone Journals, 1988; The World of the 10,000 Things, 1990. Translations: The Storm, 1978; Orphic Songs, 1984; Chickamauga, 1995. Contributions to: Numerous magazines and journals. Honours: Edgar Allan Poe Award, Academy of American Poets, 1976; PEN Translation Award, 1979; National Book Award, poetry, 1983; Brandeis Creative Arts Award, poetry, 1987; The Ruth Lilly Poetry Prize, 1993. Membership: PEN American Centre. Address: 940 Locust Avenue, Charlottesville, VA 22901, USA.

WRIGHT Derek Leslie, b. 24 Feb 1947, Wakefield, England. University Lecturer. m. Renate Lucia Mohrbach, 31 July 1981. Education: BA (1st Class), English, University of Reading, 1971; DipEd, University of Leeds, 1972; MA, American Literature, University of Keele, 1973; PhD, University of Queensland, Australia, 1986. Publications: Ayi Kwei Armah's Africa: The Sources of His Fiction, 1989; Critical Perspectives on Ayi Kwei Armah (editor), 1992; Wole Soyinka Revisited, 1993; The Novels of Nuruddin Farah, 1994; New African Writing (editor), 1995; Extra-Territorial: Poems and Stories(editor), 1996; Wole Soyinka: Life, Work and Criticism, 1996. Contributions to: Journals. Honour: Outstanding Academic Book Award, Choice, 1990. Memberships: Modern Language Association of America; Association for Commonwealth Literature and Language Studies. Address: School of Humanities, Faculty of Arts, Northern Territory University, Darwin, Northern Territory 0909, Australia.

WRIGHT George T(haddeus), b. 27 Dec 1925, New York, New York, USA. Professor; Author; Poet. m. Jerry Honeywell, 28 Apr 1955. Education: BA, Columbia College, 1946; MA, Columbia University, 1947; University of Geneva, 1947-48; PhD, University of California; Visiting Assistant Professor, New Mexico Highlands University, 1957; Instructor-Assistant Professor, University of Kentucky, 1957-60; Assistant Professor, San Francisco State College, 1960-61; Associate Professor, University of Tennessee, 1961-68; Fulbright Lecturer, University of Aix-Marseilles, 1964-65; University of Thessaloniki, 1977-78; Visiting Lecturer, University of Nice, 1965; Professor, 1968-89, Chairman, English Department, 1974-77, Regents' Professor, 1989-93, Regents' Professor Emeritus, 1993-, University of Minnesota. Publications: The Poet in the Poem: The Personae of Eliot, Yeats and Pound, 1960; W H Auden, 1969, revised edition, 1981; Shakespeare's Metrical Art, 1988. Editor: Seven American Literary Stylists from Poe to Mailer: An Introduction, 1973. Contributions to: Articles, reviews, poems and translations in many periodicals and books. Honours: Guggenheim Fellowship, 1981-82; National Endowment for the Humanities Fellowship, 1984-85; Phi Kappa Phi. Memberships: Minnesota Humanities Comission, 1985-88; Modern Language Association. Address; 2617 West Crown King Drive, Tucson, AZ 85741, USA.

WRIGHT Graeme Alexander, b. 23 Apr 1943, Wellington, New Zealand. Freelance Editor; Writer. Appointments: Managing Editor, Queen Anne Press, 1972-74; Editor, Freelance Writer, 1974-; Director, John Wisden & Co Ltd, 1983-87; Editor, Wisden Cricketers Almanack, 1986-92. Publications: Great Moments in the Olympics, 1976; Phil Read, The Real Story, 1977; Olympic Greats, 1980; Where Do I Go From Here, 1981; Test Decade, 1972-82, 1983; Botham (with Patrick Eagar), 1985; Brown Sauce, 1986; Forty Vintage Years, 1988; Betrayal, The Struggle for Cricket's Soul, 1993. Address: 14 Field End Road, Eastcote Pinner, Middlesex HA5 2QL, England.

WRIGHT Judith (Arundell), b. 31 May 1915, Armidale, New South Wales, Australia. Poet; Writer; Editor. Education: University of Sydney. Appointment: Commonwealth Literary Fund Lecturer, 1952. Publications: The Moving Image, 1946; Woman to Man, 1949; The Gateway, 1953; The Two Fires, 1955; Australia Bird Poems, 1961; Birds, 1962; Five Senses: Selected Poems, 1963; City Sunrise, 1964; The Other Half, 1966; Poetry from Australian Pergamon Poets, 1969; Collected Poems, 1942-70, 1971; Alive: Poems, 1971-72, 1973; Fourth Quarter and Other Poems, 1976; The Double Tree: Selected Poems, 1942-76, 1978; Phantom Dwelling, 1986; Essays, Books for Children, Literary Studies and Editions of Australian Poetry. Honour: D Litt, University of Melbourne, 1988. Address: PO Box 93, Braidwood, New South Wales 2622, Australia.

WRIGHT Kit, b. 1944, Kent, England. Lecturer; Editor; Poet. Education: New College, Oxford. Appointment: Fellow Commoner, Creative Arts, Trinity College, Cambridge, 1977-79. Publications: Treble Poets I, 1974; The Bear Looked Over the Mountain, 1977; Bump Starting the Hearse, 1983; From the Day Room, 1983; Real Rags and Red, 1988; Poems, 1974-83, 1988; Short Afternoons, 1989. Verse for Children: Arthur's Father, 1978; Rabbiting On and Other Poems, 1978; Hot Dog and Other Poems, 1981; Professor Potts Meets the Animals of Africa, 1981; Cat Among the Pigeons, 1987; Editor, Poems for Children. Honours: Alice Hunt Bartlett Prize; Geoffrey Faber Memorial Award; Arts Council Bursary, 1985; Hawthornden Prize; W H Heinemann Award. Address: c/o Century Hutchinson Ltd, Brookmont House, 62065 Chandos Place, London WC2N 4NW, England.

WRIGHT Laurali Rose, b. 5 June 1939, Saskatoon, Saskatchewan, Canada. Writer. m. 6 Jan 1962, 2 daughters. Education: MA, Liberal Studies, Simon Fraser University. Publications: Neighbours, 1979; The Favourite, 1982; Among Friends, 1984; The Suspect, 1985; Sleep While I Sing, 1986; Love in the Temperate Zone,

1988; Chill Rain in January, 1990; Prized Possessions, 1993; A Touch of Panic, 1994; Mother Love, 1995; Strangers Among Us, 1996. Contributions to: Professional journals, newspapers and magazines. Honours: Alberta First Novel Award, 1978; Edgar Allan Poe Best Novel Award, Mystery Writers of America, 1986; Arthur Ellis Award, Crime Writers of Canada, 1991. Memberships: International PEN; Writers Union of Canada; Authors Guild, USA. Address: c/o Writers Union of Canada, 24 Ryerson Avenue, Toronto, Ontario M5T 2P3, Canada.

WRIGHT Nancy Means, b. New Jersey, USA. Author. m. 2 sons, 2 daughters. Education: AB, Vassar College; MA, Middlebury College. Appointments: Instructor, English, various schools, 1960-87; Proctor Academy; Burlington College; Marist College, New York, 1990. Publications: The Losing, 1973; Down the Strings, 1982; Make Your Own Change, 1985; Vermonters At Their Craft, 1987; Tall Girls Don't Cry, 1990; Split Nipple, 1992; Mad Season, 1996. Contributions to: Various journals and magazines. Honours: Scholar, Bread Loaf Writers Conference, 1959; Grant for Novel in Progress Society of Children's Book Writers, 1987. Memberships: President, League of Vermont Writers, 1978-80; Poets and Writers; Authors League; Society of Children's Book Writers. Address: Box 38, Bristol, VT 05443, USA.

WRIGHT Nicholas, b. 5 July 1940, Cape Town, South Africa (British citizen). Playwright. Education: London Academy of Music and Dramatic Art. Appointments: Literary Manager, 1987, Associate Director, 1992, National Theatre, London, England. Publications: Changing Lines, 1968; Treetops, 1978; The Gorky Brigade, 1979; One Fine Day, 1980; The Crimes of Vautrin (after Balzac), 1983; The Custom of the Country, 1983; The Desert Air, 1984; Six Characters in Search of an Author (after Pirandello), 1987; Mrs Klein, 1988; Thérèse Raquin (after Zola), 1990; Also: 99 Plays, Essays, 1992. Honour: Arts Council Bursary, 1981. Literary Agent: Judy Daish Associates. Address: 2 St Charles Place, London W10 6EG, England.

WRIGHT Peter, b. 30 Mar 1923, Fleetwood, Lancashire, England. Forensic Linguist. m. Patricia May Wright, 3 Apr 1956, 1 son, 3 daughters. Education: BA, 1949, PhD, 1954, Leeds University; Advanced Diploma, London University, 1960. Appointments: Lecturer, 1965-70, Senior Lecturer, 1970-84, Honorary Senior Lecturer, Fellow in English Dialect Studies, 1984-92, Salford University; Crown or Defence, Analysing from Linguistic Angles Cases for Trial or Appeal. Publications: The Lanky Twang, 1974; The Yorkshire Yammer, 1976; Language at Work, 1978; Cockney Dialect and Slang, 1980; 8 other dialect books. Contributions to: Various Magazines and Journals. Honour: Queen's Award for Export Achievement, 1992. Memberships: Yorkshire Dialect Society; Lancashire Dialect Society; Lakeland Dialect Society. Address: 30 Broadoak Road, Stockport, Cheshire SK7 3BL, Englnd.

WRIGHT Ronald, b. 12 Sept 1948, Surrey, England. Education: MA, Archaeology and Anthropology, Cambridge University. Appointment: Snider Lecturer, University of Toronto, 1992. Publications: Cut Stones and Crossroads: A Journey in the TwoWorlds of Peru, 1984; On Fiji Islands, 1986; Time Among the Maya, 1989; Quechua Phrasebook, 1989; Stolen Continents, 1992; Home and Away, 1993. Contributions to: Numerous journals. Honours: Honorary Fellow, Trent University; Finalist, Trillium Book Awards, 1990, 1993; Winner, CBC Literary Award (essay), 1991; Gordon Montador Award, 1993; Honorary DD, Calgary. Memberships: Geographical Society, fellow; Writers Union of Canada; International PEN; Latin American Indian Literatures Association; Survival International. Literary Agent: Aiken Stone & Wylie Ltd, London SW10 0TG, England.

WRIGHT MCKINNEY Judith Arundell, b. 31 May 1915, Armidale, New South Wales, Australia. Writer. m. Jack Philip McKinney, 1 daughter. Education: University of Sydney, 1935-37. Publications: The Generations of Men, 1959; Collected Poems, 1971; The Cry for the Dead, 1981; The Double Tree, 1985; Born of Two Conquerors, 1991; Going on Talking, 1992. Contributions to: Numerous Journals and Magazines. Honours: Grace Leven Prize, 1950; Robert Frost Memorial Medal, 1970; Alice Award, 1980; Queen's Medal for Poetry, 1993. Memberships: Australian Society of Authors; PEN Australia. Address: PO Box 93, Braidwood, New South Wales 2622, Australia.

WU Duncan, b. 3 Nov 1961, Woking, Surrey, England. Academic; Writer. Education: BA, 1984, DPhil, 1991, Oxford University. Appointment: Postdoctoral Fellow, British Academy, 1991-94; Reader in English Literature, University of Glasgow, 1995-.

Publications: Wordsworth's Reading 1770-1799, 1993; Romanticism: An Anthology, 1994; William Wordsworth: A Selection, 1994; Six Contemporary Dramatists, 1994; Romanticism: A Critical Reader, 1995; Wordsworth's Reading, 1800-15, 1996; Romantic Women Poets: An Anthology, 1997. Contributions to: Journals and periodicals. Memberships: Council, Charles Lamb Society; Editor, Charles Lamb Bulletin; Keats-Shelley Memorial Association, Committee Member. Address: Department of English Literature, University of Glasgow G12 8QQ, Scotland.

WU William Lung-Shen, b. 1 Sept 1921, Hangchow, China. Aerospace Medical Engineering Design Specialist. 1 son, 1 daughter. Education: AB, Stanford University, 1943; MD, 1946; MS, Tulane University, 1955; Diploma, US Naval School of Aviation Medicine, 1956; USAF School of Aviation Medicine, 1961; University of California at Los Angeles, 1964. Appointments: Board of Directors, Emeritus Institute of Little House, Menlo Park; Member, Planning Research and Development Commission, Redwood City, California. Publications: 8 books and 100 technical papers, including: Medical Procedures Textbook for Nuclear Operations; Project Apollo Spacecraft Technical Proposal; Applicability of Metal Coordination Principles to Metal Enzymes. Honours: Sigma Xi; J Edgar Hoover Gold Distinguished Public Service Award, American Police Hall of Fame. Memberships: AIAA; IEEE, New York Academy of Sciences; Institute of Environmental Sciences; International University Foundation; International Academic Foundation. Address: Corinthian House 219, 250 Budd Avenue, Campbell, CA 95008, USA.

WUNSCH Josephine (McLean), b. 3 Feb 1914, Detroit, Michigan, USA. Author. m. Edward Seward Wunsch, 9 Aug 1940, 1 son, 2 daughters. Education: BA, University of Michigan, 1936. Publications: Flying Skis, 1962; Passport to Russia, 1965; Summer of Decision, 1968; Lucky in Love, 1970; The Aerie (as J Sloan McLean with Virginia Gillett), 1974; Girl in the Rough, 1981; Class Ring, 1983; Free as a Bird, 1984; Breaking Away, 1985; The Perfect Ten, 1986; Lucky in Love, 1987; Between Us, 1989. Address: 830 Bishop Road, Grosse Pointe Park, MI 48230, USA.

WYLDE. See: **CARTER Martin.**

WYLIE Betty Jane, b. 21 Feb 1931, Winnipeg, Manitoba, Canada. Writer; Dramatist; Poet. m. William Tennent Wylie, 2 sons, 2 daughters. Education: BA, 1950, MA, 1952, University of Manitoba. Appointments: Writer-in-Library, Burlingtin, Ontario, 1987-88; Bunting Fellow, Radcliffe College, USA, 1989-90. Publications: Over 32 books and 36 plays. Contributions to: Many periodicals. Honours: Several awards. Memberships: Dramatists Guild, USA; Playwrights Union of Canada; Writers Union of Canada. Address: c/o Writers Union of Canada, 24 Ryerson Avenue, Toronto, Ontario M5T 2P3, Canada.

WYLIE Laura. See: **MATTHEWS Patricia Anne.**

WYNDHAM Esther. See: **LUTYENS Mary.**

WYNN J(ohn) C(harles), (Jay Seawind), b. 11 Apr 1920, Akron, Ohio, USA. Professor of Pastoral Theology. m. Rachel Linnell, 27 Aug 1943, 1 son, 2 daughters. Education: BA, College of Wooster, 1941; BD, Yale University, 1944; MA, 1963, EdD, 1964, Columbia University; Post doctoral fellowship, Cornell University, 1972. Appointment: Teacher of Religious Journalism, Colgate Rochester Divinity School, 1959-69. Publications: How Christian Parents Face Family Problems, 1955; Sermons on Marriage and the Family, 1956; Pastoral Ministry to Families, 1957; Families in the Church: A Protestant Survey, 1961; Sex, Family and Society in Theological Focus, 1966; Sex, Ethics and Christian Responsibility, 1970; Education for Liberation and other Upsetting Ideas, 1977; The Family Therapist, 1987; Family Thearpy in Pastoral Ministry, 1991. Contributions to: Religious periodicals. Memberships: Presbyterian Writers Guild; American Association for Marriage and Family Therapy; Religious Education Association; National Council on Family Relations. Address: 717 Maiden Choice Lane 523, Catonsville, MD 21228, USA.

WYNNE-JONES Tim(othy), b. 12 Aug 1948, Cheshire, England. Writer. m. Amanda West Lewis, 12 Sept 1980, 1 son. Education: BA, University of Waterloo, 1974; MFA, York University, 1979. Publications: Odd's Ends, 1980; A Case of Bad Memories, 1982; Zoom at Sea, 1982; Zoom Away, 1985; I'll Make You Small, 1987; Mischief City, 1987; Fastyngange, 1988; Builder of the Moon, 1988; The Hour of the Frog, 1989; Zoom Upstream, 1994; The Book of Changes, 1995;

Some of the Kinder Planets, 1995. Honours: Seal First Novel Award, 1980; Governor-General's Award, 1993; Canadian Library Association Book of the Year for Children, 1994. Address: 142 Winona Drive, Toronto, Ontario M6G 3S9, Canada.

X

XERRI Raymond Christian, (Eco-Logija), b. 2 Feb 1969, New York, USA. Diplomat; Writer. Education: EU, Institut für Europaische Studien an der Albert-Ludwigs Universität, Freiburg-im-Breisgau, Germany, 1989-90; DDS, Mediterranean Academy of Diplomatic Studies, University of Malta, 1990-92; BA Hons, Manhattan College, Riverdale, New York, 1986-90; MA Diplomatic Studies, 1992-94; PhD Social Sciences, Victoria University of Technology, St Albans, Victoria, Australia, 1996-. Appointments: Professional Photographer, Reporter, Maltese International Newspaper, Medina, USA, 1986-90; Secretary, Executive Committee, 1991-92, Vice President of Committee, 1992-93, Qala St Joseph FC, Qala, Gozo, Malta, Qala St Joseph Newsletter, 1991-93; Founder, Chief Editor, Gozo mill-pjazza, Victoria, Gozo, Malta, 1993-94. Publications: The European Monetary System - History, the ECU and its Prospects through Maastricht and Beyond, 1992; European Union Environmental Legislation with Respect to the Mediterranean, 1994; Ecology and the Malta Ecological Society, 1995; International and Regional Organisations, 1995. Honours: Malta's National Religious Studies Award, 1978-79; Green Pen of the Year Award, 1996; Distinguished Maltese Citizens of the Twentieth Century, 1997. Memberships: Founder, Executive Director, Board Member, Malta Ecological Foundation, 1991-; Maltese-American Foundation, Medina, USA, 1987-90. Address: Stars & Stripes, 4 Zewwieqa Street, Qala GSM 104, Gozo, Malta.

Y

YAFFE James, b. 31 Mar 1927, Chicago, Illinois, USA. Professor; Writer; Dramatist. m. Elaine Gordon, 1 Mar 1964, 1 son, 2 daughters. Education: BA, summa cum laude, Yale University, 1948. Appointments: Professor, 1968-; Director, General Studies, 1981-, Colorado College. Publications: Poor Cousin Evelyn, 1951; The Good-for-Nothing, 1953; What's the Big Hurry?, 1954; Nothing But the Night, 1959; Mister Margolies, 1962; Nobody Does You Any Favors, 1966; The American Jews, 1968; The Voyage of the Franz Joseph, 1970; So Sue Me!, 1972; Saul and Morris, Worlds Apart, 1982; A Nice Murder for Mom, 1988; Mom Meets Her Maker, 1990; Mom Doth Murder Sleep, 1991; Mom Among the Liars, 1992; My Mother, the Detective, 1997. Plays: The Deadly Game, 1960; Ivory Tower (with Jerome Weidman), 1967; Cliffhanger, 1983. Other: Television plays. Contributions to: Various publications. Honour: National Arts Foundation Award, 1968. Memberships: American Association of University Professors; Authors League; Dramatists Guild; Mystery Writers of America; PEN; Phi Beta Kappa. Address: 1215 North Cascade Avenue, Colorado Springs, CO 80903, USA.

YAN Xiao Jian, b. 22 Dec 1954, Anhui, China. Author. m. Jian Ping Sun, 17 Nov 1990, 2 daughters. Education: BA, Literature, Xian Northwest China University, 1989; MA, Literature, Writers College, Beijing Normal University and Lu-xan Literature Institute, 1991. Appointment: Professional Author, Anhui Literature Institute, 1985-. Publications: Gas Lamp, 1983; All Night Shopping, 1985; Three Writers in a Small Town (short stories), 1986; Ten Years Prediction, 1987; Look Over Native Place (short stories), 1992; Bitten Itinerary (filmplay), 1994. Honours: Prize, Taiwan Government News Office, 1992; Medal, Certificate, 1993; 3 times Outstanding Award, World Writing Contest, Malaysia. Memberships: Standing Committee, Anhui Writers Association; Chinese Writers Association; Anhui Literary Institute. Address: Room 404, House 450, Luochuan Road (E), Shanghai, China.

YANKOWITZ Susan, b. 20 Feb 1941, Newark, New Jersey, USA. Writer; Dramatist. m. Herbert Leibowitz, 3 May 1978, 1 son. Education: BA, Sarah Lawrence College, 1963; MFA, Yale Drama School, 1968. Publications: Novel: Silent Witness, 1977. Plays: Slaughterhouse Play, 1971; Boxes, 1973; Terminal, 1975; Alarms, 1988; Night Sky, 1992. Screenplay: Portrait of a Scientist, 1974. Contributions to: Periodicals. Honours: Joseph Levine Fellowship in Screenwriting, 1968; Vernon Rice Drama Desk Award for Most Promising Playwright, 1969; Rockefeller Foundation Grant, 1973, and Award, 1974; Guggenheim Fellowship, 1975; MacDowell Colony Residencies, 1975, 1984, 1987, 1990; National Endowment for the Arts Grants, 1979, 1984; New York Foundation for the Arts Grant, 1989; McKnight Fellowship, 1990. Memberships: Authors Guild; Dramatists Guild; New Dramatists; PEN; Writers Guild of America. Literary Agent: Mary Harden, 850 7th Avenue, New York, NY 10019, USA.

YAOS-KEST Itamar, b. 3 Aug 1934, Hungary. Poet; Author. m. Hanna Mercazy, 21 Aug 1958, 1 son, 1 daughter. Education: BA, University of Tel Aviv. Appointment: Founder, Eked Publishing House, 1958. Publications: 15 books, 1959-92. Contributions to: Magazines. Honours: Herzel Prize, 1972; Talpir Prize, 1984; Lea Goldberg Prize, 1990; Prime Minister's Prize, 1993. Membership: Association of Hebrew Writers. Address: Merian Hahashunonout 25, Tel Aviv, Israel.

YARROW Chris. See: **MURRAY Terry.**

YEARGERS Edward K, b. 27 Apr 1938, Houma, Louisiana, USA. Professor of Biology. m. Susan Combs, 20 Feb 1993, 2 sons. Education: BS Physics, 1960; MS Biology, 1962; PhD Biophysics, 1966. Publications: Basic Biophysics for Biology, 1992; An Introduction to the Mathematics of Biology, 1996. Address: School of Biology, Georgia Institute of Technology, Atlanta, Georgia 30332, USA.

YEATMAN Ted P, (Trezevant Player), b. 16 Dec 1951, Nashville, Tennessee, USA. Writer; Historical Researcher. Education: BA, 1976, MLS, 1977, George Peabody College for Teachers. Appointments: Senior Staff Writer, Peabody Post, 1975-76; Editorial Board, Friends of the James Farm, 1984-93. Publications: Jesse James and Bill Ryan at Nashville, 1981; The Tennessee Wild West: Historical and Cultural Links with the Western Frontier (co-author),

1995; Frank and Jesse James: The Hidden Years, 1996. Contributions to: Books and journals. Memberships: Potomac Corral of Westerners; Friends of the James Farm, board of directors 1982-93, editorial board, 1984-93; Tennessee Western History & Folklore Society, co-director, 1981-. Address: 1302 The Terrace, Hagerstown, MD 21742, USA.

YEHOSHUA Abraham B, b. 9 Dec 1936, Jerusalem, Israel. Professor. m. Rivka Kirsninski, 1960, 2 s, 1 d. Education: BA, 1960; MA, 1962.Appointments: Co Editor, Keshet, 1965-72, Siman Kria, 1973-; Full Professor, University of Haifa, 1980. Publications: Death of the Old Man, 1963; Three Days and a Child, 1970; Early in the Summer of 1970, 1973; The Lover, 1978; Between Right and Right, 1981; A Late Divorce, 1984; Possessions, 1986; Five Seasons, 1988; Mister Mani, 1990; The Wall and the Mountain, 1988; Night's Babies, 1992; The Return from India, 1994. Honours: National Jewish Book Awards, 1990, 1993; Best Jewish Book of the Year Award, 1993; Israel Prize for Literature, 1995; Premio Internasional Flaiano, for A Late Divorce, 1996. Address: 102A Sea Road, Haifa, Israel 34736.

YELDHAM Peter, b. Gladstone, New South Wales, Australia. Playwright; Screen-writer. m. Marjorie Crane, 27 Oct 1948, 1 son, 1 daughter. Publications: Stage Plays: Birds on the Wing, 1969-70; She Won't Lie Down, 1972; Fringe Benefits (co-author), 1973; Away Match (co-author), 1974; Seven Little Australians, 1988; Once a Tiger, 1994. Feature Films: The Comedy Man, 1963; The Liquidator, 1965; Age of Consent, 1968; Touch and Go, 1979. Television Plays: Reunion Day; Stella; Thunder on the Snowy; East of Christmas; The Cabbage Tree Hat Boys; The Battlers. Television Series: Run from the Morning, 1977; Golden Soak, 1978; Ride on, Stranger, 1979; The Timeless Land, 1979. Also: Levkas Man, 1980; Sporting Chance, 1981; 1915, 1982; All the Rivers Run, 1983; Flight into Hell, 1984; Tusitala, The Lancaster Miller Affair, 1985; The Far Country, 1985; Captain James Cook, 1986; The Alien Years, 1987; Naked Under Capricorn, 1988; The Heroes, 1988; The Heroes, The Return, 1991; The Battlers, 1994. Novel: Reprisal, 1994; Without Warning, 1995; Two Sides of a Triangle, 1996. Honours: Sammy Award, Best Television Series in Australia, 1979; Writers Guild, Best Adaption, 1980, 1983, 1986; Penguin Award, Best Script, 1982; Writers Guild, Best Original mini-series, 1989; Order of Australia Medal, 1991. Memberships: Writers Guild, Australia; British Writers Guild. Rick Raftos Management, Sydney, Australia. Address: 21 Glover Street, Mosman, Sydney, Australia.

YEVTUSHENKO Yevgeny Aleksandrovich, b. 18 July 1933, Stanzia Zima, Siberia, Russia. Poet; Writer. m. (1) Bella Akhmadulina, div, (2) Galina Semyonovna, 1 child. Education: Gorky Literary Institute, 1951-54. Publications in English Translation: Poetry: The Poetry of Yevgeny Yevtushenko, 1953-1965, 1965; Bratsk Station, The City of Yes and the City of No, and Other New Poems, 1970; Kazan University and Other New Poems, 1973; From Desire to Desire, 1976; Invisible Threads, 1982; Ardabiola, 1985; Almost at the End, 1987; The Collected Poems, 1952-1990, 1991. Other: A Precocious Autobiography, 1963; Wild Berries (novel), 1984; Divided Twins: Alaska and Siberia, 1988. Honours: Order of the Red Banner of Labour; USSR State Prize, 1984. Memberships: International PEN; Union of Russian Writers. Address: c/o Union of Russian Writers, ul Vorovskogo 52, Moscow, Russia.

YOLEN Jane, b. 11 Feb 1939, New York, New York, USA. Author; Editor; Storyteller. m. David Wilber Stemple, 2 Sept 1962, 2 sons, 1 daughter. Education: BA, English Literature, Smith College, 1960; MEd, University of Massachusetts, 1976. Publications: Over 170 books, 1963-97. Contributions to: Many periodicals. Honours: Christopher Medal, 1979; Mythopoeic Society Awards, 1986, 1993; Smith College Medal, 1988; Caldecott Medal, 1988; Regina Medal, 1992; Kerlan Award, 1988; Keene State College Children's Book Award, 1995; World Fantasy Award, 1997. Memberships: Authors Guild; Children's Literature Association; Mystery Writers of America; Science Fiction Writers of America, president, 1986-88; Society of Children's Book Writers. Address: Phoenix Farm, Box 27, Hatfield, MA 01038, USA.

YORK Alison. See: **NICOLE Christopher Robin.**

YORK Andrew. See: **NICOLE Christopher Robin.**

YORK Georgia. See: **HOFFMAN Lee.**

YORKE Katherine. See: **ELLERBECK Rosemary Anne L'Estrange.**

YORKE Margaret, (Margaret Beda Nicholson), b. 1924. Author. Appointments: Assistant Librarian, St Hilda's College, Oxford, 1959-60; Library Assistant, Christ Church, Oxford, 1963-65; Chairman, Crime Writers Association, 1979-80. Publications: Summer Flight, 1957; Pray Love Remember, 1958; Christopher, 1959; Deceiving Mirror, 1960; The China Doll, 1961; Once a Stranger, 1962; The Birthday, 1963; Full Circle, 1965; No Fury, 1967; The Apricot Bed, 1968; The Limbo Ladies, 1969; Dead in the Morning, 1970; Silent Witness, 1972; Grave Matters, 1973; No Medals for the Major, 1974; Mortal Remains, 1974; The Small Hours of the Morning, 1975; Cast for Death, 1976; The Cost of Silence, 1977; The Point of Murder, 1978; Death on Account, 1979; The Scent of Fear, 1980; The Hand of Death, 1981; Devil's Work, 1982; Find Me a Villain, 1983; The Smooth Face of Evil, 1984; Intimate Kill, 1985; Safely to the Grave, 1986; Evidence to Destroy, 1987; Speak for the Dead, 1988; Crime in Question, 1989; Admit to Murder, 1990; A Small Deceit, 1991; Criminal Damage, 1992; Dangerous to Know, 1993; Almost the Truth, 1994; Pieces of Justice, 1994; Serious Intent, 1995; A Question of Belief, 1996; Act of Violence, 1997. Address: c/o Curtis Brown, Haymarket House, 28/29 Haymarket, London SW1Y 4SP, England.

YOSHIMASU Gozo, b. 22 Feb 1939, Tokyo, Japan. Poet; Essayist; Lecturer. m. Marilia, 17 Nov 1973. Education: BA, Keio University, 1963. Appointments: Chief Editor, Sansai Finer Arts magazine, 1964-69; Fulbright Visiting Writer, University of Iowa, 1970-71; Poet-in-Residence, Oaklands University, Rochester, Michigan, 1979-81; Lecturer, Tama Art University, 1984-; Visiting Lecturer at various institutions; Many poetry readings round the world. Publications in English Translation: A Thousand Steps and More: Selected Poems and Prose, 1964-1984, 1987. Contributions to: Anthologies and periodicals. Honours: Takami Jun Prize, 1971; Rekitei Prize, 1979; Hanatsubaki Modern Poetry Prize, 1984. Memberships: Japan PEN Club; Japan Writers Association. Address: 1-215-5 Kasumi-cho, Hachioji City 192, Japan.

YOUNG Al(bert James), b. 31 May 1939, Ocean Springs, Mississippi, USA. Writer; Poet. m. Arline June Balch, 1963, 1 son. Education: University of Michigan, 1957-61; Stanford University, 1966-67; AB, University of California at Berkeley, 1969. Appointments: Jones Lecturer in Creative Writing, Stanford University, 1969-74; Writer-in-Residence, University of Washington, Seattle, 1981-82; Co-Founder (with Ishmael Reed) and Editor, Quilt magazine, 1981-. Publications: Fiction: Snakes, 1970; Who is Angelina?, 1975; Sitting Pretty, 1976; Ask Me Now, 1980; Seduction by Light, 1988. Poetry: Dancing, 1969; The Song Turning Back into Itself, 1971; Some Recent Fiction, 1974; Geography of the Near Past, 1976; The Blues Don't Change: New and Selected Poems, 1982; Heaven: Collected Poems 1958-1988, 1989; Straight No Chaser, 1994. Other: Bodies and Soul: Musical Memoirs, 1981; Kinds of Blue: Musical Memoirs, 1984; Things Ain't What They Used to Be: Musical Memoirs, 1987; Mingus/Mingus: Two Memoirs (with Janet Coleman), 1989; Drowning in the Sea of Love: Musical Memoirs, 1995. Honours: National Endowment for the Arts Grants, 1968, 1969, 1974; Joseph Henry Jackson Award, San Francisco Foundation, 1969; Guggenheim Fellowship, 1974; Pushcart Prize, 1980; Before Columbus Foundation Award, 1982. Address: 514 Bryant Street, Palo Alto, CA 94301, USA.

YOUNG Allan (Edward), b. 21 June 1939, New York, New York, USA. Professor; Writer. m. Eleanor Podheiser, 16 Sept 1962, 1 son, 2 daughters. Education: BA, State University of New York at Binghamton, 1961; MBA, 1963, PhD, 1967, Columbia University. Appointments: Lecturer, Bernard M Baruch College, City University of New York, 1965-66; Assistant Professor, 1966-71, Associate Professor, 1971-74, Professor, 1974-, Co-Director, Entrepreneurship and Emerging Enterprises Program and Center, Syracuse University. Publications: The Contribution of the New York Based Securities Industry to the Economy of the City and State, 1985; The Financial Manager, 1987, 1994; Guidelines for the Financing of Industrial Investment Projects in Developing Countries, 1995. Contributions to: Academic and professional journals. Honours: Alexander Hamilton Chair-Fulbright Lectureship and Copnsultancy, Budapest; Trust Bank Chair in Accounting and Finance, Lincoln University, Canterbury, New Zealand; Syracuse University Award for Outstanding Research by Faculty. Memberships: Many economic and finance societies. Address: 27 Ely Drive, Fayetteville, NY 13066, USA.

YOUNG Axel. See: **McDOWELL Michael.**

YOUNG Bertram Alfred, b. 20 Jan 1912, London, England. Freelance Writer. Appointments: Assistant Editor, 1949-62, Drama Critic, 1962-64, Punch; Drama Critic, 1964-78, Arts Editor, 1971-77, Financial Times. Publications: Tooth and Claw, 1958; Bechuanaland, 1966; Cabinet Pudding, 1967; The Mirror Up to Nature, 1982; The Rattigan Version, 1986. Contributions to: Punch; Numerous Other Professional Journals and Magazines. Honour: Officer of the Order of the British Empire, 1980. Memberships: Critics Circle; Society of Authors; Garrick Club. Address: 1 Station Street, Cheltenham, Glos GL50 3LX, England.

YOUNG Carter Travis. See: **CHARBONNEAU Louis H.**

YOUNG Donald (Richard), b. 29 June 1933, Indianapolis, Indiana, USA. Writer; Editor; Photographer. Education: BA, Indiana University, 1955; MA, Butler University, 1964. Appointments: Editorial Staff, 1963-66, Senior Editor in American History and Political Science, 1967-77, Encyclopedia Americana; Editorial Staff, American Heritage Publishing Co, 1966-67; Contributor, The World Almanac and Book of Facts, 1984-; Managing Editor, Magazine and Book Division, Aperture, 1986-87; Various photography exhibitions. Publications: American Roulette: The History and Dilemma of the Vice-Presidency, 1965, 2nd edition, revised, 1974; The Great American Desert, 1980; Natural Monuments of America, 1990; The Sierra Club Book of Our National Parks (co-author), Volumes 1-5, 1990-96; Historic Monuments of America, 1990; National Parks of America, 1994. Contributions to: Books and periodicals. Honours: Indiana University Author Award, 1965; State Historical Society of Wisconsin Award of Merit, 1971. Membership: American Society of Picture Professionals. Address: 166 East 61st Street, Apt 3-C, New York, NY 10021, USA.

YOUNG Ed (Tse-chun), b. 28 Nov 1931, Tientsin, China. Children's Author and Illustrator. Education: City College of San Francisco, 1952; University of Illinois at Urbana, 1952-54; BPA, Art Center College of Design, Los Angeles, 1957; Graduate Studies, Pratt Institute, 1958-59. Publications: Over 35 books, 1962-96. Honours: Caldecott Medal, 1990; Boston Globe/Horn Book Awards, 1990, 1992. Address: c/o Shr Jung Tai Chi Chuan School, 87 Bowery, New York, NY 10003, USA.

YOUNG Hugo John Smelter, b. 13 Oct 1938, Sheffield, England. Journalist. m. (1) Helen Mason, 1966, dec, 1 son, 3 daughters. (2) Lucy Waring, 1990. Education: BA, Balliol College, Oxford. Appointments: Yorkshire Post, 1961; Chief Leader Writer, 1966-77, Political Editor, 1973-84, Joint Deputy Editor, 1981-84, Sunday Times; Political Columnist, The Guardian, 1984-; Director, The Tablet, 1985-; Chairman, Scott Trust, 1989. Publications: The Zinoviev Letter, 1966; Journey to Tranquility, 1969; The Crossman Affair, 1974; No Minister, 1982; But, Chancellor, 1984; The Thatcher Phenomenon, 1986; One of Us, 1989. Honours: Harkness Fellow, 1963; Congressional Fellow, 1964; Columnist of Year Awards, 1980, 1983, 1985; What the Papers Say Award, 1985; Honorary DLitt, 1993. Address: c/o The Guardian, 119 Farringdon Road, London EC1, England.

YOUNG Ian George, b. 5 Jan 1945, London, England. Writer; Editor. Appointments: Director, Catalyst Press, 1969-80; Director, TMW Communications, 1990-. Publications: Poetry: White Garland, 1969; Year of the Quiet Sun, 1969; Double Exposure, 1970; Cool Fire, 1970; Lions in the Stream, 1971; Some Green Moths, 1972; The Male Muse, 1973; Invisible Words, 1974; Common-or-Garden Gods, 1976; The Son of the Male Muse, 1983; Sex Magick, 1986. Fiction: On the Line, 1981. Non-fiction: The Male Homosexual in Literature, 1975, 2nd edition, 1982; Overlooked and Underrated, 1981; Gay Resistance, 1985; The AIDS Dissidents, 1993; The Stonewall Experiment, 1995. Membership: International Psychohistory Association. Address: 2483 Gerrard Street East, Scarborough, Ontario M1N 1W7, Canada.

YOUNG John Karl, b. 15 Aug 1951, Minneapolis, Minnesota, USA. Associate Professor of Anatomy. m. Paula Jean Spesock, 3 July 1977, 2 sons. Education: University of South Carolina, 1968-69; BS, Cornell University, 1972; PhD, University of California at Los Angeles, 1977; Postdoctoral Research, University of Minnesota, 1977-79. Appointment: Associate Professor of Anatomy, Howard University, Washington, DC. Publications: Cells: Amazing Forms and Functions, 1990; Hormones: Molecular Messengers, 1994; Histology on CD-ROM, 1996. Translator: B Kotlyar: Plasticity in the Nervous

System, 1992; V Dilman: Development, Aging and Disease: A New Rational for an Intervention Strategy, 1994. Contributions to: Scientific journals. Memberships: American Association of Anatomists; American Physiological Society. Address: c/o Department of Anatomy, Howard University, 520 W Street North West, Washington, DC 20059, USA.

YOUNG Michael Dunlop, (Lord Young of Dartington), b. 9 Aug 1915, Manchester, England. Sociologist. m. (1) Joan Lawson, 1945, 2 son, 1 daughters. (2) Sasha Moorsom, 1960, 1 son, 1 daughter. Education: BSc, London School of Economics; MA, Cambridge University; PhD, London University. Publications: Family and Kinship in East London, 1957; Rise of the Meritocracy, 1958; Metronomic Society, 1988; Family and Class in a London Suburb, 1960; The Symmetrical Family, 1973; Innovation and Research in Education, 1965; Learning Begins at Home, 1968; Forecasting and the Social Sciences, 1968; Life After Work (with Tom Schuller), 1990. Contributions to: New Society; New Statesman; Society; Samizdat. Honours: Honorary LittD, 1965; D Open University, 1973; Honorary DLitt, 1974; Honorary LLD, 1982; Honorary Fellow, Queen Mary College, 1983. Address: 18 Victoria Park Square, Behtnal Green, London E2 9PF, England.

YOUNG Rose. See: **HARRIS Marion Rose.**

YOUNG Wayland. See: **KENNET Wayland Hilton Young.**

YOUNG-BRUEHL Elizabeth, b. 3 Mar 1946, Elkton, Maryland, USA. Professor of Psychology; Psychoanalyst; Writer. Education: BA, 1968, MA, 1974, PhD, 1974, New School for Social Research, New York City. Appointments: Professor of Philosophy, Wesleyan University, 1974-91; Professor of Psychology, Haverford College, Pennsylvania, 1991-. Publications: Freedom and Karl Jaspers' Philosophy, 1981; Hannah Arendt: For Love of the World, 1982; Vigil, 1983; Anna Freud: A Biography, 1988; Mind and the Body Politic, 1989; Freud on Women, 1990; Creative Characters, 1991; Global Cultures, 1994; The Anatomy of Prejudices, 1996. Contributions to: Professional journals. Honours: National Endowment for the Humanities Fellowship, 1984-85; Guggenheim Fellowship, 1986-87. Membership: Authors Guild. Address: 409 West Stafford Street, Philadelphia, PA 19144, USA.

YOUNG-EISENDRATH Polly, b. 4 Feb 1947, Akron, Ohio, USA. Psychologist; Psychoanalyst; Writer. m. Edward Epstein, 13 Jan 1985, 2 sons, 1 daughter. Education: AB summa cum laude, English, Ohio University, 1965-69; Institute de Touraine, France, 1967-68; MA, Psychology, Mythology, Goddard College, 1972-74; MSW, Clinical Social Work, 1975-77, PhD, Developmental and Counseling Psychology, 1977-80, Washington University; Diploma, Jungian Analysis, Inter-Regional Society of Jungian Analysts, 1978-86; Diplomate Jungian Analyst, 1986. Appointments: Chief Psychologist, Jungian Analyst, President, Clinical Associates West, P C Radnor, 1986-94; Independent Practice as Psychologist and Jungian Analyst, Burlington, Vermont, 1994-; Clinical Associate Professor in Psychiatry, Medical College, University of Vermont, Burlington, 1996-; Numerous lectures worldwide. Publications: Author or Co-Author of numerous books, edited papers, original papers and chapters, book reviews and other publications, including: Jung's Self Psychology: A Constructivist Perspective, 1991; You're Not What I Expected: Learning to Love the Opposite Sex, 1993; A Cambridge Companion to Jung (co-editor), 1997; The Gifts of Suffering: Finding Insight, Compassion and Renewal, 1996; Gender and Desire: Uncursing, Pandora, 1997. Honours: Phi Beta Kappa; Mortar Board; Phi Kappa Phi; Various fellowships and assistantships; Madge Miller Award for Faculty Research, Bryn Mawr College, 1980-82; Junior Faculty Research Award, Bryn Mawr College, 1983-84. Memberships: International Association for Analytical Psychology; American Psychological Association; Founding Member, Independent Society for Analytical Psychology. Literary Agent: Beth Vesel, Sanford Greenburger Associates, 55 Fifth Avenue, New York City, USA. Address: 166 Battery Street, Burlington, VT 05401, USA.

YULE John, b. 11 Apr 1923, Melbourne, Victoria, Australia. Artist (Painter of Pictures); Writer. Education: Leaving Honours, Scotch College, Melbourne, 1940; Scholarship to Ormond College, University of Melbourne. Publication: The Living Canvas, 1986. Contributions to: Various publications. Address: 16 Madden St, Albert Park, Victoria 3206, Australia.

Z

ZAHNISER Ed(ward DeFrance), b. 11 Dec 1945, Washington, District of Columbia, USA. Writer; Poet; Editor. m. Ruth Christine Hope Deuwel, 13 July 1968, 2 sons. Education: AB, Greenville College, Illinois, 1967; Officers Basic Course, Defence Information School, 1971. Appointments: Poetry Editor, The Living Wilderness Magazine, 1972-75; Founding Editor, Some of Us Press, Washington, DC, 1972-75; Arts Editor, Good News Paper, 1981-; Editor, Arts and Kulchur, 1989-91; Poetry Editor, Antietam Review, 1992-. Publications: The Ultimate Double Play (poems), 1974; I Live in a Small Town (with Justin Duewel-Zahniser), 1984; The Way to Heron Mountain (poems), 1986; Sheenjek and Denali (poems), 1990; Jonathan Edwards (artist book), 1991; Howard Zahniser: Where Wilderness Preservation Began: Adirondack Wilderness Writings (editor), 1992; A Calendar of Worship and Other Poems, 1995. Contributions to: Books and periodicals. Honours: Woodrow Wilson Fellow, 1967; 1st and 2nd Prize in Poetry, West Virginia Writers Annual Competitions, 1989, 1991, 1992. Address: c/o Atlantis Rising, ARC Box G, Shepherdstown, WV 25443, USA.

ZAHORSKI Kenneth James, b. 23 Oct 1939, Cedarville, Indiana, USA. Professor of English; Director of Faculty Development. m. Marijean Allen, 18 Aug 1962, 2 daughters. Publications: The Fantastic Imagination, 2 volumes, 1977-78; Dark Imaginings, 1978; Fantasy Literature, 1979; The Phoenix Tree, 1980; Visions of Wonder, 1981; Alexander, Walton, Morris: A Primary and Secondary Bibliography, 1981; Fantasists on Fantasy, 1984; Peter S Beagle, 1988; The Sabbatical Mentor, 1994. Contributions to: Professional journals. Honours: Leonard Ledvina Outstanding Teacher Award, 1974; American Literary Association Outstanding Reference Book Award, 1979; Mythopoeic Society Special Scholarship Award, 1985; Donald B King Distinguished Scholar Award, 1987. Memberships: Professional and Organizational Development Network in Higher Education; Wisconsin Council of Teachers of English; Modern Language Association of America; National Council of Teachers of English; American Association for Higher Education. Address: 205 Arrowhead Drive, Green Bay, WI 54301, USA.

ZALBEN BRESKIN Jane, b. 21 Apr 1950, New York, New York, USA. Author; Artist; College Teacher. m. 25 Dec 1969, 2 sons. Education: BA, Art, Queen's College, City University of New York, 1971; Pratt Graphics Centre, 1972. Publications: Cecilia's Older Brother, 1973; Lyle and Humus, 1974; Basil and Hillary, 1975; Penny and the Captain, 1977; Norton's Nightime, 1979; Will You Count the Stars Without Me, 1979; All in the Woodland Early: An ABC by Jane Yolen, 1979; Oliver and Alison's Week, 1980; Oh Simple!, 1981; Porcupine's Christmas Blues, 1982, Maybe it will Rain Tomorrow, 1982; Here's Looking at You, Kid, 1987; Water from the Moon, 1987; Beni's First Chanukah, 1988; Earth to Andrew O Blechman, 1989; Happy Passover, Rosie, 1989; Leo and Blossom's Sukkah, 1990; Goldie's Purim, 1991; The Fortune Teller in 5B, 1991; Beni's Little Library, 1991; Buster Gets Braces, 1992; Inner Chimes: Poems on Poetry, 1992; Happy New Year, Beni, 1993; Papa's Latkes, 1994; Beni's First Chanukah, 1994; Miss Violet's Shining Day, 1995; Pearl Plants a Tree, 1995; Beni's Family Cookbook, 1996; Unfinished Dreams, 1996; Papa's Latkes, 1996; Pearl's Marigolds for Grandpa, 1997. Contributions to: Journals and magazines. Honours: Art Directors Club; Judge for Golden Kite Award, 1990; Sydney Taylor Honour Award, 1989; Best Books Citation, New York Public Library, 1991; International Reading Association Citation, 1993. Memberships: Society of Children's Book Writers. Agent: Curtis Brown Ltd, 10 Astor Place, New York, 10003. Address: 70 South Road, Sands Point, NY 11050, USA.

ZALYGIN Sergey Pavlovich, b. 6 Dec 1913, Durasovka, Russia. Writer; Editor; Ecologist. Education: Omsk Agricultural Institute. Appointment: Editor-in-Chief, Novy Mir Magazine, 1986-. Publications: Novels, stories, and essyas, 1941-92. Contributions to: Periodicals. Honours: State Prize, 1968; Sergey Radonezhsky Orthodox Order, 1993. Memberships: American Academy of Sciences; Russian Academy of Sciences; Russian Union of Writers. Address: 28/3 Lenin Prospect, Moscow, Russia.

ZAND Roxane, (Hakimzadeh), b. 21 Mar 1952, Tehran, Iran. Educator; Academic. m. Hakim Zadeh, 7 Nov 1978, 2 sons. Education:

B, Harvard University, 1975; DPhil, 1994. Publication: Persian Requiem. Contributions to: Jaso; Feminist Review; Nimeye Digar Feminist Quarterly. Memberships: Translators Society; Harvard Club of London. Address: 9 Templewood Avenue, London NW3 7UY, England.

ZASTROW Charles, b. 30 July 1942, Wausaw, Wisconsin, USA. Professor of Social Work; Writer. Education: BS, Psychology, 1964, MSW, 1966, PhD, Social Welfare, 1971, University of Wisconsin at Madison. Appointments: Assistant Professor, 1971-74, Associate Professor, 1974-78, Professor of Social Work, 1978-, University of Wisconsin at Whitewater; Associate Editor, International Journal of Comparative and Applied Criminal Justice, 1976-; Social Work Consulting Editor, Nelson-Hall Publishers, 1987-. Publications: The Personal Problem Solver (co-author), 1977; Talk to Yourself, 1979; Social Work with Groups, 4th edition, 1997; Social Problems, 4th edition, 1996; The Practice of Social Work, 5th edition, 1995; You Are What You Think, 1993; Introduction to Social Work and Social Welfare, 6th edition, 1996; Understanding Human Behavior and the Social Environment, 4th edition (co-author), 1997. Contributions to: Professional journals. Honour: Excellence in Teaching Award, University of Wisconsin at Whitewater, 1987. Memberships: Academy of Certified Social Workers; Council of Social Work Education; National Association of Social Workers; Register of Clinical Social Workers. Address: c/o Department of Social Work, University of Wisconsin at Whitewater, Whitewater, WI 53704, USA.

ZAWODNY Janusz K, b. 11 Dec 1921, Warsaw, Poland. University Professor. m. LaRae Jean Koppit, 18 Sept 1971, 1 son. Education: BS, Labor Economics, 1950, MA, International Relations, 1951, University of Iowa; PhD, Political Science, Stanford University, 1955; Honorary MA, Oxford University and University of Pennsylvania. Publications: Nothing But Honour: The Story of the Uprising in Warsaw, 1944; Death in the Forest: The Story of the Katyn Forest Massacre, 1962; Man and International Relations: Contribution of the Social Sciences to the Study of Conflict and Integration, 1967; Uczestnicy i Swiadkowie Powstania Warszawskiego, 1994; Several contributions to books. Contributions to: International Encyclopedia of the Social Sciences; American Scholar; Industrial and Labour Relations Review; Soviet Studies; Kultura (Paris); Terrorism: An International Journal; Political Research Organization and Design; Conflict Quarterly. Honours: Fellow, Center for Advanced Study in Behavioral Sciences, Stanford, 1961-62; Research Associate, Harvard University Center for International Affairs, 1968; Senior Associate, St Antony's College, Oxford University, 1968-69; Literary Award, Kultura, Paris, 1981. Memberships: American Philosophical Society, 1967; Institute for Advanced Study, Princeton, 1971-72. Address: 23703 Northeast Margaret Road, Brush Prairie, WA 98606, USA.

ZEAVIN Edna Arlone Jennings, b. 6 Nov 1930, San Francisco, California, USA. Freelance Writer; Teacher. m. Barney Zeavin, 30 May 1959, 2 sons, 4 daughters. Education: BS, Biological Science, 1958; MS, Biological Science, 1960, Arizona State University. Appointment: Pima College, 1986-96. Publications: Growing With Your Teen, 1989; Breathtaking Stopping the Plunder of Our Planet's Air, 1992; Cuisine from 6 Continents, 1993; Leavitt-Jennings-Roots & Branches, 1993; Trees of Time, 1996. Contributions to: The Link; Family Life Today; Bestways; Flower & Garden; Natural Health; Phoenix Home & Garden; Let's Live. Memberships: Society Southwest Authors, Secretary; National Writer's Union; Arizona Nightwriters. Address: 7901 E Mabel, Tucson, AZ 85715, USA.

ZELLER Frederic, b. 20 May 1924, Berlin, Germany (British Subject). Writer; Sculpter. m. (2) 21 Jan 1989. Education: BA, Birbeck College, London University, England. Publication: When Time Ran Out: Coming of Age in the Third Reich, 1989. Honour: National Endowment of the Arts Award, 1989. Memberships: Federation of Modern Painters and Sculptors, New York; Artists' Equity Association, New York. Literary Agent: Carole Mann Agency, New York, NY. Address: 775 Sixth Avenue, New York, NY 10001, USA.

ZEMANEK Alicja, b. 2 Aug 1949, Bielsko Biata, Poland. Scientist; Poet. m. Bogdan Zemanek, 30 July 1981. Education: Doctor, Biological Science, 1977, PhD, 1997, Jagiellonian University. Publications: Egzotyczny Ogrod na Wesotej, 1986; Listopad w Bibliotece, 1988; Dzien w Którym Zniknetam, 1990; Wakacje w Krakowie, 1991; Podobni do zagajnika olch, 1993. Contributions to: Periodicals. Memberships: Zwiazek Literatów Polskich; Polskie

Towarzystowo Botaniczne. Address: ul Kopernika 27, 31 501 Krakow, Poland.

ZEPHANIAH Benjamin (Obadiah Iqbal), b. 15 Apr 1958, Birmingham, England. Poet; Dramatist; Writer. m. Amina Iqbal Zephaniah, 17 Mar 1990. Appointment: Writer-in-Residence, Africa Arts Collective, Liverpool, 1989; Writer-in-Residence, Memphis State University, tennessee, 1991-95; Writer-in-Residence, Hay-on-Wye Literature Festival, 1991. Publications: Plays: Playing the Right Tune, 1985; Job Rocking, 1987; Delirium, 1987; Streetwise, 1990; The Trial of Mickey Tekka, 1991. Radio Play: Hurricane Dub, 1988. TV Play: Dread Poets Society, 1991. Other: Pen Rhythm, 1980; The Dread Affair, 1985; Inna Liverpool, 1988; Rasta Time in Palestine, 1990; City Psalms, 1992; Talking Turkeys, 1994; Funky Chickens, 1996; Propa Propaganda, 1996; School's Out, 1997. Contributions to: Radio, television and recordings; The Guardian; The Observer; Poetry review; New Statesman and Society; Black Parliamentarian. Honours: Nominations for Literary Chairs, Cambridge, 1987, Oxford, 1989; BBC Young Playwrights Festival Award, 1988. Address: c/o Sandra Boyce Management, 1 Kingsway House, Albion Road, London N16 0TA, England.

ZERNOVA Ruth, b. 15 Feb 1919, Tiraspol, Russia. Writer. m. Ilya Serman, 15 Nov 1943, 1 son, 1 daughter. Education: Leningrad University, 1946. Publications: Scorpionovy Yagody, 1961; Solnetshnaia Storona, 1968; Nemyie Zvonki, 1974; Jenskie Rasskazy, 1981; Dlinnye Teni, 1995. Contributions to: Short stories and articles in Russian journals and magazines. Memberships: Union of Soviet Writers, 1965-76; Union of Israeli Writers. Address: PO Box 23118, Jerusalem, Israel.

ZETFORD Tully. See: **BULMER Henry Kenneth.**

ZHANG Jie, b. 27 Apr 1937, China. Writer. Education: BA, People's University of China, 1960. Publications: Over 15 books, 1980-95. Honours: National Short Story Awards, 1978, 1979, 1983; Meodun National Novel Award, 1985; National Novella Award, 1985; Malaparte Literary prize, 1989. Memberships: American Academy of Arts and Letters; Beijing Association of Writers; Beijing Political Conference; Chinese Association of Writers; International PEN. Address: c/o International Department, Chinese Association of Writers, 2 Shatan Beijie, Beijing 1000720, China.

ZIEGLER Philip Sandeman, b. 24 Dec 1929, Ringwood, Hampshire, England. Writer. Education: New College, Oxford. Appointment: Chairman, Public Lending Rights Advisory Committee, 1995-. Publications: The Black Death, 1968; Melbourne, 1976; Diana Cooper, 1981; Mountbatten, 1985; The Sixth Great Power Barings, 1762-1929, 1988; Edward VIII, 1990; Harold Wilson, 1993; London at War, 1995. Contributions to: Newspapers and journals. Honours: Royal Society of Literature, Fellow, 1975; W H Heinemann Award, 1976; Fellow, Royal Historical Society, 1979; Honorary DLitt, Westminister College; CVO, 1994. Memberships: Royal Literary Fund. Literary Agent: Curtis Brown. Address: 22 Cottesmore Gardens, London, W8 5PR, England.

ZIFFRIN Marilyn J, b. 7 Aug 1926, Moline, Illinois, USA. Composer. Education: BM, University of Wisconsin, Madison, 1948; MA, Columbia University, 1949; Postgraduate Work, University of Chicago, 1963-65. Publication: Carl Ruggles, Composer, Painter & Storyteller, 1994. Contributions to: The New York Dictionary of Music and Musicians, 6th edition; The New Grove Dictionary of American Music. Honours: Fellow, MacDowell Colony, 1961, 1963, 1971, 1977, 1980, 1989; Residence, Virginia Center for the Creative Arts, 1987. Address: PO Box 179, Bradford, NH, USA.

ZIMMERL Richard, b. 18 Jan 1939, Vienna, Austria. Professor. m. Gertraud Nermuth, 26 June 1965, 1 son, 1 daughter. Education: Mathematics, Astronomy, Meterology, 1963, Master of Pedagogy, 1972, Oberstudienrat, 1994, University of Vienna. Appointments: Wiener Lehrerzeitung, 1966-88; Editor, Die Briefmarke, 1974; Chief Editor, Donau Post, 1985; Chief Editor, 1992. Publications: Typenkunde der Rekozettel Osterreichs, 1972; Jugendarbeit in Osterreich, 1983; Sachen Suchen, 1973. Contributions to: Schweizer Briefmarken-Zeitung; Sammler-Dienst; Briefmarken-Spiegel. Honour: Silbernes Verdienstzeichen der Republik Osterreich. Membership: Association Internationale de Journalistes Philateliques. Address: Ketzergasse 242, A-1230 Vienna, Austria.

ZINN Howard, b. 24 Aug 1922, New York, New York, USA. Professor of Political Science Emeritus; Writer. m. Roslyn Shechter, 30 Oct 1944, 1 son, 1 daughter. Education: BA, New York University, 1951; MA, 1952, PhD, 1958, Columbia University. Appointments: Instructor, Upsala College, East Orange, New Jersey, 1953-56; Visiting Lecturer, Brooklyn College, 1955-56; Chairman, Department of History and Political Science, Spelman College, Atlanta, 1956-63; Associate Professor, 1964-66, Professor of Political Science, 1966-88, Professor Emeritus, 1988-, Boston University. Publications: LaGuardia in Congress, 1959; SNCC: The New Abolitionists, 1964; The Southern Mystique, 1964; New Deal Thought (editor), 1965; Vietnam: The Logic of Withdrawal, 1967; Disobedience and Democracy, 1968; The Politics of History, 1970; Post-War America, 1973; Justice in Everyday Life (editor), 1974; A People's History of the United States, 1980, revised and abridged edition as The Twentieth Century: A People's History, 1984; Declarations of Independence, 1990; You Can't Be Neutral on a Moving Train, 1995. Contributions to: Professional journals and general periodicals. Honours: Albert J Beveridge Prize, American Historical Association, 1958; Harvard University Center for East Asian Studies Fellowship, 1960-61; Thomas Merton Award, 1991. Memberships: American Association of University Professor; Authors League. Address: 29 Fern Street, Auburndale, MA 02166, USA.

ZIOLKOWSKI Theodore Joseph, b. 30 Sept 1932, Birmingham, Alabama, USA. Professor of Comparative Literature; Writer. m. Yetta Bart Goldstein, 26 Mar 1951, 2 sons, 1 daughter. Education: AB, 1951, AM, 1952, Duke University; University of Innsbruck, 1952-53; PhD, Yale University, 1957. Appointments: Instructor to Assistant Professor, Yale University, 1956-62; Associate Professor, Columbia University, 1962-64; Professor of Germanic Languages and Literature, 1964-69, Class of 1900 Professor of Modern Languages, 1969-, Professor of Comparative Literature, 1975-, Dean, Graduate School, 1979-92, Princeton University; Various visiting lectureships and professorships. Publications: Hermann Broch, 1964; The Novels of Hermann Hesse, 1965; Hermann Hesse, 1966; Dimensions of the Modern Novel, 1969; Fictional Transfigurations of Jesus, 1972; Disenchanted Images, 1977; Der Schriftsteller Hermann Hesse, 1979; The Classical German Elegy, 1980; Varieties of Literary Thematics, 1983; German Romanticism and Its Institutions, 1990; Virgil and the Moderns, 1993; The Mirror of Justice, 1997. Editor: Hermann Hesse: Autobiographical Writings, 1972; Hermann Hesse: Stories of Five Decades, 1972; Hesse: A Collection of Critical Essays, 1972; Hermann Hesse: My Belief: Essays on Life and Art, 1974; Hermann Hesse: Pictor's Metamorphoses and Other Fantasies, 1982; Hermann Hesse: Soul of the Age: Selected Letters 1891-1962, 1991. Contributions to: Books and professional journals. Honours: Fulbright Research Grant, 1958-59; American Philosophical Society Grant, 1959; Guggenheim Fellowship, 1964-65; James Russell Lowell Prize for Criticism, 1972; American Council of Learned Societies Fellowships, 1972, 1976; Wilbur Lucius Cross Medal, Yale University, 1982; Goethe Institute Gold Medal, 1987; Henry Allen Moe Prize in Humanities, 1988; Resident Fellow, Bellagio Study Centre, Italy, 1993. Memberships: Academy of Literary Studies; American Academy of Arts and Sciences; American Association of Teachers of German, honorary life member; Association of Graduate Scholars, president, 1990-91; Association of Literary Scholars and Critics; American Philosophical Society; Authors Guild; Modern Language Association, president, 1985; Associate of Literary Scholars and Critics; International Association of Germanists; Austrian Academy of Sciences; Göttingen Academy of Sciences. Address: 36 Bainbridge Street, Princeton, NJ 08540, USA.

ZOBEL Louise Purwin, b. 10 Jan 1922, Laredo, Texas, USA. Author; Lecturer; Teacher. m. 14 Nov 1943, Dr Jerome Freemont Zobel, 1 son, 3 daughters. Education: BA, Journalism, Stanford University, 1943; MA, Communication, 1976. Appointments: Writer and Editor, United Press Bureau; Editor, Magazine, Association of College Unions, International, 1972-73; Cruise Enrichment Lecturer and Writing Teacher, Royal Viking Lines and Princess Cruises, 1974-83; Instructor, Writer's Digest Correspondence School, 1982-90; Keynote Speaker, Travel Lecturer, TV Personality. Publications: The Travel Writer's Handbook, 1980, revised, 1992; Let's Have Fun In Japan, 1982. Contributions to: Books, newspapers and magazines. Honours: Phi Beta Kappa, 1943; Sigma Delta Chi Award For Scholarship, 1943; Prizes, Writers Digest National Article Contest, 1967, 1975, 1978, 1992, 1994; National Writers Club Contest, 1976. Memberships: Women in Communication; California Writers Club; Travel Journalists Guild; International Food, Wine, and Travel Writers Association. Address: 23350 Sereno Court, Villa #30, Cupertino, CA 95014, USA.

ZUROWSKI Andrzej, b. 24 Sept 1944, Poland. Theatre Critic; Essayist. m. Magda Oller, 23 Aug 1988, 1 son, 3 daughters. Education: MA, 1967; PhD, 1973. Appointments: Chief, Artistic Programmes, Polish TV, Gdansk, 1967-90; Lecturer, University of Gdansk, 1975-77, 1986-. Publications: 14 books, 1976-97. Contributions to: Journals and periodicals. Honours: Several literary awards and medals. Memberships: International Association of Theatre Critics, vice president; Union of Polish Writers. Address: Glogowa 21, 81 589 Gdynia, Poland.

ZWICKY (Julia) Fay, b. 4 July 1933, Melbourne, Victoria, Australia. Poet. m. (1) Karl Zwicky, 1957, (2) James Mackie, 1990. Education: BA, University of Melbourne, 1954. Appointment: Senior Lecturer, University of Western Australia, 1972-87. Publications: Isaac Babel's Fiddle, 1975; Kaddish and Other Poems, 1982; The Lyre in the Pawnshop: Essays on Literature and Survival, 1974-84, 1986; Ask Me, 1990. Honours: New South Wales Premier's Award, 1982; Western Australian Premier's Award, 1991. Address: 30 Goldsmith Road, Claremont, Western Australia 6010, Australia

ZYGULSKI Zdzislaw Franciszek, b. 18 Aug 1921, Boryslaw, Poland. Art Historian; Museologist. m. Eva Voelpel, 18 Apr 1944, 1 son. Education: Doctor Degree, Jagiellonian University, Kraków, 1960; Professor Title, 1978; Full Professor, 1987. Publications: Bron w dawnej Polsee (Arms in Old Poland), 1975, 1982; Muzea na Swiecie (Museums of the World, 1982; An Outline History of Polish Applied Art, 1987; Sztuka islamu w zbirorach polskich (Art of Islam in Polish Collections), 1989; Ottoman Art in the Service of the Empire, 1992; Slawne bitwy w sztuce (Famous Battles in Art), 1996. Contributions to: Rembrandt's Lisowczyk; Bulletin de Musee National de Varsovie, 1965; Dama z gronostajem (A Study on the Lady with an Ermine, by Leonardo); Biuletyn Historii Sztuki, 1969. Honour: An Outline History of Polish Applied Art awarded as best book on Polish Culture in English, Association of Polish Art, Detroit, USA, 1991. Address: 30-112 Krakow, ul Dunin Wasowicza 12 m 5, Poland.

Appendices

APPENDIX A

LITERARY AGENTS

The following list of agents does not claim to be exhaustive although every effort has been made to make it as comprehensive as possible. In all instances, authors are advised to send preliminary letters to agents before submitting manuscripts.

ARGENTINA

Lawrence Smith Literary Agency
Aveni da de los Incas 3110
Buenos Aires 1426
Contact: *Lawrence Smith, Mrs Nancy H Smith*
Literary works accepted for translation into Spanish and Portuguese. Publications in volume or serial for representation in theatre, film, television or radio.

AUSTRALIA

Australian Literary Management
2A Armstrong Street
Middlepark, VIC 3206
Represents Australian writers in fields of fiction, non-fiction, children's books, theatre and film. Handles Australian/New Zealand rights only for a small number of American writers in conjunction with other literary agents.

Curtis Brown (Aust) Pty Ltd
27 Union Street, Paddington
Sydney, NSW 2021
Represents fiction, non-fiction, children's writers, television, screen, radio and stage; also represents directors.

Rick Raftos Pty Ltd
PO Box 445, Paddington
Sydney, NSW 2021
Contact: *Rick Raftos, Jane Rose*
Represents performing arts, writers, television, screen, radio and stage; also represents directors.

BELGIUM

Toneelfonds J. Janssens
Te Boelaerlei 107
2140 Antwerp
Contact: *Jessica Janssens*
Literary Agency specialising in plays.

BRAZIL

Karin Schindler
Caixa Postal 19051
04599 São Paulo SP
Contact: *Karin Schindler*
Handles everything for the sale of Portuguese language rights in Brazil

BULGARIA

Bulgarian Copyright Agency JUSAUTOR
17 Ernst Telman Boulevard
1463 Sofia
Contact: *Director General*
Representative of Bulgarian authors, promoting work for publication and performance abroad.

CANADA

Acacia House Publishing Services Ltd
51 Acacia Road
Toronto, Ontario M4S 2K6

Authors' Marketing Services Ltd
217 Degrassi Street
Toronto, Ontario M4M 2K8
Adult fiction and non-fiction, parental self-help, business and biography.

Bella Pomer Agency Inc
22 Shallmar Boulevard, PH2
Toronto, Ontario M5N 2Z8
Contact: *Bella Pomer*
International representation for full-length fiction and non-fiction. No cook books, how-to books or unsolicited manuscripts.

Bukowski Agency
182 Avenue Road, Suite 3
Toronto, Ontario M5R 2J1
President: *Denise Bukowski*

Kellock and Associates Ltd
11017 - 80 Avenue
Edmonton, Alberta T6G OR2
Contact: *Joanne Kellock*
Handles all non-fiction for trade market, all fiction, literary, commercial, genre and all works for children. Also acts for illustrators of books for children.

MGA/Sterling Lord Association Canada
10 St Mary Street, Suite 510
Toronto, Ontario M4Y 1P

Lucinda Vardley Agency Ltd
297 Seaton Street
Toronto, Ontario M5A 2T

DENMARK

Leonhardt Literary Agency Aps
35 Studiestraede
DK-1455 Copenhagan K
Handles all kinds of bookrights.

FRANCE

Agence Strassova
4 Rue Git-le-Coeur
75006 Paris
Handles general literature.

European American Information Services Inc
10 Rue de l'Abreuvoir
92400 Courbevoie, Paris
(US address: 110 East 59th Street
New York, NY 10022)

Representing author Catherine Nay and French publishers in North America and North American publishers and agents in France.

Francoise Germain
8 Rue de la Paix
75002 Paris
Contact: *Madame Francoise Germain*
Representation of French and foreign authors.

La Nouvelle Agence
7 Rue Corneille
75006 Paris
Representation in France for US, English, Italian and German agents and publishers as well as French authors.

Michelle Lapautre Literary Agency
6 Rue Jean Carries
75007 Paris
Contact: *Michelle Lapautre*
Representing English-language publishers, agents and authors for the sale of French translation rights.

Shelley Power Literary Agency Ltd
Le Montaud
24220 Berbigières, France
Contact: *Shelley Power*
General fiction and non-fiction. No poetry, plays or short pieces. Offers worldwide representation.

Promotion Litteraire
26 Rue Chalgrin
75116 Paris
Publishers' consultants representing leading American, French and Italian publishers, International authors, scout service, general fiction and non-fiction books, film and television scripts, film rights and properties.

GERMANY

Buro für Urheberrechte, Copyright Office, Copyright Information Center
Clara-Zetkin-Strasse 105
Berlin
Contact: *Dr Andreas Henselmann*

Corry Theegarten-Schlotterer Verlags-und Autoren-Agentur
Kulmer Strasse 3
D-8000 Munich 81
Contact: *Ms C Theegarten-Schlotterer*
Co-production of books of international interest, fiction and non-fiction, and biographies. No childrens' books.

Fralit Medium Agency
Brahmsallee 29
D-2000 Hamburg 13
Manuscripts for newspapers and book publishers, plays and features for theatre, broadcasting, television and film.

Geisenheyner and Crone International Literary Agents
Gymnasiumstrasse 31B
D-7000 Stuttgart 1
Contact: *Mr Ernst W Geisenheyner*
Representing German and foreign authors and publishers.

GPA Gerd Plesel Agentur and Veriags GmbH
Linprunstrasse 38
D-8000 Munich 2
Contact: *Gerd J Plesel*
Represents publishers and literary agencies from the English language world in general and selected ones from French and German. Also major American and British Studios for ancilliary rights.

Hans Hermann Hagedorn
Erikastrasse 142
D-2000 Hamburg 20
Contact: *Hans Hermann Hagedorn.*

Literarische Agentur Brigitte Axster
Dreieichstr 43
D-6000 Frankfurt
Contacts: *Brigitte Axster, Dr Petra Christina Hardt, Uta Angerer*
Authors agent representing English, Dutch, French and Italian publishers in German speaking countries.

Skandinavia Verlag, Marianne Weno - Michael Günther
Ithweg 31
D-1000 Berlin 37
Contact: *Michael Günther*
Represents contemporary Scandinavian playwrights.
Handles plays for radio, stage and television.

INDIA

Ajanta Books International
IUB Jawahar Nagar
Bungalow Road, Delhi 110007
Research work on Social Science and Humanity especially on Indian themes, oriental or modern.

ISRAEL

Rogan-Pikarski Literary Agency
200 Hayarkon Street
PO Box 4006
61 040 Tel Aviv
Contact: *Ilana Pikarski*
Represents major US and European publishers and agents for Hebrew volume, serial and performance and merchandising rights; also has New York agency.

ITALY

Agenzia Letteraria Internazionale
3 Via Fratelli Gabba
Milan
Represents American, English and German publishers and agencies exclusively in Italy.

Natoli and Stefan
Galleria Buenos Aires 14
I-20124 Milan
Represents fiction and non-fiction authors rights, co-editions and translations.

JAPAN

Tuttle-Mori Agency
Fuji Building, 8th Floor
2-15 Kanda Jimbocho

Chiyoda-ku
Tokyo 101
Contact: *Mr Takeshi Mori*
Largest literary agency for foreign rights in Japan.

THE NETHERLANDS

Auteursbureau Greta Baars Jelgersma
Bovensteweg 46
NL-6585 KD Mook
Contact: *Greta Baars Jelgersma*
Represents authors and publishers, and translations from the Scandinavian and modern languages. International co-printing of illustrated books and arranging profitable offers for book production. Oldest international literary agency in The Netherlands.

Prins and Prins Literary Agency
Postbus 5400
NL-1007 AK Amsterdam
Contact: *Henk Prins*
Representation in The Netherlands of foreign publishers.

NORWAY

Hanna-Kirsti Koch Literary Agency
PO Box 3043
Elisenberg
0207 Oslo 2
Contact: *Mr Eilif Koch*
Representing foreign authors in Norway.

Ulla Lohren Literary Agency
PO Box 150, Tasen
0801 Oslo 8
Contact: *Ulla Lohren*
Represents agents and publishers from Canada, UK, USA and others for Scandinavian rights in fiction, non-fiction and children's books.

POLAND

Authors' Agency
ul. Hipoteczna 2
00-950 Warsaw
Handles Polish copyrights, foreign contracts and information.

PORTUGAL

Ilidio da Fonseca Matos Literary Agency
Rua de S Bernardo 68-30,
1200 Lisbon
Contact: *Ilidio da Fonseca Matos*
Represents in Portugal: Curtis Brown Ltd; Laurence Pollinger Ltd; The New American Library; Doubleday and Company Inc; Rowholt Verla - Diogenes Verlag.

SPAIN

Andres de Kramer
Castello 30
28001 Madrid
Handles only foreign writers and foreign rights of theatrical plays and production in Spain.

Bookbank S A
Rafael Calvo 13

28010 Madrid
Represents foreign publishers and/or agents and/or writers for the sale of Spanish language and Portuguese rights. Also Spanish language authors.

Julio Fyanez Literary Agency
Via Augusta 139
08021 Barcelona
Contact: *Mr Julio Fyanez*
Represents publishers, agencies and independent authors from all countries and Spanish authors abroad. Covers Spain, Latin America, Portugal and Brazil.

Ute Korner de Moya Literary Agency
Ronda Guinardo 32-5-5
08025 Barcelona
Contact: *Ute Korner*
Represents foreign publishers, agents and authors in the Spanish and Portuguese speaking countries.

SWEDEN

D Richard Bowen
Post Box 30037
S-200 61 Malmö 30
Contact: *D Richard Bowen*
Publishers' literary and sales agent, translation rights, etc., negotiated.

Lennart Sane Agency AB
Hollandareplan
537434 Karlshamn
Contact: *Lennart Sane*
Representing US, British and Scandinavian authors, publishers and agencies for translation rights in Europe and Latin America.

Monica Heyum Literary Agency
PO Box 3300 Vendelso
S-13603 Haninge
Contact: *Monica Heyum*
Handles fiction, non-fiction and children's books.

SWITZERLAND

Dieter Breitsohl AG Literary Agency
PO Box 245
CH 8034 Zürich
or: Heimatstr 25
CH 8008 Zürich
Contact: *Dr Jutta Motz*
Handles non-fiction, psychology, psychosomatic, religion, theology and mythology.

Liepman AG
Maienburgweg 23, Postfach 572
CH-8044 Zürich
Contact: *Dr Ruth Liepman, Eva Koralnik, Ruth Weibel*
Represents American, British, Canadian, French, Dutch and Israeli publishers and agents for the German language rights and authors' manuscripts.

New Press Agency Society
Haus am Herterberg, Haldenstrasse 5
CH-8500 Frauenfeld, Herten

Paul and Peter Fritz AG Literary Agency
Jupiterstrasse 1
Postfach 8032 Zürich
Contact: *Peter S Fritz*

Represents English language authors for the German language rights and authors worldwide. No unsolicited manuscripts.

UNITED KINGDOM

Jacintha Alexander Associates
47 Emperor's Gate
London SW7 4HJ
Contact: *Jacintha Alexander, Julian Alexander*
Handles full-length general and literary fiction and non-fiction of all kinds. No plays, poetry, textbooks or science fiction. Film and television scripts handled for established clients only.

Blake Friedman Literary Agency Ltd
37-41 Gower Street
London WC1E 6HH
Contact: *Carol Blake (books), Julian Friedman (film/television), Conrad Williams (original scripts/radio)*
Worldwide representation of fiction and non-fiction, television and film rights and scripts. No juvenile projects or poetry.

Campbell Thomson and McLaughlin Ltd
1 King's Mews
London WC1N 2JA
Contact: *John McLaughlin, Charlotte Bruton*
Handles book-length manuscripts excluding children's, science fiction and fantasy. No plays, film scripts, articles or poetry. Short stories from existing clients only.

Carnell Literary Agency
Danescroft, Goose Lane, Little Hallingbury
Bishop's Stortford, Herts CM22 7RG
Contact: *Mrs Pamela Buckmaster*
Specializes in science fiction and fantasy, also handles general fiction, non-fiction and children's fantasy.

Casarotto Ramsay Ltd
National House,
60-66 Wardour Street
London W1V 3HP
Contacts: *Jenne Casarotto, Greg Hunt, Tracey Smith (Film/Television/Radio), Tom Erhardt, Mel Kenyan (Stage), Maggie Hanbury (Books)*
Handles scripts for television, theatre, film and radio, general fiction and non-fiction.

Jonathan Clowes Ltd
10 Iron Bridge House, Bridge Approach
London NW1 8BD
Contact: *Brie Burkeman*
Fiction and non-fiction plus scripts. No textbooks or children's.

Elspeth Cochrane Agency
11-13 Orlando Road
London SW4 0LE
Contact: *Donald Baker, Elspeth Cochrane*
Authors handled for theatre, films, andtelevision. Books for all types of publication.

Rosica Colin Ltd
1 Clareville Grove Mews
London SW7 5AH
Contact: *Joanna Marston*

All full length manuscripts including theatre, films, television and sound broadcasting works in the USA, European countries and overseas.

Rupert Crew Ltd
1A King's Mews
London WC1N 2JA
Contact: *Doreen Montgomery, Shirley Russell*
Representation offered to limited clientele, specialising in promoting major book projects: non-fiction, general and women' fiction.

Curtis Brown Ltd (London)
Haymarket House
28-29 Haymarket
London SW1Y 4SP
Handles a wide range of subjects including fiction, general non-fiction, children's and specialist, scripts for film, television, theatre and radio.

Felix de Wolfe
Manfield House
376-378 The Strand
London WC2R 0LR
Contact: *Felix de Wolfe*
Handles quality fiction and scripts only. No non-fiction or children's. No unsolicited manuscripts.

Eric Glass Ltd
28 Berkeley Square
London W1X 6HD
Contact: *Eric Glass, Janet Crowley*
Books, plays, screenplays and television plays. Sole agents for the Société des Auteurs et Compositeurs Dramatiques of Paris for the English speaking countries.

Elaine Green Ltd
37 Goldhawk Road
London W12 8QQ
Contact: *Elaine Green, Carol Heaton*
Handles novels, quality non-fiction and journalist's books. No original scripts for theatre, film or television.

David Grossman Literary Agency Ltd
110-114 Clerkenwell Road
London EC1M 5SA
Contact: *Address material to the company*
Fiction and general non-fiction. No verse or technical books for students. No original screenplays or teleplays.

A M Heath and Co Ltd
79 St Martin's Lane
London WC2N 4AA
Contact: *Sara Fisher, Bill Hamilton, Michael Thomas.*
Handles fiction and general non-fiction. No scripts or poetry.

David Higham Associates Ltd
5-8 Lower John Street
Golden Square
London W1R 4H4
Contact: *Anthony Goff, John Rushi (Scripts), Elizabeth Cree (Books)*
Representing professional authors and writers in all fields throughout the world.

International Copyright Bureau Ltd
22A Aubrey House

Maida Avenue
London W2 1TQ
Contact: *Joy Westendarp*
Handles scripts for television,theatre, film and radio.
No books.

M B A Literary Agents Ltd
45 Fitzroy Street
London W1P 5HR
Contact: *Diana Tyler, John Richard Parker, Meg Davis, Ruth Needham*
Represent writers in all mediums: books, television and radio. Handles fiction and non-fiction. No poetry or children's fiction. Also scripts for film, television, radio and theatre.

William Morris Agency UK Ltd
31-32 Soho Square
London W1V 5DG
Contact: *Stephen M Kenis (films), Jane Annakin (Television/Theatre), Lavinia Trevor (Books).*
Scripts handled for theatre, film, television and radio. Also fiction and general non-fiction.

Penman Literary Agency
175 Pall Mall
Leigh-on-Sea, Essex SS9 1RE
Contact: *Leonard G Stubbs*
Full length novel manuscripts. Also theatre, films, television and sound broadcasting.

Peters Fraser and Dunlop Group Ltd
503/4 The Chambers
Chelsea Harbour, Lots Road
London SW10 0XF
Contact: *Kenneth Ewing, Tim Corrie*
Agents for stage drama, television, plays and series, radio drama, fiction and non-fiction and children's books, representation for producers and directors of stage, television and film.

Laurence Pollinger Ltd
18 Maddox Street
London W1R 0EU
Contact: *Gerald J Pollinger, Margaret Pepper, Romany van Bosch.*
Author's agents for all material with the exception of original film stories, poetry and freelance journalistic articles.

Murray Pollinger
222 Old Brompton Road
London SW5 0BZ
Contact: *Murray Pollinger, Gina Pollinger, Sara Menguc*
Agents for all types of general fiction and non-fiction with the exception of plays, poetry and travel.

Rogers Coleridge and White Ltd
20 Powis Mews
London W11 1JN
Contact: *Deborah Rogers, Gill Coleridge, Patricia White, Ann Warnford Davis*
Handles fiction, non-fiction and children's books. No plays or poetry.

Tessa Sayle Agency
11 Jubilee Place
London SW3 3TE
Contact: *Rachel Calder (Books), Penny Tackaberry (Drama)*

Full length manuscripts, plays, films, television and sound broadcasting. Represented in all foreign countries.

Vincent Shaw Associates
20 Jay Mews
Kensington Gore, London SW7 2EP
Contact: *Vincent Shaw, Lester McGrath*
Handles film, television, theatre and radio only. Unsolicited manuscripts read.

Shiel Land Associates Ltd
43 Doughty Street
London WC1N 2LF
Contact: *Anthony Shiel*
Represents literary authors. Represents worldwide including translation, film, television and theatre.

Solo Syndication and Literary Agency Ltd
49-53 Kensington High Street
London W8 5ED
Contact: *Don Short*
Specialising in celebrity autobiographies and biographies. Non-fiction only except for established authors.

Tricia Sumner Agency
32 Orchard Gardens
Waltham Abbey, Essex EN9 1RS
Contact: *Tricia Sumner*
Former Deputy General Secretary of the Writers' Guild.

Peter Tauber Press Agency
94 East End Road
London N3 2SX
Contact: *Peter Tauber, Robert Tauber*
Full representation, specialising in well-researched epic women's saga fiction.

Ed Victor Ltd
162 Wardour Street
London W1V 3AT
Contact: *Ed Victor, Maggie Phillips, Sophie Hicks, Graham Greene*
Commercial fiction and non-fiction. No scripts or academic books.

Watson Little Ltd
12 Egbert Street
London NW1 8LJ
Contact: *Mandy Little, Sheila Watson*
Represents wide range of fiction and non-fiction. No poetry, short stories or articles, or books for very young children.

A P Watt Ltd
20 John Street
London WC1N 2DR
Contact: *Caradoc King, Linda Shaughnessy, Rod Hall, Lisa Eveleigh, Nick Marston, Derek Johns*
Full length works for all media including plays and telescripts. No poetry. Representation throughout the world.

UNITED STATES OF AMERICA

California

Artists Agency
10000 Santa Monica Boulevard, Suite 305
Los Angeles, CA 90067

Representation of novels and screenplays for films.

Sandra Dijkstra Literary Agency
1155 Camino Del Mar
Del Mar, CA 92014
Contact: *Sandra Dijkstra, Katherine Goodwin*
Handles quality and commercial adult fiction and non-fiction. Representation to major publishers in USA. British rights. Translations.

Renee Wayne Golden APLC
8983 Norma Place
West Hollywood, CA 90069
Contact: *Renee Wayne Golden*
Representation of selected authors.

Paul Kohner Inc
9169 Sunset Boulevard
Los Angeles, CA 90069
Non-fiction preferred to fiction. No short stories, poetry, science fiction or gothic.

Michael Larsen/Elizabeth Pomada Literary Agency
1029 Jones Street
San Francisco, CA 94109
Contact: *Elizabeth Pomada*
Handles general fiction and non-fiction for adults, self help and popular psychology.

Jack Scagnetti Talent and Literary Agency
5330 Lankershim Boulevard, No 210
North Hollywood, CA 91601
Contact: *Jack Scagnetti*
Handles screenplays, television scripts, treatments, books and major magazine articles. Franchised signatory to Writers Guild of America-West.

Singer Media Corp
Seaview Business Park
1030 Calle Cordillera, Unit 106
San Clemente, CA 92673
Contact: *Dr Kurt Singer*
Newspaper syndicate, literary agency and photo bank. Handles sophisticated modern romance novels, biographies, mysteries and horror books.

H N Swanson Inc
8523 Sunset Boulevard
Los Angeles, CA 90069
Contact: *Thomas Shanks, N V Swanson*
Represents writers for novels, screenplays, television and theatre. Worldwide representation.

Colorado

Flannery, White and Stone, A Writer's Agency
180 Cook, Suite 404
Denver, CO 80206

Connecticut

Sidney B Kramer
Mews Books Ltd
20 Bluewater Hill
Westport, CT 06880
Contact: *Sidney B Kramer, Fran Pollack*
Specializes in juvenile (pre-school - young adult), cookery, adult non-fiction and fiction, technical and medical software, film and television, etc. Prefers work of published/established authors; will accept small number of new/unpublished authors.

New England Publishing Associates Inc
PO Box 5
Chester, CT 06412
Editorial assistance and representation for non-fiction books for the adult market.

Van der Leun and Associates
464 Mill Hill Drive
Southport, CT 06490
Contact: *Patricia Van der Leun*
Handles fiction and non-fiction; specializes in illustrated books, art and science. No unsolicited manuscripts. Representation in all foreign countries.

District of Columbia

Ronald L Goldfarb and Associates
918 16th Street North West, Suite 400
Washington, DC 20006

Florida

Lighthouse Literary Agency
PO Box 2105
Winter Park, FL 32790
Director: *Sandra Kangas*

Georgia

Deering Literary Agency
1507 Oakmonth Drive
Acworth, GA 30101
Directors: *Charles and Dorothy Deering*

Hawaii

Rhodes Literary Agency
Box 89133
Honolulu, HI 96830
Handles novels, non-fiction books, magazines, poetry books, single poems, religious materials, film and television scripts, stage plays, juvenile books, syndicated materials, radio scripts, textbooks, photos, books of cartoons, etc.

Illinois

Austin Wahl Agency Ltd
53 West Jackson Boulevard, Suite 342
Chicago, IL 60604
Contact: *Thomas Wahl*
Handles film and television scripts, novels and non-fiction books.

Maryland

Columbia Literary Associates Inc
7902 Nottingham Way
Ellicott City, MD 21043

Massachusetts

Otte Company
9 Goden Street
Belmont, MA 02178
Contact: *Jane H Otte*
Handles adult fiction and non-fiction full length books. Representation in all major markets and Hollywood.

Michael Snell Literary Agency
Box 655
Truro, MA 02666

Development and sale of adult non-fiction, primarily in business, computers, science, psychology and law.

Gunther Stuhlmann, Author's Representative
PO Box 276
Becket, MA 01223
Contact: *Barbara Ward, Gunther Stuhlmann*
Representation worldwide of quality literature and non-fiction.

Michigan

Creative Concepts Literary Agency
5538 Herford
Troy, MI 48098

Minnesota

Lazear Agency Inc
430 First Avenue North, Suite 416
Minneapolis, MN 55401
Contact: *Jonathon Lazear*

Missouri

Joyce A Flaherty, Literary Agent
816 Lynda Court
St Louis, MO 63122

Montana

Phoenix Literary Agency
PO Box 669
Livingston, MT 59047

New Hampshire

Northeast Literary Agency
69 Broadway
Concord, NH 03301

New Jersey

Barbara Bauer Literary Agency
179 Washington Avenue
Matawan, NJ 07747
Contact: *Barbara Bauer*
Specializes in new and unpublished authors, quality fiction and non-fiction for children and adults.

Rosalie Siegel, International Literary Agent Inc
1 Abey Drive
Pennington, NJ 08534
Contact: *Rosalie Siegel, Pamela Walker*
Adult fiction and non-fiction, particularly quality fiction. Also French fiction and non-fiction.

New Mexico

Rydal Agency
PO Box 2247
Santa Fe, NM 87504

New York

Carole Abel Literary Agent
160 West 87th Street
New York, NY 10024
Contact: *Carole Abel*
Handles trade and mass market fiction and non-fiction books. No unsolicited manuscripts; query first. Agents in Hollywood and most foreign countries.

Dominick Abel Literary Agency Inc
146 West 82nd Street, Suite 1B
New York, NY 10024
Contact: *Dominick Abel.*

Acton, Dystel, Leone and Jaffe
928 Broadway, Suite 303
New York, NY 10010
Contact: *Jane Dystel*
Non-fiction and novels.

Marcia Amsterdam Agency
41 West 82nd Street
New York, NY 10024
Contact: *Marcia Amsterdam*
Handles adult and young adult fiction, film and television rights, screenplays and teleplays.

Julian Bach Literary Agency Inc
22 East 71st Street
New York, NY 10021
Contact: *Julian Bach, Emma Sweeney, Susan Merritt, Ann Rittenberg*
Agents for fiction and non-fiction. No science fiction or fantasy, poetry or photography.

Bethel Agency
641 West 59th Street
New York, NY 10019
Handles fiction and non-fiction, plays for theatre, film and television; sub-division handles children's books.

Brandt and Brandt Literary Agency Inc
1501 Broadway
New York, NY 10036
Contact: *Carl D Brandt, Gail Hochman*
Handles fiction and non-fiction. No unsolicited manuscripts; query first; no reading fee. Agents in most foreign countries.

Connor Literary Agency
640 West 153rd Street
New York, NY 10031
Contact: *Marlene K Connor*
Handles commercial fiction and non-fiction, illustrated books, cookbooks, self-help, ethnic subjects and how-to. Foreign agents in major countries.

Curtis Brown Ltd
10 Astor Place, 3rd Floor
New York, NY 10003
Handles fiction, non-fiction, science fiction, mystery and romance. Also children's fiction, non-fiction and theatrical, film and television. Handles general trade fiction, non-fiction, juvenile and film and television rights. Representatives in all major countries. No unsolicited manuscripts; query first.

Anita Diamant Literary Agency
310 Madison Avenue
New York, NY 10017
Contact: *Anita Diamant, Robin Rae*
Handles book manuscripts, fiction, non-fiction and foreign film rights.

Jonathan Dolger Agency
49 East 96th Street, Suite 9B
New York, NY 10128
Contact: *Jonathan Dolger*
Handles adult fiction and non-fiction, and illustrated books. No unsolicited material; query letter and SASE first.

Donadio and Ashworth Inc, Literary Representatives
231 West 22nd Street
New York, NY 10011

Ethan Ellenberg Literary Agency
548 Broadway, No 5-E
New York, NY 10012
Contact: *Ethan Ellenberg*
Handles quality fiction and non-fiction, first novels, commercial fiction, military, history and sci-fi. Query before submission of manuscripts.

Ann Elmo Agency Inc
60 East 42nd Street
New York, NY 10165
Contact: *Ann Elmo, Lettie Lee*
Handles all types of fiction, non-fiction, juveniles, plays for book and magazine publication, as well as for film, television and stage use.

Freida Fishbein Ltd
2556 Hubbard Street
Brooklyn, NY 11235
Contact: *Janice Fishbein*
Handles plays, books, film and television scripts. No short stories, poetry or young children's books.

Samuel French Inc
45 West 25th Street
New York, NY 10010
Specializing in plays.

Jay Garon-Brooke Associates Inc
101 West 55th Street, Suite 5K
New York, NY 10019
Fiction and non-fiction. No romance, western or mystery works accepted.

Max Gartenberg Literary Agent
521 5th Avenue, Suite 1700
New York, NY 10175
Contact: *Max Gartenberg*
Handles book-length manuscripts of non-fiction and fiction including all rights therein.

Gelles-Cole Literary Enterprises
320 East 42nd Street, Suite 411
New York, NY 10017
Contact: *Sandi Gelles-Cole*
Handles commercial fiction and non-fiction.

Jeff Herman Agency
500 Greenwich Street, Suite 501-C
New York, NY 10013
President: *Jeffrey H Herman*

John Hawkins and Associates Inc
71 West 23rd Street, Suite 1600
New York, NY 10010
Contact: *J Hawkins, W Reiss*
Provides all services of representation to book-length manuscripts in prose. No theatrical, film or television scripts.

International Creative Management
40 West 57th Street
New York, NY 10019

Janklow and Nesbit Associates
598 Madison Avenue
New York, NY 10022
Contact: *Lynn Nesbit*

JCA Literary Agency Inc
27 West 20th Street, Suite 1103
New York, NY 10011
Handles general fiction and non-fiction. No screen plays. Query first with SASE.

JET Literary Associates Inc
124E 84th Street, Suite 4A
New York, NY 10028
Contact: *James E Trupin*
Handles book length fiction and non-fiction only.

Asher D Jason Enterprises Inc
111 Barrow Street
New York, NY 10014
Contact: *Asher D Jason*
Handles non-fiction and fiction. Representation to all American publishers.

Lucy Kroll Agency
390 West End Avenue
New York, NY 10024
Contact: *Lucy Kroll, Barbara Hogenson*
Handles fiction and non-fiction including scripts for film, television and radio.

Peter Livingston Associates Inc
465 Park Avenue
New York, NY 10022
Contact: *Peter W Livingston, David C Johnston*
Handles serious non-fiction, business, politics, popular science, etc. Literary and commercial fiction, film and television. No poetry or children's books. Foreign rights.

Elaine Markson Literary Agency Inc
44 Greenwich Avenue
New York, NY 10011
Contact: *Elaine Markson*

McIntosh and Otis Inc
310 Madison Avenue
New York, NY 10017
Adult and juvenile fiction and non-fiction. No textbooks or scripts.

Scott Meredith Literary Agency Inc
845 Third Avenue
New York, NY 10022
Contact: *Jack Scovil, Scott Meredith*
Handles general fiction and non-fiction, books and magazines, juveniles, plays, television scripts, and film rights and properties. Accept unsolicited manuscripts; reading fee. Agents in all principal countries.

William Morris Agency
1350 Avenue of the Americas
New York, NY 10019

Jean V Naggar Literary Agency
216 East 75th Street
New York, NY 10021
Contact: *Jean Naggar*
Complete representation in all areas of general fiction and non-fiction.

Pickering Associates Inc
432 Hudson Street
New York, NY 10014
Contact: *John Pickering*

Full service literary agency with co-agents in Hollywood and all principal translation markets.

Susan Ann Protter Literary Agent
110 West 40th Street, Suite 1408
New York, NY 10018
Contact: *Susan Protter*
Principally hard and soft cover books and the various rights involved. Fiction, non-fiction, health, science, biography, history, science fiction, etc.

Rosenstone/Wender
3 East 48th Street, 4th Floor
New York, NY 10017
Contact: *Susan Perlman Cohen, Phyllis Wender.*

Russell and Volkening Inc
50 West 29th Street, No 7E
New York, NY 10001
Literary fiction and non-fiction.

Charlotte Sheedy Literary Agency Inc
611 Broadway, Suite 428
New York, NY 10012
Contact: *Charlotte Sheedy*

Shukat Company Ltd
340 West 55th Street, Suite 1-A
New York, NY 10019
Contact: *Scott Shukat, Larry Weiss*
Handles theatre musicals, plays, books (fiction and non-fiction), television and film.

Evelyn Singer Literary Agency Inc
PO Box 594
White Plains, NY 10602
Contact: *Evelyn Singer*
Exclusive representation. Handles fiction, non-fiction, for adults, young adults, children, first serial rights, foreign rights, film and television rights with sub-agents.

Philip G Spitzer Literary Agency
50 Talmadge Farm Lane
East Hampton, NY 11937
Contact: *Philip G Spitzer*
Handles general fiction and non-fiction; also screenplays.

Renee Spodheim
698 West End Avenue, No 5-B
New York, NY 10025
Contact: *Renee Spodheim*
All trade. Fiction and non-fiction. No juveniles.

Sterling Lord Literistic Inc
One Madison Avenue
New York, NY 10010
Handles full length and short manuscripts, theatre, films, television and radio. Represented in Europe by Intercontinental Literary Agency.

2M Communications Ltd
121 West 27th Street, 601
New York, NY 10001
Handles contemporary non-fiction, popular culture and celebrity biographies.

Wieser and Wieser Inc
118 East 25th Street
New York, NY 10010
Contact: *Olga Wieser*

Handles literary and commercial fiction, general non-fiction including all rights, film and television rights.

Writers House Inc
21 West 26th Street
New York, NY 10010
Represents popular and literary fiction, mainstream and genre, including thrillers, science fiction, fantasy and romance. Also juvenile and young adult.

Pennsylvania

James Allen Literary Agent (in Association with Virginia Kidd Literary Agents)
PO Box 278, 538 East Harford Street
Milford, PA 18337
Contact: *Virginia Kidd*
Handles fiction, specializing in science fiction to magazines and book publishers. Representation in foreign countries and Hollywood.

Ray Peekner Literary Agency Inc
Box 3308
Bethlehem, PA 18017
Handles general fiction, particularly mystery suspense. Quality YA.

Rhode Island

Rock Literary Agency
Box 625
Newport, RI 02840
Contact: *Andrew Rock*

Texas

Blake Group Literary Agency
One Turtle Creek Village, Suite 600
3878 Oaklawn
Dallas, TX 75219
Represents limited number of published and unpublished authors. Handles fiction, non-fiction, plays and poetry, periodicals, publishers and producers. No reading fee; SASE essential.

Gloria Stern Literary Agency
2929 Buffalo Speedway
Lamar Tower 2111
Houston, TX 77098
Contact: *Gloria Stern*
Represent 90% trade, non-fiction, mostly biography, education and women's and social issues. Also health, some self-help and serious fiction.

Utah

Bess Wallace Associates Literary Agency
Box 972
Duchesne, UT 84021
Contact: *Bess D Wallace*
Manuscripts sold, edited and typed; ghost-writing; typesetting for self publishers; writers for writing assignments; copy-editing for publishers. Query first.

Washington

Catalog (TM) Literary Agency
Box 2964
Vancouver, WA 98668

Wisconsin

Lee Allan Agency
PO Box 18617
Milwaukee, WI 53218
Handles book length novels, mysteries, thrillers, westerns, science fiction, horror, romance and young adult fiction. No television material, non-fiction, poetry, magazine articles or short stories.

APPENDIX B

LITERARY ORGANIZATIONS

Please note that while every effort has been made to include as many societies and organizations as possible, the editors acknowledge that the following list is by no means exhaustive. Many societies are organized and administered by unpaid individuals from their own homes. Not only do the addresses of secretaries change frequently, therefore, but these are difficult to trace. Secretaries of societies which have yet to be listed are consequently urged to send details for publication in future editions of the **INTERNATIONAL AUTHORS AND WRITERS WHO'S WHO** to the editors at the following address:

International Authors and Writers Who's Who
International Biographical Centre
Cambridge CB2 3QP, England

The friendly co-operation of the listed societies is gratefully acknowledged, and the future assistance of others is cordially invited.

AUSTRALIA

Australian Writers' Guild Ltd
60 Kellett Street
Kings Cross, Sydney, NSW 2011
Professional association for writers in areas of television, radio, screen and stage to promote and protect the professional interests.

Bibliographical Society of Australia and New Zealand
c/o Secretary, Miss R T Smith
76 Warners Avenue
Bondi Beach, NSW 2026
To encourage and promote research in all aspects of physical bibliography.

Children's Book Council of Australia
PO Box 420
Dickson, ACT 2602

Dickens Fellowship
29 Henley Beach Road
Henley Beach, Adelaide, SA 5022
Literary society devoted to study and appreciation of the life and works of Charles Dickens.

Poetry Society of Australia
PO Box N110, Grosvenor Street
Sydney, NSW 2000
Publications: New Poetry (quarterly); also poems, articles, reviews, notes and comments, interviews.

Society of Editors
PO Box 176
Carlton South, Vic 3053
Professional association of book editors. Regular training seminars, monthly meetings and newsletter.

BELGIUM

International PEN Club, Belgian French Speaking Centre
76 Avenue de 11 Novembre, BP7
B-1040 Brussels
Receptions of foreign writers, defense of the liberty of thought of all writers, participation at the world-wide congresses of PEN.

Koninklijke Academie voor Wetenschappen
Letteren en Schone Kunsten van Belgie
Paleis der Academien
Hertogsstrasse 1
B-1000 Brussels.

Société de Langue et de Litterature Wallonnes
Universite de Liège
B-4000 Liège
Holds meetings, lecturers, exhibitions, library, media, archives, publications.

Société Royale des Bibliophiles et Iconophiles de Belgique
4 Boulevard de l'Empereur
B-1000 Brussels
Publication of "Le Livre et l'Estampe" (Semestrial), Expositions.

BRAZIL

Academia Cearense di Letras
Palacio Senador Alencar
Rua São Paulo 51
60000 Fortaleza CE
To cultivate and develop literature and scientific achievement. Meets monthly, annual publication.

Associacao Brasileira de Imprensa (Brazilian Press Association)
Rua Araujo Porto Alegre
71-Centro-Rio de Janeiro-RJ.

Brazilian Translators Union (SINTRA)
Rua de Quitanda
194-sala 1005-Centro
CEP-20091-Rio de Janeiro-RJ

Companhia Editora Nacional
Rua Joli
294-São Paulo-SP

Sindicato de Escritores of Rio de Janeiro
Av Heitor Beltrao
353-Rio de Janeiro-RJ
CEP 20550

CANADA

Association of Canadian Publishers
2 Gloucester Street, Suite 301

Toronto, Ontario M4X 1L5
Trade association representing the interest of the Canadian-owned and operated publishing industry.

Canada Council
350 Albert Street, PO Box 1047
Ottawa, Ontario K1P 5V8

Canadian Association for Commonwealth Literature and Language Studies (CACLALS)
c/o Vice-President: Academic's Office
Wilfrid Laurier University
75 University Avenue West
Waterloo, Ontario N2L 3C5
President: Dr. Rowland Smith

Canadian Authors Association
275 Slater Street, Suite 500
Ottawa, Ontario K1P 5H9
18 branches across Canada. Annual national conference; work to protect Canadian writers, spokesman to government, sponsors awards programme; publishes periodicals.

Canadian Centre (English-speaking) PEN
24 Ryerson Avenue
Toronto, Ontario M5T 2P3
Fosters understanding among writers of all nations, fights for freedom of expression, to work for the preservation of the world's literature.

Canadian Copyright Institute
35 Spadina Road
Toronto, Ontario M5R 2S9
Established to promote the use of copyright in the public interest.

Federation Professionnelle des Journalistes du Quebec
2083 Beaudry Street, Room 302
Montreal, Quebec H2L 3G4
Representation and defense of journalists professional interest, freedom of the press, public's right to quality information, etc.

Freelance Editors' Association of Canada (FEAC)
35 Spadina Road
Toronto, Ontario M5R 2S9
Professional development seminars held twice yearly; Tom Fairly Award - award for editorial excellence by editor working on a freelance basis.

La Societé des Écrivains Canadiens de la Langue Française
1195 rue Sherbrooke Ouest
Montreal, Quebec H3A 1H9

League of Canadian Poets
24 Ryerson Avenue
Toronto, Ontario M5T 2P3

Literary Press Group
Subs of Association of Canadian Publishers
260 Kings Street East
Toronto, Ontario M5A 1K3
Promote Canadian fiction, poetry, drama and literary criticism. Sales representation across Canada.

Literary Translators Association
3492 rue Laval
Montreal, Quebec H2X 3C8

Advice to members, legal services, link between authors and translators; John Glasso Translation Prize; International Translators Conferences.

Periodical Writers' Association of Canada
24 Ryerson Avenue
Toronto, Ontario M5T 2P3
To promote and protect the interests of Canadian periodical writers.

Playwrights Union of Canada
54 Wolseley Street, 2nd Floor
Toronto, Ontario M5T 1AS

Writers' Union of Canada
24 Ryerson Avenue
Toronto, Ontario M5T 2P3
Professional association of published trade book writers.

CHINA

China PEN Centre
2 Shatan Beijie
Beijing.

DENMARK

Danish Society of Language and Literature
Frederiksholms Kanal 18A
DK-1220 Copenhagen K
Scholarly editing in Danish language, literature and history, dictionaries c. 150 titles, 750 volumes.

Dansk Fagpresse
Vesterbrogade 24, 2. sal
DK-1620 Copenhagen V

Dansk Forfatterforening (Danish Writers' Association)
Tordenskjolds gård
Strandgade 6, St.
DK-1401 Copenhagen K
Attending to social, artistic, professional and economic interests of Danish authors in Denmark and abroad.

Dansk Litteraturinformationscenter
Ameliegade 38
DK-1256 Copenhagen K
Danish Literature Information Centre

Danske Sprog-og Litteraturselskab
Frederiksholms Kanal 18A
DK-1220 Copenhagen
Publications: Standard editions of literary, linguistic and historical texts, including diaries and correspondence.

Nyt Dansk Litteraturselskab
Bibliotekscentralen
Tempovej 7-11
DK-2750 Ballerup
Works for re-publishing of titles missing in public libraries in co-operation with publishers.

FAROE ISLANDS

Rithövundafelag Färoya
Box 1124
FR-110 Tórshavn
Writers' Union of the Faroe Islands

FINLAND

Finlands PEN
PB 84
SF-00131 Helsingfors

Finlands Översättar-og Tolkforbund
Museigatan 9 B 23
FIN-00100 Helsingfors

Finlands Svenska Författareförening
Runebergsgatan 32 C 27
SF-00100 Helsingfors
Society of Swedish Authors in Finland.

Informationscentralen för Finlands Litterarur
PB 259
SF-00 171 Helsingfors
Information centre for Finnish literature and the State Literature Commission.

Kirjallisuudentutkijain Seura
Fabianinkatu 33
SF-00170 Helsinki
Publications: Kirjallisuudentutkijain Seuran Vousikirja (The Yearbook of the Literary Research Society).
Secretary: Paivi Karttunen.

Suomalaisen Kirjallisuuden Seura
PO Box 259
SF-00170 Helsinki
(Located at: Hallituskatu 1, Helsinki)

Suomen Tietokirjallijat ry
Ulvilantie 11 B, E 127
SF-00350 Helsinki

Svenska Litteratursallskapet i Finland
Mariegatan 8
SF-00170 Helsinki
Publications: Skrifter (Writings).

Svenska Osterbottens Litteraturforening
Henriksgatan 7-9 4N
SF-65320 Vasa/
Auroravagen 10
SF-65610 Smedsby
Co-owner of the publishers in Scriptum, publishing the journal Horisont, organizes writers' seminars, program evenings: lyrics, prose, music.

FRANCE

Centre National des Lettres
53 rue de Verneuil
F-75007 Paris
To uphold and encourage the work of French writers, give financial help to writers, translators, publishers and public libraries, promote translation into French.

Société des Gens de Lettres
Hotel de Massa
38 rue du Faubourg Saint-Jacques
F-75014 Paris

Société des Poetes Francais
Hotel de Messa
38 rue de Faubourg Saint-Jacques
F-75014 Paris
Lectures, prizes, defending interests of members,

loans to distinguished members in distress, quarterly bulleting.

GERMANY

Arbeitskreis für Jugenditeratur eV
Elisabethstrasse 15
D-8000 Munich 40
Encourages and coordinates all efforts to support literature for children and young people.

Association Internationale des Journalistes Philatéliques
Am Osterberg 19
D-29386 Hankensbüttel
International Association of Philatelic journalists, authors and associated societies.

Deutsche Akademie für Sprache und Dichtung
Alexandrakeg 23
D-6100 Darmstadt

Literarischer Verein in Stuttgart e V
Postfach 102251
D-7000 Stuttgart 1
(Located at: Rosenbergstr 113, Stuttgart)

PEN Zentrum
Friedrichstrasse 194. 199
Berlin 1080
Lectures, symposia, literary sessions.

HONG KONG

Composers and Authors Society of Hong Kong Ltd.
18/F Universal Trade Centre
3 Arbuthnot Road
Central Hong Kong

HUNGARY

Artisjus
Agency for Literature and Theatre
POB 67, V, Vorosmarty ter 1
H-1364 Budapest

Institute of Literary Studies of the Hungarian Academy of Sciences
Menesi ut 11-13
H-1118 Budapest
Research of history of Hungarian literature, research in literary theory, literary criticism to influence contemporary literature, source publications on the history of Hungarian literature, editing of reference books and bibliographies.

ICELAND

Rithöfundasamband Íslands (The Writers' Union of Iceland)
PO Box 949, IS-121 Reykjavík /
Hafnarstrati 9, IS-101 Reykjavík
Union of Icelandic Writers that guards copyrights, protects interests in field of literature and book-publishing, drama, textbooks, radio and television scripts etc.

INDIA

Indian Folklore Society
3 Abdul Hamid

Calcutta 700 069
To organize seminars, meetings, conference study groups and publish journals and books on Indian folklore and its allied disciplines in collaboration of Indian publications.

PEN All-India Centre
40 New Marine Lines
Bombay 400 020
National centre of International PEN, publishes The Indian PEN quarterly.

Poetry Society of India
L-67A Malaviya Nagar
New Delhi 110 017

Sahitya Akademi
35 Ferozeshah Road
New Delhi 110 001
National organization to work for the development of Indian letters, to set high literary standards, foster and co-ordinate literary activities in the Indian languages and promote through them all the cultural unity of the country.

INDONESIA

PEN Centre
c/o Jl Cemara 6
Jakarta Pusat

IRELAND

Irish Academy of Letters
School of Irish Studies
Thomas Prior House
Merrion Road
Dublin 4

Irish Book Marketing GP
Book House Ireland
165 Mid Abbey Street
Dublin 1
National association of book publishers, trade representation, training courses, national and international book fairs and promotions.

Irish PEN
26 Rosslyn, Killarney Road
Bray, County Wicklow

Poetry Ireland
Bermingham Tower
Upper Yard, Dublin Castle
Dublin
National poetry organization which organizes tours, readings and the National Poetry Competition. Publications: Poetry Ireland Review (quarterly magazine), and bi-monthly newsletter.

Society of Irish Playwrights
Room 804, Liberty Hall
Dublin 1
To foster interest in and promote contemporary Irish drama. To guard the rights of Irish playwrights.

ISRAEL

ACUM Ltd (Society of Authors, Composers and Music Publishers in Israel)
PO Box 14220
Tel Aviv 61140

PEN Centre Israel
19 Shmaryahu Lewin Street
Jerusalem 96664
Publishes a bulletin of information and translation of literature in European languages, meetings with members and receptions for guest writers.

ITALY

Istituto Lombardo Accademia di Scienze e Lettere
Via Brera 28
I-20121 Milan
Organization of conferences, meetings etc. Publications of literature and sciences, exchanged with similar associations all over the world.

Societa' Italiana Autori Drammatici (SIAD)
Via PO 10
I-00198 Rome

Societa' Italiana degli Autori et Editori (SIAE)
Viale della Letteratura 30
I-00144 Rome

JAPAN

Dickens Fellowship
Bungei-Gakubu
Seijo University
6-1-20 Seijo, Setagaya, Tokyo
Lectures, symposia, reading circles, publishing bulletins.

English Literary Society of Japan
501 Kenkyusha Bldg
9 Surugadai 2-Chome
Kanda, Chiyoda-ku, Tokyo 101
An association of scholars in the fields of English and American literature and the English language. The society's journal "Studies in English Literature" is published thrice yearly.

Japan Poets Association
c/o Eiji Kikai, 3-16-1Minami
Azabu, Minato-ku, Tokyo 105
To cultivate the mutual friendship among poets. To award H's Prize and Modern Poet Prize. Approx 500 members.

KOREA

Korean PEN Centre
186-210 Jangchung-dong 2-ka
Jung-gu, Seoul 100
Bi-annual seminars. Annual literary prize awards, publication of quarterly bulletin. Takes part in annual International PEN Congress.

MALAWI

Writers's Group
PO Box 280
Zomba
Publications: Odi The Muse.

MOROCCO

L'Union des Ecrivains du Maroc
5 rue Ab Bakr Seddik
Rabat

NEPAL

Nepal Journalists Association
PO Box 285, Maitighar
Kathmandu

NETHERLANDS

Dickens Fellowship, Haarlem Branch
26-28 Markstr
1411 EA Naarden
Branch of the Dickens Fellowship, London.
Organizes lectures, editing "The Dutch Dickensian".

Nederlandse Taalunie
Stadhoudersplantsoen 2
2517 JL The Hague

Netherlands Centre of the International PEN
Meeweg 25
1405 BC Bussum
Dutch branch of a world association of writers,
poets, essayists, novelists, editors and playwrights.

NEW ZEALAND

Arts Council of New Zealand
Old Public Trust Building
131-135 Lambton Quay, PO Box 3806
Wellington

Christchurch Dickens Fellowship
PO Box 6126
Christchurch
Study works of Dickens at regular monthly
meetings.

International Writers' Workshop NZ (Inc)
57 Baddeley Avenue
Kohimarama, Auckland
Tutored workshops, group evaluation of work.
Workshops designed to interest and encourage
writers.

New Zealand Women Writers' Society Inc
PO Box 11-352
Wellington
Stimulates and encourages creative work in
literature, fosters comradeship among members.

PEN (New Zealand Centre) Inc
PO Box 2283
Wellington
Promotion of cooperation and mutual support
among writers in all countries and encourage
creative writing in New Zealand.

NIGERIA

**West African Association for Commonwealth
Literature and Language Studies(WAACLALS)**
PO Box 622
Owerri, Imo State.
Chairman: Professor Ernest N. Emenyonu

NORWAY

**Den Norske Forfatterforening (Norwegian
Authors' Union)**
PO Box 327 Sentrum / Rådhusgate 7
N-0103 Oslo

Det Norske Videnskaps-Akademi
Drammensveien 78
Oslo 2
Publications: Skrifter Avhandlinger Arbok

NORLA - Norwegian Literature Abroad
Bygdøy Allé 21
N-0262 Oslo
Publication: Norwegian Literature
Information office for Norwegian literature.

POLAND

Instytut Badan Literackich
Nowy Swiat 72, Palac Staszica
00-330 Warsaw
Publications: Pamietnik Literacki (Literary Journal,
quarterly), Biuletyn Polonistyczny (Bulletin of Polish
Literary Scholarship).

SAP (Polish Authors'Association)
ul. Madalińskiego 15 m 16
02-513 Warsaw

**Zwiazek Literatow Polskich (Union of Polish
Writers)**
Krakoweskie Przedmiescie 87
00-950 Warsaw

RUSSIA

Russian Authors' Society
ul. Bol'Shaya Bronnaya 6A
103670 Moscow
Protects the rights and organizes legal protection
for authors in the Russian federation.
Chairman: Georgy A. Ter-Gazariants

SOUTH AFRICA

English Academy of Southern Africa
PO Box 124
Witwatersrand 2050

Institute for the Study of English in Africa
Rhodes University, PO Box 94
Grahamston 6140
Publishes English in Africa and New Coin Poetry.
Conducts research into needs of black pupils
learning English.

**Nasionale Afrikaanse Letterkundige Museum en
Navorsingsentrum**
Private Bag X20543
Bloemfontein 9300

National English Literary Museum
Private Bag 1019
Grahamstown 6140

South African Union of Journalists
Office 512-513, 5th Floor, Argon House
87 Juta Street, Johannesburg 2017

SWEDEN

**Kungl Vitterhets Historie och Antikvitets
Akademien**
Villagatan 3
S-114 32 Stockholm
Publications: Fornvannen (journal), Handlingar
(memoirs), Arkiv (archives), Arsbok (Yearbook),
Monografier (monographs).

Sveriges Författarförbund
Box 3157 / Drottninggatan 88B
S-103 63 Stockholm
Swedish Writers' Union

SWITZERLAND

Deutschschweizerisches PEN-Zentrum
Postfach 403
CH-3000 Bern 14
Swiss-German PEN centre; member of International PEN.

PEN Club Centre
Postfach 1383
CH-3001 Bern

PEN Internazionale-Centro della Svizzera Italiana e Romancia
PO Box 2126
CH-6901 Lugano 1

Schweizer Autoren Gruppe Olten
Sekretariat, Siedlung Halen 43
CH-3047 Herrenschwanden
Authors' society.

Schweizerischer Bund für Jugendliteratur
Gewerbestrasse 8
CH-6330 Cham
Promotion and diffusion of literature for children and young adults, distribution of specially developed material; further education.

Schweizerischen Schriftstellerinnen und Schriftsteller-Verband (Société Suisse des Ecrivaines et Ecrivains)
Kirchgasse 25
CH-8022 Zürich
Professional organization, founded in 1912, for the protection of writers' interests. Publications: FORUM der Schriftsteller, Dictionary of Swiss Authors.

TANZANIA

Journalists' Organization of Tanzania
PO Box 45526
Dar Es Salaam
Ludovick A. Ngatara, General Secretary

THAILAND

Siam Society
PO Box 65
Bangkok
Society promotes and tries to preserve artistic, scientific and other cultural affairs of Thailand and neighbouring countries. Publishes Journal of the Siam Society and The Siam Society Newsletter.

UNITED KINGDOM

Arvon Foundation
Totleigh Barton
Sheepwash, Beaworthy
Devon EX21 5NS
(Also at: Lumb Bank, Heptonstall
Hebden Bridge, W Yorks HX7 6DF)
Offers residential writing courses.

Association of Authors' Agents
c/o Greene and Heaton Ltd
37 Goldhawk Road
London W12 8QQ
Maintains a code of practice, provides a forum for discussion and promotes cooperation and interests of British literary agencies and agents.

Association of British Science Writers (ABSW)
c/o British Association for the Advancement of Science
Fortress House, 23 Savile Row
London W1X 1AB

Association of Golf Writers
c/o Sports Desk, The Daily Express
Blackfriars Road
London SE1 9UX

Association for Scottish Literary Studies
Department of English Literature
University of Aberdeen
Taylor Building, King's College
Aberdeen AB9 2UB
Publications: Scottish Library Journal; Scottish Literary Journal Supplement (both twice yearly).

Authors' Club
40 Dover Street
London W1X 3RB
Club for writers, publishers, critics, journalists and academics involved with literature. Administers several literary awards.

Francis Bacon Society Inc
Canonbury Tower
Islington, London N1
Publications: Baconiana (periodically), Jottings (periodically), booklets, pamphlets (list on request).

Book Trust
Book House, 45 East Hill
London SW18 2QZ
An independent charitable trust whose task is to promote reading and the using of books. Administers several major literary awards including the Booker Prize, and publishes reference and resource materials.

Book Trust Scotland
Scottish Book Centre
137 Dundee Street
Edinburgh EH11 1BG
Promotes reading and books in general, and provides a range of information and services on Scottish writers and books. Administers awards including the McVitie's Prize for Scottish Writer of the Year.

British Science Fiction Association
52 Woodhill Drive
Grove, Wantage
Oxon OX12 0DF
Promotes the reading, writing and publishing of science fiction. Activities include literary criticism, news, reviews, serious articles, meetings, writers workshop, lending library and magazine chain.
Publications: Matrix (newsletter); Vector (journal); Focus (magazine).

Commonwealth Press Union
Studio House, Hen and Chickens Court

184 Fleet Street
London EC4A 2DU

Crime Writers' Association (CWA)
PO Box 10772
London N6 4RY
Membership limited to professional crime writers, bu Associate membership is open to specialist publishers,agents and booksellers. Administers numerous annual awards.
Publication: Red Herrings (monthly newsletter)

Dickens Fellowship
Dickens House, 48 Doughty Street
London WC1N 2LF
HQ in London, over 60 branches worldwide, of Dickens enthusiasts. Organises talks, conferences, publishes "The Dickensian", concerned with preservation of buildings associated with Dickens.

Edinburgh Bibliographical Society
Department of Special Collections
Edinburgh University Library
George Square
Edinburgh EH8 9LJ
Lectures on bibliographical topics and visits to libraries.
Publication: Transaction (issued to members only).

English Association
University of Leicester
University Road
Leicester LE1 7RH
Promotes the understanding and appreciation of English language and literature. Organizes lectures and conferences, and produces a selection of publications.

Gaelic Books Council (Comhairle nan Leabhraichean)
22 Mansfield Street
Partick, Glasgow G12
Provides information about Gaelic writing and publishing. Also offers editorial services and grants to publishers and writers.

Thomas Hardy Society
PO Box 1438
Dorchester, Dorset DT1 1YH
Promotion and appreciation of works of Thomas Hardy; organizes a summer conference, lectures and walks in Wessex.

Incorporated Brontë Society
Bronte Parsonage
Haworth, Keighley
West Yorkshire BD22 8DR
The preservation of the literary works of the Bronte family and of manuscripts and other objects related to the family.

Institute of Contemporary Arts
The Mall
London SW1
Galleries, performance, music, cinema, talks, conferences, restaurant, bar, 'Bookshop'.

Johnson Society of London
255 Baring Road, Grove Park
London SE12 0BQ
To study the works of Dr Samuel Johnson, his circle, his contempories and his times through lectures and articles in 'The New Rambler'.

Keats/Shelley Memorial Association
10 Landsdowne Road
Tunbridge Wells, Kent TN1 2NJ
To promote the works of Keats, Shelley, Byron and Leigh Hunt and maintain the house in Rome where Keats died.

Kent and Sussex Poetry Society
Castens, Carpenters Lane
Hadlow, Kent TN11 0EY
Readings, workshops, discussions to promote love and understandings of poetry.

Kipling Society
2nd Floor, Schomberg House
80-82 Pall Mall
London SW1Y 5HG
Promotion of Kipling studies, discussion meetings, annual luncheon, quarterly journal.

Charles Lamb Society
1A Royston Road, Richmond
Surrey TW10 6LT
To study the life, works and times of Charles Lamb and his circle, to stimulate the Elian spirit of friendliness and humour, and form a collection of Eliana.

Lancashire Authors' Association
Heatherslade, 5 Quakerfields
Westhoughton, Bolton, Lancashire BL5 2BJ
Publications: The Record (quarterly)

Library Association
7 Ridgmount Street
London WC1E 7AE
Professional body for librarians and information managers. Numerous publications produced every year. Members receive the monthly magazine "LA Record".

Moniack Mhor (Avron Foundation of Scotland)
Teavarran, Kiltarlity,
Beauly, Inverness-shire IV4 7HT
Provides the opportunity to live and work with established writers, and participate in tutorials and workshops.

National Poetry Foundation
27 Mill Road
Fareham, Hampshire PO16 0TH
Charitable organization which encourages new writers and produces a series of books. Members receive "Pause" magazine.

National Union of Journalists
Acorn House
314 Grays Inn Road
London WC1X 8DP
Represents journalists in all sectors of publishing, providing advice and support on wages, conditions, and benefits. Publishes various guides and magazines.

Northern Poetry Library
Central Library, The Willows
Morpeth, Northumberland NE61 1TA
Books and magazines for loan, and access to text database of English poetry; Postal loans also available.

Oxford Bibliographical Society
Bodleian Library
Oxford OX1 3BG
Publications: First Series, vols I-VII, 1923-46; New Series, vol 1, 1948-.

PEN English Centre
7 Dilke Street
Chelsea, London SW3 4JE
Publications: The Pen (broadsheet, twice a year)

PEN Scottish Centre
33 Drumsheugh Gardens
Edinburgh EH3 7RN

Poetry Association of Scotland
38 Dovecot Road, Edinburgh EH12 7LE
Promotes public reading of the world's best poetry.

Poetry Library
Royal Festival Hall
South Bank Centre, Level 5
London SE1 8XX
Includes all 20th-Century poetry in English and a collection of all poetry magazines published in the UK. Also arranges functions and provides an information service.

Poetry Society
22 Betterton Street
London WC2H 9BU
Promotion of poets and poetry, including promotion of events and festivals. Also operates a series of seminars and training courses, education services and a library service, and administers the National Poetry Competition.
Publications: Poetry Review (quarterly magazine) and Poetry News (newsletter).

Publishers Association
19 Bedford Square
London WC1B 3HJ
National UK trade association representing the publishing industry. Publishes the Directory of Publishing.

Romantic Novelists' Association
Queens Farm, 17 Queens Street
Tintinhull, Somerset BA22 8PG
Membership open to published writers of romantic novels, with Associate membership open to agents, editors, publishers and booksellers. Administers two annual awards and publishes the RNA News.

Royal Society of Literature
1 Hyde Park Gardens
London W2 2LT
Lectures, discussions, readings and publications. Adminsters awards including the W H heinemann Prize.

Scottish Arts Council
12 Manor Place
Edinburgh EH3 7DD
One of the principal channels for government funding for the arts, including the administration of literary awards, bursaries, events and fellowships.

Scottish Poetry Library
Tweedale Court, 14 High Street
Edinburgh EH1 1TE
Poetry books, tapes and magazines can be borrowed in person or by post. Also provides specialist lists and bibliographies.

Scottish Publishers Association
Scottish Book Centre
137 Dundee Street
Edinburgh EH11 1BG
Provides co-operative support for Scottish publishers, and information about publishing in Scotland.

Sherlock Holmes Society of London
3 Outram Road, Southsea
Hampshire PO5 1QP
Study of the life and works of Sherlock Holmes and Dr Watson.

Society of Authors
84 Drayton Gardens
London SW10 9SB
Independent trade union which seeks to promote and protect the interests of writers and authors, and provides information and advice.
Publications: The Author (quarterly journal); The Electronic Author (twice yearly).

Society of Civil Service Authors
4 Top Street
Wing, nr. Oakham,
Rutland LE15 8SE
Encourages authorship by past and present members of the Civil Service.

Society of Freelance Editors and Proofreaders
38 Rochester Road
London NW1 9JJ
Aims to promote high editorial standards through advice, training and the introduction of recognised qualifications.

Society of Young Publishers
12 Dyott Street
London WC1A 1DF
Open to those in related occupations, members can increasetheir knowledge and experience of all aspects of publishing.

Tolkien Society
35 Amesbury Crescent, Hove
East Sussex BN3 5RD
Furthering interest in the life and works of Professor J R R Tolkien. Newsletter.

Translators Association
84 Drayton Gardens
London SW10 9SB
Subsidiary group within the Society of Authors dealing exclusively with Literary translators into the English language.

Ver Poets
Haycroft, 61/63 Chiswell Green Lane
St Albans, Herts AL2 3AL
Aim to promote poetry and help poets through information, events and publications. Holds regular competitions including the annual Ver Poets Open Competition.

H G Wells Society
English Department, Nene College
Moulton Park, Northampton NN2 7AL
Circulates newsletter and journal, Wellsian, and

organizes lectures and conferences to promote an active interest in the life and work of H G Wells.

Welsh Academy
3rd Floor, Mount Stuart House
Mount Stuart Square, Cardiff CF1 6DQ
The English language section of Yr Academi Gymreig, the national society of Welsh writers. Aims to promote Anglo-Welsh literature through readings, conferences, workshops, schools, projects. Organizes the Cardiff Literature Festival. Publishes a newsletter and numerous guides and reviews.

Welsh Book Council (Cyngor Llyfrau Cymru)
Castell Brychan
Aberystwyth, Dyfed SY23 2JB
Stimulates interest in Welsh literature and authors by disseminating grants for Welsh language publications.
Publication: Books In Wales/Llais Llyfrau (quarterly)

Welsh Union of Writers
13 Richmond Road
Roath, Cardiff CF2 3AQ
Independent union for published Welsh writers

West Country Writers' Association
Malvern View, Garway Hill,
Hereford, Hereford and Worcester HR2 8EZ

Women in Publishing
c/o The Bookseller
12 Dyott Street
London WC1A 1DF
Aims to promote the status of women in the publishing industry through networking, meetings and training. Publishes a monthly newsletter.

Women Writers Network (WWN)
23 Prospect Road
London NW2 2JU
Provides and exchanges information, support and opportunities for working writers. Also arranges functions and provides a newsletter.

The Writers' Club
PO Box 269
Redhill RH1 6GP
Newly formed club for writers, authors and journalists.

Writer's Guild of Great Britain
430 Edgware Road
London W2 1EH
Represents professional writers in film, radio, televsion, theatre and publishing. Regularly provides assistance to members on items such as contracts and conditions of work.

Yachting Journalists Association
Spinneys, Woodham Mortimer
Maldon, Essex CM9 6SX.
Promotes the awareness of all forms of leisure boating activities via the written and spoken word, ansd offers support to journalists in the field.

Yr Academi Gymreig
3rd Floor, Mount Stuart House
Mount Stuart Square, Cardiff CF1 6DQ
National society of Welsh writers which encourages writing in the Welsh language.Organizes readings, conferences and literary events. Publishes books on Welsh litereaure and an English/Welsh dictionary.
Publication: Taliesin.

UNITED STATES OF AMERICA
Arizona

Authors Resource Centre (TARC Inc)
PO Box 64785
Tucson, AZ 85728
Serves writers etc; writers' research library; literary agency; sponsors 40 workshops and seminars, publishes TARC Report for writers.

Society of Southwestern Authors
Box 30355
Tucson, AZ 85751
Organization of writers for supportive fellowship, recognition of member writers' professional achievement, and encouragement and assistance for persons striving to become writers.
Approx 125 members.

California

Society of Children's Book Writers
22736 Vanowen Street, Suite 106
West Hills, CA 91307
Offers bi-monthly 'Bulletin' MSS exchange, meetings, conferences, Golden Kite awards, insurance, grants and advice.

Writers Guild of America, West, Inc
8955 Beverly Boulevard
West Hollywood, CA 90048
Represents its membership in contract negotiation and compliance with the film and television industry.

Colorado

Associated Business Writers of America
1450 South Havana, Suite 620
Aurora, CO 80012
Association for business writers.

National Writers Association
1450 South Havana, Suite 424
Aurora, CO 80012
Association for freelance writers.

Connecticut

International PEN - Writers in Exile Center
42 Derby Avenue
Orange, CT 06477
Affiliated with International PEN to help fight for freedom of expression for writers in exile now living in the West.
Approx 135 members.
President: Clare Gyorgyey

Delaware

International Reading Association
800 Barksdale Road, PO Box 8139
Newark, DE 19714
Professional education association dedicated to the improvement of reading ability and development of the reading habit worldwide through publications, research, meetings, conferences and international congresses.

District of Columbia

Education Writers Association
1001 Connecticut Avenue North West, Suite 310
Washington, DC 20036

National Endowment for the Humanities
Public Information Office
1100 Pennsylvania Avenue North West, Room 406
Washington, DC 20506

National League of American PEN Women
Pen Arts Building
1300 17th Street North West
Washington, DC 20036

National Press Club
529 14th Street North West
Washington, DC 20045

PEN Syndicated Fiction Project
PO Box 15650
Washington, DC 20003

Washington Independent Writers
733 15th Street North West, Suite 220
Washington, DC 20005

Florida

International Society of Dramatists
Box 1310
Miami, FL 33153
Information clearinghouse for dramatists in all media: stage, screen, television and radio. Provides continually updated lists of script opportunities in English worldwide. Monthly publications. Annual playwriting award.

Illinois

American Library Association
50 East Huron
Chicago, IL 60611
Provides leadership for the development, promotion, and improvement of library and information services to enhance learning.

Illinois Writers Inc
c/o English Department
Illinois State University
Normal, IL 61761
To promote the literary arts of Illinois poets, fiction writers, and small press publishers. Publish bi-annual review and bi-monthly newsletter.

Independents Writers of Chicago
7855 Gross Point Road, Suite G-4
Skokie, IL 60077
Monthly meetings and four workshops per year dealing with the business aspects of independent writing. Writers' line job referral; insurance.

International Black Writers and Artists Inc
Box 1030
Chicago, IL 60690
Poetry readings, contests, pot lucks, workshops, annual conferences and writers picnic.

Society of Midland Authors
29 East Division Street
Chicago, IL 60610
To promote friendly contact and professional interchange among authors of the Midland, to explore topics of literary and professional interest in open monthly programmes, and honour the best of Midland writing with cash awards annually.

Indiana

Society of Professional Journalists
PO Box 77
Greencastle, IN 46135
Contact: Sandy Gretter

Maryland

The Lewis Carroll Society of North America
617 Rockford Road
Silver Spring, MD 20902
To promote interests in and be a centre for Lewis Carroll studies.

Truck Writers of North America
c/o TS and L
600 Reisterstown Road, Suite 404,
Baltimore, MD 21208

Massachusetts

American Society of Business Press Editors
PO Box 390653
Cambridge, MA 0213

Minnesota

Catholic Library Association
St Mary's College, Campus 26
700 Terrace Heights
Winoma, MN 55987
An organization of professional librarians interested in providing service according to the Catholic philosophy.

New Hampshire

MacDowell Colony Inc
100 High Street
Peterborough, NH 03458
Retreat for writers, composers, visual artists and filmmakers with professional standing in field. Colony Fellows approx: 2000.

New York

Academy of American Poets
584 Broadway, Suite 1208
New York, NY 10012
Sponsors the James Laughlin Award, the Walt Whitman Award, the Harold Morton Landon Translation Award, the Tanning Prize, the Raiziss/de Palchi Translation Award and annual college poetry prizes; workshops, classes and literary historical walking tours; award fellowships to American poets for distinguished poetic achievement.

American Podiatric Medical Writers Association
PO Box 750129
Forest Hills, NY 112375

American Society of Journalists and Authors Inc
1501 Broadway, Suite 302
New York, NY 10036
Service organization providing exchange of ideas and market information. Regular meetings with speakers from the industry, annual writers conference; medical plans available. professional

referral service, annual membership directory; first amendment advocacy group.

Author Aid Associates
340 East 52nd Street
New York, NY 10022

Brooklyn Writers' Network (BWN)
2509 Avenue K
Brooklyn, NY 11210
Seeks to improve contact between professional writers and publishing industry; newsletter; directory; conferences; workshops.

Comedy Writers' Association
PO Box 23304
Brooklyn, NY 11202-0066

International Association of Crime Writers Inc
JAF Box 1500
New York, NY 10116

International Women's Writing Guild (IWWG)
Box 810, Gracie Station
New York, NY 10028
A network for the empowerment of women through writing. Services include manuscript referral and exchange, writing conferences and retreats, group rates for health and life insurance, legal aid, regional clusters and job referrals.

Mystery Writers of America Inc
17 East 47th Street, 6th Floor
New York, NY 10017
To support and promote the mystery. Chapters around country hold monthly meetings with speakers. Sponsors the Edgar Allan Poe Awards.

PEN American Center
568 Broadway
New York, NY 10012
An international organization of writers, poets, playwrights, essayists, editors, novelists and translators whose purpose is to bring about better understanding among writers of all nations.

Poetry Society of America
15 Gramercy Park
New York, NY 10003
A service organization dedicated to the promotion of poets and poetry. Sponsors readings, lectures, contests; houses the Van Voorhis Library.

Poets and Writers Inc
72 Spring Street
New York, NY 10012
National nonprofit information center for those interested in contemporary American literature. Publish a directory of American poets and fiction writers; sponsor readings and workshops programme.

Science Fiction and Fantasy Writers of America Inc
5 Winding Brook Drive, Suite 1B
Guilderland, NY 12084
Professional association of science fiction and fantasy writers, editors, agents, anthologists; presenters of the SFFWA Nebula Awards.

Teachers and Writers Collaborative
5 Union Square West
New York, NY 10003
Teachers and writers sends professional artists into public schools to teach their art forms. Also publish books and a magazine about how to teach creative writing.

Translation Center
412 Dodge Hall, Columbia University
New York, NY 10027
Publish a magazine bi-annually. Dedicated to finding and publishing the best translations of significant works of foreign contemporary literature.

Writers Guild of America (WGA) East Inc
555 West 57th Street
New York, NY 10019
Labor union representing professional writers in motion pictures, television and radio. Membership available only through the sale of literary material or employment for writing services in one of these areas.

North Carolina

North Carolina Writers' Network
PO Box 954, Carrboro
NC 27510
Administrative Assistant: Jan Freya

Ohio

Ohioana Library Association
65 South Front Street
Columbus, OH 43215

Pennsylvania

National Book Critics Circle
400 North Broad Street
Philadelphia, PA 19103
Gives annual awards for fiction, poetry, biography/autobiography, general non fiction, criticism. Purpose: to raise the standards of book criticism and enhance public appreciation of literature.

Outdoor Writers' Association of America
2017 Cato Avenue, Suite 101
State College, PA 16801
Professional authors, journalists, broadcasters, photographers and artists who cover hunting, fishing, camping, canoeing and similar outdoor sports; workshops held at annual conference.

Texas

American Literary Translators Association (ALTA)
Box 830688, University of Texas
Richardson, TX 75083
Sponsor the Gregory Rabassa Prize for the translation of fiction from any language into English and the Richard Wilbur Prize for the translation of poetry from any language into English. Awards, which consist of the publication of the winning poems, are awarded biennially.

Science Fiction Research Association Inc
6021 Grassmere
Corpus Christi, TX 78415
Professional study of science fiction and fantasy; annual scholar award. Archives maintained at University of Kansas, Lawrence. Sponsor workshop awards and prizes.

Western Writers of America
2800 North Campbell
El Paso, TX 79902
An organization of professionals dedicated to the
spirit and reality of the West, past and present.

Virginia

American Society of Newspaper Editors
PO Box 4090
Reston, VA 22090

Associated Writing Programs (AWP)
Old Dominion University
Norfolk, VA 23529
National, non-profit organization of writers and
writers who teach.

APPENDIX C

LITERARY AWARDS AND PRIZES

The following list of Literary Awards and Prizes does not claim to be exhaustive although every effort has been made to make it as comprehensive as possible.

AT & T Non-Fiction Award
206 Marylebone Road
London NW1 6LY, England
The winner is chosen from entries submitted by publishers. Awarded to the best work of general non-fiction published by a British publisher for the first time in the 12 months between 1 April and 31 March. Entries must be written in English by living writers from the British Commonwealth or the Republic of Ireland.
Annual prize of £25,000 (first prize) - each shortlisted author receives an AT & T computer worth £1500
Administration: Booksellers Association
1988   Nairn in Darkness and Light by David Thomson
1989   Touching the Void by Joe Simpson
1990   Citizens: A Chronicle of the French Revolution by Simon Schama
1991   Invisible Woman by Claire Tomalin
1992   Wild Swans by Jung Chang
1993   Never Again: Britain 1945-51 by Peter Hennessy
1994   Edward Heath: A Biography by John Campbell
1995   Coming Back Brockens by Mark Hudson

Academy of American Poets Fellowship
584 Broadway, Suite 1208
New York, NY 10012, USA
Fellows are elected each year by majority vote of the Academy's Board of Chancellors. No applications are accepted. Each Fellow is awarded a stipend of US $20,000.
1937   Edwin Markham
1946   Ridgely Torrence
1948   Percy MacKaye
1950   e e cummings
1952   Padraic Colum
1953   Robert Frost
1954   Louise Townsend Nicholl
        Oliver St John Gogarty
1955   Rolfe Humphries
1956   William Carlos Williams
1957   Conrad Aiken
1958   Robinson Jeffers
1959   Louise Bogan
        Léonie Adams
1960   Jesse Stuart
1961   Horace Gregory
1962   John Crowe Ransom
1963   Ezra Pound
        Allen Tate
1964   Elizabeth Bishop
1965   Marianne Moore
1966   Archibald MacLeish

        John Berryman
1967   Mark Van Doren
1968   Stanley Kunitz
1969   Richard Eberhart
        Anthony Hecht
1970   Howard Nemerov
1971   James Wright
1972   W D Snodgrass
1973   W S Merwin
1974   Léonie Adams
1975   Robert Hayden
1976   J V Cunningham
1977   Louise Coxe
1978   Josephine Miles
1979   Mark Strand
        May Swenson
1980   Mona Van Duyn
1981   Richard Hugo
1982   John Ashbery
        John Frederick Nims
1983   Philip Booth
        James Schuyler
1984   Robert Francis
        Richmond Lattimore
1985   Amy Clampitt
        Maxine Kumin
1986   Irving Feldman
        Howard Moss
1987   Alfred Corn
        Josephine Jacobsen
1988   Donald Justice
1989   Richard Howard
1990   William Meredith
1991   J D McClatchy
1992   Adrienne Rich
1993   Gerald Stern
1994   David Ferry
1995   Denise Levertov
1996   Jay Wright

J R Ackerley Prize for Autobiography
English P.E.N,
7 Dilke Street
London SW3 4JE, England
Prize is awarded for Literary Autobiography, written in English and published in the year preceeding the award. Shortlisted titles are chosen by the Literary Executors of J R Ackerley; nominations are not accepted.
Annual prize of £1000
Contact: Pamela Petrie, Awards Secretary
1982   Shaky Relations by Edward Blishen
1983   Her People by Kathleen Dayus
        The High Path by Ted Walker
1984   Still Life by Richard Cobb
1985   Deceived with Kindness by Angelica

1987	After The Funeral by Diana Athill
1988	Little Wilson & Big God by Anthony Burgess
1989	The Grass Arena by John Healy
1990	Daddy, We Hardly Knew You by Germaine Greer
1991	St Martin's Ride by Paul Binding
1992	Almost a Gentleman: An Autobiography by John Osborne
1993	More Please by Barry Humphries
1994	And When Did You Last See Your Father? by Blake Morrison
1995	Something in Linoleum by Paul Vaughan
1996	The Railway Man by Eric Lomax
1997	The Scent of Dried Roses by Tim Lott

Jane Addams Children's Book Award
Jane Addams Peace Association
777 United Nations Plaza, 6th Floor
New York, NY 10017, USA
Prize awarded for a book that best combines literary merit with themes stressing peace, social justice, world community and the equality of the sexes and all races.
Award: Certificate presented annually.

1980	The Road From Home by David Kherdian
1981	First Woman in Congress: Jeannette Rankin by Florence White
1982	A Spirit to Ride the Whirlwind by Athena V Lord
1983	Hiroshima No Pika by Toshi Maruki
1984	Rain of Fire by Marion Dane Bauer
1985	The Short Life of Sophie Scholl by Hermann Vinke
1986	Ain't Gonna Study War No More: The Story of America's Peace Seekers by Milton Meltzer.
1987	Nobody Wants a Nuclear War, written and illustrated by Judith Vigna
1988	Waiting for the Rain: A Novel of South Africa by Sheila Gordon
1989	Anthony Burns: The Defeat and Triumph of a Fugitive Slave by Virginia Hamilton
1990	Long Hard Journey: The Story of the Pullman Porter by Patricia McKissak and Frederick McKissak
1991	The Book of Peace edited by Ann Durell & Marilyn Sachs
1992	Journey of the Sparrows by Fran Leeper Buss
1993	A Taste of Salt: A Story of Modern Haiti by Frances Temple
1994	Freedom's Children: Young Civil Rights Activists Tell Their Own Stories by Ellen Levine
1995	Kids at Work : Lewis Hine and the Crusade Against Child Labor by Russell Freedman
1996	The Well: David's Story by Mildred Taylor

Age Concern Book of the Year Award
c/o The Literary Editor, The Age
250 Spencer Street
Melbourne, Vic 3000 Australia
Prize is awarded to a published book of literary merit, written by living Australians.
Award of $3000 to the author of a non-fiction book and $3000 to a work of imaginative writing.
Contact: Literary Editor

Alexander Prize
Royal Historical Society
University College London
Gower Street
London WC1E 6BT, England
Offered for a paper based on original historical research of no more than 8000 words on any subject, providing an opportunity for wider recognition and gauranteed publication of their work. Candidates must be under 35 or have been registred for a higher degree in the last three years.
Prize: £250
Contact: Joy McCarthy

Alice Literary Award
c/o Federal President
Society of Women Writers (Australia)
GPO Box 2621,
Sydney, NSW 2001, Australia
Presented by the Society of Women Writers (Australia) biennially for a distinguished and long term contribution to literature by an Australian woman.

American Academy of Arts and Letters Gold Medal (Letters)
633 West 155 Street
New York, NY 10032-5699, USA

1990	C Vann Woodward
1991	Richard Wilbur
1993	Elizabeth Hardwick
1994	Walter Jackson Bate
1995	William Maxwell

Hans Christian Andersen Awards
International Board on Books for Young People
Nonnenweg 12, Postfach
CH-4003 Basel, Switzerland
The winners are selected by an international jury and announced during the IBBY Congress.
Awarded biennially to the author (Hans Christian Anderson Award for Writing established in 1956), and illustrator (Hans Christian Andersen Award for Illustration established in 1966) whose work has made a lasting contribution to children's literature.

1956	Eleanor Farjeon
1958	Astrid Lindgren
1960	Erich Kästner
1962	Meindert DeJong
1964	René Guillot
1966	Tove Jansson
	Alois Carigiet
1968	James Krüss
	José Maria Sanchez-Silva
	Jiří Trnka
1970	Gianni Rodari
	Maurice Sendak
1972	Scott O'Dell

	Ib Spang Olsen
1974	Maria Gripe
	Farshid Mesghali
1976	Cecil Bødker
	Tatjana Mawrina
1978	Paula Fox
	Svend Otto
1980	Bohumil Říha
	Suekichi Akaba
1982	Lygya Bojunga Nunes
	Zbigniew Rychlicki
1984	Christine Nöstlinger
	Mitsumasa Anno
1986	Patricia Wrightson
	Robert Ingpen
1988	Annie M G Schmidt
	Dušan Kállay
1990	Tormod Haugen
	Lisbeth Zwerger
1992	Virginia Hamilton
	Květa Pacovská
1994	Michio Mado
	Jörg Müller
1996	Uri Orlev
	Klaus Ensikat

Arts Council of Wales Book of the Year Awards/Gwobr Llyfr y Flwyddyn

9 Museum Place
Cardiff CF1 3NX, Wales
Awards are given for works of exceptional merit by Welsh authors (by birth or residence) published during the calendar year. Works may be Welsh or English, in the categories of poetry, fiction and creative non-fiction (including Literary criticism, biography and autobiography). Non-fiction works must have subject matter that is concerned with Wales.
Prize: Two first prizes of £3000 (one in Welsh, one in English), and £1000 to each of four short-listed authors.
Contact: Tony Bianchi
English Books

1992	Bonds of Attachment by Emyr Humphreys
1993	Watching the Fire Eater by Robert Minhinnick
1994	Caitlin: The Life of Caitlin Thomas by Paul Ferris
1995	Masks by Duncan Bush
1996	Gwalia in Khasia by Nigel Jenkins

Welsh Books

1992	Cilmeri by Gerallt Lloyd Owen
1993	Seren Wen ar Gefndir Gwyn by Robin Llywelyn
1994	W/J Gruffydd by Robin Chapman
1995	Unigolion by Aled Islwyn
1996	Gloynnod by Sonia Edwards

Arvon International Poetry Competition

Kilnhurst, Kilnhurst Road
Todmorden, Lancashire OL14 6AX, England
Biennial poetry competition open to anyone, for poems of any length written in the English language, and not previously published or broadcast.
First prize of £5000 with at least 15 other prizes.

Contact: David Pease, National Director

1980	The Letter by Andrew Motion
1982	Ephraim Destiny's Perfectly Utter Darkness by John Hartley Williams
1985	Rorschach Writing by Oliver Reynolds
1987	The Notebook by Selima Hill
1989	Halfway Pond by Sheldon Flory
1991	Thinking Egg by Jacqueline Brown
1993	A Private Bottling by Don Paterson
1995	Laws of Gravity by Paul Farley

Australian Literature Society Gold Medal

Association for the Study of Australian Literature Ltd
c/o English Department,
University College, ADFA
Campbell, ACT 2600, Australia
Contact: Susan Lever
Awarded annually for an outstanding Australian literary work, or occasionally, for outstanding services to Australian literature. Award was inaugurated by the ALS which was incorporated in the Association for the Study of Australian Literature (ASAL) in 1982. No nominations are required.
Prize: Winner receives a gold medal and $1000.

1983	Neighbours in a Thicket by David Malouf
1984	The People's Other World by Les Murray
1985	Archimedes and the Seagle by David Ireland
1986	Beachmasters by Thea Astley
1987	The Nightmarkets by Alan Wearne
1988	Louisa by Brian Matthews
1989	Forty-Seventeen by Frank Moorhouse (and contribution to Australian Literature)
1990	Possible Words and Collected Poems by Peter Porter
1991	Cabin Fever by Elizabeth Jolley (and contribution to Australian Literature)
1992	The Second Bridegroom by Rodney Hall (and contribution to Australian Literature)
1993	Selected Poems by Elizabeth Riddell
1994	Radiance, The Temple, and screenplay for A Map of the Human Heart by Louis Nowra (and contribution to Australian Literature)
1995	The Hand That Signed The Paper by Helen Demidenko
1996	Camille's Bread by Amanda Lohrey

Authors' Club First Novel Award

Authors' Club
40 Dover Street,
London W1X 3RB, England
The winner is selected from entries submitted by publishers and awarded to the most promising first full-length novel of the year published in the UK by a British author.
Prize: £750
Contact: Ann Carter, Secretary

1980	The Good Morrow by Dawn Lowe-Watson
1981	The Magic Glass by Dr. Anne Smith
1982	The Privileged Children by Frances Vernon
1983	Summer at the Haven by Katherine

Moore

1984	Lama, A Novel of Tibet by Frederick Hyde-Chambers
1985	Eightsome Reel by Magda Sweetland
1986	Playing Fields in Winter by Helen Harris
1987	The Levels by Peter Benson
1988	The Holy Innocents by Gilbert Adair
1989	The Silver Pigs by Lindsey Davis
1990	The Way You Tell Them by Alan Brownjohn
1991	The Book of Wishes and Complaints by Zina Rohan
1992	The Healing by David Park
1993	Season of the Rainbirds by Nadeem Aslam
1994	PIG by Andrew Cowan
1995	Walter and the Resurrection of G by T J Armstrong

Bancroft Prizes
Columbia University, 202A Low Library,
New York, NY 10027, USA

David Berry Prize
Royal Historical Society
University College London
Gower Street
London WC1E 6BT, England
Awarded to the writer of the best essay on Scottish history within the reigns of James I and James VI of between 6000 and 10,000 words.
Prize: £250
Contact: Joy McCarthy

James Tait Black Memorial Prizes
Department of English Literature, David Hume Tower
George Square, Edinburgh EH8 9JX, Scotland
Eligible works of fiction and biographies are those written in English, originating with a British publisher, and first published in Britain in the year of the award. The nationality of the writer is irrelevant.
Two prizes of £3000 each are awarded annually; one for the best biography or work of that nature, the other for the best work of fiction published in the 12-month period prior to the annual submission date of 30th September.

Biography
1980	Tennyson: The Unquiet Heart by Robert B Martin
1981	Edith Sitwell: Unicorn Among Lions by Victoria Glendinning
1982	James Joyce by Richard Ellmann
1983	Franz Liszt: The Virtuoso Years by Alan Walker
1984	Virginia Woolf: A Writer's Life by Lyndall Gordon
1985	Jonathan Swift: A Hypocrate Reversed by David Noakes
1986	Helen Waddell by D Felicitas Corrigan
1987	Victor Gollancz: A Biography by Ruth Dudley Edwards
1988	Wittgenstein: A Life: Young Ludwig (1889-1921) by Brian McGuinness
1989	Federico Garcia Lorca: A Life by Ian Gibson

1990	The Invisible Woman: The Story of Nelly Ternan and Charles Dickens by Claire Tomalin
1991	Darwin by James Moore and Adrian Desmond
1992	The Reckoning: The Murder of Christopher Marlowe by Charles Nicholl
1993	Dr Johnson & Mr Savage by Richard Holmes
1994	Under My Skin by Doris Lessing
1995	Albert Speer: His Battle with Truth by Gitta Sereny
1996	Thomas Cranmer: A Life by Diarmaid MacCulloch

Fiction
1980	Waiting for the Barbarians by J M Coetzee
1981	Midnight's Children by Salman Rusdie
	The Mosquito Coast by Paul Theroux
1982	On the Black Hill by Bruce Chatwin
1983	Allegro Postillions by Jonathan Keates
1984	Empire of the Sun by J G Ballard
	Nights at the Circus by Angela Carter
1985	Winter Garden by Robert Edric
1986	Persephone by Jenny Joseph
1987	The Golden Bird: Two Orkney Stories by George Mackay Brown
1988	A Season in the West by Piers Paul Read
1989	A Disaffection by James Kelman
1990	Brazzaville Beach by William Boyd
1991	Downriver by Iain Sinclair
1992	Sacred Country by Rose Tremain
1993	Crossing the River by Caryl Phillips
1994	The Folding Star by Alan Hollinghurst
1995	The Prestige by Christopher Priest
1996	Last Orders by Graham Swift
	Justine by Alice Thompson

Bollingen Prize in Poetry
Box 1603A,
New Haven, CT 06520, USA
Prize is awarded for the best book of poetry by an American author during the preceeding two years.
Biennial prize of $10,000

1981	Howard Nemerov and May Swenson
1983	Anthony E Hecht and John Hollander
1985	John Ashbury and Fred Chappell
1987	Stanley Kunitz
1989	Edgar Bowers
1991	Laura (Riding) Jackson and Donald Justice
1993	Mark Strand
1995	Kenneth Koch

Booker Prize For Fiction
Book Trust,
Book House, 45 East Hill,
London SW18 2QZ, England
Leading British literary award for the best full-length novel published between 1 October and 30 September in UK. Novel must be written in English and written by a citizen of Britain, the Commonwealth, Republic of Ireland or South Africa.
Annual prize of £20,000
Contact: Sandra Vince
1980	Rites of Passage by William Golding

1981   Midnight's Children by Salman Rushdie
1982   Schlindler's Ark by Thomas Keneally
1983   Life & Times of Michael K by J M
        Coetzee
1984   Hotel du Lac by Anita Brookner
1985   The Bone People by Keri Hulme
1986   The Old Devils by Kingsley Amis
1987   Moon Tiger by Penelope Lively
1988   Oscar and Lucinda by Peter Carey
1989   The Remains of the Day by Kazuo
        Ishiguro
1990   Possession by A S Byatt
1991   The Famished Road by Ben Okri
1992   The English Patient by Michael Ondaatje
        Sacred Hunger by Barry Unsworth
1993   Paddy Clarke Ha Ha Ha by Roddy Doyle
1994   How Late It Was, How Late by James
        Kelman
1995   The Ghost Road by Pat Barker
1996   Last Orders by Graham Swift

Boston Globe-Horn Book Award
c/o Boston Globe
135 William T Morrissey Boulevard
Boston, MA 02125, USA
Prize awarded for books published within the
previous year in the categories of fiction, non-fiction
and picture book.
Annual cash prize.

Micheál Brethnach Literary Memorial Award
Cló Iar Chonnachta Teo.
Indreabhán, Connemara
Co. Galway, Republic of Ireland
An annual award for the best Irish language work in
any literary form: novel, drama, poetry or short story
collection. Open to writers under 30 years of age.
Closing date for entries is 1st December each year.
Prize: IR £1000
Contact: Nóirín Ní Ghrádaigh / Deirdre N íThuathail

Bridport Prize
Bridport Arts Centre, South Street
Bridport, Dorset DT6 3NR, England
Awarded for original poems of not more than 42
lines, and short stories between 1000 and 5000
words. All entries must be written in English and
must be previously unpublished or broadcast, nor
entered in any other competition.
Prizes: First prize: £2500, Second prize: £1000,
Third prize: £500 (in each category), plus
discretionary supplementary prizes.
Contact: Peggy Chapman-Andrews

British Book Awards
Publishing News
43 Musuem Street
London WC1A 1LY, England
Established in 1988 and affectionately known as
the 'Nibbies', the British Book Awards are
announced in Publishing News in November of
each year to those who have made an impact to the
book trade. Categories include Editor, Publisher,
Author, Independent Bookseller and Children's
Book.
Prize: The Nibbie
Contact: Merric Davidson

British Fantasy Awards
2 Harwood Street
Stockport, Cheshire SK4 1JJ, England
Awarded by the British Fantasy Society at its
annual conference from votes offered by BFS
members. Categories include Best Novel and Best
Short Story. Previous winners include Ramsey
Campbell, Clive Barker and Stephen King.
Prize: Statuette.
Contact: Robert Parkinson

Buckland Award
Trustees Executors and Agency Company of New
Zealand Ltd
24 Water Street, PO Box 760
Dunedin, New Zealand
Prize is awarded annually for work of the highest
literary merit by a New Zealand writer.

Randolph Caldecott Medal
Association for Library Service to Children
50 E Huron Street
Chicago, IL 70711, USA
Prize is awarded to an illustrator of the most
distinguished American picture book for children
published in the preceding year.
Annual prize of bronze medal.

James Cameron Memorial Award
Department of Journalism
City University
Northampton Square
London EC1 0HB, England
Annual award for journalism to a reporter of any
nationality   working   for   the   British   media.
Nominations are not accepted.
Contact: Professor Hugh Stephenson
1987   David Hirst
1988   Michael Buerk
1989   Neal Ascherson
1990   John Simpson
1991   Robert Fisk and Charles Wheeler
1992   Bridget Kendall
1993   Martin Woollacott
1994   Ed Villiamy
1995   George Alagiah
1996   Maggie O'Kane

Canada-French Community of Belgium Literary Prize
The Canada Council
350 Albert Street, PO Box 1047
Ottawa, Ontario K1P 5V4, Canada
Awarded annually in alternate years to a French-
language Belgian or Canadian writer for his or her
complete works.
Prize of $5000

Canada-Japan Book Award
The Canada Council
350 Albert Street, PO Box 1047
Ottawa, Ontario K1P 5V4, Canada
Awarded annually for a book in English or French
about Japan by a Canadian author or for a book by
a Japanese author translated by a Canadian into
English or French.
Prize of $10, 000

Canada-Switzerland Literary Prize

The Canada Council
350 Albert Street, PO Box 1047
Ottawa, Ontario K1P 5V4, Canada
Awarded annually in alternate years to a Canadian or Swiss writer for a work of poetry, fiction, drama or non-fiction published in French during the preceding eight years. The prize may also be awarded for the French translation of a work written originally in English by a Canadian writer or in German, Italian or Romansh by a Swiss writer.
Prize of $2500

Canadian Authors Association Literary Awards

275 Slater Street, Suite 500
Ottawa, Ontario K1P 5H9, Canada
Four categories: fiction, non-fiction, poetry and drama. Nominations apply to book length works by Canadian writers published or produced during the previous calendar year.
One award per year in each category of a cash prize plus silver medal.
Contact: Awards Chairman

Canadian Library Association Book of the Year for Children Award

c/o Canadian Library Association
200 Elgin Street, Suite 206
Ottawa, Ontario K2P 1L5, Canada.
The award is presented annually to an author of an outstanding children's book published in Canada during the previous calendar year. The books must be suitable for children up to 14 years of age.

Melville Cane Award

Poetry Society of America
15 Gramercy Park
New York, NY 10003, USA
For a published book on poetry (in even-numbered years) alternating (in odd-numbered years) with a book of poems published within the award year.
Annual cash award.

1980	Selected Poems by Richard Hugo
1981	The Poet's Calling in the English Ode by Paul Fry
1982	The Red Coal by Gerald Stern
1983	Robert Lowell by Ian Hamilton
1984	New and Collected Poems by Alan Dugan
1985	Kenneth Patchen and American Mysticism by Raymond Nelson
1986	Triumph of Archilles by Louis Gluck
1987	Visions and Revisions of American Poetry by Lewis Turco
1988	Cemetery Nights by Steven Dobyns Memories of the Future: The Daybooks of Tina Modotti by Margaret Gibson
1989	Conrad Aiken: Poet of the White Horse Vale by Edward Butscher
1990	Harp Lake by John Hollander
1991	White Paper by J D McClatchy
1992	The 6-Cornered Snowflake by John Frederick Nims
1993	An Essay on French Verse for Readers of English Poetry by Jacques Barzan
1994	Year of the Comet by Nicholas Christopher

Carnegie Medal

The Library Association, 7 Ridgmount Street
London WC1E 7AE, England
The Library Association Carnegie Medal is awarded annually for an outstanding book for children written in English and receiving its first publication in the UK during the preceding year.
Prize: Gold medal and £1000 of books to donate.

1980	City of Gold by Peter Dickinson
1981	The Scarecrows by Robert Westall
1982	The Haunting by Margaret Mahy
1983	Handles by Jan Mark
1984	The Changeover by Margaret Mahy
1985	Storm by Kevin Crossley-Holland
1986	Granny Was a Buffer Girl by Berlie Doherty
1987	The Ghost Drum by Susan Price
1988	A Pack of Lies by Geraldine McCaughrean
1989	Goggle-Eyes by Anne Fine
1990	Wolf by Gilliam Cross
1991	Dear Nobody by Berlie Doherty
1992	Flour Babies by Anne Fine
1993	Stone Cold by Robert Swindells
1994	Whispers in the Graveyard by Theresa Breslin
1995	His Dark Material: Book 1 Northern Lights by Philip Pullman

Children's Book Award

The Old Malt Hpuse
Aldbourne, Wilts SN8 2DW, England
Contact: Marianne Adey
This annual award is judged by children themselves and the shortlist is announced at the Federation of Children's Book Group's Annual Conference. The three categories are picture books, shorter novels and longer novels.
Prizes: Shortlisted authors and illustrators receive a portfolio of children's letters inspired by their work, category winners receive a silver bowl, and the overall winner is awarded a silver and oak tree sculpture.
Best Book of the Year

1991	Threadbear by Mick Inkpen
1992	Kiss the Dust by Elizabeth Laird
1993	The Suitcase Kid by Jacqueline Wilson
1994	The Boy in the Bubble by Ian Strachan
1995	Harriet's Hare by Dick King-Smith
1996	Double Act by Jacqueline Wilson

Cholmondeley Awards

Society of Authors
84 Drayton Gardens
London SW10 9SB, England
The non-competitive award is for work generally, not for a specific book, and submissions are not required.
Annual prize of £8000 (shared).

1980	George Barker
	Terence Tiller
	Roy Fuller
1981	Roy Fisher
	Robert Garioch
	Charles Boyle
1982	Basil Bunting
	Herbert Lomas

	William Scammell
1983	John Fuller
	Craig Raine
	Anthony Thwaite
1984	Michael Baldwin
	Michale Hoffmann
	Carol Raine
1985	Dannie Abse
	Peter Redgrove
	Brian Taylor
1986	Lawrence Durrell
	James Fenton
	Selima Hill
1987	Wendy Cope
	Matthew Sweeney
	George Szirtes
1988	John Heath-Stubbs
	Sean O'Brien
	John Whitworth
1989	Peter Didsbury
	Douglas Dunn
	E J Scovell
1990	Kingsley Amis
	Elaine Feinstein
	Michael O'Neill
1991	James Berry
	Sujata Bhatt
	Michael Hulse
	Derek Mahon
1992	Allen Curnow
	Donald Davie
	Carol Ann Duffy
	Roger Woddis
1993	Patricia Beer
	George Mackay Brown
	P J Kavanagh
	Michael Longley
1994	Ruth Fainlight
	Gwen Harwood
	Elizabeth Jennings
	John Mole
1995	U A Fanthorpe
	Christopher Reid
	C H Sisson
	Kit Wright
1996	Elizabeth Bartlett
	Dorothy Nimmo
	Peter Scupham
	Iain Crichton Smith

Arthur C Clarke Award for Science Fiction

60 Bournemouth Road,
Folkestone, Kent CT19 5AZ, England
Prize established in 1986 is given annually to the best science fiction novel published in the UK of the year. Award is jointly administered and judged by the British Science Fiction Association, Science Fiction Foundation and Science Policy Foundation. Annual prize of £1000.
Administrator: Paul Kincaid

1987	The Handmaid's Tale by Margaret Atwood
1988	The Sea and Summer by George Turner
1989	Unquenchable Fire by Rachel Pollock
1990	The Child Garden by Geoff Ryman
1991	Take Back Plenty by Colin Greenland
1992	Synners by Pat Cadigan

1993	Body of Glass by Marge Piercy
1994	Vurt by Jeff Noon
1995	Fools by Pat Cadigan
1995	Fairyland by Paul J McAuley

Cló Iar-Chonnachta Literary Award

Cló Iar-Chonnachta Teo.
Indreabhán, Connemara
Co. Galway, Republic of Ireland
An annual prize for a newly written and unpublished work in the Irish language, to be awarded for a novel in 1996, a poetry collection in 1997 and a work of drama or short story collection in 1998.
Prize: IR £5000
Contact: Nóirín Ní Ghrádaigh / Deirdre N íThuathail

| 1996 | Pádraig Ó Siadhail |

Commonwealth Writers' Prize

Commonwealth Foundation, Marlborough House
Pall Mall, London SW1Y 5HY, England
Established in 1987, the Commonwealth Writers' Prize is awarded annually for a work of fiction, novel or collection of short stories - written in English by a citizen of the Commonwealth and published in the preceding year. Funded by the Commonwealth Foundation and administered by the Book Trust.
Prize of £10,000 for best book, £3000 for best first published book, eight regional prizes of £1000.
Administrator: Book Trust

1987	Summer Lightning and Other Stories by Olive Senior
1988	Heroes by Festus Iyayi
1989	The Carpathians by Janet Frame
	Women of Influence by Bonnie Burnard
1990	Solomon Gursky Was Here by Mordechai Richler Visitors by John Cranna
1991	The Great World by David Malouf
	Shape-Shifter by Pauline Melville
1992	Such a Long Journey by Rohinton Mistry
	Divina Trace by Robert Antoni
1993	The Ancestor Game by Alex Miller
	The Thousand Faces of Night by Githa Hariharan
1994	A Suitable Boy by Vikram Seth
	The Case of Emily V by Keith Oatley
1995	Captain Corelli's Mandolin by Louis de Bernières
	Seasonal Adjustments by Adib Khan
1996	A Fine Balance by Rohinton Mistry
	Red Earth and Pouring Rain by Vikram Chandra

Thomas Cook/Daily Telegraph Travel Book Awards

Thomas Cook Group
45 Berkeley Street
London W1A 1EB, England
Award for best travel book published in the previous year.
Annual award of £7500.
Contact: Alexis Coles, Corporate Affairs

1980	Tracks by Robyn Davidson
1981	Old Glory by Jonathan Raban
1982	The Sinbad Voyage by Tim Severin
1983	From Heaven Lake by Vikram Seth
1984	To The Frontier by Geoffrey Moorhouse

1985	So Far From God by Patrick Marnham
1886/87	Between the Woods and the Water by Patrick Leigh Fermor
1988	Behind the Wall by Colin Thubron
1989	Riding the Iron Rooster by Paul Theroux
1990	Our Grandmothers' Drums by Mark Hudson
1991	Hunting Mister Heartbreak by Jonathan Raban
1992	A Goddess in the Stones by Norman Lewis
	In Search of Conrad by Gavin Young
1993	The Heart of the World by Nik Cohn
1994	City of Djinns by William Dalrymple
1995	In Search of Tusitala: Travels in the South Pacific after Robert Louis Stevenson by Gavin Bell
1996	Frontiers of Heaven by Stanley Stewart

Duff Cooper Prize
54 St Maur Road
London SW6 4DP, England
Prize is awarded annually in memory of Alfred Duff Cooper, 1st Viscount Norwich (1890-1954). It consists of a copy of his autobiography, Old Men Forget, together with a cheque.
Prize: £2500.
Contact: Ms Artemis Cooper

1980	Tennyson: The Unquiet Heart by Robert Bernard Martin
1981	Edith Sitwell: A Unicorn Among Lions by Victoria Glendinning
1982	James Joyce by Richard Ellmann
1983	Collected Poems by Peter Porter
1984	Ivy Compton-Burnett by Hilary Spurling
1985	Edmund Goose: A Literary Landscape by Ann Thwaite
1986	C R Ashbee: Architect, Designer and Romantic Socialist by Alan Crawford
1987	The Fatal Shore: History of the Transporation of Convicts to Australia, 1987-1868 by Robert Hughes
1988	Serious Character: Life of Ezra Pound by Humphrey Carpenter
1989	Federico Garcia Lorca: A Life by Ian Gibson
1990	Clever Hearts: Desmond and Molly McCarthy: A Biography by Hugh & Mirabel Cecil
1991	Wittgenstein: The Duty of Genius by Ray Monk
1992	Never Again: Post-war Britain 1946-51 by Peter Hennessy
1993	A History of Warfare by John Keegan
1994	Curzon by David Gilmour
1995	Albert Speer: His Battle With Truth by Gitta Sereny
1996	Thomas Cranmer: A Life by Diarmaid McCulloch

Crime Writers' Association Awards
PO Box 10772
London N6 4RY, England
Contact: The Secretary
CWA - Gold Dagger for Fiction
Best crime fiction of the year; nominations by publishers only.

Annual prize of gold-plated dagger and cheque.

1980	The Murder of the Maharajah by H R F Keating
1981	Gorky Park by Martin Cruz Smith
1982	The False Inspector Dew by Peter Lovesey
1983	Accidental Crimes by John Hutton
1984	The Twelfth Juror by B M Gill
1985	Monkey Puzzle by Paula Gosing
1986	Live Flesh by Ruth Rendell
1987	A Fatal Inversion by Barbara Vine (Ruth Rendell)
1988	Ratking by Michael Dibdin
1989	The Wench is Dead by Colin Dexter
1990	Bones and Silence by Reginald Hill
1991	King Solomon's Carpet by Barbara Vine
1992	The Way Through the Woods by Colin Dexter
1993	Cruel and Unusual by Patricia Cornwell
1994	The Scold's Bride by Minette Walters
1995	The Mermaid's Singing by Val McDermid
1996	Popcorn by Ben Elton

CWA - Silver Dagger for Fiction
Annual award of silver dagger and cheque.

1980	Monk's Hood by Ellis Peters
1981	The Dead of Jericho by Colin Dexter
1982	Ritual Murder by S T Harmon
1983	The Papers of Tony Veitch by William McIlvanney
1984	The Tree of Hands by Ruth Rendell
1985	Last Seen Alive by Dorothy Simpson
1986	A Taste for Death by P D James
1987	Presumed Innocent by Scott Turow
1988	Toxic Shock by Sarah Paretsky
1989	The Shadow Run by Desmonde Lowden
1990	The Late Candidate by Mike Phillips
1991	Deep Sleep by Frances Fyfield
1992	Bucket Nut by Liza Cody
1993	Fatlands by Sarah Dunant
1994	Miss Smilla's Feeling for Snow by Peter Høeg
1995	The Summons by Peter Lovesey
1996	Bloodhounds by Peter Lovesey

CWA - Diamond Dagger for Fiction
Prize is awarded by Chairman and Committee for outstanding contribution to the genre.
Annual prize of Diamond Dagger plus cheque.

1986	Eric Ambler
1987	P D James
1988	John le Carré
1989	Dick Francis
1990	Julian Symons
1991	Ruth Rendell
1992	Lesley Charteris
1993	Edith Pargeter
1994	Reginald Hill

CWA - Gold Dagger for Non-Fiction
Awarde for the best non-fiction crime book published during the year.
Annual prize of gold-plated dagger and cheque.

1980	Conspiracy by Anthony Summers
1981	Prisoner With a Name, Cell Without a Number by Jacobo Timerman
1982	Earth to Earth by John Cornwell
1983	Dougle Dealer by Petr Watson
1984	In God's Name by David Yallop
1985	Killing for Company by Brian Masters

1986	Evil Angels by John Bryson
1987	Perfect Murder by Bernard Taylor and Stephen Knight
1988	The Secret Lives of Trebitsch Lincoln by Bernard Wasserstein
1989	A Gathering of Saints by Robert Lindsey
1990	The Passing of Starr by Jonathan Goodman
1991	Giordano Bruno and the Embassy Affair by John Bossy
1992	The Reckoning by Charles Nicholl
1993	Murder in the Heart by Alexandra Artley
1994	Criminal Shadows by David Canter
1995	Dead Not Buried by Martin Beales
1996	The Gunpowder Plot by Antonia Fraser

CWA John Creasey Memorial Dagger
Presented for the best crime novel by a previously unpublished author. Award established in memory of the crime writer John Creasey, founder of the Crime Writers Association. Nominations from publishers only.
Annual prize of dagger and cheque.

1980	Dupe by Liza Cody
1981	The Ludi Victor by James Leigh
1982	Caroline Miniscule by Andrew Taylor
1983	The Ariadne Clue by Carol Clemeau
	The Night the Gods Smiled by Eric Wright
1984	A Very Private Enterprise by Elizabeth Ironside
1985	The Latimer Mercy by Robert Richards
1986	Tinplate by Neville Steed
1987	Dark Apostle by Denis Kilcommons
1988	Death's Bright Angel by Janet Neel
1989	A Real Shot in the Arm by Annette Roome
1990	Postmortem by Patricia Cornwell
1991	Deep Sleep by Frances Fyfield
1992	The Ice House by Minette Walters
1993	No prize awarded
1994	Big Town by Doug J Swanson
1995	One For The Money by Janet Evanovich
1996	No prize awarded

The Last Laugh Dagger
Award for the funniest crime novel published during the year. Nominations from publishers only.
Prize: Dagger and cheque.

1994	The Villain of the Earth by Simon Shaw
1995	Sunburn by Laurence Shames
1996	Two For The Dough by Janet Evanovich

Dagger in the Library Award
Annual award established in 1995 for the crime writer most popular with library borrowers. Winner is selected in liaison with librarians, and sponsored by the NB Magazine for librarians.
Prize: Gold-plated dagger and cheque.

1995	Lindsey Davis.

The Macallan Short Story Award
6 Ainscow Avenue
Lostock, Bolton
Lancs BL6 4LR, England
Contact: Val McDermid
Award for a published crime story.
Prize: £200 and a silver-plated tie-pin/brooch

1995	Funny Story by Larry Beinhart
1996	Herbert in Motion by Ian Rankin

Danish Academy Prize for Literature
Rungstedlund
109 Rungsted Strandvej
DK-2960 Rungsted Kyst, Denmark
Contact: Allan Philip
Prize of Dkr 200,000 is currently awarded bi-annually for an outstanding work of literature.

1980	Henrik Norbrandt
1981	Dorrit Willumsen
1982	Per Højholt
1984	Jess Ørnsbro
1986	Henrik Stangerup
1988	Halfdan Rasmussen
1990	Jens Smærup Srensen
1992	Peter Laugesen
1994	Ib Michael
1996	Vibeke Grønfeldt

Dillons First Fiction Award
Dillons UK Ltd
Royal House, Princes Gate, Homer Road
Solihull, West Midlands B91 3QQ, England
Established in 1994 to encourage new novel-writing talent, this annual award is open to full-length first novels written in English and published in the Uk during the calendar year in question. Winners announced in April.
Prize: £5000
Contact: Ruth Killick / Tracey Lewis

1995	Now and Then by William Corlett

Encore Award
Society of Authors
84 Drayton Gardens,
London SW10 9SB, England
The prize has been awarded by the Society of Authors since 1990 for a second published novel.
Annual Prize: £7500

1990	A Lesser Dependency by Peter Benson
	Calm at Sunset, Calm at Dawn by Paul Watkins
1991	Richard's Feet by Carey Harrison
1992	Downriver by Iain Sinclair
1993	The Heather Blazing by Colm Toibin
1994	Afternoon Raag by Amit Chaudhuri
1995	A Goat's Song by Dermot Healy
1996	So I Am Glad by A L Kennedy

English Academy of Southern Africa
PO Box 124
Witwatersrand 2050
South Africa
Thomas Pringle Awards
Oliver Schreiner Prize

Geoffrey Faber Memorial Prize
Faber and Faber Ltd
3 Queen Square
London WC1N 3AU, England
Awarded annually since 1963, as a memorial to the founder and first Chairman of Faber and Faber, with prizes in alternate years for a volume of verse or prose fiction first published originally in UK during 2 years preceding the year of award. Eligible writers must be under 40 at time of publication, citizen of UK, Ireland, Commonwealth, or South Africa.

Prize: £1000
Contact: Sarah Gleadell/Belinda Matthews

1980	The Slant Door by George Szirtes
	Love Life by Hugo Williams
1981	Waiting for the Barbarians by J M Coetzee
1982	Why Brownlee Left by Paul Muldoon
	The Strange Museum by Tom Paulin
1983	Shuttlecock by Graham Swift
1984	In Memory of War by James Fenton
1985	Flaubert's Parrot by Julian Barnes
1986	A Quiet Gathering by David Scott
1987	Man Descending by Guy Vanderhaeghe
1988	Agrimony by Michael Hofmann
1989	Sea Music by David Profumo
1990	Shibboleth by Michael Donaghy
1991	The Fog Line by Carol Birch
1992	Madoc by Paul Muldoon
1993	The Quantity Theory by Will Self
1994	Myth of the Twin by John Burnside
1995	Their Angel Reach by Livi Michael

Eleanor Farjeon Award
Children's Book Circle
Hampshire County Library
81 North Walls
Winchester SO23 8BY, England
Prize awarded for distinguished service to children's books both in the UK and overseas. Recipients include librarians, publishers, booksellers and authors, and are chosen from nominations from members of the Children's Book Circle.
Prize: £500
Contact: Anne Marley

1981	Margaret Marshall
	Virginia Jensen
1982	Aiden & Nancy Chambers
1983	Jean Russell
1984	Shirley Hughes
1985	Bob Leeson
1986	Judith Elkin
1987	Valerie Bierman
1988	National Library for the Handicapped Children
1989	Anna Home
1990	Jill Bennett
1991	Patricia Crampton
1992	Stephanie Nettell
1993	Susan Belgrave
1994	Eileen Colwell
1995	Helen Paiba
1996	Books For Keeps

Fawcett Society Book Prize
New Light of Women's Lives
46 Harleyford Road,
London SE11 5AY, England
Prize is given to works of fiction, non-fiction or biography which offer enlightenment and understanding of women's lives. Must have first been published in Britain, Commonwealth or Ireland.
Annual prize of £2000.
Contact: Charlotte Burt

1982	Women, Power and Politics by Margaret Stacey and Marion Price

1983	Union Street by Pat Barker
	Beka Lamb by Zee Edgell
1984	The Tidy House by Caroline Steedman
1985	Here Today by Zoe Fairbairns
1986	Monuments and Maidens by Marina Warner
1987	Redhill Rococo by Sheena MacKay
1988	Iron Ladies: Why Do Women Vote Tory by Beatrix Campbell
1989	Boy Blue by Stevie Davies
1990	The Long Road to Greenham by Jill Liddington
1991	Judasland by Jennifer Dawson
1992	Cleopatra: Histories, Dreams and Distortions by Lucy Hughes-Hallett
	The Haunting of Sylvia Plath by Jacqueline Rose
1993	Wild Swans by Jung Chang
1994	Daphne du Maurier by Margaret Forster

The Kathleen Fidler Award
c/o Book Trust Scotland
Scottish Book Centre
Fountainbridge Library , 137 Dundee Street
Edinburgh EH11 1BG, Scotland
Awarded for an unpublished children's novel of not less than25,000- 28,000 words for children aged 8-12. Author must not have had a novel published previously for this age group. Entries to be typewritten, double-spaced, on one side of paper. Annual prize of £1000, plus entry published by Hodder Children's Books, and a rosewood and silver trophy, to be held for one year.
Contact: Administrative Officer

1983	Adrift by Alan Baillie
1984	Barty by Janet Collins
1985	No Shelter by Elizabeth Lutzeir
1986	Diamond by Caroline Pitcher
1987	Simon's Challenge by Theresa Breslin
1988	The Flight of the Solar Duck by Charles Morgan
1989	Mightier than the Sword by Clare Bevan
1990	Magic With Everything by Roger Burt
1991	Greg's Revenge by George Hendry
1992	Richard's Castle by Susan Coon
1993	48 Hours with Franklin by Mij Kelly
1994	Run, Zan, Run by Catherine MacPhail
1995	Edge of Danger by Claire Dudman
1996	The Falcon's Quest by John Smirthwaite

Sir Banister Fletcher Prize of the Authors' Club
Authors' Club
40 Dover Street
London W1X 3RB, England
Awarded to the best book of the year on the arts, and architecture in particular, by an author resident in Britain, and published in the UK in the preceding year. Nominations from the press and by publishers.
Prize: £750
Contact: Ann Carter, Secretary

1990	British Architectural Books and Writers 1556-1785 by Eileen Harris
1991	The Art and Architecture of Freemasonry by James Stevens Curl
1992	Bernold Lubetkin: Architecture and the Tradition of Progress by John Allan

1993   Buildings and Power by Thomas Marcus
1994   Gothic Revival by Megan Aldrich
1995   Alvar Aalto by Richard Weston

Forward Prizes for Poetry
c/o Colman Getty PR
Carrington House, 126-130 Regent Street
London W1R 5FE, England
Established in 1992, these awards are presented
for three catagories of poetry, the best poetry
collection of the year, the best first collection and
the best single published poem in English and by a
citizen of the UK or the Republic of Ireland.
Submissions by editors or publishers.
Prize £10,000 (best collection), £5000 (best first
collection) and £1000 (best single poem).
Contact: Coleman Getty PR
Best Collection
1992   The Man With Night Sweats by Thom
        Gunn
1993   Mean Time by Carol Ann Duffy
1994   Harm by Alan Jenkins
1995   GhostTrain by Sean O'Brien
1996   Stones and Fires by John Fuller
Best First Collection
1993   Nil Nil by Don Paterson
1994   Progeny of Air by Kwame Dawes
1995   Breathe Now, Breathe by Jane Duran
1996   Slattern by Kate Clanchy
Best Single Poem
1993   Judith by Vicki Feaver
1994   Autumn by Iain Crichton
1995   In Honour of Love by Jenny Joseph
1996   The Graduates by Kathleen Jamie

Mary Gilmore Award
Association for the Study of Australian Literature
Ltd
c/o English Department,
University College, ADFA
Campbell, ACT 2600, Australia
Contact: Susan Lever
Awarded for a first book of poetry published in the
preceding year. No nominations are required.
Prize: $1000
1985   The Truth About Unicorns by Doris Brett
1986   A Crowd of Voices by Stephen Williams
1987   Boy With Telescope by Jan Owen
1988   The Domesticity of Giraffes by Judith
        Beveridge
1989   The Re-arrangement by Alex Skovron
1990   In The Name of the Father by Kristopher
        Sassemussen
1991   Verandahs by Jean Kent
1992   This is the Stone by Alison Croggon
1993   The Mask and Jagged Star by Jill Jones
1994   Now, Millenium by Deborah Staines
1995   Coming Up for Light by Aileen Kelly
1996   Nervous Arcs by Jordie Albiston

Goodman Fielder Wattie Book Award
PO Box 44-146
Auckland 2, New Zealand
Book published in New Zealand in the previous
year by a New Zealand author (includes New
Zealand residents and Pacific Island countries).
Annual - 1st prize of NZ $20,000, 2nd prize of NZ

$10,000, 3rd prize of NZ $5000, Food Industry
Book Award NZ $6000

Governor General's Literary Awards
The Canada Council
350 Albert Street, PO Box 1047
Ottawa, Ontario K1P 5V8, Canada
Awarded to Canadian authors of the best books in
the English & French languages in seven
categories: fiction, non-fiction, poetry, drama,
children's literature (text), children's literature
(illustration) and translation.
Annual cash prize.

Kate Greenaway Medal
The Library Association
7 Ridgmount Street
London WC1E 7AE, England
Awarded annually for an outstanding book in terms
of illustration for children published in the UK the
preceding year.
Prize: Gold medal and £1000 of books to donate.
1990   The Whale's Song, illustrated by Gary
        Blythe
1991   The Jolly Christmas Postman, illustrated
        by Janet Ahlberg
1992   Zoo, illustrated by Anthony Browne
1993   Black Ships Before Troy, illustrated by
        Alan Lee
1994   Way Home, illustrated by Gregory
        Rogers
1995   The Christmas Miracle of Jonathan
        Toomey, illustrated by PJ Lynch

Eric Gregory Trust Fund Award
Society of Authors
84 Drayton Gardens
London SW10 9SB, England
For poets aged under 30 who are likely to benefit
from more time given to writing.
Prize: £28,000 (shared)
1986   Mick North
        Lachlan Mackinnon
        Oliver Reynolds
        Stephen Romer
1987   Peter McDonald
        Maura Dooley
        Stephen Knight
        Steve Anthony
        Jill Maughan
        Paul Munden
1988   Michael Symmons Robert
        Gwyneth Lewis
        Adrian Blackledge
        Simon Armitage
        Robert Crawford
1989   Gerard Woodward
        David Morley
        Katrina Porteus
        Paul Henry
1990   Nicholas Drake
        Maggie Hannon
        William Park
        Jonathan Davidson
        Lavinia Greenlaw
        Don Paterson
        John Wells

1991	Roddy Lumsden
	Glyn Maxwell
	Stephen Smith
	Wayne Burrows
	Jackie Kay
1992	Jill Dawson
	Hugh Dunkerly
	Christopher Greenhaigh
	Marita Maddah
	Stuart Paterson
	Stuart Pickford
1993	Eleanor Brown
	Joel Lane
	Deryn Rees-Jones
	Sean Boustead
	Tracey Herd
	Angela McSeveney
1994	Julia Copus
	Alice Oswald
	Steven Blyth
	Kate Clanchy
	Giles Goodland
1995	Collette Bryce
	Sophie Hannah
	Tobias Hill
	Mark Wormald
1996	Sue Butler
	Cathy Cullis
	Jane Griffiths
	Jane Holland
	Chris Jones
	Sinead Morrissey
	Kate Thomas

Guardian Children's Fiction Award

The Guardian
72 Dukes Avenue
London W4 2AF, England
Awarded for an outstanding work of fiction for children by a Commonwealth or British author, first published in Britain in previous year, excluding picture books and previous winners.
Annual prize of £1000.

1980	The Vandal by Ann Schlee
1981	The Sentinels by Peter Carter
1982	Goodnight Mister Tom by Michelle Magorian
1983	The Village by the Sea by Anita Desai
1984	The Sheep-Pig by Dick King-Smith
1985	What is the Truth? by Ted Hughes
1986	Henry's Leg by Ann Pilling
1987	The True Story of Spit MacPhee by James Aldridge
1988	The Runaways by Ruth Thomas
1989	A Pack of Lies by Geraldine McCaughrean
1990	Goggle-Eyes by Anne Fine
1991	The Kingdom by the Sea by Robert Westall
1992	Paper Faces by Rachel Anderson
	The Exiles by Hilary McKay
1993	Low Tide by William Mayne
1994	The Mennyms by Sylvia Waugh
1995	MapHead by Lesley Howarth
1996	Dark Materials I: Northern Lights by Philip Pullman
	The Sherwood Hero by Alison Prince

Guardian Fiction Prize

The Guardian
72 Dukes Avenue
London W4 2AF, England
The winner is chosen by a panel of five judges. Submissions are not requested. Awarded to a work of fiction by a British, Irish or Commonwealth writer and published in the UK.
Prize: £2000

1980	A Month in the Country by J L Carr
1981	Kepler by John Banville
1982	Where I Used to Play on the Green by Glyn Hughes
1983	Empire of the Sun by J G Ballard
1985	Hawksmoor by Peter Ackroyd
1986	Continent by Jim Crace
1987	The Levels by Peter Benson
1988	Sweet Desserts by Lucy Ellman
1989	Rosehill: Portraits From a Midlands City by Carol Lake
1990	Shape-Shifter by Pauline Melville
1991	The Devil's Own Work by Alan Judd
1992	Poor Things by Alasdair Gray
1993	The Eye in the Door by Pat Barker
1994	Debatable Land by Candia McWilliam
1995	Heart's Journey Into Winter by James Buchan
1996	Reading in the Dark by Seamus deane

Hawthornden Prize

42A Hays Mews, Berkeley Square
London W1X 7RU, England
For imaginative literature by a British subject under the age of 41 published during the previous year.
Annual prize of £5000
Contact: Mrs Judy Mooney

1980	Arcadia by Christopher Reid
1981	St Kilda's Parliament by Douglas Dunn
1982	Sour Sweet by Timothy Mo
1983	Allegro Postillion by Jonathan Keats
1984-87	No prizes awarded
1988	Behind the Wall by Colin Thubron
1989	Talking Heads by Alan Bennett
1990	Short Afternoons by Kit Wright
1991	The Invisible Woman by Claire Tomalin
1992	Of Love and Asthma by Ferdinand Mount
1993	The Tap Dancer by Andrew Barrow
1994	In the Place of Fallen Leaves by Tim Pears

Ernest Hemingway Foundation/PEN Award for First Fiction

PEN American Center
568 Broadway
New York, NY 10012, USA
Prize is awarded for a distinguished first novel or first collection of short fiction by a young and developing American writer.
Annual prize of $7500

1976	Parthian Shot by Loyd Little
1977	Speedboat by Renata Adler
1978	A Way of Life, Like Any Other by Darcy O'Brien
1979	Hasen by Reuben Bercovitch
1980	Mom Kills Kids and Self by Alan Saperstein
1981	Household Words by Joan Silber

1982	Housekeeping by Marilynne Robinson
1983	Shiloh and Other Stories by Bobbie Ann Mason
1984	During the Reign of the Queen of Persia by Joan Chase
1985	Dreams of Sleep by Josephine Humphreys
1986	Lady's Time by Alan V Hewat
1987	Tongues of Flame by Mary Ward Brown
1988	Imagining Argentina by Lawrence Thornton
1989	The Book by Ruth by Jane Hamilton
1990	The Ice at the Bottom of the World by Mark Richard
1991	Maps to Anywhere by Bernard Cooper
1992	Wartime Lies by Louis Begley
1993	Lost in the City by Edward P Jones
1994	The Magic of Blood by Dagoberto Gilb
1995	The Grass Dancer by Susan Power
1996	Native Speaker by Chang-rae Lee

O Henry Award
Texas Institute of Letters, Box 9032
Wichita Falls, TX 76308-9032, USA

Heywood Hill Literary Prize
10 Curzon Street
London W1Y 7FJ, England
Established in 1995 by the Duke of Devonshire, and awarded for a lifetime's contribution to the enjoyment of books. No applications are accepted.
Prize: £10,000
Contact: John Saumarez Smith

1995	Patrick O'Brian
1996	Penelope Fitzgerald

David Higham Prize for Fiction
Book Trust,
Book House, 45 East Hill
London SW18 2QZ, England
Awarded for first novel or book of short stories published in the UK in the year of the award. Author must be citizen of Britain, Commonwealth, Republic of Ireland or South Africa.
Annual prize of £1000
Contact: Sandra Vince

1980	Keep on Running by Ted Harriot
1981	A Separate Development by Christopher Hope
1982	Where I Used to Play on the Green by Glyn Hughes
1983	The Notebook of Gismondo Cavalletti by R M Lamming
1984	A Parish of Rich Women by James Buchan
1985	Family Myths and Legends by Patricia Ferguson
1986	Continent by Jim Crace
1987	The 13th House by Adam Zameenzad
1988	Life in the Palace by Carol Birch
1989	Motherland by Timothy O'Grady
1990	Soldiers and Innocents by Russell Celyn Jones
1991	O Caledonia by Elspeth Barker
1992	Halo by John Loveday
1993	Love Your Enemies by Nicola Barker
1994	The Longest Memory by Fred D'Aguilar

1995	Red Earth and Pouring Rain by Vikram Chandra
1996	The Cast Iron Shore by Linda Grant

William Hill Sports Book of the Year
Greenside House, Station Road
Wood Green, London N22 4TP, England
Sponsored by bookmakers William Hill, this is the UK's only annual sports book award. All books must be published in the UK during the year in question.
Prize: First prize: £5000 cash prize, £500 free bet with William Hill, and specially-bound copy of the book; various runners-up prizes.
Contact: Graham Sharpe

1995	A Good Walk Spoiled by John Feinstein
1996	Dark Trade by Colin McRae

Historical Novel Prize in Memory of Georgette Heyer
The Bodley Head, Random Century
20 Vauxhall Bridge Road
London SW1V 2SA, England
Awarded for full length previously unpublished historical novel set before 1939.
Annual prize of £5000.
Contact: Mrs J Black

1980	Children of Hachiman by Lynn Guest
1981	Zemindar by Valerie Fitzgerald
1982	No prize awarded
1983	Queen of the Lightning by Kathleen Herbert
1984	The Terioki Crossing by Alan Fisher
1985	Legacy by Susan Kay
1986	I Am England by Patricia Wright
1987	No prize awarded
1988	Trust and Treason by Margaret Birkhead
1989	A Fallen Land by Janet Broomfield

Richard Imison Memorial Award
Society of Authors
84 Drayton Gardens
London SW10 9SB, England
Designed to encourage talent and help maintain high standards, this award is given for the best work of radio drama, as judged by the Society of Authors Broadcasting Committee. Works must be original, the first dramatic work by the author(s) to be broadcast, and must be written specifically for radio (adaptions for works orginally intended for stage, film or television are not eligible).
Prize: £1000

1996	I Love U Jimmy Spud by Lee Hall

Ingersoll Prizes
Ingersoll Foundation, 934 N Main Street
Rockford, IL 61103, USA
T S Eliot Award for Creative Writing
For fiction, drama, poetry, essays & literary criticism.
Annual cash prize.
Richard M Weaver Award for Scholarly Letters
For a lifetime of distinguished achievements in the humanities.
Annual cash prize.

International IMPAC Dublin Literary Award
Dublin City Public Libraries

Cumberland House, Fenian Street
Dublin 2, Ireland
Awarded by an international panel of judges for a work of fiction judged to be of 'high literary merit' and published in English, either originally or in translation, during the qualifying period. Books are nominated by selected libraries in capital and major cities around the world. The award is sponsored by the managerial consultancyc company IMPAC, and administred by Dublin City Public Libraries.
Prize: IR£100,000 (shared between author and translator if the winning book is in English translation).
Contact: Brendan Teeling
1996   Remembering Babylon by David Malouf

Irish Times International Fiction Prize
Irish Times Ltd
10-16 D'Olier Street
Dublin 2, Ireland
The winners are chosen from nominations from critcis and editors. Submissions are not required. Awarded biennially since 1989 to the author of a work of fiction written in English, published in Ireland, the Uk or the US in the two years of the award.
Prize: IR£7500.
Contact: Gerard Cavanagh, Administrator, Book Prizes.
1989   Libra by Don DeLillo
1990   Possession by A S Byatt
1991   Wartime Lies by Louis Begley
1992   Mating by Norman Rush
1993   The Shipping News by Annie Proulx

Irish Times Irish Literature Prize
Irish Times Ltd
10-16 D'Olier Street
Dublin 2, Ireland
Established in 1989, three biennial prizes are awarded for works of fiction, non-fiction and poetry written by an author born in Ireland or an Irish citizen. Books are nominated by critics and editors - no submissions required.
Prize: IR£5000 for each category.
Contact: Gerard Cavanagh, Administrator, Book Prizes.
1989   The Men Who Loved Evelyn Cotton by Frank Ronan
1990   Amongst Women by John McGahern (fiction)
        Belfast Confetti by Ciaran Carson
1991   Ireland 1912-1985 by J J Lee (non-fiction)
        The South by Colm Toibin (first book)
1992   The Butcher Boy by Patrick McCabe (fiction)
        Selected Poems by Derek Mahon (poetry)
1993   An Evil Cradling by Brian Keenan (non-fiction)
        The Fallen and Other Stories by John MacKenna (first book)

Jerusalem Prize
Binyaney Ha'ooma
POB 6001

Jerusalem 91060,
Israel
The prestigious prize is awarded to a writer whose work expresses the idea of "the freedom of the individual in society".

Jewish Quarterly Literary Prizes
The Jewish Quarterly
PO Box 2078
London W1A 1JR, England
Formerly the H H Wingate Prize. Books must be published in English in the UK during the year of the award. Submissions should be of literary merit and stimulate an interest in and awareness of themes of Jewish concern. Authors must be citizens or residents of the UK, Ireland, the Commonwealth or South Africa.
Prizes: £4000 each for fiction and non-fiction categories, awarded during Jewish Book Week in February, plus expenses to attend the Jerusalem Book Fair.
Contact: Mr Gerald Don.

Kalinga Prize
c/o UNESCO
7 Place de Fontenoy
75352 Paris 07 SP, France
Awarded to popularizers of science with distinguished careers as writers, editors, lecturers, directors or producers. The winner is expected to have an understanding of science and technology, and an awareness of the scientific work of the UN and UNESCO.
Annual prize of £1000
Contact: V Zharov, Director
1980   Aristide Bastidas (Venezuela)
1981   David Attenborough (UK)
        Dennis Flanagan (USA)
1982   Oswaldo Frota-Pessoa (Brazil)
1983   Abdullah Al Muti Sharafuddin (Bangladesh)
1984   Yves Coppens (France)
        Igor Petryanov (USSR)
1985   Sir Peter Medawar (UK)
1986   Nicolai Basov (USSR)
        David Suzuki (Canada)
1987   Marcel Roche (Venezuela)
1988   Björn Kurtén (Finland)
1989   Saad Ahmed Shabaan (Egypt)
1990   Misbah-Ud-Din Shami (Pakistan)
1991   Radu Iftimovici (Romania)
        Narender Sehgal (India)
1992   Jorge Flores Valdés (Mexico)
        Peter Okebukola (Nigeria)
1993   Piero Angela (Italy)
1994   Nikolai Drozdov (Russia)
1995   Julieta Fierro Gossman (Mexico)

Gerald Lampert Award
League of Canadian Poets,
24 Ryerson Avenue
Toronto, Ontario N5T 2P3,
Canada

Harold Morton Landon Translation Award
Academy of American Poets
584 Broadway, Suite 1208

New York, NY 10012, USA
Awarded to the translator of a published translation of poetry from any language into English. Publishers may submit eligible books. Annual prize of $1000.

1976 Robert Fitzgerald for the Iliad of Homer
1978 Galway Kinnell for The Poems of François Villon
Howard Norman for The Wishing Bone Cycle
1980 Saralyn R Daly for The Book of True Love by Juan Ruis
Edmund Keeley for Ritsos in Parenthesis
1982 Rika Lesser for Guide to the Underworld by Gunnar Ekelöf
1984 Robert Fitzgerlad for The Odyssey of Homer
Stephen Mitchell for The Selected Poetry of Rainer Maria Rilke
1985 Edward Snow for New Poems (1907) or Rainer Maria Rilke
1986 William Arrowsmith for The Storm and Other Things by Eugenio Montale
1987 Mark Anderson for In the Storm of Roses by Ingeborg Bachmann
1988 Peter Hargitai for Perched on Nothing's Branch by Attila József
1989 Martin Greenberg for Heinrich von Kleist: Five Plays
1990 Stephen Mitchell for Variable Directions by Dan Pagis
1991 Robert Fagles for The Iliad of Homer
1992 John DuVal for The Discovery of America by Cesare Pascarella
Andrew Schelling for Dropping the Bow: Poems of Ancient India
1993 Charles Simic for The Horse Has Six Legs: An Anthology of Serbian Poetry
1994 Rosmarie Waldrop for The Book of Margins by Edmond Jabès
1995 Robert Pinsky for The Inferno of Dante: A New Verse Translation
1996 Guy Davenport for 7 Greeks

James Laughlin Award
(formerly the Lamont Poetry Selection)
Academy of American Poets,
584 Broadway, Suite 1208
New York, NY 10012, USA
Supports the publication of an American poet's second volume of poetry. Only manuscripts already under contract with publishers are considered. Publishers are invited to submit manuscripts by American poets who have already published one book of poems in a standard edition. Annual prize of $5000.

1954 The Middle Voice by Constance Carrier
1955 Exiles and Marriages by Donald Hall
1956 Letter from a Distant Land by Philip Booth
1957 Time Without Number by Daniel Berrigan
1958 The Night of the Hammer by Ned O'Gorman
1959 The Summer Aniversaries by Donald Justice
1960 The Lovemaker by Robert Mezey
1961 Nude Descending a Satircase by X J Kennedy
1962 Stand Up, Friend, With Me by Edward Field
1963 No award given
1964 Heroes, Advise Us by Adrien Stoutenberg
1965 The War of the Secret Agents by Henri Coulette
1966 The Distance Anywhere by Kenneth O Hanson
1967 The Marches by James Scully
1968 The Weather of Six Mornings by Jane Cooper
1969 A Probable Volume of Dreams by Marvin Bell
1970 Treasury Holiday by William Harmon
1971 Concurring Beasts by Stephen Dobyns
1972 Collecting the Animals by Peter Everwine
1973 Presentation Piece by Marilyn Hacker
1974 After Our War by John Balaban
1975 The Private Life by Lisel Mueller
1976 The Afterlife by Larry Levis
1977 Lucky Life by Gerald Stern
1978 Killing Floor by Ai
1979 Sunrise by Frederick Seidel
1980 More Trouble with the Obvious by Michael Van Walleghen
1981 The Country Between Us by Carolyn Forché
1982 Long Walks in the Afternoon by Margaret Gibson
1983 The Dead and the Living by Sharon Olds
1984 Deep Within the Ravine by Philip Schultz
1985 Victims of the Latest Dance Craze by Cornelius Eady
1986 The Minute Hand by Jane Shore
1987 The River of Heaven by Garret Kaoru
1988 Unfinished Painting by Mary Jo Salter
1989 Crime Against Nature by Minnie Bruce Pratt
1990 The City in Which I Love You by Li-Young Lee
1991 Campo Santo by Susan Wood
1992 Wildwood Flower by Kathleen Stripling Byer
1993 Stained Glass by Rosanna Warren
1994 Song by Brigit Pegeen Kelly
1995 Neither World by Ralph Angel
1996 Wise Poison by David Rivard

Grace Leven Prize for Poetry
c/o Perpetual Trustee Company Ltd
39 Hunter Street,
Sydney, NSW 2000, Australia
For recognition of the best volume of poetry published during the twelve months immediately preceding the year in which the award is made. Writers must be Australian-born and writing as Australians, or naturalised in Australia and resident in Australia for not less than ten years. Annual prize of Australian $200.

Ruth Lilly Poetry Prize
c/o Poetry
Modern Poetry Association
60 West Walton Street
Chicago, IL 60610, USA

Given to a US poet whose accomplishments warrant extraordinary recognition.
Annual prize of $75,000

1986	Adrienne Rich
1987	Philip Levine
1988	Anthony Hecht
1989	Mona Van Duyn
1990	Hayden Carruth
1991	David Wagoner
1992	John Ashbery
1993	Charles Wright
1994	Donald Hall
1995	A R Ammons
1996	Gerald Stern

Lloyds Private Banking Playwright of the Year Award

Tony Ball Associates plc
174-178 North Gower Street
London NW1 2NB, England
Awarded since 1994 to encourage new and diverse playwrighting, broadening support for the theatre and extending the links between Lloyds Private Banking and the Arts.Playwrights should be British or Irish, whose new works have been performed in the UK or Republic of Ireland for the first time in the previous year. Nominations by theatre critics form a shortlist, with winners chosen by a panel of judges.
Prize: £25,000
Contact: Stephen Harrison / Melissa Jones

1994	Dead Funny by Terry Johnson
1995	The Steward of Christendom by Sebastian Barry

Los Angeles Times Book Prizes

Los Angeles Times
Times Mirror Square
Los Angeles, CA 90053, USA

Agnes Mure Mackenzie Award

Saltire Society
9 Fountain Close, 22 High Street
Edinburgh EH1 1TF, Scotland
Awarded every third year since 1965 for a published work of Scottish historical research of scholarly importance. Nominations are invited.
Prize: Cash prize, plus a bound and inscribed copy of the winning publication.
Contact: Mrs Kathleen Munro, Administrator

Mail on Sunday / John Llewellyn Rhys Prize

Book Trust
Book House, 45 East Hill
London SW18 2QZ, England
Awarded for a work of fiction, non-fiction or poetry by an author under 35 at time of publication. Books must have been published in the UK in the year of the award in English by a citizen of Britain or the Commonwealth. Sponsored by the Mail on Sunday.
Annual First prize of £5000; £500 for shortlisted entries.
Contact: Sandra Vince

1980	The Diamonds at the Bottom of the Sea by Desmond Hogan
1981	The Laird of Abbotsford by A N Wilson
1982	An Ice-Cream War by William Boyd

1983	The Slow Train to Milan by Lisa St Aubin de Teran
1984	Dangerous Play by Andrew Motion
1985	Out of the Blue by John Milne
1986	Loving Roger by Tim Parks
1987	The Passion by Jeanette Winterson
1988	The March Fence by Matthew Yorke
1989	Sylvia Townsend Warner by Claire Harman
1990	Wittgenstein: The Duty of Genius by Ray Monk
1991	Night Geometry and the Garscadden Trains by A L Kennedy
1992	Sweet Thames by Matthew Kneale
1993	On Foot to the Golden Horn: A Walk to Istanbul by Jason Goodwin
1994	What A Carve Up! by Jonathan Coe
1995	Motel Nirvana by Melanie McGarth

Marsh Award for Children's Literature in Translation

Authors' Club
40 Dover Street
London W1X 3RB, England
Sponsored by the Marsh Christian Trust to encourage the translation of foreign children's books into English. Awarded biennially, starting in 1996, to British translators of books for 4-16 year olds, published in the UK by a British publisher. No encyclopaedias, reference works or electronic books.
Prize £750
Contact: Ann Carter, Secretary

1996	Anthea Bell for A Dog's Life by Christine Nöstlinger

Marsh Biography Award

(formerly Marsh Christian Trust Award)
Authors' Club
40 Dover Street
London W1X 3RB, England
Awarded biennialy for a significant biography by a British author, published in the UK in the two years prior to the prize. Nominations submitted by publishers.
Prize: £3500 plus a silver trophy
Contact: Ann Carter, Secretary

1987	Shackleton by Roland Huntford
1989	The Last Leopard: A Life of Lampedusa by David Gilmour
1991	Clever Hearts: The Life of Desmond and Molly MacCarthy by Hugh and Mirabel Cecil
1993	The Man Who Wasn't Maigret by Patrick Marnham
1995	Evelyn Waugh by Lady Selina Hastings

Lenore Marshall Poetry Prize

Academy of American Poets
584 Broadway, Suite 1208
New York, NY 10012, USA
Recognizes the most outstanding book of poetry published in the US in the previous year. Publishers are invited to submit books.
Annual prize of $10,000

1974	O/I by Cid Corman
1975	The Freeing of the Dust by Denise

Levertov
1976 The Names of the Lost by Philip Levine
1977 Collected Poems, 1919-1976 by Allen Tate
1978 Brothers, I Loved You All by Hayden Carruth
1979 The Poems of Stanley Kunitz,1928-1978 by Stanley Kunitz
1980 The Collected Poems of Sterling A Brown by Sterling A Brown
1981 The Bridge of Change: Poems 1974-1980 by John Logan
1982 The Argot Merchant Disaster by George Starbuck
1983 Collected Poems, 1930-83 by Josephine Miles
1984 A Wave by John Ashbery
1985 New Selected Poems by Howard Moss
1986 The Happy Man by Donald Hall
1987 The Sisters: New and Selected Poems by Josephine Jacobsen
1988 Selected Poems, 1938-1988 by Thomas McGrath
1989 God Hunger by Michael Ryan
1990 New Poems, 1980-1988 by John Haines
1991 An Atlas of the Difficult World by Adrienne Rich
1992 The Man with Night Sweats by Thom Gunn
1993 Travels by W S Merwin
1994 Winter Numbers by Marilyn Hacker
1995 Chickamauga by Charles Wright

Kurt Maschler Award
Book Trust
Book House, 45 East Hill
London SW18 2QZ, England
Annual award for works of excellence in the field of illustrated children's literature. Books must be published in the UK, and the author must be British or have been resdident in the UK for ten years.
Prize: £1000 and a bronze 'Emil' statuette.
Contact: Sandra Vince
1996 Drop Dead by Babette Cole

Somerset Maugham Awards
Somerset Maugham Trust Fund
Society of Authors
84 Drayton Gardens
London SW10 9SB, England
Awarded to a writer on the strength of a published work.
Prize: £5000 each to be used for foreign travel.
1980 The Inklings by Humphrey Carpenter
Bomer Command by Max Hastings
Arcadia by Christopher Reid
1981 Metroland by Julian Barnes
The Healing Art by A N Wilson
Hearts of Gold by Clive Sinclair
1982 Lantern Lecture & Other Stories by Adam Mars-Jones
A Good Man in Africa by William Boyd
1983 Keepers of the House by Lisa St Aubin de Teran
1984 The Last Testament of Oscar Wilde by Peter Ackroyd
The Polish Revolution: Solidarity by

Timothy Garton Ash
The Indoor Park by Sean O'Brien
1985 Dark Glasses by Blake Morrison
By the Fisheries by Jeremy Reed
Her Living Image by Jane Rogers
1986 Family Myths and Legends by Patricia Ferguson
Frontiers by Adam Nicolson
Tongues of Flame by Tim Parks
1987 The Cormorant by Stephen Gregory
Issac Campion by Janni Howker
The Lamberts by Andrew Motion
1988 The Land that Lost its Heroes by Jimmy Burns
Selling Manhattan by Carol Ann Duffy
Whore Banquets by Matthew Kneale
1989 Romantic Affinities by Rupert Christiansen
The Swimming Pool Library by Alan Hollinghurst
The Birds of the Innocent Wood by Deirdre Madden
1990 Our Grandmothers' Drums by Mark Hudson
The Automatic Man by Sam North
The Vision of Elena Silves by Nicholas Shakespeare
1991 The Other Occupant by Peter Benson
Honour Thy Father by Lesley Glaister
Four Bare Legs in a Bed by Helen Simpson
1992 But Beautiful by Geoff Dyer
Lempriere's Dictionary by Lawrence Norfolk
Householder by Gerard Woodward
1993 Jella by Dea Birkett
Bucket of Tongues by Duncan McLean
Out of the Rain by Glyn Maxwell
1994 Other Lovers by Jackie Kay
Looking for the Impossible Dance by A L Kennedy
The Crossing Place by Philip Marsden
1995 Younghusband by Patrick French
The End of Innocence by Simon Garfield
The Quenn of Sheba by Kathleen Jamie
The Dogs by Laura Thompson
1996 Truffle Beds by Katherine Pierpoint
Morven Callar by Alan Warner

McColvin Medal
c/o Library Association
7 Ridgmount Street
London WC1E 7AE, England
The winner is chosen from nominations made by Library Association members. A medal is awarded to an outstanding reference book first published in the UK during the preceding year.
1980 Guide to the Local Administrative Units of England Volume I: Southern England by Frederic A Youngs
1981 The New Grove Dictionary of Music and Musicians by Stanley Sadie (editor)
1982 The Dictionary of Blue and White Printed Pottery 1780-1880 by A W Coysh & R K Henrywood
1983 Dictionary of British Book Illustrators: The Twentieth Century by Brigid Peppin

	& Lucy Micklethwait
1984	The History of Glass by D Klein & W Lloyd (general editors)
1985	The Artist's Craft: A History of Tools,Techniques and Material by James Ayres
1986	The British Musical Theatre Volume I: 1865-1914 Volume II: 1915-1984 by Kurt Ganzl
1987	Fermented Foods of the World: A Dictionary & Guide by Geoffrey Campbell-Platt
1988	The Encyclopaedia of Oxford by Christopher Hibbert (editor)
1989	The Oxford English Dictionary Second Edition by John Simpson & Edmund Weiner (editors)
1990	William Walton: A Catalogue Second Edition by Stewart Craggs
1991	The Cambridge Encyclopaedia of Ornithology by Michael Brooke & Tim Birkhead
1992	The New Grove Dictionary of Opera by Stanley Sadie (editor)
1993	The Illustrated History of Canal and River Navigation by Edward Peget-Tomlinson

McKitterick Prize

Society of Authors
84 Drayton Gardens
London SW10 9SB, England
Annual award for a full-length work written in English and first published in the UK or previously unpublished. Open to writers over 40 who have had no previous work published other than that submitted.
Prize: £5000.

1990	Chimera by Simon Mawer
1991	A Summer to Halo by John Loveday
1992	News From a Foreign Country Came by Alberto Manguel
1993	The Tap Dancer by Andrew Barrow
1994	Zennor in Darkness by Helen Dunmore
1995	Hester by Christopher Bigsby
1996	Gagarin and I by Stephen Blanchard

Walter McRae Russell Award

Association for the Study of Australian Literature Ltd
c/o English Department,
University College, ADFA
Campbell, ACT 2600, Australia
Contact: Susan Lever
Awarded for an outstanding work of literary scholarship by a young or unestablished author. No nominations are required.
Prize: $1000.

1983	Exiles at Home by Drusilla Modjeska
1984	The Archibald Paradox by Sylvia Lawson
1985	Wild Man of Letters by Craig Munro
1986	Unbridling the Tongues of Women by Susan Magary
1987	National Fictions by Graeme Turner
1988	The Road to Botany Bay by Paul Carter
1989	Christina Stead by Susan Sheridan
1990	Black Words, White Page by Adam Shoemaker

1991	The Folly of Spring : A Study of the Poetry of John Shaw Neilson by Cliff Hanna
1992	The Life and Opinions of Tom Collins by Julian Croft
1993	The Sea Coast of Bohemia by Peter Kirkpatrick
1994	Christina Stead by Hazel Rowley
1995	The Scandalous Penton by Patrick Buckridge
1996	In Search of Steele Rudd by Richard Fotheringham

Meyer-Whitworth Award

Drama Department, Arts Council of England
14 Great Peter Street,
London SW1P 3NQ, England
Established to commemorate the Shakespeare Memorial National Theatre (SMNT) Committee of 1908, where the movement for a National Theatre joined forces with the movement to create a monument to William Shakespare. Awarded to a playwright whose work displays promise of new talent, whose writing is of individual quality and whose work 'revals the truth about the relationships of human beings with each other and the world at large' (Geoffrey Whitworth).
Plays must be written in English and have been produced in the UK in the previous 12 months.
Contact: John Johnston

Milner Award

The Friends of the Atlanta Fulton Public Library
One Margaret Mitchell Square
Atlanta, GA 30303, USA
Award to a living American author of children's books.
The winning author is awarded a specially commissioned work of the internationally famous glass sculptor, Hans Frabel, and a $1000 honorarium.

1983	Judy Blume
1984	Peggy Parish
1985	Paula Danziger
1986	Barbara Park
1987	Lois Lowry
1988	Francine Pascal
1989	John Steptoe
1990	Louis Sachar
1991	Marc Brown
1992	Barthe DeClements
1993	Matt Christopher
1994	Joanna Cole

Mitchell Prize for Art History / Eric Mitchell Prize

c/o The Burlington Magazine
14-16 Duke's Road
London WC1H 9AD, England
The Mitchell Prize is awarded for an outstanding and original contribution to the undertsanding of the visual arts, and the Eric Mitchell Prize is given for the best first book in this field. Books must be written in English, and published in the previous twleve months.
Prizes: Mitchell Prize for Art History: $15,000; Eric Mitchell Prize: $5000.
Contact: Caroline Elam, Executive Director

Mitchell Prize for Art History

1995	Colour and Culture by John Gage
1996	Roubiliac and the Eighteenth Century Monument: Sculpture As Theatre by David Bindman and Malcolm Baker

Eric Mitchell Prize

1995	Fra Angelico at San Marco by William Hood
1996	Giorgio Vasari: Art and History by Patricia Lee Rubin

National Book Awards

NBA Foundation
260 Fifth Avenue, 4th Floor
New York, NY 10001, USA
Award given annually to living American writers of books published in the USA. Categories for fiction, non-fiction and poetry.
Annual first prize of $10,000 and $1000 for short-listed works.
Contact: Executive Director

1986	Arctic Dreams by Barry Lopez
	World's Fair by E L Doctorow
1987	Paco's Story by Larry Heinemann
	The Making of the Atomic Bomb by Richard Rhodes
1988	Paris Trout by Pete Dexter
	A Bright and Shining Lie: John Paul Vann America in Vietnam by Neil Sheehan
1989	Spartina by John Casey
	From Beirut to Jerusalem by Thomas L Friedman
1990	Middle Passage by Charles Johnson
	The House of Morgan by Ron Chernow
1991	Mating by Norman Rush
	Freedom by Orlando Patterson
	What Work is by Philip Levine
1992	All the Pretty Horses by Cormac McCarthy
	Becoming A Man by Paul Monette
	New and Selected Poems by Mary Oliver
1993	The Shipping News by E Annie Proulx
	United States: Essays 1952-1992 by Gore Vidal
	Garbage by A R Ammons
1994	A Frolic of His Own by William Gaddis
	Worshipful Company of Fletchers by James Tate
	How We Die by Sherwin B Nuland
1995	Ship Fever and Other Stories by Andrea Barrett
	An American Requiem: God, My Father and the War That Came Between Us by James Carroll
1991-	Scrambled Eggs and Whiskey: Poems, 1995 by Hayden Carruth

National Book Critics Circle Awards

400 North Broad Street
Philadelphia, PA 19103, USA
For excellence in biography/autobiography, criticism, fiction, general nonfiction and poetry published for the first time during the previous year by American writers.
Annual scroll and citations.

1980	The Transit of Venus by Shirley Hazzard
	Sunrise by Frederick Seidel

	Walter Lippmann and the American Century by Ronald Steel
	Part of Nature, Part of Us: Modern American Poets by Helen Vendler
1981	Rabbit is Rich by John Updike
	A Coast of Trees by A R Ammons
	The Mismeasure of Man of Stephan Jay Gould
	A Virgil Thomson Reader by Virgil Thomson
1982	George Mills by Stanley Elkin
	Antarctic Traveller by Katha Pollitt
	The Path to Power: The Years of Lyndon Johnson by Robert A Caro
	The Second American Revolution and Other Essays 1976-82 by Gore Vidal
	12-volume edition of Byron's Letters and Journals by Leslie A Marchand
1983	Ironweed by William Kennedy
	The Price of Power: Kissinger in the Nixon White House by Seymour M Hersh
	Minor Characters by Joyce Johnson
	The Changing Light at Sandover by James Merrill
	Hugging the Shore: Essays and Criticism by John Updike
1984	Love Medicine by Louise Erdrich
1859	Dostoevsky: The Years of Ordeal 1850- by Joseph Frank
	Twentieth Century Pleasures by Robert Hass
	Weapons and Hope by Freeman Dyson
	The Dead and the Living by Sharon Olds
1985	The Accidental Tourist by Anne Tyler
	The Triumph of Achilles by Louise Gluck
	Henry James: A Life by Leon Edel
	Common Ground by J Anthony Lukas
	Habitations of the Word by William Gass
1986	Tombee: Portrait of a Cotton Planter by Theodore Rosengarten
	Less Than One: Selected Essays by Joseph Brodsky
	Kate Vaiden by Reynolds Price
	War Without Mercy: Race and Power in the Pacific War by John W Dower
	Wild Gratitude by Edward Hirsch
1987	Chaucer: His Life, His Works, His World by Donald Howard
	Dance Writings by Edwin Denby
	The Making of the Atomic Bomb by Richard Rhodes
	The Counterlife by Philip Roth
	Flesh and Blood by C K Williams
1988	The Middleman and Other Stories by Bharati Mukherjee
	The One Day by Donald Hall
	Oscar Wilde by Richard Ellmann
	Parting the Waters by Taylor Branch
	Work and Lives by Clifford Geertz
1989	Billy Bathgate by E L Doctorow
	The Broken Cord by Michael Dorris
	A First-Class Temperament by Geoffrey C Ward
	Not by Fact Alone by John Clive
1990	Bitter Angel by Amy Gerstler
	The Content of Our Character by Shelby Steele

Encounters and Reflections by Arthur Danto
Means of Ascent by Robert Caro
Rabbit at Rest by John Updike
Transparent Gestures by Rodney Jones

1993 All the Pretty Horses by Cormack McCarthy
Young Men and Fire by Norman Maclean
Collected Poems, 1946-91 by Hayden Carruth
Lincoln at Gettysburg by Gary Wills
Writing Dangerously: Mary McCarthy and Carol Brightman

1994 Opera in America by John Dizikes
Genet by Edmund White
My Alexandria by Mark Doty
A Lesson Before Dying by Ernest J Gaines
The Land Where the Blues Began by Alan Lomax

1995 The Stone Diaries by Carol Shields
The Rape of Europe: The Fate of Europe's Treasures in the Third Reich and the Second World War by Lunn H Nicholas
The Culture of Bruising: Essays on Prizefighting. Literature and Modern American Culture by Gerald Early
Shot in the Heart by Mikal Gilmore
Rider by Mark Rudman

1996 Women in Their Beds by Gina Berriault
Angela's Ashes by Frank McCourt
Bad Land: An American Romance by Jonathan Raban
Finding a Form by William Gass
Sun Under Wood by Robert Hass

National Poetry Competition

The Poetry Society,
22 Betterton Street,
London WC2H 9BU, England
Prizes awarded for an unpublished poem of less than 40 lines by anyone over the age of 16.
Prizes: £3000 (1st); £500 (2nd); £250 (3rd); plus smaller prizes.
Contact: Competition Organizer, Betty Redpath.

1985 Jo Shapcott
Ian Keenan
William Palmer
1986 Carole Satyamuri
Adam Thorpe
Bill Turner
1987 Ian Duhig
Michael Donaghy
Harry Smart
1988 Martin Reed
Ian Caws
Rodney Pybus
1989 William Scammell
Patricia Pogson
Glyn Maxwell
1990 Nicky Rice
Frances Wilson
Geoffrey Constable
1991 John Levett
Jo Shapcott
Don Paterson

1992 Steve Knight
Steve Watts
Catherine Byron

NCR Book Award for Non-Fiction

NCR Limited
206 Marylebone Road, London NW1 6LY, England
The UK's major prize for non-fiction was first awarded in 1988, and is open to books published between 1st April and 31st March, prizes being awarded in May. Books must be written in English by citizens of the UK, Republic of Ireland or the Commonwealth, and published in the UK.
Total prize money of £37,500.
Contact: Awards Administrator.

1988 Nairn: In Darkness and Light by David Thomson
1989 Touching the Void by Joe Simpson
1990 Citizens by Simon Schama
1991 The Invisible Woman by Claire Tomalin
1992 Wild Swans by Jung Chang
1993 Never Again: Britain 1945-1951 by Peter Hennessy
1994 Edward Heath: A Biography by John Campbell
1995 Coming Back Brockens by Mark Hudson
1996 The Railway Man by Eric Lomax

Neustadt International Prize for Literature

World Literature Today,
University of Oklahoma
110 Monnet Hall
Norman, OK 73019, USA
Recognizes outstanding achievement in fiction, poetry, or drama written in any language. Awarded only to a living author who has a representative portion of work in English, French and/or Spanish.
No applications are accepted.
Biennial prize of $40,000, a replica of an eagle feather cast in silver and a special award certificate.

1970 Giuseppe Ungaretti
1972 Gabriel García Márquez
1974 Francis Ponge
1976 Elizabeth Bishop
1978 Czesław Miłosz
1980 Josef Škvorecký
1982 Octavio Paz
1984 Paavo Haavikko
1986 Max Frisch
1988 Raja Rao
1990 Tomas Tranströmer
1992 João Cabral de Melo Neto
1994 Kamau Brathwaite
1996 Assia Djebar

New Venture Award

Women In Publishing
12 Dyott Street
London WC1A 1DF, England
Contact: Sheila Davies
1996 Rosemary Meleady, Big Issues

John Newbery Medal

American Library Association,
50 East Huron Street
Chicago, IL 70711, USA
To the author of the most distinguished contribution

to American literature for children published during the preceding year.

Annual award: bronze medal

Contact: The Administrator

1980	A Gathering of Days by Joan W Blos
1981	Jacob Have I Loved by Katherine Paterson
1982	A Visit to William Blake's Inn: Poems for Innocent and Experienced Travellers by Nancy Willard
1983	Dicey's Song by Cynthia Voight
1984	Dear Mr Henshaw by Beverly Cleary
1985	Hero and the Crown by Robin McKinley
1986	Sarah, Plain and Tall by Patricia MacLachlan
1987	The Whipping Boy by Sid Fleischman
1988	Lincoln: A Photobiography by Russell Freedman
1989	Joyful Noise: Poems for Two Voices by Paul Fleischman
1990	Number the Stars by Lois Lowry
1991	Maniac Magee by Terry Spinelli
1992	Shiloh by Phyllis Reynolds Naylor
1993	Missing May by Cynthia Rylant
1994	The Giver by Lois Lowry
1995	Walk Two Moons by Sharon Creech

Nobel Prize for Literature

Swedish Academy
Box 5232, Sturegatan 14
S-10245 Stockholm, Sweden

One of several celebrated prizes for outstanding achievement in various fields, founded by the chemist Alfred Nobel. The prize in the field of literature has been awarded annually since 1901 in recognition of the literary merit of a distinguished writer in world letters. Nominations are not generally accepted, as strict eligibilty controls apply. The current value of the prize is US $1,120,000 (increasing each year to cover inflation).

1901	René-François-Armand Sully Prudhomme
1902	Theodor Mommsen
1903	Bjørnstjerne Bjørnson
1904	José Echegaray and Frédéric Mistral
1905	Henryk Sienkiewicz
1906	Giosué Carducci
1907	Rudyard Kipling
1908	Rudolf Eucken
1909	Selma Lagerlöf
1910	Paul Heyse
1911	Maurice Maeterlinck
1912	Gerhart Hauptmann
1913	Rabindranath Tagore
1914	No award given
1915	Romain Rolland
1916	Verner von Heidenstam
1917	Karl Kjellerup and Henrik Pontopiddan
1918	No award given
1919	Carl Spitteler
1920	Knut Hamsun
1921	Anatole France
1922	Jacinto Benavente y Martínez
1923	W B Yeats
1924	Władysław Reymont
1925	G B Shaw
1926	Grazia Deledda

1927	Henri Bergson
1928	Sigrid Undset
1929	Thomas Mann
1930	Sinclair Lewis
1931	Erik Axel Karlfeldt
1932	John Galsworthy
1933	Ivan Bunin
1934	Luigi Pirandello
1935	No award given
1936	Eugene O'Neill
1937	Roger Martin du Gard
1938	Pearl S Buck
1939	F E Sillianpää
1940-43	No award given
1944	Johannes V Jensen
1945	Gabriela Mistral
1946	Hermann Hesse
1947	André Gide
1948	T S Eliot
1949	William Faulkner
1950	Bertrand Russell
1951	Pär Lagerkvist
1952	François Mauriac
1953	Sir Winston Churchill
1954	Ernest Hemingway
1955	Halldór Laxness
1956	Juan Ramón Jiménez
1957	Albert Camus
1958	Boris Pasternak
1959	Salvatore Quasimodo
1960	Saint-John Perse
1961	Ivo Andric
1962	John Steinbeck
1963	Georgios Seferiades
1964	Jean-Paul Sartre
1965	Mikhail Sholokov
1966	S Y Agnon and Nelly Sachs
1967	Miguel Angel Asturias
1968	Yasunari Kawabata
1969	Samuel Beckett
1970	Aleksandr Solzhenitsyn
1971	Pablo Neruda
1972	Heinrich Böll
1973	Patrick White
1974	Eyvind Johnson and Harry Martinson
1975	Eugenio Montale
1976	Saul Bellow
1977	Vicente Aleixandre
1978	Isaac Bashevis Singer
1979	Odysseus Elytis
1980	Czesław Miłosz
1981	Elias Canetti
1982	Gabriel García Márquez
1983	William Golding
1984	Jaroslav Seifert
1985	Claude Simon
1986	Wole Soyinka
1987	Joseph Brodsky
1988	Naguib Mahfūz
1989	Camilo José Cela
1990	Octavio Paz
1991	Nadine Gordimer
1992	Derek Walcott
1993	Toni Morrison
1994	Kenzaburō Ōe
1995	Seamus Heaney
1996	Wisława Szymborska

Orange Prize For Fiction
Book Trust
Book House, 45 East Hill
London SW18 2QZ, England
Established in 1996, this annual award was founded by leading women in the publishing industry to help promote and reward women writers. Full-length novels written in English by women of any nationality between 1st April and 31st March are eligible.
Prize: £30,000, and limited edition bronze figurine known as the 'Bessie'.
Contact: Sandra Vince.
1996   A Spell of Winter by Helen Dunmore

Pandora Award
Women in Publishing
12 Dyott Street
London WC1A 1DF, England
Contact: Sheila Davies
1996   Dr Anita Miller, Academy Chicago Publishers

Francis Parkman Prize
Society of American Historians Inc
Affiliate of Columbia University
603 Fayerweather Hall
New York, NY 10027, USA

PEN/Faulkner Award for Fiction
Folger Shakespeare Library
201 East Capitol Street South East
Washington, DC 20003, USA

A A Phillips Prize
Association for the Study of Australian Literature Ltd
c/o English Department,
University College, ADFA
Campbell, ACT 2600, Australia
Contact: Susan Lever
Awarded from time to time for a work of outstanding achievement in the field of Australian literary scholarship.
1986   W H Wilde, Barry Andrews and Joy Hooton for the Oxford Companion to Australian Literature
1992   Laurie Hergenham for services to Australian literature as editor of Australian Literary Studies
1995   Judith Wright for her career as poet, critic and activist.
1996   Katharine Brisbane for her career as writer and publisher on Australian theatre and drama, especially for A Companion to Theatre in Australia.

Edgar Allan Poe Awards
Mystery Writers of America
174 East 47th Street
New York, NY 10017, USA

Prix Goncourt
Restaurant Drouant
18 Place Gaillon,
75002 Paris, France
1980   Le Jardin d'Acclimatation by Yves Navarre
1981   Anne Marie by Lucien Bodard
1982   Dans la Main de l'Ange by Dominique Fernandez
1983   Les Egares by Frederick Tristan
1984   L'Amant by Marguerite Duras
1985   Les Noces Barbares by Yann Queffelec
1986   Valet de Nuit by Michel Host
1987   La Nuit Sacrée Seuil by Tahar Ben Jelloun
1988   L'Exposition Coloniale Seuil by Erik Orsenna
1989   Un Grand Pas vers le Bon Dieu Grasset by Jean Vautrin
1990   Les Champs d'Honneur by Jean Rouaud
1991   Les Filles du Calvaire by Pierre Combescot
1992   Texaco by Patrick Chamoiseau
1993   Le Rocher de Tanios by Amin Maalouf
1994   Un Aller Simple by Didier Van Caulwelaert

Pulitzer Prizes
The Pulitzer Prize Board
702 Journalism, Columbia University
New York, NY 10027, USA
21 prizes in total for newspaper journalism, literature, music and drama - for some of the prizes entrants must be an American citizen.
Annual prize of $3000.
Contact: The Administrator
Fiction
1980   The Executioner's Song by Norman Mailer
1981   A Confederacy of Dunces by John Kennedy Toole
1982   Rabbit is Rich by John Updike
1983   The Color Purple by Alice Walker
1984   Ironweed by William Kennedy
1985   Foreign Affairs by Alison Lurie
1986   Lonesome Dove by Larry McMurtry
1987   A Summons to Memphis by Peter Taylor
1988   Beloved by Toni Morrison
1989   Breathing Lessons by Anne Tyler
1990   The Mambo Kings Play Songs of Love by Oscar Hijuelos
1991   Rabbit at Rest by John Updike
1992   A Thousand Acres by Jane Smiley
1993   A Good Scent From a Strange Mountain by Robert Olen Butler
1994   The Shipping News by E Annie Proulx
1995   The Stone Diaries by Carol Shields
1996   Independence Day by Richard Ford
Drama
1980   Talley's Folly by Lanford Wilson
1981   Crimes of the Heart by Beth Henley
1982   A Soldier's Play by Charles Fuller
1983   'Night, Mother by Marsha Norman
1984   Glengarry Glen Ross by David Mamet
1985   Sunday in the Park with George by Stephen Sondheim and James Lapine
1986   No prize awarded
1987   Fences by August Wilson
1988   Driving Miss Daisy by Alfred Uhry
1989   The Heidi Chronicles by Wendy Wasserstein
1990   The Piano Lesson by August Wilson

1991	Lost in Yonkers by Neil Simon
1992	The Kentucky Cycle: Millenium Approaches by Robert Schenkkan
1993	Angels in America by Tony Kushner
1994	Three Tall Women by Edward Albee
1995	The Young Man from Atlanta by Shelby Foote
1996	Rent by Jonathan Larson

History

1980	Been in the Storm So Long by Leon F Litwack
1981	American Education: The National Experience, 1783-1876 by Lawrence A Cremin
1982	Mary Chesnut's Civil War by C Vann Woodward (editor)
1983	The Transformation of Virginia, 1740-
1790	by Rhys L Isaac
1984	No award given
1985	Prophets of Regulation by Thomas K McCraw
1986	...The Heavens and the Earth: A Political History of the Space Age by Walter A McDougall
1987	Voyagers to the West: A Passage in the Peopling of America on the Eve of the Revolution by Bernard Bailyn
1988	The Launching of Modern American Science 1846-1876 by Robert V Bruce
1989	Parting the Waters: America in the King Years 1954-63 by Taylor Branch
1990	In Our Image: America's Empire in the Philippines by Stanley Karnow
1991	A Midwife's Tale: The Life of Martha Ballard, Based on Her Diary, 1785-1812 by Laurel Thatcher Ulrich
1992	The Fate of Liberty: Abraham Lincoln and Civil Liberties by Mark E Neely Jr
1993	The Radicalism of the American Revolution by Gordon S Wood
1994	No prize given
1995	No Ordinary Time: Franklin and Eleanor Roosevelt: The Home Front in World War II by Doris Kearns Goodwin
1996	William Cooper's Town: Power and Persuasion on the Frontier of the Early American Republic by Alan Taylor

Biography

1980	The Rise of Theodore Roosevelt by Edmund Morris
1981	Peter the Great: His Life and World by Robert K Massie
1982	Grant: A Biography by William S McFeely
1983	Growing Up by Russell Baker
1984	Booker T Washington: The Wizard of Tuskegee, 1901-1915 by Louis R Harlan
1985	The Life and Times of Cotton Mather by Kenneth Silverman
1986	Louise Bogan: A Portrait by Elizabeth Frank
1987	Bearing the Cross: Martin Luther King Jr and the Southern Christian Leadership Conference by David J Garrow
1988	Look Homeward: A Life of Thomas Wolfe by David Herbert Donald
1989	Oscar Wilde by Richard Ellmann
1990	Machiavelli in Hell by Sebastian de

	Grazia
1991	Jackson Pollock: An American Saga by Steven Naifeh and Gregory White Smith
1992	Fortunate Son: The Healing of a Vietnam Vet by Lewis B Puller Jr
1993	Truman by David McCullough
1994	W E B Du Bois: Biography of a Race,
1868-	1919 by David Levering Lewis
1995	Harriet Beecher Stowe: A Life by Joan D Hedrick
1996	God: A Biography by Jack Miles

Poetry

1980	Selected Poems by Donald Justice
1981	The Morning of the Poem by James Schuyler
1982	The Collected Poems by Sylvia Plath
1983	Selected Poems by Galway Kinnell
1984	American Primitive by Mary Oliver
1985	Yin by Carolyn Kizer
1986	The Flying Change by Henry Taylor
1987	Thomas and Beulah by Rita Dove
1988	Partial Accounts: New and Selected Poems by William Meredith
1989	New and Collected Poems by Richard Wilbur
1990	The World Doesn't End by Charles Simic
1991	Near Changes by Mona Van Duyn
1992	Selected Poems by James Tate
1993	The Wild Iris by Louise Glück
1994	Neon Vernacular by Yusef Komunyakaa
1995	Simple Truth by Philip Levine
1996	The Dream of the Unified Field by Jorie Graham

General Non-fiction

1980	Gödel, Escher, Bach: An Eternal Golden Braid by Douglas R Hofstadter
1981	Fin-de-Siècle Vienna: Politics and Culture by Carl E Schorske
1982	The Soul of a New Machine by Tracy Kidder
1983	Is There No Place on Earth for Me? by Susan Sheehan
1984	The Social Transformation of American Medicine by Paul Starr
1985	The Good War: An Oral History of World War II by Studs Terkel
1986	Move Your Shadow: South Africa, Black and White by Joseph Lelyveld
	Common Ground: A Turbulent Decade in the Lives of Three American Families by J Anthony Lukas
1987	Arab and Jew: Wounded Spirits in a Promised Land by David K Shipler
1988	The Making of the Atomic Bomb by Richard Rhodes
1989	A Bright Shining Lie: John Paul Vann and America in Vietnam by Neil Sheehan
1990	And Their Children After Them by Dale Maharidge
1991	The Ants by Bert Holldobler and Edward O Wilson
1992	The Prize: The Epic Quest for Oil, Money and Power by Daniel Yergin
1993	Lincoln at Gettysburg by Garry Wills
1994	Lenin's Tomb: The Last Days of the Soviet Empire by David Remnick
1995	The Beak of the Finch: A Story of

1996 | Evolution in Our Time by Jonathan Weiner
The Haunted Land: Facing Europe's Ghosts After Communism by Tina Rosenberg

Pushcart Prize: Best of the Small Presses
Pushcart Press
Box 380
Wainscott, NY 11975, USA
Annual award for work published by a small press or literary journal.

Queen's Presentation Medals - Poetry
Buckingham Palace
London, England
The Medal is given for a book of verse published in the English language, but translations of exceptional merit may be considered. It was originally awarded only to British citizens but the scope was widened in 1985 to make Her Majesty's subjects in Commonwealth Monarchies eligible for consideration.
Award: Gold Medal.
1981 Dennis Joseph Enwright
1985 Norman MacCaig
1988 Derek Walcott
1989 Allen Curnow
1990 Sorley Maclean

Raiziss/de Palchi Translation Award
Academy of American Poets
584 Broadway, Suite 1208
New York, NY 10012, USA
Recognizes outstanding translations of modern Italian poetry into English. A $5000 book prize is awarded and a $20,000 fellowship is awarded with the winner of the latter receiving a residency at the American Academy in Rome. No applications are accepted for the book prize. Submissions for the fellowship are accepted in odd-numbered years.
Fellowship
1996 Anthony Molino for Esercizi di tipologia by Valerio Magrelli
Book Prize
1996 W S Di Piero for This Strange Joy: Selected Poems of Sandro Penna

Rhea Award for the Short Story
Dungannon Foundation
131 East 66th Street
New York, NY 10021, USA

Rhône-Poulenc Prize for Science Books
COPUS, c/o The Royal Society
6 Carlton House Terrace
London SW1Y 5AG, England
Awarded to the authors of popular non-fiction, science and technology books, written in English and which are judged to contribute most to the public understanding of science.
Prize: Rhône-Poulenc Prize £10,000; Junior Prize £10,000.
Contact: Imelda M. Topping
1988 Living With Risk by the British Medical Association Board of Science
1989 Bones of Contention by Roger Lewin

1990 The Emperor's New Mind by Roger Penrose
1991 Wonderful Life by Stephen Jay Gould
Cells Are Us by Fran Balkwill & Mic Rolph
Cell Wars by Fran Balkwill & Mic Rolph
1992 The Rise and Fall of the Third Chimpanzee by Jared Diamond
The Amazing Voyage of the Cucumber Sandwich by Peter Rowan
How Nature Works by David Burnie
1993 The Making of Memory by Steven Rose
Mighty Microbes by Thompson Yardley
1994 The Language of the Genes by Steve Jones
Eyewitness Guide: Evolution by Linda Gamlin
Science with Weather by Rebecca Heddle and Paul Shipton
The Ultimate Dinosaur Book by David Lambert
1995 The Consumer's Good Chemical Guide by John Emsley
The Most Amazing Pop-Up Science Book by Jay Young
1996 Plague's Progress by Arno Karlen
The World of Weather by Chris Maynard

Romantic Novelists' Association
Romantic Novelists Association
3 Arnesby Lane, Peatling Magna
Leicester LE8 5UN England
Major Award
Awarded for the best romantic novel of the year, published betwqeen specifc dates set each year by the RNA. Open to non-members, but authors must be based in the UK.
Prize of £5000
Contact: Jean Chapman, Organiser
1982 Zemindar by Valerie Fitzgerald
Flint and Roses by Brenda Jagger
The Unreasoning Earth by Jean Chapman
A Countess Below Stairs by Eva Ibbotson
Emma Sparrow by Marie Joseph
Mango Walk by Rhona Martin
The Black Mountains by Janet Tanner
The Avonhurst Inheritance by Sylvia Thorpe
1983 Magic Flutes by Eva Ibbotson
Gemini Girls by Marie Joseph
Antigua Kiss by Anne Weale
Celebration by Rosie Thomas
Rose Domino by Sheila Walsh
The Ravensley Touch by Constance Heaven
1984 A Highly Respectable Marriage
Margaret Normanby by Josephine Edgar
Copper Kingdom by Iris Gower
A London Season by Anthea Bell
A Heritage of Shadows by Madeleine Brent
The Silver Falcon by Sarah Hylton
The Listening Silence by Marie Joseph
1985 Sunrise by Rosie Thomas
A Winter's Child by Brenda Jagger
Silk for a Lady by Rosina Pyatt

A Fragile Peace by Teresa Crane
The Merry Maid by Mollie Hardwick
What the Heart Keeps by Rosalind Laker
At the Going Down of the Sun by Elizabeth Darrell

1986 A Song Twice Over by Brenda Jagger
Kessie by Joyce Marlow
This Side of Christmas by Louise Elliott
Company of Swans by Eva Ibbotson
Here I Stay by Barbara Michaels
Silver Shadows, Golden Dreams by Margaret Pemberton
Rachael and the Viscount by Alanna Wilson

1987 A Better World Than This by Marie Joseph
Just You Wait and See by Stan Barstow
And in the Morning by Elizabeth Darrell
Lady of Hay by Barbara Erskine
The Lushai Girl by Roberta Forrest
Tree of Gold by Rosalind Laker
Jessica by Connie Monk

1988 The Juniper Bush by Audrey Howard
Destiny by Sally Beauman
The Lodestar by Pamela Belle
Distinctions of Class by Anita Burgh
The Raging Fire by Constance Heaven
The Silver Touch by Rosalind Laker
As It Was In the Beginning by Madeleine Pollard

1989 The Peacock's Feather by Sarah Woodhouse
Daughters of the Storm by Elizabeth Buchan
Dance of the Peacocks by Elizabeth de Guise
Spring Imperial by Evelyn Hart
The Shell Seekers by Rosamunde Pilcher
The Pink Stallion by Lucy Pinney

1990 Passing Glory by Reay Tannahill
1991 Phantom by Susan Kay
1992 Sandstorm by June Knox-Mawer
1993 Emily by Cynthia Harrod-Eagles
1994 Consider the Lily by Elizabeth Buchan
1995 A Change of Heart by Charlotte Bingham

Romantic Novelists Association New Writers Award

Romantic Novelists Association
Cobble Cottage, 129 New Street
Baddesley Ensor, nr Atherstone
Warwicks CV9 2DL, England
Awarded for unpublished writers in the field of the romantic novel. Manuscripts submitted for this prize must be specifically entered for it.
Contact: Joyce Bell, Secretary

Rooney Prize for Irish Literature

Strathlin, Templecarrig
Delgany, County Wicklow
Republic of Ireland
A non-competitive prize to reward and encourage young Irish talent. Writers must be Irish, under 40 years of age, and their work must be written in Irtish or English. No applications are accepted - recipients are chosen by a panel of judges. Special awards are given on rare occasions where deemed of merit.
Prize: £5000
Contact: Barbara Norman

Rooney Prize for Irish Literature

1980	Bernard Farrell
1981	Neil Jordan
1982	Medbh McGuckian
1983	Dorothy Nelson
1984	Ronan Sheehan
1985	Frank McGuinness
1986	Paul Mercier
1987	Deirdre Madden
1988	Glenn Patterson
1989	Robert McLiam Wilson
1990	Mary Dorcey
1991	Anne Enright
1992	Hugo Hamilton
1993	Gerard Fanning
1994	Colum McCAnn
1995	Philip MacCann

Special Awards

1982	Sean O'Tuama and Thomas Kinsella
1987	Tim Robinson
1995	Vona Groarke and Conor O'Callaghan

Royal Society of Literature Award Under the W H Heinemann Bequest

Royal Society of Literature
1 Hyde Park Gardens
London W2 2LT, England
Up to three awards given annually to encourage genuine contributions to literature. Awarded for any kind of literary works, written in English and published in the previous year and submitted by publishers.
Prize: £5000
Contact: The Secretary

1979	The Older Hardy by Robert Gittings
	Live Bait by Frank Tuohy
1980	Beckford of Fonthill by Brian Fothergill
	Moortown by Ted Hughes
1981	The Unquiet Heart by Robert Martin Tennyson
	Seeing the World by Dick Davis
1982	Harold Nicolson: A Biography by James Leigh Milne
	Old Glory by Jonathan Raban
1983	The Fortunate Traveller by Derek Walcott
1984	Eleeni by Nicholas Gage
1985	Secrets of a Woman's Life: The Latter Life of Ivy Compton-Burnett by Hilary Spurling
	T S Eliot by Peter Ackroyd
1986	The Black Robe by Brian Moore
1987	The Blind Watchmaker by Richard Dawkins
1988	The Russian Album by Michael Ignatieff
1989	Elizabeth Barrett Browning by Margaret Forster
1990	Ford Madox by Alan Judd
1991	Available for Dreams by Roy Fuller
	Short Afternoons by Kit Wright
1992	Goethe: The Spirit and the Age by Nicholas Boyle
1993	Shylock by John Gross
1994	The Civilisation of Europe in the

Renaissance by John Hale

1995 Young Husband by Patrick French
Give Me Your Hand by Paul Durcan
The Handless Maiden by Vicky Feaver

Sagittarius Prize
Society of Authors
84 Drayton Gardens
London SW10 9SB, England
Establisehd in 1990, and awarded for first published novels by authors over the age of 60.
Prize: £2000.

1991 The Sea Has Many Voices by Judith Hubback
1992 Parnell and the English by Hugh Leonard
1993 The Strange Case of Mademoiselle P by Brian O'Doherty
1994 Red Branch by G B Hummer
1995 Gravity is Getting Me Down by Fred Plisner
1996 As Luck Would Have It by Samuel Lock

Saltire Society / Scotsman Scottish Literary Awards
9 Fountain Close, 22 High Street
Edinburgh EH1 1TF, Scotland
Established in 1982, the Scottish Book of the Year award is open to authors of Scottish descent or those living in Scotland, or for a book which deals with a Scottish topic. Books published between 1st September and 31st August are eligible. Since 1988, the award has been extended to include a prize for a first published work.
Prize: Scottish Book of the Year £5000; First Book of the Year, £1500.
Contact: Mrs Kathleen Munro, Administrator
Scottish Book of the Year
1988 Games with Shadows by Neal Ascherson (joint winner)
The Enchanted Glass by Tom Nairn (joint winner)
1989 A Question of Loyalties by Allan Massie
1990 From Wood to Ridge by Sorley MacLean
1991 Scottish Art: 1460-1990 by Duncan MacMillan
1992 Collected Poems by Iain Crichton Smith
1993 Robert Burns: A Biography by James Mackay
1994 Beside the Ocean of Time by George Mackay Brown
1995 The Black Sea by Neal Ascherson (joint winner)
So I Am Glad by A L Kennedy (joint winner)
1996 The Kiln by William McIlvanney
First Book
1988 The Richt Noise by Raymond Vettesse
1989 Cells of Knowledge by Sian Hayton
1990 The Ballad of Sawney Bain by Harry Tait
1991 Night Geometry and the Garscadden Trains by AL Kennedy

1992 The Adoption Papers by Jackie Kay (joint winner)
Uirsgeul: Myth by Crisdean Whyte (joint winner)
1993 Dreams of Exile (A Life of R L

Stevenson) by Ian Bell
1994 Music in a Foreign Language by Andrew Crumey
1995 Free Love by Ali Smith
1996 Slattern by Kate Clanchy

Science Fiction and Fantasy Writers of America Nebula Awards
Science Fiction and Fantasy Writers of America
5 Winding Brook Drive, Suite 1B
Guilderland, New York, NY 12084, USA
Publication during the previous calendar year, and nomination by the SFWA President.
Annual trophy.
Grand Master
1991 Lester del Rey
1993 Frederik Pohl
1995 Damon Knight
Novel
1990 The Healer's War by Elizabeth Ann Scarborough
1991 Tehanu: The Last Book of Earthsea by Ursula K Le Guin
1992 Sections of the Tide by Michael Swanwick
1993 Doomsday Book by Connie Willis
1994 Red Mars by Kim Stanley Robinson
1995 Moving Mars by Greg Bear
1996 Hobson's Choice / The Terminal Experiment by Robert J Sawyer
Novelette
1990 At the Rialto by Connie Willis
1991 Tower of Babylon by Ted Chiang
1992 Guide Dog by Mike Conner
1993 Danny Goes to Mars by Pamela Sargent
1994 Georgia on my Mind by Charles Sheffield
1995 The Martian Child by David Gerrold
1996 Solitude by Ursula K Le Guin
Novella
1990 The Mountains of Mourning by Lois McMaster Bujold
1991 The Hemingway Hoax by Joe Haldeman
1992 Beggars in Spain by Nancy Kress
1993 City of Truth by James Morrow
1994 The Night We Buried Road Dog by Jack Cady
1995 Seven Views of Olduvai Gorge by Mike Resnick
1996 Last Summer at Mars Hill by Elizabeth Hand
Short Story
1990 Ripples in the Dirac Sea by Geoffrey A Landis
1991 Bears Discover Fire by Terry Bisson
1992 Ma Qui by Alan Brennert
1993 Even the Queen by Connie Willis
1994 Graves by Joe Haldeman
1995 A Defense of the Social Contracts by Martha Soukup
1996 Death and the Librarian by Esther M Friesner

Scottish Arts Council Book Awards
c/o Scottish Arts Council
12 Manor Place,
Edinburgh EH3 7DD, Scotland

A number of book awards are given in Spring and Autumn to new and established authors in recognition of high standards of writing. Authors should be Scottish, resident in Scotland or have written works of Scottish interest. Applications from publishers only.
Contact: Literature Officer.

Smarties Book Prize
Book Trust
Book House, 45 East Hill
London SW18 2QZ, England
Award given for a children's book written in English by a citizen of the UK, or an author resident in the UK, and published in the UK in the year ending 31 October.
Formerly, an annual prize for overall winner and lesser prizes for catagory winners; Prizes awarded are currently £2500 (Gold), £1000 (Silver) and £500 (Bronze) in the three categories, with no overall winner.
Contact: Sandra Vince
1985   *Under 7's category*
        It's Your Turn Roger! by Susanna Gretz
        Over 7's category winner
        Gaffer Samson's Luck by Jill Paton Walsh
        Innovation category
        Watch It Work! The Plane by Ray Marshall and John Bradley
1986   *7-11 years category and overall winner*
        The Snow Spider by Jenny Nimmo
        6 years and under category
        The Goose That Laid the Golden Egg by Geoffrey Patterson
        Innovation category
        The Mirrorstone by Michael Palin, Alan Lee and Richard Seymour
        Village Heritage by Miss Pinnell and the children of Sapperton School
1987   *9-11 years category and overall winner*
        A Thief in the Village by James Berry
        6-8 years category
        Tangle and the Firesticks by Benedict Blathwayt
        5 years and under category
        The Angel and the Soldier Boy by Peter Collington
1988   *5 years and under category and overall winner*
        Can't You Sleep, Little Bear? by Martin Waddell
        6-8 years category
        Can It Be True? by Susan Hill
        9-11 years category
        Rushavenn Time by Theresa Whistler and Brixworth Primary School
1989   *5 years and under category and overall winner*
        We're Going on a Bear Hunt by Michael Rosen
        6-8 years category
        Bill's New Frock by Anne Fine
        9-11 years category
        Blitzcat by Robert Westall
1990   *9-11 years category and overall winner*
        Midnight Blue by Pauline Fisk

        6-8 years category
        Esio Trot by Roald Dahl
        5 years and under category
        Six Dinner Sid by Inga Moore
1991   *5 years and under category and overall winner*
        Farmer Duck by Martin Waddell and Helen Oxonbury
        9-11 years category
        Krindle Krax by Philip Ridley
        6-8 years category
        Josie Smith and Eileen by Magdaline Nabb
1992   *9-11 years category and overall winner*
        The Great Elephant Chase by Gillian Cross
        6-8 years category
        The Story of Creation by Jane Ray
        5 years and under category
        Nice Work Little Wolf by Hilda Offen
1993   *6-8 years category and overall winner*
        War Game by Michael Foreman
        9-11 years category
        Listen to the Dark by Maeve Henry
        5 years and under category
        Hue Boy by Rita Phillips Mitchell
1994   *9-11 years category and overall winner*
        The Exiles at Home by Hilary McKay
        6-8 years category
        Dimanche Diller by Henrietta Branford
        5 years and under category
        So Much by Trish Cooke and Helen Oxonbury
1995   *9-11 years category (joint winner) and overall winner*
        Double Act by Jacqueline Wilson
        9-11 years category (joint winner)
        Weather Eye by Lesley Howarth
        5 years and under category
        The Last Noo-Noo by Jill Murphy
        6-8 years category
        Thomas and the Tinners by Jill Paton Walsh
1996   *9-11 years category*
        Gold Award: The Firework-Maker's Daughter by Philip Pullman
        Silver Award: Johny and the Bomb by Terry Pratchett
        Bronze Award: Plundering Paradise by Geraldine McCaughrean
        6-8 years category
        Gold Award: The Butterfly Lion by Michael Morpurgo
        Silver Award: Harry the Poisonous Centipede by Lynne Reid Banks
        Bronze Award: All Because of Jackson by Dick King-Smith
        0-5 years category
        Gold Award: Oops! by Colin McNaughton
        Silver Award: The World is Full of BABIES! by Mick Manning and Brita Granstrom
        Bronze Award: Clown by Quentin Blake

W H Smith/Books in Canada First Novel Award
130 Spadina Avenue, Suite 603
Toronto, Ontario M5V 2M3, Canada

Prize is awarded for the best Canadian first novel published in English during the calendar year. Annual prize of $1000

1980 Gentle Sinners by W D Valgardson
1981 Obasan by Joy Kogawa
1982 Shoeless Joe by W P Kinsella
1983 Willie: A Romance by Heather Robertson
1984 Perdue: Or How The West Was Lost by Geoffrey Ursell
1985 The Story of Booby O'Malley by Wayne Johnston
1986 The Life of Helen Alone by Karen Lawrence
1987 The Butterfly Chair by Marion Quednau
1988 A Man of Little Faith by Rick Salutin
1989 The Missing Child by Sandra Birdsall
1991 Lives of the Saints by Nino Ricci
1992 Such a Long Journey by Rohinton Mistry
1993 The Afterlife of George Cartwright by John Steffler
1994 Losing Eddie by Deborah Joy Corey

W H Smith Literary Award

W H Smith plc,
Audrey House, Ely Place
London EC1N 6SN, England
Presented for an outstanding contribution to English literature in the year under review, to the author of a book written and published in English and published in the UK. Authors considered will be from the UK, Commonwealth and Republic of Ireland, but writers cannot submit work themselves. Annual award £10,000
Contact: Tricia Ryan.

1980 Selected Poems 1950-1975 by Thom Gunn
1981 The Shooting Party by Isabel Colegate
1982 Last Waltz in Vienna by George Clare
1983 Wise Virgin by A N Wilson
1984 Required Writing (Miscellaneous Pieces 1955-62) by Philip Larkin
1985 The Pork Butcher by David Hughes
1986 The Good Terrorist by Doris Lessing
1987 Collected Poems 1953-85 by Elizabeth Jennings
1988 The Fatal Shore by Robert Hughes
1989 A Turbulent, Seditious and Factious People: John Bunyan and his Church (A Biography) by Christopher Hill
1990 A Careless Widow and Other Stories by Sir Victor Pritchett
1991 Omeros by Derek Walcott
1992 The Scramble for Africa by Thomas Pakenham
1993 Daughters of the House by Michèle Roberts
1994 A Suitable Boy by Vikram Seth
1995 Open Secrets by Alice Munro
1996 Landscape and Memory by Simon Schama

Stand Magazine Short Story Competition

Stand Magazine
179 Wingrove Road
Newcastle-Upon-Tyne NE4 9DA,
England
Contact: Linda Goldsmith

Awarded for an original story of no longer than 8000 words written in English. Works must be previously unpublished and unbroadcast.
Prizes: £2500 in total prize money, including £1500 first prize.

Ian St James Awards

c/o The New Writers' Club, PO Box 60
Cranbrook, Kent TN17 2ZR, England
Presented to previously unpublished authors from any country, over the age of eighteen, for fictional short stories.
Prizes: £5,000+ in total; First prize of £2000, forty runners-up are published in The New Writer Magazine.

1990 Mothering Sunday by Annie Hedley
A Seeing Lesson by William Walker
A Whore's Vengeance by Louise Doughty
1991 Small Beginnings by Faith Addis
French Kisses by Alan Dunn
Me and Renate by Stephanie Ellyne
1992 Black Sky at Night by Jeremy Cain
Good at Things by Francesca Clementis
Me and the Stars by Peter Naylor
1993 Berlin Story by Philip Sealey
The Olive Tree by Hilary Waters
Figure of Eight by Min Dinning
Karmic Mothers by Kate Atkinson
Moira Flaherty by Juliet McCarthy
Black Lizzie Black by James Maguire
1994 The Saviour by Joshua Davidson
A is for Axe by Mike McCormack
The Food of Love by Sue Camarados
The Welfare of the Patient by Anna McGrail
Magdalen by Alison Armstrong
The Possibility of Jack by A S Penne
1995 Sweet William is the Scent by Jeanette Allee
Vessel by Heather Doran Barbieri
Barcelona by Jonathan Carr
Expect Jail by Nick Kelly
The Uncle by Maxine Rosaler
Ground No More by Hwee Hwee Tan
1996 Algebra by Josephine Corcoran
Black Water Crossing by Indira Debah
Losing Track by Tobias Hill
Constance and Louise by Beverley Strauss
Wedding Day by Julia Widdows

Sunday Times Award for Literary Excellence

The Sunday Times
1 Pennington Street
London E1 9XW, England
Established in 1987 and presented annually to fiction and non-fiction writers. Winners are chosen by a panel of judges consisting of Sunday Times writers, publishers and other leading figures from the publishing industry, and awarded at the discretion of the Literary Editor.
Award: Inscribed silver trophy.
Contact: Geordie Grieg, Literary Editor

Tanning Prize

Academy of American Poets

584 Broadway, Suite 1208
New York, NY 10012, USA
Recognizes outstanding and proven mastery in the art of poetry. No applications are accepted.
Annual prize of $100,000
1994   W S Merwin
1995   James Tate
1996   Adrienne Rich

Tom-Gallon Award
Society of Authors
84 Drayton Gardens,
London SW10 9SB, England
A biennial award for writers of limited means who have had at least one short story published.
Prize: £500.
1984   The Egg Man by Janni Howker
1986   The House of Funerals by Laurence Scott
1988   Taking Doreen Out of the Sky by Alan Beard
1990   Sister Monica's Last Journey by Richard Austin
1992   Reading the Signals by David Callard
1994   A Good Place To Die by Janice Fox

Translators Association Translation Prizes
The Translators Association
84 Drayton Gardens
London SW10 9SB, England
Contact: Kate Pool
John Florio Prize (Italian-English)
Awarded biennially for the best translation of a full-length Twentieth-Century Italian literary work into English, published by a British publisher.
Prize: £1000
Scott Moncrieff Prize (French-English)
Awarded annually for the best translation into English of a full-length French literary work originally published in the last 150 years, published by a British publisher in the preceding year.
Prize: £1000
Teixeira-Gomes Prize (Portuguese-English)
Triennial prize for translations of works from any period by a Portuguese national. Short stories and poems are eligible.The prize is also open to unpublished translations of works of Portuguese nationals.
Prize: £1000
Schlegel-Tieck Prize (German-English)
Annual award for the best translation of a full-length Twentieth-Century German literary work, published by a British publisher during the previous year.
Prize: £2200.
Bernard Shaw Prize (Swedish-English)
Triennial award funded by the Anglo-Swedish Literary Foundation for the best translation into English of a full-length Swedish work, published in the UK in the three years prior to the award.
Prize: £1000
Premio Valle Inclán (Spanish-English)
A new prize for the best translation of a full-length Spanish work from any period, published in the UK in the preceding 5 years.
Prize: 1000
Vondel Translation Prize (Dutch/Flemish-English)

Due to be first awarded in 1999 for the best translation of a Dutch or Flemish literary work into English. Translations should have been published in the UK or US during 1996-98.
Greek and Japanese translation prizes are currently under discussion.

Betty Trask Prize and Awards
Society of Authors
84 Drayton Gardens
London SW10 9SB, England
Awards are for authors under 35 and commonwealth citizens for a first novel of a traditional or romantic nature.
Annual prize of £25,000 (shared)
1984   Winter Journey by Ronald Frame
        Cold Showers by Clare Nonhebel
        A Parish of Rich Women by James Buchan
        Playing Fields in Winter by Helen Harris
        The Disinherited by Gareth Jones
        The Devil's Looking Glass by Simon Rees
1985   Legacy by Susan Kay
        A Season of Peace by Gary Armitage
        A Very Private Enterprise by Elizabeth Ironside
        Instead of Eden by Alice Mitchell
        The Standing Hills by Caroline Stickland
        The Earth Abides Forever by George Schweiz
1986   Tongues of Flame by Tim Parks
        Family Myths and Legends by Patricia Ferguson
        Mzungu's Wife by Philippa Blake
        Whore Banquets by Matthew Kneale
        The Road to Dilmun by J F McLaughlin
        The Prodigal Father by Kate Saunders
1987   Hard Luck by James Maw
        The Levels by Peter Benson
        Return Journey by Helen Flint
        Lost Time by Catherine Arnold
        Gestures by H S Bhabra
        The Pink Stallion by Lucy Pinney
1988   The General Interruptor by Alex Martin
        A Case of Knives by Candia McWilliam
        Behind the Waterfall by Georgina Andrewes
        Left of North by James Friel
        Burning Your Own by Glenn Patterson
        Small Tales of a Town by Susan Webster
1989   The Life Game by Nigel Watts
        Watercolour Sky by William Riviere
        Harry's Last Wedding by Paul Houghton
        Uncle Harry's Last Stand by Alasdair McKee
1990   Ripley Bogle by Robert McLiam Wilson
        The Wild Hunt by Elizabeth Chadwick
        No Strange Land by Rosemary Cohen
        The Vision of Elena Silves by Nicholas Shakespeare
1991   A Strange and Sublime Address by Amit Chaudhuri
        Teaching Little Fang by Mark Swallow
        Quite Contrary by Suzannah Dunn
        Honour Thy Father by Lesley Glaister
        Lives of the Saints by Nino Ricci

1992	The Dream Stone by Liane Jones
	Kissing Through a Pane of Glass by Peter M Rosenberg
	Under the Frog by Tibor Fisher
	The Last of His Line by Eugene Mullen
	Never Mind by Edward St Aubyn
1993	You'll Never Be Here Again by Mark Blackaby (unpublished)
	Pig by Andres Cowan (unpublished)
	Tommy Was Here by Simon Corrigan
	Mothers and Other Lovers by Joanna Briscoe (unpublished)
	Landing on Clouds by Olivia Fane (unpublished)
1994	Divorcing Jack by Colin Bateman
	Season of the Rainbirds by Nadeem Aslam
	After the Hole by Guy Burt
	The Game by Frances Liardet
	Some Hope by Jonathan Rix
1995	Depedence Day by Robert Newman
	The Smell of Apples by Mark Behr
	Midnight Feast by Martina Evans
	A Speck of Coaldust by Robert Manchandra (unpublished)
	Halleluja Jordan by Juliet Thomas (unpublished)
	The Latecomer by Philippa Walshe (unpublished)
	The Tennis Party by Madeleine Wickham
1996	The Debt to Pleasure by John Lanchester
	Anita and Me by Meera Syal
	The Testimony of Taliesin Jones by Rhidian Brook
	The Luxury of Exile by Louis Caron Buss

Travelling Scholarship Fund

Society of Authors
84 Drayton Gardens,
London SW10 9SB, England
Non-competitive awards enabling British writers to travel abroad
Prize: £6000

1988	Sybille Bedford
	David Harsent
	Barry Hines
	Nicholas Wollaston
1989	Roy Heath
	Adrian Mitchell
	Elizabeth North
1990	David Caute
	Roy Fisher
	David Hughes
	Robert Nye
1991	Anne Devlin
	Elaine Feinstein
	Iain Sinclair
	Emma Tennant
1993	Jim Crace
	Donald Davie
	Louis de Bernières
1994	Maurice Leitch
	Peter Levi
	Bernard MacLaverty
1995	Peter Benson
	Jenny Joseph
1996	Stewart Conn

Annette Kobak
Theo Richmond

Whitbread Book of the Year and Literary Awards

Booksellers Association
Minster House,
272 Vauxhall Bridge Road
London SW1V 1BA, England
Annual awards established in 1971 to promote and increase good English literature in each of five categories: novel, first novel, biography, children's novel and poetry. Entries are submitted by publishers, and the authors must be residents of Britain or the Republic of Ireland for at least three years. One category winner is then voted Whitbread Book of the Year by the panel of judges. Prize: £21,000 (Book of the Year); £2000 (all nominees).
Contact: Gill Cronin

Novels

1980	How Far Can You Go? by David Lodge
1981	Silver's City by Maurice Leitch
1982	Young Shoulders by John Wain
1983	Fools of Fortune by William Trevor
1984	Kruger's Alp by Christopher Hope
1985	Hawksmoor by Peter Ackroyd
1986	An Artist of the Floating World by Kazuo Ishiguro
1987	The Child in Time by Ian McEwan
1988	The Satanic Verses by Salman Rushdie
1989	The Chymical Wedding by Lindsay Clarke
1990	Hopeful Monsters by Nicholas Mosley (and Book of the Year)
1991	The Queen of Tambourine by Jane Gardam
1992	Poor Things by Alisdair Gray
1993	Theory of War by Joan Brady (and Book of the Year)
1994	Felicia's Journey by William Trevor (and Book of the Year)
1995	The Moor's Last Sigh by Salman Rushdie
1996	Every Man for Himself by Beryl Bainbridge

Biography

1980	On the Edge of Paradise: A C Benson The Diarist by David Newsome
1981	Monty: The Making of a General by Nigel Hamilton
1982	Bismarck by Edward Crankshaw
1983	Vita by Victoria Glendinning King George V by Kenneth Rose
1984	T S Eliot by Peter Ackroyd
1985	Hugh Dalton by Pen Pimlott
1986	Gilbert White by Richard Mabey
1987	Under the Eye of the Clock by Christopher Nolan (and Book of the Year)
1988	Tolstoy by A N Wilson
1989	Coleridge: Early Visions by Richard Holmes (and Book of the Year)
1990	A A Milne: His Life by Ann Thwaite
1991	A Life of Picasso by John Richardson (and Book of the Year)
1992	Trollope by Victoria Glendinning
1993	Philip Larkin by Andrew Motion
1994	The Married Man: A Life of D H Lawrence by Brenda Maddox

1995   Gladstone by Roy Jenkins
1996   Thomas Cranmer: A Life by Diarmaid MacCulloch

Children's Book
1980   John Diamond by Leon Garfield
1981   The Hollow Land by Jane Gardam
1982   The Song of Pentecost by W J Corbett
1983   The Witches by Roald Dahl
1984   The Queen of the Pharisees' Children by Barbara Willard
1985   The Nature of the Beast by Janni Howker
1986   The Coal House by Andrew Taylor
1987   A Little Lower Than the Angels by Geraldine McCaughrean
1988   Awaiting Developments by Judy Allen
1989   Why Weeps the Brogan? by Hugh Scott
1990   AK by Peter Dickinson
1991   Harvey Angell by Diana Hendry
1992   The Great Elephant Chase by Gillian Cross (and Book of the Year)
1993   Flour Babies by Anne Fine
1994   Gold Dust by Geraldine McCaughrean
1995   The Wreck of the Zanzibar by Michael Morpurgo

First Novel
1981   A Good Man In Africa by William Boyd
1982   On the Black Hill by Bruce Chatwin
1983   Flying to Nowhere by John Fuller
1984   A Parish of Rich Women by James Buchan
1985   Oranges Are Not The Only Fruit by Jeanette Winterson
1986   Continent by Jim Crace
1987   The Other Garden by Francis Wyndham
1988   The Comforts of Madness by Paul Sayer (and Book of the Year)
1989   Gerontius by James Hamilton Paterson
1990   The Buddha of Suburbia by Hanif Kureishi
1991   Alma Cogan by Gordon Burn
1992   Swing Hammer Swing! by Jeff Torrington
1993   Saving Agnes by Rachel Cusk
1994   The Longest Memory by Fred D'Aguilar
1995   Behind the Scenes at the Museum by Kate Atkinson (and Book of The Year)
1996   The Debt to Pleasure by John Lanchester

Poetry
1985   Elegies by Douglas Dunn (and Book of the Year)
1986   Stet by Peter Reading
1987   The Haw Lantern by Seamus Heaney
1988   The Automatic Oracle by Peter Porter
1989   Shibboleth by Michael Donaghy
1990   Daddy, Daddy by Paul Durcan
1991   Gorse Fires by Michael Longley
1992   The Gaze of the Gorgon by Tony Harrison
1993   Mean Time by Carol Ann Duffy
1994   Out of Danger by James Fenton
1995   Gunpowder by Bernard O'Donoghue
1996   The Spirit Level by Seamus Heaney (and Book of the Year)

Whitfield Prize
Royal Historical Society
University College London
Gower Street

London WC1E 6BT, England
Offered for an author's first book on British history published in the UK in the last three years. The winner is announced at the RHS annual reception in July.
Prize: £1000
Contact: Joy McCarthy

John Whiting Award
Drama Department, Arts Council of England
14 Great Peter Street,
London SW1P 3NQ, England
Award was inaugurated in 1965 to commemorate the contribution of playwright John Whiting (member of the Drama Panel of the Arts Council, 1955-63) to British post-war theatre. Writers who have received an award offer from the Arts Council Theatre Writing Scheme are eligible, as are those who have had a commission or première from a theatre company funded by the Arts Council or a Regional Arts Board.
Prize: £6000.
Contact: John Johnston

Whiting Writers' Awards
Mrs Giles Whiting Foundation
1133 Avenue of the Americas
New York, NY 10036, USA
Award to emergent writers in recognition of their writing achievement as well as promise for producing outstanding future work.
Annual award of $30,000

Fiction
1985   Raymond Abbott
        Stuart Dybek
        Wright Morris
        Howard Norman
        James Robison
        Austin Wright
1986   Kent Haruf
        Denis Johnson
        Darryl Pinckney
        Padgett Powell
        Mona Simpson
1987   Joan Chase
        Pam Durban
        Deborah Eisenberg
        Alice McDermott
        David Foster Wallace
1988   Lydia Davis
        Bruce Duffy
        Jonathan Franzen
        Mary La Chapelle
        William T Vollmann
1989   Ellen Akins
        Marianne Wiggins
        Tobias Wolff
1990   Yannick Murphy
        Lawrence Naumoff
        Mark Richard
        Christopher Tilghman
        Stephen Wright
1991   Rebecca Goldstein
        Allegra Goodman
        John Holman
        Cynthia Kadohata
        Rick Rofihe

Anton Shammas
1992 R S Jones
J S Marcus
Damien Wilkins
1993 Jeffrey Eugenides
Dagoberto Gilb
Sigrid Nunez
Janet Peery
Lisa Shea
1994 Louis Edwards
Mary Hood
Randall Kenan
Kate Wheeler
1995 Michael Cunningham
Reginald McKnight
Matthew Stadler
Melanie Sumner
1996 Anderson Ferrell
Cristina Garcia
Molly Gloss
Brian Kiteley
Chris Offutt
Judy Troy
A J Verdelle

Poetry
1985 Douglas Crase
Jorie Graham
Linda Gregg
James Schuyler
1986 John Ash
Hayden Carruth
Frank Stewart
Ruth Stone
1987 Mark Cox
Michael Ryan
1988 Michael Burkard
Sylvia Moss
Li-Young Lee
1989 Russell Edson
Mary Karr
C D Wright
1990 Emily Hiestand
Dennis Nurkse
1991 Thylias Moss
Franz Wright
1992 Roger Fanning
Jane Mead
Katha Pollitt
1993 Mark Levine
Nathaniel Mackey
Dionisio D Martinez
Kathleen Peirce
1994 Mark Doty
Wayne Koestenbaum
Mary Swander
1995 Lucy Grealy
James McMichael
Mary Ruefle
1996 Brigit Pegeen Kelly
Elizabeth Spires
Patricia Storace

Non-fiction
1985 Wright Morris
Austin Wright
1986 Darryl Pinckney
1987 Mindy Aloff
Gretel Ehrlich

1988 Gerald Early
Geoffrey O'Brien
1989 Ian Frazier
Natalie Kusz
Luc Sante
Tobias Wolff
1990 Harriet Ritvo
Amy Wilentz
1991 Stanley Crouch
Anton Shammas
1992 Eva Hoffman
Katha Pollitt
1993 No prize awarded
1994 Kennedy Fraser
Rosemary Mahoney
Claudia Roth Pierpont
1995 André Aciman

Plays
1986 August Wilson
1987 Reinaldo Povod
1989 Timberlake Wertenbaker
1990 Tony Kushner
1991 Scott McPherson
1992 Suzan-Lori Parks
Keith Reddin
José Rivera
1993 Kevin Kling

Walt Whitman Award
Academy of American Poets
584 Broadway, Suite 1208
New York, NY 10012, USA
Award for a first-book publication by an eminent
American poet who has not yet published a book of
poetry in a standard edition.
Annual prize of $5000
1975 Climbing into the Roots by Reg Saner
1976 The Hocus-Pocus of the Universe by
Laura Gilpin
1977 Guilty Bystander by Lauren Shakely
1978 Wonders by Karen Snow
1979 Shooting Rats at the Bibb County Dump
by David Bottoms
1980 Work, for the Night is Coming by Jared
Carter
1981 Whispering to Fool the Wind by Alberto
Ríos
1982 Jurgis Petraskas by Anthony Petrosky
1983 Across the Mutual Landscape by
Christopher Gilbert
1984 For the New Year by Eric Pankey
1985 Bindweed by Christianne Balk
1986 Fragments from the Fire by Chris
Llewellyn
1987 The Weight of Numbers by Judith
Baumel
1988 Blackbird Bye Bye by April Bernard
1989 The Game of Statues by Martha
Hollander
1990 The Cult of the Right Hand by Elaine
Terranova
1991 From The Iron Chair by Greg Glazner
1992 The Fire in All Things by Stephen Yenser
1993 Science and Other Poems by Alison
Hawthorne Deming
1994 Because the Brain Can Be Talked Into
Anything by Jan Richman

1995	Resurrection by Nicole Cooley
1996	Madonna Anno Domini by Joshua Clover

Writers' Guild Awards

The Writers' Guild of Great Britain
430 Edgware Road,
London W2 1EH, England
Originally established in 1961, and relaunched in 1991, the Writers' Guild awards are presented in five categories: radio, theatre, film, television and books (fiction, non-fiction and children's). Shortlists are prepared by juries for each categories, and presented to the Guild for the final vote.
Contact: Lisa Fortescue, Awards Co-ordinator

Fiction

1991	The Inn at the Edge of the World by Alice Thomas Ellis
1992	Persistent Rumours by Lee Langley
1993	Time and Tide by Edna O'Brien
1994	How Late It Was, How Late by James Kelman
1995	High Fidelity by Hick Hornby
1996	Promised Lands by Jane Rogers

Non-fiction

1991	Jean Rhys: Life and Works by Carole Angier
1992	Wild Swans: Three Daughters of China by Jung Chang
1993	Daphne du Maurier by Margaret Forster
1994	Genet by Edmund White
1995	William Morris: A Life for Our Times by Fiona MacCarthy
1996	I May Be Some Time: Ice and the Imagination by Francis Spufford

Children's Book

1991	Haroun and the Sea of Stories by Salman Rushdie
1992	The Secret Summer of Daniel Lyons by Roy Apps
1993	Johnny and the Dead by Terry Pratchett
1994	The Frozen Waterfall by Gayle Hicyilmaz
1995	Chandra by Frances Mary Hendry
1996	The Butterfly Lion by Michael Morpurgo

Yorkshire Post Awards

Yorkshire Post Newspapers Ltd,
PO Box 168, Wellington Street,
Leeds LS1 1RF, England
Contact: Margaret Brown

Book of the Year Award

Awarded annually for a work of fiction or non-fiction published in the UK in the year preceding the prize by a British or UK resident writer. Publisher entry only - up to four books may be submitted by any one publisher.
Prize: £1200.

1980	George Orwell - A Life by Bernard Crick
1981	Venice: The Greatness and the Fall by J J Norwich
1982	Clinging to the Wreckage by John Mortimer
1983	Battle for the Falklands by Max Hastings & Simon Jenkins
1984	Overlord: The Battle for Normandy by Max Hastings
1985	The Right of the Line by John Terraine
1986	James Anthony Eden by Robert Rhodes

1987	1914 by Lyn Macdonald
1988	The Silence in the Garden by William Trevor
1989	Citizens by Simon Schama
1990	Anthony Trollope: A Victorian in his World by Richard Mullen
1991	Engage the Enemy More Closely by Corelli Barnett
1992	Shylock by John Gross
1993	Franco by Paul Preston
1994	The Five Giants: A Biography of the Welfare State by Nicholas Timmins

Best First Work Award

Annual award for a work by a new author published during the preceding year.
Prize: £1000.

1980	The Victorians and Ancient Greece by Richard Jenkyns
1981	Churchill and De Gaulle by Francois Kersaudy
1982	Alanbrooke by David Fraser
1983	Montgomery in Europe 1943-45 by Richard Lamb
1984	Eric Linklater: A Critical Biography by Michael Parnell
1985	Pictures From The Water Trade by John David Morley
1986	Duff Cooper by John Charmley
1987	The Cartomancer by Anne Spillard
1988	The Blindfold Horse by Susha Guppy
1989	In Xanadu by William Dalrymple
1990	Epics of Everyday Life by Susan Richards
1991	Forgotten Land by Harriet O'Brien
1992	Stalin's Nose by Rory McLea
1993	The Language of the Genes by Dr Steve Jones
1994	Forgotten Land by Harriet O'Brien

Author of the Year Award

Award for an author of fiction or non-fiction born in Yorkshire.
Prize: £1000

Art and Music Awards

Two annual awards given to the authors whose work has contributed most top the understanding and appreciation of arts and music. Books should have been published in the UK in the preceding year.
Prize: £1000

APPENDIX D

AMERICAN ACADEMY OF ARTS AND LETTERS

Members of the Department with Year of Election (as of 1996), courtesy of American Academy of Arts and Letters, 633 West 155th Street, New York, NY 10032, USA.

Renata Adler	1987	Murray Kempton	1995
Edward Albee	1966	George F Kennan	1962
A R Ammons	1990	William Kennedy	1993
John Ashbery	1980	Galway Kinnell	1980
Louis Auchincloss	1965	Kenneth Koch	1996
Russell Baker	1984	Stanley Kunitz	1963
John Barth	1974	James Laughlin	1995
Jacques Barzun	1952	Denise Levertov	1980
Ann Beattie	1992	R W B Lewis	1982
Saul Bellow	1990	Alison Lurie	1989
Eric Bentley	1990	Norman Mailer	1967
Harold Bloom	1990	David Mamet	1994
Robert Bly	1987	Peter Matthiessen	1974
Paul Bowles	1981	William Maxwell	1963
John Malcolm Brinnin	1978	John McPhee	1988
Gwendolyn Brroks	1976	William Meredith	1968
Art Buchwald	1986	W S Merwin	1972
William S Burroughs	1983	Arthur Miller	1958
Hortense Calisher	1977	Czesław Miłosz	1982
Henry Steele Commager	1952	Joseph Mitchell	1970
Evan S Connell	1988	Wright Morris	1970
Robert Coover	1987	Toni Morrison	1981
Robert Creeley	1987	Joyce Carol Oates	1978
Don DeLillo	1989	Cynthia Ozick	1988
James Dickey	1972	Grace Paley	1980
Joan Didion	1981	J F Powers	1968
E L Doctorow	1984	Reynolds Price	1988
Richard Eberhart	1960	Adrienne Rich	1990
Leon Edel	1964	Philip Roth	1970
Jules Feiffer	1995	John Russell	1996
Leslie Fiedler	1988	Oliver Sacks	1996
James Thomas Flexner	1976	Meyer Schapiro	1976
Shelby Foote	1994	Arthur Schlesinger, Jr.	1961
William Gaddis	1984	Karl Shapiro	1959
John Kenneth Galbraith	1966	Sam Shepard	1986
William H Gass	1983	Charles Simic	1995
Peter Gay	1989	William Jay Smith	1975
Brendan Gill	1995	W D Snodgrass	1972
Allen Ginsburg	1973	Gary Snyder	1987
Louise Glück	1996	Susan Sontag	1979
Francine de Plessix Gray	1992	Elizabeth Spencer	1985
Julian Green	1972	Robert Stone	1994
John Guare	1989	Mark Strand	1981
Emily Hahn	1987	William Styron	1966
Donald Hall	1989	Paul Theroux	1984
Elizabeth Hardwick	1977	Anne Tyler	1983
John Hawkes	1980	John Updike	1964
Shirley Hazzard	1982	Mona Van Duyn	1983
Anthony Hecht	1970	Helen Hennessy Vendler	1993
Joseph Heller	1977	Kurt Vonnegut	1973
Edward Hoagland	1982	William Weaver	1992
John Hollander	1979	Eudora Welty	1952
Richard Howard	1983	Edmund White	1996
Ada Louise Huxtable	1977	Elie Wiesel	1996
Jospehine Jacobsen	1994	Richard Wilbur	1957
Donald Justice	1992	Garry Wills	1995
Justin Kaplan	1985	August Wilson	1995
Alfred Kazin	1965	C Vann Woodward	1970
Donald Keene	1986	Charles Wright	1995

For Product Safety Concerns and Information please contact
our EU representative GPSR@taylorandfrancis.com Taylor & Francis
Verlag GmbH, Kaufingerstraße 24, 80331 München, Germany

T - #0031 - 270225 - C0 - 234/156/41 [43] - CB - 9780948875724 - Gloss Lamination